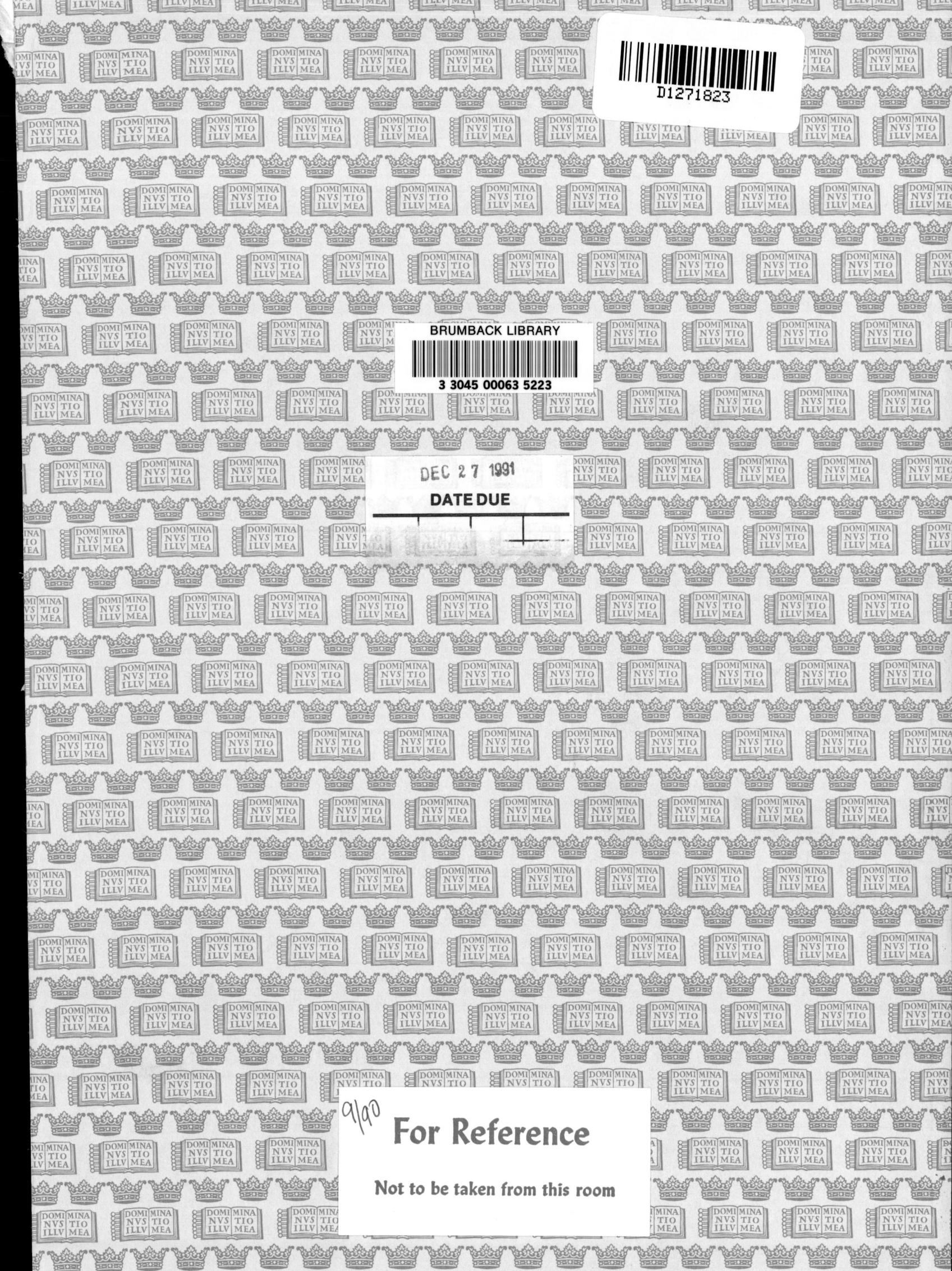

THE OXFORD ENGLISH DICTIONARY

SECOND EDITION

THE OXFORD ENGLISH DICTIONARY

First Edited by

JAMES A. H. MURRAY, HENRY BRADLEY, W. A. CRAIGIE
and C. T. ONIONS

COMBINED WITH

A SUPPLEMENT TO THE OXFORD ENGLISH DICTIONARY

Edited by

R. W. BURCHFIELD

AND RESET WITH CORRECTIONS, REVISIONS
AND ADDITIONAL VOCABULARY

THE OXFORD ENGLISH DICTIONARY

SECOND EDITION

Prepared by

J. A. SIMPSON *and* E. S. C. WEINER

VOLUME VII

Hat–Intervacuum

CLARENDON PRESS · OXFORD

1989

Oxford University Press, Walton Street, Oxford OX2 6DP
Oxford New York Toronto
Delhi Bombay Calcutta Madras Karachi
Petaling Jaya Singapore Hong Kong Tokyo
Nairobi Dar es Salaam Cape Town
Melbourne Auckland
and associated companies in
Berlin Ibadan

Oxford is a trade mark of Oxford University Press

British Library Cataloguing in Publication Data
Oxford English dictionary.—2nd ed.
1. English language-Dictionaries
I. Simpson, J. A. (John Andrew), 1953-
II. Weiner, Edmund S. C., 1950-
423
ISBN 0-19-861219-2 (vol. VII)
ISBN 0-19-861186-2 (set)

Library of Congress Cataloging-in-Publication Data
The Oxford English dictionary.—2nd ed.
prepared by J. A. Simpson and E. S. C. Weiner
Bibliography: p.
ISBN 0-19-861219-2 (vol. VII)
ISBN 0-19-861186-2 (set)
1. English language—Dictionaries. I. Simpson, J. A.
II. Weiner, E. S. C. III. Oxford University Press.
PE1625.087 1989
423—dc19   88-5330

Data capture by ICC, Fort Washington, Pa.
Text-processing by Oxford University Press
Typesetting by Filmtype Services Ltd., Scarborough, N. Yorks.
Manufactured in the United States of America by
Rand McNally & Company, Taunton, Mass.

KEY TO THE PRONUNCIATION

THE pronunciations given are those in use in the educated speech of southern England (the so-called 'Received Standard'), and the keywords given are to be understood as pronounced in such speech.

I. *Consonants*

b, d, f, k, l, m, n, p, t, v, z *have their usual English values*

g as in *g*o (gəʊ)
h ... *h*o! (həʊ)
r ... *r*un (rʌn), terrie*r* ('tɛrɪə(r))
(r) ... he*r* (hɜː(r))
s ... *s*ee (siː), su*cc*ess (sək'sɛs)
w ... *w*ear (wɛə(r))
hw ... *wh*en (hwɛn)
j ... *y*es (jɛs)

θ as in *th*in (θɪn), ba*th* (bɑːθ)
ð ... *th*en (ðɛn), ba*the* (beɪð)
ʃ ... *sh*op (ʃɒp), di*sh* (dɪʃ)
tʃ ... *ch*op (tʃɒp), di*tch* (dɪtʃ)
ʒ ... vi*s*ion ('vɪʒən), déjeuner (deʒøne)
dʒ ... *j*udge (dʒʌdʒ)
ŋ ... si*ng*ing ('sɪŋɪŋ), thi*n*k (θɪŋk)
ŋg ... fi*ng*er ('fɪŋgə(r))

(FOREIGN AND NON-SOUTHERN)

ʎ as in It. serra*gli*o (ser'raʎo)
ɲ ... Fr. cog*n*ac (kɔɲak)
x ... Ger. a*ch* (ax), Sc. lo*ch* (lɒx), Sp. fri*j*oles (fri'xoles)
ç ... Ger. i*ch* (ıç), Sc. ni*ch*t (nıçt)
ɣ ... North Ger. sa*g*en ('zaːɣən)
c ... Afrikaans baardmanne*tj*ie ('baːrtmanəci)
ɥ ... Fr. c*u*isine (kɥizin)

Symbols in parentheses are used to denote elements that may be omitted either by individual speakers or in particular phonetic contexts: e.g. *bottle* ('bɒt(ə)l), *Mercian* ('mɜːʃ(ı)ən), *suit* (s(j)uːt), *impromptu* (ım'prɒm(p)tjuː), *father* ('fɑːðə(r)).

II. *Vowels and Diphthongs*

SHORT	LONG	DIPHTHONGS, etc.
ı as in p*i*t (pıt), -n*e*ss, (-nıs)	iː as in b*ea*n (biːn)	eɪ as in b*ay* (beɪ)
ɛ ... p*e*t (pɛt), Fr. s*e*pt (sɛt)	ɑː ... b*ar*n (bɑːn)	aɪ ... b*uy* (baɪ)
æ ... p*a*t (pæt)	ɔː ... b*or*n (bɔːn)	ɔɪ ... b*oy* (bɔɪ)
ʌ ... p*u*tt (pʌt)	uː ... b*oo*n (buːn)	əʊ ... n*o* (nəʊ)
ɒ ... p*o*t (pɒt)	ɜː ... b*ur*n (bɜːn)	aʊ ... n*ow* (naʊ)
ʊ ... p*u*t (pʊt)	eː ... Ger. Schn*ee* (ʃneː)	ɪə ... p*eer* (pɪə(r))
ə ... *a*nother (ə'nʌðə(r))	ɛː ... Ger. F*äh*re ('fɛːrə)	ɛə ... p*air* (pɛə(r))
(ə) ... beat*e*n ('biːt(ə)n)	aː ... Ger. T*a*g (taːk)	ʊə ... t*our* (tʊə(r))
i ... Fr. s*i* (si)	oː ... Ger. S*oh*n (zoːn)	ɔə ... b*oar* (bɔə(r))
e ... Fr. b*é*b*é* (bebe)	øː ... Ger. G*oe*the ('gøːtə)	
a ... Fr. m*a*ri (mari)	yː ... Ger. gr*ü*n (gryːn)	aɪə as in f*iery* ('faɪərı)
ɑ ... Fr. b*â*timent (bɑtimɑ̃)		aʊə ... s*our* (saʊə(r))
ɔ ... Fr. h*o*mme (ɔm)	NASAL	
o ... Fr. *eau* (o)	ɛ̃, æ̃ as in Fr. f*in* (fɛ̃, fæ̃)	
ø ... Fr. p*eu* (pø)	ɑ̃ ... Fr. fr*anc* (frɑ̃)	
œ ... Fr. b*oeu*f (bœf) c*oeu*r (kœr)	ɔ̃ ... Fr. b*on* (bɔ̃)	
u ... Fr. d*ou*ce (dus)	œ̃ ... Fr. *un* (œ̃)	
ʏ ... Ger. M*ü*ller ('mʏlər)		
y ... Fr. d*u* (dy)		

The incidence of main stress is shown by a superior stress mark (') preceding the stressed syllable, and a secondary stress by an inferior stress mark (ˌ), e.g. *pronunciation* (prəˌnʌnsɪ'eɪʃ(ə)n).

For further explanation of the transcription used, see *General Explanations*, Volume I.

LIST OF ABBREVIATIONS, SIGNS, ETC.

Some abbreviations listed here in italics are also in certain cases printed in roman type, and vice versa.

a. (in Etym.)   adoption of, adopted from
a (as *a* 1850)   *ante*, 'before', 'not later than'
a.   adjective
abbrev.   abbreviation (of)
abl.   ablative
absol.   absolute, -ly
Abstr.   (in titles) *Abstract, -s*
acc.   accusative
Acct.   (in titles) *Account*
A.D.   *Anno Domini*
ad. (in Etym.)   adaptation of
Add.   Addenda
adj.   adjective
Adv.   (in titles) *Advance, -d, -s*
adv.   adverb
advb.   adverbial, -ly
Advt.   advertisement
Aeronaut.   (as label) in Aeronautics; (in titles) *Aeronautic, -al, -s*
AF., AFr.   Anglo-French
Afr.   Africa, -n
Agric.   (as label) in Agriculture; (in titles) *Agriculture, -al*
Alb.   Albanian
Amer.   American
Amer. Ind.   American Indian
Anat.   (as label) in Anatomy; (in titles) *Anatomy, -ical*
Anc.   (in titles) *Ancient*
Anglo-Ind.   Anglo-Indian
Anglo-Ir.   Anglo-Irish
Ann.   Annals
Anthrop., Anthropol.   (as label) in Anthropology; (in titles) *Anthropology, -ical*
Antiq.   (as label) in Antiquities; (in titles) *Antiquity*
aphet.   aphetic, aphetized
app.   apparently
Appl.   (in titles) *Applied*
Applic.   (in titles) *Application, -s*
appos.   appositive, -ly
Arab.   Arabic
Aram.   Aramaic
Arch.   in Architecture
arch.   archaic
Archæol.   in Archæology
Archit.   (as label) in Architecture; (in titles) *Architecture, -al*
Arm.   Armenian
assoc.   association
Astr.   in Astronomy
Astrol.   in Astrology
Astron.   (in titles) *Astronomy, -ical*
Astronaut.   (in titles) *Astronautic, -s*
attrib.   attributive, -ly
Austral.   Australian
Autobiogr.   (in titles) *Autobiography, -ical*
A.V.   Authorized Version

B.C.   Before Christ
B.C.   (in titles) British Columbia
bef.   before
Bibliogr.   (as label) in Bibliography; (in titles) *Bibliography, -ical*
Biochem.   (as label) in Biochemistry; (in titles) *Biochemistry, -ical*
Biol.   (as label) in Biology; (in titles) *Biology, -ical*
Bk.   *Book*
Bot.   (as label) in Botany; (in titles) *Botany, -ical*
Bp.   Bishop
Brit.   (in titles) *Britain, British*
Bulg.   Bulgarian

Bull.   (in titles) *Bulletin*

c (as *c* 1700)   *circa*, 'about'
c. (as 19th c.)   century
Cal.   (in titles) *Calendar*
Cambr.   (in titles) *Cambridge*
Canad.   Canadian
Cat.   Catalan
catachr.   catachrestically
Catal.   (in titles) *Catalogue*
Celt.   Celtic
Cent.   (in titles) *Century, Central*
Cent. Dict.   Century Dictionary
Cf., cf.   *confer*, 'compare'
Ch.   Church
Chem.   (as label) in Chemistry; (in titles) *Chemistry, -ical*
Chr.   (in titles) *Christian*
Chron.   (in titles) *Chronicle*
Chronol.   (in titles) *Chronology, -ical*
Cinemat., Cinematogr.   in Cinematography
Clin.   (in titles) *Clinical*
cl. L.   classical Latin
cogn. w.   cognate with
Col.   (in titles) *Colonel, Colony*
Coll.   (in titles) *Collection*
collect.   collective, -ly
colloq.   colloquial, -ly
comb.   combined, -ing
Comb.   Combinations
Comm.   in Commercial usage
Communic.   in Communications
comp.   compound, composition
Compan.   (in titles) *Companion*
compar.   comparative
compl.   complement
Compl.   (in titles) *Complete*
Conc.   (in titles) *Concise*
Conch.   in Conchology
concr.   concrete, -ly
Conf.   (in titles) *Conference*
Congr.   (in titles) *Congress*
conj.   conjunction
cons.   consonant
const.   construction, construed with
contr.   contrast (with)
Contrib.   (in titles) *Contribution*
Corr.   (in titles) *Correspondence*
corresp.   corresponding (to)
Cotgr.   R. Cotgrave, *Dictionarie of the French and English Tongues*
cpd.   compound
Crit.   (in titles) *Criticism, Critical*
Cryst.   in Crystallography
Cycl.   (in titles) *Cyclopædia, -ic*
Cytol.   (in titles) *Cytology, -ical*

Da.   Danish
D.A.   *Dictionary of Americanisms*
D.A.E.   *Dictionary of American English*
dat.   dative
D.C.   District of Columbia
Deb.   (in titles) *Debate, -s*
def.   definite, -ition
dem.   demonstrative
deriv.   derivative, -ation
derog.   derogatory
Descr.   (in titles) *Description, -tive*
Devel.   (in titles) *Development, -al*
Diagn.   (in titles) *Diagnosis, Diagnostic*
dial.   dialect, -al

Dict.   Dictionary; *spec.*, the *Oxford English Dictionary*
dim.   diminutive
Dis.   (in titles) *Disease*
Diss.   (in titles) *Dissertation*
D.O.S.T.   *Dictionary of the Older Scottish Tongue*
Du.   Dutch

E.   East
Eccl.   (as label) in Ecclesiastical usage; (in titles) *Ecclesiastical*
Ecol.   in Ecology
Econ.   (as label) in Economics; (in titles) *Economy, -ics*
ed.   edition
E.D.D.   *English Dialect Dictionary*
Edin.   (in titles) *Edinburgh*
Educ.   (as label) in Education; (in titles) *Education, -al*
EE.   Early English
e.g.   *exempli gratia*, 'for example'
Electr.   (as label) in Electricity; (in titles) *Electricity, -ical*
Electron.   (in titles) *Electronic, -s*
Elem.   (in titles) *Element, -ary*
ellipt.   elliptical, -ly
Embryol.   in Embryology
e.midl.   east midland (dialect)
Encycl.   (in titles) *Encyclopædia, -ic*
Eng.   England, English
Engin.   in Engineering
Ent.   in Entomology
Entomol.   (in titles) *Entomology, -logical*
erron.   erroneous, -ly
esp.   especially
Ess.   (in titles) *Essay, -s*
et al.   *et alii*, 'and others'
etc.   et cetera
Ethnol.   in Ethnology
etym.   etymology
euphem.   euphemistically
Exam.   (in titles) *Examination*
exc.   except
Exerc.   (in titles) *Exercise, -s*
Exper.   (in titles) *Experiment, -al*
Explor.   (in titles) *Exploration, -s*
f.   feminine
f. (in Etym.)   formed on
f. (in subordinate entries)   form of
F.   French
fem. (*rarely* f.)   feminine
fig.   figurative, -ly
Finn.   Finnish
fl.   *floruit*, 'flourished'
Found.   (in titles) *Foundation, -s*
Fr.   French
freq.   frequent, -ly
Fris.   Frisian
Fund.   (in titles) *Fundamental, -s*
Funk or *Funk's Stand. Dict.*   *Funk and Wagnalls Standard Dictionary*
G.   German
Gael.   Gaelic
Gaz.   (in titles) *Gazette*
gen.   genitive
gen.   general, -ly
Geogr.   (as label) in Geography; (in titles) *Geography, -ical*

Geol.	(as label) in Geology; (in titles) *Geology, -ical*
Geom.	in Geometry
Geomorphol.	in Geomorphology
Ger.	German
Gloss.	Glossary
Gmc.	Germanic
Godef.	F. Godefroy, *Dictionnaire de l'ancienne langue française*
Goth.	Gothic
Govt.	(in titles) *Government*
Gr.	Greek
Gram.	(as label) in Grammar; (in titles) *Grammar, -tical*
Gt.	Great
Heb.	Hebrew
Her.	in Heraldry
Herb.	among herbalists
Hind.	Hindustani
Hist.	(as label) in History; (in titles) *History, -ical*
hist.	historical
Histol.	(in titles) *Histology, -ical*
Hort.	in Horticulture
Househ.	(in titles) *Household*
Housek.	(in titles) *Housekeeping*
Ibid.	*Ibidem*, 'in the same book or passage'
Icel.	Icelandic
Ichthyol.	in Ichthyology
id.	*idem*, 'the same'
i.e.	*id est*, 'that is'
IE.	Indo-European
Illustr.	(in titles) *Illustration, -ted*
imit.	imitative
Immunol.	in Immunology
imp.	imperative
impers.	impersonal
impf.	imperfect
ind.	indicative
indef.	indefinite
Industr.	(in titles) *Industry, -ial*
inf.	infinitive
infl.	influenced
Inorg.	(in titles) *Inorganic*
Ins.	(in titles) *Insurance*
Inst.	(in titles) *Institute, -tion*
int.	interjection
intr.	intransitive
Introd.	(in titles) *Introduction*
Ir.	Irish
irreg.	irregular, -ly
It.	Italian
J., (J.)	(quoted from) Johnson's *Dictionary*
(Jam.)	Jamieson, *Scottish Dict.*
Jap.	Japanese
joc.	jocular, -ly
Jrnl.	(in titles) *Journal*
Jun.	(in titles) *Junior*
Knowl.	(in titles) *Knowledge*
l.	line
L.	Latin
lang.	language
Lect.	(in titles) *Lecture, -s*
Less.	(in titles) *Lesson, -s*
Let., Lett.	letter, letters
LG.	Low German
lit.	literal, -ly
Lit.	Literary
Lith.	Lithuanian
LXX	Septuagint
m.	masculine
Mag.	(in titles) *Magazine*
Magn.	(in titles) *Magnetic, -ism*
Mal.	Malay, Malayan
Man.	(in titles) *Manual*
Managem.	(in titles) *Management*
Manch.	(in titles) *Manchester*
Manuf.	in Manufacture, -ing
Mar.	(in titles) *Marine*
masc. (*rarely* m.)	masculine
Math.	(as label) in Mathematics; (in titles) *Mathematics, -al*
MDu.	Middle Dutch
ME.	Middle English
Mech.	(as label) in Mechanics; (in titles) *Mechanics, -al*
Med.	(as label) in Medicine; (in titles) *Medicine, -ical*
med.L.	medieval Latin
Mem.	(in titles) *Memoir, -s*
Metaph.	in Metaphysics
Meteorol.	(as label) in Meteorology; (in titles) *Meteorology, -ical*
MHG.	Middle High German
midl.	midland (dialect)
Mil.	in military usage
Min.	(as label) in Mineralogy; (in titles) *Ministry*
Mineral.	(in titles) *Mineralogy, -ical*
MLG.	Middle Low German
Misc.	(in titles) *Miscellany, -eous*
mod.	modern
mod.L	modern Latin
(Morris),	(quoted from) E. E. Morris's *Austral English*
Mus.	(as label) in Music; (in titles) *Music, -al; Museum*
Myst.	(in titles) *Mystery*
Mythol.	in Mythology
N.	North
n.	neuter
N. Amer.	North America, -n
N. & Q.	*Notes and Queries*
Narr.	(in titles) *Narrative*
Nat.	(in titles) *Natural*
Nat. Hist.	in Natural History
Naut.	in nautical language
N.E.	North East
N.E.D.	*New English Dictionary*, original title of the *Oxford English Dictionary* (first edition)
Neurol.	in Neurology
neut. (*rarely* n.)	neuter
NF., NFr.	Northern French
No.	Number
nom.	nominative
north.	northern (dialect)
Norw.	Norwegian
n.q.	no quotations
N.T.	New Testament
Nucl.	Nuclear
Numism.	in Numismatics
N.W.	North West
N.Z.	New Zealand
obj.	object
obl.	oblique
Obs., obs.	obsolete
Obstetr.	(in titles) *Obstetrics*
occas.	occasionally
OE.	Old English (= Anglo-Saxon)
OF., OFr.	Old French
OFris.	Old Frisian
OHG.	Old High German
OIr.	Old Irish
ON.	Old Norse
ONF.	Old Northern French
Ophthalm.	in Ophthalmology
opp.	opposed (to), the opposite (of)
Opt.	in Optics
Org.	(in titles) *Organic*
orig.	origin, -al, -ally
Ornith.	(as label) in Ornithology; (in titles) *Ornithology, -ical*
OS.	Old Saxon
OSl.	Old (Church) Slavonic
O.T.	Old Testament
Outl.	(in titles) *Outline*
Oxf.	(in titles) *Oxford*
p.	page
Palæogr.	in Palæography
Palæont.	(as label) in Palæontology; (in titles) *Palæontology, -ical*
pa. pple.	passive participle, past participle
(Partridge),	(quoted from) E. Partridge's *Dictionary of Slang and Unconventional English*
pass.	passive, -ly
pa.t.	past tense
Path.	(as label) in Pathology; (in titles) *Pathology, -ical*
perh.	perhaps
Pers.	Persian
pers.	person, -al
Petrogr.	in Petrography
Petrol.	(as label) in Petrology; (in titles) *Petrology, -ical*
(Pettman),	(quoted from) C. Pettman's *Africanderisms*
pf.	perfect
Pg.	Portuguese
Pharm.	in Pharmacology
Philol.	(as label) in Philology; (in titles) *Philology, -ical*
Philos.	(as label) in Philosophy; (in titles) *Philosophy, -ic*
phonet.	phonetic, -ally
Photogr.	(as label) in Photography; (in titles) *Photography, -ical*
phr.	phrase
Phys.	physical; (*rarely*) in Physiology
Physiol.	(as label) in Physiology; (in titles) *Physiology, -ical*
Pict.	(in titles) *Picture, Pictorial*
pl., plur.	plural
poet.	poetic, -al
Pol.	Polish
Pol.	(as label) in Politics; (in titles) *Politics, -al*
Pol. Econ.	in Political Economy
Polit.	(in titles) *Politics, -al*
pop.	popular, -ly
Porc.	(in titles) *Porcelain*
poss.	possessive
Pott.	(in titles) *Pottery*
ppl. a., pple. adj.	participial adjective
pple.	participle
Pr.	Provençal
pr.	present
Pract.	(in titles) *Practice, -al*
prec.	preceding (word or article)
pred.	predicative
pref.	prefix
pref., Pref.	preface
prep.	preposition
pres.	present
Princ.	(in titles) *Principle, -s*
priv.	privative
prob.	probably
Probl.	(in titles) *Problem*
Proc.	(in titles) *Proceedings*
pron.	pronoun
pronunc.	pronunciation
prop.	properly
Pros.	in Prosody
Prov.	Provençal
pr. pple.	present participle
Psych.	in Psychology
Psychol.	(as label) in Psychology; (in titles) *Psychology, -ical*
Publ.	(in titles) *Publications*
Q.	(in titles) *Quarterly*
quot(s).	quotation(s)
q.v.	*quod vide*, 'which see'
R.	(in titles) *Royal*
Radiol.	in Radiology
R.C.Ch.	Roman Catholic Church
Rec.	(in titles) *Record*
redupl.	reduplicating
Ref.	(in titles) *Reference*
refash.	refashioned, -ing
refl.	reflexive
Reg.	(in titles) *Register*

reg.	regular	str.	strong	*Trop.*	(in titles) *Tropical*
rel.	related to	*Struct.*	(in titles) *Structure, -al*	Turk.	Turkish
Reminisc.	(in titles) *Reminiscence, -s*	*Stud.*	(in titles) *Studies*	*Typog., Typogr.*	in Typography
Rep.	(in titles) *Report, -s*	subj.	subject		
repr.	representative, representing	*subord. cl.*	subordinate clause	ult.	ultimately
Res.	(in titles) *Research*	subseq.	subsequent, -ly	*Univ.*	(in titles) *University*
Rev.	(in titles) *Review*	subst.	substantively	unkn.	unknown
rev.	revised	*suff.*	suffix	*U.S.*	United States
Rhet.	in Rhetoric	superl.	superlative	U.S.S.R.	Union of Soviet Socialist
Rom.	Roman, -ce, -ic	Suppl.	Supplement		Republics
Rum.	Rumanian	*Surg.*	(as label) in Surgery;	usu.	usually
Russ.	Russian		(in titles) *Surgery, Surgical*		
		s.v.	*sub voce*, 'under the word'	*v., vb.*	verb
S.	South	Sw.	Swedish	*var(r)., vars.*	variant(s) of
S.Afr.	South Africa, -n	s.w.	south-western (dialect)	*vbl. sb.*	verbal substantive
sb.	substantive	*Syd. Soc. Lex.*	Sydenham Society, *Lexicon*	*Vertebr.*	(in titles) *Vertebrate, -s*
sc.	*scilicet*, 'understand' or		*of Medicine & Allied*	*Vet.*	(as label) in Veterinary
	'supply'		*Sciences*		Science;
Sc., Scot.	Scottish	syll.	syllable		(in titles) *Veterinary*
Scand.	(in titles) *Scandinavia, -n*	Syr.	Syrian	*Vet. Sci.*	in Veterinary Science
Sch.	(in titles) *School*	*Syst.*	(in titles) *System, -atic*	viz.	*videlicet*, 'namely'
Sc. Nat. Dict.	*Scottish National Dictionary*			*Voy.*	(in titles) *Voyage, -s*
Scotl.	(in titles) *Scotland*	*Taxon.*	(in titles) *Taxonomy, -ical*	*v.str.*	strong verb
Sel.	(in titles) *Selection, -s*	techn.	technical, -ly	*vulg.*	vulgar
Ser.	Series	*Technol.*	(in titles) *Technology, -ical*	*v.w.*	weak verb
sing.	singular	*Telegr.*	in Telegraphy		
Sk.	(in titles) *Sketch*	*Teleph.*	in Telephony	W.	Welsh; West
Skr.	Sanskrit	(Th.),	(quoted from) Thornton's	wd.	word
Slav.	Slavonic		*American Glossary*	Webster	*Webster's* (*New*
S.N.D.	*Scottish National Dictionary*	*Theatr.*	in the Theatre, theatrical		*International*) *Dictionary*
Soc.	(in titles) *Society*	*Theol.*	(as label) in Theology;	*Westm.*	(in titles) *Westminster*
Sociol.	(as label) in Sociology;		(in titles) *Theology, -ical*	WGmc.	West Germanic
	(in titles) *Sociology, -ical*	*Theoret.*	(in titles) *Theoretical*	*Wks.*	(in titles) *Works*
Sp.	Spanish	Tokh.	Tokharian	w.midl.	west midland (dialect)
Sp.	(in titles) *Speech, -es*	tr., transl.	translated, translation	WS.	West Saxon
sp.	spelling	*Trans.*	(in titles) *Transactions*		
spec.	specifically	*trans.*	transitive	(Y.),	(quoted from) Yule &
Spec.	(in titles) *Specimen*	*transf.*	transferred sense		Burnell's *Hobson-Jobson*
St.	Saint	*Trav.*	(in titles) *Travel(s)*	*Yrs.*	(in titles) *Years*
Stand.	(in titles) *Standard*	*Treas.*	(in titles) *Treasury*		
Stanf.	(quoted from) *Stanford*	*Treat.*	(in titles) *Treatise*	*Zoogeogr.*	in Zoogeography
	Dictionary of Anglicised	*Treatm.*	(in titles) *Treatment*	*Zool.*	(as label) in Zoology;
	Words & Phrases	*Trig.*	in Trigonometry		(in titles) *Zoology, -ical*

Signs and Other Conventions

Before a word or sense

† = obsolete

‖ = not naturalized, alien

¶ = catachrestic and erroneous uses

In the listing of Forms

1 = before 1100

2 = 12th c. (1100 to 1200)

3 = 13th c. (1200 to 1300), etc.

5-7 = 15th to 17th century

20 = 20th century

In the etymologies

* indicates a word or form not actually found, but of which the existence is inferred

:— = normal development of

The printing of a word in SMALL CAPITALS indicates that further information will be found under the word so referred to.

.. indicates an omitted part of a quotation.

- (in a quotation) indicates a hyphen doubtfully present in the original; (in other text) indicates a hyphen inserted only for the sake of a line-break.

PROPRIETARY NAMES

THIS Dictionary includes some words which are or are asserted to be proprietary names or trade marks. Their inclusion does not imply that they have acquired for legal purposes a non-proprietary or general significance nor any other judgement concerning their legal status. In cases where the editorial staff have established in the records of the Patent Offices of the United Kingdom and of the United States that a word is registered as a proprietary name or trade mark this is indicated, but no judgement concerning the legal status of such words is made or implied thereby.

hat (hæt), *sb.* Forms: 1 **hæt, hætt,** 3–8 **hatt(e,** 6 **(haitte, atte),** 3– **hat.** [OE. *hæt*, cognate with OFris. *hat*, north. Fris. *hat, hatt*, hood, head-covering; ON. *hǫttr* (genit. *hattar*, dat. *hetti*):—**hattuz*, later nom. *hattr*, hood, cowl, turban, Sw. *hatt*, Da. *hat, hatte-* hat: cf. also Icel. *hetta* (:—**hatjôn-*) hood. The OTeut. **hattuz* goes back to earlier **hadnús*, from ablaut-series *had-, hôd-*, whence OE. *hód* HOOD. Cf. Lith. *kůdas, kõdas* tuft or crest of a bird.]

I. 1. A covering for the head; in recent use, generally distinguished from other head-gear, as a man's cap (or bonnet) and a woman's bonnet, by having a more or less horizontal brim all round the hemispherical, conical, or cylindrical part which covers the head. (But cylindrical 'hats' without brims are worn by some Orientals.) **a.** as worn by men.

c **725** *Corpus Gloss.* 1318 *Mitra*, haet. *c* **893** K. ÆLFRED *Oros.* IV. x. §11 [He] bær hæt on his heafde. *a* **1300** *Cursor M.* 5314 On his heued a hatt he bar. *c* **1400** MAUNDEV. (Roxb.) xxv. 120 He doffez his hatte. *a* **1400–50** *Alexander* 2981 Some in stele plates With hard hattes on þair heddez. **1484** CAXTON *Chivalry* vi. 60 The hatte of steel or yron is gyuen to the knyght to sygnefye shamefastnes. **1556** *Chron. Gr. Friars* (Camden) 81 He was commandyd to put of hys atte. **1585** T. WASHINGTON tr. *Nicholay's Voy.* III. i. 69 b, Wearing on their heads a hygh yealow hatte made after the fashion of a suger loofe. **1694** WOOD *Life* 8 Oct. (O.H.S.) III. 469 Dr. Henry Aldrich..spoke against hatts turned up on one side. **1787** 'G. GAMBADO' *Acad. Horsemen* (1809) 29, I never admired a round hat, but with a large wig it is insupportable. **1879** *Spon's Encycl. Indust. Arts* 1102 The feature which distinguishes the 'hat' from other forms of head-dress is the possession of a brim.

b. as worn by women.

c **1470** HENRY *Wallace* I. 242 A wowyn quhyt hatt scho brassit on with all. **1500–20** DUNBAR *Poems* lxxvii. 44 Madinis..With quhyt hattis all browderit rycht brav[elie]. **1597** SHAKS. *Lover's Compl.* 31 Some [hair], untuck'd, descended her sheaved hat. **1598** —— *Merry W.* IV. ii. 78 There's her thrum'd hat, and her muffler too. **1784** COWPER *Task* I. 536 In cloak of satin trimmed With lace, and hat with splendid riband bound. **1849** C. BRONTE *Shirley* vii, 'I want to finish trimming my hat' (bonnet she meant). **1855** TENNYSON *Maud* I. xx. i, The habit, hat and feather, Or the frock and gypsy bonnet..nothing can be sweeter Than maiden Maud in either. **1864** SALA in *Daily Tel.* 10 June, By the way, they call a lady's dress here [New York] a 'robe', and a bonnet a 'hat'. **1881** GRANT WHITE *Eng. Without & Within* ii. 55 A bonnet has strings, and a hat has not.

2. With qualifying words: **a.** specifying the material, shape, or kind of hat, the place or occasion on which it is worn, etc., e.g. *beaver, felt, silk, straw hat; high, tall* (*chimney-pot, stove-pipe, top*) *hat*, the ordinary cylindrical silk hat of the 19th c.; *opera, tennis hat.* See these words; also BILLYCOCK, COCKED, CRUSH-HAT, WIDE-AWAKE, etc.

c **1430** LYDG. *Min. Poems* (1840) 105 Fyne felt hattes or spectacles to reede. **1540** *Old City Acc. Bk.* in *Archæol. Jrnl.* XLIII, iij straw hats. **1585** T. WASHINGTON tr. *Nicholay's Voy.* III. xvi. 101 Covering their head with a felt hatte. **1837** C. NEWTON in Whittock *Bk. Trades* (1842) 294 When the outer batt is considerably finer than the inner one, the retailer terms it a 'plated hat'. **1838** *Penny Cycl.* XII. 64/1 There are three descriptions or qualities of hats made of wool, viz. beaver-hats, plate-hats, and felt-hats. *Ibid.*, Silk-hats are composed of a form made of chip or of felt, and covered with woven silk plush or shag. **1839** H. AINSWORTH *Jack Sheppard* i, He wore a three-cornered hat, a sandy-coloured scratch wig. **1874** T. HARDY *Far fr. Madding Crowd* (1889) 334 He now wears..a tall hat a-Sundays. **1886** MRS. E. KENNARD *Girl in Brown Habit* viii. (1888) 67 Sooner or later, hunting hats all meet with the same fate. **1896** *Westm. Gaz.* 29 Dec. 8/1 The first high hat, it is said, was worn by John Hetherington, a haberdasher, who was in business on the Strand in London... It is to be remembered, however, that the beaver hat preceded the silk hat, and the modern top hat is only the successor of the hat with a sloping body commonly worn in the seventeenth century.

b. With the name of some person known to have habitually worn or to have been represented in such a hat, or of some artist (Rubens, Gainsborough) fond of depicting such.

1889 N. F. REDDALL *Fact, Fancy, & Fable* 309 He presented all of the refugees..with 'Kossuth' hats. **1890** CARMICHAEL *In God's Way* III. i. 127 A tall man in light clothes and with a Stanley hat on. **1891** DOBSON *Hogarth* 100 A red-haired lady in a Pamela hat and white dress. **1891** E. CASTLE *Consequences* II. 259 A young woman..with a large black Rubens hat. **1893** GEORGIANA HILL *Hist. Eng. Dress* II. 254 Anglesea hat with the bell-shaped crown. D'Orsay hat with ribbed silk binding and a large bow to the band.

3. A head-dress showing the rank or dignity of the wearer; *esp.* a cardinal's hat (see CARDINAL *sb.* III); whence *transf.*, the office or dignity of a cardinal; called also ***red hat***. More generally, any office, position, occupation; esp. in phr. ***to wear two hats***, to hold two appointments concurrently; ***wearing one's —— hat***, in one's capacity as ——.

hat of estate, cap of estate (Halliw.). †***hat of maintenance***: see MAINTENANCE.

a **1352** MINOT *Poems* (Hall) viii. 41 Cardinales with hattes rede. **1431** in Rogers *Agric. & Prices* III. 496/1 Fur to Mayor's hat. **1597–8** BP. HALL *Sat.* V. iii. 85 The red hat that tries the luckless main. **1599** SANDYS *Europæ Spec.* (1632) 150 Who..with dispensation from the Pope would resigne uppe their Hattes. **1690** *Lond. Gaz.* No. 2540/1 The Pope, in a publick Consistory, gave the Hats to nine of the new Cardinals. **1727–51** CHAMBERS *Cycl.* s.v., Pope Innocent IV. first made the hat the symbol or cognizance of the cardinals, injoining them to wear a red hat, at all ceremonies and processions, as a token of their being ready to spill their blood for Jesus Christ. **1753** *Scots Mag.* Jan. 13/2 There are..fifteen hats vacant in the sacred college. **1850** LD. HOUGHTON in Reid *Life* (1890) I. 445 Wiseman proceeds to Rome to get his hat. **18..** KNIGHT *Crown Hist. Eng.* 133 The pope bestowed on him the red hat. [**1869** S. R. HOLE *Bk. about Roses* viii. 111, I never remember to have seen a scientific botanist and a successful practical florist under the same hat.] **1884** G. B. MALLESON *Battle-Fields Germany* viii. 229 The electoral hat of Brandenburg. **1961** WEBSTER *Hat*, an office symbolized by or as if by the wearing of a special hat. **1963** *Times* 25 Apr. 13/7 They..would perform that precarious feat known in the Whitehall idiom as wearing two hats. **1965** *Observer* 31 Oct. 21/4 Even when he is wearing his ecumenical hat he is reported to be speaking as Archbishop of Canterbury. **1966** *Rep. Comm. Inquiry Univ. Oxf.* I. 27 Members of the colleges have accustomed themselves 'to wear two hats' and to act both as lecturers paid by the University and as fellows paid by their colleges. **1967** *Even. Standard* 29 Aug. 1/1 Wearing his new 'economic overlord' hat the Prime Minister summoned three key figures to Downing Street today. **1968** *Listener* 8 Feb. 177/2 Cecil Day-Lewis has two hats: one has laurel in it, the other is that of Nicholas Blake, who writes detective stories. **1972** *Village Voice* (N.Y.) 1 June 17/5, I wear two hats. Are you asking me this question as president of the Bartenders Union or as chairman of the ABC?

4. Felting, such as is used in felt hats.

1794 *Sporting Mag.* III. 193 Giving a preference to wadding made of hat.

5. Phrases and locutions: **a.** Referring to the custom of uncovering the head as a mark of reverence, courtesy, or salutation (often reduced to a momentary taking off, raising, or touching of the hat). ***hat in hand***, with the head uncovered in respect; obsequiously, servilely. Cf. CAP *sb.*[1] 4 h. ***to take off one's hat***: to doff or remove the hat, as a sign of respect. Freq. *fig.* Hence ***hats off to..***, as a command or exhortation.

1593 DONNE *Sat.* i. (R.), That, when thou meet'st one.. Dost search, and, like a needy broker, prize The silk and gold he wears, and to that rate, So high or low, dost raise thy formal hat. *a* **1659** CLEVELAND *Poems, etc.* (1677) 98 He is punctual in exacting your Hat. *c* **1660** WOOD *Life* (O.H.S.) I. 299 The common civility of a hat. **1722** DE FOE *Col. Jack* (1840) 247, I..gave you my hat as I passed you. **1725** —— *Voy. round World* (1840) 97 The governor..gave them the compliment of his hat and leg. **1848** THACKERAY *Van. Fair* (1875) III. iii. 27 To compliment Mrs. Crawley..with a profound salute of the hat. **1851** —— *Eng. Hum., Congreve* (1858) 65 John Dennis was hat in hand to Mr. Congreve. **1856** *Punch* 5 Jan. 3/2 *Quaker*, a friend who..in the art of making inflammatory speeches, takes his hat off to no man. **1857** D. LIVINGSTONE *Miss. Trav.* viii. 272 This being the only hill we had seen since leaving the Bamangwato, we felt inclined to take off our hats to it. **1863** A. J. MUNBY *Diary* 7 Mar. in D. Hudson *Munby* (1972) 151 The populace.. caught fire all at once. 'Hats off!' shouted the men: 'Here she is!' cried the women. **1881** *Harper's Mag.* Jan. 206/1 Over in Greenwood there is a stately monument, to the New York fireman,..before which I take off my hat. **1884** BLACK *Jud. Shaks.* v, Raising his hat and bowing. **1884** MRS. EWING *Mary's Meadow* i. (1886) 12 The Scotch gardener touched his hat to me. **1886** *Harper's Mag.* June 45/2 We should take off our hats to them [*sc.* the 'lady-bugs'] and wish them godspeed. **1923** *Daily Mail* 22 Jan. 6, I say in all sincerity: 'Hats off to France!' **1947** 'P. WOODRUFF' *Wild Sweet Witch* iv. 106, I take off my hat to that boy. **1972** M. FARHI *Pleasure of your Death* vii. 198 'Hats off to them.' 'Yes, of course. Hats off to all the dead.'

b. Referring to the collecting of money in a hat by street minstrels or similar performers: hence, ***to send round the hat, go round with the hat***, etc., applied contemptuously to the collection of money by personal solicitation for charitable or benevolent purposes.

1857 [Remembered in colloquial use]. **1857** KINGSLEY *Two Y. Ago* I. v. 137 A little packet, containing not one five pound note, but four... The Mumpsimus men..had 'sent round the hat' for him. **1863** W. H. GOODE *Outposts of Zion* xxi. 182 The hat for the collection was carried around by a hand disabled by a gunshot. **1870** LOWELL *Among my Bks.* Ser. I. (1882) 370 After passing round the hat in Europe and America. *a* **1878** C. J. MATHEWS in *Daily News* 11 Sept. (1894) 4/7 It was easy enough to make the hat go round, but the difficulty was to get any one to put anything in it. **1890** FENN *Lady Maude's Mania* xxx. 331 Allow me to take round the hat for coppers. **1891** *Morning Post* 10 Jan. 4/6 Dispatching men to send round the hat in America.

c. Miscellaneous phrases: ***bad hat***: a scapegrace. ***black hat*** (Australian slang): a newly-arrived immigrant. ***as black as (one's) hat***: absolutely black. ***by this hat, my hat to a halfpenny, I'll bet a hat***: common forms of asseveration. ***a brick in (one's) hat*** (U.S.): overcome with liquor. ***(his) hat covers (his) family***, etc.: said of one who is alone in the world, and has to provide only for himself. ***hats to be disposed of***: lives lost. ***I'll eat my (old Rowley's) hat***: an asseveration stating one's readiness to do this, if an event of which one is certain should not occur. ***to hang one's hat***: to take up one's quarters (in a certain place). ***to hang one's hat on***: to depend upon. ***to hang up one's hat***: see HANG *v.* 29 b. ***to be in a (the) hat***: to be in a fix. ***to make a hat of***, to make a mess of. ***my hat!***, a trivial exclamation of surprise. ***to talk through one's hat***: to make unsupported or 'wild' assertions, to talk nonsense. ***to throw one's hat into the ring***: to take up a challenge. ***to throw up one's hat***: i.e. in token of joy; cf. CAP *sb.*[1] 9. ***under one's hat***: secret, sub rosa. See also HIGH HAT.

1588 SHAKS. *L.L.L.* v. ii. 563 My hat to a halfe-penie, Pompey prooues the best Worthie. **1598** —— *Merry W.* I. i. 173 By this hat, then he in the red face had it. **1710** *Brit. Apollo* III. No. 95. 2/1 Three Stumps in her Head..as Black as my Hat. *c* **1758** CHESTERF. *Lett.* (1792) IV. cccxxxv. 131 It is by no means a weak place; and I fear there will be many hats to be disposed of before it is taken. *c* **1825** *Houlston Tracts* II. xlviii. 11 With his face as black as your hat. **1837** DICKENS *Pickw.* xlii, 'If I knew as little of life as that, I'd eat my hat and swallow the buckle whole.' **1847** *Sporting Life* V. 224/2 Warren threw his hat in the ring. **1848** *Ibid.* 1 Jan. 237/1 Curtis..threw his hat into the ring. **1849** LONGF. *Kavanagh* xxix, Her husband..often came home very late, 'with a brick in his hat', as Sally expressed it. **1854** DICKENS *Hard T.* 141 They would say, 'While my hat covers my family'..I have only one to feed. **1875** TROLLOPE *Prime Minister* (1876) I. II. xx. 335 Lopez can come in and hang up his hat whenever it pleases him. **1880** A. A. HAYES *New Colorado* (1881) viii. 118 Why that's *my* preacher. I hang my hat on him every time. **1882** MRS. CROKER *Proper Pride* III. i. 6 I'm in a most awful hat this time, and no mistake. **1882** MRS. RIDDELL *Daisies & B.* II. 239 'Hat covers his family, don't it?' 'He has no one belonging to him I ever heard of.' **1884** BESANT *Childr. Gibeon* II. xxxii, There are always bad hats in every family. **1885** C. M. YONGE *Nuttie's Father* I. xviii. 220 Nuttie..was taking in all these revelations with an open-eyed, silent horror... It was all under her hat, however, and the elder ladies never thought of her. **1887** R. M. PRAED *Longleat of Korralbyn* xxviii. 277 I'd never let it be said that a black hat had cut me out. **1887** MISS E. E. MONEY *Litt. Dutch Maiden* II. viii. 148 (Farmer) If you don't run up against him next day..you may eat your hat! **1887–9** T. A. TROLLOPE *What I remember* III. 169 The man whose estate lies under his hat need never tremble before the frowns of fortune. **1888** *N.Y. World* 13 May 12/3 Dis is only a bluff dey're makin'—see! Dey're talkin' tru deir hats. **1897** T. M. HEALY in *Daily News* 22 Jan. 3/3 The Irish farmer would throw up his hat on learning that hostilities had broken out. **1899** KIPLING *Stalky & Co.* 174 My Hat!.. That's pretty average heroic. **1902** W. N. HARBEN *Abner Daniel* 81 All this talk about the devil makin' the bad an' the Lord the good is talk through a hat. **1904** 'O. HENRY' *Cabbages & Kings* vi. 117 The governor man had a bit of English under his hat, and when the music was choked off he says: 'Ver-r-ree fine.' **1904** *N.Y. American* 18 July 2 If the Tammany leader expects to hang his hat inside Judge Parker's political headquarters, he must come here voluntarily. **1912** *Nation* 7 Mar. 226/1 When Mr. Roosevelt threw his hat into the ring the other day, he gave the signal for a contest the like of which has not been seen before in this country. **1914** C. MACKENZIE *Sinister St.* II. III. viii. 661 'My hat, what a frowst,' exclaimed Maurice. **1916** *Chambers's Jrnl.* May 302/2 Now, Joshua Billings, A.B., though officially a bad hat, was one of the best seamen in the ship. **1916** *Chums* 30 Sept. 37/2 I'm in no end of a hat, chauffeur. Can you give me a hand? **1917** W. J. LOCKE *Red Planet* xxiv. 'You dashed young idiot,' I cried, 'do you think I'm in the habit of talking through my hat?' **1923** WODEHOUSE *Inimitable Jeeves* xvii. 249 She kept it under her hat. She meant to spring it on me later, she said. **1925** J. BUCHAN *John Macnab* xv. 312 Palliser-Yeates lost at Glenraden..and now I've made a regular hat of things at Haripol. **1928** *Observer* 4 Mar. 11/2 Mr. Secretary Hoover has been forced to throw his hat into the ring for the Presidency, but he does not mean to follow it there. **1929** GALSWORTHY *Roof* iv, *Mr. B.* I suppose you think you never snore. *Mrs. B.* I know I don't. *Mr. B.* My hat! **1939** 'A. BRIDGE' *Four-Part Setting* 155 One couldn't just sit by and watch a person..make a complete hat of her life and herself and her character. **1945** M. ALLINGHAM *Coroner's Pidgin* xiv. 118 My hat! was it only last night? **1953** 'N. SHUTE' *In Wet* viii. 251 'Nothing about that in the papers, is there?' 'Not yet. Keep it under your hat.' **1956** 'A. GILBERT' *Death came Too* xiv. 152 'You,' suggested Frank, politely, 'are talking through your hat.' **1958** *Daily Mail* 6 Sept. 4/2 Some of them innocent hard-working people, others petty thieves and bad hats. **1963** N. MARSH *Dead Water* (1964) vi. 148 I'd be very grateful..if you'd keep the whole affair under your hat.

d. Also, in contexts referring to the drawing of names from (or the putting of names into) a hat in selecting opponents in a competition, etc.; also with reference to the conjuring trick of producing a rabbit from a hat.

1929 *Evening News* 18 Nov. 13/2 Dagenham..will be amongst the distinguished clubs to go into the hat. **1958** *Listener* 18 Sept. 404/1 Mr. Dulles first pulled indirect aggression out of the hat in mid-July. **1963** A. ROSS *Australia 63* v. 110 Simpson's five [wickets] were simply out of the hat. **1966** H. WAUGH *Pure Poison* (1967) xv. 93 He picked Roger out of a hat as a victim? **1971** J. MCCLUNE *Steam Pig* ii. 26, I must say you've really pulled one out of the hat this time.

II. In various technical uses.

6. a. The layer of tan-bark spread on the top of a pile of hides with interposed bark filling a tan-pit. **b.** *Metallurgy.* A depression in the tunnel-head of a smelting furnace to detain the gases (Knight *Dict. Mech.* 1875). **c.** In *Soap-making*: A depressed chamber in the bottom of a copper (see quot. 1885).

1853 C. MORFIT *Tanning, etc.* 208 When the skins have all been imbedded in the tan, they are to be covered with a six inch stratum of bark, technically termed the hat. **1885** W. L. CARPENTER *Soap & Candles* vi. 156 The copper, provided with a 'hat'..to receive impurities that subside.

d. The creamy top of hatted kit.

1831 [see HATTED *ppl. a.* c]. **1946** *Farmhouse Fare* (new ed.) 124 Hatted Kit..can..be made without milking the cow into it, although direct milking puts a better 'hat' on the Kit.

1952 F. WHITE *Good Eng. Food* IV. ii. 180 *Hatted Kit*... fresh good butter-milk, and a pint of milk hot from the cow. Mix well by jumbling... It will now firm, and gather a hat.

7. a. The pileus of a fungus.

1886 in *Syd. Soc. Lex.* **1887** *Lancet* 11 June 1215/2 Different parts of the mushroom contain more or less albumen, the 'hat'.. having twice as much as the stem.

b. *dial.* A clump of trees.

1895 DE CRESPIGNY & HUTCHINSON *New Forest* 113 The term 'hat' is still in use for a little wood crowning a hill. **1895** G. PATTERSON in *Jrnl. Amer. Folk-Lore* VIII. 29 A hat of trees. **1936** C. R. ACTON *Sport & Sportsmen of New Forest* ii. 43 A clump of trees is known as a 'Hat'; two examples being 'Crab Hat' and 'King's Hat'.

III. *attrib.* and *Comb.*

8. In sense: 'Forming part of a hat', as ***hat-brim, -crown, -leaf, -lining, -plush, -spring***; 'For supporting or holding hats', as ***hat-peg, -pin, -rail, -securer, -shelf, -shop***; also in other connexions.

1859 DICKENS *T. Two Cities* I. ii, To.. shake the wet out of his *hat-brim. **1670** COTTON *Espernon* II. VIII. 402 Leaving an orifice bigger than a *Hat Crown. *c* **1813** MRS. SHERWOOD *Stories Ch. Catech.* xvi. 142 Philip took a pair of scissars, and hid them in his hat-crown. **1829** *Blackw. Mag.* XXVI. 76 The heavy shot.. carrying off an entire whisker, a very small portion of ear, and a rather larger portion of *hat-leaf from the policeman. **1838** DICKENS *O. Twist* xliii, To hang 'em up to their own *hat-pegs. **1891** J. O. HOBBES *Some Emotions* 137 'Would you like that *hat-pin?' she said. **1888** *Illustr. Lond. News* Christm. No. 14/3 Steadying himself with one hand upon the *hat-rail of the [railway] carriage. **1892** A. CONAN DOYLE in *Strand Mag.* III. 75/1 It was pierced in the brim for a *hat-securer, but the elastic was missing. **1896** *Daily News* 21 Jan. 2/1 The programmes, and the *hat-shelves for the guests. **1892** HOWELLS *Mercy* 37 She had been one of the *hat-shop hands. **1858** SIMMONDS *Dict. Trade*, **Hat-spring Maker*, a manufacturer of springs for light opera or closing-up hats. **1794** *Sporting Mag.* III. 193 It may be preferred to *hat-wadding.

9. obj. and obj. genitive, as ***hat-bearer, -dresser, -dyer; hat-doffing, -raising, -tipping, -trimming, -turning; hat-sizing, -wearing*** adjs. Also HAT-MAKER, -MAKING.

1891 MISS DOWIE *Girl in Karp.* 216 Graceful *hat-doffings and hand-kissings. **1640** *Canterbury Marriage Licences* (MS.), John Lewknor of Canterbury, *hat-dresser. **1709** *Lond. Gaz.* No. 4580/4 Brian Thompson, of London, *Hat-dyer. **1905** *Westm. Gaz.* 11 Aug. 7/1 At Trafalgar-square there was much *hat-raising. **1908** *Ibid.* 30 Jan. 12/2 The hat-raising habit. **1921** *Dict. Occup. Terms* (1927) §549 **Hat tip sizer*, prints hat tip with size before gold leaf or bronze dust is applied by hat tip printer. **1895** *Montgomery Ward Catal.* Index, *Hat trimmings. **1905** *Daily Chron.* 23 Dec. 6/5 The success of the hat-trimming competition. **1848** SIR J. G. WILKINSON *Dalmatia, etc.* I. 167 *Hat-wearing townspeople.

10. Special combs.: **hat-body**, the unshaped or partly shaped piece of felt from which a hat is formed; **hat-brush**, a soft brush for brushing hats; **hat-card**, a card worn in the ribbon of a hat by a partisan in sport or politics; **hat-check boy, girl** *U.S.*, a cloakroom attendant; †**hat-commoner** (see quot.); **hat-conformator** = CONFORMATOR; **hat-die** = *hat-mould*; **hat-frame** (see quot.); **hat-grip**, a device for holding a hat on the head; **hat-guard**, a string or cord to prevent a hat from being blown away; **hat-homage**, †**-honour**, reverence shown by removing the hat, a phrase in use among the early Quakers; **hat leather** (see quot. 1888); **hat-mould**, the die on which a hat or bonnet is formed or shaped by pressing; **hat-pad**, a pad usually of velvet for wiping the dust off or smoothing the nap of a hat; **hat-palm** (also *chip-hat palm*), a name for *Thrinax argentea* and *Copernicia cerifera*, the leaves of which are used for making hats; **hat-piece**, (*a*) a metal skull-cap worn under the hat as defensive armour, (*b*) a coin of James VI on which the king is represented wearing a hat; **hat-plant**, an East Indian plant (*Æschynomene aspera*) of the bean family, yielding a very tough pith which is made into hats, bottles, etc.; **hat-rack**, (*a*) a rack to hold hats; (*b*) *slang*, a scraggy animal; (*c*) *slang*, the head; †**hat-respect** = *hat-honour*; **hat-roller** (see quot.); **hat-shag**, woven silk plush for silk hats; †**hat-shaker**; **hat-stand**, a standing piece of furniture for hats to be hung on; **hat-string** = *hat-guard*; **hat-tip**, the circular piece of stuff used to line the crown of a hat; **hat-tree**, (*a*) a hat-stand with projecting arms for hats and coats; (*b*) *Austral.* (see quot.); †**hat-worship** = *hat-homage*. See also HAT-BAND, -BLOCK, -BOX, etc.

1845 *Penny Cycl.* Suppl. I. 245/2 Very soft brushes, such as *hat-brushes. **1892** *Times* 24 Nov. 8/4 *Hat-cards.. were distributed and worn by hundreds on the polling day. **1917** *N.Y. Tribune* 19 June 8/4 How about the *hat check boys? **1921** WODEHOUSE *Indiscretions of Archie* xiv. 159 He paid no attention to the hat-check boy. **1959** *Guardian* 22 Dec. 5/1 He found work as a hatcheck boy. **1920** WODEHOUSE *Jill the Reckless* (1922) xv. 223 When a burglar marries a *hat-check girl, their offspring goes into the theatrical business automatically. **1938** *Times Lit. Suppl.* 3 Sept. 572/4 He.. has included all the important information.. even to.. the name of the hat-check girl in the New York restaurant. **1803** *Gradus ad Cantabr.* (Farmer), **Hat Commoner*, the son of a Nobleman, who wears the gown of a Fellow Commoner with a hat. **1858** SIMMONDS *Dict. Trade*, **Hat-frame*, cross-bars of wood placed round three or four dozen hats in sending them out for home sale. **1896** *B'ham Weekly Post* 6 June 1/8 A *hat-grip which will make it possible to wear a straw hat in a gale of wind. **1899** *Catal.* in A. Adburgham *Shops & Shopping* (1964) xxii. 261 *Hat guards. **1912** A. BENNETT *Matador* 131 William Henry commanded her to buy a hat-guard. The hat-guard cost sixpence. **1851** DIXON *W. Penn* vi. (1872) 50 *Hat-homage is our social creed. **1669** PENN (*title*) No Cross, No Crown: or Several Sober Reasons against *Hat-Honour, Titular-Respects, You to a Single Person. **1677** G. FOX in *Jrnl.* (1852) II. 206 If this hat-honour, and shewing the bare head, be an invention of men, and not from God. **1888** *Lockwood's Dict. Mech. Engin.*, **Hat leather*, the leather ring packing used for hydraulic pistons. **1940** *Chambers's Techn. Dict.* 405/1 *Hat-leather packing*, an L-section leather ring, gripped between discs to form a piston, or similarly attached to the ram of a hydraulic machine to prevent leakage. **1902** W. W. JACOBS *Lady of Barge* 221 At the hall he paused, and busied himself with the clothes-brush and *hat-pad. **1885** LADY BRASSEY *The Trades* x. 177 Sometimes called.. the thatch-palm, and the *hat-palm. **1599** in Pitcairn *Crim. Trials Scotl.* II. 99 False *hat-peiceis, pistulettis and crownis. **1664–5** PEPYS *Diary* 6 Mar., I saw him try on his buff coat and *hat-piece covered with black velvet. **1872** MARK TWAIN *Innoc. Abr.* xxxi. 241 A sort of vestibule, where they used to keep the *hat-rack. **1935** *Amer. Speech* X. 269/1 If he should try to hang his hat on the hatrack he will probably find that he will have to catch it first, for the hatrack will be found milling about in one of the pens. *Ibid.* 271/1 *Hatrack*, an old, thin cow, a nellie or canner. **1942** BERREY & VAN DEN BARK *Amer. Thes. Slang* §121/56 *Head*,.. hat rack. **1957** R. CAMPBELL *Portugal* v. 73 One trick is to deprive a hatrack of an old horse of water, and let him have a good lick of salt. **1964** L. HAIRSTON in J. H. Clarke *Harlem* 286 If you spent half as much time tryin' to put something *inside* that worthless hat-rack as you did having your brains fryed. **1669** PENN *No Cross* ix. §25 Honour was from the Beginning, but *Hat-respects, and most Titles, are of late. **1883** GRESLEY *Coal Mining Gloss.*, **Hat Rollers*, cast iron or steel rollers, shaped like a hat, revolving upon a vertical pin, for guiding incline hauling ropes round curves. **1698** *Post Man* 12–14 Apr. (N. & Q.), Joseph Briant, a *Hatshaker. **1857** HUGHES *Tom Brown* I. iv, The *hat-stand (with a whip or two standing up in it). **1892** F. M. CRAWFORD *Three Fates* II. 162 There is no more romance about her than there is in a hatstand. **1858** THOREAU *Maine W.* (1894) 118 Used for ornamental *hat-trees, together with deer's horns, in front entries. **1898** MORRIS *Austral Eng.*, *Hat-tree*, name given to a species of *Sterculia, the Bottle-trees.* **1742** *Note on Pope's Dunc.* IV. 205 The *hatworship, as the Quakers call it, is an abomination to that sect.

hat, *v.* [f. HAT *sb.*] **a.** *trans.* To cover with a hat; to furnish or provide with a hat. Also, to bestow the cardinal's hat upon.

c **1430** *Pilgr. Lyf Manhode* II. cxxii. (1869) 121 Al be it I be mantelled and wel hatted. **1598** FLORIO, *Incapellare*.. to hat one. **1852** W. JERDAN *Autobiog.* II. xiii. 164 We had.. hatted and cloaked ourselves. **1885** *Boston* (Mass.) *Jrnl.* 31 July 1/6 The Pope.. held a public consistory.. at which the newly appointed Cardinals were hatted. **1891** ANNIE THOMAS *That Affair* I. x. 171 Miss Polthuan hats and veils herself.

b. To place one's hat on (a seat) so as to claim it.

1886 *Philad. Times* 10 Apr. (Cent.), Twenty seats had.. been hatted before noon to secure them for the debate.

c. *intr.* To work alone. (Cf. HATTER *sb.* 2.) *Austral.*

1891 *Age* 25 Nov. 6/7 (Morris), Two old miners have been.. hatting for gold amongst the old alluvial gullies. **1900** H. LAWSON *On Track* 88 And he 'hatted' and brooded over it till he went ratty.

hat, obs. f. HATE *sb.* and *v.*, HIGHT *v.*, HOT *a.*; obs. pa. t. HIT; north. f. HOTE *sb.* promise; obs. var. of AT *prep.* and *rel.* (= that).

hatable, var. of HATEABLE.

‖**hatamoto** (hatamoto). [Jap.] In the Japanese feudal system, a vassal or member of the household troops of a Shogun.

1871 A. B. MITFORD *Tales of Old Japan* I. 95 *Hatamoto*. This word means 'under the flag'. The Hatamotos were men who.. rallied round the standard of the Shogun, or Tycoon, in war-time. **1899** L. HEARN *In Ghostly Japan* vi. 74 The *hatamoto* were samurai forming the special military force of the Shōgun. **1904** —— *Japan: Attempt at Interpretation* xii. 267 These two bodies of samurai formed the special military force of the Shōgun; the hatamoto being greater vassals with large incomes. **1968** J. W. HALL *Japan fr. Prehist. to Mod. Times* x. 166, 5,000 'bannermen' (*hatamoto*), who were privileged to come into the Shogun's presence.

hatare, var. HATER *sb.*[1]

'hatband, hat-band.

1. A band or narrow ribbon put round a hat above the brim.

1412–13 *Durh. MS. Alm. Roll*, Pro hatbandys de serico nigro, ijs. **1552** HULOET, Hatte bande, *spira*. **1594** H. DEANE in *Lismore Papers* Ser. II. (1887) I. 8 A hat-bande, with xviij gowlde buttons. **1623** DK. BUCKHM. in Ellis *Orig. Lett.* Ser. I. III. 146 He hath neyther chaine nor hatband. **1685** *Lond. Gaz.* No. 2094/4 A Hat, with a Black and Gold coloured Silk Hatband of the new twisted fashion. **1726** AMHERST *Terræ Fil.* xlvi. 247 Flapping hats with silver hat-bands. **1834** L. RITCHIE *Wand. by Seine* 105 Louis XI.. loaded even his hat-band with medals of the saints.

b. Phrase. ***as queer*** (***tight, odd,*** etc.) ***as Dick's*** (or ***Nick's***) ***hatband.***

(*Dick* or *Nick* was prob. some local character or half-wit, whose droll sayings were repeated. See *Notes & Queries* 8th ser. XII. 37, et seq.)

1796 GROSE *Dict. Vulg. T.* s.v. *Dick*, I am as queer as Dick's hatband; that is, out of spirits, or don't know what ails me. [*Newcastle form c* 1850. As queer as Dick's (Nick's) hat-band, that went nine times round and wouldn't meet.]

†**c.** ***gold hatband***: a nobleman at the University; a 'tuft'. *Obs.*

1628 EARLE *Microcosm.*, *Yng. Gent. Univ.* (Arb.) 45 His companion is ordinarily some stale fellow, that ha's beene notorious for an Ingle to gold hatbands. **1889** *Gentl. Mag.* June 598 Noblemen at the universities, since known as 'tufts', because of the gold tuft or tassle to their cap, were then known as gold hatbands.

2. A band of crape or other dark material worn round the hat as a sign of mourning.

1598 TOFTE *Alba* (1880) 74 To Hatband black.. This sable place doth fit you best to mourne. **1667** PEPYS *Diary* 31 Dec., My uncle Thomas, with a mourning hat-band on for his daughter Mary. **1702** *Order in Council* 8 Mar. in *Lond. Gaz.* No. 3791/4 It will be allowed as full and proper Mourning, to wear Hatbands of Black English Alamode covered with Black Crape. **1806** A. DUNCAN *Nelson's Fun.* 18 Six mourners, in scarfs and hatbands. **1886** J. K. JEROME *Idle Thoughts* (1889) 32 The undertaker's mute in streaming hat-band.

3. *Comb.*, as ***hatband-hater, -maker.***

1602 *How to Choose Gd. Wife fr. Bad* I. iii. in Hazl. *Dodsley* IX. 17 A hatband-hater, and a busk-point wearer. **1632** *Star Chamb. Cases* (Camden) 115 A. B. of London, Cittizen and Hatband-maker. **1720** *Stow's Surv.* (1754) II. v. xv. 334/1 The master, wardens, and assistants of the incorporated company of Hat-band Makers of London.

'hat-block. [See BLOCK *sb.* 4 a.] A form or mould upon which a man's hat is shaped. Hence ***hat-block maker, turner.***

1723 *Lond. Gaz.* No. 6192/9 Thomas Bossworth.. Hat-Block Turner. **1858** SIMMONDS *Dict. Trade*, *Hat-block maker*, a manufacturer of the solid wooden shapes used in blocking or forming hats.

hat-box. A box adapted to hold a hat or hats; *esp.* as in quot. 1794.

1794 W. FELTON *Carriages* (1801) I. 219 A Hat-box is a convenience for carrying hats, made of stout leather, in the exact form of a hat. **1891** MRS. OLIPHANT *Mem. L. Oliphant* II. xi. 152 Standing before a table on which his hat-box answered the purpose of a desk.

Comb. **1884** *Lond. P.O. Directory*, Hat Box Makers.

hat-case. = HAT-BOX.

1598 FLORIO, *Porta beretta*, a capcase, a hat case. **1662** DRYDEN *Wild Gallant* I. ii, The hat-case must be disposed under the bed. **1670** *Lond. Gaz.* No. 523/4 A square large Box.. with a leather Hat-case upon it. **1890** *Store Catal.* Mar. 1384 Square Hat Cases in Solid Leather.

Comb. **1884** *Lond. P.O. Directory*, Hat Case Makers.

hatch (hætʃ), *sb.*[1] Forms: 1 hæc(c, 3–7 hacche, 4 hach, hachch, 4–6 hache, 5–7 hatche, 6 acche, 6– hatch. *β.* 1 hec(c, 5 hecche, hetche, 5–6 hech(e. [OE. *hæc*, genit. *hæcce*, less commonly *hęc* (the umlaut of *a* before *cc* being generally *æ* instead of *ę*: Sievers §89. 1 Anm. 1):—WGer. **hakjā-*: cf. MLG. *heck*, DU. *hek* (in Kilian *hecke, heck*), Da. *hekke* rack in a stable, Sw. *häck*. Ulterior history and original signification obscure. The variant OE. forms gave *hatch* (sometimes *hetch*) in southern and midl. Eng.; HECK and sometimes *hack* (HACK *sb.*[2]) in north. dial.]

1. a. A half-door, gate, or wicket with an open space above; the lower half of a divided door, which may be closed while the upper half is open. Also formerly, and still dial., any small gate or wicket.

(It is doubtful whether the masc. word in quot. 1015 belongs here.)

[**1015** in Earle *Land Charters* 393 Of ðam hæcce to Dudemæres hele.. swa eft innon ðane hæcc.] **1062** in Thorpe *Dipl. Ævi Sax.* 395 Of þare hlype to þare ealden wude hæcce. *a* **1250** *Owl & Night.* 1056 Thu come sone to than hacche. **1393** LANGL. *P. Pl.* C. XVII. 335þauh ich my by-lyue sholde begge a-boute at mennes hacches. *c* **1465** *E.E. Misc.* (Warton Club) 60 Som.. lepe over the hache, They had no tyme to seche the lache. **1521** *MS. Acc. St. John's Hosp., Canterb.*, For hangyng of an acche at Syster Sawyers jd. **1595** SHAKS. *John* I. i. 171 In at the window, or else ore the hatch. **1687** T. BROWN *Lib. Consc.* in *Dk. Buckhm.'s Wks.* (1705) II. 126 Affairs were come to that pass, that he durst hardly show his Nose over his hatch. **1688** R. HOLME *Armoury* III. 336/1 An Hatch.. is a diminutive Field Gate.. only to let a single Beast in and out of the Field.. also for Milk Maids to go in and out safely without Climing or going over Stiles. **1700** TYRRELL *Hist. Eng.* II. 900 A poor.. Scholar begging for some Relief at the Kitchen-Hatch. **1879** TROLLOPE *J. Caldigate* (1880) 17 He.. passing by the well-known buttery hatches, looked into the old hall for the last time.

β. *c* **1440** *Promp. Parv.* 231/2 Hec, hek, or hetche, or a dore (*K.* hecche, *S.* heke, or hech), *antica*. *c* **1456** *Turnam. Tottenham* 205 Sum on dores, and some on hech. *a* **1529** SKELTON *Dk. Albany* 155 Go begge a byt Of brade, at ylke mannes heche.

†**b.** *fig.* esp. in proverbial phrase, ***to keep*** (***set, have***) ***a hatch before the door***: to keep silence. *Obs.*

1555 R. SMITH in Foxe *A. & M.* (1684) III. 336/2 Seeing God hath given a Tongue, And put it under power: The surest way it is to set A hatch before the door. **1579** GOSSON *Sch. Abuse* (Arb.) 53, I wish that euery rebuker shoulde place a hatch before the doore. **1588** GREENE *Pandosto* (1607) 21 Tush (quoth his wife) profite is a good hatch before the dore. **1594** *Knacke to Knowe* in Hazl. *Dodsley* VI. 535, I say no more, 'Tis good to have a hatch before the door.

c. 'Salt-making term. The door of a furnace' (*Cheshire Gloss.* 1886).

†**2.** A hay-rack; = HECK *sb.*[1] 3. *Obs.*
c **1420** *Anturs of Arth.* xxxv, Hay hely thay hade in haches vn-hiȝte [*Douce MS.* in haches on hight].

3. *Naut.* †**a.** Formerly (in *pl.*, rarely *sing.*), A movable planking forming a kind of deck in ships; hence, also, the permanent deck. *Obs.* Hence ***under hatches*** = below deck; †***over hatch*** = overboard. **b.** Now (since *deck* has become the term for the permanent covering of the hold), A trap-door or grated framework covering the openings in the deck called hatchways. (The phr. ***under hatches*** is now associated with the last sense.)
13.. *E.E. Allit. P.* C. 179 A lodes-mon lyȝtly lep vnder hachches. c **1350** *Will. Palerne* 2770 [They] busked hem boþe sone aboue þe hacches. c **1385** CHAUCER *L.G.W.* 648 *Cleopatra*, He pouryth pesyn up on the hachis sledere. **1495-7** *Naval Acc. Hen. VII* 177 For x dossen Candell.. bought & spent vnder the haches in tyme of Reparacion of the sayd Ship. **15..** *Egyngecourte* 110 in Hazl. *E.P.P.* II. 97 With theyr takyls they launched many a longe bote, And ouer hache threw them in to the streame. **1530** PALSGR. 229/2 Hatche of a shippe, *tiliac, trappe*. **1548** HALL *Chron., Hen. VIII*, 15 The Scottes foughte sore on the hatches. **1552** HULOET, Hatche of a shyppe where they walke, *pergula*. **1573-80** BARET *Alv.* H 223 The hatches, or deckes in a ship, where men stand to fight, *catastroma*. **1581** L. ALDERSEY in Hakluyt *Voy.* (1589) 178 Vp I went to the top of the hatches. **1582** N. LICHEFIELD tr. *Castanheda's Conq. E. Ind.* xxv. 64 a, Commaunded him to prison vnder the hatches. **1588** GREENE *Pandosto* (1843) 48 The maryners lay and slept upon the hatches. **1594** SHAKS. *Rich. III*, I. iv. 17 We pac'd along Vpon the giddy footing of the Hatches. **1598** W. PHILLIPS *Linschoten* in Arb. *Garner* III. 19 They have.. cabins above the hatches. **1611** COTGR., *Tillac*, the Orelop, or Arloup, or, more generally, the hatches of a ship. **1617** MINSHEU *Ductor*, The *Hatches* of a shippe, so called because they fall to like an hatch of a doore. **1700** DRYDEN *Ceyx & Alcyone* 146 Seas impell'd by winds.. Assault the sides and o'er the hatches tow'r. **1762** FALCONER *Shipwr.* II. 382 Then burst the hatches off. **1825** J. NEAL *Bro. Jonathan* II. 298 When.. we came to heave the hatches, we found him. **1869** C. GIBBON *R. Gray* vii, The object crawled along the deck to the hatchway of the hold, raising the hatch cautiously, and disappeared.
β. ? a **1400** *Morte Arth.* 3683 Owt of botes on burde was busked with stonys, Bett down of þe beste, brystis the hetches. **1513** DOUGLAS *Æneis* v. xiv. 19 Endlang the hechis lyand heir and thairis.

c. A square or oblong opening in the deck, by which cargo is lowered into the hold; a hatchway.
1793 SMEATON *Edystone L.* §99 He was going to see the covers of the Hatches of forty of the fish ships.. nailed down. **1873** *Act 36 & 37 Vict.* c. 88 Sched. 1, Hatches with open gratings, instead of the close hatches which are usual in merchant vessels.

d. *fig.* ***down the hatch***: a toasting or drinking phrase.
1931 *Amer. Mercury* Mar. 357/2 The boys didn't pester her to drink. 'Down the hatch!' they said. **1933** M. LOWRY *Ultramarine* iii. 120 'Well, let's shoot a few whiskies down the hatch, and you'll see three,' I remarked fatuously. **1935** *Yachting* Dec. 32/2 'Down the hatch!' is a toast well known ashore. **1942** T. RATTIGAN *Flare Path* I. 110 That went down the old hatch pretty quick, didn't it? **1958** B. HAMILTON *Too Much of Water* xii. 272 And so now, down the hatch, and let's.. see what we can do with the pudding and souse. **1972** *House & Garden* Mar. 130/1 Unlike the professionals, who take a small sip.. and then spit it out.. we, as amateurs, adopted the 'down the hatch' technique.

e. *Aeronaut.* An opening or door in an aeroplane or space capsule. See also quot. 1948.
1940 [see *escape hatch* s.v. ESCAPE *sb.*[1] 8]. **1943** *Coastal Command* (Ministry of Information) ix. 89 At 1.55, after the rigger has reported that all hatches are closed, the klaxon sounds. The Catalina moves slowly at first... The take-off has begun. **1943** E. V. RICKENBACKER *Seven came Through* i. 13, I helped Sergeant Alex pry open the bottom hatch in the tail and between us we dumped all that high-priority mail into the blue Pacific. **1948** PARTRIDGE *Dict. Forces' Slang* 92 *Hatch*, a bomb-hatch—the bomb-aimer's compartment, at the front of the kite, especially in 'Lanks' and 'Wimpeys'. **1956** W. A. HEFLIN *U.S.A.F. Dict.* 246/1 *Hatch*, a ship term sometimes applied to an opening or door in an aircraft, esp. one in the deck of an aircraft or in the top and bottom of the fuselage. **1962** D. SLAYTON in *Into Orbit* 26 We asked them to adapt the entry hatch and convert it into an exit, too. **1969** *Times* 23 May 1/2 The two craft are linked by a 3 ft. connecting tunnel, sealed at each end by a hatch.

4. *fig.* ***under (the) hatches***: Down in position or circumstances; in a state of depression, humiliation, subjection, or restraint; down out of sight.
c **1550** *Dice-Play* (Percy Soc.) 21 Ye have.. brought yourself.. so far under the hatches.. that ye cannot find the way to rise again. **1621** BURTON *Anat. Mel.* I. ii. iv. vi. (1651) 156 If he be poor.. he is under hatches, dejected, rejected and forsaken. **1649** MILTON *Eikon.* xxvii. 511 In this servile condition to have kept us still under hatches. **1678-9** FOULKES *Alarm Sinn.* 7 Conscience has been kept under hatches. **1710** in Hearne *Collect.* 7 Mar. (O.H.S.) II. 356 The Whigs must.. think the Church under Hatches. **1818** KEATS *Lett.* Wks. 1889 III. 143 It is impossible to live in a country which is continually under hatches.

5. *transf.* **a.** An opening in the floor of a timber-shed or other building, which is covered by a trapdoor; also, the trapdoor itself.
1888 in *Ward & Lock's Techn. Dict.*

†**b.** *Mining.* An opening made in the ground.
1671 *Phil. Trans.* VI. 2099 We sink.. an Essay hatch (an orifice made for the search of a vein). **1753** CHAMBERS *Cycl. Supp., Hatches*.. used in Cornwal, to express any of the openings of the earth, either into mines, or in search of them.

6. A flood-gate or sluice. See also quot. 1727-51.
1531-2 *Act 23 Hen. VIII*, c. 8 §1 All the sand, stones, grauell, and robell digged about.. the said tin, there to be wholly and surely kept, by the said hatches and ties, out and from the said fresh riuers or water-courses. **1587** [see FLOOD-HATCH]. **1669** WORLIDGE *Syst. Agric.* (1681) 326 *Hatches*, Flud-gates placed in the water to obstruct its Current. **1727-51** CHAMBERS *Cycl., Hatches*.. the word is particularly used for certain dams, or mounds.. to prevent the water that issues from the stream-works, and tin-washes in Cornwal, from running into the fresh rivers. **1758** *Descr. Thames* 60 The Navigation.. was impeded by Hatches, Stopps and Wears. **1840** COL. HAWKER *Diary* (1893) II. 187 The water suddenly abated, and we then opened the doors, and let it pour from the rooms as from a mill hatch. **1879** JEFFERIES *Wild Life in S. Co....* The farmers lower down the brook pull up the hatches to let the flood pass.

7. 'A contrivance for trapping salmon' (Smyth *Sailor's Word-bk.* 1867). Cf. HECK *sb.*[1] 2.
1826 J. THOMSON *Etym. Eng. Wds.* s.v., A salmon caught in a machine called a *hek* or *hatch*.

8. A wooden bed-frame. ? *Obs.*
a **1832** SCOTT (Webster 1864), A rude wooden stool, and still ruder hatch or bed-frame.

9. *attrib* and *Comb.*, as (sense 1) †***hatch-stead***; (3) ***hatch-man, -nail, -noup, -ring***; (3 c) ***hatch-head, -ladder***; **hatchback** orig. *N. Amer.*, an upward-opening rear door on a motor car (usu. giving access to storage space which can be greatly increased by folding down the rear seat); a car having such a door; **hatch-bar, hatch-deck** (see quots.); **hatch-gate**, (*a*) a wicket, (*b*) = sense 6.
1970 *N.Y. Times* Apr. 29 81/2 A *hatchback is a combination back-window-trunk lid, hinged at the roof, that swings up to allow maximum access to the trunk space. **1970** *Time* 21 Sept. 92 The basic list price of the Vega 2300 .. comes out to.. $2,197 for a 'hatchback'. **1973** *Times* 4 Oct. 43/2 The coupé, with a fashionable hatch back (the window is part of the boot lid) is pretty and practical. **1974** *Daily Tel.* 23 Oct. 14/2 A 'hatchback', or three-door, design with folding rear seat would obviously be more expensive. **1976** B. BOVA *Multiple Man* (1977) iv. 49 Little electric hatchbacks driven by young mothers out for their shopping. **1984** *Daily Tel.* 9 Oct. 10/3 The Escort is one of the few hatchbacks with a genuine Estate version. **1828** WEBSTER s.v. *Hatch*, The grate or frame of cross-bars laid over the opening in a ship's deck, now called **hatch-bars*. **1867** SMYTH *Sailor's Word-bk., Hatch-bars*, to secure the hatches. *Ibid.*, **Hatch-deck*, gun brigs had hatches instead of lower decks. **1824** MISS MITFORD *Village* Ser. I. (1863) 74 We reached the *hatch gate, with the white cottage beside it. **1867** F. FRANCIS *Angling* iii. (1880) 89 Some lock or hatch-gate. **1894** HALL CAINE *Manxman* v. iii, The sea.. washed the faces of the men as they sat in oilskins on the *hatch-head. **1465** *Mann. & Househ. Exp.* 201 Item, for iiij. c. *hache nayle, xvj. d. **1785** *Gentl. Mag.* LV. I. 429 Ventilators .. placed at the fore, main, and mizen *hatch-noup. ? c **1475** *Hunt. Hare* 261 Thei myghtt not passe the dure threscwold, Nor lope ouer the *hache-styd.

hatch, *sb.*[2] [f. HATCH *v.*[1]] The action of hatching, incubation; that which is hatched; a brood (of young). Also in phr. ***hatches, matches, and dispatches*** (occas. in *sing.*), a newspaper list of births, marriages, and deaths.
1629 GAULE *Holy Madn.* 244 A Serpent of a Difficult hatch, and dangerous. **1797-1804** BEWICK *Brit. Birds* (1847) I. 145 These birds make a second hatch. **1859** DARWIN *Orig. Spec.* ix. (1878) 240 Two hybrids from the same parent but from different hatches. **1875** WHYTE MELVILLE *Katerfelto* ii. (1876) 15 If she addles all these as she addled the last hatch, I'll forswear keeping fowls. **1878** J. PAYN *By Proxy* I. xix. 217 First came the Births, Deaths, and Marriages... The female mind.. takes an interest in the 'Hatch, Match, and Despatch' of its fellow-creatures. **1880** *Times for Year 1980* 1/1 Hatches... Matches... Despatches. **1894** *Field* 9 June 832/1 There was a good hatch of Mayfly, and the fish were taking them fairly well. **1953** M. STEEN *Anna Fitzalan* viii. 215 Dismissing reviews.. Lin turned to what Mummy called Hatches, Matches and Despatches. **1959** F. KING *So Hurt & Humiliated* 128 Glancing through the 'Hatches, Matches, Despatches' columns in *The Times* at breakfast, Emily suddenly interrupted my reading of the *Economist*. **1966** 'H. HOWARD' *Counterfeit* iii. 57 He might even be a registrar of births, marriages and deaths—the man who issued certificates for what people used to call Hatches, Matches and Despatches.
fig. **1597** SHAKS. *2 Hen. IV*, III. i. 86 Such things become the Hatch and Brood of Time. **1602** —— *Ham.* III. i. 174 There's something in his soule, O're which his Melancholly sits on brood, And I do doubt the hatch, and the disclose Will be some danger. **1624** F. WHITE *Repl. Fisher* 297 The canonizing of Saints by Popes is of a latter hatch.

hatch, *sb.*[3] Also 7 **hache.** [f. HATCH *v.*[2]] An engraved line or stroke; esp. one of those by which shading is represented in an engraving.
1658 SIR. T. BROWNE *Gard. Cyrus* ii. 110 Sculptors in their strongest shadows.. do draw their double Haches. **1662** EVELYN *Chalcogr.* v. 118 The conducting of Hatches and stroaks, whether with pen, point, or Graver. *Ibid.* v. 129 To discern an Original print from a Copy print.. is a knack very easily attain'd; because 'tis almost impossible to imitate every hatch, and to make the stroaks of exact and equal dimensions. **1747** CREED in *Phil. Trans.* XLIV. 449 Sounds of minute Duration will be expressed by the Pencils by small Hatches geometrically proportion'd to those Durations. **1811** *Self Instructor* 524 Working in hatches with a middling full pencil. **1855** tr. *Labarte's Arts Mid. Ages* iv. 180 He uses but few hatches in his shadows.

†**hatch**, *sb.*[4] *Obs.* [a. F. *hache* hatchet: see HACHE.] A hatchet.
1704 in B. Church *Hist. Philip's War* (1867) II. 132, 100 large Hatches or light Axes made pretty broad. **1716** *Ibid.* (1865) I. 33 To run upon them with their Hatches. **1810** *Naval Chron.* XXIV. 197 To demand three whale teeth and twelve hatches for their ransom.

†**hatch**, *sb.*[5] *Obs.* [? var. of HITCH.] A knot.
1688 R. HOLME *Armoury* III. 288/2 At a Hundred threds round the Reel.. Housewives make a Hatch as some call it, or a Knot, or an Hank.

hatch, *sb.*[6] *Curling.* = HACK *sb.*[1] 2 b.
a **1812** [see HACK *sb.*[1] 2 b].

hatch, *v.*[1] Forms: 3 *pa. t.* **haȝte**, 4 *pa. pple.* **y-haht, i-heyȝt**, 5 **haughte**; 4-6 **hacche**, 5 **hetch**, 5-6 **hatche**, 7 **hach**, 6- **hatch**. [Early ME. *hacche(n*, pa. t. *haȝte*, prob.:—OE. **hæccean* (not recorded): related to MHG. *hecken* (see Grimm H 746), Sw. *häcka*, Da. *hække* to hatch from the egg. Ulterior etymology unknown.]

1. *intr.* To bring forth young birds from the egg by incubation.
a **1250** *Owl & Night.* 105 Thu.. leidest thar-on thy fole ey; Tho hit bi-com that he haȝte, And of his eyre briddes y-raȝte. **1399** LANGL. *Rich. Redeles* III. 444 þis brid.. hopith ffor to hacche or heruest begynne. **1573-80** BARET *Alv.* H 226 That hath lately hatched, or brought forth.. *effœtus*. **1719** D'URFEY *Pills* (1872) VI. 316 My Hen has hatched to-day. **1879** *Daily News* 19 Apr. 3/3 Robins and hedge-sparrows are now setting or hatching-out.

2. *trans.* To bring forth from the egg either by natural or artificial heat. (Also with *forth, out.*)
a. with the young as obj.
1398 TREVISA *Barth. De P.R.* XII. i. (Tollem. MS.), Whan hire ȝonge briddes beþ newliche i heyȝt [**1495** haughte]. c **1440** *Promp. Parv.* 232/2 Hetchyd, as byrdys, *pullificatus, fetatus*. **1545** JOYE *Exp. Dan.* 2 These.. wil sitte their egges and hatche forth their chikens. **1577** B. GOOGE *Heresbach's Husb.* IV. (1586) 160 You must not take the chickins away as they be hatcht. **1653** WALTON *Angler* x. 189 Barnacles and young Goslings bred by the Suns heat and the rotten planks of an old Ship, and hatched of trees. **1774** GOLDSM. *Nat. Hist.* (1776) V. 241 In this fortress the male and female hatch and bring up their brood with security. **1890** *Spectator* 8 Feb., One of them having failed to hatch out a brood.

b. with the egg as obj.: To incubate.
1382 WYCLIF *Isa.* lix. 5 [The ey] that is hacchid, shal breken out in to a cokatrice. **1555** EDEN *Decades* 9 Sume haue alredy hatched their egges. **1698** FRYER *Acc. E. India & P.* 424 Turtles, or Tortoises.. came ashoar to lay their Eggs, which these Sands hatch. **1834** MCMURTRIE *Cuvier's Anim. Kingd.* 168 No Reptile hatches its eggs. **1846** J. BAXTER *Libr. Pract. Agric.* (ed. 4) II. 4 These eggs are hatched by the heat of the sun.

3. *intr.* for *pass.* **a.** Of the young: To come forth from the egg. **b.** Said of the egg.
1593 SHAKS. *Lucr.* 849 Why should.. hateful cuckoos hatch in sparrows' nest? **1727-51** CHAMBERS *Cycl.* s.v. *Hatching*, After this they put in the eggs to hatch. **1867** F. FRANCIS *Angling* v. (1880) 178 Larvæ rising from the bottom to hatch out. **1888** LLOYD PRYCE *Pheasant Rearing* 26 The eggs will hatch out in from twenty-three to twenty-five days.

4. *transf.* (*trans.*) Of other animals, and generally: To bring forth, bring into existence, breed.
a **1327** *Pol. Songs* (Camden) 237 Gedelynges.. Palefreiours ant pages, Ant boyes with boste; Alle weren y-haht Of an horse thoste. **1587** *Mirr. Mag., Bladud* xvii, Would you not maruell then, what monsters now doth nature hatche. **1692** RAY *Dissol. World* ii. (1732) 7 Hatching .. or quickening and bringing to Perfection the Seeds. **1791** W. BARTRAM *Carolina* 7 Serving as a nursery bed to hatch.. the infant plant. a **1845** HOOD *To Sylv. Urban* vii, Parishioners,—hatched,—husbanded,—and wived.

†**5.** *intr.* To brood (*fig.*) *Obs.*
1655 H. VAUGHAN *Silex Scint.* 62 Thick darkness lyes And hatcheth o'er thy people.

6. a. *fig.* (*trans.*) To bring to maturity or full development, esp. by a covert or clandestine process; to contrive, devise, originate and develop. Also with *up, forth.*
1549 COVERDALE, etc. *Erasm. Par. Jas.* 39 Other mennes swette hatched vp you. **1596** BELL *Surv. Popery* III. x. 436 Transubstantiation.. was first hatched by pope Innocentius the third of that name. **1605** CAMDEN *Rem.* (1637) 298 He that mischiefe hatcheth, mischiefe catcheth. **1678** WANLEY *Wond. Lit. World* v. i. §100. 468/2 The Gunpowder Treason was hatched here in England. **1778** MAD. D'ARBLAY *Diary* 23 Aug., How I wish you would hatch up a comedy between you! **1873** S. & J. HORNER *Florence* I. xviii. 274 Charged with hatching plots against the State.

b. *intr.* for *pass.* (in *to be hatching*, orig. from vbl. sb., *to be a-hatching.*)
1646 CRASHAW *Steps to Temple* 74 Who finds his warm heart hatch into a nest Of little eagles and young loves. **1654** TRAPP *Comm. Jer.* ii. 2 Treason hatching in his heart. **1741** MIDDLETON *Cicero* I. II. 140 The great dangers and plots, that were now hatching against the State.

Hence **hatched** *ppl. a.*; **hatcha'bility**, the condition or state of being likely to hatch, or able to produce eggs which will hatch.
1781 COWPER *Retirement* 64 These hatched, and those resuscitated worms. **1863** MRS. C. CLARKE *Shaks. Char.* xix. 484 They suspected it to be a hatched rumour. **1916** *Experiment Station Rec.* Feb. 178 The hatchability of eggs which are produced. **1950** *N.Z. Jrnl. Agric.* Jan. 14/1 Work is involved in keeping data about the hatchability of the eggs from each pen. **1956** *New Biol.* XXI. 116 There is evidence

that the presence of earth-worms in soil increases the hatchability of the cysts of the potato root eelworm. **1960** *Farmer & Stockbreeder* 9 Feb. 87 Greater egg production, better grading, increased hatchability.

hatch, *v.*² Also 5-6 hach(e. [a. F. *hache-r* to cut, hack, draw lines upon metal, paper, etc., f. *hache* hatchet: see HACHE; cf. CROSS-HATCH.]

1. *trans.* To cut, engrave, or draw a series of lines, generally parallel, on (a metal, wood, or paper surface); chiefly used for shading in engraving or drawing. In quot. 1598 used of 'cutting' a file.

1598 SYLVESTER *Du Bartas* II. i. IV. *Handie-crafts* 522 He hatcheth files, and hollow vices wormeth. **1661** MORGAN *Sph. Gentry* I. i. 3 Sable..is aptly expressed by lines hatchid across one another. **1703** MOXON *Mech. Exerc.* 55 This Globular end must be Hatch'd with a fine cut, by a File-cutter. **1793** SMEATON *Edystone L.* 194 Distinguished in the plan by being hatched with slant lines. **1833** J. HOLLAND *Manuf. Metal* II. 82 Having heated the steel..they hatch it over and across with the knife.

transf. **1858** HERSCHEL *Outl. Astron.* vii. §430 (ed. 5) 283 The exterior of another [moon crater] is all hatched over with deep gullies.

absol. **1601** HOLLAND *Pliny* XXXV. x. II. 535 To hach also, yea and to fill within, requireth..much labour. **1669** A. BROWNE *Ars Pict.* 101 Before that you begin to Hatch or shadow, you must draw all the outmost lines with a needle.

2. To inlay with narrow strips or lines of a different substance; to lay strips or plates of gold or silver in or on (a surface) by way of ornament. (In quot. 1480 with the material inlaid as obj.)

1480 *Wardr. Acc. Edw. IV* (1830) 160, xij yerdes of clothe of silver hached uppon satyn grounde. **1548** HALL *Chron., Hen. VIII*, 77 The fether was blacke and hached with gold. **1599** NASHE *Lenten Stuffe* (1871) 35, I might enamel and hatch ouer this deuice more artificially and masterly. **1621** HAKEWILL *David's Vow* 224 The handle or pummell hatcht or inameld. **1679** *Lond. Gaz.* No. 1395/4 A Hanger, with a Sawe on the back, hatch'd with silver. **1820** SCOTT *Monast.* xvi, The poignet being of silver exquisitely hatched.

3. *transf.* and *fig.*

a **1556** *Harpalus' Compl.* ix. in Gilfillan *Less-known Poets* (1859) I. 129 It seem'd unhap had him long hatcht In midst of his dispairs. *a* **1613** OVERBURY *A Wife* (1638) 218 A Rymer Is a fellow whose face is hatcht all over with impudence. *a* **1621** BEAUM. & FL. *Thierry & Theodoret* II. iii, A fair design..To which your worth is wedded, your profession Hatch'd in, and made one piece. **1649** G. DANIEL *Trinarch., Hen. IV*, ccxxv, His sword..Hatch't in Blood Royall. **1658** BRATHWAIT *Honest Ghost*, To State Censor A iv, A Rubrick Story, ach't in blood.

Hence **hatched** *ppl. a.* ***hatched moulding***: a kind of moulding used in Norman architecture, formed with two series of oblique parallel incisions crossing each other.

1607 MIDDLETON *Your Five Gallants* II. iii, One gilt hatcht rapier and dagger. **1842-76** GWILT *Archit.* §397 The most usual ornaments were..7. The hatched. **1846** PARKER *Gloss. Archit.* s.v. *Moulding*, The *Hatched* moulding is also not uncommon, and is found early in the style, as it can be cut conveniently without the aid of a chisel, with the pick only. **1868** G. STEPHENS *Runic Mon.* I. 223 Simple carvings, chiefly hatcht work or straight lines.

†**hatch**, *v.*³ *Obs.* [f. HATCH *sb.*¹] *trans.* To close (a door) with a hatch; to close.

1581 SIDNEY *Astr. & Stella* xxxviii, While sleepe begins with heauy wings To hatch mine eyes. **1608** SHAKS. *Per.* IV. ii. 37 'Twere not amiss to keep our door hatched.

†**hatch**, *v.*⁴ *Obs.* [var. of HACK *v.*¹] *trans.* To hoe (seed) *into* the ground; = HACK *v.*¹ 4.

1653 PLAT *Gard. Eden* 78 Hatch them into the ground with a rake striken thicke upon them.

†**hatch**, *v.*⁵ *Obs.* [Cf. HACK *v.*¹ 13.] *intr.* To cough.

1733 *Revolution Politicks* III. 63 His Holiness..when my Lord had gone a pretty way in his Speech, did mimick, hatch, and pretend to be taken with a violent Fit of Coughing.

hatch, *v.*⁶, obs. var. of HITCH *v.*

c **1440** *Promp. Parv.* 239/2 Hatchyd, or remevyd (*K.* hichid, *S.* hychyd), *amotus, remotus.*

'hatch-boat. [f. HATCH *sb.*¹ + BOAT *sb.*]

a. 'A sort of small vessel known as a pilot boat, having a deck composed almost entirely of hatches' (Smyth *Sailor's Word-bk.*). **b.** 'A kind of half-decked fishing boat; one which has a hatch or well for keeping fish' (Simmonds *Dict. Trade* 1858).

1867 J. MACGREGOR *Voy. Alone* iii. 47 The poor little hatch-boat has come near with..its scanty crew.

hatchel ('hætʃ(ə)l), *sb.* Forms: α. 4 hechele, hechil, 5 hychele, 6-7 hetchell, -ill, hichel, 7 (9- *dial.* and *U.S.*) hetchel, hitchel. β. 7-9 hatchel(l. [A parallel form to HACKLE *sb.*², q.v. for etymological relations. Of the various Eng. forms, *hechele* (*hetchel*) and *hekele*, are the earlier, and appear to be the southern and northern forms of OE. **hęcel*; while *hackle* and *hatchel* point to a parallel form **hæcel*. *Hatchel* may be merely a late variant of *hetchel* with the vowel assimilated to *hackle*; *hitchel* seems to be a casual variant.] An instrument for combing flax or hemp; = HACKLE *sb.*², HECKLE. See also HETCHEL *sb.*

α. *a* **1300** *Sat. People Kildare* xix. in *E.E.P.* (1862) 155 Ich makid on of ȝou sit opon a hechil. **14..** *Voc.* in Wr.-Wülcker 595/12 *Mataxa*, an hychele. **1530** PALSGR. 231/1 Hetchell for flaxe, *serancq, serant.* **1622** MABBE tr. *Aleman's Guzman d'Alf.* II. 261 Spindles, reeles, distaffes, and hitchels for flaxe. **1656** BLOUNT *Glossogr., Hichel.* **1869** MRS. STOWE *Oldtown Folks* xlii. 530 She don' know no more 'bout religion than an old hetchel. **1900** J. SHELTON *Salt-box House* xvii. 143 Mops were made of corn-husks bound to a handle, the husks having been drawn through a hetchel which shredded them.

β. **1611** COTGR., *Ferreur*, a flax-combe, or hatchell. **1656** W. D. tr. *Comenius' Gate Lat. Unl.* ¶385 They are..hatchelled with an iron hatchell. **1794** *Rigging & Seamanship* I. 54 *A Hatchell*..has forty sharp-pointed iron teeth, one foot long, fixed in wood. **1853** J. S. BARRY *Hist. Sk. Hanover, Mass.* 38 The hatchel, and swingling-knife, alas! are numbered..with the things that were but are not!

b. *attrib.* and *Comb.*, as ***hatchel-maker, -teeth.***

14.. *Voc.* in Wr.-Wülcker 595/14 *Mataxarius*, an hychel-maker. **1601** HOLLAND *Pliny* II. 4 Kembed with hetchell teeth of yron. **1721-2** in *Hist. Northfield, Mass.* (1875) 160 To making 36 hatchel teeth o 3 o.

hatchel, *v.* Forms: α. 4 hecchele, 5 hychele, 6 hetchyll, 7 (9- *dial.* and *U.S.*) hetchel, hitchel. β. 6 hachell, 6-9 hatchel(l. [f. prec.; cf. HACKLE, HECKLE.]

1. a. *trans.* To dress (flax or hemp) with a hatchel; to hackle.

α. *c* **1325** *Gloss. W. de Biblesw.* in Wright *Voc.* 156 La serence [*gloss* the hechele] dont pernet E vostre lyn serencet [*gloss* hechelet]. **1398** TREVISA *Barth. De P.R.* XVII. xcvii. (Tollem. MS.), [Flax] is knokked and bett..ribbed and hecchelid [**1535** heckled] and sponne. **14..** *Voc.* in Wr.-Wülcker 595/11 *Mataxo*, to hychele. **1530** PALSGR. 583/2, I hetchyll, *je cerance.* **1649** BLITHE *Eng. Improv. Impr.* (1653) 260-1 Hetchelling and dressing it up.

β. **1580** HOLLYBAND *Treas. Fr. Tong, Serancer du lin*, to hatchell flaxe. **1608** HEYWOOD *Lucrece* II. ii. (Song), She her flaxe and tow did hatchel. **1692** *Lond. Gaz.* No. 2729/4 Breaking, Swingling, and preparing it to be Hatchelled. **1883** *Harper's Mag.* Aug. 390/1 The flax is..hatchelled to..arrange the fibres for spinning.

b. *transf.*

1845 S. JUDD *Margaret* I. xiii. 100 The clouds hung low, and their floating skirts seemed to be pierced and hetchelled by the trees.

2. *fig.* To harass, worry; cf. HECKLE. *rare.*

1800 *Aurora* (Phila.) 20 Oct. (Th.), They have..hatchelled them with prosecutions, fines, and imprisonments. **1833** CARLYLE *Cagliostro* in *Misc. Ess.* (1888) V. 95 Bewritted, fleeced, hatchelled, bewildered and bedevilled. **1878** *Harper's Mag.* LVII. 576 She'll hetchel the old woman mortally, I be afraid. **1897** *Westm. Gaz.* 10 Aug. 8/1 He doesn't 'hetchel' either of them into misery. **1906** C. H. PARKHURST *Lower than Angels* 18 Mercilessly hetchelled by some prosecuting attorney.

Hence **'hatchelled** *ppl. a.*, **'hatchelling** *vbl. sb.*; also **'hatcheller**, a flax-dresser, heckler.

14.. *Voc.* in Wr.-Wülcker 595/13 *Mataxator, mataxatrix*, an hycheler. **1573** *Lanc. Wills* III. 62, xx knokes of hatchelled lyne. **1601** HOLLAND *Pliny* XIX. i, The short shuds or shives that are..parted in the hetchelling. **1611** COTGR., *Serancier*, a flax-man, a hatcheller, or comber of flax. **1656** W. D. tr. *Comenius' Gate Lat. Unl.* ¶385 That which is separated in hatchelling is hurds and tow. **1794** *Rigging & Seamanship* I. 56 Over which is the hatchelling-loft. **1798** F. LEIGHTON *Let. to J. Boucher* 17 Mar. (MS.), I have lately met with a Shropshire word new to me, viz. Hatcheler, it means a dresser of flax or hemp.

hatcher ('hætʃə(r)). [f. HATCH *v.*¹ + -ER¹.]

1. One who or that which hatches (eggs).

1632 LITHGOW *Trav.* IX. 381 The Oven producing..three or foure hundred living Chickens..the Hatcher or Curator, is onely Recompensed according to the living numbers. **1708** MOTTEUX *Rabelais* V. viii. (1737) 30 A Curse light on the Hatcher of the ill Bird. **1838** *Tait's Mag.* V. 600 Those diligent hatchers who cackle so much and sit so little.

b. *spec.* A contrivance in which eggs are hatched; an incubator.

1884 DAY in *Fisheries Exhib. Lit.* II. 84 Chester's semi-rotating hatcher. **1888** LLOYD PRYCE *Pheasant Rearing* 37 Take them [the eggs] from under the hen, and place them in the drawer of the hatcher.

2. *fig.* A contriver, deviser, plotter, covert or clandestine producer.

1581 SAVILE *Tacitus' Hist.* I. vii. (1591) 5 The crime whereof themselves were the hatchers. **1647** TRAPP *Comm. Eph.* v. 3 He found theaters to be the very hatchers of all wickednesse. **1704** SWIFT *T. Tub* ix, A great hatcher and breeder of business. **1883** SIR T. MARTIN *Ld. Lyndhurst* v. 135 His informant, as the hatchers of anecdotes too often are, was under a delusion.

hatchery ('hætʃərɪ). [f. HATCH *v.*¹ + -ERY.] A hatching establishment; *spec.* one for hatching the ova of fish by artificial means. Also *fig.*

1880 *Times* 17 Sept. 4/2 Means of introducing each year numbers of young fry from 'hatcheries'. **1884** *Harper's Mag.* Aug. 481/1 New trout and salmon hatchery opened at Linlithgow. **1885** *Times* 18 Sept. 3 The Government may..see the importance..of fish hatcheries. **1932** A. HUXLEY *Brave New World* i. 1 Central London hatchery and conditioning centre. **1932** M. A. JULL *Poultry Breeding* xi. 347 Sanitary conditions at hatcheries must be approved by the hatchery inspector. Only eggs from approved hatchery flocks may be incubated. **1942** D. MITRANY in *Agenda* I. 305 The T.V.A. is itself a hatchery of public enterprise. **1952** *Oxf. Jun. Encycl.* VI. 360/2 Some poultry-farmers do not hatch eggs from their own birds but buy day-old chicks from 'hatcheries', which are places that do nothing but incubate eggs on a very large scale.

hatchet ('hætʃɪt), *sb.* Forms: 4-6 **hachet**, 4 **acchett, hachit,** 5 **hachytt, hacchet,** 6 **hach-, hatchette,** 5- **hatchet** (7 **-ed**). [a. F. *hachette* fem. (13th c. *hacete* in Littré), dim. f. *hache* axe. In 15th c., F. had also *hachet* (masc.).]

1. A smaller or lighter axe with a short handle, adapted for use with one hand.

1375 BARBOUR *Bruce* x. 174 A ȝheman..suld dryf the vayn, and ber Ane hachit, that war scharp to scher, Vndir his belt. **1377** LANGL. *P. Pl.* B. III. 304 Alle þat bereþ..Axe, oþer hachet [C. IV. 362 acchett]. *c* **1400** MAUNDEV. (Roxb.) xxi. 94 Men hewez with a hacchet aboute þe fote of þe tree. **1474** CAXTON *Chesse* 61 He ought to haue on his gyrdel a sharpe or crokyd hatchet. **1577** B. GOOGE *Heresbach's Husb.* I. (1586) 11 b, Axes, Hatchettes, and Sithes, of all sortes. **1677** W. HUBBARD *Narrative* (1865) II. 114 The Indians..knocked the poor Maid down with their Hatchets, and gave her many Wounds. **1703** MOXON *Mech. Exerc.* 95 The Hatchet..is to Hew the Irregularities off such pieces of Stuff which may be sooner Hewn than Sawn. **1851** D. WILSON *Preh. Ann.* I. vi. 184 Hatchets or wedges are among the most abundant..relics of the Stone period.

2. Phrases. † ***to hang up one's hatchet***: to cease from one's labours; to take a rest. *Obs.* ***to take*** or ***dig up the hatchet***: to take up arms in warfare, to commence hostilities. ***to bury the hatchet***: to lay down one's arms; to cease from hostilities. (These two phrases are derived from the customs of the North American Indians.) ***to throw*** (***fling, sling***) ***the hatchet***: to make exaggerated statements. See also HELVE and BURY *v.* 2 a.

a **1327** *Pol. Songs* (Camden) 223 Hang up thyn hachet ant thi knyf, Whil him lasteth the lyf with the longe shonkes. *c* **1430** *Hymns Virg.* (1867) 69 Hange up þin hachet & take þi reste. *c* **1530** R. HILLES *Common-Pl. Bk.* (1858) 140 When thou hast well done hang up thy hatchet. **1753** G. WASHINGTON *Jrnl.* Writ. 1889 I. 21 Three Nations of French Indians..had taken up the Hatchet against the English. **1780** G. PARKER *Life's Painter* xii. 85 Many..habituate themselves by degrees to a mode of the hatchet-flinging extreme. **1794** J. JAY *Corr. & Pub. Papers* (1893) IV. 147 To use an Indian figure, may the hatchet henceforth be buried for ever. **1837** W. IRVING *Capt. Bonneville* III. 219 The chiefs met; the amicable pipe was smoked, the hatchet buried, and peace formally proclaimed. **1893** T. B. FOREMAN *Trip to Spain* 97 The ladies titter, knowing, as we do, the skipper's habit of slinging the hatchet.

3. *attrib.* and *Comb.*, as ***hatchet-edge, -head, -work***; ***hatchet-like*** adj.; ***hatchet-fashion*** adv.; **hatchet-face**, a narrow and very sharp face: so **hatchet-fist, -jaw**; **hatchet-faced** *a.*, having a hatchet-face: so **hatchet-headed** *a.*; **hatchet fish**, a member of the family Gasteropelecidæ, South American flying characins which are often kept in aquaria, or one of the family Sternoptychidæ, deep-sea clupeiform fishes found in most of the oceans of the world; also *hatchet* ellipt.; †**hatchet-fitch** (*vetch*), a leguminous plant, *Securigera Coronilla* = AX-FITCH; **hatchet-job, -work** (see HATCHET-MAN 3); **hatchet-stake**, a small anvil for bending thin sheet metal.

1858 H. MILLER *Cruise Betsy* vi. 98 The Scuir..resembled a sharp *hatchet-edge presented to the sky. **1650-66** WHARTON *Wks.* (1683) 389 Their Prodigious Ears, Short Hair, and *Hatchet-Faces. **1707** J. STEVENS tr. *Quevedo's Com. Wks.* (1709) 372 A Lanthorn Jaw'd Woman, with a Hatchet Face. **1855** MACAULAY *Hist. Eng.* xviii. (1871) II. 351 They had pulled him about and called him Hatchet-face! *a* **1700** B. E. *Dict. Cant. Crew*, **Hatchet-fac'd*, Hard-favor'd, Homely. **1824** W. IRVING *T. Trav.* I. 12 A thin hatchet-faced gentleman, with projecting eyes like a lobster. **1798** *Sporting Mag.* XII. 18 A most violent and unexpected blow of his *hatchet fist. **1597** GERARDE *Herbal* II. d. 1055 *Hatchet Fetches. *Ibid.* 1057 In English, Axseed, Axwoort, Ax-fitch, and Hatchet Fitch. **1829-55** *Loudon's Encycl. Plants* 638 Hatchet Vetch. **1931** J. R. NORMAN *Hist. Fishes* xii. 231 (*caption*) *Hatchet-fish (*Argyropelecus* sp.). **1959** P. CAPON *Amongst those Missing* 196 Hatchet-fish skimmed the water. **1960** M. BURTON *Under Sea* xi. 198 Another consumer of small prey is the 'hatchet' fish, so called because its body is flattened from side-to-side... For the most part hatchets are only a few inches long. **1962** K. F. LAGLER et al. *Ichthyology* ii. 36 Family Sternoptychidae—deepsea hatchet fishes. **1845** STOCQUELER *Handbk. Brit. India* (1854) 322 The heavy-shouldered, *hatchet-headed, zebra-striped brute before him. **1836** H. G. KNIGHT *Archit. Tour Normandy* xxiii. 199 The most common mouldings are the billet, the nail-head, the chevron, the zig-zag or embattled frette, *hatchet, nebule, star, rope, beak-head, dog-tooth. **1697** DAMPIER *Voy.* I. 85 This their digging or *hatchet work they help out by fire..making the inside of their Canoa hollow. **1849** RUSKIN *Sev. Lamps* i. §10. 20 Choose..the Norman hatchet work, instead of the Flaxman frieze and statue.

Hence **hatchet** *v. trans.*, †(*a*) to cut with a hatchet; (*b*) *transf.* to act as a hatchet-man against (someone), to do down.

1603 FLORIO *Montaigne* Ded., I..serve but as Vulcan to hatchet this Minerva from that Jupiter's bigge braine. **1700** S. PARKER *Six Phil. Ess.* 36 A large stump of a Tree..hatcheted into an Elbow Chair. **1959** 'B. O'BRIEN' *Operators & Things* (1960) i. 34 Even the Knoxes were willing to hatchet each other.

'hatchet-man. [f. HATCHET *sb.* + MAN *sb.*¹]

†**1.** A pioneer or axeman serving in a military unit. *U.S. Obs.*

1755 G. WASHINGTON *Lett.* Writ. 1889 I. 299 *note*, to detain both mulattoes and negroes..and employ them as Pioneers or Hatchetmen.

2. In the U.S., a hired Chinese assassin. Also *transf.*

1880 G. B. DENSMORE *Chinese in California* xii. 94 Some of them are called hatchet-men. They carry a hatchet with the handle cut off. **1888** *Boston Jrnl.* 3 May 1/2 The work of the hatchetmen among the enemies of the organization. **1913** J. LONDON *Valley of Moon* III. xx, Chan Chi, had been a hatchet-man of note, in the old fighting days of the San Francisco tongs. **1957** P. FRANK *Seven Days to Never* III. iii. 90 He was a hatchet man for the NKVD... He may have delivered Beria over to Malenkov and Krushchev.

3. (Now the usual sense.) A person, especially a journalist, employed to attack and destroy other people's reputations. So ***hatchet job, work.*** orig. *U.S.*

1944 *Time* 23 Oct. 20 Exuberant hatchet jobs were..done on Foster Dulles because of his Wall Street connections. **1952** *Manch. Guardian Weekly* 3 Apr. 15/4 Republican hatchet-men. **1959** *Encounter* July 83/1 One has no difficulty in recognising the familiar tones of Dr. Leavis' hatchet-men when he is attacked. **1959** *Guardian* 13 Oct. 7/4 One critic.. was the meanest son of a bitch that ever lived. His criticism was a hatchet job on every book. **1960** *News Chron.* 14 July 1/5 The Kennedy family went into action with a commando team of political hatchet-men. **1961** M. MCCARTHY *On Contrary* (1962) I. 87 The literary Communists..doing the hatchet work on artists' reputations. **1962** *Listener* 21 June 1089/1 It was difficult enough to sympathise with the hero once we'd seen him doing his hatchet work.

hatchettin ('hætʃɪtɪn). *Min.* Also **-ettine, -etin(e.** [Named after C. Hatchett, the discoverer of columbium and tantalium: see -IN.]

1. = next.

1821 *Thomson's Annals* Ser. II. I. 136 It should be distinguished by the name of Hatchetine. **1852** *W. Phillips' Elem. Introd. Min.* 627. **1861** BRISTOW *Gloss. Min., Hatchettine*, a Mineral Tallow. Occurs either flaky like spermaceti, or subgranular like bees-wax. **1881** *Pop. Educ.* VI. 50 Mineral tallow or hatchetine is the lightest of the known minerals, its specific gravity being 0.6078.

2. = CHRISMATITE.

1868 DANA *Min.* 728.

hatchettite ('hætʃɪtaɪt). *Min.* [f. as prec. + -ITE.] A yellowish-white subtransparent fossil resin or wax-like hydrocarbon found in the coal-measures of South Wales.

1868 DANA *Min.* 732 Conybeare..stated that.. hatchettite melts in warm water under 170° F.

hatchettolite ('hætʃɪtəʊlaɪt). *Min.* [f. as prec. + -LITE.] A columbate of uranium, of yellow-brown colour and resinous lustre.

1877 *Amer. Jrnl. Sc.* Ser. III. XIII. 369 Hatchettolite is doubtless a neutral columbate of uranium oxide and lime.

hatchety ('hætʃɪtɪ), *a.* [f. HATCHET + -Y.] Resembling a hatchet; thin and sharp: said of the face. Cf. *hatchet-faced.*

1851 *Fraser's Mag.* XLIII. 654 Losing had a thin hatchety face. **1873** BESANT & RICE *Little Girl* II. vi. 82 Some of them are flat-faced, some of them are inclined to be 'hatchety'. **1889** *Pall Mall G.* 11 July 3/2 The other a hatchety-faced woman.

hatching ('hætʃɪŋ), *vbl. sb.*^{1} [f. HATCH *v.*^{1}]

a. The action of HATCH *v.*^{1} in its various senses. Also, that which is hatched, a brood.

14.. *Voc.* in Wr.-Wülcker 606/6 *Pullificacio*, hacchynge. **1555** W. WATREMAN *Fardle Facions* Pref. 18 Euen from the firste hatchynge of the worlde. **1622** MABBE tr. *Aleman's Guzman d'Alf.* II. 257 Good marriages are not chickins of every dayes hatching. **1840** *Penny Cycl.* XVIII. 478/1 The twenty-one days required for the hatching of chickens. **1905** *Kynoch Jrnl.* Apr.–June 108 The hatchings at the present time are quite up to the average of a good year.

b. *attrib.* and *Comb.*

1851 MAYHEW *Lond. Labour* (1864) III. 24 A shop in Leicester Square, where Cantello's hatching-eggs machine was. **1883** *Fisheries Exhib. Catal.* 203 Model of hatching house..fitted up with miniature hatching apparatus.. Ferguson hatching jars..hatching troughs..hatching boxes [etc.]. **1884** DAY in *Fisheries Exhib. Lit.* II. 75 Carp require a hatching-pond. **1885** *Chr. World* 15 Jan. 37/3 That.. hatching-place of hellish plots of wholesale murder.

hatching, *vbl. sb.*^{2} [f. HATCH *v.*^{2} + -ING^1.] The action of HATCH *v.*^{2}: the drawing of parallel lines so as to produce the effect of shading; chiefly *concr.*, the series of lines so drawn; hatches.

In Heraldry different modes of hatching are used to represent the different tinctures or colours.

1662 EVELYN *Chalcogr.* v. (R.), Hatchings express'd by single strokes are ever the most graceful and natural; though of greater difficulty to execute, especially being any wayes oblique; because they will require to be made broader and fuller in the middle, then either at their entrance, or exit. **1688** R. HOLME *Armoury* III. 146/1 When one Hatching or Stroke in a piece of Work crosses another..this is called a Double Shadow, also a Double Hatch. **1727–51** CHAMBERS *Cycl.* s.v., The first kind of hatching in pale, or from top to bottom, signifies gules or red. **1816** SINGER *Hist. Cards* 212 The cross hatching in the print. **1870** RUSKIN *Lect. Art* vi. 163 The attempts to imitate the shading of fine draughtsmen, by dotting and hatching.

attrib. **1695** DRYDEN tr. *Du Fresny's Art Paint.* Wks. 1808 XVII. 472 Those hatching strokes of the pencil. **1798** *Characters* in *Ann. Reg.* 360 A hatching style of pencilling.

'**hatching,** *vbl. sb.*^{3} *Mining.* = HATCH *sb.*^{1}

1753 CHAMBERS *Cycl. Supp.* s.v. *Digging*, Expressing the random openings which they make in search of mines, by the word *hatching*, or *essay-hatching*.

'**hatching,** *ppl. a.* [f. HATCH *v.*^{1} + -ING^2.] That hatches, in various senses.

1856 AIRD *Poet. Wks.* 382 Yearning As if to cast some birth of shape from out Her hatching loins. **1892** MRS. H. WARD *David Grieve* II. 127 To sit at home..'like a hatching hen'.

hatchling ('hætʃlɪŋ). [f. HATCH *sb.*^{2} + -LING^1.] A very young fish or bird, etc., usually artificially hatched and not old enough to take care of itself.

1899 *19th Cent.* Sept. 399 The ova hatched out *en route*, and the hatchlings died. **1899** *Field* 16 Sept. 496 This assertion may be verified by throwing some hatchlings into a tank where fish of all sizes are mixed together. It will be seen that the strangers are at once devoured. **1955** *Sci. Amer.* Oct. 98/3 It is curious that, although the young hatchling in the nest is in great hazard of its life, once it has begun to fly it is extremely unlikely to be lost during the remainder of the dependence period. **1957** *New Scientist* 24 Oct. 9 The female octopus..laid eggs..on 6 September... The first hatchlings appeared on 16 October.

hatchment^1 ('hætʃmənt). [Shortened and altered from ACHIEVEMENT (q.v.) through the forms *atcheament, atchement, atch'ment.*] An escutcheon or ensign armorial; = ACHIEVEMENT 3; *esp.* a square or lozenge-shaped tablet exhibiting the armorial bearings of a deceased person, which is affixed to the front of his dwelling-place.

1548 HALL *Chron., Hen. V*, 50 The Hachementes wer borne onely by capitaynes. **1572** BOSSEWELL *Armorie* II. 121 b, Because ye may the better vnderstande what suche achementes bee..It might be asked of me what thys worde *acheuement* meaneth. **1602** SHAKS. *Ham.* IV. v. 214 No Trophee, Sword, nor Hatchment o're his bones. **1687** WOOD *Life* (O.H.S.) III. 216 A hatchment or achivment hanging over the great gate leading into Magd. Coll. **1747** HERVEY *Medit.* II. 62 The Hatchment suspended on the Wall, or the Crape streaming in the Air, are silent intimations. **1755** T. H. CROKER *Orl. Fur.* XLI. xxx, Orlando, to adorn his atch'ment bright Did lofty Babel thunderstruck display. **1810** W. TAYLOR in *Monthly Mag.* XXIX. 318 Ye windows dim with achments. **1864** BOUTELL *Her. Hist. & Pop.* xiii. 108 It is customary to place on a Hatchment some brief legend of a religious character.

transf. **1617** FLETCHER *Valentinian* IV. iv, My naked sword Stands but a hatchment by me; only held To shew I was a soldier. **1848** DICKENS *Dombey* xxx, With black hatchments of pictures blotching the walls.

attrib. **1864** BOUTELL *Her. Hist. & Pop.* xxix. (ed. 3) 444 Characteristics of modern hatchment-painting.

†**hatchment**^{2}. *Obs.* [f. HATCH *v.*^{2} + -MENT.] The 'hatching' with which the hilt of a sword is ornamented. (See HATCH *v.*^{2} 2.)

1616 BEAUM. & FL. *Scornf. Lady* II. ii, Five Marks in hatchments to adorn this thigh. **1649** G. DANIEL *Trinarch., Hen. V*, clxxviii, Scabbards teare From over-rusted Blades, to furbish them Worthy the Hatchment they intend to weare.

hatch-out ('hætʃaʊt). [f. the verbal phr. *to hatch out* (see HATCH *v.*^{1} 2).] The action of hatching out; also, the brood hatched out.

1898 *Westm. Gaz.* 13 May 4/1 It only depends upon climatic conditions to ensure a good hatch out. **1908** *Ibid.* 5 June 4/2 While the hatch-out is in progress the number of the fly is marvellous. *Ibid.* 14 Aug. 4/2 Partridges are more faithful to a fixed date for the hatch-out of their eggs than grouse.

hatchway ('hætʃweɪ). Also 7 **hatches way.** [f. HATCH *sb.*^{1} + WAY.]

1. *Naut.* A square or oblong opening in the deck of a ship down which cargo is lowered into the hold; also forming a passage from one deck to another. Qualified, as ***after-, fore-, main-hatchway.***

1626 CAPT. SMITH *Accid. Yng. Seamen* 11 The hatches, the hatches way, the holes in the commings. **1627** —— *Seaman's Gram.* ii. 7 The Hatches way is..where the goods are lowered that way right downe into the howle. **1745** P. THOMAS *Jrnl. Anson's Voy.* 137 On the Larboard Side, a-breast the main Hatch-way. **1833** MARRYAT *P. Simple* vi, The sentry standing by me with his lantern over the coombings of the hatchway. **1836** —— *Midsh. Easy* xii, Kicking Mr. Easthupp..down the after-lower-deck hatchway.

†**2.** An opening in a weir or sluice: cf. HATCH *sb.*^{1} 6. *Obs.*

1705 *Act 4 & 5 Anne* c. 8 Preamb., Preventing the..Fish to pass..through their Fishing Wyres and Fishing Hatchways from the Sea into the said Rivers.

3. An opening in a floor, etc. which may be closed with a hatch or trap-door. (Applied by Scott to the sliding door of a box-bed.)

1814 SCOTT *Wav.* xxxvii, Waverley had repeatedly drawn open, and they had as frequently shut, the hatchway of his cage. **1825** *Beverley Lighting Act* ii. 19 Leave open..the door, hatchway or flap-window.

4. *Comb.*, as ***hatchway-netting, -screen.***

1867 SMYTH *Sailor's Word-bk.*, *Hatchway nettings*, nettings sometimes placed over the hatchways instead of gratings, for security and circulation of air. *Hatchway-screens*, pieces of fear-nought, or thick woollen cloth, put round the hatchways of a man-of-war in time of action, to screen the passages to the magazine.

hate (heɪt), *sb.*^{1} Forms: 1–4 (6 *Sc.*) hete, (1 heate, 3 hæte), 3– hate, (3 ate, 4 het, haat(e, hat, 6 *Sc.* heyt, hait). [OE. *hęte* masc. = OS. *hęti* (:—*hati-*); cf. OHG. *haz* (*hazzes*) masc. and neut. (Ger. *hasz* m.), MDu. *hāte* fem., m., *hat* m., Du. *haat* m., ON. *hatr*, Goth. *hatis* neut.; these forms point to an OTeut. **hatoz, -izos* (:—pre-Teut. **kodos, kodesos*) which passed into an *i-* stem in WGer. In ME. *hete, het* was, under the influence of the verb, and perh. of ON. *hatr*, changed into *hate.*]

1. a. An emotion of extreme dislike or aversion; detestation, abhorrence, hatred. Now chiefly *poet.*

Beowulf (Z.) 2554 Hete wæs on-hrered. *c* **825** *Vesp. Psalter* cxxxix. 3 [cxl. 2] Ða ðohtun heatas in heortan alne deȝ. *c* **900** tr. *Bæda's Hist.* III. xv. [xxi.] (1890) 222 He forseah & on hete hæfde þa men. *c* **1200** ORMIN 4454 Ȝiff þu beresst hete and niþ. *c* **1205** LAY. 20441 Muchel hunger & hæte [*c* **1275** hate]. *c* **1250** *Gen. & Ex.* 3638 Wið-uten ate and strif. *c* **1275** LAY. 8322 þat after hate comeþ loue. *c* **1315** SHOREHAM 161 Thou areredst therne storm And alle thys hete. **1340** *Ayenb.* 8 Zenne of hate and of wreþe and of grat ire. **1382** WYCLIF *2 Sam.* xiii. 15 With to myche greet haate. **1491** CAXTON *Vitas Patr.* (W. de W. 1495) II. 221 b/2 A relygyouse that shall haue in a hate the delectacyons of the flesshe. **1513** DOUGLAS *Æneis* XIII. Prol. 129 Thus sayr me dredis I sal thoill a heyt, For the graue study I haue so long forleyt. **1570** *Satir. Poems Reform.* xviii. 107 Ȝour Inobedience hes purchessit Goddis hait. **1667** MILTON *P.L.* VII. 54 Unimaginable as hate in Heav'n. **1777** SIR W. JONES *Ess. Imit. Arts* in *Poems, etc.* 195 Where there is vice, which is detestable in itself, there must be hate. **1877** MRS. OLIPHANT *Makers Flor.* i. 10 Generations which succeeded each other in the same hates and friendships.

b. The object of hatred. *poetic.*

1592 SHAKS. *Rom. & Jul.* I. v. 140 My onely Loue sprung from my onely hate. **1594** MARLOWE & NASHE *Dido* III. ii, Here lies my hate, Aeneas' cursed brat. **1713** SWIFT *Cadenus & Vanessa* 505 Of half mankind the dread and hate.

c. In the war of 1914–18, a bombardment, a 'strafe'. *slang.*

A jocular use based upon the German 'Hymn of Hate', which was ridiculed in *Punch* 24 Feb. 1915, p. 150, in the legend of a drawing, 'Study of a Prussian household having its morning hate'.

[**1914** *Punch* 30 Dec. 530/1 Kaiser, what vigil will you keep tonight?.. While your priesthood chants the Hymn of Hate, Like incense will you lift to God your breath?] **1915** D. O. BARNETT *Lett.* 204 There are some unhealthy spots, 'Suicide Corner', 'Deadman's Alley' and others, where they drop shells regularly, trying to catch our transport at night. We call it the 'Evening Hate'. **1926** F. M. FORD *Man could stand up* II. v. 174 There is not going to be a *strafe*. This is only a little extra Morning Hate. **1927** E. THOMPSON *These Men thy Friends* 112 He was watching a spasmodic 'hate' of some violence. **1968** D. REEMAN *Pride & Anguish* x. 180 I'm going to turn in, Sub. I want a couple of hours before the night's 'hate' gets going.

d. Phr. ***to have a hate on*** or ***against*** (a person) (see quot. 1941).

1941 BAKER *Dict. Austral. Slang* 38 *Have a hate against*, actively to dislike a person or thing. **1966** 'S. WOODS' *Let's choose Executors* 62 Things have been perfectly horrid, ever since Mark started to have a hate against her. *Ibid.* 220 She seemed to have a complete hate on him.

2. a. *Comb.*, as ***hate-bearing, -maddened*** adj.; ***hate-philtre, -wile;*** **hate-love,** a conflicting emotion combining hate and love (cf. *love-hate*).

1682 N. O. *Boileau's Lutrin* I. 45 The hideous clang of her hate-bearing wing. *a* **1822** SHELLEY in *Athenæum* 2 Mar. (1895) 276/1 Why is it that we all write love-songs? why shouldn't we write hate-songs? **1884** TENNYSON *Becket* IV. ii. 165 Brew..A strong hate-philtre as may madden him. **1895** MORRIS *Beowulf* 17 He with his hate-wiles Of sudden harms framed. **1915** J. C. POWYS *Visions & Revisions* 244 This monstrous *hate-love*, caressing the bruises itself has made, and shooting forth a forked viper-tongue of cruelty from between the lips that kiss. **1921** R. GRAVES *Pier-Glass* 25 It beams on set jaw and hate-maddened eye. **1937** B. H. L. HART *Europe in Arms* xxii. 284 To use force without limit and without calculation of cost may be instinctive in a hate-maddened mob, but it is the negation of statesmanship. **1962** *Listener* 5 July 11/2 He consciously contrasts his teaching with that of the object of his hate-love.

b. Used *attrib.* or as quasi-*adj.*: designed to stir up hate, e.g. ***hate campaign;*** marked or characterized by hate; **hate mail,** letters (often anonymous) in which the senders express their hostility towards the recipient.

1916 *Daily Colonist* (Victoria, B.C.) 21 July 12/7 The official Cologne Gazette published the following excellent example of 'hate literature': 'Among those who are guilty of involving Europe in a bath of blood Lord Northcliffe is perhaps the guiltiest of all.' **1949** 'G. ORWELL' *Nineteen Eighty-Four* I. 5 The economy drive in preparation for Hate Week. **1959** *Daily Tel.* 18 May 6/2 Hence, perhaps, the decision to revert to 'Western imperialism' as target of a fresh hate-campaign in Iraq. **1966** H. WAUGH *Pure Poison* (1967) xii. 71 Have you or your wife ever received hate phone calls or hate messages before? **1967** J. D. WEAVER *Warren* xix. 331 'You should have seen the hate mail he got,' says one of his intimates. **1969** *N.Y. Rev. Books* 16 Jan. 36/1 Mr Epstein reaches the heights..of absurdity by stating that the hate literature distributed in the Ocean Hill-Brownsville teacher mail boxes may have been fraudulent. **1976** *New Yorker* 1 Mar. 21/2 In fact, the bulk of the mail from voters to the two select committees has been 'hate mail', accusing their members of treasonous conduct. **1986** *Sunday Mail* (Brisbane) 20 July 11/4 Douglas has been flooded with both hate mail from the nursing home industry and more letters from patients who claimed they were abused.

hate, haet (het), *sb.*^{2} *Sc.* Forms: 6–7 **haid,** 8–9 **haet, hait, hate,** 9 **hade.** *orig.* The words *hae't* in the phrase *Deil hae't* (South Sc. *hae'd*), 'Devil have it!' This deprecatory expression became a

strong negative (cf. DEVIL 21), and thus equivalent to 'Devil a bit', i.e. not a bit, not a whit. Hence *haet*, with an ordinary negative, as *not a haet*, came sometimes to be understood as equivalent to 'whit, atom', or 'anything, the smallest thing that can be conceived' (Jamieson).

c **1590** JAMES VI in Rowe *Hist. Kirk, Coronis* (*a* 1650), Wodr. Soc. (1842) 419 The King replyed: 'The Divill haue it aills you, but that, ye would all be alyke, and ye cannot abyde any to be ouer you'. [M'Crie *Life Knox* (1814) II. 299 *prints* 'The d——l haid ails you.] **1603** *Philotus* cvi. in Pinkerton *Scot. Poems Repr.* (1792) III. 40 For that deuyse deuill haid it dowis. **1785** BURNS *Death & Dr. H.* xv, Damn'd haet they'll kill. **1786** —— *Twa Dogs* 208 Tho' deil haet ails them, yet uneasy. **1816** SCOTT *Antiq.* xliv, Deil haet do I expect. **1819** W. TENNANT *Papistry Storm'd* (1827) 133 Fient haet ae button would keep sticket. **1825** JAMIESON s.v. *Hate, Ne'er a hate*, nothing at all; *Neither ocht nor hate*, neither one thing, nor another. *Mod. South Sc.* She has-na a haed left.

hate (heɪt), *v.* Forms: 1 hatian, 2–3 hatien, 3 hatiȝen, 3–5 haten, 4– hate, (4–5 hatte, *Sc.* 4–6 hait, 6 heit); also 2 hetien, 3 heatien. [OE. *hatian* = OFris. *hatia*, OS. *hatôn*, OHG. *hazzôn* and *hazzên*, Goth. *hatan*, a primary *ê* verb, from root *hat-* (:—*kod-*), whence also HATE *sb.*[1]]

1. *trans.* To hold in very strong dislike; to detest; to bear malice to. The opposite of *to love*.

c **897** K. ÆLFRED *Gregory's Past.* xxxiii. 222 Doð þæm wel þe eow ær hatedon. *Ibid.* xlvi. 353 Mid fulryhte hete ic hie hatode. *c* **1175** *Lamb. Hom.* 65 ȝif we hetieð us bitwene. *c* **1200** *Trin. Coll. Hom.* 5 To forleten and hatien his senne. *c* **1205** LAY. 29781 We hine hatiȝen wulleð. *a* **1240** *Sawles Warde* in *Cott. Hom.* 251 Euchan heateð oðer. *a* **1300** *Cursor M.* 12054 þai hatte vs all and has in leth. *c* **1330** R. BRUNNE *Chron. Wace* (Rolls) 11673 Wel oughte we hat hem þat hem han hated. **1382** WYCLIF *John* xv. 24 Thei han seyn and hatid me and my fadir. *c* **1440** *York Myst.* xxv. 404 Oure olde lawes as nowe þei hatte. **1508** DUNBAR *Tua mariit Wemen* 169, I hait him with my hert. **1553** GAU *Richt Vay* 72 He yat heitis his liff in this vardil he sal keip it in ye euerlestand liff. **1635** J. HAYWARD tr. *Biondi's Banish'd Virg.* 181 Shee hated her selfe for suffering her resolution to bee overcome. **1716** ADDISON *Freeholder* No. 53 Our Children.. are taught in their Infancy to hate one half of the Nation. **1832** TENNYSON *Œnone* 225 Her presence, hated both of Gods and men.

absol. *c* **1400** *Destr. Troy* 12236 þai hatid in hert, as any hed fos. *a* **1592** GREENE & LODGE *Looking Glasse* (Rtldg.) 134/1 Servants, amend, and masters, leave to hate. **1855** MACAULAY *Hist. Eng.* xv. (1880) II. 158 She hated easily; she hated heartily; and she hated implacably.

b. It is intensified by various phrases.

a **1300** *Cursor M.* 13070 Herodias him hated to ded. **1530** PALSGR. 579/2 He hateth me lyke poyson. **1573–80** BARET *Alv.* H 237 They do hate ech other deadly. **1697** DAMPIER *Voy.* I. 8 The Spaniards they hate mortally. **1699** SWIFT *Mrs. Harris' Petit.* 54 He hates to be call'd *parson*, like the *devil!*

2. To dislike greatly, be extremely averse (*to do* something). Also constr. with *vbl. sb.*

1297 R. GLOUC. (1724) 290 þys god man Seyn Dunston Hatede muche to cronny hym. **1362** LANGL. *P. Pl.* A. IV. 106 Haten to don heor harlotrie. **1607** BEAUM. & FL. *Woman Hater* II. i, I hate to leave my friend in his extremities. **1653** WALTON *Angler* To Rdr. A vj b, I hate to promise much, and fail. **1891** T. HARDY *Tess* II. 87 The easy-going who hate being bothered. **1897** D. SLADEN in *Windsor Mag.* Jan. 278/2 Dickens.. hated to have to blot his manuscripts while he was writing.

3. *Comb.*, as ***hate-Christ, hate-peace***, etc. adjs.; † **hate-light** *a.*, that hates or shuns light; † **hate-spot** *a.*, that shrinks from the slightest defilement: an epithet of the ermine, which, it was supposed, died if its fur was soiled.

1580 SIDNEY *Arcadia* (1622) 141 Which leaded are with siluer skinne, Passing the hate-spot Emerlin. **1583** BABINGTON *Commandm.* ix. Wks. (1637) 87 Through speech of hate-light pick-thankes. **1592** SYLVESTER *Du Bartas, Tri. Faith* I. 47 The Bridge it was For hate-Christ Turks the Hellespont to passe. *a* **1618** —— *Sonnets upon Peace in Fr.* xxv, Ye hate-peace Hacksters, flesht in Massacres. **1637** N. WHITING *Albino & Bellama* (N.), In this hate-light den.

hate, obs. var. HEAT; obs. north. form of HOTE promise, HOT *a.*; obs. pa. t. of HIGHT *v.*

hateable (ˈheɪtəb(ə)l), *a.* Also 7–9 **hatable**. [-ABLE.] Deserving of being hated; odious.

1611 COTGR., *Haïssable*, hatable; fit, or worthie to be hated. **1818** TODD, *Hateable*.. It should be written *hatable*. **1837** CARLYLE *Mirabeau* in *Misc. Ess.* (1872) V. 221 Really a most.. hateable, lovable old Marquis. **1883** *Harper's Mag.* Oct. 805/1 Some customs he found hateable.

hated (ˈheɪtɪd), *ppl. a.* [f. HATE *v.* + -ED.] Regarded with hatred, greatly disliked.

a **1300** *Cursor M.* 4386 (Gött.) þe most hatid of all þis land. **1590** SHAKS. *Mids. N.* III. ii. 264 Out loathed medicine; O hated poison hence! **1646** HAMMOND *View Some Except.* 137 Your hatedst enemies and your dearest friends. **1671** MILTON *P.R.* I. 47 Hell, our hated habitation. **1855** MACAULAY *Hist. Eng.* IV. 59 The hated threshold of the deserter. **1871** MORLEY *Voltaire* (1886) 9 The hated Voltaire.

hateful (ˈheɪtfʊl), *a.* [f. HATE *sb.*[1] + -FUL.]

1. Full of hate, cherishing hatred, malignant.

c **1340** *Cursor M.* 23750 (Trin.) þe world hateful & couetous. **1482** *Monk of Evesham* (Arb.) 82 Enuyus pepul, sclaunderers, hateful peple. **1530** PALSGR. 314/2 Hatefull, full of hatred, *hayneux*. **1593** SHAKS. *2 Hen. VI*, II. iv. 23 Ah Gloster, hide thee from their hatefull lookes. *a* **1618** SYLVESTER *Maidens Blush* 209 When from a Hill, his hatefull Brethren spi'd Him yet far-off. **1712** POPE *Messiah* 58 Nor ardent warriours meet with hateful eyes. **1890** *Univ. Rev.* 15 June 231 Impiteous And hateful are the gods, and void of ruth.

2. Exciting hate; odious, obnoxious, repulsive.

1382 WYCLIF *Rev.* xviii. 2 The keping of ech vnclene foul, and haatful [*odibilis*]. **1398** TREVISA *Barth. De P.R.* XII. xxviii. (1495) 430 Theyr crye is hatfull and odiouse to other byrdes. *c* **1440** *York Myst.* xxxii. 71 Youre aunsweres is hedouse and hatefull to here. **1592** SHAKS. *Rom. & Jul.* II. ii. 55 My name deare Saint, is hatefull to my selfe. **1667** MILTON *P.L.* VI. 264 These Acts of hateful strife, hateful to all. **1772** PRIESTLEY *Inst. Relig.* (1782) I. 113 No vice is universally so hateful as ingratitude. **1855** MAURICE *Learn. & Work.* 285 That mother herself who had drawn him into the hatefullest crimes.

b. as *sb.* A hateful thing. *nonce-use.*

1797 MRS. BENNETT *Beggar Girl* (1813) III. 110 A remove from the Grange, the Hall, and all the hatefuls belonging to each of them.

ˈ**hatefully**, *adv.* [f. prec. + -LY[2].]

1. With hatred; malignantly, maliciously.

1412–20 LYDG. *Chron. Troy* III. xxii, King Humerus hath a bowe take.. And hatefully therein set an arowe. **1549** COVERDALE, etc. *Erasm. Par. Gal.* v. 120 The Jewes so maliciously and hatefully persecute me. **1611** BIBLE *Ezek.* xxiii. 29 They shall deale with thee hatefully. **1897** *Advance* (Chicago) 7 Jan. 11 Who writes hatefully of folk.

2. In a way that one hates; odiously, abominably.

1632 SHERWOOD, Hatefully, *odieusement*. **1730–6** BAILEY (folio), *Hatefully*, odiously. **1754** A. DRUMMOND *Trav.* 75 The ceremony was hatefully tedious.

ˈ**hatefulness.** [f. as prec. + -NESS.] The quality of being hateful.

1. The quality of being full of hatred or strong dislike; loathing.

1548 THOMAS *Ital. Dict.* (1567), *Istomacaggine*, hatefulnesse or lothsomnesse of the stomake. **1580** SIDNEY *Arcadia* (1622) 54 The eternall hatefulnesse of my destinie made Gynecia's iealousie stop that, and all other my blessings. **1586** A. DAY *Eng. Secretary* I. (1625) 129 Those vices.. vilenesse, and execrable hatefulnesse.

2. The quality of deserving hatred; odiousness; abominableness.

1611 COTGR., *Haineuseté*, hatefulnesse, odiousnesse. **1679–1714** BURNET *Hist. Ref.* an. 1542 (R.) To inform the people of the hatefulness of vice, and the excellency of holiness. **1856** FROUDE *Hist. Eng.* I. ii. 110 Able to recognise the past in its true hatefulness.

† **hatel**, *a.* (*sb.*) *Obs.* Forms: 1 hatol, 3–4 hatel; also 1 hętol, -el, 3 hetel, heatel. [OE. *hatol, hętel* = OS. *hatul* (MDu. *hatel*), OHG. *hazzal*:—OTeut. **hatulo-*, **hatilo-*, cognate with HATE *sb.*[1], *v.*[1]: see -LE.] Full of hatred; malignant, hostile; severe, cruel; fierce, bitter.

a **850** *Kentish Gloss.* in Wr.-Wülcker 69/13 *Odiosus*, hatol. *Ibid.* 85/24 *Odiosam*, hatol. *c* **1000** ÆLFRIC *Hom.* II. 304 Mid hetelum ȝeðance. *c* **1000** *Screadunga* (Bouterwek) 17 (Bosw.) Se heahengel ðe nu is hetol deofol. *a* **1225** *Ancr. R.* 400 Lo! ich holde her hetel sweord ouer þin heaued. *a* **1225** *St. Marher.* 7 Me hatele hund quoð ha.. Me ne schendest tu nawt. *a* **1225** *Leg. Kath.* 1971 þeos heane & teos hatele tintreohe. *c* **1250** *Gen. & Ex.* 2544 Ðe eȝtenede king amonaphis, Aȝenes ðis folc hatel is. **13..** *E.E. Allit. P.* C. 481 With hatel anger & hot, heterly he callez. *c* **1386** CHAUCER *Wife's T.* 339 Pouerte is hatel [*v.r.* hateful] good.

B. *sb.* Anger; outburst of hatred.

13.. *E.E. Allit. P.* B. 200 Ne so hastyfly watz hot for hatel of his wylle.

ˈ**hateless**, *a.* [f. HATE *sb.*[1] + -LESS] Void of hate, having no feeling of hatred.

1580 SIDNEY *Arcadia* (1867) 288 Philantus.. sendeth the greeting of a hateless enemy. **1587** *Misfort. Arth.* v. i. in Hazl. *Dodsley* IV. 331 You hateless sought the safeguard of them all. **1820** SHELLEY *Lines to Reviewer* 2 What profit can you see In hating such a hateless thing as me?

† ˈ**hatelich, -ly**, *a. Obs.* [OE. *hętelíc* = OS. *hętelîk* (Du. *hatelijk*); OHG. *hazlîh* (MHG. *hazlîch, hezlîch, hezzelîch*), f. WGer. *hati-* HATE *sb.*[1]: see -LIKE, -LY[1].] Malignant, hostile; hateful.

Beowulf (Z.) 1267 Heoro-wearh hetelic. *c* **893** K. ÆLFRED *Oros.* I. viii §4 Ymb hiora hetelican forliȝnessa. *c* **1320** *Cast. Love* 682 He is so dredful and hateliche To alle.. his fon.

† ˈ**hately**, *adv. Obs.* [OE. *hętelíce* = OHG. *hazlîhho*, MHG. *hazlîche*; f. prec.: see -LY[2].] Fiercely, bitterly, scornfully, hatefully.

c **1000** ÆLFRIC *Josh.* xi. 8 Hiȝ hetelice sloh. *a* **1240** *Wohunge* in *Cott. Hom.* 281 Hu ha þe bunden swa heteli faste. *a* **1300** *Cursor M.* 14669 Hetli þai bi-hinted him. *c* **1300** *Havelok* 2655 He.. smoth godrich, and Godrich him, Hetelike with herte grim. **13..** *Guy Warw.* (A.) 10681 Guy .. hetelich smot to Colbrand. *a* **1400–50** *Alexander* 2910 So hately [*Dubl.* hetterly] þou spekis.

haten, obs. form of HEAT *v.*

hater (ˈheɪtə(r)), *sb.*[1] [f. HATE *v.* + -ER[1].] One who hates; an enemy.

1382 WYCLIF *Prov.* xxvii. 6 The gileful kosses of the hatere. *c* **1440** *Promp. Parv.* 229/2 Hatare, or he þat hatythe, *osor*. **1535** COVERDALE *Ps.* lxxx[i]. 15 The haters of yͤ Lorde shulde mysse Israel. *c* **1586** C'TESS PEMBROKE *Ps.* LXIX. ii, Haters have I, more than haires. **1606** SHAKS. *Ant. & Cl.* v. i. 9, I wore my life To spend vpon his haters. **1738** SWIFT *Polite Convers.* 102, I suppose, the Gentleman's a Women-Hater. *a* **1784** JOHNSON in Piozzi *Anecd.* (1786) 83 Dear Bathurst.. was a man to my very heart's content; he hated a fool, and he hated a rogue, and he hated a whig: he was a very good hater. **1887** RUSKIN *Præterita* II. iv. 124 A violent hater of the old Dutch school.

Hence ˈ**hatress** *nonce-wd.*, a woman that hates.

1892 *Pall Mall G.* 1 Feb. 3/3 A man-hatress, as clever girls so often are.

† ˈ**hater, ˈhatter**, *sb.*[2] *Obs.* or *dial.* Forms: *pl.* 1 **hæteru, -ra**, 3 **hateren**, 4 **hatere, hattren**, 9 *dial.* **hattern**. *sing.* 3 **hatter, heater, hetter**, 4 **hater**, 4–5 **hatere**, 5 **hatir, -yr, hattir**. [OE. *hæteru*, prob. from a sing. **hæt* (? *hǽt*): cf. MHG. *hâz* 'coat, dress, clothing', mod.Swabian *häs, hesz* (pl. *hesser*), Swiss *häs, gehäs*. The ME. plural would thus be parallel to *childer, children*; and the sing. *hater, hatter*, a new formation. (If the vowel of OE. *hæt* was orig. short, it would be in ablaut relation (*hatoz-*: *hǽtoz*) to the MHG. form.)]

1. *pl.* (and *sing.*) Clothes, clothing collectively.

c **1000** ÆLFRIC *Hom.* I. 330 He næfde ne biȝleofan, ne hælðe, ne hætera. *Ibid.* 374 Se hund.. totær his hæteru sticmælum of his bæce. *c* **1205** LAY. 30778 Alle his hateren weoren to-toren. *a* **1225** *Ancr. R.* 104 Swoti hateren. *a* **1300** *Cursor M.* 20211 Of scho did tan al hir hater. **13..** *K. Alis.* 7054 Naked they goth, withowten hater [*rime* water]. *c* **1310** *Man in Moon* in Ritson *Anc. Songs* (1877) 59 þe þornes beþ kene, is hattren to tereþ. **1876** *Whitby Gloss.*, *Hattern*, clothing of all kinds.

2. *sing.* A garment, a vestment.

a **1225** *Ancr. R.* 418 ȝe schulen liggen in on heater [*v.rr.* hatter, hetter], and i-gurd. **1393** LANGL. *P. Pl.* C. x. 157 An hater, to helye with hus bones. *c* **1440** *York Myst.* xxix. 360, I have here a hatir to hyde hym. *c* **1440** *Promp. Parv.* 229/2 Hatyr, rent clothe (*K.* hatere, *H.*, *P.* hatere, or hatyr), *scrutum, pannucia*.

† ˈ**hater**, *v. Obs.* [f. HATER *sb.*[2]] *trans.* To clothe, attire. Hence **hatering** *vbl. sb.*, clothing.

c **1200** *Trin. Coll. Hom.* 33 In to þesse wrecheliche hateringe of þisse worelde. **13..** *K. Alis.* 5922 Thinnelich hy beth y-hatered. **1377** LANGL. *P. Pl.* B. xv. 76 Freres.. folilich spenen [*v.r.* spenden] In housyng, in hateryynge.. More for pompe þan for pure charite.

haterad, -red, -reden, -redyn, -retin, -rid, -ryd, -rent, obs. ff. HATRED.

haterel(l(e, obs. ff. HATTREL.

† **haterell.** *Obs. rare*[−1]. [app. related to HATER *sb.*[2]] (?) A garment.

c **1440** *York Myst.* xxxi. 342 *i Dux.* We will with a goode will for his wedis wende, For we wotte wele anowe what wedis he schall were. *ii Dux.* Loo! here is an haterell here at youre hent, Alle faciοnndþerfore foolis to feere.

haterly, -lynge, hatirly, var. HETERLY *adv.*

† ˈ**hatesome**, *a. Obs.* [See -SOME.] Hateful.

1382 WYCLIF *Gen.* xxxiv. 30 ȝe han maad me haatsum to .. the dwellers of this loond. —— *2 Sam.* xiii. 15 And ful haatsum Amon hadde hir. —— *Prov.* i. 29 Hatesum thei hadden disciplyne. **1513** DOUGLAS *Æneis* XI. iv. 89 The caus .. that this haitsum lyfe sustene he wald.

hateworthy (ˈheɪtˌwɜːðɪ), *a.* [f. HATE *sb.*[1] + WORTHY *a.*] Worthy of hate, hateful.

1901 A. SYMONS *Poems* (1907) I. 180, I tremble lest a wrath so just avenge On him a mother so most hate-worthy. **1924** *Public Opinion* 9 May 450/3 There is nothing sinister or hateworthy in Mrs. Carlyle's slowly and deliberately formed judgement.

hatful (ˈhætfʊl). [See -FUL.] As much as a hat will contain; loosely, a considerable quantity.

1662 J. DAVIES tr. *Olearius' Voy. Ambass.* 9 Having Goosberries to sell, whereof we bought a hatful for a Copec. **1686** *Lond. Gaz.* No. 2153/3 The Soldiers divided Ducats and Dollars by Hat-fulls. **1866** MRS. H. WOOD *St. Martin's Eve* vii. (1874) 66 Mr. Pym had gone home, loudly promissing Benja a hatful of physic as a punishment for his carelessness. **1887** MISS BRADDON *Like & Unlike* xviii, I mean to earn a hatful of money by literature.

† **hath**, (?) *a. Sc. Obs.* [Cf. ON. *háð* mocking, scoffing. (Cf. HETHING.)] (?) Scornful.

c **1375** *Sc. Leg. Saints, Margaret* 435 [She] saynit hyr, & rase vp hath, & rakit to þat body rath.

Hence † **hathful** *a.*, scornful, mocking.

a **1240** *Wohunge* in *Cott. Hom.* 279 For hu mon þe ofte seide schomeliche wordes and haðfule hokeres.

hath, arch. 3rd pers. sing. pres. ind. of HAVE.

hatha-yoga (ˈhæθəˈjəʊgə). [Skr., f. *haṭha* force, violence, forced meditation + YOGA.] A system of exercises and control of breathing forming part of the Hindu religious philosophy of yoga. So **hatha-yogi(n)**, a devotee of hatha-yoga.

1911 *Encycl. Brit.* XXVI. 791/1 The physical methods and spiritual exercises recommended by theosophists are those inculcated in the systems known in Hindu philosophy as Râjâ Yoga in contradistinction to the Hatha Yoga system, which is most commonly to be met with in India, and in which the material aspects are given greater prominence. **1937** A. HUXLEY *Ends & Means* xiii. 234 The methods of Hatha Yoga, as they are called in India, are said to result in heightened mental and physical powers. *Ibid.* 247 It is possible for meditation to be practised by those who are neither extreme ascetics nor Hatha-Yogis. **1956** E. WOOD *Yoga Dict.* 62 *Hatha-yoga*, a form of yoga which is concerned chiefly with the regulation of breathing, and secondarily with other bodily disciplines or training. **1956** A. HUXLEY *Adonis & Alphabet* 32 The training of the dervish or the hatha-yogin is a long laborious affair. **1963**

Times Lit. Suppl. 11 Jan. 29/3 It may be observed that even Indian Buddha figures.. by no means express the strenuous constrictions of mediaeval Hindu Hatha-yoga. **1967** *Daily Tel.* 1 Feb. 13/5 Hatha yoga, he explained, deals with the mastery of thought and breath. 'If we control our breath we control our thought. When we control our thought we begin to understand the full meaning of life.'

†**hathel.** *Obs.* Also 5 hathil(l. [app. var. of ATHEL.] Nobel, man of worth; man. (Chiefly in alliterative verse.)

13.. *Gaw. & Gr. Knt.* 2065 His haþel on hors watz þenne þat bere his spere & launce. *c* **1350** *Wynnere & Wastoure* (Roxb. 1897) 68 Appon ynglysse tonge 'hethyng haue the hathell þat any harme thynkes'. *a* **1400–50** *Alexander* 84 Siche a somme.. þat any hathil vnder heuen ware hardy to rekyn. *Ibid.* 2086 þai haue hedid of oure hathils [*v.r.* athellys] & a hepe woundid. *c* **1420** *Anturs of Arth.* xxxviii, The hathels in hie, hor horses haue hente. *c* **1440** *York Myst.* xxxiii. 293 Why, what harmes has þis hatell here haunted? *c* **1450** *Golagros & Gaw.* 1299 All his hathillis in that heir. **1515** [see ATHEL].

hathen, hathen(n)es, obs. ff. HEATHEN, -ESSE.

hather, -ir, obs. forms of HEATHER.

hathful, *a. Obs.*: see s.v. HATH *a.*

hathi ('hɑːtɪ). *India.* Also **hotty, huttee,** etc. [Hind. *hāthī* (also Marathi, etc. *hattī*), f. Skr. *hastin* elephant, f. *hasta* elephant's trunk, hand.] An elephant. Also *attrib.*: **hathi tractor,** a kind of tractor used in the war of 1914–18.

[**1826** LEYDEN & ERSKINE tr. *Mem. Zehir-Ed-Din* 315 As for the animals peculiar to Hindustân, one is the elephant, the Hindustânis call it *Hathi.*] **1831** TYERMAN & BENNET *Voy. & Trav.* II. 375 Our bearers suddenly set up the cry of 'Huttee! huttee!' **1838** in E. Eden *Up Country* (1866) I. 269 You are of course aware that we habitually call elephants Hotties. **1860** W. H. RUSSELL *Diary India* I. 392 We came to the Ramgunga, a deep stream, which our elephant waded across... The hathi nearly floated his driver off his neck. **1890** KIPLING *Barrack-r. Ballads* (1892) 51 An' the *hathis* pilin' teak. **1922** *Glasgow Herald* 11 Feb. 10 Golden also was the head of the 'hathi' selected for this honour. **1926** *Glasgow Herald* 27 Aug. 11 There was the Hathi tractor, constructed in the first place largely from German spare parts, captured during the war. The Hathi—its title is the Indian word for elephant—had besides the strength of the elephant qualities which that intelligent animal does not possess.

Hathor ('hɑːθə(r)). Also Athor. [ad. Gr. 'Αθώρ, f. Egypt. *Ḥet-Ḥerh* the house above, or *Ḥet-Ḥeru* house of Horus.] The name of an Egyptian divinity, the goddess of love, often represented with the head or ears of a cow, used *attrib.* or *Comb.* to designate a type of column surmounted by a capital on which are carved one or more representations of the head of Hathor. So **Hathoric** (hə'θɒrɪk), *a.* Hence **Hatho'resque** *a.*, in the style of a Hathor figure.

1786 tr. *C. E. Savary's Lett. on Egypt* II. xlviii. 351 Athor, or the night, in the opinion of the Egyptian priests, represented the darkness which enveloped the chaos before the creation. **1851** W. S. W. VAUX *Handbk. Antiq. B.M.* 355 The Venus of the Egyptians was called Athor, Hathor, or Athyr, and her name implied the abode of Horus. **1857** J. GARDNER WILKINSON *Egyptians* 273 His hair is that of the milky way.. his eyes, the symbolical eyes of Athor. **1896** W. M. F. PETRIE *Koptos* i. 4/2 Below the scene is a frieze of *dad* signs alternating with figures, the lower parts of which are like the Isiac girdle tie, while above they have the human Hathor head, with cows' ears and horns... They seem as if they might be copies of some primitive Hathor idol. **1901** R. STURGIS *Dict. Archit.* I. 854/2 The columns are easily divisible into a few general types, such as the single and the clustered lotus-bud, the campaniform, the palm-capped, and the Hathor-headed. *Ibid.* II. 366/2 *Hathoric*, having to do with the Egyptian goddess Hathor. **1934** E. POUND *Eleven New Cantos* xxxix. 44 When Hathor was bound in that box afloat on the sea wave. **1960** *Times* 7 Mar. 8/3 A handsome jewelry box with an ivory inlay of Hathor beads. **1962** D. HARDEN *Phoenicians* xiii. 198 A peculiar multiple vase for offerings has.. a Hathoresque head above a long-horned cow's head.

hathorn, obs. var. HAWTHORN.

hath-pace, erron. f. HALF-PACE; cf. *harth-pace.*

a **1661** FULLER *Worthies, Montgomerysh.* IV. (1662) 47 A Hath pace of fourteen foot square, on the midst of which is placed a Dorrick Columne.

hatikvah (hə'tɪkvɑː). [ad. Heb. *ha-tikwāh* the hope.] A national song, of which the words were written by N. H. Imber (1856–1909), adopted by the Zionist movement in 1907; since 1948 the Israeli national anthem.

1925 P. GUEDALLA *Napoleon & Palestine* 63 The proceedings concluded with the singing of the Hatikvah by some of the audience. **1932** L. GOLDING *Magnolia St.* I. viii. 130 The Jewish guests thought it would balance things nicely if they sang the Jewish anthem, *Hatikvah.* **1965** *Times Lit. Suppl.* 30 Dec. 1210/5 The Jewesses of Salonika singing the Hatikvah, the Jewish anthem. **1970** I. SIEFF *Memoirs* vi. 111 We sang *Hatikvah*, and also 'God Save the King'.

hatine *ppl. a. Obs.*, called: see HIGHT.

hating ('heɪtɪŋ), *vbl. sb.* [f. HATE *v.* + -ING¹: cf. OHG. *hazzunga.*] The action of the vb. HATE; hatred, detestation, malice.

a **1000** *Lamb. Psalter* cviii. [cix.] 5 (Bosw.) Hiᵹ ᵹesetton hatunge for lufrædenne minre. *c* **1200** *Trin. Coll. Hom.* 165 Wraðe and onde and hatinge and oðer iuele lastes. *a* **1225** *Ancr. R.* 200 Rancor siue odium: þet is, hatunge. *c* **1586** C'TESS PEMBROKE *Ps.* LXIX. v, Powring out their inward hating. **1895** *Month* Oct. 201 Fond likings and fond hatings.

hatir, var. HATER *sb.*² *Obs.*, clothing.

'hatless, *a.* [f. HAT *sb.* + -LESS.] Having no hat; not wearing a hat.

c **1450** *Golagros & Gaw.* 388 He inclynand agane, Hatles, but hude. **1819** *Blackw. Mag.* V. 98 Hatted among his hatless disciples. **1848** THACKERAY *Van. Fair* xxiv, The chief clerk came rushing hatless after him.

Hence **'hatlessly** *adv.*; **'hatlessness,** hatless condition.

1890 E. DOWSON *Let.* 1 June (1967) 149 We sat & smoked for some hours hatlessly on the balcony. **1881** R. G. WHITE *Eng. Without & Within* 271 The hatlessness, the shoelessness, the rags, and the dirt. **1902** *Westm. Gaz.* 17 Oct. 2/3 Hitherto hatlessness was only *de rigueur* in the stalls and the front row of the dress circle. **1924** *Glasgow Herald* 29 May 6 Many people, who advocate hatlessness during the summer months. **1933** E. A. ROBERTSON *Ordinary Families* x. 229 He did not mind my looking out of place through hatlessness. **1960** *Guardian* 15 July 8/2 The prevailing.. hatlessness of Frenchwomen.

'hat-maker. A maker of hats.

1477 *Charter Jas. III*, in W. Maitland *Hist. Edin.* I. i. (1753) 8 The Hatmakars and Skynnars fornent thame. **1562** *Act 5 Eliz.* c. 4 §3 The Sciences, Crafts, Mysteries or Arts of .. Turners, Cappers, Hatmakers or Feltmakers. **1707** *Lond. Gaz.* No. 4322/4 Samuel Delamare, late of Wandsworth.. Hat-maker. **1875** KNIGHT *Dict. Mech.*, *Hatmakers' Battery*, a large boiler with a surrounding set of benches for a number of workmen.

'hat-making. The trade of making hats.

1547 *Act 1 Edw. VI*, c. 6 §4 Yarn.. wrought in Hats, or employed to Hat-making. **1838** *Penny Cycl.* XII. 64/2 The greatest modern improvement in hat-making.

'hat-money. [In Fr. *chapeau*, Sp. *sombrero*, app. because dropped in a hat.] (See quots.)

1676 C. MOLLOY *De Jure Maritimo* II. ix. §6 (1688) 270 Petty Averidge is another small Duty which Merchants pay to the Master.. The French Ships commonly term the Gratuity *Hat-money.* **1755** tr. *Ordenenzas di Bilbao* in Magens *Insurances* II. App. xiv. 395 By reason of what the Captain's Hat-Money [*sombrero*] or Primage is wont to vary. **1808** C. ABBOTT *Law Merch. Ships* II. vi. §3 (ed. 3) 270 The word *primage* denotes a small payment to the master for his care and trouble.. It is sometimes called the master's hat money. **1825** *Ryan & Moody's Rep.* (1827) 177 It was called *hat-money*, sometimes *pocket-money.* **1861** W. BELL *Dict. Law Scotl.*, *Hat-Money*, or primage, is a small sum.. paid along with the freight, to the master of a ship for his care. It is entirely regulated by usage.

†**'hatous,** *a. Obs. rare.* [f. HATE *sb.*¹ + -OUS, after words of OF. origin.] Hateful, odious.

c **1470** HARDING *Chron.* LXIII. xx. (1543) 52 Malga kyng of Pightes, painimes hatous.

hatred ('heɪtrɪd). Forms: α. 3–5 hatereden, (4 hatredyn, hattredin, hateretin, 4–5 hateredyn, 5 haatredyn). β. 2–4 hatrede, 4– hatred (also 4 hattred, 4–6 hatered(e, 5 haterad, -ryd, hatered, 6 haterid, *Sc.* haitred, -rid). γ. (*Sc.*) 5 hattrende, -rent, 5–6 haterent, 6 hat(te-, hait-, hettrent, het(t)rand. [Early ME., f. HATE *sb.*¹ (or *v.*) + -RED, OE. *rǣden* condition (also direction, reckoning), cf. *brōðorrǣden, frēondrǣden, lufrǣden*, etc. The historical sequence of forms must have been *hatereden, -rede, -red*, although the extant examples do not quite show this. With the Sc. form. in *-rent* cf. *kinrent, manrent.*]

The condition or state of relations in which one person hates another; the emotion or feeling of hate; active dislike, detestation; enmity, ill-will, malevolence.

α. *a* **1300** *E.E. Psalter* cviii. 5 (Mätz.) þai set againe me for godes wa, And hatereden for mi lovered. **1340** HAMPOLE *Pr. Consc.* 7394 þai salle be fulle of hateredyn þan. *c* **1440** *York Myst.* xxxii. 56, I holde it but hatereden. **1483** *Cath. Angl.* 178/1 An Hateredyn.. *inimicicia, invidea.. odium.*

β. *a* **1175** *Cott. Hom.* 233 þat ʒie hatrede and widerwardnesse aʒenes me ʒe win sceolde. *a* **1300** *Cursor M.* 27752 (Cott.) A wreth.. hattred [*v.r.* hatred] it es, and ir to strang. *Ibid.* 9666 (Gött.) þar hatered wonys, or were, or pride. **1340** HAMPOLE *Pr. Consc.* 2519 Whether he war worthy after his dede To hafe luf of God or hatrede. **1377** LANGL. *P. Pl.* B. III. 140 She.. hangeth hym for hatred [*A.* hate, *C.* haterede], þat harme dede neure. *c* **1440** *Promp. Parv.* 229/2 Haterede, idem quod *Hate.* **1477** EARL RIVERS (Caxton) *Dictes* 28 Ware that ye be no mokers for that engendreth hattered. **1553** EDEN *Treat. Newe Ind.* (Arb.) 16 All this great hatered betwene these two beastes. **1596** DALRYMPLE tr. *Leslie's Hist. Scot.* II. 131 Stryfe, haitrid and jnvie. **1667** MILTON *P.L.* II. 500 Yet live in hatred, enmity, and strife. **1773** MRS. CHAPONE *Improv. Mind* (1774) II. 28 The detestable sentiments of hatred and revenge. **1844** DISRAELI *Coningsby* I. ii, A family famous for its hatreds. **1872** DARWIN *Emotions* x. 239 Dislike easily rises into hatred. **1893** *Bookman* June 86/1 Her most vital trait was a hatred of conventionality.

γ. *c* **1375** BARBOUR *Troy-bk.* I. 422 Our-all quhar þat scho hattrende hayde. **14..** *Burgh Laws* lxx, For wroth na for haterent. **1508** DUNBAR *Tua mariit Wemen* 333 Hatrent I hid within my hert all. **1571** *Satir. Poems Reform.* xxviii. 59 Quhen Abbotschaw sic hauie haitrent tuik At the haill hous of Lennox. *a* **1572** KNOX *Hist. Ref.* Wks. 1846 I. 58 A haterent against the pride and avaritiousnes of the preastis.

hatreel, -relle, var. HATTREL *Obs.*

hatte, obs. form of HATE *v.*, HOT *a.*

hatte, obs. pa. t. of HEAT *v.*, HIGHT *v.*

hatted, *ppl. a.* [f. HAT *v.* or *sb.* + -ED.] Wearing a hat, having a hat on.

1552 HULOET, Hatted, *petasatus.* **1559** MORWYNG *Evonym.* Pref., Hens with your hatted Mercury, and with his rod also. **1607** TOURNEUR *Rev. Trag.* I. ii. Wks. 1878 II. 19 It is as easie way unto a Dutchesse, As to a Hatted-dame [= peasant woman]. **1791** MAD. D'ARBLAY *Diary* Aug., Ready hatted and cloaked. **1858** CARLYLE *Fredk. Gt.* I. v. (1872) I. 40 We will pity the crowned head, as well as the hatted or even hatless one.

b. *fig.* Capped, crowned.

1880 CHARLOTTE M. MASON *40 Shires* 376 Here and there they are hatted with trees.

c. *hatted kit*: †(*a*) A dairy vessel: ? a pail 'kit' with a cover (*obs.*). (*b*) A preparation of milk, etc., with a creamy top.

1572 *Inv. Ger. Salveyn* in *Wills & Inv. N. Counties* (Surtees 1835) 349 One buttʳ skepp, ij hattyd kitts. **1600** *Let.* in *Mem. J. Napier of Merchiston* v. (1834) 219 We sould have prepared ane fyne hattit kit, with succar, comfeits and wine. **1818** SCOTT *Br. Lamm.* xi, He has spilt the hatted kitt that was for the Master's dinner. **1831** LOUDON *Encycl. Agric.* (1857) 1048 *Hatted kitt*, a gallon of sour buttermilk is put in the bottom of the milk-pail, and a quart or more of milk drawn from the cow into it.. The new warm milk.. rises to the top and forms a creamy scum or hat over the other; whence the name.

hatten, *pa. pple. Obs.*: see HIGHT *v.*

hatter ('hætə(r)), *sb.* [f. HAT *sb.* + -ER¹.]

1. A maker of or dealer in hats. ***as mad as a hatter***: see MAD.

1389 in *Eng. Gilds* (1870) 12 Johannes de Thame ciuis, et Hatter Londonie. **1488–9** *Act 4 Hen. VII*, c. 9 No hatter nor capper.. [shall] put to sell any hatte.. above the price of xxd. **1576** GASCOIGNE *Steele Gl.* (Arb.) 80 When hatters vse to bye none olde cast robes. **1698** FRYER *Acc. E. India & P.* 331 Goats-Wool.. with which our Hatters know well how to falsify their Bevers. **1836** MARRYAT *Japhet* lxx, I.. stopped at a hatter's and purchased a hat according to the mode. **1837–40** HALIBURTON *Clockm.* (1862) 109 Sister Sall.. walked out of the room, as mad as a hatter. **1857** HUGHES *Tom Brown* II. iii, He's a very good fellow, but as mad as a hatter.

2. One who lives or works alone, orig. a miner; a solitary bushman. *Austral.* and *N.Z.*

[Cf. *hat covers his family* in HAT *sb.* 5 c.]

1853 J. ROCHFORT *Adv. Surveyor* viii. 66 The Bendigo diggings are suitable for persons working singly... Such persons are humorously called 'hatters'. **1864** ROGERS *New Rush* II. 49 Some days ago a sturdy hatter joined. **1865** B. L. FARJEON *Shadows on Snow* II. 76, I was working as a 'hatter'. **1869** R. B. SMYTH *Goldf. Victoria* Gloss. 613 *Hatter*, one who works alone.. The hatter leads an independent life, and nearly always holds a claim under the bye-laws. **1889** E. WAKEFIELD *N.Z. after 50 Yrs.* vi. 165 Miners who work alone are called 'hatters', one explanation of the term being that they frequently go mad from the solitude of their claim away in the bush, exemplifying the proverb 'As mad as a hatter'. **1890** BOLDREWOOD *Miner's Right* iv. 37 To take to fossicking like so many 'hatters'—solitary miners. **1903** 'S. RUDD' *Our New Selection* iv. 37 A weird, silent 'hatter' was there,.. the strange man who lived .. away from everybody. **1914** J. M. BELL *Wilds of Maoriland* vi. 135 At times one comes across an old hatter [near Karamea]. **1924** H. T. GIBSON *That Gibbie Galoot* xxvii. 124 The skipper [of a timber scow] I seldom saw, for he was a 'hatter' and kept to his cabin and keg. **1943** V. PALMER in *Coast to Coast 1942* 21 People on the mainland said that McGowan was a cranky old hatter who had gone off his head because his home was broken up and was now letting his mind rot in isolation. **1944** F. CLUNE *Red Heart* 66 The 'hatter' was mumbling to himself in the manner of lonely outback prowlers. **1966** *Southerly* XXVI. 108 Rueben McGrath was.. a bush 'hatter', a loner.

hatter, *v.* Now *Sc.* and *north. dial.* [? Onomatopœic, with freq. ending: cf. *batter, shatter, tatter*, etc.]

1. *trans.* To bruise with blows; to batter the edge or face of, to erode. ? *Obs.*

c **1450** *Golagros & Gaw.* 702 Helmys of hard steill thai hatterit and heuch. **1630** J. TAYLOR (Water P.) *Wks.* (N.), Where hattering bullets are fine sugred plums. **1806** J. TRAIN *Poet. Reveries* 49 (Jam.) This hatters and chatters My very soul wi' care.

2. To harass; to wear *out*, exhaust with fatigue or drudgery.

1687 DRYDEN *Hind & P.* I. 371 Religion shows a rosy-coloured face, Not hattered out with drudging works of grace. *a* **1700** DRYDEN (J.), He's hattered out with penance. *a* **1825** FORBY *Voc. E. Anglia*, *Hatter*, to harrass and exhaust with fatigue. **1850** BLACKIE *Æschylus* II. 116 From hattering chase of undeserved unrest.. She rests. **1893** *Northumbld. Gloss.* s.v., 'He wis sair hattert' is said of a person who has had a bad time of it in his circumstances generally.

hatter, dial. var. of HOTTER *sb.* and *v.*; obs. f. *hotter*, comp. of HOT *a.*; var. HETER *Obs.*

hatter, -ir, -ern: see HATER *sb.*² *Obs.*, clothing.

hattered, hattred, -redin, hat(te)rent, hattrende, -rent, obs. ff. HATRED.

hatters, *int.* [perh. the pl. of *hatter* HATER *sb.*², used as an oath. Cf. ZOUNDS, ZOOKS.] An asseveration (perh. = Christ's or holy garments).

c **1460** *Towneley Myst.* (Surtees) 113 Bot hatters! I can fynde no flesh, hard nor nesh, Salt nor fresh, Bot two tome platers. [In 19th c. use in South of Scotl.]

ˈhattery. [f. HAT *sb.* + -ERY.] **a.** Hatters' wares; hats collectively. **b.** A hat manufactory.

1823 *Chron.* in *Ann. Reg.* 120/1 Silk fabrics, hattery, jewellery and cutlery. **1871** R. S. FERGUSON *Cumbld. & Westm. M.P.'s* xi. 307 The marble works..the hatteries.

‖**hatti.** *Hist.* In full, *α.* **hatti-sherif** (ˌhatiʃəˈrif), *β.* **hatti-humaiun, -humayun** (ˌhatihuˈmɑjuːn). [Persian *khaṭṭ-i-sharīf*, *khaṭṭ-i-humāyūn*, f. Arab. *khaṭṭ* line, written line, writing + *i* (Pers.) connective + (*α.*) Arab. *sharīf* noble, honourable, sacred, and (*β.*) Pers. *humāyūn* sacred, august, royal, imperial.]

During the Ottoman Empire: a decree or edict issued by the government of Turkey, differing from a *firman* in being personally approved of by the Sultan, and bearing his special mark, which was considered to render it irrevocable.

1858 LD. MALMESBURY *Mem. Ex-minister* (1884) II. 126 He will take this opportunity, if he finds one, to urge on the Sultan the observance of the Hatti.

α. **1688** *Lond. Gaz.* No. 2320/2 The Chiaus Basha..with Tears, gave him the Hattesheriff (or Imperial Decree). **1799** TROUBRIDGE in *Naval Chron.* XXIII. 23 It was a hattesheriff. **1861** T. H. DYER *Mod. Europe* I. 9 The Sultan ..promulgated his decrees in *Firmans*, or simple commands, and *Hattischerifs* or rescripts.

β. **1876** GLADSTONE *Bulg. Horrors* 11 The reforms, which were publicly enacted in an Imperial Firman or Hatti-humayoum. **1888** *Encycl. Brit.* XXIII. 651/2 The Porte published a firman, the *Hatti-Humaiun*, professing to abolish 'every distinction making any class of the subjects of the empire inferior to any other class'.

Hattic (ˈhætɪk), *a.* Also **Kh-**. [f. Assyrian and Hittite *Hatti* + -IC.] Of or pertaining to the Hatti or their language, formerly regarded as conterminous with the Hittites, now as a section of them. Hence as *sb.*, their language. So **ˈHattian** *sb.* and *a.* **a.** One of the race of Hatti or their language. **b.** = *Hattic* adj. above. **ˈHattism**, the social and political system of the Hatti.

[**1874** *Trans. Soc. Bibl. Arch.* III. 245 The king of the Khati. **1880** CHEYNE in *Encycl. Brit.* XII. 25/1 Hittites, a warlike and powerful nation... In the Egyptian inscriptions they are called the Khita or Kheta; in the Assyrian, the Khatti; in the Hebrew Scriptures, the Khittim.] **1924** D. G. HOGARTH in *Cambr. Anc. Hist.* II. 253 Boghaz Keui..is the site of the Hattic capital. **1926** —— *Kings of Hittites* 3 The Hittite civilization of Hamath was but an outlier of 'Hattism', advanced southward along a trunk-road. *Ibid.* 8 Have any remains been revealed which manifestly are Cappadocian Hattic, wholly or in part? **1928** C. DAWSON *Age of Gods* 302 The official language of the empire has been named by its discoverers Nashili or Kanesian; but since the ruling people have always been known as the Hittites, it seems better to retain the same name for their language and to describe the native Hattic tongue as Old Hittite. **1929** J. GARSTANG *Hittite Empire* ii. 39 The suggestion of language ..would seem to indicate an original movement or series of movements from or affecting the Caucasian area, which at the same time peopled Armenia, northern Mesopotamia, and Elam, and won for the Hattians and other Hittite tribes a footing on the eastern mountains and plateau of Asia Minor. *Ibid.* 40 The Hattians themselves were an inland and not a seafaring people. **1933** E. H. STURTEVANT *Compar. Gram. Hittite Lang.* i. 29 Fortunately our use of the biblical name Hittite leaves the ancient stem free for use in its original sense; we shall call the predecessor language Hattic. **1952** O. R. GURNEY *Hittites* ii. 64 The original (Hattian?) form of the name. *Ibid.* 69 This conclusion agrees well with the linguistic evidence, according to which a group of Indo-European immigrants became dominant over an aboriginal race of 'Hattians'. **1958** *Archivum Linguisticum* X. II. 82 Bilinguals whose native language was Hattic. **1963** *Times Lit. Suppl.* 1 Feb. 72/3 The fully prehistoric 'Hattian' period.

ˈhatting, *vbl. sb.* [f. HAT *v.* and *sb.* + -ING[1].] **a.** = HAT-MAKING. **b.** Material for hats. **c.** The covering of a tan-pit with its hat of bark: see HAT *sb.* 6 a. **d.** The taking off or lifting of the hat in reverence or courtesy; giving a hat.

1796 MORSE *Amer. Geog.* I. 542 Hatting is a business long established. **1853** MORFIT *Tanning, etc.* 208 The hatting of the pit is completed. **1880** G. ALLEN in *Academy* 24 Jan. 59/1 The kneeling, bowing, and hatting of modern Europe.

†**hattir,** *a.* *Sc. Obs. rare*⁻¹. Of maple. (It renders L. *acernus*.)

1513 DOUGLAS *Æneis* II. iii. [ii.] 99 This hors..Of hattyr [**1553** haltir] geistis beildit wp.

hattock. *dial.* Also **haddock, huttock.** [app. a dim. of HAT *sb.*: see -OCK.]

†**1.** A little hat. *Sc. Obs.*

1501 DOUGLAS *Pal. Hon.* II. 153 And Quintine with ane huttok on his heid. **1662** in Pitcairn *Crim. Trials* III. 604 (*Isobel Gowdie's Confession*) I haid a little horse, and wold say 'Horse and Hattock, in Divellis name!' And than we vold flie away, quhair ve vold. *a* **1800** *Jamie Telfer* in Scott *Black Dwarf* viii, Now horse and hattock speedilie They that winna ride for Telfer's kye, Let them never look in the face o' me. **1828** SCOTT *F.M. Perth* vii, Get your boots and your beasts—horse and hattock, I say.

2. a. A shock of standing sheaves of corn, the tops of which are protected by two sheaves laid along them with their bottoms in contact in the centre, and their heads slanting downwards, so as to carry off rain. **b.** The two covering sheaves themselves, called also in various districts *headsheaves* and *hoods*. (This is prob., from the etymology, the earlier sense.) *dial.*

1674 RAY *N.C. Words* 24 Hattock, a Shock containing 12 Sheaves of Corn. **1763** R. BURN *Eccl. Law* II. 406 It [rape-seed] is never bound up in sheaves, or made into hattocks. **1805** R. W. DICKSON *Pract. Agric.* (1807) II. 280 The grain ..is mostly set up into what are provincially termed *stooks, stouks, shocks*, or *hattocks*. **1846** *Brockett's N.C. Gloss.* (ed. 3) I. 234 The huttock consists of ten sheaves of corn, set two and two upright, with two hoods, one at each end to cover them. **1849** *Jrnl. R. Agric. Soc.* X. I. 133 The wheat is.. immediately put into small 'haddocks' or 'mows'. **1879** MISS JACKSON *Shropsh. Word-bk.*, *Hattocks*, sheaves of corn inverted over the 'mow' to protect it from wet. The two end sheaves of the 'mow', which consists of eight sheaves, are taken as hattocks for the remaining six. **1893** *Northumbld. Gloss.*, *Huttock*.

†**hattrel.** *Obs.* Forms: 4 **haterel, hat-, haatreel,** 5 **haterell(e, hatrelle, hattrel.** [ME. a. OF. *haterel, hasterel, hatrel*, nape of the neck, head.] The apex or crown of the head; also, the nape of the neck; the neck.

a **1325** *Prose Psalter* cxxviii[i]. 4 Our Lord riȝtful shal keruen the haterels of the sinȝers [*cervices peccatorum*]. **1340** HAMPOLE *Pr. Consc.* 1492 Fra þe haterel oboven þe croun.. tyl þe sole of þe fot doun. *c* **1400** tr. *Secreta Secret., Gov. Lordsh.* (E.E.T.S.) 80 It wendys vp to þe haterell with attempre hete. **14..** *Nom.* in Wr.-Wülcker 674/4 *Hec vertex*, hatrelle. *c* **1440** *Partonope* 3492 Joye and sorow take hym be the haterell. *c* **1450** HENRYSON *Mor. Fab.* 35 And strake the Hattrel of his head away. *c* **1475** *Pict. Voc.* in Wr.-Wülcker 745/14 *Hic vertex*, a natrelle.

hat trick.

1. Any trick with a hat, e.g. one performed by a conjurer. (In quot. applied to securing a seat in the House of Commons by placing one's hat on it.)

1886 *Daily Tel.* 10 Apr. 5/2 He may soon acquire the hat trick and other ways of securing a place.

2. a. *Cricket.* The feat of a bowler who takes three wickets by three successive balls: orig. considered to entitle him to be presented by his club with a new hat or some equivalent.

1877 J. LILLYWHITE *Cricketers' Compan.* 181 Having on one occasion taken six wickets in seven balls, thus performing the hat-trick successfully. **1882** *Daily Tel.* 19 May, He thus accomplished the feat known as the 'hat trick', and was warmly applauded. **1896** WEST *1st Year at School* xxvi, The achievement of the hat-trick afforded Eliot the proudest moment of his life.

b. Hence *gen.*, a threefold feat in other sports or activities.

1909 *Daily Chron.* 12 Aug. 9/2 It is seldom that an apprentice does the 'hat trick', but the feat was accomplished by..an apprentice... His three successes were gained on Soldier.., Lady Carlton.., and Hawkweed. **1930** *Morning Post* 16 July 17/2 Wragg's mount..enabled his jockey to complete the so-called 'hat-trick'. **1931** *Statesman* (Calcutta) 5 Dec., British aircraft constructors are hoping that an official attempt will shortly be made on the world's height record, and the 'hat trick' accomplished by the annexation of all three of the records which really matter in aviation. **1958** *Economist* 13 Sept. 819/1 The Tories are excited because it looks as if they may flout all precedents and complete a hat-trick of wins. **1967** J. POTTER *Foul Play* (1968) ix. 100 Apart from a hat trick by our centre forward it wasn't much of a game.

hatty (ˈhætɪ), *a.* [f. HAT *sb.* + -Y[1].] Wearing showy hats; interested in wearing hats.

1909 H. G. WELLS *Tono-Bungay* III. ii. 294 They all sat about in the summer-house and in garden-chairs, and were very hatty and ruffley and sunshadey. **1959** *Star* 29 Jan. 4/2 'I'm not a hatty person really,' she confessed. 'They always take so long to put on when I'm rushing out shopping.'

hattyn: see HIGHT *v.*

†**ˈhature.** *Obs. rare*⁻¹. [irreg. f. HATE *v.* + -URE.] = HATRED.

1538 BALE *Comedy J. Baptiste* in *Harl. Misc.* (Malh.) I. 215 To appeyse thy hature.

hatyr, var. HATER *sb.*[2] *Obs.*, clothing.

hau (haʊ). *Bot.* Also **hau-tree.** The Hawaiian name for a tropical shrub or tree, *Hibiscus tiliaceus*, belonging to the family Malvaceæ.

1843 J. J. JARVES *Scenes & Scenery Sandwich Islands* iii. 117 Groves of dark-leaved *hau*. **1866** 'MARK TWAIN' *Lett. fr. Hawaii* (1967) 99 Large tracts were covered with large hau (how) bushes, whose sheltering foliage is so thick as to be almost impervious to rain. **1888** W. HILLEBRAND *Flora Hawaiian Islands* 49 A small freely branching tree... Occurs in all tropical countries and is abundant in all Pacific islands. Native name: 'Hau'. **1913** R. BROOKE *Let.* 12 Oct. (1968) 518 I'm sitting under a busy 'Hau-Tree' (pronounced 'How'). **1915** W. A. BRYAN *Nat. Hist. Hawaii* xv. 201 One of the most common, persistent and useful of the native trees..is the hau. **1935** F. B. H. BROWN *Flora S.E. Polynesia* III. 174 The native name [of *Hibiscus tiliaceus*] is..hau in the northern islands of the Marquesas,..and in Hawaii.

hau- (in ME. and 16th c.): see HAV-.

haube, obs. form of ALB.

c **1425** *Voc.* in Wr.-Wülcker 649/11 *Hec alba*, haube.

hauberd(e, -bert, obs. forms of HALBERD.

haubergeon, -gioun(e, -gyon, -jeon, -joun, obs. forms of HABERGEON.

†**haubergier.** *Obs. rare.* [a. obs. F. *haubergier* (1275 in Godefroy, in same sense).] A maker of hauberks or coats of mail.

1481 CAXTON *Godfrey* cx. 168 They were named in theyr langage Bam and Cyrra, that is..the sones of haubergyers.

hauberk (ˈhɔːbək). Forms: 3- **hauberk;** also 3 **hauberc,** 3-5 **haubert,** 4 **haberke,** 5 **hau-, hawbergh(e,** 4-6 **hawberk(e, -brek,** 5-6 **haubrek,** 6 **hawbrik, habrik.** [a. OF. *hauberc*, earlier *holberc*, later (and mod.F.) *haubert* = Pr. *ausberc*, It. *osbergo, usbergo*, med.L. *halsberga*, etc., a Com. Rom. deriv. of OHG. *halsberg*, *halsperc* masc. (also *halsberga* fem.) = OE. *healsbeorȝ*, ON. *halsbjǫrg* fem., f. *hals* neck + *-bergan* to cover, protect (cf. HARBOUR). The OE. word did not survive: the OF. form was introduced in ME. See also the deriv. HABERGEON.]

A piece of defensive armour: originally intended for the defence of the neck and shoulders; but already in 12th and 13th c. developed into a long coat of mail, or military tunic, usually of ring or chain mail, which adapted itself readily to the motions of the body.

1297 R. GLOUC. (1724) 99 Wyþ haubert noble and ryche. *Ibid.* 174 With swerd or hauberk eny batail to do. *c* **1330** R. BRUNNE *Chron. Wace* (Rolls) 10029 Hauberk wiþ plates y-burnuscht ful wel. *c* **1386** CHAUCER *Knt.'s T.* 1573 The Statue of Mars bigan his hauberk rynge. *c* **1400** *Destr. Troy* 5828 Hurlet þurghe the hawbergh, hurt hym full sore. *c* **1450** *Merlin* 118 Thei..ronnen agein hym..and smyten hym on the shelde and on the haubrek. **1495** *Act 11 Hen. VII*, c. 64 Armours Defensives, as Jakkes Salettis Brigandynes..Haubertis Curesses [etc.]. **1590** SPENSER *F.Q.* II. viii. 44 And on the haubergh stroke the Prince so sore, That quite disparted all the linked frame. **1600** FAIRFAX *Tasso* I. lxxii. 15 Some dond a curace, some a corslet bright, An hawberke some, and some a haberion. **1781** GIBBON *Decl. & F.* III. lviii. 434 His breast was defended by an hauberk or coat of mail. **1870** LOWELL *Study Wind.* 242 My ears no sweeter music know Than hauberk's clank with saddle-bow. **1887** BOWEN *Virg. Æneid* v. 259 Hauberk woven of polished chain.

†**b.** worn as a garment for penance. *Obs.*

c **1305** *Edmund Conf.* 28 in *E.E.P.* (1862) 71 Þe moder werede harde hare..and harde hauberk aboue; In suche penance heo ladde hire lyf. *c* **1386** CHAUCER *Pars. T.* ¶980 Clothing of whiche Ihesu crist is moore apayed than of heyres or haubergeons or hauberkes.

haubersion(e, haubrischoune, obs. Sc. ff. HABERGEON.

haubitzer, obs. form of HOWITZER.

hauceour, -or, obs. forms of HAWSER.

†**ˈhaucepy.** *Obs.* [a. F. *haussepié, -pied*, 'a net or engine wherewith Wolues, etc. are caught' Cotgr.; f. *hausser* to raise, lift up + *pied* foot.] A kind of trap for wolves and other wild beasts.

c **1425** *Bk. Huntynge* (*MS. Bodl.* 546, lf. 36 b), Also men takeþ hem yn puttys..and wiþ haucepys or with venemous powdres þat men gyueþ hem yn flesh.

hauch, *int.* and *sb.* *Sc.* [Cf. Ger. *hauch* breath, aspiration.] 'The forcible reiterated respiration of one who exerts all his strength in giving a stroke' (Jam.); a panting sound.

1513 DOUGLAS *Æneis* VII. ix. 79 With mony pant, and felloun hauchis and quhaikis.

hauch, hauck, obs. ff. HAUGH, HAWK.

hauchecornite (haʊkəˈkɔənaɪt). *Min.* [ad. G. *hauchecornit* (R. Scheibe 1893, in *Jahrb. d. Preuss. geol. Landesanst. und Bergakademie zu Berlin, 1891* XII. 91), f. the name of Wilhelm *Hauchecorne* (1828-1900), German geologist: see -ITE[1].] A bronze-coloured sulphide of nickel, bismuth, and antimony, $Ni_9(Bi,Sb)_2S_8$.

1893 *Jrnl. Chem. Soc.* LXIV. II. 418 Hauchecornite is of a light, bronze-yellow colour. **1950** *Amer. Mineralogist* XXXV. 440 Study of a specimen..from the original locality, Friedrich mine, Hamm a. d. Sieg, Westphalia, confirms the individuality of hauchecornite. **1968** I. KOSTOV *Mineral.* 117 (*table*) Hauchecornite.

haud, Sc. form of HOLD.

hauerite (ˈhaʊəraɪt). *Min.* [Named by Haidinger, 1846, after Von Hauer, an Austrian geologist.] Native disulphide of manganese, occurring in reddish-brown crystals, usually octahedral.

1847 *Amer. Jrnl. Sc.* Ser. II. IV. 108 Hauerite belongs to Mohs' order of blende. **1892** *Dana's Min.* 87 The hauerite crystals are sometimes coated with pyrite.

hauf, Sc. f. HALF; var. of HOWFF *Sc.*

haugh (hɑx, hɑf). *Sc.* and north *dial.* Forms: 4 **halche,** 4-6 **hawch,** 4-7 **hawgh,** 5- **haugh** (8 **haw**); also in north. Engl. **halgh** as in *Greenhalgh*. [app.

a phonetic descendant of OE. *healh, halh* 'corner, nook' (see HALE *sb.*[2]): cf. Sc. *sauch, saugh*:—OE. *sealh*; Sc. *tauch* = ME. *talȝ*.]

A piece of flat alluvial land by the side of a river, forming part of the floor of the river valley.

The original sense was perh. 'corner or nook (of land) in the bend or angle of the river'. A northern stream usually crosses and recrosses the floor of its valley, striking the base of the slope on each side alternately, and forming a more or less triangular 'haugh' within its bend, on each side in turn.

[**814** *Charter of Cœnwulf* in *Cod. Dipl.* I. 257 Of þam ȝebyhte..oð cyninges healh. **967** *Charter of Oswald* Ibid. III. 19 Sc westra easthealh.] **1375** BARBOUR *Bruce* XVI. 336 In the hawch [*v.r.* halche, hawgh] of Lyntoun-le. **1513** DOUGLAS *Æneis* XIII. Prol. 22 Amyd the hawchis, and euery lusty vaill. **1525-6** *Durh. MS. Cell. Roll*, Operantibus apud Rayls circa le haughe in bearparke. **1637-50** Row *Hist. Kirk* (1842) 330 Inundations of waters took away to the sea wholl large haughs full of shorn corne. **1726** *Dict. Rust.* (ed. 3), *Haw*..in the North it signifies a green plot of Ground in a Valley. **1786** BURNS *Scotch Drink* iii, Let husky Wheat the haughs adorn. **1799** J. ROBERTSON *Agric. Perth* 15 All the land, which has been occasionally flooded, time immemorial, is commonly called Haugh. **1809** LD. MINTO in *Scott's Fam. Lett.* (1894) I. 157, I..hope one day to see his wandering staff planted in some Teviot haugh. **1827** MACKENZIE *Hist. Newcastle* II. 743 Proposed to excavate the haughs above bridge.

b. *attrib.*, as ***haugh-land***.

1794 *Statist. Acc. Scot., Lanark.* XII. 34 (Jam.) The haugh-ground is generally ploughed 3..years for oats. **1805** *Trans. Soc. Arts* XXIII. 61 A quantity of haugh-land. *a***1852** MACGILLIVRAY *Nat. Hist. Dee Side* (1855) 255 The stream..covers all the haugh lands with its turbid waters. **1873** BURTON *Hist. Scot.* I. iii. 81 The great haugh flats.

haugh, obs. f. HOE, HAW *int.*[1] and *sb.*[4]

haught (hɔːt), *a. arch.* Forms: α. 5-6 **haute, hawt(e, 6 halt, 6-7 haut, hault(e.** β. 6- **haught.** [orig. *haut, hault* from contemporary French: see HAUT *a.*; corrupted late in 16th c. to *haught* after words like *caught, taught*, etc. in which *gh* had become mute: perh. influenced by *high, height*.]

1. High in one's own estimation; bearing oneself loftily; haughty. *arch.*

α. **1430-40** LYDG. *Bochas* v. xxiv. (1554) 138a, He was haute in his prosperitie. **1494** FABYAN *Chron.* VII. 516 Many hawte wordys were blowen on eyther partye. **1531** ELYOT *Gov.* II. v, A proude and haulte countenaunce. **1648** MILTON *Ps.* lxxx. 35 Nations proud and haut.

β. **1608** SHAKS. *Rich. II*, IV. i. 254 (2nd Qo.) *North.* My lord. *Rich.* No Lord of thine, thou haught insulting man. **1814** SCOTT *Ld. of Isles* I. xxxi, That bearing haught and high, Which common spirits fear! **1875** BROWNING *Inn Album* I. 313 As the haught high-bred bearing and dispose.

†**2.** Of exalted character, esp. in the matter of courage; high-minded, noble; lofty. *Obs.*

α. *a***1470** TIPTOFT *Cæsar* (1530) 12 He was a man of haute courage. **1556** J. HEYWOOD *Spider & F.* lix. 97 With corage hawte, Thonset to giue, this castell to assawte. **1565** GOLDING *Ovid's Met.* IV. (1593) 99 Valiant deedes and halt exploits. *a***1577** SIR T. SMITH *Commw. Eng.* II. xxvii. (1609) 97 The nature of our Nation is free, stout, hault.

β. **1590** SPENSER *F.Q.* I. vi. 29 His courage haught Desyrd of forreine foemen to be knowne.

†**3.** Of exalted rank or station; high-born, noble.

1470-85 MALORY *Arthur* II. vi, Galahad the haute [**1634** haughty] prynce. **1553** BALE *Gardiner's De Vera Obed.* F iij, In hault estate of worldly power. **1590** GREENE *Orl. Fur.* Wks. (Rtldg.) 106/1 That boast the pride of haught Latonas son. *a***1627** MIDDLETON & ROWLEY *Sp. Gipsy* II. ii, As brave a Spaniard As ever spake the haut Castilian tongue.

†**4.** High, in literal and other senses. ***of hawt grees***, tr. F. *de haute graisse*, 'full, plumpe, goodlie, fat, well-fed, in good liking' (Cotgr.). (In Bailey prob. only Fr.) *Obs.*

*c***1460** J. RUSSELL *Bk. Nurture* 409 Capon, & hen of hawt grees, þus wold þey be dight. **1587** TURBERV. *Trag. T.* (1837) 5, I know how haut thy muse doth flie. [**1731** BAILEY, *Haut*, high or shrill..*Haut Contre* (in Musick Books) signifies Counter Tenor. *Haut Dessus*, first Treble.]

5. *Comb.*, as ***haught-hearted, -minded***.

1540-1 ELYOT *Image Gov.* (1556) 23 Haulte mynded and sterne towardes the communaltee. **1547-64** BAULDWIN *Mor. Philos.* (Palfr.) 103 Th' ambicious and hautehearted felowe. **1595** *Enq. Tripe-wife* (1881) 145 Haught minded, and hot spirited Simon.

haughte, obs. pa. pple. of HATCH *v.*[1]

haughtily (ˈhɔːtɪlɪ), *adv.* Also 6 **hawt-**. [f. HAUGHTY + -LY[2].] In a haughty manner; proudly, arrogantly.

1573-80 BARET *Alv.* H 261 Hawtily, *elate..excelse.* **1611** BIBLE *Micah* ii. 3 Neither shall ye goe haughtily. *a***1720** SHEFFIELD (Dk. Buckhm.) *Wks.* (1753) II. 176 To be neither remiss, nor haughtily imperious. **1832** MACAULAY *Armada* 19 Haughtily the trumpets peal, and gaily dance the bells. **1838** DICKENS *Nich. Nick.* xvi, He..strode haughtily out of the office.

haughtiness (ˈhɔːtɪnɪs). Also 6-7 **haut-, halt-**, etc. [f. as prec. + -NESS.]

1. The quality of being haughty; loftiness of demeanour; pride, arrogance, disdainfulness.

1555 EDEN *Decades* 165 He coulde not longe abyde the hautynes of Petrus Arias. **1571** GOLDING *Calvin on Ps.* xxxi. 23 The hawltinesse wherewith they be pufft up. **1592** WARNER *Alb. Eng.* VII. xxxvii. (1612) 179 Honors made him haughtie, and his haughtines to erre. **1645** MILTON *Tetrach.* (1851) 206 To lay their hautinesse under a severity which they deserv'd. *a***1745** SWIFT *Will II*, Lett., etc. 1768 IV. 261 King William discovered so much haughtiness and disdain, both in words and gestures. **1872** J. L. SANFORD *Estim. Eng. Kings, Chas. I*, 331 The dignity of bearing..was..often replaced and travestied by a frigid haughtiness.

b. as a mock title.

1641 MILTON *Animadv.* Wks. 1738 I. 76 To send home his Haughtiness well bespurted with his own Holy-water. **1794** WOLCOTT (P. Pindar) *Ode* Wks. 1812 III. 261 Their most high Haughtinesses.

†**2.** Exalted character, loftiness, nobility, grandeur; loftiness (of courage), bravery. *Obs.*

1564 GOLDING *Justine* 77 (R.) In hautinesse of courage.. and in strength of body, he farre excelled all. **1577-87** HOLINSHED *Chron.* III. 1176/1 Which answer..moued a maruellous shout and reioising..the haltinesse thereof was so wonderfull. **1613** PURCHAS *Pilgrimage* I. ix. 44, I hope that the haughtinesse of the Attempt..shall rather purchase pardon to my slippes, then blame for my rashnesse.

†ˈ**haughtly**, *adv. Obs.* In 6 **hawt-, haute-**. [f. HAUGHT *a.* + -LY[2].] = HAUGHTILY.

1523 SKELTON *Garl. Laurel* 1117 She loked hawtly and gave on me a glum. **1581** J. BELL *Haddon's Answ. Osor.* 77b, So hautely and arrogantly enhaunced. **1586** WARNER *Alb. Eng.* III. xvi. (1589) 67 As haughtelie doest thou reuenge, as humblie I repent.

†ˈ**haughtness.** *Obs.* In 5-6 **hault(e-**. [f. HAUGHT *a.* + -NESS.] = HAUGHTINESS.

1489 CAXTON *Faytes of A.* IV. xvii. 280 Dyuerse deuyses taken by haultnesse fro the tyme ryght auncyent. **1548** UDALL *Erasm. Par. Luke* iv. 58 High solemnitie and haultenesse of countinaunce. **1594** CAREW *Tasso* (1881) 114 O how she haultnes now and pride forgoes!

haughtonite (ˈhɔːtənaɪt). *Min.* [Named 1878, after Dr. S. Haughton.] A variety of BIOTITE, in which iron replaces much of the magnesium.

1878 *Min. Mag.* V. 183 Plates of bronzy Biotite (or Haughtonite). **1881** *Academy* 6 Nov. 350 The black mica which Dr. Heddle described as Haughtonite.

haughty (ˈhɔːtɪ), *a.* Forms: α. 6 **haltie, haultie, -y, hawtie, -y, 6-7 hautie, -y.** β. 6- **haughty.** [An extension of *haut*, HAUGHT *a.*, either as in *dusk-y, worth-y*, or simply by assimilation to *doughty, mighty, naughty, weighty*, etc.]

1. High in one's own estimation; lofty and disdainful in feeling or demeanour; proud, arrogant, supercilious. (Of persons, their action, speech, etc.)

α. **1530** PALSGR. 315/1 Hawty as one that is proude, *haultain.* **1563** *Mirr. Mag., Rich. III*, x, Puft vp in pride, so hawtie then I grewe. **1570** *Satir. Poems Reform.* xxi. 55 Hautie wordis. **1659** HAMMOND *On Ps.* xlv. 4 The prides of the hautiest heathen obdurate hearts. **1667** MILTON *P. L.* IV. 858 The Fiend..like a proud Steed reind, went hautie on.

β. **1598** FLORIO, *Orgoglioso*, proude, disdainefull, haughtie. **1611** BIBLE *Ps.* cxxx. 1 Lord, my heart is not haughtie. **1667** MILTON *P.L.* V. 852 Whereat rejoic'd Th' Apostat, and more haughty thus repli'd. **1725** DE FOE *Voy. round World* (1840) 191 The cruel haughty temper of the Spaniards. **1876** ROCK *Text. Fabr.* 105 The humble broom-plant—the haughty Plantagenet's device.

b. *fig.* Of an appearance that seems to claim or assume superiority; imposing in aspect; grand, stately, dignified: often with some mixture of sense 3.

1585 T. WASHINGTON tr. *Nicholay's Voy* III. v. 78 With their great tufts of feathers upon their heads, they seem in their appearance proude and hawty. **1697** DRYDEN *Virg. Georg.* III. 641 His haughty Crest. **1700** T. BROWN tr. *Fresny's Amusem. Ser. & Com.* 86 Philosophers build those hauty Edifices they call Systems. **1850** W. IRVING *Mahomet* lv. 254 I'll carry the war into yon haughty mountains.

2. Of exalted character, style, or rank; elevated, lofty, eminent; high-minded, aspiring; of exalted courage or bravery. *arch.*

α. **1563** B. GOOGE *Eglogs, etc.* (Arb.) 72 The hawtye verse, that Maro wrote. **1576** FLEMING *Panopl. Epist.* 438 Sithence your estate is so hautie and high. **1577-87** HOLINSHED *Chron.* III. 1171/2 His stoutnesse and haltie courage. **1667** MILTON *P.L.* IX. 484 Of courage hautie, and of limb Heroic built.

β. **1578** T. N. tr. *Conq. W. India* 25 Men of haughtie corage, that no force or strength of Indians can offende. **1590** SPENSER *F.Q.* II. x. 1 Who now shall give unto me words and sound Equall unto this haughty enterprise? **1613** PURCHAS *Pilgrimage* (1614) 280 These their haughtie attempts were stayed. **1805** SCOTT *Last Minstr.* VI. xxiii, No haughty feat of arms I tell.

†**3.** High, lofty (in literal sense). *Obs.* (Often with some shade of sense 1.)

1570 B. GOOGE *Pop. Kingd.* IV. (1880) 50b, From the toppes of hawtie towres. **1576** FLEMING *Panopl. Epist.* 272 Plantes as growe in highe mountaines, in loftie and hautie places. *Ibid.* 288 Others..pufft upp in the pride of their nature, advaunce themselves to the hautie heavens. **1578** *Mirr. for Mag.* II. *Vortiger* xiii. (1610) 206 God who rules the haughtie heauen a hygh. **1621** G. SANDYS *Ovid's Met.* VIII. (1626) 156 In mind they beare Their ancient fall and haughtie places feare.

4. *Comb.*, as ***haughty-hearted, -minded, -stomached***.

1576 FLEMING *Panopl. Epist.* 5 Some..report you to be proude and hautie harted. **1605** *Tryall Chev.* I. iii. in Bullen *O. Pl.* III. 281 Were his power and spirit Ten times more hauty-ventrous. *a***1777** FAWKES tr. *Appollon. Rhod., Argonautics* III. (R.), The haughty-minded Pelias.

haugou, -gout, obs. forms of HAUT-GOUT.

Hau Hau (ˈhaʊ haʊ). *N.Z.* Also **Hauhau, Hau-hau, hau hau.** [Maori.] A follower of the Pai-Marire religion during the nineteenth-century Maori Wars. Also *attrib.* Hence ˈ**Hau-hauism.**

1865 *Richmond-Atkinson Papers* II. iii. 171 The excitement among the Hau-hau and other hostile natives was reviving. **1871** C. L. MONEY *Knocking about in N.Z.* x. 137 A large village..said to be a nest of Hau-haus. **1875** *Official Handbk. N.Z.* (ed. 2) 28/2 Many who eagerly adopted Hau-hauism at first, have since given it up. **1884** M. MARTIN *Our Maoris* xi. 169 Early in 1865 came the terrible news from the East Cape, of the Rev. Carl Volkner's murder by the fanatical Hauhaus there. [*Ibid.* 173 He proclaimed a new religion, though indeed it was a mixture of wild applications of Old Testament history with spells and incantations. A pole was set up in the pah, round which the people danced. They drew in their breaths all at once, somewhat in the way paviours used to do. This deep groan at the end of each sentence, 'Hau', gave a name to the fanatical movement which lasts to this day.] **1914** *Chambers's Jrnl.* Mar. 173/2 In religion he follows 'Hau-hauism', a strange intermingling of ideas, based largely on the Old Testament. **1930** J. COWAN in J. Reid *Kiwi Laughs* (1961) 97 They would have had his head to decorate the end of a Hauhau pole had they discovered the particular potato-pit in which he was hiding. **1949** P. BUCK *Coming of Maori* (1950) IV. iii. 474 Possession was practised by the fanatical followers of the late post-European sect known as *hauhau*, when dancing around a pole termed the *niu*. **1959** M. SHADBOLT *New Zealanders* 237 The great-grandfather was eaten in the latter stage of the Maori wars by the *Hau Hau*, that fanatic group which combined Christianity and cannibalism with apparent success.

hau-hau (hɔːhɔː), *v.* [Echoic.] *intr.* To utter the cry of a hyena.

1924 *Other Lands* Jan. 43/1 A hyena went hau-hauing down the path between the tent and the garden.

†**hauht, haht.** *Obs.* Also 3 **haȝt (aȝte).** [Cf. ON. *hætta* (:—**háhtjôn*) danger, peril, risk.] Peril, risk.

*c***1200** *Vices & Virtues* 11 Hu michel haht hit is godes forbod to brekene. —— *Ibid.* 87 Ac ðat is michel hauht, bute ðu hierof neme michele ȝieme. *c***1250** *Gen. & Ex.* 486 Of his soule beð mikel haȝt. *Ibid.* 2082 Ic am in sorȝe and haȝt. *Ibid.* 3384 Amalechkes folc fledde for aȝte of dead.

hauke, hauker, obs. ff. HAWK, HAWKER.

haukim, obs. form of HAKIM.

haul (hɔːl), *v.* Forms: 6-8 **hall**, 7 **hawle**, 7-9 **hawl**, 7- **haul.** [A variant spelling of HALE *v.*[1], in 16th c. also *hall*; representing a different phonetic development of ME. *hale* (haːl): cf. *small*, beside OE. *smæl*, ME. *smal, smale*, Sc. *smale, smail*. For the spelling *au, aw*, which dates only from 17th c., cf. *crawl*.]

1. a. *trans.* To pull or draw with force or violence; to drag, tug (*esp.* in nautical language).

1581 PETTIE tr. *Guazzo's Civ. Conv.* II. (1586) 110 If hee hung backe, hee shall be halled forward. **1597** SHAKS. *2 Hen. IV*, v. v. 37 Thy Dol..is in base Durance, and contagious prison: Hall'd thither by most Mechanicall and durty hand. **1626** CAPT. SMITH *Accid. Yng. Seamen* 27 Heaue out your top-sayles, hawle your sheates. **1667** DRYDEN *Tempest* I. i, All within, Haul catt, haul catt, haul catt, haul. **1669** STURMY *Mariner's Mag.* 17 Hawl down both Top-sails close. *c***1680** BEVERIDGE *Serm.* (1729) I. 352 See him hall'd from one judgement seat to another. **1773** GOLDSM. *Stoops to Conq.* III. (Globe) 664/1 Didn't I see him hawl you about like a milk-maid? **1798** COLERIDGE *Satyrane's Lett.* i. in *Biog. Lit.* (1882) 246 We hauled anchor, and passed gently up the river. **1810** *Sporting Mag.* XXXVI. 264 They were pushing and hawling every body about. **1853** READE *Chr. Johnstone* 160 He began to haul in the net. **1885** *Manch. Exam.* 24 Feb. 5/2 [They] would rather be stoned and hauled before the magistrates.

fig. **1725** N. ROBINSON *Th. Physick* 141 There is no Necessity always to hall in fermenting Humours to cause pain.

†**b.** To search, examine thoroughly, overhaul (cf. *drag*). *Obs. rare.*

1666 WOOD *Life* (O.H.S.) II. 83 Continually hauling taverns and alehouses [for undergraduates].

†**c.** *colloq.* To worry, torment, pester. *Obs.*

1678 R. BARCLAY *Apol. Quakers* XIV. v. 506 They went up and down..preaching..tho' daily beaten, whipped, bruised, halled, and imprisoned therefore. **1737** WHISTON *Josephus, Antiq.* XIX. i. §1 Caius..pulled and hauled its other citizens, especially the senate. **1743** GAY *Distress'd Wife* v. Wks. (1772) 328, I won't be haul'd and worried.

d. *colloq.* To bring *up* for a reprimand, to call to account. Also, ***to haul over the coals*** (see COAL *sb.* 12).

1795 NELSON 25 Nov. in Nicolas *Disp.* (1845) II. 107, I think the Admiral will be hauled over the coals for not letting me have ships. **1865** LIVINGSTONE *Zambesi* vi. 142 The first native..refused to sell his fowls at the Government prices [and] was hauled up before the irate commandant. **1882** B. D. W. RAMSAY *Recoll. Mil. Serv.* I. ix. 215 They were all young officers..and probably at times require to be hauled up sharply. **1893** ST. AUBYN *Junior Dean* xxix. 233 He was what, in figurate undergraduate language is termed 'hauled'.

e. To transport by cart or other conveyance; to cart, carry.

1741 *New Hampshire Probate Rec.* III. 43 Her fire wood from time to time shall be haul'd to Said house. **1787** WINTER *Syst. Husb.* 101 The expence of halling must be governed by the distance they are halled from. **1814** H. M. BRACKENRIDGE *Views Louisiana* 141 They are sometimes employed in hauling lead from the mines. **1852** *Trans. Mich.*

Agric. Soc. III. 179, I haul it [*sc.* manure] out in the fall, spread it and plow it in immediately after. **1880** *Harper's Mag.* Sept. 619/2 In winter I haul logs, and in summer I haul mealers. **1887** *Congress. Rec.* 10 Jan. 484/1 There is not one-tenth part of the risk in hauling dressed beef that there is in hauling live animals. **1918** F. Hackett *Ireland* ii. 46 The more fish was caught.. the less any one of them was worth. And when it came to salting them or hauling them, the same curse was in it. **1970** *Washington Post* 30 Sept. B13/4 The company sought a million-dollar contract with Ft. Rucker, Ala., to haul gasoline.

absol. **1871** R. L. Dashwood *Chiploquorgan* viii. 117 We had fifteen miles to haul along a lumber road to the mouth of Rocky brook. **1883** J. Hay *Bread-winners* vi. 96 You know Clinsty Fore, that hauls for the Safe Company? **1933** E. Merrick *True North* 338 We hauled across lots of yellow, slushy places.

f. *intr.* With *out, up.* Of bachelor seals: to come out of the water to rest on the hauling-grounds.

1869 *Overland Monthly* III. 39 To ascertain if any elephant-seal had 'hauled up' on the beach. **1894** Kipling *Jungle Bk.* 98 I've often thought we should be much happier if we hauled out at Otter Island. **1902** *Encycl. Brit.* XXXII. 488/1 The young males, or bachelors, haul out to rest and sleep on beaches adjacent to, but distinct from, the breeding-grounds. **1967** *Listener* 6 Apr. 459/1 Adult male seals hold territories on beaches where a population hauls out for breeding.

2. a. *intr.* To pull, tug (*at* or *upon* something).

1743 Bulkeley & Cummins *Voy. S. Seas* 115 All Hands haul'd. **1791** 'G. Gambado' *Ann. Horsem.* ix. (1809) 106, I ..pull'd, and haul'd, to try to turn him [a horse]. **1857** Lawrence *Guy Liv.* xiv. 129 He was hauling nervously at the reins. **1859** Reade *Love me Little* II. iv. 177 He..made the rope fast to her [the schooner's] thwart, then hauling upon it, brought the lugger alongside.

b. *intr.* for *refl.* in passive sense.

1797 Nelson in A. Duncan *Life* (1806) 42, I found..the Spanish ensign hauling down. **1871** Palgrave *Lyr. Poems* 138 Till their flag hauls down to the foe.

3. a. *Naut.* (*intr.*) To trim the sails, etc. of a ship so as to sail nearer to the wind (also ***to haul up***); hence more generally, to change or turn the ship's course; to sail in a certain course. (Also *trans.* with the ship as object; also, to sail along *a coast.*)

1557 W. Towrson in Hakluyt *Voy.* (1589) 113 We halled off our ships to fetch the winde as neer as wee coulde. ***a* 1599** H. Smith *Ibid.* (1599) I. 445 The wind being at West, we did hall the coast East northeast, and East..Wee..hald along the coast East and East southeast, and all the same night wee halled Southeast, and Southeast by East. **1697** Dampier *Voy.* (1729) I. 51 He halled into the Harbour, close to the Island. **1743** Woodroofe in Hanway *Trav.* (1762) I. ii. xxiii. 101 We haul'd round Zeloi island for Baku bay. *Ibid.* iv. lix. 272 Hauling out north north-east. **1806** A. Duncan *Nelson* 48 The enemy..hauled up on the Terpsichore's weather-beam. **1858** C. Kirton in *Merc. Marine Mag.* V. 209, I hauled in to S. 23° E., true. *Ibid.*, I told the Chief Officer to haul her off four points.

b. Phr. *to haul upon* or *to the wind*, also trans. ***to haul*** (a ship) ***on a wind***, and ***to haul the*** (***her, our***, etc.) ***wind***: to bring the ship round so as to sail closer to the wind.

1726 Shelvocke *Voy. round World* (1757) 328 Unwilling to run..into the enemy's clutches, I hauled again on a wind. **1762** Falconer *Shipwr.* ii. Argt., The ship bears up: again hauls upon the wind. **1768** Wales in *Phil. Trans.* LX. 112 At 15 h. we hauled the wind to the south-ward. **1797** Nelson in A. Duncan *Life* (1806) 40 The Spanish fleet..hauled to the wind on the larboard tack. **1806** A. Duncan *Nelson* 24 The enemy hauled their wind and made off. **1829** Marryat *F. Mildmay* xxi, My intention is to..haul dead on a wind. **1835** —— *Pirate* xiv, The Enterprise took in her topmast studding-sail, and hauled her wind. **1867** Smyth *Sailor's Word-bk.* s.v., *Haul your wind*, or *haul to the wind*, signifies that the ship's head is to be brought nearer to the wind.

c. *transf.* and *fig.* (*intr.* and *trans.*) To change one's course of action; to withdraw, retreat; to make one's way, to come or go. ***to haul off*** (chiefly *U.S.*), to withdraw or draw back a little before completing an action of any kind; ***to haul out*** (*U.S.*), to go out, depart.

1802 T. Jefferson *Writ.* (1830) III. 495 He took it in mortal offence, and from that moment has been hauling off to his former enemies. **1825** *Blackw. Mag.* XVIII. 177 Such works haul but slowly into this northern region. **1858** B. Taylor *Northern Trav.* xxii. 230 The morning looked.. threatening, but the clouds gradually hauled off to the eastward. **1866** W. H. Jackson *Diary* 30 July in *Nebr. Hist. Mag.* (1932) XIII. 156 Hauled out before sunrise and corralled at the Springs by 9 o'clock. **1867** Smyth *Sailor's Word-bk.*, *Haul my wind*, an expression when an individual is going upon a new line of action. **1870** 'Mark Twain' in *Galaxy* Oct. 572/2 Suppose he should take deliberate aim and 'haul off' and fetch me with the butt-end of it [*sc.* a gun]? **1902** A. D. McFaul *Ike Glidden* xxv. 282 The train hauled out while the officer was taking him into custody. **1930** D. Runyon in *Collier's* 20 Dec. 32/3 Then Lily hauls off and gives me a big kiss right in the smush. **1960** Wodehouse *Jeeves in Offing* vi. 63, I shall have no alternative but to haul off and bop *him* one. *Ibid.* vii. 71 A cow that looked as if it were planning, next time it was milked, to haul off and let the milkmaid have it in the lower ribs. **1961** M. McLuhan *Mech. Bride* 60/2 Looks like he's going to haul off and kiss her.

4. Of the wind: To change direction, shift, veer.

1769 Falconer *Dict. Marine* (1789), *Echars*, a wind that veers and hauls; a light and variable wind. **1840** R. H. Dana *Bef. Mast* xxxi. 111 The wind hauled to the south-ward. **1864** Lowell *Fireside Trav.* 123 The wind also is hauling round to the right quarter. **1867** Smyth *Sailor's Word-bk.*, *Haul round*, said when the wind is gradually shifting towards any particular point of the compass.

haul (hɔːl), *sb.* [f. prec. vb.]

1. a. The act of hauling; a pull, a tug; *spec.* the draught of a fishing-net.

1670 W. Hacke *Collect. Voy.* (1699) II. 82 We caught in our Sean at one Haul no less than seven Hundred. **1726** Thomson *Winter* 627 The leap, the slap, the haul. **1780** A. Young *Tour Irel.* I. 220* The largest hawl, taking 1452 salmon. **1868** Peard *Water-Farm.* viii. 87 This first haul of the net. **1871** Proctor *Light Sc.* 156 On October 5th..both the sun and the moon will give a particularly vigorous haul upon the earth's waters.

b. With *adv*, as ***haul-down***, the act of hauling down. ***haul-down promotion***: see hauling *vbl. sb.* b, quot. 1867.

1882 *Navy List* July 512/2 Haul down promotions abolished by Circular 75, of 10th November 1874.

c. *spec.* The distance over which something is hauled, freq. in phr. ***long*** (or ***short***) ***haul***. Also *fig.*

1877 W. Rockefeller *Let.* 17 Oct. in *Philadelphia Inquirer* (1879) 8 Mar. 2/c We will endeavor to deliver the oil to you at points from which you will have short hauls. **1884** *Congress. Rec.* 18 June 5314/2 The farmer has to pay for short hauls just about what they ask him [etc.]... We must study the effect..of short hauls and long hauls. **1905** *Terms Forestry & Logging* 39 *Haul*, in logging, the distance and route over which teams must go between two given points, as between the yard or skid way and the landing. **1909** H. N. Casson *Life C. H. McCormick* 213 Today it is not the long haul of wheat, but the short haul, that is more expensive. **1936** L. C. Douglas *White Banners* vi. 123 Florid, peaches-and-cream blondes weren't intended for long hauls of worry. **1957** *Sunday Times* 13 Oct. 5/6 A new building for long-haul traffic is recommended. **1962** *Listener* 15 Feb. 307/1 Both points of view are necessary at different times, but the C.R.O. one is designed for the long haul. **1968** *Times* 1 Nov. 10/3 Improvements would be certainly possible; but he gave a warning: 'This is a long haul. You cannot suddenly change the existing systems.' **1973** *Daily Tel.* 15 Jan. 19/1 Everyone knows that you don't just buy investment trusts for the short haul.

2. *concr.* **a.** A draught of fish.

1854 H. Miller *Sch. & Schm.* xx. (1860) 212 The entire haul consisted of rather more than twelve barrels. **1885** *L'pool Daily Post* 30 June 4/8 When they make good hauls of fish the price immediately drops.

b. *Rope-making.* (See first quot.)

1794 *Rigging & Seamanship* I. 55 *A Haul of Yarn* is about four-hundred threads, when warped off the winches, with a slight turn in it, to be tarred. *Ibid.* 61 It is generally tarred in hauls, as other rope. **1875** Knight *Dict. Mech.* s.v., The haul is dragged through a *grip, gape*, or sliding nipper which expresses superfluous tar.

3. *fig.* The act of 'drawing' or making a large profit or valuable acquisition of any kind; *concr.* the thing or amount thus gained or acquired.

1776 A. Adams in *J. Q. Adams' Fam. Lett.* (1876) 220, I think we made a fine haul of prizes. **1826** Scott *Jrnl.* (1890) I. 176 If I can but wheedle him out of a few anecdotes, it would be a great haul. **1891** *Lit. World* 24 Apr. 396/1 £25,000 is said to be the great haul made..as the result of his recent lecturing tour.

4. *Comb.* **haul-rope**, a rope for hauling something; **haul-seine**, a large seine that is hauled, a drag-seine.

1884 Knight *Dict. Mech.* Suppl., *Haul Seine.* **1890** O. Crawfurd *Round Calendar in Portugal* 32 I have seen the whole population of a coast hamlet..at the haul-ropes, and drawing home..the harvest of the sea.

haulabout (ˈhɔːləbaʊt). *U.S.* [f. the verbal phrase *to haul about* (haul *v.* 1).] A vessel, resembling a barge, used for coaling ships.

1903 *Trans. Inst. Naval Archit.* XLV. 221 These vessels, ..like the smaller barges, or 'coal haulabouts' as they are termed, have no means of propelling themselves.

haulage (ˈhɔːlɪdʒ). [f. as haul *sb.* + -age.]

1. The action or process of hauling or pulling; the traction or conveyance of a load in a wagon or other vehicle; the amount of force expended in hauling (quot. 1883).

1826 J. Adamson *Sk. Inform. Rail-roads* 39 The company have actually let the haulage of their coal. **1857** Smiles *Stephenson* ix. 81 The haulage was both tedious and expensive. **1883** *Manch. Exam.* 7 Nov. 5/5 The impossible gradient of one in 25..is..denounced..as the haulage would have to be trebled, and three horses employed in place of one.

2. The expense of or charge for hauling.

1864 in Webster. **1869** *Sat. Rev.* 19 June 822 He estimates his pair of cottages..at 205*l.* plus the haulage.

3. 'A traction-way' (Smyth *Sailor's Word-bk.*).

4. *attrib.* and *Comb.*, as ***haulage clip*** (see quot. 1883), ***-engine, -power, -road, -rope, -work***.

1864 *Reader* 7 May 594 The diminution of haulage power owing to the wheels becoming rail-bound. **1883** Gresley *Gloss. Coal Mining, Haulage Clip*, levers, jaws, wedges, etc., by which trams, singly or in trains, are connected to the hauling ropes. **1896** Mrs. H. Ward *Sir G. Tressady* 555 The air in the haulage road was clearing fast. **1909** *Daily Chron.* 16 Sept. 1/3 A haulage engine..was taking a load of bricks up the steep gradient. *Ibid.* 30 Sept. 1/5 The flood carried away the haulage engine at the entrance of the level.

haulbergyn, obs. form of habergeon.

†**haul-bowline, -bowling** = hale-bowline.

1867 Smyth *Sailor's Word-bk.*, *Haul-bowlings*, the old name for the able-bodied seamen.

hauld, Sc. f. hold.

hauler (ˈhɔːlə(r)). [f. haul *v.* + -er[1].] One who or that which hauls; a man employed in hauling something, e.g. coal in a mine (= haulier 1).

1674 N. Fairfax *Bulk & Selv.* Ep. Ded., Whatever is a Nonesuch, will draw enough as 'tis, without the Hogou of the stifling Haulers. **1846** Worcester, *Hauler*, one who draws. **1889** *Cent. Dict.*, *Hauler*..2. A device for catching fish, consisting of several hooks connected together and hauled through the water by a line..as, a *hauler* for bluefish. **1892** *Labour Commission* Gloss., *Drawers*, also called 'haulers', are the workmen in a coal mine who fill the tubs at the face and draw or haul them to the pit bottom.

haulier (ˈhɔːlɪə(r)). [f. haul *v.* + -ier, cf. *collier, sawyer* and hallier[1].] **1.** A man employed in hauling or pulling something; *spec.* a workman in a coal mine who pulls or drives the tubs which convey the coal from the working to the bottom of the shaft.

1577 Hanmer *Anc. Eccl. Hist.* (1585) 461 Maister..of the hauliers. **1892** *Daily News* 27 Aug. 5/4 They found in the upper roadway two hauliers or carters..overcome by the foul gas. **1893** *Times* 9 Aug. 9/2 The hauliers employed at the Prince of Wales Colliery, Risca.

2. A firm or a person engaged in road transport.

1919 *Commercial Motor* 1 May 199/1 We do not find a motor haulier keeping his vehicles in the garage because his repair department informs him that this is the best way of reducing the cost of maintenance. **1951** *Oxf. Jun. Encycl.* IV. 277/1 Hauliers often have to transfer loads from one vehicle to another at the state border. **1959** *Times Rev. Industry* May 44/3 Hauliers are afraid to work out costs properly. **1967** *Listener* 20 Apr. 539/3 Interviews with drivers and hauliers.

hauling (ˈhɔːlɪŋ), *vbl. sb.* [f. haul *v.* + -ing[1].]

a. The action of pulling, dragging, or traction.

1626 Capt. Smith *Accid. Yng. Seamen* 4 The Marshall is to..see Justice executed..ducking at Yards arme, hawling vnder the Keele. **1658–9** *Burton's Diary* (1828) III. 134 There will be hauling and pulling, and irregular proceedings. **1731** Swift *Adv. Repealing Test* Wks. 1841 II. 243/2 Pullings and haulings backward and forward. **1884** *West. Morn. News* 2 Aug. 8/1 The hauling down of the signal.

b. *attrib.* and *Comb.* **hauling-ground**, a place where bachelor seals congregate, distinguished from the rookery or ground occupied by breeding seals.

1791 *Selby Bridge Act* 3 To..make any hauling roads. **1793** Smeaton *Edystone L.* §212 The hawling track for the navigation by horses. **1837** Marryat *Dog-fiend* x, He is drawn aft by a hauling line. **1867** Smyth *Sailor's Word-bk.*, *Hauling down vacancy*, the colloquialism expressive of the promotion of a flag-lieutenant and midshipman on an admiral's hauling down his flag. **1898** D. S. Jordan *Fur Seals* I. 36 Adjoining the breeding grounds and an essential part of each rookery are what are known as the 'hauling grounds' of the bachelors, frequented by the young males of the ages of 5 years and under. **1960** *Canad. Audubon* Jan.–Feb. 2/2 Localities where sea lions come ashore for purposes other than breeding or pupping are called 'hauling grounds'.

hauling, *ppl. a.* [-ing[2].] That hauls.

1891 T. Hardy *Tess* I. 170 A driver sitting upon one of the hauling horses.

haulm, halm (hɔːm, hɑːm), *sb.* Forms: 1 **halm, healm**, 6–7 **halme, hawme, ham(e**, 7–8 **hawm**, 7–9 **haum**, 5– **halm**, 7– **haulm.** (See also helm *sb.*[3]) [OE. *healm* = OS. (MDu., Du.), OHG. (MHG., mod.G.) *halm* stem or stalk of grass, stalk of a plant. ON. *hâlmr* (Sw., Da. *halm*) straw:—OTeut. **halmo-z*, repr. a pre-Teut. **kalmos*: cf. Gr. κάλαμος, L. *calamus* reed.]

a. *collective sing.* The stems or stalks of various cultivated plants, as peas, beans, vetches, hops, potatoes, etc., now less commonly of corn or grass; *esp.* as left after gathering the pods, ears, etc., and used for litter or thatching; straw.

c **825** *Vesp. Psalter* lxxxii[i]. 14[13] Swe swe halme biforan onsiene windes. *c* **1000** *Sax. Leechd.* II. 134 ȝenim cetelhrum and berenhealm, ȝebærn & gnid togædere. *Ibid.* 148 ȝenim riȝen healm eft and beren. *c* **1440** *Promp. Parv.* 223/2 Halm, or stobyl..*stipula.* **1570** *Stanford Churchw. Acc.* in *Antiquary* Apr. (1888) 170 For hame to thatche the churche howse. **1573** Tusser *Husb.* lvii. (1878) 130 The hawme is the strawe of the wheat or the rie, which once being reaped, they mowe by and bie. **1669** Worlidge *Syst. Agric.* (1681) 282 Finish the gathering and drying of your Hops; cleanse the Poles of the Hawm. **1674** Ray *S. & E.C. Words* 68 *Haulm* or *Helm*, stubble gathered after the corn is inned. **1675** *Phil. Trans.* X. 398 These apparent tangles were the ham of the beans. **1725** Bradley *Fam. Dict.* s.v. *November*, Cut off the Asparagus Haulm when it is become Yellow. **1808** Curwen *Econ. Feeding Stock* 11 note, The potatoe top, or haulm, when properly dried, makes very good litter for cattle. **1887** *Spectator* 23 July 984/2 Peas often produce a great show of pods on short haulm in a dry summer.

b. with *a* and *pl.* A stalk or stem (of a bean, potato, grass, etc.).

c **950** *Lindisf. Gosp.* Matt. iii. 12 Ða halmas..forbernes fyres in undrysnede. **1623** Whitbourne *Newfoundland* 5 Great plenty of greene Pease and Fitches..the hawmes of them are good fodder for cattell. **1847** *Illustr. Lond. News* 24 July 61/2 The decaying haulms of the potato. **1881** Darwin *Veg. Mould* 117 A thin cylindrical object such as a haulm of grass.

c. *attrib.*

1862 T. Hughes in *Macm. Mag.* V. 241/2 They..came upon haulm walls and hurdles, within which were a flock of sheep.

haulm, *v.* [f. prec. sb.] *trans.* To lay (straw or haulm) straight for thatching. (See also HELM *v.*^{3})

1641 Best *Farm. Bks.* (Surtees) 60 Sometimes..wee have beene forced to hawme wheate and rye stubble and therewith to thatch our stackes. **1767** A. Young *Farmer's Lett. to People* 205 Haulming, at one shilling and six-pence. **1846** *Jrnl. R. Agric. Soc.* VII. I. 40 Without having to wait for haulming the stubble.

haulmy (ˈhɔːmɪ, ˈhɑːmɪ), *a.* [f. as prec. + -Y.] Having haulms; having long or large haulms.

1669 Worlidge *Syst. Agric.* (1681) Gloss., *Hawmy*, long-stalked. *Ibid.* 19 The Grass..is much discoloured, and grown so hawmy. *Ibid.* 326 Pease or other haw[m]y stuff.

haulse, haulser, obs. ff. HALSE *v.*^{2}, HAWSER.

haul-seine: see HAUL *sb.* 4.

haulster. [f. HAUL *v.* + -STER: cf. HAULER.] A man or beast that hauls; a horse used to haul.

1882 *Daily News* 23 Mar. 5/6 Four of Pickford's most magnificent haulsters were in the shaft team.

hault, haultie, haultness, obs. forms of HALT, HAUGHT, HAUT, HAUGHTY, HAUGHTNESS.

haultain, -ayn(e, -eyne, -igne, var. HAUTAIN, *Obs.*

hault-boy, -goust, obs. ff. HAUTBOY, -GOUT.

haulyard: see HALYARD.

haum(e, obs. form of HAULM, HAME.

haumed, (*Her.*): see HAWMED, HUMET.

haunce, variant of HANCE *sb.* and *v.*

haunch (hɔːntʃ, hɑːntʃ), *sb.*^{1} Forms: 4–7 **hanche, haunche**, (5 **honche**), (*Sc.* 6 **hench(e)**), 6–8 **hanch**, 6– **haunch**, (*mod.Sc.* **hainch**). [a. OF. *hanche* (ONF. *hanke*), 12th c. in Hatz.-Darm. = Pr., Sp., It., Pg. *anca* hip, buttock of the horse, med.L. *hancha* (1275 in Du Cange), prob. of German origin: cf. OHG. *anchâ* (*enchâ, einkâ*) leg, lit. joint. It is only since the 18th c. that the spelling *haunch* has displaced *hanch*.]

1. a. The part of the body, in men and quadrupeds, lying between the last ribs and the thigh; the lateral expansions of the pelvis; of a horse, that part of the hind quarters which extends from the reins or the back to the hough or ham.

a **1225** [see 6]. **1303** R. Brunne *Handl. Synne* 9108 And noþer body, ne þe arme, Bledde neuer blode, colde ne warme, But was as drye wyþ al þe haunche, As of a stok were ryue a braunche. *c* **1320** *Sir Tristr.* 1088 In þe haunche riȝt Tristrem was wounded sare. *c* **1400** *Lanfranc's Cirurg.* 176 Bonys of haunchis ben maad fast wiþ þe lattere boon of þe rigboon. **1460** *Lybeaus Disc.* 268 Thorugh herte, other thorugh honche, Wyth hys sper he wyll launche. **1500–20** Dunbar *Poems* lx. 55 With hoppir hippis, and henches narrow. **1565–73** Cooper *Thesaurus, Clunis*..the buttocke or hanche. **1595** Gosson *Quippes Upst. Gentlewom.* 151 in Hazl. *E.P.P.* IV. 256 These hoopes, that hippes and haunch do hide. **1596** Dalrymple tr. *Leslie's Hist. Scot.* VIII. 81 Strukne in the hench or he was war. **1674** tr. *Scheffer's Lapland* 130 The Rain-deer..are white not only on their belly but on their haunches. **1721–1800** Bailey, *Hanch*, the Hip, a Part of the Body. **1735** Somerville *Chase* I. 196 On their Haunches rear'd. **1831** R. Knox *Cloquet's Anat.* 118 The pelvis properly so called, or that expansion which constitutes the haunches. **1866** Geo. Eliot *F. Holt* (1868) 12 A fine black retriever..sat on his haunches, and watched him as he went to and fro.

b. The leg and loin of a deer, sheep, or other animal, prepared for, or served at, table.

1481–90 *Howard Househ. Bks.* (Roxb.) 320 For bryngenge of halff a haunche. **1573–80** Baret *Alv.* H 66 An hanch of venison. *a* **1612** Harington *Epigr.* II. li. 9, I was no ghest, Nor ever since did tast of side or haunch. **1712** Addison *Spect.* No. 482 ¶4 The best Pickle for a Walnut, or Sauce for an Haunch of Venison. **1741** *Compl. Fam. Piece* II. i. 292 When the Huntsmen come in to the Death of the Hart, they should cry, *Ware Haunch*, that the Hounds may not break in to the Deer. **1859** *All Year Round* No. 29. 57 Nowhere can the equal of a Sussex haunch or saddle be obtained.

c. The pelvis as containing the womb. (Cf. Scriptural use of *loins*.)

1598 Sylvester *Du Bartas* II. i. IV. *Handie-crafts* 778 O too fruitfull hanches! O wretched root! O hurtfull, hatefull branches! **1664** Butler *Hud.* II. iii. 693 A Vine, sprung from her hanches O'er-spread his Empire with its branches.

d. *fig.* To hinder part, the latter end.

1597 Shaks. *2 Hen. IV*, IV. iv. 92 A Summer Bird, Which euer in the haunch of Winter sings The lifting vp of day.

e. Phrases. (See quot.)

1727–51 Chambers *Cycl.* s.v., *Putting him* [a horse] *upon his haunches*..to *couple* him well, or to put him well together, or make him compact..*To drag the haunches*, is to change the leading foot in galloping.

2. The coxa or basal joint of the leg in insects, spiders, and crustaceans.

1828 Stark *Elem. Nat. Hist.* II. 314 The two anterior feet much larger than the others, with long haunches. *Ibid.*, Anterior legs with a blackish blue spot on the internal side of the haunches. **1834** McMurtrie *Cuvier's Anim. Kingd.* 302 Xyphosura..the haunches of the first six pair of feet are covered with small spines, and perform the office of jaws.

3. a. *Arch.* The side of an arch between the crown and the piers, the flank; = HANCE *sb.* 3, q.v. Hence the corresponding part of any arched figure.

1793 Sir G. Shuckburgh in *Phil. Trans.* LXXXIII. 87 *note*, When the arch had stood two years, the haunches were filled up with bricks. **1812–16** J. Smith *Panorama Sc. & Art* I. 230 Let the substance of the rope, on the convex side, be increased in some parts, for example at the haunches; it will then no longer describe a catenary. **1877** Ll. Jewitt *Half-hrs. among Eng. Antiq.* 158 The decorations upon bells consist of encircling inscriptions, usually on the haunch. **1881** Young *Every Man his own Mechanic* §1173 The sides of the arch between the crown and the piers are called its haunches or flanks.

b. The side of a made-up road.

1937 [see HAUNCHING 2].

4. *Naut.* **a.** (See quot. 1823). **b.** = HANCE *sb.* 2 a.

1823 Crabb *Technol. Dict.*, *Haunch*, (*Mar.*) a sudden decrease in the size of a piece of timber. **1867** Smyth *Sailor's Word-bk.*, *Haunch*, a sudden fall or break, as from the drifts forward and aft to the waist. The same as *hance*.

c. The end of a tenon reduced in width. So **haunched** *a.*, (of a tenon) having its end reduced in width.

1885 *Spons' Mech. Own Bk.* 276 The haunched tenon [is used] when the edge of the piece on which the tenon is formed is required to be flush with the end of the piece containing the mortice. **1904** A. C. Passmore *Handbk. Techn. Terms, Haunch*, the wide part left close to the root when part of a tenon is cut away. **1904** Goodchild & Tweney *Technol. & Sci. Dict.* 282/1 *Haunched tenon*, a tenon cut back in its width to allow for wedging. **1964** W. L. Goodman *Hist. Woodworking Tools* 53 The joints themselves are stub tenons, haunched and pinned in a very modern manner.

5. A mechanical contrivance for lowering one end of a wine-cask while drawing off the contents.

6. *attrib.* and *Comb.*, as †*haunch-evil, -hoop, -joint*; **haunch-vent** *Sc.* (see quot. 1824); (from sense 3), as ***haunch-stone***. Also HAUNCH-BONE.

a **1225** *Ancr. R.* 280 Hu ueole þe grimme wrastlare of helle breid up on his hupe, and werp, mid þe haunche turn, into golnesse. **1562** Turner A ij b, *Baths, Names of Siknesses* The sciatica or hanchevel. **1824** Mactaggart *Gallovid. Encycl.*, *Henchvents*, the same with 'gores', pieces of linen put into the lower parts of a shirt..to give 'vent' or room for the 'haunch'. **1824** R. Chambers *Trad. Edin.* (1825) II. 59 There were the breast-knots, two hainch-knots, (at which there were also buttons for looping up the gown behind). **1826** Scott *Jrnl.* (1890) I. 98 A venerable lady who always wore a haunch-hoop. **1828** —— *F.M. Perth* xxxiii, Henry..swung the ponderous implement far behind his right haunch joint. **1883** *Surv. W. Palestine* III. 407 With narrow key-stone and broad haunch-stones.

Hence **ˈhaunchless** *a.*, not having haunches. **ˈhaunchy** *a.*, having prominent haunches.

1831 Trelawny *Adv. Younger Son* xcvii. (1890) 394 Greasy and haunchy brutes. **1834** *Fraser's Mag.* IX. 300 Ill-cut, and haunchless shape.

haunch, *sb.*^{2} (*Sc.* **hainch**): see under HAUNCH *v.*^{3}

†haunch, *v.*^{1} *Obs. rare.* [f. HAUNCH *sb.*^{1}] *trans.* To bring down (a deer, etc.) upon its haunches.

1605 Camden *Rem.* (1637) 256 When the said King John saw a faire bucke haunched.

haunch, *v.*^{2} [f. HAUNCH *sb.*^{1} 4 a.] *trans.* To reduce in thickness. *intr.* Of a piece of timber: To decrease suddenly in thickness.

1794 *Rigging & Seamanship* I. 4 *Cleats*..are haunched on the back with a hollow. *Ibid.* 31 The square..haunches from thence into the round.

haunch, *v.*^{3} In *Sc.* **hainch, hench.** [f. HAUNCH *sb.*^{1} 1, in Sc. *hainch, hench.*] *trans.* To throw with an underhand movement, the arm being jerked against the haunch; 'to elevate by a sudden jerk' (Jam.).

1788 E. Picken *Poems* 75 (Jam.) To hainch a chield aboon the moon. **1825** Brockett *N.C. Gloss.*, *Haunch, Hainch*, to throw; as a stone from the hand by jerking it against the haunch. **1894** Crockett *Raiders* 110 With a pebble cunningly 'henched'.

Hence **haunch**, *Sc.* **hainch, hainsh** *sb.*, a jerked underhand throw; **hauncher**, *Sc.* **haincher, hencher**; **haunching, henching** *vbl. sb.*

1824 Mactaggart *Gallovid. Encycl.*, *Hainching*, throwing, by springing the arm on the haunch. **1843** Hardy in *Proc. Berw. Nat. Club* II. No. II. 54 The bowl..launched in the manner which in Scotland is called a *hainsh*, being precisely the fashion after which the Greek δισκος was impelled. *Ibid.* 58 The bowls were sometimes thrown by raising the arm..but more frequently they were propelled in the *hainshing* mode. **1863** J. Brown *Biggar*, in *John Leech*, etc. (1882) 328 A dextrous hencher of stones. **1894** Crockett *Lilac Sunbonnet* 310 Throwing stones at them in the manner known as 'henchin'.

ˈhaunch-bone. The bone of the haunch: sometimes applied to the *os innominatum* as a whole, but more frequently to the *os ilium*.

c **1386** Chaucer *Miller's T.* 93 He..heeld hire harde by the haunche bones. **1548–77** Vicary *Anat.* x. (1888) 84 The thye bone..the roundnes that is at the vpper ende..is receyued into the..hole of the hanche bone. **1646** Sir T. Browne *Pseud. Ep.* IV. vi. 195 The hanch bones in women..are more protuberant then they are in men. **1831** R. Knox *Cloquet's Anat.* 111 The Coxal, Iliac, or Haunch Bone..which is a double unsymmetrical bone..the largest of all the flat bones, and occupies the lateral and anterior parts of the pelvis. **1855** Ramsbotham *Obstetr. Med.* 2 The os ilium, hip or haunch bone, is the largest of the 3 divisions of the os innominatum.

haunched, *a.* [f. HAUNCH *sb.*^{1} + -ED^{2}.] Having haunches: usually in comb. See also HAUNCH *sb.* 1 c.

1611 Cotgr., *Hanchu*, big haunched..great hipt.

ˈhaunching. [f. HAUNCH *sb.*^{1} 3.] **1.** The parts of an arch belonging to the haunch collectively.

1886 *Jrnl. Franklin Inst.* Ser. III. XCI. 433 The arch was of brick while the haunching, as shown by the dotted lines, was of rubble. Above the haunching was gravel filling.

2. (See quot.)

1937 *Times* 13 Apr. p. viii/2 In such cases (of excessive camber) the process known as 'haunching' should be carried out. The haunches or sides of the road are made up with stone,..and the whole road is then dressed with a new surface dressing.

haunchman, erroneous form of HENCHMAN.

haune, obs. form of AWN.

1589 Nashe *Anat. Absurd.* 25 Least..they be choaked with the haune before they can come at the karnell.

haunk-haunk (hɔːŋkhɔːŋk). [Echoic.] The cry of a hyena. Cf. HAU-HAU *v.*

1895 B. M. Croker *Village Tales* (1896) 208 Another sound that made his heart beat very fast—the 'haunk-haunk' of a hyena.

hauns(e, haunsel, obs. ff. HANCE, HANDSEL.

haunt (hɔːnt, hɑːnt), *v.* Also 3–4 **haunten**, 4 **hauntyn, hanten**, 4–6 **haunte**, 4–7 **hant(e**, 5 **hawntyn.** [a. F. *hante-r* (12th c. in Littré), of uncertain origin: see Diez, Littré, Hatz.-Darm.

From the uncertainty of the derivation, it is not clear whether the earliest sense in F. and Eng. was to practise habitually (an action, etc.) or to frequent habitually (a place). The order here is therefore provisional.]

I. *trans.* **†1.** To practise habitually, familiarly, or frequently. *Obs.*

c **1230** *Hali Meid.* 25 Unseli horlinges unlaheliche hit haunteð in inwarde helle. *Ibid.* 33 þe nuten neauer hwat hit is & hatieð þat ha haunteð. *c* **1330** R. Brunne *Chron.* (1810) 320 þe kyng said..þe pape..haunted Maumetrie. **1362** Langl. *P. Pl.* A. Prol. 74 And leueþ hit to losels þat lecherie haunten. *c* **1375** *Minor Poems fr. Vernon MS.* (E.E.T.S.) 601 Haunte studie, þauȝ þou haue Wel conceyued þi craft. *c* **1449** Pecock *Repr.* II. xi. 214 Men woned for to haunte daili contemplacioun. **1509** Barclay *Shyp of Folys* (1874) I. 195 His preceptis hant kepe and exercyse. **1573** Tusser *Husb.* lxvii. (1878) 155 The honestie in deede I graunt, Is one good point the wife should haunt, To make hir husband thriue.

†2. To use or employ habitually or frequently; *refl.* to use, accustom, or exercise *oneself*. *Obs.*

a **1340** Hampole *Psalter* I. 1 þerfor is þis psalme mast hauntid [*v.r.* vsede] in halykirke. *c* **1340** —— *Prose Tr.* (1866) 20 Men or women the which hauntene leuefully worldely goodes. **1382** Wyclif *Exod.* xiv. 31 The greet hoond that the Lord hauntide aȝens hem. —— *1 Tim.* iv. 7 Haunte [*exerce*] thi silf to pite. **1412–20** Lydg. *Chron. Troy* II. xii, How wyues and maydens in that companie..Haunted be, and used at theyr luste. **1588** J. Mellis *Briefe Instr.* G j, Diuers and sundry goldes..which..yee may reduce into your vsuall money, such as you daily haunt. [**1893** *Northumbld. Gloss.*, *Hant*, to haunt, to accustom, as a pigeon to its dovecot.]

3. To resort to frequently or habitually; to frequent or be much about (a place).

c **1290** *S. Eng. Leg.* I. 413/381 Formest he gan haunti wakes. **1297** R. Glouc. (1724) 534 Sir Edward..hauntede tornemiens with wel noble route. **1382** Wyclif *Dan.* xiii. 6 These ofte hauntiden the hous of Joachym. *c* **1394** *P. Pl. Crede* 106 We haunten none tauernes. *c* **1400** *Destr. Troy* 2963 Hit were..semly for women, þaire houses to haunt & holde hom within. *c* **1489** Caxton *Blanchardyn* lii. 201 Takyng a waye whiche was not moche haunted. **1529** More *Dyaloge* III, Hunne had haunted heretikes lectures by nighte long before. **1538** Leland *Itin.* III. 33 The Town was hauntid with Shippes of diverse Nations. **1585** T. Washington tr. *Nicholay's Voy.* II. xxii. 59 b, The Turks wives..delight at al times to haunt the bathes. **1697** Dryden *Virg. Georg.* I. 12 Ye Nymphs that haunt the Mountains and the Plains. **1710** Whitworth *Acc. Russia* (1758) 12 The rest of the country to Astracan..is haunted by the Calmucks. **1849** Macaulay *Hist. Eng.* iv. I. 459 She was the daughter of a poor Cavalier knight who haunted Whitehall. **1897** Mary Kingsley *W. Africa* 46 It is difficult, unless you have haunted these seas, to realise the interest we take..there in currents.

4. To frequent the company of (a person), to associate with habitually; to 'run after'. (Now chiefly transferred from 5 b.)

1477 Earl Rivers (Caxton) *Dictes* 37 Yf thou haue haunted eny felowe, and thou se hys companye is not couenable vnto the, spare it. **1580** Sidney *Arcadia* (1622) 5 A man who for his hospitalitie is so much haunted, that no newes stirre, but come to his eares. **1594** Carew *Huarte's Exam. Wits.* x. (1596) 130 The preacher..who hath the conditions of a perfect Orator..is more haunted than he that wanteth them. **1691** Wood *Ath. Oxon.* (1817) III. 914 He [was] removed from Shrewsbury where he was much haunted by his party. **1713** Swift *On Himself* Wks. 1755 IV. I. 11 A certain doctor is observed of late To haunt a certain minister of state. **1890** Saintsbury *Ess.* 98 Rather given to haunting rich men.

5. *transf.* and *fig.* Of unseen or immaterial visitants. **a.** Of diseases (*obs.*), memories, cares, feelings, thoughts: To visit frequently or habitually; to come up or present themselves as

recurrent influences or impressions, *esp.* as causes of distraction or trouble; to pursue, molest.

1576 FLEMING *Panopl. Epist.* 228 One that is haunted with a fever or quivering ague. *Ibid.* 363 Heavinesse shall never haunt your heart, whiles your mind is marching with the Muses. **1594** SHAKS. *Rich. III*, I. ii. 122 Your beauty, that did haunt me in my sleepe, To vndertake the death of all the world. **1615** J. STEPHENS *Satyr. Ess.* (ed. 2) 240 He is ever haunted with a blushing weakenesse. **1724** R. WELTON 18 *Disc.* 469 He hath no secret guilt that haunts and doggs him. **1838** LYTTON *Alice* 7 Regret of another kind still seems to haunt you. **1855** BAIN *Senses & Int.* III. i. §12 A painful recollection will haunt a person through life.

b. *esp.* Of imaginary or spiritual beings, ghosts, etc.: To visit frequently and habitually with manifestations of their influence and presence, usually of a molesting kind. ***to be haunted***: to be subject to the visits and molestation of disembodied spirits.

1590 SHAKS. *Mids. N.* III. i. 107 O monstrous. O strange. We are hanted; pray masters, flye masters, helpe. **1593** —— *Rich. II*, III. ii. 158 Some haunted by the Ghosts they haue depos'd. **1602** MARSTON *Antonio's Rev.* III. ii, Bug-beares and spirits haunted him. **1660** F. BROOKE tr. *Le Blanc's Trav.* 312 They were told..how there was a Chamber haunted with spirits, and strangely molested with horrible rumblings. *a* **1679** LD. ORRERY *Herod Gt.* iii, My ghost shall haunt thee out in every place. **1722** SEWEL *Hist. Quakers* (1795) I. IV. 244 It was much talked of, that spirits haunted this dungeon, and walked there. **1847** LYTTON *Lucretia* 301 We need not that boy's Ghost amongst those who haunt us. **1871–4** J. THOMSON *City Dreadf. Nt.* VII. i, Phantoms haunt those shadowy streets.

II. *intr.* †**6.** To be wont or accustomed. *Obs.*

a **1300** *Cursor M.* 12683 Sua haunted he on knes to lij. *c* **1440** CAPGRAVE *Life St. Kath.* IV. 1223 Al her gret trost.. With þe whiche thei haunted her goddis for to calle. *c* **1560** A. SCOTT *Poems* (S.T.S.) iv. 33 Thocht bruckill wemen hantis In lust to leid thair lyvis.

7. To resort habitually; to stay or remain usually (in a place); to associate (with a person). Now usually said of the lower animals.

a **1300** *Cursor M.* 15742 Iudas wel he kneu þe stede quar iesus was hauntand. *a* **1375** *Lay Folks Mass Bk.* App. iv. 439 þer a Neddre hauntes. **1481** CAXTON *Myrr.* I. xiv. 47 (Promp. Parv.) It is good for to haunte amonge the vertuous men. **1526** TINDALE *John* xi. 34 Jesus..there haunted with his disciples. **1532–3** *Act 24 Hen. VIII*, c. 10 All maner of choughes.. breedynge or hauntynge within or vppon anye the sayde manours. **1598** SYLVESTER *Du Bartas* II. ii. III. *Colonies* 391 Where now fell Tartars hant In wandring troops. **1604** SHAKS. *Oth.* I. i. 96, I haue charg'd thee not to haunt about my doores. **1627** RUTHERFORD *Lett.* (1862) I. 35 Be diligent to know with whom she loveth to haunt. **1789** G. WHITE *Selborne* xii. (1853) 52 Some birds haunting with the missel-thrushes. **1860** HAWTHORNE *Marb. Faun* (1879) I. xvi. 158 A homeless dog, that haunted thereabouts.

†**8.** To have resort, betake oneself, go *to*. *Obs.*

a **1300** *Cursor M.* 13691 Mont oliuet it es an hill þat iesus hanted mikel till. **1525** LD. BERNERS *Froiss.* II. ccxxiii. [ccxix.] 695 There haunted into Turkey a marchaunt genouoy of the isle of Sio. **1570** *Satir. Poems Reform.* xv. 132 My counsell is expres, That to your wyfis ye hant. **1632** LITHGOW *Trav.* I. 28 To Lorett people haunt with naked feete.

haunt (hɔːnt, hɑːnt), *sb.* Also 4–6 **haunte**, 6–7, 20 **hant**. [f. HAUNT *v.*]

1. a. Habit, wont, custom, usage. Now *dial.*

c **1330** R. BRUNNE *Chron. Wace* (Rolls) 4730 Ilkaman after his auenaunt Made offrynge, as was his haunt. *c* **1449** PECOCK *Repr.* 248 So grete Evidences of the Faith..ben hadde in so greet Haunt & uce. **1621** BURTON *Anat. Mel.* II. ii. IV. (1651) 275 When once they have got a haunt of such companies, and habit of gaming. **1674** TEMPLE *Let. to Coventry* Wks. 1731 II. 307 'Tis hard for a Man to lose a good Haunt, or an ill Custom. **1855** ROBINSON *Whitby Gloss.*, *Haunt*, a habit. 'He has a sad haunt on 't', a fixed habit of doing so and so. **1894** *Hetton-le-hole Gloss.* s.v. *Hant*, 'He has a nasty hant of doing that'.

†**b.** Habitual practice or use (of anything).

c **1386** CHAUCER *Prol.* 447 Of clooth makyng she hadde swich an haunt [*Camb. MS.* hand], She passed hem of ypres and of Gaunt. *c* **1449** PECOCK *Repr.* I. xviii. 103 Summe ben ..avoutreris in greet haunt and contynuaunce. **1513** DOUGLAS *Æneis* IV. Prol. 249 Eschew thine hant, and mynniss all thi mycht. **1536** BELLENDEN *Cron. Scot.* (1821) II. 216 Than wes not usit sic hant of dise and cartis as ar now usit. **1585** T. WASHINGTON tr. *Nicholay's Voy.* III. iii. 74 For their haunt and traficke of merchandise.

†**2. a.** The act or practice of frequenting or habitually resorting to a place, etc.; resort. ***of great haunt***: much frequented. *Obs.*

c **1330** R. BRUNNE *Chron.* (1810) 223 Of Axholm to þe Ile he scaped himself alon..þer he held his haunt. *c* **1345** *Orpheo* 295 Of game they fonde grete haunt. **1393** LANGL. *P. Pl.* C. XVII. 94 A straw for þe stywes..And þey hadde non oþer haunt bote of poure peple! **1565–73** COOPER *Thesaurus* s.v. *Copiosus*, *Urbs celebris & copiosa*..a citie of great haunt and well peopled. **1600** SHAKS *A.Y.L.* II. i. 15 This our life exempt from publike haunt, Findes tongues in trees, bookes in the running brookes. **1712** ARBUTHNOT *John Bull* I. vii, John Bull..had got such a haunt about the courts of justice.

†**b.** Companionship, society, company. *Obs.*

1500–20 DUNBAR *Poems* xiv. 7 Sic hant of harlettis with thame bayth nicht and day. **1552** HULOET, Hawnte or felowshyp, *familiaritas, frequentia.*

3. *concr.* A place of frequent resort or usual abode; a resort, a habitation; the usual feeding-place of deer, game, fowls, etc.; often, a den or place frequented by the lower animals or by criminals.

c **1330** R. BRUNNE *Chron. Wace* (Rolls) 1753 In þat tyme wer here non hauntes Of no men bot of geauntes. **1398** TREVISA *Barth. De P.R.* XI. xi. (1495) 396 Snowe is noyefull to wylde beestes; for he..sheweth and dyscoueryth theyr hauntes and steppes. **1551** R. ROBINSON tr. *More's Utop.* Meter of Utopia (1895) p. xciii, Me Utopie cleped Antiquitie, Voyde of haunte and herboroughe. **1592** SHAKS. *Rom. & Jul.* III. i. 53 We talke here in the publike haunt of men. **1684** R. H. *School Recreat.* 145 To know the Haunts and Resorts of Fish, in which they are to be usually found. **1735** SOMERVILLE *Chase* II. 261 From Brake to Brake she [a hare] flies, and visits all Her well-known Haunts. **1748** *Anson's Voy.* II. i. (ed. 4) 169 This place being the usual haunt of the buccaneers and privateers. **1841** W. SPALDING *Italy & It. Isl.* I. 345 One of the most noted haunts of the ancient highwaymen. **1855** TENNYSON *Brook* 23, I come from haunts of coot and hern.

fig. **1614** BP. HALL *Recoll. Treat.* 116 Sinne where it hath gotte an haunt looketh for more. **1850** TENNYSON *In Mem.* cx, The feeble soul, a haunt of fears.

†**4.** (?) A topic, a subject of discussion. *Obs.*

1622 DONNE *Serm.* clv. (ed. Alford) VI. 213 When some ..points that beat upon that Haunt, had been ventilated. **1656** J. HARRINGTON *Oceana* (1658) 162 Appius Claudius (still upon the old haunt) would have it [etc.]. **1658** —— *Prerog. Pop. Govt.* II. v. (1660) 81 But this..is not to come off from the haunt, but to run still upon the People in a common or publick capacity.

5. *local U.S.* and *Eng.* A spirit supposed to haunt a place; a ghost. Also (occas.) in wider use.

1843 WINNEMORE & REPS *Cudjo's Wild Hunt* (song) 3 It am de hunt ob Cudjo dat nigger so bold. **1878** MRS. A. W. HUNT *Hazard of Die* I. vi. 131 Our Cordy is terrible for being afeard o' haunts. **1896** MRS. STOWE *Oldtown Folks* vi. 80 But this 'ere's a regular haunt,..they both on 'em said.. they'd seen a figger of a man. **1902** *Westm. Gaz.* 5 Feb. 2/1 This is the 'haunt' that troubles all our minds, and, especially, that comes forth..when the question is of peace by arrangement. **1933** M. EMMONS in B. A. Botkin *Treas. S. Folklore* (1949) III. ii. 540 One never knows when the most sociable of cats may turn out to be a witch or a 'ha'nt'. **1934** B. A. BOTKIN in W. T. Couch *Culture in South* xxvi. 589 A Bible or a sharp object under the pillow will keep away both 'hants' and witches. **1935** *Scribner's Mag.* XCVII. 121/2 Old Joe's daid an' gone But his hant blows de hawn. **1943** W. C. HENDRICKS *Bundle of Trouble* 98 Then the wife told the hant who her husband is, and the hant begun at the start and told it all over agin. **1952** W. R. TITTERTON in *Columba* Aug. 102/1 We had a haunt in our flat. Father Vincent came home with us that day, and blessed the place, and the haunt was no more. **1965** 'MALCOLM X' *Autobiogr.* i. 20 It was spooky, with ghosts and spirituals and 'ha'nts' seeming to be in the very atmosphere when finally we all came out of the church.

†**'haunt-dole**, *a. Obs. rare.* [f. HAUNT *v.*] That haunts doles, or the givers of doles; of or pertaining to a parasite.

a **1661** HOLYDAY *Juvenal* (1673) 38 The haunt-doal gown [*trechedipna*], Quirinus, thy Clown wears, And his oil'd neck rewards of Mast'ry bears.

'haunted, *ppl. a.* [f. HAUNT *v.* + -ED.]

1. Practised; used, habituated, or accustomed (to a course); wonted. *Obs.* exc. *dial.*

a **1325** *Prose Psalter* cxviii[i]. 15 Y shal be haunted [*exercebor*] in thy comaundement. *c* **1425** *Found. St. Bartholomew's* (E.E.T.S.) 17 Bewtyfied with hawntid and vsuall tokenys of celestiall vertu. **1513** DOUGLAS *Æneis* V. vi. 31 Hantit to ryn in wodis [*assueti silvis*] and in schawis. **1641** BEST *Farm. Bks.* (Surtees) 120 Hee..keepeth them a weeke till they be wonted and hanted togeather. **1868** ATKINSON *Cleveland Gloss.* s.v., *To be Haunted*, to grow used to, or become accustomed.

2. a. Frequented by many people, much resorted to.

1576 NEWTON *Lemnie's Complex.* (1633) 77 Their populous and great haunted Cities. **1600** J. PORY tr. *Leo's Africa* II. 359 Africke hath ever beene the least knowen and haunted parte in the world. **1838** PRAED *Home of Childhood* ii, The play-haunted lawn.

b. Frequented by noxious creatures; infested.

1822–34 *Good's Study Med.* (ed. 4) IV. 504 Few instances ..of plants and animals in perfect health being thus haunted. **1887** J. M. BROWN *Shikar Sk.* 14 A tiger-haunted jungle.

3. a. Frequented or much visited by spirits, imaginary beings, apparitions, spectres, etc.

[**1660** F. BROOKE tr. *Le Blanc's Trav.* 347 The Isle of Devills, so called because they hold it to be haunted with spirits.] **1711** ADDISON *Spect.* No. 110 ¶1, I like this Retirement the better, because of an ill Report it lies under of being haunted. **1832** W. IRVING *Alhambra* I. 110 Here was the haunted wing of the castle. **1848** DICKENS (*title*) The Haunted Man. **1859** —— The Haunted House.

b. In wider use.

1906 *Daily Chron.* 23 Feb. 3/4 The beauty-haunted eyes of such painters as Gainsborough, Romney, Botticelli. **1906** RIDER HAGGARD *Benita* vii, Staring at the white Benita and at her haunted eyes. **1908** *Westm. Gaz.* 17 Aug. 3/1 He paces the garden in this haunting, haunted fashion. **1910** A. C. BENSON *Silent Isle* xv, You become aware that some exquisite haunted quality has slipped away from the later work.

c. *Comb.*, as ***haunted-looking*** adj.

1883 LD. R. GOWER *My Remin.* II. 26 A low, long, damp, haunted-looking gallery. **1918** MRS. BELLOC LOWNDES *Out of the War?* xx. 257 Haunted-looking eyes.

Hence **'hauntedness.**

1888 MRS. JOCELYN *£100,000 versus Ghosts* II. ix. 134 That will put a stop to its hauntedness.

haunter ('hɔːntə(r), 'hɑːntə(r)). [f. HAUNT *v.* + -ER[1]. Cf. OF. *hanteur.*] One who or that which haunts, in various senses; a frequenter.

c **1440** *Promp. Parv.* 231/1 Hawntare, *frequentator, frequentatrix.* **1538** STARKEY *England* II. i. 154 Hauntarys of thes vayn plesurys, and tryfelyng thyngys. **1548** CRANMER *Catech.* 69 He that is a whore haunter. **1551** ROBINSON tr. *More's Utop.* I. (1895) 57 Dice, cardes, tables..do not al thys sende the haunters of them streyght a stealynge when theyr money is gone? **1553** T. WILSON *Rhet.* (1580) 123 To call an alehouse haunter a dronkarde. *a* **1639** WOTTON in *Reliq.* 84 (R.) Haunters of theatres. **1794** J. VAILLANT tr. *Dyer's Rep.* 254 b, The presentee was refused because he was a common haunter of taverns. **1856** RUSKIN *Mod. Paint.* IV. v. xix. §31 Plants..haunters of waste ground.

haunting ('hɔːntɪŋ, 'hɑːnt-), *vbl. sb.* [f. HAUNT *v.* + -ING[1].] The action of HAUNT *v.* †**a.** Practice, exercise. **b.** Customary resort; frequenting; visitation by fears, suspicions, imaginary beings, spirits, etc.

a **1325** *Prose Psalter* liv. [lv.] 2 Ich am made sori in my haunteyng [*in exercitatione mea*]. *c* **1400** *Rom. Rose* 6084 Telle in what place is thyn hauntyng. **1489** CAXTON *Faytes of A.* I. x. 27 The hauntyng and continuance therof be nedefull. **1558** PHAER *Æneid.* IV. Kj b, A byrd that nere the bankes of seas his haunting keepes. **1630** R. *Johnson's Kingd. & Commw.* 57 Avoid the haunting of brothell houses. **1674** tr. *Scheffer's Lapland* 126 To escape the hauntings of Ghosts. **1817** COLERIDGE *Sibyl. Leaves* (1862) 222 She had a sore grief of her own, A haunting in her brain. **1847** TENNYSON *Princ.* II. 389 I have..No ghostly hauntings like his Highness.

'haunting, *ppl. a.* [-ING[2].] That haunts, in various senses of the vb.

1388 WYCLIF *Prov.* Prol., The hauntende puple [*frequens turba*]. **1483** *Cath. Angl.* 179/2 Hawntynge, *exercens, exercitans.* **1605** SHAKS. *Macb.* I. vi. 4 The Temple-haunting Barlet [*mod. edd*, martlet]. **1836** KEBLE *Serm.* viii. Postscr. (1848) 412 Exempting them..from haunting doubts. **1887** *Pall Mall G.* 10 Sept. 3/1 We seek in vain for haunting cadences or phrases of rare felicity.

'hauntingly, *adv.* [f. prec. + -LY[2].]

†**a.** Frequently, customarily. *Obs.* **b.** So as to haunt the thoughts or memory.

c **1440** *Promp. Parv.* 231/1 Hawntyngly, or ofte, *frequenter.* **1859** FARRAR *J. Home* xv. 200 Those words rang hauntingly in Kennedy's ears. **1889** ANNIE THOMAS *That other Woman* III. ix. 152 The idea of death by drowning clung hauntingly to him all the evening.

†**haunty**, *a. Obs.* or *dial.* [Origin uncertain.] Unruly, wanton, restive.

1671 S. CLARKE *Mirror Saints & Sinners* 631 Abner, Ishbosheth's servant, grew so haughty, and haunty that he might not be spoken unto. **1674–91** RAY *N.C. Words* (E.D.S.), *Hanty*, wanton, unruly; spoken of a horse..whose provender pricks him.

haurient ('hɔːrɪənt), *a. Her.* Also 6–7 **hariant**, 7–9 **hauriant** (erron. 6 **eirant**). [ad. L. *haurient-em*, pr. pple. of *haurire* to draw (water, etc.).] Of a fish borne as a charge: Placed palewise or upright with the head in chief, as if raising it above the water to draw in the air.

1572 BOSSEWELL *Armorie* II. 64 b, Twoo Delphines d'Argent, addorsez hariant. **1587** FLEMING *Contn. Holinshed* III. 1370/1 Charged with foure leuses heads eirant. **1610** GUILLIM *Heraldry* III. xxii. (1660) 233. **1864** BOUTELL *Her. Hist. & Pop.* ix. 66 When [a fish is] in pale..as if rising to the surface for breathing, it is *hauriant.*

transf. **1855** *Fraser's Mag.* LI. 534 A flapping prawn mounts hauriant to the top.

haurl(l, variants of HARL *sbs.*[1], [3] and *v.*[1]

Hausa ('haʊsə). Also **Haussa, Hous(s)a.** [Native name.] A widespread Negroid people of the Sudan and N. Nigeria, of the Bantu family with some Hamitic mixture; also, the language of this people, used, esp. in commerce, over much of W. Africa. Also *attrib.* or as *adj.*

1820 J. G. JACKSON (*title*) Account of Timbuctoo and Housa. **1853** E. NORRIS (*title*) Dialogues and a small portion of the New Testament, in the English, Arabic, Haussa, and Bornu languages. **1879** *Encycl. Brit.* X. 59/1 An armed police force, recruited..from the Mahometan tribe of the Houssas. **1923** F. W. TAYLOR *Pract. Hausa Gram.* i. 9 Hausa occupies a position midway between the tone languages, such as Yoruba, and the stress languages, such as English. **1926** *Blackw. Mag.* Nov. 666/1 The troops were Hausas—I don't think we had begun to call them 'Waffs' then. **1957** M. BANTON *W. Afr. City* viii. 158 Some blind Hausa beggars come from Nigeria to Freetown to sing in the streets. **1959** R. C. ABRAHAM *Lang. Hausa People* i. 3 In Hausa..each word has its fixed tone, no matter what the emotional context. **1962** *Listener* 22 Feb. 335/1 A Hausaman, clad in a scarlet tarbush and flowing white robes. **1967** *Listener* 24 Aug. 230/1 There have been several uprisings already among Hausas and Yorubas trying to take revenge on Ibos. **1971** *E. Afr. Jrnl.* Mar. 8/1, I haven't worked and slaved.. to have you give me a Hausa grandson.

hause, hawse (hɔːs). *Sc.* and *north. dial.* [mod. northern dial. form of HALSE neck, used in a special sense.] A narrower and lower neck or connecting ridge between two heights or summits; a *col*; the regular name in the English Lake district and on the Scottish Border.

Generally at the head of two stream valleys which descend opposite sides of the hause, forming a pass over the ridge or mountain chain at this point; e.g. the Hause between Fleetwith and the Newlands Mountains crossed by Honister Pass, Esk Hause between Scawfell Pike and Bowfell at the head of Eskdale, Buttermere Hause, Deepdale Hause, etc.

1781 J. HUTTON *Tour to Caves* Gloss. (E.D.S.), *Hause*, see *Hose. Hose, Horse*, a deep vale between two mountains. **1786** W. GILPIN *Lakes Cumb.* (1808) I. xv. 229 The mountain over which we passed, is called, in the language of the

country, a hawse. **1822** *Lights & Shadows Scot. Life* 114 (Jam.) A storm is coming down from the Cairnibrae-hawse. **1872** Jenkinson *Guide to Eng. Lakes* (1879) 218 Between Esk Hause and Bow Fell is a mountain called Hanging Knott, which can be scaled from the top of the Hause in about twenty minutes.

hause, hauser: see HALSE, HAWSE, HAWSER.

[**hauselins,** in Cockeram (1623–31), error for HANSELINS.]

‖**hausen** (haʊz(ə)n, 'hɔːz(ə)n). Also 8 **hawson.** [Ger. *hausen*, MHG. *hûse, hûsen*, OHG. *hûso.*] The largest species of sturgeon, of the Black and Caspian Seas and their rivers, *Acipenser huso.*

1745 R. Pococke *Descr. East* II. II. 251 They say that the hawsom fish in the Danube has been taken twenty-one feet in length. **1756** Nugent *Gr. Tour* II. 210 Their larger fish are called hawsons, being about twenty feet long, and not unlike a sturgeon in the taste. **1880** Günther *Fishes, Acipenser*, the Hausen..from rivers falling into the Black Sea and the Sea of Azow..sometimes 12 feet long and yielding an inferior kind of isinglass.

‖**hausfrau** ('haʊsfraʊ). Also **house-frau.** [G.] A housewife. Also **hausvrow, huisvrouw** [after Du. *huisvrouw*].

1798 Lady A. Barnard *S. Afr. Cent. Ago* (1901) 157 This, as a careful haus-vrow, devolved on me. **1843** E. Hall *Diary* in O. A. Sherrard *Two Victorian Girls* (1966) ix. 92 [On my way] to do the haus-frau, dear Mr. Shore met me. **1848** *Wesleyan-Meth. Mag.* Aug. 886 You find the *huis-vrouw*, or 'mistress', seated at a small table. **1866** C. M. Yonge *Dove in Eagle's Nest* i. 29 Hausfrau Johanna adjured her father.. to be a true guardian and protector to the child. **1873** —— *Pillars of House* II. xiii. 40 A simple painstaking businesslike man, who had married a German hausfrau. **1918** R. Wilson *Martin Schüler* xi. 120 My sister Bertha was charming: now she is a house-frau. **1925** 'E. Barrington' *Divine Lady* II. xv. 213 Her Majesty Queen Charlotte, the prim German hausfrau. **1930** *Observer* 20 Apr. 8/4 The big German newspapers, cognisant of the power of the hausfrau. **1962** *Punch* 9 May 706/2 Women in West Germany appear to have taken a tremendous leap forward from *hausfrau* to high executive positions.

†'**hausible,** *a. Obs. rare*$^{-0}$. [f. L. *haus-*, rare ppl. stem of *haurīre* to draw (water): see -BLE.] 'That may be drawn or emptied' (Blount *Glossogr.*).

‖**hausmaler** ('haʊsmaːlər). [G., = house-painter.] One who paints undecorated china in his own house or private workshop. Hence '**hausmalerei** (-aɪ), the painting and decorating of such china.

1935 *Burlington Mag.* June 271/1 The painting on this jug bears the signature of the well-known *Hausmaler* Abraham Helmhack. *Ibid.*, Johann Schaper, the first great master of *Hausmalerei* on faience. **1938** *Ibid.* Dec. p. xviii/2 Some interesting *Hausmalerei* from the same region. **1959** G. Savage *Antique Coll. Handbk.* 68 The work of outside decorators (or *Hausmaler*), who bought white porcelain and decorated it in their homes. **1959** *Times* 6 Jan. 16/7 A Meissen hausmaler bowl. **1971** *Times* 30 Nov. 24/3 (Advt.), An important German faience Hausmaler tankard.

hausmannite ('haʊsmənaɪt). *Min.* [Named 1827, after Prof. J. F. L. Hausmann (1782–1859).] Native proto-sesquioxide of manganese, found in brownish-black tetragonal crystals; pyramidal manganese ore.

1831 *Trans. R. Soc. Edin.* XI. 128 Dr. Turner and myself propose to call the present species, Hausmannite. **1868** Dana *Min.* 162 Hausmannite..occurs with porphyry along with other manganese ores.

‖**hausse** (hoʊs). [F. *hausse*, from *hausser* to raise.] A kind of breech-sight for a cannon.

1787 J. Jeffray *MS. Th. on Guns addr. to Dk. Richm.*, I have never seen this Hausse de culasse. **1818** *Descr. Sights for Navy proposed by Congreve* 34 Neither the Hausse nor any other sort of dispart. *a* **1859** *Ordnance Man. U.S.* 112 Pendulum Hausse or tangent scale. **1887** *Rep. Chief Ordnance U.S.*, 8 Pendulum Hausses: 3 inch gun.

‖**hausse-col** (hoʊskɒl). *Armour.* [F., f. *hausse* raise + *col* neck.] A gorget of chain-mail, or (later) of plate-armour.

1821 S. R. Meyrick in *Archæol.* XX. 507 In consequence of hausse-cols, or gorgets of plate, becoming more generally worn than mail, the basnet acquired a different form. **1834** Planché *Brit. Costume* 215 The salade and the hausse-col, or gorget of steel, was still worn [under Richard III].

Haussmannize ('haʊsmənaɪz), *v.* [f. name of Baron Haussmann, who, when prefect of the Seine (1853–1870), carried out the remodelling of a great part of the city of Paris.] *trans.* To open out, widen, and straighten streets, and generally rebuild, after the fashion in which Haussmann rebuilt Paris.

1865 *Daily Tel.* 24 Oct. 5/3 The street..is now Haussmannised, open, airy, beautiful; but then, on the other hand, it is now 'up' for the fourth time within twelve months. **1884** F. Harrison *Choice Bks., etc.* (1891) 238 Paris has fewer records of the feudal ages than London; and it is hopelessly Haussmannised. **1892** *Athenæum* 3 Sept. 326/1 To remodel the thoroughfares and otherwise 'Haussmannize' the Charing Cross district.

Hence **Haussmanni'zation.**

1865 *Let.* in F. M. Whitehurst *Life in France under Napol. III* (1873) I. 85 The Budget has again attracted the public attention to the Haussmannisation of Paris. **1882** F. Harrison *Choice Bks., etc.* (1886) 276 These Attilas..of modern society..are rapidly achieving the Hausmannisation..of every mediæval city of Europe.

†**haust** (hɔːst), *sb.* [ad. L. *haustus* draught.]

1600 W. Watson *Quodlibets Relig. & St.* (1602) 339 To drinke vp the Thames at a haust.

†**haust,** *v. Obs.* [f. L. *haust-*, ppl. stem of *haurīre* to draw (water).] *trans.* To draw in, drink up, drain, absorb.

1542 Boorde *Dyetary* xi. (1870) 261 Hote breade..doth lye in the stomache lyke a sponge, haustyng vndecoct humours. **1657** Tomlinson *Renou's Disp.* v. vii. 161* When the liquor hausted to the Gurgulio is again revoked.

haust, var. HOAST *sb.* and *v.*, cough.

haustellate ('hɔːstələt), *a.* and *sb.* [ad. mod.L. *haustellāt-us*, f. *haustellum*: see -ATE[2] 2.]

A. *adj.* **1.** Provided with a haustellum or mouth fitted for sucking; of or pertaining to the *Haustellata* or suctorial insects.

1835–6 Todd *Cycl. Anat.* I. 754/1 The Haustellate Crustacea. **1877** Dawson *Orig. World* 364 The mutual relations of flowers and haustellate insects.

2. Adapted for sucking, suctorial.

1835 Kirby *Hab. & Inst. Anim.* II. xx. 316 The instrument of suction in a Haustellate mouth consists of pieces..analogous to those employed in mastication in a Mandibulate one. **1856** Carpenter *Microsc. & Rev.* §630 That which prevails among the Lepidoptera or Butterfly tribe..adapted for suction, is termed the haustellate mouth.

B. *sb.* A haustellate or suctorial insect; a member of the *Haustellata*, or suctorial insects.

1842 in Brande *Dict. Sc.*, etc.

So '**haustellated** *a.* = HAUSTELLATE *a.* 1.

1836–9 Todd *Cycl. Anat.* II. 855/2 Fabricius..divided Insects..into..the Mandibulated..and the Haustellated.

haustellation (hɔːstə'leɪʃən). [f. HAUSTELLATE *a*: see -TION.] The action of sucking.

1901 *Practitioner* Mar. 278 If a mosquito be killed on the second day after haustellation.

'**haustellous,** *a.* = HAUSTELLATE *a.* 2.

In mod. Dicts.

‖**haustellum** (hɔː'stɛləm). *Zool.* Pl. **-a.** [mod.L. dim. of *haustrum* a machine for drawing water, f. *haurīre, haust-* to draw (water).] The sucking organ or proboscis of an insect or a crustacean.

1816 Kirby & Sp. *Entomol.* (1843) I. 233 Species also of Empis whose haustellum resembles the beak of a bird. **1847** *Nat. Encycl.* I. 893 The beak, or haustellum, arises from the under part of the head. **1856–8** W. Clark *Van der Hoeven's Zool.* I. 308 An haustellum formed of setæ.

‖'**haustement.** *Obs.* An under-garment fitting the body, over which the armour was worn. (Planché *Encycl. Costume.*)

a **1483** in *Archæol.* XVII. 292 An haustement for the body with sleevis. **1821** S. R. Meyrick *Ibid.* XX. 497 The Haustement of Ajustement..was made to the shape and worn with the shirt..The doublet and haustement of this period supplied the place of the wambais and hoqueton previously worn.

‖**haustorium** (hɔː'stɔərɪəm). *Bot.* Pl. **-ia.** [mod.L., f. L. *haustor* a drawer, drainer, f. *haurīre, haust-* to draw, drain: see -ORIUM.]

A small sucker of a parasitic plant, which penetrates the tissues of the host; a specialized branch or organ of the mycelium of a fungus, whereby it attaches itself to its host.

1875 Bennett & Dyer tr. *Sachs' Bot.* 733 These haustoria and adhesive discs..are altogether indispensable for the life of the plant; for Cuscuta is nourished exclusively by the haustoria which penetrate into the tissue of the host. **1882** Vines *Sachs' Bot.* 311 The ramified mycelial filaments extend over the epidermis, crossing and re-crossing one another, and throw out haustoria at numerous points which penetrate into the cells of the epidermis.

haustrum ('hɔːstrəm). *Anat.* Pl. **haustra.** [mod. use of L. *haustrum* bucket, scoop, f. *haurīre, haust-* to draw (water).] Each of the small sacs enclosed by folds in the colon. Hence '**haustral** *a.*

[**1826** J. Lizars *Syst. Anat. Plates.* Descriptions of Plates. xi. 30 These bands purse the colon into these peculiar pouches or cells ([*Footnote*] Syn. Cellulæ seu haustra) so characteristic of this intestine.] **1889** A. Macalister *Text-bk. Human Anat.* §257. 405 Its [the colon's] cavity is to some extent sacculated, the haustra, or pouches being separated by crescentic plicæ sigmoideæ. **1913** Dorland *Med. Dict.* (ed. 7), *Haustral*, pertaining to the haustra of the colon. **1936** *Med. Rec.* 1 Jan. 28/1 The loss of haustral markings with and without dilatation, was found much less frequently. **1959** R. D. Lockhart et al. *Anat. Human Body* 522 Compared with the smooth small intestine, the large is sacculated along its length, the sacculations or haustra bulging between three equidistant longitudinal bands.

†'**hausture.** *Obs.* [f. L. type **haustūra*, f. *haust-*, ppl. stem of *haurīre*: see HAUST *v.*] The action of sucking or drinking up.

a **1650** T. Adams *Serm. Luke* xvii. 19 Wks. 1861–2 II. 199 With an avarous hausture to lick up the mud of corruption.

†**haut,** *a.* and *sb. Obs.* Also 6 **haute,** 7 **hault:** see also HAUGHT. [a. F. *haut, haute* high, height, in OF. *halt*, 14–16th c. *hault*:—L. *altum* high, the initial *h* in OFr. being due to the influence of Ger. *hoh, hoch* high. In English changed in end of 16th c. to HAUGHT, after native words in *-aught.*]

A. *adj.* High, lofty, haughty: see HAUGHT.

1430–1648 [see HAUGHT].

B. *sb.* Height; a height.

1502 *Ord. Crysten Men* (W. de W. 1506) I. iii. 31 The souerayne hautes of heuen. **1686** Goad *Celest. Bodies* I. iii. 9 The Difference arises from the difformity of the parts of the Earth amongst themselves, of Hault or Bate.

†**haut,** *v. Obs.* Also 5 **hawte.** [f. prec.] *trans.* To raise, elevate, exalt.

?*a* **1400** *Arthur* 113 He daunted þe proude & hawted þe poure. *c* **1490** *Promp. Parv.* 230/2 (MS. K.) Hawtyn ..(*Pynson* hawten or heithyn vp), *exalto, elevo.* **1583** Stanyhurst *Æneis* I. (Arb.) 23 Chiefe stags vpbearing croches high from the antlier hauted.

†'**hautain, -tein,** *a.* (*sb.*) *Obs.* Forms: 3–4 **hautein,** 3–6 **hawteyn,** 4–6 **hauteyn, -tain, hawtane, hauten.** (Also 4–6 **hawteyne,** 4–5 **-tayne,** 5 **-ten, awtayne;** 4 **hautyn,** 4–5 **-teyne,** 4–6 **-taine,** 5 **-tyng,** 5–6 *north.* **-tand,** 5 **haughten, haltyn, haultand, -tayn(e, -tigne,** 6 **haultain;** *Sc.* **haltand, -tane.**) [a. F. *hautain*, OF. *(h)altain* (11th c.), 15–16th c. *haultain*, f. *haut* high, after L. type **altān-us*: see HAUT, and for the formation cf. *sovereign*, F. *souverain*, L. type **superānus.*]

1. Holding or behaving oneself loftily; proud, arrogant: = HAUGHTY 1.

1297 R. Glouc. (1724) 66 Þe kyng, þei he hawteyn were, ches þe best won. *c* **1386** Chaucer *Pars. T.* ⁋ 540 Som tyme detraccion maketh an hauteyn man be the moore humble. *c* **1440** *York Myst.* iii. 27 For to a-bate his hautand cheere. *c* **1489** Caxton *Blanchardyn* xliv. 173 He was soo proude and so hawten. **1513** Douglas *Æneis* vi. ix. 119 Prowd and haltand in his hert. **1549** Paget in Strype *Eccl. Mem.* II. App. 114 Ye se how lofty they are and haultain in al their proceedings.

2. Of the voice: Raised, loud.

c **1350** *Will. Palerne* 2187 Herty houndes, hauteyn of cryes. *c* **1386** Chaucer *Pard. T.* 2 In chirches whan I preche, I peyne me to han an hauteyn [*v. rr.* hautyn, haunteine; *Glasgow MS.* (1476) haughten] speche. *c* **1475** *Partenay* 236 With hie hautyng voice the erle answering. *Ibid.* 2829 Raymounde gan speke with vois full hautain.

3. High-flying.

c **1385** Chaucer *L.G.W.* 1120 *Dido*, Ne gentil hawtein faucoun heroner.

4. Of exalted courage, courageous: = HAUGHTY 2.

c **1450** *Golagros & Gaw.* 923 Syne laught out suerdis.. And hewit on hard steill, wondir hawtane. **1485** Caxton *Chas. Gt.* 203 By haultayn and grete puyssaunce thou shalt surmounte thyn enemyes.

B. as *sb.* The treble in music.

c **1320** *Owain Miles* 41 Foules..breke her notes with miri gle, Burdoun and mene gret plente, And hautain with heighe steuen.

†**hautainesse.** *Obs.* In 3–4 **hautenesse,** 5 **hauteynesse.** [deriv. of HAUTAIN; the suffix may be F. *-esse* as in *justesse*, etc., or Eng. -NESS; cf. HAUGHTNESS.] Haughtiness, pride, arrogance.

1297 R. Glouc. (1724) 29 Heo was best and fairest, & to hautenesse drow lest. *c* **1425** *Eng. Conq. Irel.* (E.E.T.S.) 90 Pryde & hauteynesse he hated.

†'**hautainety.** *Obs.* In 5 **hautynete.** [a. OF. *hautaineté, -teineté* highness, hauteur, f. *hautain.*] Haughtiness.

a **1450** *Knt. de la Tour* (1868) 126 The woman defamed for her hautynete and her foly and chidinge.

†'**hautainly,** *adv. Obs.* [f. HAUTAIN + -LY[2].] **a.** Haughtily, proudly. **b.** With raised voice, loudly. **c.** Boldly, courageously.

c **1400** *Rom. Rose* 5820 That sworne hath ful hauteynly. *c* **1475** *Partenay* 1906 Ful lowde he spake And ful hautaynly. **1513** Douglas *Æneis* x. xi. 98 Richt haltandly, as curageus vnder scheyld, [She] Musturis this ymage.

hautboy, hoboy ('həʊbɔɪ). Forms: 6 **hautboi, halboie, hawboy, (howbowe),** 6–7 **hoeboy,** 6–9 **hautbois, hoboy,** 7– **hautboy,** (6–7 **ho-, how-, haut-, haugh(t)-, hoa-, hout-,** 7 **hault-, heaut-, -boie, -bois, -boy(e, hoybuck, hobo).** See also OBOE *sb.* [a. F. *hautbois* (15th c. in Hatz.-Darm., *haultbois* Cotgr. in sense 1), f. *haut* high + *bois* wood. In sense 1, from 17th c. frequent in naturalized spelling *hoboy*; the italianized spelling of the French, OBOE *sb.*, is now usual.]

1. A wooden double-reed wind instrument of high pitch, having a compass of about 2½ octaves, forming a treble to the bassoon. (Now usually OBOE *sb.*)

1575 Laneham *Let.* (1871) 7 This Pageaunt waz clozd vp with a delectable harmony of Hautboiz, Shalmz, Cornets, and such oother looud muzik. **1579–80** North *Plutarch* (1612) 451 The sound of flutes and howboyes. **1588** *Ibid.* 921 Howboyes. **1597** Shaks. *2 Hen. IV*, III. ii. 351 The Case of a Treble Hoeboy. **1600** Hakluyt *Voy.* III. 156 Winding the Cornets, Haughtboyes. **1604** Dekker *King's Entertainm.* Wks. 1873 I. 321 This song went foorth at the sound of Haultboyes. **1610** Guillim *Heraldry* IV. vi. (1611) 200 He beareth Azure three Howboies betweene as manie crosse Crosselets. **1611** Cotgr., *Haultbois*, a Hobois or Hoboy. **1695** Blackmore *Pr. Arth.* IV. 67 The lively

Hoboy, and the sweet-mouth'd Flute. **1710** STEELE *Tatler* No. 157 ¶5 The Hautboy is the most perfect of the Flute-species. **1815** ELPHINSTONE *Acc. Caubul* (1842) I. 281 Drums, trumpets, hautboys, and flutes are exempted from this proscription, as being manly and warlike.

†**b.** Humorously applied to a clyster-pipe. *Obs.*

a **1616** BEAUM. & FL. *Knt. Malta* II. iv, Wilt thou give me another glister..where's thy hoboy?

c. A reed-stop on an organ: = OBOE *sb.* 2.

c **1700** *Specif. Organ St. John's Chapel, Bedford Row* in Grove *Dict. Mus.* II. 595 Echo..25. Trumpet. 26. Hautboy. **1829** *Specif. Organ St. James's, Bermondsey* Ibid. 599 Hautboy.

d. *transf.* One who plays a hautboy.

1633 MASSINGER *Guardian* IV. ii, Wire-string and catgut men, and strong-breathed heautbois. **1686** *Lond. Gaz.* No. 2142/1, 12 English Trumpets with Silk Banners, and Six Hoe-Boys, all in Red Coats, playing by turns. **1724** RAMSAY *The Cordial*, When the hoboys are gawn by. **1773** MAD. D'ARBLAY *Early Diary* (1889) I. 199 A very fine concert.. for Mr. Fischar's (the celebrated Hautbois) benefit.

e. *attrib.* and *Comb.*

1789 BURNEY *Hist. Mus.* IV. 257 His admirable Hautbois concerto in F. **1793** BURNS *Let. to Thomson* June, Frazer, the hautboy-player in Edinburgh. **1871** HILES *Dict. Mus. T.*, *Hautboy-clarion*, a 2 ft. reed stop in an organ, also called octave-clarion. **1874** CHAPPELL *Hist. Mus.* 342 The box.. exceedingly shallow, so as only to take in hautboy reeds.

†**2.** *Forestry.* Lofty trees, as distinguished from shrubs or underwood. *Obs.*

1674 N. COX *Gentl. Recreat.* (1677) 15 Vert is of divers kinds..Some called Hautboys, serving for food and browse of and for the Game, and for the defence of them; as Oaks, Beeches, etc. Some Hautboys for Browse, Shelter, and Defence only; as Ashes, Poplars, etc. *a* **1700** B. E. *Dict. Cant. Crew, Haut-bois*, Oaks, Beaches, Ashes, Poplars, etc.

3. A species of strawberry (*Fragaria elatior*), of taller growth than the common strawberry, and having fruit of a musky flavour. Also ***hautboy strawberry***. (In this sense also spelt *hautbois*.)

1731-3 MILLER *Gard. Dict.* s.v. *Fragaria*, The Scarlet Strawberry should be planted a Foot square Plant from Plant, and the Hautboy sixteen or eighteen Inches Distance each Way. *c* **1759** *Roxb. Ball.* (1890) VII. 58 Here's fine savoys, and ripe hautboys. **1866** *Treas. Bot.* s.v. *Fragaria*, The Hautbois have plicated, rugose leaves, and the fruit has a musky flavour, which many persons greatly prefer. **1883** G. ALLEN in *Longm. Mag.* July 313 The hautboy, a taller plant, with fewer and larger blossoms and a richer flavour.

hautboyist ('həʊbɔɪɪst). [f. prec. + -IST: cf. F. *hautboïste*.] A player on the hautboy: = OBOIST.

1864 in WEBSTER. **1865** tr. *Spohr's Autobiog.* I. 45, I had the opportunity of hearing..the hautboyist Scherwenka.

Haut-Brion (o'briɔ̃). Also 7 **Hobriant, Ho Bryan,** 9 **Obryan.** [Fr., f. the name of an estate, Château *Haut-Brion*, in the commune of Pessac, near Bordeaux.] In full ***Château Haut-Brion***. A variety of fine quality claret.

1663 PEPYS *Diary* 10 Apr. (1893) III. 89 Here drank a sort of French wine, called Ho Bryan, that hath a good and most particular taste that I never met with. **1670** W. HUGHES *Compl. Vineyard* (ed. 2) 65 A sort of Claret called Hobriant-wine, of a deep red colour. *a* **1700** [see VIGNOBLE]. **1792** T. JEFFERSON *Let.* in A. Lichine *Encycl. Wines* (1967) 4/2 Bordeaux red wines. There are four crops of them more famous than the rest. These are Chateau-Margau, Tour de Segur, Hautbrion & De La Fitte. **1833** C. REDDING *Hist. Mod. Wines* 145 The first growth of this noted commune [*i.e.* Pessac] is Château Haut Brion. **1845** *Encycl. Metrop.* XXV. 1287/2 The following are the principal wines, or those most celebrated in the different countries where the vine has long been cultivated:—France... Bordeaux. Lafitte, red... Haut Brion, ditto. **1851** C. REDDING *Hist. Mod. Wines* (ed. 3) 174 In 1710, a wine called Obryan claret was sold in London at three shillings the bottle. **1888** *Encycl. Brit.* XXIV. 605/1 Château Haut-Brion, Pessac. **1935** *Punch* 28 Aug. 238/2 The Old Yquem which was not too sweet, And the Old Haut Brion so round and neat. **1959** W. JAMES *Word-Bk. Wine* 93 Haut Brion for some odd reason has always been regarded by Englishmen with a peculiar tenderness.

haute, hautely: see HAUGHT, -LY.

‖**haute Bohème** (ot boɛm). [Formed by M. Baring after HAUTE BOURGEOISIE.] A name applied to members of any fast or high-class Bohemian set.

1925 M. BARING *Cat's Cradle* I. xvii. 216 You see quite different people..people like the Svensens and all those musicians and archaeologists... *La Haute Bohème*... You never went near them before. **1939** O. LANCASTER *Homes Sweet Homes* 46 The cult of æstheticism..was only accepted whole-heartedly by..the *haute Bohème* of the day. **1954** *Design & Industries Assoc. Yearbk.* 37 The intelligentsia is.. becoming, in Maurice Baring's phrase, an Haute Boheme. **1964** M. LASKI in S. Nowell-Smith *Edwardian England* iv. 196 A fast Bohemian set, what Maurice Baring had called the *haute Bohème*.

‖**haute bourgeoisie** (ot burʒwazi). [Fr.] The French upper middle class; also extended to the upper middle class of other countries. Cf. BOURGEOISIE.

1888 *Athenæum* 4 Aug. 153/2 The haute bourgeoisie and the humble shopkeeper, citizens by nature and condition, have interests as indivisible. **1901** G. B. SHAW *Sixteen Self-Sketches* (1949) ix. 51 On the down grade from the zenith of *haute bourgeoisie* and landed gentry. **1924** A. D. SEDGWICK *Little French Girl* I. ii. 12 Alix was to tell her whether they were *petite noblesse* or *haute bourgeoisie*. **1934** A. HUXLEY *Beyond Mexique Bay* 7 A collection of the elderly *haute bourgeoisie*. **1940** F. SCOTT FITZGERALD *Let.* 14 Aug. (1964) 420 My father and Aunt Elise struggling to keep their children in the *haute bourgeoisie*. **1962** *Listener* 22 Feb. 350/1 A rich residential district for the prosperous Glasgow *haute bourgeoisie*. **1969** *N. Y. Rev. Books* 16 Jan. 34/3 The Business Council—which is about as close to an executive committee of the American *haute bourgeoisie* as one can get.

‖**haute boutique** (ot butik). [Fr., f. *haute* (fem.) high + BOUTIQUE.] (See quot. 1969.)

1966 *Guardian* 25 July 6/2 Simonetta is said to be presenting a much bigger haute boutique collection this season. **1969** *Ibid.* 14 Jan. 7/6 The class that the French call *haute boutique*—midway between couture and ready-to-wear.

haute couture: see COUTURE.

‖**haute cuisine** (ot kɥizin). [Fr., f. *haute* (fem.) high + CUISINE.] High-class (French) cooking.

1926 *Time* 5 July 12 In France, perhaps in France alone, the traditions of *la haute cuisine* survive from the days of the great gastronomes. **1928** S. BROWNE tr. *T. H. Varo de Velde's Ideal Marriage* xv. 277 The most effective dish in the *haute cuisine* is supposed to be crayfish soup. **1930** A. BENNETT *Imperial Palace* xxxvi. 246 *La Haute cuisine*. Not fifty people in the world were equipped by education and natural taste to comprehend it. **1935** *Time* 11 Mar. 22/1 If only English landladies spoke French, and if only their English cooks knew something of *haute cuisine*, Frenchmen with gold francs would be tempted across the Channel. **1951** E. DAVID *French Country Cooking* 172 Their use in what was regarded as *Haute Cuisine* became ridiculously excessive, and no dish was considered really refined without a garnish of sliced truffle. **1959** *Listener* 30 Apr. 776/3 The miracles of *haute cuisine* often arrive from a kitchen where the scales are faulty! **1962** AUDEN *Dyer's Hand* 75 It is difficult to imagine a *haute cuisine* based on algae and chemically treated grass. **1966** *Observer* 25 Sept. 46/2 An egg-based haute cuisine dinner for 6.

‖**haute école** (ot ekɔl). [Fr., = high school. Cf. SCHOOL *sb.*[1] 3 d.] The more difficult feats of horsemanship. Also *attrib.* and *transf.* (esp. in *Mus.*).

1858 *Rarey's Art of Taming Horses* i. 5 The accomplished Colonel Greenwood, who was equally learned in the *manège* of the *Haute Ecole*, and skilled in the style of the English hunting-fields. **1864** G. A. SALA *Quite Alone* I. xi. 191 She was doing the haute école. **1889** G. B. SHAW *London Mus. 1888-89* (1937) 215 The haute-école acts of the prima donna and tenor. **1896** *Strand Mag.* Mar. 334/2 Five other 'artistes'—trapezists, *haute école*, and 'bare-back' ladies. **1931** *Times Lit. Suppl.* 26 Mar. 247/3 The excellent *haute-école* rider seen at the Kingsway Opera House. **1953** G. BROOKE *Introd. Riding* vii. 69 Genuine 'Haute École', as maintained and demonstrated today. **1955** *Times* 15 Aug. 5/5 An energetic circus performer of the haute école. **1959** *Listener* 30 Apr. 776/2 Balakirev's *Islamey* is written in close imitation of Liszt's *haute école*. **1959** [see *gun-dog* (GUN *sb.* 17)]. **1960** *Times* 4 June 9/3 It is even more gratifying to hear the superbly groomed *haute école* pianism on the disc.

hautefeuillite (ot'føjaɪt). *Min.* [a. F. *hautefeuillite* (L. Michel 1893, in *Bull. de la Soc. française de Min.* XVI. 40), f. the name of P. G. *Hautefeuille* (1836-1902), French chemist.] A hydrous phosphate of magnesium and calcium that occurs in colourless crystals; possibly the same as bobierrite, the calcium being due to contamination with apatite.

1896 *Jrnl. Chem. Soc.* LXX. II. 112 (*heading*) Hautefeuillite, a new mineral from Bamle, Norway. **1937** *Amer. Mineralogist* XXII. 337 Michel..introduces the name *hautefeuillite* for a bobierrite-like mineral which, according to his analysis, differs from bobierrite..in its optical orientation. However, the redetermined optical properties of bobierrite correspond to those of hautefeuillite as given by Michel. *Ibid.* 338 Until more evidence is produced..it seems best to discard hautefeuillite as a mineral name. **1955** M. H. HEY *Index Min. Species* (ed. 2) 232 *Hautefeuillite.* $(Mg,Ca)_3PO_4.8H_2O$... Has been interpreted as a mixture of Bobierrite..and Apatite..but the H_2O is very high for this interpretation, and further study is desirable.

hautein, -en, -eyn, var. HAUTAIN *Obs.*

‖**haute noblesse** (ot noblɛs). [Fr., f. *haute* (fem.) high + NOBLESSE.] The upper stratum of the aristocracy.

1787 W. BECKFORD *Let.* 8 Nov. in *Italy* (1834) II. xxx. 146 The famous tenor singer, who entertained us..with many private anecdotes of the *haute noblesse*. **1907** M. E. BRADDON *Dead Love has Chains* ii. 23 She had friends among the *haute noblesse*..in the old St. Germain faubourg. **1934** A. WOOLLCOTT *While Rome Burns* 220 The panic among the English *haute noblesse* during the Oscar Wilde trial.

haute-pace, -pase, -pass, obs. ff. HAUT-PAS.

‖**haute-piece.** *Obs.* [F.; lit. 'high piece', 'a Poldron; or the vpper part thereof' (Cotgr.).] The shoulder-piece in plate armour; = PAULDRON.

c **1500** *Melusine* xxii. (E.E.T.S.) 145 Vryan..atteyned hym with his trenchaunt swerde betwix the heed & the sholders..and his hawtepyece fell of with the forsaid stroke. *Ibid.* xlix. 325 Thenne Geffray smote hym [the giant] with his swerd vpon the sholder, for he myght not reche his heed, and cutte the haulte piece of his harneys.

hautere, obs. form of ALTAR.

†**hau'tesse.** *Obs.* Also 4-7 **'hawtesse,** 5 **hautes,** 7 **-ess.** [a. F. *hautesse* (12th c. in Hatz.-Darm.), f. *haut* high, HAUT.] Highness, height; loftiness of rank or character, nobility; haughtiness, pride; grandeur, stateliness; length (of time).

13.. *Gaw & Gr. Knt.* 2454 Weldez non so hyȝe hawtesse, þat ho ne con make ful tame. **1399** LANGL. *Rich. Redeles* III. 13 The hertis that hautesse of yeris That pasture prikkyth, and her prevy age. *a* **1400-50** *Alexander* 2835 Hoo with þi hautes and þine vnhemed wittis, A-vaile of þi vanite and of þi vayne pride. **1415** *Crowned King* 127 So shall thy hawtesse highlich be honoured. **1660** WATERHOUSE *Arms* 217 This Perewig of hawtesse. **1667** —— *Fire Lond.* 166 Cæsar and Pompey's hautess being revived in them.

‖**hauteur** (ho'tœːr). Also 7 **haughture.** [F. *hauteur* (12th c. in Hatz.-Darm.), f. *haut* high.]

1. Loftiness of manner or bearing; haughtiness of demeanour.

a **1628** F. GREVILLE *Sidney* iii. (1652) 37 In his Spanish haughture. **1745** H. WALPOLE *Lett.* (1857) I. 413 (Stanf.) A comparison between him [Lord Chesterfield] and the *hauteur* of all other lord-lieutenants. **1792** G. WASHINGTON *Lett.* Writ. 1892 XII. 98 That your habits of expression indicated a hauteur disgusting to those, who happen to differ from you in sentiment. **1823** BYRON *Juan* XIII. xiv, Both seem'd secure—She in her virtue, he in his hauteur. **1883** S. C. HALL *Retrospect* II. 96 He seemed to think hauteur an essential feature of the clerical office.

†**2.** A height. *Obs. rare.*

1711 *Lond. Gaz.* No. 4989/2 The Enemy have drawn off all their Cannon from the Hauteurs of Wavrechin.

‖**haute vulgarisation** (ot vylgarizasjɔ̃; also freq. with (quasi-)anglicized pronunc. of second word). [Fr., f. *haute* (fem.) high + VULGARIZATION.] The popularization of abstruse of complex matters.

[**1943** *Mind* LII. 178 Mr. Skemp would refer us..to the *Timaeus* of which he regards the utterances of *Laws X* as only a 'popularised' version, in the nature of what the French call an *œuvre de haute vulgarisation*.] **1946** *Christian Sci. Monitor* 21 Dec. (Mag. Sect.) 10 Mr. Van Doren has written a work of '*haute vulgarization*'. **1958** *Times* 6 Dec. 7/7 This can only be achieved if some of the scholars themselves transform their knowledge into the *haute vulgarisation* of which Cicero himself, far more even than H. G. Wells, was the master. **1960** *Cambr. Rev.* 16 Jan. 232/3 Is the *haute-vulgarization* of archaeology, which we see happening.., a good thing? **1966** *Listener* 13 Oct. 544/2 Mrs. Thomson's edition is a model of *haute vulgarisation*. It is based on her father's..standard edition..but modernized and abridged. **1968** *Times* 9 Nov. 23/6 This book is an extraordinary mixture of lucid demonstration, mathematical wizardry and ebullient high spirits, which the two American authors define as 'haute vulgarisation'.

†**'hautful.** *a. Obs. rare.* In 5 **hawtful.** [f. HAUT + -FUL.] Exalted, lofty: = HAUGHT *a.* 3.

c **1440** HYLTON *Scala Perf.* (W. de W. 1494) II. xliv, Some tyme sheweth Jhesu..hymself as an hawtful mayster and somtyme as a reuerent fader.

‖**haut-goût** (ogu). Forms: 7 **haugou, hau-gou, hau-, hautgoust, haut-goust, haut goust, hault-gust, haut-gust, haugout, (hought-goust),** 7-8 **hautgout,** 8 **haugust,** 7- **haut-gout,** 9 **hautgoût.** See also HOGO. [F.; lit. 'high flavour', 'anything that excites the appetite, and is put into sauces, such as pepper, lemon, musk, verjuice, etc.' (Littré), as in sense 1; f. *haut* high + *goût* (formerly *goust*) taste, savour, flavour. (The 17-18th c. spellings, show that the pronunciation was sometimes anglicized ('hɔːtgʌst, 'hɔːgʌst); but *hogo* bears witness to the French form.)]

†**1.** A high or piquant flavour; a strong relish; something that gives a relish, seasoning. *Obs.*

c **1645** HOWELL *Lett.* I. v. xxxviii, He can marinat fish, make gellies, he is excellent for a pickant sawce, and the *Haugou*. *a* **1661** FULLER *Worthies, Cornwall* I. (1662) 194 [Garlick] giving a delicious Hault-gust to most meats they eat. **1663** COWLEY *Verses & Ess., Country Mouse* 18 For a *Hautgoust* there was mixt with these The swerd of Bacon, and the coat of Cheese. **1669** WORLIDGE *Syst. Agric.* (1681) 166 Our English-Tobacco..many are of Opinion that it's better than Forreign, having a more *Haut-gust*, which pleaseth some. **1743** *Lond. & Country Brew.* II. (ed. 2) 97 Which will..greatly improve the Drink, by giving it a fine Haugust, or a true Tincture of the Malt. **1752** *Milton's P.R.* I. 344 *note* (Jod.) A little book writ by a gentlewoman of Queen Elizabeth's court, where ambergris is mentioned as the hautgout of that age.

b. *fig.* 'Flavour', 'spice'. [So in French.]

1650 CHARLETON *Paradoxes* 88 Their conjecture hath ever had a strong hautgoust of absurdity. **1667** *Decay Chr. Piety* viii. ¶40 Every impertinent story or insipid jest must have the haut-goust of an oath to recommend it. **1683** KENNETT *Erasm. on Folly* 12 What stage of life is not melancholy.. unless we spice it with Pleasure, that haut goust of Folly? **1711** LADY M. W. MONTAGU *Let. to Mrs. Hewet* (1887) I. 31 Danger gives a *haut goût* to everything.

2. In later use: A 'high' or slightly putrescent flavour; a taint.

1693 CONGREVE *Juvenal, Sat.* XI. 244 (Jod.) Nor is there ever left Any unsav'ry hautgout from the holt. **1796** PEGGE *Anonym.* 185 People affect to eat venison with a haut-gout in the country. **1820** T. S. HUGHES *Trav. in Sicily* II. i. 26 (Stanf.) Oil..is relished the better for a slight taint or haut-gout. **1845** FORD *Handbk. Spain* I. 281 (Stanf.) This gives a haut goût, as putrefaction does to the aldermanic haunch.

†**3.** A highly-flavoured or seasoned dish. *Obs.*

1656-7 DAVENANT *Rutland House* Dram. Wks. 1873 III. 226 She having not known..the sufficient mystery of haut-gouts. **1664** BUTLER *Hud.* II. i. 598 Or season her, as French Cooks use Their Haut-gusts, Buollies, or Ragusts. **1693** *Humours of Town* 10 Rather..than come within forty miles

of the smell of the *Hought-goust*. **1702** MOTTEUX *Prol. to Farquhar's Inconstant*, Your rakes love hauts-goûts, like your damn'd French cheese. **1817** COLERIDGE *Sibyl. Leaves* Poems II. 312 Each haut-gout cook'd by monk or priest.

4. *attrib.*

1651 STANLEY *Excitations* Poems 93 This hau-gou Carbonade.

†**'hauther, hawther.** *Obs.* (See quots.)

1611 COTGR., *Annelet*, a gimmew, or little ring for the finger; also, a hawther. *Ibid.*, *Maille*, mayle, or a linke of mayle..also, a Hauther; or, any little ring of mettall resembling a linke of mayle. *Ibid.*, *Porte*..any entrance, or way to enter at; also, a hauther, or eye.

‖**hautin.** *Obs. rare*$^{-1}$. [F. *hautin*, also *hautaigne* (16th c. in Littré), *hautain*, deriv. of *haut* high.] A tree used as a support for a vine.

1601 HOLLAND *Pliny* I. 534 Gon this hath for currant many yeares past..That the best and most dainty Wines came of those grapes onely which grew vpon such Hautins or trees..Yea..that the higher a Vine climbed vpon these trees the better grapes it bare.

‖**haut monde** (o mɔ̃d). [Fr., lit. high world.] The fashionable world: cf. BEAU-MONDE.

1864 MRS. BEETON *Jrnl.* in N. Spain *Mrs. Beeton & her Husband* (1948) II. vi. 215 Her dress would have been the envy of many of our *haute monde* [sic]. **1894** M. BEERBOHM in *Yellow Bk.* III. 253 A certain lack of tone had crept into the amusements of the *haut monde*. **1930** *Aberdeen Press & Jrnl.* 22 Apr. 4 The Aberdeen Lido scene which depicts *haut monde* life..at the glorified Aberdeen beach of the future. **1931** *Times Lit. Suppl.* 28 May 429/1 Several ladies of the *haut monde*. **1935** *Punch* 30 Jan. 114/2 And top-hats at breakfast? Are these the manners of the *haut monde*? **1969** C. IRVING *Fake!* (1970) iii. 32 All of the *haut monde* of New York was there... You couldn't move, it was so packed.

‖**haut-pas.** Now only as Fr. (hopɑ). Forms: 5 **hautepase, haught passe, 6 hautepace, haulte pace, 7 haute pass, 7- haut-pas.** [F. *haut pas*, lit. 'high step'; in common use in 15-16th c. and anglicized in the form HALPACE, whence also the corrupted forms HALF-, HATH-, HEARTH-PACE.]

A part of the floor of a hall, etc., raised one or more steps above the level of the rest; a dais: = HALF-PACE 1.

1460 *Will of Burgate* (Somerset Ho.), The hautepase that y made for the maidens & women seruents to pray for my soule. *a* **1483** EARL RIVERS *Let.* in Gairdner *Hist. Rich. III*, (1878) App. B. 395 That the steyres of my h[a]ught passe schulbe vj fote. **1540** Haulte pace [see HALPACE]. **1548** HALL *Chron.*, *Hen. VIII.* 65 b, There was made from the West doore to the quere doore of the churche egall with the highest step, a hautepace of tymber of xii fote broade, that the kyng and the Ambassadors might be sene. **1670** F. SANFORD *Dk. Albemarle* (1722) 5 At the upper end upon a Haute-pass, a Bed of State of black Velvet was placed. **1735** in *Etoniana* x. (1865) 157 The..hall was fitted with a haut-pas at the upper end, and a chair of state upon it. **1761** GRAY *Let.* 24 Sept. in *Leisure Ho.* (1884) 752/1 Below the steps of the *haut pas* were the tables of the nobility.

‖**haut-relief** ('həʊrɪ'liːf). [F. (orəljɛf).] High relief, ALTO-RELIEVO: opp. to *bas-relief*.

1850 LEITCH *Müller's Anc. Art* §244. 251 Colossal haut-reliefs of imaginary animals. **1886** A. D. AINSLIE *Reynard* x. 241 Graved in haut relief..Rich clustered grapes.

‖**haut ton** (ho tɔ̃). [F. = high tone, the manners of the higher circles of society. (Now little used in Eng.)] High fashion; *ellipt.*, people of high fashion.

1801 *Sporting Mag.* XVII. 22 People of the *Haut Ton* are about to return to town. **1807-8** W. IRVING *Salmag.* (1824) 6 The gentlemen, who doze away their time in the circles of the *haut-ton*. *a* **1849** POE *Wks.* (1884) I. 348 (Stanf.) An air of extreme *haut ton*. **1850** *Harper's Mag.* I. 288 [It] has excited the attention of the *haut ton* abroad.

hauty, earlier spelling of HAUGHTY.

hauwitzer, obs. form of HOWITZER.

hauy, obs. form of HEAVY.

haüyne ('hɑːwɪn). *Min.* [a. F. *haüyne*; named 1807 after the French mineralogist *Haüy*.] A silicate of aluminium and sodium with calcium sulphate, occurring in certain igneous rocks in crystals or grains of various shades of blue or green.

1814 L. GMELIN (*title*) Some Account of the Mountains of Ancient Latium; in which the Mineral called Haüyne is found. **1869** PHILLIPS *Vesuv.* x. 293 Haüyne, or Latialite, occurs..in cavities of gray micaceous or augitic lava.

haüynite ('hɑːwɪnaɪt). [f. prec. + -ITE.] = prec.

1868 DANA *Min.* 332 *Haüynophyr*, a black to brown rock containing the haüynite disseminated through it.

haüynophyr ('hɑːwɪnəʊfɜː(r)). *Min.* [f. as prec. + Gr. φύρ-ειν to mix, mingle.] A name for various rocks having haüyne disseminated through them.

1865 WATTS *Dict. Chem.*, *Hauynophyr*, a name applied to the lava of Melfi on the Vulturo. **1868** [see prec.]. **1878** LAWRENCE tr. *Cotta's Rocks Class.* 133 Haüynophyr..a rock ..which essentially consists of augite and haüyne.

havage ('hævɪdʒ). *s.w. dial.* Also **haveage.** [f. HAVE *v.* + -AGE.] Lineage, parentage.

1846 *Spec. Cornish Prov. Dial.* 55, I do knaw all the havage of thee. **1865** R. HUNT *Pop. Rom. West of England* Ser. II. 245 He came of good havage. **1897** *Western Times* (Exeter) 3 Jan. 2/2 A man of Western havage, of Western education, and once Bishop of this Westernmost See.

Havana (hə'vænə). Also **Havanna(h.** [Name of the capital city of Cuba, now in Spanish *Habana*. Cf. F. *havane*]. **a.** (In full, ***Havana cigar***): A cigar of a kind made at Havana or in Cuba. (Also applied to the tobacco of which these are made.)

[**1711** *Advt.* in *Spect.* (1868) 903 Barcelona, Havana, and Old Spanish Snuff.] **1802** *Deb. Congress U.S.* 31 Mar. 229 The greater part of what we have imported came..in the shape of Havana cigars. **1826** DISRAELI *Viv. Grey* IV. v. (Stanf.), A grilled bone, Havannahs, and Regent's punch. **1833** MARRYAT *P. Simple* xvi, Having very fortunately about a couple of dozen of real Havannahs in my pocket. **1888** *Encycl. Brit.* XXIII. 426/2 Genuine ('legitimas') Havana cigars are such only as are made in the island; and the cigars made in Europe..from genuine Cuban tobacco are classed as 'Havanas'. **1972** 'A. YORK' *Expurgator* iv. 69 They lunched..on ham..on real coffee and Havana cigars.

b. *Comb.* ***havana-brown***, the shade of brown which is the colour of havana cigars.

1875 *Ure's Dict. Arts.* I. 189 Havanna brown. *Ibid.* II. 778 *Habana brown*, this name has been given to aniline-brown. **1896** *Daily News* 11 June 3/6 Floral design upon a ground of havana-brown.

c. ellipt. for *havana-brown*.

1873 *Young Englishwoman* July 338/1 Two shades of brown—Havana and maroon. **1922** *Daily Mail* 12 Dec. 7 In delightful shades of Saxe, Heliotrope, Dove Grey, or Havana. **1967** N. FREELING *Strike Out* 27 A large complicated overcheck of fuchsia, havana and off-white.

d. Havana rabbit, a variety of domesticated rabbit distinguished by its dark brown fur, bred near Utrecht about 1898, and kept for both fur and meat. Also *ellipt.*

1912 G. A. TOWNSEND *Pract. Rabbit Keeping* xx. 273 The Havana rabbit..was first introduced..into England in 1910... The originals, born in Holland, were obtained accidentally. **1953** W. K. WILSON *Mod. Rabbit Husb.* i. 14 Other fur breeds were imported, e.g. Champagnes and Havanas.

Havdal(l)ah, varr. HABDALAH.

have (hæv), *v.* Forms and Inflexions: see below. [A Common Teutonic vb.: OE. *habban, hæfde, hæfed*, = OFris. *hebba, hêde, heved, hevd*, OS. *hebbian, habda, habda, -habd, -hadd* (MDu., Du. *hebben, hadde, gehad*, MLG. *hebben*, (*hân*), *hadde, gehat*), OHG. *habên, habêta, gihabêt* (MHG. *habên, hâte, gehabet*, Ger. *haben, hatte, gehabt*), ON. *hafa, hafða, haft* (Sw. *hafva, hafvde, haft*, Da. *have, havde, havt*), Goth. *haban, habaida, habaid-*:—OTeut. stem **habê-*. On account of its correspondence in form and sense with L. *habē-re*, generally referred to a hypothetical Aryan radical form **khabhê-*. The OE., OFris., and OS. had in all parts of the present, exc. 2nd and 3rd sing. pres. Ind., the stem *habj-* (from *habē-*), reduced by gemination to *habb-* (*hæbb-, hębb-*), while these two persons and the past retained *hab-* (*hav-, haf-*); hence OE. *habban, hæbbe, habbað, hæbbende*, etc., beside *hafast* (*hæfst*), *hafaþ* (*hæfþ*), *hæfde, hæfed*. In ME. the *habb-* forms were gradually reduced by levelling to *hav-* (*have(n, I have, they have(n, having*); while the original *haf-* (= *hav-*) forms at length lost their *f(v)*, before the following consonant (*ha-st, ha-th, ha-s, ha-d*). Even the later *v*, for OE. *bb*, was worn down in colloquial and dialect speech, so that OE. *habban* passed through ME. *habben, haven, han*, to later *ha, ha'*, Sc. *hae*. These phonetic weakenings, due largely to the weakness and stresslessness of the word in many uses, both as principal verb and as auxiliary, have given rise to a very great number of historical forms for every inflected part, a number further increased by the graphic interchange of *f, v*, and *u*, and by the frequent dropping of initial *h*. The *ne plus ultra* of all these tendencies is seen in the reduction of OE. *habban* to *a*, or its entire elision, as in *I would a been*, occas. Sc. *I wad been*. In ordinary English, contracted forms are now only colloquial or metrical, in *I've, thou'st, he's, we've, I'd, he'd, we'd*. By coalescence with *ne*, this verb had also, in OE. and early ME., as in OFris., a negative form *nabban, nave*, which held in OE. the rank of an independent word (cf. *will, nill*, L. *volo, nōlo*); it is here included under the positive form.]

A. Inflexional Forms.

1. *Infinitive.*

a. *Simple Infinitive*, **have** (hæv, həv, əv). Forms: α. 1 **habban, haban,** 2-3 **habben, -eon,** 3-4 **haven,** 4-5 **havyn, hawyn, han, (hanne).** β. 1-2 **habba, hæbbe, habe,** 2-4 **habbe (abbe),** 3-4 **hafe, haf,** 3- **(haue), have** (4 **hawe,** 4-5 **haff,** 5-6 *Sc.* **haif(f, hayf,** 9 *dial.* **hab).** γ. 3-5 **ha,** 3-7 **'a, a,** 5- (now *dial.*) **hay,** 6- **ha',** 7- *Sc.* **hae.**

α. **971** *Blickl. Hom.* 107 þonne maʒon we..habban. *c* **1200** ORMIN 647 Alle þa þatt shulenn habbenn blisse. *c* **1220** *Bestiary* 196 Ðat tu milce mote hauen. *c* **1300** *Havelok* 78 He dede hem sone to hauen ricth. **13..** *Seuyn Sag.* (W.) 294 Let me of him han a sight. **1377** LANGL. *P. Pl.* B. Prol. 109 To han þat power. *c* **1440** *Promp. Parv.* 225/1 Han, or havyn, *habeo*.

β. *c* **950** *Lindisf. Gosp.* Matt. vi. 24 He scile habba. *Ibid.* xviii. 9 Ðon tuoe eʒo hæbbe. *a* **1175** *Cott. Hom.* 221 Let ham habba agenne cire. *Ibid.* 241 Hi sculen habe þat brad. *c* **1175** *Lamb. Hom.* 83 Ho ne scal..habbe nan oðer uuel. **1297** R. GLOUC. (1724) 315 þat myȝte abbe ys grace. *a* **1300** *Sarmun* xix. in *E.E.P.* (1862) 3 How hi hit mow hab and winne. *a* **1300** *Cursor M.* 8572 O riches sal þou haf god wan. **1340** *Ayenb.* 5 þou ne sselt habbe uele godes. **1340** HAMPOLE *Pr. Consc.* 98 He..Grete payne sal have. *c* **1375** *Sc. Leg. Saints*, *Petrus* 25 He wald haf refyn. *c* **1400** MAUNDEV. (Roxb.) i. 4 Men wald..hafe putte þe appel. *c* **1470** HENRY *Wallace* I. 52 How thai suld haif ane end. *Ibid.* 383 Fysche we wald hawe [*rime* gawe]. **1583** HOLLYBAND *Campo di Fior* 379 Will you have your long cloke? **1828** *Craven Dial.*, *Hab*, a corruption of have.

γ. *a* **1300** *Cursor M.* 17343 þar he o naman suld ha [*v.r.* haue] sight. *a* **1375** *Joseph Arim.* 351 þou schalt ha vengaunce. **1434** MISYN *Mending of Life* viii. (1896) 120 Begynnyng þou may ha of oþer mens wordis. *a* **1533** LD. BERNERS *Huon* lviii. 197, I wolde not a refused him. **1598** SHAKS. *Merry W.* III. iii. 231, I wold not ha your distemper. **1602** —— *Ham.* v. i. 26 Will you ha the truth on't? **1684** BUNYAN *Pilgr.* II. 27, I thought you would a come in. **1786** BURNS *Ep. Yng. Friend* iv, A man may hae an honest heart. **1828** *Craven Dial.*, Hay't, have it.

b. *Dative Infinitive* (with *to*) to **have** (tʊ hæv); in OE. **tó habbanne (hæbbenne),** ME. **to habben(n)e, habben, habbe, haven, have.**

971 *Blickl. Hom.* 59 Ælcon men..to hæbbenne. *c* **1100** *O.E. Chron.* an. 1085 He ahte to habbanne. *c* **1175** *Lamb. Hom.* 79 Me brekeð þe nute for to habbene þene curnel. *c* **1205** LAY. 145 To habben to wife. *a* **1300** *Leg. Rood* (1871) 18 Riȝt is to habbe in munde. *c* **1330** R. BRUNNE *Chron.* (1810) 14 Socour forto haue. *a* **1350** *Guy Warw.* (A.) 168 Kniȝtes to hauen & holden of pris. *c* **1375** *Sc. Leg. Saints*, *Matthew* 62 To haf na mycht. **1480** CAXTON *Chron. Eng.* cxvi, To heve a sone of his. **1560** ROLLAND *Crt. Venus* I. 122 As he thocht best to haid [= hae't]. **1562** WINJET *Cert. Tractates* I. Wks. 1888 I. 5 To haif brocht the baronis. **1583** STUBBES *Anat. Abus.* I. (1879) 75 Be sure neuer to haue good day with them. **1859** TROLLOPE *Bertrams* (1867) 287 If you knew what it is to have an empty heart.

2. *Indicative Present.*

a. *1st pers. sing.* **have.** Forms: α. 1-3 **hæbbe,** (1 **hebbe, hafu, hafo),** 2-4 **habbe,** 3 **(abbe, ab), haf,** 3- **(haue), have, (ha');** *Sc.* 4-5 **haff,** 6 **haif;** 8-9 *colloq.* **'ve,** *Sc.* **hae.** β. *north.* 4- **has, hes.**

α. *Beowulf* (Z.) 2523 Ic me on hafu bord ond byrnan. **832** *Charter* in *O.E. Texts* 447 Ic beboden hebbe. *c* **1000** *Ags. Gosp.* Matt. viii. 9 Ic hæbbe þeʒnas under me. *c* **1175** *Lamb. Hom.* 35 Swilche pine ic habbe. *c* **1205** LAY. 462 Ich abbe.. seoue þusend kempen. **1297** R. GLOUC. (1724) 205 þe pyte, þat ychabbe of þe. *a* **1300** *Fragm.* in *E.E.P.* (1862) 21 þoȝt ic ab to blinne. *a* **1300** *Cursor M.* 961 Haf I na frend. *Ibid.* 3294, I ha ben [*Fairf.*, *Trin.* haue bene] sumdel in suinc. *c* **1375** *Sc. Leg. Saints*, *Petrus* 14 One haff I tane. **1382** WYCLIF *Luke* xvi. 28, I haue fyue bretheren. **1500-20** DUNBAR *Poems* xxx. 37 In it haif I in pulpet gon. **1526** TINDALE *John* iv. 17, I have no husband. **1575** J. STILL *Gamm. Gurton* IV. i. in hazl. *Dodsley* III. 226 Alas, 'ch a lost my good nee'le. **1703** ROWE *Fair Penit.* v. i. 1852 The wrongs I ha' done thee. **1788** BURNS *Naebody*, I hae a penny to spend. **1885** F. A. GUTHRIE *Tinted Venus* viii. 95 I've a good mind to take the tram. **1892** R. KIPLING *Barrack-r. Ballads*, *Tomlinson* 73 This I ha' heard.

β. *c* **1340** *Cursor M.* 14135 (Fairf.) As I be-fore ȝou has talde. **1585** JAS. I. *Ess. Poesie* (Arb.) 13 Sen I with pen..hes servde you. *Mod. Sc.* To me that has seen him.

b. *2nd pers. sing.* **hast** (hæst, həst). Forms: α. 1 **hafast, hæfst,** 1-3 **hafest,** 2-6 **(hauest), havest,** 3 **hafuest, hæfuest, hæuest, hafust, (afest, auest), hafst,** 3- **hast,** (4 **hest,** 5-6 **haste,** 7- **'st).** β. *north.* 3-5 **haues,** 3- **has, hes,** 3-4 **hauis,** (3-5 **as),** 4 **habbes, -ez,** 5 **hauys, hais,** 5-6 **hase,** (6 **hess).**

α. *Beowulf* (Z.) 1850 þu þin feorh hafast. *a* **1000** *Cædmon's Gen.* 569 (Gr.) ȝif þu his willan hæfst. *c* **1175** *Lamb. Hom.* 25 þenne hafest þu þes hundes laȝe. *a* **1225** *Juliana* 33 þu hauest feorliche fan. *c* **1300** *St. Margarete* 144 þu hast poer ouer mi bodi. **1340** *Ayenb.* 20 þe ilke zenne þet þou hest ine þine herte. *c* **1460** *Frere & Boye* 79 in Ritson *Anc. Pop. P.* 38 Thou haste gyuen mete to me. **1588** SHAKS. *L.L.L.* v. i. 81 Thou hast it..at the fingers ends.

β. *c* **1250** *Gen. & Ex.* 1760 Qui as ðu min godes stolen? *a* **1300** *Cursor M.* 2464, I sal ta me þat þou haues left. *Ibid.* 2976 þou has anoþer mannes wijf. **13..** *Gaw. & Gr. Knt.* 327 þat þou boden habbes. *c* **1470** HENRY *Wallace* I. 262 Der sone, this lang quhar has thow beyne? *c* **1485** *Digby Myst.* (1882) IV. 400 Why haves thou not refreynyd? **1513** BRADSHAW *St. Werburge* I. 3157 Why hase thou vs lefte? *c* **1560** A. SCOTT *Poems* (S.T.S.) xxxiii. 39 Thow hess þi horne ay in þair syde. **1790** MRS. WHEELER *Westmld. Dial.* 32 What haesta the cart?

c. *3rd pers. sing.* **has** (hæz, həz, əz), orig. *north.*; *arch.* **hath** (hæθ). Forms: α. 1 **hafaþ, hæfeþ,** 1-3 **hæfþ, hafeþ,** (2 **afeð),** 2-3 **hafð, haueð, habbeð,** 2-5 **haþ,** 3 **hafueð, hæfueð, hæueð, hauið, (aueþ, abbeþ, aþ),** 4 **heþ,** 4-7 (8-9 *arch.*) **hath,** (5 **avyth, hat,** 7 **haith).** β. 1 **hæfis,** 3-5 **haues, hafs,** 4 **habbes, -ez, habes, hauis, haffys,** 4-5 **hase,** 5 **hais(e,** 6 **hace,** 3- **has,** (5- *Sc.* **hes,** 6- *colloq.* **'s).** γ. 6- *dial.* **have.**

α. *a* **1000** *Cædmon's Gen.* 635 (Gr.) þonne he his ȝeweald hafað. *c* **1000** *Ags. Gosp.* Mark iii. 30 He hæfð unclænne gast. **1154** *O.E. Chron.* an. 1154 [He] fair haued begunnon. *a* **1175** *Cott. Hom.* 237 Se gode man..godes lufe hað ȝefolȝed. *Ibid.* 239 His hlaford þe he ȝegremed afeð. *c* **1175** *Lamb. Hom.* 47 Heo hafð mid hire þreo wurdliche mihte. *Ibid.* 99 He haueð alle blisse. *c* **1200** ORMIN 3969 þatt illke mann þatt hafeþþ all god wille. *c* **1205** LAY. 1331 Hit hafð þes wurse taken.

c **1275** *Ibid.* 3369 þet auep Amari. **1297** R. GLOUC. (1724) 2 Wateres he haþ. **1340** *Ayenb.* 90 Huo þet mest heþ, mest is worþ. **1453** *Paston Lett.* No. 191 I. 260 Every man..auyth gretely to marveylle. **1583** HOLLYBAND *Campo di Fior* 53 Varro hath an excellent schoole. **1648** *Hamilton Papers.* (Camden) 226 There haith happened a misfortune this morneing. **1832** AUSTIN *Jurispr.* (1879) II. 849 In so far as meaning he hath. **1841** LANE *Arab. Nts.* I. 112 This it is which hath prevented my answering thee.

β. c **950** *Lindisf. Gosp.* Matt. viii. 20 Sunu monnes ne hæfis huer heafud ȝehlutes. *a* **1300** *Cursor M.* 15317 (Cott.) He þat has [*Gött.* hafs] his bodi clene. *c* **1300** *Ibid.* 19008 (Edin.) þe giftis..giuin us hauis he als ȝie se here. *c* **1300** *Havelok* 1980 He haues a wunde in the side. **13..** *E.E. Allit. P.* B. 995 A stonen statue þat salt sauor habbes. **1375** BARBOUR *Bruce* I. 434 Tharoff haffys he nane. *c* **1380** WYCLIF *Sel. Wks.* III. 135 Man þat hafs his spirit in his nose. *c* **1450** *St. Cuthbert* (Surtees) 886 God haues puruayde for our best. *c* **1450** *Golagros & Gaw.* 794 He is makar of man, and alkyn myght haise. *c* **1450** *Bk. Curtasye* 138 in *Babees Bk.* (1868) 303 At borde to sitt he hase no myȝt. **1513** BRADSHAW *St. Werburge* I. 1733 Eche kynge at other lysence taken hace [*rime* place]. **1598** SHAKS. *Merry W.* I. iv. 15 No body but has his fault. **1605** —— *Macb.* I. iii, 79 The Earth hath bubbles, as the Water ha's. *a* **1605** MONTGOMERIE *Misc. Poems* xxxv. 77 Quhais beutie hes me burt? **1882** TENNYSON *Promise of May* III. Wks. (1894) 799/1 *Steer.* Hes the cow cawved? *Dora.* No, Father.

γ. **1547** BALE *Sel. Wks.* (1849) 236 Of monks have it gotten a purgatory..Of the universities have it caught all the subtilties. **1559** W. CUNNINGHAM *Cosmogr. Glasse* I The Race that every man..have to runne. *Ibid.* 55 A point..is that which have no partes. *Mod. E. Anglian dial.*, Have he come? Yes, he have.

d. *plural* **have**; contracted **'ve.** Forms: *α.* 1 **habbað, hæbbað**; 2-4 **habbeð**, (2 **habeð**, 2-4 **abbeþ**, 3 **abbiþ**), 3-4 **haueþ**, (**abbeþ**), 4 **hebbeþ**, 5-6 **hath, -e.** *β. north.* 1 **habbas**, 3-4 **habbes**, (4 **-ez**), **hauis**, 3- **has**, (4 **hase, haffis, hafs,** as, 5 **hafez, hays**, 6 **haves**, 5- *Sc.* **hes**). *γ. midl.* 2 **hafen, habben**, 3 **hebben**, 3-5 (**hauen**), **haven**, 3-6 **haan**, 3-7 (*dial.* -9) **han**, (4-7 **an**). *δ.* 3- (**haue**), **have**, (3-5 **haff, haf**, 3-6 **hafe**, 5-6 **haffe**, 6- *Sc.* **hef**), *colloq.* 9 **'ve.** *ε.* 3-6 (*dial.* -9) **ha**, 6-7 **ha'**, (6 **haie**), 8- *Sc.* **hae.**

α. c **825** *Vesp. Psalter* cxiii. [cxv.] 5 Muð habbað and ne spreocað. *a* **1000** *Cædmon's Gen.* 313 (Gr.) þær hæbbað heo on æfen. *c* **1000** *Ags. Gosp. Luke* xvi. 29 Hiȝ habbað moysen and witeȝan. *c* **1175** *Lamb. Hom.* 11 Ure sunne þet we abbet idon. *a* **1225** *Ancr. R.* 20 3if ȝe habbeð neode. *c* **1275** LAY. 364 We abbeþ seue. **1340** *Ayenb.* 32 þo þet hebbeþ drede of naȝt. **1509** BARCLAY *Shyp of Folys* (1874) II. 41 Whan these caytyfes hath hurt a mannys name. **1554-9** *Songs & Ball* (1860) 9 All hathe offendyd. *a* **1555** LATIMER *Serm. & Rem.* (1845) 201 The rulers of this realm hath no better a God..than the poorest in this world.

β. c **950** *Lindisf. Gosp.* Matt. xiv. 16 Ne habbas ned. *a* **1300** *Cursor M.* 21638 (Cott.) Meracles..Has [Edin. hauis] ben in semblance and in sight. *c* **1300** *Ibid.* 23114 (Edin.) Murþerers..þat..of kirk as tint þe help. *Ibid.* 23706 (Edin.) Al þat euir hafs herd þis bok. **1340** HAMPOLE *Pr. Consc.* 57 þe creatures þat skill has nane. **13..** *E.E. Allit. P.* B. 308 Alle þat lyf habbez. *c* **1400** MAUNDEV. (Roxb.) vii. 25 þe treessez..hafez lefes of a fute brede. *c* **1420** *Avow. Arth.* xxxix, Thenne sex..Hase armut hom. **1578** *Ps. lxxvii.* in *Scot. Poems 16th C.* II. 109 Our nighbours hes mocked vs. *a* **1600** *Turnam. Tottenham* 31 We er rycher men then he, and mor gode haves. *Mod. Sc.* Thaim at hes aye gets mair.

γ. c **1175** *Lamb. Hom.* 59 His nome þet we of him hafen. *Ibid.* 69 Halde we us from uniwil, and habben feir lete and ec skil. **13..** *K. Alis.* 4940 Ne hebben hy non other fyre. *c* **1340** *Cursor M.* 15066 (Trin.) We han desired þe. **1382** WYCLIF *Luke* xvi. 29 Thei han Moyses and the prophetis. **1411** *Rolls of Parlt.* III. 650/1 The ordenance that Thomas Archebisshop of Canterbury, and Richard Lord the Grey..haven made. **1452** *Nottingham Rec.* II. 364 The said Meire and Cominalte..han putte to their comune sealle. **1579** SPENSER *Sheph. Cal.* Mar. 62 When shepheardes groomes han leave to playe. **1828** *Craven Dial., Han*, they have, an old contraction for haven. *Mod. Lancash. Dial.*, We han seen them. Han yo any?

δ. a **1300** *Cursor M.* 3591 Quen þai it haue. *c* **1330** R. BRUNNE *Chron.* (1810) 8 þe lordschip þei toke, & haf it ȝit. *c* **1470** HENRY *Wallace* I. 12 How thai haff wrocht. **1526** TINDALE *Luke* xvi. 29 They have Moses and the prophettes. **1596** DALRYMPLE tr. *Leslie's Hist. Scot.* x. 320 We hafe a true gyd. **1611** BIBLE *John* viii. 41 We haue one Father, euen God. *Mod. colloq.* They've done it; we've seen them.

ε. a **1300** *Cursor M.* 5173 Yee ha sin. *Ibid.* 5182 Ha yee broght him wit yow? **1430-40** LYDG. *Bochas* I. iii. (1544) 6 a, Some ha be lost. **1589** *Pappe w. Hatchet* B iij, Haie ye anie gold ends to sell? **1793** BURNS *Bannockburn*, Scots wha hae wi' Wallace bled. **1892** R. KIPLING *Barrack-r. Ballads, Tomlinson* 26 Give answer—what ha' ye done? *Mod. Sc.* Hae ye ocht to say for yersel?

3. *Indicative Past.*

a. *1st* and *3rd pers. sing.* **had** (hæd, həd, əd); contracted **'d.** Forms: 1-3 **hæfde, hefde**, 2 **hefede, heffede, heofde** (**efde**), 2-3 **heuede, hafde**, 2-4 **haued**, 3 **hæuede, hæfuede, hæfede, hauede, hafuede, hafede, heuede, hefuede, hefte, hafte, hauid, hædde, hadd** (**efte, afte, adde, ad**), 3-4 **hafd, hedde, hede**, 3-7 **hadde**, 3- **had** (4-5 **hade, haid**, 6 **haved**, *Sc.* 4- **hed**, 6 **hayd**).

c **825** *Vesp. Psalter* lxxvi. 6 [lxxvii. 5] Ger ece in mode ic hefde. *c* **900** tr. *Bæda's Hist.* v. xvi[ii]. (1890) 446 Osred ..ðæt rice..hæfde. *c* **1175** *Lamb. Hom.* 11 Godalmihti heofde iwriten þa ten laȝe. *Ibid.* 25 Erðon he hefde anfalde sunne. *Ibid.* 121 Al swa þe prophete heffede iboded. *c* **1200** ORMIN 113 He..haffde an duhhtiȝ wif. *c* **1205** LAY. 2624 Cnihtes he hæfde gode. *Ibid.* 4316 Anne hird-cniht he hauede. *Ibid.* 6552 þe æfre hedde kinedom. *c* **1275** *Ibid.* 15729 þisne cnaue ich hadde. *a* **1300** *Cursor M.* 9234 (Cott.) Salatiel he had to sun. *c* **1300** *Ibid.* 24824 (Edin.) He hauid al þair wil. *c* **1325** *Metr. Hom.* 103 He hafd charite inoh. **1340** *Ayenb.* 14 Hit hedde zeve heauedes. **1375** BARBOUR *Bruce* I. 38 Alexander..That Scotland haid to steyr and leid. **1382** WYCLIF *Matt.* iii. 4 Joon hadde cloth of the heeris of cameylis. **1526** TINDALE *John* xiii. 29 Judas had the bagge. **1741-2** RICHARDSON *Pamela, passim*, I'd, you'd, he'd, she'd. *Mod.* I'd seen him before.

b. *2nd pers. sing.* **hadst.** Forms: *α.* 1 **hæfdes, -est**, 2-3 **hefdest**, 3-4 **heuedest, haddist**, 4-6 **haddest**, 4 **hadest**, 6- **hadst.** *β. north.* 3-5 **hade**, 3- **had.**

c **950** *Lindisf. Gosp.* Matt. xxii. 12 Ne hæfdes ðu wede. *a* **1000** *Crist* 1383 (Gr.) þæt þu onsyn hæfdest. *c* **1175** *Lamb. Hom.* 21 þu hefdest mare deruenesse. *a* **1225** *Ancr. R.* 38 Uor þe ilke muchele blisse þet tu heuedest. *Ibid.* 40 þet tu hefdest. *a* **1300** *Cursor M.* 17046 þi sorus..þou had [*v. rr.* hade, haddist, -est] in hert. *c* **1350** *Will. Palerne* 1816 Of hardnesse hadestow neuer. **1377** LANGL. *P. Pl.* B. v. 474 And haddest mercy on þat man. **1611** BIBLE *Gen.* xxx. 30 It was little which thou hadst [WYCLIF haddist, COVERD. haddest] before I came.

c. *plural* **had**; contracted **'d.** Forms: *α.* 1 **hæfdon, hefdan**, 2 **heofdon, heoueden**, 2-3 **hefden**, (**efden**), **hafeden**, 2-5 **hæfden, hadden**, 3 **hafueden, hafden**, (**afden**), **haueden, hædden**, (**adden**), 3-4 **hedden, haden, haddyn, hadon.** *β.* 2-3 **hæfde, hefde**, 2-5 **hadde**, 3 **hafde, hauede, hafd, haued,** (**adde**), 3-4 **hade**, 3- **had**, (4- *Sc.* **haid**).

α. a **1000** *Cædmon's Gen.* 25 Hæfdon ȝielp micel. **1154** *O.E. Chron.* an. 1137 þe..men ne hadden nan more to gyuen. *a* **1175** *Cott. Hom.* 219 þa þe hi alle hafeden þisne red ..ȝefestnod. *c* **1205** LAY. 19008 þa hædden [*c* **1275** haden] heo..Merlin þer. *a* **1225** *Leg. Kath.* 1428 Clað þat ha hefden. *c* **1300** *Havelok* 238 Mikel sorwe haueden alle. *a* **1375** *Joseph Arim.* 644 þei..hedden de-deyn. *c* **1400** *Destr. Troy* 12456 þai hadon hom in hate. *c* **1450** *Merlin* 193 Alle they that eny hadden.

β. c **1175** *Lamb. Hom.* 3 Heo nomen..þe beste þet heo hefde. *c* **1205** LAY. 1933 þa hæfde þa Troinisce men ouercomen heora teonen. *c* **1275** *Ibid.* 26558 Ou [*c* **1205** hu] his iveres hadde idon. *a* **1300** *Cursor M.* 13501 (Cott.) All þai had i-nogh at ette. *Ibid.* 24326 (Edin.) Miht hafd we nan. *Ibid.* 16767 + 149 (Cott.)þai hade of him drede. *c* **1300** *Harrow. Hell* 111 þey þat haved served me. **1375** BARBOUR *Bruce* I. 514 To hald that thai forspokyn haid.

4. *Subjunctive Present.*

a. *sing.* **have.** Forms: 1 **hæbbe, hebbe**, 1-4 **habbe**, 2-3 **æbbe, abbe**; 3- **have**, etc., as Indic. present.

805 *Charter* in *O.E. Texts* 442 Gif hio bearn hæbbe. **835** *Ibid.* 448 Se ðæt min lond hebbe. *a* **1100** *O.E. Chron.* an. 675 þes papa curs..he habbe. *c* **1175** *Lamb. Hom.* 67 Bute ic þis habbe. *c* **1230** *Hali Meid.* 37 þah þu riche beo & nurice habbe. *a* **1300** *Cursor M.* 3999 (Cott.) Ar he þe half of þaa haa [*v.r.* haue] slayn. **1375** BARBOUR *Bruce* VI. 334 Bot he haf wit to steir his stede. **1382** WYCLIF *Eph.* iv. 28 That he haue wherof he schal ȝyue. **1607** BEAUM. & FL. *Woman-Hater* II. i, If he have the itch of knighthood upon him.

b. *plural* **have.** Forms: 1 **hæbben, habban, hæbbe**, 1-3 **habben**, 3-5 **haven**, 3- **have**, as Indic.

a **1000** *Guthlac* 644 (Gr.) þæt ȝe..brynewylm hæbben. *c* **1000** *Ags. Ps.* (Th.) lxix. 5 [lxx. 4] Habban þa mid wynne weorðe blisse. *c* **1175** *Lamb. Hom.* 69 Halde we us from uniwil and habben feir lete. **1362** LANGL. *P. Pl.* A. I. 8 Hauen [*B.* I. 8 haue] heo worschupe in þis world. **1431** *E.E. Wills* (1882) 88 Y wille that my parisshe chirches haue alle here duetees.

5. *Subjunctive Past* **had**: as in Indic. Past.

c **1330** R. BRUNNE *Chron. Wace* (Rolls) 12358 Nere sleighte and queyntise hadde ben. *c* **1375** *Sc. Leg. Saints, Petrus* 238 Sterand, as þai lyf had hade. **1382** WYCLIF *Acts* xxiv. 19 If thei hadden ony thing [**1526** TINDALE had ought] aȝens me. **1611** SHAKS. *Cymb.* II. iv. 147 O that I had her heere. **1891** MRS. OLIPHANT *Janet* II. v. 81, I wish I had.

6. *Imperative*: **have**

a. *sing.* Forms: 1 **hafa**, 3-5 **hafue, hafe**, 3- **have** (3-4 **haf, hab**, 4 **hawe, haa**, 4-6 **ha, a**, 6 *Sc.* **haif**).

a **1000** *Cædmon's Gen.* 2429 Hafa arna þanc. *c* **1205** LAY. 31401 Hafue þu al þi kine-lond. *Ibid.* 25787 Hafe mine godne horn. *c* **1230** *Hali Meid.* 11 Haue trust on his help. *a* **1300** *Cursor M.* 969 Of alkin fruit haf þou þe nine. *Ibid.* 3889 Haa lya in þi bedd. *a* **1300** *Fragm.* 14 in *E.E.P.* (1862) 19 Beþenche þe, man, and hab drede. *c* **1350** *Will. Palerne* 1177 A mynde on me. *c* **1460** *Towneley Myst.* (Surtees) 71 Hafe good day! **1513** DOUGLAS *Æneis* IV. Prol. 145 Haif mercy, lady. *c* **1530** H. RHODES *Bk. Nurture* 321 in *Babees Bk.* 91 Doe well, and haue well. **1589** *Hay any Work* (1844) 21 Then ha with thee. *Mod.* Have a cigar.

b. *plural.* Forms: *α.* 1 **habbaþ**, 3 **habbeoð**, 3-4 **habbeþ**, 4 **haueþ, hauithe.** *β.* 3-4 **haues, hauis, has**, 4 **haffis.** *γ.* 3- (**haue**), **have**, (4 **hab**, 4-5 **ha**).

a **1000** *Andreas* 1360 (Gr.) Habbað word ȝearu. *c* **1205** LAY. 32172 Habbeoð þat lond auer mære. *a* **1225** *Ancr. R.* 16 þis word habbeð muchel on vs. *a* **1300** *Cursor M.* 4884 Haue [*v.r.* has, haueþ] god day. *Ibid.* 9049 (Gött.) Hauis sone of me merci. *c* **1300** *Beket* 2067 His bodi habbe ȝare. **1370-80** *XI Pains of Hell* 276 in *O.E. Misc.* 230 Poul, Michael, on vs ha merci. **1375** BARBOUR *Bruce* XIII. 305 Haffis gud day! **1382** WYCLIF *Mark* xi. 22 Haue ȝe the feith of God [**1611** Haue faith in God]. *a* **1450** *Knt. de la Tour* (1868) 15 Hauithe youre loke. *c* **1475** *Babees Bk.* 183 A Trenchoure ha ye clene. *Mod.* Have your tickets ready!

7. *Present Participle* **having** ('hævɪŋ). Forms: 1 **hæbbende, habbende**, 1-3 **hæbbende**, 3 **habende**, 4-6 **hafand, hauvyng**(**e**, 6- **having** (*Sc.* **haifand, havand**).

c **1000** ÆLFRIC *Hom.* I. 250 We beoð hæbbende ðæs ðe we ær hopedon. *c* **1375** *Sc. Leg. Saints, Eugenia* 351 Hafand at hyr gret wlatsumnes. **1382** WYCLIF *Matt.* xv. 30 Hauynge with hem doumbe men. **14..** *Nom.* in Wr.-Wülcker 709/26 *Idropicus*, hafand the dropsy. **1526** TINDALE *Matt.* xxii. 24 If a man dye havinge no children. **1567** *Satir. Poems Reform.* iv. 78 Nouther to God nor honoure hauand Ee.

8. *Past Participle* **had** (hæd, həd, əd). Forms: *α.* 1 **ȝehæfed**, 3 **ihaued, ihafd** (**hihafd**), 4 **yhet**, 4-5 **yhadde, ihadde, yhad.** *β.* 1 **hæfed**, 2-4 **haued**, 4- **had** (4-6 **hadde, hade**, *Sc.* **haid**).

c **1000** ÆLFRIC *Hom.* II. 148 Æfter ðisum wordum wearð ȝemot ȝehæfd. *c* **1205** LAY. 6223 We habbeð ihaued moni burst. *c* **1275** *Ibid.* 2685 He hafde many wimmen hi-hafd. *Ibid.* 4501 Hadde hire i-wedded, and i-hafd. **1340** *Ayenb.* 40 To yelde þet hi habbeþ y-het kueadliche of oþren. **1387** TREVISA *Higden* VI. xxix, Vot-men..hadde y-hadde þe meystry. **1480** CAXTON *Chron. Eng.* lxxx. 65 Our folke haue it longe y had.

β. c **900** tr. *Bæda's Hist.* III. i[i]. (1890) 154 Is seo stow.. in micelre arwyrðnesse hæfd. *a* **1300** *Cursor M.* 2659 þat þou has had. *c* **1330** R. BRUNNE *Chron.* (1810) 8 He & his haf had þe lond. *Ibid.* 15 If he had haued myght. **1482** WARKW. *Chron.* 5 That thei shuld be hade to the Toure Hylle. **1513** DOUGLAS *Æneis* II. xi. [x] 38 In bondage with hir haid. *c* **1531** R. MORICE in *Lett. Lit. Men* (Camden) 24 Thei caused suche diligent watch to be hadde. *Mod.* Have you had enough?

9. *Negative Forms. Inf.* OE. **nabban**, ME. **nabbe**(**n, nave**(**n**; *Ind. pres.* OE. **næbbe** (**nafu**); **næfð, nabbað**, ME. **nabbe, naveþ, naþ**; *Ind. pa.* OE. **næfde**, ME. **nafde, nauede, nadde, nedde, nad**, etc. In OE. *nabban* was sometimes treated as an independent verb with pa. pple. **ȝenæfd** 'not had'.

c **888** K. ÆLFRED *Boeth.* xiv. §1 Ðonne sint hie þe pleolicran..ȝehæfd þonne ȝenæfd. *c* **1000** *Ags. Gosp.* John IX. 41 Næfde ȝe nane synne. *c* **1175** *Lamb. Hom.* 113 Moni mon nafð ehta. *c* **1205** LAY. 557 Neafde [*c* **1275** nafde] he nenne oðer. *Ibid.* 4905 Ah he neuede [*c* **1275** nadde] nenne sune. *a* **1225** *Ancr. R.* 244 Nabbe ȝe þis also? *a* **1240** *Lofsong* in *Cott. Hom.* 211 Nabbich nowðer in me wisdom ne wurschipe. *a* **1300** *Floriz & Bl.* 65 Ac rest ne miȝte he nabbe none. **13..** *Gaw. & Gr. Knt.* 1066 Naf I now..bot bare þre dayez. **1340** *Ayenb.* 210 To þe wreche fayleþ: þet he heþ and þet he neþ. **1362** LANGL. *P. Pl.* A. I. 157 ȝe naue no more merit. *Ibid.* v. 4 þat I nedde sadloker i-slept. **1393** *Ibid.* C. VII. 214 (MS. F.) Hit nad be sold. *a* **1400-50** *Alexander* 1876 þai naue no will to my notis. *c* **1420** *Pallad. on Husb.* I. 176 Necessite nath neuere halyday.

B. Signification.

From a primitive sense 'to hold (in hand)', *have* has passed naturally into that of 'hold in possession,' 'possess,' and has thence been extended to express a more general class of relations, of which 'possession' is one type, some of which are very vague and intangible. For just as the verbs *be* and *do* are the most generalized representatives of the verbal classes *κεῖσθαι* (*situs*) and *πράσσειν* (*actio*) in Aristotle's classification of verbal predications (*κατηγορίαι*), so *have* is the most generalized representative of the class *ἔχειν* (*habitus*, having). For although *have* in its primitive sense of 'hold' was a verb of action, in the sense 'possess,' and still more, in the weakened senses 2, etc. below, no notion of any *action* upon the object remains, what is predicated being merely a static relation between the subject and object. In the older languages this relation was often predicated not of the possessor but of the thing possessed, the possessor standing in the dative, thus L. *est mihi liber*, there is to me a book, I have a book. The extended use of *have* and its equivalents to express this relation is a general feature of the modern languages. Like the two other generalized verbal types *be* and *do*, *have* also tends to uses in which it becomes a mere element of predication, scarcely capable of explanation apart from the context, and at length an auxiliary verb.

General scheme of arrangement. I. As a main verb (*trans.* or *intr.*) * To *possess*, and connected uses. ** To keep in possession, *hold*, maintain, etc. *** To come into possession of, to *get*; and connected uses. **** Phrases. ***** Idiomatic uses, *had better, rather*, etc. II. As an auxiliary verb. III. Combinations.

I. As a main verb (*trans.* or *intr.*)

* *In the sense* possess, *and uses thence arising.*

1. a. *trans.* To hold in hand, in keeping, or possession; to hold or possess as property, or as something at one's disposal.

Beowulf (Z.) 814 Hine se modeȝa mæȝ Hyȝelaces hæfde be honda. *c* **888** K. ÆLFRED *Boeth.* xxiv. §4 He hæfþ on his aȝenum ȝenoh. *c* **1000** *Ags. Gosp.* Matt. xix. 22 Soþlice he hæfde mycele æhta. **1154** *O.E. Chron.* an. 1137 þa þe uurecce men ne hadden nan more to gyuen. *a* **1225** *Ancr. R.* 16 Sprengeð ou mid hali water þet ȝe schulen euer habben mid ou. *a* **1300** *Cursor M.* 5809 Quat has þou in þi hand? **1382** WYCLIF *Matt.* xiv. 17 We han nat here, no but fiue looues and two fishis. *c* **1450** tr. *De Imitatione* III. xxxvi. 106 Men askiþ hov muche a man haþ. **1483** *Lett. etc. Rich. III & Hen. VII* (Rolls 1861) I. 9 Sir William A Parre..having an axe in his hand. **1513** MORE *Rich. III* (1883) 46 My lord you haue very good strawberies at your gardayne in Holberne. **1515** BARCLAY *Egloges* (1570) A v b, But, trust me, Coridon, there is diversitie Betwene to have riches and riches to have thee. **1590** LODGE *Euphues Gold. Leg.* (1609) 56, I haue them about me. **1611** BIBLE *Luke* xxii. 31 Satan hath desired to haue you. **1631** MASSINGER *Emperor East* IV. iv, What have you there? **1700** T. BROWN tr. *Fresny's Amusem. Ser. & Com.* 26 For I have Insured more by a Thousand Pounds, than I have in her. **1818** CRUISE *Digest* (ed. 2) VI. 366 My will is that my son shall have and enjoy the manor of B. only for his life. *Mod.* How many shares have you in the company?

b. *absol.*

c **1000** *Ags. Gosp.* Matt. xxv. 29 Witodlice ælcon þæra þe hæfð man sylþ. **1382** WYCLIF *Mark* iv. 25 Sotheli it shal be ȝouen to hym that hath. **1593** DRAYTON *Idea* 867, I have, I want, Despaire, and yet Desire. **1642** ROGERS *Naaman* 115, I count my selfe the same man whether I want or have.

c. *to have and to hold*, a phrase app. of legal origin (cf. law L. *habendum et tenendum*: see HABENDUM), retained largely, as in German, Dutch, etc., on account of its alliterative form: To have (or receive) and keep or retain, indicating continuance of possession.

Beowulf (Z.) 659 Hafa nu ond ȝe-heald husa selest. **971** *Blickl. Hom.* 55 þa þe Godes rices ȝeleafan habbað & healdaþ. **1362** LANGL. *P. Pl.* A. II. 70 þe Yle of vsure..To habben and to holden. *a* **1400** *Sir Perc.* 24 He gaffe hym his

syster Acheflour, To have and to holde. **1549** *Bk. Com. Prayer, Matrimony*, I N. take thee N. to my wedded wife, to haue and to holde from this day forwarde. **1664** BUTLER *Hud., Lady's Answer* 96, I fear they'll prove so nice and coy To have, and t'hold, and to enjoy. **1839–56** BOUVIER *Law Dict.* s.v. *Habendum*, The habendum commences in our common deeds, with the words 'to have and to hold'.

2. a. To hold or possess, in a weakened sense; the relation being other than that of property or tenancy, e.g. one of kindred, relative position, etc.

The relation is often reciprocal: the father has a son, the son has a father; the king has subjects, his subjects have a king; the man has a wife, she has a husband; or it may be reciprocal to sense 1: a man has (sense 1) a house, the house has an owner or tenant.

c **1000** *Ags. Gosp.* Luke xvi. 28 Ic hæbbe fif ȝebroþru. *c* **1200** ORMIN 113 He..haffde an duhhtiȝ wif. *c* **1205** LAY. 462 Ich abbe i min castlen Seoue þusend kempen. *a* **1300** *Cursor M.* 961 Bot þe haf I na frend. **1340** *Ayenb.* 5þou ne sselt habbe god bote me. **1382** WYCLIF *Matt.* ix. 36 As sheep nat hauynge a sheperde. **1513** MORE *Rich. III* (1883) 23 Whose specyall pleasure and coumforte were to haue his brother with hym. **1568** GRAFTON *Chron.* II. 44 If we note well what enemies we have. **1601** SHAKS. *Twel. N.* I. iii. 134 Wherefore haue these gifts a Curtaine before 'em? **1601** —— *Jul. C.* I. ii. 192 Let me haue men about me, that are fat. **1708** MRS. SCOTT in *Caldwell Papers* I. (Maitland) 212 So having none but men, our ceremonys was the less. **1748** *Anson's Voy.* I. vii. 71 We had fifty-two fathom of water. **1818** CRUISE *Digest* (ed. 2) VI. 535 He having no son at the time. **1890** W. F. RAE *Amer. Duchess* I. 50 The worst Administration which we have ever had.

b. with complement or adverbial extension, particularizing the relation of the object or expressing some qualification, condition or limitation thereof.

c **1000** *Ags. Gosp.* Matt. iii. 9 We habbað abraham us to fæder. —— John viii. 41 We habbaþ anne god to fæder. *c* **1290** *Beket* 2042 in *S. Eng. Leg.* I. 165 ȝe to þe kingus wille is bodi ȝe habben al-ȝare. *a* **1300** *Cursor M.* 15317 He þat has his bodi clene. **1388** WYCLIF *1 Tim.* iv. 2 That..haue her conscience corrupt. **1474** CAXTON *Chesse* II. iv. Civb, A knyght which had to name malechete. **1526** TINDALE *Matt.* iii. 4 This Jhon had his garment off camels heer. *Ibid.* xxii. 11 A man which had not on a weddinge garment. **1583** HOLLYBAND *Campo di Fior* 183 As long as we have this monkey to our cooke. **1594** SHAKS. *Rich. III*, II. i. 112 When Oxford had me downe, he rescued me. **1634** SIR T. HERBERT *Trav.* 3 They used to have their Wives in common. **1700** S. L. tr. *Fryke's Voy. E. Ind.* 14 We still had France on the left of us. **1807** ROBINSON *Archæol. Græca* I. ii. 21 A person who had a foreigner to his mother. **1847** MARRYAT *Childr. N. Forest* v, You..have the laugh on your side now. **1852** THACKERAY *Esmond* I. iii, They had him to dine with them at the inn. **1891** MRS. NEWMAN *Begun in Jest* I. 112, I have women at work for me.

3. To possess, bear, contain, as an appendage, organ, subordinate part, or adjunct; to contain as parts of itself. (In this last shade of meaning now chiefly confined to *time*, 'Thirty days hath September', 'the year has twelve calendar months'.)

c **900** tr. *Bæda's Hist.* II. xiii. [xvi.] (1890) 144 He..hæfde blæc feax, and blacne ond wlitan. *c* **1000** *Ags. Gosp.* Mark xi. 13 An fic-treow þe leaf hæfde. *c* **1050** *Byrhtferth's Handboc* in *Anglia* VIII. 300 ȝif se monð sceal habban · xxx · nihta. *a* **1250** *Owl & Night.* 153 Þu havest wel sharpe clawe. **1382** WYCLIF *Luke* xx. 24 Schewe ȝe to me a peny; whos ymage and writynge aboue hath it? *c* **1410** *Sir Cleges* 349 Harlot, hast noo tonge? **1559** W. CUNNINGHAM *Cosmogr. Glasse* 144 A lake, is that which continually hath water. **1585** T. WASHINGTON tr. *Nicholay's Voy.* I. iii. 3 The saide Ilande hath two cities. **1592** SHAKS. *Ven. & Ad.* 389 The sea hath bounds. **1657** R. LIGON *Barbadoes* (1673) 101 The leaves.. having many veines. **1659** WILLSFORD *Scales Comm.* 113 Intercalary years, there is one day added to February, which then hath 29. **1697** DAMPIER *Voy.* I. 6 She had 12 Guns, and 150 Sea-men and Souldiers. **1704** W. PENN in *15th Rep. Hist. MSS. Comm.* App. IV. 80 Virginia has not a town bigger, if half so big, as Knightsbridge. **1887** LOWELL *Democr.* 9 If riches have wings to fly away from their owner, they have wings also to escape danger.

4. To possess, as an attribute, quality, faculty, function, position, right, etc.; to be characterized by; to hold; to be charged with. (With very various immaterial objs.)

Obsolete uses are *to have right, wrong, to have* a certain *age, so many years*.

a **1000** *Cædmon's Gen.* 280 Ic hæbbe geweald micel to ȝyrwanne godlecran stol. *c* **1000** *Ags. Gosp.* John ix. 21 Acsiað hine sylfne, ylde he hæfð. *c* **1175** *Lamb. Hom.* 25 He hefde anfalde sunne and seodðan he hauet twafald. *c* **1230** *Hali Meid.* 3 Euch meiden þat haueð meidene þeawes. *a* **1300** *Cursor M.* 6029 Þan said þe king 'i haue þe wrang, And al þis wrak on me es lang'. **1382** WYCLIF *John* viii. 57 Thou hast not ȝit fifty ȝeer. **1489** *Paston Lett.* No. 914 III. 359 Havyng the auctorite to se the Kynges money levied in the North parties. **1549** LATIMER *6th Serm. bef. Edw. VI* (Arb.) 159 The Corinthians had no suche contencions among them. **1634** SIR T. HERBERT *Trav.* 147 Eyes Diamond-like, having blacke lustre. **1697** DAMPIER *Voy.* I. 32 They have a Fashion to cut holes in the Lips. **1750** G. HUGHES *Barbadoes* 102 They have a very austere and acerb taste. **1795** *Gentl. Mag.* 543/1 Every poor family in the neighbourhood had reason to regret his departure. **1840** LARDNER *Geom.* xxi. 293 If two circles have different magnitudes, they will then have different curvatures. **1882** SHORTHOUSE *J. Inglesant* I. xiii. 243 Their policy had the desired effect.

5. To be possessed or affected with (something physical or mental); to be subjected to; to experience; to enjoy or suffer.

c **1000** *Ags. Gosp.* Mark iii. 11 Swa fela swa untrumnessa, & unclæne gastas hæfdon. *c* **1175** *Lamb. Hom.* 35 Swilche pine ic habbe. *Ibid.* 83 Hwet node efde moncun þet he Mon were? *a* **1225** *Ancr. R.* 112 Uor vuel þet he haueð. *c* **1300** *Cursor M.* 28904 (Cott. Galba) When þou sese any haue hunger or calde. **1382** WYCLIF *1 Cor.* vii. 28 Suche schulen haue tribulacioun of fleisch. **1464** J. PASTON in *P. Lett.* No. 486 II. 153 My Lord hath had gret costs syn he came hedyr. **1599** H. BUTTES *Dyets drie Dinner* Bvjb, Such as have the collicque. **1601** SHAKS. *Jul. C.* I. ii. 119 He had a Feauer when he was in Spaine. **1695** CONGREVE *Love for L.* v. ii, Hussy, you shall have a rod. **1710** LADY MANSELL in *15th Rep. Hist. MSS. Comm.* App. IV. 542, I had a tolerable night of it. **1875** JOWETT *Plato* (ed. 2) I. 94 Some patient of his, has inflammation of the lungs. **1890** W. F. RAE *Amer. Duchess* I. 123, I have had a real good time! *Mod.* He has very bad health.

6. To possess as an intellectual acquirement, to be versed in, to know; to understand, grasp with the mind.

1591 SHAKS. *Two Gent.* IV. i. 33 Haue you the Tongues? **1596** —— *Merch. V.* I. ii. 74 Hee vnderstands not me, nor I him: he hath neither Latine, French, nor Italian. **1601** —— *Twel. N.* I. iii. 131, I thinke I haue the backe-tricke. **1602** —— *Ham.* II. i. 68 You haue me, haue you not? **1619** DRUMM. OF HAWTH. *Conv. w. B. Jonson* vii. (1842) 9 He hath by heart some verses of Spenser's Calender. **1750** CHESTERF. *Lett.* (1792) III. ccxxvii. 26 Our young country-men have generally too little French. **1839** H. AINSWORTH *Jack Sheppard* iii, 'Ah! I have it', he added after a moment's deliberation. **1868** *Athenæum* 4 Jan. 21/2 A person who having no mathematics attempts to describe a mathematician.

7. a. To possess as a duty or thing to be done. With object and dative inf. expressing what is to be done by the subject.

(This is in origin a particular case of 2 b.)

971 *Blickl. Hom.* 91 Uton we forþon ȝeþencean hwylc handlean we him forþ to berenne habban. *c* **1000** *Ags. Gosp.* Luke vii. 40 Ic hæbbe ðe to secȝenne sumðing. *a* **1225** *Juliana* 9 þe þat se heh þing hefde to heden. *a* **1300** *Cursor M.* 16487 Ha we noght þar-of to do. **1382** WYCLIF *2 John* 12, I hauynge mo thinges for to wrijte to ȝou. *c* **1460** *Towneley Myst.* 181 We have other thynges at to do. **1592** SHAKS. *Ven. & Ad.* 179 Wishing Adonis had his team to guide. **1657** R. LIGON *Barbadoes* (1673) 55 He will have too much to do. **1667** MILTON *P.L.* XI. 415 He had much to see. **1742** RICHARDSON *Pamela* III. 106 Every absent Member..has it to reproach himself with the Consequences that may follow. **1816** KEATINGE *Trav.* (1817) I. 42 Condensing what they had to say into a very portable compass. **1892** *Law Rep.* Weekly Notes 165/1 The time limited..had still three years to run.

b. Hence *to have to do*: see DO *v.* 33 c, d.

c. With infinitive: To be under obligation, to be obliged; to be necessitated *to do something*. It forms a kind of Future of obligation or duty.

[Cf. the Future tense of the Romanic langs, e.g. *je parler-ai*, *je finir-ai*, I *have* to speak, to finish.]

1579 FENTON *Guicciard.* (1618) 6 He told him, he had not to beleeue, that the couetousnesse of Virginio..had moued Ferdinand. **1594** HOOKER *Eccl. Pol.* I. i. §1 We have..to strive with a number of heavy prejudices. **1596** SPENSER *State Irel.* Wks. (Globe) 657/2 This is the manner of the Spanyardes captaynes, whoe never hath to meddle with his souldiours paye. **1765** H. WALPOLE *Otranto* v. (1798) 80 Having to talk with him on urgent affairs. **1831** MRS. F. TROLLOPE *Dom. Mann. Amer.* (1894) II. 271 But 'we had to do it' as the Americans say. **1848** MRS. GASKELL *M. Barton* ix, Mary had to change some clothes after her walk home. **1883** *Manch. Exam.* 29 Oct. 5/4 In 1831 the firm had to suspend payment. **1892** LOPES in *Law Times Rep.* LXVII. 144/1, I regret to have to say that I do not believe that evidence. *Mod.* I have to go to London to-morrow.

d. *to have to be*: must be. *colloq.* Cf. GET *v.* 24, JOKE *v.* 1 b.

1967 *Weekend Mag.* 2 Dec. 2/1 That had to be the most bizarre Grey Cup game ever. **1969** V. CANNING *Queen's Pawn* ii. 8 The car had a Kent number plate MKE 800F. The woman had to be a stranger. **1971** 'A. GILBERT' *Tenant for Tomb* viii. 146 'Even your famous Mr Crook can't disprove evidence,' Ponting pointed out. 'You have to be joking,' said Gray. **1972** *Student Movement* 7 Dec. 13/2 My heart goes out to the performers who watched ⅓ to ½ of their audience leave during what had to be the most tragic selection for a Christmas program I have ever heard.

*** To keep possession of, to* hold; *and related uses.*

8. To hold, keep, retain (*in* some relation to oneself: as *to have in use*, to use (habitually); *to have in mind*, to remember; *to have in possession*, to possess; *to have it in one*: to have the ability (to do something) (cf. IN *prep.* 26); etc.

c **825** *Vesp. Psalter* lxxvi. 6 [lxxvii. 5] ȝer ece in mode ic hefde. **971** *Blickl. Hom.* 87 On bendum hie wæron hæfde. *a* **1225** *Ancr. R.* 16 Þis word habbeð muchel on vs. *a* **1300** *Cursor M.* 28456, I..has hade it in myn vsage, O mete and drink to do vtrage. **1382** WYCLIF *2 Cor.* x. 6 Hauynge in redynesse for to venge al vnobedience. *c* **1400** *Sowdone Bab.* 3243 The kinge hade wel in mynde The tresone of Genelyne. *c* **1440** *Promp. Parv.* 230/1 Have yn possessyon, *possideo.* **1462** *Plumpton Corr.* 7 Whom our Lord govern & haf in His keeping. **1551** ROBINSON tr. *More's Utop.* II. (1895) 151 But lynen clothe is..hadde more in vse. **1559** W. CUNNINGHAM *Cosmogr. Glasse* 37 The northe Pole, Still we have in sight. *c* **1600** [see IN *prep.* 26]. **1632** LITHGOW *Trav.* IX. 399 We had a Moorish Frigot in Chase. **1654** CROMWELL *Sp.* 4. Sept. in *Carlyle*, The Government hath had some things in desire. **1777** JOHNSON *Let. to Mrs. Thrale* 13 Aug., Which they have in contemplation—there's the word now. **1887** A. CONAN DOYLE *Study in Scarlet* (1893) I. ii. 32, I know well that I have it in me to make my name famous. **1889** [see IN *prep.* 26].

9. a. To hold or entertain in the mind (a feeling, opinion, etc.); to entertain, hold, cherish.

c **1000** *Gospel Nicod.* viii. in *Thwaite's Heptat.*, Buton hiȝ habbaþ andan to hym. *c* **1175** *Lamb. Hom.* 7 Ne we ne beoð iboren for to habbene nane prudu. *a* **1240** *Ureisun* in *Cott. Hom.* 185 Hwi abbe ich eni licung in oþer þing þene in þe? *a* **1300** *Cursor M.* 11161 Haf na drednes. *Ibid.* 17273 Iuus had til him envie. *c* **1400** MAUNDEV. (Roxb.) Pref. 2 What lufe he had til his sugets. **1583** HOLLYBAND *Campo di Fior* 61 Of this have not any doubt. **1656** *Artif. Handsom.* (1662) 5 Let me see..what you have against it. **1726** SHELVOCKE *Voy. round World* (1757) 227 Who..had a mind to act the madman. **1882** SHORTHOUSE *J. Inglesant* I. xv. 280, I have no doubt the Italian is at the bottom of all this.

b. Hence, To show, exhibit, exercise, exemplify (such sentiment, etc.) in action.

have a care: see CARE *sb.*[1] 3 c; *have the face*: see FACE *sb.* 7: see also DILIGENCE, HEED, MERCY, REGARD, etc.

c **1175** *Lamb. Hom.* 109 Þet he abbe ihersumnesse and ibuhsumnesse. *a* **1300** *Cursor M.* 22474 Lauerd, ha merci on all nu. *c* **1450** *St. Cuthbert* (Surtees) 4355 Of þis pure man haue hede. **1483** *Lett., etc. Rich. III & Hen. VII* (Rolls) I. 45 Havynge respecte..to othere presidentes passed afore. **1539** BIBLE (Great) *Matt.* xviii. 26 Sir, haue pacience with me, and I will paye the all. **1580** LYLY *Euphues* (Arb.) 131 All dillygence is to be had to search such a one. **1611** BIBLE *Transl. Pref.* 2 It doth certainely belong vnto Kings to haue care of Religion. *a* **1715** BURNET *Own Time* (1823) I. 341 There was less regard had to them afterwards. **1805** *Med. Jrnl.* XIV. 193 Have the goodness to permit an old friend to say a few words in his own defence. **1895** *Law Times Rep.* LXXIII. 266/2 The court will have regard to slight indications.

10. To hold in (some specified) estimation; to esteem or account as; to consider or regard as. *arch.*

c **900** tr. *Bæda's Hist.* III. ii[i]. (1890) 154 Is seo stow..in micelre arwyrðnesse hæfd. *a* **1300** *Cursor M.* 20133 Saint iohn hir keped and had ful dere. *c* **1380** WYCLIF *Wks.* (1880) 438 ȝif..he be lettid of þis preching..teche he his floc bi hooly lif and god wole haue hym excusid. **1382** —— *Luke* xiv. 18, I preie thee, haue me excusid. *c* **1475** *Rauf Coilȝear* 198 Thay haue me all at Inuy. *a* **1533** LD. BERNERS *Gold. Bk. M. Aurel.* (1534) Eiij, Truely, wyse men have hym as suspect. **1535** COVERDALE *Ps.* cxviii[i]. 51 The proude haue me greatly in derision. **1551** ROBINSON tr. *More's Utop.* I. (1895) 86 That their lawes were hadde in contempte. **1571** HANMER *Chron. Irel.* (1633) 70 They were then had in great reverence. **1728** T. SHERIDAN *Persius* vi. (1739) 95 The Athenians had him in so great Esteem.

11. a. To hold, keep up, carry on (some proceeding or performance); to engage in, maintain, or perform, as a chief actor; to engage in and perform some action.

(This has many affinities and connecting links with other senses.)

c **1100** *O.E. Chron.* an. 1085 Æfter þisu hæ fde se cyng mycel ȝeþeaht. **13..** *K. Alis.* 4766 How he hadde mony batailles With wormes. *c* **1400** MAUNDEV. (1839) xiv. 154 The Kyng had Werre, with hem of Sithie. **1456** *Sc. Acts Jas. II*, c. 7 Þat þe Demyis..sulde cum out and haif courss throu þe Realme. **1523** SIR W. BULMER in Ellis *Orig. Lett.* Ser. III. I. 327 If it pleas youe to haue spech with the said Scotishman. *a* **1535** MORE *Ibid.* Ser. I. II. 48 In eny suit that I shold after have to your Grace. **1551** T. WILSON *Logike* (1580) 79 b, Socrates sheweth that Aspasia had this talke with Zenophon and his wife. **1563** *Homilies* II. *Idolatry* I. (1859) 178 *note*, That any true Christian ought to have any ado with filthy and dead images. **1664** DRYDEN *Rival Ladies* v. ii, Why should we have recourse to desperate ways? **1714** *Lond. Gaz.* No. 5271/2 The Queen has had a Circle every Evening. **1738** SWIFT *Pol. Convers.* 45 She and I had some Words last Sunday at Church. **1845** STEPHEN *Comm. Laws Eng.* (1874) II. 257 Whenever a marriage shall not be had within three calendar months after the entry of the notice.

b. When the action or proceeding is treated as something experienced, got at, attained, or enjoyed, the sense blends with 14.

1590 LODGE *Euphues Gold. Leg.* (1609) 54 Lets haue a little sport with him. **1697** COLLIER *Immor. Stage* (1730) 35 He had, says he, an admirable Stroak at the Pathos in general. **1760** FOOTE *Minor* I. (1781) 31 Shall we have a dip in the history of the Four Kings this morning? **1847** MARRYAT *Childr. N. Forest* v, You will then have a good shot at him. **1868** W. COLLINS *Moonst.* iii, I went and had a look at the bedroom. **1891** MRS. WALFORD *Pinch of Exper.* 268 Rhoda went and had an enchanting walk.

c. Colloq. phr. ***have a nice*** (occas. ***good***) ***day*** (orig. and chiefly *U.S.*): used as a conventional formula on parting; goodbye. Cf. GOOD DAY.

1971 'D. HALLIDAY' *Dolly & Doctor Bird* v. 70 The admonitions of the freeway from the airport are wholly American: *Keep off the Median..Have a Nice Day.* **1978** P. THEROUX *Picture Palace* iii. 13 'Have a good day,' he said. 'You too.' **1980** *Redbook* Oct. 240/1 He picks up the phone, calls his old friend. What are old friends for? Have a nice day. **1985** *Eating Out in London* 87/2 What characterises a good restaurant in America is brisk service (which can, but doesn't necessarily entail the 'have a nice day' syndrome). **1986** R. BRANDON *Left, Right & Centre* xx. 118 And now if you don't mind..I have work to do. Have a nice day.

†12. *refl.* To comport oneself, behave. *Obs.*

c **1386** CHAUCER *Melib.* ¶609, I shewe yow hou ye shul haue yow..in gaderynge of richesses. *c* **1400** MAUNDEV. (Roxb.) xxvi. 123 Þai hafe þam riȝt warly and wysely. *c* **1475** *Babees Bk.* 46 How yee Babees.. Shulde haue yoursylf whenne yee be sette at mete. **1556** LAUDER *Tractate* (1864) 1 How..temporall Iugis sulde haue thame in thare officis.

13. a. To assert, maintain; to phrase it, put it (with reference to the manner).

c **1449** PECOCK *Repr.* I. xvii. 96 Also Johun vj[e] cap. it is had. *Ibid.* Thouȝ it mai be had by tho textis that God schal ȝeue and do. **1738** SWIFT *Pol. Convers.* 44 All the Town has it, that Miss Caper is to be married to Sir Peter. **1874** BLACKIE *Self-Cult.* 71 Wonder, as Plato has it, is a truly philosophic passion. **1878** *Scribner's Mag.* XV. 303/1 The fox..has run to earth, or, as we have it, 'has holed'. **1955** *Times* 18 June 6/1 One report had it that Rosario..was still in rebel hands. **1967** *Listener* 13 Apr. 485/1 The party, as the classic socialist phrase has it, is the means of activating the masses.

b. With *will*: To maintain or assert as a fact. With *will not*: To refuse to admit as a fact, etc.

c **1000** *Sax. Leechd.* III. 266 þa læwedan willað habban þone monan be þam ðe hi hine ʒeseoð. **1577** HARRISON *England* I. xix. (1881) III. 145 A traueller of my time..noteth the said street to go another waie, insomuch that he would haue it to crosse the third Auon. **1591** SHAKS. *1 Hen. VI*, III. i. 30 If I were couetous, ambitious, or peruerse, As he will haue me. **1662** STILLINGFL. *Orig. Sacr.* III. iv. §12 Stephanus..will not have him to be Hellen the son of Deucalion, but the Son of Pthius. **1712** ADDISON *Spect.* No. 271 ¶3 Some will have it, that I often write to my self. **1829** *Bengallee* 462 Nawaub, or *Nabob*, as John Bull will have it. **1864** PUSEY *Lect. Daniel* iv. 227 The Anti-Messianic interpreters will have it to be written after the event.

c. To represent as doing something. *U.S. colloq.*

1928 *Amer. Speech* June 379 William De Morgan, in *Alice for Short*, has the 'toffs' say *daw* and *flaw* for 'door' and 'floor'.

*** *To come into possession of, to get, and connected uses.*

14. a. To possess by obtaining or receiving; hence, to come or enter into possession of; to obtain, receive, get, gain, accept, take; to have learned (*from* some source); to take (food, drink). Also, to bear (a child); to give birth to (a baby). ***to let one have***, to allow one to get, to give one. ***to be had*** (*of*): to be obtained (from).

a **1000** *O.E. Chron.* an. 885 þa Seaxan hæfdun siʒe. *c* **1000** *Ags. Gosp.* Matt. xix. 16 Hwæt godes do ic þæt ic ece lif hæbbe? *a* **1123** *O.E. Chron.* an. 1101 Ealle..heora land onʒean hæfdon. *c* **1205** LAY. 10273 Seuerius wende anan to hæbbene þisne kinedom. *a* **1300** *Cursor M.* 9574 þat he moght haue forgi[u]nes. *c* **1382** BIBLE (Wycliffe) *Gen.* xviii. 10, I schall comme to þe þis tyme: þe lyf ledere & Sara þi wyf schall haue a sonne. *Ibid.* John iii. 15 That ech man that bileueth in to him, perische not, but haue euerlastinge lyf. **1429** *Will of Gerard de Braybroke* in *Trans. Essex Archæol. Soc.* (1873) V. 298 And xij poure men clothed in Russet fryse yif hit may be had or ellis in other. **1466** MARG. PASTON in *P. Lett.* No. 560 II. 291 Remember that yf the[y] wer had from you, ye kowd never gyte no moo. *c* **1489** CAXTON *Sonnes of Aymon* i. 17 Yf we can have him, I shall make hym to be shamefully hanged. **1568** GRAFTON *Chron.* II. 318 The winde was so contrarious that he could have no passage. **1582** N. LICHEFIELD tr. *Castanheda's Conq. E. Ind.* iv. 10 b, Hee shoulde haue..anye thing..that was to be had in his Countrey. **1583** HOLLYBAND *Campo di Fior* 229 [She] had two children at a birthe. **1592** SHAKS. *Ven. & Ad.* 536 You shall have a kiss. **1611** BIBLE *Transl. Pref.* 2 What thanks had he? **1632** J. HAYWARD tr. *Biondi's Eromena* 131 Would you have me marrie, when there is no man..that will have me? **1663** PEPYS *Diary* 12 Apr. (1971) IV. 101 Creede and I took a turn at White-hall; but no coach to be had and so I returned to them. *c* **1680** BEVERIDGE *Serm.*, They have it.. from his own mouth. **1736** *Gentl. Mag.* VI. *title-p.*, Sold by the Booksellers..; of whom may be had compleat setts, or any single Number. **1748** *Anson's Voy.* II. iv. 166 On their having no news of us..they were persuaded that we..had perished. **1751** LABELYE *Westm. Br.* 94 The Gentlemen of Westminster..made Application to Parliament for having a Bridge. **1765** H. GLASSE *Art of Cookery* (ed. 9) Index, Advt., Thomson's Works... N.B. *The Seasons* may be had alone. **1803** *Watering & Sea-Bathing Places* Term. Advt., And which may be had of the Booksellers. **1803** G. ROSE *Diaries* (1860) II. 35 If Lord Spencer returns he must have the Admiralty. **1861** GOSCHEN *For. Exch.* (1866) 78 The number of marks banco which are to be had for the pound. **1887** RIDER HAGGARD *Jess* xxiii, Have another egg, Jess? **1892** A. WESTLAND *Wife & Mother* i. 2 In England..it is unusual to find mothers at an earlier age than eighteen, while it is almost equally exceptional for women to have children after forty-six years of age. *a* **1899** *Mod.* There is nothing to be had here. **1915** V. WOOLF *Voyage Out* xix. 313, I have just heard that the yellow guinea-pig has had a black baby. **1926** E. O'NEILL *Great God Brown* III. ii. 75, *I* will live with Margaret happily ever after... She will have children by me! **1930** *Times Lit. Suppl.* 19 June 513/3 (Advt.), All these books may be had of any bookseller. **1946** *New Statesman* 1 June 402/2 A thousand customers have I told this day there is never a fowl to be had. **1949** 'G. ORWELL' *Nineteen Eighty-Four* 39 I'm thirty-nine and I've had four children. **1962** P. MORTIMER *Pumpkin Eater* xxi. 129 She's going to have this kid in a public ward. **1975** G. BOURNE *Pregnancy* (1981) x. 134 More and more women are having their babies in hospital: at present more than 90 per cent are delivered in a maternity unit.

b. The imperative is used *absol.* in the sense '*Here!*' '*take this!*' Now *dial.* ***have to, towards***, used in drinking to any one = here's to. *arch.*

1377 LANGL. *P. Pl.* B. xiv. 49 Haue, haukyn!..and ete þis whan þe hungreth. *a* **1529** SKELTON *El. Rummyng* 563 Have, here is for me, A cloute of London pinnes. **1596** SHAKS. *Tam. Shr.* v. ii. 37 *Petr.* Spoke like an Officer: ha to the[e] lad. [*Stage direct.*] Drinkes to Hortentio. **1639** W. CARTWRIGHT *Royal Slave* III. i, *Str.* Here's to thee Leocrates. *Leoc.* Have towards thee, Philotas. *Phil.* To thee, Archippus [pledging one the other]. **1861** RAMSAY *Remin.* Ser. II. 44 He came back in a few minutes, crying, '*Hae*'. *Mod. Sc.* He's nane sae deaf, that he canna hear 'Hae!'

c. ***to have it***: to gain the victory or advantage, to win the match; to have the superiority.

1596 SHAKS. *Tam. Shr.* v. ii. 181 Well go thy waies olde Lad, for thou shalt ha't. **1847** L. HUNT *Men, Women, & B.* I. xiv. 232 Upon the whole, the dark browns, chestnuts, etc. have it with us. **1865** DICKENS *Mut. Fr.* III. xvii, As many as are of that opinion, say Aye,—contrary, No—the Ayes have it.

d. ***to have it***: to receive (or have received) a drubbing, thrashing, punishment, reprimand; ***to let one have it***, to 'give it' one. *colloq.*

1592 SHAKS. *Rom. & Jul.* III. i. 112 They haue made wormes meat of me; I haue it, and soundly. **1816** BYRON *Ch. Harold*, Notes to IV. cxlii, When one gladiator wounded another, he shouted '*he has it*', 'hoc habet,' or 'habet.' **1848** RUXTON *Life in Far West* 8 (Farmer), I ups..and let one Injun have it, as was going plum into the boy with his lance. **1891** L. MALET *Wages of Sin* II. 102 If she catches him she'll let him have it hot. **1892** MRS. H. WARD *David Grieve* IV. i. I shall let her have it, you'll see.

e. To have sexual intercourse with, to possess sexually. Also in *colloq.* phrases ***to have it away, off (with), to have*** (a person) ***away, off.***

1594 SHAKS. *Richard III* I. ii. 230 Was ever woman in this humour woo'd? Was ever woman in this humour won? I'll have her;—but I will not keep her long. **1596** —— *1 Henry IV* III. iii. 133 Why, she's neither fish nor flesh; a man knows not where to have her. **1743** FIELDING *J. Wild* III. IV. vii. 336 'None of your Coquet Airs, therefore, with me, Madam,' said he, 'for I am resolved to have you this Night.' **1762** BOSWELL *London Jrnl.* 28 Nov. (1950) 54 In the midst of divine service I was laying plans for having women. **1820** KEATS *Let.* 1 Nov. (1931) II. 568, I should have had her when I was in health, and I should have remained well. **1894** H. JAMES *Notebks.* (1947) 170 The idea of the physical possession, the brief physical, passionate rapture..the incongruity, the nastiness, *en somme* of the man's 'having' a sick girl. **1937** in Partridge *Dict. Slang Suppl.* (ed. 6, 1967) 1169 *Have it off*..'is also used..by a man that has contrived to seduce a girl'. **1952** S. J. KAUFFMANN *Philanderer* (1953) xi. 182 It's the first time I ever had a girl from Kentucky. **1962** *Times* 23 Oct. 15/2 My wife went to France and had it off with everyone in sight. **1965** G. MELLY *Owning-Up* iv. 29, I derived iconoclastic pleasure from having it off in the public parks where fifteen years before my brother and I.. accompanied our nurse on sunny afternoons. **1967** S. BECKETT *Eh Joe* 19 You've had her, haven't you?.. You've laid her? **1967** A. WILSON *No Laughing Matter* III. 304 Having it off may make you feel very good but a diamond bracelet lasts for ever. **1968** A. DIMENT *Gt. Spy Race* ii. 28 In future please check with the duty officer if I am free. For all you knew I might be having my secretary off on the desk. *Ibid.* viii. 141 It had crossed my mind I was going to be asked to have the old fart away. **1970** G. GREER *Female Eunuch* 265 The vocabulary of impersonal sex is peculiarly desolating. Who wants to..'have it away'? **1970** *Private Eye* 13 Mar. 16 He's had more sheilahs than you've had spaghetti breakfasts. **1972** R. PERRY *Fall Guy* iii. 52 No one would dream of having it away with his mistress.

f. ***to have it in for***: to have something unpleasant in store for; to have a grudge against or dislike for (app. modelled on *to be in for*: see IN *adv.* 8).

1849 'A. HARRIS' *Emigrant Family* II. vi. 122 In consequence of a former disagreement, the speaker already '*had it in for him*' whenever a drinking bout should afford opportunity for the said 'it' becoming a transferable possession. **1888** 'R. BOLDREWOOD' *Robbery under Arms* II. xviii. 283 He 'had it in' for more than one of the people who helped the police. **1927** *Daily Mirror* 10 Dec. 2/1 If it was not for the prejudice of a certain detective-sergeant who has had it in for me since I left the police force, I should be found not guilty. **1927** WODEHOUSE *Meet Mr. Mulliner* iii. 92, I have had it in for that dog since the second Sunday before Septuagesima. **1934** A. CHRISTIE *Murder on Orient Express* II. ix. 136 A few people had it in for Cassetti all right. **1942** A. L. ROWSE *Cornish Childhood* 112 He was very unpopular with the big boys..and they had it in for him. **1961** D. G. JAMES *M. Arnold* iii. 71 He has it in for the Romantic writers, certainly. **1967** *Punch* 9 Aug. 194/2 If and when the law catches up with them, I hope it has it in for them.

g. ***to have it***: to have a solution.

1856 C. M. YONGE *Daisy Chain* I. xxvi. 275 'V.V.,' continued Meta, 'what can that mean?' 'Five, five, of course,' said Flora. 'No, no! I have it, *Venus Victrix*,' said Ethel. **1897** A. TWEEDIE *Through Finland* xviii. 307 'I have it,' said the student, after a long pause, during which we had all sought an excuse to enable us to depart without hurting the farmer's feelings. 'I will tell them.'

h. ***to have it on*** or ***over*** (a person): to have the advantage of, to be superior to; to have 'the pull' of or over. ***to have nothing on***, (*a*) to have no advantage of or superiority over; conversely, ***to have something on*** (occas. ***over***), to have an advantage over (a person); (*b*) to know nothing discreditable or incriminating about (a person), whence conversely ***to have something on*** (a person). Cf. GET *v.* 5 b.

[**1906** H. GREEN *At Actors' Boarding House* 27 I'll show 'em the Waldoff ain't got nothin' on Maggie de Shine.] **1910** S. E. WHITE *Rules of Game* v. xxiv, They think they have it on us straight enough. **1912** C. MATHEWSON *Pitching in a Pinch* 7 'Hans' Wagner of Pittsburg, has always been a hard man for me, but in that I have had nothing on a lot of other pitchers. **1917** S. MERWIN *Temperamental Henry* 31 He had it all over the banjo-strumming Thomas P. of the unpleasantly rasping voice. **1919** F. HURST *Humoresque* 298 Baby Ella herself had nothin' on you. **1922** H. TITUS *Timber* vii. 65 You know he has it on you. There is no use trying to fight the law. **1924** A. CHRISTIE *Man in Brown Suit* 6 Every one of us incriminated..and not one of us has anything on him. **1928** *Daily Express* 19 June 12 Kerensky, who tried to do what Napoleon said no man could do: run a revolution and a war simultaneously. Kerensky thought Napoleon had nothing on him. **1928** *Observer* 22 July 28/3, I have carefully analysed the pre-Olympic performances of Liddell, who won in 1924, and J. W. J. Rinkel, who we hope is going to win this year. Liddell had nothing on Rinkel in preliminaries. **1928** *Daily Express* 27 Aug. 15/3 America's heavy-weight champion of the world has nothing on Great Britain's Prime Minister. **1929** 'G. DAVIOT' *Man in Queue* iii. 30 If he thinks he has anything on me..he has another guess coming. **1930** *Publisher's Weekly* 5 July 27 Deciding that the antique hussies of history in spite of their hot reputations have nothing on her. **1936** T. S. ELIOT *Essays Anc. & Mod.* 68 Huysmans' fee-fi-fo-fum *décor* of mediævalism has nothing on Mr. Symons's 'veiled altar'. **1938** E. BOWEN *Death of Heart* I. v. 94 While you had it on me, it made it more difficult. **1941** *Punch* 9 Apr. 341/1 It has never been finally worked out which system is the more disappointing, but it is generally admitted that each has something over the other. **1947** *Penguin New Writing* XXXI. 67 He..took out his best clothes. Going to the barracks, he had to look smart, he had to show the soldiers they had nothing on him. **1960** K. HOPKINS *Dead against my Principles* xix. 129 'She is the daughter of a criminal.'.. 'Yes. But we have nothing on her.' **1962** J. BRAINE *Life at Top* x. 122, I wasn't Mark, I never could be Mark; but there at least I had it over him. **1963** M. MCCARTHY *Group* iii. 63 The *Tribune*'s typography has it all over the *Times*'s. **1967** *Listener* 28 Dec. 857/1 For a picture of sheer bloodcurdling hatred and human degradation, our playwrights have nothing on this 60-year-old music-drama inspired by Sophocles' play.

i. ***to have it off***: to rob or burgle. *Criminals' slang.*

1931 A. R. L. GARDNER *Art of Crime* 233 Bill has had it off last night. **1936** J. CURTIS *Gilt Kid* ii. 20 'I had it off last week,' he said with a wink, 'not a big job, just a little snout gaff, but I earned myself a score.' **1939** J. PHELAN *In Can* ii. 14 'Denny's 'ad it orf again,' commented one of the patrons.

j. ***to have oneself*** (something): to provide (something) for oneself, to indulge oneself with (something). *colloq.* (orig. and chiefly *U.S.*).

1929 E. WILSON *I thought of Daisy* iii. 155 Ray seems to be having himself a time with Rita Cavanagh! **1936** R. CHANDLER *Killer in Rain* (1964) iv. 49 I'm going to have me a short nap now. **1939** C. MORLEY *Kitty Foyle* 263, I went and had myself a small brandy. **1940** O. LA FARGE in *55 Short Stories fr. New Yorker* (1952) 265 He had himself two good highballs. **1957** J. OSBORNE *Entertainer* 44 We're going to have ourselves a hero, you can see that. **1966** *New Yorker* 6 Aug. 71 (Advt.), Come to Portugal and have yourself a good cry.

k. ***to have had it***: to have no chance whatever of having or doing something; to have had one's (adverse) fate finally decided, to be defeated; to be dead, to have been killed; to be ruined, broken down, useless; to have had enough. *colloq.*

1941 *New Statesman* 30 Aug. 218/3 *To have had it*, to miss something pleasant, e.g. leave. **1943** *Time* 22 Mar. 51 'You've had it,' in R.A.F. vernacular, means 'You haven't got it and you won't get it.' **1946** S. GIBBONS *Westwood* vi. 78 *That* could not be got over..as Hilda's boys would say, 'You've had it', and there was nothing she could do. **1951** L. P. HARTLEY *My Fellow Devils* 277 That was the ghastly moment, coming back to find you gone. Then I did feel I'd had it. **1952** N. COWARD *Relative Values* II. vi. 64 Of course they're still alive, but I never see a telegram come into the house without saying..'Sarah's had it!' **1954** J. B. PRIESTLEY *Magicians* ix. 175 Two more 'ave 'ad it, mate... Two-seater goes off the road an' straight over the bloody edge to Kingdom Come. **1954** D. UNWIN *Governor's Wife* 34 Conversation with an educated African is like walking a tightrope. One slip and you've had it. **1956** 'M. INNES' *Appleby plays Chicken* I. iv. 39 The heart wasn't beating... Whoever he was, the chap had had it. **1956** 'J. WYNDHAM' *Seeds of Time* 163, I was thinking: 'Well, that's that. I've had it', and deciding that I was now in..heaven. **1957** *Listener* 13 June 945/2 Here are the men who matter—the highly paid white artisan has had it, but he'll put up a big rearguard action. **1958** P. SCOTT *Mark of Warrior* 41 He was so weary he just let the men bunch up. They'd all had it. **1959** *N.Z. Listener* 12 June 21/3 He re-wound the cord and tried again: no spark. 'It's had it, I think.' **1959** *News Chron.* 10 July 4/2 In private, Labour politicians admit that they have had it. **1971** J. KILLENS in A. Chapman *New Black Voices* (1972) 58, I mean, I'd had it, for a time, with that traveling-is-broadening shit.

l. ***to have had*** (a person or thing): to have had enough of, to be fed up with. *colloq.*

1943 *N.Z.E.F. Times* 21 June, I've had the club. **1947** N. MARSH *Final Curtain* xvi. 249 We'd all..just about *had* Cedric. **1953** G. HEYER *Detection Unlimited* ii. 23 He's just about had Warrenby, muscling into every damned thing here. **1956** A. WILSON *Anglo-Saxon Att.* I. iii. 60 When you resigned in November, I'd about had politics, as much as the Labour Party'd about had you. **1965** *Sunday Mail Mag.* (Brisbane) 15 Aug. 11/1 By October..N. Dixon Campbell had utterly had that little old white schoolhouse at Pallawalla, and stamped out of it never to return.

m. ***to have it*** (***so***) ***good***: to possess (so many) advantages. Chiefly in neg. contexts. *colloq.* (orig. *U.S.*).

1946 *Amer. Speech* XXI. 243 *You never had it so good.* This is a sardonic response to complaints about the Army; it is probably supposed to represent the attitude of a peculiarly offensive type of officer. **1957** *Times* 22 July 4/6 [Mr. Macmillan's speech at Bedford on 20 July] Let us be frank about it: most of our people have never had it so good. **1957** *Glasgow Herald* 16 Nov. 5/1 Mr. Harold Macmillan, at Maidstone last night..repeated..'They have never lived so well; they have never had it so good.' **1958** *Times* 8 May 11/5 When one boy said, 'My dad says we never had it so good', he was expressing a very general acceptance of what the 'past' really meant in East London. **1958** *Times* 12 July 7/7 How long can women's magazines have it so good? **1958** *Listener* 13 Nov. 776/2 They have it so good in their garden-world. **1959** *Times Lit. Suppl.* 3 Apr. 198/2 James Bond is having it good again. **1960** J. RAE *Custard Boys* I. vii. 87 'I've never had it so good,' he told me..'during the blitz I had more business than I could handle.' **1961** C. MCCULLERS *Clock without Hands* vii. 158 From then on I never had it so good. Nobody ever had it so good. **1969** *Times* 4 Oct. 7/7 The last phrase borrowed from that campaign [*sc.* the American Presidential campaign of 1952] by a British Prime Minister was from the Democrat Party's campaign slogan of that year. The words 'never had it so good' were first used by Mr. Macmillan two years before his party won its third election in a row.

n. ***to have on***: to be prepared to accept (a person, proposition, etc.); also, to attack or fight (a person). *Austral.* and *N.Z. colloq.*

1941 BAKER *Dict. Austral. Slang* 34 *Have (someone) on*, to be prepared to fight a person: to accept a challenge to a contest or fight. **1945** —— *Austral. Lang.* vi. 120 A man who attacks another is said..to have him on. **1946** F. SARGESON *That Summer* 54 A girl came past that I thought might have

me on. **1965** —— *Memoirs of Peon* vii. 252, I didn't see why we shouldn't introduce you... But John Morgan wouldn't have it on.

o. ***have* ——, *will* ——**: in numerous expressions of the type illustrated indicating willingness to travel, etc., because one possesses an essential object, etc.

1954 B. HOPE *Have Tux, will Travel* I Hoofers, comedians and singers used to put ads in *Variety*. Those ads read: 'Have tuxedo, will travel.' This meant they were ready to go any place at any time. **1960** *Daily Mail* 13 July 6/2 Never in the whole history of moving pictures has film-making been such a mobile and international industry. 'Have talent, will travel' is the watchword now. **1961** *John o' London's* 18 May 567/3 (*heading*) Have towel, will strip. **1961** *Sunday Times* 25 June 21/2 Have honours degree, will travel. **1965** *Harrods Xmas Catal.* 43/1 *Have iron, will travel*—featherweight iron weighs only $2\frac{3}{4}$ lbs. and travels..complete with universal adapters for use with any voltage..£4. 4. 0. **1966** *Listener* 16 June 889/1 *Have Gun Will Travel* was a much better western ..than the ones they are making now. **1968** *Times* 29 Nov. p. vi/4 Have portable, will play. **1969** *Times* 14 July 5/5 The ..scene has now gone one step further towards the American dream with the opening of Have Typewriter, Will Travel.

15. a. Hence, in pregnant sense: To get or have got into one's power, or at a disadvantage; to have caught (*fig.*), to have hold upon.

1596 SHAKS. *Merch. V.* IV. i. 334 Now infidell I haue thee on the hip. —— *1 Hen. IV*, III. iii. 145 She's neither fish nor flesh; a man knowes not where to haue her. **1659** *Shuffling, Cutting & Dealing* 6 One had better sometimes play with a good gamester then a bungler, for one knowes not where to have him. **1723** STEELE *Consc. Lovers* I. i, O, I have her; I have nettled and put her into the right Temper to be wrought upon. **1744** M. BISHOP *Life & Adv.* 190 We had them [the French] all Ways, Front, and Rear, and Flank. **1892** MRS. OLIPHANT *Marr. Elinor* II. xx. 81 Women are all hypocrites alike. You never know when you have them.

b. To have caught (a person) in argument or discussion; to have put into a fix or non-plus. *colloq.*

1816 SCOTT *Old Mort.* in *Tales of Landlord* IV. vii. 125 He has you there, I think, my Lord Duke. **1820** *Examiner* No. 631. 306/1 We have you there; you must concede the solemnity of the Proclamation. **1848** THACKERAY *Lett.* 12 Aug., I eagerly seized—the newspaper (ha ha! I had somebody there). **1890** BARING-GOULD *Arminell* I. xv. 249, I admit that you have me there. **1892** *Sat. Rev.* 23 Apr. 464/2 M. Renan 'has' Leo XIII on the subject of his dallyings with the Republic.

c. To get the better of, outwit, take in, deceive, 'do'. *slang.*

1805 G. HARRINGTON *New Lond. Spy* (ed. 4) 26 (Farmer) Ten to one but you are had, a cant word they make use of, instead of saying, as the truth is, we have cheated him. **1847** DE QUINCEY *Sp. Mil. Nun* Wks. 1862 III. 65 The good señora..was not..to be had in this fashion. **1879** MISS BRADDON *Clov. Foot* xviii, There's not a real diamond among them. If you've advanced money on 'em, you've been had.

d. ***to have on***: to puzzle or deceive intentionally; to chaff, tease; to hoax. orig. *dial.*

1867 J. T. STATON *Rays fro' Loominary* 117 It looks as if somebuddy wur havin me on. **1893** FARMER & HENLEY *Slang*, *To have on*, to secure a person's interest, attention, sympathy: generally with a view to deceiving him (or her). **1895** M. MATHER *Lancs. Idylls* 46, I were nobbud hevin' her on a bit. **1928** *Daily Express* 31 Aug. 7 Speaking unjudicially and in ordinary language you are 'having him on'. **1951** L. P. HARTLEY *Travelling Grave* 52 'Of course,' said Dickie, when the boy had gone off with his *mancia*, whistling, 'he's having us on.'

16. a. To 'get' into a place or state; to cause to come or go; to take with one; to bring, lead, convey, take, put. *arch.* Also †*refl.* To betake oneself.

c **1205** LAY. 19008 Þa hædden heo mid ginne Merlin þer wiδ inne. *a* **1300** *Cursor M.* 16913 (Cott.) Ioseph wald haf awai þe rode. **1424** *Sc. Acts Jas. I* (1597) §15 That na man haue out of the realm gold nor silver. *c* **1430** *Arte Nombryng* (E.E.T.S.) 11 Euery part of the nombre multiplying is to be hade into euery part of the nombre to be multipliede. **1453** MARG. PASTON in *P. Lett.* No. 189 I. 256 This day I have had inne ij. cartfull of hey. **1484** CAXTON *Fables of Alfonce* i, He was had before the Juge. **1490** —— *Eneydos* I. 144 His knyghtes toke hym and hadde hym awaye fro the bataylle. **1577–87** HOLINSHED *Chron.* III. 800 The next daie the corps was had to Westminster. *a* **1600** *Turnam. Tottenham* 183 Thay wold have tham to Tyb. **1611** BIBLE *2 Kings* xi. 15 Haue her foorth without the ranges. **1690** W. WALKER *Idiomat. Anglo-Lat.* 230 Make haste to have away the woman. **1749** FIELDING *Tom Jones* XVII. iii, There I was had into a whole room full of women. **1889** STEVENSON *Master of B.* vi. 176 A little later he was had to bed.

b. ***have up***: to take up or cause to go before a court of justice in answer to a charge; to summon; to call to account. ***have out***: to cause to come out to a duel. ***to have it out***: see OUT *adv.* 7 b.

1749 FIELDING *Tom Jones* VIII. xi, So the fellow was had up, and Frank was had up for a witness. **1820** *Examiner* No. 638. 427/2 Sir Matthew has been had up before his brother Magistrates on charges connected with bill-broking. **1855** SMEDLEY *H. Coverdale* iii, If he feels aggrieved, he can have you out (not that I admire duelling). **1861** MISS YONGE *Stokesley Secret* xi. (1862) 169 I'd have you up for that. **1892** MRS. H. WARD *David Grieve* II. 173 The man who had let them the rooms ought to be 'had up'.

c. ***to have it away***: to escape from prison or custody. *Criminals' slang.*

1958 F. NORMAN *Bang to Rights* 48 The P.O. who was in charge of the escort that was going to..make sure no one had it away. **1965** *New Statesman* 30 July 152/3 One thing broke the monotony of this dreary sentence and that was the occasion when a geezer, three peters away from me, had it away. **1969** T. PARKER *Twisting Lane* 196 After I'd had it away three times, they decided it was no use bothering with me in these open places.

17. With object and complement: **a.** (with *adj.*, *adv.*, or *advb. phr.*): To get (something) into a specified condition. **b.** (with *pa. pple.*, or *dative inf.*): To get (something) done; to cause, procure, or oblige (something to be done, or a person to do something).

a. **1297** R. GLOUC. (1724) 541 So that the clerkes adde the stretessone iler. **1791** 'G. GAMBADO' *Ann. Horsem.* ix. (1809) 105, I have..determined to have the apple trees down. *Mod.* They are having the pavement up for the electric light.

b. **1390** ROBT. III. in *Records Priory Coldingham* (Surtees) 67 We have had den Johne of Aclyff..at spekyn wyth the byschof of Sant Andrew. **1450–1530** *Myrr. our Ladye* 33 He had gette hym a synger of psalmes. **1489** CAXTON *Faytes of A.* II. xxxv 150 Hanybal..cam by fore the cyte for to haue hyt dystroyed. **1503–4** *Act 19 Hen. VII*, c. 28 Preamb., Divers..made..pursuyte..to have the seyd atteyndours reversed. **1604** SHAKS. *Oth.* II. iii. 258 To haue their Balmy slumbers wak'd with strife. **1618** BOLTON *Florus* Ep. Ded. (1636) A iij, So desirous..to have it understood by others. **1662** J. DAVIES tr. *Olearius' Voy. Ambass.* 28 She would needs have the young Counts..go to the Inn..to Complement them. **1678** *Trials Ireland, Pickering, Grove* 24 Grove would have had the Bullets to be Champt. **1722** DE FOE *Plague* (1754) 32 To have their Fortunes told them. **1742** FIELDING *J. Andrews* I. xii, That he might have a bed prepared for him. **1845** S. AUSTIN *Ranke's Hist. Ref.* III. 571 Before their parents were compelled to have them baptized. **1886** *Manch. Exam.* 14 Jan. 5/3 He had counted the guns, or had had them counted.

18. a. ***to have something done to one***: to be subjected to the doing or infliction of it, to receive, experience, or suffer it as the action of others or of fate; to 'get' (such a thing) done (to one). Also in same sense, ***to have some one do something***, ***to have something happen to one***. ***to have it coming to one***: see COME *v.* 9 b.

13.. *K. Alis.* 940 Som the throte, and som the heorte Hadyn y-perced. *a* **1533** LD. BERNERS *Huon* ciii. 343, I haue had slayne mo then xx. M. men, besyde my thre neuewes and my yonger brother. **1568** GRAFTON *Chron.* II. 141 If they had any parte of their liberties withdrawne. **1598** SHAKS. *Merry W.* II. ii. 73, I had myselfe twentie Angels giuen me this morning. **1603** —— *Hamlet* III. iv. 206 (*Qo* 1611) For tis the sport to haue the enginer Hoist with his owne petar. **1611** —— *Cymb.* I. vi. 3 A Wedded-Lady, That hath her Husband banish'd. **1641** HINDE *J. Bruen* xxxiv. 107 Jacob had his wife Rachel to dye suddenly in his journey on his hand. **1719** DE FOE *Crusoe* II. x, Another had one of his hands..burnt. **1766** GOLDSM. *Vic. W.* i, We often had the traveller or stranger visit us to taste our gooseberry wine. **1860** *Grandmother's Money* I. 119 (Hoppe), I had a horse run away with me. **1886** *Athenæum* 30 Oct. 565/1 A man.. who certainly deserved to have his biography written.

b. with *will*, *would*, or the like: To wish, will, require that something be done (to oneself or others).

c **1205** LAY. 32197 Þa com him ufel on, Swa godd hit wolde habben idon. **13..** *Coer de L.* 112 All they gunne.. aske her what she wolde have doo. **1523** LD. BERNERS *Froiss.* I. ccclv. 573 Thenglysshmen wolde gladly haue had hym to ben maryed in Heynalt. **1535** COVERDALE *Jer.* i. 17, I will not haue the to be afrayd of them. **1591** SHAKS. *Two Gent.* III. i. 80 What would your Grace haue me to do in this? **1630** B. JONSON *New Inn* III. i. 22 Sir Pierce, I'll have him a cavalier. **1653** H. COGAN tr. *Pinto's Trav.* xlviii. 185 Good luck would have it that this young Damosel came hither. **1709** BERKELEY *Th. Vision* §33 Those who will have us judge of distance by lines and angles. **1787** 'G. GAMBADO' *Acad. Horsemen* (1809) 34, I would have you make an essay to accomplish it. **1834** MEDWIN *Angler in Wales* II. 24 As good fortune would have it.

c. with a negative, sometimes: Not to allow, bear, or suffer.

1583 HOLLYBAND *Campo di Fior* 21 Thy mother will not have it so. **1596** SHAKS. *1 Hen. IV*, II. iii. 106, I must not haue you..question me. **1697** DAMPIER *Voy.* I. p. v, [He] would by no means consent to have him chosen. **1847** TENNYSON *Princess* VII. Introd. Song ii, Yet, O my friend, I will not have thee die! **1890** E. R. ESLER *Way of Transgressors* III. xiv. 238, I will not have the merits of the poor forced upon me. *Mod.* I would not have it spoken about.

†**19. a.** *intr.* (for *refl.*) or *absol.* To betake oneself, go. *Obs.*

c **1420** *Chron. Vilod.* 937 And ouȝt of þe chapell in gret hast he hedde. **1509** BARCLAY *Shyp of Folys* (1874) II. 260 Cryeng with lowde voyce: captayne abyde, haue in. **1849** AYTOUN *Lays, Heart of Bruce* xxv, Have down, have down, my merry men all—Have down unto the plain.

†**b.** ***have over***: a call to a ferryman. *Obs.*

1590 GREENE *Never too late* Wks. (Rtldg.) 300/1 'Have over, ferryman', there cried a boy. **1637** RUTHERFORD *Lett.* (1862) I. 224 How happy are they who..can cry to Christ 'Lord Jesus, have over: come and fetch the dreary passenger.' **1756** NUGENT *Gr. Tour* II. 238 Hanover..took its present name..because of a ferry here over the Leina, Hanover..signifying as much as have-over in English.

20. *intr.* or *absol.* ***have at***: To go at or get at, esp. in a hostile way; to have a stroke at, make an attempt at. Chiefly in imperative; app. 1st pers. plural, but often singular in sense, announcing the speaker's intent to get at or attack. So with other preps. as *after*, *among*, *through*, *to*, *with*.

13.. *Gaw. & Gr. Knt.* 2288 'Haf at þe þenne', quod þat oþer. *c* **1385** CHAUCER *L.G.W.* 1383 *Hipsiphile*, Haue at the Iason now thyn horn is blowe. *a* **1529** SKELTON *Bowge of Courte* 391 Have at all that lyeth vpon the burde! **1546** J. HEYWOOD *Prov.* (1867) 65 Haue among you blynd harpers (sayde I) The mo the merier. **1575** R. B. *Appius & Virginia* in Hazl. *Dodsley* IV. 119 Have with ye, have at ye, your manhood to try. *Ibid.* 138 Well, sith here is no company, have with ye to Jericho. **1593** SHAKS *2 Hen. VI*, IV. viii. 63 Haue through the verie middest of you. **1600** —— *A.Y.L.* I. ii. 268 *Cel.* Will you goe Coze? *Ros.* Haue with you. **1602** —— *Ham.* I. iv. 89 *Mar.* Let's follow; 'tis not fit thus to obey him. *Hor.* Haue after, to what issue will this come? **1639** FULLER *Holy War* III. xi. (1647) 128 He wintered in Askelon, intending next spring to have at Jerusalem. **1777** SHERIDAN *Sch. Scand.* III. iii, *Charles S.* Careless..you shall be auctioneer; so come along with us. *Careless.* Oh, have with you, if that's the case. **1853** READE *Never too late* xvi, Well, come here and I'll have at you in the vulgar tongue.

**** *Phrases.*

21. *Have* is used in numerous phraseological expressions, which are treated under their distinctive words; e.g. *to have* ADO, *h. at* AVAIL, *h.* BUSINESS, *h. in* CHARGE, *h.* CONCERN, *h.* COURSE, *h.* DONE, *to h.* EVERYTHING, *have an* EYE *on* or *to*, *h. a* FINGER *in*, *h. at one's* FINGER ENDS, *h. a* HAND *in*, *h. in* HAND, *h. on* HAND, *h. a* HEART, *h. at* HEART, *as* LUCK *would h. it*, *h. a* MIND, *h.* ON (clothes), *have it* OUT, *h.* PART, *h.* RECOURSE, *h. under one's* THUMB, *h. in* VIEW, WHAT *h. you*, *h. the* WIND *of*, etc.

***** *Idiomatic uses.*

22. a. The past Subjunctive *had* = would have, is used idiomatically with adjectives (or adverbs) in the comparative, as *better*, *liefer*, *sooner*, *rather*; in the superlative, as *best*, *liefest*; or in the positive with 'as', *as good*, *as lief*, *as soon*, *as well*, to express preference or comparative desirability.

In the earliest form of these expressions, in OE. the adjs. *léofre*, *betre* were construed with *be* and the dative, e.g. *him wǽre betere* = it would be better for him. In ME., side by side with this, appears *have* and the nominative, in the sense 'he (I, etc.) would hold or find it better or preferable'. The use with the positive, and superlative, and the extension to *rather* are later; the use of *as soon*, *sooner*, *well*, is recent, since *liefer* and *better* began to be felt as adverbs. (See exhaustive treatment by F. Hall in *Amer. Jrnl. Philol.* II. 281.) The following instances illustrate this idiom generally; fuller illustration will be found under the several words.

[*O.E. Chron.* an. 755 Þa cuædon hie þæt him næniȝ mæȝ leofra nære. **971** *Blickl. Hom.* 25 Him wære betere þæt he næfre ȝeboren nære. *c* **1000** ÆLFRIC *Gen.* xxix. 19 Leofre me ys þæt ic hiȝ sylle þe. *c* **1330** R. BRUNNE *Chron.* (1810) 172 Better him wer..in clostre haf led his life. *c* **1386** CHAUCER *Frankl. T.* 794 Yet were hym leuere abyde. **1390** GOWER *Conf.* II. 306 He cast what thing him were best to do. *c* **1394** *P. Pl. Crede* 16 Þerfor lerne þe byleue leuest me were. **1614** W. BROWNE *Sheph. Pipe* Wks. (1772) 21 Leuer me were be slaine.]

c **1340** *Cursor M.* 6235 (Fairf.) We had leyuer [*Cott.* vs leuer ware] euermare to serue in egipte..þen in þe wildernes to dey. *c* **1340** HAMPOLE *Prose Tr.* (1866) 25 Thei had welle lever haue bene stille. *c* **1386** CHAUCER *Friar's T.* 276 An old rebekke, That hadde almoost as lief to lese hire nekke, As for to yeue a peny of hir good. *c* **1435** *Torr. Portugal* 1186 Better he had to have be away. **14..** *Chester Pl.* (E.E.T.S.) iii. 99, I had as lief thou sleppit. **1470–85** MALORY *Arthur* (1817) II. 109 Of alle knyghtes..I had levest have you. **1478** MARG. PASTON in *Paston Lett.* No. 818. III. 231, I had rather that ye never maryd in yowyr lyffe. **1485** CAXTON *Paris & V.* 47 She had as leef to deye as to lyue. **1523** LD. BERNERS *Froiss.* (1812) I. 168 They had rather that their lord therle shulde take..the kyng of Englandes doughter. *a* **1533** —— *Gold. Bk. M. Aurel.* (1546) L vij, I had rather to bee Cato. **1537** etc. [see BETTER *a.* 4 b]. **1559** etc. [see BEST *a.* 4]. **1590** SHAKS. *Com. Err.* II. ii. 36 Sconce call you it?.. I had rather haue it a head. **1595** *True Tragedie*, etc. in *First Sketches* (1843) 169, I thinke I had as good Goe with you. **1601** SHAKS. *Twel. N.* III. ii. 34, I had as liefe be a Brownist, as a Politician. **1665** COTTON *Poet. Wks.* (1765) 134 He had better, far..have been drown'd. **1712** ADDISON *Spect.* No. 287 ¶3 There had better be none at all. **1768** GOLDSM. *Good-n. Man* II. (Globe) 622/2 You had as good make a point of first giving away yourself. **1844** MOZLEY *Ess.* (1878) II. 27 You must give way; and you had as well do so voluntarily. **1844** B. BARTON *Selections* (1849) xxvii, I had almost as well never have been a child. **1847** MARRYAT *Childr. N. Forest* xx, I had rather that you had fired through his arm. **1859** TROLLOPE *Bertrams* (1867) 335 I'd as lief have an old man as a young one; perhaps liefer. **1878** W. H. MALLOCK *New Republic* 145, I had best not give her any.

b. Formerly the indicative (present and past) was also thus used.

c **1350** *Will. Palerne* 918, I haue leuer it layne. *c* **1374** CHAUCER *Troylus* II. 422 (471) Yet have I lever maken him good chere. *c* **1386** —— *Frankl. T.* 632 Yet haue I leuere to lese My lif, than [etc.]. **1390** GOWER *Conf.* I. 93 This knight hath lever for to deie. **14..** *St. Wenefrid* in Hearne *R. Brunne* Pref. Append. xv, I have lever that thou do me to dethe then [etc.]. *a* **1450** *Knt. de la Tour* (1868) 101, I haue leuer to quytte yow and gyue yow my parte. **1456–7** *Past. Lett.* No. 297 I. 407, I have lever other men go to the Dille ..than I do. **1595** SIDNEY *Apol. Poetrie* (Arb.) 61 Poesie.. like Venus..hath rather be troubled in the net with Mars, then enioy the homelie quiet of Vulcan.

c. Confusion of the two forms of expression produced ***he* (*I*, etc.) *were better*** (see BE *v.* 19), and ***him* (*me*, etc.) *had liefer*, *rather***.

13.. *Coer de L.* 3502 Hym hadde lever have ben at home. **13..** *Syr Degarre* in Utterson *Pop. Poetry* I. 139 Me had lever..That I were fayre out of this lande. *c* **1386** CHAUCER *Clerk's T.* 388 Al had hir leuer han had a knaue childe. **1593** SHAKS. *Rich. II*, III. iii. 192 Me rather had, my Heart might feele your Love, Than [etc.].

23. ***had like*** (*liked, likely*) ***to***: see LIKE. ***had need to***: see NEED.

II. As an auxiliary verb. As in the other Germanic (and Romanic) languages, the various moods and tenses of *have* are used with the pa. pple. of another verb, to form a series of compound or 'perfect' tenses of the latter, expressing action already finished at the time indicated, and answering to the Latin perfect tenses *dedi, dederam, dedero, dedisse*, etc.

This use arose directly from sense 2b, the object possessed having in agreement with it a passive participle of a transitive verb as attribute or complement; thus, *I have my work done* = 'I possess or have my work in a done or finished condition', whence, by inference of antecedent action from result, the actual sense 'I have done my work': cf. the series 'have you the article ready?', 'have you the article completed?', 'have you completed the article?' In some dialects the distinction between the original and developed forms, e.g. 'He has the house built', 'he has built the house', is still in regular use; with some past participles, as *begun, completed, done, finished*, etc., it is recognized generally. With transitive verbs the developed use was already frequent in OE.; the pa. pple., which originally agreed in number and case with the object, was sometimes left uninflected. In early ME. the usage is found with verbs of action without an object, whence it was extended to intransitive verbs, especially, at an early date, to the verb *to be* (as in French and other Romanic languages, and in opposition to continental Teutonic use), as *he has been, had been, will have been*, etc. (cf. F. *il a été*, Ger. *er ist gewesen*). Verbs of motion and position long retained the earlier use of the auxiliary *be*; and *he is gone* is still used to express resulting state, while *he has gone* expresses action. See BE 14b.

24. The present tense of *have*, forms a present of completed action, or 'present perfect'.

a. To a trans. vb. with object.

Here in origin and form belongs *I have got*, colloquially used for *I have*: see GET *v.*

832 *Charter* in Sweet *O.E. Texts* 447 Ðis..ðet ic beboden hebbe in ðisem ȝewrite. **c 1000** ÆLFRIC *Gen.* xlii. 36 Bearnleasne ȝe habbaþ me ȝedonne. —— *Exod.* v. 21 ȝe habbaþ us ȝedon laþe Pharaone. **c 1175** *Lamb. Hom.* 69 Ic habbe ifunde hu me mei in sunne ben ibunde. **c 1200** ORMIN 4458 Himm haffst tu slaȝenn. **a 1225** *Juliana* 33 Mi feader and mi moder..habbe forsake me. **a 1300** *Cursor M.* 5182 Ha yee broght him wit yow? **? a 1366** CHAUCER *Rom. Rose* 71–2 The briddes, that haven lefte her song, While thei han suffrid cold so strong. **c 1410** LOVE *Bonavent. Mirr.* xii. 30 (Gibbs MS.) Dere sone what hastow done to vs? **c 1450** *Merlin* 25 Sithe that Vortiger hath do sle oure kynge. **1584** POWEL *Lloyd's Cambria* 61 Hauing burnt Holyhed. **1652** COTTERELL *Cassandra* II. (1676) 20 An opinion that ha's mortally offended me. **1726** LEONI *Alberti's Archit.* II. 2/2 The having satisfied necessity is a very small matter. **1796** J. OWEN *Trav. Europe* I. 274 One of those objects which it is more pleasant to have seen, than to see. **1847** MARRYAT *Childr. N. Forest* vi, I've got a great deal on my hands now. **1876** MOZLEY *Univ. Serm.* v. (1877) 118 I was open to Christianity to have prohibited property and war.

b. Extended to verbs of action without object.

c 1175 *Lamb. Hom.* 77 We habbeð bigunnen ou to seggen ..hwat bi-qu[e]þ þe crede. **c 1200** ORMIN 11 Icc hafe don swa summ þu badd. **c 1400** *Apol. Loll.* 6 It is knowun þat many popis han synnyd, & ben snibbid. **1553** T. WILSON *Rhet.* (1580) 133 Els [thei] came of a meaner house then wee have dooen. **1809–10** WORDSW. in Coleridge *Friend* (1837) III. 23 Every age hath abounded in instances.

c. Extended to intransitive verbs generally. Used at an early date with *been*, pa. pple, of BE, and hence with the passive voice. With verbs of motion later, partly displacing *be* as auxiliary.

c 1205 LAY. 8325 Twien þu hafuest ibeon ouer-cummen. **1297** R. GLOUC. (1724) 3 Engelond haþ i be y nome..ylome. **c 1300** *Beket* 133 Lute we habbeth togadere ibeo. **c 1300** *St. Margarete* 180 þe were betere habbe bileued atom. **c 1300** *Harrow. Hell.* 43 Hard gates hauy gon. **c 1340** *Cursor M.* 6050 (Fairf.) Yet ys pharaon als he as bene & ay wille be. **c 1420** *Chron. Vilod.* 387 Bot rather ha stoud by hurr' futt stylt. **1523** LD. BERNERS *Froiss.* I. xviii. 24 The Englisshe.. made semblaunt to haue come to them. **1585** T. WASHINGTON tr. *Nicholay's Voy.* I. x. 12b, Having sojourned there a night. **1722** DE FOE *Plague* (1756) 174 What I found to ha' been the Case. **1826** J. WILSON *Noct. Ambr.* Wks. 1856 I. 174 Things hae really come to a queer pass. **1882** L. KEITH *Alasnam's Lady* III. 165 Why haven't you been to see me?

d. **(*I*) *have and* (*I*) *haven't***: a phrase indicating that a statement is true in some respects but not in others.

1858 TROLLOPE *Dr. Thorne* II. xiv. 282 'Have you spoken to my niece about this, Sir Louis?' 'Well, I have, and yet I haven't; I haven't, and yet in a manner I have.' **1910** J. BUCHAN *Prester John* vi. 108 'Had the man any news?' I asked. 'He had and he hadn't.' **1933** A. CHRISTIE *Ld. Edgware Dies* iii. 31 'You have a problem for me—yes?'.. 'Well,..I have and I haven't.' **1967** 'L. BRUCE' *Death of Commuter* v. 58 'You haven't got any suspicions about Mr. Parador's death, have you?'.. 'Well, I have and I haven't.'

25. The past of *have* forms a past tense of completed action or 'pluperfect'. **a.** With transitive verb and object.

a 800 *O.E. Chron.* an. 755 Oþ þæt hie hine ofslægenne [*Laud MS.* ofslæȝen] hæfdon. **a 1175** *Cott. Hom.* 221 þaða he ȝesceapen hafede. **c 1200** ORMIN 354 Hiss faderr..haffde itt all forrworrpenn. **c 1325** *Metr. Hom.* 86 That joy that he hafd tinte. **1382** WYCLIF *Wisd.* xi. 20 The hurting hadde mouȝt destroȝed them. **1582** BENTLEY *Mon. Matrones* ii. 15 Thou hadest chosen me for thy wife. **1613** PURCHAS *Pilgrimage* (1614) 393, I had thought I had ended this Chapter and our Persian Expedition. **1676** RAY *Corr.* (1848) 123, I had not blamed him had he acknowledged his authors. *Mod.* Had you met him before? Who had caused the disturbance?

b. With active verbs without object, and with intransitive and passive verbs.

c 1205 LAY. 112 Heuede Eneas..widen iwalken. **a 1240** *Lofsong* in *Cott. Hom.* 213 Hefdich ȝare so idon. **c 1275** *O.E. Misc.* 37 He hedde so longe ibeo ine wrecche lyue þisse. **a 1300** *Cursor M.* 14256 Had þou her wit vs bene Mi broþer had noght ben ded, i wen. **c 1440** *York Myst.* xv. 111 Als myn harte wolde, and I had ought. **1523** LD. BERNERS *Froiss.* I. xvi. 17 They had soiourned there in great ease. **1634** SIR T. HERBERT *Trav.* 46 The Company had no doubt been enriched..had it not beene prevented, by a Rascall. **1774** GOLDSM. *Nat. Hist.* (1776) II. 190 It did not return me sensation for sensation, as my former feelings had done. **1802** MAR. EDGEWORTH *Moral T.* (1816) I. i. 1 He had been taught to dislike politeness.

26. The compound tenses (*shall have, will have, should have*, etc.) are similarly employed.

c 1175 *Lamb. Hom.* 11 Ec crist hit walde habben idon. **a 1300** *Cursor M.* 438 If he cuth hafe born it wele. **1307** *Elegy Edw. I*, viii, So fain thou woldest hit han ywonne. **c 1420** *Chron. Vilod.* 536 þt he shulnot havy come to þt joyfull place. **1461** J. PASTON in *P. Lett.* No. 384 II. 4 Brybers that wold a robbed a ship. **1611** SHAKS. *Cymb.* II. iv. 42, I should haue lost the worth of it in Gold. **1722** DE FOE *Plague* (1756) 186 Multitudes..wou'd ha' been continually running up and down the Streets. *Ibid.*, The Person.. wou'd as certainly ha' been incurably infected.

¶ In 15th and 16th c. (and later U.S. dial.) occur many instances of redundant *have, had*, in the compound tenses.

1442 BP. BEKYNTON in *Official Corr.* II. 213 He might never have had escaped. **1470–85** MALORY *Arthur* (1817) I. 152 Had not he have be, we shold never have retorned. **c 1482** W. PASTON in *Paston Lett.* No. 867 III. 297 Sir John ..wold have largely have recompensed. **1509** J. STYLE in *Mem. Hen. VII*, 433 The sayd kyng had not so sone have returnyd. **1627–77** FELTHAM *Resolves* (1696) 37 Cleanthes might well have fail'd..had not accident have helped him. **1768** STERNE *Sent. Journ.* I. (The Monk, Calais), Nature seemed to have had done with her resentments in him. **1816** U. BROWN *Jrnl.* in *Maryland Hist. Mag.* (1915) X. 282 If this forest had never have been fired it would have been a vast..Timbered country. **1869** *Trans. Ill. Agric. Soc.* VII. 444 If said hogs had, in style of Hanlon Brothers, have stood one on the other. **1911** J. F. WILSON *Land Claimers* i. 17 'If the fire hadn't have gone out,' he mused.

III. **27.** *Comb.* (mostly *nonce-wds.*) †**have-at-all** (cf. sense 20), 'a desperate risk: a phrase taken from the practice of gamblers' (Nares); also of a person (quot. 1742). **have-been**, something that has been but is no longer; a thing belonging to the past: cf. HAS-BEEN; so ***had-been***, that had been at a former time. **have-got**: see HAVE *sb.* 2. †**have-likeness**, ? the possession of likeness or resemblance. **have-not**: see HAVE *sb.* 2. **have-on** *slang* = HAVE *sb.* 3 (cf. sense 15d). **have-something**, one who has something; so ***have-nothing***.

1622 *Good Newes & Bad N.* (N.), Her dearest knight.. What with his debts, and what with *have at all, Lay hidden like a savage in his den, For feare of bayliffes, sergeants, marshals men. **a 1634** RANDOLPH *Muses Looking-Glasse* (N.), But you will starve yourselfe, that when y' are rotten, One have at all of mine may set it flying. And I will have your bones cut into dice, And make you guilty of the spending of it. **1742** NASH in *Guide Watering Places* (1806) ix, That the younger ladies take notice how many eyes observe them.—N.B. this does not extend to the *Have at Alls*. **1874** *Daily News* 21 Oct., Swept into the *have-beens. **1892** SIR H. MAXWELL *Meridiana* 9, I am a have-been—a phantom—a mere *simulacrum*. **1835** WILLIS *Pencillings* I. xii. 93 A *had-been beautiful woman. **1674** N. FAIRFAX *Bulk & Selv.* 52 Such an *have-likeness being as needful on the behalf of the organ and object both. **1931** T. R. G. LYELL *Slang* 372 *Have* or **have on*, a swindle; a mild joke to deceive a person. **1967** *Listener* 16 Feb. 237/3 Puns, tropes, polyglot have-ons, batty new coinings. **1842** MIALL in *Nonconf.* I. 280 All the *have-somethings would be earnest to impart knowledge.

have (hæv), *sb.* [f. prec. vb.]

1. Having, possession. *Obs.* exc. as *nonce-wd.*

c 1200 *Trin. Coll. Hom.* 217 Man hoh..of þan þe god him haueð lend loc to chirche bringen..and wurðin þer-mide godes bord alse his haue beð. **a 1605** MONTGOMERIE *Misc. Poems* xlii. 11 For haif, ȝe heir, is haldin half a fill. **1860** EMERSON *Cond. Life, Wealth* Wks. (Bohn) II. 358 Want is a growing giant, whom the coat of Have was never large enough to cover.

2. *colloq.* One who *has* or possesses; one belonging to the wealthier class. Also, a nation or country that *has* or possesses; one of the wealthier nations. (Usually in *pl.*; and in conjunction with *have-not*.) Also *attrib.* and (occas.) *have-got*.

1836 LYTTON *Athens* (1837) I. 328 The division..of the Rich and the Poor—the Havenots and the Haves. **1888** BRYCE *Amer. Commw.* II. III. liii. 338 In the hostility of rich and poor, or of capital and labour, in the fears of the Haves and the desire of the Have-nots. **1896** *Westm. Gaz.* 23 Apr. 7/1 An excellent thing it was to see the Not-Have and the Have colloguing over the wrongs of the people. **1919** J. L. GARVIN *Econ. Found. Peace* xvi. 375 They contemplate a World-Federation when the international League of the Have-Nots has conquered all the Haves. **1937** E. SNOW *Red Star over China* VI. iii. 227 The Reds..radically changed the situation for..all the 'have-not' elements. **1949** KOESTLER *Insight & Outlook* xvi. 227 The equalization of the steep gradients..between have and have-not nations. **1955** *Bull. Atomic Sci.* Jan. 3/2 The proposal is for the atomic 'haves' to contribute crucial materials and at least some limited amount of technical information to the 'have nots'. **1959** *Brno Studies* I. 70 The sharp distinction..between the 'have-gots' and the 'have-nots' was soon felt in politics. **1959** *Times* 29 Sept. 18/5 Algerian oil is expected to change France from an oil 'have-not' to a 'have'. **1962** *Listener* 5 July 29/3 The greatest of the 'have' powers. *Ibid.* 30/1 The Soviet Union is a 'have' society that ought to be more generous. **1963** *Ibid.* 21 Mar. 487/1 Russia was becoming a 'have-got' power herself with a productive capacity second only to that of the United States. **1965** H. KAHN *On Escalation* xiii. 244 A 'have' nation might perceive a situation that threatened its possessions as a crisis. **1968** *Punch* 22 May 757/3 The country had a one-crop economy; the more cocoa it exported, the less the 'have' nations were willing to pay for it.

3. *slang.* 'A swindle; a *take-in*; a *do*' (Farmer *Slang*). Cf. HAVE *v.* 15c.

have, obs. pa. t. of HEAVE *v.*

haveable ('hævəb(ə)l), *a. rare.* [f. HAVE *v.* + -ABLE.] That can be had; obtainable.

a 1641 BP. MOUNTAGU *Acts & Mon.* (1642) 64 A thing not haveable in this world. **1667** WATERHOUSE *Fire Lond.* 104 No more Justice..than is haveable from a Spoyler.

†**havegooday**, obs. form of HAGGADAY [? *ha' good day*, as a form of leave-taking in going out of the door], a kind of door-latch.

1396 in C. Welch *Tower Bridge* (1894) 76 [The purchases in 1396 included a new key and a] havegooday [of iron, with two plates of iron for the same].

havek(e, obs. forms of HAWK.

†**havel**, *sb.*[1] *Obs.* Also 5 **hawvelle**. [Derivation obscure.] A term of reproach applied to a man; ? low fellow.

c 1460 *Towneley Myst.* (Surtees) 314 Ther syt thai so Alle nyghte, With hawvelle and jawvelle, Syngyng, of lawvelle, Thise ar howndes of helle. **1522** SKELTON *Why not to Court* 95 Hauell and Haruy Hatter, Jack Trauell and Cole Crafter. *Ibid.* 604 Stowpe, thou hauell, Rynne, thou iauell!

'**havel**, *sb.*[2] *local.* The beard or awn of barley.

a 1825 in FORBY *Voc. E. Anglia.*

Hence **havel** *v. trans.*, to free (barley) of the awn.

1847 *Jrnl. R. Agric. Soc.* VIII. II. 281 Machines for havelling barley, in lieu of the old-fashioned barley-choppers.

'**havel**, *sb.*[3] *local.* [cf. ON. *hafald*: see HEALD.] ? A heald or heddle.

1851 in *Illustr. Lond. News* (1854) 5 Aug. 118 (Occupations of the people) Havel and heald maker.

haveless, †**havenless**, *a. Obs.* exc. *dial.* Forms: α. 1 **hafenleas**, 3 **hauenles**, 5 *superl.* **hauenlest**, 9 *dial.* **avenless**. β. 2–4 **hafeles**, 2–5 **haueles**, 3 **haueleas**, 4 **hefles**, 4–5 **hafles**, 5 *Sc.* **hawless**, 9 *dial.* **have-**, **haiveless**. [OE. *hafenléas*, f. *hæfene* = ON. *hǫfn* (genit. *hafnar*) possession, holding, f. ON. *hafa*, OE. *haf-*, *hæf-* stem of *habban* to HAVE + -LESS. The current form rests immed. on the verb-stem: cf. Du. *haveloos*, OHG. *habalôs*.]

†**1.** Without possessions, destitute, indigent. *Obs.*

α. **c 1000** ÆLFRIC *Hom.* II. 176 Sum hafenleas man. **a 1100** *Voc.* in Wr.-Wülcker 312/21 *Inops*, hafenleas. **c 1200** *Trin. Coll. Hom.* 157 Me hit shal giuen hauenlese men. **a 1400–50** *Alexander* 1864 Oft þe hauenlest here is houen to þe sternes. β. **c 1175** *Lamb. Hom.* 111 þet hauelese monnam meie fremian. **c 1200** *Trin. Coll. Hom.* 9 Gief þe nedfulle, help þe hauelease. **a 1300** *Cursor M.* 28875 Hafe-les lete ga fra þe nan. **1390** GOWER *Conf.* II. 362 Though a man be haveles, Yet shall he nought by thefte stele. **c 1450** *St. Cuthbert* (Surtees) 5439 Bot haueles away he past. **c 1450** HOLLAND *Howlat* 982 A foule carioun, Hatit and hawless [*v.r.* hafles].

2. (*Sc.* 'hevlɪs). Without resource, shiftless, helpless; careless, slovenly. *Sc.* and *dial.*

1868 G. MACDONALD *R. Falconer* II. 83 Dinna ye think I'm the haveless crater I used to be. **1871** W. ALEXANDER *Johnny Gibb* (1873) 118 Eh, he's a haiveless man. **1879** MISS JACKSON *Shropsh. Word-bk.*, *Avenless*, shiftless, without any faculty for contriving. **1880** JAMIESON, *Haivless*, slovenly. *Banffs.*

havelock ('hævlɒk). *U.S.* [Named after Gen. Henry Havelock, distinguished in the Indian Mutiny 1857.] A white cloth covering for the cap, with a flap hanging over the neck, to be worn by soldiers as a protection from the sun's heat. ***havelock cap***, a military cap provided with a havelock.

1861 MRS. H. B. STOWE *Let.* in *Life* (1889) 365 He is a fine-looking man with black eyes and hair, set off by a white havelock. **1863** O. W. HOLMES *Inevitable Trial* in *Old Vol. Life* (1891) 116 Two years ago our women's fingers were busy making 'Havelocks'. It seemed to us then as if the Havelock made half the soldier. **1880** *Harper's Mag.* Oct. 399 A poncho and havelock cap comprise the rubber clothing outfit.

†**havelon, -ilon**, *sb. Obs. rare.* Also 4 **have-, havi-, havyloune**, 5 **havylon**, (erron. **hamylon**). [a. OF. *havellon, havillon, havrillon*, of obscure origin; possibly related to *havet* = *crochet*, a sharp change of direction.] Doubling, as of a fox; wile, guile; double-dealing.

c 1330 R. BRUNNE *Chron.* (1810) 308 Whi þat he not sped, þis skille mot it be, With hauelon þam led, to make þe purale [i.e. perambulation]. **1377** LANGL. *P. Pl.* B. x. 129 þo þat vseth þis haueloунes [*v.rr.* hauylounes, -louns, hauelons] to blende mennes wittes. **a 1422** *Venery de Twety* in *Rel. Ant.*

I. 154 If yowre houndes renne to one chace, that is to seye, rusezt or hauylon [*printed* hamylon], or croiseth.

Hence †**havelon** *v. intr.*, to double, or use wiles, as a fox. *Obs.*

13.. *Gaw. & Gr. Knt.* 1708 þe fox..trantes & tornayeez þurȝ mony tene greue; Hauilounez [*printed* Hamlounez] & herkenez, bi heggez ful ofte. **1486** *Bk. St. Albans* E vj b, And the beest begynne to renne, as herttis be wont, Or for to hauylon as doos the fox with his gyle, Or for to crosse, as the roo dooth oder while.

haven ('heɪv(ə)n), *sb.* Forms: 1 **hæfen, hæfene,** 3–5 **hauene,** 3–6 **hauen,** 3– **haven,** (4 **have,** 4–5 **heven,** *Sc.* **hawin(e, -yn(e,** 4–6 **havin, -yn,** 5 **havayn,** 6 **heaven,** *Sc.* **heiven, haevin, haivin, hevin, -yn).** [OE. *hæfen*, str. fem. and *hæfne* wk. fem. = MDu., Du. *haven*, MLG. *havene*, LG. *haven*, MHG. *hafen, haven, habene* (mod.G. *hafen*), ON. *höfn*; usually considered to be a deriv. from the root either of HAVE *v.* or of HEAVE *v.* (Goth. *hafjan* = L. *capere*), though possibly of ON. *haf*, Da. *hav*, OE. *hæf* sea.]

1. A recess or inlet of the sea, or the mouth of a river, affording good anchorage and a safe station for ships; a harbour, port.

1031 *O.E. Chron.*, þa hæfenan on Sandwic. *c* **1205** LAY. 7415 þat hauen of Douere he hauede inumen. **1297** R. GLOUC. (1724) 134 Heo wolleþ to morwe aryue atte haue [*v.r.* havene] of Tottenays. *Ibid.* 423 An hauene..þat me clupeþ Portesmouþe. **1340** *Ayenb.* 182 Nyxt þe hauene spilþ ofte þet ssip þet geþ zikerliche ine þe heȝe ze. *c* **1470** HENRY *Wallace* VII. 1068 A hundreth schippys..in hawyn was lyand thar. **1535** COVERDALE *Ps.* cvi[i]. 30 So he bryngeth them vnto the hauen where they wolde be [**1611** vnto their desired hauen]. **1552** ABP. HAMILTON *Catech.* (1884) 28 Ane skyppar can nocht gyde his schip to ane gud hevin without direction of his Compas. **1647** CLARENDON *Hist. Reb.* VII. §161 Weymouth, a very convenient Harbour and Haven. **1862** LD. BROUGHAM *Brit. Const.* xi. 152 Goods imported and exported at the havens of the realm.

2. *fig.* A place of shelter, safety, or retreat; a refuge; an asylum.

a **1225** *Juliana* 33 Lead me þurh þis lease..lif, to þe hauene of heale. *a* **1300** *Cursor M.* 25711 Penance..schal him hauen of merci win. **1547–64** BAULDWIN *Mor. Philos.* (Palfr.) 98 To the godly, death is..the port of paradise, the hauen of heauen..& harbour from all misery. **1573** TUSSER *Husb.* xxxviii. (1878) 92 Cause rooke and rauen to seeke a new hauen. **1706** WATTS *Horæ Lyr.* II. *True Courage* 44 The fair haven of eternal bliss. **1865** CARLYLE *Fredk. Gt.* XVIII. vii. (1872) VII. 215 My sole refuge and only haven..is in the arms of death.

3. *attrib.* and *Comb.*, as ***haven-finding, -keeper, -master, -mouth.*** Also HAVEN-TOWN.

c **1440** *Promp. Parv.* 230/2 Havene Kepare, or gouernare, *portunus.* **1599** E. WRIGHT (*title*) The Haven-finding Art, or the way to find any haven or place at sea, by the latitude and variation. **1600** HOLLAND *Livy* 953 (R.) To sinke them in the verie hauen-mouth, for to choke it up. **1835** *Munic. Corpor. Rep.* 2399 The Haven Master is an officer appointed under the charter of James I, by which the admiralty rights were acquired. **1870** MORRIS *Earthly Par.* II. III. 206 The fall Of the low haven-waves when night was still.

Hence **'havenful** *a.*, full of havens; **'havenward** *adv.*, towards the haven.

1616 CHAPMAN *Musæus* 364 The havenful shore he sought. **1842** TENNYSON *Golden Year* 44 Blowing havenward With silks, and fruits, and spices, clear of toll.

'haven, *v.* [f. prec. sb.]

†**1.** *intr.* To put into or shelter in a haven or port.

c **1375** *Sc. Leg. Saints, Nycholas* 310 Sa þai sailyt furth & land has sene & hawynit. **1382** WYCLIF *Acts* xx. 15 An other day we haueneden at Samum. **1535–1621** [see below].

2. *trans.* To put (a ship, etc.) into a haven.

1601 CORNWALLYES *Ess.* II. li. (1631) 322 They are never havened, and their Anchors hold not. **1795–7** SOUTHEY *Juven. Poems* Poet. Wks. II. 200 Safe haven'd from the sea. **1831** JANE PORTER *Sir E. Seaward's Narr.* I. 41 The creek, in which the good providence of God had havened us.

fig. **1820** KEATS *Eve St. Agnes* xxvii, Blissfully haven'd both from joy and pain. **1890** A. AUSTIN in *Spectator* 14 June, They havened you from strife.

Hence **'havening** *vbl. sb.* (*attrib.*, as ***havening-place***, Sc.).

1535 STEWART *Cron. Scot.* II. 601 Ane hevyning place tha fand syne in that steid. **1563** WINȜET *Wks.* (1888) II. 17, I hid me self in the heuinning place of religioun. **1621** *Sc. Acts Jas. VI*, c. 68 (1814) 658/2 The sey poirtis and havening places of Eymouth and Coldinghame.

havenage ('heɪv(ə)nɪdʒ). [See -AGE.] Harbour-dues.

1864 in WEBSTER.

havener, -or ('heɪv(ə)nə(r)). [f. HAVEN *sb.* + -ER¹, -OR.] The overseer of a haven, a harbour-master. Hence **'havenership,** the office of havener.

1495 *Act 11 Hen. VII*, c. 33 §10 Thoffice called the Havenershippe and of Collectour of our Custumes..in oure Porte of Plymouth. **1602** CAREW *Cornwall* 79 a, Speciall officers, as..Havener, Customer, Butler, Excheate, Feodary. **1885** *Law Times* 4 Apr. 403/1 Casual profits of the office of Havenor (proceeds of sale of unclaimed wreck).

†**'havenet.** *Obs.* [f. as prec. + -ET¹.] A small haven or harbour.

1538 LELAND *Itin.* I. 53 To Whiteby, wher is an havenet holp with a peere, and a great fischar Toune. **1577–87** HARRISON *England* I. xiv. (R.), A portlet or hauenet also for ships. **1610** HOLLAND *Camden's Brit.* I. 441 Shoberie a village..which sometime was a citie an Hauenet.

havenless ('heɪv(ə)nlɪs), *a.*¹ [f. as prec. + -LESS.] Without a haven; having no haven.

1398 TREVISA *Barth. De P.R.* XV. lxxx. (1495) 520 Icaria..is hauenlesse in euery syde. **1600** HOLLAND *Livy* 352 (R.) The havenlesse and harbourlesse coasts of Italie. **1867** *Contemp. Rev.* V. 145 The one great port of a havenless sea.

†**havenless,** *a.*² *Obs.*: see HAVELESS.

†**'havenlet.** *Obs.* [-LET.] A little haven.

1538 LELAND *Itin.* V. 29 A litle Havenlet, wither Alen that rennith thorough S. David Close cummith.

†**'haven-town.** *Obs.* A town having a haven or harbour; a seaport town.

c **1400** *Destr. Troy* 1789 At Mansua..A hauyn toun. **1548** HALL *Chron., Hen. VI*, 175 b, To prohibite their landyng..haven tounes were watched. **1680** MORDEN *Geog. Rect.* (1685) 186 Porto, a Haven-Town at the Mouth of the Dueras.

haveour, var. of HAVIOUR.

haver ('hævə(r)), *sb.*¹ [f. HAVE *v.* + -ER¹.] One who has or possesses; a possessor, owner. Now *rare* in *general* sense.

c **1400** *Apol. Loll.* 9 To selle is þe hauer to ȝeue his þing for price tane. *c* **1449** PECOCK *Repr.* I. 153 Hauers and vsers of ymagis. **1542** UDALL *Erasm. Apoph.* 32 b, He taught true..vertue, whiche dooeth specially aboue all other thynges commende and sette out yᵉ hauer. **1607** SHAKS. *Cor.* II. ii. 89 It is held, That Valour is the chiefest Vertue, And most dignifies the hauer. **1728** in Cramond *Ann. Banff* (1891) I. 199 Havers thereof shall be liable in ane pecuniarie punishment.

b. *Sc. Law.* One who has possession of a deed or writing which is called for by a court of justice; the holder of a document.

c **1575** *Balfour's Practicks* (1754) 188 The haver of ane manis evidentis may be chargit to deliver the samin within sax dayis to the awner. **1754** ERSKINE *Princ. Sc. Law* (1809) 395 The apparent heir may..sue havers, i.e. custodiars or possessors, for exhibition of all writings pertaining to his ancestor. **1837** *Act 7 Will. IV & 1 Vict.* c. 41 §3 The officer summoning parties, witnesses, or havers. **1868** *Act 31 & 32 Vict.* c. 100 §19 Any witness or haver requiring to be cited to attend said Court.

haver ('hævə(r)), *sb.*² *dial.* Also 5 **hafyr, havyr.** [ME. 14th c. *haver* (*hafyr*), corresp. to OS. *hab-*, *havoro* (Du., EFris. *haver*, LG. *hawer*), OHG. *habaro* (MHG. *habere, haber*, G. *haber, hafer*), ON. *hafre*, pl. *hafrar* (Sw. *hafre*, Da. *havre*):—OTeut. **habron-* wk. masc. In Eng. only northern, and presumably from Norse.] Oats.

1362 [see HAVER-CAKE]. **14..** *Nom.* in Wr.-Wülcker 726/19 *Hec avena*, hafyr. **1483** *Cath. Angl.* 178/2 Havyr, *auena.* **1562** BULLEYN *Bk. Simples* (1579) 29 In the Northe this grayne is called Hauer; the Southern people cal them Otes. **1804** R. ANDERSON *Cumberld. Ball.* 99, I mun off to deetin havver. **1864** CARLYLE *Fredk. Gt.* XII. x. (1872) IV. 218 The hay, straw, barley and haver, were eaten away.

b. = HAVERGRASS, oat-grass.

1806 J. GALPINE *Brit. Bot.* 40 Wild oat or haver.

c. *attrib.* and *Comb.*, as ***haver-bannock, -bread, -malt, -meal, -straw.*** Also HAVER-CAKE, -GRASS.

a **1804** MRS. WHEELER *Westmld. Dial.* (1821) 114 *Havver bannock, cald dumplin, and a potatoe pie. **1466–7** *MS. Hostill. Roll, Durham*, Super le *Hauerbarne infra manerium. **1641** BEST *Farm. Bks.* (Surtees) 52 The furthest roomestead in the haver barne next the East. *c* **1425** *Voc.* in Wr.-Wülcker 657/29 *Panis auenacius*, *Havyrbrede. **1889** BARING-GOULD *Pennycomequicks* x. 149 *note*, In Yorkshire cake is white bread, bread is oat-cake, Haver-bread. **1572** *Inv.* in T. D. Whitaker *Craven* (1812) 332, lx quart of *haver-malte, at viii *s.* the quarter. **1624** *Naworth Househ. Bks.* (Surtees) 217, xlj bushells of haver malt. **1785** HUTTON *Bran New Wark* II. 33 A dubbler of *haver-meal. **14..** *MS. Lincoln A.I.* 17. lf. 282 (Halliw.) Take and make lee of *havyre-straa. **1820** *Blackw. Mag.* VIII. 154 To hurkle down on a heap o' haver straw.

haver, *sb.*³, usually in pl. **havers** ('heɪvəz). *Sc.* and *north. dial.* Also **haivers.** [Origin unknown.] Foolish or senseless talk; nonsense.

1787 BURNS *To Gudewife o' Wauchope House*, Wi claivers, an' haivers, Wearing the day awa. **1824** SCOTT *Redgauntlet* Let. x, Dinna deave the gentleman wi' your havers. **1893** CROCKETT *Stickit Minister* 30 The haivers the twa o' ye talk aboot auld Tam. **1896** J. M. BARRIE *Margaret Ogilvy* vii. 141 It's a haver of a book.

haver ('heɪvə(r)), *v.* Chiefly *Sc.* and *north. dial.* Also **haiver.** [Goes with prec.] **1.** *intr.* To talk garrulously and foolishly; to talk nonsense.

1721 [see below]. **1816** SCOTT *Antiquary* xliv, He just havered on about it to make the mair of Sir Arthur. **1825** BROCKETT *N.C. Gloss.*, *Haver, Haiver*, to talk foolishly, to speak without thought. **1881** CHESNEY *Private Secret.* II. xix. 148 Hilda shuddered as her father havered on.

2. Orig. *Sc. dial.* but now in general English use: to hesitate, to be slow in deciding.

1866 W. GREGOR *Dial. Banffshire* 73 *Haiver*, to hesitate and make much ado about anything. **1955** J. BAYLEY *In Another Country* 75 It was a classic moment for polite havering, but the sensible girl did not haver: he was holding the front door open and she climbed in without more ado. **1957** *Times* 14 Nov. 13/3 No doubt the Government, in deciding to institute an inquiry.., might appear at first sight to have been havering and shifting their ground.

Hence **'havering** *vbl. sb.* and *ppl. a.*; **'haverer.**

1721 RAMSAY *Addr. Town Council Edin.* ii, Gleg-eyed friends..Receiv'd it as a dainty prize, For a' it was sae hav'ren. **1809** SCOTT *Fam. Lett.* 15 Feb. (1894) I. v. 131 A little havering and fun upon the other side of the question. **1822** *Blackw. Mag.* XI. 90 The dull, stupid, superannuated, havering Edinburgh. **1826** J. WILSON *Noct. Ambr.* Wks. 1855 II. 23 Unhappy haverers are they over tumbler or jug.

haver, var. HAGHER *a.*, skilful; obs. f. HAVIER.

'haver-cake. *north. dial.* [f. HAVER *sb.*²: see CAKE *sb.* 1 a and b.] Oatcake.

1362 LANGL. *P. Pl.* A. VII. 269 (MS. U.) A fewe Cruddes and Craym and an hauir cake [**1377** B. VI. 284 hauer cake]. **1542** BOORDE *Dyetary* xi. (1870) 259 Hauer cakes in Scotlande is many a good..lordes dysshe. **1606** PEACHAM *Art of Drawing* 68 A blew stone, such as they make Haver or Oten cakes upon. **1829** GLOVER *Hist. Derby* I. 198 Oat bread, or Haver-cake is the food of a large portion of the Derbyshire peasantry. **1855** E. WAUGH *Lanc. Life* (1857) 104 Oatmeal porridge, and oat-cake, enter largely into the diet of country people in this part of Lancashire. They used to pride themselves in the name of 'the Havercake Lads'.

'haverel ('heɪv(ə)rəl). *Sc.* and *north. dial.* Also **-al, -il, haivrel.** [f. HAVER *v.*]

1. One who 'havers' or talks without sense.

a **1818** MACNEILL *Poems* (1844) 105 Gley'd Sawnie, the haivrel. **1825** BROCKETT *N.C. Gloss.* s.v., 'Parfitly rediclous is that haveril there.' **1871** CARLYLE in *Mrs. Carlyle's Lett.* II. 103 Their only child 'Bett', a loud haveril of a lass.

2. *attrib.* or *adj.* Given to havering or foolish idle chattering.

a **1774** FERGUSSON *Drink Eclogue* 90 Ye haveril Scot! **1785** BURNS *Halloween* 32 Poor hav'rel Will fell aff the drift. **1842** MRS. CARLYLE *Lett.* I. 176 A good-hearted, rattling, clever haveral sort of woman.

'havergrass. *Obs.* exc. *north. dial.* [f. HAVER *sb.*²] 'Oat-grass'; a name for several wild grasses resembling oats; species of *Avena* and *Bromus*.

1578 LYTE *Dodoens* IV. xlvi. 505 Hauergrasse is..much like to Otes, in leaues, stemmes, and eares. **1597** GERARDE *Herbal* I. xxii. (1633) 30 Hauer-grasse hath small creeping roots. **1713** J. PETIVER in *Phil. Trans.* XXVIII. 35 Single spiked Havergrass. **1879** BRITTEN & HOLLAND *Plant-n.*, *Haver-* or *Havver-Grass*, the northern name for 'oat-grass'. *Bromus sterilis*; *Avena elatior*; *Bromus mollis.*

haversack ('hævəsæk). Also **havresack,** and as F. **havresac.** [a. F. *havresac* (1680 in Hatz.-Darm.), ad. G. *habersack* lit. 'oat-sack' (cf. HAVER *sb.*²), orig. the bag in which cavalry and horsemen carried the oats for their horses (Grimm), thence extended to a bag in which travellers and others carried personal property, and to that used by French and English soldiers.]

A bag of stout canvas, worn with a strap over the shoulder, in which a soldier carries his current day's rations. Also, any similar bag used for a like purpose by travellers, etc.

(In Cavendish's *Wolsey* edd. Singer 1827, Morley 1885, an error for *half hakks.*)

1749 SMOLLETT *Gil Bl.* II. viii. (1782) I. 198 A long sword lay by him on the grass, with an havresack, of which he had unloaded his shoulders. **1818** BYRON *Mazeppa* iv, The venerable man From out his havresack and can Prepared and spread his slender stock. **1839** *New Monthly Mag.* LVII. 257, I..strapped on my havresac. **1860** TYNDALL *Glac.* I. xi. 71 Converting my waterproof havresack into a cushion. **1868** *Regul. & Ord. Army* 36 1128 Both straps of the havresack are to be worn outside the waist belt. **1879** M. PATTISON *Milton* xiii. 165 Every private in the French army carries in his haversack the bâton of a marshal.

†**b.** 'A gunner's case for ordnance, being a leather bag used to carry cartridges from the ammunition-chest to the piece in loading'. *Obs.*

1858 in SIMMONDS *Dict. Trade.*

Haversian (hə'vɜːsɪən), *a. Anat.* [f. the name of Clopton Havers, an English anatomist (*c* 1690).] Applied to certain structures in bone discovered by Havers, as in

Haversian canal, one of the minute cylindrical passages in bone which form the channels for blood-vessels and medullary matter. ***H. glands***, the fringed vascular folds of the synovial membranes, described by Havers as mucilaginous glands, and regarded by him as the source of the synovial secretion; also called ***H. folds, H. fringes.*** ***H. lamellæ***, hollow cylinders of bone tissue surrounding and concentric with a Haversian canal. ***H. space***, the name given to a Haversian canal when large and irregular, as in growing bone and the cancellous tissue of adult bone. ***H. system***, 'term applied to the H. canal, its concentric lamellæ of bone, and the lacunæ with their canaliculi' (*Syd. Soc. Lex.*).

1836–9 TODD *Cycl. Anat.* II. 785/2 The fatty..structure named Haversian gland. **1842** E. WILSON *Anat. Vade M.* 2 The cells represent the Haversian canals, and are each surrounded by concentric lamellæ. **1845–6** TODD & BOWMAN *Phys. Anat.*, Haversian system. **1855** HOLDEN *Hum. Osteol.* (1878) 15 Almost all the compact substance of bone is made up of a multitude of these 'Haversian systems'. **1862** WOOD *Nat. Hist.* I. 9 The reptiles possess very few Haversian canals.

haversine ('hævəsaɪn). *Trigonometry.* [Abbreviation of *ha(lf) versine* (versed sine).] In nautical phraseology: Half the versed sine. (Introduced by Prof. Jas. Inman, D.D., in his

Navigation and Nautical Astronomy ed. 3, 1835. Cf. *Dict. Nat. Biog.*)

1875 BEDFORD *Sailor's Pocket Bk.* x. (ed. 2) 381 Add together the log. secants of the two first terms..and the half haversines of the two last.

havie, -y, obs. forms of HEAVY.

havier (ˈheɪvjə(r)). Also 7–9 **haver**, 8–9 **havior, -our**, 9 **heavier**. [Etymology uncertain: the earliest recorded form is *haver*, which Pegge took as = *halver*, from *half*, comparing Latin *semimas* 'castrated'. The forms in *-ier*, *-iour*, would in this case be corruptions: cf. *saviour*, *haviour*.] A gelded fallow deer. Also *attrib.*

1676 LADY CHAWORTH in *12th Rep. Hist. MSS. Comm.* App. v. 33 The finest haver deere..that ever I saw. *Ibid.*, Lady Stanhope..to whom I sent the hanch of the haver. **1796** PEGGE *Anonym.* IV. xlii. (1809) 152 *A Halfer*..means a male Fallow-deer gelded..Those that pronounce half, *hâfe*, say *hàver*; and those that speak half with *a* open, say *hauver*: but many, through ignorance of the etymon, will call it *havior*, which is very absurd. **1803** *Ann. Agric.* XXXIX. 556. **1829** *Sporting Mag.* XXIII. 369 It has been known for a havier to be hunted three times a season for ten years. **1850** LD. BRAYBROOKE in *N. & Q.* 1st Ser. I. 230/1 The word *Havior*, by which all park-keepers denote an emasculated male deer..Never having seen the word written or printed, I am guided, in attempting to spell it, by the usual pronunciation. **1891** *Field* 7 Mar. 332/1 A poll havier has no antlers, nor even the stumps, because he was added to the list in his infancy.

ˈhavil. A small kind of crab.

1857 *Illustr. Lond. News* XXXI. 70/2 A small species [of crab]..known by the French as *l'Etrille*, and called in some parts of our country grubbin, or crabbin..in London havill.

‖**havildar** (ˈhævɪldɑː(r)). *E. Ind.* Also 7 **havaldar**. [Pers. *ḥawāl-dār*, *ḥawāla-dār*, f. Arab. *ḥawālah* charge + Pers. *dār* holding, holder.] 'A sepoy non-commissioned officer, corresponding to a sergeant' (Yule).

1698 FRYER *Acc. E. India & P.* 126, I sent to the Havaldar, to know when he would pass us up the Gaot. **1788** *Gentl. Mag.* LVIII. I. 68/1 (Stanf.) A second flag, with a Sabahdaur and two Havildars, was sent in. **1839** THACKERAY *Major Gahagan* vii, The..havildars were absent. **1866** LIVINGSTONE *Last Jrnls.* ii, I left the havildar, sepoys [etc.].

having (ˈhævɪŋ), *vbl. sb.* [f. HAVE *v.* + -ING¹.]

1. The action or condition expressed by the verb HAVE; possession.

c **1375** *Sc. Leg. Saints, Johannes* 121 Of riches þe haffynge Is nocht Ill, bot þe Ill spendinge. **1579** FULKE *Confut. Sanders* 679 He would not consent to the idolatrous hauing of images. **1644** BULWER *Chirol.* 65 The covetous desire of goods and the thirst of having. **1678** BUTLER *Hud.* III. I. 743 Find all his having and his holding Reduc'd t'eternal noise and scolding. **1890** ESLER *Way Transgressors* II. 221 If a book is worth buying and having it is worth taking care of.

2. *concr.* (often in *pl.*) That which one has or possesses; possession, property, wealth, belongings.

c **1325** *Rel. Ant.* II. 119 Litel and povere is myn having. *c* **1460** *Towneley Myst.* (Surtees) 162 For nothyng Thi neghburs goodys yerne wrongwysly; his house, his rent, ne his hafyng. *a* **1652** BROME *Novella* I. ii. Wks. 1873 I. 114 Looke to my house and havings; keepe all safe. **1851** RUSKIN *Mod. Paint.* II. III. I. x. §8 Neither imagination..nor industry, nor sensibility, nor energy, nor any other good having. **1875** TENNYSON *Q. Mary* II. ii, Your havings wasted by the scythe and spade.

3. (Often in *pl.*) Behaviour, manners, demeanour, deportment. Chiefly *Sc.* (Cf. HAVE *v.* 12.)

1375 BARBOUR *Bruce* VII. 135 The kyng..Persauit weill be thair hawyng That thai lufit hym in na thing. *c* **1450** tr. *De Imitatione* II. i. 41 þe wykkyd & wondyrfull hauyngys & beringes of men. **1501** DOUGLAS *Pal. Hon.* II. xliii, The merie speiche, fair hauingis, hie renoun Of thame. **1789** BURNS *Kirks Alarm* xiii, Ye may ha'e some pretence To havins and sense. **1824** SCOTT *Redgauntlet* Let. xii, By and attour her gentle havings.

ˈhaving, *ppl. a.* [f. as prec. + -ING².]

1. That has or possesses; possessing property. (Now *rare* or *Obs.* exc. as participle.)

a **1300** *Cursor M.* 28943 Til him þat has bene hauand.. and falles in-to state o nede plight-les. **1483** *Cath. Angl.* 178/2 Havynge, *habens, possidens.*

2. Desirous of having or possessing; greedy, covetous, grasping. Now only *dial.*

1591 GREENE *Disc. Coosnage* (1592) 3 To be of a hauing and couetous mind. **1622** MABBE tr. *Aleman's Guzman d'Alf.* II. 213 To a having mind, all is too little. **1860** GEO. ELIOT *Mill on Fl.* I. vi, She's as jealous and having as can be. **1892** EMILY LAWLESS *Grania* II. ii. 91 A..spending, having brood they are.

†**ˈhavingness.** *Obs.* [f. prec. + -NESS.] **a.** The quality of having or possessing. **b.** Desire of having, covetousness.

1577 tr. *Bullinger's Decades* (1592) 609 God..by whome, in whome, and to whome all things are, being himselfe a perpetuall and most absolute ἐντελέχεια, or perfite hauingnes. **1646** J. BENBRIGGE *Vsura Accommod.* 17 Mens Havingnesse ..will be the onely Remora to this good work.

haviour (ˈheɪvɪə(r)), †**havour.** Forms: 5 hauoyr(e, -ore, 5–6 havoir, -oire, -ur(e, -eour, -your(e, 5–7 havour, -oure, 6– haviour (6 hauior); see also AVER *sb.* [Orig. a. F. *aveir*, *avoir* 'having, possession, property, estate, wealth, etc.', subst. use of *avoir*, OF. *aveir* to have. First used in Eng. in the Norman form *aveyr* (see AVER); the Central Fr. form *avoir* appeared about 1400, and displaced *aver*, exc. in the northern dialect, where that form survived in a specific sense. In 14–15th c., association with the Engl. *have*, *having*, introduced the variants *haver*, *havoir*, *havour*, and the *h* was established before 1500. At the same time the parallel *behavour* was formed on the Eng. *behave*; and in 16th c. *havour*, beside its original sense of 'possession', took also that of *behavour*. Subsequently the termination of both words passed through *-eour* to *-iour* (cf. *saviour*, and vulgar '*lovier*'); the original sense 'possession' became obs.; and, in the new sense, *haviour* came down alongside of *behaviour*, of which it may often have been viewed as a shortened by-form.]

†**1.** The fact of having; possession; a possession, property; estate, substance, wealth. *Obs.*

[**1330**, etc., in form *aveyr*, *avoir*, etc.: see AVER.] *c* **1400** *Rom. Rose* 4720 Love, it is..Wit withoute discrecioun; Havoire withoute possessioun. *c* **1440** *Promp. Parv.* 231/1 Havure, or havynge of catel, or oþer goodys (*K.* havour, or werdly good..), *averium.* **1474** CAXTON *Chesse* 94 He toke al his hauoir and put hyt in a shippe. **1475** *Bk. Noblesse* 84 After her power and havyoure. **1478** SIR J. PASTON in *P. Lett.* No. 814 III. 223 Every man off hys havore. **1523** *St. Papers Hen. VIII*, VI. 185 Prisoners of haveour takyn in the kinges armye. **1587** FLEMING *Contn. Holinshed* III. 1378/1 Persons of wealthie hauior. **1600** HOLLAND *Livy* XXIII. xli. 502 Manlius had levied of them certaine money..according to the havoir and abilitie..of each of them. **1606** WARNER *Alb. Eng.* XVI. clxiv. 409 Food, Cloath, and havour competent. **1616** J. BULLOKAR *Eng. Expos.*, *Hauoire*, possession.

2. The action of having or bearing oneself; deportment, bearing, behaviour, manner. Also *pl.* manners. *arch.* or *dial.*

1503 HAWES *Examp. Virt.* vi. (Arb.) 22 Mylde in her hauour, dyscrete of chere. **1540–1** ELYOT *Image Gov.* (1556) 4 b, Of base haviour. **1579** SPENSER *Sheph. Cal.* Apr. 66 Her heauenly haviour, her princely grace. **1599** MASSINGER, etc. *Old Law* v. i, Nearer the haviour of a funeral, Than of a wedding. **1752** FOOTE *Taste* I. Wks. 1799 I. 13 Mind your haviours. Where's your best bow? *a* **1756** WEST *Abuse Trav.* (R.), A courteous haviour, gent and debonair. *a* **1800** S. PEGGE *Anecd. Eng. Lang.* (1814) 378 Haviours, manners. 'Do you think I have forgot my haviours?'

Hence **ˈhavioured** *a.*, in Comb., as ***modest-havioured***, modestly behaved.

1878 C. & MRS. C. CLARKE *Recoll. Writers* 177 The modest-havioured woman simply sitting there.

havoc (ˈhævək), *sb.* Forms: 4–5 **havok**, 5 **hauoke, haue ok**, 6–7 **havocke**, 6–9 **havock**, 6– **havoc**. [a. AFr. *havok*, altered in some way from OF. *havot* (*c* 1150 in Du Cange, *havo*), used in same sense, esp. in phrase *crier havot*. Prob. of Teutonic origin.]

1. In the phrase ***cry havoc***, orig. to give to an army the order *havoc!*, as the signal for the seizure of spoil, and so of general spoliation or pillage. In later use (usually after Shaks.) *fig.*, and associated with sense 2.

[**1385** *Ord. War Rich. II*, in *Black Bk. Admiralty* (Rolls) I. 455 Item, qe nul soit si hardy de crier havok sur peine davoir la teste coupe. **1405** ABP. SCROPE in *Historians Ch. York* (Rolls) II. 296 Idem dominus Henricus..bona regia ubicunque fuerant inventa vastavit, et, clamando havok, fideles homines, tam spirituales quam temporales, quosdam spoliavit.] **1419** *Ord. War Hen. V*, in *Black Bk. Admiralty* (Rolls) I. 462 That noman be so hardy to crye havok upon peyn that he that is founde begynner to dye therfore. *c* **1440** *Jacob's Well* (E.E.T.S.) 207 And for his euylle dedys his godys be cryed be þe kyng 'haue ok'. *c* **1525** in Grose *Hist. Eng. Army* (1801) I. 194 Likewise be all manner of beasts, when they be brought into the field and cried havoke, then every man to take his part. **1601** SHAKS. *Jul. C.* III. i. 273 Cæsars Spirit..Shall..with a Monarkes voyce, Cry hauocke, and let slip the Dogges of Warre. **1602** —— *Ham.* v. ii. 375 His quarry cries on hauocke. **1858** BUCKLE *Civiliz.* (1869) II. i. 76 That bold and sceptical spirit which cried havoc to the prejudices and superstitions of men.

2. Devastation, destruction; esp. in phr. ***to make havoc, play havoc*** (freq. const. *with*), in which the earlier sense of spoliation or plunder has gradually passed into that of destructive devastation. Also in weakened sense: confusion and disorder, disarray. The phrases ***to work havoc, create havoc*** are also common.

1480 CAXTON *Chron. Eng.* CCXXXIX. 265 They..slowe al alyens and despoilled al hir goodes and made hauoke. **1560** BECON *New Catech.* Wks. 1844 II. 92 Whole Jewry came to havoc, and finally both destruction and desolation. **1576** FLEMING *Panopl. Epist.* 202 Make havock of them one with another. **1609** BIBLE (Douay) *Ecclus.* xxxvi. Comm., By discord al things goe to havocke. **1635** SWAN *Spec. M.* iv. §2 (1643) 66 What havock the floud had made. **1745** P. THOMAS *Jrnl. Anson's Voy.* 22 The Scurvy..made a most dreadful Havock among us. **1812** M. E. BICKNELL *Let.* 28 Oct. in *J. Constable's Corr.* (1964) II. 91 You perfectly well know, what terrible havoc it [*sc.* meeting often] makes with your time. **1868** TENNYSON *Lucretius* 22 The wicked broth Confused the chemic labour of the blood..Made havock among those tender cells. **1871** FREEMAN *Norm. Conq.* IV. xviii. 289 The work of William at this time was simple unmitigated havoc. **1900** J. MORLEY *Cromwell* I. 3 The thirst after broad classifications works havoc with truth. **1908** E. J. BANFIELD *Confessions of Beachcomber* iv. 129 Terrestrial storms work as much if not greater havoc in the shallow places of the sea as on the land. **1910** G. D. ABRAHAM *Mountain Adv.* vi. 115 The hot sun, reflected off the snow, played havoc with his complexion. **1934** G. G. COULTON *H. W. Fowler* 156 He..displayed..anxiety about the havoc made in the projected festivities. **1949** *Times Lit. Suppl.* 4 Nov. 715/2 History has played havoc with their hopes. **1961** J. E. MANSION *Harrap's French-Eng. Dict.* 705/2 The storm ..played havoc with the crops. **1961** WEBSTER s.v. *havoc*, Several small children can create havoc in a house. **1964** *Times* 5 Sept. 9/5 Surely one can make up one's mind as to which [political party] would create less havoc if they came to power. **1965** A. NICOL *Truly Married Woman* 24, I have created enough havoc in one afternoon as it is. **1966** B. KIMENYE *Kalasanda Revisited* 86 The fine, dust-like substance enveloped him in a cloud which played havoc with the delicate membranes of his eyes and nose. **1969** *Times* 25 Mar. 16/1 The noise and clatter of high-revving engines can play havoc with a driver's nerves. **1971** B. PATTEN *Irrelevant Song* 32 This creature singled out creates Havoc with intelligence.

ˈhavoc, *v.* Infl. **-ocked, -ocking.** [f. prec. sb.]

1. *trans.* To make havoc of; to devastate; to lay waste. Also *absol.*

1577 FENTON *Gold. Epist.* 171 A great Prince..entreth into the land of his enemie..to surmount and hauock his enemy. **1648** MILTON *Tenure Kings* (1649) 38 To havock and turn upside-down whole Kingdoms of men. **1667** —— *P.L.* x. 617 See with what heat these Dogs of Hell advance, To waste and havoc yonder World. **1884** TENNYSON *Becket* I. i, Those baron-brutes That havock'd all the land in Stephen's day.

2. *intr.* To make havoc, work devastation.

1796 MRS. INCHBALD *Nature & Art* xli, Remorse.. havocked on his firm inflexible mind as it would on a weak and pliant brain.

Hence **ˈhavocking** *vbl. sb.*; also **ˈhavocker**, one who havocs or makes havoc.

c **1640** J. SMYTH *Lives Berkeleys* (1883) II. 148 This lords vast havocking of his patrimony. **1680** OTWAY *Caius Marius* I. i, This Havocker..That..hunts Our senate into holes. **1824** J. SYMMONS tr. *Æschylus' Agam.* 145 The havocker meets havock in his turn.

havoir, havour, earlier forms of HAVIOUR.

havy, obs. Sc. form of HEAVY.

†**haw** (hɔː), *sb.*¹ *Obs.* exc. *Hist.* Forms: 1 **haȝa**, 3 **haȝe, hahe**, 5 **hawȝe**, 4–6 **hawe**, 7 *dial.* **haghe**, 5– **haw**. [OE. *haȝa*, corresp. to MDu. *hage*, *haghe*, Du. *haag*, in same sense (whence *'s Graven hage*, the Count's Haw, the Hague), MLG. *hage*, ON. *hagi* (Sw. *hage* pasture-field, Da. *have* garden):—OTeut. **hagon*-; co-radicate with OHG. *hag*, *hac*, enclosure, Ger. *hag* hedge, bush, coppice, fenced place; also OHG. *hagan*, MHG. *hagen* thorn, thornbush: cf. HAY *sb.*², and HEDGE.] A hedge or encompassing fence (OE.); hence, a piece of ground enclosed or fenced in; a messuage (OE.); generally, a yard, close, or enclosure, as in ***timber-haw***. See also CHURCH-HAWE.

Beowulf (Z.) 2893 Heht ðа þæt heaðo-weorc to haȝan biodan. *c* **825** *Kent. Gloss.* in Wr.-Wülcker 70/15 *Sepis*, haȝa. **1044** in Kemble *Cod. Dipl.* IV. 86 Se haȝa binnan port þe Æȝebric himsylfan ȝetimbrod hæfde. *a* **1250** *Owl & Night.* 585 Wane þu comest to manne haȝe, þar þornes boþ and ris i-draȝe. *Ibid.* 1612 Heo hongeþ me on heore hahe. *c* **1386** CHAUCER *Pard. T.* 527 Ther was a polcat in his hawe, That..hise capons hadde yslawe. **1442** in Willis & Clark *Cambridge* (1886) I. 387 For cariage of xxxj lodes of lome.. in to the tembre haw. **1457** in Arnolde *Chron.* (1811) 72 Wharfes kranes tymbre hawes. **1594** NORDEN *Spec. Brit., Essex* 10 Certayne ladinges..wher they take in wood.. which places are called vpon the Thames, westward, hawes or woodwharves. **1674** RAY *S. & E.C. Words* 68 *A Haw*, (Kent.) a close. **1726** *Dict. Rust.* (ed. 3), *Haw*..a Close or small quantity of Land near a House; as Bean-haw, Hemp-haw. **1860** *All Year Round* No. 76. 614 St. Mary, called Wool-church, because in its haw or churchyard is the beam whereby wool is appointed to be weighed.

b. *transf.*

c **1430** *Hymns Virg.* (1867) 121 Then wolle the see wytdrawe, And wend to hys owyn hawe.

c. *attrib.*, as ***haw-yard***.

1657 HOWELL *Londinop.* 58 A great Haw-yard, or garden, of old time called Coleman Haw.

haw (hɔː), *sb.*² Forms: 1 **haȝa**, 3–7 **hawe**, (5 **hawghe**, 9 *dial.* **hag, hague, haghe, haigh**), 4– **haw**. [OE. *haȝa*, in pl. *haȝan*.

App. the same word as prec.: perh. short for **hæȝberie*, i.e. hedge-berry; but this sense appears in none of the other langs., and the history of its development is not clear.]

1. The fruit of the hawthorn.

a **1000** *Gloss.* in Wr.-Wülcker 204/20 *Cinum*, haȝan. **13..** *K. Alis.* 4983 Other mete thai ne habben Bot hawen, hepen, slon, and rabben. *c* **1374** CHAUCER *Former Age* 7 They eten mast hawes and swyche pownage. **1483** *Cath. Angl.* 179/1 An Hawghe, *cinum.* **1555** EDEN *Decades* 87 He eate none other meate but only berryes and hawes. **1626** BACON *Sylva* §737 Stores of Haws and Heps do commonly portend cold Winters. **1784** COWPER *Task* I. 120, I fed on scarlet hips and stony haws. **1883** F. M. PEARD *Contrad.* xxxii, The old thorns..ruddy with a wealth of haws. **1883** *Hampsh. Gloss.*, *Hag*, a haw, or berry of the hawthorn. **1883** *Almondbury Gloss.*, *Haghe*, or *Haigh*, the haw.

†**2.** Used as a type of a thing of no value. *Obs.*

c **1000** ÆLFRIC *Gloss.* in Wr.-Wülcker 138/39 *Gignalia*, haȝan. *a* **1100** *Voc.* Ibid. 269/5 *Quisquilia*, haȝan. **1297** R. GLOUC. (1724) 524 Al nas wurth an hawe. *c* **1340** HAMPOLE

in *Relig. Pieces fr. Thornton MS.* (1867) 81 No latyn ne lawe may helpe an hawe. *c* **1386** CHAUCER *Wife's Prol.* 659, I sette noght an haw Of his proverbes. *c* **1460** J. RUSSELL *Bk. Nurture* 99 Of suche fresch lustes set not an hawe. **1593** *Jack Straw* II. in Hazl. *Dodsley* V. 394 We'll not leave a man of law, Nor a paper worth a haw.

3. The hawthorn, *Cratægus Oxyacantha.* (Also applied with qualifying words to other species of *Cratægus*, or other similar shrubs.)

[**1557** *Tottell's Misc.* (Arb.) 260 *Testament Hawthorne*, I, Sely Haw, whose hope is past.] **1821** COL. TRIMBLE in *Open Court* (U.S.A.) XI. 244 Clearing away the haw, dogwood, and pawpaws. **1850** TENNYSON *In Mem.* c, Hoary knoll of ash and haw. **1851** LONGF. *Gold. Leg.* IV. 19 Sweet is the air with the budding haws. **1884** MILLER *Plant-n.*, Haw,.. Black, *Viburnum prunifolium*. May, or Apple, *Cratægus æstivalis*. Summer, *Cratægus flava.*

†**4.** A head or ear of grass. *Obs.*

[Etymologically perh. a different word.]

1601 HOLLAND *Pliny* II. 145 Wild Otes..beareth in the haw or head certain grains hanging down, which resemble small locusts. *Ibid.* 235 Then the haw or eare that it beareth, ought to be taken away. *a* **1825** FORBY *Voc. E. Anglia, Haw*, the ear of oats.

5. *attrib.*, as ***haw-berry***, ***-blossom***; **haw-grosbeak**, the HAWFINCH.

1772–84 COOK *Voy.* (1790) V. 1787 We saw some currant, and hawberry bushes. **1838** *Penny Cycl.* XII. 67/1 *Hawfinch*. Haw Grosbeak, Grosbeak of the modern British.

haw, *sb.*[3] Also 6–7 hawe. [Etymology uncertain.] The nictitating membrane or 'third eyelid' of a horse, dog, etc., being a triangular cartilage lying just within the inner corner of the eye, which is capable of expansion, so as to sweep dust, etc. from the eye-ball.

The haw is liable to inflammation and temporary enlargement, and it was to this affected form, which the old farriers considered an 'excrescence,' that they usually applied the name.

1523 FITZHERB. *Husb.* §89 The hawe is a sorance in a horse eye, and is lyke gristell, and maye well be cutte oute, or els it wyll haue out his eye. **1587** MASCALL *Govt. Cattle* II. (1661) 131 The haw in the eye of the horse is a little white and hard gristle in the inner corner of the eye, and it will grow. **1737** BRACKEN *Farriery Impr.* (1763) 140, I take what the Farriers call the Haws, to proceed from a long and continued Defluxion of Rheum upon the Eye. **1829** *Nat. Philos., Prelim. Treat.* 30 (U.K.S.) A third eyelid..in the horse..called the haw; it is moistened with a pulpy substance..to take hold of the dust on the eyeball, and wipe it clean off. **1865** YOUATT *Horse* viii. (1872) 159 The old farriers strangely misunderstood the nature and design of the haw. **1880** *Times* 5 June 6/5 A chief point in bloodhounds was the appearance and quality of the 'haw'. **1893** H. DALZIEL *Diseases of Dogs* (ed. 3) 62 Enlargement of the haw..This membrane sometimes becomes inflamed and enlarged, interfering with the sight and preventing the eyelids from closing.

†**b.** *transf.* Applied to an excresence in the human eye. *Obs.*

c **1450** *ME. Med. Bk.* (Heinrich) 98 A charme for þe hawe in þe ye. *c* **1550** LLOYD *Treas. Health* (1585) F ij, The joyce of the Lyly rote put into thy eye taketh awaye the hawe. **1684** *Lond. Gaz.* No. 1915/4 Joshua Bugge, Aged 15 years.. having a Haw or Speck on his left Eye.

haw, *sb.*[4]: see HAW *int.*[1] and *sb.*[4]

haw, *a. Obs.* exc. *Sc.* Forms: 1 heawi, hęwi, hæwi, hawi, hæwen, 5 haa, 6– haw (8 *Sc.* haave). [OE. *háwi*, *hǽwi*, *héawi*, whence *hǽwen* blue, discoloured.] †**a.** Blue, azure; bluish, grayish- or greenish-blue; of a dull leaden blue. *Obs.* **b.** Discoloured, livid. *Sc.*

a **700** *Epinal Gloss.* 221 *C(a)erula*, haeuui [*Erf.* haui]. *c* **725** *Corpus Gloss.* 444 *C(a)erula*, heawi. *Ibid.* 981 *Glaucum*, heauui, grei. *c* **1420** *Anturs of Arth.* ii, Hur hud of a haa hew. *c* **1450** HENRYSON *Test. Cres.* 257 Hawe as the leed, of colour nothing clere. **1513** DOUGLAS *Æneis* III. i. 121 Crownit with garlandis all of haw see hewis. **16..** *Sir P. Spens* in Child *Ballads* III. lviii. (1885) 28/2 He saw the green haw sea. **1768** ROSS *Helenore* 23 (Jam.) Twa shepherds out of breath..and as haw as death. **1785** R. FORBES *Poems in Buchan Dial.* 8 (Jam.) He look'd sae haave as gin a dwam Had just o'ercast his heart.

haw, *int.*[1] and *sb.*[4] [Echoic.] An utterance marking hesitation: cf. HA *int.* 3. Usually in collocation with *hum*. See also HAW-HAW.

1679 *Hist. Somervilles* in *Ann. Lesmahagow* (1864) 73 She had a little haugh in her speech. *a* **1680** BUTLER *Rem.* (1759) I. 180 His frequent and pathetic hums and haws. *a* **1729** CONGREVE *Wks.* (1761) III. 459 (Jod.) If thro' any hums or haws, There haps an intervening pause. **1886** *Pall Mall G.* 27 Aug. 14/1 Pauses filled by a prolonged 'haw'.

haw, *int.*[2] and *sb.*[5] *dial.* and *U.S.* A call used to direct a horse or team to turn to the left.

1843 *Knickerbocker* XXI. 494 He admonishes them with his goad, and ejaculates, 'Haw'. **1843** 'R. CARLTON' *New Purchase* xxvi. 239 Whoas, gees and haws. **1856** J. C. MORTON *Cycl. Agric.* II. 723/2 Horses—terms used in directing—... Cheshire... To left. Haw. **1864** WEBSTER s.v., *Haw, haw here*;—words used by teamsters in guiding their teams. **1930** *Amer. Speech* V. 419 *Haw*, direction given to oxen to turn to the left. **1972** *Even. Telegram* (St. John's, Nwfndl.) 24 June 14/3 'Gee' tells the dogs to take a right turn, and 'Haw' means left.

haw, *v.*[1] [f. HAW *int.*[1]] *intr.* To utter 'haw!' as an expression of hesitation. Usually in the collocation ***hum (hem) and haw***: see HUM *v.*

1632 MASSINGER & FIELD *Fatal Dowry* IV. i, *Nov.* Ha? *Bella.* D'ee stand Humming and hawing now? **1739** *Joe Miller's Jests* cxiii, The Fellow was loath to speak, but humm'd and haw'd for a good Space. **1748** RICHARDSON *Clarissa* (1811) VII. 47 Such a humming and hawing caitiff. **1814** L. HUNT *Feast of Poets* 11 A whole court of Aldermen hawing and humming. **1884** W. C. SMITH *Kildrostan* 62 Public meetings where no heart is, And a chairman haws and hums.

haw, *v.*[2] *U.S.* (but Eng. *dial.* in quot. 1911). [f. HAW *int.*[2] and *sb.*[5]] **a.** *intr.* Of a horse or team: to turn to the left. Also *fig.* (see quot. 1864).

1846 *Knickerbocker* XXVII. 119 The plough-boy has hardly energy to cry out..'Gee-haw, there, I tell you to haw, now.' **1861** *Trans. Ill. Agric. Soc.* IV. 99 They were required to plow lands of about fifteen rods in length, and 'haw' about. **1864** WEBSTER s.v., *To haw and gee*, or *haw and gee about*, to go from one thing to another without good reason; to have no settled purpose; to be irresolute or unstable. (*Colloq.*) **1911** J. MASEFIELD *Everlasting Mercy* 86 Now and then he seems to stoop To clear the coulter with the scoop, Or touch an ox to haw or gee.

b. *trans.* To direct (a horse, etc.) to turn to the left. Also *fig.*

1864 WEBSTER s.v., *To haw and gee*, or *haw and gee about*, to lead this way and that at will; to lead by the nose; to master or control. (*Colloq.*) **1867** [see GEE *v.*[2] b].

Hence **hawing** *vbl. sb.*

1843 'R. CARLTON' *New Purchase* xvi. 119 After performing wonders on the journey from Philadelphia to the West in hawing and geeing. **1867** [see GEE *v.*[2] b].

haw, obs. form of AWE.

haw(e, obs. var. HOE.

Hawaiian (hə'waɪən), *a.* and *sb.* Also Hawaian. [f. *Hawaii* + -AN.] **A.** *adj.* Of or pertaining to the island of Hawaii, or to the whole group of the Sandwich Islands in the North Pacific. **B.** *sb.* **1.** A native or inhabitant of Hawaii. **2.** The language of Hawaii, belonging to the Malayo-Polynesian group.

1825 W. ELLIS *Jrnl. Tour Hawaii* 205 The account given this evening of the Hawaiian *hades.* **1859** [see *inter-island* s.v. INTER- 5]. **1864** W. D. ALEXANDER *Hawaiian Gram.* 20 What would form a long sentence in English, in Hawaiian is generally broken up into several independent propositions. **1877** T. H. STREETS *Nat. Hist. Hawaiian & Fanning Isl.* 8 The Fanning group, with the exception of the Hawaiian, were the only islands visited in the Pacific. **1877** L. H. MORGAN *Anc. Society* III. ii. 404 These are terms in Hawaiian for grandparent. **1893** *Funk's Stand. Dict.* I. 825/1 *Hawaiian*, a native..of Hawaii. **1913** R. BROOKE *Coll. Poems* (1918) 28 And new stars burn into the ancient skies, Over the murmurous soft Hawaian sea. **1921** *Nature* 20 Jan. 673/1 Some broad features of Hawaiian petrology. **1929** C. H. SMITH *Bridge of Life* ii. 29 White men, Chinese, Japanese, Hawaiians and many others slept in the common dormitory. **1936** *Discovery* June 198/2 He is bold enough to believe that the Hawaiian native practitioners can handle elemental spirits 'like tame animals'. **1957** P. WORSLEY *Trumpet shall Sound* i. 30 Sects..have also appeared amongst the.. Hawaiians. **1970** *Western Folklore* XXIX. 234 The slider occasionally covers several strings at once to produce different chords in the 'Hawaiian' style.

II. *Special Combs.* **Hawaiian goose**, a rare bird, *Branta sandvicensis*, formerly called the Sandwich Island goose; **Hawaiian guitar**, a type of guitar, usually held in a horizontal position, in which the pitch is obtained by placing a small metal bar on the strings and moving it up and down to produce *glissando* effects; hence ***Hawaiian guitarist***, ***orchestra***; **Hawaiian** (or **Hawaii**) **shirt**, a highly coloured and gaily patterned shirt.

[**1834** *Proc. Zool. Soc.* 41 A specimen was exhibited of the young of the *Sandwich Island Goose.*] **1915** W. A. BRYAN *Nat. Hist. Hawaii* xxv. 336 The nene or Hawaiian goose.. is confined to the Island of Hawaii, where it leads a life of seclusion, high up on the mountainside. **1958** E. T. GILLIARD *Living Birds of World* 80/2 One of the rarest is the néné or Hawaiian Goose (*Branta sandvicensis*) of which less than 70 wild birds are thought to survive. **1964** *Listener* 23 July 125/1 The Hawaiian goose..had it not been for special breeding studies..would have already become extinct. **1972** G. DURRELL *Catch me a Colobus* x. 219 The Hawaiian goose. .. This beautiful bird was almost extinct but, due to the sensible attitude of the Hawaiian authorities and the far-sightedness of Peter Scott, it has been saved from certain extinction. **1926** H. O. OSGOOD *So this is Jazz* 97 Practice with it..will enable the trumpeters..to imitate the violin, Hawaiian steel guitar, oboe [etc.]. **1928** *Melody Maker* Feb. 188/2, I was at first very surprised at the 'Hawaiian guitar' solos in some of the waltzes. **1935** L. MACNEICE *Poems* 13 Jazz-weary of years of drums and Hawaiian guitar. **1968** *Blues Unlimited* Nov. 20 He cannot play standard guitar, but plays a hawaiian guitar on a stand. **1959** 'F. NEWTON' *Jazz Scene* xii. 203 As he played, he pressed a knife on the strings of the guitar in a manner popularised by Hawaiian guitarists who used steel bars. **1955** L. FEATHER *Encycl. Jazz* vii. 79 The Decca company began to record him..in duets with pop singers, and even with Hawaiian orchestras. **1955** G. GREENE *Quiet American* II. i. 90, I noticed that he was wearing a Hawaii shirt, even though it was comparatively restrained in colour and design. **1962** L. DEIGHTON *Ipcress File* xviii. 114 Dalby had changed into a red Hawaiian shirt with large blue and yellow flowers across it. **1968** R. CLAPPERTON *No News on Monday* xi. 129 He was wearing a red Hawaiian shirt, unbuttoned.

haward, obs. form of HAYWARD.

hawbart, obs. form of HALBERD.

hawbe, obs. form of ALB.

c **1475** *Voc.* in Wr.-Wülcker 755/23 *Hec alba*, a hawbe.

hawberg, -berke, -brek, obs. ff. HAUBERK.

hawbergeon, -berioun, -byrschown, etc., obs. var. HABERGEON.

hawbitzer, obs. form of HOWITZER.

hawbuck ('hɔːbək). [perh. f. HAW *sb.*[1] or [2] + BUCK *sb.*[1] 2.] An unmannerly lout; a country bumpkin.

1805 *Times* in *Spirit Pub. Jrnls.* (1806) IX. 312, [I] Damned the hawbuck who quizzed us, and agreed to cross the fields towards Newington. **1851** *Beck's Florist* 32 Davy ..called all the boys in our brig a set of haw-bucks. **1855** KINGSLEY *Westw. Ho* (1861) 97 'Slife, Sir, sorrow is making a hawbuck of me. **1858** *Leeds Express* 14 Aug. 4/3 The veriest hawbuck that ever grew and flourished in the wilds of Kent.

Hawcubite ('hɔːkəbaɪt). Also Hawca-, Hawku-. One of a band of dissolute young men who infested the streets of London in the beginning of the 18th century; a street-bully, a ruffian.

1712 SWIFT *Wonderf. Proph.* Wks. 1755 III. I. 174, I am the porter, that was barbarously slain in Fleet street: by the Mohocks and Hawcubites was I slain. **1880** BREWER *Reader's Hand-bk., Hawcabite.* **1882** *Athenæum* 25 Nov. 693/1 Pounce in the 'Tender Husband'..having a wholesome distrust at his return of possible Mohocks and Hawkubites.

†'**hawdod.** *dial. Obs.* [app. f. HAW *a.* blue + DOD *sb.*[2]] A name for the Blue Cornflower, *Centaurea Cyanus* (Britten and Holland).

1523 FITZHERB. *Husb.* §20 Diuers maner of wedes, as thistyls, kedlokes, dockes..gouldes, haudoddes, dogfennel. *Ibid.*, Hawdod hath a blewe floure, and a fewe lyttell leues.. and groweth comonly in rye vpon leane grounde, and dothe lyttel hurte. **1730** in *Yorks. Diaries* (Surtees) 296 (Brit. & Hol.) A flower call'd hawdods.

hawe, obs. Sc. and north. form of HALL[1].

†**hawe-bake.** *Obs.* In the following, usually taken as = 'haw(s) baken', baked haws, equivalent to 'plain fare'; but this is doubtful.

c **1386** CHAUCER *Man of Law's Prol.* 95 But nathelees I recche noght a bene Though I come after hym with hawebake [*Camb. MS.* aw bake, *Lansdowne* halve bake] I speke in prose and lat him rymes make.

hawel, obs. form of HAIL *sb.*[1] and *v.*[1]

'**hawer.** [f. HAW *v.*[1] + -ER[1].] One who 'haws'.

1820 MISS MITFORD in L'Estrange *Life* (1870) II. 119 He is such a doubter,—such a hummer and hawer.

hawes, obs. f. *hawse*: see HALSE *sb.*

hawfinch ('hɔːfɪnʃ). [f. HAW *sb.*[2] + FINCH.] The common grosbeak, *Coccothraustes vulgaris*, a bird about six inches in length, having a large strong beak adapted for breaking the hard seeds and kernels which form its food.

1674 RAY *Collect. Words, Birds* 88. **1759** B. STILLINGFL. tr. *Biberg's Econ. Nat.* in *Misc. Tracts* (1762) 66 The cross-bill that lives on the fir-cones, and the hawfinch that feeds on the pine-cones. **1881** *Standard* 2 Mar. 5 The hawfinch some years ago was as common in Epping Forest as are pigeons in the Guildhall-yard.

hawgher, obs. form of HEIFER.

haw-haw ('hɔː'hɔː), *int.*, *sb.*, and *a.* [Echoic; cf. HA HA.]

A. *int.* An expression of hesitation uttered repeatedly in an affected tone. Also, the representation of loud or boisterous laughter.

1834 SEBA SMITH *Maj. J. Downing's Lett.* (1835) 160 'Major, call back Jany, and Barry, and Amos, and haw-haw-haw', says the Gineral.

B. *sb.* The utterance of *haw haw*; a loud or boisterous laugh, a guffaw.

1834 JAMES *Robber* i, The first indication of his coming was a peal of laughter, a loud 'Haw, haw, haw'. **1889** A. R. HOPE in *Boy's Own Paper* 10 Aug. 715/3 There was another chorus of haw-haws, which made Ronald's temper boil over.

C. *attrib.* or *adj.* Characterized by the utterance of *haw haw* as an affected expression of hesitation. Freq. applied to what is taken to resemble upper-class speech.

1841 LYTTON *Nt. & Morn.* (1851) 314 (Hoppe) 'Hush!' said the stranger, perfectly unconcerned, and regaining the dignity of his haw haw enunciation. **1866** *Cornh. Mag.* Oct. 464 The affected, lisping, and haw-haw fool. **1867** F. HARRISON *Choice Bks.* (1891) 102 Lounging with that ineffable haw-haw air of your Rotten Row. **1900** *Daily News* 8 Oct., The Censor was one of those haw-haw officers, who look down upon men like me as unnecessary upon this earth. *Ibid.* 20 Nov. 3/5 The answer I got was in Mr. Hales's 'haw-haw' style. 'Ah've nothing to dah with Mafeking.' **1913** R. BROOKE *Let.* 22 Nov. (1968) 535 Weedy Australian clerks, uncertain whether they most despise a 'haw-haw Englishman', or a 'dam nigger'. **1941** *Time* 27 Jan. 22/1 Declaring that BBC announcers were 'too haw haw' in their diction, he is responsible for the nickname 'Lord Haw-Haw' given to Nazi propagandist William Joyce. **1953** K. JACKSON *Lang. & Hist. Early Brit.* 108 The language..must have seemed..upper class and 'haw-haw'. **1968** *Listener* 9 May 615/2 Kuo-yü spoken in the next room can sound just like somewhat haw-haw English.

Hence **haw-'hawism**, the habit of affectedly uttering *haw haw*.

1867 E. YATES *Forlorn Hope* x, Forbes would assume a languid haw-hawism.

haw-haw, *v.* [f. prec.] **a.** *intr.* To utter *haw haw*; to laugh loudly or boisterously. **b.** *trans.* To laugh at. Hence **haw-hawing** *vbl. sb.*

1834 SEBA SMITH *Maj. J. Downing's Lett.* (1835) 160 He step'd up to me..throw'd his head back, and haw-haw'd right out. **1862** THACKERAY *Adv. Philip* III. xxxi. 30 It's good to see him haw-haw Bickerton. **1889** A. R. HOPE in *Boy's Own Paper* 10 Aug. 715/3 The other rustics haw-hawed at their master's repartee. **1922** Z. GREY *To Last Man* x. 226 Some of the gang haw-hawed him.

haw-haw, var. HA-HA *sb.*[2]

hawin, -yn, obs. forms of HAVEN.

hawk (hɔːk), *sb.*[1] Forms: 1 hafoc, heafoc, -uc, (haefuc, habuc, hæbuc), 2 hauek, heauek, 2-4 havek, 3 havec, 3-4 hauck, 3-7 hauk(e, 5-6 halk, 5-7 hawke, 7 haulk, 7- hawk. [Com. Teut.: OE. *habuc, heafoc* = OS. *haboc-* (in proper names) (MDu. *havic, havec, hawic,* Du. *havik,* EFris. *hâfke,* WFris. *hauck*), OHG. *habuh, hapuh,* MHG. *habech, -ich,* G. *habicht,* ON. *hauk-r,* from **hafukr* (Sw. *hök,* Da. *hög*):—OTeut. **habuko-z*; generally referred to root *hab-, haf-* to seize, as L. *accipiter* to *capere.*]

1. a. Any diurnal bird of prey used in falconry; any bird of the family *Falconidæ*. In *Nat. Hist.*, restricted to a bird of the subfamily *Accipitrinæ*, with rounded and comparatively short wings, which chases its prey near the ground; distinguished from a falcon or bird of the subfamily *Falconinæ*, which has long pointed wings and lofty flight.

hawk of the fist, the lure, the soar: see quots. 1841, 1879. *a* **700** *Epinal Gl.* 1023 *Horodius*, uualh[h]ebuc [*Erfurt* uualhhæbuc]. *c* **725** *Corpus Gl.* 1890 *Soricarius*, mushabuc. *a* **800** *Leiden Gloss.* 51 in *O.E. Texts* 112 *Accipitres* [-*iter*], haefuc. *a* **1000** *Wyrde* 86 in *Exeter Bk.* lf. 88 b (Bosw.) Sum sceal wildne fuȝol atemian heafoc. *c* **1175** *Lamb. Hom.* 49 þe habbeð feire huses..heauekes and hundes. *c* **1200** *Trin. Coll. Hom.* 179 Hundes and hauekes and hors and wepnes. *a* **1250** *Owl & Night.* 307 þe havec folȝeþ gode rede He fliht his wei. *c* **1325** *Rel. Ant.* I. 125 Y gladie for no song, Of haveke ne of hounde. *c* **1440** *Promp. Parv.* 230/2 Hawke, *falco.* **1538** STARKEY *England* II. ii. 189 Theyr haukys and theyr houndys. **1550** J. COKE *Eng. & Fr. Heralds* §8 (1877) 60 We have hawkes of the towre, as leonardes, leonerettes, fawcons, jeafawcons, hobbes, & merlyons. **1612** DRAYTON *Poly-olb.* iii. 42 His deepe mouth'd Hound to hunt, his long-wing'd Haulk to flie. **1614** BP. HALL *Recoll. Treat.* 161 The Soule, like unto some noble Hauke, lets passe the crowes. **1674** N. COX *Gentl. Recreat.* (1677) 162 The Age of a Hawk; The first year, a Soarage. The second year, an Interview. The third year, a White Hawk. The fourth year, a Hawk of the first Coat. **1727-51** CHAMBERS *Cycl.* s.v., When.. carefully looked after, she [the merlin] proves an excellent hawk. **1801** STRUTT *Sports & Past.* I. ii. 33 The books of hawking assign to the different ranks of persons the sort of hawks proper to be used by them..The eagle, the vulture, and the merloun, for an emperor..The gos-hawk, for a yeoman..The sparrow-hawk for a priest. **1841** BELANY *Falconry* 6, *Hawk of the Fist.* One that flies direct off the fist without mounting or waiting-on. *Ibid., Hawk of the Soar.* One that mounts in the air, and waits-on until the game be put up. **1879** E. D. RADCLIFFE in *Encycl. Brit.* IX. 6 The first class comprises 'falcons', 'long-winged hawks', or 'hawks of the lure';..The second class is that of 'hawks', 'short-winged hawks', or 'hawks of the fist'. **1893** NEWTON *Dict. Birds, Hawk*, a word of indefinite meaning, being often used to signify all diurnal Birds-of-Prey which are neither Vultures nor Eagles, and again more exclusively for those of the remainder which are not Buzzards, Falcons, Harriers or Kites.

b. With prefixed word indicating species, varieties, sorts used in hawking, etc.: as *brush-, field-, fishing-, game-, long-* or *short-winged*, etc. Also **black hawk**, the American rough-legged buzzard; **jack-hawk**, a male hawk; **kitchen hawk** (see quot. 1686); **musket-, small-bird-,** or **spar-hawk**, the Sparrow-hawk; **ringtail hawk** (*Falco Hudsonius*); **sharp-shinned hawk** (*U.S.*), a small species (*Accipiter fuscus*) with extremely slender shanks, also called ***pigeon hawk***. (See under their first element *duck-, fish-, lark-, mouse-, partridge-, quail-hawk*; also GOSHAWK, HOBBY-, PIGEON-, SPARROW-HAWK. etc.).

1486 *Bk. St. Albans* D iv, Ther is a Spare hawke, and he is an hawke for a prest. **1615** W. LAWSON *Orch. & Gard.* (1626) 45 If you have a..Spar-hawke in Winter to make the Black-bird stoop into a bush or hedge. **1674** N. COX *Gentl. Recreat.* (1677) 172 This is a great fault, and more incident to and worse in Field-Hawks than such as are fitted for the River. **1686** BLOME *Gentl. Recreat.* II. 29 The Lanner..is a Hawk well known..being called a Kitchin Hawk. *a* **1700** B. E. *Dict. Cant. Crew, Jack-hawk*, the Male. **1772** FORSTER in *Phil. Trans.* LXII. 382 This species [Pigeon Hawk] is called a small-bird hawk at Hudson's Bay. **1872** COUES *Key N. Amer. Birds* (1884) 528 *Accipiter fuscus*, sharp-shinned Hawk, 'Pigeon' Hawk, so-called, but not to be confounded with *Falco columbarius. Ibid.* 549 American 'Rough-legged Buzzard' 'Black Hawk'. **1873** SIR W. BULLER *Birds N. Zealand* I. 222 The continuous screaming of the Bush-Hawk is understood by the natives to be a sure indication of change.

c. Proverbs and phrases. (See also BUZZARD *sb.*[1] 1 b, HANDSAW b, HERONSEW.)

c **1386** CHAUCER *Reeve's T.* 214 With empty hand, men may none haukes tulle [allure]. *c* **1530** H. RHODES *Bk. Nurture* 740 in *Babees Bk.* 102 For empty fystes, men vse to say, cannot the Hawke retayne. **1832** J. P. KENNEDY *Swallow B.* (1860) 17, I entered Richmond between hawk and buzzard [= at twilight]. **1846** G. S. FABER *Lett. on Tractarian Secess.* 171 As different from..modern Popery, as a hawk from a handspike.

2. With qualifying word as ***night-hawk, dor-hawk, gnat-hawk, moth-hawk, screech-hawk***, applied to the goatsucker. (See these words.)

3. *fig.* Applied to a person, in various senses derived from the nature of the bird of prey: e.g. one who preys on others, a rapacious person, a sharper or cheat; one who is keen and grasping; an officer of the law who pounces on criminals (as in vagabonds' phrase, ***ware the hawk***: see WARE). Also in *Politics*, a person who advocates a hard-line or warlike policy, opp. to a *dove* (cf. DOVE *sb.* 2 f). Also *attrib.* or as quasi-*adj.*

1548 HALL *Chron., Edw. IV*, 199 b, If he might..allure the duke to his partie, that king Edward should be destitute of one of his best Hawkes. *a* **1553** UDALL *Royster D.* III. iii. (Arb.) 48 Ye were take vp for haukes. *a* **1700** B. E. *Dict. Cant. Crew, Hawk*, a Sharper. **1824** GEN. P. THOMPSON *Exerc.* (1842) III. 328 Men are hawks when they view their interests singly, and beetles when they are to lose in crowds. **1834** H. AINSWORTH *Rookwood* I. iii. (Farmer), The game's spoiled this time..the hawks are upon us. **1843** LEVER *J. Hinton* ix. (1878) 56 He..ended by becoming a hawk, where he had begun as a pigeon. **1962, 1964** [see DOVE *sb.* 2 f]. **1965** *Economist* 25 Sept. 1189/2 President Ayub's difficulties in curbing the 'hawks' in his country. **1966, 1967** [see DOVE *sb.* 2 f]. **1967** D. BOULTON *Objection Overruled* iii. 85 The committee seems to have become immersed immediately in a struggle between doves and hawks. **1969** *Guardian* 21 Feb. 10/2 The hawks at the Treasury..want to have one more hack at consumption.

4. *attrib.* and *Comb.* **a.** obvious combs., as ***hawk-cage, -hood, -perch; hawk-faced, -headed*** adjs.

1483 *Cath. Angl.* 179/1 An Hawke bage, *cassidile.* **1743-51** G. EDWARDS *Nat. Hist. Birds* 165 The Hawk-Headed Parrot. **1812** *Sporting Mag.* XXXIX. 27 The hawk-cage. **1832** G. LONG *Egypt. Antiq.* I. x. 222 The hawk-headed sphinx. **1859** TENNYSON *Enid* 280 O wretched set of sparrows..Who pipe of nothing but of sparrow-hawks! Speak, if you be not like the rest, hawk-mad. **1889** O. WILDE in *19th Cent.* Jan. 47 She has hawk-faced gods that worship her. **1891** KIPLING *Man & Beast in India* 55 The hawk-hood of soft deerskin..jesses, lures, and hawk-bells, are still regularly made in the Punjab. **1932** WODEHOUSE *Louder & Funnier* 68 Just one more of those curt, hawk-faced amateur investigators. **1936** *Discovery* Dec. 380/2 A hawk-faced negro of Benin type. **1954** 'R. CROMPTON' *William & Moon Rocket* iv. 101 Trying to look keen-eyed and hawk-faced, the two made their way round the cottage to the little back garden.

b. Special combs. **hawk-cuckoo**, an Indian cuckoo, *Cuculus* (*Hierococcyx*) *varius*, resembling a hawk in appearance; **hawk eagle**, an eagle of the genus *Nisaetus*; **hawk-eye**, (*a*) *U.S.*, colloq. appellation of a native or inhabitant of Iowa, popularly called the 'Hawk-eye State'; (*b*) (a person with) a keen eye like that of a hawk; cf. HAWK'S EYE 1; also *transf.*; **hawk-eyed** *a.*, having eyes like a hawk's; very keen-sighted; **hawk-fly**, a fly of the family *Asilidæ*, also called hornet-flies, which prey on other insects; **† hawk's-foot, -feet**, an old name for the columbine; **hawk-kite**, a kite made of silk or cotton in form of a hawk, used in shooting to make the birds lie; **hawk's meat**, food for a hawk; also *fig.* (cf. 3); **hawk-nut**, a name for the earth-nut or pig-nut; **hawk-parrot**, a parrot of the genus *Deroptyus*; **hawk-swallow**, a local name for the swift; **hawkwise** *adv.*, in the manner of a hawk.

1862 T. C. JERDON *Birds of India* I. 329 The Common *Hawk-Cuckoo..is the common Cuckoo of the plains of India. **1901** *Westm. Gaz.* 8 Aug. 8/2 The Zoological Society have lately received..a specimen of the hawk-cuckoo. **1960** M. MACDONALD *Birds in my Indian Garden* 41 It was the Common Hawk-cuckoo, whose monotonously, maddeningly reiterated phrase..gives it the nickname of Brainfever Bird. **1883** *Cassell's Nat. Hist.* III. 284 *Hawk Eagles (*Nisaëtus*), remarkable for their long legs. **1823** J. F. COOPER *Pioneers* II. 44 *Hawk-eye. **1826** —— *Last of Mohicans* III. vii. 160, I am the man..that got..the compliment of Hawk-eye from the Delawares. **1833** [see HAWK'S EYE 1]. **1839** (*title*) Hawk-eye and Iowa Patriot. **1845** [see CORN-CRACKER 1]. **186.** in F. Moore *Songs of Soldiers* (1864) 114 We have come from the prairies Of the young Hawkeye State. **1901** *Lady's Realm* X. 552/2 The most contemptuous glances of her hawk-eyes. **1911** C. HARRIS *Eve's Second Husband* 244 When he ran for Congress the hawkeye of more than one newspaper in the state was turned ..upon him. **1913** D. H. LAWRENCE *Love Poems* 45 'Er black hawk-eyes as I've Mistrusted all along! **1960** *Ottawa Citizen* 18 Nov. 5/4 Across..Canada,..74 federal hawkeyes keep a watch on hundreds of millions of dollars being paid out to unemployed persons. **1966** *Listener* 2 June 796/2 The head's wife was known behind her back as Hawk-eye from her habit of seeing everything. **1818** TODD, **Hawk-eyed.* **1849** ROBERTSON *Serm.* Ser. I. xiii. (1866) 227 The hawk-eyed deities of Egypt..implied omniscience. **1890** BOLDREWOOD *Col. Reformer* (1891) 335 The hawk-eyed Piambook had descried the stranded coach..about a mile off. **1747** GOULD *Eng. Ants* 6 The Dragon, or more properly, large *Hawk-fly. **1883** *Cassell's Nat. Hist.* VI. 86 These insects (the *Asilidæ*) ..from their habits, might very well be called 'Hawk Flies'. *a* **1500** *Sloane MS.* 5, lf. 6/1 *Columbina, pes aucipitis, idem* G[allice] *columbine*, A[nglice] *hauekesfet. *Ibid.* 10/2 *Pes aucipitis*, A[nglice] hauekesfot. **1888** LL. PRYCE *Pheasant Rearing* 161 Who can make a really satisfactory *hawk kite? **1577** HARRISON *England* II. i. (1877) I. 34 A minister taking a benefice..was inforced to paie to his patrone twentie quarters of otes, ten quarters of wheate, and sixteene yeerelie of barleie, which he called *hawkes meat. **1684** R. H. *School Recreat.* 82 Wash your Hawks-meat with the Juice thereof when you feed him. **1724** *Ray's Synops. Stirp.* 209 Earth-nut, or Kipper-nut.. by the Vulgar Pignuts..in some Places *Hawknut. **1885** SWAINSON *Prov. Names Birds* 96 Swift..*Hawk swallow. From its habit of hawking for flies. **1818** KEATS *Endym.* IV. 514 Her steed a little higher soar'd, and then Dropt *hawkwise to the Earth.

† hawk, *sb.*[2] *Obs.* [Cf. HECK *sb.*[1] 2.] A kind of fish-trap: see quots.

1669 WORLIDGE *Syst. Agric.* (1681) 252 There is a sort of Engine, by some termed a Hawk, made almost like unto a Fish-pot, being a square frame of Timber fitted to the place ..and wrought with Wire to a point almost, so that what Fish soever go through the same, cannot go back again. **1705** *Act 4 & 5 Anne* c. 8 §5 Nets, Pots, Racks, Hawks, Gins or other Devices to kill Salmon.

hawk (hɔːk), *sb.*[3] [Origin uncertain.] A plasterer's tool: see quots. Hence **hawk-boy**.

1700 MOXON *Mech. Exerc.* 12 Tools relating to Plastering ..3. A Hawke, made of Wood about the bigness of a square Trencher, with a handle..whereon the Lime and Hair being put, they take from it more or less as they please. **1823** *Builder's Perp. Price-Bk.* (Kelly) 142 Hawk-boy, per day 1*s.* 9*d.* **1842-76** GWILT *Archit.* Gloss., *Hawk*, a small quadrangular tool with a handle, used by a plasterer, on which the stuff required by him is served..He has always a boy attending on him, by whom he is supplied with the material. The boy in question is called a Hawk boy. **1892** SIR G. DUFFY in *Contemp. Rev.* Jan. 152 A plasterer called to the boy to bring him his hawk.

hawk, *sb.*[4] [f. HAWK *v.*[3]] An effort made to clear the throat; the noise made in such an effort.

1604 T. M. *Black Bk.* in *Middleton's Wks.* (Bullen) VIII. 18 After a rotten hawk and a hem, he began to spit. **1755** JOHNSON, *Hawk*..an effort to force phlegm up the throat.

hawk, dial. form of HACK *sb.*[1] 1 b.

1808-18 JAMIESON, *Hawk*, a dung fork. **1893** *Northumbld. Gloss., Hawk*, an implement or hand-tool for filling manure.

hawk (hɔːk), *v.*[1] [f. HAWK *sb.*[1]]

1. *intr.* To chase or hunt game with a trained hawk; to engage in or practise falconry.

1340-70 *Alex. & Dind.* 299 For to hauke ne hunte haue we no leue. *c* **1345** *Orpheo* 294 Every on an hauke on honed bere, And went haukyng by the rivere. **1548** LATIMER *Ploughers* (Arb.) 25 Thei hauke, thei hunt, thei card, thei dyce. **1697** R. PEIRCE *Bath Mem.* I. iv. 81 [He] went hence, to his own House, to Hawk (after the Harvest was in) for a Month. **1884** TENNYSON *Becket* 45 Where is the King?.. Gone hawking on the Nene.

b. *trans.* Cf. *to hunt a cover.*

1783 AINSWORTH *Lat. Dict.* (Morell) I. s.v., Let us first hawk this ersh, for here lieth a covey.

2. *intr.* Of birds or insects: To hunt on the wing.

1399 *Pol. Poems* (Rolls) I. 389 Thus hawkyd this egle, and hoved above. **1697** DRYDEN *Virg. Æneid* XII. 693 As the black swallow..Now hawks above, now skims along the flood To furnish her loquacious nest with Food. **1768** G. WHITE *Selborne* xxi. (1853) 89 The bird [a martin] was hawking briskly after the flies. **1852** THOMAS in *Zoologist* 3650 As daybreak advanced, I could see the fern-owls.. hawking for moths. **1879** JEFFERIES *Wild Life in S. Co.* 318 A dragon fly, hawking to and fro on the sunny side of the hedge.

b. *trans.* To pursue or attack on the wing, as a hawk does; to prey upon while flying.

1825 R. P. WARD *Tremaine* III. xvii. 316 The lark sings to the moment when she is hawked. **1868** KINGSLEY *Christmas Day* 15 Flitting bats Hawk the pale moths of winter.

3. *to hawk at*: to fly at or attack on the wing, as a hawk does. Of a person: To fly a hawk at.

1605 SHAKS. *Macb.* II. iv. 13 A Faulcon towring in her pride of place, Was by a Mowsing Owle hawkt at, and kill'd. **1633** G. HERBERT *Temple, Sacrifice* xxiii, Who does hawk at eagles with a dove? **1690** LOCKE *Hum. Und.* Ep. to Rdr. 7 He that hawks at Larks and Sparrows has no less Sport..than he that flies at nobler Game. **1872** RUSKIN *Eagle's N.* §36 Will you hawk at game or carrion?

fig. **1647** N. BACON *Disc. Govt. Eng.* I. lvii. (1739) 106 He hawked at all manner of game, France, Scotland, England, Laity, Clergy. **1820** SCOTT *Abbot* xx, To hawk at one brother with another, is less than fair play. **1886** H. SMART *Outsider* I. ii. 28 Accustomed to be welcomed with smiles, and even hawked at by young ladies on promotion.

b. *trans.* To let fly.

1709 STRYPE *Ann. Ref.* I. lii. 563 They straightway hawked at their adversaries the terrible name of the high commission.

† 4. *to hawk after* (*for*): to hunt after, to endeavour to catch or gain. *Obs.*

c **1510** MORE *Picus* Wks. 15/1 All the aduauntage that ye hawke after, and all the fauour of the court. **1548** UDALL, etc. *Erasm. Par. Matt.* xxiii. 107 To hawke for a vayne opinion of holines. **1581** MARBECK *Bk. of Notes* 1076 When we do any good deed..we should not hunt and hauke after the praise of men. **1700** ASTRY tr. *Saavedra-Faxardo* II. 98 It hawks after his Favour, with the Nets of Flattery. **1720** *Lett. fr. Lond. Jrnl.* (1721) 9 A Bookseller..hawked at the Inn for Oxford Scholars.

hawk (hɔːk), *v.*[2] Also 6 hauk(e. [app. a back formation from HAWKER *sb.*[2]]

1. *intr.* To practise the trade of a hawker.

1542-3 *Act 34 & 35 Hen. VIII*, c. 10 §2 Euill disposed persons..vse daily the craft and subtilty of hauking abroad in the Country, to Villages and to mens houses, putting the same naughty ware to sale secretly. **1676** MARVELL *Mr. Smirke* 33 The little Emissaryes..hawke about from London to Westminster with their Britches stiffe with the Copyes, and will sell them to any one. **1712** ARBUTHNOT

John Bull III. iv, To go hawking and peddling about the streets, selling knives, scissors, and shoe-buckles.

2. *trans.* To carry *about* from place to place and offer for sale; to cry in the street.

1713 SWIFT *Imit. Hor.* I. vii. 41 His works were hawk'd in ev'ry street, But seldom rose above a sheet. **1759** *Compl. Let.-writer* (ed. 6) 215 They immediately hawked it about to every surgeon. **1833** ALISON *Hist. Europe* (1849–50) I. vi. §56. 51 Inflammatory addresses were hawked in every street. **1866** ROGERS *Agric. & Prices* I. xix. 457 Salt was hawked about by retail dealers.

b. *transf.* and *fig.*

a **1745** SWIFT *Friendly Apol.* (R.), All this with design.. To hear his praises hawk'd about. **1801** MAR. EDGEWORTH *Belinda* (1832) I. ii. 28 Last winter, when I was at Bath.. this Belinda Portman was hawked about everywhere. **1847** L. HUNT *Men, Women, & B.* II. x. 237 She consented to be hawked about as a sort of nurse and overseer. **1869** LOWELL *Winter-Even. Hymn* ix, I come not of the race, That hawk their sorrows in the market-place.

3. *trans.* To traverse as a hawker with something to dispose of; to canvass.

1865 CARLYLE *Fredk. Gt.* XIII. i. V. 3 That is all her Hungarian Majesty has yet got by hawking the world, Pragmatic Sanction in hand.

4. *intr. slang.* (See quot.)

1851 MAYHEW *Lond. Labour* I. 328 They have a man.. sometimes at a fair, to hawk, or act as a button (a decoy) to purchase the first lot of goods put up.

Hence **hawked** *ppl. a.*, **'hawking** *vbl. sb.* and *ppl. a.*

1542–3 *Act 34 & 35 Hen. VIII*, c. 10 §3 No.. couerlet-makers.. shall.. vse the said craft of haukynge, or go as haukers. *a* **1700** B. E. *Dict. Cant. Crew, Hawking*, going about Town and Country, with Scotch-Cloth, &c. or Newspapers. **1708** MRS. CENTLIVRE *Busie Body* v. i, Those little Hawking Females that traverse the Park, and the Play-House, to put off their damag'd Ware. **1715** M. DAVIES *Athen. Brit.* I. 346 Hawk'd-about Tryal-Pamphlets. **1862** TROLLOPE *Orley F.* vi, I call it hawking and peddling, that going round the country with your goods on your back. It ain't trade.

hawk (hɔːk), *v.*³ Also 6–7 **hauk(e**, 7 **haulk**. [Of uncertain origin; probably echoic.]

1. *intr.* To make an effort to clear the throat of phlegm; to clear the throat noisily.

1583 [see *hawking* below]. **1602** ROWLANDS *Greenes Ghost* 9 Then they will hamme and hauke, and saie they are not euery bodie, and so take their mony. **1638** MEDE *Rever. God's House* Wks. (1672) II. 349 Nor is it lawful for us.. to hauk or hem in the Church. **1797** *Sporting Mag.* X. 272 A man.. began to hawk and spit. **1816** SCOTT *Antiq.* xxx, 'I shall prove a wretched interpreter', said M'Intyre.. coughing and hawking as if the translation stuck in his throat. **1877** ROBERTS *Handbk. Med.* (ed. 3) I. 299 There is a frequent tendency to cough and hawk.

2. *trans.* To bring *up* with a strong effort of clearing the throat.

1581 MULCASTER *Positions* xx. (1887) 84 For hauking vp of blood. **1676** WISEMAN (J.), A stinking tough phlegm which she hawked up in the mornings. **1751** SMOLLET *Per. Pic.* xiv, He hawked up, with incredible straining, the interjection ah! **1843** SIR T. WATSON *Princ. & Pract. Phys.* xxviii. (1871) 593 He hawked up in the course of the day a considerable quantity of ropy mucus.

Hence **hawking** *vbl. sb.* and *ppl. a.*

1583 STANYHURST *Æneis* Ded. (Arb.) 7 In such hauking wise, as if he were throtled with the chincoughe. **1600** SHAKS. *A. Y. L.* v. iii. 12 Shal we clap into 't roundly, without hauking, or spitting, or saying we are hoarse? **1831** TRELAWNY *Adv. Younger Son* II. 149 A gawky.. bilious, hawking Frenchman. **1892** W. H. HUDSON *La Plata* xx. 307 The violent hawking of a man clearing his throat.

hawk-bell: see HAWK'S BELL.

'hawkbill.

1. A species of turtle; = HAWK'S-BILL I.

1782 P. H. BRUCE *Mem.* XII. 424–5 Many sorts of tortoises, of which the hawk-bill is the most valuable for its fine shell. **1885** C. F. HOLDER *Marvels Anim. Life* 27, I found a hawk-bill turtle lying on the surface.

2. An instrument. (See quots.)

1875 KNIGHT *Dict. Mech.*, *Hawk-bill*, a pliers with curved nose, to hold pieces in blow-pipe soldering. *Ibid.*, *Hawk-bill-tooth-saw*, a saw having a curving, hooked saw-tooth, somewhat resembling the upper mandible of the hawk.

So **hawk-billed** *a.*, having a mouth like a hawk's beak, as the ***hawk-billed turtle*** (= HAWK'S-BILL).

hawkbit ('hɔːkbɪt). [f. HAWK(WEED) + (DEVIL'S) BIT. Called by Ray and others, '*Hieracium minus præmorsâ radice*, Hawkweed with bitten roots, Yellow Devil's bit' (after Devil's bit Scabious); the compressed form *hawkbit* was introduced by Petiver in 1713.]

A book-name for the genus *Apargia* of composite plants, resembling hawkweeds.

1713 PETIVER *Herb. Brit. Raii Catal.*, Common Hawkbit, Jagged Hawkbit [etc.]. **1825** J. E. SMITH *Eng. Flora* III. 351 **1843** W. GAZE in *Zoologist* I. 30 The autumnal hawk-bit and dandelion. **1881** G. ALLEN *Vignettes fr. Nature* xxii, Some golden heads of the autumnal hawkbit.

hawked (hɔːkt), *a.*¹ [f. HAWK *sb.*¹ + -ED: cf. *hooked*.] Curved like a hawk's beak; aquiline.

1577 HELLOWES *Gueuara's Chron.* 72 Adrian had an high bodie.. nose somewhat hawked. **1646** SIR T. BROWNE *Pseud. Ep.* VI. xi. 333 Flat noses seem comly unto the Moore, an Aquiline or hawked one unto the Persian. **1712** HEARNE *Collect.* (O.H.S.) III. 439 He had a hawk'd Nose. **1845** JAMES *Stepmother* (1846) II. xxiii. 351 A stout, well-made, hawked-faced man.

hawked (hɔːkt), *a.*² *Sc.* and *north. dial.* Also **hawkit**. [Derivation obscure.] Of cattle: 'Having white spots or streaks' (Jam.); spotted, streaked, as in ***red-hawked***.

1500–20 DUNBAR *Fenȝeit Freir* 103 He maid a hundreth nolt all hawkit. **1612–3** in *N. Riding Rec.* (1884) II. 11 A cow.. red hawked in colour. **1658** W. CHAMBERLAYNE *Love's Victory* in *Pharonnida* IV. (1850) 181 As much as the slit in our hawked bullock's ear. **1811** W. AITON *Agric. Ayrshire* xiv. 425 A cow with much white on her neck was termed a hawked cow. **1818** SCOTT *Hrt. Midl.* xxxix, I do still haud by the real hawkit Airshire breed.

hawker ('hɔːkə(r)), *sb.*¹ [OE. *hafocere*, f. *hafoc* HAWK *sb.*¹: see -ER¹ (cf. *fowler*).] One who hawks, or engages in the sport of hawking; one who tends or trains hawks; a falconer.

a **975** *Canons Edgar* in Thorpe *Anc. Laws* II. 258 We lærað þæt preost ne beo hunta, ne hafecere. **1463** *Mann. & Househ. Exp.* (Roxb.) 225 Item, the same day my mastyr gaff to the hawkerys, xij. *d.* **1601** HOLLAND *Pliny* x. viii. (R.), The hawkers and foulers when they have caught the foule, divide the bootie with the hawkes. **1893** EARL DUNMORE *Pamirs* II. 269 Hassan Beg.. enlisted the services of a professional hawker.. so off we went with our falcon.

hawker ('hɔːkə(r)), *sb.*² [app. a. MLG. *hoker*, in LG. and Ger. *höker*, Du. *heuker*, higgler, hawker, huckster, costermonger. The LG. word is usually referred to *hocken* to take upon the back, to carry pick-a-back, also, to squat, keep sitting in the same place; and has been variously explained as one that carries a pack or load on his back, and one that sits at a stall.]

A man who goes from place to place selling his goods, or who cries them in the street. In mod. use technically distinguished from *pedlar*: see quot. 1895.

1510 *Nottingham Rec.* III. 104 Pro correctione habenda de les Hawkers, iijs. iiijd. **1533** *Act 25 Hen. VIII*, c. 9 §6 Sundry euill disposed persons, which commonly beene called haukers.. goe about from place to place within this Realme, vsing buying and selling of Brasse and Pewter. **1542–3** [see *hawking*: HAWK *v.*² 1]. **1679** *Lond. Gaz.* No. 1432/4 A sort of loose and idle persons, called Hawkers, who do daily publish and sell seditious Books.. contrary to Law. **1711** BUDGELL *Spect.* No. 150 ¶1, I heard the Hawkers with great Vehemence crying about a Paper. **1785** CRABBE *Newspaper* Wks. 1834 II. 118 The rattling hawker vends through gaping streets. **1895** *Daily News* 19 Mar. 7/7 He saw defendant acting as a hawker.. He asked him if he had a licence, when he produced a pedlar's licence.. A hawker is a man who travels about selling goods with a horse and cart or van. A pedlar carries his goods himself.. The cost of a pedlar's licence is 5*s.*, and is granted by the police. Hawkers' licences are granted by the Inland Revenue, and cost 2*l.*

fig. *a* **1683** OLDHAM *Wks. & Rem.* (1686) 26 The Churches Hawkers in Divinity, Who 'stead of Lace, and Ribbons, Doctrine cry. **1855** TENNYSON *Maud* I. x. iii, This broad-brim'd hawker of holy things.

b. A horse used in hawking goods.

1719 D'URFEY *Pills* IV. 13 On Pads, Hawkers, Hunters, on Higlers and Racers.

Hence **'hawker** *v. intr.*, to act as a hawker; whence **'hawkering** *ppl. a.*

1678 BUTLER *Hud.* III. iii. 620 [He] was implacable and auker'd To all that Interlop'd, and Hawker'd. **1682** OLDHAM *Sat. to friend* Wks. (Bell) 221 They are forced to ply For jobs of hawkering divinity.

hawker, obs. form of HOOKER, a small vessel.

hawkery ('hɔːkərɪ). *nonce-wd.* [f. HAWK *sb.*¹: cf. *rookery*, and see -ERY.] A place where hawks are kept.

1832 L. HUNT *Sir R. Esher* (1850) 35 Lord Berkeley had proposed to shew them a hawkery of his in the neighbourhood.

hawkey, hawkie ('hɔːkɪ). *Sc.* and *north. dial.* [Of same origin as HAWKED *a.*², with denominative *-ie*, *-y*, as in *blacky*, *brownie*, etc.] 'A cow, properly one with a white face; often used as a general name for a cow or an affectionate name for a favourite cow' (Jam.).

1724 RAMSAY *Gent. Sheph.* II. iii, Nae mair the hawkeys shalt thou milk. **1785** BURNS *Cotter's Sat. Nt.* xi, The soupe their only Hawkie does afford. **1893** *Northumbld. Gloss.*, *Hawkie*, a white-faced cow. Also a general pet-name for the cow.

hawkey, hawkie, var. HOCKEY.

hawking ('hɔːkɪŋ), *vbl. sb.*¹ [f. HAWK *v.*¹]

1. The sport or practice of chasing birds or small animals by means of trained hawks.

c **1374** CHAUCER *Troylus* III. 1779. *c* **1375** BARBOUR *Troybk.* I. 279 Quhar-throw it fallis.. hunting and of huntinge Haboundanly thar hade þe kynge. *c* **1489** CAXTON *Sonnes of Aymon* iv. 120 Theyr fader was a hawkyng vppon the ryver. *a* **1533** LD. BERNERS *Huon* xii. 35 Desyryng me to ryde with hym an hawkynge. **1596** SHAKS. *Tam. Shr.* Induct. ii. 45 Dost thou loue hawking? **1660** H. ADIS *Fannaticks Mite* 7 He runs not to Hawkings nor Huntings. **1841** LANE *Arab. Nts.* I. 126 Hunting and hawking were common and favourite diversions of the Arabs.

fig. **1611** DEKKER *Roaring Girle* Wks. 1873 III. 166 What dost thou go a hawking after me?

2. *attrib.* and *Comb.* Relating to or used in hawking, as ***hawking-bag***, ***costume***, ***-gauntlet***, ***-glove***, ***language***, ***-pole***, ***-pouch***, ***spaniel***.

1598 FLORIO, *Falconiera*, a faulkners bagge, a hauking pouch. **1622** DRAYTON *Poly-olb.* xx, The falconers take their hawking-poles in hand. **1654** WHITLOCK *Zootomia* 185 His Tongue is not acquainted with the hawking Dialect. **1656** S. HOLLAND *Zara* (1719) 52, I can seclude Æolus and his Sons in a Hawking-bag. **1676** *Lond. Gaz.* No. 1124/4 A large well made Hawking-Spaniel. **1823** SCOTT *Quentin D.* ii, A hawking gauntlet on his left hand, though he carried no bird. **1841** ELPHINSTONE *Hist. Ind.* II. 255 Behrám took advantage of Akber's absence on a hawking party. **1888** MISS BRADDON *Fatal Three* I. i, The Chelsea lady was in hawking costume.

hawking, *ppl. a.*¹ [f. HAWK *v.*¹ + -ING².] That hawks; addicted to the sport of hawking. In Shaks. 1601, 'hawk-like, keen' (Schmidt).

1601 SHAKS. *All's Well* I. i. 105 His arched browes, his hawking eie. **1601** CORNWALLYES *Ess.* xxii, Me thinkes a drunken Cobler, and a meere hawking Gentleman rankes equally. **1855** MACAULAY *Hist. Eng.* IV. 770 His sarcastic remarks on the hunting, hawking boors.

hawking *vbl. sbs.* and *ppl. adjs.*² and ³: see under HAWK *v.*² and ³.

hawkish ('hɔːkɪʃ), *a.* [f. HAWK *sb.*¹ + -ISH.] Somewhat of the nature or appearance of a hawk. Also, inclined to favour hard-line or warlike policies. Cf. HAWK *sb.*¹ 3. Hence **'hawkishness**.

1841 CARLYLE *Misc.* (1857) IV. 245 Of temper most accipitral, hawkish, aquiline, not to say vulturish. **1859** H. KINGSLEY *G. Hamlyn* I. vi. 64 She.. was now too fierce and hawkish looking, though you would still call her handsome. **1965** *New Statesman* 17 Sept. 386/2 The very hawkish chairman of the House of Representatives Armed Services Committee.. hankers to bomb Communist China. **1967** *Guardian* 15 Feb. 6/2 Hawkishness in Bonn could undo the promise of everything that has so far been achieved. **1967** *Listener* 21 Sept. 365/2 It is.. inevitable for the newspaper to take a strong—or, as we would now say, hawkish—stand in any international dispute. **1968** *Guardian* 9 July 8/6 Sir Henry Johnson, chief of BRB, was a true hard-liner, most hawkish of hawks. **1968** *Times* 4 Nov. 1/1 President Thieu agreed to the bombing halt in advance and.. his present performance is directed at hawkish opinion within South Vietnam. **1969** *Guardian* 13 Feb. 10/1 At yesterday's student meeting [at LSE] there were signs of a new hawkishness among the moderates. **1970** *Ibid.* 4 Aug. 2/6 Withdrawal may be political dynamite, but so is hawkishness. **1972** *Listener* 6 Jan. 8/1 Pakistan's hawkish enemies in New Delhi.

hawkit, *Sc.* var. of HAWKED *a.*²

'hawk-like, *a.* Like a hawk, or like that of a hawk.

c **1611** CHAPMAN *Iliad* XXII. 121 Who, hawk-like, ayres swiftest passenger That holds a timorous dove in chace [etc.]. **1775** G. WHITE *Selborne* xliii. 109 This species may be easily distinguished from the common buzzard by its hawk-like appearance. **1892** MRS. H. WARD *D. Grieve* I. 6 With a sudden hawk-like gesture.. she tried to get hold of it.

'hawk-moth. A moth of the family *Sphingidæ* or *Sphingina*; a sphinx-moth; so called from their manner of flight, which resembles the hovering and darting of a hawk. There are many genera and species, as DEATH'S-HEAD *h.*, ELEPHANT *h.*, HUMMING-BIRD *h.*, PRIVET *h.*: see these words.

1785 M. MARTIN (*title*), The Aurelian's Vade Mecum; containing.. Catalogue of Plants affording Nourishment to Butterflies, Hawk-moths.. and Moths in the state of Caterpillars. **1847** CARPENTER *Zool.* §707 The larvæ of the Hawk-Moths have always sixteen feet. **1851** MEDLOCK tr. *Schoedler's Zool.* 565 Lepidopterous insects are.. ranked as Butterflies, Moths, and Sphinges or hawk-moths.

hawk-nose. A nose curved like a hawk's beak; an aquiline nose.

1533 UDALL *Flowers Lat. Speakyng* 192 (R.) Crokyng or bowyng inwarde, like as the bil.. of an hauke, and such we call in scorne or derision hauke-noses. **1611** COTGR. s.v. *Nez*, A high-raisd, or hawke, nose. **1680** *Lond. Gaz.* No. 1544/4 A Dapple Grey Mare.. seven years old, a Hawk Nose. **1889** BROWNING *Imperante Aug.* 122 Those sparkling eyes beneath their eyebrows' ridge (Each meets each, and the hawk-nose rules between).

'hawk-nosed, *a.* Having a nose curved like a hawk's beak.

1530 PALSGR. 315/1 Hawknosed, *becqu.* **1662** J. DAVIES tr. *Olearius' Voy. Ambass.* 271 He was.. somewhat Hawk-nos'd, as most of the Persians are. **1837** W. IRVING *Capt. Bonneville* III. 120 A fierce, game-looking set of fellows; tall and hawk-nosed, and very much resembling the Crows.

hawk-owl. A name given to: **a.** The Short-eared Owl, *Asio brachyotus*. **b.** The Day-owl, *Surnia ulula* or *funerea*. Both so called from their smaller heads, and habit of seeking their food during the day.

1743–51 G. EDWARDS *Nat. Hist. Birds* 62 The Little Hawk Owl. This Bird is rather bigger than a Sparrow-Hawk. **1802** G. MONTAGU *Ornith. Dict.* (1833) 242 The Hawk Owl comes to us in October. **1812** A. WILSON *Amer. Ornith.* VI. 64 Hawk Owl.. This is another inhabitant of both continents.. a connecting link between the Hawk and Owl tribes. **1856** KNIGHT *Cycl. Nat. Hist.* IV. 926 *Surnia funerea*.. it hunts frequently in the day-time. The smaller head.. combined with these habits, have obtained for it the name of Hawk-Owl.

'hawk's-beard. A book-name for the genus *Crepis* of composite plants, allied to the hawkweeds.

1806 J. GALPINE *Brit. Bot.* §347 *Crepis*, hawksbeard. **1861** MISS PRATT *Flower. Pl.* III. 180.

hawk's bell, hawk-bell. A small spherical bell, for fastening on the leg of a hawk.

[**1468** in Rogers *Agric. & Prices* III. 557/2, 2 hawks' bells.] **1483** *Act 1 Rich. III*, c. 12 That no merchaunt Straungier..brynge into this Realme..belles except haukes belles [etc.]. **1486** *Bk. St. Albans* D iij (heading), Of hawkys Bellys..Off spare hawke bellis ther is chooce and lyttill of charge of thaym. **1622** DRAYTON *Poly-olb.* xx, The trembling fowl that hear the jigging hawk-bells ring. **1777** ROBERTSON *Hist. Amer.* (1778) I. II. 93 They..received from them hawks-bells, glass beads or other baubles. **1832** *Westm. Rev.* XVI. 132 Beads and hawk-bells. **1835** W. IRVING *Crayon Misc.* (1849) 298 Morris-dancers, gaily dressed up with ribands and hawks'-bells.

hawk's-bill.

1. (Also ***hawk's-bill turtle***.) A species of turtle, *Chelone imbricata*, having a mouth resembling the beak of a hawk, inhabiting the Indian Ocean and the warmer parts of the Atlantic, and furnishing the tortoiseshell of commerce. Also HAWKBILL.

1657 R. LIGON *Barbadoes* (1673) 4 The Loggerhead Turtle, and the Hawks bill Turtle, of which sorts, the latter is the best. **1697** DAMPIER *Voy.* I. 103 The Hawksbill Turtle is the least kind; they are so called because their mouths [resemble] the Bill of a Hawk: On the backs of these Hawksbill Turtle grows that Shell which is so much esteem'd for making Cabinets, Combs [etc.]. **1712** E. COOKE *Voy. S. Sea* 20 There is Plenty of Tortoises, or Turtle, but not very good to eat, being a sort of Hawksbill. **1892** *Chamb. Jrnl.* 14 May 318/2 The thirteen plates of tortoise-shell on the carapace of the hawk's-bill tortoise.

2. Part of the striking action of a clock.

1875 KNIGHT *Dict. Mech.*, *Hawk's bill*, a catch-piece attached to a vibrating arm, which acts as a detent in the rack of the striking part of a clock, and assists in effecting the proper number of strokes.

3. (See quot.)

1708 *Phil. Trans.* XXVI. 78 *Gryphites*, the Hawk's Bill, or Ague-shell.

'hawk's eye. Also **hawk-eye**.

1. The eye of a hawk; hence, a sharp or keen eye like a hawk's.

1684 OTWAY *Atheist* IV. i, A plague of her Hawk's Eyes! **1687** CONGREVE *Old Bach.* I. i, I have a Hawk's Eye at a Woman's Hand. **1833** TENNYSON *Poems* 119 Your hawk-eyes are keen and bright. **1884** SPURGEON in *Sword & Trowel* July 338 There are persons in the world who seem to have hawks' eyes where anything evil is concerned.

2. A name given to some species of plover, as the golden plover and the black-bellied plover.

1813 A. WILSON *Amer. Ornith.* VII. 42 It is said, that at Hudson's Bay it [the black-bellied plover] is called the Hawk's-eye on account of its brilliancy.

hawkshaw ('hɔːkʃɔː). Also **Hawkshaw**. [Name of a detective in *The Ticket-of-Leave Man* (1863), a play by Tom Taylor, English dramatist (1817–1880); also in the comic strip *Hawkshaw the Detective*, by Gus Mager, American cartoonist (d. 1956).] A detective; also *attrib*.

[*c* **1863** T. TAYLOR in M. R. Booth *Eng. Plays in 19th Cent.* (1969) II. 77 *The Ticket-of-Leave Man*... Cast.. Hawkshaw, a detective.] **1903** 'H. MCHUGH' *Back to Woods* iii. 59 He didn't even whimper when the village Hawkshaw snapped the bracelets on his wrist. **1942** BERREY & VAN DEN BARK *Amer. Thes. Slang* §460/18 Hawk, hawkshaw, heavy foot, hot hand. **1967** N. MAILER *Cannibals & Christians* I. 40 The hawkshaw *geist* of the F.B.I. **1968** *Listener* 15 Feb. 214/1 A 'Treasury hawkshaw', charged with seizing and selling up Confederate cotton. **1973** R. TRAVERS *Murder in Blue Mountains* x. 96 The 'Hawkshaws from the Antipodes' as the [San Francisco] *Bulletin* called Roche and his men.

hawkweed ('hɔːkwiːd). [transl. of L. *hierācium* = Gr. ἱεράκιον, f. ἱέραξ hawk, falcon; but the ancient application of the name was different (see Liddell and Scott).] The common name for plants of the large genus *Hieracium* (N.O. *Compositæ*).

Also sometimes loosely applied to other yellow-flowered composites, as *Senecio hieracifolius*, *Picris hieracioides*, and the genus *Crepis* (*bastard hawkweed*).

[*c* **1000** *Sax. Leechd.* II. 56 Hafocwyrt on hluttrum ealoð.] **1562** TURNER *Herbal* II. 14 b, The nature of Hawke wede is to coule and partly to binde. **1597** GERARDE *Herbal* II. xxxii. 232 Haukeweede is also a kinde of Succorie. **1794** MARTYN *Rousseau's Bot.* xxvi. 381 Hieracium or Hawkweed is a numerous genus of this order. **1806** J. GALPINE *Brit. Bot.* 340 *Picris hieracioides*, hawkweed ox-tongue. **1849** KINGSLEY *Misc.*, *N. Devon* II. 281 Crumbling rocks, festooned with heath, and golden hawkweed.

hawky ('hɔːkɪ), *a.*[1] [f. HAWK *sb.*[1] + -Y.] Of the nature of a hawk; greedy as a hawk.

1732 ELLIS *Pract. Farmer* 98 in Britten *Old Country Wds.* (E.D.S.), [Gravel is] of a hawky voracious nature.

hawky ('hɔːkɪ), *a.*[2] *nonce-wd.* [f. HAWK *v.*[3]] Characterized by hawking.

1866 CARLYLE *Remin.* II. 204 Speech of the most haggly, hawky, pinched and meagre kind.

hawle, obs. form of HAIL *sb.*[1]

†hawler. *Obs.* [f. *hawle*, HALL *sb.*[1] + -ER; cf. HALLIER[2].] The keeper or steward of a hall.

c **1400** MAUNDEV. (Roxb.) xxx. 136 A kyng es porter, anoþer hawler, anoþer chaumberlayne.

hawling(e, var. HALLING *Obs.*, tapestry.

hawm (hɔːm), *v. dial.* [Etymol. unknown.] *intr.* To move about awkwardly; to lounge.

1847–78 HALLIWELL, *Haum*, to lounge about. *Leic. Ibid.*, *Hawming*, awkwardness. *Linc.* **1877** *N.W. Linc. Gloss.*, *Hawm*, to move about awkwardly. **1880** TENNYSON *North. Cobbler* iv, Guzzlin' an' soäkin' an' smoäkin' an' hawmin' about i' the laänes.

hawm(e, obs. forms. of HAULM.

hawmbel, -ble, etc., obs. ff. AMBLE, etc.

†hawmed, *a. Obs.* [Derivation doubtful.

It may possibly be f. *haum*, *hawm*, HAME *sb.*[2] (of the collar of a horse) as resembling them in their curvature. Another suggestion is f. *hawm*, HAULM + -ED[2]: in allusion to the prominent joints or frequent crookedness of jointed stalks.]

Of legs: Bandy, curved.

1610 HOLLAND *Camden's Brit.* I. 530 The diuels of Crowland with their..crooked and hawm'd legs [*vncis cruribus*].

hawmed, haumed, ? corrupt form of HUMET, HUMETTY.

1572 BOSSEWELL *Armorie* III. 14 b, The Hawmed in this Cote armour, is a manifeste demonstration of buriall, and is an anciente token in Armorie. **1602** CAREW *Cornwall* (1811) 373 He..beareth, a, a cross haumed s.

†hawm-legged, *a. Obs.* Also **haume-**. [See HAWMED *a.*] Bandy-legged, bow-legged.

1608 *Withals' Dict.* 286 That is hawme legged [**1634** haume-legged], legges turned outward (as some say) that hath a paire of left legges, *valgus*.

hawse (hɔːz), *sb.*[1] *Naut.* Forms: 5–7 **halse**, 6 **haulse**, 7 **hause** (**houlse**, 8 **harse**), 6– **hawse**. [A phonetic spelling of 16th c. *halse*, *haulse*, app. a. ON. *háls* neck (cf. HALSE *sb.*), *fig.* part of the forecastle or bow of a ship or boat, also, the front sheet or tack of a sail, the end of a rope, etc.]

1. That part of the bows of a ship in which the hawse-holes are cut for the cables to pass through; hence, sometimes, in *plural*, the hawse-holes themselves.

1497 *Naval Acc. Hen. VII* (1896) 313, ij peces of tymbre for the halse of the seyd ship. **1567** G. FENNER in Hakluyt *Voy.* (1589) 147 We cut our cable at the hawse. **1582** N. LICHEFIELD tr. *Castanheda's Conq. E. Ind.* lxiv. 130 To let slippe their Gabells by theyr Halsis. *a* **1608** SIR F. VERE *Comm.* 28 After many attempts to wind up the anchor I was forced to cut cable in the haulse. **1627** CAPT. SMITH *Seaman's Gram.* ii. 10 The Hauses are those great round holes before, vnder the Beak-head, where commonly is used the Cables when you come to an Anchor, the bold or high Hause is the best. **1633** T. JAMES *Voy.* 46 Our Cables froze in the hawse. **1706** PHILLIPS (ed. Kersey) s.v., A *Bold Hawse*, is when the Hole is lofty above Water. **1748** *Anson's Voy.* III. iv. 330 We were in a leaky ship, with three cables in our hawses. **1842** F. COOPER *Jack o' Lantern* I. 140 Two men appeared near the Knight-heads..looking at the vessel's hawse.

†2. A cable, a hawser. *Obs.*

1598 FLORIO, *Alzana*..a halse or cable to draw a bote or ship withall. [**1611** *Alzaniere*..a halse or halsier in a ship]. *a* **1642** SIR W. MONSON *Naval Tracts* III. (1704) 346/1 Cat-holes are over the Ports in the Gun-Room..to heave the Ship a stern by a Cable, or Hause.

3. The space between the head of a vessel at anchor and the anchors, or a little beyond the anchors, *esp.* in phr. ***athwart*** (***†thwart***) ***the hawse*** (cf. *athwart-hawse*, s.v. ATHWART C), ***to cross the hawse***, etc. Also *fig.*

1630 J. TAYLOR (Water P.) *Brave Sea-fight* Wks. III. 39/1 In the darke night they might haue chained two or three Frigots together, and turning them vpon them, vpon the Ebbe, thwart their hawse, might much haue endangered them. **1665** SIR T. HERBERT *Trav.* (1677) 332 Both fell foul one anothers houlses, through which mischance her boltsprit gave our mizen shrouds a [etc.]. **1666** *Lond. Gaz.* No. 21/4 He fell thwart the Man of Wars Halse. **1667** *Ibid.* No. 160/4 The Vice Admiral..intended then to cross the Hause. **1712** E. COOKE *Voy. S. Sea* 350 Then I lay a-thwart the Enemy's Harse. **1833** MARRYAT *P. Simple* xxxv, Nothing would suit Nelson but this four-decked ship; so we crossed the hawse of about six of them, and..were abreast of her. **1859** READE *Love me little* (Ward) ix. 112 'There are mischiefmakers behind'. 'Ay?.. I'll teach them to come across my hawse'. **1867** SMYTH *Sailor's Word-bk.* s.v., If a vessel drives at her anchors into the hawse of another she is said to 'foul the hawse' of the vessel riding there; hence the threat..'If you foul my hawse, I'll cut your cable'.

4. 'The situation of the cables before the ship's stem, when she is moored with two anchors out from forward, one on the starboard, and the other on the port bow' (Smyth *Sailor's Word-bk.* 1867). **b.** Phr. ***clear hawse***, when both cables lead directly (without crossing) to their respective anchors. ***foul***, ***open hawse*** (see quots.). ***†full hawse***, with all the cable run out (*obs.*). ***to clear the hawse***, ***fresh*** (***freshen***) ***the hawse*** (see quots.). ***cross***, ***elbow***, ***round turn in the hawse*** (see quot. 1881, and ELBOW *sb.* 2 e).

1597 J. PAYNE *Royal Exch.* 33 The ship on hull, the helme on lee, full hawse in tumbling roades. **1706** PHILLIPS (ed. Kersey), *Burning in the Hawse*, is when the Cable endures an extraordinary Stress. *Clearing the Hawse*, is the untwisting of two Cables, which being let out at two several Hawses, are wound about one another. *Riding upon the Hawse*, is when any weighty Substance falls directly before the Hawse, or lies across it. **1727–51** CHAMBERS *Cycl.* s.v., *Fresh the Hawse* when there is reason to suspect the cable may be fretted in those holes, they veer out a little, to let another part endure the stress..*Freshing the hawse* is also used when new pieces are laid upon the cable in the hawse. **1748** *Anson's Voy.* II. i. 116 These..gusts make it difficult for ships..to keep a clear hawse when anchored. **1788** *Chambers' Cycl.*, *Hawse*, *foul*, implies that the cables lie across the stern, or bear upon each other, so as to be rubbed or chafed by the motion of the vessel. **1794** *Rigging & Seamanship* II. 254* When a ship at her moorings has her cables lead strait to her anchors, without crossing, she is said to ride with an open hawse. **1881** HAMERSLY *Naval Encycl.* s.v., If from an open hawse a ship swings 180° she brings a *cross* in the hawse, a second half swing in the same direction makes an *elbow*, a third, a *round turn*, a fourth, a *round turn and an elbow*, and so on.

5. *attrib.* and *Comb.*, as **hawse-bag, -block, -bolster, -box, -boxing, -buckler; hawse-fallen** *pa. pple.*, **hawse-full** *a.*, **hawse-hook, -timber**: see quots.; **hawse-wood** = *hawse-timber*. Also HAWSE-HOLE, -PIECE, -PIPE, -PLUG.

1819 *Pantologia* s.v., **Hawse-bags*, are bags of canvas made tapering, and stuffed full of oakum..to prevent the sea from washing in at these [hawse] holes. **1867** SMYTH *Sailor's Word-bk.*, **Hawse-blocks*, bucklers, or pieces of wood made to fit over the hawse-holes when at sea, to back the hawse-plugs. **Hawse-bolsters*, planks above and below the hawse-holes. Also, pieces of canvas stuffed with oakum and roped round, for plugging when the cables are bent. *c* **1860** H. STUART *Seaman's Catech.* 55 The *hawse boxes, or deck pipe. **1867** SMYTH *Sailor's Word-bk.*, *Hawse-box*, or *Naval Hood*, pieces of plank bolted outside round each of the hawse-holes, to support the projecting part of the hawse-pipe. **1881** HAMERSLY *Naval Encycl.*, **Hawse-Boxing*..was formerly a projection left upon the hawse-timbers in the wake of the hawse-holes. **1867** SMYTH *Sailor's Word-bk.*, **Hawse-bucklers*, plugs of wood to fit the hawse-holes, and hatches to bolt over, to keep the sea from spurting in. *Ibid.* 373 To ride *hawse-fallen, is when the water breaks into the hawse in a rough sea, driving all before it. **1692** *Capt. Smith's Seaman's Gram.* I. xvi. 81 *To Ride *Hawse-full*, is when in a rough Sea the Water breaks into the Hawses. **1867** SMYTH *Sailor's Word-bk.* 373 *Riding hawse-full*, pitching bows under. *c* **1850** *Rudim. Navig.* (Weale) 123 **Hawse-hook*, the breast-hook over the hawse-holes. **1867** SMYTH *Sailor's Word-bk.*, **Hawse-timbers*, the upright timbers in the bow, bolted on each side of the stem, in which the hawse-holes are cut.

hawse, *sb.*[2], var. of HAUSE.

†hawse, *v. Obs.* Also 6 **hause**, 6–7 **halse**, 7 **haulse**. [a. F. *hausser*, in 16th c. *haulser*, OF. *halcier*, *haucier* (12th c.) = Pr. *alsar*, *ausar*, It. *alzare*, Sp. *alzar*:—late L. type **altiare*, f. *altus* high. For the initial *h* in Fr. see HAUT; and cf. HANCE *v.*] *trans.* To raise, exalt, hoist.

c **1500** *Melusine* xxiv. 166 He made to be haused a lytel galyote out of the grete galeye with viii hores. **1513** MORE *Rich. III*, Wks. 62/1 Euery thing was hawsed aboue the mesure: amercementes turned into fines, fines into raunsomes. **1548** HALL *Chron.*, *Rich. III*, 11 b, Halsed up their sailes. **1600** HOLLAND *Livy* XXV. xxv. 568 Bomilcar.. having sea-roume, halsed up sailes.

Hence **†hawse** *sb.*[3] *Obs.*, exaltation, enhancement.

c **1475** *Partenay* 498 Puttyng my hole hert..and thought ay To your honour, hawse, and encrese also.

hawse, var. of HALSE *sb.* and *v.*[2]

'hawse-hole. *Naut.* A cylindrical hole, of which there are two in the bows of a vessel, for the cable to run through. Phr. ***to enter*** (***come***, ***creep***, ***get in***) ***by the hawse-holes***: to enter the service at the lowest grade, to rise from before the mast.

1664 E. BUSHNELL *Compl. Shipwright* 8 Provided that the Rails..fall not fowl of the halshols. **1748** *Anson's Voy.* III. iv. 330 We made a great quantity of water through our hawse-holes. **1803** *Phil. Trans.* XCIII. 321 This..accident was owing to the hawse-holes being extremely large and low, the hawse-plugs not being in, and the holes being pressed under water by a crowd of sail on the ship. **1833** MARRYAT *P. Simple* xvii, Working my way up as regularly as one who gets in at the hawsehole and crawls aft to the cabin windows. **1894** C. N. ROBINSON *Brit. Fleet* 341 Very few captains and flag-officers came in at the hawseholes.

'hawse-piece. *Naut.* One of the timbers of a ship through which a hawse-hole is cut; one of the timbers which compose the bow of a vessel and whose sides look fore and aft.

1680 *Lond. Gaz.* No. 1526/4 The Adventure Pink, Dogger built..new Hawse pieces. **1769** FALCONER *Dict. Marine* (1789), *Ecubiers*..also the hawse-pieces, through which those holes are cut. *c* **1850** *Rudim. Navig.* (Weale) 123 *Hawse-pieces*, the timbers which form the bow of the ship, whose sides stand fore and aft, or nearly so; that is, parallel to the middle line of the ship.

'hawse-pipe. *Naut.* A cast-iron pipe fitted into a hawse-hole to prevent the cable from abrading the wood.

1865 *Cornh. Mag.* Apr. 465 The chain attached to the anchor, and made fast through a hawse-pipe to the bow or forepart of the vessel, acts as a pivot on which it swings. **1888** *Daily News* 16 Feb. 2/7 Abbey Home..left this morning for Dover Harbour, with hawse-pipe broken.

'hawse-plug. *Naut.* A plug made to fit into the hawse-pipe to prevent water from entering.

1627 CAPT. SMITH *Seaman's Gram.* ii. 10 They [use] a Hause-plug at Sea. **1803** [see HAWSE-HOLE]. **1886** J. M. CAULFEILD *Seamanship Notes* 8 When..heavy weather [is] expected..hawse-plugs [should be] put in.

hawser ('hɔːzə(r)). *Naut.* Forms: 4 **hauceour, hauucour, haucer,** (5 *erron.* **anwser**), 5–8 **hauser,** 6 **halsor,** 6–9 **halser, haulser,** (7 **haurser, harser, -or, hasar,** 7–8 **hasser**), 5– **hawser.** [app. Anglo-Fr. *hauceour*, f. OF. *haucier* to HAWSE, hoist; in reference to the original purpose of a hawser. Cf. obs. F. *haussérée, haulserée* 'the drawing, or haling of Barges, or great Boats vp a riuer by the force of men ashore' (Cotgr.) from same source. Evidently from an early period associated in form and sense with HAWSE *sb.*[1]: cf. sense 1 b, and HAWSE *sb.*[1] 2.]

1. A large rope or small cable, in size midway between a cable and a tow-line, between 5 and 10 inches in circumference; used in warping and mooring; in large ships now made of steel.

1338 *MS. Sacrist's Roll, Durham*, Item j cabilus magnus xl cubitorum. Item j hauceour xxx cubitorum. **1355–6** *Ibid.*, Item j hauucour et j alia corda. **1373** in Riley *Lond. Mem.* (1868) 369, 2 haucers pour boyropes, 2 touropes, 3 werpropes. **1465** *Mann. & Househ. Exp.* 200 An anwser weying iij. stone, viij. li. **1485–6** *Naval Acc. Hen. VII* (1896) 18 Cables of sundrie sortes vj, Caggyng cable j, Hauser j. *Ibid.* 36 Hawsers for the botes takle iiij. **1592–3** *Act 35 Eliz.* c. 8 Preamb., Cables, Halsors, and Cordage. **1615** CHAPMAN *Odyss.* II. 609 With well-wreath'd halsers hoise Their white sails. **1697** DAMPIER *Voy.* (1729) I. 46 Ships..have a Hasar or Rope ready to send one end ashore. **1745** P. THOMAS *Jrnl. Anson's Voy.* 178 We..carry'd out two Hawsers and Anchors to heave the Ship off. **1831** TRELAWNY *Adv. Younger Son* I. 230 He desired me to make fast a halser..to the ring-bolts of her bob-stays. **1855** SINGLETON *Virgil* II. 393 Saturnia snaps the halser. **1871** TYNDALL *Fragm. Sc.* (1879) I. vi. 205 With three huge hawsers the ship's stern was made fast.

b. Used by confusion for HAWSE *sb.*[1] 3.

1684 OTWAY *Atheist* II. i, Laying your self atwart my Harser. **1787** SIR J. HAWKINS *Johnson* 443 *note*, A barge..in great danger of running, as they call it, athwart the hawser and of oversetting.

2. *Comb.*, as ***hawser-fashion*** adv., ***hawser-like*** adj.; **hawser-bend,** a kind of hitch or knot; **hawser-clamp,** a gripper for a hawser to prevent its veering out (Knight *Dict. Mech.* 1875); †**hawser-hole** = HAWSE-HOLE; **hawser-laid** *a.*, made of three or four strands laid up into one; †**hawser-work,** towing.

1793 SMEATON *Edystone L.* 197 A rope laid *hawser fashion is a rope consisting of any number of yarns according to the strength required, which divided into three strands, and each being twisted equally, are prepared to be laid into a rope. **1802** MITCHELL in *Naval Chron.* VII. 52 Daley was looking out at the *hawser-hole. **1769** FALCONER *Dict. Marine* (1789) s.v. *Ropes*, Ropes are either cable-laid or *hawser-laid. *c* **1860** H. STUART *Seaman's Catech.* 52 When three cablets are laid up together, it is called 'hawser-laid' rope. **1875** BEDFORD *Sailor's Pocket Bk.* x. (ed. 2) 360 Running rigging is hawser-laid, right-handed. **1675** tr. *Camden's Hist. Eliz.* III. (1688) 411 The seamen, whom he encouraged at their *Halser-work.

hawslock: see HALSE *sb.* 6.

hawson, obs. form of HAUSEN.

hawt(e, obs. ff. HAUGHT; var. HAUT *v. Obs.*

hawtane, -en, var. HAUTAIN *a. Obs.*

hawtere, obs. form of ALTAR.

hawthorn ('hɔːθɔːn). Forms: 1 **haȝu-, haȝaðorn,** 3 **hawȝ-,** 4 **haȝþorn,** 4–6 **hau-, haweþorn, -thorne,** (7 **hathorn**), 5– **hawthorn.** *β.* 1 **hæȝ-, hæȝuþorn,** 5 **heiþorne,** 6 **hai-, haythorne.** [OE. *haȝa, hæȝu-, hæȝþorn*, f. *haȝa* HAW *sb.*[1] + *þorn* THORN. Cf. MDu. *hagedorn*, Du. *haagdoorn*, MHG. *hage(n)dorn, hagdorn* (Ger. *hagedorn*), ON. *hagþorn* (Sw. *hagtorn*, Da. *hagetorn*).]

1. A thorny shrub or small tree, *Cratægus Oxyacantha*, N.O. *Rosaceæ*, extensively used for forming hedges; the White-thorn. It bears white, and, in some varieties, red or pink blossom (called 'may'); its fruit, the haw, is a small round dark red berry. (Also extended to other species of *Cratægus*.)

a **800** *Erfurt Gloss.* 19 *Alba spina*, haȝudorn. *c* **950** *Lindisf. Gosp.* Matt. vii. 16 Hueðer somniȝas..of haȝaðornum fic-beamas. **13..** *Guy Warw.* (A.) 4532 Þiderward sir Gij him drouȝ, And loked vnder an hawe-þorn bouȝ. **13..** *Gaw. & Gr. Knt.* 744 Þe hasel & þe haȝ-þorne. **1377** LANGL. *P. Pl.* B. XVI. 173 A man..As hore as an hawethorne. *c* **1450** *Merlin* 681 A bussh..of white hawthorne full of floures. **1632** MILTON *L'Allegro* 68 And every shepherd tells his tale Under the hawthorn in the dale. **1657** R. LIGON *Barbadoes* (1673) 2 Nor any tree bigger than a small Hathorn. **1728–46** THOMPSON *Spring* 89 The hawthorn whitens. **1846** J. BAXTER *Libr. Pract. Agric.* (ed. 4) II. 317 The Hawthorn is justly considered the best plant for hedges.

β. a **700** *Epinal Gloss.* 19 *Alba spina*, haeȝuthorn. *c* **725** *Corpus Gloss.* 114 *Alba spina*, hea[ȝo]ðorn. *c* **1000** *Sax. Leechd.* II. 54 Hæȝþornes blostman. **14..** *Voc.* in Wr.-Wülcker 572/45 *Cinus*, an haythorne & an hawe. **1573** TUSSER *Husb.* xxxiv. (1878) 76 The box and bay, Haithorne and prim, for clothes trim. **1584** R. SCOT *Discov. Witchcr.* XII. xviii. (1886) 218 Haythorne, otherwise white[t]horne gathered on Maie daie. **1688** R. HOLME *Armoury* III. 386/2 Before..finding out of the Needle..our Fore-fathers are said to make use of an Hay-thorn, or a Thorn Prick.

2. *Angling.* Short for *hawthorn-fly*.

1884 SENIOR in *Fisheries Exhib. Lit.* II. 399 The Grannom, Yellow-dun, Hawthorn, and Sedge.

3. *attrib.* and *Comb.*, as ***hawthorn bough, bud, bush, hedge***, etc.; **hawthorn china,** a kind of Oriental porcelain, in which the decoration represents flowering branches of the Japanese plum-tree in white on a dark blue ground; **hawthorn-fly,** a small black fly appearing on hawthorn-bushes when the leaves first come out; an artificial imitation of this fly used by anglers; **hawthorn-grosbeak,** the hawfinch (? *U.S.*); **hawthorn jar, pot, vase,** etc., a jar made of hawthorn china; **hawthorn pattern,** a pattern in which the hawthorn is represented in flower; the pattern used in hawthorn china. Also HAWTHORN-TREE.

13.. [see 1]. *c* **1386** CHAUCER *Knt.'s T.* 650 Were it of wodebynde or hawethorn [*Lansdowne* heiþorne] leues. **1423** JAS. I, *Kingis Q.* xxxi, And so with treis set Was all the place, and hawthorn hegis knet. **1590** SHAKS. *Mids. N.* III. i. 4 This greene plot shall be our stage, this hauthorne brake our tyring house. **1653** WALTON *Angler* iv. 116 You may also make the hawthorn-flie, which is all black and not big, but very small, the smaller the better. *Ibid.* 118 The smal black fly, or hawthorn fly is to be had on any Hawthorn bush, after the leaves be come forth. **1770** GOLDSM. *Des. Vill.* 13 The hawthorn bush, with seats beneath the shade, For talking age and whisp'ring lovers made. **1866** D. G. ROSSETTI *Let.* 3 Aug. (1965) II. 601, I went yesterday to see Mr. Huth's hawthorn pot at Kensington, and really after that I could not become the possessor of the one you brought me, good as it is. **1890** DOROTHEA GERARD *Lady Baby* I. viii. 187 The hedges were strung with pearls of hawthorn-buds. **1892** A. T. FISHER *Rod & River* 177 The Hawthorn-fly..at times proves so good a killer that I have placed it on the list. **1896** *Daily News* 5 May 7/3 The characteristic of the Sakura silks is the design of Japanese plum blossom with a fine and delicate tracery of stems, very similar to the 'hawthorn' pattern familiar upon china. **1905** *Daily Chron.* 18 May 4/6 The enormous sum paid yesterday at Christie's for a 'hawthorn' jar. **1906** S. W. BUSHELL *Chinese Art* II. viii. 35 A typical 'hawthorn ginger jar'..decorated with rising and falling sprays of prunus blossom. **1969** M. G. EBERHART *Message from Hong Kong* xix. 169 A Hawthorn vase..its beautiful glaze, its incredible blue, the pure, amazing white of its blossoms.

Hence **'hawthorned** *a.*, furnished or planted with hawthorns. **'hawthorny** *a.*, characterized by hawthorns, redolent of the scent of hawthorn blossom.

1831 FR. A. KEMBLE *Jrnl.* in *Rec. Girlhood* (1878) III. 42 Read one of Miss Mitford's hawthorny sketches out of 'Our Village'..they always carry one in fresh air and green fields. **1885** W. P. BREED *Aboard & Abroad* 23 A narrow path, with high hawthorned inclosures on each hand.

hawthorn-tree. = HAWTHORN 1.

c **1290** *S. Eng. Leg.* I. 350/185 Onder an hawȝþorn- [*v.r.* haȝþorn-] treo. **1562** TURNER *Herbal* II. 73 b, Our haw thorn tre leseth hys leues euery yere. **1786** BOSWELL *Tour Hebrides* 27 Aug., There is a hawthorn-tree, which rises like a wooden pillar through the rooms of the castle. **1876** MACKAY *Poems, Secr. Hawthorn* i, O thou snow-white hawthorn tree!

Comb. **1787** BEST *Angling* (ed. 2) 99 The Thorn or Hawthorn Tree fly.

†**haw-tree.** *Obs.* [f. HAW *sb.*[1] or [2] + TREE.]

1. The hawthorn.

13.. *Seuyn Sag.* (W.) 905 Up to the hawe-tre he steghth. *c* **1325** *Gloss. W. de Biblesw.* in Wright *Voc.* 162 Awe-tre [*v.r.* hawethen], *ceneler.* **1388** WYCLIF *Dan.* xiii. (*Susanna*) 54 Vndur an haw tree. **1530** PALSGR. 230/1 Hawe tree, *espine blanche.* **1570** LEVINS *Manip.* 46/37 An Haw tree, *sentis.*

2. Applied by Hudson to the Whitebeam (*Pyrus Aria*) and the Service tree (*P. torminalis*).

1762 W. HUDSON *Flora Angl.* (1798) 214 *Cratægus foliis cordatis*..wild Haw-tree or Service. **1879** BRITTEN & HOLLAND *Plant-n.*

hawur, var. of HAGHER *a.*, *Obs.*, skilful.

hawvelle, var. HAVEL *sb.*[1] *Obs.*

hawves, rare obs. pl. of HALF *sb.*

hax, obs. form of AXE.

c **1475** *Voc.* in Wr.-Wülcker 807/17 *Hec securis*, a hax.

haxter, variant of HACKSTER, *Obs.*

haxyn = *ashen*, obs. plur. of ASH.

1515 *Pilton Churchw. Acc.* (Som. Rec. Soc.) 68 For ye ledde haxyn..iiij^{s}. iiij^{d}.

hay (heɪ), *sb.*[1] Forms: 1 **híeȝ, híȝ, héȝ,** (**heiȝ, hoeȝ**), 2–4 **hei,** 3–7 **hey(e,** 4 **hai,** 4–5 **heyȝ(e,** 4–7 **haye,** 5 **heiȝ(e, heygh, heey,** 6–7 **haie,** 4– **hay.** [Com. Teut.: OE. *híeȝ, híȝ, héȝ*, = OS. *houwi*, (MLG. *hoi, houwe*, MDu. *hôy, hooi, hoey*, Du. *hooi*), OHG. *hewi, houwi* (properly, nom. *hewi*, gen. *houwes*, MHG. *höu, hou, houwe*, G. *heu*), ON. *hey* (Sw., Da. *hö*), Goth. *hawi* (gen. *haujis*):—OTeut. **haujo*^{m}, app. an adj. used subst. = (that) which can be mowed, f. stem of vb. **hauw-*, OE. *heaw-* to HEW, cut down, mow.]

1. a. Grass cut or mown, and dried for use as fodder; formerly (as still sometimes) including grass fit for mowing, or preserved for mowing.

c **825** *Vesp. Psalter* xxxvi[i]. 2 Swe swe heȝ hreðlice adruȝiað. *c* **950** *Lindisf. Gosp.* John vi. 10 Uæs..gærs vel heiȝ micil on ðæm styd. *c* **975** *Rushw. Gosp.* Matt. vi. 30 þæt londes hoeȝ þæt to dæȝe is and to mærȝen *vel* marne bið in ofne sended. *c* **1000** *Sax. Leechd.* III. 178 On . vi. nihtne monan do þonne hiȝ on þin beð. *c* **1205** LAY. 24441 þer com hey, þer com gras. **1382** WYCLIF *Mark* vi. 39 He comaundide to hem, that thei schulden make alle men sitte to mete aftir cumpenyes vpon greene hey. *c* **1400** *Three Kings Cologne* 126 Seynt Elene..founde þe same heiȝe þat crist was leyde in yn þe manger. *c* **1489** CAXTON *Sonnes of Aymon* xx. 450 Ye be not worthe a botelle of heye. **1535** COVERDALE *1 Kings* xviii. 5 Go thorow the londe vnto all the welles of water & ryuers, yf happlye we maye finde hay. *c* **1645** HOWELL *Lett.* I. 47 They leave it dry many dayes like Hey. **1725** SWIFT *Lett.* Wks. 1841 II. 575, I gave over all hopes of my hay..for I reckoned the weather had ruined it. **1730–46** THOMSON *Autumn* 1270 Amid the fragrant hay. **1830** TENNYSON *Owl* I. 9 Rarely smells the new-mown hay. **1897** GRANT ALLEN in *Strand. Mag.* Oct. 404/1 Mice, shrews and lizards..can conceal themselves less easily than they were wont to do in the long hay before the cutting.

b. ***the hay***: colloq. phr. for 'bed'; esp. in phrases ***to roll in the hay*** (sense 3); ***to hit the hay*** (HIT *v.* 11 c).

1903 ADE *People you Know* 13 When he had put in a frolicsome Hour or so with the North American Review, he crawled into the Hay at 9.30 p.m. **1930** WODEHOUSE *Very Good, Jeeves* vi. 160 My experience of women has been that the earlier they leave the hay the more vicious specimens they are apt to be. **1959** N. MAILER *Advts. for Myself* (1961) 334 Al had the reputation of being great in the hay.

2. ***Burgundian*** or ***Burgundy hay***, Lucerne, or Sainfoin: see BURGUNDY, BURGUNDIAN A. ***camel's hay***, an oriental grass or rush: see CAMEL *sb.* 5.

3. Phrases and Proverbs. ***to carry hay in one's horns***: to be ill-tempered or dangerous (Lat. *fænum habet in cornu*, Horace; from an ox apt to gore, whose horns were bound about with hay). ***to look for a needle in a bottle*** (***bundle***) ***of hay***: see NEEDLE. ***to make hay***: (*a*) *lit.*, to mow grass and dry it by spreading it about and exposing it to the sun's heat; (*b*) *fig.*, to make confusion. ***to make hay of***: to throw into confusion, turn topsy-turvy, upset. ***to make hay while the sun shines***: to lose no time, to seize or profit by opportunities. ***that ain't hay*** (U.S. colloq.): that is a lot of money; similarly in other negative contexts. ***to roll in the hay*** (colloq.): to make love; hence ***a roll in the hay***, love-making; also *concr.*, a person making, or willing to make, love.

1546 J. HEYWOOD *Prov.* (1867) 6 Whan the sunne shinth make hay. **1648** HERRICK *Hesper., Oberon's Pal.* (1869) 176 He's sharpe as thorn, And fretfull carries hay in 's horne. **1673** R. HEAD *Canting Acad.* 138 She..was resolv'd..to make Hay whilest the Sun shin'd. **1703** MAUNDRELL *Journ. Jerus.* (1732) 144 No Hay being here made. **1817** MAR. EDGEWORTH *Rose, Thistle, etc.* I. ii, Oh! father, how you are making hay of my things! **1886** *Pall Mall G.* 9 June 3/2 Sussex made hay of the Gloucestershire bowling. **1891** J. M. DIXON *Dict. Idiomatic Eng. Phr.* s.v., *Between hay and grass*, in an unformed state; hobble-de-hoy. F[amiliar]. An Americanism, said of youths between boyhood and manhood. **1943** R. CHANDLER *Lady in Lake* (1944) vii. 44 Job pays eighty a month, cabin, firewood... That ain't hay. **1945** 'L. LEWIS' *Birthday Murder* (1951) iii. 39 He gets something out of it... Maybe just a good roll in the hay. **1948** C. PORTER *Always True to you in my Fashion* (song) p. 4 Mis-ter Thorne once cor-nered corn—and that ain't hay. **1949** M. MILLER *Sure Thing* (1950) 79, I thought here's a kind of pretty girl..and I bet she'd be a good roll in the hay. **1952** P. BONNER *SPQR* (1953) xxvi. 233, I had fancied her as a desirable bit for a roll in the hay. **1958** R. STOUT *Champagne for One* (1959) iv. 42 Fresh figs in March, by air from Chile, are not hay. **1959** G. FISHER *Hospitality for Murder* xvii. 137 Just over a million bucks per day, to be exact—and that ain't hay. **1963** M. McCARTHY *Group* xiv. 332 We had a few rolls in the hay... Then for him it was over. **1966** J. PORTER *Sour Cream* xiii. 166 There she was, rolling around in the hay with enough evidence for a dozen divorces. **1968** *Times* 9 Nov. 23/3 Peterson's marriage is collapsing... He..rolls in the hay with..a plump little thing. **1969** 'H. PENTECOST' *Girl Watcher's Funeral* (1970) II. i. 73, I will come into a cool two and a half million dollars. .. I will also collect executor's fees which won't be hay. **1973** *Times* 9 Mar. 18/2 A quiet girl librarian, on vodka, has fantasy dreams of rolling in the hay in frilly drawers.

4. ***attrib.*** and ***Comb.*** **a.** attributive, as ***hay-bale, -bond*** (dial.), ***-bottle, -bundle, -farm, -green, -ground, -land, -market, -mead, -meadow, -month, -season, -stalk, -wisp***; (used in the cultivation, carriage, storage, etc. of hay) ***hay-basket, -boat, -cart, -chamber, -crook, -hook, -knife, paddock*** (Austral. and N.Z.), ***-press, -shed, -spade, -wagon, -wain, -yard.*** **b.** objective genitive (as name of a person, or of a mechanical contrivance), as ***hay-baler*** (U.S.), ***-binder, -carter, -cutter*** (mechanical contrivance or person), ***-dryer, -farmer, -loader, -mower, -pitcher, -presser, -raker, -stacker, -tedder, -tier, -tosser.*** **c.** objective, as ***hay-binding, -carting, -cutting*** (orig. U.S.), ***-pitching, -tedding.*** **d.** instrumental, as ***hay-fed*** pa. pple.,

hay-feed v. **e.** parasynthetic, as ***hay-coloured***, ***-scented*** adjs.

1851 A. O. HALL *Manhattaner* 5 It was a modest commercial plain..with bits of machinery, and ploughs, and oat bags, and *hay bales. **1911** *Daily Colonist* (Victoria, B.C.) 14 Apr. 3/4 The sentence was duly carried out, the young Indian being bound to a stake with hay-bale wire. **1962** *Times* 31 May 14/7 We use haybales to build mothering-up pens. **1895** M. GRAHAM *Stories of Foot-Hills* 209 The song of the *haybalers and the whir of the threshing machine had died out of the valley. **1936** *Scrutiny* IV. IV. 443 Mark Twain's presentation of Mississippi pilots and Nevada pioneers is comparable with Davis's accounts of timber-line settlers and hay-balers. **1726** LEONI tr. *Alberti's Archit.* I. 96/1 Your Cart..Harrow, Yoke, *Hay-baskets and the like utensils. **1826-44** LOUDON *Encycl. Agric.* 384 The *hay-binding machine is an invention by Beckway for weighing and binding straw or hay. **18..** WHITTIER *Countess*, The heavy *hay-boats crawl. **1874** HARDY *Far fr. Madding Crowd* x. 89 Tending thrashing-machine, and wimbling *haybonds. **1953** A. JOBSON *Household & Country Crafts* xvi. 163 In the old days the thatcher made his own broaches, as he made his own hay-bonds. **1552** HULOET, *Haye bottell, *foenusculum*. **1653** H. MORE *Antid. Ath.* III. vi. §6 While he was making hay-bottles in the barn. **1696-7** *Act 8-9 Will. III*, c. 17 Preamb., *Hay Cartes and Straw Cartes which are dayly brought into and stand in a Street.. called the Hay-Markett. **1880** JEFFERIES *Gt. Estate* 159 We entered the meadows, where the men were at haycart. **1705** *Lond. Gaz.* No. 4187/4 A..House, with..Barns, Stables, *Hay-Chambers. **1887** *Daily News* 20 July 6/1 *Hay colour is the fashionable tint for the straw of rustic hats. **1641** BEST *Farm. Bks.* (Surtees) 37 As for stackes, they..cutte them eaven downe to the bottome with an hey-spade made for that purpose; but for pykes, they usually pull out the hey with *hey-crookes. **1653** in *Mayflower Descendant* XI. 200 One *haycutter,..00-01-06. **1838** W. B. DEWEES *Lett. fr. Texas* (1852) xxiii. 226 As it chanced there was a hay-cutter, who was at work a short distance from where the scene took place. **1867** J. N. EDWARDS *Shelby* xx. 352 Shelby marked the hay-cutters struggling over stubble and wind row. **1873** J. M. BAILEY *Life in Danbury* 21 It did seem as if I never would get out from under that hay-cutter. **1972** *Country Life* 30 Mar. 769/1 The hay-cutter or hay-knife was the proper tool for cutting into a rick. **1665** *Rowley Rec.* (Mass.) (1894) 163 John Trumble for *hay cutting. **1869** J. R. BROWNE *Adv. Apache Country* 443 Twenty settlers,..most of whom are engaged in stock-raising and hay-cutting. **1906** 'MARK TWAIN' *Autobiogr.* (1924) II. 48 Hay-cutting time was approaching. **1933** R. TUVE *Seasons & Months* iv. 165 The eleventh-century Julius A vi has..hay-cutting for July. **1634** W. WOOD *New Eng. Prosp.* (1865) 41 Very good arable grounds and *Hay-ground. **1688** R. HOLME *Armoury* III. 334/2 The *Hay Hook is..for the pulling out of Hay made either in a Rick, Stack, or Mow. **1828** WEBSTER, **Hay-knife*, a sharp instrument used in cutting hay out of a stack or mow. **1690** *Act 2 Will. & M.* Sess. II. c. 8 §15 Noe person..shall ..suffer his..Waggon Cart or Carr to stand..in the place now called the *Hay Market neere Pickadilly..loaden with Hay or Straw..after two of the Clocke. **1832** J. BREE *St. Herbert's Isle* 14 The merry *hay-month gone, now August threw Her golden mantle over every plain. **1530** PALSGR. 230/1 *Hay-mower, *fauchevr de foyn*. **1966** *Teo Reo* IX. 53 Is it not the case that wheat [in N.Z.] is grown in a wheatfield but hay is grown in a *hay paddock? **1967** *Landfall* XXI. 127 The cock pheasant strutting in a hay paddock. **1831** HOWITT *Seasons* (1837) 145 *Hay-scented fields. **1862** ANSTED *Channel Isl.* II. viii. (ed. 2) 182 The delicate hay-scented fern (*Lastræa æmula*). **1508** FISHER 7 *Penit. Ps.* cii. Wks. (1876) 146 It shall perysshe and weder awaye as a floure in the *hey season. **1865** *Atlantic Monthly* XV. 516, I used to notice her ..about Easter day, proclaiming her arrival..from the peak of the barn or *hay-shed. **1920** *Glasgow Herald* 12 Nov. 8 Farmhouses and haysheds were also fired between Killarney and Tralee. **1936** *Brit. Birds* XXX. 108 The other Martins' nests were in haysheds or under eaves. **1641** *Hay-spade [see *hay-crook*]. **1875** KNIGHT *Dict. Mech.* s.v. *Hay-knife*, The hay-spade has a sharp blade, a handle, and a tread. *Ibid.*, **Hay-stacker*, a portable derrick for the suspension of tackle in the use of the horse hay-fork in stacking. **1703** MOXON *Mech. Exerc.* 214 As small as an *Hay-stalk. **1875** KNIGHT *Dict. Mech.*, **Hay-tedder*, a machine to scatter hay to the sun and air. **1826-44** LOUDON *Encycl. Agric.* 420 *The *hay-tedding machine*, invented about 1800, by Salmon of Woburn. **1891** *Daily News* 28 Dec. 3/3 A farm labourer, *hay tier, and thatcher. **1641** BEST *Farm. Bks.* (Surtees) 37 It is very behoovefull to see that an *haywaine bee well raked. **1847-8** H. MILLER *First Impr.* xv. (1857) 260 The hay-wains..pass and repass to and from the hay-field. **1798** BERESFORD in *Ld. Auckland's Corr.* (1862) III. 403 Robbing, plundering, and burning houses, *hay-yards, corn, &c.

5. Special combs.: **hay-bag** *slang*, a woman; **hay-barrack** (*U.S.*) = BARRACK 1 b; **hay-bearded** *a.*, having a beard of the colour or texture of hay; **hay-box**, (*a*) *dial.* a hay-loft; (*b*) a box filled with hay in which food after being brought to boiling-point in a saucepan is placed to finish cooking; also *attrib.*; (*c*) a box containing hay; **hay-cap**, a piece of canvas or tarpaulin put on the top of a haycock or haystack to protect it from rain; **hay-crome**, an old kind of hay-rake (cf. CROME); see also quot. 1825; †**hay-dust**, hay-seed; **hay-goaf** (†**golph**, †**gulfe**), a hay-mow; **hay-grass**, grass preserved for hay; **hay-harvest**, the season when hay is made, hay-making time; **hay-home supper**, a meal to celebrate the successful bringing home of the hay; cf. HARVEST HOME; **hay-hut** [tr. G. *heuhütte*], a wooden hut covering a hay-stack on the mountainside; **hay-man**, a man who sells hay, a hay-salesman; **hay-pack**, a large bundle of hay packed in a sheet; **hay-plant**, an umbelliferous plant of Tibet, *Prangos pabularia*; **hay-press** *U.S.*, a press for baling hay; **hayride** *U.S.*, a pleasure ride in a hay-wagon; **hay-rig**, **-rigging**, a framework projecting from the sides of a wagon so as to increase its carrying capacity, a shelving (*U.S.*); **hay-rope**, a rope twisted of hay, a hay-band; **hay-scales** *U.S.*, a public weighing-machine for weighing loads of hay, etc.; **hay-tallat**, a HAY-LOFT; **hay-tea**, a decoction of hay used for cattle; **hay-time**, the season at which hay is made and carried; **hay-worm**, a worm or caterpillar bred in hay.

1851 MAYHEW *Lond. Labour* I. 217/2 **Haybag*, a woman. **1925** F. G. BOND *Flatboating on Yellowstone, 1877* 12, I asked a passing corporal the way to the haybag quarters. He was a married man and lived in haybag row. **1931** D. RUNYON *Guys & Dolls* (1932) viii. 159 She is nothing but an old haybag. **1939** ABBOTT & SMITH *We pointed them North* 143 A woman they called Big Ox, who was one of those old haybags that used to follow the buffalo camps. **1967** *Spectator* 10 Nov. 565/3 The weary certainty that one more stranger has paused to inspect her casually and to depart calling her a haybag. **1807** VANCOUVER *Agric. Devon* (1813) 129 This contrivance is called a *hay-barrack, in Pennsylvania, where they are equally used for the protection of hay as well as of corn. **186-.** O. W. HOLMES *Hunt after 'the Captain'* in *Pages fr. Old Vol. Life* (1891) 29 A grave, hard, honest, *hay-bearded face. **1885** B. BRIERLEY *Tales Lancs. Life* iii. 45 There's a *hay-boax theere ut I've bin in afore. **1908** *Chambers's Jrnl.* Jan. 119/2 The receptacle with its boiling contents is placed in the hay-box. **1915** *Queen* 13 Nov. 897/2 Boiled beef should be allowed thirty minutes' boiling for a large joint and three to four hours in the hay-box. **1927** *Daily Express* 6 Aug. 9/4 To feed the personnel of the force by means of new mobile hay-box cookers. **1960** *Farmer & Stockbreeder* 19 Jan. Suppl. 39/2 The hay-box fold is most useful for carrying on chicks during the spring and summer months. **1858** THOREAU *Maine W.* (1894) 116 The white *hay-caps, drawn over small stacks of beans or corn in the fields on account of the rain. **1599** NASHE *Lenten Stuffe* 40 They fell downe on their mary-bones and lift vp their *haycromes vnto him. *a***1825** FORBY *Voc. E. Anglia*, *Hay-crome*. No rustic implement is now literally called by this name, but a metaphorical use of the word is very common. The characters scrawled by an awkward penman are likened to 'hay-cromes and pitchforks'. **1607** TOPSELL *Serpents* (1658) 1715 The seed of grasse, commonly called *Hay-dust, is prescribed against the biting of Dragons. **1563-87** FOXE *A. & M.* (1684) III. 744 The poor man and woman were compelled to step into an *Hay-golph to hide themselves from their cruelty. **1604** PARSONS *3 Convers.* III. xv. 254 They two being taken togeather in a hay gulfe..were carryed to the assises at Berry. **1895** *East Anglian Gloss.*, *Hay-goaf*, hay mow. **1601** HOLLAND *Pliny* II. 286 Among the kinds of *hey-grasse. **1883** *Sunday Mag.* July 446/1 What a leap from the grass of an English meadow..to the hay-grass in Bengal! **1552** HULOET. *Hay harvest, *foenisecium*. **1824** MISS MITFORD *Village* Ser. I. (1863) 178 His master..had begun the hay-harvest that very morning. **1860** C. M. YONGE *Friarswood Post-Office* ii. 34 Mrs. King would not let him go to the *hay-home supper in the barn. **1943** F. THOMPSON *Candleford Green* iv. 69 That was the hay-home supper, a survival, though perhaps not more ancient than a couple of hundred years or so. **1903** *Daily Chron.* 23 Mar. 3/7 One sees the bright green mountain where the *hay-huts hang like birds' nests on the steep slope. **1912** D. H. LAWRENCE *Let.* 2 Sept. (1932) 56 We take rucksacks.., cook our meals by some stream—and twice we have slept in hay-huts. *c***1912** —— *Love among Haystacks* (1930) 63 There must be a hay hut somewhere near. We *can't* sleep here. **1800** G. ROSE *Diaries* (1860) I. 285 The *haymen..who sell the Kentish wheat. **1841** LEVER *C. O'Malley* cii, Already some *hay-packs were thrown in. **1892** *Pall Mall G.* 10 Feb. 3/1 We came in sight of some men, with hay-packs ready for the downward leap. **1840** *Penny Cycl.* XVIII. 490/1 The Prangos *Hay-plant is herbaceous and perennial..The crop consists of the leaves, which..have a highly fragrant smell, extremely similar to that of very good new clover hay. **1829** *20th Congress 2 Sess.* State P. No. 59, 3 [Improvement] in the *hay press [patented Jan.] 26 [1828 by] Moses B. Bliss. **1835** J. H. INGRAHAM *South-West* II. 221 A large building resembling a northern hay-press. **1872** E. EGGLESTON *Hoosier Schoolmaster* xxvi. 127 To see his new red barn with its large 'Mormon' hay-press..consumed, was too much for the Hawkins' heart to stand. **1897** *Sears, Roebuck Catal.* 151/3 Our £235,000 Belt Power Hay Press. [**1856** *Spirit of Times* 8 Nov. 154/2 The invitations he had at first received to join pic-nics, boating excursions on the river, and *haywagon rides, after a while became intermittent.] **1896** *Advance* (Chicago) 19 Mar. 414/2 Everybody being as comfortable as hay-ride etiquette permitted, the word was given, and away they went. **1906** 'MARK TWAIN' *Autobiogr.* (1924) II. 50 The remembrance of poor Susy's lost hay-ride still brings me a pang. **1915** J. WEBSTER *Dear Enemy* (1916) 274 We have had hay-rides and skating-parties and candy-pulls. **1966** *Punch* 21 Dec. 921/2 Hay-rides, an American indulgence by no means confined to Texas, are laid on by riding academies and picnic area operators. **1973** *Sat. Rev. Soc.* May 64/1 She's..become a steady patron of..hayrides ..and Ladies' Nights. **1896** *Advance* (Chicago) 19 Mar. 414/1 Two great farm wagons, provided with those wide projecting frames, technically known as *hay-rigs. **1865** THOREAU *Cape Cod* i. (1894) 4 We met several *hay-riggings and farm-wagons..each loaded with three large, rough deal boxes. **1523** FITZHERB. *Husb.* §38 Bynde her heed with a *heye rope..to the syde of the penne. **1587** MASCALL *Govt. Cattle* ii. (1661) 123 If your horse be sprained..then bind him round in a hay rope. **1773** *Rec. Early Hist. Boston* (1893) XXIII. 204 The Ground on which the *Hay Scales stands. **1844** G. W. KENDALL *Narr. Santa Fé Exped.* II. xvii. 327 They might as well say that the natives can tell the time by consulting..a pair of hay-scales. **1855** M. M. THOMSON *Doesticks* v. 34 The writer,..wearied of..the same unvarying prospect of ox-teams, hay-scales,..took the roving fever. **1893** *Citizen Guide to Brooklyn & Long Island* 8 The old hay-scales stood there, and on its roof was the first fire-bell owned by Brooklyn. **1686** N. COX *Gentl. Recreat.* IV. (ed. 2) 29 To tuck it out of the Rick by little and little, as you have occasion to use it, makes it spend much better than it would otherwise do out of the *Hay-tallet. **1869** BLACKMORE *Lorna D.* xix, Being forced to dress in the hay-tallat. **1826** LOUDON *Encycl. Agric.* (1844) 905 To make *hay-tea. **1530** PALSGR. 230/1 *Heytyme, *temps de fener*. **1776** ADAM SMITH *W.N.* I. x. I. (1869) I. 121 The demand for country labour is greater at hay-time. **1753** CHAMBERS *Cycl. Supp.* s.v., It [hay] is a proper nidus of itself, sometimes, for a much larger species of insect called the *hay-worm, whose origin and changes have not, as yet, been properly observed.

hay, *sb.*[2] Now *arch.* or *dial.* Forms: 1 **heȝe**, (**heiȝe**, **heaȝe**), 3 **heie**, 4-7 **haie**, **hey**, 5 **heyȝ**, **heȝe**, 6-7 **heye**, 4- **haye**, 5- **hay**. [OE. *heȝe* (:—**hagi-z*) a deriv. of the same root as *haȝa* HAW *sb.*[1], HAG *sb.*[2], and HEDGE. In its ME. form the word became more or less identified with Fr. *haie*:—OLG. *haga* (cf. MDu. *hāge*) hedge, a word of cognate origin.]

1. A hedge, a fence. (In some 17th c. writers distinguished as a 'dead hedge'.)

*c***725** *Corpus Gloss.* 606 *Crates*, heȝas. **845** *Charter* in *O.E. Texts* 437 Et jacit be norðan heȝe. *c***1000** ÆLFRIC *Hom.* II. 448 Wiðutan minum heȝum. *a***1250** *Owl & Night.* 817 The vox kan crope bi the heie. *a***1300** *E.E. Psalter* lxxxviii[i]. 41 [40]Þou for-dide his haies. **1412-20** LYDG. *Chron. Troy* III. xxiv, Both on hayes and in freshe greues. **1562** *Act 5 Eliz.* c. 13 §7 The Heyes, Fences, Dikes or Hedges next adjoining.. any high or common fairing Way. **1598** MANWOOD *Lawes Forest* xx. §5 (1615) 172/2 The wild beasts..must have their free passage..without any forestalling or foresetting of them..either with dogges, gunne, crosbow, longbow, dead hey, quick hey, or any maner of engin or let whatsoeuer. **1607** NORDEN *Surv. Dial.* in *Harrison's England* II. Suppl. 196 A hedge implieth quickset and trees: but a hay a dead fence, that may be made one yeere, and pulled downe another. **1801** STRUTT *Sports & Past.* I. i. 17 The game was usually enclosed with a haye or fence-work of netting. *a***1825** FORBY *Voc. E. Anglia*, *Hay*, a hedge; more particularly a clipped quickset hedge. **1867** JEAN INGELOW *Story Doom* II. 235 The golden bilhook, wherewithal He wont to cut his way, when tangled in The matted hayes. **1880** HARTING *Brit. Anim. Extinct* II. 224 Great tracts of forest were..inclosed within a pale, haye, or wall.

2. An enclosed space; an enclosure; a park.

*c***1630** RISDON *Surv. Devon* §107 (1810) 108 (Exeter) Another [religious house] was for..Nuns, which is now the kalender-hay. **1679** BLOUNT *Anc. Tenures* 57 This Hay of Hereford was a great Woodland ground near the City, and heretofore reputed a forest. **1686** PLOT *Staffordsh.* 38 The Plains or Hays below in great part being covered only with ..Ling. **1837** HOWITT *Rur. Life* v. iii. (1862) 381 Five hays, or royal parks, each fenced in, and furnished with its lodge. **1881** *Daily News* 19 Nov. 2/1 The sale of 1,270 acres to one of the Dukes of Kingston out of the hays of Bilhagh and White Lodge..[in] Sherwood Forest.

†**3.** *Mil.* An extended line of men. *Obs.* [Cf. F. *haie*.]

1684 R. H. *School Recreat.* 55 Then draw up in Hay to the Rear. **1753** *Execution Dr. A. Cameron* (Tower Rec.), The Yeoman Warders were formed into a Hay. **1867** SMYTH *Sailor's Word-bk.*, *Hay*, a straight rank of men drawn up exactly in a line.

4. *Comb.* †**hay-brier** *heybrere*, hedge-brier; **haymaids**, ground-ivy; †**hay-saule**, a hedge-stake. Also HAYBOTE, HAYWARD.

1398 TREVISA *Barth. De P.R.* XVII. cliii. (1495) 704 Sudes ..is an heysaule other a stake sharped at eyther ende. **14..** *Voc.* in Wr.-Wülcker 568/25 *Bodarius*, heybrere. **1640** PARKINSON *Theat. Bot.* v. xciii. 677 Wee in English [call it] ..Gill creepe by the ground, Catsfoote, Haymaides, and Alehoofe.

†**hay**, *sb.*[3] *Obs.* Forms: 4-7 **haie**, 5-8 **haye**, 6-7 **hey(e**, 5- **hay**. [AFr. *haie*: origin uncertain.

A conjecture is that it may have been an extension of HAY *sb.*[2] (cf. sense 1 there, quot. 1598), or of the equivalent F. *haie*; but evidence is wanting.]

A net used for catching wild animals, *esp.* rabbits, being stretched in front of their holes, or round their haunts.

1389 *Act 13 Rich. II*, Stat. I. c. 13 §1 Nene use furettes haies rees hare pipes ne cordes. *c***1440** *Promp. Parv.* 220/2 Haye, net to catche conys wythe (**1499** *Pynson* hay net, *W.* hanet). **1531** ELYOT *Gov.* II. xiv, He which entendeth to take the fierse and mighty lyon pytcheth his haye or nette in the woode, amonge great trees and thornes. **1659** T. PECKE *Parnassi Puerp.* 139 A Rabbet, who having escap'd a Weasel, fell into the Hayes. **1710** *Act 9 Anne* c. 27 §5 The pernicious Practice of driving and taking them with Hayes, Tunnells and other Nets, in the Fens, Lakes, and broad Waters. **1774** *Ms. Redsham Manor, Suff.*, Game-keeper to destroy hays, nets, and snares. **1821** *Sporting Mag.* IX. 11 Hays, nets, low-bells, hare-pipes.

fig. **1611** SPEED *Hist. Gt. Brit.* VIII. iv. §4. 389 Harold.. tooke counsel how he might traine into his Haye the sonnes of Queene Emma. *a***1643** W. CARTWRIGHT *Lady Errant* V. i, How'l you then subdue them? By policy; set Hays, and Traps, and Springs, And pitfals for 'em.

b. *Comb.* **hay-net**, in same sense.

1499 [see above]. **1813** *Sporting Mag.* XLII. 214 In his pocket were found several bag nets and a hay net. *a***1825** FORBY *Voc. E. Anglia*, *Hay-net*, a hedge-net. A long low net, to prevent hares or rabbits from escaping to covert, in or through hedges.

hay, hey, *sb.*[4] Forms: 6 **heye**, 6-8 **haye**, 7 **haie**, 6- **hay**, 7- **hey**. [Of uncertain origin: *haye d'allemaigne* is used in 15th c. Fr. by Marot.]

1. A country dance having a winding or serpentine movement, or being of the nature of a reel.

*a***1529** SKELTON *Agst. Garnesche* 170, I cannot let thè the knave to play To dauns the hay and run the ray. **1549** *Compl. Scot.* vi. 66 Thai dancit al cristyn mennis dance, the northt of scotland..ihonne ermistrangis dance, the alman haye, the bace of voragon, [etc.]. **1596** DAVIES *Orchestra* lxiv. in Arb. *Garner* V. 39 He taught them Rounds and winding Heyes to

tread. **1609** C. BUTLER *Fem. Mon.* v. (1623) L ij, They doe most nimbly bestirre themselves, sporting and playing in and out as if they were dancing the Hey. **1656** DAVENANT *Siege Rhodes* IV. Dram. Wks. 1873 IV. 418 Scourge him As boys do tops; or make him dance The Irish hey over a field of thistles Naked. **1753** HOGARTH *Anal. Beauty* xvii. 237 One of the most pleasing movements in country-dancing.. is what they call 'the hay': the figure of it, altogether, is a cypher of S's, or a number of serpentine lines interlacing or intervolving each other. ?**1810** MAR. EDGEWORTH *M. Lewis* (1849) 151 He..danced the Hays round two elbow chairs. **1881** BESANT & RICE *Chapl. Fleet* II. iv, The hymns they sang might have been a hey or a jig in a country dance.

b. *transf.* and *fig.* **to dance the hay** or **hays**: to perform winding or sinuous movements (around or among numerous objects); to go through varied evolutions like those of a dance.

1597 C. LEIGH in Hakluyt *Voy.* III. 200 Through variety of iudgements and euill marinership we were faine to dance the hay foure dayes together. **1607** CHAPMAN *Bussy D'Ambois* Plays 1873 II. 14 The King and subiect, Lord and euerie slaue Dance a continuall Haie. **1718** *Entertainer* No. 28 ⁋ 12 To make him thus dance the Hay of Scepticism and Latitude. **1813** HANSARD *Parl. Debates* XXVI. 614 Lord Ellenborough considered the Bill as a most arbitrary measure; it tended to make property dance the hays, and to alter every description of tenure. **1887** BROWNING *Parleyings, Daniel Bartoli* xv, To be duchess was to dance the hays Up, down, across the heaven amid its host.

c. Comb. ***hay-fashion*** adv.

1777 MAD. D'ARBLAY *Early Diary* (1889) II. 196 He.. made his horse dance in and out by every other tree, Hay fashion.

†**2. hay-de-guy, -guise.** Forms: 6 **hay the gy, haydeguies, -guyes, hey-day guise, heidegyes,** 6–7 **heydeguies,** 7 **haydegues, -digyes, hey-de-gay, -gey, -guize, hydegy, hy-day-gies,** *erron.* **hadegynes.** [lit. *Hay of Guy* or ? *Guise.*] A particular kind of hay or dance, in vogue in 16th and early 17th c. *Obs.*

a **1529** SKELTON *Agst. Venom. Tongues* 13 Enforce me Nothing to write but hay the gy of thre. **1579** SPENSER *Sheph. Cal.* June 27 With Heydeguyes, and trimly trodden traces. *c* **1580** *Robin Goodfellow* 101 in *Percy Rel.* (1765) III. 205 By wells and rills in meadowes greene, We nightly dance our hey-day guise. **1612** DRAYTON *Poly-olb.* v. Argt., Whilst the nimble Cambrian rills Dance hy-day-gies amongst the hills. *a* **1618** J. DAVIES *Eglogues* Wks. (1772) 112 With an heydeguies, pipt by Tom-piper, or a lorrel-lad. **1633** J. FISHER *Fuimus Troes* III. ix. in Hazl. *Dodsley* XII. 507 Be bonny, buxom, jolly, Trip haydegues belive. **1638** FORD *Fancies* IV. i, Not in a hey-de-gay of scurvy gallantry. **1694** *Ladies Dict.* 217 *Hadegynes*, a Country dance.

†**hay,** *int.* and *sb.*[5] *Obs.* [a. It. *hai* (pron. ai) thou hast (it). Cf. L. *habet*, exclaimed when a gladiator was wounded.]

A. *int.* An exclamation of hitting on opponent.

1598 B. JONSON *Ev. Man in Hum.* IV. vii, O, it must be done like lightning, hay!

B. *sb.* A home-thrust.

1592 SHAKS. *Rom. & Jul.* II. iv. 27 Ah the immortall Passado, the Punto reuerso, the Hay.

hay, *sb.*[6] [tr. F. *foin.*] The choke of an artichoke.

1877 E. S. DALLAS *Kettner's Bk. of Table* 43 Some French cooks, before sending the artichoke to table, are careful to remove the choke, or as they call it, the hay. **1958** W. BICKEL tr. *Hering's Dict. Classical & Mod. Cookery* 558 *Artichoke Béarnaise style*, blanched, hay removed, braised in white wine, [etc.]. **1960** *News Chron.* 6 July 6/6 In the middle of the vegetable is the hay or choke (what would be the flower itself if it were not an artichoke like a thistle).

Hay (heɪ), *sb.*[7] The name of William Howard *Hay* (1866–1940), U.S. physician, used *attrib.* to designate various methods of medical and dietary treatment advocated by him, as ***Hay diet***, a diet based on the belief that proteins and carbohydrates should not be eaten at the same meal.

1925 *Jrnl. Amer. Med. Assoc.* 20 June 1938/2 Hay rest cure. **1933** *Ibid.* 25 Feb. 595/2 Can you give me any information on Dr. Hay and the Hay diet which has become so popular in certain sections of our country? I believe that it is based on the idea of not eating meats and starches in the same meal! **1936** D. POWELL *Turn, Magic Wheel* II. 142, I wish you'd let me put you on a Hay diet. All proteins at once, all starches. **1937** W. H. HAY *Human Ailments* xix. 136 If you wish to end colds for all time, then merely follow the directions for building health that you will find stressed continually by the Hay System. **1937** M. OSBORNE (*title*) Meatless dishes for Hay dieters. **1969** SINCLAIR & HOLLINGSWORTH *Hutchison's Food & Princ. Nutrition* (ed. 12) viii. 193 Gastric digestion of protein is not indispensible and its importance can easily be over-estimated, as in the fallacious rationale underlying the Hay diet.

hay, *v.*[1] [f. HAY *sb.*[1]]

1. *trans.* To furnish or supply with hay; to put (land) under hay.

1708 *Lond. Gaz.* No. 4409/4 An Estate to be sold..well Hay'd and Wooded. **1857** B. TAYLOR *North. Trav.* (1858) 143 The postillion stopped..to hay his horses. **1861** *Times* 27 Sept., Part of the land is hayed, the hay put in large cocks of about four tons each.

2. *intr.* To make hay. (Chiefly in *gerund* or *pr. pple*)

1556–1677 [see HAYING *vbl. sb.*]. **1828** WEBSTER, *Hay*, to dry or cure grass for preservation. **1886** *Pall Mall G.* 21 July 1/2 A great many of the Irish voters in towns go regularly haying, harvesting, hopping.

3. *trans.* To make into hay.

1884 W. BARROWS *Oregon* 332 The bunch grass..is hayed by the sun uncut. **1893** *Times* 11 July 4/1 In making hop bines into hay the bines must be got together directly they are 'hayed'.

†**hay,** *v.*[2] *Obs.* [OE. *hęʒian*, f. *haʒa* HAW, *hęʒe* HAY *sb.*[2]] *trans.* To enclose or fence in by a hedge; to hedge.

a **1050** *Liber Scintillarum* xvi. (1889) 80 Heʒa [*sepi*] earan þine mid þornum. *c* **1425** *MS. Bibl. Reg.* 12 B I lf. 78 *Sepio* ..to heghyn. **1610** W. FOLKINGHAM *Art of Survey* II. ii. 49 Collaterage Actiue, as siding, furrowing, balking..haying, hedging or shawing. *Ibid.*, Compound Contiguall Boundage is more significant, as side-haying, head-shawing, etc.

†**hay,** *v.*[3] *Obs.* [f. HAY *sb.*[3]] *intr.* To set 'hays' or nets for rabbits, etc.

c **1440** *Promp. Parv.* 221/1 Hayyn for conys, *cassio.* **1552** HULOET, Hayen for conyes, *cassio.* **1572** *Lease Manor Hawsted, Suffolk* in *Promp. Parv.* 221 *note*, Hawking, haying [= rabbit-netting]. **1613** BEAUM. & FL. *Coxcomb* I. iii, We shall scout here, as though we went a-haying.

†**hay,** *v.*[4] *Obs.* [f. HAY *sb.*[4]] *intr.* To dance the hay. Hence **haying** *vbl. sb.*

1768–74 TUCKER *Lt. Nat.* (1852) I. 492 What pretty country-dancings, and hayings, your five million of million of corpuscles make! **1777** MAD. D'ARBLAY *Early Diary* (1889) II. 199 We danced round the room, Hayed in and out with the chairs, and all that.

hay, obs. or dial. form of HAVE.

hay, obs. var. HEIGH, HEY; see also HAYE.

hay-'asthma. [In F. *asthme de foin*, Ger. *heuasthma.*] = HAY-FEVER.

1827 SOUTHEY *Lett.* (ed. Warter) IV. 61, I escaped from the hay-asthma with a visit of one month. **1840** *Tweedie's Syst. Pract. Med.* III. 86 In cases of hay-asthma, Dr. Elliston recommends the diffusion of chlorine in the air of the patient's apartment. **1884** *Sat. Rev.* 7 June 760/1 The name 'summer catarrh' is perhaps preferable to the more commonly used 'hay fever' and 'hay asthma'.

'hay-band. [BAND *sb.*[1] 2.] A rope of twisted hay used to bind up a truss or bundle of hay.

1641 BEST *Farm. Bks.* (Surtees) 37 They twine two longe hey-bandes and cast over the toppe of it. **1836** DICKENS *Sk. Boz. Streets* (1850) 30 Decayed cabbage-leaves, broken haybands, and all the indescribable litter of a vegetable market.

'hay-barn. A barn in which hay is stored.

1577 B. GOOGE *Heresbach's Husb.* I. (1586) 13 My Hey-barne, which hath in the upper roomes my Hey, and beneath, Waynes, Cartes. **1774** JOHNSON *Tour Wales* 1 Aug. in Boswell (1848) 418/2 The hay-barn, built with brick pillars from space to space, and covered with a roof. **1842–4** H. STEPHENS *Bk. of Farm* (1891) III. 22 The hay-barns are now, as a rule, constructed entirely of iron.

'hay-bird.

1. A name given locally to various small birds that build their nests with hay, *esp.* of the genera *Sylvia* and *Phylloscopus*, as the Blackcap, Garden Warbler, and Willow-Wren.

1802 G. MONTAGU *Ornith. Dict.* (1833) s.v., A much more compact structure than the Hay-bird usually makes. *Ibid.* s.v. *Pettychaps, Lesser*, Dr. Latham says [the lesser Pettychaps] is called in Dorsetshire the Hay-bird. **1885** SWAINSON *Prov. Names Birds* 24 Blackcap..Hay bird (Northants). **1889** H. SAUNDERS *Man. Brit. Birds* 64 In many places the Willow-Wren is also known as the Hay-bird.

2. The Pectoral Sandpiper or Grass-snipe, *Tringa maculata.* (New Jersey, U.S.)

'haybote. Also 5 **heybote.** [f. HAY *sb.*[2] + BOTE, BOOT *sb.*[1]] Wood or thorns for the repair of fences; the right of the tenant or commoner to take such material from the landlord's estate, or the common. By legal writers also called HEDGE-BOTE.

?**1170** *Charter* in *Mon. Angl.* (1830) VI. i. 263–4 [H]usbotam et heybotam ad sufficientiam in bosco meo de Dicton. **1235–52** *Rentalia Glaston.* (Somerset Rec. Soc.) 83 Haybote similiter sine vasto. **1484** *Lease of Scotter Manor* (N.W. Linc. Gloss.), 12 carect subbosci pro le heybote. **1594** WEST *2nd Pt. Symbol.* §55 Housebote, haibote, and plowbote, may be demanded by the name of estovers. **1607** COWELL *Interpr.*, *Haye boote*..is used in our common lawe for a permission to take thorns and freeth to make or repair hedges. **1778** *Eng. Gazetteer* (ed. 2), *Mansfield*, Nottingh... has..the privilege of having housebote and haybote out of his majesty's forest of Sherwood. **1845** STEPHEN *Comm. Laws Eng.* I. iv. (1895) I. 251 When this allowance [of wood] is for..repairing hedges and fences, it is termed haybote or hedge-bote.

haycock ('heɪkɒk). [f. HAY *sb.*[1] + COCK *sb.*[2]] A conical heap of hay in the field.

c **1470** HARDING *Chron.* CLXXIII. ii, Walter Wareyn among the hay kockes bushed. **1523** FITZHERB. *Husb.* §25 Toward nyght make it in wyndrowes and than in smal heycockes. **1632** MILTON *L'Allegro* 90 To the tanned haycock in the mead. **1794** S. WILLIAMS *Vermont* 98 Of an oval form, resembling the construction of an haycock. **1851** D. JERROLD *St. Giles* xxx. 306 Perched upon a Kent haycock.

hay-day, obs. form of HEY-DAY.

hay-de-guy, haydigyes: see under HAY *sb.*[4]

haydenite ('heɪdənaɪt). *Min.* [Named 1822 after H. H. Hayden.] A yellowish variety of chabazite.

1822 CLEAVELAND *Min.* 478 Haydenite..occurs in reddish or garnet colored crystals. **1868** DANA *Min.* (ed. 5) 435 *Haydenite* is a yellowish variety in small crystals..from Jones's Falls, near Baltimore, Md.

†**haye.** *Obs.* Also 7 **hayen, hay.** [a. Du. *haai*, pl. *-en*, WFlem. *haaie*, in Kilian 1599 *haeye*, whence also Sw. *haj*, mod.Ger. *hai* (in 1711 *häye*), all = shark; cf. ON. *hár, hárr* 'dog-fish', and *há-* in comb. marking fish of the shark kind, as *hákarl* shark, etc.] A shark, or a particular species of shark. (Also **hay-fish.**)

1613 PURCHAS *Pilgrimage* (1614) 504 They have of Hayens or Tuberons which devour men, especially such as fish for Pearles. **1665** SIR T. HERBERT *Trav.* (1677) 6 The greedy Hayen called Tuberon or Shark. **1694** *Acc. Sev. Late Voy.* II. (1711) 139 They do not fling away the Hays in Spain, but sell them. **1705** BOSMAN *Guinea* 282 When the Haye seizes his Prey he is obliged to turn himself on his Back. **1731** MEDLEY *Kolben's Cape G. Hope* II. 193 There are in the Cape sea two sorts of Sharks. The Cape-Europeans call 'em Hayes. **1799** W. TOOKE *View Russian Emp.* III. 105 The Frozen Ocean..teems with..the sea-dog..sea-hog, hay-fish. **1867** SMYTH *Sailor's Word-bk.*, *Haye*, a peculiar ground-shark on the coast of Guinea.

hayel, obs. form of HAIL.

hayer, -yr, var. HAIRE, *Obs.*

hayesine ('heɪzaɪn). *Min.* [Named 1844, after A. A. Hayes.] A hydrous borate of calcium found in globular fibrous masses.

1844 F. ALGER *Min.* 318 Hayesine..occurs in globular masses of a fibrous structure. **1873** *Fownes' Chem.* (ed. 11) 341 Much borax is now manufactured..from..hayesine, which occurs in southern Peru.

'hayey, *a. nonce-wd.* [f. HAY *sb.*[1] + -Y; cf. *clayey.*] Of the nature of or resembling hay.

1611 COTGR., *Feneux*, hayie, full of hay.

hayfar(r)e, -fer, -fre, obs. forms of HEIFER.

hay-fever. [f. HAY *sb.*[1]] A disorder of the early summer, characterized by a catarrhal condition of the ocular, nasal, and respiratory mucous membranes, accompanied generally by asthmatic symptoms; usually caused by the pollen of grasses and some flowers, sometimes also by the dust of other substances or the odorous emanations of some fruits and animals.

First described under the name of *summer catarrh* by Bostock in *Trans. Medico-Chirurg. Soc.* 1819, X. 161, and 1828, XIV. 437. Gordon in 1829 used the names *hay-asthma, hay-fever.*

1829 GORDON in *Med. Gaz.* IV. 266. **1835** SYD. SMITH *Lett.* No. 354, I am suffering from my old complaint hay-fever (as it is called). **1840** *Tweedie's Syst. Pract. Med.* III. 84 The Summer Catarrh, hay-fever, or hay-asthma as it is termed from its supposed connexion with the effluvium of new hay. **1851** HT. MARTINEAU *Hist. Peace* (1877) III. v. ix. 379 The King enjoyed an exemption from his annual attack of hay-fever.

'hayfield. [f. HAY *sb.*[1]] A field in which haymaking is going on, or in which grass is standing to be cut for hay.

1784 COWPER *Task* I. 295 From the sun-burnt hay-field homeward creeps The loaded wain. **1853** LYTTON *My Novel* I. iv, They were now in the hayfield.

'hay-foot. [HAY *sb.*[1]] *hay-foot, straw-foot*: with right and left foot alternately (at the word of command). Also as *vb.*

In allusion to the alleged use of hay and straw to enable a rustic recruit to distinguish the right foot from the left.

1851 *Knickerbocker* XXXVIII. 79 At company-training and general-training..it was all 'hay-foot, straw-foot' with him. **1887** J. D. BILLINGS *Hardtack & Coffee* 208 Scores of men..would 'hay-foot' every time when they should 'straw-foot'. **1898** J. MACMANUS *Bend of Road* 40 Poor fool, he's off, hay foot straw foot, an' small grass grows round his heels till he's there. **1911** R. D. SAUNDERS *Col. Todhunter* vii. 98 You never got in a thousand miles of one of 'em for all your 'heppin' and 'hay-foot' and 'straw-foot' drillin'. **1911** H. S. HARRISON *Queed* i. 12 They march like little lambs when I say the word. Hay-foot—straw-foot.

hay-fork. [f. HAY *sb.*[1]] A long-handled fork used for turning over hay to dry, or in pitching and loading it.

1552 HULOET, Hay forcke, *furca, furcula.* **1573** TUSSER *Husb.* xvii. (1878) 37 Sharp sikle and weeding hooke, haie fork and rake. **1856** EMERSON *Eng. Traits* iv. (*Race*) Wks. Bohn II. 26 If a farmer has so much as a hayfork, he sticks it into a King Dag.

b. A large fork elevated by a horse and pulley in unloading hay from a wagon to a mow, or *vice versâ* (Knight *Dict. Mech.* 1875).

c. *attrib.*, as **hay-fork frame,** a frame (of a tricycle) made in the shape of a hay-fork.

1885 *Bazaar* 30 Mar. 330/2 [Tricycle] A hayfork frame carries the wheels on short independent axles.

hay-house. [f. HAY *sb.*[1]] A building in which hay is stored, a hay-barn; *spec.* a structure having a roof supported on pillars, and without side or end walls.

a **1000** *Voc.* in Wr.-Wülcker 237/36 *Fenile*, heʒhus. **1483** *Cath. Angl.* 169/2 An Hay howse, *fenerium.* **1588** *Bursar's Roll* in Willis & Clark *Cambridge* (1886) I. 26 [There were.. a] haye house [and a hen-house]. **1611** COTGR., *Foinil*, a Hay-stacke..Hay-loft, Hay-house.

†**hayhove.** *Obs.* In 4 heyhowe, hayhof, 5 heyhove, -offe, -oue, haihoue. See also ALE-HOOF. [f. HAY *sb.*² + HOVE *sb.*] The herb Ground Ivy.
c **1325** *Gloss. W. de Biblesw.* in Wright *Voc.* 162 *Eyre terestre*, heyhowe. *a* **1387** *Sinon. Barthol.* 18 *Edera nigra, Edera terrestris*, idem sunt i. hayhof. **14..** *Roy. MS. 18 A. VI*, lf. 74 b, *Edera terrestris* ys an herbe þat me clepyþ erth yuye, or heyoue. *c* **1460** J. RUSSELL *Bk. Nurture* 993 Hey hove, heyriff, herbe benet, bresewort, and smallache. **1597** GERARDE *Herbal* App., Heihow is *Hedera terrestris*.

haying ('heɪɪŋ), *vbl. sb.* [f. HAY *v.*¹ + -ING¹.] The process of making and storing hay.
1677 *Dade's Prognost.* A viij, In this Moneth [July] ply your Haying. **1864** LOWELL *Fireside Trav.* 108 The haying being over, fires blazed or smouldered against the stumps in the fields. **1882** *Times* 30 Nov. 11 The object of ensilage is to maintain the sap as nearly as possible in its original state, without..transformation into grain or straw, or the fermentation of haying.
b. *attrib.*, as *haying season, time.*
1556 WITHALS *Dict.* (1568) 2 a/1 Heying time, *fœnifacium.* **1587** FLEMING *Contn. Holinshed* III. 1542/2 Till haruest or haieng time. **1814** *Sporting Mag.* XLIV. 206 One Sunday in the haying season. **1883** MRS. ROLLINS *New Eng. Bygones* 83 In haying-time, thrice a day, a score or more of stout-limbed laborers gathered around my grandfather's board.

'**hay-jack.** [cf. HAY-BIRD.] A name given to several small birds which build their nests of hay.
a **1825** FORBY *Voc. E. Anglia, Hay-jack*, the lesser reed-sparrow, or sedge-bird of Penn. **1888** A. NEWTON in *Encycl. Brit.* XXIV. 553/1 The nests of each of these species [of Sylvia] are very pretty works of art, firmly built of bents or other plant stalks..This style of nest-building..has obtained for the builders the name of 'Hay-Jack', quite without reference to the kind of bird which puts the nests together.

hayl(e, haylle, obs. forms of HAIL, HALE.

haylage ('heɪlɪdʒ). *Agric.* [Portmanteau word f. HAY *sb.*¹ + SI)LAGE *sb.*] Silage made from grass which has been partially dried.
1960 *Times* 5 July (Agric. Suppl.) p. i/1 The preservation and mechanical feeding of grass as haylage. **1962** *Outlook on Agric.* III. 259/1 Both hay and haylage, cut at the same stage of growth, give better live weight gains in cattle than silage does. **1973** *Country Life* 28 June 1863/2 Some of the best silage, or haylage as this system is known, is made in towers.

haylce, -se, var. of HAILSE *v. Obs.*

haylemote, haylife, obs. ff. HALLMOTE, HAIRIF.

hayllyer, obs. form of HALYARD.

hayloft ('heɪlɒft, -ɔː-). [f. HAY *sb.*¹] A loft or storing place for hay over a stable or barn.
1573 TUSSER *Husb.* lxxxix. (1878) 179 Feare candle in hailoft, in barne, and in shed. **1789** P. SMYTH tr. *Aldrich's Archit.* (1818) 128 The stables with the hay-lofts placed over them. **1841** W. SPALDING *Italy & It. Isl.* III. 148 The ruined house, used as a stable and hay-loft, which stands near the Tiber at the foot of the Aventine.

haym, obs. Sc. form of HOME.

'**haymaker.** [f. HAY *sb.*¹]
1. A man or woman employed in making hay; *esp.* one engaged in lifting, tossing, and spreading the hay after it is mown.
14.. *Voc.* in Wr.-Wülcker 582/36 *Fenissa*, a heymakere. **1528** *MS. Acc. St. John's Hosp., Canterb.*, For mete & drynk for the hay makers. **1590** GREENE *Never too late* (1600) 103 A womans smile is as good to a Louer, as a sunshine day to a haymaker. **1770** WESLEY *Jrnl.* 28 July, A shower brought all the haymakers home. **1853** LYTTON *My Novel* I. iii, For the refreshment of the thirsty haymakers.
2. An apparatus for shaking up and drying hay.
1853 *Catal. R. Agric. Soc. Show Gloucester* 67 Patent Improved Double Action Haymaker. **1862** J. WILSON *Farming* 149 Haymakers are valuable implements.
3. *pl.* The name of a country-dance. Also called *haymakers' jig.*
4. a. A swinging blow. *slang* or *colloq.*
1912 ADE *Knocking Neighbors* 87 Every time he landed a crushing Hay-Maker on her Family History she countered with a short-arm Jolt. **1918** *Amer. Mag.* Apr. 113/3 'Gitteloutahere,' panted Slough, aiming a hay-maker at Doug. **1924** *Glasgow Herald* 18 July 10 It was not at all improbable that Eagan would bring over a 'haymaker' and put the Englishman out. **1925** J. J. CORBETT *Roar of Crowd* 87, I deliberately pulled my right back and swung 'hay-makers' at Choinyski, intending to miss him. **1938** I. KUHN *Assigned to Adventure* xxix. 305 Mrs. Medvedeff..emerged once more and landed a haymaker on her husband's chin. **1961** J. HELLER *Catch-22* (1962) xlii. 442 'I'm going to punch Captain Black right in the nose the next time I see him,' gloried the chaplain, throwing two left jabs in the air and then a clumsy haymaker. 'Just like that.' **1972** 'E. LATHEN' *Murder without Icing* (1973) xxii. 189 Rising from a collision, he had thrown off his glove and landed a haymaker.
b. *Cricket.* A sweeping stroke with the bat.
1954 J. FINGLETON *Ashes crown Year* 117 Davidson tried his luck with a hay-maker off Tattersall and Graveney.. took a splendid catch. **1955** *Times* 24 June 14/2 There were only a few haymakers from Wardle left.

'**haymaking,** *vbl. sb.* [f. as HAYMAKER.] **a.** The process of cutting and drying grass for hay. Also *fig.* and *transf.* The action of 'making hay' (see HAY *sb.*¹ 3).
1588 *Marprel. Epist.* (Arb.) 45 Tooke his seruants and went a heymaking. **1589** COGAN *Haven Health* (1636) 290 How that at York the Monkes of Saint Mary Abbey and the Nunnes of Clement Thorpe met together at heymaking. **1749** BERKELEY *Word to Wise* Wks. III. 447 The lightest labour, that of hay-making. **1840** DICKENS *Barn. Rudge* iv, Where there was merry hay-making in the summer time. **1882** *Daily News* (Ware), A number of men go into a friend's room, find him absent, and testify to their chagrin by disturbing the arrangements of his furniture. But hay-making of this sort is comparatively harmless and inoffensive. **1924** W. R. INGE *Lay Thoughts* (1926) 193 The hay-making of the profiteer after the war. **1971** *Weekend World* (Johannesburg) 9 May 1/2 The unrated Mexican shattered the..boxing champion's hopes of a crack at the world title with a hay-making left hook in the ninth of their ..10 round fight.
b. *attrib.* and *Comb.*, as ***haymaking season, time,*** etc.; **haymaking furnace**, an apparatus in which the heat of a coke furnace is driven by a fan through new-mown hay in order to dry it; **haymaking machine**, an apparatus for drying grass for hay.
1752 THYER *Note on Milton's L'Allegro* 92 The haymaking scene in the lower lands. **1822** SHELLEY *Chas. I*, II. 39 To catch Woodcocks in haymaking time. **1826** LOUDON *Encycl. Agric.* (1844) 420 Horse Rakes and Haymaking Machines. **1881** MISS YONGE *Lads & Lasses Langley* ii. 60 There was hay-making-machine-work going on at the farm.

hay-mow ('heɪmaʊ). Also 5 -moghte, 7 -mough. [f. HAY *sb.*¹] A rick or stack of hay; in some places applied to the pile of hay stored in a hay-house or barn, or to the compartment of a barn in which hay is stored.
1483 *Cath. Angl.* 170/1 An Hay moghte, *arconius.* **1530** PALSGR. 230/1 Heymowe, *tas de foyn.* **1620** SHELTON *Quix.* (1746) III. iv. 26 The poor Fellow thinks belike that we sleep here in a Hay-mow. **1655** MRQ. WORCESTER *Cent. Inv.* §77 Which I have tried..in a Barn, from one end to the other, on an Hay-mow. **1664** POWER *Exp. Philos.* I. 13 A little white short-leg'd Spider (which you shall find..in a sweating Hey-mough). **1838** HAWTHORNE *Amer. Note-Bks.* (1883) 198 Fields of grass beyond, where stand the hay-mows of last year. **1864** BOWEN *Logic* ix. 303 Our inability to find a needle in a hay-mow is no proof that the needle is not there. **1888** E. EGGLESTON *Graysons* 182 The hay-mow at the other end of the floor was full of men and boys.

†**hayne**¹. *Obs.* Also 4-5 heyne, 6 haine, hayn. [Origin obscure. Connexion with HAIN *v.*¹ 3 has been suggested. (The phonology shows connexion with OE. *héan* to be impossible.)] A term of reproach: A mean wretch, a niggard.
c **1386** CHAUCER *Can. Yeom. Prol. & T.* 766 He..in his sleue..hadde a siluer teyne He slyly tooke it out, this cursed heyne [*v. rr.* hayn(e, haine, *Lansd.* hyne]. *a* **1529** SKELTON *Bouge of Courte* 328 It is great scorne to see such an hayne As thou arte..With us olde seruantes suche maysters to playe. **1542** UDALL *Erasm. Apoph.* I. 51 a, Haines and niggardes of their purse. *Ibid.* II. 215 a, That sparing, pinching, and plaiyng the nygardes or haynes, belonged to cookes, and not to kinges. **1570** LEVINS *Manip.* 200/6 Hayne, *verna.*

†**hayne**². *Astrol. Obs.* [f. HAIN *v.*² to raise, elevate.] = EXALTATION 3.
1647 LILLY *Chr. Astrol.* lxx. 416 The Significator of the Man hath no manner of affliction, viz. ♀ she being in her Hayne, and free from the least manner of misfortune.

haynous, obs. form of HEINOUS.

hayr, obs. form of HAIR, HOAR; var. HAIRE.

'**hay-rack.** [f. HAY *sb.*¹]
1. A rack for holding hay for cattle.
1825 HONE *Every-day Bk.* I. 1601 A crow cawing on the hay-rack. **1888** E. EGGLESTON *Graysons* 191 [They] had to climb over a hayrack and thence down to the ground.
2. A light framework projecting from the sides of a wagon to increase its carrying capacity for hay or other bulky material; a shelving. *U.S.*

'**hay-rake.**
1. A hand-rake used in haymaking.
1725 BAILEY *Erasm. Colloq.* 552 A Boy..with a Hay-rake upon his Shoulder. **1826** LOUDON *Encycl. Agric.* (1844) 370 The hay-rake is usually made of willow, that it may be light and easy to work.
2. An implement drawn by a horse for raking hay into windrows ready for pitching.
1875 in KNIGHT *Dict. Mech.*

hayrick ('heɪrɪk). Also 5 **heyrek**, 6-8 **hayreek**. [f. HAY *sb.*¹ + RICK.] A haystack.
14.. *Voc.* in Wr.-Wülcker 582/39 *Fenile*, heyrek. **1547** BOORDE *Brev. Health* lxxiii. 24 A bocher had a sonne that fel out of a hyghe haye-rycke. **1591** PERCIVALL *Sp. Dict.*, *Almiar*, a Hay reeke. **1679** *Lond. Gaz.* No. 1451/4 Many Hay-Reeks are spoiled. **1721** CIBBER *Rival Fools* II, I'm mute as..a goose in a Hay-Reek. **1766** GOLDSM. *Vic. W.* viii, In the meadow or at the hay-rick. **1837** DICKENS *Pickw.* vii, The rich, sweet smell of the hayricks.

hayrif, var. HAIRIF, cleavers.

hayron, hayse, obs. forms of HERON, HAZE.

'**hay-seed, 'hayseed.** [f. HAY *sb.*¹]
1. a. The grass seed shaken out of hay.
1577 B. GOOGE *Heresbach's Husb.* I. (1586) 44 b, Some doo cast Hey seede, geathered from the Heyloaft or the racks, over the grounde. **1846** J. BAXTER *Libr. Pract. Agric.* (ed. 4) I. 350 With rye grass and clovers..and what are termed hay seeds, a permanent pasture of the best quality..cannot be made. *Note.* Hay seeds consist of the sweepings of hay-lofts, or the seeds and chaff obtained from hay.
b. *fig.* (cf. sense 3).
1894 W. C. RUSSELL *Good Ship Mohock* I. 43 They were fresh from a rural parish; the hayseed smelt strongly in their hair, as the sailor says.
2. The redseed, brit, etc., on which mackerel and other fish largely feed. *U.S.* (*Cent. Dict.*)
3. Humorous name for a rustic. *N. Amer., Austral.*, and *N.Z.*
1851 H. MELVILLE *Moby Dick* I. vi. 52 Ah, poor Hay-Seed! how bitterly will burst those straps in the first howling gale! **1883** *Prince Albert Times* (Sask.) 28 Dec. 3/1 Where the hay seeds may work at their farming. **1889** *Boston* (Mass.) *Jrnl.* 29 Apr. 2/2 To send a glimmer of returning reason through the mind of the frontier hay-seed. **1891** *Harper's Weekly* 19 Sept. 705/3 Dickey thought it a base presumption for an 'old hayseed' to try to enter the town's society. **1896** *Daily News* 9 July 4/2 His 'hay seed' following sent him to the U.S. Senate. **1901** *Daily Colonist* (Victoria, B.C.) 11 Oct. 4/2 It is the habit of the comic journals to print pictures about the 'hay-seeds' who are gulled by confidence men. **1916** C. J. DENNIS *Songs Sentimental Bloke* 117 *'Ayseed* (Hayseed), a rustic. **1965** F. SARGESON *Memoirs of Peon* ix. 271 He might be identified as either peasant or hayseed. *Ibid.*, Exhibiting something of the hayseed character which he lacked.

haysel ('heɪsəl). [f. HAY *sb.*¹ + ME. SELE season.] The hay season. (Proper to East Anglia.)
[**1674-5** *Watertown* (Mass.) *Rec.* 9 Mar. (1894), The town agreed to alow him for his salary 30 pounds and A fortnites time in hay-sill [*printed* hay fill].] *a* **1825** in FORBY *Voc. E. Anglia.* **1865** *Times* 14 Feb. [Lett. fr. Suffolk] Only at certain times—as in haysel and harvest. **1869** *Gd. Words* Mar. *Suppl.* 5 It was glorious weather for haysel. **1883** G. C. DAVIES *Norfolk Broads* xxxi. (1884) 240 In the period between 'haysel' (hay-harvest) and November.

haystack ('heɪstæk). [f. HAY *sb.*¹] **a.** A stack or large pile of hay built in the open air, of regular form and finished off with a pointed or ridged top. ***to look for a needle in a haystack***: see NEEDLE *sb.* 1 c.
14.. *Voc.* in Wr.-Wülcker 725/32 *Hic arconius*, a haystak. **1555** EDEN *Decades* 351 The myddlemost is lyke a heye stacke. **1688** R. HOLME *Armoury* III. 73/1 A Hay Stack is.. shaped broad at the bottom and narrow at the top. **1850** CARLYLE *Latter-d. Pamph.* vi. (1872) 205 If these rats meet a haystack, they eat their way through it.
b. *attrib.* and *Comb.*, as ***haystack roof***; **haystack boiler**, an old tall form of steam-boiler somewhat like a haystack in shape.
1855 CHAMIER *My Travels* I. iii. 42 A large white house, with a kind of haystack red roof.

haysugge. *Obs.* exc. *dial.* Forms: 1 **heȝesugge**, 3 **heisugge**, 4-5 **heysoge, -soke, -sug(ge**, 5 **eysoge, haysugge**, 9 *dial.* **haysuck, -zick.** [OE. *heȝesugge*, f. *heȝe* HAY *sb.*² + fem. form of *sugga, sucga* sucker, f. *súgan* to suck.] The hedge-sparrow.
c **1000** ÆLFRIC *Voc.* in Wr.-Wülcker 131/34 *Cicada, uicetula*, heȝesugge. *a* **1250** *Owl & Night.* 505 Thu singst worse thon the hei-sugge, þat fliȝth bi grunde among the stubbe. *c* **1381** CHAUCER *Parl. Foules* 612 Thow mortherere of the heysoge [*v. rr.* heysoke, heysug(g(e, haysugge]. **14..** *Voc.* in Wr.-Wülcker 577/16 *Cu[r]ruca*, an heysugge. *c* **1450** *Bk. Hawkyng* in *Rel. Ant.* I. 296 Eysoges..and other smale briddes. **1616** BULLOKAR *Eng. Expos.*, *Heisugge*, a bird which hatcheth the Cuckooes egges. **1890** *Gloucestersh. Gloss.*, *Haysuck* or *Hayzick*, the hedge sparrow. Generally pronounced 'Isaac'.

hayt, obs. form of HOT; var. HEIT *int.*

hayte, obs. form of AIT *sb.*¹, an islet.
1532 in W. H. Turner *Select. Rec. Oxford* 108 A certain parcel of meadow called a hayte, lying between the said meadow..on the east, and the Thames on the west.

haythe, haythen, haythorn, obs. forms of HEIGHT *v.*, HEATHEN, HAWTHORN.

Haytian, var. HAITIAN *a.* and *sb.*

haytorite ('heɪtəraɪt). *Min.* [Named 1827, from Hay Tor, in Devonshire.] A pseudomorphic chalcedony, having the form of datolite.
1827 *Philos. Mag.* Ser. II. I. 39 We contemplate calling it Haytorite in honor of its birthplace. **1868** DANA *Min.* 382 Haytorite is datolite altered to chalcedony.

hayuie, obs. Sc. form of HEAVY.

hayward ('heɪwɔːd). Also 3 **heiward**, 4 **haiward**, 5-7 **heyward**, 7 **haward**. [f. HAY *sb.*² + WARD, OE. *weard* guardian.] An officer of a manor, township, or parish, having charge of the fences and enclosures, *esp.* to keep cattle from breaking through from the common into enclosed fields; sometimes, the herdsman of the cattle feeding on the common.
a **1225** *Ancr. R.* 418 þeonne mot heo þenchen of þe kues foddre..oluhnen þene heiward. *c* **1380** WYCLIF *Sel. Wks.* III. 436 þe emperor..makede hise bishopis haywardis of þe world. **1393** LANGL. *P. Pl.* C. VI. 16 Canstow..haue an horne and be haywarde, and liggen oute a nyghtes, And kepe my corn in my croft fro pykers and þeeues? *c* **1440** *Promp. Parv.* 234/1 Heyward, *agellarius.* **1511-12** *Act 3 Hen. VIII*, c. 23 §9 The said accomptauntes..that is to saye, Feodaries

Bailliffes Reves Heywardes and Bedelles. 1607 COWELL *Interpr.*, *Haward*..signifieth with us one that keepeth the common heard of the towne. 1638 in Coffin *Hist. Newberry, Mass.* (1845) 28 Thomas Hale and John Baker are appointed hay wards till the town shall appoint new. 1654 in Picton *L'pool Munic. Rec.* (1883) I. 191 The Heyward..shall take and impound the said swyne. 1664 EVELYN *Sylva* (1776) 399 Are not 5000 Oaks worth the fencing and inspection of a Hayward? 1880 *Daily News* 18 Feb., The hayward at Corfe Castle has charge of the beautiful common which lies on the Swanage side of the village, on which the inhabitants are allowed to turn their cattle. 1884 *Century Mag.* Jan. 443/2 In some parts of Massachusetts a 'hayward' was employed to attend the cattle of a whole township. 1892 *Oxford Chron.* 23 Apr. 8 From 1810 to 1852, the time of the Cowley Inclosure, he had frequently tended the cattle as hay-ward in these grazings.

'haywire, *sb.* and *a.* [f. HAY *sb.*[1] + WIRE *sb.*]

A. *sb.* Wire for binding bales of hay, straw, etc. *N. Amer.*

1917 *Deb. House of Commons Canada* 5351/2 But the 'hay wire' did not hold. 1921 *Outing* (U.S.) Dec. 101/1 You can't run a logging camp without snuff and hay wire. 1936 D. MCCOWAN *Anim. Canad. Rockies* xii. 103 A thick mesh of hay wire. 1942 E. PAUL *Narrow St.* v. 41 The tenants bought kindling wood in little bundles... These neat little sticks had been dipped in resin at one end, and were bound with haywire.

B. *adj.* **1.** Poorly equipped, roughly contrived, inefficient, esp. ***hay-wire outfit*** (from the practice of using hay-wire for makeshift repairs). orig. *U.S.*

1905 *Forestry Bureau Bull.* (U.S.) 61 B, *Hay wire outfit*, a contemptuous term for loggers with poor logging equipment. 1931 'D. STIFF' *Milk & Honey Route* 207 A haywire outfit is something that is all tied and patched together. 1934 *N. & Q.* CLXVI. 13/1, I first heard 'hay-wire' in the summer of 1929, when I was living in northern New York State. There is also the expression 'haywire outfit', a job on which poor living accommodations are provided for the workers. Also an inefficient factory or shop. 1959 *Listener* 26 Feb. 388/2 A haywire, unpredictable, one-man business. 1968 R. D. PATTERSON *Finlay's River* 145 The..irritating, because man-made, chaos attendant on the intrusion of a haywire railroad into the ordered life of the frontier now lay behind them.

2. Of a person, circumstances, etc.: in an emotional state, tangled, involved, confused, crazy. *colloq.* (orig. *U.S.*).

1934 J. O'HARA *Appointment in Samarra* vii. 226 A married man..and absolutely haywire on the subject of another woman. 1939 W. FAULKNER *Wild Palms* 223 Now you can eat something. Or do you think that will send you haywire again? 1942 D. POWELL *Time to be Born* (1943) xiv. 330 Everything seems so haywire, lately. 1955 'E. C. R. LORAC' *Ask Policeman* viii. 89 The time element's all haywire.

b. *spec.* in phr. ***to go haywire***, to go wrong; to become excited or distracted, to become mentally unbalanced. *colloq.* (orig. *U.S.*).

1929 *N.Y. Times* 13 Oct., When some element in the recording system becomes defective it is said to have gone haywire. 1933 *Daily Express* 16 Nov. 6/4 *Haywire*, epithet applied currently in U.S. to man of confused ideas... New York's newly elect mayor La Guardia is said by his enemies to have gone all haywire. 1936 M. ALLINGHAM *Flowers for Judge* i. 15, I suppose some wives would have gone haywire by this time. 1940 N. MARSH *Surfeit of Lampreys* (1941) vii. 103 Some nice homicidal maniac..going all haywire. 1942 *Tee Emm* (Air Ministry) II. 88 If the Governor Unit should go haywire then you merely pull the little switch down to the fixed position and all is well. 1942 E. WAUGH *Put out More Flags* 42 'If anyone so much as mentions concentration camps again,' said Ambrose Silk, 'I shall go frankly haywire.' 1945 *Times* 28 May 2/1 The compasses acted normally, but over the magnetic pole, where the weather was more favourable, they 'went haywire'. 1951 M. KENNEDY *Lucy Carmichael* III. i. 149 They go haywire because they haven't had any love affair at all. 1962 *Cath. Herald* 26 Oct. 1/5 Architecture has gone haywire. Music is without harmony. 1962 A. NISBETT *Technique Sound Studio* xii. 214 Everything..going haywire at the same time.

hazan, hazzan, varr. CHAZZAN.

hazard ('hæzəd), *sb.* (*a.*) Forms: 4–6 **hasard**, 5–6 **-arde**, 6 **hazarde**, (**hassard(e**, **hazered**, *Sc.* **hasart**), 6–7 **hazzard**, 5– **hazard**. [a. OF. *hasard*, *-art* (12th c. in Hatz.-Darm.): cf. Pr., Sp., Pg. *azar*, It. *la zara*, *azzardo* (from Fr.), med.L. *azardum*, *azarum* (Du Cange).

The origin of the French word is uncertain, but its source was prob. Arabic. According to William of Tyre, the game took its name from a castle called *Hasart* or *Asart* in Palestine, during the siege of which it was invented: see Littré s.v. The true Arab name of this castle appears to have been *'Ain Zarba* (Prof. Margoliouth). Mahn proposes vulgar Arab. *az-zahr* or *az-zār* 'die' (Bocthor); but early evidence for this sense is wanting.]

1. A game at dice in which the chances are complicated by a number of arbitrary rules.

c1300 *Havelok* 2326 Leyk of mine, of hasard ok, Romanz reding of þe bok. c1380 WYCLIF *Wks.* (1880) 152 þei fallen to nyse pleies, at tables, chees & hasard. c1440 *Promp. Parv.* 228/2 Hasarde, play, *aleatura*. 1530 PALSGR. 229/2 Hasarde a dyce playe, *hasart, azart*. 1599 SHAKS. *Hen. V*, III. vii. 93 Who will goe to Hazard with me for twentie Prisoners? 1638 SIR T. HERBERT *Trav.* (ed. 2) 340 They can play at chesse, irish, passage, in and in, hazard. 1778 C. JONES *Hoyle's Games Impr.* 209 The Game of Hazard..may be played by any Number of Persons. He who takes the Box and Dice throws a Main, that is to say, a Chance for the Company, which must be above four, and not exceed nine [etc.]. 1882 SERJT. BALLANTINE *Exper.* iv. 52 The principal game played was hazard, of which there were two kinds: French hazard, in which the players staked against the bank, and English, or chicken hazard, in which they played against each other.

2. Chance, venture; a chance.

1583 STANYHURST *Æneis* III. (Arb.) 71, I viewd with wundring a grisly monsterus hazard. 1594 SHAKS. *Rich. III*, v. iv. 10 Slaue, I haue set my life vpon a cast, And I will stand the hazard of the Dye. 1597 DANIEL *Civ. Wars* II. (R.), These mighty actors..on the hazard of a bad exchange, Have ventur'd all the stock of life beside. 1641 HINDE *J. Bruen* xxxix. 121 All games depending upon hazzard or chance are to be eschewed. 1697 *Conf. at Lambeth* in W. S. Perry *Hist. Coll. Amer. Col. Ch.* I. 44 They very unfairly threw out the Bill without so much as giving it a hazard. 1843 LYTTON *Last Bar.* I. ii, On what hazards turns our fate!

3. Risk of loss or harm; peril, jeopardy.

1548 HALL *Chron., Edw. IV*, 219 In so many hasardes and ieoperdies of his life. 1576 FLEMING *Panopl. Epist.* 164 To inlarge your dominion: yea, and that without hassard and detriment. 1630 *R. Johnson's Kingd. & Commw.* 46 By preservation of himselfe from Hazards of Travell. c1645 HOWELL *Lett.* (1650) II. 33 Love..in case of distance and long absence would be in hazard to languish. 1701 PEPYS *Corr.* 4 Dec., I should not fear the hazard of sending him abroad. 1752 HUME *Ess. & Treat.* (1777) I. 284 Profits proportionable to their expence and hazard. 1855 MACAULAY *Hist. Eng.* III. 723 A service of some hazard was to be rendered to the good cause.

†**4.** That which is risked or staked. *Obs. rare.*

1596 SHAKS. *Merch. V.* I. i. 151, I do not doubt..Or to finde both, Or bring your latter hazard backe againe.

5. In various phrases belonging to prec. senses.

1340 *Ayenb.* 171 He hise heþ folliche y-spended..and al ylayd to an hazard. 1530 PALSGR. 582/2, I play at the hazarde, or put a thynge in daunger, *je hazarde*. 1548 HALL *Chron., Edw. IV*, 197b, To abyde the hasarde of hys dishonour. *Ibid.* 222 To put the estate of ye realme on [GRAFTON in] an yll hasard. 1621 BURTON *Anat. Mel.* II. iii. IV. ii. (1651) 628, I had rather marry a fair one, and put it to the hazard. 1638 SIR T. HERBERT *Trav.* (ed. 2) 91 Allured ..to runne a bold hazard with him to the gates of Death. 1741 RICHARDSON *Pamela* (1824) I. viii. 21 What a sad hazard a poor maiden..stands against the temptations of this world. 1750 JOHNSON *Rambler* No. 2 ¶15 Lest they should put their reputation in hazard. 1789 MRS. PIOZZI *Journ. France* II. 368 They would have run such hazards getting home! 1834 MACAULAY *Ess., Pitt* (1854) 304 To put both his power and his popularity to hazard.

b. ***at hazard*** (†***hazards***): (*a*) by chance, fortuitously, without design or plan; (*b*) at stake, in danger. ***at (to, with) the hazard of***, at the risk of. ***at all hazards, at every hazard***, at all risks, in spite of every peril. ***by hazard*** (F. *par hasard*) = at hazard. ***in hazard***, in peril. ***on the hazard***, at stake. ***out of hazard***, out of peril.

a1547 SURREY in *Tottell's Misc.* (Arb.) 19 In hazarde of his health. 1576 FLEMING *Panopl. Epist.* 181 Selling al at hazard. *Ibid.* 260 My reputation, and my worship hadbeene in hazard. 1640 O. SEDGWICKE *Christs Counsell* 24 He did let and suffer his spirituall estate to run on at hazards. 1641 TRAPP *Theologia Theol.* 267 S. Hierome learnt Hebrew with the hazard of his life. a1700 DRYDEN tr. *Ovid's Art Love* Wks. 1760 IV. 118 Some choose, and some at hazard seize their mate. 1726 SHELVOCKE *Voy. round World* (1757) 304 It was resolved, at all hazards, to go. 1751 JOHNSON *Rambler* No. 93 ¶10 No man can justly aspire to honour, but at the hazard of disgrace. 1801 CHARLOTTE SMITH *Solitary Wand.* II. 337 The life of Montgomeri appeared to be out of hazard. 1804 *Something Odd* I. 126 He once saved me..to the imminent hazard of his own life. 1837 SIR F. PALGRAVE *Merch. & Friar* Ded. (1844) 2 The two following examples, taken at hazard. 1838 PRESCOTT *Ferd. & Is.* (1846) I. v. 235 He determined to relieve it at every hazard. 1846 TRENCH *Mirac.* xxi. (1862) 334 Where their worldly interests were at hazard. 1876 DARWIN *Cross-Fertil.* ix. 339 Two plants taken by hazard were protected under separate nets. 1880 L. WALLACE *Ben-Hur* v. xii, Messala's whole fortune was on the hazard.

c. †***to fall into (a person's) hazard***, i.e. his power to hurt or harm: cf. DANGER *sb.* 1. (*Obs.*) ***to make a hazard***, to make a guess or venture.

1615 T. ADAMS *Two Sonnes* 75 At last they fall into the usurers hazard. 1850 B. TAYLOR *Eldorado* xi. (1862) 107 Making a hazard at the direction in which the trail ran.

6. *Tennis.* Each of the winning openings in a tennis-court. ***hazard side***, the side of the court into which the ball is served.

1599 SHAKS. *Hen. V*, I. ii. 263 We will in France..play a set, Shall strike his fathers Crowne into the hazard. 1611 COTGR., *Pelouse*..also the lower hazard in a Tennis-court. 1642 HOWELL *For. Trav.* iii. (Arb.) 20 When at the racket court he had a ball struck into his hazard. 1688 R. HOLME *Armoury* III. v. 265 They that serve upon the Pent-house, are to serve behind the Blew on the Hazard side, else it is a loss. 1702 BOYER *Dict. Royal*, *Trou*..*Le petit trou* (*au jeu de Paume*), the hazard at Tennis. 1878 J. MARSHALL *Ann. Tennis* iv. 148 The positions of these various *hazards*, on a system which can only be excused by their name, seem to have been left very much to chance, or to the individual fancy of the builders of Courts. *Ibid.* 149 That writer says 'The players on the *hazard-side* have two openings to defend, the last gallery and the grille'. 1891 *Sat. Rev.* LXXII. 690 The hazards, or winning openings, of modern tennis courts are three in number—the Dedans, the Grille, and the Winning-Gallery. To strike the ball into any one of these, at any point of the game, is to score a point.

fig. a1616 BEAUM. & FL. *Custom Country* v. iv, Our adverse fortune Bandying us from one hazard to another.

†**7.** *Billiards.* One of the holes or pockets in the sides of a billiard table. *Obs.*

1598 FLORIO, *Scaduta*, a hole or hazard at billiard boord. 1679 EVELYN *Diary* 4 Dec., A billiard-table, with as many more hazards as ours commonly have. 1688 R. HOLME *Armoury* III. 262/2 The Hazzards, the Holes in the four corners and sides of the..Billiard Table. 1751 CHAMBERS *Cycl.* s.v. *Billiards*, Hazards, or holes, on the edges and corners.

b. Hence, A stroke at billiards by which one of the balls is driven into a pocket.

losing hazard, winning hazard (see quot. 1856).

1778 C. JONES *Hoyle's Games Impr.* 197 Common Odds of the Hazards. 1836 T. HOOK *G. Gurney* III. 153 Why, you cannot make a hazard, Gilbert; what is the matter? 1850 *Bohn's Handbk. Games* 532 The full (or straight) winning hazard should first be practised. 1856 CRAWLEY *Billiards* (1859) 14 The *Winning Hazard* is one in which the object ball is struck with your own ball and sent into a pocket; the *Losing Hazard* is a stroke in which the striker's ball is pocketed from off, or after contact with, another. 1857 *Chambers' Inform.* II. 713 A white winning hazard is made when you play at the white ball and pocket it..A red winning hazard is when you pocket the red.

8. *Golf.* A general term for bunkers, furze, water, sand, loose earth, or any kind of 'bad ground'.

1857 *Chambers' Inform.* II. 693 He possibly drives his ball into some hazard—such as sand or whin-bushes—from which he is only extricated after expending several strokes in the operation. *Ibid.*, Driving it over hazards, such as bunkers, whins, etc. 1879 *Daily News* 22 Mar. 5/2 At Wimbledon certainly there are some very good 'hazards', or perilous places. 1889 LINSKILL *Golf* ii. (1895) 8 The ground should be of an undulating character, and..should abound in hazards of every description.

9. A cab-stand (in Ireland).

1882 *Times* 9 May, Being on a car 'hazard' (stand) at Parkgate-street on Saturday evening. 1884 *Freeman's Jrnl.* 5 Dec. 5/2 What about providing a hazard at each arrival platform?..the public would then know that it was beyond the power of a cab or cabman to refuse the first call.

10. *attrib.* and *Comb.*, as (from sense 1) ***hazard-bet, -board, -table***, etc.; **hazard side**: see sense 6.

1570 LEVINS *Manip.* 30/26 Hazard play, *alearum ludus*. c1710 C. FIENNES *Diary* (1888) 301 There are two hazard boards. a1737 POPE *Wks.* (1886) X. 263 Moralizing sat I by the hazard-table. 1829 *Bengallee* 109 Salary, wasted at keen Hazard-bets. 1849 MACAULAY *Hist. Eng.* II. 65 His ill luck at the hazard table was such that his estates were daily becoming more and more encumbered.

†**B.** *adj.* = HAZARDOUS. *Obs. rare.*

1601 WEEVER *Mirr. Mart.* Diij, But one of more experience..Such hazard rash proceedings did not like.

'hazard, *v.* Forms as in sb.; also *Sc.* 6 **hazsard, hasert, hazaird**, 7 **haisard**. [a. F. *hasarde-r* (1407 in Hatz.-Darm., in sense 'play at hazard'), f. *hasard*: see prec.]

1. a. *trans.* To put (anything) to the risk of being lost in a game of chance or other doubtful issue; to stake; to expose to hazard or risk.

1530 PALSGR. 582/2 It is a great folye for a man to hazarde his lyfe for the mucke of this world. 1547 J. HARRISON *Exhort. Scottes* Gj, For thinordinate gain wherof we do alwaies hazard our honoures, lifes, and countrey. 1614 SIR R. DUDLEY in *Fortesc. Papers* 11 Nor hazard the reputation of my owne workes under the discretion or skill of an other. 1634 SIR T. HERBERT *Trav.* 206 At Passage, or In and In, they [Chinese] will hazard all their worth, themselves, wives, children and other substance. 1700 T. BROWN tr. *Fresny's Amusem. Ser. & Com.* 98 When a Sick Man leaves all for Nature to do, he hazards much. When he leaves all for the Doctor to do, he hazards more. 1867 FREEMAN *Norm. Conq.* I. iv. 263 He would not hazard the prize by clutching at it too soon.

absol. 1736 LEDIARD *Life Marlborough* II. 31 Unfortunate Gamesters..hazard on, thinking to recover their Loss.

b. *refl.* To expose oneself to risk; to run or incur risks. Also *intr.* in same sense (*obs.*).

1549 *Compl. Scot.* xx. 176 ȝe maye hazsard and fecht quhen that ȝe think ȝour comodius tyme. 1567 *Satir. Poems Reform.* vii. 88 Nobillis, quha durst couragiouslie Hazaird thame self to saif vs. 1639 S. DU VERGER tr. *Camus' Admir. Events* 135 He shunnes blowes, and will not hazard himselfe, yet requires as much as wee who hazard our lives. 1653 HOLCROFT *Procopius* IV. 151 Thinke not that the Hunnes, Herulians, and Lombards will hazard to the death. 1698 FRYER *Acc. E. India & P.* 157 Not willing to hazard himself on a Voyage undertaken only for Pleasure.

2. a. *trans.* To run or take the risk of (a penalty or misfortune). Also with *inf. obj.*

1577 LD. BUCKHURST in Ellis *Orig. Lett.* Ser. I. II. 272 To hazard..your dishonor and her Ma. dislike. 1628 WITHER *Brit. Rememb.* III. 1451 What Censures thou shouldst hazzard, in thy stay. 1675 tr. *Machiavelli's Prince* (Rtldg. 1883) 282 He will hazard to be famished. 1686 N. COX *Gentl. Recreat.* IV. (ed. 2) 93 That your Adversaries being forced to follow you, may hazzard stumbling. 1703 MOXON *Mech. Exerc.* 181 Hazards the breaking of the String. 1796 *Hist. Ned Evans* I. 179 Your son would..perish in the dust before he would hazard to offend her. 1824 LANDOR *Wks.* (1846) I. 223 They hazard to..break their shins by stemming the current. 1827 C. BRIDGES *Exp. Ps. cxix.* (1830) 78 We shall be ready to hazard all consequences.

b. With *object* and *infinitive*.

1559 in Strype *Ann. Ref.* I. App. vi. 8 Hazarde..ourselves to be..drowned in the waters of schisme. 1587 FLEMING *Contn. Holinshed* III. 1292/2 Forced to..hazard himselfe to fall into the hands of naughtie people. 1659 D. PELL *Impr. Sea* 480 It hides it self, and will not hazzard its tender flower to bee shaken.

†**3.** To endanger (any person or thing). *Obs.*

1596 SPENSER *State Irel.* Wks. (Globe) 651/2 There will he lye in wayte, and..will daungerously hazarde the troubled souldiour. 1601 R. JOHNSON *Kingd. & Commw.* (1603) 172 The king of Biarma in our times greatly hazarded the states of Pagu and Siam. 1664 BUTLER *Hud.* II. i. 868 Lillies limn'd on cheeks, and roses, With painted perfumes, hazard noses. 1716 S. SEWALL *Diary* 22 Oct. (1882) III. 109 Mr. Lynde comes up from Nantasket, having..been much wearied and hazarded with the Storm. 1786 T. JEFFERSON *Writ.* (1859) I. 558 His death, with that of the king of Prussia, would hazard the tranquillity of Europe.

†**4.** To get by chance or luck; to chance upon. **1575** R. B. *Appius & Virg.* in Hazl. *Dodsley* IV. 132 Be you not afraid, And so you may happen to hazard the maid: It is but in hazard and may come by hap: Win her or lose her, try you the trap. **1664** POWER *Exp. Philos.* III. 155 Might not such Microscopes hazard the discovery of the Aerial Genii, and present even Spiritualities themselves to our view?

5. a. To take the chance or risk of; to venture upon; to adventure, venture (*to do* something). **1581** PETTIE *Guazzo's Civ. Conv.* I. (1586) 18 Who that otherwise hazardeth to enter into it, exposeth himselfe to a great danger. **1638** SIR T. HERBERT *Trav.* (ed. 2) 103 Not daring to hazard the fight, or by stratagem break out to hazard their deliverance. **1666** DRYDEN *Ann. Mirab.* xxviii, That what both love, both hazard to destroy. **1710** STEELE *Tatler* No. 175 ¶9 It is not believed.. that the Enemy will hazard a Battle for the Relief of Douay. **1753** N. TORRIANO *Gangr. Sore Throat* 84 Scarification was hazarded without being looked on as an approved Method. **1844** H. H. WILSON *Brit. India* III. 337 The Koles.. rarely hazarded an action.

b. To venture to offer (a statement, conjecture, or the like). **1758** *Monthly Rev.* 188 If one may be allowed to hazard a conjecture. **1788** FRANKLIN *Autobiog.* Wks. 1840 I. 174, I have hazarded the few preceding pages. **1816** COLERIDGE *Lay Serm.* 314 [This] justifies me.. in hazarding the bold assertion. **1860** TYNDALL *Glac.* II. xxvii. 379 He did not hazard an explanation of the phenomenon.

c. With quoted words as obj. **1881** C. E. L. RIDDELL *Sen. Partner* III. xxxiii. 110 'I met Mr. Robert the other day,' hazarded the clerk. **1903** R. LANGBRIDGE *Flame & Flood* vii. 108 'Love is so rare in this world,' she hazarded.

†**6.** *Billiards.* To 'pocket' (a ball). *Obs.* **1679** EVELYN *Diary* 4 Dec., The game being only to prosecute the ball till hazarded, without passing the port.. It is more difficult to hazard a ball.. than in our table.

Hence **'hazarded** *ppl. a.*, risked, ventured. **1596** SPENSER *F.Q.* VI. iii. 12 How to save hole her hazarded estate. **1841** D'ISRAELI *Amen. Lit.* (1867) 26 These disagreeing dates are all hazarded conjectures.

hazardable ('hæzədəb(ə)l), *a.* [See -ABLE.]

†**1.** Involving hazard; hazardous, risky. *Obs.* **1623** WINTHROP *Let.* in *New Eng.* (1825) I. 342 It is so difficult and hazardable.. I cannot tell how to convey that, or anything else to thee. **1656** S. H. *Golden Law* 47 We made it hazardable and doubtfull, by dallying with him. **1658** SIR T. BROWNE *Hydriot.* iii. 16 [It] were an hazardable peece of art.

2. That can or may be hazarded or risked. In mod. Dicts.

hazarder ('hæzədə(r)). Now *rare.* Also 4-6 **hasard-**, (5 **hass-**, 5-6 **-erd-**), 4-6 **-our**, 5 **-ar**, 5-6 **-er.** [ME. and AFr. *hasardour* = 14th c. F. *hasardeur*, f. *hasarder* to HAZARD: see -ER² 3.]

1. A player at hazard or dice; a dicer, a gamester. *a* **1300** *Cursor M.* 26854 Theif, reuer, or hazardour, hore or okerer, or Iogolour. *c* **1386** CHAUCER *Pard. T.* 268 It is reproef and contrair to honour For to be halde a comun hasardour. **14..** *Nom.* in Wr.-Wülcker 694/23 *Hic aliator*, a haserder. **1513** DOUGLAS *Æneis* VIII. Prol. 56 The hasartouris haldis thaim heryit, hant thay nocht the dice. **1533** MORE *Answ. Poysoned Bk.* Wks. 1087/2 An honest man or els a false haserder. **1556** LAUDER *Tractate* 293 None hasardours at cards nor dyce. *c* **1565** LINDESAY (Pitscottie) *Chron. Scot.* (1728) 115 A common hazarder. **1896** J. H. WYLIE *Hist. Eng. Hen. IV*, III. 397 No simoniac, adulterer, hazarder, drinker.

2. 'He who hazards' (Johnson).

†**'hazardful,** *a. Obs. rare.* [f. HAZARD *sb.* + -FUL.] Risky, hazardous, perilous. **1626** *Crt. & Times Chas. I* (1848) I. 86 How hazardful are the events of the most parts of such conferences. **1631** HEYWOOD *Eng. Eliz.* (1641) 86 Her infirmity being hazardfull, but not mortall. **1679** J. CLIDE in *Naphtali* 504, I judge the loss of my Soul to be more hazardful.

'hazarding, *vbl. sb.* [f. HAZARD *v.* + -ING¹.] The action of the vb. HAZARD in various senses. **1582** BENTLEY *Mon. Matrones* Pref. Biij b, To the hazarding of their owne liues. **1603** KNOLLES *Hist. Turks* (1638) 90 Without the hasarding of battell. *attrib.* **1552** HULOET, Hasarding house [gaming-house], *alearium, aleatorium, forum aleatorium.*

†**'hazardize,** *v. Obs. rare.* [f. HAZARD *sb.* + -IZE.] To put in hazard; to jeopardize, risk. **1628** WITHER *Brit. Rememb.* VI. 339 We will hazardize Our peace, our fame, and our posterities. **1631** BRATHWAIT *Eng. Gentlew.* (1641) 297 They make you idolize yourselves, and .. hazzardize the state of your soules.

†**'hazardize,** *sb. Obs. nonce-wd.* [For *hazardise*, f. HAZARD *sb.* + *-ise* as in *merchand-ise.*] A hazardous position, a condition of peril or risk. **1590** SPENSER *F.Q.* II. xii. 19 A.. ship Which.. Her selfe had ronne into that hazardize [*rimes* merchandize, mesprize].

†**'hazardly,** *a. Obs. rare*⁻¹. [f. HAZARD *sb.* + -LY².] Risky, dangerous. **1575** R. B. *Appius & Virg.* in Hazl. *Dodsley* IV. 123 A hazardly chance may harbour a clap.

hazardous ('hæzədəs), *a.* [f. as prec. + -OUS. Cf. F. *hasardeux*, 16th c. in Littré.]

1. Of the nature of the game of hazard; dependent on chance; casual, fortuitous. **1585** T. WASHINGTON tr. *Nicholay's Voy.* II. xii. 47 b, The adventure therof on the one side and the other was very hazardous and variable. **1653** H. MORE *Antid. Ath.* II. ix. (1712) 66 In other Generations that are more hazardous. **1791** BURKE *App. Whigs* Wks. VI. 257 They may indeed stop short of some hazardous and ambiguous excellence. **1816** SINGER *Hist. Cards* i. 9 Hazardous betting or playing for stakes. **1880** *Libr. Univ. Knowl.* (N.Y.) IV. 285 Hazardous contracts, in which the performance depends upon some uncertain future event.

†**2.** Addicted to risks; venturesome. *Obs.* **1580** SIDNEY *Arcadia* III. (1590) 323 Who was in the disposition of his nature hazzardous. **1613** PURCHAS *Pilgrimage* (1614) 769 Hazardous Mariners. **1651** HOBBES *Leviath.* II. xxiv. 129 Too hazardous in engaging the publique stock into a long, or costly war.

3. Fraught with hazard or risk; perilous; risky. ***hazardous insurance***, an insurance effected at a high premium, on a life, building, etc. exposed to more than average risks. ***hazardous occupation table***, an actuarial table showing the probability of life in trades or professions the members of which are exposed to more than average risks. **1618** BOLTON *Florus* I. xvii. (1636) 51 A most hazzardous War. **1671** MILTON *P.R.* III. 228 The enterprize so hazardous and high. **1783** WATSON *Philip III* (1839) 47 The most hazardous enterprise in which he had ever been engaged. **1856** FROUDE *Hist. Eng.* (1858) I. v. 419 To attempt to analyse the motives of a double-minded man is always a hazardous experiment.

'hazardously, *adv.* [f. prec. + -LY².] In a hazardous manner; venturesomely; perilously. **1611** COTGR., *Audacieusement*, boldly, aduenturously.. hazardously, daringly. **1664** H. MORE *Myst. Iniq.* 447 Grotius his either judgment or conscience does very hazardously lie at the stake. **1822-56** DE QUINCEY *Confess.* (1862) 252 Lord Bacon said once too boldly and hazardously [etc.]. **1883** BLACK *Shandon Bells* xxxiii, Cottages.. apparently clinging hazardously to the ascent.

'hazardousness. [f. as prec. + -NESS.] The quality of being hazardous; riskiness; perilousness. **1682** H. MORE *Annot. Glanvill's Lux O.* 219 The hazardousness of these terms. **1694** KETTLEWELL *Comp. Persecuted* 74 That no difficulties, or hazardousness of these assemblies, may make us indifferent about thy service. **1874** STUBBS *Const. Hist.* I. vi. 141 The hazardousness of their employments.

†**'hazardry.** *Obs.* Also 3 **hasarderye**, 4-6 **-drie, -drye**, (6 **hasarttrie**). [f. OF. type **hasarderie*, f. *hasardeur* HAZARDER: see -ERY.]

1. The playing at hazard; dicing; gambling. **1297** R. GLOUC. (1724) 195 Ydelnesse hem ssal brynge to synne lecherye, To tauerne, and to sleuþe, and to hasarderye. *c* **1386** CHAUCER *Pard. T.* 262 Now wol I yow deffenden hasardrye. *a* **1555** LYNDESAY *Tragedy* 306 Leif hasarttrie. **1562** LEIGH *Armorie* (1612) 78 Hazardrye and going to common Taverns. **1590** SPENSER *F.Q.* III. i. 57 Some fel to hazardry.

2. The incurring of risk; venturesomeness. *rare.* **1590** SPENSER *F.Q.* II. v. 13 Hasty wroth, and heedlesse hazardry, Doe breede repentaunce late, and lasting infamy.

haze (heɪz), *sb.* [Of obscure origin. Not known till nearly a century after HAZY *a.*, so that it may be a back-formation from that word. For the derivation, connexion with OE. *hasu, haswe* 'grey', has been suggested; but there is a long gap in time between the words, and there are difficulties both of form and early sense: see HAZE *v.*²]

1. An obscuration of the atmosphere near the surface of the earth, caused by an infinite number of minute particles of vapour, etc. in the air. In 18th c. applied to a thick fog or hoar-frost; but now usually to a thin misty appearance, which makes distant objects indistinct, and often arises from heat (*heat-haze*). **1706** PHILLIPS (ed. Kersey), *Haze*, a Rime, a thick Fog. **1721** BAILEY, *A Hase*, a thick Fog or Rime. **1755** JOHNSON, *Haze*, fog; mist. **1795** BURKE *Regic. Peace* iv. Wks. IX. 4 To trust ourselves to the haze and mist and doubtful lights of that changeable week. **1823** F. CLISSOLD *Ascent Mt. Blanc* 23 A circle of thin haze.. marked dimly the limits between heaven and earth. **1833** HT. MARTINEAU *Charmed Sea* viii. 128 Till he disappeared in the silvery night haze. **1833** M. SCOTT *Tom Cringle* xix. (1859) 526 A hot haze hung over the whole. **1849** D. P. THOMSON *Introd. Meteorol.* 114 When.. the temperature falls below the dew-point, the moisture becomes visible in the form of a haze, mist, or fog; haze when there is merely an obscuration near the surface of the earth; mist when it presents a defined outline, resting on, or hovering a few feet above the ground; fog when the humid vesicles are so numerous as to produce a general obscuration in the atmosphere. **1863** GEO. ELIOT *Romola* I. xiv, There was a thin yellow haze from incense mingling with the breath of the multitude. **1891** MRS. OLIPHANT *Jerusalem* 435 The soft hills on the other side in a haze of sunshine.

b. *transf.* Something having a misty appearance, or obscuring the view. **1879** *St. George's Hosp. Repts.* IX. 526 Ulceration [in the eye].. sufficiently deep to leave a permanent haze. **1891** DOUGALL *Beggars All* 181 The copse.. showed nothing but a haze of gray and reddish twigs.

2. *fig.* A condition of intellectual vagueness and indistinctness; the obscurity of a distant time. *a* **1797** BURKE (T.), In the fog and haze of confusion all is enlarged. **1843** MIALL in *Nonconf.* III. 489 A haze of false and wretched morality. **1873** BURTON *Hist. Scot.* I. i. 44 The annalists.. were peopling the haze with obscure persons. **1879** MCCARTHY *Own Times* II. xxix. 362 No shade or faint haze of a doubt appeared anywhere. **1888** BRYCE *Amer. Commw.* III. lxxx. 55 Nor do their moral and religious impulses remain in the soft haze of self-complacent sentiment.

3. *Comb.*, as ***haze-cradled, -hung*** adjs.; ***haze-fire***, brilliantly luminous mist. **1842** FABER *Styr. Lake, etc.* 328 The Carpathian chain, A fence of white haze-fire Compassing the plain. **1852** M. ARNOLD *Summer Night* 21 The blue haze-cradled mountains spread away. **1894** *Rev. of Rev.* Feb. 170 The low and haze-hung country.

Hence **'hazeless** *a.*, free from haze. **1874** TYNDALL in *Contemp. Rev.* Nov. 826 A calm and hazeless atmosphere.

haze (heɪz), *v.*¹ [Cf. OF. *haser* (1450 in Godef.) 'irriter, piquer, fâcher, insulter, aiguillonner'.]

1. *trans.* To affright, scare; to scold; also, to punish by blows. *dial.* **1678** LITTLETON *Lat. Dict.*, To haze or hawze one, *perterrefacio, clamore obtundo.* **1721** BAILEY, *Hase*, to afright with a sudden Noise. *Ibid.*, *Hawze*, to confound or frighten, to stun one with Noise. C[ountry Word]. **1876** *Mid-Yorksh. Gloss.*, *Haze*, to scold; also, to beat. **1881** *N. Linc. Gloss.*, *Haze*, to thrash soundly; to upbraid.

2. *Naut.* To punish by keeping at disagreeable and unnecessary hard work; to harass with overwork. **1840** R. H. DANA *Bef. Mast* viii. 18 Every shifting of the studding-sails was only to 'haze' the crew. *Note.* Let an officer once say 'I'll haze you', and your fate is fixed. You will be 'worked up', if you are not a better man than he is. **1846** J. R. BROWNE *Etch. Whaling Cruise* (1850) 187 The captain disliked him.. and continually hazed him for his awkwardness. **1893** J. A. BARRY *S. Brown's Bunyip, etc.* 283 Now then, fore-top, there, shift your pins, or I'll haze you.

3. To subject to cruel horseplay (as practised by American students); to bully. *U.S.* See HAZING 3. **1850** *Poem bef. Iadma* 22 in B. H. Hall *College Wds.* (1856) 251 'Tis the Sophomores rushing the Freshmen to haze. **1868** in G. M. Sloane *Life J. MacCosh* xiv. (1896) 216 Did you not hear that he had been hazed?.. They gagged his mouth.. shaved his head, then put him under the pump, and left him tied on the campus. *Ibid.*, I called the hazed student to my house. **1886** *Century Mag.* 905/1 Two of our roughs began to haze him. **1887** *Lippincott's Mag.* Aug. 293 The man who assists in hazing you in Freshman year, and who compels you to stand on a street-corner and scan Greek verse for the edification of the by-standers. *Ibid.*, Hazing, in its offensive signification, is practically dead and buried at Yale.

4. *intr.* To frolic, 'lark'. *U.S.* **1848** *N.Y. Com. Adv.* 2 Dec. (Bartlett), W. had been drinking and was hazing about the street at night. **1855** H. A. WISE *Tales for Marines* (ibid.), Hazin' round with Charity Bunker and the rest o' the gals.

5. ***haze about***, to roam about aimlessly; to loaf about. [? Associated with HAZY 2 b.] **1841** *Tait's Mag.* VIII. 592 It would be idle to follow [her] .. in hazing about—a capital word that, and one worthy of instant adoption—among the usual sights of London. **1870** MRS. PRENTISS *Let.* in *Life* (1882) 335 The boys are hazing about.

6. *trans.* To drive an animal (while on horseback). **1890** L. C. D'OYLE *Notches on Rough Edge of Life* 68 Bill 'hazed' 'em again, and they ran up and stood about opposite to me. **1897** *Westm. Gaz.* 8 Oct. 2/1 The beast may trip or run for dangerous ground, and it is then that a well-mounted companion is necessary to haze or ride him off. **1949** P. NEWTON *High Country Days* 95 As each raceful was finished, the calves were hazed through the gate and out into a clean yard. **1962** A. FRY *Ranch on Cariboo* xxiv. 242 A fine dust rose behind the cattle as we hazed them along the wagon tracks between the scattered trees.

haze, *v.*² [In sense 1, related to HAZE *sb.*, HAZY *a.*; perh. a back-formation from the latter; in sense 2 from the sb.]

1. *intr.* To drizzle. *dial.* **1674-91** RAY *N.C. Words* 36 *It hazes*, it misles, or rains small rain. **1808** J. BARLOW *Columb.* I. 33 O'er Valladolid's regal turrets hazed The drizzly fogs from dull Pisuerga raised. **1825** BROCKETT *N.C. Gloss.*, *Haze*, to drizzle, to be foggy.

2. *trans.* To make hazy, to involve in a haze. Hence **hazed** *ppl. a.* **1801** ANNA SEWARD *Lett.* (1811) V. 353 The noble mountains.. are here [i.e. in the picture] softened and hazed away into indistinctness. **188.** R. G. H[ILL] *Voices in Solit.* 180 The hazed sun with lurid weakness stared.

haze, *v.*³ *dial. trans.* To dry. *a* **1825** FORBY *Voc. E. Anglia*, *Haze*, to dry linen, etc. by hanging it up in the fresh air.. any thing so exposed is said to be hazed, as rows of corn or hay, when a brisk breeze follows a shower. **1863** MORTON *Cycl. Agric.* (E.D.S.), *Hazed*, surface-dried.

†**haze** = *ha' 's*, syncop. form of *have us. Obs.* *a* **1553** UDALL *Royster D.* III. iv. (Arb.) 49 Nay and ye will haze, haze.. And ye will not haze, then giue vs our geare againe.

hazel¹ ('heɪz(ə)l). Forms: 1 **hæsel, hæsil, hæsl, æsil**, 3 **hasle, asele**, 3-4 **hesel**, 4-6 **hasil**, 4-7 **-ell(e**, 4-8 **hasel(e**, 5 **hesil(l, -yl(le, -elle**, 5-6 **hasill**, 6 **-ille, -yll(e, heasle**, (*Sc.* **hissill**), 6-7 **hazell**, 6-8 **hasle**, 7 **hassel, hassle**, 7- **hazel, hazle**, (*mod.Sc.* **heezle**). [OE. *hæsel* = MDu. *hazel(are*, Du. *hazel(aar*, LG. *hassel*, OHG. *hasal* masc., *hasala* fem. (MHG., mod.G. *hasel* f.), ON. *hasl* (Sw., Da. *hassel*):—OTeut. **hasalo-z*:—pre-Teut. **kósolos* = L. *corulus, corylus*, OIr. *coll* (:—**cosl*).

ON. had also *hesli* neut. (:—**hasili-*) whence app. north. ME. *hesel, hesyl*, mod.Sc. *heezle*.]

1. a. A bush or small tree of the genus *Corylus*, having as its fruit a nut. The European species, *C. Avellana*, grows to a small tree; the North American species are *C. Americana*, a shrub forming dense thickets, and the Beaked or Cuckold Hazel, *C. rostrata*, found in Canada, etc.

There are other species, as the ***Constantinople*** or ***Turkey hazel***, *C. Colurna*, ***Japanese hazel***, *C. heterophylla*.

*a***700** *Epinal Gloss.* 236 *Corylus*, haesil [50 aesil]. *a***800** *Erfurt Gloss.* 536 *Corylus*, haesl. *c***1000** *Sax. Leechd.* II. 96 Hæsles ragu, & holen rinde niþewearde. *c***1205** LAY. 8697 Hasles [*c***1275** aseles] þer greowen. *a***1307** *Thrush & Night.* in Hazl. *E.P.P.* I. 50 Somer is comen with loue to toune.. The note of hasel springeth. **1387–8** T. USK *Test. Love* III. vi. 5 If thou desire grapes thou goest not to the Hasell. *c***1400** MAUNDEV. (Roxb.) xviii. 83 It es lyke vnto þe floure of þe hesill, þat springes oute before þe lefes. *c***1440** *Promp. Parv.* 238/1 Hesyl, tre, *corulus*. **1538** LELAND *Itin.* V. 67 The Place wher the Town was ys al over growen with Brambles, Hasylles, and lyke Shrubbes. **1578** LYTE *Dodoens* VI. lviii. 733 There be two sortes of Hasel or wood Nut trees. **1697** DRYDEN *Virg. Past.* v. 4 Beneath the grateful Shade, Which Hazles, intermix'd with Elms, have made. **1769** HOME *Fatal Disc.* v, A dell, whose sloping sides are rough With thick-grown hazel. **1861** DELAMER *Kitch. Gard.* 153 The variegated and Purple Hazels are ornamental shrubs of some esteem.

b. The wood of this tree.

1480 CAXTON *Descr. Brit.* 54 Ther is a lake that torneth hasell in to asshe and asshe in to hasell. **1634** PEACHAM *Gentl. Exerc.* xxi. 251, I leave it to their [Anglers'] owne discretion, whether to use either Haysell, or Cane. **1665** J. WEBB *Stone-Heng* (1725) 161 Hasle was the Material of which the Stakes were at first made.

c. A stick or rod of this wood.

1603 OWEN *Pembrokesh.* (1891) 276 The horsemens cudgell.. to be a hasell. **1649** G. DANIEL *Trinarch., Rich. II*, cxxxv, The Hassle soe will bend (A Rhabdomancie, was observ'd of old) Stretch'd on the Earth, vnto a Mine of Gold. **1686** N. COX *Gentl. Recreat.* IV. 71 Let the Angler fit himself with a Hazle of one piece or two set conveniently together. **1748** RICHARDSON *Clarissa* xxi. (1749) I. 144 Mr. Solmes.. fell to gnawing the head of his hazel.

d. Short for *hazel-nut*.

1601 HOLLAND *Pliny* XV. xxii. (R.), As for other nuts, their meat is solide and compact, as we may see in filberds and hazels.

e. ***oil of hazel***, a jocular name for an oil alleged to be contained in a green hazel rod, and to be the efficacious element in a sound drubbing; ***to anoint with oil of hazel***, to drub with a hazel rod. So ***sap of hazel*** in the same sense: cf. *hazel-oil*, 4 c.

*c***1678** *Roxb. Ball.* (1882) IV. 359 Take you the Oyl of Hazel strong; With it anoint her Body round.

2. Applied with qualification to other plants, as **evergreen hazel**, *Guevina Avellana*; **Australian h.**, *Pomaderris lanigera* of N.S. Wales, *P. apetala* of Victoria; WITCH or WYCH HAZEL, q.v.

3. a. The reddish brown colour of a ripe hazel-nut. **b.** *adj.* Of this colour; used esp. of eyes.

1774 GOLDSM. *Nat. Hist.* (1776) II. 82 The different colours of the eye are the dark hazle, the light hazle, the green, the blue, the grey, the whitish grey. **1805** T. HARRAL *Scenes of Life* I. 52 An eye.. the index of an intelligent soul; it was a full, bright hazel. **1829** LYTTON *Disowned* 5 Of a light hazel in their colour.

b. 1592 SHAKS. *Rom. & Jul.* III. i. 22 Thou wilt quarrell with a man for cracking Nuts, hauing no other reason, but because thou hast hasell eyes. *c***1730** SWIFT *Dick, a Maggot* 4 You know him by his hazel snout. **1743–51** G. EDWARDS *Nat. Hist. Birds* 69 The Eye of a yellowish Hazel Colour. **1805** SCOTT *Last Minstr.* VI. xix, O'er her white bosom stray'd her hazel hair. **1813** —— *Rokeby* IV. v, Her full dark eye of hazel hue. **1848** LYTTON *Harold* VIII. ii, In the quick glance of his clear hazel eye.

4. a. *attrib.* and *Comb.*, as ***hazel bank, bavin, bough, bower, -brush, bush, copse, cover, leaf, rod, staff, stick, twig, wand***, etc.; ***hazel-hooped, -leaved*** adjs.

*a***1307** *Thrush & Night*, 106 in Hazl. *E.P.P.* I. 54 Fowel, thou sitest on hasel bou. **1473** WARKW. *Chron.* (Camden) 22 (Promp.) It was lytelle as a hesylle styke. **1584** R. SCOT *Discov. Witchcr.* x. vii. (1886) 147 There must be made vpon a hazell wand three crosses. **1596** SHAKS. *Tam. Shr.* II. i. 255 Kate like the hazle twig Is straight, and slender. **1678** BUTLER *Hud.* III. ii. 1547 He's mounted on a hazel bavin. **1727–46** THOMSON *Summer* 1269 Close in the covert of a hazel copse. *c***1786** T. BLAIKIE *Diary of Scotch Gardener* (1931) 205 They have had here the famous Charlatain Lebreton who pretends by means of a hazel rod to descover Springs..; he pretend[s] to be taken with a trembling and the rod to turn round upon his hands. **1822** J. WOODS *2 Yrs. Res. Eng. Prairie Illinois* 206, I dug a piece of prairie-land to sow it on; part of it had some hazle-brush on it. **1828** J. M. SPEARMAN *Brit. Gunner* (ed. 2) 59 Budge barrels.. hazle hooped. **1855** TENNYSON *Brook* 171, I slide by hazel covers. **1858** HOGG *Veg. Kingd.* 693 Hazel rods have been supposed to have magical properties, as it was of them that the *divining-rod* was formed. **1864** *Sowerby's Eng. Bot.* III. 193 Hazel-leaved Bramble. **1880** *Encycl Brit.* XI. 549/1 The virtue of the hazel wand was supposed to be dependent on its having two forks. **1904** GOODCHILD & TWENEY *Technol. & Sci. Dict.* 282/2 *Hazel rods*. Thin rods of hazel are often used for the handles of smiths' tools.. which have to be struck by a hammer. **1932** F. L. WRIGHT *Autobiogr.* I. 46 With scattered hazel-brush and trees.

b. From sense 3.

1769–74 J. GRANGER *Biogr. Hist. Eng.* (R.), Cherry cheeked, hazel-eyed, brown haired. **1787** WINTER *Syst. Husb.* 24 Black and hazle colour soils. **1806** FORSYTH *Beauties Scotl.* IV. 228 A deep hazel-coloured loam. **1886** RUSKIN *Præterita* I. v. 141 A dark hazel-eyed, slim-made, lively girl. **1891** MRS. ALEXANDER *Wom. Heart* I. 3 Large hazel-brown eyes.

c. Special combs.: **hazel carpet**, a geometer moth, *Cidaria corylata*; **hazel crottles**, the lichen *Sticta pulmonaria*; **hazel-fly**, *Phyllopertha horticola*, also an artificial fly imitating it; **hazel-hoe**, 'a grubbing hoe for working in brush and bushes' (Knight *Dict. Mech.*); (see also quot. 1953); †**hazel-mouse** [Ger. *haselmaus*], the common dormouse (*Muscardinus avellanarius*); **hazel-oil** (*humorous*): see 1 e; **hazel-rag, -raw** = *hazel crottles*; †**hazel-rise** [cf. Ger. *haselreis*], a twig or bough of the hazel; **hazel-rough** (*U.S.*), a hazel copse; **hazel-splitter** *U.S.*, a breed of pigs; **hazel-wizard**, a diviner by means of a hazel-twig; a water-finder; **hazel-worm** [Ger. *haselwurm*], the blind-worm (*Maunder's Treas. Nat. Hist.* 1854). Also HAZEL-GROUSE, etc.

1796 WITHERING *Brit. Plants* (ed. 4) IV. 55 Lungwort. Hazel Rag, or *Hazel Crottles.. On the trunks of old trees. **1787** BEST *Angling* (ed. 2) 117 The Welchman's Button, or *Hasle-Fly. **1883** A. RONALDS *Fly-Fisher's Entomol.* (ed. 9) 104 Hazel Fly, Coch-A-Bondhu. **1895** *Montgomery Ward Catal.* 391/2 *Hazel Hoes, weight, 3 pounds, length, 10 in. .. Hazel Hoe Handles. **1953** *Brit. Commonw. Forest Terminol.* I. 75 s.v. *Hoe*. *Hazel hoe*, a fire trenching or digging tool, resembling a grub hoe but having a shorter, broader and lighter blade, a round or oval eye, and usually a straight pick-like head. **1607** TOPSELL *Four-f. Beasts* (1658) 423 Of the Nut-mouse, *Hasel-mouse, or Filbird-mouse.. so called because they feed upon Hasel-nuts and Filbirds. **1825** JAMIESON, **Hazel-oil*, a cant term, used to denote a drubbing. **1894** CROCKETT *Raiders* 46 Ye shall suffer for this, if there's hazel oil in Dumfries. **1565–73** COOPER *Thesaurus, Pulmonaria*, after some lungeworte: after other *hasel ragge. **1778** LIGHTFOOT *Flora Scot.* (1789) 831 Lungwort Lichen.. *Hazleraw, Scotis. **13..** *K. Alis.* 3293 (Bodl. MS.) Whan notte brouneþ on *hesel rys. *a***1550** *Christis Kirke Gr.* xvi, Heich Hutchon with a hissil ryss. **1893** *Advance* (Chicago) 23 Nov., Among the *hazel-roughs are still a few chewinks. **1865** *Trans. Ill. Agric. Soc.* (1868) VI. 334 [Those] who prefer the active, energetic '*hazel splitters' to the lazy Berkshire. **1930** *Amer. Speech* V. 18 *Hazel splitter*, a wild, lean range hog, a razor-back. **1843** 'R. CARLTON' *New Purchase* lii. 206 We had ceased from digging a well, after finding no water at twenty-five feet, although we had employed a great *hazel-wizzard.

'hazel², **hazle.** Also **hassell, hasel(l.** [Of uncertain origin; known first in attrib. use or comb., and in the adj. HAZELLY¹.

Markham's *hassell ground, hassell earth*, correspond to Ger. *hasselboden* 'ground consisting of gravel, reddish clay, and somewhat black earth' (Grimm), said also to be called in Switzerland *haselerde*. The latter implies connexion or association with *hasel* HAZEL¹, and some would so explain the word in Eng., with reference to the colour of hazel ground, its suitableness for hazel, or other reason.]

1. A kind of freestone: see quots. *local.*

1855 PHILLIPS *Man. Geol.* Gloss., *Hazle*, a hard, often cherty, gritstone. **1883** GRESLEY *Gloss. Coal Mining, Hazle*, a tough mixture of sandstone and shale.

2. *attrib.* and *Comb.* Consisting of a mixture of sand or gravel, clay, and earth, as ***hazel earth, ground, loam, mould, soil***, etc.

1613 MARKHAM *Eng. Husbandman* I. I. vi. (1635) 36 If it bee a rich hassell ground. *Ibid.* xiii. 83 Blacke Clay mixt with red Sand, which.. is called of Husbandmen an hassell earth. **1616** SURFL. & MARKH. *Country Farme* 556 Any mixed earths or hasell-grounds which are clayes and sands or clayes and gravells mixed together. **1686** PLOT *Staffordsh.* 341 The manner of tillage that is also given light or hasel mould. **1789** *Trans. Soc. Arts* I. 165 A field of good hazle loam. **1796** J. BOYS *Agric. Kent* (1813) 70 To make summer-fallows on light land, such as hazel loam, sand, gravel or chalk. **1846** J. BAXTER *Libr. Pract. Agric.* (ed. 4) II. 26 On all soils, except those of a deep hazel mould or sandy loam.

hazeled ('heɪz(ə)ld), *a.* [See -ED².] **a.** Full of or clad with hazel bushes. **b.** Of a hazel colour.

1651 WITTIE *Primrose's Pop. Err.* 159 Hazled cocks, which are quick for motion,.. strong to fight. **1853** G. JOHNSTON *Nat. Hist. E. Bord.* I. 263 In our hazled deans. **1857** in Miss Pratt *Flowering Plants* I. 148 Up yon hazel'd slope the farmer loudly rallies Reapers to their morning task.

†**'hazelen**, *a. Obs.* Forms: 1 **hæslen**, 4 **haselne, heslyn.** [f. HAZEL¹ + -EN⁴ (= Ger. *haseln*): cf. HALSEN *a.*] Of or pertaining to the hazel.

*c***1000** *Sax. Leechd.* II. 104 ȝenim.. hæslenne sticcan oþþe ellenne. **1388** WYCLIF *Pref. Ep.* 72 Of the haselne ȝerd. ?*a***1400** *Morte Arth.* 2504 Holtis and hare woddes with heslyne schawes.

hazel grouse. = next.

1783 LATHAM *Hist. Birds* s.v. *Grouse*, Hazel Grouse. *Haselhuhn*. **1862** MEDLOCK tr. *Schœdler's Treas. Sc.* 538 Under the section of grouse.. we note.. the black grouse (*T[etrao] tetrix*), and the hazel grouse (*T. bonasia*). **1883** *Cassell's Nat. Hist.* IV. 141 The Hazel Grouse.. does not come to England, but is found over Northern Europe and North Asia, and is a pretty bird with a fine crest.

hazel-hen. [transl. mod.G. *haselhuhn*, f. *hasel* HAZEL + *huhn* hen.] The European ruffled grouse (*Bonasia sylvestris*).

1661 LOVELL *Hist. Anim. & Min.* Introd., The.. heath-cock, hasle-hen, land duck. **1822** T. MITCHELL *Aristoph.* II. 195 Floundering in the dirt like hazle-hens. **1893** *Daily News* 11 Mar. 5/3 Ptarmigan and hazel hens are now the only inexpensive game procurable.

hazeline ('heɪzəliːn). [See -INE.] An alcoholic distillate from the Witch Hazel, *Hamamelis virginica*.

1881 NETHERCLIFT in *Brit. Med. Jrnl.* 18 June, The new product of Hamamelis Virginica called 'Hazeline'. **1882** W. SYMES in *Lancet* 4 Nov., Hazeline was highly recommended two years ago for cases of haemoptysis.

hazelly ('heɪz(ə)lɪ), *a.*¹ [cf. HAZEL².] Consisting of a mixture of sand, clay, and earth.

1587 FLEMING *Contn. Holinshed* III. 1543/1 The stuffe carried.. for the erection of the walles at Dover, was earth, being of a haselie mould, chalke and sleech. **1707** MORTIMER *Husb.* III. (1708) 53 All sorts of Land may be reduced to Sandy, Gravelly, Chalky, Stony, Rocky, Hazely, Black-earth, Marsh or Boggy, and Clay-land. **1725** BRADLEY *Fam. Dict.* s.v. *Pine*, Any dry Soil, especially light hazelly Brick Earth will do. **1796** C. MARSHALL *Garden.* xix. (1813) 383 The soil proper for carnations is a hazelly or sandy loam, procured from a pasture.

hazelly, *a.*² [f. HAZEL¹ + -Y.] Abounding in or clad with hazel bushes.

1790 BURNS *Elegy Henderson* 20 Ye hazly shaws and briery dens! **1833** *Blackw. Mag.* XXXIV. 942 The Steep and hazelly banks of the Woodburn. **1835** CLARE *Rural Muse* 158 From the hazelly wood.

hazel-nut ('heɪz(ə)lnʌt). Forms: see HAZEL and NUT. [OE. *hæselhnutu* = Du. *hazelnoot*, LG. *haselnot, hasselnöt*, OHG. *hasalnuz*, mod.G. *haselnusz*.] The nut of the hazel, a well-known fruit.

*c***725** *Corpus Gloss.* 33 *Abelena*, haeselhnutu. *c***1050** *Gloss.* in Wr.-Wülcker 345/15 *Abellana*, haslhnutu. *c***1350** *Will. Palerne* 1811 Hasel-notes, & oþer fruit.. þat in forest growen. *c***1400** MAUNDEV. (Roxb.) xvii. 79 Dyamaundes.. of þe mykilnes of hesill nuttes. **1577** B. GOOGE *Heresbach's Husb.* II. (1586) 95 b, Among Nuttes, is also.. the Hasell Nuttes, a kinde whereof is the Filberte. **1870** YEATS *Nat. Hist. Comm.* 207 The common hazel nut yields an oil most valuable for the delicate machinery of watches.

b. *attrib.* and *Comb.*, as ***hazel-nut oil, tree***, etc.

*c***1050** *Gloss.* in Wr.-Wülcker 457/14 *Nuculeus, siue nucleus*, hæslhnute cyrnel. **1762** W. HUDSON *Flora Anglica, Corylus stipulis ovatis*, etc., common Hazel-nut-tree. **1884** *Cassell's Dict. Cookery* 310 *Hazel-nut Cakes.* **1886** *Syd. Soc. Lex., Hazel nut oil*.. is pale yellow.. and is not a drying oil.

'hazel-tree. The hazel, *Corylus Avellana*.

14.. *Voc.* in Wr.-Wülcker 575/45 *Corulus*, an haseltre. **1573–80** BARET *Alv.* H 207 An hasell tree, or nut tree, a filbert tree. **1656** COWLEY *Pindar. Odes, To Mr. Hobs* Note, *Virgula Divina*, or a Divining Wand, is a two-forked Branch of a Hazel-Tree, which is used for the finding out either of Veins, or hidden Treasures of Gold and Silver. **1832** TENNYSON *May Queen* 14 On the bridge beneath the hazel-tree.

hazel-wood.

1. A wood or thicket of hazel bushes.

*c***1374** CHAUCER *Troylus* v. 1174 From hasel-wode, there Ioly Robin pleyde. **1864** TENNYSON *En. Ard.* 7 A hazel-wood By autumn nutters haunted.

2. The wood or timber of the hazel.

1573–80 BARET *Alv.* H 208 The magnificent and heroicall vertues of the haselwood. **1848** SIR J. G. WILKINSON *Dalmatia & Montenegro* I. 516 On the neighbouring mountains much hazelwood grows.

†**3.** In phrase ***hazelwoods shake***, or merely ***hazel-wood!*** (in Chaucer) app. = Of course. *Obs.*

*c***1374** CHAUCER *Troylus* III. 841 (890) A ryng quod he, ye haselwodes shaken, Ye Nece myne þat ryng moste han a stone þat myhte a dede man a-lyue maken. *Ibid.* v. 505 Ye haselwode þoughte þis Pandare, And to hym self ful sobrelich he seyde, God wot refreyden may þis hote fare.

'hazelwort. *Herb.* [An adaptation of 16th c. Ger. *haselwurtz*, OHG. *haselwurz* (also *haselwurzel*), f. *wurz* herb, WORT, *wurzel* root.] A book name in the herbalists for Asarabacca.

[**1551** TURNER *Herbal* I. Eij b, Asarum is called.. in english folfote.. and asarabacca in duche hasell wurt: because it groweth abowte hasell tree rootes.] **1578** LYTE *Dodoens* III. v. 319 This herbe.. is called in English Asarabacca, and folefoote, it may also be called Haselworte .. in Germanie Haselwurtz: in Brabant Haselwortel. **1597** GERARDE *Herbal* II. cccvi. (1633) 837. **1706** PHILLIPS (ed. Kersey), *Cabarick*, an Herb otherwise call'd Hazlewort [*mispr.* Harlewort]. So **1730–36** in BAILEY (folio). **1862** MEDLOCK tr. *Schœdler's Treas. Sc.* 460 The Pipe tree.. and the Hazelwort.

hazen ('heɪz(ə)n), *v. Obs.* exc. *dial.* Also **-an, -on.** [prob. from same source as HAZE *v.*¹: see -EN⁵.] *trans.* To scare, terrify; to scold, threaten.

1605 *Hist. Evordanus*, Night.. sent.. fantasie for to hazan idle heads. **1630** LENNARD tr. *Charron's Wisd.* III. xiv. §12 That custome.. to beat, and to box, and with strange words and out-cryes to hazen Children. **1647** HAMMOND *Power of Keys* vii. 141 To awake, and hazen, and drive those that wil not be allured and drawn. [**1893** *Wiltsh. Gloss., Hazon*, to scold or threaten. 'Now dwoan't 'ee hazon the child for 't.']

hazer ('heɪzə(r)). *U.S.* [f. HAZE *v.*¹] **1.** One who hazes or practises cruel horseplay on another.

1887 *Columbus* (Ohio) *Dispatch* 5 Sept. (*heading*) A Hazer in Trouble. **1888** *Harper's Mag.* Mar. 636/1 The hazers in college are the men.. to whom the training and instincts of the gentleman are unknown.

2. (See quots.) Chiefly *U.S.* Cf. HAZE *v.*¹ 6.

1897 E. HOUGH *Story of Cowboy* 90 Two other men, sometimes known in these days of modern ranching as 'hazers', now mount and ride up..ready to drive on the horse that is to be broken. **1965** *Wanganui* (N.Z.) *Photo News* 13 Feb. 23 In bulldogging the rider and a hazer chase the bull. **1968** *Chicago Tribune* 7 July VII. 16/2 He was the first cowboy ever to bulldog a steer. In this event, two cowboys work as a team. One, called the hazer, rides parallel with the running steer, forcing him close to the dogger.

hazily ('heɪzɪlɪ), *adv.* [f. HAZY + -LY².] In a hazy manner; dimly, indistinctly. Also *fig.*

1833 L. RITCHIE *Wand. by Loire* 31 The river..glittered hazily in the last rays of sunset. **1889** 'RITA' *Sheba* III. iii. 36 The light and the shadows seemed to swim hazily before her sight. **1894** *Advance* (Chicago) 31 May, One is so likely to think hazily of African territory.

haziness ('heɪzɪnɪs). [f. HAZY + -NESS.] The quality of being hazy.

1. Mistiness, fogginess.

1709 BERKELEY *Th. Vision* §71 Though there be no extraordinary fog or haziness. **1748** *Anson's Voy.* I. x. 106 The haziness of the weather. **1803** *Med. Jrnl.* IX. 315 The sun..being obscured by a general haziness in the atmosphere.

2. The quality of being intellectually indistinct; vagueness of mental perception; uncertainty.

1872 LIDDON *Elem. Relig.* i. 25 In no department of human knowledge is haziness deemed a merit. **1882** MASSON in *Macm. Mag.* XLV. 235 Carlyle himself seems to have become aware of the haziness of his dating of the transaction.

'hazing, *vbl. sb.* [f. HAZE *v.*¹ + -ING¹.]

1. A sound beating, a thrashing.

1825 *Gentl. Mag.* XCV. I. 396, I gave him a hazing.

2. *Naut.* See HAZE *v.*¹ 2.

1893 J. A. BARRY *S. Brown's Bunyip, etc.* 285 The process is called 'hazing'. The sufferer gets all the dirtiest and most disagreeable..jobs to be found on shipboard.

3. A species of brutal horseplay practised on freshmen at some American Colleges.

a **1860** *Harvard Mag.* I. 413 (Bartlett) The absurd and barbarous custom of hazing, which has long prevailed in the college. **1892** *Daily News* 28 June 5/3 'Hazing' at Yale has unhappily led to the death of an unfortunate young student named Rustin, and to a general denunciation of this custom as 'stupid and brutal'. **1894** *Ibid.* 16 Oct. 5/4 The freshman class of Princeton is smaller this autumn than last..due in part to the hazing outrages of recent years.

hazle, hazzle ('hæz(ə)l), *v. dial.* [freq. of HAZE *v.*³: see -LE. OF. had *hasler* as variant of *haler* to burn, to dry; but this was prob. not connected.]

a. *trans.* To dry superficially. **b.** *intr.* To become dry on the surface.

1642 ROGERS *Naaman* 886 Who by that happy wind of thine..didst hazle and drie up the forlorne dregges and slime of Noahs deluge. *a* **1825** FORBY *Voc. E. Anglia*, *Hazle*, to grow dry at top. **1881** *Leicestersh. Gloss.*, *Hazzle*, to dry slightly. 'If the clothes don't dry much, they'll hazzle'. **1893** *Sheffield Gloss.* Suppl., *Hazzle*, to dry slightly..It is better, if the ground is damp, to let the sun hazzle the surface of the land before the second harrowing.

hazle, hazly: see HAZEL¹ and ², HAZELLY *a.*²

Hazlittian (hæz'lɪtɪən), *a.* and *sb.* Also **-ean.** [f. the name of W. *Hazlitt* (1778–1830), English critic + -IAN.]

A. *sb.* An admirer of Hazlitt. **B.** *adj.* Of, pertaining to, or characteristic of Hazlitt or his work.

1923 *Nation* (N.Y.) 17 Jan. 75 [The essay] on Antony and Cleopatra is Hazlittian in its enthusiasm and its opulence of phrase. **1930** *Times Lit. Suppl.* 18 Dec. 1082/4 We know that we are in the hands of a true Hazlittian. **1931** *Ibid.* 10 Sept. 669/4 His Hazlittian freedom in misquotation. **1962** *John o' London's* 19 July 59/3, I like a certain Hazlittean waywardness to my journeyings.

hazy ('heɪzɪ), *a.* Forms: 7 **hawsey, heysey, hasie, -ey, haizy,** 8 **hazey,** 7– **hazy.** [In form, as if from HAZE *sb.* + -Y; but known nearly a century before the sb., so that their mutual relation is uncertain. The early forms also offer difficulty.]

1. Of the atmosphere, weather, etc.: Characterized by the presence of haze; misty. (orig. *Naut.*) In 17–18th c. use = foggy; but now usually applied to a kind of atmospheric indistinctness less determinate than mist or fog, and often caused by heat.

1625 *Impeachm. Dk. Buckhm.* (Camden) 7 The weather beeing thicke and hawsey, the winde highe. **1657** R. LIGON *Barbadoes* (1673) 27 Moistness of the Air..which the Seamen call a Heysey weather..as though the Sun shine out bright, yet we cannot see his body, till nine a clock. **1665** J. WEBB *Stone-Heng* (1725) 183 An hasie Morning. **1666** *Phil. Trans.* I. 241 The Air being light, though moist and a little hazy. **1694** *Acc. Sev. Late Voy.* II. (1711) 2 The Air was haizy and full of fogs and snow, so that we could not see far. *a* **1700** B. E. *Dict. Cant. Crew*, *Hazy Weather*, when it is Thick, Misty, Foggy. **1748** *Anson's Voy.* I. vii. 72 We had little wind, with thick hazy weather. **1799** VINCE *Elem. Astron.* xxi. (1810) 231 A diffused light, which made the air seem hazy. **1856** STANLEY *Sinai & Pal.* i. (1858) 64 It was too hazy to see anything in the distance.

2. *fig.* Lacking intellectual distinctness; vague, indistinct, uncertain.

1831 LAMB *Elia* Ser. II. *Newspapers 35 Yrs. Ago*, A hazy uncertain delicacy. **1862** BURTON *Bk.-Hunter* (1863) 35 His communications about the material wants of life were hazy. **1865** DICKENS *Mut. Fr.* III. iii, Some hazy idea. **1874** L. STEPHEN *Hours in Library* (1892) II. vii. 211 The chief article of Rousseau's rather hazy creed.

b. Somewhat confused with drink. *colloq.*

1824 T. HOOK *Sayings & Doings* Ser. I. *Friend of Family* II. 10 Hazy, Sir —— You understand? smoking and drinking. **1842** BARHAM *Ingol. Leg.* Ser. II. *St. Cuthbert*, Staggering about just as if he were 'hazy'.

H-bomb: see H III.

he (hiː, hɪ), *pers. pron.*, *3rd sing. masc. nom.* Forms: see below. [The simplest form of the (orig. demonstr.) base *hi-*, which supplies not only the pronoun forms *him, his, her, (h)it, (h)em*, but also the adverbs *here, hence, hither.* OE. *he, hē* was cogn. with OFris. *hi, he* (fem. *hiu*, neut. *hit*), OS. *hi, he, hie.* The other old Teutonic langs. (with OS. in the oblique cases) have parallel forms from stem *i-*: OHG. *ir, er*, Goth. *is.* Fragments of a *hi-* stem, in sense 'this', are found, however, in Gothic, in dat. *himma*, acc. m. and n. *hina, hita*; they differ only in the initial *h* from the corresponding inflexions of *is* 'he'. In OHG. the East Franconian had also *her* in place of the usual OHG. *er*, 'he'. In English, the typical form in all ages has been *he*, from which emphasis probably produced *heo, hye, hee*, and tonelessness *hă, ă*, which last long prevailed in representations of familiar speech, as in the dramatists, and is still a prevalent dialect form. In OE. the base *he* supplied all parts of the third personal pronoun, singular and plural; it was thus inflected:

SING.	MASC.	FEM.	NEUT.	PLURAL
Nom.	he, *he*	híо, héo, híe, hí	hit	hí, hí e, héo, hiȝ
Acc.	hiene, hine (hyne)	hie, hí (héo)	hit	hí, híe, héo, hiȝ
Dat.	him (hym)	hiere, hire (hyre)	him	him, heom (hym)
Gen.	his (hys)	hiere, hire (hyre)	his	hiera, hira, heora

1. In all the cognate languages, even in the early period, certain parts of the *hi-* or *i-* stem were lost, and supplied by the corresponding parts of the demonstrative base *syă*, a derivative of *să*, SE. This extended to English also in the 11th or 12th c. when the fem. *hio, heo*, became supplanted by the fem. demonstrative *sio, syo*, which appears as *sco, scho* = *sho* in northern, and *scæ* = *shæ* in midl., now SHE, q.v. In the south and west *heo* (*ho, hoo*) survived in literature till the 15th c. and is still native in the dialects in various forms; but *she* has been the only literary Eng. form since the introduction of printing. In the oblique cases HER remains.

2. The original plural has been supplanted by a plural of the demonstrative *that.* In the northern dial. *c* 950, the OE. *þá*, plural of *þæt*, was often used instead of *hia, hi*; within the next two centuries the equivalent ON. *þei-r* must have been adopted, as it appears *c* 1200 in full use in Orm. as *þeȝȝ*, whence the later *they, thei, thay, thai*, which gradually spread south, and before 1500 superseded *hi, hy*, first in the nominative, and then also in the other cases, so that the plural forms are now *they, them, their.* But a relic of the earlier pronoun survives, in southern dialect and colloquial use, in the dat.-accus. *hem*, commonly written *'em.*

3. The original accusative forms have everywhere, except in the neuter, been replaced by an extended use of the dative: this began in the midl. dial. before 1000, and was completed in the southern by 1350. In this change, the analogy of the 1st and 2nd persons was followed (see ME). Traces of the original acc. sing. masc. *hine* remain as *en, 'n* (*un*), in southern dialects: see HIN.

4. In the neuter the acc. *hit* remained, and also displaced the dative *him*; in all constructions *hit* lost its initial *h* between 12th and 15th c. in Standard English; and in 16–17th c. the original neuter genitive *his* was displaced first by *it*, and then by *it's, its.*

5. The genitive cases *his, hire, hire,* (*their*), were treated after 1100, on the earlier analogy of *mine, thine, our, your*, as adjectives, and inflected to agree with substantives; the plurals *his-e, hir-e* were still used by Wyclif. Like the other possessives, they also developed two forms, an adjective and an absolute, the latter being *hers, theirs* (the *-s* of which was originally the possessive *'s*); *hisis* was used by Wyclif, but in mod.Eng. *his* and *its* take no additional *s* in the absolute form. *Hisn, hern, theirn* (perhaps by false analogy with *my, mine*) appear in 16th c. in midl. counties, but are now only dialectal. The changes which these, originally genitives of the Personal Pronoun, have undergone, make it more convenient in modern grammar to treat them separately as Possessive Pronouns.

The present inflexion of this pronoun (with its derived possessives) is therefore:

SING.	MASC.	FEM.	NEUT.	PLURAL
Nom.	he	[she]	it	[they]
Acc. } *Dat.* }	him	her	it	[them]
Possess. adj.	his	her	its	[their]
absol.	his	hers	its	[theirs]

The following explanations and illustrations refer only to the nominative singular masculine HE; the other inflexional parts are treated separately, each in its alphabetical place. So also the now colloq. 'EM, formerly HEM 'them', the obs. or dial. HEO (*hoo*) 'she', HI 'they', HIN (dial. *'en, 'un*) 'him', the ME. HEMEN (dial. *min, mun*) 'them', the early ME. HISE 'her', and HISE 'them', and the dial. HISN, HERN, THEIRN.]

A. Forms.

α. 1– **he** (6–7 **h'**); β. 2–3 **hi**; γ. 2 **heo**, 3–4 **ȝe, ghe**; δ. 3 **hæ**; ε. 3–4 **ha**, 4 **ho**; ζ. 3 **e**, 3–9 (*dial.*) **a**; η. 4–5 **hye**, 6 **hie**; θ. 4–7 **hee.**

α. *c* **893** K. ÆLFRED *Oros.* I. i. §13 He cwæð þæt he bude on þæm lande. *c* **1386** CHAUCER *Prol.* 636 Thanne wolde he speke and crie as he were wood. **1598** MARSTON *Sco. Villanie* x. H iij b, H'ath made a common-place booke out of plaies. **1647** WARD *Simp. Cobler* 85 And when h' hath done, 'tis good to lay 't aside.

β. *c* **1175** *Lamb. Hom.* 29 And cweðen in his þonke þar hi bið. *a* **1200** *Moral Ode* 221 Neure in helle hi com.

γ. *a* **1175** *Cott. Hom.* 217 Heo [God] is hefone liht. *Ibid.* 225 Heo and his wif þa bearn ȝestriende. *a* **1250** *Owl & Night.* 874 Mid mine songe ich hine pulte That ghe groni for his gulte. *c* **1315** SHOREHAM 123 Tho ȝe [Jesus] was bote twelf wynter ald.

δ. *c* **1205** LAY. 23113 Hæ hafeð al his kineriche bi-queðe her Loððe.

ε. *c* **1250** *Kent. Serm.* in *O.E. Misc.* 27 Goþ, ha seide, into bethleem. *Ibid.* 30 Ha maket of þo watere wyn. *c* **1320** R. BRUNNE *Medit.* 573 Þey hye hym, and ho goþ withoutyn any stryfe. **1340** *Ayenb.* 30 Ha beat and smit and wyf and children,..ase ha were out of his wytte.

ζ. *c* **1205** LAY. 15636 E [*c* **1275** he] wende þat he ilad weore limen for to leosen. *c* **1250** *Meid. Maregrete* lxiv, E cleped forð malcus is monquellere. **1250–1610** [A *pron.*]. **1756** A. MURPHY *Apprentice* I. i, I got as far as the jesuit before a went out of town. **1864** TENNYSON *North. Farmer* (Passim).

η. **13..** *Guy Warw.* (A.) 6376 And for he him so miseise y-seye Of prisoun aschaped, bliþe was hye. *c* **1560** A. SCOTT *Poems* (S.T.S.) iii. 40 Maist witt hes hie that moniest owrsylis. **1596** DALRYMPLE tr. *Leslie's Hist. Scot.* I. 50 The hie Salmonte haueng castne the meltis, and the sche salmonte the Rounis.

θ. *a* **1300** *Cursor M.* 17288 + 165 His name neuend hee. *c* **1386** CHAUCER *Cook's T.* 2 Of a craft of vitailliers was hee. *c* **1440** [see B 2]. **1567** [see B 7]. **1575** LANEHAM *Let.* (1871) 23 Hee waz so loth to cum forward. **1611** BIBLE *Transl. Pref.* 1 Hee was no babe, but a great clearke. **1644** MILTON *Areop.* (Arb.) 37 That whereof before hee was so scrupulous.

B. Senses and constructions.

I. As proper masculine pronoun of the third person, nominative case.

1. a. The male being in question, or last mentioned: Used of persons and animals of the male sex.

c **893** K. ÆLFRED *Oros.* I. i. §13 Ohthere sæde..þæt he ealra Norðmonna norþmest bude. He cwæð þæt he bude on þæm lande norþweardum wiþ þa Westsæ. *c* **1000** *Ags. Ps.* (Th.) ix. [x.] 8 Drihten þurhwunað on ecnesse. And he ȝearwað his dom-setl, and he demð ealre eorþan swyðe emne. *c* **1175** *Lamb. Hom.* 7 Þis witeȝede dauid..Þis he witeȝede bi drihtene þurh þene halie gast. *c* **1220** *Bestiary* 146 Ðe neddre..If he naked man se, ne wile he him noȝt neggen, oc he fleð fro him als he fro fir sulde. **1388** WYCLIF *Gen.* iii. 6 And sche..eet, and ȝaf to hir hosebonde, and he eet. *a* **1400–50** *Alexander* 1141 Þan drafe he sa to Damac with dukis and princes. *c* **1620** A. HUME *Brit. Tongue* (1865) 28 He is the noat of the male; as, he is a gud judge; he is a wyse man; he is a speedie horse. **1667** MILTON *P.L.* IV. 297 For contemplation hee and valour form'd, For softness shee and sweet attractive Grace; Hee for God only, shee for God in him. **1678** CUDWORTH *Intell. Syst.* I. i. §40. 49 He will go about to prove that there is something besides He-knows-not-what. **1697** DRYDEN *Virg. Georg.* IV. 700 He first, and close behind him follow'd she. **1835** J. H. NEWMAN *Par. Serm.* (1837) I. viii. 122 Our Saviour spake of man as he is.

b. In some northern dialects (Westmorland, Cumberland, etc.), *he* is used instead of *thou* or *you*, in addressing a boy or inferior (cf. Ger. *Er* so used): e.g. 'Well, Joe! where has he been? what is this he has brought me?'

2. Of things not sexually distinguished:

†**a.** Things grammatically masculine. *Obs.* **b.** Things personified as masculine, as mountains, rivers, oak-trees, etc.

It is not easy to say when grammatical gender ceased to be used, this differing according to dialect. In dialect speech, *he* is still used for most things of definite shape, without any feeling of personification.

a **1200** *Moral Ode* 144 Swines brede is swiðe swete . swa is of wilde dore . alto dore he is abuh[t]. *c* **1320** *Cast. Love* 40, Ichulle tellen him Wherfore þe world was i-wrouht, And aftur how he was bi-tauht. *c* **1386** CHAUCER *Can. Yeom. Prol. & T.* 314 The Philosophres stoon Elixer clept..With al oure sleighte he wol nat come vs to. *c* **1440** CAPGRAVE *Life St. Kath.* v. 1379 Yet was this fyre soo horryble that hee.. Brent men eke. *c* **1449** PECOCK *Repr.* 4 This present book.. he schal have v. principal parties. *Ibid.* 8 An argument if he be ful and foormal..is mad of twey proposiciouns. **1523** FITZHERB. *Husb.* §126 The better the stake wyll be dryuen whan he is well bounden. **1551** TURNER *Herbal* I. C vj a, Dyll..hath..a spokye top as fenell hath, whome he doth represent wonders nere. **1593** SHAKS. *Rich. II*, III. iii. 65 The blushing discontented Sunne..When he perceiues the enuious Clouds are bent To dimme his glory. **1598** GRENEWEY *Tacitus' Descr. Germanie* iv. 265 That, euerie nation as he was strong, should not set himselfe in possession. **1697** DRYDEN *Virg. Georg.* II. 409 Jove's own Tree..Full in the midst of his own Strength he stands..His Shade protects the Plains, his Head the Hills commands. **1823** BYRON *Island* III. i, The flashing..Which robes the cannon as he wings a tomb. **1832** TENNYSON *New Year's Eve* ii, Tonight I saw the sun set: he set and left behind The good old year.

3. Peculiar constructions: **a.** Used pleonastically along with its noun. Common in ballad style, and now in illiterate speech.

c **1000** *Prose Life St. Guthlac* v. (1848) 32 Moyses ærest and Helias hi fæston, and swylce eac se Hælend.. he fæste. **1297** R. GLOUC. (1724) 120 Þe kyng he sende aftur hem. *a* **1300** *Cursor M.* 4055 Ioseph he sagh a night in sueuen. *c* **1430** *Syr Tryam.* 744 The kyngys sone of Armony..To Tryamowre he ranne. **15..** *Chevy Chase* 74 The first man that did answer make, Was noble Percy hee. **1782** COWPER *Gilpin* 85 'Fair and softly', John he cried, But John he cried in vain. **1839** LONGF. *Wreck of Hesperus* iii, The skipper he stood beside the helm.

¶**b.** Erroneously for objective *him.*

1560–2 WHITEHORNE *Arte Warre* (1573–4) II. 36 a, These instrumentes helpeth much more him that besiegeth a towne then he that is besieged. **1594** MARLOWE & NASHE *Dido* v. ii, Yet he, whose heart['s] of adamant or flint, My

HE 35 HEAD

tears nor plaints could mollify a whit. **1642** tr. *Perkins' Prof. Bk.* xi. §770. 338 It behoveth not he to be ready upon the land to make the feoffment.

c. In s.w. dialects *he* is the emphatic objective, beside the unemphatic *'en, 'un.* 'I zeed un drow it tu *hee*', I saw him throw it to *him.*

1863 BARNES *Dorset Dial.* 23 Gi'e the money to *I*, not *he.* **1878** ELWORTHY *Grammar of W. Somerset* 34 Our objective *him* is always *un, n*, unless it is emphatic, when it is *ee*.. *uur ded·n zai noa·ürt tü ee*, 'she did not say anything to *he*'.

d. he self: earlier form of *himself* nom., *he himself*: see SELF.

II. As Antecedent pronoun. followed by relative, etc.: = OE. *se, þe*; Fr. *celui*; Ger. *derjenige, der.* (The neuter is *that*, the plural *they* or *those.*)

4. a. The or that man, or person of the male sex (*that* or *who*...). Hence *Indefinitely*, Any man, any one, one, a person (*that* or *who*).

a **1240** *Sawles Warde* in *Cott. Hom.* 259 He sit on heh þat is ow on helpe. *a* **1300** *Cursor M.* 3693 If þou be he i luue sa wele. *c* **1380** *Sir Ferumb.* 2186 þis is he þat fader myn ordeyneþ my lord to be. **1382** WYCLIF *Ps.* xciii[i]. 9 He that plauntede the ere, shal he not heren? *c* **1400** MAUNDEV. *Prol.* (1839) 2 He that wil pupplische ony thing. **1523** LD. BERNERS *Froiss.* I. ix. 8 As he that was yong and lusty desiryng all honoure. **1526** TINDALE *Matt.* xi. 15 He that hath eares to heare, let him here. **1581** PETTIE *Guazzo's Civ. Conv.* II. (1586) 77 There is not he, who is not glad with all his heart to be honoured. **1590** SPENSER *F.Q.* I. i. 43 He that the stubborne Sprites can wisely tame. **1590** SHAKS. *Mids. N.* II. i. 34 Are you not hee, That frights the maidens of the Villagree? **1712** ADDISON *Spect.* No. 441 ¶4 He who considers himself abstractedly. **1842** TENNYSON *Vision of Sin* 127 He that roars for liberty. **1859** —— *Elaine* 1083 He makes no friend who never made a foe.

b. Followed by a prepositional phrase; as 'he of Modena', 'he of the sevenfold shield', 'he with the scar on his face'. *arch.*

1598 SHAKS. *Merry W.* I. i. 173 He in the red face had it. **1644** MILTON *Areop.* (Arb.) 39 If he of the bottomlesse pit had not long since broke prison. *a* **1821** KEATS *2nd Sonn. to Haydon*, Great spirits now on earth are sojourning; He of the cloud, the cataract, the lake.

III. As demonstrative pronoun.

5. *he and he*: this and that, the one and the other, both. *arch.*

a **1300** *Cursor M.* 16161 For he and he had samen ben, forwit selcuth wrath. *c* **1381** CHAUCER *Parl. Foules* 166 It likyth hym at wrastelyng for to be, And demyn ȝit wher he do bet or he. **1513** DOUGLAS *Æneis* VI. xii. 68 And gan begyn desyre, baith he and he, In bodeis ȝit for to returne agane. **1535** STEWART *Cron. Scot.* I. 371 Talkand thai raid togidder to the toun, Hand for hand rycht hamelie he and he. *c* **1620** A. HUME *Brit. Tongue* vii. (1865) 18 He snapped me on this hand and he on that. **1848** CLOUGH *Bothie* iii. 20 Arthur.. Leapt from the ledges with Hope, he twenty feet, he thirty. **1876** TENNYSON *Harold* Introd. Sonn., But he and he, if soul be soul, are where Each stands full face with all he did below.

IV. As *sb.* (not changing in the objective).

6. a. Man, person, personage. *any he*: any person whatever. *arch.* and *poet.*

c **1384** CHAUCER *Ho. Fame* III. 979 And nat so sone departed nas That he fro him, thoo he ne mette With the thrid. **1472** SIR JOHN PASTON in *Lett.* No. 703 III. 59, I mente weell by my trowthe to hyr..as any he that owythe heer best wyll in Ingelond. **1538** BALE *Thre Lawes* 1439, I am no other but euen the very he. **1574** tr. *Marlorat's Apocalips* 25 The way, truth, and lyfe, and to be short, the only he that can saue vs for euer. **1652–62** HEYLIN *Cosmogr.* III. (1673) 150/1 Who..challenged the proudest He of the Macedonians, to a single combat. **1682** BUNYAN *Holy War* (Cassell) 275 He has shewed as much honesty and bravery of spirit as any he in Mansoul. **1742** FIELDING *J. Andrews* (L.), The best he in the kingdom. **1880** G. MEREDITH *Trag. Com.* (1881) 230 He—that great *he*—covers all.

b. = IT *pron.* 1 f. Also a game of this type.

1810 *Gammer Gurton's Garland* III. 31 One-ery, two-ery, Ziccary zan; Hollow bone, crack a bone, Ninery ten:.. Stick, stock, stone dead, Blind man can't see, Every knave, will have a slave, You or I must be *He.* **1863** *Boy's Handy Bk. of Sports* I. 8 Touch is a very simple game... One of the ten or twelve..is chosen..to use the approved schoolboy expression..'*he*'. **1893** *Funk's Stand. Dict.*, *He*, sometimes, the leader of a game, or one who takes some special part in it. **1900** E. V. & E. LUCAS *What shall we do Now?* 113 For a short time 'He' is a good warming game. It is the simplest of all games. The 'He' runs after the others until he touches one. The one touched then becomes 'He'. **1902** *Little Folks* Aug. 113/1 Let's play 'Touch last'. Look out, I'm 'He'! **1924** W. DE LA MARE *Ding Dong Bell* 23 'Twas life's bright game And Death was 'he'. **1937** HULL & WHITLOCK *Far-Distant Oxus* ii. 40 It was not real hide-and-seek..but a wild game of 'he'. **1960** S. H. COURTIER *Gently dust Corpse* iv. 43 The youngsters had played a game of hide-and-seek. In the course of one of Pete's turns as 'he'..he sallied into the hall. **1969** I. & P. OPIE *Children's Games* ii. 64 We played He and I was had, so I had to be he.

7. a. Opposed to *she*: Male. (Also as adj.: see 8.)

c **950** *Lindisf. Gosp.* Mark x. 6 From fruma..scæftes woepen mon *vel* hee and hiuu *vel* wifmon worhte hia god. —— *Luke* ii. 23 Eȝhuelc he *vel* woepen-mon to-untynes hrif ..haliȝ drihtne ȝe-ceiȝed. *c* **1000** ÆLFRIC *Gram.* vii. (Z.) 18 Ælc nyten byð oððe he oððe heo. *Ibid.* 19 *Hic coruus* ðes hremn, swa hwæðer swa hit byð, swa he, swa heo. **1567** MAPLET *Gr. Forest* 105 It is also carefull in laying vp store for Winter, both the Hee and Shee. **1888** *Sat. Rev.* 20 Oct. 467/1 Any one not a poet, whether he or she, might toil, [etc.].

b. A male. (With pl. *hes, he's, †hees.*)

1575 LANEHAM *Let.* (1871) 53 The hées to sum laughing, but the shées to more sport. **1649** MILTON *Eikon.* x. Wks. (1851) 415 The dissolute rabble of all his Courtiers..both Hees and Shees, if ther were any Males among them. **1701** ROWE *Amb. Step-Moth.* IV. i. 1725 The greatest he..Must have confest Woman's superior Wit. **1776** S. J. PRATT *Pupil of Pleasure* I. 225 Unprotected by some ostensible he or she. **1801** C. K. SHARPE *Corr.* 12 Jan. I. 102 Good spouses to the *shes*, and none at all to the *hes!* **1875** JOWETT *Plato* (ed. 2) III. 331 Do we divide dogs into hes and shes, and take the masculine gender out to hunt?

V. *attrib.* (Now generally hyphened to following noun; sometimes written separately like an adjective.)

8. a. Male. (Now confined to the lower animals, as *he-goat*; in 16–18th c. with nouns denoting persons; this is now contemptuous.) † *he-she*: see quots. 1661, 1754.

a **1300** *Cursor M.* 6067 A clene he lambe, wit-vten sake. **14..** *Voc.* in Wr.-Wülcker 571/24 *Catta*, a hecatte. **1509** *Test. Ebor.* (Surtees) 10 Oon he swan. **1535** COVERDALE *Dan.* viii. 5 Then came there an hegoate from the west. **1579** FULKE *Refut. Rastell* 759 Be there hee Angels and she Angels also? **1580** HOLLYBAND *Treas. Fr. Tong, Vn Amoureux*, a hee louer. *Amoureuse*, a shee louer. *Ibid.*, *Barbier*, a hee barber. **1596** [see A ŋ]. **1605** *Jeronimo* in Hazl. *Dodsley* IV. 357 I'll be the he-one then, and rid thee soon Of this dull, leaden, and tormenting elf. **1620** SHELTON *Quix.* IV. xxi. 171 Thou and thy Wife, with two of thy He-friends, and two of her She-friends. *a* **1661** FULLER *Worthies* (1840) I. iv. 15 Pope Joan ..this He-she..is generally believed born at Metz. **1665** PEPYS *Diary* 11 June, My aunt James and he-cosen Harman. **1692** WASHINGTON tr. *Milton's Def. Pop.* viii. (1851) 193 You now make He-Saints, and She-Saints, at your pleasure, as if you were a true genuine Pope. **1734** FIELDING *Univ. Gallant* I. Wks. 1882 X. 44 A woman..may speak to one of her husband's he-friends there. **1754** J. SHEBBEARE *Matrimony* (1766) II. 88 A He-she Thing! a Disgrace to his Sex. **1813** MOORE *Post-bag* iii. 8 A He-cook, of course!.. ne'er keep a She-cook. **1829** MARRYAT *F. Mildmay* xxii, Great he-fellows of footmen. **1836** *Hansard's Parl. Deb.* Ser. III. XXXII. 1201 The appropriate language of a noble Lord ..who..said, 'I have not risen to defend these he-pensioners, and she-pensioners, whom I find in this list'. **1855** SINGLETON *Virgil* I. 46 Safe is thy he-goat.

b. Sometimes with names of plants. **he-oak**, an Australian tree, *Casuarina stricta*; also *C. suberosa*. Cf. SHE-OAK, applied to other species.

1626 BACON *Sylva* §608 For the difference of Sexes in Plants, they are oftentimes by name distinguished; as *Male-Piony, Female-Piony*..*He-Holly, She-Holly.* **1876** *Forest & Stream* 13 July 375/3 'Wattle' in large variety, he-oak, she-oak, and very many others. **1880** FISON & HOWITT *Kamilaroi* 252 They chose a tall He-oak, lopped it to a point.

c. Of things. Cf. *male* and *female screw.*

1816 *Specif. J. Welch's Patent* No. 4052 The claws or prongs of the he part received or inserted in the she part.

d. *spec.* **he-man** orig. *U.S.*, a particularly strong, virile, or masterful man. Also *attrib.* So **he-male; he-mannish** *a.*

1832 J. K. PAULDING *Westward Ho!* I. 101 A young fellow who could..tree a rackoon with any he man that ever breathed in all out of doors. **1909** J. R. WARE *Passing Eng.*, *He-male*, a full shape of male, and resulting from calling female she-male. **1922** C. E. MULFORD *Tex* xiv. 207 Yo're about th' best he-man I've seen since I looked into a looking-glass. **1924** A. J. SMALL *Frozen Gold* vii, He's such a great big he-male-masculine man. **1926** *Times Lit. Suppl.* 25 Feb. 147/4 That was in the late nineties, when the 'real he-men' ..had not attained the softer exterior of the civilization they despised. **1926** S. LEWIS *Mantrap* v. 48 Woodbury was a zealot at showing how lusty and he-mannish he could be. **1931** W. HOLTBY *Poor Caroline* vi. 111 'And how was our friend Johnson?' asked Basil. 'More he-mannish, dirty and businesslike than ever.' **1931** L. STEFFENS *Autobiogr.* I. 406 The rulers of his city, who knew what he knew and knew also what a he man was, held him to be the First Citizen of Pittsburgh. **1931** *Punch* 22 July 60/1 One of their [*sc.* the Americans'] hundred-per-cent he-men. **1934** *N.Z. Alpine Jrnl.* V. XXI. 412 Mt Whitcombe is the 'he-man' peak of the Ramsay and Lyell Valleys. **1937** D. L. SAYERS *Busman's Honeymoon* v. 93 Strong, he-man stuff. **1955** W. GADDIS *Recognitions* I. vi. 204 That wonderful he-man aroma that girls really go for. **1961** *Times* 2 Mar. 15/5 Why is the American way of life now so infantilist..when it was notoriously he-mannish?

e. *He Bible*: the first of the two issues of the Bible printed in 1611, so called from its rendering of Ruth iii. 15.

1878 [see *She Bible* (SHE *pers. pron.* 13)]. **1888** J. R. DORE *Old Bibles* (ed. 2) 329 A 'He' Bible used as 'copy' at one printing office, and a 'She' Bible at another. **1911** A. W. POLLARD *Records English Bible* iii. 72 The first edition of the translation is frequently called the He-Bible and the second the She-Bible.

Hence **he** *v. trans.*, to speak to or of (a person) as 'he'.

1741 RICHARDSON *Pamela* I. 17, I must *he* and *him* him now; for he has lost his Dignity with me.

†he, *int.*[1] *Obs.* [Cf. F. *hé*, and HEH.] An exclamation used to draw attention or express emotion.

13.. *K. Alis* 880 He! fyle asteynte horesone! To misdo was ay thy wone.

he (hiː), *int.*[2] [A natural exclamation: cf. L. *he, hæ*, Ger. *he*, etc.; also HA, HO.] Repeated, as *he, he*, or in combination with *ha, ha*, etc.: A representation of laughter expressing a closer utterance than *ha, ha*, or *ho, ho*, usually affected or derisive.

c **1000** ÆLFRIC *Gram.* xlviii. (Z.) 279 *Ha ha* and *he he* ȝetacniað hlehter on leden and on englisc. **1567** *Triall Treas.* E iij, We, he, he, he, he! ware the horse heles, I saye. **1599** SHAKS. *Much Ado* IV. i. 23 How now! interiections? why then, some be of laughing, as ha, ha, he. **1675** WYCHERLEY *Country Wife* II, He! he! he! he's my wife's gallant; he! he! he! **1831** T. L. PEACOCK *Crotchet Castle* ii, Pray, sir, what do you mean by Ha! ha!?.. Precisely, sir, what you mean by He! he!.. You need not dispute about terms; they are two modes of expressing merriment. **1854** THACKERAY *Rose & Ring* vii, 'O, ho, ho! ha, ha, ha! he, he, he!' And he nearly choked himself with laughing.

Hence **he-he** *v.*, to utter *he he* in laughter.

1848 THACKERAY *Bk. Snobs* xxxii, This was said with much archness and he-he-ing.

he, obs. form of EYE, HIGH.

heach, var. HETCH.

head (hɛd), *sb.*[1] Forms: 1 **héafod, -ud, -ut,** 1–2 **heofod,** 2 **hefed, -et, heavet,** 2–3 **heafd, hæfed,** 2–4 **hefd, heaved,** 2–5 **heved,** 3 **hæfd, heifd, hafed, hafd, hafved, hæfved, hefved, hæved, (hæhved), hevod, hevd,** 3–5 **hevid, -yde,** 3–6 **heed,** 3–8 **hed,** 4 **hewid(e, -yd(e,** 4–7 **hede,** 6– **head;** (5–6 **heede, hedd(e,** 6 **heade,** 5– (*Sc.*) **heid,** 6 **heide, heyd).** [Com. Teut.: OE. *héafod* = OFris. *hâved, hâfd, hâvd, hâd*, OS. *hôbid* (LG. *höved, höfd*, MDu. *hôvet(d)*, Du. *hoofd*), OHG. *houbit, haubit* (MHG. *haubet*, G. *haupt*), ON. *haufuð*, later *hǫfuð* (Sw. *hufvud*, Da. *hoved*), Goth. *haubiþ*:—OTeut. **haubud-, -iđo* (with suffix ablaut). Notwithstanding a close consonant correspondence with L. *caput, capit-*, the difference of the root vowel makes it very difficult to identify the words, or to refer them to a common root. Some refer the Teutonic word to an ablaut stem *heub-, haub-, hub-*, whence OHG. *hûba*, Ger. *haube*, OE. *húfe*, head-covering, cap. The phonetic development of the word in Eng. has been *héafod, hêved, hêvd, hêd, hed* ('hɛːəvəd, 'hɛːvəd, hɛːvd, hɛːd, hɛd); in *Sc.* (hɛːd, heːd, hiːd, hid). In some dialects a diphthongal ('heːəd) has developed as ('hɪəd, hɪ'ɛd, hjɛd, jɛd).]

I. The literal sense, and directly connected uses.

1. The anterior part of the body of an animal, when separated by a neck, or otherwise distinguished, from the rest of the body; it contains the mouth and special sense-organs, and the brain.

a. In man, the upper division of the body, joined to the trunk by the neck.

c **825** *Vesp. Psalter* iii. 4 Uphebbende heafud min. *c* **975** *Rushw. Gosp.* John xiii. 9 Honda and heofod. *c* **1000** *Ags. Gosp.* Matt. v. 36 Ne ðu ne swere þurh ðin hëafod. *c* **1175** *Lamb. Hom.* 29 Ʒif þin hefet were offe. *c* **1200** *Trin. Coll. Hom.* 205 Uppen his holi hafde. *c* **1205** LAY. 1596 He gurde Suard on þat hæfd. *c* **1230** *Hali Meid.* 3 Lustne me wið earen of þin heaued. **1297** R. GLOUC. (1724) 17 And smot hym vpon þe hed. *a* **1300** *K. Horn* 641 Þat heued i þe bringe. *a* **1300** *Cursor M.* 528 (Cott.) Mans hefd has thirls seuen. *c* **1340** *Ibid.* 5314 (Trin.) On his heede his hatt he bare. **1382** WYCLIF *Matt.* v. 36 Neither thou shalt swere by thin heued. *c* **1400** *Lanfranc's Cirurg.* 2 From þe heed to þe foot. *c* **1450** *St. Cuthbert* (Surtees) 924 His fete vpwarde, his heued doune. **1450** *Paston Lett.* No. 93 I. 125 Oon of the lewdeste of the shippe badde him ley down his hedde. **1526** TINDALE *Matt.* viii. 20 The sonne of the man hath not wheron to leye his heede [**1557** *Geneva* head]. **1530** PALSGR. 230/1 Heed of a man or beest, *teste.* **1535** COVERDALE *Mark* vi. 24 Ihon baptistes heade. **1546** J. HEYWOOD *Prov.* (1867) 70 God sende that hed (said she) a better nurs. For whan the head aketh, all the bodie is the wurs. **1610** SHAKS. *Temp.* III. ii. 40 Keepe a good tongue in your head. **1726–7** SWIFT *Gulliver* II. viii. (1865) 130, I had like to have gotten one or two broken heads for my impertinence. **1818** SCOTT *Rob Roy* viii, As if I had brought the Gorgon's head in my hand. **1859** GEO. ELIOT *A. Bede* xxvii. 233 He'd leave his head behind him, if it was loose.

b. In lower animals.

c **1000** ÆLFRIC *Gen.* iii. 15 Heo tobryt þin [the serpent's] heafod. *c* **1250** *Gen. & Ex.* 3151 Heued and fet..lesen fro ðe bones and eten. **1390** GOWER *Conf.* I. 93 He his hors heved aside Tho torned. *c* **1430** *Two Cookery-bks.* 9 Take fayre garbagys of chykonys, as þe hed, þe fete, þe lyuerys. **1577–87** HOLINSHED *Chron.* (1808) VI. 412 The great and venomous hydra was thus shortened of one of his heds. **1735** SOMERVILLE *Chase* III. 407 He [a stag]..tosses high his beamy Head. **1870** ROLLESTON *Anim. Life* 246 The asexual 'head' or 'nurse' [of the tapeworm] is armed with a double circlet of spines. **1888** ROLLESTON & JACKSON *Anim. Life* 333 *Coelomata*..A shorter anterior region or head which is preoral, and a longer postoral region, the body.

fig. **1865** GOSSE *Land & Sea* (1874) 5 An envious sea curled up its green head right over the quarter.

c. As a measure in comparing persons' heights, as *taller by a head*; *to cut shorter by the head*, i.e. to behead. So in *Racing*, as *to win by a head*, i.e. by the length of the horse's head. (See also *head and shoulders*, 50 b.)

13.. *Sir Gawain & Green Knight* 333 Þe stif mon hym bifore stod vpon hyȝt, Herre þen ani in þe hous by þe hede and more. **14..** *ME. Metrical Paraphrase Old Testament* 5160 He was cumly to ken, of breyd and heyghnes als, A bowe all oþer men both be þe hede and þe hals. **1548** HALL *Chron.*, *Hen. VI.* 166 b, Beyng taken..was made shorter by the hedde. **1588** SHAKS. *L.L.L.* v. i. 44 Thou art not so long by the head as honorificabilitudinitatibus. *a* **1674** CLARENDON *Hist. Reb.* XIII. §69 Near the head higher than most tall Men. **1800** *Sporting Mag.* XVI. 104/2 The first heat was..won by Omen, beating Play or Pay by only half a head. **1805** *Ibid.* XXVI. 270/2 He [*sc.* a race-horse]..won his race by a head. **1823** 'J. BEE' *Slang* 94 *Head* (turf), 'won by a head', or 'half-a-head':..is by so much that one horse comes in before another. **1847** TENNYSON *Princ.* III. 163 She stood Among her maidens, higher by the head. **1875** JOWETT

Plato (ed. 2) I. 480 A is taller by a head than B. **1886** *World* 17 Nov. 21 To be beaten by a head or a neck.

d. A headache, esp. such a condition caused by a blow or over-indulgence in liquor.

[**1857** G. A. Lawrence *Guy Liv.* iii. 23 Pale men with splitting heads..after a heavy drink.] **1869** Trollope *Phineas Finn* I. xxiii. 189 Don't you know how one feels sometimes that one has got a head? And when that is the case one's armchair is the best place. **1888** Kipling *Plain Tales fr. Hills* 15 The 'head' that followed after drink. **1889** E. Dowson *Let.* 18 Feb. (1967) 36, I have not felt myself since my generous allowance of the potent green on Thursday... To day for the first time I awoke without a head. **1889** *St. James's Gaz.* 10 Aug. 3/2 He is decidedly feverish, and, in the pleasing vernacular of the modern youth about town, he has a 'head' on him. **1906** *'Varsity* 17 May 323/3 One has not gone to bed over-night to wake up with a 'head' consequent on over-indulgence in the flowing bowl. **1919** *Punch* 22 Jan. 67 *Sailor.* The only time I smoked it [*sc.* opium] was in China, an' for three days I 'ad an 'ead on me like a smoke barrage. **1928** R. Macaulay *Keeping up Appearances* xxv. 291 'God, I've got a head.' 'You look rotten..better go straight to bed.' **1938** D. Smith *Dear Octopus* ii. ii. 64 She was lying down with a head. **1954** I. Murdoch *Under Net* x. 131 It was no use..my trying to think it all out,..especially with the head I still had. **1961** J. Wade *Back to Life* xi. 164, I get one of those blinding heads. **1973** B. Graeme *Two & Two make Five* ii. 12 'How long have you been suffering these heads?' 'For months now..they have become more frequent.'

e. *a good* or *strong head*: see strong *a.* 2 d; *a good* (or *bad*, etc.) *head for heights*: a feeling of security (insecurity) when at an unaccustomed distance above the ground.

c **1810** W. Hickey *Mem.* (1960) ii. 36, I replied that I could drink as much as the best of them and..I had, for such a youngster, a tolerable strong head. **1822** [see strong *a.* 2 d]. **1932** E. Bowen *To North* xiii. 131 Markie had a good head; if he had been very drunk he was not drunk now. **1935** *Discovery* Dec. 351/2 A silly old man who tried to please a ridiculous enthusiast of a girl by climbing about on towers when he had no head for heights. **1947** A. Menen *Prevalence of Witches* ix. 159 Most people have a bad head for heights. **1954** I. Murdoch *Under Net* vi. 98, I..looked at the drop, and decided that I was not a daring fellow. I have no head for heights.

2. a. As the seat of mind, thought, intellect, memory, or imagination; cf. brain *sb.* 3. Often contrasted with *heart*, as the seat of the emotions: see heart 9. Formerly (rarely) in reference to disposition (quot. *a* 1450). (See also in phrases, 33–70.)

c **1374** Chaucer *Troylus* iii. 845 (894) Discrecioun out of ȝoure heuid is gon. *c* **1380** Wyclif *Sel. Wks.* III. 134 Monnis hond helpis his heved. *a* **1450** *Knt. de la Tour* 22 Thei that haue an euelle hede and wolde chide. **1559** W. Cunningham *Cosmogr. Glasse* 159 There is now an other dout entred into my hed. **1573–80** Baret *Alv.* H 271 They remembred, or it came into their heads. **1703** T. N. *City & C. Purchaser* 46 To set their Heads to work at it. **1708** Swift *Death Partridge* Wks. 1755 II. i. 258 He had often had it in his head. **1802** Mar. Edgeworth *Moral T.* (1816) I. xix. 153 Accounts..which he kept in his head. *c* **1820** *Houlston Juvenile Tracts* No. 17 *Forethought* 3 We ought not to expect old heads to grow on young shoulders. **1863** Mrs. Gaskell *Sylvia's L.* (1877) 282 Tell him, Sylvie..for my head's clean gone. **1870** Freeman *Norm. Conq.* (ed. 2) I. App. 696 The story..was running in the heads of those who devised it. **1887** Edna Lyall *Knight-Errant* xvi. (1889) 144 Your head will be turned with all this triumph. **1892** *Daily Tel.* 29 Mar. 573 Whether he bowls with his head, as it is called, or turns himself into a catapult.

b. As a part essential to life; hence, in phrases, = life.

a **1000** *Laws Edgar* iv. c. 2 §11 (Schmid) Sy he þeof and þolige heafdes. *c* **1205** Lay. 28148 Min hafued beo to wedde þat isæid ich þe habbe Soð buten lese. **1382** Wyclif *Dan.* i. 10 ȝe shuln condempne myn hed to the kyng. **1559** *Mirr. Mag., Dk. Clarence* xv, The peril of my hed. **1749** Fielding *Tom Jones* v. iv, Many 's the man would have given his head to have had my lady told. **1887** P'cess Christian *Mem. Margrav. Baireuth* 42 Proofs enough against this scoundrel, Fritz, to cost him his head.

c. ***to have a (good) head (up)on one's shoulders***: to be sensible, able, proficient; ***to have a head for*** (figures, etc.): to be adept at; ***to have an old head on young shoulders***: see shoulder *sb.* 2 c.

1812 M. Edgeworth *Absentee* in *Tales Fash. Life* (1848) II. xvi. 244 Lady Dashfort, who had always..'her head upon her shoulders'. **1883** [see shoulder *sb.* 2 c]. **1886** Mrs. C. Praed *Miss Jacobsen's Chance* I. xvi. 312 That young man hasn't got a head on his shoulders. **1930** J. B. Priestley *Angel Pavement* vi. 301 You say I haven't a head for business. **1931** *Times Lit. Suppl.* 1 Oct. 742/2 He had a head for figures. **1932** A. J. Worrall *Eng. Idioms* 42 Young Brown will go far; he has a good head on his shoulders. **1939** G. B. Shaw *Good King Charles* i. 61 It is not your fault that you have no head for politics.

3. A representation, figure, or image of a head.

c **1430** Lydg. in Turner *Dom. Archit.* III. 39 Gargoyle, & many hydous heede. **1585** T. Washington tr. *Nicholay's Voy.* ii. iii. 33 The statue of a woman..certaine yeeres before the head had been taken away. *a* **1719** Addison *Paria* Wks. 1871 II. 13 A head of Titian by his own hand. **1727–51** Chambers *Cycl.* s.v., Vert, a chevron gules, between three Turks heads, couped, side-faced, proper. **1801** Strutt *Sports & Past.* iv. ii. 296 Any other coin with a head impressed upon it. **1849** Macaulay *Hist. Eng.* x. II. 650 William and Mary must be king and queen. The heads of both must appear together on the coin.

b. The obverse side of a coin, when bearing the figure of a head; the reverse being called the *tail*; in phr. ***head(s) or tail(s)***, used in tossing a coin to decide a chance. ***heads I win, (and) tails you lose***, I win whatever happens. *colloq.*

1684 Otway *Atheist* ii. i, As Boys do with their Farthings ..go to Heads or Tails for 'em. **1801** Strutt *Sports & Past.* (1810) 296 One person tosses the halfpenny up and the other calls at pleasure head or tail. **1832** A. Fonblanque *Eng. under 7 Admin.* (1837) II. 302 They would play the toss up with the creditor on the terms 'Heads I win, tails you lose'. **1838** De Morgan *Ess. Probab.* 82 In 100,000 tosses, between what limits is it 99 to 1 that the heads shall be contained? **1846** Dk. Rutland in *Croker Papers* (1884) III. xxiv. 59 A game which a sharper once played with a dupe, intituled, 'Heads I win, and tails you lose'. **1853** De Quincey *Autobiog. Sk.* Wks. I. 189 'We tossed up', to settle the question..'Heads' came up. **1909** F. M. Ford *Let.* 29 Jan. (1965) 33 This is an arrangement for Wells of an entirely 'Heads, I win. Tails, you lose'. **1958** *Times* 17 Oct. 17/1 The heads-I-win, tails-you-lose sort of argument between the conscious and the unconscious.

c. A postage-stamp: so called from the figure of the sovereign's head. (Cf. *queen's head*, queen *sb.* 15 b.) *colloq.* or *dial.*

1840 R. H. Barham *Let.* 30 July in R. H. D. Barham *Life* (1870) II. viii. 99 One of those abominable little heads which the wisdom of our Post Office people has invented. **1854** R. S. Surtees *Handley Cross* (rev. ed.) xix. 147 Take that to the Post, and mind you don't pick the 'ead off. **1859** *Punch* 17 Dec. 243/1 We signed it and sealed it, and put it into a hangvelop, and stuck a ned on it, and put it into the Post. **1927** G. Sturt *Small Boy in Sixties* i. 2 One very curious request would sometimes come from a villager; the man or woman asking for 'a head'.

4. In reference to, and hence denoting, the hair on the head. (See also *head of hair*, 44.)

13.. *K. Alis.* 1999 His hed was crolle, and yolow the here. **1530** Palsgr. 662/1, I holde best to polle my heed. *Ibid.* 694/2 You muste nedes rounde your heed for shame or you go home. **1565–73** Cooper *Thesaurus*, *Crines emissi*,..heare cast abroade as a woman loosing hir heade. **1775** Sheridan *Rivals* i. i, He'll never forsake his bob, though all the college should appear with their own heads! **1832** Tennyson *Sisters* vi, I curl'd and comb'd his comely head.

†5. The hair as dressed in some particular manner; applied esp. in the 18th c. to the heads of powdered and pomaded hair drawn up over a cushion or stuffing, and dressed with gauze, ribbon, etc., then worn; hence, a head-dress. *Obs.*

1494 Fabyan *Chron.* vii. ccxxiv. 251 For that tyme clerkes vsed busshed and brayded hedys. **1696** *Lond. Gaz.* No. 3199/4 A striped Muslin Head, laced with a fine small edging. **1712** Arbuthnot *John Bull* iv. viii, To buy..some high-heads of the newest cut, for my daughters. **1712** Addison *Spect.* No. 323 ¶7 At my toilette, try'd a new head. **1752** Johnson *Rambler* No. 191 ¶9 Ladies..asked me the price of my best head. **1753** Miss Collier *Art Torment.* i. ii. 70 *note*, Blushing is full as much out of date as high-heads. **1792** *Northampton Merc.* 20 Dec., The ladies now wear the lappets to their gauze heads worked with aces of spades, hearts, diamonds, and clubs, and call them quadrille heads. **18..** Mrs. Markham *Hist. France* xxxix. (1855) 539.

b. A horse's headstall.

1897 *Price List*, Best Billeted Weymouth Heads and Reins, with Noseband..Double-Rein Snaffle Head and Reins.

6. *Venery.* The 'attire' or antlers of a deer, roebuck, etc.

c **1420** *Venery de Twety* in *Rel. Ant.* I. 151 He [a hart] goth wexyng tyl he comes to .xxxij. yere..his hed aftir that tyme wexith no furthere. *a* **1547** Surrey *Descr. Spring* 6 The hart hath hung his old head on the pale. **1611** Markham *Countr. Content.* i. iv. (1668) 24 The Red Deer is said the first year to have no head. *Ibid.*, Stags yearly cast their Heads in March, April, May or June. **1674** N. Cox *Gentl. Recreat.* (1677) 87 The Rain-deer..intrapped with Nets..by reason of his great and spreading Head. **1892** *Chamb. Jrnl.* 14 May 318/2 The state of a deer's antlers, by which his age is known, is spoken of as his 'head'.

b. Phr. ***of the first head***: said of a deer, etc. at the age when the antlers are first developed; hence *fig.* of a man newly ennobled or raised in rank.

c **1420** *Venery de Twety* in *Rel. Ant.* I. 151 The .vj. yere a hert at the fyrst hed..for alleway we calle of the fyrst hed tyl that he be of .x. of the lasse. **1486** *Bk. St. Albans* E iv b, Robucke of the first hede he is at the iiij. yere. **1509** Barclay *Shyp of Folys* (1874) I. 36 A fox furred Jentelman: of the fyrst yere or hede. **1603** Holland *Plutarch's Mor.* 439 Reproching him..that he was a new upstart, and a gentleman of the first head. **1774** Goldsm. *Nat. Hist.* ii. v. (1862) I. 329 The buck is called..the fifth year, a buck of the first head. **1824** Scott *St. Ronan's* xxxi, But here is my lord, just upon us, like a stag of the first head.

7. Put for the person himself: **a.** in reference to his mind or disposition (cf. 2 a), or to some quality or attribute.

1551 T. Wilson *Logike* (1580) 88 b, Some heddes are verie bolde to enter farther than witte can reache. **1573–80** Baret *Alv.* P 476 A pleasant companion, a merrie head. **1579** Spenser *Sheph. Cal.* Gen. Argt., Sauing the leaue of such learned heads. *a* **1635** Naunton *Fragm. Reg.* (Arb.) 21 Pestered with the admission of too many young heads. **1794** Gouv. Morris in Sparks *Life & Writ.* (1832) I. 424 Montesquieu..is certainly one of their best heads. **1828** Scott *F.M. Perth* xv, The swaggering Smith, and one or two other hot heads. **1840–1** De Quincey *Rhetoric* Wks. 1862 X. 57 Different crowned heads..bidding against each other. **1887** P'cess Christian *Mem. Margrav. Baireuth* 281 Those wise heads came to the conclusion that there was hope.

b. in enumeration: An individual person. ***per head***: for each person.

1535 Coverdale *1 Chron.* xiii. [xii.] 23 This is the nombre of the heades harnessed vnto the warre which came to Dauid vnto Hebron. *Ibid.* xxiv. [xxiii.] 24 Counted after the nombre of ye names heade by heade. *a* **1687** Petty *Pol. Arith.* viii. (1691) 105 Forty Millions, that is 4*l.* per Head. **1748** H. Walpole *Lett. to Montagu* xxx, A play at Kingston, where the places are two-pence a head. **1847** Mrs. Sherwood *Life* xxi. 355 An anna a head for each boy. **1869** Freeman *Norm. Conq.* III. xi. 57 Except by taking the votes not by heads, but by tribes, cities, or cantons.

c. As a unit in numbering cattle, game, etc. (Plural, after a numeral, *head.*)

1513 Douglas *Æneis* viii. i. 96 Wyth thretty heyd..of grysis syne. **1533** in Weaver *Wells Wills* (1890) 105, x hed of shepe and lams. **1677** W. Hubbard *Narrative* (1865) II. 186 Thirteen Head of Neat Cattel were also killed by them. **1772** *Ann. Reg.* 160/2 The low grounds were laid under water, and many head of cattle drowned. **1856** Olmsted *Slave States* 219 Next year, twenty head of black men, direct from Africa, were landed from a Dutch ship, in James River, and were immediately bought by the gentlemen of the Colony. **1865** Trollope *Belton Est.* xvi. 183 Every head of cattle about the place had died.

d. An indefinite number or collection of animals, esp. of game.

1601 *Death Earl of Huntington* iv. ii. in Hazl. *Dodsley* VIII. 292 This howling like a head of hungry wolves. **1852** C. W. H[oskyns] *Talpa* 5 Adapted for the.. accommodation of a better and larger head of stock. **1862** *Lond. Rev.* 26 July 69 Everything has been lost sight of except the possible head of pheasants to be bagged next Christmas. **1894** *Times* 16 Apr. 7/3 Shooting tenants ought to be obliged to wire-in their woods where they kept a large head of rabbits.

e. A drug-addict or drug-taker; freq. with defining word prefixed, as hophead, *pot-head*; also *transf. slang* (orig. *U.S.*).

1911 [see hophead 1]. **1936** L. Duncan *Over Wall* i. 21, I saw the more advanced narcotic addicts.., laudanum fiends, and last but not least, the veronal heads. **1955** *U.S. Senate Hearings* (1956) viii. 4164 Terms for morphine addicts: 'Hype', 'Hygelo', 'Head' , [etc.]. **1959** N. Mailer *Advts. for Myself* (1961) 438 There was a horde: movie stars who left early,..councillors, pot-heads (discreet to be sure), hoodlums, [etc.]. **1966** *Observer* 25 Sept. 21/6 You've been to the delicatessen, of course, that's where the acid-heads and pot-heads assemble. **1969** *It* 11–24 Apr. 3/3 Berlin is alive with heads, dropping acid and STP in cinemas, parks, buses. *Ibid.* 18–31 July 9/4 Nightride was taken from a spot so convenient to many music heads and put on at an awkward hour. **1970** K. Platt *Pushbutton Butterfly* xiii. 149 A punchy Hell's Angel tea-head. **1973** *Daily Mail* 3 Apr. 19/4 *Heads*, habitual users of drugs, divided into acid heads (LSD) and potheads (cannabis).

II. A thing or part of a thing resembling a head in form or position.

8. The upper or principal extremity of various things, esp. when rounded, projecting, or of some special shape.

a. The striking or cutting part of certain weapons and instruments (as distinct from the shaft or handle): as of an ax, spear, arrow, hammer, club, etc. **b.** The rounded or knobbed extremity of a pin, nail, screw, etc., opposite to the point. **c.** The extremity of a bone, at which it articulates with another bone; esp. when rounded. **d.** The relatively fixed end of a muscle (usually consisting of a tendon) by which it is attached to a bone; the origin of a muscle. (A muscle may have more than one head; e.g. the biceps.) **e.** The bulb at the end of a tube as in a thermometer. (Cf. bolthead 2.) **f.** The rounded part of a comet, comprising the nucleus and coma, as distinct from the *tail*. **g.** *Music.* That part of a note (in modern notation round or oval) which determines its position on the stave, as distinct from the *stem* or *tail*. **h.** That part of a lute, violin, etc. above the neck, in which the tuning-pins are inserted; usually of a rounded form, and often artistically carved. **i.** The upper end or point of a violin-bow; also, the projecting part at the handle end in which the hairs are inserted. **j.** The upright timber of a gate at the opposite end from the hinges (opposite to the *heel*); each of the two upright pieces at the ends of a hurdle. **k.** The flat end of a barrel, cask, or similar vessel; the membrane stretched across the top or end of a drum. **†l.** The capital of a column. *Obs.* **m.** The cover of an alembic or crucible. **n.** A cover or hood for a carriage. **o.** A collective trade-name for the larger plates of tortoiseshell (usually thirteen) on the carapace of the hawk's-bill turtle. (Cf. foot *sb.* 17.) **p.** The upper member or part of various other things: see quots. **q.** = pommel *sb.* 5. Cf. *leaping-head* (leaping *vbl. sb.* b). **r.** The closed end of a cylinder of a pump or engine, esp. an internal-combustion engine; a cylinder-head or cylinder-cover. **s.** Of a bicycle frame (see quot. 1904). Also *attrib.* **t.** Of an explosive shell.

a. 13.. *Coer de L.* 2201 King Richard..Let him make an ax..The head was wrought right wele; Therin was twenty pounde of stele. *c* **1386** Chaucer *Sir Thopas* 171 His spere it was of fine Ciprees..The heed ful scharpe ygrounde. *c* **1400** *Rom. Rose* 1784 This arowe..I anoon dide al my crafte For to drawen out the shafte..But in myn herte the heed was lefte. *a* **1533** Ld. Berners *Huon* viii. 19 A spere with a sharpe hed. **1545** Ascham *Toxoph.* (Arb.) 123 A shaft hath three principall partes, the stele, the fethers, and the head. **1556** in W. H. Turner *Select. Rec. Oxford* 248 The hedd of the mase fell of. **1562** [see hammer-head 1]. **1611** Bible *Deut.* xix. 5 A stroke with the axe..and the head slippeth from the helue. **1858** Simmonds *Dict. Trade*, *Head*, ..the striking part of a hammer. **1896** Park *Golf* Gloss., *Head*, the lowest part of the golf-club.

b. 1542–3 *Act 34 & 35 Hen. VIII*, c. 6 Pinnes..such as.. haue the heads soudered fast to the shanke. **1565–73** Cooper *Thesaurus* s.v. *Acus*, Thou hast hitte the nayle on the heade. **1694** Moxon *Mech. Exerc.* 119 Those Chissels Joyners use have their wooden heads made hollow to receive the Iron Sprig..to endure the heavy blows of the Mallet they lay upon the head of the Chissel. *Ibid.* 157 That the Head of the Rivet be on the outside. **1711** *C.M. Lett. to Curat* 83 Which drives the Nail to the Head. **1774** Goldsm. *Nat. Hist.* (1776) VII. 153 Little protuberances..as large as a pin's head. **1879** Thomson & Tait *Nat. Phil.* I. i. §424 Measured by means of a divided head fixed perpendicularly to the screw at one end.

c. 1727–51 Chambers *Cycl.* s.v., When a bone has a round tip, or end, which advances, or projects forward..it is called

the head of the bone. **1793–1804** J. BELL *Anat. Hum. Body* (1829) I. 35 The head of each rib has..a small articulating surface. **1871** HUXLEY *Vertebr. Anim.* 155 Head of the hyomandibular which articulates with the skull.

d. 1727–51 CHAMBERS *Cycl.*, *Head* is also used for the extreme of a muscle, which is fastened or inserted into the stable-bone.. The head of a muscle is always a tendon. **1877** ROSENTHAL *Muscles & Nerves* (1881) 13 The ends are spoken of as the head and tail, of the muscle.

e. 1664 POWER *Exp. Philos.* 120 Take a long Tube, with a Head like a Weather-Glass, onely open at both ends. **1665** R. HOOKE *Microgr.* Pref. C b, I prepare a pretty capaceous Bolt-head..with a small stem about two foot and a half long ..and then fit the whole..that almost half the head..may lye buried in a concave Hemisphere cut into the Board.

f. 1727–51 CHAMBERS *Cycl.* s.v. *Comet*, Their tail is a very thin, slender vapour, emitted by the head, or nucleus of the comet. **1878** NEWCOMB *Pop. Astron.* III. v, Nucleus and coma..are together called the *head* of the comet.

g. 1727–52 CHAMBERS *Cycl.* s.v. *Note*, There are three things to be considered in these [musical] notes: 1. The quantity, i.e. the size and figure, of the head. 2. The quality, i.e. the colour, of the head; whether it be white or black, or full or open. **1888** STAINER & BARRETT *Dict. Mus. T.*

h. 1611 COTGR., *Ioug*..the head of a Lute, Violl, etc. **1727–51** CHAMBERS *Cycl.* s.v., The head of a lute, theorbo, or the like, is the place where the pins, or pegs, are screwed, to stretch or slacken the strings.

i. 1836 DUBOURG *Violin* ix. (1878) 280 Their bend..is so regulated as to cause the nearest approach made by the stick to the hair to be exactly in the middle, between the head and the nut. **1879** GROVE *Dict. Mus.* I. 264 The bow now [13th c.] gradually loses more and more the actual bow-shape; the head is distinct from the stick.

j. 1641 BEST *Farm. Bks.* (Surtees) 15 To a barre [= hurdle] belongeth two heads..into which the 4 spelles are to bee putte. **1826** LOUDON *Encycl. Agric.* (1831) 500 When gates are hung to open one way only, their heels and heads generally rest against the hanging and falling post. **1854** *Jrnl. R. Agric. Soc.* XV. II. 251 The head, heel, and top rail of a gate should be of oak.

k. 1390–1 in *Exped. Earl Derby* (Camden) 41 Hans Couper pro barelhedes et pro imposicione eorundem in dictos barellos, v scot. **1428** *Surtees Misc.* (1888) 2 He opend ye heued of ye other barell. **1567** GOLDING *Ovid's Met.* XII. 155 As a man should pat Small stones vppon a dromslets head. **1659** WILLSFORD *Scales Comm.* 159 The diameter at the bung 30, and at the head or either end 21 inches. **1691** RAY *Creation* II. (1701) 271 A membrane..stretched like the head of a drum. **1799** G. SMITH *Laboratory* I. 22 A paper cylinder with two small heads or bases. **1835** MARRYAT *Pacha* ii, I was directed to take the head out of the cask.

l. 1552 HULOET, Heade or chapiter of a pyller. **1660** BLOOME *Archit.* A, The Corinthian head.

m. 1594 PLAT *Jewell-ho.* II. 3 Let the bucket, or cooler in the head containe as much more colde water, as our ordinarie Limbecks doe. **1727–51** CHAMBERS *Cycl.*, *Alembic* ..consisting of a matrass or body, fitted with a roundish head, terminating in a sloping tube. **1758** REID tr. *Macquer's Chym.* I. 230 Fill therewith a crucible..heat it till it melts: then set it on fire, and when its whole surface is lighted place it under a large glass head. **1800** HENRY *Epit. Chem.* (1808) 91 An alembic of pure silver, furnished with a glass head.

n. 1794 W. FELTON *Carriages* (1801) I. 202 Heads to phaetons, &c. are found great conveniencies for sheltering from the sun, wind, or rain. **1851** *Voy. to Mauritius* v. 174 A 'bogy'—a gig with a head but no back. **1868** RUMPF *Techn. Dict.* s.v., Head of a carriage (covering which may be taken down).

o. 1892 *Chamb. Jrnl.* 14 May 318/2.

p. 1535 COVERDALE *1 Kings* x. 19 Ye heade of the seate was rounde behynde. **1659** WILLSFORD *Scales Comm.*, *Archit.* 30 A post with a turn'd or carv'd head. **1663** GERBIER *Counsel* 22 Cover the top of Chimneyes..the smoake holes can be.. made on the sides of the heads of them. *Ibid.* 29 The middle part of the head of the Windowes. **1706** PHILLIPS (ed. Kersey), *Head of an Anchor*, the Shank or longest part of it. **1848–52** *Dict. Archit.* IV. 34 *Head of a Down Pipe*, a sort of small cistern..which receives the water directly from the gutter and conveys it into the..down pipes. **1867** SMYTH *Sailor's Word-bk.* s.v. *Capstan*, Capsterns..agree in having a horizontal circular head, which has square holes around its edge, and in these long bars are shipped. **1868** RUMPF *Techn. Dict.*, *Head*, cap of a wind-mill. **1869** SIR E. J. REED *Shipbuild.* 252 The rudder generally tapers considerably from the head to the heel. **1886** BARING-GOULD *Court Royal* II. xxxii. 181 Captain Otley..put the silver head of his cane to his mouth. **1887** RUSKIN *Præterita* II. viii. 271, I offered to design the entire window head.

q. 1850 S. C. WAYTE *Equestrian's Manual* VI. 166 There are people who say *no* to the off head being cut off, as if in case a lady is nervous she cannot steady herself so well as when the head is left on. *Ibid.*, The saddler must have the head (or what we call the pummel) of the saddle to begin upon, and the further that can be carried forward the better. **1891** A. T. FISHER *Through Stable & Saddle-Room* xiii. 117 In some provincial, but nowadays in no well-made London saddles, the head of the saddle is cut back towards the seat. **1963** E. H. EDWARDS *Saddlery* xiv. 96 The head and gullet are strengthened with steel plates and there is also a steel reinforcement laid on to the underside of the tree from the head to the cantle.

r. 1884, 1895 [see *cylinder head* s.v. CYLINDER *sb.* 9 b]. **1904** A. B. F. YOUNG *Compl. Motorist* iv. 111 The cylinders consist of two separate parts. The body of the cylinder proper is a cast-iron liner... The head—containing the vertical valves and ignition-plug—is a separate casting. **1907** R. B. WHITMAN *Motor-Car Princ.* i. 5 While in the great majority of steam engines the steam acts first on one side of the piston and then on the other, in an automobile gasoline engine the pressure is exerted on only one side, the combustion of the mixture taking place between the piston and the closed end, or head, of the cylinder. **1965** P. H. SMITH *High-Speed Two-Stroke Petrol Engine* xiii. 258 On air-cooled engines, non-detachable heads are generally confined, in the case of iron castings, to the simplest and cheapest industrial engines.

s. 1887 BURY & HILLIER *Cycling* (1889) xiv. 321 Beneath the head and between the forks is placed the trouser guard. **1902** *Captain* VII. 82/1 That going from the head to the crank bracket is made duplex. **1904** GOODCHILD & TWENEY *Technol. & Sci. Dict.* 282/2 *Head* (Cycles), the socket or hollow tube through which the tube carrying the front fork runs. **1959** *Sears, Roebuck Catal.* Spring & Summer 1017/1 Universal Head Bearing Set... Fits all bicycles.

t. 1898 [see *war-head* (WAR *sb.*[1] 11)]. **1899** *Kynoch Jrnl.* Oct.–Nov. 17/1 The head [of a shrapnel shell] is attached to the body by means of small rivets.

9. a. Any rounded or compact part of a plant, usually at the top of the stem:

e.g. a compact mass of leaves (as in the cabbage and lettuce), of leaf-stalks (as in the celery), of flower-buds (as in the cauliflower), or of flowers, esp. of sessile florets upon a common receptacle, as in the *Compositæ* (= CAPITULUM); one of the young shoots of asparagus; an ear of corn; the 'cap' or pileus of a mushroom, etc.; the capsule of the poppy. Also applied to the compound bulb of garlic, and formerly to a simple bulb, as in the onion.

c **1000** *Sax. Leechd.* I. 376 Nim þes leaces heafda and dryȝ swiðe. *c* **1440** *Promp Parv.* 232/1 Heed of a garlek, lely, or oþer lyke (*Harl.* or of a leke), *bulbus*. **1565** J. SPARKE in *Hawkins' Voy.* (1878) 57 The head of mayis. **1577** B. GOOGE *Heresbach's Husb.* II. (1586) 56 The great Cabbedge with broad leaves and a great head. *Ibid.* 61 Garliche groweth both of the head and the seede, as the Onyon and other of this kind dooth. **1620** VENNER *Via Recta* vii. 135 The great, hard, and compacted heads of Cole, commonly called Cabbage. **1665** R. HOOKE *Microgr.* 128 Resembling the head of a mushroom. *a* **1697** AUBREY *Wilts* (1862) 198 The mowers..have always a pound of beefe and a head of garlick every man. **1697** DRYDEN *Virg. Georg.* I. 425 Bearded Grain: While yet the Head is Green. *a* **1732** GAY (J.), How turneps hide their swelling heads below, And how the closing colewor ts upwards grow. **1794** MARTYN *Rousseau's Bot.* vi. 67 An aggregate or capitate flower, or a head of flowers. **1866** *Treas. Bot.* 842/2 A decoction of poppy-heads. **1880** GRAY *Struct. Bot.* v. 147 A Head or Capitulum is a globular cluster of sessile flowers, like those of Red Clover.

b. The rounded leafy top of a tree or shrub.

1523 FITZHERB. *Husb.* §133 And euery boughe wyll haue a newe hede. **1596** SPENSER *F.Q.* VII. vii. 8 Most dainty trees, that..seeme to bow their bloosming heads full lowe. **1712** J. JAMES tr. *Le Blond's Gardening* 157 Your Trees..should be cut..by taking off their Heads. **1794** COWPER *Needless Alarm* 11 Oaks..that had once a head. **1861** MISS PRATT *Flower. Pl.* V. 80 A large tree..with a bushy head.

10. A collection of foam or froth on the top of liquor, esp. ale or beer.

1545 ASCHAM *Toxoph.* (Arb.) 117 Newe ale..wil sone lease his pith, and his head, afore he be longe drawen on. **1707** MORTIMER *Husb.* I. (1708) 574 Stirring of it twice a day, and beating down the Head or Yeast into it. **1760–72** tr. *Juan & Ulloa's Voy.* (ed. 3) I. 50 Palm-wine..bears a greater head than beer, and is of a very inebriating quality. **1810–20** B. SILLIMAN *Jrnl. Trav.* (ed. 3) III. 89 The porter drinkers of London reject the liquor unless it foams, or *has a head*, as they call it.

b. A collection of cream on the surface of milk.

[**1589** COGAN *Haven Health* cxcv. (1636) 179 Creame..is indeed the very head or heart of Milke.] **1848** *Jrnl. R. Agric. Soc.* IX. II. 480 The extent of surface in the large milk-pans produces a large 'head' of cream. **1888** ELWORTHY *W. Somerset Word-bk.* s.v., 'I ont break my head vor nobody' —meaning, now that the head or cream has begun to rise, I will not disturb it. *Mod.* (Devonshire Farmer's Wife) Would you prefer raw head or scald head?

11. Various technical uses.

a. A bundle of flax or silk: see quots. **b.** A tile of half the usual length, used at the eaves of a roof. **c.** Local name for certain geological formations: see quots. **d.** *Gold-mining.* A rammer for crushing quartz. **e.** (*pl.*) *Tin Manuf.* (See quot.) **f.** *Curling* and *Bowls.* (See quots. 1897.) **g.** A device designed to convert variations in an electrical signal into variations in the motion of a stylus (in the making of a gramophone record) or *vice versa* (in the playing of one). Also, a device in which a small electro-magnet is similarly used to produce or respond to variations in the magnetization of magnetic tape as the tape is moved past it. Freq. with defining word(s), as ***cutting head, erase head, magnetic head*** (see the defining words).

a. 1704 *Dict. Rust.*, *Head of Flax*..signifies twelve Sticks of Flax tied up to make a bunch. **1858** SIMMONDS *Dict. Trade*, *Head*,..a bundle of flax measuring probably two feet in length, and weighing a few pounds; in the North of Europe 18 head of hemp or flax are about 1 cwt. **1876** TOLHAUSEN *Techn. Dict.*, *Head of silk*.

b. 1703 T. N. *City & C. Purchaser* 165 *Heads*,..a Term used by Bricklayers, by which they mean ½ a Tile in length, but to the full breadth of a Tile; these they use to lay at the Eaves of a Roof.

c. 1846 *Jrnl. R. Agric. Soc.* VII. II. 452 'Heads' or prominent parts of the substratum of sand rising up through the substratum of brick earth in the manner that 'heads of marl' shoot up towards the surface. **1876** H. B. WOODWARD *Geol. Eng.* (1887) 485 During later Tertiary times, a great part of the country was dry land, and then no doubt much 'head' or subaërial detritus was formed. **1882** GEIKIE *Text-Bk. Geol.* III. II. ii. §1. 340 'Brick-earth', 'head' and 'rain-wash'..earthy deposits, sometimes full of angular stones, derived from the subaerial waste of the rocks of the neighbourhood. **1930** L. M. DAVIES in P. O'Connell *Science of To-Day* (1959) II. xii. 75 'Head' is a term applied to this rubble-drift where it masks an old raised beach. **1934** *Antiquity* VIII. 305 The angular deposit..corresponds to what is termed 'head' in Devon and Cornwall.

d. 1890 *Goldf. Victoria* 7 Forty additional heads will be shortly added to the crushing power, bringing the battery up to sixty heads. **1896** *Daily News* 11 Mar. 11/5 The new ten heads are running well, but the old 10-head mill has been giving trouble.

e. 1879 *Cassell's Techn. Educ.* III. 98 (*Tin-washing*) The rack or frame..consists of a long table on a slight incline down which the slimes are carried by a gentle stream of water.. The purest ore called 'heads' collects at the upper part of the table.

f. 1828 *Kilmarnock Treat. Curling* (1883) 79 Head (probably a corruption of *heat*,) that portion of the game in which both parties play all their stones once. **1877** *Encycl. Brit.* VI. 713 [Curling Rules.] All matches to be of a certain number of heads. **1897** *Encycl. Sport* I. 129/1 (Bowls) *End* —One delivery of all the bowls upon the two sides, after which the jack is again 'set'. Also called Head. *Ibid.* 264/1 (Curling) *Head*, the portion of the game in which all the players have delivered their stones, and have counted the winning shot or shots. **1969** R. WELSH *Beginner's Guide Curling* xvi. 104 All matches shall be of a certain number of Heads, or Shots, or by Time as may be agreed on, or as fixed by the Umpire at the outset.

g. 1951 *Catal. Exhibits S. Bank Exhib., Festival of Brit.* 143/1 Gramophone pick-up with interchangeable heads. **1960** COOKE & MARKUS Electronics & Nucleonics Dict. 207/1 *Head.* 1. The photoelectric unit that converts the sound track on motion-picture film into corresponding audio signals in a motion-picture projector. 2. Cutter. 3. Magnetic head. **1962** L. DEIGHTON *Ipcress File* xxvii. 172 He laid a huge shiny L.P. on the..turntable and delicately applied the diamond head. **1962** A. NISBETT *Technique Sound Studio* 255 *Head*, transducer which converts electrical energy into magnetic or mechanical energy, or vice versa. Thus we have a tape recording and reproducing heads and disc cutter and pick-up heads. The electromagnet used for erasing tape is also called a head. **1963** *Which?* Jan. 8/2 The pick up is composed of two parts—an arm, and at the end of the arm..a head. The head contains the cartridge, and set into the cartridge is the stylus. **1964** *Honeywell Gloss. Data Proc.* 29/1 *Head*, a device that reads, records or erases information in a storage medium, e.g., a small electromagnet used to read, write or erase information on a magnetic drum or tape, or the set of perforating, reading or marking devices and block assembly used for punching, reading or printing on paper tape. **1964** F. L. WESTWATER *Electronic Computers* (ed. 2) iv. 68 Each track must have its read/write head.

12. The top, summit, upper end (of an eminence, or erection, as a pole, pile, mast, sail (cf. FOOT *sb.* 18 d), staircase, ladder, etc.).

a **1300** *Cursor M.* 16577 Apon þe hefd o þis rode, ouerthwart was don a brede. *c* **1425** *Craft Nombrynge* (E.E.T.S.) 7 þen write þe articulle þat is ten ouer þe figuris hed of twene as þus $\frac{1}{322}$. **1542** RECORDE *Gr. Artes* 135 b, 30 is represented by the ioynynge together of ye headdes of the foremost fynger and the thombe. **1548** *Compl. Scot.* vi. 51 Ane man beand on the hede of ane hil. **1602** SHAKS. *Ham.* v. i. 276 The skyish head Of blew Olympus. **1627** CAPT. SMITH *Seaman's Gram.* v. 19 The head of the fore top-Mast. **1711** W. SUTHERLAND *Shipbuild. Assist.* 114 The upper Part is called the Head of the Sail. **1712** J. JAMES tr. *Le Blond's Gardening* 17 From the Head of these Steps you have a general View of the Garden. **1797** MAD. D'ARBLAY *Lett.* Dec., I then accompanied her to the head of the stairs. **1810** SCOTT *Lady of L.* I. i, But when the sun his beacon red Had kindled on Benvoirlich's head. **1882** NARES *Seamanship* (ed. 6) 9 *Head*..The upper end of a spar.

13. a. The top of a page or writing; hence, Something, as a title, written at the top of a page, section, etc.; a heading.

1586 A. DAY *Eng. Secretary* To Rdr. (1625) A iv, Peruse but the head of every page, and there you shall finde what in the same page is contained. **1659** WILLSFORD *Scales Comm.* 58 Being stated (as in the head of the table). *Ibid.*, *Archit.* 9 Contracted to heads in necessary particulars. **1685** LOCKE *Comm.-Pl. Bk.* Wks. 1812 III. 311 The heads of the class appear all at once, without the trouble of turning over a leaf. **1712** ADDISON *Spect.* No. 273 ¶2 Without seeing his name at the head of it. *a* **1854** E. FORBES *Lit. Papers* vii. (1855) 189 The heads of chapters are ornamented with artistic woodcuts. **1866** BRANDE & COX *Dict. Sc. etc.* II. 101 In Printing.. The divisions and subdivisions of a work, when they are set in lines and chapters are also called heads.

b. The top of a book. Cf. HEADBAND 3.

1835 J. HANNETT *Bibliopegia* 26 The book is now taken between the hands and well beaten up at the back and head on a smooth board, to bring the sheets level and square. **1876** *Encycl. Brit.* IV. 43/1 The object of the binder in this operation is to make every page of uniform size, presenting a smooth and equal 'head', 'tail', and 'fore-edge'. **1930** *Godfrey's Catal.* No. 134. 26/1 Folio, old sheep (roughly repaired at head and heel).

c. A headline in a newspaper.

1911 H. S. HARRISON *Queed* xviii. 230 The Chronicle that afternoon shrieked it under a five-column head. **1915** J. WEBSTER *Patty & Priscilla* xi. 170 A life-size portrait of her ..appeared in a New York evening paper, and scare-heads three inches high announced..that the champion athlete.. was at death's door. **1962** *Amer. Speech* XXXVII. 200 A *Saturday Evening Post* editorial head: 'Good News.' **1967** *Guardian* 2 Nov. 8/7 'Ebullient Mr Brown hits out,' said the (changed) head on the last edition.

14. The maturated part of a boil, abscess, etc., at which it tends to break. Chiefly in phrases, as to ***come to a head***, to suppurate: see also 31.

1611 COTGR., *Aboutir*, to wax ripe, or draw to a head, as an impostume. **1697** DRYDEN *Virg. Georg.* III. 691 To lance the Sore, And cut the Head. **1737** BRACKEN *Farriery Impr.* (1756) I. 15 Suppuration, or coming to a Head, as it is vulgarly called. **1871** DIAZ *W. Henry & Lett.* 134 Come to a head—like a boil or a rebellion.

15. The upper end of something on a slope or so regarded; e.g. that end of a lake at which a river enters it; the higher end of a valley, the inner extremity of a cave, gulf, etc.; that end of a bed, grave, etc. towards which a person's head lies; that end of a table at which the chief seat is (cf. 26).

847 *Charter* in *O.E. Texts* 434 Fram smalan cumbes heafde to græwanstane. *c* **1290** *S. Eng. Leg.* I. 6/179 þe heued of þis valeie. *a* **1300** *Cursor M.* 17288 + 219 þat one at þe fote of þe graf, þat other at the hede. *c* **1380** WYCLIF *Wks.* (1880) 49 Vndir here beddis hed. *c* **1400** MAUNDEV. (Roxb.) xiii. 58 At þe heued of þis see of Galile..es a castell. **1548** HALL *Chron.*, *Hen. IV*, 32 b, He caused his crowne to be set on the pillowe at his beddes heade. **1676** WALTON & COTTON *Angler* xx. (Chandos) 341 The head of the pond. **1786** MAD. D'ARBLAY *Diary* 17 July, I was offered the seat ..at the head of the table. **1830** LYELL *Princ. Geol.* I. 286 A point which must..be considered the head of its delta. **1860** TYNDALL *Glac.* I. xiv. 98 A crevasse that extended quite round the head of the valley. **1862** STANLEY *Jew. Ch.* (1877) I. viii. 159 At the head of the Gulf.

16. *spec.* The source of a river or stream. Now chiefly in FOUNTAIN-HEAD, q.v.

1375 BARBOUR *Bruce* II. 589 Till þai come to þe hed off tay. **1480** CAXTON *Descr. Brit.* 9 The riuers Seuarn and dee almost to the heedes. **1538** LELAND *Itin.* (1768) II. 51 The Hed of Isis in Coteswalde risith about a Mile a this side Tetbyri. **1541** *Act 33 Hen. VIII*, c. 35 Cleane running water, issuyng out of the heades of freshe springes. **1625** N. CARPENTER *Geog. Del.* II. ix. (1635) 142 Nilus in Africke is thought to haue his first head in the mountaines of the Moone. **1718** WATTS *Ps.* CXIV. ii, Jordan beheld their March and fled With backward Current to his Head. **1854** *Jrnl. R. Agric. Soc.* XV. II. 426 Where the spring head has been boggy. **1871** PHILLIPS *Geol. Oxf.* iii. 25 The refreshing rivulet which has been honoured by the name of 'Thames Head' or 'the very head of Isis'.

b. *fig.* Source, origin: usually FOUNTAIN-HEAD.

1548 CRANMER *Catech.* 206 b, The wel and heade, out of the which al these euylle do spring is original synne. **1586** A. DAY *Eng. Secretary* II. (1625) 96, I will go to the head of the matter. **1720** WATERLAND *Eight Serm.* 112 By referring all Things to one Head and Fountain. **1817** COLERIDGE *Biog. Lit.* 80 Acquiring facts at the fountain head.

17. A body of water kept at a height for supplying a mill, etc.; the height of such a body of water, or the force of its fall (estimated in terms of the pressure on a unit of area). Sometimes, the bank or dam by which such water is kept up.

1480 CAXTON *Chron. Eng.* ccxxxvii. 261 Brekyng hir fisshponde hedes and lete the water of hir pondes, stewes and riuers renne out. **1530** PALSGR. 506/2, I damme or make the heed of a water. **1563** *Act 5 Eliz.* c. 21 §1 Any Hedd or Heddes, Damme or Dammes, of any Pondes, Pooles, Motes, Stanges, Steues, or severall Pittes. **1723** *Royal Proclam.* in *Lond. Gaz.* No. 6135/2 Heads of Fish-Ponds. **1769** *De Foe's Tour Gt. Brit.* I. 274 Here is a very large Pond, or Lake of Water, kept up to an Head by a strong *Battre d' Eau*, or Dam. **1791** R. MYLNE *2nd Rep. Thames* 15 Millers.. working their Heads of Water in a spendthrift way. **1814** *Gen. Rep. Agric. State Scotl.* xiii. §4 II. 671 Heads, or banks of earth, for the confinement of water in artificial lakes or ponds. **1832** *Examiner* 289/1 He has dammed the stream to give it head. **1861** SIR W. FAIRBAIRN *Mills* I. 178 The head of water is 132 feet. **1878** HUXLEY *Physiogr.* 181 At certain seasons the head of water attains to as great a height as forty feet.

b. *transf.* The difference of pressure (per unit of area) of two columns of fluid (liquid or gaseous) of different densities communicating at the base; the pressure (per unit of area) of a confined body of gas or vapour.

1862 *Times* 27 Mar., The 'Merrimac'.. made direct for the 'Cumberland' under a full head of steam. **1889** 'MARK TWAIN' *Yankee at Crt. K. Arthur* (Tauchn.) I. 141 By the time I had got a good head of reserved steam on.

c. A high tidal wave, usually in an estuary; = BORE *sb.*³ 2, EAGRE.

1570 *Tarlton's Jests* App. 127 At twelve a clock at night, It [the rushing river] flowde with such a hed. **1807** SOUTHEY *Espriella's Lett.* III. 380 The tide [in the Parrot] instead of rising gradually, flows in a head. **1854** *Jrnl. R. Agric. Soc.* XV. I. 5 [The] river came down with a 'head' similar to the tidal phenomenon on the Severn.

d. *Founding.* (See quots.)

1858 SIMMONDS *Dict. Trade, Feeder*,.. a large head or supply of fluid iron to a runner or mould in heavy castings. **1867** GWILT *Archit.* §2265 h, Cannon, pipes, columns, &c., are stronger when cast in a vertical than in a horizontal position, and stronger still when provided with a *head* or additional length, whose weight serves to compress the mass of iron in the mould below it. **1869** [see DEADHEAD *sb.* 2]. **1884** KNIGHT *Dict. Mech.* Suppl., *Head* , over the thickest part of heavy castings, a large flow-gate or riser for the metal is placed. Through this the contracting mass below is fed from time to time with hot metal, while a boy keeps the head open with a feeding or working rod.

18. The foremost part or end; the front. (See also AHEAD.)

a. The front of a procession, army, or the like.

c **1205** LAY. 8671 Þer com Julius teon forn aȝæien heore hæued. **1375** BARBOUR *Bruce* IX. 610 And syne schir Eduardis cumpany.. Set stoutly in the hedis agane. **1618** BOLTON *Florus* IV. ii. (1636) 288 Caesar.. ranne like a mad-man into the head of the battell. **1796** *Instr. & Reg. Cavalry* (1813) 116 If gradual and inconsiderable changes of direction are to be made during the march of the column, the head will, on a moveable pivot, effect such change. **1863** KINGLAKE *Crimea* I. xiv, The head of the vast column of troops.

b. The front, outer or projecting end of a fortification, a pier, etc.

1706 PHILLIPS (ed. Kersey), *Head of a Work* (in *Fortif.*), the Front of it next the Enemy, and farthest from the Body of the Place. **1727–51** CHAMBERS *Cycl.*, *Head of the Camp* is the front, or foremost part, of the ground an army is encamped on; or that which advances most towards the field, or enemy. **1758** BORLASE *Nat. Hist. Cornwall* iv. 53 The Seyn-boats, riding at the head of the pier. **1823** CRABB *Technol. Dict.*, *Head* (*Gunn.*), the fore part of the cheeks of a gun or howitz carriage.

c. The front part of a plough which bears the share. (Cf. *plough-tail*.)

1842–4 H. STEPHENS *Bk. Farm* (1871) I. 76 The attachment of the sock is with the lower end of the head of the plough. *Ibid.* 488, I caused to be fitted to the plough.. a shifting head with unequal sides. **1844** *Loudon's Encycl. Agric.* 391 The materials with which ploughs are constructed is, generally, wood for the beam and handles, cast iron for the head.

†**19. a.** The beginning (of a word, writing, etc.). **b.** *Astrol.* The commencement of a zodiacal sign, i.e. the point where the sun enters it. *Obs.*

1340 HAMPOLE *Pr. Consc.* 486 E es þe first letter and þe hede Of þe name of Eve. **1382** WYCLIF *Ps.* xxxix. 8 [xl. 7] In the hed of the boc it is write of me, that I do thi wil. *c* **1391** CHAUCER *Astrol.* I. §17 In this heued of cancer is the grettest declinacioun northward of the sonne. **1816** SCOTT *Antiq.* xxi, 'When she [the moon] is in her fifteenth mansion, which mansion is in de head of Libra.'

c. (*a*) *Phonetics.* The initial stressed element(s) in a sequence of sounds before the nucleus. (*b*) *Linguistics.* (See quot. 1964¹.)

1922 H. E. PALMER *Eng. Intonation* v. 17 Any syllable or syllables preceding the nucleus in the same Tone-Group is termed the 'Head' of the group. **1961** R. B. LONG *Sentence & its Parts* i. 20 Headed units are made up of (1) contained heads and (2) contained modifiers which attach to these heads. **1964** R. H. ROBINS *Gen. Ling.* vi. 236 The word or group sharing the syntactic functions of the whole of a subordinative construction is called the head, and the other components are subordinate. Thus in English adjective noun groups, the noun is head and the adjective subordinate. In adverb adjective groups the adjective is head and the adverb subordinate..; in *reasonably clever boys*, *boys* is head and *reasonably clever* is subordinate, and within this latter group *clever* is head and *reasonably* is subordinate. **1964** M. SCHUBIGER in D. Abercrombie et al. *Daniel Jones* 263, I am using the term head for the first stressed element pitched high. **1964** *Amer. Speech* XXXIX. 37 Nice city home... All the ten fine old stone houses. In these sequences the noun is more intimately tied to the head than is the adjective. *Ibid.* 38 A noun that has 'widespread' use as attributive to many different heads is an adjective.

20. The thick end of a chisel or wedge, opposite to the edge.

1793 SMEATON *Edystone L.* §238 [see 46]. **1842** *Chambers' Inform.* II. 24 Here the wedge is seen to taper from a thick end or head.. to a thin edge or point.

21. The fore part of a ship, boat, etc.; the bows.

1485 *Naval Acc. Hen. VII* (1896) 50 Sheves of Iren in the bote Hede. **1582** N. LICHEFIELD tr. *Castanheda's Conq. E. Ind.* xxx. 73 b, The Shippes laye with their beake heads close to the same [land]. **1697** DRYDEN *Virg. Æneid* VI. 4 They turn their heads to sea, their sterns to land. **1795** NELSON in Nicolas *Disp.* (1846) VII. p. xxx, We are getting on very fast with our caulking; our head is secured. **1834** M. SCOTT *Cruise Midge* vi. (1867) 108 We were riding with our head up the river. **1847** GROTE *Greece* (1862) III. xxxviii. 374 They were moored by anchors head and stern. **1867** SMYTH *Sailor's Word-bk.*, *Head*,.. the whole fore-part of a ship, including the bows on each side.

b. Phrases. ***by*** (***down by***) ***the head***, with the head lower in the water than the stern; hence *fig.* (*slang*), slightly intoxicated. ***head on***, with the head pointed directly towards something: see ON *adv.*

1769 FALCONER *Dict. Marine* U u iv, The vessel is too much by the head. *Ibid.* (1789), *Orser*, to row against the wind, or row head-to-wind. **1860** *Times* 17 Dec. 10/5 He said he was a little by the head, but not drunk. **1894** HALL CAINE *Manxman* v. iii, The boat was brought head to the wind.

c. *spec.* The work fitted in front of the stem in some (mostly obsolete) types of ships, including the knee of the head, the figure-head, rails, etc. Also used simply for FIGURE-HEAD.

1676 *Lond. Gaz.* No. 1130/4 A square stern'd Sloop with a Deck, a small Head, and the Figure of a Cat thereon. **1703** *Ibid.* No. 3968/1 The Privateer.. carried away her Head and Boltsprit. **1711** W. SUTHERLAND *Shipbuild. Assist.* 161 *Head of a Ship*, that part which is fasten'd to the Bow or foremost part of the Ship without-board. **1804** A. DUNCAN *Mariner's Chron.* Pref. 19 A Head is an ornamental figure erected on the continuation of a ship's stem. *c* **1850** *Rudim. Navig.* (Weale) 123 *Head*.. particularly applied to all the work fitted afore the stem, as the figure, the knee, rails, etc. **1867** SMYTH *Sailor's Word-bk.*, *Head*,.. in a confined sense that part on each side of the stem outside the bows proper which is appropriated to the use of the sailors for wringing swabs, or any wet jobs.

d. A ship's latrine (in the bows). Often (in the U.K., usually) in *pl.* In the U.S. also used of W.C.s ashore.

1748 SMOLLETT *R. Random* I. xxviii. 253 The madman.. took an opportunity, while the centinel attended him at the head, to leap over-board. **1905** *Trans. Inst. Naval Archit.* XLVII. I. 29 The W.C.s for officers, and the seamen's head for the crew, are to be fitted where shown on the drawings. **1938** C. S. FORESTER *Ship of Line* 21 You'll clean out the heads of this ship every day. **1952** 'E. BOX' *Death in Fifth Position* (1954) iv. 85, I saw Louis coming out of the head with a blond footman. **1957** *Partisan Rev.* 328 Yet it had happened and here I was, talking about algebra to a lot of boys who might.. be popping off needles every time they went to the head. **1965** J. R. HETHERINGTON *Selina's Aunt* 48 The rating who cleans them is Captain of the Heads. **1972** *Daily Colonist* (Victoria, B.C.) 20 Jan. 28/2 The head, or ship-board bathroom, for women crew members is to be the same one that male crew members now use exclusively.

22. A projecting point of the coast, esp. when of considerable height; a cape, headland, promontory. Now usually in place-names.

c **1155** *Newminster Cartul.* (Surtees) 45 Usque ad Gladenehefde. **1461** *Liber Pluscardensis* IX. xxxiii, Apud locum qui Sanct Abbis Heid vocatur. **1577–87** HOLINSHED *Chron.* I. 5/1 The name of an head of land in Britaine called *Promontorium Herculis*. **1606** SHAKS. *Ant. & Cl.* III. vii. 52 Our ouer-plus of shipping will we burne, And with the rest full mann'd, from th' head of Action Beate th' approaching Cæsar. **1843** MACAULAY *Armada* 38 High on St. Michael's Mount it shone: it shone on Beachy Head. **1893** W. T. WAWN *S. Sea Islanders* 162 Hardly were we within the 'Heads', when the wind dropped.

b. A projecting point of a rock or sandbank.

1775 ROMANS *Hist. Florida* App. 34, 1½ miles E. from the land are a parcel of dangerous sunken heads called the Hen and Chickens. **1846** MᶜCULLOCH *Acc. Brit. Empire* (1854) I. 61 The Bunt Head, on the west side [of the Goodwin Sands] is very dangerous.

23. *Coal-mining.* An underground passage or level for working the coal: = HEADING 11.

1664 POWER *Exp. Philos.* 177 If a Pistol be shot off in a head remote from the eye of a pit, it will give but a little report. **1894** *Times* 15 Aug. 13/3 He knew that gas existed in one of the heads, and fences were placed there to indicate that it was dangerous.

24. An end, extremity (of anything of greater length than breadth). *Obs.* exc. in certain special uses, as of a stone or brick in a building (cf. HEADER 5), or of a bridge.

c **1400** *Destr. Troy* 1672 At the tother hede of þe halle was .. A wonderfull werke. *c* **1400** MAUNDEV. (1839) xxii. 242 His Lond.. durethe so ferre, that a man may not gon from on Hed to another, nouther be See ne Lond, the space of 7 ȝeer. **1452** in Willis & Clark *Cambridge* (1886) I. 336 [A messuage] abbuttyng at the one heved vpon the high strete and at the other heved vpon the said College. **1622** *Ibid.* II. 74 The east hed abutting upon the strete and the west hed upon the buildings belonging to Katherine Hall. **1703** T. N. *City & C. Purchaser* 29 If a Barn consist of a Floor, and 2 Heads, where they lay Corn, they say a Barn of 2 Bays. **1735** J. PRICE *Stone-Br. Thames* 4 A House on each Head of the Bridge.. to receive the Toll. **1793** SMEATON *Edystone L.* §82 Two Headers or bond pieces; whose heads being cut dovetail-wise, adapted themselves to and confined in the stretchers. **1843** MACAULAY *Lays Anc. Rome*, *Horatius* xxxv, As that great host, with measured tread.. Rolled slowly towards the bridge's head.

III. Various figurative uses arising from preceding senses.

25. A person to whom others are subordinate; a chief, captain, commander, ruler, leader, principal person, head man.

c **897** K. ÆLFRED *Gregory's Past.* xvii. 112 Ða ic ðe ȝesette eallum Israhelum to heafde. *c* **1100** *O.E. Chron.* an. 1087 Hine þe wæs ærur heafod to þam unræde. *c* **1200** ORMIN 362 He wass Preost Hæfedd off alle preostess. *a* **1240** *Sawles Warde* in *Cott. Hom.* 247 Þat heaued prof is þe feont [fiend]. *a* **1300** *Cursor M.* 17288 + 172 He ordend him hede of heli kirk. *c* **1330** R. BRUNNE *Chron.* (1810) 2, I rede we chese a hede, þat vs to werre kan dight.. For werre withouten hede is not wele, ve fynde. *c* **1380** WYCLIF *Sel. Wks.* III. 339 Heed of þis Chirche is Crist, boþe God and man. *c* **1460** FORTESCUE *Abs. & Lim. Mon.* xv, Thai all haue an hed, or a cheef to rule þe counsell. **1521** FISHER *Wks.* (1876) 314 The heed of the vnyuersall chirche is the pope. **1532–3** *Act 24 Hen. VIII*, c. 12 Preamb., This Realme of Englond is an Impire.. governed by oon Supreme heede and King. **1579** SPENSER *Sheph. Cal.* June 83 The soueraigne head Of shepheards all. **1667** MILTON *P.L.* IX. 1155 Why didst not thou the Head, Command me absolutely not to go? **1686** J. DUNTON *Lett. fr. New-Eng.* (1867) 106 Madam Brick is a Gentlewoman whose Head [i.e. Husband] has been cut off, and yet she lives and walks. **1725–51** CHAMBERS *Cycl.* s.v., A dean is the head of his chapter. **1793** A. HAMILTON *Wks.* (1886) VII. 71 The President and heads of departments ought to be near Congress. **1838** PRESCOTT *Ferd. & Is.* (1843) I. iv. 198 The head of the house of Mendoza. **1888** BRYCE *Amer. Commw.* I. v. 47 That a single head is not necessary to a republic might have been suggested to the Americans by.. ancient examples.

b. *spec.* The master or principal of a college or 'house' in a university; also short for HEADMASTER.

1565 in Strype *Parker* (1821) III. 127 All Heddes, and all other Scholers.. shal weare in ther cherches or chappels.. surplesses and hodes. **1576** in Nichols *Progr. Q. Eliz.* (1823) II. 111 The said Vice-chauncelor and hedds of Colledges. **1583** *Ibid.* 406 Reverend Doctors and heads of houses all on horse-backe. **1631** T. ADAMS in *Lett. Lit. Men* (Camden) 147 From the Vice-Chancellour and Heads of your famous University. **1705** HEARNE *Collect.* 7 Sept. (O.H.S.) I. 42 He never knew any Fellow turn'd out in the Heads Absence. **1780** V. KNOX *Lib. Educ.* (R.), In the presence of heads of houses, public officers, doctors, and proctors. **1847** TENNYSON *Princ.* IV. 360 Delivering seal'd dispatches which the Head Took half-amazed. **1889** A. R. HOPE in *Boy's Own Paper* 3 Aug. 697/3 Who could.. mix on equal terms with those ineffable beings the head's daughters.

c. A collection of persons holding a position of command or leadership; in quot. 1665, translation of CAPUT 3, q.v.

1665 J. BUCK in Peacock *Stat. Cambridge* (1841) App. B 66 The V.C. readeth all the graces, some one of the Head holding the Posers Bill to stay those whose names are not in the said Bill.

d. Applied to things or places: The chief city, capital; the chief or most excellent part.

c **893** K. ÆLFRED *Oros.* II. i. §3 Sameramis.. ȝetimbrede þa burȝ Babylonie, to þon þæt heo wære heafod ealra Asiria. **1340** HAMPOLE *Pr. Consc.* 4081 Bygyn at Rome; For it es heved of all cristendome. **1480** CAXTON *Descr. Brit.* 18 This Cite was hede and chief Cyte of alle Venedocia. **1589** COGAN *Haven Health* cxcv. (1636) 179 Creame.. is indeed the very head or heart of Milke. **1611** BIBLE *Isa.* vii. 8 The head of Syria is Damascus.

26. Position of leadership, chief command, or greatest importance; chiefly in phr. ***at*** (†***in***) ***the head of***. (Sometimes with mixture of sense 18 a.)

a **1300** *E.E. Psalter* xvii[i]. 44 (Mätz.) Þou sal In heved of genge me set with al. *a* **1400** *Relig. Pieces fr. Thornton MS.* (1867) 5 Oure gastely ffadire þat hase heuede of vs. **1563–87** FOXE *A. & M.* (1841) I. 341 Thus Rome first began to take a head above all other churches. **1599** *Broughton's Let.* ix. 32 To keepe their wiues from soueraintie, and not suffer them .. to take head and ouerrule. **1636** MASSINGER *Bashf. Lover* I. ii, Tho' you charged me I' the head of your troops. **1662** H. MORE *Philos. Writ.* Pref. Gen. (1712) 23 Certain opinions of his.. in the head of which he names this of the Praeexistence of the Soul. **1678** LADY CHAWORTH in *12th Rep. Hist. MSS. Comm.* App. v. 51 Having such a Prince as the Duke of Yorke at the head of our Armies. **1735–8**

Bolingbroke *On Parties* 22 Some leading Men..who thought it better to be at the Head of a Sect, than at the Tail of an Establishment. **1845** M. Pattison *Ess.* (1889) I. 7 At the head of the class of the pictorial historians stands Augustin Thierry. **1849** Macaulay *Hist. Eng.* vii. II. 166 At twenty-one..he was placed at the head of the administration. **1894** H. Drummond *Ascent Man* 143 Anatomy places Man at the head of all other animals that were ever made.

b. ***head of the river*** (in Bumping races): the position of being first boat; also said of the boat, crew, or college, which gains this position in a race or series of races, such as the Oxford 'Eights'.

1853 C. Bede *Verdant Green* x, The placing of the Brazen-face boat at the head of the river. **1897** *Whitaker's Alm.* 632/1 On the first night New College bumped Magdalen and went head of the river.

c. *Rugby Football.* In full ***loose head***: in the front row of the scrummage the forward closest to the scrum half as he puts the ball into the scrummage; ***to win the ball against the head***, to hook the ball notwithstanding the fact that the opposition front row holds the advantage by having a player in the loose-head position.

1917 in P. Jones *War Lett.* (1918) 259 We used to spend hours arguing over anything, from free-will to the 'loose-head'. **1959** *Times* 7 Sept. 16/2 A heel against the loose head was a prelude to Coventry's next try. **1960** *Times* 30 Nov. 3/6 He even managed to win the ball against the head in a five-yard scrummage.

27. One of the chief points of a discourse; the section of it pertaining to any such point; hence, a point, topic; a main division, section, chapter of a writing; a division of a subject, class, category.

(Partly arising from sense 13, and often associated with it, as in the phr. ***under this head.***)

c **1500** *Melusine* xxiv. 185 This gentylman thanne reherced to them fro hed to hed..all thauenture of theire vyage. **1573–80** Baret *Alv.* H 271 Set this on my head in your booke, or write that you haue lent it, or deliuered it to me. **1607** Shaks. *Timon* iii. v. 28 As if they labour'd To bring Man-slaughter into forme, and set Quarrelling Vpon the head of Valour. **1632** J. Lee *Short Surv.* A iij, The Contents or principall heads handled in this whole Discourse. **1652** Gataker *Antinom.* 5 We were acknowledged to agree in those two heds. **1725** De Foe *Voy. round World* (1840) 209 He made me many compliments upon that head. **1773** Goldsm. *Stoops to Conq.* ii. (Globe) 653/2 Make yourself easy on that head. **1838** Thirlwall *Greece* IV. xxxii. 241 The accusation comprised several heads. **1849** Macaulay *Hist. Eng.* I. 306 The expenditure under this head must have been small indeed. **1868** Helps *Realmah* xv. (1876) 411, I have very little to say upon this head. **1875** Jowett *Plato* III. 603 The heads of our yesterday's discussion.

28. Turning of the head, backward change of the course: = heading *vbl. sb.* 4. ? *Obs.*

1607 Topsell *Four-f. Beasts* (1658) 208 The wandring hares..making heads upon the plain ground, to the confusion of the dogs. *Ibid.* 211 In her course she taketh not one way, but maketh heads like labyrinths to circumvent and trouble the Dogs. **1798** *Sporting Mag.* XI. 3 After much manœuvring, *heads* and *doubles*, as well as equally good racing in view, she [the hare] was killed in the rickyard of the Sun Inn.

29. Advance against opposing force; resistance; insurrection: in certain phrases, as ***to make*** or ***gain head*** (see 52); ***to bear*** or ***keep head against***, to resist successfully, hold one's own against.

1597 Daniel *Civ. Wars* ii. xi, If any hardier than the rest ..offer head that idle fear to stay. **1602** Shaks. *Ham.* iv. v. 101 Young Laertes, in a Riotous head, Ore-beares your Officers. **1612** Hayward *Ann. Eliz.* (Camden) 43 Unable.. to beare head against this storme. **1806–7** J. Beresford *Miseries Hum. Life* (1826) i. Introd., This 'gypsy-jargon'.. Which is gaining head upon us every hour. **1818** Keats *Isabella* xxvii, The bream Keeps head against the freshets.

†**30.** A body of people gathered; a force raised, esp. in insurrection. (See also *to make a head*, 57 b). *Obs.*

1588 Shaks. *Tit. A.* iv. iv. 63 The Gothes have gather'd head. **1596** —— *1 Hen. IV*, i. iii. 284 To saue our heads, by raising of a Head. **1631** Gouge *God's Arrows* i. §69. 115 Korah..impudently gathered an head against Moses and Aaron. **1661** Pepys *Diary* 8 Jan., Some talk to-day of a head of Fanatiques that do appear about Barnett.

31. Issue, result; conclusion, summing up; culmination, crisis; maturity; pitch, height; strength, force, power (gradually attained): in various phrases, as ***to come, grow, gather to a head; to bring, draw to a head; to gather head.***

App. a blending of various senses: often, in reference to evils, consciously *fig.* from 14. Cf. also F. *venir à chef*, *mettre à chef*, and the derivative, *achever*, achieve.

1340 *Ayenb.* 183 He yeþ red huerby me comþ to guode heauede and to guode ende of þet me nimþ an hand. **1579** Gosson *Sch. Abuse* (Arb.) 31 Sith these abuses are growne too head and sinne so rype. **1596** Spenser *State Irel.* Wks. (Globe) 673/2 To keepe them from growing to such a head. **1598** Hakluyt *Voy.* I. 56 To take away the head or force from the fire. **1614** Bp. Hall *Recoll. Treat.* 166 There (which is the heade of all thy felicitie,) thine eyes shall see him whom now thine heart longeth for. **1662** Pepys *Diary* 31 Oct., Some plots there hath been, though not brought to a head. **1678** Littleton *Lat. Dict.* s.v., To draw to a head, or to sum up, *recapitulor, in summam colligo.* **1771** Wesley *Wks.* (1872) VI. 156 Vice is risen to such a head, that it is impossible to suppress it. **1814** Scott *Ld. of Isles* iii. ix, Where valiant Lennox gathers head. **1855** Prescott *Philip II*, I. ii. vi. 207 Religious troubles in France had been fast gathering to a head. **1878** Bosw. Smith *Carthage* 281 The revolt of Sardinia was stamped out before it came to a head. **1887** T. Hardy *Woodlanders* I. ix. 168 It might bring things to a head, one way or the other. **1888** R. F. Horton *Inspir. & Bible* vi. (1889) 170 But it is time to draw to a head this somewhat lengthened discussion.

IV. Phrases.

* *With a preposition.*

32. ***at*** or ***in the head of***: see sense 26.

†**33. of one's own head.** Out of one's own thought, device, or will; of one's own accord, spontaneously. *Obs.* or *arch.*

1375 Barbour *Bruce* ii. 121 Tak him as off thine awyne heid, As I had gevyn thar-to na reid. **1420** in Ellis *Orig. Lett.* Ser. iii. I. 69, I of myn owne heuede have wryte vn to hym a lettre. **1548** Hall *Chron., Hen. VIII*, 27 The master carpenter would woorke all of his awne hedde without counsayll. **1613** Sir H. Finch *Law* (1636) 181 He that entereth into land of his owne head, and receiueth the profits of it. **1687** Wood *Life* 30 May, The Bishop sent it of his owne head. **1775** Sheridan *Rivals* v. iii, It [the pistol] may go off of its own head. **1800** T. Jefferson *Writ.* (1859) IV. 313, I do not propose to give you all this trouble merely of my own head, that would be arrogance. **1831** Lamb *Elia* Ser. ii. *Newsp. 35 Yrs. Ago*, He never went in of his own head.

34. off one's **head.** Out of one's mind or wits, crazy. *colloq.*

a **1845** Hood *Turtles* iii, He 'was off his head'. **1872** Black *Adv. Phaeton* xiii. 177 He is off his head: he does not know what he says. **1883** M. Pattison *Mem.* (1885) 156 One poor girl went off her head in the midst of all.

35. on or **upon..head.**

a. ***on one's head***: said of evil, vengeance, etc., or of blessing, etc. figured as falling or descending upon a person; also of guilt, 'blood' (see blood *sb.* 3 c), or responsibility of any kind, figured as resting upon him.

[*c* **825** *Vesp. Psalter* vii. 17 Sie ȝecerred sar his in heafde his.] **13..** *Coer de L.* 1732 On his head falleth the fother. **1388** Wyclif *Josh.* ii. 19 The blood of hym schal be on his heed, that goith out at the dore of thin hows. **1598** Shaks. *Merry W.* ii. i. 191 What hee gets more of her then sharpe words, let it lye on my head. **1611** —— *Wint. T.* v. iii. 123 You Gods looke downe, And from your sacred Viols poure your graces Vpon my daughters head. **1735** Pope *Prol. Sat.* 348 The distant threats of vengeance on his head. **1869** Freeman *Norm. Conq.* III. xii. 253 If Harold sinned, his guilt was on his own head.

†**b.** ***on one's own head*** = of one's own head, 33.

1340 Hampole *Pr. Consc.* 8874 Yhit wille I ymagyn, on myne awen hede, Ffor to gyf it a descripcion. **1579** Tomson *Calvin's Serm. Tim.* 1/2 That he [S. Paul] thrust not in himselfe, vppon his owne head, but that he was appointed of God. **1656** Bramhall *Replic.* iii. 133 If the persons so banished will return on their own heads. *a* **1667** Jer. Taylor *Serm. Titus* ii. 7–8 Wks. 1831 IV. 179 Let no man, on his own head, reprove the religion that is established by law. **1707** Freind *Peterborow's Cond. Sp.* 123 He had quitted the army in discontent and upon his own head.

†**c.** ***on head***: Straight forward; towards the front, or in front; ahead. *Obs.*

1579 Gosson *Sch. Abuse* (Arb.) 44 It runnes on head. **1590** Spenser *Muiop.* 420 Some vngracious blast..perforce him [the butterfly] droue on hed. **1672** H. Savile *Engagem. w. Dutch Fleet* 4 Sir F. Holles in the Cambridge, came..on Head of us. **1708** Motteux *Rabelais* iv. lxiii. (1737) 256 We were becalm'd, and could hardly get o' head. **1741** *Compl. Fam.-Piece* ii. i. 288 To make forth on Head.

†**d.** ***on*** (***upon***) ***head*** (***a, the head***): Headlong, precipitately, hastily, rashly, inconsiderately. *Obs.*

1555 W. Watreman *Fardle Facions* i. iii. 36 Roilyng and rowmyng vpon heade, heather and thether. **1565–73** Cooper *Thesaurus, Abruptum ingenium*, a rashe braine that doth all things on heade. **1579–80** North *Plutarch* (1676) 129 So went Lucius upon a head to present battle to the Enemy. **1622** Bacon *Hen. VII*, Wks. 1825 III. 306 Rebels contrariwise run upon an head together in confusion. **1674** N. Cox *Gentl. Recreat.* (1677) 207 The Faulcon..is apt presently to fly on head at the check.

e. ***to do it*** (***standing***) ***on one's head***: to do it with ease. *slang.*

1896 G. B. Shaw *Our Theatres in Nineties* (1932) ii. 227 Of course, Mr Waring does the thing on his head, so to speak; but how can I compliment an actor who has done what he has done on stuff like that? **1897** Conrad *Nigger of Narcissus* i. 7 It's a 'omeward trip... Bad or good I can do it hall on my 'ed. **1922** A. A. Milne *Red House Myst.* xvi, Right, old boy. Leave it to me. I can do this on my head. **1923** *Westm. Gaz.* 19 Mar., Mr. Wells, assuming the best Cockney accent, intimated that he could 'do it on 'is 'ead'. **1944** M. Sharp *Cluny Brown* xvi. 109 If there was one thing Betty could do on her head, it was handle a compliment. **1968** J. M. White *Nightclimber* viii. 60 The climb he wanted me to attempt was a simple one. At Cambridge I could have done it standing on my head.

36. out of..head.

a. From one's own mind, imagination, or invention. (Somewhat *colloq.*)

1719 De Foe *Crusoe* ii. xii, It came from you, and not out of my own head. **1875** Jowett *Plato* (ed. 2) I. 288 Were not all these answers given out of his own head?

b. Out of one's mind. Chiefly *U.S.*

1825 J. Neal *Bro. Jonathan* I. 267 You are out o' your head, I guess. **1878** H. James Fr. Poets & Novelists 428 Pathelin pretends to be out of his head. **1902** C. E. Jefferson *Quiet Hints Preachers* xiii. 103 If they could not understand what was going on they..might think Christians out of their head.

37. over...head.

a. Over one's head, up aloft; cf. overhead.

1590 Spenser *F.Q.* ii. ix. 46 The roofe hereof was arched over head. **1704** Addison *Italy* (1733) 278 Bridge..coped over Head. **1768** J. Byron *Narr. Patagonia* (ed. 2) 188 It was dry over head. **1834** M. Scott *Cruise Midge* viii. (1867) 134 A faint distant strain of solemn music seemed now to float over head.

b. To such a depth that the head is submerged.

1653 Baxter *Worc. Petit. Def.* 35 That silly women shall be dipt over head in a Gumble-stool for scolding?

c. ***over*** (one's) ***head***: *lit.* above one, e.g. in the sky or air, or affording shelter; also of something (e.g. waves) rising and overwhelming one; hence *fig.* of danger or evil impending, or of some overwhelming or oppressive force.

1530 Palsgr. 595/2 They have jombled so over my heed to nyght I coulde nat slepe. **1568** Grafton *Chron.* II. 2 The daungers hangyng over theyr heades. **1816** Scott *Antiq.* xli, Dinna be cast down—there's a heaven ower your head. **1883** Mrs. Hungerford *Rossmoyne* III. v. 156 You will have the roof burned over your head one of these dark nights. **1886** *Cassell's Mag.* Dec. 12 That the father and child might have a roof over their heads.

d. ***over*** (some one's) ***head***: passing over (a person) who has a prior right, claim, etc.; said esp. in reference to the promotion of a person into some position above another who is considered to have a better right to it.

c **825** *Vesp. Ps.* lxv[i]. 12 Ðu onsettes men ofer heafud ur. **1550** Lever *Serm.* (Arb.) 142 They take one anothers ferme ouer their heades. **1635** R. N. *Camden's Hist. Eliz.* an. 7. i. 59 [He] devorcing his first wife, marryed over her head in her life time. *a* **1661** Fuller *Worthies* (1840) I. vi. 25 The younger being often brought over the head of the elder to be principal. **1887** *Times* 31 Oct. 9/3 It is no compliment..that an ex-diplomatist should be chosen for promotion over their heads.

e. ***over*** (one's) ***head***: (of time) past, over.

1576 Fleming *Panopl. Epist.* 24 Persuade your self..that her uttermost houre passed over head. **1634** Rutherford *Lett.* (1862) I. 141 When all these strokes are over your head, what will ye say to see your wellbeloved. **1708** Burnet *Lett.* (ed. 3) 118, I have now another Month over my Head. **1755** Ramsay *Ep. to J. Clerk* 69 Now seventy years are o'er my head. **1886** H. Smart *Outsider* I. ii. 26 Ere many more days were over her head!

f. ***over*** (one's) ***head***: beyond one's comprehension or intellectual capacity (cf. sense 2 a).

1622 Bacon *Holy War* Ep. Ded. Misc. Wks. (1629) 86 It flies too high ouer Mens Heads. **1837** Lytton *E. Maltrav.* (1886) 111 Talking over the heads of the company. **1886** H. Smart *Outsider* II. ii. 20 Welstead quickly became cognizant that his wife was over his head.

38. to (one's) **head. a.** To one's face; directly to the person himself. *Obs.* exc. *dial.*

1603 Shaks. *Meas. for M.* iv. iii. 147 And to the head of Angelo Accuse him home and home. **1607** T. Rogers 39 *Art.* Pref. §31 (1625) The 22..Brethren tell K. James to his head, how the Subscription..is more then the Law requireth. *a* **1825** Forby *Voc. E. Anglia* s.v., We say, 'I told him so to his head', not to his face, which is the usual phrase.

b. ***to go to*** (some)one's ***head***: (*a*) to intoxicate; cf. go *v.* 37 b; (*b*) to make one vain or proud.

1912 A. Lunn *Oxf. Mountaineering Essays* ix. 233 The delight of watching distant hills..went to my head like wine. **1939** A. Christie *Ten Little Niggers* x. 143 He's played God Almighty for a good many months every year. That must go to a man's head eventually. **1942** —— *Body in Library* xii. 108 He settled a large sum of money on Frank... It went to Frank's head.

** *With another substantive.*

39. head and ears.

a. ***by the head and ears***: roughly, violently, as one drags a beast; see ear *sb.*[1] 1 c. (Cf. 50 a.)

1590 Nashe *Pasquil's Apol.* i. C b, They have all vowed to hale thee out of thy trenches by the head and eares. **1873** *Punch* 17 May 200 An..utterly irrelevant story, lugged in by head and ears.

b. ***over head and ears***: completely immersed; also *fig.* deeply immersed or involved (e.g. in love, in debt). Rarely ***head and ears.***

1530 Palsgr. 725/2 He souced him in the water over heed and eares. **1576** Fleming *Panopl. Epist.* 353 That Man.. should lye..and shrowde himselfe, head and eares, in slouthfulnesse. **1581** Mulcaster *Positions* xxvii. (1887) 104 To dippe their new borne children into extreme cold water ouer head and eares. **1663, 1768** [see ear *sb.*[1] 1 c]. **1665** Manley *Grotius' Low C. Warres* 875 The Commonwealth ..would run over head and ears in debt. **1690** W. Walker *Idiomat. Anglo-Lat.* 233 He is over head and ears in love. **1749** Fielding *Tom Jones* iv. iii, The poor lad plumped over head and ears into the water. **1867** Trollope *Chron. Barset* II. liii. 103 You are over head and ears in debt.

¶ Also corruptly ***head over ears*** (cf. 'head over heels', 46 b).

1887 Caroline Fothergill *Enthusiast* II. 95 He was head over ears in debt when he married her. **1912** G. B. Shaw *Let.* 22 Dec. in *Times* (1968) 19 Oct. 19/5, I plunged in head over ears and..wrote off my 56 years.

40. head in the air. ***to go about with one's head in the air***: to assume a pose of superiority. Hence ***head-in-air***, designating either one who is absent-minded and dreamy or one who is a snob or a 'highbrow', or the actions of such persons.

1848 *English Struwwelpeter* (ed. 4) 21 (*title*) The story of Johnny Head-in-Air. **1903** *Trawl* May 7 The Laureate crost over the lawn with the dreamy head-in-air gait that was known through five parishes round. **1906** Rider Haggard *Benita* iv, On the ship I always thought him rather a head-in-air kind of swell, but he was a splendid fellow. **1942** J. Pudney *Dispersal Point* 24 Do not despair For Johnny-head-in-air; He sleeps as sound As Johnny underground.

41. head...foot.

a. ***from head to foot***: all over the person; *fig.* completely, thoroughly, 'all over'. (Also *head to foot, head and foot.*)

a **1300** *Cursor M.* 16435 Fra the hefd vnto þe fote, Oueral þe blod vte-wrang. **1382** Wyclif *Lev.* xiii. 12 If..the rennynge lepre..couer al the flesh, fro the heed vnto the feet. **1602** Shaks. *Ham.* I. ii. 228 *Ham.* From top to toe? *Both.* My Lord, from head to foote. *Ibid.* II. ii. 478 Head to foote. **1762–71** H. Walpole *Vertue's Anecd. Paint.* (1786) II. 188 He..leaves..to Lord Rothes the King's picture from head to foot. **1784** R. Bage *Barham Downs* I. 269 He overthrew it head and foot. **1886** Tennyson *Promise of May* III. A gentleman?.. That he is, from head to foot.

†**b.** ***neither head nor foot***: = 'neither head nor tail', 51. *Obs.*

1563–87 Foxe *A. & M.* (1837–41) V. 479 When the bishop..looked on the writing, he pushed it from him, saying, 'What shall this do? It hath neither head nor foot'. **1566** Gascoigne *Supposes* II. i. (D.), I find neither head nor foot in it.

42. head and front. A Shaksperian phrase, orig. app. denoting 'summit, height, highest extent or pitch' (cf. 12, 31); sometimes used by modern writers in other senses.

1604 Shaks. *Oth.* I. iii. 80 It is most true: true I haue married her; The verie head, and front of my offending, Hath this extent; no more. **1813** Scott *Let. to J. Ballantyne* 25 July in *Lockhart*, The head and front of your offending is precisely your not writing explicitly. **1888** Burgon *Lives 12 Gd. Men* II. xii. 375 He was the head and front of every movement for good in his neighbourhood.

43. head and girth. See girth *sb.*[1] 1 b.

44. head of hair. The covering or growth of hair on the head, esp. when long or copious. (See 4.)

1586 J. Hooker *Girald. Irel.* in Holinshed (1808) VI. 328 This head of haire they call a glibe. **1602** Marston *Ant. & Mel.* III. Wks. 1856 I. 36, I have a good head of haire. **1717** Lady M. W. Montagu *Let. to C'tess Mar* 1 Apr., I never saw in my life so many fine heads of hair. **1859** Jephson *Brittany* viii. 131 It was a head of hair more than a yard long ..which he had bought.

45. head to head.

a. Face to face; in private conversation. (F. *tête-à-tête.*) Also *transf.*

c **1728** Earl of Ailesbury *Mem.* (1890) 595 An account of a long discourse..I had head to head with the Baron of Renswoode. **1799** *Sporting Mag.* XIII. 311/1 The contest here commenced,..the horses never being more than a length asunder, and generally head to head. **1858** Hogg *Life Shelley* II. 453 Head to head, as the French have it, he was by no means silent. **1950** J. Dempsey *Championship Fighting* 63 Short range. That's the head-to-head slugging range. **1956** *Nature* 4 Feb. 206/2 There is the so-called head-to-head or head-to-tail arrangements. **1966** *B.B.C. Handbk. 1966* 14 Much of the time the BBC's competition is merely head-to-head. **1972** *Times* 17 Apr. 24/1 Until December the Gallup poll did not even pit McGovern in head-to-head polls with President Nixon and Wallace.

b. As *sb.* A conflict or contest (between two adversaries) at close quarters; a confrontation. *colloq.* (orig. *U.S.*).

1970 *Atlantic Monthly* Nov. 65/2 It [*sc.* the Sheridan tank] cannot stand against any of the Russian tanks in a head-to-head, and its highly sophisticated mechanisms make it difficult to use in places like jungles or deserts.

46. head...heel(s.

a. ***from head to heel***: = from head to foot, 41 a.

c **1400** *Destr. Troy* 7720 Fro þe hede to þe hele herit as a capull! **1781** Cowper *Anti-Thelyphthora* 184 So polished and compact from head to heel. **1843** Macaulay *Lays Anc. Rome, Regillus* xxiii, And many a curdling pool of blood Splashed him from heel to head. **1847** Tennyson *Princ.* v. 29 Disprinced from head to heel. **1886** Mrs. Hungerford *Lady Branksmere* I. iv. 96 A tall figure..clothed from head to heel in sombre garments.

b. ***head over heels***: a corruption of *heels over head*, frequent in modern use: see heel *sb.*[1] Also *fig.* (In quot. 1924 with contextual omission of *heels.*)

1771 *Contemplative Man* I. 133 He gave [him] such a violent involuntary kick in the Face, as drove him Head over Heels. **1834** D. Crockett *Narr. Life* i. 20, I soon found myself head over heels in love with this girl. **1840** Thackeray *Paris Sk.-bk.* (1869) 32 Why did you..hurl royalty..head-over-heels out of yonder Tuileries' windows? **1887** Rider Haggard *Jess* i. 4 Away he went head-over-heels like a shot rabbit. **1924** Galsworthy *White Monkey* II. vi. 158 They were head over—the family feud stopped that [marriage].

c. ***head over tip*** = *head over heels.*

1824 P. Egan *Boxiana* IV. 260 A first-rate *swell*, who was extremely eager to get on board, lost his footing, and went *head* over *tip* into the water. **1906** E. Dyson *Fact'ry Ands* xv. 202 Er stream iv water..sluices ther red-'eaded girl..'ead-over-tip down ther front stairs.

47. head of horns. The horns of a deer, etc. as forming the adornment of the head. (See 6.)

1626 Bacon *Sylva* §757 To make an Oxe or a Deere haue a Greater Head of Hornes. **1786** Burns *Calf*, That you may wear A noble head of horns.

48. heads and points. Said of nails, wedges, etc. placed alternately in opposite directions, so that the head of one lies against the point or edge of the next; hence *transf.* of persons lying; also of whales (see quot. 1889).

1611 Cotgr. s.v. *Bechevet*, *Teste a teste Bechevet*, the play with pins, called, heads and points. **1612** Capt. Smith *Map Virginia* 21 On these round about the house, they lie heads and points one by other against the fire. **1793** Smeaton *Edystone L.* §238 The two wedges in each groove would then lie Heads and Points. **1889** *Cent. Dict.* s.v., *To blow heads and points*, to run..hither and thither, spouting and blowing ..said of whales when attacked.

49. heads and posts. Leather heads placed on posts for use in cavalry exercises.

1895 *Army & Navy Co-op. Soc. Price List* 15 Sept. 1456 Heads and Posts. For Military Tournaments. **1902** *Encycl. Brit.* XXVI. 156/1 Courses for jumping and 'heads and posts' exercise. **1907** *Yesterday's Shopping* (1969) 1017/2 Heads and Posts..for Military Tournaments.

50. head and shoulders.

a. ***by head and shoulders*** (sometimes with ellipsis of *by*): by force, violently; with *thrust, push, drag, bring* (*in*), etc.; *fig.* of something violently and irrelevantly introduced into a speech or writing.

1581 Sidney *Apol. Poetrie* (Arb.) 65 All theyr Playes.. thrust in Clownes by head and shoulders. **1647** Ward *Simp. Cobler* 24 Any, whom necessity..thrusts out by head and shoulders. **1679** *Hist. Jetzer* 20 The Lecturer brought in this whole affair by the head and shoulders into his Sermon. **1768–74** Tucker *Lt. Nat.* (1852) II. 116 He..hunts perpetually for texts..introduces them by head and shoulders upon the most trifling occasions. **1887–9** T. A. Trollope *What I remember* II. iii. 44, I must drag the mention of the fact in head and shoulders here, or else I shall forget it.

b. (with *taller, higher*, etc.) By the measure of the head and shoulders (cf. 1 c); hence *fig.* (in reference to intellectual or moral stature), considerably, by far.

1864 Webster s.v., He is head and shoulders above them. **1885** D. C. Murray *Rainbow Gold* II. iv. v. 124 Job walked leisurely among them, head and shoulders higher than his neighbours.

c. A portrait in which only the head and shoulders are shown. Freq. *attrib.*

1865 D. G. Rossetti *Let.* 30 July (1965) II. 562, I fear all I could undertake with prospect of bringing it to a conclusion without unreasonable delay would be a 'head and shoulders' portrait. **1897** H. B. Wheatley *Hist. Portraits* viii. 173 Stoop himself made an etching of this portrait... The picture is described as 'Head and shoulders'. **1902** *Daily Chron.* 7 July 3/5 A head and shoulders portrait of Lady Morshead in white dress and fichu. **1968** R. Sawkins *Snow along Border* xv. 121 The picture was a head-and-shoulders portrait of a man of about thirty.

d. ***head-and-shoulder target***, a target representing a head and shoulders.

1899 *Westm. Gaz.* 23 Nov. 2/2 A hostile force in entrenchments is represented by rows of 'head and shoulder' targets. **1901** *Ibid.* 11 Sept. 3/1 Not only were there the usual head-and-shoulder dummies, but there were several 'surprise' targets.

51. head or tail.

a. Either one thing or another; anything definite or intelligible. (With negative expressed or implied.) Now always *to make head or tail of.*

1651 Baxter *Inf. Bapt.* 213 On a loose sheet or two that had neither head nor taile. **1679** Marg. Mason *Tickler Tickl.* 7 Their Tale..had neither head nor Taile. **1729** Fielding *Author's Farce* III. i, Pray what is the design or plot? for I could make neither head nor tail on 't. **1890** J. H. McCarthy *Fr. Rev.* II. 88 It is difficult to make head or tail of the whole business.

b. *head*(*s or tail*(*s*: see sense 3 b.

*** *With a verb.* (*to come to a head*: see senses 14, 31. *to* beat *one's head*, break *Priscian's h.*, eat *one's h. off*, hide *one's h.*, knock *on the h.*, turn *h.*, etc.: see the verbs.)

52. get head. To gain force, ascendency, or power; to attain to vigour. (Cf. 26, 31.)

1625 Sanderson *12 Serm.* (1637) 226 The times were such, as wherein sin had gotten head. **1631** Gouge *God's Arrows* iii. §84. 341 Whereas..Haman..got some head, the Lord had warre with him. **1722** De Foe *Plague* (1884) 252 A great Fire..gets a Head. **1812** *Sporting Mag.* XXXIX. 92 Hydrophobia..will occur and get head even in the coldest weather.

53. get one's head down. To have a sleep.

1943 in Hunt & Pringle *Service Slang* 35. **1958** 'N. Shute' *Rainbow & Rose* 61 I'll have to get my head down for a bit, though, before going out again.

54. have one's head examined (or need one's **head examining**). A jocular phrase suggesting that one is 'off one's head'.

1949 'J. Tey' *Brat Farrar* xxvi. 239 Of all the 'old soldier' tricks to fall for!.. I ought to have my head examined. **1954** J. Symons *Narrowing Circle* xxxii. 145 Giue me credit fer a bit of sense... If I'd behaved in the way you suggest I should need my head examining. **1965** R. McDowell *Hound's Tooth* (1967) vii. 69, I let Bowman persuade me to call in the state police... I should've had my head examined. **1966** J. Bingham *Double Agent* ii. 25 If you think these chaps know nuclear secrets..you want your head examined. **1972** *N.Y. Times* 3 Nov. 22/6 Anyone who votes for Nixon ought to have his head examined.

55. keep one's head. To keep one's wits about one, retain self-control, keep calm: the opposite of *to lose one's head*, 56 b. (Cf. 2 a.)

1717 Prior *Alma* III. 186 Richard, keep thy head, And hold thy peace. **1876** Trevelyan *Macaulay* I. i. 22 If only the man in the post of responsibility..can contrive to keep his head.

b. ***to keep one's head above ground***: to keep oneself in life; so ***to keep one's head above water***; also *fig.* = out of debt or insolvency.

1627 Drayton *Moon-Calf* Wks. (1753) 513 Scarce their heads above ground they could keep. **1712** Arbuthnot *John Bull* IV. i, I have almost drowned myself, to keep his head above water. **1886** Tennyson *Promise of May* III. Farmer Dobson, were I to marry him, has promised to keep our heads above water.

56. lose one's head.

a. *lit.* To have one's head cut off, be beheaded (as a form of capital punishment).

c **1386** Chaucer *Knt.'s T.* 849 Namoore vp on peyne of lesynge of youre heed. **1484** Caxton *Fables of Æsop* II. iii, Which haue been cause of theyr dethe and to lese theyre heedes. **1594** Shaks. *Rich. III*, IV. iv. 242 Vp to some Scaffold, there to lose their heads. **1888** Baring-Gould *Eve* I. iii. 31 Copplestone..escaped losing his head for the murder by the surrender of thirteen manors.

b. *fig.* To lose self-possession or presence of mind, to become confused.

1847 Tennyson *Princ.* Concl. 59 The gravest citizen seems to lose his head. *a* **1849** Poe *Marginalia* lxxiv. (D.), It has now and then an odd Gallicism—such as 'she lost her head', meaning she grew crazy. **1855** Macaulay *Hist. Eng.* IV. 121 He lost his head, almost fainted away on the floor of the House.

57. make head.

a. (in sense 29): To advance, press forward, esp. in opposition to some person or thing: also formerly ***to make a head.*** Usually, ***to make head against***: to advance against; to resist; to rise in insurrection or revolt against; to resist successfully, advance in spite of.

1577–87 Holinshed *Chron.* (1808) VI. 82 That..they might the better make head against both Romans and Britons. **1640** tr. *Verdere's Romant of Romants* I. 50 That done, he made head to the Giants, who battered him. **1667** Milton *P.L.* II. 992 That mighty leading Angel, who of late Made head against Heav'ns King. **1821** Byron *Sardan.* III. i. 89 [They] make strong head against The rebels. **1840** Dickens *Barn. Rudge* xxxiv, They made head against the wind.

†**b.** ***to make a head*** (sense 30): to raise a body of troops. *Obs.*

1593 Shaks. *3 Hen. VI*, II. i. 141 In the Marches heere we heard you were, Making another Head, to fight againe. **1627** Drayton *Miseries Q. Marg.* 153 That Warwick..Had met the Duke of York, and made a head Of many fresh and yet unfought-with bands. **1648** Evelyn *Mem.* (1857) III. 8 To make a handsome head, and protect such as shall recruit.

58. open one's head. To speak. *U.S. slang.*

1849 *Neal's Sat. Gaz.* (Phila.) 17 Feb. 1/1 But don't you open yer head about it to no other indiwiddiwal—for I want to supprise the Wiggletown folks, and make 'em open ther eyes a leetle. **1885** H. Jackson *Zeph* ii. 44 He never opens his head to nobody. **1895** *Century Mag.* Sept. 674/1 I'm glad you didn't open your head about it. **1898** M. Deland *Old Chester Tales* 307 Jones said..that he hardly opened his head for the whole twenty-one miles.

59. put (a thing) **in** or **into** (a person's) **head**: to suggest it to his mind, make him think of it; formerly also, to remind him of it. So ***to put out of one's head***, to cause one to forget.

1548 Hall *Chron., Hen. VI*, 158 b, Puttyng into mens heades secretely his right to yᵉ crown. **1682** Claverhouse in Napier *Life* (1859) I. I. 135 What those rebellious villains they call *ministers* put in the heads of the people. **1735** Pope *Ep. Lady* 178 She bids her footman put it in her head. **1816** Scott *Antiq.* xliii, You said something just now that put every thing out of my head. **1844** *Hawkstone* ix. (1846) 127 If you had not put it into my head, I should never have done it!

†**b.** Hence, by corruption, ***to put*** (a person) ***in the head of*** (a thing): to suggest the idea of it to him; to remind or put in mind of. *Obs.*

1613–18 Daniel *Coll. Hist. Eng.* 60 (D.) Putting the king in head that all these great castles..were onely to entertaine the partie of Maude. **1668** Pepys *Diary* 31 Jan., Griffin did ..put me in the head of the little house by our garden..to make me a stable of. **1749** Fielding *Tom Jones* IX. vi, And now you put me in the head of it, I verily and sincerely believe it was the devil.

60. put a head on. 'To punch or assault another, and figuratively to silence, or shut up another' (Clapin). *U.S. slang.* (Cf. 1 d.)

1868 F. Whymper *Trav. Alaska* 283 One calls the other a 'regular dead beat!' at which he, in return, threatens to 'put a head on him!' **1869** *Overland Monthly* III. 63 The gentlemanly proprietor of the premises had kindly volunteered to 'put a head' on the man who fired the pistol. **1876** *Scribner's Monthly* Nov. 142/2 Threats, profanely emphasized, 'to put a head on' me! **1911** R. W. Chambers *Common Law* ii. 46 Kelly will put a head on you!

61. show one's head. To show oneself publicly; to appear abroad. Cf. *to show one's face* (see face *sb.* 2 b).

1551 T. Wilson *Logike* (1580) 49 This manne..durst not once for his life shewe his hedde, for feare. **1593** Shaks. *Rich. II*, V. vi. 44 With Caine go wander through the shade of night, And neuer shew thy head by day, nor light. **1610** *Crt. & Times Jas. I* (1849) I. 122 He hath scarce shewed his head ever since. **1775** J. Q. Adams in *Fam. Lett.* (1876) 50 The Tories there durst not show their heads.

62. take...head.

†**a.** ***to take*** (*a*) ***head***: to make a rush forward, to start running. *Obs.*

1674 N. Cox *Gentl. Recreat.* (1677) 129 Having broken out of a Forest and taken head end-ways, he [a boar] will not be put out of his way either by Man, Dog..or any thing. **1760–72** H. Brooke *Fool of Qual.* xvii. (1792) IV. 5 So I took a head, and ran into the country as fast as my feet would carry me.

†**b.** ***to take a head***: to make insurrection; to raise a tumult. (Cf. 29.) *Obs.*

1678 Littleton *Lat. Dict.* s.v., To take a head, *tumultuor.*

†**c.** ***to take*** (one) ***in the head***: to come into one's mind, occur to one. *Obs.*

1581 G. PETTIE tr. *Guazzo's Civ. Conv.* I. (1586) 12b, Moved either by some sodaine toie which taketh them in the head. **1591** F. SPARRY tr. *Cattan's Geomancie* 38 He..will not do any thing but that which taketh him in the head. **1609** HOLLAND *Amm. Marcell.* (Farmer), Now, it tooke him in the head..to set first upon Constantino. *a*1632 T. TAYLOR *God's Judgem.* I. I. xx. (1642) 70 It took him in the head to ..visit Rome.

d. ***to take into*** (***in***) ***one's head***: to conceive the idea or notion of; to have (something) occur to one's mind: usually, ***to take it into one's head*** (*that...*, or *to do* something).

1711 ADDISON *Spect.* No. 47 ¶7 When every Body takes it in his Head to make as many Fools as he can. **1837** DISRAELI *Venetia* (Tauchn.) I. x. 66, I took it into my head to walk up and down the gallery. **1876** E. JENKINS *Blot on Queen's Head* 17 Little Ben had taken it into his head..that the sign-board ..could be improved.

**** *With adverb.*

63. head first, head foremost: with the head first or foremost; hence *fig.* precipitately, headlong, hastily. (Also with hyphen, or as one word.)

[**1625** HART *Anat. Ur.* I. i. 8 [She] thrust him..his head foremost, into an ouen.] **1697** [see FOREMOST *a.* 3d]. *a*1813 A. WILSON *Loss o' the Pack* in Chambers *Pop. Hum. Scot. Poems* (1862) 86 Frae that day forth I never mair did weel, But drank, and ran headforemost to the deil! **1828** WEBSTER, *Headfirst, adv.* with the head foremost. *a*1845 HOOD *Submarine* iv, Down he went, Head-foremost. **1877** [see FIRST 3b]. **1884** *Pall Mall G.* 24 Apr. 3/1 The..Dean..plunged headforemost into the controversy.

***** *Various figurative and proverbial phrases.*

64. ***to give*** (a horse) ***the head***, also ***to let him have his head***: not to check or hold him in with the bridle; to give him freedom, let him go freely. So ***to take the head***, to throw off control or restraint. Hence *fig.* in reference to persons.

1579 GOSSON *Sch. Abuse* (Arb.) 24 You are no sooner entred, but libertie looseth the reynes, and geues you head. **1597** J. PAYNE *Royal Exch.* 29 Thrusting theme to rashenes, vnrulines, and to take ouermoche heade and bridle. **1597** SHAKS. *2 Hen. IV*, I. i. 43 With that he gaue his able Horse the head. **1703** STEELE *Tend. Husb.* I. i, What a Fool have I been to give him his Head so long. **1886** MRS. LYNN LINTON *Paston Carew* xxxiv, He had yielded so far to the necessities of the case as to give Lady Jane her head. **1886** BESANT *Childr. Gibeon* III. 148 She let him have his head for a bit.

†**65.** ***to give one's head for the polling*** or ***washing***: to yield tamely without resistance. *Obs.*

*c*1583 J. HOOKER *Descr. Excester* (1765) 82 Such a one as would not give his Head for the polling, nor his Beard for the washing. **1663** BUTLER *Hud.* I. iii. 256 For my Part it shall ne'er be sed, I for the washing gave my Head.

66. ***to lay*** (†***run, put,*** †***cast,*** †***draw***) ***their heads together***: to consult or take counsel together.

*c*1381 CHAUCER *Parl. Foules* 554 The watyr foulis han here hedis leid Togedere..They seydyn sothly al be on assent How that [etc.]. **1523** LD. BERNERS *Froiss.* I. cxv. 137 Whenne they sawe hym, they began to murmure, and began to ron togyder thre heedes in one hood, and sayde, beholde yonder great maister. **1526** SKELTON *Magnyf.* 572 Nay, let vs our heddes togyder cast. **1551** ROBINSON tr. *More's Utop.* I. (1895) 70 They will laye theyr heddes togither and conspire agaynst the weale publyque. **1682** BUNYAN *Holy War* 122 And there lay their heads together and consult of matters. **1886** BARING-GOULD *Court Royal* I. i. 17 We'll put heads together and consider what is to be done.

†**67.** ***in spite of*** or ***maugre his head***: in spite of himself: notwithstanding all he can do. *Obs.*

*c*1386 CHAUCER *Wife's T.* 31 Of which mayde anon, maugree hir heed By verray force birafte hire maydenhed. *c*1449 PECOCK *Repr.* I. x. 52 He schal consente in his witt.. amagrey his heed. **1568** GRAFTON *Chron.* II. 114 He gave them all to the French men in spight of their heades. **1600** HOLLAND *Livy* XXX. xxx. 760 You pulled me maugre my head out of Italie.

68. ***to talk*** (etc.) a person's ***head off*** (humorous): i.e. until he is too weary to reply, or thoroughly sick and tired of it, *ad nauseam*. So ***to beat his head off***, i.e. to beat him out and out; etc.

1855 THACKERAY *Newcomes* vi, He pretends to teach me billiards, and I'll give him fifteen in twenty and beat his old head off. **1872** MRS. OLIPHANT *Mem. Montalembert* I. 29 In society in the evenings yawns his weary head off. **1894** G. B. SHAW *Let.* 3 Dec. (1965) 467 You could, at your worst, talk the heads off most of them. **1897** D. GERALD *Spotless Reput.* vii. (ed. 2) 88 If it were not for the standing danger of having one's head talked off one's shoulders. **1931** H. CRANE *Let.* 11 Sept. (1965) 379 Yesterday we..worked our heads off digging into the side of a small hill. **1951** J. CORNISH *Provincials* 11 As term progressed, Saturdays and Sundays ..we would sit in our den..talking our heads off. **1965** W. SOYINKA *Road* 17 The bishop sermonized his head off.

69. Prov. ***two heads are better than one*** (cf. sense 2a, and Eccl. iv. 9).

1546 J. HEYWOOD *Prov.* (1867) 18 Two heddis are better than one. **1591** SPENSER *M. Hubberd* 82 Two is better than one head. **1772** FOOTE *Nabob* I. Wks. 1799 II. 289 Here comes brother Thomas; two heads are better than one; let us take his opinion. **1818** SCOTT *Rob Roy* viii, O certainly; but two heads are better than one, you know.

70. ***to put a pistol to*** one's ***head***: to commit suicide by shooting; ***to put a pistol to*** (someone's) ***head***: to coerce (someone). Also *fig.*

1841 C. DICKENS *Let.* 26 Feb. (1969) II. 220 Put a penny pistol to Chapman's head, and demand the blocks of him. **1853** THACKERAY *Newcomes* (1854) I. ix. 91 I'm blowed if I don't put a pistol to my 'ead, and end it, Mrs. G. **1896** A. E. HOUSMAN *Shropshire Lad* xliv. 67 And early wise and brave in season [you] Put the pistol to your head.

V. Attributive uses and Combinations.

* *Simple attrib. or as adj.* (Often hyphened.)

71. At the head (sense 26); in the position of command or superiority; chief, principal, capital.

*c*1000 ÆLFRIC *Hom.* II. 420 Abiathar, ðæra Iudeiscra heafod biscop. *c*1200 ORMIN 299 Aaron wass hæfedd preost. *Ibid.* 8469 Ȝerrsalæm was hæfedd burrh Off Issrææless riche. *a*1225 *Ancr. R.* 392 Uour heaued luuen me iuint iðisse worlde. *a*1300 *Cursor M.* 22229 Þe kingrikes o grece and pers war hefd kingrikes. *c*1400 *Destr. Troy* 10902 Thurgh helpe of þat hynd, and hir hede maidons. **1548** HALL *Chron., Hen. VII*, 58b, London..the hed citie of hys realme. *Ibid., Hen. VIII*, 10 The lord Stuard nor the head officers could not cause them to abstaine. **1588** SHAKS. *L.L.L.* IV. i. 43 Which is the head Lady? **1658** A. FOX *Wurtz' Surg.* I. vi. 22 Having cleared the two head points..I will touch also other abuses. **1711** SHAFTESB. *Charac.* (1737) I. 318 How the inferiour imps appear, when the head-goblin is securely laid. **1752** J. LOUTHIAN *Form of Process* (ed. 2) 82 At the Market Cross of the Head-burgh of the Shire, Stewarty, or other Jurisdiction. **1805** G. COLMAN *John Bull* I. i. 17 *Dan.* .. I be head-waiter and hostler:—only we never have no horses, nor customers. **1822** BYRON *Vis. Judgem.* lxxxix, He ..scribbles as if head clerk to the Fates. **1823** L. MINOR *Jrnl.* 29 Nov. in *Atlantic Monthly* (1870) XXVI. 171/1 It is a singular spectacle to see a man, who has occupied such high and varied stations, bustling about a tavern at once as landlord, barkeeper, and head waiter. **1842** TENNYSON *Will Waterproof* i, O plump head-waiter at The Cock. **1971** *Good Food Guide* 484 Rich, male, business customers..will receive highly skilled attention from everybody, starting with the headwaiter and sommelier and going down to the busboy.

†**b.** Applied *spec.* to the 'cardinal virtues' and the 'deadly sins'; see CARDINAL *a.* 2. *Obs.*

*c*1000 ÆLFRIC *Hom.* II. 592 Þa heafod leahtras sind mansliht, cyrc-bræce [etc.]. *c*1175 *Lamb. Hom.* 103 Nu beoð .viii. heofod sunnan. *Ibid.* 105 Nu beoð .viii. heafod mihtan þe maȝen ouercumen alle þas sunnan þurh drihtnes fultum. *c*1200 ORMIN 10213 Grediȝnesse iss hæfedd plihht. *a*1300 *Cursor M.* 10010 Four vertus principals, þe quilk man clepes cardinals; All oþer vertus o þam has hald, For-þi er þai hede vertus tald. **1357** *Lay Folks Catech.* 448 The seuen heued synnes or dedely synnes. *c*1440 HYLTON *Scala Perf.* (1494) II. xi, Of pryde or enuye, of couetyse or lechery, or of ony other hede synne. **1654** GATAKER *Disc. Apol.* 67 His Popish reckoning of the seven Hed-sins.

†**c.** as adj. in superl., ***headest*** = chiefest. *Obs. rare.*

1577 B. GOOGE *Heresbach's Husb.* IV. (1586) 181b, To kill the heddest of the dissention, and to appease the fury of the fighters. **1658** J. JONES *Ovid's Ibis* 101 Content is a lesson too hard for the headst Of the highest forme a King.

72. Situated at the head, top, or front (see senses 12–24); †initial (quot. 1387); coming from the front, meeting one directly in front, as ***a head wind***.

1387 TREVISA *Higden* (Rolls) IV. 299 Þe heed lettres of þe vers spelep þis menynge. **1627** CAPT. SMITH *Seaman's Gram.* ix. 41 If your course be right against it, you shall meet it right a head, so we call it a head Sea. **1659** WILLSFORD *Scales Comm., Archit.* 8 Part of..[the] head wall..is brick. **1796** *Instr. & Reg. Cavalry* (1813) 153 The head division of each..regiment. **1799** J. ROBERTSON *Agric. Perth* 107 This fence..because it ran across the head of every farm.. was called..the head-dyke. **1824** W. IRVING *T. Trav.* I. 53, I was kept by storms and head winds for three long days. **1886** R. BROWN *Spunyarn & Spindrift* ix. 67 A head-sea began to heave up. **1893** W. T. WAWN *S. Sea Islanders* 226 The vessel paid off under the weight of her head canvas.

** *Combinations.*

73. General Comb. **a.** *attrib.*, 'of or for the head', as ***head-affection, -attire, -brush, -covering, -end, -fillet, -flannel,*** †***-hair, -knot, -notion, -rest, -shake,*** †***-top, -vein, -wing, -wrap, -wrapping***, etc.

1862 J. B. HARRISON *Lett. Dis. Children* iii. 47 In relation to *head affections. **1601** HOLLAND *Pliny* II. 533 With their hoods and other *head attire of sundry colours. **1837** CARLYLE *Fr. Rev.* II. I. v, Duel and *head-breakage. **1596** NASHE *Saffron Walden* Wks. (Grosart) III. 135 His case of *head-brushes and beard-brushes. **1860** FAIRHOLT *Costume Eng.* (ed. 2) 482 The Anglo-Saxon *head-coverings were very simple. **1545** ASCHAM *Toxoph.* (Arb.) 127 The *head ende would euer be downwardes, and neuer flye strayght. **1676** COTTON *Walton's-Angler* (Chandos ed.) 155 It must not be at the head-end of the worm. **1861** MRS. BEETON *Bk. Househ. Managem.* 1021 The infant..must not be exposed to strong light, or too much air; and in carrying it about the passages, stairs, &c., the nurse should always have its *head-flannel on. **1880** Advt. in L. Higgin *Handbk. Embroidery* 106 Babies' Headflannels, from £1 3*s.* *c*1000 ÆLFRIC *Gloss.* in Wr.-Wülcker 156/30 *Capilli*, *heafodhær. **1398** TREVISA *Barth. De P.R.* v. lxvi. (Add. MS. 27,944), If a man is withoute hed-her. **1717** PRIOR *Alma* II. 332 Her scarf pale pink, her *head-knot cherry. *c*1200 *Trin. Coll. Hom.* 163 Þe *haued line [linen] sward, and hire winpel wit. **1642** ROGERS *Naaman* 23 Absolon is snatcht up, by his long *head locks. **1884** H. N. HUDSON *Stud. Wordsw.* 243 The *head-logic grows so..as to stifle and crush the heart-logic. **1886** H. P. WELLS *Amer. Salmon Fisherman* 84 *Head-nets, to go over the hat and tuck in under the shirt-collar. **1801** W. HUNTINGTON *Bank of Faith* Ded. 22 Filled with *head notions from commentators rather than the grace of God in their hearts. **1853** *Handbk. Photogr.* App. §37. 72 Instruments have been constructed called *head-rests, to assist the sitter. **1884** *Health Exhib. Catal.* 102/2 Invalids' Bedstead and Mattress, with adjustable headrest. **1602** SHAKS. *Ham.* I. v. 174 With Armes encombred thus, or this [*Fol.* thus] *head shake; Or by pronouncing of some doubtfull Phrase. **1696** *Lond. Gaz.* No. 3188/4 Two laced *Head-Suits. **1583** STANYHURST *Æneis* II. (Arb.) 65 A certeyn lightning on his *headtop glistered harmelesse. **1838** ELWIN *Bk. Fam. Crests* II. 17 The *head-trappings of their horses. **1600** ROWLANDS (*title*) The Letting of Humours Blood in the *Head-Vaine. **1610** HEALEY *St. Aug. Citie of God* 273 [Mercury] had *head-wings also behind each of his eares. **1896** *Godey's Mag.* Feb. 202/1 Fastening..a sombre *head-wrap over her..hair. **1905** *Daily Chron.* 15 May 3/3 A hood of this kind..will avoid any necessity for the wearing of those head-wraps. **1887** RIDER HAGGARD *She* xvii. 198, I looked up at Ayesha, whose *head-wrapping had slipped back.

b. *objective* and *obj. genitive*, as ***head-breaking, -combing, -hanging, -purging, -scratching*** (also *fig.*), ***-shaking, -splitting***, sbs. and adjs.; ***head-breaker, -maker, -scratcher*** (also *fig.*), ***-shaker***. Cf. SHAKE *v.* 6b.

*c*1515 *Cocke Lorell's B.* (Percy) 11 Dyssymulynge beggers, *hede brekers. **1843** BETHUNE *Sc. Fireside Stor.* 8 To use your utmost endeavours to promote *head-breaking. **1845** HOOD *Craniol.* i, By simple dint of *Head-combing. **1545** ASCHAM *Toxoph.* (Arb.) 137, I woulde wyshe that the *head makers of Englande shoulde make their sheafe arrowe heades more harder poynted. **1591** SPENSER *Muiopot.* 197 Veyne-healing Verven, and *hed-purging Dill. **1936** J. B. PRIESTLEY *They walk in City* 375 A pair of tweezers and a *head-scratcher from Ur of the Chaldees. **1969** E. H. PINTO *Treen* ii. 26 The plain lignum vitae, English head scratcher ..was typical of that 18th-century elegance which accepted public poking of wigs and itching heads as normal. **1971** *Daily Colonist* (Victoria, B.C.) 22 July 1/1 Now, the head-scratcher is how interest rates can be going up. **1926** J. S. HUXLEY *Ess. Biologist* v. 178 It was a hard nut for them, and there was much *head-scratching. **1958** *Times* 22 Oct. 14/3 It is now that the Rugby football captains get down to their real head-scratching. **1973** *Times* 3 July 23/4 If it is cleared without reference, then there will be more head scratching. **1927** H. G. WELLS in *Sunday Express* 1 May 12/3 The Gummidge chorus is never silent; the thoughtful *headshaker moping for a return to medievalism casts his daily shadow on every patch of sunshine. **1958** *Times Lit. Suppl.* 14 Mar. 140/3 Even the contemplative Henry James became a head-shaker. **1869** GEO. ELIOT *Lett.* (1955) V. 54 Best love to Sara—and some *headshaking at her tendency to work too hard. **1961** *Times* 11 Mar. 3/3 Both new works caused widespread discussion and much head-shaking. **1847** L. HUNT *Men Women & B.* II. ix. 189 In very solemn, *head-shaking style. **1883** BLACK *Shandon Bells* xxvii, There is to be a tremendous *head-smashing when he and Murtough meet. **1903** W. J. LOCKE *Where Love Is* (1904) i. 3 Discussing the functions of art and other such *head-splitting matters. **1953** W. STEVENS *Let.* 8 Dec. (1967) 804, I sat..listening to platitudes propounded as if they were head-splitting perceptions. **1647** WARD *Simp. Cobler* 57 Importable *head-tearings and heart-searchings.

c. *locative*, as ***head-felt, -wise, -wrong*** adjs.; *instrumental*, as ***head-lined, -lugged*** adjs.; *similative*, etc., as ***head-high, -like*** adjs.

1880 T. W. ALLIES *Life's Decis.* 137 Heart-felt and *head-felt difficulties. **1842** WILSON *Ess., Streams* (1856) 32 The ancient Moss with its heather *head-high..is now drained. **1874** *Pop. Encycl.* s.v., The so-called head of..tape-worms is only the end of attachment, the globular hook-bearing mass being *headlike on a long neck. **1606** SYLVESTER *Du Bartas* II. iv. I. *Trophies* 514 *Head-lined helmes, heaw'n from their trunks. **1605** SHAKS. *Lear* IV. ii. 42 (1st Qo.) A gracious aged man Whose reuerence euen the *head-lugd beare would lick. **1673** PENN *Life* Wks. 1782 I. 43 Carnal *head-wise opposers..skilled in science falsely so called. **1863** MRS. C. CLARKE *Shaks. Char.* xvii. 415 The headlong and *headwrong Richard II.

74. Special Comb.: †**head-angles**, vertical or opposite angles; **head arrangement** *Jazz* (see quot. 1946); **head-axe** (*Whaling*), an axe used in cutting off the head of the whale; **head-ball** *Cricket*, a cunningly-bowled ball; so **head bowler, bowling**; **head-bay**, the water-space just above a lock in a canal; **head betony**: see BETONY b; also a name for *Pedicularis Canadensis* (Cent. Dict.); †**head-bone** (OE. *héafod bán*), the skull; **head-boom** (*Naut.*), a boom at the ship's head, a jib-boom or flying-jib-boom; **head-bound** *ppl. a.*, wearing a turban, turbaned; **head boy**, the senior pupil in a school, the captain of the school; †**head-brand** (ME. *hedbronde*), a brand or log placed at the back of the fireplace to keep the fire in during the night; **head-butt**, a forceful thrust with the top of the head into the chin or body of another; hence as *v. trans.*, to attack (another) by butting with the head; also **head-butting** (*transf.* in quots.); **head-cap** (*Bookbinding*), the leather cap over the head-band; **head-carry** *v.*, to carry (a load) on one's head; **head-case** (*Entomol.*), that part of a chrysalis which covers the head of the insect; **head-cell** (*Bot.*), a cell at the end of the manubrium in the *Characeæ*; **head centre**: see CENTRE *sb.* 8; **head-chair**, a chair with a high back forming a rest for the head; **head-cheese** (*U.S.*), pork-cheese, brawn; **head-chute** (*Naut.*), a tube leading from the ship's head down to the water, for conveying refuse overboard; **head-clause** *Gram.*, the principal clause; **head-coal**, the upper portion of a thick seam of coal which is worked in two or more lifts (Gresley *Coal-mining Terms*); **head-collar**, the leather headstall of a horse; **head-cone** (*Zool.*), one of two or three conical appendages surrounding the mouth of certain pteropods; **head-cover** *Mil.*, protection for the head, *spec.* a shield for protection against gun-fire; *Fortif.*

(see quot. 1892); **head-cowl** (*Zool.*), one of the two coverings on the head of certain pteropods; **head-cracker** (*Whaling*) = *head-spade*; **head-cringle** (*Naut.*), a cringle at the upper corner of a sail (Smyth *Sailor's Word-bk.*); **head dip** *Surfing* (see quots.); **head doctor** *slang*, a psychiatrist; **head-earing** (*Naut.*), an earing attached to a head-cringle (*ibid.*); †**head-edging**, ? an ornamental edging to a head-dress; **head-feast**, a feast in celebration of successful head-hunting; **head-fish** (*U.S.*), 'a sun-fish of the family *Molidæ*' (*Cent. Dict.*); **head-fold** (see quots.); **head-footed** *a.* (tr. CEPHALOPODA), having the organs of locomotion attached to the head; **head-form**, (*a*) the form of the head, *spec.* in reference to the ratio of its breadth to its length; (*b*) the first word in a dictionary or glossary entry, lemma; †**head-fountain** = FOUNTAIN-HEAD; **head-frame**, the frame of a head-block in a saw-mill; also, a structure at the head of a shaft in a mine, a gallows-frame; **head-gate** (see quot.); **head girl** (see quot. 1963); also *transf.*; †**head-height** (*Arch.*) = HEADWAY 3; **head-hid** *a.*, having the head or source hidden; **head-house** (*Mining*), the 'house' or structure forming a shelter for the *head-frame*; †**head-hung** *a.*, hanging the head, despondent; **head-hunt** *v. trans.* (chiefly *pass.*), to seek (a person) as a senior executive or other skilled employee by 'head-hunting', sense b below; **head-hunter**, (*a*) one who practises head-hunting; (*b*) orig. *U.S.*, an employment agent or agency specializing in the recruitment of managers and other skilled personnel by identifying and approaching preferred candidates; one who recruits using these methods; **head-hunting**, (*a*) the practice, among certain savage tribes, of making incursions for the purpose of procuring human heads as trophies, etc.; so *head-hunting* adj.; (*b*) the action or practice of seeking to fill a senior executive position, etc., by approaching directly a preferred candidate employed elsewhere, rather than by general advertisement; **head-kidney** (*Embryol.*), the foremost of the three parts of the rudimentary kidney in a vertebrate embryo, the pronephros; **head-knee** (*Naut.*): see quot.; **head-knife** (*Whaling*), a knife used in cutting off the head of the whale (Knight *Dict. Mech.*, *Supp.*); **headlamp**, one of the headlights of a (motor) vehicle; **head-lease** (*Law*), a lease granted directly by the freeholder; **head-ledge** (*Ship-building*), one of the thwart-ship pieces which frame the hatchways and ladderways; **head-lessee** (*Law*), a person to whom a head-lease is granted; **head-lining** (*U.S.*): see quot.; **head-load**, a load carried on the head; so **head-load** *v.*; **head-lobe**, an appendage on the head of the embryo in certain molluscs; **head-lock, -locking**, (*a*) (see quots.); (*b*) *Wrestling* (see quot. 1961); **head-louse**, the common louse (*Pediculus capitis*), which infests the hair of the head; †**head mass penny**: see quots.; **head-matter** (*Whaling*), the substance obtained from the head of the sperm whale, consisting of oil and spermaceti, also called shortly *head*; **head metal** *Founding*, the head of metal at the upper end of a cylindrical casting (see DEADHEAD 2 a); **head-netting** (*Naut.*), 'an ornamental netting used in merchant ships instead of the fayed planking to the head-rails' (Smyth *Sailor's Word-bk.*); **head-page** (*Printing*), a page on which the beginning of a book, chapter, etc. is printed; †**head-polles** *sb. pl.*, a name for the swan, crane, and bustard, ? as the chief or largest of fowl used for the table (F. *poule*); **head-post**, (*a*) one of the posts at the head of a four-post bedstead; (*b*) the post nearest to the manger in a stable; **head-pump** (*Naut.*), a small pump at the head of a ship, communicating with the sea, and used for washing the decks; **head-reach** *v. intr.* (*Naut.*), to shoot ahead, as a sailing vessel while tacking; also *trans.*; **head-register** (see quots. and REGISTER *sb.*[1] 8 b); also *attrib.*; **head-rent** (*Law*), rent payable to the freeholder; **head resistance**, resistance of a fluid to the movement of a body through it; **headrest**, a support or rest for the head attached to the (front) seat of a motor vehicle, etc.; a head restraint; **head restraint**: see RESTRAINT *sb.* 1 c; **head-ridge** (*Sc.*), **head-rig**) = HEADLAND 1; **head-right** *U.S.*, an inheritable right to land, formerly granted by the state of Texas to the heads of immigrating families; **head-ring**, (*a*) see quot. 1794; (*b*) a decoration consisting of a leaflet of palm fixed to the hair, worn by Nguni men after marriage; **head-scarf, headscarf**, a scarf worn instead of a hat; hence **head-scarved** *a.*; **headset**, (*a*) a pair of earphones; (*b*) a combination of earphones and a microphone as worn by a telephone exchange operator; **head-shaking**, a display by certain birds at mating or egg-laying (see also sense 73 b); so **head-shake** *v.*; **head-shield** (*Zool.*), a horny plate on the head of a snake, lizard, tortoise, or armadillo; **head-shrinker**, (*a*) a head-hunter who preserves and shrinks human heads; (*b*) *slang* (orig. *U.S.*) a psychiatrist; so (sense (*a*)) **head-shrinking** *vbl. sb.*; **head-shy** *a.*, of animals: afraid of having the head touched; so **head-shyness**; **head-sill**, (*a*) the upper part of the frame of a door or window; (*b*) a piece at each end of a saw-pit, on which the end of the log rests; †**head-silver** = HEAD-MONEY 1 (*obs.*); **head-skin** (see quot.); **head-spade** (*Whaling*), an instrument with a long handle and steel blade, used in cutting the bone which joins the whale's head to the body; **head start**, an advantage at the beginning of a race; also *transf.*; *spec.* (with capitals) the name of an educational and welfare programme in the United States; **head-station** (*Austral.* and *N.Z.*): see quot. 1881; **head-stool**, a kind of small pillow, formerly used to rest the neck or cheek upon without disturbing the hair or head-dress; †**head-strain** = HEAD-STALL *sb.*[1] 2; **head-stream, -tributary**, a head-water stream or tributary; **head teacher**, the principal teacher or administrator of a school; a headmaster or headmistress; **head-territ** = *head-ring* (*a*); **head-tie**, a head-band or scarf worn by women, esp. among peoples of African origin; **head-timber** (*Ship-building*), one of the upright pieces of timber which support the frame of the head-rails; **head-tin**: see quot.; **head-tone** = HEAD-NOTE 2; **head-tree** (*Coal-mining*), 'a piece of wood about a foot long set across the head of an upright prop to support the roof in a pit: cf. *crown-tree*' (*Northumb. Gloss.*); **head-turner**, 'a machine for rounding and beveling barrel-heads' (Knight *Dict. Mech.*, *Supp.*); **head-up** *Aeronautics*, used *attrib.* of a visual display system by which the pilot is able to read his instruments without averting his eyes from the aircraft's course; also, such a system in a motor vehicle; **head-valve**, in a steam-engine, 'the delivering valve, the upper air-pump valve' (Knight *Dict. Mech.*, *Supp.*); **head-veil**, a veil worn over the head and falling behind it, not over the face; **head-wall** *Phys. Geogr.*, the steep slope at the head of a glaciated valley, esp. a cliff that rises abruptly from the floor of a cirque; †**head-well** = HEAD-SPRING, FOUNTAIN-HEAD; **head-word**, (*a*) a word written or printed at the top or beginning of a chapter, paragraph, etc.; a word forming a heading; (*b*) *Gram.* a word modified by another word or words; (*c*) = HEAD *sb.*[1] 19 c(*b*); = *head-form* (*b*); **head-yard** (*Naut.*), one of the yards on the foremast.

1570 BILLINGSLEY *Euclid* I. xv. 24 If two right lines cut the one the other: the *hed angles shal be equal the one to the other. **1946** R. BLESH *Shining Trumpets* (1949) xi. 251 '*Head' arrangement. *footnote.* A memorized, not written arrangement, that leaves ample room for improvisation. **1949** L. FEATHER *Inside Be-bop* iii. 21 He'd help to set up ideas for head arrangements. **1958** N. D. HINTON in *Publ. Amer. Dialect Soc.* xxx. 46 Head arrangement, a musical arrangement which is not written down and never has been, but is known by all the members of the ensemble. **1968** *Jazz Monthly* Feb. 21/1 The functional scoring of *John's idea*, *Shorty George* and *Cherokee* was the work of Jimmy Mundy, ..the remainder probably being head arrangements. **1874** SCAMMON *Mar. Mammals* 232 The rest of the cutting gear.. which consists of toggles, spades..*head-axes, etc. **1870** *Baily's Monthly Mag.* July 295 Alfred Shaw..is one of the few bowlers..qualified to attempt a '*head ball'. **1902** *Westm. Gaz.* 11 Aug. 7/1 Self-restraint that not even the most tempting 'head-balls' of Lockwood and of Rhodes could overcome. *c* **1000** *Sax. Leechd.* II. 126 Monnes *heafod ban bærn to ahsan. *c* **1205** LAY. 1467 He smot Numbert..þat his hæfd-bon to-brec. *a* **1400** *Sir Perc.* 1190 He..Made the Sarazenes hede bones Hoppe, als dose hayle stones, Abowtte one the gres. *a* **1616** BEAUM. & FL. *Knt. of Malta* I. iii, *Head-bound infidels. **1870** F. GALE in *New Sporting Mag.* New Ser. LX. 35, I must..see another little square man..before I believe that a better *head bowler ever lived than Lillywhite. **1867** G. H. SELKIRK *Guide Cricket Ground* ii. 28 *Head Bowling. **1851** THACKERAY *Eng. Hum., Steele* (1853) 120 The person to whom he has looked up with the greatest wonder and reverence, was the *head boy at his school..Addison was always his [Steele's] head boy. **1972** P. CAVE *Mama* (1974) iii. 16 Hurling it at Mick's head, he crouched low and went in for another *head-butt. **1977** *Western Morning News* 1 Sept. 5/8 Mr. Chadwick tried to head butt him and he hit him with a glass. **1985** *Times* 4 Oct. 3/3 He lost control, head-butted his wife and strangled her with the flex from a tape recorder. **1986** *Los Angeles Times* 21 July III. 4/2 A head butt in the 10th round.. opened a cut at the corner of Gonzales' right eye. **1946** *Sat. Even. Post* 30 Mar. 45 The climax of the rivalry..was an all-out *head butting between Amon Carter, of Fort Worth, and Banker Robert Thornton, of Dallas. **1980** *Outdoor Life* (Northeast ed.) Oct. 130/2 In an epic head-butting with the Corps, Derrick fought almost single handed to stop the Richard B. Russell Dam on the Savannah River. **14..** *Voc.* in Wr.-Wülcker 607/33 *Repofocilium*, an *hed-bronde. **1888** *Arts & Crafts Catal.* 87 The *head-band* and **head-cap*, the fillet of silk worked in buttonhole stitch at the head and tail, and the cap or cover of leather over it. **1957** R. CAMPBELL *Portugal* 84 Trundling, *head-carrying, or pedalling their various contraptions. **1968** *Times* (Pakistan Suppl.) 6 Apr. p. v/5 For eight or more hours a day, he head-carries his dish of earth from one spot to another and his pay is about three rupees, or roughly 4*s.* **1826** KIRBY & SP. *Entomol.* III. 249 The *Head-case covers and protects the head of the inclosed imago. **1887** K. GOEBEL *Morphol. Plants* 58 Each *head-cell is surmounted by six smaller cells (secondary head-cells). **1841** *Southern Lit. Messenger* VII. 39/2 The animal..may be traced in the stewed chine and souse, the *head cheese and sausages. **1860** BARTLETT *Dict. Amer.*, *Head-Cheese*, the ears and feet [*ed.* **1877** scraps of the head and feet] of swine cut up fine, and after being boiled, pressed into the form of a cheese. **1891** H. FREDERICK *Copperhead* (1894) 255 Reducing what remained of the [pig's] head into small bits, to be seasoned..and then fill other pans as head-cheese. **1942** C. MORLEY *Thorofare* (1943) xli. 159 Yes, Ma'am, over here we call it headcheese, but I remember my old gramp called it brawn. **1970** C. MAJOR *Dict. Afro-Amer. Slang* 65 *Headcheese*, various cheap grades of pork meat prepared and sold as lunch meat. **1928** H. POUTSMA *Gram. Late Mod. Eng.* (ed. 2) 38 A subordinate statement with modal *may* often stands with a *head-clause containing *possible*. **1957** R. W. ZANDVOORT *Handbk. Eng. Gram.* I. iv. 62 The *perfect of experience*..is not unknown in other languages, at least in head-clauses, though an adjunct expressing repetition is usually added. **1890** LD. LUGARD *Diary* 26 Mar. (1959) I. iv. 160 Along the top [of the Stockade] a log for *head cover, and line below it for firing. **1892** F. IRWIN *Fortification* (ed. 2) 37 Always place head-cover on wall when firing over the top. **1916** 'BOYD CABLE' *Action Front* 229 It's a good foot and a half I have of head-cover. **1923** KIPLING *Irish Guards in Gt. War* I. 24 The Battalion..next day quietly improved trenches and head-cover. **1852** TODD *Cycl. Anat.* IV. 174/2 The *head-cowls are shown partially folded back, so as to display the conical appendages (*head-cones) which the cowls enclose and protect. **1962** *Austral. Women's Weekly* Suppl. 24 Oct. 3/2 **Head dip*, trick riding—putting head in and out of a wave while riding it. **1963** *Observer* 13 Oct. 15/5 The 'head dip', in which the rider bends double and dips his head into the wave at his feet. **1956** 'E. MCBAIN' *Cop Hater* (1958) xxi. 177 'What's the matter with this guy?' 'Nothing that a *head doctor couldn't cure,' Byrnes said. **1959** M. DOLINSKY *There is no Silence* vii. 114, I was impressed in spite of my previous opinions about 'head doctors'. **1971** 'A. BLAISDELL' *Practice to Deceive* xiv. 210 Getting let loose by some damn-fool head doctor. **1731** *Chron.* in Thackeray *Four Georges* ii. (1861) 96 Her Majesty..wore a flowered muslin *head-edging. **1882** H. DE WINDT *On Equator* 82 These '*Head Feasts' are general among the aboriginal tribes throughout the island of Borneo. **1843** *Proc. Amer. Phil. Soc.* IV. 11 A fish found upon Squam Beach N.J. called by the fishermen the *Head-fish. **1890** BILLINGS *Med. Dict.*, **Head-fold*, a fold of the blastoderm under the cephalic end of the embryo. **1893** A. M. MARSHALL *Vert. Embryol.* 226 The head of the embryo is lifted up above the yolk-sac by an anterior constriction or head fold. **1851** RICHARDSON *Geol.* viii. 248 [The head] is surrounded by a circle of fleshy processes, or feet, from whence the name of the class, '*head-footed', is derived. **1885** J. BEDDOE *Races of Britain* xiii. 259 The principal ethnical elements in Britain are too much alike in *headform to yield their differences to an average constructed on but a few living heads. **1903** *Biometrika* II. 505 We are ignorant..of the characters of such a race, of its variability, for instance in head-, nose- or hair-form. **1927** PEAKE & FLEURE *Peasants & Potters* 128 There can be little doubt that profile and head-form have subtle..interrelations. **1935** *Proc. Prehist. Soc.* I. 4 The particulate inheritance of the several genes determining head-form. **1962** K. MALONE in Householder & Saporta *Probl. Lexicogr.* 112 Here such verbs are listed in full, and the irregular forms of each verb are entered against the head-form. **1688** NORRIS *Theory Love* I. iii. 24 The Heart is ..the *Head-fountain of Life. **1878** *Sci. Amer.* XXXVIII. 291 The *head frame..is supported by track wheels secured to axles. **1875** KNIGHT *Dict. Mech.*, **Head-gate* (Hydraulic Engineering), (*a*) one of the upper pair of gates of a canal-lock. (*b*) a crown-gate, flood-gate, water-gate, by which water is admitted to a race, run, sluice, etc. **1846** C. M. YONGE in *Mag. for Young* 2 Sept. 196 At school..she went to..the *head girl. **1919** A. BRAZIL (*title*) The Head Girl at the Gables. **1941** *Brit. Jrnl. Psychol.* Jan. 194 The 'head-girls' [in a factory] wear an overall different in colour. **1963** BARNARD & LAUWERYS *Handbk. Brit. Educ. Terms* 104 *Head boy/girl*, a boy or girl appointed or elected as a leader of the other pupils, and who traditionally in public schools has considerable responsibilities for the maintenance of discipline acting through prefects. **1964** M. DRABBLE *Garrick Year* xii. 179, I was a prefect, but I wasn't head girl. **1620–55** I. JONES *Stone-Heng* (1725) 40 There could not possibly be a convenient *Head-height remaining a Passage underneath. **1625** K. LONG tr. *Barclay's Argenis* I. xii. 33 A land where *head-hid Nile his streames divides. **1631** SHIRLEY *Love in Maze* IV. ii, You must not be so *head-hung. **1632** —— *Bird in Cage* III. ii, Gentlemen, be not head-hung, droop not. **1969** *Sunday Times* 2 Nov. 30/5 The new ex-Slater managing director, Allan Baxter (*head-hunted by KIM) wanted to carry out his own programme before coming back for consultation. **1985** *Daily Tel.* 1 Oct. 19/3 Mr Bullock..was headhunted from Flymo to revive Neill. **1853** H. KEPPEL *Ind. Archip.* I. 141 A chief named Dungdong..had..adopted the Dyak costume, and become a notorious *head-hunter. **1961** *Fortune* June 129/1 McCulloch had no compunction about using these executive recruiting firms. They were, he knew, often derisively called 'body snatchers', 'head hunters', 'flesh peddlers', and 'pirates'. **1985** *Investment Chron.* 8–14 Nov. 26/2 My latest head-hunter story: a Brit being considered for an international fund management job asked for £50,000, half for himself and half for his wife. **1853** H. KEPPEL *Ind. Archip.* I. 129 Some..Dyaks have..stated that they would give up *head-hunting, were it not for the taunts and gibes of their wives and sweethearts. **1965** *Fortune* Sept. 236/2 Fifteen years ago there were less than a dozen 'head-

hunting' firms of any consequence, most of them adjuncts of management-consultant operations. 1966 Times 4 May 12/1 The polite word for head-hunting is the 'search' method of executive selection. 1984 J. Archer First among Equals xix. 223 Head-hunting seemed to be the next move. 1884 Rajah Brooke in Pall Mall G. 1 Mar. 2/1 The *head-hunting Dyaks. 1880 Rep. Brit. Assoc. 644 The hypothesis of Gegenbauer and Fürbringer as to the relation of the *head-kidney to the hinder part of the excretory system. 1867 Smyth Sailor's Word-bk., *Head-knees, pieces of moulded compass timber fayed edgeways to the cutwater and stem, to steady the former. 1885 Kipling Phantom' Rickshaw in Quartette 96 It [sc. a rickshaw] lay in readiness in the Mall, and..with a lighted *head-lamp. 1912 Motor Man. (ed. 14) iii. 123 Paraffin Head-lamps. 1961 Times 25 Apr. 17/3 The first British production car to be fitted with two pairs of twin headlamps. 1972 Country Life 7 Dec. 1592/3 The brakes were effective..and wipers and headlamps very good. 1882 Law Rep. 8 Queen's Bench Div. 329 The contract of a sub-tenant to perform the covenants of the *head-lease. 1819 Rees Cycl. s.v., *Head-ledges, are the thwart-ship pieces which frame the openings in the decks. 1869 Sir E. Reed Shipbuild. xv. 275 Half round iron is riveted to the upper edges of the plate coamings and head-ledges. 1845 Disraeli Sybil (1863) 132 There are no land-lords, *head-lessees, main-masters, or butties in Wodgate. 1864 Webster, *Head-lining, the lining of the head or hood of a carriage; the oil-cloth or other textile lining of the roof of a railway car (U.S.). 1927 W. H. Todd Tiger, Tiger! 20 Carrying *head-loads of sand. 1957 M. Banton W. Afr. City iv. 67 Head-loading someone's baggage or helping to take goods out of a lorry. 1959 Times (Ghana Suppl.) 9 Nov. p. iv/1 Much of the cocoa starts its journey to the coast by being head-loaded along the bush tracks. 1971 J. Spencer Eng. Lang. W. Afr. 29 Head-load (a term now surely becoming obsolescent with the advent of mechanical modes of transport). 1854 Woodward Mollusca (1856) 99 The..eggs of the fresh-water limneids..are not hatched until the young have passed the larval condition, and their ciliated *head-lobes.. are superseded by the creeping disk, or foot. 1901 Dorland Med. Dict. (ed. 2), *Head-lock, the locking together of the chins in twin labor. 1905 F. R. Toombs How to Wrestle (1906) 107 Secure a head lock by putting your left forearm ..on the defensive man's head. 1934 J. M. Cain Postman always rings Twice x. 109 He's the only one in this town can throw the headlock on Sackett. 1957 Encycl. Brit. XXIII (caption, facing p. 804), Jim Browning..with a headlock on Danno O'Mahoney. 1961 J. S. Salak Dict. Amer. Sports 220 Headlock, a hold in which the wrestler encircles the opponent's head with one or both arms. 1973 Times 16 Mar. 2/2 They dragged me out of the house and struck me on the head and legs, holding me in a headlock. 1890 Billings Med. Dict., *Head-locking, in twin labor, one child being born by the breech, its chin catches upon the chin of the second child presenting by the head. 1547 Boorde Brev. Health §273 *Head lyce, body lyce, crabbe lyce. 1861 Hulme tr. Moquin-Tandon ii. vi. i. 292 The Head (or Common) Louse..is found on the head, in people who are neglectful of their person. c 1460 Towneley Myst. (Surtees) 104 To gyf alle in my cofer, To morne at next to offer Her *hed mas penny. 1514 in Eng. Gilds (1870) 144 For a hedmesse penny, a penny. 1791 Phil. Trans. LXXXI. 44 A cargo of 76 tons of spermaceti oil and *head-matter. 1874 C. M. Scammon Marine Mammals iii. 239 The oil taken from the case of the Sperm Whale is..when put into casks.. known as head, or head-matter. 1888 Lockwood's Dict. Mech. Engin. s.v., When the casting is removed from the mould the *head metal is turned off, leaving the actual casting smooth and free from these foreign impurities. 1960 R. Lister Decorative Cast Ironwork 229 Head metal, the metal in a feeding head. 1838 Timperley Printer's Man. 114 *Head page, the beginning of a subject. 1553-4 Act Comm. Council Lond. (Journal 16, fol. 334-5) That theare be no Swanne, Crane, nor bustarde, which are wonte to be called *hed polles. 1875 Knight Dict. Mech., *Head-post, a stanchion by the manger in a stable. 1879 Butcher & Lang Odyss. 382 Beginning from this head-post, I wrought at the bedstead till I had finished it. 1840 R. H. Dana Bef. Mast xiv. 33 The crew rig the *head-pump, and wash down the decks. 1858 Merc. Marine Mag. V. 310 Lying *head reaching, under close-reefed stormsails. 1892 Outing (U.S.) Apr. 57/1 Soon she had head-reached them all, Shadow included, and showed to the front of the fleet. 1938 C. S. Forester Ship of Line 276, I want to hear instantly if they alter course, or if they headreach upon us. 1890 Billings Med. Dict., *Head-register, register in which the pitch is raised by shortening the vocal chords; second falsetto in females. 1909 H. Klein Phono-Vocal Method 37 The blending of the medium and head registers will be practised upon the same plan. 1966 H. L. Shorto in C. E. Bazell In Memory of J. R. Firth 407 Henderson found that in Cambodian a sequence of head-register consonant and chest-register vowel..was the mark of a secondary pattern. 1859 Rules 15 July (Landed Estates Act Ireland 1858) §31 What sums are due for arrears of rates, cess, taxes, *head rents, quit rents. 1889 J. J. Welch Text Bk. Naval Archit. iii. 53 This [fluid] resistance is due:—..(2) To the opposition offered to the passage through the water..of projections such as the keel and bilge keels, and of the comparatively flat parts of the ship at the ends: this is known as direct or *head resistance. 1891 Railroad & Engin. Jrnl. LXV. 465/1 The head or hull resistance will probably be found to be the chief element which will limit the possible speed of flying machines. 1909 Westm. Gaz. 1 July 4/1 Allowing a coefficient of ·3 for the pointed ends, the total head-resistance would be reduced to 3,324 lb. 1922 R. Glazebrook Dict. Appl. Physics I. 717/1 A second form of eddy resistance developed by a ship, sometimes called 'head resistance', is due to such features as..web supports to the propeller shafts, thick stems, and stern posts. 1934 Discovery Dec. 352/2 Another cowl known as a Townend Ring..produces..a reduction in head resistance. 1959 J. L. Nayler Dict. Aeronaut. Engin. 128 Head resistance, a term used for the resistance, or drag at no yaw, of the front part of a projectile, the remainder of the drag being due to skin friction and base drag. 1961 Mod. Plastics Encycl. XXXIX. 392/2 The low cost and ease of fabrication of the dies..has made the technique useful for producing such novelties as soap dishes,..*head rests, etc. 1986 Christian Science Monitor 27 Jan. 25/1 The minivan is not a car and therefore does not have to meet the same safety standards as an automobile. Among other things, no front-seat headrests. 1765 A. Dickson Treat. Agric. (ed. 2) 452 The earth of a *head-ridge. 1875 W. McIlwraith Guide Wigtownshire 42 A path along the head-rigs of some fields. 1703 in Amer. Speech (1961) XXXVI. 152 *Head-right. 1799 in O. A. Rothert Hist. Muhlenberg County (1913) 45 Colonel William Campbell's head-right..adjoining the lands [etc.]. 1837 Laws of Texas (1838) I. 266 So much of the vacant lands.. to be surveyed and sectionized..as will be sufficient to satisfy all claims..for scrip sold, soldiers' claims, and head rights. 1898 H. S. Canfield Maid of Frontier i. 13 He owned the headright of 160 acres on which his house was built. 1794 W. Felton Carriages (1801) II. Gloss. 189 *Head Ring, or Head Territ, a ring, placed on the top of the bridle of the wheel harness, through which the leading reins pass, when four horses are drove in hand. 1866 C. Barter Alone among Zulus v. 51 When a [Zulu] soldier has attained a certain standing he receives the royal permission to marry, and adopt the head-ring as a mark of manhood. 1952 S. G. Millin Burning Man xxv. 227, I have worn the head-ring of a married man for three years. 1921 G. B. Shaw Back to Methuselah iii. 101 (stage direction) A handsome negress is trying on a brilliant *head scarf. 1955 G. Freeman Liberty Man i. i. 18 Maureen came out adjusting her headscarf. 1962 D. Harden Phoenicians vii. 103 A bearded priest with a head-scarf. 1960 M. Sharp Something Light ii. x. 91 A *head-scarved plumpish figure. 1970 Guardian 13 July 9/3 Head-scarfed refugees. 1921 Telegr. & Teleph. Jrnl. Dec. 46/2 Supervisor (speaking on *head-set of bewildered learner). 1942 Tee Emm (Air Ministry) II. 84 The pilot.. should see that his headset plug is firmly in. 1955 'N. Shute' Requiem for Wren 64 A telephone headset strapped across his beret. 1957 Spaceflight I. 71/2 Each seat in the auditorium was fitted with a headset and switchbox, by means of which one could select the language one desired. 1970 N. Armstrong et al. First on Moon iii. 63 They had to be checked out: the communications consoles, the technician headsets, the purge ventilators. 1930 J. S. Huxley Bird-Watching & Bird Behaviour iv. 70 It is doubtless very enjoyable to *head-shake together. Ibid. v. 95 The head-shaking ceremony. 1959 Bannerman Birds Brit. Isles VIII. 217 The second important display is 'head-shaking'. The bird..waggles its head from side to side at another... Birds already paired together frequently head-shake together. 1893 H. N. Hutchinson Extinct Monsters 31 The eyes are placed on the margin of the *head-shield. 1926 G. M. Dyott On Trail of Unknown xii. 173 (heading) The *head shrinkers. Ibid. 190 In the process of head-shrinking, the hair retains its original length and..looks longer than it did on the original man. 1950 Time 27 Nov. 19 Anyone who had predicted that he would end up as the rootin'-tootin' idol of U.S. children would have been led instantly off to a headshrinker. 1957 A. Maney in G. Oppenheimer Passionate Playgoer (1958) 381 Marcus Heiman, head of the United Booking Office, turned the play over to his psychiatrist. That headshrinker said a play glorifying a drunkard conflicted with public interest. 1958 Spectator 22 Aug. 241/2 The head-shrinkers would doubtless say it is the universal human search for a father-figure that is behind it. 1959 T. B. Morris Death among Orchids xiii. 121 There are still cannibals... But the worst of them are now..the head-shrinkers. 1968 New Scientist 8 Feb. 289/1 Dr. Louis West..may eventually be taking the caviare out of headshrinkers' mouths with his development of the robot psychiatrist. 1970 I. Reed in A. Chapman New Black Voices (1972) 516 A vocabulary that calls things by their names: 'headshrinker' and 'egghead'. 1900 M. H. Hayes Among Horses in Russia iv. 82 They weren't *head-shy, and liked their manes to be scratched. Ibid., Every horseman knows that 'head-shyness' is one of the worst of vices. 1952 J. Steinbeck East of Eden 384 A few strokes on the nose will make a puppy head-shy. 1694 Moxon Mech. Exerc. 144 The Window Frames are so framed, That the Tennants of the *Head-sell, Ground-sell, and Transum, run through the outer Jaums about four Inches. 1467 Rolls Parlt. V. 582 Hidage, Beaupleder, Frithsilver, *Hedesylver. 1565-73 Cooper Thesaurus, Capitatio..headsilver: subsidie. 1874 C. M. Scammon Marine Mammals i. viii. 75 This [whale's nostril], with the 'case,' is protected by a thick, tough, elastic substance called the '*head-skin,' which is proof against the harpoon. 1886 in Amer. Speech (1950) XXV. 34/1 Fifteen paces, *head start. 1911 W. James Some Probl. Philos. xi. 180 Owing to the tortoise's head-start, the tortoise's path is only a part of the path of Achilles. 1935 F. Scott Fitzgerald Let. (1964) 6 You and Peaches (who isn't selfish, I think) had a superficial head-start with prettiness. 1962 Economist 18 Aug. 620/2 The research data needed to give them a head-start in the market. 1965 Mrs. L. B. Johnson White House Diary 3 Feb. (1970) 235 Sarge [Shriver] asked me if I would consider and sponsor the program Head Start. 1968 Times 9 Oct. 10/7 If we can give them a head start—..they're going to do as well as other children. 1970 Washington Post 30 Sept. 133/1 Volunteers are urgently needed for Head Start and day care programs throughout the Washington area. 1973 Black World Mar. 37 Effective or not, the Poverty Program, Headstart, compensatory education programs,..and so on were efforts toward establishing justice for Blacks. 1973 J. Pattinson Search Warrant ii. 37 He decided to spend the night in Philadelphia... The other man had a head start anyway. 1862 R. Henning Let. 19 Oct. (1966) 111 It is a most eligible spot for a *head-station, and the two carpenters have already begun putting up the store. 1881 A. C. Grant Bush-Life Queensland I. 42 A headstation, as the homestead and main buildings of a station are invariably called. 1895 G. Chamier South-Sea Siren xi. 161 [The house] was used as the head-station for a sheep run. 1936 A. Russell Gone Nomad iii. 14, I had left the head station at sunrise and ridden all day. 1598 Florio, Testiera,..the headstall of a bridle, a *headstraine. 1658 Hist. Christina Q. Swedland 371 With Furniture of Velvet..twisted with Silver, with buckles, bridles, and head-strains of the same metall. 1817 S. R. Brown Western Gaz. 8 Navigation..can be pursued up the Coose to one of its *head streams. 1899 A. H. Keane Man Past & Present 190 Northwards..about the Irawadi head-streams. 1908 Athenæum 11 Apr. 456/3 From its head-streams in the glens. 1956 D. L. Linton Sheffield p. xxiv, Turning southwards round the headstreams of the Don our boundary passes above the long Woodhead tunnel. 1825 E. Weeton Jrnl. 10 Apr. (1969) II. 346 Miss Jackson, the *head teacher, came past, and the whole train of boarders. 1975 Language for Life (Dept. Educ. & Sci.) xxvi. 531 Head-teachers have a vitally important role in the promotion of successful language work and reading in the school. 1857 M. Griffith Autobiogr. Female Slave i. 17 One gave a yard of ribbon, another a half-paper of pins, a third presented a painted cotton *head-tie. 1956 in Cassidy & Le Page Dict. Jamaican Eng. (1967) 222/2 [Head-tie] a head scarf. 1967 W. Soyinka Kongi's Harvest 52 You see yourself How the courtesan is one hour escalating Her brocade head-tie. 1973 Trinidad Guardian 1 Feb. 11/1 She was wearing black shoes, a flowered dress and headtie. c 1850 Rudim. Navig. (Weale) 124 *Head-timbers, the pieces that cross the rails of the head vertically. They are bolted through their heels to the cutting-down of the knee, and unite the whole together. 1753 Chambers Cycl. Supp. s.v., When the [tin] ore has been pounded and twice washed, that part of it which lies uppermost or makes the surface of the mass in the tub, is called the *Head-tin. 1747 Hooson Miner's Dict. G iij b, If the Wholes be too soft..we put a Sill under them..and drive them fast up against the *Head-tree. 1851 Greenwell Coal-trade Terms Northumb. & Durh. 30 Head-tree, a piece of a crowntree, a foot long, placed upon a prop to support the roof; the head-tree being to extend the bearance of the prop. 1925 N. E. Odell in E. F. Norton Fight for Everest, 1924 iii. 292 A far-flung *head tributary of the Dzakar Chu. 1960 Times 15 Dec. 4/3 Mr. Naish said that some 1,200 hours of laboratory 'flying' with the *head-up device used in conjunction with the flight simulator had shown that accuracy in following flight directions was twice as good as with the normal instruments. 1968 New Scientist 8 Aug. 273/1 A new term has found its way into the cockpits of military aircraft in the past few years. It is 'head-up display'. It connotes a system whereby the pilot can see what tale his instruments are telling without taking his eyes off the scene ahead. Ibid. 273/2 Head-up flying is a bonus derived from the application of electronics in many new ways. 1972 Drive Spring 43/2 Road-speed reflected in the windscreen glass by the safety-first 'head up' display. 1972 Times 14 Sept. 31/1 At present only the drivers of a handful of experimental cars (and the pilots of supersonic aircraft) get the benefit of head-up displays... Smiths are working on head-up displays for family cars. 1896 L. Eckenstein Woman under Monast. 115 The dark *head-veil is given up for white and coloured head-dresses. 1904 Jrnl. Geol. XII. 570 The canyons, at their heads, were abnormally deep.. and their *head walls..stood as nearly upright, apparently, as scaling of the rock would permit. 1910 Geogr. Jrnl. XXXV. 154 Perhaps because of their small size these cliff glaciers have not developed cirques, though a Bergschrund parallels the generally straight head-wall. 1954 W. D. Thornbury Princ. Geomorphol. xv. 367 A cirque headwall may be as much as 2000 to 3000 feet high and is notably steep and free from talus at its base, even in empty cirques. c 1250 Gen. & Ex. 868 On *heued-welle of flum iordan. 1823 Crabb Technol. Dict., *Head word. 1898 Sweet New Eng. Gram. ii. §1759 Thus pre-adjunct or pre-adjective position means that the adjunct-word precedes its head-word. 1939 English Studies XXI. 71 It [sc. the genitive] was pinned down..to its head-word, first either in front or in post-position, eventually only in front position. 1940 Ibid. XXII. 88 Headwords, attributes and adjuncts, the terms representing their relative importance or ranks within the sentence, headwords coming first. 1957 S. Potter Mod. Ling. v. 115 In the phrase good men there are two ranks: men is the head-word or primary and good is the attribute or secondary. 1957 R. W. Zandvoort Handbk. Eng. Gram. ii. ii. 104 The headword need not be repeated if it occurs earlier or later in the sentence: She put her arm through her mother's. 1961 R. B. Long Sentence & its Parts v. 121 But in true phrasal passives the auxiliaries set the time for actions whose semantic centers are the head-word participles. 1964 M. Schubiger in D. Abercrombie et al. Daniel Jones 258 Restrictive relative clauses preceded by their head-words. 1966 English Studies LXVII. 211 Head-words..appear in their West-Saxon variant. 1967 Listener 26 Oct. 545/3 (Advt.), 97,000 headwords. 1762 Falconer Shipwr. ii. Argt., The *head yards braced aback.

Head (hɛd), *sb.*² The name of Sir Henry *Head* (1861–1940), English neurologist, used *attrib.* and in the possessive with reference to his work on sensation, etc.

1908 Jrnl. Nerv. & Mental Dis. XXXV. 576 (title) On the hyperesthetic areas (Head's zones) in visceral disease. Ibid. 577 His experience would not corroborate Dr. Bloomfield's as to the great value of Head's test. Ibid., Dr. McCarthy asked in what percentage of tuberculous cases Dr. Ludlum found the distinct Head sign. Ibid. 578 Head's lines cannot be elicited in chronic cases. Ibid., That patient still shows Head's lines. 1910 Practitioner Jan. 119 Some of the headache of pyorrhœa alveolaris may be reflex (cf. Head's areas). 1913 Dorland Med. Dict. (ed. 7) s.v. Zone, Head's zones, areas of cutaneous sensitiveness associated with diseases of the viscera: called also zones of hyperalgesia. 1941 Brit. Jrnl. Psychol. XXXII. i. 6 Physiological experiments upon the action of the vagus nerve in respiratory movements..[which were recorded] by the use of a strip of the diaphragm (known henceforth as 'Head's strip'). 1961 Brain LXXXIV. 530 He [sc. Head] devised the preparation which is known as the 'Head's diaphragm slip preparation'. Ibid. 533, I suggest the possibility that this gasping response in the newborn baby is in fact Head's Paradoxical Reflex. Ibid. 532 The Head Reflex is carried in small unmyelinated fibres.

head, *sb.*³ Colloq. abbrev. of headlight.

1959 I. Jefferies 13 Days vi. 75 He..flashed his heads just as I got abreast. 1969 'A. Hall' Striker Portfolio ix. 112 My undipped heads catching the Mercedes full across the screen. 1971 —— Warsaw Document xxii. 279 The patrol-car coming at us with the heads full on.

head (hɛd), *v.* Forms: 4–5 hefd(en, heued, (5 hefed), 4–6 hedde, hede, hed, 5–6 heed, 6 heade, *Sc.* heid, 6– head. [f. head *sb.*¹; in many senses having no connexion with each other, but formed independently on the sb. and its phrases, at various times. Not in OE., which had, however, in sense 1, *behéafdian* to behead.]

I. To take off the head.

1. *trans.* To cut off or remove the head of; to decapitate, behead. †**a.** a person. *Obs.*

a **1300** *Cursor M.* 7587 Daui..hedded him wit his aun brand. *Ibid.* 20990 Hefdid he was wit dint o suord. **1375** BARBOUR *Bruce* IV. 30 The king..gert draw hym, & hede, & hing. *c* **1400** MAUNDEV. (Roxb.) xiv. 62 Þare es a kirk of sayne George, whare he was heuedid. **1548** HALL *Chron., Hen. VI*, 160 Hym..caused..to be hedded, and his head to be fixed on a poole. **1603** SHAKS. *Meas. for M.* II. i. 251 If you head and hang all that offend that way. **1608–33** BP. HALL *Medit. & Vows* (1676) 397 Are we headed? so was John Baptist.

b. an animal.

c **1470** in *Hors, Shepe & G., etc.* (Caxton 1479, Roxb. repr.) 33 A pigge heded & syded. **1800** *Naval Chron.* III. 284 They head and gut the fish.

2. To lop off the branches forming the head of (a tree or plant); to top, poll. Also, *to head down*.

1523 FITZHERB. *Husb.* §132 Excepte thou hede thy trees & cut of the toppes. **1649** BLITHE *Eng. Improv. Impr.* (1653) 172 [The Lime-tree] being headed and set in walks in roes, makes a very gallant shady walk. **1712** J. JAMES tr. *Le Blond's Gardening* 145 The Willow..is headed every three or four Years. **1769** *Projects* in *Ann. Reg.* 120/1 Your fruit tree is planted and headed down. **1789** *Trans. Soc. Arts* I. 111, I was obliged to head them [Ash trees] the first year. **1882** *Garden* 11 Mar. 169/3 Stocks intended for grafting are headed down in readiness for that operation.

II. To put a head on; to form a head.

3. a. *trans.* To put a head on; to furnish or fit with a head; to fit with an arrow-head.

(The first quot. is, from its date, very doubtful: Chaucer may have written *hedid*: see HEADED *ppl. a.*)

[*c* **1374** CHAUCER *Troylus* II. (993) 1042 Yf a peyntour wolde peynte a pyk With asses feet and hede it [*MS. Gg.* 4. 27 hedit] as an ape.] **1530** PALSGR. 582/2 Heed your arowes with Strande heedes. **1589** R. HARVEY *Pl. Perc.* (1860) 31 Like two drums which are headed, the one with a sheeps skin the other with a woulfes hide. **1697** DRYDEN *Virg. Georg.* I. 357 Let him..whet the shining Share..Or sharpen Stakes, or head the Forks. **1766** POSTLETHWAYT *Dict. Trade* (ed. 3) s.v. *Fisheries*, The Coopers put the finishing hand to all, by heading the casks. **1797** *Monthly Mag.* III. 300 Engines, to cut and head nails. **1854** H. MILLER *Sch. & Schm.* (1858) 510 Acquiring the ability..of heading a pin with the necessary adroitness. **1856** *Jrnl. R. Agric. Soc.* XVII. II. 363 The..fence..is..then headed or finished with 2 feet of grass sods.

b. To close *up* (a barrel or cask) by fitting the head on; to enclose (something) in a barrel or cask by this means.

1611 COTGR., *Foncer*, to head a peece of Caske. **1641** S. SMITH *Herring-Busse Trade* 10 [He] then fills them up, and Heads up the Barrels. **1727** BRADLEY *Fam. Dict.* s.v. *Herrings*, In a fresh Barrel..close packed and headed up by a sworn Cooper. **1800** COLQUHOUN *Comm. Thames* ii. 59 To open and again head-up the casks. **1833** *Fraser's Mag.* VIII. 57, I was going to pack my most valuable seeds, and head them up in flour-barrels.

c. To form or constitute the head or top of.

1637 DAVENANT *Brit. Triumph.* Dram. Wks. 1872 II. 279 His hook was such as heads the end of pole. **1686** PLOT *Staffordsh.* 389 The Mangers were..so placed that the range of them headed the end of the barn. **1870** MRS. GATTY *Parables fr. Nat.* Ser. v. (1871) 67 Carved oaken finials headed the divisions of the open sittings.

4. a. To furnish with a heading or head-line; to place a title, name, etc. at the head of. **b.** To stand at the head or form the heading of (a page, list, etc.). See also HEADED 6.

1832 TENNYSON *Dream Fair W.* 201 Heaven heads the count of crimes With that wild oath. **1844** *Hawkstone* (1846) I. iii. 34 Mr. Lomax very liberally headed it [a subscription-list] with two pounds. **1877** 'H. A. PAGE' *De Quincey* II. xviii. 80 We have so headed this chapter. **1885** *Manch. Exam.* 13 July 5/2 At the last general election Mr. L. headed the poll with 4,159 votes.

5. *to head a trick* (at cards): to play a card of a higher value.

1863 PARDON *Hoyle's Games* 130 (All Fours) It is not incumbent on the player to head the trick with one of the same suit or a trump.

6. *intr.* To form a head; to come or grow to a head. Also with *out*, *up*.

c **1420** *Pallad. on Husb.* XI. 156 Now leek, ysowe in veer, transplaunted be That hit may hede. **1577** B. GOOGE *Heresbach's Husb.* II. (1586) 60 b, If you will not have it [onion] seede but head, plucke off the blade still close by the ground. **1606** MARSTON *Fawne* II. i, I charge you check Your appetite and passions to our daughter, Before it head. **1768** G. WASHINGTON *Writ.* (1889) II. 242 All my early wheat..was headed and heading. **1864** LOWELL *Fireside Trav.* 289 The crop of early muscle that heads out under the forcing-glass of the gymnasium. **1872** O. W. HOLMES *Poet Breakf.-t.* i. (1885) 23 Cabbages would not head.

7. Of a stream: To have its head or source, to take its rise, to rise. Chiefly *U.S.*

1762 J. BARTRAM in Darlington *Mem.* (1849) 423, I believe Haw River..heads in the high hills on the south side of the bottom. **1814** BRACKENRIDGE *Jrnl.* in *Views Louisiana* 220 The Kansas, a very large river..heads between the Platte and the Arkansas. **1881** *Academy* 21 May 366/1 The upper waters of the Cubango, the great artery which heads..in the highlands of Bihé..and dies of drought in the Ngami Lake. **1887** R. MURRAY *Geol. Victoria* 9 [These rivers] head from a range which forms the divide between their waters and those of the Morwell.

8. *trans.* (with *up*): To collect (water) so as to form a head. Also *fig.*

1829 I. TAYLOR *Enthus.* x. 281 The means of diffusing religious knowledge long..accumulated and headed up above the level of the plains of China. **1867** SMYTH *Sailor's Work-bk., Heading up the land water*, when the flood-tide is backed by a wind, so that the ebb is retarded, causing an overflow.

III. To be at the head, to lead.

9. *trans.* To be the head, chief, captain, or ruler of; to be or put oneself at the head of. Also with *up*. Chiefly *N. Amer.*

a **1400** *Minor Poems fr. Vernon MS.* (E.E.T.S.) liii. 188 Hir herte holliche on him þat þe heuene hedes. **1669** DRYDEN *Tyrannic Love* II. i, They head those holy factions which they hate. **1696** PRIOR *To the King* 73 Heading his troops, and foremost in the fight. **1727** POPE, etc. *Art of Sinking* 96, I in person will my people head. **1864** BRYCE *Holy Rom. Emp.* xvii. (1875) 303 The reforming party in the church, headed by Gerson. **1959** E. LIPSKY *Scientists* 178 Bronco and I feel you're the logical one to head up the committee. **1968** *Globe & Mail* (Toronto) 17 Feb. B7 (Advt.), Company..requires capable and professional person..to head up real estate department. **1971** *Daily Tel.* 21 Oct. 10 (Advt.), We need women who can head up the book department of several of our branches throughout England and Wales.

10. To go in front or at the head of; to lead; to go before, precede; *fig.* to surpass, outdo, excel.

1711 BUDGELL *Spect.* No. 116 ¶7 The old Dogs, which had hitherto lain behind, now headed the Pack. *a* **1763** SHENSTONE *Ess.* (1765) 14 Some find their account in heading a cry of hounds. **1884** *Manch. Exam.* 8 Apr. 4/7 The Cambridge crew..took the lead from the first, were never headed, and won by upwards of three lengths. *Ibid.* 11 June 5/2 [He] has headed all the records of mountaineering by a long stretch.

IV. To direct the head, advance, face, etc.

11. a. *intr.* To direct the head or front in a specified direction; to face, front.

1610 W. FOLKINGHAM *Art of Survey* II. ii. 49 Confrontage Actiue may enter the Plot with these or the like Epithetons, Abutting, Heading, facing, fronting..etc. Or Passiue headed, faced, etc. **1850** SCORESBY *Whaleman's Adv.* iii. (1859) 34 Sing out when we head right! **1880** C. C. ADLEY *Rep. Pioneer Mining Co., Lim.* 2 Oct. 1 Two strong veins..heading on in the direction of the main lode. **1897** tr. *Nansen's Farthest North* II. 566 The Fram lay moored..with her bow heading west.

b. To have an upward inclination or slope: opp. to *dip*.

1802 PLAYFAIR *Illustr. Hutton. Th.* 409 The secondary strata..are not horizontal, but rise or head towards the west, dipping towards the east.

c. *trans.* To cause to take a specified direction.

1610 [see 11].

d. To point towards with the head, to face.

1887 FLORENCE MARRYAT *Driven to Bay* III. viii. 126 The ..ship..drifted along idly, with her nose heading every point except the one she was wanted to follow.

12. *intr.* **a.** To move forward or advance towards (a particular point); to shape one's course in a specified direction; to make *for*. (Especially of a ship.) Also *fig.*

1835 WILLIS *Pencillings* I. xxiv. 167 We head for Venice. **1840** R. H. DANA *Bef. Mast* iv. 7 We saw a small, clipper-built brig..heading directly after us. **1887** SIR R. H. ROBERTS *In the Shires* ii. 23 Out [the fox]..comes, heading down the field for the main road. **1884** *Harper's Mag.* Dec. 96/2 Wagons were coming into view, heading for the court-house. **1903** G. B. SHAW *Man & Superman* II. 56, I rather think Rhoda is heading for a row with Ann. **1922** H. CRANE *Let.* 7 Nov. (1965) 104 Matty's trans[lations] from Soupault in the last *Broom* are undoubtedly clever, but I don't see how he can rave so... Where is he headed for, anyway?

†**b.** *to head it*: to make head, advance; cf. 13.

1684 BUNYAN *Pilgr.* II. 137 That which heads it against the greatest opposition, gives best Demonstration that it is strongest.

c. *trans.* To direct the course of.

1885 *Manch. Exam.* 16 Feb. 4/7 The vessel was then headed for Brodick. **1888** B. W. RICHARDSON *Son of a Star* III. xi. 200 Joshua heads his troops towards Caesarea Philippi.

13. *trans.* **a.** To move forward so as to meet; to advance directly against, or in opposition to the course of; to face, front, oppose; to attack in front.

1681 TATE in *Dryden's Abs. & Achit.* II. 597 At once contending with the waves and fire, And heading danger in the wars of Tyre. **1769** FALCONER *Dict. Marine* (1789), *Franchir la lame*, to head the sea; to sail against the setting of the sea. *Ibid.* E ee ij b, The wind heads us, or takes us a-head. **1877** CLERY *Min. Tact.* v. 63 Headed and attacked in flank. **1881** MISS BRADDON *Asph.* III. 34 In a district where he has to cover his face with a muffler, and head the driving snow.

b. To get ahead of so as to turn back or aside; now often with *back*, *off*; also *fig.*

1716 B. CHURCH *Hist. Philip's War* (1865) I. 133 Concluding that if they headed him and beat him back, that he would take back in his own Track. **1812** *Sporting Mag.* XXXIX. 232 The fox being repeatedly headed, the hounds ran into him. **1822** SCOTT *Fam. Lett.* 6 Mar. (1894) II. xviii. 136 The Bavarian General..tried to head back Bony in his retreat from Leipsic. **1841** J. F. COOPER *Deerslayer* v. 29 But 'head him off', as you say of the deer. **1891** R. H. SAVAGE *My Offic. Wife* iii. 35 To head my rival off I indulged in a tremendous flirtation. **1893** SELOUS *Trav. S.E. Africa* 75, I saw that I must head my eland before she crossed the valley.

c. *N.Z.* (See quot. 1933.)

1933 L. G. D. ACLAND in *Press* (Christchurch, N.Z.) 28 Oct. 15/7 A dog goes round to the far side of a mob of sheep and stops them. This is called heading... The owner would also say 'I can head with him'. **1934** J. LILICO *Sheep Dog Mem.* 27 [The dogs] would head, lead, huntaway, force and back, though, of course, they were best at rouseabout work. **1947** P. NEWTON *Wayleggo* (1949) v. 52 This dog would 'head a nor'wester'.

14. To go round the head of (a stream or lake).

a **1657** BRADFORD *Plymouth Plant.* x. 81 They..headed a great creake. **1766** J. BARTRAM *Jrnl.* 12 Jan. in Stork *Acc. E. Florida* 33 Soon came to a little lake which we headed. **1866** HUXLEY *Lay Serm.* (1870) i. 14 It is shorter to cross a stream than to head it.

V. 15. *trans.* To strike or drive with the head.

1784 *Laura & Aug.* II. 29 Old Crabtree..headed and handled the door so dexterously, that he sprained his collar-bone. **1887** [see HEADING *vbl. sb.* 5]. **1897** ROSEBERY in *Westm. Gaz.* 12 Apr. 4/1 The way in which the [football] players headed the ball.

-head (hɛd), *suffix*, later form of ME. **hêde, hêd**, found already in 12th c., but not known in OE., though pointing etymologically to an OE. **-hǣdu*, *-o* (obl. cases *-hǣde*) fem., beside OE. *-hád* masc., corresp. to OHG. *-heit* masc. and fem.

This suffix was orig. an independent subst. (OTeut. **haidu-z* masc. in Goth. *haidus* m., manner, way (see HAD *sb.*, HEDE), which, after coming to be used only in comb., was practically only a suffix of condition or quality. In its primary use, *-hede* appears to have been appropriate to adjs. as *boldhede, biterhede, drunkenhede, fairhede, falshede*, etc., but it was soon extended to sbs., as in *knyghthede, manhede, maydenhede, wommanhede* (all in Chaucer), being thus used indiscriminately with *-hôd* (*-hode, -hood*) from OE. *-hád*. In Cursor M. *fadirhede, faderhade, preistes hede, pristis hade*, occur as MS. variants. This led the way finally to the obsolescence of *-hede, -head*, and the substitution, even in adjs., of *-hood*, as in mod. *falsehood, likelihood*, etc. One or two special forms in *-head*, e.g. *godhead, maidenhead* (distinguished from *godhood, maidenhood*), only remain. In Scotch, on the contrary, *-hede, -heid*, remained the current form, but is now more or less obsolescent. See also HAD *sb.*, HEDE *sb.*, and -HOOD.

headache (ˈhɛdeɪk). Forms: see HEAD *sb.*[1] and ACHE *sb.* Also 5–8 **-ake**, 7–9 **-ach**.

1. a. An ache or continuous pain, more or less deep-seated, in the cranial region of the head.

c **1000** *Sax. Leechd.* II. 20 Wiþ heafod ece hundes heafod ȝebærn to ahsan..leȝe on. *a* **1225** *Ancr. R.* 370 Ase þauh heo were betere to þolien golnesse brune þen heaued eche. **1398** TREVISA *Barth De P.R.* v. ii. (1495) 104 Also heed ache cometh of grete fastinge and abstynences. **1581** SIDNEY *Apol. Poetrie* (Arb.) 44 How many head-aches a passionate life bringeth vs to. **1653** BAXTER *Chr. Concord* 119, I like not him that will cure the Headach by cutting the Throat. **1779** FORREST *Voy. N. Guinea* 154 Having a severe head-ake. **1779–81** JOHNSON *L.P., Pope* Wks. IV. 90 His most frequent assailant was the headach. **1845** DARWIN *Voy. Nat.* vii. (1879) 128, I was confined..to my bed by a headach. *a* **1861** MRS. BROWNING *Ld. Walter's Wife* vii, Will you vow to be safe from the headache on Tuesday? **1884** OUIDA *P'cess Napraxine* i. (1886) 5 No doubt, it is utterly wrong, and would give [him] a sick headache.

b. Phr. ***to be no more use than*** (or ***as good as***) ***a*** (***sick***) ***headache***: said of something quite useless. *colloq.*

1915 D. O. BARNETT *Lett.* 153 Shrapnel is for defenders, to stop an advance of infantry, but no more use against prepared positions than a sick headache. **1927** D. L. SAYERS *Unnatural Death* I. v. 50 That woman..was no more use than a headache—to use my brother's rather vigorous expression. **1931** W. HOLTBY *Poor Caroline* vi. 225 The Tona Perfecta's no more use to any company today than a sick headache. **1963** *Guardian* 3 Dec. 5/5 The car's contract of sale gives no undertaking or guarantee except the usual one—and that is as good as a sick headache.

c. A troublesome or annoying problem. *colloq.* (orig. *U.S.*).

1934 M. WESEEN *Dict. Amer. Slang* 347 Headache, anxiety; worry. **1937** *Punch* 1 Dec. 610/1 My headache is this—the Big Guy, my boss, won't go to the movies and see for himself what a newspaper girl can do. **1939** G. B. GILBERT *Forty Years a Country Preacher* 77 The new rectory was both beautiful and expensive, but it proved to be a great headache. **1942** 'H. HABE' *Thousand shall Fall* ix. 181, I asked him how we were expected to transport all these goods. He shrugged his shoulders. 'That's your headache!' **1945** *Times* 11 Jan. 2/4 Commander Bower continued: 'The biggest headache of all is undoubtedly Poland.' **1952** N. STREATFEILD *Aunt Clara* 251 They're my headache, not yours. **1968** *New Scientist* 25 Jan. 205/1 The single-celled organism *Euglena* is rather a headache for those who would like to divide living things neatly into plants and animals.

2. A rustic name for the wild poppy (*Papaver Rhœas*), from the effect of its odour.

a **1825** FORBY *Voc. E. Anglia*, *Head-ache*, the wild field-poppy. Any one, by smelling it for a very short time, may convince himself of the propriety of the name. **1827** CLARE *Sheph. Cal.* 47 Corn-poppies..Call'd 'Head-achs' from their sickly smell. *Mod.* (*Northampton*), The barley field is red with head-aches.

3. *Comb.* **headache-tree**, a verbenaceous shrub, *Premna integrifolia*, found in the East Indies and Madagascar, the leaves of which are used to cure headache (*Treas. Bot.* 1866); **headache-weed**, a shrub, *Hedyosmum nutans* (N.O. *Chloranthaceæ*), found in the West Indies (Miller *Plant-n.*, 1884).

So **head-aching** *sb.*, aching of the head, = HEADACHE 1; *adj.*, causing headache.

1679–80 MARLBOROUGH in Wolseley *Life* (1894) I. 228, I never had so long a fit of headaching. **1824** LADY GRANVILLE *Lett.* (1894) I. 259 She, an excellent, head-aching woman. **1860** GEO. ELIOT in *Life* (1885) II. 155 Written in six weeks, even with headaching interruptions.

headachy (ˈhɛdeɪkɪ), *a.* [f. HEADACHE + -Y.]

1. Suffering from or subject to headache.

1795 LADY NEWDIGATE *Let.* Aug. in A. E. Newdigate-Newdegate *Cheverels* (1898) xi. 154 Want of sleep..makes me feel Languid & headachy in a Morning. **1813** JANE AUSTEN *Let.* 29 Jan. (1952) 298, I was rather headachey that day & could not venture on anything sweet except jelly. **1833** HT. MARTINEAU *Briery Creek* vi. 136 Mrs. Temple

arose, head-achy and feverish. *a* **1834** LAMB *Final Mem.* I. To Coleridge, From your afflicted, headachey, sore-throatey, humble servant. **1897** MARY KINGSLEY *W. Africa* 234, I go, dead tired and still head-achy..with my host.

2. Accompanied with or producing headache.

1828 LADY GRANVILLE *Lett.* (1894) II. 26 The consequence..is the heavy headachy *accablement.* **1862** RAWLINSON *Anc. Mon.* I. 44 The wine, 'sweet but headachy'.

Hence **headachiness**.

1862 GEO. ELIOT *Let.* 1 May (1956) IV. 28 In a moment of feverish headachiness I transgressed my own rule. **1872** —— in *Life* (1885) III. 149 Dragged back into headachiness by a little too much fatigue.

headage ('hɛdɪdʒ). [f. HEAD *sb.*[1] 7c + -AGE.] The number of animals; = HEAD[1] *sb.* 7c. Also *attrib.*

1957 *Liverpool Daily Post* 30 Jan. 5/9 Abbey-Cwm-Hir.. Fox Destruction Society have decided to pay headage money on rabbits and carrion crows, as well as foxes, that are killed in the society's area. **1960** *Farmer & Stockbreeder* 5 Jan. 91/1 A headage price [for a steer] of 22,356 dollars. **1962** *Times* (Agric. Suppl.) 3 July p. ii/3 Winter reserves of fodder to carry a greatly increased headage of stock. **1972** *Guardian* 30 Dec. 4/7 'Headage' subsidies for sheep flocks are ruled out by the EEC commission.

headband ('hɛdbænd).

1. a. A band worn round the head, a fillet.

1535 COVERDALE *Isa.* iii. 20 Headbandes, rynges and garlandes. **1677** *Govt. Venice* 120 Coyfe of white Linnen.. like the Headband which the Conservators of their Laws wore at Athens during their Office. **1725** BRADLEY *Fam. Dict.* s.v. *Sleeping*, To promote Sleep, take common Roses with the white of an Egg well beaten..and make an Headband or Fillet of it. **1853** HICKIE tr. *Aristoph.* (1872) II. 547 Let me wear the head-band as conqueror.

b. tr. L. *capistrum* a halter. (Cf. FILLET 1 c.)

1782 ELPHINSTON tr. *Martial* I. civ. 77 A beast, like Calydon's of yore, Boasts headbands never bristler wore.

c. The band connecting a pair of receivers or ear-phones.

1913 *Work* 17 May 145/3 Double Receivers, with adjustable head-band. **1962** A. NISBETT *Technique Sound Studio* 256 *Headphones*, a pair of electro-acoustic transducers..held to the ears by a headband.

2. A band round the top of trousers or drawers.

1818 SCOTT *Hrt. Midl.* xxviii, Giving the head-band of his breeches a..hoist with one hand. **1834** M. SCOTT *Cruise Midge* x. (1863) 180 The iron-hook was..passed through the head-band of his nether garment.

3. *Bookbinding.* An ornamental band or fillet (usually of silk or cotton) fastened to the inner back of a bound book at the head and tail; also, the material of which this is made.

1611 COTGR., *Trenchefile*, the head-band of a booke. **1727–51** CHAMBERS *Cycl.* s.v. *Book-binding*, The headband ..is an ornament of silk of several colours..placed at each extreme of the back, across the leaves. **1817** DIBDIN *Bibl. Decameron* II. 526 His great error lay in double head-bands, and brown-paper linings. **1892** ZAEHNSDORF *Binding of Bk.* 11 In cheap work this headband, bought by the yard, is fastened on by glue..In early times this headband was twisted as the book was sewn, and..laced into the wooden boards.

4. *Arch.* The band of mouldings on the inner contour of an arch; = ARCHIVOLT.

1723 CHAMBERS tr. *Le Clerc's Treat. Archit.* I. 57 The Archivolte or Head-Band.

5. *Printing.* **a.** A thin slip of iron forming the top of the tympan of a printing-press. **b.** A printed or engraved band of decoration at the head of a page or chapter. (*U.S.*)

1841 SAVAGE *Dict. Print.* 310. **1845** *Encycl. Metrop.* VIII. 774/2 These tympans are light square frames covered with parchment. They consist of three slips of thin wood with a *headband* or top slip of thin iron.

Hence **'headbander**, the person who fastens on the headbands of books; **'headbanding**, the process of fastening these; also *concr.* the headband.

1707 *Phil. Trans.* XXV. 2401 Bookbinding shall be handled in all its Parts..Folding, Sewing, Headbanding. **1873** SPON *Workshop Rec.* (1875) 396 *Headbanding*, there are two kinds, stuck on and worked. **1892** ZAEHNSDORF *Binding of Bk.* 11 Headbanding next follows, and is the work of women, it is the silk or cotton finish at the edges, head and tail. *Ibid.* 18 *Headbander*, the person who works the fine silk or cotton ornament at head or tail of the book.

head-block ('hɛdblɒk).

†**1.** A log put at the back of the chimney to keep the fire in by night: cf. *head-brand* in HEAD *sb.*[1] 74.

1642 FULLER *Holy & Prof. St.* v. xix. 439 These Netherlands being like the head-block in the chimney, where the fire of warre is alwayes kept in (though out every where else).

2. In a saw-mill: The device for holding the log upon the carriage, while it is sawn.

1864 WEBSTER, *Head-block* (*Saw-mill*), the movable cross-piece of a carriage on which the log rests. **1878** *Sci. Amer.* XXXVIII. 291 An improved head block..for saw mills.

3. The piece which connects the wheel-plate or 'fifth wheel' of a carriage with the fore-body.

1875 in KNIGHT *Dict. Mech.* **1884** *Ibid.* Suppl., *Head Block Plate* (*Carriage*), an iron resting on the fore-axle and supporting the head block.

4. (See quot. 1905.)

1853 *Trans. Mich. Agric. Soc.* IV. 35 G. S. Snyder, Lancaster O. improved head block for setting logs on saw mills. **1905** *Terms Forestry & Logging* 39 *Head block*, the log placed under the front end of the skids in a skid-way to raise them to the desired height.

head-board ('hɛdbɔəd).

1. A board at the head or upper end of anything, as a bedstead, a grave, etc.

1730 SOUTHALL *Bugs* 34 Deal Head-Boards..avoid. **1869** R. B. SMYTH *Goldf. Victoria* Gloss., *Head-Board*, a wedge of wood, or part of a slab, placed against the hanging-board. **1895** HOFFMAN *Beginn. Writing* v. 65 The head-board, erected to the memory of a woman, has displayed upon it various articles used by her in life. **1897** MARY KINGSLEY *W. Africa* 412 A big wooden bedstead of the native type—a wooden bench without sides, but with a head- and foot-board.

2. *Naut.* (*pl.*) 'The berthing or close-boarding between the head-rails' (Smyth *Sailor's Word-bk.*).

headborough ('hɛd,bʌrə). Forms: 5 -borwe, 5–7 -borow, 6–7 -borowe, -boroughe, 7 -burrowe, -burrough, 8 -bourg, 6– -borough.

Originally, the head of a *friðborh*, tithing, or frank-pledge (see BORROW *sb.* 3); afterwards a parish officer identical in functions with the petty constable; = BORROWHEAD, BORSHOLDER, TITHINGMAN.

c **1440** *Promp. Parv.* 231/2 Heed borow (*K.*, *H.* hedborwe), *plegius capitalis.* *c* **1515** *Cocke Lorell's B.* (Percy Soc.) 10 Constables, hede borowes, and kâters. **1536** *Act 28 Hen. VIII*, c. 10 Euery..counstable, hedborowe, thyrdboroughe, borsolder, and euery other lay officer. **1596** SHAKS. *Tam. Shr.* Induct. i. 11, I must go fetch the Headborough. *Beg.* Third, or fourth, or fift Borough, Ile answere him by Law. **1642** ROGERS *Naaman* 228 Oh! yee Headburrowes, and Officers of Townes, let this truth of God convince yee. **1722** DE FOE *Plague* (1884) 301 There died six and forty Constables and Headboroughs. **1766** ENTICK *London* IV. 389 The officers stand thus; 6 church-wardens..3 headboroughs. **1855** MACAULAY *Hist. Eng.* xi. III. 11 The Whig theory is..that the right of a king is divine in no other sense than that in which the right of a..judge, of a juryman, of a mayor, of a headborough, is divine.

b. *transf.* An official holding a similar position in foreign countries.

1555 W. WATREMAN *Fardle Facions* I. iv. 47 The headborough of the Citie (whom we call the Mayour). **1598** HAKLUYT *Voy.* I. 152 Two other headboroughs, one of Dantzick, and the other of Elburg. **1843** BORROW *Bible in Spain* xlix. (1872) 283, I was visited by various alguazils, accompanied by a kind of headborough who made a small seizure of Testaments and Gypsy Gospels.

head-chief. *U.S.* [HEAD *sb.*[1] 71.] The paramount chief of an Indian tribe.

1806 J. ORDWAY in *Jrnls. Lewis & O.* (1916) 355 The head chief..informed us that the most of our horses and pack Saddles were Safe. **1837** R. M. BIRD *Nick of Woods* I. 236 From the head-chief to the commoner. **1881** *Harper's Mag.* Apr. 670/2 White Eagle, head-chief of the Poncas. *a* **1918** G. STUART *40 Yrs. on Frontier* (1925) I. 96 The head chief proposed to meet the interpreter unarmed and talk with him.

head-cloth ('hɛdklɒθ, -ɔː-). [See CLOTH *sb.* 1.]

1. A cloth or covering for the head; in *pl.* the pieces composing a head-dress.

a **1000** *Voc.* in Wr.-Wülcker 199/13 *Capitale*, heafodclaþ, *uel* wangere. *a* **1225** *Ancr. R.* 424 Hore heued cloð sitte lowe. **1552** *Inv. Ch. Goods Surrey* 46 Item iiij or HED-CLOTHES. **1653** H. MORE *Antid. Ath.* III. vii. (1712) 106 The Spirit.. stuck two pins in the Maid's head cloaths, and bid her keep them. **1707** MRS. CENTLIVRE *Platon. Lady* III. Wks. 1760 II. 214 Head-cloaths to shorten the Face, Favourites to raise the Forehead. **1741** RICHARDSON *Pamela* (1811) I. 12 (D.) Two suits of fine Flanders laced head-clothes. **1886** W. J. TUCKER *E. Europe* 426 A..bodice of coloured prints with a cotton head-cloth to match.

2. A piece of cloth at the head of a bed.

1730 SOUTHALL *Bugs* 34 Head-Cloths lined with Deal, or Rails of that Wood.

3. 'A canvas screen for the head of a ship' (*Cent. Dict.*).

head-court. *Hist.* A chief court (of justice); *spec.* in Scotland, a court or meeting of the freeholders of a county, anciently held thrice a year, in later times once a year; now obsolete.

This court was for some time, under an act of 1681 and Act 16 Geo. II, c. 11, used as a court for the registration of county voters, a function which it ceased to have after the Reform Act of 1832.

1545 BRINKLOW *Compl.* 22 Gret and wayghty matters, which may be brought to one head court of the reame. **1609** SKENE *Reg. Maj.* 55 Advocat to the kings heid court. **1748** *Act 20 Geo. II*, c. 50 §18 Whereas the ancient usage of the vassals of the king and other subject superiors, being obliged to give suit and presence, or to appear at head courts at certain times of the year, has of a long time been useless. **1773** ERSKINE *Inst. Law Scotl.* I. iv. §5 All freeholders were bound to attend the three head-courts which were held by the Sheriff yearly. **1820** SCOTT *Monast.* Introd. Ep., The laird..had to attend trustee meetings, and lieutenancy meetings, and head-courts.

head-dress ('hɛddrɛs). Any dress or covering for the head; *esp.* an ornamental attire for the head worn by women.

1703 *Lond. Gaz.* No. 3743/4 Lost..a Deal Box..having in it..three Head-Dresses. **1773** MRS. CHAPONE *Improv. Mind* (1774) II. 111 As ridiculous as an old woman with a head-dress of flowers. **1877** M. M. GRANT *Sun-Maid* vii, It is the old national head-dress of the women of Russia.

transf. **1712** ADDISON *Spect.* No. 265 §3 Among Birds.. the Male..very often appears in a most beautiful Head-dress; whether it be a Crest, a Comb, a Tuft of Feathers, or a natural little Plume.

'head-dresser. = HAIRDRESSER. Also, one who makes head-dresses (*obs.*).

1727 DEFOE *Compl. Eng. Tradesman* II. II. v. 166 Now we see..the Millenary Trade separated into innumerable little Commode Shops, Head Dressers and such like People. **1859** TROLLOPE *Bertrams* ix. 81 No stray jagged ends would show themselves if by chance she removed her bonnet, nor did it even look as though it..required to be afresh puffed out by some head-dresser's mechanism. **1927** *Daily Tel.* 24 May 17/3 The 'head-dressers' shops are nests of decoy birds.

†**head-dressing.** *Obs.* The dressing or attiring of the head; *concr.* a head-dress.

1568 in *Antiq. Rep.* (1808) II. 394 She hathe a new Devyce of Heade dressyng. **1678** *Lond. Gaz.* No. 1325/4 A laced Apron, a laced Head-dressing.

headed ('hɛdɪd), *a.* and *pa. pple.* [f. HEAD *sb.*[1] and *v.* + -ED.]

1. Having a head (of a specified kind). **b.** Of a stag: Having a 'head' of horns.

c **1374** [See HEAD *v.* 3.] **1399** LANGL. *Rich. Redeles* II. 11 þe seson was paste For hertis y-heedid so hy and so noble. **1579–80** NORTH *Plutarch* 133 (R.) Schinocephalos, as much as to say, headed like an onion. **1607** TOPSELL *Four-f. Beasts* (1658) 249 Setting their horses in a double front, so as they appeared headed both wayes. **1670** NARBOROUGH *Jrnl.* in *Acc. Sev. late Voy.* I. (1694) 59 They are..headed and beaked like a Crow. **1876** JAS. GRANT *One of the 600* ix. 75 Headed like a snake.

c. Frequent in parasynthetic combinations, as ***bare-headed***, ***clear-headed***, ***light-headed***, ***many-headed***, etc., q.v. under the first element.

c **1386** CHAUCER *Wife's Prol.* 645 He..hire forsok for terme of al his lyf Noght but for open-heueded he hir say Lokynge out at his dore vpon a day. **1553** EDEN *Treat. Newe Ind.* (Arb.) 15 They are all naked..and go beare headed. **1863** E. V. NEALE *Anal. Th. & Nat.* 16 Clearest headed thinkers.

2. Of things: Furnished with a head; tipped, as an arrow, etc. (Often as pple., const. *with.*)

c **1450** HENRYSON *Test. Cress.* 168 Flanis fedderit with yse, and heidit with hail-stanis. *c* **1470** HENRY *Wallace* x. 853 With speris hedyt weill. **1624** T. SCOTT *Vox Dei* To Rdr. 5 All the arrowes they shoote..are both headed and feathered. **1670** NARBOROUGH *Jrnl.* in *Acc. Sev. Late Voy.* I. (1711) 98 A Cane..headed with Silver. **1830** TENNYSON *Poet* iii, The viewless arrows of his thoughts were headed And wing'd with flame.

3. Of a plant: Having a head, grown to a head.

1577 B. GOOGE *Heresbach's Husb.* II. (1586) 60 The headed, or sette Leeke. **1641** BEST *Farm. Bks.* (Surtees) 51 Good chinnell-oates, that are large and well headed. **1753** CHAMBERS *Cycl. Supp.* s.v. *Brassica*, The headed cabbage. **1822** J. FLINT *Lett. Amer.* 227 Oats, at that time, were headed out and luxuriant.

4. That has come to a head or matured, as a boil.

1600 SHAKS. *A.Y.L.* II. vii. 67 All th' imbossed sores, and headed euils.

†**5.** Of flints: = Faced: see FACE *v.* 14.

1671 EVELYN *Diary* 17 Oct., Buildings of flints so exquisitely headed and squared. **1717** TABOR in *Phil. Trans.* XXX. 554 A very firm..Wall, made of Roman Brick, squar'd Stone and headed Flint. *Ibid.*, Pitch'd with small Flint and Stones, Pointed at their lower ends, and Headed at their upper ends.

6. Furnished with a heading, written or printed. (Usually as pple., followed by *with*, or simply by the word or words which constitute the heading.)

1838 GLADSTONE *State in Rel. Ch.* vii. §30 (L.) Prayers.. headed with the promise that such and such religious advantages shall be given to all who devoutly recite them. **1838** DE MORGAN *Ess. Probab.* 69 A column headed t. **1884** *L'pool Mercury* 18 Feb. 5/6 The following five-lined whip, headed 'Most important', has been issued to members of the Opposition. **1894** *Daily News* 9 Apr. 2/7 A letter on the headed notepaper of a firm in New Bond-street.

header ('hɛdə(r)). Forms: 5 **hevedare, hefdare, heder(e, -are, 6 heeder, 7 (9) headder, 6– header.** [f. HEAD *v.* and *sb.*[1] + -ER[1].]

1. One who or that which removes the head. †**a.** One who beheads; a headsman, executioner.

1432–50 tr. *Higden* (Rolls) V. 113 Alban..conuertede his heder in to the feithe of Christ. *c* **1440** *Promp. Parv.* 231/2 Hedare, or hefdare..*decapitator.* **1519** HORMAN *Vulg.* 136 An hangeman or an heeder is odiose to loke vpon.

b. One who removes the heads of fish; also, a machine used for this purpose.

1623 WHITBOURNE *Newfoundland* 82 Skilfull headders, and splitters of fish. **1809** *Naval Chron.* XXI. 21 The headder cuts open the fish, tears up its entrails, and..breaks off its head.

c. A kind of reaping-machine which cuts off only the heads of the grain; also, a machine for gathering the heads of clover for the seed.

1874 KNIGHT *Dict. Mech.*, *Clover-seed Harvester*,..it is known as a header. **1883** *Harper's Mag.* Aug. 389/1 Here are ..no 'headers' devouring fields and delivering sacks of clean grain. **1884** *Ibid.* Sept. 503/1 The use of 'headers' rather than the ordinary mowers and reapers.

2. a. One who puts a head on something, e.g. casks, nails, pins, etc. **b.** An apparatus for shaping the mouth end of a cigar.

1755 JOHNSON, *Header*, one that heads nails or pins, or the like. **1858** SIMMONDS *Dict. Trade, Header*, a cooper who closes casks. **1870** *Eng. Mech.* Mar. 599/1 A 'header'.. shapes the head or mouth end of the cigar.

†3. One who makes head against or resists something; an opponent. *Obs. rare.*

1537 HILSEY in Strype *Eccl. Mem.* (1721) I. App. lxxxviii. 232 The headers of that truth that God techyth cannot escape just judgment.

4. a. One who heads or leads a party, etc.; a leader. *rare.*

1818 TODD, *Header*..2, one who heads a mob or party. **1882** W. B. WEEDEN *Soc. Law Labor* 94 The header, captain, intertaker..must conduct the operation.

b. 'A ship's mate or other officer in charge of a whale-boat; a boat-header' (*Cent. Dict.*).

c. = *heading dog* (HEADING *vbl. sb.* 4b). *N.Z.*

1938 R. M. BURDON *High Country* x. 107 Dogs are usually kept in the proportion of three or four huntaways to one header now. **1958** *Landfall* XII. 17 Watching him work the new sheep dog, I see the taut thread of his whistle run from his mouth to the pricked quivering ears of the header. **1973** *Times* 13 Oct. 14/4 Early British sheep dogs were less versatile, They were divided into those which fetched the sheep and those which drove them away, as still occurs in New Zealand with header and hunt-away.

5. a. *Building.* A brick, or stone, laid with its head or end in the face of the wall; opp. to *stretcher*, which is laid lengthwise. Also applied to sods, etc., similarly placed in fortification.

1688 R. HOLME *Armoury* 261 *Header*, is the laying the end of a Brick in the outside of a wall. **1700** MOXON *Mech. Exerc.* 36 The Header half the length of the Stretcher. **1725** W. HALFPENNY *Sound Building* 51 The Course..consists of two Streachers and one Header. **1793** SMEATON *Edystone L.* §82 The tail of the header was made to..bond with the interior parts. **1851** J. S. MACAULAY *Field Fortif.* 63 The third kind of revetment..made with sods of unequal sizes, called headers and stretchers. **1884** *Milit. Engin.* I. II. 73 Making good the interval between parapet and gabions with filled sandbags, header, and stretcher.

b. A top layer. *U.S.*

1867 *Trans. Ill. Agric. Soc.* VI. 641 Prime Pork—Shall be packed with a header of side cuts, the regular width, three half heads.

c. *Engin.* (See quot. 1940.)

1930 *Engineering* 25 July 121/1 They contain four headers, which are turned from solid mild-steel forgings. **1940** *Chambers's Techn. Dict.* 406/2 *Header*, a box or manifold supplying fluid to a number of tubes or passages, or connecting them in parallel. **1958** W. HRYNISZAK *Heat Exchangers* vii. 132 The function of the headers is either to distribute the gas over the matrix (inlet header), or to collect it from the matrix (outlet header) with the minimum possible loss of pressure not used for heat transfer purposes.

d. *Hedging.* (See quot.)

1941 *Archit. Rev.* LXXXIX. 85/2 The 'pleaches' too are rammed down, and when several yards are ready the two men work in the headers, which are slender and straight rods, twisted over and across, in and out of the stakes.

6. *Pugilism.* A blow on the head.

1818 *Sporting Mag.* II. 279 The latter almost instantly surprised Johnson with another header.

7. A plunge or dive head foremost. *colloq.*

1849 ALB. SMITH *Pottleton Leg.* 298 A 'header' from the bank through a thin coat of ice. **1859** W. H. GREGORY *Egypt* I. 276 Four blacks one after the other took a header into the boiling current. **1873** G. C. DAVIES *Mount. & Mere* xiv. 113 The delights of a header off a rock ten feet high, and an unknown depth of clear, cold water below.

transf. and *fig.* **1860** HUGHES *Tom Brown at Oxf.* (1870) II. iv. 59 Till we..take our final header out of this riddle of a world. **1870** H. MEADE *N. Zealand* 286 The mast..took a clear header overboard. **1891** *Spectator* 25 July, The world in general goes a header for the new system.

8. One who dives head foremost. *rare.*

1848 CLOUGH *Bothie* III. 20 There they bathed, of course, and Arthur, the glory of headers, Leapt from the ledges with Hope, he twenty feet, he thirty.

9. *Mining.* **a.** A collier or coal-cutter who drives a head (see HEAD *sb.*¹ 23).

1883 GRESLEY *Gloss. Coal-mining.*

b. = HEADING *vbl. sb.* 11.

1877 R. W. RAYMOND *Statistics of Mines* 165 The header had reached..a length of 12,259 feet.

10. *Needle Manuf.* A person who turns the needles all one way for drilling (*Cent. Dict.*).

11. *Association Football.* A ball which is headed. Also, one who heads the ball (see HEAD *v.* 15).

1906 L. V. LODGE in B. O. Corbett *Ann. Corinthian Football Club* 188 A back must be not only a good kick and sound tackler, but at the same time an accurate header. *Ibid.* 189 A really high-class header, by a skilful movement of the neck.., can move the ball a surprising distance. **1927** *Daily Express* 20 Apr. 13/2 Trotter gave the home club the lead with a beautiful header, following a free kick well taken by Leach. **1955** *Times* 13 Aug. 4/3 Yashin brought off a wonderful one-handed save to push out Wilshaw's header, which looked a certain goal. **1969** *Times* 8 Oct. 13/3 It was Marsh who came closest to scoring, when Kelly, using his left arm like a scythe, turned a header over the bar.

12. *attrib.* and *Comb.*: **header-board**, a diving-board; **header brick** = HEADER 5; so **heading brick**.

1913 E. F. BENSON *Thorley Weir* i, The nude figure of a boy on the header-board in the act of springing from it into the water. **1897** F. C. MOORE *How to build Home* vii. 110 A 'header' brick is one laid in the wall so that only its end shows. **1901** J. BLACK *Illustr. Carp. & Build., Scaffolding* 24 Cavities in the brickwork obtained by leaving out 'header' bricks at proper intervals. *Ibid.* 26 A 'heading' brick.

headfast ('hɛdfɑːst, -æ-), *sb. Naut.* Also 7 -fest. [f. HEAD *sb.*¹ + FAST *sb.*²] A rope or chain at the head of a vessel, to make her fast to a wharf, buoy, or other point.

c **1569** HAWKINS *3rd Voy.* (1878) 77 So leesing her hedfasts, and hayling away by the stearne fastes shee was gotten out. **1635** *Voy. Foxe & James to N.W.* (Hakluyt Soc.) I. 146 They cut the head-fest from the sterne of their ship. **1724** DE FOE *Tour Gt. Brit.* I. 98 The Ships ride here..with their Head-fasts on Shore. **1837** COLQUHOUN *Comp. Oarsman's Guide* 31 The *painter* is the rope attached to the stem to make fast by, and is otherwise called the *headfast*.
attrib. **1876** T. HARDY *Ethelberta* (1890) 349 A strong pull from a headfast rope might drag the erection completely over.

Hence **'headfast** *v. trans.*, to make fast with a headfast.

1889 *Daily News* 9 Nov. 6/4 The point in the river at which the barge may be headfasted.

head-foremost, headforemost, *adv. phr.* and *a.* **A.** *adv. phr.* See *head foremost*, s.v. HEAD *sb.*¹ 63. **B.** *adj.* Headlong, precipitate. *rare.*

1871 *Member for Paris* I. 180 That headforemost kind of rhetoric which capsizes a jury.

headful ('hɛdfʊl), *sb.* [f. HEAD *sb.*¹ + -FUL 2.] As much as the head contains or will hold.

1589 COGAN *Haven Health* (1636) 234 A headfull of vapours. **1633** FORD *'Tis Pity* I. ii, I'll undertake, with a handful of silver, to buy a headful of wit at any time. **1884** *Century Mag.* XXIX. 54 For all his headful of knowledge.

head-gear ('hɛdgɪə(r)).

1. That which is worn on the head; a hat, cap, bonnet, or head-dress of any kind.

1539 *Inv. R. Wardrobe* (1815) 53 (Jam.) Item, ten heid geiris of fedderis for hors. **1621** BURTON *Anat. Mel.* III. ii. III. iii, Glittering attires, counterfeit colours, headgears, curled hairs. **1729** SOMERVILLE *Ep. to Ramsay* 65 In her tartan plaid And all her richest headgear trimly clad. **1875** J. H. BENNET *Winter Medit.* I. iii. (ed. 5) 76 The peculiar headgear used in India as a protection against the sun. **1888** J. PAYN *Myst. Mirbridge* I. iii. 47 His headgear—a billy-cock-hat.

2. The parts of the harness about a horse's head.

1875 KNIGHT *Dict. Mech.*, *Head-gear*, the bridle of a horse. The head-stall and bit.

3. *Mining.* Apparatus at the head of a shaft. (See also quot. 1881.)

1841 *Collieries & Coal Trade* (ed. 2) 200 The erection of head-gear will depend much..upon the description of machinery to be employed. **1875** R. F. MARTIN tr. *Havrez Winding Mach.* 97 An iron head gear consisting of two vertical lattice girder legs and two struts. **1881** RAYMOND *Mining Gloss.*, *Head-gear*, that part of deep-boring apparatus which remains at the surface.

4. The rigging on the fore part of a vessel.

headgrow, dial. form of EDGROW.

†**'headhood.** *Obs. rare.* In 5 heedhode. [f. HEAD *sb.*¹ + -HOOD.] = HEADSHIP.

c **1449** PECOCK *Repr.* 439 If Crist wolde Petir or hise Successouris to stonde in Heedhode of al the chirche in Erthe.

headily ('hɛdɪlɪ), *adv.* [f. HEADY + -LY².] In a heady manner; headlong, precipitately, hastily, rashly; violently, impetuously; †eagerly.

c **1450** *Merlin* 119 Antor..met hym so hedlyche with a grete spere, that bothe the tymbir and stelen heede shewed thourgh his shuldre. **1565** GOLDING *Ovid's Met.* Epist. (1593) 10 A person sage and wise..who headily will nothing enterprise. **1683** R. GROVE *Perswas. Communion* 17 Why should we run so headily into opposite Parties? **1736** L. WELSTED *Scheme Provid.* iv. Wks. (1787) II. 454 The multitude..ran readily into mischief.

headiness ('hɛdɪnɪs). [f. as prec. + -NESS.] The quality or condition of being heady.

1. Rashness, hastiness, precipitancy; unruliness, self-will, obstinacy, headstrongness.

1475 *Bk. Noblesse* 79 Usid after his owne wilfulnesse and hedinesse and without counceile. **1579** SPENSER *Sheph. Cal.* Ded., Of witlesse headinesse in iudging, or of heedelesse hardinesse in condemning. **1768–74** TUCKER *Lt. Nat.* (1852) II. 414 The rationalist, who complains so loudly of the headiness and hastiness of zeal. **1865** W. G. PALGRAVE *Arabia* I. 85 Famous for headiness and the spirit of contradiction.

2. The quality of going to the head; intoxicating quality.

1603 HOLLAND *Plutarch's Mor.* 65 b, He was not able to beare his drinke nor resist the least headinesse and strength thereof. **1655** GURNALL *Chr. in Arm.* I. x. §2 (1669) 56/1 Water to dash this strong wine of joy, and take away its headiness.

heading ('hɛdɪŋ), *vbl. sb.* [-ING¹.]

I. The action of HEAD *v.*, in various senses.

1. The cutting off or removal of the head: **a.** of persons: beheading, decapitation. *arch.*

a **1300** *Cursor M.* 22860 Men..wit hefding draght, or hanging spilt. **1494** FABYAN *Chron.* II. xxxvii. 27 By heddyng, fleyng, brennynge, & other cruel execucions. **1555** W. WATREMAN *Fardle Facions* I. v. 66 To be periured was headyng. **1692** WAGSTAFFE *Vind. Carol.* xv. 102 Their frequent Headings and Gibbettings. **1893** *Athenæum* 9 Sept. 346/1 Plots and rumours of plots, with their consequences of headings and hangings.

b. of trees, etc.

1552 HULOET, Headynge, or choppynge, or clyppynge of any thynge, *truncatio*. **1707** MORTIMER *Husb.* I. (1708) 335 As 'tis a large tree you must avoid heading of them if you can. **1843** *Jrnl. R. Agric. Soc.* IV. II. 396 Heading-down, that is, removing all the branches to within a foot or two of the main forks or the stem of the tree. **1886** G. NICHOLSON *Dict. Gard.* s.v., Heading-down will be requisite with fruit-trees which it is intended to graft.

2. The action of furnishing or fitting with a head.

1390–1 in *Exped. Earl Derby* (Camden) 22 Pro hedynge iiij doliorum pro floure imponendo. **1463** *Mann. & Househ. Exp.* (Roxb.) 193 For hopyng and hedyng and settyng in of hedys of pypys and barells. **1599** MINSHEU, *Enastadura*, heading with iron.

3. The process of forming a head or coming to a head; *fig.* culmination. Also *heading-up*. (See HEAD *sb.*¹ 9 a, 17, 31; HEAD *v.* 6, 8.)

1819 REES *Cycl.* s.v. *Brassica*, The true purple kind is superior both in size and perfectness of heading. **1857** P. FREEMAN *Princ. Div. Serv.* II. 98 It was..the heading-up and the final effort of a form of thought, which..had for near a century past been gathering momentum. **1873** F. ROBERTSON *Engin. Notes* 12 The heading up of the water.

4. a. A facing or advancing in a particular direction; the doubling of a hare, etc. (= HEAD *sb.*¹ 28).

1607 TOPSELL *Four-f. Beasts* (1658) 107 Remembring and preventing..the subtile turnings and headings of the hart. *Ibid.* 120 The nature of this hare is sometimes to leap and make headings, sometimes to tread softly. **1860** *Merc. Marine Mag.* VII. 98 With your present heading you will run aground.

b. *N.Z.* Of a farm dog: see quot. 1933. Hence *heading dog*. Cf. HEAD *v.* 13 c.

1913 A. I. CARR *Country Work & Life N.Z.* xix. 33 A new hand, if he intends to qualify for the work [as shepherd] is wise in investing in a good huntaway or a heading dog. **1933** L. G. D. ACLAND in *Press* (Christchurch, N.Z.) 28 Oct. 15/7 A dog goes round to the far side of a mob of sheep and stops them. This is called heading. Hence heading dog, one whose work this is. **1947** P. NEWTON *Wayleggo* (1949) 13 The heading dog is bred to run out silently, cast round sheep, and bring them back to his master. **1968** *N.Z. News* 28 Aug. 16/1 The heading dog brings sheep up to the shepherd and holds them at one spot. **1972** P. NEWTON *Sheep Thief* v. 40 He told her of his successes on the dog trial grounds. His old huntaway, Sam, was his particular pride, and he also had high hopes for his little heading dog, Smoke.

c. *Aeronaut.* (See quot. 1951.)

1935 T. C. LYON *Pract. Air Navigation* 29 *Compass heading*, the true course plus or minus variation and deviation, and *including* allowance for wind. **1951** *Gloss. Aeronaut. Terms* (*B.S.I.*) III. 7 *Heading*, the direction of the longitudinal axis of an aircraft defined by the angle it makes with a specified meridian. **1968** *New Scientist* 18 Apr. 133/1 The aircraft's heading is defined by the localizer's two overlapping beams.

5. *Football.* The action of striking or driving the ball with the head.

1887 *Sporting Life* 28 Mar. 4/5 Their kicking and heading being perfection. **1887** M. SHEARMAN *Athletics & Footb.* (Badm. Libr.) 347 Heading is often quicker than 'footing' when the ball is high in the air.

II. Concrete senses.

6. a. A distinct or separable part forming the head, top, or front of a thing; **b.** in *Needlework*; **c.** in *Mining*: see quots.

1676 MOXON *Print Lett.* 40 The Heading is made like the Heading of k. **1870** F. R. WILSON *Ch. Lindisf.* 81 The east window has [a] low four-centred arched heading. **1875** KNIGHT *Dict. Mech.*, *Heading*..(*Fireworks*), the device of a signal-rocket, such as a *star-heading*, a *bounce-heading*.

b. 1875 KNIGHT *Dict. Mech.*, *Heading*..(*Sewing*), the extension of a line of ruffling above the line of stitch. **1882** CAULFEILD & SAWARD *Dict. Needlework*, *Heading*, a term used sometimes instead of Footing, to distinguish the edge of the lace that is upon the side of the lace sewn to the dress from the edge that is left free. **1886** *Queen* 22 Jan. 114 Two curtains..with headings made in soft silk.

c. 1831 RAYMOND *Mining Gloss.*, *Headings*, in ore-dressing, the heavier portions collecting at the upper end of a buddle or sluice, as opposed to the tailings, which escape at the other end, and the middlings, which receive further treatment.

d. The highest part; that which is at the top.

1846 *Jrnl. R. Agric. Soc.* VII. I. 56 The middle or heading of the stetch would grow little. **1883** GRESLEY *Gloss. Coal-mining*, *Heading*,..the top portion above the tub sides of the load carried.

7. Material for the heads of casks.

1682 T. A. *Carolina* 6 With this [cedar] they make Heading for their Cask. **1752** J. MACSPARRAN *Amer. Dissected* (1753) 26 Barrel and Hogshead Staves and Heading. **1772** *Ann. Reg.* 230/2 Bounties..to be allowed upon the importation of white oak staves and heading. **1774** J. Q. ADAMS *Diary* 17 Aug. Wks. 1850 II. 344 They had vast forests, and could make their own heading, staves, and hoops. **1858** SIMMONDS *Dict. Trade*, *Heading*, pieces of wood suited for closing sugar hogsheads, and other casks.

8. a. The title or inscription at the head of a page, chapter, or other division of a book, manuscript, etc.; cf. HEAD *sb.*¹ 13.

dead heading (*Printing*), the numbers indicating the pagination; *live heading*, the running title at the top of the page (Tolhausen *Technol. Dict.* 1874).

1849 FREESE *Comm. Class-bk.* 53 The Heading..should be written the whole width of the paper on which the account is to be made out. **1867** FREEMAN *Norm. Conq.* (1870) I. App. 667 This is the date given in the heading of one of the manuscripts. **1885** SIR R. BAGGALLAY in *Law Times Rep.* LII. 672/1 A group of sections, the heading of which is 'Official Receivers and Staff of Board of Trade'.

b. *fig.* A division, section of a subject of discourse, etc.; cf. HEAD *sb.*¹ 27.

1859 DARWIN *Orig. Spec.* v. (1873) 122 The principle discussed under the last heading may be applied to our present subject. **1862** TROLLOPE *Orley F.* xxxii, The woman Bolster is in the next room, And I..will take down the headings of what evidence she can give.

9. A fancy striped border at the end of a piece of calico, or the like.

†10. ? A bank or dam: cf. HEAD *sb.*[1] 17. *Obs.*

1662 DUGDALE *Hist. Imbanking* xlv. 234/1 The Hevedinges of Spalding, on Westone Side, had used and ought to be whole, but then were cut through in divers places. **1793** *Southburn Inclos. Act* 14 Cuts, drains.. headings, trays. **1832** *Holderness Drainage Act* 13 Dams, mounds, headings, cloughs.

11. A horizontal passage driven through in preparation for a tunnel, for working a mine, or for draining, ventilating, or other purpose; a drift or drift-way; also, the end of a drift or gallery.

1819 REES *Cycl.*, *Headings* are small soughs or tunnels driven underground to collect and draw off the springs of water from any tunnel, deep cutting, or other large work. **1838** F. W. SIMMS *Pub. Wks. Gt. Brit.* 32 The heading must be carried through before any part of the main tunnel is commenced. **1878** F. S. WILLIAMS *Midl. Railw.* 422 The bottom of the landslip..was drained by underground headings of great depth.

12. A top layer or covering: in various technical applications.

1777 MACBRIDE in *Phil. Trans.* LXVIII. 115 Ooze is then poured on, to fill up interstices; and the whole crowned with a sprinkling of bark, which the tanners call a heading. **1846** WORCESTER, *Heading*..foam on liquor. **1869** R. B. SMYTH *Goldf. Victoria* Gloss., *Headings*, coarse gravel or drift overlying the washdirt. **1873** *Q. Rev.* CXXXV. 143 The lignite is covered by a thick heading of sand [etc.].

13. A mixture for producing a 'head' on beer, etc.

1861 WYNTER *Soc. Bees* 85 The heading..is a mixture of half alum and half copperas ground to a fine powder.

14. Homespun cloth. *Southern U.S.*

1878 N. H. BISHOP *Voy. Paper Canoe* 236 A roll of homespun for a pillow, which the women called 'heading'.

III. 15. *attrib.* and *Comb.* **a.** From sense 1 a: used for beheading, as ***heading axe***, ***block***, ***hill***, ***man***, †***stead***, ***sword***. **b.** from sense 8, as ***heading-line***. **c.** In the names of tools used in various trades for making or manipulating the 'head' of an article, as ***heading chipper***, ***chisel***, ***circler***, ***hammer***, ***jointer***, ***planer***, ***saw***, ***tool***, etc. **d. heading-course**, a course of bricks lying transversely or consisting of headers; **heading-joint** (see quot.); †**heading-stone**, a faced or pitched stone; cf. HEADED 5. Also HEADING-KNIFE, etc.

1513 DOUGLAS *Æneis* VI. xiv. 46 So bryme and felloun with the *heding ax. **1679** in *Daily News* 1 Jan. (1894) 5/6 [A] 'heading axe' [does not appear in the Tower Inventories before the year 1679.] *a* **1533** LD. BERNERS *Gold. Bk. M. Aurel.* (1546) Diij, There shoulde be no nede of ..*headdyng blockes for traitours. **1875** KNIGHT *Dict. Mech.*, **Heading-chisel*, a chisel for cutting down the head of a mortise, a mortise-chisel. *Ibid.*, **Heading-circler* (*Coopering*), a machine for cutting down and dressing the pieces to form the head of a cask. **1659** WILLSFORD *Scales Comm.*, *Arch.* 2 The length of 2 bricks or 18 inches for the *heading course. **1776** G. SEMPLE *Building in Water* 116 The Parapets..must rest on a heading Course of cut Stone. **1874** TOLHAUSEN *Technol. Dict.*, **Heading-hammer* (*needlemaking*). *a* **1800** *Young Waters* xiv, They hae taen to the *heiding-hill His lady fair to see. **1823** CRABB *Technol. Dict.*, **Heading Joint* (*Carpent.*), the joint of two or more boards at right angles to the fibres. **1874** TOLHAUSEN *Technol. Dict.* s.v., *Heading-line, head-margin, running title. **1890** CHILD *Ballads* VII. ccviii. 125/2 He orders the *heading-man to make haste. *c* **1375** *Sc. Leg. Saints*, *Cristofore* 594 Christofore furth þan haf þai lede, Furth one to þe *heding stade. **1766** ENTICK *London* IV. 424 St. James's-square..is neatly paved with *heading-stone all over. **1513** DOUGLAS *Æneis* VI. xiv. 30 *Heding swerd, baith felloun, scherp and gair. **1564-5** *Burgh Rec. Edin.* (Rec. Soc.) 3 Feb. (Jam. Suppl.), His tua handit sword to be vsit for ane heiding-sword. **1868** MORRIS *Earthly Par.* I. 120 Make sharp thy fearful heading sword. **1852** APPLETON *Dict. Mech.* I. 695 The *heading tools..are made of all sizes and varieties of forms. **1875** KNIGHT *Dict. Mech.*, *Heading-tool* (*Forging*), a tool used in swaging heads on stems of bolts.

heading, *ppl. a.* [f. as prec. + -ING[2].] That heads or forms a head.

1819 REES *Cycl.* s.v. *Brassica*, Of the..common heading cabbage, the varieties are numerous. **1826** LOUDON *Encycl. Agric.* (1831) 515 The sheaves are set on end in pairs..and covered..by what are called heading sheaves.

heading-knife. A knife used for heading. Applied **a.** to various kinds of knives used by coopers, saddlers, curriers, etc.; **b.** to a knife for removing the heads of fishes.

1574 in Rogers *Agric. & Prices* III. 580/2 (*Carpenter's tools*) 23 heading knives. **1880** TURNER *Catal. Tool Wks.* (Sheffield) 10 Cowpers Heading Knives.

heading-machine. **a.** A kind of harvester; = HEADER 1 c. **b.** A machine for forming heads, as for casks, pins, bolts, etc.

1875 KNIGHT *Dict. Mech.*, *Heading-machine* (*Agriculture*), a machine for cutting off the heads of grain in the field. **1884** *B'ham Daily Post* 23 Feb. 2/4 Heading-machine, for bicycle spokes.

†**'headish**, *a. Obs. rare.* [f. HEAD *sb.*[1] + -ISH.] Heady, headstrong.

1530 PALSGR. 315/1 Heedysshe or heedstronge, *testu.*

headkerchief ('hɛdkətʃɪf). *rare.* Also **headkercher.** A kerchief for the head.

1540 COVERDALE *Fruitf. Less.* iii. Wks. (Parker Soc.) I. 327 The clothes wherein the Lord was wrapped, the head-kerchief, every thing folden together in his several place. **1577** FRAMPTON *Joyful News* (1580) 3 They doe perfume therewith their head kerchers, when they doe goe to sleepe. **1851** LAYARD *Pop. Acc. Discov. Nineveh* 78 Over his Kiffiah or headkerchief was folded a Turban. **1896** *Westm. Gaz.* 14 Dec. 2/1 The costumes and headkerchiefs are infinitely picturesque and varied in colour.

headland ('hɛdlənd). [f. HEAD *sb.*[1] + LAND *sb.*[1]]

1. A strip of land in a ploughed field, left for convenience in turning the plough at the end of the furrows, or near the border; in old times used as a boundary. Called in Scotland, *headrig*, †*headroom.*

In some districts the headland is left only at the two ends of the ridges or 'lands', but in others it runs parallel to the fence, round the whole field; it is ploughed last, with furrows parallel to the fence, which at the head and foot of the regular furrows of the field cross these at right angles.

956 *Charter of Eadwig* in Earle *Land Charters* 291 On þæt heafod lond of þe heafodon andlang fura. *c* **1000** ÆLFRIC *Voc.* in Wr.-Wülcker 147/18 *Limites*, hafudland. **14..** *Voc.* ibid. 584/8 *Forarium*, an hedelonde. **1483** *Cath. Angl.* 180/1 An Hede lande, *auiseges*, *artifinium.* **1573** TUSSER *Husb.* xxi. (1878) 58 Now plough vp thy hedlond, or delue it with spade. **1598** KITCHIN *Courts Leet* (1675) 209 Custom to turn his Plough upon the Head-land of another is a good Custom. **1637** *Watertown* (*Mass.*) *Rec.* 26 Feb. (1894) 3 There shalbe two Rod of hadland lying next to every mans particular meddow. **1669** WORLIDGE *Syst. Agric.* (1681) 327 Head-land, that which is ploughed overthwart at the ends of the other Lands. **1863** FAWCETT *Pol. Econ.* I. vi. 81 After the centre of the field has been ploughed, the head-lands will remain to be ploughed separately.

2. A point of land projecting into the sea or other expanse of water; a cape or promontory: now usually, a bold or lofty promontory.

1527 R. THORNE in Hakluyt *Voy.* (1589) 253 An head lond called Capo verde. **1555** EDEN *Decades* 350 A rounde hyll ouer the hedde lande. **1595** SPENSER *Col. Clout* 283 An high headland thrust far into the sea. **1622** R. HAWKINS *Voy. S. Sea* (1847) 179 In all the coast from head-land to head-land. **1769** *De Foe's Tour Gt. Brit.* III. 312 The Cape or Head-land of St. Bees..still preserves its Name. **1856** KANE *Arct. Expl.* I. ix. 102 Lofty headlands walled it in.

attrib. **1887** BOWEN *Virg. Æneid* III. 699 The towering bluffs of Pachynum's headland brow.

headle, variant of HEDDLE.

headless ('hɛdlɪs), *a.* [See -LESS.]

1. Without a head; having no head; deprived of the head, beheaded.

(*Headless hood*, in quot. 1579, is explained in the Globe ed., followed by recent Dicts., as = *heedlesshood*; but Spenser elsewhere always distinguishes *headless* and *heedless*.)

c **1000** ÆLFRIC *Voc.* in Wr.-Wülcker 159/1 *Truncus*, heafodleas bodiȝ. **13..** *Seuyn Sag.* (W.) 1333 The heuedles bodi.. Was i-drawe thourgh eueri strete. *c* **1489** CAXTON *Sonnes of Aymon* xiv. 331 Hym that never shall come agayn, but he be hedles. **1579** SPENSER *Sheph. Cal.* Feb. 86 Cuddie, I wote thou kenst little good, So vainely taduance thy headlesse hood. **1596** —— *F.Q.* IV. iii. 20 The headlesse tronke, as heedlesse of that stower, Stood still awhile. **1773-91** HOOLE *Orl. Fur.* XLII. (R.), The headless trunk of Agramant. **1862** D. WILSON *Preh. Man* II. xix. 126 Headless figures are the symbols of the dead.

†**b.** In grimly jocular phr. ***to hop headless*** = to have the head struck off, to be beheaded. *Obs.*

c **1330** R. BRUNNE *Chron. Wace* (Rolls) 1082 Hedles schal þou hop. *c* **1330** *King of Tars* 1039 Hou the Sarazins that day Hopped hedles for heore pray. **1596** DALRYMPLE tr. *Leslie's Hist. Scot.* VII. 9 Mony ane of the cheif nobilitie..the Bruse gart hap heidles. **1635** R. N. tr. *Camden's Hist. Eliz.* I. 111 Lest she saw ere long those on whom she most leaned, hop headlesse.

c. Having no head, or having lost the head (in various senses, see HEAD *sb.*[1] II); without the top.

headless cross (*spec.*) = *tau cross*; see CROSS *sb.* 18.

c **1420** *Pallad. on Husb.* I. 881 Brenne heer and ther the heedles garlek stelis. **1513** DOUGLAS *Æneis* VI. xiii. 12 That lenys him apon his heidless speir. **1563** in *Vicary's Anat.* (1888) App. iii. 163 There shalbe CC blew hedles Crosses made with all convenient spede. **1693** C. MATHER *Wond. Invis. World* (1862) 137 Several Poppets..with headless Pins in them, the Points being outward. **1884** *Milit. Engin.* I. II. 86 Each cylinder is made of gabions or headless casks, placed end to end, and lashed together.

d. Having no part distinctly organized as a head; = ACEPHALOUS 3.

1880 BASTIAN *Brain* vii. 107 Sedentary animals, though they may possess a Nervous System, are often headless. **1883** *American* VI. 46 It [the oyster] is a headless creature.

2. Having no chief or leader. **b.** Subject to no ecclesiastical head. (Cf. ACEPHALI 2.)

c **1330** R. BRUNNE *Chron. Wace* (Rolls) 6617 A lond hedles in tyme of nede. **1529** MORE *Comf. agst. Trib.* III. Wks. 1260/1 Now to this great glory can ther no man come hedlesse. Our head is Christ. **1565** T. STAPLETON *Fortr. Faith* 93 b, Headles heretikes bicause they were vnder no bishops. **1598** BARRET *Theor. Warres* II. i. 28 Not to send them out like headlesse men. *a* **1647** SIR R. FILMER *Patriarcha* ii. §17 (Rtldg.) 41 It will lie in the hands of the headless multitude. **1855** MILMAN *Lat. Chr.* XIII. ix. (L.), He..would..appeal to Christendom against the decrees of a headless council.

3. Wanting in brains or intellect; brainless.

1526 *Pilgr. Perf.* (W. de W. 1531) 225 That the kyng of heuen wolde marry his onely eternall sone to a hedles woman. **1549** CHEKE *Hurt Sedit.* (1641) 22 Neither.. touched of headlesse Captaines, nor holden of brainlesse Rebels. **1884** *Pall Mall G.* 12 Sept. 4/2 A landowner, perfectly heartless and headless.

b. Of things, actions, etc.: Senseless, stupid.

1586 J. HOOKER *Girald. Irel.* in *Holinshed* II. 86/1 Their bare words or headlesse saiengs. *a* **1619** FOTHERBY *Atheom.* I. ix. §2 (1622) 62 Headlesse Old-wiues Tales. **1701** J. LAW *Counc. Trade* Introd. (1751) 12 The main hazard..will be, of a rash, raw, giddy and headless direction.

Hence **'headlessness**, headless condition.

1876 L. TOLLEMACHE in *Fortn. Rev.* Jan. 112 This singular example of sanitary headlessness.

'headlet. *Obs.* or *dial.* [f. HEAD *sb.*[1] + -LET.] A little or miniature head.

1577 HARRISON *England* III. viii. (1878) II. 55 The heads [of the crocus] are said to child, that is, to yeeld out of some parts of them diuerse other headlets. **1847-78** HALLIWELL, *Headlets*, buds of plants. *West.*

headlight ('hɛdlaɪt). orig. *U.S.* Also with hyphen. A powerful light carried on the front of a locomotive or on the mast-head of a vessel; each of two powerful lamps carried on the front of a motor vehicle. Also *attrib.* and *fig.*

1861 *Remin. Life Railroad Engineer* 124, I saw the glimmer of his head-light when he first turned the curve. **1862** in *U.S. Pat.* 35486. **1891** C. ROBERTS *Adrift Amer.* iii. 55 The great head-light which forms such a noticeable feature of American engines at night. **1904** A. B. F. YOUNG *Compl. Motorist* (ed. 2) xii. 257 On dark nights it is advisable, when driving in the country, to carry on such cars a single head-light of greater power... On very fast cars two of these head-lights should be carried. **1907** *Autocar* 28 Dec. 1067/2 The thief calmly took the large valuable head light off and disappeared. **1929** *Evening News* 18 Nov. 4/4 He had almost reached the high road when the headlights of an automobile swung round a corner. **1959** *Sears, Roebuck Catal.* Spring & Summer 1103/3 Chrome-plated headlight shields. **1963** *Times* 13 Mar. 10/6 It has transistorised ignition, a.c. electrical generator, automatic headlight dipper, [etc.]. **1971** *Daily Tel.* 11 Feb. 11/2 It is only when they commit some offence that they are caught in the headlights of history. **1973** 'M. INNES' *Appleby's Answer* IV. xx. 172 The sound of a motor engine..and the sudden appearance of wavering headlights.

'headline, *sb.*

1. *Naut.* **a.** One of the ropes that make a sail fast to the yard. **b.** See quot. 1794.

1626 CAPT. SMITH *Accid. Yng. Seamen* 15 Diuerse other small cordage, as head lines. **1627** —— *Seaman's Gram.* v. 22 Head lines, are the ropes that make all the sailes fast to the yard. **1794** *Rigging & Seamanship* I. 169 *Head-line*, is the line sewed along the upper edge of flags to strengthen them.

2. *Printing.* †**a.** See quot. 1676. †**b.** See quot. 1823. **c.** The line at the top of a page in which the running title, pagination, etc., are given; a title or sub-title in a book, newspaper, etc. ***to make*** or ***hit the headlines***: to be given prominent notice in the newspapers.

1676 MOXON *Print Lett.* 6 The Head-line is the upper line that bounds the Short Letter. **1823** CRABB *Technol. Dict.* s.v. *Head*, *Head-line*, the line which is drawn across the top or head of a page. **1824** J. JOHNSON *Typogr.* II. vi. 133 Head-lines are generally set in small capitals of the same fount, or in Italics. **1825** HANSARD *Typogr.* 411 Having..placed the head-line at the top, and signature or direction line at bottom. **1890** DILKE *Probl. Greater Brit.* I. 78 The amazing headlines which are so conspicuous a feature in the leading journals of New York. **1934** M. WESEEN *Dict. Amer. Slang* (1935) xvii. 257 *Hit the headlines*, to become famous; to gain notoriety. **1939** *War Illustr.* 21 Oct. 181 He [*sc.* Winston S. Churchill] 'hit the headlines' in 1899 with a dramatic escape from captivity in a Boer armoured train. **1944** F. CLUNE *Red Heart* 12 It was just another tragedy of the Outback, the sort of thing that doesn't make headlines in the City newspapers, but it wrings the hearts of people who really know. **1948** *Manch. Guardian Weekly* 29 Jan. 11 The publication..hit the headlines here last night. **1957** 'J. WYNDHAM' *Midwich Cuckoos* 12 Before that it [*sc.* the village] hit the headlines —well, anyway, the broad-sheets—when Black Ned, a second-class highwayman, was shot on the steps of The Scythe and Stone Inn by Sweet Polly Parker. **1968** *Globe & Mail* (Toronto) 3 Feb. 35/1 Anybody who gets his picture on the cover of the magazine [sc. *Time*] immediately breaks a leg, or hits the headlines in embarrassing fashion about the date of publication.

d. *Broadcasting.* Usu. in *pl.* A summary of important news items, given at the beginning or end of a news bulletin.

1908 'O. HENRY' *Gentle Grafter* 39 He shows me a machine..with two things for your ears..I puts it on and listens. A female voice starts up reading headlines of murders, accidents and other political casualties. 'What you hear,' says the farmer, 'is a synopsis of to-day's news..wired in to our Rural News Bureau and served hot to subscribers.' **1934** *B.B.C. Year-Bk.* 82 They [*sc.* Topical Talks] were given five minutes every evening in which to deal with the 'head line' of the day, and were tacked on like a tail to the news bulletins. **1941** *B.B.C. Gloss. Broadc. Terms* 14 Headline News: Brief statements giving, within the space of not more than five minutes, salient news items without comment or background material. **1971** 'D. HALLIDAY' *Dolly & Doctor Bird* i. 6, I watched the news headlines on television.

3. **a.** A line or rope attached to the head of an animal, as a bullock (*Cent. Dict.*).

b. A line fastening the head of a vessel to the shore.

1876 'MARK TWAIN' *Tom Sawyer* ii. 29 Get out that headline! **1877** J. HABBERTON *Jericho Road* i. 9 The head-line was cast off as the pilot's bell rang. **1958** E. S. LAND *Winning War with Ships* 105, I 'went ashore with the headline', contacted the Italian Admiral, and cooled off somewhat.

4. A base-line in surveying.

1656 *Doc. & Rec. New Hampshire* I. 221 From the said head lyne we measured for the length..6 miles & a halfe. **1704** *New Hampshire Probate Rec.* I. 514 All my land..up as far as the southern hills, viz. as far as to butt against Andrews head line.

5. *Palmistry.* A line of the head (cf. LINE *sb.*^{2} 8 b).

1867 A. R. CRAIG *Bk. of Hand* xxiii. 189 If a line sets out from the head line, and rises straight to the mount of Jupiter, crosses it, and cuts the roots of the forefinger, it is excessive pride. **1894** 'MARK TWAIN' in *Century Mag.* Feb. 554/2 Wilson began to study Luigi's palm, tracing life lines, heart lines, head lines, and so on. [**1911** *Encycl. Brit.* XX. 650/1 s.v. *Palmistry.* A line starting above the head of the second metacarpal bone and crossing the hand to the middle of its ulnar border is the line of the head.] **1934** *Cassell's Mod. Encycl.* 733/1 The principal lines on the palm are named life line, head line, heart line, fate line, and line of Apollo.

6. *attrib.* and *Comb.*

1909 *Daily Chron.* 19 Aug. 3/1 His ingenuity is amazing, ..and not merely amazing in the headline sense of that ill-used word. **1933** *Amer. Speech* Dec. 6/2 'Headline English' has become almost a menace to standard English usage nowadays. **1958** *Times* 11 Aug. 11/3 She..is usually to be seen..at Broadway first nights,..at headline parties. **1963** *Times* 11 June 17/4 The headline-maker, of course, has been the contract from United Airlines, of the United States, which has taken delivery of its 20-plane medium-range jet fleet from France. **1965** *Economist* 2 Oct. 57/3 He still uses that unfortunate American headline-verb 'to score' (meaning 'to attack').

Hence **'headline** *v. trans.*, to furnish with a headline; **'headlined** *ppl. a.*, furnished with a headline.

1891 *Punch* 25 Apr. 196/2 A daily newspaper gave a headlined account of the speech. **1897** *Literary Guide* 1 July 199/1 The book is head-lined with the announcement that [etc.]. **1912** *Out West* Apr. 237/2 A big headlined, illustrated ..story, the pride of some reporter's heart. **1953** *Manch. Guardian Weekly* 12 Feb. 3 The 'New York Herald Tribune' headlined this story to-day. **1958** *Listener* 20 Nov. 811/2 The answer..faithfully reported and perhaps headlined the next day in the local press. **1964** *Melody Maker* 28 Nov. 4/2 Nashville Teens, Kinks and Hullaballoos will be headlined in the 10-day Christmas holiday show..at Brooklyn's Fox Theatre.

'headliner. [In sense 1, f. prec. + -ER^1.]

1. a. One who writes headlines.

1891 *Pall Mall G.* 27 Oct. 2/2 The *Times* is becoming quite smart as a 'head-liner'. **1892** *Columbus* (Ohio) *Disp.* 2 Aug., The headliner of the Journal.

b. One whose name appears in a headline; a chief personage or performer. *U.S.*

1896 *N.Y. Dramatic News* 4 July 10/3 That clever pair.. were the headliners..last week. **1905** *Daily Chron.* 11 Feb. 3/5 They..secure good 'head-liners' or 'stars' at paralysing salaries. **1907** *Chicago Tribune* 8 May 7 The 'Headliners' on the program will be James Whitcomb Riley, George Ade, etc. **1914** *Boston Herald* 23 June 8/4 The headliner at B. F. Keith's. **1966** R. STOUT *Death of Doxy* (1967) xii. 140 Julie's dressing room..was about six by eight, par for a headliner in a place with a four-dollar cover charge. **1970** *Globe & Mail* (Toronto) 26 Sept. 35/1 He is the centre on a checking line, a headliner on the penalty-killing unit.

2. One engaged in head-lining (HEAD *sb.*^{1} 74).

1963 *Times* 5 Mar. 13/1 A typical example were the headliners, who fitted the roof linings in vehicles.

headli'nese. [-ESE.] The elliptical style of language characteristic of the headlines, esp. in popular newspapers.

1927 C. G. MARSHALL *Private Let.* (G. & C. Merriam Co. files) 12 Aug., In the headlines of general newspapers you see time after time such words as 'Probe', 'Quiz', 'Tilt', 'Pact', etc. In Newspaper offices such language is referred to as 'Headlinese'. We banned it from the headlines of The [United States] Daily. **1934** *Times Lit. Suppl.* 1 Feb. 66/3 They recognize that the difficulty nowadays is to keep the headline 'from shouting too loudly', and they cannot condemn too heartily mere 'headlinese'. **1935** H. STRAUMANN *Newspaper Headlines* 256 An essential feature of present-day headlinese is the typographical make-up. **1966** *Listener* 2 June 811/3 In headlinese you don't marry, you wed... You don't advance arguments against, you score.

†**'headling,** *sb. Obs.* Forms: 1 héafod-, -ud-, 3 heuedling. [f. HEAD *sb.*^{1} + -LING^1: cf. DARLING.] In OE., Equal, fellow, mate; in quot. 1275, Chieftain: cf. Ger. *häuptling.*

c **950** *Lindisf. Gosp.* Matt. xxiv. 49 Gif..yfle ðrael.. ongann slae heafudlinges his. *c* **1275** LAY. 9986 Hadden hii anne heuedling [*c* **1205** to here-toȝe].

†**'headling,** *adv.* (*a.*) *Obs.* [f. HEAD *sb.*^{1} + -LING^2: cf. OE. *bæcling.*]

A. *adv.* 1. With the head foremost; headlong.

13.. *K. Alis* 2261 Heore hors hedlyng mette. **1382** WYCLIF *Matt.* viii. 32 Al the droue wente heedlynge [**1526** TINDALE hedlinge] in to the see. *c* **1410** *Sir Cleges* 354, J schall..put the out hedlynge. **1540** CRANMER *Bible* Pref., To tumble a man heedlinge downe the hyll.

2. Without thought or regard; precipitately.

1421-2 HOCCLEVE *Dialog* 647 Thou wilt nat haaste, I trowe, Vn-to thy penne and ther-with wirke heedlynge. **1526** *Pilgr. Perf.* (W. de W. 1531) 51 To renne hedlynge.. vpon all ieopardyes. **1603** KNOLLES *Hist. Turks* (1621) 170 The rest of his discomfited armie flying headling back againe to Constantinople.

B. *adj.* Precipitate.

c **1510** BARCLAY *Mirr. Gd. Manners* (1570) Bv, In sentence remise is lesser iniury, Then in headling sentence pronounced hastely.

†**'headlings,** *adv. Obs.* Also 4-6 -es, -is. [f. prec. with adverbial genitive *-es*: see -LINGS.]

1. = HEADLING 1.

c **1400** *Destr. Troy* 7485 [He] hurlit hym doun hedlynges. **1535** COVERDALE *2 Kings* ix. 33 Cast her downe headlinges. **1550** —— *Spir. Perle* vi. (1588) 66 In a slippery and sliding place he might fall headlings ouer & ouer.

2. = HEADLING 2.

c **1380** WYCLIF *Sel. Wks.* III. 150 þei gon hedlingis to helle. **1558** BP. WATSON *Sev. Sacram.* xx. 127 Whether so euer the fleshe and the deuyll leadeth hym, thyther he runneth headlynges. **1596** DALRYMPLE tr. *Leslie's Hist. Scot.* I. 118 Mony walde be drawne heidlings into the deip swallie of al abhominable vice.

headlong ('hɛdlɒŋ), *adv.* and *a.* Also 5-6 hedlong. [Alteration of the earlier HEADLING, by erroneous assimilation to -LONG: cf. *sidelong.*]

A. *adv.* 1. Head foremost, in falling or plunging; head downmost.

1482 *Monk of Evesham* xli. (Arb.) 85 Oftyn times he fylle down hedlong. **1548** UDALL, etc. *Erasm. Par. Matt.* iv. 32 To cast a man hedlong into the ryver. **1594** BLUNDEVIL *Exerc.* III. I. xxiv. (ed. 7) 330 Capricornus..riseth right up, and goeth downe headlong. **1658** J. JONES *Ovid's Ibis* 36 Achæus whom his subjects took And hang'd him headlong in the golden brook. **1725** POPE *Odyss.* VIII. 556 To plunge it headlong in the whelming wave. **1887** BOWEN *Virg. Æneid* v. 176 Headlong into the waters the laggard helmsman he threw.

fig. **1602** T. FITZHERBERT *Apol.* 28 a, He casts him selfe head-long to hel. **1652** COTTERELL *Cassandra* III. (1676) 34 He plunged himself headlong into his grief.

2. Head foremost, as in rushing forward; with ungoverned speed; with blind impetuosity.

1576 GASCOIGNE *Philomene* (Arb.) 117 The harbrainde colte Which headlong runnes and for no bridle bydes. **1697** DRYDEN *Virg. Georg.* III. 140 He bears his Rider headlong on the Foe. **1719** YOUNG *Revenge* I. i, Darting headlong to thy arms, I left The promis'd fight. **1884** *Chr. World* 11 Sept. 678/4 A train ran off the line, and went headlong into a morass.

b. *fig.* With unrestrained course; without regard to where one is going; precipitately.

1530 TINDALE *Answ. More* I. xxix, They..runne headlong vnto al mischief. **1665** MANLEY *Grotius' Low C. Warres* 129 This cast the Duke head-long upon Counsels, dangerous, and full of desperation. **1721** BERKELEY *Prev. Ruin Gt. Brit.* Wks. 1871 III. 205 To see their country run headlong into all those luxurious follies. **1875** JOWETT *Plato* (ed. 2) V. 362 He among us who would be divine..should not rush headlong into pleasures.

B. *adj.* 1. Of heights, etc.: Such as one might fall headlong from; precipitous. Now *rare.*

c **1550** CHEKE *Matt.* viii. 32 Bi an hedlong place in to ye see. **1692** E. WALKER *Epictetus' Mor.* (1737) lx, You tumble down a headlong Precipice. **1816** BYRON *Ch. Har.* III. xli, Like a tower upon a headlong rock. **1854** HAWTHORNE *Eng. Note-bks.* (1879) I. 890 Such a headlong hill.

2. Plunging downwards head foremost, as when one falls or dives: a. of actions.

c **1586** C'TESS PEMBROKE *Ps.* LXXIII. v, They fell with headlong fall. **1608-11** BP. HALL *Medit. & Vows* I. §60 The descent..[is] easie and headlong. **1856** MRS. BROWNING *Aur. Leigh* I. 617 Headlong leaps of waters. **1897** MARY KINGSLEY *W. Africa* 612 Taking a headlong dive into the deep Atlantic.

b. *poet.* of a person, etc.

1663 BUTLER *Hud.* I. ii. 870 The Friendly Rug preserv'd the ground, And headlong Knight from bruise or wound. **1855** LONGF. *Hiaw.* viii. 124 Down..Plunged the headlong Hiawatha.

c. Hanging head downmost. *rare.*

1710 POPE *Windsor For.* 210 Oft in her glass the musing shepherd spies The headlong mountains and the downward skies.

3. Rushing forward impetuously; wildly impetuous. Of actions or agents.

1590 SPENSER *F.Q.* II. xi. 18 Nor bounds nor banks his headlong ruine may sustayne. **1613** J. DENNIS *Secr. Angl.* I. in Arb. *Garner* I. 158 The rivers making way..With headlong course into the sea profound. **1715-20** POPE *Iliad* XII. 120 The moving legions speed their headlong way. **1718** *Freethinker* No. 88 ¶4 At her Call, he plunged into the headlong Stream. **1849** MACAULAY *Hist. Eng.* I. 122 They saw a brigade of their countrymen..drive before it in headlong rout the finest infantry of Spain. *Ibid.* 540 Wild mountain passes..torn by headlong torrents.

4. *fig.* Characterized by unrestrainable or ungoverned haste; precipitate, madly impetuous; rash, reckless. Of persons, their actions, etc.

1566 T. STAPLETON *Ret. Untr. Jewel* IV. 58 Of most high wickednes or of hedlonge arrogancie. **1586** J. HOOKER *Girald. Irel.* in *Holinshed* II. 89/2 The lord Thomas being youthfull, rash, and headlong. **1640** YORKE *Union Hon.* 29 The headlong crew of London favour the rebelles. **1791** COWPER *Odyss.* II. 322 Injurious Mentor! headlong orator! **1810** SCOTT *Lady of L.* I. xxi. The sparkling glance..Of hasty love, or headlong ire. **1884** *Manch. Exam.* 7 Oct. 5/1 Rash and headlong leaders.

Hence †**'headlongwise** *adv.*, in a headlong way, precipitately. *Obs.*

1600 HOLLAND *Livy* 29 Should still run on end, and headlongwise fall unto such base varlets.

†**'headlong,** *v. Obs.* [f. prec.]

1. *trans.* To cast headlong; to precipitate.

c **1586** C'TESS PEMBROKE *Ps.* LXII. ii, To headlong him their thoughtes devise. **1622** H. SYDENHAM *Serm. Sol. Occ.* II. (1637) 170 That place from which he was headlonged. ?*a* **1655** T. ADAMS *Wks.* (1861-2) III. 93 (D.) Our own sinful ignorance that headlongs us to confusion.

2. *intr.* To proceed in a headlong fashion.

1654 TRAPP *Comm. Esther* vi. 14 [They] hurried and headlonged in a turbulent manner.

†**'headlongly,** *adv. Obs.* [f. HEADLONG *a.* + -LY^2.] In headlong manner; = HEADLONG *adv.*

1610 R. ABBOT *Old Way* 29 Warning vs..to doe nothing headlongly and rashly. *a* **1612** DONNE *Βιαθανατος* (1644) 94 In France the Lawes abound against Duells, to which they are headlongly apt. **1653** *Consid. Dissolv. Crt. Chancery* 16 They were not hurried, or headlongly driven on.

'headlongness. *rare.* [see -NESS.] Headlong quality or speed; precipitateness, rashness.

1580 *Apol. Pr. Orange* in *Phenix* (1721) I. 517 By the Head-longness or Hastiness of some. **1865** *Pall Mall G.* 23 Dec., It..saves him from any dangerous headlongness of impulse.

'headlongs, *adv. Obs.* exc. *dial.* [An alteration of the earlier HEADLINGS.] = HEADLONG *adv.*

[*c* **1400** *Destr. Troy* 10980 [MS. 16th c.; cf. HEADLINGS 1] He hurlit down hedlonges to the hard erthe.] **1546** BALE *Eng. Votaries* I. (1560) 21 She should haue bene brought into a high mountaine & there throne down headlonges. **1551** ROBINSON tr. *More's Utop.* I. (1895) 101 To rome hedlonges the contrary waye. **1558** BP. WATSON *Sev. Sacram.* xxvi. 166 To runne hedlonges without bridle, from one crime to another. **1859** GEO. ELIOT *A. Bede* vi. 135 That's the road you'd all like to go, headlongs to ruin.

†**'headly,** *a. Obs.* Also 1 héafodlíc, 4 hauedliche, hedly. [f. HEAD *sb.*^{1} + -LY^1.] Chief, principal; capital; (of sins) deadly.

971 *Blickl. Hom.* 37 þæt we us healdan..wiþ þa heafodlican leahtras. **1340** *Ayenb.* 15 þe zeuen hauedliche zennes. *c* **1380** WYCLIF *Sel. Wks.* III. 162 þis weddyng is broken by iche hedly synne. [**1599** SHAKS. *Hen. V*, III. iii. 32 The filthy and contagious Clouds Of headly Murther, Spoyle, and Villany. *Fols.* 2, 3, 4 heady.]

†**headly,** *adv. Obs.* Also 4 heedli. [f. HEAD *sb.*^{1} + -LY^2.] In a heady manner; impetuously; precipitately; headily.

1388 WYCLIF *Judg.* v. 22 The strongeste of enemyes fledden with bire, and felden heedli. **1477** NORTON *Ord. Alch.* iv. in Ashm. (1652) 45 Headly they proceed as men well nigh madd.

head-man, headman, head man. Forms: see HEAD *sb.*^{1} [OE. *héafodman*: cf. MHG. *houbetman, houptman*, Ger. *hauptmann*, ON. *höfuðsmaðr*, Sw. *hufvudman*. See HEAD *sb.*^{1} 71.]

1. Chief man, chief, leader. In various contextual applications.

c **1000** ÆLFRIC *Voc.* in Wr.-Wülcker 155/20 *Primas*, heafodman, *uel* þegn. *a* **1123** *O.E. Chron.* an. 1101 þa wurdon þa heafodmen wiðerræden toȝeanes þam cynge. *c* **1175** *Lamb. Hom.* 123 ȝif þa hefdmen of þissere worlde hefden icnawen crist. *c* **1200** ORMIN 297 Moysæs wass hæfedd mann Off Issraæle þeode. *a* **1400-50** *Alexander* 441 To be halden heuydman of all þe hale werde. **1548** UDALL, etc. *Erasm. Par. John* vii. 50 An headman, & a doctor of the lawe. **1609** SKENE *Reg. Maj.* 164 All Lords, and heidmen of all parts of this Realme. **1791** W. BARTRAM *Carolina* 489 The head men, or chiefs of the whole nation, were convened. *a* **1825** FORBY *Voc. E. Anglia*, *Head-man*, the chief hind on a farm. **1844** H. H. WILSON *Brit. India* I. 407 The landholders and head-men of the villages. **1873** *Act 36 & 37 Vict.* c. 88 §2 The term 'foreign state' includes any foreign nation..sovereign, prince, chief, or headman.

†2. = HEADSMAN 2. *Obs. rare.*

1673 [R. LEIGH] *Transp. Reh.* 69 Probationer for the headmans office. **1816** BYRON *Parisina* xv, The headman [*some edd.* headsman]..Feels if the axe be sharp and true.

'head-mark. *Sc.* [f. HEAD *sb.*^{1} + MARK *sb.*]

1. The peculiarity of head, face, and features, which distinguishes each individual of a species: said primarily of sheep, and opposed to any artificial mark as of a brand or 'buist'. Hence *to know by head-mark*: to know by personal appearance, recognize by face.

1727 P. WALKER *Remark. Passages* 169 (Jam.) K. James VI ..knowing them all by head-mark. **1805** FORSYTH *Beauties Scotl.* II. 180 An intelligent shepherd knows all his sheep from personal acquaintance, called head-mark, and can swear to the identity of a sheep as he could to that of a fellow-servant. **1816** SCOTT *Antiq.* xl. *note.* He knew every book, as a shepherd does the individuals of his flock, by what is called head-mark. **1888** BRYCE *Amer. Commw.* II. lx. 426 In cities where people do not know their neighbours by headmark.

2. A headland marking the limits of fields.

1820 D. TURNER *Normandy* II. 101 Not a fence to be seen; nor do there even appear to be any balks or head-marks.

head master, ,head'master. The principal master of a school, having assistant masters under him.

1576 FLEMING *Panopl. Epist.* 357 The head maister of the schole lysteneth. **1656** BLOUNT *Glossogr.*, *Gymnasiarch*, the head Master of the place where Champions did exercise, also the head Master of a School. **1791** BOSWELL *Johnson* 29 Apr. an. 1778, We were all as quiet as a school upon the entrance of the head-master. **1829** LYTTON *Devereux* I. iii, The head-master publicly complimented him.

Hence **head'master** *v.*, to act as headmaster; also *transf.*; **head'masterdom** (*nonce-wd.*), the world or sphere of headmasters; **head'masterly** *a.*; **head'mastership**, the position or office of headmaster.

1827 ARNOLD *Let.* 21 Oct. in Stanley *Life & Corr.* ii. (1890) 48 Wishing to procure for me the head-mastership at Rugby. **1892** *Pall Mall G.* 21 Jan. 2/2 The successful removal of Uppingham to Borth by Mr. Thring was always regarded as one of the greatest triumphs in the annals of

headmasterdom. **1940** J. H. JAGGER *English in Future* vi. 73 No novelist has *headmastered* his countrymen as frequently as Mr. H. G. Wells. **1959** R. FULLER *Ruined Boys* 154 The school..so brilliantly headmastered. **1964** *English Studies* XLV (Suppl.). 9 Further headmasterly duties took him to Klagenfurt. **1965** G. HOUSEHOLD *Olura* 175 A headmasterly grief that there should be nigger-lovers in the upper forms. **1967** *Guardian* 4 Oct. 1/4 A headmasterly chat.

head mistress, ˌhead-ˈmistress. The principal mistress of a school, having assistant mistresses under her.

1872 (May) *Prospectus School Women's Educ. Union*, The School will be under the general superintendence of a qualified Head Mistress, who will have the same powers and duties as the Head Master of a Public School. **1881** *Macm. Mag.* XLIV. 483 The attendant soon brought the head-mistress.

Hence **head-mistress-ship**, the position or office of head mistress.

ˈhead-money. Money paid for or by each person or head.

1. A fee, tax, etc. paid per head; a poll tax; a capitation fee.

1530 PALSGR. 230/1 Heed money, *truaige*. *a* **1618** RALEIGH *Rem.* (1644) 101 He used David's Law of Capitation or Head-money, and had of every Duke ten marks. *a* **1716** *Politia United Prov.* in Somers *Tracts* (1810) III. 632 All the people of the land..pay yearly for head money..x^d. **1794** J. GIFFORD *Louis XVI.* 119 An ancient custom..by which a kind of poll-tax was levied upon the subjects of either nation in the other, called, in England, *head-money*; in France, *argent du chef*. **1819** REES *Cycl.* s.v. *Head*, Capitation.. called also *poll* and *head-money*.

2. A sum paid for each prisoner taken at sea, for each slave recovered, or for each person brought in certain circumstances.

1713 *Lond. Gaz.* No. 5099/3 Her Majesty's Bounty for the Head-Money of the Prisoners taken in the..St. Francis. **1868** *Every Boy's Ann.* (Rtldg.) 219 The freed Africans were made over to the civil authorities, and the ship's company.. received the head money allowed by government. **1893** W. T. WAWN *S. Sea Islanders* 67 A small sum per head for all recruits [Polynesian labourers] brought to Queensland.. The practice of paying 'head-money' was stopped 10th March, 1884.

†3. Payment for redemption from death. *Obs.*

a **1533** LD. BERNERS *Huon* xlii. 142 To pay me for a knowlege euery yere .iiii. drams of gold for thy hed money.

ˈheadmost, *a.* [f. HEAD *sb.*¹ + -MOST.]

1. Most forward or advanced in order or progression. a. Said *esp.* of the foremost ship of a line.

1628 DIGBY *Voy. Medit.* 36 My sattia (that was headmost by much) kept sight of her all night. **1727** A. HAMILTON *New Acc. E. Ind.* II. I. 226, I kept in the headmost Jonk, and a good Officer in the sternmost. **1797** NELSON in A. Duncan *Life* (1806) 40 The Excellent was engaged with the headmost, and..leewardmost of the Spanish division. **1850** SCORESBY *Whaleman's Adv.* v. (1859) 72 Each striving to be headmost in the chase.

b. Foremost of any advancing series.

1676 MARVELL *Mr. Smirke* 62 [65] They..would joyn, and at least be the Headmost in the Persecution of their own former Party. **1810** SCOTT *Lady of L.* I. ii, Then, as the headmost foes appeared. **1856** MRS. STOWE *Dred* II. xxi. 216 They saw the headmost squirrel walk into Dred's hand.

2. Topmost. Chiefly *dial.*

1798 H. TOOKE *Purley* (1829) I. ix. 423 Where you may use indifferently..Topmost, Upmost or Headmost. *Mod. Sc.* Gang up the glen to the heidmost house.

†**ˈhead-mould**¹. *Obs.* [f. MOULD skull.] The skull. Only in **head-mould-shot**: see quot. 1719. So **head-mould-shottenness**: see quot. 1684.

1684 tr. *Bonet's Merc. Compit.* IX. 321 Seiriasis, or, An Inflammation of the Brain, and of its Membranes, attended with a Hollowness of the Mold of the Head..It may be called Head-mold-shottenness most properly. **1719** QUINCY *Phys. Dict., Head-Mould-shot*, is when the Sutures of the Skull, generally the Coronal, ride; that is, have their Edges shoot over one another. **1781** *Gentl. Mag.* LI. 633 (*Lond. Bills of Mortality*) Headmouldshot, Horseshoehead, and Water in the Head..20.

head-mould², **-moulding.** *Arch.* A variant of HOOD-MOULD, -ING, given in some mod. Dicts.

1875 KNIGHT *Dict. Mech.*, Head-molding. **1889** *Cent. Dict.*, Head-mold, -molding.

ˈhead-note.

1. *Law.* A summary prefixed to the report of a decided case, stating the principle of the decision, with, latterly, an outline of the facts.

1855 SIR R. B. CROWDER *Comm. Bench Rep.* XVI. 491 The head note or the side or marginal note of a report, is a thing upon which much skill and exercise of thought is required. **1885** *Law Rep.* 14 Q. Bench Div. 812 The facts..may be gathered from the above head-note.

2. *Mus.* A note produced in the second or third register of the voice: cf. HEAD-VOICE.

1869 in *Eng. Mech.* IX. No. 220. 259 The result will be the emission of a firm, clear, sharp head note. **1889** *Grove's Dict. Mus.* IV. 322 The peculiarity of the female voice is the possession of a large range of fine head-notes in the place of the male falsetto.

3. A note or comment inserted at the head of the text.

1863 D. G. ROSSETTI *Let.* (1965) II. 472 Alteration of the last part to suit the new plan of head-notes to Part II. *Ibid.* 479, I am glad you like the headnote plan. **1965** *Listener* 17 June 905/3 A headnote to each poem. **1972** *Times* 4 Mar. 12/7 Since performance details for individual [crossword] puzzles are likely to interest many more readers than they may distress, it is hoped that those in the latter category will agree to turn a blind eye to head-notes to puzzles.

head office. [f. HEAD *sb.*¹ 71 + OFFICE *sb.* 8.] The principal, controlling office of a firm or organization, where the chief administration is carried out, policy decisions made, etc. Also *attrib.*

1869 *Bradshaw's Railway Man.* XXI. (Advt.), London & County Banking Company... Head Office. 21, Lombard Street. *Ibid.* 390 Head office accounts, local. **1933** A. G. MACDONELL *England, their England* vi. 70, I was warned by telephone, my Lord, from our Head Office. **1941** F. THOMPSON *Over to Candleford* xiv. 214 I'll speak to Head Office. **1952** A. BRIGGS *Hist. Birmingham* II. 54 In 1881 an export representative was sent out to Australia and New Zealand with his first head office in Sydney, and later on new offices were opened at Melbourne, Adelaide, and Brisbane. **1972** *Woman* 4 Mar. 10/2 If you ever feel you have been badly treated [by the bank], *complain*—first to the branch and, if that's no good, then wake up head office. **1972** C. WATSON *Broomsticks over Flaxborough* xi. 150 In this trade you get used to being buggered about a bit by head office.

head-on, *adv.* and *a.* orig. *U.S.* [HEAD *sb.*¹ 21 b.] A. *adv.* (ˈhead-ˈon). With the head pointed directly towards or running full against or towards something. Also *fig.* B. *adj.* (ˈhead-on). Of a collision: involving the direct meeting of the fronts of two vehicles in the same track, or of the head of a vehicle with an object. Also *fig.*

1840 R. H. DANA *2 Yrs. bef. Mast* ii. 15 The two vessels stood 'head on', bowing and curveting at each other. **1903** C. E. MERRIMAN *Lett. from Son* 33 It's a case of head-on collision with your pride. **1904** *N.Y. Evening Post* 11 May 2 A head-on collision between north and southbound passenger trains. **1907** *Westm. Gaz.* 16 Sept. 5/2 New York, September 16.—A head-on collision between two passenger trains. **1916** H. BARBER *Aeroplane Speaks* 46 Gliding just over the trees and head on to the wind. **1930** *Daily Express* 8 Sept. 1/3 When the vehicles collided head-on. **1932** *Economist* 20 Feb. 400/2 At the same time, a head-on collision between the chamber and the Senate is an unusual occurrence. **1952** *Manch. Guardian Weekly* 15 May 2 The General will here run head-on into the irony of the destiny he has chosen. **1954** J. STEINBECK *Sweet Thursday* 166 Despair and humour crashed head-on in Doc. **1957** *Economist* 9 Nov. 492/1 He is known to be working..to present foreign aid next year in a way that will meet head-on and in good time any indiscriminate renewal of the economy drive. **1958** E. L. MASCALL *Recovery of Unity* i. 4 It shows directly how a head-on theological conflict can arise from the unquestioned assumption of a common premiss. **1961** *Lancet* 5 Aug. 325/1 The Government had a head-on collision with the medical profession in 1956. **1973** *Listener* 14 June 790/3 The coming of the Renaissance..was a head-on collision with the medieval system.

†**ˈhead-pan.** *Obs.* [OE. *héafodpanne*, f. *héafod* HEAD¹ + *panne* PAN.] Skull, brain-pan.

c **1000** *Ags. Gosp.* Matt. xxvii. 33 On þa stowe þe ys ȝenemned golgotha, þæt is, heafod-pannan stow [*Lindisf. G.* heafudponnes stowa]. *c* **1000** *Sax. Leechd.* I. 370 Hundes heafodpanne ȝecnucad. **13..** *Sir Beues* (A.) 2876 A karf ato his heued pan.

ˈhead-penny. *Obs.* exc. *Hist.*

1. A poll tax or capitation fee. Cf. HEAD-MONEY.

c **1200** ORMIN 3293 He shollde þær forr himm Hiss hæfedd-peninng reccnenn. **1444** *Act 23 Hen. VI*, c. 7 La somme de lx li. & pluis, appellez hede peniez. *c* **1460** *Towneley Myst.* (Surtees) 70 Byd ych man com to you holly, And bryng to you a heede penny. **1624** CAPT. SMITH *Virginia* IV. 167 A Penny vpon euery Poll, called a head-penny.

2. A personal or individual ecclesiastical payment or offering.

1550 CROWLEY *Inform. & Petit.* 11 b, .I. d. to the curate, which he called an heade penye, and .vi. d. to .ii. clarkes. **1635** PAGITT *Christianogr.* 182 First-fruits, Redemption of the first-borne, head-pence, and such like, were by his Laws reserved to the use and benefit of the priests.

headphone (ˈhɛdfəʊn). [f. HEAD *sb.*¹ + *phone* of TELEPHONE (see -PHONE).] = *ear-phone* (*a*) and (*c*), s.v. EAR *sb.*¹ 17.

1914 *Work* 7 Mar. 506/1 Electrolite Head-phones. *Ibid.* 28 Mar. 576 We..consider our Headphones a perfect treat. **1926** C. SIDGWICK *Sack & Sugar* xxi. 250 At present they only had head-phones. **1926** *Proc. Musical Assoc. 1926–7* 19 Many seem to have the headphones permanently attached to themselves. **1929** *Strand Mag.* Aug. 152 Women whose head-phones appear so appropriate. **1965** *Listener* 20 May 743/2 These side plaits were gathered into nets..in something like our head-phone style. **1970** J. EARL *Tuners & Amplifiers* iii. 76 Headphones..can nowadays give a subjective impression of quality, spaciousness and stereo effect equally as good as the best loudspeakers.

ˈhead-piece. The piece that covers or forms the head.

1. A piece of armour for the head, a helmet.

1535 LATIMER *Serm., Insurrect. North* (1844) 31 Take also the helmet or head-piece of health. *a* **1627** HAYWARD *Edw. VI* (1630) 37 He finding the Earle..without his helmet.. tooke of his owne headpeece and put it on the Earles head. **1697** DRYDEN *Æneid* VII. (1886) 176 The shining headpiece and the shield. **1843** MACAULAY *Lays Anc. Rome, Lake Regillus* xxviii, Mamilius smote Herminius Through head-piece and through head. **1874** BOUTELL *Arms & Arm.* 106 The head-pieces of these warriors.

2. Any covering for the head; a cap.

1552 *Inv. Ch. Goods Surrey* (1869) 90 Vj amyses or hed peases. **1605** SHAKS. *Lear* III. ii. 26 He that has a house to put's head in, has a good Head-peece. **1824** MISS FERRIER *Inher.* xvii, His ordinary head-piece, a striped woollen nightcap. **1824** MISS MITFORD *Village* Ser. I. (1863) 213 A fine plain clear-starched caul..was plaited on a Scotch gauze head-piece.

3. The head, skull, cranium. *arch.*

1579 SPENSER *Sheph. Cal.* May 241 In his headpeace he felt a sore payne. **1627** F. E. *Hist. Edw. II* (1680) 89 One and the self-same Hood doth fit the head-piece of divers Actors. **1836–8** B. D. WALSH *Aristoph., Acharnians* II. ii, I will speak, sir, with my head-piece On a butcher's chopping-block.

b. The figure-head of a ship.

1807–8 SYD. SMITH *Plymley's Lett.* Wks. 1859 II. 136/1 A wooden image of Lord Mulgrave, going down to Chatham, as a head-piece for the Spanker gun-vessel.

4. The head, as seat of the intellect; brain.

1588 FRAUNCE *Lawiers Log.* I. i. 2 Not lurking in the obscure head-pieces of one or two loytering Fryers. **1613** *Crt. & Times Jas. I* (1849) I. 262 The hurt..which was feared had somewhat crazed his headpiece. **1741** RICHARDSON *Pamela* (1824) I. 79 You have an excellent head-piece for your years. *c* **1817** HOGG *Tales & Sk.* V. 231 An easy, good-natured, and gentlemanly being..with no great head-piece. **1890** BOLDREWOOD *Col. Reformer* (1891) 402 With a real good headpiece too, though there's not much book-learning in it.

b. A man possessed of brains; a man of intellect.

1656 *Burton's Diary* (1828) I. 309 Of all the head-pieces that were there, he was thought to give the strongest reasons. **1720** GAY *Poems* (1745) I. 226 Is not this Steward of mine a pure ingenious fellow now..a rare head-piece? **1803** CHALMERS *Let.* in *Life* (1851) I. 475 Exhibiting yourself..as a great philosopher, a wonderful head-piece.

5. † a. The protective covering of the forehead of a barded horse (*obs.*). b. A halter, a headstall.

1530 PALSGR. 230/1 Head pece of harnesse, *armet, chafrayn*. **1611** COTGR., *Chanfrain de Cheval d'armes*, the front-stall, head-peece, or forhead-piece, of a barbed horse. **1632** SHERWOOD, The head-peece of a bridle. **1678** LITTLETON *Lat. Dict.* s.v., The head-piece of a bridle, *capistrum*. **1844** ALB. SMITH *Adv. Mr. Ledbury* (1856) I. iii. 20 Horses [with] head-pieces and bearing-reins.

6. The top piece or part of various things.

a. The lintel of a door or window. b. The head-board of a bed. c. The upper part of a section of a made mast. d. The top part of a yoke for attaching cattle.

1611 COTGR., *Linteau*, the lintell or headpeece ouer a doore. **1726** LEONI *Alberti's Archit.* II. 46/1 The Windows ..Their head-piece may be upon a line with the top of the Columns. **1794** *Rigging & Seamanship* I. 27 The heel-piece ..coaks on to the heel of the lower tree, and the head-piece to the upper tree. **1807** VANCOUVER *Agric. Devon* (1813) 473 A button or knob at each end..put into the circular holes of the flat head-piece [of a yoke].

7. *Printing.* A decorative engraving placed at the top of the first page of a volume and at the beginning of books, chapters, etc.

1718 *Freethinker* No. 70 ¶1, I am at a Loss for a Head-Piece to my Paper; to speak in the Printer's Language. **1762–71** H. WALPOLE *Vertue's Anecd. Paint.* (1786) I. 156 This and several head-pieces in the same book were designed by Holbein. **1866** BRANDE & COX *Dict. Sc., Lit. etc.* II. 101 Headpieces have been revived of late years; they are mostly copied from old works.

†**ˈhead-place.** *Obs.*

1. The residence occupied by the owner of a property containing several messuages; the capital messuage.

1463 *Bury Wills* (Camden) 20, I will y^t my newe hous..be deseverid and partyd froom the hefd place. *Ibid.* 21 The seid hefd place or whoo that ocupyeth it, to paye the hool rente.

2. A head or chief division of a subject.

1559 BP. SCOT in Strype *Ann. Ref.* I. App. vii. 15 For the better understanding of the same [reasons], I will brynge them unto three head-places.

ˈhead-plate.

†1. *Coach-building*: see quot. 1794. *Obs.*

1794 W. FELTON *Carriages* (1801) I. 171 Head Plates..are ornaments made to fix on the upper quarters of a coach or chariot, and on the flats of a chaise head. *Ibid.* 172 Fig. 21, a fashionable bead-rim head-plate for a crest to go in. **1809** *Sporting Mag.* XXXIII. 276 The crests, in raised silver, will be placed in a garter in the head-plates.

2. *Artillery.* 'The plate which covers the breast of the cheeks of a gun-carriage' (Knight *Dict. Mech.* 1875).

3. *Saddlery.* 'The plate strengthening the point or cantle of a saddle-tree' (*Ibid.*).

1874 in TOLHAUSEN *Technol. Dict.*

4. *Entom.* The chitinous upper surface of the head of a caterpillar or other larva.

1836 SHUCKARD *Man. Entomol.* §53. 37 Larvæ with a distinct corneous head-plate.

headquarter (ˈhɛdˌkwɔːtə(r)), *v.* Usu. in *pass.*: to be provided with headquarters.

1903 *Daily Mail* 3 Sept. 4/4 The off-scourings of civilisation which are headquartered in Constantinople. **1958** P. SCOTT *Mark of Warrior* III. 203 We can take it that Blake's headquartered on the ridge. **1963** *Time & Tide* 28 Mar. 24/2 The society is headquartered in Westminster. **1971** W. TUCKER *This Witch* (1972) v. 55 The refugee camps ..are really terrorist camps as well. The Al Fatah are headquartered there.

ˈhead-ˈquarters, *sb. pl.* Also **headquarters.** (Rarely *sing.* **head-quarter.**) [f. HEAD *sb.*¹ 71.]

1. *Milit.* a. The residence, permanent or temporary, of the commander-in-chief of an

army; the place whence a commander's orders are issued.

1647 CLARENDON *Hist. Reb.* VI. §80 Edge-hill..where the head-quarters of the earl was. **1660** *Trial Regic.* 158 The head-quarters of the Army were at Windsor. **1767** T. HUTCHINSON *Hist. Mass.* II. iii. 279 To repair to the head quarters on the..western frontiers. **1837** W. IRVING *Capt. Bonneville* I. 12 He..was on his way to report himself at head-quarters, in the hopes of being reinstated in the service.

b. The officers belonging to head-quarters.

1812 in A. H. Craufurd *Craufurd & Light Div.* (1891) 218 Lord Wellington and the whole of head-quarters moved in the mournful procession. **1893** FORBES-MITCHELL *Remin. Gt. Mutiny* 5 It turned out to be the Mauritius with head-quarters on board.

c. 'The man of war, or transport, which carries the staff on an expedition' (Smyth *Sailor's Word-bk.*).

2. A chief or central place of residence, meeting, or business; a centre of operations.

1780 A. YOUNG *Tour in Ireland* 382 A good line in which to view these objects is..to make Dobbin's inn, at Ballyporeen, the head quarters, and view them from thence. **1809** J. M'MAHON in G. L. Wardle *Charges against Duke of York* 235 Although he has returned to town for the season as his head-quarters, he makes two or three days excursions from it as often as he can. **1834** G. CRABBE Jun. *Life G. Crabbe* ix. 270 Mr. Crabbe, in subsequent years, made Hampstead his head-quarters on his spring visits. **1836** DICKENS *Let.* ?22 Aug. (1965) I. 168, I shall be at head quarters by 12 Wednesday Noon. **1851** D. JERROLD *St. Giles* xix. 202 Whereupon the canvassing party returned to their head-quarters. **1860** TYNDALL *Glac.* I. xxiii. 161 The Mattmark hotel, which was to be my head-quarters for a few days. **1888** BURGON *Lives 12 Gd. Men* I. ii 178 Sound guidance..and a strong continuous impulse from head-quarters. **1922** E. WALLACE *Crimson Circle* v. 34, I didn't think that head-quarters had much use for private men like you. *Ibid.* vi. 37 We view with consternation the seeming helplessness of police head-quarters to deal with this criminal gang. **1929** A. CHRISTIE *Partners in Crime* xi. 107 The local Inspector of Police had unemotionally arrested the second footman who proved to be a thief well known at headquarters.

3. *attrib.*, usually in form *head-quarter*.

1879 LUBBOCK *Addr. Pol. & Educ.* i. 5 For recruiting expenses, headquarter expenses, or non-effective charges. **1887** RIDER HAGGARD *Jess* 194, I must drive round by the headquarter camp to explain about my going.

'head-race. The race or flume which brings water to a mill-wheel. Cf. *tail-race.*

1846 KANE tr. *Rühlman's Turbines* 12 Head race and tail race. **1873** *Act 36 & 37 Vict.* c. 71 §17 No person shall catch ..any salmon..in the head race or tail race of any mill.

'head-rail¹.

1. One of the rails at the head of a ship.

1823 in CRABB *Technol. Dict.* c **1850** *Rudim. Navig.* (Weale) 123 *Head-rails*, those rails in the head which extend from the back of the figure to the cat-head and bow, and which are not only ornamental to the frame, but useful to that part of the ship.

2. The upper horizontal piece of a door-frame.

1874 TOLHAUSEN *Technol. Dict.*, Head-rail, *linteau en cloison.* **1875** KNIGHT *Dict. Mech.*

3. Usu. in *pl.* Teeth. *slang.*

1785 GROSE *Dict. Vulg. T.*, *Head rails*, teeth; sea phrase. **1854** 'C. BEDE' *Verdant Green* II. iv. 31 Your head-rails were loosened there, wasn't they? **1935** A. J. POLLOCK *Underworld Speaks* 52/1 *Head rails*, the teeth.

'head-rail². *Obs.* exc. *Hist.* [OE. *héafodhrægl* (Sweet), f. *héafod* head + *hrægl* garment, dress.] The kerchief or head-dress of women in Old English times.

1834 PLANCHÉ *Brit. Costume* 35 The head-dress of all classes is a veil or long piece of linen or silk wrapped round the head and neck..The Saxon name for it appears to have been hæfodes rægel (head-rail) or wæfles. **1860** FAIRHOLT *Costume Eng.* (ed. 2) 43 The hood, coverchief, or head-rail (the latter being the genuine Saxon name).

'head-roll. †**1.** A phylactery. *Obs.*

1583 GOLDING *Calvin on Deut.* xlvi. 275 Men must haue Gods lawe continually in their sight and make as it were a headroll thereof.

2. A roll or list of names of individuals.

1864 BURTON *Scot Abr.* I. iii. 114 Froissart gives a head-roll of those whose names he remembered. **1877** W. BRUCE *Comm. Rev.* 306 Names which hold an honorable place in the annals and headrolls of the Church.

'headroom. †**1.** *Sc.* = HEADLAND 1. *Obs.*

1572 in *Peebles Burgh Rec.* (1872) 337 It is statute..that the haill inhabitantis..euery ane to big their awne heid-roome betuix the Tolbuth to Peblis brig. c **1575** *Balfour's Practicks* 439 All landis..In Scotland's partis, has merchis thre; Heid-roume, water, and monthis bord..Heid-roume is to the hill direct, Fra the haugh callit in effect.

2. Room above the head; overhead space. Also *fig.*

1851 J. S. MACAULAY *Field Fortif.* 190 The frames.. should be set..perpendicular to the slope; more head-room is thus obtained. **1876** *Encycl. Brit.* IV. 267/2 Sufficient light, and headroom of at least 48 inches, being provided. **1902** *Eng. Dial. Dict.* s.v. *Head* sb. II, *Head-room*, of ceilings, staircases, etc.: sufficient height over-head. **1908** *Installation News* II. 68/1 Arrangements are being made to provide 15 feet headroom. **1933** *Punch* 18 Oct. 421/1 In the two-decker Underground trains..the upper deck would have less than six feet of head-room. **1958** *Economist* 20 Dec. 1103/2 Greater 'headroom' to make..increases in passenger fares..was the main object of the application by the Transport Commission. **1960** *Farmer & Stockbreeder* 15 Mar. 157, 14 ft. clear headroom.

'head-rope.

†**1.** One of the stays of a mast. *Obs.*

? a **1400** *Morte Arth.* 3668 Thane was hede-rapys hewene þat helde vpe þe mastes. c **1475** *Pict. Voc.* in Wr.-Wülcker 805/5 *Hec antemnis*, a hedrope.

2. 'That part of the bolt-rope which terminates any sail on the upper edge, and to which it is accordingly sewed. Also, the small rope to which a flag is fastened, to hoist it to the mast-head, or head of the ensign staff' (Smyth *Sailor's Word-bk.*).

1627 CAPT. SMITH *Seaman's Gram.* v. 22 The Robbins are little lines reeued into the eyelet holes of the saile vnder the head ropes. **1762-9** FALCONER *Shipwr.* II. 207 To each yard-arm the head-rope they extend. **1861** *Chamber's Encycl.* II. 205 A head-rope along the top edge.

3. A rope along the top of a fishing-net.

1883 *Cassell's Nat. Hist.* V. 94 The floating barrel fixed to the head-rope of a pilchard-net.

4. A rope for leading a horse, or for tying him up. Also for other animals.

1854 H. H. WILSON tr. *Rig-veda* II. 115 The halter and the heel-ropes of the fleet courser, and the head-ropes. **1936** P. FLEMING *News from Tartary* 328 The camels' headropes were fixed not to nose-pegs but to gaily decorated halters. **1957** P. KEMP *Mine were of Trouble* viii. 137 Hold on to the mules' head-ropes!

†**'head-roping.** *Obs.* = HEAD-ROPE 3.

1615 E. S. *Britains Buss* in Arb. *Garner* III. 630 Round about the head and two sides of each net, but not at the bottom, must be set a small cord, about the bigness of a bow-string, which is called [the] Head-roping or Nostelling.

head-sail. *Naut.* A general name for any of the sails belonging to the foremast and bowsprit.

1627 CAPT. SMITH *Seaman's Gram.* vii. 32 All head Sailes, which are those belonging to the fore Mast and Boltspret, doe keepe the Ship from the wind, or to fall off. **1670** NARBOROUGH *Jrnl.* in *Acc. Sev. Late Voy.* I. (1694) 21, I braced the Head-sails to the Mast. **1806** A. DUNCAN *Nelson* 123 The enemy appeared in great confusion, being reduced to his head-sails. **1875** BEDFORD *Sailor's Pocket-bk.* vi. (ed. 2) 221 Her sails should be much reduced, a half-lowered foresail or other small head-sail being sufficient.

'head-sheet.

†**1.** (?) A sheet put at the head of a bed. *Obs.*

1423 in *Rolls of Parlt.* IV. 228 Item, 1 Hedeshete de Reyns veilx, de 11 toelx. c **1460** J. RUSSELL *Bk. Nurture* 925 Boþe hedshete & pillow also. ? c **1475** *Sqr. lowe Degre* 843 Your headshete shall be of pery pyght, With dyamondes set and rubyes bryght.

2. *Naut.* A sheet belonging to the head-sails.

c **1860** H. STUART *Seaman's Catech.* 6 The men..to.. stand firmly on the head sheets.

headship ('hɛdʃɪp). [f. HEAD *sb.*¹ + -SHIP.] The position or office of head, chief, principal, or supreme governor; chiefship, leadership; the first place or position; supremacy, primacy.

1582 BENTLEY *Mon. Matrones* III. 272 Knocke Sisera of Roome in the temples of his usurped headship. **1654** GATAKER *Disc. Apol.* 54 Hedship of one of the principal Colledges. **1660** R. COKE *Power & Subj.* 73 Henry the Eighth, (who being of all mortal men the most unfit for a Churchman, ascribed to himself the Headship of the Church). **1736** NEAL *Hist. Purit.* III. 342 As to the Supremacy, he thinks such an Headship as the Kings of England claim..is not to be justified. **1861** HUGHES *Tom Brown at Oxf.* xiv, The prize is the headship of the river. **1870** ROGERS *Hist. Gleanings* Ser. II. 113 The headship of a college is the best prize which the fellows of the society have to bestow. **1886** RUSKIN *Præterita* I. vii. 209 Keeping..the headship of her class [in school].

'headsman. [f. *head's*, genitive of HEAD *sb.*¹ + MAN: cf. *draughtsman.*]

1. A chief, leader, head man. Now *rare.*

? a **1400** *Morte Arth.* 281 Thei..Hyngede of þeire heddysmene by hundrethes at ones. **1536** BELLENDEN *Cron. Scot.* (1821) II. 478 Mony othir noblis and heidismen. **1602** *2nd Pt. Return fr. Parnass.* IV. iii. 1864 The worshipfull headsmen of the towne. **1890** BOLDREWOOD *Miner's Right* xix. 183 One boss or headsman.

2. One who beheads; an executioner.

1601 SHAKS. *All's Well* IV. iii. 342 Come headesman, off with his head. **1625** K. LONG tr. *Barclay's Argenis* I. vi. 14 Brought upon the scaffold to offer her tender necke to the Headsmans axe. **1814** SCOTT *Ld. of Isles* v. xxvi, The griesly headsman's by his side.

3. The man in command of a whaling boat, who steers till the whale is struck, and then moves to the head of the boat.

1839 T. BEALE *Sperm Whale* xiii. 157 The crew of the boat ..consists of the headsman, boatsteerer and four hands.. The headsman..has the command of the boat. *Ibid.* 164 The line is running through the groove at the head of the boat..the headsman, cool and collected, pours water upon it as it passes. **1854** *Chamb. Jrnl.* I. 53 We gain on one fine fellow, which our headsman is steering for.

4. *Mining.* A labourer in a colliery who pushes coal from the workings to the tramway; a 'putter'.

1841 *Collieries & Coal Trade* (ed. 2) 227 These (who push a tram singly) are called hewing putters or headsmen: the others are two to a tram, and are called headsmen and foals. **1851** GREENWELL *Coal-trade Terms Northumb. & Durh.* 30 This little boy is called a foal. He sometimes assists the headsman by pushing the tub beside him.

'headspring.

1. The fountain-head or main source of a stream.

1430-40 LYDG. *Bochas* I. xii. (1544) 23 a, From one hed-spring There ran out riuers and stremes of al cunning. **1586** HOLINSHED *Chron.* (1808) VI. iv. 40 The riuer of the Banne flowed from this head spring. **1691** T. H[ALE] *Acc. New Invent.* p. lxii, The great winding of the River..and the low-lying of the Head-springs of it. **1876** BANCROFT *Hist. U.S.* III. iii. 54 The land was not less fertile to the very head-springs of the river.

2. *fig.* The chief source of anything; the quarter whence anything originates.

c **1450** in *Pol. Rel. & L. Poems* (1866) 47 Hede-spryng and welle of perfite continence! **1577** tr. *Bullinger's Decades* (1592) 630 As the Sunne is the headspring of the light and the heat: so is the Father the headspring of the Son. **1698** NORRIS *Pract. Disc.* (1707) IV. 30 Faith being..the Head-Spring of all that is good in us. **1859** MILL *Liberty* ii. 46 The two headsprings of ethical as of all other philosophy.

head-stall, headstall ('hɛdstɔːl), *sb.*¹ [f. HEAD *sb.*¹ + STALL, OE. *steall* position, standing position, standing place, place, stall for horses, etc.

Possibly applied first, as in *finger-stall*, to a closed place or case made to contain a part, and thence extended to the open casing of a *head-stall*.]

†**1.** (?) See quot. *Obs.*

1404 *Mann. & Househ. Exp.* (Roxb.) 264 Item, for a hedstalle for the taberet, iiij. *d.*

2. The part of a bridle or halter that fits round the head.

1480 *Wardr. Acc. Edw. IV* (1830) 153, x hedstalles and x broderayns for x hobyes and palfreys. **1592** GREENE *Art Conny Catch.* II. 5 A litle white leather head-stal and rains. **1684** EVELYN *Diary* 17 Dec., The reins and headstalls were of crimson silk. **1715-20** POPE *Iliad* VIII. 676 And fix'd their headstalls to his chariot-side. **1852** R. S. SURTEES *Sponge's Sp. Tour* vi. 25 The collar-shanks were neatly coiled under the headstalls.

3. A bandage worn by ancient flute-players to prevent undue distension of the cheeks in blowing.

1753 CHAMBERS *Cycl. Supp.*, *Head-Stall*, among antient musicians. **1888** in STAINER & BARRETT *Dict. Mus. T.*

Hence **head-stall** *v. nonce-wd. trans.*, to put a headstall on (a horse).

1616 SURFL. & MARKH. *Country Farme* 92 You must first beat him from these faults, before you goe about to head-stall him.

†**head-stall,** *sb.*² *Obs.* A choir-stall for a chief official, having its back against the screen, i.e. facing east.

c **1515** in Willis & Clark *Cambridge* (1886) I. 483 Karving and ioynyng for x hedstalles with their tabernacles of them.

'head-stick.

†**1.** An ancient piece of artillery. *Obs.*

1549 *Compl. Scot.* vi. 41 Slangis, and half slangis, quartar slangis, hede stikkis, murdresaris.

2. *Naut.* 'A short round stick with a hole at each end, through which the head-rope of some triangular sails is thrust, before it is sewed on. Its use is to prevent the head of the sail from twisting' (Smyth *Sailor's Word-bk.*).

1794 *Rigging & Seamanship* I. 128 The hoist-rope is put through the holes in the head-stick.

3. *Printing.* (See quot.)

1841 SAVAGE *Dict. Print.* 310 *Head stick*, pieces of furniture put at the head of pages when a form is imposed, to make the margin at the head of the page.

headstock. [f. HEAD *sb.*¹ + STOCK *sb.*]

1. Name applied to the bearings or supports of revolving parts in various machines.

a. The framing which supports the gudgeons of a wheel or axle. **b.** That part of a lathe which carries the mandrel or live stock. **c.** The framework in which the carriage of a spinning-mule runs. **d.** The head which supports the cutters in a planing machine. **e.** (*pl.*) *Mining.* A frame over a shaft, carrying the pulleys for the hoisting cables; a gallows-frame. **f.** The stock of a bell. **g.** The horizontal end members in the under-frame of a railway carriage or truck. **h.** (See quot.¹)

a. 1731 BEIGHTON in *Phil. Trans.* XXXVII. 6 A quadruple Crank..the Center..is fixed in Brasses at each End in two Head-stocks.

b. 1812-16 J. SMITH *Panorama Sc. & Art* I. 55 An accommodation of a few inches is obtained by screwing H further through or out of the headstock. **1863** SIR W. FAIRBAIRN *Mills* II. 9 A large headstock, carrying a hollow spindle through which is inserted a mandrill.

c. 1851 L. D. B. GORDON in *Art Jrnl. Illustr. Catal.* p. vi**/1 In some Mules the headstock is placed in advance of the roller-beam, towards the middle of its length. **1879** *Cassell's Techn. Educ.* IV. 395/2 Seven..to nine hundred spindles..arranged..upon the 'carriage'..in one long row, which is interrupted at the middle..by the 'headstock'.

d. 1863 SIR W. FAIRBAIRN *Mills* II. 11 A headstock carrying two cutters, one for roughing, and the other for finishing.

e. 1869 *Eng. Mach.* 19 Nov. 238/1 It..was taking the chair and men..over the headstocks. **1882** *Pall Mall G.* 25 Jan. 8/2 The engineman..failed to pull up in time to prevent the ascending empty cage from being wound over the headstocks.

f. 1688 R. HOLME *Armoury* III. 461/2 A Bell Azure hanging by its Headstock and Gugions in an Arch. **1881** *Standard* 20 Dec. 2/1 In ordinary peals the bells are swung well upwards, and..every headstock is provided with a stop, to prevent the bell accidentally turning over. **1882** *Ibid.* 20 Mar. 2/4 The bell is secured to the headstock by iron straps passing through its canons and bolted above the stock.

g. 1888 *Lockwood's Dict. Mech. Engin.*, *Headstock.* (2) The end timbers in the under frame of a railway truck. **1928** *Daily Express* 29 Dec. 9/4 The interval between headstocks

of coaches should be as small..as practicable for necessary freedom of movement.

h. **1927** T. WOODHOUSE *Artificial Silk* 108 Occasionally both reeds are placed on what is termed a dividing head or headstock. *Ibid.* 112 Fig. 50 illustrates the delivery or headstock end with the weaver's beam partially filled with the sheet of sized and dried threads.

2. *Sc.* (See quots.)

1834 H. MILLER *Scenes & Leg.* (1858) 420 The schoolmaster would call on the boys to divide and choose for themselves 'Head-stocks', *i.e.*, leaders, for the yearly cock-fight. **1854** —— *Sch. & Schm.* iii. (1857) 50, I contributed in no degree to the success of the *head-stock* or leader.

'headstone, head stone.

1. (*head stone*) The chief stone in a foundation; the cornerstone of a building. Also *fig.*

1535 COVERDALE *Ps.* cxvii[i]. 22 The same stone which the buylders refused, is become the heade stone in the corner [WYCLIF the hed of the corner]. **1649** MILTON *Eikon.* 1 His first foundation and as it were the head stone of his whole Structure. **1870** ROSSETTI *Poems* (1872) 37 Thou headstone of humanity, Groundstone of the great Mystery.

2. (*'headstone*) An upright stone at the head of a grave; a gravestone.

1775 ASH, *Headstone*..a gravestone set up at the head with an inscription. **1787** *Sederunt Managers Kirk Canongate* 22 Feb. in *Burns' Wks.* (1856) II. 35 The said managers..grant power and liberty to the said Robert Burns to erect a headstone at the grave of the said Robert Fergusson. **1833** TENNYSON *Poems* 3 Come only, when the days are still, And at my headstone whisper low, And tell me if the woodbines blow. **1866** GEO. ELIOT *F. Holt* i. 5 The churchyards, with their grassy mounds and venerable headstones.

†**'headstoops,** *adv. Obs.* In 5 hedstoupis. [f. HEAD *sb.*¹ + *-stoupes* an advb. genitive, from root of ME. *stoupen*, OE. *stúpian*, to STOOP: lit. 'with the head falling'.] Head downmost; headlong.

c **1400** *Destr. Troy* 6638 Mony hurlit doun hedstoupis to þe hard vrthe. *Ibid.* 7434 Hedstoupis of his horse he hurlit to ground.

headstrong ('hɛdstrɒŋ), *a.* [f. HEAD *sb.*¹ + STRONG *a.*; lit. strong of or in head.]

1. Of persons: Determined to have one's own way or to pursue one's own course; wilful, obstinate; violently self-willed.

1398 TREVISA *Barth. De P.R.* VI. xvi. (1495) 200 An euyl seruaunte and heedstronge settyth more by hymself than of his lorde. **1530** PALSGR. 315/1 Heedstrong, selfe wylled, *effronté, estourdi.* **1590** GREENE *Never too late* (1600) 15 To tie a headstrong girle from loue, is to tie the Furies again in fetters. **1692** BENTLEY *Boyle Lect.* ix. 335 They were too stiff-necked and headstrong. **1720** GAY *Poems* (1745) I. 172 The headstrong coursers tore the silver reins. **1856** EMERSON *Eng. Traits, Char.* Wks. (Bohn) II. 61 They are testy and headstrong through an excess of will and bias.

2. Of things, actions, etc.: Characterized by or proceeding from wilfulness or obstinacy.

1586 T. B. *La Primaud. Fr. Acad.* I. To Rdr., That none through any headstrong conceit should be wedded to private opinions. **1676** HALE *Contempl.* I. 317 Commonly our own choice is headstrong and foolish. **1796** H. HUNTER tr. *St. Pierre's Stud. Nat.* (1799) II. 25 Dangerous and headstrong passions. **1871** R. ELLIS *Catullus* xv. 14 Should..humour headstrong Drive thee wilfully..to such profaning.

Hence **'headstrongly** *adv.*

a **1639** W. WHATELEY *Prototypes* I. xix. (1640) 224 He will head strongly like a madded beast runne on in his owne race.

'headstrongness. [f. HEADSTRONG + -NESS.] The quality or condition of being headstrong; wilfulness, obstinacy.

1625 K. LONG tr. *Barclay's Argenis* v. iii. 339 The head-strongnesse of any bad men. **1741** RICHARDSON *Pamela* (1824) I. xcviii. 483 A little sort of perverseness and head-strongness. **1867** R. PALMER *Life P. Howard* 131 He followed out his views with a headstrongness that wrought great troubles.

'headswoman. *dial.* [f. *head's* genitive case: cf. HEADSMAN sense 1.] A midwife.

a **1825** in FORBY *Voc. E. Anglia* **1857** in DUNGLISON.

head-tire ('hɛdtaɪə(r)). Now *arch.* or *dial.* Attire for the head; a head-dress.

1560 BIBLE (Genev.) 1 *Esdras* iii. 6 An head tyre of fine linnen. **1653** HOLCROFT *Procopius* I. xiii. 20 The King..took from him his Head-tire of gold and pearl, which tied up his hair. **1847** MRS. SHERWOOD *Life* xxiii. 378, I see this tyrant now, in her smart head-tire, seated in her elbow chair. **1855** ROBINSON *Whitby Gloss.*, *Head-gear* or *Head-tyre*, the head dress and its adornments. **1885** BIBLE (R.V.) *Isa.* iii. 20 The headtires, and the ankle chains.

'head-voice. One of the higher registers of the voice in singing or speaking; applied both to the second register (that immediately above the *chest-voice*), and to the third register or falsetto.

1849 DICKENS *Dav. Copp.* xxxvi, He has a remarkable head-voice. **1880** B. HARTE *J. Briggs's Love Story* ii, Come here! she cried in a small head voice not unlike a bird's twitter. **1896** R. J. LLOYD *Gen. of Vowels* in *Jrnl. Anat. & Physiol.* XXXI. 239 Here..in singing up the scale, the 'chest' voice changes into the 'head' voice.

'head-ward, *sb. Obs.* exc. *Hist.* [OE. *héafodweard*: cf. ON. *hǫfuðvǫrðr* body-guard.] The guarding or protection of the lord's head or life; attendance as a guard upon the lord or king.

c **1000** *Rect. Sing. Pers.* in Thorpe *Anc. Laws* (1840) I. 432 Heafod-wearde healdan and hors-wearde. **1861** PEARSON *Early & Mid. Ages Eng.* 206 *note*, He must..do heed-ward and horse-ward, go post far and near, as he is told. **1883** GREEN *Conq. Eng.* 331 To keep 'head-ward' over the manor at nightfall, or horse-ward over its common field..were tenures by which the villagers held their land.

headward ('hɛdwəd), *adv.* and *a.* Also 9 **-wards.** [f. HEAD *sb.*¹ + -WARD.]

†**A.** *orig.* in phrase. **a.** ***to the headward,*** toward the head, in the direction of the head. **b.** Of a ship: In advance, ahead. *Obs.*

1387 TREVISA *Higden* (Rolls) III. 323 A briȝt swerd..and þe poynt dounward evene to his hevedward. **1662** HOBBES 7 *Problems* vi. Wks. 1845 VII. 44 The ship will gain the space DF to the headward. **1674** N. FAIRFAX *Bulk & Selv.* 130 Why earthworms are limed so much to the headward.

B. *adv.* Towards or in the direction of the head.

1798 H. TOOKE *Purley* (1829) I. ix. 423 Where you may use indifferently either *Upward, Topward,* or *Headward.* **1862** M. B. EDWARDS *John & I* xxix. (1876) 221, I was thrown headwards from my seat. **1883** A. MACLEAN in *Memorial Vol.* 295 They are robust enough headward.

C. *adj.* Being in the region or direction of the head. ***headward erosion***: erosion of a stream at its head, in such a way that the length of the stream is increased.

1667 T. COXE in *Phil. Trans.* II. 452 The heart-ward part of the Vein..and the head-ward part of it. **1894** *Nation* (N.Y.) 13 Sept. 195/1 Headward growth of branches. **1916** H. F. CLELAND *Geol.* iv. 99 A valley is lengthened at its upper end and is cut back by the water which flows in at its head... This is called headward erosion. **1922** C. A. COTTON *Geomorphol. N.Z.* I. 72 They [*sc.* insequent streams] rapidly eat their way back into the interfluves by headward erosion. **1937** WOOLDRIDGE & MORGAN *Physical Basis Geogr.* xii. 162 With the progress of time it [*sc.* down-cutting] proceeds backwards, *i.e.* headwards, from the lowest point. The grading of a stream course thus involves headward erosion. **1944** A. HOLMES *Princ. Physical Geol.* II. x. 153 The torrent tract..evolves into the valley tract, and each gradually migrates inland as the source continues to recede by headward erosion. **1965** F. J. MONKHOUSE *Dict. Geogr.* 154/2 *Headward erosion*, the cutting back upstream of a valley above its original source by rainwash, gullying and spring-sapping. **1968** [see DISSECTION 7].

†**head-wark, -werk.** *Now dial.* Also 6 rarely -work. [OE. *héafodwærc* masc., ON. *hǫfuðverkr* headache, f. *hǫfuð* head + *verk* work; cf. *verkja* to ache, pain, 'virkir mik i hǫfuðit', it aches me in the head. OE. *weorc* neut., besides 'work', had the senses 'hardship, pain, grief'.]

1. Pain in the head, headache. Cf. dial. *belly-wark.*

c **1000** *Sax. Leechd.* II. 18 Wið heafod wærce ȝenim rudan. *c* **1350** in *Archæol.* XXX 350 All hys hedwerk awey xal synke. *c* **1450** *St. Cuthbert* (Surtees) 2580 Alle hir hedewerk went away. **1483** *Cath. Angl.* 180/1 Þe Hedewarke. *a* **1510** DOUGLAS *King Hart* II. lvii, Heid-werk, Hoist, and Parlasy. **1549** *Compl. Scot.* vi. 37 Caterris, hede verkis, ande indegestione. **1629** Z. BOYD *Balm Gilead* 59 (Jam.) A toothache, or an head-worke, as we say.

attrib. *c* **1440** *Promp. Parv.* 232/2 Heedwarke sufferere.

2. The Common Corn Poppy; = HEADACHE 2.

1863 PRIOR *Plant-n.*, *Headache*, or *Head-warke*, from the effect of its odour, the red field-poppy, *Papaver Rhœas.*

head water, head-water.

1. a. *pl.* ***head waters***: The streams from the sources of a river.

[**1535** COVERDALE *Gen.* ii. 10 A ryuer..there deuyded it selfe in to foure heade waters.] **1802** *R. Brookes' Gazetteer* (ed. 12) s.v. *Lexington*, Lexington..on the head waters of the Elkhorn river. **1862** D. WILSON *Preh. Man* I. viii. 271 The head-waters of the Mississippi. **1878** HUXLEY *Physiogr.* 4 The main stream splits up into a number of smaller streams, forming the 'head-waters' of the river.

attrib. **1895** *Educ. Rev.* Nov. 356 The whole river-system, its dismembered headwater streams excepted.

b. *ellipt.* = ***head-water-mark.***

1908 *Westm. Gaz.* 29 Apr. 6/3 The Thames has risen rapidly during the night, and is now 2 ft. 6 in. above head-water at Windsor.

2. ***head-water-mark***, a mark showing the 'head' (cf. HEAD *sb.*¹ 17) to be allowed above a weir, etc.

1894 *Act 57–8 Vict.* c. clxxxvii. §75 [They] shall..prevent the waters of the Thames being at any place above the level of any head-water-mark for the time being fixed.

headway. [In I. short for *ahead-way*; in II. f. HEAD *sb.*¹ + WAY *sb.*]

I. 1. Of a ship: Motion ahead or forward; rate of progress.

1748 *Anson's Voy.* II. i. 112 By means of the head-way we had got, we loofed close in. **1769** FALCONER *Dict. Marine* (1789) Rrij, The head-way..is..feeble. **1809** W. IRVING *Knickerb.* (1849) 88 She made as much leeway as headway. **1865** DICKENS *Mut. Fr.* I. i, The boat made slight headway against it [the tide].

2. *transf.* and *fig.* Advance, progress (in general).

1775 ASH, *Headway*, the act of moving forward, the motion of advancing. **1837** CARLYLE *Fr. Rev.* II. IV. i, There is rearing, rocking, vociferation; not the smallest headway. **1887** JESSOPP *Arcady* v. 159 Rarely, except in the open parishes, do the demagogues make headway.

II. 3. *Arch.* Room over head; the clear height of a doorway, arch, tunnel, or the like.

1775 ASH, *Headway*,..room for the head to pass. **1842–76** GWILT *Archit.* Gloss., *Headway of Stairs*, the clear distance, measured perpendicularly, from a given landing place or stair to the ceiling above. **1861** SMILES *Engineers* II. 355 The strength as well as lightness of a bridge of this material..is of great moment where headway is of importance. **1892** *Pall Mall G.* 23 Feb. 3/3 The bridge has a clear headway of 20 ft. 6 in. above high water.

4. *Mining.* (Also ***headways.***) A narrow passage or 'gallery' connecting the broad parallel passages or 'boards' in a coal mine.

1708 J. C. *Compl. Collier* (1845) 41 This Headways..or first working..is carried on, according to the Grain of the Coal, as it lies along the Grain, and not cross the Grain. *Ibid.* 42 A Yard and a Quarter broad or wide for a Headways. **1839** *Penny Cycl.* XV. 247 A series of broad parallel passages or bords..communicating with each other by narrower passages or 'headways'. **1881** RAYMOND *Mining Gloss.* s.v., The headways are the second set of excavations in post-and-stall work.

5. The interval of time or the distance between two consecutive trains, trams, buses, etc., running on the same route and in the same direction. orig. *U.S.*

1895 in *Funk's Standard Dict.* **1900** *Jrnl. Soc. Arts* 2 Mar. 315/1 The headway between the carriers is fixed say at ten or twenty seconds. **1930** *Oxford Times* 21 Mar. 17/4, I think Route 2 should have a six-minute headway between 8 a.m. and 10.30 a.m. *Ibid.*, Until the headway was closed to 15 minutes in the morning, and 12 minutes in the afternoon, serious inadequacy existed. **1970** *Courier-Mail* (Brisbane) 17 Dec. 1/3 The 30-minute headway between each bus reduced to a 50-minute head-way. **1971** *Mod. Railways* May 193/3 Page 105 of the March *Modern Railways* indicates a new 17.11 Paddington to Bristol, first stop Didcot, thus providing a second 3 min headway to Didcot East Junction with the existing 17.15 to Worcester.

6. *Comb.* **headways course**: see quots.

1851 GREENWELL *Coal-trade Terms Northumb. & Durh.* 30 *Headways Course*, a line of walls or holings, extending from side to side of a pannel of boards. **1883** GRESLEY *Gloss. Coal-mining*, *Headways Course*, when a set of headings or walls extend from side to side of a set of boards, they are said to be driven headways course.

headwear ('hɛdwɛə(r)). [f. HEAD *sb.*¹ + WEAR *sb.* 3.] = HEAD-GEAR 1.

1896 J. C. HARRIS *Sister Jane* 39 Gi' me my bonnet. It's all the head-wear I've got left. **1900** *Daily News* 27 Mar. 4/2 They were most easily classified by their headwear. Caps, bowlers, and felt hats were there in almost equal proportions. **1904** W. M. GALLICHAN *Fishing & Trav. Spain* vii. 76 He was much interested in my wife's hat. Such headwear had never been seen in Coria. **1937** *Discovery* Apr. 106/2 The head wear is the Kalpak, a tall cap, not unlike a busby in principle. **1939–40** *Army & Navy Stores Catal.* p. xxxviii/5 Headwear, Naval, Military and Tropical.

'head-work. [f. HEAD *sb.*¹ + WORK *sb.*]

1. a. Mental work; brain-work.

1837 DICKENS *Pickw.* liv. 587 How the blazes you can stand the head-work you do, is a mystery to me. **1843** MAURY in Mrs. Corbin *Life* (1888) 46 Destroying myself with over-much head-work. **1859** GEO. ELIOT *A. Bede* III. xxxiii, His headwork was so much more important to Burge than his skill in handicraft. **1869** J. MARTINEAU *Ess.* II. 49 The art..is not hand-work, but head-work.

b. The practice of carrying loads on the head.

1840 R. H. DANA 2 *Yrs. bef. Mast* xiv, For we soon found that..'head-work' was the only system for California.

c. Skill in games and sports.

1851 J. PYCROFT *Cricket Field* ii. 22 There is a deal of head-work in bowling. **1898** B. J. ANGLE in W. A. Morgan *'House' on Sport* 42 His quickness of foot and tricky head-work quickly demoralised the majority of his opponents. **1898** K. S. RANJITSINHJI *With Stoddart's Team* (ed. 3) iv. 84 The English bowling..aimed at steadiness, rather than head work and sting. **1958** F. C. AVIS *Boxing Ref. Dict.* 52 *Headwork*, craftiness in boxing.

2. *Arch.* 'An ornament for the keystone of an arch' (1864 in Webster citing Gwilt).

3. *pl.* **a.** Apparatus for controlling the flow of water in a river or canal. **b.** (See quot. 1905.)

1891 *Scribner's Mag.* X. 468 The river flowing between firm banks, could be permanently controlled by head-works of masonry. **1903** *Sci. Amer. Suppl.* 10 Jan. 22597/3 Headworks can be placed more easily along the banks of smaller streams, or dams built across their beds, raising and controlling the waters. **1905** *Terms Forestry & Logging* 40 *Headworks*, a platform or raft, with wind-lass or capstan, which is attached to the front of a log raft or boom of logs, for warping, kedging, or winding it through lakes and still water, by hand or horse power. **1963** *Times* 19 Apr. 14/6 Smoothly it flowed, the head-works of a carefully planned series of canals. **1971** N. SMITH *Hist. Dams* i. 10 The headworks of the irrigation canal.

Hence **'head-ˌworker**, one who works with his head or brain.

1873 B. STEWART *Conserv. Force* (U.S. ed.) viii. 224 The head-worker is not equally fitted to be a hand-worker.

heady ('hɛdɪ), *a.* Forms: 4–5 hevedi, -y, hedi, 4–6 hedy, 6 heedye, heddie, -y, 6–7 headie, -ye, headdy, 6– heady. [f. HEAD *sb.*¹ + -Y. Allied in orig. sense to *headling* adv.]

1. Headlong, precipitate, impetuous, violent; passionate; headstrong; 'hurried on with passion' (J.). **a.** Of motion, action, personal qualities.

1382 WYCLIF *Judg.* v. 15 Into hevedi fallynge [*quasi in præceps*] and helle, he ȝaf hym silf to peryl. **1460** *Paston Lett.* No. 349 I. 514 With here hevedy and fumows langage. **1545** RAYNOLD *Byrth Mankynde* Prol. (1634) 8 They that giue so precipitate and heady judgements. **1561** T. NORTON *Calvin's Inst.* II. ii. (1634) 118 Raging with headie lust. **1579** LYLY *Euphues* (Arb.) 145 That hot and heady humor which he is by nature subiect vnto. *a* **1656** BP. HALL *Rem. Wks.* (1660) 149 Carried with an heady and furious impetuousnesse. **1749** JOHNSON *Van. Hum. Wishes* 281 His

heady rage. **1871** R. ELLIS *Catullus* xv. 11 Let luxury run her heady riot. **1886** STEVENSON *Dr. Jekyll* 112.

b. Of a person. (In early use, also, domineering, overbearing (quots. 1494, 1526); passionately desirous of something, 'keen' *upon* (quot. 1540).)

1494 FABYAN *Chron.* VII. 342 Noo wonder thoughe ye kyng were thus hedy or greuouse to ye cytie. **1526** *Pilgr. Perf.* (W. de W. 1531) 70 The fyfthe condicyon that becometh a prynce, is, that he be not heddy to his subgectes. **1526** TINDALE *2 Tim.* iii. 4 Traytours, heddy, hye mynded, gredy apon voluptousnes more then the lovers of god. **1540** in Strype *Eccl. Mem.* I. App. cxv. 324, I wold have men not be heady upon flesh at such times as yt is forbydden them. **1545** ASCHAM *Toxoph.* (Arb.) 85 Wales being headye, and rebelling many yeares agaynst vs. **1690** LOCKE *Govt.* II. xviii. §205 Mischiefs that may happen..when a heady Prince comes to the Throne. **1751** JOHNSON *Rambler* No. 184 ¶6 Passions by which the heady and vehement are seduced and betrayed. **1888** RIDER HAGGARD *Col. Quaritch* xii, He was too heady a man to reason overmuch.

c. Of a stream or current: Impetuous, violent.

1599 SHAKS. *Hen. V*, I. i. 34 Neuer came Reformation in a Flood, With such a heady currance scowring faults. **1636** FEATLY *Clavis Myst.* xxxii. 428 Like as a headie streame glides by the bankes. **1837** *Blackw. Mag.* XLI. 602 Swept.. by the currents of the heady ocean.

2. a. Apt to affect or 'go to' the head; having an intoxicating or stupefying quality. Also, that affects or turns the head; that turns one giddy.

1577 HARRISON *England* II. xviii. (1877) I. 295 There is such headie ale. **1652–62** HEYLIN *Cosmogr.* II. (1682) 128 All heady and intoxicating Drinks are by Law prohibited. **1664** EVELYN *Sylva* II. vii. (1812) II. 161 They are driven from their haunts, for a time, by garlic, and other heady smells. *a* **1774** W. HARTE *Charit. Mason* (R.), Both ways deceitful is the wine of Power, When new, 'tis heady, and, when old, 'tis sour. **1848** H. ROGERS *Ess.* I. vi. 278 Just the man to be easily intoxicated with this heady liquor. **1893** Q. [Couch] *Delectable Duchy* 39 The yellow was out on the gorse, with a heady scent like a pineapple's. **1898** *Atlantic Monthly* Apr. 501/1 He would sit on a heady scaffold. **1924** A. I. I. FINCH in G. I. Finch *Making of Mountaineer* xii. 177 Up and down we seemed to go, and once round a little natural balcony that hung out over space but proved not in the least heady.

fig. **1669** PENN *No Cross* viii. §1 His [Nebuchadnezzar] Successes and Empire were too Heady for him.

†**b.** Affected in the head; giddy. *Obs. rare.*

1628 WITHER *Brit. Rememb.* VIII. 820 Some sheep are headdy; some get the staggers; some the scab.

c. Headachy (cf. HEAD *sb.*^{1} 1 d).

1872 GEO. ELIOT *Let.* 4 June (1956) V. 277 George, being a little heady, and unable to occupy his mornings with writing, is going tomorrow to see the aquarium. **1934** *Air Rev.* Nov. 60, I was feeling a little 'heady' as..a good sea was running, and I was making an effort to eat some nice fat, greasy beef. **1955** E. HILLARY *High Adventure* 69 In the morning I felt thick and heady and a sharp cough rasped my sore throat. **1965** 'J. LYMINGTON' *Green Drift* iv. 63, I was feeling very heady and tired. *Ibid.* 64 'Do you still have this heady feeling?' 'Yes, I think it must be the heat. Thundery.'

†**3.** Having a large head. *Obs. rare.*

1552 HULOET, Headye, or hauynge a great heade, *capito.*

†**4.** Of a tenure: In chief (*in capite*); held direct of the crown. *Obs. nonce-use.*

1599 MARSTON *Sco. Villanie* I. ii. 179 Tenure..All to be headdy, or free-hold at least.

5. *Comb.*, as ***heady-rash, -minded*** adjs.

1590 SHAKS. *Com. Err.* v. i. 216 Nor headie-rash prouoak'd with raging ire. **1598** R. BERNARD tr. *Terence, Hecyra* IV. i, What are you so headie-minded that you wish the death of the child?

heaf. *north. dial.* [Modification of *heft*, HAFT, *sb.*^{2}, *v.*^{3}] Accustomed pasture-ground (of sheep).

c **1525** *Survey St. Bees Priory* in *Monast. Angl.* (1821) III. 579/1 A pasture for shepe upon the morez or hefe called Sandwith Marshe. **1852** *Jrnl. R. Agric. Soc.* XIII. II. 265 (Cumberland) Some shepherds are at the daily pains of taking a few stones of hay..five or six miles to their sheep-heaf, and thus induce the sheep to keep their heaf in all weathers. **1886** *Pall Mall G.* 9 Aug. 4/1 Some of the largest farms have most extensive 'heafs', and graze from two to four thousand sheep. **1894** R. S. FERGUSON *Hist. Westmld.* xviii. 290 A Herdwick sheep is very much attached to its own 'heaf', or that part of the fell where it generally goes.

heaft, rare obs. form of HAFT *sb.*^{1}

heah, *adv.* A representation of a colloq. pronunciation of HERE *adv.* Freq. used in Black English.

1927 A. P. RANDOLPH in A. Dundes *Mother Wit* (1973) 200 Bin heah too long. **1937** C. HIMES *Black on Black* (1973) 139 A nickel victrola in the rear blared a husky, negroid bellow: 'Anybody heah wanna buy.' **1970** R. D. ABRAHAMS *Positively Black* p. ix, Everybody 'round heah is talkin' 'bout 'ligion, gittin' happy an' shoutin'. **1973** *Black World* June 61 Yo ole man in heah?

heake, erron. form of HECK *sb.*

†**heaking-time.** *Obs. rare*$^{-1}$. ? Time to draw in the HAKING, or the fish caught in it.

1599 NASHE *Lenten Stuffe* 20 Now it is high heaking-time, and bee the windes neuer so easterly aduerse, and the tyde fled from vs, wee must violently towe and hale in our redoutable Sophy of the floating Kingdom of Pisces, etc.

†**heal, hele,** *sb. Obs.* exc. *Sc.* Forms: 1 **hælu, hælo, hæl,** 2–3 **hæle,** 2–6 **hele,** 2–7 **heale,** 4–5 **heel(e,** 6–7 **heal;** also 4 **hel,** *Sc.* **heile, heyle,** 5 **helle, (ȝele),** 5 *north.*, 5–7 *Sc.* **heill,** 6 *Sc.* **heil,** 7–8 *Sc.* **heal(l,** 9 *Sc.* **hale.** [OE. *hælu, hælo, hæl*, corresp. to OS. *hêli* (MDu. *heile*), OHG. *heilî, hailî, hêlî* (MHG. *heile*), Goth. **hailei, -ein*, from *hail-s*, OE. *hál* adj. HALE, WHOLE; one of the abstr. fems. in WGer. *-î*, from earlier *-în*, which in OE. changed this ending to *-u*. Cf. the doublets HAIL *sb.*^{2}, HALE *sb.*^{1}]

1. Sound bodily condition; freedom from sickness; health.

a **1000** *Crist* 1654 þær is..hælu butan sare. *c* **1000** *Sax. Leechd.* I. 342 Him cymð god hæl. *c* **1175** *Lamb. Hom.* 145 þer scal beon..hele wið-uten unhele. *a* **1300** *Cursor M.* 23465 Hele [*Edin.* hel] wit-vten seke or sare. *c* **1400** tr. *Secreta Secret., Gov. Lordsh.* (E.E.T.S.) 66 Kepyng of hele ys mor bettir and mor precious þan any medicyne. **1431** *E.E. Wills* (1882) 87 Beyng yn goode heale and yn my full wittes. *c* **1460** J. RUSSELL *Bk. Nurture* 351 To preserue your lord in heele [*rime* euery deele]. **1508** DUNBAR *Poems* iv. 1, I that in heill wes and glaidnes, Am trublit now with gret seiknes. *a* **1553** UDALL *Royster D.* III. iii. (Arb.) 46 He was your right good maister while he was in heale. **1606** WARNER *Alb. Eng.* XVI. ciii. 405 That thou beest, Pegge, in better heale than I my selfe am now I wish. **1721** RAMSAY *Answ. Burchet's Epist.* 31 I'll wish ye weel, And aft in sparkling claret drink your heal. **1795** BURNS *To Mr. Mitchell* v, My heal and weal I'll tak a care o't.

b. Recovery from sickness, healing, cure. (In quots. 1470–85, 1687, A cure, remedy.)

c **1175** *Lamb. Hom.* 29 Ane wunde..oðer hwile hit is on wane of his hele. *c* **1290** *S. Eng. Leg.* I. 16/514 Heore hele huy hadden riȝt þere. *c* **1340** *Cursor M.* 19754 Crist ȝyue þe hele of þi wo. **1470–85** MALORY *Arthur* XVII. xi, And she myght haue a dysshe ful of blood of a mayde..that blood shold be her hele. **1687** P. MADAN *Tunbridge Waters* in *Harl. Misc.* (1808) I. 586 A common heal, A free-cost health.

2. Well-being, welfare, safety; prosperity.

c **950** *Lindisf. Gosp.* Matt. v. 47 Gif ȝie hælo beadas broðero. **13..** *E.E. Allit. P.* A. 16 þat wele þat wont watz.. heuen my happe & al my hele. *c* **1386** CHAUCER *Frankl. T.* 359 Arueragus with heele and greet honour..Is comen hoom. **1412–20** LYDG. *Chron. Troy* I. v, Where thrugh thin honor worship & thin hele Was lost. **1522** SKELTON *Why nat to Court* 768 To cause the commune weale Longe to endure in heale. *a* **1605** MONTGOMERIE *Sonn.* lviii. 14 Revenge, revert, revive, revest, reveall, My hurt, my hairt, my hope, my hap, my heall.

b. ***good heal***, welfare, fortune; whence ME. (*to*) ***godere hele***, to good fortune, to welfare; fortunately.

c **1175** *Lamb. Hom.* 57 Godere hele þu hit scalt iseon. *c* **1205** LAY. 3597 ȝef þu heo þus dalest, to godere þire hæle. **1297** R. GLOUC. (1724) 368 þat goder hele al Engelond was heo euere ybore.

c. ***evil heal***: disaster, harm. (*to*) ***evil hele, wrother heal***, unfortunately, disastrously. Cf. HAIL *sb.*^{2} 2, HALE *sb.*^{1} b.

c **1175** *Lamb. Hom.* 33 Hwet seið þe dusie? to ufele hele wes ic iboren. *c* **1205** LAY. 490 To wroþer heore hele habbeð heo such werc idon. *a* **1330** *Otuel* 211 Sarazin, nere thou messager Wrother hele come thou her. *c* **1340** *Cursor M.* 6583 (Trin.) Ful euelhele brake ȝe þe day.

3. Spiritual health, well-being, or healing; salvation. Cf. SOUL-HEAL.

901–9 *Charter of Eadweard* in Kemble *Cod. Dipl.* V. 163 Ic ðær mynster on ȝestaðolode for mine saule hælo. *c* **1000** *Ags. Gosp.* Luke xix. 9 To-dæȝ þisse hiw-rædene ys hæl ȝeworden. *c* **1200** *Trin. Coll. Hom.* 41 He..bihat us to mede eche hele. *a* **1225** *Ancr. R.* 430 To alle uolkes heale. *a* **1300** *Cursor M.* 11341 Do me to rest nu seruand þin, for nu min ei has sen þin hel. *c* **1400** MAUNDEV. (Roxb.) x. 39 Godd.. has wroȝt hele in myddes of þe erthe. **1578** *Ps. lxvii.* in *Scot. Poems 16th C.* II. 128 Thy sauing heill and righteousnes.

heal (hiːl), *v.*^{1} Forms: 1 **hǽlan,** 2–3 **hælen,** 2–6 **hele(n,** 3 **(helien), healen,** 4 **haile,** 4–5 **heel(e,** (*Sc.* **heile, heyle, hel),** (5 **ȝele**), 6–7 **heale,** (*Sc.* **heil(l),** 7– **heal.** [A Com. Teut. vb.: OE. *hǽlan* = OFris. *hêla*, OS. *hêlian* (MDu. *hêlen, heilen*, Du. *heelen*, LG. *helen*), OHG. *heilan* (Ger. *heilen*), ON. *heil* (Sw. *hela*, Da. *hele*), Goth. *hailjan*, deriv. of *hail-s*, OTeut. **hailo-z*, OS. *hál*, HALE, WHOLE.]

1. *trans.* To make whole or sound in bodily condition; to free from disease or ailment, restore to health or soundness; to cure (*of* a disease or wound).

c **1000** *Ags. Gosp.* Matt. x. 8 Hælað untrume. *c* **1175** *Lamb. Hom.* 91 Heo weren iheled from alle untrumnesse. *a* **1300** *Cursor M.* 13261 He..heild mani þat war seke. *c* **1325** *Metr. Hom.* 130 The prophet Helesius Of leper heled an hethen man. *c* **1375** *Sc. Leg. Saints, Petrus* 117 He heilys sek men And quyknyse dede. **1382** WYCLIF *Luke* iv. 23 Leeche, heele thi silf. *c* **1400** MAUNDEV. (1839) vi. 69 The drye tree..heleþ him of the fallynge euyll. *c* **1450** *St. Cuthbert* (Surtees) 1066 How aungel Raphael helyd his kne. **1607** SHAKS. *Timon* II. i. 24, I..must not breake my backe, to heale his finger. **1842** TENNYSON *Morte d'Arth.* 264 Where I will heal me of my grievous wound. **1846** TRENCH *Mirac.* Introd. (1862) 20 Christ, healing a sick man with his word.

b. *absol.* To perform or effect a cure.

c **1000** *Ags. Gosp.* Matt. xii. 10 Ys hyt alyfed to hælenne [*c* **1160** *Hatton G.* to hælen] on reste-daȝum? *c* **1000** *Sax. Leechd.* I. 342 Wið eaȝena dymnysse ȝenim foxes geallan.. hyt hæleþ. *c* **1375** *Sc. Leg. Saints, Symon & Judas* 32 Of fewire and parlesy, Vith word þu heilis. *c* **1400** MAUNDEV. (1839) xi. 124 þe Oyle..heleþ of many sykenesses. *c* **1450** tr. *De Imitatione* III. lv. 132 þe heuenly leche of soules, þat smytist & helist. **1611** BIBLE *Deut.* xxxii. 39, I wound, and I heale. **1732** POPE *Ep. Bathurst* 234 As Poison heals, in just proportion us'd. **1827** KEBLE *Chr. Y.* Visit. Sick iii, As if one prayer could heal.

c. *spec.* To touch for the 'king's evil'.

1503–4 in Pegge *Curialia Misc.* (1818) 127 For heling 3 seke folks 20. 0..for heling 2 seke folks 13. 4. **1661** PEPYS *Diary* 13 Apr., I went to the Banquet-house, and there saw the King heale.

2. To cure (a disease); to restore to soundness (a wound); also ***to heal up, over.*** Also *absol.*

c **1000** *Ags. Gosp.* Matt. x. 1 Ðæt hiȝ..hældun [*c* **1160** *Hatton G.* helden] adle, and ælce untrumnysse. *c* **1205** LAY. 23072 For heo sculde mid haleweie helen [*c* **1275** heale] his wunden. **1398** TREVISA *Barth. De P.R.* VI. xxi. (1495) 209 To kepe helthe and to heele sykenesse. *c* **1450** *Golagros & Gaw.* 882 Thai hynt of his harnese, to helyn his wound. **1590** SPENSER *F.Q.* III. v. 42 O foolish physick..That heales up one, and makes another wound! **1676** WISEMAN *Surg.* (J.), A fontanel had been made in the same leg, which he was forced to heal up. **1781** COWPER *Expostulation* 153 They saw distemper healed, and life restored. **1863** WHYTE MELVILLE *Gladiators* ix. (1864) 62 Mere scratches, skin deep, and healed over now.

3. *fig.* To restore (a person, etc.) from some evil condition or affection (as sin, grief, disrepair, unwholesomeness, danger, destruction); to save, purify, cleanse, repair, mend.

c **825** *Vesp. Psalter* cxlvii. 3 Se haeleð ȝeðreste on heortan. *c* **1000** *Ags. Ps.* (Spl.) xliii. 4 [xliv. 3] (Bosw.) Earm heora ne hælþ hiȝ. *c* **1175** *Lamb. Hom.* 95 He ne com na to demane moncun..ac to helenne. *c* **1205** LAY. 15871 ȝif ich þi wærc [a ruined wall] hæle. **1382** WYCLIF *2 Chron.* vii. 14, I schal ..ben mercyable to the synnes of hem, and helyn their lond. **1535** COVERDALE *2 Kings* ii. 22 So the water was healed. **1650** JER. TAYLOR *Holy Living* (1834) 190 Let it alone, and the thing will heal itself. **1719** DE FOE *Crusoe* II. xii, Our ship was..healed of all her leaks. **1847** TENNYSON *Princ.* III. 49 Heal me with your pardon.

b. To cure, repair, amend (any evil condition compared to a disease or wound).

c **1200** *Trin. Coll. Hom.* 173 Elch sinne..bute hit be here forgieue oðer mid bote iheled. **1340** HAMPOLE *Pr. Consc.* 1724 þe gastly woundes of syn Thurgh penaunce may be heled. **1526** *Pilgr. Perf.* (W. de W. 1531) Gb, Sacramentes of the chirche: the whiche cureth, releueth & heleth all defautes. **1600** SHAKS. *A.Y.L.* III. v. 117 Faster then his tongue Did make offence, his eye did heale it vp. **1720** OZELL *Vertot's Rom. Rep.* II. XIV. 348 Octavia, Antony's Wife and Cæsar's Sister..at various Times, heal'd up their Breaches. **1849** MACAULAY *Hist. Eng.* II. 135 Something might have been done to heal the lacerated feelings..of the Irish gentry. **1887** TREVELYAN in *Times* 7 Mar. 10/6 The breach in our ranks might be healed tomorrow.

4. *intr.* (for *refl.*) To become whole or sound; to recover from sickness or a wound; to get well. (Said of the person, of the part affected, or of a wound or sore.)

a **1375** *Joseph Arim.* 681 þe arm helede a-ȝeyn hol to þe stompe. *a* **1400–50** *Alexander* 2817, I sall hele all in hast. **1530** PALSGR. 595/1 Whan thy wounde begynneth to heale, it wyll ytche. **1606** SHAKS. *Tr. & Cr.* III. iii. 229 Those wounds heale ill, that men doe giue themselues. **1803** *Med. Jrnl.* IX. 432 He suffered the issues to heal. **1888** *Gardening* 11 Feb. 685/1 The incisions in the crowns soon heal over.

heal, *v.*^{2} to cover: see HELE *v.*^{2}

heal(e, dial. forms of HALE *a.*

'healable, *a. rare*$^{-0}$. [f. HEAL *v.*^{1} + -ABLE.] That may be healed; curable, remediable.

1570 LEVINS *Manip.* 2/26 Healeable, *sanabilis.* **1611** COTGR., *Guarissable*, healeable, cureable, recouerable.

heal-all ('hiːlɔːl). [f. HEAL *v.* + ALL. Cf. ALL-HEAL.]

1. Something that heals or is reputed to heal all diseases; a universal remedy; a panacea. Also *fig.*

1577 B. GOOGE *Heresbach's Husb.* IV. (1586) 191 It was called in the olde time Panacea or Healeal. *a* **1878** LEWES *Study Psychol.* (1879) 150 Forgiveness is contemplated as a heal-all. **1891** *Lit. World* 4 Sept. 159 Unlike many other popular economic heal-alls, co-operation does not involve any fundamental economic fallacy.

2. *Herb.* A popular name of various plants, including *Rhodiola rosea*, *Valeriana officinalis*, *Prunella vulgaris*, and *Collinsonia canadensis*.

1853 G. JOHNSTON *Nat. Hist. E. Bord.* 82 (Britt. & Holl.) *Rhodiola rosea.* Often to be met with in gardens, where it is sometimes called *Heal-all*, for the leaves are applied to recent cuts of a slight nature. **1884** MILLER *Plant-n.*, Heal-all, *Collinsonia canadensis* and *Rhodiola rosea*.

†**'heal-bite.** *Obs.* [f. as prec. + BITE *sb.*] = HEAL-DOG, q.v.

heald (hiːld). *Weaving.* [app. the same word as OE. *hęfeld*, *hęfeld*, *hefel*, ON. *hafald*, a deriv. of **hafjan*, *hębban*, *hef-* to raise, with instrumental suffix; cf. OE. *nǽdl*, ME. *nedel*, and *nelde*, needle. But the OE. word appears to be applied to the threads of the warp or woof themselves.]

= HEDDLE.

a **700** *Epinal Gloss.* 602 *Liciatorium*, hebild [*Corpus* hebelȝyrd]. *c* **725** *Corpus Gloss* (*O.E.T.*) 1232 *Licium*, hebeld. *Licia*, hebeldðred. *c* **1000** *Sax. Leechd.* I. 320 Gewrið to anum hefel-þræde. *c* **1050** *Supp. Ælfric's Voc.* in Wr.-Wülcker 187/13 *Licium*, hefeld. **1483** *Cath. Angl.* 181/1 An Helde, *trama*. **1760** *Specif. Patent J. Stell* No. 753 The lashes, harness or healds which contain the warp. **1824** *Ann. Reg.* 270* An improved method of making healds to be made in the weaving of cotton, silk, woollen, and other cloths. **1851** *Art Jrnl. Illustr. Catal.* p. vii**/1 Placed in the healds or 'heddles' of the loom. **1864** *Chambers' Encycl.* VI. 189 In the case of plain weaving the threads of the warp are divided alternately by the loops of each heald.

b. *attrib.* and *Comb.*, as ***heald-cord, -knitter, -ing, -machine, -maker, -shaft, -thread, -yarn.***

1851 in *Illustr. Lond. News* (1854) 5 Aug. 118 [Occupations of the people] heald maker, heald knitter. **1862** *Chamber's Encycl.* V. 276 The manufacture of heald

yarns..employs the chief attention of several manufacturers. **1864** *Ibid.* VI. 189 Six heald-threads and six warp-threads are shown. **1874** TOLHAUSEN *Technol. Dict.*, Heald-cord, cross string..*embarbe.*

heald, var. HIELD *v.* to lean, incline to one side.

heald(e, obs. forms of HOLD *v.*

healder (ˈhiːldə(r)). [f. HEALD + -ER[1].] An operative who draws the warp yarn through the eyes of a heald. So **ˈhealding** *vbl. sb.*

1881 *Instr. Census Clerks* (1885) 64 Woollen cloth manufacture... Healder. **1888** R. BEAUMONT *Woollen & Worsted Cloth Manuf.* 138 After healding the work of loom mounting is comparatively simple, the only operation requiring attention being that of sleying.

†**heal-dog.** *Obs.* [f. HEAL *v.* + DOG *sb.*[1]] A name formerly given to species of Alyssum, called also *heal-bite.*

1551 TURNER *Herbal* I. C j a, Alysson of Dioscorides and Plyny may be named in English helebyte or heledog, of the property that it hath in helyng of the bityng of madde dogges. **1597** GERARDE *Herbal* II. cxviii. §2. 380 Mad-woort or Moonewoort is called..of some Heale dog. **1611** COTGR., *Alysson*, the hearbe Madwort..heale dog.

healed (hiːld), *ppl. a.* [f. HEAL *v.*[1] + -ED[1].] Restored to health, cured. Also *fig.*

a **1300** *Cursor M.* 13863 Iesus..par spak he wit þis heeld man. **1597** SHAKS. *2 Hen. IV*, I. ii. 167, I am loth to gall a new-heal'd wound. *a* **1831** A. KNOX *Rem.* II. 150 To give evidence of a healed mind.

†**ˈhealend.** *Obs.* Forms: 1–3 **hǽlend**, 2 **helend(e**, **halende**, 3 **helind(e**, **halind**, **healend**, **-ent**. [OE. *hǽlend*, *hélend* = OS. *hêljand*, *hêleand*, *hêland*, OHG., MHG. *heilant*, G. *heiland*: substantival form of pres. pple. of OE. *hǽlan*:—OTeut. **hailjan* to heal, save.] One that 'heals' or saves; the Saviour. In OE. regularly used instead of the proper name Jesus.

c **1000** *Ags. Gosp.* Matt. i. 1 Her is on cneorisse-boc hælendes cristes dauides suna. *Ibid.* 16 Se hælend þe is ȝenemned crist. *c* **1000** ÆLFRIC *Hom.* II. 214 Iesus is Ebreisc nama, þæt is on Leden 'Saluator', and on Englisc 'Hælend'. *c* **1175** *Lamb. Hom.* 3 Þe helend nehlechede toward ierusalem. *c* **1200** ORMIN 3355 Ȝuw iss borenn nu to daȝȝ Hælennde off ȝure sinness. *c* **1205** LAY. 9144 A child..þat scolde beon ihaten Hælend [*c* **1275** Helare]. *a* **1225** *Ancr. R.* 112 Þe luuewurðe Louerd and helinde, of heouene.

healer[1] (ˈhiːlə(r)). [f. HEAL *v.*[1] + -ER[1].]

1. One who heals (wounds, diseases, the sick, etc.); a leach, doctor; also, one who heals spiritual infirmities; in early use, Saviour = prec.

c **1175** *Lamb. Hom.* 83 Ȝef he hefde on his moder ibroken hire meidenhad, ne mihte nawiht brekere bon icloped helere. *c* **1275** *Passion Lord* 115 in *Old Eng. Misc.* 40 He com to þe Gywes..And chepte heom to sullen, vre helare. *c* **1440** HYLTON *Scala Perf.* (W. de W. 1494) I. xliv, This name Jhesu is nouȝt elles for to saye upon englisshe but heler. **1611** BIBLE *Isa.* iii. 7, I will not be a healer. **1680** OTWAY *Complaint* (R.), In vain you strive To act a healer's part. **1859** C. BARKER *Assoc. Princ. Middle Ages* i. 9 Healers of the sick in their hospitals.

2. A healing substance; a remedy.

1523 FITZHERB. *Husb.* §43 Terre of hym-selfe is to kene, and is a fretter, and no healer. **1658** A. FOX *Wurtz' Surg.* II. xxv. 151 The said Hearb..is an extraordinary healer. **1674** R. GODFREY *Inj. & Ab. Physick* 5 This can no waies be better, and safelier done than by Spirituous, Valiant, and Innocent Healers, seconded by a regular Diet.

healer[2]: see HELER, coverer.

healewei, -wi, var. of HALEWEI, *Obs.*

healfang: see HALSFANG, *Obs.*

†**healful**, *a. Obs.* Forms: see HEAL *sb.* [f. HEAL *sb.* + -FUL.] Fraught with health, well-being, safety, salvation; wholesome, salutary.

c **1340** HAMPOLE *Prose Tr.* 1 Ihesu es als mekyll to be mene als saueoure or helefull. *c* **1375** *Sc. Leg. Saints, Pelagia* 206 [He] Iniungit hyr heileful pennance. **1387** TREVISA *Higden* (Rolls) I. 305 Þis lond haþ hoot welles and heleful. *c* **1400** MAUNDEV. (Roxb.) xv. 67 Þe Ewangels, in þe whilk es helefull teching and sothefastnes. *a* **1563** BALE *Sel. Wks.* (Parker Soc.) 122 Healful remedies to know and to withstand the privy suggestions and the apert temptations of the fiend.

ˈhealing, *vbl. sb.*[1] [f. HEAL *v.*[1] + -ING[1].]

1. The action of the vb. HEAL; restoration to health; recovery from sickness; curing, cure.

c **1000** *Gosp. Nicod.* x, Ne be hælinge, ne reste daȝa ȝewemminge. *c* **1340** *Cursor M.* 13871 (Trin.) Of sekenes hastou helynge. *c* **1400** *Lanfranc's Cirurg.* 68 Of þis heelyng ..hise neiȝeboris hadden greet wondir. **1546** J. HEYWOOD *Prov.* (1867) 71 It is yll healyng of an olde sore. **1611** BIBLE *Nahum* iii. 19 There is no healing of thy bruise: thy wound is grieuous. **1860** ELLICOTT *Life Our Lord* v. 213 Numerous healings..performed in the plain of Gennesareth. **1880** *Daily News* 7 Dec. 5/4 The wound is already showing signs of healing.

b. *spec.* The touching by English sovereigns for the king's evil.

(An *Office for the Healing* was formerly often printed with the Prayer-book. A MS. copy, said to be of 1559, is in the Bodleian Library.)

1676 *Lond. Gaz.* No. 1082/4 Lost in the Banketing-house at Whitehall..presently after the Healing, a Ring, with an Onyx-Stone. **1707** *Bk. Com. Prayer* Y vi (*title*), At the Healing. **1876** BLUNT *Annot. P.B.* 580 The Office used at the Healing. *Ibid.*, Two silver touch-pieces for distribution at the healing.

2. *transf.* and *fig.* Mending, reparation; restoration of wholeness, well-being, safety, or prosperity; spiritual restoration, salvation.

a **1225** ST. MARHER. 19 Fulht of fonstan healunge. **1611** BIBLE *Mal.* iv. 2 Vnto you that feare my Name, shall the Sunne of righteousnesse arise with healing in his wings. **1704** F. FULLER *Med. Gymn.* (1711) 100 It seems to promise enough, and carry more Healing with it. **1861** MAY *Const. Hist.* i. (1882) I. 9 A new reign..was favourable to the healing of political differences.

3. *attrib.* and *Comb.*, as ***healing action***, ***art***; **healing-box**, the box containing the chrism for unction (Ogilvie, 1885); †**healing-coin**, **-gold**, the money given to those that were touched for the king's evil; **healing-pyx** = *healing-box.*

1683 *Treasury Warrant* 17 Nov. (Halliwell), Privy purse healing-gold £500. **1824** SCOTT *St. Ronan's* vii, It covered more of the healing science than the gowns of a whole modern university. **1857** *Chambers' Inform.* I. 777 If the healing action is languid, some stimulating ingredient may be added. **1857** MAYNE REID *War Trail* xxvii. 124 Ample practice in the healing art.

healing, *vbl. sb.*[2], covering: see HELING.

ˈhealing, *ppl. a.* [f. HEAL *v.* + -ING[2].]

1. That heals or cures; curative; salutary.

1398 TREVISA *Barth. De P.R.* XVII. xxiv. (1495) 618 The apples of the cypresse tree..ben soure and heelyng. **1605** SHAKS. *Macb.* IV. iii. 156 To the succeeding Royalty he leaues The healing benediction. **1611** BIBLE *Jer.* xxx. 13 Thou hast no healing medicines. **1712–14** POPE *Rape Lock* IV. 56 A branch of healing Spleenwort in his hand. **1824** SCOTT *St. Ronan's* i, An analysis of the healing waters.

2. *transf.* and *fig.*

1659 *Burton's Diary* (1828) IV. 331, I should be glad that this question might be a healing question among us. **1667** MILTON *P.L.* IX. 290 To whom with healing words Adam reply'd. **1701** ROWE *Amb. Step-Moth.* II. i. 535 By his Concurrence, Help, and healing Counsels To stop those wounds. **1767** T. HUTCHINSON *Hist. Mass.* II. iii. 228 He made the following mild and healing speech to them. *a* **1859** MACAULAY *Hist. Eng.* V. 281 Some Lords..came down to give a healing vote.

3. Of a wound: That cicatrizes or closes.

1857 *Chambers' Inform.* I. 777 The best dressing for a healing wound. **1888** *Daily News* 4 Oct. 6/2, I saw six.. healing sores on the left forehead.

4. *Comb.*: **healing blade**, **leaf**, (*a*) the Common House-leek, *Sempervivum tectorum*; (*b*) the Greater Plantain, *Plantago major*; **healing-herb**, the Common Comfrey, *Symphytum officinale*; †**healing-horn**, ? hartshorn; **healing-oil**, the chrism used in the rite of extreme unction (Lee *Gloss. Eccl. & Liturg. Terms*).

1657 REEVE *God's Plea* 317 Ivory, Furs, Musks, Sables, healing-horns, Bezarstones, etc., come not there from Beasts? **1799** *Ess. Highland Soc.* III. 389 (Jam.) The uniformly successful treatment of sheep affected with this disorder..by giving them a decoction of the Dewcup and Healing leaf boiled in buttermilk. **1877** A. W. BENNETT tr. *Thomé's Struct. Bot.* (1882) 43 In direct contrast to the generating tissues are the healing-tissues, tuberous tissues, or cork-tissues.

Hence **ˈhealingly** *adv.*

1864 in WEBSTER. **1886** MISS BROUGHTON *Dr. Cupid* III. ii. 39 The lovely common sights of early morning touch healingly upon his bruised brain.

†**healless**, *a. Obs.* In 4–5 **heleles**. [f. HEAL *sb.* + -LESS.] Deprived of health or well-being.

c **1374** CHAUCER *Troylus* v. 1593 How myght a wyght in torment and in drede, And heleles [*ed.* **1561** healelesse] yow sende as yet gladnesse.

healm, -et, obs. forms of HELM, HELMET.

†**healme.** *Obs.* [a. obs. F. *heaulme*, *heaume* helmet, 'the Helmet cherrie, Heart-cherrie, French cherrie' (Cotgr.): see HELM.] A kind of cherry.

1574 HYLL *Planting* 86 Ye may well begin to graffe..at Christmas..and principally the healme or great Cherrie. **1575** *Art of Planting* 15 The great healme cherry.

†**healmier.** *Obs.* [a. obs. F. *healmier*, *heaulmier* 'the Heart-cherrie tree' (Cotgr.), f. prec.]

1575 *Art of Planting* 15 The great Cherry (called Healmier).

†**healness.** *Obs.* In 3 **heilnesse**. [OE. *hǽlnes*, f. *hǽle*, by-form of *hál* whole + -ness.] Welfare; salvation.

c **897** K. ÆLFRED *Gregory's Past* xxxvi. 246 Nu is hiersumnesse tima & nu sint hælnesse daȝas. *c* **1250** *Gen. & Ex.* 2068 Heilnesse and blisse is ðer-in.

healp, obs. form of HELP.

healsfang: see HALSFANG.

healsome, *a. Obs.* exc. *Sc.* [ME. *helsum*, f. *hele*, HEAL *sb.* health + -SOME. Cf. HALESOME; Ger. *heilsam*, ON. *heilsamr.*] Wholesome, salutary; healthful.

c **1375** *Sc. Leg. Saints, Cecile* 150 Sene þat þu Has trewit heilesum consel now. *c* **1400** *Apol. Loll.* 6 It is helsum to þe pope..þat þe peple be riȝtly enfourmid, how þei owe to accept þe pope as þe vicar of Crist. *c* **1450** HENRYSON *Mor. Fab.* 3 Helsome and good to mans sustenance. *c* **1560** A. SCOTT *Poems* (S.T.S.) xv. 1 Vp, helsum hairt! thy rutis rais, and lowp! **1785** BURNS *Cotter's Sat. Nt.* 92 The healsome parritch, chief o' Scotia's food.

Hence **healsomeness**, wholesomeness.

1818 SCOTT *Hrt. Midl.* ix, The healsomeness of the food.

health (hɛlθ), *sb.* Forms: 1 **hǽlþ**, 3–5 **helþe**, 4–5 **heelthe (elth(e)**, 4–6 **helth(e**, 6 **healthe (hellthe)**, 6– **health.** [OE. *hǽlþ* = OHG. *heilida*, *-itha*, *-idha*:—WGer. type **hailiþa*, f. *hail-s* WHOLE, HALE: see -TH[1].]

1. a. Soundness of body; that condition in which its functions are duly and efficiently discharged.

c **1000** ÆLFRIC *Hom.* II. 540 Ure lichamana hælðe we awendað to leahtrum. *c* **1205** LAY. 29992 Þa weoren Æluriches wunden..alle iheled, ah þe helðe was neoðered for lurre of his monnen. **1377** LANGL. *P. Pl.* B. XIV. 298 Þe fyfte [pouerte] is moder of helthe. **1483** CAXTON *Gold. Leg.* 190 b/1 A preest..had lost the helthe of one of his handes that he myght synge no masse. **1559** *Mirr. Mag., Salisbury* xxxvi, Whan helth and welth is hyest. **1593** SHAKS. *2 Hen. VI*, III. i. 82 All health vnto my gracious Soueraigne. **1626** MASSINGER *Rom. Actor* v. ii, I, that feel myself in health and strength. **1709** ADDISON *Tatler* No. 75 ¶3 With a..Flush of Health in his Aspect. **1815** JANE AUSTEN *Emma* v, One hears sometimes of a child being 'the picture of health'; now Emma always gives me the idea of being the complete picture of grown-up health. **1851** CARPENTER *Man. Phys.* (ed. 2) 253 The accumulation of nutritive matter in the blood is so far from being a condition of health, that it powerfully tends to produce disease.

b. Colloq. phr. ***for one's health***, used esp. in neg. contexts or with negative implication, e.g. ***to be not doing*** (something) ***for one's health***: to have a serious purpose in doing something, to be doing something for one's material advantage. orig. *U.S.*

1887 G. H. DEVOL *Forty Yrs. a Gambler* 133 We called it ours, for we had fitted it up just to suit us; and for fear someone would use it when we were out traveling for our health, we paid for it all the time. **1900** *Congress. Rec.* 5 Feb. 1520/2, I am not making this speech for fun, nor for my health, nor as an oratorical exercise. **1900** J. K. JEROME *Three Men on Bummel* iv. 96 What d'ye think I'm running this shop for—my health? **1909** *Westm. Gaz.* 5 July 2/2 We ..doubt if it can really be said that Tariff Reformers are 'in it for their health' (to use a very expressive Americanism) or anybody else's. **1914** WODEHOUSE *Man Upstairs* 229 What is it that makes men do perilous deeds? Why does a man go over Niagara Falls in a barrel? Not for his health. **1927** G. K. CHESTERTON *Coll. Poems* 90 He will learn..Whether the Health Ministry Are in it for their health. **1944** L. A. G. STRONG *Director* 31 I'm not in this job for my health, any more than you are. **1955** L. P. HARTLEY *Perfect Woman* ix. 86 You ought to have sold several hundredweight, at least, or several tons if you want to persuade the Inspector that you're not in business for your health.

2. a. By extension, The general condition of the body with respect to the efficient or inefficient discharge of functions: usually qualified as *good*, *bad*, *weak*, *delicate*, etc.

1509 HAWES *Past. Pleas.* XXXIV. iv, Your lady..is in perfect health. **1590** SPENSER *F.Q.* III. ix. 26 Her crased helth. **1633** G. HERBERT *Temple, Church Porch* xxiii, Amidst their sickly healths. **1638** BAKER tr. *Balzac's Lett.* (vol. III.) 34 Ignorant of the state of your health. **1782** MISS BURNEY *Cecilia* iii. 32 The ill health of her uncle had hitherto prevented her. **1802** *Med. Jrnl.* VIII. 210 She enjoyed very tolerable health. **1827** G. BEAUCLERK *Journ. Marocco* xvi. 190 Our healths slightly improved.

b. ***bill of health***: see BILL *sb.*[3] 10; formerly in Scotch Law, an application by an imprisoned debtor to be allowed to live out of prison, on the ground of bad health (Bell *Dict. Law Scot.*). ***board of health***, (*a*) in the United Kingdom: a Government Board which existed 1848–58 for the control of matters affecting the public health: its duties are now discharged by the Local Government Board; (*b*) in the United States: the name of boards of commissioners for controlling sanitary matters, esp. in reference to contagious and infectious diseases. ***office***, ***officer of health***: see *health-office*, *-officer* in 8.

1617 MORYSON *Itin.* I. 74 Hee must bring to the Confines a certificate of his health..Neither will the Officers of health in any case dispence with him. *Ibid.* 252 Appoint chiefe men to the office of providing for the publike health, calling the place where they meete, the Office of Health.

†**3.** Healing, cure. *Obs.*

c **1000** ÆLFRIC *Hom.* II. 28 Gif we wyllað ealle ða wundra and hælða awritan..ȝefremode þurh ðone wuldorfullan cyðere Stephanum. **1382** WYCLIF *Acts* iv. 22 The man..in the which this sygne of heelthe was maad. —— *1 Cor.* xii. 9 To another, grace of heelthis. **1483** CAXTON *Gold. Leg.* 88 b/2 Holy oylle..moche vayllable to thelthe of sykenesses of many men. **1555** EDEN *Decades* 74 The diseased woman obteyned healthe of the fluxe of her bludde.

4. Spiritual, moral, or mental soundness or well-being; salvation. *arch.*

c **1000** *Sax. Leechd.* III. 236 Þam arist rihtwisnysse sunne, and hælþ is on hyre fiðerum. *c* **1250** *Old Kent. Serm.* in *Old Eng. Misc.* 32 Greded gode..þet he us yeue gostliche helþe in ure saule. **1382** WYCLIF *Ps.* xxvi[i]. 1 The Lord my liȝting and myn helthe. —— *Luke* ii. 30 Myn yȝen han seyn thin helthe. **1526** TINDALE *Luke* xix. 9 Iesus sayd vnto hym: This daye is healthe come vnto this housse. **1552** *Bk. Com. Prayer* Gen. Confess., There is no health in vs. **1616** R. C. *Times' Whistle* IV. 1620 He hath made sale of his soules dearest health. **1744** HARRIS *Three Treat.* III. XI. (1765) 185 That Health, that Perfection of a Social State. **1887** EDNA LYALL *Knt.-Errant* xxiii. 224 As you value the health of your own souls.

†**5. a.** Well-being, welfare, safety; deliverance.

c **1250** *Gen. & Ex.* 2344 Ic am iosep, dredeð ȝu noȝt, for ȝure helðe or hider broȝt. **1382** Wyclif *2 Sam.* xxiii. 12 He smoot the Philisteis, and the Lord made a greet heelth. **1535** Coverdale *1 Sam.* xiv. 45 Ionathas..that hath done so greate health in Israel this night. **1602** Shaks. *Ham.* i. iv. 40 Be thou a Spirit of health, or Goblin damn'd. *c* **1611** Chapman *Iliad* xv. 683 There is no mercy in the wars, your healths lie in your hands.

†**b.** ***evil health***: bad luck, hurt, disaster. *Obs.*

c **1477** Caxton *Jason* 30 Thenne cam agaynst him the king of Poulane, but that was to his euill helthe. *c* **1500** *Melusine* xxxvi. 287 To theire euyl helthe they haue recountred geffray.

6. A salutation or wish expressed for a person's welfare or prosperity; a toast drunk in a person's honour. See also drink *v.* 14.

1596 Shaks. *Tam. Shr.* iii. ii. 171 Hee calls for wine, a health quoth he. **1602** Marston *Ant. & Mel.* iv. Wks. 1856 I. 46 Your drunken healths, your houts and shouts, Your smooth God save's. **1675** Cocker *Morals* 9 By drinking others healths, to lose their own. **1713** Addison *Cato* ii. ii, Cæsar sends health to Cato. **1795** Wolcott (P. Pindar) *Convention Bill* Wks. 1812 III. 378, I like not healths; too oft they carry treason. **1855** Macaulay *Hist. Eng.* xvii. IV. 7 As often as any of the..princes proposed a health, the kettle drums and trumpets sounded.

†**7.** Healthiness, wholesomeness, salubrity. *Obs.*

1387 Trevisa *Higden* (Rolls) II. 13 Bretayne passeþ Irlond in faire weder and nobilte but noȝt in helþe.

8. *attrib.* and *Comb.* **a.** simple attrib., as ***health-biscuit***, ***-card***, ***certificate***, ***-culture***, ***-drop***, ***-recuperation***, ***-token***; **b.** obj. and obj. gen., as ***health-building***, ***-drinker***, ***-drinking***, ***-giver***, ***-screening***, ***-seeker***, ***-wishing***; ***health-bearing***, ***-boding***, ***-giving***, ***-hunting***, ***-promising***, ***-restoring***, ***-saving*** adjs.; **c.** instrumental, as ***health-flushed***, ***-proud*** adjs. **d.** Special Comb.: **health-board** = board of health; **health camp** *N.Z.*, a camp open (for exercise, outdoor life, etc.) to children below the average in physique, etc.; **health care** orig. *U.S.*, care for the general health of a person, community, etc., esp. that provided by an organized health service; freq. *attrib.*; **health centre** (cf. centre *sb.* 6 a), a local headquarters of medical services, *spec.*, a local centre for a group practice; **health club**, an establishment where one can do exercises, have massage, etc.; **health exhibition**, a public exhibition of sanitary appliances and the like; **health farm** orig. *U.S.*, a place to which people resort in the hope of improving their health; **health food**, food chosen for its dietary or health-giving properties; **health-guard**, an officer appointed to enforce quarantine regulations (Smyth *Sailor's Word-bk.* 1867); **health insurance**, insurance against financial loss through illness; **health laws**, the statutes regulating general sanitary conditions by the appointment of Boards of Health (Bouvier *Law Dict.* 1856); †**health-offering**, peace offering; **health-office**, the department having the administration of the health laws; **health-officer**, an officer charged with the administration of the health laws and sanitary inspection; **health physics**, that branch of radiology which is concerned with the health of those working with radioactive material; **health-resort**, a place to which people resort for the benefit of their health; **health-roll**, a list showing the state of health of a company of people, as of a ship's crew; **health salt**, freq. in *pl.*, name given to a number of salts, sold under various brand-names, obtained from or mixed with mineral water or other beverages; **health service**, name given generally or specifically to the aggregate of public (as opposed to private) medical facilities available to members of a community; **health visitor**, a specially trained nurse concerned with the welfare of sick or old people, expectant mothers, etc., in their homes.

1905 *Daily Chron.* 25 Apr. 4/5 An uneatable *health biscuit..stood by his bedside. **1888** Miss A. K. Green *Behind Closed Doors* iii, He is on the *Health Board. **1598** Sylvester *Du Bartas* ii. ii. i. *Ark* 383 O sacred Olive! ..*Health-boading branch. **1896** *Westm. Gaz.* 5 Aug. 6/3 The time that you can devote to *health-building. **1925** *N.Z. Educ. Gaz.* 1 May 68/1 The teachers decided to hold a '*health camp' for the twenty-six children. **1963** *Evening Post* (Wellington) 26 Oct., A woman doctor whose name will always be remembered in New Zealand as the pioneer of the health camp movement, Dr. Elizabeth Catherine Gunn, M.B.E., died in Wellington today. **1940** Auden *Another Time* 96 And his *Health-card shows he was once in hospital but left it cured. **1970** T. Lilley *Projects Section* x. 123 You will not..have inoculations to bring your Health Card up to date. **1940** *Health Care for Children* (U.S. Bureau Publ. Assistance) iv. 30 State and local agencies will need to make available to the staff information in regard to the facilities for *health care. **1954** Z. Stich *Health Care in Czechoslovakia* 15 Health care has been made available to all citizens... The number of hospitals has increased and a dense network of health centres has been established. **1963** in J. B. Grant *Health Care for Community* i. 6 The family rather than the individual must become the unit of health care. **1973** *Black World* Jan. 13/2 Persons interested in redesigning American health-care systems have been moving toward fulfilling the specific needs of identifiable segments of the population. **1985** *Globe & Mail* (Toronto) 9 Oct. A23/3 The OMA committee..has been working since the spring of 1984 with women's groups and health-care workers across the province. **1552** Huloet, *Health causynge..*sospitalis.* **1916** *Public Health Nurse Q.* (U.S.) Jan. 27 Historically the first *Health Center started under that name was begun by the New York Health Committee in 1913. *Ibid.* 33 This Health Center..illustrates two fundamental principles, namely a definite area is selected for the field of operation; [etc.]. **1918** *Lancet* 29 June 922/2 With the removal of the medical officer of health from the jurisdiction of the borough council that official will need a new office in the town, with laboratories, museum, library, and lecture hall. This I call for want of a better title the future 'Health Centre' of the borough. **1934** T. S. Eliot *Rock* ii. 72 Libraries and health centres and milk for the children. **1968** *Brit. Med. Bull.* XXIV. 198/1 With the era of the medical team and health centre upon us, the necessity for adequate documentation already exists. **1972** *Times* 22 Feb. 3/1 Some 3,000 family doctors will be practising from more than 500 health centres by the end of 1974. **1938** F. G. Hobson *Med. Pract. Residential Schools* p. xv (*heading*) Organization of medical services. A. *Health Certificates. B. Records. **1960** J. Betjeman *Summoned by Bells* vii. 66 My health certificate, photographs of home. **1961** *Economist* 27 May 872/1 The active gymnasia ('*health clubs') are much of a type. **1962** *Which?* Oct. 303/1 These health clubs, which have been fashionable in the United States for many years, have appeared in this country over the last three. **1964** S. Bellow *Herzog* (1965) 84 Herzog had met him in the steam bath at Postl's Health Club. **1970** L. Sanders *Anderson Tapes* xliv. 121 We were in the steam room of that health club the Doc's got on West Forty-eighth Street. **1606** Marston *Fawne* iv. Wks. 1856 II. 72 Favour-wearers, sonnet-mongers, *health-drinkers. **1633** Prynne *Histrio-Mastix* Title-p., Sundry particulars concerning Dancing, Dicing, *Healthdrinking. **1813** Shelley *Q. Mab* vi. 52 Until pure *health-drops, from the cup of joy, Fall like a dew of balm upon the world. **1884** *Nature* 388/2 Preparations for..the International *Health Exhibition. **1927** E. Hemingway *Men without Women* (1928) 115 Jack started training at Danny Hogan's *health farm over in Jersey. **1928** Wodehouse *Money for Nothing* ix. 196 What if that health-farm was a mere blind for more dastardly work? **1966** G. B. Mair *Kisses from Satan* v. 55 He was going to enter one of the most fashionable health farms in the world. **1969** *Guardian* 18 Aug. 7/5 Their health farm..is the place where they go once a year..and..lose 10 lb. or 15 lb. in two weeks. **1882** W. D. Howells *Mod. Instance* xxviii, I put the camp on a *health-food basis. **1884** E. W. Nye *Baled Hay* 75, I have had occasion to thoroughly investigate the subject of so-called health food, such as gruels, beef tea. **1939** 'G. Orwell' *Coming up for Air* iv. v. 261 Health-food cranks. **1962** J. B. Priestley *Margin Released* i. iii. 26 Another shop, specialising in health foods, had a line in mashed dates and coconut. **1965** *Observer* 18 Apr. 45/2 Health food shops, where everything is free range, unsprayed, naturally fertilized. **1972** *New York* 8 May 49 *Health Food.* As used to describe stores, this term has taken on a generic meaning, encompassing everything from organic, natural, and specialized diet foods to whole wheat and other products mass-produced and refined. **1382** Wyclif *Ps.* lxiv. [lxv]. 6 God, oure *helthe ȝiuere. **1882** Edna Lyall *Donovan* xxi. (1887) 257 It drew him away from the thought of weakness and soul-disease to the Health-giver. **1588** Shaks. *L.L.L.* i. i. 236 The moste wholesome Physicke of thy *health-giuing ayre. **1876** Bancroft *Hist. U.S.* VI. lv. 433 Health-giving truth. **1901** *Index-Catal. Library Surg.-General's Office U.S. Army* Ser. 2. VI. 849/1 (*heading*) *Health-insurance. **1911** *Act 1 & 2 Geo. V* c. 55. 1 (*heading*) National Health insurance... All persons so insured..shall be entitled..to the benefits in respect of health insurance and prevention of sickness. **1916** *Machinery* July 1018/1 Booklet entitled 'Health Insurance'. **1941** J. S. Huxley *Uniqueness of Man* p. ix, Subsidized housing..health insurance..free education ..are all symptoms of..change. **1535** Coverdale *Ezek.* xliii. 27 The prestes shal offre their burntoffringes and *healthoffringes vpon yᵉ aulter. *Ibid.* xiv. 15, xlvi. 12. **1856** Bouvier *Law Dict.* I. 581 **Health Officer*, the name of an officer invested with power to enforce the health laws. **1804** tr. *Volney's View Soil U.S.* 252 The establishment of lazarettoes and *health-offices. **1860** Mill *Repr. Govt.* xv. (1865) 116/1 It is ridiculous that a surveyor, or a *health officer..should be appointed by popular suffrage. **1946** R. S. Stone in *Proc. Amer. Philos. Soc.* XC. 13/2 The term '*Health-Physics' has been used..to define that field in which physical methods are used to determine the existence of hazards to the health of personnel. *Ibid.* 16/1 The instrument development problems that faced the Health-Physics section were numerous. **1961** *Engineering* 26 May 734/2 The syllabus will include lectures..with..instruction in health physics. **1753** Miss Collier *Art Torment.* 164 People may be *health-proud as well as purse-proud. **1865** R. B. Grindrod *Malvern* 29 No other *health resort in England which presents such a combination of hygienic advantages. **1891** Freeman *Sk. fr. French Trav.* 181 Royat, a village which has become a health-resort. **1715** Rowe *Lady Jane Gray* i. i, [He] Try'd ev'ry *health-restoring herb and gum. **1856** Kane *Arct. Expl.* I. xx. 256 His *health-roll makes a sorry parade. **1900** *Confectioners' Union Hand-bk.* 169 Gums, jellies, lozenges..*health salt, etc. **1921** D. H. Lawrence *Sea & Sardinia* 46 Like a health-salts.. advertisement. **1962** A. Nisbett *Technique Sound Studio* x. 177 Health salts do fine for fizzy drinks. **1888** M. B. Edwards *Parting of Ways* III. xi. 179 A..*health-saving invention. **1966** *New Scientist* 1 Dec. 499/2 Whether Britain goes ahead with an intensive programme of *health screening is a decision for the politicians. **1968** *Daily Tel.* 22 Nov. 25 A £250,000 health-screening centre aided by computers in a new building..adjoining Harley Street. **1832** *Chambers's Edinb. Jrnl.* I. 113/2 When a *health-seeker takes a walk, he keeps his coat wide open. **1953** Dylan Thomas *Under Milk Wood* (1954) 23 There is little to attract the hillclimber, the healthseeker, [etc.]. **1935** *Economist* 7 Sept. 456/2 Twenty-five years ago only the germ of our present *health services existed, in the form of the old Poor Law and a rudimentary Old-Age Pension scheme. **1938** B. Webb *Let.* Jan. in K. Martin *Editor* (1968) iii. 73 The organisation of a public Health Service. **1958** *Times Lit. Suppl.* 12 Dec. 717/2 The Health Service and the welfare state...have brought appalling drabness into the doctor's life. **1883** W. H. Bishop *House Merch. Prince* iii. (1885) 40 They went..to the *health springs of Colorado and Florida. **1901** *Health visitor [see visitor 1 c]. **1905** *Westm. Gaz.* 3 Apr. 12/2 An audience of health visitors, district visitors, charity organisation visitors. **1917** *New Witness* 28 June 202/1 The bare idea that a Health Visitor should attempt to force her way into a French-woman's house would be regarded with horror. **1965** *Listener* 30 Sept. 483/1, I would think it most important by means of..the health visitor..to make assessments of the food which they require. **1970** G. Greer *Female Eunuch* 19 The revolutionary woman must know her enemies, the doctors, psychiatrists, health visitors. **1886** Annie Edwardes *Playwright's Dau.* ii. 21 The companion of her father's Italian *health-wanderings. **1613** Selden *On Drayton* Wks. III. 838 (Jod.) An usual ceremony among the Saxons..as a note of *health-wishing.

†**health**, *v. Obs.* [f. prec. sb.] *intr.* To drink a health or healths. Also *to health it.*

1611–1696 [see healthing *vbl. sb.* 2]. **1633** Heywood *Eng. Trav.* iv. Wks. 1874 IV. 72 Goe, health it freely for my good successe. **1636** W. Sampson *Vow Breaker* ii. i, They now are healthing, and carrowsing deepe.

ˈ**healtheries**, *sb. pl. colloq.* [f. health *sb.* + -ery.] A name familiarly given to the Health Exhibition held in London in 1884; suggested by the *Fisheries* of the preceding year.

1884 *Daily News* 30 May, The Shakspeare show..will be more attractive to poetic souls than the Healtheries. **1884** *Pall Mall G.* 12 Aug. 2/1 If the Fisheries spoiled the early Promenades last year, it is probable that the Healtheries will do so with these..this year.

healthful (ˈhɛlθfʊl), *a.* [f. health *sb.* + -ful.]

1. Promoting or conducive to bodily health; health-giving, wholesome, salubrious.

1398 Trevisa *Barth. De P.R.* xiv. xii. (1495) 473 Mount Effraym was most helthfull in ayre. **1559** W. Cunningham *Cosmogr. Glasse* 180 These famous, and helthfull rivers, the Rhine, Danuby. **1694** *Acc. Sev. Late Voy.* ii. (1711) 212 The Country seems much subject to Earthquakes, else very healthful. **1709–10** Steele *Tatler* No. 128 ¶4 Cleanliness and healthful Industry wait on all your Motions. **1877** Thorold in *Gd. Words* XVIII. 16/1 The cheapest and healthfullest route..is by steamer.

b. Bestowing, promoting, or conducive to moral or spiritual welfare or prosperity; salutary, saving.

1382 Wyclif *2 Macc.* iii. 32 He offride for helthe of the man an helthful sacrifice [*hostiam salutarem*]. *c* **1410** Love *Bonavent. Mirr.* (Gibbs MS.) lf. 121 In þat furst makynge of þis helþfulle sacramente. **1560** Becon *New Catech.* Wks. 1844 II. 201 His glorious passion and healthful death. **1596** Dalrymple tr. *Leslie's Hist. Scot.* v. 281 King Gregorie.. setis out helthfull and gud lawis. **1642** *Declar. Lords & Com.* 23 Nov. 2 Healthfull for the present State of this Kingdome. **1862** D. Wilson *Preh. Man* II. xxiii. 369 Healthful elements of European civilization.

2. Of persons, their actions, etc.: Full of or characterized by health; enjoying good health; healthy. Now *rare.*

1550 Coverdale *Spir. Perle* xv. Wks. (Parker Soc.) I. 138 When a man hath been a long season healthful and without any manner of sickness. **1667** D'chess Newcastle *Life Dk. N.* (1886) III. 208 By this temperance he finds himself very healthful. **1754–81** Johnson *L.P., Cave*, He was generally healthful, and capable of much labour. **1862** Miss Yonge *C'tess Kate* i. (1880) 2 Kate was tall, skinny, and brown, though perfectly healthful.

b. Marked by intellectual or moral soundness.

1601 Shaks. *Jul. C.* ii. i. 319 Such an exploit haue I in hand Ligarius, Had you a healthfull eare to heare of it. **1744** Armstrong *Preserv. Health* i. (R.), In healthful body how A healthful mind the longest to maintain. **1831** Macaulay *Ess., Ld. Nugent's Hampden* (1887) 205 A mind so great..so healthful and so well proportioned. **1884** *Manch. Exam.* 14 Nov. 5/7 The Chinese will continue to be a clog upon the healthful progress of the world.

ˈ**healthfully**, *adv.* [f. healthful *a.* + -ly².] In a healthful manner: see the adj.

1398 Trevisa *Barth. De P.R.* xviii. lxxiv. (1495) 829 A wesell brent to asshes is helthfully done in medycyn. **1581** Marbeck *Bk. of Notes* 74 They therby are stirred to hate themselues, and so are healthfullie killed. *a* **1642** Sir W. Monson *Naval Tracts* iv. (1704) 394/1 The Island [is] Healthfully seated. *a* **1687** Petty *Pol. Arith.* vi. (1691) 97 New England..where People live long, and healthfully. *a* **1791** Wesley *Husb. & Wives* v. Wks. 1811 IX. 81 An admonition..healthfully sharp. *a* **1864** Hawthorne *S. Felton* (1879) 14 Living healthfully in the open air.

ˈ**healthfulness.** [f. as prec. + -ness.] The condition or quality of being healthful; wholesomeness, salubrity, healthiness.

1561 T. Norton *Calvin's Inst.* iv. xiii. 86 They refreshe their body, so much as suffiseth for life and healthfulnesse. *a* **1568** Coverdale *Ghostly Ps.* l. Wks. (Parker Soc.) II. 575 Thou God of all my healthfulnesse. **1661** Lovell *Hist. Anim. & Min.* Introd., According to the healthfulnesse of the place, in which they live. **1863** Bates *Nat. Amazon* i. (1864) 20 The healthfulness of the climate. **1878** Bayne *Purit. Rev.* iv. 110 Solid ability and moral healthfulness.

ˈ**healthily**, *adv.* [f. healthy *a.* + -ly².] In a healthy manner.

1632 Sherwood, Healthfully, or healthilie, *sainement, salubrement, salutairement.* **1726** Leoni *Alberti's Archit.* I. 3/2 Where they might live the most healthily. **1847** Emerson *Repr. Men, Swedenborg* Wks. (Bohn) I. 333 Behmen is healthily and beautifully wise, notwithstanding the mystical narrowness. **1868** Lynch *Rivulet* cxlvii. ii, His wind, that bloweth healthily, Thy sicknesses to heal.

'healthiness. [f. as prec. + -NESS.] Healthy quality or condition, salubrity: see the adj.
1670 NARBOROUGH *Jrnl.* in *Acc. Sev. Late Voy.* I. (1711) 96 A good Testimony of the healthiness of the Country. 1748 *Anson's Voy.* 313 All these advantages were greatly enhanced by the healthiness of its climate. 1884 SEELEY in *Contemp. Rev.* Oct. 503 'Werther'..has certainly no advantage in healthiness of tone.

†**'healthing,** *vbl. sb.* [f. HEALTH *sb.* or *v.*]
1. The furthering or imparting of health. *rare.*
1581 MULCASTER *Positions* xlv. (1887) 298 The helping, and healthing of all studentes.
2. The drinking of healths; toasting.
1611 BP. HALL *Serm.* xxiv. Wks. 1837 V. 324 What bouzing, and quaffing, and whiffing, and healthing is there. 1654 TRAPP *Comm. Esther* i 8 This detestable healthing and carousing too too common in all parts of Christendom. 1696 O. HEYWOOD *Let.* in *Thoresby's Corr.* (Hunter) I. 229, I prefer this exercise to ranting, railing, healthing.

†**'healthist.** *Obs. nonce-wd.* [f. HEALTH *sb.* + -IST.] One who is addicted to drinking healths.
1640 BP. HALL *Chr. Moder.* I. i. §3 The Greeks drink in small cruses at the beginning of their feasts, and in large bowls at the latter end: an order ill imitated by the lavish Healthists of our time.

healthless ('hɛlθlɪs), *a.* Now *rare.* [see -LESS.]
1. Without health, out of health; destitute of bodily, mental, or spiritual health: unhealthy.
1568 T. HOWELL *Arb. Amitie* (1879) 97 Why doe I seeke to heate my helthlesse hart? 1635 QUARLES *Embl.* III. iii. (1718) 139 Restore health to my healthless soul. 1651-3 JER. TAYLOR *Serm. for Year* I. xiii. 165 It may be for the lust of thy youth thou hast a healthlesse old age. 1857 MRS. MATHEWS *Tea-t. Talk* I. 48 [Her] healthless condition had kept her many years in painful retirement.
2. Not conducive to health; unwholesome, insalubrious.
1650 JER. TAYLOR *Holy Living* I. i. §16 Like him whose.. meat [is] nothing but sauces; they are healthless, chargeable, and useless. 1855 SINGLETON *Virgil* II. 354 Who dwell In ..ancient Pyrgi, and Graviscæ healthless.
Hence **'healthlessness,** unhealthiness; unwholesomeness.
1655 JER. TAYLOR *Unum Necess.* vi. §7 (R.) There is such a certain healthlesness in many things to all..that to supply a need is to bring a danger. 1660 —— *Duct. Dubit.* II. iii.-viii. §7 Fasting..is the best..unless it be altered by the inconveniences or healthlessness of the person.

healthsome ('hɛlθsəm), *a.* Now *rare.* [f. HEALTH *sb.* + -SOME.]
†1. Full of health; possessing good health; healthy. *Obs.*
1563 *Homilies* II. *Sacrament* I. (1859) 444 A stomach.. which is healthsome and sound. 1635 R. CAREW in *Lismore Papers* (1888) Ser. II. III. 225 Some say he is yᵉ healthsomer for it [sickness].
2. Bestowing health (bodily, mental, or spiritual); wholesome; salutary.
1538 BALE *Comedy Johan Baptiste* in *Harl. Misc.* I. 105 Thys helthsome counsell maketh my hart joyfull and glad. 1573 TUSSER *Husb.* xi. (1878) 27 And healthsom aire inuest thee. 1610 HOLLAND *Camden's Brit.* I. 63 That healthsome light of Jesus Christ shone..upon the Britans. 1707 SLOANE *Jamaica* I. 45 A stream of hot water, which..becomes cool and healthsome. 1891 H. C. HALLIDAY *Someone must suffer* II. xiii. 240 The healthsome joys of the covered-cart.
Hence **'healthsomely** *adv.*; **'healthsomeness.**
1563 GOLDING *Cæsar* (1565) 271 He..made so many iorneyes..for chaunge of the places for healthsomnesse. 1579 FULKE *Heskins' Parl.* 498 He did helthsomly or profitably consecrate his bodie and bloud. 1582 BENTLEY *Mon. Matrones* ii. 16 Wellspring of all healthsomnes.

'healthward, *a.* [f. HEALTH *sb.* + -WARD.] Tending in the direction of health.
1884 *Pennsylv. Sch. Jrnl.* XXXII. 382 There is a strong healthward tendency in the constitution. 1886 *Brit. Med. Jrnl.* 25 Sept. 585/2 If we can do nothing to help nature on her healthward course.

healthy ('hɛlθɪ), *a.* [f. HEALTH *sb.* + -Y.]
1. Possessing or enjoying good health; hale or sound (in body), so as to be able to discharge all functions efficiently.
1552 HULOET, Healthye or healthfull, *incolumis, saluber, salutifer, salutaris, sanus.* 1581 PETTIE *Guazzo's Civ. Conv.* I. (1586) 23 Healthie men..are properly those, who have yᵉ foure humours so equally tempered in them..that one thing exceede not another. 1670 NARBOROUGH *Jrnl.* in *Acc. Sev. Late Voy.* I. (1711) 96 The Spaniards are well-complexioned People..and seem to be mighty healthy. a1715 BURNET *Own Time* II. 535 He is of a very vigorous and healthy constitution. 1815 W. H. IRELAND *Scribbleomania* 15 My abstinence keeps me quite healthy. 1879 HARLAN *Eyesight* v. 57 Healthy eyes, if given anything like a fair chance, will take care of themselves.
2. a. Conducive to or promoting health; wholesome, salubrious; salutary. Also *fig.*
1552 [see sense 1]. 1577 B. GOOGE *Heresbach's Husb.* I. (1586) 8b, Best is it..in good and healthy places, to set the house toward the East. a1704 LOCKE (J.), Gardening or husbandry, and working in wood, are fit and healthy recreations for a man of study or business. 1748 WESLEY *Let. conc. Tea* in Besant *London* (1892) 372 A Mixture of Herbs ..healthier as well as cheaper than Tea. 1871 NAPHEYS *Prev. & Cure Dis.* I. v. 135 Healthy dwelling-houses.
fig. 1884 *Chr. World* 11 Sept. 682/4 The deep, wide, and healthy influence which he exerted upon society.
b. In ironical use.
1831 S. SMITH *Life & Writings Major J. Downing* 149 Major Eaton, it won't be healthy for you to come on to these steps to-night. 1902 C. HYNE *Mr. Horrocks Purser* 251, I want to impress on them that they'll find it more healthy not to try for more. 1916 'BOYD CABLE' *Action Front* 179 'Additional artillery support would be useful a—a—a.' 'Sounds healthy, don't it?' said the sergeant reflectively.
3. a. Denoting or characteristic of health or sound condition (*lit.* and *fig.*); opp. to *morbid.*
1597 SHAKS. *2 Hen. IV*, I. ii. 4 He said..the water it selfe was a good healthy water. 1709 STEELE *Tatler* No. 77 ¶1 With a fresh, sanguine, and healthy Look. 1790 BURKE *Fr. Rev.* 34 The healthy habit of the British constitution. 1878 H. M. STANLEY *Dark Cont.* II. vii. 199 An interchange of small gifts served as a healthy augury for the future. 1897 *Daily News* 7 June 9/4 The cutlery trade is in a very healthy state.
b. *spec.* in *Med.*: see quots.
1807-26 S. COOPER *First Lines Surgery* 2 By healthy inflammation, is meant that which is not characterized and modified by any particular disease in the part or constitution. 1854 MAYNE *Expos. Lex.*, *Healthy Pus*, term applied to pus discharged from abscesses which are the result of phlegmonous inflammation; or from wounds and ulcers in the healing state; formerly termed laudable pus.
4. *Comb.*, as ***healthy-looking***, ***-minded*** adjs; ***healthy-mindedness.***
1800 SIR M. HUNTER *Jrnl.* (1894) 176 The farmers are healthy-looking. 1851 MAYNE REID *Scalp Hunt.* ii. 17 Displaying healthy-looking, sun-tanned throats. a1882 H. JAMES *Lit. Remains* (1885) 117 In a pluralistic philosophy the healthy-minded moralist will always feel himself at home. *Ibid.*, The feeling of *action*..makes us turn a deaf ear to the thought of *being*; and this deafness and insensibility may be said to form an integral part of what in popular phrase is known as 'healthy-mindedness'. 1886 MRS. C. PRAED *Miss Jacobsen's Chance* I. ii. 33 She was as thoroughly discontented with her own lot as any fairly healthy-minded girl can be. 1906 *Westm. Gaz.* 25 Jan. 12/2 The spirit which animated Japan was chivalry and healthy-mindedness. 1931 *Times Lit. Suppl.* 19 Feb. 122/1 So well supplied is the Victorian era with names standing for stability, sanity and healthy-mindedness.

healve, obs. form of HELVE.

†**heam.** *Obs.* or *dial.* [A dial. variant of HAME *sb.*¹] The amnion of an animal (= CAUL *sb.*¹ 5 b); the secundine.
1681 WALLER *Advice to Painter* II. 2 (Brand) Then draw a Haw-thorn Bush, and let him place The Heam upon't. 1726 *Dict. Rust.* (ed. 3), *Heam* (in Beasts) is the same thing with the after-birth in women.

heam, var. HAME², EME, uncle.

†**hean, hene,** *a. Obs.* Forms: 1 héan, 3 hæne, heane, 3-4 hene, 4 heyne. [Com. Teut. adj.: OE. *héan* = OHG. *hôni*, Goth. *hauns* contemptible, base, humble: cf. Lettish *kauns* shame, disgrace, dishonour.] Mean, abject, poor; humble, lowly.
Beowulf (Z.) 1275 þa he hean ȝe-wat, dreame be-dæled. c825 *Vesp. Psalter* ix. 39 [x. 18] Doem ðæm freondleasan and ðæm heanan. c1205 LAY. 3172 Heo hold me for hæne [c1275 wrecche]. *Ibid.* 12136 Hermes heo worhten and hene lond makeden. c1230 *Hali Meid.* 13 Who makeð out..of heane hine, of fa freond. c1325 *Pol. Songs* (Camden) 150 Me halt hem ful hene. c1400 *Apol. Loll.* 26 To stere men to be heuy of þer mysse and to desire to be heyne.

†**hean, hene,** *v. Obs.* Forms: 1 híenan, hýnan, hénan, 2-4 hene(n, 3 heanen, hænen. [Com. Teut.: OE. *híenan* = OFris. *héna* (MDu. *hônen*. Du. *hoonen*), OHG. *hônen* (MHG. *hœnen*, Ger. *höhnen*), Goth. *haunjan*, f. *haun-s* adj.: see prec. (From the OHG. came OF. *honir* to dishonour, pa. pple. *honi*, in 'honi soit qui mal y pense'.)] *trans.* To treat with contumely; to insult, humiliate, debase, lower.
Beowulf (Z.) 2320 Geata leode hatode ond hynde. c950 *Lindisf. Gosp.* Luke x. 16 Seðe iuih teleð *vel* ȝeheneð mec henes. c1175 *Lamb. Hom.* 13 Stala and steorfa swiðe eow scal hene. c1205 LAY. 6874 Al his folc he hatede and al he hit hænde. c1230 *Hali Meid.* 13 Vre flesch is ure fa & heaneð us & harmeð. c1410 *Chron. Eng.* 1030 (Ritson *Metr. Rom.* II. 313) Heo heveden him in henyng, Ant seiden he wes traitour.

†**'heanling.** *Obs.* In 3 heanlung. [f. HEAN *a.* + -LING.] A base, abject, or humble person.
a1225 *St. Marher.* 14 Heanlunges makeð ham wið heouenlich hirð.

heap (hiːp), *sb.* Forms: 1 héap, 2- heap, (2 hap, 3 hæp, 3-5 hep, 4 (*Ayenb.*) hyeap, hyap, 4-7 heep, hepe, 5 hype, heppe, 6 *Sc.* heip, 6-7 heape). [OE. *héap* = OFris. *hâp*, OS. *hôp* (MDu., MLG., LG. *hôp*, Du. *hoop*), OHG. *houf* (MHG. *houf*), ON. *hópr* (Sw. *hop*, Da. *hob*) adopted from LG.; wanting in Gothic; :—OTeut. **haupo-z.* In ablaut relation to OHG. *hûfo*, MHG. *hûfe*, Ger. *haufe*:—**hûpon-*; from stem **hup-*, pre-Teut. **kub-*: cf. L. *cumbĕre*, *cubāre*.]
1. a. A collection of things lying one upon another so as to form an elevated mass often roughly conical in form. (A heap of things placed regularly one above another is more distinctively called a *pile.*)
c725 *Corpus Gloss.* 1912 (O.E.T.) *Strues*, heap. c897 K. ÆLFRED *Gregory's Past.* xlviii. (Sw.) 367 Galað on Ebreisc, ðæt is on Englisc ȝewitnesse heap. a1225 *Ancr. R.* 314 Heo gedereð al þet greste on one heape. 1340 *Ayenb.* 139 Zuo hit is of þe hyeape of huete y-þorsse. 1382 WYCLIF *Song Sol.* vii. 2 An hep [1388 heep] of whete. 1398 TREVISA *Barth. De P.R.* XIII. iii. (1495) 442 Hepes of grauell and erthe. c1450 *Mirour Saluacioun* 1470 Of..twelue stones fro the bank.. Thai made a hepe. 1535 COVERDALE *Ps.* lxxviii[i]. 1 They haue..made Ierusalem an heape of stones. 1574 J. DEE in *Lett. Lit. Men* (Camden) 39 An heap of old papers and parchments. 1611 BIBLE *Josh.* iii. 13 The waters of Jordan.. shall stand upon an heape. 1774 GOLDSM. *Nat. Hist.* (1776) I. 252 The waters will..be attracted by the moon, and rise in an heap. 1854 RONALDS & RICHARDSON *Chem. Technol.* (ed. 2) I. 111 Coking in Heaps or Ridges.—The oldest and still very common method of preparing coke is in meiler or heaps. 1860 TYNDALL *Glac.* II. viii. 266 At first sight, these sand-covered cones appear huge heaps of dirt. 1881 RAYMOND *Mining Gloss.*, *Heap* (*Newc.*), the refuse at the pit's mouth.
b. *fig.* of things immaterial.
c1200 ORMIN 4330 All þiss þrinne taless hæp. a1300 *Cursor M.* 26021 Scailand a hepe es samen o sin. 1340 *Ayenb.* 130 He yziȝþ þane greate heap of his zennes.
†c. Mass, main body. *Obs.*
1608 SHAKS. *Per.* I. i. 33 Her countless glory..which, without desert, because thine eye Presumes to reach, all thy whole heap must die. 1709 STEELE *Tatler* No. 87 ¶8 If we consider the Heap of an Army, utterly out of all Prospect of Rising and Preferment.
d. *fallacy of the heap*: see quot. 1768-74.
1768-74 TUCKER *Lt. Nat.* (1852) II. 140 Their sophism of the sorites, or argument of the heap; because, say they, if you drop a number of things upon one another you can never tell precisely when they begin to make a heap. 1893 *Oxford Mag.* 1 Nov. 39/1 Mr. A.'s contention..seems to us based on a *petitio principii*, or on the fallacy of the heap.
e. Usually preceded by a defining word: a slovenly woman. *colloq.* (orig. *dial.*).
1806 A. DOUGLAS *Poems* 125 She jaw'd them, misca'd them For clashin' claikin' haips. 1810 J. COCK *Simple Strains* II. 91 Foul fa' the sly bewitchin' heap Cou'd turn hersel' in ony shape. 1922 JOYCE *Ulysses* 300 The fat heap he married is a nice old phenomenon with a back on her like a ball-eye. 1957 J. FRAME *Owls do Cry* 106, I may be *forced* to [sell-out], if that lazy heap doesn't help me.
f. A battered old motor vehicle. *colloq.* (orig. *U.S.*).
1926 *Clues* Nov. 161/1 *Heap*, automobile. 1928 R. J. TASKER *Grimhaven* iii. 28 Once in a while some fellow who really did own a good car would come up to be topped, but, as a rule, I've noticed that kind never have much to say about their heaps. 1935 R. CHANDLER *Killer in Rain* (1964) 7, I got out of the Chrysler... I went back to my heap. 1951 J. KEROUAC *On Road* (1958) 79 He gunned the heap to eighty. 1959 J. BRAINE *Vodi* xiv. 190 Bought two old heaps today. Just junk really, a '28 Chrysler and a '27 Essex. 1967 A. HUNTER *Gently Continental* xi. 166 Stody too has driven away in his modest heap. 1969 C. F. BURKE *God is Beautiful, Man* (1970) 56 You will be like a guy who paid no attention to his heap and it broke down in the traffic.
2. a. A heaped measure of capacity. b. A pile or mass of definite size, varying with the commodity.
1674 JEAKE *Arith.* (1696) 70 Usage in some places hath continued Measure by heap, although some Statutes order it by Strike. 1813 R. KERR *Agric. Surv. Berw.* 448 (Jam.) In Berwickshire..four fills [of a firlot with potatoes], heaped by hand as high as they can go, called heaps, are counted as one boll. 1823 CRABB *Technol. Dict.*, *Heap* (*Print.*), any number of reams or quires as is set out by the warehouse keeper for the pressmen to wet is called a heap..'The heap holds out,' i.e. it has the full intended number of sheets. 1855 ROBINSON *Whitby Gloss.*, *Heeap* or *Heap*, a quarter of a peck measure. 1862 MIALL *Title Deeds Ch. Eng.* 39 *note*, Barley and oats were titheable by the heap or cock.
3. A great company (esp. of persons); a multitude, a host. An early sense in the Teutonic langs.; now only as in 4.
Beowulf (Z.) 400 þryð-lic þeȝna heap. 971 *Blickl. Hom.* 81 Se halȝa heap hehfædera and witȝena. a1175 *Cott. Hom.* 219 He ȝescop tyen engle werod oðer hapes..Her beoð niȝen anglen hapes. c1275 LAY. 10300 þo wes Seuarus heap mochel ibolded. c1290 *S. Eng. Leg.* I. 63/331 An hep of foules grete i-novȝ. 1340 *Ayenb.* 267 Ich yzeȝ to þe blyssede heape of confessours. 1377 LANGL. *P. Pl.* B. x. 309 An heep [C. hepe] of houndes at his ers, as he a lorde were. 1477 EARL RIVERS (Caxton) *Dictes* 105 A great heep of sheep. 1535 COVERDALE *Ezek.* xxxviii. 22 Fyre and brymstone, wil I cause to rayne vpon him and all his heape. 1590 SPENSER *F.Q.* I. iv. 16 The heapes of people, thronging in the hall, Doe ride each other, upon her to gaze. 1594 SHAKS. *Rich. III*, II. i. 53 Among this Princely heape, if any heere..Hold me a Foe.
4. a. Hence, in later colloquial use: A large number or quantity; a (great) deal, 'a lot'.
a1661 FULLER *Worthies* (1840) III. 53 No county in England hath such a heap of castles together. a1682 SIR T. BROWNE *Tracts* (1684) 116 This heap of artificial terms first entring with the French Artists. 1697 DAMPIER *Voy.* (1729) I. 389 The Principal of a heap of Islands. 1741 RICHARDSON *Pamela* (1824) I. 64 What a heap of hard names does the poor fellow call himself! 1818 KEATS *Lett.* Wks. 1889 III. 166 A man on the coach said the horses took a 'hellish heap o' drivin''. 1867 TROLLOPE *Chron. Barset* II. xlv. 12 She lives in a big house, and has a heap of servants. 1884 BESANT *Childr. Gibeon* II. xxxii, He got into trouble a heap of times.
b. *pl.* in same sense. Cf. the like use of 'lots'.
a1547 SURREY *Poems, Compl. Lover*, What pleasant life, what heapes of ioy these litle birdes receue. 1622 SPARROW *Bk. Com. Prayer* (1661) 170 For the antiquity of this Feast, heaps of Testimonies might be brought. 1856 WHYTE MELVILLE *Kate Cov.* i, We're in heaps of time. 1872 BLACK *Adv. Phaeton* iii. 25 He has..knocked heaps of things to smithereens.
c. *absol.* and as *adv.* A great deal, much; a 'lot'. (*sing.* and *pl.*) *colloq.*
a1834 DOW *Serm.* (Bartlett), To go to church in New York in any kind of tolerable style costs a heap a-year. 1848 RUXTON *Life in Far West* 223 (Farmer) He pronounced himself a heap better. 1852 MRS. STOWE *Uncle Tom's C.* x. 80 It's nature I should think a heap of him. 1871 W. ALEXANDER *Johnny Gibb* viii. (1873) 46 'Aw wudna care a

great heap, gin we can 'gree aboot the waages.' **1887** MRS. H. MARTIN *Amor Vincit* I. 5 You will find some one somewhere you think heaps better than me.

d. In the representation of the speech of North American Indians used adverbially and as quasi-adj.: very, very much, a great deal.

1832 W. IRVING *Jrnl.* (1919) III. 180 'Look at these Delawares,' say the Osages, 'dey got short legs—no can run —must stand and fight a great heap.' **1848** *Blackw. Mag.* LXIII. 719 An Indian is always a 'heap' hungry or thirsty —loves a 'heap'—is a 'heap' brave—in fact, 'heap' is tantamount to very much. **1850** 'M. TENSAS' *Louisiana 'Swamp Doctor'* 42 Whoop! whiskey lour! Injun big man, drunk heap. **1867** *Harper's Mag.* July 137/1 Disturb the game and you make the Indian 'heap big mad'. **1872** 'MARK TWAIN' *Roughing It* (1873) xxxix. 276 'Heap' is 'Injun-English' for 'very much'. **1902** —— in *Harper's Mag.* Jan. 270/2 Billy explained..'she heap much hungry'. **1958** B. CERF *Shake well before Using* 17 President Coolidge posed later in the regalia of a heap-big chief. **1968** MRS. L. B. JOHNSON *White House Diary* 21 June (1970) 688 His favorites among the presents were..the gift wrappings, or maybe the rubber canoe that said 'Heap Big Indian Lyn'.

e. ***a heap sight*** (U.S. *dial.* and *colloq.*): see HEAP *sb.* 4c and SIGHT *sb.*[1] 2.

1874 E. EGGLESTON *Circuit Rider* i. 14 He 'lows there was a heap sight more corn. **1888** G. W. CABLE *Bonaventure* 49 He's..a heap sight happier than us. **1906** *Smart Set* June 107/1, I care a heap sight too much for Ummy to let him go through what I know's comin'. **1911** R. D. SAUNDERS *Col. Todhunter* x. 152 You're a heap-sight smarter man than I gave you credit for bein'.

5. Phrases. †**a.** ***by, in heaps***: in crowds, in large quantities, in great numbers. **b.** ***in (of) a heap***: (of a body falling or lying) in a mass, in a state of collapse, having the appearance of a shapeless inert mass. **c.** †***on heap*** (4–5 ***an hepe***): in a heap or mass, together; = AHEAP. †***on a heap, on heaps***: in a prostrate mass, prostrate. †**d.** ***to heap***: together, into one mass. **e.** ***all of*** (†***on***) ***a heap***: all in a mass falling or fallen; so †***all on*** (***upon***) ***heaps***; ***to strike all of*** (†***on***) ***a heap*** (colloq.): to paralyze, prostrate mentally, cause to collapse; also, ***to knock all of a heap***.

a. 1523 LD. BERNERS *Froiss.* I. clxxxiii. (R.), They..slewe and hanged them vpon trees by heapes. **1568** GRAFTON *Chron.* II. 259 They..walked in the streetes in heapes. **1641** MILTON *Reform.* II. Wks. (1847) 14/1 The inhabitants..are enforced by heaps to forsake their native country. *a* **1700** DRYDEN *Ceyx & Alcyone* 174 The sailors run in heaps, a helpless crowd. **1799–1805** S. TURNER *Anglo-Sax.* (1836) I. III. i. 157 [Hengist] is affirmed..to have butchered in heaps the people who fled to the mountains and deserts.

b. 1840 MRS. BROWNING *Drama of Exile* Poems 1844 I. 23 What is this, Eve? thou droppest heavily In a heap earthward.

c. *a* **1000** *Wonders of Creation* in *Codex Exon.* (Thorpe) 350 Gewiteð þon..forð mære tungol, faran on heape. *c* **1205** LAY. 28292 Þa heo weoren þer on hepe an hunddred þusende heðene and cristene. *c* **1325** *Gloss. W. de Biblesw.* in Wright *Voc.* 158 *En monceus*, on hepe. *c* **1420** *Liber Cocorum* (1862) 15 Gar hit on hepe to renne. **1590** SPENSER *F.Q.* III. iv. 16 He tombled on an heape, and wallowd in his gore. **1607** SHAKS. *Timon* IV. iii. 101 When I haue laid proud Athens on a heape. **1611** BIBLE *Ps.* lxxix. 1 They haue layd Ierusalem on heapes.

d. *a* **1300** *Sarmun* xxxiv. in *E.E.P.* (1862) 5 Sei, sinful man, whi neltou leue þat al þing sal come to hepe. *c* **1374** CHAUCER *Boeth.* IV. pr. vi. 105 (Camb. MS.) Puruyance embraceth alle thinges to hepe. *c* **1391** —— *Astrol.* I. §14 A litel wegge ..þat streyneth alle thise parties to hepe. **1393** LANGL. *P. Pl.* C. XI. 189 And ȝut were best to bee aboute and brynge hit to hepe, That alle londes loueden, and in on lawe by-leouede. **14..** *Voc.* in Wr.-Wülcker 590/26 *Invicem*, to geder, to hepe. *c* **1475** *Rauf Coilȝear* 83 Bot, micht we bring this harberie this nicht weill to heip. **1480** CAXTON *Descr. Brit.* 12 Gadrith to hepe grete hepes of grauel.

e. 1588 SHAKS. *Tit. A.* II. iii. 223 Lord Bassianus lies embrewed heere, All on a heape. **1653** H. MORE *Antid. Ath.* I. xi. (1712) 34 That lies like a Net all on heaps in the Water. **1711** *Brit. Apollo* III. No. 133. 2/1 A Young Woman.. struck me all on a heap. **1741** RICHARDSON *Pamela* I. 205 This alarm'd us both; and he seem'd quite struck of a Heap. **1759** STERNE *Tr. Shandy* I. xxi, The story..is long and interesting..it would be running my history all upon heaps to give it you here. **1818** SCOTT *Rob Roy* xxiv, The interrogatory seemed to strike the honest magistrate, to use the vulgar phrase, all of a heap. **1875** JOWETT *Plato* (ed. 2) III. 120 Some one who..will not be struck all of a heap like a child by the vain pomp of tyranny. **1887** RIDER HAGGARD *Jess* 3 It..struck her horse upon the spine..so that it fell all of a heap on to the veldt. **1898** W. J. LOCKE *Idols* xiii, It knocked the prosecution all of a heap. **1928** *Manch. Guardian Weekly* 7 Sept. 183/3 Its owner's anxiety to knock the critics all of a heap.

6. *attrib.* and *Comb.*: **heap-cloud** = CUMULUS 2; **heap-flood**, a heavy sea; **heap-measure** = heaped measure; **heap-keeper, heap-stead** (see quots.).

1561 *Burgh Rec. Aberdeen* (Spalding Club) I. 335 To be mesourit with ane straik mett corresponden to the hep messour. **1583** STANYHURST *Æneis* I. (Arb.) 21 One ship.. was swasht wyth a roysterus heapeflud. **1858** SIMMONDS *Dict. Trade, Heap-keeper*, a miner who overlooks the cleaning of coal on the surface. **1883** GRESLEY *Gloss. Coal Mining, Heap-stead*, the entire surface works about a colliery shaft. **1889** *Nature* XXXIX. 26 The common cumulus or heap-cloud, which is the commonest cloud of the day-time in fine weather.

heap (hiːp), *v.* Forms: see the sb. [OE. *héapian*, corresp. to OHG. *houfôn*, MHG. *houfen*, mod.G. *haufen, häufen*; deriv. of the corresp. sb.]

1. *trans.* To make, form, gather, or cast into a heap; to pile *up*, amass, accumulate; to pile one thing *upon* another so as to form a heap. Often with *up, together, on.*

c **1000** *Ags. Gosp.* Luke vi. 38 God ȝemet..ȝeheapod and ofer-flowende. *a* **1225** *Ancr. R.* 314 Heo..heapeð.. togederes al þet was er bileaued. *c* **1375** *Sc. Leg. Saints, Johannes* 207 He þat mony heppis ay, Is seruand þare-to nycht and day. **1483** *Cath. Angl.* 183/1 To Heppe, *accumulare*. **1538** STARKEY *England* I. i. 6 Lyke vnto ryches hepyd in corneys. **1590** SPENSER *F.Q.* III. vii. 47 The Titans which did make Warre against heven, and heaped hils on hight To scale the skyes. **1611** BIBLE *Job* xxvii. 16 Though he heape vp siluer as the dust. **1611** —— *Ezek.* xxiv. 10 Heape on wood, kindle the fire. **1860** TYNDALL *Glac.* I. xxvii. 198 The snow had been heaped in oblique ridges across my path.

b. *intr.* for *pass.* (Chiefly *U.S.*)

1873 LOWELL *Among my Bks.* Ser. II. 273 A stripe of phosphorescence heaping before you in a star-sown snow. **1890** *Harper's Mag.* Nov. 865/1 Fallen avalanches heap whitely at intervals below.

2. *transf.* and *fig.* To amass, accumulate; to add many things together or one thing to another. Often with *up, together*. Also *absol.*

c **900** [see HEAPING *vbl. sb.*]. *c* **1200** ORMIN 4331 All þiss þrinne taless hæp Iss hæpedd aȝȝ wiþþ ehhte. *c* **1320** R. BRUNNE *Medit.* 865 þey wounded here, and heped harm vp on harmes. **1382** WYCLIF *Hab.* ii. 5 He shal hepe togidere to hym alle peplis. **1529** S. FISH *Supplic. Beggars* (E.E.T.S.) 13 [They] haue heped to him benefice vpon benefice. **1582** N. T. (Rhem.) *2 Tim.* iv. 3 According to their owne desires they will heape to themselues maisters, hauing itching eares. *a* **1605** MONTGOMERIE *Sonn.* xxxiv. 5 More hevynes within my hairt I heep. **1711** STEELE *Spect.* No. 260 ¶1 The Circumstances which are heaped up in my Memory. **1845** M. PATTISON *Ess.* (1889) I. 3 Generations of antiquaries have heaped together vast piles of facts.

†**b.** *refl.* and *intr.* for *refl.* (or *pass.*) *Obs.*

c **1400** *Destr. Troy* 3548 Thes harmes so heterly hepit in his mynde. **1508** DUNBAR *Tua Mariit Wemen* 334 And ȝit hatrent I hid within my hert all; Bot quhilis it hepit so huge [etc.]. **1535** COVERDALE *Ezek.* xxxix. 17 Heape you together and come. **1581** PETTIE *Guazzo's Civ. Conv.* II. (1586) 53 b, The preasse of people which heapeth together at the judgement place.

3. *trans.* To furnish with a heap or heaps; to fill, load, cumber, with a heap or heaps. Also with *up*.

1526 *Pilgr. Perf.* (W. de W. 1531) 54 Your measure.. heped & fylled vnto it flowe ouer. **1530** PALSGR. 583/1 Heape this busshell as hye as you can. **1542–3** *Act 34 & 35 Hen. VIII*, c. 9 §1 The mouth & hole channell of the saide hauen is so heaped and quarred with stones. **1667** MILTON *P.L.* v. 391 With these various fruits the Trees of God Have heap'd this Table. **1790** A. WILSON *Death* Poet. Wks. 63 Frowning dread Stalked o'er the world, and heapt his way with dead. **1824** MACAULAY *Ivry* v, The field is heaped with bleeding steeds, and flags, and cloven mail.

†**b.** *intr.* for *refl.* and *pass. Obs.*

1398 TREVISA *Barth. De P.R.* XIV. ii. (1495) 465 The erthe hyght Tellus, for we take fruyte therof, and hight ops, for he hepyth wyth fruyte. *c* **1400** *Destr. Troy* 3688 The heuyn in hast hepit with cloudis.

4. *trans.* To deal or bestow in heaps or large quantities. Const. *upon*.

1573–80 BARET *Alv.* H 303 To heape euill upon him, *conglomerare mala in aliquem*. **1590** SPENSER *F.Q.* III. vii. 33 Yet he perforce him held, and strokes upon him hept. **1613** SHAKS. *Hen. VIII*, III. ii. 175 Your great Graces Heap'd vpon me (poore Vndeseruer). **1671** MILTON *Samson* 276 To heap ingratitude on worthiest deeds. **1861** BRIGHT *Sp. on India* 19 Mar., To heap insults on his memory.

5. To load, charge, or overwhelm (a person) *with* (something in large quantities).

1583 STANYHURST *Æneis* I. (Arb.) 21 Hee..sees thee Troians wyth seas and rayne water heaped. *Ibid.* II. 58 Pat fals thee turret, thee Greeks with crash swash yt heapeth. **1751** JOHNSON *Rambler* No. 91 ¶14 Some were..heaped by Patronage with the gifts of Fortune. **1874** KINGSLEY *Lett.* (1878) II. 427 We are received with open arms, and heaped with hospitality.

heaped (hiːpt), *ppl. a.* [f. prec. + -ED[1].]

1. Gathered or thrown into a heap; piled *up*.

c **1440** *Promp. Parv.* 235/2 Heepyd, *cumulatus*. **1592** WYRLEY *Armorie, Ld. Chandos* 95 As lurcking sparke in hept straw inclosed. **1632** MILTON *L'Allegro* 147 A bed Of heaped Elysian flowers. **1820** SHELLEY *Vision Sea* 128 The heaped waves behold The deep calm. **1881** BESANT & RICE *Chapl. Fleet* I. xii, Heaped-up piles of fruit and vegetables.

2. Having its contents piled up above the brim instead of being levelled. ***heaped measure***, a dry measure used for certain commodities which are heaped up in a cone above the brim of the measure.

1530 PALSGR. 315/1 Heaped, as thynges that be measured, *comble*. **1581** LAMBARDE *Eiren.* IV. iv. (1588) 455 If any person have bought..corne by heaped measure. **1659** WILLSFORD *Scales Comm., Archit.* 5 The common allowance for lime is one quarter, or 8 bushels (heap'd measure) to every 1000 of bricks. **1740** BERKELEY *Let. to T. Prior* 8 Feb. Wks. 1871 IV. 263 A heaped spoonful of rosin. **1866** ROGERS *Agric. & Pr.* I. x. 168 When the bushel is described as heaped, nine struck bushels are reckoned as equal to eight heaped. **1896** *Whitaker's Alm.* 424 Coke, apples, potatoes.. are still sold by heaped measures and the sack of three bushels.

3. *fig.* Accumulated; stored *up*.

1402 HOCCLEVE *Let. of Cupid* 407 Hir heped vertu hath swich excellence. **1513** DOUGLAS *Æneis* I. Prol. 228 In mair hepit malice. **1847** DISRAELI *Tancred* IV. iv. (1871) 264 All the heaped-up lore of ages. **1865** NEALE *Glor. Parad.* 66 O how dear, how heaped, the rapture!

'heaper. [f. HEAP *v.* + -ER[1].] One who heaps up or accumulates.

c **1490** *Promp. Parv.* 235/2 (MS. K.) Hepar, *cumulator*. **1548** UDALL *Erasm. Par. Luke* xxiii. (1551) 377 b, An heaper of sinnes vpon sinnes. **1755** RAMSAY *Ep. to J. Clerk* 9 May, Tho' I ne'er was a rich heaper, To make that up I live the cheaper. **1861** DASENT *Burnt Njal* I. 90 Heaper up of piles of dead.

†**heap-full**, *a. Obs.* [f. HEAP *sb.* (in advb. relation) + FULL *a.*] Full and heaped up.

1530 PALSGR. 549/2 Fyll your busshell heape full. *Ibid.* 849/2 Heape full, or heaped full, *a comble*. **1769** *Projects* in *Ann. Reg.* 115/2 A corn-bushel heap-full.

'heaping, *vbl. sb.* [f. HEAP *v.* + -ING[1].]

1. The action of the verb HEAP; making into a heap; accumulation. Also *concr.*

c **900** tr. *Bæda's Hist.* v. xiv. [xiii.] (1890) 440 In heapunge eowerre niðerunge. *c* **1440** *Promp. Parv.* 235/2 Hepynge, *cumulacio*. **1571** GOLDING *Calvin on Ps.* lxv. 7 In that unmeasurable heaping of the earth. *a* **1631** DONNE in *Select.* (1840) 30 This better resurrection is a heaping euen of that fulness. **1712** ADDISON *Spect.* No. 549 ¶1 Grown old in the heaping up of riches. **1853** KANE *Grinnell Exp.* xx. 156 Circular mounds or heapings-up of the crumbled limestone.

2. *Comb.* †**heaping figure**, a rhetorical figure in which epithets, etc. are heaped up. *Obs.*

1589 PUTTENHAM *Eng. Poesie* III. xix. (Arb.) 243 The Latines called it Congeries and we the heaping figure.

heaping, *ppl. a. U.S.* [f. HEAP *v.*] Of a spoonful: heaped. Also *fig.* mounting up.

1838 *Congress. Globe* June 470/2 App., The amount of money..is a very high and heaping price. **1868** L. M. ALCOTT *Lit. Women* xi, Amy..took a heaping spoonful, choked..and left the table precipitately. **1908** *Smart Set* June 25/1 Aunt Natica waddled off..to fetch Thorndyke a heaping portion of the *dulce*. **1965** C. D. EBY *Siege of Alcázar* (1966) xi. 221 He had just been served a heaping ration of rice and beans, a special treat.

†**'heaply**, *adv. Obs. rare*$^{-0}$. [f. HEAP *sb.* + -LY[2].] In heaps.

1552 HULOET, Heape upon heape, and heapelye.

†**heap-meal**, *adv.* [OE. *héap-mælum*, f. HEAP *sb.*: see -MEAL.] In heaps; in large quantities or numbers. (Also ***by heap-meal.***)

c **897** K. ÆLFRED *Gregory's Past.* xlvi. 348 Hu hie hie gadriað heapmælum. *c* **1000** ÆLFRIC *Numb.* i. 3 Telle þu and Aaron heapmælum. *c* **1000** —— *Saints' Lives* (E.E.T.S.) II. 282 Þa hæþenan..feollon heap-mælum ealle to þæs halȝan weres cneowum. **1610** HOLLAND *Camden's Brit.* I. 71 And thereon powre the same forth by heap-meale.

heapy ('hiːpɪ), *a.* [f. HEAP *sb.* + -Y. Cf. Ger. *häufig* frequent.] Full or consisting of heaps.

1552 HULOET, Heapye or full of heapes, *aceruosus*. **1557** *Tottell's Misc.* (Arb.) 242 My heapy doubtes and trembling feares are fled. **1725** POPE *Odyss.* XIX. 515 With wither'd foliage strew'd, a heapy store! **1869** PHILLIPS *Vesuv.* iv. 128 Lava lying in heapy ridges.

hear (hɪə(r)), *v.* Pa. t. and pa. pple. **heard** (hɜːd). Forms: *Inf.* 1 **híeran, hýran, héran**, 2–5 **heren**, 4–5 **heere(n**, 3–6 **here**, 6–7 **heare**, 6– **hear**; also 3 (*Lay.*) **hæren**, (*Orm.*) **herenn**, 3–4 **heoren**, 3–5 *s.w.* **hure(n**, 4 **hyere(n, hiere(n**, 4–5 **hir(e**, *s.w.* **huyre**, *Sc.* **heyre**, 4–6 **her, hyre**, 5 *2nd sing.* **harst**; *Sc.* 5–6 **heire**, 5– **heir**. *Pa. t.* 1 **híerde, hýrde, hérde**, 2–6 **herde**, 4–6 **herd, hearde**, 4– **heard**; also 3 **heorde**, (*Orm.*) **heorrde**, 3–4 **herede**, 3–5 **hirde, hurde**, 3–6 **harde**, 4–7 (*Sc.* -9) **hard**. *Pa. pple.* 1 **ȝehíered, -hýred, -héred**, 2 **hered**, 2–6 **herd**, 6– **heard**; also 3 (*Orm.*) **herrd, heorrd**, 3–5 **hurd**, 4 **y-hyerd**, 5 **y-herd**, 4–6 **harde**, 4–7 (*Sc.* -9) **hard**. [Com. Teut. vb.: OE., early WS. *híeran*, late WS. *hýran*, Anglian *héran* (:—**hēarjan*) = OFris. *hêra, hôra* (:—**hôrja*) (WFris. *hearren*, Satl. *hêra*), OS. *hôrjan, hôrean* (MLG., MDu. *hôren*, Du. *hooren*), OHG. *hôrren* (MHG. *hœren*, Ger. *hören*), ON. *heyra* (Norw. *höyra*, Sw. *höra*, Da. *höre*), all:—**haurjan* = Goth. *hausjan* :— OTeut. **hauzjan*. Beside the simple vb., OE. had, like the other old Teutonic langs., the compound *ȝehíeran* (Goth. *gahausjan*) in the same sense, but perhaps with greater implication of completeness of action. In some uses *ȝehíeran* was more frequent in OE. than the simple vb., so that the latter is rare or not evidenced; it occurs more frequently in Old Northumbrian, and becomes commoner after 1200, perhaps under Norse influence. The pa. pple. in *ȝe-*, in early ME. southern dialect, may belong to either verb. See YHERE.

Cognates of *hauzjan* outside Teutonic are unknown. Conjectures of its relationship to the root *auz-* EAR, to L. *audire*, and Gr. ἀκούειν, are all extremely doubtful.]

1. a. *intr.* To perceive, or have the sensation of, sound; to possess or exercise the faculty of audition, of which the specific organ is the ear. The proper verb to express this faculty or function.

c **950** *Lindisf. Gosp.* Matt. xiii. 15 Ðy læs eȝum hia ȝeseað and earum herað [*Ags. G.* ȝehyron]. —— 16 Eadȝo biðon..

earo iuere forðon héras hia [*Ags. G.* hiȝ ȝehyraþ]. *c* **1200** ORMIN 15501 And dumbe menn and dæfe he ȝaff To spekenn wel and herenn. *c* **1375** *Sc. Leg. Saints, Mathou* 62 Als þai tuk fra men þe sycht, And for to here to haf na mycht. **1382** WYCLIF *Matt.* xi. 15 He that hath eeris of heerynge, heere he. **14..** *Voc.* in Wr.-Wülcker 566/44 *Audio*, to huyre. **1526** TINDALE *Matt.* xi. 15 He that hath eares to heare, let him here. **1599** SHAKS. *Much Ado* IV. i. 89 Leonato, I am sorry you must heare. *c* **1600** —— *Sonn.* xxiii, To heare with eies belongs to loves fine wit. **1611** BIBLE *Deut.* iv. 28 Ye shall serue gods..which neither see, nor heare. **1785** REID *Int. Powers* II. i, We cannot see without eyes, nor hear without ears. *Ibid.*, The ear is not that which hears; but the organ by which we hear. **1875** JOWETT *Plato* I. 54 [He] whispered..so that Menexenus should not hear. *a* **1898** *Mod.* He does not hear readily; he is dull of hearing.

b. *to hear of both ears, not to hear of that ear* (see EAR *sb.*[1] 3 d), *on that side* (see quot. 1617).

1548 HALL *Chron., Hen. IV*, 16 b, The kyng was required to purchase his deliverance..but he could not heare on that side. *a* **1617** BAYNE *On Eph.* i, If he have no mind to perform it, we say, hee cannot heare on that side. **1624** BP. MOUNTAGU *Gagg* Pref. 9 We should have heard thereof on both eares to a purpose.

2. a. *trans.* To perceive (sound, or something that emits or causes sound); to have cognizance of by means of the ear or auditory sense.

c **950** *Lindisf. Gosp.* Matt. xiii. 17 ȝewillnadon..ȝehera ða ilco ȝe heres and ne herdon [*Ags. G.* ȝehyran þa þing þe ȝe ȝehyrað, and hiȝ ne ȝehyrdon]. *c* **1175** *Lamb. Hom.* 47 Þeos ilke weord..god ha beoð to heren [cf. 49 for to iheren godes weordes]. *c* **1200** *Vices & Virtues* 11 He it ne herde. *c* **1200** ORMIN 10850 Þær wass þe Faderr heorrd anan Off heoffne Þurrh an steffne. *a* **1300** *Cursor M.* 2849 Sir loth wijf þis cri sco hard. **1382** WYCLIF *Luke* x. 24 Many prophetis and kyngis wolden..heere tho thingis, that ȝe heere, and thei herden not. *c* **1440** *Gesta Rom.* lix. 243 (Harl.) He harde a voyse seing to him, 'Whi erte thowe so hevy?' **1538** STARKEY *England* I. i. 20 Thyngys wych we se, fele, or her. **1563** W. FULKE *Meteors* (1640) 27 Although the lightning appeare unto us, a good pretty while before the thunderclap be heard. **1596** SHAKS. *1 Hen. IV*, II. ii. 35 Lay thine eare close to the ground, and list if thou can heare the tread of Trauellers. **1694** *Acc. Sev. Late Voy.* II. (1711) 44 So great a noise, that one can hardly hear his own words. **1715** DE FOE *Fam. Instruct.* I. i. (1841) I. 15 How can he hear what I say? **1860** TYNDALL *Glac.* I. xxvii. 215 The men shouted.. and I distinctly heard them through the falling snow.

b. predicated of the ear.

[*c* **825** *Vesp. Psalter* ix. 38 [x. 17] Lustas heortan heora ȝeherde eare ðin.] *c* **1375** *Sc. Leg. Saints, Egipciane* 428 Na þine eris to her it sa lange ma nocht thole. **1382** WYCLIF *1 Cor.* ii. 9 Y3e sy3 not, ne eere herde..what thingis God made redy bifore to hem that louen him. **1586** B. YOUNG *Guazzo's Civ. Conv.* IV. (1586) 191 Ladie Lelias eares are to daintie to heare anie reasons. *a* **1835** MRS. HEMANS *Better Land* iv, Ear hath not heard its deep songs of joy.

c. *not to hear day nor door*: not to hear anything distinctly. *Sc.*

1768 ROSS *Helenore* 86 (Jam.) That day nor door a body cudna hear. **1816** SCOTT *Old Mort.* viii, 'She's as deaf as Corra-linn—we canna mak her hear day nor door.'

3. a. As with other verbs of perception, the subst. or pronominal object may be followed by an *inf.*, *pres. pple.* (orig. *vbl. sb.* with *a-*), or *pa. pple.*, expressing an action performed or suffered by it.

The infin. now takes *to* after the passive, but not after the active vb.: *we heard him groan*; *he was heard to groan*. But exceptions to both rules are to be met with: see ¶

a **1000** *Beowulf* (Z.) 1346 Ic þæt lond-buend leode mine.. secȝan hyrde. *c* **1200** ORMIN 901 Godd..wollde himm sellf þa belless herenn ringenn. **1297** R. GLOUC. (1724) 279 He hurde angles synge an hey. *c* **1340** *Cursor M.* 550 (Trin.) Of þese þinges I haue herde seide Was adames body to gider leide. *c* **1375** *Sc. Leg. Saints, Petrus* 58 As he mycht heyre þe cok craw. *c* **1440** *Gesta Rom.* ii. 6 (Harl. MS.) Whenne þe seruauntis hirde hire lord crye. **1508** DUNBAR *Tua Mariit Wemen* 117 Quhen I heir nem-myt his name. **1551** T. WILSON *Logike* (1580) 33 As I heard once a doctor of Divinitie..earnestly defendyng his cause with examples. **1597** SHAKS. *2 Hen. IV*, V. v. 113, I heare a Bird so sing. **1651** HOBBES *Leviath.* II. xxvi. 141 To assemble the people..to heare it read. **1716** ADDISON *Freeholder* No. 11 (Seager), Mr. Motteux has been heard to say it more than once. **1737** POPE *Hor. Epist.* II. ii. 93 A Poet begs me, I will hear him read. **1782** COWPER *Gilpin* 206 Whereat his horse did snort, as he Had heard a lion roar. **1850** TENNYSON *In Mem.* x. 2, I hear the bell struck in the night. *Mod.* I heard a clock striking; I heard the clock strike three.

¶**1574** tr. *Littleton's Tenures* 8 b, Yf that childe..bee harde crye. **1647** W. BROWNE tr. *Gomberville's Polexander* I. 180, I heare the magnanimous Benzaida to accuse the ingratefull Nephizus.

b. Hence, by ellipsis of such objects as *people*, *persons*, *some one*, before the infinitives *say*, *speak*, *talk*, *tell*, the phrases *to hear say*, *hear tell*, etc., of which some are still in dialectal or colloquial, and occasionally literary, use. Formerly also with pa. pple., as *to hear told* (*obs.*).

a **1000** *Beowulf* (Z.) 582 No ic wiht fram þe swylcra searo-niða secgan hyrde. *a* **1123** *O.E. Chron.* an. 1114 Ða þe munecas of Burch hit herdon sæȝen. *c* **1220** *Bestiary* 584 He hauen herd told of ðis mere..half man and half fis. **1297** R. GLOUC. (1724) 391 Kyng Macolon hurde telle her-of in Scotlonde. **1465** SIR J. PASTON in *Paston Lett.* No. 531 II. 244 When Debnam herd sey how that I began to gadyr sylvyr. *c* **1470** HENRY *Wallace* IV. 379, I her spek of that man. *a* **1533** LD. BERNERS *Huon* lxv. 225 Ye neuer herd speke of a trewere nor more noble man. **1589** COGAN *Haven Health* (1636) 139, I have heard tell of a bishop of this land, that would have eaten fryed frogs. **1603** KNOLLES *Hist. Turks* (1638) 322 He was..neuer afterwards seene or heard tell of. **1640** tr. *Verdere's Rom. Romants* II. 71 The burning Knight, of whom it may be you have heard talk. *Ibid.* III. 59 Hee would by no means hear speak of sleeping till Florisbell had related [etc.]. **1861** GEO. ELIOT *Silas M.* vi, We heared tell as he'd sold his own land. **1892** G. F. X. GRIFFITH tr. *Fouard's St. Peter* 131 Even those who had heard tell of his conversion did not know [etc.].

c. Hence the gerundial phrase †(*by*) *hearing say*, (by) hearing it said (by) hearsay. *Obs.* or *dial.*

c **1330** R. BRUNNE *Chron.* (1810) 304 Edward vnderstode, þorgh oft heryng say, How [etc.]. **1491** CAXTON *Vitas Patr.* (W. de W. 1495) I. xxxvii. 49 a/2 He sayde soo by heryng saye. **1525** LD. BERNERS *Froiss.* II. cxxvii. [cxxiii.] 361, I knowe nothyng of the mater but by heryng saye. *a* **1533** —— *Gold. Bk. M. Aurel.* (1546) B v b, Thei wrote by heryng saie. *Mod. Sc.* They knew by hearing tell of it.

d. *to like to hear oneself speak, talk* (and similar phrases): to be fond of talking; *to hear oneself think*: usu. in neg. contexts, not to be able to think because there is too much noise going on.

1592 SHAKS. *Rom. & Jul.* II. iv. 156 Pray what sawcie Merchant was this?..*Rom.*: A Gentleman Nurse that loves to heare himselfe talke. **1781** GEORGE III *Lett.* (1927) V. 304 Considering the great love modern Orators have of hearing themselves speak. **1920** R. MACAULAY *Potterism* VI. iii. 226, I wish everyone would shut up, so that we could hear ourselves think. **1927** H. T. LOWE-PORTER tr. *Mann's Magic Mountain* II. vii. 779 You won't be able to hear yourselves think. **1934** J. E. MANSION *Harrap's French & Eng. Dict.* 272/1 *Discoureur... C'est un grand d.*, he likes to hear himself talk. **1962** *New Yorker* 12 May 38/1 You have to wear earplugs to hear yourself think.

4. To exercise the auditory function intentionally; to give ear, hearken, listen. **a.** *intr.*

[*c* **1000** *Ags. Gosp.* Matt. xv. 10 ȝehyrað and onȝytaþ.] *c* **1340** *Cursor M.* 271 *heading* (Trin.) Hereþ now of þe trinite dere And of þe makyng of þis world here. **1382** WYCLIF *1 Sam.* iii. 9 Spek, Lord, for thi seruaunt herith. *c* **1460** *Towneley Myst.* (Surtees) 17 Harstow, boy? ther is a podyng in the pot. **1482** WARKW. *Chron.* (Camden) 27 A castelle that spekethe, and a womane that wille here, thai wille be gotene bothe. **1611** BIBLE *2 Sam.* xx. 16 Then cried a wise woman out of the Citie, Heare, heare. **1702** ROWE *Tamerl.* I. i. 443 When first thy moving Accents Won me to hear.

b. *trans.* To listen to (a person or thing) with more or less attention or understanding; to give ear to, hearken to; to give audience to. Orig. with dative of the person or thing. *to hear out*, to listen to to the end: see OUT; *to hear out*: also, to distinguish (the sounds of something heard).

a **1000** *Juliana* 371 (Gr.) He minum hraðe leahtrum ȝelenge larum hyreð. *c* **1160** *Hatton Gosp.* John viii. 47 Se þe is of gode he herð [*Ags. G.* ȝehyrð] godes word. *c* **1200** *Trin. Coll. Hom.* 127 And bigan þat folc..to here his wise lore. *c* **1205** LAY. 1329 Ne bið na man weri heora songes to heræn. *c* **1230** *Hali Meid.* 3 Her me, dohter. *a* **1300** *Cursor M.* 20510 Sittes stell now..And hers [*Fairf.* heris] now þis mirines. *c* **1440** *Gesta Rom.* lvi. 239 (Harl. MS.) He that hurithe the doctrine of the ioyes of paradys. **1475** *Bk. Noblesse* 79 He.. disdeyned to hire theym. **1611** BIBLE *1 Sam.* xxiv. 9 Wherfore hearest thou mens words? **1617** MORYSON *Itin.* I. 137 There is a Chamber [in the Vatican]..wherein Ambassadours are heard. *Ibid.* III. 32 The Pharises..were to be heard, as sitting in the chaire of Moses. **1637** SHIRLEY *Gamester* III. (Dodsley *O. Pl.* 1780 IX. 63) It will be inconvenient to hear out your currranto. **1749** FIELDING *Tom Jones* XIV. iii, I desire only to be heard out. **1841** LANE *Arab. Nts.* I. 81 Hear my story, O fisherman. **1875** JOWETT *Plato* (ed. 2) I. 363 There was an agreement between us that you should hear me out. **1922** R. S. WOODWORTH *Psychol.* x. 230 By careful attention and training we can 'hear out' the separate overtones from the total blend.

c. With two objects, as *to hear* (one) *his lessons*: to listen to the recitation of his lessons.

1804 LADY HUNTER in *Sir M. Hunter's Jrnl.* (1894) 202, I ..have heard George and James their lessons. **1811** L. M. HAWKINS *C'tess & Gertr.* (1812) II. 256 He hears some of the younger ones their lessons. **1894** BLACKMORE *Perlycross* 111 Three pupils, and not a lesson have I heard them.

5. a. *trans.* To attend and listen to (a lecture, sermon, play, musical performance, etc.); to form one of the audience at.

a **1300** *Cursor M.* 9764 (Gött.) He mote þaim giue his benisoun, þat wil gladly here þis sarmoun. *c* **1375** *Lay Folks Mass Bk.* App. iv. 2 Hou mon scholde here hys masse. **1470–85** MALORY *Arthur* XVII. ix, Vpon the morowe whan they had herde masse. **1548** HALL *Chron., Hen. VIII*, 9 He and the Quene heard evensong. **1596** SHAKS. *Tam. Shr.* Induct. ii. 136 They thought it good you heare a play. **1827** HALLAM *Const. Hist.* (1876) I. ii. 95 Many persons were sent to prison for hearing mass.

b. 'To be a hearer of; to sit under the preaching of; as, what minister do you hear? (A colloquial use of the word.)' Webster, 1828. Also *absol.*

1783 COWPER *Let.* 8 Sept., There are, however, many who have left the Church, and hear among the Dissenters.

6. *trans.* To listen to judicially in a court of law; to give (one) a hearing; to try (a person or a case).

c **1160** *Hatton Gosp.* John vii. 51 Demð ure eæ aniȝene man bute hyne man ær hyre [*Ags. G.* ȝehyre]? **1382** WYCLIF *Deut.* i. 17 The litil ȝe shulen here as the more. **1484** *Lett. etc. Rich. III* (Rolls) I. 79 If any persone wolle come and compleyn of any of the said baillieffes that they shalbe herd. **1609** SKENE *Reg. Maj.* Table 62 He quha first accuses, is first hard. **1613** SHAKS. *Hen. VIII*, V. iii. 120 His Royall selfe in Iudgement comes to heare The cause. **1709** ADDISON *Tatler* No. 121 ⁋1 They are so in haste, that they never hear out the Case. **1844** H. H. WILSON *Brit. India* I. 115 Three Judges were appointed to the special duty of hearing appeals from the courts below. **1891** *Law Reports* Weekly Notes 202/1 The plaintiff ought to have had an opportunity of being heard before he was dismissed.

7. a. To listen to with compliance or assent; to accede to, grant (a request or prayer). Chiefly in scriptural use.

971 *Blickl. Hom.* 49 Gif him mon þonne hyran nelle, þonne mot se mæsse-preost hit wrecan. *c* **1175** *Lamb. Hom.* 63 Ah lauerd god her ure bone. *a* **1300** *Cursor M.* 10499 'Anna', he said, 'herd es þi bone, þou salt haf child and þat wel sone'. **1382** WYCLIF *Matt.* xviii. 15 3if he shal heere thee, thou hast wonnen thi brother. —— *Luke* i. 13 Thi preier is herd. **1450–1530** *Myrr. our Ladye* 188 Though ye deserue not to be harde for youre selfe, yet that he wylle graunte you youre askynges. **1562** WINȜET *Four Scoir Thre Quest.* Wks. 1888 I. 91 That altar, vpon the quhilk the prayaris of all acceptit and hard be our heuinly Father are offerit. **1568** GRAFTON *Chron.* II. 73 The king..sent to Rome with his excuse, which the Pope woulde in no wise heere. **1697** DRYDEN *Virg. Georg.* IV. 656 Orpheus' dying Pray'rs at length are heard. **1827** KEBLE *Chr. Y.* St. Peter's Day ii. 1 The prayer is heard.

b. *to hear of*, with *will* (*would*) and negative: to refuse to listen to, entertain the notion of, consent to, or permit.

1584 POWEL *Lloyd's Cambria* 274 He would in no case heare of reconciliation. **1658** W. BURTON *Itin. Anton.* 150 The learned Antiquary will not hear of it. **1785** MRS. S. BOYS *Coalition* I. 143 She would not hear of it. **1796** CHARLOTTE SMITH *Marchmont* IV. 347 He would by no means hear of her going. **1879** MRS. OLIPHANT *Within Precincts* (Tauchn.) II. xxix. 237 Mother would not hear of her staying.

c. *to hear to*, to listen to, to hear of. *U.S.*

1833 H. BARNARD in *Maryland Hist. Mag.* (1918) XIII. 379, I made a move to depart—but they would not hear to that. **1869** MRS. STOWE *Oldtown Folks* xx. 243 She has her own ways and doings, and she won't hear to reason. **1915** E. POOLE *Harbor* 202 When I tried at last to turn our talk to our affairs at home, at first she would not hear to it.

†**8.** To obey. *Obs.* (Only OE., ME., and *arch.*) Orig. with *dative*.

c **950** *Lindisf. Gosp.* Mark iv. 41 Hua..is ðes þæte ec wind and sæ herað him. *c* **1000** ÆLFRIC *Exod.* xiv. 31 Þæt Israhelisce folc..hyrdon Gode and Moise his þeowe. *c* **1380** WYCLIF *Serm.* Sel. Wks. I. 214 [Crist] ordeynede many folk to here alweie þis newe lawe. **1700** PRIOR *Carmen Seculare* 215 The fiery Pegasus disdains To mind the Rider's Voice, or hear the Reins. *a* **1729** CONGREVE *Ode to Godolphin* (T.), The beast..Whom soon he tam'd to use, and taught to hear the reins.

†**9.** *intr.* To be subject (*to*); to belong. *Obs.* [So MHG. *hœren*, beside *gehœren*.]

c **893** K. ÆLFRED *Oros.* I. i. §22 Þas land eall hyrað to Denemearcan. **940** *Chart. Eadmund* in *Cod. Dipl.* III. 415 Se haȝa æt Wiltune ðe hyrð into Wiliȝ. *c* **1205** LAY. 24062 Þa hafuenes alle, þe herden to þan londes. ? *a* **1300** *Shires of Eng.* in *O.E. Misc.* 146 Her-to hereþ viii store schire.

10. a. *trans.* To learn or get to know by hearing; to receive or obtain as information; to be told; to be informed of.

c **950** *Lindisf. Gosp.* Luke xvi. 2 Huætd ðis ic hero from ðe? [*Ags. G.* Hwi ȝehyre ic þis be þe?] *c* **1160** *Hatton Gosp.* ibid., Hwi here ich þis be þe? *c* **1250** *Gen. & Ex.* 1370 Sum good tiding heren or sen. *c* **1290** *Beket* 814 in *S. Eng. Leg.* I. 130 To court eft-soone he wende, For-to heore [*v.r.* hure] þe kingus wille. *a* **1300** *Cursor M.* 4192 His fader of him hirs na tiþand. *c* **1450** *Merlin* 32, I shall often..brynge soche tidinges as thow shalt put in thi boke, And wite it well, peple shulbe glad euer to heiren it. **1529** MORE *Dyaloge* I. Wks. 159/1 The Jewes that were vnworthy to hyre it, were offended. **1568** GRAFTON *Chron.* II. 377 The next newes that was heard of him, was, that he was slaine in Lorraine. **1667** MILTON *P.L.* IX. 888 Adam, soon as he heard The fatal Trespass don by Eve. **1781** COWPER *Conversation* 804 Great changes and new manners have occurred, And blest reforms, that I have never heard. **1893** W. T. WAWN *S. Sea Islanders* 53 The inquiry over, I heard nothing more about the matter.

b. with *obj. clause*.

a **1000** *Beowulf* (Z.) 2173 Hyrde ic þæt he ðone heals-beah Hyȝde ȝesealde. *c* **1050** *Byrhtferth's Handboc* in *Anglia* (1885) VIII. 321 We habbað on gastlicum ȝewritum oft ȝe-hyred þæt us ys beboden. *c* **1160** *Hatton Gosp.* John ix. 32 Ne herde [*Ags. G.* ȝehyrde] we næfre..þæt anyȝ un-tynde þas eaȝen. *c* **1200** *Trin. Coll. Hom.* 63 Nu ȝe hauen herd þat ure drihten bit turnen to him, hereð nu o hu uele wise. **1382** WYCLIF *Gen.* xlii. 2, I haue herd that wheet is sold in Egipte. **1559** W. CUNNINGHAM *Cosmogr. Glasse* 5 Let me here what you call Cosmographie. **1591** SHAKS. *Two Gent.* IV. ii. 113, I likewise heare that Valentine is dead. **1670** LADY M. BERTIE in *12th Rep. Hist. MSS. Comm.* App. v. 21, I am very sorry to heare that the small pox increases so as to fright you from Exton. **1674** N. COX *Gentl. Recreat.* (1677) 193 Garlick I have heard will do the like. **1746** *Tom Thumb's Trav.* 32 The courteous Behaviour of the Inhabitants, which, I hear, is habitual to them. **1808** *Sketches of Character* (1813) I. 198, I hear there are no lodgings to be had.

11. a. *absol.* or *intr.* To be informed, learn; to receive information or tidings *of*, or obtain news concerning; to receive a message or letter *from*. Also, (pregnantly) to receive a reprimand *from*.

c **1320** *Cast. Love* 1371 Ȝe habbeþ i-herd nou riht Of his strengþe and of his miht. *c* **1400** *Destr. Troy* 1866 Ne I hardely herde of hym hade in my lyue. *a* **1400–50** *Alexander* 2667 As sone as Darye þe derfe of þis dede heris. *a* **1533** LD. BERNERS *Huon* cxxvii. 466 They neuer had hard of suche a myracle. **1548** HALL *Chron., Hen. V*, 78 Therle of Suffolk.. hearing of their doynges. **1611** SHAKS. *Cymb.* IV. iii. 36–8, I heard no Letter from my Master..Nor heare I from my Mistris, who did promise To yeeld me often tydings. **1776** *Trail of Nundocomar* 23/1 Would you not have heard if he had been so ill as not to be able to come out? **1830** SOUTHEY *Lett.* (1856) IV. 168, I too had been looking to hear from you. **1837** DICKENS *Pickw.* ii, You shall hear from me in the morning, sir. *Mod.* When did you hear from your son in South Africa? We hear from him regularly every mail. He has never been heard of since. **1907** *Munsey's Mag.* Dec. 307/1 If those louts up at the castle neglected to have dinner

ready.., they would hear from him... If they didn't [spring at his word] they always heard from him.

b. *to hear of it*: to be spoken to about it; to be called to account for it. *colloq.*

1596 SHAKS. *1 Hen. IV*, I. iii. 124 Send vs your Prisoners, or you'l heare of it. **1658** GURNALL *Chr. in Arm.* Verse 15. xiv. §3 (1669) 161/2 We.. look to find them at hand on the shelf, clean and fit for use, or our servants shall hear of it. *Mod.* You'd better not do it again, or you'll hear of it.

c. *to have heard of*: to have become or been made aware of (a fact, etc.) in the course of one's experience; to have heard tell of. Freq. in negative contexts, often with *never*.

1907 G. B. SHAW *John Bull's Other Island* I. 8 Have you ever heard of Garden City? **1925** F. SCOTT FITZGERALD *Great Gatsby* i. 12 'Who with?' I told him. 'Never heard of them,' he remarked decisively. **1954** W. FAULKNER *Fable* 34, I have heard of your United States Coca-Cola. **1986** *N.Y. Times* 16 Apr. A2/4 Similarly, he said he had never heard of Dr. Jesa Vidic.

†**12. a.** To be reported or spoken (well or ill) of. [After Gr. *εὖ, κακῶς ἀκούειν*, L. *bene, male audire*.]

1583 BABINGTON *Commandm.* ix. (1637) 85 Desire ever.. rather to heare well, than to be rich: yea.. to leave unto thy posterity an honest report and name, before heaps of any riches. **1590** SPENSER *F.Q.* I. v. 23 O! what of gods then boots it to be borne, If old Aveugles sonnes so evill heare? **1652** BP. HALL *Invis. World* II. i, Aristotle himself is wont to hear ill for his opinion of the soul's mortality. **1658–9** *Burton's Diary* (1828) IV. 147 You have been three days upon it. It hears ill abroad. **1706** STANHOPE *Paraphr.* III. 502 If such Indulgences hear ill in the World, and naturally expose a Man to Censure and Disrepute.

b. *to hear rather*: to prefer to hear, to prefer to be addressed or called. (A Latinism.)

1667 MILTON *P.L.* III. 7 Or hear'st thou rather pure Ethereal stream Whose Fountain who shall tell? **1829** LAMB *Let. to V. Novello* Oct., Dear Fugueist—or hear'st thou rather Contrapuntist?

13. a. The imperative **hear!**, now usually repeated, **hear! hear!** (formerly ***hear him! hear him!***) is used as an exclamation to call attention to a speaker's words, and hence has become a general expression of approbation or 'cheering'.

It is now the regular form of cheering [CHEER *sb.*¹ 8] in the House of Commons, and expresses, according to intonation, admiration, acquiescence, indignation, derision, etc.

1689 SIR E. SEYMOUR 19 Feb. in Cobbett *Parl. Hist.* V. 122, I see gentlemen speak here under great disadvantages .. When gentlemen speak with reflections, and cry 'hear him, hear him', they [the former] cannot speak with freedom. **1689** SIR H. CAPEL *ibid.*, When Seymour was in the Chair, I have heard 'Hear him, hear him', often said in the house. **1762** FOOTE *Orators* II. Wks. 1836 II. 176 *Ter.* Dermot, be easy— *Scam.* Hear him— *Tire.* Hear him— *Ter.* Ay, hear him, hear him. **1768** LD. J. CAVENDISH *Sp. Ho. Com.* 8 Dec. in Sir H. Cavendish *Deb.* (1841) I. 96 Let us.. give a dispassionate attention to everything that passes. [Hear!] That very word 'hear!' I dread of all others. **1769** SIR F. NORTON *Sp.* ibid. 432 The common law is as much the law as the statute law. [Mr. Grenville called out hear! hear!] If the hon. gentleman will hear, by and by he will hear. **1770** G. GRENVILLE *Sp.* 16 Feb. ibid. 461 The House will be obliged to you [the Speaker] for your information. [Hear, Hear!] *Mr. Speaker*, I beg the House will be silent. I am sure that is disorderly. **1783** *Gentl. Mag.* LIII. II. 822 As to himself, he was free to acknowledge.. the hand which he had in it (A cry of *Hear him! Hear him!*) By the cry of *Hear Him!* said his Lordship, gentlemen seem to think I am going to make a confession. **1803** in Stanhope *Life Pitt* (1862) IV. 49 When he [Pitt] sat down there followed three of the.. most enthusiastic bursts of applause I ever heard.. as far as I observed, however, it was confined to the parliamentary 'Hear him! Hear him!' **1812** *Parl. Deb.* 5 May in *Examiner* 11 May 292/2 Orders were sent off to Mr. Henry to withdraw from the United States.—(*Hear, hear!*) **1865** LOWELL *Scotch the Snake* Prose Wks. 1890 V. 251 One Noble Lord or Honorable Member asking a question, and another Noble Lord or Honorable Member endeavoring to dodge it, amid cries of Hear! Hear!

b. Hence as sb. **hear, hear!** (formerly ***hear-him***), a cheer. Also **hear-hear** *v. intr.*, to shout '*hear! hear!*'; *trans.*, to acclaim with shouts of '*hear! hear!*'; to cheer. Hence **hear-'hearer**.

1727 POPE, etc. *Art of Sinking* 115 The *hear him* of the house of commons. **1736** BOLINGBROKE *Patriot.* (1749) 48 With repeated hear-hims ringing in his ears. **1836** *Westm. Rev.* Apr. 233 The *hear hims* are more fervent than on almost any other occasion. **1837** DICKENS *Pickw.* vii, I thank my honourable friend, if he will allow me to call him so—(four *hears*, and one certainly from Mr. Jingle)—for the suggestion. **1855** —— *Dorrit* I. xxxiv, Hearing, and ohing, and cheering. **1868** DISRAELI *Sp.* in *Ho. Com.* 3 Apr., If the hear-hearers have their way. **1879** SIR G. CAMPBELL *White & Black* 374 The members seemed generally very quiet; there was little 'Hear, hearing!' **1883** *Standard* 3 Apr. 5/4 He .. 'hear, hears' the member for Northampton. **1895** *Daily News* 3 Dec. 3/1 Mr. Morley's explanation of his position.. was received with sympathetic hear, hears.

hear(e obs. ff. HAIR, -E, HEIR, HERE, HIGHER.

hearable ('hɪərəb(ə)l), *a.* [f. HEAR *v.* + -ABLE.] That can be heard, audible.

c **1449** PECOCK *Repr.* I. xiv. 74 That he haue sure knowing of heereable treuthis and that bi heering of eeris. **1483** *Cath. Angl.* 184/1 Hereabylle, *audibilis.* **1851** RUSKIN *Let. to F. D. Maurice* (1889) 9 He is to me Visible and Hearable. **1885** W. C. RUSSELL *Strange Voy.* I. viii. 106 It was necessary to scream to make one's words hearable.

hearb, hearce, heard, obs. ff. HERB, HEARSE, HERD.

heard (hɜːd), *ppl. a.* [pa. pple. of HEAR *v.*] Perceived by the ear.

1483 *Cath. Angl.* 183/2 Herde, *auditus.* **1819** KEATS *Grecian Urn* 11 Heard melodies are sweet, but those unheard Are sweeter.

heard-say, obs. var. of HEARSAY.

hearer ('hɪərə(r)). [f. HEAR *v.* + -ER¹.]

1. One who hears; an auditor, listener.

a **1340** HAMPOLE *Psalter* v. 11 þai shew stynkand wordes þat corumpis þe herers. **1382** WYCLIF *Jas.* i. 23 An herere of the word, and not a doere. **1529** MORE *Dyaloge* I. Wks. 150/2 The fruit of stryfe among the hyrers. **1599** SHAKS. *Much Ado* I. i. 309 Thou wilt be like a louer presently, And tire the hearer with a booke of words. *a* **1734** NORTH *Exam.* III. vii. §19 (1740) 517 As in the proverbial Court at Dover, all Speakers and no Hearers. **1758** JOHNSON *Idler* No. 49 ¶1 He knows me to be a very patient hearer. **1875** JOWETT *Plato* (ed. 2) I. 151 Those who are present.. ought to be impartial hearers of both the speakers.

†**b.** One who hears causes; a judge. *Obs.*

1535 COVERDALE *Judg.* xi. 10 The Lorde be hearer betwene vs.

2. One who receives oral instruction, or attends lectures or sermons; a disciple. Cf. AUDIENT.

1686 J. DUNTON *Lett. fr. New-Eng.* (1867) 59 Mr. Burroughs.. formerly a hearer, and still a great lover, of my Reverend Father in Law, Dr. Samuel Annersly. **1838** THIRLWALL *Greece* V. 251 He was for a time one of Plato's hearers. **1888** *Pall Mall G.* 2 Apr. 14/1 The non-matriculated students, or 'hearers', at the four [Swiss] universities are about four hundred in number.

3. *Eccl. Hist.* [tr. L. *audiens*.] One admitted to hear the Scriptures read and receive instruction, but not to the common worship of the church: applied to catechumens and penitents of the second order.

1697 tr. *Dupin's Eccl. Hist.* II. 109 This sort of Catechumens were called Hearers, because they heard the Instructions which were given in the Church. *a* **1711** KEN *Hymnotheo* III. Poet. Wks. 1721 III. 76 Within the hallow'd Door on either Hand, The Penitents advanc'd to Hearers stand. **1722** J. BINGHAM *Chr. Antiq.* VI. 534 St. Basil says expressly, they were hearers only, and not allowed to be present at any prayers whatsoever.

hear-hear, *v.*, etc.: see HEAR *v.* 13 b.

'hearing, *vbl. sb.* [f. HEAR *v.* + -ING¹.]

1. a. The action of the verb HEAR; perception by the ear or auditory sense; the faculty or sense by which sound is perceived; audition.

c **1230** *Hali Meid.* 13 Fif wittes, sihðe & heringe [etc.]. *a* **1300** *Cursor M.* 13107 þe def has hering, blind has sight. **1375** BARBOUR *Bruce* I. 10 Suth thyngis.. Tyll mannys heryng ar plesand. **1398** TREVISA *Barth. De P.R.* III. xviii. (1495) 64 Alway the heryng is gendred by ayre smytte. **1509** FISHER *Fun. Serm. C'tess Richmond* Wks. (1876) 305 Her herynge sholde haue dulled more and more. **1548** HALL *Chron., Edw. IV*, 232 b, Fayning that he was thycke of hearyng. **1588** SHAKS. *L.L.L.* II. i. 75 Aged eares play treuant at his tales, And yonger hearings are quite rauished. **1597** GERARDE *Herbal* (1633) 856 Ground-Iuy is commended.. for them that are hard of hearing. **1772** PRIESTLEY *Inst. Relig.* (1782) II. 154 Captivating.. at the first hearing. **1828** STARK *Elem. Nat. Hist.* II. 224 The organ of hearing is not manifest in insects.

b. *in one's hearing*, in such a position or way as to be heard by one. *within hearing*, *out of hearing*, at such a distance as to be heard, or not heard; within, or out of, hearing distance.

1388 WYCLIF *Ezek.* ix. 5 He seide to hem in myn heryng, Go 3e thorou3 the citee.. and smytte 3e. *c* **1470** HENRY *Wallace* x. 455 Quhen that the Bruce out off thair heryng wer. **1568** GRAFTON *Chron.* II. 200 [He] cursed his sonne in the hering of those that had the guyding of them. **1590** SHAKS. *Mids. N.* II. ii. 152 What, out of hearing, gone? No sound, no word? **1596** —— *Merch. V.* v. i. 241 In the hearing of these manie friends I sweare to thee. **1615** G. SANDYS *Trav.* 9 Where stood that renowned Citie of Corinth, in hearing of both Seas. **1766** GOLDSM. *Vic. W.* xxx, As soon as we came within hearing, I called out to him by name. **1791** BOSWELL *Johnson* (1831) III. 79 It was not said in his hearing. **1862** D. WILSON *Preh. Man* II. xxiii. 361 Within the hearing of Niagara's voice.

2. The action of actively giving ear, listening (e.g. to a lecture, sermon, play, etc.); *spec.* attendance at preaching (*dial.*); audience. Also *fig.*

a **1225** *St. Marher.* 2 Hercnið alle þe mahen, ant herunge habbeð. *c* **1340** *Cursor M.* 13708 (Trin.) þei 3af hering to him vchone. **1529** MORE *Dyaloge* I. Wks. 168/2 To gyue diligent hyrynge.. and faithfull obedience to the churche. **1568** GRAFTON *Chron.* II. 390 At that tyme the Archebishop had no further heeryng. **1602** SHAKS. *Ham.* III. ii. 161 We begge your hearing Patientlie. **1604** HIERON *Preacher's Plea* Wks. 1624 I. 539 To draw the people to hearing upon the weeke-dayes. **1791** COWPER *Let.* 26 June, He.. has a mother between seventy and eighty, who walks every Sunday eight miles to hearing, as they call it, and back again. **1856** FROUDE *Hist. Eng.* (1858) I. ii. 170 New doctrines ever gain readiest hearing among the common people.

3. a. The listening to evidence and pleadings in a court of law; the trial of a cause; *spec.* a trial before a judge without a jury. **b.** (*Sc. Law.*) ***hearing in presence***, 'a formal hearing of counsel before the whole thirteen Judges' (Bell *Dict. Law Sc.* 1861).

1576 FLEMING *Panopl. Epist.* 357 The Usher.. is willing to give us the hearing, and to determine the controversie. **1603** SHAKS. *Meas. for M.* II. i. 141 I'll take my leaue, And leaue you to the hearing of the cause. **1690** WOOD *Life* 15 Jan. (O.H.S.) III. 322 There was to be a hearing between the University and City of Oxon on the 15 January [*note*, at the barr of the house]. **1705** HEARNE *Collect.* 17 Nov., On ye 14th Instant.. came on the Hearing of yᵉ Election of St. Albans. **1768** BLACKSTONE *Comm.* (1800) III. 453 The cause is again brought to hearing on the matters of equity reserved, and a final decree is made. **1818** CRUISE *Digest* (ed. 2) IV. 554 The cause was twice heard in Ireland, on the last of which hearings, before Lord Middleton.. he decreed a perpetual injunction against Lord Forbes. **1891** *Law Reports* Weekly Notes 80/1 [They] attended the hearing before the registrar.

4. Knowledge by hearing or being informed; esp. in phr. ***to come to one's hearing***.

c **1450** LONELICH *Grail* lvi. 322 So long they spoken of this thing.. that it cam to hire lordis hering. *a* **1533** LD. BERNERS *Huon* lxxxviii. 281 The brute therof came to the heryinge of duke Raoull. **1617** MORYSON *Itin.* II. iii Upon the hearing of his Lordships returne.

5. Something heard; report, rumour, news. *dial.*

a **1300** *E.E. Psalter* cxi[i]. 7 Of ivel hering noght drede sal he. **1382** WYCLIF *Ezek.* vii. 26 Trublynge togidre shal come vpon trublynge togidre, and herynge vpon heryynge. *c* **1440** *Jacob's Well* xxxiv. (E.E.T.S.) 220 þin erys, þat first spak dyshonest herynges of bacbytyng, flateryng, lesynges, & rybaudrye. ? *a* **1500** *Sir Beues* 3680 (Pynson) The pope [of] that heryng was ful glad. **1596** SHAKS. *Tam. Shr.* v. ii. 182 Tis a good hearing, when children are toward, But a harsh hearing, when women are froward. **1611** —— *Cymb.* III. i. 4 Whose remembrance.. will to Eares and Tongues Be Theame, and hearing euer. **1666** PEPYS *Diary* 4 Aug., De Ruyter dares not come on shore.. Which is a very good hearing. **1840** DICKENS *Barn. Rudge* xlviii. (1892) 348 This is a pleasant hearing. I thank Heaven for it.

6. A 'lecture', a scolding. *dial.*

1816 SCOTT *Old Mort.* xiv, 'After she had gi'en us a hearing on our duties.' **1824** MISS FERRIER *Inher.* xli, [She] left the room for the purpose.. of giving her a good hearing.

7. *attrib.* and *Comb.*, as ***hearing-day***, ***-distance***, ***-organ***, ***-tube***; **hearing aid**, a sound-amplifier for the hard of hearing; **hearing-fee**, the fee paid by a suitor to an official of the court before the case is heard; **hearing-trumpet** = EAR-TRUMPET.

1922 *Lancet* 11 Mar. 462/2 These electrical instruments should go far towards destroying the too general prejudice against the use of *hearing aids. **1950** *Lancet* 11 Nov. 532/2 Practical courses.. on audiometry and hearing-aids. **1951** *Consumer Reports* Jan. 13/1 Hearing aids and batteries are.. supplied without charge. **1960** 'H. CARMICHAEL' *Seeds of Hate* ii. 18 A grey-haired woman who wore a hearing aid. **1969** B. PATTEN *Notes to Hurrying Man* 57 Much later on in life I wear my hearing-aid. **1860** FITZROY in *Merc. Marine Mag.* VII. 343 What is called 'a good *hearing-day', may be mentioned among the signs of wet. **1887** *Cassell's Fam. Mag.* 141/2 You must pay 2*s.* for every pound you sue for, for *hearing-fee. **1895** *Daily News* 4 Dec. 6/2 So poor that she actually could not pay the hearing-fee. **1725** WATTS *Logic* II. v. §1 Mediums which assist the Hearing, such as Speaking-Trumpets, *Hearing-Trumpets. **1856** LD. COCKBURN *Mem.* i. (1874) 41 A small hearing trumpet fastened by a black ribbon to a button-hole of his coat.

8. hearing say, *gerundial phr.*: see HEAR *v.* 3 c.

'hearing, *ppl. a.* [f. HEAR *v.* + -ING².] That hears: see the verb.

a **1300** *Cursor M.* 27989 þe eres o þe herand. **1382** WYCLIF *Prov.* xx. 12 The herende ere, and the seende e3e. **1676** WYCHERLEY *Pl. Dealer* III. i, If it had not been for me, thou hadst been yet but a hearing counsel at the bar. **1884** A. J. ELLIS in *Athenæum* 12 Jan. 55/1 A school.. for teaching deaf-mute infants in.. association with hearing infants.

hearing, obs. form of HERRING.

†**'hearingless**, *a. Obs.* [f. HEARING *vbl. sb.* + -LESS.] Destitute of the faculty of hearing; deaf.

1398 TREVISA *Barth. De P.R.* III. xviii. (Tollem. MS.) Ambrose sayeþ þat men of þe contray þere þe ryuer Nilus ariseþ ben heringles [**1582** void of hearing].

heark, obs. form of HARK.

hearken, harken ('hɑːk(ə)n), *v.* Forms: 1 **hercnian, heorcnian**, 2–3 **hercnen**, (*Orm.* **herrcnenn**), 3 **hærcnien**, 3–4 **heorknien, herknen, herkin**, 3–6 **herken**, 4 **herkon**, 4–5 **herkyn**, 5 **harkyn**, 6 **harcken**; 4– **harken**, 6– **hearken**. [OE. *hercnian, heorcnian, hyrcnian*, formed with suffix *-n-* from **heorci-an*, the OE. type of HARK *v.*

The spelling *harken*, which agrees with that of HARK, and is at once more regular and of earlier standing, is the accepted one in modern American Dictionaries, and is preferred by some good English writers; but in current English use it is much less frequent than *hearken*. The preference for the latter spelling is probably due to association with HEAR, supported by the analogy of *heart* and *hearth*.]

1. *intr.* To apply the ears to hear; to listen, give ear. Const. *to* (†*of*), in OE. and ME. with dative.

a **1000** *Life St. Guthlac* (1848) 42 Guðlac.. eode þa sona ut and hawode and hercnode. *c* **1000** ÆLFRIC *Hom.* I. 422 Ypolitus.. heora wordum heorcnode. *c* **1175** *Lamb. Hom.* 59 Hercnið alle to þis writ. *c* **1205** LAY. 19668 Heo.. hærcneden 3eorne of þas kinges hærme. *a* **1300** *Cursor M.* 966 He said, 'adam, now wel sais þou I sal þe tell, and herken [*Gött.* harkin] now'. **13..** *Gaw. & Gr. Knt.* 1708 þe fox.. Hauilounez, & herkenez, bi heggez ful ofte. *c* **1386** CHAUCER *Knt.'s T.* 668 His felawe That was so neih to herken of his sawe. **1489** CAXTON *Faytes of A.* II. xxxvii. 155 They ought often to herken yf they can here eny noyse or smytynge of hamers. **1530** PALSGR. 579/1 Harken here at this hole. **1550** CROWLEY *Inform. & Petit.* 255 Herken you possessioners. **1592** SHAKS. *Ven. & Ad.* 868 She hearkens for his hounds and for his horn. **1697** DRYDEN *Virg. Georg.* IV. 564 But

aged Nereus harkens to his Lore. **1718** LADY M. W. MONTAGU *Let. to Lady Rich* 10 Oct., It is full employment enough to hearken, whether one answers or not. **1774** GOLDSM. *Nat. Hist.* (1776) IV. 50 Whenever it is whistled to, it stops to hearken. **1832** TENNYSON *Œnone* 23 Dear mother Ida, harken ere I die.

†**2.** *intr.* To listen privily; to play the eavesdropper; to eavesdrop. *Obs.*

1382 WYCLIF *Ecclus.* xxi. 27 [24] The folie of a man to herknen thurȝ the dores. **1535** COVERDALE *ibid.*, A foolish man standeth herkenynge at the dore. **1588** *Nottingham Rec.* IV. 219 By harckeninge of our howses with drawen weapens.

3. *intr.* To apply the mind to what is said; to attend, have regard; to listen with sympathy or docility. Const. *to.*

c **1230** *Hali Meid.* 39 Hercne his read. **1535** COVERDALE *Exod.* vi. 9 But they herkened not vnto him, for very anguysh of sprete, and for sore laboure. **1549** LATIMER *Ploughers* (Arb.) 25 No man wyll herken to it. **1651** HOBBES *Leviath.* III. xxxvi. 224 Josiah not hearkning to them, was slain. **1667** MILTON *P.L.* IX. 1134 Would thou hadst heark'nd to my words, and stai'd. **1777** ROBERTSON *Hist. Amer.* (1778) II. VI. 205 Instead of hearkening to some of his officers. **1870** BRYANT *Iliad* I. I. 12 To him Who hearkens to the gods, the gods give ear. **1896** A. AUSTIN *Eng. Darl.* II. iv, They would not harken.

†**b.** with *on.* *Obs.*

1523 LD. BERNERS *Froiss.* I. cclxxiii. 414 The people..had great desyre to harken on the promysses that the duke of Amiens made vnto them. **1580** SIDNEY *Arcadia* (1627) 434 Harkening on euery rumour.

4. *trans.* To hear with attention, give ear to (a thing); to listen to; to have regard to, heed; to understand, learn by hearing; to hear, perceive by the ear. Now only *poet.*

c **1000** ÆLFRIC *Hom.* II. 440 Heo ȝesæt æt Godes fotum, his word heorcniende. *c* **1200** ORMIN 11723 Forr ȝuw birrþ herrcnenn Godess word. *a* **1225** *Ancr. R.* 82 Nout one þeo þet hit spekeð, auh þeo þet hit hercneð. *c* **1374** CHAUCER *Boeth.* III. pr. i. 50 (Camb. MS.) For thow seyst þat thow art so desirous to herkne hem. *a* **1400–50** *Alexander* 2304 In-to þe temple he turned tythandis to herken. **1529** MORE *Comf. agst. Trib.* III. Wks. 1232/2 When they heare it, harken it but as they woulde an idle tale. **1610** SHAKS. *Temp.* I. ii. 122 This King of Naples being an Enemy To me inueterate, hearkens my Brothers suit. **1832** TENNYSON *New-Year's Eve* 39 Tho' I cannot speak a word, I shall harken what you say.

b. With personal obj. (orig. dative as in 1; but this afterwards levelled with the accusative or objective). *Obs.* exc. *dial.*

1297 R. GLOUC. (1724) 308 Kyng Edmond..lende vp hys sseld, & herkned hym ynou. *c* **1400** *Destr. Troy* 9238 Sho herknet hym full hyndly. *Ibid.* 9264 Long he stode..Doun hengond his hed, herkonyng the qwene. *c* **1500** *Melusine* lvi. 334 Raymondyn herkned hym gladly. **1583** STANYHURST *Æneis* III. (Arb.) 76 Who would Cassandra then harcken? **1890** *Yorksh. Clergyman*, What do you come to church for? *Boy.* To harken yo.

†**5.** *intr.* ***hearken to***: Listen, give ear. [As if from a compound vb. *to-hearken*; cf. Ger. *zuhorchen*, imper. *horch zu!* Cf. *go to*, from vb. TO-GO.] *Obs.*

1526 TINDALE *Mark* iv. 3 He..sayde vnto them in his doctrine: Herken to. Beholde, The sower went forth to sowe. —— *Acts* vii. 2 Brethren, and fathers, harken to. **1535** COVERDALE *2 Chron.* xviii. 27 Herken to, all ye people.

†**6.** *intr.* To seek to hear tidings; to make inquiries, to inquire *after*, ask *for*. *Obs.*

1523 LD. BERNERS *Froiss.* I. ccciii. 450 There abode styll the Englysshmen to harken after other newes. **1575** LANEHAM *Let.* (1871) 36 A this day allso waz thear such earnest tallk and appointment of remoouing, that I gaue ouer my noting, and harkened after my hors. **1599** SHAKS. *Much Ado* V. i. 216 *Clau.* Harken after their offence my Lord. *Prince.* Officers, what offence haue these men done? *a* **1670** HACKET *Abp. Williams* I. (1692) 19, I hearkened no more after it: for I reckon'd it was done. **1783** JOHNSON *Let. to Miss S.A. Thrale* 18 Nov., I hearken every day after a letter from her. **1830** DE QUINCEY *Bentley* Wks. VII. 41 To abstain from hearkening after libels upon himself.

†**7.** *intr.* To lie in wait; to wait. *Obs.*

[Cf. **1523** in 6.] **1580** R. HITCHCOCK *Politic Plat* in Arb. *Garner* II. 159 People who daily do harken when the world should amend with them. **1584** STAFFORD in Motley *Netherl.* (1868) I. iii. 70 The king hearkeneth to see the end, and then to believe as he seeth cause. **1596** SHAKS. *Tam. Shr.* I. ii. 260 The yongest daughter whom you hearken for, Her father keepes from all accesse of sutors. **1633** T. STAFFORD *Pac. Hib.* I. xv. (1810) 167 Whether it were..the hearkening after a Ship, to arrive in those parts..that occasioned his delatory excuses.

†**8.** *trans.* To get to hear of; to search *out* or find by inquiry. *Obs.*

1590 SIR T. COCKAINE *Hunting* B iij, Your Hounds.. harken them foorth of such a kinde as bee durable. **1606** *Wily Beguiled* in Hazl. *Dodsley* IX. 226 If I can hearken out some wealthy marriage for her. **1607** DEKKER *Knt.'s Conjur.* (1842) 57 It is some ease to Syr Timothy..to harken out the worst that others haue endured. **1609** B. JONSON *Sil. Wom.* I. ii, He has imploied a fellow..to harken him out a dumbe woman. **1637** R. HUMPHREY tr. *St. Ambrose* I. 118 Hunting and hearkening out places of mart where hee may best vent them.

†**9.** *intr.* To have regard or relation. *Obs. rare.*

1734 POPE *Ess. Man* IV. 40 There's not a blessing Individuals find, But some way leans and hearkens to the kind.

10. To talk in one's ear, to whisper. *Obs.* exc. *Sc.*

1612 DRAYTON *Poly-olb.* xii. 200 This harkneth with his friend, as though with him to break Of some intended act. *Mod. Sc.* What are ye herk'ning thegither aboot? He herk'nt to me to gang and fetch them.

hearkener, harkener (ˈhɑːk(ə)nə(r)). Also 4–5 herkner(e, 6 harkner. [f. HEARKEN *v.* + -ER[1].] One who listens or gives ear; a listener.

1340 *Ayenb.* 58 Þe herkneres do wel lheȝe. *c* **1422** HOCCLEVE *Learn to Die* 547 Thyn herkners and thyn Auditours. **1423** JAS. I *Kingis Q.* clvi, There sawe I..The fery tigere..The herknere bore. **1477** EARL RIVERS (Caxton) *Dictes* 101 The predication is not to be lawded that endureth ouer the power of the herkeners. **1550** CROWLEY *Epigr.* 1421 An herkener of fables and lyes. **1811** W. TAYLOR in *Monthly Rev.* LXV. 486 The starers..or harkeners are satirized.

†**b.** An eavesdropper; a scout. *Obs.*

1549 COVERDALE, etc. *Erasm. Par. Tim.* v. (R.), Babling tale-tellers & curious herkeners. **1580** HOLLYBAND *Treas. Fr. Tong, Escouteur*..a harkner, a scout, an eavesdropper.

hearkening, harkening (ˈhɑːk(ə)nɪŋ), *vbl. sb.* [In OE. *heorcnung*, f. *heorcnian* to HEARKEN + -ING[1].] The action of the vb. HEARKEN; giving ear, hearing with attention; listening; giving attention.

c **1000** ÆLFRIC *Hom.* I. 26 Deafum [he forȝeaf] heorcnunge. *Ibid.* 96 We sceolon..awendan [ure] earan from yfelre heorcnunge. *a* **1225** *Ancr. R.* 104 Auh hold wiðinnen þin hercnung, þi speche, & tine sihðe. *c* **1375** *Lay Folks Mass Bk.* (MS. B.) 28 To him þou gyue gode herknynge. **1583** STANYHURST *Æneis*, etc. (Arb.) 131 Toe graunt mee Gratius harckning. *a* **1715** BURNET *Own Time* (1766) II. 29 The ill effects of his not harkening to their address. **1885** STEVENSON *Dynamiter* 185 The sound was gone, nor could his closest hearkening recapture it.

†**b.** Searching *out*; inquiry; discovery. *Obs.*

a **1483** *Liber Niger* in *Househ. Ord.* (1790) 53 The Steward ..specially owith to have herkenyng uppon this clerkes demeanyng in the countries for oppressions. **1602** FULBECKE *1st Pt. Parall.* 66 His eares to be open for the harkning out of their offences.

hearn(e, hearon, obs. ff. HERN, HERON.

hearsay (ˈhɪəseɪ). Forms: see HEAR *v.* and SAY *v.* Also 6 **heard say.** [subst. use of phr. *to hear say*: see HEAR 3 b.]

1. That which one hears or has heard some one say; information received by word of mouth, usually with implication that it is not trustworthy; oral tidings; report, tradition, rumour, common talk, gossip.

c **1532** DEWES *Introd. Fr.* in Palsgr. 1075, I knowe nothyng of it but by here say. **1553** GRIMALDE *Cicero's Offices* (*c* 1600) 14 b, I have heard nothing but by heard say. **1577** HELLOWES *Gueuara's Chron.* 315 Thou speakest by heare-saye, rather then by anye experience. **1577** HARRISON *England* II. ix. (1877) I. 199 So much as I have gathered by report and common heare-saie. **1589** R. HARVEY *Pl. Perc.* (1590) 11 Heresay is too slender an euidence to spit a mans credit vpon. **1600** HOLLAND *Livy* XXXIX. vi. 1026 Things..which by bare heeresay were reported to haue beene done. **1631** GOUGE *God's Arrows* V. vii. 417 The whole world was made to tremble at the heare-say of them. **1642** ROGERS *Naaman* 117 The hearsay of Christ wrought all these things in them. *a* **1708** BEVERIDGE *Thes. Theol.* (1710) II. 298 Not meerly upon hearsay or tradition. **1761** *Gilbert's Law Evidence* 112 Hearsay is good evidence to prove, who is my grandfather, when he married, what children he had, etc. of which it is not reasonable to presume that I have better evidence. **1769** SIR W. DRAPER in *Junius Lett.* xxvi. 121 Is it hearsay, or the evidence of letters, or ocular? **1847** JAMES *J. Marston Hall* ix, I gave him stronger proof than mere hearsay.

b. With *a* and *pl.* A report received; a rumour, a piece of gossip.

a **1642** SIR W. MONSON *Naval Tracts* IV. (1704) 428/1 This Report seems to be a Hearsay of a second Person. **1699** BENTLEY *Phal.* Introd. 7, I am asham'd to see a Person tell such little Hear says. **1730** BERKELEY *Let. to T. Prior* 7 May Wks. 1871 IV. 183 A hearsay, at second or third hand. **1840** CARLYLE *Heroes* i, Wrappage of traditions, hearsays, mere words. **1847** LONGF. *Ev.* II. i. 33 Sometimes a rumour, a hearsay..came.

2. *attrib.*, passing on one side into an *adj.*, on the other giving rise to *combinations*: (*a*) Of the nature of hearsay; (*b*) founded or depending upon what one has heard said, but not within one's direct knowledge, as ***hearsay account, censure, declaration, knowledge, report, rumour, tale***; (*c*) of hearsay, speaking from hearsay, as ***hearsay author, babbler, witness,*** †***hearsay-man.***

1580 SIDNEY *Arcadia* I. x. 139 Poet. Wks. 1873 II. 33 [Those] whose metall stiff he knew he could not bend With hear-say pictures. **1602** CAREW *Cornwall* (1811) 59, I can in these tin cases plead but a hearsay experience. **1646** SIR T. BROWNE *Pseud. Ep.* III. xxv. 171 An hearsay account by Bellonius. **1683** TRYON *Way to Health* 361 These Hear-say-men or Book-Philosophers, called, The Learned, are as ignorant as any..of the true knowledge of God in themselves. **1738** BIRCH *Life Milton* App. M.'s Wks. I. 94 All the Evidence was two hear-say Depositions taken in 1642, from Persons who were told so by the common Soldiers of the Irish. **1787** M. CUTLER in *Life, etc.* (1888) I. 254 We had both of us an hearsay knowledge of each other. **1814** CHALMERS *Evid. Chr. Revel.* i. 44 The report of hearsay witnesses. **1816** SINGER *Hist. Cards* 149 To promulgate hearsay reports. **1826** in *Sheridaniana* 315 The crude opinions of the hearsay babbler. **1859** TENNYSON *Vivien* 800 She blamed herself for telling hearsay tales.

b. ***hearsay evidence***: evidence consisting in what the witness has heard others say, or what is commonly said, as to facts of which he has himself no original or personal knowledge.

1753 W. STEWART in *Scots Mag.* Mar. 135/1 Hearsay-evidence is..rejected in law. **1768** BLACKSTONE *Comm.* III. xxiii. (1800) 368 Yet in some cases (as in proof of any general customs, or matters of common tradition or repute) the courts admit of hearsay evidence. **1848** WHARTON *Law Lex.* s.v. *Hearsay Evidence*, The exceptions to the general rule of the inadmissibility of hearsay evidence are..(1) dying declarations; (2) hearsay in questions of pedigree; (3) hearsay on questions of public right, customs, boundaries, [etc.]. **1878** LECKY *Eng. in 18th C.* II. vi. 148 Hear-say evidence of the loosest kind was freely admitted.

Hence **ˈhearsay** *v. intr.* (*nonce-wd.*), to tell what one has heard; to repeat rumours. †**hearsaying** (in 4 **hyere zigginge**), hearsay, report = *hearing say*: see HEAR 3 c.

1340 *Ayenb.* 117 He ne may noþing wel conne bote ase me kan þe batayle of troye be hyere-ziggynge. **1837** CARLYLE *Fr. Rev.* III. VI. vii, Men riding and running, reporting and hearsaying.

hearse (hɜːs), *sb.* Forms: 4–5 **heers(e,** 5 **heerce,** 5–6 **hers,** 5–6 (9) **herce,** 6 **hearce, herst,** 7 **hierce,** 4–9 **herse,** 6– **hearse.** [Formerly *herse*, a. F. *herse* (12th c. in Littré) = It. *erpice*:—L. *hirpic-em* (*hirpex*) large rake used as a harrow; ? cf. Gr. ἅρπαξ grappling-iron. See HERSE, under which the sense 'harrow' and its immediately derived senses are treated.]

†**1. a.** A triangular frame somewhat similar in form to the ancient harrow, designed to carry candles, and used at the service of *Tenebræ* in Holy Week. **b.** A candlestick used at the *Benedictio ignis* on Easter Eve. *Obs.*

[**1287** *Synod of Exeter* xii. in Wilkins *Conc.* (1737) II. 139 Vas ad aquam benedictam. Hercia ad tenebras.] **1563** *Inv. Chr. Ch., Canterb.* (Chapter Libr. Canterb.), Item a heade for the hearse of coper and gylte to carrye the iij. lyghts to the fier vppon Estereuen.

2. a. An elaborate framework originally intended to carry a large number of lighted tapers and other decorations over the bier or coffin while placed in the church at the funerals of distinguished persons; also called *castrum doloris, chapelle ardente*, or *catafalco.*

[**1291** *Acc. Executors Q. Eleanor* in *Gloss. Archit.* (1845) I. 199 Pro meremio ad hercias Dominæ Reginæ, apud Westmonasterium.] *c* **1368** CHAUCER *Compl. Pite* 15 Adown I fell when I sawe the herse, Dede as stone. [**1399** *Test. Rich. II* in Rymer *Fœdera* VIII. 75 Ita..quod, pro prædictis Exequiis, iv Herciæ..per Executores nostros congrue præparentur.] *c* **1400** *Destr. Troy* 8753. *a* **1450** *Le Morte Arth.* 3532 By-fore a tombe, that new was dyghte..There-on an herse, sothely to saye, Wyth an C tappers lyghte. **1485** *Will* in *Ripon Ch. Acts* (Surtees) 277 That there be byrnyng on herse v serges, ilkoone of a pownde of waxe. **1526** *MS. Acc. St. John's Hosp., Canterb.*, Payd for strykyng of iiij tapers for the herst *jd.* **1548** HALL *Chron., Hen. VIII*, 1 b, The body was taken out, and caried into the Quire, and set under a goodly Herce of waxe, garnished with Banners, Pencelles, and Cusshions. *a* **1678** MARVELL *Wks.* III. 510 And starrs, like tapers, burn'd upon his herse. **1814** SCOTT *Ld. of Isles* Concl., That one poor garland, twined to deck thy hair, Is hung upon thy hearse, to droop and wither there! **1849** ROCK *Ch. of Fathers* II. vii. 495 There used to be put up in the church a 'hearse', which was a lofty framework of wood..with four or eight posts..and ceiled. **1896** PEACOCK in Andrews *Church Gleanings* 218 It was the custom in the case of rich families to erect one of these hearses in every church where it [the body] rested for the night.

b. A permanent framework of iron or other metal, fixed over a tomb to support rich coverings or palls, often adapted to carry lighted tapers.

1552 *Berksh. Ch. Goods* 10 A herse of Irone. **1846** PARKER *Gloss. Archit.* 129 There is a brass frame..over the effigy of Richard, earl of Warwick, in the Beauchamp chapel at Warwick, which is called a herse in the contract for the tomb. **1851** TURNER *Dom. Archit.* II. v. 242 The Sheriff of Southampton is commanded to repair the herces in the king's chapel. **1866** PEACOCK *Eng. Ch. Furniture* 128 A very graceful iron hearse of this kind..in Tanfield Church.

c. A temple-shaped structure of wood used in royal and noble funerals, after the earlier kind (2 a) went out of use. It was decorated with banners, heraldic devices, and lighted candles; and it was customary for friends to pin short poems or epitaphs upon it.

c **1575** J. HOOKER *Life Sir P. Carew* in *Archæol.* XXVIII. 145 The nexte daye his herse was sett vpe, beinge made after the forme of a felde bedd, covered with blacke..garnyshed with scogeons and with yelowe pynyons full of blacke lyons. **1598** *Remembrance of Eng. Poets* in *Barnfield's Poems* (Arb.) 119 Whose Fame is grav'd on Rosamond's blacke Herse. *c* **1621** ? B. JONSON *Epit. C'tess Pembroke*, Underneath this sable herse Lyes the subject of all verse. **1639** HORN & ROB. *Gate Lang. Unl.* xcvii. §962 Gravestones (toombs) and herses are rear'd up, and epitaphs..written on them. **1659** PECKE *Parnassi Puerp.* 119 Shall I to pin upon thy Herse, devise Eternal Praises; or weep Elegies? *a* **1667** COWLEY *Voy. W. Harvey* Wks. 1710 I. 27 Be this my latest Verse With which I now adorn his Herse. **1898** ANDREWS *Church Treasury* 280 The last herse used in this country was the one under which her effigy [that of Mary II] was placed.

3. A light framework of wood used to support the pall over the body at funerals. It fitted on to the parish bier, and was probably adapted to carry lighted tapers.

1566 in Peacock *Eng. Ch. Furniture* (1866) 36 Item a hearse—sold to John Banton..who hathe put it to prophane use. **1896** PEACOCK in Andrews *Church Gleanings* 216 Of these hearses, not a single example is known to have come down to our time.

†**4.** A hearse-cloth, a funeral pall. *Obs.*

1530 PALSGR. 230/2 Herce for a deed corse of silke, *poille*. **1581** W. STAFFORD *Exam. Compl.* I. (1876) 16 All other

Marchaundize that wee buy from beyond the Sea..and all Hearses, and Tapestry. **1603** KNOLLES *Hist. Turks* (1621) 1200 This coffin of the great Sultan..covered with a rich hearse of cloth of gold downe to the ground.

5. A bier; a coffin; vaguely, a tomb, grave. *Obs.* or *arch.*

1601 SHAKS. *Jul. C.* III. ii. 169 Stand from the Hearse, stand from the Body. **1610** G. FLETCHER *Christ's Vict.* I. xliv, One touch would rouze me from my sluggish hearse. **1616** BULLOKAR, *Hearse*, a buriall coffin couered with blacke. **1623** LISLE *Ælfric on O. & N. Test.* Ded. xxix, But, wheth'r I live, or be first laid on herse. **1625** —— *Du Bartas, Noe* 132 As thou my cradle wert, so wilt thou be my herse. **1651** DAVENANT *Gondibert* I. v. (R.), When she with flowres lord Arnold's grave shall strew..She on that rival's hearse will drop a few. *a* **1700** DRYDEN *Meleager* 325 Ah! hadst thou died, my son, in infant years, Thy little hearse had been bedewed with tears. **1849** LONGF. *Blind Girl* iii, Decked with flowers a simple hearse To the churchyard forth they bear.

†**6.** The solemn obsequy in a funeral. *Obs.* (Perh. only an error.)

1579 SPENSER *Sheph. Cal.* Nov. 60 O heauie herse [*gloss.* Herse, is the solemne obsequie in funeralles]. *Ibid.* 70 The earth now lacks her wonted light, And all we dwell in deadly night, O heauie herse.

†**7.** A dead body, a corpse. *Obs.*

1530 PALSGR. 230/2 Herce, a deed body, *corps.* **1609** HEYWOOD *Brit. Troy* III. lxxxvi. 72 Bold Archas pierses Thrugh the mid-hoast and strewes the way with herses. **1633** MAY *Hen. II*, v. 775 Her hearse at Godstow Abbey they enterre.

8. a. A carriage or car constructed for carrying the coffin at a funeral. (The current use.)

1650 B. *Discolliminium* 2 It is hung about with as many.. trappings, as Coll. Rainsboroughs Herse and horse were at his fine Funerals. **1672** WOOD *Life* (O.H.S.) II. 245 Thomas Moor hath a hearse..for the carrying of dead corps to any part of England. **1706** HEARNE *Collect.* 4 Dec., He was very decently interr'd, being carried in a Hearse, and the Company in Mourning Coaches. **1722** DE FOE *Plague* (Rtldg.) 35 They saw Herses and Coffins. **1850** MRS. CARLYLE *Lett.* II. 128 A hearse too, with plenty of plumes, and many black coaches. **1881** BESANT & RICH *Chapl. Fleet* I. 294 A hearse stopped before our door.

b. *transf.* A vehicle for carrying pianofortes.

1812 COLERIDGE *Lett.* II. 584 Musical Instrument Manufacturers, whose grand pianoforte hearses he [a horse] now draws in the streets of London.

9. *Comb.*, as ***hearse-light*** (see 1, 2); ***hearse-driver, -man, -plume*** (sense 8); **hearse-cover**, a pall; **hearse-house**, a dead-house; a building in which a hearse is kept; **hearse-like** *a.*, like a hearse; mournful. Also HEARSE-CLOTH.

1885 R. W. DIXON *Hist. Ch. Eng.* III. 451 Three *hearse-covers..eight stall-cloths. **1829** G. GRIFFIN *Collegians* III. xxxiii. 60 ''Twill be a great funeral,' said the *hearse-driver. **1841** J. S. BUCKINGHAM *Amer.* II. 322 The Whig authorities of New-Haven, have removed Mr. Willoughby..from the place of hearse-driver, and appointed another person in his place. **1851** H. MELVILLE *Moby Dick* III. xiii. 90 The old hearse-driver, he must have been. **1922** JOYCE *Ulysses* 590 Sober hearse-drivers a speciality. **1870** F. R. WILSON *Ch. Lindisf.* 101 A vestry, with a *hearse-house beyond it..has been built in modern times. **1895** PRYCE *Burden of Woman* 91 The hearse-house or dead-house of the church (the lowest room of a tower where in old days the bodies of strangers who had lost their way and perished were placed for possible identification pending burial). **1555** *Churchw. Acc. St. Helens, Abingdon* (Nichols 1797) 141 For making the *herse lyghtes. **1566** in Peacock *Eng. Ch. Furniture* (1866) 127 The sepulcre and herse lightes wᵗ all the bookes of papistrie rent and burned. **1625** BACON *Ess., Adversitie* (Arb.) 505 If you Listen to Davids Harpe, you shall heare as many *Herselike Ayres, as Carols. **1839** BAILEY *Festus* xxiii. (1848) 289 It steals Hearselike and thieflike round the universe. **1893** J. W. BARRY *Stud. in Corsica* 170 It [the corpse] is..abandoned to the *hearseman. **1848** ELIZA COOK *Lines among Leaves* viii. 3 Like *hearse-plume waved about.

hearse, var. of HEARST *sb.*

hearse, *v.* [f. HEARSE *sb.*]

1. *trans.* To lay (a corpse) on a bier or in a coffin; to bury with funeral rites and ceremonies. **b.** (in recent use) To carry to the grave in a hearse.

1592 *Nobody & Someb.* in Simpson *Sch. Shaks.* (1878) I. 319 We will forbeare our spleene..till you have hearsd your husbands bones. **1596** SHAKS. *Merch. V.* III. i. 93 Would she were hearst at my foote, and the duckets in her coffin. *c* **1611** CHAPMAN *Iliad* XVIII. 199 Then the Grecians spritefully drew from the darts the corse, And hears'd it, bearing it to fleet, his friends with all remorse Marching about it. **1827** POLLOK *Course T.* VII. 295 Richly hearsed With gloomy garniture of purchased wo. **1854** GILFILLAN *Life Blair* in *Beattie's, Blair's*, etc. *Wks.* 126 He lashes the proud wicked man whom he sees pompously hearsed into Hell. **1855** SINGLETON *Virgil* II. 81 In his own resting place consign him first, And hearse him in the grave.

c. To enclose or contain as in a bier or tomb; to entomb.

1608 DAY *Hum. out of Br.* III. iv, Please you survey the cell, go in and see, I'me hearst, and none but sorrowe lies with me. **1764** CHURCHILL *Ep. to Hogarth* 452 Worth may be hears'd but Envy cannot die. **1796** W. TAYLOR in *Monthly Mag.* II. 489 Shall marble hearse them all? **1819** WIFFEN *Aonian Hours* (1820) 160 Murmurs deep, not loud, Swelled in the gale when earth thy relics hearsed.

2. *fig.* To furnish with something hearse-like.

1646 CRASHAW *Steps to Temple* (R.), The house is hers'd about with a black wood, Which nods with many a heavy headed tree. **1864** LONGF. *Hawthorne* vi, The hill-top hearsed with pines.

Hence **hearsed** *ppl. a.*, placed on, in, or under a hearse.

1602 SHAKS. *Ham.* I. iv. 47 Tell Why thy Canoniz'd bones Hearsed in death, Haue burst their cerments.

'hearse-cloth. [f. HEARSE *sb.*] A black cloth to cover a bier or coffin; a funeral pall.

1522 *Churchw. Acc. St. Marg. Westm.* (Nichols 1797) 9 Sir Robert Danby Curett..of him, for his herst-cloth 2*s.* **1530** PALSGR. 231/1 Herse clothe, *poille.* **1642** FULLER *Holy & Prof. St.* IV. ix. 282 No more then a dead corps is affected with a velvet herse-cloth over it. **1650** R. STAPYLTON *Strada's Low C. Warres* x. 22 Foure Mourners..each of them holding in their hands a corner of the Herse-Cloth. **1829** HEATH *Grocers' Comp.* (1869) 14 *note*, The Fishmonger's Company have preserved their herseclothe or pall..at their Hall.

'hear-so, *sb. nonce-wd.* [f. HEAR *v.* + SO *adv.*] One who has heard so: one who knows by hearsay.

1639 J. CLARKE *Paræmiologia* 309 One eye-witnesse is better than two heare-so's.

hearst. *Hunting.* Also 7–8 **hearse.** A hind of the second or third year.

1674 N. COX *Gentl. Recreat.* (1677) 7 A Hinde..is called the first year, a Calf. The second year, a Hearse; and sometimes we say Brockets Sister. **1774** GOLDSM. *Nat. Hist.* II. v. (1862) I. 324 The female is called a hind..the second year she is a hearse. **1877** 'STONEHENGE' *Brit. Sports* (1886) 134 According to the Devonshire Hunt—Deer under one year are called Calves; till three, the male a Brocket, and the female a Hearst.

†**'hearsum, hersum,** *a. Obs.* Forms: 1 **híer-, hér-, hýrsum, héarsum,** 2 **hersam,** 2–4 **hersum,** 3 **hærsum, (horsom).** [OE. *híersum* = OFris. *hârsum*, OHG. *hôrsam*, f. stem of *híeran*, Goth. *hauzjan* to HEAR: see -SOME. *Héarsum* was a later OE. by-form.] Ready to hear; obedient, compliant; dutiful, devout.

c **900** tr. *Bæda's Hist.* I. xiv. [xxv.] (1890) 58 Se þe him hyrsum beon wolde. *a* **1000** *Guthlac* 677 þæt ȝe..him hearsume..siþþan wæron. *Ibid.* 697 Gearwe stodon hæftas hearsume. *c* **1200** *Trin. Coll. Hom.* 51 þat israelisshe folc.. was hersum godes hese. *c* **1205** LAY. 19395 He hæhte his cnihtes leoue beon hærsume [**1275** horsom] Loðe. **13..** *Gaw. & Gr. Knt.* 932 To þe hersum euensong of þe hyȝe tyde.

Hence †**'hersumlecg** (mod. type **hearsomledge*), †**'hersumnesse**, obedience.

c **900** tr. *Bæda's Hist.* v. xxii[i]. (1891) 478 Ealle þas mæȝþe ..Æþelbolde Mercna cyninge in hyrsumnesse under þeodde seondon. *a* **1175** *Cott. Hom.* 223 Mid edmodnisse and mid hersamnisse. *c* **1175** *Lamb. Hom.* 107 ȝif þe ȝunge bið butan hersumnesse. *c* **1200** ORMIN 2521 All full off haliȝ mahhtess, Off herrsummleccg, off rihhtwisleccg. *c* **1205** LAY. 29731 Austin..hehte heom comen..& don him hersumnesse.

†**'hearsum, 'hersum,** *v. Obs.* Forms: 1 **héar-, hýr-, hérsumian,** 2–3 **hersumien, -sumen.** [OE. *híer-, héarsumian* = OHG. *hôrsamôn*; f. *híersum* adj.: see prec.] *trans.* To obey, be obedient to; to revere. (In OE. with dative.)

c **900** tr. *Bæda's Hist.* II. vi. (1890) 116 Hwæðre he..þæm godcundan bebodum þeowode ond hearsumede. *c* **1000** *Ags. Gosp.* Matt. viii. 27 Windas and sæ him hyrsumiað [*Hatton G.* her-]. *c* **1175** *Lamb. Hom.* 11 Hine ȝe scule wurþian and hersumen. *a* **1225** *Leg. Kath.* 249 [He] hereð and hersumeð seheliche schaftes.

hearsy ('hɜːsɪ), *a.* [f. HEARSE *sb.* 8 + -Y¹.] Resembling or characteristic of a hearse; funereal.

1901 'A. HOPE' *Tristram of Blent* v. 57 Mr. Gainsborough was obviously a man who would not waste his chance of a funeral;..it would need startling measures to keep him from a funeral. 'I hate hearsey people,' grumbled Harry as he threw the letter down. **1908** HARDY *Dynasts* III. VI. vi. 476 Full-clothed in black, with nodding hearsy plumes.

heart (hɑːt), *sb.* Forms: 1–3 **heorte,** 3–6 **herte,** 4–6 **harte,** 4–7 **hert, hart,** 6– **heart.** (Also 1 *north.* **hearta,** 2–3 **horte, hierte,** 3 *Orm.* **heorrte, herrte,** 3–4 *s.w.* **hurte,** 4 **huerte, ert,** 4–6 **hertte, hartt, herth,** 6 **hearte,** 6–7 *Sc.* **hairt**). [Com. Teut.: OE. *heorte* (Northumb. *hearta*) = OFris. *herte, hirte*, OS. *herta* (MLG. *herte*, MDu. *hert(e, hart(e*, Du. *hart*), OHG. *herza* (MHG. *herze*, Ger. *herz*), ON. *hjarta* (Sw. *hjerta*, Da. *hjerte*), Goth. *hairtô*:—OTeut. **herton-*; orig. a weak neuter, which became in OE. and OFris. a weak fem., in MLG. and MDu. fem. or neuter. Radically related to L. *cor, cord-*, Gr. *καρδ-ία, κραδ-ία* (also *κῆρ* from *κηρδ-*); OIr. *cride*, Lith. *szird-ìs*, OSlav. *srĭdĭ-tse, srŭdĭ-tse* (Russ. *serd-tse*, Boh. *srd-ce*) heart; root *kerd-, kr̥d-*.]

General arrangement. I. The simple word. *The bodily organ, its function, etc., 1–4. **As the seat of feeling, etc., 5–13. ***Put for the person, 14–16. ****Something having a central position, 17–19. *****The vital part or principle, 20–22. ******Something of the shape of a heart, 23–30. II. Phrases. *With governing preposition, 31–39. **With verb and preposition, 40–44. ***With governing verb, 45–49. ****With another noun, 50–52. *****In exclamations, 53. ******Proverbial phrases, 54. III. Attributive uses and Combinations, 55–56.

I. The simple word. * *The bodily organ, its function, region,* etc.

1. a. The hollow muscular or otherwise contractile organ which, by its dilatation and contraction, keeps up the circulation of the blood in the vascular system of an animal.

c **1000** *Sax. Leechd.* III. 42 Gif þin heorte ace. *c* **1175** *Lamb. Hom.* 121 He wes..mid speres orde to þere heorte istungen. *a* **1300** *K. Horn* 872 He smot him þureȝ þe herte. **1382** WYCLIF *2 Kings* ix. 24 The arewe is sent out thoruȝ his hert. *c* **1440** *Promp. Parv.* 237/2 Hert, ynwarde parte of a beste. **1483** *Cath. Angl.* 177/1 A Harte, *cor, cordialis, corculum.* **1548** HALL *Chron., Hen. VI*, 183 [He] stacke the erle to yᵉ hart with his dagger. **1548–77** VICARY *Anat.* vii. (1888) 56 The Hart..is the principal of al other members, and the beginning of life. **1607** SHAKS. *Cor.* I. i. 140, I send it through the Riuers of your blood Euen to the Court, the Heart. **1615** CROOKE *Body of Man* 357 The vse of this *Mediastinum* or bound-hedge is first to hold the hart vp suspended. **1664** POWER *Exp. Philos.* 58 Perfect Animals have an incessant motion of their Heart, and Circulation of their Bloud. **1812** *Morn. Chron.* in *Examiner* 25 May 336/2 After the body of Bellingham was opened, it was noticed that his heart continued to perform its functions..for four hours. **1841–71** T. R. JONES *Anim. Kingd.* (ed. 4) 556 A heart is present in all the Brachiopoda. **1872** MIVART *Elem. Anat.* i. 4 The Heart..is rhythmically contractible and propulsive. **1887** H. S. CUNNINGHAM *Cœruleans* I. 145 Camilla's heart went pit-a-pat. **1897** MARY KINGSLEY *W. Africa* 297, I saw a sight that made my heart stand still.

fig. *a* **1822** SHELLEY *Ode to Heaven* 44 Drops which Nature's mighty heart Drives through thinnest veins. **1842** TENNYSON *Locksley Hall* 140 Tho' the deep heart of existence beat for ever like a boy's. **1866** LONGF. *Killed at Ford* i, The heart of honor, the tongue of truth.

b. ***right*** (***left***) ***heart***, the right (or left) side of the heart.

1886 *Cassell's Fam. Mag.* Nov. 722 Those who suffer from chronic rheumatism have often weak right hearts.

c. A diseased or disordered heart: often with defining word; as ***athletic heart***, simple hypertrophy of the heart with no disease of the valves; ***fatty heart*** (see FATTY *a.* 5); ***smoker's heart***, a disordered condition of the heart due to excessive tobacco-smoking.

1862 W. H. WALSHE *Pract. Treat. Dis. Heart* (ed. 3) II. 320 Patients..often express themselves, 'they have a heart', (the mildest form of cardiac paræsthesia). **1871** DA COSTA in *Amer. Jrnl. Med. Sci.* LXI. 17, I noticed cases of a peculiar form of functional disorder of the heart, to which I gave the name of irritable heart. **1886** FAGGE & PYE-SMITH *Princ. Med.* II. 41 Rather more than a century ago Haller described the 'hairy' heart as occurring especially in bold and adventurous men. **1888** *Science* (N.Y.) 9 Nov. 223/2 The frequent existence of what is known as 'smoker's heart' in men whose health is in no other respect disturbed. **1902** *Daily Chron.* 3 Nov. 8/4 [He] has been forbidden to row again..owing to his having developed 'a heart'. **1908** *Westm. Gaz.* 29 Oct. 14/1[He] failed to qualify before the Medical Board of the police on the ground that he had an 'athletic heart'. **1929** E. BOWEN *Joining Charles* 125 Cottesby the cow-herd, a greyish-faced man, had 'a heart'. **1965** 'W. HAGGARD' *Hard Sell* i. 4 He's got a heart, by the way, and I'm afraid this might finish him. **1971** *Current Slang* (Univ. S. Dakota) VI. 6 Slow down or you'll give me *a heart.*

2. Considered as the centre of vital functions: the seat of life; the vital part or principle; hence in some phrases = life. *Obs.* or *arch.*

c **825** *Vesp. Psalter* xxi[i]. 27 Herȝað dryhten ða soecað hine leofað heorte heara in weoruld weoruldе. *a* **1325** *Prose Psalter* ciii[i]. 15 And wyn glade mannes hert. **1382** WYCLIF *Ps.* ci[i]. 5, I am smyten as heiȝ, and myn herte driede. **1382** —— *Gen.* xviii. 5, I shal sett a morsel of breed, and ȝoure herte be coumfortid. **1535** COVERDALE *Ibid.*, A morsell of bred, to comforte youre hertes withall. **1548** HALL *Chron., Edw. IV*, 213 Commaundyng, upon pein of the harte, that no man should once passe the sea with hym. *c* **1601** SIR C. HATTON in *Hatton Corr.* (1878) 2 Beecause hee hath nothinge deerer then his harte. **1611** BIBLE *Ps.* civ. 15 Bread which strengtheneth man's heart. *a* **1618** RALEIGH *Lett.* (1651) 109 That the King (though I were not pardoned) had granted my heart under the Great Seal. **1743** BULKELEY & CUMMINS *Voy. S. Seas* 97 Desiring no more than to go off Heart in Hand from this Place to the Southward. [**1871** *Speaker's Comment.* Gen. xviii. 5 The heart considered as the centre of vital functions, is put by the Hebrews for the life itself. To support the heart therefore is to refresh the whole vital powers and functions.]

3. *transf.* **a.** The region of the heart; breast, bosom.

c **1450** HOLLAND *Howlat* 477 He..it hyng About his hals full hende, and on his awne hart. **1535** COVERD. *Exod.* xxviii. 29 Thus shall Aaron beare the names in yᵉ brestlappe of iudgment vpon his hert. **1590** SPENSER *F.Q.* II. vi. 26 He.. ever held his hand upon his hart. **1592** SHAKS. *Rom. & Jul.* III. v. 192 Lay hand on heart, aduise. **1611** BIBLE *Exod.* xxviii. 30 The Urim and the Thummim..shall bee vpon Aarons heart, when he goeth in before the Lord. **1717** POPE *Eloisa* 123 Let me..Pant on thy lip, and to thy heart be press'd. **1887** H. S. CUNNINGHAM *Cœruleans* II. 226 He pressed her to his heart.

b. Hence in *fig.* expressions.

1886 DOWDEN *Shelley* I. vi. 280 Godwin..had indeed taken the young disciple to his heart. **1887** EDNA LYALL *Knt.-Errant* xviii. 162 He hugged his old conviction to his heart.

4. The stomach. *Obs.* or *dial.* Chiefly in phr. ***next the heart***: on an empty stomach, fasting (*obs.* or *dial.*). Cf. Fr. *avoir mal au cœur*: to be sick (bilious).

1542 UDALL *Erasm. Apoph.* (1877) 359 (D.) A newe founde diete, to drinke wine in the morning nexte the harte. **1589** COGAN *Haven Health* (1636) 189, I have knowne some maidens to drinke vinegar next their heart to abate their colour. **1647** R. STAPYLTON *Juvenal* vi. 637 (D.) The Romans held it ominous to see a Blackamoore next their hearts in a morning. **1674** R. GODFREY *Inj. & Ab. Physic* 116 So much is it the mode still to call the Stomach the Heart, that people frequently say their Hearts were at their Mouths, when on a sudden fright or surprisal their

Stomach's have been mov'd. a1825 Forby *Voc. E. Anglia*, *Heart*, the stomach. 'A pain at the heart' means the stomach-ache.

*** As the seat of feeling, understanding, and thought.*

5. a. = mind, in the widest sense, including the functions of feeling, volition, and intellect.

c825 *Vesp. Psalter* lxxx. 13 [lxxxi. 12] Ne forleort hie efter lustum heortan heara. c1000 *Ags. Gosp.* Luke ii. 51 His modor ȝeheold ealle þas word, on hyre heortan smeaȝende. c1175 *Lamb. Hom.* 25 He seið mið þa muðe þet nis naut in his heorte. a1225 *Leg. Kath.* 2142 Do nu þenne hihendliche þat tu hauest on heorte. 1390 Gower *Conf.* II. 225 His hert and tunge must accorde. 1558 Knox *First Blast* (Arb.) 36 A principle..depelie printed in the hart of man. 1607 Shaks. *Cor.* III. i. 257 His Heart's his Mouth; What his Brest forges, that his Tongue must vent. 1611 Bible *1 Kings* viii. 18 Thou diddest well that it was in thine heart. 1635 Sanderson *Serm.* II. 306 The heart..is..very often in Scripture..taken more largely, so as to comprehend the whole soul, in all its faculties, as well the apprehensive as the appetitive; and consequently taketh in the thoughts, as well as the desires, of the soul. 1729 Butler *Serm., Love Neighbour* Wks. 1874 II. 159 The whole system, as I may speak, of affections (including rationality), which constitute the heart, as this word is used in Scripture and on moral subjects. 1886 H. Conway *Living or Dead* II. ix. 180 Capable of any villainy that the heart of man could devise.

b. In this relation spoken of as having ears, eyes, etc., meaning those faculties of the mind, understanding, or emotional nature, that have some analogy to these bodily organs. Cf. *heart of heart(s.*

c1025 *Rule St. Benet* (Logeman) 1 Ahyld eare heortan þinre. c1200 Ormin 3899 Wiþþ innwarrd heorrtess tunge. c1230 *Hali Meid.* 3 Opene to vnderstonde þe ehne of þin heorte. c1400 *Apol. Loll.* 36 Wiþ þe eeris and een of his hert, he schuld vnderstond hem. 1604 *Act 1 Jas. I*, c. 1 Vpon the knees of our hearts to agnize our most constant faith, obedience and loyaltie to your Maiestie. 1620 Sir T. Matthews tr. *St. Augustine's Confess.* I. v, Behould the eares of my hart, are set before thee; open thou them, O Lord. 1735–8 Bolingbroke *On Parties* 13 The Parliament acknowledged, on the Knees of their Hearts (such was the Cant of the Age) the indubitable Right, by which..the Crown descended to Him.

6. a. The seat of one's inmost thoughts and secret feelings; one's inmost being; the depths of the soul; the soul, the spirit.

c1000 *Ags. Gosp.* Matt. xii. 34 Soþlice of þære heortan willan se muþ spicþ. a1300 *Cursor M.* 43 Vr dedis fro vr hert tas rote. 1382 Wyclif *Matt.* xii. 34 Sothely the mouth spekith of the grete plente of the herte. 1508 Dunbar *Tua Mariit Wemen* 162, I sall a ragment reveil fra [the] rute of my hert. 1548–9 (Mar.) *Bk. Com. Prayer* Communion, Vnto whom all hartes bee open. 1580 Hollyband *Treas. Fr. Tong*, *Contre son cueur*, dissemblingly, or against his heart. 1611 Bible *Judg.* v. 16 For the diuisions of Reuben there were great searchings of heart. 1627–8 Feltham *Resolves* (1636) 366 Rather than have poured out his heart with such indiscretion. 1794 Mann in *Lett. Lit. Men* (Camden) 440 Excuse my laying my heart open to you and exposing my feelings as they are. 1886 Baring-Gould *Crt. Royal* xviii. I. 283, I like you to speak out of your heart freshly what you think.

b. ***double heart, two hearts***: phrases indicating duplicity or insincerity; see double *a.* 5, and cf. 51 b.

1382 Wyclif *1 Chron.* xii. 33 Fyfty thousand camen in to help, not in double hert. 1594 T. B. *La Primaud. Fr. Acad.* II. Ep. to Rdr. 4 Men of two harts, or of a double heart. 1611 [see 51 b].

7. Intent, will, purpose, inclination, desire. *Obs.* exc. in phr. ***after one's own heart.***

c825 *Vesp. Psalter* xix. (xx.) 4 Selle ðe dryhten efter heortan ðinre. c1175 *Lamb. Hom.* 3 Heo urnen on-ȝein him ..mid godere heorte and summe mid ufele þeonke. c1290 *S. Eng. Leg.* I. 10/330 Muche aȝein heore heorte it was. 1387 Trevisa *Higden* (Rolls) VI. 437 He hadde þe money aȝenst herte. c1470 Henry *Wallace* I. 386 Waith suld be delt, in all place, with fre hart. c1485 *Digby Myst.* (1882) III. 47 Now have I told yow my hart. 1535 Coverdale *1 Sam.* xiii. 14 The Lorde hath soughte him out a man after his owne hert. 1568 Grafton *Chron.* II. 200 Mawgre the heart and minde of all his Barons. 1584 R. Scot *Discov. Witchcr.* xv. v. (1886) 330 They..may be forced to yeeld in spight of their harts. 1883 Mrs. Hungerford *Rossmoyne* I. vi. 120, I am going to give you a mission after your own heart.

†8. Disposition, temperament, character. *Obs.*

a1225 *Ancr. R.* 384 Auh swote and schir heorte is god to alle þinges. 1307 *Elegy Edw. 1*, i, Alle that beoth of huerte trewe. 1402 Hoccleve *Let. of Cupid* 36 Fful herd yt is to know a manys hert. c1489 Caxton *Sonnes of Aymon* ix. 205 They had the herte so fell that they wolde take none amendes. 1548 Hall *Chron., Hen. VII*, 40 To whom at the fyrst he shewed his good hart. 1599 Shaks. *Much Ado* II. i. 324 In faith Lady you haue a merry heart. 1603 —— *Meas. for M.* v. i. 389 Not changing heart with habit. 1611 Bible *Ecclus.* iii. 27 An obstinate heart shall be laden with sorrowes.

9. a. The seat of the emotions generally; the emotional nature, as distinguished from the intellectual nature placed in the *head*.

In earlier use often referring to the physical organ; in later mostly *fig.*

Beowulf (Z.) 2463 Heortan sorȝe. c1050 *Byrhtferth's Handboc* in *Anglia* VIII. 317 Him mæȝ beon þe glædre his heorte. c1275 *Passion Our Lord* 6 in *O.E. Misc.* 37 Heore heorten weren so colde. c1350 *Leg. Rood* (1871) 88 Vp he rase with hert ful light. 1413 *Pilgr. Sowle* (Caxton) I. iii. (1859) 4 The syght..gladyd moche my harte. 1548 Latimer *Ploughers* (Arb.) 20 Breakynge their stonie hertes. 1596 Shaks. *Merch. V.* III. ii. 64 Tell me where is fancie bred, Or in the heart, or in the head. c1600 —— *Sonn.* xlvi. 1 Mine eye and heart are at a mortal war How to divide the conquest of thy sight. a1700 Dryden tr. *Ovid's Art Love* I. Wks. 1808 XII. 252 Tears will pierce a heart of adamant. 1735 Pope *Ep. Lady* 250 To raise the Thought, and touch the Heart be thine! 1784 Cowper *Tiroc.* 897 One comfort yet shall cheer thine aged heart. 1824 Scott *St. Ronan's* xvi, With zeal honourable to his heart and head. 1867 Trollope *Chron. Barset* II. l. 71 Her heart was too full to speak. 1884 Ouida *P'cess Napraxine* vi. (1886) 67 In her it was a thirst of the mind, in him it was a hunger of the heart. 1886 H. Conway *Living or Dead* II. ix. 193 If the man had a soft place in his heart I felt sure I was finding it.

†b. The feeling or sentiment which one has in regard to a thing. *Obs.*

1596 Shaks. *Merch. V.* I. ii. 141 If I could bid the fift welcome with so good heart as I can bid the other foure farewell, I should be glad of his approach. 1603 Knolles *Hist. Turks* (1621) 356 Above others, his heart was greatest against the Hungarians.

10. a. More particularly, The seat of love or affection, as in many fig. phrases: ***to give, lose one's heart (to), to have, obtain, gain a person's heart.*** Hence = Affection, love, devotion. ***near, nearest, one's heart***, close or closest to one's affection.

c1175 *Lamb. Hom.* 5 We sulen habben ure heorte and habben godne ileafe to ure drihten. 1297 R. Glouc. (1724) 24 Kyng Locryne's herte was al clene vp hire y went..[He] thoȝte hire to spouse, so ys herte to hire droȝ. c1330 R. Brunne *Chron.* (1810) 253 Sir Edward..His herte gaf tille dame Blanche, if hir wille wer þerto. 1382 Wyclif *Prov.* xxiii. 26 Gif, sone myn, thin herte to me. c1450 *Merlin* 24 So hadde Vortiger the hertys of the peple. 1590 Spenser *F.Q.* I. xii. 40 Thrise happy man..Possessed of his Ladies hart and hand. 1610 Shaks. *Temp.* III. i. 65 The verie instant that I saw you, did My heart flie to your seruice. 1676 Wycherley *Pl. Dealer* II. i. (1735) 43, I have an Ambition ..of losing my Heart before such a fair Enemy. 1711 Addison *Spect.* No. 18 ¶4 The Lover..gained the Heart of his Princess. 1884 Edna Lyall *We Two* xxv, Lady Caroline will quite lose her heart to you. 1886 Baring-Gould *Crt. Royal* xxxiii. II. 195 In matters of the heart..I am confused. 1887 Edna Lyall *Knt.-Errant* ix. 69 She..won all hearts. 1888 Burgon *Lives 12 Gd. Men* I. Pref. 28 Important for the cause which was nearest to his heart.

b. Kindly feeling; cordiality, heartiness. *rare.*

a1656 Bp. Hall *Life* in *Sat.* (1824) p. lv, His welcome to Waltham could not but want much of his heart without me. 1827 Scott *Jrnl.* 7 Mar., I must say, too, there was a heart, —a kindly feeling prevailed over the party.

c. Susceptibility to the higher emotions; sensibility or tenderness for others; feeling. (Often qualified by indef. article or *no*.)

1735 Pope *Ep. Lady* 159 With ev'ry pleasing, ev'ry prudent part, Say, what can Chloe want?—She wants a Heart. 1839 C. L. H. Pependiek *Crt. Time Q. Charlotte* (1887) II. 55 A total want of heart or filial affection. a1845 Hood *Lady's Dream* xvi, But evil is wrought by want of Thought, As well as want of Heart! 1847 Tennyson *Princ.* vi. 218 Our Ida has a heart. 1886 Mrs. Alexander *By Woman's Wit* II. viii. 266 Which would have been pain and humiliation to a woman of real heart and delicacy.

d. ***to have a heart*** (colloq.), to be merciful. Freq. in *imp.*: come off it, be reasonable, show some pity!

1917 Wodehouse & Bolton (*play title*) Have a heart. 1928 *Observer* 1 Jan. 4 We only sigh for old delights, and in homely phrase beseech him..to 'have a heart'. 1936 P. Bottome *Level Crossing* xviii. 225 'Have a heart!' Nelly told her crossly. 1950 W. Stevens *Let.* 28 June (1967) 683 If you use the things..I shall have to go out and drown myself... Have a heart. 1967 J. B. Priestley *It's Old Country* xix. 209 'You haven't made any plans for him, have you?' 'How could I?.. Have a heart!' 1970 *New Yorker* 12 Sept. 50/3 Spare us a reefer, beautiful. Have a heart.

11. a. The seat of courage; hence, Courage, spirit. Especially in ***to pluck up, gather, keep (up), lose heart.*** See also 48, 49, *to have the heart, take h.*

c825 *Vesp. Psalter* cxi[i]. 8 Getrymed is heorte his. a1000 *Cædmon's Gen.* 2348 (Gr.) Heortan strange. c1250 *Gen. & Ex.* 3253 On and on kin, als herte hem cam, ðat folc ilc in his weiȝe nam. 1375 Barbour *Bruce* I. 28 King Robert..That hardy wes off hart and hand. 1390 Gower *Conf.* II. 12 He hath the sore, which no man heleth, The whiche is cleped lacke of herte. a1400–50 *Alexander* 470 'Nay', quod þe comly kyng 'cache vp þine hert'. 1450 W. Somner in *Four C. Eng. Lett.* 4 Thanne his herte faylyd him. 1481 Caxton *Godfrey* cxlix. 221 They ran on them with grete herte, and slewe them som of them. 1530 Palsgr. 661/2 Plucke up thy herte, man, thou shalte be set at large to morowe. 1596 Spenser *State Irel.* (Globe) 659 To give harte and encouradgement to all such bold rebells. 1607 Shaks. *Cor.* II. iii. 212 Why, had your Bodyes No heart among you? a1700 Dryden *Hector & Androm.* 48 Thy dauntless heart.. will urge thee to thy fate. 1776 Burke *Corr.* (1844) II. 107 You have, however, heart to the last. 1850 Merivale *Rom. Emp.* (1865) I. x. 435 The Germans lost heart. 1863 Mrs. Gaskell *Sylvia's L.* (1877) 247 Now, good-by..and keep a good heart. 1867 Freeman *Norm. Conq.* I. v. 376 Æthelred seems to have plucked up a little heart. 1885 *Sat. Rev.* 24 Jan. 103/2 Its younger members, if brainless, are not without heart and pluck. 1886 F. L. Shaw *Col. Cheswick's Camp.* II. i. 14 You put heart into me again.

b. The source of ardour, enthusiasm, or energy. So ***to have one's heart in, put one's h. into*** (a thing).

1780 Mad. D'Arblay *Lett.* 22 Jan., I have so little heart in the affair, that I have now again quite dropped it. 1853 Lytton *My Novel* I. xii, His whole heart was in the game. 1886 Mrs. Lynn Linton *Paston Carew* I. x. 181 A man who puts his heart into all he does.

12. The seat of the mental or intellectual faculties. Often = understanding, intellect, mind, and (less commonly) memory. *arch.* exc. in phrase ***by heart***: see 32.

c950 *Lindisf. Gosp.* John xii. 40 Ofblindade eȝo hiora & onstiðade hiora hearta þæte ne ȝeseað mið eȝum & ongeattað mið hearta. c1175 *Lamb. Hom.* 121 þe deofel ablende heore heorte þet heo ne cunnan icnawen ure helend. a1200 *Moral Ode* 285 Ne mai non heorte it þenche, ne no tunge ne can telle. c1300 *Beket* 1199 His hurte him ȝaf that hit was he. 1415 *Rolls of Parlt.* IV. 85/1 As free mak I the, as hert may thynk, or eygh may see. 1576 Gascoigne *Steele Gl.* (Arb.) 50 And me they found..Whose harmelesse hart, perceivde not their deceipt. 1602 Shaks. *Ham.* I. v. 121 Would heart of man once think it? 1611 Bible *Hosea* vii. 11 Ephraim is like a silly dove without heart [1885 *R.V.* understanding]. —— *Luke* xxiv. 25 O fooles, and slow of heart to beleeue all that the Prophets haue spoken.

13. The moral sense, conscience. Now only in phrase ***my (his, etc.) heart smote me (him, etc.).***

1382 Wyclif *2 Sam.* xxiv. 10 Forsothe the herte of Dauid smoot hym, aftir that the puple is noumbred. 1382 —— *1 John* iii. 20 For if oure herte shal reproue us, God is more than oure herte. a1699 Lady Halkett *Autobiog.* (1875) 3 That my owne Hart cannott challenge mee.

**** Put for the person.*

14. a. Used as a term of endearment, often qualified by *dear, sweet* (see sweetheart), etc.; chiefly in addressing a person.

c1305 *St. Kenelm* 142 in *E.E.P.* (1862) 51 Allas, heo seide ..þat mie child, mie sweete hurte, scholde such þing bitide. c1350 *Will. Palerne* 1649 Whi so, mi dere hert? *Ibid.* 1655 Mi hony, mi hert, al hol þou me makest. c1374 Chaucer *Compl. Mars.* 138 Alas whan shall I mete yow, herte dere? c1440 *Partonope* 792 As ye byn hir hert swete. 1494 *Will of Combe* (Somerset Ho.), My last derest hart & lady. c1500 *Melusine* xlv. 318 Adieu, myn herte, & al my joye. a1553 Udall *Royster D.* I. iii. (Arb.) 25 Howe dothe sweete Custance, my heart of gold, tell me how? 1676 Beale *Pocket-bk.* in H. Walpole *Vertue's Anecd. Paint.* (1786) III. 139 My dear heart and self and son Charles saw at Mr. Walton's the lady Carnarvon's picture. 1677 *Epist. to Yng. Maidens*, Sweet Hearts..I have..composed this little Book, as a Rich Storehouse for you. 1719 Hamilton *Ep. to Ramsay* 24 July x, Do not mistake me, dearest heart. 1855 Tennyson *Maud* I. xviii. viii, Dear heart, I feel with thee the drowsy spell.

†b. ***dear heart***: a boon companion. *Obs.*

1663 Dryden *Wild Gallant* I. i, He's one of your Dear Hearts, a debauchee. *Ibid.* II. i, That you were one of the errantest Cowards in Christendom, though you went for one of the dear Hearts.

15. a. As a term of appreciation or commendation: Man of courage or spirit. Often in nautical language: cf. hearty C. 2.

c1500 *Melusine* xxi. 141 Whan the noble hertes herde hym saye thoo wordes they held it to grete wysedome of hym. 1600 Nashe *Summer's Last Will* Wks. (1883–4) VI. 104 What cheere, what cheere, my hearts? 1610 Shaks. *Temp.* I. i. 6 Heigh my hearts, cheerely, cheerely my harts. 1627 Capt. Smith *Seaman's Gram.* xiii. 61 Courage my hearts for a fresh charge. 1684 Meriton *Praise Yorksh. Ale* (1697) 14 Come here my Hearts, Said he. 1780 Cowper *Table T.* 23 History..Tells of a few stout hearts that fought and died. a1845 Hood *Storm* iv, Come, my hearts, be stout and bold. 1863 Kingsley *Water-Bab.* vii, They were all true English hearts; and they came to their end like good knights-errant.

b. ***Hearts of Steel***: the name of an agrarian organization formed by the Protestant tenants in Ulster in 1770.

1772 *Petition* in Froude *Irel. 18th C.* v. ii. (1881) II. 133 It is not wanton folly that prompts us to be Hearts of Steel, but the weight of oppression. 1780 A. Young *Tour Irel.* I. 217 The hearts of steel lasted 3 years; began in 1770 against rents and tythes. 1807 Vancouver *Agric. Devon* (1813) 468 The insurgent banditti of Tories, Hearts of Steel, Peep-o'day Boys, White Boys, etc. 1882 Lecky *Eng. in 18th C.* IV. 393 In the North the disturbances of the Hearts of Steel had just broken out.

†16. As a term of compassion: ***poor heart!*** (cf. *poor soul, poor body*). *Obs.*

1599 Shaks. *Hen. V*, II. i. 123 A poore heart, hee is so shak'd of a burning quotidian Tertian. 1668 Pepys *Diary* 27 Dec., My wife and I fell out a little..she cried, poor heart! which I was troubled for. 1682 Bunyan *Holy War* (Cassell) 91 Wherefore the town of Mansoul (poor hearts!) understood him not. 1749 Fielding *Tom Jones* XI. ii, The poor little heart looked so piteous, when she sat down.

***** Something having a central position.*

17. a. The innermost or central part of anything; the centre, middle.

a1310 in Wright *Lyric P.* viii. 31 That ys in heovene hert in-hyde. a1325 *Prose Psalter* xlv[i]. 2 þe mounteins shul be born in-to þe hert of þe see. 1530 Palsgr. 34 The herte of Fraunce. 1581 Mulcaster *Positions* xl. (1887) 228 In the hart of a great towne. 1658 Cokaine *To W. Dugdale* Poems 112 Our Warwick-shire the Heart of England is. 1674 N. Fairfax *Bulk & Selv.* 71 A bore through the heart or centre of the earth. 1722 De Foe *Plague* (1884) 30 The Heart of the City. 1855 C. Bronte *Villette* vi. 44, I got into the heart of city life. 1871 L. Stephen *Playgr. Europe* v, We soon found ourselves in the very heart of the glacier.

b. The part of any time or season when its character becomes most intense (usually the middle part); the height, depth.

1764 *Mem. G. Psalmanazar* 168 To send me away in the heart of a severe winter. 1844 Disraeli *Coningsby* VIII. i, It was the heart of the London season.

18. *esp.* A central part of distinct conformation or character, as **a.** The pith of wood, the white tender part of a cabbage or the like, the core of an apple, etc., the receptacle or other central part of a flower; **b.** The central strand of a hawser-laid rope, round which the other strands are twisted; **c.** The central solid portion or core of a twisted column (Knight *Dict. Mech.* 1875).

1578 Lyte *Dodoens* III. lxi. 402 The Roote..hauing in the middle a little white, the whiche men call the Harte of

Osmunde. **1596** SHAKS. *Merch. V.* I. iii. 102 A goodly apple rotten at the heart. **1681** W. ROBERTSON *Phraseol. Gen.* (1693) 715 The heart or pith of a tree, *medulla.* **1707** *Curios. in Husb. & Gard.* 45 A Flower is compos'd of..the Cup..the Leaves, and the Heart. **1841** *Penny Cycl.* XX. 155/2 Ropes formed in the most common manner, with three strands, do not require a heart, or central strand. **1866** *Treas. Bot.* 166/1 Cabbage..eaten in a young state..before the heart has become firm and hard. *Ibid.* 166/2 The heart, or middle part of the plant [Large-ribbed Cabbage] has..been found very delicate. **1875** BEDFORD *Sailor's Pocket Bk.* x. (ed. 2) 360 Shroud-laid rope, 4 strands and a heart.

19. a. *spec.* The solid central part of a tree without sap or alburnum. Cf. HEARTWOOD.

c **1400** MAUNDEV. (Roxb.) ix. 35 Treesse..failed in þaire hertes and become holle within. **1523** FITZHERB. *Husb.* §126 Get the stakes of the hert of oke. **1577** B. GOOGE *Heresbach's Husb.* II. (1586) 103 The Elme..(as it is all hart) it maketh good tymber. **1659** WILLSFORD *Scales Comm., Archit.* 16, 3 kinds, *viz.* heart of Oak, sap and Deal lath. **1760** *New Song* in *Universal Mag.* Mar. 152 Heart of oak are our ships, heart of oak are our men.

b. Hence fig. ***heart of oak***: a stout, courageous spirit; a man of courage or valour; a man of sterling quality, capable of resistance or endurance. (Cf. F. *cœur d'or*; also sense 15.) Also *attrib.*

1609 *Old Meg of Herefordsh.* (N.), Yonkers that have hearts of oake at fourescore yeares. **1691** WOOD *Ath. Oxon.* II. 221 He was..a heart of oke, and a pillar of the Land. **1760** [see 19]. **1832** TENNYSON *Buonaparte* 1 He thought to quell the stubborn hearts of oak. **1870** DICKENS *E. Drood* xii, A nation of hearts of oak. **1895** *Q. Rev.* Oct. 320 Thrashers, Whiteboys, Heart-of-Oak-boys..and other off-spring of agrarian and political discontent.

***** *The vital part or principle.*

20. The vital, essential, or efficacious part; essence. (Often combined with other notions.)

c **1533** LATIMER *Serm. & Rem.* (1845) 237 God looketh not to the work of praying, but to the heart of the prayer. **1598** SHAKS. *Merry W.* II. ii. 233 Now (Sir John) here is the heart of my purpose. **1653** BAXTER *Meth. Peace Consc.* 44 The Heart of saving faith is this Acceptance of Christ. **1840** MRS. BROWNING *Drama Exile* Poems 1844 I. 52 And from the top of sense, looked over sense, To the significance and heart of things. **1871** DARWIN *Life & Lett.* (1887) III. 147 Mr. Huxley's unrivalled power in tearing the heart out of a book. **1889** JESSOPP *Coming of Friars* iii. 122 The church of a monastery was the heart of the place.

21. a. Of land, etc.: Strength, fertility; capacity to produce or effect what is required of it; 'proof' (of grass, etc.). ***in (good, strong, etc.) heart***: in prime condition. ***out of heart***: in poor condition, unproductive.

1573 TUSSER *Husb.* xix. (1878) 49 Land out of hart, Makes thistles a number foorthwith to vpstart. **1594** PLAT *Jewell-ho.* I. 59 A fruitfull molde, and such as giueth hart vnto the earth. **1620** MARKHAM *Farew. Husb.* II. xi. (1668) 49 This..shall maintain and keep the earth in good heart. **1649** BLITHE *Eng. Improv. Impr.* (1653) 139 To Till it forth of heart is just as if you work an Ox off his legs. **1697** DRYDEN *Virg. Georg.* I. 108 That the spent Earth may gather heart again. **1704** SWIFT *Batt. Bks.* Misc. (1711) 231 Their Horses large, but extreamely out of Case and Heart. **1727–51** CHAMBERS *Cycl.* s.v. *Hops,* If the hops be in good heart, manuring and pruning is most adviseable. **1805** FORSYTH *Beauties Scotl.* I. 263 The soil being kept in heart, or rich..by superior agriculture. **1807** VANCOUVER *Agric. Devon* (1813) 212 The produce of upland hay varies according to the season, the heart, and condition, the land may be in. **1856** *Jrnl. R. Agric. Soc.* XVII. II. 528 Such grass affords, as the farmers say, 'no heart'—'no proof' in it. **1895** W. RYE *Ibid.* Mar. 5 In 1787 the heart of the land was so improved that Coke began to sow wheat.

b. Hence, generally, ***in heart***: in good or sound condition.

1626 BACON *Sylva* §305 The Lees..keepe the Drinke in Heart, and make it lasting. **1703** *Art & Myst. Vintners* 11 The Lee, tho' it makes the Liquor turbid, doth yet keep the Wine in heart.

22. The best, choicest, or most important part.

1589 COGAN *Haven Health* cxcv. (1636) 179 Creame..is indeed the very head or heart of Milke. **1603** KNOLLES *Hist. Turks* (1621) 528 To deliver into his power the castle with the heart of the citizens.

****** *Something of the shape of a heart.*

23. A figure or representation of the human heart; esp. a conventionalized symmetrical figure formed of two similar curves meeting in a point at one end and a cusp at the other. Also, an object, as a jewel or ornament, in the shape of a heart.

1463 *Bury Wills* (Camden) 35 The seid broche herte of gold to be hange, naylyd, and festnyd vpon the shryne. **1593** SHAKS. *2 Hen. VI,* III. ii. 107, I tooke a costly Iewell from my necke, A Hart it was bound in with Diamonds. **1720** MRS. MANLEY *Power of Love* I. (1741) 20 The Justs ended with his receiving a Heart of Diamonds from the Dutchess. **1766** PORNY *Heraldry* (1787) 150 A Man's Heart Gules, within two equilateral triangles braced Sable. **1828–40** BERRY *Encycl. Her.,* Hearts are..met with in coat-armour, borne in several ways. **1834** L. RITCHIE *Wand. by Seine* 104 At the foot of the tomb was another heart in white marble.

24. a. A playing card bearing one or more conventionalized figures of a heart; one of the suit marked with such figures; *pl.* the suit of such cards.

1529 LATIMER *1st Serm. on Card* (1886) 27 Now turn up your trump, your heart (hearts is trump, as I said before), and cast your trump, your heart, on this card. **1599** *Hist. Pope Joan* A j b in Singer *Hist. Cards* 259 Like the ace of hearts at Mawe. **1648** HERRICK *Hesper., Oberon's Palace* (1869) 177 With peeps of hearts, of club and spade. **1712–14** POPE *Rape Lock* III. 79 Clubs, diamonds, hearts, in wild disorder seen. *Mod.* I couldn't follow suit; I hadn't got a heart.

b. ***Hearts***, a card-game for three or four players, similar in principle to whist but without partners or a trump suit: the object of the game is to avoid taking a trick containing a Heart or the Queen of Spades.

1886 'THE MAJOR' (*title*) The game of hearts. Rules of the game. How to play hearts. **1907** *Yesterday's Shopping* (1969) 361/1 *Invitation Cards...* At Home, Progressive Hearts —— o'clock. R.S.V.P. **1930** W. S. MAUGHAM *Writer's Notebk.* (1949) 231 In the evening the guests collect and play hearts for infinitesimal sums. **1943** 'C. DICKSON' *She died a Lady* viii. 67 You don't call playing bridge or hearts on Saturday night a very Bohemian sort of life, do you? **1946** A. CHRISTIE *Hollow* viii. 75 Do you think Hearts or Bridge or Rummy? **1959** J. D. SALINGER in *New Yorker* 6 June 101 At all card games, without exception—Go Fish, poker, cassino, hearts, old maid..—he was absolutely intolerable.

†**25.** The sole of a horse's foot. *Obs.*

1523 FITZHERB. *Husb.* §100 Morfounde..appereth vnder the houe in the hert of the fote. **1737** BRACKEN *Farriery Impr.* (1757) II. 210 He has got a Prick thro' the Sole or Heart of the Foot (as it is called).

26. *Naut.* A triangular wooden block pierced with one large hole through which a lanyard is reeved, used for extending the stays; a kind of dead-eye.

1769 FALCONER *Dict. Marine, Heart,* a peculiar sort of dead-eye, somewhat resembling the shape of a heart..only furnished with one large hole in the middle, whereas the common dead-eyes have always three holes. **1804** A. DUNCAN *Mariner's Chron.* Pref. 17. **1882** NARES *Seamanship* (ed. 6) 37 Lanyards, rove through iron-bound hearts.

27. *Mach.* A heart-shaped wheel or cam used for converting a rotary into a reciprocating motion.

1875 in KNIGHT *Dict. Mech.*

28. Short for *heart-shell* (see 56).

1750 R. POCOCKE *Trav.* (1888) 153, I found in the Quarries several of those bivalve petrifyed shells, call'd hearts.

29. Short for *heart-net* (see 56).

30. In names of trees and plants.

black-heart, white-heart, varieties of cultivated Cherry (see BLACK *a.* 19, WHITE *a.*). ***bleeding-heart*** (see BLEEDING *ppl. a.* 5). ***floating heart***, an American name for *Limnanthemum* (*Treas Bot.* 1866).

1664 EVELYN *Kal. Hort.* (1729) 219 Black Cherry, Morellos, Black Heart, all good. **1803** J. ABERCROMBIE *Ev. Man his own Gardener* (ed. 17) 674/1 Cherries..White heart, Black heart, Bleeding heart.

II. Phrases.

* *With governing preposition.*

31. at heart. In one's inmost thoughts or feelings; in one's actual character or disposition; inwardly, secretly; at bottom; in reality.

1735 POPE *Ep. Lady* 216 But every Woman is at heart a Rake. **1780** COWPER *Table T.* 191 Patriots, who love good places at their hearts. **1849** MACAULAY *Hist. Eng.* II. 222 It was certain that the King at heart preferred the Church-men to the Puritans. **1855** *Ibid.* xii. III. 153 Rice was charged to tell James that Mountjoy was a traitor at heart. **1855** PRESCOTT *Philip II,* II. viii. (1857) 296 One cannot doubt that Philip was at heart an inquisitor.

32. by heart. In the memory; from memory; by rote; so as to be able to repeat or write out correctly what has been learnt. Cf. F. *par cœur.*

c **1374** CHAUCER *Troylus* v. 1494 She told ek al þe prophesies by herte. **1528** GARDINER in Pocock *Rec. Ref.* I. I. 103 [We] rehearsed by heart the chapter *Veniens.* **1573–80** BARET *Alv.* H 202 To learne by harte, or without booke..To say by harte. **1645** FULLER *Good Th. in Bad T.* (1841) 15, I had said them [prayers] rather by heart than with my heart. **1682** WHELER *Journ. Greece* v. 367 The Tragedians got their Plays by heart. **1709** PRIOR *Hans Carvel* 13 Whole Tragedies she had by Heart. **1739** CHESTERF. *Lett.* (1792) I. xliii. 138 Pray get these verses by heart against the time I see you. **1885** *Law Times* LXXIX. 339/2 Few lawyers know by heart the complicated statutes relating to Church matters.

†**33. for one's heart.** For one's life; to save one's life. See FOR *prep.* A. 9 c. *Obs.*

34. from one's heart. Out of the depths of one's soul; with the sincerest or deepest feeling.

1594 T. B. *La Primaud. Fr. Acad.* II. 93 And wee know..that hee speakes from his heart. **1651** SIR E. NICHOLAS in *N. Papers* (Camden) I. 249, I wish from my hart Mr. Attorney had come away. **1665** BOYLE *Occas. Refl.* III. vi. (1845) 159 In such kind of Sermons, there is little spoken, either from the Heart, or to the Heart. **1840** CARLYLE *Heroes* ii. (1858) 234 If a book come from the heart, it will contrive to reach other hearts.

35. in...heart.

a. ***in (one's) heart***: in one's inmost thoughts or feelings; inwardly; secretly; at heart.

c **1000** *Ags. Gosp.* Matt. xxiv. 48 Ȝyf se yfela þeowa ðencþ on hys heortan and cwyþ, min hlafurd uferað hys cyme. *a* **1175** *Cott. Hom.* 219 [He] cweð an his herto, þat he wolde and eaðe mihte bien his sceoppende ȝelic. *a* **1300** *Cursor M.* 2959 (Gött.) Abraham syhid in his hert ful sare. *a* **1325** *Prose Psalter* lii[i]. 1 Þe vnwys seid in his hert, God nis nouȝt. **1390** GOWER *Conf.* I. 64 Many one Which spekeþ of Peter and of John And thenkeþ Judas in his herte. **1548** HALL *Chron., Hen. VI.* 127 b, Whiche thyng in his harte, he moste coveted and desired. **1611** BIBLE *Transl. Pref.* 2 They..wish in their heart the Temple had neuer bene built. **1849** MACAULAY *Hist. Eng.* vi. II. 105 Julian had..pretended to abhor idolatry, while in heart an idolater.

†**b.** ***in all one's heart*** (transl. L. *in toto corde*): with all one's heart (39 a). *Obs.*

c **825** *Vesp. Psalter* ix 1 Ic ondetto ðe dryhten in alre heortan minre. **1382** WYCLIF *Ibid.,* I shal knoulechen to thee, Lord, in al myn herte. **1382** —— *Jer.* xxiv. 7 Thei shal turne aȝeen to me in al ther herte.

c. ***in heart***: in good spirits. So in phr. ***to put in*** (or ***into***) ***heart***: to restore to good spirits.

1596 SHAKS. *Tam. Shr.* IV. v. 78 Well, Petruchio, this has put me in heart. **1614** RALEIGH *Hist. World* II. v. iii. §15. 442 His Armie must have somewhat to keep it in heart. **1719** DE FOE *Crusoe* II. v, Whether they were still in heart to fight. **1832** HT. MARTINEAU *Ella of Gar.* viii. 100 To put you in heart again.

d. In good condition: see 21.

36. near, next one's heart: see 10, 4.

†**37. of (all one's) heart.** With all one's heart; sincerely, earnestly. *Obs.* (Cf. F. *de tout mon cœur.*)

c **1380** WYCLIF *Sel. Wks.* III. 431 To holde religioun of Crist and love hym of hert siþ..Cristis religioun stondiþ in love of God of al our herte. *c* **1400** *Apol. Loll.* 47, I cnowlech of mowþ & hert, me to hold þe same feiþ of þe sacrament of þe Lordis bord.

38. out of heart.

a. In low spirits; discouraged, disheartened.

1586 J. HOOKER *Girald. Irel.* viii. in *Holinshed* II. 9/2 Perceuung them to be somewhat dismaied and out of heart. **1690** W. WALKER *Idiomat. Anglo-Lat.* 234 After he had lost his boy, he grew quite out of heart. **1711** tr. *Werenfels' Disc. Logomachys* 143 Pray, dear Good Sir, don't be out of Patience, or out of Heart. **1882** TENNYSON *Promise of May* III. Wks. (1894) 300/1 What is it Has put you out of heart? **1891** *Spectator* 11 Apr. 497 The Regent is evidently out of heart.

b. In poor condition: see 21.

39. with...heart.

a. ***with*** (OE. *mid*) ***all one's heart, with one's whole heart,*** †***with heart***: with great sincerity, earnestness, or devotion; now chiefly in weakened sense, with the utmost goodwill or pleasure.

971 *Blickl. Hom.* 13 Herede heo hine..mid ealre heortan. *c* **1000** ÆLFRIC *Hom.* I. 420 Ȝelyfst ðu mid ealre heortan? *c* **1220** *Bestiary* 171 To helden wit herte ðe bodes of holi k[i]rke. *c* **1470** HENRY *Wallace* IV. 20 He luffyt him with hart and all hys mycht. **1509** HAWES *Past. Pleas.* XXVII. xxxix, With all my herte I wyll, quod he, accepte Hym to my servyce. **1535** COVERDALE *Jer.* xxiv. 7 They shal returne vnto me with their whole herte. **1598** SHAKS. *Merry W.* I. i. 86, I thank you alwaies with my heart, la: with my heart. **1606** —— *Tr. & Cr.* III. iii. 294 God buy you with all my heart. **1653** WALTON *Angler* ii. 44 Take one with all my heart. **1851** MAYNE REID *Scalp Hunt.* vii. 60 That I will promise you, with all my heart.

b. ***with a heart and a half***: with great pleasure, willingly. ***with half a heart***: half-heartedly, with divided affection or enthusiasm.

1636 MASSINGER *Gt. Dk. Florence* IV. ii, Such junkets come not every day. Once more to you With a heart and a half, i faith. **1855** MACAULAY *Hist. Eng.* III 587 Some naval officers..though they served the new government, served it sullenly and with half a heart. **1885** TENNYSON *Let. to S. Cox* 5 Aug., I thank you, as the Irishman says, 'with a heart and a half', for your volume of Expositions.

** *With verb and preposition.*

40. find in one's heart. To feel inclined or willing; to prevail upon oneself (to do something): now chiefly in negative and interrogative sentences.

c **1440** [see FIND *v.* 10 c]. **1530** PALSGR. 687/1 Thoughe you can nat fynde in your herte to honour hym for his owne sake. **1638** F. JUNIUS *Paint. of Ancients* 316 Yet can these men finde in their hearts to boast. **1665** BOYLE *Occas. Refl.* IV. viii, [One] that can find in his Heart to destroy Armies, and ruine Provinces. **1834** M. SCOTT *Cruise Midge* vii. 122 Neither of us could find it in our hearts to speak. **1883** E. BLACKWELL *Booth* iv. 45 They could hardly find in their heart to disturb its peaceful surface.

41. a. have at heart. To have as an object in which one is deeply interested.

1711 STEELE *Spect.* No. 20 ¶1 The Correction of Impudence is what I have very much at Heart. **1712** ADDISON *Italy* Wks. 1721 II. 138 The Pope has this design extremely at his heart. **1850** MERIVALE *Rom. Emp.* (1865) I. v. 199 The Romans had no object more at heart than to obtain possession of this key to Gaul. **1875** JOWETT *Plato* (ed. 2) I. 206 A matter which we have very much at heart.

b. So, conversely, ***to be at the heart of.***

1824 SCOTT *St. Ronan's* iii, The interests of the establishment being very much at the heart of this honourable council.

42. lay to heart. To take into one's serious consideration, as a thing to be kept carefully in mind; to think seriously about; to be deeply affected by or concerned about (a thing); *rarely,* to impress it seriously upon another.

1602 DEKKER *Satirom.* Wks. 1873 I. 234 Captaine, I'm sorry that you lay this wrong so close unto your heart. **1605** SHAKS. *Macb.* I. v. 15 Lay it to thy heart, and fare-well. **1611** BIBLE *Mal.* ii. 2 If yee will not lay it to heart, to giue glory vnto my name. **1802** BEDDOES *Hygëia* II. v. 21 Many writers ..have laid it to the heart of mothers not to commit to hirelings the task of nurse. **1853** TRENCH *Proverbs* 141 It contains..a lesson which I should do wisely and well at this present time to lay to heart. **1884** *Century Mag.* Oct. 942/2 Do not lay it to heart, my child.

†**43. put** or **set to** or **on the heart**: earlier equivalents of prec. *Obs.*

1382 WYCLIF *Mal.* ii. 2 Ȝif ȝe woln not putte on the herte, that ȝe ȝeve glorie to my name. *c* **1400** *Apol. Loll.* 24 If ȝe wil not sett to þe hert to ȝef glory to my name. *Ibid.* 34 Son of man, putt to hert, and see wiþ þin een..alle þings þat I spek to þe.

44. take to heart. To take seriously; to be much affected by; to grieve over; †to be zealous, solicitous, or ardent about (*obs.*).

a **1300** *Cursor M.* 24010 þat mast i tok til hert. **1535** COVERDALE *Eccl.* vii. 2 There is the ende of all men, and he that is lyuinge taketh it to herte. **1586** J. HOOKER *Girald. Irel.* in *Holinshed* (1808) VI. 299 Whose death he is said to haue taken greatlie to hart. **1621** BURTON *Anat. Mel.* II. iii. VII. (1651) 352 But why shouldst thou take thy neglect, thy canvass so to heart? *a* **1626** BACON (J.), If he would take the business to heart, and deal in it effectually, it would succeed well. *a* **1647** CLARENDON *Hist. Reb.* VIII. §257 It was very vehemently pressed by many persons..and amongst those who took it most to heart, sir John Stawel was the chief. **1822** LAMB *Elia* Ser. I. *Dream Children*, Though I did not cry and take it to heart as some do..yet I missed him all day long. **1865** TROLLOPE *Belton Est.* vi. 60 She had no idea when she was refusing him that he would have taken it to heart as he had done.

*** *With governing verb.*

45. break the heart of.

a. To kill, crush, or overwhelm with sorrow. See BREAK *v.* 7 c.

b. To accomplish the hardest part of (a task), to 'break the back of'.

1684 J. SCOTT *Chr. Life* (ed. 3) 383 You must by this time have broken the Heart of the Difficulty of your Warfare. **1828** *Craven Dial.* s.v., 'To break the heart of a business', to have almost finished it.

46. cry (*eat, fight, plague, slave, tease, tire, weary, weep*, etc.) **one's heart out**: to cry (etc.) violently or exhaustingly: see the verbs.

1606 SHAKS. *Tr. & Cr.* III. ii. 54 Nay, you shall fight your hearts out ere I part you. **1712** SWIFT *Let. to Mrs. Dingley* 25 Jan. (Seager), They have never paid him a groat, though I have teazed their hearts out. **1885** EDNA LYALL *In Golden Days* III. vii. 142, I could weep my heart out. **1886** MISS YONGE *Mod. Telemachus* I. i. 15 Making him weary his very heart out.

47. eat one's heart: to suffer or pine away from vexation or longing. See EAT *v.* 8 c.

1581 PETTIE *Guazzo's Civ. Conv.* I. (1586) 47 b, If you thinke to stoppe everie ones mouth: Which were to eate up your heart, as they say. **1591** SPENSER *M. Hubberd* 904 To eate thy heart through comfortlesse dispaires. **1603** HOLLAND *Plutarch's Mor.* 15 'Eat not thy heart', that is to say, offend not thine owne soule, nor hurt and consume it with pensive cares. **1890** W. A. WALLACE *Only a Sister?* xviii. 155 Why, there's poor Aikone..eating his heart out and getting no further.

48. a. have...heart. ***to have the heart***: to be courageous or spirited enough, to prevail upon oneself (to do something); also (in mod. use and chiefly in negative sentences), to find it in one's heart, to be hard-hearted enough.

a **1300** *Cursor M.* 11805 Hu had he hert to sced þair blod? **1413** *Pilgr. Sowle* (Caxton) IV. xxxviii. (1859) 63, I am soo full of sorow, and of heuynes, that I haue no herte to speke to yow. **1489** CAXTON *Faytes of A.* I. vi. 12 All thoost shold haue the better herte to fyghte. **1594** SHAKS. *Rich. III*, I. ii. 15 Cursed the Heart, that had the heart to do it. **1657** *North's Plutarch* Add. Lives (1676) 44 The Turks being discouraged..had not the heart to defend themselves. **1716** ADDISON *Freeholder* No. 30 (Seager) One cannot have the heart to be angry at this judicious observer. **1780** MAD. D'ARBLAY *Diary* 6 Dec., I had no heart to leave..Mr. Thrale in a state so precarious. **1840** DICKENS *Barn. Rudge* xlviii, Have you the heart to say this of your own son, unnatural mother! **1882** TENNYSON *Promise of May* III. Wks. (1894) 798/2, I hadn't the heart or face to do it.

b. *have, put* (*one's*) *heart in, into*: see 11 b.

49. take heart. To pluck up courage. (Also with qualifying adj.) ***to take heart of grace***, etc.: see HEART OF GRACE.

13.. *Coer de L.* 5757 They wer bolde, her herte they tooke. **1530** PALSGR. 748/1, I take herte, *je prens couraige.* **1590** SPENSER *F.Q.* III. x. 26 Take good hart, And tell thy griefe. **1600** SHAKS. *A.Y.L.* IV. iii. 174 Take a good heart, and counterfeit to be a man. **1663** BUTLER *Hud.* I. iii. 35 Took heart again and fac'd about, As if they meant to stand it out. **1840** DICKENS *Barn. Rudge* (Libr. ed.) II. ix. 76 Take heart, take heart. We'll find them.

**** *With another noun.*

50. heart and hand. (Also ***with h. and hand.***) With will and execution; readily, willingly.

a **1547** SURREY *Poems, Lover describeth* (Aldine) 79 And all the planets as they stand, I thank them too with heart and hand. **1847–78** HALLIWELL s.v., *To be heart and hand*, to be fully bent. **1884** *Times* (weekly ed.) 19 Sept. 5/3 The woman said she would have admitted me 'heart and hand', only that her orders were peremptory.

51. heart...heart.

a. ***heart of hearts*** (orig. more correctly, ***heart of heart, heart's heart***): the heart's core; the centre or depth of one's heart; one's inmost heart or feelings. Usually ***in one's heart of hearts.***

1602 SHAKS. *Ham.* III. ii. 78, I will weare him In my hearts Core: I, in my Heart of heart. **1605** SYLVESTER *Du Bartas* II. iii. III. Law 1287 O Israel..in thy heart's-heart (not in Marble) beare His ever-lasting Law. **1606** SHAKS. *Tr. & Cr.* IV. v. 171 From heart of very heart, great Hector welcome. *a* **1649** DRUMM. OF HAWTH. *Poems* Wks. (1711) 39/1 Him deep engrave In your heart's heart, from whom all good ye have. **1806** WORDSW. *Intim. Immort.* 190 Yet in my heart of hearts I feel your might. **1867** TROLLOPE *Chron. Barset* II. lxxiii. 293 That she should be admitted to his heart of hearts. **1895** *Q. Rev.* Oct. 298 In his heart of heart Froude would have admitted that.

b. ***a heart and a heart***, a Hebraism = duplicity, insincerity. (Cf. 6 b.)

c **825** *Vesp. Psalter* xi. 3 [xii. 2] Welure faecne in heortan and heortan spreocende. **1382** WYCLIF *Ps.* xi[i]. 2 Ther treccherous lippis in herte and herte speeken. **1583** HARSNET *Serm. Ezek.* (1658) 137 God doth abhor a Heart and a Heart, and his soule detesteth a double minded Man. **1611** BIBLE *1 Chron.* xii. 33 They were not of double heart [*Heb.* without a heart and a heart]. **1633** EARL MANCH. *Al Mondo* (1636) 86 A heart and a heart God cannot abide.

[***heart and part***: error for *art and part*: ART 16.]

c. ***heart-to-heart***: used to denote conversation, discussion, etc. of real frankness and sincerity; usually *attrib.* but also *absol.* as *sb.*

1867 *Mission Life* 1 Mar. 190 The visitation of an Australian Bishop..is a hand-to-hand and heart-to-heart visit to each Clergyman, and to his people with him. **1894** *Advance* 11 Oct., A kind of public religious 'orphanage', where no true heart-to-heart 'mothering'..was possible. **1902** A. H. LEWIS *Wolfville Days* xi. 152 He don't own no real business to transact; he's out to have a heart-to-heart interview with the great Southwest. **1902** KIPLING *Traffics & Discov.* (1904) 22 He began by a Lydia Pinkham heart-to-heart talk about my health. **1906** *Daily Chron.* 5 Mar. 6/4 A heart-to-heart discussion of the solar plexus and its part in the emotional economy of man. **1910** S. E. WHITE *Rules of Game* v. xvi. 444 Let's have a heart-to-heart, and find out how we stand. **1918** E. M. ROBERTS *Flying Fighter* 201 After a heart-to-heart talk, I induced him to let me remain in the Flying Service. **1925** WODEHOUSE *Carry on, Jeeves* ix. 221 He and Jeeves had had a heart-to-heart chat in the kitchen. **1934** J. E. NEALE *Queen Eliz.* ii. 31 Parry came back to have heart-to-heart talks with Mistress Ashley and to probe Elizabeth's mind. **1948** A. WAUGH *Unclouded Summer* xv. 252, I have the girls up there in the evenings for 'heart-to-hearts'. **1951** L. MACNEICE tr. *Goethe's Faust* 50 All this needs a little explaining And will keep till our next heart-to-heart. **1955** W. GADDIS *Recognitions* I. v. 180 Baby, I just make a few notes on them and write these heart-to-heart confessions.

52. heart and soul.

a. The whole of one's affections and energies; one's whole being.

1883 RITA *After Long Grief* xxvi. 160, I saw that you were mine, heart and soul, as ever. **1884** *Times* (Weekly ed.) 26 Sept. 6/2 The earnest actor who has heart and soul in his work.

b. *advb.* With all one's energy and devotion.

1798 COLERIDGE *Lett.* (1895) 261 Read it heart and soul. **1845** M. PATTISON *Ess.* (1889) I. 4 Entering heart and soul into the dust and heat of the Church's war with the world. **1888** BURGON *Lives 12 Gd. Men* II. xi. 329 He threw himself, heart and soul, into every requirement of the time.

c. *attrib.* Devoted and enthusiastic.

1836 DARWIN in *Life & Lett.* (1887) I. 275 The heart-and-soul manner in which he put himself in my place.

***** *In ejaculations of surprise and exclamatory invocations.*

53. † ***God's heart!***, † ***Ods heart!***, ***'s heart***, or simply † ***heart!*** (*obs.*). Also, ***for God's heart, heart of God!, Ads my heart!***, † ***my heart!*** (*obs.*), ***dear heart!*** The commonest expressions now are: ***Lord*** (***God***) ***bless my*** (***your***, etc.) ***heart!*** elliptically, ***bless my*** (etc.) ***heart!*** See BLESS *v.*[1] 9 and cf. LIFE, SOUL.

c **1386** CHAUCER *Miller's T.* 629 Help, water! water, help! for goddes herte. **1573** *New Custom* II. iii. in Hazl. *Dodsley* III. 37 Heart of God, man, be the means better or worse, I pass not. **1596** SHAKS. *1 Hen. IV*, III. i. 252 Heart! you swear like a comfit-maker's wife. **1605** *Tryall Chev.* III. i. in Bullen *O. Pl.* III. 306 S'hart, what a name's that! **1681** DRYDEN *Sp. Friar* II. i, Heart! you were hot enough, too hot, but now. **1701** CIBBER *Love makes Man* II. i. 27, I can't bear this! 'Sheart, I could cry for Madness! **1728** VANBR. & CIB. *Prov. Husb.* II. i. 42 Odsheart! this was so kindly done of you naw. **1732** FIELDING *Miser* v. i, Bless her heart! good lady! **1741** RICHARDSON *Pamela* I. 84 Ad's my Heart! I think it would be the best Thing. **1844** DICKENS *Christmas Carol* 161 Dear heart alive, how his niece by marriage started! **1862** MRS. SEWELL *Patience Hart* xxv. 166 Bless your heart, child; you are a good girl. **1886** MISS BROUGHTON *Dr. Cupid* II. vii. 164 She can no longer look upon me as a child, bless her old heart!

****** *Proverbial phrases and locutions.*

54. a. ***one's heart †is in*** (***at***) ***one's heel***(***s*** or ***hose***, † ***is at the bottom of***, or ***turns into, one's hose, sinks in one's shoes***, etc.; ludicrous intensifications of 'the heart sinks', connoting extreme fear or dejection. (See BOOT *sb.*[3] 1 b.) **b.** ***to have one's heart in one's mouth, one's heart leaps into one's mouth*** (***throat***), referring to the violent beating and apparent leaping of the heart under the influence of a sudden start. So, ***to bring one's h. into one's mouth, make one's h. leap out of one's mouth.*** **c.** † ***to wear one's h. in one's mouth***, † ***to have one's h. at one's tongue's end***: to be always ready to speak what is in one's mind. † ***to carry one's mouth in one's h.***: to do the opposite of this, to conceal one's thoughts, keep silence. **d.** ***one's h. is in its right place***: one's sympathies are rightly engaged, one means well. † **e.** ***to have one's h. upon one's pouch***: to be set upon one's private profit. **f.** ***to wear one's h. upon one's sleeve***: to expose one's feelings, wishes, intentions, etc. to every one. **g.** ***to do one's heart good***: to make one feel better, gladdened, strengthened, etc. (see also GOOD).

a. *c* **1430** *Hymns Virg.* 91 Myn herte fil doun vnto my too. **1546** J. HEYWOOD *Prov.* (1867) 30 Your hert is in your hose all in dispaire. **1548** UDALL *Erasm. Par. Luke* xxii. 174 b, Petur beeyng feared with this saiyng of a woman..as if his herte had been in his hele clene gon. **1563–87** FOXE *A. & M.* (1631) III. XI. 253/2 When the Bishop heard this, by and by his heart was in his heeles, and..he with the rest of the Court betooke them to their legges. *c* **1600** *Timon* I. v, My hart is at the bottome of my hose. **1642** [see BOOT *sb.*[3] 1 b.] **1682** N. O. tr. *Boileau's Lutrin.* II. 174 Chear up, and pluck thy Heart out of thy Hose! **1888** MRS. H. WARD *R. Elsmere* II. 153 An expression which sent the sister's heart into her shoes.

b. 1548 UDALL *Erasm. Par. Luke* xxiii. 199 Hauyng their herte at their verai mouth for feare, they did not belieue that it was Iesus. **1601** W. PARRY *Trav. Sir A. Sherley* 16 It had been an easie matter to have found a company of poore hearts neere their maisters mouthes. **1716** ADDISON *Drummer* I. i. (D.), I fell across a beam that lay in the way, and faith my heart was in my mouth; I thought I had stumbled over a spirit. **1809** W. IRVING *Knickerb.* (1861) 154 Antony..sounded a charge with such a tremendous outset ..that it was enough to make one's heart leap out of one's mouth only to be within a mile of it. **1856** WHYTE MELVILLE *Kate Cov.* xiii, A ring at the door-bell brings everybody's heart into everybody's mouth. **1887** EDNA LYALL *Knt.-Errant* xviii. 158 Francesca's heart leapt into her mouth.

c. *c* **1590** NASHE *Pasquil's Apol.* I. C ii b, I will carrie my mouth in my hart..there is a time for speech, and a time for silence. **1592** —— *P. Penilesse* Wks. 1883–4 II. 5 A hare braind little Dwarfe..that hath his hart at his tongues end.

d. *a* **1809** MALKIN tr. *Gil Blas* (K. O.), Heart lies in the right place. **1886** SCHMITZ tr. *Stinde's Buchholtz Fam.* 51 Your heart is in its right place; if only you had the right words on your tongue.

e. 1583 GOLDING *Calvin on Deut.* clxxxviii. 1171 Hee was such a one as had his tongue to sale, and his heart vppon his powche.

f. 1604 SHAKS. *Oth.* I. i. 64 'Tis not long after But I will weare my heart vpon my sleeue For Dawes to pecke at. **1862** SALA *Seven Sons* II. xi. 282 A..ready-tongued man, wearing..his heart upon his sleeve. **1891** SMILES *J. Murray* II. xxxiv. 449 He did not wear his heart upon his sleeve.

g. 1590 SHAKS. *Mids. N.* I. ii. 73, I will roare that I will doe any mans heart good to heare me. **1824** SCOTT *St. Ronan's* vii, It's done me muckle heart's good.

III. Attributive uses and Combinations.

55. a. *attrib.* Of, for, or pertaining to (*a*) the physical heart, as ***heart-action, attack, -beating, condition, -disease, failure, -murmur, -pulse, rate, -shape, -shock, -strain, -stroke, -tube, -valve, -wall***; (*b*) the heart as the seat of emotion, etc., as ***heart-agony, -anguish***, † ***-brest*** (= burst), ***-burst, -corruption, -grief, -grudge, -hardness, -hate, -heaviness, -ill, -lift*** (so ***-lifter***), ***-religion, -service, -sorrow, -springs, -worship, -wound***, etc., etc.; also, with vbl. sbs.: ***heart-bleeding, -heaving, -longing, -pining, -rising, -sinking***, etc.

1887 *Cassell's Fam. Mag.* July 467/2 A belladonna plaister ..to quieten pain and *heart-action. **1807** WORDSW. *White Doe Rylstone* II. 102 That dimness of *heart-agony. **1710** PHILIPS *Pastorals* IV. 162 Who can relieve *Heart-anguish sore. **1935** D. L. SAYERS *Gaudy Night* xxi. 444 She's had rather a nasty *heart-attack, but she's better now. **1593** NASHE *Christ's T.* Wks. 1883–4 IV. 248 This holy Father (with no little commiserate *hart-bleeding) beholding [etc.]. *c* **1340** *Cursor M.* 4283 (Trin.) What is more *herte brest þen want of þing þat men loue best. **1845** P. J. BAILEY *Festus* (ed. 2) 258 Like a horse Put to his *heart-burst speed, sobbing up hill. **1896** A. MORRISON *Child of Jago* xiii. 134 Dicky..had been afflicted to heart-burst by his father's dodging and running. *a* **1711** KEN *Psyche* Poet. Wks. 1721 IV. 211 To temper all the Sisters *Heart-complaints. **1946** *Mod. Lang. Notes* Nov. 442 *Heart condition. **1958** *Listener* 13 Nov. 778/2 Before cleaning a car..be certain you haven't a heart condition. **1971** D. O'CONNOR *Eye of Eagle* viii. 53 He has a heart condition—nothing very serious. **1878** BROWNING *La Saisiaz* 116 From the *heart-deeps where it slept. **1868** MILMAN *St. Paul's* xi. 275 Elizabeth had no.. comprehension of the *heart-depth of that Puritanism which thus opposed or slighted her mandates. **1864** TENNYSON *Sea Dreams* 264 He suddenly dropt dead of *heart disease. **1894** 'O. HENRY' *Compl. Wks.* (1928) 797 'Read this,' he said, 'here is proof that Marie Cusheau died of *heart failure.' **1906** *Lancet* 13 Jan. 96/2 Dr. C. Bolton.. read a paper entitled 'The Treatment of Heart Failure in Diphtheria'. **1960** I. A. STANTON *Dict. for Med. Secretaries* 68/1 Occasionally heart failure denotes a sudden cessation of heart action, but generally it merely means insufficient circulation. **1580** HOLLYBAND *Treas. Fr. Tong, Tristesse et douleur de cueur*, sorowe, or *hartgriefe. **1671** MILTON *Samson* 1339 In my midst of sorrow and heart-grief To show them feats, and play before their god. **1577–87** HOLINSHED *Chron.* I. 53/2 Which..was to them an occasion of *hartgrudge. *c* **1550** CHEKE *Matt.* xix. 8 Moosees did suffer iou to loos iour-selves from yo[r] wiifes for iour *harthardnes. **1863** A. B. GROSART *Small Sins* (ed. 2) 50 *note*, The gushing lip-kindness with heart-hardness of many. **1875** TENNYSON *Q. Mary* III. iv, A fierce resolve and fixt *heart-hate. *a* **1806** FOX *Hist. Jas. II*, iii. 210 (Jod.) With a *heart-hatred of popery, prelacy, and all superstition. **1600** SHAKS. *A.Y.L.* v. ii. 51 The more shall I to morrow be at the height of *heart heauinesse. **1751** SMOLLETT *Per. Pic.* (1779) I. viii. 65 Frequent palpitations, *heart-heavings, and alterations of countenance. **1678** BUNYAN *Pilgr.* 115 A life of holiness, *heart-holiness. **1892** G. E. WOODBERRY *Introd. Lamb's Elia* p. xiii, That mournful fancy, that affection for things unrealized, which betray *heart-hunger. *a* **1605** MONTGOMERIE *Flyting w. Polwart* 302 The hunger, the *hart-ill, and the hoist still thee hald. **1893** 'MARK TWAIN' in *Cosmopolitan* Nov. 61/2 Oh, the *heart-lift that was in those words! **1967** 'LA MERI' *Sp. Dancing* (ed. 2) 7 Yet who can reflect in the immutable phrase the heartlift in watching emotion in motion? **1901** KIPLING *Kim* x. 260 You will find one small silver amulet..a *heart-lifter. **1959** *New Statesman* 25 Apr. 576/3 The heart-lifter that I chanced to hear was well up to her standard. **1884** HUDSON *Stud. Wordsw.* 243 The head-logic grows so out of proportion as to stifle and crush the *heart-logic. **1742** YOUNG *Nt. Th.* VI. 263 *Heart-merit wanting, mount we ne'er so high, Our Height is but the Gibbet of our name. **1798** SOTHEBY tr. *Wieland's Oberon* (1826) II. 21, I, who in every *heart-pulse feel her glow. **1936** *Discovery* 291/2 Adrenalin, by increasing the *heart rate..facilitates the passage of the current. **1961** *Lancet* 22 July 190/1 An increase in heart-rate may also

increase potassium efflux. **1758** *S. Hayward's Serm.* p. viii, How truly his mind was bent in pursuit of *heart-religion. **1583** GOLDING *Calvin on Deut.* xxxvii. 222 Ye must looke whether ye haue not some *hartrisings and eagernesse in you. **1668** *Phil. Trans.* III. 859 The Interception of the *Heart-sap may have an effect analogous to the boring at the Heart. **1842** W. HOWITT *Rural & Dom. Life Germany* v. 62 The gingerbread was all made up into *heart-shapes. **1863** G. SETON *Law Her. Scotl.* v. 192 This form.. tending to the pear-shape and heart-shape. **1850** ROBERTSON *Serm.* Ser. III. vi. (1864) 95 The man who has received the *heart-shock from which.. he will not recover. **1660** BAXTER *Call Unconverted* 158 They charge them with *heart-sins, which none can see but God. **1842** MANNING *Serm.* (1848) I. 38 A heart-sin, indulged in secret, which eats into their whole spiritual life. **1743** D. BRAINERD *Let.* 30 Apr. in J. Edwards *Life D. B.* (1765) 265 There seems to be little of the special workings of the divine Spirit among them yet; which gives me many a *heart-sinking hour. **1879** CHR. ROSSETTI *Seek & F.* 312 Moments of keenest fear and utmost heart-sinking. **1903** B. HARRADEN *Kath. Frensham* xviii. 278 She, with.. perseverance, dug a hole in their frozen *heart-springs. **1907** KIPLING *Bk. of Words* (1928) 36 A people.. whose heart-springs go down deep into the fabric. **1906** *Med. Ann.* 241 *Heart-strain in growing boys. **1909** *Daily Chron.* 21 Aug. 6/2 Heartstrain and contraction of the joints. **1887** T. HARDY *Woodlanders* III. xxi, They could read each other's *heart-symptoms like books. **1509** HAWES *Past. Pleas.* XVI. xxii, To devyde my joye and my *hert torment. **1881** *Trans. Obstetr. Soc. Lond.* XXII. 78 An abnormal amount of tension on the primitive *heart-tube. **1932** *Gray's Anat.* (ed. 25) 1437 *Heart valves. **1963** *Daily Tel.* 21 Sept. 9/5 (*heading*) Heart valve operation. *Ibid.*, The limited number of heart valve replacement operations so far carried out. **1856** R. A. VAUGHAN *Mystics* (1860) I. 21 *Heart-weariness, the languishing longing for repose. *c* **1400** *Destr. Troy* 10979 Pantasilia.. Hit hym so heturly with a *hert wille, þat he hurlit down hedlonges to the hard erthe. **1630** SANDERSON *Serm.* II. 262 The lip-worship they may have.. but the *heart-worship they shall never have. **1839** P. J. BAILEY *Festus* 269 Her *heart-wound. **1902** *Temple Bar* CXXVI. 111 It rained upon his bleeding heart-wound like balm. **1906** *Westm. Gaz.* 3 Aug. 10/2 The faint, fine smell of new-mown grass Stabs like a heart-wound as I pass.

b. *objective* and *objective genitive*, as ***heart-biting, -conner, -disposer, -searcher, -wringing*** sbs.; ***heart-affecting, -cheering, -dulling, -easing, -freezing, -fretting, -hardening, -holding, -melting, -moving, -purifying, -shaking, -sickening, -stirring, -swelling, -tearing, -warming, -wounding, -wringing***, etc., etc., adjs.

1829 I. TAYLOR *Enthus.* v. (1867) 101 The *heart-affecting elements of piety and virtue. **1587** GOLDING *De Mornay* xii. 166 Consider.. the *hart-bitings.. which he indureth. **1659** D. PELL *Impr. Sea* 304 One of the dreadfullest, and *heart-bleedingest conditions that can bee seen. **1644** VICARS *Jehovah-Jireh* 5 The Suns.. *heart-cheering bright beams. **1781** COWPER *Hope* 714 In darkness and *heart-chilling fears. **1563** MAN *Musculus' Commonpl.* 45 a, He that made man.. is aptly called Cardiognostes, that is, The *hart-conner. **1645** QUARLES *Sol. Recant.* v. 67 The *heart-corroding Fangs Of griping Care. **1654** TRAPP *Comm. Esther* v. 2 God the great *Heart-disposer so ordered it. **1593** SHAKS. *Lucr.* 1782 *Heart-easing words. **1632** MILTON *L'Allegro* 13 In Heav'n ycleap'd Euphrosyne, And by men, heart-easing Mirth. **1621** BURTON *Anat Mel.* I. ii. IV. v, Sequestred from all company, but *heart-eating melancholy. **1730–46** THOMSON *Autumn* 40 A gayly-checker'd *heart-expanding view. **1596** SPENSER *F.Q.* IV. v. 45 Disquiet and *hart-fretting payne. **1748** SMOLLETT *Rod. Rand.* lxi. (1804) 439 *Heart-gnawing cares corrode my pensive breast. **1607** SHAKS. *Cor.* IV. i. 25 Thou hast oft beheld *Heart-hardning spectacles. **1897** J. L. ALLEN *Choir Invisible* xvi. 240 Universal fellowship with seeding grass and breeding herb and every *heart-holding creature of the woods. **1913** E. F. BENSON *Thorley Weir* iv, Things fairer and more heart-holding. *a* **1711** KEN *Hymnotheo* Poet. Wks. 1721 III. 112 *Heart-melting Zeal. **1784** BURNS *Commonpl. Bk.* Sept., There is.. a heart-melting tenderness, in some of our ancient ballads. **1593** DRAYTON *Essex* Wks. 1753 II. 590 *Heart-moving music. **1581** SIDNEY *Apol. Poetrie* (Arb.) 23 This *hart-rauishing knowledge. **1594** SPENSER *Amoretti* xxxix, A melting pleasance.. me revived with *hart-robbing gladnesse. **1907** *Tatler* 22 May 132/2 A *heart-shaking tragedy. **1911** KIPLING *Diversity of Creatures* (1917) 130 The heart-shaking jests of Decay. **1918** V. WOOLF in *Times Lit. Suppl.* 31 Jan. 55/1 Effective and heart-shaking ghost stories. **1945** W. S. CHURCHILL *Victory* (1946) 223 The decision.. remained nevertheless a heart-shaking risk. **1814** SCOTT *Wav.* xxvii, The long and *heart-sickening griefs which attend a rash and ill-assorted marriage. **1820** *Edin. Monthly Rev.* Apr. 449 Can anything be more heart-sickening to such a philanthropist? **1902** *London Mag.* VIII. 432/2 It was heart-sickening, as his great form with its yellow skin and black stripes, as his blazing eyes, his flashing teeth and his outspread claws rose toward us through the air. **1848** BLAKEY *Free-w.* 91 These *heart-stirring and delightful emotions. **1814** JANE AUSTEN *Mansf. Park* III. vi, Her happiness was of a quiet, deep, *heart-swelling sort. **1884** W. JAMES *Coll. Ess. & Rev.* (1920) 258 In listening to poetry.. we are often surprised at the.. heart-swelling and the lachrymal effusion that unexpectedly catch us. **1916** 'BOYD CABLE' *Action Front* 149 Thirty-six solid hours of physical stress and *heart-tearing strain. **1920** *Glasgow Herald* 21 Oct. 6 The latest phases of the heart-tearing Irish tragedy. **1590** SPENSER *F.Q.* III. ii. 5 With *hart-thrilling throbs and bitter stowre. **1580** SIDNEY *Arcadia* III. (1724) II. 431 What a *heart-tickling joy it is. **1899** *Daily News* 20 Apr. 5/7 They are a *heart-warming cordial. **1966** *Times* (Austral. Suppl.) 28 Mar. p. viii/4 Perth.. friendly enough to give.. migrants.. a heartwarming impression of their new country. **1872** BLACK *Adv. Phaeton* xxiii. 327 What bitterness and grievous *heart-wringing. **1932** H. CRANE *Let.* 12 Apr. (1965) 408 The Mexican singer.. is generally shrill but capable of heart-wringing vibrations.

c. *locative* and *instrumental*. In, at, from, with the heart; as to the heart: as ***heart-blow; heart-angry, -burdened, -chilled, -deadened, -dear, -deep, -drawn, -free, -full, -happy, -hardened, -heavy, -hungry, -sorrowing, -true, -weary, -wounded, -wrung***, etc., adjs.; ***heart-eat*** vb.

1622 MABBE tr. *Aleman's Guzman D'Alf.* II. 160, I was *heart-angry with my selfe, that I had told him so much. **1731** MEDLEY *Kolben's Cape G. Hope* I. 362 The *coup-de-grace*, or *heart-blow, as it is called, not being given them, they were taken alive from the wheel. **1646** CRASHAW *Delights Muses* (1652) 102 The *heart-bred lustre of his worth. **1597** SHAKS. *2 Hen. IV*, II. iii. 12 My *heart-deere-Harry. **1609** ARMIN *Maids of More-Cl.* (1880) 100 It is my loue.. that makes me step *Heart-deepe in disobedience to my mother. **1871** SWINBURNE *Songs bef. Sunrise, Blessed among Women* 106 Heavens own heart-deep blue. **1851** D. JERROLD *St. Giles* xi. 111 A deep, *heart-drawn sigh broke from him. **1630** BRATHWAIT *Eng. Gentlem.* (1641) 197 They.. cannot see.. anything which likes them, but with a greedy eye they *heart-eat it. **1830** I. TAYLOR *Unitar.* 111 *Heart-fallen and sick of the profitless usages of devotion. **1748** RICHARDSON *Clarissa* (1811) II. 167 If indeed she be hitherto innocent and *heart-free. **1886** W. S. GILBERT *Ruddigore* (1887) 4 Rose is still heart-free. **1876** T. HARDY *Ethelberta* (1890) 168 She was *heartfull of many emotions. **1623** PENKETHMAN *Handf. Hon.* IV. i, If thou would'st be *heart-happy, wealth despise. **1661** R. DAVENPORT *City Night-cap* I. in Hazl. *Dodsley* XIII. 107 She that is lip-holy Is many times *heart-hollow. **1591** GREENE *Maiden's Dreame* xlii, *Heart-holy men he still kept at his table. **1880** W. S. GILBERT *Patience* 15 Do you know what it is to be *heart-hungry? **1727–46** THOMSON *Summer* 892 The *heart-shed tear, th' ineffable delight Of sweet humanity. **1594** SHAKS. *Rich. III*, II. ii. 112 You clowdy Princes, and *hart-sorowing-Peeres. **1601** CHESTER *Love's Mart.*, *K. Arth.* xcvii, *Heart swolne heauinesse. **1602** WARNER *Alb. Eng.* XI. lxviii, And theare did him the *heart trew King most kindly intertaine. **1840** MRS. NORTON *Dream* 12 Sinking *heart-weary, far away from home. **1791** BURNS *Ae Fond Kiss* in *Wks.* (1871) 294 Deep in *heart-wrung tears I'll pledge thee. **1820** *Ellen Fitzarthur* 93 Floods of heart-wrung tears. **1948** C. DAY LEWIS *Poems 1943–47* 70 One heart-wrung phantom still.. Shadows my noontime still.

d. *similative*, as ***heart-fashioned, -leaved*** adjs. Also HEART-SHAPED.

1756 SIR J. HILL *Brit. Herbal* 359 The lower lip.. is short, broad, and heart-fashioned. **1822–34** *Good's Study Med.* (ed. 4) I. 630 The three species of cinchona.. the lance-leaved.. heart leaved.. and oblong leaved.

56. a. Special Combs.: †**heart-bag**, the pericardium; **heart-balm**, (*a*) something that soothes a person's emotions; (*b*) *U.S. slang*, alimony; **heart-bearer**, †(*a*) a name of the Franciscan friars; (*b*) a name of the moth *Anorta cordigera*; **heart-bird**, the Turnstone, *Strepsilas interpres* (*U.S.*); **heart-block** [BLOCK *sb.* 19 d] *Med.* (see quot. 1906); **heart brass**, a brass sepulchral tablet in which a heart is represented (see quot. 1912); **heart-cake**, a heart-shaped cake; **heart-cam** (see quot.); **heart-clot**, a clot of blood or fibrin formed in the heart, usually after death; **heart-cockle**, a bivalve mollusc, *Isocordia cor*, so called from its shape; **heart-hurry** *Med.*, tachycardia (see also quot. 1897); †**heart-lath**, a lath made from the heartwood of the oak; **heart-line** *Palmistry* = *line of the heart* (LINE *sb.*[2] 8 b); **heart-lung** *attrib.*, involving or consisting of the heart and the lungs, esp. when removed together for physiological experimentation; ***heart-lung machine***, a machine to which a patient's blood supply is connected during an operation and which by-passes and takes over the functions of the heart and the lungs; **heart-moth**, the moth *Dicycla Oo*; **heart-motion**, the motion generated by a heart-cam; **heart-net, -piece** (see quots.); †**heart-pit**, the hollow in the middle of the breast at the bottom of the breast-bone; †**heart-purse, heart-sac**, the pericardium; **heart-rot**, a disease which causes decay in the heart of a tree; also, a fungous disease of beetroots etc.; **hearts-and-flowers** orig. *U.S.*, undue sentimentality, cloying sweetness; also *attrib.*; **heart-seine, -shake** (see quots.); **heart-shell** = *heart-cockle*; †**heart-side**, the left side; **heart-sound** (see quots.); **heart-strand**, the central strand of a rope: cf. 18 b; †**heart-strength**, the central strength or fortress; **heart-stroke**, (*a*) the impulse of the contraction of the heart, apex-beat; (*b*) = angina pectoris; **heart-talk**, a heart-to-heart talk; **heart-thimble** (*Naut.*), a heart-shaped thimble; **heart-throb**, (*a*) *lit.* a pulsation of the heart; (*b*) *colloq.* (orig. *U.S.*) something or (esp.) someone that thrills the heart, a lover: freq. used of film stars and other entertainers; also *attrib.*; **heart-trace**, 'the record on smoked paper made by the needle of a cardiograph' (*Syd. Soc. Lex.*); **heart transplant**, an operation in which a heart from one person is transplanted into the body of another; similarly of two animals; a heart so transplanted; also *attrib.* and *fig.*; **heart-urchin**, a sea-urchin of the genus *Spatangus*, being heart-shaped; a spatangoid; **heart-warm** *a.*, warm-hearted, genuinely affectionate; **heart-wheel** = *heart-cam*; †**heart-white**, the white spot on a butt or target; **heart-worm**, a parasitic nematode worm which infests the hearts of some carnivores, or the disease caused by this worm; also *transf.*; **heart-yarn**, the soft yarn in the centre of a rope.

1668 CULPEPPER & COLE *Barthol. Anat.* II. vi. 100 The Watry Vapors of both the Ventricles, are congealed into the water of the *Heart-bag. **1922** JOYCE *Ulysses* 352 There were wounds that wanted healing with *heartbalm. **1938** WODEHOUSE *Summer Moonshine* x. 126 This Miss Prudence Whittaker is suing this T. P. Vanringham for breach of promise and heart balm. **1561** DAUS tr. *Bullinger on Apoc.* (1573) 116 b, The secte of the Fryers Minors (otherwyse called *hartbearers). **1844** DE KAY *Zool. N. York* II. 216 Known under the name of Brant-bird, *Heart-bird, Horse-foot Snipe, and Beach-bird. **1903** *Lancet* 22 Aug. 523/1 The jugular pulsations correspond to independent auricular contractions which are not propagated to the ventricles—a state of '*heart-block'. **1906** *Brit. Med. Jrnl.* 27 Oct. 1107/1 The term 'heart-block' is applied to that condition where the stimulus for contraction passing from auricle to ventricle, is stopped or 'blocked' on account of some defect in those muscle fibres. **1966** *Lancet* 31 Dec. 1441/1 Patients who had partial heart block while on P.G.I. therapy alone.. reverted to sinus rhythm. **1971** *Jrnl. Gen. Psychol.* Jan. 13 Magnesium sulphate was superior to sodium amytal and ether. Its main drawback was its tendency to produce heart block. **1907** H. W. MACKLIN *Brasses of England* VIII. 205 The typical form of a *heart brass is seen when this device is placed by itself in the midst of a monumental slab. **1912** J. S. M. WARD *Brasses* 80 Heart brasses proper fall into two main divisions: (*a*) plain, sometimes inscribed or with scrolls, (*b*) held by hands, usually coming out of a cloud. **1956** A. C. BOUQUET *Church Brasses* VII. 114 There is a large heart brass at Melton Mowbray, Leicestershire. **1756** MRS. BROOKE *Old Maid* No. 36 (1764) 294 Delicate *heart-cakes, a penny a-piece. **1885** *Old Lond. Cries* 29 'Spanish Chestnuts'; 'Ripe Turkey Figs'; 'Heart Cakes'. **1875** KNIGHT *Dict. Mech.*, **Heart-cam*, a form of cam which serves for the conversion of uniform rotary motion into uniform rectilinear reciprocating motion. **1874** DUNGLISON *Med. Dict.* s.v. *Polypus*, Fibrinous concretions found in the heart, *Heart clots. **1854** WOODWARD *Mollusca* II. 300 The *heart-cockle burrows in sand by means of its foot. **1891** *Lancet* 18 July 118/2 (*title*) Paroxysmal *heart hurry associated with visceral disorders. **1897** *Med. Times & Hosp. Gaz.* XXV. 33/2 By acceleration of the heart or 'heart-hurry', is meant a persistent increase of the pulse above eighty in a woman, well above seventy beats per minute in a man, and above ninety in a child. Heart-hurry is divided into two kinds; they are tachycardia and palpitation. **1479** *Churchw. Acc. St. Mary Hill, Lond.* (Nichols 1797) 94 For 4 cwts. of *Hertlaths. **1617** in Willis & Clark *Cambridge* (1886) I. 205 The studies to bee lathed with hart lath. **1727** BRADLEY *Fam. Dict.* s.v. *Building*, Heart Laths of Oak are one shilling and ten pence a bundle or hundred. **1893** BEERBOHM *Let.* 14 Oct. (1964) 76 He has no *heart-line on his right hand. **1894** 'MARK TWAIN' in *Century Mag.* Feb. 554/2 Wilson began to study Luigi's palm, tracing life lines, heart lines, head lines, and so on. **1956** N. D. FORD *Life in your Hands* v. 40 The Head and Heart lines join in forming one straight line.. The Fate line begins well clear of the Heart line. **1912** *Jrnl. Physiol.* XLV. 213 The *heart-lung preparation should serve therefore for investigations on the normal gaseous metabolism of the heart. *Ibid.* 214 The apparatus consisted of the heart-lung circulation apparatus as described by Knowlton and Starling, and of a respiration apparatus. **1925** *Ibid.* LX. 103 (*title*) A closed circuit heart lung preparation. **1945** *Amer. Jrnl. Physiol.* CXLIV. 191 No details of the experiments on the heart-lung preparation need be presented. *Ibid.*, The results of the thirty-two heart lung experiments can be summarized as follows. **1959** *Daily Tel.* 24 Apr. 13/3 In the party is Dr. Denis Melrose, inventor of the heart-lung machine which bears his name. This makes possible the by-passing of heart and lungs, and enables the operating surgeon to work on a heart which is bloodless, clear and stopped. **1961** *Lancet* 22 July 187/1 (*heading*) Variable atrial venting for the Melrose heart-lung machine. **1968** J. H. BURN *Lect. Notes Pharmacol.* (ed. 9) 37 Another way of demonstrating the action of ouabain on the ventricular contraction is in the heart-lung preparation of the dog. **1869** E. NEWMAN *Brit. Moths* 381 The *Heart Moth.. appears on the wing in July, and has occurred in the New Forest. **1829** E. IRVING *Tales Times Mart.* in *Anniversary* 283 Her spinning wheel was of the upright construction, having no heck, but a moveable eye which was carried along the pirn by a *heart-motion. **1884** KNIGHT, *Dict. Mech.* Suppl., **Heart-Net*, a [fishing] net with a leader and a bowl or pound, between which is a heart-shaped funnel. **1884** F. J. BRITTEN *Watch & Clockm.* (ed. 4) 121 **Heart Piece*, a heart-shaped cam used in chronographs to cause the chronograph hand to fly back to zero. **13..** *K. Alis.* 2250 He hit him thorugh theo *heorte put. **1615** CROOKE *Body of Man* 426 Hee thinketh that the water which is found in the *heart purse is a portion of our drinke. **1847** J. BROWN *Forester* v. 193 That disease, now so prevalent among our larch plantations, generally termed the **heart-rot* —or, as some writers term it, *dry-rot*. **1882** *Encycl. Brit.* XIV. 311/2 A far more formidable enemy [of larches] is the disease known as the 'heart-rot'. **1909** *Cent. Dict.* Suppl. 571/2 *Heart-rot*.. of beets. **1919** W. E. HILEY *Fungal Dis. Common Larch* v. 80 Heart-rot of trees is caused by fungi which grow saprophytically on the dead wood. **1945** *New Biol.* I. 52 Heart rot of swedes. **1955** AUDEN *Shield of Achilles* I. 19 An oak with heart-rot. **1968** *Gloss. Terms Timber Preservation* (*B.S.I.*) 10 *Heart rot*, a type of decay characteristically confined to the heart-wood. **1896** *Daily News* 29 Dec. 3/2 The heart had been slowly bleeding into the pericardium or '*heart-sac'.. and no help would have availed to save her life. [**1908** A. WOOLLCOTT *Lett.* (1946) 13 Taking dinner with the mother of the girl I hope to marry some day, and she played '*Hearts and Flowers' for me.] **1942** BERREY & VAN DEN BARK *Amer. Thes. Slang* §265.1 *Sentimentality*, hearts and flowers. **1964** *Times* 16 Apr. 6/7 We are nearly betrayed into a hearts-and-flowers ending in domestic compromise. **1967** *Listener* 11 May 626/2 Hearts-and-flowers confrontations between.. pop singer.. and a girl friend. **1884** KNIGHT *Dict. Mech.* Suppl., **Heart Seine* (Fishing), a species of seine, with a leader, heart, and pound secured by stakes so that the upper edge is floated at the surface and the lower touches the bottom. **1875** LASLETT *Timber* 25 Timber having much *heart-shake. **1884** *Spon's*

Mech. Own Bk. (1886) 167 'Heartshakes': splits or clefts in the centre of the tree; common in nearly every kind of timber. **1753** CHAMBERS *Cycl. Supp.*, *Heart-shells..always expressing what we call the figure of a Heart. **1580** SIDNEY *Arcadia* III. (1724) II. 664 Closing her eyes, and turning upon her *heart-side. **1876** *Clin. Soc. Trans.* IX. 111 *Heart-sounds were clean and free from murmur. **1886** *Syd. Soc. Lex.*, *H[eart] sounds* .. are two in number, one dull and prolonged, the other shorter, sharper, and terminating more abruptly. They have been likened to the syllables tŭb, dŭp. *c* **1860** H. STUART *Seaman's Catech.* 52 The standing rigging is often made with four strands and a *heart strand. **1618** BOLTON *Florus* III. x. (1636) 205 Then assaulting the *heart-strengths of the Warre, he destroyed Avaricum. **1860** *Chambers's Encycl.* I. 254 Subject to fits of the *heart-stroke. **1874** DUNGLISON *Med. Dict.* s.v. *Heart*, The Beating or Impulse of the heart, Heart-stroke, Apex beat..against the parietes of the chest is mainly caused by the systole of the heart, which tends to project forwards. **1912** F. M. HUEFFER *Panel* I. ii. 31, I want a regular—what you might call—*heart-talk with Miss Delamere. **1882** NARES *Seamanship* (ed. 6) 37 The shroud is turned in round a *heart thimble. **1839** P. J. BAILEY *Festus* 62 We should count time by *heart-throbs. **1846** WHITTIER *Lines* 2 He.. felt the heart-throb of the free. **1908** *Modern Song Favorites: High Voices* 2 (*title*) Heart-Throbs. **1912** J. LONDON *Let.* 19 Nov. (1966) 368 I've not much heart-throb left for my fellow beings. **1914** G. BURGESS *Burgess Unabridged* 7 The 'jacket' of the 'latest' fiction..tells of 'thrills' and 'heart-throbs'. **1926** *Atlantic Monthly* Mar. 390/1 Word has gone out to the writers..that the heart throb is what the reading world now pulsates to. **1928** J. P. MCEVOY *Show Girl* (title-p.), Cast... Also..the Heart-throb Poet. **1930** WODEHOUSE *Very Good, Jeeves* ix. 227 She has got that way..from a lifetime of writing heart-throb fiction for the masses. **1943** 'A. A. FAIR' *Double or Quits* (1949) vii. 72 She's easy on the eyes, but she's a little too anxious to have it understood I'm her heart throb. **1958** G. MITCHELL *Spotted Hemlock* ii. 16 He was quite a heart-throb, you know. **1959** D. DU MAURIER *Breaking Point* 202 A heart-throb, a lover, someone with wide shoulders and no hips. **1966** *Listener* 23 June 911/2 Rudolph Valentino was the great heart-throb of the silent screen in the nineteen-twenties. **1952** *Surg. Forum 1951* 217 An arterial supply from the host was anastomosed to a pulmonary vein of the *heart transplant and an outlet for the left ventricular output of the heart transplant was provided. **1960** *Ibid.* X. 103 Forty-eight puppy heart transplants are reported. **1963** *Surg. Gynecol. & Obstetrics* CXVII. 361/2 If a renal graft fails to function for several days after transplantation, the host can be supported by dialysis. A heart transplant at the present time enjoys no such privilege and must function vigorously immediately. **1967** *Times* 4 Dec. 1/7 The heart transplant operation, the first in the world, took Groote Schuur's surgical team five hours. **1968** *Guardian* 11 Sept. 1/5 Some of the gravest criticisms yet were yesterday levelled against the over-eagerness of heart-transplant surgeons to get hold of donors. **1973** *N.Y. Times Bk. Rev.* 21 Jan. 2 It is a real heart-transplant into English of the great Alexandrian love-poet and voluptuary. **1843** EMBLETON in *Proc. Berw. Nat. Club* II. No. 11. 51 *Amphidotus cordatus.* Common *Heart Urchin. **1855** KINGSLEY *Glaucus* (1878) 167 The great purple heart-urchin (*Spatangus purpureus*), clothed in pale lilac horny spines. **1787** BURNS *Farew. Brethren St. James's Lodge*, Adieu! a *heart-warm, fond adieu! **1834** M. SCOTT *Cruise Midge* (1863) 200 A shout of heartwarm and heart-felt gratitude. **1806** O. GREGORY *Mech.* (1807) II. 203 *Heart wheel is the name given in England to a well-known method of converting a circular motion into an alternating rectilinear one..contrived we believe by Sir Samuel Morland about the year 1685. **1875** *Ure's Dict. Arts* III. 997 The periphery of the heart-wheel..is seen to bear upon friction wheels. **1600** *Look about You* xiv. in Hazl. *Dodsley* VII. 426 Ay, there's the But, whose *heart-white if we hit, The game is ours. **1888** J. S. STALLYBRASS tr. J. Grimm's *Teut. Mythol.* IV. 1659 Stories of the *heart-worm. *Ibid.* 1660 The miser's heart-worm. **1955** W. W. DENLINGER *Compl. Boston* 94 Heart worms..in dogs are rare. **1957** *Encycl. Brit.* XVI. 207/2 *Dirofilaria immitis* (cause of heartworm in dogs). **1959** *Listener* 5 Nov. 796/1 The professional intimate, the confidential heart-worm with the hypodermic technique, is one of the horrors of television. **1965** E. J. L. SOULSBY *Textbk. Vet. Clin. Path.* I. iv. 100 *Dirofilaria immitis* is the heartworm and is parasitic in the.. dog, fox, wolf and various other wild carnivores. **1867** SMYTH *Sailor's Word-bk.* s.v., The *heart-yarn or centre, on which four-stranded rope is formed.

b. In names of trees and plants: **heart-cherry**, a heart-shaped variety of the cultivated cherry; **heart-clover**, *Medicago maculata*; **heart-leaf**, (*a*) = prec.; (*b*) an American species of *Limnanthemum*, also called *floating heart*; **heart-liver** = *heart-clover*; †**heart-nut**, a name for the Cashew-nut, *Anacardium*; **heart of the earth**, a popular name of Self-heal, *Prunella vulgaris*; **heart-pea**, **heart-seed**, a name for plants of the genus *Cardiospermum*, especially of *C. Helicacabum*, from the heart-shaped scar which marks the attachment of the seed; †**heart-trefoil** = *heart-clover*.

1596 GERARDE *Catal. Arborum* (1876) 29 *C[erasus] cordata maiora.* Great *hart Cherrie. **1655** MOUFET & BENNET *Health's Improv.* (1746) 294 Heart-Cherries, because they are made like a Heart..are the firmest of all other. *c* **1000** *Sax. Leechd.* I. 16 *Herba chamedris* þæt is *heortclœfre. **1794** Heart-clover [see CLOVER *sb.* 2]. **1854** THOREAU *Walden* ix. (1886) 178 A few small *heart-leaves and potamogetons. **1794** MARTYN *Flora Rustica* III. lxxvi, *Heart Medick*.. others call it Heart Claver or Clover, which has been corrupted into *Heart Liver. **1568** TURNER *Herbal* III. 51 Anacardium maye be called in Englishe *Hartnut of the likenes that it hath with an hart. **1597** GERARDE *Herbal* II. lii. §2. 271 The blacke winter Cherrie is called..in English the Indian hart, or *hart Pease. **1731–68** MILLER *Gard. Dict.*, *Cardiospermum*, Hart Pea; by the inhabitants of America called Wild Parsley. *Ibid.*, *Heart-seed with smooth leaves. **1866** *Treas. Bot.* 222 The common Heartseed..sometimes called also Winter Cherry, or Heart Pea. **1597** GERARDE *Herbal* (1633) 1189 The *Hart Trefoile hath..leaues ioined together by three on little slender foot-stalks, euery little leafe of the fashion of a heart, whereof it took his name. **1656** W. COLES *Art of Simpling* 89 Heart Trefoyle is so called.. also because each Leafe containes the perfect Icon of an Heart, and that in its proper colour, viz. a flesh colour.

heart (hɑːt), *v.* Forms: 1 hyrtan, hiertan, 3 hirten, 3–5 hert(e-n, 5–6 hart, 6– heart. [OE. *hiertan*, *hyrtan*:—**hertjan*, **heortjan*, f. *hert*, *heort*, HEART *sb.* (Cf. MHG. *herzen*, MDu. *herten* in same sense.)]

1. *trans.* To give heart to, put heart into (a person, etc.); to inspire with confidence, embolden, encourage, inspirit, animate; = HEARTEN 1. *arch.*

c **897** K. ÆLFRED *Gregory's Past.* viii. 53 Mid oðrum worde he hierte. *c* **1205** LAY. 25941 Beduer heo gon hirten mid hendeliche woorden. *c* **1250** *Gen. & Ex.* 1980 His sunes comen..And hertedin him. *a* **1300** *Cursor M.* 27296 þat þe preist..hert þe sinful wel. *c* **1400** *Ywaine & Gaw.* 1889 He herted so his cumpany, The moste coward was ful hardy. *c* **1410** LOVE *Bonavent. Mirr.* 115 (Gibbs MS.) þis one thyng schulde stire & herte þin intencioun. **1540** HYRDE tr. *Vives' Instr. Chr. Wom.* (1592) Cj, Those that bee apt, should bee harted and encouraged. **1580** SIDNEY *Arcadia* III. Wks. 372 Growing now so hearted in his resolution. **1681** COLVIL *Whigs Supplic.* (1751) 189 To sing and pray.. hearts them more when danger comes, Than others trumpets and their drums. **1830** TENNYSON *Poems* 33 A grief not uninformed and dull, Hearted with hope.

b. Const. *to* and *inf.*, or *subord. cl.*

1398 TREVISA *Barth. De P.R.* XVIII. i. (1495) 737 All beestys of the erthe ben..hertyd to gendre. *c* **1449** PECOCK *Repr.* II. v. 165 That he mai therbi be hertid..for to serue God. **1450–1530** *Myrr. our Ladye* 262 Martyrs she harted to suffer ioyfully trybulacyons. **1600** FAIRFAX *Tasso* IX. liii. 169 Harting the Pagans that they shrinked not. **1848** *Fraser's Mag.* XXXVIII. 315 It was long before I was hearted to herd again in the woods by myself.

†**2.** To supply with physical strength or stimulus; to put (land) into good heart. Cf. HEARTEN *v.* 3 b, HEART *sb.* 21. *Obs.*

1573 TUSSER *Husb.* xlviii. (1878) 106 The land is well harted with helpe of the fold, for one or two crops.

3. To take to heart, establish or fix in the heart. (See also HEARTED 5.)

1604 SHAKS. *Oth.* I. iii. 373, I hate the Moore. My cause is hearted; thine hath no lesse reason. **1633** T. ADAMS *Exp. 2 Peter* ii. 6 There is one thing, if we hear it, and heart it, enough to fright us all.

b. To establish as central or essential. *rare.*

1884 BROWNING *Ferishtah, Two Camels* 84 The richness hearted in such joy Is in the knowing what are gifts we give.

†**c.** To utter with the heart or sincerely. *Obs.*

1642 S. ASHE *Best Refuge for Oppresed* 48 It will not be sufficient to say a Prayer..or to word it before the Lord; but we should rather heart it before God in holy prayer.

4. *Building.* To fill up the central space within (a piece of masonry) with rubble or similar material. Also with *in*.

1776 G. SEMPLE *Building in Water* 49 We..laid a Course of large flat Stones, and filled and hearted them in close about the Pile. *Ibid.* 79 They hearted their Walls with their Spawls and smallest Stones. **1892** *Gd. Words* Feb. 103/1 It was enough to 'heart' the embankment with clay, and protect it outside with heavy stonework.

5. *intr.* Of a plant, *esp.* cabbage, lettuce, etc.: To form a 'heart' or close compact head; to have the leaves growing into a firm dense globe.

1866 *Treas. Bot.* 166/1 Cabbages are preferred when.. thoroughly hearted and blanched. *Ibid.* Heading or hearting cabbages. **1887** *Gardening* 17 Dec. 569/1 The cabbages heart sooner by two or three weeks.

heart-ache (ˈhɑːteɪk). [f. HEART *sb.* + ACHE.]

1. Pain in the heart; formerly = HEARTBURN 2.

c **1000** *Sax. Leechd.* I. 192 Wið heort ece, ȝenim þysse ylcan wyrte. **1685** *Cooke's Marrow Chirurg., Physic* II. v. 526 Heart-ach Fever is caused by the Pancreatick Juice getting a corroding quality.

2. Pain or anguish of mind, esp. that arising from disappointed hope or affection.

1602 SHAKS. *Ham.* III. i. 62 The Heart-ake, and the thousand Naturall shockes That Flesh is heyre too. **1749** FIELDING *Tom Jones* V. vi, Many bitter heart-achs, that Fortune seems to have in store for me. **1875** J. H. BENNET *Winter Medit.* II. xi. (ed. 5) 373 The anxieties and heartaches that are inseparable from our arduous career.

So ˈ**heart-aching** *vbl. sb.* = HEART-ACHE; ˈ**heart-aching** *ppl. a.*, causing heart-ache, distressing.

1650 HUBBERT *Pill Formality* 227 Many a groan, many a sigh, and heart-aking. **1703** ROWE *Ulyss.* IV. i. 1751 If ever maid was yet belov'd..With such Heart-aking, eager, anxious Fondness. **1882** SERJT. BALLANTINE *Exper.* xxiii. 229 The heart-aching that is concealed within the glare and tinsel exposed to the audience.

heart-bag, -bird, etc.: see HEART *sb.* 56.

ˈ**heart-beat.** [See BEAT *sb.*[1] 6.] A beat or pulsation of the heart; *fig.* an emotion; *transf.* an extremely brief space of time.

1850 MARG. FULLER *Wom. 19th C.* (1862) 211 Those who do not know one native heart-beat of my life. **1855** LONGF. *Hiaw.* xxi. 218 Speaking many tongues, yet feeling But one heart-beat in their bosoms. **1883** *Harper's Mag.* Mar. 584/1 In another heart-beat the whole..valley was afloat.

ˈ**heart-blood, heart's-blood.** Blood from the heart; blood shed in death, life-blood; hence, vital energy, life.

a **1240** *Ureisun* in *Cott. Hom.* 191 Al min heorte blod to ðe ich offrie. *a* **1300** *Cursor M.* 17136 For þe i gaf mi hert blode. **1579** SPENSER *Sheph. Cal.* Feb. 243 My hartblood is welnigh frorne. **1688** BUNYAN *Heavenly Footman* (1886) 151 Thy sins are washed away with His heart-blood. *a* **1723** *Ld. Thomas & Fair Ellinor* xvii. in Allingham *Ballad Bk.* (1864) 239 O dost thou not see my own heart's blood Run trickling down by my knee? **1815** T. JEFFERSON *Writ.* (1830) IV. 250 The cement of this Union is the heart-blood of every American. **1878** B. TAYLOR *Deukalion* III. v. 128 The gush of human heart's-blood comes to dim My crystal eyesight.

b. *fig.*

1606 SHAKS. *Tr. & Cr.* III. i. 34 The mortall Venus, the heart blood of beauty. **1627** CRESWELL *Sp.* in Rushw. *Hist. Coll.* (1659) I. 506 Justice..is the Life and the Heart-blood of the Commonwealth. **1875** LOWELL *Wks.* (1890) IV. 397 Creations which throbbed with the very heart's-blood of genius.

ˈ**heart-bond.** [See BOND *sb.*[1] 7, 13.] **a.** A union of hearts, betrothal. **b.** (See quot. 1851.)

1823 in CRABB *Technol. Dict.* **1851** *Dict. Archit.*, *Heart-bond*, the construction of walling in which two stones side by side form the width of the wall, and a third stone of an equal breadth is put over the joint in the course above. **1887** W. S. GILBERT *Ruddigore* 32 Our plighted heart-bond gently bless.

ˈ**heart-bound,** *ppl. a.* [See BOUND *ppl. a.*[2]] Bound in heart, having the heart bound:

a. Having the heart enchained or entirely devoted (*to* an object). †**b.** Having the heart shut up or fast-closed (*to* a person); pitiless, hard-hearted (*obs*).

1580 SIDNEY *Arcadia* (1622) 92 Her, who both them did possesse As heart-bound slaues. **1616** T. ADAMS *Serm.* Wks. 1861 I. 169 The most laxative prodigals, that are lavish..to their lusts, are yet heart-bound to the poor. **1618** T. GAINSFORD *Hist. P. Warbeck* in *Select. Harl. Misc.* (1793) 82 Because she should not think him barren of education, nor heart-bound to his ambitious designs.

ˈ**heart-break,** *sb.* (*a.*) [See BREAK *sb.*[1]]

A breaking of the heart; great and overpowering sorrow, such as breaks the heart; overwhelming distress of mind.

1583 BABINGTON *Commandm.* vii. (1637) 64 Those griefes, cares, heart-breakes, and sorrowes, which are incident daily to married folks. **1598** SHAKS. *Merry W.* V. iii. 11 Better a little chiding, then a great deale of heart-breake. **1624** HEYWOOD *Gunaik.* III. 130 [This] deformitie being a sorrow to the father, and almost a heart-breake to the daughter. **1828** SCOTT *Aunt Marg. Mirr.* i, The poor girl..died of heart-break.

†**B.** *adj.* Heart-breaking. *Obs.*

1586 WARNER *Alb. Eng.* IV. xxii. 105 Shunne Jelousie that hart-breake loue. **1599** T. M[OUFET] *Silk-wormes* 63 The hart-breake crush of melancholies wheele.

So ˈ**heart-break** *v.* (*nonce-wd.*) *trans.*, to break the heart of. ˈ**heart-breaker**, (*a*) one who breaks hearts; (*b*) a curl, a love-lock: by Butler used contemptuously of Samson's long hair. ˈ**heart-breaking** *vbl. sb.* = HEART-BREAK *sb.* ˈ**heart-breaking** *ppl. a.*, causing intense sorrow or crushing grief, extremely distressing; hence ˈ**heart-breakingly** *adv.*

1792 BURNS *What can a young Lassie do* iv, I'll cross him, and wrack him, until I *heart-break him. **1663** BUTLER *Hud.* I. i. 253 Like Sampson's *Heart-breakers, it grew In time to make a Nation rue. *a* **1687** COTTON *Poet. Wks.* (1765) 124 A red Heart-breaker next she mow'd off, A Wart that Dido was full proud of. **1863** *N. & Q.* 3rd Ser. IV. 301 We don't refer to the ball-room butterfly..but to the regular professional heart-breaker. **1606** SHAKS. *Ant. & Cl.* I. ii. 74 It is a *heart-breaking to see a handsome man loose-Wiu'd. *c* **1610** SIR J. MELVIL *Mem.* (1683) 56 They took them to the fields to her Majesty's great dissatisfaction and heart-breaking. **1885–6** SPURGEON *Treas. Dav.* Ps. cxli. 5 Head-breaking and heart-breaking attend the anointings of the riotous. **1591** SPENSER *Teares Muses* 6 Making your musick of *hart-breaking mone. *a* **1711** KEN *Hymns Evang.* Poet. Wks. 1721 I. 163 Nothing can more Heart-breaking Grief excite, Than utmost Love, repaid with utmost Spite. **1886** ANNIE THOMAS *Reigning Favourite* III. ix. 169 Dull, level tones that were *heart-breakingly significant.

ˈ**heart-broke,** *a.* Archaic variant of next.

1636 W. DENNY in *Ann. Dubrensia* (1877) 14 At last downe falls The heart-broke Hare. **1711** SWIFT *Let. to Mrs. Johnson* 9 Feb. Wks. 1778 XIV. 164 They say the old King is almost heart-broke. **1850** MRS. BROWNING *Seraphim* Poems I. 116 He seemeth dying..heart-broke by new joy too sudden and sweet.

ˈ**heart-broken,** *a.* [f. HEART *sb.* + BROKEN.] Having a broken heart, broken-hearted; overwhelmed with anguish, despair, or crushing grief.

c **1586** C'TESS PEMBROKE *Ps.* LI. vii. The sacrifice that God will hold respected, Is the heart-broken soule. **1694** WOOD *Life* 14 Sept., Benjamin Wood..died of a feaver, and hart-broken. **1752** YOUNG *Brothers* IV. i, He views, with horror, what mad dreams have done, And sinks, heart-broken, on a murder'd son. **1872** BAKER *Nile Tribut.* xviii. 319 They were heart-broken at the idea of losing their animal.

b. *transf.* Said of a person's feelings, acts, etc.

1832 J. M. REYNOLDS *Miserrimus* (1833), I stood before you in heart-broken penitence. **1834** CAMPBELL *Life Mrs. Siddons* II. vi. 139 To make us weep over the heart-broken death of Katharine. **1844** MARG. FULLER *Wom. 19th C.* (1862) 60 In low heart-broken tones [he] tells her of Heaven's will.

Hence ˈ**heart-**ˌ**brokenly** *adv.*, -ˌ**brokenness**.

1881 D. C. MURRAY *Joseph's Coat* xxviii, Quite heart-brokenly penitent. **1882** J. PARKER *Apost. Life* I. 95 Who has felt heart-brokenness on account of sin?

heartburn ('hɑːtbɜːn), *sb.* Also 3 herte-bren. [f. HEART *sb.* + BURN *sb.*[3] Sense 2 translates Gr. καρδιαλγία in Galen: cf. HEART *sb.* 4.]

†**1.** Burning of heart; fire of passion. *rare.*

c **1250** *Gen. & Ex.* 4054 Ðe ȝinge wimmen of ðin lond .. ðe cumen brewen herte-bren.

2. An uneasy burning sensation in the lower part of the chest, due to putrefactive fermentation of the food in the stomach; cardialgy.

1597 GERARDE *Herbal* II. cxxxvi. 414 Small stonecrop .. is good for the hart-burne. **1620** VENNER *Via Recta* vii. 142 It is of singular force against the heart-burne. **1710–11** SWIFT *Lett.* (1767) III. 105 Congreve's nasty white wine has given me the heart-burn. **1789** W. BUCHAN *Dom. Med.* (1790) 419, I have frequently known the heart-burn cured .. by chewing green tea. **1880** BEALE *Slight Ailm.* 93 Chalk or magnesia is taken for the relief of the Heartburn.

3. Rankling jealousy, discontent, or enmity; = HEART-BURNING *sb.* 1.

1621 G. SANDYS *Ovid's Met.* II. (1626) 42 Faire Herse's happy state such heart-burne breeds In her black bosom. **1748** RICHARDSON *Clarissa* (1811) II. 78 Not without a little of the heart-burn. **1862** H. AÏDÉ *Carr of Carrlyon* II. 253 Was so poor a triumph worth the exchange to an existence of struggle, and heartburn, and unrest?

†**'heart-burn,** *v. Obs.* [f. HEART *sb.* + BURN *v.*; cf. HEART-BURNING *sb.*]

1. *trans.* To affect with heartburning; to render jealous or grudging.

c **1540** tr. *Pol. Verg. Eng. Hist.* (Camden) I. 86 Not being able to reconcile them .. for the greate hatred which harte-burned them. **1599** SHAKS. *Much Ado* II. i. 4 How tartly that Gentleman lookes, I neuer can see him, but I am heart-burn'd an howre after. **1669** SHADWELL *R. Sheph.* II. Wks. 1720 I. 241, I had been most abominably heart-burnt, if I had kept it in: this Love-passion [etc.].

2. To regard or treat with jealous enmity.

1612 T. TAYLOR *Comm. Titus* ii. 4 To quippe, raile, heart-burne their betters. **1612–15** BP. HALL *Contempl., N. T.* IV. iv, He once reverencd him .. whom now he heart-burns as an enemy.

heart-burning ('hɑːtbɜːnɪŋ), *sb.* [f. HEART *sb.* + BURNING *vbl. sb.*]

1. A heated and embittered state of mind, which is felt but not openly expressed; jealousy or discontent rankling in the heart; grudge.

1513 MORE *Rich. III*, Wks. 38/1 A long continued grudge and hearte brennynge betwene the Quenes kinred and the kinges blood. **1661** MARVELL *Corr.* xxxii. Wks. 1872–5 II. 76 Lest there should be any new feud or hart-burning occasiond thereby. **1809** W. IRVING *Knickerb.* (1861) 107 Which outrages occasioned as much vexation and heart-burning as does the modern right of search on the high seas.

b. *pl.* Feelings of this description; grudges.

1605 *2 Vnnat. & Bloodie Murthers* (Collier) 31 Their seuerall seruants could not agree one with another, but would expresse their heart-burnings. **1768** BOSWELL *Corsica* ii. (ed. 2), 120 There was nothing but heart-burnings, and miserable dissensions. **1874** BURNAND *My Time* iii. 23, I was manager of a theatre where there were neither heart-burnings nor jealousies.

†**2.** = HEARTBURN *sb.* 2. *Obs.*

1591 PERCIVALL *Sp. Dict., Azedia*, sharpnes, sowernes of stomack, hartburning. **1635** SWAN *Spec. M.* vi. §4 (1643) 262 Lettice .. cooleth a hot stomach called heart-burning. **1747** WESLEY *Prim. Physic* (1762) 74 The Heart Burning, a sharp gnawing Pain at the Orifice of the Stomach.

attrib. **1607** TOPSELL *Serpents* (1658) 749 The hearts of them that die of the heart-burning disease.

'heart-burning, *ppl. a.* [f. HEART *sb.* + BURNING *ppl. a.*] That inflames, kindles, or consumes the heart; distressing the heart.

1588 SHAKS. *L. L. L.* I. i. 280 Thine in all complements of deuoted and heart-burning heat of dutie. **1590** SPENSER *F. Q.* II. vii. 22 Disloyall Treason, and hart-burning Hate. **1821** BYRON *Juan* v. xxiv, Swallowing a heart-burning sigh.

heart-cake, -cam, -cherry, -clover, -cockle, etc.: see HEART *sb.* 56.

hearted ('hɑːtɪd), *ppl. a.* [f. HEART *sb.* and *v.*: see -ED[1], [2].]

1. Having a heart; *esp.* in parasynthetic comb., as FAINT-HEARTED, HARD-HEARTED, etc., q.v.

c **1205** [see HARD-HEARTED]. *a* **1225** *Ancr. R.* 118 Mine leoue sustren .. lokeð þet ȝe beon .. swete & swote iheorted. *a* **1529** SKELTON *Col. Cloute* 169 They are good men Much herted like an hen. **1577–87** HOLINSHED *Chron.* III. 1176/1 Which answer of so noble an hearted princesse .. mooued a maruellous shout. *c* **1825** BEDDOES *Torrismond* I. iii, If this man should be Vain, selfish, light, or hearted with a stone. **1860** DELAMER *Kitch. Gard.* 56 In cutting a hearted cabbage.

†**2.** Sagacious, wise, prudent; = HEARTY *a.* 2.

1388 WYCLIF *Job* xxxiv. 10 Therfor ȝe men hertid [*gloss.* that is, vndirstondinge] here ȝe me.

†**3.** Full of heart, spirited, courageous. *Obs.*

1538 LELAND *Itin.* V. 26 Coltes .. better fed then harted or apt for War. **1595** SOUTHWELL *St. Peter's Compl.* 7 O coward troups, far better arm'd then harted.

4. Having the shape of a heart; cordate.

1834 PLANCHÉ *Brit. Costume* 199 The steeple head-dress, which succeeded the horned or hearted shape. *a* **1864** LANDOR (Webster), With hearted spear-head.

5. Fixed or established in the heart.

1604 SHAKS. *Oth.* III. iii. 448 Yield vp (O Loue) thy Crowne, and hearted Throne To tyrannous Hate. **1850** TALFOURD *Lett. Lamb* vii. 67 A deep and hearted feeling of jealousy.

Hence **-heartedly, -heartedness** in comb.

1583 [see HARDHEARTEDNESS]. **1585** T. WASHINGTON tr. *Nicholay's Voy.* I. xix. 23 So fainte heartedlie to surrender themselves. **1884** J. PARKER *Apost. Life* III. 93, I ask for great-heartedness—all but infinite heartedness, that will listen to all kinds of people.

hearten ('hɑːt(ə)n), *v.* Also 6–7 harten. [Extended form of HEART *v.*: see -EN[5] 2.]

1. *trans.* To put heart into, give heart to (a person, etc.); to inspire with confidence, embolden, encourage; to rouse to fresh energy or enthusiasm; to inspirit, animate, cheer.

1526 R. WHYTFORD *Martiloge* (1893) 182 Saynt Cicily hertned them vnto martyrdom. **1553** T. WILSON *Rhet.* 115 b, Because I have halfe weried the reader with a tedious matter, I wil harten him agayne with a merye tale. **1650** FULLER *Pisgah* II. 61 Where God .. heartened his own people .. by drying up the waters of Jordan. **1777** BURKE *Let. Sheriffs Bristol* Wks. III. 156 One of a noisy multitude to halloo and hearten them into doubtful and dangerous courses. **1855** BROWNING *Gram. Funeral* 76 Hearten our chorus! **1859** SMILES *Self-Help* xi. (1860) 293 Encounter with difficulties will train his strength .. heartening him for future effort.

b. Const. *inf.*

1579–80 NORTH *Plutarch* (1676) 945 This [token] did hearten him .. to follow his purpose. **1683** *Apol. Prot. France* iii. 9 [They] heartened him by their advice to pursue his Hellish Design of stabbing the King. **1881** ELIZ. R. CHAPMAN *Master of All* I. 77 The slant rays .. heartened the robins to chirp their merriest.

c. *refl.*

1571 GOLDING *Calvin on Ps.* vii. 1 Too thentent he may harten himselfe unto boldnesse. **1708** STANHOPE *Paraphr.* (1709) IV. 503 Let us hearten our selves with their Assistance against Temptations. **1806–7** J. BERESFORD *Miseries Hum. Life* (1826) XI. Concl., How long a time you will require to hearten yourself for the next consultation.

2. With adv. **a.** ***to hearten on***: to encourage, inspirit, incite, stimulate.

1555 W. WATREMAN *Fardle Facions* II. x. 221 The princes and capitaines .. crye vnto their men, and harten them on. *a* **1690** RUSHW. *Hist. Coll.* (1721) V. 358 The Train-Band .. kill'd a Ballad-Singer with one Arm, that was heartning on the Women [rioters]. **1878** BOSW. SMITH *Carthage* 259 Heartening on his men, till he dropped exhausted from his saddle.

b. ***to hearten up***: to animate, cheer up.

1590 MARLOWE *Edw. II*, III. ii, Hearten up your men. **1674** R. GODFREY *Inj. & Ab. Physic* 76 The Doctor heartned him up, and admonisht him not to let in fears. **1724** DE FOE *Mem. Cavalier* (1840) 185 They boasted of the victory to hearten up their friends. **1849** GROTE *Greece* II. lx. (1862) V. 292 Marshalling the troops, heartening up their dejection.

c. *refl.* and *intr.* for *refl.* To rouse oneself from despondency; to take fresh heart or courage, regain one's spirits, cheer up.

1708 MOTTEUX *Rabelais* IV. xxiv. (1737) 101 Who is fain to drink to hearten himself up. **1874** T. HARDY *Far fr. Madding Crowd* (1889) 308 Do hearten yourself up a little, ma'am. **1883** *Sunday Mag.* Dec. 751/2, I heartened up a good bit. **1891** ATKINSON *Last Giant Killers* 136 'Hearten up, my sweet', he said.

†**3.** To give physical strength or stimulus to: **a.** To strengthen with food or nourishment. *Obs.*

1586 A. DAY *Eng. Secretary* I. (1625) 110 Good Ale, which inwardly must hearten him. **1616** SURFL. & MARKH. *Country Farme* 82 Peacocks are verie sicke when they moult, and then they must be heartened with Honey, Wheat, Oates, and Horse-beanes. **1693** SIR T. P. BLOUNT *Nat. Hist.* 118 Messengers .. take of it [opium] to hearten themselves. **1748** *Anson's Voy.* II. viii. 220 Of great service both in lengthning out our store of provision, and in heartning the whole crew with .. palatable food. **1792** OSBALDISTON *Brit. Sportsman* 74/1 A composition given to hearten and strengthen them.

†**b.** To put (land) into good heart; to fertilize with manure. Cf. HEART *v.* 2. *Obs.*

1594 PLAT *Jewell-ho.* I. 49 These being returned vppon the grounds .. do helpe in some measure to harten them again. **1601** CORNWALLYES *Disc. Seneca* (1631) 34 But rather hearten our soils and make us shoot up. **1622** MAY *Virg. Georg.* (J.), The ground one year at rest; forget not then With richest dung to hearten it again.

†**c.** To supply (liquor) with stimulant quality.

1697 DAMPIER *Voy.* I. 293 Makes most delicate Punch; but it must have a dash of Brandy to hearten it, because this Arack is not strong enough.

4. *transf.* in weaker sense: To strengthen, help on, further, promote. *Obs.*

1615 T. ADAMS *Spir. Navig.* 4 Somewhat to hearten the probability of this opinion. **1649** BP. HALL *Cases Consc.* Addit. i. (1654) 384 His offensive marriage with his Neece is hartned by a sophisticall pleader.

Hence **'heartened** *ppl. a.* **'heartener**, one who heartens, encourages, or cheers. **'heartening** *vbl. sb.*, encouragement, stimulus, renewal of strength or spirits. **'heartening** *ppl. a.*, that heartens, stimulates, etc.: see senses of vb.

1649 *Lanc. Tracts* (Chetham Soc.) 223 The *heartned old man quickly left me. **1601** F. GODWIN *Bps. of Eng.* 514 He was a great *hartner of King John against the Pope. **1896** *Advance* (Chicago) 12 Nov. 662 What the world most greatly needs is hearteners, not disheartеners. **1581** MULCASTER *Positions* xxxvii. (1887) 151 Without any either greate feare, or much *heartening. **1616** SURFL. & MARKH. *Country Farme* 109 Which exceedeth all other kinds of dung in goodnesse, for the great substance, strength, and heartening which it giueth vnto the ground. **1816** J. BALLANTYNE in Smiles *J. Murray* (1891) I. xviii. 467, 'I am .. confident of the success of this work'. This is no bad heartening. **1613–16** W. BROWNE *Brit. Past.* II. ii, They turn'd them tow'rds the *hart'ning sound. **1796** MRS. GLASSE *Cookery* xiv. 217 This is a pretty heartening dish for a sick or weak person. **1895** J. SMITH *Message Exod.* v. 67 A new, living and most heartening message from the Unseen.

†**'hearter.** *Obs. rare*$^{-1}$. [f. HEART *v.* + -ER[1].] One who heartens or encourages; an abettor.

c **1550** *Vpchering of Messe* 29 in *Skelton's Wks.* (1843) I. App. iii. p. cxiii, Plewmen, smythes, & carters. With such as be their hartars.

'heart-felt, *a.* [f. HEART *sb.* + *felt*, pa. pple. of FEEL *v.*] Felt in the heart; appealing to or proceeding from the innermost self; hence, thoroughly sincere, genuine, real.

1734 POPE *Ess. Man* IV. 168 The soul's calm sunshine, and the heartfelt joy. **1783** MAD. D'ARBLAY *Diary* 3 Oct., I have been repeating internally, all day long, these heart-felt lines. **1861** GEN. P. THOMPSON *Audi Alt.* III. clxxviii. 215 Honest and heartfelt enemies of Slavery. **1888** BURGON *Lives 12 Gd. Men* I. Pref. 17 Of great religious earnestness, and consistent heartfelt piety.

heartful ('hɑːtfʊl), *sb.* [f. HEART *sb.* + -FUL 2]. As much as a heart can contain: chiefly *fig.*

1637 RUTHERFORD *Lett.* (1862) I. 253 So that I may get my heartful of my Lord Jesus. **1839** BAILEY *Festus* xx. (1848) 264 It is a handful of eternal truth Make ye a heartful of it. **1860** O. W. HOLMES *Elsie V.* (1861) 302 If she is of the real woman sort, and has a few heartfuls of wild blood in her.

'heartful ('hɑːtfʊl), *a.* [f. HEART *sb.* + -FUL 1.] Full of heart; characterized by deep emotion or sincere affection; hearty.

1375, etc. [implied in next]. **1535** COVERDALE *Ezek.* xxvii. 32 They shall mourne for the with hertfull sorow. **1820** BYRON *Mar. Fal.* IV. i. 206 Happy, heart-full hours! **1881** PALGRAVE *Vis. Eng., Sir Hugh Willoughby*, The heartful prayers, the fireside blaze and bliss.

'heartfully, *adv.* [f. prec. + -LY[2].] With the whole heart; with entire affection, enthusiasm, or devotion; cordially, heartily; earnestly.

1375 BARBOUR *Bruce* III. 510 Thai welcummyt him mar hartfully. *c* **1475** *Rauf Coilȝear* 891, I rid that thow hartfully forsaik thy Mahoun. **1513** BRADSHAW *St. Werburge* I. 1443, I pray you hertfully Take no dysplesure. *c* **1565** LINDESAY *Chron. Scot.* (1728) 35 Douglas .. was received right heartfully by the King. **1612** WOODALL *Surg. Mate* Wks. (1653) 292 To animate and inable us the more heartfully to serve him. **1890** MRS. LAFFAN *Louis Draycott* II. III. iv. 85, I worked harder, and more heartfully.

'heartfulness. [f. as prec. + -NESS.] Heartful quality; sincerity of affection, cordiality.

1611 COTGR., *Cordialité*, cordiallnesse, heartinesse, heartfulnesse. **1823** *Examiner* 586/1 An additional tinge of acidity, and a consequent negation of what we hope we may be allowed to call heartfulness. **1845** G. MURRAY *Islaford* 157 Whose heartfulness has warmth enough To give the thing a soul.

hearth[1] (hɑːθ). Forms: 1 heorð, **herth,** (4 erþe), 4–6 **herth(e,** 5–7 **harth(e,** 6– **hearth.** [OE. *heorð* str. masc. = OFris. *herth, herd,* OS. *herth,* (MDu. *heert, haart(d),* MLG. *hert,* Du. *haard,* LG. *heert, heerd*); OHG., MHG. *hert,* Ger. *herd* floor, ground, fireplace:—WGer. **herþoz.* (In Sc. and north. dial. still rimes with *earth.*)]

1. a. That part of the floor of a room on which the fire is made, or which is beneath the fire-basket or grate; the paved or tiled floor of a fireplace.

a **700** *Epinal Gloss.* 5 *Arula*, fyrpannae *vel* herth. *c* **725** *Corpus Gloss.* 906 *Fornacula*, cyline, heorðe. *c* **1000** *Azariah* 176 Hweorfað nu æfter heorðe. **1382** WYCLIF *Jer.* xxxvi. 23 He kutte it .. and threȝ it in to the fyr, that was vpon the herth. *c* **1425** *Voc.* in Wr.-Wülcker 657/1 *Hoc focarium*, harthe. *c* **1440** *Promp. Parv.* 237/2 Herthe, where fyre ys made, *ignearium*. **1486** *Nottingham Rec.* III. 258 Baceford ston for to make þe chymney harth with. **1573–80** BARET *Alv.* H 328 The Hearth wherein fire is kept, *focus*. **1596** DALRYMPLE tr. *Leslie's Hist. Scot.* I. 95 Thay bake it at the harth. **1634** *Althorp MS.* in Simpkinson *Washingtons* App. 65 The stone for the harth in the Great Chamber. **1750** GRAY *Elegy* vi, For them no more the blazing hearth shall burn. **1838** THIRLWALL *Greece* II. 98 The sacred fire, which was kept constantly burning on the public hearth of the colony, was taken from the altar of Vesta. **1849** JAMES *Woodman* ii, A pile of blazing logs on the hearth.

fig. **1594** T. B. *La Primaud. Fr. Acad.* II. To Rdr. 7 The heart is the harth from whence proceedeth all that inset and natiue heate. **1866** B. TAYLOR *Icarus* Poems 247 Hearths of air Whereon the Morning burns her hundred fires.

b. A portable receptacle for fire, or flat plate on which it may be made.

1618 BOLTON *Florus* (1636) 321 Carrying, for as it were his crest, a chafing-dish or little hearth upon his helmet, and the coales thereof kindling with the motion of his body. **1665** *Sir T. Roe's Voy. E. Ind.* 359 They .. bake it upon small round iron hearths, which they carry with them. **1845** E. ACTON *Mod. Cookery* vii. 191 The hot plates, or *hearths* with which the kitchens of good houses are always furnished.

c. 'Applied to the ship's fire-place, coppers, and galley generally' (Smyth *Sailor's Word-bk.* 1867).

2. As typical of the household or home; the home, 'fireside'. Often in the alliterative phrase ***hearth and home***.

c **1000** *Laws Edgar* II. c. 2 (Schmid) Be ælcum friȝan heorðe. *c* **1000** ÆLFRIC *Hom.* II. 262 He sceolde bebeodan Israhela folce þæt hi namon æt ælcum heorðe anes ȝeares lamb. **1585** T. WASHINGTON tr. *Nicholay's Voy.* I. xii. 13 b, This towne doth not now containe above 300 harthes. **1607**

SHAKS. *Cor.* IV. v. 85 Now this extremity, Hath brought me to thy Harth. **1817** BYRON *Manfred* III. iv, A grove which.. twines its roots with the imperial hearths. **1838** THIRLWALL *Greece* V. 35 To fight for their hearths and altars. **1857** MAYNE REID *War Trail* (Rtldg.) 141 Puissant defenders of the hearth and home.

3. Technical. **a.** The fireplace of a smith's forge. **b.** The floor in a reverberatory furnace on which the ore, or in a puddling furnace on which the iron, is exposed to the flame. **c.** The hollow at the bottom of a blast-furnace through which the molten metal descends to the crucible. **d.** A portable brazier or chafing-dish used in soldering. **e.** In cylinder glass manufacture: A spreading frame.

open-hearth furnace, a form of regenerative furnace of the reverberatory type used in some processes of making steel; hence ***open-hearth steel***.

1398 TREVISA *Barth. De P.R.* VI. xxix. (Tollem. MS.), þe eyer þat bloweþ in þe erþe [1535 forge] is hoot and dry; hit heteþ and dryeþ smeþis. **1645** G. BOATE in *Nat. Hist. Irel.* (1726) 76 The [melted] iron itself descendeth to the lowest part of the furnace called the hearth; the which being filled .. they unstop the hearth, and open the mouth therof. **1693** LISTER in *Phil. Trans.* XVII. 866 Those Bars which are wrought out of a Loop, taken up out of the Finnery Harth, or second Forge, are much better Iron than those which are made in the Bloomary or first Harth. *Ibid.* 867 Set in the Smiths Forge or Harth, a Crucible, or Dish of Crucible Metal. **1872** RAYMOND *Statist. Mines & Mining* 125 The furnaces must be differently constructed.. the walls must come down straight to the hearth, or contract gradually. **1875** *Ure's Dict. Arts* II. 996 The puddling furnace.. is divided interiorly into three parts; the fireplace, the hearth, and the flue. **1883** CRANE *Smithy & Forge* 10 The smith's hearth, when of the largest description, is a kind of trough of brick-work about six feet square, elevated several inches from the floor of the smithy. **1894** *Harper's Mag.* Jan. 412 It may be crucible, Bessemer, or open-hearth steel.

4. *attrib.* and *Comb.*, as **a.** ***hearth-broom***, ***-brush***, ***-fire***, ***-holder***, ***-light***, ***-place***, ***-side***, ***-staff***, ***-tool***; ***hearth-baken*** adj.; **b.** **hearth-book**, a book containing a list of hearths for the purpose of the HEARTH-TAX; **hearth-bottom**, the stone which forms the bed of a blast-furnace; **hearth-cake**, a cake baked on the hearth; **hearth-cinder**, the slag formed on the refinery-hearth; **hearth-cricket**, the common house-cricket; **hearth-ends**, particles of unreduced lead ore from a blast-furnace; **hearth-fellow**, a fireside companion; **hearth-fly**, a kind of artificial fly used in angling; **hearth-plate**, a cast-iron plate forming the hearth of a reverberatory furnace; †**hearth-stock**, = HEAD-BLOCK 1; **hearth tidy**, a pan for containing the ashes that fall from a fireplace; **hearth-warming**, a merry-making to handsel a new house; a house-warming; †**hearth-yeld** = HEARTH-PENNY. Also HEARTH-MONEY, -PENNY, -RUG, -STONE, -TAX.

c **1000** ÆLFRIC *Voc.* in Wr.-Wülcker 153/36 *Subcinericeus, uel focarius*, *heorðbacen hlaf. **1769** R. PRICE *Observ. Revers. Payments* (1792) II. 276 According to the *hearth-books of Lady-day 1690. **1880** *Encycl. Brit.* XIII. 299/2 This is the *hearth bottom, formerly made of one or more large slabs of sandstone. **1951** *Good Housek. Home Encycl.* (1956) 269/2 Sunk or hearth-bottom grates, in which the fuel rests on a bed of fire clay. **1781** BURNEY in Boswell *Johnson* July, He cut some bristles off his *hearth broom. **1752** G. WHITE *Petty Cash Acc.* in *Selborne* (1878) II. 317 Cinder-sifter and *hearth-brush. **1617** MORYSON *Itin.* III. 155 They vulgarly eate *harth Cakes of Oates. *a* **1781** R. CHALLONER *Medit.* (1843) I. 379 That hearth-cake of the prophet Elias, with which he was fed. **1789** G. WHITE *Selborne* xlvii. (1853) II. 286 Cats catch *hearth-crickets and.. devour them. **1870** J. PERCY *Metall. Lead* 289 The *hearth-ends.. consist of particles of ore, projected from the hearth partly by the action of the blast, but chiefly by decrepitation of the ore, and of particles of fuel and lime. **1895** MORRIS *Beowulf* 110 For the fall of their lord, e'en they his *hearth-fellows. **1784** M. UNDERWOOD *Dis. Childr.* (1799) I. 294 The warm ashes of a *hearth-fire. **1787** BEST *Angling* (ed. 2) 106 The *Hearthfly Dubbed with the wool off an aged black ewe, mixed with some grey colt's hair. **1837** CARLYLE *Fr. Rev.* II. VI. ii, So many householders or *hearthholders do severally fling down their crafts and industrial tools. **1723** *Pres. State Russia* II. 375 The *Hearth-place is in the middle of the Tent. **1875** *Ure's Dict. Arts* II. 997 Cast-iron *hearth-plates, resting upon cast-iron beams. **1803** MARY CHARLTON *Wife & Mistress* IV. 170 Let 'em all get to their own *hearth-side. **1863** W. PHILLIPS *Speeches* xix. 443 Soldiers .. at their very hearth-sides. **1688** R. HOLME *Armoury* III. 321/1 The *Hearth-staff.. is to open and stir up the Fire, and cast out the Cinders that come from the Iron. **1703** MOXON *Mech. Exerc.* 10 With your Hearth-staff stir up the Fire. *c* **1440** *Promp. Parv.* 237/2 *Herthe stok or kynlyn .. *repofocilium*. **1920** *Ironmonger* 18 Dec. 95 Saucepans, *hearth tidies, curbs, plate racks. **1830** W. CARLETON *Irish Peasantry* (1836) II. 198 Among the peasantry no new house is ever put up without a *hearth-warming, and a dance. *c* **1300** *Battle Abbey Custumals* (1887) 10 Pro Romescot et *hertȝeld iiij *d*.

Hence **'hearthing** (*nonce-wd.*): cf. FURNACING.

1612 STURTEVANT *Metallica* (1854) 109 By their new kind of furnacing and hearthing.

†**hearth**[2]. *Obs. rare.* In 4 *Kent.* **hyerþe**. [f. OE. *hier-an* to hear + -TH[1].] = HEARING.

1340 *Ayenb.* 91 þe vif wyttes of þe bodye be zyȝþe be hyerþe be smellinge be zuelȝynge and be takynge.

heart-heaviness: see HEART *sb.* 55 a.

hearthless ('hɑːθlɪs), *a.* [f. HEARTH[1] + -LESS.] Without a hearth.

1817 BYRON *Lament Tasso* ix, While thou, Ferrara!.. shalt .. view thy hearthless halls. **1818** SHELLEY *Rev. Islam* VI. xlvi, A heap of hearthless walls.

'hearth-money. *Hist.*

†**1.** Used by Coke for the ancient CHURCH-SCOT.

1660 R. COKE *Power & Subj.* 175 Let the Hearth-money be first paid to the Church by every Freeman. [*Cnut's Laws* I. c. 11 §1 (Schmid) And ga ælc cyric-sceat into þam ealdan mynstre be ælcon friȝan heorðe 'and let each church-scot go to the mother church for each free hearth'.]

2. A tax upon hearths or fireplaces; *esp.* a tax of two shillings per annum on every fire-hearth in England and Wales, imposed by Act 13 & 14 Chas. II, repealed by 1 Wm. and M.; = CHIMNEY-MONEY.

1663 *Act 15 Chas. II*, c. 13 Title, An Additionall Act for the better ordering and collecting the Revenue ariseing by Hearth Money. **1664** EARL ORRERY *State Lett.* (1743) I. 155 The payments of hearth and chimney money. **1689** LUTTRELL *Brief Rel.* (1857) I. 506 The king sent a message to the commons, signifyeing that the duty of hearth-money becomeing a greivance to the people, he left it to their consideration. **1733** BERKELEY *Let. to T. Prior* 19 Apr. Wks. 1871 IV. 206 The number.. had been lately and accurately taken by the collectors of hearth-money. **1780** A. YOUNG *Tour Irel.* II. 66 The number of people at Corke mustered by the clergy, by hearth-money, and by the number of houses. **1855** MACAULAY *Hist. Eng.* xi. III. 36 Importuned by the common people to relieve them from the intolerable burden of the hearth money.

hearth-pace, erron. f. HALF-PACE; cf. *hath-pace*.

1667 PRIMATT *City & C. Build.* II. (1680) 146 A Pair of Hearth-pace Stairs.

hearth-penny. *Hist.* Also 1 **heorðpeniȝ**, **-pening**, 3 **hert-**, **hurt-**, **hurdpeny**, **hurpeny**. [So called because chargeable on every dwelling-house.]

1. The payment also called Peter's pence and Rome-scot, anciently made to the Pope.

c **1000** *Edgar's Laws* II. c. 4 (Schmid) Sy ælc heorð-peniȝ agifen be Petres mæsse-dæȝe. **1235–52** *Rentalia Glaston.* (1891) 13 Et dat hurdpeny sicut Jordanus. *Ibid.* 76 Edit[ha] .. reddit xijd. de Gabulo et viijd. ad lardarium et hertpeni. **1660** R. COKE *Power & Subj.* 159 Let the Hearth-penny be paid before the Feast of S. Peter. **1889** *Archæol. Rev.* Aug. 43 It was called Rome-scot, Rome-penny, Hearth-penny.

†**b.** perh. = *sulh-ælmesse*, or plough-alms, an ecclesiastical tax on ploughed land (Schmid). *Obs.*

c **1000** *Rectitud. Sing. Pers.* in Schmid *Gesetze* App. iii. 372 Sylle [cot-setla] his heorð-pæniȝ on halȝan þunres-dæȝ, eal swa ælcan friȝean men ȝebyreð.

'hearth-rug. a. A rug laid before a fireplace to protect the carpet or floor.

1824 SCOTT *St. Ronan's* viii, A setter is.. fitter for his place on the hearth-rug than a pointer. **1835** DICKENS *Sk. Boz, Brokers & Mar.-Store*, A bright red, blue, and yellow hearth-rug. **1869** TROLLOPE *He Knew, etc.* i. (1878) 6 He would sometimes come in and eat his biscuit standing on the hearth-rug.

b. *attrib.* (*a*) fireside, domestic; (*b*) resembling a hearth-rug.

1901 *Daily Chron.* 31 July 7/2 Turning the hearthrug favourite into the streets is certainly better than shutting it up, slowly to starve in an unoccupied house. **1902** *Ibid.* 2 Sept. 5/2 The sparrow is far too 'fly' a bird for the hearth-rug-bred cat. **1909** *Westm. Gaz.* 20 July 5/1 The inelegant, cumbrous, and shaggy hearth-rug coats.

'hearth-stead. [f. STEAD place.] The place of a hearth; fireside; hence, = homestead.

c **1475** in Horstmann *Altengl. Legenden* (1881) p. cxxi. *note*, þe herthstede þat has bene all wynter browne & blake with þe smok. **1585** T. WASHINGTON tr. *Nicholay's Voy.* II. x. 44 The village containeth about two or three hundred hearthsteds. **1834** SOUTHEY *Doctor* xxxiv. II. 17 The most sacred spot upon earth to him was his father's hearth-stead. **1851** BORROW *Lavengro* I. 180 Northmen.. flocked thither across the sea to found hearthsteads on its fertile soil.

hearthstone ('hɑːθstəʊn), *sb.*

1. The flat stone forming the hearth; a variety of stone used for this purpose. Also put symbolically for the fireside or home.

c **1325** *Gloss. W. de Biblesw.* in Wright *Voc.* 170 *Hastre*, the hert-ston. *c* **1475** *Pict. Voc.* in Wr.-Wülcker 779/9 *Hoc focarium*, a hartstone. *a* **1491** J. ROSS *Hist. Reg. Angl.* (1716) 130 *Locum antiquæ prophetiæ*.. The hare shall kendyll on the harthestone. **1634–5** BRERETON *Trav.* (Chetham Soc.) 22 Adorned with such stones a yard and dim. high, as are our best hearthstones in England. **1725** RAMSAY *Gent. Sheph.* I. ii. Song 5, A bleezing ingle and a clean hearth-stane. **1821** BYRON *Juan* III. cvii, Whate'er of peace about our hearth-stone clings. **1847** EMERSON *Poems, Good-Bye* 15, I am going to my own hearth-stone.

2. A soft kind of stone used to whiten hearths, door-steps, etc.; a composition of powdered stone and pipeclay used for this purpose.

1851 MAYHEW *Lond. Labour* I. 27/1 The hearthstone-barrow, piled up with hearth-stone, Bath-brick, and lumps of whiting. **1896** *Daily News* 9 Sept. 7 Those who mined for what London housekeepers know as 'hearthstone'.

3. *Comb.*, as ***hearthstone-maker***, ***-seller***, ***-woman***.

1858 SIMMONDS *Dict. Trade*, *Hearth-stone Maker*.

'hearthstone, *v.* [f. prec. sb.] *trans.* To whiten with hearthstone. Also *absol.*

1840 *P. Parley's Ann.* I. 151 Mosette.. with her wet feet left many black marks in the hearth-stoned kitchen. **1887** MISS BRADDON *Like & Unlike* III. xiv. 255 He.. washed and hearth-stoned steps and window sills.

'hearth-tax. = HEARTH-MONEY 2.

1689 EVELYN *Diary* 8 Mar., In the mean time to gratify the people, the Hearth Tax was remitted for ever. **1807–8** SYD. SMITH *Plymley's Lett.* Wks. 1859 II. 140/2 Ireland does not contain at this moment less than five millions of people. There were returned in the year 1791 to the hearth tax 701,000 houses. **1846** MCCULLOCH *Acc. Brit. Empire* (1854) II. 405 A hearth-tax, or duty proportioned to the number of fire-places in a house, was established in this country [England] at a very early period.

hearthward ('hɑːθwəd), *adv.* and *a.* [see -WARD.] **A.** *adv.* Towards or in the direction of the hearth. **B.** *adj.* Directed towards the hearth.

1847 in J. Brown *Horæ Subs.* (1882) 408 Folks look hearth-ward then. **1852** *Meanderings of Mem.* I. 206 Hag of the hearthward cringe and tripod stool.

†**'heartikin.** *Obs.* Also 6 **hartykyn**. [f. HEART *sb.*: see -KIN.] Little heart: a term of endearment. ***ods-heartikins!***, a minced oath (= God's heart); cf. HEART *sb.* 53, and BODIKIN 2.

1540 PALSGR. *Acolastus* Hartykyn (Halliw.). **1741** RICHARDSON *Pamela* I. xxviii. 45 Ads-heartikins! you young gentlemen are made of iron and steel, I think. **1751** SMOLLETT *Per. Pic.* lxvii. (1779) II. 230 Odds heartlikins! had I known. *Ibid.* lxxviii. III. 43 Oddsheartikins! this may be some London apprentice running away.

heartily ('hɑːtɪlɪ), *adv.* [f. HEARTY *a.* + -LY[2]. Cf. also HEARTLY *adv.*] In a hearty manner.

1. With full or unrestrained exercise of real feeling; with genuine sincerity; earnestly, sincerely, really; with goodwill, cordially.

a **1300** *Cursor M.* 20054 Qua hertili hers or redis it. *c* **1385** CHAUCER *L.G.W.* 1492 *Hypsipyle*, Myn lady quod he thanke I hertyly. **1596** SHAKS. *Merch. V.* IV. i. 243 Most heartily I do beseech the Court To giue the iudgement. **1631** T. POWELL *Tom All Trades* 142 To bid all his guests welcome right heartily. **1717** LADY M. W. MONTAGU *Let. to Lady Rich* 17 June, I really could not forbear laughing heartily at your letter. **1751** JOHNSON *Rambler* No. 174 ¶14 No man heartily hates him at whom he can laugh. **1868** FARRAR *Silence & V.* ii. (1875) 47 To repent heartily is to be forgiven wholly.

2. With courage, zeal, or spirit; spiritedly, zealously.

c **1330** R. BRUNNE *Chron. Wace* (Rolls) 15954 þe hertiloker on þem he brak. **1612** in *Crt. & Times Jas. I* (1849) I. 168 Taking his cause, to seeming, very heartily. **1719** DE FOE *Crusoe* I. i, The Men rowing very heartily. **1875** JOWETT *Plato* (ed. 2) V. 55 The people never fought heartily for their masters.

3. With good appetite; to the satisfaction of appetite, abundantly, amply.

a **1613** OVERBURY *A Wife* (1638) 210 He breaks his fast heartilest while hee is making a grave. **1725** DE FOE *Voy. round World* (1840) 275 We made no dinner this day, having fed heartily in the morning. **1733** CHEYNE *Eng. Malady* II. ix. §7 (1734) 215 Advice to Persons of weak Nerves.. to drink a Bottle heartily every Day. **1874** DASENT *Half a Life* III. 172 No man.. ever devoured his food more heartily.

4. Abundantly, plenteously; to the full, completely, thoroughly; exceedingly, very.

1686 N. COX *Gentl. Recreat.* v. (ed. 3) 67 Follow the Dogs three quarters speed, that he may sweat heartily. **1719** DE FOE *Crusoe* II. v, They.. were.. heartily beaten. **1727** ARBUTHNOT *John Bull* III. vi, Old Lewis Baboon was.. heartily sick in mind of his last Law-Suit. **1839** JAMES *Louis XIV*, II. 244 The citizens had.. become heartily tired of the war.

heartiness ('hɑːtɪnɪs). [f. as prec. + -NESS.] The quality of being hearty; genuine sincerity of feeling, earnestness; enthusiasm, zeal; cordiality and friendliness of manner; goodness of appetite; strength, healthiness, vigour, etc.

1530 PALSGR. 229/2 Hartynesse, *magnanimité*. **1548** UDALL *Erasm. Par. Luke* vii. (R.), The lustie freashnes & hertinesse of spirit in him. **1647** JER. TAYLOR *Lib. Proph.* §20 (R.) Idolatry.. which yet they hate and disavow, with much zeal and heartiness of perswasion. *a* **1715** BURNET *Own Time* (1766) II. 13 The duke [of York] with a seeming heartiness gave his consent. **1862** LYTTON *Str. Story* II. 30 Strahan.. rushed up to me with the heartiness of old college days. **1882** A. W. WARD *Dickens* i. 14 Half achieving his task by the very heartiness with which he set about it.

hearting ('hɑːtɪŋ), *vbl. sb.* [f. HEART *v.*]

1. The action of the verb HEART; the imparting of courage; encouragement, animation, cheer.

c **1250** *Gen. & Ex.* 1982 'Nai! nai!' quat he, 'helpeð it noȝt, Mai non herting on me ben wroȝt.' *c* **1350** *Leg. Rood* (1871) 88 He.. was ful glad, For he so gude herting þan had. *c* **1440** *York Myst.* xvii. 115 ȝis certis, such hartyng haue we hadde. **15..** *Surtees Misc.* (1888) 68 'Marye, that's ill hartinge', saies my Lord Charlls Howeward. **1637–50** ROW *Hist. Kirk* (1842) p. xxii, In hairting.. of him to byd still langer.

2. *Building.* The filling up of a central space within masonry with rubble or similar material; *concr.*, the material so used.

1858 *Illustr. Times* 7 Aug., The small materials used for the hearting of the breakwater. **1862** SMILES *Engineers* III. 405 Built of ashlar, with a hearting of rubble.

3. The growing to a heart; as 'the hearting of a lettuce'. Also *attrib.*

1858 R. HOGG *Veg. Kingd.* 67 Cabbages..assuming the headed or hearting character.

†**'heartist.** *nonce-wd.* A fencer who can pierce the heart.

a **1625** FLETCHER *Love's Pilgr.* IV. ii, Where is there a man now living in the Town That hath a steady hand?..is there Ever a good heartist, or a member percer, or a Small-gut man left?

heartland ('hɑːtlænd). [f. HEART *sb.* 17 + LAND *sb.*] A (usually extensive) central region of homogeneous (geographical, political, industrial, etc.) character. Also *transf.*

1904 H. J. MACKINDER in *Geogr. Jrnl.* XXIII. 434 But trans-continental railways are now transmuting the conditions of land-power, and nowhere can they have such effect as in the closed heart-land of Euro-Asia, in vast areas of which neither timber nor accessible stone was available for road-making. **1919** —— *Democratic Ideals & Reality* 96 Taken together, the regions of Arctic and Continental drainage measure nearly a half of Asia and a quarter of Europe, and form a great continuous patch in the north and centre of the continent..inaccessible to navigation from the ocean... Let us call this great region the Heartland of the Continent. **1947** *Landfall* I. 298 We are in the frontier West, the heartland of the American myth. **1949** 'G. ORWELL' *Nineteen Eighty-Four* II. 189 The territory which forms the heartland of each super-state always remains inviolate. **1959** A. J. TOYNBEE *Hellenism* 2 The matrix of the Indo-European languages, somewhere in the heartland of the Old World. **1966** *New Statesman* 13 May 674/3 Mr Heath..is right to make the attempt even if it means some ill-feeling in the Conservative heartlands. **1968** POWELL & WALLIS *House of Lords in Middle Ages* viii. 123 King John planned a concerted attack on the French heartland from east and west. **1972** *Observer* 30 July 9/8 Chobham Farm container depot and Midland Cold Storage nestling within a few hundred yards of each other, lie at the very heartland of British trade unionism.

heart-leaf: see HEART *sb.* 56 b.

heartless ('hɑːtlɪs), *a.* [f. HEART *sb.* + -LESS.]

1. *lit.* Without a heart.

1586 J. HOOKER *Girald. Irel.* (1808) VI. 319 None hartlesse liues. **1603** DRAYTON *Odes* iv. 19 It cannot two Brests fill, One must be heartlesse still. **1753** *Scots Mag.* July 315/1 A shapeless, helpless, heartless body.

2. Destitute of courage, enthusiasm, or energy; spiritless; out of heart, disheartened, dejected.

c **1330** R. BRUNNE *Chron. Wace* (Rolls) 11564 þorow ildelnesse of þes Are Bretons feble & herteles. **1380** *Lay Folks Catech.* (Lamb. MS.) 1375 Hertles in eny gostly good. *a* **1420** HOCCLEVE *De Reg. Princ.* 644, I hertles was ay thurghe myne impressede drede. **1596** DALRYMPLE tr. *Leslie's Hist. Scot.* VI. 313 The kingis capitane was sa hartles at the sycht of sik a multitude. **1666** *Lond. Gaz.* No. 65/1 Their own Seamen being poor heartless fellows. *a* **1795** AIKIN *Evenings at Home* xvii. (1858) 227 Whence, cold and heartless, home he slunk, Involved in sore disgrace. **1799–1805** WORDSW. *Prelude* IX. 515 A hunger-bitten girl.. Was busy knitting in a heartless mood Of solitude.

b. Without warmth or zeal; not heartfelt, hearty, or zealous.

1658 *Whole Duty Man* v. § 22. 47 Slight and heartless petitions. **1706** E. GIBSON *Assize Serm.* 28 These ill impressions make subjects cold and heartless in their service. *a* **1822** SHELLEY *Falsehood* 96 Heartless scraps of godly prayer.

†**3.** Without understanding; foolish. *Obs.*

1382 WYCLIF *Prov.* xii. 8 Who forsothe is veyn and herteles [Vulg. *excors*] shal ben open to despising. *c* **1440** *Promp. Parv.* 237/2 Hertles, or vnherty, *vecors.* **1509** BARCLAY *Shyp of Folys* (1874) II. 211 O hertles folys, haste here to our doctryne. **1611** [see HEARTLESSLY].

4. Destitute of feeling; lacking in affection or friendliness; callous, unfeeling, unkind, cruel.

(The current sense, which, however, is not recognized in Johnson, Todd, Webster 1828; it is doubtful whether the Shaks. quotation belongs here.)

1599 SHAKS. *Pilgr.* 279 How sighs resound through heartless ground. **1816** SHELLEY *Alastor* 690 Heartless things Are done and said i' the world. **1864** TENNYSON *Aylmer's Field* 368 Leolin cried out the more upon them —Insolent, brainless, heartless! **1887** RUSKIN *Præterita* II. vi. 189 He made up his mind that I was heartless and selfish.

5. Of land: Without fertility, sterile.

1594 PLAT *Jewell-ho.* I. 38 In an hartlesse peece of ground. **1611** R. FENTON *Usury* II. xiii. 95 The land if it want a Iubile will in time grow hartlesse. **1641** BEST *Farm. Bks.* (Surtees) 37 Growndes that are mossy and heartlesse. **1839** MURCHISON *Silur. Syst.* I. xii. 154 Of so cold and heartless a quality as almost to defy improvement.

6. Of food or drink: Without stimulating or sustaining power.

1657 AUSTEN *Fruit Trees* I. 131 Wine that was [not] worth the drinking being so small, and heartlesse. **1674** R. GODFREY *Inj. & Ab. Physic* 90 Following Heartless Slops and Spiritless Small-beer. **1688** BURNET *Persec. Piedmont* 39 Bad Bread, black and heartless, without Substance. **1869** BLACKMORE *Lorna Doone* lvi, Their wretched heartless stuff, such as they call claret.

7. Of plants or trees: **a.** Without heartwood or core. **b.** Not forming a heart or compact mass of leaves.

1731 S. HALES *Stat. Ess.* I. 13 The motion of the sap..in the heartless vegetable would otherwise be very slow. **1859** W. H. RUSSELL in *Times* 24 Mar. 9/4 Spongiose and heartless timbers are of no good. **1883** *Leisure Ho.* 149/1 Heartless..cabbages.

'heartlessly, *adv.* [f. prec. + -LY².] In a heartless manner: †**a.** Foolishly. †**b.** Without spirit, dejectedly. **c.** Without feeling, callously, cruelly; insincerely.

1611 COTGR., *Bestement*..witlesly; dully; heartlesly. **1629** J. COLE *Of Death* 95 We must not heartlesly lye downe, but courageously beare [our cross]. **1886** RUSKIN *Præterita* I. vii. 210, I was stupidly and heartlessly careless of the past history of my family.

'heartlessness. [f. as prec. + -NESS.] The state or fact of being heartless: †**a.** Lack of energy or spirit, dejection; **b.** Lack of feeling; insincerity; callous cruelty.

1591 PERCIVALL *Sp. Dict.*, *Descorazinamiento*, heartlesnesse..sluggishnesse. **1647** BP. HALL *Christ Myst.* I. § 10 (R.) A disconsolate heartlessnesse, and sad dejection of spirit. **1658** *Whole Duty Man* i. §39. 8 Their negligence and heartlesness when they are at them. *a* **1836** MRS. SHERWOOD *Nun* v. 121 Our ceremonies; there is a sameness and heartlessness in them. **1891** *Leeds Merc.* 25 May 5/2 There..cannot be the shadow of excuse for the heartlessness of the atrocity.

heartlet ('hɑːtlɪt). [f. HEART *sb.* + -LET.] A little heart or core; a nucleus.

1826 GOOD *Bk. Nat.* (1834) I. 164 We find the seed to consist internally of a corculum, or heartlet.

'heartlike, *a.* and *adv.*

A. *adj.* Like or having the appearance of a heart.

1616 SURFL. & MARKH. *Country Farme* 343 Garden plummes and hartlike cherries. **1776** DA COSTA *Conchol.* 275 (Jod.) The two shells do not close, but leave a large oval or heart-like gap. **1839** BAILEY *Festus* (1854) 309 Shaped Out of one ruby heartlike.

B. *adv.* Like or after the manner of a heart.

1844 MRS. BROWNING *Vis. Poets* lxiii, His brain beat heart-like.

heartlikins: see HEARTIKIN.

†**'heartliness.** *Obs. rare.* [f. HEARTLY *a.* + -NESS.] Cordiality, heartiness, sincerity.

1435 MISYN *Fire of Love* I. xv. 32 Both in excellence of wark and hartlynes in lufe. **1452** *Declaration* in Tytler *Hist. Scot.* (1864) II. 387, I..shall take thay personnes in heartlines and friendship.

†**'heartling.** *Obs.* [f. HEART *sb.* + -LING.] Little or dear heart: cf. HEARTIKIN.

ods heartlings!: a minced oath (= God's heart!).

1598 SHAKS. *Merry W.* III. iv. 59 Odd's-hart-lings, that's a prettie iest indeede.

†**'heartly,** *a. Obs.* Forms: 4 **hertelyche,** 4–5 **hertli, -ly,** 4–6 **hertely,** 5 **hertlie, (hertelysshe),** 5–6 **hartlie, -ly,** 6 **heartly.** [f. HEART *sb.* + -LY¹; cf. MHG. *herzelich*, Du. *hartelijk*, ON. *hjartaligr.*]

1. Proceeding from or seated in the heart; expressive of real feeling; earnest, genuine, sincere; = HEARTY 4.

1340–70 *Alex. & Dind.* 961 ȝe han hertely hate to oure hole peple. **1388** WYCLIF *Job* viii. 21 Til thi mouth be fillid with leiȝtir, and thi lippis with hertli song. **1483** CAXTON *Cato* I j b, When the persone hath the herte fulle of hertelysshe loue. *c* **1489** —— *Sonnes of Aymon* xix. 429 He toke for it suche a hertly sorowe.

2. Showing genuine friendliness or warmth of affection; cordial, affectionate, kindly; = HEARTY 3.

c **1385** CHAUCER *L.G.W.* 2124 *Ariadne*, This lady smylith ..at his hertely wordis. **1563** WINȜET *Four Scoir Thre Quest.* Wks. 1888 I. 96 As..hertlie mother, haifand compassioun of hir tribulit sones. **1573** *Let.* in *Wodr. Soc. Misc.* 289 Efter maist hartlie commendatioun. **1600** *Gowrie's Conspir.* in *Select. Harl. Misc.* (1793) 193 Without any welcomming of his maiestie, or anie other hartlie forme of entertainement.

3. Courageous, spirited.

1340–70 *Alex. & Dind.* 95 As þe heie heuene goodus wiþ herteli þouhtus So a-wecchen my wit. *c* **1430** *Syr Gener.* 3634 With hertli corage and manful chere. **1535** STEWART *Cron. Scot.* II. 598 To caus his men no forder for to fle, Bot turne agane with hartlie mynd and will.

4. Vigorous, severe, sore.

? *a* **1400** *Morte Arth.* 1835 Of his hertly hurte helyde he neuer. *Ibid.* 2551 Hittes one hellmes fulle hertelyche dynttys.

†**'heartly,** *adv. Obs.* Forms: 2–3 **heort(e)liche,** 3 **hertelike, -li,** 4 **hert(e)lich,** 4–6 **herte-, hert-, hartly,** etc., 5–7 **hartely.** [f. HEART *sb.* + -LY². Perhaps in some instances merely a variant of HEARTILY.]

1. With the heart; earnestly, sincerely; cordially; = HEARTILY 1.

a **1225** *Juliana* 75 Wel him þe..heorteliche sikeð ofte for his sunnen. *a* **1240** *Ureisun* in *Cott. Hom.* 185 Wend me heorteliche and turn me allunge to þe. *a* **1300** *Cursor M.* 20045 All þat..herteli it heres or redes. **1393** LANGL. *P. Pl.* C. XI. 84 He..helpeth herteliche alle men of þat he may aspare. *c* **1420** CDL. BEAUFORT in Ellis *Orig. Lett.* Ser. I. I. 8 Trusty & welle belouid, I grete ȝow herttely well. **1548** HALL *Chron., Edw. IV*, 198 He..hartely thanked the lady for her consent. **1583** STANYHURST *Æneis* I. (Arb.) 17 A labor and a trauaile too plowswayns hertelye welcoom. **1664–5** LD. WINDSOR in *Hatton Corr.* (1878) 46 Which I am hartely glad are so much.

2. With courage or spirit; courageously; vigorously, with might and main; = HEARTILY 2.

a **1300** *Cursor M.* 16814 + 7 Iosephe of abaramathy, Vnto pilat hertly went. *c* **1380** WYCLIF *Wks.* (1880) 298 Aȝen errours þat þey sowen men shulden speke hertliche. *c* **1450** *Golagros & Gaw.* 849 Thai..girdit out suerdis..And hewit on hard steill, hartlie but houne.

3. With good appetite; = HEARTILY 3.

1589 L. WRIGHT *Summons for Sleepers* Epistle to Rdr., The first friend..deuoured his apple hartely, sound and rotten together.

4. In heart: opp. to *in body, in spirit.*

a **1225** *Ancr. R.* 40 And stien nu heortliche, & hwon ich deie gostliche, a domesdeie al licomliche, into ðe blisse of heouene.

heart of grace, *phrase.* Forms: 6 **herte a gresse;** 6 **hart a grasse, hart of grease, grasse, grace,** 6–7 **hart at grasse;** 6–7 **heart of grasse, h. at grasse,** 7 **h. to grasse, a grasse,** 7–8 **h. a grace,** 6– **heart of grace.** [Not known before 1530: origin and early form uncertain.

The simple *take heart* (= F. *prendre cœur*) is as old or older. The words *heart, hart,* were both written *hert(e, hart* in 16th c. Hence it has been surmised that *take herte a gresse*, or *hart of grease*, was orig. a punning or sportive expansion of *take herte*, after the earlier *herte of gresse, hart of grease*, fat hart (see HART 1 b); and that when the expression became proverbial, attempts were made to put sense into it by substituting *grass* and *grace.* Of course, *heart of grace* might be the original, and all the other forms popular corruptions of it; but it is not easy to explain *grace* in such a connexion; there is no corresponding F. *cœur de grâce.* In any case, the number and variety of the forms show that the analysis was not clear even in the 16th c.]

a. in phrase ***to take h. of gr., h. a gr.***, to pluck up courage. Cf. *take heart* (HEART 49).

1530 PALSGR. 748/1, I take herte a gresse, as one doth that taketh a sodayne courage upon hym, *je prens cueur en pance.* **1548** UDALL, etc. *Erasm. Par. Matt.* xxii. 106 They takyng hart of grace agayne. **1560** BECON *New Catech.* Wks. (1564) 516 a, They [evil wives] shame not to answer..They haue bene made dolts and foles long inough: it is now high time to take hart of grease vnto them. There is no worme so vile, but if it be troden vpon it will tourne again. **1562** J. HEYWOOD *Prov. & Epig.* (1867) 140 Thou takest hart of grasse, wyfe, not hart of grace. **1567** MAPLET *Gr. Forest* 43 The Fir tree..being cut, eyther hindred or hurt..it by and by taketh hart a grasse, and groweth..a little beneath his top. **1583** GOLDING *Calvin on Deut.* clvii. 971 When he seeth that we take heart of grasse against him. **1600** HOLLAND *Livy* 115 The Commons should take heart of grasse and hold up head againe. **1673** R. HEAD *Canting Acad.* 141 His wife.. took heart a-grace. **1712** ARBUTHNOT *John Bull* IV. iv, He was afraid to venture himself alone with him. At last he took heart of grace. *a* **1734** NORTH *Exam.* II. v. §10 (1740) 321 The Loyallists began to chear up, and to take Heart-a-grace. **1823** SCOTT *Quentin D.* vi, The peasants, who at first shrunk from him in horror..took heart of grace as he got to a distance. **1861** HUGHES *Tom Brown at Oxf.* xxxiv, In a day or two, however, Tom began to take heart of grace. **1890** *Times* 14 Oct. 6/2 The non-union labourers..took heart of grace and applied for work.

b. Hence ***to get, give, keep, gather h. of gr.***

1587 HIGINS in *Mirr. Mag., Sir N. Burdet* xv, By our losses they gate heart of grasse. **1591** HARINGTON *Orl. Fur.* XXI. xxxix, His absence gaue him so much heart of grace. **1856** KANE *Arct. Expl.* II. xxi. 213 But they kept heart of grace. **1870** MORRIS *Earthly Par.* II. III. 297 She gathered heart of grace to meet The few words they might speak together.

†**c.** Also 16–17th c. ***to take heart*** (***hart***) ***at grass, to grass.*** *Obs.*

1576 FLEMING *Panopl. Epist.* 80 Taking courage and hart at grasse. **1579** LYLY *Euphues* (Arb.) 65 Rise therefore Euphues, and take heart at grasse, younger thou shalt neuer be. **1602** CAREW *Cornwall* 134 b, Our Foyens tooke heart at grasse, and..stiffly refused to vaile their bonets. **1631** WEEVER *Anc. Fun. Mon.* 866 Animated by his manly prowesse, they tooke heart to grasse, as the prouerbe is.

d. In other expressions.

(In 1609 perh. associated with *herb of grace*, rue.)

1609 W. M. *Man in Moone* (1849) 3 After I had eaten a little heart a grasse, which grew at my feete, I feared not. **1703** R. WILKINSON IV. *Vice Reclaimed* G ij b, I will hide my self in thy Bosom, and be not far from thy Heart of Grace.

heart-pea, -piece, -pit, -purse: see HEART *sb.* 56.

'heart-piercing, *a.* [See PIERCE *v.*] That pierces, or is fitted to pierce, the heart; *fig.* that appeals keenly to the heart or emotions. Hence **'heart-piercingly** *adv.*

1590 SPENSER *F.Q.* III. xi. 30 The point of his hart-percing dart. **1647** TRAPP *Comm. Matt.* xiii. 4 The Pharisees were not a button the better for all those heart-piercing sermons of our Saviour. **1715–20** POPE *Iliad* XIV. 569 Heart-piercing anguish struck the Graecian host. *a* **1797** MARY WOLLSTONECR. *Posthum. Wks.* (1798) I. 50 So heart-piercingly pathetic in the little airs they would sing. **1870** MORRIS *Earthly Par.* I. II. 460 That sweet heart-piercing melody.

'heart-quake. [See QUAKE, and cf. *earthquake.*] Palpitation of the heart; *fig.* sudden and violent emotion, as of terror, delight, etc.

1561 HOLLYBUSH *Hom. Apoth.* 6 b, Somtyme commeth it [palsy] of..swounynge, hartquake, and superfluitye of bloode. *c* **1611** CHAPMAN *Iliad* VII. 188 Heartquakes shook the joints Of all the Trojans. *a* **1711** KEN *Anodynes* Poet. Wks. 1721 III. 427 When I a Heart-quake feel within, And Pains, Mementos of my Sin. **1819** BYRON *Juan* II. clxxxvi, Each kiss a heart-quake. **1884** BROWNING *Ferishtah, Two Camels* 117 How a lip's mere tremble..cheek's just change of colour..effect a heartquake.

So **'heart-quaking** *vbl. sb.* = prec.; **'heart-quaking** *a.*

1398 TREVISA *Barth. De P.R.* VII. xxxii. (1495) 246 Herte quakinge other Cardiacle comyth of defawte of the herte. *a* **1649** DRUMM. OF HAWTH. *Poems* Wks. (1711) 25 This great heart-quaking dolor wail and mourn.

ˈheart-qualm. [See QUALM.] An attack of palpitation or faintness of heart; also *fig.*; cf. prec.

c **1621** S. WARD *Life of Faith* (1627) 33 Vsing it..for swones and heart qualmes only. **1635** SWAN *Spec. M.* (1670) 205 Borage..doth greatly hinder swooning and heart-qualms. **1673** JANEWAY *Heaven on E.* (1847) 180 To be cured of these heart-qualms.

ˈheart-rending, *a.* [See REND *v.*] That rends the heart; terribly distressing. So **ˈheart-rending** *vbl. sb.*, terrible distress, pangs of anguish; **ˈheart-rendingly** *adv.*

a **1687** WALLER (J.), Heart-rending news..That death should licence have to rage among The fair [etc.]. **1798** MALTHUS *Popul.* (1817) II. 45 The heart-rending sensation of seeing his children starve. **1810** T. JEFFERSON *Writ.* (1830) IV. 154, I had..heard of the heart-rending calamity. **1854** J. S. C. ABBOTT *Napoleon* (1855) I. xxi. 343 As a..mother, I must feel the heart-rendings of those who will apply to me. **1873** BLACK *Pr. Thule* xx. 333 The trouble and heartrending of sleepless nights. **1890** *Temple Bar Mag.* 468 He..heard her heart-rendingly beg him not to go.

†**ˈheart-root.** *Obs.* Rarely **heart's-root.** [See ROOT *sb.*]

1. (Also pl. *heart-roots.*) The depth or bottom of the heart; the seat of the deepest emotion or most genuine feelings.

c **1200** *Trin. Coll. Hom.* 151 þe teares þe man wepeð..walleð of þe heorte rotes, swo water doð of welle. *a* **1300** *Cursor M.* 14892 He luued þaim in his hert rote. *c* **1386** CHAUCER *Wife's Prol.* 471 It tikleth me aboute myn herte roote. **1413** *Pilgr. Sowle* (Caxton 1483) IV. xxxi. 80 He draweth a depe sighe fro the herte rote. **1583** BABINGTON *Commandm.* iv. (1637) 39 Lamenting the same euen from our heart roots. **1650** S. CLARKE *Eccl. Hist.* I. (1654) 41, I..am sorry from the heart-root. **1822** SCOTT *Nigel* xxvii, Bash and Battie, blessings on the heart's-root of ye!

2. A sweetheart; a beloved one.

1522 SKELTON *Why not to Court* 664 He ys the kynges derlyng And his swete harte rote. **1555** BRADFORD in Coverdale *Lett. Mart.* (1564) 322 Praye for me myne own hart roote in the Lord. *a* **1765** *Old Robin of Portingale* xxvii. in Child *Ballads* III. lxxx. (1885) 241/2 Euer alacke, and woe is me, Here lyes my sweete hart-roote!

3. The tap-root of a tree. *rare.*

1668 *Phil. Trans.* III. 863 The best [wood] is found in the midst of the Tree, nourish'd by the Heart-root, which goes straight down into the Ground.

4. ? = HEARTWORT.

1617 MINSHEU *Ductor*, Harts-roote, *radix cordialis*: namque radix hujus herbæ confortat et corroborat cor.

ˈheart-scald, -scad. *Sc.* and *north. dial.* [See SCALD *sb.*] **a.** = HEARTBURN. **b.** *fig.* Disagreeable sensation, disgust, aversion.

1629 Z. BOYD *Last Battell* 1266 (Jam.) What an heart-scald should this bee vnto us, that wee have so long neglected this best part. *a* **1774** FERGUSSON *Cauler Water* Poems (1845) 25 Tho' cholic or the heart-scad tease us. **1822** SCOTT *Nigel* xiv, A look..that suld give her a heart-scald of walking on such errands. **1825** BROCKETT *N.C. Gloss*, *Heart-scad*, any thing disagreeable or contrary to your expectation or wishes. **1886** in *Syd. Soc. Lex.*

ˈheart-searching, *a.* [See SEARCH *v.*] That searches or rigorously examines the heart or feelings. So **ˈheart-searching** *sb.*; **ˈheart-searcher.**

1647 WARD *Simp. Cobler* 57 Into what importable..heart-searchings you will be ingulfed. **1685** BAXTER *Paraphr. N.T.* Matt. x. 11 Ministers being not heart-searchers, must pronounce God's Blessing on Men, on uncertainties. *a* **1708** BEVERIDGE *Thes. Theol.* (1711) III. 6 To fear Him..as an heart-searching God. **1863** I. WILLIAMS *Hymn*, '*Lord in this* [etc.]', Fill me with heart-searching fears. **1885** *Athenæum* 28 Nov. 697/1 The somewhat superfluous heart-searchings he has undergone.

heartsease, heart's-ease (ˈhɑːtsiːz). [See HEART *sb.* and EASE.]

1. (prop. as two distinct words.) Ease of heart; tranquillity or peace of mind; freedom from care and trouble; blithesomeness.

14.. *Chaucer's Clerk's T.* 378 (MSS. Corp.; Lansd.) And wisly bringe hem alle in hertes eese [*v.r.* reste and ese]. **1444–60** *Paston Lett.* No. 330 I. 443 To his plesaunce, and to your herts ease. *a* **1569** KINGESMYLL *Confl. Satan* (1578) 50 He is at heartesease both in mind and bodie. **1591** *Troub. Raigne K. John* II. (1611) 84 Hap and hearts-ease braue Lordings be your lot. **1748** RICHARDSON *Clarissa* III. iii. 32 In mere wantonness and heartsease I was for buffetting the moon. **1855** LONGF. *Hiaw.* x. 265 Songs of happiness and heart's-ease.

2. As name of a flower or plant. In 16th c. applied both to the Pansy and the Wallflower; at length restricted to the former.

The origin and occasion of the name are not clear. By the mediæval herbalists the pansy and wallflower or wall-gilliflower (as well as the stock gilliflower and other plants) were included in their genus *Viola*. Of the 16th c. herbalists, Turner 1548–51 has 'heart's ease' only as a name of the wallflower; Lyte in 1578, both of the wallflower ('viola lutea') and 'pances' ('viola tricolor'). But Palsgrave 1530 applies it only to the pansy, and this appears to be the general usage from R. Greene onward.

a. The Pansy (*Viola tricolor*); more esp. the small wild form. Also extended to kindred species, as the ***mountain heart's-ease*** (*V. lutea*).

1530 PALSGR. 229/2 Hartysease, a floure. *Ibid.* 231/1 Hertes-ease, *menve pensee.* **1578** LYTE *Dodoens* II. ii. 149 This floure is called..in English Pances, Loue in idleness, and Hartes ease. **1671** SALMON *Syn. Med.* III. xxii. 440 Viola Flammea, Herba Trinitatis..Hearts-ease, it is Emollient, helps Epilepsies. **1821** CLARE *Vill. Minstr.* II. 97 True-love-lies-bleeding, with the hearts-at-ease. **1828** MOORE *Ill Omens* iii, She stole through the garden, where heart's-ease was growing. **1862** HUXLEY *Lect. Wrkg. Men* 132 Hearts-ease and red clover..are fertilized by the visits of the bees.

allusively. **1599** *Life Sir T. More* Commend. Ep. in Wordsw. *Eccl. Biog.* (1853) II. 47 The golden marygold of obedience, hearts-ease of a settled conscience. **1684** BUNYAN *Pilgr.* II. 100 This Boy..wears more of that Herb called Hearts-ease in his Bosom.

†**b.** The Wallflower (*Cheiranthus Cheiri*). *Obs.*

1548 TURNER *Names of Herbes* 80 Viola..There are diuerse sortes of Leucoion. One is called in english, Cheiry, Hertes ease or wal Gelefloure..it hath yealowe floures. **1562** —— *Herbal* II. 163 b, Viola..that hath the yelow floure..is called..in Englishe Wal gelouer or hartis ease. **1562** BULLEYN *Def. agst. Sickness* (1579) 46 This herbe [Viola alba]..is commonly called Sweete William or Harts ease. **1578** LYTE *Dodoens* II. iii. 151 The yellow Gillofer is called..in English Wall floures and Hartes ease.

c. *locally* in *U.S.* The common Persicary or Peachwort (*Polygonum Persicaria*).

d. An ornament resembling a pansy flower.

a **1542** Q. KATH. HOWARD in Burnet *Hist. Ref.* III. App. III. lxxii. (1715) III. 171 He gave me a Heart's-Ease of Silk for a New-Year's Gift.

3. *slang.* (See quots.)

a **1700** B. E. *Dict. Cant. Crew*, *Hearts-ease*, a Twenty shilling piece; also an ordinary sort of Strong Water. **1785–96** GROSE *Dict. Vulgar T.*

ˈheart-shaped, *a.* Having the shape of a heart, especially the conventional form (HEART 23); cordate.

1776 J. LEE *Introd. Bot.* (ed. 3) Gloss. 408 *Cordatum folium*, the Heart-shaped Leaf. **1824** MISS MITFORD *Village* Ser. I. (1863) 100 Heart-shaped and triply folded, and its root Creeping like beaded coral. **1866** MISS YONGE *Dove in Eagle's N.* i. (1880) 2 The heart-shaped shepherd's purse.

ˈheart-sick, *a.* [f. HEART *sb.* + SICK *a.*]

1. Sick at heart; *fig.* depressed and despondent, esp. through 'hope deferred' or continued trouble.

1526 SKELTON *Magnyf.* 1640 Yet I am not harte seke. **1638** BAKER tr. *Balzac's Lett.* (Vol. II.) 127 The League is dead, and Spaine heartsicke. **1784** COWPER *Task* II. 244 Chatham, heart-sick of his country's shame. **1793** *Resid. France* (1797) I. 442 Faint and heart-sick with the unhealthy air. **1862** MRS. H. WOOD *Mrs. Hallib.* III. xxiv. (1888) 444, I have concealed our troubles until I am heart-sick.

2. Pertaining to or characterized by heart-sickness.

1591 GREENE *Maiden's Dr.* v, So was this Hinde with Hart-sicke pains enthralled. **1644** VICARS *Jehovah-Jireh* 21 To recover the Kingdom of its heart-sick diseases. **1667** MILTON *P.L.* XI. 482 Qualmes Of heart-sick Agonie. **1857** W. COLLINS *Dead Secret* VI. i, With a heart-sick consciousness of the slur that was cast on her birth.

3. (See quot.)

1725 BRADLEY *Fam. Dict.*, *Heart-Sick*, a Distemper incident to Oxen, and may be known by the frequent panting of the Flanks.

Hence **ˈheart-sickness,** heart-sick condition.

1726 *Dict. Rust.* (ed. 3) s.v., Heart-sickness in Oxen. **1841** LYTTON *Nt. & Morn.* I. v, Catherine was..deadly pale with heart-sickness and dismay.

heartsome (ˈhɑːtsəm), *a.* Chiefly *Sc.* [f. HEART *sb.* + -SOME.]

†**1.** Courageous, spirited, bold. *Obs.*

1567 *Satir. Poems Reform.* iii. 101 Now euerie Dowglas of ane hartsum mynde, Think on dame Margaret.

2. That gives heart or cheer; that rejoices the heart; animating.

1596 DALRYMPLE tr. *Leslie's Hist. Scot.* I. 49 The citie [Aberdeen] enioyes..a schip read, or hartsum hauining place. **1634** RUTHERFORD *Lett.* (1862) I. 110 Pray for well-cooked meat and an hartsome Saviour. **1726** E. ERSKINE *Serm.* Wks. 1871 I. 288 What a lightsome and heartsome dwelling place the believer has. **1879** STEVENSON *Trav. Cevennes* (1895) 191 Overhead the heartsome stars were set in the face of the night. **1889** *Harper's Mag.* Dec. 121/2 The wild thyme..filled all the air with heartsome fragrance.

3. Full of cheer or gladness; cheerful, merry, joyous, blithe.

1724 RAMSAY *Tea-t. Misc.*, *Polwart on Green*, With sangs and dancing keen We'll pass the heartsome day. **1799–1805** WORDSW. *Prelude* VII. 29 Ye heartsome Choristers, ye and I will be Associates. **1895** CROCKETT *Sweetheart Trav.* 129 He was a heartsome cleric, and gave us jovial greeting.

ˈheartsomely, *adv. Sc.* [f. prec. + -LY².] With good heart or cheer; cheerily, blithely.

1732 E. ERSKINE *Serm.* Wks. 1871 II. 150 How heartsomely doth faith lay claim to these treasures. **1831** CARLYLE in Froude *Life* (1882) II. 184, I can sit down with a clear conscience and talk heartily and heartsomely.

ˈheart-sore, *sb.* [f. HEART *sb.* 55 a + SORE *sb.*]

1. Pain or grief of heart; a cause of such pain.

c **1200** *Trin. Coll. Hom.* 207 *Cordis contricio*..þat is herte sor for mannes ȝene sinne. **1535** STEWART *Cron. Scot.* (1858) I. 17 With siching, sobbing, and with greit hart-sair. **1590** SPENSER *F.Q.* II. i. 2 That godly knight..His onely hart-sore and his onely foe. **1601** BP. W. BARLOW *Defence* 114 As Ægina to Athens, λημη, the eiesore thereof; so is this to Rome, the hartsoare thereof. **1835** MISS MITFORD *Country Stories* (1850) 154 Chalcott mill..was to Mrs. Deborah not merely an eye-sore, but a heart-sore.

†**2.** A disease of horses, etc. (obs. F. *encœur*).

1616 SURFL. & MARKH. *Country Farme* 139 The Enceur marg. The hartsore or swelling of the kernels of the hart.

heart-sore, *a.* [f. HEART *sb.* 55 c + SORE *a.*] Sore or grieved at heart; characterized by grief.

1591 SHAKS. *Two Gent.* I. i. 30 With hart-sore sighes. **1856** LEVER *Martins of Cro' M.* 412 Heartsore with the cares of wealth. **1862** TROLLOPE *Orley F.* xiii. (1866) 98 Every word that the dear, good, heart-sore woman spoke, told the tale of her jealousy.

ˈheart-spoon. *Obs.* or *dial.* [See SPOON *sb.*]

a. The depression at the end of the breast- or brisket-bone, called also *spoon of the brisket* or *stomach.* **b.** The pit of the stomach; the navel or midriff.

c **1386** CHAUCER *Knt.'s T.* 1748 He feeleth thurgh the herte spoon the prikke. *a* **1728** KENNETT *Etym. Angl.* Lansd. MS. 1033 lf. 174/2 Ha's varra seek, it warks at his heart-speaun. **1821** SCOTT *Kenilw.* xx, I will whet my dagger on his heart-spone, that refuses! *a* **1825** FORBY *Voc. E. Anglia*, *Heart-spoon*, the pit of the stomach.

ˈheart-strike, *v. rare.* [See STRIKE *v.*] *trans.* To strike to the heart, make a deep impression upon the feelings of. So **ˈheart-stricken** *ppl. a.* (= HEART-STRUCK b); **ˈheart-strickenly** *adv.*

a **1637** B. JONSON tr. *Horace' Art Poetry* 136 If they seeke to heart-strike us That are spectators, with their miserie. **1797** T. PARK *Sonn.* 6 Heart-stricken deeply by some barbed grief. **1837** HAWTHORNE *Twice-Told T.* (1851) I. iii. 44 Cruel! cruel! groaned the heart-stricken bride. **1846** LANDOR *Wks.* (1853) I. 571/2 *note*, So heart-strickenly and desperately was I ashamed.

heart-strings (ˈhɑːtstrɪŋz), *sb. pl.* [f. HEART *sb.* + STRING in sense 'sinew, tendon'.]

1. In old notions of Anatomy, the tendons or nerves supposed to brace and sustain the heart.

1483 *Cath. Angl.* 177/1 An Hartstringe, *precordia.* **1530** PALSGR. 229/2 Hartestrynges, *ueines de cuevr.* **1587** GOLDING *De Mornay* xv. 238 The head..heart..Liuer..the Sinewes, Heartstrings, and Vaines come from those parts. **1643** PRYNNE *Rome's Master-P.* (1644) 34 Stabbing [him] first in the mouth, next in the heart-strings. **1881** ROSSETTI *Ball. & Sonn.* (1882) 33 Once she sprang as the heifer springs With the wolf's teeth at its red heart-strings.

2. *transf.* and *fig.*

1601 HOLLAND *Pliny* I. 30 To seek out gemmes..we plucke the very heart-strings out of her [the earth]. **1652** R. SAUNDERS *Balm to heal Rel. Wounds* 72 The heart-strings of..his..arguments are cut. **1659** RUSHW. *Hist. Coll.* I. 537 The Priviledges of this House..are the Heart-strings of the Commonwealth. **1896** *Daily News* 4 June 6/2 The engineer..holding in his firm grasp the heartstrings of the ship.

b. *esp.* The most intense feelings or emotions; the deepest affections; the heart.

1596 SPENSER *F.Q.* IV. vi. 29 Her hart did leape and all her hart-strings tremble. *a* **1625** FLETCHER *Nice Valour* I. i, The falsest woman, That ever broke man's heart-strings. **1742** FIELDING *J. Andrews* I. xiii, A young woman, whom he loved as tenderly as he did his heartstrings. **1857** LIVINGSTONE *Trav.* Introd. 3 By his..winning ways he made the heartstrings of his children twine around him.

c. Often with allusion to stringed instruments of music.

1602 *2nd Pt. Return fr. Parnass.* V. i. 1982 [A fiddler sings] How can he play whose heart stringes broken are? **1869** SPURGEON *Treas. Dav.* Ps. cxi. 2 Our heart-strings are evermore getting out of tune. **1887** LADY M. MAJENDIE *Precautions* III. ii. 47, I will play on your heart-strings as I used to do.

ˈheart-struck, *ppl. a.* Struck to the heart:

†**a.** Keenly affecting or distressing the heart (*obs.*). **b.** Smitten with mental anguish or dismay.

1605 SHAKS. *Lear* III. i. 17 His heart-strooke injuries. **1667** MILTON *P.L.* XI. 264 Adam at the newes Heart-strook with chilling gripe of sorrow stood. **1785** BURNS *Cotter's Sat. Nt.* 61 Wi' heart-struck anxious care. **1818** MISS MITFORD in L'Estrange *Life* (1870) II. 43 Were you not heart-struck at the awful catastrophe?

heartward (ˈhɑːtwəd), *a.* and *adv.* [See -WARD.] Towards or in the direction of the heart; as concerns the heart.

1667 T. COXE in *Phil. Trans.* II. 452 The heart-ward part of the Vein to receive the Maingy Dog-blood. **1862** FROUDE in *Fraser's Mag.* May, Some silent heartward way. **1883** A. MACLEAN in *Memorial Vol.* 295 What a wasting disease we soon discover heartward.

heartwater (ˈhɑːtˌwɔːtə(r)). *Vet.* [f. HEART *sb.* + WATER *sb.*: so called from the characteristic accumulation of straw-coloured fluid in the pericardium of the heart.] A febrile disease of sheep, goats and cattle, caused by the virus *Rickettsia* (= *Cowdria*) *ruminantium*, transmitted by the bont tick (or other closely related ticks), and occurring in various parts of Africa, esp. South Africa, and in Madagascar.

1882 S. HECKFORD *Lady Trader in Transvaal* xiv. 134 The Nell family..swore it had died of what they call here 'heart-water'. **1896** R. WALLACE *Farm. Ind. Cape Col.* xx. 380 Heart-water in sheep is another obscure disease of a specific nature, which seems to be unknown in other sheep countries. **1905** *Rep. Brit. Assoc.* 282 An old-time supposition that *A*[*mblyomma*] *hebræum* was associated with a disease called 'heartwater', which had practically put a stop to the farming of sheep and angora goats in several south-eastern districts. **1930** *Discovery* Aug. 265/2 Heartwater in sheep was..caused by the bite of a tick,

Amblyomma hebraeum. **1949** *Cape Argus* 11 Aug. 3/6 They dealt with heartwater..in the Union.

'heart-whole, *a.* [See WHOLE.]

1. Uninjured at the heart; having the spirits or courage unimpaired; undismayed.

1470–85 MALORY *Arthur* IX. xxxiv, Neuer drede the, for I am herte hole, and of this wounde I shal soone be hole. **1591** HORSEY *Trav.* (Hakl. Soc.) 201 He is as hartt hole as ever he was. **1656** LD. HATTON in *Nicholas Pap.* (Camden) III. 280, I haue not heard from..the good Earle of N... I hope he is hart whole. **1721** NAISH in *Phil. Trans.* XXXI. 226 Dying daily by Piecemeal; but Heart-whole, as he express'd it. **1843** SIR T. WATSON *Princ. & Pract. Phys.* (1871) I. xxviii. 600 The mental faculties are clear, and the patients serene, and what is called heart-whole, to the last.

2. Having the affections free; with the heart unengaged.

1600 SHAKS. *A.Y.L.* IV. i. 49 Cupid hath clapt him oth' shoulder, but Ile warrant him heart hole. **1712** STEELE *Spect.* No. 288 ¶1 Your (yet Heart-whole) Admirer, and devoted humble Servant, Melainia. **1862** MRS. RIDDELL *World in Ch.* (1865) 314 Having passed heart-whole through a succession of London seasons.

3. Whole-hearted; free from hypocrisy or affectation; sincere, genuine.

1684 BUNYAN *Pilgr.* II. 141 Any Pilgrim..if he keeps Heart-whole towards his Master. **1879** FARRAR *St. Paul* (1883) 353 The Philippians were heart-whole in their Christian faith. **1886** MRS. HUNGERFORD *Lady Branksmere* I. i. 18 Such a gay, pretty, heart-whole laugh!

b. Thorough, thorough-paced, unmitigated.

1811 LAMB *Guy Faux* Misc. Wks. (1871) 370 This arch-bigot, this heart-whole traitor.

Hence **'heartwholeness.**

1882 H. G. MERIVALE *Faucit of B.* III. II. xiv. 69 That same heartwholeness..had been exposed to some dangerous siege-work. **1888** MRS. H. WARD *R. Elsmere* III. 4 Calmly certain of her own heart-wholeness.

'heart-wise, *adv.* [See -WISE.] After the manner or shape of a heart.

1727 BRADLEY *Fam. Dict.* s.v. *Horse Shoe*, Leaves..made Heartwise and divided by a crooked line. **1865** SWINBURNE *Ball. of Life* 12 Shaped heartwise.

'heart-wood. 1. A name for the central part of the timber of exogenous trees, hardened and matured by age; duramen.

1801 KNIGHT in *Phil. Trans.* XCI. 351 Ossified within the heart-wood. **1876** *Oxford Bible-Helps* 113 Ebony..is the heart-wood of the date-tree. **1880** GRAY *Struct. Bot.* iii. §3. 80 In all trees which have the distinction between the sap-wood and heart-wood well marked, the latter acquires a deeper colour.

2. The Tasmanian iron-wood, *Notelæa ligustrina.*

1889 J. H. MAIDEN *Useful Native Plants Austral.* 579 The heart-wood yields a very peculiar figure; it is a very fair substitute for Lignum-Vitæ. **1902** G. S. BOULGER *Wood* II. 221 *Notelæa ligustrina*... South-eastern Australasia. Known also as 'Heartwood' in Tasmania...exceedingly hard and close-grained.

heartwort ('hɑːtwɜːt). Also hert-, hart-. [From form of leaves (or ? seeds).]

1. The plant *Aristolochia Clematitis*, also called Birthwort.

c **1350** *O.E. Med. Gloss.* in *Archæol.* XXX. 409 Hert-wort, see Wodebron. Wodebron, bot. *Fraximis* [? *fraxinus*]. **1548** TURNER *Names of Herbes* 15 Astrolochia or round hertworte. *Ibid.*, Aristolochia longa..bryngeth furth fruite lyke blacke peares and seede lyke mennes hertes. **1565–73** COOPER *Thesaurus*, *Aristolochia*..Called astrologe or hartworte. **1578** LYTE *Dodoens* III. i. 314 Called..of some Byrthwort and Hartwort. **1607** TOPSELL *Four-f. Beasts* (1658) 269 Take of Aristoloch, otherwise called round Hart-wort, one ounce. **1610** MARKHAM *Masterp.* II. clxxiii. 483 Aristolochia, which we call birthwort, or hartwort.

†**2.** = HARTWORT, q.v. *Obs.*

†**3.** A species of Mint. *Obs.*

1597 GERARD *Herbal* (1633) 681 The fourth [species] is called..in English, Hart-woort, or Heart-mint.

†**4.** A local name of Melilot. *Obs.*

1640 PARKINSON *Theat. Bot.* 120 In some places of Essex they call it *Hartwort*, because [it causes] heart burne or paines of the heart.

hearty ('hɑːtɪ), *a.* (*adv.*) and *sb.* Forms: see HEART *sb.* [f. HEART *sb.* + -Y[1].] **A.** *adj.* Full of heart.

1. a. Full of courage; courageous, bold (*obs.*). In later use coloured by senses 4 and 5: Zealous; energetic or thorough in one's support or action.

c **1380** WYCLIF *Serm.* Sel. Wks. I. 286 Made hem herti to die for þe love of þe treuþe. *c* **1400** *Destr. Troy* 3813 The hertist to helpe of all the high kynges. *Ibid.* 8203 Triet men ..herty to stryke. **1509** HAWES *Past. Pleas.* XXVIII. lix, Dame Minerve..Dyd me endue with harty hardynes. **1568** GRAFTON *Chron.* II. 2192 Valiaunt Capteynes and hartie Souldiours. **1684** DRYDEN *Epil. to Constantine* 23 Such hearty rogues against the king and laws. **1704** *Col. Rec. Pennsylv.* II. 166 Persons hearty to the English Interest and Government. **1709** SWIFT *Adv. Relig.* Wks. 1755 II. I. 119 Declaring himself hearty for the government. **1776** ADAM SMITH *W.N.* I. i. (1869) I. 10 When he first begins the new work he is seldom very keen and hearty. **1855** MACAULAY *Hist. Eng.* xix. IV. 259 Two of the allied powers, and two only, were hearty in the common cause.

†**b.** As an epithet of compliment: ? Great-hearted, magnanimous, noble. *Obs.* (But perh. = prec. 'bold, courageous'.)

1552 LATIMER *Wks.* (1844) I. 356 Esay, that hearty prophet, confirmeth the same. *Ibid.* 515 Judas Machabeus, that hearty captain. **1596** DALRYMPLE tr. *Leslie's Hist. Scot.* VI. 312 Thay namet him a hartie horsman [L. *generosi equitis*] or a noble rydar.

†**2.** Possessed of understanding; wise, prudent, sagacious. *Obs. rare.*

1382 WYCLIF *Deut.* i. 13 3yue 3e of 3ow wise men and herti [Vulg. *gnaros*]. —— *Job* xxxiv. 10 Therfore, herty [Vulg. *cordati*] men, hereth me.

3. a. Full of kindly sentiment or goodwill; exhibiting warmth of affection or friendly feeling; cordial, kind-hearted, genial, cheery.

c **1440** *Promp. Parv.* 238/1 Herty, *cordialis.* *c* **1490** *Plumpton Corr.* 83 In the most hartyest wyse I recommend me to you. **1513** MORE in Grafton *Chron.* (1568) II. 757 No one thing..gat him..more hartie favor among the common people. **1712** ADDISON *Spect.* No. 269 ¶5 Our Salutations were very hearty on both Sides. **1853** LYTTON *My Novel* v. ii, There was no hearty welcoming smile on his face. **1856** KANE *Arct. Expl.* I. iii. 30 Madame Christiansen..was hearty and warm-hearted as ever.

b. Merry, blithe; = HEARTSOME 3. *Sc.*

1768 ROSS *Helenore* 117 (Jam.) Come, deary, gie's a sang, And let's be hearty with the merry thrang.

4. a. Proceeding from the heart; heartfelt, genuine, sincere.

1479 *Office Mayor Bristol* in *Eng. Gilds* 415, I shal aske theym forgevnes in as herty wyse as I can. **1526** *Pilgr. Perf.* (W. de W. 1531) 245 b, With herty thankes. **1546** in *Vicary's Anat.* (1888) App. iii. 129 Att the hartye desyer of the hole court. **1601** BP. W. BARLOW *Serm. Paules Crosse* 36 His repentance was so harty, that [etc.]. **1771** *Junius Lett.* lv. 292 He is a true and hearty christian. **1875** T. W. HIGGINSON *Hist. U.S.* xxiv. 239 Jefferson had a very hearty faith in it.

b. Existing in the heart; belonging to the inner feelings. *rare.*

1550 J. COKE *Eng. & Fr. Heralds* i. (1877) 55 Perceyvyng ..the sayde boke to be compyled of harty malyce. **1674** BREVINT *Saul at Endor* 124 Tho they keep still their hearty thoughts, they do quite reform their Language; they are ashamed to say in England, what they are proud to do at Rome. **1880** G. MEREDITH *Trag. Com.* (1881) 60 His inmost hearty devil was glad of a combat.

5. Giving unrestrained expression to the feelings; vehement, vigorous.

a **1661** FULLER *Worthies, Cambridge* (1840) I. 318 Such hearty laughters and other passionate gestures. **1727** SWIFT *Gulliver* II. iii, After an hearty fit of laughter. **1823** SCOTT *Peveril* xx, The captain bestowed a hearty curse. **1840** DICKENS *Barn. Rudge* xxxviii, Mr. Dennis gave him a hearty slap on the back. **1874** L. STEPHEN *Hours in Library* (1892) I. ii. 48 Who provoked Fielding to a coarse hearty burst of ridicule.

†**6.** Of disease: Violent, severe. *Obs.*

a **1639** SPOTTISWOOD *Hist. Ch. Scot.* VI. (1677) 411 The Chancellor..contracted a hearty sickness.

7. In sound health, having good appetite and spirits; vigorous, hale. Also *euphem.* tipsy (*Sc.*).

1552 HULOET, Hartye not beynge sycke, *sanus, valens in corpore.* **1662** R. MATHEW *Unl. Alch.* §22. 13 He was hearty and eat his meat. **1727** *Philip Quarll* (1816) 41 He awoke in the morning refreshed and hearty. **1818** *Edin. Even. Courier* 8 Oct. (Jam.), The pannel was hearty, but knew what he was about, and could walk very well. **1828** *Craven Dial.* s.v. *Hearty*, Shoe's feaful hearty to her meat. **1844** W. H. MAXWELL *Sports & Adv. Scotl.* xxxiii. (1855) 266 His honour was riding home hearty. **1858** LONGF. *M. Standish* v. 73 Square built, hearty, and strong, with an odour of ocean about him.

8. Of food or drink: Yielding good nourishment; strengthening, invigorating.

1617 MARKHAM *Caval.* VI. 17 This foode is verie hartie. **1776** ADAM SMITH *W.N.* I. xi. (1869) I. 171 Bread of oat-meal is a heartier food for labouring people than wheaten bread. **1796** MRS. GLASSE *Cookery* xv. 265 It is a very hearty drink. **1871** NAPHEYS *Prev. & Cure Dis.* I. ii. 58 Mutton and lamb have the reputation of being less hearty..than beef.

9. Of a meal or portion of food or drink: Satisfying to the appetite; abundant, ample, full.

1593 *Bacchus Bountie* in *Harl. Misc.* (1809) II. 308 They applied themselves to the harty carouse. **1596** SPENSER *F.Q.* IV. iii. 48 Ech drunk an harty draught. **1653** WALTON *Compl. Angler* 73 So here's to you a hearty draught. **1721** RAMSAY *To a friend at Florence*, Of all those dainties take a hearty meal. **1837** W. IRVING *Capt. Bonneville* III. 124 In a hearty and prolonged repast.

10. Of soil, land, etc.: In good heart, well fitted to bear crops.

1573 TUSSER *Husb.* xix. (1878) 49 Thistles so growing.. signifieth land to be hartie and strong. **1719** LONDON & WISE *Compl. Gard.* 314 Stronger and more hearty Lands. **1871** BEEVER *Daily Life Farm* Sept. 182 There was plenty of wet hearty muck put underneath.

11. Of timber: Consisting of heart-wood; strong, durable.

1624 WOTTON *Archit.* I, Oake and the like true hartie timber. **1776** G. SEMPLE *Building in Water* 115 Hearty and sound red Fir. **1884** *West. Morn. News* 30 Aug. 1/5 The oak is..clean, and very hearty.

12. *Comb.*, as ***hearty-hale, -mild.***

1591 SPENSER *Muiop.* 198 Sound Savorie, and Bazil hartie-hale. **1592** SYLVESTER *Tri. Faith* I. xv, Repentance, Hope, and hearty-milde Humility.

B. *adv.* or quasi-*adv.* = HEARTILY.

1753 FOOTE *Eng. in Paris* Prol., At your tragedy sure they laugh'd hearty enough. *a* **1863** THACKERAY *Fatal Boots* viii, I don't think I ever..ate more hearty.

C. *sb.* **1.** The adj. used *absol.*

c **1400** *Destr. Troy* 10053 Hard was the hurtelyng tho herty betwene.

2. A hearty fellow; a brave, vigorous man; *esp.* in phr. ***my hearty! my hearties!*** used in addressing sailors. Hence, a sailor, a jack-tar.

1839 MARRYAT *Phant. Ship* xli, You might..have let me had a side-rope, my hearties. **1841** LEVER *C. O'Malley* xxxvi, Monsoon, my hearty, how goes it? **1890** W. C. RUSSELL *My Shipmate Louise* II. xvi. 38 The lively hearty in the bows hooked-on.

3. At some English universities, used to denote an extrovert who enters heartily into college life and sports; an athletic (as distinguished from an æsthetic) man. Also in more general use (see quot. 1955).

1925 *Weekly Dispatch* 22 Nov. 9/2 The leaders in the sport ['debagging'] are a band of 'hearties' who hail mostly from Magdalen and 'The House'. **1928** in L. MacNeice *Strings are False* (1965) 274 Capell was knocked down in the Broad the other day by a hearty. **1930** *Times Lit. Suppl.* 24 July 610/4 At English universities undergraduates classify themselves into the mutually exclusive categories of 'aesthetes' and 'hearties'. **1934** C. LAMBERT *Music Ho!* iii. 216 The sheer anger aroused in 'hearties' of the Beachcomber order by such different manifestations of contemporary depression as jazz songs and the poetry of Eliot. **1955** *Times* 12 May 11/4 A hearty has come to mean an oppressively cheerful, muscular and back-slapping personage who is prostrating company. **1959** *News Chron.* 19 Aug. 4/3 There is no trace of the horse-play hearty in his make-up. **1964** C. MACKENZIE *My Life & Times* III. iv. 130 To go back to the noise in Trinity quad on that Saturday evening in 1903. 'Oh, these hearties!' I said... From that moment, at first as a term for Trinity men and later more generally, 'hearties' became current.

†**heascen,** *v. Obs.* Also 1 **hyscan, hiscan.** [OE. *hyscan*, f. *husc* insult, scorn, mockery.]

1. *trans.* To mock, deride, taunt.

c **1000** *Ags. Ps.* (Spelm.) ii. 4 (Bosw.) Seðe eardaþ on heofonum hyscþ hy. *c* **1000** *Lamb. Psalter* xxxii[i]. 10 (Bosw.) He hiscþ ȝeþeahtas eldra. *a* **1225** *Juliana* 5 Hire fleshliche feader..heascede mest men þe weren cristene.

2. *intr.* To rail, utter taunts.

c **1000** *Wulfstan* 235/25 Þonne hyscte he on ða godcundan lareowas. *c* **1230** *Hali Meid.* 31 Inker eiðer heasci wið oðer.

hease, variant of HEEZE.

heast, obs. form of HEST, HIGHEST *a.*

heat (hiːt), *sb.* Forms: 1 **hǽto, hǽtu, hǽte,** 2–3 **hæte,** 2–6 **hete,** 3, 6–7 **heate,** 6– **heat,** (4–5 **hette, heite,** 4–6 **heete,** *Sc.* **heit,** 4–5 **het,** 5 **heyte,** 5–6 **heet).** [OE. *hǽtu, hǽto*, str. fem., also *hǽte* wk. fem.; the former = OFris. *hête*, MDu. *hête, heete, heite*, OHG. *heizî*:—OTeut. **haitîn-*, f. **haito-* HOT: cf. *brede, heal* sbs.; *hǽte* corresponds to a type **haitjôn-*. Other words from same root (*hit, hît, hait*), differing in ablaut-grade and suffix, are Ger. *hitze*, OHG. *hizza*, OS. *hittia*, Du. *hitte*:—OTeut. **hitjâ-*, also ON. *hite* masc., and Goth. *heitô* fever.]

1. a. The quality of being hot; that quality or condition of matter which produces the sensation described in b; often regarded as a substance or thing contained in or issuing from bodies: *esp.* In ordinary use, A high or sensible degree of this quality; the condition of being hot; high temperature; warmth.

c **825** *Vesp. Psalter* xviii. 7 [xix. 6] Ne is se ðe hine ahyde from haeto his. **971** *Blickl. Hom.* 51 Þære sunnan hæto þe þas eorþan hlyweþ. *c* **1200** *Trin. Coll. Hom.* 119 Fir haueð on him þre mihtes, on to giuende hete, oðer to giuende liht [etc.] *c* **1200** ORMIN 1487 Þu..grindesst itt, annd cnedesst it, And harrdnesst itt wiþþ hæte. *a* **1300** *Cursor M.* 2248 Þe hette [*v.r.* hete] o þe sun. *c* **1375** *Sc. Leg. Saints, Magdalena* 116 Þe gret heit of þe sone. *c* **1440** *Promp. Parv.* 238/1 Hete, *calor, estus.* **1547** J. HARRISON *Exhort. Scottes* G vij a, If there should bee twoo sonnes, it wer perill least their two heates should burne vp al the arth. **1553** GAU *Richt Vay* 108 As heit procedis fra yᵉ fyr. **1585** T. WASHINGTON tr. *Nicholay's Voy.* I. viii. 7 b, The..stoves of Germanie in the whiche with a small heate they do breed and hatch their egges. **1665** R. HOOKE *Microgr.* 39 A Thermometer, thus marked and prepared, will be the fittest Instrument to make a Standard of heat and cold. **1731** ARBUTHNOT *Aliments* 6 The Heat in Land Animals helps likewise to the Solution of the Aliment. **1870** JEVONS *Elem. Logic* xxxiii. 291 Heat means ordinarily the excess of temperature above the ordinary mean.

b. The sensation or perception of this quality or condition; one of the primary sensations, produced by contact with or nearness to fire or any body at a high temperature, and also by various other causes, e.g. by any agency that quickens the circulation of the blood.

(In early use not easily separable from that which causes the sensation, the external or internal quality (senses 1, 4); see esp. quots. 1225, 1375 in 4 c.)

a **1704** [see 2]. **1794** J. HUTTON *Philos. Light*, etc. 19 When we approach the fire, our sense informs us in a particular manner; and this we name *heat*, which is then purely a sensation. **1855** BAIN *Senses & Int.* I. i. §6 We can neither feel nor know heat, except in the transition from cold. **1865–72** WATTS *Dict. Chem.* III. 15 The word Heat is used in common language, both as the name of a particular kind of sensation, and to denote that condition of matter in which it is capable of producing this sensation in us.

c. With adjectives of colour, used in reference to the appearance of metals and some other substances when at certain high temperatures, as BLUE *heat*, RED *heat*, WHITE *heat*; also with other defining words, as ANIMAL *heat*, BLOOD-HEAT, FEVER *heat*, etc.: see these words.

1703 MOXON *Mech. Ex.* 8 Several degrees of Heats Smiths take of their Iron..As first, a Blood-red Heat. Secondly, a White Flame Heat. Thirdly, a Sparkling, or Welding Heat.

2. a. In *Physics*, formerly supposed to be an elastic material fluid (CALORIC *sb.*), of extreme subtility, attracted and absorbed by all bodies; now held to be a form of ENERGY, viz. the kinetic and potential energy of the invisible molecules of bodies, capable of being transmitted from one body to another, whether in contact (see CONDUCTION 6, CONVECTION) or separated (see RADIATION): in the latter case, the energy during the transmission takes the form of **b.** ***radiant heat***, which is not properly heat at all, but the energy of vibration of the intervening ether, being identical, within a certain range of wave-length, with light.

1626 BACON *Sylva* §99 It is certaine, that of all Powers in Nature, Heat is the chiefe. **1665** R. HOOKE *Microgr.* 37 Heat is a property of a body arising from the motion or agitation of its parts; and therefore whatever body is thereby toucht must necessarily receive some part of that motion, whereby its parts will be shaken. *Ibid.* Table 248 Experiments to shew, that bodies expand by heat. **1695** WOODWARD *Nat. Hist. Earth* III. i. 121 *note*, Heat and Fire differ but in degree: and Heat is Fire, only in lesser quantity. Fire I shall shew to be a Fluid consisting of Parts extremely small and light and consequently very subtile, active, and susceptive of Motion. *a* **1704** LOCKE *Elem. Nat. Phil.* xi. (R.), Heat is a very brisk agitation of the insensible parts of the object; which produces in us that sensation, from whence we denominate the object hot: so what in our sensation is heat, in the object is nothing but motion. **1760** J. BLACK *Inq. Nat. Heat* 529 But heat is evidently not passive; it is an expansive fluid, which dilates in consequence of the repulsion subsisting among its own particles. **1833** N. ARNOTT *Physics* (ed. 5) II. 10 Heat cannot be exhibited apart, nor proved to have weight or inertia. *c* **1860** FARADAY *Forces Nat.* iii. 79 Whenever we diminish the attraction of cohesion we absorb heat. **1862** H. SPENCER *First Princ.* II. viii. §66 That mode of force which we distinguish as Heat, is now generally regarded by physicists as molecular motion. **1879** THOMSON & TAIT *Nat. Phil.* I. I. §385 The Dynamical Theory of Heat..is based upon the conclusion from experiment that heat is a form of energy.

b. **1794** G. ADAMS *Nat. & Exp. Philos.* I. iv. App. 157 The nature and properties of what has been called *radiant* heat. **1800** HERSCHEL in *Phil. Trans.* XC. 291 If we call *light*, those rays which illuminate objects, and *radiant heat*, those which heat bodies, it may be inquired, whether light be essentially different from radiant heat? *a* **1832** SIR J. LESLIE *Dissert.* in *Encycl. Brit.* (ed. 7) I. 646/2 Scheele pursued a similar path ..[That] which streams immediately from its source in rectilineal directions..he designated [*c* 1775] by the phrase Radiant Heat, which has since become a favourite appellation. **1834** MRS. SOMERVILLE *Connect. Phys. Sc.* xxv. (1849) 240 Radiant heat passes through the gases with the same facility as light. **1869** E. A. PARKES *Pract. Hygiene* (ed. 3) 309 Radiant heat from an open fire.

c. ***latent heat*** (Physics): the heat required to convert a solid into liquid or vapour, or a liquid into vapour; which, as it does not raise the temperature and so become sensible to the touch as warmth, was regarded as being absorbed and remaining latent in the resulting liquid or vapour.

Now viewed as the energy absorbed during the change of state, partly in increasing the molecular potential energy of the body, and partly in compressing external bodies.

c **1757** J. BLACK *Lect.* (1803) I. 157 Considered as the cause of warmth, we do not perceive its presence; it is concealed or latent, and I gave it the name of *latent heat.* **1765** REID *Let.* Wks. I. 42/2, I have attended Dr. Black's lectures hitherto. His doctrine of latent heat is the only thing I have yet heard that is altogether new. **1787** KEIR in *Phil. Trans.* LXXVII. 277 The heats absorbed and rendered latent, as some late philosophers express themselves. **1799** *Phil. Mag.* III. 419 A great quantity of vaporific, or, as it is called, latent heat, is carried off by the steam of water. **1830** LYELL *Princ. Geol.* I. 466 A portion of the steam is at first condensed into water, and the temperature of the water is raised by the latent heat evolved.

d. ***specific heat*** (Physics): the heat required to raise the temperature of a given substance to a given extent (usually one degree); it is calculated relatively to some standard substance, usually water (see quot. 1871), and forms a measure of the given substance's ***capacity for heat***.

a **1832** SIR J. LESLIE in *Encycl. Brit.* (ed. 7) I. 645/2 The best series of experiments on the distribution of heat among different bodies was performed before the year 1784 by Professor Gadolin of Abo, who, rejecting the notion of *Capacity*, introduced the unexceptionable expression, *Specific Heat.* **1842** BRANDE *Dict. Sci.*, etc., s.v., The term *specific heat* is applied to the quantity of thermometric heat required to raise different substances to the same temperature..The specific heat of water being = 1, that of oil is 0·5. **1863** TYNDALL *Heat* (1870) 139 As the specific heat increases, the atomic weight diminishes, and *vice versa.* **1871** MAXWELL *The. Heat* iii. 66 The Specific Heat of a body is the ratio of the quantity of heat required to raise that body one degree to the quantity required to raise an equal weight of water one degree. **1881** *Nature* No. 627. 15 Platinum has a specific heat of only ·032.

e. ***atomic heat, molecular heat*** (Chem.): the product of the specific heat of a substance into its atomic or molecular weight: see quots.

1850 GRAHAM *Elem. Chem.* I. 139 The *atomic heat* of bodies, as it is named by this chemist [M. Regnault, 1841], is obtained by multiplying the observed specific heat of each body by its equivalent. **1865–72** WATTS *Dict. Chem.* III. 37 Within certain classes of allied compounds..the molecular heats of the substances..or the products of their specific heats into their molecular weights..are approximately equal ..As a rule, the molecular heat of solid compound bodies increases with the number of atoms contained in their molecule.

3. *spec.* **a.** A hot condition of the atmosphere or physical environment; hot weather or climate: often spoken of as an agent perceptible by its effects (cf. COLD *sb.* 1 a).

c **825** *Vesp. Hymns* viii. 8 Bledsiað cele and hætu dryhten. *c* **1000** *Ags. G.* Matt. xx. 12 Gelice us þe bæron byrþena on þises dæᵹes hæton. **1340** HAMPOLE *Pr. Consc.* 1438 Now es cald, now es hete, Now es dry, and now es wete. **1382** WYCLIF *Gen.* viii. 22 All the daies of the erthe, seed and ripe, coold and hete, somer and wynter, nyȝt and day, shulen not rest. *c* **1420** *Pallad. on Husb.* I. 41 If hit [water] be cole in hete an luke in colde. *c* **1470** HENRY *Wallace* IV. 2 In September..Quhen passyt by the hycht was off the hette [*v.r.* heit]. **1593** SHAKS. *Lucr.* 1145 Some dark deep desert.. That knows not parching heat nor freezing cold. **1697** DRYDEN *Virg. Georg.* IV. 581 Weary with his Toil, and scorch'd with Heat. **1799** *Med. Jrnl.* I. 78 Throughout a great part of September, the heat continued with little sign of abatement. **1870** LOWELL *Study Wind.* 4, I had not felt the heat before, save as a beautiful exaggeration of sunshine.

b. (with *pl.*) An instance of this condition; a hot period or season.

1390 GOWER *Conf.* III. 106 The cheles bothe and eke the hetes. **1448** *Prose Chron.* in *R. Glouc.* (1724) 520 This yere [1252] was a gret hete and droughthe in Engelond. **1526** SKELTON *Magnyf.* 12 After a hete oft cometh a stormy colde. **1573–80** BARET *Alv.* H 333 The great heates are abated. **1760–72** tr. *Juan & Ulloa's Voy.* (ed. 3) II. 267 The heats not being excessive, nor the colds severe. **1856** STANLEY *Sinai & Pal.* i. I. 19 The chief resorts of the Bedouin tribes during the summer heats.

c. A hot place; a fire.

1382 WYCLIF *Acts* xxviii. 3 An eddre, whanne she cam forth fro the heete, assailide his hond. *a* **1400** *Sir Perc.* 862 He keste the wiche in the hete. **1611** BIBLE *Acts* xxviii. 3 There came a Uiper out of the heat, and fastened on his hand.

d. High temperature produced by fermentation or putrefaction, as in a hotbed; hence applied *concr.* to a hotbed, esp. in phr. ***in heat.***

c **1400** MAUNDEV. (1839) v. 49 Thei..coveren hem [Eyren of Hennes, etc.] with Hete of Hors Dong, with outen Henne, Goos or Doke, or any other Foul. **1664** EVELYN *Kal. Hort.* (1729) 189 The Dung..must have pass'd its first Heat, lest apply'd before, it burn the Plant. **1724** MILLER *Gard. Dict.* s.v., All Heat of Hot-Beds, Mr. Bradley says, proceeds from fermentation. **1796** C. MARSHALL *Garden.* xix. (1815) 385 Some chuse to forward them on heat, in March and April. **1887** *Gardening* 3 Dec. 531/1 Those that are wanted to come in early may at once be put in heat. **1887** *Ibid.* 17 Dec. 567/3 Strike them..in a moderate bottom-heat.

4. As a quality or condition of animal bodies.

a. The normal high temperature of the body in warm-blooded animals; the warmth characteristic of a living body (***natural heat, vital heat***).

1340–70 *Alex. & Dind.* 328 Whan we holde waxen, Whan mihte lakken our limus & lesen our hete, We schulle forleten oure lif. **1390** GOWER *Conf.* I. 251 The life hath lost his kindely hete, And he lay dede as any stone. **1563** W. FULKE *Meteors* (1640) 31 The vitall heat is quite extinguished. **1697** DRYDEN *Æneid* III. 397 Astonished at the sight, the vital heat Forsakes her limbs.

b. High temperature in the body arising from a disordered condition, as in inflammation or fever; inflamed or feverish state.

c **1000** *Sax. Leechd.* I. 82 Gif se lichoma hwær mid hefighere hæto sy ᵹebysᵹod. *Ibid.* 84 Wiþ wunda hatum ᵹenim þonne weᵹbrædan þa wyrt. *c* **1205** LAY. 30550 Þa iwarð þe king..hafde þat uuel hate. *a* **1535** MORE *Wks.* 572 (R.) No more then the heate of a feuer is a right natural heate. **1573–80** BARET *Alv.* H 333 It helpeth the head ach, the burning heat of the eies, and other inflammations. **1597** GERARDE *Herbal* (1633) 171 The iuyce [of onions] taketh away the heate of scalding with water or oyle. **1782** MISS BURNEY *Cecilia* I. viii. 272 The burning heat of his skin. **1862** J. B. HARRISON *Lett. Dis. Children* 192 There is room for more apprehension..if there be no febrile heat.

c. A condition of the body in which the general surface temperature is higher than usual, producing the sensation described under 1 b; the state of feeling hot.

a **1225** *Leg. Kath.* 1701 Ne eileð þer na mon..nowðer heate ne chele nowðer hunger ne þurst. *c* **1375** *Sc. Leg. Saints, Paulus* 912 He tholit..bath gret hungir & het. *c* **1489** CAXTON *Sonnes of Aymon* xx. 452 For there nys noo man so oolde, but he sholde soone gete hete there wythin a lityll while. **1573–80** BARET *Alv.* H 333 When they were in heate with drinking. **1612** DRAYTON *Poly-olb.* ii, Where over-toil'd, her heat to cool, She bathes her in the pleasant Pool. **1887** P'CESS CHRISTIAN *Mem. Margrav. Baireuth* 383 The soldiers..having got into a fearful state of heat, threw themselves into cold water.

d. with *a* (rarely in *pl.*): An instance of this bodily condition. †***to catch*** or ***get a heat***: to become hot or warm (*obs.*).

a **1400–50** *Alexander* 3803 A litill drysnynge of dewe ..[he] bringis it to oure balde kyng to brigge with his hetis. **1508** DUNBAR *Tua mariit Wemen* 222 Me think ther haldin ȝow a hete, as ȝe sum harme alyt. *a* **1529** SKELTON *Dyuers Balettys* Poet. Wks. 1843 II. 22 After her cold she cought a hete. **1589** PUTTENHAM *Eng. Poesie* III. xxiv. (Arb.) 302 When she walketh apace for her pleasure, or to catch her a heate in the colde mornings. **1887** RITA *Lady Nancye* I. ix. 37 To commence, he was in a profuse heat.

†**5.** In mediæval physiology, as a quality of 'elements', 'humours', and bodies in general: see HOT *a. Obs.*

1390 GOWER *Conf.* III. 100 The drie coler with his hete By wey of kinde his propre sete Hath in the galle. **1398** TREVISA *Barth. De P.R.* III. xiv. (1495) 58 Bi hete and wete the vertue inmutatiua werkyth the softer substaunce. **1610** BARROUGH *Meth. Physick* I. ii. (1639) 2 By heat in this Chapter is meant a hot distemper without any kind of humour. **1626** BACON *Sylva* §758 Doues are the fullest of Heat and Moisture amongst Birds.

6. The quality of being 'hot' in taste; strength or pungency of flavour.

1586 B. YOUNG *Guazzo's Civ. Conv.* IV. 190 b, She caused the heate of the wine to be delayed with water. **1599** SHAKS. *Hen. V*, III. vii. 21 The heat of the Ginger. **1626** BACON *Sylva* §863 The Root [orris root] seemeth to haue a Tender dainty Heat.

7. a. A redness or eruption on the skin, accompanied by a sensation of heat, or indicating inflammation.

1597 GERARDE *Herbal* (1633) 999 The ripe Straw-berries ..take away..the rednesse and heate of the face. **1676** *Lond. Gaz.* No. 1146/4 A black brown [Nag] having a little heat on his fore-feet. **1711** ADDISON *Spect.* No. 57 ¶ 5, I have seen a Woman's Face break out in Heats, as she has been talking against a great Lord. **1773** (*title*), The History of a Gentleman cured of Heats in the Face.

b. ***prickly heat***: a skin disease common in hot climates (*Lichen tropicus*), characterized by minute papulæ formed by the hyperæmia of the sweat follicles.

1736 WESLEY *Wks.* (1872) I. 37 She had only the prickly heat, a sort of rash, very common here in summer. **1874** DUNGLISON *Med. Dict.*, Prickly Heat, *Lichen Tropicus.* The pimples are bright red..with heat, itching, and scratching.

†**8. a.** A heating (in phr. ***to give a heat to***). *Obs.* exc. as in b.

c **1430** *Two Cookery-bks.* 22 Sette it on þe fyre, an ȝif it an hete. **1500–20** DUNBAR *Poems* xxvi. 77 Thay gaif thame in the fyre a heit. **1545** ASCHAM *Toxoph.* II. (Arb.) 114, I woulde desyre all bowyers to season theyr staues well, to woorke them and synke them well, to giue them heetes conuenient and tylleryriges plentye.

b. A single operation of heating, as of iron in a furnace; hence *concr.* the quantity of metal heated at one operation.

1594 GREENE & LODGE *Looking Glasse* Wks. (Rtldg.) 119, I have left my master striking of a heat and stole away. **1602** *Life T. Cromwell* I. ii. 79 You idle knaves..What, not a heat among your work to-day? **1703** MOXON *Mech. Exerc.* 9 But if it be not..throughly welded at the first Heat, you must reiterate your Heats so oft. **1831** J. HOLLAND *Manuf. Metal* I. 84 It [the..metal] is piled loosely in the middle of the furnace, and is called a heat. **1888** *Sci. Amer.* 21 Apr. 246/3 A field bakery of this kind can deliver 17,928 loaves of bread for nine 'heats', each loaf forming two rations. **1892** *Labour Commission* Gloss. s.v. *Heats*, The quantity of metal or steel placed in a puddling mill or Siemens furnace is called a *heat*.

†**c.** A run given to a race-horse by way of exercise in preparation for a race. *Obs.*

[**1577** B. GOOGE *Heresbach's Husb.* III. (1586) 123 b, Then walke him to chafe him, and put him in a heate.] **1670** EVELYN *Diary* 22 July, The jockeys breathing their fine barbs and racers, and giving them their heats. **1683** *Markham's Masterp. Revived* Title-p., Containing Methods for the Training of Horses up for Racing, with their Heats and Courses. **1727–51** CHAMBERS *Cycl.* s.v., Two heats in a week are reckoned a just measure for any horse..The jockeys lay it down as a rule, that one of the heats be given on the same day of the week whereon the horse is to run his match.

9. *fig.* A single intense effort or bout of action; one continuous operation; a stroke, a 'go'. Chiefly in phr. ***at a heat.*** (Sometimes associated with 8 b.)

c **1380** *Sir Ferumb.* 2762 Capouns y-bake al-so tok he foure in þilke hete. *c* **1400** *Destr. Troy* 10288 Miche harme, in þat hete, happit to falle. **1676** DRYDEN *Aurengz.* II. i, I'll strike my fortunes with him at a heat, And give him not the leisure to forget. **1681** —— *Sp. Friar* Ep. Ded., Neither can a true just play, which is to bear the test of ages, be produced at a heat. **1726** LEONI *Alberti's Archit.* III. 26/2 One..shewed him a piece of Painting, with a boast, that he had done it at a single heat. **1823** J. BADCOCK *Dom. Amusem.* p. iv, The new articles..having been 'thrown off at a heat', stood particularly in want of re-revision. **1855** MOTLEY *Dutch Rep.* viii. (1858) II. 12 On one occasion he hanged twenty heretics, including a minister, at a single heat.

10. a. A single course in a race or other contest. (See also DEAD HEAT *sb.*)

a **1663** VISCT. FALKLAND *Marriage Nt.* II. in Hazl. *Dodsley* XV. 129 And will ride his heats as cleanly as a dieted Gelding. **1673** DRYDEN *Marr. à-la-Mode* IV. i, I take heat after heat, like a well-breath'd Courser. **1675** *Lond. Gaz.* No. 1026/4 The second Plate will be Run for on the same Moor, by three Heats. **1697** *Ibid.* No. 3315/4 The same day in the morning will be run for, by Women, a Smock of 5*l.* value, 3 Heats, half a mile each Heat. **1751** SMOLLETT *Per. Pic.* lxxxviii. (Farmer), Seeing his antagonist distanced in the first and second heats. **1801** STRUTT *Sports & Past.* II. ii. 82 These contests are extended to two or three heats or trials. **1873** BENNETT & 'CAVENDISH' *Billiards* 12 He won three heats of 100 up, and in the second heat made 22 spot-hazards.

b. *transf.* and *fig.*

1685 DRYDEN *Epil. to Albion & Albanius* 4 Feigned Zeal, you saw, set out the speedier pace; But the last heat, Plain Dealing won the race. **1705** STANHOPE *Paraphr.* II. 222 He that gives out, at the last Heat, loses the Benefit of all his labours and successes in the former. **1817** BYRON *Let. to Murray* 5 Apr., As for 'Manfred', the first two acts are the best; the third so so; but I was blown with the first and second heats. **1849** THACKERAY *Pendennis* iv, Pen had started in the first heat of the mad race.

†**c.** The ground on which a heat is run; a race-course. *Obs.*

1682 *Lond. Gaz.* No. 1741/4 The Plates are run for 3 times round the Round-Heat. **1701** *Ibid.* No. 3751/8, 3 Plates will be run for on the new Heat upon Epsom Downs.

11. a. Intensity or great warmth of feeling; fervour, ardour, animation, vehemence, eagerness, excitement, passion, rage.

*c*825 *Vesp. Hymns* xi. 9 Se rehta ȝeleafa mid hætu walle. *c*1200 ORMIN 13855 Off all soþ lufess hæte. *c*1375 *Sc. Leg. Saints, Katherine* 386 In ire & in gret het. *c*1380 WYCLIF *Serm.* Sel. Wks. I. 104 Dewe of grace..wiþ þe hete of charite. 1481 CAXTON *Reynard* (Arb.) 110 Fooles that in hete hasten hem so moche. 1526 *Pilgr. Perf.* (W. de W. 1531) 107, I wyll..not departe for all this intemperate heate. 1580 SIDNEY *Ps.* VI. i, While thou art in the heate of thy displeasure. 1604 SHAKS. *Oth.* I. ii. 40 It is a businesse of some heate. 1649 MILTON *Eikon.* (1770) 21 He was sorry to hear with what popular heat elections were carried in many places. 1694 F. BRAGGE *Disc. Parables* IV. 155 Many a man injures another in suddain heat and passion. 1834 L. RITCHIE *Wand. by Seine* 66 A lady, who spoke with some heat, and great volubility. 1862 MRS. H. WOOD *Mrs. Hallib.* III. iii. (1888) 323 It was done in the heat of passion. 1958 *Listener* 30 Oct. 709/2 The heat is being pumped into utterly different quarrels. 1962 *Ibid.* 5 Apr. 587/1 His foreign minister..had set himself the task of taking the heat out of inter-Arab exchanges. 1964 *Ann. Reg. 1963* 100 This merely added more heat to the argument.

b. (with *pl.*) An instance of this: an access of feeling or intensity.

*c*1200 *Trin. Coll. Hom.* 111 He is sendere of alle holie heten. 1340 *Ayenb.* 124 Temperance aye þet zouþ aye þe wykkede hetes. 1474 CAXTON *Chesse* III. iii. (1883) 103 That he..myght eschewe the heetes and occasions of lecherye. 1565 JEWEL *Def. Apol.* (1611) 238 Amplifications, or heats of speech, the better to stirre vp, and to enflame the minds of the Hearers. 1711 ADDISON *Spect.* No. 261 ¶6 When the first Heats of Desire are extinguished. 1856 W. ARTHUR *Tongue of Fire* ii. (1885) 27 The very head whose heats of ambition and of vindictiveness He had rebuked.

c. (with *pl.*) A fit of passion or anger; †a quarrel, angry dispute (*obs.*).

1549 W. WRIGHTMAN in Tytler *Edw. VI & Mary* (1839) I. 170 He was in a great heat. 1570–6 LAMBARDE *Peramb. Kent* (1826) 329 Betweene whom and the predecessors of these Monks there had beene great heats for the erection of the same. 1664 POWER *Exp. Philos.* III. 184 A vexatious dispute..which..signified no more than a Heat 'twixt two Oyster-wives in Billingsgate. 1733 POPE *Hor. Sat.* II. i. 136 Fond to spread friendships, but to cover heats. 1804 WELLINGTON in Gurw. *Desp.* III. 107 To keep alive heats and animosities. 1887 EDNA LYALL *Knt.-Errant* xii. 106 Vexed! I was never in such a heat in my life.

†d. As a personal quality: Passionateness, excitability, ardour of temperament. *Obs.*

1689 BURNET *Tracts* I. 44 One sees in them a heat, and bigotry beyond what appears either in France or Italy. 1712 ADDISON *Spect.* No. 440 ¶6 The Man of Heat replied to every Answer of his Antagonist with a louder Note than ordinary. 1718 HICKES & NELSON *J. Kettlewell* III. cxix. 483 She should not choose People of Heat for her Companions.

e. *U.S. slang.* A state of intoxication caused by alcohol or drugs, esp. in phr. ***to have a heat on.***

1912 D. LOWRIE *My Life in Prison* vii. 77 A few years ago this dump was full of dope. Every other man y'r met had a heat on, an' lots o' young kids what came here strong an' healthy went out with a habit. 1931 D. RUNYON *Guys & Dolls* (1932) ii. 41 The party is going big along toward one o'clock when all of a sudden in comes Handsome Jack Maddigan with half a heat on, and in five minutes he is all over the joint, drinking everything that is offered him.

12. a. The intense or violent stage of any action; greatest vehemence or intensity; height, stress (e.g. of conflict, debate, etc.).

1588 Q. ELIZ. in Nichols *Progr.* (1823) II. 536 Being resolved, in the midst and heat of the battle, to live or die amongst you all. 1607 SHAKS. *Cor.* IV. iii. 19 To com vpon them, in the heate of their diuision. 1695 *Lond. Gaz.* No. 3098/2 The heat of the Action lasted about two hours. 1722 DE FOE *Plague* (1754) 42 At the first Heat of the Distemper. 1838 PRESCOTT *Ferd. & Is.* (1843) I. iii. 187 In the very heat of the war against the insurgent Catalans. 1944 'N. SHUTE' *Pastoral* ix. 206 He wants to get you both off the station on leave till the heat goes off. 1970 E. R. JOHNSON *God Keepers* (1971) xii. 132 There was a lot of merit in having the ranking man right where the heat was going to be.

b. *slang* (orig. *U.S.*), in various interconnected senses, notably (*a*) a gun (? as an instrument of 'heat'); also ***heater***; (*b*) in phr. ***to turn on*** (or ***give***) ***the heat***, to use a gun, hence *fig.*, ***to turn the heat on*** (someone), to apply pressure on; (*c*) involvement with or pursuit by the police; a police officer, the police.

1928 *Amer. Mercury* May 80/1 The greatest difficulty for such a mob was to avoid another's *heat*. *Ibid.*, It's not so much your own heat you got to watch, but you're apt to run into a bunch of hoosiers out looking for another outfit just hot from some caper. 1929 *Sat. Even. Post* 13 Apr. 54/3 A pistol may be a heat... A man shooting a gun is fogging... 'I fogged away with my heat until I pooped that dummy.' 1929 *Detective Fiction Weekly* 9 Nov. 651/2 Aw, put up your heaters. If you bump me you don't git anywheres. 1930 *Amer. Mercury* Dec. 456/1 Either take our beer or it's plenty of heat for yours. 1931 G. IRWIN *Amer. Tramp & Underworld Slang* 96 *Heat*, the state of mind of the police or public following a crime or series of crimes, when the people are 'hot under the collar' or 'all heated up'. More lately, any trouble, as 'in hot water'. 1931 D. RUNYON *Guys & Dolls* (1932) iii. 58 Maybe you remember John the Boss, and the heat which develops around and about when he is scragged in Detroit? 1932 W. R. BURNETT *Silver Eagle* i. 7 'He don't even pack a heater.' 'Don't what?' 'He don't carry a gun.' 1934 H. N. ROSE *Thesaurus of Slang* iii. 16/2 Cover One with a Gun (v. phr.): to turn on the heat. 1936 J. G. BRANDON *Pawnshop Murder* xxv. 246 You planted yourself in a safe spot to give Lou the heat. 1936 H. COREY *Farewell, Mr. Gangster* xiv. 174 But the word went out that the government heat was on. The FBI was known to be relentless in its pursuit. *Ibid.* ii. 14 During the heat on the bank robbers the field agents almost lost the habit of sleep. 1937 E. H. SUTHERLAND *Professional Thief* 238 *Heat*, danger in general; an investigation; a policeman. 1938 J. CURTIS *They drive by Night* xix. 211 The bleeding heat's on here for me. 1939 R. CHANDLER *Big Sleep* xiv. 110 Then he leaned back..and held the Colt on his knee. 'Don't kid yourself I won't use this heat, if I have to.' 1944 W. R. BURNETT *Nobody lives Forever* xvii. 137 Jim..took out his gun..and ..tossed it down a manhole-grating... 'I was hoping that I'd never have to use that heater.' 1957 *Listener* 24 Oct. 637/2 The moment seemed opportune to 'turn the heat' on Turkey. 1967 W. MURRAY *Sweet Ride* x. 168 He got busted last week and he don't take that too kindly. Guess he figured you was heat. 1969 *New Yorker* 19 July 20 Out the door comes this great big porcine member of the heat, all belts and bullets and pistols and keys. 1970 C. MAJOR *Dict. Afro-Amer. Slang* 65 *Heat*, law-enforcement officer. 1972 WODEHOUSE *Pearls, Girls, & Monty Bodkin* xi. 178 And Dolly, drop the heater and leave that jewel case where it is, I don't want any unpleasantness.

13. Sexual excitement in animals, especially in the female, during the breeding season; usually in phr. ***at*** or ***in heat.***

1768 G. WASHINGTON *Writ.* (1889) II. 243 Music was also in heat and served promiscuously by all the Dogs. 1794 S. WILLIAMS *Vermont* 102 The female is in heat in the winter, and bears her young in..March. 1836–9 TODD *Cycl. Anat.* II. 441/2 This state of excitement, generally named 'the heat', lasts for a longer or shorter period.

14. *Comb.* **a.** *attrib.*, as ***heat-capacity, -chart, -cloud, -flame, -flow, -focus, -force, -haze, -insulation, -insulator, -lamp, -mist, -power, -ray, -retrogression, -shock, -supply, -test, -trap, -value***; (sense 4 b) ***heat-pimple, -rash.*** Also ***heat-like*** adj. or adv.; ***heat-labile, -sensitive, -stable*** adjs.

1875 *Wond. Phys. World* II. iv. 311 The *heat-action of the sun. 1902 *Encycl. Brit.* XXXIII. 279/2 The *heat-capacity of the water. 1892 E. REEVES *Homeward Bound* 42 Weather, wind and *heat charts. 1895 KIPLING *2nd Jungle Bk.* 140 When the *heat-cloud sucks the tempest. 1881 WATTS *Chem.* VIII. II. 1017 The axis of greatest *heat-conduction in uniaxial crystals is parallel to the direction of easiest cleavage. *Ibid.*, The *heat-conductivity of mercury. 1871 tr. *Schellen's Spectr. Anal.* iii. 11 No soot is deposited ..by the non-luminous *heat-flame. 1902 *Encycl. Brit.* XXXIII. 297/1 *Heat-flow due to Conduction. 1925 J. JOLY *Surface-Hist. Earth* vi. 104 Steady heat-flow to the surface. 1955 *Times* 11 July 2/6 A research group investigating problems of heat flow in supersonic aircraft. 1971 I. G. GASS et al. *Understanding Earth* iii. 67/1 The 'heat flow'—the rate of escape of interior heat from the Earth's surface. 1884 *Times* (weekly ed.) 12 Sept. 17 Wind-mills.. with those unwieldy arms swaying around in the *heat-haze. 1899 *Daily News* 12 Jan. 6/2 The flat, endless continent, fading away in the heat-haze. 1901 'LINESMAN' *Words by Eyewitness* (1902) 30 The ranks of little kopjes across the river slumbered in the heat-haze. 1960 C. DAY LEWIS *Buried Day* ii. 43 Summer lanes Whose sound quivers like heat-haze endlessly. 1902 *Encycl. Brit.* XXXIII. 283/2 Expansion or compression under the condition of *heat-insulation, represented by curves called Adiabatics. 1937 *Discovery* Feb. 35/1 Double walls of canvas enclosing an air space, which acted as a perfect *heat insulator. 1946 *Nature* 27 July 121/1 One vital *heat-labile system in the earliest stages of the chain of activity preceding cell division. 1964 *Oceanogr. & Marine Biol.* II. 342 A hot-water extract (containing the substrate but not the heat-labile enzyme). 1839 BAILEY *Festus* xxiii. (1848) 292 As a spiritual quality.. Hidden or open, *heatlike doth inhere In all existence. 1901 H. W. WILSON *With Flag to Pretoria* I. vi. 91 Indistinct lines of Boer entrenchments, flickering through the *heat-mist. 1940 W. EMPSON *Gathering Storm* 48 The heat-mists that my vision hood Shudder precisely with the throng. *a*1665 in Walton *Life Hooker* H.'s Wks. 1888 I. 77 His face full of *heat-pimples. 1905 *Westm. Gaz.* 26 Aug. 13/2 The practical science of *heat-power-production. 1956 A. H. COMPTON *Atomic Quest* 52, 10,000 kilowatts of heat-power. 1887 SAINTSBURY *Hist. Elizab. Lit.* xii. (1890) 450 They were only harmless *heat-rashes, not malignant distempers. 1866 BRANDE & COX *Dict. Sci., etc.*, **Heat Rays*, applied to the red rays of the spectrum, and to other rays which fall outside the red end of the spectrum, and which are consequently invisible. 1887 WARD tr. *Sachs' Phys. Plants* xxxix. 696 The least refrangible heat-rays. 1880 S. HAUGHTON *Phys. Geogr.* vi. 312 Periods of *heat-retrogression (such as the glacial). 1946 *Nature* 10 Aug. 194/1 Electronics have brought a contribution in the evaporation of solutions of *heat-sensitive materials such as penicillin. 1964 N. G. CLARK *Mod. Org. Chem.* i. 5 This may cause the decomposition of one or more of the heat-sensitive components. 1946 *Nature* 23 Nov. 763/1 The production in certain varieties of apples, of diploid pollen by *heat-shock treatment of the pollen mother cells. 1956 *Ibid.* 4 Feb. 227/2 In *Drosophila*, heat-shock at an appropriate stage results in the development of the cross-veinless phenotype. 1946 *Ibid.* 23 Nov. 760/1 *Heat-stable enzyme. 1964 M. HYNES *Med. Bacteriol.* (ed. 8) xxiii. 339 *R. prowazeki* and *R. mooseri*..are differentiated by specific heat-labile major antigens, but share a common heat-stable antigen. 1901 *Kynoch Jrnl.* Feb.–Mar. 57/1 The *Heat-Test of Nitro Explosives. 1906 W. DE MORGAN *Joseph Vance* xviii, I think of the *sole di marzo* blazing on the roses in that Tuscan *heat-trap. 1887 *Chambers's Jrnl.* 24 Sept. 623/1 The exact *heat-value of different kinds of liquid fuel. 1962 *Economist* 21 July 256/1 The main use of this gas should be to fuel power stations (at a 'heat value' parity price with coal or oil).

b. *objective* and *obj. genitive*, as ***heat-absorbing, -absorption, -economizer, -evolution, -forming, -giver, -giving, -loss, -making, -measurer, -producer, -production, -radiator*** (= RADIATOR b), ***-regulator, -regulating, -resistant, -resisting, -storage, -tempering*** adjs.

*a*1618 SYLVESTER *Posthumi* Sonn. xiii. Wks. 1880 II. 323 The timely sweet heat-temp'ring showers. 1800 HERSCHEL in *Phil. Trans.* XC. 310 If the coloured rays themselves are not of a heat-making nature. 1857 *Chambers' Inform. People* I. 739/1 The proportion of nutritive to the heat-forming principle in loaf-bread is 10 to 46. 1864 *Proc. Amer. Phil. Soc.* IX. 343 The heat-absorbing capacity of aqueous vapor. 1867 *Trans. Ill. Agric. Soc.* VI. 53 Heat Radiator [exhibited]. 1874 DUNGLISON *Med. Dict.* s.v. *Aliment*, Liebig divides them [aliments] into two classes..flesh formers and heat givers. 1877 ESTES *Half-hour Recreat. Pop. Sc.* Ser. II. 148 An accurate Heat-Measurer. 1879–81 WATTS *Dict. Chem.* VIII. II. 1018 The heat-conducting power of water. 1884 *Jrnl. Nerv. & Mental Dis.* XI. 141 He believed the central nervous system to have an immediate influence on heat-production. 1897 *Daily News* 8 Jan. 9/1 Infra-red waves or the invisible rays beyond the red end of the spectrum..being calorific or heat-producing. 1897 *Allbutt's Syst. Med.* II. 26 The paralysis of the heat-regulating centres. 1899 CALLENDAR & BARNES in *Rep. Brit. Assoc.* 626 The external heat loss is more regular and certain. 1899 *Daily News* 21 July 4/4 A heat-resisting alloy. 1902 *Encycl. Brit.* XXXIII. 280/1 Heat-evolution is reckoned as positive, heat-absorption as negative. *Ibid.* XXVI. 508/1 The heat-loss can be reduced to a minimum. 1904 GOODCHILD & TWENEY *Technol. & Sci. Dict.* 283/2 *Heat radiator*, a device by which the cooling of the cylinder of a motor cycle or of the condenser of a car is promoted. 1904 *Daily Chron.* 29 Nov. 4/5 The heat-regulating mechanism of the body. 1905 *Daily Chron.* 14 July 4/4 Animal foods rich in fat..are heat-producers of the first order. 1927 HALDANE & HUXLEY *Animal Biol.* iii. 87 If we put our man..into a calorimeter for a day and measure his heat-production. 1934 *Archit. Rev.* LXXV. 24/2 With the removal of weight from partitions and external walls came a reduction in thickness of material, with a consequent loss of sound and heat-resisting qualities. 1935 *Archit. Rev.* LXXVIII. 129 A double window was evolved with central heating between the two glass lines to minimize the heat loss occasioned by the lavish use of glass. 1951 *Good Housek. Home Encycl.* 263/1 All heat-storage cookers have insulated hot-plate covers. 1960 *Farmer & Stockbreeder* 22 Mar. Suppl. 11/3 The steel-reinforced, heat-resistant handle. 1961 WHITBY & HYNES *Med. Bact.* (ed. 7) ii. 17 The ultimate test of a sterilizer is to show that live spores are killed. The spores must be carefully chosen—soil bacteria are often too heat-resistant for the purpose. 1962 *Gloss. Terms Glass Industry* (*B.S.I.*) 8 *Heat-resisting glass*, a glass able to withstand high thermal shock. 1964 L. MARTIN *Clinical Endocrinol.* (ed. 4) vii. 227 A varicocœle may also upset the heat-regulating mechanism and this is aggravated by a suspensory bandage. 1964 R. F. FICCHI *Electr. Interference* viii. 151 As ground current flows through the ground rod electrode, heat is generated that follows the well known I^2R heat-loss pattern.

c. *instrumental*, as ***heat-clouded, -concreted, -cracked, -crazed, -hazed, -killed, -laden, -misted, -oppressed, -set*** adjs. (so ***heat-setting*** vbl. sb. and adj.); ***heat-seal*** vb. (so ***heat-sealed, -sealing*** ppl. adjs.); also with meaning 'against or from heat', as ***heat-insulated, -isolated, isolation, -proof*** adjs.

1598 SYLVESTER *Du Bartas* II. i. III. *Furies* 470 Heat-concreted sand-heaps. 1605 SHAKS. *Macb.* II. i. 39 A false Creation Proceeding from the heat-oppressed Braine. 1859 LD. LYTTON *Wanderer* (ed. 2) 179 The glimmer Of day thro' the heat-clouded window. 1876 GEO. ELIOT *Dan. Der.* liv. IV. 102 Heat-cracked clay. 1894 M. DYAN *All in Man's Keeping* I. vi. 98 The deep heat-misted valley. 1902 *Encycl. Brit.* XXXIII. 288/1 If the system is heat-isolated. *Ibid.* The difficulty of realizing experimentally the condition of heat-isolation. 1906 *Daily Colonist* (Victoria, B.C.) 6 Jan. 5/6 Get a 34-inch poker for your air-tight heater; they are nicely made and have the Alaska heat-proof handle. 1909 *Daily Chron.* 21 Jan. 4/7 Glasses treated in this manner become heat-proof, and may last for years. 1913 E. F. BENSON *Thorley Weir* iii, Over all lay a grey heat-hazed sky. 1920 H. G. WELLS *Outline Hist.* 21 This novel covering of feathers, this new heat-proof contrivance that life had chanced upon. 1926 *Daily Colonist* (Victoria, B.C.) 23 July 1/4 In Jersey City, three heat-crazed dogs attacked two young boys. 1946 *Nature* 27 July 121/1 In heat-killed grain there was no change in nucleolar size. 1952 E. J. LABARRE *Dict. Paper* (ed. 2) 125/2 Heat-sealing papers include several types of paper coated with wax, varnish..which will adhere when pressed together with heat. 1957 *Textile Terms & Defs.* (ed. 3) 88 (s.v. *Setting*), In order to ensure that the crimp is not readily removed..the fibre may be set to impart permanency of crimp, and the operation is known as heat-setting. 1961 *Lancet* 9 Sept. 592/1 This is heat-sealed across its width. 1962 J. T. MARSH *Self-Smoothing Fabrics* ii. 8 During the early investigations into the finishing of nylon fabrics, it was found that a heat-setting process had a stabilising effect. 1963 A. J. HALL *Textile Sci.* iii. 130 The yarn becomes bulky, with each filament having heat-set small loops closely but irregularly spaced. *Ibid.* v. 221 The pin or clip chains over the greater part of their travel run through a heat-insulated chamber. 1964 *Discovery* Oct. 17/1 So impervious to water-vapour is the laminate, even along heat-sealed seams, that less than 0.012 grams per square metre can be leaked through samples every 24 hours.

d. Special combs.: **heat-apoplexy, -asphyxia** = ***heat-stroke***; **heat balance**, the distribution of the flow of heat and other forms of energy into and out of a system in which there is no change in internal energy; also, an account or record of such a distribution, esp. as a means of evaluating the efficiency of boilers, etc.; **heat barrier** *Aeronaut.*, the limitation on the speed of aircraft, etc., due to heating by air friction; **heat bump**, a protuberance on the skin supposed to be due to heat; **heat-centre** *Physiol.*, any of several areas within the central nervous system which control the regulation of the body temperature; **heat coil** *Electr.*, a device fitted in a telephone exchange to protect the lines against small harmful currents; **heat cycle**, a cycle of operations or states in a heat engine; **heat-death** (see quot. 1930[2]); **heat-energy**, that form of energy which is manifested in heat; **heat-engine**, an engine in which the motive power is

produced by heat, a thermodynamic engine; **heat equator** = *thermal equator* (see EQUATOR 3 b); **heat exchanger**, a device used for the transference of heat from one medium to another; so **heat exchange, heat exchanging**; **heat-factor** = ENTROPY; **heat-fever**, fever caused by exposure to heat; **heat filter**, any device that selectively removes heat radiation but permits the passage of light, **heat flash** (see quot. 1958); **heat-lightning**, summer lightning, occurring in hot weather; **heat-pipe**, a closed, evacuated tube containing around its inner surface a wire mesh or other wick saturated with a working liquid, which through the capillary action of the wick and the higher vapour pressure of the liquid when heated makes possible the rapid conduction of heat away from a source; **heat-potential**, term used by Rankine for the rate of isometric variation with temperature of the external work done by a body per unit mass during its isothermal expansion to any volume from a standard volume; **heat-pump**, a heat-engine working in reverse (such as a refrigerator), in which work supplied to it is used to transfer heat from a colder to a hotter body; **heat-seeker**, (*a*) a heat-seeking missile; (*b*) a device which detects infra-red radiation and the direction from which it comes and supplies the information to the control system of a heat-seeking missile, etc.; **heat-seeking** *ppl. a.* (of a missile, etc.) using the infra-red radiation emitted by a target to home on it; **heat-set, heat-setting ink** (see quots.); see also *heat-set* adj., *-setting* vbl. sb. and adj. sense 14 c above; **heat-shield** (see quots.); **heat-sink** (see quot. 1965²); **heat-spectrum**, the spectrum of heat-rays, visible and invisible; **heat sponge**, a type of heat sink; **heat-stroke**, an affection of the nervous system, frequently fatal, caused by exposure to excessive heat; **heat tinting** (see quot. 1958); **heat tonality, tone, toning** *Physical Chem.* [tr. G. *wärmetönung*], the sum of the heat produced in a chemical reaction and of the work done by the system, expressed in heat-units; the heat of reaction at constant volume (*disused*); **heat transfer**, the transfer of heat from one medium to another; **heat-unit**, a unit quantity of heat; usually reckoned as the amount of heat required to raise the temperature of a unit weight (pound, gramme, etc.) of water one degree. See also HEAT-DROP, -SPOT, -WAVE.

1874 DUNGLISON *Med. Dict.*, *Coup de soleil*, .. an affection produced by the action of the sun on some region of the body .. has been called heat or solar asphyxia, heatstroke, *heat apoplexy. **1891** *Daily News* 21 Sept. 6/1 Two men were seized with heat apoplexy. **1898** B. DONKIN *Heat Efficiency of Steam Boilers* xiv. 239/2 An approximate '*heat balance', or statement of the distribution of the heating value of the coal among the several items of heat utilised and heat lost, may be included in the report of a test. **1954** *Jrnl. Meteorol.* XI. 8/1 The heat balance between the surface of the earth and the atmosphere .. involves a flux of latent heat and of sensible heat, in addition to the radiational items. **1971** *Nature* 25 June 540/1 Ecologists are therefore interested in ways of inferring the temperature of a leaf from a knowledge of its heat balance. **1953** H. HABER *Man in Space* 66 The designers of the Sky-rocket had to be on guard against not only the sonic barrier. With its high rate of speed their craft might run into an obstacle more serious than buffeting shock waves: the *heat barrier. **1953** *Sci. Amer.* Dec. 80/1 This is the heat barrier: the heating of a plane by the friction and piling up of air on aircraft surfaces at supersonic speeds. **1954** *Times* 5 Mar. 11/5 They might well find that [the ultimate limits of manned aircraft] were very high and that in the same way as the sound barrier had been overcome the problems of the heat barrier would be solved also. **1957** [see BARRIER *sb.* 4 b]. **1970** J. CHAPLIN *Wings & Space* 146/1 There is no way to break through the heat barrier as there is with sound. **1927** W. E. COLLINSON *Contemp. Eng.* 57 Spots, which, it is hoped, are *heat-bumps. **1884** *Jrnl. Nerv. & Mental Dis.* XI. 141 Tscheschichin was the first to announce the existence of an inhibitory *heat-centre in the nervous system. **1907** *Practitioner* June 771 The action of the heat-centres being sluggish. **1968** M. MONNIER *Functions Nerv. Syst.* I. xv. 422 Successful protection from cold is possible through the central nervous co-ordination of several biophysical and chemical mechanisms. This is accomplished by the so-called heat center in the posterior hypothalamus. **1900** K. B. MILLER *Amer. Telephone Pract.* (ed. 3) xxiii. 275 A device to afford protection against currents such as these [*sc.* sneak currents] .. is termed a *heat coil. **1971** *Gloss. Electrotechnical Power Terms (B.S.I.)* III. ii. 13 *Heat coil*, a thermal device to protect apparatus from damage by external currents. **1894** B. DONKIN *Text-bk. Gas, Oil, & Air Engines* I. ii. 13 (*heading*) *Heat 'cycles' and classification of gas engines... Engineers have agreed to designate as a 'cycle' the successive operations taking place in a heat motor. **1930** *Engineering* 8 Aug. 187/3 The following .. trends were .. observable: .. design and operation on more efficient heat cycles [etc.]. **1930** J. JEANS *Mysterious Universe* i. 13 The second law of thermodynamics predicts that there can be but one end to the universe—a '*heat-death' in which the total energy of the universe is uniformly distributed, and all the substance of the universe is at the same temperature. **1959** J. BLISH *Clash of Cymbals* iii. 73 Any cyclical theory of the universe, any continuous and eternal systole/diastole from monobloc to heat-death and back again. **1973** *Nature* 11 May 65/1 What lies ahead is, in Clausius's later term, 'a heat death'. **1876** P. G. TAIT *Rec. Adv. Phys. Sci.* 138 We are led to speak of the availability of an amount of *heat-energy. **1893** *Jrnl. Soc. Arts* 8 Sept. 897/1 The practically unavoidable waste of heat energy. **1902** *Encycl. Brit.* XXXIII. 283/2 The whole of its intrinsic heat energy might theoretically be recovered in the form of external work. **1915** *Chambers's Jrnl.* Jan. 43/1 For all the heat-energy wasted .. the consumer has had to pay. **1968** R. A. LYTTLETON *Mysteries Solar Syst.* ii. 77 The release exceeds the gentle loss of heat-energy arising from the very slow processes of conduction within the Earth. **1904** GOODCHILD & TWENEY *Technol. & Sci. Dict.* 283/2 *Heat Equator. **1911** M. I. NEWBIGIN *Mod. Geogr.* iv. 87 Those regions of the earth which are directly beneath the vertical rays of the sun are heated most intensely... This belt of high temperature is called the heat equator. **1902** G. E. DAVIS *Handbk. Chem. Engin.* II. ii. 132 (*caption*) Diagrammatic sketch of *heat-exchanging tanks. *Ibid.* 133 (*heading*) Heat exchangers... In no case would the cold water be heated to the temperature of the original hot water. **1908** *Sci. Abstr.* A. XI. 203 For snow the average total daily heat-exchange is 19 gm. cals. per cm.² **1915** *Chem. Abstr.* IX. 2332 (*heading*) Heat exchange apparatus wherein the one agent flows through one tube and the other agent flows through an annular chamber surrounding the said tube. **1924** R. SELIGMAN *Brit. Pat.* 223,033, In some .. descriptions of heat exchanging or sterilising apparatus .. it has been proposed in order to obtain a tight jointing to groove and tongue the rims. *Ibid.*, The plates would be working in parallel and the heat exchange effected by counter current. **1947** *Science News* IV. 33 A heat exchanger, then, is merely a means whereby the heat which would normally be wasted is used for combustion. **1952** *Ibid.* XXV. 87 This is done by means of the heat exchanger, which by various means effects the transfer of heat from the gases leaving the turbine to the air entering the combustion chamber. **1958** *Engineering* 28 Feb. 284/1 As an aid in securing high thermal efficiency from gas-turbine plants, use is frequently made of a heat exchanger, whereby the turbine exhaust heat is used to preheat the combustion gas. **1959** *Listener* 29 Oct. 732/3 Twelve heat exchangers for the new Bradwell (Essex) nuclear power station. **1967** M. CHANDLER *Ceramics in Mod. World* v. 157 Where refractories are used to store and transfer heat, as in heat exchangers, the most important property required is high heat capacity. **1859** RANKINE *Steam Eng.* 310, ϕ is called the *thermodynamic function* of the substance for the kind of work in question; and in some papers, the **heat-factor*. **1549** *Compl. Scot.* xi. 24 The lord sal sende pestilens on the, the *heyt feueir, drouht. **1898** W. E. WOODBURY *Encycl. Dict. Photogr.* 367, I have taken a powerful projection lantern and set it as near to the microscope as the intervening *heat-filter will permit. **1962** *Which?* Mar. 68/2 The heat filter prevents much of the heat radiated from the lamp, from reaching the slide. **1958** *Chambers's Techn. Dict.* Suppl. 984/1 **Heat flash*, intense heat radiation from an elevated A or H bomb, detection of which, by heat-sensitive paint, gives the precise indication of ground-zero. **1961** 'C. E. MAINE' *Man who owned World* x. 118 Central London was a wilderness of fused stone and leaning skeletal buildings, blackened and oxidised by nuclear heat flash. **1834** C. A. DAVIS *Lett. J. Downing* ii. 17 You may just as well try to paint a flash of *heat-lightning in dog-days. **1849** THOREAU *Week Concord Riv.* 275 Friendship is .. remembered like heat lightning in past summers. **1890** JULIA P. BALLARD *Among the Moths* 122 Like the play of miniature heat-lightning. **1964** G. M. GROVER et al. in *Jrnl. Applied Physics* XXXV. 1990/1 We will refer to devices of this general class, for brevity, as '*heat pipes'. *Ibid.* 1991/1 A liquid sodium heat pipe for operation at about 1100°K was constructed. **1969** *New Scientist* 19 June 641/1 A heat pipe is one of the major components of the most powerful and efficient radioisotope-heated power generator yet built. *Ibid.*, The advantage of the heat pipe is that the outside surface is at the same temperature along the whole of its length. **1853** RANKINE in *Trans. R.S.E.* XX. 569, I shall call this function a *heat-potential. **1894** J. A. EWING *Steam-Engine* iv. 118 By a refrigerating machine or *heat-pump is meant a machine which will carry heat from a cold to a hotter body. *Ibid.*, Any heat-engine will serve as a heat-pump if it be forced to trace its indicator diagram backwards. **1948** E. F. OBERT *Thermodynamics* xiv. 520 The reversed heat-engine cycle is called a refrigerator (and, also a heat pump) when the evaporator is used for cooling purposes .. ; the same cycle is called a heat pump (but not a refrigerator) when the condenser is used for heating purposes. **1957** *Encycl. Brit.* XIX. 55/2 The heat-pump system .. is a conventional refrigeration system where the heat rejected by the refrigerant at the condenser is utilized for heating during the winter while the evaporator absorbs heat from .. any .. low-grade heat source. **1966** *McGraw-Hill Encycl. Sci. & Technol.* VI. 369/1 Unless the price of electric energy is low .. the heat pump cannot be justified solely as a heating device. However, if there is also need for comfort cooling .. in the summer, the heat pump, to do both the cooling and heating, becomes attractive. **1956** W. A. HEFLIN *U.S. Air Force Dict.* 248/1 **Heat seeker*, a guided missile or the like incorporating a heat-seeking device for homing on heat-radiating machines or installations, such as an aircraft engine or blast furnace. *Colloq.* **1961** *Flight* LXXX. 716/2 Other features include a wide-angle heat-seeker behind the hemispherical glass nose, and extreme system simplicity. **1984** *Pacific Defence Reporter* Aug. 61 It is an all-aspect heat seeker that can perform 30 g maneuvers, and can be launched in a very wide envelope. **1986** *Rotor & Wing Internat.* Feb. 84 Texas Instruments is developing an enhanced signal processor using very high speed integrated circuits .. for the missile's infrared heat-seeker. **1956** *Heat-seeking [see *heat-seeker* above]. **1966** *Sunday Times* 25 Sept. 2/7 The MiG 17 does not carry heat-seeking missiles but is an excellent plane in low-level combat. **1985** *Daily Tel.* 22 Nov. 32/6 This equipment can be used to counter heat-seeking missiles such as the Soviet SA-7 Grail shoulder-fired weapon, now extensively deployed in Third World countries. **1941** *Inland Printer* Nov. 42/1 The new presses .. would enable us to print the body of the magazine entirely with the improved *heat-set inks. **1947** R. BURNS *Printing Inks* v. 249 (*heading*) Heat-setting inks. The fresh prints are exposed to intense heat from gas flames or radiant surfaces for a very short period. **1963** KENNEISON & SPILMAN *Dict. Printing* 91 *Heat-set inks*, printing inks manufactured in a special way to induce quicker drying... The vehicle of these inks is such that it vaporizes rapidly when the paper is heated after printing. **1957** W. E. CLASON *Elsevier's Dict. Electronics* 226 **Heat shield*, a metallic surface surrounding a heat radiating element e.g. a hot cathode in order to reduce the radiation loss. **1962** J. GLENN et al. in *Into Orbit* 245 *Heatshield*, as used in Project Mercury missions .. consists of a coating of ablative material on the rounded base of the capsule which evaporates during re-entry and carries off much of the heat in the form of a gas. **1968** *Times* 16 Dec. 7/3 Reentry speed was slightly faster than expected for Apollo 8 and the heat shield on the space-craft was charred to a depth of three-quarters of an inch. **1956** *Jrnl. Brit. Interplan. Soc.* XV. 302 The determination of optimum sink temperature is beyond the scope of this paper, particularly since thorough analysis of the entire radiation *heat sink problem has been previously presented. **1957** W. E. CLASON *Elsevier's Dict. Electronics* 226 *Heat sink*, used with power transistors to dissipate heat. **1959** *Listener* 28 May 930/1 By mounting the transistor on a relatively large piece of metal, which in turn is fixed to what is called a heat sink—something into which unwanted heat can be shot—the powers that transistors can handle .. have been greatly increased. **1961** *Aeroplane* C. 372/2 For the Mach 2 aircraft the air supply from the main engines can be cooled by using the fuel as a heat sink. **1965** *New Scientist* 20 May 507/1 Satisfactory control of the rate and extent of cooling of the patient is obtained by regulating the temperature of the heat sink. **1965** W. H. ALLEN *Dict. Technical Terms for Aerospace Use* 132/2 *Heat sink*, (1) in thermodynamic theory, a means by which heat is stored, or is dissipated or transferred from the system under consideration; (2) a place toward which the heat moves in a system; (3) a material capable of absorbing heat; a device utilizing such a material and used as a thermal protection device on a spacecraft or reentry vehicle; (4) in nuclear propulsion, any thermodynamic device, such as a radiator or condenser, that is designed to absorb the excess heat energy of the working fluid. **1972** *Sci. Amer.* Mar. 118/2 All power transistors .. must be mounted on heat sinks that have large cooling fins. **1949** A. R. WEYL *Guided Missiles* 15 For short ranges, cooling of the heated walls may be avoided, either by the '*heat sponge' principle (absorption and conduction of heat through walls of substantial thickness) [etc.]. **1958** A. G. HALEY *Rocketry* iii. 57 The American Rocket Society .. developed a 'heat sponge' motor, wherein blocks of aluminum absorbed large amounts of heat. **1874** *Heat-stroke [see *heat-apoplexy*]. **1891** *Lancet* 11 July 82 Heat-stroke is not a frequent disease in the British Navy .. the cases .. generally arise in the Red Sea in the persons of cooks, stewards, bakers, and occasionally stokers. **1910** C. H. DESCH *Metallogr.* vii. 149 Stead has devised an electrical heater, by means of which the *heat-tinting can be carried on on the stage of the microscope. **1958** A. D. MERRIMAN *Dict. Metallogr.* 121/2 *Heat tinting*, a method of distinguishing and of identifying the micro-constituents of a polished surface of a metallographic specimen. The method is based on the fact that temper colours or heat tints .. appear when oxidation begins on a polished surface that is being heated. **1895** C. S. PALMER tr. *Nernst's Theoret. Chem.* III. iv. 435 Instead of using the '*heat-toning' (heat tonality) to determine the ratio of distribution, one may employ .. the changes in the volumes .. of the solutions, on neutralisation. *Ibid.* IV. i. 491 The sum of the heat produced in the reaction, and of the external work performed, .. we will call the 'heat-toning' (Wärmetönung) of the reaction... This 'heat-toning' represents the change of the total energy .. of the system. **1902** H. C. JONES *Elem. Physical Chem.* 286 Since we have reactions which evolve heat .., and also reactions in which heat is absorbed .., the heat tone may be positive or negative. **1934** A. J. MEE *Physical Chem.* xv. 608 The term 'heat tonality' is sometimes used to denote the amount of heat associated with a chemical reaction. **1940** GLASSTONE *Physical Chem.* iii. 192 At one time the heat of reaction at constant volume was called the 'heat tone' (Wärmetönung) of the reaction; although this term is still used in German scientific literature, its significance is now equivalent to the general expression 'heat of reaction', the qualification of constant volume or pressure being added. **1937** *Jrnl. R. Aeronaut. Soc.* XLI. 121 He had been very interested in discovering the relationship between *heat transfer and friction. *Ibid.*, It was well known that a flat plate and a rough surface produced comparatively the same rate of heat transfer. **1958** *Times Rev. Industry* Apr. 9/1 The relative virtues of .. heat-transfer media. **1966** W. A. HEFLIN *Second Aerospace Gloss.* 60/2 *Heat transfer*, the transfer of heat within a substance or structure by radiation, conduction, or convection.

heat (hiːt), *v.* Forms: 1 hǽtan, (haten, hatten), 2–5 hete(n, 3 heaten, (3rd sing. pres. hat), 4–6 *Sc.* het, 5 heete, hette, 6–7 heate, 6– heat. Pa. t. and pple.: see below. [Com. Teut.: OE. *hǽtan* = MDu. *heeten, heten, heiten*, Du. *heten*, LG. *hêten*, OHG. and MHG. *heizan*, Ger. *heizen*, ON. *heita* (Da. *hede*):—OTeut. **haitjan*, f. **hait-oz* HOT. The pa. t. and pple. underwent in ME. various shortenings, some of which are still dialectal; the literary language now recognizes only *heated*.]

A. Illustration of Forms of Pa. t. and Pa. pple.

1. *Pa. t.* α. 1 **hǽtte, hætte**; β. 3–4 **hatte**; γ. 4 **hette**, 4–5 **hett**, 5–7 (*dial.* -9) **het**; δ. 6–7 **heat**; ε. 6– **heated**.

α. *c* **1000** *Shrine* 16/15 Ðæs swanes wif hætte hire ofen.
β. *c* **1330** R. BRUNNE *Chron. Wace* (Rolls) 15729 Þe ffeuere agu ful sore hym hatte.
γ. *c* **1381** CHAUCER *Parl. Foules* 145 That on me hette, that othir dede me colde. *c* **1430** LYDG. *Min. Poems* (Percy Soc.) 40 She het his bak. *c* **1450** *St. Cuthbert* (Surtees) 3491 He hett water and wescht his fete. **1616** MARLOWE & CHAPMAN *Musæus* III. Wks. (Rtldg.) 291/2 Her blushing het her chambers.
δ. **1607** TOPSELL *Four-f. Beasts* (1658) 203 He first of all heat the Goats dung. **1665** R. HOOKE *Microgr.* 35 Others .. I heat red hot .. and then suffered them to cool.
ε. **1583** STANYHURST *Æneis* III. (Arb.) 75 Thee fields .. thee dogstar Sirius heated.

2. *Pa. pple.* α. 1 **ȝehǽt(ed, -hǽtt**; β. 3–4 **yhat, ihatte**, 5–6 **hatte**; γ. 4 **i-het**, 4–6 **hett, -e**, 5–6 (*dial.

-9) het; δ. 5 heet, 6-7 heat, -e, 7 *Sc.* hete; ε. 6- heated.

β. **1387** TREVISA *Higden* (Rolls) II. 61 The water..is i-hatte kyndeliche. *c* **1410** LOVE *Bonavent. Mirr.* vi (Gibbs MS.), In þat cold tyme þe chyld..hadde nede to be hatte [*v.r.* hette] in þat manere. **1528** PAYNEL *Salerne's Regim.* G ij b, Hit be..hatte vpon the coles.

γ. **1387** TREVISA *Higden* (Rolls) II. 17 ȝif he is i-froted and i-het. *c* **1400** tr. *Secreta Secret., Gov. Lordsh.* (E.E.T.S.) 71 Hit ys cold and nedith to be het. **1575** TURBERV. *Faulconrie* 310 When ye have well het it in the fire. **1583** BABINGTON *Commandm.* vii. (1590) 316 So shall the wrath of God.. cause hell to bee hette 70 times 7 times hotter.

δ. *c* **1449** PECOCK *Repr.* III. viii. 330 The wil is heete and inflamyd into loue. **1560** BIBLE (Genev.) *Dan.* iii. 19 That they shulde heate the fornace at once seuen times more then it was wonte to be heate [**1611** heat]. **1595** SHAKS. *John* IV. i. 61 The Iron of it selfe, though heate red hot. **1662** GURNALL *Chr. in Arm.* Verse xviii. lv. 424/1 To make some sinful impression upon the Saint when he is heat.

ε. *c* **1553** T. WILSON *Rhet.* (1567) 100 a, So sone as the Sunne had somewhat heated hym.

B. Signification. **I.** *trans.*

1. To communicate heat to; to make hot, to warm; to raise the temperature of.

c **1000** *Sax. Leechd.* I. 370 Wið toþ wræce..hæt scenc fulne wines. *c* **1000** *Laws Ordeal* in Schmid *Gesetze* 414 ȝif hit þonne wæter sy, hæte man hit. *c* **1200** *Trin. Coll. Hom.* 109 þe sunne..hat alle þing, þe on eorðe wecseð. *c* **1375** *Sc. Leg. Saints, Thomas* 588 [He] is þe fyre gert het þem wele. *c* **1430** *Two Cookery-bks.* 12 Hete it hote, but let it nowt boyle. **1590** SHAKS. *Com. Err.* IV. iv. 33 When I am cold, he heates me with beating. **1664** POWER *Exp. Philos.* 161 If you bore with a Wimble..till you heat it soundly. **1707** MORTIMER *Husb.* (1708) 141 As fast as you pick your Hops, dry them, for their lying undried heats them, and changes their Colour. **1834** COLERIDGE *Table-t.* 5 July, Like emerging from a sick room heated by stoves, into an open lawn.

†**b.** *fig.* To keep (a place) 'warm' by frequenting it. *Obs. rare.*

1606 HOLLAND *Sueton.* 71 Wee haunted I say and heat the dicing house.

†**c.** (?) To run swiftly over, as in a race. *Obs.*

1611 SHAKS. *Wint. T.* I. ii. 96 You may ride's With one soft Kisse a thousand Furlongs, ere With Spur we heat an Acre.

2. To produce the sensation of heat in, cause to feel hot or warm; to bring into a condition of bodily heat, to inflame. Also *absol.*

1601 HOLLAND *Pliny* II. 180 Ammoniack..hath vertue to mollifie, to heat, discusse, and dissolue. **1606** SHAKS. *Ant. & Cl.* I. iii. 80 You'l heat my blood no more. **1738** WARBURTON *Div. Legat.* II. *note* Wks. 1811 II. 346 Men heated with wine. **1887** H. AÏDÉ *Passages in Life Lady* III. xii. 55 His blood was heated.

3. *fig.* To rouse to intense emotion; to excite in mind or feeling; to inspire with ardour or eagerness; to inflame with rage or passion.

a **1225** *Ancr. R.* 404 Sturieð ou euer cwicliche ine gode werkes, & þet schal heaten ou. *a* **1340** HAMPOLE *Psalter* xxii. 7 Hetand & strenghtand me withinen. *c* **1400** *Destr. Troy* 2054 His harme, as a hote low, het hym with in. **1596** SHAKS. *Merch. V.* III. i. 60 He hath..cooled my friends, heated mine enemies. **1638** F. JUNIUS *Paint. of Ancients* 180 Nothing heateth their forward spirits so much as the.. applauses of all sorts of men. **1719** DE FOE *Crusoe* II. iii, This ..discourse had heated them. **1855** MACAULAY *Hist. Eng.* xviii. IV. 163 Officers who heated each other into fury by talking against the Dutch.

II. *intr.* **4.** To contract heat, become hot or warm, rise in temperature.

a **700** *Epinal Gloss.* 206 *Calentes*, haetendae. *c* **725** *Corpus Gloss.* 357 *Calentes*, hatende. **1398** TREVISA *Barth. De P.R.* XVI. viii. (1495) 557 Noo thynge ouercometh the adamas.. also it heetyth neuer. *c* **1440** *Promp. Parv.* 238/2 Hetyn, or waxyn hoote, *caleo*. **1613** PURCHAS *Pilgrimage* (1614) 432 They set a Kettle of water over the fire to heat. **1707** MORTIMER *Husb.* I. iv. (1708) 35 You must take care..that it do not lie thick, because it will heat. **1828** WEBSTER s.v., Green hay heats in a mow, and green corn in a bin. **1884** S. P. THOMPSON *Dynamo-Electr. Mach.* (1888) 113 The first machines constructed heated too much.

b. To have or get the sensation of heat, to grow hot; to become inflamed physically.

a **1300** *K. Horn* 608 þe sarazins he smatte þat his blod hatte. **1596** SHAKS. *Merch. V.* I. i. 81 Let my Liuer rather heate with wine. **1826** SCOTT *Jrnl.* (1890) I. 185 In walking I am like a spavined horse, and heat as I go on.

5. *fig.* To become inflamed or excited in mind or feeling; to wax warm.

a **1225** *Juliana* 21 His heorte feng to heaten. **1648** W. ASHHURST *Reasons agst. Agreement* Pref., I thought it.. unsafe, to let so great dis-satisfactions lye privately heating together. **1859** KINGSLEY *Misc.* (1860) I. 249 Heating into a sneerer. **1880** G. MEREDITH *Trag. Com.* (1881) 238 As I waned, she waned; as I heated, so did she.

Hence **'heatable** *a.*, capable of being heated.

1570 LEVINS *Manip.* 2/32 Heatable, *calefactabilis*.

'heat-drop. Usually in *pl.*: **a.** A few drops of rain ushering in a hot day. Also *fig.*, e.g. of tears. **b.** Drops of sweat.

1651 C. CARTWRIGHT *Cert. Relig.* I. 55 No more considerable in respect of the whole, then so many heat-drops of error, can stand in competition with a cloud of witnesses. **1663** COWLEY *Cutter Coleman St.* IV. i, Nothing at their Command beside their Tears, And we, vain Men, whom such Heat-drops deceive. **1839** BAILEY *Festus* viii. (1848) 92 Weep if you can, and call the tears heat-drops. **1887** BARING-GOULD *Red Spider* xxii. (1888) 166 Her brow was pearled with heat-drops.

heated ('hi:tɪd), *ppl. a.* [f. HEAT *v.* + -ED[1].]

1. a. Made hot; having the temperature raised.

1617 MORYSON *Itin.* III. 97 A long Table furnished with these often heated meats. **1697** DRYDEN *Æneid* IX. 799 The heated lead half melted as it flew. **1842** *Penny Cycl.* XXII. 484/1 These tubes..increase considerably the heated surface in contact with the water. **1858** LARDNER *Hand-bk. Nat. Phil.* 182 A balloon..containing 23000 cubic feet of heated air. **1881** *Print. Trades Jrnl.* XXXI. 38 Heated bearings in machinery may be relieved..by the use of graphite as a lubricator.

b. ***heated term***, the hot season of the year. *U.S.*

1855 *N.Y. Herald* 26 Dec. 3/4 Our 'heated terms' are over, and we now begin to look out for the approach of the 'northers'. **1867** *Congress. Globe* 5 July 487/1, I think we could go on now during the heated term..better than.. during the cold season. **1873** J. H. BEADLE *Undevel. West* 793 The average of the 'heated term', one day with another, is there recorded at eighty-four degrees. **1949** *Chicago Tribune* 11 Sept. 43/5 What a month ago appeared to be a trivial item of conversation during the heated term has become a raging topic among scientists.

2. Inflamed, excited (physically or mentally); fevered, impassioned, angry.

1593 SHAKS. *3 Hen. VI*, II. i. 124 But whether 'twas the coldnesse of the King..That robb'd my Soldiers of their heated Spleene. **1751** JORTIN *Serm.* (1771) I. i. 1 When the heated imagination is let loose. *a* **1839** PRAED *Poems* (1864) II. 23 Morning cools my heated brain. **1886** *Manch. Exam.* 28 Sept. 5/3 These heated phrases..are the outcome of a bitter disappointment.

Hence **'heatedly** *adv.*, in a heated manner, with warmth of temper.

1862 H. AÏDÉ *Carr of Carrlyon* II. 90 Mrs. Courteney, (said Carr, rather heatedly,) do you not place enough confidence in me to say candidly what this..is? **1885** *Manch. Exam.* 12 Sept. 5/2 The decision..was heatedly discussed.

†**'heaten,** *v. Obs.* Also 5 hatne-n. [f. HEAT *v.* or *sb.* + -EN[5].] = HEAT *v.* **a.** *intr.* **b.** *trans.*

a. *c* **1400** *Destr. Troy* 9153 All hatnet his hert, as a hote fyre. *Ibid.* 9304 Now hatnis his hert all in hote loue.

b. **1559** MORWYNG *Evonym.* 363 Dry fomentacions do drye..and heaten more. *Ibid.* 366. **1788** D. GILSON *Serm.* 346 The malignant spirit that heatened her veins.

heater ('hi:tə(r)). [f. HEAT *v.* + -ER[1].]

1. a. A person or thing that heats; a heating agent.

a **1500** *Medulla Gram.*, *Ciniflo*, a fyre blower, an yryn heter. **1638** RAWLEY tr. *Bacon's Life & Death* (1650) 64 Heaters from without, during the assimilation after sleep. **1664** EVELYN *Kal. Hort.* (1729) 228 Common Stoves, Pans of Charcoal, and other included Heaters. *a* **1691** BOYLE *Wks.* V. 104 (R.) Camphire..is..a great heater of the blood. **1803** *Naval Chron.* XV. 56 Cabin keepers, oakum boys, and pitch heaters. **1894** *Daily News* 28 Dec. 2/6 The electric current ..in its various capacities of a chemist, a heater, an illuminator, a messenger, and a power.

b. *slang.* A gun (see HEAT *sb.* 12 b).

2. *spec.* The name of various contrivances for imparting heat.

a. A piece of iron, which is made hot and placed in a cavity in a box-iron, smoothing-iron, tea-urn, etc. **b.** An instrument used in encaustic painting for burning in the wax. **c.** A stove used for heating a room, lobby, or office. Also, a usual name for a domestic electric or gas fire. **d.** A vessel or other contrivance in which something is placed to be heated. **e.** A pan in which cane or maple juice is heated as part of the process in sugar manufacture.

1666 in *Essex Inst. Hist. Coll.* XXV. 147 It. boxe Iron & heaters. **1744** B. FRANKLIN *Acc. Fire-Places* 27 You..may.. warm the Flat-Irons, heat Heaters [etc.]. **1755–73** JOHNSON, *Heater*, an iron made hot, and put into a box-iron, to smooth and plait linen. **1759** COLEBROOKE in *Phil. Trans.* LI. 44 An ironing box, charged with an hot heater. **1807–26** S. COOPER *First Lines Surg.* (ed. 5) 244 An apparatus, consisting of a stand, an iron heater on which the mercurial powder is thrown, and a tube for conducting the smoke to the part affected. **1848** WORNUM in *Lect. Paint.* 221 *note*, Burning in with a heater (*cauterium*) the ordinary wax colours. **1880** *Girl's Own Paper* 13 Nov. 108/1 A box-iron with three heaters. **1883** *Harper's Mag.* Dec. 45/2 A great heater, with its ample rotundity and glowing heart..stood there.

f. A triangular structure resembling in form the heater of a box-iron.

1797 J. A. GRAHAM *Descr. Sk. Vermont* 119 There are two arches..with a pier in the centre..with the addition of a heater, or triangular front. **1899** DICKINSON & PREVOST *Cumbld. Gloss.* 379 *Heater bit* is the triangular piece of ground, generally grass-grown, at the junction of three roads; so called because of resemblance to the iron heater in a box-iron.

g. A device used for the indirect heating of the cathode of a thermionic valve.

1940 *Chambers's Techn. Dict.* 407/2 *Heater*, the conductor carrying the current for heating an equipotential cathode, generally enclosed by the cathode. **1945** *Electronic Engin.* XVII. 454 Radio receivers and other electronic devices may have the valve heaters connected in series.

h. A device used for heating the interior of a motor car. Also *attrib.* and *Comb.*, as ***heater-demister, -fan.***

1939–40 *Army & Navy Stores Catal.* 266/1 *Car heater*... A robust and reliable heater. **1948** *Motor Man.* (ed. 33) xii. 232 (*heading*) Car heaters. The use of car heaters has spread in recent months, largely owing to the spur of the export trade. **1961** *Which?* (Reports on Cars) 14 Heater efficiency is measured and compared, and the results analysed for average interior temperatures and effective distribution of heat. **1962** *Ibid.* Oct. 310/2 Most modern cars can have a built-in heater-demister which blows warmed air into the car. **1969** S. HYLAND *Top Bloody Secret* ii. 163 The [car] engine was silent, but the heater-fan was still humming.

3. *attrib.* and *Comb.*, as ***heater-shape, -shaped*** adjs., etc.; **heater-piece** *U.S.*, a gore or triangular piece of land; **heater-shield,** a triangular shield with curved sides, like the shape of a flat iron heater.

1821 SCOTT *Let. to J. Ballantyne* 20 July in *Lockhart*, A three cornered, or heater shield. **1847** C. BOUTELL *Monumental Brasses* 37 The shield is small, flat, and heater-shaped. **1859** BARTLETT *Dict. Amer.*, *Heater piece*, a gore or triangular piece of land, so called probably, from a flat iron, the form of which it resembles. **1863** D. G. MITCHELL *My Farm* 243 Waal—kinder like to have a little 'heater' piece, the boys, you see, hoe it out in odd spells. **1863** G. SETON *Law Her. Scotl.* v. 192 About the middle of the thirteenth century, when the heater-shape was almost universally adopted. **1874** BOUTELL *Arms & Arm.* x. 193 The shield assumed the 'heater' form. **1917** A. C. FRYER in *Trans. Bristol & Glouc. Archaeol. Soc.* XL. 41 A half angel vested in alb and holding a heater-shaped shield.

'heatful, *a. rare.* [f. HEAT + -FUL.] Full of heat or warmth; producing heat. *lit.* and *fig.*

1591 SYLVESTER *Du Bartas* I. ii. 977 Bright-flaming, heat-full Fire. *Ibid.* I. v. 90 The banefull Hare, And heat-full Oyster. **1622** MABBE tr. *Aleman's Guzman d'Alf.* II. 302 In his heatfull humour, set on fire with filthy Lust. **1627–77** FELTHAM *Resolves* II. lv. 271 Their Loves that by frequent Intercourses, were heatful and alive between them.

heath (hi:θ), *sb.* Forms: 1-3 **hæð**, 3-4 **heþ**, 4-6 **heth, -e, heeth**, 6 **heyth**, 4- **heath.** [OE. *hǽð* (:—**haiþi-*), corresponding, exc. in the formative suffix, with MLG. *hêde*, MDu. *hêde*, *heide*, Du. *heide*, *hei*, OHG. *heida* (only as in sense 2), MHG., G. *heide*, ON. *heiðr*, Goth. *haiþi* fem., gen. *haiþjôs* field, open untilled land, pasture, open country, from pre-Teut. root **kait-*. A cognate has been suggested in L. *bū-cētum* cow-pasture.]

1. a. Open uncultivated ground; an extensive tract of waste land; a wilderness; now chiefly applied to a bare, more or less flat, tract of land, naturally clothed with low herbage and dwarf shrubs, esp. with the shrubby plants known as heath, heather or ling.

In ME. often contrasted with *holt* or *wood*.

a **1000** *Cædmon's Exod.* 118 þy læs him westengryre, har hæð..ferhð ȝetwæf(de). *c* **1205** LAY. 12819, I wude i wilderne, inne hæðe & inne uærne. *c* **1330** R. BRUNNE *Chron. Wace* (Rolls) 8864 Ffro stede to stede þey fledde to sculk, On heþ & hilles to hyde in hulk. *c* **1386** CHAUCER *Prol.* 6 Whan Zephirus..Inspired hath in euery holt and heeth The tendre croppes. *c* **1400** *Destr. Troy* 1350 The Troiens.. Fleddon..Ouer hilles & hethes into holte woddes. **1412–20** LYDG. *Chron. Troy* I. iii, On holte and hethe the merye somers daye. **1530** PALSGR. 231/1 Hethe a playne, *lande*. **1535** COVERDALE *Jer.* xii. 12 The distroyers come ouer the heeth euery waye [**1611** upon all high places through the wilderness]. **1568** GRAFTON *Chron.* II. 383 [They] met the King on the Hethe on this side Shene. **1626** BACON *Sylva* §834 Some Woods of Orenges, and Heathes of Rose Mary, will Smell a great way into the Sea. **1674** N. COX *Gentl. Recreat.* (1677) 46 As for high Downs or Heaths, the best are about Marlborough, Salisbury, Cirencester, and Lincoln. **1784–92** BELKNAP *Hist. New Hampsh.* in Morse *Amer. Geog.* (1796) I. 366 A large area, called the plain. It is a dry heath, composed of rocks covered with moss. **1792** A. YOUNG *Trav. France* (1794) 20 An uninteresting flat, with many heaths of ling. **1815** DUC DE LEVIS *Eng. 19th Cent.* I. 12 A Common..the English distinguish these uncultivated lands ..into heaths and pastures. **1872** E. W. ROBERTSON *Hist. Ess.* 246 At a comparatively recent period..in many parts of England..the Common of modern days was known as 'the heath' or 'the waste'.

†**b.** *transf.* Part of a garden left more or less in the wild state. *Obs.*

1625 BACON *Ess.*, *Gardens* (Arb.) 558 Gardens..to be diuided into..A Greene in the Entrance; A Heath or Desart in the Going forth; And the Garden in the middest.

2. A name given to plants and shrubs found upon heaths or in open or waste places. †**a.** In early times vaguely applied or identified. *Obs.*

a **700** *Epinal Gloss.* 1007 *Thymus*, haeth. *a* **800** *Erfurt Gloss.* 269 *Calomacus*, haeth. *Ibid.* 2012 *Thymus*, haedth. *a* **1387** *Sinon. Barthol.* (Anecd. Oxon.) 30 *Mirix, Mirica, idem*, bruer heath, *sive* genesta. *Ibid.* 33 *Paliurus*, heth.

b. The ordinary name for undershrubs of the Linnæan genus *Erīca*, of which the common native species are *E.* (now *Calluna*) *vulgaris*, ***common heath***, heather, or ling, *E. cinerea* ***fine-leaved heath*** (the 'common heath' of some parts), and *E. tetralix* ***cross-leaved heath.*** By botanical writers sometimes limited to the modern genus *Erica*, sometimes extended to other cognate genera of *Ericaceæ*.

The name *heath* seems native to the south and middle of England: see HEATHER. Since the 'common heath' is now separated from the genus *Erica*, botanical writers sometimes distinguish it from the 'true heaths' by its northern names LING and HEATHER; but locally all three names include all the native species. Of early botanical writers, Turner mentions only *E. vulgaris*, Lyte (transl. Dodoens), *E. vulgaris* and *tetralix*, distinguished as 'long heath' and 'smal heath'.

c **1000** *Sax. Leechd.* I. 354 Wið liþa sare..smeoce mid hæþe, and þæt ylce on wine drince. *c* **1325** *Know Thyself* 30 in *E.E.P.* (1862) 131 What is al þat forþ is past Hit fareþ as fuir of heth. *c* **1440** *Promp. Parv.* 238/2 Hethe or lynge, fowaly, *bruarium*. **1548** TURNER *Names of Herbes* (E.D.S.) 35 Erice is called in greeke Ereice, it is named in english Heth, hather, or ling..it groweth on frith and wyld mores; some vse to make brusshes of heath. **1578** LYTE *Dodoens* VI. xvi. 677 There is in this Countrie two kindes of Heath, one ..is called long Heath. The other..smal Heath. **1610** SHAKS. *Temp.* I. i. 70 Now would I giue a thousand furlongs of Sea, for an Acre of barren ground: Long heath, Browne firrs, anything. **1686** PLOT *Staffordsh.* 379 They frequently

used the *Erica vulgaris*, heath, or ling instead of hopps to preserve their beer. **1728–46** Thomson *Spring* 513 Oft with bolder wing they [bees] soaring dare The purple heath, or where the wild-thyme grows. **1794** Martyn *Rousseau's Bot.* xix. 258 Common Heath..is distinguished by the anthers being terminated with an awn, and lying within the flower. *Ibid.*, Fine-leaved Heath has crested anthers lying within the corolla. **1834** Mrs. Somerville *Connect. Phys. Sc.* xxvii. (1849) 307 Heaths are exclusively confined to the Old World. **1858** R. Hogg *Veg. Kingd.* 482 The *Common Heath*, or *Ling*, of the hills of Britain, is *Calluna vulgaris*..With Heath, cottages are thatched, besoms are made, and faggots are composed to burn in ovens. *Ibid.* 483 The Heaths [of] our greenhouses are all natives of the Cape of Good Hope, and embrace upwards of six hundred species and varieties.

c. With distinctive additions, applied to other species of *Erica*, and allied genera; and popularly to some other plants.

The three less common British species are the ***ciliated, Cornish***, and ***Mediterranean heaths*** (*E. ciliaris, vagans, Mediterranea*); other species are ***Sicilian, Spanish, tree***, and ***winter h.*** **American false heath**, *Hudsonia ericoides*. **black-berried h.** the Crowberry, *Empetrum nigrum*; **Irish** or **St. Dabeoc's h.**, *Menziesia polifolia*; **Australian h.**, *Epacris grandiflora*; **Otago h.**, *Leucopogon Fraseri*; **sea heath**, *Frankenia levis*; **Tasmanian h.**, *Epacris exserta*. † **heath of Jericho**, Rose of Jericho, *Anastatica Hierochuntina*.

1617 Minsheu *Ductor*, Heath of Jericho, *erica Hiericontœa*, quod similitudinem aliquam habeat cum erica.

d. In two passages (*Jer.* xvii. 6, xlviii. 6) in Coverdale's and later versions of the Bible, applied to some desert plant, identified variously with Tamarisk, or with Savin, *Juniperus Sabina*.

1535 Coverdale *Jer.* xvii. 6 He shall be like the heeth, that groweth in the wildernes [**1382** Wyclif iencian trees, **1388** bromes, **1611** heath, **1885** (*R.V.*) *marg.* Or, a tamarisk]. *Ibid.* xlviii. 6 Get you awaye..and be like vnto the heeth in yᵉ wildernes [Wyclif, **1611** and *R.V.* as before].

3. Short for *heath butterfly, moth*: see 5 c.

1827 *Butterfly Collector's Vade Mecum* 68 *Hipparchia Typhon*, Scarce Heath. *H. Pamphilus*, Small Heath ..*H. Tithonus*, Large Heath. **1832** J. Rennie *Butterflies & Moths* 101 The Brown Heath (*F[idonia] atomaria*, Haworth).. Common. *Ibid.* 102 The Grey Heath (*F. ericetaria*, Stephens) appears in August. **1871** E. Newman *Brit. Butterflies* (1874) 93 The Large Heath, *Epinephele Tithonus*. *Ibid.* 101 The Small Heath, *Cœnonympha Pamphilus*.

4. *attrib.* and *Comb.* **a.** simple attrib., as ***heath-bank, -besom, -broom, -bush, -field*** (*a* 1000), ***-fire, -flower, -ground, -honey, -land, -man, -mould, -mutton, -pony, -snail, -soil, -tribe***. **b.** obj. and obj. gen., as ***heath-cropping*** adj., ***-keeper, -tramper***. **c.** locative and instrumental, as ***heath-bred, -clad, -grown, -roofed, -thatched*** adjs. **d.** ***heath-like*** adj.

1813 Coleridge *Remorse* iii. i, Stretched on the broad top of a sunny *heath-bank. **1610** J. Heath *Epigr.* in *Brit. Bibl.* (1812) II. 250 That *Heath-bred Muse. **1874** *P.O. Lond. Trades Directory*, *Heath Broom Makers. **1470–85** Malory *Arthur* xxi. iv, Ryght soo came an adder oute of a lytel *hethe busshe. **1766** J. Cunningham *Day* vii, On the *heath-clad hill. *c* **909** *Charter of Eadweard* in *Cod. Dipl.* V. 177 Ðonan to higgeate; ðæt utt on ðone *hæðfeld. **1787** G. White *Selborne* vii. 20 About March or April..vast *heath-fires are lighted up. **1810** Scott *Lady of L.* i. xviii, A foot more light..Ne'er from the *heath-flower dashed the dew. **1824** Miss Mitford *Village* Ser. i. (1863) 101 The ruddy glow of the heath-flower. **1523** Fitzherb. *Husb.* §2 Some sande..and in many places *heeth grounde. **1653** Walton *Angler* 222 Ploughing up heath-ground. **1577** B. Googe *Heresbach's Husb.* iv. (1586) 184 *Heath Hony, a wilde kind of Hony..being gathered..while the Heath is in floure. **1895** *St. James' Gaz.* 10 Sept. 9/2 An auxiliary *heathkeeper in the employment of the London County Council. **1819** Rees *Cycl.*, *Heath-plough*, a plough for preparing *heath-land for planting. **1936** *Discovery* Jan. 25/1 Only about 50,000 acres of Breckland remain at the present moment as heathland. **1954** M. Beresford *Lost Villages* vi. 200 This was forest, scrub or rough heathland. **1966** M. R. D. Foot *SOE in France* xii. 407 Bourgoin was too wily a fighter to be rounded up methodically in his heathland base. **1864** Thoreau *Cape Cod* vii. (1894) 159 A barren, *heath-like plain. **1861** Delamer *Fl. Gard.* 118 In pots, Heaths must have *heath-mould. **1771** Smollett *Humph. Cl.* (1820) 166 As much superior in flavour..as my *heath-mutton is to that of St. James's Market. **1804** J. Grahame *Sabbath* (1808) 67 Yon *heath-roofed shielin. **1832** Carlyle *Remin.* i. 51 This little *heath-thatched house. **1853** C. A. Johns *Flowers of Field* (1885) 392 *Ericaceæ*, the *Heath Tribe.

5. a. Special Combs.: **heath-ale, -beer**, a traditional beverage said to have been anciently brewed from the flowers of heather; **heath-blooms**, a name given by some to the plants of the Natural Order *Ericaceæ*; †**heath-coal**: see heathen-coal; **heath-cropper**, *lit.* one that crops or feeds on heath; a sheep or pony, living on open heath or down; hence, a person who inhabits a heath; **heath-fowl** = heath-bird; **heath-game**, grouse or moorfowl; **heath-stone**, see quots; **heath-tax**, a tax to defray the expenses of repairing the course at Newmarket; **heath-throstle, -thrush**, the Ring Blackbird or Ring-ouzel, *Turdus torquatus*.

1801 J. Leyden *Elfin-King* xxi, The cup..With *heath-ale mantling o'er. **1828** Scott *Rev. Ritson's Hist.* Wks. (1849) 356 The genuine heath-ale of the Picts. **1858** R. Hogg *Veg. Kingd.* 479 *Ericaceæ*, *Heath-blooms. **1819** Rees *Cycl.* s.v. *Sheep*, **Heath-cropper*, a small ill-shaped breed.. of sheep..found abundantly..within the precincts of the forest of Windsor. **1863** Kingsley *Water Bab.* ii. 62 You are a heath cropper bred and born. **1893** H. J. Moule *Old Dorset* 109 They tramped, or rode their shaggy heath-croppers. **1804** J. Grahame *Sabbath* (1839) 6/2 The *heath-fowl's plumes. **1823** in *Joanna Baillie's Collect. Poems* 287 Conceal'd 'mong the mist, where the heath-fowl was crying. **1711** *Act 9 Anne* c. 27 §3 *Heath-Game or Grouse. **1773** Barrington in *Phil. Trans.* LXIII. 229 The claws of our common Grous, or Heath-game. **1447–8** in Willis & Clark *Cambridge* (1886) I. 399 Ragge *hethstones and Flints to be purveid for the seid werkes. **1813** G. Robertson *Agric. Surv. Kincard.* 3 (Jam.) There is a variety..known under the name of Heathens or heath-stone, and is I think what is otherwise called Gneiss. **1851** *Dict. Archit.*, *Heath-stone*, a name given by builders to a description of sandstone that occurs in irregular masses in the Bagshot sands. **1856** in 'Stonehenge' *Brit. Sports* (1886) 510 The payment of *Heath Tax shall not be taken to confer on the person paying the same any legal rights which shall interfere..with the absolute control the Club now has over all persons using or going on to their grounds. **1676** Lister in *Ray's Corr.* (1848) 125 *Heath-throstle..the Ring-ouzle is so called with us in Craven. **1804** Charlotte Smith *Conversations* II. 54 Bashful..The *heath-thrush makes his domicile.

b. In names of trees and plants: applied to any species which grows on heaths, as ***heath bedstraw, hair-grass, mouse-ear, rush***; †**heath-bramble**, the Dewberry, *Rubus cæsius*; **heath-corn** (*U.S.*), Buckwheat, *Polygonum Fagopyrum*; **heath-cup**, an erect herb, *Artanema fimbriatum* (N.O. *Scrophulariaceæ*), native of the East Indies and Australia, cultivated for its large blue flowers; **heath-cypress**, a Club-moss, *Lycopodium alpinum*; **heath-fern**, the Sweet Mountain Fern, *Lastrea Oreopteris*; **heath-grass**, *Triodia decumbens*; **heath-honeysuckle**, Australian name for a flowering shrub, *Banksia serrata*; †**heath-rose**, the Rose of Jericho, *Anastatica Hierochuntina*.

1578 Lyte *Dodoens* vi. iv. 661 The lesser berie is called.. in Englishe, a heare Bremble, or *heath Bramble..The fruite is called a Dewberie, or blackberie. **1551** Turner *Herbal* i. I iv a, *Chamaecyparissus*..may be called in English *hethe cypres because it groweth amonge hethe, or dwarf cypres. **1777** Robson *British Flora* 264 *Lycopodium alpinum* ..Cypress Wolfsclaw, Heath Cypress. **1863** Kingsley *Water Bab.* ii. (1889) 50 Heaps of fallen limestone..with holes between them full of sweet *heath-fern. **1578** Lyte *Dodoens* i. lx. 87 The small [Pilosella]..may be called in English..*Heath mouse-eare. **1597** Gerarde *Herbal* (1633) 1387 The Rose of Jerico..in English, the *Heath Rose.

c. In names of butterflies and moths: see quots. and cf. sense 3.

1832 J. Rennie *Butterflies & Moths* 137 The Heath Rivulet (*E[mmelesia] ericetata*..) appears in June. **1871** E. Newman *Brit. Butterflies* (1874) 46 The Heath Fritillary.. is fond of basking on thistles. **1883** *Cassell's Nat. Hist.* VI. 67 The Heath Moths, or *Fidonidæ*, fly by day.

Hence **heath** *v. trans.*, to cover with heath.

1862 *Macm. Mag.* Sept. 426 How was it lichened and mossed, ferned and heathed..and brought to such a show of verdure and softness?

'heath-bell.

1. The bell-shaped flower of the Heath: cf. heather-bell.

1808 Scott *Marm.* iii. Introd. ix, Let the wild heath-bell flourish still. **1810** —— *Lady of L.* iii. v, Heath-bell with her purple bloom. **1840** Miss Costello *Summer amongst the Bocages* I. 128 Before the smell of steam has taken the place of the perfume of the heath-bell.

2. Applied to other bell-shaped flowers growing on heaths, esp. the Blue-bell (*Campanula rotundifolia*).

1804 J. Grahame *Sabbath* (1808) 67 Thinly strewed with heath-bells up and down. **1821** Clare *Vill. Minstr.* II. 135 Last lingering of the flowery kind, Blue heath-bells tremble 'neath the sheltering furze. **1824** L. Hunt *Mirr. Months* in Hone *Every-day Bk.* II. 1284 Even the elegant and fragile heathbell, or harebell, has not yet quite disappeared.

'heath-berry. A name vaguely applied to various berries growing on heaths, esp. the Bilberry and Crowberry.

c **1000** *Sax. Leechd.* II. 344 Ꝺenim..hæþ berȝian wisan.. do þas wyrta in an fæt. **1670–1** Narborough *Jrnl.* in *Acc. Sev. Late Voy.* i. (1711) 124 A-shore there is great Store of Heath-berries..and small Black-berries. **1772–84** Cook *Voy.* (1790) V. 1909 Berries of different species, such as cranberries, hurtle-berries, bramble-berries, and heath-berries. *a* **1792** S. Hearne *Journ. North. Ocean* in Southey *Comm.-pl. Bk.* IV. 167 Heathberries grow close to the ground.

'heath-bird. A bird which lives on heaths; *spec.* the Black Grouse, of which the male is the heath-cock and the female the heath-hen.

1683–4 W. Penn *Let. to Dk. Ormonde* 9 Jan. in *Academy* (1896) 11 Jan. 36/3 Phesants, heath-birds, Pidgeons and Patredges, innumerably. **1810** Scott *Lady of L.* iii. xii, Like heath-bird, when the hawks pursue. **1842** Faber *Styrian L.* 151 A heath-bird that lies on the Cheviot moor.

heath-cock. The male of the heath-bird or Black Grouse (*Tetrao tetrix*), the Blackcock; in N. America, the Canada grouse and other species.

1590 R. Payne *Descr. Irel.* (1841) 7 Great store of wild Swannes, Cranes..Heathcocks, Plouers. **1674** Ray *Collect. Words, Birds* 85 The common Heath cock, Black game or Grous. **1789** G. White *Selborne* vi. (1853) 26 That was the heath-cock or black-game. **1810** Scott *Lady of L.* i. xxxv, Until the heath-cock shrilly crew. **1893** [see heath-hen].

heathen ('hiːðən, -ð(ə)n), *a.* and *sb.*[1] Forms: 1 **hǽðen, hǽþen, héðen,** 2–3 **hæðen, heðen,** 2–5 **heþen,** 2–6 **hethen** (3 **heaðen, heaþen, eþen,** 3–4 **haþen, hethene,** 4 **heiþen, -in, heyþen, heȝthen, haiþen, -in, heþyn, -in, heden, -in,** 4–5 **haythen,** 5 **heþun, -on(e, -ynne,** 6 *Coverd.* **heithen**), 6– **heathen.** [OE. *hǽðen* = OFris. *hêthin, -en*, OS. *hêðin* (MDu., Du. *heiden*), OHG. *heidan* (MHG. *heiden*, Ger. *heide*), ON. *heiðinn* (Sw., Da. *heden*); cf. Goth. *haiþnô* Gentile or heathen woman.

As this word is used in all the Germanic langs. in the sense 'non-Christian, pagan', which could only have arisen after the introduction of Christianity, it is thought probable that, like some other terms of Christian origin (e.g. *church*), it was first used in Gothic, and thence passed to the other tribes. This is supported by the use by Ulfilas, in Mark vii. 26, of the fem. form *haiþnô* (Vulg. *mulier gentilis*, all OE. versions *hǽðen*). The word has generally been assumed to be a direct derivative of Gothic *haiþi*, heath, as if 'dweller on the heath', taken as a kind of loose rendering of L. *pāgānus* (orig. 'villager, rustic', later, after Christianity became the religion of the towns, while the ancient deities were still retained in rural districts, 'pagan, heathen'). But in this there are difficulties chronological and etymological, esp. in reference to the form and use of the suffix; and Prof. S. Bugge (*Indog. Forsch.* V. 178) includes this among several words which point to Armenian influence on the language of Ulfilas; he takes *haiþnô* as indicating a masc. *haiþans*, which he refers to Armenian *het'anos* 'heathen', ad. Gr. ἔθνος 'nation', pl. 'nations, Gentiles, heathens'. This would explain the OHG. form *heidan*, while in OE., etc., the suffix was, as in *cristen*, levelled under the ordinary *-in, -en*, from *-în*. But even so, the stem-vowel has prob. to be explained by assimilation to *haiþi* heath.]

A. *adj.* **1.** Applied to persons or races whose religion is neither Christian, Jewish, nor Muslim; pagan; Gentile. In earlier times applied also to Muslims; but in modern usage, for the most part, restricted to those holding polytheistic beliefs, esp. when uncivilized or uncultured.

971 *Blickl. Hom.* 15 He bið ȝeseald hæþnum mannum. *c* **1000** Ælfric *Hom.* I. 206 Se ȝetigeda assa and his fola ȝetacniað twa folc, þæt is Iudeisc and hæðen. **1154** *O.E. Chron.* an. 1137 Næure hethen men werse ne diden þan hi. *a* **1200** *Moral Ode* 295 in *Trin. Coll. Hom.* 229 Þar beð þe haðene men þe waren laȝe-lease. *c* **1200** Ormin 7286 Þatt hæþenn follc, Kalldisskenn follc, Wass warr off Cristess come. **1297** R. Glouc. (1724) 397 Wyllam..an eþene kyng com to. *c* **1300** *Cursor M.* 19740 (Edin.) Baþe to haiþin [*v.rr.* heþen, heþin, heiþen] folc and iues. **1340** Hampole *Pr. Consc.* 5508 Haythen men..þat never baptem ne right trouthe tuke. **1377** Langl. *P. Pl.* B. xv. 450 A barne..Til it be crystened in crystes name and confermed of þe bisshop, It is hethene as to heueneward..Hethene is to mene after heth and vntiled erthe. ? *a* **1400** *Arthur* 435 Lat not þe heþone Men Destroye þe puple crystien. **1563** W. Fulke *Meteors* (1640) 13 Helena was of the Heathen men taken as a Goddesse, the daughter of Jupiter and Leda. **1627** Sanderson *Serm.* I. 263 Abimelech, an heathen-man, who had not the knowledge of the true God of heaven to direct him. **1708** Swift *Remarks* Wks. 1883 VIII. 142 Made familiar to such practices by the heathen priests. **1825** Scott *Talism.* vi, I did the heathen Soldan injustice. **1870** B. Harte *Heathen Chinee* 17 He went for that heathen Chinee.

2. Of things: Pertaining to such persons or races, or to their religion and customs.

826 *Charter of Ecgberht* in *Cod. Dipl.* V. 83 Andlang dic to ðem heðenum biriȝelsum. *c* **1000** Ælfric *Hom.* I. 98 On hæðenum daȝum. *a* **1225** *Leg. Kath.* 53 þe temple..of hise heaðene godes. **13..** *Sir Beues* (A.) 547 Me ȝhe solde in to heþenlonde. *a* **1400–50** *Alexander* 5673 Out of haythen Spayn. **1485** Caxton *Malory's Arthur* Pref. 2 In al places crysten and hethen. **1662** Stillingfl. *Orig. Sacr.* i. ii. §1 Having already shewed a generall defect in the ancient Heathen Histories. **1708** Swift *Remarks* Wks. 1883 VIII. 118 The same authority..may abolish Christianity, and set up the Jewish, Mahometan, and heathen religion. **1722** Wollaston *Relig. Nat.* ix. 208 Even the Heathen world believed that the souls of men survived their bodies. **1879** Farrar *St. Paul* (1883) 3 The victorious enemy of heathen philosophy and heathen worship had passed his boyhood amid the heathen surroundings of a philosophic city.

3. *transf.* Religiously or otherwise on a level with heathens.

1856 Emerson *Eng. Traits, Race* Wks. (Bohn) II. 22 A country of extremes—dukes and chartists, Bishops of Durham and naked heathen colliers.

B. *sb.* (or *adj.* used *subst.*)

1. One who holds a religious belief which is neither Christian, Jewish, nor Muslim; a pagan.

c **1000** *Ags. Gosp.* Mark vii. 26 Soðlice þæt wif wæs hæðen sirofenisces cynnes. **13..** *Coer de L.* 6297 He..slowgh ther many a hethene. **1682** Evelyn *Diary* 24 Jan., The Russian Ambassador..behav'd himselfe like a clowne, compared to this civil heathen. **1720** Watts *Div. Songs* vi, That I was born of Christian race, And not a Heathan or a Jew. **1727** Swift *Gulliver* iii. i, I was sorry to find more mercy in an heathen than in a brother Christian. **1873** Edith Thompson *Hist. Eng.* iii. §1 Though himself a heathen, he [Æthelbert] had agreed to allow his wife, as being a Christian, free exercise of her religion.

b. The adj. plural, ***the heathen*** (cf. the *faithful*), is now collective; in O.T. = the Gentiles, or people who did not worship Jehovah, the God of the Jews.

c **1000** Ælfric *Saints' Lives* (E.E.T.S.) II. 322 Þa hæþenan swa dydon. *a* **1131** *OE. Chron.* an. 1128 Betwenen ða cristene and þa heðene. *c* **1200** *Vices & Virtues* (1888) 51 And beuall þo haðene mid his leðre meneȝinges. *c* **1340** *Cursor M.* 21254 (Fairf.) Þen come þe heiþen wiþ mikel wrange þat cristen men to pine was prest. **1535** Coverdale *Ps.* lxxviii[i]. 1 O God, yᵉ Heithen are fallen in to thine heretage. —— *2 Esdras* ii. 7 Scatred abrode amonge the Heithen. **1671** Milton *Samson* 1430 And spread his name

Great among the Heathen round. **1852** Mrs. Stowe *Uncle Tom's C.* xxviii, It would certainly be a greater self-denial to receive heathen among us than to send missionaries to them.

c. The sb. plural, *heathens*, is mostly individual.

1630 Prynne *Anti-Armin.* 135 Heathens.. want the true knowledge of God. **1736** Wesley *Wks.* (1872) I. 25 My brother and I.. went to pay our first visit in America to the poor Heathens. **1845** R. Jebb in *Encycl. Metrop.* II. 692/1 Among the speculations of the more enlightened heathens we find the love of mankind at large highly commended. **1857** Maurice *Ep. St. John* iii. 38 Showing you how both Heathens and Jews were taught.

2. *transf.* One that has no more religion, enlightenment, or culture than a pagan.

1818 Scott *Rob Roy* xv, Puir frightened heathens that they are. **1870** Dickens *E. Drood* viii, My ideas of civility were formed among Heathens.

3. Applied humorously to persons belonging to places bearing the name 'Heath', as Blackheath.

1891 *Pall Mall G.* 16 Nov. 1/2 Blackheath crossed over with a goal to love.. The Oxonians.. got two goals, while the Heathens were unable to score. **1894** *Westm. Gaz.* 15 Jan. 6/2 Blackheath v. London Scottish.. a victory for the Heathens.

C. *Comb.*, as ***heathen-minded*** adj.; ***heathen-like*** adj. and adv.

1565 Jewel *Def. Apol.* (1611) 21 Thus prophanelie and Heathen-like he writeth. **1889** R. B. Anderson tr. *Rydberg's Teut. Mythol.* 104 Heathen-heroic songs. **1895** *Dublin Rev.* Oct. 318 A society of heathen-minded Humanists.

heathen, *sb.*[2] = *heath-stone*: see heath 5.

†**heathen-coal.** *Obs.* (See quot. 1697.)

c **1697** Kennett *Etym. Angl.* Lansdowne MS. 1033 lf. 174/2 At Amblecot in Staffordsh... the second measure is called *Heath* or tough-coal: and the 12th or lowest of all, is called *Heathen-coal.* **1712** Bellers in *Phil. Trans.* XXVII. 542 The Heathen-Coal. **1719** F. Hauksbee *Phys. Mech. Exp.* Suppl. 319 The Heathen-Coal.

heathendom ('hiːðəndəm). [OE. *hǽðendóm* = MLG. *heidendôm*, OHG. *heidentuom*, Ger. *heidentum*, Du. *heidendom*, ON. *heiðindómr* (Sw. *hedendom*); f. heathen + -dom. The old word appears to have died out before 1400; in modern use app. formed anew after *Christendom*. Not in Johnson, Todd 1818, Webster 1828.]

1. The belief and practice of the heathen; = heathenism 1.

c **1000** *Laws of Edw. & Guth.* §1 (Schmid) Hi ȝecwædon þæt hi ænne God lufian woldon, and ælcne hæðendom ȝeorne aweorpan. *c* **1200** Ormin 18855 þiss þessterrnesse iss hæþenndom And dwillde inn hæfedd sinness. *c* **1200** *Vices & Virtues* (1888) 31 Ða unwraste ileaue of hæðen-dome. *a* **1225** *Leg. Kath.* 35 And dreien cristene men.. alle to heaðendom. **1701** J. Law *Counc. Trade* (1751) 233 Improvement of human society, beyond what it could possibly attain to in Heathendom. **1850** Hawthorne *Scarlet L.* xx, The many precious souls he hath won from heathendom. **1867** Freeman *Norm. Conq.* (1876) I. iv. 179 Whatever traces of heathendom may have cloven to Rolf himself.

b. *transf.* The condition of being unenlightened and untouched by Christian influences.

1850 Kingsley *Cheap Clothes & Nasty* in *Alt. Locke* (1879) p. lxiii, He trims his paletots, and adorns his legs, with the flesh of men and the skins of women, with degradation, pestilence, heathendom, and despair.

2. The domain or realm of the heathen; heathen people collectively; the heathen world.

1860 Trench *Serm. Westm. Abb.* ix. 96 Thick darkness rested over the whole of heathendom. **1861** E. Gaskell *Boyle Lect.* 32 The mighty work of subjugating all heathendom to the faith of the crucified Nazarene.

'heatheness. *rare.* [f. heathen + -ess.] A female heathen, a heathen woman.

1876 *Contemp. Rev.* XXVII. 962 The proud heatheness humbly submitted to baptism.

heathenesse ('hiːðəˌnɛs). *arch.* Forms: 1 **hǽðe(n)nes, -nys,** 3 **hæðenesse, heþinesse,** 3–5 **heþen-, hethenesse, -es, -isse, -nes,** etc., 6 **heathennesse, heath-, heythnesse,** 6–7, 9 **heathenesse, -(n)ess.** [OE. *hǽðennes, -nys*, f. *hǽðen* heathen + -ness. From an early date one of the two *n*'s was generally omitted, so that the word was sometimes treated as analogous to such words of French origin as *noblesse*, *Lyonesse*.]

1. The quality or condition of being heathen; the belief and practice of the heathen; heathenism.

c **900** tr. *Bæda's Hist.* iii. xxii. [xxx.] (1890) 250 He to hæðenisse [*v.r.* hæðennysse] wæs ȝehwyrfed. *c* **1205** Lay. 29388 And forsaken godes mæsse, and luuien hæðenesse. **1388** Wyclif *1 Chron.* xxii. 2 Alle conuersis fro hethenesse to the lawe of Israel. *c* **1430** *Life St. Kath.* (1884) 35 Aftur I had leyde be-syde me þe errour of hethenesse. **1540** Hyrde tr. *Vives' Instr. Chr. Wom* (1592) Bb v, When we couple.. Paganisme and heathennesse, unto Christianitie: and the devill to God. **1581** Marbeck *Bk. Notes* 627 Then shall the vnfruitfull, rough and woodye heathnesse.. bee tourned vnto the religion of Christes congregation or Church. **1848** Lytton *Harold* i. i, Merriments, savouring of heathenesse.

2. Heathendom, the heathen world; the lands outside Christendom, including, in Middle English, Muslim lands.

c **1205** Lay. 16631 þe wes in hæðenesse king of muchele mæhte. **1297** R. Glouc. (1724) 480 Saladin nom the holi croys, & to hethenesse it ber. *a* **1300** *Cursor M.* 2102 Asie.. es þe best, for þar in es Bath haly land and hethyenes. *c* **1380** *Sir Ferumb.* 2187 In al heȝenis ys no Sarsyn wikkeder þan is he. **1480** Caxton *Chron. Eng.* ccxxxviii. 263 His fame.. sprang so ferre that it come in to hethnes and barbarye. **1599** Hakluyt *Voy.* II. 161 Divers provinces of Christendome and of Heathenesse. **1828** *Blackw. Mag.* 399 The event was not such as could bear trumpeting in Heathenesse.

†**'heathenhede.** *Obs.* [See hede, -head.] = heathendom 2.

a **1300** *Cursor M.* 7024 (Cott.) Kinges four of haithen-hede. *Ibid.* 19864 (Gött.) þe mete þai ete in haiþen-hede.

†**'heathenhood, -hode.** *Obs.* [See -hood.] = heathendom 1.

c **1275** *Serving Christ* 38 in *O.E. Misc.* 91 Al þes world is bi-heled myd heþene-hode.

†**heathenic,** *a.* and *sb. Obs.* In 6 **heathnick,** 7 **hethnike.** Var. of ethnic assimilated to *heathen*. So †**heathnical** *a.* = ethnical.

1554 Hooper in Strype *Eccl. Mem.* (1721) III. App. xxvii. 78 The sword of the heathnicks and gentils. **1583** Stubbes *Anat. Abus.* i. (1879) 177 Beare baiting and other exercyses.. These Hethnicall exercyses vpon the Sabaoth day. *Ibid.* 185 More then Hethnicall impieties. **1632** Lithgow *Trav.* ix. 397 Whose presence to me after so long a sight of Hethnike strangers was exceeding comfortable.

heathenish ('hiːðənɪʃ), *a.* Also 6 **heathnish,** (**etnyshe**). [OE. *hǽðenisc* = OHG. *heidanisc, -inisc* (G. *heidnisch*), ON. *heiðneskr* (Sw. *hednisk*, Da. *hedensk*). In modern use prob. a new formation: see -ish.]

1. Of or pertaining to the heathen. Now *rare*.

c **893** K. Ælfred *Oros.* iii. iii. §1 Him man worhte anfiteatra, þæt mon mehte þone hæðeniscan pleȝan þærinne don. **1550** Bale *Image Both. Ch.* Biij, All her hethnyshe ceremonyes, supersticions, and sorceryes. **1597** Hooker *Eccl. Pol.* v. lxxviii. §2 The most eminent part both of Heathenish and Jewish seruice did consist in sacrifice. **1677** Hale *Prim. Orig. Man.* ii. v. 167 The various Denominations of those Heathenish Deities. **1774** J. Bryant *Mythol.* II. 475 The heathenish temples.

†**2.** = heathen *a.* 1. [Cf. *Jewish*.] *Obs.*

1535 Coverdale *1 Kings* Contents, Salomon displeaseth God with the loue of Heythenysh wemen. **1581** J. Bell *Haddon's Answ. Osor.* 92 b, All nations and people, as well Heathenishe, as the Jewes also themselves. *a* **1652** J. Smith *Sel. Disc.* vi. 297 The heathenish philosopher Plutarch. **1718** Lady M. W. Montagu *Let. to C'tess Bristol* (1887) I. 239 She was too good a christian to kill herself, as that heathenish Roman did. [**1882–3** Schaff *Encycl. Relig. Knowl.* III. **1941** A heathenish slave bought of a heathen.]

3. *transf.* and *fig.* **a.** Heathen-like; unchristian, uncivilized, barbarous; unworthy of a Christian. **b.** *colloq.* Abominable, disgusting, offensive, 'beastly'. (Cf. Christian *sb.* 3.)

1593 Nashe *Harvey-Greene Tractates* Wks. (Grosart) II. 206 O Heathenish and Pagan Hexamiters. **1604** Shaks. *Oth.* v. ii. 313 Most Heathenish, and most grosse. *c* **1700** T. Browne in *Four C. Eng. Lett.* 147 Tobacca, though it be a heathenish weed. **1718** *Freethinker* No. 3 ¶1, I may not appear a strange, heathenish Creature to the Ladies. **1859** Miss Cary *Country Life* (1876) 218 It was heathenish in the mowers to laugh. **1866** Geo. Eliot *F. Holt* (1868) 39 That's a heathenish, Brutus-like sort of thing. **1882** Mrs. Pitman *Mission L. Greece & Pal.* 251 The heathenish noises I now hear from a garden near by us.

'heathenishly, *adv.* [f. prec. + -ly².] In a heathen, unchristian, pagan, or barbarous manner.

1561 Daus tr. *Bullinger on Apoc.* (1573) 84 A thousand yeares after the incarnation of Christ, the Byshops began to defile the Lordes supper.. too heathenishly. **1580** *Ord. of Prayer* in *Liturg. Serv. Q. Eliz.* (1847) 574 The Sabbath days and holy days.. spent full heathenishly, in taverning, tippling [etc.]. **1611** Beaum. & Fl. *King & no K.* i. i, 'Tis heathenishly done of 'em in my conscience. **1749** Fielding *Tom Jones* vii. xv, He was heathenishly inclined to believe in, or to worship the goddess Nemesis. **1836** *Chamb. Jrnl.* 24 Dec. 383 The burial place of the royal family heathenishly styled the 'Pantheon'.

'heathenishness. [f. as prec. + -ness.] Heathenish quality or condition; barbarity.

1571 Golding *Calvin on Ps.* x. 16 Horrible was the heathnishnesse, when the land that was given for an heritage to God's people did foster ungodly and wicked inhabiters. **1633** Prynne *2nd Pt. Histrio-M.* iv. i. (R.), The obscenity.. heathenishnesse, and prophanenesse of most play-bookes. **1880** Miss Bird *Japan* I. 135 Singing.. which sounds like the very essence of heathenishness.

heathenism ('hiːðənɪz(ə)m). [See -ism.]

1. The religious or moral system of heathens; heathen practice or belief; paganism.

1605 Bacon *Adv. Learn.* ii. xiv. §9 The heresy of the Anthropomorphites.. and the opinion of Epicurus, answerable to the same in heathenism, who supposed the gods to be in human shape. **1645** Milton *Tetrach.* (1851) 152 If we be not lesse zealous in our Christianity, then Plato was in his heathenism. **1707** *Curios. in Husb. & Gard.* Pref. 6 A Relick of Heathenism. *a* **1719** Addison *Chr. Relig.* §5. 8 (Seager) He brought over multitudes both from heresy and heathenism. **1868** Freeman *Norm. Conq.* (1876) I. App. 650 The whole.. country relapsed into heathenism.

b. With *a* and *pl.* A heathen belief or characteristic.

1843 J. Martineau *Chr. Life* (1867) 202 Cast out as a dead heathenism. **1860** Emerson *Cond. Life, Worship* Wks. (Bohn) II. 397 Witness the heathenisms in Christianity.

2. *transf.* Unchristian state of things; heathenish condition; unchristian degradation or barbarism.

1742 Fielding *J. Andrews* (L.), Ay, there is nothing but heathenism to be learned from plays. **1895** Miss Montresor *Into Highways & Hedges* iii. ii. (ed. 4) 302 Fitting ornaments for the 'heathenism' of luxury. *Mod.* The practical heathenism of our great cities.

†**'heathenist.** *Obs.* [f. heathen + -ist.] One holding or supporting heathenism.

1551 Abp. Browne *Serm.* in *Harl. Misc.* V. 567 These sorts will turn themselves into several Forms; with the Heathen a Heathenist; with Atheists, an Atheist; with the Jews, a Jew. **1570** Dee *Math. Pref.* 21 Could the Heathenists finde these vses, of these.. Mighty Corporall Creatures.

'heathenize, *v.* [f. heathen + -ize.]

1. *trans.* To render heathen or heathenish.

1681 H. More *Exp. Dan.* iii. 74 Endeavouring to Heathenize the People of God again. **1827** Hare *Guesses* (1859) 84 Till very lately we sent out our colonists, not so much to christianize the Heathens, as to be heathenized by them.

2. *intr.* To practise heathenism; to become heathen or heathenish.

1769 [see below]. **1850** S. R. Maitland *Eruvin* (ed. 2) 174 The Christians, instead of judaizing, began to heathenize. **1861** Trench *Sev. Ch. Asia* 74 These.. do not judaize but heathenize, seeking to throw off every yoke.

Hence **'heathenized** *ppl. a.*; **'heathenizing** *vbl. sb.* and *ppl. a.*

1769 W. Jones (of Nayland) *Wks.* (1810) I. 203 By the proud Arian or the heathenizing moralist. **1856** Miss Winkworth *Tauler's Life & Serm.* (1857) 75 To combat the heathenizing philosophers of Christendom. **1857–8** Sears *Athan.* vii. 64 A heathenized Christianity. **1893** E. Bellasis *Mem. Serjt. Bellasis* 157 The result.. must be the heathenizing of the rising generation.

†**'heathenly,** *a. Obs.* [f. heathen + -ly¹. Cf. OHG. *heidanlîh*, MHG. *heidenlîch*.] Heathen-like, heathenish, heathen.

1415 Hoccleve *To Sir J. Oldcastle* 21 Fro cristen folk to hethenly couyne. **1579** Lyly *Euphues* (Arb.) 176 Which hath made me.. of an heathenly Pagan a heauenly Protestant. **1591** Horsey *Trav.* (Hakl. Soc.) 158 The manner.. of this mariage was so streinge and heathenly.

'heathenly, *adv.* [f. as prec. + -ly².] After the manner of the heathen; barbarously.

1382 Wyclif *2 Macc.* xv. 2 Do thou not so feersly and heithenly. —— *Gal.* ii. 14 If thou, sithen thou ert a Jew, lyuest hethenli [**1388** hethenlich] and not Jewly. **1579** J. Jones *Preserv. Bodie & Soule* i. xxxix. 87 Them that teach with the desperate and damnable Turkes, or that do beleeue as his Ienesaries are instructed al too Heathenly. **1776** W. C. Combe *Diaboliad* 6 *note*, Mercury.. is (Heathenly speaking) the presiding Genius of rogues, sharpers, &c.

heathenness: see heathenesse.

†**'heathenous,** *a. Obs. rare*⁻¹. Heathen.

1613 Purchas *Pilgrimage* (1614) 715 That huge Heathenous Tract of the unknowne South Continent.

heathenry ('hiːðənrɪ). [f. heathen + -ry.]

1. Heathen belief, practice, or custom; heathen character or quality; heathenism.

1577–87 Holinshed *Chron.* II. 28/1 In conuerting the Iland from heathenrie to christianitie. **1583** Stubbes *Anat. Abus.* i. (1879) 144 It is all one, as if they had said, bawdrie, hethenrie, paganrie. **1856** T. A. Trollope *Girlh. Cath. de Med.* iii. 46 Aghast on his arrival in Rome at the utter heathenry around him. **1868** *Contemp. Rev.* VIII. 166 Some of our brilliant imitators of Greek poetry seem to pursue it mainly for its heathenry.

2. Heathen people. (Cf. *Irishry*.)

a **1890** R. F. Burton in Lady Burton *Life* (1893) I. 292 My Goanese boys, being 'Christians'.. will not feed with the heathenry.

†**'heathenship.** *Obs.* or *arch.* [OE. *hǽðenscipe*; f. heathen + -ship.]

1. Heathenism, heathendom.

a **1000** *O.E. Chron.* an. 634 For þan heðenscipe þe hi druȝon. *c* **1000** Ælfric *Hom.* II. 504 Martinus.. awende his moder of manfullum hæðenscipe. *c* **1205** Lay. 12114 And summe heo godd wið-soken and to haðenescipe token. *Ibid.* 14862 Hengestes laȝen.. and his hæðene-scipe þæ he hider brohte. [**1832** Thorpe tr. *Cædmon's Par.* 229 And would not swerve from the Lord of hosts.. into heathenship.]

2. Gentilism; uncircumcision. *rare literalism.*

1535 Coverdale *1 Cor.* vii. 18 Yf eny man be called beynge Circumcysed let him take no Heythenshippe vpon him. Yf eny man be called in the Heythenshippe let him not be circumcysed.

†**'heatheny,** *a. Obs. rare.* [f. heathen *sb.* + -y.] Heathen, heathenish.

1580 Sidney *Ps.* x. ix, Who hast the heath'ney folk destroy'd From out Thy land.

heather ('hɛðə(r)). Forms: 4, 6 **hathir,** 5 **had(d)yr,** 6 **haddir, hedder,** 6–7 **hadder,** 6–8 **hather,** 8 **hether,** 8– **heather.** [Of uncertain origin: commonly viewed as related to *heath*; but the form *heather* appears first in 18th c., and the earlier *hadder* seems on several grounds to discountenance such a derivation. The word

appears to have been originally confined to Scotland (with the contiguous part of the English Border); the northern Engl. equivalent, as in Yorkshire, etc., being *ling*, from Norse. The word *heath*, on the other hand, seems to be native only in Southern and Midland counties, and never to have been applied to the Yorkshire or Scottish 'moors'; it is only in comparatively recent times that the southern English *heath* and the Sc. *hadder*, *hedder*, have been associated, and the spelling *heather* thence introduced. On the analogy of *adder*, *bladder*, *ladder*, now in Sc. *èther*, *blèther*, *lèther*, and of Eng. *feather*, *together*, *weather*, we should expect *heather* to go back through *hedder*, *hadder*, to a type *hædder* or *hæddre*.]

1. a. The Scotch name, now in general use, for the native species of the Linnæan genus *Erica*, called in the north of England, LING; especially *E.* (now *Calluna*) *vulgaris*, ***common heather***, and *E. cinerea*, ***fine-leaved heath*** or ***lesser bell-heather***.

Some recent botanical writers have essayed to limit the originally local names *heath*, *ling*, *heather*, to different species; but each of these names is, in its own locality, applied to all the species there found, and pre-eminently to that locally most abundant. On the Yorkshire and Scottish moors, the most abundant is *E. vulgaris*, which is therefore the 'common ling' of the one, the 'common heather' of the other. But in other localities, esp. in the south-west, *E. cinerea* is the prevalent species, and is there the 'common heath'. Scottish distinctions are ***dog-heather***, ***he-heather*** (*E. vulgaris*), ***carlin h.***, ***she-heather*** (*E. cinerea*).

1335 *Compotus Procuratoris de Norham* (Durham Treasury MS.), In strauue et hathir emptis pro coopertura domus molendini. *c* **1470** HENRY *Wallace* v. 300 In heich haddyr Wallace and thai can twyn. *Ibid.* XI. 898 Hadyr and hay bond apon flakys fast. **1500–20** DUNBAR *Poems* lxvi. 86 Greit abbais grayth I nill to gather, Bot ane kirk scant coverit with hadder. **1548** Hather [see HEATH 2 b]. **1572** *Satir. Poems Reform.* xxxii. 19 With Peittis, with Turuis, and mony turse of Hedder. **1578** LYTE *Dodoens* VI. xvi. 678 Heath, Hather, and Lyng is called in high and base Almaigne, Heyden. **1607** NORDEN *Surv. Dial.* (N.), Heath is the generall or common name, whereof there is one kind, called hather, the other ling. **1621** BURTON *Anat. Mel.* III. ii. VI. i. (1651) 546 Those Indian Brachmanni..lay upon the ground covered with skins, as the Redshanks do on Hadder. **1633** HART *Diet Diseased* I. xxvii. 126 In the Northerne..places of this Island..They dry their malt with ling, or heath, called there hadder. **1674–91** RAY *N.C. Words* 135 *Hadder*, Heath or Ling. **1725** BRADLEY *Fam. Dict.* s.v. *Plague*, They are to give them Hather or Hadder to eat. *c* **1730** BURT *Lett. N. Scotl.* xiii. (1754) I. 297 The Surface of the Ground is all over Heath, or, as they call it, *Heather*. **1866** *Treas. Bot.* 199/1 *Calluna*. The true 'Heather' of Scotland, called also Ling and Common Heath. **1873** BLACK *Pr. Thule* 3 Set amid the browns and greens of the heather.

b. Phr. ***to set the heather on fire***: to make a disturbance. ***to take to the heather***: to become an outlaw or bandit.

1818 SCOTT *Rob Roy* xxxv, It's partly that whilk has set the heather on fire. **1896** *Westm. Gaz.* 28 July 1/3 A woman.. informed against the murderer, who at once 'took to the heather'.

2. Applied with distinctive additions to other plants.

Himalayan heather, *Andromeda fastigiata* (Miller, 1884); **monox heather**, the Crowberry; **silver** or **sponge heather**, the moss *Polytrichum commune*. (Britten & Holl. *Plant-n.*)

3. *attrib.* and *Comb.* **a.** Of, pertaining to, consisting of, or made from heather, as ***heather-ale***, ***-bed***, ***-beer***, ***-besom***, ***-bloom***, ***-blossom***, ***-brae***, ***-brake***, ***-bush***, ***-cow*** (COW *sb.*²), ***-honey***, ***-knoll***, ***-land***, ***-roof***, ***-top***, ***-tuft***, ***-wine***. **b.** Of the colour or appearance of heather: applied to fabrics, etc., of a mixed or speckled hue thought to resemble that of heather, as ***heather-mixture***, ***-stockings***, ***-suit***, ***-tweed***, ***-wool***. **c.** ***heather-clad***, ***-covered***, ***-mixed***, ***-sweet*** adjs. **d.** **heather-cat**, a cat living wild and roaming among the heather; hence *fig.* applied to a person; **heather-grass** = *heath-grass*, *Triodia decumbens*; **heather-owl**, the Short-eared Owl, *Asio accipitrinus*.

1820 SCOTT *Monast.* xxv, Halbert Glendinning.. expressed himself unwilling to take any liquor stronger than the *heather ale, which was at that time frequently used at meals. **1724** RAMSAY *Gentl. Sheph.* II. i, And skulk in hidings on the *heather braes. **1855** KINGSLEY *Heroes, Theseus* I. 196 Beneath whose shade grew..purple *heather-bushes. **1886** STEVENSON *Kidnapped* xvi. 153 He's here and awa; here to-day and gone to-morrow; a fair *heather-cat. **1895** CROCKETT *Men of Moss Hags* xvi, That daft heather-cat of a cousin of mine. **1886** G. ALLEN *Maimie's Sake* ii. 12 To climb the *heather-clad hill. **1818** SCOTT *Br. Lamm.* xxix, What good can the poor bird do..except pine and die in the first *heather-cow or whin-bush she can crawl into? **1826** *Blackw. Edin. Mag.* XX. 412/1 *Heather-honey of this blessed year's produce. **1863** KINGSLEY *Water Bab.* (1879) 146 He..smelt..the wafts of heather honey off the grouse moor. **1935** *Jrnl. Physical Chem.* XXXIX. 213 The term 'heather honey' is used to describe any honey derived largely from the nectar of *Calluna vulgaris*, *Erica cinerea*, and allied species. **1971** *Country Life* 28 Oct. 1107/2 The drawback to heather honey is that it is difficult to extract. **1971** *Harrod's Xmas Catal.* 59/3 'Double Scotch' Honey is a unique blend of Scottish heather honey and rare old malt whisky. **1863** J. G. BAKER *N. Yorksh.* 181 A considerable extent of the surface yet remains as *heatherland. **1885** MABEL COLLINS *Prettiest Woman* xxvi, He changed his '*heather-mixture' for clothes more suitable to Piccadilly. **1819** REES *Cycl.* s.v., *Heather-roofs are frequently met with in the district of Cowal. **1876** MRS. ALEXANDER *Her Dearest Foe* I. 278 Tom entered, in a bright purple-tinted '*heather suit'. **1824** SCOTT *St. Ronan's* ii, A head like a *heather-tap.

heather-bell. **a.** A name given to *Erica tetralix* (or spec. to its blossom), and sometimes also to *E. cinerea*. (In quot. 1725 app. = HEATH-BELL 2.)

1725 RAMSAY *Gentl. Sheph.* II. iv, Blue heather-bells Bloom'd bonny on moorland. **1785** BURNS *To W. Simpson* 56 Her moors red-brown wi' heather bells. **1808** SCOTT *Marm.* I. Introd. 18 Away hath passed the heather-bell, That bloomed so rich on Needpath-fell.

'heather-bleat. *Sc.* [Perversion, after *heather*, of the OE. name *hæfer-blǣte*, goat-bleater, f. *hæfer* goat + *blǣtan* to bleat: from the noise which it makes in flight, associated in many languages with the bleating of a goat (Newton, Dict. Birds 885; Swainson, Prov. Name Birds 192). So Ger. *himmelziege*, Fr. *chèvre-volante*, Gaelic *meannan-adhair* air-kid, *gabhair-adhair* sky- or air-goat, etc.] The Snipe.

[*c* **1000** ÆLFRIC *Gloss.* in Wr.-Wülcker 116/41 *Bicoca*, hæferblæte, *uel* pur. *Ibid.* 260/3. *c* **1050** *Ags. Gloss.* ibid. 361/17 *Bugium*, hæferblæte.] **1824** MACTAGGART *Gallovid. Encycl.*, *Heather-bleet*, the mire snipe. **1894** CROCKETT *Raiders* xxxvi, The snipe (which is called the heather-bleat). *Ibid.*, Farther off a heatherbleat whinnied.

'heather-,bleater. *Sc.* and *north. dial.* Also -blut(t)er, -bluiter, -blooter; corrupted *earn-bleater*, *hammer-bleat*, *-er*. [as prec., with second element conformed to agent-nouns in -ER.] = prec.

a **1617** BUREL *Pilgremer* in Watson *Collect.* (1706) II. 27 (Jam.) The Hobie and the Hedderbluter. **1791** *Statist. Acc. Scotl.*, *Ayrsh.* II. 72 (Jam.) A bird, which the people here call a hether blutter. **1820** SCOTT *Monast.* iv, What saw she in the bog, then..forby moor-cocks and heather-blutters? **1893** *Northumbld. Gloss.*, *Heather-bleater*..It is also called *mire-bleater* and *gutter-snipe*.

heathered ('hɛðəd), *a.* [f. HEATHER + -ED².] Covered with heather.

1831 J. WILSON in *Blackw. Mag.* XXIX. 319 A treeless but high-heathered rock. **1849** AYTOUN *Lays, Island of Scots* xi, Scotland's high and heathered hills. **1884** Q. VICTORIA *More Leaves* 133 A lovely drive with pink heathered hills to the right.

heathery ('hi:θərɪ), *sb.* [f. HEATH + -ERY: cf. *pinery*, *fernery*.] A collection of heaths; a place in which heaths are grown.

1804 H. C. ANDREWS (*title*) The Heathery, or Monograph of the Genus Erica. **1849** *Beck's Florist* 10, I know from experience that Heaths will thrive as well in a greenhouse.. as they would do in a heathery. **1850** *Ibid.* Feb. 33 A skilful disposition of the plants in the Heathery.

heathery ('hɛðərɪ), *a.* Also 6 hadrie. [f. HEATHER + -Y.] Covered with or abounding in heather; of the nature or appearance of heather.

1535 STEWART *Cron. Scot.* I. 340 In craig and cleuche, and mony hadrie hill. **1710** EARL CROMERTIE in *Phil. Trans.* XXVII. 296 The Surface is covered with a heathy, and (as they call it) a heathery Scurf. **1804** J. GRAHAME *Sabbath* 152 Flowers that strangers seem Amid the heathery wild. **1810** SCOTT *Lady of L.* I. ii, The antlered monarch of the waste Sprung from his heathery couch in haste.

Hence **'heatheriness.**

1862 SHIRLEY *Nugæ Crit.* I. 67 The romance of the moor has been recently disturbed, and even the gor-cock has begun to lose the old racy heatheriness.

'heath-hen. **a.** The female of the HEATH-COCK; the Grey-hen. **b.** Applied in N. America to species of grouse.

1591 *Shuttleworth Acc.* (Chetham Soc.) 66 A lade of Alexander Bradshawes wᶜʰ broughte hethe henes iiijd. **1670** D. DENTON *Descr. New York* (1845) 5 Wild Fowl there is great store of, as Turkies, Heath-Hens, Quails. **1728–46** THOMSON *Spring* 699 O'er the trackless waste The heath-hen flutters. **1893** NEWTON *Dict. Birds*, *Heath-cock* and *Heath-hen*, originally names by which..the Black-cock and Grey-hen were called; but on the North American continent ..applied to one or more species of grouse.

'heathless, *a. rare.* [f. HEATH + -LESS.] Devoid of heath.

1804 J. GRAHAME *Sabbath* 247 There on the heathless moss outstretch'd he broods.

heathnick, -ical: see HEATHENIC.

heath-pea ('hi:θpi:). Also 8 -pease. A tuberous-rooted leguminous plant, *Lathyrus macrorrhizus* (*Orobus tuberosus*), called also CARMELE. Also **heath-peaseling.**

1706 PHILLIPS (ed. Kersey), *Heath-pease*, or *Wood-pease*, a kind of wild Pease. **1755** JOHNSON, *Heath-peas*, a species of bitter Vetch. **1800** GARNETT *Tour Scotl.* I. 337 The *Orobus tuberosus*, or heath-peasling. **1808** *Med. Jrnl.* XIX. 77 Heath peaseling..The roots, when boiled, are savoury and nutritious. **1863** PRIOR *Plant-n.*, *Heath-pea*.

'heath-poult. Also -polt, -powt. = HEATH-BIRD; more *spec.* the female or young.

1678 RAY *Willughby's Ornith.*, The Merlin..They fly also Heath-pouts with it. **1687** *Lond. Gaz.* No. 2263/4 It is His Majesties Will and Pleasure, That no Person do..presume to Hawk at any Heath-Poult, in any year before the 20th day of July. **1825** *Sporting Mag.* XVI. 422 [He] had the good fortune..to get 16 shots at heath-poults, or black game. **1884** JEFFERIES *Red Deer* ii. 33 Heath-poults, the female of black game, fly like a great partridge. **1887** *Pall Mall G.* 4 Oct. 5/1 The young heath-poults are at first extremely tender creatures.

Heath Robinson (hi:θ 'rɒbɪnsən). [f. the name of the humorous artist W. *Heath Robinson* (1872–1944).] Used *attrib.* or *ellipt.* of any absurdly ingenious and impracticable device of the kind illustrated by this artist. Hence **,Heath-Robinso'nesque**, **,Heath-'Robinsonish** *adjs.*; **,Heath 'Robinsonism.**

1917 'CONTACT' *Airman's Outings* i. 12 The movable mounting for the observer's gun in the rear cockpit... We called it the Christmas Tree, the Heath Robinson, the Jabberwock, the Ruddy Limit, and names unprintable. **1930** *Telegr. & Teleph. Jrnl.* June 180/2 The tour commenced at the principal machine shop. Here one is introduced to what on first acquaintance appears to be a Heath Robinson nightmare. **1931** D. L. SAYERS *Five Red Herrings* xiii. 137 'Not very lively,' he mused; 'better, I think, for a Heath Robinson picture.' **1934** *Discovery* Nov. 328/2 This 'Heath-Robinson' jumble of wooden sheds, sluices, and water troughs looks ridiculous, yet it works all right. **1951** R. CAMPBELL *Light on Dark Horse* xiii. 175 In the bay was the Heath-Robinsonesque, palm-crested fortress of Goree. **1960** L. DAVIDSON *Night of Wenceslas* xiii. 207 It was surely a bit of a Heath-Robinsonish way of passing valuable secrets. **1962** *New Scientist* 29 Mar. 762/2 Certain general principles of heathrobinsonism. **1963** *Times* 26 Feb. 9/5 Some of the devices look somewhat Heath Robinson and rather like a film set, but of their serious purpose the visitor is left in no doubt. **1968** N. FREELING *This is Castle* III. iii. 163 The English talked about things being 'Heath-Robinson' to this day, quite rightly—he recalled the man from his own childhood, a caricaturist who filled his drawings with wonderful complicated mechanisms made out of every kind of rubbish-tip junk held together with knotted bits of string.

heathwort ('hi:θwɜ:t). Lindley's name for a plant of the Nat. Ord. *Ericaceæ*. Also *attrib.*

1847 in CRAIG. **1866** *Treas. Bot.* 461/1 Shrubby plants belonging to the heathwort order.

heathy ('hi:θɪ), *a.* Also 5 hethy. [f. HEATH + -Y.] Abounding in or covered with heath; of, pertaining to, or of the nature of heath; heathery.

a **1450** *Fysshynge w. Angle* (1883) 11 The tawney colour for those waters that ben hethy or morysshe. **1545** BRINKLOW *Compl.* iv. B vj, Such heathy, woddy and moory ground, as is vnfrutefull for corne or pasture. **1667** *Phil. Trans.* II. 525 It is Heathy, Ferny and Furzy. **1809** SHELLEY *Zastrozzi* iv. Pr. Wks. 1888 I. 18 The wild berries which grew amid the heathy shrubs. **1873** BLACK *Pr. Thule* ii, An illimitable prospect of heathy undulations.

heating ('hi:tɪŋ), *vbl. sb.* [f. HEAT *v.* + -ING¹.]

a. The action of the verb HEAT; imparting of heat, warming; becoming hot; *techn.* 'in the iron and steel industry, Getting the steel hot for rolling' (*Labour Comm. Gloss.* 1892).

1398 TREVISA *Barth. De P.R.* VII. xlix. (1495) 263 Bathynges and heetynges whyche dyssolue and departe and melte the matere. **1545** ASCHAM *Toxoph.* (Arb.) 115 Well seasoned..wyth hetynges and tilleryinges. **1592** SHAKS. *Ven. & Ad.* 742 Sickness, whose attaint Disorder breeds by heating of the blood. **1665** R. HOOKE *Microgr.* 37 A gradual heating and cooling does anneal or reduce the parts of Glass to a texture that is more loose. **1858** GREENER *Gunnery* 175 The loss of strength by heating or softening. **1884** S. P. THOMPSON *Dynamo-Electr. Mach.* 105 There is another cause of heating in field-magnet cores.

b. *attrib.* and *Comb.*, as ***heating apparatus***, ***appliance***, ***arrangement(s)***, ***power***, ***stove***; **heating element** (see ELEMENT *sb.* 4 c); **heating furnace** (see quot.); **heating pan**, a pan in which substances are warmed in various manufacturing processes.

1611 COTGR., *Chauffage*,..heating stuffe, or stuffe to heat with. **1811** A. T. THOMSON *Lond. Disp.* (1818) p. xxxviii, Chemical effects..independent of its heating power. **1860** TYNDALL *Glac.* II. ii. 240 Beyond the red..we have rays possessing a high heating power. **1861** W. FAIRBAIRN *Mills* I. 270 Feed-water Heating Apparatus. **1873** *Leisure Hour* 18 Jan. 48/1 Cisterns in the upper parts of a house should be emptied, if the heating arrangement has been neglected. **1881** RAYMOND *Mining Gloss.*, *Heating-furnace*, the furnace in which blooms or piles are heated before hammering or rolling. **1902** *Encycl. Brit.* XXVI. 510/2 It [*sc.* a temperature of 20°C] is readily attainable at any time in a modern laboratory with adequate heating arrangements. **1923** R. G. COLLINGWOOD *Roman Brit.* 54 The discovery of skeletons huddled inside the heating-arrangements beneath the floors.

'heating, *ppl. a.* [f. HEAT *v.* + -ING².] That heats or makes hot, in various senses.

1591 PERCIVALL *Sp. Dict.*, *Caluroso*, hot, heating. **1601** HOLLAND *Pliny* II. Table, Heating medicines. **1732** ARBUTHNOT *Rules of Diet* 258 Truffles..are heating. **1812** L. HUNT in *Examiner* 7 Dec. 771/1 To have..his warmth in an argument traced to a heating diet.

b. ***heating surface***, the total surface of a steam boiler, exposed on one side to the fire, on the other to water; the fire-surface: see quots. ***heating-tube***, a water tube in a boiler surrounded by flame.

1854 RONALDS & RICHARDSON *Chem. Technol.* (ed. 2) I. 259 The grate is large in proportion to the consumption of fuel, as well as the heating surface. **1861** W. FAIRBAIRN *Mills* I. 261 The efficient heating surface is obtained by deducting from the total heating surface one-half the area of vertical

portions, and one-half the area of horizontal cylindrical flues. **1894** *Times* 23 July 6/4 Boilers, which have an aggregate heating surface of 7,890 square feet, with a grate area of 189.

Hence **'heatingly** *adv.*, in a heating manner.

1668 WILKINS *Real Char.* 303 Heatingly. Illuminatingly.

heatless ('hi:tlɪs), *a. rare.* [f. HEAT *sb.* + -LESS.] Destitute of heat.

1596 WILLOBIE *Avisa* (1880) 154 This Not-seene Nimph, this heatlesse fire. **1664** DRYDEN *Rival Ladies* v. iii, The heatless Beams of a departing Sun. **1680** J. CHAMBERLAINE *Birth Christ* 3 My Wife is likewise known, Through heatless age, past hopes to have a Son. **1887** T. HARDY *Woodlanders* III. xii. 243 Bright but heatless sun.

heatronic (hi:'trɒnɪk), *a.* [f. HEAT *sb.* + ELECT)RONIC *a.*] (See quot. 1943.)

1943 *Plastics Engin.* Mar. 87/1 Heatronic molding is announced as a most significant advance in the art of molding plastics. This process is the result of..research involving the application of electronics to the molding of thermosetting materials. **1944** *Electronic Engin.* XVII. 40 Space is devoted to discussing the physical properties of heatronic mouldings.

heat-spot. **a.** A red spot on the skin, a freckle. **b.** *Physiol.* A spot or point of the skin at which the sensation of heat can be produced.

1882-34 *Good's Study Med.* (ed. 4) IV. 479 The blushing halo by which they are surrounded, is popularly called a heat-spot. **1887** G. T. LADD *Physiol. Psychol.* xiii. 315 The sense of locality connected with the cold-spots is about twice as fine..as that connected with the heat-spots.

heat treatment. **a.** The specialized application of heat to various substances to produce a desired metallurgical or physical condition, e.g. hardness, softness, toughness. Hence **heat-treat** *v.*; **heat-treatable** *a.*; **heat-treated** *ppl. a.*; **heat-treating** *vbl. sb.*

1895 H. M. HOWE in *Trans. Amer. Inst. Mining Engin. 1894* XXIV. 746, I..call your attention to two directions in which very important progress may be..hoped for—pyrometry and the heat-treatment of steel. *Ibid.* 747 In the hardening and tempering of tools, in the annealing of steel castings,..and in the manufacture of guns, projectiles, and armor, we have already extensive and careful if empirical heat-treatment. **1899** *Jrnl. Iron & Steel Inst.* LIV. 147 The simple heat treatment had converted the more or less brittle annealed material into tough and strong steel. **1904** F. W. HARBORD *Metallurgy of Steel* xxxix, (*title*) Heat treatment of steel. **1908** *Chem. Abstr.* II. 1121 The Structure of Metals. Changes Produced by Working and by Heat Treatment. **1908** *Westm. Gaz.* 2 June 4/2 The wonderful effect of heat-treating [of steel]. *Ibid.*, With these alloying materials added to steel small gears can be made that, if properly heat-treated, they will be so tough and strong as to make it impossible to break out a tooth even with a sledge-hammer. **1946** *Nature* 27 July 120/2 Plants from heat-treated grain were..somewhat shorter in the straw. **1947** *Hansard, Commons* 4 Dec. 559 Mr. Lambert asked the Minister of Education the number of rural schools..in which the children are supplied with heat-treated milk. **1947** *Food & Drugs Statut. Rules & Orders* DCXII. (*heading*) The ice cream (heat treatment, etc.) regulations, 1947. *Ibid.*, The mixture shall be subjected to heat treatment as follows [etc.]. **1950** J. G. DAVIS *Dict. Dairying* 332 *Heat treatment of milk.* The term is a general one covering any of the ordinary commercial heating methods by which the keeping quality of milk is enhanced and pathogenic organisms destroyed. **1956** *Nature* 25 Feb. 360/1 He invented the heat-treatment which has for decades been applied as compulsory routine at every ginnery in the country. *Ibid.* 3 Mar. 436/2 The specimen [of an alloy] had been heat-treated. **1960** *Farmer & Stockbreeder* 5 Jan. 64 All seed grown from heat-treated stocks. **1960** *Times* (Roy. Soc. Number) 19 July p. xxi/3 Heat-treatable aluminium alloys. **1963** *B.S.I. News* Feb. 17/1 Fifteen different steels..were heat-treated by the National Engineering Laboratory. **1971** *Nature* 26 Nov. 231/1 Heat treatment (57°C for 30 s in summer) disrupted the layer into irregular globules.

b. The therapeutic use of heat, esp. radiant and infra-red heat.

1934 J. E. MANSION *Harrap's Fr. & Eng. Dict.* 837/2 *Thermothérapie*, heat cure, heat treatment, thermotherapy. **1967** *Listener* 5 Oct. 427/2 He asked for..heat treatment, which my wife should apply herself.

heat-wave. **a.** A wave of radiant heat; one of those vibrations of the ether that produce heating effects: see HEAT *sb.* 2 b. **b.** A 'wave' or access of excessive heat in the atmosphere, esp. when regarded as passing from one place to another.

1878 J. FISKE in *N. Amer. Rev.* CXXVI. 35 The sum-total of motion is ever the same, but its distribution into heat-waves, light-waves, nerve-waves, &c., varies. **1893** R. S. BALL *In the High Heavens* xii, (*heading*) The 'Heat Wave' of 1892. *Ibid.* The culmination of what had been somewhat absurdly designated 'the great heat-wave'..The so-called heat-wave then seems to have travelled eastward.

heaume (həʊm). *Obs.* or *arch.* [a. F. *heaume* (om):—OF. *helme*: see HELM *sb.*[1]] A massive helmet, reaching down to the shoulders, worn in the 12th and 13th centuries, sometimes over a smaller close-fitting one.

1572 BOSSEWELL *Armorie* II. 122 Whiche of heraltes is proprely called blazon, heawme, and timbre. **1610** GUILLIM *Heraldry* VI. v. (1660) 394. **1706** PHILLIPS (ed. Kersey), *Heaulme* or *Heaume*, a Term in Heraldry for an Helmet or Head-piece. **1834** PLANCHÉ *Brit. Costume* 186 The great crested helmet or heaume was now [temp. Hen. V] only worn for the tournament. **1858** MORRIS *Near Avalon* Poems 239 Their heaumes are on, whereby, half blind, They pass by many sights.

heauto- (hi:ɔ:təʊ), before a vowel **heaut-**, comb. form of Gr. ἑαυτοῦ of oneself, used occas. instead of the more common AUTO-[1]: as in **heau'tandrous** *a.* [Gr. ἀνδρ-, ἀνήρ man] (see quot.). **he,auto'morphism** [Gr. μορφή form] = AUTOMORPHISM 1. **heau'tophany** [Gr. -φανία, f. φαίνειν to show], self-manifestation. **he,auto'phonics** [Gr. φωνή sound] = AUTOPHONY.

1837 J. F. PALMER in *J. Hunter's Wks.* IV. 35 *note*, Three kinds of hermaphroditism. First, the cryptandrous .. Second, the *heautandrous, in which the male organs are developed, but so disposed as to fecundate the ova of the same individual. **1870** ROLLESTON *Anim. Life* 248 The act of self impregnation observable in these heautandrous hermaphrodites. **1886** SULLY *Handbk. Psychol.*, *Heautomorphism, in default of science, is ever the first resource of explanation; i.e. we judge of others by ourselves. *a* **1834** COLERIDGE *Notes Eng. Divines* (1853) I. 257 If there be one other subject graced by the same total *heautophany, it is in the pouring forth of his [Jeremy Taylor's] profound common sense on the ways and weaknesses of men.

heave (hi:v), *v.* Pa. t. and pple. **heaved** (hi:vd), **hove** (həʊv). Forms: 1 **hebban, hæbban**, 2-4 **hebbe(n**, 3-5 **hefe(n**, 3-6 **heve(n**, 6- **heave**; also 3 **heoven**, (*3rd pres. sing. Ind.* **hefð, hefieð**), 4 **heeve**, 5 **heff(e**, 5-6 *Sc.* and *north.* **heive**, 6 *Sc.* **heif.** Pa. t. and pple.: see below. [A Com. Teutonic strong vb.: OE. *hębban* (*hefþ*), *hóf*, *hafen* (*hæfen*) = OFris. *heva*, *hôf*, *heven* (*hevet*), OS. *hębbian* (*hęffian*), *hof* (*huof*), *haban* (MLG. *heven*, *hov*, *hafen*, LG. *hefen*, *heffen*, *hôf*, *hafen*, MDu. *heffen*, *hoef* (*hief*, *huef*), *gehaven*, *geheven*, Du. *heffen*, *hief*, *geheven*), OHG. *hęffen* (*hęvit*), *huob*, *haban* (*hapan*) (MHG. *heben* (*heven*, *hefen*), *huop*, *huoben*, *gehaben*, also *hebte*, *gehebt*, mod.G. *heben*, *hob*, *gehoben*), ON. *hefja*, *hóf*, *hafenn* (Sw. *häfva*, *hof*, *häfwen*, and *häfde*, *häfd*, Da. *hæve*, *hævde*, *hævd*), Goth. *hafjan*, *hôf*, *hafans*:—OTeut. **hafjan*, *hôf* (pl. *hôbun*), *habano-*, corresp. to L. *capĕre*, *capio*, to take. Originally belonging to the same ablaut-series as *shake*, *shave*, but subseq. affected by many changes. The present stem *hafj-* had orig. a formative *j* (= L. *-i-* in *cap-i-o*), which caused umlaut of the stem vowel, giving OE. *ę*, ME. *e*, lengthened by position to *ē*, *ea*. The WGer. gemination of *fj*, giving *bb* in OS. and OE., affected all parts of the present stem, exc. 2nd and 3rd sing. pres. Ind. and sing. Imp., giving *hębbe*, *hębbað*, *hębban*, *hębbende*, beside *hęfest*, *hęfeþ*, *hęfe*. In ME. the *bb* forms were retained (in the south) till 14th c., but were at length everywhere reduced by levelling to *f* (later *v*). The pa. t. *hóf* came down as *hove*; but in ME. this was largely displaced by a type *hæf*, *heaf*, *hêf*, *hêve*, and another *haf*, *have*, both of which survived till 15th c. The OE. pa. pple. *hafen* was by the 12th c. abandoned for *hofen* (later *hoven*, *hove*), with *o* from the pa. t.; there are also traces of *heven* (cf. OFris. and Du.). But, beside these strong inflexions, there appeared also in late OE. (as in some of the other langs.) weak inflexions *hefde*, *hefod*; these gained ground in ME., and esp. in mod.Eng., in which *heaved* is now the general form, though *hove* remains in certain uses. The original sense, as evidenced by various derivatives, as well as by L. *capĕre*, was 'take', whence, through 'take up', came that of 'lift, raise', already developed in Com. Teut.

The close correspondence to Latin is seen in comparing *capio*, *capis*, *capit*, *capiunt* with OTeut. **hafjô*, *hafis*, *hafiþ*, *hafjanð*, OLG. *hebbiu*, *hebis*, *hebið*, *hebbiað*, OE. *hębbe*, *hęfes(t)*, *hęfeþ*, *hębbað*. Since *heave* is thus certainly cognate with *capĕre*, it must be originally quite distinct from *have*, if the latter is = L. *habēre*. The two verbs however come close together in various forms in most of the langs., and their derivatives have probably influenced each other, so that it is difficult in some instances to know whether these belong to *hafjan* 'heave' or *habên* 'have'.]

A. Inflexional Forms.

1. Present tense stem (with consonant-exchange).

α. *Beowulf* (Z.) 655 Ic hond and rond hebban mihte. *a* **1225** *Ancr. R.* 290 Uorte hebben up hire þreo uingres. **1297** R. GLOUC. (1724) 17 Þat an oþer scholde hebbe vn neþe. *Ibid.* 455 Our [= your] herten hebbeþ vp. *c* **1380** *Sir Ferumb.* 1248 Sche gan þo hebbe and pynge.

β. *c* **1000** *Ags. Ps.* (Th.) lxxiii. 4 [lxxiv. 3] Hefe þu þine handa. *c* **1200** ORMIN 11865 He wile hemm hefenn upp. *a* **1225** *Ancr. R.* 32 Hwon þe preost hefð up Godes licome. *c* **1230** *Hali Meid.* 25 Þat tu schuldest þin heorte heouen þiderward. **13..** *E.E. Allit. P.* A. 472 Þy self in heuen ouer hyȝ þou heue. **13..** *Gaw. & Gr. Knt.* 1346 And heuen hit vp al hole. *a* **1400** *Prymer* (1891) 65 Hefeth up ȝoure handes.

2. Past Tense. α. 1-5 **hóf**, 3- **hove**; (3 *pl.* **hofen, hoven, huven**), 4 **hoif, hoef**, 6 *Sc.* **huif, huve.** β. 2-4 **hef**, 3 **hæf, heaf, heof**, 4 **heef**, 5 **heve**; *pl.* 3 **heven, hefven, heoven**, 4-5 **hevyn.** γ. 4-5 **haf**, 4 **have.** δ. 1 **hefde**, 2-5 **hevede**, 4-6 **heved**, (*Sc.* 4 **hewid, -it, heywit**, 5 **heyffyt**, 6 **huit**), 6- **heaved.** ε. 6 **heft(e.**

α. *c* **1000** *Ags. Ps.* (Th.) cxxii[i] 1 To ðe ic mine eaȝan hof. *a* **1300** *Cursor M.* 11114 Þis ilk was Ion.. þat after-ward hof [*v.r.* hoif] iesu crist. *Ibid.* 28240 Childir þat ic houe o funt. *c* **1400** *Destr. Troy* 5259 [He] hof vp his hond. **1786** tr. *Beckford's Vathek* 93 The surface hove up into heaps. **1872** BLACKIE *Lays Highl.* 16 His prayerful hands he hove. [See also senses 20-22.]

β. *c* **1200** *Trin. Coll. Hom.* 35 He..hef his honde. *c* **1205** LAY. 1914 He..him grimliche heaf [*c* **1275** heof]. *Ibid.* 16509 Aldolf..hæf [*c* **1275** hefde] hæhȝe his sweord. *Ibid.* 23195 Heo..hefuen hine to kinge. *c* **1374** CHAUCER *Boeth.* I. pr. i. 2 (Camb. MS.) She hef hyr heued heyere. **13..** *Minor Poems fr. Vernon MS.* liii. 262 Þen Susan..Heef hir hondus on hiȝ. *c* **1420** *Chron. Vilod.* 640 Þey..hevyn up þe ston.

γ. *a* **1300** *Cursor M.* 17913 (Gött.) Quen i haf [*v.rr.* haue, heef] þat sacles. *c* **1340** *Ibid.* 10479 (Laud) She hafe [*v.rr.* heef, lift] hir hondes vp. *c* **1386** CHAUCER *Knt.'s T.* 1570 And Arcita anon his hand vp haf. *c* **1430** *Pilgr. Lyf Manhode* III. i. (1869) 138 She haf it hye to hire tunge.

δ. *c* **1000** ÆLFRIC *Gen.* xlviii. 14 He hefde þa his swiþran hand ofer Ephraimes heafod. *c* **1200** *Trin. Coll. Hom.* 111 He dranc..and þarfore heuede siðen up þat heued. *c* **1375** *Sc. Leg. Saints, Katerine* 350 Þane hewid scho wpe bath hir handis. *c* **1470** HENRY *Wallace* XI. 544 Þai..Heyffyt wp thar handis. *c* **1489** CAXTON *Sonnes of Aymon* xvii. 392 He..heved his handes.

ε. **15..** *How marchande did his wyfe betray* 42 in Hazl. *E.P.P.* I. 198 Tho..He heft hyt in hys purs. **1590** SPENSER *F.Q.* I. xi. 39 His raging blade he hefte. **1596** *Ibid.* IV. iii. 12 The other halfe..Cambell fiercely reft, And backe at him it heft [*rime* cleft].

3. Past Participle. α. 1 **hafen, hæfen.** β. 2-4 **hofen**, 2-9 **hoven**, 4-5 **hovin, -yn, -un**, 4 **ihove**, 4- **hove.** γ. 3 **heven.** δ. 1 **hefod**, 2-5 **heved**, 3 **iheved, (efed)**, 4 *Sc.* **heywit**, 5 **hevyd, hewede**, 6 **heyved**; 6- **heaved**, 7 **heft.**

α. *a* **1000** *Christ* 651 He wæs upp-hafen engla fæðmum. *a* **1000** *Andreas* 1157 Þa wæs wop hæfen.

β. *c* **1200** *Trin. Coll. Hom.* 167 Hie þis dai was houen in to heuene. *a* **1300** *Cursor M.* 17962 (Gött.) Houen [*v.rr.* hovyn, hofen] sal he be in flom iordane. **1303** R. BRUNNE *Handl. Synne* 55 (Mätz.) Ȝyf a man have hove a chylde. **1382** WYCLIF *Gen.* xxiv. 63 Whan he had houun vp the eyen. **1599** *Broughton's Let.* ii. 8 You are so houen and lifted vp. **1787** WINTER *Syst. Husb.* 162 To be hove out of the ground. **1853** FELTON *Fam. Lett.* i. (1865) 3 The ship was hoven to.

γ. *a* **1300** *E.E. Psalter* xii. 3 [xiii. 2] When sal mi fa heven over me be?

δ. *c* **888** K. ÆLFRED *Boeth.* xxxvi. §2 Siððon þu ofer þone bist ahefod. *c* **1200** *Trin. Coll. Hom.* 111 Ure helende þe was þis dai heued on hegh. *c* **1375** *Sc. Leg. Saints, Magdalena* 926 And fand þe magdelane..He [high] heywit vpe with angel hand. **1382** WYCLIF *Gen.* xiii. 10 His eyen heued vp.

B. Signification.

I. Transitive senses.

1. To lift, raise, bear up. (Often with *up.*)

a. Formerly in general sense; now only *arch.* or *dial.*

971 *Blickl. Hom.* 149 Hie hofan þa bære. *c* **1000** ÆLFRIC *Hom.* I. 516 Þæt hi ðe healdon, and on heora handum hebban. *c* **1200** ORMIN 16705 All swa se Moysæs Hof upp þe neddre i wesste. *a* **1350** *Childh. Jesus* 102 (Mätz.) Joseph..of þat best þat heo sat on Softeliche haf hire adoun. **1382** WYCLIF *Gen.* xiv. 14 Heue vp thin eyen. *c* **1386** CHAUCER *Prol.* 550 Ther nas no dore þat he ne wolde heue of harre. **1470-85** MALORY *Arthur* XXI. iv, He swouned ofte tymes, and syr Lucan..and syr Bedwere oftymes heue hym vp. **1493** *Festivall* (W. de W. 1515) 6 b, Heve up thy heed, & be mery. **1596** SPENSER *F.Q.* VI. viii. 10 His hand was heaved up on hight. **1639** E. SPENSER in *Lismore Papers* Ser. II. (1888) IV. 75 He heaved vp his sticke with an intent..to haue strooken me. **1671** MILTON *Samson* 197 How could I once look up, or heave the head. **1702** POPE *Dryope* 45 Her trembling hand she heaves To rend her hair. **1712** J. JAMES tr. *Le Blond's Gardening* 174 Moles..do a great deal of Mischief to the young Plants, in heaving the Earth. **1803** BEDDOES *Hygëia* x. 63 It pitched him between two walls, so close that he could not heave an arm. **1855** ROBINSON *Whitby Gloss.*, *To Heave the Hand*, to bestow charity in mites, amounting to little more than..the mere motion of the hand in the act.

b. In modern use: To lift with exertion (something heavy); to raise with effort or force; to hoist.

1715-20 POPE *Iliad* II. 250 Murmuring they move, as when old Ocean roars, And heaves huge surges to the trembling shores. **1793** SMEATON *Edystone L.* §98 Our boat, which the seamen were heaving into the sloop, filled with water. **1863** A. C. RAMSAY *Phys. Geog.* xv. (1878) 236 For a space they have been heaved nearly on end. **1865** KINGSLEY *Herew.* xix, Who heaved up a long tybill, or double axe.

c. *absol.*

1593 SHAKS. *3 Hen. VI*, v. vii. 23 This shoulder was ordain'd so thicke, to heaue. **1607** TOPSELL *Four-f. Beasts* (1658) 390 Of the Mole or Want..When they heave, they do it more for meat than for breath.

2. *transf.* and *fig.* To raise. **a.** In various figurative senses directly related to 1.

a **1000** *Cædmon's Exod.* 573 Hofon here þreatas hlude stefne. *c* **1000** *Ags. Ps.* (Th.) xxiv. [xxv.] 1 To ðe ic hæbbe..min mod. *c* **1205** LAY. 11280 Scottes huuen up muchelne ræm. **13..** *E.E. Allit. P.* A. 314 Man to god wordez schulde heue. *a* **1375** *Lay Folks Mass Bk.* App. iv. 552 Hef up ȝor hertes in-to heuen. *a* **1400-50** *Alexander* 3014 Ser Dary..Heuyd vp a huge ost. **1526** *Pilgr. Perf.* (W. de W. 1531) 290 It is so violent, that it heueth and lyfteth vp the spiryt to god. **1824** W. IRVING *T. Trav.* II. 12 The resolution..heaved a load from off my heart. **1851** W. PHILLIPS *Woman's Rights* in *Speeches* (1863) 28 Strong political excitement..heaves a whole nation on to a higher platform of intellect and morality.

†**b.** To raise, exalt, lift up, elevate (in feeling, dignity, station, etc.); to extol. *Obs.*

c **825** *Vesp. Psalter* xcviii[i]. 9 Hebbað up dryhten god urne. *c* **1200** *Trin. Coll. Hom.* 213 He hefieð his lichame, and

heneð his soule. *c* **1205** LAY. 23183 We scullen..hebben hine to kinge. *a* **1225** *Ancr. R.* 156 Heo schal..holden hire stille, & so hebben hire sulf buuen hire suluen. *a* **1300** *K. Horn* 1267 þu me to kniȝt houe. *a* **1400–50** *Alexander* 3290 Oure lord..heues him to welthis. **1450–1530** *Myrr. our Ladye* 290 Lorde thou art..heyued aboue all thynges wythouten ende. **1581** PETTIE *Guazzo's Civ. Conv.* I. (1586) 43 b, Ambition..heaveth those that followe it to the high degree of dignitie and honour. **1596** BP. W. BARLOW *Three Serm.* i. 127 Rich men, who..haue bene houen and lifted vp with their heapes of riches. **1641** MILTON *Ch. Govt.* I. vi, For the prevention of growing schisme the Bishop was heav'd above the Presbyter.

†**c.** To set up, erect, institute. *Obs.*

c **1200** ORMIN 16840 Þeȝȝ..hofenn þurrh hemm sellfenn upp..Settnessess.

†**3.** *spec.* To lift (a child) from the font (formerly the duty of a sponsor at baptism); to stand sponsor to; hence *transf.* to baptize, christen. *Obs.* (Ger. *ein kind aus der taufe heben*, med.L. *levare de sacro fonte*.)

c **1200** ORMIN 10881 Whase shall i Crisstenndom Beon hofenn upp. **1303** R. BRUNNE *Handl. Synne* 9698 Ȝe þat chyldryn heue, ȝe shul nat forȝete ne leue, To teche hyt paternoster and crede. *c* **1340** *Cursor M.* 168 (Fairf.) Of baptist seynt Ioan þat ihesus hoef in flume Iordan. **1340** HAMPOLE *Pr. Consc.* 3126 When he was hoven at funtstane. **1480** CAXTON *Chron. Eng.* cxii. 94 Edelwold..prayd hym to heue a sone of his at fontstone. **1535** LYNDESAY *Satyre* 781 Wee mon all thrie change our names. Hayif me, and I sall baptize thee. **1571** *Satir. Poems Reform.* xxviii. 39 Hammiltoun he me huif..Ane sorie Surname.

†**b.** *transf.* To present for confirmation. *Obs.*

c **1315** SHOREHAM 18 Hym selve no man hebbe schel To the bischoppynge..That hi ne hebbe hare oȝe child.

†**4.** To lift and take away, carry off, remove, convey. *Obs.*

a **1240** *Lofsong* in *Cott. Hom.* 205 Summe tide ich habbe iheued of oðer monnes mid woh and mid unriht. **1387** TREVISA *Higden* (Rolls) II. 153 Flemmynges..were ihoue þennes and i-putte to Hauerforde. *c* **1440** *York Myst.* xxx. 134 Heue me fro hyne. **1580** SIDNEY *Arcadia* II. xxviii. 31 Poems 1873 II. 72 Thy words..had almost heaued me Quite from my selfe. **1603** DRAYTON *Bar. Wars* v. lii, His onely Daughter, whom (through false Pretext) Stephen, Earl of Bulloyn, from the kingdom heaves. **1648** MILTON *Observ. Art. Peace* (1851) 568 Since thir heaving out the Prelats to heave in themselves, they devise new ways [etc.]. **1649** G. DANIEL *Trinarch., Hen. IV*, cclxxxvi, To arrogate all Ill, They heave the Peerage; for that Pale throwne downe In breakes the Herd, to the vnfenced Crowne.

†**b.** *Thieves' Cant.* To 'lift', to rob. *Obs.*

1567 HARMAN *Caveat* 84 To heue a bough, to robbe or rifle a boeweth. **1609** DEKKER *Lanthorne & Candle-lt.* C iij b, If we heaue a booth we cly the Ierke. **1673** R. HEAD *Canting Acad.* 39 *Heave a booth*, to rob an house. *Ibid.* 78 They will not stick to heave a Booth; that is rob a Booth at a Fair. *a* **1700** B. E. *Dict. Cant. Crew.*

c. *Mining* and *Geol.* To move away or displace (a vein or stratum): said of another vein or stratum intersecting it.

1728 NICHOLLS in *Phil. Trans.* XXXV. 403 The Load is frequently intercepted by the crossing of a Vein of Earth, or Stone..one Part of the Load is moved a considerable Distance to one Side..the Part of the Load which is moved, is, in their Terms, said to be heaved. **1758** BORLASE *Nat. Hist. Cornwall* ix. 157 Guessing..that the lode is heaved, or more properly speaking, started. **1815** W. PHILLIPS *Outl. Min. & Geol.* (1818) 163 North and south veins..always divide tin or copper veins, and generally alter their course; or in the language of the miner, heave them out of their place. **1884** J. PRESTWICH *Geol.* I. 318 The 'cross-courses'.. are of later date than the veins which they frequently displace or *heave*.

†**5.** *fig.* To 'move'; to rouse the feelings of, agitate; to urge, press. *Obs.*

c **1400** *Destr. Troy* 8962 Hit heuet hym hogely of þat hard chaunce. **1593** DRAYTON *Essex* Wks. 1753 II. 616 The king to marry forward still I heave.

6. To cause to swell up or bulge out; to swell.

1573 TUSSER *Husb.* xlix. (1878) 108 Tom Piper hath houen and puffed vp cheekes, if cheese be so houen, make Cisse to seeke creekes. **1621** AINSWORTH *Annot. Pentat.* Lev. vi. 21 So fried that it may be hoven as with bubbles. **1730–46** THOMSON *Autumn* 923 Glittering finny swarms, That heave our friths, and crowd upon our shores. **1808** *Trans. Soc. Arts* XXVI. p. vii, Cattle hoven or swollen by this disorder. *a* **1825** FORBY *Voc. E. Anglia* s.v. *Hoven*, Cattle are hoven by eating too much green clover in a moist state..Turnips are hoven by rank and rapid growth in a strong wet soil.

7. To cause to rise in repeated efforts.

1612 J. TAYLOR (Water P.) *Wks.* (1872) Introd. 12 The surges up and down did heave us. **1719** YOUNG *Revenge* I. i, O what a doubtful torment heaves my heart! **1810** SCOTT *Lady of L.* II. xxxiii, The death-pangs of long-cherished hope..Convulsive heaved its chequered shroud. **1832** DE LA BECHE *Geol. Man.* (ed. 2) 111 The water was observed.. to be heaved up and agitated. **1836** J. GILBERT *Chr. Atonem.* iii. (1852) 83 When pity is heaving his bosom with emotion. **1851** ELIZ. WETHERELL *Old Helmet* xi. 201 The swelling tide of thought and emotion which heaved the whole assembly.

8. To utter (a groan, sigh, or sob; *rarely*, words) with effort, or with a deep breath which causes the chest to heave; to 'fetch'.

1600 SHAKS. *A.Y.L.* II. i. 36 The wretched annimall heau'd forth such groanes. **1605** —— *Lear* IV. iii. 27 Once or twice she heaued the name of father Pantingly forth. *c* **1718** PRIOR *Answ. to Cloe* 6 Heave thou no sigh, nor shed a tear. **1820** W. IRVING *Sketch Bk.* I. 343 He heaved a deep sigh. **1824** MISS FERRIER *Inher.* liii, 'Miss Pratt!' heaved the Earl.

intr. for *pass.* **1821** CLARE *Vill. Minstr.* I. 166 Thy sigh soon heaves, thy tears soon start.

9. To throw, cast, fling, toss, hurl (esp. something heavy, that is lifted and thrown with effort). Now only *Naut.* and *colloq.*

a **1592** GREENE *Orpharion* Wks. (Grosart) XII. 68 The Pirats had heaued me ouer boord. **1596** SPENSER *F.Q.* IV. iii. 12 The other halfe [of the spear]..Out of his headpeece Cambell fiercely reft, And with such furie backe at him it heft. **1627** CAPT. SMITH *Seaman's Gram.* ix. 44 He that doth heaue this lead..doth sing fadome by the marke. **1663** GERBIER *Counsel* 57 There is..so much Stone heaved thereon. **1725** DE FOE *Voy. round World* (1840) 116 They hove over their grappling in five fathom water. **1727–51** CHAMBERS *Cycl.*, *Heave*, at sea, signifies to throw away, or fling, any thing, over-board. **1744** M. BISHOP *Life & Adv.* xxvi. 248 The Captain..by heaving the Lead found us to be but three Fathom Water. **1828** *Craven Dial.*, *Heave*, to pour corn from the scuttle before the wind instead of cleansing it by the fan. **1833** MARRYAT *P. Simple* xiv, The body..was hove overboard. **1833** M. SCOTT *Tom Cringle* xiv. (1859) 329 With a swing he hove the leathern noose at the skipper and whipped it over his head. **1863** KINGSLEY *Water Bab.* i. (1889) 4 Tom was just hiding behind a wall, to heave half a brick at his horse's legs.

10. *Naut.* To haul up or raise by means of a rope; and, more generally, to haul, pull, draw with a rope or cable; to haul a cable; to weigh (anchor); to unfurl (a flag or sail; also, *to heave out*); to cause (a ship) to move in some direction, as by hauling at a rope (e.g. at the anchor-cable when she is aground, or at the sail-ropes so as to set the sails to the wind).

1626 CAPT. SMITH *Accid. Yng. Seamen* 27 Heaue out your top-sayles, hawle your sheates. **1633** T. JAMES *Voy.* 95 We heau'd home our Anker. **1692** *Capt. Smith's Seaman's Gram.* I. xvi. 77 *To heave out the Flag*, is to wrap it about the Staff. **1697** DRYDEN *Æneid* v. (1886) 109 With iron poles they heave her off the shores. **1711** W. SUTHERLAND *Shipbuild. Assist.* 161 *To Heave*, to hale or pull by turning round the Capstan. **1748** *Anson's Voy.* II. i. 112 The capstan was so weakly manned, that it was nearly four hours before we hove the cable right up and down. **1779** FORREST *Voy. N. Guinea* 365 On the 23d, got a hauser..and hove the vessel off the ground. **1867** SMYTH *Sailor's Word-bk.*, *Heaving astern*, causing a ship to recede or go backwards, by heaving on a cable or other rope fastened to some fixed point behind her. This more immediately applies to drawing a vessel off a shoal. **1893** W. T. WAWN *S. Sea Islanders* 5 The anchor was hove up for good.

absol. **1840** MARRYAT *Poor Jack* xxvii, We hove up [i.e. the anchor] and made sail. **1856** KANE *Arct. Expl.* II. xvi. 176 Poor fellows not yet accustomed to heave together. **1867** SMYTH *Sailor's Word-bk.*, *Heave and rally*, an encouraging order to the men at the capstan to heave with spirit, with a rush, and thereby force the anchor out of the ground. *Ibid.*, *Heaving in*, shortening in the cable.

II. Intransitive senses.

†**11.** To remove, shift to another place. *Obs.*

c **1205** LAY. 27490 Þa hæf þat fiht of þan studen þer heo ær fuhten.

†**12.** To be moved or agitated in mind; to feel vexation. *Obs.*

c **1400** *Destr. Troy* 12815 Hir hade leuer haue lost all hir lond hole..Thus heuet þat hynd to hir hede lord. *Ibid.* 13426 Pirrus heivet in hert for his hegh chaunse, And myche dut hym for deth of his derf graunser.

13. To rise, mount, come up, spring up. Now *Obs.* exc. in spec. uses: see following senses.

c **1325** *Body & Soul* 252 in *Map's Poems* (Camd.) 343/1 The hed haf up and the swire. *c* **1385** CHAUCER *L.G.W.* 1196 *Dido*, And vp-on courseris..Hire ȝonge knyghtis houyn al a-boute. *c* **1420** *Pallad. on Husb.* x. 75 Out of molde er colde eek must hit heuen. **1638** SUCKLING *Goblins* IV. (1646) 38 Pox on that noise, he's earth't, Prethee let's watch him and see Whether hee'le heave agen. **1725** POPE *Odyss.* XXIII. 194 The huge trunc rose, and heav'd into the sky. **1808** J. BARLOW *Columb.* II. 238 And temples heave, magnificently great. **1853** KANE *Grinnell Exp.* xxxii. (1856) 279 This ice seems to heave up slowly against the sky.

b. ***heave and set***: to rise and fall, as a floating object upon the waves.

1509 HAWES *Past. Pleas.* XXI. i, Quadrant it was, and did heve and sette At every storme whan the wind was great. *a* **1661** HOLYDAY *Juvenal* 232 Sometimes the one end.. sometimes the other..is mounted-up by the waves; and this is called the heaving and setting of a ship. **1727–51** CHAMBERS *Cycl.* s.v., When a ship, being at anchor, rises and falls by the force of the waves, she is also said to *heave and set*. **1867** in SMYTH *Sailor's Word-bk.*

14. To rise above the general surface, or expand beyond the ordinary size; to swell up, bulge out.

1629 GAULE *Holy Madn.* 94 Marke how he heaves, as though hee almost scorn'd to tread. **1655** H. VAUGHAN *Silex Scint.* I. *Rules & Lessons* (1858) 73 True hearts spread and heave Unto their God. **1697** DRYDEN *Virg. Past.* x. 109 Alders, in the Spring, their Boles extend; And heave so fiercely, that their Bark they rend. **1711** ADDISON *Spect.* No. 127 ¶2 Their Petticoats, which began to heave and swell before you left us, are now blown up into a most enormous Concave. **1750** GRAY *Elegy* iv, That yew-tree's shade, Where heaves the turf in many a mould'ring heap. **1850** *Jrnl. R. Agric. Soc.* XI. I. 152 It [cheese] is too strong-tasted, and inclined to heave, or get hollow and full of eyes.

15. To rise with alternate falling, as waves, or an object floating on them, the breast in deep breathing, etc. Also *fig.*

1618 J. TAYLOR (Water P.) *Navy Land Ships* Wks. (1872) 8 Ships do wallow and heave, and sit upon the sea. **1713** ADDISON *Cato* III. ii, My blood runs cold, my heart forgets to heave. **1746** WESLEY *Princ. Meth.* 46 His Breast heaving at the same Time, as in the Pangs of Death. **1827–35** WILLIS *Confessional* 3 When heaved the long and sullen sea. **1850** TENNYSON *In Mem.* xi, Dead calm in that noble breast Which heaves but with the heaving deep. **1856** STANLEY *Sinai & Pal.* ii. (1858) 124 They actually heave and labour with the fiery convulsions that glow beneath their surface. **1884** *Expositor* Mar. 207 The dangerous forces in a community which heaved with discontent.

16. To draw in the breath with effort; to pant, gasp.

1678 DRYDEN & LEE *Œdipus* IV. i, While we fantastic dreamers heave and puff. **1697** DRYDEN *Virg. Georg.* III. 756 He heaves for Breath; which, from his Lungs supply'd, And fetch'd from far, distends his lab'ring side. **1811** W. R. SPENCER *Poems* 21 And horse and horseman heave for breath.

17. To make an effort to vomit, to retch; *fig.* to feel loathing. Also *trans.*, ***to heave the gorge***.

1601 [see HEAVING *vbl. sb.*]. **1604** SHAKS. *Oth.* II. i. 236 Her delicate tendernesse wil find it selfe abus'd, begin to heaue the gorge, disrellish and abhorre the Moore. **1755** JOHNSON, *Heave*..4, to keck; to feel a tendency to vomit. **1868** ATKINSON *Cleveland Gloss.*, *Heave and throw*, to retch and end by vomiting. **1894** MRS. LYNN LINTON *One too Many* I. 120 It makes me heave to hear you.

†**18.** To make an effort to lift or move something; to push or press with force; to put forth effort, endeavour, labour, strive. ***heave at***: to aim at, strive after. *Obs.*

c **1374** CHAUCER *Troylus* II. 1240 (1289) But þer-on was to heuen and to done. *c* **1380** *Sir Ferumb.* 1248 As sche wolde þe dore to-breke, sche gan þo hebbe and pynge. *c* **1422** HOCCLEVE *Jereslaus' Wife* 912 The wynd ful sore in the sail bleew & haf. **1535** COVERDALE *Matt.* xxiii. 4 But they them selues wil not heaue at them with one of their fyngers. **1674** N. FAIRFAX *Bulk & Selv.* 121 It asks some time to heave or pend in, before it actually starts. **1742** YOUNG *Nt. Th.* VII. 399 Souls immortal must for ever heave At something great.

†**b.** ***heave at*** (fig.): to meditate or threaten an attack upon; to take up a position of hostility to; to oppose; to aim at with hostile intent. *Obs.* (Frequent in 17th c.)

1546 BALE *Sel. Wks.* (Parker Soc.) 165 John Frith is a great mote in their eyes, for so turning over their purgatory, and heaving at their most monstrous mass or mammetrous mazan, which signifieth bread or feeding. **1592** NASHE *P. Penilesse* (ed. 2) 15 a, He was spite blasted, heaued at, and ill spoken of. **1655** FULLER *Ch. Hist.* III. i. §22 His adversaries heaved at him, to cast him out of his Bishoprick. **1674** P. WALSH *Quest. conc. Oath Alleg.* Pref., Then they shrewdly heav'd at me again.

19. To pull or haul (*at* a rope, etc.); to push (*at* the capstan so as to urge it round and haul in the cable); to move the ship in some direction by such means; of the ship, to move or turn in some direction.

1626 CAPT. SMITH *Accid. Yng. Seamen* 27 Break ground or way Anchor, heaue a head. **1727–51** CHAMBERS *Cycl.* s.v., *To heave at the capstan* signifies to turn it about. **1749** *Naval Chron.* III. 88 Did you observe her heave up in the wind? **1794** *Rigging & Seamanship* II. 338 The chaser heaves about as soon as the vessel he is in pursuit of is on his beam. **1853** KANE *Grinnell Exp.* (1856) 513 Heaving ahead between an iceberg and a heavy field of ice. **1867** SMYTH *Sailor's Word-bk.*, *Heave about*, to go upon the other tack suddenly. *Ibid.*, *Heaving ahead*, is the act of advancing or drawing a ship forwards by heaving on a cable or rope made fast to some fixed point before her.

transf. **1857** HUGHES *Tom Brown* II. vi, Make the most of it; heave ahead, and pitch into me right and left. **1881** ROSSETTI *Ball. & Sonn.* (1882) 293 Then one great puff of wings, and the swarm heaves Away with all its din.

III. Phrases.

20. From senses 10 and 19: ***to heave a-peak***: see quots. and A-PEAK. ***to heave*** (the ship) ***in stays***: to bring her head to the wind in tacking; also *intr.* of the ship. ***to heave short***: 'to heave in on the cable until the vessel is nearly over her anchor' (Smyth). ***to heave taut***: to heave at the capstan until the cable is taut.

1726 SHELVOCKE *Voy. round World* 19 Which done, I hove apeak on my anchor. **1727–51** CHAMBERS *Cycl.* s.v. *Peek*, The ship being about to weigh, comes over her anchor, so that the cable hangs perpendicularly between the hause and the anchor; the bringing of a ship into which position they call *heaving a-peek*. **1769** FALCONER *Dict. Marine* (1776), *Heave-short. Ibid.*, *Heaving-taught.* **1795** NELSON 13 Mar. in Nicolas *Disp.* II. 14 At one PM the Frigate hove in stays and got the Ça Ira round..As soon as our after-guns ceased to bear, the Ship was hove in stays. **1832** MARRYAT *N. Forster* xi, The frigate [was] unmoored, and hove 'short stay a-peak'. **1839** —— *Phant. Ship* xviii, They had laid an anchor out astern, and hove taut. **1893** W. T. WAWN *S. Sea Islanders* 88 Towards sundown, the chain was hove short.

b. ***heave down***: to turn (a ship) over on one side by means of purchases attached to the masts, for cleaning, repairing, etc.; to careen. (Also *intr.* of the ship.) The part thus raised above the water is said to be *hove out*.

1745 P. THOMAS *Jrnl. Anson's Voy.* 271 They could not.. use it as a Help for heaving down by. **1748** *Anson's Voy.* I. v. 55 The Commodore..ordered the *Tryal* to be hove down. *Ibid.* II. iii. 140 There are two coves..where ships may conveniently heave down. *Ibid.* III. vii. 367 They..hove out the first course of the *Centurion's* starboard side, and had the satisfaction to find, that her bottom appeared sound and good. **1769** FALCONER *Dict. Marine* U u ij, To heave down or careen a ship. **1798** NELSON 7 Sept. in Nicolas *Disp.* III. 116 The place where large ships heave down. **1836** E. HOWARD *R. Reefer* liv, The ship had been hove down.

c. ***heave to***: to bring the ship to a standstill by setting the sails so as to counteract each other; to make her lie to. (*a*) *trans.* with the ship as obj. (*b*) *intr.* or *absol.*

a. **1775** DALRYMPLE in *Phil. Trans.* LXVIII. 397 Hove the ship to. **1833** M. SCOTT *Tom Cringle* xv. (1859) 357 'Shorten sail..and heave the ship to', said the Captain. **1884** LADY BRASSEY in *Gd. Words* Mar. 163/1 We remained hove-to all the next day.

fig. **1887** STEVENSON *Misadv. J. Nicholson* iv, [He] was at last hove-to, all standing, in a hospital.

b. 1781 BLAGDEN in *Phil. Trans.* LXXI. 337 Soon afterwards we hove-to in order to sound. 1835 SIR J. ROSS *Narr. 2nd Voy.* vi. 79 This obliged us to heave to. 1860 MAURY *Phys. Geog. Sea* xix. §807 Took in fore and mizen top-sails; hove to under close-reefed main top sail and spencer.

transf. 1832 MARRYAT *N. Forster* iii, We must 'heave-to' in our narrative awhile.

21. *intr.* (from sense 13.) ***heave in sight***: to rise into view, become visible, come in sight, as an object at sea when approaching or approached; hence (*colloq.*) *transf.* in general sense.

1778 J. SULLIVAN in Sparks *Corr. Amer. Rev.* (1853) II. 205 Those ships were out of sight yesterday morning, but I hear they afterwards hove in sight again. 1816 'QUIZ' *Grand Master* I. 24 The Table-mountain heaves in sight. 1830 GALT *Lawrie T.* III. ix. (1849) 115 A most tremendous he-bear hove in sight. 1874 GREEN *Short Hist.* v. §1. 223 The great Spanish ships heave in sight, and a furious struggle begins. 1878 BOSW. SMITH *Carthage* 103 They hove in sight of the enemy.. to the west of the promontory of Ecnomus.

heave (hiːv), *sb.* [f. prec. vb.]

1. a. An act of heaving, in various senses; a lift; an effort to lift or move something, a push, shove, pressure; a swelling or rising up; rhythmical rising (and falling), as of waves, the breast, etc.; the utterance of a sigh, etc. with a deep breath; an effort to vomit; a throw, cast. ***heave of the sea***: the force exerted by the swell of the sea in quickening, retarding, or altering a vessel's course.

a1571 JEWEL *On Thess.* iv. 6 When his heaves renew, the heat increaseth, his heart panteth. 1602 SHAKS. *Ham.* IV. i. 1 There's matters in these sighes. These profound heaues You must translate. 1612–15 BP. HALL *Contempl., O.T.* xx. viii, Judah was at a sore heave. 1640 tr. *Verdere's Rom. of Romants* III. 188 The Gyant.. gave him such twitches, and terrible heaves, that he had.. like to have overthrown him. 1663 BUTLER *Hud.* I. i. 411 After many strains and heaves, He got up to his Saddle Eaves. 1684 T. BURNET *Th. Earth* I. 186 Only to have given it an heave at one end, and set it a little to rights again. a1734 NORTH *Lives* II. 59 Divers heaves were made at the Duke of Lauderdale. 1755 JOHNSON, *Heave*.. 3. Effort to vomit. 1833 C. STURT 2 *Exped. S. Australia* II. 164 [A channel] so narrow that we passed over it between the heaves of the lead. 1834 M. SCOTT *Cruise Midge* (1863) 18 The vessel rolled about on the heave of the sea. 1877 SPURGEON *Serm.* XXIII. 140 It took them a long pull and a great heave to haul the uncomely lump of marble into its place. 1893 STEVENSON *Catriona* 296 There went through me so great a heave of surprise that I was all shook with it.

†b. ***heave and shove***: *fig.* great exertion or effort. *Obs.*

1600 HOLLAND *Livy* IV. xxv. 155 They obtained at length with much heaue and shoue, that there should be militarie Tribunes chosen. 1612 DRAYTON *Polyolbion* IV. 56 Mongst Forrests, Hills, and Floods, was ne're such heaue and shoue Since Albion weelded Armes against the sonne of Ioue.

c. *Wrestling.* A chip performed by bringing the right arm round the opponent's right shoulder preparatory to a throw. ***Cornwall heave***, a heave in which a wrestler places one hand in front and one behind his adversary, and falls with him.

1889 W. ARMSTRONG *Wrestling* 224 The Heave, Cornwall and Devon. *Ibid.* 230 The principal Cornish and Devon chips are.. the Back-heave, the Belly-heave, the Heaving-toe. 1898 *Encycl. Sport* II. 548/2 One way to stop the heave is to cross click your man and then ply the crossbuttock.

2. *Mining* and *Geol.* A horizontal displacement or dislocation of a vein or stratum, at a 'fault'.

1801 *Chron.* in *Ann. Reg.* 436 The heave of the copper lode is about eighteen or twenty inches to the right, in the language of the Cornish miner. 1874 J. H. COLLINS *Metal Mining* 30 These heaves.. are sometimes of great extent, occasionally as much as 70 fathoms. 1882 GEIKIE *Text Bk. Geol.* (1885) 514 Sections to show the variation of horizontal displacement or Heave of Faults. 1890 *Goldfields Victoria* 12 The reefs here have taken a north-west 'heave'.

3. *pl.* A disease of horses, in which the breathing is laborious; broken wind.

1828 WEBSTER, *Heaves*. 1837–40 HALIBURTON *Clockm.* (1862) 86, I blow like a horse that's got the heaves. 1855 — *Nat. & Hum. Nat.* II. 122 It gave him the heaves.. it made his flanks heave like a blacksmith's bellows.

4. *concr.* A raised place; a swelling, an undulation. *nonce-use.*

1882 G. MACDONALD *Warlock o' Glenwarlock* (Cent.), Crossing a certain heave of grass.

5. *Comb.*: **heave-gate** *local*, a gate which is opened by being lifted out of the sockets or mortises.

1736 PEGGE *Kenticisms* (1876), *Heave-gate*, when the rails, with the pales nailed to them, may be taken out of their mortises, and then put in again. 1876 in G. L. Gower *Surrey Provincialisms*. 1887 I. R. *Lady's Ranche Life Montana* 27, Instead of gates out here, they generally have bars, which you have to let down,.. like the 'heave gates' in Sussex. 1907 'J. HALSHAM' *Lonewood Corner* 149, I perched myself on the heave-gate between the two fields. 1959 F. DONALDSON *Child of Twenties* vii. 107 A very easy hunting country, mainly a question of jumping the local Sussex heave-gates and small fences.

heaved (hiːvd), *ppl. a.* [wk. pa. pple. of HEAVE *v.*: see also HOVE.] Lifted, swollen, etc.

1578 BANISTER *Hist. Man* I. 35 Lyke a round heaued, or swelled thing. 1591 GREENE *Maidens Dreame* 49 With heavèd hands she poureth forth these plaints. 1670 DRYDEN *2nd Pt. Conq. Granada* III. ii, With heaved-up hands. 1676 — *Aurengz.* IV. i, Heard you that sigh? from my heaved heart it past. 1816 L. HUNT *Rimini* I. 47 With heaved-out tapestry the windows glow. 1871 R. ELLIS *Catullus* lxiv. 368 Dankly that high-heav'd grave shall gory Polyxena crimson.

heave ho, *int.* and *sb.* Formerly also **heave and how** (**hoe**, etc.); **heave-low** (**-law, -logh**). [app. the imperative of HEAVE *v.*, (?) with HO *int.* Cf. also HEY HO.] **a.** A cry of sailors in heaving the anchor up, etc.; also used as the burden of a song. †***with heave and how*** (***ho***), *fig.* with force, with might and main (*obs.*).

13.. *Coer de L.* 2522 They rowede hard, and sungge ther too: 'With heuelow and rumbeloo'. 1494 FABYAN VII. 420. a1500 *Ortus Vocab., Celeuma est clamor nauticus, vel cantus vel* heuylaw romylawe (*ed.* 1518 *ut* heue and howe, rombylow). a1529 SKELTON *Bowge of Courte* 252 Heue and how rombelow, row the bote, Norman, rowe! 1558 PHAER *Æneid* VI. Riij, Heaue and hoaw for ioy they sing. 1591 HARINGTON *Orl. Fur.* XXXVII. lxxxix, Though they seeme in punishing but slow, Yet pay they home at last, with heaue and how. 1600 NASHE *Summer's Last Will* 243 Here enter.. 3. maids, singing this song, daunsing: Trip and goe, heaue and hoe, Vp and downe, to and fro. 1611 COTGR. s.v. *Cor, A cor & à cry*,.. by might and maine, with heaue and hoe; eagerly, vehemently, seriously. 1803 DIBDIN *Songs* II. 254 To the windlass let us go, With yo heave ho! 1885 C. F. HOLDER *Marvels Anim. Life* 175 Yells,.. snatches of song, and heave-hoys rent the air.

b. orig. *U.S. slang.* A snub or dismissal.

1944 D. RUNYON *Runyon à la Carte* (1946) vi. 107 A most obnoxious character.. tries to claim the deuce as a sleeper and gets the heave-o from Nathan Detroit. 1952 B. CERF *Good for Laugh* (1953) 152 I'll bet that new girl.. gave you the heave-ho. 1962 WODEHOUSE *Service with Smile* vii. 112 If I were you, I think I would reconsider this idea of yours of giving Bill Bailey the old heave-ho. 1966 *New Yorker* 22 Oct. 52 Do we keep him on or give him the heave-ho? 1973 *Guardian* 20 Jan. 1/5 Mr Heath's prices and incomes package was given the old heave-ho by.. the TUC Economic Committee.

Hence **heave-ho** *v. intr.*, to cry 'heave ho!'; also *v. trans.*, to heave or lift with force.

1840 R. H. DANA *Bef. Mast* xxv. 81 They were heave-hoing, stopping and unstopping, pawling, catting, and fishing, for three hours. 1964 *New Yorker* 18 Jan. 84 A groaning mass of men heave-ho'd the snow car up the ramp. 1968 *Listener* 5 Dec. 768 During a rehearsal of *Billy Budd*, a singer was asked why he was just lolling about in the wings, not heave-hoing with the rest of them. 1971 *Guardian Weekly* 7 Aug. 17 The [Congolese] women who, apparently 12 months pregnant, nonetheless are constantly hauling and heave-hoing on this packing case of merchandise or that basket full of provisions.

heaveless ('hiːvlɪs), *a.* [f. HEAVE *sb.* or *v.* + -LESS.] Free from heavings: that does not heave.

1784 JERNINGHAM *Matilda* in Evans *Old Ball.* II. xlii. 252 Yes, Yes! his little life is fled, His heaveless breast is cold. 1853 *Tait's Mag.* XX. 532 The tents that round and far like a heaveless ocean lay.

heaven ('hɛv(ə)n), *sb.* Forms: 1 **heben, hefen, -on, heofon, -un, -en, hiofon, -un, heafen; heofene, -one**; 2 **heofone, hefene**, 2–3 **heofene, heouene, houene**, 3 **heauene, heofne, heoffne, heffene, heuone**, 3–5 **heuene**, 4 **hefen, heyuen, heiuen, -in**; 4–5 **hevyn, hewyn(e, -in(e**, 4–6 **heven, heuin**, 5 **heuon, -un**, 6 **heavin**, 6– **heaven**. [OE. *heben, hefen, -on, heofon, -un*, str. masc. = OS. *heban*, MLG. *heven* (Schiller-Lüb.), LG. *hêben, hêwen, hæwen*; in late OE. also *heofone* weak fem. (app. after *eorðe*, in *heofonan and eorðan*). The OE. form in *eo* was caused by *u*-umlaut before the ending *-un, -on*. Southern ME. had usually *hevene*, even in nom., perh. from *heofone* fem.; the more northern form in 13–14th c. was *heven*, i.e. *hêven*, whence *c* 1525 *heaven* with (ɛː), now shortened as in *bread*. Ulterior etymology unknown: not connected with *hafjan* to HEAVE, the *e* being radical.

The LG. **hebana-*, **hebuna-*, was app. an entirely different word from Goth. *himins*, ON. *himinn* (:—**himina-*), and OHG. *himil* (:—**himila-*), whence Ger. *himmel*, Du. *hemel*; at least no connexion between them can, in the present state of our knowledge, be assumed. The alleged ON. *hifinn*, sometimes cited as a connecting form, has no existence (see Bugge *Archiv* II. 214). The existence of *himil* beside *heban* in OS. was possibly due to High German missionaries. The mod.Da., Sw., and Norw. *himmel* are also from German.]

1. a. The expanse in which the sun, moon, and stars, are seen, which has the appearance of a vast vault or canopy overarching the earth, on the 'face' or surface of which the clouds seem to lie or float; the sky, the firmament. Since 17th c. chiefly poetical in the sing., the plural being the ordinary form in prose: see c.

Beowulf (Z.) 1571 Swa of hefene hadre scineð rodores candel. a1000 *Boeth. Metr.* xxi. 77 Hiofones leohtes hlutre beorhto. c1000 ÆLFRIC *Gen.* i. 8 And God het þa fæstnisse heofenan. a1123 *O.E. Chron.* an. 1106 Wæron ȝesewen tweȝen monan on þære heofonan. c1275 LAY. 27455 Ase heauene [c1205 heouene] wolde falle. a1300 *Cursor M.* 22694 Al that es vnder heuen [*v.r.* heiuin]. c1375 *Sc. Leg. Saints, Petrus* 89 þane lyftyt he his Ene to hewin. 1387–8 T. USK *Test. Love* III. iv. (Skeat) l. 94 The heuens iye, which I clepe yᵉ sonne. a1400–50 *Alexander* 84 Any hathill vnder heuen. 1508 DUNBAR *Gold. Targe* 89 A gounn Rich to behald.. Off ewiry hew under the hevin. 1535 COVERDALE *Eccl.* iii. 1 All that is vnder the heauen. 1585 T. WASHINGTON tr. *Nicholay's Voy.* I. vi. 4 The ordinaunce.. made such a great noyse and thunderyng that it seemed the heaven would have fallen. 1656 STANLEY *Hist. Philos.* v. (1701) 187/2 Stars and Constellations; some fixed for the ornament of Heaven. a1700 DRYDEN *Ovid's Met.* I. Wks. 1808 XII. 63 Heaven's high canopy, that covers all. 1796–7 COLERIDGE *Poems* (1862) 35 Still burns wide Heaven with his distended blaze. 1860 TYNDALL *Glac.* I. xv. 101 A serene heaven stretched overhead.

b. Things of great height are said by hyperbole to reach to heaven; opposite points of the sky are said to be a whole heaven apart. Also *fig.*

c1000 ÆLFRIC *Deut.* i. 28 Micle burȝa and oþ heofun fæste. c1175 *Lamb. Hom.* 93 Swa hehne þet his Rof astiȝe up to heofena. 1382 WYCLIF *Deut.* i. 28 Greet citees, and in to heuene wallid [1611 walled vp to heauen]. 1576 FLEMING *Panopl. Epist.* 147 Advauncing you with praises above hilles and mountaines, yea to the very heaven. 1731 POPE *Ep. Burlington* 59 That.. helps th' ambitious Hill the heav'ns to scale. 1864 TENNYSON *Sea Dreams* 100 Trees, As high as heaven. 1885 J. L. DAVIES *Soc. Quest.* 372 There must always remain a whole heaven of difference between the position of those who know nothing of nature.. and that of those who recognise light and guidance.. as coming to men from the living God.

c. The plural *heavens* was formerly used, esp. in Biblical language (transl. Heb. pl. *shāmayim*) in the same sense as the sing.; it is now the ordinary prose form for the visible sky. Hence *maps of the heavens, planisphere of the heavens, globe of the heavens*, etc.

c825 *Vesp. Psalter* viii. 4 [3] Ic ȝesie heofenas werc fingra ðinra. 1382 WYCLIF *Ps.* xviii[i]. 1 Heuenes tellen out the glorie of God. 1535 COVERDALE *Zech.* viii. 12 The grounde shal geue hir increase, and the heauens shal geue their dew. 1590 SHAKS. *Com. Err.* I. i. 67 What obscured light the heauens did grant. 1625 N. CARPENTER *Geog. Del.* I. iv. (1635) 77 The Heauens.. are carryed in 24 houres from East to West. 1812 WOODHOUSE *Astron.* i. 1 If, on a clear night, we observe the Heavens, they will appear to undergo a continual change. 1891 *Law Times* XC. 441/2 The *Spectator*.. seemed to think the heavens must fall because the Press questioned the capacity of a judge.

2. a. By extension (in accordance with Biblical use) the region of the atmosphere in which the clouds float, the winds blow, and the birds fly; as in the more or less poetical expressions, ***the clouds, winds, breath, fowls of heaven***.

Rain or *dew* of heaven, so called as falling (or supposed to fall) from the clouds.

c1000 ÆLFRIC *Gen.* xxvii. 28 Sylle þe God of heofenes deawe. 1382 WYCLIF *Job* xxxv. 11 The bestis of the erthe.. the foulis of heuene. — *Dan.* vii. 2 Loo! foure wyndis of heuen fouȝten in the mydil see. 1563 W. FULKE *Meteors* (1640) 49 b, The water that commeth from Heaven, in raine. 1596 SHAKS. *Merch. V.* IV. i. 78 The Mountaine Pines.. fretted with the gusts of heauen. 1733 POPE *Ess. Man* III. 38 The birds of heav'n shall vindicate their grain. 1864 TENNYSON *Aylmer's Field* 429 Tears, and the careless rain of heaven, mixt Upon their faces. 1870 — *Window* 146 Be merry in heaven, O larks, and far away. *Mod.* Exposed to every wind of heaven.

b. In reference to the atmospheric conditions of a country, the clear or cloudy sky, etc., = climate.

1581 PETTIE *Guazzo's Civ. Conv.* I. (1586) 26 Everie.. Countrie, by the nature of the place, the climate of the Heaven, and the influence of the starres hath certaine vertues. 1596 DALRYMPLE tr. *Leslie's Hist. Scot.* I. 44 The clemencie of the hevin, and gentlenes of the wethir. 1697 DRYDEN *Virg. Past.* x. 94 Not tho' beneath the Thracian Clime we freeze; Or Italy's indulgent Heav'n forego. 1847 TENNYSON *Princ.* Prol. 12 Flowers of all heavens.. Grew side by side.

3. a. The 'realm' or region of space beyond the clouds or the visible sky, of which the latter is popularly or poetically viewed as the 'floor'. *Esp.* in the collocation ***heaven and earth***, as constituting the universe.

c1000 ÆLFRIC *Gen.* i. 1 On anginne ȝesceop God heofenan and eorþan. c1250 *Gen. & Ex.* 40 In firme bigining, of noȝt Was heuene and erðe samen wroȝt. 1382 WYCLIF *Mark* xiii. 31 Heuene and erthe schal passe, forsothe my wordis schulen not passe. 1596 SHAKS. *Merch. V.* v. i. 58 Looke how the floore of heauen Is thicke inlayed with pattens of bright gold. 1823 F. CLISSOLD *Ascent Mt. Blanc* 23 A circle of thin haze.. marked dimly the limits between heaven and earth. 1842 TENNYSON *St. Agnes' Eve* iii, All heaven bursts her starry floors. 1862 TROLLOPE *Orley F.* xix. (1866) 149 Papa.. would move heaven and earth for her if he could. 1887 *New Antigone* xix. (1888) II. 97 Nothing in heaven or earth would have stayed her hand now.

b. The plural is sometimes used for the realms or regions of space in which the heavenly bodies move.

1678 CUDWORTH *Intell. Syst.* (1837) I. 683 Lifted up far above the starry heavens. 1726 tr. *Gregory's Astron.* I. 95 The Planets and Comets move in the Heavens very freely. 1838 NICHOL (*title*) Views of the Architecture of the Heavens. 1860 RUSKIN *Mod. Paint.* VII. iv. V. 152 The Heavens, for the great vault or void, with all its planets, and stars, and ceaseless march of orbs innumerable.

†c. *transf.* A model showing the motions of the heavenly bodies; an orrery, a planetarium. *Obs.*

1600 NASHE *Summer's Last Will* Wks. 1885 VI. 88 Euery man cannot, with Archimedes, make a heauen of brasse. 1605 VERSTEGAN *Dec. Intell.* ii. (1628) 52 The heauen of siluer which.. was sent vnto Soliman the great Turke wherein all the planets had their seuerall courses.

4. In the language of earlier cosmography: Each of the 'spheres' or spherical shells, lying above or outside of each other, into which astronomers and cosmographers formerly

divided the realms of space around the earth. These generally corresponded to the spaces supposed, according to the Ptolemaic system, to be comprised within the successive orbits of the seven planets (including the sun and moon), the fixed stars, and other spheres. Their number varied according to computation from seven to eleven.

1340 HAMPOLE *Pr. Consc.* 7567 Sere hevens God ordaynd for sere thyng.. þese hevens er oboven us heghe.. Ane es þat we þe sterned heven calle.. Ane other es þat clerkes calles cristallyne [etc.]. **1398** TREVISA *Barth. De P.R.* VIII. ii. (1495) 296 Heuens ben seuen namyd in this manere Aereum Olimpium Igneum Firmamentum Aqueum, Imperium, Celum. *c* **1400** tr. *Secreta Secret., Gov. Lordsh.* (E.E.T.S.) 95 þer ar nyne heuens, oon in erthe, þe oþer amonge hem seluyn, ilk oon amonge oþer; þe firste & þe soueraryne of þe speres, is þe spere couerant, and þanne with-ynne þat þe spere of þe sterrys; after þat þe spere of Saturne, and so to þe spere of þe mone, vnder whom ys þe spere of þe elemenz, þat er fyre, Eyre, water, and erthe. þe Erthe þanne ys yn þe myddyl stede of þe oþer elementz. **1559** W. CUNNINGHAM *Cosmogr. Glasse* 210 Whatsoever is conteined within the circuit of the heaven of the Mone. **1594** BLUNDEVIL *Exerc.* III. I. iii. (ed. 7) 280 What doth the celestiall part containe? The eleven Heavens and Spheares. *Ibid.* 281 In ascending orderly upwards.. The first is the Spheare of the Moone.. The fourth, the Spheare of the Sunne.. The seventh, the Spheare of Saturne. The eighth, the Spheare of the fixed stars, commonly called the firmament. The ninth is called the second movable or Christal heaven. The tenth is called the first movable. And the eleventh is called the Imperiall heaven, where God and his Angels are said to dwell. **1783** HOOLE *Orl. Fur.* XIII. (Brewer), Sometimes she deemed that Mars had from above Left his fifth heaven, the powers of men to prove. **1832** TENNYSON *Mariana in the S.* 92 Deepening thro' the silent spheres Heaven over Heaven rose the night.

fig. **1599** SHAKS. *Hen. V*, Prol. 2 O For a Muse of Fire, that would ascend The brightest Heauen of Inuention.

5. a. The celestial abode of immortal beings; the habitation of God and his angels, and of beatified spirits, usually placed in the realms beyond the sky; the state of the blessed hereafter. Opposed to *hell*.

c **1000** *Ags. Gosp.* Matt. vi. 9 Fader ure þu þe eart on heofene. *c* **1175** *Lamb. Hom.* 45 Grið on eorðe and grið on hefene. *Ibid.* 79 Engles in houene. *c* **1200** ORMIN 3263 To brukenn heffness blisse. *c* **1205** LAY. 21442 þu woldest to hæuene. *a* **1300** *Cursor M.* 24783 (Cott.) He suar be þe king of heuen. *c* **1375** *Sc. Leg. Saints, Petrus* 16 To þe I gyff þe keys of hewyne. *c* **1470** HENRY *Wallace* XI. 1236 Scotland he fred, and brocht it off thrillage, And now in hewin he has his heretage. **1500–20** DUNBAR *Poems* lxxxi. 100 Sufficience dwellis nocht bot in heavin. **1544** *Suppl. to Hen. VIII*, 21 Teache the people to gett heuen with fastynge. **1581** PETTIE *Guazzo's Civ. Conv.* III. (1586) 157b, Marriages (as they saie) are made in heaven, and are guided by destinie. **1622** BACON *Hen. VII*, Wks. 1825 III. 275 Stirring both heaven and hell to do him mischief. **1667** MILTON *P.L.* I. 263 Better to reign in Hell, then serve in Heav'n. **1803–6** WORDSW. *Intim. Immort.* v. 9 Heaven lies about us in our infancy. **1855** BROWNING *An Epistle* 141 Heaven opened to a soul while yet on earth, Earth forced on a soul's use while seeing heaven. **1858** SEARS *Athan.* III. ix. 326 Heaven is not the firmament overhead, but the condition of the redeemed after death, of which the blue serene gives us the appropriate symbol. **1879** CHR. ROSSETTI *Seek & F.* 22 Heaven is the presence of God: the presence of God, then, is heaven.

b. Also in *plural*. [In its origin a literalism of transl.—L. *cæli*, Gr. *οὐρανοί*, Heb. *shāmayim*: cf. 1 c.]

c **950** *Lindisf. Gosp.* Matt. vi. 9 Fader urer ðu arð in heofnum *vel* in heofnas [*Vulg.* in cælis]. *c* **1000** *Ags. Gosp.* Matt. xviii. 18 Swa hwylce swa ȝe ȝe-bindað ofer eorþan þa beoþ ȝebundene on heofonum. *c* **1380** WYCLIF *Wks.* (1880) 42 Heiris and kyngis of þe kyngdom of heuenys. **1548** UDALL, etc. tr. *Erasm. Par. Acts* 16a, He.. sitteth and reigneth in high heauens aboue. **1596** DALRYMPLE tr. *Leslie's Hist. Scot.* x. 386 Leiuing the course of this lyfe tha pas to the heuinis. **1611** BIBLE *Heb.* iv. 14 Wee haue a great high Priest, that is passed into the heauens.

c. By the Jews (at least in later times) seven heavens were recognized; the highest, called also 'heaven of heavens,' being the abode of God and the most exalted angels. Thence also the seven heavens of Muhammad.

This division was probably of Babylonian origin, and founded on astronomical theories (cf. 4).

c **1000** ÆLFRIC *Deut.* x. 14 Heofon and heofuna heofun. *c* **1375** *Sc. Leg. Saints, Paulus* 948 Paule.. thocht þat he was rewyst ewine.. to þe thred hewyne, & syne in paradis. **1382** WYCLIF *Ps.* cxiii. [cxv] 16 The heuene of heuene [*c* **1430** *MS. S.* heuenys] to the Lord; the erthe forsothe he ȝaf to the sones of men. **1382** —— *2 Cor.* xii. 2, I woot a man in Crist .. rauyschid til to the thridde heuene. **1560** BIBLE (Genev.) *Ps.* cxlviii. 4 Praise ye him heauens of heauens, and waters, that be aboue the heauens. **1611** BIBLE *1 Kings* viii. 27 The heauen and heauen of heauens cannot conteine Thee. **1688** PRIOR *Ode Exod.* iii. 106 The Heaven of Heavens, the high abode, Where Moses places his mysterious God. **1734** SALE *Koran* (1764) II. 178 And we have created over you seven heavens. **1841** LANE *Arab. Nts.* I. 20 According to the common opinion of the Arabs there are seven Heavens, one above another. **1858** W. MUIR *Mahomet* II. 219 From Jerusalem he seemed to mount upwards, and ascend from one Heaven to another.

d. The seat of the celestial deities of heathen mythology.

1382 WYCLIF *Jer.* vii. 18 Thei make sweete cakis to the quen of heuene. **1588** SHAKS. *Tit. A.* IV. iii. 40 With Ioue in heauen, or some where else. *a* **1700** DRYDEN *Ovid's Met.* I. Wks. 1808 XII. 69 Against beleaguered heaven the Giants move. **1791** COWPER *Iliad* XI. 60 Aurora, now on the Olympian height Proclaiming, stood new day to all in heaven. **1841** ELPHINSTONE *Hist. Ind.* I. iv. 169 The heaven of Siva is in the midst of the eternal snows and glaciers of Keilas, one of the highest and deepest groups of the stupendous summits of Himalaya.

e. *transf.* and *fig.*

1810 MONTGOMERY *W. Indies* III. 23 In the clear heaven of her delightful eye, An angel-guard of loves and graces lie.

6. a. The power or majesty of heaven; He who dwells above; Providence, God. (With capital H.)

c **1000** *Ags. Gosp.* Luke xv. 21 Fæder, ic synȝude on heofon, and beforan ðe. **1388** WYCLIF *Dan.* iv. 23 [26] Aftir that thou knowist that the power is of heuene. **1593** DRAYTON *Essex* Wks. 1753 II. 602 Envy.. Affecting the Supremacy of Heaven. **1640** tr. *Verdere's Rom. Romants* i. 3 The heaven takes care of your quiet. **1667** MILTON *P.L.* I. 212 The will And high permission of all-ruling Heaven. **1692** DRYDEN *St. Euremont's Ess.* 347 Sometimes Heaven ordains, and Nature makes an opposition. **1816** SCOTT *Bl. Dwarf* iii, 'For Heaven's sake, no', said his companion. **1819** SHELLEY *Cenci* v. iv. 57 Sweet Heaven, forgive weak thoughts! **1885** EDNA LYALL *In Golden Days* III. xiv. 299 How in heaven's name did you manage it all?

b. Also in *plural*. The powers above; the gods; God.

1579 G. HARVEY *Letter-bk.* (Camden) 62, I hope in the heavens my chin will on day be so favorable and bountifull unto me. *c* **1592** MARLOWE *Massacre Paris* I. iii, The Heavens forbid your highness such mishap! **1611** BIBLE *Dan.* iv. 26 After that thou shalt haue knowen that the heauens doe rule. **1640** tr. *Verdere's Rom. Romants* i. 174 The heavens.. made me yesterday seek to save you. **17..** *Siege of Aubigny* 118 Whatever power the Heavens have favoured me with. **1859** TENNYSON *Geraint & Enid* 893 She was ever praying the sweet heavens To save her dear lord whole from any wound.

c. In asseverations: ***by*** (***†through, before, 'fore***) ***heaven***, (***heavens***). Cf. BY *prep.* 2.

The sense in **c** and **d** is somewhat indefinite, probably including the place and its Divine Lord or inhabitants: cf. Matt. v. 34, xxiii. 22.

[*c* **1000** *Ags. Gosp.* Matt. xxiii. 22 Seþe swerað on heofonan [*Lind.* on heofne, *Rushw.* be heofune, *Vulg.* in cælo], he sweryð on godes þrymsetle, and on þam þe ofer þæt sitt.] *c* **1400** *Destr. Troy* 8313, I may not hate hym, by heuyn, þat me in hert tes. **1610** B. JONSON *Alch.* I. Wks. (Rtldg.) 240/2 Not I, by heaven. *Ibid.* 241/2 Fore heaven, I scarce can think you are my friend. **1716** ADDISON tr. *Ovid* Wks. 1753 I. 176 By heav'n the story's true. **1752** MRS. LENNOX *Fem. Quix.* VIII. iii. II. 187 'By Heavens!' cried Glanville.. 'there's no bearing this'. **1859** TENNYSON *Merlin & Vivien* 341 By Heaven that hears, I tell you the clean truth. **1887** A. C. GUNTER *Mr. Barnes of N.Y.* xviii. (1888) 135 He commenced to strut and hector about.. and cry, By Heavens.

d. In exclamations expressing surprise, horror, etc. (Also in *pl.*). Often with qualifications, as *good, gracious, great.* Also ***Heaven and earth!***; ***Heavens above, alive!***; ***Heavens to Betsy!*** (U.S.).

1588 in Nichols *Progr. Q. Eliz.* (1823) II. 559 O Heavens! O Earth! O never-dying Fame! **1610** SHAKS. *Temp.* I. ii. 59 O the heuens, What fowle play had we. **1709** STEELE *Tatler* No. 23 ¶7 Heavens! Is it possible you can live without Remorse? **1752** MRS. LENNOX *Fem. Quix.* VIII. iii. II. 187 Good Heavens! cried Mr. Glanville.. quite out of patience, I shall go distracted! *Ibid.* IX. i. 209 Oh, heavens!.. this must .. be a very notable adventure. *a* **1777** DODD *Fanny Melmouth* (1799) 96 'Heaven and earth!' exclaimed Miss Melmouth, 'what will become of me?' **1801** AMELIA OPIE *Father & Dau.* (1809) 102 Gracious Heaven! who are you? **1819** MRS. MARCET *Conv. Nat. Phil.* ii. (1851) 36 Heavens, Emily, what an idea! **1877** FRITH *Autobiog.* II. iv. 75 Great heaven! What a place to stop at! **1892** R. T. COOKE *Huckleberries fr. New England Hills* 173 'Heavens to Betsey!' gasped Josiah. **1895** A. W. PINERO in M. R. Booth *Eng. Plays of 19th Cent.* (1969) II. 275 They say Orreyed has taken to tippling at dinner. Heavens above! **1913** 'S. ROHMER' *Mystery of Fu-Manchu* xix. 205 The eyes—heavens above, the huge green eyes! **1914** *Dialect Notes* IV. 74 *Heavens to Betsy!* Common Exclamation among women. **1957** M. SUMMERTON *Sunset Hour* i. 56 Heavens alive, it's ten past one. I haven't been up so near dawn for years. **1958** HAYWARD & HARARI tr. *Pasternak's Dr. Zhivago* II. viii. 246 But Heavens above! You misunderstood us. What are we talking about? **1968** 'E. V. CUNNINGHAM' *Cynthia* (1969) xi. 130 'Oh, heavens to Betsy, I am scared, Harvey,' Lucille whispered.

e. ***Heaven knows.*** (*a*) Used to emphasize the truth of a statement. (*b*) Used to imply that something is unknown to the speaker, and probably also to others. Freq. with *what, where, who.* Cf. GOD 10.

[**1605** SHAKS. *Macbeth* v. i. 52 Shee ha's spoke what shee should not, I am sure of that: Heauen knowes what shee ha's knowne.] **1711** ADDISON *Spect.* No. 164 ¶5 Heaven only knows how dear he was to me whilst he liv'd. **1805** WORDSWORTH *Prelude* XI. 141 Not in Utopia—subterranean fields,—Or some secreted island, Heaven knows where! **1872** GEO. ELIOT *Middlemarch* IV. VIII. lxxiv. 198 She invites clergymen and heaven-knows-who. *a* **1916** 'SAKI' *Square Egg* (1924) 125 From privates in the Regular Army to Heaven-knows-what in some intermediate corps. **1936** *Delineator* CXXIX. 48/3 It was clearly apart from the spirituals.. and heaven knows, was unlike any music that America had been playing before. **1967** *Listener* 26 Jan. 117/1 Heaven knows, there are old excuses for it. **1969** *Ibid.* 13 Mar. 351/2 Heaven knows, he'd been through this often enough in the past.

7. *fig.* **a.** A place like or compared to heaven; a place of supreme bliss.

1377 LANGL. *P. Pl.* B. x. 300 For if heuene be on this erthe .. It is in cloistere or in scole. **1546** J. HEYWOOD *Prov.* (1867) 33 They that be in hell, wene there is none other heven. **1590** SHAKS. *Mids. N.* II. i. 243, I follow thee, and make a heauen of hell. **1660** *Sp. in Ho. Comm.* 14 Nov. in Cobbett *Parl. Hist.* (1808) IV. 145 England, that was formerly the heaven, would be now the hell for women. **1667** MILTON *P.L.* I. 254 The mind is its own place, and in it self Can make a Heav'n of Hell, a Hell of Heav'n. **1725** POPE *Odyss.* VI. 22 A heav'n of charms divine Nausicaa lay. **1810** SCOTT *Lady of L.* II. viii, Ere Douglasses, to ruin driven, Were exiled from their native heaven. **1831** CARLYLE *Nibelungen-Lied* in *Misc. Ess.* (1872) III. 142 Here for eleven days.. there is a true heaven-on-earth.

b. A state of bliss or supreme felicity.

c **1374** CHAUCER *Troylus* II. 777 (826) It an heuene was hire voys to here. **1546** J. HEYWOOD *Prov.* (1867) 70 Husbandes are in heauen whose wiues scold not. **1596** SPENSER *Hymn to Love* 244 What heauens of ioy, then to himselfe he faynes. **1604** MIDDLETON & DEKKER *1st Pt. Honest Wh.* I. i. (Dalbiac) O what a heaven is love! O what a hell! **1625** BACON *Ess., Truth* (Arb.) 501 Certainly, it is Heauen vpon Earth, to haue a Mans Minde Moue in Charitie, Rest in Prouidence, and Turne vpon the Poles of Truth. **1678** BUTLER *Hud.* III. i. 935 And like an Anchorite, gives over This World for th' Heaven of a Lover? **1792** S. ROGERS *Pleas. Mem.* I. 59 The clock.. That faithful monitor, 'twas heaven to hear, When soft it spoke a promised pleasure near.

c. In same senses: ***heaven of heavens, seventh heaven, third heaven.*** (*fig.* from 5 c.)

1824 SCOTT *St. Ronan's* xxvi, He looked upon himself as approaching to the seventh heaven. **1883** RITA *After Long Grief* xxii, Lady Ramsey was in the seventh heaven of delight. **1885** J. H. MCCARTHY *Camiola* I. vii. 156 The heaven of heavens into which he presumed, an earthly guest, was the West End of London.

†8. *transf.* [from 7]. A quintessence. *Obs.*

1460–70 *Bk. Quintessence* 2 Philosophoris clepen þe purest substaunce of manye corruptible þingis elementid, quinta essentia, þat is to seie, mannys heuene. *Ibid.* 13 How þat ȝe may wiþ oure heuene drawe out euery 5 essencia from alle þingis aforeseid.

9. *transf.* [from 1]. A canopy; the covering over a stage. [F. *ciel*, Ger. *himmel*.] In the 19th c. quots. directly fig. from sense 1.

1486 *Surtees Misc.* (1888) 54 In the entre.. shalbe craftely conceyvid a place in maner of a heven.. under the heven shalbe a world desolaite. **1611** COTGR., *Volerie*,.. a place ouer a stage which we call the Heauen. **1612** HEYWOOD *Apol. Actors* II. D ij b, The couerings of the stage, which wee call the heauens.. were Geometrically supported by a Giant-like Atlas. **1821** SHELLEY *Prometh. Unb.* III. iii. 140 Bright golden globes Of fruit, suspended in their own green heaven. *a* **1822** —— *Two Fragm. Love* ii. 3 Under a heaven of cedar boughs.

10. *attrib.* and *Comb.* **a.** Simple attrib.: in sense 'of heaven'. (Many of the early ME. instances in *hevene* are prob. examples of the genitive case: cf. *Lady-day, Lady-chapel, Bride-well*, etc.).

a **1000** *Phœnix* 173 Under heofun-hrofe. *c* **1000** ÆLFRIC *Past. Ep.* in Thorpe *Laws* II. 382 Into his fæȝeran heofon-healle. *c* **1220** *Bestiary* 227 If he leue haue of ure heuen louerd. *c* **1250** *Gen. & Ex.* 101 Ðe firmament.. mai ben hoten heuene-Rof. *Ibid.* 281 Al ðe ðhinges.. Twen heuone hil and helle dik. *Ibid.* 1547 Heuene dew, and erðes fetthed. *a* **1300** *Cursor M.* 8290 (Gött.) An angel com fra heuen trone. *Ibid.* 18741 (Cott.) þe toþer us come fra heuen ture. **1390** GOWER *Conf.* III. 102 Under the heven cope. *c* **1440** *Gesta Rom.* II. lvi. 373 (Add. MS.) The Ioye of heuyne life. **1591** SYLVESTER *Du Bartas* I. ii. 555 Many Heav'n-floods in our Floods do lose. **1667** MILTON *P.L.* XII. 52 Ere the Tower Obstruct Heav'n Towrs. **1844** MRS. BROWNING *Rhapsody of Life's Progr.* viii, On the Heaven-heights of Truth. **1870** MAX MÜLLER *Sc. Relig.* (1873) 172 We have in the Veda the invocations *dyaûs pitar*.. and that means.. Heaven-Father! **1882** J. PARKER *Apost. Life* I. 43 God came down in the great heaven-wind and the great heaven-fire.

b. Obj. and obj. gen., as ***heaven-climber, -worshipper; heaven-assailing, -defying, -kissing, -rending, -threatening***, etc. adjs. (Mostly since 1600: their number is practically limitless.)

1602 SHAKS. *Ham.* III. iv. 59 Mercurie New lighted on a heauen-kissing hill. **1602** CAREW *Cornwall* (1811) 272 Set forth, against that heaven-threatening Armada. **1645** QUARLES *Sol. Recant.* xi. 60 When that blood pleads, heav'n will not lend an eare If heav'n-engaging Charity be not there. *a* **1671** MARVELL *Poems, Billborow Hill*, The cliff Of heaven-daring Teneriff. **1780** COWPER *Table-t.* 418 Perjury, that Heaven-defying vice. **1818** KEATS *Endym.* I. 284 Giving out a shout most heaven-rending. **1827** KEBLE *Chr. Y.* Whitsun Mond., Heaven-assailing cries. **1880** G. MEREDITH *Trag. Com.* (1881) 252 The whole Alpine.. heaven-climbers.

c. Instrumental and locative, as ***heaven-accepted, -begot, -descended, -dyed, -fallen, -forsaken, -given, -made, -protected, -sprung, -taught***, etc. adjs. (The number of these is unlimited: nearly all since 1600.) Also HEAVEN-BORN, HEAVEN-SENT.

1591 SHAKS. *Two Gent.* III. ii. 72 Much is the force of heauen-bred Poesie. **1600** S. NICHOLSON *Acolastus* (1876) 57 Diuine Aurora full as faire as she, Whose heauen-di'de face the Graces still admire. **1606** SYLVESTER *Du Bartas* II. iv. III. *Magnificence* 386 Words of the Heav'n-prompted stile. **1659** W. CHAMBERLAYNE *Pharonnida* III. iii. (1820) II. 52 The heaven-built pillars of his soul. **1667** MILTON *P.L.* x. 535 All yet left of that revolted Rout Heav'n-fall'n, in station stood. **1693** TATE in *Dryden's Juvenal* Sat. xv. (1697) 374 Prometheus Ghost is sure o'er-joy'd to see His Heav'n-stol'n Fire from such disaster free. **1715–20** POPE *Iliad* IX. 803 The fall of Heaven-protected Troy. **1718** ROWE tr. *Lucan* 314 The Heav'n-instructed Shipman thus replies. **1727–46** THOMSON *Summer* 1010 Who heaven-inspired To love of useful glory rais'd mankind. **1742** YOUNG *Nt. Th.* III. 2 Reason, that Heav'n-lighted Lamp in Man. **1777** POTTER *Æschylus* (1779) I. 60 (Jod.) Heav'n-sprung, or mortal? if permitted, say. **1787** BURNS *Verses in Kenmore*, Here poesy might wake her heav'n-taught lyre. **1849** HARE *Par. Serm.* II. 227 In the free heaven-lit atmosphere of the Gospel. **1865** PUSEY *Truth Eng. Ch.* 256 The Heaven-controlled Seer.

d. Adverbial, 'to or toward heaven', as ***heaven-affianced, -aspiring, -dear, -devoted, -erected, -translated***, etc. **e.** Similative, as ***heaven-clear, -sweet***, etc. **f.** Parasynthetic, as ***heaven-hued***, etc. adjs. See also HEAVEN-HIGH, -WIDE, etc.

1591 SYLVESTER *Du Bartas* I. 667 Heav'n-bent souls. **1597** SHAKS. *Lover's Compl.* 215 The heaven-hued sapphire. **1598** SYLVESTER *Du Bartas* II. ii. II. *Babylon* 564 Mong the Heav'n deer spirits. **1607** J. DAVIES *Summa Totalis* Kj b, Then (with that Heu'n-rapt Saint) rapt Muse ascend. *a* **1711** KEN *Christophil* Poet. Wks. 1721 I. 526 A Heav'n-aspiring Mind. *a* **1711** —— *Hymnotheo* Ibid. III. 155 With a Heav'n-erected Look. **1772** W. HODSON *Ded. Temp. Solomon* 19 This Heav'n-devoted Shrine. **1821** LAMB *Leisure*, The heaven-sweet burthen of eternity. **1839** BAILEY *Festus* xx. (1848) 253 The Heaven-affianced spirit. **1858** HAWTHORNE *Fr. & It. Jrnls.* II. 126 This heaven-aspiring tower.

11. Special combinations: †**heaven-bow**, rainbow; **heaven-bridge**, bridge of the dead; **heaven-burster** (see quot.); **heaven-gazer**, (*a*) one who gazes at the sky, who studies the stars, an astrologer; (*b*) a fish, the star-gazer; so **heaven-gazing**; **heaven-god**, a celestial deity, a god of the heaven or sky; **heaven-plant** = *heaven-tree*; **heaven-send**, something received as sent specially from heaven, a godsend; **heaven-tree**, a mythical tree, which figures in some Malay and Polynesian beliefs, as reaching from the under-world to the earth, or from earth to heaven; **heaven-worshippers**, a Judæo-Christian sect (*Cœlicolæ*) of the fourth and fifth centuries. Also HEAVEN-BLISS, etc.

c **1320** *Cast. Love* 743 For *heuene-bouwe is abouten i-bent, Wiþ alle þe hewes þat him beþ i-sent. **1865** TYLOR *Early Hist. Man.* 352 Like the *Heaven-Bridge, the Heaven-Gulf which has to be passed on the way to the Land of Spirits, has a claim to careful discussion. *Ibid.* xii. 349 The Polynesians..still call foreigners '*heaven-bursters', as having broken in from another world outside. **1535** COVERDALE *Isa.* xlvii. 13 The *heauengasers & the beholders of starres. **1611** COTGR., *Tapecon*, the Heauen-gazer; a scalelesse sea-fish..hauing..a great head, on whose top his eyes (wherewith he lookes directly vpward) are placed. **1593** NASHE *Christ's T.* Wks. 1883–4 IV. 82 Excessiue staring, and stedfast *heauen-gazing. **1871** TYLOR *Prim. Cult.* II. 235 The Aztec Tlaloc was no doubt originally a *Heaven-god, for he holds the thunder and lightning. **1865** —— *Early Hist. Man.* xii. 346 A story..which contains the episode of the **heaven-plant.* **1811** H. MARTYN in *Mem.* III. (1825) 436 This was a *Heaven-send. **1887** *Century Mag.* Nov. 45/2 The man who has been away, is a heaven-send in a village. **1865** TYLOR *Early Hist. Man.* 348 *note*, In the Samoan group..there was a *heaven-tree, where people went up and down, and when it fell it stretched some sixty miles.

'heaven, *v.* [f. prec. sb.] *trans.* To make heavenly in character, to transport or transform into heaven; also, to bless with heaven, beatify, render supremely happy.

1627–47 FELTHAM *Resolves* I. xlviii. 153 They are idle Divines that are not heav'ned in their lives, above the unstudious man. **1637** RUTHERFORD *Lett.* (1862) I. 225 Surely I were rich enough, and as well heavened as the best of them, if Christ were my heaven. *a* **1650** T. ADAMS *Pract. Wks.* (1861) I. 194 (D.) He heavens himself on earth, and for a little pelf cozens himself of bliss. **1655** H. VAUGHAN *Silex Scint.* I. *Search* (1858) 34 He heav'nd their walks, and with his eyes Made those wild shades a Paradise. **1839** BAILEY *Festus* xxxvi. (1848) 365 Heaven our spirits, Hallow our hearts.

heaven, obs. form of HAVEN.

†**heaven-bliss.** *Obs.* [perh. *heaven* was here orig. genitive case.] The bliss of heaven.

a **1300** *Cursor M.* 2692 (Gött.) Vr lauerd went him to heuen blis. *c* **1320** *Cast. Love* 113 Of heuene-blisse heo beoþ i-flemed. **1583** STANYHURST *Æneis* II. (Arb.) 62 Her deitee to the Saincts dooth luster in heunblisse.

'heaven-born, *a.*

1. Of celestial birth, of divine origin.

1595 J. WEEVER *Epigr.* IV. xxii. (1599) E vj, Some heaven born goddesse. **1629** MILTON *Nativity* 30 While the Heaven-born child All meanly wrapped in the rude manger lies. **1794** COLERIDGE *Monody on Chatterton* 16, I weep that heaven-born Genius so should fall. **1863** I. WILLIAMS *Baptistery* I. vi, The immortal shoot Of heaven-born virtue.

2. Of such original genius or ability as to seem specially prepared or designed by Heaven for the work. Now often *sarcastic.*

1789 in *Parl. Hist.* XXVII. 1080 (*Ho. Lords* 17 Jan.) The duke [of Chandos] parodying what Mr. Pitt's father had said of General Wolfe, pronounced the present Chancellor of the Exchequer a heaven-born minister. **1789** BURKE *Sp. Ho. Com.* 6 Feb. Speeches 1816 III. 394 The present minister, he understood, had been called 'a heaven-born minister' in another place. **1827** SCOTT *Jrnl.* 27 Aug., He is a heaven-born teacher. **1858** J. B. NORTON *Topics* 265 The same Heaven-born amateurs still occupy the bench, and the quality of their judgments cannot but be the same.

'heaven-directed, *a.*

1. Directed or pointing towards the sky.

1732 POPE *Ep. Bathurst* 261 Who taught that heav'n-directed spire to rise?

2. Directed or guided by Heaven; divinely guided.

1738 POPE *Epil. Sat.* II. 214 O sacred weapon!..To all but Heav'n-directed hands deny'd. **1823** E. IRVING *Orac. God* 152 The force of heaven-directed will.

'heavenful. [See -FUL.] As many, or as much, as would fill heaven.

1637 RUTHERFORD *Lett.* I. xlv. (1675) 96 The blessing of that House-ful or Heaven-ful of Dyvours, shall rest for ever upon him. **1884** J. PARKER *Apost. Life* III. 15 He is a host, an army, a whole heavenful..of human nature.

heaven-gate. The gate or portal of heaven.

c **1250** *Gen. & Ex.* 1620 Her, heuenegate amongus us. *c* **1440** *Jacob's Well* (E.E.T.S.) 269 þin obedyens schal be þin heuene-keye, þat schal opyne to þe heuen-gatys. **1688** BUNYAN *Jerus. Sinner Saved* (1886) 48 To see so vile a one knock at heaven-gates for mercy. **1844** MRS. BROWNING *Mournful Mother*, Until ye two give meeting Where the great Heaven-gate is.

heaven-high, *a.* and *adv.* As high as heaven.
A. *adj.* Reaching or piercing the clouds, very lofty. **B.** *adv.* To the height of heaven, to an immense height.

a **1000** *Cædmon's Dan.* 553 þæt þu ȝesawe..heofonheanne beam. *c* **1515** *Cocke Lorell's B.* (Percy) 13 They songe and daunsed full merely, With swerynge, and starynge heven- hye. *a* **1618** J. DAVIES *Exstasie* Wks. (Grosart) 93 (D.) Their Heav'n-high roofes shal be embattelled With adamant in gold enuelloped. **1864** BROWNING *Abt Vogler* i, Each from the other heaven-high, hell-deep removed. **1878** —— *La Saisiaz* 382 World-wide heaven-high sea.

'heavenhood. *rare.* [See -HOOD.] Heavenly quality or character; heavenliness.

1878 G. D. BOARDMAN *Creative Week* 63 (Cent.) Ripe, rich fruits of heavenhood. **1888** MAX MÜLLER *Nat. Relig.* ii (1889) 30 This is the heavenhood of heaven.

†**'heavenish**, *a. Obs.* [See -ISH.] Of or pertaining to heaven; celestial, heavenly.

c **1374** CHAUCER *Troylus* V. 1813 Ful of heuenyssh melodye. *c* **1374** —— *Compl. Mars* 30 Lord a-bove..by heuenysh [*v. rr.* -yssh(e] reuolucion. *c* **1391** —— *Astrol.* I. §21 This forseide heuenissh zodiak is cleped the cercle of the signes. *c* **1450** *Mirour Saluacioun* 964 Ffor thilk flece be it self wete of this hevenyshe dewe. **1577** B. GOOGE *Heresbach's Husb.* IV. (1586) 180 b, Hony dewe, cleaving to the leaves..loosing much of his heavenishe Vertue.

Hence †**'heavenishly** *adv. Obs.*

c **1386** CHAUCER *Knt.'s T.* 197 As an Aungel heuenysshly she soong.

'heavenize, *v. rare.* [See -IZE.] *trans.* To render heavenly, imbue with heavenly principles.

a **1656** BP. HALL *Soliloquies* lxxx, O my soul, if thou be once soundly heaveniz'd in thy thoughts and affections, it shall be otherwise with thee.

†**heaven-king.** *Obs.* King of heaven: applied to God or Christ.

971 *Blickl. Hom.* 201 Ic eom heahengel Heofoncyninges. *c* **1175** *Lamb. Hom.* 61 Hwilch wurðin(g) eow haueð idon þe heouenking. *a* **1300** *Cursor M.* 14921 (Gött.) þat for vs gaf iesus, heuene king. *c* **1440** *Generydes* 2642 For loue of hevyn kyng, Tell me the trougth. **1591** SYLVESTER *Du Bartas* I. vii. 105 The Heav'n-King's glorious Prayse.

'heavenless, *a. rare.* [See -LESS.] Having no portion in heaven.

1652 WARREN *Unbelievers* (1654) 22 Write this man..hopelesse, heavenlesse. **1839** BAILEY *Festus* xx. (1854) 375 As do idolators their heavenless gods, We deify the things which we adore.

'heavenlike, *a.* (*adv.*) [See -LIKE.]

A. *adj.* Like heaven; heavenly, divine.

1548 UDALL, etc. *Erasm. Par. Mark* viii. (R.) Menne farre aboue the common sorte, or as you woulde saye, heauenlyke felowes. **1610** *Histrio-m.* I. 176 The Harmonie of musick is so Heavenlike that I love it with my life. **1816** COLERIDGE *Statesm. Man.* (1817) 355 O how heaven-like it is to sit among brethren at the feet of a minister who speaks under the influence of love!

B. *adv.* After the manner of heaven.

1876 SWINBURNE *Erechth.* 1590 Who behold Thee made so heavenlike happy?

heavenliness ('hɛv(ə)nlɪnɪs). [f. HEAVENLY *a.* + -NESS.] The state or quality of being heavenly in origin, nature, or character.

1530 PALSGR. 231/1 Hevenlynesse, *celestialeté.* **1587** GOLDING *De Mornay* xxvii. 418 One further marke of the heauenliness of our Scriptures. *a* **1665** J. GOODWIN *Filled w. the Spirit* (1867) 367 By the holiness and heavenliness of his life and conversation. **1702** C. MATHER *Magn. Chr.* v. i. (1852) 183 The heavenliness of the matter, the efficacy of the doctrine. **1856** VAUGHAN *Mystics* (1860) I. VI. iv. 182 Now we feel that in heavenliness of nature he has gone beyond his former self.

b. As a title: Celestial highness, divinity.

1596 DAVIES *Orchestra* (R.), Goddess of women, sith your heavenliness Hath now vouchsaf'd itself to represent To our dim eyes.

heavenly ('hɛv(ə)nlɪ), *a.* (*sb.*) Forms: see HEAVEN *sb.*: in 1–4 -líc, 2–4 -lich, -lik, 4–5 -li, 4– -ly (also 3 heueliche, 5 hefly). [OE. *heofonlíc*: see HEAVEN and -LY¹.]

1. a. Of, in, or belonging to heaven, as the abode of God; divine, celestial.

971 *Blickl. Hom.* 11 Dæl-nimende þæs heofonlican rices. *c* **1000** *Ags. Gosp.* Luke ii. 13 Mycelnes heofonlices werydes. *c* **1175** *Lamb. Hom.* 113 We ne maȝen habben þene heouenlichen eþel. *c* **1275** *Passion our Lord* 638 in *O.E. Misc.* 55 Ye beon byweued of heueliche myhte. *c* **1375** *Sc. Leg. Saints, Paulus* 859 Hevinlyk Ioy and lestand bliss. **1382** WYCLIF *Matt.* vi. 14 ȝoure heuenly fadir shal forȝeue to ȝou ȝoure trespassis. *c* **1450** *Golagros & Gaw.* 265 Hevinly god!..how happynis this thing? **1526** *Pilgr. Perf.* (W. de W. 1531) 1 Takyng on vs the iourney to the heuenly Jerusalem. **1611** BIBLE *Transl. Pref.* 3 A showr of heauenly bread. **1713** GAY *Epist.* iii, In her notes the heavenly choir descends. **1840** DE QUINCEY *Style* II. Wks. 1861 X. 247 Under a heavenly afflatus.

b. Belonging to the heaven of the heathen gods.

1483 *Cath. Angl.* 185/1 Heuenly, *celestis.* **1596** SHAKS. *Merch. V.* III. v. 84 If two gods should play some heauenly match, And on the wager lay two earthly women. **1678** CUDWORTH *Intell. Syst.* (1837) I. 645 The heavenly Venus.

2. Of or belonging to the natural heaven or sky; now chiefly in the phrase ***heavenly bodies***, i.e. the stars, planets, comets, etc. Formerly also, Coming from the clouds or atmosphere, as 'heavenly dew'.

1387 TREVISA *Higden* (Rolls) I. 271 þe ouer party þerof hatte Celica, þat is, heuenliche and hiȝe, for hiȝe mountaignes þat beeþ þerynne. **1390** GOWER *Conf.* I. 34 Lo, first the hevenly figures. The sonne and mone eclipsen both. *c* **1450** HOLLAND *Howlet* 431 The colour of asure, ane hevinliche hewe. **1508** DUNBAR *Gold. Targe* 23 The rosis.. powderit brycht with hevinly beriall droppis. **1535** COVERDALE *Jer.* viii. 2 The Sonne, the Moone and all the heauenly hooste. **1607–12** BACON *Ess., Empire* (Arb.) 308/1 Princes are like the heavenly bodyes, which cause good, or evill tymes, and which have much veneration, but noe rest. **1677** HALE *Prim. Orig. Man.* II. iii. 145, 372 Astronomical miles, or 25 Heavenly degrees. **1874** ESTES *Half-hour Recreat.* Ser. I. 96 Of the physical constitution of the heavenly bodies.

3. Having relation to heaven and divine things; divine, sacred, holy, blessed.

c **1375** *Sc. Leg. Saints, Machor* 1101 Lang sermonyng Of haly lyf & hewinlik thing. **1447** BOKENHAM *Seyntys* (Roxb.) 31 She was so enflawmyd with heuenly hete. **1588** SHAKS. *L.L.L.* V. ii. 356 A breaking..Of heauenly oaths, vow'd with integritie. **1655** FULLER *Ch. Hist.* IX. vii. §13 Instructing them by his heavenly preaching. **1814** SOUTHEY *Roderick* xxv. 312 Never man enjoyed a heavenlier peace. **1879** R. K. DOUGLAS *Confucianism* iii. 72 The Sage..pursues the heavenly way without the slightest deflection.

4. a. Having the excellence, beauty, or delight that belongs to heaven; of more than earthly or human excellence; divine. Of music: Such as that of the heavenly choirs.

1460–70 *Bk. Quintessence* 22 ȝe schulen haue an heuenly medicyn to cure perfiȝtly þis sijknesse. *c* **1470** HENRY *Wallace* VIII. 1193 Quhar byrdis blythly sang..in hewynly armony. **1559** MORWYNG *Evonym.* 94 Quintessence they name to be the chief and the heavenliest power or vertue in any plant, metall, or beast. **1588** SHAKS. *L.L.* IV. iii. 227 Who sees the heauenly Rosaline That..Bowes not his vassall head? **1712** STEELE *Spect.* No. 443 ⁋1 A graceful Person, an exalted Mien, and Heavenly Voice. **1779** MAD. D'ARBLAY *Diary* 26 May, Our journey was delightfully pleasant, the day being heavenly. **1860** TYNDALL *Glac.* I. xxv. 188 The gush of the direct sunlight could add nothing to this heavenly beauty.

b. *colloq.* Excellent, particularly enjoyable.

1874 L. TROUBRIDGE *Life amongst Troubridges* (1966) ix. 88 We had a most heavenly bathe. **1931** R. LEHMANN *Let. to Sister* 11 The heavenly mixing of paints and distempers. **1940** N. MITFORD *Pigeon Pie* viii. 127 Sophia felt at once extremely dowdy. 'You are lucky,' she said, 'the way you always have such heavenly things.'

5. *absol.* in pl. ***the heavenlies***: a literal rendering of Gr. (ἐν) τοῖς ἐπουρανίοις (Eph. i. 3, iii. 10), variously translated '(in) heavenly places' or 'things', in Rhemish Vers. 'in the celestials'.

1844 MRS. BROWNING *Drama Exile* Poems I. 102 Thy speech is of the Heavenlies. **1872** SPURGEON *Treas. Dav.* Ps. lxi. 7 In him we are made to sit together in the heavenlies. **1875** E. WHITE *Life in Christ* II. xii. 138 Against spirits of wickedness in the heavenlies, or aerial regions.

6. *Comb.*, as ***heavenly-seeming, -dewed*** adjs.

1580 SIDNEY *Arcadia* II. vii. 44 Poems 1873 II. 52 The second sweetly-fenced ward, Her heavenly-dewed tongue to gard. **1785** BURNS *Vision* II. 2, I view'd the heavenly-seeming Fair.

7. heavenly fruit, the genus *Diospyros*, the Fruit of Jove (Loudon *Encycl. Plants*, 1855, 870).

'heavenly, *adv.* In 1 -líce, 2–5 -liche. [OE. *heofonlíce*: see HEAVEN and -LY².]

1. a. From or by heaven. **b.** In a heavenly manner or degree; divinely; qualifying an *adj.*

c **1000** ÆLFRIC *Gram.* xxxviii. (Z.) 239 *Cælitus*, heofonlice. *c* **1380** WYCLIF *Sel. Wks.* III. 343 Joon lovede Crist more heuenliche. *c* **1430** *Pilgr. Lyf Manhode* II. cxxii. (1869) 121 þat I be a brid, hye raueshed, heuenlich contemplatyf. **1508** DUNBAR *Tua mariit Wemen* 11 Vnder ane holyn hewinlie grein hewit. **1590** SPENSER *F.Q.* I. Introd. iv, O Goddesse heavenly bright! **1604** SHAKS. *Oth.* V. ii. 135 Oh she was heauenly true. **1717** POPE *Eloisa* 297 Oh virtue heav'nly fair.

c. Usually hyphened to adjs. used *attrib.*

1580 SIDNEY *Arcadia* III. ii. 18 Poems 1873 II. 115 Captiuing snares Which heau'nly-purest gifts defile. *c* **1630** MILTON *On Time* 19 Our heavenly-guided soul. **1717** POPE *Eloisa* 2 Where heav'nly-pensive contemplation dwells. **1850** TENNYSON *In Mem.* lxxxvii, Azure orbits heavenly-wise. **1868** LD. HOUGHTON *Select. fr. Wks.* 213 To seem So heavenly-happy in my dream.

2. To the extent of heaven, as in ***heavenly wide***, as far apart as the two poles, differing *toto cælo.*

1674 HICKMAN *Hist. Quinquart.* (ed. 2) 107 But indeed his Opinion and the Remonstrants Opinion, seem to be heavenly wide.

'heavenly-ˌminded, *a.* Having the thoughts and affections set on things above; holy, devout.

a **1656** Bp. Hall *Soul's Farew. to Earth* ix. (Jod.), They are of the heavenly minded with far greater ardency of spirit affected. *a* **1661** Fuller *Worthies, Norfolk* (1840) II. 465 This heavenly-minded man Archbishop Whitgift. **1869** W. P. Mackay *Grace & Truth* (1875) 211 To be more holy, more Christ-like, more heavenly-minded.

Hence **ˌheavenly-'mindedness.**

1647 Ward *Simp. Cobler* 42 Hope, zeale, heavenly-mindednesse. **1835** Longf. *Outre-Mer* Pr. Wks. 1886 I. 205 Many a pure soul, through heavenly-mindedness..has fled from the temptations of the world to seek..a closer walk with God.

'heaven-pointing, *a.* [heaven 10 d.] Pointing upward to heaven.

1884 Symonds *Shaks. Predec.* ix. 333 One heaven-pointing pyramid.

† **heaven-queen.** *Obs.* [Orig. two words with *heuene* in genitive.] The, or a, queen of heaven; *spec.* a title of the Virgin Mary.

c **1230** *Hali Meid.* 11 Meidenhad is heuene cwen and worldes alefnesse. *a* **1300** *Cursor M.* 20140 þe levedi, þat es heuen quene, hir langed sare hir sun cum to. *c* **1386** Chaucer *Can. Yeom. Prol. & T.* 536 Sire oste, in faith, and by þe heven [*v.r.* heuenes] quene, It was anoþer Chanon.

† **heavenric, -rich.** *Obs.* Forms: 1 heofon-, 2 heofen-, 2–3 heouen-, 2–5 heuen-, heven- (see heaven); 1 -ríce, 2–5 -riche, 3–5 -ryche, 3–4 -rike, 4 -ryke. [OE. *heofonríce* = OS. *hebanrîki*, f. *heofon*, heaven + *ríce* kingdom, realm; cf. OS. *himilrîki*, OFris. *himelrîk*, OHG. *himilrîchi*, ON. *himinríki*. (The form in Ags. Gosp. is *heofona ríce* kingdom of the heavens.)] The kingdom of heaven; heaven as the place of the blessed.

971 *Blickl. Hom.* 9 Heofonrices duru..belocen standeþ. *a* **1000** *Christ* 1259 Bið him hel bilocen, heofonrice aȝiefen. *c* **1200** Ormin 3489 To cumenn upp Till heofennrichess blisse. *c* **1200** *Vices & Virtues* (1888) 7 Ðe angel was ȝedriuen ut of heuene riche for modinesse. **1340** Hampole *Pr. Consc.* 1898 Here lyves nan, under hevenryke, þat can telle..what þe ded es lyke. **13..** *Gaw. & Gr. Knt.* 2423 Of alle þyse oþer, vnder heuen-ryche. *c* **1450** *Hymns Virg.* 119 In erthe and in heuyn-ryche.

heavens! *int.*: see heaven *sb.* 6 d.

heavens, *adv. dial.* and *colloq.* Employed as an intensive.

1858 Dickens in *Househ. Words* Xmas no. 21/1 A shy company though its raining Heavens hard. **1870** —— *E. Drood* i. 2, I got Heavens-hard drunk for sixteen years afore I took to this. **1878** Miss Braddon *Open Verd.* xxxviii. 260 'It'll rain 'eaven's 'ard presently.' **1888** D. C. Murray *Weaker Vessel* xv, It was raining heavens hard.

'heaven-sent, *a.* Sent from heaven; providentially sent. Cf. *heaven send*, heaven *sb.* 11.

a **1649** Drumm. of Hawth. *Poems* Wks. (1711) 37/2 If you your heaven-sent good could duly prize. **1777** Potter *Æschylus* (1779) I. 52 (Jod.) How relate the heav'n-sent tempest That burst upon my head? **1875** Jowett *Plato* (ed. 2) I. 341 He is their heaven-sent friend.

heavenward ('hɛv(ə)nwəd), *adv.* and *a.* [f. heaven *sb.* + -ward.]

A. *adv.* Towards heaven, in the direction of heaven. Orig. *to heaven-ward*: cf. toward.

c **1250** *Gen. & Ex.* 3025 Moyses..warp es vt til heuene-ward. *c* **1350** *Will. Palerne* 102 To-heuene-ward he loked. **1390** Gower *Conf.* II. 151 How such thing to the hevenward Among the goddes mighte falle. *c* **1400** *Melayne* 135 He sawe a bryghtenes of a beme Up un-to hevenwarde glyde. *c* **1440** *Jacob's Well* (E.E.T.S.) 172 þin herte is raysyd in sorwe in heueneward. **1580** Sidney *Arcadia* iii. xvi. 2 Poems 1873 II. 130 Your heads to heav'nward heaue. **1634** Habington *Castara* (Arb.) 89 When Pelion..saw, that raine which fell But now from angry Heaven, to Heaven ward swell. **1646** Jenkyn *Remora* 28 Shall we run with the swiftness of the Roe earthward, and go a dull Asses trot heaven-ward? **1681** Flavel *Meth. Grace* xxxi. 533 They would move..heavenward. **1784** Cowper *Task* vi. 818 Heav'n-ward all things tend. **1838** Marg. Fuller *Wom. 19th C.* (1862) 360 Above the heavenward-pointing spire. **1860** Tyndall *Glac.* i. xvi. 106 The other summits, without a trace of cloud..pointed heavenward.

B. *adj.* Directed towards heaven; tending or conducting towards heaven.

1795 Southey *Joan of Arc* v. 24 The reverend man..with heaven-ward eye Call'd on the God of Justice. **1799** Campbell *Pleas. Hope* ii, I smile on death, if Heaven-ward Hope remain. **1828** Moore *If thou'lt be mine* iii, Like streams that come from heavenward hills.

Hence **'heavenwardly** *adv.*, **'heavenwardness.**

1838 *Blackw. Mag.* XLIV. 612 The expansivity and soaring heavenwardness of the gases. **1839** Bailey *Festus* xix. (1848) 202 Echoes of Light, reacting heavenwardly.

heavenwards ('hɛv(ə)nwədz), *adv.* [f. prec. with advb. gen. *-s*: see -wards.] Towards heaven, in the direction of heaven.

1650 W. Brough *Sacr. Princ.* To Rdr., Using them..as..guides and helps to heaven-wards. **1670** Brooks *Wks.* (1867) VI. 229 What trade did you drive Christ-wards, and heaven-wards, and holiness-wards? **1860** Pusey *Min. Proph.* 418 Weighing it down that it should not rise Heavenwards.

† **'heavenware.** *Obs.* Forms: 1 heofonwara, 2 houene-, 2–3 heueneware. [OE. *heofonwara* pl., f. *-wara* 'people'.] The inhabitants of heaven.

c **1000** Ælfric *Hom.* I. 36 Cristes acennednys ȝegladode heofenwara, and eorðwara, and helwara. *c* **1175** *Lamb. Hom.* 139 Sunnedei blisseð to-gederes houeneware and horðe ware. *a* **1225** *Ancr. R.* 244 (MSS. T. & C.) Al heuene ware and helle ware.

'heaven-ˌwide, *adv.* and *a.*

A. *adv.* By the width of the heavens, as far as the east is from the west.

c **1611** Chapman *Iliad* xxiii. 299 Hurl'd about This way and that..all heaven wide of his end. **1857–8** Sears *Athan.* vii. 62 This principle clears the pneumatology of the Bible heaven-wide of the slough of naturalism.

B. *adj.* As wide or broad as the heavens.

1883 J. Parker *Apost. Life* II. 71 This heaven-wide principle. **1891** *Pall Mall G.* 18 Nov. 3/3 An appearance of heaven-wide difference of opinion.

'heave-ˌoffering. In the Levitical law: An offering which was 'heaved' or elevated by the priest when offered; also used of other offerings, e.g. those for the construction of the tabernacle.

The word is used in Tindale's version of the Pentateuch and the Bible of 1611 to render Heb. *t'rūmāh* (in 1611 also frequently rendered simply 'offering' or 'oblation'), which was taken by some Rabbis to mean 'elevation', from *rōmem* to lift up.

1530 Tindale *Exod.* xxv. 3 This is the heueoffrynge [**1611** offering] which ye shall take of them. [*Table exp. Words*, Heveoffringe, because they were hoven vp before the Lorde.] —— *Numbers* xv. 20 Ye shall geue a cake of the first of youre dowe vnto an heue offerynge: as ye do the heue offerynge of the barne, euen so ye shall heue it. **1611** Bible *Exod.* xxix. 27 Thou shalt sanctifie the brest of the waue-offering, and the shoulder of the heaue offering, which is waued, and which is heaued vp of the ramme of the consecration. **1653** Milton *Hirelings* Wks. (1851) 252 He..passes, by Deed of Gift, this Tenth to the Levite; yet so as offer'd to him first a Heav-offering, and consecrated on his Altar.

heaver ('hiːvə(r)). [f. heave *v.* + -er¹.]

1. A person who heaves (in various senses: see the verb); *spec.* a labourer employed in landing goods at a dockyard. (See also ballast-*heaver*, coal-heaver.)

1586 J. Hooker *Girald. Irel.* in *Holinshed* II. 84/1 Notwithstanding the pushes giuen against him by secret heauers that enuied his fortune. **1673** R. Head *Canting Acad.* 69 Padders, Booth-heavers, and the like. **1696** Luttrell *Brief Rel* (1857) IV. 96 The heavers of coales from the ships to the lighters. **1824** *Examiner* 70/2 Mere heavers of the leg, kickers of the ankle. **1881** Miss Jackson *Shropsh. Word-bk.* s.v. Heler, 'The heler's as bad as the heaver'; which is analogous to 'The receiver's as bad as the thief'.

2. Something that heaves; an apparatus for heaving or lifting, a lever; *spec.* (*Naut.*) a wooden bar or staff used for twisting or tightening a rope or strap.

1598 Florio, *Toladro*, an instrument, heauer, or engine to mount any piece of ordinance vp into the carriage. **1615** Crooke *Body of Man* 775 The fourth Muscle is called *Leuator* or the Heauer. *a* **1700** B. E. *Dict. Cant. Crew*, *Heaver*, a Breast. **1769** Falconer *Dict. Mar.* (1776), *Heaver*, a name given by seamen to a wooden staff, employed by them as a lever on many occasions. **1794** *Rigging & Seamanship* I. 190 The strap is nippered, with a heaver, round the block. **1867** Smyth *Sailor's Word-bk.*, *Heaver*, a wooden bar or staff, sometimes tapered at the ends; it is employed as a lever or purchase.

heaves, a disease of horses: see heave *sb.*³

heave shoulder. In the Levitical law: The shoulder of an animal 'heaved' or elevated in sacrifice (cf. heave-offering). Also *transf.* and *fig.*

1530 Tindale *Lev.* vii. 34 The wauebrest and the heue-shulder I haue taken of the childern of Israel..and haue geuen it vnto Aaron the prest and vnto his sonnes; to be a dutie for euer of the children of Israel. **1647** *Husbandm. Plea agst. Tithes* 38 Then the custome is (in some Parishes) for the Parson to have a tenth joynt, a heave shoulder, or a shake breast. *a* **1659** Bp. Brownrig *Serm.* (1674) I. xxi. 278 'God', said Gregory, 'requires..the heave-shoulder and arm of Obedience'.

† **heave-shouldered**, *a. Obs. rare.* With raised shoulders; high-shouldered.

1599 Nashe *Lenten Stuffe* in *Harl. Misc.* VI. 157 Captaines that wore a whole antient in a scarfe, which made them goe heave-shouldred, it was so boysterous.

heave thigh, substituted by the Revisers of 1885 for heave shoulder in the Bible of 1611.

1885 Bible (R.V.) *Lev.* vii. 34 The wave breast and the heave thigh [*marg.* Or, shoulder].

ˌheavier-than-'air, *attrib. phr. Aeronautics.* Designating a flying-machine whose weight is greater than the weight of the air which it displaces, and whose lift is not dependent on light gases; also applied to the use of such a machine or machines in flight.

[**1870** tr. *Marion's Wonderful Balloon Ascents* ii. ix. 162 To form a 'Free Association for Aerial Navigation by means of Machines heavier than Air'. **1879** *Encycl. Brit.* IX. 309/2 Weight, however paradoxical it may appear, is necessary to flight. Everything which flies is vastly heavier than the air.] **1903** *Westm. Gaz.* 18 Sept. 9/3 The only example of the heavier-than-air machine. [**1904** *Chambers's Jrnl.* 1 Oct. 699/1 All who have sought to sail the skies divide themselves..into..the 'lighter-than-airites' and the 'heavier-than-airites'.] **1908** H. G. Wells *War in Air* viii. §2 The most efficient heavier-than-air fliers. **1909** A. Berget *Conquest of Air* ii. ii. 155 Many persons ask aviators why their 'heavier-than-air' apparatus is not provided with parachutes. **1909** *Flight* 19 June 356/1 Any heavier-than-air type of machine. **1909** *Daily Chron.* 9 Sept. 1/6 For a long time, Mr. Cody has practised heavier-than-air flying on Laffan's Plain. **1927** C. L. M. Brown *Conquest of Air* 21 When heavier-than-air flight was an accomplished reality. **1961** C. B. Smith *Testing Time* ii. 27 The War Office instructed O'Gorman to concentrate entirely on airships. They admitted that 'heavier-than-air dirigibles' might one day have military uses.

heavily ('hɛvɪlɪ), *adv.* Forms: 1 **hefiȝlíce, hefilíce, hefelíce,** 3 **hefilike, heui(c)liche,** *Orm.* **hefiȝlike,** 4 **hevyleche,** 4–6 **hevely, hevyly, -li,** 5 *Sc.* **hevaly, hewyly,** 5–6 **havelie.** 6 **hevily,** *Sc.* **hewilie,** 6– **heavily.** [OE. *hefiȝlíce* adv., from *hefiȝ* heavy: see -ly².]

1. In a heavy manner; with or as with weight, *lit.* and *fig.*; ponderously, massively; burdensomely, oppressively.

c **1320** *Cast. Love* 1671, I-charged with synne so hevyleche. **1375** Barbour *Bruce* vii. 209 His fut he set Apon his man weill hevaly. **1613** Purchas *Pilgrimage* (1614) 802 They did sound a long time upon Trumpets, Cornets, and Flutes, very heavily. **1622** Mabbe tr. *Aleman's Guzman d'Alf.* II. 188 This..will light heavilier vpon you then you are aware. **1712** Steele *Spect.* No. 268 ¶2 A Gentleman leaning upon me, and very heavily. **1837** W. Irving *Capt. Bonneville* III. 150 The horses were too heavily laden to travel fast. **1871** Freeman *Norm. Conq.* (1876) IV. xvii. 57 On the great house of..Eadward his hand fell more heavily. **1886** Mrs. Alexander *By Woman's Wit* I. vii. 207 Mrs. Ruthven did not find time hang heavily on her hands.

2. With heavy, laborious, or dragging movement; laboriously, sluggishly; without elasticity or animation.

c **1000** *Ags. Gosp.* Matt. xiii. 15 Hiȝ hefelice mid earum ȝehyrdon. **1398** Trevisa *Barth. De P.R.* iii. xvii. (1495) 63 The humour by nyghte meuyth heuyly. **1496** *Dives & Paup.* (W. de W.) i. lix. 101/2 Yf the seruyce be sayd so hauenly [*Pynson* hauely] & dedely. **1611** Bible *Exod.* xiv. 25 And broke off their charet wheeles, that they draue them heauily. **1697** *Lond. Gaz.* No. 3288/3 The..Fireship sailing very heavily. **1709** Steele *Tatler* No. 72 ¶6 He read his Discourse..so heavily, and with so little Air of being convinced himself. **1760** Milles in *Phil. Trans.* LI. 538 Burn heavily, leaving a large quantity of brownish ashes. **1824** Miss Ferrier *Inher.* lxvii, Breakfast passed very heavily. **1887** H. Erroll *Ugly Duckling* III. vii. 122, 'I think I'll be off now', said Lambert getting heavily up.

3. With sorrow, grief, displeasure, or anger; grievously. *Obs.* or *arch.*

c **1000** Ælfric *Gen.* xxi. 11 Abraham þa undernam hefiȝlice þas word. *c* **1380** Wyclif *Serm.* Sel. Wks. II. 26 Jesus..tok it hevely. **1388** —— *Mark* xiv. 4 There weren summe that beren it heuyli with ynne hem silf. **1483** *Vulgaria abs Terentio* 8 a, I fere me lest my fadyr bere heuyly that ȝister-day j com not to hym. **1591** Spenser *Teares Muses* 35 [They] Hearing them so heavily lament, Like heavily lamenting from them went. *a* **1674** Clarendon *Hist. Reb.* xiii. §124 Berkley..took this refusal very heavily. **1777** Burke *Corr.* (1844) II. 169 Any mistake or neglect of mine is..heavily taken. **1816** Byron *Siege Cor.* xix, There he sate all heavily.

4. With great force or violence; forcibly, violently; intensely, deeply, strongly; severely.

c **897** K. Ælfred *Gregory's Past.* xxiv. 179 Ða weras mon sceal hefiȝlecor and stiðlecor læran, and ða wif leohtlecor. *c* **1000** *Ags. Gosp.* Luke xi. 53 þa ongunnun..þa ægleawan hefilice him aȝen standan. *c* **1200** Ormin 8236 He wass..Biforr þe Romanisshe king Full hefilike wreȝedd. **1375** Barbour *Bruce* iii. 235 It ranyt sa hard and hewyly. **1500–20** Dunbar *Poems* xxxv. 6 Off Fortoun I complenit hevely. **1548** Hall *Chron., Hen. VI*, 95 b, Thei had been hevyly thretened for the tyme of his absence. **1588** Shaks. *L.L.L.* i. ii. 155 Thou shalt be heauily punished. *a* **1661** Fuller *Worthies, Northampton* (1840) II. 533 Lately the earl of Oxford was heavily fined. **1798** Malthus *Popul.* (1878) 128 Merchants..complain heavily of this inconvenience. **1876** Green *Stray Stud.* 223 The strong tendency to national unity told heavily against judicial inequality.

5. To a large or heavy amount.

1819 *Scotsman* 30 Jan. 40/3 Oatmeal..sold heavily at fully more money. **1847** *Jrnl. R. Agric. Soc.* VIII. i. 64 Farm-yard manure is used heavily. **1850** *Ibid.* XI. ii. 613, I stock heavily. **1859** Darwin in *Life & Lett.* (1887) II. 164, I have ..corrected so heavily, as almost to have rewritten it. **1864** *Jrnl. R. Agric. Soc.* XXV. ii. 271 The county is heavily wooded.

6. *Comb.*: often equivalent to parasynthetic comb. of the adj., as ***heavily-booted***, having heavy boots.

1883 A. Thomas *Mod. Housewife* 131 Trodden by heavily-booted feet. **1883** Ld. R. Gower *My Remin.* II. 79 A large and heavily-veined nose. **1904** *Westm. Gaz.* 27 Aug. 6/2 This heavily-scented, image-laden atmosphere. **1905** *Daily Chron.* 20 Oct. 8/5 Those heavily-jetted waistbelts. **1906** *Ibid.* 11 June 5/2 A good deal of heavily-jewelled..speech. **1907** B. von Hutten *Halo* i. i, Very long, half-closed, heavily-lashed eyes. **1927** A. Conan Doyle *Case Bk. S. Holmes* xi. 293 A strong, heavily-moustached face and angry eyes. *c* **1909** D. H. Lawrence *Collier's Friday Night* (1934) i. 9 Then he drags his heavily-shod feet to the door on right. **1938** *Daily Tel.* 18 Jan. 6/3 As the heavily-policed funeral was marched down the street every window was flung open and red flowers showered down. **1961** *B.S.I. News* Feb. 6/1 Fast heavily-trafficked roads.

heaviness ('hɛvɪnɪs). Forms: 1 **hefiȝnes, (hæfiȝnes, hæfnis),** 3–5 **heuenes, -nis, -nys,** 3–6 **hevinesse,** 4 *Sc.* **hewynes,** 4–6 **hevynesse,** 5

euynes, 6 hevines, heueneys, *Sc.* havines, 6–7 heavines(se, 6– heaviness. [OE. *hefiȝnes*: see HEAVY *a.* and -NESS.] The state or quality of being heavy: in the various senses of the adj.; esp. **a.** Weightiness, ponderousness; gravity; weight or force of impact.

c **1340** *Cursor M.* 23235 (Fairf.) Is heuenis of dint.. Als hit ware dintis of a stiþi þat smiþþis smitis in þaire smeþi. *c* **1440** *Promp. Parv.* 239/1 Hevynesse of wyghte, *ponderositas*. **1545** ASCHAM *Toxoph.* (Arb.) 126 What heuynes doth in a stripe euery man by experience can tell. **1600** J. PORY tr. *Leo's Africa* II. 63 Having.. on the one side of their horses a great weight.. to counterpoize the heavines of their drums on the other side. **1674** N. FAIRFAX *Bulk & Selv.* 153 A perpendicular from the centre of heaviness.

b. Burdensomeness, oppressiveness, severity; †a grievance.

c **950** *Lindisf. Gosp.* Matt. xx. 12 We ða ðe beron hefiȝnise ðæs dæȝes & hæto. *a* **1225** *Ancr R.* 132 þe heuinesse of hire flesche & flesches unðeawes binimeð hire hire vluht. *c* **1400** *Destr. Troy* 1800 The harmys and þe heuenys hym happit of yow. **1548** HALL *Chron., Hen. VI*, 95 The causes and matters of hevinesse, declared in articles. *Ibid.* 97 There were caste many hevinesses and sedicious billes, under the names of suche laborers. **1582** N. LICHEFIELD tr. *Castanheda's Conq. E. Ind.* lxxiii. 150b, The heauinesse of my losse beeing such. **1638** ABP. SYMSON in Spurgeon *Treas. Dav.* Ps. vi. 2 And only lament the heaviness of his sickness.

†**c.** Enraged feeling, displeasure, anger. *Obs.*

c **1386** CHAUCER *Melib.* ¶782 He hath swich heuynesse and swich wratthe to vs ward. **1431** in *Eng. Gilds* (1870) 279 If any man be at heuynesse with any of his bretheryne. **1502** ARNOLDE *Chron.* (1811) 291 My sayd Lorde of Gloucester bare heuynes vnto my Lorde off Winchester. **1548** HALL *Chron., Hen. VI*, 98b, Never.. take.. querelles, displeasures or hevinesses.. one against the other. **1590** SPENSER *F.Q.* I. v. 6 The instruments of wrath and heavinesse.

d. Oppressed condition of the body, members, or senses; torpor, drowsiness; dullness; want of animation.

c **888** K. ÆLFRED *Boeth.* xxxv. §1 Nan hæfiȝnes ðæs lichoman, ne nan unþeaw. *a* **1225** *Ancr. R.* 270 ȝif þet tu muhtest wel wakien, he.. leið on þe heuinesse. **1382** WYCLIF *Luke* xxii. 45 He fond hem slepinge for heuynesse. **1398** TREVISA *Barth. De P.R.* III. xviii. (1495) 65 Callyd defnes and.. heuynesse of heringe. **1577** B. GOOGE *Heresbach's Husb.* IV. (1586) 190b, The dumpishe heavinesse, that proceedeth of Melancholy. **1700** DRYDEN *Sigism. & Guisc.* 204 A welcome heaviness That seiz'd his eyes. **1885** *Manch. Exam.* 18 Feb. 3/3 The terrible dryness and heaviness which make themselves manifest on every page.

e. Dejectedness of mind; †sadness, grief.

c **1275** *XI Pains of Hell* 45 in *O.E. Misc.* 212 Hou dredful is hel.. In þe wyche is heuenes with-out gladnes. *c* **1386** CHAUCER *Frankl. T.* 100 Hire freendes.. Conforten hire in al þat euer they may Al for to make hire leue hire heuynesse. *c* **1440** *Generydes* 4625 Hir joy was turnyd into hevynes. **1513** MORE in Grafton *Chron.* (1568) II. 756 He was with great funerall honor and heavynesse of his people.. enterred at Windsore. **1610** SHAKS. *Temp.* v. i. 200 Let vs not burthen our remembrances, with A heauinesse that's gon. **1742** RICHARDSON *Pamela* IV. 215 So much Heaviness had I lost, and so much Joy had I received! **1879** DIXON *Windsor* II. viii. 92 Richard, in seeming heaviness of heart, broke up his Court.

heaving (ˈhiːvɪŋ), *vbl. sb.* [f. HEAVE *v.* + -ING[1].] The action of the verb HEAVE, q.v., in various senses.

a **1300** *E.E. Psalter* cxl[i]. 2 Heving of mi hend. *a* **1310** in Wright *Lyric P.* x. 36 Ne kepte heo non heuyng here. **1523** SKELTON *Garl. Laurel* 250 With heuynge and shouynge, haue in and haue oute. **1601** HOLLAND *Pliny* II. 62 The sicke heauing of the stomacke. *Ibid.* 277 They shall not be sea-sicke nor giuen to heauing, as commonly they be that are at sea. **1611** SHAKS. *Wint. T.* II. iii. 35 'Tis such as you That creepe like shadowes by him, and do sighe At each his needlesse heauings. **1709** STEELE *Tatler* No. 82 ¶4 The silent heaving of the Waves. **1758** REID tr. *Macquer's Chem.* I. 391 A reduction of the Lead, which is always attended with a sort of effervescence, and such a considerable heaving, that.. most of the mixture runs over the crucible. **1802** PLAYFAIR *Illust. Hutton. Th.* 255 The heaving of one vein by another. **1805** FORSYTH *Beauties Scotl.* II. 279 A.. mode of fishing, called heaving or hauling, is standing in the stream.. with a bag or net fixed to a kind of frame... Whenever a fish strikes against the net, they.. instantly haul up the mouth of the net above water. **1847** EMERSON *Poems, Threnody* 101 When thou didst yield thy innocent breath In birdlike heavings unto death.

b. The rustic custom, formerly observed at Easter, of heaving or lifting into the air persons of the opposite sex.

1787 *Public Advertiser* 13 Apr. (Brand), The counties of Shropshire, Cheshire, and Lancashire boast of one [custom] of equal antiquity, which they call Heaving. **1800** F. LEIGHTON *Let. to J. Boucher* 17 Feb. (MS.), With respect to the custom of heaving at Easter.. The men heave the women on Easter Monday; the women heave the men on the Tuesday. **1826** HONE *Every-day Bk.* I. 425 Lifting or heaving differs a little in different places. In some parts the person is laid horizontally, in others placed in a sitting position on the bearers' hands. Usually, when the lifting or heaving is within doors, a chair is produced.

c. A name for certain diseases of animals: see quots.

1799 *Med. Jrnl.* I. 116 The pox of swine, called also by the London feeders, the heavings. **1883** *Standard* 19 Apr. 2/3 The disease from which ewes die, about three days after parturition.. generally called 'inflammation', or sometimes 'heaving', is due to a disease which is analogous to puerperal fever in women.

†**d.** *heaving of the maw*: name of an old game at cards. *Obs.*

a **1612** HARINGTON *Epigr.* IV. 12 Then thirdly follow'd heauing of the Maw, A game without Civility or Law, An odious play, and yet in Court oft seene, A sawcy knave to trump both King and Queene.

e. With adv. *heaving-down*, *heaving-to*: see HEAVE *v.* 20

1799 NELSON 6 Mar. in Nicolas *Disp.* (1843) III. 280 The Emerald.. having been on shore and got so much damage as to require heaving down. **1833** M. SCOTT *Tom Cringle* i. (1876) 4 Heaving to was impossible. **1875** BEDFORD *Sailor's Pocket-bk.* v. 146 Conveniences for heaving down.

f. *attrib.* and *Comb.*: **heaving-day** (see quots., and b above); †**heaving-house**, (?) a gambling-house, for dice-play; **heaving-line** (*Naut.*), a line, usually from 5 to 10 fathoms long, used for casting from a vessel to enable a hawser to be hauled ashore or to another vessel; **heaving-net**, a net that is heaved or hauled up; see quot. 1805 in a.

1584 *Order* in *Descr. Thames* (1758) 63 No Fishermen, Garthmen, Petermen.. shall avaunce or set up any Wears, Engines.. Heaving Nets, except they be 2 Inches in the Meish. **1579** T. F. *Newes fr. North* xiv. (1585) F iv, I call to witnesse the Theaters, Curtaines, Heauing-houses, Rifling boothes, Bowling alleyes, and such places. **1826** HONE *Every-day Bk.* I. 425 Easter Monday and Easter Tuesday were known by the name of *heaving day*, because on the former day it was customary for the men to heave and kiss the women, and on the latter day for the women to retaliate on the men. *Ibid.*, The women's heaving-day was the most amusing.

ˈ**heaving**, *ppl. a.* [f. as prec. + -ING[2].] That heaves, in various senses; see the verb.

1606 SHAKS. *Tr. & Cr.* II. ii. 196 The performance of our heauing spleenes. **1697** DRYDEN *Virg. Georg.* III. 166 The Youthful Charioteers with heaving Heart Rush to the Race. **1714** GAY *Trivia* II. 193 The heaving tide In widen'd circles beats on either side. **1833** HT. MARTINEAU *Fr. Wines & Pol.* iv. 66 A heaving ocean of upturned faces. **1887** BOWEN *Virg. Æneid* v. 33 Over the heaving billows the ships of the Teucrians go.

Heaviside (ˈhɛvɪsaɪd). *Physics.* The name of O. *Heaviside* (1850–1925), English physicist, used attrib. to designate concepts proposed by him; esp. ***Heaviside layer***, an ionized layer in the upper atmosphere able to reflect long radio waves (now usu. called *E layer of the ionosphere*); ***Heaviside-Lorentz units*** (H. A. Lorentz, 1853–1928, Dutch physicist), or ***Heaviside rational units***, units of electric charge or magnetic pole defined in a certain manner which simplifies many formulæ; ***Heaviside unit function***, a function which is zero when its argument is negative, and unity when its argument is positive; used esp. in *Electr. Communication*.

1911 *Encycl. Brit.* XXVII. 744/2 It will be seen.. that the Heaviside rational units are all incommeasurable with the practical units. **1912** *Proc. R. Soc.* A. LXXXVII. 95 Both long and short waves are propagated through the lower and middle atmosphere in straight lines to great heights and reflected at the Heaviside layer. **1913** *Year-Bk. Wireless Telegr.* 395 The conductivity, and consequently the reflecting power, of the Heaviside layer depends greatly on the presence of local electro-motive forces. **1926** R. W. HUTCHINSON *Wireless* vii. 131 It is clear that if the earth were surrounded by a spherical conductor some distance away from it the waves would travel between this conducting surface and the conducting surface of the earth, and they would follow the curvature of the earth... Such a conductor does exist and it is known as the Heaviside layer. **1937** *Discovery* Mar. 65/2 The well known Heaviside and Appleton layers which play such an important part in carrying broadcasting to long distances. **1940** *Chambers's Techn. Dict.* 407/2 *Heaviside unit function*, a step in which the change in amplitude is unity. **1955** O. KLEIN in W. Pauli *N. Bohr* 99 The units are the usual ones, $\hbar = c = 1$ and Heaviside-Lorentz units for the electromagnetic quantities. **1963** JERRARD & MCNEILL *Dict. Sci. Units* 14 The Heaviside-Lorentz units were the earliest rationalized units, they were proposed by Heaviside in 1883 and used by him in a classical paper on electrical theory published nine years later.

†ˈ**heavisome**, *a. Obs.* or *dial.* Also 5 **heuisum, evysum.** [f. HEAVY *a.* + -SOME.] Of heavy mood, doleful, sad; dull, gloomy.

1435 MISYN *Fire of Love* II. iv. 77 Heuisum longyng of þis exile me castis downe. *c* **1450** *Cov. Myst.* (Shaks. Soc.) 365 Sory and evysum ye ben alway: Your myrthe is gon. **1561** T. NORTON *Calvin's Inst.* I. 60 A heauisome mistinesse is cast before our eyes. **1825** BROCKETT, *Heavisome*, dark, dull, drowsy. So **1828** *Craven Dial.*

Hence †ˈ**heavisomely** *adv. Obs.*, sadly.

1382 WYCLIF *Ecclus.* vi. 26 Vnderlei thi shulder, and ber it, and ne bere thou heuysumli in the bondis of it.

†ˈ**heavity.** *Obs.* In 5 **hevyte, -ee.** [irreg. f. HEAVY *a.* + -TY.] Heaviness of heart, sorrow.

14.. *Chaucer's L.G.W.* 1736 (MS. Fairfax) *Lucrece*, And eke the teeres ful of hevytee [*v. rr.* oneste, honeste, -ee, heuynesse] Embelysshed hir wifely chastitee. *c* **1440** *Partonope* 2466 The french departed wyth grete heuyte.

heavy (ˈhɛvɪ), *a.*[1] (*sb.*) Forms: 1 **hefiȝ, hefeȝ,** (*north.* **hæfiȝ**), 2–3 **hefeȝ,** 2–4 **hevi,** 3 (*Orm.*) **hefiȝ,** (**evi**), 4 **heve,** 4–6 **hevy,** *Sc.* **hewy,** 5–6 (**evy**), **hevye,** 6 **hevey,** (*Sc.* **havy, -ie, hawy(e, hayvie**), 6–7 **heavie, -ye,** 6– **heavy.** [OE. *hefiȝ* = OS. *hębig* (MDu. *hevich*, Du. *hevig*), OHG. *hębîg, hęvîg, hęvîch*, MHG. *hebec*, ON. *höfugr, höfigr*:—OTeut. **habigo-*, **habugo-*, f. **hafi-z*, OE. *hefe* weight, f. **hafjan*, to HEAVE.]

A. *adj.* **I.** In the primary physical sense, and uses connected therewith.

1. a. Of great weight; weighty, ponderous. The opposite of *light*.

c **1000** *Ags. Gosp.* Matt. xxiii. 4 Hiȝ bindað hefiȝe byrþyna.. and lecgeað þa uppan manna exla. *c* **1200** *Vices & Virtues* (1888) 95 Ic am heui, al so he ðe is imaked of ierðe. *a* **1300** *Cursor M.* 17288 + 99 Who sal vus helpe To remou þat heuy stone? **13..** *Gaw. & Gr. Knt.* 289 þis ax, þat is heue innogh. **1486** *Bk. St. Albans* D iij, Looke.. that thay be not to heuy ouer hir power to weyr. **1592** TIMME *10 Eng. Lepers* C iv b, [A coate] too colde for winter, and too heavie and hote for sommer. **1665** R. HOOKE *Microgr.* 204 It [the ant] was able to grasp and hold a heavy body, three or four times the bulk and weight of its own body. **1765** A. DICKSON *Treat. Agric.* (ed. 2) 158 Bad tradesmen make this plough heavy and clumsy. **1853** W. GREGORY *Inorg. Chem.* (ed. 3) 24, 1 atom of oxygen will be eight times heavier than 1 atom of hydrogen.

fig. *a* **1340** HAMPOLE *Psalter* iv. 3 þe weght of wickednes þ[t] makis ȝoure herts heuyere þan lede. **1340** —— *Pr. Consc.* 2868 For syn es swa hevy and swa harde, þat it drawes þe saul ay dunwarde. *a* **1786** COWPER *Yearly Distr.* iv, Each heart as heavy as a log.

b. *to lie, sit heavy upon* or *at*: chiefly *fig.*

1594 SHAKS. *Rich. III*, v. iii. 118 Let me sit heauy on thy soule to morrow. **1638** BAKER tr. *Balzac's Lett.* (Vol. II.) 32, I have something, I know not what, lies heavy at my heart. **1721** BERKELEY *Prev. Ruin Gt. Brit.* Wks. III. 209 This public calamity that lies so heavy on the nation. *c* **1726** A. EVANS *Elegy on Vanbrugh*, Lie heavy on him, earth! for he Laid many heavy loads on thee! **1849** MACAULAY *Hist. Eng.* I. 287 These burdens did not lie very heavy on the nation.

c. Weighty because of the quantity present; hence, in large quantity or amount, abundant. Also of timber: consisting of large trees (*U.S.*).

1728 POPE *Dunc.* I. 78 Heavy harvests nod beneath the snow. **1795** *Gentl. Mag.* 539/1 Another sharp frost and heavy snow. **1835** *Penny Cycl.* III. 464/1 The early-sown crops are.. in general the heaviest. **1843** *Yale Lit. Mag.* VIII. 406 In this patch of 'heavy timber'. **1853** B. F. TAYLOR *Jan. & June* (1871) 252 [The storm] went crashing on, into the heavy timber. **1857** LIVINGSTONE *Trav.* xix. 373 Virgin soil does not give such a heavy crop as an old garden.

d. *techn.* Possessing (appreciable) weight. In *Physics*, applied to bodies whose weight may not be disregarded in calculations.

1871 TAIT & STEELE *Dynamics of a Particle* (ed. 3) iv. Example 46 A heavy particle is projected from a given point with a given velocity.

2. a. Possessing great weight in proportion to bulk; of great specific gravity.

a **1000** *Boeth. Metr.* xx. 266 Eorþe is hefiȝre oðrum ȝesceaftum. **1382** WYCLIF *Prov.* xxvii. 3 Heuy is the ston, and charjous is the grauel. *c* **1440** *York Myst.* xviii. 20 Hevye as leede. **1530** PALSGR. 315/1 Heavy as golde is or any thyng that wayeth moche, *massif*. **1695** WOODWARD *Nat. Hist. Earth* Pref., According to the Order of their Gravity those which are heavyest lying deepest in the Earth. **1838** T. THOMSON *Chem. Org. Bodies* 608 An oil, deeper coloured.. but equally heavy.

b. Of bread, pastry, etc.: That has not properly 'risen', and is consequently dense and compact.

1828 WEBSTER, *Heavy*.. 25. Not raised by leaven or fermentation; not light; clammy; as heavy bread. **1837–42** WHITTOCK, etc. *Bk. Trades* 17 Kneading.. is.. indispensable, or the dough would be in lumps and the bread heavy. **1859** GEO. ELIOT *A. Bede* II. (ed. 5) 208 If the bread turned out heavy. **1887** BARING-GOULD *Red Spider* xxix. (1888) 218 The pasty is heavy.

c. Applied to elements whose specific gravity is relatively great; ***heavy metal*** (see also sense 6 b), a metal of high specific gravity (see quot. 1955).

1864 *Jrnl. Chem. Soc.* XVII. 126 In support of the view that thallium is one of the heavy metals, the following reasons may be given. **1868** LOCKYER *Elem. Astron.* iii. (1879) 59 Platinum, the heaviest metal. **1903** *Jrnl. Physiol.* XXIX. 165 Most of the heavy metals when injected directly into the circulation give rise to increased movements of plain muscle throughout the body. **1922** F. W. ASTON *Isotopes* viii. 101 The nucleus of the atom of an ordinary element (not hydrogen).. is very small compared with the atom itself. Its dimensions can be roughly determined by actual experiment in the case of the heavy elements. **1936** *Discovery* Feb. 36/1 Heavy elements, such as gold, silver, and lead. **1936** R. P. BELL tr. *Bjerrum's Inorg. Chem.* 213 The metals fall naturally into two groups: the light metals with densities below four, and the heavy metals with densities above seven... The heavy metals have their electrons more firmly bound and are less electropositive than the light metals. **1946** *Monthly Notices R. Astron. Soc.* CVI. 357 Material at any point.. on the other side of the curve is composed almost entirely of heavy elements, the main mass of the elements in the latter case having atomic weight greater than 50. **1955** *Chem. & Engin. News* 2 May 1902/2 Karl F. Heumann wonders what is meant by 'heavy metal'. One authority says it is any metal having a specific gravity greater than 4.0. Another says it is sometimes applied to those of sp. gr. 5.0 or over... Has 'heavy metal' ever been officially defined? **1961** *Jrnl. Chem. Educ.* XXXVIII. 67/1 The present treatment will be restricted to the main process responsible for the heavy elements, of mass number *A* greater than 70. **1972** *Science* 14 Apr. 161 (*title*) Enrichment of heavy metals and organic compounds in the surface microlayer of Narragansett Bay, Rhode Island.

d. *Physics.* Of hydrogen: consisting of the isotope deuterium (which is of greater mass than protium, the normal isotope). Of a compound of hydrogen: having some or all of the hydrogen isotope present as deuterium. So **heavy water,**

deuterium oxide, D_2O, or a mixture of this with ordinary water; **heavy-water-moderated** *a.*, of a nuclear reactor: employing heavy water as a moderator; **heavy water reactor**, a nuclear reactor in which the moderator is heavy water.

This usage is occas. extended to the isotopes of other elements to designate an isotope that is of greater mass than the normal isotope.

1933 *Nature* 22 Apr. 590/2 Heavy water freezes when surrounded by melting ice. **1933** *Jrnl. Chem. Physics* June 344/2 Let us make an estimate of the amount of the heavy hydrogen isotope in ordinary water. **1933** *Discovery* July 211/1 For the first time in history a chemical element has been divided into two completely different parts. A new 'heavy' hydrogen has been separated from the old. **1933** *Science* 29 Dec. 602/1 In fact, if there were only two waters, two ammonias, and so forth, the names 'light water', 'heavy water', 'light ammonia' and 'heavy ammonia' would be very satisfactory indeed. **1934** *Discovery* Jan. 1/1 There is one part only of heavy hydrogen to 35,000 parts of light hydrogen. **1934, 1935** [see DEUTERIUM]. **1936** *Punch* 23 Sept. 337/1 'Heavy-water', the newly-discovered fluid, costs £120 a teaspoonful. **1937** *Discovery* Oct. 317/1 The value of heavy nitrogen for research in physiological chemistry is inestimable. **1938** *Encycl. Brit. Bk. of Year* 320/1 'Heavy water' or deuterium oxide is now manufactured commercially and is an article of commerce. **1938** R. W. LAWSON tr. *Hevesy & Paneth's Man. Radioactivity* (ed. 2) xx. 187 The properties of 'heavy hydrogen' or 'deuterium'..differ..strongly from those of the much more abundant ordinary hydrogen. **1941** in M. Gowing *Britain & Atomic Energy* (1964) App. ii. 395 We know that Germany has taken a great deal of trouble to secure supplies of the substance known as heavy water. **1945** H. D. SMYTH *Gen. Acct. Devel. Atomic Energy Mil. Purposes* i. 11 A frequently used 'beam' source of neutrons results from accelerated deuterons impinging on 'heavy water' ice. **1946** *Electronic Engin.* XVIII. 142 The deuteron..which is the nucleus of heavy hydrogen, or deuterium. **1947** CROWTHER & WHIDDINGTON *Science at War* 145 The slow neutrons produced by the uranium and heavy-water system would transmute many uranium atoms into the new element plutonium. **1955** *Ann. Reg. 1954* 393 Dimple (deuterium moderated pile, low energy) was Britain's first heavy water reactor. **1956** *Nature* 4 Feb. 205/2 Three enriched-uranium heavy-water-moderated..reactors are under construction. **1958** *Listener* 28 Aug. 294/2 Producing heavy water from electricity from the proposed Aswan High Dam. **1964** M. GOWING *Britain & Atomic Energy* ii. 73 Meanwhile doubts grew about the wisdom of pressing the Americans too hard about the heavy water project.

3. Great with young; gravid, pregnant. Also *fig.*

c **1375** *Sc. Leg. Saints, Magdalena* 396 Suppose with barne scho hewy ware. *a* **1684** LEIGHTON *Comm. 1 Pet.* Wks. 1835 I. 345 When they are big and heavy with some inward exercise of mind. **1884** JEFFERIES *Red Deer* ii. 32 Two of them were heavy in calf.

4. Increased in weight by the addition of something; laden *with*. Also *fig.*

1622 BACON *Hen. VII*, Wks. 1825 III. 324 His men heavy and laden with booty. **1726** LEONI *Alberti's Archit.* I. 65/2 Winds..from the West..are heavyest at Sun-rise. **1840** MISS MITFORD in L'Estrange *Life* (1870) III. vii. 109 The very air heavy with the rich perfume of the seringas and acacias. **1888** L. MALET *Couns. Perfect.* 63 The words seeming to her heavy with meaning. *Ibid.* 290 This hour, heavy though it was with possible sorrow.

5. a. Applied technically to classes of goods, manufactured articles, breeds of animals, etc. of more than a defined or usual weight. Hence **b.** *transf.* Connected or concerned with the manufacture, carriage, etc. of such articles. Esp. in phr. ***heavy industry***. Hence ***heavy-industrial*** adj. Also ***heavy chemicals***: see CHEMICAL *a.* 6 b.

1617 MORYSON *Itin.* III. 56 They have not heavy luggage. *Ibid.* 95 They have a race of heavy Horses. **1883** MRS. CROKER *Pretty Miss Neville* xiii. (1884) 110 Your heavy baggage—is it all right? **1887** *Daily News* 2 May 2/7 In heavy woollens..there is a little more doing. **1895** *Ibid.* 3 Jan. 5/3 Precedence is as usual given to the exhibition of heavy horses, colloquially known as 'shires'.

b. 1888 *Lit. World* 7 Sept. 179/1 The father became a curate in the Heavy Woollen District of Yorkshire. **1894** *Daily News* 19 Mar. 3/7 Those engaged in the heavy steel trades. **1896** *Westm. Gaz.* 9 July 6/1 The passenger lines have secured gains on increases a year ago, but on some of the 'heavy' lines less satisfactory results are shown. **1932** *Times* 5 Jan. 11/2 The Central Committee of the Communist Party has decided to reorganize the Union Supreme Economic Council, which is to be styled Commissariat of Heavy Industries. **1938** *Archit. Rev.* LXXXIII. 117/2 The majority of 'heavy' industries are of the latter type. **1938** *Times* 17 Feb. 16/1 The comparatively high price of iron and steel in Japan (a result of the artificial character of heavy-industrial growth in a country with insufficient ore and unsuitable coal). **1944** J. S. HUXLEY *On Living in Rev.* I. iii. 6 The deliberate encouragement of heavy industry under a Five Year Plan, at the expense of all other kinds of enterprise which would have flourished in a *laisser-faire* economy, is the most clear-cut example. **1957** L. F. R. WILLIAMS *State of Israel* 44 The raw materials required by her expanding heavy and light industries.

6. a. Applied to ordnance of the larger kind. Also applied to aerial bombs.

1727–51 CHAMBERS *Cycl.* s.v. *Artillery*, There was no attacking such a place for want of heavy artillery. **1813** WELLINGTON in Gurw. *Desp.* X. 479, I have not by me the state of the heavy ordnance and stores which were sent. **1828** WEBSTER s.v., *Heavy metal*, in military affairs, signifies large guns, carrying balls of a large size, or it is applied to large balls themselves. **1844** H. H. WILSON *Brit. India* II. 24 Heavy guns were brought up..and preparations were made to carry the fort by storm. **1889** *Cent. Dict.*, s.v. *Artillery*, *Heavy Artillery* [U.S.], all artillery not formed into batteries or equipped for field evolutions. **1917** 'CONTACT' *Airman's Outings* 206 A line of narrow-nosed buses, with heavy bombs fitted under the lower planes, ready to leave for their objective.

b. fig. ***heavy metal***: see quot.

1882 OGILVIE s.v., *Heavy metal*, guns or shot of large size; hence, *fig.* ability, mental or bodily; power, influence; as, he is a man of heavy metal; also, a person or persons of great ability or power, mental or bodily; used generally of one who is or is to be another's opponent in any contest; as, we had to do with heavy metal. (Colloq.)

7. *Mil.* Carrying heavy arms or equipment; heavily armed or equipped: said chiefly of soldiers (who are themselves usually specially selected for their height and weight). ***heavy (marching) order***: see quot. 1883. (Cf. B. 1.) Also of military aircraft, descriptive of a large type of bombing aeroplane.

1836 *Penny Cycl.* VI. 389/1 The heavy cavalry in general carry carabines, pistols and swords; and the light cavalry very small carabines, pistols, and sabres. **1838** THIRLWALL *Greece* V. 43 To raise an army of 20,000 heavy infantry and 500 cavalry. **1844** *Regul. & Ord. Army* 55 To be frequently paraded, and exercised at least once a week in Heavy Marching Order. **1869** E. A. PARKES *Pract. Hygiene* (ed. 3) 394 The soldier..when he marches in time of peace in heavy order, carries his pack, kit, haversack. **1883** H. P. SMITH *Gloss. Terms & Phr.*, *Heavy order* or *heavy marching order*, that of a soldier equipped and carrying, besides his arms and ammunition, complete kit, and great coat, amounting altogether to about 60 pounds. **1885** TENNYSON (*title*) Charge of the Heavy Brigade. **1921** *Flight* XIII. 615/2 The S.E.5's made the first attack, and dropped about 40 25-lb Cooper bombs, with the object of..preparing the way for the heavy bombers. **1939** *War Illustr.* 18 Dec. 459 Described as modern heavy bombers, these 'planes of the Red Air Force are certainly larger than any standard bomber in the British Air Force.

II. Expressing the action or operation of things physically weighty.

8. Having great momentum; striking or falling with force or violence.

1375 BARBOUR *Bruce* II. 369 He him-selff..Sa hard and hewy dyntis gave. **1500–20** DUNBAR *Poems* lxix. 7 With haill, and hevy schouris. **1590** SPENSER *F.Q.* I. viii. 18 The stroke upon his shield so heavie lites. **1663** BUTLER *Hud.* I. ii. 871 Like feather-bed betwixt a wall And heavy brunt of cannon ball. **1805** in Nicolas *Nelson's Disp.* (1846) VII. 166 *note*, The Enemy opened a very heavy fire on the Royal Sovereign. **1857** HUGHES *Tom Brown* I. v, They mean heavy play and no mistake. **1865** GOSSE *Land & Sea* (1874) 5 A heavy sea running outside. **1888** MRS. ALEXANDER *Life Interest* I. x. 198 A heavy thunderstorm came on.

9. a. Of ground, a road, etc.: That clings or hangs heavily to the spade, feet, wheels, etc., and thus impedes motion or manipulation; soft and tenacious. Also *transf.*

1577 B. GOOGE *Heresbach's Husb.* I. (1586) 22 b, If you breake up newe ground, yf it be riche, heavie, and prepared for seede, it suffiseth to plowe it once. **1710** S. SEWALL *Diary* 1 Dec. (1879) II. 294 The ways were heavy. **1720** DE FOE *Capt. Singleton* vi. (1840) 105 The sand was nowhere so deep and heavy. **1827** WHATELY *Logic* I. III. (1836) 181 Universally what are called heavy soils are specifically the lightest. **1837** *Boston Herald* 3 Jan. 2 Scarcely any of the mail-coaches arrived in London before half-past 8 o'clock, owing to the heavy state of the roads. **1855** THOREAU *Cape Cod* iii. (1894) 34 That we should find it very 'heavy' walking in the sand. **1864** *Lillywhite's Cricket Ann.* 44 The ground was so heavy from recent rains.

b. *Golf.* Of a ball: lying in sand.

1886 H. HUTCHINSON *Hints Game Golf* 39 When lying 'heavy'..bear in mind that it is better to hit the ball with the iron than to miss it with a spoon.

10. That weighs upon the stomach; difficult of digestion.

1574 NEWTON *Health Mag.* L ij, Mullets and Barbilles..fried..are heauie and hard to digest. **1661** LOVELL *Hist. Anim. & Min.* Introd., The flesh of the males is more strong, dry, and heavy of digestion. **1708** SWIFT *Remarks* Wks. 1883 VIII. 127 It may lie heavy on her stomach, that she will grow too big to get back into her hole. **1842** J. WILSON *Ess.*, *Health* (1856) 172 Bacon is a coarse and heavy food.

11. ***heavy in, on (upon) hand***: said of a horse that bears or hangs on the bit. Also *fig.*

1682 *Lond. Gaz.* No. 1708/4 A Spring Snaffle, that Commandeth with the greatest ease imaginable, all hard-mouthed Run-away Horses..and those that ride heavy in hand. **1831** JOHNSON *Sportsm. Cycl.* s.v., A horse is said to be heavy in hand, when from want of spirit he goes sluggishly on, bearing his whole weight upon the bit. **1857** G. LAWRENCE *Guy Liv.* xi. 106 Poor Bella! how heavy on hand she will find him.

III. Weighty in import, grave, serious.

12. Of great import; weighty, important; serious, grave. Now *rare* or *Obs.*

971 *Blickl. Hom.* 101 Eac we maᵹon ᵹeþencean þæt þæt hefiᵹre is þæt man [etc.]. *c* **1000** *Ags. Gosp.* Matt. xxiii. 23 Ge forleton þa þing þe synt hefeᵹran [*c* **1160** *Hatton G.* hefeᵹeren], þære æ dom, and mildheortnysse, and ᵹeleafan. *a* **1225** *Ancr. R.* 76 For þe seldspeche hire wordes weren heuie, and hefden much mihte. **1596** SHAKS. *1 Hen. IV*, II. iii. 66 Some heauie businesse hath my Lord in hand. **1601** —— *All's Well* II. v. 49 Trust him not in matter of heauie consequence. **1890** *Spectator* 6 Dec., To make a graver, and, if we may be allowed the adjective, a heavier speech.

13. Grave, severe, deep, profound, intense.

c **1000** *Eccl. Inst.* xxvii. in Thorpe *Anc. Laws* II. 424 Hwa ..on swa hefiᵹe scylde ᵹehreose. *c* **1050** *Byrhtferth's Handboc* in *Anglia* VIII. 320 Wið hefiᵹum synnum. *a* **1123** *O.E. Chron.* an. 1106 Ðises ᵹeares eac wæron swiðe hefiᵹe and sinlice ᵹewinn betwux þam Casere..and his sunu. *c* **1175** *Lamb. Hom.* 51 Ulcne mon..þet lið in heuie sunne. *c* **1200** ORMIN 10028 Full of hefiȝ dwilde. **1594** HOOKER *Eccl. Pol.* I. i. §1 A number of heauie preiudices, deepely rooted in the hearts of men. **1596** DALRYMPLE tr. *Leslie's Hist. Scot.* III. 196 *margin*, The hayuie hatred and Jnuie of the Pechtes towarde the Scottis. **1603** KNOLLES *Hist. Turks* (1621) 827 A dead march sounded, and heavy silence commanded to be kept through all the campe. **1801** STRUTT *Sports & Past.* II. i. 50 In the sixteenth century we meet with heavy complaints respecting the disuse of the long-bow. **1820** SHELLEY *Œdipus* I. 371 The heaviest sin on this side of the Alps! **1861** DICKENS *Lett.* (1880) II. 138 You have read in the papers of our heavy English frost.

b. Of an amatory relationship: intense, intensive; spec. ***heavy petting***, non-coital physical contact between two people, involving sexual stimulation of the genitals.

1952 M. R. RINEHART *Pool* xii. 111 He has a sort of heavy date here with a girl called Janey. **1959** 'M. NEVILLE' *Sweet Night for Murder* vii. 76 Duncan was making a very heavy pass at Cathy. **1960** 'M. CAINE' *S Man* 126 What is called 'heavy petting' in which frank exploration of each other's bodies is permitted. **1968** M. RICHLER *Cocksure* xviii. 111 His thirteen-year-old daughter was the only girl in the fifth form to stop at..*heavy* petting. **1972** *Daily Tel.* 29 Jan. 2/6 Heavy petting between boys and girls is not discouraged and intercourse is described in some detail.

IV. Having the aspect, effect, sound, etc. of heaviness.

14. a. Of the sky, clouds, etc.: Overcast with dark clouds; lowering, gloomy.

1583 STANYHURST *Æneis* III. (Arb.) 89 Thee welken is heauye. **1596** BP. W. BARLOW *Three Serm.* Ded. 82 Who so obserued our heauie heauens. **1876** MRS. ALEXANDER *Her Dearest Foe* I. 304 A mild, heavy day.

b. *fig.*, esp. in phr. ***to make heavy weather of***: to make (unnecessary) fuss or labour over.

1915 [see WEATHER *sb.* 2 c]. **1955** *Times* 21 July 8/5 The Geneva conference ran into heavy weather this morning, but made some ground later. **1957** *Listener* 24 Oct. 664/1 He makes rather heavy weather of the difference. **1960** V. GIELGUD *To Bed at Noon* I. xii. 92 Aren't you making rather heavy weather out of nothing?

15. Having comparatively much thickness or substance; thick, coarse; also, massive in conformation or outline; wanting in gracefulness, lightness, elegance, or delicacy. ***heavy face*** (***type***): see FACE *sb.* 22.

1818 SCOTT *Rob Roy* vi, The good humour and content which was expressed in their heavy features. *Ibid.* xix, We feel that its appearance is heavy, yet that the effect produced would be destroyed were it lighter or more ornamental. **1859** JEPHSON *Brittany* v. 54 The church, like most of the purely monastic buildings..is heavy. **1886** F. L. SHAW *Col. Cheswick's Camp.* I. x. 217 With heavy renaissance porch and wide spreading flight of granite steps. **1891** [see FACE *sb.* 22]. *a* **1898** *Mod.* The heavy lines of the drawing. Make a heavier stroke. His handwriting is heavy and clumsy. **1898** J. SOUTHWARD *Mod. Printing* I. xxii. 140 The first would be called a *light face*, and the second a *heavy face*.

16. Having a sound like that made by a weighty object; loud and deep.

1810 SCOTT *Lady of L.* I. i, The deep-mouthed blood-hound's heavy bay Resounded up the rocky way. **1819** SHELLEY *Julian* 97 Listen well If you hear not a deep and heavy bell. **1845** *Hawkstone* (1846) I. xxvii. 383 One heavy tramp he could hear close at his side.

†**17. a.** Of an accent: = GRAVE. *Obs.*

1589 PUTTENHAM *Eng. Poesie* II. vi[i]. (Arb.) 92 To the lowest and most base because it seemed to fall downe rather then to rise vp, they gaue the name of the heauy accent.

b. Of a line in Old English verse: containing more than the normal number of stressed elements. Also, more generally, opp. to LIGHT *a.*[1] 12.

1893 J. LAWRENCE *Chapt. Allit. Verse* 46 Verses with double alliteration are as a rule heavier than those with single. **1948** *Mod. Philol.* XLVI. 81 These heavy and extra-heavy verses, are the exceptions. **1958** A. J. BLISS *Metre of Beowulf* 8 There are also many verses which contain three stressed elements instead of the normal two: blæd | wide | sprang 18 b... All verses of this kind are here termed 'heavy' verses.

V. Having the slow or dull action of what is weighty.

18. Of persons, their qualities, etc.: Ponderous and slow in intellectual processes; wanting in facility, vivacity, or lightness; †slow of understanding, inapprehensive, dull, stupid (*obs.*).

c **1300** *Cursor M.* 27789 (Cott. Galba) Slewth..makes a man lath for to lere, And heuy in hert sarmon to here. **1340** *Ayenb.* 31 Þe man is zuo heui þet ne louep bote to ligge and resti and slepe. *a* **1400–50** *Alexander* 2708 Bot parde, þi prouidence impossible it semes, A heuy As to be houyn vp to þe sternes. **1604** SHAKS. *Oth.* II. i. 144 Oh heauy ignorance: thou praisest the worst best. **1667** PEPYS *Diary* (1877) V. 71 The heaviest man in the country. *a* **1700** B. E. *Dict. Cant. Crew*, *A heavy Fellow*, a dull Blockish Slug. **1709** STEELE *Tatler* No. 132 ¶1 A Set of heavy honest Men, with whom I have passed many Hours with much Indolence. **1873** LOWELL *Among my Bks.* Ser. II. 259 If there is anything worse..it is a heavy man when he fancies he is being facetious.

19. Acting or moving slowly, clumsily, or with difficulty; wanting in briskness or alacrity; slow, sluggish; unwieldy. **a.** of material objects.

a **1400–50** *Alexander* 5572 With heuy hedis and hoge as horses it were. **1538** STARKEY *England* I. iii. 79 Of them..we haue ouer many, wych altogyddur make our polytyke body vnweldy and heuy, and, as hyt were, to be greuyd wyth grosse humorys. **1595** SHAKS. *John* III. iii. 43 If that surly spirit melancholy Had bak'd thy bloud, and made it heauy, thicke. **1674** N. COX *Gentl. Recreat.* (1677) 214 More creese than the Lanner, and more heavy and sluggish in her flight. *a* **1700** DRYDEN *Pyth. Phil.* Wks. 1808 XII. 221 His heels too

heavy, and his head too light. **1808** Wellington in Gurw. *Desp.* IV. 45, I understand that some of the transports you have with you are heavy sailers. **1844** Mrs. Browning *Brown Rosary* II. 77 He flapped his heavy wing all brokenly and weak. **1962** *Which?* (Car Suppl.) Oct. 117/1 The Riley 4/72's steering was somewhat heavy and imprecise. *Ibid.* 119/2 The Ford Taunus foot brake was not too heavy at 30 mph but needed a great deal of pressure for gentle stops at 60 mph.

b. of abstract things.

1590 Shaks. *Mids. N.* v. i. 375 The heauy gate [gait] of night. **1595** —— *John* iv. i. 47 Still and anon cheer'd vp the heauy time. **1690** Locke *Hum. Und.* To Rdr., The diversion of some of my idle and heavy Hours. **1816** Byron *Parisina* xx, Sleepless nights and heavy days.

c. Time is said *to lie* or *hang heavy*, when its passage seems slow and tedious.

1703 Farquhar *Inconstant* v. iii, My time lies heavy on my hands. **1794** Mann in *Lett. Lit. Men* (Camden) 444 My time does not hang heavy on my hands. **1833** Tennyson *Clara Vere de Vere* 65 If Time be heavy on your hands, Are there no beggars at your gate, Nor any poor about your lands?

d. Of market conditions.

1831 *Lincoln Herald* 30 Sept. 1 The oat trade is heavy, and this grain may be quoted full 1*s.* per qr. under our last quotation. **1843** *Times* 20 May 7/3 The English securities were heavy again to-day. **1935** *Economist* 2 Feb. 261/2 Japanese bonds were heavy. **1962** S. Strand *Marketing Dict.* 339 *Heavy market*, a market of declining prices.

e. *heavy going*: see going *vbl. sb.* 4 a.

20. a. Of things, esp. artistic or literary productions: Wanting in vivacity; dull; ponderous; tedious, uninteresting.

1601 Holland *Pliny* II. 533 Polygnotus the Thasian.. represented much variety of countenance, far different from the rigorous and heauy looke of the visage beforetime. **1638** F. Junius *Paint. of Ancients* 61 Without such a force of phantasie the whole labour of their braines will be but a heavie, dull, and life-lesse piece of worke. **1708** Swift *Remarks* Wks. 1883 VIII. 111 It may still be a wonder how so heavy a book..should survive to three editions. **1846** Wright *Ess. Mid. Ages* II. xix. 257 The longer poems..of the first half of the fourteenth century are dull and heavy. **1863** Mrs. C. Clarke *Shaks. Char.* xv. 383 This play..has been denominated a 'heavy one', which means that it is not distinguished by various and rapid action, or abrupt and startling incident.

b. Of newspapers, journals, etc.: serious, addressed to the serious-minded.

1874 Trollope *Way we live Now* (1875) I. xxx. 187 Old Splinter,..who had written for the heavy quarterlies any time this last forty years, professed that he saw through the article. **1967** *Listener* 7 Dec. 743/1 The editors of the heavy dailies.

c. orig. in Jazz and popular music, used in various senses to designate something profound, serious, etc. *colloq.*

1937 B. Goodman *This Thing called Swing* 9 *Mugging heavy*: soft swing with a heavy beat. **1940** *Swing* July 17 Very fast semi-boogie blues in Gabriel with nasty, heavy off-beat drumming. **1958** Blesh & Janis *They all played Ragtime* vi. 117 *Victory Rag*, a 'heavy' number of great difficulty, went on the market in 1921. **1959** 'F. Newton' *Jazz Scene* xiv. 261 Jazz is not simply an ordinary music, light or heavy. **1969** *Rolling Stone* 28 June 38/4 Bass player wanted for heavy blues-rock band. **1969** *It* 4–17 July 10/2 The Rolling Stones..are well supported by such swingin' outfits as..the very heavy Third Ear Band. **1970** *Time* 17 Aug. 32 Marcuse is heavy stuff. **1971** *It* 2–16 June 2/1 The Bournemouth drug squad (reputed to be one of the heaviest squads in the country). **1972** *Last Whole Earth Catalog* (Portola Inst.) 30/1 Not heavy stuff about what is terrible or what should happen, but how to remake life and stay alive in the process. **1972** *Southerly* XXXII. 101 We talk about this and that and where's the heavy dope scene now.

d. *heavy metal*, a type of loud, vigorous rock music characterized by the use of electronically amplified instruments (typically guitar, bass, and drums), a heavy (usu. fast) beat, intense or spectacular performance, and often a clashing, harsh musical style; formerly identified with *hard rock*. Freq. *attrib.* or as *adj. phr.*

[**1964** W. S. Burroughs *Nova Express* 66 At this point we got a real break in the form of a defector from The Nova Mob: Uranian Willy The Heavy Metal Kid.] [**1968** M. Bonfire *Born to be Wild* (*sheet music*) 2, I like smoke and lightning, Heavy metal thunder.] **1973** *Crawdaddy* Nov. 81/2 They find no comfort in glitter or Heavy Metal – Black Sabbath, Black Oak Arkansas and their ilk. **1975** Carr & Tyler *Beatles* 76 By far the best of the four [songs] was Lennon's heavy-metal 'Hey, Bulldog'. **1976** *New Musical Express* 17 Apr. 14/5 The superb 'Action'..easily the strongest piece of commercialized heavy-metal to appear throughout 1975. **1977** *Rolling Stone* 13 Jan. 5/2 Heavy metal kings Black Sabbath inspire some of the most rabid followers in all of rock fandom. **1980** *Daily Mirror* 10 Apr. 12/2 The names of Heavy Metal groups like Deep Purple and Motorhead are inscribed on the back of his leather jacket. **1985** *Sounds* 27 July 29/4 It's a strange and dangerous music, this heavy metal. **1986** *Daily News* (N.Y.) 23 May 36/3 It's not Sergio Valente Queens, it's heavy metal, but very polite. They wear stiletto heels and all that hair.

21. a. In *Theatrical phrase*: Sober, serious; relating or pertaining to the representation of sombre or tragic parts; as *heavy villain*, *heavy business*.

1814 Jane Austen *Mansf. Park* I. xv. 301 'Anhalt' is a heavy part. **1823** *Drama* IV. 209 Mr. Hillington takes the heavy line of business. **1826** Disraeli *Viv. Grey* v. xii, The regular dramatic performance was thought too heavy a business for the evening. *a* **1828** J. Bernard *Retrosp. Stage* (1830) I. 13 The Company consisted of a heavy man, who played the tyrants in tragedy. **1833** R. Dyer *9 Yrs. of Actor's Life* 237 This gentleman possesses natural requisite and acquired talents of the first order in heavy tragedy. **1838** Dickens *Nich. Nick.* xxii, I played the heavy children when I was eighteen months old. **1858** H. J. Byron *Maid & Magpie* 35 Such a heavy villin. **1860** G. Vandenhoff *Dramatic Rem.* 176 There was no heavy lady for the Emilias and Lady Macbeths. **1868** Helps *Realmah* viii. (1876) 230 As the heavy villain at the Surrey Theatre would say. **1870** T. A. Brown *Hist. Amer. Stage* 54/1 In California she played all lines of business, from walking ladies to heavy, and juvenile leading. **1884** [see lead *sb.*² 7]. **1885** W. C. Day *Behind Footlights* 113 Practising attitudes before the cheval glass we have the heavy gentleman, chronic villain of the footlights. **1901** C. Morris *Life on Stage* 40 Then came the leading lady, the first old woman (who was sometimes the heavy woman). **1909** J. R. Ware *Passing Eng.* 151/2 *Heavy merchant*, man who plays the villain. **1941** *Picturegoer* 26 July 6/1 John [Barrymore] started off in heavy drama.

b. Also, ponderously dignified; stern, repressive, unbending: esp. *heavy father*, *heavy uncle*, which are also used as attrib. phrases (= sternly paternal or avuncular). orig. *Theatrical slang.*

1849 Thackeray *Pendennis* I. xxix. 281 Those parts in the drama, which we called the heavy fathers. **1853** 'C. Bede' *Verdant Green* v. 42 He took an affectionate farewell of his son, somewhat after the manner of the 'heavy fathers' of the stage. **1858** H. J. Byron *Maid & Magpie* 4 A Fine Specimen of the good old Heavy Father of Melodrama. **1864** H. Morley *Jrnl.* (1866) 339 A heavy father in broad farce. **1898** Rider Haggard *Doctor Therne* iii, Sir John..received me in his best 'heavy-father' manner. **1931** *Daily Express* 31 Jan. 15/2 The heavy uncle attitude. **1931** *Times Lit. Suppl.* 13 Aug. 613/4 The Venetian Pantalone becomes the Atellane 'heavy father' Pappus. **1956** 'M. Westmacott' *Burden* II. iii. 83 Really, Laura dear, you might be at least fifty. A heavy Victorian father rather than a sister.

VI. That weighs or presses hardly or sorely on the senses or feelings.

†**22. a.** Of persons: Oppressive; troublesome, annoying; angry; severe, violent. *Obs.*

c **825** *Vesp. Psalter* liv. 4 [lv. 3] Onhældon in mec unrehtwisnisse and in eorre hefie werun me. *c* **1000** *Ags. Ps.* (Th.) liv. [lv.] 3 Wurdon me þa on yrre yfele and hefiȝe. **1382** Wyclif *Luke* xviii. 5 Netheles for this widowe is heuy [*gloss*, or diseseful] to me, I schal venge hir. **1388** *Ibid.* xi. 7 Nyle thou be heuy to me. *c* **1400** *Destr. Troy* 12320 Eneas with anger was angardly heuy With Antenor the traytor. **1452** in *Paston Lett.* I. Introd. 72, I..am informed that the King, my sovereign lord, is my heavy lord, greatly displeased with me. **1476** Sir J. Paston *Ibid.* No. 771 III. 153 It is demyd that my lady wolde herafftr be the rather myn hevy lady ffor that delyng. **1579–80** North *Plutarch* (1676) 902 Above all others Fabius Maximus was his heavy Enemy. **1628** Hobbes *Thucyd.* (1822) 38 You would have been no less heavy to the confederates than we. **1703** J. Logan in *Pa. Hist. Soc. Mem.* IX. 225 Who groan to find their deliverer prove so heavy.

†**b.** *heavy friend*: a troublesome or evil friend; an enemy. So *heavy father*. *Obs.*

c **1510** Barclay *Mirr. Gd. Manners* (1570) F iij, If this ioconde person would alter his visage, And counterfayt in chere an heavy father sage. **1554** in Strype *Eccl. Mem.* III. xxiii. 193 Sir, I perceive that thou art my heavy friend. **1600** Holland *Livy* xlii. xiv. 1124 He..was an heavier friend unto Asia than Antiochus had bene. **1611** Speed *Hist. Gt. Brit.* ix. xx. §4 Some..thinke him to haue beene an heauy Father to the Common-wealth. **1621** Molle *Camerar. Liv. Libr.* I. iii. 8 This woman while she liued was an heauie friend of mine.

c. *heavy man*: a criminal or law-breaker. *U.S. slang.*

1926 J. Black *You can't Win* xx. 302 It was the kind of safe that discouraged the 'heavy man' (safe breaker). **1963** H. L. Mencken *Amer. Lang.* (ed. 4) 730 *Heavy man*, one transporting narcotics.

23. Hard to bear, endure, or withstand; oppressive, grievous, sore; distressful.

a **1000** *Laws Ælfred* I. c. 49 §3 (Schmid) þæt ure ȝeferan sume..eow hefiȝran [wisan budan] to healdanne. *c* **1200** Ormin 1442 Harrd and hefiȝ pine. **1340** Hampole *Pr. Consc.* 4583 Þe days þat er ille and hevy. *c* **1440** *Promp. Parv.* 239/1 Hevy and grevows, *gravis*. **1567** *Satir. Poems Reform.* xi. 21 My hauie hap and piteous plicht. **1592** Timme *10 Eng. Lepers* D ij, Wherewithall they carie the heavie vengeance of God. **1607** Shaks. *Cor.* v. vi. 143 Ile..endure Your heauiest Censure. **1667** Milton *P.L.* xii. 103 Who for the shame Don to his Father, heard this heavie curse. **1703** Maundrell *Journ. Jerus.* (1732) 145 Let. p. 2 [They] hold their own Slaves in the heaviest Bondage. **1844** *Mem. Babylonian P'cess* II. 46 Universally regarded as a heavy calamity. **1867** Trollope *Chron. Barset* I. xl. 349 The world has been very heavy on him.

24. a. Hard to perform or accomplish; requiring much exertion; laborious, toilsome.

c **1250** *Gen. & Ex.* 2565 For al ðat swinc heui & sor. *c* **1391** Chaucer *Astrol.* Prol., Curio[u]s enditing and hard sentence is ful heuy atones for swich a child to lerne. **1577–87** Holinshed *Scot. Chron.* (1805) II. 288 Certain factious persons did beat into their ears, how heavie a journie that would be unto them. **1611** Bible *Exod.* xviii. 18 This thing is too heauy for thee; thou art not able to performe it thy selfe alone. **1855** Macaulay *Hist. Eng.* III. 537 The work, he said, was heavy; but it must be done. **1887** Ruskin *Præterita* II. v. 170 The day had been a heavy one.

b. *heavy-duty* (see duty 6), used *attrib.*, of a machine, material, etc., designed to deal with heavy materials or to be suitable to stand up to hard wear. Also *transf.*

1914 *Engineering* 4 Dec. 670/2 (*caption*) Heavy-Duty Drilling-Machine. **1935** *Discovery* July 202/1 Fireproof materials can be substituted for practically every form of heavy duty cloth. **1958** *Listener* 20 Nov. 839/3 The heavy-duty rubber tyre. **1964** *English Studies* XLV. 426 Special attention has been given to 'heavy-duty' words such as *have*. **1969** *Computers & Humanities* III. 137 A stand-alone device which consists of a magnetic tape unit, keyboard, and heavy-duty selectric typewriter.

25. a. Causing or occasioning sorrow; distressing, grievous, saddening; sad, sorrowful.

c **1374** Chaucer *Compl. Mars* 12 The glad nyght ys worthe an heuy morowe. *c* **1489** Caxton *Sonnes of Aymon* xxii. 492 Your departyng is so hevy to me that I trowe I shall deye for sorow. **1568** Grafton *Chron.* II. 626 Where he without great solempnitie kept a heavie Christmasse. **1600** Holland *Livy* 1241 These proved in effect to be unfortunate and heavie presages [*auspicia tristia*] unto Mancinus. **16..** *Chevy Chase* II. 19 in *Percy's Reliq.*, It was a hevy syght to se. **1719** De Foe *Crusoe* II. x, This was a heavy piece of news to my nephew. **1827** Carlyle *Misc.* (1857) I. 30 To the great body of mankind this were heavy news.

†**b.** *heavy hill*: the ascent to Tyburn; the way to the gallows. *Obs.*

1577 Gascoigne *Arraignm. Lover* in *Brit. Bibl.* (1810) I. 76 Thou must go hence to Heavy Hill; And there be hang'd all but the head. **1678** Dryden *Kind Keeper* iv. i, I saw you follow him up the heavy hill to Tyburn.

26. Oppressive to the bodily sense; overpowering.

c **1375** *Sc. Leg. Saints, Ninian* 702, And vaknit as of hewy slepe. **1697** Dryden *Virg. Georg.* iv. 583 His Eyes with heavy Slumber overcast. **1845** Mrs. S. C. Hall *Whiteboy* ii. 9 The heavy smell of the oil. *Mod.* The poppy has a heavy smell.

VII. Weighed down mentally or physically.

27. a. 'Weighed down' with sorrow or grief; sorrowful, sad, grieved, despondent.

a **1300** *Cursor M.* 12625 Wit heui hert and druppand chere. *c* **1330** R. Brunne *Chron.* (1810) 18 He felt him heuy & ferly seke. *c* **1400** *Sowdone Bab.* 400 Tho sorowede alle the Citesyns And were full hevy than. *c* **1450** *St. Cuthbert* (Surtees) 7369 Þe bischop semed to be heuy, þe kirke was left sa unsemely. **1526** *Pilgr. Perf.* (W. de W. 1531) 87 Consyderyng some persones to be iocunde and mery, some sadde and heuy. **1634** Rutherford *Lett.* (1862) I. 113 Her husband is absent and I think she will be heavy. **1725** Pope *Odyss.* ix. 117 With heavy hearts we labour thro' the tyde, To coasts unknown, and oceans yet untry'd. **1859** Tennyson *Elaine* 1284 For this most gentle maiden's death Right heavy am I. **1863** Fr. A. Kemble *Resid. in Georgia* 34 With a heart heavy enough.

b. Expressing or indicative of grief, doleful.

a **1225** *Ancr. R.* 342 Heui murnunge. *c* **1275** *XI Pains of Hell* 170 in *O.E. Misc.* 216 Poule he weppid with heue chere. **14..** Hoccleve *Min. Poems* (1892) 67, I walkid..Besyde a groue in an heuy musynge. **1568** Grafton *Chron.* II. 217 Then answered he with heavie chere: alas, alas, am not I here in prison, and at your owne will? **1603** Knolles *Hist. Turks* (1621) 82 With floods of teares abundantly running down their heavie countenances. **1827** Pollok *Course T.* II, Who farther sings, must change the pleasant lyre To heavy notes of woe.

28. 'Weighed down' by sleep, weariness, or some physical depression or incapacity; hence, *esp.* weary from sleep, sleepy, drowsy.

1382 Wyclif *Exod.* xvii. 12 The hoondes of Moyses weren heuy. *c* **1385** Chaucer *L.G.W.* 885 *Thisbe*, On hire he caste hise hevy dedly eyen. *c* **1440** *Promp. Parv.* 239/1 Hevy a-slepe.., *somnolentus*. **1526** Tindale *Matt.* xxvi. 43 He..founde them aslepe agayne. For there eyes were hevy. **1587** Turberv. *Trag. T.* (1837) 152 And stole upon the heavie prince, That slumbring long had byn. **1620** Venner *Via Recta* v. 86 It will make the head heauy by repleating it with vapors. **1760** C. Johnston *Chrysal* (1822) II. 247, I thought I had overslept myself—I am so heavy. **1843** Hood *Song of Shirt* i, With fingers weary and worn, With eyelids heavy and red.

VIII. Transferred from action to agent.

29. That does what is expressed heavily (in various senses).

1816 *Sporting Mag.* XLVIII. 181 The heavy betters began to quake at this change of things. **1856** Froude *Hist. Eng.* (1858) II. viii. 305 To pardon so heavy an offender. **1884** *Sword & Trowel* Jan. 25, I have been a very heavy drinker. **1887** A. C. Gunter *Mr. Barnes of N.Y.* (1888) 95 Miss Anstruther..returns to the hotel a heavy loser. **1888** *Gardening* 25 Feb. 712/2 A heavy cropper and a good table Potato.

IX. 30. In other specialized uses (chiefly technical from I): **heavy bag**, a punch-bag; **heavy-clay**, *lit.* (see 9); *fig.* an agricultural labourer; **heavy drawer**, in coining, a drawer into which coins exceeding the standard weight are dropped; **heavy drift-ice**, **heavy ice** (see quot.); **heavy-earth** = baryta; **heavy franc**, name given to the new franc, equivalent to 100 old francs, introduced in France in 1960; **heavy gunner**, *fig.* = *heavy swell*; **heavy mineral** (see quot. 1971); **heavy oil**, any oil of high specific gravity, orig. such an oil obtained from the distillation of coal-tar (cf. *dead oil* s.v. dead *a.* D. 2); **heavy pine**, a name of the *Pinus ponderosa*; **heavy-sizing**, **-wood** (see quots.); **heavy sugar** *U.S. slang*, 'big money' (see sugar *sb.* 2 c); **heavy swell** *colloq.* (with pun on *heavy swell* in sense 8), a man of showy or impressive appearance; one dressed in the height of fashion; **heavy-wooded pine**, the western yellow pine, *Pinus ponderosa*.

1950 J. Dempsey *Championship Fighting* 41 Canvas or leather 'dummy bag'—sometimes known as the '*heavy bag'. **1869** *Daily News* 8 Sept., These unfortunate *heavy-clays never dream of bettering their condition. **1887** *Pall Mall G.* 2 June 5/1 Should the coin being weighed prove too heavy, the pan into which it falls goes down, and the coin slips into a '*heavy' drawer. **1958** *Times* 29 Dec. 6/4 (*headline*) The '*Heavy' Franc... A new monetary unit is to be created [in France] worth 100 francs. It will be introduced gradually during the next 12 months. **1959** *Observer* 11 Oct. 3/8 The new 'heavy franc', which officially comes into use next January. **1890** Boldrewood *Col.*

Reformer (1891) 136 We can always find out and trace our '*heavy gunners'. **1835** Sir J. Ross *Narr. 2nd Voy.* Explan. Terms p. xv, **Heavy-ice*, that which has a great depth in proportion, and not in a state of decay. **1893** A. Geikie *Text-bk. Geol.* (ed. 3) ii. ii. 129 These *heavy minerals constitute sometimes as much as 4 per cent of the Bagshot sand. **1939** *Proc. Prehist. Soc.* V. 109 A heavy-mineral analysis of a sample of the sand. **1971** I. G. Gass et al. *Understanding Earth* xiii. 166/2 Rather more satisfactory from the point of view of recognising parent rocks is the presence of a small proportion (often less than 1%) of what are known as 'heavy minerals'. These have a greater specific gravity than the common minerals quartz and feldspar (hence the name), and are separated by breaking up the rocks and floating off the lighter minerals in a heavy liquid (bromo-form, S.G. 2.89 is commonly used). Assemblages of heavy minerals may be characteristic of certain groups of parent rocks. **1849** *Heavy oil [see *dead oil* s.v. dead *a.* D. 2]. **1913** V. B. Lewes *Oil Fuel* 129 The heavy tar oil, or 'creosote oil' forms a fairly good liquid fuel. The specific gravity is usually in the neighbourhood of 1.1, hence its name of 'heavy-oil', being heavier than water. *Ibid.* 180 Heavy oil engines. **1936** *Discovery* Feb. 37 Locomotives driven by heavy oil and electricity. **1880** *Nature* XXI. 299 Unscrupulous manufacturers introduced the practice of '*heavy-sizing'—that is, in plain terms, of substituting cheap mineral substances for cotton. **1926** Maines & Grant *Wise-Crack Dict.* 9/2 **Heavy sugar papa*, sweet old man with fat purse. **1928** *Flynn's* 4 Feb. 437/1 Johns with heavy sugar. **1819** *Heavy swell [see swell *sb.* 9 a]. **1830** Lady Granville *Lett.* (1894) II. 60 The people at Melton.. asking 'Who's that heavy swell?' **1883** Mrs. Croker *Pretty Miss Neville* xlii. (1884) 385 You ought to make a good match, you know, and marry some heavy swell with heaps of coin. **1884** Miller *Plant-n., Baroxylon rufum*, Red *Heavy-wood. **1836** P. & C. Lawson *Agriculturalist's Manual* 354 Pinus ponderosa—*Heavy Wooded Pine... Introduced by Mr. Douglas from the west coast of North America in 1828. **1858** J. A. Warder *Hedges & Evergreens* ii. 250 *Pinus ponderosa*, or Heavy-wooded Pine, has leaves from nine inches to a foot long. **1866** 'Senilis' *Pinaceæ* 125 *Pinus Ponderosa*: The Heavy-Wooded Pine. Introduced from North America nearly forty years ago. **1923** Dallimore & Jackson *Handbk. Coniferæ* 437 *Pinus ponderosa*, Douglas. Western Yellow Pine... Big Pine; Bull Pine; Heavy Pine; Heavy-wooded Pine.

31. *Comb.*, mostly parasynthetic, unlimited in number, as heavy-armed, -handed, etc.; also ***heavy-blossomed***, ***-browed***, †***-cheered***, ***-eyed***, ***-faced***, ***-fisted***, ***-footed***, ***-framed***, ***-fruited***, ***-heeled***, ***-jawed***, ***-jowled***, ***-lidded*** (so ***heavy-liddedness***), ***-limbed***, ***-lipped***, ***-mettled***, ***-mouthed***, ***-paced***, ***-priced***, ***-scented***, ***-set***, ***-shotted***, ***-shuttered***, ***-tailed***, ***-winged***, ***-witted***, etc.; also ***heavy-looking***, ***-seeming***. **heavy-faced**, having a heavy face (see face *sb.* 22 and sense 15 above); **heavy-timbered**, (*a*) thickly furnished with growing trees; (*b*) large-limbed.

1842 Tennyson *Locksley Hall* 163 Droops the *heavy-blossom'd bower, hangs the *heavy-fruited tree. **1377** Langl. *P. Pl.* B. xx. 2 *Heuy-chered I ȝede and elynge in herte. **1917** F. S. Henry *Printing for School & Shop* vii. 90 *Heavy-faced types are appropriate in printed matter for the iron and steel industry. **1625** Gill *Sacr. Philos.* viii. 116 As fast as our *heavy-footed reason can follow our faith. **1824** Miss Ferrier *Inher.* xvii, The great awkward heavy-footed maidservant. **1957** T. Gunn *Sense of Movement* 13 Here is a room with heavy-footed chairs. **1898** *Daily News* 14 Mar. 7/2 A *heavy-framed colt. *a* **1963** J. Fountain in B. James *Austral. Short Stories* (1963) 2nd Ser. 274 His heavy-framed bike loaded with packages. **1593** Shaks. *Rich. II*, iii. ii. 15 Let.. *heauie-gated Toades lye in their way. **1688** Bunyan *Heavenly Footman* (1886) 146 What, do ye think that every *heavy-heeled professor will have heaven? **1944** A. L. Rowse *Eng. Spirit* 88 That earlier Tudor type.. clean-shaven and *heavy-jowled. **1919** V. Woolf *Night & Day* xxvii. 390 Camels slanted their *heavy-lidded eyes at her. **1961** *New Yorker* 25 Feb. 129/1, I remember experiencing spells of heavy-liddedness during a fairly recent stage presentation of this talkfest. **1632** Sherwood, :*Heauie-looking, *halbrenné*. **1888** E. J. Goodman *Too Curious* iv, A dull, heavy-looking girl. **1598** Grenewey *Tacitus' Ann.* iii. vi. 73 He seemed drousie and *heauie metled. **1815** *Sporting Mag.* XLVI. 263 *Heavy-mouthed horses. **1906** *Westm. Gaz.* 4 Jan. 2/1 The *heavy-scented buds. **1908** *Ibid.* 7 Aug. 3/1 Never was such clover!.. heavy-scented, rich, and generous. **1938** D. Runyon *Furthermore* vii. 130 He is a *heavy-set guy. **1850** Tennyson *In Mem.* vi, His *heavy-shotted hammock-shroud. **1702** Vanbrugh *False Friend* i The dull, *heavy-tailed maukin melts him down with her modesty. **1831** J. W. Peck *Guide for Emigrants* ii. 40 The wide, level, and *heavy timbered alluvions, are.. unhealthy. **1861** Whyte Melville *Market Harb.* 7 Deep-ribbed, heavy-timbered hounds. **1903** S. E. White *Conjuror's House* iv. 39 The fort itself, a medley of heavy-timbered stockades and square block-houses. **1908** *Westm. Gaz.* 25 Aug. 7/1 A dark, heavy-timbered wood.

B. *sb.* [absolute use of the adj.]

1. a. *pl.* ***heavies***: heavy cavalry; the Dragoon Guards. Rarely in *sing.*

1841 Lever *C. O'Malley* lviii, We'd better call out the 'heavies' by turns. **1849** Thackeray *Pendennis* xlix, Have you.. never happened to be listening to the band of the Heavies at Brighton? **1876** Voyle *Milit. Dict.* (ed. 3) 86 In the British service there are 7 regiments of heavies, viz. the dragoon guards. The weight the horse of the heavies has to carry is over 19 stone. **1895** *Daily News* 19 Dec. 5/3 Old soldiers.. representing the Household Cavalry, the heavies, Lancers, Hussars.

b. ***the heavies***, the heavy artillery.

1908 *Daily Chron.* 6 Aug. 6/4 The excellent firing of the 4·7 guns by the First and Seconds (or, as they are more familiarly called, 'the Heavies'). **1916** 'Boyd Cable' *Action Front* 113 The Heavies as well as the Field guns were to bombard. **1918** E. M. Roberts *Flying Fighter* 57 Soon the field artillery and the 'heavies' woke up again.

c. A heavy bomber.

1943 *Time* 15 Nov. 26/2 Another co-ordinated series of punches.. cost the Allies only ten heavies, two Marauders and five fighters. **1944** *Even. Standard* 16 Dec. 1/4 Heavy bombers could be heard massing for an attack... Wave after wave of 'heavies' went out. **1961** W. Vaughan-Thomas *Anzio* viii. 164 In cold blood the heavies may not have done vital damage to the Germans forming up on the ground.

d. ***the heavies***, the serious newspapers, journals, etc. (see sense A. 20 b).

1950 C. Woodham-Smith *F. Nightingale* 310 In 1857 great influence was exercised by 'the heavies'—the quarterlies and the reviews. **1962** *Guardian* 5 Dec. 7/4, I was reading the Sunday papers... I picked up one of the two Heavies. **1962** 'O. Mills' *Headlines make Murder* viii. 89 All three 'heavies', *The Times*, *Telegraph* and.. *Guardian*. **1971** *Author* LXXXII. 101 The popular press, thrown off balance and uncertain of its role, lost out to the heavies and the provincials.

2. a. A stage wagon for the conveyance of goods.

1847 De Quincey *Schlosser's Lit. Hist.* Wks. VIII. 53 The very few old heavies that had begun to creep along three or four main roads.

b. Anything particularly large and weighty of its kind.

1897 *Daily News* 25 Nov. 5/1 Amongst the elephantine heavies is Mandarin, who killed a keeper during his last residence at Olympia. **1908** *Pall Mall Gaz.* 27 Mar. 12/3 Firms.. which have specialised in the manufacture of 'heavies' [*sc.* motor vehicles]. **1935** *Amer. Speech* X. 271/1 *Heavies*, very heavy beef cattle, more than two years old. **1960** *Farmer & Stockbreeder* 15 Mar. 6/2 Of the uncertified beasts, lightweights were more plentiful than heavies. **1965** *Listener* 8 Apr. 537/1 The 'heavies' are on the march. By 1970 there will be 120 trucks for every 100 there are now on our inadequate roads. **1968** *Times* 25 Oct. 25/3 (*heading*) 60 mph for 'heavies' [*sc.* motor vehicles].

c. A heavyweight boxing-match or boxer.

1913 J. G. B. Lynch *Compl. Amat. Boxer* 221, I remember in the finals of the heavies at the All-India Championship of 1909 seeing Private Clohessy.. take on Bombardier Wells. **1950** J. Dempsey *Championship Fighting* 16 Top-flight heavies like Frank Moran.

d. *pl. Racing.* Horses' work-shoes.

1930 *Times* 24 Mar. 4/2 It is almost impossible to tell by watching a horse walk in the parade ring whether he is plated, or whether he is carrying, to use a racing term, 'the heavies'.

e. A strongly built person, usu. of violent disposition.

1936 [see come *v.* 13 d]. **1962** R. Cook *Crust on its Uppers* i. 22 A good solid heavy like Chas to deal with the writ-servers. **1970** G. Greer *Female Eunuch* 194 Cherry is surrounded by threatening creatures, mostly the nightclub heavies. **1972** *Catholic Herald* 28 Jan. 2/5 Sit down, we want to talk to you... We are going out to get the 'heavies'. **1973** *Times* 12 July 4/1 Prostitutes were threatened with 'heavies' working for a man named Kenny Lynch.

3. Short for heavy wet. *slang.*

1823 *Spirit Pub. Jrnls.* (1824) 441 A drop of any thing beyond a pint of heavy. **1850** Kingsley *Alt. Locke* ii, Here comes the heavy. Hand it here to take the taste of that fellow's talk out of my mouth.

4. ***to do the heavy***: to swagger, to make a fine show. *slang.*

1884 *Gd. Words* June 399/2 Your ordinary thief, if he have a slice of luck, may 'do the heavy' while the luck lasts.

5. esp. *Theatr.* Short for *heavy actor*, *villain*, etc. Cf. sense A. 21.

1880 F. Belton *Random Recoll. Old Actor* viii. 132 Robertson (the celebrated author of 'Caste' 'School' etc. for 'second heavies'). **1906** S. Ford *Shorty McCabe* (1908) 70 So far it's as good as playin' leading heavy in 'The Shadows of a Great City'. **1928** *Observer* 22 July 15/2 The fun succumbed to a bucolic lethargy that was only partially shaken off by the retreat to Half Moon Street and the assault of the sentimental heavies. **1937** 'C. McCabe' *Face on Cutting-room Floor* vii. 53, I asked.. who the man was... 'That's Vic's new heavy.' **1961** J. McCabe *Mr. Laurel & Mr. Hardy* (1962) ii. 49, I always played a 'heavy'—you know, the villain. *Ibid.* ii. 57 The villains in those days were always called 'heavies'. Their trade-mark was usually *heavy* eyebrows and moustache make-up. **1962** J. D. Salinger *Franny & Zooey* 143 I'm sick to death of being the heavy in everybody's life... They're as happy as pigs till I show up. I feel like those dismal bastards Seymour's beloved Chuang-tzu warned everybody against. **1966** *Listener* 15 Dec. 890/2 Two of the chief characters are avowed communists, and yet are not the heavies plotting to overthrow the free world. **1973** J. Wainwright *Pride of Pigs* i. 178 Two of the heavies dived for Tallboy.

6. *pl.* The heavy trades or industries (see heavy *a.* 5); also, stocks or shares in such a trade or industry.

1900 *Westm. Gaz.* 26 Jan. 11/1 Hope for the Heavies. **1902** *Daily Chron.* 20 May 3/6 The ratio of working expenses for the past half-year on the North British railways was 49 per cent., compared with 65 per cent., or more, on the four 'heavies'. **1922** *Daily Tel.* 12 June 2/3 The prices of the other comparable 'heavies'—Great Western and London and North-Western—have also gone ahead.

heavy ('hiːvɪ), *a.*[2] [f. heave *sb.* 3 + -y.] Of a horse: Suffering from the heaves.

1864 in Webster, and in mod. Dicts.

heavy ('hɛvɪ), *adv.* [OE. *hefiȝe* = OHG. *hebîgo*, *hevîgo*; f. *hefiȝ* heavy *a.*] = heavily *adv.*

1. In a heavy manner; with weight, *lit.* and *fig.*; ponderously; massively; burdensomely, oppressively.

c **1000** *Ags. Ps.* (Th.) lvii[i]. 2 Forþan ðæs wite eft, on eowre handa, hefiȝe ȝeeode. *a* **1225** *Ancr. R.* 32 Heo liggeð mid iren heuie iveotered. *c* **1470** Henry *Wallace* x. 426 Hewy cled in to plait off maill. **1582** N. Lichefield tr. *Castanheda's Conq. E. Ind.* lxxviii. 158 b, The Boates went verye heavie laden with theyr furniture. **1600** J. Pory tr. *Leo's Africa* ii. 383 Holding their hands heavie over such as shewed themselves repugnant. **1611** Bible *Isa.* xlvi. 1 Your carriages were heauie loaden. **1703** Moxon *Mech. Exerc.* 17 Lean heavy upon it. **1790** Burke *Fr. Rev.* Wks. 1808 V. 403 The least likely to lean heavy on the active capital employed. **1828** Southey *Ess.* (1832) II. 231 The mortality.. fell heaviest upon the poor.

2. With laborious movement; slowly, sluggishly; laboriously.

1701 *Lond. Gaz.* No. 3715/4 Stolen.. a sorrel Gelding.. trots heavy. **1798** Nelson 7 Sept. in Nicolas *Disp.* (1845) III. 116 The Culloden sails so heavy, by having a sail under her bottom in order to stop her leak. **1803** *Naval Chron.* X. 157 The third [boat], from rowing heavy, did not get up.

†**3.** With displeasure or anger. See also *bear heavy*, bear *v.*[1] 16. *Obs.*

c **1380** Wyclif *Sel. Wks.* III. 359 Many men þenken ful hevy wiþ þis sentence. **1382** —— *Mark* x. 14 Whom whanne Jhesus hadde seyn, he baar heuye. **1430–40** Lydg. *Bochas* v. xxv. (1554) 138 b, Hatefull also to euery creature, And heauy borne of worthy kynges three. *c* **1565** Lindesay (Pitscottie) *Chron. Scot.* (1728) 38 The king took very heavy with this high contempt.

†**4.** Gravely, seriously. *Obs.*

1563 Winȝet *Four Scoir Thre Quest.* Wks. 1888 I. 106 Thai hef failȝeit hauelie.. and ȝe fer hauiar.

5. Now chiefly hyphened to participles which it qualifies. See also heavy-laden.

1553 Brende *Q. Curtius* 133 (R.) Dimichas y[t] were footemen, heauye-harnised, but yet rydyng on horsebacke. **1669** Dryden *Tyran. Love* iv. i, Gross, heavy-fed.. And shotted all without. **1836–48** B. D. Walsh *Aristoph., Clouds* i. iv, The pipe's heavy-echoing booming. **1840** Marryat *Poor Jack* x, A heavy-pulling boat. **1840** R. H. Dana *Bef. Mast* xv. 37 A large, heavy-moulded fellow. **1885** Howells *Silas Lapham* (1891) I. i. 45 Lapham's idea of hospitality was.. to bring a heavy-buying customer home to pot-luck.

†**heavy**, *v. Obs.* Forms: 1 **hefiȝian, hefeȝian**, 3 **heuegy, heueȝi**, 3–4 **heuien**, 4–6 **hevie, -ye**, (5 **euye**), 6 **heauy**, *Sc.* **hewie**. [OE. *hefiȝian*, *hefeȝian* = OHG. *hevîgôn*:—OTeut. **hebigôjan*, f. **hebigo-*, OE. *hefiȝ* heavy *a.*]

1. *trans.* To make heavy, burdensome, or oppressive.

c **825** *Vesp. Psalter* xxxi[i]. 4 Deȝes and naechtes ȝehefeȝad is ofer me hond ðin. *a* **1300** *E.E. Psalter* ibid., For over me, bathe dai and night, Hevied es þi hand of might. *c* **1440** *Promp. Parv.* 239/1 Hevyyn, or makyn hevy in wyghte, *gravo, aggravo, pondero.*

2. To weigh down; to burden; to oppress, grieve, distress.

c **897** K. Ælfred *Gregory's Past.* liv. 419 Se hund wile aspiwan ðone mete ðe hine hefiȝað on his breostum. *c* **900** tr. *Bæda's Hist.* iv. xxi. [xix.] (1890) 320 Heo wæs eft hefiȝad mid þæm ærrum sarum. *c* **1000** *Ags. Gosp.* Matt. xxvi. 43 Soðlice heora eaȝan wæron ȝehefeȝode. *c* **1200** *Trin. Coll. Hom.* 79 Þe fule lustes heuien þe sowle. **1382** Wyclif *2 Sam.* xiv. 26 Onys in the ȝeer he was doddid, for the heere heuyde [**1388** greuede] him. *c* **1430** *Pilgr. Lyf Manhode* i. xlix. (1869) 30 It is not matere of wratthe; it shulde not heuy yow of no thing. **1465** *Paston Lett.* No. 508 II. 200 Thei had hevyed the peple that dwelle ther and that gretly. **1553** Gau *Richt Vay* 62 Cum to me al ȝe quhilk ar hewit (that is with sine). **1581** Mulcaster *Positions* xx. (1887) 88 Darke and cloudie aire heauyeth.

3. *intr.* To grow heavy or weighty.

c **897** K. Ælfred *Gregory's Past.* xxi. 163 Hu sio byrðen wiexþ and hefeȝaþ. *c* **1305** *St. Christopher* 96 in *E.E.P.* (1862) 62 Eueree as he bar þis child: hit gan to heuye faste.

4. To become heavy through weariness or grief.

a **1000** *Guthlac* 956 in *Exeter Bk.* lf. 46 b, Leomu hefeȝedon, sarum ȝesohte. *c* **1275** Lay. 18408 Nou non hii solle heueȝi and suþþe hii solle sleape. **1382** Wyclif *Mark* xiv. 33 He.. bigan for to drede, and to heuye [**1388** be anoyed].

heavy-armed ('hɛvɪɑːmd), *a.* Bearing heavy armour or arms.

1836 *Penny Cycl.* VI. 388/2 The employment of artillery in the field deprived this heavy armed cavalry of all the advantages it possessed over the soldiers who fought on foot. **1843** Liddell & Scott *Greek Lex.*, 'Οπλίτης, a heavy-armed foot-soldier, man-at-arms, who carried a pike and a large shield. **1875** Jowett *Plato* (ed. 2) I. 74 As the heavy-armed Spartans did at the battle of Plataea.

'heavy-'handed, *a.*

1. a. Having the hands heavy from physical incapacity or weariness. **b.** 'Clumsy; not active or dextrous' (Webster 1828).

a **1633** Austin *Medit.* (1635) 137 If we grow weary (like Moses who was heavy-handed) yet let Aaron and Hur.. lift them up againe. **1647** Trapp *Comm. Hebr.* v. 11 Slow-paced and heavy-handed.

2. Having the hands laden; full-handed.

1864 Burton *Scot Abr.* I. iii. 117 They came back heavy-handed with droves and flocks.

3. a. Oppressive; overbearing.

1883 Mrs. Croker *Pretty Miss Neville* xvi. (1884) 143 Some day Nemesis will arrive heavy-handed, in the shape of a couple of pretty grown-up daughters.

b. Of a joke, humour, etc.: clumsy.

1910 A. C. Benson *Diary* 7 Dec. (1926) 199 Their jokes are very heavy-handed, and generally involve discomfort for the victim. **1934** *Amer. Speech* IX. 158/2 The work of heavy-handed humorists.

Hence **heavy-'handedness**, heaviness of hand; the opposite of lightness of hand.

1892 *Athenæum* 26 Nov. 736/2 The dialogue gives an impression of heavy-handedness.

'heavyhead. *rare.* A dull, stupid fellow.
1399 LANGL. *Rich. Redeles* III. 66 A! hicke hevyheed! hard is þy nolle To cacche ony kunnynge.

'heavy-'headed, *a.*
1. Having a heavy or large head.
1684 *Lond. Gaz.* No. 1910/4 A dark Iron gray Gelding.. heavy headed. 1771 MAD. D'ARBLAY *Early Diary* 8 May, A very civil, heavy-headed man of the Law..listened with attentive admiration. 1865 H. H. DIXON *Field & Fern* ix. 243 Some of the heavy-headed [rams] grow sadly weary. 1886 *Hurst & Hanger* II. viii. II. 15 The glorious hunters' moon, rising above the heavy-headed elms.
2. Dull, stupid.
1590 MARLOWE *Edw. II*, v. ii, To dash the heavy-headed Edmund's drift. 1603 KNOLLES *Hist. Turks* (1621) 604, I would not bee accounted so base minded, or heavy headed. 1825 J. NEAL *Bro. Jonathan* I. 191 He stood..regarding his vulgar, heavy-headed..brother opposite.
3. Drowsy, sleepy; = HEAVY *a.* 28.
1552 HULOET, Heuy headed, *grauedinosus.* 1560 ROLLAND *Crt. Venus* Prol. 31 Heuie heidit, and seindill in game or glew. 1600 HOLLAND *Livy* 735 (R.) Some that had taken their load of wine, and were heauie-headed and sleepie. 1602 SHAKS. *Ham.* IV. i. 17 This heavy-headed revel.. Makes us traduced and tax'd of other nations. 1887 *Cassell's Fam. Mag.* 94/2 No wonder they are heavy-headed, and tired of a morning.

'heavy-'hearted, *a.*
1. Having a heavy heart; grieved, sad, melancholy.
*c*1400 *Cato's Mor.* 235 in *Cursor M.* p. 1672 Heuy herted men and stille studious men. 1535 COVERDALE *Neh.* ii. 2 Thou art not sicke, that is not yᵉ matter, but thou art heuy harted. 1766 SMOLLET *Trav.* I. v. (Jod.), I am a little heavy-hearted at the prospect. 1888 MRS. OLIPHANT *Joyce* I. xvi. 304 The old man..saw nothing as he jogged onward heavy-hearted.
2. Proceeding from or caused by a heavy heart; sad, doleful.
1562 J. HEYWOOD *Prov. & Epigr.* (1867) 151 Lyght purses Make heauy hartes, and heuy harted curses. *a*1656 HALES *Gold. Rem.* (1688) 210 Sad and heavy-hearted thoughts. 1851 H. MELVILLE *Whale* xxii. 117 We gave three heavy-hearted cheers.
Hence **heavy-'heartedness,** sadness.
1860 PUSEY *Min. Proph.* 269 Deep was the sleep..not of heartlessness, but of heavy-heartedness.

†**'heavyingly,** *adv. Obs. rare.* [f. *heavying,* pr. pple. of HEAVY *v.*] Heavily, severely.
1434 MISYN *Mending Life* (E.E.T.S.) 107 Qwhos cold mynd heviyngly we reprefe.

heavyish ('hɛvɪɪʃ), *a.* [f. HEAVY *a.* + -ISH.] Somewhat heavy, in various senses.
1736 BYROM *Jrnl. & Lit. Rem.* (1856) II. I. 47 A little heavyish, I fancied, with drinking wine. 1784 MAD. D'ARBLAY *Diary* 17 Apr., I am only heavyish, not ill. 1876 SMILES *Sc. Natur.* iv. (ed. 4) 280 Having put a heavyish stone at the bottom of the trap.

'heavy-'laden, *a.*
1. Laden or loaded heavily; bearing a heavy burden. Also *fig.*
*c*1440 *Jacob's Well* xxxvii. (E.E.T.S.) 236 þou art full of fruyte of vertuys, heuy ladyn wyth gode werkys. 1697 DRYDEN *Virg. Georg.* II. 287 No toiling Teams from Harvest-labour come So late at Night, so heavy laden home. 1784 COWPER *Task* I. 242 He dips his bowl into the weedy ditch, And heavy-laden brings his bev'rage home. 1859 MRS. CARLYLE *Lett.* III. 13 One of Pickford's heavy-laden vans.
2. Weighed down with trouble, weariness, etc.; oppressed.
1611 BIBLE *Matt.* xi. 28 Come vnto mee all ye that labour, and are heauie laden. 1871 CARLYLE in *Mrs. Carlyle's Lett.* I. 47, I was sickly of body and mind, felt heavy-laden, and without any hope.
Hence **heavy-'ladenness.**
1877 A. EDERSHEIM in Spurgeon *Treas. Dav.* Ps. cxxxvii. 3 The cure of weariness, and the relief of heavy-ladenness, lies in this—to take the cross upon ourselves.

heavy spar. [transl. of Ger. *Schwerspat,* the name given by Werner in 1774.] The native sulphate of barium, barytes; also improperly applied to barium carbonate, and sometimes to the sulphate and carbonate of strontia (Page *Geol. Terms*).
1789 A. CRAWFORD in *Med. Commun.* II. 353 The muriated barytes..was obtained by the decomposition of the heavy spar. *Ibid.* 356 Heavy spar from the lead mines of Derbyshire. 1805–17 R. JAMESON *Char. Min.* (ed. 3) 107 Heavy spar, and actyonite afford examples of the hexahedral prism. 1845 ATKINSON in *Proc. Berw. Nat. Club* II. No. 13. 137 It is calc-spar, in a setting of heavy-spar or sulphate of baryta. 1892 *Dana's Min.* 903 The septaria of Durham.. have the veinings lined with brown heavy spar.

heavy-weight. Also **heavyweight. a.** A person or animal of more than the average weight; *spec.* a jockey, etc., of more than the average weight; a professional boxer weighing over 12 st. 7 lb., or *transf.*, a horse which carries more than the average weight.
1857 G. LAWRENCE *Guy Liv.* iii. 17 The horses he kept were well up to his weight, and he stood A I. in Jem Hill's estimation, as the best heavy-weight that had come out of Oxford for many a day. 1877 'PUGNUS' *Hist. Prize Ring* II. 104 For such a heavy weight, Hooper had a particularly small foot, of which he was very proud. 1888 W. DAY *Horse* Index 447 Heavy-weight carriers, how to breed. 1888 *Encycl. Brit.* XXIV. 691/1 Heavy weights [amateur] to be over 11 stone 4 lb. 1889 [see FEATHER-WEIGHT 3]. 1910 [see WELTER WEIGHT 2]. 1917 *Sat. Rev.* 10 Nov. 373/2 Thanks to the muscle, he has become a champion heavy-weight. 1928 [see CRUISER 4]. 1954 F. C. AVIS *Boxing Dict.* 52 *Heavyweight,* a standard weight division for professional boxers weighing more than 12 st. 7 lb.; for amateurs, 12 st. 10 lb.
b. *fig.* 'A person of weight or importance; one of much influence' (*Cent. Dict.*). *U.S. colloq.*
c. A work of large size or serious content. Cf. HEAVY *a.*[1] 20 a, b.
1928 BLUNDEN *Undertones of War* x. 111 When I saw scattered about the porch and the doorstep,..a number of volumes,..I could not but snatch up four or five... The heavyweight was..a treatise on Country Houses. 1963 *Punch* 3 Apr. 488/2, I have managed to convert my wisp of a *conte* into a heavyweight.
d. *attrib.* Also as *adj.*, particularly heavy of its kind.
1895 *Montgomery Ward Catal.* 283/1 Ladies' jersey knit ribbed vests, heavy weight Egyptian cotton. 1909 *Westm. Gaz.* 2 Mar. 5/2 In a variety of cloths, serges, and heavy-weight cashmere. 1931 *Bombay Chron.* 14 Oct. 1 Heavy-weight championship. 1934 G. B. SHAW *Too True to be Good* I. 40 Oh, sweetiest, why did you tell me that this heavyweight champion was a helpless invalid? 1958 *Times* 26 Sept. 6/3 Heavyweight American and Continental trucks and buses are not being exhibited. 1963 *Times Lit. Suppl.* 4 Jan. 16/5 Figgins's heavyweight version of Caslon's (1816) Sanserif in 1832. 1972 *Guardian* 31 Oct. 11/5 Underwear: Heavy-weight tights in nylon.

heavy wet. *slang.* [See WET *sb.*] Malt liquor.
1821 EGAN *Tom & Jerry* 75 (Farmer) The soldiers and their companions were seen tossing off the heavy wet and spirits. 1823 *Spirit Pub. Jrnls.* (1824) 57 One pint of heavy wet was then distributed to every domestic in the establishment. 1843 CARLYLE *Past & Pr.* I. v, They..have loved their own appetites, ambitions, their coroneted coaches, tankards of heavy-wet.

heaw, obs. form of HEW.

heawin, obs. form of HEAVEN *sb.*

heban, obs. form of EBON, ebony.

†**hebawde.** *Sc. Obs. rare.* [? ad. F. *hibou* owl.] An owl.
1513 DOUGLAS *Æneis* VII. Prol. 105 Hornit Hebawde, quhilk clepe we the nycht owle, Within hir caverne hard I schout and ȝowle.

hebbe(n, obs. forms of HEAVE *v.*

hebberman, var. of EBBERMAN, *Obs.*
1630 *Ord. Preserv. Brood Fish Thames* in *Descr. Thames* (1758) 75 No hebberman shall fish for Smelts before the twenty-fourth Day of August. *Ibid.* 76 No Hebberman shall work any higher for Whitings than Dartford Creek. 1670 BLOUNT *Law Dict.*, *Hebber-man,* a Fisherman below London-bridge, who fishes for Whitings, Smelts, &c. commonly at Ebbing-water, and therefore so called. 1839–40 THACKERAY *Catherine* xiv, The ferries across the river, and..the pirates who infest the same—namely tinklermen, petermen, hebbermen, trawlermen.

hebbing, obs. form of EBBING.
1475 *Rolls Parlt.* VI. 159/1 Fishgarthes..Lokkes, Hebbyng weeres..and dyvers other ympedyments dayly been made. 1590 *Cal. St. Papers, Dom. Ser.* 692 Regulations for hooks, lamperne rods, and hebbing nets.

hebdomad, -ade ('hɛbdəmæd, -eɪd). Also 6 ebd-. [ad. L. *hebdomas, hebdomad-*, a. Gr. ἑβδομάς (-αδ-) the number seven, a period of seven days.]
†**1.** The number seven viewed collectively; a group composed of seven. *Obs.*
1545 JOYE *Exp. Dan.* x. (R. s.v. *Heavy*), I Daniel was so heuey by thre hebdomads of dayes. 1552 HULOET, *Ebdomade,* Vide in number of 7. 1603 SIR C. HEYDON *Jud. Astrol.* 411 (Stanf.), 9 Hebdomades of yeares. 1678 CUDWORTH *Intell. Syst.* I. iv. §20. 376 The Tetrad is an arithmetical mediety betwixt the Monad and the Hebdomad. 1837 SOUTHEY *Doctor* IV. Inter-ch. xiv. 57 Like the hebdomad, which profound philosophers have pronounced to be..a motherless as well as a virgin number.
2. The space of seven days, a week: used particularly in reference to the '70 weeks' of Daniel's prophecy.
1600 W. WATSON *Quodlibets Relig. & St.* (1602) 201 (Stanf.) In this Babylonian transmigration Daniels Hebdomades beginning to take their place. 1662 GLANVILL *Lux Orient.* ii. (1682) 15 Those of creation being concluded within the first Hebdomade. 1890 E. JOHNSON *Rise Christendom* 413 The Passion was consummated in the time of the seventieth Hebdomad.
3. In some Gnostic systems, a group of seven superhuman beings; also a title of the Demiurge.
1837 WHEWELL *Hist. Induct. Sc.* (1857) I. 223 The intellectual gods..evolve the intelligible, and at the same time intellectual triads, into intellectual hebdomads. 1853 W. E. TAYLER *Hippolytus* II. iv. 97 Seven powers are supposed to have originated from the First Cause of all, which hebdomad formed, with their author, the first ogdoad ..or root of all existence. 1881 CHR. WORDSWORTH *Ch. Hist.* I. 195 In the next lower sphere [below the Ogdoad, in the system of Basilides] called the Hebdomad, or sphere of seven, is the second Archon, or Ruler.

hebdomadal (hɛb'dɒmədəl), *a.* (*sb.*) [ad. L. *hebdomadāl-is*, f. *hebdomad-*: see prec. and -AL[1].]
†**1.** Consisting of or lasting seven days. *Obs.*
1613 SELDEN on *Drayton's Poly-olb.* xi. (T.), They had their original of later time than this hebdomadal account. 1646 SIR T. BROWNE *Pseud. Ep.* IV. xii. 212 Hebdomadall periods or weeks. 1651 BIGGS *New Disp.* Pref. 11 When he [God] was about his hebdomadal work of the Hexameron Fabrick.
b. Changing every week; fickle, changeable.
1796 BURKE *Regic. Peace* iv. Wks. IX. 5 Listening to variable, hebdomadal politicians, who run away from their opinions without giving us a month's warning.
2. Meeting, taking place, or appearing once a week; weekly.
Hebdomadal Council: the representative board of the University of Oxford, which meets weekly, and takes the initiative in all matters to be brought before the University; it has taken the place of the earlier Hebdomadal Meeting of Heads of Houses.
1711 STEELE *Spect.* No. 17 ¶2 Several of these Hebdomadal Societies. 1818 SCOTT *Rob Roy* iv, His hebdomadal visitants were often divided in their opinion. 1846 MᶜCULLOCH *Acc. Brit. Empire* (1854) II. 333 In the reign of Elizabeth..the regent masters were deprived of the initiative in legislative measures in the House of Convocation in Oxford, which was transferred to the hebdomadal meeting of heads of houses. 1849 SIR J. STEPHEN *Eccl. Biog.* (1850) II. 403 The whole tribe of party writers, diurnal and hebdomadal. 1854 [see COUNCIL 11 b]. 1880 FOWLER *Locke* ii. 16 A letter to the Hebdomadal Board from Lord Clarendon, then Chancellor of the University.
B. *sb.* (*ellipt.*) A periodical appearing once a week, a 'weekly'. (*pedantic* or *humorous.*)
1835 *Blackw. Mag.* XXXVIII. 637 Accounts..have occasionally appeared in the journals and hebdomadals. 1838 B. CORNEY *Controversy* 4 Let its appearance be proclaimed in the diurnals, in the hebdomadals, etc. 1885 *Advance* (Chicago) 18 June, A fit contemporary of our Eastern hebdomadals.

heb'domadally, *adv.* [f. prec. + -LY[2].] Once a week; weekly. (*humorous* or *affected.*)
1816 G. COLMAN *Br. Grins, Lond. Rurality* (1872) 318 The secondary Cit..From London jogs hebdomadally down And rusticates in London out of town. 1827 *Blackw. Mag.* XXII. 603 He..is seen hebdomadally in the pulpit. 1880 MRS. C. READE *Brown Hand & White* I. ii. 60 The leader she hebdomadally supplies to the advanced weekly.

†**heb'domadar, -er.** *Sc. Obs.* [ad. eccl. L. *hebdomadārius* (see HEBDOMADARY *sb.* and *a.*): cf. *ordinar, testamentar*, etc., also F. *hebdomadaire.*] In the Scotch Universities: The name given to one of the superior members whose weekly turn it was to superintend the discipline of the students; also, in Grammar Schools, the master who took 'duty' for the week.
1700 *Order* 23 Oct. in *Aberdeen Counc. Reg.* (1872) 330 Upon every play day the hebdomader for that week shall goe along with the scholars to the hill when they get the play. 1807 J. HALL *Trav. Scotl.* I. 114 The masters in their turns exercised the office of what was called Hebdomader. His business was to preside and say grace at the college table and to go round and call at every chamber at six o'clock in the morning to see if the students had got up [etc.]. 1840 in Bulloch *Hist. Aberdeen Univ.* (1895) 179 Professor Gordon happened to be the hebdomadar.

hebdomadarian (hɛbdɒmə'dɛərɪən). [f. HEBDOMADARY *sb.* and *a.* + -IAN.] = HEBDOMADARY *sb.*
1898 W. ST. CLAIR BADDELEY *Cotteswold Shrine* 75 At a signal given by the hebdomadarian of the week they returned to the Cloister. 1949 M. BALDWIN *I leap over Wall* vi. 139 The 'hebdomadarian' (such was the official title of the 'Great Week' keeper in the *Ceremonial*) was continually in evidence.

hebdomadary (hɛb'dɒmədərɪ), *sb.* and *a.* Also 5–6 **ebdomadary, -edary.** [ad. eccl. L. *hebdomadāri-us*, f. *hebdomas* HEBDOMAD.]
A. *sb. R.C. Ch.* A member of a chapter or convent, who took his (or her) weekly turn in the performance of the sacred offices of the Church.
1432–50 tr. *Higden* (Rolls) I. 113 The mansiones also of the ebdomadaries, prestes, and minstres. 1450–1530 *Myrr. our Ladye* 127 Yt ys always sayde of the ebdomedary..to whome yt longeth rather to gyue blyssynge then to aske yt in that offyce. 1864 GREENSHIELD *Ann. Lesmahagow* 13 While engaged in such services as they performed by weekly turns, monks were called 'Hebdomadaries'. 1877 J. D. CHAMBERS *Div. Worship* 90. 1888 'BERNARD' *From World to Cloister* 29 The voice of the Hebdomadary was heard, as he prayed.
B. *adj.* Hebdomadal, weekly; doing duty for a week.
1625 N. CARPENTER *Geog. Del.* II. vi. (1635) 97 Marriners make six degrees of change in the tides..The second Hebdomedary, or weekely. *a*1631 DONNE *Serm.* lxi. 614 An Hebdomadary righteousnesse, a Sabbatarian Righteousnesse is no righteousnesse. *a*1711 KEN *Hymns Evang.* Poet. Wks. 1721 I. 7 Hebdomadary Priests neglect their turns. 1892 *Speaker* 30 July 141/1 Mr. Pinkerton, of the hebdomadary picnics.

†**hebdo'madic,** *a. Obs.* [f. Gr. ἑβδομαδ- HEBDOMAD + -IC.] Pertaining to the days of the week.
*a*1681 WHARTON *Dominical Lett.* Wks. (1683) 68 Seven Hebdomadick [*printed* Hebdomaick] Letters used be, And those are A. B. C. D. E. F. G.

'hebdomary. Also ebd-. A shortened form of HEBDOMADARY *sb.*
*c*1450 *Rules St. Saviour & St. Bridget* xlvi. in Aungier *Syon Monast., etc.* (1840) 362 The ebdomary is bounde..to absteyn thynges that wyke that myght lette her to performe her office. 1706 PHILLIPS (ed. Kersey), *Ebdomadarius*..the Ebdomary or Weeks-man, an Officer in Cathedral Churches. 1879 E. WATERTON *Pietas Mariana* 260 The

hebdomary, i.e., the canon of the week, who sang the daily High Mass.

†**hebdo'matical**, *a. Obs. rare.* [f. late L. *hebdomatic-us*, irreg. ad. Gr. ἑβδομαδικός weekly + -AL[1].] Weekly; hebdomadary.

a **1659** MORTON *Episc. Ch.* (1670) 142 Far from the conceipt of a Deambulatory, Hebdomatical (or peradventure Ephemeral) Office.

heb'domically, *adv.* [f. Gr. ἕβδομ-ος seventh + -IC + -AL[1] + -LY[2].] According to the hebdomad or mystical number seven: cf. HEBDOMAD 3.

1837 WHEWELL *Hist. Induct. Sc.* (1857) I. 223 The intellectual gods produce all things hebdomically.

‖**Hebe**[1] ('hiːbiː). [a. Gr. ἥβη youthful prime, puberty; name of the daughter of Zeus and Hera.]

1. The goddess of youth and spring, represented as having been originally the cup-bearer of Olympus; hence applied *fig.* to: **a.** A waitress, a barmaid; **b.** A woman in her early youth.

1606 SYLVESTER *Du Bartas* II. iv. III. *Magnificence* 862 Here, many a Hebê fair, here more than one Quick-seruing Chiron neatly waits vpon The Beds and Boords. **1815** SCOTT *Guy M.* xliv, Shortly after, the same Hebe brought up a plate of beef collops. **1889** MRS. WALFORD *Stiff-n. Generation* I. ii. 35 'Good heavens! what a perfect Hebe!'

2. *Astron.* Name of the sixth of the asteroids.

1858 HERSCHEL *Outl. Astron.* (ed. 5) 335 The discovery of Astræa and Hebe by Professor Hencke in 1845 and 1847.

3. *Bot.* [mod.L. (P. Commerson in A. L. Jussieu *Genera Plantarum* (1789) 105).] A member of a large genus of shrubs so called, mostly native to New Zealand, belonging to the family Scrophulariaceæ, and formerly included in the genus *Veronica*.

[**1921** F. W. PENNELL in *Rhodora* XXIII. 2 The austral distribution, with its suggestion of genetic remoteness, emphasizes *Hebe's* claim to recognition as a genus. **1927** COCKAYNE & ALLAN in *Trans. N.Z. Inst.* LVII. 13 A species is usually transferred to *Hebe* only when.. we are pretty well convinced it is valid.] **1961** *Amat. Gardening* 21 Oct. 5/1 The hebes, as the shrubby veronicas are now called. **1972** *Country Life* 23 Mar. 690/1 Our hebes have come through remarkably well: even the tenderest kinds like Simon Deleaux and Andersonii Variegata.

4. *attrib.* and *Comb.*, as ***Hebe bloom***; ***Hebe-like*** adj.; **Hebe's cup**, Heidelberg Punch (*Cassell's Dict. Cookery*); **Hebe vase**, a small vase like a *cotyliscos* of the kind which Hebe is represented as bearing (Brewer *Dict. Phr. & Fable*).

1838 LYTTON *Alice* VI. vi, A certain melancholy in her countenance.. I am sure not natural to its Hebe-like expression. **1842** TENNYSON *Gard. Dau.* 136 Her violet eyes, and all her Hebe bloom.

Hebe, hebe[2] (hiːb). Also Heeb. [abbrev. of HEBREW *sb.* 1.] A derogatory term for a Jew.

1932 J. T. FARRELL *Studs Lonigan* (1936) iv. 71 He should've been a nigger or a hebe instead of Irish. **1946** MEZZROW & WOLFE *Really the Blues* 374/2 *Heeb*, Jewish person. **1950** T. SUGRUE in M. Hay *Foot of Pride* p. xx, He might go through the whole of his life without expressing more than a casual distaste for 'the Hebes'. **1953** E. F. RUSSELL *Somewhere a Voice* (1965) 11 Lastly there was Sammy Finestone... A typical Hebe. **1972** *National Observer* (U.S.) 27 May 17/4 They will be followed close upon their heels by miserly Hebes, and cheating kikes.

hebe- (hiːbiː), used as combining form of Gr. ἥβη youth, also puberty, down of puberty, taken in senses **a.** Pubescence (in botanical terms), as in **hebe'anthous** *a.* [Gr. ἄνθος flower], having the corolla of the flower pubescent (Mayne *Expos. Lex.* 1854). **hebe'carpous** *a.* [Gr. καρπός fruit], having pubescent fruit (ibid.). **hebecladous** (hiː'bɛklədəs), *a.* [Gr. κλάδος branch], having pubescent branches (ibid.). **hebegynous** (-'ɛdʒɪnəs) *a.* [Gr. γυνή female: see -GYNOUS], having pubescent ovaries (ibid.). **hebe'petalous** *a.*, having pubescent petals (ibid.). **b.** Puberty, as in **hebe'phrenia** [Gr. φρήν mind], a form of insanity incident to the age of puberty (*Syd. Soc. Lex.* 1886). **hebe'phreniac** *a.* and *sb.*, (a person) affected with hebephrenia; also **hebe'phrenic** *a.* and *sb.*

1883 W. A. HAMMOND *Treat. Insanity* 556 Hebephrenia ..is the term applied to the insanity of pubescence. **1948** *Brit. Jrnl. Psychol.* XXXIX. 89 Hebephrenia is featured by silliness, incongruity, mannerisms etc. **1956** C. P. SNOW *Homecomings* 348 He lay on his back, his legs relaxed, like a figure on a tomb or one in a not disagreeable state of hebephrenia. **1884** *Jrnl. Nerv. & Mental Dis.* XI. 303 Imperative conceptions are relatively frequent among hebephreniacs. **1885** *Ibid.* XII. 516 (*heading*) Autopsy findings in a hebephreniac. **1908** *Practitioner* Jan. 12 The patient may gradually become imbecile and demented—the hebephrenic type. **1915** C. R. PAYNE tr. *Pfister's Psychoanalytic Method* 542 Dementia praecox (in catatonic, hebephrenic and paranoid forms). **1938** S. BECKETT *Murphy* 168 A hebephrenic playing the piano intently. **1973** 'E. MCBAIN' *Let's hear It* v. 59 He considered them [*sc.* the police] obsolete and essentially hebephrenic.

heben, hebeny, -yf, obs. ff. EBON, EBONY.

†**'hebenon, hebon, hebona.** Names given by Shakspere and Marlowe to some substance having a poisonous juice.

Commentators have variously identified the word with *ebon*, *henbane*, and Ger. *eibe*, *eibenbaum* the yew. Gower has *hebenus* app. in a similar sense.

[**1390** GOWER *Conf.* II. 103 Of hebenus that slepy tre.] *c* **1592** MARLOWE *Jew of Malta* III. Wks. (Rtldg.) 164/1 In few, the blood of Hydra, Lerna's bane, The juice of hebon, and Cocytus' breath. **1602** SHAKS. *Ham.* I. v. 62 Vpon my secure hower thy Vncle stole With iuyce of cursed Hebenon [*Qos.* hebona] in a Violl. **1789** E. DARWIN *Bot. Gard.* II. *Loves Pl.* III, Brews her black Hebenon, and stealing near, Pours the curst venom in his tortured ear.

Heberden's nodes ('hɛbədənz nəʊdz). *Med.* [f. the name of William *Heberden*, Eng. physician (1710–1801), who described the condition.] Nodular enlargements of the terminal joints of the fingers due to osteoarthritis.

1889 D. DUCKWORTH *Treat. Gout* iv. 72 (*heading*) Heberden's nodes in a case of gout—..patient has noticed a gradual increase in size of the joints of the fingers... Heberden's nodes, both hands. **1911** *Encycl. Brit.* XXIII 239/1 What are termed 'Heberden's nodes' are small hard knobs about the size of a pea frequently found upon the fingers near the terminal phalangeal joints... These nodes are.. a manifestation of arthritis. **1961** R. D. BAKER *Essent. Path.* xxi. 578 In the hands the hypertrophy of the bones about the distal interphalangeal joints is known as Heberden's nodes. **1972** H. L. JAFFE *Metabolic, Degenerative & Inflammatory Dis. Bones & Joints* xxv. 757 With advancing age, the incidence of Heberden's nodes increases.

†**hebescate**, *v. Obs. rare.* [irreg. f. L. *hebescĕre* to grow dull.] *trans.* To make dull or blunt.

1657 TOMLINSON *Renou's Disp.* 570 Such affections.. as stupifie the senses or hebescate motion.

hebetant ('hɛbɪtənt), *a.* [ad. L. *hebetānt-em*, pr. pple. of *hebetāre* to HEBETATE.] Making dull.

1801 LAMB *Curious Fragm.* iv. Poems, etc. (1884) 202 Who disallows the use of meat in a morning as gross, fat, hebetant.

hebetate ('hɛbɪteɪt), *v.* [f. L. *hebetāt-*, ppl. stem of *hebetāre*, f. *hebes*, *hebet-* blunt, dull. Cf. F. *hébéter* (16th c. in Littré).]

1. *trans.* To make dull or obtuse; to blunt.

1574 NEWTON *Health Mag.* 53 To hebetate or dull the memorie. **1694** F. BRAGGE *Disc. Parables* III. 90 It.. effeminates the soul, and dispirits and hebetates the body. **1851** CARLYLE *Sterling* I. viii. (1871) 51 Men's souls were blinded, hebetated. **1887** LOWELL *Democr., etc.* 118 Desultory reading.. hebetates the brain.

2. *intr.* To become dull or inert.

1832 *Examiner* 673/2 Allowing it [the clergy] to cram, and surfeit, and pall, and hebetate, with forbidden wealth.

Hence **'hebetated, 'hebetating** *ppl. adjs.*

1735 THOMSON *Liberty* III. 381 Of narrow gust and hebetating sense. **1826** *Blackw. Mag.* XIX. 659 Patients with callous appetites and hebetated tongues. **1864** CARLYLE *Fredk. Gt.* IV. 186 The hebetated old gentleman.

'hebetate, *a. Bot.* [ad. L. *hebetāt-us*, pa. pple. of *hebetāre*: see prec.] Having a dull or blunt and soft point (Gray *Bot. Text-bk.* 1. Gloss.).

hebetation (hɛbɪ'teɪʃən). [ad. late L. *hebetātiōn-em*, n. of action f. *hebetāre* to HEBETATE. Cf. 15th c. F. *hébétation*.] The action of making or fact of being made blunt or dull; blunted or dulled condition.

1623 COCKERAM II, *Dulnesse*, hebetude, hebetation. **1755** JOHNSON, *Hebetation.* 1. The act of dulling. 2. The state of being dulled. *c* **1865** in *Circ. Sc.* I. 363/1 A hebetation of the senses.. supervenes.

hebetative ('hɛbɪteɪtɪv), *a.* [f. L. *hebetāt-*, pa. ppl. stem of *hebetāre*: see -IVE.] Having the quality of making dull.

1834 *Tait's Mag.* I. 586 Hebetative and instupifying qualities.

hebete ('hɛbiːt), *a. rare.* [ad. L. *hebes*, *hebet-* blunt, dull.] Dull, stupid, obtuse.

1743 J. ELLIS *Knowl. Div. Things* (1811) 325 Observe how hebete and dull they are. **1840** E. FITZGERALD *Lett.* (1889) I. 56, I am becoming more hebete every hour.

†**hebete**, *v. Obs. rare.* [a. F. *hébéter* (14th c. in Hatz.-Darm.), ad. L. *hebetāre*: see HEBETATE.] *trans.* To make dull.

1597 LOWE *Chirurg.* (1634) 53 It hebeteth and maketh grosse the spirits of olde folkes and children.

'hebetin. [? f. L. *hebes*, *hebet-* + -IN.] Anhydrous silicate of zinc, the same as WILLEMITE.

1865–72 WATTS *Dict. Chem.* III. 138. **1868** DANA *Min.* (ed. 5) 262.

'hebetize, *v. rare.* [f. L. *hebes*, *hebet-* blunt, dull + -IZE.] *trans.* To make dull; to blunt.

1845 *Vulgar Errors Adapted* 102 The ignorance of the patient thus hebetizing, as it were, the art of the doctor.

hebetude ('hɛbɪtjuːd). [ad. L. *hebetūdo*, n. of quality f. *hebes*, *hebet-* blunt, dull: cf. F. *hébétude* (1535 in Hatz.-Darm.).] The condition or state of being blunt or dull; dullness, bluntness, obtuseness, lethargy.

c **1621** S. WARD *Life Faith* (1627) 62 Motion as well as health.. driues away all lassitude, hebetude, and indisposition. **1665** G. HARVEY *Advice agst. Plague* 10 According to their grosseness or subtility, activity, or hebetude. **1787** SIR J. HAWKINS *Life Johnson* 258 That appearance of hebetude which marked his countenance when living. **1833** CHALMERS *Const. Man* I. iii. 165 A hebetude, if it may be so termed, of the moral sensibilities. **1918** E. POUND *Let.* 3 Apr. (1971) 133 There is *something* in his [*sc.* Jules Romains's] work. It is not the hebetude of a lignified cerebrum. **1955** W. GADDIS *Recognitions* II. vi. 564 The robe was too big. Nevertheless, the pattern was so conservative, and the material so fine, that this seemed rather a mark of luxuriance than some deliberate hebetude on the part of the giver.

hebetudinous (hɛbɪ'tjuːdɪnəs), *a.* [f. L. *hebetūdo*, *-tūdin-*: see prec. and -OUS.] Inclined to hebetude; dull, obtuse.

1820 L. HUNT *Indicator* No. 37 (1822) I. 291 Dull, uninformed, hebetudinous. **1834** H. AINSWORTH *Rookwood* III. v, His person was heavy and hebetudinous.

Hence **hebetudi'nosity**, dullness, obtuseness.

1884 *St. James's Gaz.* 22 Aug. 5/1 [His] intellectuals are clogged in the peculiar manner which constitutes hebetudinosity.

†**'hebolace**: see HERBELADE.

hebra ('hɛbrə). Also **chevra(h)**. Pl. **hebras, hebroth, chevroth.** [Heb. *ḥebrāh*, association, society; group as small religious community.] (See quot. 1959.)

1880 *Jewish Chron.* 6 Feb. 9/2 The poorer classes prefer to belong to one of the numerous *Hebras* which.. abound in the East End. *Ibid.* 4/1 Many of these unattached Jews are not wealthy... They.. have their *Hebras*, their customs and peculiarities. **1892** I. ZANGWILL *Childr. Ghetto* I. I. ii. 44 Even in the smallest *Chevrah* the high hat comes next in sanctity to the Scroll of the Law. **1918** C. G. MONTEFIORE *Liberal Judaism & Hellenism* v. 259 This oligarchic tendency is counteracted by the little Synagogues and the *Chevras*. **1959** F. M. WILSON *They came as Strangers* III. iii. 195 Thousands of Jews were too poor to be seat-holders in the synagogue, so they formed *chevras*, which were partly Friendly Societies, and partly groups for public worship and the study of the Talmud. **1960** *Economist* 25 June 1331/1 Here and there are the little *chevras* or conventicles whose continued existence so much annoyed the big synagogues. **1960** L. P. GARTNER *Jewish Immigrant* vii. 186 In the *hebra* ..a Jew associated himself with fellow Jews.. for.. worship and study and conviviality.

Hebræan (hiː'briːən). Also 6–8 Hebrean. [f. L. *Hebræ-us*, a. Gr. Ἑβραῖ-ος (see HEBREW) + -AN.]

†**1.** A Hebrew, a Jew. *Obs.*

1509 BARCLAY *Shyp of Folys* (1874) II. 3 Kynge Assuerus ..Whiche commaundyd all the hebreans to be slayne.

†**2.** A Hebrew scholar, Hebraist. *Obs.*

1637–50 ROW *Hist. Kirk* (1842) 466 His father being a great Hebrean, and the man that first broght the knowledge of Hebrew letters to Scotland. *c* **1770** WESLEY *Wks.* (1872) XII. 464 The best Hebraean I ever knew. **1801** W. TAYLOR in *Monthly Mag.* XII. 214 The translators of the bible were better Hebræans than Anglicists.

3. One of a school of religionists in Holland, whose system rested on the interpretation of certain hidden truths in the Hebrew language.

1882–3 SCHAFF *Encycl. Relig. Knowl.* II. 1604 Mysticism entered into various combinations.. producing, in the 18th century, the Hebraeans in Holland, the Hutchinsonians and Jumpers in England.

Hebraic (hiː'breɪk), *a.* [ad. late L. *Hebraic-us*, a. Gr. Ἑβραϊκός, f. a stem Ἑβρα-: see HEBREW. Cf.F. *hébraïque* (15th c. in Hatz.-Darm.).] Pertaining or relating to the Hebrews or their language; having a Hebrew style or quality; Hebrew.

c **1384** CHAUCER *H. Fame* III. 343 The Ebrayke Iosephus the olde. **1530** PALSGR. 315/1 Hebrayke, belongyng to the countrey, speche of Hebrewe, *hebraicq*. **1632** LITHGOW *Trav.* 290 Making merry with our Hebraick friends. **1669** GALE *Crt. Gentiles* I. I. x. 54 Plato affirmes..that the Hebraic language was the Mother of al Languages. **1730** BOLINGBROKE *Hist. Eng.* i. (1752) 8 (Jod.) Reducing the immense antiquity of the Ægyptians within the limits of the Hebraick calculation. **1847** EMERSON *Repr. Men, Swedenborg* Wks. (Bohn) I. 323 His perception of nature.. is mystical and Hebraic.

He'braical, *a.* Now *rare.* [f. as prec. + -AL[1].] = prec.

1601 DEACON & WALKER *Answ. Darel* 20 An hebraicall iterating or doubling of one and the selfesame matter, to make it more notoriouslie and expreslie apparant. **1877** DAWSON *Orig. World* ii. 55 Cosmological conclusions similar to the doctrines of that Hebraical school.

He'braically, *adv.* [f. prec. + -LY[2].] In Hebrew fashion; after the manner of the Hebrews or the Hebrew language (e.g. with reference to the fact that Hebrew is written from right to left, or 'backwards').

1720 SWIFT *Adv. Yng. Poet* Wks. 1841 II. 297 The.. modern device of consulting indexes, which is to read books Hebraically and begin where others usually end. **1836** T. HOOK *G. Gurney* (1850) I. vii. 129 Contingencies and consequences hebraically obscure to my comprehension.

†Hebra'ician. *Obs.* [f. Hebraic + -ian, after *physician, logician,* etc.] = Hebraist 1.
1610 Healey *St. Aug. Citie of God* 577 A great Hebraician sayth they were called Hebrewes, *quasi travellers*, for so the word intends. **1675** T. Tully *Let. Baxter* 25 Pagnine, Buxtorf &c. are very good Hebraicians. **1705** Hickeringill *Priest-cr.* iv. (1721) 216 He himself also was a great Hebraition.

Hebraicism (hi:'breɪɪsɪz(ə)m). *rare.* [f. as prec. + -ism.] = Hebraism 2.
1852 Robertson *Serm.* Ser. iii. xv. 183 What..was called Judaism, and in modern times is called Hebraicism.

He'braicize, *v.* *rare*⁻⁰. [f. as prec. + -ize.] *trans.* = Hebraize *v.* 2.
1882 in Ogilvie.

He'braico-, comb. form of L. *Hebraicus*, used in sense: Hebraically, Hebrew and ——.
1820 T. Moore *Mem.* (1853) III. 145 [I] wrote a verse or two of my Hebraico-Hibernian Melody.

Hebraism ('hi:breɪɪz(ə)m). [a. F. *hébraïsme* (1567 in Hatz.-Darm.) or ad. mod.L. *Hebraismus* = late Gr. Ἑβραϊσμός, f. Ἑβραΐζειν to Hebraize: see Hebrew and -ism.]
1. A phrase or construction characteristic of the Hebrew language; a Hebrew idiom or expression.
1570 Levins *Manip.* 146 Hebraisme, *hæbraismus.* **1645** Milton *Tetrach.* (1851) 237 The New Testament, though ..originally writt in Greeke, yet hath nothing neer so many Atticisms as Hebraisms, and Syriacisms. **1712** Addison *Spect.* No. 405 ¶3 Our Language has received innumerable Elegancies and Improvements, from that Infusion of Hebraisms, which are derived to it out of the Poetical Passages in Holy Writ. **1844** Stanley *Arnold* (1858) I. vi. 228 To fill our pages with Hebraisms.
2. A quality or attribute of the Hebrew people; Hebrew character or nature; the Hebrew method of thought or system of religion, Judaism.
1847 Emerson *Repr. Men, Swedenborg* Wks. (Bohn) I. 326 The book had been grand, if the Hebraism had been omitted, and the law stated without Gothicism. **1872** Chr. Wordsworth *Comm. Rev.* Pref. 149 *note*, The design of the Apocalypse is not to Hebraize Christianity but to Christianize Hebraism. **1888** Mrs. H. Ward *R. Elsmere* III. 12 In Hebraism of feature, and swarthy smoothness of cheek.
b. Applied by Matthew Arnold to that mode of human thought and action of which the ancient Hebrew is taken as the type; the moral, as opposed to the intellectual, theory of life: cf. Hellenism.
1869 M. Arnold *Cult. & Anarchy* iv. (1875) 133 Self-conquest, self-devotion, the following not our own individual will, but the will of God, *obedience*, is the fundamental idea of this form, also, of the discipline to which we have attached the general name of Hebraism.

Hebraist ('hi:breɪɪst). [f. stem *Hebra-* in Hebraic, Hebraize: see -ist. Cf. F. *hébraïste*.]
1. One versed in the Hebrew language; a Hebrew scholar.
1755 in Johnson. **1817** Coleridge *Biog. Lit.* 55 A very learned man and a great Hebraist. **1883** A. Roberts *O.T. Revis.* viii. 173 The celebrated Hebraist, Gesenius.
2. One who has the qualities of the Hebrew people; an adherent of the Hebrew system of thought or religion.
1879 Farrar *St. Paul* I. 26 St. Paul was a 'Hebraist' in the fullest sense of the word. **1887** Swinburne in *19th Cent.* XXI. 423 This splendid poetic style..what modern criticism would define as that of a natural Hebraist.
3. A Jew of Palestine, who used the Hebrew Scriptures, as opposed to a Hellenistic or Grecian Jew.
1892 G. F. X. Griffith tr. *Fouard's St. Peter* 62 [The Hellenists] were better prepared than were the Hebraists for the teachings of Jesus.
4. One who maintains that the New Testament was written in Greek that contained Hebrew idioms.
1859 E. Masson tr. *Winer's Gram. N.T. Diction* I. i. 25 Various..scholars (the Purists) perseveringly endeavoured to demonstrate that the style of the N.T. entirely reaches the standard of classical Greek purity..while others (the Hebraists) maintained..that it exhibits a..predominant Hebrew tincture. **1906** J. H. Moulton *Gram. N.T. Greek* (1908) 3 The Hebraist went absurdly far in recognising Semitic influence where none was really operative. **1907** [see purist 2].

Hebra'istic, *a.* [f. prec. + -ic.] Of or pertaining to Hebraists; marked by Hebraism; of a Hebrew quality, Hebraic.
1846 in Worcester. **1856** Mrs. Stowe *Dred* I. xix. 257 Giving a Hebraistic coloring to their habitual mode of expression. **1873** Symonds *Grk. Poets* xii. 422 The separation between the Greeks and us is due..principally to the Hebraistic culture we receive in childhood. **1882–3** Schaff *Encycl. Relig. Knowl.* II. 964/1 In the New Testament..words..are often used with more Hellenic than Hebraistic signification.
Hence **Hebra'istical** *a.* = prec.; **Hebra'istically** *adv.*
1846 Worcester, *Hebraistical.* **1864** *Kitto's Cycl. Bibl. Lit.* II. 105 Οἱ ἔξω, those without, which is Hebraistically used in the N.T.

Hebraize ('hi:breɪaɪz), *v.* [ad. Gr. Ἑβραΐζειν to speak Hebrew, to imitate Jews, f. stem Ἑβρα- in Ἑβρα-ικός, etc.: see Hebrew. Cf. F. *hébraïser*.]
1. *intr.* To use a Hebrew idiom or manner of speech.
1645 Milton *Tetrach.* (1851) 237 The Evangelist heer Hebraizes. **1699** [see below]. **1862** Lowell *Biglow P.* Poems 1890 II. 329 If they [Puritans] Hebraized a little too much in their speech, they showed remarkable practical sagacity as statesmen and founders.
b. To follow Hebraism as an ideal of mind and conduct. See Hebraism 2 b.
1869 M. Arnold *Cult. & Anarchy* [see Hellenize 1 b]. *Ibid.* v, We have fostered our Hebraizing instincts, our preference of earnestness of doing to delicacy and flexibility of thinking, too exclusively.
2. *trans.* To make Hebrew; to give a Hebrew character or quality to.
1816 G. S. Faber *Orig. Pagan Idol.* II. 292 What they hebraized into Sabaoth was, I believe, no other than the Indian Seba. **1869** [see below]. **1873** Tristram *Moab* xiv. 276 An attempt to Hebraize a foreign sound.
Hence **'Hebraized** *ppl. a.*, **'Hebraizing** *vbl. sb.* and *ppl. a.*; also **Hebrai'zation**, the action of Hebraizing; **'Hebraizer**, one who Hebraizes.
1699 Bentley *Phal.* 412 We must impeach him not only for Atticizing, but for Hebraizing too. **1869** *Daily News* 1 Feb., A deeply Hebraized Christianity. **1869** M. Arnold *Cult. & An.* iv. (1882) 143 The Reformation has been often called a Hebraising revival. **1882** Farrar *Early Chr.* I. 256 The stern old Hebraisers—the Hebrews of Hebrews—who taught in the schools of Palestine and Jerusalem. **18..** *N. York Courier-Jrnl.* (Cent.), The next decade will see a more extensive Hebraization of the wholesale trade of New York than ever.

†Hebreish, *a.* and *sb.* *Obs.* In 1 ebreisc, (ebrisc), 1–2 hebreisc, 3 ebreisch, ebris(se. [f. L. *Hebræ-us* (med.L. *Ebrē-us*), Gr. Ἑβραῖος Hebrew: see -ish.] = Hebrew.
c **1000** *Ags. Gosp.* John xix. 20 Hit wæs awriten ebreisceon stafon, & grecisceon & leden stafon. *c* **1050** *Byrhtferth's Handboc* in *Anglia* VIII. 322 Pasca is ebreisc nama & he ʒetacnað oferfæreld. *a* **1225** *Ancr. R.* 302 Boðe heo speleð on an Ebreische ledene. *c* **1250** *Gen. & Ex.* 73 Ðis ik wort in ebrisse wen He witen ðe soðe ðat is sen.

Hebrew ('hi:bru:), *sb.* and *a.* Forms: (1 (*pl.*) Ebréas), 3–6 Ebreu, 4 Ebru, Ebrewe, Hebru, Hebreu, *Sc.* Hebrow, 4–6 *Sc.* (*pl.*) Hebreis, 4–7 Ebrew, 5–7 Hebrewe, 6 Ebrue, Hebrieu, 6–7 Hebrue, 4– Hebrew. [ME. *Ebreu*, a. OF. *Ebreu*, *Ebrieu* (nom. *Ebreus*, 12th c. in Hatz.-Darm.), ad. med.L. *Ebrēus* for cl.L. *Hebræus*, a. Gr. Ἑβραῖος, f. Aramaic *ʿebrai*, corresp. to Heb. *ʿibrī* 'a Hebrew', lit. 'one from the other side (of the river)'; f. *ʿēber* the region on the other or opposite side; f. *ʿābar* to cross or pass over. Cf. the LXX, Gen. xiv. 13 Ἄβρὰμ ὁ περατής, 'Abram the passer-over' or 'immigrant', for *Abrām haʿibrī* 'Abram the Hebrew'. At the revival of learning the initial H was resumed after cl.L. in French and English. (The OE. *Ebréas* was immediately from med.L. *Ebrēi*.)
To the Aramaic form on which the Greek word was fashioned is due the stem Ἑβρα-, *Hebra-*, in *Hebraic, Hebraist, Hebraize*, etc.]
A. *sb.*
1. A person belonging to the Semitic tribe or nation descended from Abraham, Isaac, and Jacob; an Israelite, a Jew. (Historically, the term is usually applied to the early Israelites; in modern use it avoids the religious and other associations often attaching to *Jew*.)
[*c* **1000** Ælfric *Gen.* xl. 15 For þam þe ic wæs dearnunga forstolen of Ebrea lande.] *c* **1375** *Sc. Leg. Saints, Thomas* 73 þare is bot a god but drede, þat of hebreis þe god Is. *c* **1450** tr. *De Imitatione* iii. xliii. 114 Not seruaunt, but a veray hebrewe. **1553** Gau *Richt Vay* 35 As it is writine in the vi chaiptur to the Hebreis. **1585** T. Washington tr. *Nicholay's Voy.* iii. xii. 93 Of nature an Hebrew. **1591** Shaks. *Two Gent.* ii. v. 57 If not, thou art an Hebrew, a Iew, and not worth the name of a Christian. **1671** Milton *Samson* 1319 Thou know'st I am an Ebrew. **1845** Maurice *Mor. & Met. Philos.* in *Encycl. Metrop.* II. 558/1 The difference between the Hebrews and Greeks generally.
†b. Hebrew race or stock. *Obs.*
c **1375** *Sc. Leg. Saints. Thomas* 59 A madyne com amange þam all Of hebrow borne In-to þe land. *Ibid.* 65 He of hebrow ves a manne. **1382** Wyclif *Gen.* xl. 15 Theuelich Y am had awey fro the loond of Hebrew [**1388** Ebrews].
2. The Semitic language spoken by the Hebrews, and in which most of the books of the Old Testament were written; it became extinct in vernacular use three or four centuries B.C., but survived liturgically, and is still cultivated by educated Jews throughout the world.
(In the New Testament applied to the Aramaic or Syriac, the vernacular language of the Hebrews of the time.)
a **1225** *Ancr. R.* 136 Vor Iudit on Ebreu is schrift an Englis. *a* **1300** *Cursor M.* 2179 Al men spak bot wit on tong, þat es hebru, al for to sai. *c* **1400** Maundev. (Roxb.) xxix. 132 þai can speke na langage bot Ebrew. *Ibid.* All þe Iews..lere for to speke Hebrew. **1526** Tindale *John* xix. 17 A place.. which is named in hebrue, Golgatha. **1645** Milton *Colast.* Wks. (1851) 345 As if hee knew both Greek and Ebrew. **1796** H. Hunter tr. *St. Pierre's Stud. Nat.* (1799) III. 732 The Doctor of the highest reputation for learning, who understood Hebrew, Arabic and the Hindoo Language. **1842** Prichard *Nat. Hist. Man* 143 Even the language of Numidia is supposed by Gesenius to have been a pure, or nearly pure, Hebrew.
b. *colloq.* Unintelligible speech: cf. *Greek*.
1705 Vanbrugh *Confederacy* i. ii, *Mon.* If she did but know what part I take in her sufferings —— *Flip.* Mighty obscure! *Mon.* Well, I say no more: but —— *Flip.* All Hebrew! **1816** Lady L. Stuart *Let.* 5 Dec. in *Scott's Fam. Lett.* (1894) I. 394 Even I..found a great many words absolute Hebrew to me.
B. *adj.* Belonging to the Hebrews; Israelitish, Jewish: **a.** in reference to the nation.
1483 *Cath. Angl.* 179/2 Hebrewe, *hebreus.* **1604** R. Cawdrey *Table Alph., Hebrew*, from Hebers stock. **1681** Dryden *Abs. & Achit.* 128 Which Hebrew priests the more unkindly took. **1851** Gallenga *Italy* 123 He is said to be of Hebrew extraction, the son of a converted Jew.
b. in reference to the language; of persons: learned in Hebrew, as a *Hebrew scholar*. (In the New Testament = Aramaic: see A. 2.)
a **1300** *Cursor M.* 406 In a dale..þat ebron hatte, in hebru nam. **1526** Tindale *Luke* xxiii. 38 His superscripcion was written over him in greke, latin, and ebrue letters. **1591** Sylvester *Du Bartas* i. i. 198 Turks Characters, nor Hebrew points to seek. **1611** Bp. Hall *Serm.* iii. Wks. (1837) 50 The Maccabees had four Hebrew letters in their ensign. **1663** Butler *Hud.* i. i. 59 For Hebrew roots, altho' they're found To flourish most in barren ground. **1895** W. A. Copinger in *Trans. Bibliogr. Soc.* II. ii. 112 Hebrew type is found in a book printed by Fyner, at Esslingen in 1475.. but no work was, I believe, wholly printed in this character till 1477.
c. ***Hebrew character, Hebrew letter***: collectors' names for a kind of moth and of shell respectively, so called from their markings.
1756 T. Amory *J. Buncle* (1770) I. xiii. 51 The Hebrew letter, another voluta, is a fine curiosity. **1843** Humphreys *Brit. Moths* (1858–9) 41 *Semiphora Gothica* (the Hebrew Character)..appears to be double-brooded.
Hence **'Hebrew-wise** *adv.*, in Hebrew fashion; in the manner of Hebrew writing, from right to left, backwards.
1689 Prior *Ep. to Fleetwood* 61 The God makes not the poet; but The thesis, vice-versâ put, Should Hebrew-wise be understood; And means, the Poet makes the God. **1774** Burney *Hist. Mus.* (1789) I. vii. 100 The opinion of some that the Greek scale and music should be read Hebrew wise.

'Hebrewdom. [See -dom.] The Hebrew community; the spirit or quality of the Hebrew people.
1843 T. Parker in J. Weiss *Life* I. 214 The culmination of Hebrewdom, the blossom of the nation. **1889** *Advance* (Chicago) 28 Feb., He must have enough of Hebrewdom in him..his spirit and attitude must be sufficiently Hebraic.

Hebrewess ('hi:bru:ɛs). [See -ess.] A female Hebrew, a Jewess.
1535 Coverdale *Jer.* xxxiv. 9 Euery man shulde let fre go his seruaunt and handemayde, Hebrue and Hebruesse [**1611** Hebrewesse]. **1849** *Tait's Mag.* XVI. 749 He was willing to abandon the great Otha, although only for another idol—namely, the young Hebrewess.

Hebrewish ('hi:bru:ɪʃ), *a.* [See -ish.]
†a. = Hebrew *a.* (*obs.*). **b.** Somewhat Hebrew; having something of a Hebrew character.
a **1225** *Ancr. R.* 136 On Ebreuwische ledene, Oloferne is þe ueond, þet makeð uet kelf & to wilde, feble & unstrong. *a* **1655** Vines *Lords Supp.* (1677) 37 The expression is Hebrewish.

'Hebrewism. [See -ism.] = Hebraism.
1611 Florio, *Ebraismo*, an Hebrewisme. **1684** N. S. *Crit. Enq. Edit. Bible* xiv. 137 The Hebrewisms are..more frequent. **1873** Geo. Eliot in Cross *Life* III. 216 This is, to me, pre-eminently true of Hebrewism and Christianity. **1886** A. B. Bruce *Mirac. Elem. Gosp.* ix. 342 He has discovered the defects of Hebrewism.

'Hebrewist. *rare*⁻⁰. = Hebraist 1.
In mod. Dicts.

Hebrician (hi:'brɪʃ(ɪ)ən). Now *rare* or *Obs.* Also 6 Hebrecyon, Hebretian, 6–7 Hebrecian, Hebritian. [Another form of Hebraician: cf. *algebrician*. (In early form perh. assimilated to *Grecian*.)]
†1. A Hebrew. *Obs.*
1542 Boorde *Dyetary* xxii. (1870) 287 Wherfore the Hebrecyon doth say, 'why doth a man dye?' **1565** Calfhill *Answ. Treat. Crosse* (1846) 108 It is the last letter of twenty-two among the Hebritians. **1570** Levins *Manip.* 19/30 Hebretiane, *hæbreicus*.
2. One versed in Hebrew, a Hebrew scholar.
1571 Golding *Calvin on Ps.* xviii. 2 Some Hebretians interpret it to seeke mercy. **1582** G. Martin *Disc. Corrupt. Script. Her.* in Fulke *Def.* (1843) 122 The great Grecians and Hebricians of the world. *a* **1661** Fuller *Worthies, Suffolk* iii. (1662) 70 He was an excellent Hebrician and well skilled in Cabalistical Learning. **1702** C. Mather *Magn. Chr.* iii. i. (1852) 254 The third chapter of Isaiah..might therefore have puzzled a very good Hebrician. **1883** C. F. Adams *Coll. Fetich* 22 Not to make learned Hebricians, but to teach..the Hebrew alphabet.

Hebrid ('hɛbrɪd), *a.* [ad. *Hebrides*: see next.] = Hebridean *a.* Also **'Hebridal** *a.*
1748 Thomson *Cast. Indol.* i. xxx, A shepherd of the Hebrid Isles. **1841** W. Yarrell *Brit. Fishes* (ed. 2) II. 133 The Hebridal Smelt, *Osmerus Hebridicus*..is at once clearly distinguishable from our long-known and highly-esteemed favourite, the common Smelt. **1923** *United Free Ch. Mission*

Rec. July 275 From many a Hebrid isle..from plain manses and luxurious mansions these men and women have come.

Hebridean (hɛbrɪ'diːən, hɪ'brɪdɪən), *a.* and *sb.* Also 6–9 -ian. [f. *Hebrides*, an alteration, said to have originated in an accidental misprint, of L. *Hebudes* (Pliny), Gr. Ἔβουδαι (Ptolemy).]

A. *adj.* Of or pertaining to the Hebrides, a group of islands off the west coast of Scotland. **B.** *sb.* A native or inhabitant of the Hebrides.

1623 COCKERAM, *Hebridean wave*, the Irish sea. **1632** LITHGOW *Trav.* 494 The desperate courage of these awfull Hebridians. **1641** in J. Sylvester tr. *Du Bartas's Weeks* 331/1 *Hebridian Wave*, the Sea about the Isles Hiberides, to the North from Ireland. **1775** JOHNSON *West. Isl.* 221 Such intelligence the Hebridians probably receive from their transmarine correspondents. **1780** J. JOHNSTONE (*title*) Anecdotes of Olave the Black, King of Man, and the Hebridian Princes of the Somerled Family. **1810** SCOTT *Fam. Lett.* 10 June (1894) I. 181, I intend to take the Hebridian character and scenery..for my subject. **1828** J. TYTLER *Hist. Scot.* I. i. 29 Dugal and other Hebridean chiefs. **1833–4** J. PHILLIPS *Geol.* in *Encycl. Metrop.* VI. 561/1 The Zetland Isles, which are in some measure to be viewed as a prolongation to the Hebridian group. *a* **1856** H. MILLER *Cruise Betsey* (1858) vi. 90 The penetrating powers of a true Hebridean drizzle. **1887** H. B. WOODWARD *Geol. Eng. & Wales* (ed. 2) 38 The Lewisian (or Hebridean) group. **1897** R. H. STORY *Apostolic Ministry Scot. Church* v. 154 The beehive cells, the remains of which may still be seen in Eilean Naomh and other Hebridean isles. **1911** *Encycl. Brit.* XXIV. 416/1 The oldest rocks of Scotland and of the British Isles are known..as Archean, and consist chiefly of gneiss (called..Lewisian and Hebridean). **1926** *Chambers's Jrnl.* Sept. 577/2 Our comely Hebridean. **1972** *Daily Tel.* 29 Jan. 16/5 The Hebridean processes of cloth-treatment are in danger of falling into oblivion.

hec, obs. form of HECK *sb.*

hecatarchy ('hɛkətɑːkɪ). *nonce-wd.* [f. Gr. ἑκατ-όν hundred + -αρχία rule, after *heptarchy*.] Government by a hundred rulers; = HECATONTARCHY (with play on HECATE).

1884 BLACKMORE *Tommy Upm.* II. xx. 273 Any other man, of any English era, from Heptarchy to Hecatarchy (that last child of Hecate).

‖**Hecate** ('hɛkətiː). Also 5 Ecate, Echate, 7 Hecat, Heccat. [a. Gr. Ἑκάτη, fem. of ἕκατος far-darting, an epithet of Apollo. (Always disyllabic, like Fr. *Hécate*, in Shaks., exc. in one passage (see 1 d); so also once in Milton.)]

1. In ancient Greek mythology, a goddess, said to be of Thracian origin, daughter of Perses and Asteria; in later times more or less identified with several others, esp. with Artemis, and thus **b.** with the moon; also, with Persephone the goddess of the infernal regions, and hence **c.** regarded as presiding over witchcraft and magical rites.

a. 1638 F. JUNIUS *Paint. of Ancients* 133 Theagenes..was wont to consult an image of Hecate, which he had ever about him. *Ibid.* 165 Statues of Diana or Hecate, set up at the meeting of three severall ways.

b. *c* **1420** *Pallad. on Husb.* XI. 253 But let not Ecate this craft espie [*marg.* luna].

c. 1573 G. HARVEY *Letter-bk.* (Camden) 141 Yet had I rather serve Hecate then any sutch. **1590** SHAKS. *Mids. N.* v. i. 391 And we Fairies, that do runne, By the triple Hecates teame, From the presence of the Sunne. **1605** —— *Lear* I. i. 112 The miseries of Heccat and the night. **1605** —— *Macb.* III. v. 1 Enter the three Witches, meeting Hecat. 1. Why how now Hecat, you looke angerly? **1634** MILTON *Comus* 135 Stay thy cloudy ebon chair, Wherein thou ridest with Hecat', and befriend Us thy vowed priests. *Ibid.* 535 Doing abhorred rites to Hecate In their obscured haunts.

d. *transf.* Applied vituperatively to a woman: = Hag, witch.

1591 SHAKS. *1 Hen. VI*, III. ii. 64, I speake not to that rayling Hecate, But vnto thee Alanson, and the rest. **1634** SIR T. HERBERT *Trav.* 169 An old Tartarian Hecate my servant. **1753** SMOLLETT *Ct. Fathom* xxi. (1817) IV. 100 (Stanf.) This declaration had its effect upon the withered Hecate.

e. Hecate supper (Gr. Ἑκάτης δεῖπνον), a meal set out by rich persons at the foot of the statue of Hecate on the thirtieth of each month, which became a kind of dole for beggars and paupers, in later times of offal or miserable food (Liddell and Scott).

1820 W. TOOKE tr. *Lucian* I. 429 Lupines, and a Hecate-supper.

2. *Astr.* Name of the 100th asteroid, discovered in 1868.

Hence **Heca'tæan** [Gr. ἑκαταῖ-ος: see -AN], **He'catic** [see -IC], **'Hecatine** [see -INE] *adjs.*, belonging to Hecate, magical.

1635 QUARLES *Embl.* II. ix, 'Twas neither Hecatæan spite, Nor charm below, nor pow'r above. **1678** CUDWORTH *Intell. Syst.* 293 From that Operation about the Hecatine Circle. **1792** T. TAYLOR *Proclus* I. 24 *note*, Nicephorus..informs us, that the hecatic orb is a golden sphere [etc.].

hecatolite ('hɛkətəʊlaɪt). *Min.* [f. Gr. Ἑκάτη as 'the moon'; see HECATE 1 b.] = MOONSTONE.

1868 DANA *Min.* (ed. 5) 354.

hecatologue ('hɛkətəʊlɒg). *nonce-wd.* [f. Gr. ἑκατ-όν hundred + λόγος word, after *decalogue*.] A code of a hundred rules.

1894 BLACKMORE *Perlycross* 241 Of all offences upon the Sergeant's Hecatologue, mutiny was the most heinous.

hecatomb ('hɛkətuːm, -tɒm), *sb.* [ad. L. *hecatombē*, a. Gr. ἑκατόμβη, properly, 'an offering of a hundred oxen' (f. ἑκατόν hundred + βοῦς ox), but even in Homer meaning simply 'a great public sacrifice' not necessarily confined to oxen. Cf. F. *hecatombe* (15–16th c. in Hatz.-Darm., 1611 in Cotgr.).]

1. A great public sacrifice (properly of a hundred oxen) among the ancient Greeks and Romans, and hence extended to the religious sacrifices of other nations; a large number of animals offered or set apart for a sacrifice.

a **1592** H. SMITH *Wks.* (1867) II. 391 Augustus had been very liberal in making the great sacrifice called hecatomb. **1599** MARSTON *Sco. Villanie* II. v. 198 Ile offer to thy shrine, An Hecatombe, of many spotted kine. **1659** T. PECKE *Parnassi Puerp.* 157 For many Laurel wreaths, the Prince of Rome, The Gods presented with an Hecatomb. **1791** COWPER *Iliad* I. 121 A whole hecatomb in Chrysa bled. **1820** BYRON *Mar. Fal.* I. ii. 231 Great expiations had a hecatomb. **1843** PRESCOTT *Mexico* (1850) I. 48 His altars reeked with the blood of human hecatombs in every city of the empire.

2. *transf.* and *fig.* A sacrifice of many victims; a great number of persons, animals, or things, presented as an offering, or devoted to destruction; *loosely*, a large number or quantity, a 'heap'.

1598 MARSTON *Pygmal.* v. 156 O Hecatombe! O Catastrophe! From Mydas pompe, to Irus beggery! **1646** G. DANIEL *Poems* Wks. 1878 I. 85 Whole Hecatombes of Tribute Rhimes. **1713** PARNELL *Guardian* No. 66 ¶6 A hecatomb of reputations was that day to fall for her pleasure. **1821** SHELLEY *Prometh. Unb.* I. 7 Hecatombs of broken hearts. **1879** GEO. ELIOT *Theo. Such* xi. 197 Some of us might be offering grateful hecatombs by mistake.

Hence **'hecatomb** *v. trans.*, to furnish with a hecatomb.

a **1745** SWIFT *Misc. Poems* (1807) 37 Bid a hundred sons be born, To hecatomb the year. **1808** J. BARLOW *Columb.* IV. 230 What altars hecatomb'd with Christian gore!

hecatomped (hɛkə'tɒmpɪd), *a.* [ad. Gr. ἑκατόμπεδ-ος of a hundred feet long, f. ἑκατόν hundred + πεδ- ablaut-grade of πούς, ποδ- foot.] Measuring a hundred feet in length and breadth; a hundred feet square. So **heca'tompedon** [Gr. ἑκατόμπεδον], a temple of these dimensions, as the Parthenon at Athens; hence **heca'tompedism** (irreg. *hecatompedonism*), applied to the system of exact proportions in architecture.

1703 SAVAGE *Let. Antients* cxlvi. 343 I'll pass over..the Hecatomped Temples. **1773** MELMOTH *Cato* 239 (Jod.) The Athenians, after they had completed the building of the temple called the Hecatompedon, exempted from all future toil those beasts of burden, whose labours had assisted in carrying on that sacred edifice. *a* **1854** COCKBURN *Ess., Pagan or Chr.* in *Mem.* (1860) 72 Admirers of Grecian Hecatompedonism and the mathematical exactness of a fixed series of Ratios in the proportions of a structure. *Ibid.* 193.

hecatonstylon (ˌhɛkətɒn'staɪlən). [f. Gr. ἑκατόν hundred + στῦλος column, pillar, app. after F. *hécatonstyle*.] A building having a hundred pillars or columns.

1842 in BRANDE *Dict. Sci.*, etc. Hence in mod. Dicts.

† **heca'tontad.** *Obs. rare.* [ad. Gr. ἑκατοντάς, -αδ- a group of a hundred.] A hundred.

1680 H. MORE *Apocal. Apoc.* 147 Sixteen Hecatontads or Centuries of furlongs.

hecatontarchy (hɛkə'tɒntɑːkɪ). [ad. Gr. ἑκατονταρχία the post or command of a centurion, f. ἑκατοντ(α)- comb. form of ἑκατόν hundred + -αρχία, ἀρχή rule, sovereignty.] Government by a hundred rulers.

1660 S. FORD *Loyal Subj. Exhult.* 37 One whiles we were under a Saxon Heptarchy again..sometimes under an Hecatontarchy (give me leave to frame a new name for a new thing). *a* **1670** HACKET *Abp. Williams* II. (1692) 202 What would come to pass if the choice of a governor or governors were referred to the thousands and millions of England? Beware a Heptarchy, again beware a hecatontarchy. **1852** GROTE *Greece* II. lxxvi. (1856) X. 98 The omnipotent Hekatontarchy named by the partisan feelings of Agesilaus.

† **'hecatontome.** *Obs. nonce-wd.* [f. Gr. ἑκατόν hundred + τόμος tome, volume.] A collection of a hundred volumes.

1641 MILTON *Animadv.* (1851) 246 A better confutation of the Pope and Masse than whole Hecatontomes of controversies.

hecatophyllous (ˌhɛkətəʊ'fɪləs), *a. Bot. rare.* [f. Gr. ἑκατόν hundred + φύλλον leaf + -OUS.] Having leaves consisting each of a hundred leaflets.

1854 in MAYNE *Expos. Lex.* **1886** in *Syd. Soc. Lex.*

hecceitie, obs. form of HÆCCEITY.

1625 GILL *Sacr. Philos.* XII. 202 The difference of men must be in their hecceities, or numerall diversitie of their bodies onely. **1654** GATAKER *Disc. Apol.* 68 All other Doctrines, that bear the tru mark and hecceitie of corruption.

hecche, hecchele, obs. ff. HECK, HATCHEL.

† **'hecco.** *Obs.* The woodpecker: cf. HICKWALL.

1604 DRAYTON *Owle* 206 The sharp-nebd Hecco stabbing at his braine. **1612** —— *Poly-olb.* xiii. 215 The laughing Hecco, then the counterfetting Jay.

hecfer, -forde, obs. ff. HEIFER.

hech (hɛx, hɛç), *int. Sc.* [Sc. form of HEIGH.] An exclamation expressive of various feelings, chiefly of surprise, sorrow, or fatigue.

1777–1808 J. MAYNE *Siller Gun* I. 113 Hech, sirs! what crowds were gather'd roun'. **1816** SCOTT *Antiq.* xliv, Hech, sirs! guide us a'! to burn the engines? that's a great waste. **1823** W. TENNANT *Cdl. Beaton* 171 (Jam.) Hech, man! is that possible? **1871** C. GIBBON *Lack of Gold* i, Hech, sirs, but it's a sorry thing to come to this pass.

Hence **hech** *v.*, to utter the exclamation *hech!*

c **1750** *Mary Hamilton* xiii. in Child *Ballads* (1889) III. VI. clxxiii. 392 Monie a lady fair Siching and crying, Och how! .. What need ye hech and how, ladies? What need ye how for me?

hech, Sc. var. HIGH *a.*

hech, obs. form of EACH.

1297 R. GLOUC. (1724) 240 Seynt Peter..tormented hym sore ynou, þat hech lyme hym oke.

heche: see HATCH, HECK.

hechele, -il, obs. forms of HATCHEL.

hechewal, obs. form of HICKWALL.

hechima (he'tʃiːma). [Jap.] The sponge-gourd (see SPONGE *sb.*[1] 13 c).

1883 *Trans. Asiatic Soc. Japan* XI. 13 (*heading*) Luffa petola, Ser. Hechima... Young fruit as food: and fibres of ripe fruit as brushes and sponges. **1889** J. J. REIN *Industries of Japan* i. 72 (*heading*) 21. *Luffa petola*, Ser., Jap. Hechima, Tô-guwa. The long cylindric fruit resembles a long straight cucumber.

hecht, obs. Sc. form of HIGHT.

heck (hɛk), *sb.*[1] Chiefly *Sc.* and *north. dial.* Forms: 1 hec, 4–5 hek, hekke, (5 hec, heke), 6– heck (6 hekk, 7 hecke, heake); other forms, see HATCH *sb.*[1] [OE. *hęc* (in *fodder-hęc*, Anglia IX. 265), also *hæc*:—WGer. **hakjâ*: cf. in same sense MLG. *heck*, Du. *hek* fence, rail, gate, in Kilian *hecke*. *Heck* is a northern form, the southern being *hetch*. The OE. variant *hæc* (cf. Sievers *Ags. Gr.*, ed. 3, §89) gave in southern and midl. Eng. the form HATCH: see also HACK *sb.*[2]]

1. a. The lower half of a door; also, an inner door; = HATCH *sb.*[1] 1. *north. dial.*

13.. *Minor Poems fr. Vernon MS.* xxiv. 231 Of paradys he opened the hekke. *c* **1425** *Voc.* in Wr.-Wülcker 668/4 *Hoc ostiolum*, hek. *c* **1440** *Promp. Parv.* 231/2 Hec, hek, or hetche, or a dore. *c* **1460** *Towneley Myst.* (Surtees) 106 Good wyff, open the hek. Seys thou not what I bryng? **1483** *Cath. Angl.* 181/1 An Heke (*A.* hekke), *antica.* **1570** LEVINS *Manip.* 54/9 An Heck, hatch, *portella.* **1674–91** RAY *N.C. Words* 36 The *Heck*, the Door. Steck the Heck. *Ibid.* 133 The Hollen is a wall about 2½ yards high, used in Dwelling Houses to secure the family from the blasts of wind rushing in when the heck is open. **1703** THORESBY *Let. to Ray* (E.D.S.), *Heck*, the heck is ordinarily but half a door, the lower half. **1788** W. MARSHALL *Yorksh.* Gloss. (E.D.S.), *Heck*,..also the inner or entry-door of a cottage; formerly, in all probability made like a *heck*. **1876** *Whitby Gloss.*, *Heck*, a door, or rather a door in halves as a top and bottom; especially the lower half door. **1893** *Northumbld. Gloss.*, *Heck, heck-door*, the inner door between the entry or lobby, and the house or kitchen.

b. (See quots.) *north. dial.*

1825 BROCKETT, *Heck*..the passage into a house. **1847–78** HALLIWELL, *Heck*, the division from the side of the fire in the form of a passage in old houses.

2. A grating or frame of parallel bars in a river to obstruct the passage of fish, or other solid bodies, without obstructing the flow of the water: variously applied to an apparatus of this kind used to catch fish at a weir, and in Sc. and north Eng., to the bars or spars of which this is composed, also to a horizontal series of bars laid alongside the top of a dam or weir to prevent salmon from jumping over it, and to a grating of vertical bars set in a mill-race to prevent solid floating substances or fish from passing over or under the mill-wheel; = HATCH *sb.*[1] 7.

1424 *Sc. Acts Jas. I*, c. 12 þat ilk hek of þe forsaid crufis be þre inche wyde as it is requirit in þe auld statutis. **1472** *Act 12 Edw. IV*, c. 7 Hebbyngwerez, estakez, kideux, hekkez ou flodegates. **1531–2** *Act 23 Hen. VIII*, c. 18 title, Fisshegarthes, piles, stakes, heckes, and other ingins sett in the Ryver & Water of Ouse & Humbre. *c* **1575** *Balfour's Practicks* (1754) 543 All sic cruives and maskis and heckis thairof, sall have at the leist twa inche in lenth, and thre inche in breidth, swa that the smolt or fry may frelie swim up and down the water. **1623** *N. Riding Rec.* (1885) III. II. 199 Matthew Harland presented for suffering his salmon heckes to stand in the Eske in unseasonable times. *a* **1724** in Hearne *R. Glouc.* (1724) Gloss. s.v. *Hext*, Grates, sett in Rivers or Waters before Fludgates, which are called Hecks. **1804** *Act 43 Geo. III*, c. xlv. §15 No person shall use any grate heck or other engine or device..in any fishery..

whereof the bars or staps shall be otherwise than perpendicular and of an oval shape. **1820** *Aberdeen Jrnl.* 2 Aug. (Jam.), To put proper hecks on the tail-races of their canals, to prevent salmon or grilse from entering them. **1863** *N.B. Daily Mail* 12 Sept., It is in the power of the Commissioners to order hecks above and below mill-wheels. **1870** *Law Rep.* 5 Com. Pleas 717 Besides the perpendicular hecks placed in the apertures of the weir or dam, there were also a set of horizontal hecks.. along the top of the weir. *Ibid.* 718 This coop was legal in all its parts.. both in the coop-hecks and the weirhecks.

3. A rack made with parallel spars to hold fodder, either fixed in a stable, or movable, so as to be placed in a field, cattle-yard, or sheep-fold (***stand-heck***); = HACK *sb.*[2] 2, HATCH *sb.*[1] 2. ***at heck and manger***: in comfortable circumstances, in plenty, 'in clover'. *Sc.* and *north. dial.*

c **1420** *Anturs of Arth.* 448 (Thornton MS.) Haye hendly, heuyde in hekkes [*v.r.* haches] on hyghte. **1521** in *Archæol.* XVII. 203 A rowm.. which I have orissed with Hek and Mangeor for xx horse. **1620** MARKHAM *Farew. Husb.* ii. 13 The soyle of yong Cattell made in the Winter time by feeding at stand Heakes. **1663** *Inv. Ld. J. Gordon's Furniture*, The stables all in order, with heck and manger. **1748** tr. *Renatus' Distemp. Horses* 99 The Rack or Heck as the common People call it. **1814** SCOTT *Wav.* lxiv, '[He] maintained puir Davie at heck and manger maist feck o' his life.' **1824** MISS FERRIER *Inher.* II. 237 (D.) Six horses.. had been living at heck and manger. **1877** *N.W. Linc. Gloss.*, *Heck*, a rack for fodder in a stable or field.

4. = HAKE *sb.*[3] 1. *Obs.* or *dial.*

1403 *Nottingham Rec.* II. 20, j. chesehek, ijd. **1611–14** [see CHEESE *sb.*[1] 7].

5. (See quots.) Also ***heck-board***. *local.*

1825 BROCKETT, *Heck-board*, a loose board at the back part of a cart. **1862** *Jrnl. R. Agric. Soc.* XXIII. 216 One-horse carts, with hecks and shelvings. **1883** *Almondbury Gloss.*, *Heck*,.. the rail or hurdle placed in front and behind a cart, used in housing hay.

6. A 'shuttle' or sluice in a drain; = HATCH *sb.*[1] 6. *local.*

1877 *N.W. Linc. Gloss.*

7. A contrivance in a spinning-wheel, and hence, also, in a warping-mill, by which the yarn or thread is guided to the reel or reels: see quots.

1824 MACTAGGART *Gallovid. Encycl.*, *Heck*,.. the toothed thing which guides the spun-thread on to the pirn, in spinning-wheels. **1829** E. IRVING *Tales Times Mart.* in *Anniversary* 283 Her spinning wheel was of the upright construction, having no heck, but a moveable eye which was carried along the pirn by a heart-motion. **1883** H. P. SMITH *Gloss. Terms & Phr.*, *Heck*,.. an apparatus by which the threads of warps are separated into sets for heddles.

8. *attrib.* and *Comb.*, as ***heck-door***, ***-stake*** (see sense 1), ***-stave***; **heck-board** (see sense 5); **heck-box**, a box used to divide the warp threads into two alternate sets, one for each heddle or heald; **heck-stead**, **-way** (*dial.*), a doorway; **heck-stower**, one of the spars of a heck: see also quot. 1876.

1875 KNIGHT *Dict. Mech.*, s.v. *Heck*, The *heck-box slides vertically on a bar as the reel rotates, and thus disposes the warp spirally on the reel. **1811** AITON *Agric. Surv. Ayrsh.* 115 (Jam.) The cattle.. turning the contrary way by the *heck-door to the byre or stable. **1888** *Sheffield Gloss.*, *Heck-doors*, small wooden doors opening into a farmyard. **1876** *Whitby Gloss.*, **Hecksteeak*, the door-stake or night-bar. **1416–17** *Durh. MS. Terr. Roll.*, *Hekstaues pro ovibus in le Holme. **1876** *Whitby Gloss.*, **Hecksteead*, or *Heckway*, the doorway. **1401–2** *Durh. MS. Terr. Roll.*, *Hekstaures pro le Holme. **1641** BEST *Farm. Bks.* (Surtees) 121 Younge trees.. in fower or five yeares space.. will serve for flayle-hande-staffes, cavinge-rake-shaftes, hecke-stowers [etc.]. **1876** *Whitby Gloss.*, *Heckstower*, the portable beam across the middle of the hatchway (i.e. the opening through the shop floor into the cellar) for supporting the lid.

†**Heck**, *sb.*[2] *Obs. rare*$^{-1}$. Short for HECTOR *sb.*

1707 E. WARD *Hud. Rediv.* II. III. 20 Behind these came two Bully Hecks, With feather'd Cock'd up Cordebecks [cf. quot. 1598 s.v. HECTOR *sb.* 1].

heck (hɛk), *sb.*[3] and *int. dial.* and *colloq.* Euphemistic alteration of *hell.* (Also ***hecky*** in dial. use.)

[**1865** [J. A. FERGUSON] *Wot Aw seed ut th' Preston Eggsibishun* 88 (E.D.D.), Well, aw'll go to ecky, he cried. **1878** J. ALMOND *Bunch of Watercresses* 21 Where the hecky could he go to?]

1887 T. DARLINGTON *Folk-sp. S. Cheshire* s.v., What the heck are yō up to? **1922** S. LEWIS *Babbitt* xiv. 178 How it feels, by heck, to be up at five-thirty. **1925** *Blackw. Mag.* Oct. 545/1, I couldn't make out what in heck was going on. **1928** M. WALSH *While Rivers Run* ii. § 3 By heck! what a kick he must have in that right of his. **1930** *Daily Express* 23 May 10/3 Does the borough council care? By heck, it doesn't! **1932** J. T. FARRELL *Studs Lonigan* (1936) iii. 68 He would have the heck of a time explaining his shiner to the old lady. **1933** *Punch* 11 Jan. 52/1 He insisted on St. Isinglas because he thought everything here was so well organised. The heck it is. **1936** M. H. BRADLEY *Five Minute Girl* xiii. 236 He had certainly played heck with that party. **1956** E. POUND tr. *Sophocles' Women of Trachis* 17 That fellow was lying, one time or the other, One heck of a messenger! **1957** I. CROSS *God Boy* (1958) i. 12 Heck now, I started off with Dad talking to me.. and here we are no further on. *Ibid.* xii. 95 People go all the way the heck over to France. **1966** *Guardian* 5 Feb. 6/4 Sometimes he sings for sheer fun and the heck of it. **1973** D. WESTHEIMER *Going Public* i. 15 It's a heck of a responsibility.

heck, *v.* [Echoic. Cf. HACK *v.*[1] 13.] *intr.* To cough slightly; to imitate the noise of a cough.

1892 P. H. EMERSON *Son of Fens* 44 They had seen me, and they hecked when they came in.

So †**'hecking** *ppl. a.* = HACKING *ppl. a.* 2.

1642 FULLER *Holy & Prof. St.* II. ii. 55 An hecking cough which ever attendeth that disease. **1750** *Phil. Trans.* XLVI. 438 A short, low, hecking, hoarse Cough. **1799** BEDDOES *Contrib. Phys. & Med. Knowl.* 536 A hard cough, which had succeeded to a short hecking cough.

heckberry, var. HAGBERRY.

heckel, -ill, obs. forms of HECKLE.

heckelphone ('hɛkəlfəʊn). Also **-phon**. [ad. G. *heckelphon*, f. name of Wilhelm *Heckel* (1856–1909), an instrument-maker of Biberich, after *saxophone*.] A baritone oboe.

1905 *Westm. Gaz.* 14 Dec. 8/2 A new instrument, called appropriately the 'Heckelphon', answered from the orchestra. **1914** C. FORSYTH *Orchestration* 228 Strauss has made use of the Heckelphon in.. *Salome.* **1940** G. JACOB *Orchestral Technique* (ed. 2) i. 3 Some very fully scored modern symphonic and operatic works employ quadruple woodwind, such exotics as the bass flute and heckelphone sometimes being added to the flute and oboe group respectively. **1966** *Guardian* 22 Apr. 12/5 A heckelphone (a kind of outsize 'baritone' oboe).

heckfare, -fer, -furth, etc., obs. ff. HEIFER.

heckle ('hɛk(ə)l), *sb.* Also 5–7 **hek-, hekk-, heck-, -el(l, -il(l, -yl(l.** [A parallel form (:—OE. **hęcel*) of HACKLE, q.v. for etymological relations. Another parallel form is HATCHEL, with variants *hetchel, hitchel.*]

1. An instrument for combing or scutching flax or hemp; = HACKLE *sb.*[2] 1.

c **1425** *Voc.* in Wr.-Wülcker 668/32 *Hec mataxa*, hekylle. *c* **1440** *Promp. Parv.* 234/1 Hekele (*Harl.* heykylle), *mataxa.* **1485** *Inv.* in *Ripon Ch. Acts* (Surtees) 372, ij hekels pro lino. *a* **1529** SKELTON *El. Rummyng* 295 Som layde to pledge.. Theyr hekell and theyr rele. **1570** LEVINS *Manip.* 125/30 An Heckyl, *pecten.* **1615** MARKHAM *Eng. Housew.* II. v. (1668) 135 When your Hemp hath been twice swingled, dryed and beaten, you shall then bring it to the heckle. **1808** *Char.* in *Ann. Reg.* 101 To determine.. whether long or short heckles make least refuse in dressing the flax. **1863** SIR W. FAIRBAIRN *Mills* II. 197 [Baxter's] machine consists generally of six gradations of heckles.

fig. **1788** BURNS *Ep. to H. Parker* 3 A land unknown to prose or rhyme; Where words ne'er crost the Muse's heckles. *? a* **1800** *Rob Roy* xii. in Child *Ballads* VII. ccxxv. 246/1 He was a hedge unto his friends, A heckle to his faes, ladie.

2. a. The long shining feathers on the neck of certain birds, esp. the cock; = HACKLE *sb.*[2] 3.

c **1450** HENRYSON *Mor. Fab.*, *Sir Chanticleer* 58, I beheld your fedderis fair and gent, Your beike, your breist, your Hekill & your Came. **1513** DOUGLAS *Æneis* XII. Prol. 156 Phebus red fowle.. Oft streking furth his hekkyll, crawand cleir. **1893** *Daily News* 8 Apr. 7/1 For Guildersmalsen, January, 1795, the men of the 'Forty Twa', were rewarded with 'the glorious red heckle' or vulture plume, which has ever since been the distinctive badge of the Black Watch.

b. ***to set up (one's) heckle.*** See HACKLE *sb.*[2] 3 b.

1601 DEACON & WALKER *Answ. to Darel* 79 If.. you begin (like a cowardlie crauen) so soone to set vp the heckle.

3. *Angling.* An artificial fly; = HACKLE *sb.*[2] 4. Also ***heckle-fly***.

1808–18 JAMIESON, *Heckle*.. A fly, for angling, dressed merely with a cock's feather. **1825** BROCKETT, *Heckle, Heckle-flee*, an artificial fly for fishing.

4. a. One who heckles. See HECKLE *v.* 3. *Sc.*

1830 GALT *Lawrie T.* IV. xi. (1849) 183 What was the use of argolbargoling with such a heckle?

b. The action of heckling.

1905 *Westm. Gaz.* 29 Apr. 3/2 Our congratulations to.. Mr. Davies on his.. successful heckle. **1944** H. VAN ZELLER *Ezechiel* viii. 69 We again look for some sort of an apologia, an objection or two, a mild heckle, a question.

5. *attrib.* and *Comb.*, as ***heckle-maker, -pin, tooth*** (sense 1); ***heckle-fly*** (sense 2); ***heckle-headed*** adj. ***to be on the heckle-pins***, to be in painful anxiety or uneasiness.

c **1450** HENRYSON *Mor. Fab.*, *Lion & Mouse* 32 His hude of skarlet, bordowrit with silk, In hekle wyss vntill his girdill doun. **1483** *Cath. Angl.* 181/1 (MS. A) Hekylle makere, *mataxarius.* **1770** in A. N. Palmer *Wrexham* (1893) Introd. 11 One heckel-maker. *c* **1785** *J. Thompson's Man* 15 Crook-backed, heckle-headed.. lap-lugged, ill-haired. **1808–18** JAMIESON s.v. *Heckle* v., *To come o'er the heckle-pins*, to be severely examined. **1835** URE *Philos. Manuf.* 209 [They] present their heckle points radially from their axes. **1863** SIR W. FAIRBAIRN *Mills* II. 198 The short.. fibres.. are taken out by the heckle teeth. *Ibid.*, The bite of the holder is quite close up on the points of the heckle-pins. **1872** C. GIBBON *For the King* xix, The poor lad was on heckle-pins.

heckle, dial. var. of HICKWALL.

heckle ('hɛk(ə)l), *v.* Forms: 5 **hekel, -ylle, -le,** 5–6 **heckel(l, (hecle),** 6– **heckle.** [f. prec. sb.; cf. HACKLE, HATCHEL *vbs.*]

1. *trans.* To dress (flax or hemp) with a heckle, to split and straighten out the fibres; = HACKLE *v.*[3]

c **1440** *Promp. Parv.* 234/1 Hekelyn, *mataxo.* **1530** PALSGR. 582/2 My father was a hosyer and my mother dyd heckell flaxe. **1535** [see HATCHEL *v.* 1 *a*, quot. 1398]. **1616** SURFL. & MARKH. *Country Farme* 567 Heckle it through a finer heckle, then spinne it. **1794** A. YOUNG *Agric. Suffolk* (1797) 122 The buyer heckles it [the hemp].. he makes it into two or three sorts: *long strike, short strike,* and *full tow.* **1835** URE *Philos. Manuf.* 213 A system of machines for scutching and heckling flax was specified by patent.. in July, 1833.

b. *transf.* To scratch.

1508 DUNBAR *Tua Mariit Wemen* 107 With his hard hurcheone skyn sa heklis he my chekis.

2. *intr.* for *refl.* To undergo heckling.

1733 P. LINDSAY *Interest Scot.* 153 This Kind of Lint heckles away almost to nothing, and is indeed in Appearance very fine.

3. *trans.* To catechize severely, with a view to discover the weak points of the person interrogated. Long applied in Scotland to the public questioning of parliamentary candidates. Also *absol.*

1808–25 JAMIESON, *To Heckle*, 2. To tease with questions, to examine severely. **1880** *Punch* 28 Aug., To heckle with questions and bother with Bogeys Appear the Fourth Party's preposterous rules. **1886** *Leeds Mercury* 12 Mar. 5/2 The audience proceeded to 'heckle' him in a way dear to Scotch constituencies. **1891** E. W. GOSSE *Gossip in Library* xxiii. 298 On the hustings, Lord John Manners was a good deal heckled.

†**4.** *intr.* To wrangle. Cf. HAGGLE *v.* 2. *Obs.*

1596 J. MELVILL *Diary* (Wodrow Soc.) 302 And ther they heckled on, till all the hous and clos baith hard much of a large hour.

5. *trans.* To 'dress', chastise. *dial.*

1828 *Craven Dial.*, *Heckle*, to beat, to chastise. **1855** ROBINSON *Whitby Gloss.*, *A Heckling*, a scolding undergone; the ordeal of being 'called over the coals'.

Hence **'heckled** *ppl. a.*, dressed (as flax) with a heckle; **heck'lee** *nonce-wd.*, one who undergoes heckling or hostile interrogation; **heckling** *ppl. a.*, that heckles.

1863 SIR W. FAIRBAIRN *Mills* II. 198 Heckled flax. **1888** BESANT *Herr Paulus* I. 296 'Permit me one more question', this heckling Professor continued. **1893** STEVENSON *Catriona* 89 He answered, with a heckling laugh. **1895** *Daily Tel.* 17 July 5/1 As a 'hecklee'—if the term be permissible—the Liberal candidate for East Fife leaves little to be desired.

'heckleback. [f. HECKLE *sb.*; cf. HACKLE *sb.*[2] 2.] Local name of the fifteen-spined or sea stickleback.

1710 SIBBALD *Fife* (1803) 128 (Jam.) Our fishers call it Stronachie or Heckleback.

†**heckled**, *a. Obs.* [? f. HECKLE *sb.* 2.] ? Having a border or fringe like the heckle of a cock.

c **1450** HENRYSON *Test. Cres.* 244 His hude was reid, heklit atouir his croun. *a* **1568** ? LICHTOUN *Quha douttis dremes* 73 in *Bannatyne MS.* (1887) 291 Ane heklit hud maid of the wyld wode sege Trest weill this pundlar thocht him no manis pege.

heckler ('hɛklə(r)). [f. HECKLE *v.* + -ER[1].]

1. A dresser of flax or hemp.

c **1440** *Promp. Parv.* 234/1 Hekelare, *mataxatrix.* **1720** *Lond. Gaz.* No. 5882/10 Robert Pickering, Heckler. **1851** MAYHEW *Lond. Labour* (1861) II. 306 The hecklers or flax-dressers, can unfold 'a tale of wo' on this subject.

2. One who severely questions another; *spec.* one who catechizes a parliamentary candidate.

1885 *Manch. Exam.* 13 Oct. 5/2 A lively bout between.. the Liberal candidate.. and some hecklers whom he encountered at Delph. **1889** *Spectator* 16 Nov., Mr. Morley's 'heckler', Mr. Laidler, who signs himself 'Bricklayer'.

†**'hecklester.** *Obs. rare.* [See -STER.] A dresser of flax or hemp: originally feminine.

c **1475** *Voc.* in Wr.-Wülcker 795/9 *Hec matatrix*, a hekylster [*printed* hok-]. *c* **1481** CAXTON *Dialogues* (E.E.T.S.) 44/40 Roberte the hekelester Hath no more hempe, And hath lost her hekell.

heckling ('hɛklɪŋ), *vbl. sb.* The action of HECKLE *v.*

1. The splitting and separation of the fibres of flax and hemp.

1495 *Trevisa's Barth. De P.R.* (W. de Worde) XVII. clx. 708 Wyth moche brakyng, heckelynge [*MS. Bodl.* hechelinge] and robbyng, hardes ben departyd fro the substaunce of hempe and of flexe. **1618** *Naworth Househ. Bks.* (Surtees) 93 To ij women for heckling ix dayes, ij^{s} iij^{d}. **1863** SIR W. FAIRBAIRN *Mills* II. 197 Heckling.. consists in effectually completing the process commenced in scutching.

2. Severe catechizing or cross-examination.

1879 SIR G. CAMPBELL *White & Black in U.S.* 245 There was no opposition and no heckling. **1888** *Times* 10 Oct. 5/1 He underwent another severe heckling to-day before a *juge d'instruction.*

3. *attrib.* and *Comb.* (from sense 1), as ***heckling-machine, -shop***, etc.

1842 *Penny Cycl.* XXII. 349/2 Machinery for spinning tow.. has a different heckling apparatus. **1863** SIR W. FAIRBAIRN *Mills* II. 197 Heckling machines are various, according to the quality of the flax. **1876** SMILES *Sc. Natur.* iii. (ed. 4) 50 The boys were first put into the heckling shop. **1894** H. SPEIGHT *Nidderdale* 304 Many of the old 'heckling-mills' are now.. abandoned.

'heckum-'peckum. (See quot.)

1867 F. FRANCIS *Angling* vi. (1880) 251 The great trout fly for the lakes, known through all the South of Scotland as the *Heckum Peckum.* **1886** *World* 25 Aug. 9 The 'Zulu' and the 'heckum-peckum' are the only two flies for the loch.

heckyl(l, obs. forms of HECKLE *sb.*

hecogenin (hɛkəʊ'dʒɛnɪn). *Chem.* [f. mod.L. *Hec(htia*, name of a genus of plants + -o + -GENIN.] A steroid glycoside (see quot. 1965) occurring in various plants, as *Hechtia texensis* and *Agave* species, obtained commercially from sisal waste and used commercially as a precursor

in the manufacture of cortisone and other steroid hormones.

1943 R. E. Marker et al. in *Jrnl. Amer. Chem. Soc.* LXV. 1199/2 We first isolated from *Hechtia texensis* (S. Wats.) a new steroidal sapogenin having the composition $C_{27}H_{42}O_4$ . . which we have named hecogenin. **1952** *Sci. News* XXV. 115 More than 100,000 tons of fibre are produced yearly from sisal, . . and . . approximately the same amount of waste material, containing 0.04 per cent to 0.1 per cent of hecogenin, are available. **1965** Pollock & Stevens *Dict. Org. Compounds* (ed. 4) III. 1809/1, 3β-Hydroxy-5α-spirostan-12-one (Hecogenin). **1972** *Materials & Technol.* V. xx. 752 Hecogenin is extracted from sisal waste.

hecseite, obs. form of hæcceity.

‖**hectare** ('hɛktɛə(r) or as F. ɛktar). Also **hectar**, **hecatare**. [F., irregularly f. Gr. ἑκατόν hundred (see hecto-) + are *sb.*³, ad. L. *ārĕa*.] In the Metric system, a superficial measure containing 100 ares, or 2·471 acres.

1810 *Naval Chron.* XXIV. 301 Hectar, square hectometer. **1839** W. Chambers *Tour Belgium* 81/1 The third . . contains 138 mines in an extent of 32,777 hectares. **1881** Darwin *Veg. Mould* 159 There must exist 133,000 living worms in a hectare of land.

hectastyle, erron. form of hexastyle.

hecte, var. hekte.

hectic ('hɛktɪk), *a.* and *sb.* Forms: α. 5 etik(e, 5–6 etyk(e, 6 eticke, ethyke, hetique. β. 7 hecticke, -ique, 7–8 hectick, 7– hectic. [ad. (through Fr.) late L. *hectic-us*, a. Gr. ἑκτικός habitual, hectic, consumptive, f. ἕξις habit, state of body or mind. The earlier forms *etik*, etc., were a. OF. *étique* (13th c. in Littré) = It., Sp. *etico*, Romanic forms from *hectic-us*; the later agree with F. *hectique* (Paré, 16th c.).]

A. *adj.*

1. a. Belonging to or symptomatic of the bodily condition or habit: applied to that kind of fever which accompanies consumption or other wasting diseases, and is attended with flushed cheeks and hot dry skin.

1398 Trevisa *Barth. De P.R.* vii. xxxv. (1495) 248 The feuer etyk hurtyth and greuyth the sadde membres. **1562** Turner *Herbal* ii. 103 a, In consumyng agues which ar called hectice. **1578** Lyte *Dodoens* i. xlix. 71 Such as are fallen into Consumtions and Feuer Hetiques. **1604** R. Cawdrey *Table Alph.*, *Hecticke*, inflaming the hart, and soundest parts of the bodie. **1611** Cotgr. s.v. *Ectique*, Thence is a feuer called Hecticke, when it hath possessed all parts of the bodie, without any alteration in it selfe. **1719** Quincy *Phys. Dict.*, *Hectick* . . it is only joined to that kind of Fever which is slow and continual, and ending in a Consumption. **1807–26** S. Cooper *First Lines Surg.* (ed. 5) 34 Hectic fever is more or less remittent, but never wholly intermittent.

b. Belonging to or symptomatic of this fever.

1642 Rogers *Naaman* 541 No hectique disposition upon the body so sapes away the strength thereof. **1651** Davenant *Gondibert* ii. v. (R.) The hectick heate Of Oswald's blood doubled their pulses pace. **1807** Crabbe *Par. Reg.* iii. 923 All the rose to one small spot withdrew: They call'd it hectic; 'twas a fiery flush. **1831** Brewster *Nat. Magic* xiii. (1833) 326 This action on the lungs . . oppresses them with a hectic cough. **1885** Edna Lyall *Gold. Days* I. x. 283 Like the hectic beauty of one dying of consumption.

c. Affected with hectic fever; consumptive.

1664 *Phil. Trans.* I. 24 All of them in time . . become paralitick and dye hectick. **1771** Smollett *Humph. Cl.* (1820) 100 Thin, puny, yellow, hectic figures. **1850** Kingsley *Alt. Locke* iv, A pretty, hectic girl of sixteen. **1860** Piesse *Lab. Chem. Wonders* 54 Many young people with hectic cheeks.

2. *fig.* **a.** Wasting, consuming. **b.** With reference to the hectic flush.

1603 Florio *Montaigne* (1634) 495 All enjoyings are not alike. There are some hecticke, faint and languishing ones. **1819** Shelley *Ode W. Wind* 4 The leaves . . Yellow, and black, and pale, and hectic red. **1826** Mrs. Hemans *For. Sanct.* ii. xii, Day's last hectic blush. **1886** Dowden *Shelley* I. iii. 99 Thrill with vehement and hectic feeling.

†**3.** In etymological sense: Habitual, constitutional. *Obs.*

1641 Milton *Ch. Govt.* ii. iii. (1851) 162 That hectick disposition to evill, the source of all vice. **1654** H. L'Estrange *Chas. I* (1655) 5 He seemed naturally to affect a majestique carelesnesse, which was so hectique, so habitual in him as [etc.].

4. Stirring, exciting, disturbing; characterized by a state of feverish excitement or activity. *colloq.*

1904 Kipling *Traffics & Discov.* 210 Didn't I say we never met in pup-pup-puris naturalibus, if I may so put it, without a remarkably hectic day ahead of us? **1922** *Westm. Gaz.* 19 Aug., The hectic undulations of the mark. *Ibid.* 7 Nov., Those hectic inconsidered actions which kept the country in a state of crisis for some ten days. **1922** *Daily Mail* 21 Nov. 11 As additional excitements to the hectic finishes one horse was killed and the judge mistook the winner of the Leycester Nursery. **1925** Fraser & Gibbons *Soldier & Sailor Words* 117 *Hectic show*, an Air Force expression for flying very low. **1968** *Daily Mirror* 20 Aug. 9/2 Stretch bikini bottoms and loose towelling tops in hectic colours.

B. *sb.* (ellipt. use of the adj.) **1. a.** A hectic fever.

1398 Trevisa *Barth. De P.R.* xvi. v. (Tollem. MS.), It helpeþ tisik and etik. *c* **1400** *Lanfranc's Cirurg.* 279 Or þe patient falle into etikis. **1519** Horman *Vulg.* 37 b, He is in an eticke or a consumption. **1602** Shaks. *Ham.* iv. iii. 68 Like the Hecticke in my blood he rages, And thou must cure me. **1651** Wittie tr. *Primrose's Pop. Err.* ii. 88 In them that have the consumption, the lungs especially are affected, and the whole body in hecticks. **1845** Budd *Dis. Liver* 237 She had much hectic and sweating.

b. *fig.*

c **1430** Lydg. *Æsop* iii. 26 in *Herrig's Archiv* LXXXV. 25 With suche false etykes many man is shent. **1647** *Case Kingdom* 2 This heat of Presbytery proved . . an Hectique in the body Politique of Scotland. **1742** Young *Nt. Th.* iv. 77 Wishing, that constant hectic of a fool. **1879** Geo. Eliot *Theo. Such* 30, I have often had the fools' hectic of wishing about the unalterable.

2. A person affected with hectic fever; a consumptive person.

a **1653** G. Daniel *Idyll* ii. 126 The Hecticke has yᵉ Day To cease in, but drinks Marrow. **1687** Willis *Tunbridge* in *Harl. Misc.* (1808) I. 587 As for hecticks, they are commonly of a fine texture of body. *c* **1800** K. White *Time* 102 The hectic, lull'd On Death's lean arm to rest.

3. A hectic flush; *transf.* a flush or heightened colour on the cheek; also *fig.*

1768 Sterne *Sent. Journ.* (1778) I. 17 (Monk Calais), A hectic of a moment pass'd across his cheek. **1847** De Quincey *Sp. Mil. Nun* xvi. (1853) 41 One man's cheek kindled with the hectic of sudden joy. **1890** W. C. Russell *Ocean Trag.* III. xxxii. 193 Overhead the sky had fainted into a sickly hectic.

hectical ('hɛktɪkəl), *a.* [f. as prec. + -al¹.] = hectic *a.* (*lit.* and *fig.*)

1614 Wotton *Let. to Sir E. Bacon* 8 June in *Reliq. Wotton.* (1685) 433, I will keep it from being hectical. **1626** Jackson *Creed* viii. xii. §6 Hecticall, pestilentiall, or other feevers. **1765** Huxham in *Phil. Trans.* LV. 8 With the thin, tender, and hectical, it seldom agrees. **1806** *Med. Jrnl.* XV. 568 The hectical symptoms precluded all hopes . . from the trial of any other means.

hectically, *adv.* [f. as prec.] **a.** In the sense of hectic *a.* 1. **b.** With feverish activity. *colloq.*

1761 Johnson *Ascham* Wks. IV. 635 He was for some years hectically feverish. **1908** *Daily Chron.* 18 May 3/5 So many pictures in the Salons look as if they had been painted hectically a month before the exhibitions opened. **1972** *Daily Tel.* 15 Jan. 11 A hectically social couple of my acquaintance.

†**hective**, *a.* *Obs.* [Altered from hectic, or corresp. Fr., after adjs. in -ive, as costive.] = hectic *a.*

1634 T. Johnson *Parey's Chirurg.* x. xxxi (1678) 261 An hective Fever [*la fièvre hectique*] easily follows upon these kinds of Wounds. **1642** Fuller *Holy & Prof. St.* i. ii. 55 Being guilty of no Greek, and being demanded why it was called an hective fever; because, saith he, of an hecking cough which ever attendeth that disease. **1709** Steele *Tatler* No. 34 ¶5 Of a very spare and hective Constitution.

hecto-, hect-, a non-etymological contraction of Gr. ἑκατόν hundred, first used as a combining form in French words, esp. in the Metric system of weights and measures to express a hundred times the unit.

hectocotyl, -e (hɛktəʊ'kɒtɪl). *Zool.* Also in L. form **hectocotylus**. [ad. mod.L. *Hectocotylus*, name given by Cuvier to what he took for a genus of parasitic worms (see def. below), f. hecto- + Gr. κοτύλη small cup, hollow thing (cf. cotyle 2 b).]

A modified arm in male dibranchiate Cephalopods, which serves as a generative organ, and in some species is detached and remains in the pallial cavity of the female; in this position formerly mistaken for a parasite, to which the name *Hectocotylus octopodis* was given by Cuvier.

1854 Woodward *Mollusca* (1856) 65 Dr. Albert Kölliker has suggested that the real males . . are the *hectocotyles*, previously mistaken for parasitic worms. The *hectocotyle* of *octopus granulatus* was described by Cuvier, who obtained several specimens from octopods captured in the Mediterranean. **1877** Huxley *Anat. Inv. Anim.* viii. 538 The male is very much smaller than the female, and gives rise to a Hectocotylus.

Hence **hecto'cotylize** *v. trans.*, (*a*) to convert or modify into a hectocotyle; (*b*) to impregnate with a hectocotyle. **hectocotyli'zation**, the process of hectocotylizing. **hecto'cotylism**, the formation of a hectocotyle.

1870 Nicholson *Zool.* 272 The arm so affected . . is said to be 'hectocotylised'. **1877** Huxley *Anat. Inv. Anim.* viii. 530 The male Cephalopods are distinguished . . by the asymmetry of their arms, one or more of which, on one side, are peculiarly modified, or hectocotylised. *Ibid.* 534 There is thus a kind of hectocotylisation in the Tetrabranchiata. **1878** Bell *Gegenbaur's Comp. Anat.* 327 This 'hectocotylised arm' is not developed, as are the others, by a process of free gemmation, but it is formed in a vesicle, from which it is not let loose till it is mature. *Ibid.* 386 Hectocotylism is the cause therefore of a functional adaptation.

hectogramme, -gram ('hɛktəʊgræm). [ad. F. *hectogramme* (ɛktɔgram): see hecto- and gram².] In the Metric system, a weight containing 100 grammes, or 3·52 oz. avoirdupois.

1810 *Naval Chron.* XXIV. 302 Hectogram = 3 oz. 2 gros. 12·1 gr.

hectograph ('hɛktəʊgrɑːf, -æ-), *sb.* Also **hekto-**. [f. hecto- + Gr. -γραφος writing.] An apparatus for multiplying copies of writing: = chromograph 2. Also applied to the process of taking copies by means of this.

1880 *Printing Times* 15 Feb. 43/2 A multiplying process based upon the use of the glue plate . . used in the hektograph and other similar processes. **1882** *Times* 13 Feb., The manner in which the political 'hectograph' manufactures, reproduces, and multiplies 'public opinion'. **1884** *Standard* 6 May, The police discovered the first number of a new Socialist paper . . printed by hectograph.

Hence **'hectograph** *v. trans.*, to reproduce by means of the hectograph; **hecto'graphic** *a.*, pertaining to, or produced by, the hectograph.

1887 *Pall Mall G.* 18 Apr. 1/1 The hektographed resolutions of executive committees. *Ibid.* 27 May 7/2 By means of hectographic placards. **1890** *Times* 27 Mar. 5/4 They had helped to hectograph this address to the Russian people.

hectography (hɛk'tɒgrəfɪ). [f. hectograph *sb.*: see -graphy.] The use of the hectograph.

1889 J. H. Scrine *Mem. E. Thring* 31 Splice 3 pens together, . . and execute the task . . by fraudulent hectography.

hectoid ('hɛktɔɪd), *a.* [irreg. f. hect-ic + -oid.] Of a hectic appearance.

1871 W. A. Hammond *Nervous Syst.* I. xvi. (Cent.), The skin was red with a hectoid flush.

hectolitre, -liter ('hɛktəʊliːtə(r)). [F. *hectolitre* (ɛktɔlitr): see hecto- and litre.] In the Metric system, a measure of capacity containing 100 litres, or 3·531 cubic feet, or about 2¾ bushels.

1810 *Naval Chron.* XXIV. 301 Hectolittre = 2·9203 cubic feet. **1860** *All Year Round* No. 69. 448 A hectolitre contains a trifle more than a three-bushel English corn-sack. **1891** *Daily News* 31 Oct. 2/3 Russia has usually a crop of about 200 million hectolitres of oats.

hectometre, -meter ('hɛktəʊmiːtə(r)). [F. *hectomètre* (ɛktɔmɛtr): see hecto- and metre.] In the Metric system, a measure of length containing 100 metres, or 328·089 feet.

1810 *Naval Chron.* XXIV. 301 Hectometer, 100 M. **1869** Roscoe *Elem. Chem.* 24 The multiples of the metre . . are called decametres, hectometres, and kilometres.

Hector ('hɛktə(r)), *sb.* [L. *Hectŏr*, Gr. Ἕκτωρ, son of Priam and Hecuba, husband of Andromache, 'the prop or stay of Troy'; in origin, as adj. ἕκτωρ = holding fast, f. ἔχειν to have, hold.]

1. Name of a Trojan hero celebrated in the Iliad; hence *transf.* A valiant warrior like Hector.

1387 Trevisa *Higden* (Rolls) II. 255 ȝif we wil mene þat þey beeþ . . hardy, we clepeþ hem *Hectores*. **1525** Ld. Berners *Froiss.* II. cxliii. (R.) Thus he [Duglas] went euer forwarde lyke a hardy Hector. **1548** Hall *Chron.*, *Hen. VI*, 164 b, Thys English Hector and marcial flower. **1598** Shaks. *Merry W.* i. iii. 12 Said I well (bully Hector?). **1621–51** Burton *Anat. Mel.* To Rdr. (1676) 18/1 Every Nation hath their Hectors, Scipios, Cæsars and Alexanders.

2. (Now usu. with lower-case initial.) A swaggering fellow; a swash-buckler; a braggart, blusterer, bully.

(Frequent in the second half of the 17th c.; applied *spec.* to a set of disorderly young men who infested the streets of London. Cf. '*bully Hector*' 1598 in 1.)

1655 Sir E. Nicholas in *N. Papers* (Camden) II. 256 The Earle of Anglesie and his two Hectors upon Sunday morning last fought a duell with Collonel Dillan . . and two Irishe Captains . . His Lordships Hectors had no hurt, and yᵉ Irishe came of untoucht. *a* **1658** Cleveland *To the Hectors* 1 You Hectors! tame Professors of the Sword! **1693** Luttrell *Brief Rel.* (1857) III. 2 On Sunday night last 3 hectors came out of a tavern in Holborn, with their swords drawn, and began to break windows. *a* **1716** Blackall *Wks.* (1723) I. 333 Surely this blustering Hector is not one of the Sons of Adam. **1849** Macaulay *Hist. Eng.* iii. I. 361 The Muns and Tityre Tus had given place to the Hectors, and the Hectors had been recently succeeded by the Scourers.

3. Name of a species of butterfly (*Papilio Hector*).

1863 Wood *Illustr. Nat. Hist.* III. 508 The Hector forms a fine contrast to the preceding insect [the Sarpedon], its colours being almost wholly black and flaming crimson.

Hence **Hec'torean, -ian** *a.* [f. L. *Hectŏre-us* + -an], belonging to Hector. **'hectorism**, the quality or practice of a hector or bully. **'hectorly** *a.*, of the nature of a hector, blustering, insolent. **'hectorship**, a trait characteristic of a hector.

1715–20 Pope *Iliad* xviii. 18 Warn'd to shun Hectorean force in vain. **1673** O. Walker *Educ.* (1677) 82 Men mis-like a vice for a seemingly-like but really-contrary virtue—as hectorisme for valour. **1675** J. Smith *Chr. Relig. Appeal* ii. 15 A desperate Principle of Hectorism. **1676** Shadwell *Virtuoso* iv. i. Wks. (1720) 375 My wife with a hectorly fellow here! *a* **1677** Barrow *Serm.* Wks. 1686 III. xxxi. 336 Presumptuous transgression of God's law, (Hectorly profaneness). **1858** Carlyle *Fredk. Gt.* iii. x. (1872) I 198 His other Hectorships I will forget.

hector ('hɛktə(r)), *v.* [f. prec. sb. (sense 2).]

1. *intr.* To play the hector or bully; to brag, bluster, domineer. Also, *to hector it*.

1660 Hickeringill *Jamaica* (1661) 80 For which he needs not venture life nor limb, Nor Hector it, nor list under Sir Hugh. **1681** —— *Def. Fullwood's Leges Angliæ* 5 While I

hector and rant and call names. **1723** SWIFT *Stella at Wood-Park* 6 Don Carlos made her chief director, That she might o'er the servants hector. **1764** FOOTE *Mayor of G.* I. (1783) 25 She does now and then hector a little. **1863** MRS. C. CLARKE *Shaks. Char.* vi. 145 John not only allows himself to be bamboozled, but..to be hectored over. **1882** MISS BRADDON *Mt. Royal* III. vii. 141 He blustered and hectored as of old.

2. *trans.* To intimidate by bluster or threats; to domineer over; to bully; to bring or force *out of* or *into* something by threats or insolence.

1664 PEPYS *Diary* 22 Feb., Our King did openly say..that he would not be hectored out of his right and pre-eminencys by the King of France. **1670** DRYDEN *Conq. Granada* II. i, But [Fortune] she's a drudge, when hector'd by the Brave. **1722** DE FOE *Col. Jack* (1840) 27 You shan't be hectored by him. **1749** FIELDING *Tom Jones* x. viii, We are..not to be hectored, and bullied, and beat into Compliance. **1824** W. IRVING *T. Trav.* II. 37, I was hectored and lectured in my own green-room. **1850** —— *Mahomet* xxiii. (1853) 131 But suffers himself to be..hectored out of his crafty policy.

Hence **'hectoring** *vbl. sb.* and *ppl. a.*; **'hectoringly** *adv.*, in a hectoring manner; also **'hectorer**, one who hectors.

1664 BUTLER *Hud.* II. i. 352 The Hect'ring Kill-Cow Hercules. **1678** CUDWORTH *Intell. Syst.* 176 Ranting and hectoring atheists. **1788** T. JEFFERSON *Writ.* (1859) II. 443 A mere piece of hectoring to frighten Russia. **1827** J. F. COOPER *Prairie* I. xii. 175 Ah! you are a hectorer with the boys, when need calls! **1849** C. BRONTË *Shirley* i, He grew a little insolent, [and] said rude things in a hectoring tone. **1913** W. J. LOCKE *Stella Maris* xx. 251 He..questioned her further, almost hectoringly. **1963** *Punch* 27 Feb. 315/3 His adopting a hectoringly superior manner.

hectostere ('hɛktəʊstɪə(r), Fr. ɛktɔstɛr). [F. *hectostère*: see HECTO- and STERE.] In the Metric system, a measure of capacity containing 100 steres, or 3531·65 cubic feet. (Little used even in Fr.)

1864 in WEBSTER.

hecup, obs. form of HICCUP.

hed, hedd(e: see HEAD *sb.*¹, HEED, HIDE *v.*¹

hedder, obs. form of HEATHER, HITHER.

heddir, obs. form of ADDER.

c **1400** *Apol. Loll.* 97 Def heddir stuppend her ȝeris.

heddle ('hɛd(ə)l), *sb. Weaving.* Also 6 hedel(l)e, *Sc.* heidle, 8–9 hiddle, 9 ? *dial.* haddle. [app.:—OE. **hefedl*, earlier form of *hefeld*: see HEALD.] In *plural*, The small cords (or in recent use, wires) through which the warp is passed in a loom after going through the reed, and by means of which the warp threads are separated into two sets so as to allow the passage of the shuttle bearing the weft.

A leaf of heddles consists of a set of parallel cords of the width of the webs stretched vertically between two horizontal shafts of wood, and forming in their centre loops or eyes through which the warp-threads pass.

1513 DOUGLAS *Æneis* VII. i. 29 With subtell slais and hir heidlis [**1553** hedeles] sle, Rych lenȝe webbis natly weiffis sche. **1523** SKELTON *Garl. Laurel* 791 To weve in the stoule some were full preste, With slaiis, with tavellis, with hedellis well drest. **1792** A. ADAM *Rom. Antiq.* 523 The principal parts of the machinery of a loom, vulgarly called the Caam or Hiddles, composed of eyed or hooked threads, through which the warp passes. **1831** G. R. PORTER *Silk Manuf.* 215 The depression of each treadle will correspondingly influence the position of its heddle. **1875** *Ure's Dict. Arts* III. 979 In every species of weaving..the whole difference of pattern or effect is produced, either by the succession in which the threads of warp are introduced into the heddles, or by the succession in which those heddles are moved in the working.

b. *Comb.*, as *heddle-beam*, *-maker*, *-thread*, *-twine*, *-yarn*; **heddle-eye, -hook, -lever**: see quots.

1794 A. MARTIN *Agric. Surv. Renfr.* 257 (Jam.) Heddles ..are made of very strong thread called heddle-twine. **1852** APPLETON *Dict. Mech.* 257 The heddle-beam. **1864** WEBSTER, *Heddle-eye*, the eye or loop formed in each heddle to receive a warp-thread. **1875** KNIGHT *Dict. Mech.*, *Heddle-hook*, a hook used in heddling the warp-threads. **1885** G. A. GRIERSON *Bihar Peas. Life* 74 Heddle-levers..the upper levers to which the heddles are attached.

Hence **heddle** *v. trans.*, to draw (warp-threads) through the eyes of a heddle.

1864 WEBSTER, *Heddling*. **1875** [see b above].

heddre, var. EDDRE *Obs.*, bloodvessel, vein.

a **1300** *Vox & Wolf* 43 in Hazl. *E.P.P.* I. 59 Hy ne miȝtte non lengour libe, Bote here heddre were i-take.

†**hede.** *Obs.* Also hed. [ME. *hede*:—OE. type **hǣdu* (acc. *hǣde*) fem., beside *hád* masc.; corresp. to MHG. *heit* fem., OHG. *hait*, *heit*, m. and f., 'person, order, rank, position', Goth. *haidus*, masc., 'manner, way'. See HAD *sb.*, -HEAD *suffix*.]

1. Rank, order, condition, quality.

a **1300** *Cursor M.* 21220 [Barnabas] wan vn-to þe apostlis hede. *Ibid.* 21700 Suld haf þe preistes hede wit dome. *a* **1400** *Sir Perc.* 1103 Blode rede was his stede, His aktone and his other wede, His cote of the same hede.

2. By entering into combination with qualifying adj., or with sb., it became a suffix, ME. *-hede*, mod.Eng. *-head*, Sc. *-heid*: see -HEAD.

a **1100** *O.E. Chron.* an. 1070 Þurh heora druncen hed on an niht for bærnde þa cyrce. *c* **1250** *Gen. & Ex.* 56 On miȝt and on godfulhed. *Ibid.* 1852 Sichem tok hire maiden-hed. *a* **1300** *Cursor M.* 6949 (Gött.) His sone Elyazar was neist, And bar þe state of his fadir hede. *c* **1440** HYLTON *Scala Perf.* (1494) II. xlvi, The fairhede of angels. **1535** COVERDALE *Zech.* xi. 14 The brotherheade betwixte Iuda and Israel. **1585** JAS. I *Ess. Poesie* (Arb.) 54 Chyldheid.

hede, obs. form of HEAD *sb.*¹, HEED.

hedebo ('hɛdɛbəʊ). [ad. Dan. *hedebobroderi*, f. *hede* heath + *bo* dwelling + *broderi* embroidery.] (See quots.)

1932 D. C. MINTER *Modern Needlecraft* 49/2 The drawing of threads..forms the basis of various interesting forms of embroidery. This network..is sometimes used as a contrast for parts of a richly embroidered surface. This kind of work is known as *Hedebo work*, and is usually executed almost entirely in white. **1957** M. B. PICKEN *Fashion Dict.* 171/1 *Hedebo embroidery*, Danish embroidery of cut and drawn work.

hedell, heden, obs. ff. HIDEL, HEATHEN.

hedenbergite ('hɛdənbəgaɪt). *Min.* [Named by Berzelius, 1819, after Ludwig Hedenberg: see -ITE.] A black crystalline variety of PYROXENE.

1822 CLEAVELAND *Min.* 615 Hedenbergite..occurs in masses composed of shining plates. **1868** DANA *Min.* (ed. 5) 215 Iron-lime pyroxene; hedenbergite.

hedeous, -ows, obs. forms of HIDEOUS.

heder ('hiːdə(r)). *dial.* Also 6–7 hidder, 8 heeder. [f. HE + (?) DEER: cf. SHEDER.] A male sheep; *spec.* one from eight or nine months old till its first shearing.

1579 SPENSER *Sheph. Cal.* Sept. 211 He would haue deuoured both hidder & shidder [*gloss.* He & she, Male and Female]. **1633** J. FISHER *Fuimus Troes* III. ix. in Hazl. *Dodsley* XII. 507 Hidder, eke, and shidder. **1799** A. YOUNG *Agric. Linc.* 235 (E.D.S.) They are forced to sell their heeders, and joist their sheeders in the spring. **1851** *Jrnl. R. Agric. Soc.* XII. II. 333 A lamb eight or nine months old, and until his first shearing, is called a 'heder' or 'sheder'..or 'lamb-hog'. *Ibid.* 341 The 'heder' hogs being grazed on the seeds, and the 'sheders' on grass.

heder, obs. form of HITHER.

heder, var. CHEDAR.

hederaceous (hɛdə'reɪʃəs), *a.* [f. L. *hederāce-us*, f. *hedera* ivy.] Pertaining or allied to ivy.

1727 BAILEY vol. II, *Hederaceous*, of or belonging to Ivy. **1755** in JOHNSON. Hence in mod. Dicts.

Hence **hede'raceously** *adv.*, after the manner of ivy.

1683 *Phil. Trans.* XIII. 107 Many several sorts growing up Hederaciously together.

hederal ('hɛdərəl), *a.* [f. L. *heder-a* ivy + -AL¹.] Of or pertaining to ivy.

1656 BLOUNT *Glossogr.* s.v., The Hederal Crown or Garland was given to Poets, and excellent Musitians. **1706** in PHILLIPS (ed. Kersey). **1721** in BAILEY. Hence in mod. Dicts.

hederated ('hɛdəreɪtɪd), *a.* [f. L. *hederāt-us* in same sense (f. *hedera* ivy) + -ED.] Adorned or crowned with ivy.

a **1661** FULLER *Worthies*, *Yorkshire* III. (1662) 207 He [Gower] appeareth there neither laureated nor hederated Poet..but only rosated, having a Chaplet of four Roses about his head.

hederic (hɪ'dɛrɪk), *a. Chem.* [f. L. *heder-a* ivy + -IC.] Of or pertaining to ivy; as in **hederic acid**.

1865–72 WATTS *Dict. Chem.* III. 138 *Hederic acid*, an acid contained, according to Posselt (Ann. Ch. Pharm. lxix. 62) in the seeds of ivy (*Hedera helix*)..It appears to belong to the family of the tannic acids. **1886** *Syd. Soc. Lex.*, *Hederic acid* ..consists of colourless bitter crystals, soluble in alcohol, but insoluble in water and ether.

hede'riferous, *a.* [f. L. *hedera* ivy + -FEROUS.] Bearing or producing ivy.

1656 in BLOUNT *Glossogr.* **1721** in BAILEY. In mod. Dicts.

'hederiform, *a.* [ad. medical L. *hederiform-is*, f. *hedera* ivy + *forma*: see -FORM. Cf. F. *hédériforme*.] Resembling ivy.

1656 BLOUNT *Glossogr.* s.v. *Vein*, *Hederiform vein*, a certaine veine which passes down along by the sides of the womb. **1886** in *Syd. Soc. Lex.*

hede'rigerent, *a.* [f. L. *hederiger* ivy-bearing + -ENT, after L. *gerent-em* bearing.] Bearing or wearing ivy.

1871 M. COLLINS *Mrq. & Merch.* III. iii. 96 The hederigerent Maenads of old. *a* **1876** —— *Th. in my Gard.* (1880) I. 269 Nymphs, hederigerent, wine that's refrigerant, These are the joy of the poets and gods.

hederine ('hɛdəraɪn). *Chem.* [mod. f. L. *hedera* ivy + -INE; in F. *hédérine*.] A bitter alkaloid obtained from the seeds of the ivy.

1865–72 WATTS *Dict. Chem.* III. 138.

Hence **hede'rinic** = hederic (acid).

hede'rose, *a.* [ad. L. *hederōs-us*, f. *hedera* ivy: see -OSE.]

1727 BAILEY vol. II, *Hederose*, full of Ivy. In mod. Dicts.

hedg(e, obs. forms of EDGE *sb.*

a **1535** MORE *How Sergt. wd. be Frere* 118 in Hazl. *E.P.P.* III. 123 He bare it out, Even unto the harde hedge. **1581** J. BELL *Haddon's Answ. Osor.* 437 b, Supported to yᵉ hard hedg.

hedge (hɛdʒ), *sb.* Forms: 1 *hecg (*dat.* hegge), 3–6 hegge, 4 hegg, 5–6 hege, 6 *Sc.* haige, 5 hedche, 7 hedg, 4– hedge; *β.* 4–6 heg. [OE. **hęcg*, *hęgg* str. fem., corresp. to EFris. *hegge*, MDu. *hegghe*, Du. *hegge*, *heg*, OHG. *hegga*, *hecka* (MHG. *hegge*, *hecke*, Ger. *hecke*):—OTeut. **hagjâ-*; a deriv. of the same root as OE. *haga* HAW *sb.*¹ and *hęge* HAY *sb.*² Cf. also HAG *sb.*²]

1. a. A row of bushes or low trees (e.g. hawthorn, or privet) planted closely to form a boundary between pieces of land or at the sides of a road: the usual form of fence in England.

A hedge is called *quickset* or *dead* according as it is planted of living or dead plants. (See these adjs.)

785 *Charter* in *Cart. Sax.* (Birch) I. 339 Æt þære lange hegge ænde. **855** *O.E. Chron.* an. 547 He ȝetimbrade Bebban burh, sy wæs ærost mid hegge be tined. *a* **1250** *Owl & Night.* 17 Þe nihtegale..sat up one faire boȝe..In ore waste þicke hegge. **1297** R. GLOUC. (1724) 211 Hii come among narwe heggys. *c* **1330** R. BRUNNE *Chron. Wace* (Rolls) 16428 Any leues or rotes seþ, þat henged on heg or on heþ. **1382** WYCLIF *Eccl.* x. 8 Who scatereth the hegg [**1388** hegge]. **1382** —— *Mark* xii. 1 A man plauntide a vyneȝerd, and puttide aboute an hegge. *c* **1440** *Promp. Parv.* 232/1 Hedge (*K.*, *S.* hegge), *sepes*. **1481** CAXTON *Reynard* xxx. (Arb.) 75 The serpent stode in an hedche. **1483** *Cath. Angl.* 180/1 Hege, *ubi* a garthe. **1508** DUNBAR *Goldyn Targe* 34 On every syde the hegies raise on hicht. **1508** —— *Tua Mariit Wemen* 13 That in haist to the hege so hard I inthrang. **1550** CROWLEY *Epigr.* 10 b, Two beggars that vnder an hedge sate. **1556** *Chron. Gr. Friars* (Camden) 59 The commyns..within the realme ryssyd and pullyd up heggys and palys. **1577** B. GOOGE *Heresbach's Husb.* II. (1586) 50 b, Columella..preferreth the quickeset hedge before the deade. **1653** WALTON *Angler* ii. 62 But turn out of the way..towards yonder high hedg. **1774** GOLDSM. *Nat. Hist.* (1776) V. 142 To take shelter in the first tree or hedge that offers. **1806** FORSYTH *Beauties Scotl.* IV. 73 Hedge and ditch is the most common mode of fencing property. **1826–44** LOUDON *Encycl. Agric.* 475 Dead hedges..are principally intended for temporary purposes.

b. Locally or spec. applied to other fences.

1850 *Beck's Florist* 25 If we examine the stone walls, or, as they are called, 'hedges'. **1868** KIRK *Chas. Bold* III. v. iii. 428 The Burgundians erected a palisade, called in the military language of the time a 'hedge'. **1887** HALL CAINE *Deemster* xvi, One..had jumped to the top of the broad turf hedge.

2. A fishing weir of faggots or of wattle-work.

1653 WALTON *Angler* vi. 135 They [salmon] will force themselves over the tops of Weirs, or Hedges, or stops in the water. **1714** *Act 1 Geo. I*, Stat. II. c. 18 § 14 If any person.. make, erect, or set any bank, dam, hedge or stank, net or nets, cross the said rivers or any part thereof.

3. *trans.* Said of any line or array of objects forming a barrier, boundary, or partition.

1523 LD. BERNERS *Froiss.* I. cxxx. 157 The frenche kynge wolde fayne haue come thyder..but there was a great hedge [*grand'haye*] of archers before hym. **1578** BANISTER *Hist. Man* I. 10 A [Processe]..which..into the nostrels discendyng, constituteth the hedge, or partition of the nose. **1617** MORYSON *Itin.* II. 95 These three Countries being an hedge betweene the English Pale, and the North. **1638** SIR T. HERBERT *Trav.* (ed. 2) 183 Towring in a hedge of hills from Armenia to the furthest part of Indya. **1808** SCOTT *Marmion* VI. xviii, Flashing on the hedge of spears. **1855** HT. MARTINEAU *Autobiog.* (1877) II. 121 Hedges of police from our little street to the gates of the Abbey.

4. *transf.* and *fig.* A barrier, limit, defence; a means of protection or defence.

1340 *Ayenb.* 240 Hardnesse of liue þet is a strang heg aye þe wyckede bestes. *c* **1380** WYCLIF *Serm.* Sel. Wks. III. 29 Þus was Poul constreyned to crepe out of his hegge, and holde þe sect of Crist, forsakinge þe sect of Pharisees. **1526** *Pilgr. Perf.* (W. de W. 1531) 65 As hedges, or stoppes to lette those thynges that myght hurt perfeccyon. **1617** MORYSON *Itin.* II. 72 It might appeare by that hedge which he diligently put to all his answers, that he spake..only to cleere himselfe. **1649** *Belfast Presbytery* in *Milton's Wks.* (1851) II. 550 Their strong oppositions to Presbyterial Government (the Hedg and Bulwark of Religion). **1825** SCOTT *Jrnl.* 19 Dec., He talks of..making sales of our interest..which would put a hedge round his finances. **1879** FARRAR *St. Paul* I. 148 The Pharisees regarded it as the main function of their existence to raise a hedge around the Law.

5. *spec. Betting.* [f. HEDGE *v.* 8.] The act of hedging; a means of hedging. Also *Commercial*, *Financial*, and *transf.* (cf. HEDGE *v.* 8 c).

1736 FIELDING *Pasquin* III. i, *S.* That's laying against yourself, Mr. Trapwit. *T.* I love a hedge, sir. **1801** *Sporting Mag.* XVIII. 100 To make a hedge; to secure a bet, or wager, laid on one side, by taking the odds on the other. **1805** WINDHAM *Speeches Parl.* 26 Mar. (1812) II. 298 What, in the sporting language was called 'a hedge', the effect of which was, that there was a chance the Right Honourable Gentleman would at all events win. **1857** HUGHES *Tom Brown* I. viii, The horse is no use to you. He won't win, but I want him as a hedge. **1917** A. W. ATWOOD *Exchanges & Speculation* xiv. 196 The local elevator companies..place their hedges as soon as they begin to accumulate supplies of grain. **1955** *Times* 8 June 9/2 Your board are keenly aware of the need that the group should continue to build up, in the form of profitable interests elsewhere, 'hedges' against catastrophe in British Guiana. *Ibid.* 29 June 11/3 As for the hedge of going into television itself that may save the property but it will not save the Press. **1957** *Economist* 12 Oct. 152/2 In France, wool was probably taken into stock as a hedge against currency devaluation and the pressure of credit restriction is also at work there. **1958** *Punch* 19 Nov. 669/2 A good unit trust group..provides the best way of

combining the safety of numbers with the promise of participating in the economic growth that lies before us and of providing a hedge against inflation. **1959** *Ibid.* 19 Aug. 54/2 The share of these companies would seem to be a perfect election hedge.

6. Phrases and proverbs. **a.** ***to hang (be hung) on (in) the hedge***: to be put on one side, to be 'on the shelf'. ***to be on the right (better, safer) or wrong side of the hedge***: to be in a right or wrong position. ***to take a sheet off a hedge***: to steal openly. ***to take hedge***: to depart. ***the only stick left in one's hedge***: one's only resource. ***by hedge or by stile*** (see quot. 1700). ***to be on the hedge*** = to 'sit on the fence'.

c **1510** *Hickscorner* 17 Ye whan my soule hangeth on the hedge cast stones. **1600** HOLLAND *Livy* LXIX. Epit. 1246 One who ever loved to be on the better side of the hedge [L. *secundam fortunam transire*]. **1630** *R. Johnson's Kingd. & Commw.* 27 He durst as well take a sheet of an hedge, as come within the cracke of a pistoll. **1638** FORD *Lady's Trial* IV. ii, They durst not give the souse, And so took hedge. *a* **1641** BP. MOUNTAGU *Acts & Mon.* (1642) 64 That much talked of, and employed distinction..of implicite, and explicite, faith..may be hanged on the hedge, for any use is of it. **1644** VICARS *Jehovah-Jireh* 196 Those two Regiments were the onely stick they now had left in their hedge. **1653** BAXTER *Worc. Petit. Def.* 24 If you say, We have too much in any of these particulars; then we are on the safer side the hedge. **1666** PEPYS *Diary* 27 Oct., The business of money hangs in the hedge. *a* **1700** B. E. *Dict. Cant. Crew, By Hedge or by Style*, by Hook or by Crook. **1816** AINSWORTH *Lat. Dict.* s.v., To be on the wrong side of the hedge, or mistaken, *hallucinor, erro.*

b. Other locutions of obvious meaning.

1546 J. HEYWOOD *Prov.* (1867) 56 Where the hedge is lowest, men maie soonest ouer. **1563** WINȜET *Wks.* (1888) II. 54 The serpent sal byte him quha cuttis the haige. **1591** LYLY *Endym.* III. iii, Some men may better steale a horse, then another looke over the hedge. *a* **1656** BP. HALL *Rem. Wks.* (1660) 223 Men are still apt to climb over the hedg where it is lowest. **1869** HAZLITT *Prov.* 201 Hedges have eyes and walls have ears. **1892** *Daily News* 4 July 3/1 The fog ..hanging like a heavy pall 'as thick as a hedge'.

7. *attrib.* and *Comb.* **a.** Simple attrib., 'of or for a hedge', as ***hedge-bottom, -cricket, -fence, -flower, -fruit, -knife, -plant, -scissors, -shears, spade, -stake, -tree, -weed, -wren.*** **b.** objective and obj. gen., as ***hedge-breaker, -breaking, -clipper, -cutter, -cutting, -maker.*** **c.** instrumental, as ***hedge-bound.***

1644 DIGBY *Nat. Bodies* I. xxxvi. (1645) 386 Hares..hide themselves in *hedge bottomes, or in woods. **1816** *Ainsworth's Lat. Dict.* s.v., She lays her eggs in hedge bottoms. **1631** *Star Chamb. Cases* (Camden) 62 As *hedge-breakers or breakers of the peace they put them in the stockes. **1785** J. PHILLIPS *Treat. Inland Navig.* 19 Poor people who now destroy all the hedges..will find *hedge-breaking a losing trade. **1871** W. H. BEEVER *Daily Life Farm* i. 6 Heaps of fire-wood and *hedge-clippings. **1601** SHAKS. *All's Well* IV. i. 2 He can come no other way but by this *hedge corner. **1820** KEATS *To Autumn* in *Lamia*, etc. 139 *Hedge-crickets sing. **1881** *Encycl. Brit.* XII. 234/1 A new instrument for clipping hedges, Ridgway's *hedge-cutter. **1960** *Farmer & Stockbreeder* 2 Feb. 80/1 There was a record entry of nearly 100 mechanical hedge-cutters. **1971** P. GRESSWELL *Environment* 125 The mechanical hedge-cutter clears the young saplings. **1899** *Westm. Gaz.* 22 Dec. 1/3 *Hedge-cutting competitions have a..useful effect in checking the use of barbed wire. *a* **1774** HARTE *Eulogius* in Chalmers *Eng. Poets* (1810) XVI. 386 Deck'd..With poor *hedge-flow'rs. **1647** TRAPP *Comm. Matt.* xv. 27 Those that are hunger-starved are glad to feed upon *hedge-fruit. **1846** WORCESTER, **Hedge-knife*, an instrument for trimming hedges. **14..** *Nom.* in Wr.-Wülcker 697/21 *Hic septor*, a *hegmaker. **1758** BORLASE *Nat. Hist. Cornwall* 229 Hill and *hedge plants. **1887** *Gardening* 10 Dec. 553/2 Laurustinus is used here largely as a hedge plant. **1833** J. HOLLAND *Manuf. Metal* II. 44 [Pruning instruments] resembling common *hedge-shears. **1602** *2nd Pt. Return fr. Parnass.* I. ii. 326 They haue some of them beene the old *hedgstakes of the presse. **1843** *Zoologist* I. 97, I generally have a stout hedge-stake or clothes-prop to try the soundings with. **1611** COTGR., *Marmaux, Arbres mar.*, *Hedge-trees, wild trees. **1591** F. SPARRY tr. *Cattan's Geomancie* 73 A number of thieves and *hedge walkers. **1866** *Treas. Bot.* 1064/1 *Sisymbrium officinale*..a common *hedge-weed. **1844** H. STEPHENS *Bk. of Farm* (1871) II. 473 A small useful implement is the *hedge weed-hook..which pulls out the weeds between the hedge-roots. **1899** *Westm. Gaz.* 21 July 2/3 The swallow does not fear us, the *hedge-wren does not flout us. **1907** *Academy* 9 Feb. 131/2 The hedge-wren..Is out in the open.

8. a. Born, brought up, habitually sleeping, sheltering, or plying their trade under hedges, or by the road-side (and hence used generally as an attribute expressing contempt), as ***hedge-bantling, -brat, -chaplain, -curate, -doctor, -lawyer, -parson, -player, -poet, -wench, -whore***, etc. Also HEDGE-PRIEST. **b.** Done, performed, produced, worked, under a hedge, in by-ways, or clandestinely, as ***hedge-marriage, -notes, -press, -rimes.*** **c.** Of such kind as is met with by the way-side; of mean, inferior, 'common', 'third-rate' quality, and generally as a contemptuous adjunct, as ***hedge-alehouse, -inn, -lodging, -tavern, -wine***, etc. Also HEDGE-SCHOOL.

c **1530** *Jyl of Breyntford's Test.* 331 A hedge Curat, with as moche wit as a calf. **1546** BALE *Eng. Votaries* II. (1550) L iij, They..continued vnder the slender name of secular priests or hedge chaplains. **1583** STANYHURST *Æneis* IV. (Arb.) 108 A runnagat hedgebrat. **1590** R. W. *3 Lds. & 3 Ladies Lond.* in Hazl. *Dodsley* VI. 421 This blindfold buzzardly hedge-wench. **1641** BROME *Jovial Crew* V. Wks. 1873 III. 435 Hedge-birds said you? Hedge Lady-birds, Hedge Cavaliers, Hedge Souldier, Hedge Lawyer, Hedge Fidlers, Hedge Poet, Hedge Players, and a Hedge Priest among 'em. **1656** W. D. tr. *Comenius' Gate Lat. Unl.* §804. 251 Hee doth not rashly venture upon the cure (as Quack-salvers, and Hedg-doctors are wont). **1711** SWIFT *Rem. Let. to 7 Lds.* Wks. 1814 IV. 196 These hedge-writers (a phrase I unwillingly lend him, because it cost me some pains to invent) seldom speak a word against any of the late ministry. **1738** THYER in *Byrom's Rem.* (1856) II. I. 198, I find your curiosity tempted into a hedge bookseller's in some bye-lane. **1751** SMOLLETT *Per. Pic.* lxxxvii. (1779) IV. 34 This hedge inamorata. **1815** SCOTT *Guy M.* xxxi, She ran out into a horrid description of a hedge-ruffian. **1822** —— *Nigel* xvii, A hedge-parson, or buckle-beggar, as that order of priesthood has been irreverently termed. **1855** MRS. GASKELL *North & S.* (ed. 2) I. 183 Not hedge-lawyers, as Captain Lennox used to call those men in his company who questioned and would know the reason for every order.

b. *a* **1667** COWLEY *Answ. Verses fr. Jersey* 13 Such Base, Rough, Crabbed, Hedge-Rhimes, as ev'n set the Hearers Ears on Edge. **1679** MULGRAVE *Ess. Sat.* in *Dryden's Wks.* (1821) XIII. 53 When they began to be somewhat better bred..they left these hedge-notes for another sort of poem, somewhat polished. **1724** SWIFT *Drapier's Lett.* Wks. 1755 V. II. 7 Corrector of a hedge-press in some blind alley about Little Britain. **1847–78** HALLIWELL, *Hedge-marriage*, a secret clandestine marriage. *North.*

c. **1594** NASHE *Terrors Nt.* Wks. 1883–4 III. 267 Hedge wine and leane mutton. **1688** SHADWELL *Sqr. Alsatia* I. i, Is not rich generous wine better than your poor Hedge-Wine stum'd? *a* **1700** B. E. *Dict. Cant. Crew, Hedge-Tavern* or *Ale-house*, a Jilting, Sharping Tavern, or Blind Alehouse. **1711** SWIFT *Lett.* (1767) III. 203, I was forced to go to a little hedge place for my dinner. **1748** SMOLLETT *Rod. Rand.* (1812) I. 38 A small hedge alehouse. **1816** SCOTT *Fam. Lett.* 26 Aug. (1894) I. xii. 368 Otterbourne..is an indifferent sort of hedge inn.

d. Hence passing into an *adj.* with sense 'Mean, third-rate, paltry, despicable, rascally'.

1596 NASHE *Saffron Walden* Wks. 1883–4 III. 38 Rascally hedge rak't vp termes. *a* **1734** NORTH *Exam.* III. viii. §78 (1740) 643 These are hedge Objections. When nothing can be said against the Matter, they fall upon the Manner, and in Circumstances not material. *a* **1745** SWIFT (J.), The clergy do much better than a little hedge, contemptible, illiterate vicar can be presumed to do.

9. Special combs.: **hedge-accentor**, the hedge-sparrow; †**hedge-binding**, something used to bind together the bushes composing a hedge; **hedge-born** *ppl. a.*, born under a hedge, of low or mean birth; **hedge-brow** (see quot.); **hedge-bush**, a bush used to make a hedge, *spec.* hawthorn; **hedge-carpenter**, one whose business is to repair fences; so **hedge-carpentering**; **hedge-chafer**, the cockchafer; **hedge-chanter, -chat**, the hedge-sparrow; **hedge-clause** *U.S.*, a safeguarding clause in a contract; **hedge-crocus**, an itinerant quack-doctor: see CROCUS 4; **hedge-fence**, a hedge serving as a fence; **hedge-fight**, a fight under cover of hedges or other shelters, as opposed to a pitched battle; **hedge-fire**, firing from a hedge; †**hedge-frog**, a toad; **hedge-green**, the green headland in a ploughed field; **hedge-grown** *a.* (see quots.); **hedge-hook**, a bill-hook for trimming hedges; **hedge-hop** *v. colloq.*, to fly in an aircraft at low levels so as to suggest hopping over hedges; so **hedge-hopper, -hopping** *vbl. sb.* and *ppl. a.*; also *fig.*; **hedge-planter**, 'a frame for holding plants in order as to distance and position while being set in the furrow prepared for them' (Knight *Dict. Mech.* 1875); **hedge-popping**, shooting from behind a hedge; **hedge-pulling**, the pulling of firewood out of a hedge; **hedge-rise** (see quot.); **hedge-rustic**, the moth *Luperina Cespitis*; **hedge selling** (see 5 above and HEDGE *v.* 8 c); **hedge-shrew**, ? the shrew-mouse; **hedge trimmer** (see TRIMMER 3); **hedge trimming**, (*a*) (see TRIMMING *vbl. sb.* 1 b); (*b*) (see TRIMMING *vbl. sb.* 1 c); **hedge-warbler**, the hedge-sparrow; **hedge-wise** *adv.*, in the fashion of a hedge. Also HEDGE-BILL, etc.

a **1825** FORBY *Voc. E. Anglia*, **Hedge-accentor*, the hedge-sparrow. **1611** BEAUM. & FL. *Knt. Burn. Pestle* II. iv, He came and basted me with a *hedge-binding. **1591** SHAKS. *1 Hen. VI*, IV. i. 43 Like a *Hedge-borne Swaine, That doth presume to boast of Gentle blood. **1750** W. ELLIS *Mod. Husb.* III. I. 37 (E.D.S.) Where bushes, or other trumpery, that grew near hedges, have been grubbed up, which we call *hedge-brows. **1576** FLEMING *Panopl. Epist.* 351 The pricking Blackthorne, the *hedge bushe, the Bryer, the bramble. **1859** W. S. COLEMAN *Woodlands* (1862) 38 The Maple, from its valuable qualities as a hedge-bush. **1888** T. HARDY *Wessex T.* I. 29 'You may generally tell what a man is by his claws', observed the *hedge-carpenter, looking at his own hands. **1878** JEFFERIES *Gamekeeper at H.* iii. 55 *Hedge-carpentering was..a distinct business, followed by one or two men in every locality. **1797** BEWICK *Brit. Birds* (1847) I. 79 Rooks are fond of the erucæ of the *hedge-chafer. **1882** A. HEPBURN in *Proc. Berw. Nat. Club* IX. No. 3. 504 The Redbreast and *Hedgechanter were plentiful. **1821** CLARE *Vill. Minstr.* I. 91 No music's heard the fields among; Save where the *hedge-chats chittering play. **1928** *Sat. Even. Post* 10 Mar. 185/2 In the Wall Street language ..*hedge clauses..signify that if the representations turn out to be wrong the banker shall not be held accountable. **1851** MAYHEW *Lond. Labour* I. 424 **Hedge crocusses*—men who sell corn salve, or 'four pills a penny', to cure anything, and go from house to house in the country. **1662** *Portsmouth* (R.I.) *Rec.* 396 The said fence..provided that it be a *hedge fence. **1778** *Essex Inst. Hist. Coll.* LII. 13 Seeing this hedge fence, they might take it to be a breastwork thrown up to annoy them. **1826–44** LOUDON *Encycl. Agric.* 475 Hedge fences are of two kinds: either..of dead materials, or..of living plants. **1724** DE FOE *Mem. Cavalier* (1840) 213 It was a kind of a *hedge-fight, for neither army was drawn out in the field..They fought twice through the town..and in the hedges and lanes with exceeding fury. **1859** TENNENT *Ceylon* II. VIII. v. 372 A *hedge-fire of musketry was kept up in the rear of the terrified elephants. **1580** HOLLYBAND *Treas. Fr. Tong, Vn verdier*..a kinde of tode or *hedge frogge. **1601** HOLLAND *Pliny* II. 450 The hedge frog, otherwise called a toad. **1732** W. ELLIS *Gloss. to Pract. Farmer* s.v. *Baulks of grass* (E.D.S.), Those which some call *hedge-greens; they lie next to the hedges in ploughed fields, and serve to turn the plough-horses on. **1820** KEATS *Fancy* in *Lamia*, etc. 124 The first *Hedge-grown primrose that hath burst. **1900** *Daily Express* 3 Aug. 2/7 Barley is not so good this year, for it has come up irregularly..; barley of this character is known with us as a 'hedge-grown crop'. **1890** *Sale Catal. Suffield House near Derby*, *Hedge hook and mittens. **1926** *Nat. Geogr. Mag.* Jan. 18/2 Back he'd go 'upstairs' under a 200-foot ceiling, and *hedge-hop along 20 miles or so, to the next emergency field. **1928** *Daily Express* 21 May 10/3 They can 'hedge-hop' with skill or fly to the greater heights with as much impunity as a man pilot. **1940** 'GUN BUSTER' *Return via Dunkirk* II. xi. 171 A German plane hedge-hopped right over us. **1962** L. DEIGHTON *Ipcress File* vii. 49 The machine [*sc.* a helicopter]..hedge-hopped in 100 m.p.h. gallops towards the sea. **1940** H. E BAUGHMAN *Aviation Dict.* 96/1 **Hedge-hopper airplane* (slang), any small, under-powered plane with enough power and lift to get off the ground a few feet for a brief period of time. **1957** R. W. ZANDVOORT et al. *Wartime Eng.* 127 *Hedge-hopper*, a low-flying aircraft. **1919** R. H. REECE *Night Bombing with Bedouins* 23 The British sport of '*hedge-hopping', i.e., flying close to the ground and 'zooming' up over trees. **1939** *War Illustr.* 11 Nov. 286 The German pilot's story of his eventful pursuit of a hedge-hopping English 'plane. **1955** *Amer. Speech* XXX. 72 Hedge-hopping..took on a special meaning in the 1952 presidential campaign—using an airplane in political campaigning. **1957** L. DURRELL *Bitter Lemons* 100 My own ambitions were more hedge-hopping and my means forbade me to indulge in such delightful fantasies. **1875** 'STONEHENGE' *Brit. Sports* I. I. i. §5. 8 Some *hedge-popping boy is made to bear the blame. **1887** C. J. R. TURNER *Vagrants & Vagrancy* 205 Six women were in the year 1800 stripped to the waist and flogged..for '*hedge pulling' under the Acts of 1766 and 1768. **1828** *Craven Dial.*, **Hedge-rise*, underwood for making hedges. **1862** E. NEWMAN *Brit. Moths* (1874) 297 The *Hedge Rustic..appears on the wing in August. **1920** J. STEPHENSON *Princ. Commercial Corr.* II. xiii. 151 Further liquidation and some *hedge selling caused another decline. **1930** *Daily Express* 8 Sept. 2/7 A reaction occurred owing to liquidation, hedge selling, a bearish crop estimate. **1964** *Financial Times* 12 Mar. 2/7 Selling was stop loss, together with some hedge selling. **1841** BROWNING *Pippa Passes* Concl. 12 But winter hastens at summer's end, And fire-fly, *hedge-shrew, lob-worm, pray, How fare they? **1870** *Trans. Ill. Agric. Soc.* VIII. 18 For want of opportunity there had been no test made of the *Hedge Trimmer, entered by D. Oliver, of Galesburg, Ill. **1961** *Times* 26 May 16/7 Hedge-trimmers and verge-cutters are a common part of the roadside scene. **1859** *Trans. Ill. Agric. Soc.* III. 362, I believe that the men are..here present, who will live to see ..*hedge trimming &c., done by steam. **1960** *Farmer & Stockbreeder* 12 Jan. 63/2 Disposing of hedge-trimmings. **1797–1804** BEWICK *Brit. Birds* (1847) I. 179 *Hedge Warbler. Hedge Sparrow. **1727** BRADLEY *Fam. Dict.* s.v. *Garden fences*, Rather to be handprun'd with a Knife than clipt or struck up *Hedgewise with a Hook.

10. In names of plants and fruits growing in hedges, as ***hedge-apple, -mallow, -nut, -pear, -rose***; **hedge-bedstraw**, the white-flowered species, *Galium Mollugo*; **hedge-bell(s, hedge-bindweed**, the Greater Bindweed, *Convolvulus* (or *Calystegia*) *sepium*; also erron. the Field Bindweed, *C. arvensis*; **hedge-cactus** *U.S.*, a cactus (*Cereus peruvianus*) grown as a hedge-plant; †**hedge fumitory**, *Corydalis claviculata*; **hedge-garlic**, *Sisymbrium Alliaria* (*Alliaria officinalis*), also called garlic mustard, a common cruciferous weed with an odour like garlic; **hedge-laurel**, name of various species of *Pittosporum*, a genus of shrubs or small trees found in Australia and New Zealand; **hedge-maids**, a local name of Ground Ivy = *haymaids*; **hedge-mushroom**, *Agaricus arvensis*; **hedge-mustard**, the cruciferous plant *Sisymbrium officinale*, a common weed with small yellow flowers; also applied to plants of the genus *Erysimum*; **hedge-nettle**, name for labiate plants of the genus *Stachys*, esp. *S. sylvatica*, also called *hedge woundwort*; **hedge-parsley**, common name of the genus *Torilis*, esp. *T. Anthriscus*, an umbelliferous weed with finely-divided leaves; also applied to various species of *Caucalis*; **hedge-peak, -pick, -speak**, local names for the wild hep, the fruit of the dog-rose; also for the sloe, *esp.* a small kind of sloe; **hedge pink**, the Soapwort, *Saponaria officinalis*; **hedge-taper**, the Great Mullein = HAG-TAPER; **hedge-thorn**, a thorn-bush growing in a hedge, *esp.* the hawthorn; **hedge-vine** (*heg-vine*), name given by Turner to *Clematis Vitalba*; **hedge violet**, *Viola sylvatica*; **hedge woundwort**, *Stachys sylvatica*.

1617 MINSHEU *Ductor*, **Hedge-apple*..Vi[de] Crab, or Arbut. **1597** GERARDE *Herbal* II. cccxvii. (1633) 863 Called in English Bindeweed and *Hedgebels. **1883** J. H. BEADLE

Western Wilds xxxvi. 593 There is..the *hedge cactus, with which Mexicans fence their fields. **1578** LYTE *Dodoens* I. xv. 24 Henfoote or *hedge Fumeterre..is of the same nature and vertue as the other Fumeterre. **1836** *Penny Cycl.* V. 251 The common *hedge mallow. **1671** SALMON *Syn. Med.* III. xxii. 399 *Hedge Mustard..opens the Lungs, and cures an old cough. **1678** LITTLETON *Lat. Dict.*, *Hedge-nettle, *Galeopsis.* **1794** MARTYN *Rousseau's Bot.* iv. 45 Strong smelling and stinking as hedge nettle. **1869** J. G. FULLER *Flower Gatherers* 277 There are several other species of the Hedge-nettle, some of them without hairs. **1620** VENNER *Via Recta* vii. 127 The common *Hedge, or Hasell-nut. **1830** *Withering's Brit. Plants* (1845) 143 *Torilis anthriscus*, Upright *Hedge-parsley. **1889** JEFFERIES *Field & Hedgerow* 159 The broad hedge-parsley leaves, tunnelled by leaf-miners. **1630** J. TAYLOR (Water P.) *Wks.* (N.), The bullesse, *hedg-peake, hips, and hawes, and sloes, Attend his appetite where e'er he goes. **1678** E. HOWARD *Man of Newmarket* (N.), I judge it is with men as it is with plants; take one that blossoms too soon, 't will starve a sloe or hedg-peake. *a* **1722** LISLE *Observ. Husb.* (1757) 432 The slow, or hedge-peak-bush is apt to die in the hill country. **1609** SIR R. SHIRLEY in *Harl. Misc.* (Malh.) III. 95 Their victuals..are acorns and *hedge-pears. **1875** TENNYSON *Q. Mary* III. iv, Like the wild *hedge-rose Of a soft winter, possible, not probable. **1847–78** HALLIWELL, **Hedge-speaks*, hips. *Glouc.* **1855** *Househ. Words* X. 172 That's the very bush..it's grow'd to almost a tree, and bears hedge-speakes. **1893** *Wiltsh. Gloss.* s.v. *Sloe*, In N. Wilts, at Huish, *Slōns* are large and *Hedge-speāks* small. **1585** LUPTON *Thous. Notable Th.* (1601) 2 An hearb called Mullen, some calls it *Hedge taper. **1640** PARKINSON *Theat. Bot.* 1026 The Hawthorne is called.. Hawthorne or *Hedgethorne, Whitethorne and May or May-bush. **1548** TURNER *Names of Herbes* (1881) 81 It mayе be called in Englishe *Heguine or Downiuine.

hedge, *v.* Forms: 4–5 hegge(n, -yn, 5 hedgyn, 5–6 hege, 6– hedge. [f. HEDGE *sb.*]

1. *trans.* To surround with a hedge or fence as a boundary, or for purposes of defence. Also with *in, about. to hedge off*: to fence off with a hedge.

[*c* **1000** *Rectitud. Sing. Pers.* c. 2 in Schmid *Gesetze* 372 On sumon he sceal..bytlian, and burh heȝeȝian.] **1388** WYCLIF *Matt.* xxi. 33 An hosebonde man..plauntide a vynȝerd, and heggide it aboute. *c* **1449** PECOCK *Repr.* v. vi. 517 Heggis and wardis..for to close and kepe and hegge yn. **1483** *Cath. Angl.* 180/1 To Hege, *ubi* to close. **1526** *Pilgr. Perf.* (W. de W. 1531) 53b, Defensed & hedged about with the sacramentes of Chrystes chirche. **1652** ASHMOLE *Theat. Chem.* 214 Heggyd and dychyd to make yt sure and strong. **1698** FRYER *Acc. E. India & P.* 37 Pallisadoes..hedge in at least a Mile of ground. **1755** SMOLLETT *Quix.* (1803) I. 233 Till you hedge in the sky, the starlings will fly. **1796** H. HUNTER tr. *St.-Pierre's Stud. Nat.* (1799) I. 443 In need of being watered, and of being hedged round. **1897** *Advance* (Chicago) 14 Jan. 58/3 A portion of the home-park is hedged-off for her particular diversions.

2. *intr.* or *absol.* To construct hedges or fences.

1393 LANGL. *P. Pl.* C. VI. 19 Heggen oþer harwen..oþer swyn oþer gees dryue. *c* **1440** *Promp. Parv.* 232/2 Hedgyn, or make an hedge..*sepio.* **1573** TUSSER *Husb.* xx. (1878) 59 No season to hedge. *a* **1845** HOOD *Lay of Labourer* ii, To hedge, or dig the ditch.

3. a. *trans.* To shape (trees) to form hedges.

1765 EARL HADDINGTON *Forest-trees* 15 The hedging of trees, in my opinion, takes away much of the beauty they have in their natural shape.

b. To arrange so as to form a barrier.

1812 *Examiner* 25 May 332/1 As well..oppose the inundations of the mountain torrent by hedging up piles of chaff. **1868** MENKEN *Infelicia* 15, I know that ye [Philistines] are hedged on the borders of my path.

†**4.** *fig.* To bound, limit, define. *Obs.*

c **1440** *York Myst.* xli. 206 The lawe is hedgyd for theme right playn, That they muste be puryfied agayne. **1551** T. WILSON *Logike* (1567) 74b, For, this worde [wife] in the firste Proposicion, is hedged with her circumstaunce, that is to saie, adultrie, whiche causeth diuorcement.

5. a. To surround as with a hedge or fence. Also with *in, about, around.*

c **1500** *Babees Book* 375 The ffirst cours: brawne, with the bory shed, lying in a felde, hegge about with a scriptur, sayng on this wyse; Welcombe you bretheren godely in this hall. **1581** SIDNEY *Astr. & Stella* lxxv, The floure-de-luce.. strongly hedg'd of bloudy lyons' pawes. **1595** SHAKS. *John* II. i. 26 England hedg'd in with the maine, That Water-walled Bulwarke. **1602** —— *Ham.* IV. v. 123 There's such Diuinity doth hedge a King. **1659** D. PELL *Impr. Sea* 36 *note*, They would hedge him about with Pearl. **1710** STEELE *Tatler* No. 197 ¶3 Hedged in by Logical Terms. **1894** *Nature* 26 July 295 A pursuit which is further hedged about with a formidable and unwieldy terminology.

b. To hem *in*, so as to prevent escape or free movement; to confine, restrict.

1549 LATIMER *1st Serm. bef. Edw. VI* (Arb.) 27, I will hedge strongly thy waye. **1568** GRAFTON *Chron.* II. 2 The Duke..seeyng all the country ready set to hedge him in. **1596** SHAKS. *Merch. V.* II. i. 18 If my Father had not scanted me, And hedg'd me by his wit to yeelde my selfe His wife who wins me by that meanes. **1612** T. TAYLOR *Comm. Titus* ii. 12 This excellent grace hedgeth his heart. *a* **1732** T. BOSTON *Crook in Lot* (1805) 77 To hedge you up from courses of sin. **1828** D'ISRAELI *Chas. I*, II. v. 108 The King was hedged in by the most thorny difficulties. **1860** TYNDALL *Glac.* I. x. 66, I found myself so hedged in by fissures [etc.]. **1863** MRS. RIDDELL *World in Ch.* (1865) 66 'By Jove, I am getting hedged', thought the young man.

†**c.** In reference to trade; to restrict or confine to one's own use; to monopolize. *Obs.*

1701 J. LAW *Counc. Trade* (1751) 110 Persuaded..that by the meer means or ways of monopoly, praeemption and exclusion, they could hedge in the herring, code and other sorts of fish, as some of the same stamp..that they can thus not only hedge in their wool, but hinder it or anything like it to grow elsewhere. *Ibid.* 149 They are at least as incapable of hedging in the herring, white, and other sorts of fish, as our ancestors have been. **1832** *Westm. Rev.* XVII. 273 The attempt to hedge-in gold and silver.

6. a. To obstruct as with a hedge; also *hedge up.*

1535 COVERDALE *Job* xix. 8 He hath hedged up my path. **1620** J. WILKINSON *Courts Leet* 119 If any high-waies or foote-pathes to Church, Mill, or Market bee stopped or hedged up. **1854** J. S. C. ABBOTT *Napoleon* (1855) II. xiv. 259 The path of the army seemed now entirely hedged up. **1864** D. G. MITCHELL *Sev. Stories* 227 The difficulties which hedged all approach.

†**b.** *hedge out*: to shut or keep out, to exclude.

1549 LATIMER *4th Serm. bef. Edw. VI* (Arb.) 109 Naye ye be hedged out of that lybertye. **1606** SHAKS. *Tr. & Cr.* III. i. 65 Nay this shall not hedge vs out, weele heare you sing certainely. **1670** MILTON *Hist. Eng.* II. Wks. (1847) 496/2 Lollius Urbius..drew another wall of turves..to hedge out incursions from the north. **1701** J. LAW *Counc. Trade* (1751) 256 Money..[is] capable of being hedged out, but never of being hedged in, by restraints, coercions, and prohibitions.

†**7.** *hedge in.* **a.** To secure (a debt), app. usually by including it in a larger one for which better security is obtained. *Obs.*

1616 B. JONSON *Devil an Ass* III. i, Some pretty ring or jewel, Of fifty or threescore pound.—Make it a hundred, And hedge in the last forty, that I owe you, And your own price for the ring. *c* **1620** DONNE *Let. to Sir H. Goodyere* Wks. VI. 382 You think that you have Hedged in that Debt by a greater, by your Letter in Verse. **1667** WATERHOUSE *Fire Lond.* 165 To inforce him to hedg in his first Debt by addition of money lent.

†**b.** To introduce and include within the limits of something else; to thrust in, intrude, insinuate. (Perh. in some later instances associated with *edge in*, EDGE *v.*[1] 6 b.) *Obs.*

1664 J. WILSON *Cheats* III. ii, Pox o' these bonds! I must persuade him to take another £1000, and hedge all into one good mortgage. **1665** J. WEBB *Stone-Heng* (1725) 163 He could never..have any pretence, to hedge in other Antiquities at his Pleasure. *a* **1700** DRYDEN (J.), I pr'y thee, let me hedge one moment more Into thy promise. **1729** SWIFT *Direct. Servants, Footman* (1745) 47 When you are sent on an Errand, be sure to hedge in some business of your own. *a* **1764** LLOYD *Ep. to Colman* Poet. Wks. 1774 I. 167 Proud to hedge in my scraps of wit.

8. a. *trans.* To secure oneself against loss on (a bet or other speculation) by making transactions on the other side so as to compensate more or less for possible loss on the first. Formerly also with *in, off.* Also *fig.* (In origin app. related to 7 a.)

1672 VILLIERS (Dk. Buckhm.) *Rehearsal* (1714) 31 Now, Criticks, do your worst, that here are met; For, like a Rook, I have hedg'd in my Bet. *a* **1700** B. E. *Dict. Cant. Crew*, *Hedge*, to secure a desperate Bet, Wager or Debt. *a* **1734** NORTH *Exam.* III. vi. §65 (1740) 471 Abetting on one Side or the other, to hedge (as they call it) their own Stake. **1774** *Westm. Mag.* II. 583 He..contrived now-and-then prudently to hedge in a bet, by which means he soon found himself in possession of a sum which placed him above the abject dependence of a waiter. **1813** *Sporting Mag.* XLI. 4, I kept hedging my bets as I laid them. **1820** *Ibid.* New Ser. VI. 79 This..induced most of the sporting men to hedge off their bets. **1887** E. J. GOODMAN *Too Curious* xi, Backing the horse named and dexterously hedging his other investments.

b. *absol.* or *intr.*

1676 MARVELL *Mr. Smirke* I, [Some] like cunning Betters, sate judiciously hedging, and so ordered their matters that which side soever prevailed, they would be sure to be the Winners. *a* **1677** BARROW *Serm.* (1686) III. 397 This rooking trick, to hedge thus, and save stakes, to play fast and loose, to dodge and shuffle with God, God doth not like. **1761** COLMAN *Jealous Wife* v. ii, When one has made a bad bet, it is best to hedge off, you know. **1819** *Sporting Mag.* IV. 76 No man should venture to bet, who could not hedge well. **1855** MACAULAY *Hist. Eng.* xvii. IV. 57 Godolphin..began to think..that he had betted too deep on the Revolution, and that it was time to hedge. **1894** WOLSELEY *Marlborough* II. lxxviii. 316 He played for averages..when, therefore, the stakes became high he invariably 'hedged' against all serious loss.

c. To insure against risk of loss by entering into contracts which balance one another. Also *trans.*, to operate in (a commodity) in this way.

1909 I. FISHER *Elimination of Risk* 12 An important method of shifting risks is 'hedging', whereby a dealer, for instance in transporting wheat, may be relieved of the risk of a change of price. **1917** A. W. ATWOOD *Exchanges & Speculation* xiv. 195 Hedging..consists in matching a purchase with a sale, or vice versa; in other words, it consists in making a purchase or sale for future delivery to offset and protect an actual merchandising transaction. *Ibid.* xiv. 197 It makes little difference to an elevator if wheat rises or falls fifty cents a bushel, provided its holdings have been hedged. **1957** *Times* 19 Dec. 16/1 We have drawn the attention of the stockholders to the difficulty in hedging our unsold stocks against a fall in cotton content value.

9. *intr.* To go aside from the straight way; to shift, shuffle, dodge; to trim; to avoid committing oneself irrevocably; to leave open a way of retreat or escape.

1598 SHAKS. *Merry W.* II. ii. 26, I, I, I my selfe sometimes, leauing the feare of heauen on the left hand..am faine to shuffle: to hedge, and to lurch. **1606** —— *Tr. & Cr.* III. iii. 158 If you giue way, Or hedge aside from the direct forth right. **1611** COTGR., *Harceler*, to haggle, hucke, hedge, or paulter long in the buying of a commodity. **1861** O. W. HOLMES *Pages fr. Old Vol. Life, Bread & Newsp.* (1891) 12 Prophesy as much as you like, but always hedge. **1866** *Lond. Rev.* 8 Dec. 623 He has hedged with such dexterity upon this point that his clergy must be sorely puzzled to determine how far they may go in ritualistic observances. **1888** 'CUSHING' *Blacksm. Voe* I. 245 For a while the miller hedged and dodged, but being pressed hard he finally admitted the truth. **1894** WOLSELEY *Marlborough* II. 291 It was..natural to him to trim and hedge in politics.

hedge-bank. [See BANK *sb.*[1] 1.] The bank or ridge of earth on which a hedge is planted; the slope beneath a hedge by a wayside.

1776–96 WITHERING *Brit. Plants* (ed. 3) III. 362 Woods, mountainous heaths, walls, and hedge banks. **1854** P. J. SELBY *Observ. Wasps* in *Hist. Berwick. Nat. Club* III. 181 [It] makes its nest in hedge-banks. **1900** *Daily News* 21 Sept. 3/2 Deeply laid roads and high, steep hedge banks. **1909** *Westm. Gaz.* 6 Mar. 16/3 A network of tiny marks..crossing and recrossing from hedge-bank to stack. **1937** *Discovery* Apr. 120/2 Feverfew, commonly found about hedgebanks.

hedgeberry, hedge-berry. A 'berry' or fruit growing in a hedge, as the blackberry; *spec.* applied to the hagberry or bird-cherry, *Prunus Padus*, and the common wild cherry, *P. avium.*

1623 MIDDLETON *More Dissemblers* v. ii, Black in mouth, Like boys with eating hedge-berries. **1657** COLES *Adam in Eden* (Britten & Holl.), In Westmerland and Lancashire they call it [bird-cherry] the Hedge-berry-tree. **1866** *Treas. Bot.* 572/2 Hedgeberry, *Cerasus avium.*

hedge-bill. [See BILL *sb.*[1] 4.]

1. A bill for lopping and pruning hedges.

1497 *Naval Acc. Hen. VII* (1896) 98 Sithes..vj, ffelling axes..xxiiij, Hegge billes..xxv. **1576** FLEMING *Panopl. Epist.* 356 Let us gett a hedgebill and fall to repayring broken fences. **1823** SCOTT *Peveril* x, The peasant-boy.. with a hedge-bill in his hand.

2. A collector's name of a moth.

1832 J. RENNIE *Conspectus Butterfl. & Moths* 220 The Hedge Bill (*P*[*lutella*] *subfalcatella*, Stephens).

'hedge-bird.

1. Any bird that lives in or frequents hedges.

1884 JEFFERIES in *Chamb. Jrnl.* 1 Mar. 130/1 The hedge-sparrows..are early in spring joined by the whitethroats, almost the first hedgebirds to return.

2. *transf.* A person born, brought up, or accustomed to loiter under a hedge; a vagrant; a sturdy vagabond; a footpad. Cf. *gaol-bird.*

1614 B. JONSON *Barth. Fair* II. i, Out, you rogue, you hedge-bird, you pimp. **1670** G. H. *Hist. Cardinals* I. I. 6 His garb spoke him rather a Hedge-bird. **1706** ESTCOURT *Fair Examp.* v. i, I know there's some Business a-foot by this Hedge-bird's cackling. **1877** SPURGEON *Serm.* XXIII. 287 They were highwaymen and hedge-birds.

hedgebote ('hɛdʒbəʊt). *Law.* Also 6 -butt, -bot, 6–8 -boot. [See BOOT *sb.*[1] 5.] = HAYBOTE.

1565 *Lease Manor Pollington, Yorksh.* (MS.), Lessees may take housebutt, henbutt, firebutt, hedgebutt and ploughbutt. **1579** RASTELL *Expos. Diff. Words, Haybote or Hedgbot* is necessarie stuffe to make and mend hedges, which lessee for yeres, or for life, of common right may take vpon the ground to him leased. **1716** *Lease of Lands in Brumby* in *N.W. Linc. Gloss.*, To have..sufficient house-boot, hedgeboot..and Stakeboot yearly. **1767** BLACKSTONE *Comm.* II. iii. (1799) 34 Hay-bote or hedge-bote is wood for repairing of hays, hedges, or fences. **1845** [see HAYBOTE].

†**'hedge-creeper.** *Obs.*

1. 'One that skulks under hedges for bad purposes' (J.); a hedge-bird; a sneaking rogue.

1548 W. PATTEN *Exped. Scotl.* in Arb. *Garner* III. 140 A dozen or twenty of their hedge-creepers, horsemen that lay lurking thereby. **1594** NASHE *Unfort. Trav.* 11 A sneaking eauesdropper, a scraping hedgecreeper. **1688** BUNYAN *Jerus. Sinner Saved* (1886) 35 These poor, lame, maimed, blind, hedge-creepers and highwaymen, must come in. **1708** MOTTEUX *Rabelais* (1737) V. 217 Rovers, Ruffian-Rogues, and Hedge-Creepers.

2. A hobgoblin, pixy.

c **1580** J. JEFFERE *Bugbears* III. iii. 50 Wood-crepers, hedg-crepers, and the whyte and red fearye.

†**'hedge-creeping,** *a.* *Obs.* That creeps or sneaks by hedges; clandestine, base; cf. HEDGE *sb.* 8.

1579 J. STUBBES *Gaping Gulf* B ij, To set vp a thousande hyll alters for hedgecreeping Priestes. **1597** BP. HALL *Sat.* IV. v. 107 Some base hedge-creeping Collybist. **1602** F. HERRING *Anat.* 6 The croaking and hedge-creeping Quack-saluer. **1656** *Artif. Handsom.* (1662), Like the hedge-creeping light of glo-worms.

hedged (hɛdʒd), *ppl. a.* [f. HEDGE *v.* or *sb.* + -ED.] Enclosed with or as with a hedge. Also with *in.*

c **1440** *Promp. Parv.* 232/2 Hedgyd (*K.*, *S.* heggyd), *septus.* **1625** K. LONG tr. *Barclay's Argenis* IV. xx. 313 Over ditches and hedged fields. **1824** MISS MITFORD *Village* (1863) 257 A real cottage..with its hedged-in garden. **1891** ELIZ. R. PENNELL *Stream of Pleas.* 44 Long walks through hedged-in lanes.

hedgehog ('hɛdʒhɒg). Also 5 heyghoge, 6 hediock, 7 hedgehock. [f. HEDGE *sb.* + HOG: named from its frequenting hedgerows and from its pig-like snout.]

1. An insectivorous quadruped of the genus *Erinaceus*, armed above with innumerable spines, and able to roll itself up into a ball with these bristling in every direction; an urchin.

a **1450** *Fysshynge w. angle* (1883) 2 Wen he wenyt hyt be a hare ful often hit ys a heyghoge [**1496** hegge hogge]. **1535** COVERDALE *Isa.* xxxiv. 15 There shall the hedghogge buylde, digge, be there at home. **1579** LYLY *Euphues* (Arb.) 373 Thou arte..not vnlyke vnto the Hedgehogge, who euermore lodgeth in the thornes, bicause he himselfe is full of prickells. **1656** BP. HALL *Occas. Medit.* (1851) 136 The fox knows many pretty wiles, but the hedgehog knows one

great one. **1864** Tennyson *Aylmer's F.* 850 The hedgehog underneath the plantain bores. **1889** *Pall Mall G.* 6 Feb. 1/2 You need a tolerably thick skin when you go to bed with a hedgehog.

fig. **1642** R. Carpenter *Experience* II. iii. 142 In.. desire to be delivered of a hedghog that wounds and teares them in their tender inside. **1828** Hawthorne *Fanshawe* vii. (1879) 108 Her firmness, decision, and confident sagacity—which made her a sort of domestic hedgehog. **1876** Eliz. Wetherell *Daisy in Field* xiv. 173 That hedgehog of thoughts began to stir and unfold and come to life.

2. Applied to various animals armed with spines, as (*a*) the Tenrec of Madagascar; (*b*) the Porcupine Ant-eater of Australia; (*c*) ***sea-hedgehog***, the Porcupine-fish *Diodon hystrix*; also the Sea-urchin.

1598 Florio, *Hechinometri*, a kinde of sea hedgehog. **1737** Ozell *Rabelais* I. 350 The Shells of Sea-hedge-hogs are.. call'd Coquecigruës. **1863** Wood *Illustr. Nat. Hist.* III. 337 The Urchin-Fish or Sea Hedgehog is a good example of the genus Diodon, or Two-toothed fishes.. remarkable for the tremendous array of spiny points which it bears on its skin.

3. A name for prickly seed-vessels or burs borne by plants, and for the plants which bear them, e.g. *Ranunculus arvensis*, *Medicago Echinus* (*M. intertexta*), *Echinaria capitata*.

1711 J. Petiver in *Phil. Trans.* XXVII. 387 Hard Bur Hedgehogs.. The Fruit of this resembles our Xanthium or Lesser Burdock. **1794** Martyn *Rousseau's Bot.* xxv. 369 Hedgehogs, whose legumes are closely armed with long spines pointing out every way. **1864** H. Trimen in *Jrnl. Bot.* II. 79 *R*[*anunculus*] *Arvensis*..called 'Hedgehogs' (I suppose from its muricated fruit) by the country people. **1866** *Treas. Bot.* 572/2 Hedgehog, *Medicago intertexta*. **1880** Jefferies *Gt. Estate* 132 The curious prickly seed-vessels of the corn buttercup—the 'hedgehog'—whose spines, however, will not scratch the softest skin.

4. Applied to other things likened to a hedgehog: †**a.** A disease of sheep. *Obs.* †**b.** A kind of military firework. *Obs.* **c.** (See quot. 1794.) **d.** A kind of vagrant rabbit. **e.** A kind of dredging-machine. **f.** A dish in cookery.

1607 Topsell *Four-f. Beasts* (1658) 476 Of the Warts and Cratches of Sheep. This disease is called by the vulgar shepheards the Hedghog. **1672** T. Venn *Milit. Discipl.* III. III. xv. 13 To make Hedg-hogs, or balls, you must fill them with the same receipts you do your Arrows and Pikes [etc.]. **1723** J. Nott *Cook's & Confect. Dict.* 28 (*heading*) To make a hedge-hog. *Ibid.*, Almonds,.. Eggs,.. Cream,.. Butter.. stirring, till it is stiff enough to be made in the Form of a Hedge-hog; then stick it full of blanch'd Almonds,.. like the Bristles of a Hedge-hog. **1794** W. Felton *Carriages* (1801) II. Gloss., *Hedge Hog*, a leather stuck full of nails, to buckle on the pole with the points upward, to prevent the horses gnawing it. **1838** *Civil Engin. & Archit. Jrnl.* Dec. 391/1 (*title*) A machine called a hedgehog for removing mud etc. in rivers. **1846** *P. Parley's Ann.* VII. 325 The hedgehog is a sort of vagabond rabbit. **1855** Eliza Acton *Mod. Cookery* (1863) 480 An *Apple Hedge-Hog*, or *Suédoise*, this dish is formed of apples, pared, cored without being divided, and stewed tolerably tender in a light syrop. **1856** S. C. Brees *Gloss. Terms*, *Hedgehog*, a machine for removing mud and silt from rivers and streams. It is somewhat similar in shape to a road or garden roller, consisting of a wheel revolving on an axle, to which drawing shafts are fixed. Timber stocks are projected from the cylinder with iron spades bolted thereto, which act upon the bottom of the river, clearing away all obstructions. **1960** *Good Housek. Cook. Bk.* 405/2 Hedgehog cake.

g. A fortified position 'bristling' with guns pointing in all directions.

1942 *Daily Tel.* 22 May 1/2 The German infantry has been used to being led by tanks and, throughout the past winter, to holding strong points called 'hedgehogs'. **1943** *Times* 16 Dec. 4/1 The Germans fought with the utmost ferocity for their old 'hedgehog' position. **1952** *Time* 29 Sept. 18/1 Holdfast's strategists had developed their plan after studying German tactics in the long retreat from Stalingrad (in which the Germans first used the word 'hedgehog').

h. (See quot. 1947.)

1947 *Jane's Fighting Ships 1946–7* 6 Anti-Submarine Weapons.. include the 'hedgehog', a salvo of 24 depth charges each containing 32 lb. of explosive fired ahead of a ship from a spigot mortar. **1968** D. McLachlan *Room 39* xiv. 329 The dangers of underwater hedgehogs to the Mulberry floating harbours [had not] been closely examined.

†**5.** Applied to a person who is regardless of others' feelings; often as a term of obloquy. *Obs.*

1594 Shaks. *Rich. III*, I. ii. 102 Do'st grant me Hedge-hogge. **1605** *Tryall Chev.* III. i. in Bullen *O. Pl.* III. 306 My name, sir, is Bow wow. S'hart, what a name's that! the Hedge-hog mocks us. **1660** *Mrs. Rump* 2 Thou Dam'd Hedgehock.

6. *attrib.*, passing into *adj.*: Of, belonging to, or resembling a hedgehog.

1610 Guillim *Heraldry* III. vii. (1660) 135 Unlike to those Hedge-hogge holy-ones whose Sharpe censures.. pierce thorow all those who converse with them. **1774** Goldsm. *Nat. Hist.* (1776) IV. 99 Animals of the Hedge-hog kind. **1891** N. Cory *Lett. & Jrnls.* (1897) 461 The tilting, hedge-hog, ransom age. **1930** *Engineering* 14 Nov. 615/2 An elevator.. delivered the clay into small hedgehog rollers.

7. a. General Comb., as ***hedgehog-hooked*** adj., ***-hunting***, ***-like*** adj. or adv.

1606 Sylvester *Du Bartas* II. iv. I. *Tropheis* 74 His hands and arms, and bosom bristled were (Most Hedg-hog-like) with wyer insteed of haire. **1678** *Narr. Murder Godfrey* 4 There had been several Soldiers thereabout.. a Hedghog-hunting. **1792** Wolcott (P. Pindar) *Ode to Acad. Chair* Wks. 1812 III. 48 Most hedgehog-like thou bristlest up my hair. **1793** Martyn *Lang. Bot.*, Hedge-hog-hooked, *Echinato-uncinata spica*. A spike beset with prickles.

b. Special Comb.: **hedgehog cactus**, a plant of the genus *Echinocactus*, globular and spiny; **hedgehog caterpillar** (*U.S.*), see quot.; **hedgehog converter, transformer** *Electr.*, a type of transformer (no longer used) with open magnetic circuit, in which the ends of the iron wire core assume a bristling appearance; **hedgehog crystal** (see quot.); **hedgehog fish** = *porcupine fish*; **hedgehog fruit**, the prickly fruit of an Australian tree, *Echinocarpus Australis*; also the tree itself; **hedgehog fungus** = *hedgehog mushroom*; **hedgehog gooseberry**, a variety of gooseberry covered with stiff hairs; **hedgehog grass**, † (*a*) a kind of sedge (*Carex flava*) having prickly fruit; (*b*) name of various grasses of which the spikelets form burs, esp. *Cenchrus tribuloides* of N. America; **hedgehog holly**, a variety of holly with spines on the surface of the leaves (Miller *Gard. Dict.* 1724); **hedgehog liquorice**, name for *Glycyrrhiza echinata*, an Italian plant from which liquorice is made (*Gerarde's Herbal* 1633); **hedgehog medick**, a species of *Medicago* with prickly pods, as *M. Echinus* (*M. intertexta*), *M. maculata*; **hedgehog mushroom**, an edible fungus of the genus *Hydnum*, having prickly hymenium; **hedgehog parsley**, a name for burparsley, *Caucalis daucoides*; **hedgehog plant** = sense 3; **hedgehog pudding**, a pudding stuck over with blanched almonds (*Cassell's Dict. Cookery*); **hedgehog rat**, a rodent of the subfamily *Echinomyinæ* (see quot.); **hedgehog shell**, the shell of *Murex erinaceus*, having prickly projections; **hedgehog soup** (see quot., and cf. *hedgehog pudding*); **hedgehog stone**, popular name of a brown iron ore occurring in rock crystals; **hedgehog thistle** = *hedgehog cactus*; **hedgehog trefoil**, ? = *hedgehog medick*; **hedgehog wheat**, a race of hardy dwarf wheats, grown in mountainous districts of Europe, having dense short ears and awned glumes.

1872 C. V. Riley *Noxious Insects* 143 The larva of this insect (*Arctia Isabella*).. is familiarly known by the name of the *Hedgehog Caterpillar. It is thickly covered with stiff black hairs on each end and with reddish hairs on the middle of the body. **1886** *Syd. Soc. Lex.*, **Hedgehog-crystals*, the globular masses of sodium urate found in the urine, which are provided with points or prickles. **1851** P. H. Gosse *Nat. Sojourn Jamaica* 244 Specimens of the *Hedgehog-fish, or Sea Porcupine (*Diodon*), are frequently carried home by mariners. **1887** C. F. Holder *Liv. Lights* 138 The chantarelle and the *hedgehog fungus are esteemed by many. **1676** Worlidge *Cyder* (1691) 229 The *Hedgehog Gooseberry is a large fruit, well tasted, and very hairy. **1597** Gerarde *Herbal* I. xiv. §1. 15 *Hedgehog grasse hath broade, long and stiffe flaggie leaues.. and at the top of euerie stalke groweth certaine round and pricking knobs, fashioned like an Hedgehog. **1884** Miller *Plant-n.*, Hedgehog Grass, *Panicum stagninum*. **1861** Miss Pratt *Flower. Pl.* II. 92 The *Hedge-Hog Medick (*Medicago intertexta*). **1854** Mayne *Expos. Lex.*, *Hedgehog Mushroom, common name for the *Hydnum erinaceum*. **1879** Prior *Plant-n.*, *Hedgehog parsley, from its prickly burs, *Caucalis daucoides*. **1884** Miller *Plant-n.*, *Hedge-hog-plant, *Anthyllis erinacea* and *Echinaria capitata*. **1884** Kingsley *Stand. Nat. Hist.* V. 89 The *Echinomyinæ*, or *Hedge-hog Rats, as they may be collectively termed.. the pelage is usually harsh, or bristly, or even mixed with spines. **1863** Wood *Illustr. Nat. Hist.* I. 370 The British Woodcock or *Hedgehog Shell.. is a native of our seas.. much smaller than the thorny woodcock. **1769** Mrs. Raffald *Eng. Housekpr.* (1778) 6 Blanch a few Jordan almonds.. stick them round the edge of the rolls slantways, then stick them all over the top of the rolls.. when dished up pour the soup upon the roll.. some French cooks give this soup the name of *hedge-hog soup. **1849** J. Nicol *Min.* 403[Goethite] occurs enclosed in rock crystal.. the Stachelschweinstein, *Hedgehogstone. **1597** Gerarde *Herbal* (1633) 1177 Of the Melon or *Hedge-hog Thistle. **1856** Knight *Cycl. Nat. Hist.* II. 466 *Echinocactus*, a genus of.. Cactaceæ.. known by the name of Hedgehog Thistles. **1902** *Encycl. Brit.* XXVIII. 117/2 The wire.. used.. to form the core of his '*hedgehog' transformers. **1706** Phillips (ed. Kersey), **Hedge-hog-Trefoil*, a kind of Herb. **1909** Webster, *Hedgehog wheat. **1921** J. Percival *Wheat Plant* 307 Club, Dwarf, Cluster or Hedgehog Wheat, *Triticum compactum*.

'hedgehogged, *a.* [transl. L. *echīnātus*, f. *echīnus* hedgehog: see -ED[2].] Set with prickles.

1793 Martyn *Lang. Bot.*, Hedge-hogged Pericarp, *Echinatum pericarpium*.

hedgehoggy ('hɛdʒhɒgɪ), *a.* [f. HEDGEHOG + -Y.] Of the nature of a hedgehog; externally repellent; difficult to get on with. Hence **'hedgehogginess**.

1858 Motley in *Corr.* (1889) I. 266 'Why is it that we English, when we meet abroad, are so very friendly, and when we reappear in London are so very hedgehoggy?' I told her that the reason why there was no hedgehogginess on this occasion was because I was not an Englishman. **1866** Ruskin *Eth. Dust* (1883) 101 So your hedgehoggy readers roll themselves over and over their Bibles, and declare that whatever sticks to their own spines is Scripture. **1882** Spurgeon in *Chr. World Pulpit* XXII. 163 Get near some of those dear hedgehoggy brethren, and go and make a pillow of them.

hedge-hyssop. A name given by early herbalists to *Gratiola officinalis*, a scrophulariaceous plant of Central Europe, formerly noted for its medicinal properties; extended to various British plants supposed to resemble this in appearance or properties, e.g. *Scutellaria*, *Lythrum hyssopifolium*.

1578 Lyte *Dodoens* VI. xii. 673 Hedge Hysope is founde in certayne places of Germanie and Fraunce.. It groweth in Hedges, and wilde places. Some do call it in Latine, *Gratia Dei*, howbeit it is nothing like *Gratia Dei*, or *Gratiola*. ? *a* **1605** Middleton *Witch* III. iii, Hedge-hyssop too: how near he goes my cuttings! **1633** Johnson *Gerarde's Herbal* 564 (Britten & Holl.) It [*Polygala*] is vulgarly known in Cheapside to the herbe-women by the name of Hedge-Hyssop; for they take it for *Gratiola*, or Hedge-Hyssop, and sell it to such as are ignorant for the same. **1640** Parkinson *Theat. Bot.* xxvii. 220 *Gratiola vulgaris*, true hedge Hyssope. *Ibid.* 221 *Gratiola cœrulea*, *sive latifolia major*, the greater broade leafed or blew flowred hedge Hyssope. **1796** Withering *Brit. Plants* (ed. 3) II. 442 *Lythrum*.. *hyssopifolium*.. Grasspoly, Small Hedge-hyssop. **1893** McCarthy *Red Diamonds* II. 43 The deadly fox-glove, and its less deadly cousin, the hedge hyssop.

hedgeless ('hɛdʒlɪs), *a.* [f. HEDGE *sb.* + -LESS.] Destitute of hedges.

1802 W. Taylor in Robberds *Mem.* (1843) I. 412 The hedgeless sweeps of field. **1873** Miss Broughton *Nancy* I. 164 The endless, treeless, hedgeless German flats.

hedgeling ('hɛdʒlɪŋ). [f. as prec. + -LING.]

1. A young or dwarf hedge.

1787 W. Marshall *Norfolk* I. 103 The hedgling is defended on one side by a deep ditch.

2. A young hedge-bird. (Cf. *fledgeling*.)

1833 Aird *Wks.* (1856) 337 The callow hedgelings chirping through the briar.

'hedgelong, *a.* [f. as prec. + *-long*, OE. *-lang*: cf. ALONG.] Extending alongside of a hedge.

a **1758** Dyer *Poems* (1761) 55 (Jod.) On the hedgelong bank Sow frequent sand.

hedge-pig. 1. = HEDGEHOG.

1605 Shaks. *Macb.* IV. i. 2 Once the Hedge-Pigge whin'd. **1889** *Pall Mall G.* 31 May 2/2 Hedge pigs are egg eaters, and will also dine off young birds.

2. A corrupt form of *hedge-pick*, *-peak*, *-speak*, dial. name of the sloe. See HEDGE *sb.* 10.

'hedge-priest. [See HEDGE *sb.* 8 a.] An illiterate or uneducated priest of inferior status. (*contemptuous.*)

1550 J. Coke *Eng. & Fr. Heralds* §167 (1877) 107 In Fraunce.. the most parte of your sperituual men.. be symple persons, hedge priestes not lerned. *a* **1568** Ascham *Scholem.* II. (Arb.) 136 Therefore did som of them at Cambridge.. cause hedge priestes fette oute of the contrie to be made fellowes in the vniuersitie. *a* **1617** Bayne *On Eph.* (1658) 8 In times of superstition every hedge-priest's blessing was highly esteemed. **1874** Green *Short Hist.* iii. §1. 116 The whole body of the clergy, from Pope to hedge-priest.

hedger ('hɛdʒə(r)). [f. HEDGE *sb.* or *v.* + -ER[1].]

1. One who makes, repairs, or trims hedges.

c **1515** *Cocke Lorell's B.* (Percy Soc.) 11 Hedgers, dykers, and mowers. **1634** Milton *Comus* 293 The swinkt hedger at his supper sat. **1791** Boswell *Johnson* 3 Apr. an. 1776, A pair of large gloves such as hedgers use. **1848** Mill *Pol. Econ.* I. ii. §1 The hedgers and ditchers, who made the fences necessary for the protection of the crop.

2. One who hedges; a shuffler.

1728 *Wodrow Corr.* (1843) III. 401 The *Go ons* and *Non liquets*, too often hedgers and skulkers. *a* **1845** Hood *Ode to Rae Wilson* xix, A black-leg saint, a spiritual hedger.

3. One who 'hedges' in betting.

1873 *Slang Dict.* s.v., The hedger.. cannot lose, providing his information or judgement lead to the required result.

hedgerow ('hɛdʒrəʊ). Forms: see HEDGE *sb.* and ROW *sb.* [OE. *heggerǽw*, *-réw*, f. HEDGE *sb.* + ROW *sb.* OE. had also *heȝerǽw*.]

1. A row of bushes forming a hedge, with the trees, etc. growing in it; a line of hedge.

940 *Charter of Eadmund* in *Cod. Dipl.* VI. 229 Of Stanforde on ðe olde heggerewe on sondermede. **1577** B. Googe *Heresbach's Husb.* II. (1586) 97 Cheryes growing wilde in the Woodes, and Hedgerowes. *a* **1661** Fuller *Worthies* (1840) I. 549 Made of apples, here [Gloucester] grown in hedge-rows. **1769** N. Nicholls *Corr. w. Gray* (1843) 100 There are many fine trees in the hedge-rows. **1849** Macaulay *Hist. Eng.* I. 281 Rich corn land and meadow, intersected by green hedgerows.

2. *attrib.* and *Comb.*, as ***hedgerow-bird***, ***-carpenter***, ***-elm***, ***-oak***, ***-shrub***, ***-thief***, ***-timber***, ***-tree***.

1632 Milton *L'Allegro* 57 By hedge-row elms, on hillocks green. **1781** Cowper *Retirement* 419 Her hedge-row shrubs, a variegated store. **1807** Vancouver *Agric. Devon* (1813) 115 The common Devonshire plough, made by a hedge-row carpenter. **1878** Stevenson *Inland Voy.* 43 The hedges were of great height, woven about the trunks of hedgerow elms. **1892** A. Birrell *Res Judic.* ii. 48 His family tree.. was indeed of the most ordinary hedge-row description.

Hence **hedgerowed** ('hɛdʒrəʊd) *a.*, traversed by hedgerows.

1830 *Blackw. Mag.* XXVIII. 163 That rich and beautifully hedgerowed country.

hedgery ('hɛdʒərɪ). [f. HEDGE *sb.* + -ERY.] Hedges collectively.

1880 MRS. WHITNEY *Odd or Even* xxvi. 275 The kindly tangles of its broken hedgery.

'hedge-school. A school held by a hedge-side or in the open air, as was once common in Ireland; hence, a poor, mean, low-class school.

1807 *Edin. Rev.* X. 53 The lower Irish are sufficiently well taught, even in their hedge-schools. **1807** T. HORNE tr. *Goede's Trav.* II. 81 Bristol [has] a few charity-schools, and two hedge-schools with only one master. **1830** W. CARLETON *Traits Irish Peasantry* (1836) II. 142 The worthy pedagogue selected the first green spot on the sunny side of a quick-set-thorn hedge..and there..carried on the work of instruction. From this circumstance the name of Hedge School originated. **1845** R. W. HAMILTON *Pop. Educ.* viii. (ed. 2) 194 The hedge-school, a name of contempt for institutions in which the smatterings of knowledge could only be obtained. **1879** *Cassell's Techn. Educ.* IV. 394/1 The workmen are Irish; taken from common hedge schools.

Hence **hedge-'schoolmaster**.

1830 W. CARLETON *Traits Irish Peasantry* (1836) II. 248 What was Plato himself but a hedge schoolmaster? **1851** THACKERAY *Eng. Hum.* vi, Paddy Byrne, the hedge-schoolmaster, took him in hand.

'hedge-side. The side of a hedge. Also *attrib.*, sometimes with sense of HEDGE *sb.* 8c.

1568 GRAFTON *Chron.* II. 296 [He] layed him under a hedge side for to refreshe hym. **1821** CLARE *Vill. Minstr.* I. 208 By hedge-side coolly led, Brooks curl o'er their sandy bed. **1848** KINGSLEY *Lett.* (1878) I. 174 The commonest hedge-side leaf. **1851** D. JERROLD *St. Giles* xiii. 135 Maid-of-all-work at a hedge-side hotel.

'hedge-sparrow. A common British and European bird (*Accentor modularis*), belonging to the *Sylviidæ*, or Warblers.

1530 PALSGR. 230/1 Hedge sparowe, a byrde. **1629** MASSINGER *Picture* II. ii, Soldiers—that, like the foolish hedge sparrow, To their own ruin, hatch this cuckoo, peace. **1774** G. WHITE *Selborne* xli. 106 Hedge-sparrows frequent sinks and gutters in hard weather, where they pick up crumbs and other sweepings. **1897** *Times* 2 Jan. 8/3 The so-called hedge sparrow is not a sparrow at all, the colour of the upper parts being its only similarity with that bird..it has nothing whatever in common with true sparrows.

'hedge-wood. †**a.** Wood for hedge-bote (*obs.*). **b.** Trees or timber grown in hedgerows. **c.** Firewood gathered from hedges.

1602 FULBECKE *2nd Pt. Parall.* 52 The termor hath.. hedge-wood, and fire-woode belonging to his tearme of common right: and he may cut wood for that purpose. **1707** MORTIMER *Husb.* I. (1708) 610 Plant timber-Trees or Coppice-Wood, or Hedge-wood. **1785** J. PHILLIPS *Treat. Inland Navig.* 19 Coals purchased will be cheaper..than hedge-wood stolen.

hedging ('hɛdʒɪŋ), *vbl. sb.* [f. HEDGE *v.*]

1. The action of the verb HEDGE; the construction or repair of hedges.

*c***1380** WYCLIF *Serm.* Sel. Wks. I. 28 For dichying and hegging, and delvynge of tounes. **1481-93** *Howard Househ. Bks.* (Roxb.) 366 For woode makynge and hedgynge. **1663** GERBIER *Counsel* (1664) 52 Charges for hedging, forty shillings. **1818** CRUISE *Digest* (ed. 2) III. 53 No tithes shall be paid of *sylva cædua* employed in hedging, or for fuel.

2. *concr.* Matter forming or made into a hedge.

1517 *Domesday Inclos.* (1897) I. 249 One acre of Errable land, with hedgyng and Dikyng. **1801** R. GILL *Tint Quey* in Chambers *Pop. Hum. Scot. Poems* (1862) 176 Whilk..had, by light o' day, Within the hedging made its way.

3. The securing of, or limiting the possible loss on, a debt, bet, or the like: see HEDGE *v.* 7, 8.

*a***1631** DONNE *Serm.* V. cxxviii. 301 All your Hedgings in of Debt, all your crafty Bargains. *c***1770** C. ANSTEY *Hor. Imit.* Wks. (1808) 191 Hedging and odds and bets their theme. **1816** *Sporting Mag.* XLVII. 277 In a manner that will render the practice of hedging off rather precarious. **1824** MISS MITFORD *Village* Ser. I. (1863) 172 An affair of bettings, and hedgings, and cheatings. **1917** [see HEDGE *v.* 8c]. **1940** *Economist* 11 May 863/1 Much of the apparent speculation taking place in markets..is, in fact, justifiable hedging either against receipts of sterling..or against the holding of sterling assets... But over and above such hedging some outright speculation is also proceeding. **1954** *Ibid.* 22 May 642/2 The Liverpool market should..offer Lancashire a satisfactory hedging medium. **1958** *Spectator* 13 June 785/1 The tenacity of the 'inflation hedging' investor.

4. Shuffling, dodging.

1722 *Wodrow Corr.* (1843) II. 645 Where was a great deal of hedging and political disputing. **1728** *Ibid.* III. 407 The plain shiftings and hedgings I have observed before the committee. **1826** CARLYLE in Froude *Life* (1882) I. 352 Persuaded that he shall go to heaven, when his hedging here below is done.

5. *attrib.* and *Comb.*, as ***hedging time***; esp. = used in hedging, as ***hedging cuff***, ***glove***, ***hook***, ***money***.

1521 in Rogers *Agric. & Prices* III. 565/4, 3 pr. hedging cuffs & gloves @ /6. **1530** PALSGR. 230/1 Hedgyng glove, *moufle*. **1611** COTGR., *Hayeson*, hedging time, or, the season to make hedges in. **1827** in Hone *Every-day Bk.* II. 905 With..his bill-hook and hedging mittens in his hand. **1906** KIPLING *Puck of Pook's Hill* 235, I was cheated..over a pair of hedging-gloves.

'hedging-bill. [BILL *sb.*[1] 4.] A bill with a long handle used in cutting and trimming hedges.

1497 *Naval Acc. Hen. VII* (1896) 116 Ffelling axes..xxx, Heggyng billes..xxiiij. **1523** FITZHERB. *Husb.* §5 An husbande muste haue an axe, a hachet, a hedgyngebyll. **1681** WORLIDGE *Dict. Rust.* (E.D.S.), A *Bill* is an edg-tool, at the end of a stale or handle; if short then it is called a *Hand-bill*; if long then a *Hedging-bill*. **1712** J. JAMES tr. *Le Blond's Gardening* 173 Cutting the Palisade..with the Hedging-Bill. **1827** DE QUINCEY *Murder* Wks. 1862 IV. 53 One author contends..for a hedging-bill.

hedgingly, *adv.* [f. *hedging*, pr. pple. of HEDGE *v.* + -LY[2].] So as to hedge (see HEDGE *v.* 8).

1894 *Sat. Rev.* 12 May 488 The contention which the Chancellor of the Exchequer merely hedgingly threw out on the first night of the debate.

hedgy ('hɛdʒɪ), *a.* [f. HEDGE *sb.* + -Y.] †**a.** Of or belonging to a hedge (*obs.*). **b.** Characterized by abundance of hedges.

1597-8 BP. HALL *Sat.* III. i, Or search'd the hopeful thicks of hedgy rows, For briery berries, or haws, or sourer sloes. **1643** NICHOLAS *Let.* in Carte *Ormonde* (1735) III. 173 Between the rivers of Severne and Avon, in a woodland and hedgy country. **1890** *Times* 10 Sept. 5/1 The hedgy nature of the country rendered it impossible for cavalry to act in force.

c. Of behaviour (see HEDGE *v.* 9).

1928 D. H. LAWRENCE *Lady Chatterley* iv. 38 Clifford was much more hedgey and nervous. **1955** 'C. H. ROLPH' *Women of Streets* 154 *Personality*: Suspicious, hedgy, aggressively defensive.

hedious, hedoes, obs. forms of HIDEOUS.

hedir(e, obs. form of HITHER.

†**hedley medley.** *Obs.* [A riming jingle upon *medley*. Cf. *hugger-mugger*.] A jumble, confusion; an impersonation of confusion.

1646 J. HALL *Poems* I. 7 Strange hedly Medly! who would make his swine Turn grey-hounds, or hunt foxes with his kine?

hedonal ('hiːdənəl). *Chem.* [a. G. *hedonal* (H. Dreser 1899, in *Verh. d. Ges. deutsch. Naturf. und Ärzte* II. 48), f. Gr. ἡδονή pleasure + -AL.] A white crystalline compound, $C_6H_{13}O_2N$, that has been used as a hypnotic and an anæsthetic; methyl-propyl-carbinol urethane.

1900 *Brit. Med. Jrnl.* epit. 21 July 12/1 (*heading*) Hedonal. Schüler..publishes 21 cases in which this new hypnotic was used in Krafft-Ebing's clinic. Hedonal is methyl-propyl-carbinol-urethan, a white crystalline body. **1905** *Med. Ann.* 191 Hedonal has been used by Vargas in the treatment of chorea. **1927** *Observer* 27 Mar. 13/1 Drugs such as hedonal may be injected..to facilitate or produce surgical anaesthesia. **1971** MCCOMISH & BODLEY *Anaesthesia for Neurol. Surg.* i. 15 The vogue for hedonal [as an anæsthetic] did not last long because the war in 1914 stopped supplies from Germany, and toxic effects later became apparent.

hedonic (hiː'dɒnɪk), *a.* and *sb.* [ad. Gr. ἡδονικός pleasurable, f. ἡδονή pleasure.]

A. *adj.* **1.** Of or relating to pleasure. (In first quot. applied to the Cyrenaic school of philosophers: see B. 1.) In wider use, chiefly in *Psychol.*: of, pertaining to, or involving pleasurable or painful sensations or feelings, considered as affects. Spec. ***hedonic tone***, the degree of pleasantness or unpleasantness associated with an experience or state, esp. considered as a single quantity that can range from extreme pleasure to extreme pain.

1656 STANLEY *Hist. Philos.* IV. (1701) 134/1 Aristippus.. Instituted a Sect called Cyreniack from the place, by some Hedonick, or voluptuous, from the Doctrine. *a***1866** J. GROTE *Exam. Utilit. Philos.* xi. (1870) 182 'Hedonic' knowledge. **1880** *Mind* V. 88 The defects of Mill's Hedonic philosophy. **1901** G. F. STOUT *Man. Psychol.* (ed. 2) I. i. 63 When we wish to say that pleasure or displeasure belongs to this or that mental process, we say that the process is pleasantly or unpleasantly toned. Hedonic-tone is a generic term for pleasure and the reverse, considered as attributes of this or that mental process. *Ibid.*, Anger has hedonic-tone, mostly of an unpleasant kind. **1932** J. G. BEEBE-CENTER *Psychol. Pleasantness & Unpleasantness* i. 6 In the present volume..the general algebraic variable, whose positive values correspond to pleasantness and whose negative values correspond to unpleasantness, will be called hedonic tone. **1940** *Jrnl. Exper. Psychol.* XXVI. 233 The oscillations of hedonic tone in his case are slight, and the tone rises continuously from the beginning, in spite of pain and fatigue. *Ibid.* 227 While Ss worked Es took their tapping rate every minute..and in a number of cases called at stated intervals for a rating on a previously agreed hedonic scale. **1952** D. J. O'CONNOR *John Locke* 51 By pleasure and pain Locke..is referring to what the psychologists nowadays call the hedonic tone of our experiences which can be roughly measured on a scale ranging from very pleasant through mildly pleasant, neutral, mildly unpleasant to very unpleasant. **1961** P. T. YOUNG *Motivation & Emotion* v. 153 The sign, intensity, and temporal changes of affective processes can be represented upon the hedonic continuum.

2. *Zool.* Of or pertaining to sexual activity; ***hedonic gland***, any of various specialized glands found in many reptiles and amphibia that serve, apparently by secreting an attractive-smelling substance, to attract members of the opposite sex.

1901 H. GADOW *Amphibia & Reptiles* x. 443 All the recent Crocodilia possess two pairs of skin-glands, both secreting musk... The use of these strongly scented organs, which are possessed by both sexes, is obviously hedonic. *Ibid.* 658/2 (*index*) Hedonic glands (ἡδονή, lust). **1931** G. K. NOBLE *Biol. Amphibia* vi. 137 The secretions of the hedonic glands of newts and plethodontid salamanders have no recognizable odor and yet they seem to function in holding the attention of the female during courtship. **1960** H. M. SMITH *Evol. Chordate Struct.* xiii. 344 A large number of integumentary glands of spotty distribution among vertebrates are of hedonic function.

B. *sb.* †**1.** One who maintains that pleasure is the proper end of action; applied to the ancient Greek school of philosophers (Gr. οἱ ἡδονικοί) otherwise called CYRENAICS. *Obs.*

1678 CUDWORTH *Intell. Syst.* 75 Our Fellow-Atheists, the Hedonicks and Cyrenaicks.

2. *pl.* **hedonics**: The doctrine of pleasure; that part of ethics which treats of pleasure.

1865 J. GROTE *Treat. Mor. Ideas* ii. (1876) 14 The unideal form of eudæmonics of which I have spoken is *hedonics*, or a science of *indolentia*. *a***1866** —— *Exam. Utilit. Philos.* ii. (1870) 181 Hedonics, or the science of human pleasure. **1879** *Mill Hill Mag.* June 6 And now one rises to bepraise John Stuart Mill's hedonics.

So **he'donically** *adv.*

1951 H. A. MURRAY in Parsons & Shils *Toward Gen. Theory Action* IV. iii. 456 The kinds of events that are hedonically negative and the kinds that are hedonically positive. *Ibid.* 457 The aim of all needs is hedonically positive (in the imagination). **1961** P. T. YOUNG *Motivation & Emotion* ii. 49 It is reasonable to assume that playful behavior is generally enjoyable, hedonically positive.

hedonical, *a.* *rare*$^{-1}$. = HEDONIC *a.*

1897 B. RUSSELL *Essay Foundations Geom.* iii. 158 They would leave Geometry in a position no better than that of the Hedonical Calculus, in which we depend on a purely subjective measure. In recent Dicts.

hedonism ('hiːdənɪz(ə)m). [f. Gr. ἡδονή pleasure + -ISM. Cf. F. *hédonisme* (Littré *Suppl.*).] The doctrine or theory of ethics in which pleasure is regarded as the chief good, or the proper end of action.

1856 SEELYE tr. *Schwegler's Hist. Philos.* (1864) 71 Hedonism, the philosophical doctrine of the Cyreneans that pleasure is the chief good. **1873** SYMONDS *Grk. Poets* v. 138 As mere hedonism—the simple love of sensual pleasure—grew, so did the songs and the style of Anacreon gain in popularity. **1879** H. SPENCER *Data of Ethics* 151 Distinguishing Hedonism into the two kinds, egoistic and universalistic, according as the happiness sought is that of the actor himself or is that of all. **1897** G. G. FINDLAY in *Expos. Times* Feb., Hedonism, or the pleasure theory of life ..is the great heresy in morals.

hedonist ('hiːdənɪst). [f. as prec. + -IST.] One who maintains the doctrine of hedonism; one who regards pleasure as the chief good.

1856 DE QUINCEY *Confess.* (ed. 2) 251 In Professor Wilson's word, 'Gentlemen, I am a Hedonist; and if you must know why I take opium, that's the reason why'. (*Note*) Professor Wilson coined the English word *Hedonist*. **1874** L. STEPHEN *Hours in Library* I. 390 If a man chances to be a Hedonist, he should show the good temper which is the best virtue of the indolent. **1876** PATER in E. Gosse *Crit. Kit-Kats* (1896) 258, I wish they wouldn't call me 'a hedonist'; it produces such a bad effect on the minds of people who don't know Greek.

attrib. **1878** DOWDEN *Stud. Lit.* 402 This devotion to beauty, to beauty alone..was a kind of hedonist asceticism. **1896** MRS. H. WARD *Sir G. Tressady* 361 George's hedonist temper was almost at the end of his patience.

hedo'nistic, *a.* [f. prec. + -IC.] Pertaining to hedonists, or of the nature of hedonism.

1866 MILL in *Edin. Rev.* CXXIII. 341 Sokrates.. inculcates the ordinary duties of life on hedonistic grounds, and recommends them by the ordinary hedonistic inducements. **1875** JOWETT *Plato* (ed. 2) IV. 30 The Utilitarian or hedonistic mode of speaking. **1894** *Thinker* V. 571.

Hence **hedo'nistically** *adv.*, according to hedonism, in reference to hedonism.

1874 SIDGWICK *Meth. Ethics* II. v. §4. 156 The moral pain ..would be so great as to render the whole remainder of life hedonistically worthless. **1886** —— *Outl. Hist. Ethics* iv. §6. 181 *note*, Shaftesbury interprets the 'good' of the individual hedonistically, as equivalent to pleasure, satisfaction, delight, enjoyment.

hedo'nology. *rare.* [f. Gr. ἡδονή pleasure + -(O)LOGY.] = HEDONICS.

*a***1866** J. GROTE *Exam. Utilit. Philos.* xxi. (1870) 345 Hedonics, or hedonology, the science of human pleasure.

hedo'nometer. *humorous.* [f. as prec. + -METER.] An apparatus for measuring pleasure.

1880 *Sat. Rev.* No. 1312. 763 Who will construct a hedonometer for us which shall give the exact values in coin ..of a '47 signboard and a bottle of '47 port? **1887** *Jus* 6 May 14/2 Who is a competent judge, and where is his 'hedonometer'?

hedous, -ly, obs. forms of HIDEOUS, -LY.

†**'hedral**, *a.* *Obs.* *rare.* [f. Gr. ἕδρα seat, base + -AL[1].] Of or pertaining to the base of a solid.

1690 W. LEYBOURN *Curs. Math.* 326 The Diametre of the Basial or Hedral ambient Circle of the Hexaedron.

hedrumite ('hɛdrəmaɪt). *Petrogr.* [a. G. *hedrumit* (W. C. Brögger 1890, in *Zeitschr. f. Kryst. und Min.* XVI. 40), f. *Hedrum*, the name of a village north of Larvik, Norway + -ITE[1].] A hypabyssal porphyritic igneous rock having a trachytic texture and consisting essentially of a potash-feldspar with small amounts of pyribole and usu. also nepheline.

1896 J. F. KEMP *Handbk. Rocks* 141 *Hedrumite*, a name proposed by Brögger for certain syenitic rocks that are poor or lacking in nepheline, but that have a trachytic texture. **1920** A. HOLMES *Nomencl. Petrol.* 116 *Hedrumite*... A

leucocratic variety of alkali-syenite containing accessory nepheline. **1938** A. JOHANNSEN *Descr. Petrogr. Igneous Rocks* IV. I. 25 Hedrumites.. are essentially pulaskite-porphyries with a coarse trachytic texture. Brögger defined them as the mineralogical and chemical hypabyssal-trachytoid-equivalents of the pulaskites. **1964** *Mineral. Abstr.* XVI. 574/1 Senonian hedrumites cutting somewhat earlier andesites and pyroclastics have been found.. in Bulgaria.

hedur, -yr, obs. forms of HITHER.

hedus, obs. form of HIDEOUS.

hedychium (hɪˈdɪkɪəm). [mod.L. (J. G. Koenig in A. J. Retzius *Observationes Botanicæ* (1785) III. 73), f. Gr. ἡδύς sweet + χιών snow, in allusion to the fragrant white flowers of one species.] A perennial herb of the genus so called, belonging to the family Zingiberaceæ, native to tropical Asia, and bearing showy flowers in a terminal spike; the garland-flower. Also, a fibre obtained from a species of this plant.

1822 *Curtis's Bot. Mag.* XLIX. 2300 Roots of this undescribed species of *Hedychium* were sent by Dr. Wallich of Calcutta, to our friend Mr. Kent. **1894** A. K. NAIRNE *Flowering Plants W. India* 339 *Hedychium*, with long and slender filament and broad lateral staminodes, is.. a garden plant with pure white, fragrant flowers. **1920** CROSS & BEVAN *Text-bk. Paper-Making* (ed. 5) 171 *Hedychium coronarium*. Hedychium has lately come into prominence as a paper-making fibre. **1952** F. KINGDON-WARD *Plant Hunter in Manipur* 237 During the long summer.. Hedychium, with several species and in many bright colours, comes into bloom.

hedyphane (ˈhɛdɪfeɪn). *Min.* [Named *Hedyphan* by Breithaupt, 1830, f. Gr. ἡδύς sweet + -φανής appearing (cf. Gr. ἡδυφαής sweet-shining) in reference to its brilliant lustre.] A colourless variety of mimetite, containing calcium; a variety of green lead ore.

1832 C. U. SHEPARD *Min.* 222 Hedyphane. **1852** BROOKE & MILLER *Min.* 483 Breithaupt's hedyphane is a massive variety of mimetite.

hee, obs. form of EYE, HE, HIGH.

Heeb, var. HEBE, HEBE².

heebie-jeebie(s (ˌhiːbɪˈdʒiːbɪ(z)). *slang* (orig. *U.S.*). Also **heebies, heeby-jeebies**, etc. A feeling of discomfort, apprehension, or depression; the 'jitters'; delirium tremens; also, formerly, a type of dance.

1923 W. DE BECK in *N.Y. American* 26 Oct. 9/3 You dumb ox—why don't you get that stupid look offa your pan—you gimme the heeby jeebys! *Ibid.* 10 Nov. 10/1, 31,000 shares! Worthless stock of 'the Belgian Hair Tonic Company' wiped out! Every cent I had in the world... It gives me the heebie jeebies. **1924** H. C. WITWER in *Cosmopolitan* Oct. 114/2 That discovery gave my new found friend the hibby jibbys. **1926** MAINES & GRANT *Wise-Crack Dict.* 9/2 *Heebie-jeebies*, alcoholic shimmy. **1926** *Bulletin* 13 Dec. 5/5 The latest dance, the 'Heebie-Jeebies' is said to represent the incantations made by Red Indian witch doctors before a human sacrifice. **1927** *Punch* 2 Feb. 116/1 It is interesting to observe that in spite of artificial sunlight, television, winter sports and the heebie-jeebie there are still some stalwarts who stand by the old traditional amusements of the English people. **1927** *Weekly Dispatch* 1 May 8 The Heebie Jeebies is rich in haunch movements. *Ibid.* 3 May 3/7 A terrible girl in the next gallery, painted in the fearsome and fashionable 'pink and putty' manner, had given him what an American present might have called the 'heeby-jeebies'. *Ibid.* 17 Aug. 3/2 Does this work never give you the heeby-jeebies? Does it never depress you? **1929** R. C. ANDREWS *Ends of Earth* 89, I thought I had the 'hebe-jibies' and stepped up very gingerly. **1934** R. NICHOLS *Fisbo* 37 It would have given the downright heebee-jeebee To even the dullest of the dull *amœbæ*. **1959** J. FLEMING *Miss Bones* viii. 94 You've given me the heeby jeebies... It'll be the end of me. **1971** R. DENTRY *Encounter at Kharmel* iii. 57 That little creep.. gives me the screaming heebies. **1972** WODEHOUSE *Pearls, Girls & Monty Bodkin* ix. 138 He was suffering from an ailment known to the medical profession as the heeby-jeebies, and anything having the appearance of a hitch in the programme might lead to a total collapse.

heed (hiːd), *v.* Forms: 1 **hédan**, 2–3 **heden**, 4–5 **hede**, 5 **heede (heyd)**, 4– **heed**. *Pa. t.* 1 **hédde**, 3 **hedd(e**, 5 **hedit, -yt, -ut**, 6– **heeded**. *Pa. pple.* 4 **hed, hedit**, etc. [OE. *hédan* = OS. *hôdian*, *huodian* (MDu., Du. *hoeden*, LG. *höden*, *höen*), OHG. *huotan* (MHG. *hüeten*, Ger. *hüten*):—WGer. **hôdjan*, deriv. of **hôdâ*, sb. str. fem., OFris. *hôde*, *hûde*, OHG. *huota*, MHG. *huote*, Ger. *hut* fem., heed, guard, care, keeping; not recorded in OE., where its form would have been *hód*.]

†**1.** *intr.* (In OE.) To take charge, take possession, take. Const. with *genitive*.

c **1000** ÆLFRIC *Hom.* I. 330 Lazarus ne moste.. hedan ðæra crumena. *Ibid.* II. 114 We hedað þæra crumena ðæs hlafes. *c* **1000** *Rectitud. Sing. Pers.* c. 5 in Schmid *Gesetze* 376 þonne him forð-sið gebyrige, hede se hlaford þæs he læfe, bute hwet friges sy.

2. *intr.* To have a care, pay attention, take notice. Const. in OE. and ME. with *genitive*; subseq. with *of*, later *to*, *for*. *arch.* and *dial.*

Beowulf (Z.) 2697 Ne hedde he þæs heafolan. *c* **1000** *Inst. Polity* §10 in Thorpe *Laws* II. 316 Bisceopum gebyreð þæt hi.. ne hunda ne haveca hedan to swyðe. *a* **1300** *Fragm. Sev. Sins* 33 in *E.E.P.* (1862) 19 Nel he of oþir þing hede. *c* **1400** *Destr. Troy* 2663 Hedis to þat, and puttis of þat purpos. *Ibid.* 11531 Euer hedyng in hert of the hegh treason. *a* **1400–50** *Alexander* 3094 Hefys nott your hert to hye, bott hedes to your ende. **1477** EARL RIVERS (Caxton) *Dictes* 2 Whan I had heeded and loked vpon it. *a* **1618** SYLVESTER *Paradox agst. Libertie* 800 Much strength and many men unto their hoordes to heed. **1690** PENN *Rise & Progr. Quakers* (1834) 60 Never heed, the Lord's power is over all weakness and death. **1828** SCOTT *F.M. Perth* xxvi, Heed no longer for me, my lord. **1868** ATKINSON *Cleveland Gloss.* s.v., *Never heed*, don't concern yourself, never mind.

3. *trans.* To care for, concern oneself about; to take notice of, give attention to, to mind; to regard. (In Engl. now chiefly literary; in common use in Sc.)

a **1225** *Juliana* 8 As þe þat heh þing hefde to heden. *c* **1340** *Cursor M.* 3085 (Trin.) Oure lord him ȝaf his lawe to hede. *c* **1400** *Destr. Troy* 10339 He hedut no hathell. **1553** T. WILSON *Rhet.* 54 (R.) That man should be punished who little heedeth the maintenaunce of his tillage. **1592** WEST *1st Pt. Symbol.* §48 In the persons two thinges are to bee heeded. **1759** HURD *Retirem.* II. (R.), Which seem to be not perceived, or not heeded, by other men. **1816** J. WILSON *City of Plague* II. iii. 104 Heed not that foolish wretch—go on, go on. **1870** BRYANT *Iliad* I. I. 11 Domineer Over thy Myrmidons; I heed thee not. *Mod. Sc.* Never heed them!

†**4.** To observe, see, behold, take note of. Also *intr.* To look. (Cf. F. *regarder*.) *Obs.*

c **1205** LAY. 17801 Heo leopen to þan bedde, & þene king hedden. **13..** *E.E. Allit. P.* A. 1050 þe hyȝe trone þer moȝt ȝe hede. *a* **1400–50** *Alexander* 678 He.. to þe heuyn lokis, Hedis heterly on hiȝe, beholde on a sterne. *Ibid.* 1527 Who so wates fro withowte & within hedes.

heed, *sb.* Forms: 3–6 **hede**, 4–5 **hed**, 4–6 *Sc.* **heid**, 5 **hedde, (ȝed, -e)**, 5–6 **heede, heade**, 5– **heed**. [app. f. HEED *v.*: there is no corresponding OE. sb.: see prec.]

1. Careful attention, care, observation, regard. (Now chiefly literary.)

a **1300** *Cursor M.* 4248 (Gött.) Ioseph held euer his in hede. **1357** *Lay Folks Catech.* 200 Our gastly fadirs that has hede of us. **1553** T. WILSON *Rhet.* (1567) 54 b, Good hede would be had, that nothing be doubtfully spoken. **1575** LANEHAM *Let.* (1871) 50 With great art and heed.. thyther conueyd, and thear erected. **1590** SHAKS. *Com. Err.* IV. i. 101, I will.. teach your eares to list me with more heede. **1634** SIR T. HERBERT *Trav.* 5 Swimming so without heed, that some were in apparant danger. **1782** COWPER *Gilpin* 72 Full slowly pacing o'er the stones With caution and good heed. **1867** FREEMAN *Norm. Conq.* (1876) I. App. 701, I look on this account as worthy of all heed.

b. Esp. in phr. ***to take* (†*nim*) *heed*.**

c **1305** *St. Dunstan* 25 in *E.E.P.* (1862) 35 His freond nome þerto hede. *c* **1305** *St. Swithin* 47 Ibid. 44 He þoȝte on þat þe godspel saiþ, þat me takþ of lute hede. **13..** *Sir Beues* (A.) 1030 Beues of hem nam gode hede. **1340** HAMPOLE *Pr. Consc.* 592 Bot proud man of þis tas na hede. *c* **1420** *Pallad. on Husb.* I. 177 Necessite hath neuere haly-day: Tak hede of that. *c* **1425** *Seven Sag.* (P.) 279 Of falsnesse non heed he nam, Bot at the last out hit kame. *c* **1450** *Cov. Myst.* (Shaks. Soc.) 368 Tak hede at Aaron. **1526** TINDALE *Mark* iv. 24 Take hede what ye heare. **1535** COVERDALE *Ps.* xxxvii. 37 Kepe innocency, and take hede vnto the thinge that is right. **1548** HALL *Chron., Hen. VIII*, 6 b, Every man toke muche hede to them that daunsed. *a* **1592** H. SMITH *Wks.* (1867) II. 33 Take heed is a good staff to stay upon. *c* **1689** PRIOR *Ode* 13 Take heed, my dear, youth flies apace. **1875** JOWETT *Plato* (ed. 2) I. 65 Let us take heed, and be on our guard against deceptions.

c. later, ***to give, pay heed* (*to*).**

1504 ATKYNSON tr. *De Imitatione* III. iii. 197 My sone, gyue hede to my wordes. **1526** TINDALE *1 Tim.* i. 4 Nether geve hede to fables. *a* **1774** PEARCE *Wks.* III. xi. (R.), Every christian is bound to give diligent heed to the reading, and the study of them. **1844** THIRLWALL *Greece* VIII. 443 Damocritus however paid no heed to their advice. **1870** MORRIS *Earthly Par.* I. I. 423 These unto thee will call To help them, but give thou no heed at all.

†**2.** That which one heeds. *Obs. rare.*

1588 SHAKS. *L.L.L.* I. i. 82 Who dazling so, that eye shall be his heed, And giue him light that it was blinded by.

3. *Comb.*, as ***heed-giving, -taking***.

1545 ASCHAM *Toxoph.* I. (Arb.) 53 Companions of shoting, be prouidens, good heed giuing, true meatinge, honest comparison. **1577** HARRISON *England* II. vi. (1877) I. 152 They fall into this for want of heedtaking. **1619** W. SCLATER *Exp. 1 Thess.* (1630) 218 Circumspection; diligent heed-taking to our selues.

heed, obs. form of HEAD *sb.*¹

†**heedely, heedly**, *adv.* *Obs.* [f. HEED *sb.* + -LY²; but prob. orig. a variant of HEEDILY: cf. *hastely*, *hastly*, *hastily*.] = HEEDILY.

1548 GEST *Pr. Masse* D iij, Let vs hedely beware lest christ iudge vs by our mouth. **1577** B. GOOGE *Heresbach's Husb.* IV. (1586) 166 b, The Hennes must be.. heedely looked to. **1583** STANYHURST *Æneis* III. (Arb.) 82 Too the eende in thye trauayl thow mayst the more heedlye be lessond.

heeder (ˈhiːdə(r)). One who heeds.

1849 J. STERLING in *Fraser's Mag.* XXXIX. 410 If they found a heeder.

heeder, obs. form of HEDER.

heedful (ˈhiːdfʊl), *a.* [f. HEED *sb.* + -FUL.] Full of heed; careful, attentive, watchful, mindful.

1548 UDALL, etc. *Erasm. Par. Mark* xi. (R.), God.. loueth wakeful & hedeful persones. **1577** B. GOOGE *Heresbach's Husb.* I. (1586) 40 You must be very heedefull in the weedyng of it. **1607** ROWLANDS *Guy Warw.* 46 On every side they cast a heedful eye. **1725** POPE *Odyss.* I. 397 Heedful of advice. **1875** WHITNEY *Life Lang.* viii. 142 If use were heedful of incongruities.

ˈ**heedfully**, *adv.* [f. prec. + -LY².] In a heedful manner; attentively, carefully.

1561 T. NORTON *Calvin's Inst.* III. 326 Let vs be hedefully bent to this most earnest thing. **1610** SHAKS. *Temp.* I. ii. 78 *Pros.* Do'st thou attend me? *Mira.* Sir, most heedefully. **1634** T. JOHNSON *Parey's Chirurg.* XXVI. xviii. (1678) 640 Cauteries heedfully used, strengthen and dry the part. **1870** MORRIS *Earthly Par.* III. IV. 32 Heedfully He guarded it, that none came in.

ˈ**heedfulness.** [f. as prec. + -NESS.] The quality of being heedful; attentiveness, carefulness.

1561 T. NORTON *Calvin's Inst.* Pref., To moue you to willingnesse and hedefulnesse. *a* **1677** BARROW *Wks.* (1830) I. 130 A circumspect heedfulness not to provoke any man. **1832** HT. MARTINEAU *Ella of Gar.* xi. 133 Fergus waited upon them both with all the quiet heedfulness of a girl.

†ˈ**heedily**, *adv.* *Obs.* [f. HEEDY + -LY².] Heedfully; with attention.

1577 B. GOOGE *Heresbach's Husb.* III. (1586) 114 b, The shape and proportion of the Horse, ought heedily to be considered. **1589** PUTTENHAM *Eng. Poesie* III. iv. (Arb.) 156 This part in our maker or Poet must be heedyly looked vnto. **1612** BRINSLEY *Lud. Lit.* 23 Writing English heedily, in true Orthography. **1656** W. D. tr. *Comenius' Gate Lat. Unl.* §501. 147 Heedily receiv information concerning it.

†ˈ**heediness.** *Obs.* [f. as prec. + -NESS.] Heedfulness, attentiveness; caution.

1596 SPENSER *F.Q.* V. vi. 34 By Gods grace, and her good heedinesse, She was preserved. **1620** BP. HALL *Hon. Mar. Clergy* I. §29 *Prætextu cautionis*, in pretence of heedinesse.

ˈ**heeding**, *vbl. sb.* [f. HEED *v.* + -ING¹.] The action of the verb HEED; attention; care.

1678 BUTLER *Hud.* III. ii. 1320 Your constant Method of Proceeding, Without the Carnal Means of Heeding. **1699** LISTER *Journ. Paris* 108 With a little heeding 'tis yet very legible.

heedless (ˈhiːdlɪs), *a.* [f. HEED *sb.* + -LESS.] Without heed; paying no heed or attention; careless, inattentive, regardless.

1579 SPENSER *Sheph. Cal.* July 15 Though one fall through heedless hast, Yet is his misse not mickle. **1624** GEE *Foot out of Snare* in Somers *Tracts* (1810) III. 53 To make havock and spoil of the harmelesse and heedelesse flock of Christ. **1764** GOLDSM. *Trav.* 161 There in the ruin, heedless of the dead, The shelter-seeking peasant builds his shed. **1857** BUCKLE *Civiliz.* I. xiii. 730 Despising unsupported authority, and heedless of tradition.

¶ Undeserving of attention. *Obs.*

1611 SPEED *Theat. Gt. Brit.* (1614) 145/1 A man.. may well esteem them [certain legendary histories] as heedlesse as vncertaine.

[**heedlesshood**, a supposed synonym of *heedlessness*, which some would read for 'headelesse hood', in Spenser *Sheph. Cal.*: see HEADLESS *a.* 1.]

ˈ**heedlessly**, *adv.* [f. HEEDLESS + -LY².] In a heedless manner; carelessly, inattentively.

1682 SIR T. BROWNE *Chr. Mor.* I. §30 Post not heedlesly on. **1710** STEELE *Tatler* No. 212 ¶3 Our Women run on so heedlesly in the Fashion, that [etc.]. **1861** MRS. H. WOOD *East Lynne* (1885) 24, I think the woman did it heedlessly; not mischievously.

ˈ**heedlessness.** [-NESS.] The quality of being heedless; carelessness, inattention, disregard.

1581 PETTIE *Guazzo's Civ. Conv.* I. (1586) 13 b, If through heedlesnesse you resalute not a friend, he will speake no more to you. **1673** *Lady's Call.* I. v. ¶56. 50 Thro heedlesness, and want of looking before us. **1789** BENTHAM *Princ. Legisl.* ix. §12 What heedlessness is in the case of an unadvised act, rashness is in the case of a misadvised one. **1823** SCOTT *Peveril* xxxiv, I tripped on, showing a bold heedlessness of his displeasure.

hedling, var. of HEADLING.

†**heedy**, *a.* *Obs.* [f. HEED *sb.* + -Y.] Heedful, attentive, careful, cautious.

1548 GEST *Pr. Masse* Ded., Rather heady than heedy. *Ibid.* A vij, Therfore good reader gyue heedy attendaunce therto. **1581** MARBECK *Bk. of Notes* 1058 Worldly men are more heedy in their affaires of this world. **1645** USSHER *Body Div.* (1647) 237 That we have a carefull and a heedy watch to all things that may advance God's glory.

heef, obs. pa. t. of HEAVE.

heegh, heeȝ, obs. forms of HIGH *a.*, HIE *v.*¹

hee-haw (ˈhiːˌhɔː), *sb.* Also **hiu haw, he-haw (he-hawn** *U.S.*). [Echoic.]

1. A conventional representation of the bray of a jackass; a name for this.

1815 W. H. IRELAND *Scribbleomania* 84 *note*, The chants were interrupted at intervals with an Hiu Haw, in imitation of the Ass's braying. **1831** S. WARREN *Diary Physic.* xvi. (1832) I. 379 An Ass.. opened on us with an astounding hee-haw! hee-haw! hee-haw! **1878** BROWNING *Poets Croisic* cxx, To.. estimate applause As just so many asinine he-haws. **1884** C. D. WARNER in *Harper's Mag.* Dec. 14/2 He-hawn, sire Ass, you sing.

2. A loud unrefined laugh.

1843 THACKERAY *Miss Tickletoby* iii, If to laughter he was minded, out they burst in loud hee-haws. **1872** ANNE THACKERAY *Men's Wives* 402 All the boxes began to roar with great coarse heehaws at Titania hugging Bottom's long ears.

Hence **hee-haw** *v. intr.*, to bray, as an ass.

1821 CLARE *Vill. Minstr.* I. 44 Ass after ass still hee-haws through the town. **1831** S. WARREN *Diary Physic.* xvi. (1832)

I. 379 Away sprung the jackass..hee-hawing incessantly. **1859** THACKERAY *Virgin.* (Ogil.), Suppose thou art making an ass of thyself..are there not people in England who heehaw too? **1884** C. D. WARNER in *Harper's Mag.* Dec. 14/2 The ass *he-hawned*, or brayed..The people *he-hawned* or brayed thrice, in like manner.

heel (hi:l), *sb.*¹ Forms: 1 **héla, hǽla, (hél),** 3 **heale,** 3-6 **hele,** 4-5 **heill,** 4-7 **heele,** 5-7 **heille,** (5 **hyelle,** 6 **helle, hiele,** 7 **eel),** 6-7 **heal(e,** 4- **heel.** [OE. *héla, hǽla* wk. masc. = OFris. *hêla* fem., MDu. *hiele* m. and f., Du. *hiel* m.; cf. ON. *hǽll* m. (Sw. *häl*, Da. *hæl*):—**hâhil*:—**hanhil*, deriv. of **hanh-*, in OE. *hóh* hough, heel.]

I. 1. a. The projecting hinder part of the foot, below the ankle and behind the hollow of the foot.

c **850** *Lorica Gloss.* 57 in *O.E. Texts* 173 *Talos*, helan. *Ibid.* 59 *Calcibus*, helum. *c* **1100** *Ags. Voc.* in Wr.-Wülcker 266/8 *Calx*, hela, hoh niþeweard. *a* **1225** *Ancr. R.* 112 A lutel ihurt i þen eie derueð more þen deð a muchel iðe hele, vor þet fleschs is deadure þere. *c* **1300** *Havelok* 898 Sparede he neyther tos ne heles. **1375** BARBOUR *Bruce* XVI. 596 The gilt spuris, richt by the heill. *c* **1485** in *E.E. Misc.* (Warton Club) 7 Undure my hyelle is that me grevys, Fore at my hart I fele no sowre. *a* **1529** SKELTON *P. Sparowe* Wks. (1843) 86 To se her treade the grounde With heles short and rounde. **1599** NASHE *Lenten Stuffe* 24 A fift, of an inflamed heale. **1641** J. JACKSON *True Evang. T.* I. 17 A Serpent, a Basilisk, biting the heele, and stinging the face. **1711** BUDGELL *Spect.* No. 77 ¶8 His Stockings are about his Heels. **1842** TENNYSON *Morte d'Arthur* 286 Then Francis..drove his heel into the smoulder'd log.

b. The heel armed or fitted with a spur.

c **1400** *Destr. Troy* 6394 Ector..toke his horse with his helis, hastid before. *c* **1620** Z. BOYD *Zion's Flowers* (1855) 62 It's time to lend my horse a heele. **1663** BUTLER *Hud.* I. iii. 484 Then ply'd, With iron heel, his courser's side. **1792** OSBALDISTON *Brit. Sportsm.* 395 The word heel is taken for the spur itself; hence they say..'he knows the heels; he obeys the heels; he answers the heels; he is very well upon the heels'. **1888** MRS. KENNARD *Glorious Gallop* 92 She gave Galopard a slight touch of the heel, and trotted briskly on.

c. Put for the foot as a whole.

a **1225** *Juliana* 30 þat hit urne endelong hire leofliche bodi dun to þe helen. *a* **1225** *St. Marher.* 13 þe meiden dude swa, leowsede ant leoðede a lutel hire hele. **1586** J. HOOKER *Girald. Irel.* Ep. Ded. Aij b in *Holinshed* III, His bodie hanged by the heeles at Corke. **1590** SPENSER *F.Q.* II. xii. 46 His looser garment..flew about his heeles in wanton wize. **1637** MILTON *Lycidas* 34 Rough Satyrs danced, and Fauns with cloven heel From the glad sound would not be absent long. *c* **1718** PRIOR *Hans Carvel* 118 He..was carried off to bed: John held his heels, and Nan his head. **1859** GEO. ELIOT *A. Bede* I. xi, For ye're a stirring body in a mornin', an' ye've a light heel.

d. *Cribbage*, etc. (See quots.)

1796 *Grose's Dict. Vulg. T.* s.v., *To turn up his heels*, to turn up the knave of trumps at the game of all-fours. **1850** *Bohn's Hand-bk. Games* 275 (*Cribbage*) Should the turn-up card itself be a Knave, the dealer immediately scores two points ..which by way of antithesis with 'his nob', are called 'two for his heels'. **1882** *Society* 11 Nov. 9/1 In cribbage parlance, it was one for her nob and two for her heels.

e. ***heel of Achilles, Achilles' heel***: the only vulnerable spot (in allusion to the story of the dipping of Achilles in the river Styx: cf. *tendon of Achilles* s.v. TENDON a).

1810 COLERIDGE *Friend* 431 Ireland, that vulnerable heel of the British Achilles! **1864** CARLYLE *Fredk. Gt.* IV. XVII. ii. 522 Hanover,..the Achilles'-heel to invulnerable England. **1897** G. B. SHAW *Let.* 2 July (1965) 777 Divorce is the Achilles heel of marriage. **1930** L. D. BRONSHTEIN tr. *Trotsky's Life* xxv. 262 By his verbal artifices, he only discloses his own Achilles' heel. **1944** *Times* 19 June 5/6 Military observers have dubbed Viipuri the Achilles' heel of the Finnish defences. **1957** A. E. COPPARD *It's Me, O Lord!* ii. 17 The three R's, the third of which..was..my Achilles heel. **1972** *Catholic Herald* 28 Jan. 1/5 It is this refusal to condemn which is the Achilles heel of contemporary Christian psychology.

f. *Horsemanship.* Management by the heel (in quot. the spurred heel).

1728 CHAMBERS *Cycl.* s.v., This horse understands the Heels well. **1792** [see sense 1 b above].

2. In quadrupeds and other vertebrates:

a. *Anatomically*, The part of the hinder limb which is the analogue of the human heel; the calcaneal part of the tarsus, whatever its shape or position; in digitigrade and ungulate quadrupeds, and in birds, this is elevated above the ground, and is popularly called *knee* or *hock*, also ***heel of the hock***.

1792 OSBALDISTON *Brit. Sportsm.* 93/2 These are of a wenny nature, and grow on the point of the elbow and the heel of the hock. **1874** COUES in Baird, etc. *Hist. N.A. Birds* III. 545 The heel (*calcaneus*) is at the top of the tarsus.

b. *popularly.* (*a*) In quadrupeds, the hinder part of the hoof; also, each of the projections on the coffin-bone.

1674 N. COX *Gentl. Recreat.* (1677) 72 Seek for his Slot: If he findes the Heel thick, and the Toe spreading broad, it argues an old Deer. **1727-51** CHAMBERS *Cycl.*, *Heel of a horse*, is the lowest hind part of the foot, comprehended between the quarters, and opposite to the toe. **1831** YOUATT *Horse* (1848) 378 On either side [of the coffin-bone]..are projections called the wings, or heels of the coffin-bone.

(*b*) More commonly applied (in *pl.*) to the two hind feet. Also, the hoof or whole foot. See 3 a, c.

c **1000** *Sax. Leechd.* I. 346 Wið wambe wræce ʒenim haran helan. *c* **1420** *Anturs of Arth.* 386 (Douce MS.) His horse in fyne sandel was trapped to þe hele. **1535** COVERDALE *Gen.* xlix. 17 Dan shalbe..an edder in the path, and byte the horse in the heles [WYCLIF feet]. **1577** B. GOOGE *Heresbach's Husb.* III. (1586) 152 b, After that, hanging him [Hog] up by the heeles, you shall plucke [etc.]. **1607** TOPSELL *Four-f. Beasts* (1658) 245 They must not be afraid of other Horses ..but..rush into the battle, fighting (as is said) with heels and mouth. *a* **1700** DRYDEN *Ovid's Met.* XII. Wks. 1808 XII. 170 He falls; and lashing up his heels, his rider throws. **1847** TENNYSON *Princ.* Prol. 44 She trampled some beneath her horse's heels. *c* **1875** MARY JEWRY *Every-day Cookery* 128/2 Put two thoroughly clean cow-heels into a stew pan. **1877** A. B. EDWARDS *Up Nile* iv. 91 The donkey kicks up his heels and brays.

(*c*) In birds, the hinder toe or hallux, the spur.

1611 MARKHAM *Countr. Content.* I. xix. (1668) 82 A sharp heel'd cock, though it be a little false, is much better than the truest cock which hath a dull heel, and hitteth seldome. **1792** OSBALDISTON *Brit. Sportsm.* 346 His narrow heel, or sharpness of heel, is known no otherwise than by observation in fighting. **1863** BATES *Nat. Amazon* viii. (1864) 237 Swarms of goatsuckers..descend and settle on a low branch..and then, squatting down on their heels, are difficult to distinguish from the surrounding soil.

3. Pregnant uses in reference to the heel or hind foot of man or beast. **a.** As the instrument of kicking: hence ***to raise*** or ***lift the heel against, to make a heel.*** In *Rugby Football*: a heeling of the ball from the scrummage; cf. HEEL *v.*¹ 5 b.

c **950** *Lindisf. Gosp.* John xiii. 18 Seðe brucað mec mið þæt hlaf he ahefeð onʒæʒn mec hel his. *a* **1225** *Ancr. R.* 136 Mi leof is ivetted..& smit me mid his hele. **1382** WYCLIF *John* xiii. 18 He that etith my breed, schal reyse his heele aʒens me. **1535** COVERDALE *Ps.* xl[i]. 9 Yee euen myne owne familier frende.. hath lift vp his hele agaynst me. **1590** SHAKS. *Com. Err.* III. i. 15, I should kicke being kickt, and being at that passe, You would keepe from my heeles, and beware of an asse. **1728** RAMSAY *Fables & T., Ass & Brock* 9 Replied the Ass, and made a heel. **1732** POPE *Ep. Bathurst* 68 With spurning heel. *a* **1822** SHELLEY *Ode Naples* 112 Fair Milan..lifts her heel To bruise his head. **1937** *Times* 15 Feb. 5/3 A quick heel and the ball went through the hands of [etc.].

b. As the instrument of trampling down or crushing.

1601 HOLLAND *Pliny* XVIII. v, That the lords eie is far better for the land, than his heele. **1819** SHELLEY *Cenci* IV. iv, Our innocence is as an armed heel To trample accusation. **1838** PRESCOTT *Ferd. & Is.* (1842) I. x. 440 The green crop had no time to ripen ere it was trodden down under the iron heel of war. **1867** GOLDW. SMITH *Three Eng. Statesmen* (1882) 218 Too hasty in setting his heel on the agents of tyranny and corruption. **1879** H. GEORGE *Progr. & Pov.* v. ii. (1881) 257 Those classes upon whom the iron heel of modern civilization presses.

c. ***heels***: as the hindmost parts displayed by a fugitive; hence as the means of flight. ***to have*** or ***get the heels of***: to outrun.

1523 LD. BERNERS *Froiss.* I. cli. 180 Suche as had their horses by them mounted and shewed their horses heles, and thenglysshmen after them in chase. **1583** STUBBES *Anat. Abus.* I. (1879) 96 He showes them a faire pair of heeles, and away goeth he. **1583** STOCKER *Hist. Civ. Warres Lowe C.* I. 96 a, The rest, full of lyfe in the heeles, saued them selues. **1599** SHAKS. *Hen. V*, III. v. 34 Saying, our Grace is onely in our Heeles, And that we are most loftie Run-awayes. **1612-15** BP. HALL *Contempl.*, *O.T.* XIX. viii, Many a one hath had better counsell from his heeles, then from his elbows. **1647** W. BROWNE tr. *Gomberville's Polexander* II.-IV. 197 One squadron..he routed and put to their heeles. *c* **1685** VILLIERS (Dk. Buckhm.) *Conf.* Wks. 1705 II. 49 Father, your zeal has got the heels of your Discretion. **1719** DE FOE *Crusoe* I. xx, Friday..had..the heels of the bear. **1730-6** BAILEY (folio) s.v., One Pair of Heels is worth two Pair of Hands, that is, it is better to run for it, than be beaten, where a Man has not the Courage or Force to withstand his Enemy. **1832** MARRYAT *N. Forster* xi, Be smart, my lads, for she has the heels of us.

4. In insects: **a.** The terminal extremity of the tibia; **b.** The base of the first tarsal joint, when it is curved to join the tibia; the 'calx' of Kirby, by him limited to the heels of the four posterior tarsi; **c.** Leach's name for the bristles forming the strigilis (*Century Dict.*).

1826 KIRBY & SPENCE *Introd. Entomol.* III. 386 *Calx* (the Heel). The curving part of the *Planta*..by which it inosculates with the *Tibia*.

5. a. The part of a stocking that covers the heel; **b.** The thick part of the sole of a boot or shoe which raises the heel, esp. as ***high heel***.

1577-87 HOLINSHED *Chron.*, *Irel.* III. 89/2 He..bare it awaie in the heele of his stocke. **1596** SHAKS. *Tam. Shr.* IV. i. 136 Gabrels pumpes were all vnpinkt i'th heele. **1634** SIR T. HERBERT *Trav.* 146 Their shooes..are usually sharpe at the toe..the heeles shod with thin Iron. **1671** A. WOOD *Life & Times* (1892) II. 226, 4*d* given to see a man at the King's Head 7 foot and an half high... He had a night gowne on, which made him seem taller, and high heels. **1709** STEELE *Tatler* No. 7 ¶16 One of his Shoes had lost an Heel. **1714** GAY *Trivia* I. 31 The wooden Heel may raise the dancer's bound. **1753** in Fairholt *Costume* (1860) 304 But mount on French heels when you go to a ball. **1849** MACAULAY *Hist. Eng.* I. 397 She determined..whether his heels must be high or low. **1882** CAULFEILD & SAWARD *Dict. Needlework* 305/1 Upon the ease with which the heel fits the wearer much of the comfort of the stocking depends. *a* **1898** *Mod.* She wears high heels. Slippers have no heels. **1950** G. BARKER *News of World* 10 Heavy my heart walks ahead on the pavements With her high-heel shoe my martyrdom on stone.

6. ***the heel of Italy***: the S.E. extremity of that country (which in shape resembles a leg and foot).

1717 BERKELEY *Tour in Italy* Wks. 1871 IV. 556 No mountains in the heel of Italy. **1869** RAWLINSON *Anc. Hist.* 335 The heel of Italy (Iapygia).

7. A part of a thing which has the position or shape of the human heel; the hinder end of the base; a protruding hinder or lower extremity.

a. *generally.* **b.** The lower or handle end of a pike, violin bow, etc., or of the blade of a sword, etc.; the crook in the head of a golf-club; the top corner of the butt of a gun when in firing-position at the shoulder; the hinder part of a ploughshare. **c.** *Naut.* The after end of a ship's keel; the lower end of a rudder, mast, or piece of timber. **d.** *Arch.* 'The lower end or foot of a rafter where it rests on the wall or plate' (Knight *Dict. Mech.*); also, a cyma reversa. **e.** *Horticulture.* A projecting bit of older wood taken off with a cutting. **f.** *Silversmiths' work.* The small projecting part at the back of the bowl of a spoon. **g.** The vertical timber of a gate which bears the hinges; the harre. **h.** *Conch.* The part of a bivalve shell which bears the joint or hinge. **i.** ***heel of the hand***: The lower part of the palm, next the wrist. **j.** ***heels of a horse-shoe***: The turned up extremities; the calkins. **k.** The lower part of the back of a book. **l.** (See quot.) **m.** (See quots.)

a. 1707 MORTIMER *Husb.* (1708) 256 In Hertfordshire they have a particular Sort of Spade..the Teeth of which being Iron and broad, rakes out the Mould and spreads it; and at the other side there is a kind of heel or knob.

b. 1591 GARRARD *Art Warre* 55 The heele and tippe of their pikes would be equally bolden. **1807** A. YOUNG *Agric. Essex* (1813) I. 139 The plough heel, comprising the position of the breast behind, and forming, together with the end of the rest, that wedge which fills up the furrow. **1812** *Examiner* 31 Aug. 552/1 Two hairs on the heel of it [a razor]. **1856** MRS. C. CLARKE tr. *Berlioz' Instrument.* 12 With the heel of the [violin] bow. **1857** *Chambers' Inform.* II. 696/2 *Heel*, the crook of the head [of a golf-club] where it joins the shaft. *c* **1860** H. STUART *Seaman's Catech.* 11 On the stock [of a rifle] is a..heel. **1881** GREENER *Gun* 432 Most gun-stocks are twisted over, that is to say, the toe of the butt is more out of truth with the barrels than the heel. **1890** *Gloucestershire Gloss.*, *Heel*, the lower part of a scythe blade. **1933** L. G. D. ACLAND in *Press* (Christchurch) 28 Oct. 15/7 *Heel*, the corner of a shear blade, next the grip.

c. 1602 MARSTON *Ant. & Mel.* I. Wks. 1856 I. 16 Now gustie flawes strook up the very heeles Of our maine mast. **1769** FALCONER *Dict. Marine* (1789), *Talon de la quille*, the after-end of the keel, into which the foot of the stern-post is tenented: this is also called the ship's heel. **1840** R. H. DANA *Bef. Mast* xxx. 107 The tightest ship..will leak more or less round the heel of the bowsprit. **1858** *Merc. Marine Mag.* V. 19 She..went with her heel upon the rocks.

e. 1882 *Garden* 4 Feb. 85/3 [They] propagate readily from cuttings made of ripened wood, taken off with a 'heel'. **1889** *Co-op. News* 6 Apr. 349 The slips [of currant-bush] being about ten inches long, and having a 'heel' if possible.

f. 1879 *Cassell's Techn. Educ.* IV. 413/1 The next operation is stamping upon it the little projection which in trade parlance is called the 'heel', and which seems to indicate the juncture of the bowl with the stem.

g. 1854 *Jrnl. R. Agric. Soc.* XV. II. 250 The head and heel [of gate], called here the 'har', are usually made of elm. **1893** *Ibid.* Mar. 38 A gate is a rectangular frame consisting of 'heel' and 'head' and top and bottom rails.

h. 1692 RAY *Dissol. World* 115 It seems strange to me that two shells should be so adapted together at the heel as to shoot out to the same extension and the upper and nether valve be of different Figure. **1836** *Penny Cycl.* V. 312 The heel of the larger valve deeply notched up to the border of articulation.

i. 1704 J. PITTS *Acc. Mahometans* ix. (1738) 222 A hole made in the Heel of each hand. **1887** D. GRAHAM in Buck *Hand-bk. Med. Sc.* IV. 645/1 The heel of the operator's hand will be used for vigorous friction of the palm. **1888** ELWORTHY *W. Somerset Word-bk.*, *Heel of the hand*, the part of the hand on which it rests in the act of writing.

j. 1831 YOUATT *Horse* (1848) 421 The heels of the shoe should be examined as to their proper width. **1886** *Pall Mall G.* 17 Aug. 14/1 The shoes of the horses have neither toes nor heels, which seems to be a peculiarity of Paris farriery.

k. 1930 *Godfrey's Catal.* No. 134. 26 Small piece gone from heel, and joint becoming tender.

l. 1880 E. D. COPE in *Amer. Naturalist* XIV. 836 Stages in the following modification of parts:—..(6) In the obliteration of the inner tubercle of the lower sectorial. (7) In the extinction of the heel of the same.

m. 1888 *Lockwood's Dict. Mech. Engin.*, *Heel*, the thick or broad end of a wedge-shaped piece, the broad end of a railway switch for example. **1957** R. LISTER *Decorative Wrought Ironwork* i. 12 The anvil's parts are known by special names... The part of the face and body that terminates in a thick wedge-shaped end is the *heel*.

8. The crust at the bottom (also, sometimes, the top) of a loaf; the rind of a cheese.

1362 LANGL. *P. Pl.* A. VIII. 181, I nolde ȝeue for þi pardoun one pye hele. **1611** COTGR., *Esquignonner*, to cut, or breake off a lumpe, cantle, crustie heele, or peece from a loafe of bread. *a* **1774** FERGUSSON *Rising of Session* vii, I wat weel They'll stoo the kebbuck to the heel. **1814** SCOTT *Wav.* lxiv, The heel o' the white loaf that came from the bailie's. **1849** DICKENS *Dav. Copp.* xi, The heel of a Dutch cheese. **1879** MISS JACKSON *Shropsh. Word-bk.*, *Heel*, the top crust of a loaf cut off, or the bottom crust remaining.

9. The latter or concluding part of a period of time; also, of a book or writing; in *Astrol.*, of a zodiacal sign: cf. HEAD *sb.*¹ 19 b.

1584 R. SCOT *Discov. Witchcr.* XIII. vii. (1886) 243 That it be not doone in the end, declination, or heele (as they terme it) of the course [of the planet]. **1599** NASHE *Lenten Stuffe* 47 So but seldome should they meete in the heele of the weeke at the best mens tables, vppon Fridayes and Satterdayes. **1636** B. JONSON *Eng. Gram.* I. vi, I will promise..to giue, in the heel of the Book, some spur and incitement to that which I so reasonably seek. **1758** J. RUTTY *Spir. Diary* (ed. 2) 122 Nine hours spent in bed: it is a great deal in the heel of the evening. **1803** WELLINGTON in Owen *Wellesley's Desp.* 787 The corps..in a close pursuit at the heel of the day, lost many men. **1847** CALHOUN *Wks.* IV. 363 The Senate's resolution—passed at the very heel of the session.

II. Phrases. * *With prep.* or *adv.*

10. at, on, upon, †**in** (one's) **heel(s.** Close behind; in close pursuit or immediate

attendance; also *fig.* ***at the hard heels of***, at the very heels of: see HARD *a.* 21.

13.. *Gaw. & Gr. Knt.* 1899 Renaud com..& alle þe rabel in a res, ryȝt at his helez. **1390** GOWER *Conf.* I. 18 There bene also somme as men saie, That folwen Simon ate heles. *a* **1555** LATIMER *Serm. & Rem.* (1845) 229 It is but a superstition to think that a Pater Noster cannot be well said without an Ave Maria at its heel. **1571** GOLDING *Calvin on Ps.* xlix. 13 Death preaceth hard at your heeles. **1579** GOSSON *Sch. Abuse* (Arb.) 26 Our auncestours, which pursued vertue at the harde heeles, and shunned vyce. **1607** SHAKS. *Timon* I. i. 27 *Painter.* When comes your Booke forth? *Poet.* Vpon the heeles of my presentment sir. **1646** TRAPP *Comment. Numb.* xxxii. 23 The guilt will haunt you at heels, as a bloodhound. **1650** CROMWELL *Lett.* 30 July in *Carlyle*, I marching in the heel of them with the residue of the army. **1674** N. COX *Gentl. Recreat.* III. (1677) 13 To have your Dog at your heels. *a* **1687** PETTY *Pol. Arith.* Pref., The Hollanders are at our heels, in the race of Naval Power. **1749** FIELDING *Tom Jones* XVIII. x, Unavailable repentance treads on his heels. **1782** COWPER *Gilpin* 204 Away went Gilpin, and away Went post-boy at his heels. **1827** POLLOK *Course T.* v, So swift trode sorrow on the heels of joy! **1853** M. ARNOLD *Poems, Sohrab & R.*, Ruksh, his horse, Follow'd him like a faithful hound at heel. **1860** TYNDALL *Glac.* I. xvi. 112, I..kept close at his heels.

11. down at heel (*adv.* and *adj.*): **a.** having the heels of one's boots or shoes quite worn down; taken as a symptom of destitution: cf. 12. Also **down-at-heels** *attrib.*; **down-at-heeledness**. **b.** said of shoes or slippers, when negligently slipped on so that the heel part is crushed down under the foot; also, of persons so wearing their shoes; and *fig.* slovenly, slip-shod.

1732 *Gentl. Instr.* (ed. 10) 212 (D.) Sneak into a corner.. down at heels and out at elbows. **1835** LONGF. *Outre-Mer* Prose Wks. 1886 I. 120 Thus the unhappy notary ran gradually down at the heel. **1840** BARHAM *Ingol. Leg., St. Odille*, Her shoes went down at heel. **1860** *All Year Round* No. 57. 158 Down-at-heel self-neglect. **1875** TENNYSON *Q. Mary* I. i, Fray'd i' the knees, and out at elbow..and bursten at the toes, and down at heels. **1880** *World* 8 Dec. 2 Shuffling down-at-heel sentences. **1886** *Pall Mall G.* 7 Dec. 11/2 If ignorance is bad, assuredly down-at-heel dilettantism is worse. **1906** *Daily Chron.* 22 Dec. 3/2 A down-at-heels party hailed him as a countryman, and asked 'the lend of the loan of twopence'. **1919** C. ORR *Glorious Thing* iv. 37 The old down-at-heel slippers she kept for working. **1924** Down-at-heeledness (see DAVERDY *a.*). **1956** E. C. HISCOCK *Around World in Wanderer III* vi. 68 To hear once more the shrill scream of pigs protesting their passage aboard some down-at-heel schooner. **1963** A. LUBBOCK *Austral. Roundabout* 31, The usual two-storey bush pub, rather scruffy and down-at-heel.

12. out at heels (*adv.* and *adj.*): with stockings or shoes worn through at the heel; also, of persons wearing such; *fig.* in unfortunate or decayed circumstances; in trouble or distress.

1553 WILSON *Rhet.* (1567) 82 b, Some riche snudges..go with their hose out at heles. **1588** FRAUNCE *Lawiers Log.* I. iv. 27 To affectate such woordes as were quite worne out at heeles and elbowes long before the nativitie of Geffray Chawcer. **1605** SHAKS. *Lear* II. ii. 164 A good mans fortune may grow out at heeles. **1676** WYCHERLEY *Pl. Dealer* III. (1735) 74 Go look out the Fellow..that walks with his Sword and Stockings out at Heels. **1747** W. HORSLEY *Fool* (1748) II. No. 83. 254 My present Situation being, as I may say, a little out at Heels.

13. to heel. Of a dog: close behind, in behind; under rule. Also as a word of command: ***heel!*** Also *fig.*

1810 *Sporting Mag.* XXXVI. 149 They will back, or come to heel, as commanded. **1849** JAMES *Woodman* xiii, To heel, good dog. **1870** HUXLEY *Lay Serm.* iii. (1874) 35 Whose passions are trained to come to heel. **1873** G. C. DAVIES *Mount. & Mere* vi. 45 We did so, the dogs, a spaniel and a retriever, keeping to heel. **1878** C. HALLOCK *Amer. Club List & Sportsman's Gloss.* p. vi, *Heel*, the order to dogs to come behind the gunner. **1923** D. L. SAYERS *Whose Body?* ix. 200 The dog..barked... 'Heel,' said the man in velveteen, violently. The animal sidled up, ashamed. **1935** G. HEYER *Death in Stocks* ii. 13 She..was chiefly occupied in keeping back a powerful bull-terrier... 'Shut up, you fool!' commanded the girl. '*Heel!*' **1971** M. TRIPP *Five Minutes with Stranger* I. vi. 64 She was saying 'Heel' in a voice that would have quelled a riot in hell.

** *With another substantive.*

14. heel and toe. a. *adv.* With proper walking, as opposed to running; also as *adj.* and *sb.* **b.** Of dancing (also ***heel over toe***).

1820 W. IRVING *Sketch Bk., Christm. Eve* (1865) 251 Master Simon..was endeavoring to gain credit by the heel and toe, rigadoon, and other graces of the ancient school. **1827** T. HAMILTON *Cyril Thornton* (1845) 277 With that sort of walk, generally called heel and toe, he led his fair partner to her station. **1837** DICKENS *Pickw.* xl, Bravo—heel over toe—cut and shuffle. **1861** HUGHES *Tom Brown at Oxf.* xiv, They returned to college, having done a little over fifteen miles, fair heel and toe walking. **1883** BLACK *Shandon Bells* iii, A curious clamping and shuffling, as if some one were doing a heel-and-toe step on a wooden floor. **1892** A. M. *Yoshiwara Episode* 33 He spent the best part of the day in a healthy heel-and-toe to Ojigoku.

c. Of motoring. Also as *vb.* (see quot. 1962). So **heeling-and-toeing** *vbl. sb.*

1937 O. STEWART *Learn to Drive* viii. 63 A method of gear changing..is that which employs heel-and-toe operation of clutch and accelerator pedals at the same time. **1962** *Which?* (Suppl.) July 96/2 If you want to, you can 'heel-and-toe'—work brake and accelerator at the same time. **1966** T. WISDOM *High-Performance Driving* viii. 73 Use of the 'heel-and-toe' technique..reduces the time and distance taken to complete the slowing-down and gear-change operations. **1966** R. MAXWELL in T. Wisdom *High-Performnce Driving* viii. 72 Heeling and toeing..involves double-declutching into a lower gear while braking. **1973** 'J. ASHFORD' *Double Run* xiv. 114 With heel-and-toe braking and gear changing he flicked down through the gears.

15. a. heels over head. With the heels in the air and the head downmost; upside down; ***to turn heels over head***, to turn a somersault.

13.. *E.E. Allit. P.* C. 269 He [Jonas] glydez in by þe giles, þurȝ glaymande glette..Ay hele ouer hed hourlande aboute. **1768** ROSS *Helenore* 64 (Jam.), I couped Mungo's ale Clean heels o'er head. *Ibid.* 86 (Jam.) Now by this time the house is heels o'er head. **1814** WORDSW. *Excurs.* VIII. 387 They.. An uncouth feat exhibit, and are gone Heels over head. **1864** CARLYLE *Fredk. Gt.* IV. 523 A total circumgyration, summerset, or tumble heels-over-head in the Political relations of Europe. **1886** TENNYSON *Locksley Hall 60 Y. After* 135 Tumble Nature heel o'er head.

attrib. **1887** *Century Mag.* Nov. 49/1 What'll happen if you go on in this heels-over-head way?

b. So (*Sc.*) ***heels over gowdy***.

1796 BURNS *Poem on Life* 37 Soon, heels-o'er-gowdy! in he gangs. **1819** W. TENNANT *Papistry Storm'd* (1827) 150 Heels-over-gowdie whurlin'.

*** *With a verb.*

†16. cast or **throw at..heel(s.** To cast under foot, reject with contempt. *Obs.*

1555 W. WATREMAN *Fardle Facions* App. 350 Those that ..threwe not at their hieles those thinges that Moyses had taughte them. **1576** GASCOIGNE *Steele Gl.* (Arb.) 56 Wherein I see, a corps of comely shape..Is cast at heele, by courting al to soone. *a* **1628** PRESTON *Breastpl. Faith* (1630) 24 They resist it, casting it at their heeles. **1659** D. PELL *Impr. Sea* 593 The States of England throw not their dear and costly purchased Victories at their heels.

17. dig in one's **heels**: see DIG *v.* 11 c.

18. kick one's **heels.** To stand waiting idly or impatiently. Cf. *to cool one's heels*, s.v. COOL *v.* 5.

1760 FOOTE *Minor* II. (1781) 51 To let your uncle kick his heels in your hall. **1833** MARRYAT *P. Simple* xiii, I'll trouble him [not] to leave me here kicking my heels.

19. lay, set, clap by the heels. To put in irons or the stocks; to fetter, arrest, or confine; also, *fig.* to overthrow, disgrace. So ***to have by the heels***; and, of the person confined, ***to lie*** or ***be tied by the heels***.

c **1510** *Hickscorner* in Hazl. *Dodsley* I. 170, I will go fetch a pair of gyves, For in good faith he shall be set fast by the heels. **1584** R. SCOT *Discov. Witchcr.* III. xv. (1886) 51 One of Q. Maries justices..laid an archer by the heeles. **1654** G. GODDARD *Introd. Burton's Diary* (1828) I. 160 When they had seized upon him and clapped him by the heels. **1700** LUTTRELL *Brief Rel.* (1857) IV. 638 The lord cheif justice.. will lay the undersherif by the heels. **1781** MAD. D'ARBLAY *Diary* Aug., I supposed you would have finished it [a play] in your last fit of sickness..pray go on with it when you are tied by the heel next. **1865** KINGSLEY *Herew.* II. xvi. 274 Tell him Hereward has..half a dozen knights safe by the heels. **1889** *Baltimore* (Md.) *Sun* 19 Nov., The bold offender ..would have been quickly set by the heels.

20. take to one's **heels**; formerly ***to (be)take himself to his heels, to take one's heels***. To run away.

1542 UDALL *Erasm. Apoph.* I. 127 When this Manes had taken his heeles and renne awaye from his maister. **1548** HALL *Chron., Hen. VII*, 49 So deceavyng his kepers [he] toke him to his heeles. **1583** STUBBES *Anat. Abus.* II. (1882) 54 They..betake them to their heeles as to their best refuge. **1590** SHAKS. *Com. Err.* I. ii. 95 Nay, and you will not sir, Ile take my heeles. **1600** HOLLAND *Livy* XXXIII. xxxvi. 845 The Gaules..turned their backe, tooke them to their heeles, and ran away. **1659** B. HARRIS *Parival's Iron Age* 7 The Tartars ..as soon as they..find the Poles advancing, betake themselves to their heels. **1690** W. WALKER *Idiomat. Anglo-Lat.* Pref. 1 Let us take our heels and run away. **1809** W. IRVING *Knickerb.* VII. xi. (1849) 440 The rabble incontinently took to their heels. **1889** JESSOPP *Coming of Friars* ii. 93 The beholders would have..taken to their heels and run for their lives.

21. trip (***kick, strike, throw***) **up** a person's **heels.** To trip up, upset, or overthrow (him); also *fig.*

1600 SHAKS. *A.Y.L.* III. ii. 225 It is yong Orlando, that tript vp the Wrastlers heeles, and your heart, both in an instant. **1618** J. TAYLOR (Water P.) *King's Majesty* Wks. (1872) 3 Thy Constancy hath trip'd up Fortune's heel. **1678** BUNYAN *Pilgr.* I. 174 It shall go hard but they will throw up his heels. **1706** ADDISON *Rosamond* vii. Wks. 1721 I. 123 Death has tripped up my heels. **1887** BARING-GOULD *Gaverocks* III. 58, I wish it were in my power to kick up his heels.

†22. turn one's **heels.** To run away. *Obs.*

1586 J. HOOKER *Girald. Irel.* XXV. in *Holinshed* III. 19/1 He turneth a faire paire of heeles and runneth awaie. *Ibid., Irel.* 142/1 [They] turned their heeles, forsooke the field, and dispersed themselues into the woods. *c* **1620** Z. BOYD *Zion's Flowers* (1855) 120 Big looking minions..make hast To turne their heeles.

23. turn on (*upon*) one's **heel.** To turn sharply round, turn back or away.

1751 FIELDING *Amelia* III. IX. vii. 283 Instead..of attempting to follow her, he turned on his Heel, and addressed his Discourse to another Lady. **1757** W. THOMPSON *R.N. Advoc.* 38 L——d V——e..turn'd short on his Heel, telling me he knew nothing of the Matter. **1782** MISS BURNEY *Cecilia* I. 61 Sir Robert..turned upon his heel, and was striding out of the room. **1834** M. SCOTT *Cruise Midge* viii, He turned round on his heels, and marched out of the cabin. **1887** EDNA LYALL *Knt.-Errant* xii. 102 Carlo had turned sharply round on his heel and left him without a word.

24. turn (***kick, tumble***) **up** a person's **heels.** To knock (him) down; to lay low; to kill. So ***to turn (kick, lay, tip, topple) up one's heels***, to die.

c **1500** *Maid Emlyn* (Halliw.), He toke a surfet with a cup, That made hym tourne his heels up. **1577–87** HOLINSHED *Chron., Irel.* III. 93/2 He strake him with his bullet full in the forehead..and withall turned vp his heeles. **1599** NASHE *Lenten Stuffe* 13 Of which [sickness]..seauen thousand and fifty people toppled vp their heeles there. **1604** DEKKER *Honest Wh.* Wks. 1873 II. 8, I would not for a duckat she had kickt vp her heeles. **1611** COTGR., *Passer oultre*, to tipe vp the heeles, to die. *c* **1620** Z. BOYD *Zion's Flowers* (1855) 155 Nowe Shechem's gone, he hath laid up his heeles. **1641** BEST *Farm. Bks.* (Surtees) 29 Oftentimes (after a longe declininge and goinge backe) [they] turne up theire heeles. **1648** GAGE *West. Ind.* vi. 17 Our men with one reasonable Cup of Spanish Sacke presently tumbled up their heeles, and left them like swine. **1688** BUNYAN *Heavenly Footman* (1886) 148 He hath turned up their heels, and hath given them an everlasting fall. **1845** BROWNING *Flight Duchess* xvii. 33 His heels he'll kick up, Slain by an onslaught fierce of hiccup.

**** *Other phrases.*

25. †a. ***to bless the world with one's heels***, to be hanged. **†b.** ***to cast*** or ***lay (one's) heels in one's neck***, to leap headlong or recklessly. **c.** ***to run back the heel, run*** or ***hunt heel, hunt it by the heel, take it heel***, to run back on the scent; to hunt or run counter; also ***to run heel-way*** (27 c). **d.** ***with the heels foremost*** or ***forward***, as a corpse is carried.

a. 1566 PAINTER *Pal. Pleas.* 63 The three theues were conueied foorth, to blesse the worlde with their heeles.

b. 1599 NASHE *Lenten Stuffe* 8 His yeomen bolde cast their heeles in their necke, and friskt it after him. **1676** COTTON *Walton's Angler* II. 281 These stones are so slippery I can not stand!.. I think I were best lay my heels in my neck and tumble down!

c. 1674 N. COX *Gentl. Recreat.* (1677) 16 When the Hounds or Beagles hunt it by the Heel, we say, they *Hunt Counter.* **1781** P. BECKFORD *Hunting* (1802) 148 A fault.. which such hounds must of necessity sometimes be guilty of; that is, running back the heel. **1828** *Sporting Mag.* XXII. 232, I cannot help challenging a stale scent, or, speaking more technically, taking it heel. **18..** *Rec. N. Devon Staghounds* 45 (Elworthy) The whole pack took it heel, and were stopped before they reached the edge of the covert. **1888** ELWORTHY *W. Somerset Word-bk., Heel*, hounds following the scent in the wrong direction are said to 'be running heel.' **1897** D. H. MADDEN *Diary Silence* 51 He was merely hunting counter (or heel, as it is now called). **1923** *Times* 17 Jan. 5/5 The old Melbreak hounds will never run heel. **1946** M. C. SELF *Horseman's Encycl.* 455 When hounds hit the line and run it backwards they are said to 'run heel'.

d. 1670 G. H. *Hist. Cardinals* II. II. 147 He was clapt in Prison, and came not out but with his heels forward. **1701** CIBBER *Love makes Man* IV. ii, *Car.* How came you hither, Sir! *D. Lew.* Faith, like a Corpse into Church, Boy, with my Heels foremost.

III. *attrib.* and *Comb.*

26. General, as ***heel-back, -beam, -catcher, -chaser, -dance, -end, -kicker, -leather, -loop, -stitch, -strap***; ***heel-clacking, -clicking, -sliding, -treading*** vbl. sbs. and ppl. adjs.; ***heel-fast, -free, -hurt*** adjs.

1936 *Times* 9 Jan. 4/1 A quick *heel-back from a loose scrummage. **1827** STEUART *Planter's G.* (1828) 242 Others.. have added what they denominate a '*Heel-beam' 18 in. out from the axle or cross-bar..in front of the axle, and next to the draught-bar, to which the horses are put. **1646** TRAPP *Comm. Gen.* XXV. 26 *Calcanearius*, an *heel-catcher, or supplanter. **1938** DYLAN THOMAS *Let.* 1 June (1966) 199 It's the dog among the fairies..the wizard's *heel-chaser. **1922** JOYCE *Ulysses* 515 A firm *heelclacking is heard. **1928** BLUNDEN *Undertones of War* 155 Strutting with redoubled vanity and *heel-clicking. **1970** R. PARKES *Death Mask* v. 64 The abrupt, heel-clicking return of Castilla. **1951** KOESTLER *Age of Longing* I. iv. 58 Loose, springy limbs which seemed specially designed for the Kaukasian *heel-dance. **1807** VANCOUVER *Agric. Devon* (1813) 119 At the *heel-end [in a drill-plough] of this sole, a perpendicular bar is inserted. **1887** FLO. MARRYAT *Driven to Bay* III. xv. 241 Clinging to the heel end of the spar. **1896** *Ch. Times* 2 Apr. 403 Rogues who are lying *heel-fast in gaol. **1948** B. VESEY-FITZGERALD *Bk. Dog* 223 Ten minutes a day for three days and most puppies will be '*heel-free' in the pen. *a* **1569** KINGESMYLL *Man's Est.* ix. (1580) 45 Wee are but *heele hurted, but he shall be wounded in the head. **1926** D. H. LAWRENCE *Let.* 19 Jan. (1932) 647 Murry..wrote me impertinently..that I was a professional *heel-kicker. **1794** W. FELTON *Carriages* (1801) II. 123 A *heel-leather to shelter the legs behind. **1880** *Turner & Co.'s Catal. Tools* (Sheffield) 66 Common brown Skate Straps, with *heel loops. **1859** DICKENS *Haunted Ho.* VIII. 48 There ensued such toe-and-heeling.. and double-shuffling, and *heel-sliding. *c* **1740** FIELDING *Ess. Conv.* Wks. (1840) 640 Three dancing-masters..the *heel sophists. **1882** CAULFEILD & SAWARD *Dict. Needlework* 306/2 Place together the pin holding the *heel stitches and those holding the foot stitches.

27. Special combinations: **a.** in *Shoemaking* (see sense 5), as **heel-blank** (also *blank heel*), a set of 'lifts' built up into a heel for attachment to a shoe; **heel-block**, a block used in fastening a blank heel or a 'lift' to a shoe; **heel-breast**, in a shoe, the inside edge of the heel, adjoining the waist; so **heel-breaster**, an operator who cuts heel-breasts; also, the tool used; **heel-breasting**, the cutting of heel-breasts; **heel-cutter**, a tool for cutting out the 'lifts' which form the heel of a boot or shoe; **heel-fastener** (see quot.); **heel-iron** = HEEL-PLATE 2; **heel-lift**, one of the pieces of leather, etc., of which the heel of a shoe is built up; **heel-maker**, one who makes the heels of shoes; **heel-parer**, one who shapes and trims heel-blanks; **heel-quarters**, the part of the shoe round the heel, the counter; **heel-scourer**, one who scours the surface of heels; **heel-seat**, the part of the sole to which the blank heel is

attached; **heel-shave**, a tool like a spoke-shave, used to shape the heel; **heel-tip** = HEEL-PLATE 2 (Simmonds *Dict. Trade* 1858); **heel-trimmer**, a machine for trimming and shaping the edges of the 'lifts' or heel-blank.

1600 DEKKER *Gentle Craft* Wks. 1873 I. 23 Hoe, boy, bring him an *heele-blocke, heers a new-journeyman [shoemaker]. *a* **1666** A. BROME *On Death Josias Shute* 32 He was no whirligig lect'rer of times, That from a heel-block to a pulpit climbs. **1921** *Dict. Occup. Terms* (1927) §429 *Scourer*..designated according to parts upon which he works, *e.g.* bottom or naumkeag scourer, heel scourer, *heel-breast scourer. **1905** *Westm. Gaz.* 30 Oct. 7/3 The same firm have several other novelties, including an automatic Louis *heel-breaster. The uninitiated may like to know that 'heel-breasting' is the operation of bevelling out the curve on the inside edge of the heel to the familiar half-moon or other shape. **1921** *Dict. Occup. Terms* (1927) §414 *Heel breaster*; cuts breast on front of heel square. **1888** *Penton & Son's Shoe Mercery Catal.*, **Heel Fastener*, a Metal Plate for placing between the Sock and Innersole and attaching firmly all round the Seat of Shoe to Wood Heel. **1875** KNIGHT *Dict. Mech.* 1094/2 The *heel-lifts are cut to graduated size, and merely require beveling after attachment. **1660** *Chas. II Esc. fr. Worcester* in *Harl. Misc.* (1744–6) IV. 423/1 A Captain of the Rump, one Broadway, formerly a *Heel-maker. **1723** *Lond. Gaz.* No. 6196/8 Joseph Cook..Heelmaker. **1881** *Instr. Census Clerks* (1885) 76 *Heel Parer. **1904** *Daily Chron.* 11 June 8/6 Boot Trade.—Wanted good heel parers and heel scourers. **1798** COLERIDGE *Satyrane's Lett.* in *Biog. Lit.* (1817) 252 Countrywomen and servant girls..with slippers without *heel-quarters, tripped along the dirty streets. **1921** *Heel scourer [see *bottom-scourer* s.v. BOTTOM *sb.* 19]. **1885** *Harper's Mag.* Jan. 284/2 The crude heel is pressed upon the '*heel seat' of the shoe.

b. *Nautical* (see sense 7 c), as **heel-brace**, 'a piece of iron-work applicable to the lower part of a rudder, in case of casualty to the lower pintles' (Smyth *Sailor's Word-bk.*); **heel-chain**, a chain for holding out the jib-boom; **heel-jigger**, a jigger or light tackle fastened to the heel of a spar to assist in running it in and out; **heel-knee**, 'the compass-piece which connects the keel with the sternpost' (Smyth); **heel-lashing**, 'the rope which secures the inner part of a studding-sail-boom to the yard; also, that which secures the jib-boom' (Smyth); **heel-tackles**, 'the luff purchases for the heels of each sheer previous to taking in masts, or otherwise using them' (Smyth).

1847 A. C. KEY *Recov. H.M.S. Gorgon* 24 The upper purchase was hauled taut, and heel tackles clapped on. *c* **1860** H. STUART *Seaman's Catech.* 74 The heel of the jib-boom has a sheave for the heel rope to reeve through, a score for the heel chain.

c. In other uses: **heel bug**, a harvest mite, *Trombicula autumnalis*, or the skin disease it causes in horses; **heel-cap**, a cap or protective covering for the heel of a shoe or stocking; whence **heel-cap** *v. trans.*, to put a heel-cap on (a shoe or stocking); **heel-clip**, a part of a sandal used when a horse has cast a shoe; **heel-dog**, one that comes or keeps to heel; a retriever; **heel-fly**, 'a bot-fly, *Hypoderma lineata*, that attacks the heels of cattle in Texas' (Funk); **heel-joint** (*Ornith.*), the joint between the *crus* or leg and the tarsometatarsus or shank of a bird, the suffrago; †**heel-lifter**, a runaway; **heel-pad**, (*a*) a pad in the heel of a boot; (*b*) see quot. 1874; **heel-ring**, the ring securing the blade of a plough (Halliwell 1847–78); that by which the blade of a scythe is fixed on the snathe; **heel-string**, the *Tendo Achillis* (*Syd. Soc. Lex.*); **heel-tool** (see quot.); **heel-tree**, the swingle-tree of a harrow (Halliw.); **heel-way** *adv.*, backward on the scent (see sense 25 c); **heel-wedge**, (*a*) a wedge used to fasten the coulter; (*b*) a wedge used to tighten the heel-ring of a scythe (Halliw.).

1920 *Vet. Rec.* 6 Nov. 218/1 *Heel bug, or harvester, *Leptus autumnalis*, is an annual source of trouble to thoroughbreds in training. **1931** *Daily Tel.* 22 May 19/7 Lady Marjorie is suffering from lameness in the off-hind heel, due to variola, which is a similar complaint to heel-bug. **1950** W. E. LYON *First Aid Hints Horse Owner* (rev. ed.) iv. 87 Heel Bug. As a rule only well-bred horses with thin skins are affected. The heels will be swollen and painful: lameness may also be present. **1954** P. SMYTHE *Jump for Joy* v. 83 She had contracted a heel bug disease. **1968** G. LAPAGE *Vet. Parasitol.* (ed. 2) xxxii. 771 *T[rombicula] autumnalis* may be the cause of 'heel-bug' of racehorses. **1813** W. BEATTIE *Fruits Time Parings* 34 [He] *heel-caps his hose. **1859** J. BROWN *Rab & F.* 8 His heavy shoes..heel-capt and toe-capt. **1831** YOUATT *Horse* (1848) 429 The *heel clips are two clips at the heels of the side bars. **1887** *Field* LXX. 569/3 Any man..would with ease dispose of twenty '*heel' dogs ere he was asked for one 'Hold up' one. **1889** FARMER *Americanisms*, **Heel Fly*, an insect pest which infests cattle on Western ranches. **1583** STOCKER *Hist. Civ. Warres Lowe C.* I. 132 b, Amongest the lustie *heele lifters..a good manie ..were driuen to returne. **1874** COUES *Gloss.* in Baird, etc. *Hist. N.A. Birds* III. 545 **Heel-pad*, pterna, tuber..The posterior portion of pelma, immediately under the foot-joint, and frequently prominent. (But *heel-pad* should not be used in this connection, since the heel (*calcaneus*) is at the top of the tarsus, and not at the bottom, where the *heel-pad* lies.) **1894** *Westm. Gaz.* 12 July 3/3 The knees are squeezed in a vice..and heel-pads inserted in the boots. **1849–50** WEALE *Dict. Terms*, **Heel tool*, a tool used by turners for roughing out a piece of iron, or turning it to somewhat near the intended size: it has a very acute cutting edge and an angular base or heel. **1873** *N. & Q.* 4th Ser. XII. 198/1 There is a sporting phrase, to 'run *heel-way', when, after a check, hounds take up the scent in the wrong direction, running back towards the start. **1523** FITZHERB. *Husb.* §4 In the settyng of the culture: and with the dryuinge of his syde wedges, forewedge and *helewedge.

heel (hiːl), *sb.*[2] *Naut.* [A later form of HIELD, after HEEL *v.*[2]] An act of heeling or inclining to one side; the amount of such inclination on the part of a ship.

1760 C. JOHNSTON *Chrysal* (1822) II. 252 When the ship takes a heel. **1819** BYRON *Juan* II. li, She gave a heel, and then a lurch to port. **1862** *Standard* 24 Apr., An average of 2 deg. of deviation for each degree of heel! **1882** W. H. WHITE *Naval Archit.* (ed. 2) 151 The Devastation..was made to reach a heel exceeding 7 degrees, by four hundred men running eighteen times across her deck.

heel (hiːl), *sb.*[3] *slang* (orig. *U.S.*). [Of doubtful origin though prob. f. HEEL *sb.*[1] (cf. sense 3).] Among criminals: a double-crosser, a sneak-thief; more generally: a dishonourable or untrustworthy person, a rotter.

1914 JACKSON & HELLYER *Vocab. Criminal Slang* 43 *Heel*, ..An incompetent; an undesirable; an inefficient or pusillanimous pretender to sterling criminal qualifications. **1916** *Lit. Digest* 19 Aug. 425/1 She..is said to be running a respectable 'scatter' in Dayton, Ohio, for reformed pickpockets and 'heels' or 'pennyweighters', the argot for sneak-thieves and shoplifters. **1929** *Sat. Even. Post* 13 Apr. 54/4 If a crook becomes an informer, then he is a rat or a heel. **1932** J. T. FARRELL *Studs Lonigan* xvi. 354 Studs watched him give the college handshake, thought what a heel O'Brien had turned into. **1949** 'J. TEY' *Brat Farrar* xvii. 157 Signing a paper didn't make him any more of a heel than he was being at the moment. **1949** R. GRAVES *Seven Days in New Crete* 67 She had not only treated me foully but managed at the same time to put me in the wrong and make me feel a thorough heel. **1957** L. P. HARTLEY *Hireling* 225 It doesn't matter how she feels, does it, when she's lost her fiancé—though he was a heel and she's well rid of him? **1958** *Times Lit. Suppl.* 26 Dec. 749/5 John Augustus Grimshawe was a heel about money and women.

heel (hiːl), *v.*[1] [f. HEEL *sb.*[1]]

1. *intr.* To move the heel, tap or touch the ground with it in a rhythmical manner in dancing; also *trans.* to perform (a dance) with the heels. Also *to heel it.*

1606 SHAKS. *Tr. & Cr.* IV. iv. 88, I cannot sing, Nor heele the high Lauolt. **1828** *Examiner* 679/1 Our English Sailor again toed and heeled, almost as neatly as life. **1845** MRS. S. C. HALL *Whiteboy* iv. 30 [He] performed a most characteristic and animated jig in the dust, covering the buckle—heeling and toeing—whirling his whip. **1863** RUSSELL *Diary North & South* I. 273 The men [negroes].. shuffled and cut and heeled and buckled to each other with an overwhelming solemnity.

2. a. *trans.* To furnish with a heel or heel-piece; to add or put a heel to.

1605 ROWLANDS *Hell's Broke Loose* 18 Hendrick the Botcher, cease from heeling Hose. **1612** WEBSTER *White Devil* I. ii, For want of means..I have been fain to heel my tutor's stockings. **1888** CORNEY GRAIN *Autobiog.* 14 One Gibson, who soled and heeled shoes in the world.

b. To arm (a game-cock) with a gaff or spur; hence (*U.S. slang*), to furnish or arm (a person) with something, esp. with a weapon: see HEELED 2.

1755 JOHNSON, *To heel*, v.a., to arm a cock. **1873** J. MILLER *Life amongst Modocs* 301 This was his signal to 'heel' himself and come upon the ground. **1881** LD. DUNRAVEN in *19th Cent.* Nov. 688 We ain't much 'heeled' for chairs. *Note*, A bird is said to be heeled when his spurs are put on and he is ready for the fight.

3. To catch or take by the heel (*nonce-use*); to fasten or secure by the heels.

a **1638** MEDE *Wks.* (1672) I. 226 My brother may well be called an Heeler, for he hath heeled me these two times. Now..to come behind a man and take him by the heel was foul play. **1887** *N.Y. Evening Post* 14 Jan. (Cent.), One would heel him (rope him [a calf] by the hind feet), while the other roped him about the neck. **1889** FARMER *Americanisms* s.v., In cowboy vernacular to heel is to lariat or secure an animal by the hind leg.

4. To follow at the heels of, chase by running or nipping at the heels; also *absol.* to follow at a person's heels.

18.. *Sportsman's Gaz.* 448 (Cent.) See that he [the collie] ..is staunch on point and charge, heels properly. **1889** BOLDREWOOD *Robbery under Arms* (1890) 12 The old dog had been heeling him up too, for he was bleeding up to the hocks. **1893** J. A. BARRY *S. Brown's Bunyip*, etc. 197 Cattle-dogs were heeling his horses. **1940** E. C. STUDHOLME *Te Waimate* (1954) xvi. 138 Two good dogs, one of which frightened the beasts by heeling them up (biting their heels) and the other by pulling their tails. **1947** R. B. KELLEY *Sheep Dogs* (ed. 2) xv. 178 Dogs that heel when forcing can be made relatively harmless by removing their canine..teeth. **1966** 'J. HACKSTON' *Father clears Out* 14 Our half-bred sheep-dog, which for years had poked about the kindly heels of callers' nags, got it in the ribs. 'No mong's going to heel that horse.'

5. a. To urge on with the heel.

1886 R. F. BURTON *Arab. Nts.* I. 386 So he made towards his steed and mounted and heeled him on. *Note*, Arab[ic], 'kicked' him, i.e. with the sharp corner of the shovel-stirrup.

b. *Rugby Football.* (*intr.* or *absol.*) To pass the ball *out* at the back of the scrimmage with the heels, so that it may be picked up. Also *trans.*

1892 *Stratford-on-Avon Herald* 18 Nov. 2/2 First get mastery in the scrums, and then you will heel out properly. **1893** *Daily News* 14 Dec. 2/6 Oxford were well content to only hold the scrummage, and heeled out quickly. **1930** R. CAMPBELL *Poems* 11 See the fat nouns like porky forwards sprawl Into a scrum that never heels the ball. **1936** *Times* 9 Jan. 4/3 In the earlier scrummages the Navy's forwards heeled the ball with commendable cleanness. **1955** *Times* 22 Aug. 3/2 One of those [*sc.* abilities] is to heel out sufficiently cleanly to offer the halves a chance to open up the play.

c. *Golf.* (*trans.*) To strike (the ball) with the 'heel' of the club.

1857 *Chambers' Inform.* II. 695/1 When standing too near, the ball is often 'heeled', or struck with that part of the club-head nearest the shaft. **1880** A. LANG *Ballades Blue China*, *Golf* 4 Ye may heel her and send her agee.

6. *Shipbuilding.* (*intr.*) To rest with the heel or lower end *on* something.

c **1850** *Rudim. Navig.* (Weale) 147 The stern-timber.. heels upon the end of the..transom. **1869** SIR E. J. REED *Shipbuild.* v. 88 The pillars heeling on the floors and lowest tie plate are $3\frac{1}{2}$ inches in diameter.

7. *intr.* To run back on the scent, to run heel.

1898 *Daily News* 5 Oct. 6/6 One or two of the best hounds showed a disposition to heel—i.e.—go back on the line if they chanced to lose it.

heel (hiːl), *v.*[2] Chiefly *Naut.* [A corruption of earlier *heeld*, HIELD *v.*, due perh. in part to the final *d* being regarded as the pa. t. suffix. But cf. MDu. and Du. *hellen* for earlier **helden*, in OS. *-heldian*, LG. *hellen*, in MLG. *helden, hellen*, and ON. *halla, hella*, Sw. *hälla* (= Da. *hælde*), in which also the dental is merged in prec. *l*.]

1. *intr.* Of a ship: To incline or lean to one side, as when canted by the wind or unevenly loaded. Also of other things (quot. 1887).

[**1530** see HIELD *v.* I.] *c* **1575** J. HOOKER *Life Sir P. Carew* (1857) 33 (MS. reading) The Mary Rose beganne to heele that is to say leane on the one syde. *Ibid.*, The sayde Mary Rose thus heelynge more and more was drowned. **1659** SOMNER *Saxon Dict.* s.v. *Hylding*, As we say, the ship heeles, when it lies or leanes to one side. **1682** WHELER *Journ. Greece* III. 286 The Wind abated nothing of its force..making the Vessel often heel. **1782** COWPER *Royal George* 7 Eight hundred of the brave..Had made the vessel heel. **1854** H. MILLER *Sch. & Schm.* (1858) 15 Our cargo is shifting..I could hear the coals rattle below; and see how stiffly we heel to the larboard. **1887** *Times* (weekly ed.) 14 Oct. 18/2 The balloon then heeled over, and..there was a large rent in the silk near the escape valve.

fig. **1858** CARLYLE *Fredk. Gt.* VIII. iii. II. 308 Grumkow himself..is now heeling towards England. **1865** *Ibid.* XVIII. ii. VII. 119 The Austrian Battle..has heeled fairly downwards, and is in an ominous way.

2. *trans.* To cause (a ship) to heel; to lay (her) on her side; †to careen. Also *absol.*

1667 PEPYS *Diary* 30 June, The Dutch did heele 'the Charles' to get her down. **1684** W. HACKE *Coll. Voy.* (1699) 8 Here we heeled our Ships and scraped them. **1697** DAMPIER *Voy.* I. 363 At the S.E. end of the Island we heel'd and scrubb'd also. **1772–84** COOK *Voy.* (1790) V. 1872 The commodore was determined to heel the ship in our present station. **1853** KANE *Grinnell Exp.* xlix. (1856) 461 The Rescue was heeled over considerably by the floes.

Hence **'heeling** *vbl. sb.*; also *attrib.*, as in ***heeling error*** (see quot. 1893).

1668 WILKINS *Real Char.* 283 When it doth lean too much on one side: or doth turn too much on each side..Heeling.. Rolling. **1785** FRANKLIN *Lett.* Wks. 1840 VI. 477 In heeling they are not so subject to take in water as our boats. **1893** *Standard* 15 Mar. 3/5 The error of the compass caused by the heeling of the vessel..Comparatively few compasses are properly adjusted for heeling error.

heel (hiːl), *v.*[3] [A corruption of earlier HELE, HEAL *v.*[2]] With *in* = HELE *v.*[2] 2 (*a*). Hence **'heeling-'in** *vbl. sb.*

1857 *Rep. Comm. Patents 1856* (U.S.): *Agric.* 93 In nurseries, fruit-trees are often taken up and 'heeled in'. **1882** *Gardener's Chron.* 4 Mar. 295 Lay or 'heel them in' sufficiently deep to cover the naked portion of the stems. **1928** *Forestry* II. 54 A group of thirty young elms which had been 'heeled-in' temporarily in the nursery. **1953** H. L. EDLIN *Forester's Handbk.* iv. 59 The bundles [of plants] are then *heeled in* —that is, set in a trench to keep their roots moist—until needed. **1957** *N.Z. Timber Jrnl.* Aug. 59/1 *Heeling in*, placing plants temporarily in a shallow trench, the roots covered with soil to prevent loss of moisture before planting.

heel, heele, obs. forms of HEAL, HELE *v.*[2]

heelaman, -oman, varr. HIELAMAN.

'heel-ball, *sb.*

1. The ball or under part of the heel.

1796 S. DINSMOOR in Morse *Amer. Geog.* I. 667 One of these tracks was very large..the proximate breadth behind the toes seven inches, the diameter of the heel-ball five.

2. A polishing substance, composed principally of hard wax and lamp-black, used by shoemakers to give a shining black surface to the sole-edges of new boots and shoes; used also for taking rubbings of monumental brasses, etc.

1822 R. G. WALLACE *Fifteen Years Ind.* 142 Heel balls, shirts, and nankeen for the use of the soldiers. **1842** *Few Words to Churchw.* (Camb. Camden Soc.) I. 11 There is a way of taking copies of them [brasses] by laying thin paper upon them, and rubbing it over with black lead, or with what is called heel-ball. **1861** *Sat. Rev.* 22 June 647 What the upholsterers call 'lining paper', and what the shoe-makers call 'heelball', form the weapons of a brass-rubber.

Hence **heel-ball** *v.*, to polish with heel-ball.

1851 MAYHEW *Lond. Labour* I. 369 The old shoes are to be cobbled up, and the cracks heel-balled over. **1870** *Daily*

News 10 Nov., The Prussian troops have heel-balled the eagle on their helmets.

'heel-bone. The bone of the heel; the *calcaneum* or *os calcis*.

1598 FLORIO, *Calce*..the heelebone of a mans leg. **1741** MONRO *Anat. Bones* (ed. 3) 297 The internal Side of the Heel-bone is hollowed. **1836–9** TODD *Cycl. Anat.* II. 339/2.

heeld(e, var. HIELD *v.*

heeled (hiːld), *ppl. a.* [f. HEEL *sb.*^{1}, *v.*^{1} + -ED.]

1. Furnished with a heel or heel-like projection; esp. in *comb.*, as ***long-heeled***.

1562 J. HEYWOOD *Epigr.* (1867) 134 A hart in a heelde hose, can neuer do weele. **1698** FRYER *Acc. E. India & P.* 245 Persian Boots (which are low-heel'd and good cordovan Leather). **1704** *Lond. Gaz.* No. 4034/4 A short Negro Man, long Heel'd. **1711** 'J. DISTAFF' *Char. Don Sacheverellio* 3 A pair of Red-heel'd Shoes. **1854** WOODWARD *Mollusca* (1856) 299 Foot large, heeled.

2. a. Provided, equipped; armed, esp. with a revolver. *slang* (orig. *U.S.*).

1866 'MARK TWAIN' *Lett. fr. Hawaii* (1967) 86 In Virginia City, in former times, the insulted party..would lay his hand gently on his six-shooter and say, 'Are you heeled?' **1873** J. H. BEADLE *Undevel. West* 351 To travel long out West a man must be, in the local phrase, 'well heeled'. **1883** *Leisure Hour* 282/2 The ratio of 'heeled' citizens increased.. the meekest-looking individual having one [revolver]. **1887** A. A. HAYAS in *Jesuit's Ring* 227 You fellows would want to go well heeled. **1915** A. CONAN DOYLE *Valley of Fear* II. i. 153 'Halloa, mate!' said he. 'You seem heeled and ready.' **1928** 'I. HAY' *Poor Gentleman* xvii. 284 A scattered shot or two rang out—doubtless some of the defenders were 'heeled'. **1956** 'E. MCBAIN' *Cop Hater* (1958) v. 47 'Were you heeled when they pulled you in?'..'We didn't even have a water pistol between us.'

b. Provided with money. Usu. preceded by *well*. *slang* (orig. *U.S.*).

1880 *Pacific Metropolis* (San Francisco) 12 June 8/4 His friends want him to go 'heeled' and so they've got up the biggest sort of a bill for..next Wednesday night. **1897** E. W. BRODHEAD *Bound in Shallows* 153, I ain't so well-heeled right now. **1936** J. CURTIS *Gilt Kid* v. 51 He had done a gaff and was well heeled with dough. **1965** G. MCINNES *Road to Gundagai* x. 176 Dr. Crapp was a prominent dentist... He was therefore obviously well heeled. **1968** *Daily Tel.* (Colour Suppl.) 19/1 Though the million and a quarter left by his grandfather has been spread among a large family he is still well-heeled enough.

3. *Golf.* Struck or given with the 'heel' of a club.

1890 HUTCHINSON *Golf* 63 The tendency of the 'heeled' ball to fly to the right. **1891** *Field* 7 Mar. 349/1 A heeled tee stroke at this point is sure to lie in tufty grass.

4. *heeled bet*: in card games (see quot.).

1923 L. H. DAWSON *Hoyle's Games Modernized* 274 A 'heeled Bet' is said to be one in which the counters of the stake are placed diagonally across from one card to another signifying that the punter is playing both cards to win.

heeler^{1} ('hiːlə(r)). [f. HEEL *v.*^{1} or *sb.*^{1} + -ER^{1}.]

1. a. One who puts heels on shoes; cf. *soler*.

1665 *Canterbury Marriage Licences*, George Robinson of Canterbury, heeler. **1884** L. GRONLUND *Co-oper. Commw.* viii. 179 The 'heelers' among the operatives in a shoe-factory.

b. (See quot.: cf. HEEL *v.* 2 b).

1831 JOHNSON *Sportsman's Cycl.*, *Heeler*, is the person who affixes the spur to the heel of a game cock.

2. A fighting cock, that uses his spurs or 'heels'.

1688 R. HOLME *Armoury* II. 252/1 A Heeler, or a Bloody-heel Cock..strikes or wounds much with his spurs. **1815** *Sporting Mag.* XLVI. 24 Mark them for steady fighters, good heelers..and deep game.

3. a. One who has light heels; a quick runner.

1828 *Craven Dial.*, *Heeler*, a quick runner, active.

b. (See quots.)

1929 F. BOWEN *Sea Slang* 66 *Heeler*, a fast sailing ship. **1961** F. H. BURGESS *Dict. Sailing* 114 *Heeler*, a light fast sailing boat with a good performance; it is said to possess a good, or clean, pair of heels.

4. a. One who catches by the heels; one who trips up, undermines, or supplants.

a **1638** [see HEEL *v.*^{1} 3]. **1850** J. T. WHEELER *Anal. O. Test. Hist.* 14 Jacob signifying a heeler or one who heels or strikes up his adversary.

b. A working dog that urges animals, esp. cattle, onwards by nipping at their heels. Also (quot. 1888), a nip on the heels. Also ***blue heeler*** (BLUE *a.* 12 a). *Austral.*

1888 'R. BOLDREWOOD' *Robbery under Arms* xii, He fetches him [*sc.* the horse] such a 'heeler' as gave him something else to think of for a few miles. **1928** 'BRENT OF BIN BIN' *Up Country* 11 Bert's heelers and kangaroo dogs chased the packhorses ahead. **1940** F. D. DAVISON *Woman at Mill* III. 214 As thick as the hair on a heeler's back. **1945** [see *Australian cattle-dog* s.v. AUSTRALIAN B *adj.* b]. **1959** A. UPFIELD *Bony & Black Virgin* vii. 58 Bluey, the heeler dog, laid himself in the trough. **1966** 'J. HACKSTON' *Father clears Out* 116 Patting the Queensland heeler..that was..to be rechristened later on, 'lousy mongrel'. **1968** K. WEATHERLY *Roo Shooter* 139 He [*sc.* a dog] was a heeler, and it was his nature to attack from the rear.

5. One who follows at the heels of a leader or 'boss'; an unscrupulous or disreputable follower of a professional politician. *U.S.*

a **1877** *N.Y. Herald* in Bartlett *Dict. Amer.* (1877) s.v., The politician, who has been a heeler about the capital. **1888** BRYCE *Amer. Commw.* II. III. lxiii. 451 By degrees he rises to sit on the central committee, having..surrounded himself with a band of adherents, who are called his 'heelers', and whose loyalty..secured by the hope of 'something good', gives weight to his words. **1901** *Daily Chron.* 6 Nov. 6/2 The assurance of the Tammany 'Heelers' was less blatant than usual. **1933** H. G. WELLS *Shape of Things to Come* III. 311 The specialist demagogue, sustained by his gang and his heelers, his spies and secret police.

6. One who heels (cf. HEEL *v.*^{1} 5 b).

1898 MACLAGAN & JEFFERY in W. A. Morgan *'House' on Sport* 157 An English [Rugby football] team is an amalgam of heelers, wheelers, pushers (scarce), and sprinters.

heeler^{2}. *colloq.* [f. HEEL *v.*^{2} + -ER^{1}.] A lurch to one side; also, a boat inclined to lurch.

1894 *Times* 6 Aug. 5/2 The wind came off in hard puffs. Each took a regular heeler as they crossed the mouth of the Medina. **1926** R. CLEMENTS *Stately Southerner* 106 The ship herself was a heeler.

'heeling, *vbl. sb.*^{1} [f. HEEL *v.*^{1} + -ING^{1}.]

1. The action of HEEL *v.*^{1}, in various senses.

[**1691** J. WILSON *Belphegor* IV. iii, One cobbling of old shoes; another heeling of stockings.] **1859** GEO. ELIOT *A. Bede* II. 186 'She'll know nothin' o' narrowin' an' heelin', I warrand.' **1896** *Daily News* 21 Feb. 3/5 There was none of the fashionable heeling-out for your Yorkshire forward. **1963** *Times* 14 Feb. 3/4 They were helped, it is true, by the quicker heeling, although perhaps hindered by their stand-off half's unwillingness to part with the ball until too late.

2. *concr.* **a.** The heel-piece of a stocking. **b.** *Naut.* The (square) lower end of a mast or spar; the heel.

1591 SPENSER *M. Hubberd* 213 His hose broken high aboue the heeling. **1794** *Rigging and Seamanship* I. 29 The heeling is to be square. **1823** CRABB *Technol. Dict.*, *Heeling*, the square part left at the lower end of a mast.

3. *attrib.*, as ***heeling-machine***, a machine for attaching the heel to a boot or shoe. ***heeling dog***, a heeler (HEELER 4 b).

1880 *Times* 21 Sept. 4/4 There are other varieties of heeling machines, which also attach the heel with one stroke. **1947** P. NEWTON *Wayleggo* 101 Jim had the severest heeling dog I have seen.

'heeling, *vbl. sb.*^{2}: see under HEEL *v.*^{2}

heelless ('hiːllɪs), *a.* [f. HEEL *sb.*^{1} + -LESS.]

a. Having no heel. **b.** Not using the heel.

1841 *Tait's Mag.* VIII. 61 Heelless stockings and ragged jerkin. **1857** *Chamb. Jrnl.* VIII. 1 Villagers in heelless boots. **1866** *Cornh. Mag.* Mar. 309 The red man..steps on ahead with that easy, light-toed, heelless step which has taken these mountain men up many a smoke-wreathed hill.

'heel-piece, *sb.*

1. The piece forming or covering the heel.

a. The part of a shoe, etc. which forms its heel; a piece added to the heel.

1709 *Brit. Apollo* II. No. 65. 2/2 A pair of Heel-pieces. **1733** SWIFT *On Poetry* 173 Like a Heel-piece to support A Cripple with one Foot too short. **1858** SIMMONDS *Dict. Trade* 192/1 Heeling..putting new heel-pieces to boots.

b. Armour for the heel; that part of the solleret which bore the spur.

1828 WEBSTER, citing CHESTERFIELD.

c. The piece forming the heel of a mast or the like.

1794 *Rigging & Seamanship* I. 27 The heel-piece..coaks on to the heel of the lower tree, and the head-piece to the upper tree.

d. *Shipbuilding.* An angle-bar joining the heels of a frame across the keel.

1904 A. C. HOLMS *Pract. Shipbuilding* I. 471 The frame heel pieces are usually fitted when the frames are screwed up ready for riveting.

e. *Electr.* The iron bar connecting the soft iron cores in an electro-magnet.

1904 M. M. KIRKMAN *Telegr. & Telephone* 29 The magnet is constructed of a bar or heel piece of soft iron, into which are screwed two pencil-shaped pieces of iron which form the cores of the magnets.

2. *fig.* The end-piece; the conclusion.

1761 LLOYD *Cobbler Tessington's Let.* 16 And then it griev'd me sore to look Just at the heel-piece of his book. **1786** *Francis, Philanthr.* III. 176 That great furnisher of theatric heel-pieces.

Hence **heel-piece** *v. trans.*, to put a heel-piece on.

1712 ARBUTHNOT *John Bull* III. vii, Some blamed Mrs. Bull for new heelpiecing of her shoes. **1826** MISS MITFORD *Village* Ser. II. (1863) 442, I don't think he has had so much as a job of heel-piecing to do since [etc.].

heel-plate.

1. The plate on the butt-end of a gun-stock.

1847 *Infantry Man.* (1854) 34 Bring the firelock..to the shoulder, pressing the centre part of the heel-plate..into the hollow of it. **1881** GREENER *Gun* 257 The heel-plates are either of buffalo horn or ebonite.

2. A metal plate protecting the heel of a shoe.

1895 *Montgomery Ward Catal.* 526/1 Star heel plates, for preventing boots and shoes from wearing off at the heels. **1905** *Daily Chron.* 27 Dec. 4/7 The accident was through A wicked heel-plate on my shoe. **1959** *Sears, Roebuck Catal.* Spring & Summer 565/1 Home shoe repair outfit, includes ..6 pairs of heel plates.

3. A plate to support the heel of the boot in a metal skate; also, 'a slotted plate fixed on a boot-heel, to which a skate may be locked' (*Funk's Standard Dict.* 1893).

1890 D. ADAMS *Skating* 5 A metal sole and heel-plate screwed on to the boot with ordinary screws, is unquestionably the best and firmest. **1895** G. A. MEAGHER *Figure & Fancy Skating* 19 A perfect skate should be all of one piece. This is effected by welding the toe and heel plates on to the blade itself.

heel-post. **a.** The post to which a door or gate is fastened. **b.** *Ship-building.* The post which supports a propeller shaft at the outer end, nearest the screw (Webster 1864). **c.** The outer post which supports a stall-partition in a stable.

1846 *Loudon's Encycl. Cott. Archit.* Gloss., *Heel-posts*, to which the stalls of a stable are attached. **1875** KNIGHT *Dict. Mech.*, *Heel-post*..(2) That stile of a gate to which the hinges are attached. (3) The post to which a door or gate is hung. (4) The quoin-post of a lock-gate. **1893** *Jrnl. R. Agric. Soc.* Mar. 58 Additional security may be given to the heel-post..by nailing on to it slabs of timber.

heel-rope, *sb.* A rope attached to the heel of anything: *spec.* **a.** A rope rove through a sheave at the heel of the bowsprit or jib-boom, in order to haul it out; a rope temporarily attached to the heel of a rudder to move or secure it. **b.** A rope by which the heels of a horse are fastened so as to prevent kicking.

1794 *Rigging & Seamanship* I. 172 *Heel-rope* is to haul out the bowsprits of cutters, etc. **1854** H. H. WILSON tr. *Rig-veda* II. 115 The halter and the heel-ropes of the fleet courser. **1869** SIR E. J. REED *Shipbuild.* xiii. 251 Heel-ropes are usually fitted to large iron rudders. **1886** *Army & Navy Co-op. Soc. Price List* Sept. 1525 Heel Ropes, V Shape, with Leather Leg Strap. **1893** W. T. WAUN *S. Sea Islanders* 173, I..rove a heel rope to the main-top-mast.

Hence **heel-rope** *v.*, to fasten with a heel-rope.

1890 R. KIPLING in *Fortn. Rev.* XLVII. 357 Even the stallion too long heel-roped, forgets how to fight.

'heel-tap, *sb.*

1. One of the thicknesses or 'lifts' of leather (or other material) of which a shoe-heel is made.

1688 R. HOLME *Armoury* III. 324/2 A false quarter shooe ..hath one of the Heel Taps cut off. **1797** WOLCOTT (P. Pindar) *Out at Last* Wks. 1812 III. 494 With heeltaps, toe-caps, soles for worn out fame. *c* **1850** *Nat. Encycl.* I. 240 The imports of Herat..lemon-juice, and ivory heel-taps. **1954** J. STEINBECK *Sweet Thursday* 136 Run up the street to Wildock's and get new heel-taps on these [shoes].

2. a. The liquor left at the bottom of a glass after drinking; also, the fag-end of a bottle. ***heel-tap glass***, one without shank or foot.

1780 BANNATYNE *Mirror* No. 76 ¶ 13 Having, it seems, left a little more than was proper in the bottom of his glass, he was saluted with a call of 'No heeltaps!' **1820–36** [see DAYLIGHT 3]. **1840** DICKENS *Old C. Shop* lxii, 'Toss it off, don't leave any heeltap.' **1859** L. OLIPHANT *Earl Elgin's Miss. to China* I. 203 Obliging us to turn over our glasses each time as a security against heel-taps. **1933** C. ST. J. SPRIGG *Fatality in Fleet St.* v. 55 Wait, I have still a heel-tap. I must drink a toast.

attrib. **1897** *Pall Mall Mag.* June 158 Old heel-tap glasses with toasts engraved round the rim.

b. *fig.* The last or end part of anything.

1894 BLACKMORE *Perlycross* 75 Her heart was full again, and the heel-tap of a sob would have been behind her words.

Hence **heel-tap** *v. trans.*, (*a*) to add a piece of leather to the heel of (a shoe); also *fig.*; (*b*) to delay. So **heel-tapping** *vbl. sb.*

1763 *Brit. Mag.* IV. 38 A great club who sit till break of day to heel-tap the nation; which, they say, is also run out at the toes. **1909** *Westm. Gaz.* 15 May 2/3 He riveted china, and clumped or heel-tapped boots. **1958** M. MCMINNIES *Visitors* 491 Twenty-four hours to git—and no heel-tapping. **1968** *Daily Colonist* (Victoria, B.C.) 19 Dec. 4/8 To put it bluntly the government is heel-tapping and will continue to do so until and unless all those affected make themselves heard.

heelthe, obs. form of HEALTH.

heel-way. Erroneous rendering of *hele-waȝes* in '*The Grave*': see quot. *a* 1200 s.v. HELEWOU.

1838 LONGF. *The Grave* ii, The heel-ways are low, The side-ways unhigh.

heemantic (hiːɪ'mæntɪk), *a.* *Heb. Gram.* In 7 **hem-, hæem-.** [f. Heb. *heĕmantīv* a mnemonic term containing all the letters in question.] Applied to those Hebrew letters which are used in the formation of derivative words and inflexional forms.

a **1638** MEDE *Wks.* (1672) I. 281 Gog..signifies the very same with Magog, for Mem is but an Hemantick letter. *a* **1646** J. GREGORY *Assyr. Mon.* Posthuma (1650) 189 Gir signifying in the Persian tongue an arrow, to which if wee add the Hemantick letter Tau, we have the word entire Tiger or Tigris. **1674** BOYLE *Grounds Corpusc. Philos.* 40 Hæemantic letters. **1681** H. MORE *Exp. Dan.* 137 The Hemantik ה being prefixt.

heeme, var. EME, *Obs.*, uncle.

Heemrad ('hiːmræt, 'heɪmrɑːd). *Hist.* Also **-raad, -raat.** Pl. **-ra(a)den.** [Du., f. *heem* village, home + *raad* council.] A local petty court or council assisting the landdrost in South Africa and also formerly in Holland; also, a member of this council.

1801 J. BARROW *Trav. S. Afr.* i. 12 A civil magistrate called a *Landrost*, who, with his *Hemraaden*, or a council of country burghers, is vested with powers to regulate the police of his district, [etc.]. **1823** W. W. BIRD *State of Cape of Good Hope in 1822* ii. 23 An Englishman has been rarely called to the office of heemrad. **1876** *Encycl. Brit.* V. 47/2 Prior to 1827 there existed in the several districts of the colony an institution established by the Dutch called the Board of Landrost and Heemraaden. **1888** THEAL in J. P. Fitzpatrick *Transvaal* (1899) 10 The abolition in 1827 of the courts of landdrost and heemraden. **1900** *Westm. Gaz.* 19

Dec. 3/2 Lord Caledon, after our second annexation of the Cape, revived an old kind of elected Councils, named Heemraden, for the government of the inland districts. **1970** *S. Afr. Panorama* Feb. 45/2 In 1682 local administration was set up in the form of four Heemraden.

heende, obs. f. END *sb.*; var. HEND *a. Obs.*
c **1440** CAPGRAVE *Life St. Kath.* Prol. 177 Of her lyffe & also of her heende.

heeng, obs. pa. t. of HANG *v.*

heenge, obs. form of HINGE *sb.*

heep(e, obs. forms of HEAP, HIP.

heer (hɪə(r)). *Sc.* Also **hier**. [Origin obscure: connexion with ON. *herfa* skein has been suggested.] A measure of linen or woollen yarn containing two cuts, 'the sixth part of a *hesp* or hank of yarn, or the twenty-fourth part of a *spyndle*' (Jamieson).
1777 J. ANDERSON *Observ. Nat. Industry* in *Farmers' Mag.* (1856) Jan. 44 It was so coarse that they could not undertake to draw above 'forty heeres' from a pound of it. **1792** *Statist. Acc. Scotl., Forfarsh.* IV. 19 (Jam.) A woman could spin at an average only 3½ hiers in a day.—A hier is 240 threads, or rounds of the reel, each . . 91 inches long.

heer(e, var. HERE *sb. Obs.*, host; obs. ff. HAIR, HAIRE *sbs.*, HERE *adv.*, HIGHER *a.*

heerce, obs. form of HEARSE *sb.*

heerd(e, obs. forms of HERD *sb.*[1] and [2].

heerdes, obs. form of HARDS, HURDS.

heerin(g, -(r)yng, dial. and obs. ff. HERRING.

heern, heerse, obs. ff. HERON, HEARSE.

heest, Sc. and north. form of HIGHEST *a.*

heet(e, obs. forms of HEAT, HIGHT *v.*

heeze, heize (hiːz), *v. Sc.* and *north.* Forms: 4–6 heis, hese, 6 heiss, heise, 6–9 hease, 8–9 heeze, 9 heize. [orig. identical with *hysse, hyse, hyce*, early forms of HOISE *v.*; cf. Icel. *hisa*, Da. *hisse*, *heise*, LG. *hiesen, hissen*, Du. *hijschen*; Fr. *hisser.*] *trans.* To hoist, raise, elevate, push or pull up: generally with the notion of exertion. Also *fig.*
1513 DOUGLAS *Æneis* V. xiv. 6 Than all sammyn, with handis, feit, and kneis, Did heis thar saill, and trossit doun ther teis. *Ibid.* IX. viii. 112 All sammyn haistand wyth a pavis of tre Hesit togidder abuf thar heidis hie. **1549** *Compl. Scot.* vi. 41 The marynals began to heis vp the sail, cryand, heisau, heisau. **1589** R. BRUCE *Serm.* (1843) 166 To have our hearts heased and our minds lifted vp to the heavens. **1721** RAMSAY *Answ. Bourchet* 19 Up to the stars I'm heez'd. **1780** J. MAYNE *Siller Gun* III. 135 Heeze up his carcass on a chair. **1893** *Northumbld. Gloss., Heeze*, . . to hoist, to elevate.

heeze, heize, *sb. Sc.* [f. HEEZE *v.*] The act of hoisting or raising; a lift.
1513 DOUGLAS *Æneis* III. ii. 120 With mony heis and how. *Ibid.* III. viii. 111 With mony heis and haill. **1790** SHIRREFS *Poems* 77 (Jam.) I'll gie the match a heeze. *a* **1832** SCOTT in *Lockhart* xvi, As Scott has confessed, 'the popularity of Marmion gave him such a heeze he had for a moment almost lost his footing'.
Hence **'heezy**, in same sense.
1719 RAMSAY *Answ. Hamilton's 1st Ep.* iii, When Hamilton . . Lends me a heezy. **1815** SCOTT *Guy M.* xiii, If he had stuck by the way, I would have lent him a heezie. **1824** MACTAGGART *Gallovid. Encycl., Heezie*, a mighty lift.

hef, hefe, heffe, obs. ff. HEAF, HEAVE *v.*

hefd, hefed, -et, obs. forms of HEAD *sb.*[1]

hefen, heffne, obs. forms of HEAVEN.

heffalump ('hɛfəlʌmp). A child's word for 'elephant'.
Now commonly in adult use.
1926 A. A. MILNE *Winnie-the-Pooh* v. 66 He would go up very quietly to the Six Pine Trees now, peep very cautiously into the Trap, and see if there *was* a Heffalump there. **1928** —— *House at Pooh Corner* iii. 43 He guessed what had happened. He and Piglet had fallen into a Heffalump Trap. **1958** *Spectator* 22 Aug. 241/1 The Conservatives are not going to leap into the heffalump-trap in which their opponents . . reside. **1959** *Manch. Guardian* 14 July 6/3 Hannibal's heffalumps can hardly have had any such protection against the weather.

heffarth, -forth, hef(fe)ker, heffour, -fre, obs. forms of HEIFER.

hefful, dial. form of HICKWALL.

Hefner ('hɛfnə(r)). *Physics.* The shortened name of F. F. von *Hefner*-Alteneck (1845–1904), German electrical engineer, used *attrib.* to designate esp. a lamp devised by him and formerly used as a photometric standard and the intensity of light obtained from it, as **Hefner candle** (see quot. 1943); **Hefner (amyl** or **amyl-acetate) lamp**, a lamp of standard dimensions and with standard parts burning amyl acetate. Also *Hefner flame, kerze* (G., = candle), *standard, unit.* Also occas. in full *Hefner-Alteneck lamp*, etc.
1891 *Jrnl. Soc. Chem. Industry* X. 685/2 A discussion on the subject of amyl acetate, the fuel of the Hefner lamp, has recently taken place. **1896** *Electrician* 2 Oct. 738/2 The standard of light will be either the Vernon-Harcourt or the Hefner-Amyl-Acetate. **1898** *Electr. Rev.* XLII. 795/1 As a result of the investigations of the German Reichsanstalt, the Hefner lamp alone fulfils all technical requirements. The light of the Hefner lamp is designated a Hefner candle. *Ibid.*, The Hefner candle was accepted as the international unit of light by the Electrical Congress at Geneva in 1896. **1901** *Phil. Trans. R. Soc.* A. CXCVI. 26 Knowing the value of the energy of the visible light of the Hefner standard, the heating effect of the rays can be deduced. *Ibid.* 37 The chief source of difficulty in the comparison is the difference in colour between the light from the Hefner lamp and a fluorescent screen. **1902** *Encycl. Brit.* XXX. 235/2 For accurate scientific purposes the best standard is the Hefner-Alteneck or amyl-acetate lamp. **1911** *Ibid.* XXI. 526/2 Various experimental investigations into the properties of the Hefner flame. **1914** S. E. SHEPPARD *Photo-Chem.* 23 Viollé's unit was found by Lummer to equal 26 Hefner units. *Ibid.* 24 The light-unit 1 HK (Hefner-Kerze or Hefner candle) is taken as the mean of protracted observations on a Hefner lamp at the Physik. Techn. Reichsanstalt in Charlottenburg. **1917** G. MARTIN *Industr. & Manuf. Chem.* II. 357 The Hefner candle power is equal to about 0·9 British standard candle. **1943** *Gloss. Terms Electr. Engin.* (*B.S.I.*) 112 *Hefner candle*, a unit of luminous intensity equal to that of the Hefner lamp burning under specified conditions of atmospheric pressure and humidity. It is the official unit of luminous intensity in Germany and is accepted internationally as equivalent to 0·9 candle. **1963** JERRARD & MCNEILL *Dict. Sci. Units* 30 Germany, however, continued to use the Hefner candle (Hefnerkerze HK) unit which was derived from the Hefner lamp and had a luminous intensity of about 0·9 International candles.

heft (hɛft), *sb.*[1] [A late deriv. of HEAVE *v.*; app. analogical: cf. *weave, weft, thieve, theft*, etc., also *heft* pa. pple. = *heaved.* In sense 1, there was perh. immediate association with *heavy*.]
I. 1. a. Weight, heaviness, ponderousness. *dial.* and *U.S.*
1558 PHAER *Æneid* VII. S iij b, A swarme of bees beset the bowes . . and fast with feete in cluster clung . . and on the top with heft they hung. **1567** TURBERV. in Chalmers *Eng. Poets* II. 583/1 Or never crusht his head with Helmets heft. **1598** GRENEWEY *Tacitus' Ann.* XV. xiii. 240 Weighing downe with the heft of her bodie. **1655** MRQ. WORCESTER *Cent. Inv.* §56 That all the Weights . . shall be perpetually . . equal in number and heft to the one side as the other. **1848** LOWELL *Biglow P.* Ser. I. iv. 135 Constitoounts air hendy to help a man in, But arterwards don't weigh the heft of a pin. **1864** 'E. KIRKE' *Down in Tennessee* viii. 107 I's six foot three, . . weigh a hun'red an' eighty, kin whip twice my heft in Secesh, bars, or rattlesnakes. **1867** *Pennsylv. School Jrnl.* No. 16107 The books have a heft,—a feeling of weight and solidity,—that the book fancier especially prizes. **1879** MISS JACKSON *Shropsh. Word-bk., Heft*, . . a heavy weight. A *dead heft* is a weight that cannot be moved. **1966** H. ROTH *Button, Button* (1967) iv. 84 He was more on the lean side than supplied with heft. **1972** *Sci. Amer.* Dec. p. ii/2 Go ahead, pick it up. The heft tells you it's solid sterling silver.
fig. **1878** MRS. STOWE *Poganuc P.* iii. 24 Come to a sermon —wal, ain't no gret heft in't.
†**b.** Force (of falling blows). *Obs.*
1659 W. CHAMBERLAYNE *Pharonnida* v. v. (1820) 98 Each nimble stroke, quick . . fell; yet with a heft So full of danger, most behind them left Their bloody marks.
†**2.** *fig.* Stress, pressure of circumstances; 'need, emergency' (Nares). *Obs.*
1586 *Mirr. Mag., K. Forrex* v, Far apart from vs we wisedome left: Forsooke each other at the greatest heft.
3. The bulk, mass, or main part. *U.S. colloq.*
1816 PICKERING *Vocab.* 104 A part of the crop of corn was good, but the heft of it was bad. **1849** *N.Y. Herald* 5 Feb. (Bartlett), He's to his shop the heft of his time. **1884** *Harper's Mag.* Oct. 740/1 The heft of Mr. Lane's means was placed in the boat and the house.
II. †**4.** A heave, a strain; a heaving effort. *Obs.*
1611 SHAKS. *Wint. T.* II. i. 45 He cracks his gorge, his sides, With violent Hefts.
5. The act of lifting; a lift. *dial.*
1881 BLACKMORE *Christowell* iii, The sturdy parson seized the bigger of the two ash staves, and . . gave the stuck wheel such a powerful heft, that the whole cart rattled. **1888** 'P. CUSHING' *Blacksm. of Voe* I. Prol. 12 Giving a sudden mighty heft that was intended to do the work. **1895** *E. Anglian Gloss., Heft*, or *Hift*, a lift or a push.

‖**heft** (hɛft), *sb.*[2] Pl. **hefte.** [G.] A number of sheets of paper fastened together to form a book; *spec.* a division of a serial work; a part of a serial publication, a fascicle.
1886 *Athenæum* 9 Oct. 464/1 This treatise forms the fifth *Heft* of the second volume. **1892** *Rev. Reviews* Jan. 58/1 There is another interesting article . . in Heft 14 of the *Gartenlaube.*

heft, *sb.*[3] *local.* [Var. of HAFT *sb.*[2] 2.] (The sheep in) a settled or accustomed pasture-ground.
1960 WILLIAMSON & BOYD *St. Kilda Summer* 84 The Hirta flock is divided into hefts, more or less discrete groups each restricted to its own particular range. **1961** *New Scientist* 9 Nov. 341/2 The natural unit in hill sheep farming is the heft—the group of sheep that habitually graze within the confines of a particular area of hill ground. **1971** *Country Life* 28 Oct. 1166/1 Anticipated difficulties from depriving the hefted sheep of their age-old hefts or heafs have not occurred.

heft, *v.*[1] *dial.* and *U.S. colloq.* [app. f. HEFT *sb.*[1]]
1. To lift, lift up; to remove by lifting. Also *absol.*
a **1661** FULLER *Worthies* (1840) III. 106 Hence hefted over into Flanders. **1789** DAVIDSON *Seasons* 3 (Jam.) The eagle . . to the beetling cliff he hefts his prey. **1858** O. W. HOLMES *Aut. Breakf.-t.* xii. (1883) 260 The Governor hefted the crowns. **1882** JEFFERIES *Bevis* III. xvi. 254 With this considerate ease Bevis was to 'heft' his gun to the shoulder. **1913** R. W. SERVICE *Rhymes of Rolling Stone* 40 And here they must make the long *portage*, and the boys sweat in the sun; And they heft and pack, and they haul and track, and each must do his trick. **1932** W. FAULKNER *Light in August* xiv. 308 He was hefting the bench leg. **1960** J. MACLAREN-ROSS *Until Day she Dies* ii. 36 'Can't see anybody,' I said, hefting the case.
2. To lift for the purpose of trying the weight.
1816 PICKERING *Vocab.* 104 *To heft*, . . to lift any thing in order to judge of its weight, is not in the dictionaries. **1828** WEBSTER s.v. *Heft* n., We sometimes hear it used as a verb, as, to heft, to lift for the purpose of feeling or judging of the weight. **1872** O. W. HOLMES *Poet Breakf.-t.* xii. (1885) 303, I should like to 'heft' it in my own hand. **1894** BLACKMORE *Perlycross* 58 He . . 'hefted it' (that is to say, poised it carefully to judge the weight, as one does a letter for the post).
fig. **1878** MRS. STOWE *Poganuc P.* iii. 24 Come to heft him, tho', he don't weigh much 'longside o' Parson Cushing.
3. *intr.* To weigh, have weight.
1851 S. JUDD *Margaret* (1871) 241, I remember the great hog up in Dunwich, that hefted nigh twenty score. **1893** C. M. YONGE *Treasures in Marshes* ii. 11, I do believe it is [gold]. Brass never would heft so much.

heft, *v.*[2] Chiefly *Sc.* [prob. a. ON. *hefta* to bind, fetter, hold back, restrain, f. *haft* handcuff, fetter; cf. Ger. *heften* to make fast: see HAFT *v.*[2] and [3].] To restrain, retain (milk or urine).
1808–25 JAMIESON, *To heft*, to confine nature, to restrain. A cow's milk is said to be heftit, when it is not drawn off for some time. . . One is said to be heftit, when, in consequence of long retention, the bladder is painfully distended. **1842** H. STEPHENS *Bk. of Farm* (1849) 522/2 The impropriety of *hefting* or holding the milk in cows until the udder is distended.

heft, var. of HAFT *sb.*[1] and [2], *v.*[1] and [3].

heft, obs. pa. t. and pple. of HEAVE.

hefty ('hɛftɪ), *a.* orig. *dial.* and *U.S.* [f. HEFT *sb.*[1] + -Y.]
1. Weighty, heavy; hard, grievous. Also, large or significant in size, and as *advb.*, 'powerfully', exceedingly.
1867 F. H. LUDLOW *Fleeing to Tarshish* 167, I reckon I could forgive him . . but I'm afeard it'd come hefty on me. **1871** *N.Y. Tribune* 21 Jan., He is, as a Yankee would say, a little hefty for the ideal lover. **1875** *My Opinions & Betsey Bobbett's* 372, I never looked well in the saddle any way, being so hefty. **1890** P. H. EMERSON *Diary* 25 Nov. in *On Eng. Lagoons* (1892) xxii. 100 Rum night this, hefty weather, don't it blow and snow. **1898** KIPLING *Land & Sea T.* (1923) 135 What are we going to do? It's hefty damp here. **1905** *Daily Chron.* 18 Sept. 8/2 When an American girl does that, you can guess there's something 'mighty hefty' weighing her down. **1908** *Daily Chron.* 1 July 3/3 Mr. Barnes of New York was hefty with the trigger. **1925** E. F. NORTON *Fight for Everest, 1924* 39 The bucolic bumpkin with coarse features and slow brain fails no less than the 'hefty' giant. **1930** J. B. PRIESTLEY *Angel Pavement* ii. 85 It's a hefty commission all right. **1930** *Diary of Public School Girl* 32 Played in a game with Highlands. Got some good hefty bangs. **1958** *Oxf. Mag.* 22 May 461/1 Slighter than Hitchcock but heftier than Chaplin. **1959** *Manch. Guardian* 29 Jan. 5/5 You may protect yourself in respect of the very hefty bill for any medical treatment if someone falls ill . . while you are abroad. **1972** *Sunday Times* 30 Jan. 63/5 On top of the hefty basic wage is a bonus system from the pool of tips. **1972** *Sunday Tel.* 6 Feb. 14/6 This hefty book, written in brisk journalese, brings Capone to life.
2. *dial.* Violent. [Cf. Ger. *heftig.*]
1886 MRS. F. H. BURNETT *Little Ld. Fauntleroy* xi. (1887) 222 A hefty un she was—a regular tiger-cat.
3. *U.S.* Easy to lift or handle.
1885 *American* IX. 232 It should be hefty, light and of a form that can be easily held in the hand.

heg, obs. form of HAG, HEDGE, HIGH.

hegberry, dial. form of HAGBERRY.

hege, obs. form of HAY, HEDGE, HEY, HIGH.

Hegelian (hiː'giːlɪən, heɪ'geɪlɪən), *a.* and *sb.* [f. the name of the German philosopher Georg Wilhelm Friedrich Hegel (1770–1831).]
A. *adj.* Of, pertaining to, or connected with Hegel or his philosophy.
1838 *Penny Cycl.* XII. 99/1 The thought . . independent of its subject matter, or, in the Hegelian terminology, of all its contents. **1845** MAURICE *Mor. & Met. Philos.* in *Encycl. Metrop.* II. 671 Something which should be a substitute for the Hegelian system. **1875** JOWETT *Plato* (ed. 2) I. xviii, The Kantian and Hegelian philosophies.
B. *sb.* One who holds the philosophical system of Hegel.
1843 MILL *Logic* V. iii. 364 Whether in the Vedas, in the Platonists, or in the Hegelians, mysticism is neither more nor less than ascribing objective existence to the subjective creations of the mind's own faculties. **1864** in WEBSTER. **1881** *Nation* (N.Y.) No. 834. 443 All these facts . . are mostly admitted by Hegelians. **1891** [see THING *sb.*[1] 14 e].

He'gelianism. [f. prec. + -ISM.] The philosophical system of Hegel.
A system of Absolute Idealism (as distinguished from the Subjective Idealism of Kant), in which pure being is regarded as pure thought, the universe as its development, and philosophy as its dialectical explication.
1846 J. D. MORELL *Hist. View Philos.* II. II. v. 160 It is in the department of theology chiefly, that the great battle of Hegelianism has been, and is still being fought. **1860** MANSEL *Proleg. Log.* ix. 299 *note*, [Michelet] professes to

discover in Aristotle's Metaphysics an anticipation of Hegelianism. **1865** *Sat. Rev.* 12 Aug. 214 For this spice of Hegelianism, or identification of opposites, the British mind, it might be thought, was hardly prepared.

So **Hege'lese**, the language or jargon of Hegel; **He'gelianize** *v. trans.*, to render Hegelian; **He'gelianizing** *ppl. a.* and *vbl. sb.*, rendering Hegelian; **'Hegelism** = HEGELIANISM; **'Hegelize** *v. intr.*, to do like Hegel; **'Hegelizer** = HEGELIAN *sb.*

1856 *Mem. F. Perthes* II. xxv. 376 It Hegelized and Straussized too much. **1864** WEBSTER, *Hegelism.* **1879** W. JAMES *Let.* 3 Sept. in R. B. Perry *Tht. & Char. of W. J.* (1935) II. 15 Poor Palmer has gone abroad to steep himself I suppose still more deeply in that priggish English Hegelism. **1881** *Nation* (N.Y.) No. 834. 443 Hegelism is.. essentially passive, receptive, feminine. **1886** *Mind* XI. 258 The chief point about the law of development is its containing what in Hegelese might be called *Aufgehobensein.* **1887** LOWELL *Democr., etc.* 169 When the obvious meaning of Shakespeare has been rewritten into Hegelese. **1887** A. SETH in *Mind* Jan. 94 The Hegelianising of Kant may be best illustrated from the section on the 'Deduction of the Categories'. **1890** W. JAMES *Princ. Psychol.* I. vi. 163 The Hegelizers amongst them will take high ground at once, and say that the glory and beauty of the psychic life is that in it all contradictions find their reconciliation. *Ibid.* xii. 464 A conception, according to the Hegelizers in philosophy, 'develops its own significance'. **1910** *Mind* XIX. 123 The Hegelianising of poetry. **1945** K. R. POPPER *Open Society* II. xxii. 196 These Hegelianizing theories. **1970** A. MACINTYRE *Marcuse* ii. 35 The counterpart to Marcuse's Hegelianizing of Marx is a total neglect of Engels.

hegemon ('hiːdʒɪmɒn, 'hɛ-). [a. Gr. ἡγέμων leader.] A leading or paramount power.

1904 *Forum* Jan.–Mar. 347 (Cent. Dict. Suppl.), The *hegemon* of the western hemisphere is the United States. **1920** *Public Opinion* 2 July 6/1 Japan.. asserting her ambition to become hegemon of a far East on which white influence shall be reduced to a vanishing point. **1936** W. J. ENTWISTLE *Spanish Lang.* v. 135 He was king of León as others were sovereigns elsewhere in the Peninsula, but he alone was hegemon and the successor of those who had ruled all Spain from Toledo.

†**hege'moniac.** *Obs.* = HEGEMONIC *sb.*

1656 STANLEY *Hist. Philos.* VIII. (1701) 318/2 Profit is a part of Virtuous, as being the Hegemoniack thereof. *Ibid.* A virtuous man being the whole, in respect of his Hegemoniack, which is profit, is not different from profit.

hegemonic (hɛdʒɪ'mɒnɪk, hiːg-), *a.* and *sb.* [ad. Gr. ἡγεμονικός capable of command, leading, authoritative, ἡγεμονικόν, neut. used subst., authoritative principle, f. ἡγεμών leader, chief.]

A. *adj.* Ruling, supreme.

hegemonic functions, 'the functions of the highest value in the animal economy' (*Syd. Soc. Lex.*).

1656 STANLEY *Hist. Philos.* VIII. (1701) 332/2 The Supream or Hegemonick part of the Soul. **1800** J. JOHNSTONE *On Madness* 2 (T.) All maniacks have a predominant idea, which.. is hegemonick in most of their propositions. **1893** HUXLEY *Evol. & Ethics* 26 The one supreme hegemonic faculty.. the pure reason.

B. *sb.* The ruling or supreme part, the master-principle.

1678 CUDWORTH *Intell. Syst.* 3 In animals, the members are not determined by themselves, but by that which is the Hegemonick in every one. **1837** WHEWELL *Hist. Induct. Sc.* (1857) III. 354 Who placed the hegemonic or master-principle of the soul, in the heart. [**1848** J. H. NEWMAN *Loss & Gain* 177 Spirit, or the principle of religious faith or obedience, should be the master principle, the hegemonicon.]

hege'monical, *a.* [f. as prec. + -AL[1].] = prec.

a **1619** FOTHERBY *Atheom.* I. xi. §5 (1622) 120 The most Prince-like and Hegemonical part of his soule. **1678** CUDWORTH *Intell. Syst.* 859 Mind.. hath a natural imperium and dominion over all—it being the most hegemonical thing.

hegemonist (hɪ'dʒɛmənɪst). [f. HEGEMON(Y + -IST.] An advocate of hegemony. Also **he'gemonizer**.

1898 *Pall Mall Gaz.* 12 Feb. 4/1 This Prince Kraft was also, it would seem, the earliest Prussian hegemonist, who has so far, and as such, revealed himself to us. **1921** *Pilgrim* Apr. 273 It does not.. follow that the resistance of England to the previous hegemonisers would be condemned.

hegemony (hiː'dʒɛmənɪ, 'hɛdʒiːmənɪ, 'hiː-; *or with g hard*). [ad. Gr. ἡγεμονία, f. ἡγεμών leader. Cf. F. *hégémonie.*] Leadership, predominance, preponderance; esp. the leadership or predominant authority of one state of a confederacy or union over the others: originally used in reference to the states of ancient Greece, whence transferred to the German states, and in other modern applications.

1567 MAPLET *Gr. Forest* 29 Keeping our selues free from blame in this Aegemonie or Sufferaigntie of things growing vpon yᵉ earth. **1847** LEWES *Hist. Philos.* (1867) I. 278 Philip ..claimed for Macedon the hegemony of Greece. **1847** GROTE *Greece* II. xliv. (1862) IV. 16 The headship, or hegemony, was in the hands of Athens. **1860** *Times* 5 May 9/2 No doubt it is a glorious ambition which drives Prussia to assert her claim to the leadership, or as that land of professors phrases it, the 'hegemony' of the Germanic Confederation. **1887** LECKY *Eng. in 18th C.* VI. 41 A universal Republic under the guidance and hegemony of France.

hegge, obs. form of HAG, HEDGE.

heggle, dial. form of HAGGLE.

hegh, *int.* Variant of HEH, HECH, HEIGH.

1722 DE FOE *Col. Jack* (1840) 59 Hegh, hegh, hegh, the rogues.. have got away my bag! **1816** SCOTT *Antiq.* xxvi, Hegh, sirs, can this be you, Jenny?

hegh, heȝ, obs. forms of HIGH *a.*

hegh, obs. form of HEY, HIE.

heght, heȝt(e, heȝþe, obs. forms of HEIGHT.

heght, heȝt(e, obs. forms of HIGHT *v.*

heȝthen, obs. form of HEATHEN.

‖**hegira, hejira** ('hɛdʒɪrə, *erron.* hiː'dʒaɪrə), **hijra(h** ('hɪdʒrə). Also 7 **hegire, hegyra, hegeira.** [a. med.L. *hegira* (F. *hégire*, Sp. *hegira*, It. *egira*), ad. Arab. *hijrah* departure from one's country and friends, spec. *al hijrat* the flight of Muhammad from Mecca to Medina; f. *hajara* to separate, go away. The more correct form, directly from Arabic, is *hijrah.*]

1. The flight of Muhammad from Mecca to Medina in 622 A.D., from which the Muslim chronological era is reckoned; hence, this era.

The era is reckoned to begin with 16th July 622, though the actual date of Muhammad's flight is now believed to have been nearly a month earlier. As the era is reckoned by lunar years of 354 and 355 days, it progresses more rapidly than the Christian era, founded upon the solar year.

1590 L. LLOYD *Consent of Time* 709 (Stanf.) Neither the Arabians of their Hegyra. **1600** J. PORY tr. *Leo's Africa* II. 381 From this flight the Mahumetans fetch the originall of their Hegeira. **1681** L. ADDISON *Disc. Tanger* 15 The last Month of the 1073 year of the Hegira. **1788** MARSDEN in *Phil. Trans.* LXXVIII. 414 The era of the Mahometans, called by them the Hejerà, or Departure. **1800** *Asiatic Ann. Reg.* I. 121/1 These transactions occurred in the 38th year of the Hejira. **1839** *Penny Cycl.* XV. 299/1 This retreat happened on the 16th of July, 622, and has been adopted as the Mohammedan æra called Hejra.

2. *transf.* Any exodus or departure.

1753 H. WALPOLE *Corr.* (1837) I. 205, I perceived how far I was got back from the London hegira. **1850** W. IRVING in *Life & Lett.* (1864) IV. 77, I am sorry to find my hegira from town caused you so much regret and uneasiness. **1886** SEELEY *Short Hist. Napoleon I*, i. 16 With this Hijra [flight of the Buonapartes from Corsica to France, 1793] the first period of Napoleon comes to an end.

Hence **hegiric, hejiric** *a.*, pertaining to the Muslim era; ‖**hijrī (hegiree)** *a.*, of the Hijra.

1827 G. S. FABER *Calendar of Proph.* (1844) II. 296 The Hejiric Year 699. **1849** SIR H. M. ELLIOT *Bibl. Index Histor. Moham. Ind.* I. 48 During the first four Centuries of the Hijrī Era.

heglar, obs. var. of HIGGLER.

hegtaper, obs. form of HAG-TAPER.

1587 MASCALL *Govt. Cattle* (1627) 236 The iuyce of hegtaper called Foxegloue, put into his eare.

hegumen (hɪ'gjuːmən). [ad. med.L. *hēgūmenus*, a. Gr. ἡγούμενος chief of an abbey, abbot, pr. pple. of ἡγεῖσθαι to lead, command, used subst. Also in Greek form. Cf. F. *hégoumène* (Littré *Suppl.*).] In the Greek Ch.: The head of any religious community; *spec.* the head of a monastery of the second class, corresponding to the abbot of a second-class convent; also, the second person in authority in a large monastery, corresponding to a prior in the West.

1662 J. DAVIES tr. *Olearius' Voy. Ambass.* III. (1669) 104 (Stanf.) They have *Archimandrites*, *Kelari's*, and *Igumeni's*, who are their Abbots, Priors, and Guardians. **1772** J. G. KING *Gr. Ch. in Russia* 376 The probationer takes up the scissars.. and delivers them.. to the hegumen. **1820** T. S. HUGHES *Trav. Sicily* II. v. 113 (Stanf.) The hegumenos, or prior, in full robes. **1850** NEALE *Eastern Ch.* I. 887 The catechetical discourse.. is read by the Hegumen or Ecclesiarch, the brethren standing.

heh (heɪ), *int.* [Cf. Fr. *hé* and HE *int.*[1]] An exclamation used to express emotion, as sorrow or surprise, or to attract attention.

1475 *Bk. Noblesse* 41 Heh allas! thei did crie, and woo be the tyme they saide. **1719** RAMSAY *Answ. to Hamilton* 10 July iii, Ha heh! thought I, I canna say But I may cock my nose the day. **1724** —— *Gentle Sheph.* I. ii, Heh! lass, how can ye loe that rattle-skull? **1806** MRS. OPIE *Black Pelisse* (1846) 186, I suppose it was that very money which she gave ..Heh! was it not so, Julia?

heh, obs. form of HIGH.

he-haw, -n, var. of HEE-HAW.

Hehner ('heɪnə(r)). The name of the chemist Otto *Hehner* used attrib. in ***Hehner number, value*** (see quots.).

1909 WEBSTER *Hehner value*, a number expressing the percentage of insoluble fatty acids in an oil or fat. **1913** G. MARTIN *Industr. & Manuf. Chem.* I. iv. 64 Hehner Value. —This test devised by Hehner indicates the percentage of insoluble fatty acids which can be separated from oil or fat. .. Thus butter usually has a Hehner value ranging from 85–88. **1915** *Chem. Abstr.* IX. 531 (*heading*) A new modification for making the Hehner number determination. **1918** T. H. POPE tr. *Villavecchia's App. Anal. Chem.* I. 382 Insoluble, Fixed Fatty Acid Number. (Hehner Number.)

hehte, heicht, obs. ff. HIGHT *v.*, HEIGHT.

Heian ('heɪən), *a.* [Jap.] Of or pertaining to a period in Japanese history from the late 8th to the late 12th century A.D.

1893 F. BRINKLEY tr. *Hist. Empire Japan* iii. 104 The people called the new capital 'Heian-kyo'... The interval.. from 794 to 1186 A.D.—is known in history as the 'Heian Epoch'. **1909** *Westm. Gaz.* 30 Dec. 9/1 It has been decided to arrange the pictures in strict historical sequence, commencing with examples of the Heian period. **1911** *Encycl. Brit.* XV. 259/1 All the pastimes of the Nara epoch were pursued with increased fervour and elaboration in the Heian (Kiōto) era. **1959** *Chambers's Encycl.* VIII. 41/2 (*title*) The Heian Period. *Ibid.*, A new capital was built on the site of the present city of Kyoto. It was given the auspicious name of Heian-kyō (the 'city of peace and tranquillity'). **1960** *Times* 1 Mar. 9/7 Professor Sakamoto.. in Heian court robes. **1967** *Listener* 14 Dec. 791/2 In Japan quite a lot of Heian literature has been preserved. **1970** *Oxf. Compan. Art* 609 During the later Heian or Fujiwara period an easier, milder Buddhist sect prevailed. **1973** *Times Lit. Suppl.* 2 Mar. 237/2 The Heian period, perhaps the apogee of Japanese culture, was essentially peaceful.

heiar, -ast, obs. ff. HIGHER, -EST.

heiau ('heɪaʊ). [Hawaiian.] A temple.

1825 W. ELLIS *Jrnl. Tour Hawaii* 51 Tamehameha.. finished the heiau, dedicated it to his god of war. **1920** *Nature* 15 July 628/1 There are shorter notes on heathen prayers and the ceremonial erection of the *heiau* or god's house. **1954** J. SHERIDAN in J. Macdonald *Lethal Sex* (1962) 160 Sacred regions where ancient *heiaus* still stand.

heicht, var. HICHT *Sc.*

heid(e, Sc. ff. HEAD *sb.*[1]

Heidelberg ('haɪdəlbɜːg, ‖'haɪdəlbɛrx). The name of a German city used *attrib.* to denote a jaw found at Mauer near Heidelberg in 1907, or the type of prehistoric man (*Homo heidelbergensis*) indicated by this jaw.

1911 A. KEITH in *Nature* 25 May 414/1 The Heidelberg mandible was found in 1907 embedded in the Mauer sand beds. **1912** W. L. H. DUCKWORTH *Prehistoric Man* 10 The Heidelberg or Mauer jaw. **1927** R. S. LULL *Org. Evol.* xxxviii. 677 The Heidelberg man represents the oldest recorded European race, geologically speaking. **1964** K. P. OAKLEY *Frameworks for Dating Fossil Man* 108 He considered that the horizon of the Heidelberg jaw was at the base of the 30-m terrace which he equated with the Mindel-Riss Interglacial.

Heidsieck ('haɪdsiːk). [Name of the original producer and exporter.] The proprietary name of a brand of champagne.

1853 E. K. KANE *U.S. Grinnell Exped.* ix. 64 We tapped a bottle of Heidsiek.., and all hands spliced the main-brace. **1877** *Trade Marks Jrnl.* 29 Jan. 249/1 Charles Heidsieck. Charles Heidsieck, Reims (Marne), France; champagne merchant... Wine. **1890** KIPLING *Life's Handicap* (1891) 163 The King's Peg.. liqueur brandy for whisky, and Heidsieck for soda-water. **1904** A. BENNETT *Great Man* xxv. 284 He was intoxicated.. though not with the Heidsieck. **1920** G. SAINTSBURY *Notes on Cellar-Bk.* v. 70 The earliest pages of my book show Pommery itself and Heidsieck Monopole. **1956** A. L. SIMON *Know your Wines* 82 Heidsieck & Co. are a firm of producers and shippers of Reims. It started as a man's name. **1959** *Trade Marks Jrnl.* 26 Aug. 731/1 Heidsieck... Champagne wines. Kunkelmann et Compagnie.., Reims, France; wine shippers. **1965** O. A. MENDELSOHN *Dict. Drink* 163 *Heidsieck*, old-established champagne of Reims, not to be confused with Piper-Heidsieck.

heiduc, var. HEYDUCK.

heie, obs. f. HIGH, HIE.

heif, obs. Sc. f. HEAVE.

heifer ('hɛfə(r)). Forms: α. 1 **heahfore, heafor, heahfru,** 4 **hayfre,** (? **heyffer**), 5 **heyfre, hayfare,** (**hawgher**), 5–6 **heyghfer,** 6 **heighfer, hayfer, -farre, heyffer, heyfar, haifer, -ir, hafir,** 6–8 **heyfer,** 7 **heifar,** 6– **heifer.** β. 5 **hekfore, -fere, hekefeer, hefker,** 6 **heffeker, effker, hec(k)fare, -forde, -forthe, -furthe, hek-, heke-, heckefar,** 7 **heckfer, heicfar,** 9 *dial.* **heifker.** γ. 5 **heffre,** 6 **heffour, effer, heffarth, -orth.** [OE. *heahfore* (prob. *héahfore*), *heahfru, -fre*, of obscure etymology; not found outside English.

As to the form, *héahfore* might perh. mean 'high-farer', i.e. high-goer or high-stepper (*-fōre* unstressed form of *-fare*, fem. of *-fara*, f. *faran* to fare, go). But the applicability of such a name is not apparent; and the form *héahfru, -fre*, remains without satisfactory explanation. The difficulties of form and sense are increased by connecting, as some suggest, *-fare, -fru*, with OE. *fearr*, OHG. *far(r, farro* bull.]

1. a. A young cow, that has not had a calf.

α. *c* **900** tr. *Bæda's Hist.* IV. iv. (1890) 272 In Scyttisc ȝenemned Inisbofinde, þæt is ealond hwitre heahfore. *c* **1000** ÆLFRIC *Lev.* iii. 1 Bringe unwemme fear oþþe heafre. *c* **1000** —— *Voc.* in Wr.-Wülcker 120/29 *Annicula, uel vaccula*, heahfore. *Ibid.* 120/35 *Altilium*, fæt heahfore. *c* **1000** *Ags. Voc.* Ibid. 274/20 *Antile*, heahfru. *a* **1327** in *Pol. Songs* (Camden) 239 With lowe lacede shon Of an hayfre hude. **1387** TREVISA *Higden* IV. 451 An hoyffer [? heyffer; *v.rr.* heyfre, heffre].. enyed a lomb [*vitula agnum peperit*]. **14..** *Voc.* in Wr.-Wülcker 624/14 Hayfare, *iuuenca.* *c* **1483** CAXTON *Dialogues* (E.E.T.S.) 10/17 Flessh of moton or of lambe Of an hawgher or of a calfe. **1526** TINDALE *Heb.* ix. 13 The asshes off an heyfer. **1548** *Will of J. Plume* (Somerset Ho.), A blake bulloke otherwyse called a Hayfer. **1555** EDEN *Decades* 4 Heyghfers and such other of bothe kindes. **1560**

BIBLE (Genev.) *Deut.* xxi. 4 Let the Elders of that citie bring the heifer vnto a stonie valley. **1577** B. GOOGE *Heresbach's Husb.* III. (1586) 131 b, Oxen, Kine, and Hayfarres. **1587** HARRISON *England* III. i. (1878) II. 2 For the steere and heighfer. **1697** DRYDEN *Virg. Georg.* IV. 781 Four fair Heifars yet in Yoke untry'd. **1767** A. YOUNG *Farmer's Lett. People* 232 Two steers, or heifers, may be kept and fatted in the place of one cow. **1863** P. BARRY *Dockyard Econ.* 121 The Greek philosophers sat on their stools chewing the facts in much the same fashion as heifers chew their grass.

β. **1407** in Kennett *Par. Antiq.* (1818) II. 212 De debili vitulo cujusdam hekfore vendito. *c* **1425** *Found. St. Bartholomew's* (E.E.T.S.) 41 A yonge hefker alone leuyng, Lay yn thryssheholde. *c* **1440** *Promp. Parv.* 234/1 Hekfere, beeste..*juvenca.* **1510** *Will of Parker* (Somerset Ho.), Yong mete callid Heffekers. **1529** *Acc. Metyngham Coll.* (B.M. Add. MS. 27404), For xx kien and for xx heckforthes. **1570** *Bury Wills* (Camden) 156 One blacke heckforde of two yeares age. **1570** LEVINS *Manip.* 29/1 Heckfare, *bucula.* **1572** *Will of R. Gibson* (Somerset Ho.), To Mary Pye, one heck-furthe. **1583** GOLDING *Calvin on Deut.* cxx, Take a young Hekfar from the droue. **1606** in Maddison *Linc. Wills* Ser. II. 23 To my sister Harrington one Heckfer. *a* **1825** FORBY *Voc. E. Anglia, Heifker*, a heifer. This is the pronunciation of the word, whatever may be its orthography.

γ. **1387** Heffre [see in *a*.]. **1525** *Test. Ebor.* (Surtees) V. 210 A heffour in calf. **1552** HULOET s.v. *Yonge*, Yonge cowe or heffarth, *iunix.*

b. *to plough with one's heifer*: derived from the story of Samson (Judges xiv. 18).

1560 BIBLE (Genev.) *Judg.* xiv. 18 If ye had not plowed with my heiffer, ye had not founde out my ridle. **1655** SIR E. NICHOLAS in *N. Papers* (Camden) II. 172 If he doe not, wee will plough with his heifer as well as with others. **1663** J. SPENCER *Prodigies* (1665) 15 Some few which had their own heifer to plough withal. **1677** GILPIN *Demonol.* (1867) 63.

c. *fig.* Wife.

1609 B. JONSON *Sil. Wom.* II. v, Her, whom I shall choose for my heicfar.

d. A woman, a girl. *depreciatory slang.*

1835 A. B. LONGSTREET *Georgia Scenes* 143 He rushed into the Kitchen in a fury. 'You infernal heifer!' said he to Aunt Clory. **1853** T. C. HALIBURTON *Sam Slick's Wise Saws* II. xii. 282, I have half a mind to marry that heifer, tho' wives are bothersome critters when you have too many of them. **1940** M. MARPLES *Pub. Sch. Slang* 115 Charwomen were satirically known as heifers at Charterhouse. **1964** O. E. MIDDLETON in C. K. Stead *N.Z. Short Stories* (1966) 201 Was that heifer of Blackie's the same one he had a fortnight ago? **1973** *Black World* Jan. 62/2 That heifer that been trying to get next to my man Lucky since the year one.

2. *Comb.*, as ***heifer calf, yearling***; †**heifer-bud**, a weaned she-calf of the first year; **heifer dust** *slang*, (*a*) nonsense (see also quot. 1927[2]); (*b*) (see quot. 1945); **heifer-paddock** *Austral. slang*, a girls' school.

1507 *Will of Walter* (Somerset Ho.), Juvencas voc. *heffer-buddes. **1865** H. H. DIXON *Field & Fern* vii. 140 The brothers only sell a few *heifer calves. **1927** 'J. BARBICAN' *Confess. Rum-Runner* xxiii. 256 Even if they do get pinched, they always have some *heifer dust ready about laying a trap for a ship. **1927** *Dialect Notes* V. 449 *Heifer dust act, the*, an arrest and cross-questioning by the police. **1941** BAKER *Dict. Austral. Slang* 35 *Heifer dust*, nonsense. **1945** —— *Austral. Lang.* vi. 123 Other Australianisms for girls or young women include:..a bit of heifer dust. **1885** MRS. C. PRAED *Sketches Austral. Life* ii. 50 Next year I shall look over a *heifer-paddock in Sydney, and take my pick. **1865** H. H. DIXON *Field & Fern* vii. 133 Deacon Milne bought the *heifer yearling.

Hence **'heiferhood**, the state or age of a heifer.

1886 *All Year Round* 14 Aug. 36 The cows never get a run after they have once grown out of heiferhood.

heigh (heɪ, heː), *int.* (*sb.*) [Cf. also HE *int.*[1], HECH, HEGH, HEH, HEY.] **A.** *int.* An exclamation used as a call of encouragement.

1599 B. JONSON *Ev. Man out of Hum.* II. i, They'll leap from one thing to another, heigh! dance and do tricks in their discourse. **1610** SHAKS. *Temp.* I. i. 6 Heigh my hearts, cheerely, cheerely my harts. **1611** —— *Wint. T.* IV. iii. 2 When Daffodils begin to peere, With heigh the Doxy ouer the dale. **1750** WESLEY *Wks.* (1872) IX. 75 Now, heigh for the Romans! **1871** J. MILLER *Songs Italy* (1878) 116 Heigh boot and heigh horse, and away with a will.

b. As an expression of inquiry: cf. *eh?*

1848 THACKERAY *Van. Fair* (1878) II. xvi. 173 Heigh ha? Run him through the body. Marry somebody else, hay?

B. *sb.* Used as a name for the exclamation.

1573-80 BARET *Alv.* H 369 An Heigh, or shrill sound, *extentus sonus.* **1575** LANEHAM *Let.* (1871) 61 What..with my Spanish sospires, my French heighes. **1595** *Enq. Tripe-wife* (1881) 146 Shall he run vp and downe the town, with friskes, and heighs, and fillops, and trickes.

heigh, obs. form of HAY, HIE *v.*[1], HIGH *a.*

heighday, -go-mad, -pass, -presto, etc.: see HEY-.

heighfer, obs. form of HEIFER.

heigh-ho ('heɪhəʊ), *int.* (*sb.*, *v.*) Forms: 6 heyhow, -hough, heihow, heigh hoe, heigh-how, 7 hey ho, heyho, hai-ho, 6- heigh ho, 7- heigho, heigh-ho. [f. HEIGH, HEY *int.* + HO.]

A. *int.* An exclamation usually expressing yawning, sighing, languor, weariness, disappointment.

a **1553** UDALL *Royster D.* II. i. (Arb.) 33 Ah for these long nights, heyhow, when will it be day? **1590** SHAKS. *Mids. N.* IV. i. 209 Hey ho, Peter Quince? **1599** —— *Much Ado* II. i. 332, I may sit in a corner and cry, heigh ho for a husband. **1609** BUTTER *Man in Moon* in *Brit. Bibl.* (1812) II. 89 Heigh-ho how he sigheth, and beateth his brest. **1633** MASSINGER *Guardian* v. ii, We'll talk of that anon.—Heigh ho! (Falls asleep.) **1776** *Maiden Aunt* III. 151 Heigh, ho! —Be merciful on that trying occasion. **1801** MAR. EDGEWORTH *Angelina* ii. (1832) 22 Heigh-ho! must I sleep again without seeing my Araminta? **1842** MIALL in *Nonconf.* II. 832 Heigho! This is a world of ups and downs. **1871** W. H. BEEVER *Daily Life Farm* 40 Heigh-ho! this dreary day!

B. *sb.* An utterance of *heigh-ho!*; a loud or audible sigh.

?*c* **1600** *Distracted Emp.* III. i. in Bullen *O. Pl.* III. 208 Dreames sonnetts to the tune of syghes and heyhos. *a* **1616** BEAUM. & FL. *Bonduca* I. ii, Ay me's! and hearty hey hoes! Are sallads fit for soldiers. **1795** *Fate of Sedley* I. 149, I bid her farewell as a lover, and left her with a low bow and an heigho.

C. *v.* To utter *heigh-ho!*, to sigh audibly.

1824 GALT *Rothelan* III. 241 She began to sob, and wipe her dry eyes, and heighho. **1852** M. W. SAVAGE *R. Medlicott* I. 11 It was just the sort of house which youthful couples.. heigh-ho'd for as they passed. **1868** ATKINSON *Cleveland Gloss., Heigh how*, to yawn, as when weary.

heiȝre, variant of HAIRE, *Obs.*

height (haɪt), **highth** (haɪθ), *sb.* Forms: *α.* 1 híehþo, héhþu, héahþu, hýhð; 3-4 heȝþe, 3-5 heiȝþe, 4-5 heiȝthe, heyȝth(e), (5 hekþe, heyeth, heth, 5-6 heygth, heyth(e), 6-9 heighth, (6 heyghth, heighthe, hyghth, hyethe, 6-7 heith, 6-8 heigth, 9 *Glouc. dial.* hecth); also 3-4 hihþe, hiȝþe, 7-9 highth (9 *W. Som. dial.* 'uyth). *β.* 4-5 heȝt(e, height(e, (heyt), *Sc.* heycht; 4-5 heght, heyȝte, heyhte, (*Sc.* hecht); 4-6 heyght, *Sc.* heicht, 5 heghte, heihte, heyȝte, heyghte, 4- height (5-6 heighte, heyght); also 3-5 hiȝt, (4-5 -te), 3-9 hight, (4 hiht, hithte, hit, 4-5 hyȝt(e, 4-6 *Sc.* hycht, 4-7 *Sc.* hicht, 5 highte, hyghte, 5-6 hyght). [OE. *híehþo* (also later *héahþu*) = OLG. **hôhitha* (MDu. *hogede, hochte, hoochte*, Du. *hoogte*, MLG. *hogede*, LG. *högte*), OHG. *hôhida* (MHG. *hoehede*), Goth. *hauhiþa*, f. *hauh-* HIGH + abstr. ending *-iþa*: see -TH[1]. From the 13th c. the final *-th* after *-ȝ*, *-gh* varied with *t* (cf. *drought, drouth*). In ME. the forms in *-t* were predominant in the north, and since 1500 have increasingly prevailed in the literary language; though *heighth*, *highth* were abundant in southern writers till the 18th c., and are still affected by some. The stem-vowel has generally been *ē*, *ey*, *ei*, though forms in *i* occur from 13th c., esp. in northern writers, *hicht* being the typical Sc. form from 14th c.; in Eng. *hight* is found from 15th c., and was very common in 16th and 17th c.; *highth* was also very common in 17th c. and was the form used by Milton. The *hei-* forms come lineally down from OE. (Anglian *héhþo*); the *hi-* forms are due in the main to later assimilation to HIGH. Current usage is a compromise, retaining the spelling *height* (which has been by far the most frequent written form since 1500), with the pronunciation of *hight*.]

I. The quality of being high.

1. a. Distance or measurement from the base upwards; altitude; stature (of the human body); the elevation of an object above the ground or any recognized level (e.g. the sea).

α. *c* **1290** *S. Eng. Leg.* I. 266/190 Fram þe eorþe heo was op i-houe þe heiȝþe of fet þreo. **1398** TREVISA *Barth. De P.R.* XVII. xviii. (1495) 613 A shrub that neuer growyth passynge the heyeth and quantyte of two cubytes. *c* **1511** *1st Eng. Bk. Amer.* (Arb.) Introd. 33/2 This people ben .xx. Cubettes of heythe. **1548** HALL *Chron., Hen. VIII*, 77 The same Trees were..in heighth from the foote to the toppe .xxxiiii. foote of assise. **1570** DEE *Math. Pref.*, Poure in water, handsomly, to the heith of your shorter line. **1673** RAY *Journ. Low C.* 76 Stakes or Poles of about a mans highth. **1756** BURKE *Subl. & B.* II. x, The Medium betwixt an excessive length or heighth and a short or broken quantity. **1809** ROLAND *Fencing* 22 It depends on the person's heighth. **1890** *Glouc. Gloss.*, Hecth, height.

β. *a* **1300** *Cursor M.* 1419 Of a nellen heght þai ware. *Ibid.* 1677 (Gött.) Fiftene [elne] on..heit. **1382** WYCLIF *Gen.* xi. 4 A citee and a towr, whos heiȝt [1388 hiȝnesse] fulli ateyne vnto heuene. *a* **1400-50** *Alexander* p. 282 All þe housez of þat Cyte were of one hight. **1591** SHAKS. *Two Gent.* IV. iv. 169, I know she is about my height. **1664** POWER *Exp. Philos.* 108 So the same Cylinder of 29 inches is raised by a Column of the height of the whole Atmosphære it self. **1868** LOCKYER *Elem. Astron.* ix. (1879) 323 The average height of the tide round the islands in the Atlantic and Pacific Oceans is about 3½ feet.

b. *fig.* (Often in reference to Eph. iii. 18.)

1526 *Pilgr. Perf.* (W. de W. 1531) 220 b, What is the length, the brede, the heyght & depnes of yᵉ crosse of Chryst. **1667** MILTON *P.L.* VIII. 413 To attaine The highth and depth of thy Eternal wayes. **1672** BP. PATRICK *Dev. Chr.* (1676) 258 O the heighth, the depth, the breadth of thy love in Christ Jesus. **1850** HARE *Mission Comf.* Pref. 9 The progressive unfolding of the truth, in its world-embracing highth and depth and breadth and fulness.

c. Of type: the distance from the foot to the face, called by printers ***height to paper.***

1683-4 J. MOXON *Mech. Exerc. Printing* (1962) 157 If he finds that the edge of the Liner just touch..as well all the parts of his Proof-Letters as they do upon his old Letters, He concludes his Matrice is Sunk to a true Height against Paper. **1771** P. LUCKOMBE *Hist. Printing* 243 They [*sc.* imperfections] are seldom exact to the prior sorts, but differ from them, sometimes in thickness, height to paper, or depth of Body. **1888** *Encycl. Brit.* XXIII. 698/2 The height of type varies slightly with different founders, the mean being $\frac{11}{12}$ in. **1890** A. OLDFIELD *Pract. Man. Typogr.* xxii. 164 Each letter should be of exactly the same height to paper; the height of type being 11-12ths of an inch. **1900** H. HART *Cent. Typogr.* 23 Five packets of types of the same face, but cast on a Pica body and Dutch 'height-to-paper', were found at the Oxford Press in 1898.

2. The quality of being comparatively high; great or considerable altitude or elevation.

a **1300** *Cursor M.* 1380 (Gött.) Cedir [es] a tre of hit [*v.rr.* heght, heȝt], widuten make. **1553** EDEN *Treat. Newe Ind.* (Arb.) 22 The sea in certaine chanels is of such heigth and depth, that no anker may come to the bottome therof. **1563** W. FULKE *Meteors* (1640) 1 Those bodies..named of their height *Meteors.* **1634** SIR T. HERBERT *Trav.* 107 But the height did not so amate us, as the danger of descending. **1796** H. HUNTER tr. *St.-Pierre's Stud. Nat.* (1799) III. 39 The height and the tumult of those tides of Cook's great River.

3. The elevation of a heavenly body, the pole, etc., above the horizon; = ALTITUDE 5.

1551 ROBINSON tr. *More's Utop.* II. (Arb.) 165 The subleuation or height of the pole in that region. **1559** W. CUNNINGHAM *Cosmogr. Glasse* 89 A Table of the sonnes height, for every degree of the signes in the Zodiake. **1726** tr. *Gregory's Astron.* I. 352 From the Altitudes and Azimuths observed, and the Height of the Pole.

†**4.** The diameter of a bullet; the bore of a gun.

1588 E. YORK *Ord. Marshall* in *Stow's Surv.* (1754) II. v. xxxi. 570/1 Some men..brought hither the name of the Height of the Bullet for the Piece. **1590** SIR J. SMYTH *Disc. Weapons* 18 b, Bullets for the field being smaller and lower ..than the heighths of the peeces by a bore. **1669** STURMY *Mariner's Mag.* v. 49 How by knowing the weight of one Bullet, to find the weight of another Bullet, the height being given. **1678** PHILLIPS (ed. 4), *Caliber*, in Gunnery the height of the bore in any peice of Ordnance.

†**5. a.** *Geog.* = LATITUDE. *Obs.*

(Cf. the expression *high latitude.*)

1585 T. WASHINGTON tr. *Nicholay's Voy.* II. vi. 35 Cituated betweene the Iles of Samos and Lesbos, about the height of Erithase. **1604** E. G. tr. *D'Acosta's Hist. Indies* 16 The ignorant suppose this Crosse to be the southerne Pole, for that they see the Navigators take their heigth thereby. **1622** PEACHAM *Compl. Gent.* 208 Spain lyeth..in the same height and parallel with the Azores Islands. **1694** *Acc. Sev. Late Voy.* Introd. (1711) 6 They sailed..until they came to the height of 15 degrees of South Latitude.

†**b.** More generally: Position (at sea) in the parallel of, alongside of, and, hence, *off* some place. (F. *à la hauteur de.*) *Obs.*

1604 E. G. tr. *D'Acosta's Hist. Indies* 58 Vasco de Gama, who in the heigth of Mosambique, met with certaine Mariners. **1673** *Lond. Gaz.* No. 751/4 Growing extreamly leaky at the height of the Isle of Wight, they were forced yesterday to run her on shoar. **1711** *Ibid.* No. 4911/2 Six.. Men of War are cruising off the Hight of Lisbon. **1753** HANWAY *Trav.* (1762) I. VII. lxxxvi. 403 The 20th we reached the height of Gotland.

†**6.** High pitch (of the voice or of a musical note).

1597 MORLEY *Introd. Mus.* 3 Shewing the heigth and lownes of euery note. **1697** DRYDEN *Virg. Past.* v. 24 Such is his Voice..in sweetness and in height.

†**7.** Exalted rank, estate, or degree. *Obs.*

1375 BARBOUR *Bruce* I. 608 God of mycht Preserwyt him till hyer hycht. *a* **1400-50** *Alexander* 3584 To put away oure pouerte & pas to ȝoure hiȝtes. *c* **1600** SHAKS. *Sonn.* xxxii, Exceeded by the hight of happier men. **1699** BURNET 39 *Art.* ii. (1700) 46 To be next to God, seems to be the utmost heigth, to which even the Diabolical Pride could aspire. *a* **1718** PENN *Life* Wks. 1726 I. 160 Such by crying down all Heighth, raise themselves up higher than ever.

8. High degree of any quality. *Obs.* or *arch.*

1601 HOLLAND *Pliny* II. 276 Suffered to seeth gently and leisurely to the height or consistence of honey. **1629** DAVENANT *Albovine* III. F iv, It works with hight, like new Mighty wine! as if 'twould split the Caske. **1659** STANLEY *Hist. Philos.* III. III. 22 Heighth of ambition causeth many men to go astray. **1662** COKAINE *Ovid* v. ii, I am Become enamour'd on her to that height, That I must marry her or I shall die! **1762** *Gentl. Mag.* 142 To such a heighth is licentiousness risen. **1770** GILPIN *Wye* (1789) 84 A gentleman..raised these mines to their greatest height. **1823** J. BADCOCK *Dom. Amusem.* 138 The fusion is to be raised to the tempering height.

9. Haughtiness; *hauteur.* orig. *Sc. Obs.* Also sometimes in good sense: Loftiness of mind, magnanimity. *arch.*

c **1450** HOLLAND *Howlat* 965 For my hicht I am hurt, and harmit in haist. **1533** BELLENDEN *Livy* III. (1822) 255 Thay war instruckit with sa prideful counsel, that thay couth nocht dissimill thare hicht. **1596** DALRYMPLE tr. *Leslie's Hist. Scot.* VIII. 63 This man..of hicht and pryde contemned al creature. **1650** CROMWELL *Let.* 2 Apr. in *Carlyle* Let. cxxx, A very resolute answer, and full of height. **1653** DOROTHY OSBORNE *Lett.* vii. (1888) 50 The worst of my faults was a height..that was..the humour of my family. **1662** STILLINGFL. *Orig. Sacr.* Ded. 4 If there by any such thing in the World as a true height and magnanimity of spirit. **1820** LAMB *Elia* Ser. I. *Christ's Hosp.* 35 *Yrs. Ago*, With something of the old Roman height about him.

II. Semi-concrete senses.

10. A high point or position.

1563 W. FULKE *Meteors* (1640) 33 b, It..negligently letteth them fall from a great height. **1667** MILTON *P.L.* I. 92 Into what Pit thou seest From what highth fal'n. **1697** DRYDEN *Virg. Georg.* III. 434 They take their Flight Thro' Plains, and mount the Hills unequal height. **1839** G. BIRD *Nat. Philos.* 78 A mass of water..falling from a given height. **1849** HARE *Par. Serm.* II. 468 Mounting from strength to strength, from highth, to a higher highth! **1893** *Bookman* June 85/2 There are critics who reach classical heights and metaphysical depths which he does not attempt.

11. The highest part *of* anything; the top, summit.

α. *a* **1000** *Cædmon's Genesis* 321 Heoldon englas forð heofonrices hehðe. **1388** Wyclif *Dan.* xi. 45 He schal sette his tabernacle..on the noble hil and hooli; and he schal com til to the heiȝthe [**1382** heeȝ] therof. *c* **1440** *Promp. Parv.* 233/2 Heythe (*S.* heyght, *Pynson* heighte),..*culmen, cacumen, sublimitas, summitas.* **1517** Torkington *Pilgr.* (1884) 30 We went vnto the hyethe and tope of thys.. Mounte. **1548** Hall *Chron., Hen. V*, 65 b, On the top and heigth of the same was set a great Egle of golde. **1667** Milton *P.L.* ii. 190 He from heav'ns highth All these our motions vain, sees and derides.

β. *c* **1375** *Sc. Leg. Saints, Jacobus minor* 167 And stabliste hym one þe maste heycht Of þe tempil. **1486** *Surtees Misc.* (1888) 55 On the hight of Ouse brigge. *a* **1533** Ld. Berners *Huon* cxxxi. 483 And so came to the heyght of the mountayne. *a* **1649** Drumm. of Hawth. *Poems* Wks. (1711) 15 Phœbus mounting the meridian's hight. **1712–14** Pope *Rape Lock* v. 53 Triumphant Umbriel on a sconce's height Clapp'd his glad wings, and sate to view the fight. **1788** Cowper *On Mrs. Montague's Feather-hangings* 35 Like sunbeams on the golden height Of some tall temple playing bright.

fig. **1667** Milton *P.L.* ix. 510 Her who bore Scipio the highth of Rome.

12. The highest point, the utmost degree (of something immaterial); extremity; summit; zenith.

α. *a* **1050** *Liber Scintill.* i. (1889) 4 Mæȝ soðes ȝebedes ys hyhð soðre lufe. *c* **1491** *Chast. Goddes Chyld.* 61 He that wyll come to the heyth of contemplacion..euermore he must areyse his herte vpwarde. **1611** B. Jonson *Catiline* iii. iv, The heighth of wickednesse. **1697** Dampier *Voy.* I. 370 Now was the heighth of the Easterly Monsoon. **1704** in B. Church *Hist. Philip's War* (1867) II. 164 Carrying the Remainder into Captivity in the heighth of Winter. **1714** Swift *Pres. St. Affairs* Wks. 1755 II. i. 210 Those who professed the heighth of what is called the church principle. **1726** Leoni tr. *Alberti's Archit.* Pref. 8 The heigth of Beauty.

β. **1375** Barbour *Bruce* ix. 508 In-to the takyn that he was set In to the hicht of cheuelry. *c* **1475** *Rauf Coilȝear* 496 Quhill half the haill day may the hicht haue. **1632** J. Hayward tr. *Biondi's Eromena* 66 God..grant your Majestie the height of felicity. **1697** Dampier *Voy.* I. 414 The height of the Storm is commonly over when the Corpus Sant is seen aloft. **1718** *Freethinker* No. 79 ¶3 Ceasing to be the Height of Folly, it became the Height of Wickedness. **1766** Fordyce *Serm. Yng. Wom.* (1767) I. ii. 48 A young lady dressed up to the height of the present fashion. **1841** Macaulay *Let. to Napier* in Trevelyan *Life* (1876) II. ix. 130 He was in the height of his popularity. **1923** T. E. Lawrence *Lett.* (1938) 407 Knewstub..thinks it's the height of John.

III. Concrete senses. Something that is high.

†**13.** The regions above; the heavens. *Obs.*

a **900** Cynewulf *Elene* 1087 Fæder ælmihtiȝ, wereda wealdenð..haliȝ of hiehðo. *a* **1000** *Guthlac* 796 in *Exeter Bk.*, On eorðan ecan lifes hames in heahþu. *a* **1000** *Christ* 414 *ibid.*, þe in heahþum sie a butan ende ece herenis. *a* **1050** *Liber Scintill.* lviii. (1889) 180 þænne hyhð [*celsitudo*] heofenlic byð openud. *a* **1400** *Prymer* (1891) 23 Wonderful is the lord in heyȝthis. **1535** Coverdale *Ecclus.* xliii. 1 The glory of the heyth, is the fayre and cleare firmament. **1553** Gau *Richt Vay* 48 He is passit wp to the heicht and led the presoners with hime. **1615** Bedwell *Moham. Imp.* i. §29 So is God in the height, and in the earth, by Christ his word.

14. a. A high or lofty rising ground; an eminence. ***height of land***, a watershed or ridge of high land dividing two river basins (*N. Amer.*).

1375 Barbour *Bruce* x. 52 Thai had..The hicht abovyn thair fayis tane. *c* **1470** Henry *Wallace* v. 781 Syn lychtyt for to gang Towart a hicht, and led thar hors a quhill. **1585** T. Washington tr. *Nicholay's Voy.* i. xii. 13 b, Caused upon a height..towardes the West, a great castle too be builded. **1615** W. Lawson *Orch. & Gard.* (1626) 5 The wind will blow fatnesse from the heights to the hollowes. **1725** in G. Sheldon *Hist. Deerfield* (1895) I. 559 They told us they wd travel to the hight of land by black river. **1727** Swift *Gulliver* iii. i, I stood upon a height about two hundred yards from the shore. **1804** W. Tennant *Ind. Recreat.* (ed. 2) II. 390 The country was..diversified with heights and swells. **1805–9** J. J. Henry *Camp. agst. Quebec* (1812) 36 On this lake, we obtained a full view of those hills which were then, and are now, called the 'Heighth of land'. **1860** H. Y. Hind *Narr. Canad. Red River Exped.* II. 225 The Vermilion Pass, which was traversed by Dr. Hector presents on the whole the greatest natural facilities for crossing the mountains without the aid of engineering work, as the rise to the height of land is gradual from both sides. **1875** *Encycl. Brit.* II. 201/1 In the north it [*sc.* the watershed] is found in a stretch of country, called the Height of Land, that lies between the White and the Green Mountains, and gives birth to the Connecticut and a number of smaller streams. **1887** C. Ransome *Short Hist. Eng.* viii. ii. 349 When morning broke, Montcalm..saw the British drawn up on the Heights of Abraham close to Quebec. **1902** *Encycl. Brit.* XXXI. 330/2 Beyond the Height-of-Land the Winnipeg and English rivers flow westward to Lake Winnipeg. **1918** H. Bindloss *Agatha's Fortune* xxv, It was hardly a range of hills, but rather what prospectors call a 'heighth' of land. **1930** G. L. Wood *Pacific Basin* 5 Behind the peninsula of California the height of land is a thousand miles from the sea.

†**b.** = eminence 2 a.

c **1400** *Lanfranc's Cirurg.* 150 þe ligament of þe þrote is clepid emanence eiþir þe heiȝþe [*MS.B.* hekþe] of þe epiglote.

15. *Her.* (See quot.)

1847 *Gloss. Heraldry* 134 *A plume of feathers* strictly consists of three..If there be more rows than one they are termed *heights*.

IV. Phrases.

16. at (..) height. ***at the height*** (arch.), †***at height*** (*obs.*): at the highest point or degree. (Cf. 12.) Now usually ***at its height***.

1375 Barbour *Bruce* xiii. 713 Kyng robert now wes weill at hycht. **1594** Shaks. *Rich. III*, i. iii. 41, I feare our happinesse is at the height. **1684** R. H. *School Recreat.* 32 Golden Rain, or Streams of Fire, that will when at height, descend in the Air like Rain. **1709** Mrs. D. Manley *Secret Mem.* (1736) III. 199 Luxury reigns at the height. **1839** Marryat *Phant. Ship* x, The gale was..at its height. **1849** Macaulay *Hist. Eng.* iii. I. 397 Her military glory was at the height.

†**17. in (..) height.** *Obs.*

a. ***in height***: on high, aloft.

a **1340** Hampole *Psalter* vii. 8 And for that in heght [*in altum*] agayn ga. **1617** Moryson *Itin.* iii. 109 Plants Elme Trees..and likewise plants Vines, which shoote up in height upon the bodies of those trees.

b. ***in height***, (*Sc.*) ***into height***: aloud; openly; in an open or evident manner.

1375 Barbour *Bruce* v. 487 Him thoucht nocht speidfull for to fair Till assale hym into the hicht. *c* **1375** *Sc. Leg. Saints, Machor* 1425 Lof god in hicht, & blissis hyme with all ȝour mycht. ? *a* **1500** *Chester Pl.* (E.E.T.S.) 243/350 Why I say this..I shall tell you sone in height.

c. ***in the height***: in the highest degree.

1599 Shaks. *Much Ado* iv. i. 303 Is a not approued in the height a villaine?

d. ***in height, in the*** (***its***, etc.) ***height*** = 16.

1606 Shaks. *Ant. & Cl.* iii. x. 21 Anthony..Leauing the Fight in heighth, flyes after her. **1662** Stillingfl. *Orig. Sacr.* i. iv. §11 When Learning was in its height in Greece. **1722** De Foe *Plague* (1884) 219, I must..speak of the Plague as in its height.

†**18. on** or **upon height.** *Obs.*

a. On high, aloft (of position or direction).

a **1300** *Cursor M.* 13620 'Blisce him', þai said, 'þat wons on hight'. **1340–70** *Alex. & Dind.* 123 þe tres..spronngen on hiȝþe. *c* **1475** *Rauf Coilȝear* 37 Amang thay Montanis on hicht. **1526** Skelton *Magnyf.* 428 To Tyburne, where they hange on hyght. **1540–1** Elyot *Image Gov.* (1549) 90 The crosse..beyng lifte vp on height.

b. Aloud.

c **1375** *Sc. Leg. Saints, Petrus* 249 He sad on hicht, þat all mycht heyre: 'pece be till ȝow'. *c* **1386** Chaucer *Knt.'s T.* 926 He..spak thise same wordes al on highte. *c* **1460** *Otterbourne* 34 in *Percy's Reliq.*, The Skottes they cryde on hyght. **1596** Spenser *F.Q.* vi. vi. 24 And with reprochfull words him thus bespake on hight.

19. to the height. To the highest or utmost degree; to the extremity; to the utmost. *Obs.* exc. in literary use.

[**1375** Barbour *Bruce* v. 183 Syne he drew him to the hicht, To stynt bettir his fais mycht.] **1606** Shaks. *Tr. & Cr.* v. i. 3 Let vs Feast him to the hight. **1613** —— *Hen. VIII*, i. ii. 214 By day and night Hee's Traytor to th' height. **1660** Sharrock *Vegetables* 136 It is his interest..to improve his ground to the height. **1765** T. Hutchinson *Hist. Mass.* I. 57 Carrying antinomianism to the heighth. **1798** W. Clubbe *Omnium* 114 His Colonel..Goes to the Serjeant, praises to the height. **1820** Lamb *Elia* (1823) 8 While he held you in converse, you felt strained to the height in the colloquy. **1871** Tennyson *Last Tournament* 658 For once—ev'n to the height—I honour'd him.

V. 20. *Comb.*, as ***height-growth***, ***-increaser***; **height-board**, †(*a*) ? = *height-rule*; (*b*) 'a stair-builders' gage for the risers and treads of a stairway' (*Cent. Dict.*); †**height-rule**, a rule for measuring the bores of guns.

1672 T. Venn *Milit. Discipl.* iii. i. xxi. 51 Furnished with all necessary things for his Artillery..viz...Rammers, Spunges, Worms, Tampions, height-board, Auger-bit [etc.]. **1692** *Capt. Smith's Seaman's Gram.* ii. iii. 92 A Gunner's Height-Rule of Wood, or Brass. **1889** *Nature* 12 Dec. 122 Different species have a different mode of height-growth..Scotch pine and beech..make the principal height-growth during the first period of their life.

†**height, hight,** *a.* *Sc.* and *north. dial. Obs.* Forms: 4–6 **heycht**, 4–7 **hecht**, 5–6 **hight**, 6 **heicht**, **hicht**, **hycht**. [app. a variant form of *heich* high.] = high: in various senses.

1375 Barbour *Bruce* iii. 707 Sum [schippys] wald slyd fra heycht to law. *c* **1375** *Sc. Leg. Saints, Jacobus* 360 Hyr palace, hecht & square. *c* **1460** *Towneley Myst.* (Surtees) 158 A floure, that shalle spryng up fulle hight. **1504** *Bury Wills* (Camden) 95 To the hyght aughter..xxs. **1560** Rolland *Crt. Venus* iii. 291 The words scharp quhilk scho thocht al to hicht. *a* **1572** Knox *Hist. Ref.* Wks. 1846 I. 166 He is heychtar then the heavins. **1610** Holland *Camden's Brit.* i. 155 The Scots are divided into Hechtlandmen and Lawlandmen.

Hence †**heightly, heichtlie** *adv.*, highly.

a **1575** *Diurn. Occurr.* (Bannatyne) 265 Quhairat the lord Seytoun wes heichtlie movit.

height, *v.* *Obs.* or *arch.* Forms: α. 5–6 **heyghte**, 6–9 *Sc.* **hicht**, 7– **height**. β. 6 **hayth(e**, **heyth**, 7 **heighth**, 9 *arch.* **highth**. [f. height *sb.*]

1. *trans.* To make high, heighten; to raise aloft or on high. *arch.*

1515 Barclay *Egloges* ii. (1570) A vj b/2 Strengthing our bankes and heyghting them agayne, Which were abated with floudes or great rayne. **1530** Palsgr. 577/1 I haythe, I lyfte on heythe, *je haulce*..Hayth this tester a lytell, *haulces ce ciel vng peu*. **1890** L. Lewis *Prov. Gennad.* 84 A mightier yet Liveth for us and thee—far highthed above.

2. To raise in amount, degree, quality, or condition; to increase, augment; to elevate, exalt. *arch.*

1528 Roy *Rede Me* (Arb.) 100 Their farmes are heythed so sore That they are brought vnto beggery. **1572** *Satir. Poems Reform.* xxxiii. 245 ȝe hicht yair maills; yair pleuchs ȝe dowbil on yame. **1622** Peacham *Compl. Gent.* ii. 18 Heighthing with skill his Image to the life. **1719** *Wodrow Corr.* (1843) II. 439, I am determined, if I get five hundred subscriptions, not to height the price, for all this addition. **1786** *Harvest Rig* in Chambers *Pop. Hum. Scot. Poems* (1862) 60 Weel may the shearers now pretend To height their fee! **1825–80** Jamieson s.v., Provisions are said to be hichted, when the price is raised.

†**3.** To bring or come to its height. *Obs. rare.*

1648 *Hunting of Fox* 14 When..that rebellion [was] ripned, and heighted a while with successe.

¶ Erroneously for hight *v.*[3], to adorn, confused with this verb.

1495 Wynkyn de Worde's ed. *Trevisa's Barth. De P.R.* v. lxvi. 183 Heeres..ben made to heyghte [*MS. Bodl.* hiȝte] the hede. **1861–2** ed. *T. Adams' Wks.* I. 400 When we are heighted [*ed.* **1630** highted] with his righteousness, and shining with his jewels. —— *Ibid.* I. 421.

Hence **heighting** *vbl. sb.*, heightening, increase.

1494 Fabyan *Chron.* vi. clvi. 145 It stondith at no sertente for heyghtyng and lowyng of theyr coynes.

heighted (ˈhaɪtɪd), *a.* [f. height *sb.* + -ed[2].] Having a (certain) height; as ***moderately heighted***, of a moderate height.

1892 *Temple Bar Mag.* Nov. 428 The range of moderately heighted, delicately varied Carnarvonshire mountains.

heighten (ˈhaɪt(ə)n), *v.* Forms: α. 6 **heythen**, 7 **highthen**, **heighthen**, 7–8 **heigthen**. β. 6–8 **highten**, 6– **heighten**. [f. height *sb.* + -en[5]; or perh. extended form of height *v.*: see -en[5].]

1. *trans.* To give or add height to; to make high or higher; to elevate.

1530 Palsgr. 582/2 This balke is heythened two foote. **1577** B. Googe *Heresbach's Husb.* i. (1586) 42 They may heyghten it, or let it downe as they list. **1617** Moryson *Itin.* ii. 169 The ditches..should bee deepned, and the trenches highthned. **1763** J. Brown *Poetry & Mus.* vi. 119 The Buskin and Masque..the first hightened the Stature, as the second inlarged the Visage. **1871** Freeman *Norm. Conq.* IV. xviii. 125 That church..had been simply repaired and heightened.

2. To render high or higher in amount or degree; to increase, raise, augment, intensify.

1523 Fitzherb. *Surv.* Prol., That..the owners therof do nat heyghten their rentes of their tenauntes. **1639** Fuller *Holy War* iv. vii. (1647) 180 Men heightened their looking for great matters from him. **1643** Denham *Cooper's H.* 48 In whose face Sate Meekness, heightned with Majestick Grace. **1750** Johnson *Rambler* No. 1 ¶14 It heightens his alacrity to think in how many places he shall hear what he is now writing. **1776** Adam Smith *W.N.* i. ix. (1869) I. 103 It would be necessary to heighten the price. **1853** Soyer *Pantroph.* 93 The leaves of wormwood are used in salad to ..heighten the flavour. **1876** Tait *Rec. Adv. Phys. Sc.* vi. (ed. 2) 135 The boiling point of water is heightened by pressure.

b. To augment in description.

1731 Swift *Answ. Simile* Wks. 1755 IV. 223 Your poets, Chloe's beauty hightning, Compare her radiant eyes to lightning. **1867** Freeman *Norm. Conq.* I. vi. 526 A story, somewhat heightened in details.

3. *spec.* To render (a colour) more luminous: the opposite of to *deepen*. Also sometimes, to render more intense; to deepen.

1622 Peacham *Compl. Gent.* cxiii. (1634) 127 To heighten or deepen [the shadows] as your body appeareth neerer or farther. **1665** R. Hooke *Microgr.* 69 The Red is diluted.. and the Blue heightned. **1756** C. Lucas *Ess. Waters* I. 129 A pink color..is heightened to a crimson. **1799** G. Smith *Laboratory* I. 382 Shade them with deep ochre, and heighten them with masticot and white. **1854** Fairholt *Dict. Terms Art* s.v., To heighten a tint is to make it lighter and more prominent, by means of touches of light opaque colour, placed upon it.

†**4.** To exalt in feeling or condition; to elate, excite. *Obs.*

1604 *Twelve Patriarchs* 83 The single-hearted man.. desireth not shift of apparel, nor heightneth himself long time. **1607** Shaks. *Cor.* v. vi. 22, I rais'd him..who being so heighten'd, He watered his new Plants with dewes of Flattery. *a* **1656** Ussher *Ann.* (1658) 757 Being heighthened with this victory he entred the pallace. **1667** Milton *P.L.* ix. 793 Satiate at length, And hight'nd as with Wine. **1676** Marvell *Mr. Smirke* 71 The people of God did glory and heighten it self in the doing of good things. **1692** O. Walker *Hist. Illustr.* 236 They..made Caracalla Augustus..which so heightned him, that he continually sought to kill his Father.

5. *intr.* To become high or higher; to increase in height; to rise. Now *rare*.

1567 Maplet *Gr. Forest* 32 The Balme tree..heightneth neuer aboue two cubites. **1659** D. Pell *Impr. Sea* 507 The flood hath heightned and carried you off clear. **1832** J. H. Newman *Lett.* (1891) I. 298 As we rode up the carriage-way, the Rock seemed to heighten marvellously.

b. To rise in amount or degree.

1803 [see heightening *ppl. a.*]. **1860** Pusey *Min. Proph.* 238 Obadiah's description heightens as it goes on. **1869** Freeman *Norm. Conq.* III. xi. 9 The public anxiety heightened at every stage of the disorder.

heightened (ˈhaɪt(ə)nd), *ppl. a.* [f. prec. + -ed[1].] Raised, elevated, exalted; elated; increased, augmented; intensified.

1647 Clarendon *Hist. Reb.* i. §67 Without mentioning any particular ground for his so heightened Displeasure. **1701** J. Woodward *Relig. Soc.* iv. 84 Numerous and heightened enormities. *a* **1732** T. Boston *Crook in Lot* (1805) 80 A humbled spirit is better than a heightened condition. **1873** M. Arnold *Lit. & Dogma* (1876) 38 Holiness is but a heightened righteousness.

b. *Her.* (See quot.)

1873 Boutell & Aveling *Heraldry* 159 *Heightened*, having a decorative accessory or another charge placed above or higher in the field.

heightener ('haɪt(ə)nə(r)). [f. as prec. + -ER[1].] One who or that which heightens or intensifies.
a **1656** BP. HALL *Rem. Wks.* (1660) 121 This disappointment is a just heightner of his griefe. **1863** MRS. C. CLARKE *Shaks. Char.* iii. 65 A heightener of his dramatic and poetical effects.

heightening ('haɪt(ə)nɪŋ), *vbl. sb.* [f. as prec. + -ING[1].] The action of the verb HEIGHTEN.

1. Raising, elevation.
1598–9 in Willis & Clark *Cambridge* (1886) II. 486 For the hightning of the greate Tower. **1631** WEEVER *Anc. Fun. Mon.* 428 The heighthening of the ground for garden plots. *a* **1683** OLDHAM *Poems* (1697) 39 (Jod.) You'r low And must some height'ning on the place bestow.

2. *transf.* and *fig.* Augmentation, increase, intensification; exaggeration. Also with *a* and *pl.*: An instance of this; sometimes, a means of augmenting.
1629 DEKKER *Lond. Tempe* Wks. 1873 IV. 119 The Dutch-mans thunder, and the Spaniards lightning, To whom the sulphures breath giues heate and heightning. **1658** *Whole Duty Man* iii. §5 (1673) 28 A great heightning of the Sin. **1752** MRS. LENNOX *Fem. Quix.* I. i, These native charms were improved with all the heightenings of art. **1818** HAZLITT *Eng. Poets* i. (1870) 4 Without the heightenings of the imagination.

b. *spec.* in *Art*: see HEIGHTEN *v.* 3. With *a* and *pl.*: An instance of this; *concr.* the colouring which produces the heightened effect.
1662 EVELYN *Chalcogr.* iv. (R.), Had he performed his heightenings with more tendernesse, and come sweetly off with the extremities of his hatchings. **1700** PEPYS in *Academy* (1890) 6 Sept. 200/3 To..embellish y[e] same with its just Heightenings and Shadowings. **1855** tr. *Labarte's Arts Mid. Ages* iv. 161 A few heightenings of white and gold.

'heightening, *ppl. a.* [f. as prec. + -ING[2].] That heightens (*trans.* and *intr.*): see HEIGHTEN *v.*
1768 BEATTIE *Minstr.* II. xl, To joy each heightening charm it can impart. **1803** JANE PORTER *Thaddeus* ii. (1831) 15 The palatine observed the heightening animation of his features.

heighth, heiȝþe, heigth, obs. ff. HEIGHT.

heih, obs. form of HIGH *a.*

heik, var. HIKE *v.* and *sb.*

||**heil** (haɪl), *int.* [Ger., = hail!] Used in the expression *Heil Hitler!* by the Germans during the Nazi regime. Also *transf.*, and as *sb.* So **heil** *v.*, to give the Nazi salute; **heiled** *ppl. a.* ***ski-heil!***: good skiing!
1927 E. HEMINGWAY *Men without Women* (1928) 182 'Ski-heil!' said the innkeeper. 'Heil!' we said. **1937** *Nation* 31 July 114/2 The weekly scene of heiling. **1937** A. S. NEILL *That Dreadful School* i. 20 In the absence of a government I herewith declare myself Dictator. Heil Neill! **1938** [see CLICK *v.*[1] 2 a]. **1939** *Journal* (Topeka, Kans.) 20 Apr. 1/7 Germany heils Hitler on fiftieth birthday. **1939** S. SPENDER tr. *Toller's Pastor Hall* I. 48 Extending your arm like a crane and yelling, 'Heil Hitler.' **1940** *Time* 15 Apr. 43/1 One of the most widely heiled of German sculptors. **1942** E. WAUGH *Put out More Flags* iii. §5. 234 An obnoxious young man.. said 'Heil Mosley.' **1961** J. HELLER *Catch-22* (1962) xxiii. 241 When the Germans marched into the city, I danced in the streets..and shouted, '*Heil* Hitler!' until my lungs were hoarse. **1965** EVA-LIS WUORIO *Z for Zaborra* vi. v. 175 The man..gave..a sharp salute. 'Leader and blood brother,' he heiled.

heil(e, obs. f. HAIL *a.* and *v.*[2]; Sc. var. HEAL.

heil, obs. form of HEEL.

†**heild,** *v. Sc. Obs.* Also 6 **held.** [Var. of HELE *v.*[2], due to phonetic reduction of *-ld* to *-l* (cf. HEEL *v.*[2]), and consequent writing of *-ld* for original *-l.*]

1. *trans.* To cover; to shield, protect; to hide.
1508 DUNBAR *Tua Mariit Wemen* 14, I was heildit with hawthorne, and with heynd leveis. **1513** DOUGLAS *Æneis* IV. v. 140 His schulderis heildit with new fallin snaw. *Ibid.* X. xiii. 102 Thai cast dartis thikfald thar lord to held. **1550** LYNDESAY *Sq. Mel.* 378 Ane quaif of gold, to heild his hair.

2. *intr.* for *refl.* To take shelter.
1535 STEWART *Cron. Scot.* II. 598 Ane passage wes that tyme quhair he micht heild.

Hence †**heilding (heildyne),** *vbl. sb.*, covering.
15.. *Barbour's Bruce* XVII. 598 Stalwart heildyne aboyne it haid.

heild: see HEAL, HELE, HIELD, HOLD.

heilding, variant of HILDING, *Obs.*

heildom. *nonce-wd.* [Pseudo-archaic, formed by Scott from *heal*, HALE *a.* + -DOM.] Health.
a **1806** SCOTT *Contn. Sir Tristr.* ii, But never thai no might ..Bring Tristrem..To heildom ogayn.

heilesum, obs. var. of HEALSOME.

heill, Sc. var. HEAL, HELE *v.*[2]; obs. f. HEEL.

heilnesse: see HEALNESS.

||**Heilsgeschichte** ('haɪlzgə,ʃɪçtə). *Theol.* [Ger.] Sacred history, *spec.* the history of God's saving work among men; history seen as the working out of God's salvation. So **'heilsgeschichtlich** *a.*
1938 C. H. DODD *History & Gospel* v. 168 The whole of history is in the last resort sacred history, or *Heilsgeschichte.* **1952** G. E. WRIGHT *God who Acts* v. 115 Biblical faith may be treated in such a way as to preserve its history-centred (or as the Germans call it, *heilsgeschichtlich*) nature. **1957** D. M. BAILLIE *Theol. Sacraments* ii. 69 It is bound up with the rediscovery that the Christian message is a *Heilsgeschichte*, a sacred story, running on from eternity through history to eternity again, with Christ as its central and determinative point. **1959** GUTHRIE & HALL tr. *Cullmann's Christology N.T.* i. 9 There can be no *Heilsgeschichte* without Christology; no Christology without a *Heilsgeschichte* which unfolds in time.

†**heily,** *a. Sc. Obs.* Also **helie, -y, hiely.** [prob. identical with OE. *héalíc*: see HIGHLY *a.*] Haughty, proud.
[*a* **1000** *Cædmon's Gen.* 294 His engel..Spræc healic word dollice wið drihten sinne.] **1500–20** DUNBAR *Poems* xxvi. 25 Heilie harlottis on hawtane wyiss Come in with mony sindrie gyiss. **1501** DOUGLAS *Pal. Hon.* III. xxix, Roboam quhilk throw his helie pride, Tint all his leigis hartis. **1513** —— *Æneis* IX. x. 13 Rycht proud and hely [**1553** hiely] in his breist and hart. **1552** ABP. HAMILTON *Catech.* (1884) 63 Thai..that ar in thair wordis prydful, helie, vaine glorious.

heily, obs. form of HIGHLY.

heimin ('heɪmɪn). [Jap., f. *hei* level (horizontal), common + *min* people.] In Japanese society of the feudal period, the common people, including the peasantry, craftsmen, and traders, as contrasted with the court aristocracy and samurai (the warrior class).
1875 *Trans. Asiatic Soc. Japan* (1884) III. II. 104. **1891** A. M. BACON *Jap. Girls & Women* ix. 228 The great héimin class includes not only the peasants of Japan, but also the artisans and merchants. **1904** *Daily Chron.* 30 Mar. 4/5 Of those not Samurai, the heimin, or commoners, the peasantry ranked first. **1904** L. HEARN *Japan: Attempt at Interpretation* xii. 271 The Buddhist (like the Shintō) priests, though forming a class apart, ranked with the samurai, not with the heimin. **1951** D. H. JAMES *Rise & Fall Jap. Empire* iii. 119 The profession of arms, previously the privilege of Samurai, was extended to heimin (commoners).

||**heimisch** ('haɪmɪʃ), *a.* orig. *U.S.* Also **haimish, heimische, heimishe, heymish.** [a. Yiddish *heymish* domestic, homelike.] Homely; unpretentious. Hence **'heimischness,** homeliness.
1964 S. BELLOW *Herzog* (1965) 35 A politician..still found me good company, *heimisch*, and took me along to the races. **1968** L. ROSTEN *Joys of Yiddish* 148 *Haimish, haimisher,..haimisheh,..*informal, cozy,..having the friendly characteristics..that exist inside a happy home,.. unpretentious; putting on no airs... Jews put a high value on being *haimish.* **1970** L. M. FEINSILVER *Taste of Yiddish* II. 111 *Heymish*, homey, friendly, informal. *Ibid.* 279 This conveys the sense of good talk in congenial company—the 'Heymishness' of herd warmth. **1970** 'E. QUEEN' *Last Woman* I. 8, I own..a guest cottage... It's all terribly *heimisch.* **1973** *Times* 3 Feb. 13/4 Another word that may confuse is *heimishe*, which is Yiddish, and means roughly.. home cooking' or 'traditional' cooking. *Ibid.*, The heimishe cooking at Leslie's is only part of a large suburbanized menu.

||**Heimweh** ('haɪmveɪ). [Ger.] Home-sickness.
a **1721** PRIOR *Essay upon Opinion* in *Dialogues of Dead* (1907) 199 The Swiss are remarked to have a Distemper, which they call the Hemvie, a desire of going home, and where ever They are in Service they get leave to return to their Canton at least once in Some Years, and certainly desire to Dye there. **1756, 18..** [see HOME-SICKNESS]. **1845** R. FORD *Handbk. Trav. Spain* II. 695 If debarred a hope of return, they [*sc.* the Asturians] pine from Nostalgia or Heimweh. **1850** GEO. ELIOT *Let.* 9 Feb. (1954) I. 328, I have a little *Heimweh* 'as it regards' my friends. **1912** R. BROOKE *Let.* 24 June (1968) 389 Writing about Grantchester gave me a bit of *Heimweh.* **1920** D. H. LAWRENCE *Let.* in C. Mackenzie *My Life & Times* (1966) V. 170 Heimweh or nostalgia there, for the North. **1971** *Guardian* 25 Nov. 13/4 The *Heimweh* of absences.

||**Heimwehr** ('haɪmvɛə(r)). [Ger., f. *heim* home + *wehr* defence.] Formerly, the German or the Austrian Home Defence Force. Also *attrib.*
1931 *Ann. Reg. 1930* 184 The usual collisions between Heimwehr and Socialists recommenced, in consequence of the revival of the Heimwehr policy of holding provocative marches. **1938** *Times Lit. Suppl.* 15 Jan. 34/4 A *Heimwehr* officer in the late twenties. **1939** *War Illustr.* 2 Dec. 384/2 Prince von Starhemberg, formerly leader of the Austrian Heimwehr, has been deprived of German citizenship. **1957** *Times Lit. Suppl.* 20 Dec. 771/4 He was later in charge of several *Heimwehr* newspapers—the organs of Austrian Fascism.

heind, obs. pl. of HAND; var. HEND *a. Obs.*

Heinesque (haɪ'nɛsk), *a.* [f. the name of H. *Heine* (1799–1856), German poet + -ESQUE.] Of, pertaining to, or resembling the style of Heine.
? **1892** E. DOWSON *Let.* ?Jan. (1967) 222 Where would appreciation of the Heinesque style come in? **1899** *Academy* 24 June 677/1 A grimly tragic vignette of peasant life, with a Heinesque turn at the close. **1907** *Daily Chron.* 2 Aug. 3/3 His Heinesque moods are steeled through with a strong man's virility. **1915–16** *Musical Assoc. Proc.* 158 Beethoven is never sinister, never even Heinesque, if I may use the word.

Heinie ('haɪnɪ). *N. Amer. slang.* Also **Heine, Hiney.** [f. the German Christian name *Heinrich.*] A German (soldier).
1904 'No. 1500' *Life in Sing Sing* xiii. 249/1 *Hiney*, a German. **1917** *Daily Chron.* 25 Aug. 1/7 The Canadians call their enemy Heine and not Fritz. **1918** *Daily Mirror* 12 Nov. 6/4 An Irish terrier of my acquaintance was perfectly certain that the maroons meant a visit from Heinie. **1925** FRASER & GIBBONS *Soldier & Sailor Words, Heine* (or *Hiney*). **1929** E. W. SPRINGS *Above Bright Blue Sky* 227 'There, you're all right,' the sergeant soothed him. 'Those yellow-bellied Heinies can't kill you. We got ten of 'em this morning.' **1931** [see DUTCHMAN 1 a]. **1961** *Listener* 20 Apr. 684/1 It's not the Russians we should be congratulating..but the Heinies. Sure, we got Von Braun, but the Russians grabbed all the rest of the German rocket guys.

heinous ('heɪnəs), *a.* Forms: 4–8 **heynous,** 5 **-nȝous, -nos, heneus,** 5–7 **haynous(e,** 5–9 **hainous,** 6 **h(e)yghnous(e, heighnous, heynouse, hanouse, hainus,** 6– **heinous.** [a. F. *haineux*, in OF. *haïnos, haïneus* (12th c. in Hatz.-Darm.), f. *haine* hatred, f. *ha-ïr* to hate.]

1. Hateful, odious; highly criminal or wicked; infamous, atrocious: chiefly characterizing offences, crimes, sins, and those who commit them.
c **1374** CHAUCER *Troylus* II. 1568 (1617) So heynous þat men myghte on it spete. *c* **1489** CAXTON *Blanchardyn* liv. 215 To kill a man is hainous murder. **1512** *Act 4 Hen. VIII*, c. 2 Preamble, Felonies..don in more heynous open & detestable wyse. **1513** MORE *Rich. III*, Wks. 54/1 Worthye to bee punished as heighnous traitors. **1529** —— *Dyaloge* III. Ibid. 209/2 The more heyghnouse, odiouse, & abhominable that the crime is, the more slow should we be to beleue it. **1549** CHEKE *Hurt Sedit.* (1641) 52 Set murther aside, it is the hainousest fault to a private man. **1555** W. WATREMAN *Fardle Facions* II. ix. 192 Thei compted none offence more heinous then thefte. **1648** *Shorter Catech. Westm. Assemb.* (1718), *Q.* 83. Are all Transgressions of the Law equally hainous? *A.* Some Sins in themselves, and by reason of several aggravations, are more hainous in the sight of God than others. **1667** MILTON *P.L.* X. 1 The hainous and despightfull act Of Satan done in Paradise. **1683** *Col. Rec. Pennsylv.* I. 87 A Heynous and Grevious Crime. **1705** STANHOPE *Paraphr.* II. 436 The Heinousest of Malefactors. **1772** *Junius Lett.* lxviii. 357 You are guilty of a heinous aggravation of your offence. **1845** R. JEBB in *Encycl. Metrop.* II. 710/1 Heinous offenders, whose crimes afford proof of an incorrigibly bad disposition. **1869** FREEMAN *Norm. Conq.* III. xii. 251 A sin of the most heinous dye.

b. *transf.* from crimes or offences to the accusation or charge, or view taken of them.
1548 HALL *Chron., Hen. VI*, 167 b, Against whom..wer laied diverse and heinous articles of high treason. **1555** in Strype *Eccl. Mem.* (1721) III. App. xlvi. 138 Who had..just and heynouse matter agaynst theym. **1818** SCOTT *Hrt. Midl.* ii, Contraband trade..is not usually looked upon..in a very heinous point of view. **1875** STUBBS *Const. Hist.* III. xviii. 148 The greater and more heinous charges included in the first bill.

†**2.** Grievous, grave, severe. *Obs.*
1541 R. COPLAND *Guydon's Quest. Chirurg.*, To clense the blode of haynous superfluytees. **1552** LATIMER *Serm. & Rem.* (1845) 54 It shall be a heinous sentence unto them, when he shall say unto them..'Go, ye cursed, into everlasting fire'. **1645** MILTON *Tetrach.* (1851) 225 These men.. will suffer the worst and hainousest inconveniences to follow. **1675** BROOKS *Gold. Key* Wks. 1867 V. 200 That the sufferings of Christ have been..very great and heinous.

†**3.** Expressing or denoting hatred; full of hate, malicious. *Obs.*
? *a* **1400** *Morte Arth.* 268 [He] said what hym lykyde, Hethely in my halle, wyth heynȝous wordes. *a* **1547** SURREY *Æneid* II. 92 To wreke Their hainous wrath wyth shedyng of my bloud. **1578** T. N. tr. *Conq. W. India* 264 The heinous and injurious words which he had heard. **1580** SIDNEY *Arcadia* I. (1590) 49 Which hee..tooke in so hainous maner.

heinously ('heɪnəslɪ), *adv.* [f. prec. + -LY[2].]

1. In a heinous manner or degree; hatefully, odiously; atrociously, infamously.
c **1440** *York Myst.* xxviii. 294 Euen like a theffe heneusly. *a* **1529** SKELTON *Poems agst. Garnesche* 144 Your brethe..so haynously doth stynke. **1598** HAKLUYT *Voy.* I. 56 She answered, that she had rather die, then so haynously transgresse the law. **1670** BAXTER *Cure Ch. Div.* Pref. III. §5 When God hath been so heinously dishonoured by it.

†**2.** Grievously, severely, sorely; esp. in phr. ***to take heinously***: to take in ill part, to be grievously offended at. *Obs.* **b.** In late use, as a strong intensive: Very badly, shockingly, dreadfully.
1552 LATIMER *Serm. & Rem.* (1845) 24 God will plague and most heinously punish them. **1632** BROME *Northern Lasse* I. vii. Wks. 1873 III. 19 Tell your Cuz how hainously I take it. **1649** MILTON *Eikon.* 43 Lest the Parlament.. might have resented too hainously his doings. **1663** COWLEY *Cutter Coleman St.* IV. vi, I'm hainously mistaken if thou beest not cheated of it within these three Years. **1709** STEELE *Tatler* No. 50 ¶7 Lest you should think your self neglected, which I have Reason to believe you would take heinously ill. **1792** COWPER *Let.* 10 Mar., I told you..how heinously I am unprovided with the means of being so. **1826** SCOTT *Woodst.* iii, They are heinously impoverished.

'heinousness. [f. as prec. + -NESS.] The state or quality of being heinous; extreme wickedness, infamousness, atrociousness.
1563 *Homilies* II. *Repentance* II. (1859) 537 Sorrow and grief..for the heinousness of sin. *a* **1653** GOUGE *Comm. Heb.* x. 26 The heighnousnesse of Apostacy. **1716** ADDISON *Freeholder* No. 20 (1751) 112 To extenuate the Hainousness of the Rebellion. **1875** JOWETT *Plato* (ed. 2) V. 181 The heinousness of offences is apt to depend on accidental circumstances.

†**heinsby.** *Obs. rare.* ? = HAYNE *sb.*[1], mean wretch, niggard.

1546 J. HEYWOOD *Prov.* (1867) 31 Men say also, children and fooles can not ly. And both man and child saieth, he is a heinsby.

heintzite ('haɪntsaɪt). *Min.* [ad. G. *heintzit* (O. Luedecke 1890, in *Zeitschr. f. Kryst. und Min.* XVIII. 485), f. the name of W. H. *Heintz* (1817–80), German chemist: see -ITE[1].] A borate of potassium and magnesium, at first also called HINTZEITE and now regarded as the same as kaliborite.

1891 *Jrnl. Chem. Soc.* LX. I. 528 For the new borate, Milch proposes the name of *hintzeite*, after Professor Hintze, of Breslau; whilst Luedecke proposes that of *heintzite*, after Heintz, the discoverer of pinnoite. **1892** *Ibid.* LXII. II. 791 The author [*sc.* O. Luedecke]..admits that the chemical composition of kaliborite and heintzite is practically identical, both containing about the same percentage of boric acid, potash, magnesia, and water. This does not, however, prove them to be the same mineral. Whilst kaliborite occurs in badly-formed, crystalline crusts on the surface of pinnoïte, heintzite, which is found on the inside, forms well-made crystals with shining faces, and is readily cleavable in three directions. **1951** C. PALACH et al. *Dana's Syst. Min.* (ed. 7) II. 368 Heintzite (and hintzeite, the two names being proposed simultaneously for the mineral) was later shown to be identical with kaliborite.

heir (ɛə(r)), *sb.* Forms: α. 3–4 eir(e, 3–5 eyr, ayr, 3–7 air, 4 eier, ere, eeyre, 4–5 eyre, 4–6 ayre, aire, are, 5 ayer, 5–6 eyer. β. 4–7 heire, 4– heir (also 4 hair, 4–5 heyr, hayre, 4–6 haire, here, 4–7 heyre, 5 hoir, heyer, 5–7 heier, 6 heire, hayer, *Sc.* hear). [ME. *eir, eyr*, etc., a. OF. *eir, heir* (central Fr. *oir*, later *hoir*) later AFr. *heyr* (Britton) = Pr. *her*:— late L. *hērem* (found beside *hērēdem*) from nom. *hēres* heir.]

1. a. The person who is entitled by law to succeed another in the enjoyment of property or rank, upon the death of the latter; one who so succeeds; in general use, one who receives or is entitled to receive property of any kind as the legal representative of a former owner.

The word is correctly applied to either a male or a female, although, in the latter sense, HEIRESS has been in general use since 17th c. In *Law* a person is not called an heir to any property until, through the death of its possessor, he becomes entitled to it (*nemo est heres viventis*). As to the limitations of the word in Common Law and in the Civil Law and systems founded thereon, see quots. 1651, 1861, 1876.

c **1275** LAY. 23115 Þat þe king of Cisille his dead and eyr naueþ he nanne. **1297** R. GLOUC. (1724) 469 Henri is eldoste sone, & is eir al so. *a* **1300** *Cursor M.* 2565 He þin ere [*v.rr.* ayr(e] sal noght be. *c* **1300** *Beket* 24 For the Princes heir heo was. **13..** *E.E. Allit. P.* B. 52 To marie his here dere. *Ibid.* 666 Sende to Sare a soun & an hayre. *c* **1330** R. BRUNNE *Chron.* (1810) 56 Com Edward, Eilred sonne..Right heyre of þe lond. *c* **1380** *Sir Ferumb.* 3483 He ys myn ayr after my ded To broke myn heritage. **1382** WYCLIF *Matt.* xxi. 38 This is the eire; cume ȝe, slea we hym. *c* **1386** CHAUCER *Man of Law's T.* 668 Crist whan him lust may sende me an hair [*v.rr.* heir(e, haire, eyr]. **1417** *Surtees Misc.* (1888) 12 Thomas Duffeld sonne and ayre unto Richard Duffeld Esquier. *c* **1475** *Partenay* 5554 Disherite shall be your hoires manyfold. **1475** *Bk. Noblesse* 2 Dame Maude, Emperes, soule doughter and heire to..Henry the first. *c* **1510** MORE *Picus* Wks. 9/1 The heyre of his landes he made the poore people of the hospitall of Florence. **1556** LAUDER *Tractate* 520 The better is ȝouris, Ȝour Hearis, and als ȝour Successouris. **1582–8** *Hist. Jas. VI* (1804) 200 The aires of the Lord Fleeming..and utheris that were slaine. **1590** SPENSER *F.Q.* I. ii. 23 The onely haire Of a most mighty king. **1634** SIR T. HERBERT *Trav.* 133 Fatima, daughter and heire of their greatest Prophet Mahomet. **1651** G. W. tr. *Cowel's Inst.* 128 The Civillians and wee have a different acceptation of the word Heire; for they call him an Heir whom the Testator nominates in his Will: And we him, who is next of Kin to the party deceased, to whom a Fee doth of right belong, after the death of the Ancestor. *a* **1693** LD. DELAMER *Wks.* (1694) 95 For this word Heir to the Crown was not heard of till Arbitrary Power began to put forth. **1712** *Lond. Gaz.* No. 5009/4 Sarah Lewis..Heir to the said Rebecca Warren. **1756–7** tr. *Keysler's Trav.* (1760) III. 53 The heirs of the founder being, by his will, obliged to have it twice a year carefully cleaned. **1767** BLACKSTONE *Comm.* II. xiv. 201 An heir..is he upon whom the law casts the estate immediately on the death of the ancestor. *Ibid.* 208 By law no inheritance can vest, nor can any person be the actual complete heir of another, till the ancestor is previously dead ..Before that time the person who is next in the line of succession is called an heir apparent, or heir presumptive. **1828** J. JEKYLL *Corr.* (1894) 177 The prospect..of Lady Ellenborough presenting him with a heir or a heiress. **1841** ELPHINSTONE *Hist. Ind.* I. 29 On failure of heirs, the property of others escheats to the King. **1861** W. BELL *Dict. Law Scotl.* s.v., The term heir does not mean merely the heir-at-law; it means also the heir by destination; nor does it mean the heir in heritage only; it is likewise applied to the person who succeeds to the moveable estate. **1876** DIGBY *Real Prop.* x. 385 *note*, The word 'heir' in English law has a sense far more limited than the word 'haeres' in Roman law. The 'heir' is the person on whom the real estate of a deceased intestate devolves. He is opposed to the devisee who is the person to whom real property is left by will, and to the executor or administrator who succeed to the personal estate.

b. With qualifications:

heir-at-law: the person who succeeds another by right of blood in the enjoyment of his property; in English law confined to one who has such a right in real property, and distinguished from executors or administrators. ***heir of blood***: see quot. 1658. ***heir of the body***: an heir who is a direct descendant: see BODY *sb.* 12b. ***heir in capite***: the heir to land held directly of the sovereign. ***heir of conquest*** (Sc. Law): the heir of an ancestor who acquired the estate in question by purchase and not by succession (see CONQUEST *sb.* 6). ***heir by custom***: one who succeeds by virtue of a particular or local custom, *e.g.* Borough English, under which the youngest son succeeds his father. ***heir-designate***, one who has been designated as a person's heir. ***heir by destination*** (Sc. Law): 'the person who is entitled to succeed, failing the person to whom an estate is disponed' (Bell *Dict. Law Scotl.*). ***heir by devise***: 'he who is made, by will, the testator's heir or devisee, and has no other right or interest than the will gives him' (Wharton *Law Lex.*). ***heir of entail*** = *heir in tail*. ***heir female***: an heiress; also an heir (male or female) whose rights are derived through a female or females. ***heir general*** = *heir-at-law*: used to include heirs female as well as heirs male. ***heir of inheritance***: see quot. 1658 s.v. *heir of blood*. ***heir of inventory*** (Sc. Law) = *beneficiary heir* (see below). ***heir of line*** (Sc. Law) = *heir-at-law*. ***heir male***: an heir who is a male, and who traces his descent from the ancestor in question wholly through males. ***heir portioner*** (Sc. Law): see quots. ***heir of provision*** = *heir by destination*. ***heir presumptive***: he who, if the ancestor should die immediately, would be his heir, but whose right of inheritance may be defeated by the contingency of some nearer heir being born. ***heir special***: (*a*) = *heir by custom*; (*b*) one to whom an estate passes by virtue of letters patent or a deed of entail. ***heir in tail*** (Sc. *of entail, of tailȝie*): the person who succeeds or is entitled to succeed to an entailed estate by virtue of the deed of entail; tenant in tail in remainder. See also HEIR-APPARENT.

beneficiary heir (Sc. Law): an apparent heir in heritage who enters upon his predecessor's estate subject to a formal inventory being made, in order to avoid liability for debts beyond the amount stated in such inventory. ***collateral heir***: see COLLATERAL *a.* 4. ***conventional heir***: one who is entitled by virtue of a contract. ***forced heir*** (Civ. Law): a person who cannot be disinherited. ***last heir***: see quot. 1607. ***right heir*** = *heir-at-law*.

1729 JACOB *Law Dict.* s.v. *Discent*, If he devise Lands to one who is *Heir at Law, the Devise is void, and he shall take by Discent. **1858** BRIGHT *Sp. Reform* 27 Oct., If a man received landed property..as heir-at-law it paid no legacy duty. **1853** *Bouvier's Law Dict.* s.v., *Beneficiary heirs are those who have accepted the succession, under the benefit of an inventory regularly made. **1658** PHILLIPS, **Heire of Blood* in Common Law, is he who succeedeth by right of blood in any mans Lands or Tenements in fee, but heir of Inheritance is he that cannot be defeated of his inheritance upon any displeasure. **1439** *E.E. Wills* (1882) 125 And if he die withouten *heire of his body, then to Rauf his brother, and his issue. *a* **1626–1788** [see BODY *sb.* 12b]. **1883** *Wharton's Law Lex.* (ed. 7) s.v. *Tail*, An estate granted to a man and the heirs of his body should descend to the issue. **1839** KEIGHTLEY *Hist. Eng.* I. 131 The *heir 'in capite', on coming of age was bound to take Knighthood or pay a fine to the King. **1909** *Daily Chron.* 6 Sept. 3/3 Her relatives, *heirs-designate of Charles Dorrien in the scrap of paper lying in his widow's writing-desk. **1961** B. FERGUSSON *Watery Maze* xii. 311 The meeting in Carthage on Christmas Day, with Churchill presiding, and Eisenhower and Wilson as his heir-designate. **1861** W. BELL *Dict. Law Scotl.* 806/2 An *heir of entail in possession was empowered to disentail the estate. *c* **1575** *Balfour's Practicks* (1754) 227 Ane *air male or female may enter to his blanch landis at ony time. **1611** COTGR., *Hoir de quenouille*, an inheritrix, heire female, daughter and heire. *a* **1674** CLARENDON *Hist. Reb.* XIV. §113 Having lately fallen to Heirs Females. **1491** *Act 7 Hen. VII*, c. 15 She was *heire generall to John Mountagu late Erle of Salesbury. *c* **1575** *Balfour's Practicks* (1754) 232 The ȝounger brother-german..sould be servit and retourit air general or universal to him, and not the elder. *a* **1715** BURNET *Own Time* I. 458 In England, Spain and Sweeden, the heir general did succeed: whereas it was only the heir male in France and Germany. **1791** BOSWELL *Johnson* Jan. an. 1776, My father had declared a predilection for heirs-general, that is, males and females indiscriminately. **1873** DIXON *Two Queens* IV. XIX. v. 31 All parties in the suit.. should know which lands were settled on the heirs male, which on the heirs general. **1607** COWELL *Interpr.* (1672), **Last heyre*..Is he to whom Land comes by Escheat, for want of lawful Heirs, that is, the Lord of whom they held in some cases, but in others the King. *c* **1575** *Balfour's Practicks* (1754) 325 The *airis of line..sould be first warnit and discussit..befoir the airis of tailȝie. **1888** MISS LEE *Imperf. Gentl.* I. 59 John Scudamore, heir of line of that Sir Alan Scudamore..who married Joan. **1375** BARBOUR *Bruce* xx. 130 Ȝif it fell that his sone davy Deit but [= without] *air male of his body Gottyn. **1463** *Bury Wills* (Camden) 24 To him and to his eyris male. **1697** LUTTRELL *Brief Rel.* (1857) IV. 172 He cutting of the entail from the heirs males. **1814** SCOTT *Wav.* lxiv, From a romantic idea of not prejudicing this young man's right as heir-male. **1655** in Z. Boyd *Zion's Flowers* (1855) App. 29/2 The *Airs portioners of umquhile Mr. Zacharie Boyd. **1838** *Erskine's Inst. Law Scotl.* 834 Each heir-portioner has an equal interest in the succession, in so far as it is divisable. **1628** LE GRYS tr. *Barclay's Argenis* 334 The souldier..with a new oath bound himselfe to the *presumptiue heir. **1683** *Brit. Spec.* 272 Apparent (or according to the new-coyned Distinction, Presumptive) Heir of the Crown is His Royal Highness James [etc.] **1875** STUBBS *Const. Hist.* III. xviii. 202 The duke of Clarence, the heir-presumptive to the throne. [*c* **1180** GLANVILL IX. i, Recipere homagium recti heredis.] *c* **1330** R. BRUNNE *Chron.* (1810) 56 Hardeknoute's broþer on his moder side, *Right heyre of þe lond. **1411** in *E.E. Wills* (1882) 20 And for defawte of issue of þe forseyd William, y wille þat þe remaynder be to my ryte heirs. **1628** COKE *On Litt.* 8b, For the benefit and safety of right heires. **1872** *Spectator* 21 Sept. 1203 *Laissez-faire* management, supineness because of the interest of the *heir-in-tail. *c* **1575** *Balfour's Practicks* (1754) 325 The *airis of tailȝie may be callit and persewit in supplement. **1685** *Sc. Acts Jas. II*, c. 26 It shall not be Lawfull to the Airs of Tailȝie to sell annalȝie or Dispone the said Lands.

2. *transf.* One who possesses, or is entitled at some future time to possess, any gift, endowment, or quality in succession to another. The idea of succession is very often lost, so that the word frequently means little more than one to whom something (*e.g.* joy, punishment, etc.) is morally due.

a **1300** *Cursor Mundi* 23555 For þai ar airs al wit[h] crist. **1426** AUDELAY *Poems* 12 Ayres of heven blys. **1548–9** (Mar.) *Bk. Com. Prayer, Priv. Bapt.*, By the lauer of regeneracion in Baptisme, made the childe of God, and heire of euerlastyng life. **1602** SHAKS. *Ham.* III. i. 63 The Heart-ake, and the thousand Naturall shockes That Flesh is heyre too. **1703** POPE *Thebais* 31 Thou, great Heir of all thy father's fame. **1820** BYRON *Mar. Fal.* IV. ii. 314 Such examples will find heirs. **1836** J. GILBERT *Chr. Atonem.* i. (1852) 19 Before the first born of the human race became the heir of failure and of its bitter fruits. **1842** TENNYSON *Locksley Hall* 178, I the heir of all the ages, in the foremost files of time. **1873** HAMERTON *Intell. Life* VII. v. (1876) 250 Heirs of a nobility of spirit.

†**3.** *fig.* That which is begotten; offspring; product. *Obs.*

1413 *Pilgr. Sowle* (Caxton) I. xv. (1859) 12, I am adredde lest charyte be dede, withouten heyer, or yssue of hir seed. **1593** SHAKS. *Ven. & Ad.* Ded., Dedicating my unpolishd lines to your Lordship..But if the first heire of my inuention proue deformed, I shall be sorry it had so noble a God-Father.

heir, *v.* [f. prec. sb.] **a.** *trans.* To inherit; to be heir to (a thing or person); to acquire by inheritance or succession.

c **1330** R. BRUNNE *Chron. Wace* (Rolls) 13483 Þey wonne þe londes þat we now heyre. *c* **1611** CHAPMAN *Iliad* v. 161 Not one son more To heir his goods. **1639** G. DANIEL *Ecclus.* xl. 49 His Children shall but heir him; vnto them Shall be noe Sons. **1703** POPE *Thebais* 544 Two fair daughters heir'd his state and throne. **1813** SCOTT *Trierm.* II. xvii, She is the loveliest maid, beside, That ever heir'd a crown. **1867** J. B. ROSE *Æneid* 13 Pygmalion, her brother, heired the throne.

fig. *c* **1611** CHAPMAN *Iliad* To Rdr. 149 No tongue hath the Muse's utterance heir'd. **1715–20** POPE *Iliad* XVI. 223 The son confess'd his father's heavenly race, And heir'd his mother's swiftness in the chase.

b. *intr.* To inherit. *rare.*

1900 J. HASTINGS *Dict. of Bible* III. 270 The younger brother, instead of himself heiring, raises up heirs to the deceased.

heir, -e, obs. ff. HAIR, HAIRE, HER *sb.*, HERE *sb.*, HERE *adv.*, HIGHER.

†**heirage.** *Sc. Obs.* In 5 herage. Inheritance, succession.

1478 *Act. Dom. Conc.* 15 (Jam.) Ony accioun that outher of thaim has again other for herage of landis.

heir apparent. Formerly also **apparent heir.** [See APPARENT *a.* 4.] The heir (of one still alive) whose right is indefeasible, provided he outlives his ancestor, at whose death he is *heir-at-law*.

1375, 1494–1711 [see APPARENT *a.* 4]. **1530** PALSGR. 230/1 Heyre apparaunt, *monsievr*. **1555** BRADFORD in Strype *Eccl. Mem.* (1721) III. App. xlv. 131 Thoughe the Quene.. disheryt the right heyres apparant. **1614** SELDEN *Titles Hon.* 168 A designation..of the next Apparant Heire or successor. **1765** BLACKSTONE *Comm.* I. iv. 223 The prince of Wales, or heir apparent to the crown. **1844** WILLIAMS *Real Prop.* (1877) 96 A man may have an heir apparent, or an heir presumptive, but until his decease he has no heir.

attrib. **1596** SHAKS. *1 Hen. IV*, II. ii. 46 Go hang thy selfe in thine owne heire-apparant-Garters.

Hence **heir-a'pparency, heir-a'pparentish** *a.*, **heir-a'pparentship** *nonce-wds.*

1858 CARLYLE *Fredk. Gt.* VII. iv. II. 284 Cannot you renounce the Heir-Apparentship, then? **1882** H. C. MERIVALE *Faucit of B.* I. iv, To keep him out of his elder's heir-apparentish influence.

heirby, obs. Sc. form of HEREBY *adv.*

heird(e, obs. forms of HERD *sb.*

heirdom ('ɛədəm). [f. HEIR *sb.* + -DOM.] Succession by right of blood; the state or dignity of an heir; inheritance; an inheritance.

1597–8 BP. HALL *Sat.* IV. iii, Or if..Thy wealthy heirdom thou haue buried. **1645** *Sacred Decretal* 13 [We] wisely converted the purchase of their blood..even to the heirdome of Sir Johns. **1790** BURKE *Fr. Rev.* 30 Whether the heir *per capita* gave way when the heirdom *per stirpes* took place, or the Catholic heir when the Protestant was preferred. **1831** *Crayons fr. Commons* 103 That Duke, the foremost of his peers Who draws his heirdom from a thousand years. **1841** LONGF. *Childr. Lord's Supper* 125 To the heirdom of heaven be ye welcome.

heireftir, obs. Sc. form of HEREAFTER *adv.*

heiress ('ɛərɪs). [f. HEIR *sb.* + -ESS. Introduced app. in 17th c.] A female heir. Also *fig.*

1659 B. HARRIS *Parival's Iron Age* 14 The Heiress of the house of York. *Ibid.* 84 His first wife was the Princesse, who was heiresse to Sexan. **1690** EVELYN *Diary* 20 Dec., One Johnson, a knight, was executed at Tyburn for being an accomplice with Campbell..in stealing a young heiress. **1749** FIELDING *Tom Jones* XIV. v, [He] would have had us consider ourselves as highly as if we had been the richest heiresses. **1769** BLACKSTONE *Comm.* IV. xv. 208 Their forcible abduction and marriage; which is vulgarly called stealing an heiress. **1878** B. TAYLOR *Deukalion* I. iii, Heiress of gifts interpreted as woe.

b. *Comb.*, as ***heiress-hunting***, ***-portioner***, etc.

1861 W. BELL *Dict. Law Scotl.* s.v. *Executors*, Heiresses-portioners who succeed *ab intestato* to equal portions..of the heritable estate. **1886** BARING-GOULD *Crt. Royal* I. vii. 111 He must go about the country heiress-hunting.

Hence '**heiresshood, -ship** (*nonce-wds.*), the state or position of an heiress.

1862 T. A. TROLLOPE *Marietta* I. 78 This heiress-ship was known to be a very important matter. **1884** MRS.

Houstoun *Caught in Snare* II. viii. 98 The fact of her heiresshood. **1889** Mrs. Oliphant *Poor Gentl.* III. vi. 109 Mab with her heiress-ship had been thrown at his head.

heiretrice: see HERETRIX.

heirfoir, -fra, obs. Sc. ff. HEREFORE, -FROM *adv.*

heirie, heyre, var. of AIRE *sb.* and *v. Obs.* = AERIE; esp. a swan's breeding-place.

[**1250** *Concher Bk. of Selby* (Yorks. Rec. Soc.) I. 267 Unam haeram cignorum.. in stagno suo, viz. duos cignos haerarias veteres cum sequela sua.] **1552** *Will of Claymonde* (Somerset Ho.), The swannes heyres & Singnetts. *c* **1560** *Order for Swans* in *Arch. Inst. Lincoln* (1850) 306 Such ground where any swan shall heiry. *Ibid.* 309 If any Heirie be leyed with one Swan. *Ibid.*, When they do heire.

heiriff, dial. var. of HAIRIF.

heirless ('ɛəlɪs), *a.* [f. HEIR *sb.* + -LESS.] Without an heir.

a. Of persons: Having no one to succeed in the enjoyment of property or title.

c **1425** Wyntoun *Cron.* IV. ii. 20 Mony by rycht lyne deyd ayrles. **1845** Costello *Valley of Meuse* 119 Albert of Moha, heirless and broken in spirit. **1892** T. A. Cook *Old Touraine* I. 110 The heirless Duke of Orleans.

b. Of things: Having no one to inherit them on the death of the present possessor.

1611 Shaks. *Wint. T.* v. i. 10 Heire-lesse it hath made my Kingdome. **1739** G. Ogle *Gualth. & Gris.* 54 To feast on Heirless Crowns with eager Views. **1881** Palgrave *Vis. Eng.* 233 Mine, an heirless sceptre: His, an exile life!

heirloom ('ɛəlu:m). Forms: see HEIR, LOOM; also 6 **hare-, earlome (ayrlime)**. [f. HEIR *sb.* + LOOM tool, utensil.] A chattel that, under a will, settlement, or local custom, follows the devolution of real estate. Hence, Any piece of personal property that has been in a family for several generations.

[**1424** *E.E. Wills* (1882) 56, I wull he haue my grete maser þe which I call ȝele, for þe terme of his life, and so from heir to heyr lome]. **1472** *Wolley Charter* (B.M.) ix. 49 In allowance and recompence of all the heir lomes and of all other goodes that he demaunded of in the right of.. his father. **1513** *Test. Ebor.* (Surtees) V. 39, I will that my best standyng maser.. and my best salt.. remayne evermore for heyerlomys to the heire male. **1526** *Lanc. Wills* (Chetham Soc.) I. 21 That my son Thomas have all heyr lomes that of right after the custome and usage of the shyre of Chester belongeth to hym to have. **1569** *Ibid.* II. 251 One standinge cuppe of silver.. wheare upon ys graven this word earlome. **1569** *Wills & Inv. N.C.* (Surtees 1835) 309 That the standinge bed in yᵉ perler wᵗʰ a trendell bed and a longsetle shall remayne styll vnto him as ayrlimes. **1628** Coke *On Litt.* 18 b, In some places chattels as heirloomes (as the best bed, table, pot, pan, cart, and other dead chattels moveable) may go to the heire. **1765** Blackstone *Comm.* II. xxviii. 427 Heir-looms are such goods and personal chattels, as, contrary to the nature of chattels, shall go by special custom to the heir along with the inheritance. **1777** Sheridan *Sch. Scand.* III. iii, Learning that had run in the family like an heirloom! *c* **1820** S. Rogers *Italy, Ginevra* 240 Alone it hangs Over a mouldering heir-loom its companion, An oaken-chest half eaten by the worms. **1872** Jenkinson *Guide Eng. Lakes* (1879) 126 A glass cup, called.. 'The Luck of Muncaster'.. is carefully preserved as a precious heirloom, and a harbinger of the family's fortunes.

b. *fig.* Anything inherited from a line of ancestors, or handed down from generation to generation.

1612 Drayton *Poly-olb.* xi. (R.), He [Edward the Confessor].. obtain'd by earnest pray'r, This tumour by a king might cured be alone: Which he an heir-loom left unto the English throne. **1834** L. Ritchie *Wand. by Seine* 187 The name of a town, a village, or hamlet, is an heir-loom inherited from our ancestors. **1875** Stubbs *Const. Hist.* III. xxi. 592 Political wisdom is the heirloom of no one class of society.

heirof, obs. Sc. form of HEREOF *adv.*

heirship ('ɛəʃɪp). [f. HEIR *sb.* + -SHIP.]

1. The state, condition, or rights of an heir; right of inheritance; inheritance.

1478 [see 2]. *c* **1575** *Balfour's Practicks* (1754) 231 Gif he hes takin or ressavit airschip of ony movabill gudis pertening to his predecessour. **1691** Wood *Ath. Oxon.* I. 224 He came into England, purposely to resign up his Heirship of his Estate at Sherburn. **1757** W. Thompson *R.N. Advoc.* 56 They are reported to have been.. driven from their.. legal Heirship. **1884** Chitty in *Law Rep.* 26 Ch. Div. 546 The only heirship there referred to was the heirship to the Earldom.

b. *fig.* (Cf. *heritage*.)

1697 C. Leslie *Snake in Grass* (ed. 2) 210 To set up their Heirship to any Kingdom they please; when their King (the Son of God) Commands them. **1816** Byron *Parisina* xiii, I could not claim The lawful heirship of thy name. **1833** Medwin in *Fraser's Mag.* VII. 33 What is the lot of man But misery?—'tis the heirship of his birth.

†**2.** ***heirship movables, goods*** (*Sc. Law*), the best of certain kinds of movable goods (such as furniture, horses, cows, farming utensils, etc.), belonging to his predecessor, which the heir was entitled to take besides the heritable estate. *Obs.* (The right was abolished in 1868 by Act 31–2 Vict. c. 101.)

1478 *Act. Dom. Conc.* 15 (Jam.) Ony accioun.. for herage of landis, or movable gudis of areschip pertening to ane are. *c* **1575** *Balfour's Practicks* (1754) 236 Ane bastard may not be ane air, nor crave airschip gudis. *a* **1646** Sir T. Hope *Minor Practicks* (1734) 538. **1838** *Erskine's Inst. Law Scotland* 834 The heirship-movables fall also to the eldest [heir-portioner] alone. **1861** W. Bell *Dict. Law Scot.* 421 *Heirship Moveables* are the moveables to which the heir in heritage is entitled, in order that he may not succeed to a house and land completely dismantled.

heirship, var. of HERSHIP *Obs.*, devastation.

heise, variant of HEEZE *v.*, to hoist.

Heisenberg ('haɪzənbɜ:g). The name of Werner *Heisenberg* (b. 1901), German physicist, used esp. with reference to his matrix theory of quantum mechanics, and to the 'uncertainty principle' deduced by him in 1927.

1932 W. T. Stace *Theory of Knowl. & Existence* xiv. 381 Heisenberg's Principle of Indeterminacy.. lays it down that an electron may have a determinate position or a determinate velocity, *but not both.* **1951** *Physical Rev.* LXXXII. 922/1 Note that these Schrödinger equations have been obtained from the Heisenberg picture. **1955** W. Pauli *Niels Bohr* 38 We.. restrict ourselves to the discussion of the field operators (Heisenberg-representation). **1965** Phillips & Williams *Inorg. Chem.* I. i. 3 As this [*sc.* wave mechanics] provides a relatively simple method of representing atoms and molecules in pictorial terms, we use it in preference to such alternatives as Heisenberg's matrix mechanics which can be shown to be equivalent. **1968** *Peace News* 18 Oct. 6/3 A kind of Heisenberg effect which is far more serious than anything in the physical or biological sciences: the very act of observation distorts that which is being observed. **1968** J. J. C. Smart *Betw. Sci. & Philos.* 12 Some scientific results (Heisenberg's uncertainty principle, for example) do *not* bear on the problem of free will.

heist (haɪst). *slang* (orig. *U.S.*). [Repr. U.S. local pronunc. of HOIST *v.* and *sb.*] A hold-up, a robbery; also *attrib.* and *Comb.* Also as *vb.*, to hold up, rob, steal. So **'heister**, a robber, a hijacker; a shoplifter. Cf. HIST *v.*[2] 2, HOIST *v.* 6 and *sb.* 5.

1927 *Dialect Notes* V. 449 *Heister*, n. (1) A nickname. Suggested etymon, Ger. 'heissen'. (2) A shoplifter. **1930** E. D. Sullivan *Chicago Surrenders* (1931) xiv. 229 Any such giant 'heist'. **1931** [see HOIST *v.* 6]. **1943** P. Cheyney *You can always Duck* xi. 170 If you think I'm gonna be heisted by a cheap thug like you, you made a mistake. **1947** S. J. Perelman *Westward Ha!* (1949) x. 123 His new ballpoint fountain pen.. had been heisted by the attendants. **1953** 'S. Ransome' *Drag Dark* (1954) ii. 22 Any heister.. would face a bit of a problem in moving his loot. **1955** D. W. Maurer in *Publ. Amer. Dial. Soc.* XXIV. 18 Very peaceful when he ain't on the heist. *Ibid.* 92 Thus a *heist mob* is one which brooks no interference and robs the victim willy-nilly. **1965** *Punch* 11 Aug. 199/2 Six years ago Jim Tempest was one of a bunch of tearaways heisting cars round the North Circular. **1967** 'D. Shannon' *Chance to Kill* (1968) i. 7 The pair of heist boys had been busy... Since ten days they had .. hit four liquor stores, three small markets, two bars, and a drugstore, for a total take of around eighteen hundred bucks. **1968** 'E. Trevor' *Place for Wicked* ii. 22 A heist was when you took a motor with the idea of doing a repaint and flogging it with a bent log-book you'd got from a breaker.

heist, obs. Sc. f. HEST.

heisugge, obs. f. HAYSUCK.

heit, obs. Sc. f. HATE, HEAT, HOT; see HIGHT *v.*

heith, obs. f. HEIGHT.

heithen, heiþen, obs. ff. HEATHEN, HETHEN.

heithing, heithorne, obs. ff. HETHING, HAWTHORN.

‖**hei-tiki** (heɪ'tɪkɪ). *N.Z.* [Maori, f. *hei* to hang + *tiki* the first created being.] A greenstone neck-ornament worn by Maoris.

1835 W. Yate *Acc. N.Z.* (ed. 2) 151 The *hei-tiki* being taken off the neck, laid down.. and then wept and sung over. **1843** E. Dieffenbach *Trav. N.Z.* II. iv. 55 Around the neck both sexes generally wear a figure cut out of jade. This they call E' Tiki: it has an enormous head, very large eyes, and monstrous and disproportionate arms and legs. **1880** *Encycl. Brit.* XIII. 540/1 The hideous breast ornament termed *hei tiki.* **1887** *Col. & Indian Exhib., Rep. Col. Sect.* 74 Heitikis or native deities. **1936** 'R. Hyde' *Check to your King* 153 Queer little amulets, some of which, the hei-tikis, were in the shape of the human embryo. **1949** P. Buck *Coming of Maori* (1950) II. xii. 295 The term *tiki* was applied to the carved human figures set up at the gable end of important houses. When the ornaments in human form were made, they were also termed *tiki* but, to distinguish them from the larger wooden *tiki*, the nephrite ornaments were termed *hei tiki*, *hei* meaning to tie around the neck.

heive, -en, obs. ff. HEAVE, HEAVEN, HAVEN.

heivol, obs. f. HIGHFUL *a.*

heixt(e, obs. ff. HIGHEST.

heize: see HEEZE.

hejalap: see JALAP.

hejeen, var. HYGEEN, HAJEEN.

hejira, variant of HEGIRA.

hek, heke, obs. forms of HECK.

†**heke**[1]. *Obs. rare*$^{-1}$. A horse (of some kind).

a **1400** *Morte Arthur* 2284 Hekes and hakkenays and horses of armes.

†**heke**[2]. *Obs. rare*$^{-1}$. [Cf. HACK *sb.*[1] 2 and *v.*[1] 2 a.] A chilblain.

c **1450** *Alphita* (Anecd. Oxon.) 144 Quod fit in talo [h]yeme maxime propter frigus et dicitur pernio a pernicie, anglice *heke* uel *moule*.

hek(e)far, -feer, etc., obs. forms of HEIFER.

hekel, -ill, -elare, obs. ff. HECKLE, HECKLER.

†**hekemose.** *Obs.* [Cf. *heckymal, hackmall* dial. names of the Titmouse.] A bird: prob. the Titmouse.

14.. *Voc.* in Wr.-Wülcker 585/1 *Frondator*, an hekemose. [*Ibid.* 640/28 *Hic frondator*, tytmase. 702/3 *Hic frondator*, a sterkyng.]

hekistotherm (hɪ'kɪstəʊθɜ:m). *Bot.* [ad. F. *hékistotherme* (A. de Candolle 1874, in *Archives des Sciences physiques et naturelles* L. 14), f. Gr. ἥκιστο-ς smallest + θέρμη heat.] A plant which can grow in very cold environments, as the arctic and antarctic lichens and mosses. Hence **hekisto'thermic** *a.*

1875 J. H. Balfour *Man. Bot.* (ed. 5) 817 Hekistotherms, plants requiring a very small amount of heat, as arctic or antarctic plants. **1909** Groom & Balfour tr. *Warming's Oecology of Plants* 36 Hekistothermic: plants living beyond the limits of tree-growth, where the annual mean temperature sinks below 0° C. **1934** H. Gilbert-Carter tr. *Raunkiaer's Life Forms of Plants* ii. 6 A fourth group, Hecistotherms, comprises plants belonging to the cold regions. They have the lowest heat demand of all plants, will grow where the summer is short, and are able to endure a long and very cold winter. **1965** F. J. Monkhouse *Dict. Geogr.* 155/2 *Hekistotherm*, a plant such as reindeer moss or lichen, which can exist where the mean temperature of the warmest month is under 50° F.

hekk-: see HECK-.

hekst, obs. f. HIGHEST, superl. of HIGH *a.*

hekte ('hɛktiː). Also **hecte**. [Gr. ἕκτη the sixth (of a stater), fem. (sc. μοῖρα part) of ἕκτος sixth.] A Greek silver coin.

1872 B. V. Head in *Synopsis Contents Brit. Museum* (Dept. Coins & Medals) 37 The work upon many of these staters and hektæ is exceedingly fine. **1906** G. F. Hill *Hist. Greek Coins* 17 A few specimens of an electrum *hekte*, or sixth of the stater. **1921** *Brit. Mus. Return* 79 An electrum hecte with the type of a crouching lion and a hemihecte with the type of a winged monster. **1933** C. Seltman *Greek Coins* vii. 113 The staters of Cyzicus, and her *hektai*, or 'sixths',.. testify.. to the large issues of these states.

hel, obs. form of HEAL, HELE, HELL.

HeLa ('hi:lə). [f. the name, *He*nrietta *La*cks, of the patient from whom the original tissue was taken (cf. *Obstetr. & Gynecol.* XXXVIII (1971). 945).] Designating a strain of human epithelial cells maintained in tissue culture and derived originally from tissue from a carcinoma of the cervix. Occas. *absol.*

1953 W. F. Scherer et al. in *Jrnl. Exper. Med.* XCVII. 695 This cellular strain, designated as strain HeLa by one of the authors (G. G[ey]) when he obtained it from an epidermoid carcinoma of the cervix has been maintained in continuous serial culture passage *in vitro* from February 8, 1951, until the present. *Ibid.* 705 Cultures of strain HeLa cells are capable of producing large quantities of poliomyelitis virus. **1959** *Laboratory Invest.* VIII. 278 Since the human cancer cell strain HeLa is in such wide use as an in vitro system for the study of cell processes, it appeared to be of value to study.. aspects of DNA physiology in these cultures. *Ibid.* 283 The variability in DNA synthesis in HeLa is small in this medium. **1965** C. H. Andrewes *Common Cold* viii. 65 A few lines of cells.. have been growing happily for years and these have been sent all round the world, so that the best-known lines, such as HeLa cells from a human cancer.. are used in hundreds of laboratories.

Helanca (hɛ'læŋkə). [Proprietary term.] (See quot. 1964.)

1944 *Trade Marks Jrnl.* 15 Nov. 544/2 Helanca. Textile yarns. Heberlein & Co. A.G. (a Joint Stock Company organized under the laws of Switzerland), Wattwil, Canton of St. Gallen, Switzerland. **1946** J. V. & S. L. Sherman *New Fibers* xii. 229 An interesting new type of viscose rayon, known as 'Helanca', was used extensively in Switzerland during the war as a substitute for wool. It is a yarn mechanically and chemically treated to produce a permanent wool-like effect. *Ibid.* 230 Helanca yarns are available in a wide variety of colors. **1959** *Times* 7 Dec. 13/2 Elasticised cloth (generally wool and Helanca) gives the greatest comfort as well as best and smartest fit. **1960** *Guardian* 26 Aug. 6/5 The brown and white Helanca bikini was lovely. **1964** *Which?* Sept. 286/1 *Helanca*, wide range of bulked and stretched yarns (made from a number of man-made fibres).

heland, obs. form of HIGHLAND.

†**helas**, *int. Obs.* [a. F. *hélas*, the later form of *ha las, a las* ALAS.] An exclamation expressing grief, sorrow, etc.; alas!

1484 Caxton *Fables of Æsop* III. xix, Helas for god & for pyte I praye yow that ye wylle hyde me. *a* **1529** Skelton *Col. Cloute* 1022 Helas, I say, helas! Howe may this come to passe. **1610** Holland *Camden's Brit.* I. 300 But if of Edward King (helas) our Hector wailes the death. **1753** Lady Luxborough *Let. to Shenstone* 24 June, Helas!—Lady Plymouth, Lady Archer, &c. are in the neighbourhood, and I in my chimney-corner.

helbow(e, obs. forms of ELBOW *sb.*
c **1325** *Gloss. W. de Biblesw.* in Wright *Voc.* 147 Helbowes, *coudes.* *c* **1475** Wr.-Wülcker 749/6 *Hic cubitus*, a helbowe.

helco-, combining form of Gr. ἕλκος 'festering wound, ulcer', used to form technical terms with sense 'ulcer': as in **'helcoid** *a.*, resembling an ulcer (Mayne *Expos. Lex.* 1854). **hel'cology**, the doctrine of, or a treatise on ulcers (Mayne). ||**hel'coma**, an old term for ulceration (*Syd. Soc. Lex.*). **helcoph'thalmia, -my**, ophthalmia with ulceration (Mayne). **'helcoplasty** [Gr. πλαστ-ός formed], the operation of grafting on an ulcer a piece of healthy skin from another part or person (Dunglison *Med. Dict.*). ||**hel'cosis** [Gr. ἕλκωσις], ulceration. **helcotic** (hɛl'kɒtɪk) *a.* [Gr. ἑλκωτικός ulcerating], of or belonging to ulceration (Mayne).
1876 *Wagner's Gen. Pathol.* 283 The doctrine of ulcers belongs for the most part to special surgery, where helcology has attained to great perfection.

†**'helctic**, *a.* *Obs.* [ad. Gr. ἑλκτικός fit for drawing, f. ἑλκτός, verbal adj. of ἕλκειν to draw, drag.] That serves to draw, drawing.
1658 W. BURTON *Itin. Anton.* 54 Who with I know not what Helktique Instruments..have removed Cataractonium out of Yorkshire.

†**'helcysm.** *Obs. rare*$^{-0}$. [a. L. *helcysma*, a. Gr. ἕλκυσμα silver dross.]
BLOUNT *Glossogr.*, *Helcysm*, the froth and filth of silver; the dross and scum of that metal.

held (hɛld), *ppl. a.* [pa. pple. of HOLD *v.*] Kept in, restrained, detained. Also with adverbs.
c **1611** CHAPMAN *Iliad* xxiv. 275 With held vp hands. **1820** KEATS *Lamia* I. 300 While, like held breath, the stars drew in their panting fires. *a* **1850** ROSSETTI *Dante & Circ.* II. (1874) 287 Still whispering under my held breath. **1891** *Pall Mall G.* 2 Feb. 2/1 The coda with its held notes for the bass clarinet and bassoon deserves close attention. **1906** *Westm. Gaz.* 28 Dec. 7/2 A long string of 'held-up' cars.

†**held, helde**, *sb.* *Obs.* [Late OE. *helde* fem., allegiance, fealty: cf. OE. *hyldo*, *hyld* favour, grace, loyalty, allegiance = OS. *huldi*, OHG. *huldî* (Ger. *huld*), Goth. type **hulþei*, f. *hulþs*, OHG., OS., OE. *hold* gracious, kind.]
1. Grace, favour, kindness.
a **1000** *Cædmon's Gen.* 301 Hyld hæfde his ferlorene. *c* **1175** *Lamb. Hom.* 69 God..ȝefe us mihte þurh his held þet ure leue beo ure sceld. *a* **1310** in Wright *Lyric P.* x. 37 Y-here thou me nou, hendest in helde.
2. Loyalty to the liege lord, allegiance.
a **1000** *Laws of Edgar* IV. c. 12 (Schmid) For eowrum hyldum, þe ȝe me symble cyddon. *c* **1100** *O.E. Chron.* an. 1097 He þær on þæs cynges Willelmes heldan to cynge ȝesette. **1297** R. GLOUC. (1724) 285 Understonde þe bet efsone, and hold me þyn helde. *a* **1300** *Floriz & Bl.* 397 Þat he þe bere al þe helde þat man schal to his louerd ȝelde.

held, obs. erron. form of YIELD *v.*

†**helde.** *Herb. Obs.* An old name of Tansy.
c **1000** *Sax. Leechd.* II. 86 Genim..heldan & betonican colonan. *c* **1000** ÆLFRIC *Voc.* in Wr.-Wülcker 133/33 *Tanaceta*, helde. *c* **1265** *Names of Plants* in Wr.-Wülcker 556/17 *Tanesetum*, i. *tanesie*, i. helde.

helde, obs. form of HEALD, HIELD, HILD.

||**Heldentenor** ('hɛldəntɛ'nɔə(r)). [Ger.] A powerful tenor voice suited to the singing of heroic roles in opera; a person with such a voice.
1926 *Times* 18 May 6/3 Herr Melchior..has..the physical energy of voice and action which is the essential qualification of the *helden* tenor. **1931** *Gramophone* Suppl. Oct. 16/1 A *Heldentenor* whose career..has been almost exclusively restricted to the embodiment of Wagner's greatest heroes. **1947** N. CARDUS *Autobiogr.* III. 234 A fearsome imitation of the latest Heldentenor at Covent Garden. **1962** J. B. PRIESTLEY *Margin Released* III. iii. 175 The help he gave the *Heldentenor* Melchior. **1962** *Listener* 5 Apr. 617/1 Mr Thomas has the commanding quality of a real *Heldentenor*, not a pushed-up baritone as are many Wagnerian tenors. **1973** *Times* 20 Mar. 16/8 Mr Lauritz Melchior, whom English opera goers remember as the greatest Wagnerian *Heldentenor* of his generation between the wars, died in Santa Monica, California.

helder, *adv.* *Obs.* exc. *dial.* [ME. = ON. comp. *heldr* (Sw. *heller*, Da. *heller*).] More; rather.
13.. *Gaw. & Gr. Knt.* 430 And nawþer faltered ne fel þe freke neuer þe helder. *a* **1400–50** *Alexander* 1016 My couatyng is elder [*v.r.* helder] þe sadnes of slike men þan swyftnes of childir. *Ibid.* 4657 Þat gome is gods gud frend & god neuire þe hildire. **1674** RAY *N.C. Words* 25 *Heldar*, rather, before. *c* **1840** in *Almondbury & Huddersf. Gloss.* s.v., [One of 'some masons setting a flag'] It's elder slack yet. **1857**, **1874** [see ELDER *adv.*].

Helderberg ('hɛldəbɜːg). *Geol.* The name of a range of hills in New York State, used *attrib.* to designate a group of strata found there and later also the lower division of the Lower Devonian in North America and the fossils, etc., typical of it. Hence **Helder'bergian** (-bɜːg-, -bɜːdʒ-), *a.*
1840 W. W. MATHER in *Geol. Surv. State N.Y.* (Assembly No. 50) 212 The subjoined nomenclature of these rock groups is presented as local, and one of convenience merely. ..(3) The next in order is the Helderberg group, which is composed of various strata of common and hydraulic limestones..interstratified with grits and shales. **1880** J. DANA *Man. Geol.* (ed. 3) III. ii. 236 The Lower Helderberg period..is so named because its beds are well displayed in the Helderberg Mountains, south of Albany, beneath Devonian beds called the 'Upper Helderberg'. *Ibid.*, The Helderberg rocks outcrop also over a large area in western Ohio. **1906** CHAMBERLIN & SALISBURY *Geol.* II. 454 From this intermediate or transitional assemblage the Helderberg fauna seems to have taken its origin. *Ibid.* 455 The capulid shells which abound at some localities in the Helderbergian ..faunas. **1949** C. O. DUNBAR *Hist. Geol.* x. 207 Two stages [of the American Devonian] are recognized, the Helderbergian and the Deerparkian, each with several formations. The Helderberg stage includes only limestone and calcareous shales.

†**'heldest**, *adv.* *Obs.* [superl. of HELDER, ON. *helzt.*] Most, foremost, soonest.
a **1400–50** *Alexander* 1855 (Dubl. MS.) In howre-selfe to sitte all-þar heldest [*v.r.* heist]. *Ibid.* 2509 When we hope all þe heldest [*v.r.* althire-hiȝest] to herye hym with armes.

heldest, -ast, obs. forms of ELDEST.
c **1375** *Sc. Leg. Saints, Nycholas* 104 His heldast douchtyre. *a* **1400–50** *Alexander* 2319 Heldest child.

helding, obs. form of HILDING.

†**hele**, *v.*[1] (*str.*) *Obs.* Forms: 1 helan (2nd sing. hilest, 3rd sing. hilþ), 2–3 heole(n, 2–4 hele (2nd sing. hilest), (3 hale), 4 hel. *Pa. t.* 1 hæl, pl. hǽlon, 4 hal. *Pa. pple.* 1 holen (Bosw.), 3 iholen, 4 holn, hole, ihole. [Com. Teut. str. vb. of ablaut series *hel-*, *hal-*, *hul-* (*hol-*): OE. *helan*, *hæl*, *hǽlon*, *holen* = OFris. *hela*, OS., OHG. *helan* (MLG., MDu., Du. *hēlen*, MHG. *heln*, Ger. *hehlen*) to hide, conceal, cover up; Aryan root *kel-* in L. *celāre* to hide, *oc-cul-ĕre* to hide, Gr. καλ-ύπτειν to hide. (See note below.) The present stem of this strong vb. blended in ME. with that of the derivative OE. *hęlian* (see next), so that the strong inflexions did not survive the 14th c. Weak inflexions occur beside the strong in MDu. *helen*, and alone in MLG., mod.Ger., and Du.]
trans. To hide, conceal; to keep secret.
c **825** *Vesp. Psalter* xxxix. 11 [xl.] 10 Ne hel ic mildheortnisse ðine..from ȝesomnunge micelre. *c* **893** K. ÆLFRED *Oros.* VI. xxxiii. §2 He hit hæl swiþe fæste wið his broðor. *c* **1175** *Lamb. Hom.* 57 Ne þu naȝest for to stele ne nan þef þe for to heole. *a* **1200** *Moral Ode* 161 in *Trin. Coll. Hom.* 225 Al sal þar ben þanne cuð þat men luȝen her and halen. *a* **1225** *Ancr. R.* 146 Ȝif þi god dede were iholen. *c* **1230** *Hali Meid.* 47 Ȝif þu wel hiles te under godes wenges. *a* **1300** *Cursor M.* 28135 Ic ha þam holn al wit my pride. **1340** *Ayenb.* 26 Þe kueades þet were y-hole and yroted ine þe herte. **13..** *K. Alis.* 4203 My coppe thow hast y-stole, And undur thy barm hole.
[*Note.* The Teutonic ablaut-series *hel-*, *hal-*, *hǽl*, *hul-* (*hol-*), has an extensive family of derivatives:
I. From *e* grade: OE. *helan*, HELE *v.*[1], HELE *sb.*; HELM[1].
II. From *a* grade (with umlaut): **haljan*, OE. *hęlian*, HELE *v.*[2]; Goth. *halja*, OE. *hęl(l)*, HELL *sb.*
III. From *u(o)* grade: OE. *hulu*, HULL 'husk'; OE. *hol*, Sc. *holl*, HOWE 'hollow'; OE. *hol*, HOLE; HOLLOW *a.*, *sb.*, *v.*
IV. From *u* grade (with umlaut): Goth. *huljan*, OE. **hyllan*, ON. *hylja*, ME. *hyll*, *hule*, *hile*, HILL *v.*]

hele, heal (hiːl), *v.*[2] (*wk.*) *Obs.* exc. *dial.* Forms: 1 helian, 2–4 helie(n, 2–5 hele, 4–5 heyle, *Sc.* heile, 4–7 hell(e, 5 heele, *Sc.* heill, 6–9 heal, 7 heale, 8– heel, 9 hele. *Pa. t.* 1 -ode, 2–4 -ede, 3–5 -ed, 4 helled, heild, *Sc.* helit, heylyt, 4–5 helet(e, 6–9 healed. *Pa. pple.* 3 ihæled, iheoled, 3–5 (i)heled, -id, -yd, yheled, 4 *Sc.* helit, 5 -ud, -ut, 6–9 healed. [OE. *hęlian*, a later form of *hęllan* (Sievers, ed. 2. §400. 2) = OS. *bi-helljan*, OHG. *bi-hellen*:—**haljan*, f. ablaut stem *hal-* of *helan*: see prec. etym. and note.]
†**1.** *trans.* To hide, conceal; to keep secret. *Obs.*
c **975** *Canons Edgar* §47 in Thorpe *Anc. Laws* II. 254 Ðæt ænig ȝehadod man his sceare ne heliȝe. *c* **1000** ÆLFRIC *Gen.* xxxviii. 15 Heo helode hire nebb. *c* **1200** *Trin. Coll. Hom.* 197 Þat heued þat he helede. *a* **1225** *Ancr. R.* 410 Mei ich.. helien Abraham þing þet ich þenche uorto donne? **1375** BARBOUR *Bruce* IV. 373 Syne [thai] it helit weill eneuch. *c* **1440** *Gesta Rom.* xxxiii. 129 (Harl. MS.) Hele the cors of this dede man in some prive place of thin house. *c* **1440** *Bone Flor.* 989 They made them to swere they schulde be lele, And syr Emers counsell heyle. **1483** CAXTON *Gold. Leg.* 189 b/2 But the preest alwey heled his synne. **1570** *Satir. Poems Reform.* xviii. 35 Heill nor conceill, reset nane of thay lownis. ? **16..** *Bold Burnet's Dau.* ix. in Child *Ballads* II. lii. (1884) 453/2 Although I would heal it neer sae well, Our God above does see.
†**b.** *absol.* or *intr.* To practise concealment, keep a secret, keep silence. *Obs.*
13.. *Guy Warw.* (A.) 351 No longer hele y nille, Al that soþe tellen y wille. *c* **1400** *Rom. Rose* 2522 To hele wel is no folye. *c* **1450** *Erle Tolous* 1034 The abbot seyde..that he wolde hele, And ellys he were wode.
2. To cover, cover in. Still in local use, esp. in senses (*a*) to cover (roots, seeds, etc.) with earth; (*b*) to cover with slates or tiles, to roof.
a. *c* **1200** *Trin. Coll. Hom.* 195 Anes kinnes neddres is þe mid hire lichame heleð hire heued þane he beð of harme offered. *Ibid.* 197 Þat heued þat he helede wið þe deules eginge. *c* **1205** LAY. 18405 Heo leggeð i þissen felden Ihæled [*c* **1275** iheled] in heore telden. **1375** BARBOUR *Bruce* IX. 128 Snaw had helit all the land. *c* **1400** *Three Kings Cologne* 52 Derkenes schulle heele þe erþe. **1497** *Will of Dynham* (Somerset Ho.), A Matynsbooke helid with purpill veluet. **1572** BOSSEWELL *Armorie* II. 42 When his [the lion's] necke and shoulders be healed with heare and mayne. **1625** USSHER *Answ. Jesuit* 287 In this Countrie, with them that retaine the ancient language..to hell the dead, is as much as to cover the dead. **1674** RAY *S. & E.C. Words*, Heal, to cover; *Suss.* As, 'to heal the fire'; 'to heal a house'; 'to heal a person in bed'. **1773** W. TADMAN in R. Dossie *Mem. Agric.* (1782) III. 102 [It] destroys the small weeds, lets in the earth, and heels the seeds. **1861** *Jrnl. R. Agric. Soc.* XXII. II. 275 At the time of earthing the potatoes by the double mould-plough, turnip seed is sown, and thus 'heled'.
b. **1387** TREVISA *Higden* (Rolls) II. 17 Brent tyle to hele wiþ hous and cherches. **1393** LANG. *P. Pl.* C. VIII. 237 Alle þe houses beþ heled..With no lede, bote with loue. **1458** *Yatton Churchw. Acc.* (Som. Rec. Soc.) 100 It. for a Plomer to hely the batylmente for the styple. **1674** [see prec.]. **1703** T. N. *City & C. Purchaser* 275 They Rip, and Heal, and Counter-lath, for 3*s.* per Square. **1894** [see next].
Hence **heled** *ppl. a.*, covered, roofed.
c **1400** *Three Kings Cologne* 23 A strete þat þan was clepede þe couerid or þe helid strete. **1578** LYTE *Dodoens* I. xxxii. 46 Olde tyled, or stone healed houses. **1894** *W. Sussex County Times* 5 May 4/2 For Sale, a Block of Four Freehold Brick-built Slate-healed Modern Cottages.

hele, *sb.* *Obs.* exc. *dial.* [f. HELE *v.*, in various senses.] †**a.** ? Concealment. (OE.) †**b.** A hiding-place (*obs.*). **c.** Cover (*dial.*).
a **1000** *Inst. Polity* xii. in Thorpe *Anc. Laws* II. 320 Hi.. mid yfelan helan earme men beswicað. **13..** *K. Alis.* 4959 Ac from her frendes hy stelen An gon to wode and maken hem helen, And crepen thereinne. **1894** BLACKMORE *Perlycross* III. 106 The man..had gone home..keeping under hele with his oilskins on.

hele, obs. f. HALE *a.*, HEAL *sb.* and *v.*, HEEL *sb.*[1]

helegug, obs. form of ELIGUG.

heleles: see HEALLESS.

†**Helena** ('hɛlɪnə). *Obs.* [a. L. *Helena*, a. Gr. Ἑλένη female proper name. The Greek *Helen* was the sister of Castor and Pollux, the name given to double meteors at sea; but there was perh. association also with Gr. ἑλένη torch.] A meteoric light seen about the masts of ships: cf. CORPOSANT.
1563 W. FULKE *Meteors* (1640) 11 b, Seen on the land, is called..*Ignis fatuus*..That which is seene on the Sea, if it be but one, is named Helena, if it be two, it is called Castor and Pollux. **1601** HOLLAND *Pliny* I. 18 But if they appeare two and two together, they bring comfort with them..as by whose comming, they say, that dreadfull, cursed, and threatning meteor called Helena is chased and driuen away.

helend(e, var. HEALEND *Obs.*, Saviour.

helen-flower. An anglicized form of *Helenium*, a genus of composite plants.
1884 MILLER *Plant-n.*, *Helenium*..Dark purple Helen-flower..Autumn Helen-flower or Sneezewort.

helenge, var. ELENGE *a. dial.*, lonely.

helenin ('hɛlɪnɪn). *Chem.* [f. botanical name *Helen-ium* + -IN.] A colourless crystalline substance (C_6H_8O) obtained from the root of elecampane (*Inula Helenium*).
1838 T. THOMSON *Chem. Org. Bodies* 498 When the root of elecampane is distilled, the helenin passes with the water under the form of a yellowish oil. **1886** *Syd. Soc. Lex.* s.v., According to Valenzuela, helenin is very useful in bronchitis.
Hence **'helenene**, a yellow oily hydrocarbon obtained by distilling helenin with phosphoric anhydride (Watts *Dict. Chem.* 1865).

helenium (hɛ'liːnɪəm). [mod.L., f. Gr. ἑλένιον, possibly commemorating Helen of Troy.]
1. An early name for elecampane, the European herb *Inula helenium*, of the family Compositæ.
1608 TOPSELL *Serpents* 5 Helen..planted the same there ..called..after her owne Name Helenium, which the skilfull Herborists at this day affirme to grow in Pharus. **1777** R. WESTON *Universal Botanist* II. 380 Many of the Varieties of the Helenium of Vaillant, are arranged under Aster and Inula. **1931** M. GRIEVE *Mod. Herbal* I. 279/1 Elecampane was known to the ancient writers on..natural history... *Inula*, the Latin classical name for the plant, is considered to be a corruption of the Greek word *Helenion*, which in its Latinized form *Helenium*, is also now applied to the same species.
2. [Adopted by Linnæus in *Hortus Cliffortianus* (1737) 418.] A plant of a large genus of North American annual or perennial herbs so called, belonging to the family Compositæ; a sneezeweed.
1789 W. T. AITON *Hortus Kewensis* III. 227 (*heading*) Smooth Helenium. *Nat[ive]* of North America. **1900** J. M. ABBOTT in W. D. Drury *Bk. Gardening* viii. 272 Heleniums are valuable composite plants for back positions in mixed borders. **1961** *Amateur Gardening* 16 Sept. 7/2 Despite the epithet 'autumnale', many of the heleniums are summer-flowering plants.

helepole ('hɛlɪpəʊl). *Anc. Hist.* [a. F. *hélépole*, ad. late L. *helepolis* = Gr. ἑλέπολις city-taking, used as fem. sb. = a besieging engine, f. ἑλ- to

take + πόλις city.] An ancient besieging engine, a kind of movable tower.

[**1569** J. SANFORD tr. *Agrippa's Van. Artes* 33 b, Ye engins called..tolleons, Walking toures, Heliopolins.] **1770** LANGHORNE *Plutarch* (1879) II. 950/1 His engines, called *helepoles*, were a pleasing spectacle to the very towns which he besieged. **1845** *Encycl. Metrop.* XIV. 793 The moveable towers employed by the ancients in their sieges, and which they called *Helepoles*.

heler, healer (ˈhiːlə(r)). *Obs.* exc. *dial.* Also 8–9 heeler. [f. HELE *v.*²]

1. a. One who covers up or conceals. **b.** A thing that covers; a cover, covering, coverlet.

1398 TREVISA *Barth. De P.R.* v. vi. (1495), The eye lyddes that ben the helers and couerars of the eyen. *Ibid.* v. viii, A byrde in stede of an eye lydde hath an heler to couere and kepe the syghte. **1879** MISS JACKSON *Shropsh. Word-bk.* s.v., A proverbial saying heard in the neighbourhood of Stoddesden:—'The heler's as bad as the heaver'. **1888** ELWORTHY *W. Somerset Word-bk.* 334 *Heler*, a horse-cloth; coverlet. 'Better nit put the haler 'pon th' 'oss'. *Ibid.* 335 'The heler's so bad as the stealer.'

2. A slater or tiler: = HELLIER.

1674 RAY *S. & E. C. Words* s.v. *Heal*, In the West he that covers a House with slates is called a Healer or Hellier. **1703** T. N. *City & C. Purchaser* 82 Squares of..Tyling in the Healers, or Bricklayer's Work.

3. The upper half of a drain tile, when made in two semicylindrical parts (the under part being the 'gutter tile').

1846 J. BAXTER *Libr. Pract. Agric.* (ed. 4) I. 231, 1300 tiles with heelers, at 5*s.* per 100.

†**heleth.** *Obs.* Forms: 1–3 hæleþ, heleþ, 3 haleþ; also 7 *pseudo-arch.* health. [OE. *hæleð, hęleð* = OSax. *hęliþ*, late OHG. *hęlid*, Ger. *held* hero.] A warrior, hero, man.

Beowulf (Z.) 191 Ne mihte snotor hæleð, wean onwendan. *c* **1205** LAY. 1779 þa heleðes weren bliðe. *Ibid.* 11989 Hæleð. [**1612** DRAYTON *Poly-olb.* viii, They under false pretence of amity and chear, The British Peers invite, the German healths to view At Stonehenge.]

helewei, -wi, var. of HALEWEI *Obs.*

†**helewou, -wow, -wogh, helowe-wall.** *Obs.* [f. HELE, covering + OE. *wáȝ*, ME. *woȝ, wow*, WOUGH, wall.] An end-wall; (? also = roof-wall).

a **1200** *Grave* 17 in Thorpe *Anal.* 153 Ðe hele-waȝes beoð laȝe, sid-waȝes unheȝe. [*c* **1205** LAY. 25887 He nom þare halle wah [*c* **1275** hilewoþ] and helden hine to grunde.] *a* **1300** in Horstm. *Altengl. Leg.* (1875) 90 Side walles hit hedde to, ac non helewou þer nas; hit was opun at eiþer ende, to go in al þat wolde. *c* **1325** *Femina* (MS. Trin. Coll. Cambr. B. 14. 39 lf. 122 b) *Et pluis pur lever le meisere* and more to rere uppe the helewoghes. **1425** in Kennett *Par. Antiq.* II. 25 Et in solutis eidem dominæ pro quodam helowe wall unius domus apud Curtlyngton annuatim ii. den. **1695** *Ibid.* Gloss., *Helowe-wall*, the hell-wall or end wall that covers and defends the rest of the building.

helf, obs. form of HALF *sb.*

helgramite: see HELLGRAMMITE.

heli, obs. form of HOLY.

heli-, combining form, repr. the first element of HELICOPTER (cf. Gr. ἕλιξ), used (*a*) in the names of types of helicopters or aircraft resembling helicopters, as **helibus**, a helicopter with accommodation for a large number of passengers; (*b*) = 'helicopter', as **heliborne** *a.*, carried by helicopter; **heli-lift** *v.*, to transport by helicopter; **helipad**, a 'pad' or landing-ground for a helicopter; **helipod**, a 'pod' or container borne by a helicopter and carried e.g. to forward battle-areas for use as an operating theatre, workshop, etc. See also HELIDROME, HELIPORT.

1949 *News-Age-Herald* (Birmingham, Ala.) 13 Nov. A18/3 There is much work..to be done before the combination of the jetliner and the helibus can be fully utilized. **1956** *Britannica Bk. of Year* 493/1 Helicar, a combination of automobile and helicopter. **1960** *Times* 29 Oct. 4/5 A Rotodyne helicopter lifting the ' helipod', which contains two operating theatres. **1961** *New Scientist* 8 June 583/3 The principles of the helicopter and the ducted air flying platform are combined in a vehicle named 'Helipod' and designed by an American business man. **1961** *Aeroplane* CI. 822/2 There are now 487 established heliports or helipads in the U.S.A., Canada and Puerto Rico. **1966** *Guardian* 2 Apr. 14/2 Military requests for a hard 'helipad' that could be laid swiftly in jungles on mud, sand, grass, or dusty surfaces. **1966** *Atlantic Monthly* Oct. 14 Man for man, the U.S. troops may lack some of their enemies' jungle skill, but the rapid availability of firepower and heliborne mobility have tipped the scales decisively in their favor. **1966** *New Statesman* 14 Oct. 549/1 Heli-lifted Medivac Attends the WIA. **1968** *Guardian* 29 Feb. 5/5 Hovercraft and heli-buses would transport people and goods. **1968** *Courier-Mail* (Brisbane) 5 June 2/6 Because of the heliborne capability of the Government forces it was no longer possible for the Viet Cong to concentrate anywhere in company strength. **1969** I. KEMP *Brit. G.I. in Vietnam* xii. 197 A 'heliborne' assault in the jungle near Song Be mountain. **1970** *Guardian* 12 Sept. 11 The Israelis..could heli-lift a half brigade to Dawsons Field. **1973** *Observer* (Colour Suppl.) 3 June 34/2 Units of the elite First Cav, the new heliborne division.

heliac (ˈhiːlɪæk), *a.* [ad. late L. *hēliac-us*, a. Gr. ἡλιακός, f. ἥλιος the sun. Cf. F. *héliaque.*]

1. Pertaining to the sun, solar.

1808 J. BARLOW *Columb.* II. 431 Quito bow'd; and all the heliac zone Felt the same sceptre, and confirm'd the throne.

2. = HELIACAL 1.

1775 ASH, *Heliac*, emerging from the lustre of the sun, falling into the lustre of the sun. **1839** J. TAYLOR *Poems & Transl.* 203 The Heliac settings and Heliac risings of the constellations.

heliacal (hɪˈlaɪəkəl), *a.* [f. as prec. + -AL¹.]

1. *Astron.* Said of the rising of a star when it first emerges from the sun's rays and becomes visible before sunrise, or of its setting when it is last visible after sunset before being lost in the sun's rays.

1607 A. BREWER *Lingua* III. vi, Setting of stars, chronic, and heliacal. **1631** WIDDOWES *Nat. Philos.* (ed. 2) 6 Apparent rising is called Heli[a]cal which is of stars getting out of the sun beames; and so if the star get into the sun beames at setting. **1728** NEWTON *Chronol. Amended* 15 By observing the Heliacal Risings and Setting of the stars, they found the length of the Solar year. **1834** *Nat. Philos., Astron.* vii. 169/2 (U.K.S.) The Egyptian rural year was determined by the heliacal rising of Sirius.

†**b.** *heliacal year*, the year reckoned from the heliacal rising of Sirius, the canicular year; ***great heliacal year***, the canicular cycle: see CANICULAR 3.

1662 STILLINGFL. *Orig. Sacr.* I. vi. §1 In 1461 years, which was the great Heliacall year, it returns to the same beginning.

2. Relating to or produced by the sun, solar. *rare.*

1801 W. TAYLOR in *Monthly Mag.* XII. 224 That the headaches and other symptoms of heliacal injury might not ensue. **1871** BLACKIE *Four Phases* i. 21 Then the whole of your lofty heliacal philosophy is only a blaze of lies.

heliacally (hɪˈlaɪəkəlɪ), *adv.* [f. prec. + -LY².] In the way of heliacal rising or setting: see prec. 1.

1589 FLEMING *Virg. Georg.* I. 8 *note*, Cosmically not heliacally: for these two, rising and setting are ascribed to the stars. **1646** SIR T. BROWNE *Pseud. Ep.* IV. xiii. 222 From the rising of this [the dog-] starre, not cosmically, that is, with the Sun, but Heliacally, that is, its emersion from the rayes of the Sunne, the Ancients computed their canicular dayes. **1834** *Nat. Philos., Astron.* vii. 169/2 (U.K.S.) The age of Hesiod..may be determined by the fact that he mentions that Arcturus rose heliacally sixty days after the winter solstice.

Heliæan (hiːlɪˈiːən), *a.* [f. Gr. Ἡλιαία + -AN.] Belonging to the *Heliæa*, a public hall in ancient Athens, in which was held the chief law-court, before which were tried all offences liable to public prosecution.

1807 ROBINSON *Archæol. Græca* I. xxv. 106 Carry him to be tried at the Heliæan court. **1830** tr. *Aristoph., Wasps* 119 When you eat the paunch procured by an Heliæan old stager.

helianthaceous (hiːlɪænˈθeɪʃəs), *a.* *Bot.* [f. mod.L. HELIANTH-US + -ACEOUS.] Allied to the genus *Helianthus* of composite plants.

helianthemum (hiːlɪˈænθɪməm). *Bot.* [mod.L. (J. P. de Tournefort *Elemens de Botanique* (1694) I. vi. 214), f. Gr. ἥλι-ος sun + ἄνθεμον flower.] A plant of the very large, widely-distributed genus of evergreen shrubs or herbs so named, belonging to the family Cistaceæ; also called *rock-rose, sun-rose*, or *frost-weed*.

1822 LOUDON *Encycl. Gard.* 1406/1 *Helianthemum*, sun-rose..and cistineæ..grow in sandy loam and peat. **1827** R. SWEET *Cistineæ* 43 They were both sent from the Brazils.. as two distinct species, one marked *Helianthemum*, 19, the other 48. **1900** M. THORN in W. D. Drury *Bk. Gardening* xi. 436 Helianthemums (Sun Roses)..are charming plants of dwarf habit. **1934** V. RENDALL *Wild Flowers in Lit.* 67 The flower was called *Helianthemum*, 'sun-flower' in Greek, because the blossoms open out in sunshine. **1958** *Listener* 26 June 1058/3 Helianthemums are ideal plants for a new garden.

helianthoid (hiːlɪˈænθɔɪd), *a.* and *sb.* *Zool.* [f. mod.L. *Hēlianthoidea*, neut. pl. of *Hēlianthoides*; f. *Hēlianthus*: see next and -OID.]

A. *adj.* **a.** Resembling the *Helianthus* (Mayne *Expos. Lex.* 1854). **b.** Belonging to the *Helianthoidea*, an order of *Actinozoa*, comprising the sea-anemones. **B.** *sb.* One of the *Helianthoidea*. Also **helian'thoidean** *a.* and *sb.*

1865 H. SPENCER *Princ. Biol.* IV. xiii. §246 (1867) II. 167 Solitary polypes—hydroid or helianthoid—mostly stationary, and when they do move, moving with any side foremost.

‖**helianthus** (hiːlɪˈænθəs). *Bot.* [mod.L., f. Gr. ἥλι-ος sun + ἄνθος flower.] The botanical genus including the common sunflower (N.O. *Compositæ*); a plant of this genus.

1776 MARTYN *Rousseau's Bot.* xxvi. 400 Jerusalem artichoke is also a species of Helianthus. **1804** J. GRAHAME *Sabbath* (1839) 9/2 Like helianthus, borne on downy wings To distant realms. **1834** MRS. SOMERVILLE *Connect. Phys. Sc.* xxvi. (1849) 294 The leaves of a single plant of helianthus three feet high exposed nearly forty feet of surface. **1851** MAYNE REID *Scalp Hunt.* i. 10 Yonder is golden yellow, where the *helianthus* turns her dial-like face to the sun.

Hence **heli'anthic** *a.*, of or belonging to Helianthus, as in ***helianthic acid***, obtained from sunflower seeds. **heli'anthin**, an aniline dye of orange yellow colour.

heliast (ˈhiːlɪæst). *Gr. Antiq.* [ad. Gr. ἡλιαστής, f. ἡλιάζεσθαι to sit in the court Ἡλιαία.] One of the qualified citizens of ancient Athens chosen to sit as judges in the Heliæan court; a dicast.

1807 ROBINSON *Archæol. Græca* I. xxxv. 127 Set in the stocks five days and as many nights, if the heliasts so order it.

heli'astic, *a.* [ad. Gr. ἡλιαστικός, f. ἡλιαστής: see prec.] Of or pertaining to the Heliasts.

1647 N. BACON *Disc. Govt. Eng.* I. iv. (1739) 10 They executed their Commission in Circuits, like unto the Athenian Heliastick or Subdial Court. **1807** ROBINSON *Archæol. Græca* I. xxxv. 125 The heliastic court alone was to pass sentence upon him.

helical (ˈhɛlɪkəl), *a.* and *sb.* [f. L. *helix, helic-em* (see HELIX) + -AL¹.] **A.** *adj.* Belonging to or having the form of a helix; screw-shaped; spiral. Also *Comb.*, as ***helical gear, tube; helical-cut*** adj.

1613 M. RIDLEY *Magn. Bodies* 27 A Helicall and Spirall vertue to move on the Cilinder of her Axis in Spirall lines. **1641** WILKINS *Math. Magick* I. ix. (1648) 57 A helicall revolution about a Cylinder. **1789** *Trans. Soc. Arts* I. 217 The mean helical angles of Archimedean or Water Screws. **1884** F. J. BRITTEN *Watch & Clockm.* 16 For marine chronometers helical springs, in which both ends curve inwards, are universally used. **1888** *Lockwood's Dict. Mech. Engin., Helical gear*, toothed gear in which the wheel-teeth instead of being at right angles with their faces are set at some other angle therewith. **1904** GOODCHILD & TWENEY *Technol. & Sci. Dict.* s.v. *Cycles*, A form of tube known as 'helical', which is formed from a thin steel band or ribbon, wrapped into the form of a tube and brazed at the edges. **1908** *Westm. Gaz.* 28 May 4/2 The live axle is chiefly noticeable for its helical-cut driving pinion. *Ibid.* 18 Nov. 5/1 Several of the wheels have helical-cut teeth. **1958** *Which?* I. III. 30 The new..[drill] has..helical gears, which give quieter running and longer life.

B. *sb.* = *helical gear.*

1913 *Lockwood's Dict. Mech. Engin.* (ed. 4) s.v. *Helical gear cutting*, Double helicals are cut in the same way if the teeth are staggered and divided at the apex.

helically (ˈhɛlɪkəlɪ), *adv.* [f. prec. + -LY².] In a helical manner, spirally. Also *Comb.*

1664 EVELYN *Sylva* (1776) 543 Such as we sometimes find so helically twisted. **1676** *Phil. Trans.* XI. 594 Turn'd helically like a Snail-shell. **1878** THURSTON *Growth Steam-eng.* 74 Flues helically traversing the masonry setting. **1908** *Westm. Gaz.* 14 Nov. 14/2 Helically-cut half-time gear-wheels to ensure silence. **1962** [see DELAY *sb.* 3].

helicampana, obs. form of ELECAMPANE.

‖**Helice** (ˈhɛlɪsiː). *Obs.* [a. L. *Helicē*, Gr. ἑλίκη lit. 'winding', from its revolution round the pole; mod.F. *Hélice.*] A poetical appellation of the constellation Ursa Major.

1596 FITZ-GEFFRAY *Sir F. Drake* (1881) 33 The Cynosura of the purest thought, Faire Helice, by whom the heart is taught. **1631** WIDDOWES *Nat. Philos.* (ed. 2) 8 Helice the greater Beare hath 27 Starres.

heliced (ˈhiːlɪst), *a.* *rare.* [f. HELIX, pl. *helices*, in F. *hélice* + -ED².] Adorned with helices.

1875 LEWIS & STREET in *Encycl. Brit.* II. 411/2 Terminates in a foliated and heliced acroterium.

helices (ˈhɛlɪsiːz), pl. of HELIX.

helichryse (ˈhɛlɪkraɪs). = next.

1893 SYMONDS *In the Key of Blue* 10 While curling through lush grass one spies Tendrils of honeyed helichryse.

‖**helichrysum** (hɛlɪˈkraɪsəm). Also -os, -on. [L., *helichrȳsum*, also *helichrȳsos* = Gr. ἑλίχρυσος, f. ἕλιξ spiral + χρυσός gold.]

1. A creeping plant with yellow flowers, so called by the ancients: variously identified as *Gnaphalium stœchas* and *Tanacetum annuum*.

1551 TURNER *Herbal* I. C ij a, The ryght Elichryson groweth in Italy..and it may be called in englysh, flour amor, or yelowe flour amor. **1850** LEITCH *Müller's Anc. Art* §298. 335 A carved cup..surrounded at the rim with a wreath of ivy and helichrysos, beneath with acanthos.

2. *Bot.* A large genus of composite plants, having mostly yellow flowers, of persistent character, whence called *Everlastings* or *Immortelles*.

1664 EVELYN *Kal. Hort.* (1729) 227 [Plants] least patient of cold..*Balsamum, Helichryson.* **1882** *Garden* 11 Feb. 91/1 Helichrysums are not very particular as to soil.

heliciform (ˈhɛlɪsɪfɔːm), *a.* [ad. mod.L. *heliciform-is*, f. *helix* HELIX; see -FORM.] Having the form of the snail's shell; spirally wound (Mayne *Expos. Lex.* 1854).

helicin (ˈhɛlɪsɪn). *Chem.* [mod. f. L. *helix* spiral, also a kind of willow + -IN.]

1. The glycoside of salicylic acid.

1859 FOWNES *Man. Chem.* 444. **1865** WATTS *Dict. Chem.* III. 139. **1873** *Fownes' Chem.* (ed. 11) 642 Helicin, $C_{13}H_{16}O_7$, is a white, crystalline, slightly bitter substance, produced by the action of very dilute nitric acid upon salicin.

2. An oily substance extracted from snails.

1854 Mayne *Expos. Lex.*, *Helicin*, name given by Oscar Figuier for a peculiar substance which he discovered in the garden snail. **1861** Hulme tr. *Moquin-Tandon* II. III. ii. 85 An oil with a sulphurous odour.. to which he has given the name of Helicine.

helicine ('hɛlɪsaɪn, -ɪn), *a. Anat.* [f. as prec. + -INE.] **a.** Spiral, coiled; applied to certain small arteries of the penis and clitoris. **b.** Pertaining to the helix of the ear.

1833 Dunglison cited in Worcester. **1836–9** Todd *Cycl. Anat.* II. 446/1 Passage of the blood from these helicine arteries.

helicinian (hɛlɪ'sɪnɪən), *a.* and *sb. Zool.* [f. mod.L. *Helicīna* (f. *helix*) + -IAN.]

A. *adj.* Spiral; said of a shell. **B.** *sb.* One of the *Helicina*, a family of Gastropods in De Férussac's classification.

1838 *Penny Cycl.* XII. 106/2 *Helicidæ*, The fifth order [of gastropods] contains two families:—1st The Helicinians.. 2nd The Turbicinians.

helicite ('hɛlɪsaɪt). *Geol.* [f. L. *helix*, *helic-* HELIX + -ITE.] A fossil snail-shell.

1828 in Webster. **1852** Th. Ross *Humboldt's Trav.* II. xvi. 7 The same little helicites.. are found in layers of three or four feet thick as far inland as Turmero.

helicity (hiː'lɪsɪtɪ). [f. L. *helix*, *helic-em* (see HELIX) + -ITY.] **1.** *Physics.* The projection of the spin angular momentum of an elementary particle on the direction of its linear momentum.

1958 *Physical Rev.* CIX. 1017/1 Our result seems compatible with.. 100‰ negative helicity of the neutrinos emitted in orbital electron capture. **1968** M. S. Livingston *Particle Physics* vii. 142 Helicity must be defined relative to a particular coordinate system. For example, if an electron is emitted from a beta decay process with velocity $v = 0{\cdot}95c$ and is observed in the laboratory to have left-handed helicity, its helicity would be reversed if viewed from a coordinate system moving parallel to the particle with velocity $v = 0{\cdot}99\ c$. **1970** *New Scientist* 19 Mar. 545/2 A particle has helicity + 1 if it is seen as spinning counter-clockwise while approaching an observer, while if the observer sees the particle as spinning clock-wise, it has helicity − 1.

2. *Biochem.* Helical character.

1965 *Biochem. & Biophys. Res. Communications* XIX. 231 We observe that the degree of helicity in native and denatured *a* lactalbumin are the same. **1970** *Nature* 25 July 336/2 The side chains in a series of water-soluble glutamine derivatives, the helicity of which can be controlled.

helico- ('hɛlɪkəʊ), comb. form of Gr ἕλιξ HELIX, in names of chemical substances occurring in snails.

1914 J. A. Mandel tr. *Hammarsten & Hedin's Physiol. Chem.* (ed. 7) 174 Another phosphoglycoprotein is helicoproteid, obtained by Hammarsten from the glands of the snail Helix pomatia. **1917** *Jrnl. Chem. Soc.* CXII. I. 421 Helicorubin is thus closely related to hæmoglobin, and acts without doubt in the intestine of the snail as a respiratory pigment.

helicograph ('hɛlɪkəʊgrɑːf, -græf). [f. *helico-*, combining form of Gr. ἕλιξ HELIX + -GRAPH.]

1851 *Dict. Archit.* s.v., An instrument.. for describing the volutes and scroll work found in Grecian architecture, and called the screw helicograph.

helicogyrate (-'dʒaɪəreɪt), *a. Bot.* [f. as prec. + GYRATE.] Surrounded by an obliquely placed ring, as some spore-cases. Also said of the ferns.

1857 Berkeley *Cryptog. Bot.* §595 Fée.. includes the helicogyrate ferns also in the general denomination of Polypodiaceæ. **1866** *Treas. Bot.*, *Helicogyrate*, having a ring or gyrus carried obliquely round it; as in the spore-cases of *Trichomanes*.

helicoid ('hɛlɪkɔɪd), *a.* and *sb.* Also 7 -oeid. [mod. ad. Gr. ἑλικοειδής of winding or spiral form, f. ἕλιξ HELIX + εἶδος shape: see -OID. Cf. F. *hélicoïde* (1704 in Hatz.-Darm.).]

A. *adj.*

1. Having the form of a helix; screw-shaped; spiral. Chiefly in *Zool.* of shells, and in *Bot.* of forms of inflorescence, etc. ***helicoid parabola***, in *Geom.* a spiral curve formed by twisting the common parabola so that its axis becomes a circle, the ordinates still remaining perpendicular to the axis and in the same plane with it.

1704 J. Harris *Lex. Techn.*, *Helicoid Parabola*, or the *Parabolick Spiral*, is a Curve which arises from the Supposition of the Axis of the common *Apollonian Parabola's* being bent round into the Periphery of a Circle. **1796** Hutton *Math. Dict.*, *Helicoid Parabola*, or the *Parabolic Spiral*. **1835** Lindley *Introd. Bot.* (1848) I. 324 The cyme.. is helicoid or scorpioid. **1849** Dana *Geol.* App. i. (1850) 721 The fusiform helicoid cavity. **1875** Bennett & Dyer *Sachs' Bot.* 521 *The Unilateral Helicoid Cyme* is a sympodial cyme in which the median plane of each of the successive axes.. is always situated on the same side.

2. *Zool.* Belonging to or resembling the *Helicidæ*, gastropodous molluscs including the snail.

1876 tr. *Beneden's Anim. Parasites* 37 Molluscs.. with a helicoid shell, similar to that of a small natica.

B. *sb.* **1.** Something of a helicoid or spiral form.

1699 Garth *Dispens.* 80 Shells, Some Helicoeids, some Conical appear, These Miters emulate, Those, Turbans are. **1959** *New Scientist* 5 Mar. 515/2 Inside the silencer cylinders there are two helicoids which have the effect of mincing the air flow passing through the cylinder.

2. *Geom.* †**a.** = Helicoid parabola: see A. 1. *Obs.* **b.** A warped surface generated by a moving straight line which always passes through or touches a fixed helix.

1842 Brande *Dict. Sc., etc.* 547/1 [This] spiral curve.. is the helicoid. **1855** Davies & Peck *Math. Dict.*, *Helicoid*, a warped surface, which may be generated by a straight line moving in such a manner that each point of it shall have a uniform motion in the direction of a fixed straight line, and at the same time a uniform angular motion about it.

helicoidal (hɛlɪ'kɔɪdəl), *a.* [f. as prec. + -AL[1].] = HELICOID *a.* 1.

1864 in Webster. **1883** *Brit. Assoc. Rep.* 405 The formation of the right and left-handed helicoidal crystals.

'helicoidly, *adv.* [f. HELICOID *a.* + -LY[2].] In a helicoid manner, spirally.

1849 Dana *Geol.* App. i. (1850) 720 A fusiform chamber helicoidly divided.

helicometry (hɛlɪ'kɒmɪtrɪ). *Geom.* [f. *helico-*, comb. form of Gr. ἕλιξ HELIX + -METRY.] The measurement of spirals.

1706 Phillips (ed. Kersey), *Helicometry*, or *Helicosophy*, a Mathematical Art, which teaches how to measure or draw all Spiral Lines upon a Plain, and shews their respective Properties. **1811** *Encycl. Londin.* s.v.

Helicon ('hɛlɪkɒn). Also (senses 2, 3) **helicon.** [L. *Helicōn* = Gr. Ἑλικών. In sense 2b there seems to be association with HELIX.]

1. Name of a mountain in Bœotia, sacred to the Muses, in which rose the fountains of Aganippe and Hippocrene; by 16th and 17th c. writers often confused with these. Hence used allusively in reference to poetic inspiration.

a **1529** Skelton *Agst. Garnesche* 99, I gaue hym drynke of the sugryd welle Of Eliconys waters crystallyne. **1567** Harman *Caveat* (1869) 28 Eloquence haue I none; I neuer was acquaynted with the muses; I neuer tasted of Helycon. **1579** Spencer *Sheph. Cal.* Apr. 42 You Virgins, that on Parnasse dwell, Whence floweth *Helicon*, the learned well. **1600** *title* England's Helicon [ed. 2.. or the Muses Harmony.] **1631** Milton *Epit. M'chess Winchester* 56 Here be tears of perfect moan Wept for thee in Helicon. **1651** Randolph, etc. *Hey for Honesty* v. Wks. (1875) 481 Poor shallow scoundrels.. that never drank any Helicon above a penny a quart. **1892** *Bookman* Nov. 57/1 Any question of his precise place in England's Helicon.

2. a. An ancient acoustical instrument consisting of strings stretched over a resonance-box and capable of being adjusted to different lengths. **b.** A large brass wind-instrument of a spiral form.

1875 Knight *Dict. Mech.*, *Helicon*, a form of wind-instrument of metal, resembling a French-horn, but having keys and valves. **1961** J. Richardson tr. *'Ilf' & 'Petrov's' Twelve Chairs* (1965) 257 The most powerful machine in the band was the helicon, encircled three times by a brass serpent.

3. In various techn. senses (see quots.).

[**1961** P. Aigrain in *Proc. Internat. Conf. Semiconductor Physics (Prague 1960)* 225 Le temps d'atténuation des ondes basse fréquence.. que nous proposons d'appeler 'hélicon'.] **1962** *Electronics* 9 Feb. 26/1 He'll talk about active homogenous semiconductor developments including the Ecole [Normale Supérieure, Paris]'s helicon. Defined as devices without p-n junctions that amplify or oscillate by an action similar to that of a traveling-wave tube, these devices are expected to have a bright future. **1966** *New Scientist* 20 Jan. 155/3 The type of plasma-wave currently exciting most attention is called a helicon. It is transverse and circularly polarized.. and moves along the direction of a magnetic field. **1968** *Ibid.* 17 Oct. 13/2 One might also single out for their promise the intriguing 'helicon waves' which result from the interaction between electromagnetic radiation and a 'gas' of electrons within a solid.

Heliconian (hɛlɪ'kəʊnɪən), *a.* [In sense 1, f. L. *Helicōni-us* = Gr. Ἑλικώνιος, f. Ἑλικών (see prec. and -IAN). In sense 2, f. mod.L. *Helicōnia*, a genus of butterflies.]

1. Pertaining to Helicon, or to the Muses.

1557 Grimald in *Tottell's Misc.* (Arb.) 107 Th Heliconian Nymphs. **1590** Spenser *F.Q.* II. xii. 31 Th' Heliconian maides. **1635** J. Taylor (Water P.) *Life T. Parr* Wks. (1872) 17 He.. ne'er did taste the Heliconian cup. **1779** Cowper *Let. to J. Hill* 14 Nov., Your approbation of my last Heliconian present encourages me to send you another. **1868** Tennyson *Lucretius* 224 Shutting reasons up in rhythm, Or Heliconian honey in living words, To make a truth less harsh.

2. *Entom.* Belonging to the genus *Heliconia*, or family *Heliconiidæ* of butterflies. Also **Helico'nideous, 'Heliconine, 'Heloconoid** *adjs.*

1826 Kirby & Sp. *Entomol.* (1828) III. xxxv. 645 In several of the Heliconian butterflies the greater part of both wings is transparent. **1867** A. R. Wallace *Nat. Select.* iii. (1871) 85 Every species of Napeogenes mimics some other Heliconideous butterfly. **1887** —— in *Fortn. Rev.* Sept. 355 The immense variety of the Heliconoid butterflies.

helicopter ('hɛlɪkɒptə(r)). [ad. F. *hélicoptère*, f. Gr. ἕλικος, ἕλιξ spiral, HELIX + πτερόν wing.] An aircraft which derives its lift and propulsive power principally from the action of one or more lifting screws or rotor-blades, usu. engine-driven, revolving horizontally: modern helicopters are highly-manœuvrable machines used for short or medium-range flights. Also *attrib.* and *Comb.* Also formerly in Fr. form.

[**1861** G. L. M. de Ponton *Brit. Pat. 1929*, The required ascensional motion is given to my aerostatical apparatus (which I intend denominating aeronef or helicoptere,) by means of two or more superposed horizontal helixes combined together.] **1887** tr. *Verne's Clipper of Clouds* iv, We can look forward to such contrivances.. which we can call streophores, helicopters, orthopters.. by means of which man will become the master of space. **1908** O. & W. Wright in *Century Mag.* Sept. 641/2 Several years later we began building these hélicoptères for ourselves. **1909** *Westm. Gaz.* 28 Jan. 4/2 Mr. Howard Wright's helicopter, with which flying tests have been satisfactorily carried out, is now *en route* for Italy. *Ibid.* 2 Mar. 4/1 The Gobron engined Breguet helicopter aeroplane. **1921** *Glasgow Herald* 11 Nov. 6 Recently the Aero Club of France.. offered a prize.. to the first helicopter pilot in France to take a machine 25 metres up in the air. **1923** *Ibid.* 5 May 8 (*heading*) Helicopter Flight. **1927** C. L. M. Brown *Conquest of Air* 39 The helicopter method of flight. **1958** *Jane's Fighting Ships 1957–8* 9 Official illustrations of the new.. helicopter carrier. **1959** *Daily Tel.* 24 Apr. 20/7 He was opening the helicopter station built in Battersea. *Ibid.*, It is intended primarily to be experimental and to assist in the development of helicopter services for London rather than as a permanent station. **1961** *Ibid.* 11 Oct. 25/7 The men are normal infantry, not specialist helicopter-borne troops. **1963** *Economist* 30 Mar. 1213/1 Several helicopter-carriers and three anti-submarine hunter-killer air groups. **1967** *Courier-Mail* (Brisbane) 17 Mar. 4 The petrol drums.. were blasted alight by tracer bullets from R.A.A.F. helicopter gunships hovering 60 ft. above the treetops. **1973** *Guardian* 24 Feb. 2/2 Three helicopter carriers had arrived in the Gulf of Tonkin to join the US naval fleet.

Hence **'helicopt, 'helicopter** *vbs. trans.* and *intr.*, to fly with or as with a helicopter; to transport by helicopter; **heli'copterist** (now *rare*), one who uses a helicopter.

1923 *Daily Mail* 12 Feb. 7 M. Raoul de Pescara, the helicopterist. **1926** *Spectator* 10 Apr. 665/1 An albatross, helicoptering over the masthead, signalled the land. **1959** *Time* 23 Mar. 15 He might be helicoptered up to Camp David. **1961** *Aeroplane* CI. 121/2 The sequence is then: brakes off.. and helicopt away. **1962** *New Scientist* 3 May 230/1 The rotor on its long spindle helicoptered up and out of its case into the air. **1965** *Sunday Times* 10 Oct. 44/3 They build it on deck, and then helicopt it ashore. **1968** *Radio Times* 10 Oct. 31/1 We joined her [*sc.* the aircraft-carrier] off Singapore, helicoptering over the rubber forest.

†**heli'cosophy.** *Obs.* [f. *helico-*, comb. form of Gr. ἕλιξ HELIX, after *philosophy*.] That part of geometry which treats of spirals.

1570 Dee *Math. Pref.* 34 Helicosophie, is nere Sister to Trochilike. **1696** Phillips, *Helicosophy*, a mathematical Art which demonstrates the designing of all spiral Lines.

helictite (hɛ'lɪktaɪt). [f. Gr. ἑλικτός twisted: after STALACTITE.] A distorted twig-like form of stalactite.

1882 H. C. Hovey *Celebrated Amer. Caverns* xi. 186 The term 'Helictite' has been suggested as appropriate to these contorted growths. **1941** *Illustr. London News* CXCIX. 186 (*caption*) The roof of the first grotto or chamber, festooned with stalactites of varied shapes and structure, some tree-like, termed helictites. **1954** W. D. Thornbury *Princ. Geomorphol.* xiii. 337 There is found in portions of some caves a form known as a helictite. It is unusual in that its growth does not necessarily extend along vertical lines. **1971** *Islander* (Victoria, B.C.) 24 Jan. 5/3 Helictites are the amazing coral-like stalactites which grow in every direction, seemingly to defy the law of gravity.

helidrome ('hɛlɪdrəʊm). [f. HELI- after AERODROME.] A landing-site for helicopters.

1951 *Daily Tel.* 5 June 4/6 Helidrome, rotorport, helistop and helihalt are among recent verbal coinage[s] to signify a helicopter station. **1952** *Times* 10 Oct. 7/4 What.. is a 'helidrome'? So far as I can see it is either a place where marsh-meadows run.. or a place where [s]nails run.. But in either case the word ought to be 'helodrome'. **1953** *Listener* 25 June 1040/2 One can almost hear the sound of rockets being fired from the space ships moored at the South Bank helidrome to herald in the twenty-first century. **1966** *Punch* 6 July 8/2 The Director.. with a personal helidrome at Great Yarmouth.

helie, -y, var. HEILY, HIGHLY *a. Obs.*

Heligoland trap ('hɛlɪgəʊlænd træp). [f. *Heligoland*, a German island in the North Sea: see TRAP *sb.*[1]] A type of trap used to catch birds for banding or ringing.

1935 *Brit. Birds* XXVIII. 310 The few hundred Pipits which have been caught since a Heligoland trap was put into operation on Skokholm in August, 1933. **1960** E. Ennion *House on Shore* iv. 40 Variety in the design of Heligoland and crow traps at the various Observatories is as nothing compared with the diversity found among their smaller.. types of trap.

heling, healing, *vbl. sb.* Now *dial.* Also 6- helling. [f. HELE *v.*[1] and [2] + -ING[1].]

1. The action of covering; covering up, concealing; the covering in of a house, roofing with slate, tiles, or the like.

a **1200** *Lofsung* in *Cott. Hom.* 207 Bi his spotlunge and bufettunge and his heliunge. *a* **1225** *Ancr. R.* 150 Þe heliunge is þe god dedes lif, & halt hit ine strencðe. **1357** *Lay Folks Catech.* 222 All wrangwise takyng.. hiding or helyng of othir men godes. **1451** *Churchw. Acc. Yatton* (1890) 94 For helyng of Synt Jamys ys Chapell. **1554** *Ibid.* 166 The tyler for yᵉ hellyng of yᵉ Church. **1609** Skene *Reg. Maj.* 6 Fraudfull heiling and concealing of treasure. **1669**

WORLIDGE *Syst. Agric.* (1681) 237 Healing with Lead or flat Stone is not to be approved of, by reason of its weight. **1703** T. N. *City & C. Purchaser* 275 For Ripping, and Healing again.. Bricklayers reckon 3*s.* 6*d.* per Square.

2. *concr.* A covering; a cover, roofing.

13.. *K. Alis.* 6188 Above, and byneothe, is heore heolyng. **1375** BARBOUR *Bruce* v. 11 The heling of thar hevede That vikkit vyntir had thame revede. **1387** TREVISA *Higden* (Rolls) II. 283 Sche hidde hir armes and hir þyȝhes wiþ dyuers helynges. *Ibid.* III. 273 þe helynge [of the palace] liche to þe firmament. **1498** *Will of Whytmor* (Somerset Ho.), My portouse wᵗ a rede helyng. **1543** *Will of J. Mors* (Ibid.), Fetherbedde, a bolster.. twoo blankettes a Helyng a matres. **1674** RAY *N. C. Words* 24 A *Bed-Healing* (*Derb.*), a coverlet: it is also called absolutely a Hylling in many places. **1703** T. N. *City & C. Purchaser* 169 Of the weight of this sort of Healing. **1838** MRS. BRAY *Trad. Devonsh.* I. 306 Slaters with us.. are called *helliers* and the slate roof of a house is termed the *helling*. **1853** *N. & Q.* 1st Ser. VIII. 44/2 Another Devonianism. The Cover of a book is called its healing.

†**b.** Clothing. *Obs.*

1382 in *Wyclif's Sel. Wks.* III. 519 Ynowȝ for liflode and heling. *c* **1400** *Apol. Loll.* 43 Fode & heling hauing, wiþ hem I schal be content.

3. *Comb.*, as ***heling-coster, -net, -stone.***

1447 *E.E. Wills* (1882) 131 All my.. helyng Costurs of hallys. **1558–9** *Act 1 Eliz.* c. 17 §1 No person.. shall use any Heling Nett or Trymle Bote. **1602** CAREW *Cornwall* 6 b, For covering of houses there are three sorts of Slate, which from that use take the name of *Healing-stones.*

helio¹ ('hiːlɪəʊ), colloq. abbrev. of HELIOGRAPH *sb.* and *v.* **a.** *gen.*

1893 R. KIPLING *Many Invent.* 30, I used to put my signaller under arrest to prevent him reading the helio-orders. **1897** *Daily News* 4 Sept. 5/4 Messages had to be helio'd under a hot fire at short range.

b. *spec.* = HELIOGRAPH *sb.* 4 b.

1886 KIPLING *Departm. Ditties* (1904) 23 All honour unto Bangs, for n'er did Jones thereafter know By word or act official who read off that helio. **1901** 'LINESMAN' *Words by Eyewitness* (1902) 32 Then another helio, spelt out painfully by the frowning, staring signallers, 'Very hard pressed'.

helio². [colloq. abbrev. of HELIOTROPE.] = HELIOTROPE 1 d.

1894 *T. Eaton & Co. Catal.* Spring & Summer 31/3 Pink, sky and helio. printed pique vest. **1922** *Daily Mail* 22 Nov. 5 Very exceptional value with Blue or Black or Helio border. **1928** *Ibid.* 31 July 1/3 Dainty.. Dressing Jackets in Pink, Apple and Helio.

helio-, combining form of Gr. ἥλιος sun, occurring in various scientific and other terms, most of which are entered in their alphabetical places; others of rarer occurrence are placed here. **helio'arkite** *a.* [cf. ARKITE], relating to the sun and Noah's ark, as objects of worship; ‖**helioco'metes** [mod.L., f. Gr. κομήτης comet], an appearance of rays of light extending from the sun like a comet's tail; **helio-dæ'monic** *a.*, relating to the sun and dæmons; **helio-e'lectric** *a.*, relating to electric force emanating from the sun; **helio-en'graving** = HELIOGRAVURE; **helio'fugal** *a.* [after *centrifugal*; cf. F. *héliophuge*], tending away from the sun; **heli'olater** [Gr. -λατρης worshipping], a worshipper of the sun; so **heli'olatrous** *a.*, worshipping the sun; **heli'olatry** [Gr. λατρεία worship], sun-worship; **heli'ologist**, one versed in heliology; **heli'ology**, the science of the sun's energy and action; **heli'ophilous** *a.* [φίλος loving], fond of or attracted by sunlight; **helio'phobia** [Gr. -φοβία fear], dread of or shrinking from sunlight, photophobia; so **'heliophobe** [Gr. -φοβος fearing], one affected with heliophobia; **helio'phobic** *a.*, fearing or shunning sunlight; **heli'ophyllite** *Min.* [ad. G. *heliophyllit* (G. Flink 1888, in *Öfversigt af kongl. Vetenskaps-Akad. Förh.* XLV. 575), f. Gr. φύλλον leaf: so called because of its colour and structure], a yellowish oxychloride of lead and arsenic, probably dimorphous with ecdemite; **helio'polar** *a.*, pertaining to the pole of the sun's rotation; **helio'tactic** *a.*, responding to sunlight by movement; characterized by heliotaxis; **helio'taxis**, phototaxis due to the rays of the sun; **helio'therapy**, the treatment of disease by exposure to the sun's rays; ˌ**heliozin'cography** (see quots.).

1804 *Edin. Rev.* III. 314 Seats of the *Helio-arkite superstition. **1838** MRS. BRAY *Trad. Devonsh.* I. 148 The ceremonies of the Helioarkite procession. **1727–51** CHAMBERS *Cycl.*, **Heliocometes*, comet of the sun; a phænomenon sometimes observed at the setting of the sun; thus denominated by Sturmius and Pylen.. in regard it seems to make a comet of the sun, being a large tail, or column of light, fixed or hung to that luminary, and dragging after it at his setting. **1866** *Cornh. Mag.* Mar. 293 Notions about an arkite idolatry and a *Helio-dæmonic worship. **1884** *Nature* 8 May 47/2 The *helio-electric theory of the perturbations of terrestrial magnetism. **1886** *Sci. Amer.* 24 July 49/2 The *helio-engraving by etching was brought to a high degree of completion by Klic, of Vienna, in 1883. **1885** CLERKE *Pop. Hist. Astron.* 387 The '*heliofugal' power by which Comets' tails are developed. **1828** WEBSTER, **Heliolater. Ibid.*, **Heliolatry.* **1890** GLADSTONE *Impreg. Rock* (1892) 66 According to *heliologists, the process does not even yet appear to be absolutely completed. **1886** *Spectator* 24 Apr. 545/1 The evolution of *heliology. **1885** *Syd. Soc. Lex.*, **Heliophobe*, one whose eyes suffer from the sun's rays. **Heliophobia*, the fear of the sun's rays on the retina, such as occurs in albinism. **1886** J. RATTRAY in *Trans. R. Soc. Edin.* XXXII. 598 A *heliophobic spore may often find enough of shade among the rhizoids of other pre-existing weeds. **1890** *Jrnl. Chem. Soc.* LVIII. I. 459 On specimens of the so-called rhodotilite from Pajsberg a yellow mineral has been observed... The author names this mineral *heliophyllite. **1968** I. KOSTOV *Mineral.* II. vii. 467 Ekdemite is tetragonal, dimorphous with heliophyllite which is orthorhombic pseudotetragonal. **1902** *Science* 7 Feb. 223/2 The vector diagram in *heliopolar coordinates takes the form of a conical surface around the Sun. **1898** *Jrnl. R. Microsc. Soc.* 422 The progressive movements of the larvæ of the gooseberry mite (*Bryobia ribis* Th.) are always positively *heliotactic. **1904** *Biol. Bull.* VI. 253 The mating habits of these highly heliotactic males and wingless females. **1898** *Jrnl. R. Microsc. Soc.* 422 (*heading*) *Heliotaxis of larval mites. **1890** BILLINGS *Med. Dict.* I. 627/2 **Heliotherapy*, treatment of disease by exposure to sunlight. **1903** *Lancet* 11 July 104/1 The fundamental principles and practical applications of helio-therapy and phototherapy. **1921** *Glasgow Herald* 15 July 10 For the information of medical practitioners interested in heliotherapy. **1928** A. HUXLEY *Let.* 23 May (1969) 297 My medical uncle.. says that he has known TB of the intestine greatly benefited by heliotherapy. **1903** *Nature* 19 Nov. 60 Two new methods have now superseded photo-zincography; one of these, '*heliozincography', was worked out by the Ordnance Survey... The first method consists in reproduction direct on a sensitised zinc plate in contact with a reversed negative. **1936** H. S. L. WINTERBOTHAM *Key to Maps* xix. 196 We have seen above how work from paper may go direct to the zinc by a process known as vandyking. To do the same with a negative and a sensitized sheet of zinc is known as heliozincography.

heliocentric (ˌhiːlɪəʊ'sɛntrɪk), *a.* (*sb.*) [f. HELIO-: see CENTRIC. Cf. F. *héliocentrique*. Opposed in both senses to GEOCENTRIC.]

1. Referred to the sun as centre; considered as viewed from the centre of the sun: as the ***heliocentric latitude, longitude, place,*** etc. of a planet, i.e. that in which it would appear to an observer placed at the centre of the sun.

1685 *Phil. Trans.* XV. 1217 It was necessary.. to make a Table of ♃'s Heliocentrick places, to which the Parallaxes being applied, give the Geocentrick. **1703** GREGORY *Ibid.* XXIII. 1318 Finding the Heliocentrick and Geocentric places of a Comet. **1786** *Ibid.* LXXVI. 429, I have here given its heliocentric and geocentric longitudes and latitudes. **1833** HERSCHEL *Astron.* v. 210 When we speak of the heliocentric longitudes and latitudes of objects, we suppose the spectator situated in the sun.

2. Having, or taking, the sun as centre: as the ***heliocentric*** (or Copernican) ***system*** of astronomy. (See B.)

1834 *Nat. Philos.* III. Gloss. s.v. *Geocentric* (U. K. S.), The moon's orbit is Geocentric; but the orbits of the other planets, and of the earth itself, are Heliocentric. **1892** WESTCOTT *Gospel of Life* 12 The heliocentric view of our system.. is more religious and, in the fullest sense, more scriptural than the geocentric view which it displaced. *fig.* **1871** R. H. HUTTON *Ess.* II. 285 It [poetry of the Old Testament] is what one might call a heliocentric, as distinguished from a geocentric, representation of life.

†**B.** *sb.* One who takes the sun as a centre. *Obs.*

1667 A. NOWEL in Josselyn *Voy. New Eng.* (1674) 48 This assertion is not expugned by Geocentricks.. nor oppugned by Heliocentricks.

Hence ˌ**helio'centricism**, the heliocentric theory; ˌ**heliocen'tricity**, heliocentric quality.

1865 F. HALL in H. H. Wilson tr. *Vishṇu Purāṇa* II. 242 *note*, The heliocentricism taught in this passage.. is remarkable. **1878** *N. Amer. Rev.* CXXVI. 163 Our readers who are ignorant of astronomy may as well refuse to acknowledge the heliocentricity of things. **1885** W. W. ROBERTS *Pontif. Decrees* Introd. 21 The Pope said in effect that heliocentricism was a heresy.

helio'central, *a. rare.* [f. as prec. + -AL¹.] = HELIOCENTRIC. Hence **helio'centrically** *adv.*, as viewed from the centre of the sun.

1686 GOAD *Celest. Bodies* II. i. 122, I have reason to believe the Planetary motions to be Heliocentrical. **1726** tr. *Gregory's Astron.* I. 471 The Earth.. when it is in Conjunction with any other Planet Heliocentrically. **1960** V. NABOKOV *Bend Sinister* ii. 18 They of the solar side saw heliocentrically what you telurians [*sic*] saw geocentrically.

heliochrome ('hiːlɪəʊkrəʊm). [f. HELIO- + Gr. χρῶμα colour.] A photograph representing an object in its natural colours. So **helio'chromic** *a.*, pertaining to *helio-chromy*. **helio-'chromoscope**, a device for superposing three specially prepared photographs of an object so as to produce an image in the natural colours. **helio'chromotype** = HELIOCHROME. **'heliochromy**, the production of images of objects in the natural colours by a photographic process.

1853 R. HUNT *Man. Photogr.* xii. 176 The name of *Heliochromes has been given to these naturally coloured photographs.. the colours soon faded. **1855** LACAN *Pref. Niépce de St. Victor's Researches* 17 His *heliochromic investigations. **1892** *Daily News* 4 May 5/5 To reproduce them [the natural colours] to the eyes it is sufficient to superpose the three images, one with red light, one with green, and one with blue violet. This is accomplished in.. a device called a *heliochromoscope about the size of a hand stereoscope. **1875** KNIGHT *Dict. Mech.*, **Heliochromotype*, a sun-picture in the natural colors: long desired, partially obtained, but always fugitive—so far. **1855** tr. *Niépce de St. Victor's Researches* 43 *Heliochromy. **1892** *Daily News* 5 May 6/5 Mr. Fred. E. Ives, of Philadelphia, gave an exhibition.. of his 'composite heliochromy', the name of his process of coloured photography.

heliochryse ('hiːlɪəʊkraɪs). [ad. L. *hēliochrȳsos, -on*, a variant form in Pliny for *helichrȳsos, -on* (see HELICHRYSUM), app. taken by later writers as derived from Gr. ἥλιος sun + χρυσός gold.] Poetic name for some bright yellow flower: ? a sunflower or marigold. (See also HELICHRYSE.)

1593 B. BARNES *Parthenophil* Sonn. xcvi. in Arb. *Garner* V. 394 To whom, for need, Parthenophe did lend At Nature's suit, rich Heliochrise, which shined In her fair hair. *Ibid.* Madr. xxiii. *Ibid.* 404 In his hand, a wreath of Heliochrise He brought, to beautify those tresses. **1689** T. PLUNKET *Char. Gd. Commander* 55 The Heliochryse.. His Golden Leaves expandeth out of love To Phoebus.

helio-dæmonic: see HELIO-.

heliodon ('hiːlɪəʊdɒn). [f. HELI(O- + Gr. ὁδός way, path.] A mechanical apparatus for demonstrating the sun's apparent motion, used in astronomy or in architectural design.

1909 in WEBSTER. **1932** DUFTON & BECKETT in *Jrnl. Sci. Instrum.* IX. 253 In the Heliodon, the apparatus which is the subject of the present paper, the representation of the motion of the sun is simplified. **1964** *New Scientist* 30 Jan. 288/1 Models of a building.. with an artificial Sun would be of immense value... Although individual machines were given such names as 'sunshine analyser' or 'solarometer', the generic name for them is 'heliodon'.

heliodor ('hiːlɪəʊdɔə(r)). *Min.* Also **-dore**. [a. G. *heliodor*, f. Gr. ἥλιο-ς sun + δῶρον gift.] A richly coloured variety of golden beryl found in South West Africa.

1913 *Mineral. Mag.* XVI. 362 *Heliodor*... Trade-name for a golden beryl of gem-quality from German South-West Africa. **1952** L. G. GREEN *Lords of Last Frontier* (1953) xviii. 185 Heliodore is found only on the barren slopes of Rossing Mountain... Apparently it does not exist anywhere else in the world. German prospectors discovered the first deposit.. and the lovely greenish-yellow opalescent stones were set in the form of a cross. **1959** *Chambers's Encycl.* II. 281/2 The pink morganite, the golden heliodor and the green emerald are among the most attractive of coloured gems.

helio-electric, etc.: see HELIO-.

Heliogabalus (ˌhiːlɪəʊ'gæbələs). [Latinized f. *Elagabal*, Syro-Phœnician sun-god.] The adopted name of Varius Avitus Bassianus, Roman Emperor A.D. 218–222, famed for folly and profligacy, used allusively. Also ˌ**Helioga'balian** (-gə'beɪlɪən) *a.*, resembling the character or tastes of Heliogabalus. ˌ**Helio'gabalize** *v. intr.*, to act like Heliogabalus.

1589 GREENE *Menaphon* (1880) 71 For his dissolute life he seemed another Heliogabalus. **1618** J. TAYLOR (Water P.) *Pennilesse Pilgr.* sig. F3ʳ Had I beene a Sardanapalus, or a Heliogabalus, I thinke that.. the great trauell ouer the Mountaines had tamed me. **1624** BURTON *Anat. Mel.* (ed. 2) I. ii. II. ii. 63 What Fagos, Epicures, Apitios, Heliogables our times affoord? **1859** *National Mag.* V. 142/1 In California.. the Celestials.. make a Heliogobalian [*sic*] kind of dish of rats' brains. **1893** W. S. GILBERT *Utopia Ltd.* I. 5 His Majesty is one of the most Heliogabalian profligates that ever disgraced an autocratic throne. **1930** D. H. LAWRENCE *Phoenix II* (1968) 492 Perhaps the mentality of a boy of fourteen.. is more wholesome than the mentality of the young cock-taily person.. whose mind has nothing to do but play with the toys of life... Heliogabulus [*sic*], indeed!

heliogram ('hiːlɪəʊgræm). [f. HELIOGRAPH 4, after *telegram*.] A message transmitted by a heliograph (see next, sense 4).

1881 *Nature* XXIV. 176 The sight of those who receive the heliogram gets.. soon fatigued. **1897** LD. ROBERTS *41 Yrs. India* II. li. 225 Brigadier-General Massy was informed in reply to his heliogram, that [etc.].

heliograph ('hiːlɪəʊgrɑːf, -græf), *sb.* [f. HELIO- + -GRAPH, Gr. -γραφος writing, writer.]

1. a. Name given to an engraving obtained by a process in which a specially prepared plate is acted on chemically by exposure to light. Also *attrib.*

The name was originally given to the process invented by Niépce de St. Victor in 1826.

1853 R. HUNT *Man. Photogr.* i. 12 Niepce.. had also succeeded in rendering his Heliographs, when once formed, impervious to the further effects of the solar rays. **1875** tr. *Vogel's Chem. Light* i. 11 Copper plate impressions of this kind have been found amongst the papers left behind by Niépce, which he called 'heliographs'.. as far back as 1826. This method.. is still in use.. especially in the printing of paper money. **1896** *Daily News* 18 Dec. 7/6 Miniature paintings by Fouquet.. copied by the heliograph process.

†**b.** A photograph (Webster, 1864). *Obs.*

2. An apparatus for taking photographs of the sun.

1848 *Jrnl. R. Agric. Soc.* IX. II. 326 This latter instrument includes a *heliograph* and *nebulograph*, worked by one and the same clock-movement. **1865** *Reader* 9 Sept. 291/3 The Kew heliograph, in charge of Mr. De La Rue, continues to be worked by a qualified assistant.

3. An instrument for measuring the intensity of sunlight.

1851 R. HUNT *Photogr.* 210 The number of lines marked on the paper.. will furnish a comparative measure of the intensity of solar light.. and may be registered as so many

degrees of the Heliograph, the name Mr. Jordan has given his instrument.

4. a. An apparatus for signalling by means of a movable mirror which reflects flashes of sunlight to a distance. Cf. HELIOTROPE 4. Also *attrib.*

1877 ATKINSON *Ganot's Physics* (ed. 8) §509 *Mance's Heliograph.* The reflection of light from mirrors has been lately applied by Mance in signalling at great distances by means of the sun's light. **1880** *Rep. Brit. Assoc.* 461 The author claims to have contrived a heliograph, or sun-telegraph, by which the rays of the sun can be directed on any given point with greater ease than by those at present in use. **1880** *Times* 9 Oct. 5/4 On the 27th of August, about 9 a.m., a flash was seen in the far distance. In a moment our heliograph was on, and we found, to our great delight, it was from General Roberts. **1897** *Daily News* 18 Sept. 5 They hope to secure heliograph connection with General Blood's force shortly.

b. A message sent by heliograph.

1899 *Pall Mall Mag.* Nov. 319, I have just received a heliograph that the Basutos have bands out through .. the valley.

'heliograph, *v.* [f. prec. sb.]

1. *trans.* To communicate by heliograph: see prec. 4. Also with *obj. clause* and *absol.*

1880 *Standard* 24 Apr. 5/5 General Stewart heliographed an account of the battle to Brigadier Ross. **1888** *Athenæum* 7 Jan. 10/2 There were all the means for heliographing at Korti. **1893** R. KIPLING *Many Invent.* 29 We used to heliograph to them.

2. To photograph by heliography.

1883 R. HALDANE *Workshop Receipts* Ser. II. 192/1 When the cloth tracings have to be heliographed, raw sienna is also added to the ink.

heliographer (hi:lɪ'ɒgrəfə(r)). [f. prec. + -ER: cf. *photographer.*] One who practises heliography; one who makes or works a heliograph: see the various senses of these words.

1875 tr. *Vogel's Chem. Light* xix. 281 The failure of heliographers, lithographers, and photographers who tried to work by combining the two arts.

heliographic (hi:lɪəʊ'græfɪk), *a.* [f. HELIO- + -GRAPHIC. Cf. F. *héliographique.*]

1. Pertaining to the description of the sun.

heliographic latitude or ***longitude***: the latitude or longitude of points on the sun's surface, referred to the sun's equator and to a meridian passing through the node of this with the ecliptic. (Cf. *geographic.*)

1706 PHILLIPS (ed. Kersey) s.v. *Charts, Heliographick Charts*, Descriptions of the Sun's Body, and of its *Maculæ*, or Spots. **1879** NEWCOMB & HOLDEN *Astron.* 289 The heliographic latitude of the spot, or its angular distance from the solar equator.

2. †**a.** Belonging to photography; photographic.

1840 *Proc. Amer. Phil. Soc.* I. 181 Dr. Patterson exhibited some specimens of the Heliographic Art (Daguerreotype). **1855** tr. *Niépce de St. Victor's Researches* i. 44 The heliographic images coloured by its light.

b. Belonging to photographic engraving: see HELIOGRAPH 1, HELIOGRAPHY 3.

1851 R. HUNT *Photography* ix. 107 Producing a better effect than was given by the Heliographic process in several hours. **1855** LACAN *Pref. Niépce de St. Victor's Researches* 21 The remarkable works which heliographic engraving has produced. **1858** *Photogr. Notes* III. 260/2 The heliographic image formed by the sensitive varnish acted on by the light. **1875** tr. *Vogel's Chem. Light* i. 12 Printed off from heliographic plates.

3. Pertaining to or obtained by the signalling apparatus called a heliograph (see HELIOGRAPH 4).

1880 *Standard* 8 Apr. 5/3 Hughes's Brigade is in heliographic communication with Khelat-i-Ghilzai. **1897** LD. ROBERTS *41 Yrs. India* II. liv. 258 The more perfect heliographic apparatus which is now available.

So **helio'graphical** *a.* = HELIOGRAPHIC; **helio'graphically** *adv.*, by means of a HELIOGRAPH (sense 4 in quot.).

1884 *Sat. Rev.* 26 Jan. 120 How the relieving force first came heliographically into communication with Candahar.

heliography (hi:lɪ'ɒgrəfɪ). [f. HELIO- + -GRAPHY. Cf. F. *héliographie.*]

1. The description of the sun. (Cf. *geography.*)

1730–6 BAILEY (folio), *Heliography*, a Description of the Sun. **1798** C. PALMER (*title*) A Treatise on the Sublime Science of Heliography satisfactorily demonstrating our great orb of light, the sun, to be absolutely no other than a body of Ice! **1867–77** G. F. CHAMBERS *Astron.* VII. vii. 712 So much useful work has been done in heliography.

†**2.** The process or art of obtaining permanent images of objects by the chemical action of light on prepared surfaces; photography. *Obs.*

1840 *Penny Cycl.* XVIII. 113 s.v. *Photogenic Drawings*, Such apparatus is named after its inventor the Daguerrotype, and the process itself either photogeny, photography, or heliography (sun-drawing). **1840** (*title*) Handbook of Heliography.

3. Name of a process of engraving in which a specially prepared plate is acted upon chemically by exposure to light.

1845 *Athenæum* 22 Feb. 202 The process by which these pictures were procured, called by its discoverer *Heliography*. **1875** tr. *Vogel's Chem. Light* i. 10 One of the finest applications of photography, that of *heliography*, or the combination of photography with copper-plate printing.

1880 *Daily News* 2 Dec. 5/2 Heliography, it seems, makes no impression on the paper as types do.

4. The system of signalling by means of the HELIOGRAPH (sense 4).

1887 *Advance* (Chicago) 10 Nov. 718 Heliography is a sort of telegraphic system of communication by means of flashes of sunlight reflected from mirrors.

heliogravure (hi:lɪəʊ'greɪvjʊə(r)). [a. F. *héliogravure*, f. HELIO- + *gravure* engraving.] A process of engraving by means of the action of light on a sensitized surface; an engraved plate, or an engraving, thus obtained; photogravure. Also *attrib.*

1879 FURNIVALL *New Shaks. Soc. Rep.* 7 A héliogravure reproduction by M. Dujardin, of Virtue's engraving. **1881** *Athenæum* 16 Apr. 521/2 The medium of reproduction .. is besides somewhat antiquated in these days of autotype and heliogravure. **1883** *Pall Mall G.* 29 Nov., Phototype, heliogravure, woodcuts, photo and chromo lithography, have been each used according to need.

helioid ('hi:lɪɔɪd), *a.* [f. Gr. ἥλιος sun + -OID.]

1886 *Syd. Soc. Lex.*, *Helioid*, resembling the sun. Applied to a body that is round, and has it circumference radiated with hair-like points.

heliolater, -logy, etc.: see HELIO-.

heliolite ('hi:lɪəʊlaɪt). *Min.* [a. F. *heliolite* (1797), f. HELIO- + -LITE.] Sun-stone, a variety of orthoclase containing albite or oligoclase.

heliolithic (ˌhi:lɪəʊ'lɪθɪk), *a.* [f. HELIO-, after *eolithic*, etc.] Designating a civilization characterized by megaliths and sun-worship.

1915 G. E. SMITH *Migr. Early Culture* 4 The habit of megalithic building and sun-worship (a combination for which it is convenient to use Professor Brockwell's distinctive term 'heliolithic culture'). **1916** *Church Q. Rev.* Jan. 283 The world-wide migration of this 'heliolithic culture'. **1925** *Bull. John Rylands Libr.* IX. 402 There is no known heliolithic temple in the Thames Valley. **1929** W. DEEPING *Roper's Row* xxxvi, But assuredly Ruth belonged to the old heliolithic people. She had something of the south in eyes, hair, temperament.

heliometer (hi:lɪ'ɒmɪtə(r)). [ad. F. *héliomètre* (1747 in Hatz.-Darm.), f. HELIO- + Gr. μέτρον measure, -METER.]

1. An astronomical instrument originally devised for measuring the diameter of the sun; now much used in determining the angular distance between two stars. Also *attrib.*

It consists of a telescope, having the object-glass divided into two parts, each of which can be made to slide past the other and thus superpose the two images produced.

1753 SHORT in *Phil. Trans.* XLVIII. 165 M. Bouguer had read .. in the year 1748, a memoir, in which he describes an heliometer; which is an instrument, consisting of two objective glasses, for measuring the diameters of the planets. **1836** *Penny Cycl.* V. 269 An invention of his in 1748, which he calls the *heliometer*, and which is in fact the first *double object glass micrometer*, and was properly so called. **1874** *Monthly Not. R. Astron. Soc.* XXXIV. 279 The planet Juno at the opposition of 1874 appears to be very favourably situated for a trial of this method .. and the Repsold Heliometer, with which the transit is to be observed, a suitable instrument. **1893** SIR R. BALL *Story of Sun* 334 The heliometer of six inches aperture at the Yale Observatory. **1893** D. GILL (*title*) Heliometer observations for determination of stellar parallax made at the Royal Observatory, Cape of Good Hope. **1905** *Astrophysical Jrnl.* XXII. 103 The heliometer measures made in connection with transits of Venus in 1874 and 1882.

†**2.** Name given to a complex form of portable sun-dial, used for ascertaining solar time, latitude, length of day, times of sunrise and sunset, etc. *Obs.*

1875 KNIGHT *Dict. Mech.*

So **heliometry** (hi:lɪ'ɒmɪtrɪ), the art or practice of using the heliometer.

heliometric (hi:lɪəʊ'mɛtrɪk). *a.* [f. prec. + -IC: cf. F. *héliométrique.*] Pertaining to, or obtained or made by, the heliometer; relating to measurement of the sun. Also **helio'metrical** *a.*; hence **helio'metrically** *adv.*

1881 *Athenæum* 4 June 753/2 Heliometric observations of Mars. **1882** *Standard* 9 Dec. 5/4 At Harvard more than eight hundred heliometrical measurements were made. **1883** *Science* I. 94 [They] do not maintain a steady contact together when heliometrically observed. **1886** C. A. YOUNG *Recent Adv. in Solar Astron.* in *Pop. Sci. Mo.* XXX. 25 The publication of the photographic and heliometric results is waited for with much interest.

helion ('hi:lɪɒn). *Nuclear Physics.* [ad. F. *hélion* (G. Fournier 1930, in *Jrnl. de Physique et le Radium* I. 196, f. HELI(UM + -ON[1].] **a.** The nucleus of the normal helium isotope (^{4}He), consisting of two protons and two neutrons; an alpha-particle. **b.** The nucleus of the helium isotope ^{3}He, consisting of two protons and one neutron.

1930 *Sci. Abstr.* A. XXXIII. 969 Equilibrium tends to be conserved between the number of helions (helium nuclei) in the nucleus and the number of free nuclear electrons. **1964** L. PAULING in *Nature* 4 Jan. 61/1, I suggest that the word helion be used for the α-particle, the nucleus of the helium atom. **1965** *New Scientist* 14 Oct. 87/2 The helium nucleus, or helion, consisting of two neutrons and two protons. **1972** *Nature* 8 Dec. 325/1 In the case of deuterons, the low binding energy makes it easy to calculate the deuteron-nucleus potential from the constituent neutron-nucleus and proton-nucleus optical potentials, but for the more tightly bound helions, tritons and α particles this cannot yet be done with sufficient accuracy.

heliophilous, -phobia, etc.: see HELIO-.

heliopore ('hi:lɪəʊpɔə(r)). [ad. mod.L. *Heliopora*, f. Gr. ἥλιος sun + πόρος pore: see MADREPORE.] A coral of the genus *Heliopora*; a sun coral.

helioscope ('hi:lɪəʊskəʊp). [a. F. *hélioscope* (1671 in Hatz.-Darm.), f. HELIO- + -SCOPE.] An apparatus for observing the sun without injury to the eye, or a telescope fitted with such an apparatus; the intensity of the light being reduced by smoked or coloured glass, by reflectors, or by other means.

1675 *Phil. Trans.* X. 441 A Description of Helioscopes and some other instruments. **1761** SHORT *Ibid.* LII. 178 A reflecting telescope of 18 inches focus, with a helioscope adapted to it. **1869** PHIPSON tr. *Guillemin's Sun* (1870) 85 What are called *helioscopes*, which are merely composed of two prisms, or two pieces of glass cut wedge-shaped, one white and transparent and the other black or coloured.

So **helio'scopic** *a.*, belonging to the helioscope, or to observation of the sun; **heli'oscopy**, the use of the helioscope, observation of the sun.

1869 HERSCHEL *Astron.* III. (ed. 10) 75 Helioscopy. **1881** C. A. YOUNG *Sun* 65 Other forms of helioscopic eyepiece.

‖**heliosis** (hi:lɪ'əʊsɪs). [mod.L., a. Gr. ἡλίωσις exposure to the sun, f. ἡλιοῦσθαι to be exposed to the sun, also to suffer sunstroke, f. ἥλιος sun.]

1. *Med.* **a.** = INSOLATION. **b.** Sunstroke.

1854 MAYNE *Expos. Lex.*, *Heliosis*, the warming of the body in the sun's rays; insolation. **1882** QUAIN *Dict. Med.*, *Heliosis* .. is also employed as a synonym for the sunstroke.

2. *Bot.* (See quot.)

1866 *Treas. Bot.*, *Heliosis*, a term applied to the spots produced upon leaves by the concentration of the rays of the sun through inequalities of the glass of conservatories, or through drops of water resting upon them.

[**heliospherical**, in recent Dicts., app. an error for HELISPHERICAL.]

heliostat ('hi:lɪəʊstæt). Also **heliostata, -state.** [a. mod.L. *heliostata*, F. *héliostat* (1764 in Hatz.-Darm.), f. HELIO- + στατός standing.]

An apparatus consisting of a mirror turned by clockwork so as to reflect the light of the sun in a fixed direction. (Also applied to a simpler apparatus worked by hand, properly a *porte-lumière.*)

1747 J. T. DESAGULIERS tr. *Gravesande's Nat. Phil.* II. v. ii. 107 *An Heliostate*, Whereby the Sun's Rays are fix'd. This Machine consists of two principal Parts .. The first is a plane metallick Speculum, supported by a Stand, the other is a Clock which directs the Speculum. *c* **1790** IMISON *Sch. Art* I. 271 The *Heliostata* to take off the inconveniences which arise from the motion of the earth, in making experiments on the solar light. **1803** YOUNG in *Phil. Trans.* XCIV. 16 For performing this experiment with very great accuracy, a heliostate would be necessary. **1841** *Proc. Amer. Phil. Soc.* II. 97 A simple form of the Heliostat, or instrument for throwing a stationary beam of light into a darkened room.

Hence **helio'static** *a.*, pertaining to a heliostat.

1881 *Nature* 29 Sept. 514 Phenomena developed by heliostatic star-disks.

heliothid (hi:lɪ'ɒθɪd), *sb.* and *a.* *Entom.* [f. mod.L. *Heliothidæ*, f. generic name *Heliothis.*]

A. *sb.* A moth of the family *Heliothidæ*. **B.** *adj.* Belonging to or having the character of the *Heliothidæ*.

1884 *Science* 11 July 44/2 Even Agrotis takes a distinct heliothid tendency in the tuberculate front and heavily armed fore-tibia of the western species.

heliotrope ('hi:lɪəʊtrəʊp, 'hɛlɪəʊtrəʊp). Forms: α. 1 **eliotropus**, 4 **elitropium, -ius, eliotropia**, 6 **helytropium, heliotropion, -ius**, 6–7 **-ium**; see also HELIOTROPIAN *sb.* β. 6– **heliotrope**. [Formerly in Lat. form *hēliotropium*, etc., a. Gr. ἡλιοτρόπιον (also ἡλιοτρόπος) a plant which turns its flowers and leaves to the sun, heliotrope; also a green stone streaked with red, bloodstone, and a kind of sundial; f. ἥλιος sun + -τροπος turning, τρέπειν to turn. In current form, a. F. *héliotrope* (16th c. in Hatz.-Darm.).]

1. a. A name given to plants of which the flowers turn so as to follow the sun; in early times applied to the sunflower, marigold, etc.; now, a plant of the genus *Heliotropium* (N.O. *Ehretiaceæ* or *Boraginaceæ*), comprising herbs or shrubs with small clustered purple flowers; esp. *H. Peruvianum*, commonly cultivated for its fragrance.

α. *c* **1000** *Sax. Leechd.* I. 254 Deos wyrt þe man eliotropus and oðrum naman sigilhweorfa nemneð. **1398** TREVISA *Barth. De P.R.* XVII. liv. (1495) 635 *Elitropium* is a drye herbe and .. it beeryth and tornyth the leyf abowte wyth the meuynge of the sonne. **1549** *Compl. Scot.* vi. 57 Siklyik, ther is ane eirb callit helytropium, the quhilk the vulgaris callis

soucye; it hes the leyuis appin as lang as the soune is in our hemispere, and it closis the leyuis, quhen the soune passis vndir our orizon. *c* **1590** GREENE *Fr. Bacon* xvi. 58 Apollo's heliotropion then shall stoop And Venus hyacinth shall vail her top. **1603** B. JONSON *King's Coronation Entertain.* Wks. (Rtldg.) 528/2 Her chaplet [was] of Heliotropium, or turnsole.

β. *a* **1626** BACON *Wks.* (1857) III. 832 Flowers of heliotrope. **1645** G. DANIEL *Poems* Wks. 1878 II. 32 The Heliotrope may live with the last Sun. **1664** EVELYN *Kal. Hort.* (1729) 215 Star-wort, Heliotrop, French Marigold. **1796** H. HUNTER tr. *St.-Pierre's Stud. Nat.* (1799) II. 89 The French or Peruvian heliotrope. **1861** WHYTE MELVILLE *Good for Nothing* II. 169 The sweet heliotrope exhaled her dying fragrance ere she sank to decay.

attrib. **1676** MARVELL *Mr. Smirke I bis*, As the Heliotrope Flower that keeps its ground, but wrests its Neck in turning after the warm Sun.

b. *fig.* (Also *attrib.*)

1603 B. JONSON *Sejanus* IV. v, Good Heliotrope! Is this your honest man? Let him be yours so still; he is my knave. **1669** *Addr. Yng. Gentry Eng.* 99 With free expansions, and heliotrope conversions to that Eternal light. **1746–7** HERVEY *Medit.* (1818) 149 Let us all be heliotropes (if I may use the expression) to the Sun of Righteousness.

c. Applied, with qualifying words, to other plants, as **false** or **summer heliotrope**, *Tournefortia heliotropioides*; **winter heliotrope**, *Nardosmia* (*Petasites*, or *Tussilago*) *fragrans*.

1866 *Treas. Bot.* 777 *Nardosmia*, a name under which the Winter Heliotrope . . and some allied Northern species of *Tussilago*, have been separated generically. **1884** MILLER *Plant-n.*, Summer Heliotrope.

d. A shade of purple like that of the flowers of the heliotrope. Also *attrib.*

1882 *World* 21 June 18/1 A white cotton with violet sprig and bonnet of heliotrope. **1886** *Truth* XXI, It is lined with heliotrope satin. **1887** *Daily News* 5 July 5/5 A costume of that peculiar mauve known as heliotrope.

e. A scent imitating that of the heliotrope.

1865 *Public Opinion* 7 Jan. 20 Many scents, however, are imitations—heliotrope, for instance, having no relation to that flower.

2. *Min.* A green variety of quartz, with spots or veins of red jasper; also called BLOODSTONE; anciently credited with various 'virtues', as that of stanching blood, rendering the wearer invisible, etc. (As to the origin of the name see quot. 1601.)

α. **1390** GOWER *Conf.* III. 112 There sitten five stones mo . . Jaspis and elitropius. **1398** TREVISA *Barth. De P.R.* XVI. xl. (1495) 566 *Eliotropia* is a precyous stone and is grene and spronge wyth red dropes and veynes of colour of blood. **1601** HOLLAND *Pliny* II. 627 The pretious stone Heliotropium . . is a deepe green in maner of a leeke . . garnished with veins of bloud: the reason of the name Heliotropium is this, For that if it be throwne into a pale of water, it changeth the raies of the Sun by way of reuerberation into a bloudie colour . . Magitians . . say, that if a man carrie it about him . . he shall goe inuisible.

β. **1587** GOLDING tr. *Solinus' Polyhistor* (1590) Sijb (Stanf.), The precious stone called Heliotrope. **1740** tr. *Barba's Metals* 120 The Heliotrope in his fine green Substance hath Veins of the purest Blood. **1814** CARY *Dante's Inf.* XXIV. 91 Nor hope had they of crevice where to hide, Or heliotrope to charm them out of view. **1884** F. J. BRITTEN *Watch & Clockm.* 215 Chrysoprase, Heliotrope, and Jasper are forms of silica either amorphous, translucent, or opaque.

3. An ancient kind of sun-dial.

1669 GALE *Crt. Gentiles* I. I. vii. 36 Phenicians . . communicated the knowledge of the Heliotrope taken from Ahaz's dial. **1753** CHAMBERS *Cycl. Supp.*, *Heliotrope, Heliotropium*, among the antients, an instrument or machine, for shewing when the sun arrived at the tropics and the æquinoctial line. **1789** WHITE *Selborne* xliv, Two heliotropes; the one for the winter, and the other for the summer solstice. **1875** KNIGHT *Dict. Mech.*, *Heliotrope* . . The ancient Greek *polos* or *heliotrophion* was a basin in the middle of which was a perpendicular staff or finger, whose shadow indicated on lines the twelve parts of the day.

4. An apparatus with a movable mirror for reflecting the rays of the sun, used for signalling and other purposes, esp. in geodesic operations: cf. HELIOGRAPH *sb.* 4.

1822 *Gentl. Mag.* II. 358 The inventor of the Heliotrope . . had full proof of the great advantage to be derived from it. **1858** *Merc. Marine Mag.* V. 145 Of all signals, the heliotrope —a movable mirror, placed so as to be directed by a telescope—is the most perfect.

heliotroper ('hiːlɪəʊtrəʊpə(r)). [f. prec. + -ER.] One who manages a HELIOTROPE (sense 4).

1864 in WEBSTER. **1883** *Times* 31 July 10, I was doing service as a heliotroper all alone on the top of Arc Dome. **1887** J. T. WALKER in *Encycl. Brit.* XXII. 698/2 Heliotropers were also employed . . to flash instructions to the signallers.

†**helio'tropian**, *sb. Obs.* Also heli-, helli-. [A corruption of *heliotropion*, HELIOTROPE (sense 1), frequent about 1600.]

1. = HELIOTROPE 1.

1590 GREENE *Never too late* (1600) 48 As the yron follows the Adamant . . and the Helitropian the beames of the sun. **1624** HEYWOOD *Gunaik.* I. 35 The gods . . changed her into an Heliotropian, which is called the Suns flower, which still inclines to what part soever he makes his progresse. **1649** LOVELACE *Poems* 147 The noble Heliotropian Now turnes to her, and knowes no Sun.

2. = HELIOTROPE 2.

1638 SIR T. HERBERT *Trav.* (ed. 2) 22 With Agats, Helitropians, Jasper.

helio'tropian, *a. rare.* Also 7 *erron.* heli-. [f. L. *hēliotropium* HELIOTROPE + -AN.] Pertaining to or of the nature of the heliotrope (1 and 2).

1640 HOWELL *Dodona's Gr.* (1645) 5 Most of her Plants have the Heliotropian quality of the Marigold and Tulip, who follow the motion of the Sunne. **1670** WALTON *Lives* I. 55 He caused . . figures thus drawn to be ingraven very small in Helitropian Stones.

heliotropic (hiːlɪəʊ'trɒpɪk), *a. Bot.* [f. Gr. ἥλιος sun + -τροπος turning + -IC; or ad. F. *héliotropique.*] Bending or turning in a particular direction under the influence of light; pertaining to or marked by heliotropism. Said of, or in reference to, growing parts of plants, which may be ***positively heliotropic***, i.e. bend towards the light (the most usual case), or ***negatively heliotropic*** (APHELIOTROPIC), i.e. bend away from it, or DIAHELIOTROPIC, q.v.

1875 BENNETT & DYER *Sachs' Bot.* 676 The fact of heliotropic curvature towards the side which receives the most light. *Ibid.* 677 There are a much smaller number which bend in the opposite direction, *i.e.* become concave on the shaded side. In order to distinguish between them the former are termed *positively*, the latter *negatively heliotropic*. **1880** C. & F. DARWIN *Movem. Pl.* 418 Heliotropic movements are determined by the direction of the light.

So **helio'tropical** *a.* (*rare*$^{-0}$) = prec.; hence **helio'tropically** *adv.*

1875 BENNETT & DYER tr. *Sachs' Bot.* 676 The observation that leaves, some roots, Fungi . . etc., curve heliotropically, indicates that their growth is retarded by light. **1891** *Athenæum* 27 June 832/3 The action of light and gravitation on the protoplasm of heliotropically and geotropically curving cells and hyphæ.

heliotropin (hiːlɪəʊ'trəʊpɪn). *Chem.* Also -ine. [f. HELIOTROP(E 1: see -IN^1.] A colourless crystalline compound, $C_8H_6O_3$, present in the heliotrope and other plants, that has a strong smell of heliotropes and is made synthetically for use in perfumes. Also called *piperonal*.

1881 *Chemist & Druggist* 15 Sept. 396/2 (*heading*) Heliotropine... Messrs. Schimmel & Co., of Leipsic, now prepare pure heliotropine in crystals... The heliotropine prepared by them is . . suitable for preparing perfumes. **1943** *Thorpe's Dict. Appl. Chem.* (ed. 4) VI. 191/1 Most of the artificial heliotrope perfumes contain modifiers of the geraniol type, the basic ingredients being heliotropin, with a little vanillin, coumarin and dimethylhydroquinone. **1963** *New Scientist* 4 Apr. 30/3 Two Japanese scientists have produced . . aromas for cosmetics and foodstuffs similar to the heliotropin . . obtained by chemical synthesis.

heliotropism (hiːlɪ'ɒtrəʊpɪz(ə)m). *Bot.* [mod. f. Gr. ἥλιος sun + -τροπος turning: see -ISM. In F. *héliotropisme* (1832, De Candolle, *Physiol. Végét.* II. 844), mod.L. and Ger. *heliotropismus.*]

The property, exhibited by growing parts of plants, of bending or turning in a particular manner under the influence of light. The most usual case (to which some restrict the term) is that of bending towards the light (***positive heliotropism***); that of bending away from it is distinguished as ***negative heliotropism*** or APHELIOTROPISM; that of taking a direction at right angles to it, as ***transverse heliotropism*** or DIAHELIOTROPISM.

1854 MAYNE *Expos. Lex.*, *Heliotropismus*, term for that faculty by which certain plants constantly turn their flowers to the sun: heliotropism. **1875** BENNETT & DYER *Sachs' Bot.* 677 Both positive and negative heliotropism occur not only in organs containing chlorophyll, but also in those that are colourless. *Ibid.* 775 The positive heliotropism of twining internodes is generally feeble. **1880** *Nature* XXI. 438 The Electric Light . . produced heliotropism in plants exposed to it. **1880** C. & F. DARWIN *Movem. Pl.* 5 Authors speak of positive and negative heliotropism . . but it is much more convenient to confine the word heliotropism to bending towards the light.

heli'otropy. *rare.* [f. HELIO- + Gr. -τροπία turning. Cf. F. *héliotropie.*] = prec.

1883 *Nat. Educ.* XXIV. No. 6. 6 The author applies the name selenotropy to these motions, as contrasted with heliotropy produced by the sun.

heliotype ('hiːlɪəʊtaɪp). [f. HELIO- + Gr. τύπος impression, print, TYPE.] A picture obtained by printing from a film of gelatine which has been sensitized with bichromate of potash and exposed to light under a negative; also, the process by which such a picture is produced. Also *attrib.*

1870 *Echo* 4 Nov., *Art* . . presents its readers with four splendid heliotype pictures. **1874** ABNEY *Instr. Photogr.* xlii. (1886) 297 In the heliotype process a film of gelatine is prepared on a glass plate, from which it is stripped when dry, and printed in the ordinary manner. *Ibid.* 303 The great secret of producing a good heliotype is to have first-rate rollers at command. **1883** R. HALDANE *Workshop Receipts* Ser. II. 188/2 The most important of the many modifications of the collotype process is the 'heliotype' invented by Ernest Edwards.

So **'heliotyped** *ppl. a.*, produced by the heliotype process; **heliotypic** (-'tɪpɪk) *a.*, of or belonging to the heliotype process; **'heliotypy** (-taɪpɪ), the heliotype process.

1883 *Fisheries Exhib. Catal.* 327 Heliotyped Drawings.

heliozoan (hiːlɪəʊ'zəʊən), *a.* and *sb. Zool.* [f. mod.L. *Heliozōa* sb. pl., f. Gr. ἥλιος sun + ζῷον animal.] **A.** *adj.* Belonging to the *Heliozoa* or sun-animalcules, a group of marine Radiolarians. **B.** *sb.* One of the *Heliozoa*.

helio'zoic, *a.* [f. as prec. + -IC.] = prec. A.

1881 CARPENTER *Micros.* xii. (ed. 6) 595 So does the Heliozoic type seem to culminate in the marine *Radiolaria*.

helipad, helipod: see HELI-.

heliport ('hɛlɪpɔət). [f. HELI- after AIRPORT.] A landing-place for helicopters.

1948 *Amer. Aviation* 1 June 20 The helicopter is a marvelous vehicle. It just plops down anywhere. All but three of the 12 stops were made right inside towns on small fenced-off portions of vacant lots which have been designated by the super-name of 'heliports'. **1950** *N.Y. Times* 28 Nov. 46/3 (*heading*) Construction of City's first aerial heliport begun atop Port Authority's headquarters. **1955** *Economist* 5 Mar. 813/2 Plans for the first commercial heliport on Manhattan Island in New York City now await only the final approval of the city and port authorities. **1958** *Times* 15 May 16/5 A committee appointed by the Helicopter Association of Great Britain have come to the conclusion that there is an immediate need for a London 'heliport'. **1959** *Daily Tel.* 24 Apr. 20/7 'Guinea pig' heliport is opened. **1971** *Guardian* 17 Nov. 15/1 A public inquiry into a proposal for a heliport at Shadwell Basin on the Thames . . opens today.

helipterum (hɛ'lɪptɛrəm). *Bot.* [mod.L. (A. P. de Candolle *Prodromus* (1837) VI. 211), f. Gr. ἡλι-ος sun + πτερόν wing, in allusion to the feathery pappus.] A shrub or herb of the genus so called, belonging to the family Compositæ, native to South Africa and Australia, and including several plants described as everlastings or immortelles (q.v.).

1862 *Curtis's Bot. Mag.* LXXXVIII. 5350 Major Sandford's Helipterum... Whether it be a true *Helipterum* or a *Helichrysum* I will not venture to say. **1886** G. NICHOLSON *Illustr. Dict. Gardening* II. 131/2 Helipterums may be raised from seeds. **1962** *Amateur Gardening* 7 Apr. 3/1 Catalogues may list the attractive little rhodanthes either separately or under helipterum, which is their proper name.

heli'spheric, *a. rare*$^{-0}$. = next (Webster 1828).

helispherical (hɛlɪ'sfɛrɪkəl), *a.* [irreg. f. HELIX + SPHERICAL.] Winding spirally upon a sphere.

helispherical line: the line traced upon the terrestrial sphere by a ship sailing constantly towards the same point of the compass (other than the four cardinal points), which winds spirally round the pole, continually approaching but never reaching it; otherwise called the *loxodromic curve* or *rhumb-line*.

a **1646** J. GREGORY *Posthum.* (1650) 285 (T.) They are helispherical lines, as they call them. **1659** MOXON *Tutor Astron.* I. (1686) 9 The Rhumbs are neither circles nor streight Lines, but Helispherical or Spiral lines. **1796** HUTTON *Math. Dict.*, *Helispherical line* is the Rhumb line in Navigation.

helium ('hiːlɪəm). *Chem.* [mod.L., f. Gr. ἥλιος sun, with the termination already used in *selenium*, *tellurium*, etc.] **a.** One of the chemical elements, a transparent gas, first actually obtained by Prof. Ramsay in 1895, its existence in the sun's atmosphere having been inferred by Lockyer in 1868 from a certain line (D_3) in the spectrum of the solar prominences. (Cf. CORONIUM.) Symbol He.

1872 W. THOMSON in *Rep. Brit. Assoc.* p. xcix, Frankland and Lockyer find the yellow prominences to give a very decided bright line not far from D, but hitherto not identified with any terrestrial flame. It seems to indicate a new substance, which they propose to call Helium. **1878** NEWCOMB *Pop. Astron.* III. ii. 266 This hydrogen is always mixed with another substance, provisionally called helium. **1884** *Longm. Mag.* Apr. 599 The orange-yellow tint of helium. **1895** *Daily News* 28 Mar. 7/7 As he had anticipated, argon was given off and not nitrogen, but mixed with it he found what appeared to be another gas. This gas is no other than the hypothetical Helium, whose existence has only been inferred up to the present from a line D 3 in the solar spectrum. **1897** LOCKYER *Sun's Place in Nat.* iv, The Discovery of Helium. **1955** *Sci. Amer.* Oct. 61/1 Helium is an ideal cooling gas, because it has a high specific heat and does not capture neutrons, but it is very expensive and is not available in large quantities in Great Britain. **1958** *Chambers's Techn. Dict.* 984/2 *Helium*, proposed coolant for reactors because of negligible cross-section for neutrons.

b. *attrib.* and *Comb.*, as ***helium atom***, ***content***, etc.; **helium star**, a star which exhibits the helium lines in its spectrum.

1903 A. M. CLERKE *Probl. Astrophysics* 93 A helium-envelope surrounds the sun to a depth of five thousand miles. *Ibid.* 94 Now that the helium-spectrum has been unravelled. **1904** GOODCHILD & TWENEY *Technol. & Sci. Dict.* 284/2 *Helium stars*, stars the spectra of which show prominently the lines of the gas helium. **1920** *Discovery* Apr. 111/1 Helium determinations never can provide data for more than a *minimum* estimate [of the age of a mineral]. All that the helium-ratio can tell us is that the age of the mineral to which it refers is greater than a certain minimum value. **1921** *Ibid.* Sept. 236/1 The B or helium stars are on the crest of the evolutionary curve, at the meridian of stellar life. **1926** R. W. LAWSON tr. *Hevesy & Paneth's Man. Radioactivity* xxvi. 216 (*heading*) Age determination from the helium content. **1938** *Ibid.* (ed. 2) xxv. 267/2 When the 'helium method' was first applied to minerals, it gave values for the age which were mostly only about one-half or one-third of the values found by the 'lead method'. **1940**

Chambers's Techn. Dict. 409/1 *Helium diving bell*, a diving bell in which the nitrogen in the compressed-air is replaced by helium, thus reducing tendency to the bends. **1956** A. H. Compton *Atomic Quest* iii. 163 The only plans for a production plant..were those of Moore's helium-cooled reactor. **1957** *Gloss. Terms Nucl. Sci.* (Nat. Res. Council U.S.) 7/1 s.v. *Age*, If the age is calculated from the relative number of atoms of a stable radiogenic end product and radioactive parent present, the method is designated by the name of the end product. Examples are the lead age and helium age of a uranium-containing and/or thorium-containing mineral. **1957** *Technology* Mar. 14/2 In the hydrogen bomb the energy generated is derived from the fusion of hydrogen atoms into helium atoms. **1958** F. E. Zeuner *Dating Past* (ed. 4) 329 Were there not certain difficulties connected with the gaseous nature of helium, age estimates could be carried out with the helium generated by radioactive substances just as well as with the lead. The amount of helium present is determined and compared with the amount of uranium (and thorium) contained in the mineral, in other words, the helium-ratio is determined. *Ibid.* 427 A sample of magnetite from Larder Lake District ..has yielded a helium-age of 2,400 million years. **1960** *Nature* 24 Sept. 1077/1 At the meeting of the International Committee of Weights and Measures held in Sevres, during September 29–October 3, 1958, the recommendation was adopted that the '1958 Helium-4 Vapour Pressure Scale of Temperatures'..should be used as the international standard scale of temperature between 1° and 5·2°K.

helix ('hɛlɪks, 'hiːlɪks). Pl. helices ('hɛlɪsiːz), helixes. [a. L. *helix*, a. Gr. ἕλιξ anything of spiral form.]

1. Anything of a spiral or coiled form, whether in one plane (like a watch-spring), or advancing around an axis (like a corkscrew), but more usually applied to the latter; a coil, a spiral, as an electromagnetic coil of wire, the thread of a screw, a tendril, etc. In *Geom.*, the curve formed by a straight line traced on a plane when the plane is wrapped round a cylinder; more generally, a curve on any developable surface (e.g. a cone) which becomes a straight line when the surface is unrolled into a plane; distinguished from *spiral*, which is applied only to plane curves.

1643 Sir T. Browne *Relig. Med.* I. §17 The lives..of men ..and the whole world, run not upon a Helix that still enlargeth, but on a Circle. **1664** Power *Exp. Philos.* I. 8 [The butterfly's tongue] being drawn up into an Helix, and retracted into the mouth. **1792** T. Taylor *Proclus* I. 134 The helix..is described about a sphere or a cone. **1826** Henry *Elem. Chem.* I. 195 A copper wire, by being rolled round a solid rod, was twisted into a spiral so as to form a *helix*. **1837** Brewster *Magnet.* 156 An electro-magnetic helix enclosing a bar-magnet. **1854** J. Scoffern in *Orr's Circ. Sc., Chem.* 195 Take a flat helix of..wire. *c* **1860** Faraday *Forces Nat.* 189 Three wheels of magnets and two sets of helices. **1882** Vines *Sachs' Bot.* 866 The tendrils.. form a spiral..or..a helix narrowing conically upwards.

2. *Arch.*, etc. A spiral ornament, a volute; *spec.* applied to the eight smaller volutes under the abacus of the Corinthian capital.

1563 Shute *Archit.* D iij d, Helices, the which..haue but halfe the height of the other great Helices, or Volutas. **1664** Evelyn tr. *Freart's Archit.* 128 At the extreams of the leaves do issue the *Caules*, and *Codds* breaking from the *Helices*. **1789** P. Smyth tr. *Aldrich's Archit.* (1818) 98 The greater one, under the horn of the abacus, is called the volute; the smaller one, under the flower, the helix. **1857** Birch *Anc. Pottery* (1858) II. 5 The development of the helix or ornament of the antefixae is very remarkable.

3. *Anat.* The curved fold or prominence which forms the rim of the external ear.

1693 Blancard *Phys. Dict.* (ed. 2), *Helix*, the Exterior brim of the Ear, so called from its Winding. **1705** *Phil. Trans.* XXV. 1979 The Prominence called *Helix* ends in the Lobe of the Ear, which it constitutes. **1873** Darwin in *Life & Lett.* III. 324–5 The leaf on one side looks just like the helix of a human ear.

4. *Zool.* A genus of molluscs with spiral shells, of which the common snail (*Helix hortensis*) is a typical example.

1820 Scoresby *Acc. Arctic Reg.* I. 180 Helices, and other genera of Mollusca. **1830** Lyell *Princ. Geol.* I. 384 Terrestrial shells, chiefly helices. **1866** Tate *Brit. Mollusks* iv. 94 The Helices do not live to a venerable age.

helixin ('hiːlɪksɪn). [f. helix + -in[1].] **a.** *Chem.* A crystalline glucoside found in the seeds and leaves of ivy, *Hedera helix*, later called *hederin*. **b.** An antibiotic produced from species of *Streptomyces*, a genus of actinomycete fungi.

1894 C. E. Sohn *Dict. Active Princ. Plants* 56/2 (*heading*) Hedera helix (Ivy);..Helixin G. (Hedera Glucoside). *Ibid.*, Fehling's solution not reduced till the Helixin has been boiled with acid. **1952** C. Leben et al. in *Mycologia* XLIV. 160 A name, helixin, is tentatively proposed for the antibiotic produced... The name was suggested by the helical nature of the spore chains produced by the antibiotic organism. *Ibid.* 167 Helixin appears to be an antibiotic potent primarily against fungi.

helixoid ('hɛlɪksɔɪd). *Geom.* [f. helix (sense 1) + -oid.] = helicoid *sb.* 2.

1876 *Catal. Sci. App. S. Kens.* §106 The developable helixoid..is the surface swept out by the right line tangents of the helix.

helk, obs. form of hulk.

hell (hɛl), *sb.* Forms: 1–7 hel, 1– hell, 2–6 helle. [OE. *hel(l*, obl. cases *helle*, str. fem. = OFris. *helle*, *hille*, OS. *hellja*, *hella*, MDu. *helle*, Du. *hel*), OHG. *hella* (MHG. *helle*, mod.G. *hölle*), ON. *hel*, gen. *heljar*, Goth. *halja*:—*OTeut.* **haljâ* str. fem., lit. 'the coverer up or hider', f. *hel-*, *hal-*, *hul-* to hide, conceal, hele. In ON. also the proper name of the goddess of the infernal regions, 'the ogress Hel, the Proserpine of Scandinavian mythology' (Vigfusson).]

1. The abode of the dead; the place of departed spirits; the infernal regions or 'lower world' regarded as a place of existence after death; the grave; Hades. **a.** In Jewish and Christian use.

In the Bible of 1611, translating Heb. *shĕōl* (31 times), which is also rendered *the grave* (31 times), *the pit* (3 times); in N. T. rendering Gr. ᾅδης Hades (10 times), as well as γέεννα gehenna (12 times); once (2 Pet. ii. 4) 'cast downe to hel' represents ταρταρώσας pa. pple., 'put in Tartarus.' In the Revised Version, in O. T., *hell* has been retained in the prophetical books, with *Sheol* in the margin; elsewhere *Sheol* is substituted in the text, with *grave* in the margin (exc. in Deut. xxxii. 22, Ps. lv. 15, lxxxvi. 13, where *pit* is retained in the text, with *Sheol* in the margin); in N. T., Hades has everywhere been put for Gr. ᾅδης, and *hell* reserved for γέεννα.

c **825** *Vesp. Psalter* liv. 16 [lv. 15] Cyme deað ofer hie and astiȝen hie in helle lifȝende. *c* **1000** Ælfric *Gen.* xxxvii. 35 Ic fare to minum sunu to helle. *a* **1340** Hampole *Psalter* xv. 10 Þou sall noght leue my saule in hell. **1382** Wyclif *Gen.* xlii. 38 Ȝe shulen lede doun myn hoore heeris with sorwe to helle. **1502** *Ord. Crysten Men* I. vii. (W. de W. 1506) 68 For before that he styed up in to the heuyns he dyscended in to the helles. **1529** More *Suppl. Soulys* Wks. 320/2 *Descendit ad inferna*: that is to say he discended down beneth into the lowe places. In stede of which low places ye english toung hath euer vsed thys word hel. **1535** Coverdale *Job* xiv. 13 O that thou woldest kepe me, and hyde me in the hell, vntill thy wrath were stilled. —— *Acts* ii. 31 His soule was not left in hell [**1881** *R. V.* Hades]. **1649** Jer. Taylor *Gt. Exemp.* III. Ad §16. 170 Our Lord descended into hell..that is into the state of separation and common receptacle of spirits. *a* **1748** Watts *Improv. Mind* II. v. §2, I will explain the word hell to signify the state of the dead, or the separate state of souls.. and..that the soul of Christ existed three days in the state of separation from his body, or was in the invisible world. *a* **1848** R. W. Hamilton *Rew. & Punishm.* iii. (1853) 113 The real conception of hell, is that which is unseen, the invisible state.

b. In Greek and Latin mythology.

c **1384** Chaucer *H. Fame* I. 441 Cybile And Eneas..To helle went for to see His ffader Anchyses. *a* **1529** Skelton *P. Sparowe* 1337 By the feryman of hell, Caron with his beerd hore. **1708** Pope *Ode St. Cecilia* 83 He sung, and hell consented To hear the Poet's prayer. *a* **1822** Shelley *Orpheus* 67 Returning from drear Hell.

c. In Scandinavian mythology.

1770 Percy tr. *Mallet's North. Antiq.* II. 151 The Gods.. dispatched messengers throughout the world begging of every thing to weep, in order to deliver Balder from Hell. **1865** Max Müller *Chips* (1880) II. xxv. 287 To Northern nations Hell was a cold place, a dreary region of snow and frost.

2. The infernal regions regarded as a place of torment; the abode of devils and condemned spirits; the place or state of punishment of the wicked after death.

In N. T. rendering γέεννα gehenna: see note to 1.

c **888** K. Ælfred *Boeth.* xv, Swa byrnende swa þæt fyr on þære helle, seo is on þam munte ðe Ætne hatte. *c* **1020** *Rule St. Benet* (Logeman) 36 Na mid eȝe helle ac mid cristes lufan. *c* **1175** *Lamb. Hom.* 61 From hwonne þe engles a-dun fellen in to þe þosternesse hellen. *a* **1225** *Ancr. R.* 150 Þenne nis hit to nout so god ase to þe fure of helle. **1297** R. Glouc. (1724) 506 Thouȝtes he adde inowe, Leste the deuelen of helle al quic to helle him drowe. *a* **1300** *Cursor M.* 478 Lucifer..þat formast fell, thoru his ouergart in to hell. *c* **1400** Maundev. (Roxb.) viii. 29 Þe entreez and þe ȝates of hell. **1522** Skelton *Why not to Court* 590 As ferce and as cruell As the fynd of hell. **1667** Milton *P.L.* x. 230 Within the Gates of Hell sate Sin and Death. **1731** Pope *Ep. Burlington* 148 Who never mentions Hell to ears polite. **1827** Pollok *Course T.* v, Leagues, though holy termed, first made In Hell. **1856** R. A. Vaughan *Mystics* (1860) II. 16 Not fully God's is he who cannot live, Even in hell, and find in hell no hell.

3. a. Represented as a living being: chiefly as a poetical personification.

c **1000** *Nicodemus* xxvi, Seo hell þa swiþe grymme and swyðe eȝeslice andswarode. *a* **1300** *Cursor M.* 18025 Helle ȝaf to satan vnswere. **1382** Wyclif *Isa.* v. 14 Therfore helle spredde abrod his soule, and openede his [*16th c. vers.* her] mouth with oute any terme.

b. The powers of inhabitants of hell; the wicked spirits; also, the kingdom or power of hell.

1297 R. Glouc. (1724) 322 Heuene & helle & ech þyng mot nede hys heste do. **1559** *Mirr. Mag., Clifford* x, Hel haleth tirauntes downe to death amayne. **1593** Shaks. *2 Hen. VI*, IV. viii. 63 In despight of the diuels and hell, haue through the verie middest of you. **1667** Milton *P.L.* vi. 867 Hell heard th' unsufferable noise, Hell saw Heav'n ruining from Heav'n and would have fled Affrighted. **1845** S. Austin *Ranke's Hist. Ref.* III. 193 He had fought against Satan and hell.

c. A hellful, an infernal company, a devilish assembly.

1594 Shaks. *Rich. III*, I. iii. 227 Some tormenting Dreame Affrights thee with a Hell of ougly Deuills. **1598** Sylvester *Du Bartas* II. i. II. *Imposture* 71 'Tis that old Python which..doth fire A hell of Furies in his fell desire. **1652** Bp. Hall *Myst. Godl.* §13 There is now a hell of the spirits of error broken loose into the world.

4. Something regarded as resembling hell:

a. A place or state of wickedness, suffering, or misery. (In quot. 1586 applied to a person.)

c **1374** Chaucer *Anel. & Arc.* 166 The helle Which suffereth faire Anelyda. *a* **1420** Hoccleve *De Reg. Princ.* 1034, I am right siker it hathe ben an helle, You for to herken me thus jangle and clappe. **1555** J. Philpot in Foxe *A. & M.* (1631) III. xi. 541/2 Afterward [he] felt such a hell in his conscience, that hee could scarce refraine from destroying himselfe. **1586** A. Day *Eng. Secretary* I. (1625) 42 He was called the hell of the world, the plague of the commonweale. **1597** Shaks. *Lover's Compl.* 288 What a hell of witchcraft lies In the small orb of one particular tear! *c* **1600** —— *Sonn.* cxx, You've pass'd a hell of time. **1667** Milton *P.L.* iv. 78 In the lowest deep a lower deep Still threatning to devour me opens wide, To which the Hell I suffer seems a Heav'n. **1719** Young *Busiris* I. i, I fear no farther hell than that I feel. **1833** Chalmers *Const. Man* (1835) I. ii. 133 They kindle a hell in the heart of the unhappy owner. **1849** Macaulay *Hist. Eng.* iii. (1871) I. 207 The prisons were hells on earth. **1867** Smyth *Sailor's Word-bk.*, *Hell-afloat*, a vessel with a bad name for tyranny. **1903** Kipling *Five Nations* 51 Yes, we shall be perfectly pleased with our work, And that is the perfectest Hell of it! **1944** *Living off Land* v. 103 A boggy area is hell to plough through with a wheeled vehicle. **1951** N. Balchin *Way through Wood* viii. 111, I should think he'd be pretty average hell to live with. **1971** H. E. Bates *Blossoming World* xv. 176 If the times had been bad for writers in 1926,..they were now hell.

b. A place of turmoil and wild discord.

1818 Byron *Ch. Har.* iv. lxix, The hell of waters! where they howl and hiss, And boil in endless torture.

†**c.** A yawning depth, an abyss. *Obs.*

c **1620** Z. Boyd *Zion's Flowers* (1855) 148 The tossed ship from Hells goes to the skye.

d. *a hell of a* ——, an infernal ——; also, an exceedingly bad, great, loud, etc.: cf. *a devil of a* —— (devil 14). Also ***the hell of a*** —. Cf. helluva.

1776 J. Leacock *Fall Brit. Tyranny* iv. vii, This is a hell of a council of war. **1778** in S. Curwen *Jrnl.* (1842) x. 207 After travelling in the heat of the season in a hell of a climate. **1806** M. L. Weems *Lett.* (1929) II. 354 I've had a hell of a time in your service. **1810** *Morn. Post* 26 June in *Spirit Pub. Jrnls.* (1811) XIV. 278 They all knew what a hell of a row had been kicked up. **1897** 'Mark Twain' *Following Equator* xxxi, It's a charming town, with a hell of a hotel... It's the worst hotel in Australia. **1910** R. W. Service *Ballads of Cheechako* 133 Lord! it's a hell of a night. *a* **1918** McCudden *Five Yrs. R.F.C.* (1919) 232 There was immediately a Hell of a yell. **1920** C. E. Mulford *J. Nelson* xii. 126 You must 'a' had one h—l of a time gettin' out. **1923** —— *Black Buttes* ii. 24 He was a hell of a trail-boss, an' he had a hell of an outfit, if you leave it to me! **1931** J. Betjeman *Mount Zion* 20 And we each had a couple of toy balloons and made the hell of a din. **1942** N. Coward *Blithe Spirit* I. ii. 34 Pedalling off down the drive at the hell of a speed. **1944** *Living off Land* vii. 155 The Abo thinks himself a hell of a feller, the same as you do. **1947** 'N. Shute' *Chequer Board* i. 3, I had the hell of a headache. **1964** E. A. Nida *Toward Sci. Transl.* ix. 215 In Bassa, a language of Liberia, the English phrase *hell of a* has been borrowed through Pidgin English as an attributive meaning 'tremendous, great, and important', so that a Bassa churchgoer can quite appropriately tell the pastor that his latest message was 'a helava sermon'. **1969** *New Yorker* 14 June 44/3 His forehand is a hell of a weapon.

e. Used in the genitive (esp. with *own*), or as ***hells*** quasi-adverbially, with intensive force.

1926 E. Hemingway *Fiesta* (1927) I. vii. 65 You've got hell's own drag with the concierge. **1962** 'J. Le Carré' *Murder of Quality* i. 10 He's entertaining every don... Hells extravagant. **1963** C. Bingham *Coronet among Weeds* ii. 25 They sit about and..talk about their ancestors. Ancestors are hell's boring. **1968** 'M. Underwood' *Man who killed too Soon* ix. 84, I had a puncture. I had hell's own time changing the wheel.

†**5.** A part of a building, etc., which for its darkness or discomfort, or for a similar reason, was compared to hell; the name of a part of the old law courts at Westminster, app. used at one time as a record office; also, a place of confinement for debtors; hence, a sponging-house. *Obs.*

1322–3 *Ely Sacrist's Roll* in Stewart *Ely* (1868) 275 Camera in Infirmaria quæ vocatur Helle. **1474** Caxton *Chesse* III. iii. (1860) 3 Men of the lawe..that longe to the courtes of the chaunserye, kynges benche, comyn-place, cheker, ressayt, and helle, and the bagge berars of the same. **1590** Shaks. *Com. Err.* IV. ii. 40 One that before the Iudgment carries poore soules to hel. **1598** Florio, *Secreta*, ..also the name of a place in Venice where all their secret records and ancient euidences be kept, as hell is in westminster hall. **1628** R. S. *Counter-Rat* xxi, Aske any how such newes I tell, Of Wood-streets hole, or Poultries Hell. *a* **1661** Fuller *Worthies* II. (1662) 236 There is no redemption from Hell. There is a place partly under, partly by the Exchequer chamber, commonly called Hell.. formerly this place was appointed a prison for the King's debtors, who never were freed thence, untill they had paid their uttermost due demanded of them.

6. The name for the 'den' to which captives are carried in the games Barley-break and Prisoner's Base.

1557, **1608** [see barley-break]. **1580** Sidney *Arcadia* I. (1627) 87 The two that in mid place, Hell called, were, Must striue with waiting foot, and watching eye To catch of them, and them to Hell to beare, That they, as well as they, Hell may supplye. *a* **1641** Suckling (R.), Love, Reason, Hate, did once bespeak Three mates to play at barley-break.. Love coupled last, and so it fell That Love and Folly were in hell. **1835** *Penny Cycl.* III. 466/2 s.v. *Barley-Break*, When all had been taken in turn, the last couple was said *to be in hell*, and the game ended.

7. a. A place under a tailor's shop-board, in which shreds or pieces of cloth, cut off in the process of cutting out clothes, are thrown, and looked upon as perquisites. (So Ger. *hölle*: see Grimm.) Also sometimes applied to a place where refuse type is thrown by printers.

1592 Greene *Upst. Courtier* (1871) 30 He can cast large shreds of such rich stuff into hell, under his shopboard. **1606**

DAY *Ile of Guls* I. iii. (1881) 15 Like a Taylers hell; it eates up part of euery mans due. **1704** SWIFT *T. Tub* iii. (1709) 57 The Taylor's Hell is the Type of a Critic's Common-place-book. **1805** *Spirit Pub. Jrnls.* (1806) IX. 245 *note*, Hell, a place so termed by the knights of the needle, wherein they stow their cabbage.

b. Also designating similar receptacles for waste.

1872 *Saddl. Harn. & Carriage Builder's Gaz.* 1 Dec. 207/2 Each smith shop has what is termed the 'hell', and in cutting off a set of tires, if the farmer is not present, the largest half of the end cut off finds its way to the 'hell.' **1886** *Encycl. Brit.* XXI. 345/2 A useful adjunct to the many saw-mills, which produce more waste than can be consumed in raising the necessary steam, is the 'slab-burner' or 'hell'.

8. A gaming-house; a gambling-booth. (= F. *enfer*, Mercier *Tableau de Paris* 1783, cxcviii.)

1794 *Sporting Mag.* III. 130 A noted gambling-house in Dame-street, Dublin..known by the name of *Hell.* **1812** SIR R. WILSON *Diary* I. 38 Then to the conversazione, which is no other than a great gambling hall, or *hell* in classical terms. **1823** BYRON *Juan* XI. xxix, Don Juan.. Pursued his path, and drove past some hotels, St. James's Palace and St. James's 'Hells'! **1870** STEINMETZ *Gaming Table* I. v. 102. **1882** STEVENSON *New Arab. Nts.* I. 107 The proprietor of a hell.

9. In imprecations, wishes of evil, and expressions of impatience or irritation: used similarly to *devil* (DEVIL 14–20). See also 4 d. ***hell's bells!***: an expression of anger or annoyance. ***what the hell!***, = what does it matter?, who cares? Also used in expressions of strong disagreement of the type 'Will I hell!' = 'I won't'.

1596 SHAKS. *Merch. V.* III. ii. 21 Let Fortune goe to hell for it, not I. **1678** DRYDEN *All for Love* II. i, Hell, death! this eunuch pandar ruins you, You will not see her? **1691** —— *K. Arthur* II. ii, By hell, she sings them back, in my despite. **1816** 'QUIZ' *Grand Master* VI. 142 Gentlemen, you may go to H—ll. **1836** M. SCOTT *Cruise Midge* I. xiii. 72 So, good men, go to hell all of you. **1836** MARRYAT *Midsh. Easy* xviii, What the hell are you making such a howling about? **1842** J. WILSON *Ess., Streams* (1856) 39 Not, at least, for mine—no—hell and furies! not for mine! **1872** GEO. ELIOT *Middlemarch* II. III. xxiii. 21 But, what the hell! the horse was a penny trumpet to that roarer of yours. **1893** *St. Louis Republic* 8 July 16/3 The dealer..said: 'Say, Rick, do you know this gentleman? He's been playing mighty lucky.' Rickebaugh glanced at the great stack of chips..and sarcastically remarked: 'Lucky h—!' **1902** R. H. DAVIS *Capt. Macklin* 295 'Then why in hell didn't you say so!' he roared. **1912** Z. GREY *Riders of Purple Sage* i. 10 To hell with your Mormon law! **1912** E. HUBBARD *Age of Rubber* 11 Goshity gosh, helzbelz, there ain't no such animile. **1913** *Maclean's Mag.* Mar. 45/1 'To hell with 'em,' he grated. **1919** *Thrill Bk.* 1 May 13/1 '*Mister*!' I corrected him in his own tone... 'Mister, was it?' he rumbled... 'Mister— hell!' **1920** S. LEWIS *Main Street* 352 Hell's bells,..no harm in being polite. **1925** N. COWARD *Fallen Angels* III. 83 *Maurice*: We are great friends—they confide in me. *Fred*: The hell they do! **1925** *New Yorker* 22 Aug. 5/1 Where the hell is my comb? **1927** D. L. SAYERS *Unnatural Death* III. xxi. 244 Hell's bells. Here's somebody at the door. **1931** E. LINKLATER *Juan in Amer.* II. xvii. 183 'We'll all see her,' shouted the Snake's Hips. 'Will you hell!' said Rosy. **1931** G. B. SHAW *Too True to be Good* (1934) I. 46 *The Patient*... Doesn't that tempt you? *The Nurse*. Tempt me hell! I'll see you further first. **1932** J. MAXWELL (*title*) Hell's bells and mademoiselles. **1933** *Atlanta Jrnl.* 21 Jan., I've abandoned it completely. The hell with it. **1936** R. LEHMANN *Weather in Streets* II. 235 As if she'd decided to say at last, 'Oh, what the hell! Let them rip.' **1942** N. COWARD *Blithe Spirit* I. ii. 42 *Mrs. Bradman*: Ought we to pick it up or leave it where it is? *Dr. Bradman*: How the hell do I know? **1943** F. J. BELL *Condition Red* 38 Carrier, hell! It's a goddamn submarine! **1957** *New Yorker* 5 Oct. 37/2 'The hell with organization,' Todd said. **1958** *Engineering* 4 Apr. 424/3 If *we* can't do it how the hell can I expect Government to do it? *Ibid.* 425/1 Why the hell haven't we got a computer? **1959** M. HASTINGS *Hour-Glass to Eternity* II. i. 154 Hell's bells! You talk and I'll spill the beans. **1961** *John o' London's* 18 May 567/3 The hell with realism. **1962** P. GREGORY *Like Tigress at Bay* vi. 70, I wish to hell I was out of it. **1962** *Sunday Express* 1 Apr. 19/5 Am I dressed for ease and comfort? Am I *hell*? **1968** *Landfall* XXII. 195 Why in hell didn't you get John to build it for you? **1968** A. MACLEOD *Dam* xiv. 140 'Hell's teeth!' he swore furiously.

10. Phrases and Proverbs. (Cf. DEVIL.)

* *gen.*

1590 SIR J. SMYTH *Disc. Weapons* Proeme *iij b, They verifie the olde Proverb, which is, That such as were never but in Hell, doo thinke that there is no other Heaven. **1600** S. NICHOLSON *Acolastus* (1876) 38 Before my hell of foule mishap breake loose. **1617** MORYSON *Itin.* III. 53 England.. is said to be the Hell of Horses, the Purgatory of Servants, and the Paradise of Weomen. **1632** HAUSTED *Rivall Friends* v. x, Fye, fye, Hell is broke loose upon me. *a* **1633** G. HERBERT *Jac. Prud.* (Chandos) 363 Hell is full of good meanings and wishings. **1640** H. MILL *Night's Search* i. 8 He sets out sin (most lively) black as hell. **1678** DRYDEN *Œdipus* II. i, Since hell's broke loose, why should not you be mad? **1775** JOHNSON in *Boswell* (1887) II. 360 Sir, Hell is paved with good intentions. **1780** COWPER *Progr. Err.* 609 He that will be cheated to the last, Delusions strong as Hell shall bind him fast. **1784** —— *Task* v. 862 Fables false as hell ..lure down to death The uninformed and heedless souls of men. **1821** BYRON *Vis. Judgm.* lviii, Their..cries..realised the phrase of 'hell broke loose'.

** *With another substantive.*

b. not a chance, hope, in hell: no possibility; also, ***a snowball's chance in hell*** and similar phrases.

1923 O. ONIONS *Peace in Our Time* iii. 37 'I rather fancied Lovelightly.' 'Lovelightly? Not a hope in Hell!' **1931** *Amer. Speech* VI. 435 As much chance as a snowball in hell. **1961** K. VONNEGUT *Sirens of Titan* (1962) v. 129 The Army of Mars didn't have the chance of a snowball in hell. **1963** J. T. STORY *Something for Nothing* iii. 79 'What are the chances of a job here, then?' Albert asked. 'For you—not a chance in hell.' She spoke matter-of-factly. **1966** J. PORTER *Sour Cream* vii. 94 One telephone call from Melkin..and Babak wouldn't have a snowball's chance in hell. **1972** *Listener* 27 Jan. 126/2 Poor Robert's empirical doubts don't stand a snowflake's chance in hell.

c. hell and (or **or**) **high water**: any great difficulty or obstacle.

1915 *Everybody's Mag.* June 69/2 He'll be one of us in spite of hell and high water. **1918** C. E. MULFORD *Man fr. Bar-20* xii. 120 Logan found out that he was a *real* man, a *gun*-man, an' not scared of h—l an' high water. **1939** A. KEITH *Land below Wind* I. ii. 26 'Let empires be built!'—and, come hell or high water, they build 'em. **1939** P. I. WELLMAN *Trampling Herd* viii. 93 'In spite of hell and high water'..is a legacy of the cattle trail when the cowboys drove their horn-spiked masses of longhorns through high water at every river and continuous hell between. **1962** *Sunday Times* 12 Aug. 27/7 A superb instinct for working with the camera guided her to rough out a public image which, come hell or high water, she was not going to change.

d. hell for leather: at breakneck speed, orig. used with reference to riding on horseback; also (usu. with hyphens) *attrib.* or as *adj.*

1889 KIPLING *Story of Gadsbys* (1891) 116 Here, Gaddy, take the note to Bingle and ride hell-for-leather. **1893** —— *Many Invent.* 47, I perceived a gunner-orf'cer in full rig'mentals perusin' down the road, hell-for-leather, wid his mouth open. **1915** D. O. BARNETT *Lett.* 176 The little English plane went humming back, hell-for-leather. **1927** *Sunday Express* 10 July 4 A long line of stage coaches starting on a hell-for-leather race. **1928** H. W. FREEMAN *Joseph & His Brethren* vi. 48 Charging down hell for leather with your sabres all flashing in the sun. **1930** *Daily Express* 6 Sept. 8/7 That magnificent, hell-for-leather, boiling verse. **1963** *Times* 21 Feb. 3/2 Australia's plan was to make 90 during the afternoon, if they could, without losing too many wickets and to go hell for leather afterwards.

e. hell on wheels: someone or something regarded as resembling hell; also *attrib.* or quasi-*adj.*

1843 *Quincy* (Ill.) *Herald* 10 Mar. 1/4 Hell-upon-Wheels! ..the most appropriate name for that craft [*sc.* a steam-boat]. **1868** S. BOWLES in F. L. Paxson *Hist. Amer. Frontier* (1924) iii. 497 'Hell on Wheels' was the appropriate name that Samuel Bowles of the Springfield *Republican* bestowed upon the town he visited in 1868. **1897** P. WARUNG *Tales of Old Regime* 50 To look up an' know heaven's above, an' not the roof of a hell-on-wheels—oh, that'll be grand! **1945** WYNDHAM LEWIS *Let.* 13 Mar. (1963) 381 We learn here that the 'Hell-on-wheels' outfit has reached the Elbe. Hooray! **1966** J. PEARL *Crucifixion P. McCabe* (1967) ii. 24 He's hell on wheels on Monday mornings. **1968** S. CHALLIS *Death on Quiet Beach* xii. 174 You don't pull any imitation disease over the immigration doctors. Those guys are hell on wheels.

f. hell's delight: pandemonium.

1823 'J. BEE' *Slang* 95 Kicking up hell's delights. **1835** *Sessions Paper* Apr. 959 She said if I went out, she would kick up *hell's delight*. **1888** 'R. BOLDREWOOD' *Robbery under Arms* II. xix. 287 If these fellows are half drunk they'll.. play hell's delight. **1918** W. J. LOCKE *Rough Road* xi. 131 Just listen to the hell's delight that's going on over yonder. **1958** L. A. G. STRONG *Light above Lake* 26 Once let anything bad go wrong with them, and you'd hell's delight to mend it. **1961** M. KELLY *Spoilt Kill* iii. 134 There'll be hell's delight ringing round all the hotels till we find him.

*** *With a verb.*

g. to beat, blast, knock, etc., **hell out of** (a person): to pound heavily, thrash, 'beat up'; also *fig.* to achieve supremacy over.

1922 JOYCE *Ulysses* 247 His old fellow welted hell out of him. **1925** [see GANG *v.*[2] 2 b]. **1937** E. AMBLER *Uncommon Danger* viii. 110 Are you going to be sensible or do I knock hell out of you first? **1945** C. ISHERWOOD *Prater Violet* 95 If anybody says you're not, I'll help you beat the hell out of him. **1958** P. SCOTT *Mark of Warrior* II. 166 How did we interrogate Mr Baksh? Beat the hell out of him, I hope? **1965** *Times* 15 Apr. 12/1 Given the response of which our people are capable..we shall be ready to knock hell out of you.

h. when, till, until hell freezes (**over**): advb. phr. indicating a date in the impossibly distant future, for ever.

1919 J. A. FISHER *Let.* 13 June in *Henry Bristow Ltd. Catal.* (1973) No. 203.9 Yours till hell freezes. **1931** *Amer. Speech* VI. 435 Till hell freezes over. **1949** *Romance Philol.* II. 105 We have the meaning 'forever' in 'I'll wait until Hell freezes over' and the meaning 'never' in 'I'll do it when Hell freezes over'. **1961** 'A. A. FAIR' *Stop at Red Light* (1962) ii. 36 If their suspicions once get aroused, they'll investigate until hell freezes over. **1962** *Listener* 1 Nov. 704/1 'I am prepared,' Mr Stevenson rasped out, 'to wait for an answer till hell freezes over.' **1966** *Guardian* 17 Aug. 9/2 The Texan chairman..declared that he would..open the hearing today even if it meant going to gaol 'until hell freezes'.

i. to get hell: to be given hell, to be reprimanded, dressed down.

1938 E. BOWEN *Death of Heart* III. iv. 382 'I was using the telephone in Miss Paullie's study, and she came in and caught me...' 'So then you got hell, I suppose.' **1951** WODEHOUSE *Old Reliable* ii. 32, I would only get hell from Emily Post.

j. to get the (or **to**) **hell out** (**of** a place): to make a hasty retreat.

a **1911** D. G. PHILLIPS *Susan Lenox* (1917) II. x. 257 Get the hell out... I want to sleep. **1929** E. LINKLATER *Poet's Pub* vii. 83 Get to hell out of this, you accidental offspring of a Marine sentry. **1934** W. SAROYAN *Daring Young Man* (1935) 262 Get the hell out of here, I reply quietly. **1944** 'BRAHMS' & 'SIMON' *Titania has Mother* xii. 147 'Get to hell out of here,' he roared. **1952** 'J. TEY' *Singing Sands* ix. 139 You want her to get the hell out of here. **1961** J. HELLER *Catch-22* (1962) vi. 57 He..felt that any who did not share this confidence he had placed in them could get the hell out. The only way they could get the hell out, though..was by flying the extra ten missions. **1972** WODEHOUSE *Pearls, Girls, & Monty Bodkin* v. 67 You ought to be in bed. Get the hell out of here, Bodkin.

k. to give (a person) **hell**: to give him 'a bad time'.

1851 *Harper's Mag.* III. 461/1 Riley shouted, 'Forward and give them h-ll.' **1863** O. W. NORTON *Army Lett.* (1903) 161 We have met the enemy and given them hell. *a* **1917** E. A. MACKINTOSH *War, the Liberator* (1918) 141 You swine, I'll give you hell for this. **1940** N. MARSH *Surfeit of Lampreys* (1941) xv. 235 Gabriel would give me hell and we would both get rather angry with each other.

l. hell to pay: great trouble, discord, pandemonium.

1807 LD. PAGET *Let.* 29 July in A. Paget *Paget Papers* (1896) II. 311 Did you not know..that there has been hell to pay between the Dukes of York and Cumberland. **1811** WELLINGTON in Gurw. *Desp.* VIII. 235 Unless the design has been altered..we shall have the Emperor in Spain and hell to pay before much time elapses. **1956** WALLIS & BLAIR *Thunder Above* (1959) iv. 42 I got you all in this mess... There'll be hell to pay.

m. to play hell (**with**): to upset, confuse; to alter for the worse; to make a fuss; also † ***to play hell and tommy*** (***with***).

1803 G. COLMAN *John Bull* III. ii. 39 I'll be good to the landlord, but I'll play hell with his wife! **1832–4** DE QUINCEY *Cæsars* Wks. 1862 IX. 135 Lord Bacon played Hell and Tommy when casually raised to the supreme seat in the council. **1879** MCCARTHY *Donna Quixote* xxxii, I've played hell-and-tommy already with the lot of them. *a* **1911** D. G. PHILLIPS *Susan Lenox* (1917) I. xiii. 218 Don't drink..it'll play hell—excuse me—it'll spoil your looks. **1927** H. CRANE *Let.* 19 Dec. (1965) 312 Port every night for dinner is playing hell with my waistline. **1937** T. RATTIGAN *French without Tears* I. 22 As a matter of fact it would rather amuse me to see you play hell with the Commander. **1959** *Listener* 4 June 979/1 Wingate and his Chindits would play hell with the Japanese communications. **1960** 'A. BURGESS' *Right to Answer* xix. 201 E talks about gross neglect..and e plays ell. **1960** L. COOPER *Accomplices* II. v. 119 The firm..wanted delivery and were playing hell about it.

n. to raise hell: to create a disturbance; to cause great trouble. (The slogan 'Kansas should raise less corn and more hell' is attributed to Mrs Mary Ellen Lease (1853–1933) but proof is lacking. See *Kansas Quarterly* Fall 1969, 52–58.)

1896 *Emporia Weekly Gaz.* 20 Aug., We have decided to send three or four harpies out lecturing, telling the people that Kansas is raising hell and letting the corn go to weeds. *a* **1911** D. G. PHILLIPS *Susan Lenox* (1917) II. viii. 214 What hell Jim will raise when he finds I spent the night working in this house. **1959** M. SCOTT *White Elephant* iii. 24 He would go home, ring Bert and 'raise hell'.

**** *Other phrases.*

o. (**just**) **for the hell of it**: out of (pure) devilry, (merely) for fun.

1934 'J. SPENSER' *Limey breaks In* x. 166 Both of them were of the mischievous type that misbehaves 'just for the hell of it'. **1939** R. CHANDLER in *Sat. Even. Post* 14 Oct. 74/3, I wouldn't be telling you just for the hell of it. **1951** W. STEVENS *Let.* 7 Sept. (1967) 726, I assume that he is merely doing it for the hell of it. **1959** P. MCCUTCHAN *Storm South* xiii. 197 The kind of bloke you'd expect to find taking passage in a venture like ours, just for the hell of it.

p. like hell: recklessly, desperately; extremely, very much: freq. as a mere intensive; also ironically, to indicate emphatic contradiction: not at all, on the contrary.

1855 THACKERAY *Newcomes* I. xxix, I tried every place.. and played like hell. **1892** KIPLING *Lett. of Travel* (1920) 66 'Hit, old man?' 'Like hell,' he said. **1922** D. H. LAWRENCE *England, my England* 231 'And I shall miss thee, Jack.' ..'Miss you like hell.' **1925** F. LONSDALE *Last of Mrs. Cheyney* I. 19 *Maria*: Enjoying the concert, Willie? *Willie*: Like hell! **1930** D. HAMMETT *Maltese Falcon* xx. 260 'You can't say that.' 'Like hell I can't,' Spade said. **1941** H. MACINNES *Above Suspicion* ix. 76 'I've quite enjoyed it here.' Like hell I have, she added under her breath.

q. merry hell: a disturbance, upheaval, great trouble; severe pain.

a **1911** D. G. PHILLIPS *Susan Lenox* (1917) II. xi. 279 We don't dare let you off... They'd send down along the line, to have merry hell raised with us. **1922** S. LEWIS *Babbitt* xix. 229 I've come to raise particular merry hell. *c* **1926** 'MIXER' *Transport Workers' Song Bk.* 13 We don't get drunk to fight the boss Or kick up merry hell. **1931** D. L. SAYERS *Five Red Herrings* xxii. 248, I am supposed to have faked an alibi, suborned my friends and played merry hell generally. **1938** S. V. BENÉT *Thirteen O'Clock* IV. 268 If you think it was all romance..you're wrong. A lot of it was merry hell. **1944** J. H. FULLARTON *Troop Target* 86 This arm's giving me merry hell. **1961** B. FERGUSSON *Watery Maze* iv. 102 The Special Boat Squadron..was to play merry hell in the Eastern Mediterranean during the next two years. **1963** M. DUGGAN in *Landfall* Mar. 9 Watching mum with a shoehorn wedging nines into sevens and suffering merry hell.

r. to hell and gone: used hyperbolically = 'a long way', 'for ever', etc.

1938 S. J. PERELMAN in *New Yorker* 15 Oct. 17/2 Zarah Trenwick just got blasted to hellangone in her tepee at the Gayboy. **1944** N. MAILER in *Cross-Section* 332 Picking up two-foot piles of plates and lugging them to hell and gone. **1957** M. MILLAR *Soft Talkers* 39 That's my business. I can contradict myself to hell and gone if I feel like it. **1972** R. LOCKRIDGE *Preach No More* ii. 24 Name's Manuel something... Lives to-hell-and-gone downtown.

11. *attrib.* and *Comb.* **a.** Simple attrib., as ***hell-babe, -bond, -bound, -brew, -cauldron, -deed, -fiend, -flame, -pack, -pain, -pot, -powers, -pride, -queen, -rake, -rook, -shout, -spell, -spurge, -torment, -worm.***

In OE. and early ME. combinations, such as *helle bealu*, *helle déofol*, *helle fýr*, *helle* is the genitive, 'of hell'. OE. had a few real compounds, as *hellcræft*, *helldeofol*, *helldor*.

1838 DICKENS *O. Twist* l, 'Open the door of some place where I can lock this screeching *Hell-babe.' **1667** MILTON *P.L.* II. 644 *Hell bounds high reaching to the horrid Roof. **1923** WODEHOUSE *Inimitable Jeeves* viii. 69 'Have some lemon squash,' I said... The *hell-brew appeared to buck him up, for he resumed in a slightly more pally manner. **1935** *Discovery* Sept. 264/2 The dart poison..is indeed a hell-brew. **1740** E. BAYNARD *Health* (ed. 6) 46 Some little *Hell-Cub. **1546** *Supplic. Poore Comm.* (E.E.T.S.) 90 Thys more then *hell darkenesse. **1652** BENLOWES *Theoph.* x. lxxviii. 189 Thou..with *hell-deeds souls to hell dost sink. **1678** W. DILLINGHAM *Serm. Funer. Lady Alston* 25 So fall down like a Log into *Hell-flames. **1923** R. GRAVES *Whipperginny* 56 Twenty swans glide out With *hell-packs loathlier yet to amaze the night. **1601** SHAKS. *All's Well* II. iii. 245, I would it were *hell paines for thy sake. *a* **1711** KEN *Preparatives* Poet. Wks. 1721 IV. 47 *Hell-Pow'rs the Voice shall quiv'ring hear. **1944** BLUNDEN *Shells by Stream* 50 Passions armed with horror and *hell-pride. **1918** D. H. LAWRENCE *New Poems* 63 Out of the *hell-queen's cup, the heaven's pale wine. **1794** R. F. GREVILLE *Diary* 28 Aug. (1930) 309 His M. order'd Me to call at Farmer Sherring's where I order'd two of those Broad Rakes called *Hell Rakes. **1879** G. M. HOPKINS *Poems* (1918) 44 The *hell-rook ranks. **1834** L. RITCHIE *Wand. by Seine* 206 There was also the *hell-sauce, composed of pepper. **1813** PLUNKETT in *Ho. Com.* 25 Feb., Assailed by the *Hell-shout of 'No Popery'. **1605** SYLVESTER *Du Bartas* III. iii. III. *Law* 752 Think'st..with thy *Hel-spels thus To crosse our Counsels. **1849** D. G. ROSSETTI *Let.* 18 Oct. (1965) I. 74 *Hell-spurge of geomaunt and teraphim. *a* **1603** A. W. in Farr *S. P. Eliz.* (1845) II. 452 Me..He..Brought from *hell-torments to the ioyes of heauen.

b. Objective and obj. genitive, as ***hell-confounding***, ***-deserving***, ***-raising***, ***-raking***, ***-roaring***, ***-tearing*** adjs.; ***hell-buster***, ***-keeper***, ***-raiser***, ***-raker*** sbs. Also ***hell-rake*** vb.

1929 J. B. PRIESTLEY *Good Companions* III. iii. 2 They're all damned good, but the last two are real *hell-busters. **1648** JOS. BEAUMONT *Psyche* 20 (T.) His Lord's almighty name..Of *hell-confounding majestie made up. **1758** S. HAYWARD *Serm.* 21 To rescue *hell-deserving sinners. **1859** *Art Taming Horses* ix. 151 The 'pals' of fighting men and *hell-keepers. **1914** *Emporia* (Kans.) *Gaz.* 13 Jan., He is a..rip-snorting *hell-raiser. **1925** S. LEWIS *Martin Arrowsmith* iii. 20 Young men technically known as 'hell-raisers' looked forward to his lectures on physiology. **1928** *Daily Express* 1 June 9 She dislikes the 'hell-raiser' that he likes to make the public believe he is. **1971** *Guardian* 24 July 10/6 The ex-hell raiser of the Bevanite group [*sc.* Michael Foot]..seemed to have settled comfortably into the new role of Left-wing Whip. **1922** S. LEWIS *Babbitt* iii. 25 When it comes to..a lot of *hell-raising all the while.., it's too rich for my blood! **1936** W. STEVENS *Let.* 27 Jan. (1967) 307 Any form of hell raising is simply out. **1966** WODEHOUSE *Plum Pie* ix. 215 She's the hell-raising type, always apt to be starting something. **1915** J. E. FLECKER *Old Ships* 5 The pirate Genoese *Hell-raked them till they rolled Blood, water, fruit and corpses up the hold. **1816** SCOTT *Old Mort.* xli, A' thae *hell-rakers o' dragoons wad be at his whistle in a moment. **1606** SYLVESTER *Du Bartas* II. iv. I. *Trophies* 674 Whose *Hell-raking, Nature-shaking Spell. **1960** *Spectator* 17 June 870 Chatter nostalgically but amusingly about the hellraking times at Balliol. **1920** J. GREGORY *Man to Man* iv, Your *hell-roaring old grand-dad. **1915** W. J. LOCKE *Jaffery* xxi, These *hell-tearing fellows.

c. Instrumental and locative, as ***hell-assisted***, ***-begotten***, ***-brewed***, ***-engendered***, ***-enkindled***, ***-girt***, ***-governed***, ***-hatched***, ***-haunted***, ***-hired***, ***-instructed***, ***-kindled***, ***-mouthed***, ***-plumed***, ***-sprung***, ***-spun***, ***-taught***, etc., adjs.

a **1711** KEN *Hymnotheo* Poet. Wks. 1721 III. 378 The Brute..His *Hell-assisted Inchantation slights. **1751** SMOLLETT *Per. Pic.* (1779) I. xi. 94 A *Hell-begotten brat. **1667** MILTON *P.L.* II. 697 And reck'n'st thou thy self with Spirits of Heav'n, *Hell-doom'd. **1581** SIDNEY *Astr. & Stella* xlviii, Let not mine eyes be *hel-driv'n from that light. **1594** SHAKS. *Rich. III*, I. ii. 67 This good Kings blood, Which his *Hell-gouern'd arme hath butchered. **1600** ROWLANDS *Lett. Humours Blood* 3 For ther's no habite of *hell-hatched sinne, That we delight not to be clothed in. **1691** DRYDEN *K. Arthur* IV. i, Bound to the fate of this *hell-haunted grove. **1934** DYLAN THOMAS *Let.* 11 May (1966) 126 Today I complain again for a *hell-mouthed mist is blowing. **1876** G. MEREDITH *Vittoria* iii. 35 Those *hell-plumed Tyrolese. **1647** TRAPP *Marrow Gd. Auth.* in *Comm. Ep.* 610 Hell was long since said by one to be paved with the shaven crowns of those *hell-sprung locusts. **1797** *College* 33 Foul myst'ry drew Around her *hell-spun web.

d. Similative, 'like or as hell', as ***hell-black***, ***-dark***, ***-deep***, ***-hued***, ***-purple***, ***-red*** adjs.; also ***hell-like*** adj.

1605 SHAKS. *Lear* III. vii. 60 With such a storme as his bear head, In *Hell-blacke-night indur'd. **1904** SWINBURNE *Poems* VI. 392 Till murder dawns Blood-red from hell-black treason's heart of hate. **1598** HAKLUYT *Voy.* (N.), To guide the ship in the *helle-darke night. **1592** SYLVESTER *Triumph Faith* Ded., *Hell-deepe-founded Monuments. **1632** MASSINGER *Maid of Hon.* IV. iv, So horrid oaths, And hell-deep imprecations. **1733** E. ERSKINE *Serm.* Wks. 1871 II. 178 We are become *hell-hued, black like the Ethiopian. **1563** B. GOOGE *Eglogs* (Arb.) 83 From whence these *Hellike torments sprying. **1625** J. PHILLIPS *Way to Heaven* 39 That fearefull and hell-like torment in Purgatory. **1923** D. H. LAWRENCE *Birds, Beasts & Flowers* 57 At her white ankles Hell rearing its husband-splendid, serpent heads, *Hell-purple, to get at her.

12. Special combs.: **hell-box**, a term for a box for holding damaged or broken type; **hell-broth**, a decoction of infernal character or prepared for an infernal purpose; †**hell-cart**, an early nick-name for a hackney carriage: see quots.; **hell-devil**, Satan; also 'the hellgrammite-fly' (Funk); **hell-diver** *U.S.*, a grebe; the dabchick; **hell-dog** = HELL-HOUND; **hell-door**, the gate or entrance of hell; a place that may lead to hell; **hell-driver**, (*a*) *slang*, a coachman (*Dict. Cant. Crew*, *a* 1700); (*b*) one who drives a motor vehicle in a very fast or dare-devil manner; hence ***hell-driving***; **hell-god**, a god of the infernal regions, an infernal deity (so **hell-goddess**); **hell-hag**, a diabolical or vile woman, a hell-cat; †**hell-hated** *a.*, hated or abhorred as hell; **hell-hole, -house**, the hole or mansion of hell, an infernal hole or house; **hell-kite**, a kite of hell, a person of hellish cruelty; **hell-matter**, the broken or battered type in the 'hell-box'; †**hell-moth**, a term applied to a prostitute; **hell-mouth**, the mouth or jaws of hell; **hell-pit**, the pit or abyss of hell, the bottomless pit; **hell-receptacle** = *hell-box*; **hell's angel** (usu. in *pl.*), name given in the 1950s in the U.S. (later to similar people elsewhere) to a member of a group of lawless, usually leather-jacketed, motor-cyclists notorious for their disturbances of civil order in California (featured, but there called 'Black Rebels', in a 1954 film entitled 'The Wild One'); also earlier casual uses, e.g. (in *pl.*) as the name of a film about air-battles in the 1914–18 war (quot. 1930) and (in *sing.*) as the name of a Flying Fortress aeroplane (quot. 1943); **hell-ship**, a hell-afloat (cf. HELL *sb.* 4 a); **hell-wain**, a phantom wagon seen in the sky at night (Halliwell); †**hell-ware**, the inhabitants of hell.

1889 BARRÈRE & LELAND *Dict. Slang* I. 458/1 **Hell-box*, the receptacle for bad, broken, or 'battered' letters, which are eventually melted down. **1909** 'MARK TWAIN' *Is Shakes. Dead?* vii. 73 If a man should..say '..empty..the imposing stone into the hell-box..' I should..know that the writer was only a printer theoretically, not practically. **1605** SHAKS. *Macb.* IV. i. 19 For a Charme of powrefull trouble, Like a *Hell-broth, boyle and bubble. **1861** LOWELL *Wks.* (1890) V. 86 The caldron where the hell-broth of anarchy was brewing. **1630** J. TAYLOR (Water P.) *A Thiefe* 52 Wks. II. 121/1 Then upstart *Helcart-Coaches were to seeke, A man could scarce see twenty in a weeke. **1634** *Withals' Dict.* 417/1 *Rhedæ meritoriæ*, coaches that bee hyred for money. Herein doe the Women that bee called *Meritoriæ*, such Hyrelings..ride..and therefore they cal them *Helcarts*, such Coaches that be so employed. **1654** GAYTON *Pleas. Notes* II. i. 36 The Ladies in the Hell Carts screem'd out for their Hector. **1839–40** W. IRVING *Wolfert's R.* (1855) 179 He could live under water like that notable species of wild-duck, commonly called the *hell-diver. **1940** E. T. SETON *Trail of Artist-Naturalist* 89, I traced them to the pied-bill grebe, or little helldiver. *a* **1225** *Ancr. R.* 290 Sweng hem aȝean..þene *helle dogge. *a* **1618** SYLVESTER *Panthea* Invoc. iii. in Wks. 1880 II. 343/2 Make these pure Hell-Dogs in their Dens to couch. **1814** SOUTHEY *Roderick* III. Poet. Wks. 1838 IX. 31 This hell-dog turn'd aside Toward his home. *a* **1000** *Guthlac* 559 in *Exeter Bk.*, Wuldres cempan halig husulbearn æt *hel-dore. *a* **1200** *Moral Ode* 182 in *Trin. Coll. Hom.* 225 Brecð nafre eft crist helle dure. **1681** OTWAY *Soldier's Fort.* IV. i, Ay, that's Hell-door, and my Damnation's in the Inside. **1942** BERREY & VAN DEN BARK *Amer. Thes. Slang* §723/2 *Automobile racer*,..*hell driver. **1971** *Cape Times* 13 Feb. 7/6 The helldriver with the 99-to-1 chance of becoming the first Cape Times *hell-driving champion. *Ibid.*, One of the hottest nights of helldriving. *c* **888** K. ÆLFRED *Boeth.* xxxv. §6 Ða pohte he [Orfeus] þæt he wolde ȝesecan *helle godu. *a* **1618** SYLVESTER *Maiden's Blush* 52 Much to know is given Unto that Hell-God, by the God of Heaven. **1655** BP. J. RICHARDSON *On O.T.* 281 (T.) A corroding disease it [envy] is; an *hel-hag that feeds upon its marrow, bones and strongest parts. **1817** COLERIDGE *Sibyl. Leaves* (1862) 265 It roused the Hell-Hag. **1605** SHAKS. *Lear* V. iii. 147 Backe do I tosse these Treasons to thy head, With the *hell hated Lye ore-whelme thy heart. **13..** *E.E. Allit. P.* B. 223 Hurled in-to *helle-hole. **1866** J. C. GREGG *Life in Army* xxi. 184 All the whiskey shops, even down to the lowest hell-hole, adopt the decent name..of a 'Coffee-house'. **1882** M. ARNOLD *Irish Ess.* 71 Our 'Hell-holes', as Cobbett calls our manufacturing towns. **1891** G. M. HOPKINS *Let.* 15 June (1956) 63 Liverpool too, 'hellhole' though it is. **1896** *Tablet* 28 Mar. 490 Vice and cruelty..made of old Goa the hell-hole of India. **1945** J. B. PRIESTLEY *Three Men in New Suits* ii. 26 Go and drudge in some hell-hole of an office. *a* **1000** *Guthlac* 677 in *Exeter Bk.*, In *helle hus. **1659** D. PELL *Impr. Sea* 491 In ships which are meer Hell-houses of swearing and prophaneness. **1605** SHAKS. *Macb.* IV. iii. 217 All my pretty ones?..Oh *Hell-Kite! All? What, All my pretty Chickens? **1849** JAMES *Woodman* viii, There is no knowing what such hell kites may do. **18..** MARK TWAIN *Printer in N.Y. Sun* (Farmer *Amer.*), I put the good type in his case and the broken ones among the *hell-matter. **1602** ROWLANDS *Greene's Ghost* 4 Is there not one appointed for the apprehending of such *hell-moths [harlots and curtizans], that eat a man out of bodie and soule? *a* **1175** *Cott. Hom.* 239 Wat sceol se wrecce don þe..iseȝð.. under him *helle muð open. **1546** COVERDALE *Lord's Supper* Wks. 1844 I. 453 But after this detestable opinion was invented, this unhappy custom proceedeth out of it, as out of an hell-mouth. **1623** MIDDLETON *More Dissemblers* IV. ii, Hell-mouth be with thee! *c* **1200** ORMIN 10215 Forr *helle pitt niss næfre full. **1553** T. WILSON *Rhet.* (1580) 170 Procuryng his passe porte to poste it to hell pitt, there to be punished. **1876** J. GOULD *Letter-press Printer* 156 **Hell receptacle*, the receptacle for broken or battered letters; the old metal box; the shoe. **1930** (*film title*) *Hell's Angels. **1943** *Examiner* (San Francisco) 8 Aug. 3/1 The ten-man crew which manned the flying fortress, 'Hell's Angel', on her thirty-three raids across the English channel. **1957** *Chronicle* (San Francisco) 3 June 5/1 It also attracted several hundred cyclists who are not American Motorcycle Association members, but who belong to such clubs as the Vampires, Scavengers and Hell's Angels group that rides in the Bay Area. **1957** *Call-Bulletin* (San Francisco) 9 Aug. 3/4 Police raiders cracked down last night on the Hell's Angels, a hard-riding motorcycle outfit whose members have had brushes with the law in the past. **1958** *Ibid.* 1 Aug. 11/1 The main wheel of the 'Hell's Angels' motorcycle club is a more or less conservative delivery man during the week, but Fridays he ..combs his hair into a wild mane, gets into black denims and motorcycle boots, plus a red-fringed vest with the club's death's-head emblem, fastens his pierced ear-lobe and dyes his blonde handlebar mustache with heliotrope pencil. **1967** G. LEGMAN *Fake Revolt* 21 The hoodlum drug-addicts and homosexual motorcyclists..who've had two 'Hell's Angels' movies already exposing (*read*: glorifying) them. **1968** *Listener* 22 Feb. 253/2 The Hell's Angels—those much-publicised outlaw motor-cyclists, noted for their wearing of leather jackets and Nazi insignia, whose hunting ground is mainly California. **1969** *Oz* Apr. 3/2 Hell's Angels were moved in on the 3rd floor as a protection against external aggression. **1971** *New Scientist* 11 Feb. 331/2 The Hell's Angels created rather than prevented disorder when Mick and the Stones were dispensing their magic. **1927** *Observer* 21 Aug. 15/2 *Hell-ships they must be if three and four months' passages..is anything from which to form an opinion. **1934** *Times Lit. Suppl.* 18 Oct. 713/2 The Dovenby Hall, a notorious hell-ship in her day. **1971** D. NIVEN *Moon's a Balloon* (1972) vii. 93 The troopship was a hell-ship of about 11,000 tons. **1584** R. SCOT *Discov. Witchcr.* VII. xv. (1886) 122 They have so fraied us with bull beggers..the man in the oke, the *hell waine, the fier drake..and such other bugs, that we are afraid of our own shadowes. *c* **1000** ÆLFRIC *Hom.* II. 362 Ealle ȝesceafta, heofonwara, eorðwara, *helwara, onbuȝað..ðam Hælendum Criste. *c* **1200** *Trin. Coll. Hom.* 53 Biforen alle heueneware and herðeware, and ec helleware.

hell, *v.*[1] *Obs.* exc. *dial.* [A by-form of ME. *held*, HIELD *v.*: cf. HEEL from *hield*; prob. immediately a. ON. *hella*, Sw. *hälle*, Da. *hælde*, to pour, cognate with HIELD *v.*] To pour. *trans.* and *intr.*

a **1340** HAMPOLE *Psalter* Prol. 3 þai drope swetnes in mannys saule and hellis delite in þaire thoghtis. *Ibid.* xxi. 13 As water .i. am helt. *Ibid.* lxviii. 29 Hell on þaim þi wreth. *a* **1400–50** *Alexander* 3813 As all þe watir of þe werd ware in þaire wambs hellid. **1483** *Cath. Angl.* 182/1 To Helle in, *jnfundere*..To Helle oute, *fundere*, *effundere*. **1821** *Harvest* 17 in *Borrowdale Let.* 9 Gash the sickle went into me hand: Down hell'd the bluid. **1828** *Craven Dial.*, *Helle*, to pour out. [So in Northumberland, Lonsdale, Swaledale Glossaries.]

†**hell**, *v.*[2] *nonce-wd.* [f. HELL *sb.*] In various, chiefly *slang*, uses: **a.** *trans.* To place in or as in hell, to cause to have their hell. **b.** To make into a hell. **c.** To give (a person) hell. **d.** To hurry, to go 'hell for leather', to 'fly' *around* (esp. in some activity disapproved of by the speaker).

a **1650** T. ADAMS *Pract. Wks.* (1861) I. 231 (D.) The dead in sin are hell'd here by the tormenting anguish of an unappeasable conscience. **1897** O. WISTER *Lin McLean* (1898) 60 A man was liable to go sporting and helling around till he waked up. **1903** P. F. ROWLAND *New Nation* 34 The raging bush-fires that hell the Australian plains. **1924** KIPLING *Debits & Credits* (1926) 242 *That's* not his real trouble... I wonder what's really helling him. **1928** J. P. MCEVOY *Show Girl* 166 You were in the show business and throwing your best years away helling around. **1929** W. FAULKNER *Sound & Fury* 243 She had to come helling in there at twelve, worrying me about that letter. **1929** —— *Sartoris* (1933) II. 53 Men can't stand anything... Can't even stand helling around with no worry. **1959** E. FENWICK *Long Way Down* x. 83 Had his supper..just like he always did. I missed *mine*, helling up here this way. **1960** F. SULLIVAN *Let.* 9 Jan. in *Groucho Lett.* (1967) 147 That oppressed and downtrodden share-cropper, Massa Nunnally Johnson, is hellin' around with Ava Gardner, making a picture. **1969** 'E. LATHEN' *Come to Dust* xvii. 172 'If he did any helling around, it wasn't here,' the janitor continued.

hell, *v.*[3] [a. Ger. *hellen* in same sense (see Grimm), f. *hell* clear.] *trans.* To add lustre to, to burnish (gold or silver).

1799 G. SMITH *Laboratory* I. 99 To Hell Gold, or Gilt Work. Take two ounces of tartar, two ounces of sulphur.. and it will give it a fine lustre. *Ibid.* 91 Unwrought gold and silver..undergo several operations, and are heightened by gilding wax, colouring and helling.

hell, obs. form of HELE *v.*[2], to conceal, cover.

he'll (hiːl), colloq. contraction of *he will*.

He'lladian, *a.* and *sb. rare.* [f. Gr. Ἑλλαδ-, stem of Ἑλλάς Hellas, Greece + -IAN.] **A.** *adj.* = HELLENIC *a.* 1. **B.** *sb.* A Hellene or Greek.

1811 in *Encycl. Londin.*

Helladic (hɛˈlædɪk), *a.* [ad. Gr. Ἑλλαδικ-ός of or from Greece: see -IC.] **a.** Of or pertaining to Hellas or Greece; Grecian, as opposed to Asiatic.

1801 FUSELI in *Lect. Paint.* ii. (1848) 387 The Helladic and the Ionian schools. **1850** LEITCH *Müller's Anc. Art* §139. 115 Zeuxis, Parrhasius and their followers, under the general name of the Asiatic school, were opposed to the Grecian (Helladic) school.

b. *Archæol.* Denoting the Bronze Age cultures of Greece, lasting from about 2800 to 1200 B.C. Also *absol.*

1921 WACE in *Jrnl. Hellenic Studies* XLI. II. 260 Early Helladic pottery. *Ibid.* 265 With the Third Late Helladic Period Mycenae reached the zenith of its dominion and riches. **1925** V. G. CHILDE *Dawn Europ. Civilisation* v. 74 The first metal-using culture therefore is called Early Helladic. **1927** PEAKE & FLEURE *Priests & Kings* 113 The sub-periods range from Early Helladic I to Late Helladic III. **1940** *Antiquity* XIV. 244 Deposits earlier than the

beginning of Late Helladic III, the fourteenth century B.C. **1971** J. L. CASKEY in *Cambr. Anc. Hist.* (ed. 3) I. II. xxvi(*a*). 783 There has been a question whether material elements of the latest Stone Age culture persisted for a time alongside the earliest Helladic, since pottery of both types was found together.

hellandite ('hɛləndaɪt). *Min.* [ad. G. *hellandit* (W. C. Brögger 1903, in *Nyt Mag. f. Naturvid.* XLI. 213), f. the name of A. *Helland* (1846–1918), Norwegian geologist: see -ITE[1].] A hydrous borosilicate of the rare earths and calcium, samples of which also contain aluminium, manganese, and iron, perhaps as impurities, that is found in pegmatite veins in Norway.

1903 *Jrnl. Chem. Soc.* LXXXIV. II. 657 Both in crystalline form and chemical composition, hellandite is analogous to guarinite. **1924** J. W. MELLOR *Inorg. & Theoret. Chem.* V. 512 Brownish-red hellandite from Lindvikskollan near Kragerö, Norway. **1964** *Mineral. Abstr.* XVI. 644/2 Hellandite is a boro-silicate with more than 10% B_2O_3 in addition to the known major constituents.

hellarne, obs. form of ELDER *sb.*[1]

hellbender ('hɛl,bɛndə(r)). *U.S.* [f. HELL *sb.* + BENDER, one who or that which bends.]

1. The menopome or American salamander, an ugly and repulsive amphibian, from one to two feet in length, of which two species (*Menopoma alleghaniensis, M. horrida*) are found in the Ohio and Mississippi valleys.

1812 B. S. BARTON (*title*) Memoir concerning an Animal of the Class Reptilia or Amphibia, which is known by the name of Alligator and Hellbender. **1863** WOOD *Illustr. Nat. Hist.* III. 185 A large array of names, among which are Tweeg, Hellbender, Mud Devil, and Ground Puppy. **1893** LELAND *Mem.* II. 179 That extraordinary fish lizard.. known as the hell-bender from its extreme ugliness.

2. A protracted and reckless debauch or drunken frolic.

1889 FARMER *Americanisms.*

'hell-bent, *a.* and *adv. colloq.* (orig. *U.S.*). [HELL *sb.* 11 d, BENT *ppl. a.* 3.] 'Fiendishly', doggedly, or recklessly determined (*on* or *upon* a certain course). Also *advb.* determinedly, recklessly.

1835 *Knickerbocker* VI. 12 A large encampment of savages,..'hell-bent on carnage'. **1840** *Pol. Song* (Cent. Dict.), Maine went Hell-bent For Governor Kent. **1904** *Boston Herald* 2 Aug. 6 The Populist Democrats are going 'hell-bent', as the old song says, for Roosevelt. **1910** W. M. RAINE *B. O'Connor* ii. 21, I know your kind—hell-bent to spend what you cash in. **1910** C. E. MULFORD *Hopalong Cassidy* xxviii. 184 As soon as we lick this aggregation of trouble-hunters, what's left will ride hell-bent for that valley. **1912** L. J. VANCE *Destroying Angel* ix, Unless you're hell-bent upon sticking around here. **1918** C. E. MULFORD *Man fr. Bar-20* xv. 152, I was hell-bent to get down here,.. an' now I'm hell-bent to get back again. **1926** B. CRONIN *Red Dawson* vi, Shaw sending the coach hell-bent round the curve of Jumping Lead. **1935** A. SQUIRE *Sing Sing Doctor* iii. 32 We'll always have people hell bent on doing what they want to. **1957** *Times* 27 Dec. 6/1 Sir Edmund Hillary's message.. went on to say: 'We are heading hellbent for the Pole, God willing and crevasses permitting.' **1967** *Spectator* 24 Nov. 633/1 This report has been widely used to sustain the charge that the French government was hell-bent on feeding speculation against the pound. **1968** *Times* 31 Oct. 11/3 It is now becoming.. clear that an intelligent plan may have to be drawn, according to which those elements hell-bent on.. embarrassing the School will have to be expelled from it. **1973** *Times* 31 July 1/3 A minority of Unionist Party members.. feel obliged to vote with those who are hell-bent on destroying the first democratically elected assembly the Ulster people have had since the dissolution of Stormont.

'hell-born, *a.* Born of or in hell; of infernal origin.

1593 SHAKS. *Lucr.* 1519 That jealousy itself could not mistrust.. Or blot with hell-born sin such saintlike forms. **1667** MILTON *P.L.* II. 687 Retire, or taste thy folly, and learn by proof, Hell-born, not to contend with Spirits of Heav'n. **1752** YOUNG *Brothers* IV. i, Hell-born impostor! **1851** GLADSTONE *Glean.* IV. ix. 7 The hell-born spirit of revenge.

'hell-bred, *a.* Bred or engendered in hell.

1590 SPENSER *F.Q.* I. xi. 40 What outrage and what cries .. The hell-bred beast [the dragon] threw forth unto the skies. **1640** BROME *Sparagus Gard.* II. v. Wks. 1873 III. 149 Oh thou hel-bred Rascall thou. *a* **1711** KEN *Hymns Festiv.* Poet. Wks. 1721 I. 300 His very Temper seem'd on fire With Hell-bred Ire.

'hell-cat. [f. HELL *sb.* + CAT: possibly suggested by *Heccat*, HECATE.] An evil or spiteful woman; a furious vixen; a witch.

a **1605** MIDDLETON *Witch* II. ii, The whorson old hellcat would have given me the brain of a cat. **1632** CHAPMAN & SHIRLEY *Ball* III. ii, We cannot be too bitter, she's a hell-cat. **1837** MARRYAT *Dog-fiend* II. i. (L.), A hell-cat, who hates me as she does the devil.

b. Applied to a man: see quots.

a **1700** B. E. *Dict. Cant. Crew, Hell-cat*, a very Lewd Rakehelly Fellow. **1845** DISRAELI *Sybil* VI. vi, The Hell-cats [Chartist agitators] as they call themselves, halt at every town, and offer fifty pounds for a live policeman.

helleboraster (,hɛlɪbɒ'ræstə(r)). [mod.L., f. *hellebor-us* hellebore + -ASTER.] The Fetid Hellebore or Bear's foot (*Helleborus fetidus*).

1663–4 E. BROWNE in *Sir T. Browne's Wks.* (1848) III. 402, I saw Helleboraster in flower. **1823** *Mechanics' Mag.* No. 11. 175 To try helleboraster, milk-thistle, henbane, etc.

hellebore ('hɛlɪbɔə(r)). Forms: 5 el(l)ebre (-bur, -byr, eleure), 6–7 el(l)ebor(e, 6–8 hellebor, (7 helebore, -bour), 6– hellebore. Also in L. form helleborus, -um. [ad. L. *elleborus*, in 14th c. F. *ellebore* (Oresme), a. Gr. ἐλλέβορος, more rarely ἐλλ-. (The native L. equivalent was *veratrum.*) The initial *h* has been restored in Botanical Latin and in Eng. after the prevailing Gr. form.]

1. A name given by the ancients to certain plants having poisonous and medicinal properties, and esp. reputed as specifics for mental disease; identified with species of *Helleborus* and *Veratrum*; now, in botany, applied to the species of *Helleborus*, (N.O. *Ranunculaceæ*), including the Christmas Rose and its congeners: **a.** the plant; **b.** the drug.

c **1420** *Pallad. on Husb.* I. 1044 This wermot, and eleure [*eleborus*]. *c* **1440** *Promp. Parv.* 138/1 Elebre, herbe (*K., P.* elebyr), *eleborus.* **1561** T. NORTON *Calvin's Inst.* IV. xix. (1634) 730 *margin*, Anticyra where groweth Hellebor, a good purgation for phrenticke heads. **1718** QUINCY *Compl. Disp.* 30 Plants, which abound less with Rosin, such as Hellebore. **1882** *Garden* 28 Jan. 56/2 Hellebores.. are at present almost the only occupants in flower in outdoor gardens.

b. *c* **1400** *Lanfranc's Cirurg.* 83 Sle [worms] wiþ þe ius of calamynte.. eiþer wiþ decoccioun of elebre. **1599** MARSTON *Sco. Villanie* I. i. 172 As methodist Musus kild with Hellebore. **1652** BP. HALL *Invisible World* II. i, These errors are more fit for hellebore than for theological conviction. **1692** E. WALKER *Epictetus' Mor.* xxxviii, As whether.. Hellebore can purge a Mad-man's Head. **1830** SCOTT *Demonol.* vii. 204 Wretches fitter for a course of hellebore than for the stake. **1884** TENNYSON *Becket* IV. ii. 165 Such strong hate-philtre as may madden him—madden Against his priest beyond all hellebore.

2. With qualifying word, denoting: **a.** species of the genus *Helleborus*: **black hellebore**, (*a*) of the ancients, *H. officinalis*; (*b*) of some moderns, the Christmas Rose, *H. niger*; **green hellebore**, also called ***bastard*** or ***wild black h.***, *H. viridis*; **stinking** or **fetid hellebore**, *H. fetidus*; **Oriental** or **East Indian hellebore**, *H. orientalis*; **b.** of the genus *Veratrum* (N.O. *Melanthaceæ*), sometimes called ***false hellebore***: **white hellebore** (of the ancients), *V. album*; **swamp hellebore**, *V. viride*, also called ***American*** or ***green hellebore***. **c. winter hellebore**, the Winter Aconite, *Eranthis hyemalis.*

[**1390** GOWER *Conf.* III. 130 His [Argol's] herbe, which is him betake, Is hote eleborum the blacke. **1398** TREVISA *Barth. De P.R.* XVII. lv. (1495) 635 Eleborus.. the Romayns calle this herbe Veratrum.. and therof is two manere of kyndes: whyte and blacke.] **1578** LYTE *Dodoens* III. xxiv. 348 White Ellebor vnprepared, and taken out of time and place ..is very hurtfull to the body. **1590** SPENSER *F.Q.* II. vii. 52 Dead sleeping Poppy, and black Hellebore. **1747** WESLEY *Prim. Physic* (1762) 34 In the fit, blow Powder of White Hellebore up the nose. **1778** G. WHITE *Selborne* Let. xli. (1875) 249 *Helleborus fœtidus*, stinking hellebore, bear's foot, or setterwort.. women give the leaves powdered to children troubled with worms. *Helleborus viridis*, green hellebore. **1858** HOGG *Veg. Kingd.* 737 White Hellebore (*Veratrum album*), a native of the Alps and Pyrenees, is a violent emetic and cathartic. **1875** H. C. WOOD *Therap.* (1879) 536 Black Hellebore has been used by some as a purgative emmenagogue, but is now very rarely if ever employed.

3. *attrib.* and *Comb.*, as ***hellebore-root.***

1792 OSBALDISTON *Brit. Sportsm.* s.v. *Herbes*, They put into a horse's counter a piece of hellebore-root. **1878** tr. *Ziemssen's Cycl. Med.* XVII. 742 Hellebore-poisoning.. results from the joint action of the two active principles contained in the plant.

Hence ,**hellebo'raceous** *a.*, botanically related or akin to the hellebores (*Syd. Soc. Lex.* 1886); **'helleborate** *a.*, mixed or prepared with hellebore; **hellebo'rein**, **helle'boresin**, **hellebo'retin**, and **he'lleborin**, chemical principles derived from hellebore: **helle'boric**, *a.*, of or pertaining to hellebore; † **hellebo'rose** *a.*, 'full of hellebore' (Bailey vol. II. 1727); **helle'borous** *a.*, of the nature of hellebore; † **hellebory** (**elebory**) = HELLEBORE.

1587 MASCALL *Govt. Cattle* (1627) 35 Take the roots of white elebory, otherwise called neesing powder. **1609** BP. W. BARLOW *Answ. Nameless Cath.* 4 An Eleborous purge to make him disgorge the gall of his bitternesse. **1633** HART *Diet Diseased* III. xi. 272 His helleborate medicines. **1811** BYRON *Hints fr. Hor.* 473 Tuns of helleboric juice. **1872** WATTS *Dict. Chem.* VI. 695 *Helleborin*, $C_{36}H_{42}O_6$, and *Helleboreïn*, $C_{26}H_{44}O_{6}$, two glucosides existing in the roots of *Helleborus niger* and *H. viridis*.. Helleborin.. occurs but .. sparingly in black, more abundantly in green hellebore.. Helleboreïn is much more abundant in black than in green hellebore, but occurs in considerably larger quantity than helleborin, even in the latter.. By boiling with dilute acids, it is resolved into helleboretin, $C_{14}H_{20}O_3$, which separates as a dark violet-blue precipitate, and glucose.. [Helleborin] is resolved by boiling with dilute acids, or more completely with a concentrated solution of zinc chloride, into glucose and helleboresin, $C_{30}H_{38}O_4$. **1876** HARLEY *Mat. Med.* (ed. 6) 768 The activity of the root is due to two glucosides, helleborin, and helleborein.

helleborine ('hɛlɪbɒraɪn). *Bot.* [mod. ad. Gr. ἐλλεβορίνη a plant like hellebore: see -INE: cf. F. *elleborine.*] An orchidaceous plant of the genus *Epipactis* (formerly called *Serapias*), or of the closely-allied genus *Cephalanthera.*

1597 GERARDE *Herbal* II. cvi. §1. 357 Helleborine is like vnto white Hellebore, and for that cause we haue giuen it the name of Helleborine. **1778** LIGHTFOOT *Fl. Scot.* (1789) I. 527 *Serapias longifolia Lin.*.. Marsh Helleborine. **1778** G. WHITE *Selborne* (1853) II. xl. 266, *Serapias latifolia*, helleborine. **1833** SMITH & SOWERBY *Eng. Bot.* 2775 Purple-leaved Helleborine.. was discovered in Worcestershire in 1807. **1900** *Daily Express* 22 June 2/7, I was surprised.. to find the large white helleborine.. flowering in plenty. **1951** V. S. SUMMERHAYES *Wild Orchids Brit.* vii. 123 The helleborines have rather tall slender stems.

attrib. **1748** *Phil. Trans.* XLV. 159 The most elegant Flower of all the helleborine Tribe.

helleborism ('hɛlɪbɒrɪz(ə)m). *Med.* [mod. ad. Gr. ἐλλεβορισμός a curing by hellebore, f. ἐλλεβορίζειν to HELLEBORIZE.] **a.** The treatment of diseases (esp. insanity) by hellebore. **b.** 'The symptoms produced by the charging of the system by hellebore, or by its too free administration' (*Syd. Soc. Lex.* 1886). **c.** A purgative made from hellebore.

1621 BURTON *Anat. Mel.* II. v. I. iii, That famous Helleborisme of Montanus, which he so often repeats in his consultations and counsells. **1640** CHILMEAD tr. *Ferrand's Erotomania* 169 (T.) In vain should the physician attempt, with all his medicines and helleborisms, the cure of those that are sick with love. **1883** J. B. WOOD *Addr. Hahnemann* 5 His public thesis, on the Helleborism of the Ancients.

'helleborize, *v.* [mod. ad. Gr. ἐλλεβορίζ-ειν to dose with hellebore: see -IZE.] *trans.* To treat or dose with hellebore, as for madness.

a **1856** SIR W. HAMILTON (Ogilvie), I am represented.. as one who would be helleborised as a madman for harbouring the absurdity.

† **'hellen**, *a. Obs. rare.* [f. HELL *sb.* + -EN[4].] Of or belonging to hell; infernal, hellish.

a **1225** *Ancr. R.* 150 þis world.. is al biset of helle muchares [*MSS. T., C.* hellene mucheres]. *c* **1230** *Hali Meid.* 41 þat teameð hire in horedom of þe laðe vnwiht, þe hellene schucke. **13..** *E.E. Allit. P.* C. 306 Out of þe hole þou me herde, of hellen wombe I calde, and þou knew myn vncler steuen.

Hellene (hɛ'liːn, 'hɛliːn). Also 7–8 **Hellen**. [a. Gr. Ἕλλην a Greek. The pl. occurs first in Homer, as the name of a Thessalian tribe of which Hellen was chief; in the historical period it was the name applied to themselves by all Greeks.] A Greek: **a.** An ancient Greek, of genuine Grecian race. **b.** A subject of the modern kingdom of Greece or Hellas.

1662 STILLINGFL. *Orig. Sacr.* III. iv. §12 Although the name of Hellens at last spread its self over all the people of Greece, yet it was at first peculiar to that part of Thessaly called Pthiotis. **1835** THIRLWALL *Greece* I. 379 A general congress of the Hellenes. **1896** *Whitaker's Alm.* 550/2 George, second son of the present King of Denmark.. elected King of the Hellenes.. 1863.

Hence **He'llenedom**, the Grecian realm or world; † **He'llenish** *a.* = HELLENISTIC.

1659–60 JER. TAYLOR in *Evelyn's Diary* (1852) III. 128 The word is used by the Hellenish Jews to signify any place of spiritual and immaterial pleasure. **1891** *Q. Rev.* July 188 Athens, even in the first Christian centuries the Capital of Hellenedom.

Hellenian (hɛ'liːnɪən), *a.* and *sb. rare.* [f. Gr. Ἑλλήνι-ος HELLENIC + -AN.]

A. *adj.* Grecian; HELLENIC.

1813 T. BUSBY *Lucretius* V. 917 The Chaldean Magi.. whose pride To vanquish the Hellenian doctrine tried. **1830** tr. *Aristoph., Knights* 100 Hellenian Jove, thine is the prize of victory!

B. *sb.* = HELLENE, in the Homeric sense.

c **1611** CHAPMAN *Iliad* (1843) I. II. 69 In Hellade where live the lovely dames, The Myrmidons, Helenians, and Achives, rob'd of fames. *a* **1846** B. R. HAYDON *Autobiogr.* (1927) III. xvi. 308 Two complete subjects of combat,—viz. between the Centaurs and Lapithæ, and between the Amazons and Hellenians.

Hellenic (hɛ'liːnɪk, -'lɛnɪk), *a.* (*sb.*) [ad. L. *Hellēnicus*, a. Gr. Ἑλληνικ-ός: see HELLENE and -IC.] **A.** *adj.* **1.** Of or pertaining to the Hellenes or Greeks, ancient or modern; Greek, Grecian.

1644 MILTON *Areop.* (Arb.) 42 So great an injury they then held it to be depriv'd of Hellenick learning. **1835** THIRLWALL *Greece* I. 63 Before the name and dominion of the Pelasgians had given way to that of the Hellenic race. **1879** FARRAR *St. Paul* ii. 30 The glamour of Hellenic grace. **1897** *Daily News* 22 Feb. 9/1 The Hellenic regular troops round Canea. **1936** A. THIRKELL *August Folly* viii. 240 Everyone had a suggestion to make for spending the gift.. Mrs. Tebben thought an Icelandic or Hellenic cruise. **1971** A. CHRISTIE *Nemesis* vii. 76 They had been on an Hellenic cruise last year and a tour of bulbs in Holland the year before.

2. *Typogr.* Designating a variety of Greek type.

1927 *Greek Printing Types* (Exhib. B.M.) 3 It is thus only natural that the Graeco-Latin founts should now make way for more directly Hellenic styles of type. *Ibid.* 21 Thucydides, Funeral Oration of Pericles (part). Printed with 12-point 'New Hellenic' type.

B. *sb.* **a.** The Greek language. **b.** *pl.* Writings on Greek subjects.

1847 LANDOR (*title*) Hellenics. **1855** (*title*) Xenophon's Hellenics, or Grecian History. **1870** ANDERSON *Missions Amer. Bd.* III. i. 11 They repaired to the Greek College in Scio, for the purpose of studying the Modern Hellenic.

Hence **He'llenicize** *v.*, to make Greek, to Græcize.

1854 BADHAM *Halieut.* 467 Resolved..to hellenicize the name.

Hellenism ('hɛlɪnɪz(ə)m). [a. Gr. *Ἑλληνισμ-ός* imitation of the Greeks, use of a pure Greek idiom, f. *Ἑλληνίζειν* to HELLENIZE: see -ISM.]

1. A peculiarity of the Greek language; esp. a phrase, idiom, or construction used or formed in the Greek manner.

1609 HOLLAND *Amm. Marcell.* Annot. C iij a, Yee must admit here a Synecdoche, the plurall for the singular, a usuall figure in Hellenisme. **1614** SELDEN *Titles Hon.* 198 That age, about Alexius his time, generally affected Hellenisme and such words of Greeke as they could get them. **1646** GREGORY *An Order Comm., Oriens* 79 This was but an Hebraisme in the old, and but an Hellenisme in the new Testament. **1712** ADDISON *Spect.* No. 285 ⁋9 Virgil is full of the Greek Forms of Speech, which the Criticks call Hellenisms. **1771** MACPHERSON *Introd. Hist. Gt. Brit.* 244 Their language, though tinctured with Hellenisms, is radically different from the Greek. **1841** D'ISRAELI *Amen. Lit.* (1867) 128 When Greek was first studied..it planted many a hellenism in our English.

2. Conformity to Hellenic speech and ideas; imitation or adoption of Greek characteristics, e.g. by the Jews of the Dispersion, by the later Romans, etc.; the principle of Hellenizing.

1862 MERIVALE *Rom. Emp.* (1865) VII. lv. 34 The Hellenism which Nero vaunted was apostasy from the goddess Roma. **1879** FARRAR *St. Paul* vii. 126 Hellenist.. means, in the first instance, one who 'Græcises' in language or mode of life..Now this hellenism expressed many shades of difference, and therefore the exact meaning of the word Hellenist varies with the circumstances under which it is used. *Ibid.* 130 That detestation which had once burned in the Jewish heart against Hellenism.

3. The national character or spirit of the Greeks; Grecian culture.

1865 GROTE *Plato* Pref. 12 New foreign centres of rhetoric and literature—Asiatic and Alexandrian Hellenism—were fostered into importance by regal encouragement. **1869** SWINBURNE *Ess. & Stud.* (1875) 188 Their exquisite Hellenism of spirit. **1876** GLADSTONE *Homeric Synchr.* 197 A Poet with the intense Hellenism and Autochthonism of Homer. **1881** *Daily News* 1 Feb. 3/3 Hellenism (they say) has educated us and prepared us for the enjoyment of liberty.

b. Applied by Matthew Arnold to that form of culture, or ideal of life, of which the ancient Greek is taken as the type: see quot. 1869, and cf. HEBRAISM.

1869 M. ARNOLD *Cult. & Anarchy* iv. (1875) 136 To get rid of one's ignorance, to see things as they are, and by seeing them as they are to see them in their beauty, is the simple and attractive ideal which Hellenism holds out before human nature; and from the simplicity and charm of this ideal, Hellenism, and human life in the hands of Hellenism ..are full of what we call sweetness and light. *Ibid.* 143 As the great movement of Christianity was a triumph of Hebraism and man's moral impulses, so the great movement which goes by the name of the Renascence, was an up-rising and re-instatement of man's intellectual impulses and of Hellenism. **1869** *Contemp. Rev.* XI. 150 Mr. Arnold treats of the great rival forces Hebraism and Hellenism which between them divide the world.

4. Greek nationality; the Hellenic race or 'world' as a political entity.

1883 SEELEY *Expans. Eng.* 239 The Macedonians, through their close relationship with the Greeks, brought all Hellenism in their train. **1886** *Manch. Exam.* 29 Jan. 4/7 The Government believes it to be its duty to safeguard Hellenism, whose future is menaced. **1897** *Daily News* 22 Feb. 9/1, I shall have the whole of Hellenism on my side.

Hellenist ('hɛlɪnɪst). [ad. Gr. *Ἑλληνιστής* a follower of the Greeks in language, etc., one who Hellenizes, f. *Ἑλληνίζειν* to HELLENIZE: see -IST.]

1. One who used the Greek language, though not a native Greek. Applied *esp.* to those Jews of the Dispersion who used the Greek language and were more or less affected by Greek influences.

1613 PURCHAS *Pilgrimage* (1614) 137 The Hebrewes and Hellenists often disagreed. **1653** HAMMOND *Annot. Acts* vi. 1 (R.) These Jews understood Greek, and used the Greek Bible, and therefore are called Hellenists. **1879** FARRAR *St. Paul* vii. 125 It is to these Greek-speaking Jews that the term Hellenist..properly applies..It means one who 'Græcises' in language or mode of life..It is therefore..the..antithesis ..to strict 'Hebrews'. **1881** N. T. (R. V.) *Acts* vi. 1 There arose a murmuring of the Grecian Jews [*marg.* Hellenists] against the Hebrews.

attrib. **1789** GIBBON *Autobiog.* (1896) 141 The corrupt dialect of the Hellenist Jews.

2. One skilled in the Greek language and literature; a Greek scholar.

1680 DALGARNO *Didascolocophus* 126 (T.) But if all this do not satisfy the critical Hellenist, then I must add [etc.]. **1837** HALLAM *Hist. Lit.* I. III. §3 In Italy..there were still professors of it [Greek] in the university; but no one Hellenist distinguishes this [17th] century. **1880** *Contemp. Rev.* XXXVII. 479 An Oxford Hellenist (as we venture to call any person with considerable knowledge of Greek).

3. One of the Byzantine Greeks who contributed to the revival of classical learning in Europe in the 15th century.

In mod. Dicts.

Hellenistic (hɛlɪ'nɪstɪk), *a.* [f. prec. + -IC.] Of or pertaining to the Hellenists; using the Greek language and following Greek modes of thought or life. **a.** Applied to the modified form of the Greek language, with many foreign elements, current in Egypt, Syria, and other countries, after the time of Alexander the Great.

1706 PHILLIPS (ed. Kersey), *Hellenistical*, or *Hellenistick*, belonging to Greece. **1727–51** CHAMBERS *Cycl.* s.v., Salmasius rejects the common opinion of the learned touching the Hellenistic language. **1827** G. S. FABER *Expiatory Sacr.* 111 Through the Hellenistic use of a well-known Hebrew idiom. **1837–9** HALLAM *Hist. Lit.* (1855) II. 373 He [Salmasius] says..in the last age (i.e. prior to 1643) the very name of Hellenistic was unknown to scholars. **1881** WESTCOTT & HORT *Grk. N.T.* Introd. §398 The term Hellenistic was coined to denote the language of Greek-speaking Jews.

b. Of or pertaining to the ancient Greeks of this later age, when the true Hellenic characteristics were modified by foreign elements; belonging to the school of Greek art after the time of Alexander.

1874 MAHAFFY *Soc. Life Greece* x. 297 Menander, whose essentially refined and social temper belonged more properly to the Platonic than the Hellenistic age.

Hence **Helle'nisticism**, the Hellenistic condition or stage of history.

1897 *Daily Chron.* 24 May, This change in the world's history, the change from Hellenism to Hellenisticism, is regarded by the essayist as an almost unmixed blessing.

Hellenistical (hɛlɪ'nɪstɪkəl), *a.* [f. as prec. + -AL[1].] = HELLENISTIC.

1656 BLOUNT *Glossogr.*, *Hellenistical*, pertaining to Greece, or the Grecians. **1661** FELL *Life Hammond* (R.), Into the importance of the hellenistical dialect he had made the exactest search. **1770** *Monthly Rev.* 94 This is a merely hellenistical sense of the word.

Hence **Helle'nistically** *adv.*, in a Hellenistic manner; in Hellenistic Greek.

1646 J. GREGORY *Notes & Obs.* 59 *Shakar*..is often rendered by the LXX *ἀδικία*, which therefore may beare the same signification Hellenistically in this place. **1819** G. S. FABER *Dispensations* (1823) I. 348 It bears such a sense Hellenistically.

Hellenization (ˌhɛlɪnaɪ'zeɪʃən). [f. next + -ATION.] The action of hellenizing or condition of being hellenized; the giving of a Greek character to anything.

1873 A. W. WARD tr. *Curtius' Hist. Greece* II. iii. I. 446 In Sicily also the Hellenisation of the coast had made progress. **1881** *Athenæum* 8 Oct. 465/3 The gradual Hellenization of the Byzantine Empire in the language, customs, and the national character.

Hellenize ('hɛlɪnaɪz), *v.* [mod. ad. Gr. *Ἑλληνίζ-ειν* to speak Greek, to make Greek, f. *Ἕλλην* HELLENE.]

1. *intr.* To use the Greek language; to adopt Greek or Hellenistic habits; to become, or live as, a Greek or Hellenist.

1613 [see HELLENIZING *vbl. sb.* below]. **1646** SIR T. BROWNE *Pseud. Ep.* IV. i. 279 Such [of the Jews] as did Hellenize and dispersedly dwell out of Palestine with the Greeks. **1653** HAMMOND *Annot. Acts* vi. 1 (R.) So saith Phavorinus..to hellenize is to speak Greek, and to have skill in the Greek learning. **1806** *Edin. Rev.* VII. 493 In Alexandria..the Egyptian superstitions..condescended to hellenize a little. **1879** FARRAR *St. Paul* ii. 27 There had been ..Hellenistic Jews who Hellenised in matters far more serious than the language which they spoke.

b. *nonce-use.* To adopt Hellenism (sense 3 b).

1869 M. ARNOLD *Cult. & Anarchy* Pref. (1875) 47 Now and for us, it is a time to Hellenise, and to praise knowing; for we have Hebraised too much, and have over-valued doing.

2. *trans.* To make Greek or Hellenistic in form or character.

1799 W. TAYLOR in Robberds *Mem.* I. 290 Perhaps I shall one day have to hellenize the jargon. **1845** *Blackw. Mag.* LVII. 514 To Anglicize Pindar is not the adventure. It is to Hellenize an English reader. *a* **1873** LYTTON *Pausanias* 274 Why should not Asia be Hellenized?

Hence '**Hellenized** *ppl. a.*; '**Hellenizing** *vbl. sb.* and *ppl. a.*; '**Hellenizer**, one who affects the Greek language and ways.

1613 PURCHAS *Pilgrimage* (1614) 137 The Hellenists were so called of hellenizing or vsing the Greeke tongue in their Synagogues. **1844** W. KAY in *Fleury's Eccl. Hist.* III. 29 *note*, Pelagius is only a Hellenized form of Morgan. **1846** TRENCH *Mirac.* v. (1862) 177 There were numbers of hellenizing Jews just in these parts. **1854** KEIGHTLEY *Mythol. Greece & Italy* (ed. 3) 462 Some of the Hellenisers said she was Minerva. **1861** J. G. SHEPPARD *Fall Rome* vi. 283 Leontius, the candidate for the throne selected by the Heathenizers, or Hellenizers, for the names have the same import. **1869** *Contemp. Rev.* XI. 151 Mr. Arnold, a Hellenizer by every instinct of his nature.

Hellenophile ('hɛlɪnəfaɪl), *a.* and *sb.* Also **Hellenophil** (-fɪl). [f. HELLENE + -O + -PHIL, -PHILE.] = PHILHELLENE *a.* and *sb.* Also **Helleno'philic** *a.*

1897 E. A. BARTLETT *Battlefields of Thessaly* iii. 60 A little splutter of Hellenophile and Radical agitation in this country. **1898** [see ARMENO-]. **1959** *Encounter* July 48/1 A few Greek and hellenophil critics acclaimed Kazantzakis's poem as a masterpiece. **1966** *Listener* 6 Jan. 34/3 Another Hellenophile's reluctant conversion to the myth of the old Turkey. **1970** *Nature* 21 Nov. 711/1 Travers reports the discovery of another such protein, which in the Hellenophilic tradition of Harvard he duly names psi.

‖**heller**[1] ('hɛlər). Also 6–7 **haller.** [Ger. *heller*, in MHG. *häller, haller*, 'usually assumed to be named from the imperial city *Schwäbisch-Hall*, where it was first coined' (Kluge).]

A small coin formerly current in Germany, worth half a pfennig; also a coin = $\frac{1}{100}$ of a crown ($\frac{1}{10}$ of a penny) issued in Austria between 1893 and 1916.

1575 *Brieff Disc. Troubl. Franckford* (1642) 134 The summe which they gave growed to so much as thirteene, not Sallers but Hallers or Pennings. **1617** MORYSON *Itin.* I. 287 (Stanf.) At Nurnberg..two haller make one pfenning. **1842** MOTLEY *Corr.* (1889) I. iv. 102 The sister gave two hellers a day to the workmen. **1895** *Baedeker's Eastern Alps* Introd. 11 The new Austrian monetary unit is the Crown (Krone) = 100 Heller. These new coins, however, are still comparatively rare.

heller[2] ('hɛlə(r)). *U.S. slang.* [f. HELL *v.*[2] + -ER[1].] One who 'hells around'.

1895 W. C. GORE in *Inlander* Nov. 67 Heller, a remarkable person. 'He is a heller at foot-ball.' **1933** *Amer. Speech* VIII. I. 81/2 *Heller*, one who is unusually daring or aggressive, intensified usually as *a regular heller*. **1939** J. STEINBECK *Grapes of Wrath* viii. 107 Tom grinned affectionately at him. 'Ain't he a heller?' he said. **1959** *Listener* 17 Dec. 1086/1 Jack Harrick, the old hillbilly satyr or 'heller'.

Hellespont ('hɛlɪspɒnt). [ad. Gr. *Ἑλλήσποντ-τος*; explained as sea (*πόντος*) of Helle (*Ἕλλη*), daughter of Athamas, said to have been drowned in it.] The ancient name for the Strait of the Dardanelles; hence, in allusion to the story of Leander, something that separates lovers.

1591 SHAKS. *Two Gent.* I. i. 22 & 26 *Val.* Some shallow Storie of deepe loue, How yong Leander crost the Hellespont..You are ouer-bootes in loue, And yet you neuer swom the Hellespont. **1657** *Lust's Domin.* II. iii. in Hazl. *Dodsley* XIV. 123 Your wife..She's the Hellespont divides my love and me.

Hence **Helle'spontiac**, **Helle'spontine** *adjs.*, of, pertaining to, or situated on the Hellespont.

1649 STANLEY *Europa*, etc. 29 Because the Hellespontiack power they slight. **1840** THIRLWALL *Greece* VII. lvii. 225 Arridæus was appointed to the Hellespontine Phrygia.

hell-fire, hell fire. [Orig. two words, *helle* being genitive case; in later use usually hyphened. In N.T. versions rendering Gr. *γέεννα τοῦ πυρός* lit. gehenna (or hell) of fire, i.e. fiery hell.]

1. The fire of hell.

a **1000** *Boeth. Metr.* viii. 101 Etne..þæt mon helle fyr hateð wide. *c* **1000** *Ags. Gosp.* Matt. xviii. 9 Asend on helle fyr [**1382** WYCLIF, fijr of helle; **1526** TINDALE, hell fyre; **1582** *Rhem.* hel of fire]. *a* **1225** *Ancr. R.* 150 Iwurð, buten ende, helle fures fode. *a* **1300** *Cursor M.* 2894 Þat ȝee in hell fire for brin. **1526** TINDALE *Matt.* v. 22 In daunger of hell fyre. *a* **1600** HOOKER *Eccl. Pol.* v. App. 1 §34 Devils were not ordained of God for hell-fire, but hell-fire for them. **1860** EMERSON *Cond. Life, Fate* Wks. (Bohn) II. 316 Neither.. hell-fire, nor ichor..can get rid of this limp band. **1915** W. S. MAUGHAM *Of Human Bondage* xxviii. 122 He could go his way without the intolerable dread of hell-fire. **1972** P. M. HUBBARD *Whisper in Glen* vi. 59 Abomination was one of the devalued words. No one had used it wholly seriously. Mrs Haskell did, so that there was the reek of hell-fire to it.

2. A member of a Hell-fire club.

1720 in Malcolm *Mann. & Cust. Lond.* (1808) 149 The Hell-Fires..fly at Divinity. The third person of the Trinity is what they peculiarly attack..calling for a Holy-Ghost-pye at the Tavern.

3. *attrib.* **Hell-fire club**, name given to clubs of reckless or abandoned young men, chiefly about the beginning of the eighteenth century. (See N. & Q. 12 May 1860, 27 Aug. 1892, etc.)

1721 (*title*) The Hell Fire Club, kept by a Society of Blasphemers. **1755** *Connoisseur* No. 54 The Mohocks, and the members of the Hell-Fire-Club, the heroes of the last generation..struck out mighty good jokes from all kinds of violence and blasphemy. **1821** DE QUINCEY *Richter* Wks. (1863) XIII. 124 When a member of the Hell-fire club, he actually tied a poor man to the spit, and, having spitted him, proceeded to roast him. **1825** R. CHAMBERS *Trad. Edinb.* II. 259. **1881** *Haydn's Dict. Dates, Hell-fire clubs*, three of these associations were suppressed 1721. **1952** R. CAMPBELL *Lorca* 10 The hell-fire sermons of the local priest. **1957** J. S. HUXLEY *Relig. without Revelation* (new ed.) ii. 31 A Hell-fire revivalist preacher. **1957** *Economist* 21 Dec. 1046/3 He reacted violently..against the hellfire faith which had laid waste his childhood. **1972** P. M. HUBBARD *Whisper in Glen* xviii. 175 The old woman tried to purge her own indiscretions by giving her daughter a hell-fire upbringing.

4. *advb.* In profane use: 'Damned'.

1760 C. JOHNSTON *Chrysal* (1761) II. I. i. 2 The weather in summer is *hell-fire* hot, in winter *hell-fire* cold. Now what sense can the very Devil himself..make of such contradictions?

hell-fired, *a.*

1. 'Set on fire of hell' (Jas. iii. 6).

a **1711** KEN *Christophil* Poet. Wks. 1721 I. 447 Blasphem'd by ev'ry Hell-fir'd Tongue.

2. As an intensive: 'Damned'. Cf. ALL-FIRED.

1756 W. Toldervy *Two Orphans* III. 157 Sir..he is a h—ll-fir'd good creature. **1833** J. Neal *Down-Easters* I. 79 See what a hell fired noise it [*sc.* the watch] makes. **1972** J. S. Hall *Sayings from Old Smoky* 80 It was the hell-firedest wreck I've ever seen!

'hellful. [f. hell *sb.* + -ful.] As many as hell could hold.

1637 Rutherford *Lett.* (1862) I. 218 Christ hath..casten the knot so fast that the fingers of the devils and hell-fulls of sins cannot loose it. **1884** J. Parker *Apost. Life* III. 15 A host, an army, a whole..hellful of human nature.

hell-gate, *pl.* **hell-gates.** [Orig. two words.] The portal or entrance of hell.

c **1000** Ælfric *Hom.* I. 228 Ure Hælend Crist tobræc helle ȝatu. *c* **1160** *Hatton Gosp.* Matt. xvi. 18 Helle ȝate ne maȝen on-ȝean þa. *c* **1320** *Cast. Love* 1341 Helle-ȝates he al to-breek. *c* **1460** *Towneley Myst.* (Surtees) 314 Oure porter at helle gate Is halden so strate. **1590** Spenser *F.Q.* ii. vii. 25. **1626** Shirley *Brothers* ii. i, Mouths, that day and night Are open, like hell-gates, to feed. **1667** Milton *P.L.* ii. 746 The Portress of Hell Gate. **1892** Kipling *Barrack-Room Ballads* 195 He yearned to the flare of Hell-gate there as the light of his own hearth-stone. **1934** T. S. Eliot *Rock* i. 47 The Heart of Man..Swinging between Hell Gate and Heaven Gate.

'hellgrammite, 'helgramite. *U.S.* The larva of a neuropterous insect, *Corydalus cornutus*, the hellgrammite fly, allied to the May-fly, used as a favourite bait for the black bass. Also *transf.*

1866 *Wilkes' Spirit of Times* 14 July 315/3 There is another bait for bass called *kill-devil*—a sort of indescribable Barnum-what-is-it thing... An old friend of mine denominated them hell gramites. **1878** C. Hallock *Amer. Club List & Sportsman's Gloss.* p. vi, *Helgramite*, the dobson. **1884** J. S. Kingsley *Stand. Nat. Hist.* II. 156 They are much sought after as fish-bait, having a very tough integument, so that one larva suffices to catch several fish; and they are called by fishermen 'crawlers', 'dobsons', and sometimes, we hope rarely, 'hellgrammites'. **1894** *Outing* (U.S.) XXIV. 228/2 Helgramites (purchasable at most any of the tackle stores during the bass season). **1935** O. Nash *Primrose Path* (1936) 122 This human hellgrammite that I think we could all dispense with. **1957** *Times* 11 Oct. 12/6 A helgramite net—a flat wire tray that will catch any insects swept down by the current.

'hellhoffite. *Chem.* [from the name of the inventor Hellhoff.] An explosive, a solution of a nitrated organic combination (naphthaline, phenol, benzene, etc.), in fuming nitric acid.

1885 *Times* (weekly ed.) 28 Aug. 9/4 A new explosive.. hellhoffite..invented by Hellhoff and Gruson. *Ibid.*, A quantity of hellhoffite poured into a bowl could not be exploded by a lighted match. **1895** Cundill & Th. *Dict. Explos.* Pref. 42.

† **'hellhood.** *Obs.* The state or personality of an infernal being; usually as an ironical title.

1625 Fletcher & Shirley *Nt. Walker* ii. ii, We might have done some fine thing To have made thy hel-hood laugh. **1630** J. Taylor (Water P.) *Nauy Land Ships* Wks. i. 92/1 To sacrifice themselues..and all that they esteeme dearest vnto them, to his infernall Hell-hood.

'hell-hound. [Orig. two words, *helle* in genitive case.]

1. Hound or dog of hell; esp. in Greek and Latin mythology, Cerberus, the watch-dog of Hades.

c **888** K. Ælfred *Boeth.* xxxv. §6 þa sceolde cuman þære helle hund, þæs nama..wæs Ceruerus. **1006** *Charter* in *Cod. Dipl.* III. 350 Sy he toren of hellehundes toðum on ðam eȝeslicum hellewitum. **1340–70** *Alex. & Dind.* 792 ȝe ben to þe helle-hond holliche i-like, Tri-cerberus þe tenful of wham i tolde haue. *c* **1440** *Jacob's Well* (E.E.T.S.) 167 þe helle-huntere, wyth his helle-houndys, com ny. **1667** Milton *P.L.* x. 630 My Hell-hounds to lick up the draff and filth Which man's polluting Sin with taint hath shed On what was pure. **1821** Shelley *Prometh. Unb.* i. 408 But hark, the hell-hounds clamour.

2. A fiend; a fiendish person: as a term of execration.

c **1420** *Metr. Life St. Kath.* (Halliw.) 10 Thou false cursyd Sarasyn..Helle hounde, thou fowle wyghte. *a* **1529** Skelton *P. Sparrowe* 89 From that hell hounde, That lyeth in cheynes bounde. **1532** More *Confut. Tindale* Wks. 446/1 Neither Luther, Tyndal, nor Huskin, nor all yᵉ hel houndes that yᵉ deuyl hath in hys kenell. **1633** T. Stafford *Pac. Hib.* i. ii. (1810) 39 Tyrone with his Hell-hounds being not farre from Corke. **1712** Steele *Spect.* No. 533 ¶2, I am sure these shameless hell-hounds deserved it highly. **1777** Earl Chatham *Sp. in Ho. Lords* 18 Nov., These horrible hell-hounds of savage war. **1879** Browning *Ivàn Ivànovitch* 208 Hellhounds, we baulk you!

3. *attrib.* and *Comb.*

1719 De Foe *Crusoe* ii. ix, Villains! hell-hound dogs! **1790** *By-stander* 46 Of the hell-hound breed. **1811** W. Taylor in *Monthly Mag.* XXXII. 117 To account and apologise for the hell-hound-hearted mangling fury.

'hellicat, *a.* and *sb.* *Sc.* [app. a fanciful alteration by Scott of *halokit* (halok); perh. with some notion of *hell-cat.*]

A. *adj.* Lightheaded, giddy, extravagant; rompish.

1815 Scott *Guy M.* xxxii, I dare sae now it had been on some hellicat errand or other. **1816** —— *Antiq.* xxxix, I want to see what that hellicate quean Jenny Rintherout's doing. **1894** Crockett *Raiders* (ed. 3) 32 That hellicat..lassie, who had called me a sheep.

B. *sb.* A wicked creature: cf. hell-cat.

1816 Scott *Bl. Dwarf* ix, Let us but get puir Grace out o' that auld hellicat's clutches. **1893** Stevenson *Catriona* 268 It's highly possible the hellicat would try and gar me to marry her when he turned up.

† **'hellick,** *a.* *Obs. rare.* [OE. had *hel-líc* hellish, infernal, f. *hel* + *-líc* -like. It is not clear whether the 16th c. use was a revival of the OE.] Of or belonging to hell; hellish, infernal.

c **1000** Ælfric *Hom.* I. 380 Ða hellican fynd. *Ibid.* II. 78 Scyldiȝ he wæs to hellicere susle. **1581** J. Studley tr. *Seneca's Hippolytus* 67 b, Who when the hellicke hound From Tartares griesly gates in chaynes he dragd above the ground. *Ibid.* 73 The Hellick Tyrant knowes his perfect tale.

hellier ('hɛljə(r)). Now *dial.* Also 5–6 **helyer, helier,** 5, 9 **hillyer.** [ME. *helyer*, f. hele *v.*, to cover: cf. *sawyer*, etc.] A slater or tiler.

c **1450** T. Walsingham *Hist. Angl.* an. 1381 in Camden *Anglica, Hibernica*, etc. (1602) 252 Ductor..dictus Walterus Helier, vel Tyler. *Ibid.* 265 Walterus Tyler vel vt quidam dicunt Walterus Helyer. **1467** *Ordin. Worcester* in *Eng. Gilds* (1870) 398 Tylers called hillyers. **1562** *Act 5 Eliz.* c. 4 §30 The Art..of a Smith..Bricklayer, Tyler, Slater, Helier, Tyle-maker. **1625** Ussher *Answ. Jesuit* 287 He that covereth the house with tile or slate, is from thence commonly called a hellier. **1669** S. Colepress in *Phil. Trans.* IV. 1009 The most experienced Helliers (or Coverors with Slat). **1725** *Lond. Gaz.* No. 6400/8 Francis Budd, late of Horwood, Hellier. **1888** Elworthy *W. Somerset Word-bk.*, *Hellier*, a slater; one who *heles* roofs..A thatcher is never called a *hellier.* [Hence the surnames *Hellier, Helyar, Hillyer, Hilliard, Helyard.*]

hellier, obs. form of halyard.

helling, dial. form of heling, covering, roof.

hellion, hellyon ('hɛljən). *U.S. colloq.* [prob. variant of hallion, hallyon, with assimilation to hell *sb.*] A troublesome or disreputable person; a mischievous child.

1846 J. J. Hooper *Adv. Simon Suggs* i. 18 The 'oudacious' little hellions! **1857** *Jrnl. Discourses* V. 135/2 We are going to dig a cache..and put all the whining men and women into it... We want to be released from such poor hellyons. **1896** J. C. Harris *Sister Jane* 136 If dey ever was a hellian he wuz one. **1906** 'O. Henry' *Four Million* 8 Jawn, did ye ever see a straighter-nosed gang of hellions in the days of your life? **1919** H. L. Wilson *Ma Pettengill* vii. 225 Three children that was known to be hellions. **1941** H. G. Wells *You can't be too Careful* iii. xxii. 218 That vision of Swedenborg's where all the damned and blessed fly of their own accord to the particular places appointed for them, hellions of every sort to their hells and the blessed to their heavens. **1957** M. Mezzrow in S. Traill *Concerning Jazz* 26 Baby Dodds, our drummer in Nice, is a wonderful person, but in his younger days he was a real hellion, and would fight at the drop of a hat. **1973** J. Wainwright *Pride of Pigs* 83 They were young animals..pure, down-to-earth hellions.

hellish ('hɛlɪʃ), *a.* (*adv.*) [f. hell *sb.* + -ish.]

1. Of, belonging or pertaining to hell or the infernal regions; infernal.

1530 Palsgr. 315/1 Hellysshe, belongyng to helle, *tartaricque, infernal.* **1590** Spenser *F.Q.* i. ii. 2 Who, all in rage..gan threaten hellish paine. **1687** *Death's Vis.* Pref. (1713) 11 The Fury and Hideousness of that Hellish Prince. **1727** De Foe *Syst. Magic* i. ii. (1840) 48 The last is truly called diabolical and hellish magic.

b. Belonging to Hades.

1579 Spenser *Sheph. Cal.* Oct. 30 His musicks might the hellish hound did tame. *a* **1704** T. Brown *Praise Drunkenness* Wks. 1730 I. 37 In vain does Hercules boast of all his victories, of his Hydra..and the hellish Cerberus.

2. Of the nature or character of hell and infernal things; befitting or worthy of hell; diabolical, fiendish.

1569 *Commem. Boner* in *Skelton's Wks.* (1843) I. Introd. 125 Romishe derision, And hellishe deuision. **1604** Shaks. *Oth.* v. ii. 368 To you, Lord Gouernor, Remaines the Censure of this hellish villaine. **1712** Steele *Spect.* No. 402 ¶3, I sit down and describe my present Disposition with so hellish an Aspect. **1798** Coleridge *Anc. Mar.* ii. iii, I had done a hellish thing, And it would work 'em woe. **1826** Scott *Woodst.* xii, But we heard hellish noises.

b. As an intensive: cf. *infernal, devilish.*

1798 *Courier* in *Spirit. Pub. Jrnls.* (1799) II. 307 Why did you ride at such a hellish rate?

B. *adv.* Infernally; execrably. Sometimes a mere coarse intensive: cf. *devilish.*

1613 Purchas *Pilgrimage* (1614) 481 A mouth O hellish wide. **1768** Foote *Devil on Two Sticks* i. Wks. 1799 II. 251 You make a little free with our condition..as, hellish dull, damn'd clever, hellish cold. **1792** Charlotte Smith *Desmond* II. 37 You've got a hellish clever trotting mare.

'hellishing, 'hellishun, *a.* and *adv.* *slang* (chiefly *Austral.* and *N.Z.*). Used as intensive adj. or adv.: terrible; very. Cf. *hangashun* s.v. hang *sb.* 6.

1931 *Amer. Speech* VI. 434 He seems to be in a hellishin' hurry about something. This is a hellishin' fine time to tell us about it. **1941** Baker *Dict. Austral. Slang* 35 *Hellishun*, an intensive used widely by children. **1950** *Landfall* IV. 38 It's hellashin funny. **1967** K. Giles *Death & Mr. Prettyman* vii. 145 The journey was as hellishing as he remembered. **1968** E. McGirr *Lead-Lined Coffin* iii. 114, I don't know that anybody..has any knowledge of how hellishing thorough we are.

hellishly ('hɛlɪʃlɪ), *adv.* [f. hellish *a.* + -ly².] In a hellish manner; infernally, devilishly; execrably. Sometimes merely intensive.

c **1580** J. Jeffere *Bugbears* i. ii. 50 in *Archiv Stud. Neu. Spr.* (1897) XCVIII. 308 Amedeus is so hellishely bent on the muck of this world. **1631** R. H. *Arraignm. Whole Creature* xiii. §3. 218 The Divell..horribly yea hellishly disquieting them. **1754** Richardson *Grandison* (1810) VI. xxxi. 221 If he had not interposed so hellishly as he did..I had been the husband of Miss Byron in two hours. **1778** *Learning at a Loss* I. 152 A dark Chesnut..gets on hellishly, a remarkable Gift of going.

hellishness ('hɛlɪʃnɪs). [f. as prec. + -ness.] The quality of being hellish; infernal or damnable nature or disposition.

1608 Machin *Dumb Knt.* iv. in Hazl. *Dodsley* X. 182, I was..star-cross'd with some hag's hellishness. **1648** Gage *West Ind.* xiv. 82 Outward seeming and frothy sanctity, and inward hellishnesse. **1826** in Cobbett *Rur. Rides* (1885) II. 192 Enough to convince any one of the hellishness of this system! **1854** Duff in G. Smith *Life* xxi. (1881) 342 Such utter absolute hellishness I never saw surpassed.

hellite ('hɛlaɪt). [f. hell *sb.* + -ite.]

1. An inhabitant of hell.

1866 D. Forbes *Hindūstānī Dict.* 45 s.v. *'a'rāf*, The poet Sa'dī says that 'to those in heaven A'rāf would seem hell, but the hellites would call A'rāf paradise'.

2. The proprietor of a 'hell' or gaming-house.

1824 *Times* 9 Oct. in *Westm. Rev.* (1829) XI. 319 The hellites at all the 'hells'..resort to every species of cheating. **1838** Jas. Grant *Sk. Lond.* 355 In all the gaming-houses of any note, there are unprincipled reckless persons in the pay of the hellites. **1870** A. Steinmetz *Gaming Table* II. iv. 93.

hell-kettle. A deep black gulf or abyss; a name locally applied to holes or pools popularly supposed to be bottomless.

1577 Harrison *England* i. xxiv. (1881) iii. 164 What the foolish people dreame of the hell kettles, it is not worthie the rehearsall.. There are certeine pits, or rather three little pooles, a mile from Darlington..which the people call the kettles of hell, or the diuels kettles. **1634** *Relat. Short Survey* (in Longstaffe *Darlington*), The three..deepe pitts called Hell Kettles, we left boyling by Darlington. **1698** Fryer *Acc. E. India & P.* 250 An huge Casm, or Hell-Kettle was left where the mountain had emptied its self.

† **'hellness.** *Obs. nonce-wd.* [f. hell *sb.* + -ness, after highness.] A title for a person of diabolical character: = hellhood.

1605 Sylvester *Du Bartas* ii. iii. iv. *Captaines* 1007 There's not a king among ten thousand kings But..gildeth those that glorifie his Folly, That sooth and smooth, and call his Hell-ness holy.

hello (hə'ləʊ), *int.* and *sb.* [var. of hallo, q.v.] An exclamation to call attention; also expressing some degree of surprise, as on meeting any one unexpectedly.

A. as *int.* **a.** Also as a greeting.

1883 *Breadwinners* 241 Hello, Andy! you asleep. **1888** Black *Adv. House-boat* xxiii, Hello—here's more about evolution. **1967** *Listener* 5 Oct. 427/2 'Hello,' I thought, 'Now she's overdoing it.' **1971** *Farmer & Stockbreeder* 23 Feb. 3/3 Next week..we shall say hello again to most of you, and to 100,000 new readers as well.

b. Used as an answer to a telephone call.

1892 Kipling *Lett. of Travel* (1920) 94 A..millionaire.. clawing wildly at the telephone... 'Hello!.. Yes. Who's there?' **1922** S. Lewis *Babbitt* iv. 41 On the telephone they said only: '..Oh, Hello, 343?' **1973** J. Wainwright *Pride of Pigs* 169 She..picked up the receiver, waited for the S.T.D. pips to stop, said 'Hello?' and..recognised her brother's voice.

B. as *sb.*

1897 Mary Kingsley *W. Africa* 45 The amount of 'Hellos' 'Are you theres?' and 'Speak louder, pleases'..that must at such times be poured out and wasted..before the break [in telephonic connexion] is realised.

Comb. **1889** 'Mark Twain' *Connecticut Yankee* 176 The humblest..hello-girl..could teach the highest duchess. **1895** *Critic* 6 Apr. 263/2 The awful nuisance of the central [telephone] office, and..what is familiarly known as the 'hello-girl'. **1928** *Daily Chron.* 4 Feb. (*headline*) Brave Hello Girls. **1971** *New Scientist* 17 June p. iv, That was the day we said Goodbye to the Hello girls.

Hence **hello** *v.*, to shout *hello!*

1895 *Critic* 6 Apr. 263/2 There will be no helloing girl to ask you every minute, 'Have you finished?' while you are straining your ears to hear what the person you are talking to is saying.

† **hellu'ation.** *Obs. rare*$^{-0}$. [ad. L. *helluātiōn-em* (*hēl-*), n. of action f. *helluārī* to gormandize (see next).] 'A devouring gluttony' (Blount *Glossogr.* 1656).

† **hellue,** *v.* *Obs. rare*$^{-0}$. In 6 helue. [ad. L. *helluārī* (*hēl-*), f. *helluo* (see next).] To gormandize, guzzle.

1570 Levins *Manip.* 59/11 Helue..*potitare, deglutire.*

‖ **helluo** ('hɛljuːəʊ). Also 7 helluoh. [L. *helluo*, *hēluo* a gormandizer.]

1. A glutton, gormandizer; *transf.* and *fig.* a greedy devourer.

1583 Stubbes *Anat. Abus.* i. (1879) 102 The insaciablest Helluo, the deuouringest glutton, or the greediest cormorant that is. **1631** R. H. *Arraignm. Whole Creature* v. 32 They eate like gurmundizing Helluohs. **1678** Cudworth *Intell. Syst.* i. iv. 425 Thereby making him to be a Helluo and Devourer of Gods. *a* **1734** North *Exam.* iii. vi. §63 (1740) 470 To let an Helluo loose upon the Revenue, which should be too hard for all Retrenchment. **1822** T. Taylor *Apuleius* viii. 184 In this ludicrous way the crier treated that helluo.

2. *Zool.* A genus of beetles belonging to the family *Carybidæ.*

† **'helluous**, *a.* [irreg. f. prec.] Gluttonous.

1641 J. JOHNSON *Acad. Love* 2 Shee, making me the cadaver of her love to feed her helluous gorge.

Hence **hellu'osity**, gluttony.

1799 *Public Characters* 101 So voracious and insatiable is his helluosity. **1830** *Fraser's Mag.* I. 748 The helluosity of my reading, and omnivorous voracity with which I digest.. all manner of languages.

helluva ('hɛləvə). Used freq. to represent 'hell of a'. Cf. HELL *sb.* 4 d.

1910 C. E. MULFORD *Hopalong Cassidy* xxvi. 176, I got money—helluva lot of money. **1934** E. POUND *Eleven New Cantos* XXXV. 24 It must be one helluva country. **1959** 'H. CARMICHAEL' *Stranglehold* ii. 25 Be a helluva thing if I've left it just too late. **1959** 'M. M. KAYE' *House of Shade* ii. 26 It looks like saving you a helluva headache. **1967** *Crescendo* Dec. 33/1 Although she may not be as good a jazzer as Humph, she's certainly one helluva lot prettier. **1968** *Times* 23 Oct. 10/8 It's very unfortunate looking like him: he must have a helluva life.

hellward ('hɛlwəd), *adv.* and *a.* [f. HELL *sb.* + -WARD: orig. *to hellward.*]

A. *adv.* Towards hell: **a.** Downward, towards the centre of the earth. **b.** Towards the place of final punishment.

1377 LANGL. *P. Pl.* B. XVIII. 114 A wenche..Cam walkynge in þe wey, to-helle-ward she loked. *c* **1440** *Jacob's Well* (E.E.T.S.) 170 þe depthe of þi skete of contricyoun muste be depe in sorwe downward, to helle-warde. **1623** LISLE *Ælfric on O. & N. Test.* Pref. ¶3 We are hoisted sometime to heaven with a billow of presumption, and dung downe againe with abysse of despaire to helward. **1675** HOBBES *Odyssey* (1677) 125 Then of the ram and ewe let out the blood Into the pit; their heads to hell-ward place. **1726** W. BROOME *Ep. to Elijah Fenton* 97 Trees.. Root hell-ward, and thence flourish to the skies. **1789** BURNS *Ode in Mem. Mrs. Oswald*, Doom'd to share thy fiery fate, She, tardy, hell-ward plies. **1831** CARLYLE *Sart. Res.* III. iii, Magician and Wizard to lead us hellward.

B. *adj.* Directed or conducting to hell.

1829 MOIR in *Blackw. Mag.* XXV. 632 Still man thinks that hellward paths can e'er lead up to Heaven.

'hell-weed, 'hellweed. A name given to certain plants, noxious as weeds, and difficult to eradicate: **a.** the species of Dodder (*Cuscuta*) parasitic on cultivated plants; **b.** Hedge Bindweed, *Convolvulus sepium*; **c.** *Ranunculus arvensis.*

1640 PARKINSON *Theat. Bot.* 10 *Cuscuta* as it is generally called..is called of the Country people *Hell-weede*, because they know not how to destroy it. **1670** [see DEVIL'S-GUTS]. **1829** GLOVER *Hist. Derby* I. 109 *Cuscuta europæa*, greater dodder, hell weed or devil's guts. **1879** PRIOR *Plant-n., Hell-weed*, dodder, so called from the trouble and ruin it causes in flax fields.

† **'helly**, *a.* (*adv.*) *Obs.* [f. HELL *sb.* + -Y (or ? -LY).] **A.** *adj.* Of or belonging to hell; of the nature of hell; hellish, infernal, devilish. Revived in literary example.

1532 MORE *Confut. Tindale* Wks. 423/2, I call heartely to yᵉ spirite of God to quenche the foule fyrebrond of yᵉ helly light. **1556** J. HEYWOOD *Spider & F.* lxvi, No worldlie sight More like hell then was sight of that hellie fight. **1563** BALDWIN in *Mirr. Mag., How Collingbourne was Executed* (1815) II. 366 Helley haunts, & ranke pernicious ylles. **1583** STANYHURST *Æneis* IV. (Arb.) 103 His rod..by which from the helly Bocardo Touzt tost souls he freeth. **1613** *Acc. Anglesea* (Halliw.) 39 Authority conferr'd upon him to keep this helly trade. **1934** DYLAN THOMAS *Let.* 11 May (1966) 127 Every doubt and misgiving that an hereditary.. imagination, an hereditary thirst..are capable of conjuring up out of their helly deeps.

B. *adv.* Hellishly, infernally.

1600 TOURNEUR *Transf. Metamorph.* lviii, With poyson hellie blacke. *a* **1762** LADY M. W. MONTAGU *Poems* (1785) 53 No rake helly gay, Or laughing, because he has nothing to say.

helm (hɛlm), *sb.*[1] Forms: 1– **helm**; also 3 **hælm, healm**, 4–7 **helme**, 6 **healme**. [Com. Teut.: OE. *helm* str. masc. = OFris., OS. (LG., MDu., Du.), OHG. (MHG., Ger.) *helm*, ON. *hjalmr* (Sw., Da. *hjelm*), Goth. *hilms*:—OTeut. **helmo-z*:—pre-Teut. **kelmo-s*, f. root *kel-* to cover, conceal (see HELE *v.*). OF. *helme* (mod.F. *heaume*) masc., It. *elmo*, Sp. *yelmo*, are from OHG. Senses 7 and 8 are prob. from Norse.]

I. 1. That part of the armour which covers the head; a helmet. Now *poet.* and *arch.*

c **725** *Corpus Gloss.* 422 *Cassium*, helm. *c* **1000** ÆLFRIC *Voc.* in Wr.-Wülcker 143/27 *Crista*, helmes camb. *a* **1175** *Cott. Hom.* 243 þa beoð sceold helm and brenie. *c* **1205** LAY. 25813 Hælm [*c* **1275** healm] an his hafde. *c* **1375** *Sc. Leg. Saints, Cristofore* 549 þane gert þe kinge ane helme tak. **1483** CAXTON *Gold. Leg.* 65 b/2 A helme of brasse on his heed. *a* **1533** LD. BERNERS *Huon* liv. 182 There was brought him a good harneis, helme, sheld, & spere. **1667** MILTON *P.L.* VI. 840 O're Shields and Helmes, and helmed heads he rode. **1715–20** POPE *Iliad* v. 5 High on his helm celestial lightnings play. **1870** MORRIS *Earthly Par.* II. III. 345 Methought I had a helm upon my head Wrought all of gold.

fig. *c* **1200** *Trin. Coll. Hom.* 193 Habbeð rihte bileue to brunie, and hope to helme. **1382** WYCLIF *Isa.* lix. 17 The helm of helthe in his hed.

b. *Her.* = HELMET 2.

1864 BOUTELL *Her. Hist. & Pop.* xiv. 165 A large helm surmounted by the lion crest.

† **2.** *transf.* Put for a man in armour. *Obs.*

a **1400–50** *Alexander* 5498 Ser Bedwyn þe bald with many briȝt helmes. **1470–85** MALORY *Arthur* VI. vi, The kyng of Northgaly's with eyght score helmes. **1548** HALL *Chron., Hen. V*, 47 In the Vaward wer eight thousande Healmes of Knightes and Esquiers and foure thousande Archers.

† **3.** Christ's crown of thorns. *Obs.*

c **1000** ÆLFRIC *Hom.* II. 252 Mid þyrnenum helme his heafod befengon. *c* **1175** *Lamb. Hom.* 147 Ure helende.. hefde uppen his hefde þornene helm. *a* **1400** *Leg. Rood* (1871) 142 þorw-out his helm þe harde hat þe þornes in-to his flesch gan crepe.

II. 4. The crown, top, or summit of anything; in OE. *esp.* the leafy top of a tree. *Obs.* exc. *dial.*

c **888** K. ÆLFRED *Boeth.* xxxiv. §10 He onginþ of ðam wyrtrumum and swa upweardes grewþ..oþ ðone helm. *c* **1000** ÆLFRIC *Hom.* II. 150 His orf læswode mid treowenum helme. *a* **1100** *Voc.* in Wr.-Wülcker 243/33 *Frondea robora*, ȝebufe beamas *uel* helmas. **1893** *Northumbld. Gloss., Helm*, the top (crest) or head of a thing. 'Helm o' the hill'..a considerable eminence on the old post road a few miles south of Felton.

† **5.** The head or cap of an alembic or retort.

1594 PLAT *Jewell-ho.* II. 5 Those glasses which they call bodies..fitted to their helmes. **1610** B. JONSON *Alch.* II. i, She'll mount you up, like quick-silver Over the helm. **1686** PLOT *Staffordsh.* 102 That its oil or sulphur came over the Helm upon the first heat. **1718** J. CHAMBERLAYNE *Relig. Philos.* (1730) II. xviii. §7 Distil it with a glowing Iron Pot, upon which there is an Iron Helm or Head.

III. † **6.** A covering. (Only in OE.) *Obs.*

a **1000** *Riddles* iv. 64 (Gr.) Under lyfte helm.

7. A roofed shelter for cattle, etc.; a shed. *north.*

1501 *Searcher's Verdicts* in *Surtees Misc.* (1888) 22 For his kid helme upon þe tenement or ground. **1641** BEST *Farm. Bks.* (Surtees) 58 The Greate Helme in the Staggarth helde 43 [loades], the Helme in the Foregarth helde 23. **1674–91** RAY *N.C. Words* 36 An *Helm*, a Hovel. **1855** ROBINSON *Whitby Gloss., Helm*, a hovel, an open shed for cattle in a field. **1863** MRS. TOOGOOD *Yorksh. Dial., Helm*, a cart or cattle shed.

8. (Also ***helm-cloud.***) The local name in Cumberland and Westmorland of a cloud which forms over a mountain top before or during a storm; esp. that which accompanies the ***helm-wind*** (also occas. called the *helm*), a violent wind which in certain circumstances rushes down the escarpment of the Pennines near Cross Fell, when a helm-cloud lies over the summit. ***helm bar***, a roll of cloud suspended in the air to the leeward of the helm-cloud.

1777 NICOLSON & BURN *Hist. Westm. & Cumb.* I. 7 It is called a Helm-wind. *Ibid.*, A rolling cloud..hovers over the mountain tops..When this cloud appears, the country people say the helm is up..This helm..continues in its station, although a violent roaring hurricane comes tumbling down the mountain. **1787** J. CLARKE *Surv. Lakes* Introd. xl, A black streak of cloud..continually fed from the white one, which is the real Helm: this is called the Helm-bar, from its being supposed to bar or obstruct the winds that burst upon the vallies beneath as soon as it wholly vanishes. *Ibid.*, Such is the Helm-Wind generated in that enormous cloud, which, like a helmet, covers the summit of Cross-fell. **1801** COLERIDGE *Poems* II. 159 Ancient Skiddaw ..Thus spake from out his helm of cloud. **1885** *Nature* 23/1 Whenever the helm-wind was blowing, there was an easterly wind. **1886** *Jrnl. R. Meteor. Soc.* 2 On certain occasions, when the wind is from some Easterly point, the Helm suddenly forms..Small portions of thin vaporous clouds are seen travelling from the Helm Cloud to the Bar. **1888** *Encycl. Brit.* XXIV. 515/2 Here for weeks at a time prevails a kind of cyclone, revolving on a horizontal axis parallel to the escarpment,—the 'helm-wind'. **1888–9** J. G. GOODCHILD in *Trans. Cumb. & Westm. Assoc.* XIV. 44 The Helm Wind descends with greatest force in the neighbourhood of the highest elevation of the Escarpment, being strongest along a zone extending a few miles on each side of Cross Fell, and gradually diminishing in force in proportion to the distance on either side.

IV. 9. *attrib.* and *Comb.*, as ***helm-bearing, -decked, -mover***; **helm bar, helm-cloud, helm-wind** (see sense 8); **helm-guard**, 'a chain attaching the helm to the girdle or to the mammelière' (*Cent. Dict.*).

a **1100** *Voc.* in Wr.-Wülcker 243/40 *Frondigeris coronis*, helmberendum wuldorbeagum. *c* **1611** CHAPMAN *Iliad* II. 725 Helm-deck'd Hector. *Ibid.* VI. 277 The great helm-mover thus received the authoress of his kind.

helm (hɛlm), *sb.*[2] Forms: 1 **helma**, 4–7 **helme**, (7 **helmne**, 8 *Sc.* **hellim**), 6– **helm**. [OE. *helma* wk. masc., corresp. in stem to ON. *hjálm* str. fem. With sense 3, cf. MHG. *helm* handle.]

1. The handle or tiller, in large ships the wheel, by which the rudder is managed; sometimes extended so as to include the whole steering gear.

c **725** *Corpus Gl.* 4 *Clavus*, helma. *c* **1050** *Voc.* in Wr.-Wülcker 182/6. *c* **1330** R. BRUNNE *Chron. Wace* (Rolls) 12060 Roperes, helmes, right for to stande. *c* **1440** *Promp. Parv.* 235/1 Helme, or þe rothere of a schyp. *c* **1515** *Cocke Lorell's B.* (Percy) 12 Some stered at the helme behynde, Some whysteled after the wynde. **1634** SIR T. HERBERT *Trav.* 5 Many times the ships will feele no helme. **1656** BLOUNT *Glossogr., Helme* of the Rudder of a ship, is a handle of wood, put on the Rudder for a man to govern the same, and direct the ship. **1669** STURMY *Mariner's Mag.* I. 17 The Helmne is hard a weather, mind at Helmne what is said to you carefully. **1757** GRAY *Bard* II. ii, In gallant trim the gilded Vessel goes; Youth on the prow, and Pleasure at the helm. *a* **1796** BURNS (*Song*), When Guilford good our Pilot stood, An' did our hellim thraw, man. **1826** H. N. COLERIDGE *West Indies* 76 There was no one on deck but the man at the helm and himself.

b. Use or turning of the helm, space through which the helm is turned.

1892 *Pall Mall G.* 23 Feb. 7/1 Many of the witnesses disagree as to the amount of helm which was given to the ship. **1894** *Times* 17 Mar. 5/4 Very little helm, three or four spokes either to port or starboard, would have done it.

c. Phrases. ***down with the helm, down helm***, the order to place the helm so as to bring the rudder to windward. ***up with the helm, up helm***, the order to place the helm so as to bring the rudder to leeward. See also ALEE, AMIDSHIPS, BEAR *v.* 37, EASE *v.* 9, FEEL *v.* 12, OVER, PORT, STARBOARD, WEATHER.

1769 FALCONER *Dict. Marine* (1789) s.v. *Amidships*, Put the helm amidships, i.e. in the middle. **1833** M. SCOTT *Tom Cringle* xv. (1859) 380 Down with the helm and let her come round, said I. **1840** WILLIS in *Longfellow's Life* (1891) I. 371 So I up helm for my sister's house in Brighton. **1859** GEN. P. THOMPSON *Audi Alt.* II. xc. 66 See if he does not up helm, and make the best run of it he can. **1875** BEDFORD *Sailor's Pocket Bk.* vi. (ed. 2) 215 If caught in a hard sudden squall, down helm at once..A tendency to carry lee helm should be counteracted at once. **1880** *Boy's own Bk.* 316 *Helm's-a-lee*, the call of the helmsman when his helm is hard down in tacking.

2. a. *fig.* That by which affairs, etc., are guided.

c **888** K. ÆLFRED *Boeth.* xxxv. §4 Mid þæm helman and mid þæm stiorroþre hi godnesse. *a* **1529** SKELTON *Bowge of Crt.* 250 Holde up the helme, loke up, and lete God stere. **1607** SHAKS. *Cor.* I. i. 79 You slander The Helmes o' th State. *c* **1645** HOWELL *Lett.* V. I. xxxi. (1754) 226 Bishop Laud..sits at the Helm of the Church. **1679** *Establ. Test* 2 'Tis dangerous meddling with the Helm of State. **1770** LANGHORNE *Plutarch* (1879) I. 216/1 Fabius came to the helm, when Rome experienced the worst..turn of fortune. **1840** ARNOLD *Hist. Rome* II. 33 The elderly men, who generally held the tribuneship, now abandoned the helm in despair.

b. *transf.* Any part which is used like a helm.

1660 MRQ. WORCESTER *Cent. Inv.* Exact Def. 15 The [Water-commanding] Engine consisteth of the following Particulars..5. A Helm or Stern with Bitt and Reins, wherewith any Child may guide, order, and controul the whole Operation. **1860** G. H. K. *Vac. Tour* 162 Salmon.. give a series of sharp sculling strokes with their broad helms, which sends them sheer out of the water.

† **3.** A handle, helve. *Obs.*

c **1430** *Syr Gener.* 3729 Like mattokes wer here wepens wroght, With long helmes of yren stoute. **1589** NASHE *Martins Months Minde* 45 Let them once cut a helme for their hatchet, but of a braunch of you, and they will cut downe all the wood handsmooth. **1615** CHAPMAN *Odyss.* V. 312 A great axe..In which a fair well-polish'd helm was put.

4. *attrib.* and *Comb.*, as **helm circle**, the smallest circle in which a ship can be turned; **helm-coat**: see COAT *sb.* 8; **helm-man** = HELMSMAN q.v.; **helm-port** (see quot.); † **helm-stock**, the tiller (cf. Du. *helmstok*).

1884 *West. Morn. News* 2 Aug. 8/1 The diameter of the *helm circle of the Defence is..500 yards. *c* **1850** *Rudim. Navig.* (Weale) 124 **Helm-port*, that hole in the counter through which the head of the rudder passes. *Helm port transom*, the piece of timber placed athwart the inside of the counter timbers at the height of the helm-port. **1513** DOUGLAS *Æneis* V. xiv. 62 Our burd hym kest amyde the flowand se, Rycht all togiddir with the *helmstok of tre.

helm, *sb.*[3] *dial.* Also 6 **helme**, 8 **healm**, 9 *dial.* **h)ellum, elam, elm.** [app. related to HAULM, OE. *healm*, but the phonology is not clear. In sense 2, Du. and LG. have also *helm*, in Holstein *halm*, in Heligoland *hallem*; some Du. dialects have *helm, hellem, hellim* in the general sense of *halm*, straw.

It has been suggested that *helm* might be a special southern development of OE. *healm* HAULM.]

1. The stalk of corn; the stalks collectively, straw; *esp.* as made up in bundles or laid straight for thatching. (In this sense perh. confused with YELM q.v.)

1437 [see *helm-bote* in 3]. **1578** LYTE *Dodoens* IV. viii. 461 Barley hath helme or strawe, lyke wheaten strawe. **1669** WORLIDGE *Syst. Agric.* (1681) 238 The best..is called Helm, that is, long and stiff Wheat-straw (with the Ears cut off) bound up in bundles unbruised. **1674** RAY *S. & E. C. Words* 68 *Haulm* or *Helm*, stubble gathered after the corn is inned. *a* **1722** LISLE *Husb.* Gloss. (E.D.S.), *Helm, halm*, or straw prepared for thatching. [**1862** J. R. WISE *New Forest* (1863) 282 [In the New Forest] three elams make a bundle ..[In Wiltshire] the measurement is somewhat different, five elams forming a bundle. **1866** BLACKMORE *Cradock Nowell* xxxiii, The wind..brought an 'elam' of thatch to shelter her.]

b. = HAULM *sb.* a.

1888 ELWORTHY *W. Somerset Word-bk., Hellum*, the stalk of beans, pease, vetches, potatoes, clover, etc...Not..straw of any kind..A coarse kind of stalk is implied.

2. A name for the Bent-grass of the sandhills. ? *Obs.* or *alien.*

1640 PARKINSON *Theat. Bot.* 1200 The Italians, and Spaniards call it *Sparto*..The Dutch *Halm.* And we in English, Helme, and Matweede. **1897** *Contemp. Rev.* June 863 Swarms of rabbits lie out in the 'helm', buckthorn bushes and little dwarf pine copses [in Holland].

3. *Comb.*, as ***helm-sheaf***; **helm-bote** (in quot. *-bought*), the right of cutting helm in a common field for thatching.

1437 *Churchw. Acc.* (Som. Rec. Soc. vol. 4) 178 Uno homini locato pro le stubel vocato helmebought falcando

hoc pro dicta domo pistrine cooperienda. **1563–87** FOXE *A. & M.* (1684) III. 855 Good store of Helme-sheaves.

helm, *v.*[1] [OE. *helmian*, f. HELM *sb.*[1]] *trans.* To furnish or cover with a helm. (Chiefly *poet.*)

a **1000** *Andreas* 1307 (Gr.) Niht helmade..beorȝas steape. *c* **1000** ÆLFRIC *Gram.* xliii. (Z.) 256 *Galea*, helm. *Galeatus*, ȝehelmod. *c* **1374** CHAUCER *Troylus* II. 544 (593) Maris þe god þat helmyd is of stel. **1525** LD. BERNERS *Froiss.* (1812) II. clxviii. 472 Anone, they were agayne helmed, and ran togider. **1691** DRYDEN *Arthur* I. i. (R. Sup.), Now again you helm your hoary head. **1795** SOUTHEY *Joan of Arc* VII. 498 Then from the bank He sprung, and helm'd his head. *a* **1839** PRAED *Poems* (1864) II. 366 Now saddle my steed and helm my head.

helm, *v.*[2] [f. HELM *sb.*[2]] *trans.* To guide with or as with a helm; to steer. Chiefly *fig.*

1603 SHAKS. *Meas. for M.* III. ii. 151 The businesse he hath helmed, must..giue him a better proclamation. **1607** MARSTON *What you will* II. i. C iij b, Fate helmeth all. **1808** J. BARLOW *Columb.* I. 613 The steerman gaily helms his course along. **1884** TENNYSON *Becket* I. iii, No forsworn Archbishop Shall helm the Church. **1890** RIDER HAGGARD & LANG *World's Desire* 41 He helmed the ship towards these.

intr. or *absol.* **1666** *Lond. Gaz.* No. 31/4 The Conquerors ..helmed a weather, and stood for the Southward Cape.

helm, *v.*[3] *dial.* [f. HELM *sb.*[3]; but see YELM *v.*] *trans.* To lay (straw) in order for thatching.

a **1722** LISLE *Husb.* (1752) 236 Straw is heaped up together in order to be helmed. **1762** FORSTER in *Phil. Trans.* LII. 475, I had a woman..helming of straw, i.e. laying it straight, for the thatcher.

ˈhelmage. *rare.* [f. HELM *v.*[2] + -AGE.] Guidance, direction, management.

1864 in WEBSTER.

helm bar, -cloud: see HELM *sb.*[1] 8.

helmed (hɛlmd), *ppl. a.* [f. HELM *v.*[1] or *sb.*[1] + -ED.] Wearing a helm; helmeted.

c **1205** LAY. 26744 Ihelmede þeines. **1382** WYCLIF *Ezek.* xxxviii. 5 Men of Persis..alle sheeldid and helmyd. **1583** STANYHURST *Æneis* I. (Arb.) 33 In coach runs helmed Achilles. **1629** MILTON *Nativity* 112 The helmed Cherubim, And sworded Seraphim. **1883** OMAN in *Academy* No. 577. 371/3 The helmed Aphrodite of Corinth.

helmet (ˈhɛlmɪt), *sb.* Forms: 5– **helmet**, (6 **helmette**, **healmet**, *Sc.* **hewmet**, **hewmond**, **heumont**, 7 **helmit**). [a. obs. F. *healmet*, *helmet*, dim. of *helme* (see HEAUME and HELM *sb.*[1]).]

1. A defensive cover for the head; a piece of armour, usually made of, or strengthened with, metal, which covers the head wholly or in part.

It has varied greatly in shape and material at different periods; the name is still given to the stiff hat of domed or conical form, made of metal or strengthened with bars of metal, worn by many troops.

1470–85 MALORY *Arthur* VI. ix, [He] gate hym by the Bauowre of his helmet, and plucked hym doune on his knees. **1513** DOUGLAS *Æneis* IX. vii. 194 Mesapus rich hewmet [ed. 1553 hewmond] schynand brycht. **1563** WINȜET *Wks.* (1890) II. 6 For a waippin and a werklume, for a speir or a spade, a heumont or a hemmir. **1590** SPENSER *F.Q.* II. xi. 22 Upon his head he wore an Helmet light, Made of a dead mans skull, that seemed a ghastly sight. **1789** BELSHAM *Ess.* I. vii. 139 Virtue is..a Minerva, armed with helmet, spear, and shield. **1858** LARDNER *Hand-bk. Nat. Phil.* 374 The helmet and cuirass worn by cavalry is a cooler dress than might be imagined, the polished metal being a good reflector of heat.

fig. **1509** HAWES *Past. Pleas.* XXVII. lii, The helmet mekenes, and the shelde good fayth. **1526** TINDALE *Eph.* vi. 17 Take the helmet off heelth.

†**b.** *transf.* Put for a man in armour. *Obs.*

c **1500** *Melusine* xxiv. 189 Men of armes, to the nombre of foure thousand helmets. *Ibid.* xxx. 225 A houndred helmets of Hongery..valyaunt knightes & good men of werre.

c. Extended to other (non-military) defensive or protective kinds of head-gear, such as those worn by policemen, firemen, and divers, and the felt or pith hat worn in hot climates.

1842 BRANDE *Dict. Sc.*, etc., s.v. *Diving*, A helmet of thin sheet copper, which covers the head of the diver. [**1858** cf. *helmet-maker* in 9.] **1882** OGILVIE s.v., Helmets of white felt, with folds of linen wrapped round them, are worn in India and other hot climates as a protection against the sun. The name helmet is also given to a kind of hat worn by policemen. **1885** *Times* 20 Feb. 6/1 Officers and men were attired in red serge tunics..sun helmets and puggarees.

2. A representation of a helmet; esp. in *Her.* The figure of a helmet placed above the escutcheon in an achievement and supporting the crest.

1610 GUILLIM *Heraldry* IV. xv. (1611) 231 The bearing of Helmets after these seueral manners. **1617** MORYSON *Itin.* III. 263 They take to themselves coates of Armes..yet not with open Helmets, as Gentlemen beare them, but with closed Helmets, after the manner used by the Citizens in Germany. **1847** *Gloss. Heraldry* s.v., Helmets of different forms are placed above shields of arms to denote the rank of the bearers.

3. The upper part of a retort; = HELM *sb.*[1] 5.

1599 A. M. tr. *Gabelhouer's Bk. Physicke* 25/1 Distille therout a water, with a glasse helmet as we are used to distille the stronge waters. **1660** BOYLE *New Exp. Phys. Mech.* viii. 64 We took a Glass Helmet or Alembick..such as Chymists use in Distillations. **1683** PETTUS *Fleta Min.* I. (1686) 121 Put in it fifty pounds of Quicksilver..and place an Helmet upon it. **1858** SIMMONDS *Dict. Trade*, *Helmet*,..the upper part of a retort.

4. A kind of fancy pigeon: see quot. 1735.

1676 COTTON *Walton's Angler* iv. 76 Of the tame [pigeons] there be helmits and runts, and carriers, and cropers. **1735** J. MOORE *Columb.* in Tegetmeier *Pigeons* xix. (1867) 164 They are called Helmets, from their heads being covered with a plumage which is distinct in colour from the body, and appears somewhat like a helmet to cover the head. **1833** R. MUDIE *Feathered Tribes Brit. Isles* (1841) I. 74.

5. (in full *helmet-shell*.) The shell of a mollusc of the genus *Cassis*.

1753 CHAMBERS *Cycl. Supp.*, *Cassis lævis*, the smooth helmet shell, a name given by Rumphius, though very improperly, to the genus of shells called dolia and conchæ globosæ. **1756** P. BROWNE *Jamaica* (1789) 408 The..real Conques come next after the Helmets. **1776** DA COSTA *Conchol.* 290 A Helmet, *Cassis*. **1863** WOOD *Illustr. Nat. Hist.* III. 381 Cameos..that are cut from the Horned Helmet-shell are white.

6. A collector's name for a fossil echinoderm, *Galerites albogalerus*; cf. *helmet-stone* in 9.

1887 H. B. WOODWARD *Geol.* (ed. 2) 405.

7. *Bot.* The arched upper part of the corolla (or calyx) in some flowers, esp. labiates and orchids; the galea.

1793 MARTYN *Lang. Bot.*, Helmet, *Galea*. The upper lip of a ringent corolla. **1862** DARWIN *Fertil. Orchids* ii. (1885) 59 The whole upper part of the helmet answers to the minute oval bit of membrane to which the caudicle of Orchis is attached. **1866** *Treas. Bot.* I. 335/2 s.v. *Coryanthes*, At the foot of the column are two fleshy feet, from whose toe perpetually distils a clear honey-like fluid, which drops into the hollow of the helmet.

8. An appendage of the stipes of the maxilla of some insects, as the cockroach; the galea.

1828 STARK *Elem. Nat. Hist.* II. 313 A corneous and dentated portion..covered by another piece of a membranous consistence, and arched, called the *galea* or helmet.

9. *attrib.* and *Comb.*, as ***helmet-bonnet***, ***-cone***, ***-crown***, ***-feather***, ***-hat***, ***-head***, ***-maker***, ***-shape***; ***helmet-shaped***, ***-strewn***, ***-tubed*** adjs.: **helmet-beetle**, a beetle of the family *Cassididæ*, having a dilated thorax forming a kind of helmet covering the head; **helmet-bird**, a bird of the genus *Corythaix*, a turakoo; † **helmet-cherry**, a kind of cherry: cf. HEALME; **helmet-cockatoo**, *Callocephalon galeatum*, 'an iron-grey bird with a bright red head' (Newton); **helmet-crab**, a species of King-crab, *Limulus longispinus*; **helmet-flower**, a name for Monkshood or Aconite, and for orchids of the genus *Coryanthes*; **helmet-hornbill**, a species of Hornbill, *Buceros galeatus*; **helmet-quail**, a quail of the American genus *Lophortyx*, having an elegant curved crest; **helmet-shell**: see sense 5; **helmet-stone**: see sense 6.

1816 PRISC. WAKEFIELD *Nat. Hist. Ins.* iv. 35 The larvae of the genus *Cassida* or *Helmet Beetle. **1794** W. ROBERTS *Looker-on* No. 87 ¶6 Still see my *helmet bonnet unimpaired. **1611** COTGR., *Heaulme*,..the *Helmet cherrie, Heart-cherrie. **1777** WARTON *Poems* 70 (Jod.) Wearing in death his *helmet-crown. **1832** TENNYSON *Lady of Shalott* iii, The helmet and the *helmet-feather Burn'd like one burning flame together. **1597** GERARDE *Herbal* (1633) 972 Blew *Helmet-floure, or Monks-hood. **1629** PARKINSON *Paradisi* xxvi. 216 The poisonfull Helmet flower. **1893–6** NEWTON *Dict. Birds* 434 The *Helmet-Hornbill, a native of Sumatra and Borneo. **1858** SIMMONDS *Dict. Trade*, **Helmet-maker*, a maker of defensive coverings for the head, worn by soldiers, firemen, etc. **1813** SCOTT *Trierm.* II. viii, Steel from spur to *helmet-plume. **1776** WITHERING *Brit. Plants* (1796) I. 283 Melampyrum..Upper lip *helmet-shaped, compressed. **1835** LINDLEY *Introd. Bot.* (1848) I. 335 If the corolla is very irregular with one petal very large and helmet-shaped, it is sometimes called cassideous. **1753** CHAMBERS *Cycl. Supp.*, *Galea*,..a genus of..sea hedgehogs, whose shape is that of a large elevated helmet..This genus, when fossile, is called in English the *helmet stone. **1793** MARTYN *Lang. Bot.*, *Helmet-tubed Petal, *Galeato-tubulatum petalum*.

Hence **ˈhelmetful**, as much as a helmet will hold; **ˈhelmetless** *a.*, having no helmet.

1863 WHYTE MELVILLE *Gladiators* III. xx. (1864) 416 He would give all his share of spoil for a helmetful of water. **1891** R. KIPLING *Light that failed* ii, A helmetless soldier was firing over Dick's head.

ˈhelmet, *v.* [f. HELMET *sb.*] *trans.* To furnish with a helmet.

a **1661** FULLER *Worthies* (1840) I. 165 Helmeted on their heads and crested like a lark. **1807** WORDSW. *White Doe* v. 137, I helmeted a brow though white, And took a place in all men's sight. **1889** *Spectator* 9 Nov. 637/2 Rock-panoplied giants..helmeted with eternal snow.

helmet-crest.

1. (Also *helmet crest*.) The crest of a helmet.

1509 HAWES *Past. Pleas.* XXXIII. viii, Upon his first head in his helmet crest. **1676** HOBBES *Iliad* (1677) 244 Lycon him hit upon the helmet-crest. **1814** SCOTT *Ld. of Isles* III. vi, The honoured pledge you gave..shall wave upon my helmet-crest.

2. A crested humming-bird of the genus *Oxypogon*.

1863 WOOD *Illustr. Nat. Hist.* II. 241 The Helmet-crests are very curious birds, and are at once known by the singular pointed plume which crowns the top of the head.

helmeted (ˈhɛlmɪtɪd), *ppl. a.* [f. HELMET *sb.* or *v.* + -ED.] Wearing a helmet. In *Bot.* helmet-shaped, galeate.

1552 HULOET, Helmeted, *galeatus*. **1612** *Two Noble K.* I. i, Unto the helmeted Bellona use them. **1831** DON *Gard. Dict.* Gloss., *Galeate*, helmeted. **1862** J. GRANT *Capt. of Guard* vii, They knelt..on the green sward, bowing all their helmeted heads.

†**helmeˈtier, helmettier.** *Obs. rare.* [see -IER.] A soldier wearing a helmet.

1600 HOLLAND *Livy* XLIV. xxxiii. 1191 He ordained that the helmettiers or morioners [*galeatos*] should stand upon their feet, having their shields upright before them.

Helmholtz (ˈhɛlmhɒlts). *Physics.* The name of H. L. F. von *Helmholtz* (1821–1894), German scientist, used attributively with reference to various devices and theories invented by him. Also **Helmˈholtzian** *a.*

1890 W. JAMES *Princ. Psychol.* II. xx. 170 The Helmholtzian theory is probably not the last word in the physiology of hearing. **1920** G. B. SHAW *How to become Mus. Critic* (1960) 311 The Helmholtzian chords of Scriabin. **1930** R. PAGET *Human Speech* 8 The ocarina is, I believe, the only well-known wind instrument which operates on the principle of the 'Helmholtz' resonator. **1940** *Chambers's Techn. Dict.* 409/2 Helmholtz galvanometer, Helmholtz resonance, Helmholtz resonator. **1962** CORSON & LORRAIN *Introd. Electromagn. Fields* v. 215 A pair of Helmholtz coils consists of two identical circular current loops placed coaxially so as to obtain uniformity of the magnetic induction *B* in the region midway between the loops.

helminth (ˈhɛlmɪnθ). [ad. Gr. ἕλμινς, ἑλμινθ- (comb. form ἑλμινθο-) maw-worm, intestinal worm; in mod.F. *helminthe*.]

1. A worm, esp. an intestinal worm.

1852 DANA *Crust.* I. 6 Certain Vermes, as the Helminths. **1867** J. HOGG *Microsc.* II. iii. 565 The Fluke belongs to the order *Trematoda*, which signifies that they are internal parasites, suctorial worms or helminths. **1887** F. J. BELL in *Rep. Brit. Assoc.* 770 (*title*) A Note on the Relations of Helminth Parasites to Grouse Disease.

2. *Min.* A variety of chlorite occurring in felspar and quartz.

1861 in BRISTOW *Gloss. Mining*.

helminthagogue (hɛlˈmɪnθəgɒg), *a.* and *sb.* *Med.* [f. Gr. ἑλμινθ- (see prec.) + ἀγωγός drawing forth.]

A. *adj.* 'Having power to expel intestinal worms' (*Syd. Soc. Lex.* 1886); anthelmintic.

1854 in MAYNE *Expos. Lex.*

B. *sb.* A medicine for expelling intestinal worms.

1704 in J. HARRIS *Lex. Techn.* **1706** PHILLIPS (ed. Kersey), *Helminthagogues*, or *Helminthicks*, Medicines that drive out Worms, or cause them to be voided.

So **helminthagogic** (-əˈgɒdʒɪk), *a.* = prec. A.

1727 BAILEY vol. II, *Helminthagogick*, expelling Worms.

helminthiasis (hɛlmɪnˈθaɪəsɪs). *Path.* [mod.L., f. Gr. ἑλμινθιᾶν to suffer from worms, f. ἑλμινθ- HELMINTH: see -ASIS.] A diseased condition characterized by the presence of worms in the body.

1811 in HOOPER *Med. Dict.* **1865** *Pop. Sc. Rev.* IV. 165 Introducing this parasite (*Bilharzia hæmatobia*) and its terrible helminthiasis into this country. **1876** tr. *Wagner's Gen. Pathol.* 109 The disposition to helminthiasis.

helminthic (hɛlˈmɪnθɪk), *a.* and *sb.* [f. Gr. ἑλμινθ- HELMINTH + -IC.] **A.** *adj.* Pertaining to a helminth or intestinal worm.

1755 JOHNSON, *Helminthick*, relating to worms. **1822–34** *Good's Study Med.* (ed. 4) I. 278 An hepatic disease, which gradually changed to violent helminthic symptoms in the stomach.

B. *sb.* = HELMINTHAGOGUE *sb.*

1704 in J. HARRIS *Lex. Techn.* **1706** in PHILLIPS.

helˈminthite. *Geol.* [f. as prec. + -ITE.] 'Applied to those long sinuous tracks so common on the surfaces of many flaggy sandstones, and which are usually considered as worm-trails' (Page *Hand-bk. Geol. Terms* 1859).

helminthoid (hɛlˈmɪnθɔɪd), *a.* [f. as prec. + -OID.] Resembling or of the nature of a helminth; vermiform.

1854 in MAYNE *Expos. Lex.* **1864** W. AITKEN *Sc. & Pract. Med.* (ed. 3) I. 807 Helminthoid Entozoa which have been discovered infesting the human body.

helˈmintholite. [f. Gr. ἑλμινθο- HELMINTH + -LITE.] †**1.** *Palæont.* (See quot.) *Obs.*

1846 WORCESTER cites HAMILTON. **1882** OGILVIE, *Helmintholite*, a fossil worm, with or without shell.

2. *Min.* (See quot.)

1865–72 WATTS *Dict. Chem.* III. 141 *Helmintholite*, a variety of limestone, generally of a dark colour, and distinguished by the beautiful red and green iridiscence of the fossil shells which it contains. It is found in Carinthia, at Halle in the Tyrol, and other localities, and is made into a variety of ornamental articles.

helˈmintholith. *Path.* [f. as prec. + Gr. λίθ-ος stone.] 'A calcareous concretion produced from an intestinal worm or other entozoon' (*Syd. Soc. Lex.* 1886).

helminthology (hɛlmɪnˈθɒlədʒɪ). [f. as prec. + -LOGY.] That branch of zoology, or of medical science, which treats of helminths.

1819 in *Pantologia*. **1822–34** *Good's Study Med.* (ed. 4) I. 265 *note*, Persons unacquainted with helminthology. **1864**

T. S. COBBOLD (*title*) Entozoa: an Introduction to the Study of Helminthology, with reference more particularly to the Internal Parasites of Man.

So **helmintho'logic, helmintho'logical** *adjs*., pertaining to helminthology; **helmin'thologist**, one versed in helminthology.

1822 J. FLEMING *Philos. Zool.* II. 416 (L.) Few parts of either England or Scotland have been surveyed by the eye of the helminthologist. **1828** WEBSTER, *Helminthologic, Helminthological.* **1862** T. S. COBBOLD in *Intell. Observer* No. I. 25 Our recent helminthological discoveries. **1876** *Beneden's Anim. Parasites* Introd., All helminthologists, with few exceptions, looked upon worms in the interior of the body as formed without parents in the same organs which they occupy.

helminthous (hɛl'mɪnθəs), *a.* [f. HELMINTH + -OUS.] Infested with intestinal worms; predisposed to helminthic diseases.

1854 MAYNE *Expos. Lex., Helminthodes,*..helminthous. **1861** HULME tr. *Moquin-Tandon* II. VII. 332 Improper nourishment greatly favours the appearance of the Helmintha... It appears also that the nature of the constitution ('helminthous') has great influence.

helmitol ('hɛlmɪtɒl). [a. G. *helmitol* (E. Eichengrün 1902, in *Pharm. Zeitschr.* XLVII. 866/2).] A proprietary name of a derivative of hexamethylenetetramine that has been used as a urinary antiseptic and in the treatment of rheumatism.

1903 *Jrnl. Chem. Soc.* LXXXIV. I. 195 Helmitol..forms colourless crystals. **1908** *Practitioner* Jan. 64 The newer drugs, urotropine, hetraline, helmitol, are useless in gleet. **1933** A. J. CLARK *Appl. Pharmacol.* (ed. 5) ii. 50 Hexamethylenetetramine anhydromethylene citrate (helmitol) yields formaldehyde with alkalis as well as with acids, but it is doubtful whether it yields formaldehyde in alkaline urines. **1967** *Martindale's Extra Pharmacopoeia* (ed. 25) II. 1524/1 Proprietary preparations of formamol were formerly marketed in Great Britain under the name helmitol (Bayer Products).

helmless ('hɛlmlɪs), *a.*[1] [f. HELM *sb.*[1] + -LESS.] Without a helm or helmet.

1600 FAIRFAX *Tasso* III. xxvi, Clorinda..helmlesse to the forrestward gan hie. **1814** BYRON *Lara* II. xvi, The cloven cuirass, and the helmless head.

'helmless, *a.*[2] [f. HELM *sb.*[2] + -LESS.] Without a helm or steering gear; rudderless. Also *fig.*

1824 BYRON *Def. Transf.* I. i. 116 The desert-ship, The helmless dromedary. **1850** TENNYSON *In Mem.* iv, My will is bondsman to the dark; I sit within a helmless bark.

'helmlet. *nonce-wd.* [f. HELM *sb.*[1] + -LET.] A small helm or helmet.

1883 SWINBURNE *Les Casquettes* xi. in *Eng. Illustr. Mag.* Oct. 18 No touch may loosen the black braced helmlets For the wild elves' heads of the wild waves wrought.

helmsman ('hɛlmzmæn). Also 7 **helmeman**. [f. HELM *sb.*[2] + MAN.] The man at the helm who steers the ship; a steersman. Also *fig.*

1622 R. HAWKINS *Voy. S. Sea* (1847) 84 A good helme man may be overcome with an imagination, and so mis-take one poynt for another. **1627** CAPT. SMITH *Seaman's Gram.* ii. 12 The Rudder is so turned to and fro as the Helmesman pleaseth. **1798** COLERIDGE *Anc. Mar.* v. xi, The helmsman steered, the ship moved on. **1860** *Merc. Marine Mag.* VII. 147 The helmsman, and others of the watch.

Hence **'helmsmanship**, the function of a helmsman. Also **'helmswoman, 'helmsgirl** *nonce-wds.*, a woman or girl who steers.

1890 *World* 13 Aug. 28/2 The Squadron..encouraged amateur helmsmanship. **1870** *Daily News* 17 May, A helmsgirl at the stern in a pilot jacket and straw hat.

†**'helmster**. *Obs. rare*$^{-1}$. [irreg. f. HELM *sb.*[2]] The helm, tiller.

1594 *Knack to Know a Knave* in Hazl. *Dodsley* VI. 571 While I am master of the bark, I mean to keep the helmster in my hand.

helmstok: see HELM *sb.*[2] 4.

helm-wind: see HELM *sb.*[1] 8.

†**helo**, *a.* *Obs.* or *dial.* Forms: 7 **helo(e, helaw,** 7–9 **halo, hala,** 8–9 **healo**. [Etymology unknown.] Bashful, modest, shamefaced.

1611 COTGR. s.v. *Coiffé, Il est né tout coiffé,*..hee is verie maidenlie, shamefacde, heloe. *Ibid., Honteux,* shamefast, bashfull, helo, modest. **1674** RAY *N.C. Words* 25 *Heloe* or *Helaw,* bashful, a word of common use. **1688** SHADWELL *Sqr. Alsatia* III. (1720) 57 *Hack*... Kiss her, I say. *Lolp.* I am so hala; I am ashamed. *c* **1746** J. COLLIER (Tim Bobbin) *Lanc. Dial.* (1862) 87 *Healo,* bashful. **1828** *Craven Dial., Halo, Healo,* bashful, modest.

helobious (hɪ'ləʊbɪəs), *a.* *rare*$^{-0}$. [f. mod.L. *helobius* (f. Gr. ἕλος marsh + -βιος living) + -OUS.] Living in marshes; palustrine.

[**1854** MAYNE *Expos. Lex., Helobius.*] **1889** in *Cent. Dict.*

helocerous (hiː'lɒsərəs), *a.* *Entom.* [f. Gr. ἧλος nail + κέρας horn + -OUS.] Having club-shaped antennæ; clavicorn.

1854 MAYNE *Expos. Lex., Helocerus,*..applied by Dumeril to a Family..of the *Coleoptera,* comprehending those in which the *antennæ* represent an oblong mass composed of *laminæ,* which seem perforated by a central axis; helocerous.

heloderm ('hiːləʊdɜːm). *Zool.* [ad. mod.L. *hēloderma,* f. Gr. ἧλος nail + δέρμα skin.] A large and repulsive-looking venomous lizard of the genus *Heloderma,* having its skin studded with warts or tubercles like heads of nails. There are two species, found in Mexico and Arizona.

1882 *Proc. Zool. Soc.* 632 Sir Joseph Fayrer made the subjoined remarks..I was present when the Heloderm bit two Guinea-pigs in the hind leg. **1895** *Westm. Gaz.* 17 Aug. 3/3 Mr. Tyrrell does not think the heloderm's poisonous bite would kill a man unless in exceptional cases.

Hence **helo'dermatoid** *a.*, having the form or character of a heloderm; **helo'dermatous** *a.*, having a warty skin like a heloderm.

‖**helodes** (hɪ'ləʊdiːz), *a.* and *sb.* *Med.* [mod.L., a. Gr. ἑλώδης marshy, f. ἕλος marsh.]

A. *adj.* Marshy, marsh-; (of fevers) produced by marsh miasma. **B.** *sb.* A fever so produced; a marsh-fever.

1730–6 BAILEY (folio), *Helodes,* a particular kind of Fever, accompanied with colliquative Sweats, the Tongue being dry and hard. **1753** CHAMBERS *Cycl. Supp., Helodes*..In medicine..used as a characteristic epithet in certain fevers. **1811** HOOPER *Med. Dict.* **1886** *Syd. Soc. Lex., Helodes*.. Also, a term for marsh fever.

helodont ('hiːləʊdɒnt), *a.* *Palæont.* [f. Gr. ἧλος nail + ὀδοντ-tooth.] Having teeth shaped like a nail or spike; (of a tooth) of this shape.

1886 J. W. DAVIS in *Geol. Mag.* (N.S.) III. 151 A number of small helodont teeth are scattered over some of the pieces of limestone.

helophyte ('hɛləfaɪt). *Bot.* [mod. f. Gr. ἕλος marsh + φυτ-όν plant.] A marsh plant.

[**1902** F. E. CLEMENTS *Syst. Nomencl. Phytogeogr.* 6 Helium, a marsh formation; helia, a group of marsh formations; helophyta, marsh plants; helophilus, marsh-loving.] **1909** GROOM & BALFOUR tr. *Warming's Oecology of Plants* xxxiv. 131 There is a group of plants, marsh plants (*helophytes*), which..develop their lower parts..in water or at least in soaking soil, but have their assimilatory organs mainly adapted to existence in the air. **1913** *Jrnl. Ecol.* I. 17 Another division [of plants] is characterised by semi-aquatic dormant buds—helophytes and hydrophytes. The helophytes or marsh-plants do not include all so-called marsh species. **1926** TANSLEY & CHIPP *Study of Vegetation* ii. 22 The marsh plants (*Helophytes*) and water-plants (*Hydrophytes*), whose [perennating] buds are situated at the bottom of the water or in the subjacent soil. **1960** N. POLUNIN *Introd. Plant Geogr.* xv. 505 Marsh-plants (*helophytes*..) and water-plants (*hydrophytes*) are much alike in their morphological and anatomical characteristics.

‖**helosis** (hɪ'ləʊsɪs). *Path.* [mod.L., f. Gr. εἰλ-εῖν to roll.] (See quots.)

1706 PHILLIPS (ed. Kersey), *Helosis,* a turning back of the Eye-lid. **1811** HOOPER *Med. Dict., Helosis,* an eversion or turning up of the eyelids. **1874** in DUNGLISON.

helot ('hɛlət, 'hiːlət). Forms: 6 **Hylote,** 6–7 **Ilot(e,** 7 **El(y)ot,** 7– **Helot,** 9 **helot**. [ad. L. *Hēlōtes,* a. Gr. Εἵλωτες (pl. of Εἵλως), also *Hīlōtæ* (*Ilōtæ,* Livy), a. Gr. Εἱλῶται (pl. of Εἱλώτης); traditionally taken as deriv. of Ἕλος Helos, a town in Laconia whose inhabitants were enslaved. (The capital H is now usual only in the original historical sense; so in the derivatives.)]

Gr. Antiq. (*Helot*) One of a class of serfs in ancient Sparta, intermediate in status between the ordinary slaves and the free Spartan citizens.

drunken Helot: in allusion to the statement (Plutarch *Lycurg.* xxviii), that Helots were, on certain occasions, compelled to appear in a state of intoxication, in order to excite in the Spartan youth repugnance to drunken habits.

1579 GOSSON *Sch. Abuse* (Arb.) 48 If Lycurgus..take counsel of Apollo..he shalbe charged to leaue those precepts to the white liuered Hylotes. **1586** T. B. *La Primaud. Fr. Acad.* I. (1589) 194 Well, if yee thinke it good, divide the rest amongst the Ilots. **1630** BRATHWAIT *Eng. Gentlem.* (1641) 100 Like those base Elyots slaved to ebriety. *a* **1653** G. DANIEL *Idyll* iii. 166 The Rest Like drunken Helots, either Act the Jest Their Rigours shall impose. **1779** JOHNSON in *Boswell* 1 Apr., In that respect he would be like the drunken Helot. **1846** GROTE *Greece* II. vi. (1888) II. 291 The Helots..were Coloni or serfs bound to the soil, who tilled it for the benefit of Spartan proprietors.

b. *transf.* (*helot*) A serf, a bondsman.

[**1579** GOSSON *Sch. Abuse* (Arb.) 48, I coulde wishe it in England, that there were greater preferment for the valiant Spartanes, then the sottishe Hylotes.] **1823** BYRON *Age of Bronze* vi, Slaves of the east, or helots of the west. **1862** D. WILSON *Preh. Man* II. xxiv. 404 The Saxon helot of the Conquest grew into the sturdy English freeman. **1877** FARRAR *Days of Youth* ii. 17 God's heroes may be the world's helots.

c. *Comb.*, as ***helot-like*** adj.

a **1873** LYTTON *Pausanias* 84 The rigid and helot-like slavery to which the native Bithynians were subjected.

'helotage. [f. prec. + -AGE.] = HELOTISM 1.

1831 CARLYLE *Sart. Res.* III. iv. *heading.* **1957** K. A. WITTFOGEL *Oriental Despotism* 414 The helotage-based societies of ancient Greece. **1962** *Listener* 27 Sept. 478/3 Spartan helotage barely lasted into the second century B.C.

helotism ('hɛlətɪz(ə)m, 'hiː-). [f. as HELOTAGE + -ISM.] **1.** The condition of a Helot or helot; the system of serfage which prevailed in Sparta; a system under which a class of the community are treated as a permanently inferior order.

1823 *Blackw. Mag.* XIV. 533 Lamenting over the Helotism of Ireland. **1845** McCULLOCH *Taxation* I. iii. (1852) 105 Providing..for the exaltation of a few individuals by the irremediable helotism of the great majority. **1846** GROTE *Greece* II. vii. (1849) II. 591 The subsequent state of Helotism into which they were reduced.

2. *Biol.* [ad. Sw. *helotisme* (E. Warming *Plantesamfund* (1895) II. iv. 85), prob. after G. *helotenthum* (S. Schwendener *Die Algentypen der Flechtengonidien* (1869) 4).] A form of symbiosis in which one organism makes use of another as if it were a slave, by causing it to function to its own advantage; used *esp.* of the relationship of the fungus and alga in a lichen by those who regard it as neither mutualism nor parasitism.

1900 B. D. JACKSON *Gloss. Bot. Terms* 119/2 *Helotism,* Warming's term for the relation of the symbionts in the Lichen thallus. **1909** GROOM & BALFOUR tr. *Warming's Oecology of Plants* 85 The symbiosis between lichen-fungi and algae is obviously most correctly interpreted as helotism. **1932** FULLER & CONARD tr. *Braun-Blanquet's Plant Sociol.* i. 6 The original individualities of fungus and alga are lost and merged in a new and more aggressive organism, so that the term helotism does not seem any more fortunate than the term mutual parasitism. **1962** C. J. ALEXOPOULOS *Introd. Mycology* (ed. 2) xxii. 539 Botanists of a middle-of-the-road group..state that the fungus holds the alga imprisoned in a state of slavery, helotism being the word used, thus granting that the fungus has the upper hand.

helotize ('hɛlətaɪz, 'hiː-), *v.* [f. as prec. + -IZE.] *trans.* To reduce to the condition of a Helot.

1846 GROTE *Greece* II. vi. (1862) II. 140 Helotising the inhabitants. *a* **1873** LYTTON *Pausanias* (1875) 106 Those galling chains of custom and of country which helotize affection, genius, nature herself.

helotry ('hɛlətrɪ, 'hiː-). [f. as prec. + -RY.]

1. Helots or serfs collectively; a class of helots.

1829 SOUTHEY *Sir T. More* (1831) I. 174 Down to the poorest hovel in which his helotry are stalled. **1829** MACAULAY *Ess., Southey* (1887) 126 The helotry of Mammon are not, in our day, so easily enforced to content themselves as the peasantry of that happy period. **1835** *Tait's Mag.* II. 521 The priesthood have been called in to supply to a trampled helotry..the want of natural leaders.

2. The condition of Helots; serfdom; slavery.

1873 SYMONDS *Grk. Poets* xii. 400 Who can forget the stories of Spartan Helotry? **1882** *Gd. Words* 748 The ancient system of slavery and helotry.

help (hɛlp), *v.* Pa. t. **helped** (hɛlpt), *arch.* **holp** (həʊlp); pa. pple. **helped**, *arch.* **holpen** ('həʊlpən, -p(ə)n). Forms: 1 **helpan,** 2–4 **helpen,** 3–7 **helpe,** 4– **help.** (Also 3 **halp-, healp-, heolp-, elp,** 6 **healp(e.)** *Pa. t.* and *pple.*: see below. [Com. Teut. str. vb.: OE. *helpan, healp* (*hulpon*), *holpen* = OFris. *helpa,* OS. *helpan* (Du., LG. *helpen*), OHG. *helfan* (Ger. *helfen*), ON. *hjálpa* (Sw. *hjelpa,* Da. *hjelpe*), Goth. *hilpan, halp* (*hulpum*), *hulpans*: OTeut. ablaut series *help-, halp-, hulp-* (*holp-*). The expected pre-Teut. form is **kelb-*: a root *kelp-* in same sense appears in Lith. *szèlpti* to help. Of the strong inflexions, the normal ME. pa. t. sing. was *halp*; the pl. was *holpen* (with *o* of pa. pple.), later *holp(e,* which *c* 1500 was extended also to the sing., and continued in frequent use till 17th c.; it is now a rare archaism exc. in U.S. dial. use. The pa. pple. *holpen,* kept alive by biblical and liturgical use, is still employed by poets and archaists (and occurs also in U.S. dial.); from 14th to 17th c. it occurs shortened to *holp(e.* The weak inflexion *helped* is found from *c* 1300, and has gradually become the usual form. For other points see the Forms below.]

A. Illustrations of Forms of Pa. t. and Pa. pple.

1. *Strong past tense.* **a.** *1st* and *3rd sing.* α. 1 **healp,** 2–3 **hėlp,** 5 **huelp.** β. 3–5 **halp.** γ. 6–7 **holpe,** 6– **holp;** (*U.S. dial.*) **holpen.**

α. *c* **897** K. ÆLFRED *Gregory's Past.* v. 45 He..his healp. *c* **1175** *Lamb. Hom.* 79 A preost..him nawiht ne help. *a* **1300** *Floriz & Bl.* 761 Ho him rodde and help. *c* **1410** *Chron. Eng.* 558 in Ritson *Metr. Rom.* He huelp hire brother.

β. *c* **1200** ORMIN 1342 Hemm itt hallp. *c* **1305** *Judas* 108 in *E.E.P.* (1862) 110 He halp menie man. **1470–85** MALORY *Arthur* II. xiii, Her blood halpe not the lady. **1480** CAXTON *Chron. Eng.* xiii. 15 His yongest doughter halp hym.

γ. **1523** LD. BERNERS *Froiss.* I. ccxx. 283 The kyng of Cypre holpe them. **1559** *Mirr. Mag., Warwicke* xvii, I lyke wyse hym refused: And holpe vp Henry. **1571** CAMPION *Hist. Irel.* xv. (1633) 48 Who..holpe the Saxons. **1859** TENNYSON *Guinevere* 45 Lancelot holp To raise the Prince. **1890** *Dialect Notes* I. 68 *Holp*.., for *helped.* 'He holp me out of the scrape.' **1927** *Amer. Speech* II. 357/2 He holpen me over the creek. [**1931** *Amer. Speech* VI. 230 Such old forms of English as..'holp' for 'help', and 'effen' for 'if' may be heard in the ordinary speech of the natives [of Oregon].] **1940** W. FAULKNER *Hamlet* I. ii. 47 'Help him up.' So the nigger holp Ab onto the horse. **1962** E. B. ATWOOD *Regional Vocab. Texas* vi. 118 Items of nonstandard 'grammer' are usually considerably more frequent..in the less-educated group: for example *clum* (climbed), *throwed, holp(ed).*

b. *2nd sing.* 1–3 **hulpe,** (3 **holpe**). *Subj.* 1–3 **hulpe.**

c **1000** *Ags. Ps.* (Th.) lxx[i]. 20 Đonne ðu..hulpe min. *c* **1200** ORMIN 12033 But iff þatt Godd himm hullpe þær. *c* **1205** LAY. 8931 þu me hulpe [*c* **1275** holpe].

c. *plural.* α. 1 **hulpon.** β. 3–4 **holpen.** γ. 4–7 **holpe,** 6–7 **holp,** (4 **hylpe**). δ. 4 **halp.** ε. 5 **heelp.**

α, β, γ. *a* **1000** *Christ* 1353 in *Exeter Bk.*, ðe hyra hulpon. *c* **1000** *Shrine* 162/16 (Bosw.) Ða steortas hulpan ealle ðæs hæfdes. *c* **1250** *Gen. & Ex.* 3382 Hise benes hem holpen wel. *c* **1320** R. BRUNNE *Medit.* 922 Anone runne to alle..and hylpe. **1377** LANGL. *P. Pl.* B. VI. 108 To erie þis halue acre holpyn hym manye. **1382** WYCLIF *1 Esdras* x. 15 Mosollam, and Sebethai, Leuitus, holpen hem. **1600** HOLLAND *Livy* VII. x. 255 Then his feeres and companions holpe to arme the younge Gentleman. **1605** *Lond. Prodigal* I. i, These hands of mine holp to wind him.

δ. **13..** *Guy Warw.* (A.) 2217 No his tvifold armes halp him nouȝt.

ε. **1483** CAXTON *Gold. Leg.* 130/1 All men..heelp them.

2. *Strong pa. pple.* α. 1– holpen, (4–5 -yn(e). β. 4–7 holpe, (4 hulpe), 6–7 holp.

c **1200** ORMIN 6201 Eȝȝþer birrþ þurrh oþerr beon Hollpenn. *c* **1340** HAMPOLE *Prose Tr.* (1866) 28 Nede for to be lukede to and holpyne by þe. **1382** WYCLIF *Ps.* lxxxv[i]. 17 Thou Lord hast holpe me. *c* **1385** CHAUCER *L.G.W.* 1984 *Ariadne*, He shal ben holpyn. **1526** TINDALE *Luke* i. 54 He ..hath holpen his servaunt Israhel. **1581** RICH *Farew. Milit. Prof.* (1846) 14 We have..holpe them at many a pinche. **1607** TOPSELL *Four-f. Beasts* (1658) 120 The Hound must be holp..with the voyce..of the Hunter. **1676** HOBBES *Iliad* I. 378 If you have holpen Jove with word or deed. **1856** MRS. BROWNING *Aur. Leigh* 24, I who was Entreated thus and holpen. **1881** 'MARK TWAIN' *Prince & Pauper* xix. 221 Of a truth I was right—he hath holpen in a kitchen.

3. *Weak pa. t.* and *pple.* α. 3– helped, (4–5 -id, -yd, -et, -it, -yt), 6–9 helpt. β. 6–7 holpt.

α. *a* **1300** *Cursor M.* 20184 Freindes..me helped. *a* **1300** *E.E. Psalter* xxvii[i]. 7 In him hoped mi hert, and helped [*v.r.* hulpen] am I. **1676** HOBBES *Iliad.* I. 553, I would have helpt you once.

β. **1583** STANYHURST *Æneis* II. (Arb.) 52 Downe Menelaus is holpt. **1607** TOPSELL *Four-f. Beasts* (1658) 22 By drinking asses milk they be holpt.

B. Signification.

1. *trans.* To furnish (a person, etc.) with what is serviceable to his efforts or his needs; to aid, assist. **a.** To add one's own action or effort to that of (another) so as to make it more effectual; to further the action or purpose of. (See also 5 b).

In OE. construed with genitive or dative (as if = to be a helper *of*, helpful *to*), of which the former became obs. and the latter ceased to be distinguishable from the accusative.

c **897** K. ÆLFRED *Gregory's Past.* v. 44 He nyle..helpan ðæs folces mid ðæm þe he [God] his healp. *a* **1000** *Hymns* vii. 44 (Gr.) Ðu moneȝum helpst. *c* **1000** *Ags. Ps.* (Th.) lxx. 20 [lxxi. 21] Ðonne..ðu hulpe min. *a* **1035** *Laws Cnut* II. c. 68 [69] (Schmid) Helpan aa þam raðost, þe helpes betst behofað. *a* **1067** *Charter Eadweard* in *Cod. Dipl.* IV. 206 Gode geuðe mine saule to helpene. *c* **1205** LAY. 9263 And þe eorl Aruiragus Mid æðele help his broðer. **1382** WYCLIF *Rev.* xii. 16 The erthe helpide the womman. **1480** CAXTON *Chron. Eng.* ccxxxviii. 263 He worshyped halp and mayntened holy chirche and hir mynystres. **1484** —— *Fables of Æsop* III. vi, Fortune helpeth bothe the good and euylle folke. **1577–87** HOLINSHED *Chron.* I. 4/2 They faine.. that Jupiter holpe his sonne Hercules, by throwing downe stones from heauen in this battell. **1700** GREGORY in *Collect.* (O.H.S.) I. 322 Machines for the helping and enlarging the sight (as telescopes). **1865** RUSKIN *Sesame* §30 *note*, A nation in its youth may be helped by laws, as a weak child by backboards.

b. To supply or relieve the wants or necessities of; to succour.

c **950** *Lindisf. Gosp.* Matt. xx. 30 Milsa us *vel* help usiȝ sunu dauides. *c* **1000** ÆLFRIC *Hom.* II. 442 We sceolon earmra manna helpan. *c* **1175** *Lamb. Hom.* 79 Þer com a prost bi þe weie and him nawiht ne help. *c* **1200** *Trin. Coll. Hom.* 9 Help þe hauelease. *c* **1205** LAY. 28394 Heo him heolpen At heȝere neoden. **1340** HAMPOLE *Pr. Consc.* 3567 Þe saules, þat til purgatory wendes, May be helped thurgh help of frendes. **1578** TIMME *Caluine on Gen.* 276 Who would haue suffered him rather to perish with hunger an hundred times than that they would haue holpen him in his need. **1601** SHAKS. *Jul. C.* I. ii. 111 Helpe me Cassius, or I sinke. **1733** POPE *Hor. Sat.* II. i. 137 To help who want, to forward who excel.

c. In *subj. pres.*, in invocations and oaths: *esp.* in ***so help me God***, the customary formula in a solemn oath; and in ***God help him*** (***them***, etc.), often a parenthetical exclamation of pity for the helpless condition of the person spoken of. Also ellipt. *so **help me***, and as a variant *so **help me bob***. Cf. SWELP.

c **1175** *Lamb. Hom.* 33 Ah swa me helpe drihten, þe ilke mon þe wule fulien alle his sunne lustes..ne kimeð he nefre inne heoueneriche. *c* **1250** *Gen. & Ex.* 2528 And he ðat ðise lettres wrot, God him helpe weli mot, And berȝe is sowle fro sorȝe & grot Of helle pine. *c* **1369** CHAUCER *Dethe Blaunche* 550, I wolde as wys god helpe me soo Amende hyt yif I kan or may. **1508** DUNBAR *Tua Mariit Wemen* 159, I hait him with my hert, sa help me our Lord! **1605** SHAKS. *Macb.* IV. ii. 59 Now God helpe thee, poore Monkie. **1617** MORYSON *Itin.* III. 190, I N N. sweare..that I will..and give my Voice ..as God helpe me, [etc.]. **1821** P. EGAN *Life in London* II. iii. 229 She tripped me up, my Lord, so help me bob, it is true. **1847** TENNYSON *Princ.* III. 67, I never knew my father, but she says (God help her) she was wedded to a fool. **1868** *Act 31–2 Vict.* c. 72 §2, I..do swear that I will be faithful and bear true allegiance to Her Majesty Queen Victoria, her heirs and successors, according to law. So help me God. **1869** TROLLOPE *Vicar of Bullhampton* (1870) iii. 20 Just go home to father's, sir; not a foot else, s' help me. **1936** L. C. DOUGLAS *White Banners* iv. 69 That he would never again.. so help him..fritter away precious time. **1939** JOYCE *Finnegans Wake* 118 So holp me Petault, it is not a miseffectual whyacinthinous riot of blots and blurs.

d. *absol.* or *intr.* To afford aid or assistance; often in *imper.* as a cry for assistance.

(See note to 1 as to OE. constr.)

a **1225** *Ancr. R.* 320 Cause is, hwi þu hit dudest, oðer hulpe þerto. *c* **1330** R. BRUNNE *Chron.* (1810) 44 Help knyghtes, if ȝe may, I may no ferrer go. **1375** BARBOUR *Bruce* II. 416 Schir philip..gan cry: 'Help, help! I have the new maid king!' *c* **1420** *Chron. Vilod.* 447 Dan Benna halp ryȝt well þerto. **1589** COGAN *Haven Health* (1636) 176 Yet the goodnesse of the pasture helpeth much to the goodnesse of the milke. **1591** *Troub. Raigne K. John* (1611) 19 Help hands, I haue no lands, Honor is my desire. **1611** BIBLE *2 Sam.* xiv. 4 Shee fell on her face to the ground, and did obeysance, and said, Helpe, O king. **1811** BYRON *Hints fr. Hor.* 817 Help, Christians, as ye hope for grace!

†**2. a.** *trans.* To benefit, do good to; to be of use or service to, to profit. *Obs.* (exc. as implied in 1.)

c **1000** *Inst. Polity* in Thorpe *Anc. Laws* II. 332 Þonne helpe ȝe wel þam þe ȝe lærað, ȝif hi eowrum larum fyliȝean willað. *a* **1200** *Moral Ode* 297 Ne mai heom noþer helpen þer i-bede ne almesse. *c* **1340** *Cursor M.* 1439 (Fairf.) Ne muȝt ham help na hali-hede, Attyn to hel þai most nede. *c* **1470** HENRY *Wallace* III. 237 Bot loss our men, it helpis ws rycht nocht. **1535** COVERDALE *1 Macc.* ii. 13 What helpeth it vs then to lyue? **1581** PETTIE *Guazzo's Civ. Conv.* I. (1586) 2 b, To consider the things that helpe him, and the things that hurt him. **1582** N. T. (Rhem.) *Matt.* xxv. 9 *margin*, We shal not be holpen by other mens deserts at the day of iudgement. **1648** GAGE *West Ind.* vi. 17 Iron, Knives, or such things which may help them in their Wars.

†**b.** *absol.* or *intr.* To be of use or service; to avail. Often quasi-*impersonal.* *Obs.* (exc. as implied in 1 d.)

c **1000** *Sax. Leechd.* II. 134 Wiþ fefre eft hylpð syndriȝo marubie to drincanne. *c* **1205** LAY. 16181 Heo rohten, þat heo inoh hafden, þeh hit lutel hulpe. *a* **1300** *Cursor M.* 20271 Lat be weping, it helps noght. *c* **1386** CHAUCER *Knt.'s T.* 1962 What helpeth it to tarien forth the day? *c* **1477** CAXTON *Jason* 76 b, Appollo..dyde all that he coude but yt halpe not ner profited no thing. **1553** T. WILSON *Rhet.* (1580) 192 A similitude, whiche beyng dilated helpeth well for amplification. **1747** WESLEY *Prim. Physic* (1762) 97 Mustard, and Juice of Scurvy Grass, help in a cold Scurvy. [**1756** BURKE *Subl. & B.* II. iv, In reality, a great clearness helps but little towards affecting the passions.]

3. *refl.* **a.** To put forth needed effort in one's own behalf; to do of oneself what is needed; to extricate oneself from a difficulty.

a **1225** *Leg. Kath.* 2103 Ha ne mahen nowðer Helpen ham seoluen, Ne heom þat ham seruið. *c* **1275** LAY. 30390 For niþing worþe þe mon þat nele him seolue heolpe. *a* **1300** *Cursor M.* 16255 If þou wil noght help þi-self, men haldes þe for quede. **1551** T. WILSON *Logike* (1580) 74 b, God will helpe them..if thei helpe theimselves. **1597** SHAKS. *2 Hen. IV*, III. ii. 247 She is old, and cannot helpe her selfe. **1860** EMERSON *Cond. Life, Fate* (1861) 14 He helps himself on each emergency by copying or duplicating his own structure, just so far as the need is. **1873** F. W. ROBINSON *Little Kate Kirby* I. iv. 45, I don't think that I shall require your assistance, or that I shall be unable to help myself. **1881** S. R. GARDINER *Introd. Eng. Hist.* viii. §3. 153 He [Cromwell] had no pleasure in ruling by force. But he could not help himself.

†**b.** with *of* or *with*: To make use of, avail oneself of. *Obs.* (= F. *se servir de*).

1489 CAXTON *Faytes of A.* II. xx. 133 We have holpen us of the saynges of the boke of Vegece. *c* **1489** —— *Sonnes of Aymon* xxiv. 528, I byleve that this devyll helpeth himself wyth som devilry. **1581** PETTIE *Guazzo's Civ. Conv.* II. (1586) 50 b, I judge them mervailous unfortunate that cannot helpe themselves with those qualities they are indued withall, at such time. **1628** DIGBY *Voy. Medit.* 64 Through ..a dishonest desire to helpe himselfe of my being there.

c. with *to*: see 7, 8.

4. *trans.* To make (an action, process, condition, etc.) more effectual; to assist in bringing about; to further, promote. See *help forward, help on*, in 5.

1559 *Mirr. Mag., Hen. VI*, xiv, The other sinne, through humours holpe, which god doth highly hate. *a* **1626** BACON *Sylva* §364 If you make the Earth narrower at the bottome than at the Top..it will helpe the Experiment. **1667** MILTON *P.L.* VI. 656 Thir armor help'd thir harm. **1700** S. L. tr. *Fryke's Voy. E. India* 355 We were forced to Eat Bacon ..Raw, and afterwards help the Digestion of it with Indian Brandy. **1874** GREEN *Short Hist.* ii. §6. 90 The troubles of the time helped here as elsewhere the progress of the town.

5. With *infin.* or *clause*:

a. With *infin.* alone. (This may either arise through ellipsis of the object in b, or may be a use of sense 4 with inf. obj.)

In this and b the infinitive has normally *to*, which however from 16th c. is often omitted: this is now a common *colloq.* form.

c **1175** *Lamb. Hom.* 37 To seke gan, and þa deden helpen to buriene. *c* **1320** R. BRUNNE *Medit.* 922 And hylpe þat precyus body to bere. **1387** TREVISA *Higden* (Rolls) VI. 135 Theodorus..halp to putte Wilfridus out of his bisshopricke. *c* **1410** LOVE *Bonavent. Mirr.* l. 104 (Gibbs MS.), I halp to burye hym. **1548** UDALL *Erasm. Par. Luke* 6 b, To helpe garnishe his mother tongue. **1598** BARCKLEY *Felic. Man* (1631) 220 He proved so good a scholler that it holpe to work the destruction of his owne soule and many others. *c* **1611** CHAPMAN *Iliad* XIII. (R.), Many helpfull men That..would then Helpe beare his mighty seven-fold shield. **1625** BURGES *Pers. Tithes* 18 Yet is hee still..bound to help maintaine his Minister, if he be in want. **1735** POPE *Ep. Arbuthnot* 248 He help'd to bury whom he help'd to starve. **1853** LYNCH *Self-Improv.* iii. 58 All the leaves that helped nourish it. **1862** TYNDALL *Mountaineer* vi. 55 Such thoughts had a dynamic value, and helped to lift me over the rocks. **1941** *Punch* 2 July 13/3 Sir Kingsley Wood..asked the House for another £1,000,000,000, to help pay for the next three months of war.

b. With *obj.* and *inf.* To aid or assist (a person *to do* something). (See sense 1.)

c **1200** ORMIN 1342 Forr hemm itt hallp biforenn Godd To clennsenn hemm off sinne. *a* **1300** *Cursor M.* 28363 Or help oþer men to sing. **1362** LANGL. *P. Pl.* A. VII. 99 To heren þis half-Acre helpen him ful monye. *c* **1430** LYDG. *Compl. Bl. Knt.* xxvi, But who shal helpe me now for to compleyne. *a* **1539** COVERDALE *Remains* (1846) 575, I wyll helpe synners turne to the. **1662** J. DAVIES tr. *Olearius' Voy. Ambass.* 400 The Envoy help'd him to put it on. **1697** DAMPIER *Voy.* I. 214 Every Ships company made [canoas] for themselves, but we all helped each other to launch them. **1852** M. ARNOLD *Empedocles on Etna* I. i, I would fain stay and help thee tend him. **1855** MACAULAY *Hist. Eng.* xi. III. 49 The hereditary enemies of his house had helped him to mount a throne. **1936** *Punch* 1 Apr. 375/1, I suppose you two fellows wouldn't help me get the stuff into the coal-cellar, would you? **1940** *Ibid.* 5 June 620/3 The collection of waste-paper that's going to help us win the war. **1971** D. E. WESTLAKE *I gave at Office* (1972) 121 None of the locals.. had any desire to help us off-load the plane.

†**c.** With *obj. cl.*: To procure or assist in procuring (*that* something should be done). *Obs.*

c **1410** HOCCLEVE *Mother of God* 136 Helpith me þat I may my lyf amende. *c* **1440** *Gesta Rom.* i. 1 (Harl. MS.), I woll wite, if þou cowde helpe þat he were ded by ony Crafte. **15..** *Merch. & Son* 49 in Hazl. *E.P.P.* I. 136 Be yowre bettur avyse, Helpe y had a gode maystyr to teche me marchandyse.

6. a. Elliptically with adverbs or prepositions: = to help to proceed, go, come, or 'get' (*away, down, forward, in, off, on, out, up*, etc.; *to, into, out of*, etc.). See also 7.

c **1200** *Trin. Coll. Hom.* 103 Aris, louerd, and elp me up. *c* **1300** *Cursor M.* 25390 (Cott. Galba) Askinges seuyn þat helpes vs to þe blis of heuyn. **1393** LANGL. *P. Pl.* C. III. 38 Trewe charite That most helpeþ men to heuene. **1535** COVERDALE *Matt.* x. 21 Chyldren shall aryse agaynst their fathers & mothers & shall helpe them to deeth. **1586** HOLINSHED *Chron., Irel.* III. 89/2 It was holpen forward by Thomas Canon. **1588** SHAKS. *Tit. A.* II. iii. 209 Why dost not comfort me and helpe me out, From this vnhallow'd and blood-stained Hole? **1598** —— *Merry W.* III. iii. 149 Helpe mee away. **1611** —— *Cymb.* v. iv. 179 A Hangman to helpe him to bed. *a* **1635** NAUNTON *Fragm. Reg.* (Arb.) 54 To help on his Catastrophe. **1781** COWPER *Charity* 522 Strange! how the frequent interjected dash, Quickens a market, and helps off the trash. **1871** R. ELLIS *Catullus* x. 8 Had it helped me to profit or to money. **1886** *Miss* FOTHERGILL *Borderland* xxix. (1887) 337, I am thankful to be helped forward a bit. **1886** G. T. STOKES *Celtic Ch.* (1888) 349 You can all do something to help on that work.

b. With adverb (or adverbial phrase) followed by *with*: = to help (a person) to put, take, or get something (*on, off, up, down*, etc.); esp. in reference to clothing, e.g. *to help* a person *on* (or *off*) *with* his coat = to help him to get it on (or off).

c **1300** *Havelok* 901 Þan men haueden holpen him doun With þe birþene of his croun. **1553** T. WILSON *Rhet.* (1580) 170 Helpe me of with my bootes and my spurres. **1570** *Durham Depos.* (Surtees) 166 He..helpt the said Holmes on with his mess clothes. **1698** WANLEY in *Lett. Lit. Men* (Camden) 258, I did all in my power..to help her off with above £400 worth of her books. **1886** F. W. ROBINSON *Court. Mary Smith* VI. iv, If you will help me on with my coat. *a* **1898** *Mod.* Help me up the hill with this load.

c. ***help out*** or ***through***: to afford assistance in completing something; to eke out, supplement. Also *absol.*

1618 BOLTON *Florus* I. iii. (1636) 10 Horatius..helping out his valour with his wit. *a* **1632** FAIRFAX (J.), Boldest hearts good fortune helpeth out. **1711** ADDISON *Spect.* No. 59. ¶6 She..helps out his Verse, and furnishes him with Rhymes. **1722** DE FOE *Plague* (1756) 125 They have given me a Bag of Bread too, and a Salt Fish and some Flesh; so all helps out. **1722** WOLLASTON *Relig. Nat.* ix. 194 To expect omnipotence should interpose to help out a bad cause. **1815** SCOTT *Guy M.* xliv, I will sit wi' you..and help ye out wi' your bottle. **1874** MRS. WALFORD *Mr. Smith* xxx. (1876) 261, I looked to you, and you wouldn't say a word to help me out. **1917** *Dialect Notes* IV. 413 *Holp* v. tr., to help. 'I axed him to *holp* me out.'

d. To render assistance in dealing *with*.

1924 A. D. SEDGWICK *Little French Girl* I. v, If he sat there ..not helping with the water-cans, the baskets of flowers, the scissors, it was because he loved her and wanted to watch her. **1933** *Punch* 26 July 104/2 'Poetry. I believe people use it in exams to remember rules..and things...' 'That wouldn't help with Greek and Latin,' said Charles.

e. Phr. ***to help the police in*** (or ***with***) ***their inquiries***: to be questioned by the police in connection with a crime, often regarded as having the implication of being the chief suspect; also ***to help the police, to help with inquiries***.

1957 *Times* 3 Sept. 4/3 The police are anxious to trace an itinerant photographer... It is believed that he may be able to help them in their inquiries. **1970** *Guardian* 10 Nov. 20/4 A man was helping police last night after the body of Susan Young, aged 12..was found. **1971** 'J. FRASER' *Death in Pheasant's Eye* xxvi. 162 What's the deadline for arresting Stanley Robinson? At the moment he's 'helping with enquiries'. **1972** V. C. CLINTON-BADDELEY *To study Long Silence* ii. 72 In newspaper language..the man who is 'helping the police' is the chap who's being badgered into a confession. **1973** *Sunday Times* 14 Oct. 1/1 A 17-year-old girl..was found battered to death... Later, a man was helping police with their inquiries.

7. ***help*** (a person) ***to*** (also †***with***): to help him to attain to, to aid in obtaining; hence, to furnish, provide, or present with. ***help oneself to***: to provide oneself with, take for oneself; *euphem.* to appropriate (something not one's own), to steal. Also simply *to **help oneself***. Cf. next.

c **1380** WYCLIF *Wks.* (1880) 78 Goddis lawe helpeþ hem not her-to. **1458** in Turner *Domest. Archit.* III. 43 Gentil Jeffray, That clothed many a pore man to bed and to rige,

And hathe holpe to rentis to holde up this waye. **1535** COVERDALE *1 Macc.* viii. 13 Whom they wolde helpe to their kyngdomes. **1568** GRAFTON *Chron., Hen. VIII*, an. 19 (R.), The emperor's dominions had holpen them with corne. **1585** T. WASHINGTON tr. *Nicholay's Voy.* II. i. 31 b, Desiring him too helpe him with a barrell of fresh water, for that theirs began to stinke. **1601** SHAKS. *Twel. N.* IV. ii. 87 Helpe me to a Candle, and pen, inke, and paper. **1674** tr. *Scheffer's Lapland* 142, I have not met with any one that could help me to the exact shape of them. **1708** SWIFT *Sacram. Test* Wks. 1755 II. I. 127, I will help you to enough of them. **1868** *Every Boys' Ann.* viii. (Rtldg.) 138 Not quite as bad as the ants, who walked in and helped themselves. **1883** E. BLACKWELL *Booth* iv. 31 They helped themselves freely to the furniture of an uninhabited house.

8. a. To serve (a person) with food at a meal. Const. *to*.

1688 MIEGE *French Dict.* s.v. *Help*, Shall I help you to a piece of Veal? **1711** ADDISON *Spect.* No. 119 ¶4 He will not help himself at Dinner 'till I am served. **1741** RICHARDSON *Pamela* II. 110 So I carv'd it in a Trice, and helped the Ladies. **1762** GOLDSM. *Cit. W.* xxxiii, I begged to be helped from a piece of beef. **1828** SCOTT *F.M. Perth* vi, He did not help himself to any food. **1881** C. GIBBON *Heart's Prob.* xi. (1884) 171 Maurice.. helped himself to a bumper of sherry.

absol. **1888** BESANT *Fifty Years Ago* vii. 121 The host sat behind the haunch of mutton, and 'helped' with zeal.

b. *transf.* To serve, distribute (food) at a meal.

1805 EMILY CLARK *Banks of Douro* II. 191 A goose.. which [she] carved and helped to every person that chose to have any of it. **1829** MARRYAT *F. Mildmay* iv, My father.. was in the very midst of helping his soup. **1876** BESANT & RICE *Gold. Butterfly* II. 53 There's a fate in it.. it is helped, and must be eaten. **1889** J. K. JEROME *3 Men in Boat* 221, I want a spoon to help the gravy with. **1919** V. WOOLF *Night & Day* xxxi. 2 She behaves very oddly. She forgets to help the pudding. **1938** M. K. RAWLINGS *Yearling* i. 11 Ma Baxter sat at the table waiting for them, helping their plates.

c. help-yourself, used *attrib.* esp. of a restaurant or cafeteria where one serves oneself, or of the meal obtained there; also as *sb.* Also *transf.*

1894 M. FRY *Let.* in E. H. Jones *Margery Fry* (1966) v. 37 Then at 1 is lunch.. a help-yourself meal and you get up and come away as soon as you've done without waiting for anyone else. **1923** [see CAFETERIA]. **1955** T. H. PEAR *Eng. Social Diff.* 183 The 'help yourself' cafeteria system. **1959** R. POSTGATE *Good Food Guide* 280 There is an à la carte menu and a 'help-yourself' lunch for the hasty at 6/6. **1961** *Times Lit. Suppl.* 13 Oct. 712/5 Up to a point he has invented the help-yourself novel. **1967** 'A. GILBERT' *Visitor* iii. 38, I got a cup of coffee and a sandwich at a help-yourself, and went back to the flat.

9. To succour in some distress or misfortune (cf. 1 b); hence, to deliver, save, set free, relieve (*from*, *of*); *spec.* to relieve or cure of a disease, or of some evil condition. *Obs.* or *arch.*

a **1225** *Ancr. R.* 110 He ne help him suluen in his muchele pine. *a* **1300** *Cursor M.* 5727 (Gött.) He helpid þaim of þair wa. *c* **1386** CHAUCER *Merch. T.* 1126, I haue yow holpe on bothe youre eyen blynde. —— *Frankl. T.* 577 Thanke yow lord and lady myn Venus That me han holpen fro my cares colde. *c* **1420** *Pallad. on Husb.* VII. 6 This helpith whete From auntys and fro mys. **1577** B. GOOGE *Heresbach's Husb.* I. (1586) 15 To use such remedies.. as have holpen others of like diseases. **1579** LYLY *Euphues* (Arb.) 100 Doth not Tryacle as well poyson as helpe, if it be taken out of time? **1594** PLAT *Jewell-ho.* III. 59 To helpe beere that beginneth to soure. **1683** SALMON *Doron Med.* III. 647 Some have been helpt of blindness by the use thereof. **1832** TENNYSON *Mariana in South* iii, Mother, give me grace To help me of my weary load. **1870** —— *Victim* i, Help us from famine And plague and strife!

10. a. To relieve or cure (a malady, etc.); to remedy, amend. *Obs.* or *arch.*

c **950** *Lindisf. Gosp.* Mark ix. 24 Ic ȝelefo, help un-ȝeleaffulnise minne. **1398** TREVISA *Barth. De P.R.* IV. iii. (1495) 83 The Tysyk and Etyk and other suche euylles may vneth be holpe by socour of medycynes. *c* **1410** HOCCLEVE *Mother of God* 33 Helpe my distresse. **1412–20** LYDG. *Chron. Troy* I. vi, All her ill was holpe and remedyed. **1576** BAKER *Jewell of Health* 130 b, This helpeth poysoning and comforteth al the members. **1594** PLAT *Jewell-ho.* III. 72 How to helpe smoking Chimnies. **1633** *Treas. Hid. Secrets* cv, This soveraigne water helpeth the Toothache. **1733** POPE *Ess. Man* III. 51 He only knows, And helps, another creature's wants and woes. **1842** TENNYSON *Locksley Hall* 105 But the jingling of the guinea helps the hurt that Honour feels.

b. To mend, repair. *Obs.* or *dial.*

1518 *Churchw. Acc. St. Michael Spurriergate, York*, For helpyng ye sacrynbell at Mary Mawdland alter. **1527** *Ibid.*, Paid for helpyng of Sir Herry surples. **1847–78** HALLIWELL, *Help*, to mend, or repair.

11. a. To remedy, obviate, prevent, cause to be otherwise. (With *can*, *cannot*, or some equivalent.)

In earlier use usually in passive 'it cannot be helped', later in active with personal subject 'I cannot help it' = I cannot do anything to remedy or prevent it.

1589 COGAN *Haven Health* (1636) 175 But this last inconvenience may bee holpen, as he teacheth afterward. **1591** SHAKS. *Two Gent.* III. i. 241 Cease to lament for that thou canst not helpe. **1605** BACON *Adv. Learn.* II. ii. §7 Deficient they are no doubt.. but the deficience cannot be holpen. **1659** D. PELL *Impr. Sea* 401 If so bee that ships bee cast away.. it cannot bee helped. **1668** PEPYS *Diary* 18 June, One thing there is.. which I fear will touch me; but I shall help it, I hope. **1711** STEELE *Spect.* No. 43 ¶3 If other People are not of our Opinion, we can't help that. **1865** TROLLOPE *Belton Est.* viii. 87 How can I help it that I am not a man and able to work for my bread? **1890** BESANT *Demoniac* v. 60 You do not believe. Well, we cannot help that. **1963** *Sunday Express* 3 Mar. 2/5 You are aware that the archdeacon swears that he never wears pyjamas?—I can't help that.

b. To prevent oneself from, avoid, refrain from, forbear; to do otherwise than. (With *can*, *cannot*.) Usually with *vbl. sb.* (rarely *infin.*), or *it* = doing it.

(For quot. 1894: cf. BUT C. 7 b.)

1697 in W. S. Perry *Hist. Coll. Amer. Col. Ch.* I. 39, I was very unwilling to take a Scotch Schoolmaster if I could have holpen it. **1711** STEELE *Spect.* No. 155 ¶2, I.. cannot help hearing the improper Discourses. **1741** CHESTERF. *Lett.* (1792) I. lxxvii. 213 He could not help thinking in verse, whether he would or not. **1757** MRS. E. GRIFFITH *Lett. Henry & Frances* (1767) I. 187, I can't help frequently to haunt and revisit these dear scenes. **1772** H. WALPOLE *Last Jrnls.* (1859) I. 38, I thought he should not offend the King if he could help it. **1808** COBBETT *Pol. Reg.* XIII. 528 No man can help being a coward or a fool. **1862** CARLYLE *Fredk. Gt.* X. iii. III. 238 Not one of us could help laughing. **1865** KINGSLEY *Herew.* II. xvi. 276 He could not help to weep and sigh, but yet himself he would not forget. **1883** *Manch. Guard.* 22 Oct. 5/6 A few such blunders as these could scarcely have been helped. **1894** HALL CAINE *Manxm.* I. ix. 43 She could not help but plague the lad. **1928** *Manch. Guardian Weekly* 5 Oct. 263/4 If clairvoyants are to be attached to police stations they can hardly help but become officials. **1952** G. SARTON *Hist. Sci.* I. xxi. 526 They were brutally raped by conquistadors.. who could not help increase geographic knowledge.

c. Idiomatically with negative omitted (*can* for *cannot*), after a negative expressed or implied.

1862 WHATELY in *Gd. Words* Aug. 496 In colloquial language it is common to hear persons say, 'I won't do so-and-so more than I can help', meaning, more than I can not help. **1864** J. H. NEWMAN *Apol.* 25 Your name shall occur again as little as I can help, in the course of these pages. **1879** SPURGEON *Serm.* XXV. 250, I did not trouble myself more than I could help. **1885** EDNA LYALL *In Golden Days* III. xv. 316, I do not believe we shall be at the court more than can be helped.

help (hɛlp), *sb.* Forms: 1 help, helpe, 2– help, (2–7 helpe, 4 heelpe, hilp, hylp, 5 (?) holp, 6 healpe). [OE. *help* = OFris. *helpe*, OS. *helpa* (MDu. and MLG. *helpe*, *help*), OHG. *helfa*, *hilfa* (MHG. *helfe*, *hilfe*), ON. *hjalp* (Sw., Da. *hjelp*):—OTeut. **helpâ* str. fem.; f. stem of *helpan* to HELP. In OE. the sb. was also str. masc. or neut. (gen. *helpes*) and weak fem. (acc. *helpan*). The continental langs. have also a form from the ablaut-grade *hulp-*, OHG. *hulfa*, MG. *hulfe*, OLG. *hulpa*, MDu. *hulpe*, *hulp*, Du. *hulp*, Ger. *hülfe*.]

1. a. The action of helping; the supplementing of action or resources by what makes them more efficient; aid, assistance, succour.

Beowulf (Z.) 1552 Nemne him heaðo-byrne helpe ȝefremede. **971** *Blickl. Hom.* 105 Hwa him to hæle and to helpe and to feorhnere on þas world astaȝ. *c* **1175** *Lamb. Hom.* 13 Ʒe me þenne clepiað and helpes me biddað. *a* **1225** *Juliana* 33 Habbe ich þin anes help. *a* **1300** *Cursor M.* 122 Al þis werld, or þis bok blin, Wit cristes help I sal ouerrin. *c* **1380** WYCLIF *Sel. Wks.* III. 28 Þou art goon out in heelpe of þi folk. *c* **1380** *Sir Ferumb.* 1030 Wiþ þe hilp of god almiȝt. *Ibid.* 3208 Hylp on hem nys none. **1477** EARL RIVERS (Caxton) *Dictes* 7 By whiche ye atteyne helpe of the holy gost. **1513** DOUGLAS *Æneis* VIII. ix. *heading*, Evander sendis his son.. in help of Eneas. **1634** SIR T. HERBERT *Trav.* 88 Calling out for helpe. **1712** ADDISON *Spect.* No. 281 ¶4 By the help of our Glasses [we] discern'd in it Millions of little Scars. **1779** JOHNSON *L.P.*, *Pope* Wks. IV. 91 He.. neither went to bed nor rose without help. **1849** MACAULAY *Hist. E.* ii. I. 208 To learn that the princes of the House of Stuart needed his help, and were willing to purchase that help by unbounded subserviency.

b. With *a* and *plural*. An act of helping, an aid. (Now *rare*, or merged in sense 2.)

a **1300** *Cursor M.* 23759 His helpes and vr wittes eke. *c* **1400** *Destr. Troy* 7166 All the Troiens.. Helit þere hurt men þurgh helpis of leches. **1549** COVERDALE, etc. *Erasm. Par. Jas.* 37 Let vs distruste oure owne helpes and the helpes of this worlde. **1707** *Curios. in Husb. & Gard.* 27 The Helps we have receiv'd from the Microscope. **1775** BURKE *Corr.* (1844) II. 72, I am perfectly sensible of the greatness of the difficulties, and the weakness and fewness of the helps. **1883** STEVENSON *Treas. Isl.* II. xii, I'll ask you, later on, to give us a help.

†c. ***at help***: in the quarter for helping, in (our, etc.) favour.

1602 SHAKS. *Ham.* IV. iii. 46 The Barke is readie, and the winde at helpe.

2. *transf.* Any thing or person that affords help; a source or means of assistance; an aid.

c **893** K. ÆLFRED *Oros.* III. ii[i]. §1 (Sweet) 100 Crist is eaðmodeȝra help and ofermodiȝra fiell. *c* **1230** *Hali Meid.* 13 Ha is us swiðe god freond and help. **1340** HAMPOLE *Pr. Consc.* 3586 Four maners of helpes er general.. þat es to say, prayer and fastyng, And almus dede and messyng. **1388** WYCLIF *Gen.* ii. 18 It is not good that a man be aloone; make we to hym an help lijk to hym self. **1577** B. GOOGE *Heresbach's Husb.* II. (1586) 53 Some require staies and helpes to clime by, as Hoppes, Lupines, and Pease. **1586** T. B. *La Primaud. Fr. Acad.* I. (1589) 453 To give him [Adam] a wife for a faithfull companion.. and a helpe like unto him-selfe. **1611** BIBLE *Ps.* xlvi. 1 God is our refuge and strength: a very present helpe in trouble. **1611** —— *Acts* xxvii. 17 They vsed helps, vnder-girding the ship. **1657** M. LAWRENCE *Use & Pract. Faith* 73 He looks at a meet help as a portion promised from God. **1722** DE FOE *Relig. Courtsh.* (1840) 187 A husband will be a sorry help to a wife, if he is not a help in the religious part of her life. **1843** G. BUCKLE in *Fleury's Eccl. Hist.* II. 80 *note*, Their business is.. only to be a decent help to their own sex. **1874** BLACKIE *Self-Cult.* 1 Books are no doubt very useful helps to knowledge.

3. A person, or company of persons, whose office it is to render help. **†a.** *gen.* Assistant; adjutant.

c **1250** *Gen. & Ex.* 3409 And taȝte him.. Vnder him helpes oðere don. **1533** BELLENDEN *Livy* v. (1822) 475 To put all thare gudis and cariage togidder under ane helpe.

†b. An ally; *pl.* allies, auxiliary troops. *Obs.*

c **1400** *Destr. Troy* 10803 For hope þat he hade of a helpe sone. *c* **1450** *Merlin* 113 Fro hens-forth thei hym deffien and his helpes. *c* **1489** CAXTON *Blanchardyn* lii. 197 Wold Subyon or not, & all his helpes, the noble lady.. was taken oute of his power. **1593** SHAKS. *3 Hen. VI*, II. i. 178 Now if the helpe of Norfolke, and my selfe.. Will but amount to fiue and twenty thousand.

c. A person employed to give assistance in household or other manual work; in *U.S.*, a hired labourer or servant, esp. a domestic servant.

In U.S. app. originally a person giving temporary or occasional assistance: cf. J. R. LOWELL *Among my Books* Series I. (1870) 251.

lady help, a lady engaged as assistant and companion to the mistress of a house. ***mother's help***, a young woman employed to help in the nursery, but in a position reckoned superior to that of a nurse-maid.

1645 *Mass. Col. Rec.* II. 139 (Bartlett) Such of his servants and helps as have been employed about yᵉ attendance of yᵉ court. **1743** ELLIS *Mod. Husb.* III. II. 2 Next to them [*sc.* hired servants] we should be provided with auxiliary Helps. **1807** C. W. JANSON *Stranger in Amer.* 87, I am Mr ——'s *help*. I'd have you know.. that I am no *sarvant*. **1815** *Massachusetts Spy* 23 Aug. (Th.), Our lady and gentleman 'hired helps' do not understand who is meant when their master is inquired for. **1818** H. B. FEARON *Sk. Amer.* 80 Servants, let me here observe, are called 'helps'. If you call a servant by that name they leave you without notice. **1824** *Examiner* 200/2 The hiring of 'a help', *anglicè* a servant,—a word rejected in America. **1830** GALT *Lawrie T.* VII. iii. (1849) 322 At this moment.. the help, or maiden servant, came. **1838** J. F. COOPER *Amer. Democrat* 122 Those who aid their masters in the toil may be deemed 'helps', but they who perform all the labor do not assist.. but they do it themselves. **1861** THACKERAY *Four Georges* i. (1862) 38 Fourteen postillions, nineteen hostlers, thirteen helps. **1883** *New Eng. Jrnl. Educ.* XVII. 54 The Boston 'help' reads Dante while she prepares the succulent pork and beans. *a* **1899** *Mod. Advertisements.* Wanted, Lady Help. Wanted, Two superior domestic helps to undertake the duties of cook and housemaid. Wanted, young girl, as useful help. Mother's Help wanted immediately, to assist with two children and housework. **1899** *Westm. Gaz.* 4 Aug. 2/3 Judge: What is a 'help'? Plaintiff: Well, she's a cook-housemaid-barmaid. **1949** 'J. TEY' *Brat Farrar* xi. 84 Lana, their 'help'.. 'obliged' only because her 'boy friend' worked in the stables. **1971** [see DAILY *a.* 1 b].

d. The labour of hired persons; *collect.* the body of servants belonging to a farm or household. orig. *U.S.*

1817 J. BRADBURY *Trav. Amer.* 318 Ask one of them the reason, he replies, 'I want help'. **1850** LYELL *2nd Visit U.S.* II. 303 The lady's sister.. was obliged to milk the cow.. such was the scarcity of 'help'. **1888** BRYCE *Amer. Commw.* III. xciv. 316 How simply the rooms are furnished, and how little 'help'.. is kept. **1896** HOWELLS *Impr. & Exp.* 204 We were seven hundred and fifty at table, and the help who served us were three hundred and fifty. **1959** S. GIBBONS *Pink Front Door* xviii. 221 The months when she had been without help had established Molly's unexpected visits as a habit. **1962** P. MORTIMER *Pumpkin Eater* xi. 106 'We got help. I don't know why it's called help.' 'You mean servants?' 'We don't call them servants.'

†4. Avail, boot, good, use. *Obs. rare.*

1562 PILKINGTON *Wks.* (Parker Soc.) 30 There is no help to be disobedient and strive against him, for he will have the victory.

5. †a. Relief, cure, remedy. *Obs.* exc. as in b.

c **1000** *Sax. Leechd.* II. 262 Ʒif þas fultumas ne syn helpe, læt blod þonne. *c* **1375** *Sc. Leg. Saints*, *Petrus* 44 Sindry oþir, at war leile, Throw his schadow gat helpe and heile. **1581** PETTIE *Guazzo's Civ. Conv.* I. (1586) 3 Not Aesculapius himself.. can.. give you the least helpe.. so long as [etc.]. **1611** SHAKS. *Wint. T.* III. ii. 223 What's gone, and what's past helpe Should be past greefe. **1674** tr. *Scheffer's Lapland* 8 Thir only help against these [winds] is to convey themselves into dens and caves.

b. Means of obviating or avoiding something; in phr. ***there is no help for it*** = it cannot be helped (see HELP *v.* 11).

1581 PETTIE *Guazzo's Civ. Conv.* I. (1586) 26 There is no helpe in it, but you must settle your selfe to like of such men with their imperfections. **1669** HOLDER *Speech* (J.), There is no help for it, but he must be taught accordingly to comply with that faulty way of writing. **1863** MRS. CARLYLE *Lett.* III. 162 It is their way and there is no help for it. **1887** FRITH *Autobiog.* II. v. 112, I was really sorry to dispel my old friend's illusion; but there was no help for it.

6. A portion of food served; a 'helping'.

1809 MALKIN tr. *Gil Blas* X. iii, Between every succeeding help my servants.. filled our large glasses.. with wine. **1873** MISS THACKERAY *Wks.* (1891) I. 124 He asked her for a second help of cold pie at luncheon.

7. *attrib.* and *Comb.*, as ***help-girl***, ***-giver***, ***-work***; **† help-ale** [see ALE 3], a rustic festival or merry-making in celebration of the completion of some work (e.g. haymaking) done with the help of neighbours (*obs.*); **help-mate** *Chess*, a type of chess problem in which Black is required to play so that White may give mate in a certain number of moves.

1577–87 HOLINSHED *Chron.* (1807) I. 233 The superfluous numbers of idle wakes, guilds, fraternities, church-ales, *helpe-ales, and soule-ales. **1643** WITHER *Campo Musæ* 42 Yea, baser then our Countrey Help-Ales are. **1675** R. FANE *Let.* 19 Apr. (MS.), Going to every feast and help ale within five miles round. **1863** MRS. GASKELL *Cousin Phillis* in *Cornhill Mag.* Nov. 633 Betty.. carried off the great dish to the kitchen, where an old man.. and a *help-girl, were awaiting their meal. *c* **1586** C'TESS PEMBROKE *Ps.* LXXI. iii, O my God, my sole *help-giver. **1897** ROWLAND & ROWLAND

Problem Art 91 Another class of problems..in which *both players concur* in endeavouring to effect the speediest mate —..which we term *Help-mate Problems. **1913** A. C. WHITE *Sam Loyd* 31 Whether Loyd was the inventor of the Help-mate problem..I do not know. **1966** *New Statesman* 11 Nov. 718/3 'Help-mate'..Black moves first and helps White to mate in a given number of moves. **1855** BROWNING *Saul* vii, Then I played the *help-tune of our reapers. **1883** *Harper's Mag.* Jan. 207/1 John Chinaman is in force here, as everywhere, for all *help-work.

helpable ('hɛlpəb(ə)l), *a. rare.* [f. HELP *v.* + -ABLE.] Capable of being helped or aided. Hence **helpa'bility**, capacity of being helped.
1833 J. S. MILL *Lett.* (1910) I. 48, I believe I am the least *helpable* of mortals. **1887** E. GOSSE in *Daily News* 10 Mar. 3/3 The first thing to be done was to distinguish the helpable from the unhelpable author. **1891** *Charity Organis. Rev.* Aug. 334 The main question was helpability. *Ibid.*, To use the refuges for helpable cases.

help-ale: see HELP *sb.* 7.

helped (hɛlpt), *ppl. a.* [f. HELP *v.* + -ED¹.] That has been helped, aided, or assisted. Also with advs., as ***helped-out***.
1905 *Daily Chron.* 15 May 3/5 The dowagers of to-day, with their helped-out complexions and Venetian red hair. **1910** E. M. ALBANESI *For Love of Anne Lambart* 104 But this is no helped success, this is real.

†**'helpend.** *Obs.* Also 4 **-inde.** [Substantival form of OE. pres. pple. of HELP *v.*] A helper.
971 *Blickl. Hom.* 105 Ealra gasta Nergend, and ealra saula Helpend. **13..** *Guy Warw.* (A.) 556 'God', he seyd, 'be mine helpinde!'

helper ('hɛlpə(r)). [f. HELP *v.* + -ER¹.]
1. One who (or that which) helps or assists; an auxiliary. (Also with adverbs, as ***helper-off***.)
a **1300** *E.E. Psalter* xxix. 11 [xxx. 10] Laverd mi helper made es he. **1382** WYCLIF *Gen.* ii. 20 To Adam forsothe was not foundun an helper like hym. **1494** FABYAN *Chron.* I. xcix. (R.), Wherfore the kynge sayd after in game, that seynt Martyn was a good helper at nede. **1598** BARRET *Theor. Warres* IV. iii. 110 He hath all the officers of the regiment for helpers. **1601** SHAKS. *All's Well* IV. iv. 21 It hath fated her to be my motiue And helper to a husband. **1670–98** LASSELS *Voy. Italy* I. 104 Gilding, mosaic work, and such like helpers off of bare walls. **1824** L. MURRAY *Eng. Gram.* (ed. 5) I. 145 *Must* is sometimes called in for a helper, and denotes necessity: as, 'We must speak the truth'. **1850** LYTE *Hymn*, '*Abide with me*' i, When other helpers fail, and comforts flee, Help of the helpless, O abide with me.
2. A person employed to assist in some kind of work; an assistant; *spec.* a groom's assistant in a stable.
1686 N. COX *Gentl. Recreat.* v. (ed. 3) 94 You must have two or three Helpers, and..see that they..rub him dry all over. **1731** *Gentl. Mag.* in Hone *Every-day Bk.* (1827) II. 955 One of the helpers in the king's stables. **1837** DICKENS *Pickw.* ix, Two sleepy helpers put the wrong harness on the wrong horses. **1851** GREENWELL *Coal-trade Terms Northumb. & Durh.*, *Helper up*, a lad employed to assist the barrowman out of a dip place. **1892** *Labour Commission* Gloss., *Helpers*, the persons in the blast furnace industry who help the keeper to mould the beds, run the metal in, and generally assist at the front of the furnace.
b. An assistant minister: among the early Methodists, and in Scottish churches. Now *colloq.*
1780 WESLEY in *Four C. Eng. Lett.* 232 You seem not well to have considered the Rules of a Helper, or the rise of Methodism. **1791** —— *Wks.* (1872) VIII. 309 Q. 25. What is the office of a Helper? *A.* In the absence of a Minister, to feed and guide the flock. **1849** MRS. OLIPHANT *Marg. Maitland* xii, On that particular Sabbath I can scarce say I got much more from Mr. Wallace himself, the helper.
3. *Hop-growing.* (See quot.)
1750 W. ELLIS *Mod. Husb.* IV. iii. 60 (E.D.S.) The common number of [hop] poles to each hill are three, but.. some add a fourth, called a *helper*: this *helper* is a larger pole than the rest.
Hence **'helper** *v. trans.* (*Hop-growing*), to support with a 'helper' (see 3); **'helperess** (*nonce-wd.*), a female helper; **'helpership**, the office or position of a helper.
1881 WHITEHEAD *Hops* 35 The plants are 'helpered' by short, slight pieces of old poles up which the bines are trained to go. **1886** H. F. LESTER *Under two Fig Trees* 196 [To] act as a sort of lay helperess. **1893** W. WALLACE *Scotl. Yesterday* 178 His successor in the 'helpership' had no objection to his 'Veesiting'.

†**helpfellow.** *Obs.* A companion who renders help; a helpmate.
1549 COVERDALE *Erasm. Par. 1 Thess.* iii. 4 A tried minister of God and a helpe felowe of our office. **1571** GOLDING *Calvin on Ps.* lxxiii. 25 As helpfelowes unto God.

helpful ('hɛlpfʊl), *a.* [f. HELP *sb.* + -FUL.] Full of help; having the quality of rendering or affording help; useful, serviceable, profitable.
a. of persons.
c **1340** *Cursor M.* 14395 (Trin.) Her owne lord ful of blis þat so helpful [*earlier MSS.* helpand] was to his. **1382** WYCLIF *1 Macc.* ii. 21 God be helpful to us. *c* **1611** CHAPMAN *Iliad* XIII. (R.), But Aiax Telemonius, had many helpfull men. **1796** BURKE *Corr.* IV. 404 My friend and kinsman, Nagle, who has indeed been very helpful to me. **1858** MRS. CARLYLE *Lett.* II. 353 Charlotte is much kinder and helpfuller than Anne was.
b. of things.
1382 WYCLIF *1 Macc.* iv. 56 Helpful thingis of heryingis. *c* **1450** *Cov. Myst.* (Shaks. Soc.) 77, I holde it helpfful that on of us with ȝow be had. **1599** MINSHEU *Sp. Gram.* 21 Called *Verbum auxiliarium*, a helpfull verbe. **1602** SHAKS. *Ham.* II. ii. 39 Heauens make our presence and our practises Pleasant and helpfull to him. *a* **1779** WARBURTON *Wks.* IX. iii. (R.), A pursuit or an abhorrence of what is helpful or hurtful. **1883** *Congregationalist* Sept. 729 One of the ablest, helpfullest books on the subject.

helpfully ('hɛlpfʊlɪ), *adv.* [f. prec. + -LY².] In a helpful manner; so as to help.
1832 *Fraser's Mag.* VI. 271 Two maidens caught her helpfully in their arms. **1868** GEO. ELIOT *Sp. Gipsy* v. 358 Grave white-turbaned Moors Move helpfully.

helpfulness ('hɛlpfʊlnɪs). [f. as prec. + -NESS.] The quality or condition of being helpful.
1643 MILTON *Divorce* II. xvii. (1851) 107 A disability of future helpfulnesse, or loyalty, or loving agreement. *a* **1791** WESLEY *Husb. & Wives* iii. 1 Wks. 1811 IX. 62 The Effects of Nuptial Love are three, Pleasingness, Faithfulness, Helpfulness. **1860** TYNDALL *Glac.* II. 439 In a spirit of mutual helpfulness, encouragement, and goodwill.

helping ('hɛlpɪŋ), *vbl. sb.* [-ING¹.]
1. The action of the verb HELP; help, aid, assistance, succour.
c **1205** LAY. 23748 þe heȝe heueneliche king stonde me an helping. *a* **1300** *Cursor M.* 5304 (Gött.) Thanck him of his gret helping. **1382** WYCLIF *1 Cor.* xii. 28 Aftirward vertues, aftirward graces of heelingis, helpingis. **1523** LD. BERNERS *Froiss.* I. ccxxxix. 347 [He] wolde make..greatter warre then euer he had done before, with the helpynge of the bastarde Henry. **1616** SURFL. & MARKH. *Country Farme* 413 But such sweet Apples..stand not in need of hauing any sowre Apples mixt with them, to the helping of them to make good Cider. **1846** TRENCH *Mirac.* xiii. (1862) 241 The law of all true helping.
†**b.** Use, service, function. *Obs.*
c **1400** *Lanfranc's Cirurg.* 26 þer ben þre helpingis of þe arteries. **1548–77** VICARY *Anat.* ii. (1888) 18 The Bone.. hath diuers formes..for the diuersitie of helpings.
†**2.** A means of help, an aid; an ally. *Obs.*
13.. *Guy Warw.* (A.) 3242 þer-fore ne wonde þou no-þing Nouȝt for him no his helping. *c* **1380** *Sir Ferumb.* 1283 þou for me schalt don a þyng..And ther-to ben myn helpyng. **1555** L. SAUNDERS in Coverdale *Lett. Mart.* (1564) 205 Yea howe all thynges haue bene holpynges vnto vs.
3. The action of serving food at a meal; *concr.* a portion of food served at one time (= HELP *sb.* 6).
1824 LAMB *Elia* Ser. II. *Capt. Jackson*, Carving could not lessen, nor helping diminish it. **1865** TROLLOPE *Belton Est.* xxiv. 286 There was some little trouble as to the helping of the fish. **1883** BESANT *All in Gard. Fair* II. i, A pretty fair slice, a large helping. **1893** Q. [COUCH] *Delect. Duchy* 286 Holding out his plate for a second helping of the pasty.

helping, *ppl. a.* [f. as prec. + -ING².] That helps; rendering assistance; helpful; auxiliary. (Chiefly in phr. ***a helping hand***.)
a **1300** *Cursor M.* 29303 þe sext [case of cursing] es þaa men..þat helpand es to sarazines Gain cristen men. **1389** *Eng. Gilds* (1870) 5 þe forsaide bretherhede shul be helpyng aȝeins þe rebelle & vnboxhum. *c* **1450** tr. *De Imitatione* III. xlv. 115 It is sone amendid, whan it pleasiþ þe to put to an helping honde. **1590** *Recorde's, etc., Gr. Artes* (1640) 370 When time shall fall fit..you shall not want my helping hand. **1705** STANHOPE *Paraphr.* I. 58 All lend their helping hand. **1824** L. MURRAY *Eng. Gram.* (ed. 5) I. 109 Auxiliary or helping Verbs, are those by the help of which the English verbs are principally conjugated. **1883** S. C. HALL *Retrospect* II. 31 Ready to hold out a helping hand to those whose struggles for fame were just beginning. **1892** DAVIDSON *Heb. Gr.* 50 The helping vowel between the stem and the suffix seems in all cases traceable to *i* or *a*.
Hence **'helpingly** *adv. rare.*
1611 COTGR., *Subsidiairement*, subsidiarily, helpingly. **1884** *Harper's Mag.* Jan. 263/1 Saints..who..watch over and guard helpingly sinful men on earth.

helpless ('hɛlplɪs), *a.* [f. HELP *sb.* + -LESS.]
1. Destitute of help; having no assistance from others; needy. (Of persons, their condition, etc.)
c **1175** *Lamb. Hom.* 129 Drihten alesde þene wrechan..þe wes al helples. *c* **1200** *Vices & Virtues* (1888) 23 Ðat ðu naked ware and helpleas. *c* **1460** *Towneley Myst.* (Surtees) 182, I will not leyf you all helples, as men withoutten freynd. **1590** SHAKS. *Com. Err.* I. i. 158 Hopelesse and helpelesse doth Egeon wend. **1694** KETTLEWELL *Comp. Persecuted* 141 Helper of the Helpless..be thou my Fortress. **1715–20** POPE *Iliad* VI. 513 A widow I, an helpless orphan he. **1841** ELPHINSTONE *Hist. Ind.* I. 379 Even to their families when they have left them in a helpless condition.
†**b.** Destitute (*of*). *Obs.*
1362 LANGL. *P. Pl.* A. VIII. 83 Olde men and hore, þat helples beoþ of strengþe. *a* **1700** DRYDEN (J.), Helpless of all that human wants require.
2. Having no resources in oneself; unable to help oneself; shiftless. (The ordinary current sense.)
1620 QUARLES *Div. Poems, Jonah*, This naked portraiture before thine Eye Is wretched, helplesse man, man born to die. **1666** DRYDEN *Ann. Mirab.* cxxx, One dire shot..Close by the board the Prince's main-mast bore..All three now helpless by each other lie. **1807** CRABBE *Par. Reg.* I. 655 Strange names our rustics give To helpless infants. **1855** MACAULAY *Hist. Eng.* xvi. III. 631 Tyrconnel looked on in helpless despair. **1871** R. ELLIS *Catullus* xvii. 18 Helpless as alder Lies, new-fell'd in a ditch.
3. Affording no help; unavailing, unprofitable. (The opposite of *helpful*.) Now *rare.*
1590 SHAKS. *Com. Err.* II. i. 39 Thou..With vrging helpelesse patience would releeue me. **1592** —— *Ven. & Ad.* 604 As those poor birds that helpless berries saw. **1732** POPE *Ess. Man* II. 154 A sharp accuser, but a helpless friend. **1858** CARLYLE *Fredk. Gt.* VII. ii. II. 242 Incondite dateless helpless Prussian Books.
†**4.** Admitting no remedy; that cannot be helped.
1590 SPENSER *F.Q.* I. iv. 49 Helplesse hap it booteth not to mone. *Ibid.* vii. 39 Such helpless harmes yts better hidden keep.

helplessly ('hɛlplɪslɪ), *adv.* [f. prec. + -LY².] In a helpless manner; without help or remedy; without being able to help oneself.
1594 KYD *Sp. Trag.* III. Hj a, But if he be thus helplesly [*later edd.* haplesly] distract. **1755** in JOHNSON. **1855** DICKENS *Lett.* (1880) I. 404 They all stood looking at it helplessly. **1875** STUBBS *Const. Hist.* II. xiv. 71 The king was helplessly in debt.

helplessness ('hɛlplɪsnɪs). [f. as prec. + -NESS.] The state or condition of being helpless; want of aid or resource; inability to help oneself.
1731 BAILEY vol. II, *Helplessness*, destituteness of help. **1742** WARBURTON *Note Pope's Ess. Man* III. 225 (Jod.) From their helplessness in distress. **1779–81** JOHNSON *L.P.*, *Milton* Wks. II. 167 The mind sinks under them in passive helplessness. **1863** GEO. ELIOT *Romola* II. ii, He was in one of his most wretched moments of conscious helplessness.

†**helply,** *a. Obs.* Also 3–5 **-lich,** 4–6 *Sc.* **-lyk(e,** 6 *Sc.* **-like.** [f. HELP *sb.* + -LY¹.] Affording help; helpful, serviceable.
a **1300** *Sarmun* i. in *E.E.P.* (1862) 1 Soch wirkes to wirche þat helplich to ure soules be. *c* **1350** *Med. MS.* in *Archæol.* XXX. 396 It is helply to the body ageyn venym and poysoun. *c* **1380** WYCLIF *Sel. Wks.* I. 27 God be helplich to me þat am synful. **1413** *Pilgr. Sowle* (Caxton 1483) IV. xxxii. 81 The armes of a man ben the moost helpely members. *c* **1500** *Auchinleck Chron.* (Asloan MS.) 56 Ane richt gud man and helplyk to the place. **1533** BELLENDEN *Livy* I. (1822) 36 The favour of Goddis apperit to thame sa supportabill and helplie in all thair besines. **1553** Q. KENNEDY in *Wodr. Soc. Misc.* (1844) 148 Helplyke to men.

helpmate ('hɛlpmeɪt). [f. HELP *sb.* or *v.* + MATE; prob. influenced in origin by next.] A companion who is a help, or who renders help; an assistant, coadjutor, partner, consort. Chiefly applied to a wife or husband.
1715 M. DAVIES *Athen. Brit.* I. 278 The Jesuits..notable Helpmates to the Monks in that kind of Forgery. **1722** DE FOE *Relig. Courtsh.* II. i. (1840) 187 A woman is to be a helpmate, and a man is to be the same. **1766** PENNANT *Zool.* (1776) I. 57 In Minorca the ass and the hog are common help-mates, and are yoked together in order to turn up the land. **1815** SCOTT *Guy M.* xliv, She next addressed her amiable help-mate. **1849** MACAULAY *Hist. Eng.* iii, A waiting woman was generally considered as the most suitable helpmate for a parson.

helpmeet ('hɛlpmiːt). [A compound absurdly formed by taking the two words *help meet* in Gen. ii. 18, 20 ('an help meet for him', i.e. a help (HELP *sb.* 2) suitable for him) as one word.
Already in the 17th c. the Scripture phrase is found with the two words improperly hyphened; which led the way to the use of *help-meet*, *helpmeet*, without 'for him'. But its recognition as a 'word' is chiefly of the 19th c.: it is unknown to Johnson, Todd, Richardson, and to Webster 1832. In the 17th c. they used more grammatically *meet help*, *meet-help*: cf. *sweet heart*, *sweetheart*.]
A fitting or suitable helper; a helpmate: usually applied to a wife or husband.
[**1382** WYCLIF *Gen.* ii. 18 Make we to hym help like hym. [**1388** an help lijk to hym silf]. *Ibid.* 20 an helper like hym. **1535** COVERD. *ibid.* an helpe, to beare him company. **1611** BIBLE *ibid.* I will make him an helpe meet for him (marg. *Hebr.* as before him). **1885** (R.V.) an help meet for (*or* answering to) him.]
1673 DRYDEN *Marr. à la M.* IV. i, If ever woman was a help-meet for man, my Spouse is so. **1696** *Feltham's Resolves*, etc. *On Eccl.* 322 An help-meet for man [*ed.* **1661** an help meet for man.] **1718** *Entertainer* No. 15 ¶6 Socrates had the like Number of Helpmeets; and Athenæus concludes it was no Scandal in those Times. **1739** R. BULL tr. *Dedekinds' Grobianus* 174 Or on your Help-meet let the Blame recoil. **1766** FORDYCE *Serm. Yng. Wom.* (1767) I. iv. 142 What..if, hoping to find a help meet, we should wed our ruin? **1805** E. DE ACTON *Nuns of Desert* I. 22 Much more passed on this subject between Selwyn and his helpmeet. **1849** CLOUGH *Amours de Voy.* I. vii. 150 But for Adam there is not found an help-meet for him. **1863** MRS. C. CLARKE *Shaks. Char.* i. 31 His piteous anguish to his help-meet in crime—'Oh, full of scorpions is my mind, dear wife!' **1870** FREEMAN *Norm. Conq.* (ed. 2) I. App. 716 No help-meet for him is found. **1873** SMILES *Huguenots Fr.* II. ii. (1881) 363 A true helpmeet for him, young, beautiful, rich, and withal virtuous. **1881** LADY HERBERT *Edith* 19 Mrs. Murray was the model of all that is contained in the old-fashioned word of 'help-meet' to her husband.
transf. **1879** *Cassell's Techn. Educ.* IV. 249/2 Gutta percha ..has..sufficient specialities to render it a valuable help-meet to its elder brother [caoutchouc].

'helpship. *nonce-wd.* The function or position of a 'help' (see HELP *sb.* 3 c).
1715 M. DAVIES *Athen. Brit.* I. 297 *Botal*, Helpship. **1849** CARLYLE *Misc.* (1872) VII. 93 The state of American helpship.

†**'helpster.** *Obs. rare.* [f. HELP-ER: see -STER.] A female helper.
a **1400** *Prymer* (1891) 113 Godes moder marye..be to me synful wrechche a meeke helpestre in alle þynges.

†**'help-tire.** *Obs.* *rare*⁻¹. [f. HELP *v.*] Something that helps one who is tired.
c **1611** CHAPMAN *Iliad* V. 253 My powers are yet entire And scorn the help-tire of a horse.

helpworthy ('hɛlpwɜːðɪ), *a. rare.* Worthy or deserving of help.

1889 MACKAY-SMITH in *Harper's Mag.* Jan. 213/2 Our preaching..fails in helpfulness to helpworthy people.

† **'helpy**, *a. Obs. rare.* [f. HELP *sb.* + -Y; if not an error for *helply*.] Helpful.

c **1440** *Gesta Rom.* xcii. 420 (Add. MS.) 'Blessyd be god', he saide, 'and þis helpy lady'. **1450–1530** *Myrr. our Ladye* 78 Yf ye calle vpon thys moste helpy name Marye..the fende flyeth a waye fro hym.

helre(n, obs. forms of ELDER *sb.*[1]

helsum, obs. form of HEALSOME *a.*

helt, obs. 3 sing. pres. and pa. t. and pple. of HIELD *v.*

helt(e, obs. forms of HILT.

helter, -ir, -yr, obs. forms of HALTER *sb.*

helter-skelter ('hɛltə'skɛltə(r)), *adv.*, *a.*, *sb.*, and *v. colloq.* [A jingling expression vaguely imitating the hurried clatter of feet rapidly and irregularly moved, or of many running feet.

In its form it resembles *hurry-scurry*; but the latter is a jingle upon the intelligible *hurry*, while no satisfactory explanation of *helter* (other than its echoic suggestiveness) has been offered. Cf. also *harum-scarum*.]

A. *adv.* In disordered haste; confusedly, tumultuously, pell-mell.

1593 NASHE *4 Lett. Confut.* 27 Helter skelter, feare no colours, course him, trounce him. **1597** SHAKS. *2 Hen. IV*, v. iii. 98 Helter-skelter haue I rode to thee, and tydings do I bring. **1598** FLORIO, *Alla rinfusa*, pelmell, helterskelter. **1668** R. L'ESTRANGE *Vis. Quev.* (1708) 210 All running helter-skelter, to and again, like mad. *a* **1704** T. BROWN *Declam. Adverbs* Wks. 1730 I. 40 Neither diligently enough, nor carefully..but helter skelter, slap-dash, confusedly. **1872** BAKER *Nile Tribut.* xvii. 294 Away we all went, helter skelter, through the dry grass.

B. *attrib.* or *adj.* Characterized by disorderly haste or headlong confusion.

1785 *Span. Rivals* 25 'Tis a helter-skelter journey we have taken. **1798** COLERIDGE *Poems, Mad Ox* xv. 89 This helter-skelter crowd. **1842** S. LOVER *Handy Andy* iii, A wild helter-skelter sort of fellow. **1894** *Albion Citizen* (Michigan) 290 Something can be done on the harem-scarem helter-skelter plan.

C. *sb.* **a.** A helter-skelter run or flight.

1713 C'TESS WINCHELSEA *Misc. Poems* 57 Dost think.. That, when he proffers Aid and Shelter, Will rudely fall to Helter-Skelter? **1851** LONGF. *Gold. Leg.* v. *Foot of Alps*, Such a helter-skelter of prayers and sins! **1887** T. A. TROLLOPE *What I remember* I. xiii. 266 The helter-skelter that ensued..furnished Paris with laughter for days afterwards.

b. (Also ***helter-skelter lighthouse***.) A tower-like structure used in fun fairs and pleasure-grounds, with an external spiral passage for sliding down on a mat.

1906 *Westm. Gaz.* 1 June 10/2 The World's Manufacturing Company, examples of whose 'helter-skelter' lighthouses are at Earl's Court, Blackpool, Southport, and other places. **1907** *Daily Chron.* 4 Sept. 2/7 All sorts of fearsome things..from a helter-skelter..to a smashing saloon and a 'coker nut' alley. **1927** *Sunday Express* 5 June 4 They will travel on the merry-go-rounds.. They will go down with the mats on the helter-skelter, and up with the swings. **1945** G. MILLAR *Maquis* i. 8, I began to feel that I was sitting on a mat on top of a helter-skelter. That somebody would give me a push and I would be away with..nobody at the bottom to pick me up. **1968** D. BRAITHWAITE *Fairground Archit.* 24 Vertical features like the 'Big Wheel', 'Helter Skelter' and 'Chair-o-Planes'..are valuable advertising symbols.

† **D.** *vb. trans.* To throw away or *off*, in disordered haste. *Obs.*

1600 *Look About You* xvii. in Hazl. *Dodsley* VII. 436 Here are two crack'd groats To helter-skelter at some vaulting house. **1782** MRS. E. BLOWER *Geo. Bateman* III. 116 He has helter-skeltered off his horseman's coat, palmer's weeds, or what not.

helter-skelteriness. *rare.* [f. *helter-skeltery + -NESS.] Random hastiness.

a **1849** POE *Marginalia* Introd., While the picturesqueness of the numerous pencil-sketches arrested my attention, their helter-skelteriness of commentary amused me.

helthe, obs. form of HEALTH.

heluc, -uation: see HELLUE, -UATION.

helve (hɛlv), *sb.* Forms: 1 **hielf, helfe,** 3 *Orm.* **hellfe,** 4–5 **hilve,** 6 **healve,** 4– **helve.** [OE. *hielfe* (*hylfe, helfe*) masc. or neut.:—**halbjo-*, corresp. in stem to MDu. *helf* n., *helve* n. and fem., MLG. *helf, helve* n., OHG. *halb, halp* masc., MHG. *halp*, pl. *helbe*:—OTeut. type **halbi-* neut., from a root which appears also in HALTER.]

1. A handle of a weapon or tool, as an axe, chisel, hammer, etc.

c **897** K. ÆLFRED *Gregory's Past.* xxi. 166 ȝif..sio æcs ðonne awint of ðæm hielfe. *c* **1000** ÆLFRIC *Voc.* in Wr.-Wülcker 142/21 *Manubrium*, hæft and helfe. *c* **1200** ORMIN 9948 þatt bulaxess hellfe. *c* **1380** *Sir Ferumb.* 4655 A mayl of Ire..þe hilues lengþe was viij fet. **1497** *Naval Acc. Hen. VII* (1896) 117 Halberdes with blak helves. **1574** R. SCOT *Hop Gard.* (1578) 27 Made with a rounde hole to receive a helue like to the helue of a Mattock. **1598** BARRET *Theor. Warres* v. iii. 134 These iron tooles are to haue handles, and healues. **1609** F. GREVIL *Mustapha* III. ii, Vile Caine! that (like the Axe) do'st goe about, To cut thy selfe an helve to weare thee out. **1785** H. MARSHALL in Darlington *Mem.* (1849) 544 By twisting a withe of Hickory round the stone, they make a helve, and so cut and bruised the bark round the trees. **1831** J. HOLLAND *Manuf. Metal* I. 85 The shaft or helve is nine feet in length.

b. Phrases. ***to throw the helve after the hatchet***: after losing or risking so much, to risk all that is left; to go the whole length regardless of loss or damage. Also, by confusion, ***to throw the hatchet after the helve***. ***to put the axe in the helve***: see AXE *sb.*[1] 5.

1546 J. HEYWOOD *Prov.* (1867) 80 Here I sende thaxe after the helue awaie. **1577–87** HOLINSHED *Chron.* (1807–8) IV. 338 Rather throw the helve after the hatchet, and leave your ruines to be repared by your prince. *a* **1610** HEALEY *Theophrastus* (1636) 59 Wel come on, hatchet after helve, Ile even loose this too. **1685** COTTON tr. *Montaigne* (1711) 222, I abandon myself through despair..and as the saying is, throw the Helve after the Hatchet. **1824** SCOTT *St. Ronan's* xxvi, Monsieur Martigny will be too much heartbroken to make further fight, but will e'en throw helve after hatchet.

2. (Also ***helve-hammer***.) A tilt-hammer, the helve of which oscillates on bearings, so that it is raised by a cam carried by a revolving shaft, and falls by its own weight.

1858 SIMMONDS *Dict. Trade, Helve-hammer.* **1879** *Cassell's Techn. Educ.* I. 410 Before the introduction of Nasmyth's patent, the only assistance which steam had given to human labour in forging was the helve or tilt-hammer..It is..a lever of the first order. **1881** RAYMOND *Mining Gloss., Helve*, a lift-hammer for forging blooms. **1894** *Harper's Mag.* Jan. 422 The helve-hammer and the trip-hammer are essentially the same—each consists of a heavy head attached to a beam mounted on gudgeons, which is lifted at..intervals by a cam carried by a revolving shaft.

helve, *v.* Now *rare.* [f. prec. sb.] *trans.* To furnish or fit with a helve.

c **1440** *Promp. Parv.* 235/1 Helvyn, or heftyn, *manubrio.* **1542** *MS. Acc. St. John's Hosp., Canterb.*, For helving the mattok *jd.* **1633** T. JAMES *Voy.* 66 The 2 hatchets to be new helu'd. **1861** LOWELL *P.-&-S. Rebell.* Prose Wks. 1890 V. 78 To edge it with plan and helve it with direction.

helve, obs. form of HALF *sb.*

helvellic (hɛl'vɛlɪk), *a.* [tr. G. *helvellasäure* helvellic acid (Boehm & Külz 1885, in *Arch. f. exper. Path. u. Pharm.* XIX. 414), f. mod.L. *Helvella*, a genus of ascomycetous fungi: see -IC.] ***helvellic acid***, a poisonous acid, $C_{12}H_{20}O_7$, present in some fungi of the sub-family Helvellæ.

1906 H. B. SHAW in Allbutt & Rolleston *Syst. Med.* (ed. 2) II. I. 871 Helvellic acid and extracts of the Helvella produce nausea, vomiting, hæmoglobinuria, icterus,..and uræmia. **1947** F. A. & F. T. WOLF *Fungi* II. xv. 351 There occurs in *Helvella esculenta* a water-soluble, heat-labile, hemolytic principle that has been identified as helvellic acid, $C_{12}H_{20}O_7$. **1953** J. RAMSBOTTOM *Mushrooms & Toadstools* vi. 54 *Gyromitra esculenta, Helvella crispa*..and several other Discomycetes contain helvellic acid, which has a strong dissolving action on the red corpuscles of the blood.

† **helvenac**, *a. Obs.* [ad. L. *helvenācus* pale yellow, yellowish, f. *helvus* light bay.] Applied to a kind of grape (obs. F. *helvenaque* Cotgr.).

1601 HOLLAND *Pliny* II. 154 The wines made of the Heluenake grapes.

helvendel, var. of HALFENDEAL, *Obs.*

helver ('hɛlvə(r)). [f. HELVE.] 'In *mining*, the handle or helve of a tool' (Annandale).

Helvetian (hɛl'viːʃ(ɪ)ən), *a.* and *sb.* [f. *Helvētia* (sc. *terra*) ancient name of Switzerland, f. L. *Helvētius* pertaining to the Helvētii, a people of the ancient Gallia Lugdunensis. Cf. F. *Helvétien*.]

A. *adj.* **a.** Pertaining to the ancient Helvetii. **b.** Pertaining to Helvetia or Switzerland; Swiss.

1559 W. CUNNINGHAM *Cosmogr. Glasse* 57 *margin*, Helvetian miles. **1591** SYLVESTER *Ivry* 375 Th' Helvetian Bands alone, Loth to disgrace their ancient valour known. *c* **1645** HOWELL *Lett.* (1650) I. 345 Some embracing the Waldensian..and some the Helvetian confession. **1842** *Penny Cycl.* XXIII. 427/2 The 21st legion..appropriated to its own use certain moneys destined to pay the Helvetian garrison.

B. *sb.* **a.** One of the ancient Helvetii. **b.** An inhabitant of Helvetia or Switzerland; a Swiss.

1593 *Bacchus Bountie* in *Harl. Misc.* (1809) II. 308 He came from Friburgum, an Helvetian. **1842** *Penny Cycl.* XXIII. 427/2 The Helvetians appear for the first time in history about 110 B.C.

Helvetic (hɛl'vɛtɪk), *a.* and *sb.* [ad. L. *Helvēticus*, f. *Helvētia* (see prec.). Cf. F. *Helvétique*.]

A. *adj.* Helvetian, Swiss.

1708 *Lond. Gaz.* No. 4399/2 The whole Helvetick Body think fit to stand upon their Guard on this Occasion. **1711** *C.M. Lett. to Curat* 71 The Church of Geneva and the Helvetick Church. **1727–51** CHAMBERS *Cycl.* s.v., The Helvetic body comprehends the republic of Switzerland, consisting of thirteen cantons, which make so many particular commonwealths. **17..** HOPKINS in Bancroft *Hist. U.S.* (1876) V. ii. 351 The German body votes by states; so does the Helvetic; so does the Belgic.

B. *sb.* A Swiss Protestant; a Zwinglian.

helvetium (hɛl'viːʃɪəm). *Chem.* [ad. G. *helvetium* (W. Minder 1940, in *Helvetica Physica Acta* XIII. 152), f. mod.L. *Helvet(ia* Switzerland + -IUM.] Earlier name for ASTATINE. Cf. also ALABAMINE and ANGLO-HELVETIUM. (*Disused.*)

1940 *Times* 13 Aug. 3/2 The Swiss scientist, Dr. W. Minder, of Berne University, has now succeeded in isolating element '85', which, in honour of his Fatherland, he has named 'Helvetium'. He has proved that 'Helvetium' is produced in small quantity from the decomposition of actinium, which is radio-active.

Hel'vidian. [f. *Helvidius*, who lived in Rome in the fourth century.] One of a sect who denied the perpetual virginity of the mother of Jesus.

1727–51 CHAMBERS *Cycl.* s.v., The Helvidians are called, by the Greeks, Antidicomarianites.

helvin, -ine ('hɛlvɪn). *Min.* [mod. (Werner, 1817) f. L. *helvus* light bay + -IN.] A honey-yellow or greenish silicate of glucinum and manganese, occurring in regular tetrahedral crystals.

1818 T. THOMSON *Ann. Philos.* XII. 311 Helvin..was discovered in..Saxony. **1849** J. NICOL *Min.* 234 Helvine occurs at Schwarzenberg..in beds in gneiss. **1865–72** WATTS *Dict. Chem.* III. 141 Helvin affords the only known example of a native compound of a silicate with a sulphide.

† **helvine**, *a. Obs.* Also 7 *erron.* helvian. [ad. L. *helvin-us* yellowish (*helvinum vinum* Pliny) f. *helvus* light bay.] Applied to some kind of wine: cf. HELVENAC.

1601 HOLLAND *Pliny* I. 411 The Eugenian Vines, and the smaller Heluine. **1623** COCKERAM, *Heluian wine*, Claret wine.

helvite ('hɛlvaɪt). *Min.* [f. as HELVIN + -ITE.] = HELVIN.

1868 DANA *Min.* (ed. 5) 264 Helvite. **1877** WATTS *Fownes' Chem.* (ed. 12) I. 394 This somewhat rare metal [beryllium] occurs as a silicate..in beryl, emerald, euclase, leucophane, helvite, and several varieties of gadolinite.

helvolic (hɛl'vɒlɪk), *a. Biochem.* [f. mod.L. *helvola* yellowish, the name of the mutant variety of fungus, characterized by its buff colour, from which the acid was first isolated: see -IC.] ***helvolic acid***, an antibiotic with the probable formula $C_{32}H_{42}O_8$ produced by some strains of the fungus *Aspergillus fumigatus*. Also called *fumigacin*.

1943 E. CHAIN et al. in *Brit. Jrnl. Exper. Path.* XXIV. 119 A new antibiotic has been isolated in the crystalline state from culture filtrates of *Aspergillus fumigatus*, mut. *helvola* Yuill. It has been named helvolic acid. **1944** *Jrnl. Bacteriol.* XLVII. 392 Helvolic acid is apparently identical with the fumigacin from which the gliotoxin fraction has been removed. **1949** H. W. FLOREY et al. *Antibiotics* i. 66 Helvolic acid..had some protective action against streptococcal infection in mice, but its other properties made it unsuitable for use in man. **1953** J. RAMSBOTTOM *Mushrooms & Toadstools* xxiii. 289 Fumigacin (helvolic acid) produced by *Aspergillus fumigatus* has all the necessary qualities except that bacteria readily acquire resistance to it. **1965** P. K. C. AUSTWICK in Raper & Fennell *Genus Aspergillus* vii. 106 *Aspergillus fumigatus* is known to produce three antibiotics that are toxic to experimental animals: fumigatin,..helvolic acid,..and gliotoxin.

helxine (hɛlk'saɪnɪ, hɛl'zaɪnɪ). *Bot.* [mod.L. (E. Requien 1825, in *Annales des Sciences Naturelles* V. 384), f. Gr. ἑλξίνη pellitory, a related plant.] *Soleirolia soleirolii*, a creeping, perennial herb of the family Urticaceæ, native to Corsica and Sardinia, formerly called by the generic name *Helxine*.

1873 MRS. HOOKER tr. *Le Maout & Decaisne's Gen. Syst. Bot.* II. 667 Flowers [of Urticaceæ]..very rarely solitary and axillary (*Helxine*). **1924** L. H. BAILEY *Man. Cultivated Plants* 241 Helxine..making a matted moss-like covering. **1964** M. FISH *Ground Cover Plants* v. 44 If one happened to have a dark, dank courtyard which needed the softening influence of tender green, nothing could be more charming than helxine. **1969** O. POLUNIN *Flowers of Europe* 58 *Soleirolia soleirolii*..(*Helxine*)..Native of Mediterranean islands; naturalized in Western Europe.

hely, obs. form of HIGHLY, HOLY.

helynge, var. ELENGE *a. Obs.*, tedious, dreary.

hem (hɛm), *sb.*[1] Also 4 **hemm, hemn,** 4–5 **heme,** 4–7 **hemme,** 6 **hembe.** [OE. *hem(m*, recorded in one vocabulary, and not found in the other older Teutonic langs.; but NFris. has *heam* 'hem, edge, border', and Fris. a dim. *hämel*. App. from the same root as HAM *sb.*[2], and NorthGer. *hamm* enclosure; the radical sense being 'border'.]

1. a. The border or edging of a piece of cloth or article of apparel. In earlier times including a fringe or other marginal trimming.

c **1000** ÆLFRIC *Gloss.* in Wr.-Wülcker 125/13 *Limbus*, stemning, *uel* hem. *a* **1300** *Cursor M.* 21136 Qua rin moght titest on his hemm [*Trin.* who myȝte furste touche his hem]. **13..** *Guy Warw.* (A.) 3664 Men miȝt wade ouer þe scho hem In þe blod þat of hem kem. *c* **1380** WYCLIF *Serm.* Sel. Wks. I. 59 If y touche þe hemn of þe cote of Jesus. **1382** — *Deut.* xxii. 12 Litil cordis in the hemmes thow shalt make bi foure corners of thi mantil. — *Matt.* xxiii. 5 Thei alargen her

filateries..and magnyfie hemmys. **1483** *Cath. Angl.* 182/2 Hem (*A.* hemmes), *fimbria, limbus, limbulus, lacinia, ora.* *c* **1515** *Cocke Lorell's B.* (Percy Soc.) 2 As sone as the hemme is tore The sho is lost for euer more. **1553** EDEN *Treat. Newe Ind.* (Arb.) 14 Ye hemme or edge of his cloke is beset with all maner of..Iewelles. **1833** HT. MARTINEAU *3 Ages* iii. 85 The country was chalky, and whitened the hems of her petticoats. **1846** TRENCH *Mirac.* vii. (1862) 194 This hem, or blue fringe on the borders of the garment, was put there by divine command.

†**b.** By extension: the skirt of a tunic or gown.

c **1205** LAY. 4995 Heo nom hire on anne curtel..Hire hem heo up i tæh. *c* **1275** *Luue Ron* 167 in *O.E. Misc.* 98 Þe hwile þu hyne [mayden-hod] witest vnder þine hemme þu ert swetture þan eny spis. **14..** *Nom.* in Wr.-Wülcker 679/8 *Hoc gremium*, a heme.

2. *spec.* (in current use). A border made on a piece of cloth by doubling or turning in the edge itself, and sewing it down, so as to strengthen it or prevent ravelling, as in a handkerchief or a tablecloth; a piece of hemming.

1665 HOOKE *Microgr.* 141 The upper side of the leaf, that by a kind of hem or doubling of the leaf appears on this side. **1758** J. S. *Le Dran's Observ. Surg.* (1771) 201, I took the Hem of a Piece of..Linen. **1758** JOHNSON *Idler* No. 13 ⁋10 Molly asked me the other day whether *Ireland* was in *France*, and was ordered by her mother to mend her hem. **1842** *Father Oswald* 145, I..wear Spectacles..only when I am doing open hem by candlelight. **1877** BRYANT *Poems, Song of Sower* v, By whom the busy thread, Along the garment's even hem And winding seam is led.

†**3.** The edge, border, rim, margin of anything.

c **1200** *Trin. Coll. Hom.* 25 Swo diȝeliche [he] hit al dihte þat on elche feinge is hem onsene. **13..** *E.E. Allit. P.* A. 1000 Iasper hyȝt þe fyrst gemme..He glente grene in þe lowest hemme. ?*a* **1400** *Morte Arth.* 1648 Hovande one þe hye waye by þe holte hemmes. **1607** SHAKS. *Timon* v. iv. 66 Timon is dead, Entomb'd vpon the very hemme o' th' Sea. **1674** N. FAIRFAX *Bulk & Selv.* 82 Imagine we now two Angels..over against each other, in the hem or rim of the world.

fig. **1649** G. DANIEL *Trinarch., Hen. IV*, ccclxxxvii, The Refractions of his Spirit Gild Only the Hemme of Life. **1878** BROWNING *La Saisiaz* 39 Knowledge stands on my experience: all outside its narrow hem, Free surmise may sport and welcome!

4. In technical uses: †**a.** A socket at the head of a still or the end of a length of pipe, etc., which serves to receive the end of a tube or pipe. *Obs.* **b.** The partition which divides the hearth from the fireplace in a reverberatory furnace; the firebridge. **c.** The outer edge of a millstone. **d.** *Archit.* See quot. 1823.

1559 MORWYNG *Evonym.* 53 A blynde limbek is that which hath no nose nor beake, nor limbe or hembe. **1693** G. POOLEY in *Phil. Trans.* XVII. 676 A Hearth..divided from the Oven it self by a Hem or Partition made open at the top. **1710** J. HARRIS *Lex. Techn.* s.v. *Hem*, The Ovens wherein..Calamine is baked, have..a Partition open at the Top, by which the Flame passes over, and so..bakes the Calamine. This partition is called the Hem. **1712** J. JAMES tr. *Le Blond's Gardening* 195 The Joint [of a pipe] which is made with a Hem, or Collar is secured with Mastick and Hemp. **1802** *Trans. Soc. Arts* XX. 275 Each millstone is..eleven inches thick in the hem, and thirteen at the eye. **1823** P. NICHOLSON *Pract. Build.* 586 *Hem*, the projecting and spiral parts of the Ionic capital.

5. *Comb.* **hem-line**, the outline of the hem, hence the height from the ground, of a woman's skirt.

1923 *T. Eaton & Co. Catal.* Spring & Summer 34 The modish uneven hemline. **1927** *Vanity Fair* Sept. 4/3 Liberty of opinion, in skirt lengths, hemlines, waistlines,..was convincingly demonstrated. **1929** *Daily Tel.* 16 Jan. 8/4 It is admitted that the hem lines of 1928 changed the whole contour of the evening mode as they flounced and floated in uneven length to the ground. **1957** *New Yorker* 30 Mar. 98/3 This year, she puts a minute and completely absurd circular godet, only three inches deep, at the hemline in front—to allow for striding, they say. **1958** *T.V. Times* 10 Oct. 21/2 Other girls put up their hem-lines a couple of inches as Paris dictates. **1971** R. GARRETT *Spiral* x. 94 She fidgeted with the hemline of her skirt.

hem (h(ə)m, hɛm), *int.* and *sb.*² Also 6–7 **hemme**, 8 **hemm**, 9 **h'm**. [A vocalized representation of the sound made in clearing the throat with a slight effort, consisting in a guttural or glottal aspiration followed by nasal murmur with the lips closed, more closely represented by *hm* or *h'm*. In spontaneous utterance, the actual sound is used; but, in reading, even the interjection is usually pronounced *hem*, as the sb. and vb. regularly are. See also AHEM, HUM.]

A. *int.* An interjectional utterance like a slight half cough, used to attract attention, give warning, or express doubt or hesitation. Also used to represent the slight clearing of the throat of a hesitating or non-plussed speaker.

1526 SKELTON *Magnyf.* 213 Hem, syr, yet beware of Had I wyste! *a* **1536** *Calisto & Melib.* Bj b, Now forward now mume now hem. **1550** CROWLEY *Epigr.* 260 When he mette his frendes, than woulde he saye but, hem. **1552** HULOET, *Hemme*, a note of blamynge, disdeynynge, marueylynge, shewynge, or of taciturnitye. **1600** SHAKS. *A.Y.L.* I. iii. 20 *Cel.* Hem them away. *Ros.* I would try if I could cry hem, and haue him. **1614** BEAUM. & FL. *Wit at Sev. Weap.* I. ii, *Oldc.* Sed quod est tibi nomen?..*Pris.* Hem, hem. *Witty.* He's dry; he hems; On quickly. **1763** C. JOHNSON *Reverie* II. 151 Hem! ahem! In the first place, said he, clearing his voice. **1855** DICKENS *Dorrit* I. viii, Gardens are—hem—are not accessible to me.

B. *sb.* The utterance of this sound; the sound itself as a fact.

1547 BOORDE *Brev. Health* lxxi. 20 After every sygh make an hem, or cough after it, and use myrth and mery company. **1658** SIR R. TEMPLE in *5th Rep. Hist. MSS. Comm.* 172/1 My friend heard them all give a general hemme after Goffe's speech in token of satisfaction. **1679** JONES in *Trials Green, etc. Murder Sir E. Godfrey* 10 Whenever a man should come before and make an hem, it should be a sign to Berry to open the Gate. **1712** ADDISON *Spect.* No. 269 ⁋3 My friend..is not a little pleased with any one who takes notice of the strength which he still exerts in his morning hemms. **1824** MISS FERRIER *Inher.* vii, Lord R.'s air, looks, manners, hems, all portented a story. **1848** C. BRONTË *J. Eyre* xviii, I heard a hem close at my elbow.

†**hem, 'em** (əm), *pers. pron.*, *3rd pl.*, *dat.-acc.* Forms: see below. [1. Originally OE. *him, hiom, heom*, dat. pl. in all genders of HE, = OFris. *him* (*hiam*), MDu. *hem, him, hom*, dat.; *hem, him*, acc. (Cf. Goth., OHG., OS. *im* in same sense.) 2. In 10th c. *him, heom* began in north midl. dial. to be substituted for the acc. pl. HI, *hia*, etc.; by 1150 the dative had quite supplanted the accusative in midl. dial., and was encroaching on it in south., and by 1350 *hem* had supplanted *hi* in south. also, the dative and accusative being thus identified under the form *hem*. (Cf. the history of HIM, ME.) 3. In 10th c. we see *þǽm* dat. pl. of the demonstrative THAT, THE, sometimes used in the north instead of *him, heom* (perhaps as more emphatic); by 1200 we find *þezzm, þeym* (from ON. *þeim* = OE. *þǽm, þám*) beside *hemm* in Ormin (north midl.); and *þaim, thaim*, was the regular northern ME. form. In 15th c. *theym* and *hem* are both used by Caxton, as more and less emphatic. After 1500 *them* is the standard form, *hem* (usually written *'em*) surviving only as a subordinate weak form, chiefly colloquial, in which capacity it is still used in the south (see 'EM). In the 13th c. *hem* was sometimes combined as *-m* with another pronoun, as *hem* = *he 'em, him* = *hi hem*; and in 14th c. was appended to vbs. as *sendem*, identical with modern *send 'em*. In some s.w. dialects, *them* has not yet displaced *hem, 'em*; but in the north no trace of *hem* has been left for 700 years. See also HEMEN.]

A. Forms.

α. 1 **him, hiom**, 1–4 **heom, hym**, 3–4 **him.** β. 2–5 **hom.** γ. 2–5 **ham**, (3–4 **ȝam**). δ. 2–7 **hem**, (3 *Orm.* **hemm**, 6–7 **'hem**). ε. 3–4 **huem.** ζ. 3–7 **am**, 3–5 **-em**, 7– **em, 'em** (**um**).

α. *c* **825** *Vesp. Psalter* cvi[i]. 5 Sawul heara in him asprong. *a* **900** *O.E. Chron.* an. 866 Hie him friþ namon [*Laud MS.* hi heom wið frið ȝenamon]. *c* **1000** *Psalms* (Cott.) l. 57 (Gr.) Þæt hio cerrende Criste herdon and hiom lif mid þe langsum begeton. *c* **1000** *Ags. Gosp.* Matt. xxii. 29 Ða andswarode se hælend hym [*Lindisf.* him, *Rushw.* to heom, *Hatt.* heom]. *c* **1000** *Nicodemus* xii, Ða com he to hym þær þær hiȝ heora ȝesomnunga hæfdon and cwæþ to hym. Hu come ȝe hyder? *a* **1050** *O.E. Chron.* (MS. C.) an. 1016 Hi gislas him betwynan sealdon [*Laud MS.* (1123) heom betweonan]. *Ibid.* an. 1020 Maneȝa bisceopas mid heom. *a* **1250** *Owl & Night.* 1517 Mid heom þu holdest, and heom biwerest. **1258** *Proclam. Hen. III*, Alle oþer þe moare dæl of heom. *c* **1330** R. BRUNNE *Chron. Wace* (Rolls) 1470 Coryneus..meintened hym [*v.r.* þam] in pes & were. *c* **1340** *Cursor M.* 2734 (Trin.) Abraham led him [*v.rr.* þam, þaim, ham] inwey. *Ibid.* 16810 (Laud) They comyn as he hym [*v.rr.* þam, þaim, hem] bad. *c* **1380** *Sir Ferumb.* 4995 Þus barouns by-gunne hym þanne to doute.

β. *c* **1175** *Lamb. Hom.* 77 Þet hwile ne studed hom nawiht. *c* **1205** LAY. 21177 Nu fusen we hom to [*c* **1275** to heom]. *c* **1440** in *Househ. Ord.* (1790) 425 Take raw ȝolkes of eyren and bete hom wel. ?*c* **1475** *Hunt. Hare* 82 Sum of hom had no taylys.

γ. *c* **1175** *Lamb. Hom.* 44 Ic ham ȝeue reste. *c* **1275** LAY. 1989 Neþ him he ȝam [*c* **1205** heom] lende. *c* **1315** SHOREHAM 135 Manye of ham. *c* **1380** *Sir Ferumb.* 2650 Somme of ȝam. *c* **1425** *Seven Sag.* (P.) 310 Saye that I ham gretyng sende.

δ. *a* **1131** *O.E. Chron.* an. 1123 Þa bed se cyng heom þæt hi scoldon cesen hem ærce biscop. *c* **1200** ORMIN 150 Itt turrneþþ hemm till sinne. *c* **1386** CHAUCER *Prol.* 379 A Cook they hadde with hem. *c* **1400** *Apol. Loll.* 11 If money or sum oþer þing be ȝeuen to hem. **1579** SPENSER *Sheph. Cal.* May 27 Tho to the greene Wood they speeden hem all. **1598** B. JONSON *Ev. Man. in Hum.* Prol., Except we make 'hem such. **1616–61** HOLYDAY *Persius* 323 To stuff Thy swelling cheeks, to break 'hem with a puff. **1661** MARVELL *Corr.* xxix. Wks. 1872–5 II. 70 The mayor and alderman or any six of hem.

ε. *c* **1300** *Prov. Hending* xxxv. in *Salomon & S., etc.* (1848) 279 Of þi soule huem ys eþe. *a* **1310** in Wright *Lyric P.* 106 Me knelede huem by-fore. *a* **1327** *Pol. Songs* (Camden) 237 The devel huem afretye! *a* **1400** *Geste K. Horn* 54 in Ritson *Metr. Rom.* (Mätz.), Huem wes ful wo.

ζ. *c* **1200** *Trin. Coll. Hom.* 57 Er þanne he hem forlete, and shewe em his prest. *c* **1275** LAY. 11549 [þe] king am [*c* **1205** heom] axede read. *c* **1340** *Cursor M.* 5758 (Fairf.), I am þine eldres god..For I am [*v.rr.* þam, þaim, hem] led. *c* **1380** *Sir Ferumb.* 3065 Þan þus doþþepers of fraunce torndem to þat ferde. *Ibid.* 3098 Þer na ascapedem non. *c* **1430** *Two Cookery-bks.* 20 Take Rys, and wasshem clene. **1605** CHAPMAN *All Fooles* Plays 1873 I. 136 Goe Dame, conduct-am in. **1685** in *Bagford Ball.* (1878) App., They having Money, she'd ease 'um. **1692** WASHINGTON *Milton's Def. Pop.* M's. Wks. 1738 I. 485 You have deserved well of 'em. **1711** J. GREENWOOD *Eng. Gram.* 67 *Q.* Have all Languages the Articles? *A.* No: For the Latin is without 'em. **1832** TENNYSON *Death of Old Year* ii, The New-year will take 'em away. **1863** BARNES *Dorset Dial.* 22 'Da seem to em, that we be under em.'

B. Signification.

1. *Dative.* (To) them. (Lat. *iis.* Ger. *ihnen.*)

a **855** *O.E. Chron.* an. 755 Þa cuædon hie þæt hem [*Laud MS.* heom] næniȝ mæȝ leofra nære þonne hiera hlaford. *a* **1154** *Ibid.* (Laud MS.) an. 1140 Æfre þe mare he iaf heom, þe wærse hi wæron him. *a* **1200** *Moral Ode* 388 Wel hem is. *c* **1340** *Cursor M.* 26 (Fairf.) Þe þinges þ at ham likes best. **1387** TREVISA *Higden* (Rolls) I. 235 Hem semede þat þe legges were to feble. *c* **1420** *Chron. Vilod.* 359 Forȝeeve hem þat gret mysdede. *Ibid.* 905 He forȝaff hit hom. **1460** CAPGRAVE *Chron.* 122 He acorded with them to pay hem ȝerely x thousand pound. **1599** [see 'EM].

b. Governed by *prep.* Them. (With many prepositions the dative is original, but in others it answers to an OE. accusative, as in 2, with which it is now classed as a simple objective.)

c **900** *Juliana* 81 in *Exeter Bk.*, Ic are æt him æfre finde. *a* **1175** *Cott. Hom.* 219 Þa be-com godes grama ofer ham alle. *c* **1200** *Trin. Coll. Hom.* 121 Mildheorte is ure louerd..toȝenes heom. *c* **1200** *Harrow. Hell* 132 Moni of hem. *c* **1340** *Cursor M.* 8118 (Trin.) He helde hem to hem for to kis. **1417** *E.E. Wills* (1882) 27 Atte þe value of xx. li. amonge hame. **1426** AUDELAY *Poems* 1 Fore hom that here serven the fynd. **1485** CAXTON *Paris & V.* 12 For eyther of hem mayntened. **1661** [see A. δ]. **1672–1750** [see 'EM].

2. *Accusative.* Them. (L. *eos, eas, ea*, Ger. *sie.*)

c **975** *Rushw. Gosp.* Matt. ii. 8 Sendende heom [*Ags. G.* hi, *Hatt.* hye] to bethlem. *Ibid.* xx. 32 And cliopade heom [*Lindisf.* ceiȝde hia; *Ags. G.* clypode hiȝ; *Hatt.* clypede hyo]. *a* **1131** *O.E. Chron.* an. 1124 And brohton hem to þone kinge. *c* **1175** *Lamb. Hom.* 17 Hit is riht þet me hem spille. *a* **1225** *Ancr. R.* 8 Eueriche mon ham mot nede holden. *c* **1340** *Cursor M.* 3968 (Fairf.) He dalt ham [*v.rr.* þam, þaim, hem] in twyn. *c* **1394** *P. Pl. Crede* 96 Let hem forþ pasen. *c* **1430** *Two Cookery-bks.* I. 37 Take Perys, & seþe ham, & Pike ham & stampe ham, & draw hem þorw a straynoure. **1477** *Paston Lett.* No. 807 III. 211 Ye chal not leke wel be them whan ye see hem. **1605** MARSTON, etc. *Eastw. Ho.* III. ii, They goe forth on holydayes and gather 'hem by the Sea-shore. **1702–1868** [see 'EM].

3. *Reflexive* and *Reciprocal Pron.* (*dat.* and *acc.*) Themselves, to themselves; (to) each other.

c **1000** *Ags. Gosp.* Mark i. 27 Hi betwux him cwædon [*c* **950** *Lindisf.* bituih him. *c* **1160** *Hatton* hyo be-tweoxe heom cwæðen]. *a* **1175** *Cott. Hom.* 225 Þa cweðen hi betwxe ham þat hi woldan. *c* **1200** ORMIN 13736 Þeȝȝ baþe hemm hidden. *c* **1380** WYCLIF *Sel. Wks.* III. 121 Men þat ben ypocritis hyen hom in holynes. *c* **1430** *Freemasonry* 7 A cownsel togeder they cowthe hem take. *c* **1450** *Merlin* 149 Yef thei sholde hem arme. **1579** [see A. δ].

Hence, †**hems** (i.e. *them's*: so MDu. *hems* = *hare, haer*) = their, their own. *Obs. rare.*

c **1410** LOVE *Bonavent. Mirr.* lviii. ff. 113 (Gibbs MS.) To putte awey fro here hertes alle manere..of mysbeleue to boþe hems [*v.rr.* thayre, theyrs] and oure grete profyte.

hem, *v.*¹ Also 5 **hemne**, 5–7 **hemme, hemm**, 7 **hemb.** [f. HEM *sb.*¹ Not known before 15th c. Sense 3 is usually taken to be the same word, though this is not certain. Quot. 1583 approaches the sense of Ger. *hemmen.*]

1. *trans.* To edge or border (a garment or cloth); to decorate with a border, fringe, or the like.

c **1440** *Promp. Parv.* 235/2 Hemmyn garmentys, *limbo, fimbrio.* **14..** *Voc.* in Wr.-Wülcker 599/25 *Orare*, to hemny. **1486** *Bk. St. Albans, Her.* Dj a, Here folowis an odir cros hemyt or borderit. *c* **1540** *Pilgr. T.* 175 in *Thynne's Animadv.* (1865) App. i. 82 With a blak fryng hemyd al about. **1548** UDALL *Erasm. Par. Luke* vi. (R.), Walkyng vp and downe in hys habite garded hemmed with hys brode phylacteries. **1590** SPENSER *F.Q.* II. iii. 26 All the skirt about Was hemd with golden fringe. **1666** J. DAVIES *Hist. Caribby Isles* 114 The ends of the sleeves..and the bottom of it are hemm'd in with a very thin black skin.

2. To turn in and sew down the edge of (a piece of stuff). *intr.* To do the particular kind of sewing which is used in this operation.

1530 PALSGR. 583/1, I hemme a shyrte or a smocke..Hemme my kercher, I praye you. **1758** JOHNSON *Idler* No. 15 ⁋2 She is..hemming a towel. **1775** —— in *Boswell* 14 Apr., A man would not submit to learn to hem a ruffle, of his wife, or his wife's maid. *a* **1845** HOOD *I'm not a single Man* iv, One used to stitch a collar then, Another hemmed a frill. **1875** *Plain Needlework* 13 These pieces should be hemmed on each side, thus making twelve yards of hemming.

intr. **1867** TROLLOPE *Chron. Barset* I. xxiii. 194 [She] sat ..hemming diligently at certain articles of clothing.

fig. **1663** J. SPENCER *Prodigies* (1665) 202 The contexture of this Discourse will..be the less subject to ravel out, if I hem it with the Speech of our learned..Annotator.

3. To confine or bound by an environment of any kind; to enclose, shut in, limit, restrain, imprison. Now rarely without advb. extension, most usually *in*, also *about, round, up*; *hem out*, to shut out.

1538 LELAND *Itin.* III. 23 A Creeke of Salt Water..hemmith in a peace of Mr. Reskymer's Parke. **1580** SIDNEY *Ps.* v. v, Thy work it is such men safe in to hemm With kindest care. **1583** STANYHURST *Æneis*, etc. (Arb.) 135 The northern frostye gale hemd the riuer. **1594** MARLOWE & NASHE *Dido* II. i, His band of Myrmidons..which hemm'd me about. **1640** G. SANDYS *Christ's Pass.* III. 259 Late hemb'd with Auditors whose store Incumbred the too-narrow Shore. **1667** MILTON *P.L.* IV. 979 Th' Angelic Squadron..began to hemm him round With ported Spears. **1697** DRYDEN *Æneid* IV. 55 On ev'ry side..hemm'd with warlike Foes. **1788** COWPER *Corr.* (1824) II. 150 You will find it pleasant..at least not to be hemmed around by business. **1840** DICKENS *Barn. Rudge* lxii, The angle of the wall into which I had hemmed him back. **1876** R. F. BURTON *Gorilla L.* I. 166 The tall black trees which hem in the

village. **1878** Bosw. Smith *Carthage* 133 The Carthaginians were..hemmed up in the north-western corner of the island.

hem, *v.*² [f. HEM *int.*]

1. *intr.* To utter the sound described under HEM *int.*; to give a short sharp cough as a signal, etc.; to clear the throat; to stammer or hesitate in speech; to express disapproval of a speaker by factitious coughing.

1470–85 [see HEMMING *vbl. sb.*²]. **1530** Palsgr. 583/1, I hemme, I coughe, *je tousse*. Whan you here me hemme, than come. **1553** T. Wilson *Rhet.* 62 Hackyng and hemmyng as though our wittes and our senses were a woll gatheryng. **1602** Shaks. *Ham.* iv. v. 5 She speaks much of her father..and hems and beats her heart. *a* **1612** Harington *Epigr.* ii. xxv. (R.), His tongue so vainly did and idly chatter, The people nought but hem, and cough, and spatter. **1679** *Trials Green, etc. Murder Sir E. Godfrey* 19 Some body hem'd, and that was the Sign. **1710** Addison *Tatler* No. 155 ¶2, I heard some body at a Distance hemming after me. **1748** Richardson *Clarissa* (1811) I. 103, I arose; the man hemming up for a speech, rising, and beginning to set his splay feet..in an approaching posture. **1848** C. Bronte *J. Eyre* xx, Jane, if any one is about, come to the foot of the stairs and hem.

b. In combination, as ***hem and hawk***, ***hem and haw***, ***hem and ha***. Cf. *hum and haw*, HUM *v.*

1580 Babington *Exp. Lord's Prayer* (1596) 61 Wee gape and we yawne, we hem and we hawke. **1604** [see HA *v.*]. **1786** Mad. D'Arblay *Lett.* 16 Oct., I hemmed and hawed—but the Queen stopped reading. **1833** Marryat *P. Simple* lxi, You would have done better, to have hemmed or hawed, so as to let your officers know that you were present. **1855** Thackeray *Newcomes* II. 285 The old Colonel..hems and hahs, and repeats himself a good deal.

†**2.** *trans.* To utter or read *out* or *over* with frequent hems or coughs. *Obs.* ***hem in***: to throw in or interject with a hem. *Obs.*

1553 T. Wilson *Rhet.* 117b, Some coughes at euery woorde. Some hemmes it out. **1567** R. Edwards *Damon & Pythias* in Hazl. *Dodsley* IV. 69 Then follow me, and hem in a word now and then. *a* **1693** Urquhart *Rabelais* iii. xv. 128 Their Matines were hem'd over only with three Lessons.

3. To remove, clear *away* with a hem or cough. Also *fig.*

1600 Shaks. *A.Y.L.* i. iii. 19 *Ros.* These burs are in my heart. *Cel.* Hem them away. **1800** Mrs. Hervey *Mourtray Fam.* III. 201 Emma..tried in vain to hem away a rising sigh.

Hence **'hemming** *ppl. a.*

1606 *Choice, Chance*, etc. in *Brit. Bibl.* (1812) II. 559 *note*, Made him with a hemming sigh, ilfauouredly sing the ballad.

hem, obs. by-form of HOME; var. HIM *pron.*

hem, Sc. var. HAME².

1808–18 Jamieson, *Hem*, a horse-collar. **1847–8** H. Miller *First Impr.* v. 73 Not a piece of hem-mounting or trace-chain, not a cart-axle or wheel-rim, was secure.

hema-, hemato-, variant spelling of HÆMA-, HÆMATO-, q.v.: common in U.S., less frequent in Great Britain, exc. in the commercial spelling of *hematite* (see HÆMATITE).

he-man: see HE *pers. pron.* 8 d.

hemantick, -ik, obs. forms of HEEMANTIC.

hematist, obs. var. of AMETHYST.

1638 Sir T. Herbert *Trav.* (ed. 2) 108 Calcedons, Hematists, Pearl.

hemble: see HEMEL.

†**heme**, *sb. Obs. rare.* [perh. a deriv. of OE. *hám* HOME; cf. next.] ? A man; ? a householder.

a **1250** *Owl & Night.* 1115 For children gromes heme and hine Hi þencheþ alle of þire pine. *a* **1327** *Pol. Songs* (Camden) 156 An heme in an herygoud with honginde sleven.

†**heme**, *a. Obs. rare.* [? f. *hám* HOME.] ? Fitting, suitable, agreeable.

a **1310** in Wright *Lyric P.* viii. 32 In rude were roo with hem roune, That he mihte henten ase him were heme.

So **'hemely** *adv.*, ? fittingly, fitly.

13.. *Gaw. & Gr. Knt.* 1852 While he hit hade hemely halched aboute.

heme, var. HÆM.

hemel, hemmel ('hɛm(ə)l). *north. dial.* Also **hammel**, 8–9 **hemble**. [Etymol. uncertain: possibly a dim. formation from root of HAM *sb.*² (Cf. also HELM *sb.*¹ 7.)] A cow-shed; a close for cattle, partly covered.

1717 in *N. Riding Rec.* VII. 284 A messuage or dwelling house with a stable, a barn, a hemble or cowhouse, on the backside of the said messuage. **1806** R. Kerr *Agric. Surv. Berwick* 503 (Jam.) Sheds are named hemmels. **1812** J. Sinclair *Syst. Husb. Scot.* i. 21 Small open sheds, or what, in Berwickshire, are called *Hammels* or *Hemmels*, with separate straw-yards attached. **1825** Brockett, *Hemmel*, a shed or covering for cattle. **1850** *Jrnl. R. Agric. Soc.* XI. i. 30 Cattle hemels..are highly favourable to health. **1851** H. Stephens *Bk. Farm* (1855) I. 242 The hammels [are occupied] by the two-year-olds, or such as are fattening for the butcher. **1893** W. Fream *Youatt's Compl. Grazier* (ed. 13) 171 The litter used in hammels is..less by one-third than that required for stall-feeding.

hemelytrum: see HEMIELYTRUM.

†**hemen, hymen, -yn**, *pron. Obs.* exc. *dial.* [A form of the 3rd person pronoun dative-accusative plural, found in s.w. before 1400 (many instances in *Sir Ferumbras*). It appears to have been formed from the dat.-acc. pl. HEM, *hym* (perh. for its clearer differentiation from 3 sing. masc. *him, hym*), by addition of the southern pl. ending *-en* (*-yn*); cf. the double plurals *childr-en, brethr-en, ky-en, kyne*, also of southern origin; and the analogous mod.Ger. dat. pl. *ihn-en*, from MHG. *în*, OHG. *im, in*, differentiated from the acc. sing. *ihn* by the same suffix. Already in 14th c. the metre shows that it was often reduced in pronunciation and combination to *'men, 'myn*, which, with the spelling *min, mun*, is still characteristic of Devonshire dialect.] = THEM.

1. *Dative.* To them.

c **1380** *Sir Ferumb.* 1395 Ryche garnymentz forþ sche drow, & by-tok hymen [= 'men] for to were. *Ibid.* 1963 So þow schalt hemen alle schewe, þat þay buþ al mys-went.

b. after preposition. Them.

c **1380** *Sir Ferumb.* 1567 A cryede to hymen wel an heȝ, & þus he hymen grette. *Ibid.* 1672 Euerech of hymen þan tok an hed. *Ibid.* 1749 With hymen schalt þou al þyng fynde þat þov hast to ous y-said. **1866** 'N. Hogg' *Poems* Ser. ii. 6 An zlayp'd way bothe aw-min under tha close.

2. *Accusative.* Them.

c **1380** *Sir Ferumb.* 3542 To holde hymen [= 'men] þo with-inne. *Ibid.* 4239 þan clepede he hemen þat were most worthyest. *Ibid.* 4261 Ylefte hymen murye, & in god aray. **1746** *Exmoor Scolding* 270 (E.D.S.) If e'er tha comst to Hewn only to zey men. *Ibid.* 419 Twonty Nobles a Year and a Puss to put min in. **1866** 'N. Hogg' *Poems* Ser. ii. 3 Ma spurrit..Zeth 'Doant put min inta rime.' *Ibid.* 6 Hur'd car'd min upstairs.

3. *refl.* Themselves, to themselves.

c **1380** *Sir Ferumb.* 2476 þe amerel & is host..armede hymen ecchon. *Ibid.* 3022 Ac hymen duste doun on þe fon.

‖**hemera**¹. *Obs.* Pl. **-æ**; in 6 *erron.* **hæmerae**, 7 **hæmere**. = EPHEMERA 1 (q.v.).

c **1590** Greene *Fr. Bacon* x. 124 The flies haemerae..take life with the sun and die with the dew. **1614** *Scou. Venus* (1876) 21 As the flies Hæmere we do see To leaue their breath their life being scarce begunne.

hemera² ('hɛmərə). *Palæont.* and *Geol.* Pl. **-æ**. [mod.L., f. Gr. ἡμέρα day.] A period of geological time in which any particular species was most abundant as represented in strata; an interval between times when two successive species were dominant. Hence **'hemeral** *a.*

1893 S. S. Buckman in *Q. Jrnl. Geol. Soc.* XLIX. 481 For a palaeontological purpose... I propose the term 'hemera'... I wish to use it as the chronological indicator of the faunal sequence. **1898** —— *Ibid.* LIV. 443 The hemeral names are taken from the names of ammonites. *Ibid.*, The shortest geological time-division is a hemera: that is, the time during which a particular species..had dominant existence. *Ibid.* 448 The genera *Dactylioceras* and its allies..almost disappear with the close of the hemera *bifrontis*. **1902** —— in *Geol. Mag.* Dec. 555 A 'hemera' was designed to mark the time from..when one species or set of species becomes dominant to the time when another..does so. **1920** *Q. Jrnl. Geol. Soc.* LXXVI. 63 The range of strata which Mr. Richardson has divided into seven or at the most eight hemeræ cover, according to my more detailed subdivisions, thirty-two hemeræ, and should afford a good test as to whether this more detailed method of dating makes for greater precision. **1933** W. J. Arkell *Jurassic Syst. Gt. Brit.* i. 20 Nine years later, finding that there were still some who considered that a hemera was simply a subdivision of a zone, Buckman published a fresh explanation. *Ibid.* 27 In the course of an argument with Buckman over his insertion of an excessive number of hemeræ into the time-table of the Corallian rocks, I attempted to justify my view..that many of his hemeral indices lived side by side on the same sea-bed. **1966** D. T. Donovan *Stratigr.* vii. 160 Several other time terms have been proposed but have never achieved general recognition. Perhaps the most notorious is the *hemera*. *Ibid.* 161 Hemerae were much used by English Jurassic workers for about forty years, but hardly at all by anyone else.

hemeragie, obs. form of HÆMORRHAGY.

‖**hemeralopia** (ˌhɛmərə'ləʊpɪə). *Path.* [mod.L., a. Gr. type *ἡμεραλωπία, f. ἡμεράλωψ, f. ἡμέρ-α day + ἀλα-ός blind + ὤψ eye: cf. NYCTALOPIA. (In mod.F. *héméralopie*.) The Gr. ἡμεράλωψ appears in Galen as the contrary of νυκτάλωψ, i.e. ὁ τῆς νυκτὸς ἀλαός that is blind by night.]

'Day-blindness'; a visual defect in which the eyes see indistinctly, or not at all, by daylight, but tolerably well by night or artificial light. (But used by many in the sense of 'night-blindness', NYCTALOPIA.)

'Day-blindness' is the etymological meaning of the word, and the sense in which ἡμεράλωψ, as the contrary of νυκτάλωψ, was used by Galen. But, as NYCTALOPIA was, from an early date, taken by some in the opposite sense, these also reversed the etymological sense of *hemeralopia*, and used it as = 'night-blindness', 'day-sight', as if the word were *hemeropia*. 'With the exception of Copland and Henry Power, all or most modern authors..have used the term in the sense of *night-blindness*. The Royal College of Physicians of London have reverted to the true meaning of the word in their "Nomenclature of Diseases"' (*Syd. Soc. Lex.*). But the *Medical Dictionary* of F. P. Foster, New York, 1891, continues the non-etymological sense of 'day-vision, night-blindness'. The word was rightly used by Paré in 16th c.: *Œuvres* xv. 3 (Littré) Le contraire est quand on voit mieux de nuit que de jour, et se peut dire hemeralopia en grec, œil de chat en francois.

1706 Phillips (ed. Kersey), *Hemeralopia*, a Faculty when one sees clearer in the Night than in the Day. **1814** R. W. Bampfield in *Med. Chirurg. Trans.* V. 32 (*title*) A Practical Essay on Hemeralopia, or Night Blindness, commonly called Nyctalopia. **1822–34** *Good's Study Med.* (ed. 4) III. 144 The confusion which has taken place among earlier writers in distinguishing the disease by two directly opposite terms, nyctalopia and hemeralopia. *Ibid.* 145 It [hemeralopia] is the *luscitas* of Beer; the day-blindness of various other writers. **1858** Copland *Dict. Pract. Med.* II. 896 One terming night-blindness nyctalopia, and another hemeralopia, while day-blindness has been equally designated by both terms. **1878** tr. *Ziemssen's Cycl. Med.* XVII. 205 Hemeralopia and scurvy have been very frequently found existing in the same person.

Hence **hemera'lopic** *a.*, affected with or subject to hemeralopia.

1878 tr. *Ziemssen's Cycl. Med.* XVII. 205 Usually the scurvy is developed first, the patients subsequently becoming hemeralopic. **1880** *Libr. Univ. Knowl.* (N.Y.) X. 757 [He] was the first of the family known to be hemeralopic; his children..were all affected with night-blindness.

hemerine ('hɛməraɪn), *a. Med.* [ad. Gr. ἡμεριν-ός, f. ἡμέρα day.] Of or belonging to a day; daily; applied to a fever = quotidian.

1854 in Mayne *Expos. Lex.* **1886** in *Syd. Soc. Lex.*

Hemerobaptist (ˌhɛmərəʊ'bæptɪst). *Eccl.* [ad. eccl. L. *Hēmerobaptista*, pl. *-æ*, a. Gr. ἡμεροβαπτισταί (Eusebius), f. ἡμέρα day + βαπτιστής BAPTIST.]

A Jewish sect which practised daily baptism as a spiritual means of cleansing from sin; also an early obscure Christian sect who followed the same practice. Also *attrib.*

1577 Hanmer *Anc. Eccl. Hist.* (1585) 556 The Hemerobaptists were Iewes in all points. **1580** Fulke *Retent.*, etc. 314 A great number of the old heresies, in which the papists consent with the ancient hereticks; the Valentinians, in their cross;..the hemerobaptists, in their holy water. **1600** O. E. *Reply to Libel* ii. iii. 46 The Hemerobaptistes for these continual washings..are by Epiphanius numbred in the catalogue of Jewish heretickes. **1727–51** Chambers *Cycl.* s.v. **1895** *Bible Soc. Rec.* (N.Y.) Nov. 167/1 The interesting little community of the Sabeans, the descendants of the Hemero-baptists of the first centuries. **1897** *Expositor* Aug. 145 The spread of Hemerobaptist principles had developed widely after the destruction of the temple and the Jewish polity.

So **Hemero'baptism**, †**Hemerobapti'zation**, the practice of daily baptism.

1653 R. Bailie *Disswas. Vind.* (1655) 81 This..was enough for any Hemerobaptization, and more. **1897** *Expositor* Aug. 147 There appear to be no clear intimations of Hemerobaptism in the Ignatian epistles.

hemerobian (hɛmə'rəʊbɪən), *a.* and *sb. Zool.* [f. mod.L. *Hemerobi-us*, a genus of neuropterous insects, a. Gr. ἡμερόβιος, f. ἡμέρα day + -βιος living.]

A. *adj.* Pertaining to the genus *Hemerobius* or the family *Hemerobiidæ* of neuropterous insects. **B.** *sb.* An insect of this genus or family; a day-fly.

1842 Brande *Dict. Sci.*, etc., *Hemerobians*.

‖**hemero'callis.** [mod.L., ad. L. *hemerocalles*, Gr. ἡμεροκαλλές a kind of lily, f. Gr. ἡμέρα day + κάλλος beauty, adopted by Linnæus in his *Hortus Cliffortianus* (1737) 128 as the name of a genus.]

A herbaceous perennial plant of the genus so called, belonging to the family Liliaceæ, mostly native to temperate, eastern Asia, and bearing corymbs of yellow or orange, trumpet-shaped, short-lived flowers; a DAY-LILY.

a **1656** Bp. Hall *Wks.* (1837–9) VIII. 183 (D.) The hemerocallis is the least esteemed, because one day ends its beauty. **1664** Evelyn *Kal. Hort.* (1729) 205 May..Flowers in Prime..yellow Hemerocallis, striped Jacinth, early Bulbous Iris. **1900** L. H. Bailey *Cycl. Amer. Hort.* II. 728/1 The flowers of Funkia are borne in racemes; of Hemerocallis in corymb-like panicles. **1938** F. Perry *Water Gardening* xvi. 271 Hemerocallis have some economic qualities, for in the Orient the flower petals are gathered. **1970** *Observer* 23 Aug. 25/4 In the Orient hemerocallis flowers are often used for food.

†**hemerology** (hɛmə'rɒlədʒɪ). *Obs. rare*$^{-0}$. [ad. L. *hēmerologium*, a. Gr. ἡμερολόγιον, f. ἡμέρα day + λόγος account.] (See quots.)

1656 Blount *Glossogr.*, *Hemerologe* (*hemerologium*), a Kalendar or Register declaring what is done every day, a Day-book. **1658** Phillips, *Hemerology*, a Calender, or Book wherein are registered the passages of every day.

hem-fell, *v.* = FELL *v.* 6.

1880 *Plain Hints* 20 Two hems crossing each other (which is the case if gathers are hemmed in and hem-felled), must result in a twisted appearance of the belt.

hemi- ('hɛmɪ-, 'hiːmɪ-), *prefix.* [a. Gr. ἡμι-, combining element, from earlier *σᾱμι- = L. *sēmi-*, Skr. *sāmi-*, OTeut. *sâmi-*, OE. *sam-*, all meaning 'half-'. Several Gr. words containing this element were in use as technical terms in later L., e.g. *hēmicyclium, hēmīna, hēmisphærium, hēmistichium*. In the modern

langs. they are very numerous, not only in terms adopted or adapted from Gr. (directly or through L.), but in new formations, scientific or technical, from Greek, or on Greek analogies. Words formed from Latin have the corresponding prefix SEMI-; but there are instances of hybridism in the use of both prefixes.]

a. Half-; one half, the half, pertaining to or affecting one half; *esp.* in *Anat.*, *Biol.*, and *Path.* Pertaining to one of the two halves (right and left) of the body, or of any of its symmetrical organs.

b. In *Crystallography*, denoting that a crystal has only half the number of faces which belong to the corresponding holohedral or perfect form; hemisymmetrical; as ***hemi forms, hemi-icositetrahedron, -octahedron*** (hence ***-octahedral*** adj.), ***-scalenohedron, -trisoctahedron,*** HEMIHEDRON, etc. (See also HEMIDOME, -PRISM, -PYRAMID.)

c. In *Chemistry*, formerly applied to binary compounds in which the combining proportion of the electro-negative or chlorous radical, was supposed to be one half that of the electro-positive or basylous radical, as in 'hemichloride of copper', Cu_2Cl (now Cu″Cl or Cu_2Cl_2, cuprous chloride), 'hemioxide of copper', Cu_4O (now Cu_2O, cuprous oxide). These were called ***hemi-compounds.*** So ***hemi-hydrate,*** a compound of one molecule of hydroxyl (HO) with two molecules of an element or radical. Now frequently used to form the name of a derivative body, in which some constituent is present in half the proportion, or in a smaller proportion, than in other members of the group, as in ***hemibromhydrin,*** $2C_3H_8O_3 + HBr - 4H_2O$ (compared with *monobromhydrin*, $C_3H_8O_3 + HBr - H_2O$), or which forms one of the two substances into which a body may be split up, as in *hemialbumin, hemicollin.*

The following are compounds of *hemi-* in less general use; words of greater importance follow in their alphabetic places.

‖**hemia'blepsia** *Path.* [see ABLEPSY] = HEMIANOPSIA. **hemi-'acetal** *Chem.*, any of a class of compounds having the general formula R·CH(OH)(OR′), differing from an acetal in having an -OH group in place of one of the -OR groups. **hemial'bumin** *Chem.*, a substance thought to be one of the two original constituents of ordinary albumin; it is converted on digestion into **hemi'albumose**, which is probably an antecedent of *hemipeptone.* ‖**hemi'algia** *Path.*, unilateral pain. **hemi'amb, -iambus** *Pros.*, an iambic dimeter catalectic. ˌ**hemiambly'opia** *Ophthalm.*, amblyopia of half of the field of vision; hence ˌ**hemiambly'opic**, one suffering from hemiamblyopia. ‖**hemianæs'thesia** *Path.* [ANÆSTHESIA], loss of sensation in one side of the body; hence **hemianæs'thesic** *a.* ‖**hemianal'gesia** *Path.* [ANALGESIA], insensibility to pain on one side of the body (*Quain's Dict. Med.*, 1883). **hemia'natropous** *a. Bot.* [ANATROPOUS], half-anatropous; = HEMITROPOUS. ˌ**hemiangio'carpic, -'carpous** *adjs.*, designating a fungus in which the hymenium is enclosed during the early part of its development; characteristic of such a fungus. **hemia'taxy** *Path.* [ATAXY 2], ataxy of a limb on one side of the body. **hemi'atrophy** *Path.* [ATROPHY], atrophy of one side of the body or an organ. **hemi'catalepsy** *Path.*, catalepsy affecting one side of the body. **hemi'central** *a. Anat.*, of or pertaining to the *hemicentrum*, one of the pair of lateral elements which compose the *centrum* of a vertebra. **hemice'phalic** *a. Anat.*, of or pertaining to the *hemicephalum* or sinciput (Mayne *Expos. Lex.* 1854). **hemi'cerebral** *a. Anat.*, of or pertaining to a *hemicerebrum*, i.e. either of the two CEREBRAL hemispheres. **hemi'chordate** *a. Biol.*, partly or imperfectly chordate, as the anomalous genus *Balanoglossus*; *sb.*, a hemichordate animal. ‖**hemicho'rea** *Path.*, chorea affecting one side of the body. ˌ**hemico'lectomy** *Surg.*, excision of part of the colon, *esp.* of the right or left half. **hemi'collin** *Chem.* [COLLIN], a peptone-like body formed along with semiglutin, when a solution of gelatin is boiled for a long time. **hemi'crystalline** *a.*, half or incompletely crystalline. **'hemiˌdemi'semiˌquaver** *Mus.*, a note of half the length of a demisemiquaver, also the symbol for this note, resembling a quaver, but with four hooks. **hemidia'pente** *Anc. Mus.* [DIAPENTE], a diminished or imperfect fifth. **hemi'ditone** *Anc. Mus.* [DITONE], a minor third. **'hemidrachm** ('hɛmɪdræm) [ἡμίδραχμον], an ancient Greek coin, a half-drachma. **hemi-e'lliptic, -ical** *adjs.*, half-elliptic; 'applied to the recess of the vestibule of the external ear'. **hemi-ence'phalic** *a. Anat.*, of or pertaining to a ***hemiencephalon,*** or lateral half of the ENCEPHALON or brain. **hemi-'epilepsy** *Path.*, an epilepsy producing convulsions on one side of the body only. **hemi'facial** *a. Anat.*, of or pertaining to one side of the face. **he'migamous** *a. Bot.* [γάμος marriage], said of grasses, having one of the two florets of a spicule neuter, and the other unisexual. **hemige'ometer** *Entom.*, a caterpillar of the *Noctuidæ*, which in its mode of progression resembles the true geometer caterpillars. **hemiglyph** ('hɛmɪglɪf) *Arch.*, the half-glyph or -groove at the edge of the triglyph in the Doric entablature. **hemi'gnathous** *a. Ornith.* [γνάθος jaw], having one mandible much shorter than the other, as in the genus *Hemignathus* of sun-birds. **hemiholo'hedral** *a. Cryst.*, having half the number of planes in all the octants; sometimes said of the parallel hemihedral forms of the isometric system. **hemihydrate** *Chem.*: see c above. **hemihy'pertrophy**, unilateral or partial hypertrophy. **hemi'karyon** *Cytol.* [a. G. *hemikaryon* (T. Boveri 1905, in *Jenaische Zeitschr. f. Naturwiss.* XXXIX. 447), f. Gr. κάρυον: see KARYO-] (see quot.); so ˌ**hemikary'otic** *a.* **hemi'ligulate** *a. Bot.*, half-ligulate: said of the irregular corolla of a composite flower, when it has only one lip of the limb. **hemi'mellit(h)ene, -ine** *Chem.* = *trimethylbenzine.* **hemime'llitic** *Chem.*, a crystalline tri-basic acid $C_9H_6O_6$: see c above, and MELLITIC. **hemi'obol(e), -o'bolion** *Numism.* [ἡμιωβόλιον], an ancient Greek coin, half an obol. **hemiocta'hedron** *Cryst.*, a tetrahedron considered as to its relation to the octahedron: see b above; hence **hemiocta'hedral** *a.* **hemio'logamous** *Bot.*: see quot. **'hemione** *Zool.* [ad. L. *hemionus*, Gr. ἡμίονος, f. ὄνος ass], the dziggetai. **hemi'orthotype** *a. Cryst.* [ORTHOTYPE] = monoclinic. **hemi'palmate** *a. Biol.* [PALMATE], half- or partially webbed, semipalmate (Mayne, 1854). ‖**hemipara'plegia** *Path.* [παραπληγία stroke on one side], paralysis of one lower limb. **hemi'parasite** *Bot.* [G. (F. Johow 1890, in *Verhandl. Deutsch. Wissensch. Ver. Santiago* II. II. 67)], a facultative parasite, e.g. certain fungi; also a plant which is partially parasitic, drawing water and mineral nutrients but not synthesized foods from its host, e.g. certain higher plants, as the mistletoe; hence ˌ**hemipara'sitic** *a.* ‖**hemipa'resis** *Path.* [πάρεσις slackening], paresis or impairment of muscular strength affecting one side of the body; hence **hemipa'retic** *a.* **hemi'penis** *Zool.*, one of the paired eversible copulatory organs in snakes and lizards. **hemi'peptone** *Chem.*, a variety of peptone derived from hemialbumose by a continuance of the digestive process: see *hemialbumin.* **hemi'petalous** *a. Bot.*, applied to a state intermediate between monopetalous and polypetalous, in which the petals have partly coalesced. **'hemiphrase** *Mus.*, a half-phrase, usually occupying only one measure. **hemi'pinic** *a. Chem.*, in *h. acid*, a dibasic crystalline acid, $C_{10}H_{10}O_6$, formed by the decomposition of Opianic acid, $2C_{10}H_{10}O_5$. **hemi'pinnate** *a. Bot.*, half or partly pinnate. **'hemiplane** *Geom.*, half a plane. **hemi'protein** *Chem.*: see quot. 1878 under *hemialbumin.* **hemi'rhamphine** *a. Ichth.*, (a fish) having the upper jaw very short in comparison with the lower, as in the genus *Hemirhamphus*, or half-bills. **hemi'saprophyte** *Bot.* [ad. G. *hemisaprophyt* (F. Johow 1889, in *Jahrb. f. wissensch. Bot.* XX. 479)], a facultative saprophyte, being alternatively either parasitic or autotrophic; hence ˌ**hemisapro'phytic** *a.* **hemi'septal** *a. Anat.*, of or pertaining to a *hemiseptum*, or lateral half of a septum or partition, as those in the heart and brain. **'hemisome** *Biol.* [σῶμα body], one half of the body of an animal. **'hemispasm** *Path.*, a spasm affecting one side only of the body. **he'mitrichous** *a. Bot.* [τριχ- hair], half clothed with hairs (*Treas. Bot.* 1866). **hemi'triglyph** *Arch.*, a half triglyph (Gwilt *Arch.*). **'hemitype**, a half-type, that which is hemitypic. **hemi'typic** *a. Zool.*, partially typical of a given group, of an intermediate type.

1893 *Jrnl. Chem. Soc.* LXIV. I. 563 (*heading*) *Hemi-acetals derived from substituted chloranils. **1964** N. G. CLARK *Mod. Org. Chem.* xiv. 273 Hemi-acetals are generally unstable intermediates in the formation of true acetals. **1876** tr. *P. Schützenberger's Ferment.* 145 The hemiproteïdin or *hemialbumin formed by the action of boiling dilute sulphuric acid on albumin. **1878** KINGZETT *Anim. Chem.* 365 When albumin is boiled with dilute sulphuric acid for a few hours it gives two kinds of syntonin, one of which he names hemiprotein..the other he terms hemialbumin. **1883** FOSTER *Phys.* App. (ed. 4) 719 The *hemialbumose..was.. isolated by Meissner; it is apparently the body called by him A-peptone. **1844** BECK & FELTON tr. *Munk's Metres* 272 Many Anacreontic poems which are written in *hemiambs. **1890** W. JAMES *Princ. Psychol.* I. ii. 44 According to Loeb, the defect is a dimness of vision ('*hemiamblyopia') in which (however severe) the centres remain the best seeing portions of the retina. **1947** F. B. WALSH *Clin. Neuro-Ophthalm.* i. 56/1 Along with hemiamblyopia, hemiachromatopsia is evidence for early and partial involvement of the primary visual pathways. **1960** H.-L. TEUBER et al. *Visual Field Defects* vi. 64 (*caption*) The hemiamblyopia was more disturbing to this patient than an outright hemianopia. **1933** *Mind* XLII. 386 In *hemiamblyopics there is a tendency for a displacement, towards the sound side, of stimuli falling on the amblyopic area. **1878** A. HAMILTON *Nerv. Dis.* 100 *Hemianæsthesia is quite marked. **1880** BASTIAN *Brain* xxv. 547 In many cases of Hemi-anæsthesia, the viscera remain at least as tender as ever under firm pressure. **1857** HENFREY *Bot.* I. ii. 130 Another condition is..the *amphitropous* or *heterotropous*, or **hemianatropous*, intermediate between orthotropous and anatropous. **1866** *Treas. Bot.* 579/2 *Hemianatropous*, an ovule which is anatropal, with half the raphe free. **1902** *Encycl. Brit.* XXVIII. 558/2 Gymnocarpic and *Hemiangiocarpic:—*Hymenomycetes.* **1900** B. D. JACKSON *Gloss. Bot. Terms*, **Hemiangiocarpous*, when the hymenium of some Fungi is for some time covered with a membrane, the gonidiophore is so termed. **1902** *Encycl. Brit.* XXVIII. 561/1 The Discomycetes and their immediate allies are termed Hemiangiocarpous, because however much their fructifications are closed at first, they ultimately open and expose the layers of asci. **1928** C. W. DODGE tr. *Gäumann's Compar. Morphol. Fungi* xxv. 410 In the second, or hemiangiocarpous, stage..the sporiferous tissue is differentiated from the tissue in the interior of the fundaments. **1967** M. E. HALE *Biol. Lichens* ii. 32 Henssen has recently traced consistent hemiangiocarpous development in a group of genera. **1886** W. R. GOWERS *Man. Dis. Nerv. Syst.* I. 299 *Hemiatrophy of the Tongue. **1885** *Athenæum* 28 Nov. 704/2 A species of Balanoglossus obtained..at Herm, Channel Islands, being the first recorded instance of the occurrence of this *hemichordate in any part of the British seas. **1926** R. J. E. SCOTT *Gould's Med. Dict.* 596/1 *Hemicolectomy. **1963** *Lancet* 19 Jan. 133/1 A man, aged 53, had had right hemicolectomy performed eight months previously on account of carcinoma of the cæcum. **1881** PRITCHARD tr. *Eder's Emuls. Photogr.* 44 Semi-glutin, by standing, reduces silver nitrate without precipitating it, while *hemi-colline causes a flaky precipitate of the same. **1863** WATTS *Dict. Chem.* I. 669 **Hemi-Compounds* ..are often called *di-compounds.* **1894** *Athenæum* 19 Sept. 391/1 He..describes the principal igneous rocks in groups under the three heads, Holocrystalline, *Hemicrystalline, and Highly Glassy Rocks. **1853** SHELTON *Rector St. Bardolph's* ii. 22 Many a *hemi-demi-semi-quaver. **1959** D. COOKE *Lang. Mus.* iii. 133 A bass of rushing hemi-demi-semi-quavers. **1823** CRABB *Technol. Dict.*, **Hemidiapente*, an imperfect fifth. **1774** BURNEY *Hist. Mus.* I. 30 (Jod.) The chromatick proceeded by two successive semitones and a *hemiditone, or minor third. **1841** H. H. WILSON *Ariana Antiqua* 268 *Hemidrachm. Head of king, with fillet, to the right. **1836–9** TODD *Cycl. Anat.* II. 530 The hemispherical and *hemi-elliptical depressions are separated by a ridge or pyramidal eminence. **1837** *Penny Cycl.* VIII. 200/1 Let us suppose two diagonal lines to be drawn through opposite angles, and crossing each other on the faces of the Cube. It may be observed..that the solid angles at the extremities of all these diagonals are truncated to produce the octahedron; but it sometimes happens that the solid angles at the extremities of only one of those diagonals on one plane, and a transverse diagonal on a parallel plane, are truncated, producing a four instead of an eight-sided secondary figure; these are termed **hemi* forms, from their presenting only half the number of planes which might be expected from the symmetry of the primary crystal. **1842** BRANDE *Dict. Sci., etc.*, **Hemigamous.* **1816** KIRBY & SP. *Entomol.* (1828) II. xxii. 286 Other *hemigeometers..have only six prolegs. **1909** WEBSTER, *Hemihydrate. **1946** *Nature* 6 July 13/2 Calcium sulphate exists in three states of hydration, anhydrite, gypsum, and the lower hydrate, generally known as hemihydrate or plaster of Paris. **1965** *New Scientist* 18 Mar. 709/2 Gypsum is calcined to form the hemi-hydrate which sets after wetting to re-form gypsum. **1900** DORLAND *Med. Dict.* 294/1 *Hemihypertrophy. **1922** *Proc. R. Soc. Med.* XV Child. 51 Forty cases..of complete hemihypertrophy where all the structures on one side of the body were involved. **1964** S. DUKE-ELDER *Syst. Ophthalm.* III. xvii. 1028 Facial hemihypertrophy is a much rarer condition which may involve the whole of one side of the body. **1895** STORY-MASKELYNE *Crystallogr.* §180 The *hemi-icositetrahedron, or tetrahedrid pyramidion..called also the trigonal dodecahedron, or twelve-icoscelohedron. **1925** E. B. WILSON *Cell* (ed. 3) 1132 **Hemikaryon*, a nucleus containing the haploid number of chromosomes. *Ibid.* ix. 728 (*caption*) Karyoplasmic relation in embryos of the sea-urchin..stage of haploid (*hemikaryotic) dwarf, from merogonic egg-fragment. **1873** *Fownes' Chem.* (ed. 11) 833 Mellophanic acid undergoes similar transformations, resulting in the formation of *Hemimellitic and Phthalic acids. **1877** WATTS *Ibid.* (ed. 12) II. 554 Hemimellitic acid ..crystallises in colourless needles somewhat sparingly soluble in water. **1889** MUIR & MORLEY *Watts' Dict. Chem.* (rev. ed.) 671/1 **Hemimellithene*,..formed by distilling (*a*)-cuminic acid with lime. *Ibid.*, Hemimellithene may also be isolated from coal-tar oil. **1956** *Nature* 18 Feb. 301/2 The great variety of organic compounds contained in this latest issue [of a text-book] may be indicated by mentioning azelanitrile,..hemimellitine, [etc.]. **1921** *Brit. Mus. Return*

81 A gold *hemiobol of the fourth century B.C. **1941** *Antiquity* XV. 302 Issues of tetrobols and hemiobols. **1837** DANA *Min.* i. (1844) 40 The resulting form is a tetrahedron or *hemi-octahedron. **1868** *Ibid.* Introd. (ed. 5) 27 *Monoclinic System*..The octahedral planes are all *hemioctahedral. **1842** BRANDE *Dict. Sci., etc.*, **Hemiologamous*, a term employed in speaking of grasses when in the same spikelet one of two florets is neuter, and the other hermaphrodite, as in several species of Panicum. **1891** *Jrnl. R. Microsc. Soc.* 70 Each of these classes, except the last, may be again divided into Holoparasites and *Hemiparasites. **1900** B. D. JACKSON *Gloss. Bot. Terms* 120/1 *Hemiparasite*, a facultative saprophyte, a parasite which can exist as a saprophyte. **1927** Hemiparasite [see FACULTATIVE *a.* 1 c]. **1960** N. POLUNIN *Introd. Plant Geogr.* xiv. 437 There are..two main synusiae in the tropical rain forest—the root-parasites growing on the ground..and the semi-parasites (often termed hemi-parasites) growing epiphytically on the trees. **1970** *Nature* 21 Mar. 1162/1 Annual hemiparasites characteristically form haustorial connexions (root grafts) with most of the plants that surround them. **1902** *Encycl. Brit.* XXV. 439/2 Loranthaceæ and Santalaceæ are chiefly *hemiparasitic. **1970** *Nature* 21 Mar. 1161/2 The hemiparasitic flowering plants that live in annual grasslands are of special interest. **1893** *Funk's Stand. Dict.*, *Hemiparesis. **1952** M. E. FLOREY *Clin. Appl. Antibiotics* ii. 37 One patient developed hemiparesis and prolonged convulsions. **1909** WEBSTER, *Hemipenis. **1913** G. A. BOULENGER *Snakes of Europe* ix. 83 Each hemipenis is lodged in a cavity on each side of the base of the tail. **1965** R. & D. MORRIS *Men & Snakes* viii. 190 Male snakes possess two hemipenes. Only one hemipenis is inserted at a time and apparently males do not switch from one to the other during the same mating bout. **1883** FOSTER *Phys.* App. (ed. 4) 718 In..normal peptic and tryptic digestion..*hemipeptone [is preceded] by a hemi-albumose. **1873** *Fownes' Chem.* (ed. 11) 739 *Hemipinic Acid is also produced by oxidation of opianic acid and of narcotine. **1892** G. B. HALSTED *Elem. Synth. Geom.* 5 Any straight line in a plane cuts it into two parts called *hemiplanes. **1876** tr. *P. Schützenberger's Ferment.* 65 *Hemi-protein is also soluble in dilute alkalis, and precipitated by acids. **1895** *Ann. Bot.* IX. 337 The structure of the stele in absorbing rhizome-axes of *hemi- and holo-saprophytes is frequently remarkably like that of a root. **1900** B. D. JACKSON *Gloss. Bot. Terms* 120/2 *Hemisaprophyte*, a facultative parasite. **1909** GROOM & BALFOUR tr. *Warming's Oecology of Plants* II. xxv. 90 *Hemisaprophytes* have the external appearance and structure of normal plants. **1927** Hemisaprophyte [see FACULTATIVE *a.* 1 c]. **1895** *Ann. Bot.* IX. 337, I have already shown that in a *hemisaprophytic Orchid (*Corysanthes*) there is an atrophy in the leaves of the absorbing rhizome. **1895** STORY-MASKELYNE *Crystallogr.* §273 Of the *hemiscalenohedron, instances are met with on certain crystals of phenakite, dioptase, and ilmenite. **1871** SIR T. WATSON *Lect. Princ. & Pract. Phys.* (ed. 5) I. xxv. 484 The phenomena of *hemispasm—of convulsions limited to the limbs of one side. *a* **1883** C. H. FAGGE *Princ. & Pract. Med.* (1886) I. 534 Hemispasm—the 'mobile counterpart' of hemiplegia.

hemianopia (ˌhɛmɪəˈnəʊpɪə). *Ophthalm.* [mod.L., f. HEMI- + Gr. ἀν priv. + -ωπία sight.] = HEMIANOPSIA. Hence **hemiaˈnopic** *a.*, of, pertaining to, or characterized by hemianopia; also as *sb.*, a person with hemianopia.

1882 *Ophthalmic Rev.* I. 253 The more exactly the cause of a homonymous hemianopia can be localised in the cortex of one occipital lobe, the more improbable becomes the theory of Charcot and Landolt. **1889** G. A. BERRY *Dis. Eye* xi. 340 Hemianopia may be to the right or left, and partial or complete. *Ibid.* 341 Ferrier's experiments, which led him to localise the visual centres in the angular gyri, have given rise to the hemianopic symptoms. **1891** F. TAYLOR *Man. Pract. Med.* (ed. 2) 161 A transient hemianopia may occur in cerebral hæmorrhage. **1898** *Nature* 13 Jan. 255/1 Hallucinations connected with hemianopia. **1908** *Practitioner* Oct. 558 Hysterical hemianopia. **1943** *Mind* LII. 363 This seems ruled out by the experiments of Gelb and Goldstein on hemianopics, who saw a field of vision of the normal shape, though the receptive area had been severely damaged. **1964** S. DUKE-ELDER *Parsons' Dis. Eye* (ed. 14) iv. 37 A lesion in the optic tract will produce a hemianopic reaction involving both eyes. **1966** D. G. COGAN *Neurol. Visual Syst.* xiv. 265 The most common complaint of patients with hemianopia, aside from collision with objects on the blind side, is the difficulty with reading.

‖**hemiaˈnopsia.** *Path.* Also **hemianopsy.** [mod.L., f. HEMI- + Gr. ἀν- priv. + ὄψις sight.] Half-blindness, being a loss of perception of one half the field of vision.

1883 *Ophthalmic Rev.* II. 82 The above named recent works on hemianopsia and the decussation of the optic nerve contain much of interest. **1884** *Encycl. Brit.* XVII. 785/1 Hemianopsia means loss of one-half of the visual field. **1885** STIRLING tr. *Landois' Hum. Phys.* II. 786 When it is spoken of as paralysis of one-half of the retina, the term *hemiopia* is applied to it; when, with reference to the field of vision, the term *hemianopsia* is used. **1891** J. HUTCHINSON in *Archives Surg.* II. 303 Persisting vertical hemianopsia. **1893** *Brit. Med. Jrnl.* 18 Nov. 1107/1 There was..complete blindness of one eye and diminished vision, but no hemianopsia of the other. **1908** *Practitioner* Jan. 15 Attacks of aphasia, monoplegias, hemiplegias, word-blindness, and word-deafness, or hemianopsy. **1962** L. S. SASIENI *Optical Dispensing* viii. 200 Hemianopsia spectacles.

hemibranch (ˈhɛmɪbræŋk). *Zool.* [f. HEMI- + Gr. βράγχια gills.] **a.** An incomplete gill. **b.** A fish of the order *Hemibranchii*, having the branchial apparatus incomplete. Hence **hemibranchiate** (-ˈbræŋkɪət) *a.*, half-gilled; *sb.*, a hemibranch.

1880 *Libr. Univ. Knowl.* (N.Y.) VII. 431 The hemibranchiates..have imperfect gills or branchiae. **1891** *Nature* 17 Sept. 483/2 The spiracular gill of Elasmobranchs should be described as the hyoid hemibranch, and the opercular gill of the higher fishes as the first branchial hemibranch.

†ˈ**hemicade.** *Obs. rare*$^{-0}$. [ad. L. *hēmicadium*, Gr. ἡμικάδιον, f. κάδος *cadus*, CADE.] 'A half Hogshead' (Blount *Glossogr.* 1656).

ˈ**hemicarp.** *Bot.* [f. HEMI- + Gr. καρπός fruit.] A half-fruit; one of the two carpels which constitute the fruit of the *Umbelliferæ*.

1854 in MAYNE *Expos. Lex.* **1870** BENTLEY *Bot.* 312 Each half-fruit is termed a hemicarp or mericarp.

hemicellulose (hɛmɪˈsɛljuːləʊs). [a. G. *hemicellulose* (E. Schulze 1891, in *Ber. d. Deut. Chem. Ges.* XXIV. 2286), f. HEMI- + CELLULOSE *sb.*] Any of various non-cellulosic polysaccharides, of simpler composition than cellulose, that are major constituents of the cell walls of many plants and are characterized by undergoing hydrolysis by acids more readily than cellulose to give a variety of simple sugars and other carbohydrates and by being extractable with dilute alkaline solutions.

1891 *Jrnl. Chem. Soc.* LX. 1179 Those constituents of the cell which dissolve easily in dilute mineral acids, with formation of glucose, he [*sc.* E. Schulze] calls hemicelluloses. **1921** A. L. SMITH *Lichens* v. 212 In *Cladonia rangiferina*..the cell-membranes of the hyphae contained, as hemicelluloses, pentosans in small quantities and galactan. **1948** *New Biol.* IV. 87 Interspersed in the meshes of the cellulose, which constitutes approximately 50 per cent of the weight of the dry wood, are a number of other substances which apparently serve to stiffen the framework, principally hemicelluloses..and the more complex carbohydrate lignin. **1963** R. R. A. HIGHAM *Handbk. Papermaking* ii. 33 Hemi-celluloses are found in two main groups, i.e., those associated mainly with the plant cellulose and centred largely in the structure of the fibre and those associated with lignin, in the middle lamella and primary walls of fibres. *Ibid.*, The presence of hemi-celluloses in papermaking pulps is very important, as they assist in internal fibrillation of the fibres, but owing to their short chain structure they easily become broken down during digestion and are lost in the form of by-products.

hemicentral, -cerebral, etc.: see HEMI-.

ˈ**hemicircle.** *Obs.* or *arch.* [f. HEMI- + CIRCLE *sb.*] A half circle, semicircle.

a **1618** J. DAVIES *Extasie* 25 Wks. (Grosart) I. 89 Her Browes two hemi-circles did enclose Of Rubies. **1625** N. CARPENTER *Geog. Del.* I. v. (1635) 106 Euery oblique Horizon will diuide the Equatour into two equall hemicircles. **1875** J. H. BENNET *Winter Medit.* II. xi. (ed. 5) 358 A hemi-circle of the majestic granite mountains.

So **hemiˈcircular** *a.*, semicircular.

1656 BLOUNT *Glossogr.*, *Hemicircular*, halfe round. **1895** LUNN *How to visit Italy* 92 Two grand hemi-circular colonnades.

†**hemicrane.** *Obs.* Also 6 -cran, 7 -crain, -cranie, -y. [a. obs. F. *hemicraine* (Cotgr.), ad. L. *hēmicrānia*, a. Gr. ἡμικρανία, f. ἡμι- HEMI- + κρανίον skull. *Hemicranie* is an adaptation of the L.] = next.

c **1550** LLOYD *Treas. Health* (1585) C iv, Hyera hermetis purgeth the hemicran. *Ibid.* D j, Oyle of fystikes healeth the hemicrane and watchynges. **1600** VAUGHAN *Direct. Health* (1633) 87 Here-hence springs the Head-ache..which last we call the Hemicrany or Megrim, possessing but the one side of the Head. **1651** BAXTER *Inf. Bapt.* 135 Cephalalgies, Hemicranies, Phthises. **1657** *Physical Dict.*, *Hemicrania*, or *hemicrane*, a kind of head-ach, when but one side of the head is grieved.

‖**hemicrania** (hɛmɪˈkreɪnɪə). *Path.* [L.: see prec.] **1.** Headache confined to one side of the head; megrim.

1657 [see prec.]. **1661** LOVELL *Hist. Anim. & Min.* 151 The bones help the Hemicrania. *a* **1801** W. HEBERDEN *Comm.* xvii. (1806) 93 The hemicrania, or pain of one half of the head. **1872** GEO. ELIOT in J. W. Cross *Life* III. 157, I am ..struggling with hemicrania and *malaise*.

2. 'Also a term used in Teratology to denote imperfect development or total defect of one side of the brain and its coverings' (*Syd. Soc. Lex.*).

hemiˈcranic, *a.* [ad. L. *hēmicrānic-us* = Gr. ἡμικρανικός.] Pertaining or subject to hemicrania.

1656 BLOUNT *Glossogr.*, *Hemicranick*.., subject to the sickness called Megrim or Hemicrain. **1854** in MAYNE.

hemicryptophyte (hɛmɪˈkrɪptəʊfaɪt). *Bot.* [ad. Da. *hemikryptofyte* (C. Raunkiaer 1904, in *Bot. Tidsskrift* XXVI, p. xiv), f. HEMI- + CRYPTO-: see -PHYTE.] (See quot. 1932.) Also *attrib.* Hence ˌ**hemicryptoˈphytic** *a.*

1913 *Jrnl. Ecol.* I. 24 The *Anemone nemorosa* facies of the beech-wood is geophytic since the 0·1 sq. m. readings show geophytes 82 per cent., hemicryptophytes 18 per cent. *Ibid.* 25 The contrast between spruce hemicryptophytic wood and beech geophytic wood. **1932** FULLER & CONARD tr. *Braun-Blanquet's Plant Sociol.* xii. 291 Hemicryptophytes ..plants with perennial shoots and buds close to the earth's surface. **1938** J. R. CARPENTER *Ecol. Gloss.* 130 *Hemicryptophyte climate*, the climate of the greater part of the cold temperate zone. **1964** V. J. CHAPMAN *Coastal Veget.* vi. 150 A hemicryptophyte flora.

hemicycle (ˈhɛmɪsaɪk(ə)l). Also 7 -cicle. [a. F. *hémicycle* (1557 in Hatz.-Darm.), ad. L. *hēmicyclium*, a. Gr. ἡμικύκλιον, f. ἡμι- HEMI + κύκλος circle.] A half circle, semicircle; a semicircular structure, as an orchestra or apse-like recess.

1603 B. JONSON *King's Coron. Entertain.* Wks. (Rtldg.) 531/2 Upon the right hand of her..in a hemicycle was seated Esychia, or Quiet. **1638** SIR T. HERBERT *Trav.* (ed. 2) 170 The scaberd of his sword was red..the blade formed like a hemi-cicle. *c* **1790** COWPER *Notes P.L.* I. 616 Thus forming themselves into a hemicycle or half moon figure, that all might hear him. **1861** BERESF. HOPE *Eng. Cathedr. 19th C.* 155 Earlier and larger churches seem to have been contented with the single hemicycle.

hemicyclic (hɛmɪˈsɪklɪk), *a.* *Bot.* [ad. F. *hémicyclique* (Littré), ad. Gr. ἡμικυκλικ-ός, f. ἡμικύκλιον (see prec.).] Applied to flowers which have the parts arranged spirally in such a manner that the transition from one series to another (e.g. from petals to stamens) occurs at the completion of a turn of the spiral; also to those which have some parts arranged spirally (*acyclic*) and others in whorls (*cyclic*).

1875 BENNETT & DYER tr. *Sachs' Bot.* 533 In hemicyclic flowers those members at least which are arranged in whorls may possibly be distributed symmetrically. **1878** [see ACYCLIC *a.* 1].

hemicyˈlindrical, *a.* Having the form of half a cylinder, divided in the direction of its axis.

1854 in MAYNE *Expos. Lex.* **1880** *Libr. Univ. Knowl.* (N.Y.) V. 771 The articular surface of the condyles is hemicylindrical. **1883** BUCHAN & STEWART in *Encycl. Brit.* XVI. 162/2 By means of a hemicylindrical lens.

hemiˈdactyl, *a.* and *sb.* *Zool.* [f. HEMI- + Gr. δάκτυλος finger.] **A.** *adj.* Having an oval disk at the base of the toes, as in the saurian genus *Hemidactylus* (Webster 1864). **B.** *sb.* A saurian of this genus; a gecko. Hence **hemiˈdactylous** *a.* = A. (Mayne *Expos. Lex.* 1854).

1863 WOOD *Nat. Hist.* III. 72 The Spotted Gecko, or Spotted Hemidactyle, a rather pretty species of Gecko.

ˈ**hemi-ˌdemi-ˈsemi:** used as adj. and sometimes as a combining form in imitation of the use in *hemidemisemiquaver* (s.v. HEMI-).

1929 J. LAIRD *Idea of Value* ix. 302 Even believers in the 'unconscious'..seem commonly to hold that the 'unconscious' is at least hemi-demi-semi conscious. **1958** *Spectator* 3 Jan. 14/3 What is the point of ideological compromises and hemi-demi-semi pro-Soviet hedging? **1965** O. BARFIELD in J. Gibb *Light on C.S. Lewis* p. xiii, Hemi-demi-semitone of alteration in the pitch of his voice.

hemidemisemiquaver, etc.: see HEMI-.

hemidesmus (hɛmɪˈdɛsməs). *Bot.* [mod.L. (R. Brown, 1809) f. HEMI- + Gr. δεσμός bond; so named in allusion to the incomplete coherence of the anthers with the stigma.] A small, swimming herb of the genus so named, belonging to the family Asclepiadaceæ, and native to India and Ceylon; *esp.* a plant of ***hemidesmus indicus***, the root of which is used as a substitute for sarsaparilla; also, a syrup prepared therefrom. Hence **hemiˈdesmic** *a.*

1809 R. BROWN in *Mem. Wernerian Nat. Hist. Soc.* I. 56 Hemidesmus..whose name is derived from the partial connection of the stamina, is composed of *Periploca Indica*, and two very nearly related unpublished species. **1844** *Pharm. Jrnl.* III. 239 The root of hemidesmus indicus has for some years been sold in this country under the name of Smilax Aspera. **1880** GARROD & BAXTER *Mat. Med.* 311 Hemidesmus Root... It..contains a peculiar volatile, crystallizable substance, with acid properties: this has been called hemidesmic acid. **1898** *Revised Brit. Pharmacop.* 4 The retention of hemidesmus is noteworthy, and a tribute to the St. Bartholomew's school of physic. **1968** D. C. GUNAWARDENA *Genera et Species Plantarum Zeylaniae* 122 Hemidesmus... Anther connective prolonged, covering over stigma.

hemidome (ˈhɛmɪdəʊm). *Cryst.* [f. HEMI- + DOME *sb.* 5 b.] A pair of parallel and equal faces, parallel to the orthodiagonal in the monoclinic (or monosymmetrical) system (in which two such pairs constitute a dome). Hence **hemidoˈmatic** *a.*, of or pertaining to a hemidome.

1868 DANA *Min.* Introd. (ed. 5) 27 *Monoclinic System*.. The domes parallel to the orthodiagonal are hemidomes, the planes in front at top being unlike in inclination those in front below, each being a hemidome. **1879** RUTLEY *Study Rocks* x. 88 When the light falls obliquely either on the basal plane..or the hemidome of a monoclinic felspar.

‖**hemi-elytrum** (hɛmɪˈɛlɪtrəm). *Zool.* Pl. **-a**. Also *erron.* **hemelytrum**. [mod.L., f. Gr. ἡμι- HEMI- + ἔλυτρον ELYTRUM, sheath.] The fore wing of an insect, which is coriaceous at the base and membranous at the end, as in the *Hemiptera* and *Heteroptera*.

1826 KIRBY & SP. *Entomol.* (1828) IV. xlvii. 387 Wings covered by Hemelytra or Tegmina. **1870** NICHOLSON *Zool.* 210 In some of the Hemiptera..the apices [of the anterior wings] remain membranous, and to these the term 'hemelytra' is applied. **1888** ROLLESTON & JACKSON *Anim. Life* 500 The fore wings may be converted into wing covers ..as in the hemi-elytra of *Dermaptera* and elytra of *Coleoptera*.

Hence **hemi-'elytral** *a.*, pertaining to or of the nature of a hemielytrum.

hemigamous, -gnathous: see HEMI-.

hemihedral (hɛmɪ'hiːdrəl, -'hɛdrəl), *a. Cryst.* Also **hemiedral.** [f. HEMI- c + Gr. ἕδρα seat, base + -AL.] Of a crystal: Having half the number of planes required by the highest degree of symmetry belonging to its system; thus, a tetrahedron is the hemihedral form corresponding to the holohedral octahedron.

1837 [see HEMIHEDRON]. **1839–47** TODD *Cycl. Anat.* III. 806/1 Triple phosphate..generally occurs in hemihedral six-sided prisms. **1850** DAUBENY *Atom. Th.* viii. (ed. 2) 264 All the crystals..were alike hemiedral..that is, half of their similar planes or angles were modified independently of the other half. **1878** GURNEY *Crystallogr.* 39 When the crystal has dissimilar faces at the two ends of the same axis of symmetry, the form to which those faces belong is called *hemihedral*.

Hence **hemi'hedrally** *adv.*

1837 DANA *Min.* ii. 19 Minerals, whose crystals are hemihedrally modified, are invariably thus modified, if the secondary planes occur, in which the hemihedrism may take place.

hemihedron (hɛmɪ'hiːdrən, -'hɛdrən). *Cryst.* [f. HEMI- c + Gr. ἕδρα after *hexahedron*, etc. Cf. F. *hémièdre*.] A form or crystal of a hemihedral type.

1837 DANA *Min.* ii. 19 This species of hemihedral Crystal has been called the *inclined hemihedron*. **1895** STORY-MASKELYNE *Crystallogr.* §137 A form of the hemi-symmetrical kind will be termed a semiform or a hemihedron. *Ibid.* §176 Holo-systematic haplohedral forms; or holotesseral hemihedra.

So **hemi'hedrism, hemi'hedry** [cf. F. *hémiédrie*], the property or quality of crystallization in hemihedral forms.

1837 DANA *Min.* ii. 19 The first species of hemihedrism gives rise to solids, whose opposite planes are not parallel. *Ibid.*, Examples of the first kind of hemihedrism, in which half the angles of the cube are modified. **1864–72** WATTS *Dict. Chem.* II. 143 This kind of hemihedry is strikingly exhibited in apatite. **1883** *Nature* 1 Feb. 317/1 Some remarks on hemihedry in crystals.

he'milogous, *a. Chem.* [f. HEMI- + *ana-logous*.] (See quot.)

1865–72 WATTS *Dict. Chem.* III. 141 *Hemilogous Series*, a name applied by Shiel..to series of organic compounds, the terms of which differ from one another by *n*CH.

‖**hemimetabola** (ˌhɛmɪmɪ'tæbələ), *sb. pl. Entom.* [mod.L. neut. pl. (sc. *insecta*), f. Gr. ἡμι- HEMI- + μετάβολος changeable.] A division of Insects comprising those which undergo incomplete metamorphosis.

1870 NICHOLSON *Zool.* (1880) 341 Insects are divided into sections, called respectively *Ametabola, Hemimetabola*, and *Holometabola*. **1888** ROLLESTON & JACKSON *Anim. Life* 508 In the *Hemi-metabola*, the larva may differ notably from the adult in the structure of the antennæ, eyes, mouthparts..as well as in the absence of wings.

Hence **hemimeta'bolic, hemime'tabolous** *adjs.*, of the nature of the *Hemimetabola*; undergoing incomplete metamorphosis. **hemime'taboly**, incomplete metamorphosis.

1870 ROLLESTON *Anim. Life* Introd. 113 The adult insect, whilst gaining certain organs which the larva does not possess, such as wings, loses certain others, which the larva does possess, such as the provisional structures making up the 'mask' of the *Libellulidæ*..Such insects are called 'Hemimetabolous'. **1875** BLAKE *Zool.* 281 In the hemimetabolic insects there is a metamorphosis, which consists of 3 stages.

hemimeta'morphic, *a. Biol.* [f. HEMI- + METAMORPHIC.] = HEMIMETABOLIC. Hence **hemimetamor'phosis**, incomplete or partial metamorphosis; hemimetaboly.

1880 DAY *Fishes Gt. Brit.* I. Introd. 91 In some pelagic forms Hemimetamorphosis may occur, or very considerable alterations in their growth and development.

hemimorphic (hɛmɪ'mɔːfɪk), *a. Cryst.* [f. HEMI- + Gr. μορφή shape + -IC.] Of a crystal: Having unlike planes or modifications at the ends of the same axis. So **hemi'morph**, a hemimorphic crystal. **hemi'morphism**, the property of being hemimorphic. **hemi'morphous** *a.* = HEMIMORPHIC. **'hemimorphy** = HEMIMORPHISM.

1864 WEBSTER, *Hemimorphic*. **1868** DANA *Min.* (ed. 5) 407 Calamine..Orthorhombic; hemimorphic-hemihedral. **1878** LAWRENCE tr. *Cotta's Rocks Class.* 32 Tourmaline is Rhombohedral, eminently hemi-morphous. **1879** RUTLEY *Study Rocks* x. 138 The crystals when heated and freely suspended, exhibit polar electricity, a phenomenon which usually accompanies hemimorphism. **1886** *Syd. Soc. Lex.*, *Hemimorphy*. **1895** STORY-MASKELYNE *Crystallogr.* §140 *Hemimorphism* is the term for a particular case of haplohedral mero-symmetry. One-half or, it may be, one-fourth of the faces of the original form are present in the hemimorphic form: but these all lie on one side of a systematic plane, the symmetral character of which is in abeyance. *Ibid.* §272 Hemimorphous forms are not rare in the Hexagonal system, but they occur most often as hemimorphs of hemisymmetrical types of crystal.

hemimorphite. *Min.* [f. as prec. + -ITE.] Kenngott's name (1853) for hydrous silicate of zinc, the crystals of which are hemimorphic. Now generally used in place of earlier names such as *calamine*.

1868 J. D. DANA *Syst. Min.* (ed. 5) v. 409 Unfortunately, Brooke & Miller, in 1852, reversed Beudant's use of these names [sc. *calamine* and *smithsonite* for the silicate and carbonate of zinc], with no good reason; and in 1853, Kenngott, on account of the confusion of names, as he says, introduced for the silicate the new name *Hemimorphite*, and so added to the confusion. **1910** *Encycl. Brit.* VII. 583/1 Two hemihedral or hemimorphic crystals (e.g. of diamond or of hemimorphite) are often united in twinned positions. **1951** A. N. & H. WINCHELL *Elem. Optical Mineral.* (ed. 4) II. x. 482 Hemimorphite is found in veins with smithsonite and sphalerite.

hemin, var. HÆMIN.

‖**hemina** (hɪ'maɪnə). Also (anglicized or as F.) 7 **hemine**, 8 **emine, (esmine)**. [L. *hēmīna*, a. Gr. ἡμίνα, f. ἡμι- half-. Cf. F. *emine, hemine* 'a measure that containes three Possons; and comes to, in weight, about seuen and a halfe of our moderne ounces' (Cotgr.).] A liquid measure (orig. ancient Sicilian) of about half a pint; also, a measure for corn (see above, and quot. 1756).

1601 HOLLAND *Pliny* xx. xix, Five heads of the Poppy being sodden in three hemines of wine. **1661** LOVELL *Hist. Anim. & Min.* 3 The Ephemera feaver is cured by 3 drops taken from an Asses eare..in two hemina's of water. **1745** A. BUTLER *Lives Saints* (1836) I. 377 *note*, The hemina of wine allowed by St. Bennet. **1756** R. ROLT *Dict. Trade & Comm.*, *Hemina, Emine*, or *Esmine*, is a great corn measure..At Marseilles the hemina of corn weighs 75 lb...and in Barbary it is computed equal to 9 bushels.

heming, var. of HEMMING *sb. Obs.*

Hemingwayesque (ˌhɛmɪŋweɪ'ɛsk), *a.* [f. the name of Ernest *Hemingway* (1898–1961), American novelist + -ESQUE.] Characteristic of the works of E. Hemingway. So ˌ**Heming'wayan** *a.*; ˌ**Hemingway'ese; 'Hemingwayish** *a.*

1942 H. HAYCRAFT *Murder for Pleasure* viii. 171 Hemingwayesque courage and fatalism. **1957** J. KEROUAC *On Road* (1958) vii. 41 Composing his latest Hemingwayan short story. **1959** *Times Lit. Suppl.* 4 Sept. 505/3 His father, a Hemingwayish figure. **1964** *Listener* 28 May 882/2 Plain unvarnished Hemingwayese looks decidedly mannered. **1970** *English Studies* LI. 491 In *Ernest Hemingway, A Life Story*..Carlos Baker has adopted his subject's deliberately simple declarative style. The opening and closing of the book are archly Hemingwayesque; some parts of the 640 pages that come between are simply Hemingwayese.

hemioctahedron, etc.: see HEMI-.

‖**hemiolia** (hɛmɪ'əʊlɪə). *Mus. Obs.* exc. *Hist.* Also 6 **hemiola**, 7 **hemiolion, hemolios**, 8 **hemiolius**. [med.L. *hemiolia*, a. Gr. ἡμιολία (sc. διάστασις interval, in Plato), fem. of ἡμιόλιος 'in the ratio of one and a half to one', f. ἡμι- HEMI- + ὅλος whole.] In mediæval music. **a.** A perfect fifth, so called because produced by shortening a string to two-thirds of its length. **b.** Three notes in the place of two; a triplet.

1597 MORLEY *Introd. Mus.* 30 That proportion which the musitions falselie termed *Hemiola*, when in deede it is nothing else but a round *Tripla*. **1603** HOLLAND *Plutarch's Mor.* 1358 (Stanf.) The proportion of the Musicke or Symphonie Diatessaron, is Epitritos or Sesquitertiall, that is to say, the whole and a third part over: of Diapente, Hemolios or Sesquialterall..the whole and halfe as much more. **1651** J. F[REAKE] *Agrippa's Occ. Philos.* 182 Harmony contains three consents in tune, Diapason, Hemiolion, Diatessaron. **1727–51** CHAMBERS *Cycl.* **1880** in Grove *Dict. Mus.* I. 727.

‖**hemi'opia, hemi'opsia.** *Path.* Also (anglicized) **hemiopy, -opsy.** [mod.L., f. HEMI- + Gr. ὤψ, ὠπ- eye, ὄψις sight.] = HEMIANOPSIA. So **hemi'opic** *a.*

1811 HOOPER *Med. Dict.*, *Hemiopsia*, a defect of vision, in which the person sees the half, but not the whole of an object. **1831** BREWSTER *Newton* (1855) I. x. 230 The curious disease of hemiopsy, or amaurosis dimidiata, in which the patient sees with each eye only half of an object, being blind to the other half. **1838** *Penny Cycl.* XII. 114/2 *Hemiopia*. **1854** MAYNE *Expos. Lex.*, *Hemiopia, Hemiopsia*..hemiopy: hemiopsy. **1864–70** T. HOLMES & HULKE *Syst. Surg.* (1883) II. viii. 77 Transient hemiopsia is often an initial symptom of megrim. **1873** *Arch. Sci. & Pract. Med.* I. 293 (*title*) Hemiopic and sector-like defects in the field of vision. **1890** W. JAMES *Princ. Psychol.* I. ii. 42 A hemiopic disturbance of vision is one in which neither retina is affected in its totality, but in which, for example, the left portion of *each* retina is blind, so that the animal sees nothing situated in space towards its right.

hemipalmate, -phrase, etc.: see HEMI-.

hemi'plectic, *a. Path.* [f. HEMI- + Gr. πληκτικός of a striking kind.] = HEMIPLEGIC.

1891 in F. P. FOSTER *Med. Dict.*

‖**hemiplegia** (hɛmɪ'pliːdʒɪə). *Path.* [Late L., a. Gr. ἡμιπληγία (rare, for ἡμιπληξία), f. ἡμι- HEMI- + πληγή stroke, f. stem of πλήσσειν to strike.]

Paralysis of one side of the body; usually caused by a lesion in the opposite side of the brain.

1600 HOLLAND *Pliny* XLI. xvi. 1105 The Consull..fell downe in a fit of Apoplexie: which turned into an *Hemiplegia* or dead palsey all the one side of his bodie. **1754** CHESTERF. in *World* No. 92 ¶5 Though they have not yet lost one half of themselves by a hemiplegia. *a* **1754** MEAD *Wks.* 481 (Jod.) On dissection of the bodies of apoplecticks who had been seized with an hemiplegia, he always found the cause of the disease in the opposite side of the brain. **1876** tr. *Wagner's Gen. Pathol.* 291 In old Hemiplegias the epidermis is often dry, rough, and scaly.

Hence **hemi'plegiac** *a.*, affected with or subject to hemiplegia; *sb.*, one so affected. **hemi'plegian** *a.* = prec.

1782 W. HEBERDEN *Comm.* lxix. (1806) 352 In one hemiplegiac the motion of the parts began to return. **1835–6** TODD *Cycl. Anat.* I. 805/1 In hemiplegiac subjects. **1842** SYD. SMITH *Lett. Locking in Railw.* Wks. 1859 II. 324/1 Most absurd..is this hemiplegian law—an act..to protect one side of the body and not the other.

hemiplegic (hɛmɪ'plɛdʒɪk, -pliː-), *a. Path.* [f. prec. + -IC.] Pertaining to or characterized by hemiplegia; affected with or subject to hemiplegia. Also *sb.*, one who is affected by hemiplegia (see also quot. 1970).

1822–34 *Good's Study Med.* (ed. 4) III. 478 Hemiplegic palsy. *Ibid.* 480 The jaundice affecting the hemiplegic side alone. **1861** T. J. GRAHAM *Pract. Med.* 602 The convulsion is hemiplegic. **1878** *Smithsonian Inst. Rep.* 419 *note*, A hemiplegic person has the will to move the paralysed limbs, but not the power. **1890** *Retrospect Med.* CII. 155 Convalescent hemiplegics. **1970** *New Scientist* 3 Sept. 473/1 It would enable amputees and hemi-plegics—persons paralyzed below the waist—to walk about under their own power.

hemiplegy ('hɛmɪplɛdʒɪ). *rare.* Also **hemiplege.** [ad. late L. *hēmiplēgia* (see above). (In mod.F. *hémiplegie*, 1752).] = HEMIPLEGIA.

1755 in JOHNSON. **1802** *Med. Jrnl.* VIII. 312 To ascertain, whether in hemiplegies the primitive cause continues to act in the brain. **1864** *Gd. Words* 723/1 A twist or a hemiplege of the reasoning faculty.

†**'hemiplexy.** *Obs.* [ad. mod.L. *hēmiplēxia*, a. Gr. ἡμιπληξία a stroke on one side, f. ἡμι- HEMI- + πληγή stroke.] = HEMIPLEGIA.

1576 BAKER *Jewell of Health* 161 b, It prevayleth against the palsie of the members, left after an Apoplexie, or Hemiplexie. **1656** in BLOUNT *Glossogr.*, *Hemiplexy*.

hemipod, -pode ('hɛmɪpɒd, -pəʊd). [ad. mod.L. *hēmipodius* (Temminck's generic name), f. Gr. ἡμι- HEMI- + πούς, ποδ-ός foot.] A member of the genus *Hemipodius*, or *Turnix*, of three-toed quail-like birds; a bush-quail, ortygan.

1862 *Trans. Zool. Soc.* V. 149 Certain border-groups..the Sand-Grouse, the Hemipodes, and the Tinamous. **1886** *Encycl. Brit.* XX. 147 One species, *T[urnix] sylvatica*, inhabits Barbary and southern Spain, and under the name of Andalucian Hemipode has been included..among British Birds as a reputed straggler. **1893** NEWTON *Dict. Birds*, *Hemipode*, a recognized English rendering of Temminck's generic name *Hemipodius* (1815)..for a small group of birds some of which Anglo-Indians often call 'Bustard-Quails' or 'Button-Quails'.

So **hemi'podiine** *a.*, allied to the Hemipodes.

1862 *Trans. Zool. Soc.* V. 189 The Galline, Columbine, or Hemipodiine types.

hemiprism ('hɛmɪprɪz(ə)m). *Cryst.* [HEMI-.] A pair of parallel faces, parallel to the vertical axis of the crystal in the triclinic system (in which two such pairs constitute a prism).

1864 DANA in Webster, *Hemiprism*, a form, in the monoclinic and triclinic systems of crystallization, that comprises but one face of a prism and its opposite. **1882** A. H. GREEN *Phys. Geol.* (ed. 3) 70 The prisms will be Hemiprisms.

Hence **hemipri'smatic** *a.*, of the nature of a hemiprism.

1837 DANA *Min.* (1844) 324 Hemi-prismatic Kouphone-Spar. **1879** RUTLEY *Study Rocks* x. 87 In both systems there are hemiprismatic cleavages.

hemipter (hɪ'mɪptə(r)). [ad. F. *hémiptère*, f. L. *hēmiptera*: see next.] One of the *Hemiptera*.

1828 WEBSTER s.v., The hemipters form an order of insects with the upper wings usually half crustaceous and half membranaceous, and incumbent on each other. **1863** DANA *Man. Geol.* 420 Hemipters have the outer wings coriaceous for about half their length only.

‖**Hemiptera** (hɪ'mɪptərə), *sb. pl. Entom.* Rarely in sing. **Hemipteron.** [mod.L., neut. pl. of *hēmipterus*, f. *hēmi-*, ἡμι- HEMI- + πτερόν wing, in reference to the structure of the wings.] A large order of Insects, comprising a wide variety of different kinds, characterized by a suctorial mouth, and in the largest group (the HETEROPTERA), by wings coriaceous at the base and membranous at the tip. Also called

Rhynchōta. Well-known examples are bugs, lice, and plant-lice.

1816 KIRBY & SP. *Entomol.*, Hemiptera. **1834** MCMURTRIE *Cuvier's Anim. Kingd.* 403 These Hemiptera, also called pseudo-aphides..live on the trees and plants from which they derive their nourishment. **1885** H. O. FORBES *East. Archipelago* viii. 251 A singular case of ants milking a winged Hemipteron, which of course could not be kept in captivity.

Hence **he'mipteral** *a.*, hemipterous. **he'mipteran** *adj.*, hemipterous; *sb.*, one of the *Hemiptera*. **he'mipterist**, a student or collector of *Hemiptera*.

1828 WEBSTER, *Hemipteral*. **1865** DOUGLAS & SCOTT *Brit. Hemiptera* 6 The instruments of capture used by the Coleopterist will be those wanted by the Hemipterist. **1877** HUXLEY *Anat. Inv. Anim.* vii. 424 The absence of palps.. suggesting that the Hemipteran mouth is the extreme term of a series of modifications. **1878** *Pop. Sci. Monthly* Aug. 512 That terrible microscopic hemipteran, the chinch-bug.

hemipterous (hɪˈmɪptərəs), *a. Entom.* [f. HEMIPTERA + -OUS.] Pertaining to or characteristic of the *Hemiptera*.

1816 KIRBY & SP. *Entomol.* (1843) I. 257 The hemipterous order of insects. **1880** *Athenæum* 30 Oct. 574/1 Specimens of..an Hemipterous insect supposed to be damaging the hops grown near Canterbury.

hemi'pyramid. *Cryst.* [HEMI-.] A figure consisting of two pairs of parallel faces intersecting all three axes in the monosymmetric system (in which four such pairs constitute a pyramid). Hence **hemipy'ramidal** *a.*, of or pertaining to a hemipyramid.

1854 MAYNE *Expos. Lex.*, *Hemipyramidal.. Hemirhombohedral.*

hemirhamphine, etc.: see HEMI-.

hemisect, *v.* [f. HEMI- + L. *sect-*, ppl. stem of *secāre* to cut.] *trans.* To bisect, esp. longitudinally, or into the right and left halves. So **hemi'section**, the action or process of thus bisecting.

1878 FOSTER *Phys.* III. v. §3. 487 In the frog, after hemisection of the cord below the brachial plexus. **1885** *Science* 11 Sept. 223/1 A hemisected skeleton showing the variation in size of the neural and hæmal cavities. **1895** *Athenæum* 30 Mar. 412/1 The Changes in Movement and Sensation produced by Hemisection of the Spinal Cord in the Cat.

hemi'spheral, *a. rare.* [f. next + -AL¹.] Of or pertaining to a hemisphere.

1839 BAILEY *Festus* xxix. (1854) 475 The great galactic line of life Which parts the hemispheral palm of Heaven.

hemisphere (ˈhɛmɪsfɪə(r)). Forms: α. 4–5 hemy-, hemi-, -sperie, -ye, 4–6 emy-, emi-, (eme)sperie, -ry, 6 hemispherie, -ye. β. 5 h)emyspere, 6 emispere, hemispher, 6–7 -sphære, 7–8 hemisphear(e, 6– hemisphere. [In form *hemispherie*, etc., ad. late L. *hēmisphærium*, a. Gr. ἡμισφαίριον, f. ἡμι- HEMI- + σφαῖρα SPHERE; in form *hemisphere*, through OF. *emispere*, *-sphere* (13–14th c.), mod.F. *hémisphère*.]

1. *generally.* A half sphere; one of the halves of a sphere or globe formed by a plane passing through the centre.

1585 T. WASHINGTON tr. *Nicholay's Voy.* II. xviii. 51 Al made of very cleare glasse..in forme of a rounde Hemisphere. **1664** POWER *Exp. Philos.* I. 11 In one of our Critical Observations, I could see more then a hemisphere of the eye at once. **1796** HUTTON *Dict. Math.* s.v., The centre of gravity of a Hemisphere, is five-eighths of the radius distant from the vertex. **1837** M. DONOVAN *Dom. Econ.* II. 331 A hemisphere of the cocoa-nut shell is used as a lamp to burn its own oil. **1895** STORY-MASKELYNE *Crystallogr.* §325 The sphere of projection is divided into hemispheres by a single symmetral plane.

b. ***Magdeburg hemispheres***, a contrivance invented by Otto von Guericke of Magdeburg to demonstrate the pressure of the air.

It consists of two strong hollow nicely-fitting brass hemispheres, each of which is furnished with a handle, and one with a cock to be adjusted to an air-pump. When they are fitted together and the air has been exhausted, great force is required to separate them.

1815 in HUTTON *Math. Dict.* **1858** LARDNER *Hand-bk. Nat. Phil.* 179 Two of the strongest men will be unable to tear the hemispheres asunder, provided they are of a moderate magnitude, owing to the amount of the pressure with which they are held together.

2. *spec.* Half of the celestial sphere; in early quots., esp. that half of the heavens seen above the horizon, the sky above us; in *Astron.*, usually, one of the halves into which the celestial globe is divided by the equinoctial or by the ecliptic. (The earliest sense in Eng.)

α. *c* **1374** CHAUCER *Troylus* III. 1390 (1439) (Harl. MS.) Ther god..þe for thyn haste..So fast ay to our hemysperie [*v. rr.* emesperie, hemy-spere] bynde! *c* **1391** —— *Astrol.* I. §18 The cercle þat deuydeth the two Emysperies, þat is, the partie of the heuene a-boue the Erthe & the partie be-nethe. *c* **1400** MAUNDEV. (Roxb.) xx. 90 We schuld hafe sene all þe roundeness of þe firmament, þat es to say bathe þe emisperies, þe vppermare and þe nedermare. **1412–20** LYDG. *Chron. Troy* I. v, With the brightnes of his beames merye For to reioyse all our Hemisperie. **1509** HAWES *Past. Pleas.* I. x, When cleare Dyana..Gan for to ryse, lightyng our emispery.

β. [Cf. quot. *c* 1374 in α.]. *a* **1532** ?LYDG. *Goodly Balade* 27 (Skeat, *Chaucerian Pieces* 406) The rude night, that.. shadoweth our emispere [*rime* dere]. **1549** *Compl. Scot.* vi. 38 The sternis & planetis..durst nocht be sene in oure hemispere. **1604** R. CAWDREY *Table Alph.*, *Hemisphere*, halfe of the compasse of heauen, that we see. **1607** J. DAVIES *Summa Totalis* D ij b, Fal'n to rest beneath our Hemyspheare. **1725** BRADLEY *Fam. Dict.* s.v. *Shepherd*, The Sun keeps on the Left Hand of the Hemisphear. **1892** R. S. BALL *In Starry Realms* xxi. 304 The number of stars in the northern hemisphere alone is upwards of three hundred thousand. We may assume that the southern hemisphere has an equally numerous star-population.

3. One of the halves of the terrestrial globe, esp. as divided by the equator (***Northern*** and ***Southern hemispheres***). Also the halves containing Europe, Asia, and Africa (***Eastern hemisphere***), and America (***Western hemisphere***), respectively.

α. **1551** RECORDE *Cast. Knowl.* (1556) 280 No generall eclipse, whiche should extende to all the worlde, namely for that hemispherye. **1555** EDEN *Decades* (Arb.) 51 Neyther dydde any..trauerse the Equinoctial line to thinferiour hemispherie or halfe globe of the earthe and sea. **1561** —— *Arte Nauig.* I. xiv. 14 b, Also called yᵉ Hemisphery.

β. **1559** W. CUNNINGHAM *Cosmogr. Glasse* 125 *A Card*, for halfe the face of th' Earth whiche..wyll conveniently serve for our Hemisphere. **1624** DONNE *Serm.* xvii. 167 The Western Hemisphere the land of Gold and Treasure; The Eastern Hemisphere the Land of Spices and Perfumes. **1633** G. HERBERT *Temple, Sacrifice* vii, These drops..A Balsome are for both the Hemispheres. **1646** SIR T. BROWNE *Pseud. Ep.* VI. vii. 312 The ancient Cosmographers doe place the division of the East and Westerne Hemisphere, that is the first terme of longitude in the Canary or fortunate Islands. **1753** *Adventurer* No. 99 ⁋9 When Columbus had engaged king Ferdinand in the discovery of the other hemisphere. **1833** HERSCHEL *Astron.* (1858) 186 It is a fact..that London occupies nearly the center of the terrestrial hemisphere.

b. ***hemisphere of vision, h. of illumination.***

1812 WOODHOUSE *Astron.* xxiii. 241 The illuminated hemisphere, called, for distinction, the Hemisphere of *Illumination*. *Ibid.* 242 The hemisphere which he sees, called the Hemisphere of *Vision*.

4. A map or projection of half the terrestrial globe or the celestial globe.

1706 PHILLIPS (ed. Kersey) s.v., The Maps or Prints of the Heavens pasted on Boards or Cloth are also sometimes call'd *Hemispheres*, but more commonly *Planispheres*. **1858** HAWTHORNE *Fr. & It. Jrnls.* (1872) I. 25 There was a map—a hemisphere of the world—which his father had drawn.

5. *Anat.* Each of the halves of the cerebrum of the brain. (See CEREBRAL.)

1804 ABERNETHY *Surg. Obs.* 188 Inflammation operating probably chiefly on the left hemisphere of the brain. **1831** R. KNOX *Cloquet's Anat.* 409 This surface of the brain has been regarded..as formed of several distinct regions, which they have named Lobes, and which occupy the base of the hemispheres. **1846** OWEN *Comp. Anat. Vertebr.* viii. 181 *note*, Influenced by the inapplicability of the term 'hemispheres' to parts which are more commonly spheres or spheroids. **1873** MIVART *Elem. Anat.* ix. 366 A very deep fissure running from before backwards, and dividing the visible part of the brain into two lateral halves termed *hemispheres*.

6. *transf.* and *fig.* A realm or region of action, life, or thought; = 'sphere'. In earlier quots. directly *fig.* from 2.

1503 HAWES *Examp. Virt.* xiv. (Arb.) 66 It may well glad thyn emyspery. **1608** D. T. *Ess. Pol. & Mor.* 38 b, When.. the starre of merit shal appear within the compasse of their Hemisphere, and offer presents. **1699** GARTH *Dispens.* II. 16 To guild, by turns, the Gallick Hemisphear. **1856** DOVE *Logic Chr. Faith* v. i. §2. 265 To surmise the possibility, as beyond the hemisphere of my knowledge. **1863** MRS. C. CLARKE *Shaks. Char.* iii. 75 He is a cheering..gleam coming across the dark hemisphere of treachery, mistrust and unkindness.

hemispherectomy (ˌhɛmɪsfɛˈrɛktəmɪ). *Surg.* [f. HEMISPHER(E 5 + -ECTOMY.] Excision of a cerebral hemisphere.

1950 *Jrnl. Neurol. & Psychiatry* XIII. 243/1 Over a period of five years..12 hemispherectomies were performed on patients suffering from infantile hemiplegia. *Ibid.* 263/1 Because of the ventricular distortion, hemispherectomy was carried out. **1956** E. L. MASCALL *Christ. Theol. & Nat. Sci.* vi. 252 There are no *theoretical* problems for Christian faith ..in the remarkable psychological effects of operations such as pre-frontal leucotomy, lobotomy and hemispherectomy.

'hemisphered, *a. rare.* [f. HEMISPHERE + -ED².]

1. Formed as a hemisphere.

1665 HOOKE *Microgr.* 178 The eyes of Crabs..are Hemispher'd, almost in the same manner as these of Flies. **1839** BAILEY *Festus* ix. (1854) 106 The hemisphered abysses here.

2. Having a cerebral hemisphere (of such a kind).

1871 HUXLEY in Darwin *Desc. Man* vii. (1883) 203 The Lemurine, short hemisphered, brain.

hemi'spheric, *a.* [f. HEMISPHERE + -IC. Cf. F. *hémisphérique* (16th c.).]

1. = HEMISPHERICAL 1: chiefly in technical use.

1585 T. WASHINGTON tr. *Nicholay's Voy.* II. xxi. 58 Great bodies of building round and strongly set up vawtwise in form of the Hemispherike. *a* **1728** WOODWARD *Fossils* (J.), A pyrites, placed in the cavity of another of an hemispherick figure, in much the same manner as an acorn in its cup. **1774** G. WHITE in *Phil. Trans.* LXIV. 197 In about ten or twelve days is formed an hemispheric nest. **1852** TH. ROSS *Humboldt's Trav.* I. vi. 239 Mimosas, with hemispheric tops. **1870** HOOKER *Stud. Flora* 355.

2. = HEMISPHERICAL 2.

1889 TALMAGE in *Voice* (N.Y.) 28 Feb., Corrupt legislation, which at times makes our State and National capitals a hemispheric stench. **1896** *Westm. Gaz.* 16 Jan. 5/2 The Olney doctrine of the Hemispheric Sovereignty of the United States.

hemispherical (hɛmɪˈsfɛrɪkəl), *a.* [f. as prec. + -AL¹.]

1. Of or pertaining to a hemisphere; of the form of or resembling a hemisphere.

1624 WOTTON *Archit.* in *Reliq.* (1672) 32 Hemispherical Vaults..be..the securest. **1685** BOYLE *Effects of Mot.* ix. 114 A hollow vessel..of an almost Hemispherical figure. **1794** MARTYN *Rousseau's Bot.* xvi. 194 The capsule is.. covered with a hemispherical lid. **1831** BREWSTER *Optics* xxxix. 325, I have proposed to use a hemispherical lens. **1879** *Cassell's Techn. Educ.* I. 186 The seeds..are hemispherical, with one side convex and the other flat.

2. Of or belonging to one hemisphere of the earth; extending over a hemisphere.

1872 O. W. HOLMES *Poet Breakf.-t.* x. 334, I suppose we are getting over our hemispherical provincialism. **1884** (*U.S. Senator*) in *Pall Mall G.* 7 June 1/2 The American idea is hemispherical rather than continental.

Hence **hemi'spherically** *adv.*, with a hemispherical form.

1846 DANA *Zooph.* (1848) 524 Hemispherically shrubby-cespitose.

hemi'spherico-, combining form of HEMISPHERIC *a.*, joined adverbially with adjectives, as **hemispherico-conical, -conoid** *adjs.*, conical, etc. but with an approach to the hemispheric form.

1831 DON *Gard. Dict.* Gloss., *Hemispherico-conical*, a shape between a globe and a cone. **1851** LEIGHTON *Brit. Lichens* 23 The slightly raised hemispherico-conoid black apex only visible.

hemispheroid (hɛmɪˈsfɪərɔɪd). [f. HEMI- + SPHEROID, or f. HEMISPHERE + -OID. Cf. F. *hémisphéroïde* (1732 in Hatz.-Darm.).] The half of a spheroid; a figure approaching a hemisphere.

1727–51 CHAMBERS *Cycl.* s.v. *Hemispheroidal*, The cacao opens, when yellow and ripe, into two large hemispheroids. **1752** BEVIS in *Phil. Trans.* XLVIII. 397 The hemispheroid of the earth formed by the section..of the circle of declination. **1823** J. BADCOCK *Dom. Amusem.* 209 The shape of his pontons..was an oblong hemispheroid.

ˌhemisphe'roidal, *a.* [f. prec. + -AL¹.] Having the form of a hemispheroid.

1727–51 CHAMBERS *Cycl.* **1881** G. MACDONALD *Mary Marston* I. ii. 21 A large hemispheroidal carbuncle.

†**hemi'spherule.** *Obs.* A half spherule; a small hemispherical lens.

1696 W. S. GRAY in *Phil. Trans.* XIX. 281, I was wont to Grind them [glasses] and Polish them on a brass Plane, and so reduce them to Hemispherules. **1756** AMORY *J. Buncle* (1770) II. 81 They have them [microscopes] of all kinds, of one and more hemispherules.

hemistich (ˈhɛmɪstɪk). *Pros.* Also 7 **hemistique, -estique**, 7–8 **hemistick**, 8 **-estich**; 7–8 in L. form **hemistichium**. [ad. late L. *hēmistichium*, ad. Gr. ἡμιστίχιον, f. ἡμι- HEMI- + στίχος row, line, verse. Cf. F. *hémistiche* (16th c. in Hatz.-Darm.), *hémistique* in Cotgr.] The half or section of a line of verse, as divided by the cæsura or the like; also, a line of less than the usual length. *spec.* Such a half-line or line in Old English verse.

1575 LANEHAM *Let.* (1871) 40 In the skro vndergrauen.. iz thear a proper woord, an hemistichi, well squaring with al the rest..*Lac, Caseus infans.* **1609** DOD & CLEAVER *Expos. Prov. ix. & x.* 88 The first hemistich, or former part of the verse. **1621** BURTON *Anat. Mel.* III. iv. I. ii, According to that hemistichium of Petronius, *primus in orbe deos fecit timor*. **1635–56** COWLEY *Davideis* I. *14th Note*, I am far from their opinion, who think that Virgil himself intended to have filled up these broken Hemestiques. **1711** ADDISON *Spect.* No. 39 ⁋5, I do not dislike the Speeches in our English Tragedy that close with an Hemistick or Half Verse. **1823** J. BOSWORTH *Elem. Anglo-Saxon Gram.* 246 The question, as to whether the two hemistichs shall be regarded as one or two lines, is evidently that of a writer or printer, not of a singer or reciter. **1837–9** HALLAM *Hist. Lit.* (1847) II. 169 The occasional hemistich and redundant syllables break the monotony of the measure. **1857** C. PATMORE in *North Brit. Rev.* XXVII. 148 Each hemistich contains two accented syllables. **1888** A. S. COOK *Judith* p. 1, The line of poetry consists of two hemistichs, separated by the cæsura. **1925** M. D. CLUBB *Christ & Satan* p. xv, The mark most consistently..employed is the metrical point, indicating the pause between hemistichs. **1970** *Jrnl. Eng. & Gmc. Philol.* LXIX. 86 One would not expect *þā* to provide the only alliteration in the second hemistich.

Hence **'hemistichal** *a.*, pertaining to a hemistich.

1824 *Warton's Hist. Eng. Poetry* (1840) I. 15 *note*, The reader will observe the constant return of the hemistichal point, which I have been careful to preserve.

hemi'symmetry. *Cryst.* [HEMI- b.] Same as HEMIHEDRISM. Hence **hemisy'mmetrical** *a.*, hemihedral.

1881 THUDICHUM *Ann. Chem. Med.* II, Hemisymmetry in the Chemical Constitution of Gelatin. **1895** STORY-MASKELYNE *Crystallogr.* §271 A few forms exhibit, in the defalcation of their alternate faces, the gyroidal hemi-

symmetry, which, however, must be held really to dominate the structure of the entire crystal. *Ibid.* §280 Hemi-symmetrical crystals afford abundant examples of twin-structure.

hemisyste'matic, *a.* *Cryst.* [HEMI- b.] (See quot.)

1878 GURNEY *Crystallogr.* 54 A hemisystematic form. **1895** STORY-MASKELYNE *Crystallogr.* §139 A *hemi-systematic form* is a form in which only half the origin-planes or normals are extant, the correlative half being absent.

'hemitery. *Path.* [ad. mod.L. *hemiteria*, F. *hémitérie*, f. HEMI- + Gr. τέρας monster.]

A general term for a malformation that does not amount to monstrosity.

1879 tr. *De Quatrefages Hum. Spec.* 252 With man, as with animals, varieties have appeared at times which may be classed among hemitery.

†**'hemitone.** *Mus. Obs.* [ad. L. *hēmitonium*, ad. Gr. ἡμιτόνιον, f. HEMI- + τόνος TONE.] Half-tone, SEMITONE.

1694 *Phil. Trans.* XVIII. 71 In the Chromatick the Degrees were Hemitones and Trihemitones. **1760** STILES *Ibid.* LI. 724 But, should we admit more tones than these, as they do, who augment their excesses by hemitones, the meses of two tones must..be applied to the place of one sound.

hemitrichous, -triglyph, etc.: see HEMI-.

†**hemitri'tæan**, *a.* *Obs. Med.* [f. late L. *hēmitritæ-us*, ad. Gr. ἡμιτριταῖος (Hippocrates) semi-tertian, f. ἡμι- HEMI- + τριταῖος on the third day, lasting three days, f. τρίτος third: see -AN. Cf. F. *hémitritée.*]

Semi-tertian: said of an intermittent fever that combines the symptoms of a quotidian and a tertian fever, consisting of a paroxysm occurring every day with a second stronger one every other day.

1651 J. F[REAKE] *Agrippa's Occ. Philos.* 374 It will cure the Hemitritean Feaver. **1657** G. STARKEY *Helmont's Vind.* 259, I leave out the names of Feavers Hemitritean.

hemitropal (hɪˈmɪtrəpəl), *a.* [f. as next + -AL[1].] = HEMITROPOUS 2.

1864 in WORCESTER (citing A. GRAY). **1866** *Treas. Bot.* 581/1 *Hemitropal*, a slight modification of the anatropal ovule, in which the axis of the nucleus is more curved.

hemitrope (ˈhɛmɪtrəʊp), *a.* and *sb.* *Cryst.* [ad. F. *hémitrope* (1801 Haüy), f. HEMI- + Gr. -τροπος turning.] **A.** *adj.* = HEMITROPIC.

1805–17 R. JAMESON *Char. Min.* (ed. 3) 225 *Hemitrope*.. that is, one-half turned round, when it is composed of two halves of one and the same crystal, of which the one-half appears to be turned upon the other one-half of the circumference. Example, Twin-crystal of felspar. **1823** H. J. BROOKE *Introd. Crystallogr.* 89 A hemitrope crystal.. resembling one of the varieties of the common spinelle. **1895** STORY-MASKELYNE *Crystallogr.* §159 In the hemitrope position..one pair of the faces forms a re-entrant angle.

B. *sb.* A hemitropic crystal.

1805–17 R. JAMESON *Char. Min.* (ed. 3) 176 Haüy has given to these reversed crystals the name hemi-tropes, denoting one half reversed. **1895** STORY-MASKELYNE *Crystallogr.* §157 Repetition of the twinning on similar twin-faces may indeed occur..Such crystals are triple, quadruple, &c. hemitropes (or triplings, fourlings, &c.).

So **'hemitropism, he'mitropy**, hemitropic crystallization.

1845 *Encycl. Metrop.* IV. 578 A variety of cases of hemitropism. **1879** RUTLEY *Study Rocks* x. 92 Due to hemitropy or a half revolution of one of the halves of the crystal. **1895** STORY-MASKELYNE *Crystallogr.* §163 It results from the law of hemitropy that each pair of corresponding faces on the two crystals lies in one zone with the twin-plane and that the faces make equal angles with it.

hemitropic (hɛmɪˈtrɒpɪk), *a.* *Cryst.* [f. as prec. + -IC.] Said of a composite or twin crystal: see quots.

1886 F. W. RUDLER in *Geol. Mag.* III. 267 The edges of the hemitropic lamellæ are too blurred to allow the exact angles to be taken. **1895** STORY-MASKELYNE *Crystallogr.* §154 Two crystals are said to be hemitropic or twinned when, presenting identical forms, they are united together in such a way that, if we conceive one of them as being turned through half a revolution round a particular line which wil' be termed the twin-axis..corresponding faces and edges in the two crystals would become parallel. *Ibid.* §159 In the case of two hemitropic diplohedral crystals, the twin plane becomes in a crystallographic sense a plane of symmetry to the twin-structure; but..each crystal in the hemitropic group retains its individuality, notwithstanding the mutual interpenetration of the crystals.

he'mitropous, *a.* [f. as prec. + -OUS.]

1. *Cryst.* = HEMITROPIC (Mayne *Expos. Lex.*).

2. *Bot.* Said of an ovule having a form intermediate between the anatropous and orthotropous, so that the hilum lies halfway between the base and the apex.

1860 in WORCESTER (citing A. GRAY).

hemitype, -typic: see HEMI-.

hemixis (hɛˈmɪksɪs). *Biol.* Also **hemimixis**. [f. HEMI- + Gr. μίξις mixing, f. μ(ε)ίγνυμι to mix: see MIXO-.] In *Paramecium*, any of several types of change in the macronucleus, such as fission or elimination of chromatin, which take place without involving the micronucleus. So **he'mictic** *a.*, of, pertaining to, or characterized by hemixis.

1936 W. F. DILLER in *Jrnl. Morphol.* LIX. 18 The attempt at interpreting the varied cytological conditions which P. aurelia exhibits under different circumstances has led to the discovery of a hitherto undescribed sexual reproductive process which corresponds to autogamy as it is known in other animals, and to a group of asexual phenomena which will be called 'hemixis'. *Ibid.* 36 It is proposed to group these reorganizations together..and refer to them collectively by the term 'hemixis'. By this term is meant a series of autonomous changes which the macronucleus undergoes in vegetative life, exclusive of binary fission. *Ibid.*, No genetic relationships are necessarily implied between the varieties of hemictic phenomena. **1940** L. H. HYMAN *Invertebrates* I. iii. 176 In hemimixis the macronucleus undergoes degenerative changes. **1953** R. WICHTERMAN *Biol. Paramecium* iii. 90/2 Hemictic animals with the two micronuclei may show variable numbers and sizes of macronuclear fragments. **1961** MACKINNON & HAWES *Introd. Study Protozoa* iv. 292 A variety of nuclear changes may occur [in *Paramecium*] without the intervention of a micronucleus; they are collectively known as hemixis..and their significance is uncertain.

hemizygous (hɛmɪˈzaɪgəs), *a.* *Biol.* [f. HEMI- + HOMO)ZYGOUS *a.*] Having a single unpaired allele at a particular genetic locus, as at all the loci in an XO pair of sex-chromosomes and some of the loci in an XY pair, rather than having two paired alleles, one on each homologous chromosome, as normally occurs in a diploid. So **hemi'zygote**, a hemizygous organism; **hemizy'gotic** *a.*, hemizygous; **hemi'zygously** *adv.*, in a manner characteristic of a hemizygote.

1921 W. A. LIPPINCOTT in *Amer. Naturalist* LV. 570, I should like to suggest the noun *hemizeuxis* (a half yoking) and the corresponding adjective *hemizygous* (half yoked). Should such a suggestion prove acceptable there would be the three adjective series: homozygous, heterozygous, and hemizygous, referring to the three possible conditions with respect to any single gene, namely, 'like mates', 'differing mates', and 'no mate'. **1935** H. J. MULLER in *Jrnl. Genetics* XXX. 407 The terms 'hemizygous' and 'hemizygote' (Serebrovsky) refer to the condition of being haploid for a given gene when the genome as a whole is diploid; its usual usage is in connection with sex-linked genes in the sex in which they are haploid. *Ibid.*, The normal gene, although apparently quite dominant to white and to the other mutants, must in reality be incompletely so, and the heterozygotes, being like uncompensated hemizygotes, must have a definitely lower average survival rate. **1939** C. H. WADDINGTON *Introd. Mod. Genetics* ii. 62 Muller has suggested that it would be better to speak of factors in haploid organisms such as male bees as hemizygous; and this word can also be used for factors (e.g. in an unpaired *X* chromosome) for which there is no allelomorph in a normal diploid. **1961** *Lancet* 16 Sept. 626/2 In a hemizygous XO female, a recessive gene could express itself as in a heterozygous XY male. **1965** J. A. SERRA *Mod. Genetics* I. iv. 103 The genes for haemophilia and for colour-blindness have no allele in the Y chromosome, that is the males are hemizygotic for these factors. *Ibid.* 109 The yellow-black pair of alleles in cats producing either yellow or black hemizygous males but giving patched black and yellow or 'tortoise-shell' females when these are heterozygous. *Ibid.* 111 Such a character is transmitted from father to son and because there is no corresponding allele in the X chromosome, it manifests itself hemizygously.

hemlock (ˈhɛmlɒk), *sb.* Forms: α. 1 **hymlice, hymlic, hemlic**, 3 **hemeluc**, 5 **hem(e)lok**, 6 **hemlake**, 6–7 **hemlocke**, 7 **hemloc, hemblock**, 6– **hemlock**. β. 5 **humlok(e, humblok, homeluk, -lok**, 6 **humlocke, homlo(k)ke, -lock(e**, 5–9 (*dial.*) **humlock**. [OE. *hymlice* weak fem., *hymlic, hemlic*, str. masc.; of obscure origin: no cognate word is found in the other langs.

The form *hym-* is app. the original, that in *hem-* being Kentish. The later *hum-, hom-*, probably come from *hym-*; the ordinary form in mod.Sc. is *humlo*'.]

1. a. The common name of *Conium maculatum*, a poisonous umbelliferous plant, having a stout branched stem with purplish spots, finely divided leaves, and small white flowers; it is used medicinally as a powerful sedative. **b.** Also in rural use applied to the large *Umbelliferæ* generally: in south of Scotland esp. to *Angelica sylvestris*, and to *Heracleum Sphondylium*, 'Hairy Humlo'.

It is not clear how far back these uses go. The OE. *hymlice* was a medicinal plant (prob. *Conium*); but the ME. the plant is chiefly referred to as a weed; the definite references to it as poisonous appear to begin with the 16th c. herbalists.

a **700** *Epinal Gloss.* 185 *Cicuta*, hymblicæ [*a* **800** *Erfurt* Huymblicæ]. *c* **725** *Corpus Gloss.* 463 *Cicuta*, hymlice. *c* **1000** ÆLFRIC *Gloss.* in Wr.-Wülcker 136/1 *Cicuta*, hemlic. *c* **1000** *Sax. Leechd.* II. 18 Do to hymlican and eofor þrotan. *Ibid.* II. 74 Nim weax & hemlic, ʒetrifula. *Ibid.* III. 50 Wyll in buteran nyoðerweardne hymlic. *c* **1265** *Voc.* in Wr.-Wülcker 558/3 *Herba benedicta*, *i.* herbe beneit, *i.* hemeluc. *c* **1400** MAUNDEV. (Roxb.) xiv. 65 It es gude to sawe in humbloks and nettles and swilk oþer wedes. **14..** *Voc.* in Wr.-Wülcker 571/34 *Cecuta*, hemlok. *c* **1425** *Voc.* ibid. 645/21 *Hic tipus*, homelok. *c* **1450** *Alphita* 40/1 *Cicuta*.. *angl.* hemelok *uel* hornwistel. **1483** *Cath. Angl.* 191/2 An Humlok, *cicuta, harba benedicta, intubus.* *a* **1500** *Songs & Carols* (1847) 10 (Mätz.) Whan brome wyll appelles bere, And humloke hony in feere, Than sek rest in lond. **1549** COVERDALE, etc. *Erasm. Par. Jas.* iii. (R.), What is it elles than the poison of humlocke myxed with wyne? **1551** TURNER *Herbal* I. K iv, In sum places men vse to eate the yong stalkes of homlokkes in sallattes. **1573** TUSSER *Husb.* xxxiii. (1878) 74 Thy garden twifallow, Stroy hemlock and mallow. **1578** LYTE *Dodoens* III. xxiv. 452 Hemlocke is very euyl, dangerous, hurtful, and venemous. **1597** GERARDE *Herbal* 904 (Britten & H.) The leaues shoote foorth of the ioints and branches like unto wilde Homlocks. **1599** SHAKS. *Hen. V*, v. ii. 44 Her fallow Leas, The Darnell, Hemlock, and ranke Femetary, Doth root vpon. **1605** —— *Macb.* IV. i. 25 Roote of Hemlocke, digg'd i' th' darke. **1635** SWAN *Spec. M.* vi. §4 (1643) 266 Hemlock..is meat to storks, and poyson to men. **1699** GARTH *Dispens.* II. (1700) 14 Baneful Hemlock, and cold Aconite. **1758** J. G. COOPER *Apol. Aristippus* (R.), Deadly hemlock's pois'nous weed. *c* **1800** *Yng. Tamlane* lv. in Scott *Minstr. Scot. Bord.*, Their oaten pipes blew wondrous shrill, The hemlock small blew clear; And louder notes from hemlock large, And bog-reed, struck the ear.

c. With qualifying words, applied to various other umbelliferous plants with finely-divided leaves, as **bastard hemlock**, *Anthriscus sylvestris* (*Syd. Soc. Lex.*); **lesser h.**, Fool's Parsley, *Æthusa Cynapium*; **mountain h.**, *Levisticum officinale* (Miller *Plant-n.*); **water h.**, various species of *Cicuta* and *Œnanthe*.

1764 CROKER, etc. *Dict. Arts & Sc.*, *Cicuta-Aquatica*, long-leaved water hemlock, a poisonous plant..growing in many meadows and watery places. **1788** J. LEE *Introd. Bot.* (ed. 4) 273 *Cicuta*, Water Hemlock. **1794** MARTYN *Rousseau's Bot.* xvii. 231 The waters afford other poisonous herbs as Water Hemlock. **1796** WITHERING *Brit. Plants* (ed. 3) II. 305 Fool's Parsley, or Ciceley, Lesser Hemlock.

2. a. A North American tree, *Abies canadensis*, more fully ***hemlock fir, h. spruce***, 'so called from the resemblance of its branches in tenuity and position to the leaves of the common hemlock'.

1776 C. CARROLL *Jrnl. Miss. Canada* in B. Mayer *Mem.* (1845) 49 Several rocky islands appear in the lake [George, N.Y.], covered with a species of cedar here called hemlock. **1830** LYELL *Princ. Geol.* xiv. (1847) 197 Forests of spruce-fir and hemlock, a kind of fir somewhat resembling our yew in foliage. **1841–4** EMERSON *Ess.*, *Nature* Wks. (Bohn) I. 224 The stems of pines, hemlocks, and oaks, almost gleam like iron on the excited eye. **1847** LONGF. *Ev.* Prel. 1 The murmuring pines and the hemlocks, Bearded with moss, and in garments green, indistinct in the twilight. **1856** BRYANT *Poems, Catterskill Falls* iv, The long dark boughs of the hemlock fir. **1892** *Garden* 27 Aug. 200 One came upon finely-developed specimens of the Hemlock Spruce..the Indian Cedar..and such-like ornamental trees. **1927** M. DE LA ROCHE *Jalna* xviii. 213 She stood..looking at the sombre shapes of the hemlocks. **1932** *Atlantic Monthly* Mar. 331/2 We come to that hidden glade, under the beeches, under the hemlocks.

b. ***ground hemlock***: a Canadian species or variety of Yew (*Treas. Bot.* 1866).

3. A poisonous potion obtained from the common hemlock. (Believed to have been the poison by which Socrates was put to death.)

1601 HOLLAND *Pliny* II. 235 The..law of the Athenians, wherby malefactors..were forced to drink that odious potion of Hemlock. **1626** BACON *Sylva* §643 The Death that is most without Paine, hath beene noted to be, vpon the Taking of the Potion of Hemlock. **1820** KEATS *Ode to Nightingale* 2 A drowsy numbness pains My sense, as though of hemlock I had drunk. **1874** BLACKIE *Self-Cult.* 21 Plato was twenty-nine years old when Socrates drank the hemlock.

4. *attrib.* and *Comb.*, as ***hemlock draught, -drinker***; ***hemlock-like*** adj.; (sense 2) ***hemlock forest, lumber***, etc.; also **hemlock chervil**, *Torilis Anthriscus*; **hemlock dropwort**: see DROPWORT 2; **hemlock parsley**, a North American umbelliferous plant resembling hemlock, but not poisonous; there are two species *Conioselinum Canadense* and *C. Fischeri*; **hemlock pitch**, the resinous exudation of the Hemlock spruce; **hemlock stork's-bill**, *Erodium cicutarium*; **hemlock tree** = sense 2.

1761 WATSON in *Phil. Trans.* LII. 91 This plant is called, by..Mr. Ray, Small *hemlock-chervil with rough seeds. **1849** RUSKIN *Sev. Lamps* v. §3. 138 Architecture..being especially dependent..on the warmth of the true life, is also peculiarly sensible of the *hemlock cold of the false. **1597–8** BP. HALL *Sat.* iv. (1824) 38 Socrates his poison'd *hemlock draught. **1824** BYRON *Def. Transf.* I. i. 228 Be air, thou *hemlock-drinker! **1856** OLMSTED *Slave States* 155 An agreeable resinous odor, resembling that of a *hemlock forest. **1862** *Chambers' Encycl.* V. 306 A..liquid, having.. a penetrating *hemlock-like odour. *Ibid.*, Two priests ate *hemlock-root by mistake; they became raving mad. **1813** HOGG *Witch of Fife* vii, Mine [steed] was made of ane *humlocke schaw, An a stout stallion was he. **1861** MISS PRATT *Flower. Pl.* II. 45 *Erodium cicutarium* (*Hemlock Stork's-bill).

hemlock (ˈhɛmlɒk), *v.* [f. the sb.] *trans.* To poison with hemlock. Hence **'hemlocked** *ppl. a.*

1846 THACKERAY *Cornhill to Cairo* v. 66 Of the race of Englishmen who come wondering about the tomb of Socrates, do you think the majority would not have voted to hemlock him? **1908** L. ABERCROMBIE *Interludes & Poems* 18 The slave Fate who serves Gods..fetched Skill'd poison,.. and with this stew Hemlock'd the wine of Heaven. **1934** DYLAN THOMAS *Let.* 11 May (1966) 129 A twisted veil of evil ..coils up from the pit to the top of the hemlocked world.

hemmed (hɛmd), *ppl. a.* [f. HEM *v.*[1] + -ED.]

Furnished with a hem or border; sewed with a hem. ***hemmed in***: shut in, confined, imprisoned.

c **1460** *Towneley Myst.* (Surtees) 311 With thare hemmyd shoyn, Alle this must be done. **1730** A. GORDON *Maffei's Amphith.* 339 The young Men..wore a hemm'd Gown. **1824** SCOTT *Redgauntlet* Let. xii, I ken him by his hemmed cravat. **1894** *Westm. Gaz.* 27 June 7/1 With a mere hemmed-in Sierra Leone (and Egypt) to represent its once wide dominions.

hemmel: see HEMEL.

hemmer ('hɛmə(r)). [f. HEM *v.*[1] + -ER[1].] One who hems; in earlier times, one who makes or trims borders of garments.

1483 *Cath. Angl.* 182/2 An Hemmer, *limbator.* **1598** FLORIO, *Orlatrice*, a seame-stresse, a welter, a hemmer. **1852** MISS MITFORD *Recoll.* I. 301 The hemmer of flounces ..seemed flurried and fatigued.

b. An 'attachment' to a sewing-machine for doing hemming (Knight *Dict. Mech.* 1875).

†'**hemming**, *sb. Obs.* [a. ON. *hemingr* (*hǫmungr*) 'the skin of the shanks of a hide', f. *hǫm* shank.] The skin or hide of a deer's shank; a rough shoe or brogue made from this.

c **1050** *Gloss.* in Wr.-Wülcker 468/31 *Pero*, hemming *i.* ruh sco. *c* **1320** *Sir Tristr.* 476 Þe heminges swiþe on est He schar and layd bi side. *c* **1425** WYNTOUN *Cron.* VIII. xxix. 274 At sa gret myschef he wes, That hys Knychtis weryd Rewylynys Of Hydis, or of Hart Hemmynys.

hemming ('hɛmɪŋ), *vbl. sb.*[1] [f. HEM *v.*[1] + -ING[1].] **a.** The action of the vb. HEM[1]; the making or providing of a firm neat border to any article of clothing, upholstery, or the like; that which is hemmed; a fringe, the border of a garment. Also ***hemming-in***.

German hemming, a substitute for top-sewing (Caulfeild & Saward *Dict. Needlework* 1882).

a **1300** *E.E. Psalter* xliv. 14 [xlv. 13] Doghtres of kinges.. In gliterand gilted hemminges. **1502** *Privy Purse Exp. Eliz. of York* (1830) 7 Payed for the hemmyng of a kertelle of the Quenes of damaske iiij*d.* **1530** PALSGR. 230/2 Hemmyng or hemme of a garment, *ourelevre.* **1642** FULLER *Holy & Prof. St.* I. ix. 23 Many favours which God giveth us ravell out for want of hemming. **1888** *Illustr. Lond. News* 14 Apr. 384/1 The exquisitely fine hemming and stitching shown at Lord Aberdeen's house. **1905** *Fabian News* Mar. 14/2 It is enacted that 'he who receives relief must submit to the hemmings in of his personal liberty which the law imposes'.

b. *attrib.*

1858 *U.S. Patent 21,355* (*title*) Improvement in hemming guides for sewing machines. *a* **1865** in M. Johnson *Amer. Advertising* (1960), Patent binding folders and hemming guides on hand. **1932** D. C. MINTER *Mod. Needlecraft* 196/2 *For Machining Hems.*—Screw on the hemming foot in place of the presser foot. **1972** *Canad. Antiques Collector* Mar.-Apr. 32/2 A hemming bird, ornate and beautifully made..brought over..one hundred and fifty years ago from Scotland.

hemming, *vbl. sb.*[2] [f. HEM *v.*[2] + -ING[1].] The action of the verb HEM[2]; coughing, clearing of the throat.

1470–85 MALORY *Arthur* XI. viii, She coughed soo lowde that syre launcelot awaked and he knew her hemynge. **1553** BECON *Reliques of Rome* (1563) 263 b, It might chaunce to be cast out by spitting or hemmyng. **1609** *Ev. Woman in Hum.* II. i. in Bullen *O. Pl.* IV, Hem, hem. A pox on your hemmings, do you think we care for your hemmings? **1786** MAD. D'ARBLAY *Diary* 6 Oct., At length a prodigious hemming showed the preparation in the Colonel for a speech. **1896** in Sir. A. Otway *Pref. to Autobiog. Ld. Clarence Paget* 5 With his 'hemming' and 'hawing', and other tokens of oratorical imperfection.

hemmir, obs. Sc. form of HAMMER.

hemmorhoid(e, obs. forms of HÆMORRHOID.

hemo-, variant spelling of HÆMO-, usual in U.S., and not unfrequent in Great Britain in words of more general use, as *hemorrhage*, *hemorrhoid*.

hemp (hɛmp), *sb.* Forms: 1 **hænep, henep,** 4– **hemp,** (4–7 **hempe,** 6 **hemppe**). [OE. *hęnep, hænep* = OLG. **hanap*, **hanip*, MDu. and Du. *hennep*, LG. *hemp*, OHG. *hanaf, -if, -uf* (MHG. *hanef*, Ger. *hanf*), ON. *hampr* (Sw. *hampa*, Da. *hamp*):—OTeut. **hanpi-z*, **hanapi-z*, cogn. with Gr. κάνναβις, L. *cannabis*: cf. also Lith. *kanapės*, OSlav. *konoplja*, Pers. *kanab*. The word is perh. not Aryan, but adopted in Greek, Germanic, etc. from some common source.]

1. An annual herbaceous plant, *Cannabis sativa*, N.O. *Urticaceæ*, a native of Western and Central Asia, cultivated for its valuable fibre.

It is a diœcious plant, of which the female is more vigorous and long-lived than the male, whence the sexes were popularly mistaken, and the female called ***carl*** or ***winter h.***, the male ***fimble*** (i.e. female), ***barren***, or ***summer h.***: see CARL HEMP and FIMBLE.

(The quotations from the *Saxon Leechdoms* appear to refer to some wild British plant, perh. the ***wild hemp*** of 5.)

a **1000** *Gloss.* in Wr.-Wülcker *Voc.* 198/12 *Cannabum*, hænep. *Ibid.* 198/15 *Cannabin*, hænep. *c* **1000** *Sax. Leechd.* I. 16 Herba chamepitys þæt is henep [*v.r.* hænep]. *Ibid.* 228 Deos wyrt þe man cannane silfatica, & oþrum naman henep nemneþ. *c* **1325** [implied in HEMPSEED]. *c* **1440** *Promp. Parv.* 235/2 Hempe, *canabum.* **1523** FITZHERB. *Husb.* §146 In Marche is tyme to sowe flaxe & hempe. **1551** TURNER *Herbal* I. Hjb, Hempe..is profitable for many thynges..and specially to make stronge cables, and roopes of. **1578** LYTE *Dodoens* I. l. 72 Hempe is called in Greeke κάνναβις..in English Hempe, Neckeweede, and Gallow-grasse. **1794** MARTYN *Rousseau's Bot.* xxix. 456 Hemp has a five parted calyx in the flowers which bear stamens, but in the pistilliferous ones it is one-leaved, entire and gaping on the side. **1883** *Harper's Mag.* Oct. 715/2 Land that will grow hemp will grow anything.

b. **1523**, etc. [see CARL HEMP]. **1577**, etc. [see FIMBLE]. **1597** GERARDE *Herbal* II. ccxxxviii. (1633) 709 The male is called Charle Hempe and Winter Hempe. The female Barren Hempe, and Sommer Hempe. **1753** CHAMBERS *Cycl. Supp.* s.v., The male Hemp, or summer Hemp, which bears no seeds, and is called by the farmers *Fimble-hemp*, will have its stalks turn white in July. *Ibid.*, The remaining plants, which are the female Hemp, called by the farmer *Karle-hemp*, are to be left till Michaelmas.

2. The cortical fibre of this plant, used for making cordage, and woven into stout fabrics.

c **1300** *Havelok* 782 Hemp to maken of gode lines And stronge ropes to his netes. ? *a* **1366** CHAUCER *Rom. Rose* 1233 A sukkenye, That not of hempe ne [? hempene] heerdis was. **1404** *Nottingham Rec.* II. 22, xlv. strykes de hempe, iiij*d.* **1550** CROWLEY *Epigr.* 1139 Newe halters of hemppe. **1634** SIR T. HERBERT *Trav.* 105 Long, deepe prams, sowed together with hempe and cord. **1662–3** PEPYS *Diary* 18 Feb., Casting up..accounts of 500 tons of hemp brought from Riga. **1722** SEWEL *Hist. Quakers* VII. (1795) II. 10 Committed to Bridewell and required to beat hemp. **1881** *Daily News* 18 Apr. 2/8 Tows and hemps move off very freely.

3. In allusion to a rope for hanging.

† ***stretchhemp***, a person worthy of the gallows. † ***to wag hemp***, to be hanged.

1532 MORE *Confut. Tindale* Wks. 715/1 To mocke the sacrament the blessed body of god, and ful like a stretch hempe, call it but cake bred. *Ibid.*, Tindall..feareth not (like one yt would at length wagge hempe in the winde) to mocke at all such miracles. **1599** SHAKS. *Hen. V*, III. vi. 45 Let not Hempe his Wind-pipe suffocate. **1654** WHITLOCK *Zootomia* 60 Of no small use to purge a Common-wealth, without the expence of Hemp. **1849** JAMES *Woodman* xxviii, If his people catch me, I shall taste hemp. **1864** LOWELL *Fireside Trav.* 56 [He] express[ed] a desire for instant hemp rather than listen to any more ghostly consolations.

b. (See quot.) Cf. HEMPY *sb.*

1785 GROSE *Dict. Vulg. T.* s.v., *Young hemp*, an appellation for a graceless boy.

4. A narcotic drug obtained from the resinous exudation of the Indian hemp; bhang; hashish.

1870 YEATS *Nat. Hist. Comm.* 195 Hemp is employed in other forms besides churrus as a narcotic. **1893** *Nation* (N.Y.) 9 Feb. 108/1 Its votaries have taken to opium and hemp, the latter of which Sir Lepel Griffin says is far more injurious than tobacco.

5. With qualifying words, applied to numerous other plants yielding a useful fibre, or otherwise resembling hemp: as **African hemp**, (*a*) = *bowstring hemp* (*a*); (*b*) *Sparmannia africana* (Miller *Plant-names*). **American false h.**, *Datisca hirta* (Miller *Ibid.*). **bastard h.**, name given to the British plants Hemp-nettle and Hemp Agrimony (Britten & Holland). **Bengal h.**, **Bombay h.**, **Madras h.**, *Crotalaria juncea* (Miller). **bowstring h.**, (*a*) a plant of the genus *Sanseviera*, esp. *S. guineensis*, a liliaceous plant of tropical Africa, the leaf-fibres of which are used by the natives for bowstrings and for making ropes; (*b*) in India, *S. Roxburghiana*; also *Calatropis gigantea* (N.O. *Asclepiadaceæ*). **brown Indian h.**, *Hibiscus cannabinus* (Miller). **Canada** or **Indian h.**, *Apocynum cannabinum*, a N. American perennial (J. Smith *Dict. Econ. Pl.*). **Cretan h.**, *Datisca cannabina* (Miller). **holy h.**, an old name for *Galeopsis Ladanum* (Miller). **Indian h.**, a tropical variety of Common Hemp, *Cannabis Indica*. **jute** or **plant h.**, *Corchoris capsularis* (Encycl. Brit.). **Kentucky h.**, *Urtica* (*Laportea*) *Canadensis* and *U. cannabina* (Miller). **Manilla h.**, the fibre of *Musa textilis*, of the Banana family. **mountain h.**, *Hyoscyamus insanus* (Syd. Soc. Lex.). **nettle h.** = HEMP-NETTLE. **Peruvian h.**, *Bonapartea juncea*. **Queensland h.**, the tropical weed *Sida rhombifolia* (N.O. *Malvaceæ*), called also Paddy or Native Lucerne, and Jelly Leaf. **ramie h.**, *Bœhmeria nivea*. **sisal h.**, the fibre of species of *Agave*, esp. *A. Sisalana*. **Virginian h.**, **willow h.**, *Acnida cannabina*, an amarantaceous marsh plant, native of eastern U.S. **water h.**, a name given to *Eupatorium cannabinum* and *Bidens tripartita*, in U.S. to *Acnida cannabina*. **wild h.**, *Eupatorium cannabinum* (Gerarde), and *Galeopsis Tetrahit* (Britten & Holland).

1597 GERARDE *Herbal* II. ccxxviii. 573 This wilde Hempe called *Cannabis spuria*, and also *Cannabina Spuria*, or bastarde Hempe. *Ibid.*, In English wilde hempe, Nettle hempe, bastard hempe. *Ibid.* II. ccxxix. 574 The bastarde or wilde Hempes, especially those of the water, are called commonly *Hepatorium Cannabinum*..in English, water Hempe, bastard and water Agrimonie. **1611** COTGR., *Chanure sauvage*, Bastard Hempe, wild Hempe, Nettle Hempe. **1688** R. HOLME *Armoury* II. 72/2 The bastard Hemp is with several Burs, or hairy Knobs at a distance on the stalk. **1744** J. WILSON *Synops. Brit. Pl.* 95 *Lamium cannabino folio vulgare*..Nettle Hemp, or rather Hemp-leav'd dead Nettle. **1796** WITHERING *Brit. Plants* (ed. 3), *Bidens tripartita*, Trifid Doubletooth, Water Hemp, Water Agrimony. **1866** *Treas. Bot.* 350/2 *Crotalaria juncea*..This plant is extensively cultivated in..India, on account of the valuable fibre yielded by its inner bark, which is known by the names of Sunn-hemp, Bombay Hemp, Madras Hemp, Brown Hemp, etc. *Ibid.* 1015/2 The Bowstring Hemps..are stemless perennial plants. **1897** MORRIS *Austral Engl.* 195 *Queensland Hemp*...is not endemic in Australia.

6. ***attrib.*** and ***Comb.***

a. ***attrib.*** Of hemp; made of hemp, hempen.

a **1400–50** *Alexander* 2224 Oure pepill..Halis vp hemp cordis. **1549** *Privy Council Acts* II. 349/1 Hemp ropes, mᵗ weight. **1599** *Acc. Bk. W. Wray* in *Antiquary* XXXII. 243 A p[air] of hempe shetes. **1630** B. JONSON *New Inn* I. iii, He may, perhaps, take a degree at Tiburne..And so goe forth a Laureat in hempe circle! **1662–3** PEPYS *Diary* 24 Feb., Captn. Cocke and I upon his hemp accounts till 9 at night. **1668** T. THOMPSON *Eng. Rogue* II. i, You have no remedy against a hemp halter I hope. **1875** R. F. MARTIN tr. *Havrez Winding Mach.* 32 The wires..in each strand must be twisted round a hemp core. **1893** *Daily News* 2 Mar. 5/4 Inquiry..into the trade in all preparations of hemp drugs in Bengal.

b. Comb., as ***hemp-close***, ***-cock***, ***-garth***, ***-hammer***, ***-harvest***, ***-harvester***, ***-heckle***, ***-knocker***, ***-plant***, ***-plot***, ***-ridge***, ***-seller***, ***-smoker***, ***-spinner***, ***-stalk***, ***-top***; ***hemp-leaved***, ***-like***, ***-packed***, ***-producing*** adjs.; **hemp-beater**, a person employed in beating the rotted stems of hemp, so as to detach the fibre; an instrument used in doing this; **hemp-brake**, an instrument for bruising or breaking hemp; **hemp-bush**, an Australian Malvaceous plant, *Plagianthus pulchellus*, yielding a hemp-like fibre; **hemp-cake**, the residue of crushed hempseed, after extraction of the oil; **hemp-dike**, **-dub**, **-pit** (*dial.*), a small pond for steeping green hemp; **hemp-hards**, **-hurds**: see HARDS; **hemp-hatcheler**, **-heckler** = HEMP-DRESSER; **hemp-oil**, the oil pressed out of hempseed; **hemp-palm**, a palm, *Chamærops excelsa*, of China and Japan, the fibres of which are made into cordage; † **hemp-roll** (see quot.); **hemp-sick** *a.* (cf. HEMPEN 1 b, quot. 1785); **hempwort**, any plant of the Hemp family; **hemp-yard**, a piece of ground on which hemp is grown, a hemp-garth or hemp-close.

1615 E. S. *Brit. Buss* in Arb. *Garner* III. 653 Will convert ..our vagabonds..into lusty *hempbeaters. **1725** VANBR. *Prov. Wife* IV. iii, That fist of her's will make an admirable hemp-beater [in Bridewell]. **1886** *Syd. Soc. Lex.* s.v., Hempbeaters, carders, and spinners..suffer from dust arising from the material. **1873** BOUTELL & AVELING *Heraldry* Gloss., **Hemp-brake* or *Hackle*, an instrument for bruising hemp. **1878** *Ure's Dict. Arts* IV. 364 *Hemp cake is chiefly used for adulterating linseed cake. **1698** FROGER *Voy.* 58 The Fields..are like those of our *Hemp-Closes. **1669** WORLIDGE *Syst. Agric.* xii. (1681) 250 Stick them on the tops of *Hemp-cocks or Wheat-sheaves. **1877–89** *N.W. Linc. Gloss.*, **Hemp-croft*, *-garth*, *-yard*, the gardens attached to old cottages commonly went by one of these names, as they were in former days used mainly for growing hemp. **1878** *Cumberld. Gloss.* **Hemp dub*, a small pond used for steeping green hemp. **1627** *Merton Reg.* II. 296 Unum *Hempegarth simul cum libertate communii. **1663** *MS. Indent. of Barlby* (Yorksh.), An orchard, a hemp-garth, two gardens. **1637** NABBES *Microcosm.* v, The shrieks of tormented ghosts [are] nothing to the noise of *hemp-hammers. **1707** MORTIMER *Husb.* v. xi. 120 'Tis a very great help to the Poor; the *Hemp-harvest coming after the other Harvest. **1724–7** RAMSAY *Tea-t. Misc.*, *Bob of Dumblane*, Lend me your braw *hemp heckle. **1579** LANGHAM *Gard. Health* (1633) 300 Apply it with *Hempe-hurds to the heate of the Liuer and stomach. **1586** *Praise of Mus.* 76 That petie and counterfait Musick which..*hemp-knockers [make] wᵗ their beetels. **1744** *Hemp-leaved [see sense 5]. **1712** tr. *Pomet's Hist. Drugs* I. 158 The burnt Oil they make use of in *Hemp-Oil. **1839** R. S. ROBINSON *Naut. Steam Eng.* 39 This kind..keeps steam-tight with far less friction than the *hemp-packed piston. **16..** *Add. MS.* 31028 lf. 7 (N.W. Linc. Gloss.) Drowned in a *hempe pitt near a little sink of hempe. **1832** G. A. HERKLOTS tr. *Cust. Moosulm. India* Gloss., *Gunja*..the leaves or young leaf-buds of the *hemp plant. **1678** BUTLER *Hud.* III. ii. 43 Like Thieves that in a *Hemp-plot lie Secur'd against the Hue and Cry. **1824** MACTAGGART *Gallovid. Encycl.*, **Hemp-riggs*, ridges of fat land whereon hemp was sown in the olden time. **1696** J. F. *Merchant's Ware-ho.* 23 The next..Linnen, is called *Hemp Roles, it is always brought into England brown, and is a strong coarse Linnen..and..when whited very good for Sheets for Poor People. **1785** *Life Miss Davis* 5 He..was convicted and hanged..and her *hemp-sick husband laid in the earth. **1875** KNIGHT *Dict. Mech.* 1099/2 *Hemp-stalks are beaten to remove the bark and cellular pith from the fiber. **1853–5** *Cassell's Pop. Educ.* IV. 29/1 Cannabinaceæ or *Hempworts. **1378** *Durham MS. Cell. Roll*, In plumbo empto pro uno aqueducto in le *Hempyard. **1725** BRADLEY *Fam. Dict.* s.v. *Hemp*, Pigeons dung is good for Hemp Yards.

Hence **hemp** *v. trans.* (*rare*), to halter, to hang.

a **1659** CLEVELAND *Lenten Litany* II. i, That if it please thee to assist Our Agitators and their List, And Hemp them with a gentle twist.

hemp-'agrimony. *Herb.* **a.** A book-name for *Eupatorium cannabinum*, a composite plant with dull red flowers; also extended to other species. **b.** ***water hemp-agrimony***, a book-name for *Bidens* or Bur-Marigold.

1760 J. LEE *Introd. Bot.* 304 Hemp agrimony, Eupatorium. **1778** LIGHTFOOT *Flora Scot.* (1789) 461 *Bidens*, Water-hemp-agrimony, or Bur-marygold. *Ibid.* 464 *Eupatorium cannabinum*, Hemp-agrimony, Dutch-agrimony. **1893** E. H. BARKER *Wand. by South. Waters* 268 Hemp-agrimony made the bees sing a drowsy song. **1908** *Westm. Gaz.* 31 Aug. 2/3 Nature had..enriched the banks with..meadow-sweet and hemp-agrimony. **1971** *Country*

Life 17 June 1520/1 The muzzy mauve hemp-agrimony (*Eupatorium purpureum*).

'hemp-dresser. One who hackles hemp.

a **1659** CLEVELAND *Times* 81 No zealous Hemp-dresser yet dipp'd me in The Laver of Adoption from my Sin. **1723** *Lond. Gaz.* No. 6171/10 Benjamin Bellamy.. Hempdresser.

b. *pl.* The name of a kind of country-dance.

1756 AMORY *J. Buncle* (1770) II. 25 We..had the hemp-dressers one night, which is, you know..the most difficult, and laborious of all the country dances. **1827** in Hone *Every-day Bk.* II. 122, I have 'footed it' away in Sir Roger de Coverley, the hemp-dressers, &c.

hempen ('hɛmpən), *a.* (*sb.*) Also 4–5 **hempyn(e, -pene, (6–7 hempton, 7 hemton), 6–8 hemping.** [f. HEMP *sb.* + -EN[4]. Not recorded in OE.; but cf. OHG. *hanafîn* (Ger. *hänfen*), LG. *hempen*.]

1. Made of hemp; of or pertaining to hemp. ***hempen homespun***, homespun cloth made of hemp; hence, one clad in such cloth, one of rustic and coarse manners.

1375 BARBOUR *Bruce* x. 360 He gert sym of the ledows.. Of hempyn rapis ledderis ma. **1398** TREVISA *Barth. De P.R.* XIX. lxii. (1495) 898 The weke is made of hempen threde. *c* **1440** [see HEMPY *a.* 1]. **1535** LATIMER *Serm. Insurr. in North* (1844) 29 It is no knot of an hempton girdle. **1558** PHAER *Æneid* v. 552 But [he] hyt the hemping corde, and of the knot the bands he brast. **1590** SHAKS. *Mids. N.* III. i. 79 What hempen home-spuns haue we swaggering here? **1651** *Miller of Mansf.* 8 Good browne hempton sheetes. **1669** WORLIDGE *Syst. Agric.* (1681) 44 A very great succour to the poor, the Hempen Harvest coming after other Harvests. **1703** *Wakes Colne, Essex, Overseers' Acc.* (MS.), 6 yards of hempinge cloth for two shifts for Suzan Beets. **1776** ADAM SMITH *W.N.* I. x. II. (1869) I. 128 Weavers of linen and hempen cloth. **1887** BOWEN *Virg. Æneid* II. 236 Hempen cords cast over its neck.

fig. **1675** COTTON *Poet. Wks.* (1765) 297 Coarse hempen Trash is sooner read Than Poems of a finer Thread.

b. In humorous phrases and locutions, referring to the hangman's halter.

a **1420** HOCCLEVE *De Reg. Princ.* 454 Ware hem of hempyn lane! For stelthe is meeded with a chokelewe bane. *a* **1529** SKELTON *Agst. Garnesche* 162 Stop a tyd, and be welle ware Ye be nat cawte in an hempen snare. **1593** SHAKS. *2 Hen. VI*, IV. vii. 95 Ye shall haue a hempen Caudle then, and the help of hatchet. **1594** NASHE *Unfort. Trav.* 67, I..scapde dauncing in a hempen circle. **1606** DEKKER *Sev. Sinnes* VII. (Arb.) 44 Lamentable hempen Tragedies acted at Tiburne. **1632** RANDOLPH *Jealous Lovers* (N.), Shall not we be suspected for the murder, And choke with a hempen squincey? *a* **1700** B. E. *Dict. Cant. Crew*, *Hempen-widdow*, one whose Husband was Hang'd. **1785** GROSE *Dict. Vulg. T.* s.v., A man who was hanged is said to have died of a hempen fever. **1837** SIR F. B. HEAD *Narrative* viii. (1839) 208 What could they be worth to him but a hempen neck-cloth?

2. Resembling hemp.

1651 J. F[REAKE] *Agrippa's Occ. Philos.* 100 It makes a Hempen colour. **1772–84** COOK *Voy.* IX. IV. iii. (R.), Made of the bark of a pine-tree beat into a hempen state.

B. *sb.* Hempen cloth.

1777 ROBERTSON *Hist. Amer.* (1783) I. 255 They found Balboa..wearing coarse hempen used only by the meanest peasants.

†**'hempenly,** *a. nonce-wd.* [f. prec. + -LY[1].] Relating to or connected with hemp.

1609 PAULE *Life Abp. Whitgift* 40 A choise broker for such souterly wares, and in regard of his hempenly trade, a fit person to cherish up Martins birds.

hemph, obs. var. HUMPH *int.*

hempie: see HEMPY.

hemping: see HEMPEN.

hempland. Land appropriated to the growth of hemp; a piece of land formerly so applied.

1526 *MS. Acc. St. John's Hosp., Canterb.*, Rec...for ferme of hempland iiij*d.* **1670** EACHARD *Cont. Clergy* 93 A couple of apple-trees, a brood of ducklings, a hempland, and as much pasture as is just able to summer a cow. **1735** *N. Riding Rec.* IX. 131 The other closes and parcells of ground called Hemplands. **1846** E. SPURDENS *E. Anglian Words* (E.D.S.), *Pightle*, the little man's little field: called in Suffolk a *hempland*, without respect to the produce.

†**hempling,** *a. Obs.* Also 6 -lynne. [f. HEMP: cf. *hemping* = HEMPEN.] Of hemp, hempen.

1492 *Churchw. Acc. Walberswick, Suffolk* (Nichols 1797) 190 Two hempnling toweles. **1594** in *Archæol.* XLVIII. 136 Item v hemplynne square clothes.

'hemp-nettle. *Herb.* A name for the genus *Galeopsis* (N.O. *Labiatæ*), and esp. the common species *G. Tetrahit*; cf. *nettle-hemp* in HEMP 5.

1801 WITHERING *Brit. Plants* (ed. 4). **1861** S. THOMSON *Wild Fl.* III. (ed. 4) 251 Another lipped flower is the..hemp-nettle. **1863** BARING-GOULD *Iceland* 242 In the grass grew the common hempnettle.

hempseed ('hɛmpsiːd). The seed of hemp. ***a caudle of hempseed*** = 'hempen caudle' (HEMPEN 1 b).

c **1325** *Gloss. W. de Biblesw.* in Wright *Voc.* 156 *Canoys*, hempseed. *c* **1532** DEWES *Introd. Fr.* in *Palsgr.* 915 Hempe sede, *canebuise*. **1588** *Marprel. Epist.* (Arb.) 17 He hath prooued you to haue deserued a cawdell of Hempseed. **1694** *Phil. Trans.* XVIII. 36 Of a grey colour, and a convex figure, like the half of an Hempseed. **1714** GAY *Sheph. Week* Thursday 31 This hempseed with my virgin hand I sow, Who shall my true-love be, the crop shall mow. **1838** T. THOMSON *Chem. Org. Bodies* 429 Oil of Hempseed is obtained by expression from the seeds of..hemp.

b. A gallows-bird.

1597 SHAKS. *2 Hen. IV*, II. i. 64 Do, do thou Rogue: Do thou Hempseed.

c. *attrib.*, as **hempseed bird**, a bird fed on hempseed; **hempseed calculus** (*Path.*), name given by Wollaston to some varieties of the mulberry-calculus.

1611 CORYAT *Crudities* 15 Many gold Finches, with other birds which are such as our hempseede birds in England. **1864–70** T. HOLMES & HULKE *Syst. Surg.* (1883) III. 237 The dumb-bell crystals often unite into a mass and form the nucleus of a concretion called the hemp-seed calculus. *Ibid.* 246 The small, smooth, globular 'hemp-seed calculus'.

'hempstretch. *nonce-wd.* A person hanged. Cf. *stretch-hemp*, HEMP 3.

a **1843** SOUTHEY *Comm.-pl. Bk.* I. 369 One of the men who were hanging..asked him..to cut the rope. He did so, and Hempstretch fell on his feet.

'hempstring. *lit.* String or cord made of hemp. Hence *transf.*, one who deserves the halter.

1566 GASCOIGNE *Supposes* IV. ii, If I come neere you, hempstring, I will teache you to sing sol fa. **1606** CHAPMAN *Mons. D'Olive* Plays 1873 I. 241 A perfect yong hempstring. *Van.* Peace, least he overheare you! **1885** HOWELLS *S. Lapham* I. i. 40 He cut the heavy hemp-string with his penknife.

†**'hemptery.** *Obs.* Also hemptre, -teren. [? for *hempery, hempry*.] Hempen fabric.

1570 *Bury Wills* (Camden) 156, I beqwethe to my dawghter Jone..one payer of shetes of hempteren..to my dawghter Anne..one payer of sheets of hemptery..to John Kanam my sonne..one payer of shetes of hemptre.

hempton, obs. form of HEMPEN.

†**'hemp-tree.** *Obs.* An old name of the Chaste Tree, *Vitex Agnus-castus*.

1548 TURNER *Names of Herbes* G viij b, Vitex is..a tree and hath leaues lyke Hemp..Wherfore it may be called in englishe Hemp tree, or Chast-tree, or Agnus tree. **1597** GERARDE *Herbal* (1633) 1388. **1611** COTGR., *Amerine*, Agnus castus..chast or hempe tree.

'hempweed.

†**1.** Some kind of sea-weed; ? = DULSE. *Obs.*

1620 MARKHAM *Farew. Husb.* iii. 28 You shall gather from the bottome of the Rocks (where the seydge of the Sea continually beateth) a certaine blacke weede, which they call Hemp-weede, hauing great broad leaues.

2. = HEMP-AGRIMONY, and other species of *Eupatorium*.

1796 WITHERING *Brit. Plants* (ed. 3) III. 707 *Eupatorium cannabinum*,..Hemp Agrimony, Dutch Agrimony, Water Agrimony, Water Hemp, Common Hempweed. **1862** ANSTED *Channel Isl.* (1865) 177 The hemp-weed or hemp-agrimony, a common plant enough. **1886** *Syd. Soc. Lex.* s.v., Aromatic hempweed, *Eupatorium aromaticum*. Round-leaved Hempweed, *Eupatorium rotundifolium*.

hempy, hempie ('hɛmpɪ), *a.* and *sb.* [f. HEMP *sb.* + -Y.]

A. *adj.* **1.** Made of, like, or of the nature of hemp; hempen; having or producing hemp.

c **1440** *Promp. Parv.* 235/2 Hempyne, or hempy.., *canabeus*. **1572** J. JONES *Bathes Buckstone* 10 b, Such [euill ayre] as commeth of Hempy grounds, as in Holland. **1611** COTGR., *Chanureux*, Hempen, Hempie, of Hempe. *c* **1645** HOWELL *Lett.* II. 54 'Twixt the rind and the Tree there is a Cotton, or hempy kind of Moss, which they wear for their Clothing.

2. *Sc.* and *north.* Worthy of the hangman's halter; usually jocular, meaning merely Mischievous, giddy, often in scrapes.

1816 SCOTT *Old Mort.* xlii, I was a daft hempie lassie then, and little thought what was to come o't. **1825** BROCKETT, *Hempy*, mischievous—having the qualities likely to suffer by cat o' nine tails, or by the halter. Applied jocularly to giddy young people of both sexes. **1885** RUNCIMAN *Skippers & Sh.* 110 Noted as the most 'hempy' boy in the..district.

B. *sb.* One who deserves to be hanged; one for whom hemp grows. Usually jocular: A mischievous giddy boy or girl.

1718 RAMSAY *Christ's Kirk* III. xviii, He had gather'd seven or aught Wild hempies stout and strang. **1818** SCOTT *Hrt. Midl.* l, 'Where did you get the book, ye little hempie?' said Mrs. Butler. **1864** J. HARDY in *Proc. Berw. Nat. Club* 181 This hempie of a bird has taken to colonising. **1893** CROCKETT *Stickit Minister* (1894) 259 She had been a big-boned 'hempie' at the Kirkland School.

hemrod, -roid, obs. ff. HÆMORRHOID, EMEROD.

hemselve(n, self(e, themselves: see SELF.

'hem-stitch, *v.* [f. HEM *sb.*[1] + STITCH *v.*] *trans.* To hem with an ornamental stitch of a particular kind, giving the effect of a row of stitching (see quot. 1882); to ornament with this stitch.

1839 MRS. PAPENDIEK *Crt. Q. Charlotte* (1887) I. i. 28 The tucks and hems being hem-stitched with Valenciennes lace. **1852** MRS. STOWE *Uncle Tom's C.* xv, A hemstitched pocket-handkerchief. **1874** MRS. H. WOOD *Mast. Greylands* xvii. 196 Half-a-dozen handkerchiefs..that Mrs. Castlemaine had given to her to hem-stitch. *Ibid.* xxii. 254 Diligently pursuing the hem-stitching of the handkerchief. **1882** CAULFEILD & SAWARD *Dict. Needlework*, *Hem-stitch*, a term in needlework, designating the mode of producing a delicate kind of open-work, by drawing together certain threads in the material of the stuff, to be sewn in small successive clusters.

Hence **'hem-stitch** *sb.*, ornamental needle-work of this kind.

1853 MRS. BROWNING *Let.* Dec. in *Pall Mall G.* (1892) 15 Aug. 2/3 You give the facts, as facts, without using them as the confirmatory hemstitch of a preconceived theory. **1874** MRS. H. WOOD *Mast. Greylands* xix. 220 The work is really beautiful: it is the broad hem-stitch..four or five rows of it.

hemton, obs. form of HEMPEN.

†**hemule, hemuse.** *Venery. Obs.* [A word of uncertain form. The Bk. of St. Albans has *hemule*; the 16–17th c. and later writers (whose information seems to be entirely derived from the Bk. of St. Albans) have *hemuse*: an *l* and a 'long *s*' are easily confused in 15th c. writing. No etymology is known.] A roebuck of the third year.

1486 *Bk. St. Albans* E iv b, The Roobucke..The first yere ..is a kyde..The thirde yere an hemule loke ye hym call. **1576** TURBERV. *Venerie* 143 The fawne of a Rowe is called the first yeare a kidde: the second a gyrle: the third yeare an hemuse. **1598** MANWOOD *Lawes Forest* iv. §5 (1615) 44/2 A Roe is called..The third yeere, a Hemuse. **1660** HOWELL *Parly Beasts* 62 (D.) Those pretty fawns, prickets, sorrells, hemuses, and girls, whereof som are mine.

hemward, toward them: see HEM *pron.* and -WARD.

hen (hɛn), *sb.* Forms: 1 hen(n, hæn(n, 2–5 henn, 3–7 henne, (5 hene), 3– hen. [OE. *hęnn* str. f., corresp. to OLG. **hęnna* (MDu. *henne*, Du. *hen*), OHG. *hęnna* (Ger. *henne*):—WGer. **hannja*, deriv. of *hano*, OE. *hana* cock.]

1. a. The female of the common domestic or barn-door fowl, the male of which is the COCK.

As in the domestic state the females greatly exceed in number the cocks kept, and their economic importance is more prominent, the word *hens* is also used in some connexions as = 'domestic fowls' without regard to sex.

c **950** *Lindisf. Gosp.* Matt. xxiii. 37 Suæ henne somnigas cicceno hire under feðrum. *c* **1000** *Ags. Gosp.* Ibid., Swa seo henn hyre cicenu under hyre fyþeru ȝegaderað. *c* **1000** *Sax. Leechd.* II. 40 Wiþ þon ilcan ȝenim hænne rysele. *c* **1050** *Byrhtferth's Handboc* in *Anglia* VIII. 309 Oft seo brodiȝe henn þeah heo sarlice cloccige. *a* **1225** *Ancr. R.* 66 Þe hen hwon heo haueð ileid, ne con buten kakelen. *c* **1308** *Pol. Songs* (Camden) 199 Gees no hen nad ic noȝt. **1340** *Ayenb.* 38 Þe little þyeues þat steleþ..hire capons, hennen, frut of hire gardins. **1390** GOWER *Conf.* III. 280 As a cock among the hennes. *c* **1430** *Two Cookery-bks.* 14 Take Conynge, Hen, or Mawlard. **1577** B. GOOGE *Heresbach's Husb.* IV. (1586) 170 b, Fesantes..are better to bee brought up under a Henne. **1601** HOLLAND *Pliny* x. lvi. (R.), A man shall know a good and kindly hen by her comb, when it is streight and upright. **1774** GOLDSM. *Nat. Hist.* III. III. ii. (R.), A common hen, if moderately fed, will lay above a hundred eggs from the beginning of spring to the latter end of autumn. **1847** TENNYSON *Princ.* v. 318 'Boys!' shriek'd the old king, but vainlier than a hen To her false daughters in the pool.

b. Proverbial and other expressions. ***like a hen with one chick(en)***: indicating extreme solicitude or fussiness about a small matter; **(as) mad as a wet hen**: very angry; **(as) scarce** (occas. **rare**) **as hen's teeth** (orig. *U.S.*): very scarce.

1508 DUNBAR *Tua mariit Wemen* 269 That hurtis ȝow nought worth a hen. **1553** T. WILSON *Rhet.* (1580) 223, I knewe a Prieste that was as nice as a Nonnes Henne, when he would saie Masse. **1595** G. DELAMOTHE *Treasure French Toung* 19 He is as busie as a henne that hath but one chicken. **1601** HOLLAND *Pliny* Ep. to Vespas., As the proverb goeth, looke to drinke there or else no where a good draught of hens milke. **1670** J. RAY *Coll. Eng. Prov.* 203 As busie as a hen with one chicken. **1732** T. FULLER *Gnomologia* 25 As busy as a Hen with one Chick. **1766** GOLDSM. *Vic. W.* xii, I'll warrant we'll never see him sell his hen of a rainy day. **1823** J. DODDRIDGE *Logan* 42 Every body that was not ax'd was mad as a wet hen. **1854** A. E. BAKER *Gloss. Northampt.* I. 320 'As busy as a hen with one chick.' Unnecessarily solicitous or active over trifles. **1858** in N. E. Eliason *Tarheel Talk* (1956) 276 As scarce as hen's teeth. **1863** 'E. KIRKE' *Southern Friends* 250 [Horses are] scarcer than hen's teeth round here. **1881** A. PARKER *Oxfordshire Words* (Suppl.) s.v., To be as busy as a hen with one chick is to make a great fuss over a little work. They also say 'as proud as a hen with one chick'. **1893** *Congress. Rec.* 2 Oct. 2044/1 North of Mason and Dixon's line, colored county officials are scarce as hen's teeth. **1904** E. F. BENSON *Challoners* x, Karl is devoted to him, just like a beautiful old hen in spectacles with one chicken. **1907** *Amer. Mag.* Feb. 339/1 He just looked at me and then flounced out, mad as a wet hen. **1962** *Listener* 5 July 8/2 A good guide for Western leaders, among whom communiqués were 'as scarce as hens' teeth'. **1969** *Times* 12 June 3 (Advt.), Stoppages are as rare as hen's teeth.

2. With qualifying words: † ***hen of grease***, fat hen: see GREASE. † ***hen of Guinea***: the Guinea hen. † ***Our Lady's hen***: a name formerly given to the wren and the lark. ***Pharaoh's hen***: the Egyptian vulture (*Neophron Percnopterus*). ***Port Egmont hen***: the Great Skua of the Falkland Isles. ***sea hen***: a name of the *Uria Troile*, Foolish Guillemot (Pennant *Brit. Zool.* 1768 II. 410).

1552 HULOET, Hennes of Genny, *meleagrides*. **1604** DRAYTON *Owl* Wks. (1793) 565/2 The Hedge Sparrow, and her compeer the Wren, (Which simple people call our Lady's-Hen). *c* **1878** *Helps Study Bible* 185 *Gier Eagle* (Lev. xi. 18), the 'Egyptian vulture' or 'Pharaoh's hen'. **1878** LECKY *Eng. in 18th C.* II. v. 28 The lark was known as Our Lady's hen.

3. a. The female of various other birds; in a wider sense, of any bird = *hen-bird*. See also 7.

?*c* **1325** in *Rel. Ant.* I. 168 Partriche, fesant henne ant fesant cocke. *c* **1420**, *c* **1475** [see COCK *sb.*[1] 9]. **1540** HYRDE tr. *Vives' Instr. Chr. Wom.* II. vii. (R.), I my selfe..haue seene the cocke swan kill his hen, because she followed another

cocke. **1577** B. GOOGE *Heresbach's Husb.* IV. (1586) 167 Turky Cockes..the Hennes may compare with either the goose, or the Pehen. **1600** SHAKS. *A.Y.L.* IV. i. 151 More iealous..then a Barbary cocke-pidgeon ouer his hen. **1766** PENNANT *Zool.* (1776) I. 267 The hen [of the blackcock] lays seldom more than six or seven eggs. **1879** J. A. TAYLOR *Mount. & Moor* 219 An old blackcock crowing on a birch-tree with a dozen hens below it.

b. Forming the second element in the name of female birds of various species, as GUINEA HEN, GREY-HEN, HEATH-HEN, MOOR-HEN, PEA-HEN, WATER-HEN, etc. q.v.

In some of these the name of the male is in *-cock*, as *heath-cock*, *peacock*, etc.

4. A female fish or crustacean.

1747 H. GLASSE *Art of Cookery* xxi. 164 Cock Lobster is known by the narrow back Part of the Tail... The Hen is soft, and the back of her Tail broader. *a* **1855** G. JOHNSTON *Fishes Berwicksh.* (in Yarrell), The Cock and Hen Paidle spawn toward the end of March and in April. At that season the Hen..deposits her spawn among the rocks. **1895** *Westm. Gaz.* 31 May 5/3 A splendid salmon..The fish (a hen) was taken with a net.

5. *fig.* Of persons. **a.** Used for wife, woman, female. *humorous* or *low colloq.* **b.** A hen-hearted person of either sex.

c **1626** *Dick of Devon.* IV. iii. in Bullen *O. Pl.* II. 79 One of the soldiers..sayes th'are dainty Hennes. **1632** BROME *North. Lass* I. v. Wks. 1873 III. 10 Are you the Cockbawd to the Hen was here? **1685** *Roxb. Ball.* (1891) VII. 474 She is the Cock and I am the Hen. **1785** GROSE *Dict. Vulg. T.*, *Hen*, a woman. A cock and hen club; a club composed of men and women. *c* **1880** G. MEREDITH *Old Chartist* in *Daily News* (1897) 21 Sept. 6/1 But if I go and say to my old hen: I'll mend the gentry's boots, and keep discreet. **1897** MARY KINGSLEY *W. Africa* 650 The Krumen are silly hens not to go and wipe out Liberia on shore.

6. A kind of bivalve shell-fish, *Venus mercenaria*. Also *locally*, A fresh-water mussel. Cf. HEN-CLAM.

1603 OWEN *Pembrokesh.* (1892) 126 Perywinkles, hens and diuerse other shell fish [still in local use (Editor's note)]. **1623** WHITBOURNE *Newfoundland* 9 Lobsters, Crafish, Muskels, Hens, and other varieties of Shelfish. **1686** J. DUNTON *Lett. fr. New-Eng.* (1867) 178 Their black Money ..is made of the shell of a Fish, which the English call Hens, but the Indians Poquauhock. **1864** THOREAU *Cape Cod* v. (1894) 100 The sea-clam, or hen, was not easily obtained.

7. *attrib.* in sense of 'female': **a.** of birds.

c **1000** *Sax. Leechd.* I. 92 Nim þonne þa corn and ȝewurp to sumum henfuȝule. **1154** *O.E. Chron.* an. 1131 þær æ fter swulten þa henne fuȝeles. **1616** SURFL. & MARKH. *Country Farme* I. xxi. 85 The Henne Partridge is so fruitfull that [etc.]. **1660** BOYLE *New Exp. Phys. Mech.* Wks. 1772 I. 97 Soon after we got a hen sparrow. **1760** EDWARDS in *Phil. Trans.* LI. 835 The whole upper side nearly resembles that of a hen-pheasant. **1773** BARRINGTON in *Phil. Trans.* LXIII. 264 It is for the same reason that no hen-bird sings. **1818** KEATS *Endym.* III. 1020 The hen-dove shall not hatch Her ready eggs.

b. of fishes, crustacea, etc.

1865 J. G. BERTRAM *Harvest of Sea* xiii. (1873) 266 There are the cock and hen lobster. **1886** R. C. LESLIE *Sea-painter's Log* 21 The hen crab is known from the male by her much wider waistcoat.

8. *Comb.*, as ***hen-court***, ***-dam***, ***-hutch***, ***-keep***, ***-killer***, ***-loft***, ***-run***, ***-trough***, ***-yard***; ***hen-brained***, ***-feathered***, ***-footed***, ***-headed***, ***-house***, ***-like***, ***-tailed***, ***-toed*** adjs.; **hen-and-egg**, used *attrib.* of the unresolvable problem of the 'first cause' (freq. in somewhat trivial contexts); cf. CHICKEN *sb.*[1] 6 b; **hen-balk**, a hen-roost; **hen-blindness**, nyctalopia; **hen-cackle** *N.Z. slang* (see quots.); **hen-corn** (see quots.); **hen-driver**, the hen-harrier; **hen-fish**, †(*a*) a kind of shell-fish: see sense 6; (*b*) a local name of the bib or pout; **hen-flesh**, the roughness of the skin arising from chilliness or shivering, goose-flesh; **hen-frigate**, 'a ship wherein the captain's wife interfered in the duty or regulations' (Smyth *Sailor's Word-bk.* 1867): cf. HEN-PECKED b; **hen-fruit** chiefly *U.S. slang*, eggs; also ***hen's fruit***; †**hen-harm**, the hen-harrier; **hen-party**, a gathering consisting only of women; **hen-plant**, a name for two common species of Plantain (*Plantago lanceolata*, *P. major*); †**hen's bill**, an old name of Sainfoin (Gerarde *Herbal* 1597, Index); **hen scratch** *U.S.*, 'a chicken feed made from grain for scattering in litter or on the ground to induce chickens to scratch' (*Dict. Americanisms*); **hen-scratch** *v.*, to scratch in the manner of a hen; also *transf.*; **hensure** *a.* [joc. formation after COCK-SURE *a.*], = COCK-SURE *a.* 5; so ˌ**hen'sureness**.

1931 A. L. ROWSE *Politics & Younger Generation* 146 It is the old *hen-and-egg argument, that there is no knowing which comes first. **1951** W. EMPSON *Struct. Complex Words* 436 But firstly, there is a typical hen-and-egg problem. *a* **1963** L. MACNEICE *Astrology* (1964) ii. 39 The old hen-and-egg dilemma (did god or planet come first?). **1674–91** RAY *N.C. Words* 135 **Hen bawks*, a Hen Roost, from the Bawks of which it consists. **1893** *Northumb. Gloss.*, *Hen-baak*, *-balk*, *-boak*, a hen roost. **1822–34** *Good's Study Med.* (ed. 4) III. 148 Hens..cannot see to pick up small grains in the dusk of the evening, and so employ this time in going to roost; on which account the disease is sometimes called *hen-blindness. **1923** W. DE LA MARE *Riddle* 93 Poor *hen-brained things, they came to be fed. **1965** A. GARNER *Elidor* xix. 147 You landed us in enough trouble yesterday with your hen-brained ideas. **1939** J. PASCOE *Unclimbed N.Z.* ii. 33 All the lasting Alpine partnerships in Canterbury have been formed on the easy expeditions. '*Hen-cackles' we call these expeditions. **1941** BAKER *N.Z. Slang* vi. 57 Hen-cackle ..is applied by mountaineers to a mountain that is easy to climb. Doubtless there is a wider application of the term since a mere hen-cackle, a trifle, seems to have been the origin of the application. **1790** *Trans. Soc. Enc. Arts*, etc. VIII. 32 Wheat sown too long on the same spot, without changing the seed, will generally become smutt and *hen-corn. **1891** *Sheffield Gloss.* Supp., *Hen corn*, poor, thin, ill-fed wheat; corn which is not round and plump. 'It will grow nothing but hen corn'. **1853** MRS. CARLYLE *Lett.* II. 244 A perfectly empty *hen-court. **1678** T. JONES *Heart & Right Sov.* 201 No more than duck-chickens [hear] their *hen-dam, recalling them from their connatural element. **1674** N. COX *Gentl. Recreat.* (1677) 161 Of inferiour sort are these.. The Forked Kite and bold Buzzard, The *Hen-driver, &c. **1868** DARWIN *Anim. & Pl.* I. 253 This bird..has begot both *hen-feathered and male-feathered offspring. **1603** OWEN tr. *Hor. Sat.* II. iv. in *Pembrokesh.* (1892) 125 *Henfishe best are in Lucrina Lake. **1835–59** *Yarrell's Brit. Fishes* (ed. 3) I. 541 The Bib or Pout..is brought to Belfast Market..under the name of *Henfish*. *c* **1425** *Voc.* in Wr.-Wülcker 662/3 *Caro gallinacia*, *heneflesch. **1854** MISS BAKER *Northampton Gloss.*, Hen-flesh. **1892** D. JORDAN ['Son of the Marshes'] *Within Hour Lond.* (ed. 2) 153 They know all the fowl, web-footed and *hen-footed. **1785** GROSE *Vulg. T.* s.v., *Hen frigate..a sea phrase..applied to a ship, the captain of which had his wife on board, supposed to command him. **1854** *Harper's Mag.* Jan. 280/2 A young lady is said to have asked a gentleman at the table of a hotel 'down East' to pass her the '*hen fruit'. She pointed to a plate of eggs. **1873** C. G. LELAND *Egypt. Sketch-Bk.* 71 Their 'hen-fruit', as it is elegantly termed in America. **1887** *Boston Guide* (Farmer), If he confines his Hen Fruit to the vintage of '87. **1942** *Sunday Chron.* 1 Mar. 1/1 To him [*sc.* a ward-room steward] egg and bacon is 'hen's fruit and hog's body'. **1611** COTGR., *Ian le blanc*, a *Hen-harme, or white Kite. **1912** *Dialect Notes* III. 578 *Hen-headed*, brainless. 'That *hen-headed cuss can't do anything you tell him.' **1938** A. H. BILL *Astrophel* iv. 76 Elizabeth, always short of money.., railed against the required outlay like a hen-headed housewife over a coal bill. **1960** *Farmer & Stockbreeder* 16 Feb. 152/1 A *hen-housed average of 104·4 eggs per bird in 112 days. **1826** CARLYLE *Lett.* (1888) I. 41 All the farm-produce that he should need, horse-keep and *hen-keep [etc.]. **1611** COTGR. s.v. *Adventurier*, An idle..rogue; a hedge-creeper, *henne-killer. **1868** DARWIN *Anim. & Pl.* I. 252 Several of these *hen-like sub-breeds having been long propagated. **1888** *Harper's Mag.* Jan. 191 Wings outspread after a protective, hen-like fashion. **1592** NASHE *P. Penilesse* (1842) 68 Hauing no roome for his *hen-loft but the tester of his bed. **1887** W. WESTALL *Her two Millions* xxvii, It was a '*hen party' to which his wife had gone. **1960** *Guardian* 15 Feb. 4/3 A hen-party can be a very pleasant, relaxing affair, particularly for the older woman. **1897** *Westm. Gaz.* 3 Aug. 2/1 Eulogistic accounts of his *hen-run and his kitchen-garden. **1929** J. B. PRIESTLEY *Good Companions* I. i. 20 He was now 'on his own' at Wabley, the proud proprietor of a large hen-run. **1887** V. PYKE *Hist. Early Gold Discoveries in Otago* 35 Peter was only **hen-scratching* on the edges of the creek. **1921** D. H. LAWRENCE *Sea & Sardinia* 267 It was a small, stony, hen-scratched place of poor people. **1931** *Daily News-Jrnl.* (Murfreesboro, Tenn.) 15 Apr. 4/2 Corn,.. White oats,..Hen Scratch. **1957** V. J. KEHOE *Technique Film & T.V. Make-Up* vii. 86 Facial lining for old age and other character make-ups should not look like 'hen scratchings'. **1929** D. H. LAWRENCE *Assorted Articles* (1930) 72 There are the women who are cocksure, and the women who are *hensure. *Ibid.* 76 The lovely henny surety, the hensureness which is the real bliss of every female, has been denied her. **1951** M. MCLUHAN *Mech. Bride* 64/1 The old age reserved for the hensure types. **1868** DARWIN *Anim. & Pl.* I. 252 A *hen-tailed sub-breed of Hamburghs was recently much esteemed. **1937** PARTRIDGE *Dict. Slang* 388 **Hen-toed*, with one's feet turned in as one walks. **1955** I. PEEBLES *Ashes* 36 He stands at the wicket rather hen-toed. **1701** J. CUNNINGHAM in *Phil. Trans.* XXIII. 1207 A small frame about 3 or 4 foot long not much larger than a *Hen-trough. **1816** M. L. WEEMS *Lett.* (1929) III. 166 Yr. Bible carts had been here as thick as weasels in a *hen yard selling Bibles at nearly half price. **1876** *Scribner's Monthly* Apr. 813/2 The best places in which to look for Jacobean sideboards..are found to be the hen-yard. **1960** *Farmer & Stockbreeder* 2 Feb. 121/1 The breeders have been housed in the henyard previously used for layers.

†**hen, henne**, *adv.* *Obs.* Forms: α. 1 *hionane, heonane, -one, 2–3 heonene, 3 hinene, hennene, hinne, heonne, honne, 3–4 hunne, 3–5 henne, (4 hanne). β. 1 *hinan, hionan, heonan, -on, -un, 2 *heonen, (honen, henon), 2–3 henen, (3 hennen, heonnen, honnen, hunnen). γ. 1 (-hina), hiona, heona, 2–3 heone, 4–5 hene, hen. δ. 4–6 HYNE, q.v. [OE. **hionane*, *hionan* = OS. and OHG. *hinana*, *hinan*, MDu. *henen*, MHG. *hinnen*, *hinne*, Ger. *hinnen*; cf. also OHG. *hina*, MHG. *hine*, *hin*, Ger. *hin*, MLG. *hen*, MDu. *hēne*, *hin*, Du. *heen*; adverbial formations from root *hi-* 'this', of HE pron. The various OE. types gave a great number of forms in ME., all which are now obsolete, leaving only the later extended form *henne-s*, *hen-s*, HENCE, and the Sc. HYNE.]

= HENCE: of place, time, or inference.

α. *a* **1000** *Cædmon's Gen.* 791 Nu þu hie grimman meaht heonane ȝehyran. *c* **1000** *Ags. Gosp.* Matt. xvii. 20 Gyf..ȝe cwædon to þissum munte far heonone [*Lindisf. G.* heona, *Rushw. G.* heonan, *Hatton G.* heonen]. *c* **1175** *Lamb. Hom.* 11 We moten heonene feren. *c* **1205** LAY. 7122 Uncuðe leoden..beoð idriuen hennene. *Ibid.* 19119 þenne maȝen we ..heonene [*c* **1275** hinne] iwenden. *a* **1225** *Leg. Kath.* 1393 Ear we faren henne. *a* **1250** *Owl & Night.* 66 Alle ho the driveth honne. *c* **1290** *S. Eng. Leg.* I. 226/238 þat is hunne meni a myle. *Ibid.* 236/584 'Wend heonne', heo seiden. **1297** R. GLOUC. (1724) 476 Wende we henne anon. *a* **1300** *St. Michael* 98 in *Treat. Science* (1841) 134 More..Than hit beo hunne to the mone. **13..** *Sir Beues* (A.) 1237 Beues, þow most hanne To Brademond. *c* **1374** CHAUCER *Troylus* IV. 1218 (1246) þat day is not fer henne. *c* **1440** *Partonope* 173 But two yere henne and one half a yere.

β. *c* **825** *Vesp. Psalter* xcii[i]. 2 Hionan from weorulde. *c* **1000** *Ags. Gosp.* Matt. ix. 24 Gað heonun [*Hatton G.* Gað heonen]. *c* **1200** *Trin. Coll. Hom.* 161 Seðen hie henen wenden. *c* **1205** LAY. 5822 Ʒif we hennen [*c* **1275** hinne] fareð þus. *Ibid.* 5968 Heonnen [*c* **1275** hinene] he wule buȝen in to Bruttæine.

γ. [*a* **800** *Leiden Gloss.* 255 in *O.E. Texts* 117 *Citra*, bihina.] *c* **950** *Lindisf. Gosp.* Luke iv. 9 Asend ðeh heona aduna [*Rushw. G.* hiona of dune]. *c* **1340** *Cursor M.* 18080 (Fairf.) Do now go hen fro me sathon. *Ibid.* 20388 (Fairf.), I was farrer hen..ferre out in anoþer lond. *c* **1386** CHAUCER *Reeve's T.* 113, I pray yow spede vs heythen [*Camb.* hene] that ye may. **1426** AUDELAY *Poems* 9 And bryng thi lyf to good endyng, here and hen.

Hence †**hen-**, **henneforth**, **-forthward**(**s**, **forward** *adv.*, henceforth, henceforward. †**hen**(**en**)**sith** *sb.*, departure hence, death. †**henward, heoneward** *adv.*, away from here, hence.

c **1000** ÆLFRIC *Gen.* viii. 21 Nelle ic nateshwon awirȝean þa eorþan heonon forþ for mannum. *a* **1175** *Cott. Hom.* 225 Ic nelle henon forð mancyn mid watere adrenche. *a* **1225** *Leg. Kath.* 2099 Him we kennið..heonne forðwardes. **13..** *Guy Warw.* (A.) 593 Henne forward ne reche y me Of mi liif whare it be. *c* **1380** WYCLIF *Serm.* Sel. Wks. I. 170 To be hise frendis from henneforþ. **1382** —— *Phil.* iii. 1 Henne forthward, my britheren, haue ȝe ioye in the Lord. **14..** *Tundale's Vis.* 2292 Fro syn henforward thou the absteyne. *c* **1410** LOVE *Bonavent. Mirr.* xliii. lf. 93 (Gibbs MS.) Now henne forwarde be plesede and welwylled to hem for my loue.

a **1000** *Cod. Exon.* (Th.) 450 Heofona hyrde, æfter heonan siþe, godum dædum. *c* **1200** *Trin. Coll. Hom.* 185 Sorehful is ure hider cume, and sorilich ure henen sið.

971 *Blickl. Hom.* 115 þæt þeos world is scyndende and heononweard. *a* **1225** *Leg. Kath.* 1915 Me longeð heonneward. *a* **1225** *Ancr. R.* 98 Aris up; hie þe heoneward.

†ˈ**henad.** *Obs.* [ad. Gr. ἑνάς, ἑνάδ- unit, f. ἕν one.] A unit, monad (in the Platonic philosophy).

1678 CUDWORTH *Intell. Syst.* I. iv. §36. 556 One Goodness, Many Goodnesses, and one Vnity or Henade, Many Henades. *Ibid.* 626 That there must be a single Monad or Henad, standing alone by itself. **1792** J. TAYLOR tr. *Proclus* II. 267 There must be an order of Henades prior to that of intellects.

Hence †**he'nadical** *a.*, relating to a henad.

1678 CUDWORTH *Int. S.* 556 Henadical (or Monadical) Gods.

hen and chickens. (Beside the literal sense, this has the following transferred uses.)

1. A name for the Pleiades.

[**1535** COVERD. *Job* ix. 9 *note*, Some call these seuen starres, the clock henne with hir chekens.] **1613** PURCHAS *Pilgrimage* (1614) 68 That Constellation, called by the vulgar, the Hen and chickens, and of the learned Pleiades.

2. A name for several plants. **a.** ***hen-and-chicken***(*s* ***daisy***: a cultivated variety or monstrous form of the daisy, in which smaller flower-heads grow from the edge of the main flower-head.

1794 MARTYN *Rousseau's Bot.* xv. 163 The main flower is surrounded by a set of very small ones..as in the Hen and Chicken Daisy. **1861** DELAMER *Fl. Gard.* 81 Proliferous or Hen-and-Chicken Daisies. **1884** V. STUART *Egypt* 164 The curious compound daisy called Hen-and-chickens.

b. A name for a variety of Polyanthus; also for a species of Houseleek (*Sempervivum globiferum*); also (locally) for Ground Ivy, London Pride, Columbine, Bird's-foot Trefoil, and Daffodil. (See Britten & Holland *Plant-n.*).

3. The name of a children's game.

1894 A. B. GOMME *Trad. Games Eng. Scotl. & Irel.* I. 201 Hen and Chicken... The game is played in the usual manner of 'Fox and Goose' games. One is chosen to be the Hen, and one to be the Fox. The rest are the Chickens. **1969** I. & P. OPIE *Children's Games in Street & Playground* xi. 311 It was played..under the names 'Fox and Chickens'..and 'Hen and Chickens'.

ˈ**henatrice.** *nonce-wd.* A humorous feminine of COCKATRICE.

a **1843** SOUTHEY *Doctor* cc. (1847) VI. 366 It is affirmed that there is no female Basilisk, that is, no Henatrice, the Cock laying only male eggs.

henbane (ˈhɛnbeɪn). Also 3 **hennebone**, 4 **henebon**, 5 **henneban**(**e**, **henban**, (**hen**(**n**)**esbane**), 6 **henbayne**. [f. HEN *sb.* + BANE. Cf. HENBELL.]

1. The common name of the annual plant *Hyoscyamus niger*, a native of Europe and northern Asia, growing on waste ground, having dull yellow flowers streaked with purple, viscid stem and leaves, unpleasant smell, and narcotic and poisonous properties; also extended to the genus as a whole.

c **1265** *Voc.* in Wr.-Wülcker 559/9 *Iusquiamus*..i. hennebone. **1398** TREVISA *Barth. De P.R.* XVII. lxxxvii. (Tollem. MS.), Aristotel..seyeþ þat þe seed of hen bane is poyson. **14..** *Rel. Ant.* I. 55 For the goute..tak leves of the henbane. **1578** LYTE *Dodoens* III. xxiii. 448 Of Henbane are three kindes..that is, the blacke, the yellowe, and the white. **1630** J. TAYLOR (Water P.) *Praise Hempseed* Wks. III. 68/2 No cockle, darnell, henbane, tare or nettle Neere where it is can prosper spring or settle. **1796** COLERIDGE *To Friend writing no more Poetry* 33 In the outskirts, where pollutions grow, Pick the rank henbane. **1872** OLIVER *Elem. Bot.* II. 213 Henbane..a viscid weed of waste places about villages, with dingy, purple-veined, yellow flowers.

2. The drug extracted from this plant.

1840 DICKENS *Barn. Rudge* ix, The prospect of finding any-body out in anything would have kept Miss Miggs awake under the influence of henbane. **1859** MRS. CARLYLE *Lett.* III. 3 The henbane I took in despair last night.

3. *attrib.* and *Comb.*

1398 TREVISA *Barth. De P.R.* XII. xxxiii. (1495) 433 The sperrowe etyth venemous thynges wyth hote growinge henban seed. **1687** DRYDEN *Hind & P.* III. 1081 Henbane juice to swell them till they burst. **1866** *Sowerby's E. Bot.* VI. 108 The baneful effects of the Henbane exhalations.

†**'henbell.** *Obs.* In 1-5 **henne-belle.** [f. HEN *sb.* + BELL *sb.*[1]; from the bell-shaped calyx.] Earlier name of HENBANE.

c **1000** ÆLFRIC *Voc.* in Wr.-Wülcker 134/5 *Simphoniaca*, henne-belle. *c* **1000** *Sax. Leechd.* I. 94 Ðeos wyrt þe.. sume men henne-belle hatað. *a* **1500** *Sloane MS.* 5. 6/2 *Cassialago, simphoniaca, iusquiamus*.. A[nglice] hennebelle. **1597** GERARDE *Herbal* App. to Table.

†**henbilt.** *Obs.* A kind of fishing net (or the cable belonging to it).

1630 *Ord. Preserv. Brood Fish Thames* in *Descr. Thames* (1758) 74 That every Trinck Cable be no more than twenty Fathom long at the most; or any Henbilt above twenty-two Fathom long.

henbit ('hɛnbɪt). [f. HEN *sb.* + BIT *sb.*[2]: app. a 16th c. transl. of the Low German name: see quot. 1578.] Name given to two common weeds. †**a.** Ivy-leaved Speedwell (*Veronica hederifolia*); also distinguished as ***small henbit.*** *Obs.*

1578 LYTE *Dodoens* I. xxxv. 51 The fourth kinde [of Chickweed] (called of the base Almaignes Hoenderbeet) that is to say Henbit, hath many rounde and hearie stemmes. **1597** GERARDE *Herbal* II. clxxxii. §3. 492 Iuie Chickweede or small Henbit. **1713** DERHAM *Phys.-Theol.* (J.), In a scarcity in Silesia a rumour was spread of its raining millet-seed; but it was found to be only the seeds of the ivy-leaved speedwell, or small henbit.

b. A species of Dead-nettle (*Lamium amplexicaule*), with irregularly cut or incisocrenate leaves; formerly distinguished as ***greater henbit.*** Also ***henbit nettle, h. dead-nettle.***

1597 GERARDE *Herbal* II. clxxxii. 492 The great Henbit hath feeble stalkes leaning towarde the grounde, whereon do growe.. leaues like those of the dead Nettell. **1778** LIGHTFOOT *Flora Scot.* (1789) I. 309 *Lamium amplexicaule* .. Great Henbit.. In cultivated ground, frequent. **1861** S. THOMSON *Wild Fl.* III. (ed. 4) 229 The example given.. is the.. henbit, or dead-nettle.

hence (hɛns), *adv.* Forms: 3-4 **heonnes**, 3-5 **hennes**, (3 **hinnes, hunnes**, 4 **hennus, henys**, 4-5 **hennys, -is**); 4-6 **hens**, (5 **hense, henes, -us**, 6 *Sc.* **henss, ynce**); 6- **hence.** [ME. *hennes*, etc., f. the earlier *henne*, HEN *adv.*, with adverbial genitive suffix *-es, -s*, as in *-ward, -wards*, etc. The spelling *hence* is phonetic, to retain the breath sound denoted in the earlier spelling by *s*, as in *once, twice, mice, pence, defence*, etc.]

I. Of place. **1.** (Away) from here, from this place; to a distance.

c **1275** LAY. 1581 Are we hinnes [*c* **1205** heonne] wende. *c* **1290** *S. Eng. Leg.* I. 41/231 Ich it wolle hennes lede. *c* **1300** *Beket* 998 Go hunnes. *c* **1330** R. BRUNNE *Chron. Wace* 15662 To Cornewaille þey fledden hennes. **1382** WYCLIF *Gen.* xlii. 15 ȝe shulen not goon hens, to the tyme that ȝoure leest brother come. *c* **1400** *Sowdone Bab.* 1922 Elles come we nevere hennys oute. *c* **1440** *York Myst.* xxii. 3 High you hense. **1559** *Mirr. Mag., Dk. Suffolk* xii, In wit and learning matcheles hence to Grece. *c* **1560** A. SCOTT *Poems* (S.T.S.) xx. 57 Thairfoir go hens in haist. **1591** SHAKS. *Two Gent.* I. ii. 60 How churlishly, I chid Lucetta hence. **1634** SIR T. HERBERT *Trav.* 214 Hence our journey led us homewards in five dayes sayle. **1808** SCOTT *Marm.* VI. xxiii, Hence might they see the full array of either host.

b. At a distance from here; away.

c **1330** *Assump. Virg.* 328 (B.M. MS.), I was fer hens atte my prechinge. **1393** LANGL. *P. Pl.* C. VI. 80 Lyf-holynesse and loue, han ben longe hennes. **1562** J. HEYWOOD *Prov. & Epigr.* (1867) 177 Ye haue tarid longe hence. **1595** SPENSER *Col. Clout* 22 Whilest thou wast hence. **1611** SHAKS. *Wint. T.* IV. iii. 86, I haue a Kinsman not past three quarters of a mile hence.

c. with redundant *from* (†*fro*).

c **1340** *Cursor M.* 1264 (Trin.) Þi gate Fro hennes to paradis ȝate. **1388** WYCLIF *Gen.* xlii. 15 ȝe schulen not go fro hennus. **1477** EARL RIVERS (Caxton) *Dictes* 146 Socrates was .. boren in a ferre Contre from hens. **1526** TINDALE *Luke* iv. 10 Cast thy silfe doune from hens. **1593** SHAKS. *Rich. II*, III. iii. 6 Richard, not farre from hence, hath hid his head. **1704** ADDISON *Italy* Wks. 1804 V. 149 We sailed from hence directly for Genoa. **1792** T. JEFFERSON *Writ.* (1859) III. 489 It being impossible to prescribe them from hence. **1820** W. IRVING *Sketch Bk.* I. 171 From hence I was conducted up a staircase to a suite of apartments.

2. with ellipsis of vb. of motion, chiefly as a command: ***hence!*** go hence, depart. ***hence with***: go away with, take away.

1573-80 BARET *Alv.* H. 392 Hence, away, *apage te.* **1583** STANYHURST *Æneis* II. (Arb.) 66 Let vs hence. **1593** SHAKS. *Ven. & Ad.* 382, I pray you hence, and leave me here alone. **1610** —— *Temp.* I. ii. 474 Hence: hang not on my garments. **1611** —— *Wint. T.* II. iii. 67 Hence with her, out o'dore. **1637** MILTON *Lycidas* 18 Hence with denial vain and coy excuse. **1769** GRAY *Ode for Music* 12 Hence, away, 'tis holy ground! **1855** BROWNING *Gram. Funeral* 112 Hence with life's pale lure!

3. *spec.* From this world, from this life.

c **1315** SHOREHAM 83 That no fend ous ne schende Nou, ne wanne the tyme comthe Thet we scholle hennes wende. *c* **1450** *Lay Folks Mass Bk.* (MS. F.) 121 And for the saules that hennes be past. **1583** STUBBES *Anat. Abus.* II. (1882) 86 When God shall call them hence to himself. **1611** BIBLE *Ps.* xxxix. 13 Before I goe hence, and be no more. **1875** JOWETT *Plato* (ed. 2) I. 443 They go from hence into the other world.

†**b.** Elsewhere (than in this world); in the next world. *Obs.*

1426 AUDELAY *Poems* 11 Hit schal be ponysched here or henus evere trespasse. **1595** SHAKS. *John* IV. ii. 89 This must be answer'd either heere or hence. **1602** —— *Ham.* III. ii. 232 Both heere, and hence, pursue me lasting strife, If once a Widdow, euer I be Wife.

II. Of time.

4. From this time onward, henceforward, henceforth. Also with *from* (†*fro*). *arch.* and *poet.*

c **1380** WYCLIF *Serm.* Sel. Wks. II. 17 From hens bigan Jesus to preche. *c* **1384** CHAUCER *H. Fame* III. 194 Fro hennes in to domes day. **1588** SHAKS. *L.L.L.* V. ii. 826 Hence euer then, my heart is in thy brest. **1604** —— *Oth.* III. iii. 379 From hence Ile loue no Friend, sith Loue breeds such offence. **1633** P. FLETCHER *Purple Isl.* XII. lxxxviii, Hence mayst thou freely play. **1818** SHELLEY *Rev. Islam* IX. xvi, That the rule of men was over now, And hence, the subject world to woman's will must bow.

†**b.** (At some time in the past reckoned) from now; in quot. 1393 = since, ago. *Obs. rare.*

1393 LANGL. *P. Pl.* C. VI. 35 Whanne ich ȝong was.. meny ȝer hennes. **1610** BP. HALL *Recoll. Treat.* (1614) 738 But you leape backe.. from hence to the Apostles times.

c. (At some time in the future) from now.

1590 SHAKS. *Com. Err.* III. i. 122 Ile meet you at that place some houre hence. *a* **1735** ARBUTHNOT (J.), Let not posterity a thousand years hence look for truth in the voluminous annals of pedants. **1885** *Manch. Exam.* 12 Oct. 5/1 We have to.. think of what our position will be five years hence.

III. Of issue, result, consequence, etc.

5. From this, as a source or origin.

1597 SHAKS. *Lover's Compl.* 110 Controversy hence a question takes, Whether the horse by him became his deed, Or he his manage by the well-doing steed. *a* **1641** SUCKLING *Love's World* 15 Poems (1648) 11 My Flora was my Sun.. All other faces borrowed hence Their light and grace. **1667** MILTON *P.L.* VII. 366 Hence [from the sun] the Morning Planet guilds his horns.

b. ***from*** (†***of***) ***hence***: from this world.

1382 WYCLIF *John* xviii. 36 Now forsothe my kyngdom is not of hennis [TINDALE and **1611** from hence].

6. (As a result) from this fact or circumstance. Also with *from.*

1608 D. T. *Ess. Pol. & Mor.* 107 Hence proceeded that pleasant Motto of the Græcian Courtizan. **1613** PURCHAS *Pilgrimage* (1614) 62 Hence it is, saith R. Moses, that the Law of Moses forbiddeth these rites. **1725** POPE *Odyss.* XII. 252 Learn courage hence! **1771** GOLDSM. *Hist. Eng.* II. 280 From hence he has been accused, by historians, of avarice. **1884** W. C. SMITH *Kildrostan* 46 You have fallen out, and hence your thoughts are sad.

7. (As an inference) from this fact or circumstance; from these premisses or data; for this reason; therefore.

1586 YOUNG *Guazzo's Civ. Conv.* IV. 226 From hence, saide Lord John, we may know, that if [etc.]. **1660** BARROW *Euclid* (1714) 27 *Coroll.* Hence, All right-lined figures of the same species have the sum of their angles equal. **1695** *Enq. Anc. Const. Eng.* 77, I grant it; but what do you infer from hence? **1774** GOLDSM. *Nat. Hist.* (1776) III. 253 From hence, therefore, we may conclude, that the size in these animals is not sufficient to make a distinction among them. **1840** LARDNER *Geom.* 210 Hence, the surface of the entire sphere is equal to the surface of the entire cylinder. **1864** BOWEN *Logic* vi. 167 *Rule.* Both Contraries may be false, but both cannot be true. Hence, to posit A is to sublate E; to posit E is to sublate A. *Mod.* It is so with men generally, and hence we assume it to be so with you.

IV. 8. *Comb.* **a.** with sb., as ***hence-departure, -going***; **b.** with pa. pple., as ***hence-brought, -got***, etc.; **hence-meant**, intended, purposed, or planned from this place. *Obs.* or *arch.*

a. 1611 SHAKS. *Cymb.* III. ii. 65 From our hence-going, And our returne. —— *Wint. T.* I. ii. 450 My people did expect my hence departure Two dayes agoe.

b. 1589 WARNER *Alb. Eng.* VI. xxxiii, As if by miracle preseru'd by Forraines long From hence-ment Treasons. **1602** *Ibid.* XIII. lxxix, Much have we done, hence-outed. **1610** HEALEY *St. Aug. Citie of God* 122 Even building the Capitoll up with hence-got spoiles. *a* **1649** DRUMM. OF HAWTH. *Poems* Wks. (1711) 37 That Rhine with hence-brought beams his bosom warms.

†**hence**, *v.* *Obs. rare.* [f. prec.] **a.** *trans.* To order hence or away. **b.** *intr.* To go hence, depart.

1580 SIDNEY *Arcadia* (1622) 95 With that his dog he henc'd his flocke he curst. **1614** SYLVESTER *Panaretus* 1281 Here-with the Angell henc't, and bent his flight Tow'rds Our Sad Citie.

hence, *sb.* *U.S.* [HENCE *adv.* 3 b and 4 c.] **a.** The other world. **b.** The future.

1884 E. W. NYE *Baled Hay* 26 All-wool delaine that was worn by one who is now in the golden hence. **1904** F. LYNDE *Grafters* xviii. 233 Now suppose you hint.. that more.. developments may be safely predicted in the immediate hence.

†**hence-along**, *adv.* *Obs.* [See ALONG *a.*[1]] 'Along of' or because of this; for this reason.

1592 NASHE in *Smith's Wks.* (1866-7) I. 17 Hence-along did it proceed that thou wast such a plausible pulpit man.

henceforth ('hɛnsfɔəθ, hɛns'fɔəθ), *adv.* [f. HENCE *adv.* + FORTH *adv.*] From this time forth; from now onwards.

c **1350** *Will. Palerne* 1050 ȝe may mete eft dernli hennes-forþ eche day. *c* **1386** CHAUCER *Sqr.'s T.* 650 But hennes forth I wol my proces holde. **1590** SPENSER *F.Q.* II. i. 17 Or why should ever I henceforth desyre To see faire heavens face? **1664** BUTLER *Hud.* II. iii. 1165 I'll make him henceforth to beware And tempt my fury, if he dare. **1719** YOUNG *Busiris* IV. i. (1757) 59 Henceforth let no man trust the first false step Of guilt. **1874** GREEN *Short Hist.* viii. §2. 478 A power had at last risen up in the Commons with which the Monarchy was henceforth to reckon.

b. With *from* (†*fro*). *arch.*

c **1380** WYCLIF *Serm.* Sel. Wks. I. 35 Make covenaunt wiþ him to leve oure synne from hennsforþ. *c* **1450** *Merlin* 22 They haue fro henes-forth loste ther trauayle. **1526** TINDALE *2 Tim.* iv. 8 From hence forth is layde vppe for me a croune of rightewesnes. **1595** SHAKS. *John* I. i. 159 From hence-forth beare his name Whose forme thou bearest. **1676** HOBBES *Iliad* I. 72 And to destroy us from henceforth forbear.

†**'hencefor'thon**, *adv.* *Obs.* [f. as prec. + FORTH ON.] Henceforth, henceforward.

c **1489** CAXTON *Sonnes of Aymon* ii. 59 Ye shall now here & vnderstande from the hensfourthon a terryble and a pyetous songe. *Ibid.* xiv. 350 We shall have peas in Fraunce fromhens forthon. *c* **1500** *Melusine* i. 17 From hens fourthon I wil bigynne & shew the trouth of thystory.

†**hence-forthward**, *adv.* *Obs. rare.* = next.

c **1391** CHAUCER *Astrol.* I. §1 From hennes-forthward, I wol clepe the heyhte of any thing þat is taken by thy rewle, the altitude.

hence'forward, *adv.* [f. HENCE *adv.* + FORWARD.] From this time forward; henceforth.

1388 WYCLIF *Phil.* iii. 1 Hennus forward, my britheren, haue ȝe ioye in the Lord. *a* **1450** *Knt. de la Tour* (1868) 50 Ye aught hennys forward kepe you welle from falling in suche perille. **1592** SHAKS. *Rom. & Jul.* IV. ii. 22 Hence-forward I am euer rul'd by you. **1699** BENTLEY *Phal.* 128 Henceforward he will not make so many awkward Jests upon Lexicons and Dictionaries. **1790** BURKE *Fr. Rev.* 4 Henceforward we must consider them as a kind of privileged persons. **1877** MRS. OLIPHANT *Makers Flor.* i. 19 They were friends henceforward as long as Guido's life lasted.

b. with *from* (†*fro*). *arch.*

1472 *Presentm. Juries* in *Surtees Misc.* (1888) 25 If he do so from hensforward. **1542-5** BRINKLOW *Lament.* (1874) 90 Bestow them therfore from hence forwarde vppon the trew image of Christe. **1685** J. SCOTT *Chr. Life* II. vi. (R.), Let us from hence-forward beware of them. **1845** STODDART in *Encycl. Metrop.* I. 42/1 From henceforward for 1500 verses .. we hear nothing further of this second person.

†**hence'forwards**, *adv.* *Obs.* [f. as prec. + FORWARDS.] = prec.

c **1400** *Rom. Rose* 7304 Yhe, sir, from hens forewardis. **1643** in Caryl *Sacr. Covt.* 28 He may be enabled to overcome that temptation from henceforwards. *c* **1705** VANBRUGH *Mistake* II. Wks. (Rtldg.) 444/2 Henceforwards all your interest shall be mine. *a* **1773** CHESTERF. (Mason), My letters will henceforwards be principally calculated for that Meridian.

†**hence-from**, *adv.* *Obs. rare.* [An inversion of *from hence*: cf. *herefrom, hitherto.*] From this (place, source, or fact).

1666 J. SMITH *Old Age* (1676) 131 Hence-from all the spirits of a man are enlivened. *Ibid.* 183, I find no Translator to vary hencefrom but some few into Vulgar Tongues.

hench, Sc. form of HAUNCH *sb.*[1] and *v.*[3]

†**hench-boy.** *Obs.* Also **hinch-boy.** [f. *hench-* in HENCHMAN + BOY.] A page of honour, a boy attendant.

In the 17th c. they ran on foot beside the mayor, sheriffs, etc.

1611 MIDDLETON & DEKKER *Roaring Girl* II. i, You'd have it for a hench-boy, you shall. **1616** B. JONSON *Masque Christmas* Wks. (Rtldg.) 602/1 He said grace as prettily as any of the sheriff's hinch-boys, forsooth. **1636** DAVENANT *Witts* in Dodsley *O. Pl.* (1780) VIII. 420, I will match my Lord Mayor's horse, make jockeys Of his hench-boys, and run 'em through Cheapside. **1661** K. W. *Conf. Charact., Univ. Beadle* (1860) 70 Much of kin to those hinch-boys, who on my lord mayor's day at London, were wont to run before my lady marice in velvet caps. *a* **1683** OLDHAM *Poet. Wks.* (1686) 64 When in Solemn State he pleas'd to ride, Poor Scepter'd Slaves ran Henchboys by his side.

hencher, Sc. form of HAUNCHER.

henchman ('hɛnʃmən). Pl. **-men.** Forms: α. 4 (**hengestmannus**), **henxst-**, 4-5 **henxt-**, 4-7 **henx-, hensman**, 5 **henxe-, heyns-, heynce-**, 5-6 **hense-**, 6 **hence-, henxceman.** β. 5-6 **henche-**, 6 **hensh(e-**, 6-7, 9 **henchman.** γ. 5 **hansemane**, (*pl.*) **anschamen**, 6 **hauns-, hansh-, haunch-**, 8 **hanchman.** [A compound of the word which appears in OE. as *hengest, hengst* (in Layamon *hængest*: see HENGEST), OHG. *hengist*, MHG. *hengest*, Ger. *hengst*, OFris. *hengst*, MLG. *hengest, hingest, hinxt*, MDu. *henxt, heynst, henst*, LG. and mod.Fris. *hingst*, Du. *hengst* 'male horse' (at different periods, and in the various langs. = 'stallion', 'gelding', and 'horse' generally) + MAN; but it is not clear how or

whence the compound made its appearance in the 14th c.

The latinized *hengestmannus* in 1360, suggests immediate formation from OE. *hengest*; but there is the difficulty that no trace of the latter appears after *c* 1205 (exc. as an element of proper names, where OE. *Hengestes* became *Hinx-*, *Hinks-*, *Hinckes-* in accordance with the normal phonetic change of OE. *eng* to later *ing*). On the other hand though *hengest* was also MLG., and *henxt*, *heynst*, *henst* the MDu. forms, and Hans Wynsele in quot. 1377 was evidently of 'Dutch' or German nativity, no example of the compound *hengestman*, or *henxtman*, is found in these languages. (Mod.G. *hengstmann*, 'groom of a stallion', is recent and technical.) As to the original sense, the *Promp. Parv.* renders *heyncemann* by med.L. *gerolocista*; a contemporary L.-E. glossary, Wr.-Wülcker 586/21, has '*gerolotista*, sompturman' (cf. also 582/11 '*Falerarius*, a sompterhors; *falerator*, a sompterman'). *Gerolocista* (in Du Cange also *gerulasista*) was app. a deriv. of L. *gerulus* 'carrier, porter', also 'sumpter-horse': cf. *Promp. Parv.*, 'Male horse [OF. *male*, F. *malle* trunk], *gerulus*, *somarius*'; 'somer hors, *gerulus*, *somarius*, *summarius*.' These equivalents seem to point to the sense 'attendant on a sumpter-horse'; perh. the original meaning was simply 'attendant on a horse', 'groom', which might rise to be an honourable title, as in the current 'Groom-in-waiting', 'Groom-of-the-chamber': cf. also the history of *marshal*, originally 'horse-servant', 'groom'. The '*hengestmanni*, Mustard and Garleke', of 1360, the 'harlottez and hansemene' in *Morte Arthur*, and the 'henxmen and lackies' of P. Holland (1 b), were apparently of the rank of ordinary grooms; but in connexion with the English court, the word came to connote a position of honour, and the royal henchmen of the 15–16th c. were usually young men of rank. In its historical sense, the word appears to have become obs. by 1650 (see sense 1); for the modern use see sense 2. (See the discussion of this word in *N. & Q.* 7th s. II, III, 8th s. III, etc.; also Skeat, *Student's Pastime*, several articles.)]

1. a. ? A groom. **b.** A squire, or page of honour to a prince or great man, who walked or rode beside him in processions, progresses, marches, etc.; also, one who, on occasion, fulfilled the same office to a queen or princess. In later 16th c. use, app. = HENCH-BOY. *Obs.* (exc. *Hist.*) since 17th c.

Henry, Earl of Derby, afterwards Henry IV, had in his retinue, in his Expedition to Prussia and Palestine 1392–3, 'two henxmen', to whom there are many references in the Accounts (edited by Miss L. Toulmin Smith for Camd. Soc.), cited in quot. 1392. In 1402, two 'henxtmen' accompanied Henry's daughter Blaunche from Cologne to the parts of Almaine, whither she went as a bride. From the 14th cent., henxmen or henchmen formed part of the regular household or suite of English kings and queens, their number rising from three under Henry VI to seven under Edward IV and Richard III, under the command of the Master of the Horse. At the coronation of Richard III in 1483, his queen had also five henchmen riding on 'womens sadelles'. In 15–16th c. nobles and knights also had their henchmen, usually three. The royal henchmen or 'chyldren of honor' were abolished by Queen Elizabeth in 1565 (see quot.); and the word, though still frequent in transferred and analogical uses *c* 1600, app. became obs. in English use by 1650. (Cf. also HENCH-BOY, which continued in practical use to *c* 1675.)

1360 *Issue Roll* 224 (34 Ed. III Easter) Memb. 20 Mustardo Garlek' et duobus sociis suis hengestmannis domini Regis..cuilibet eorum, vj. *s.* viij. *d.* per breve de privato sigillo. **1377–80** *Roll of Liveries* by Wardr. Keeper, 1–3 Rich. II, memb. 23 (*Accts. Excheq.* Q. R., Bundle 400 No. 4) Hans Wynsele, henxstman domini regis pro vestura et apparat' suis. **1392** *Earl Derby's Expedition* (Camden) 163 Diuersis hominibus pro tribus equis ab ipsis conductis pro equitacione domini et ij henksmen apud Dansk. *Ibid.* 280 Pro panno..empto ibidem pro ij henksmen..Item pro factura ij gounarum pro dictis hensmen. ? *a* **1400** *Morte Arth.* (Thornton MS. *c* 1425) 2662 Tak heede to þis hansemane, þat he no horne blawe. *Ibid.* 2743 Þat es fully to fewe to feghte with theme alle, ffore harlottez and hansemene salle helpe bott littille. **1402** *Roll of Expenses* for P'cess Blaunche (Q.R., Bundle 404 No. 11) Alberto Blike et Petro Stake, henxtmen domine euntibus cum domina de Colonia versus partes Alman'. *c* **1440** *Promp. Parv.* 233/2 Heyncemann (*H.* henchemanne), *gerolocista*, *duorum generum*. *c* **1450** HOLLAND *Howlat* 648 Robyn Redbrest nocht ran, Bot raid as a hensman. **1463** *Mann. & Househ. Exp.* (Roxb.) 234 Payd ffor..iij. bowys for the heynsmen of my lorddys of Norfolke, ij. *s.* **1463–4** *Rolls Parlt.* V. 505/2 Provided also, that Hensh-men, Herawdes, Purcyvauntes, Swerdeberers to Mayers, Messyngers and Mynstrelles..be not comprised in this Acte [regulating apparel]. **1480** *Wardr. Acc. Edw. IV* (1830) 167 John Cheyne Squier for the Body of oure said Souverain Lorde the King and Maister of his Henxmen for th' apparaile of the saide Maister and vij of the Kinges Henxemen ayenst the feste of Midsomer. **1481–90** *Howard Househ. Bks.* (Roxb.) 431 Item, for makyng of ij. gownes of tawney for the said anschamen, price ij. *s.* viij. *d.* **1483** *Wardr. Accts. Coronation Rich. III* (Grose *Antiq. Repertory* 1779, II. 254) To vij of our sayde Souverain Lorde the Kyngs henxemen, that is to wit, The Lorde Morley, Thomas Dane [etc.] for theire apparail agenst the day of the grete solempnitee..viij doubletts. *Ibid.* 258 To v henxemen of our saide Souverain Lady the Quene, ryding in the said v womens sadelles covered in crymysyn cloth of gold. **1488** *Ld. Treas. Acc. Scotl.* in Pitcairn *Crim. Trials* I. 114* For liverayis to viij Hensemen of þe Kingis. *a* **1500** *Flower & Leaf* xxxvi, And every Knight had after him ridinge Three henchemen on him awaitinge. **1530** PALSGR. 230/2 Henchman, *paige dhonnevr, emfant dhonnevr*. **1538** LELAND *Itin.* IV. 17 Turwith now being yn the Courte a late a haunchman hath maried the Heir Generale of the Eldest House of the Oxenbridges. **1548** UDALL, etc. *Erasm. Par. Mark* xi. lf. 180 The solemne pompe, passing the pompe of any worldly prince, of such as go before the Bishop, of his hensemen, of Trumpettes of sundry tunes [etc.]. **1548** HALL *Chron., Edw. IV*, 190 b, So nere pursued, that certain of his henxmen or folowers wer taken [**1568** GRAFTON Henchmen and folowers]. *Ibid., Hen. VIII*, 9 The chyldren of honor called the Henchemen, whiche were freshely disguised, and daunced a morice before the king. **1555** EDEN *Decades* 256 Clement Adams scole mayster to the Queens henshemen. **1565** F. ALEN *Let. to Earl Shrewsbury* 11 Dec. in Lodge *Illustr. Hist.* (1791) I. 358 Her highnes hath of late, whereat some doo moche marvel, dissolved the auncient office of the henchemen. **1578** in Nichols *Progr. Q. Eliz.* (1823) II. 138 There attended upon him three henchmen in white and greene. **1587** FLEMING *Contn. Holinshed* III. 1949/2 Behind him rode sir John Dudleie maister of hir horsses, leading hir spare horsse trapped in rich tissue downe to the ground; after them followed henxmen and pages of honor. **1590** SHAKS. *Mids. N.* II. i. 121, I do but beg a little changeling boy, To be my Henchman. **1601** ? MARSTON *Pasquil & Kath.* I. 337 Profound toung'd Master Puffe, hee that hath a perpetuitie of complement, hee whose phrases are as neatly deckt as my Lord Maiors hens-men. **1607** COWELL *Interpr.*, *Henchman* or *Heinsman*, is a German word..It is vsed with vs for one that runneth on foote attending vpon a man of honour or worship. [So in Blount 1656.] **1616** J. BULLOKAR *Eng. Expos.*, *Henchman*, a page of honour, neere attendant to a Prince, or other great personage. *a* **1618** RALEIGH *Rem.* (1644) 17 Nobles to attend the Court; which was well imitated by our Train of Henchmen, if they were of the Nobler sort.

c. *transf.* (Rendering L. *minister*, *agaso*, *accensus*, *armiger*, *ministrator*.)

1600 HOLLAND *Livy* XLIII. v. 1159 To send presents..two bard horses with their henxmen and lackies [*agasonibus*]. **1601** —— *Pliny* II. 540 Prince Clytus..hasting to a battell, calling vnto his squire or henxman for his helmet. **1606** —— *Sueton.* 238 He served Caius as his henxman at a chariot running.

d. *fig.*

1594 J. DICKENSON *Arisbas* (1878) 34 Rough Boreas winters Hench-man..scourged the plaines with a troupe of tempests. *a* **1592** GREENE *Orpharion*, *Orpheus' Song* Wks. (Rtldg.) 316/2 Of Hesper, henchman to the day and night.

2. The personal attendant, 'right-hand man', or chief gillie of a Highland chief; hence, generally, a trusty follower or attendant who stands by the side of his chief or leader, and supports him in every case of need.

This sense begins app. with Burt, who spells *hanchman*, and explains it as derived from *hanch*, i.e. HAUNCH; hence Scott (who edited Burt) has *hanchman* in *Waverley*, but elsewhere, in the same sense, uses *henchman*, thus identifying Burt's and his own 'hanchman' with the obsolete Eng. 'henchman'; the rest of the world has taken the word from Scott. It does not appear whence or how Burt got the word: there is no term corresponding to 'haunch-man' in Gaelic (Burt himself, a few sentences on, calls the same individual simply *gilly*), and it is uncertain whether he himself invented the term, or really found the obs. Eng. *henchman* retained in a modified sense in some part of the Highlands. In any case, association between *henchman* and *haunchman* was very natural; *haunch* in Scotch is pronounced *hainch*, *hench* (see HAUNCH *sb.*[1], *v.*[2]), 'haunchman', if it existed, would be pronounced *hainchman* or *henchman*, and the Eng. 'henchman', if in any way known, would be there naturally taken as = 'man at the hench or haunch'.

c **1730** BURT *Lett. N. Scotl.* (1754) II. xxi. 157 The Foster-brother, having the same Education as the young Chief, may besides that..become his *Hanchman*..This Officer is a Sort of Secretary, and is to be ready upon all Occasions, to venture his Life in Defence of his Master; and at Drinking-bouts he stands behind his Seat, at his Haunch, from whence his Title is derived, and watches the Conversation. *Ibid.*, A Youth who was *Hanchman*, not understanding one Word of English, imagin'd his Chief was insulted, and thereupon drew his Pistol..and snap'd it at the Officer's Head. **1814** SCOTT *Wav.* xvi, He counted upon his fingers the several officers of his chief's retinue—'there is his *hanchman* or right-hand man; then his *bàrdh* or poet; then his *bladier* or orator,..then his *gilly-more* or armour-bearer ..then his *gilly-casfluich* [etc.].'

1810 SCOTT *Lady of L.* II. xxxv, 'Malise, what ho!'—his henchman came. **1823** BYRON *Juan* XI. xiii, And roar'd out ..Unto his nearest follower or henchman. **1831** SCOTT *Cast. Dang.* ii, I have been his henchman, and can vouch for it. **1835** LYTTON *Rienzi* II. i, A page, who..was the especial henchman of the Lord of the Castle. **1855** MACAULAY *Hist. Eng.* xiii. III. 335 The henchman was an excellent orderly: the hereditary piper and his sons formed the band: and the clan became at once a regiment. **1865** *Cornh. Mag.* July 119 One Jacobus Battus, a faithful brother-scholar, and henchman. **1883** S. C. HALL *Retrospect* II. 272 He could still make a good cast over the river..and aided by his henchman land a salmon.

fig. **1811** SCOTT *Fam. Lett.* 14 Aug. (1894) I. 227, I have the Tweed for my henchman for about a mile.

b. A stout political supporter or partisan; *esp.* in U.S. 'A mercenary adherent; a venal follower; one who holds himself at the bidding of another' (*Cent. Dict.*).

1839 *Morn. Herald* 2 Sept. in *Spirit Metrop. Conserv. Press* (1840) II. 446 Such Liberals as Lord John Russell, and his henchman, Mr. Hawes. **1867** GOLDW. SMITH *Three Eng. Statesmen* (1882) 196 Horsley, the leading political bishop of the day, and a sort of ecclesiastical henchman of Pitt. **1875** *N. Amer. Rev.* CXX. 127 A henchman of his, who had a place on the police force, being arraigned before the Commissioners. **1880** *St. James' Gaz.* 11 Oct., The excuses made for him by the scribes who are his henchmen. **1884** *Sat. Rev.* 14 June 768/2 It is contended by the Government henchmen that there is..a strong Romanist and Nationalist ..party in Ulster. **1891** *Boston* (Mass.) *Jrnl.* 28 Nov. 2/3 These charges are the result of a conspiracy among Hill's henchmen in Syracuse.

henchwoman. *nonce-wd.* [after HENCHMAN.] A female attendant, a waiting-woman.

1889 *Mod. Society* 24 Aug. 1031/2 She told her faithful hench-woman and scribe to tear up the letter.

hen-clam. [f. HEN *sb.* 6 + CLAM.] The name given on the Atlantic coast of North America to two large species of clam, *Mactra* (or *Spisula*) *solidissima* and *M. ovalis*. On the Pacific coast, the name is transferred to *Pachyderma crassatelloides*.

1884–5 J. S. KINGSLEY *Stand. Nat. Hist.* I. 278 *Mactra solidissima* and the closely allied *M. ovalis* are known along our northern coasts as hen-clam, sea-clam, and surf-clam.

hen-coop ('hɛnkuːp). **a.** A coop or pen of basket-work, wire-work, or the like, in which poultry are kept.

1697–1703 DAMPIER *Voy.* 1676 (R.) With provision chests, hen-coops and parrot cages, our ships were full of lumber. **1831** TRELAWNEY *Adv. Younger Son* (1890) 49 Grill a hen-coop full of fowls. **1859** GEO. ELIOT *A. Bede* I. xv, She stooped down to put the soaked bread under the hen-coop.

b. *attrib.*

1898 *Daily News* 28 Sept. 5/3 The huge hen-coop crinoline disfigured the women. **1937** E. SITWELL *I live under Black Sun* 296 There came a sound of crazy hen-coop laughter.

hencote. Now *dial.* [f. HEN *sb.* + COTE *sb.*[1]] A place for keeping fowls; a hen-house.

c **1425** *Voc.* in Wr.-Wülcker 670/35 *Hoc gallinarium*, henecote. **1865** B. BRIERLEY *Irkdale* I. 129 Exploring some secret recess of the hencote. **1893** *Morn. Post* 23 Oct. 3/2 People ..asserted their right to a common by formally destroying a hencote and shippon, which the owner..declined to remove.

†**hen-cub, -cubb.** *Obs.* [See CUB *sb.*[2]] = HEN-COOP.

1699 J. DICKENSON *Jrnl. Trav.* 4 Some of which [Sea-Birds] were, by force of Wind, blown into and under our Hen-Cubbs.

†**hend, hende,** *a.* and *adv.* *Obs.* Forms: (1 **ʒehende**), 3–6 **hende**, (3 **ende**), 4 **heind**, 4–5 **heende**, **hind(e**, 4–6 **hend**, **hynd(e**, 5–6 **heynd(e**. [app. an aphetic form of OE. *ʒehęnde* adj. (and adv.), near, convenient, lit. at hand, handy, corresp. to OHG., MHG. *gehende*, *gehente*:—WGer. type **gahandja-z*, f. *hand-* HAND. Cf. also ON. *-hęndr*, -handed (in comb.).]

A. *adj.*

1. Near, at hand. (In ME. only predicative, and thus not easily distinguishable from the adverb; see B. 1, where all the quots. are placed.)

[*c* **1000** ÆLFRIC *Hom.* I. 456 Þa ferdon hi to ʒehendre byriʒ, þær ðær oðer deofol wæs ʒewurðod. *c* **1000** *Ags. Gosp.* Mark i. 38 Fare we on ʒehende tunas. So *c* **1160** *Hatton Gosp.*]

2. Ready to hand, convenient, handy. *rare.*

[*c* **893** K. ÆLFRED *Oros.* III. vii. §6 (1883) 116 Þæt hie þær ʒehendaste wæren on ʒehwelc lond þonan to winnane.] **1508** DUNBAR *Tua Mariit Wemen* 14, I was heildit with hawthorne, and with heynd leveis. **1513** DOUGLAS *Æneis* V. xii. 113 Follow the counsale is maist ganand and hend, That agit Nautes gaif the, thi trew frend. *Ibid.* VII. iii. 40 For to remane heyr is oure cuntre heynd.

3. Ready or skilful with the hand, dexterous; expert, skilful, clever.

c **1205** LAY. 18707 An ald man swuðe hende..muche wisdom wes mid him. *c* **1300** *Havelok* 2628 Roberd saw þat dint so hende. **13..** *Guy Warw.* (A.) 173 He was hende and wele y-tauʒ t, Gij to lern forʒat he nauʒt. **1494** FABYAN *Chron.* 6 Thorough that connynge and parfyte memorye Of thynges taken whan I was yonge and hynde. **1508** DUNBAR *Gold. Targe* 191 Dame Hamelynes..That hardy was, and hende in archery. *a* **1550** *Christis Kirke Gr.* x, Ane hasty hensure, callit Hary, Quha wes ane archer heynd.

4. Pleasant in dealing with others; courteous, gracious; kind, gentle, 'nice'. (Of persons; less commonly of speech, action, etc.).

A conventional epithet of praise, very frequent in Middle English poetry.

c **1205** LAY. 14357 Rouwenne þe hende sat bi þan kinge. *c* **1250** *Hymn to God* 25 in *Trin. Coll. Hom.* 259 Þat bred of hele & of lif, ihesu crist þe hende. *a* **1300** *Cursor M.* 967 O-mang þine oþer werkes hend [*v.r.* hende] O þi winning giue me þe tend. *Ibid.* 2337 For he was theuful bath and hind [*v. rr.* hende, hend] Vr lauerd him hild his priue freind. *c* **1386** CHAUCER *Friar's Prol.* 22 A sire ye sholde be hende And curteys as a man of youre estaat. *c* **1400** *Destr. Troy* 475 So hardy, so hynd in hall for to se. *c* **1450** *St. Cuthbert* (Surtees) 4448 Þou hase a hende hert. *c* **1450** *Mirour Saluacioun* 4655 One thi hoegest mercy Jhesu curtays & heende. *c* **1460** *Towneley Myst.* (Surtees) 53 So is his mercy heynd [*rime* feynd]. **1513** DOUGLAS *Æneis* Pref. 456, I say na mair, bot gentill redaris hend, Lat all my faltis with this offence pas by. **1522** *World & Child* in Hazl. *Dodsley* I. 250 Now I am dubbed a knight hend. **1616** BULLOKAR *Eng. Expos.*, *Hend* (obs.), gentle. *a* **1765** *Sir Cawline* xxxvi. in Child *Ballads* 111, 'But away, away!' sayd the hend soldan, 'Thou tarryest mee here all day!'

5. Pleasing to the sight; comely, fair, 'nice'.

c **1205** LAY. 3559 Metes and drinches, and hende claðes. *c* **1305** *Judas Isc.* 39 in *E.E.P.* (1862) 108 Þo he seʒ hit fair and hende: he let hit nemne Iudas. Hit nis noʒt al god þat is fair. *c* **1350** *Med. MS.* in *Archæol.* XXX. 371 Yon it growyth comely hende Be twyn veye as men wend. **14..** *Stac. Rome* 366 in *Pol. Rel. & L. Poems* 126 In þat mynster þat ys so hende. *c* **1450** HOLLAND *Howlat* 893 The farest foule of the firth, and hendest of hewes.

6. *absol.* or as *sb.* Gentle, courteous, or gracious one or ones (see 4); applied conventionally, chiefly to ladies or persons of noble rank. (Cf. similar use of *bright*, *fair*, etc.)

a **1300** *Cursor M.* 18751 Til his disciplis badd þat heind [*v.r.* hende] Fra iursalem þai suld noght weind. *c* **1400** *Destr. Troy* 3851 For the helpe of these hende, & hertely of other. *Ibid.* 8380 In a halle þat was hoge, þere þe hend lay. *c* **1475** *Rauf Coilyear* 970 His wyfe wald he nocht forʒet..He send

efter that hende. **1508** DUNBAR *Tua Mariit Wemen* 32 Alkin hewis under hewin, that ony heynd knew. *a* **1549** *Murning Maidin* 57 in *Laneham's Let.* (1871) Introd. 151 In hy eftir that heynd I ȝeyd, And in my armes could hir hent.

B. *adv.*

1. Near, at hand. (When used after the verb *to be*, or similarly, this may be considered a predicative adjective: see A. 1.)

[*c* **1000** ÆLFRIC *Gen.* xix. 20 Nu ys her ȝehende an ȝehwæde burh.] *c* **1250** *Gen. & Ex.* 3370 Amalec, ysmaeles sune, was ðor hende rafadim wune. *c* **1300** *Havelok* 359 Raþe he sende After prestes fer an hende. *c* **1330** R. BRUNNE *Chron. Wace* (Rolls) 8844 He scorned þem on his langage, 'So fer for stones to make passage..Ffor þey no stones hender fond'. *c* **1380** *Sir Ferumb.* 3616 'Ihesu lord'..'þat syttest on þy maieste, And seest boþe fer & hende'. **1456** *Paston Lett.* No. 284 I. 390 Devyle seyd ye were hender the londes at the begynning of your sute thanne ye be now. ?**1507** *Communyc.* (W. de W.) Biij, That houndes of hell come me not hende.

2. Courteously, kindly; gently. (Sometimes used merely for the sake of rime or alliteration.)

c **1340** *Cursor M.* 9134 (Trin.) Of salomon now we ende þat regned fourty wyntur hende. *c* **1350** *Will. Palerne* 2713 Of þis hert and þis hinde hende now listenes. *a* **1400-50** *Alexander* 212 Bot will ȝ e herken hende, now sall ȝe here. *c* **1450** HOLLAND *Howlat* 477 He gart hallowe the hart, and syne couth it hyng, About his hals full hende, and on his awne hart.

†**hend,** *v. Obs.* [perh. shortened from OE. *ȝehęndan* to handle, take hold of, f. HAND; perh. directly from the corresp. ON. *hęnda* (Sw. *hända*, Da. *hende*); cf. OFris. *hęnda* in same sense.] *trans.* To lay hold of, seize; to take; to grasp, hold.

c **1275** LAY. 21365 And Colgrim ȝam hende [*c* **1205** hente] and fulde þe Bruttus. **13..** *Coer de L.* 4033 They..toke the temple of Apolyn. They felde it down, and hende Mahoun. *c* **1460** in *Pol. Rel. & L. Poems* 192 That bondis of helle can me nat hende. **1596** SPENSER *F.Q.* v. xi. 27 As if that it she would in peeces rend, Or reave out of the hand that did it hend.

hend(e, obs. pl. of HAND; obs. f. END; obs. Sc. f. HIND *a.*

hendeca-, before a vowel **hendec-**; sometimes erron. **endeca-**. **a.** Combining form of Gr. ἕνδεκα eleven, occurring in scientific or technical words, as **hendecachord** (hɛn'dɛkəkɔːd) *Mus.* [after *tetrachord, hexachord*], a series or scale of eleven notes; hence **hendeca'chordal** *a.*, relating to such a scale. **hendeca'colic** *a. Pros.*, consisting of eleven cola (see COLON² 1). **hendecagynous** (hɛndɪ'kædʒɪnəs) *a. Bot.* [see -GYNOUS], having eleven pistils. **hendeca'hedron** *Geom.* [Gr. ἕδρα seat, base], a solid figure contained by eleven faces. **hende'candrous** *a. Bot.* [see -ANDROUS], having eleven stamens. **hendecaphyllous** (-'fɪləs) *a. Bot.*, (of a leaf) consisting of eleven leaflets. **'hendecarchy** (-ɑːkɪ) [after *heptarchy*], government by eleven persons. **hendecasemic** (-'siːmɪk) *a. Pros.* [cf. DISEMIC], of the value of eleven moræ or units of time.

1760 STILES in *Phil. Trans.* LI. 771 Two other suppositions, viz. that either the *hendecachord or disdiapason was here meant. **1842-3** *Smith's Dict. Gr. & Rom. Antiq.* 646 A *hendecachordal system, consisting of three tetrachords. **1847** CRAIG, **Endecagynous*. *Ibid.*, **Endecaphyllous*. **1663** *Flagellum, or O. Cromwell* (1672) 164 England being now cantoned under this *Hendecharchy.

b. *Organic Chem.* Occas. used in place of the synonymous and more usual prefix *undeca-* to denote the presence in a molecule of eleven carbon atoms, as in **'hendecane**, undecane; **hende'coic acid**, undecoic acid.

1889 MUIR & MORLEY *Watts' Dict. Chem.* II. 673/1 n-*Hendecane* $C_{11}H_{24}$... Formed by the action of HI and phosphorus at 230° upon hendecoic (undecylic) acid. **1943** *Thorpe's Dict. Appl. Chem.* (ed. 4) VI. 204/1 (*heading*) Hendecoic acids (undecoic acids), $C_{11}H_{22}O_2$. **1960** *Handbk. Chem. Soc. Authors* iii. 49 Greek numeral roots are used, except that 9 (alone or in combination) is rendered by the Latin nona (not the Greek ennea) and 11 by the Latin undeca (not the Greek hendeca).

hendecagon (hɛn'dɛkəgən). Also erron. **en-**. [f. Gr. ἕνδεκα- (see prec.) + -γωνον, f. γωνία angle.]

a. *Geom.* A plane figure having eleven sides and eleven angles. †**b.** *Fortif.* A fort with eleven bastions (*obs.*).

1704 J. HARRIS *Lex. Techn.*, *Endecagon*, a plane Figure in Geometry of eleven Sides and Angles. *Ibid.*, *Hendecagon. Ibid.*, *Hendecagon*, in Fortification, 'tis taken for a Place defended by 11 Bastions.

Hence **hendecagonal** (hɛndɪ'kægənəl) *a.*, of the form of, or relating to, a hendecagon.

hendecasyllabic (ˌhɛndɪ-, hɛnˌdɛkəsɪ'læbɪk), *a.* and *sb. Pros.* Also erron. **en-**. [f. as next: see also SYLLABIC.]

A. *adj.* Of a 'verse' or line of poetry: Consisting of eleven syllables.

1727-51 CHAMBERS *Cycl.* s.v., Sapphic and Phaleucic verses are, *hendecasyllaba*, or *hendecasyllabic*. **1819-20** R. WATT *Bibliogr. Brit.* I. 136 f, Spanish poetry owes to him [Boscan] the introduction of the hendecasyllabic verse. **1824** *Edin. Rev.* XL. 448 Specimens of the Italian Endecasyllabic verse. **1845** *Encycl. Metrop.* XXV. 818 Amand Daniel invented the Hendecasyllabic metre, which was chosen by Dante for his earlier compositions.

B. *sb.* A hendecasyllabic verse. (Usually in *pl.*)

1836 LANDOR *Peric. & Asp.* Wks. 1846 II. 373 How greatly more noble and more sonorous are those hendecasyllabics commencing the Scollion on Harmodius and Aristogiton. **1873** WAGNER tr. *Teuffel's Hist. Rom. Lit.* II. 128 Martial..frequently uses hendecasyllabics and choliambics.

hendecasyllable (ˌhɛndɪ-, hɛnˌdɛkə'sɪləb(ə)l). *Pros.* Also erron. **en-**. [f. L. *hendecasyllabus*, a. Gr. ἑνδεκασύλλαβ-ος, after SYLLABLE.] A 'verse' or line of eleven syllables; = prec. B.

1746 MELMOTH *Pliny* IV. xiv. (R.), I design to give these trifles the title of hendecasyllables. **1775** TYRWHITT *Ess. Versif. Chaucer* III. §7 *note* in *Chaucer's Wks.*, As the French Alexandrin may be composed of twelve or thirteen syllables, and the Italian Hendecasyllable of ten, eleven, or even twelve. **1823** tr. *Sismondi's Lit. Eur.* (1846) I. viii. 264 The verses, thus interlinked, are all endecasyllables. **1871** R. ELLIS *Catullus* Pref. xiii, Had Sir Philip Sidney written.. every hendecasyllable like 'Where sweet graces erect the stately banner'.

†**'hendelaik.** *Obs. north. dial.* [f. *hende*, HEND *a.* + -LAIK *suffix* = ON. *-leikr* action, function.] Courtesy, civility.

c **1300** *Havelok* 2793 And brouthen hire, þat..ne hauede per, Of hende-leik, fer ne ner. **13..** *E.E. Allit. P.* B. 860 Harlotez with his hendelayk he hoped to chast. *a* **1400-50** *Alexander* 2715 (Ashm.), I haue herd of þi hendlaike [*Dubl.* hynlake]. *Ibid.* 2718 (Dubl.) Qwat bounte þou schewys, What curtasy and hyndlake [*Ashm.* kyndlaike].

hendely, hendeness: see HENDLY, -NESS.

†**henden,** *adv. Obs.* Also **enden.** [f. *hende*, HEND *a.* and *adv.*, with advb. suffix as in *aboven*, etc.] Near; = HEND *adv.* 1.

c **1200** *Trin. Coll. Hom.* 167 Ne mihte no man for stenche cumen him enden. *c* **1250** *Gen. & Ex.* 3361 It was a stede henden ðor-bi.

‖**hendiadys** (hɛn'daɪədɪs). *Gram.* [Late or med.L. *hendiadys*, f. the Gr. phrase ἓν διὰ δυοῖν 'one by means of two'.

The Gr. phrase is app. not found in Gr. grammarians, but is frequent in Servius on Virgil; in late MSS. of Servius, it appears latinized as *endyadis, endyadys*; Papias (12-13th c.) has *endiadis*.]

A figure of speech in which a single complex idea is expressed by two words connected by a conjunction; e.g. by two substantives with *and* instead of an adjective and substantive.

1586 A. DAY *Eng. Secretary* II. (1625) 83 Hendiadis, when one thing of it selfe intire, is diversly laid open, as to say, On iron and bit he champt, for on the iron bit he champt. **1589** PUTTENHAM *Eng. Poesie* III. xvi. (Arb.) 188 Another manner of speach when ye will seeme to make two of one..which therefore we call the figure of Twynnes, the Greekes Endiadis. **1621** T. BEDFORD *Sinne unto Death* 21 Whether we..make it an Endiadis, with Bullinger [etc.]. **1871** *Publ. Sch. Lat. Gram.* II. v. §215 Hendiadys. **1887** CLARK & WRIGHT *Hamlet* 123 *Law and heraldry*, a kind of hendiadys, meaning 'heraldic law', 'jus fetiale'.

hendir, obs. Sc. form of HINDER.

†**'hendly,** *a. Obs.* [f. HEND *a.* + -LY¹.] = HEND *a.* 4.

c **1205** LAY. 8169 I-sæh he enne hendlicne mon. *Ibid.* 25942 Mid hendeliche worden. *c* **1450** *Golagros & Gaw.* 358 It hynderis neuer for to be heyndly of speche.

†**'hendly, hendely, hendily,** *adv. Obs.* Forms: see HEND *a.*, HENDY. [f. HEND *a.*, HENDY *a.* + -LY².]

1. Courteously, kindly, gently, graciously.

c **1205** LAY. 1227 Heo..hendiliche hire hond on his heued leide. *a* **1300** *Floriz & Bl.* 334 Ansuare him wel hendeliche. *a* **1300** *Cursor M.* 7396 And hailsed hendli [*v.rr.* hendly, hendely] þat prophete. *c* **1380** WYCLIF *Serm.* Sel. Wks. II. 53 Crist heendly reprovede Jewis. **1393** LANGL. *P. Pl.* C. IV. 30 Mede hendiliche by-hyht hem þe same. ?*a* **1400** *Morte Arth.* 15 Herkynes me heyndly and holdys ȝow stylle. *c* **1420** *Chron. Vilod.* 285 Mekelyche and hendlyche, as y ȝ ow sayde. **1480** CAXTON *Chron. Eng.* xlix. 33 Conan Meridok thanked him hendly.

2. Finely, neatly, gracefully; nicely.

1340-70 *Alisaunder* 187 Hondes hendely wrought, helplich, sweete. *a* **1400-50** *Alexander* 883 Heraudis on heȝe hors hendly a-rayed.

†**'hendness, hendeness, hendiness.** *Obs.* [f. as prec. + -NESS.] Courtesy, gentleness.

c **1300** *Thrush & Night.* 101 in Hazl. *E.P.P.* I. 54 Hote hendinese and curteysi. **1377** LANGL. *P. Pl.* B. XX. 144 And helde holynesse a iape and hendenesse a wastour [C. XXIII. 145 hendynesse]. **1393** *Ibid.* C. III. 81 Mede ys y-maried more for hure richesse þan for holynesse oþer hendenesse. *a* **1510** DOUGLAS *K. Hart* I. xv, Conning, Kyndnes, Heyndnes, and Honestie.

†**'hendship.** *Obs.* [f. HEND *a.* + -SHIP.] Courtesy, kindness.

c **1300** *St. Margarete* 189 Maide for þin hendeschipe þu haue merci of me. **1340-70** *Alex. & Dind.* 277 Haþel, for þin hendschipe haue vs exkused.

†**'hen-dwale.** *Obs.* [f. HEN *sb.* + DWALE *sb.*² 2.] = HENBANE.

c **1450** *Alphita* (Anecd. Oxon.) 30 *Caniculata, iusquiamus* ..henbane uel hennedwole. *Ibid.* 84 Hennedewole.

†**hendy,** *a. Obs.* Also 3 **hendi.** [f. HEND *a.* + -Y. (OE. had *-hendiȝ* in *list-hendiȝ* skilful-handed.)] = HEND *a.* (with various shades of meaning).

c **1205** LAY. 4833 An oðer stret he makede swiðe hendi. *a* **1225** *Ancr. R.* 186 þeonne beo ȝe his hendi children þet cusseð þe ȝerden þet he haueð ou mid iðrosschen. *c* **1275** *XI Pains of Hell* 289 in *O.E. Misc.* 155 He is curteys and hendy. *c* **1375** *Sir Beues* (E.) (1886) 181/1 When Iosyan saw3 þat hendy kny3t, In here herte sche wax full ly3t.

b. *absol.* or as *sb.*

a **1310** in Wright *Lyric P.* v. 27 He haveth me to hede this hendy a-non.

†**hene,** *v. Obs.* [OE. *hǽnan*, f. *hán* stone, HONE.] *trans.* To stone.

c **1000** *Ags. Gosp.* John x. 32-3 For hwylcum þæra weorca, wylle ȝe me hæ nan?.. Ne hæne we þe for godum weorce. *c* **1160** *Hatton G.* ibid., For hwilcen þare weorken wille ȝe me stænen?.. Ne hene we þe for goden weorkan. *a* **1300** *Leg. Rood* (1871) 40 Our giwes him ladde wiþþoute þe toun, and henede [*v.r.* stened] him wiþ stones.

henebon, obs. form of HENBANE.

hen-egg. Forms: see EGG. [In OE. two words, with *henne* in genitive; later treated as a compound; in mod.Eng. *hen's egg* is more commonly used.] The egg of a hen.

c **1000** *Sax. Leechd.* II. 38 Hænne æges ȝeolocan. **13..** *Coer de L.* 2841 For an hen..Men gaff off penys fiften schillings. For an hen-ay penys unlevene. **1387** TREVISA *Higden* (Rolls) VI. 75 Oon hen ey. **1620** VENNER *Via Recta* v. 83 Neither must this be vnderstood of all kindes of Egges, but of Hen-Egges onely. **1641** FRENCH *Distill.* i. (1651) 39 Take Hen-egs boyled hard. [**1660** BOYLE *New Exp. Phys. Mech.* Wks. 1772 I. 57 We likewise conveyed hens eggs into the receiver.] **1763** WESLEY *Jrnl.* 2 Nov. (1827) III. 150 Some of the hail-stones were larger than hen-eggs. **1837** M. DONOVAN *Dom. Econ.* II. 149 The albumen of a duck-egg coagulates with less heat than that of the hen-egg. **1900** *Daily News* 23 July 5/1 When they [*sc.* hailstones] attain the size of hen-eggs..the matter is beyond a joke. **1961** *Ann. Reg. 1960* 508 The guaranteed prices for..hen eggs..were reduced.

heneicosane (hɛ'naɪkəʊseɪn). *Chem.* Also henicosane. [f. Gr. ἑν-, εἷς one + εἴκοσι twenty + -ANE.] Any of the hydrocarbons of the paraffin series having twenty-one carbon atoms, *esp.* the unbranched isomer (n-*heneicosane*). Hence **heneico'sanic, -cosa'noic, -co'soic acid,** the saturated fatty acid, $C_{20}H_{41}COOH$, derived from *n*-heneicosane.

1889 MUIR & MORLEY *Watts' Dict. Chem.* II. 674/1 *Henicosane* $C_{21}H_{44}$.. Formed by reduction of the dichloride..of the ketone. **1915** *Jrnl. Chem. Soc.* CVII. 738 Heneicosoic acid, $CH_3{\cdot}[CH_2]_{19}{\cdot}CO_2H$, is readily soluble in ether. **1924** *Jrnl. Biol. Chem.* LIX. 920 n-Heneicosanic Acid ..melted at 75-76°C. **1945** A. N. SACHANEN *Chem. Const. Petroleum* iv. 232 The heneicosanes substituted in position 11 ($C_{10}H_{21}.CHR.C_{10}H_{21}$) have low melting points (below −7°C). **1951** KIRK & OTHMER *Encycl. Chem. Technol.* VI. 257 Heneicosanoic acid, $C_{21}H_{42}O_2$, has been reported to occur in Japanese wax and earth-nut oil, but the evidence presented indicates that it is not found in natural fats and waxes.

henen, obs. var. of HEN, hence.

henequen ('hɛnɪkɛn). Also **-quin, hennequen.** [ad. Sp. *jeniquen, geniquen*, from the native name.] The fibrous product known as *sisal hemp*, obtained from the leaves of species of *Agave*, esp. *Agave Ixtli* of Yucatan; also, the plant itself.

1880 *Libr. Univ. Knowl.* (N.Y.) IX. 777 The hennequen plant..from which is prepared Sisal hemp. **1884** F. A. OBER *Trav. Mexico* 28 (Stanf.) The road passes through the henequen plantations. **1888** *Encycl. Brit.* XXIV. 758 The chief cultivated plants [in Yucatan] are maize, the sugarcane ..and especially henequen..It is..used chiefly for the manufacture of coarse sackcloth, cordage, and hammocks.

henes, obs. form of HENCE, HIGHNESS.

henforth, -forward: see HEN *adv.*

heng, ME. inflexion of HANG *v.*

henge¹, hange (hɛndʒ, hændʒ). Now *dial.* [An early form of HINGE *sb.* q.v., f. *hang* vb.] The 'pluck' (heart, liver, etc.) of an animal.

1469 *Househ. Ord.* (1790) 96 Every sheepe to be brought in whoole, except the hedde and the henge. **1787** GROSE *Provinc. Gloss.*, *Hanje*, or *Hange*, the head, heart, liver and lights of any animal, called in Somersetshire the purtenance. **1888** ELWORTHY *W. Somerset Word-bk.*, *Hange*, the pluck, *i.e.* the liver, lungs, and heart of any animal. In dressing sheep, the head is usually left attached by the windpipe; this is always called a 'sheep's head and hange'.

henge² (hɛndʒ). [f. STONE)HENGE.] **1.** In particular reference to the name *Stonehenge*: something 'hanging' or in suspense. **2.** *Archæol.* A term (first applied by T. D. Kendrick) for classes of monuments more or less akin to the stone circle of Stonehenge. Also *attrib.*

1740 W. STUKELEY *Stonehenge* ii. 8 Pendulous rocks are now called henges in Yorkshire, and I have been informed of another place there called Stonehenge, being natural rocks. So that I doubt not, Stonehenge in Saxon signifies the hanging stones. **1742** in Defoe *Tour Gt. Brit.* (ed. 3) I. v. 257 The present Name [*sc.* Stonehenge] is Saxon, tho' the Work is beyond all Comparison older, signifying a hanging Rod or Pole, *i.e.* a Gallows, from the hanging Parts,

Architraves, or rather Imposts; and pendulous Rocks are still in Yorkshire called Henges. **1932** KENDRICK & HAWKES *Archæol. in Eng. & Wales* vii. 83 (*heading*) The 'henge' monuments. **1936** *Proc. Prehist. Soc.* II. 1 A new monument of the 'henge' class. **1951** *Field Archæol.* (*Ordnance Survey*) (ed. 3) 17 The critical event in the modern study of 'henges' was the discovery of the site known as 'Woodhenge' from the air, two miles east-north-east of Stonehenge... The term henge monument..is an unsatisfactory term since, on strict etymological grounds, it should only be applied to sites which contain a 'hanging' element like the lintels of Stonehenge. **1967** *Antiquaries Jrnl.* XLVII. 166 The term 'henge' is applied to those monuments which enclose a circular or oval area by means of a bank and *internal* ditch and which possess one or two opposed entrances (Atkinson, Piggott, and Sandars, 1951, p. 82).

henge, obs. f. HINGE; obs. inflexion of HANG *v.*

†'**hengest**, *Obs.* Also 1 **hencgest, hengst,** 2 **hængest.** [OE. *hęngest, hęngst* = OFris. *hengst, hingst, hangst*, MDu. *henghest, henxt*, etc. (Du. *hengst*), OHG. *hęngist* (mod.G. *hengst*), LG. (Sw., Da.) *hingst.* (See also HENCHMAN.) The sense has varied in different langs. and at different periods, as stallion, gelding, and horse generally.] A male horse; usually a gelding.

(Also the proper name of the reputed founder of the Saxon or Jutish kingdom of Kent; and in various place-names, as OE. *Hengestesbróc, Hengestesgeat, Hengestesheáfod, Hengestesigе*, now *Hinxbrook, Hinxgate, Hinxhead, Hinksey.*)

a **1000** *Ags. Voc.* in Wr.-Wülcker 274/8 *Cabullus*, hengest. *c* **1000** ÆLFRIC *Voc.* Ibid. 119/37 *Canterius*, hengst. **1002** in *Dipl. Angl. Ævi Sax.* (Th.) 548 An hundred wildra horsa, and xvi. tame hencgestas. *c* **1205** LAY. 3546 Ich bi-tæche þe anne hængest, godna and strongna.

hengle, obs. form of HINGLE, hinge.

hengwite, var. HANGWITE, *Obs.*

'**hen-,harrier.** *Ornith.* Also 6–7 **-harrow(er.** [f. HEN *sb.* + HARRIER: in reference to its preying on poultry.] A European bird of prey, *Circus cyaneus*, also called Blue Hawk, Blue Kite.

The female is known as the Ring-tailed Hawk.

1565–73 COOPER *Thesaurus, Rubetarius*, a kinde of haukes called an henne harroer. **1688** R. HOLME *Armoury* II. 236/1 A Henharrow, or Henharrier, is the Male of a Ring-tail. **1691** RAY *Collect. Words* Pref. (E.D.S.) 3 There is a sort of puttock called a hen-harrier, from chasing, preying upon, and destroying of poultry. **1774** G. WHITE *Selborne* xl. 101 Hen-harriers breed on the ground, and seem never to settle on trees. **1849** MAUNDER *Treas. Nat. Hist.* 309/1 The Hen-Harrier feeds on birds and reptiles.

'**hen-hawk.** *Ornith.* A name given in U.S. to various species of hawks or buzzards, esp. to the Red-tailed and Red-shouldered hawks, *Buteo borealis* and *B. lineatus.* ***blue hen-hawk***, the adult American goshawk.

1806 W. CLARK in Lewis & Clark *Orig. Jrnls.* (1905) IV. 131, I have observed..a hawk of an intermediate size with a long tail and blewish coloured wings, remarkably swift in flight and very ferce. Sometimes called in the Un. States the hen Hawk. **1819** D. THOMAS *Trav. W. Country* 210 The Hen-Hawk is not very numerous. **1855** LONGF. *Hiaw.* xiv. 116 Crane and hen-hawk, And the cormorant. **1860** BARTLETT *Dict. Amer., Hen-hawk* (*Falco lineatus*), the popular name of the Red-shouldered Hawk of naturalists. **1884** ROE *Nat. Ser. Story* iv, The American goshawk is the dreaded blue hen hawk of New England.

'**hen-heart.** One who has the heart of a hen; a chicken-heart, coward.

c **1440** *York Myst.* xxxiii. 198 A! henne-harte!

'**hen-,hearted,** *a.* Timorous or cowardly, faint-hearted, chicken-hearted, pusillanimous.

1522 SKELTON *Why not to Court* 164 They kepe them in theyr holdes, Lyke henherted cokoldes. **1638** H. RIDER tr. *Horace's Epodes* xvi, The hen-hearted and despairing wretch. **1708** MOTTEUX *Rabelais* IV. lxvi. (1737) 272 The Hen-hearted Rascal is so cowardly. **1815** SCOTT *Guy M.* xxviii, Are you turned hen-hearted, Jack?

'**henhood.** *nonce-wd.* The condition of a hen.

1829 SOUTHEY *Pilgr. Compost.* Poet Wks. VII. 265 From which two milk-white chicken To Cock and Henhood grew.

'**hen-house. a.** A small house or shed in which poultry are shut up for the night.

1512–13 *Durham MS. Cell. Roll*, Eidem pro..bordyng lez henhowse. **1577** B. GOOGE *Heresbach's Husb.* IV. (1586) 162b, Let the front of your Henne house stande alwaies towardes the East. **1616** SURFL. & MARKH. *Country Farme* 17 Your Henne-house, and roomes for other Fowles, fashioned foure-square like a tower. **1740** MRS. DELANY *Life & Corr.* (1861) II. 120 You'll find me as errant a country Joan as ever frequented a hen-house or dairy. **1887** ADELINE SERGEANT *Jacobi's Wife* III. vi. 85 A little deserted building which had once been used as a hen-house.

b. *fig.* A house or establishment inhabited chiefly by women.

1785 GROSE *Dict. Vulg. T., Hen house*, a house where the woman rules. **1931** W. FAULKNER *Sanctuary* xxi. 193 She's got two daughters... I'm heading for the hen-house. **1963** P. MOYES *Murder à la Mode* ii. 29 'You know what this place is, don't you, sir?' The sergeant was plunged in gloom. 'Fashion magazine. Ruddy hen-house.'

henid ('hɛnɪd). *Philos.* [ad. G. *henide*, coined by Weininger on the basis of Gr. ἑν- one; cf. HENISM.] In the philosophy of Otto Weininger (1880–1903): see quots. Hence **he'nidical** *a.*

1906 tr. *O. Weininger's Sex & Character* II. iii. 99, I propose for psychical data at this earliest stage of their existence the word Henid (from the Greek ἕν, because in them it is impossible to distinguish perception and sensation as two analytically separable factors, and because, therefore, there is no trace of duality in them)... The very idea of a henid forbids its description; it is merely a something. **1909** J. LONDON *Martin Eden* xxxvii. 322 By some henidical process—henidical, by the way, is a favourite word of mine which nobody understands—by some henidical process you persuade yourself that you believe in the competitive system and the survival of the strong. **1914** —— *Let.* 10 Sept. (1966) 428 The word henid was coined by a crazy German philosopher... All persons possess henids. **1915** —— *Jacket* xiv. 160 'I'll—' he began explosively, proving, by his inability to conclude the remark, that he thought in henids. **1946** D. ABRAHAMSEN *Mind & Death of Genius* 112 Weininger introduces a special name for the psychological data at the earliest stage, before clarification has begun. He calls the vague perception the henid. *Ibid.* 113 According to Weininger, the henid is the form of perception known to the lower types of organism. In mankind development from the henid to the completely differentiated form of perception and idea is possible.

henism ('hɛnɪz(ə)m). [f. Gr. εἷς, ἑν- one + -ISM.] The doctrine that there is but one kind of substance, whether mind or matter; = MONISM. Cf. DUALISM.

1881 MAX MÜLLER *Kant's Pure Reason* I. 187 We have seen how the unreconciled and irreconcilable elements in the Cartesian dualism ended in leading by a double road to Henism, according to which either matter or mind..had the right to existence alone conceded to it. **1882** *Mind* Apr. 281 One would enter a mild protest against the new term, Henism.

Henle ('hɛnlɪ). *Anat.* The name of F. G. J. *Henle* (see HENLEAN *a.*) used in the possessive and with *of* adjunct to designate numerous anatomical structures, as: **a.** ***Henle's layer*** (or ***layer of Henle***), a single layer of cubical cells in the inner root sheath of the hair follicle, between Huxley's layer and the outer root sheath. Formerly also called ***Henle's sheath*** etc. (cf. sense c).

1853 BUSK & HUXLEY tr. *Kölliker's Man. Human Histol.* I. 186 The outermost layer [of the inner root-sheath of the hair], which alone was formerly known, the inner root-sheath of Henle, is formed of elongated cells without nuclei. **1860** G. BUCHANAN tr. *Kölliker's Man. Human Microsc. Anat.* 109 (*caption*) A portion of the root of a dark hair..f. outer fenestrated layer (*Henle's* layer). **1892** H. E. CLARK *Wilson's Anatomist's Vade Mecum* (ed. 11) 70 The inner root-sheath [of a hair] is again divisible into..an outer layer (Henle's sheath). **1970** T. S. & C. R. LEESON *Histol.* (ed. 2) xiii. 263/2 Henle's layer..is a single layer of flattened, clear cells which contain hyaline fibrils.

b. ***Henle's loop*** (or ***loop of Henle***), a portion of a uriniferous tubule from where it passes from the cortex of the kidney into the medulla to where it returns into the cortex, also *spec.* the central part of this where it forms a distinct loop at its deepest point in the medulla. Also called ***Henle's*** (***looped***) ***tube*** or ***tubule*** etc.

1867 *Quain's Elem. Anat.* (ed. 7) II. 930 The tubes in question have been designated looped tubes of Henle. **1877** W. TURNER *Introd. Human Anat.* II. xi. 785 Each intermediary tube..descends..into the medullary pyramid, where it turns on itself, forms a loop, known as the looped tube of Henle, and reenters the cortex as the ascending limb of the looped tube. **1885** [see LOOP *sb.*[1] 4 a]. **1890** BILLINGS *Med. Dict.* I. 631/2 *Henle's loop*, loop of Henle. *Ibid., Henle's tubules*, looped tubules of Henle. **1970** T. S. & C. R. LEESON *Histol.* (ed. 2) xvi. 374/2 The loop of Henle consists of the straight part of the proximal tubule in the descending limb, a thin segment in descending and ascending limbs, and the straight part of the distal tubule in the ascending limb.

c. ***Henle's sheath*** (or ***sheath of Henle***) (see quot. 1942). Cf. sense a.

[**1878** M. L. RANVIER *Lecons Histol. Syst. Nerveux* I. x. 159 Nous pouvons vous montrer sous un de ces microscopes des nerfs composés d'un seul tube nerveux qui possèdent une membrane enveloppante; j'appellerai cette membrane, gaîne [= sheath] de Henle, du nom de l'auteur qui l'a découverte.] **1887** *Buck's Handb. Med. Sci.* V. 145/1 The sheath in this form has been named the sheath of Henle (Ranvier). There is a space between the nerve-fibre and the sheath. **1890** BILLINGS *Med. Dict.* I. 631/2 *Henle's sheath*, a continuation of the fibrous tissue of the perineurium. **1942** O. LARSELL *Anat. Nervous Syst.* iv. 48 A delicate sheath of connective tissue fibers, continuous with the endoneurium of the nerve trunk, is intimately associated with and surrounds the neurolemma of most individual peripheral fibers. This is usually called the sheath of Henle.

d. ***Henle's gland*** (or ***gland of Henle***), any of numerous gland-like structures in the conjunctiva of the eye-lid (see quot. 1933).

1890 BILLINGS *Med. Dict.* I. 631/2 *Henle's glands*, short tubular glands said to be found on the palpebral conjunctiva. **1933** E. WOLFF *Anat. Eye & Orbit* iii. 105 Henle's 'Glands' occur in the palpebral conjunctiva between the tarsal plates and the fornices. They are probably not true glands, but folds of mucous membrane cut transversely. **1961** S. DUKE-ELDER *Syst. Ophthalm.* II. iii. 115 The epithelial depressions between them were originally described by Henle (1866) as glands (the *glands of Henle*) and were termed conjunctival crypts by Dubreuil (1908).

Henlean ('hɛnli:ən), *a. Anat.* [f. *Henle*, a German anatomist and pathologist (1809–85): see -AN.] In ***Henlean membrane***, the elastic fenestrated membrane forming the outer layer of the innermost coat of an artery.

1886 in *Syd. Soc. Lex.*

Henley ('hɛnlɪ). The name of a town on the Thames, in Oxfordshire, used alone or *attrib.* to designate the annual regatta held there since 1839. Hence '**Henleyite**, a Henley enthusiast.

1839 *Times* 6 June 3/5 Henley Regatta..takes place on Friday, the 14th. **1861** T. HUGHES *Tom Brown at Oxf.* II. 218 You know the Leander are to be at Henley... There will be a splendid race for the cup. **1868** *Broadway* I. 104/2 Roland rowed his man—a Henley winner—down. **1887** [see REGATTA 2 *attrib.*]. **1893** *Isis* 29 Apr. 130/2, I have heard nothing more about the Henley arrangements. *Ibid.* 3 June 207/2 The Oxford arrangements for Henley are now getting into rather a more settled condition. **1901** *Westm. Gaz.* 2 July 7/2 Henleyites..will be depressed to hear that the Meteorological Office forecasts..rainy and colder weather. **1902** *Encycl. Brit.* XXXII. 307/1 A motion was proposed at the October meeting of the Henley Stewards to exclude foreign crews from the regatta. **1959** *Chamber's Encycl.* VII. 13/2 Henley Royal Regatta (1851—— formerly Henley Regatta, 1839).

henmost, Sc. form of HINDMOST.

hen-mould. *local.* A kind of soil or earth: see quot.

1712 MORTON *Northampt.* I. I. §25. 37 *Hen-mould*..is of a much like Constitution to the Moory-Land above described. 'Tis a black, hollow, spungy, and mouldering Earth, which is usually found..at and nigh the Bottoms of Hills. **1753** CHAMBERS *Cycl. Supp., Hen-mould Soil.*

henna ('hɛnə). Also 7 **hena, hanna, hina,** 8–9 **hinna(h,** 9 **hennah.** [a. Arab. *ḥennāɛ.* See also ALCANNA.] **a.** The Egyptian Privet, *Lawsonia inermis* (N.O. *Lythraceæ*); the shoots and leaves of this plant used, esp. by eastern nations, as a dye for parts of the body, or made into a cosmetic with catechu.

1600 J. PORY tr. *Leo's Africa* I. 22 They have no oyle of olives, but of another kinde which they call Hena..in colour it is as beautifull as gold. **1613** PURCHAS *Pilgrimage* (1614) 637 Their women..with a certaine colour in their hand called Hanna, which will staine. **1678** J. PHILLIPS tr. *Tavernier's Trav.* (1684) I. I. 44 (Stanf.) Another sort of Water with which they dye their Hands and Nails red, which they squeeze out of a certaine Root call'd Hina. **1748** *Phil. Trans.* XLV. 570 Called Henna, or Alhenna, and, by Corruption, Alkanna. **1791** NEWTE *Tour Eng. & Scotl.* 50 A large quantity of the herb hinna is sent by the bride-groom to the house of the bride. **1872** BAKER *Nile Tribut.* i. 3 The henna grows in considerable quantities on the left bank of the river.

b. *attrib.* and *Comb.*, as ***henna-scented*** adj.; (with reference to dyeing or staining with henna) ***henna-dyeing***; ***henna-coloured, -dyed, -haired, -tipped, -tressed*** adjs.

1954 M. MEAD *Growing up in New Guinea* 143 *Henna-coloured betel juice. **1920** *Chambers's Jrnl.* May 299/1 He..showed a handful of his *henna-dyed beard. **1906** *Daily Chron.* 27 June 6/4 From tight-lacing to *henna-dyeing the frisky matron is a study in successful artifice. **1885** BIBLE (R.V.) *Song Sol.* i. 14 My beloved is unto me as a cluster of *henna-flowers. **1907** *Daily Chron.* 31 Dec. 3/1 His American trotting-car and his *henna-haired wife. **1858** CARPENTER *Veg. Phys.* §369 The *Henna-juice..is a very permanent brown dye. **1923** *Chambers's Jrnl.* 306/2 Their henna-tipped fingers are loaded with rings. **1841** LANE *Arab. Nts.* I. iii. 137 (Stanf.) Sprigs of the *henna-tree. **1939** R. CAMPBELL *Flowering Rifle* I. 24 Amongst her Modern Southeys, henna-tressed.

hennaed ('hɛnəd). [f. HENNA + -ED[2].] Dyed or stained with henna.

1924 *Countries of World* II. 1145/1 A slim hand with hennaed nails. **1925** H. V. MORTON *Heart of London* 53 Maud's hennaed hair. **1961** A. WILSON *Old Men at Zoo* vii. 309 Her dark hennaed hair.

henne, obs. form of HEN *sb.*, *adv.*

'**hennery.** [f. HEN *sb.* + -ERY.] An establishment or place for rearing poultry; a place where hens are kept: cf. *rookery.*

1859 *All Year Round* No. 32. 125 Why not establish extensive henneries, hatch by steam? **1877** E. G. SQUIER *Peru* (1878) 45 Sometimes the roofs are used as grand henneries. **1884** ROE *Nat. Ser. Story* vi, I was soon covering the hennery with my gun.

hennes, obs. form of HENCE.

‖**hennin** ('hɛnɪn). *Hist.* [a. obs. F. *hennin* (see Godefroi).] A head-dress worn by women in France in the 15th century, of high and conical shape, with a muslin veil depending from it.

1852 JAMES *Agnes Sorrel* I. 51 An elderly woman in an extravagantly high *hennin*..the head dress of the times. **1885** *Mag. of Art* Sept. 480/1 Ladies' head-dresses grew so prodigious as to bear comparison with the hennins of the Fifteenth Century.

'**hennish,** *a. rare.* [f. HEN *sb.* + -ISH.] Of or pertaining to a hen.

1595 SOUTHWELL *St. Peter's Compl.* 12 Well might a Cocke correct me with a crowe, Whom hennish cackling first did ouer-throwe.

hennus, -ys, obs. forms of HENCE.

henny (ˈhɛnɪ), *a.* and *sb.* [f. HEN *sb.* + -Y.]
A. *adj.* Of or pertaining to a hen; hen-like; having the plumage or figure of a hen: said of the males of some breeds of fowls.
1885 *Encycl. Brit.* XIX. 644 There is a tendency towards the assumption of the female plumage by the males, and distinct breeds of 'henny' Game [fowls] are known.
B. *sb.* A hen-like male fowl.
1868 DARWIN *Anim. & Pl.* I. 252 Males in certain sub-breeds have lost some of their secondary masculine characters, and from their close resemblance in plumage to the females, are often called hennies. **1884** *St. James' Gaz.* 27 Nov. 5/2 Some males are known as 'hennies'.

Henoch (ˈhiːnɒx). The name of E. H. *Henoch* (1820–1910), German pædiatrician, used in the possessive and occas. *attrib.* to designate esp. purpura associated with abdominal symptoms, as ***Henoch('s) purpura***; also used *attrib.*, in combination with the name of Schönlein (see SCHÖNLEIN), to designate purpura associated with both the abdominal symptoms of Henoch's purpura and the articular symptoms of Schönlein's purpura, as ***Henoch-Schönlein*** (or ***Schönlein-Henoch***) ***purpura, syndrome.***
1893 DUNGLISON *Dict. Med. Sci.* (ed. 21) 522/1 *Henoch's purpura*, purpura complicated with infection of the intestines. **1896** *Intercolonial Med. Jrnl. Australasia* I. 364 (*title*) A case of Henoch's purpura hæmorrhagica. **1897** *Brit. Med. Jrnl.* 18 Dec. 1800/1 Henoch's purpura. Dr. Dreschfeld made some observations on the symptoms, pathology, and treatment of this disease, cases of which, though not under that name, had been repeated, observed and described in English journals. **1908** *Practitioner* June 824 Gastro-intestinal crises are common with both Henoch's purpura and angioneurotic oedema. **1947** *Gastroenterology* IX. 610 My working diagnosis in this case was Henoch's Purpura. **1948** *Q. Jrnl. Med.* XLI. 95 (*title*) The Schönlein-Henoch syndrome (anaphylactoid purpura). **1952** *Arch. Dis. Childhood* XXVII. 480 (*title*) The Schoenlein-Henoch syndrome in childhood with particular reference to the occurence of nephritis. **1959** *Brit. Med. Jrnl.* 19 Dec. 1385/2 (*heading*) Familial incidence of the Henoch-Schönlein syndrome. **1966** DUNLOP & ALSTEAD *Textb. Med. Treatm.* (ed. 10) 502 (*heading*) Henoch-Schönlein purpura. *Ibid.*, In this condition,..abdominal symptoms,..(Henoch purpura), and pain and swelling in joints (Schönlein purpura), may occur together. **1967** A. C. ALLEN *Skin* (ed. 2) xvii. 661/1 In Henoch's purpura..the prominent symptoms are recurrent abdominal pain..and colic, associated with moderate fever and with melena, tenesmus, and mucus in the stools. **1968** *Gastroenterology* LIV. 260 (*title*) Gastro-intestinal and roentgenological manifestations of Henoch-Schoenlein purpura.

‖**henopœia.** *Obs.* [a. Gr. type *ἑνοποιΐα, f. ἑνοποιεῖν, f. εἷς, ἑν- one + ποιεῖν to make.] A figure of speech by which a number of things are considered as one.
1685 H. MORE *Illustr.* 75 The whole succession..being looked upon but as one Beast, by a Prophetick Henopoeia whatever befell any particular King is referred to the Beast.
So †**henopoˈetic**, †**henopoˈetical**, *adjs.* [Gr. type *ἑνοποιητικός], involving henopœia; unifying.
1664 H. MORE *Myst. Iniq.*, etc. 219 Henopoetick Types of a Multitude collected into one Government. *Ibid.* 322 To him that considers how Collective and Henopoetical, as I may so speak, the Prophetick Types are.

henotheism (ˈhɛnəʊθiːɪz(ə)m). [f. Gr. εἷς, ἑνό-ς one + θε-ός god + -ISM.] The belief in one god as the deity of the individual, family, or tribe, without asserting that he is the only God: considered as a stage of religious belief between polytheism and monotheism. See quots.
1860 MAX MÜLLER *Semitic Monotheism* in *Sel. Ess.* (1881) II. 415 The latter form of faith, the belief in One God, is properly called monotheism, whereas the term of henotheism would best express the faith in a single god. **1879** P. LE PAGE RENOUF *Lect. Orig. Relig.* 217 The nature of Henotheism as distinct from Monotheism was explained in last year's lectures as a phase of religious thought in which the individual gods invoked are not conceived as limited by the power of others. **1880** GLADSTONE in *19th Cent.* No. 38. 721 Henotheism, the affirmative belief in one God, without the sharply-defined exclusive line which makes it a belief in Him as the only God. **1886** TIELE in *Encycl. Brit.* XX. 367/1 From this primitive naturism sprang..*henotheism*, not the henotheism of Max Müller, or of Hartmann, or of Asmus, but a practical henotheism, *i.e.* the adoration of one God above others as the specific tribal god or as the lord over a particular people, a national or relative monotheism.
So ˈ**henotheist**, one who worships according to henotheism. **henotheˈistic** *a.*
1880 GLADSTONE in *19th Cent.* No. 38. 721 The region of ideas, in which..Iris had been born, was the henotheistic region. **1882** MAX MÜLLER *India* 182 If the Veda had taught us nothing else but this henotheistic phase. **1884** *Athenæum* 22 Nov. 653/2 The Moquis would probably be claimed as 'Henotheists' by the person who believes in 'Henotheism'. **1897** *Edin. Rev.* July 225 The worshipper of one out of a number of gods; the Henotheist of Prof. Max Müller.

henotic (hɛˈnɒtɪk), *a.* [a. Gr. ἑνωτικός serving to unite, f. ἕνωσις unification, f. ἕν one. Cf. F. *hénotique.*] Tending to make one; unifying; reconciling, harmonizing.
1878 GLADSTONE *Glean.* (1879) III. 226 Nor, I believe, has any country produced a greater number of Henotic writers; the theological peacemakers, who..have striven..to close the breaches of Christendom.

ˈ**hen-peck,** *v. colloq.* [A back-formation from HEN-PECKED in its participial use.] *trans.* Of a wife: To domineer over or rule (the husband).
1688 *Loyal Litany* iii. in *3rd Collect. Poems* (1689) 30/2 From being Henpeck'd worse at home..*Libera nos.* **1753** MURPHY *Gray's Inn Jrnl.* No. 52 ¶3 An uxorious Gentleman, who is sometimes a little Henpecked by his Wife. **1819** BYRON *Juan* I. xxii, But—oh! ye lords of ladies intellectual..have they not hen-peck'd you all? **1852** THACKERAY *Esmond* I. vii, That my lady was jealous and henpecked my lord.

ˈ**hen-peck,** *sb. rare.* [f. prec.]
†**1.** **a.** A wife who domineers over her husband. *Obs.*
c **1801** T. SELWYN *Warn. to Batchelors* ix. (MS.), Their Mac Tabs and their Henpecks may prate as they please.
b. A husband so domineered.
1765 GARRICK *Let.* 23 May in *Corr. Garrick* (1831) I. 185 More of the sneaking hen-peck, than of the tender enamoured husband.
2. = Hen-pecking, the domineering of a wife.
1833 CARLYLE *Diderot* in *Misc. Ess.* (1888) V. 23 Dying of heartbreak coupled with henpeck.
So **hen-peckery**, the state or condition of being henpecked.
1838 DICKENS *O. Twist* xxxvii, He had fallen..to the lowest depth of the most snubbed hen-peckery. **1869** *Harper's Mag.* Mar. 508/2 Husbands flee from hen-peckery, and wives desert bearish husbands. **1958** *Daily Mail* 15 July 3/4 Charmian Eyre..remains disarmingly human at the height of henpeckery.

hen-pecked (ˈhɛnpɛkt), *ppl. a. colloq.* [lit. pecked by a hen or hens: alluding to the plucking of some of the feathers of the domestic cock by his hens.] **a.** Domineered over by, or subject to the rule of, a wife.
a **1680** BUTLER *Rem.* (1759) II. 104 The henpect Man rides behind his Wife, and lets her wear the Spurs and govern the Reins. **1690** DRYDEN *Amphitryon* II. ii, Was ever poor deity so hen-pecked as I am! **1697** —— *Virg. Past.* III. 49 A Step-dame too I have, a cursed She Who rules my hen-peck'd Sire and orders me. **1712** STEELE *Spect.* No. 479 ¶5 Socrates, who is by all Accounts the undoubted Head of the Sect of the Hen-peck'd. **1820** W. IRVING *Sketch Bk.* I. 59 An obedient henpecked husband. **1923** D. H. LAWRENCE *Kangaroo* i. 4 A little red-faced man, rather beery and hen-pecked looking. **1930** G. B. SHAW *Apple Cart* Interlude 57 *Orinthia*: Why are you so afraid of your wife? You are the laughing stock of London, you poor henpecked darling. **1939** —— *In Good King Charles's Golden Days* I. 57 What! that henpecked booby! *Ibid.* 58 He may be henpecked: what married man is not?
b. *transf.* Cf. *hen-frigate* in HEN *sb.* 8.
1695 CONGREVE *Love for L.* IV. xiii, I believe he that marries you will go to Sea in a Hen-peck'd Frigat.

hen-plant: see HEN *sb.* 8.

Henrician (hɛnˈrɪʃ(ɪ)an), *a.* and *sb. Eccl. Hist.* [ad. med.L. *Henriciān-us*, f. *Henricus* Henry.]
A. *adj.* **1.** Pertaining to Henry VIII of England or the ecclesiastical measures of his reign.
1893 R. W. DIXON *Hist. Ch. Eng.* xv. III. 39 The chief articles of the Henrician settlement of religion.
2. Of or pertaining to the Henricians (B. 1).
1894 *Dublin Rev.* Apr. 317 Many of the citizens had embraced the Henrician heresy.
B. *sb.* **1.** One of the followers (in Switzerland and Southern France) of Henry of Lausanne, a religious and moral reformer of the 12th century.
1579 FULKE *Heskins' Parl.* 115 Petrobrusians, and Henricians, that denied the body of Christe to be consecrated, and giuen by the priestes, as it was by Christe him selfe. **1889** S. J. EALES *St. Bernard* I. 61 The zeal of Bernard..was exercised chiefly against the heresy of the Henricians.
2. A supporter of the opinion and practice of the Emperor Henry IV of Germany, in opposition to Pope Gregory VII.
1874 J. H. BLUNT *Dict. Sects* (1886) 183/2 *note.*
3. A supporter of the ecclesiastical policy of Henry VIII. Hence **Henricianism** (hɛnˈrɪʃ(ɪ)ənɪz(ə)m), the ecclesiastical policy of Henry VIII.
1828 E. NARES *Mem. Ld. Burghley* I. IV. 53 The king's supremacy, which, like a true *Henrician*, he was very careful to maintain. **1900** F. W. MAITLAND *Coll. Papers* (1911) III. 159 Calvin had spoken ill of Henricianism. **1903** —— in *Camb. Mod. Hist.* II. 555 A Reformed religion, or some northern version of Henricanism [*sic*]. **1946** A. L. ROWSE *Use Hist.* 180 Yet we cannot be grateful enough to the (sometimes unattractive) Henricians and Elizabethans who pushed us through it.

Henri Deux (ɑ̃ri dø). [Fr., = Henri II.] Designating the style of Renaissance architecture or art developed in France during the reign of Henri II, king of France 1547–59; *spec.* the purest style of the French Renaissance.
1863 W. CHAFFERS *Marks Pott. & Porc.* 89 The following is a list of all the pieces of Henri II. ware now known to be extant. **1873** *Young Englishwoman* May 234/2 The Henri II. hat is very becoming to a young face. **1881** C. C. HARRISON *Woman's Handiwork* II. 104 Modern English potters have put within our reach reproductions of that exquisite (so-called 'Henri Deux') faïence bequeathed to the world by the lady Hélène de Hangest-Genlis—the ware of the Chateau d'Oiron. **1884** KNIGHT *Dict. Mech.* Suppl. s.v., Henri-Deux Ware (*Faïence d'Oïron*). **1960** R. G. HAGGAR *Conc. Encycl. Cont. Pott. & Porc.* 397 Saint-Porchaire earthenware *tazza* with inlaid decoration in coloured clays (so-called Henri Deux Ware), c. 1540.

Henrietta (hɛnrɪˈɛtə). *Disused.* [Female name.] Designating a light-weight dress fabric, sometimes with a silk warp.
1851 *Illustr. Catal. Gt. Exhib.* III. 494/2 Henrietta cloths, with silk warp and worsted weft. **1862** *Illustr. Catal. Internat. Exhib., Industr. Dept., Brit. Div.* II. No. 4018 Paramatta, or Henrietta Cloth, twill. **1890** *Advt.* (Ann Arbor, Mich.) 1 Mar., We offer a 46-inch Black Silk Warp Henrietta. **1901** *Daily News* 23 Feb. 6/7 Henrietta cloths, which wear so well and drape so charmingly. **1908** *Sears, Roebuck Catal.* 933/1 Cotton henrietta cloth..having all the appearance and touch of an imported all wool henrietta.

hen-roost. [f. HEN *sb.* + ROOST *sb.*] **a.** A place where domestic fowls roost at night.
a **1100** *Gerefa* in *Anglia* IX. 262 ȝe eac henna hrost. **1611** COTGR., *Poulailler*, a Henne-house, or Henne-roost. **1620** J. WILKINSON *Coroners & Sherifes* 120 Walkers by night to steale..Hennes from Henrouse, or any other thing. **1711** ADDISON *Spect.* No. 130 ¶1 If a Man prosecutes them [Gipsies] with Severity, his Hen-roost is sure to pay for it. **1855** MACAULAY *Hist. Eng.* xviii. IV. 150 A boy who had robbed a henroost.
b. *fig.* A source of plunder: in allusion to a political speech referring to 'the robbing of hen-roosts'.
1909 *Westm. Gaz.* 16 Apr. 5/1 Mr. Lloyd George's now historic reference to 'hen-roosts'. **1928** *Britain's Industr. Future* (*Lib. Ind. Inq.*) V. xxix. §2. 420 Apart from the public hen-roosts which Mr. Churchill has raided, it is impossible for an outsider to estimate what private hen-roosts inside the Treasury he has also helped himself to.

Henry[1] (ˈhɛnrɪ). The name of Benjamin Tyler *Henry* (1821–98), American inventor, used attrib. to designate a breech-loading magazine rifle or parts thereof, subsequently used in the Martini-Henry rifle. Also *ellipt.*
1859 G. A. JACKSON *Diary* 25 Jan. in F. Hall *Hist. Colorado* (1890) II. 522 Packed up our things for the trip and got Oakes' Henry rifle for Phil. **1869** in *Frontier* (1929) IX. 157 One of them..lost one of our Henry carbines. **1880** *Encycl. Brit.* XI. 282/1 In the Henry action the barrel does not move, but is closed at the breech end by a sliding vertical block. *Ibid.* 282/2 The combination of the Martini breech action with the Henry barrel. *Ibid.* 283/2 Henry rifling. **1902** *Ibid.* XXXII. 242/1 In 1861 the Henry grooving for a cylindrical bullet, a modification of the Whitworth, first appeared. **1927** C. M. RUSSELL *Trails plowed Under* 71, I guess his weapon's a Henry. **1964** H. L. PETERSON *Encycl. Firearms* 180 (*caption*) Iron-frame Henry rifle and brass-frame Henry rifle.

Henry[2] (ˈhɛnrɪ). The name of William *Henry* (1774–1836), English chemist, used in ***Henry's law*** (see quot. 1940).
1886 *Syd. Soc. Lex.*, H[enry]'s law. **1910** *Encycl. Brit.* XIII. 302/1 The conclusion he reached ('Henry's law') being that 'water takes up of gas condensed by one, two or more additional atmospheres, a quantity which, ordinarily compressed, would be equal to twice, thrice, &c. the volume absorbed under the common pressure of the atmosphere'. **1940** *Chambers's Techn. Dict.* 411/1 *Henry's Law.* The amount of a gas absorbed by a given volume of a liquid at a given temperature is directly proportional to the pressure of the gas. **1966** PHILLIPS & WILLIAMS *Inorg. Chem.* II. xix. 43 Oxygen dissolves as atoms (obeying Henry's law) in molten silver.

henry[3] (ˈhɛnrɪ). *Physics.* The name of Joseph *Henry* (1797–1878), American physicist, used (pl. **henrys, henries**) to designate the practical unit of inductance, now incorporated in the International System of Units, i.e. the inductance of a circuit in which an electromotive force of one volt is produced by a current changing at the rate of one ampere per second. Abbrev. H or (*rare*) h. Also ˈ**henrymeter** (see quot. 1940).
1893 *Electrician* 29 Sept. 577/2 There was the proposal [at the International Electrical Congress] to christen the unit of self-induction as the *henry* in honour of Joseph Henry its discoverer. **1915** *Proc. IRE* III. 223 The transformer is made up of coils having an inductance of the order of a henry or more. **1929** K. HENNEY *Princ. Radio* iv. 62 The coils used in radio apparatus vary from inductances of the order of microhenries to very large ones having over 100 henries in inductance. **1940** *Chambers's Techn. Dict.* 411/1 *Henrymeter*, an obsolete apparatus for measuring inductance; in it an alternating current was passed through the inductance under test and a standard inductance in series, the voltage drop across the two being compared. **1947** *Jrnl. Inst. Electr. Engin.* XCIV. 342/1 From the 1st January the units employed [at the National Physical Laboratory] will be those derived from the centimetre, gramme and second, i.e. the so-called 'absolute' units. The effects of this change may be seen from the following table:..One international henry = 1·00049 'absolute' henrys. **1952** *Electronic Engin.* XXIV. 465 A 10 henry A.F. choke has been provided in the cathode circuit.

Henry: see GOOD HENRY.

Henry Clay. The name of an American statesman (1777–1852) used to designate a type of cigar.
1867 in *Amer. Speech* (1965) XL. 130. **1884** *Harper's Mag.* Sept. 647/1 The dealer..asked him if he would 'like to 'ave

a 'Enry Clay'. **1888** KIPLING *Departmental Ditties* (1890) 105 There's peace in a Laranaga, there's calm in a Henry Clay. **1893** *Harper's Mag.* Dec. 34/1 And bring some cigars—Henry Clays. *Ibid.*, My father was always a Henry Clay man. **1922** JOYCE *Ulysses* 243 He removed his large Henry Clay decisively. **1969** L. GROW tr. *Davidoff & Lambert's Connoisseur's Bk. Cigar* 71 Henry Clay (now planted in the Canary Islands) has changed its name; its owners have struck the new name of Don Miguel.

Henry-sophister: see HARRY-SOPH.

hen's-bill: see HEN *sb.* 8.

hens(e), henns, obs. forms of HENCE.

hen's-foot. Also 6 henfoote, 7 hens-feet. [From the supposed resemblance of the divided leaves to a hen's claws.] Name given to two different plants: †**a.** [tr. L. *pes gallinaceus* (Pliny).] The Climbing Fumitory, *Corydalis claviculata*. *Obs.*

1578 LYTE *Dodoens* I. xv. 24 Called.. Hedge Fumeterre, and Hennes foote... Henfoote or hedge Fumeterre. **1601** HOLLAND *Pliny* II. 236 The first Capnos, which in Latine is commonly called *Pedes Gallinacei*, *i.* hens feet.

b. [L. *pes pulli*.] Bur-parsley, *Caucalis daucoides*.

1597 GERARDE *Herbal* II. ccccxliii. (1633) 1023 In English bastard Parsley or Hennes foot. **1776–96** WITHERING *Brit. Plants* (ed. 3) II. 289 *Tordylium Anthriscus*... Hedge Parsley or Hens-foot... Horses are extremely fond of it.

Henslovian (hɛn'sləʊvɪən), *a. Bot.* [f. *Henslow*, an English botanist (1796–1861).] In ***Henslovian membrane***, the cuticle of plants, discovered by Henslow (*Treas. Bot.* 1866).

hensman, obs. form of HENCHMAN.

†**hensour.** *Sc. Obs.* Also 6 hensure. [Origin unknown: see conjectures in Jamieson. The form of the word suggests OFr. derivation.]

'Perhaps a giddy young fellow' (Jam.); perh. = henchman.

(The sense was app. obscure to Henry Charters in 1602.)

15.. *Christs K. on Gr.* x, Ane haisty hensure callit Hary Quha wes ane archer heynd. **1535** LYNDESAY *Satyre of Thrie Estaitis* (Bann. MS.) 2651 Thir juglars, jestouris and ydill hensouris Thir carriouris and thir quynte sensouris [E.E.T.S. 2605 *from ed.* 1602, Thir Iugglars, Iestars, and idill cuitchours, Thir carriers, and thir quintacensours].

†**hent**, *v.* *Obs.* exc. *arch.* or *dial.* Forms: 1 hentan, 3–6 **hente(n**, 4–9 **hent**; 4–5 **hint**, 5 **hynt(e**. *Pa. t.* 3–6 **hente**, 4–9 **hent**; 4–6 **hint, hynt**. *Pa. pple.* 3–4 **yhent**, 3–7 **hent**, 4–5 **hente**, 5 **ihent**; 4–6 **hint**, 5 **hynt, hyntyd**, 6 *Sc.* **hyntit**. [OE. *hentan* (also *ȝehentan*), of obscure formation.

It is probably related to Gothic *hinþan* to seize. Its resemblance, both in form and sense to HEND *v.* is also noteworthy. But in both cases the phonological relations are difficult.]

1. *trans.* To lay hold of, seize, grasp; to take or hold in one's hand; to catch. *arch.*

(In OE. *intrans.* with *genitive* or *prep.*)

a **1000** *Laws Edward & Guthrum* vi. §6 (Schmid) Beo he þonne utlah, and his hente mid hearme ælc þara þe riht wille. *c* **1200** *Trin. Coll. Hom.* 209 Ðe sinfulle haueð leid grune me to henten. **1297** R. GLOUC. (1724) 185 Ȝyf he nadde wyþ þe selde somdel þe dunt yhent Syker he hym adde aslawe. *a* **1300** *Cursor M.* 3841 Abute hir hals þan he hir hent [*v.r.* hint]. *Ibid.* 21624 A wessel.. Sett vnder þat licure to hint. *c* **1330** R. BRUNNE *Chron.* (1810) 41 Alle about þei robbed, & tok þat þei mot hent. **14..** HOCCLEVE *Min. Poems* (1892) 71 þat in the feendes net we be nat hent. *c* **1450** *Merlin* 101 He hente the swerde be the hiltes and drough it oute. **1530** PALSGR. 583/1, I hente, I take by vyolence or to catche, *je happe*. This terme is nat utterly comen. **1536** BELLENDEN *Cron. Scot.* II. 355 Scho hint his hors be the renyeis. **1579** SPENSER *Sheph. Cal.* Feb. 195 His harmefull Hatchet he hent in hand. **1611** SHAKS. *Wint. T.* IV. iii. 133 Iog-on, Iog-on, the foot-path way, And merrily hent the Stile-a. **1651** W. CARTWRIGHT *Ordinary* V. iv. in Hazl. *Dodsley* XII. 311 Hent him, for dern love hent him. [**1885** BURTON *Arab. Nts.* (1887) III. 77 Then he hent in hand two stones.]

absol. ? *a* **1500** *Chester Pl.* (E.E.T.S.) vii. 263 Hent on! and hould that thou hase! **1566** DRANT *Horace* A iii, When hande nil houlde or hente.

2. To lay hold of and take away, lift, or move in some way; to snatch, carry off; to take (*away*, *off*, *out*, *up*, etc.), put (*on*).

a **1300** *Cursor M.* 13236 þis bodi vte of erth þai hint [*v.r.* hent]. **13..** *Gaw. & Gr. Knt.* 983 þe lorde.. Hent heȝly of his hode, and on a spere henged. *c* **1400** *Rowland & O.* 1194 Ane Actone one he hent. *c* **1440** *York Myst.* xxiii. 77 Lord god!.. þat.. wolde.. hendly hente me oute of hell. **1579** SPENSER *Sheph. Cal.* Nov. 169 Dido nis dead, but into heauen hent. **1589** PEELE *Tale of Troy* Wks. (Rtldg.) 553/2 Her heart was from her body hent. **1647** H. MORE *Song of Soul* III. III. vii, For a time into high heaven hent.

b. *fig.* To lift *up*, pluck *up* (heart). (Cf. also 5.)

c **1400** *Destr. Troy* 9739 Therfore hent vp your hert & your high wille. *c* **1450** *St. Cuthbert* (Surtees) 4484 Right so þi frendes als faste Heuy hertis sall hente.

3. a. To get at with a blow; to strike, hit.

c **1250** *Gen. & Ex.* 2715 Moyses.. hente ðe cherl wið hise wond, And he fel dun in dedes bond. **13..** *Coer de L.* 6783 That other he hint upon the hood.

b. To get to, arrive at, reach, occupy.

c **1330** R. BRUNNE *Chron.* (1810) 39 Tuo outlandes kynges on þis lond hauens hent. *c* **1440** *Bone Flor.* 139 The furste hauyn that ever they hente. *c* **1475** *Partenay* 5272 When of lusignen the faire Cite hent. **1603** SHAKS. *Meas. for M.* IV. vi. 14 The generous, and grauest Citizens Haue hent the gates.

4. To seize, affect (as an influence or condition).

1390 GOWER *Conf.* I. 141 The vanite of pride him hente. *c* **1400** *Rom. Rose* 1730 Therwithalle such colde me hente. *a* **1547** SURREY in *Tottell's Misc.* (Arb.) 8 There might I se how Ver had euery blossom hent. **1613–16** W. BROWNE *Brit. Past.* II. i, Men, whose watchfull eyes no slumber hent.

5. To get, take, receive, obtain, gain, meet with; to experience, suffer, 'catch' (harm, etc.); to 'take' (courage, etc.); to apprehend, perceive.

1297 R. GLOUC. (1724) 204 Uerste he was sore adrad.. And naþeles he hente herte. *a* **1330** *Otuel* 1195 þou ne sschalt hente no vileinie, Of no man of king charles lond. *c* **1386** CHAUCER *Prol.* 301 Al þat he myghte of his freendes hente, On bookes and his lernynge he it spente. *c* **1450** *Mirour Saluacioun* 1412 Of some man.. the Baptisme of watere he hent. *c* **1460** *Towneley Myst.* (Surtees) 122 So that I no harmes hent. **1591** GREENE *Maiden's Dr.* l, Then thought I straight such friends are seldom hent.

b. *to hent upon* (or *in*) *hand*: to take in hand, undertake. *to hent one's way*: to take one's way.

c **1400** *Destr. Troy* 7969 To hent vppon hand soche a hegh charge. **1486** *Bk. St. Albans* E vij b, Ayen the water his way eeuen iff he hent. **1590** SPENSER *F.Q.* III. vii. 61 Great labour fondly hast thou hent in hand.

6. *intr.* To take one's way, go. *pseudo-archaism.*

1579 *Poor Knt.'s Pal.* G iv, To seas he hent, whose washinge waves did cause him to returne. **1714** *Orig. Canto Spencer* xlvi, Strait without Word or Answer forth he hent.

7. *dial.* (See quots.) [perh. not this word.]

1677 [see HENTING 2]. *a* **1722** LISLE *Husb.* (1757) Gloss. (E.D.S.), *Hint*, to lay up; to put together. **1794** T. DAVIS *Agric. Wilts* in *Archæol. Rev.* (1888) Mar., A barn process, well hinted—well secured. **1828** *Craven Dial.*, *Hent*, to plow up the bottom of the furrow.

†**hent**, *sb.* *Obs.* Also 6 hint. [f. HENT *v.*]

1. The act of seizing; a clutch, grasp.

1500–20 DUNBAR *Poems* xxxiii. 88 Scho was so cleverous of hir cluik.. Scho held thame at ane hint.

2. *fig.* That which is grasped or conceived in the mind: conception, intention, design.

1600 HOLLAND *Livy* XXV. xiv. 557 So [they] put the Consull out of his hent [*consilia ducis disjecit*].

¶It is doubtful whether in the following we have sense 1 or 2, or whether *hent* is for *hint* in its Shaksperian sense.

1602 SHAKS. *Ham.* III. iii. 88 Vp Sword, and know thou a more horrid hent When he is drunke asleepe: or in his Rage.

†**hent**, *prep.* and *conj. adv.* *Obs.* [? f. HEN *adv.* hence + TO, corresp. to OFris. *hent*, MHG. *hinze*, *hinz*, LG. *hento*, *hente*.] Till, until.

A. *prep.* (also *hent to*, *hento.*)

1426 AUDELAY *Poems* 14 He kepis not to restore That he takys amys to no maner mon, Hent his endyng. *Ibid.* 74 Thenke theron and thenke not erke, Hent to the last endyng. **1573** *Durham Depos.* (Surtees) 252 The brother did put him of warke hento suche tyme as he brought answear from that wyfe.

B. *conj. adv.*

14.. *Cast. Love* (Hal.) 1479 [Thei] nere never i-wyst ne holden Hent [*early MS.* er] he himselvyn come wolde. **1426** AUDELAY *Poems* 15 We were put in paradise to have wele withoutyn woo, Hent we had unblest brokyn the commaundmentis of our kyng.

hent, obs. form of HINT.

Hentenian (hɛn'tiːnɪən), *a.* [f. the name of John *Henten* or *Hentenius* (1499–1566), a theologian of the Dominican order at Louvain: see -IAN.]

Of or pertaining to Henten, or to the editions of the Vulgate (Louvain 1547, often reprinted) prepared by him.

1902 H. J. WHITE in J. Hastings *Dict. Bible* IV. 880/2 The various Hentenian editions remained for some years as the standard text of the Roman Church, but were still private publications. **1930** S. ANGUS in *Intern. Stand. Bible Encycl.* V. 3061/2 Hentenian critical ed. (Louvain, 1547).

†**henter.** *Obs.* [f. HENT *v.* + -ER[1].] One who seizes, a grasper.

c **1374** CHAUCER *Boeth.* I. pr. iii. 7 (Camb. MS.) Rauyneres and henteres of fowleste thinges.

henting, *vbl. sb.* [f. as prec. + -ING[1].]

1. The action of the verb HENT; laying hold, seizing; grasp, apprehension.

c **1440** *Promp. Parv.* 58/1 Cahchynge, or hentynge.., *apprehencio*. **1471** RIPLEY *Comp. Alch.* IX. iv. in Ashm. (1652) 174 These of our Secretts have som hentyng. **1508** DUNBAR *Flyting w. Kennedie* 8 Hell sould nocht hyd thair harnis fra harmis hynting.

2. *Agric.* (See quot.) [perh. a different word.]

1677 PLOT *Oxfordsh.* 246 They have also a way of sowing in the Chiltern Country, which is called sowing Hentings, which is done before the Plough, the Corn being cast in a straight line just where the plough must come, and is presently ploughed in. **1733** TULL *Horse-Hoeing Husb.* (ed. 2) xi. 116 They call the Top of a Ridge, a Veering; they call the two Furrows that are turn'd from each other at the Bottom, between two Ridges, a Henting, i.e. an Ending.

hentriacontane (ˌhɛntraɪə'kɒnteɪn). *Chem.* [f. Gr. ἑν-, εἷς one + τριάκοντα thirty + -ANE.]

A hydrocarbon of the paraffin series, $C_{31}H_{64}$, *esp.* the solid unbranched hydrocarbon $CH_3{\cdot}(CH_2)_{29}{\cdot}CH_3$ present in petroleum and many natural waxes.

1887 *Jrnl. Chem. Soc.* LII. I. 124 The most soluble portion of the extract melting.. at 67°, is probably identical with normal hentriacontane, $C_{31}H_{64}$. **1950** J. BONNER *Plant Biochem.* xxiv. 366 Commercial candelilla wax (*Euphorbia* sp.) contains.. 50–60% of a paraffin, *n*-hentriacontane.

henus, obs. form of HENCE.

henware ('hɛnwɛə(r)). *Sc.* Also **hens-ware.** [app. f. HEN *sb.* + WARE *sb.*] The edible seaweed *Alaria esculenta*, also called *badderlocks*.

1808–18 JAMIESON, *Hens-ware, Henware.* **1865** GOSSE *Land & Sea* (1874) 63 The henware.. a large plant, much resembling the oar-weed, but of paler colour.

'**henwife.** Chiefly *Sc.*

1. A woman who has charge of fowls; sometimes applied contemptuously to a man.

a **1500** *Colkelbie Sow* 844 He.. chairgeit sone his hen-wyfe to do hir cure And mak thame fruct; than to set them [eggs] scho fure. **1500–20** DUNBAR *Poems* v. 24 Scho.. wes our Ladyis hen wif: And held Sanct Petir at stryfe, Ay quhill scho wes in hevin. **1816** SCOTT *Old Mort.* ii, A half-witted lad.. who had a kind of charge of the poultry under the old henwife. **1831** JANE PORTER *Sir E. Seaward's Narr.* II. 138 A single 'henwife'.. being found quite enough for the business. **1897** *Pall Mall Mag.* 108, I am the hen-wife here.

†**2.** *Venus' hen-wife*, a bawd. *Obs.*

1513 DOUGLAS *Æneis* IV. Prol. 188 With Venus henvifis quhat wyse may I flite?

†'**henwile.** *Sc. Obs.* [app. f. HEN *sb.* + WILE.] A petty or contemptible wile or stratagem.

a **1662** R. BAILLIE *Lett.* (1775) II. 80 (Jam.) Their old unhappy and unprofitable way of hen-wiles. **1697** CLELAND *Poems* 55 (Jam.) Seeks out raw shifts, and poor hen wiles. **1728** P. WALKER *Life Peden* Pref. (ed. 3) 23 Jurants sitting at the Head.. as if they were to communicate, using that Hen-wyle to get the Tables full.

henwoodite ('hɛnwʊdaɪt). *Min.* [f. the name of W. J. *Henwood*, of Penzance (1805–1875); see -ITE.] A hydrous phosphate of aluminium and copper, of bright blue colour, found in Cornwall.

1878 in *Ure's Dict. Arts* IV. (Supp.). **1887** DANA *Man. Min.* 220.

henys, obs. form of HENCE.

†**heo**, *dial.* **hoo**, *pers. pron., 3rd sing. fem., nom. Obs.* exc. *dial.* Forms: see below. [OE. *hiu*, *hío*, *héo*, fem. of HE; = OFris. *hiu*. In Goth., OS., and OHG., the fem. of the parallel pronominal stem *i-s*, *i-r*, was lost and supplied by a form *sî*, *siu*, Ger. *sie*. A like substitution took place later in Fris. and Eng.; in the latter, the northern and e. midl. dialects about the 12th c. exchanged *hio*, *heo*, *hyo*, *ȝho*, *ȝhe* for the forms, northern *sco*, *scho*, *sho*, e. midl. *scæ*, *sȝe*, *sche*, SHE. But *heo* in various forms survived in the south and w. midl. as a literary word till the 15th c., and is still vernacular from Lancashire to Devon and Sussex, under the forms *hoo*, *hŭh* (the latter often mistaken for the objective *her*), *ŭh*, *ŭ*.]

The original feminine pronoun corresponding to *he*; the place of which is now taken by SHE. Used of women, and of animals or things grammatically feminine.

α. 1 **híu, híuu, hío, héo**, 2 **hio**, 2–5 **heo**, 2 **hyo**; 2–3 **ȝho**, 3 **ȝeo, ȝo, ȝoe.**

855 *O.E. Chron.* (Parker MS.) an. 718 Hio wæs forgifen Norþan hymbra cyninge. *c* **910** *Ibid.* an. 910 Heo ȝeherȝade swiðe micel on þæm norð here. *c* **950** *Lindisf. Gosp.* Matt. xv. 27 Soð hiu cweð [*c* **975** *Rushw. G.*, & hiu cweþ; *c* **1000** *Ags. G.*, ða cwæð heo; *c* **1160** *Hatton G.*, ða cwæð hyo]. *c* **950** —— Mark x. 6 Hee and hiuu. *c* **975** *Rushw. Gosp.* Matt. ix. 24 Hio slepeþ [*Ags. G.*, heo slæpð; *Hatton G.*, hyo slæpð]. *c* **1175** *Lamb. Hom.* 111 Heo hi wernað wið drunkenesse. *c* **1205** LAY. 182 He wes king and heo quen. *c* **1300** *Beket* 24 The Princes heir heo was. *c* **1330** *King of Tars* 76 To god heo made hire preyers. **1362** LANGL. *P. Pl.* A. II. 5 'Loke on þe lufthond', quod heo. *c* **1450** MYRC 396 That heo a-vow no maner þynge.

c **1200** ORMIN 2037 þe laffdiȝ Marȝe ȝho barr child Wiþþutenn weddedd macche. *c* **1275** LAY. 1149 Ȝeo was cwene [*c* **1205** heo wes quen] of alle wodes. **1297** R. GLOUC. (1724) 436 Ȝoe was worþy to be ycluped, Mold þe god quene Vor al þe godenesse, þat ȝoe dude her to Engelond. *a* **1300** *Fall & Passion* 81 in *E.E.P.* (1862) 15 Al hir ioi was ago, þo ȝo him sei dei in rode.. þat del, neuer such nas þer none.. as ȝho makid an seint Jon.

β. 1 **híæ**, 1 **híe**, 2–3 **hie**, 3–4 **ȝhe, ȝe, hye.**

c **975** *Rushw. Gosp.* Matt. xv. 23 Forlet hiæ forþon þe hiæ cæȝeþ æfter us. *a* **1000** *Cædmon's Gen.* 822 þa spræc Eue eft, idesa scienost, wifa wliteȝost, hie wæs ȝeweorc godes. *c* **1200** *Trin. Coll. Hom.* 161 Hie is þe heuenliches kinges dohter. *c* **1250** *Gen. & Ex.* 2626 Ȝhe kepte it wel in fostre wune, Ȝhe knew it for hire owen sune. *c* **1250** *Old Kent Serm.* in *O.E. Misc.* 29 Hye spac to þo serganz þet seruede of þo wyne. *a* **1275** *Prov. Ælfred* 292 *Ibid.* 121 Swo hie ne þochte. *a* **1300** *Fall & Passion* 82 in *E.E.P.* (1862) 15 For to wep ȝe nad no mo bot iiii bitter teris of blode. *c* **1325** *Lai le Freine* 114 That hye nil, no hye ne schal. *c* **1330** *Florice & Bl.* (1857) 572 Ȝhe said anon right Ȝhe had i-waked al this night.

γ. 1 **hi**, 2–4 **hi**, 4–5 **hy.**

a **1000** *Crist* 559 in *Exeter Bk.*, Hafað nu se halȝa helle bireafod ealles þæs gafoles þe hi ȝear-daȝum.. unryhte swealȝ. *a* **1175** *Cott. Hom.* 223 Hi is ælra libbinde moder. *Ibid.* 227 Hi.. warð mid cylde. *a* **1250** *Owl & Night.* 32 Me hi halt loþlich and fule. **1340** *Ayenb.* 26 þeruore is hy doȝter of prede. *Ibid.* 28 Hi ys contrarious to þe holy goste. *c* **1460** *Launfal* 352 Sche badd hym aryse anoon; Hy seyde to hym, Syr gantyl knyght.

δ. 2–5 **he**, 4 **hey**, 5 **hee.**

c **1175** *Lamb. Hom.* 103 þa oðer sunne [is] forliger..þet is ihaten fornicatio. He buleð þene mon. *c* **1200** *Trin. Coll. Hom.* 159 Lusteð nu wich maiden..and hwat he hatte, and hware he was fet. *a* **1300** *St. Michael* 203 in *Treat. Science*, etc. (1841) 136 The sonne..sent a-doun hire hete..and of fersch water he draweth up the breth. *c* **1380** WYCLIF *Sel. Wks.* III. 413 Crist askid þo womman watir to drinke, and ȝitte he was an alien, for he was a Samaritan. *a* **1400** *Pol. Rel. & L. Poems* 229 Hey endetz shameliche Hey draweþ dredfulliche. *c* **1420** *Chron. Vilod.* 1119 And thongede hurr' heyȝelyche..þat hee had delyveryd hym. *a* **1450** *Le Morte Arth.* 584 Ther-for he dude on a Russet cote..And made heore self þo a Nonne.

ε. 3–4 **ha, a.**

c **1205** LAY. 28219 þa wile a [the queen] beoð aliue. *a* **1225** *Leg. Kath.* 136 þus hwil ha [*v.r.* a] wiste hire. **1387** TREVISA *MS. Cott. Vesp.* D. vii. 29 b, He..prayede hys wyf þat hue wolde helpe..bote a dude þe contrary.

ζ. 2–5 **ho**, 3–5 **hoe.**

c **1175** *Lamb Hom.* 77 þe sunne streonþ þe lome þet ho spret in to al þis wide worlde. *c* **1205** LAY. 42 He hoe [boc] ȝef þare æðelen Ælienor. **1297** R. GLOUC. (1724) 13 Ho wende from al hire kyn. **13..** *Gaw. & Gr. Knt.* 1001 þe olde auncian wyf heȝest ho syttez. *c* **1420** *Sir Amadace* (Camden) lxvi, Ho kissutte hur lord. *c* **1420** *Chron. Vilod.* 376 In yche werk þ^t^ hoe wrouȝt.

η. 4–5 **hue.**

1307 *Elegy Edw. I*, iv, Ich biquethe myn herte aryht.. Over the see that hue be diht. **1340–70** *Alex. & Dind.* 562 While hue liuede alse. **1393** LANGL. *P. Pl.* C. II. 10 Ich was aferd of hure face, thauh hue faire were.

θ. 5–9 **hoo.**

a **1440** *Sir Degrev.* 686 Natheles hoo was wel paid. **1674** RAY *N.C. Words* 26 *Hoo, he*, in the Northwest parts of England most frequently used for she. *c* **1815** *Lancash. Ballads & Songs* 169 Hoo says hoo can tell when hoo's hurt. **1867** E. WAUGH *Owd Blanket* 72 Th' mistress said hoo thought hoo'd suit 'em.

b. Opposed to *he*: female, feminine.

c **950–1000**: see HE 7. **13..** *E.E. Allit. P.* B. 337 Ay þou meng with þe malez þe mete ho-bestez.

he-oak: see HE *pron.* 8 b.

heold, obs. pa. t. of HOLD *v.*

heole, variant of HELE *v.*¹ *Obs.*

heom, var. HEM *pron.*, *Obs.* (= them); obs. f. HOME.

heonene, heonne(n, heonnes, obs. ff. HEN *adv.*, HENCE.

heore, obs. forms of HER *pron.*

heortology (hiːɔːˈtɒlədʒɪ). [ad. G. *heortologie*, F. *héortologie*, f. Gr. ἑορτή feast: see -OLOGY.] The science or study of the origin, meaning, growth, and history of the religious feasts and seasons of the Christian year. Hence **heortoˈlogical** *a.*, of or pertaining to heortology; **heorˈtologist**, one who studies heortology.

1900 *Expositor* Nov. 348 We are to regard the statement of the calendars as the conjecture of a heortologist. **1901** J. R. HARRIS in *Soc. Hist. Theology* 31 Oct. 5 The Study of Christian Heortology... The problems that belong to the region of Christian Heortology. **1913** J. R. MCKEE (*title*) The Church's year, a handbook of heortology. **1918** E. BISHOP *Liturg. Hist.* 258 Recalling too how the recent heortologist Dr. Kellner considers that the mention of the feast in the Irish calendars does not prove the celebration of the feast.

heou, heow, obs. ff. HUE.

heoven, obs. inf. and pa. t. of HEAVE; obs. f. HEAVEN.

hep (hɛp), *a. slang* (orig. *U.S.*). [Of unknown origin.] Well-informed, knowledgeable, 'wise *to*', up-to-date; smart, stylish. Hence as *sb.*, the state of being 'hep'. Also as *vb.*, to pep *up*; **hepped** *ppl. a.* (often with *up*); ***to be hepped on***, to be enthusiastic about, 'bitten with'. Cf. HEP-CAT, HIP *a.*

1908 *Sat. Even. Post* 5 Dec. 17/1 What puzzles me is how you can find anybody left in the world who isn't hep. **1914** JACKSON & HELLYER *Vocab. Criminal Slang* 43 *Hep*,... Sapiency; understanding... Derived from the name of a fabulous detective who operated in Cincinnati. **1918** WODEHOUSE *Piccadilly Jim* xi. 118 'You see in me a confidant. I am hep.' 'You know—' 'Everything.' **1923** —— *Adv. Sally* xiii. 148 He was aware that women were seldom hep to the really important things in life. **1927** P. MARKS *Lord of Himself* 47 You're pleased because the top-notchers wanted me, but that doesn't make you think I'm a top-notcher. I'm just getting hep. There you have it. **1938** 'J. SPENSER' *Crime against Society* xxiv. 235 The coppers are hep and we've got to stage a cover-up. **1941** *Amer. Speech* XVI. 154/1 'Tis said that back in the 1890's Joe Hep ran a saloon in Chicago... Although he never quite understood what was going on, he thought he did... Hence his name entered the argot as an ironic appellation for anyone who thought he knew but didn't. The ironic sense has now largely disappeared..in..to get hep to. **1951** M. MCLUHAN *Mech. Bride* 68/2 His failure to be hep to success doctrines. **1956** D. KARP *All Honorable Men* 107 You know how hepped on the matter of wasting time the whole Board is. **1957** C. MACINNES *City of Spades* I. iii. 19 Where can I get a shirt like that?..It's hep. Jumble style, but hep. **1958** N. D. HINTON in *Publ. Amer. Dial. Soc.* xxx. 40 In the swing period 'hep' was widely used by musicians to mean 'in the know', 'possessed of good taste', or to indicate simple understanding... The boppers quickly changed the word to 'hip'. Use of 'hep' was then regarded as a sign that the speaker was not the right sort. **1958** *Punch* 27 Aug. 270/1 And when I stood up and he began to get hep I noticed that his shoes were cunningly low cut. **1959** 'M. M. KAYE' *House of Shade* xviii. 246 Are you, in the distressing jargon of the age, 'hep'? **1959** *Guardian* 16 Oct. 10/6 Columns of drug-hepped, ragged men. **1959** *News Chron.* 14 July 4/4 A slightly hepped-up version of the old deck chair and concert party formula. *Ibid.* 21 July 1/6 The pills were being taken ..to give the addicts a form of 'hep'. **1959** T. GRIFFITH *Waist-high Culture* (1960) 238 A California chemist who is hep to every current allusion and is an asset to any party. **1960** *News Chron.* 6 July 3/1 Even some of the classics.. have been hepped up to circus style. **1960** *Guardian* 12 Aug. 8/3 Not even its bitterest critics could accuse the Labour party of being 'hep'. **1962** *Listener* 6 Sept. 350/2 'I wasn't hepped on becoming a painter,' he [*sc.* Henry Miller] said. **1970** *Cape Times* 28 Oct. 1/8 Are you hep to what the Beatles are saying? **1972** J. L. DILLARD *Black English* iii. 119 It is, of course, a commonplace of the jazz language that *hep* is a white man's distortion of the more characteristically Negro *hip*.

hep (hɛp), *int.* [Said to be f. the initials of *H*ierosolyma *E*st *P*erdita; or, the cry of a goatherd.] Usu. ***hep, hep!*** The cry of those who persecuted Jews in the 19th century. Also *attrib.*

1839 *Penny Cycl.* XIII. 122/1 They [*sc.* the Jews] were massacred at the cry of 'Hep', 'Hep', the initials of the words 'Hierosolyma est perdita'. **1879** GEO. ELIOT *Impressions of Theophrastus Such* xviii. 313 (*heading*) The Modern Hep! Hep! Hep! **1930** D. PHILIPSON *Reform Movement in Judaism* (rev. ed.) i. 25 The *hep hep* cry resounded in the streets of.. Frankfort and Würzburg. *Ibid.* vi. 108 A violent anti-Jewish literary campaign ensued..which culminated in the.. disgraceful hep-hep outbreaks of the year 1819. **1971** *Encycl. Judaica* VII. 1227/1 Hamburg Jews were molested during the Hep! Hep! riots of 1819.

hep, variant form of HIP *sb.*², the fruit of the rose-tree.

hep, obs. form of HEAP, HIP *sb.*¹

‖**hepar** (ˈhiːpɑː(r)). *Chem.* and *Med.* [med.L., a. Gr. ἧπαρ liver, in reference to its colour.]

1. An old name for a metallic sulphide, having a reddish-brown or liver colour. Also, for compounds of sulphur with other substances. (Cf. HEPATULE.)

1796 KIRWAN *Elem. Min.* (ed. 2) II. 321 Molybdenous Acid..takes Sulphur from its Hepars. **1799** —— *Geol. Ess.* 397 Glauber is found..frequently in the state of a hepar. **1800** HENRY *Epit. Chem.* (1808) 149 [Sulphurets] have, for the most part, a reddish brown or liver colour; and hence were formerly called *hepars*, or *livers* of sulphur.

2. Also more fully, ***hepar sulphuris*** or ***hepar sulphur***: **a.** (*H. s. kalinum*) Old name for *potassa sulphurata*. **b.** (*H. s. calcareum*) The name commonly given in homœopathy to calcium sulphide.

a. 1693 SALMON *Bates' Disp.* (1715) 436/1 Le Febure makes this Hepar Sulphuris thus: ℞ Of the best Sulphur in fine Pouder ℥iv. Salt of Tartar very dry, as much: Mix them together..till all be reduced to a Mass, which is called the Liver of Sulphur. **1742** *Phil. Trans.* XLII. 73 That sort of *Hepar*, formed by the Union of the Caustic Salt with the Sulphur of the Ashes of the Glass-wort. **1873** *Fownes' Chem.* (ed. 11) 327 Liver of sulphur, or hepar sulphuris, is a name given to a brownish substance, made by fusing together.. potassium carbonate and sulphur.

b. 1866 *Allshorn's Handy-bk. Homœop. Pract.* 22 Hepar Sulphuris, Sulphuret of Lime, Proto-Sulphuret of Calcium, or Liver of Sulphur, is prepared by trituration. **1885** *Pall Mall G.* 26 Feb. 6/2 Patti, I am told, puts a great deal of dependence upon hepar-sulphur. **1887** *Homœop. World* 11 Nov. 503 If the patient has been already dosed with Mercury, Hepar is the remedy.

heparin (ˈhɛpərɪn). *Biochem.* [f. HEPAR + -IN¹.] A sulphated polysaccharide present in various body tissues and organs, esp. the liver, lungs, and muscles, and used therapeutically as an anti-coagulant.

1918 HOWELL & HOLT in *Amer. Jrnl. Physiol.* XLVII. 328 A phosphatid, not previously described, which exists in various tissues but is found in greatest abundance in the liver. This phosphatid is designated as *heparin* to indicate its origin from liver... This substance was [previously] described under the name of antiprothrombin. **1933** *Jrnl. Biol. Chem.* CII. 435 Dog liver contains approximately twice as much heparin as does beef liver. **1946** *Nature* 24 Aug. 270/1 Even drastic blood changes brought about by the injection of dicoumarol or heparin had only a slight effect on the rate of growth of the bugs. **1968** A. WHITE et al. *Princ. Biochem.* (ed. 4) xxxi. 732 Many tissues of the body contain heparin since it specifically originates in the metachromatic granules of mast cells.

Hence ˌ**heparini'zation**, the process of heparinizing; ˈ**heparinize** *v. trans.*, to treat with heparin and thus reduce the clotting power of the blood; ˈ**heparinized** *ppl. a.*

1940 J. E. R. MCDONAGH *Universe through Med.* 24 Snake venom has the same action in this condition as has calcium in making heparinised blood coagulate. **1943** *Science* 2 July 20/1 In all experiments in which heparinized whole blood or plasma was administered the lipemia was abolished. **1956** *New Eng. Jrnl. Med.* 29 Nov. 1027/2 General heparinization carries with it the risk of serious hemorrhage from bleeding lesions elsewhere in the body as well as at the operative site. **1959** *Lancet* 11 July 25/1 The risk of heparinising a patient who is receiving a coumarin drug. **1961** *Ibid.* 14 Oct. 858/1 The principle of regional heparinisation is to supply anticoagulated blood to the artificial kidney, whilst not interfering with the normal coagulation of blood in the patient.

hepat-, before a vowel = HEPATO-, comb. form of Gr. ἧπαρ, ἡπατ- liver: as in **hepaˈtalgia**, pain affecting the liver, neuralgia of the liver (Hooper *Med. Dict.* 1811); hence **hepaˈtalgic** *a.*, of or belonging to hepatalgia (Mayne *Expos. Lex.* 1854). **hepaˈtectomy**, excision of (a part of) the liver; also **hepaˈtectomized** *ppl. a.* **hepatemˈphraxis** [Gr. ἔμφραξις stoppage], obstruction of the liver (Craig 1847); hence **hepatemˈphractic** *a.* (Mayne 1854). **hepaˈtoma**, a tumour of the liver (see quot. 1934).

1900 DORLAND *Med. Dict.* 296/2 Hepatectomy. **1910** *Practitioner* Mar. 383 Hepatectomy under these conditions does not appear to add to the gravity of the prognosis. **1946** *Nature* 31 Aug. 310/2 The so-called xanthorubin, a yellow compound present in the serum of hepatectomized dogs. **1905** H. D. ROLLESTON *Dis. Liver* 457 The term 'hepatoma' was suggested by Sabourin to describe the transitional stage between adenoma and carcinoma. **1912** *Ibid.* (ed. 2) 474 This condition [*sc.* primary carcinoma developing in a cirrhotic liver] was described..as Hepatoma by Rénon, Géraudel, and Monier-Vinard who insist that it is not a carcinoma. 'Hepatoma', also employed by Sabourin..is a confusing title. **1934** *Brit. Jrnl. Surg.* XXI. 684 The next advance of note was made by Yamagiura in 1911. He.. made two simple divisions: (1) Hepatoma, i.e., carcinoma of hepatic cells; and (2) Cholangioma, i.e., carcinoma of bile-ducts. The term 'hepatoma' had previously been used by Sabourin in reference to a condition of nodular hyperplasia which in his opinion was a transitional stage between adenoma and carcinoma. Most modern writers, however, accept Yamagiura's interpretation, and use it as a term for primary carcinoma of the liver cells. **1971** *New Scientist* 17 June 668/3 From one strain of a mouse hepatoma they have a factor which they describe as being 'a heat stable molecule of low molecular weight'.

†**hepaˈtarian**, *a. Obs. rare.*⁻⁰ [f. L. *hēpatāri-us*, f. *hepat-*: see prec. and -AN.] Of or pertaining to the liver, hepatical (Blount *Glossogr.* 1656).

hepatic (hɪˈpætɪk), *a.* and *sb.* Also 4–8 **ep-**. [ad. L. *hēpatic-us*, a. Gr. ἡπατικός of or belonging to the liver.]

A. *adj.* **1.** Of or pertaining to the liver.

e.g. ***hepatic artery, ducts, plexus, vein; hepatic apoplexy, colic, disorder, disease, flux.***

1599 A. M. tr. *Gabelhouer's Bk. Physicke* 178/1 Phlebotomise..in his right Arme, the Hepaticke or Livervayn. **1621** BURTON *Anat. Mel.* I. i. III. iv, Melancholy, which Laurentius subdivides into three parts..Hepatick, Splenatick, Meseriack. **1719** QUINCY *Phys. Dict.*, *Hepatick Flux*, is a bilious Looseness, occasioned by overflowing of Choler. **1742** EAMES in *Phil. Trans.* XLII. 32 A Discharge of Bile..'tis but thin and diluted, and such as in other Animals is usually called Hepatic Bile. **1773** *Gentl. Mag.* XLIII. 604 His lordship's bilious and hepatic complaints. **1806** *Med. Jrnl.* XV. 577 The hepatic artery being very small, comparatively with the size of the liver. **1827** ABERNETHY *Surg. Wks.* I. 60 Hepatic disorder may disturb the sensorium. **1831** R. KNOX *Cloquet's Anat.* 479 The original filaments..follow the pyloric artery, to cast themselves into the hepatic plexus. **1866** HUXLEY *Phys.* v. (1872) 118 The hepatic duct, which conveys away the bile brought to it..from the liver. **1877** *Encycl. Brit.* VI. 140 *Hepatic colic*..where a biliary calculus or gall stone passes down from the gall bladder into the intestine.

†**2.** Affected with liver complaint. *Obs.*

1398 TREVISA *Barth. De P.R.* XVII. viii. (Tollem. MS.), Licoure þat it is sodde inne helpeþ and socoureþ frenetik men, and epatik.

3. Acting on the liver, good for the liver.

1671 SALMON *Syn. Med.* III. xxii, Mountain-mint..is Pectoral and Hepatick. **1819** REES *Cycl.* s.v. *Tabella*, We have cordial, stomachic..and hepatic tablets.

4. Liver-coloured, dark brownish-red; as in ***hepatic aloes, tanager.***

hepatic cinnabar, cinnabar mixed with idriolite, carbon, and earthy matter. ***hepatic pyrites***, decomposed liverbrown tessular crystals of iron pyrites (Bristow *Gloss. Min.*).

c **1420** *Pallad. on Husb.* XI. 361 With aloes tweyne vncis epatike. **1589** COGAN *Haven Health* (1636) 92 Take..of Aloes Epaticke, of white Sugar-Candie, of each the weight of two pence. **1796** KIRWAN *Elem. Min.* (ed. 2) II. 388 Compact Brown Iron Stone or Hepatic Iron Ore. **1811** A. T. THOMSON *Lond. Disp.* (1818) 21 The Cape aloes have a.. more disagreeable odour than the Socotrine and Hepatic.

5. Of or pertaining to a hepar; sulphurous. † ***hepatic air*** or ***gas***, sulphuretted hydrogen.

1651 BIGGS *New Disp.* ¶ 165 This balsamick hepatick salt. **1786** *Phil. Trans.* LXXVI. 118 Hepatic Air is that species of permanently elastic fluid which is obtained from combinations of sulphur with various substances, as alkalies, earths, metals, etc. **1788** *Ibid.* LXXVIII. 384 If nitrous air be mixed with hepatic air volatile alkali will be formed. **1789** *Ibid.* LXXX. 67 Upon applying heat to the sulphur thus blackened, I have perceived an hepatic smell. **1794** G. ADAMS *Nat. & Exp. Philos.* I. xii. 500 Inflammable air possesses the property of dissolving sulphur, in which case it contracts a very fetid smell, and forms hepatic air. *Ibid.* 497 Hepatic gas. **1800** tr. *Lagrange's Chem.* II. 365 [It] exhales a hepatic odour capable of altering the splendor of silver.

†**6.** ***hepatic moss***, a liverwort: see HEPATICA 2.

1824 GREVILLE *Flora Edin.* Introd. 15 Hepaticæ, Liverworts, Hepatic Mosses. Most of the plants of this order have a considerable affinity with the true mosses.

B. *sb.* **1.** A medicine that acts on the liver and increases the secretion of bile.

1486 *Bk. St. Albans* C v b, Yeue hir epatike with the flesh of a chycon. **1671** SALMON *Syn. Med.* III. xv. 358 You must use cooling Hepaticks. **1707** FLOYER *Physic. Pulse-Watch.* 419 The Bitters are Hepatics. **1886** in *Syd. Soc. Lex.* **1908** *Chambers's Jrnl.* Sept. 671/2 An East Indian Aloes used to.. be quoted in trade papers under the distinction of 'Hepatic'.

2. *Bot.* Usu. in *pl.* = HEPATICA.

1939 *Nature* 2 Sept. 416/2 The three smallest plants which have left recognizable fragments are a fungus and two liverworts or, as they are often called, hepatics, a group allied to the mosses but of simpler construction. **1964** V. J. Chapman *Coastal Veget.* vi. 152 It is here also that some hepatics..can be found.

‖**hepatica** (hɪˈpætɪkə). *Bot.* [med.L., fem. (quasi *herba hēpatica*) of *hēpatic-us*: see prec.]

1. A subgenus or section of the genus *Anemone*; esp. the common spring-flowering *Anemone* (*Hepatica*) *triloba*, a native of continental Europe, cultivated in Britain, the three-lobed leaves of which were fancied to resemble the liver.

1578 Lyte *Dodoens* I. xl. 58 The leaues of *Hepatica* are broade, and diuided into three partes..Amongst the leaues groweth fayre azured or blew floures, euery one growing vpon a single stemme. *Ibid.* 59 [It] may be called in English *Hepatica*, Noble Agrimonie, or Three leafe Lyuerwurte. **1664** Evelyn *Kal. Hort.* (1729) 192 January..Flowers in Prime..Hepatica, Primroses, Laurus-tinus. **1803** J. Abercrombie *Ev. Man Own Gard.* 688/1 Hepaticas, single white, single blue, single red, Double red, Double Blue. **1882** *Garden* 11 Mar. 155/1 The fine single blue American Hepatica..is a stronger and more vigorous species.

2. The old name in the herbalists for Common Liverwort, *Marchantia polymorpha*, a lichen-like plant which creeps over wet rocks and damp ground, rooting from the lower surface of the leaf. Hence pl. ***Hepaticæ***, a group of Cryptogams allied to the Mosses, containing plants which have no operculum, and as a rule possess elaters; of which the Common Liverwort is an example.

The group was proposed and named by the French botanist Adanson (*Familles des Plantes*, 1763).

1548 Turner *Names of Herbes* 48 Lichen is called in englise Liuerwurte, in duch Steinliberkraut, in french Hepatique, the Poticaries cal it Hepatica. **1578** Lyte *Dodoens* III. lxx. 411 This herbe is called in Greeke λειχὴν: in Latine *Lichen*: in Shoppes *Hepatica*..in Englishe Liuerwurt and Stone Liuerwort. **1796** Withering *Brit. Plants* (ed. 3) I. 349 The Cryptogamia Class..may be divided into the following orders or assemblages:—1. Miscellaneæ; 2. Filices; 3. Musci; 4. Hepaticæ; 5. Algæ; 6. Fungi. *Ibid.* 363 Hepaticæ..Female fructifications inclosed in a veil which splits open at the top, and discharges the capsule. **1867** J. Hogg *Microsc.* II. i. 308 The little group of *Hepaticae* or Liverworts which is intermediate between Lichens and Mosses. **1880** C. R. Markham *Peruv. Bark* 273 His vast collection of mosses and hepaticæ from the valley of the Amazons.

†**heˈpatical**, *a. Obs.* [f. as HEPATIC + -AL[1].] = HEPATIC *a.* 1.

1611 Cotgr., *Hepatique*, hepaticall. **1651** Bedell in *Fuller's Abel Rediv.* 74 He dropt into an Hepaticall flux. **1732** Arbuthnot *Rules of Diet* 323 They degenerate into Hepatical Fevers. *Ibid.* 342 The hepatical Artery and the Vena Porta, carry the Blood into the Liver.

B. *sb.* = HEPATIC B.

1671 Salmon *Syn. Med.* III. xv. 357 Hepaticals are such Medicines as are dedicated to the Liver.

hepatico- (hɪˈpætɪkəʊ), combining form of HEPATIC, = HEPATO-.

For further examples see medical dicts.

1910 *Practitioner* Mar. 384 The hepatico-cystic confluence. *Ibid.* 385 Vautrin put a drain in the hepatic duct, thus making a hepaticostomy. **1933** *Med. Rec.* 18 Jan. 52/2 Hepaticocholangiogastrostomy..should be used only when other methods are impracticable.

hepatiˈcologist. A botanist who devotes his attention to the *Hepaticæ* or Liverworts.

1895 *Naturalist* 111 Work..performed by the distinguished hepaticologist, Dr. Richard Spruce.

heˈpaticous, *a.* [f. as HEPATIC + -OUS.] **a.** Of a liver colour. **b.** Lobed like the liver.

1886 *Syd. Soc. Lex.*

hepatin (ˈhɛpətɪn). *Biochem.* Also (sense 1) -ine. [f. HEPAT- + -IN[1].] †**1.** = GLYCOGEN. *Obs.*

1858 F. W. Pavy in *Guy's Hosp. Rep.* IV. 316 [In calling it glucogenic] we are giving a name..to a substance which implies a purpose to which the facts..show it does not naturally administer in the living animal... I therefore propose to call it hepatine—a term which..cannot convey an erroneous impression..and which, nevertheless, is strictly pertinent. **1860** —— in *Phil. Trans. R. Soc.* CL. 608, I have made some analyses to show..how much sugar is formed for the hepatine that disappears. **1865** W. B. Carpenter *Man. Physiol.* (ed. 4) I. iii. 108 The conversion of hepatine into sugar seems to be promoted by the presence of a 'ferment' not merely in the liver itself, but also in the blood circulating through it. *Ibid.* II. viii. 454 There is evidence that Hepatin may be formed in the Liver at the expense of Albuminous substances.

2. [a. G. *hepatin* (S. S. Zaleski 1886, in *Zeitschr. f. physiol. Chem.* X. 494)], an iron-containing protein reported to occur in liver.

1886 *Jrnl. Chem. Soc.* L. 1054 Iron..is found in all the morphological constituents of the liver tissue in organic combinations, both with albuminates and with nucleïn. In the iron-nucleïn group of compounds, one is present which gives the ordinary tests for iron in contradistinction to the others which do not; from this latter group one compound, hepatin, has been isolated. **1891** W. D. Halliburton *Text-bk. Chem. Physiol. & Path.* xxv. 551 The quantity of iron in the blood-free liver was found to vary between wide limits, but it was constantly found in organic combinations in the liver-cells, especially with nuclein; and one of the iron-nuclein compounds named hepatin was isolated. **1914** G. M. Niles *Diagn. & Treatm. Digestive Dis.* xiv. 357 Other somewhat vaunted preparations are gasterin and hepatin, which are obtained from the gastric juice of dogs through gastric fistulas.

†**hepatite**[1] (ˈhɛpətaɪt). *Obs.* Also 4 **epetite**. [ad. L. *hēpatītis*, a. Gr. ἡπατῖτις.] An early name for a precious stone (*hepatitis gemma* Pliny) said to resemble the liver in some respect.

c **1305** *Land Cokayne* 94 in *E.E.P.* (1862) 158 Chalcedun and epetite. **1601** Holland *Pliny* II. 630 Some [stones] there be which bear the names of certain members of the body; as for example, Hepatites, of the liuer. **1706** Phillips, *Hepatites*, a precious Stone of the shape of the Liver.

hepatite[2]. *Min.* [Named by Karsten, 1800 (*Hepatit*), from the older name *lapis hepaticus*.] A name applied to varieties of Barytes emitting a fetid, sulphurous, or hepatic odour when rubbed or heated; liver-stone.

1802–3 tr. *Pallas' Trav.* (1812) I. 145 They form cavities ..filled up with dun hepatite of the spath kind. **1816** R. Jameson *Syst. Min.* (ed. 2) II. 288 It is named hepatite from the disagreeable sulphureous odour it exhales when rubbed.

hepatitis (hɛpəˈtaɪtɪs). *Path.* [a. Gr. ἡπατῖτις adj., of or pertaining to the liver: see -ITIS.] Inflammation of the liver.

1727–51 Chambers *Cycl.* s.v., The hepatitis bears a near resemblance to the pleurisy. **1788** J. C. Smyth in *Med. Commun.* II. 173 Phrenitis, Pleuritis, Hepatitis, Nephritis. **1819** B. E. O'Meara *Expos. Trans. St. Helena* 28 Hepatitis, with its usual train of distressing symptoms, followed. **1879** A. Flint *Clinical Med.* III. 370 Diffuse, or parenchymatous hepatitis and yellow atrophy of the liver are considered as one affection. **1938** Yater & Ault in W. M. Yater *Fund. Internal Med.* IV. 375 The differential diagnosis of the various types of hepatitis brings into consideration the differentiation of the causes of jaundice. **1955** Gaiger & Davies *Vet. Path. & Bacteriol.* (ed. 4) xxxiii. 644 Apart from the specific forms of hepatitis met with in tuberculosis,..the two main forms of inflammation met with are suppurative hepatitis due to bacterial activity within the liver tissue and chronic interstitial hepatitis due to blood-borne toxins and other agents. **1959** *Chamber's Encycl.* VII. 23/2 Acute infective hepatitis is the newer name for a condition long known in medical practice as catarrhal jaundice. **1963** L. Schiff *Dis. Liver* (ed. 2) xii. 370/1 At least two forms of viral hepatitis are recognized: the naturally occurring type referred to as infectious hepatitis (catarrhal jaundice, infectious jaundice, etc.), and homologous serum hepatitis (transfusion jaundice, yellow fever vaccine jaundice, syringe jaundice, postarsphenamine jaundice, etc.). *Ibid.* xiv. 453 (*heading*) Toxic and drug-induced hepatitis.

hepatization (hɛpətaɪˈzeɪʃən). [f. HEPATIZE.]

†**1.** *Chem.* Impregnation with sulphuretted hydrogen. (See HEPATIC 5.) *Obs.*

1796 Kirwan *Elem. Min.* (ed. 2) II. 455 These [expedients] were Torrefaction, Sulphurization, Hepatization.

2. *Path.* Consolidation of the lung tissue, so that it becomes solid and friable somewhat like liver, being first of a red and afterwards of a grey colour. Applied also to the state of any texture which has been converted into a liver-like substance (Mayne *Expos. Lex.* 1854).

1822–34 *Good's Study Med.* (ed. 4) II. 130 In the second stage [of Pneumonia] or that of hepatisation, the crepitous feel is entirely lost. **1862** H. W. Fuller *Dis. Lungs* 249 The third [stage] that of grey hepatization, or diffused suppuration of the pulmonary tissue. **1866** A. Flint *Princ. Med.* (1880) 161 In the second stage, usually called the stage of red hepatization..The solidified lung is of a brownish-red color, non-crepitant, and presents an appearance not unlike that of the liver, whence the name hepatization.

hepatize (ˈhɛpətaɪz), *v.* [f. Gr. ἧπαρ, ἡπατ- liver + -IZE: corresp. in form to Gr. ἡπατίζ-ειν to be like the liver, to be liver-coloured.] Hence **hepatized** (ˈhɛpətaɪzd), *ppl. a.*

trans. †**a.** *Chem.* To impregnate with sulphuretted hydrogen. *Obs.* **b.** *Path.* To convert (the lungs) by engorgement and effusion into a substance resembling liver.

1786 *Phil. Trans.* LXXVI. 142 Hepatised water in a well closed vessel effects a solution of iron in a few days. **1822–34** *Good's Study Med.* (ed. 4) IV. 377 Some form of hepatised ammonia being employed. *Ibid.* II. 134 Sometimes the hepatised portions are exactly circumscribed by a lobule.

hepato-, repr. Gr. ἡπατο-, combining form of ἧπαρ liver; as in **hepatocele** (ˈhɛpətəʊsiːl) [Gr. κήλη tumour], hernia of the liver; ˌ**hepatoˈcellular** *a.*, of or pertaining to hepatic cells; **hepato-colic** (-ˈkɒlɪk) *a.* [Gr. κόλον COLON[1]], relating to the liver and the colon (*Syd. Soc. Lex.*); **hepatocystic** (-ˈsɪstɪk) *a.* [see CYST], pertaining to the liver and the gall-bladder, or uniting the two (Mayne *Expos. Lex.* 1854); **hepatoduodenal** (-ˈdiːnəl) *a.*, pertaining to the liver and the duodenum; **hepatoenteric** (ˈhɛpətəʊɛnˈtɛrɪk) *a.*, pertaining jointly to the liver and the intestine; **hepatoˈflavin** *Biochem.*, a substance first isolated from liver and later found to be the same as RIBOFLAVIN; **hepatogastric** (-ˈgæstrɪk) *a.*, pertaining to both the liver and the stomach (Craig 1847); **hepatogenic** (-ˈdʒɛnɪk), **hepatogenous** (hɛpəˈtɒdʒɪnəs) *adjs.* [see -GEN], originating from the liver; **hepaˈtography** [see -GRAPHY], the description of the liver, its attachments and functions (Dunglison); **hepato-lenticular degeneration** [tr. F. *dégénérescence hépato-lenticulaire* (H. C. Hall, 1921)], a progressive disease of the nervous system (see quot. 1955); Wilson's disease; **ˈhepatolith** [Gr. λίθος stone], a gall-stone (*Syd. Soc. Lex.*); hence **hepatoˈlithic** *a.*, of the nature of a gall-stone; **hepatolithiasis** (-lɪˈθaɪəsɪs), the formation of stone-like concretions in the liver (Craig 1847); **hepaˈtology** [see -LOGY], that part of medical science which treats of the liver (Dunglison 1833–46); hence **hepaˈtologist**, a student of hepatology; **hepatoˈlogical** *a.*, of or belonging to hepatology (Mayne); ˌ**hepatomeˈgalia**, **-ˈmegaly**, abnormal enlargement of the liver; **hepatopancreas** (ˌhɛpətəʊˈpænkriːəs) *Biol.*, Klaus's name for the glandular organ, called the liver in Invertebrates, in reference to its twofold functions of secretion and digestion; **hepaˈtopathy** [Gr. πάθος suffering], disease of the liver (Mayne); **hepato-ˈportal** *a.* [see PORTAL], of or pertaining to the hepatic portal system, as distinguished from *reniportal*; **hepato-ˈrenal** *a.* [see RENAL], relating to the liver and kidneys; **hepatoˈrrhœa** [Gr. ῥοία a flow], a flow or discharge from the liver; **hepaˈtoscopy** [Gr. -σκοπία inspection], inspection of the liver; divination by inspection of the liver of an animal; hence **hepaˈtoscopist**, one who practises hepatoscopy; ˌ**hepatoˌsplenomeˈgalia**, **-ˈmegaly**, abnormal enlargement of the liver and spleen; **hepaˈtotomy** [Gr. -τομία cutting], dissection of the liver (Mayne); **hepatoˈtoxic** *a.*, having a toxic effect on the liver; so ˌ**hepatotoˈxicity**; **hepatoˈtoxin**, (*a*) any substance which has a toxic effect on the liver; (*b*) an antibody produced by injecting liver tissue into an animal; ˌ**hepato-umˈbilical** *a.* [L. *umbilicus* navel], connecting the liver and the navel.

1811 Hooper *Med. Dict.*, *Hepatocele, an hernia in which a portion of the liver protrudes through the abdominal parietes. **1940** E. Rosenthal *Dis. Digestive Syst.* iii. 212 Jaundice may be i. Mechanical ii. Functional (*hepato-cellular) iii. Hæmolytic. **1949** Kantor & Kasich *Handbk. Digestive Dis.* (ed. 2) xvii. 415 The hepato-cellular and the obstructive forms of jaundice make up more than 95 per cent of the cases encountered in clinical practice. **1962** *Lancet* 13 Jan. 67/1 Patients with hepato-cellular disease are faced with the prospect of hepatic coma and death every time they have a haemorrhage. **1738** Amyand in *Phil. Trans.* XL. 322 *Hepaticystic Ducts. **1766** Hunter *Ibid.* LVI. 309 The hepatocystic ducts..enter the gall-bladder at its anterior end or fundus. **1880** J. W. Legg *Bile* 89 Schiff..tied all the structures in the *hepato-duodenal ligament, save the hepatic artery. **1933** K. G. Stern in *Nature* 18 Nov. 784/1 The isolation in a crystalline state of the lyochrome from horse liver, to be designated as '*hepatoflavin', has been achieved. **1936** *Jrnl. Nutrition* XI. 75 Fractions prepared from liver extract which were rich in vitamin G (B_2) and from which the hepatoflavin had been removed..were very active in the cure of black tongue. **1943** M. E. Rehfuss *Indigestion* xxiv. 392 The terms lactoflavin, ovoflavin, hepato-flavin, and so on serve to indicate the source of the particular riboflavin under discussion. **1960** A. E. Bender *Dict. Nutrition* 62/1 *Hepatoflavin*, name given to substance isolated from liver, shown later to be riboflavin. **1876** tr. *Wagner's Gen. Pathol.* 551 *Hepatogenic Icterus in the duodenum. **1886** *Syd. Soc. Lex.*, *Hepatogenic icterus*, jaundice produced by the absorption of bile already formed in the liver. **1875** H. C. Wood *Therap.* (1879) 109 That the icterus is not really *hepatogenous, but haemic in origin. **1897** Allbutt *Syst. Med.* II. 400 True hepatogenous jaundice, with bile pigment in the urine and decolouration of the fæces. **1922** *Lancet* 29 Apr. 849/2 This is an account of the disease known as progressive lenticular degeneration, which Dr. Hall christens *hepato-lenticular degeneration. **1925** *Brain* XLVIII. 332 It would be better to adopt Hall's terminology, and refer to the condition as hepato-lenticular degeneration... This title fails to indicate the peculiar type of the disease in the liver..but it indicates..that the lenticular disease is a sequel to liver damage. **1945** *Archives Internal Med.* LXXV. 151/1 Wilson in 1912..first clearly defined the condition now most widely known as hepatolenticular degeneration. **1955** S. Sherlock *Dis. Liver & Biliary Syst.* xiii. 339 Hepatolenticular degeneration is a rare disease of young people characterised by portal cirrhosis of the liver, bilateral softening and degeneration of the lenticular nuclei of the basal ganglia of the brain, and greenish-brown pigmented rings in the periphery of the cornea. **1854** Mayne *Expos. Lex.*, *Hepatolithicus*, of or belonging to a *hepatolith, *hepatolithic. **1888** *Sci. Amer.* LVIII. 98 Dr. Harley, the English *hepatologist and nephrologist. **1893** Dunglison *Dict. Med. Sci.* (ed. 21) 524/1 *Hepatomegalia. **1910** Collins & Liebmann tr. *Dieulafoy's Text-bk. Med.* II. viii. i. 1916 He [*sc.* Glénard] found that hepatomegalia is the most frequent of the organic changes in diabetes. **1904** Stedman *Dunglison's Dict. Med. Sci.* (ed. 23) 527/1 *Hepatomegaly. **1937** J. L. Kantor *Synopsis Digestive Dis.* xxi. 230 Cancer of the liver must be differentiated from other conditions causing hepatomegaly. **1969** Hepato-megaly [see *hepatotoxicity* below]. **1884** Sedgwick tr. *Claus' Zool.* I. 59 In the Invertebrata the secretions of many glands, which are generally called 'liver', but which would be more appropriately termed *hepatopancreas. **1886** *Syd. Soc. Lex.*, **Hepato-renal ligament*, a reflection of the peritonæum extending from the

transverse fissure of the liver to the kidney. **1947** AUDEN *Age of Anxiety* (1948) vi. 121 Peace was promised by the public *hepatoscopists. **1727–51** CHAMBERS *Cycl.* s.v. *Divination*, *Hepatoscopy, or the consideration of the liver. **1928** C. DAWSON *Age of Gods* xiii. 307 The practice of Hepatoscopy or divination from the liver of the sacrificial victim, which reached Asia Minor from Mesopotamia, was carried by the Etruscans to Italy. **1957** *Encycl. Brit.* XI. 451/1 The theory underlying hepatoscopy consists of the belief (1) that the liver is the seat of life, or the soul of the animal; and (2) that the liver of the sacrificial animal..took on the same character as the soul of the god to whom it was offered. **1930** *Chem. Abstr.* XXIV. 886 In *hepatosplenomegalia and hepatic cirrhosis, the urobilin increased in the urine and feces. **1939** STEDMAN *Med. Dict.* (ed. 14) 496/2 Hepatosplenomegaly. **1961** *Lancet* 19 Aug. 434/2 Physical examination revealed considerable hepatosplenomegaly. **1940** *Jrnl. Amer. Med. Assoc.* 28 Dec. 2264/2 (*heading*) Alleged *hepatotoxic action of stilbestrol. **1961** *Lancet* 16 Sept. 623/1 Each of the drugs which has caused jaundice is a derivative of hydrazine, itself a potent hepatotoxic agent in laboratory animals. **1972** *Nature* 4 Feb. 279/1 Both compounds..have been reported to be hepatotoxic, carcinogenic, teratogenic and neurotoxic. **1952** *New Eng. Jrnl. Med.* 20 Nov. 797 (*heading*) The *hepatotoxicity of intravenous aureomycin. **1969** *Nature* 19 Apr. 223/2 Increase in size of the liver (hepatomegaly) is not a reliable indication of hepatotoxicity. **1904** STEDMAN *Dunglison's Dict. Med. Sci.* (ed. 23) 527/1 **Hepatotoxin*, a cytotoxin having a specific action on the cells of the liver. **1909** J. G. ADAMI *Princ. Path.* I. III. viii. 489 Ciliated epithelium was shown to have its cytotoxin.., as have kidney cells (nephrotoxin), liver cells (hepatotoxin), pancreatic, adrenal, in fact, every form of animal cell that has been tested. **1929** *Chem. Abstr.* XXIII. 5509 Hepatotoxins, prepd. by immunizing rabbits with emulsions of rabbit and rat livers, were injected into rabbits and rats. **1951** A. GROLLMAN *Pharmacol. & Therapeutics* xxvii. 607 Because of their lipotropic action, choline and, to a lesser extent, methionine ..have been used therapeutically in cirrhosis of the liver,.. and as a prophylactic in poisoning by hepatotoxins. **1963** G. KLATSKIN in L. Schiff *Dis. Liver* (ed. 2) xiv. 453/1 Hepatotoxins, a heterogeneous group of naturally occuring and synthetic chemical agents, produce a variety of lesions in the liver that are classified as forms of toxic hepatitis.

'hepatoid, *a.* [ad. Gr. ἡπατοειδής liver-shaped: see HEPATO- and -OID.] 'Like to the liver in colour or in function' (*Syd. Soc. Lex.* 1886).

Hepburn ('hɛpbɜːn, 'hɛbɜːn). The name of J. C. *Hepburn* (1815–1911), Amer. physician and missionary, used *attrib.* in ***Hepburn system***, a Romanized transcription of Japanese characters. So **Hep'burnian** *a.*

[**1867** J. C. HEPBURN (*title*) A Japanese and English dictionary.] **1937** *Mélanges Ling. et Phil. offerts à J. van Ginneken* 357 The Nipponsiki or Japanese system versus the Hepburnian system. *Ibid.* 358 It was this Hepburn system ..which was adopted by the Romajikai. **1950** D. JONES *Phoneme* 38 The old (Hepburnian) Roman writing of Japanese. **1961** T. LANDAU *Encycl. Librarianship* (ed. 2) 369/1 These [Japanese] sounds are transcribed into Roman letters, either by the Hepburn system..or by the Japanese system of 'New spelling'... The outside world sticks to the Hepburn system.

hep-cat ('hɛpkæt). *slang* (orig. *U.S.*). [f. HEP *a.* + CAT *sb.*[1] 2 c.] An addict of jazz, swing music, etc.; one who is 'hep'; = HIPSTER[1].

1938 in *Amer. Speech* (1939) XIV. 140 *Hep cat*,..guy who knows what it's [*sc.* swing music is] all about. *a* **1940** F. SCOTT FITZGERALD *Last Tycoon* (1949) v. 127 Suddenly they were at work again—taking up this new theme in turn like hepcats in a swing band and going to town with it. **1955** *Sci. News Let.* 1 Oct. 221/2 This is not cool chatter between some young hep-cats in a smoke-filled jazz joint. **1957** C. MACINNES *City of Spades* II. xii. 184 You's the hep-cat what stole Mr. Vial's puss-cat! **1959** *Listener* 9 Apr. 646/2 The lament at a local hep-cat's funeral. **1959** *News Chron.* 14 Oct. 8/6 The jazz-loving 'hep-cat'. **1961** *Times* 20 May 5/1 Mr. Louis Armstrong and his fellow hepcats.

†**hepe**. *Obs. rare.* [Identical with MHG., MLG. *hepe*, early mod.Du. *heepe*, Du. *heep* sickle-shaped pruning-knife or bill; other forms of which are MHG., MLG. *heppe*, mod.Ger. *heppe*, *hippe*, OHG. *habba*, *happa*, *hęppa*:—**happja*:—OTeut. **habjôn*, f. pre-Teut. root *kop-*, whence prob. Gr. κοπίς chopper, cleaver, broad curved knife. As there is no cognate word in OE., its appearance in Gower, and this app. in a proverbial phrase (cf. 'by hook or by crook' under HOOK), is not easy to account for.]

A curved pruning-knife.

1390 GOWER *Conf.* II. 223 So what with hepe and what with crok(e) They make her maister often winne.

hepe, obs. form of HEAP, HIP.

‖**Hephæstus** (hɪ'fiːstəs). Romanized spelling of Gr. Ἥφαιστος the god of fire, identified by the Romans with Vulcan. Hence **He'phæstian** *a.*, of, or belonging to, or made by Hephæstus. **He'phæstic** *a.*, relating to fire; also, relating to the forge or use of the smith's hammer.

1658 PHILLIPS, *Hephæstian* mountains, certain burning mountains in Lycia. **1854** KEIGHTLEY *Mythol. Anc. Greece & Italy* (ed. 3) 434 Arrayed in Hephæstian armour. **1869** *Lancet* I. 427 Cases of hemiplegia among Sheffield smiths were described..as due to the use of the hammer, and termed..'hephaestic hemiplegia'.

hephthemimer (hɛfθɪ'mɪmə(r)). *Anc. Pros.* [ad. late L. *hephthemimerēs* (*-is*) (Diomedes, Servius), a. Gr. ἑφθημιμερής 'containing seven halves', f. ἑπτ(α- seven + ἡμι- half + μέρος part, -μερης -partite. So mod.F. *hephthémimère*. Also commonly used in the Latin form; sometimes contracted *hephthemim*.] A group or catalectic colon of seven half-feet; the part of a hexameter line preceding the cæsura when this occurs in the middle of the fourth foot, as in 'Inferretque deos Latio · genus unde Latinum'.

Hence **hephthe'mimeral** *a.*, of or pertaining to a hephthemimeris, as in ***hephthemimeral cæsura***: see the example above.

1706 PHILLIPS (ed. Kersey), *Hephthemimeris*. **1727–41** CHAMBERS *Cycl.*, *Hephthemimeris*, in the Greek and Latin poetry, a sort of verse consisting of three feet and a syllable; that is, of seven half feet. **1871** *Public Sch. Lat. Gram.* §226. 464–5 Next in power to the penthemimeral is the hephthemimeral or semiseptenarian caesura. *Ibid.*, In this verse, *Quid faciat | laetas | segetes | quo sidere terram*..the principal pause is at the hephthemimeris. *Ibid.* §232. 470 Trochaic Hephthemimer.

Hepialid (hiːpɪ'ælɪd), *a.* and *sb.* *Zool.* Formerly also **epialid**. [ad. mod.L. *Hepialidæ*, f. *Hepialus* (J. C. Fabricius, *Systema Entomologiæ* (1775) 589), a. Gr. ἠπίολος moth; sometimes *Epialidæ*, *Epialus*, perhaps through confusion with Gr. ἠπίαλος nightmare: see -ID[3].] (Of or pertaining to) a moth of the family Hepialidæ, the ghost-moths or swifts.

1888 *Proc. Linnean Soc. N.S.W.* II. 1015 We have drawn up a description of the finely coloured Hepialid which was exhibited at the June meeting. **1895** *Funk's Stand. Dict.*, *Ghost-moth*, an epialid moth, especially *Epialus humuli*. *Ibid.*, *Swift*, n... 2. An epialid or ghost-moth. **1900** *Trans. Ent. Soc.* III. 411 (*title*) Life histories in the Hepialid group of Lepidoptera. **1931** *Ann. Appl. Biol.* XVIII. 54 The larva of a Hepialid moth, *Oncopera intricata*.

hepper. A local name of a smolt, or young salmon of the second year.

1861 *Act 24 & 25 Vict.* c. 109 §4 All migratory fish of the genus salmon, whether known by the names hereinafter mentioned, that is to say, salmon..pink, last spring, hepper, last brood, gravelling..or by any other local name. **1885** F. DAY *Fishes Gt. Brit.* II. 69 From one to two years old before it..has gone to the sea it is known as a..skegger, gravelling, hepper..in Wales.

Hepplewhite ('hɛp(ə)lwaɪt). The name of George *Hepplewhite* (died 1786), who was succeeded by A. *Hepplewhite* and Co., used *attrib.* to designate an English style of furniture of the latter part of the eighteenth century, characterized by lightness, delicacy, and graceful curves, being an adaptation of current French styles.

1897 K. W. CLOUSTON *Chippendale Period Eng. Furnit.* vii. 177 The Hepplewhite commode has long been obsolete or transformed into the modern cabinet with mirror back. **1900** *Jrnl. Soc. Arts* 23 Mar. 380/1 Hepplewhite and Sheraton furniture should be studied by designers for *motifs*. **1901** *Connoisseur* Dec. 272/2 Six Hepplewhite arm-chairs. **1903** *Chambers's Jrnl.* 20 June 460/1 Three..ball-and-claw Hepplewhite chairs. **1957** *Encycl. Brit.* XI. 453/1 The smaller Hepplewhite pieces are much prized by collectors.

hepster ('hɛpstə(r)). *slang* (orig. *U.S.*). Now *rare.* [f. HEP *a.* + -STER.] = HEP-CAT. Cf. HIPSTER[1].

1938 in *Amer. Speech* (1939) XIV. 140/2 Cab Calloway's Cat-alogue, a 'hepster's' dictionary. **1948** [see BOP *sb.*[2]]. **1958** *Spectator* 21 Nov. 702/1 Yet although jazz seems to have burst out of the locked treasure casket over which an egghead minority of hepsters crooned for so many years, it still remains a curiously unreal cult.

hepta-, before a vowel **hept-**, combining form of Gr. ἑπτά seven, occurring as the first element of many compounds in Greek, some of which have descended through Latin into the modern langs., while many more have been taken directly from Greek, or formed on Greek analogies. Normally, *hepta-* is combined with elements of Greek origin, but in some instances (chiefly on account of the inconvenience of L. *septem*) it is combined with L. or other elements, as ***heptangular***, ***heptavalent***. In *Chem.* it indicates the presence of seven atoms of an element, as *heptacarbon* (see below), ***heptachloride***, ***heptoxide***, ***heptachlorotoluene***, etc.

hepta'capsular *a.* *Bot.* [L. *capsula* CAPSULE], having seven capsules, cells, or cavities (Bailey 1730–6). **hepta'carbon** *a.* *Chem.*, containing seven carbon atoms, as in ***heptacarbon compounds***, ***series***: cf. HEPTANE. †**heptace** ('hɛptəsiː) *Cryst.* [Gr. ἀκή point], a summit of a polyhedron formed by the concurrence of seven faces (Kirkman). **'heptachlor** *Chem.*, a chlorinated hydrocarbon, $C_{10}H_5Cl_7$, used as an insecticide. **heptachronous** (hɛp'tækrənəs) *a.* [late L. *heptachronus*, a. Gr. ἑπτάχρονος, f. χρόνος time], in ancient prosody = *heptasemic*. **hepta'colic** *a.* [Gr. ἑπτάκωλ-ος of seven verses or members, f. κῶλον COLON], in ancient prosody: of seven cola or members, as 'a heptacolic period'. **hepta-compound**, *Chem.*, a compound containing seven atoms of any element or radical; esp. a heptacarbon compound. **hepta'decane** *Chem.* [Gr. δέκα ten: see -ANE], any of the hydrocarbons of the paraffin series having seventeen carbon atoms, *esp.* the unbranched isomer. **hepta-hexa'hedral** *a.* *Cryst.*, having seven ranges of six faces each. **hepta'hydrate**, *Chem.*, a compound containing seven molecules of water ($7H_2O$). **,heptahy'drated** *a.* *Chem.*, containing seven molecules of water. **hepta'hydric** *a.* *Chem.*, containing seven hydroxyl groups. **hepta(i)'cosane** *Chem.* [Gr. εἴκοσι twenty: see -ANE], any of the hydrocarbons of the paraffin series having twenty-seven carbon atoms, *esp.* the unbranched isomer, which is present in tobacco oil and many natural waxes. ‖**hep'tameron** [Gr. ἑπταήμερ-ος, neut. -ον, of seven days, f. ἡμέρα day], a seven days' work; title of a collection of stories, represented (after the pattern of the Decameron of Boccaccio) to have been told on seven successive days, made by Queen Margaret of Navarre, *a* 1549. **hep'tameter** *Pros.* [late L. *heptametrum*, a. Gr. ἑπτάμετρον, f. μέτρον measure], a verse consisting of seven feet or measures; cf. *heptapody*. **hepta'metrical** *a.*, consisting of seven feet or measures. **hep'tangular** *a.*, having seven angles. **hepta'petalous** *a.* *Bot.*, having seven petals. †**hep'taphony** [f. Gr. ἑπτάφων-ος seven-voiced, having a sevenfold echo], the union of seven sounds (Blount *Glossogr.* 1656). **hepta'phyllous** *a.* *Bot.* [Gr. ἑπτάφυλλ-ος seven-leaved], having seven leaves or calyx sepals (Webster 1828). **heptapodic** (-'pɒdɪk) *a.* *Pros.* [Gr. -ποδος -footed], consisting of or containing seven metrical feet; so **hep'tapody**, a measure or verse consisting of seven feet. **heptasemic** (-'siːmɪk) *a.* [late L. *heptasēm-os*, a. Gr. ἑπτάσημ-ος of seven times], in ancient prosody: containing seven units of time or moræ. **heptasepalous** (-'sɛpələs) *a.* *Bot.*, having seven sepals. **hepta'spermous** *a.* *Bot.* [Gr. σπέρμα seed], bearing seven seeds. **heptastich** ('hɛptəstɪk) *Pros.* [Gr. στίχος line], *sb.*, a group of seven lines of verse; *a.*, seven lines long. **heptastichous** (-'æstɪkəs) *a.* *Bot.*, having seven leaves in the spiral row. **heptastrophic** (-'strɒfɪk) *a.* *Pros.* [Gr. στροφή turning, STROPHE], consisting of seven strophes or stanzas. **'heptastyle** *Archit.* [Gr. στῦλος pillar], (a building or portico) having seven columns in front. †**hepta'technist** [Gr. τέχνη art], a professor of the Seven Arts (cf. ART 7), a Master of Arts. **hepta'tomic** *a.* *Chem.* [ATOMIC], containing or equivalent to seven atoms. **heptatonic** (-'tɒnɪk) *a.* *Mus.* [Gr. ἑπτάτον-ος seven-toned], consisting of seven notes. **heptavalent** (-'ævələnt) *a.* *Chem.* [L. *valēnt-em* having power or value], combining with or capable of replacing seven atoms of hydrogen or other univalent element or radical. **'heptose** [a. G. *heptose* (E. Fischer 1890, in *Ber. d. Deut. Chem. Ges.* XXIII. 934): see -OSE[2]], any of a group of monosaccharides, $C_7H_{14}O_7$, present in some plants and as constituents of some bacterial polysaccharides.

1866 ODLING *Anim. Chem.* 109 *Heptacarbon compounds such as the benzoic residue of hippuric acid. **1949** *Jrnl. Econ. Ent.* XLII. 328/1 *Heptachlor, a close relative of chlordan, gave results superior to chlordan. **1961** *New Scientist* 6 July 9/2 British manufacturers of agricultural chemicals have agreed with the Government to restrict the use of three pesticides..aldrin, dieldrin and heptachlor. **1963** R. CARSON *Silent Spring* x. 140 Heptachlor, after a short period in the tissues of animals or plants or in the soil, assumes a considerably more toxic form known as heptachlor epoxide... The Food and Drug Administration took action which had the effect of banning any residues of heptachlor or its epoxide in food. **1968** M. PYKE *Food & Society* viii. 119 [They] found not only DDT and its breakdown products, but BHC, heptachlor and dieldrin as well in the tissues of penguins. **1880** *W.A. Miller's Elem. Chem.* III. (ed. 5) 317 A small quantity of ..*heptachlorotoluene. **1866** ODLING *Anim. Chem.* 66 *Heptacompounds, including oil of bitter almonds, and the benzoic, salicic, and gallic acids. **1882** *Jrnl. Chem. Soc.* XLII. 1272 *Heptadecane (from margaric acid, or from the ketone $C_{17}H_{34}O$, obtained from barium palmitate) crystallizes in large hexagonal plates. **1805–17** R. JAMESON *Char. Min.* (ed. 3) 204 A crystal is *hepta-hexahedral, when its surface consists of seven ranges of planes, disposed six and six above each other. **1874** GUTHRIE in *Proc. Phys. Soc. Lond.* I. 67 On cooling such a solution..the *heptahydrate crystallizes out. **1895** G. LUNGE *Sulphuric Acid* (ed. 2) II. 22

The anhydrous salt..if protected from the air is changed into *heptahydrated..salt. **1892** E. F. SMITH tr. *V. von Richter's Chem. Carbon Compounds* (ed. 2) 49 The *heptahydric aldehydes, $C_7H_{14}O_7$, resemble the sugars in their behavior. **1968** J. A. MONICK *Alcohols* v. 442 Perseitol ..is a heptahydric alcohol with a 7-carbon atom straight-chain that contains seven hydroxyl groups. **1889** MUIR & MORLEY *Watts' Dict. Chem.* II. 675/1 **n*-Heptaicosane $C_{27}H_{56}$. **1901** *Jrnl. Chem. Soc.* LXXIX. I. 986 The results of the analysis..indicate that the second hydrocarbon is in all probability heptacosane, $C_{27}H_{56}$. **1961** L. F. & M. FIESER *Adv. Org. Chem.* iv. 110 Beeswax contains heptacosane ($C_{27}H_{56}$) and hentriacontane ($C_{31}H_{64}$). **1727–41** CHAMBERS *Cycl.*, **Heptameron*..is chiefly used as a title..The Heptameron of Margaret de Valois..is a very ingenious piece, in the manner of Boccace's Decameron. **1894** H. H. GIBBS (*title*) Colloquy on Currency: a Heptameron. **1814** SOUTHEY in *Q. Rev.* XII. 84 It revived the old long verse, which he calls the *heptametrical seven-footed line. **1706** PHILLIPS (ed. Kersey), **Heptangular Figure* is that which consists of seven Angles. **1752** SIR J. HILL *Hist. Anim.* 203 (Jod.) The middle of the body heptangular. **1775** J. JENKINSON *Brit. Plants* Gloss., **Heptaphyllous*. **1870** BENTLEY *Bot.* 216 *Heptasepalous. **1882–3** in Schaff *Encycl. Relig. Knowl.* III. 1945 Of *heptastichs there is only one example [Prov. xxiii. 6–8]. From this heptastich..we see that the proverb of two lines can expand itself to the dimensions of seven and eight lines. **1891** DRIVER *Introd. Lit. O. Test.* (1892) 375 Several pentastichs and hexastichs, a heptastich and an octastich also occur. **1843** *Civil Engin. & Archit. Jrnl.* VI. 167/1 The temple of the giants, at Agrigentum (*heptastyle). **1909** A. MARQUAND *Greek Archit.* vi. 313 Another classification of temples notes merely the number of columns exhibited in the façade... The Theseion at Athens was hexastyle; the Temple at Thorikos, heptastyle. **1680** T. LAWSON (*title*) A Mite in the Treasury, being a Word to Artists, especially *Heptatechnists, the Professors of the Seven Liberal Arts. **1886** CROOKES in *Rep. Brit. Assoc.* 573 Fluorine mon- and *heptatomic. **1890** *Athenæum* 4 Jan. 24/1 A *heptatonic scale [in Java], consisting of semitones, three-quarter tones, and minor thirds. **1893** *Ibid.* 23 Dec. 890/3 A certain series of notes..chosen to form the chromatic, heptatonic, pentatonic, or whatever sequential basis may be required. **1890** *Jrnl. Chem. Soc.* LVIII. I. 598 The author proposes to employ the terms pentose, *heptose, octose, &c., for the sugars..and heptonic acid, octonic acid, &c., for the acids of the series, according to the number of carbon-atoms in the compounds. **1916** Heptose [see BIOSE]. **1952** J. K. N. JONES in E. M. Rodd *Chem. Carbon Compounds* IB. xx. 1264 Heptose sugars may exist in ketose and aldose forms. **1960** *Adv. Carbohydrate Chem.* XV. 288 Whereas, in the Enteric group of bacteria, there is as yet no evidence for the presence of heptoses other than L-*glycero*-D-*manno*-heptose, this is not true of other Gram-negative groups. **1869** ROSCOE *Elem. Chem.* 235 This substance is Manganese *Heptoxide.

heptachord ('hɛptəkɔːd), *a.* and *sb.* *Mus.* [ad. Gr. ἑπτάχορδ-ος seven-stringed, f. ἑπτά seven + χορδή string, CHORD. Cf. F. *heptacorde.*]

†**A.** *adj.* Seven-stringed. *Obs.*

1727–41 CHAMBERS *Cycl.* s.v., In the antient poetry, Heptachord verses were those sung or played on seven chords; that is, in seven different notes, or tones; and probably on an instrument with seven strings.

B. *sb.* **a.** A musical instrument of seven strings. **b.** A series of seven notes, formed of two conjunct tetrachords. **c.** The interval of a seventh.

1765 CROKER, etc. *Dict. Arts & Sc.*, *Heptachord*,..was applied to the lyre, when it had but seven strings. **1775** ASH, *Heptachord*, a musical instrument of seven strings, a poetical composition played or sung on seven chords or notes. **1774** BURNEY *Hist. Mus.* I. 35 Forming then the whole system of the octachord, or heptachord. *Ibid.* 205 If these two strings were tuned fourths to each other, they would furnish that series of sounds which the ancients called a heptachord, consisting of two conjunct tetrachords. **1861** T. L. PEACOCK *Gryll Gr.* xxii. 197 If..these two heptachords should harmonize into a double octave.

heptad ('hɛptæd). [ad. Gr. ἑπτάς, ἑπταδ-, the number seven collectively.]

1. The sum or number of seven; a group of seven.

1660 STANLEY *Hist. Philos.* IX. (1701) 383/2 The Heptad was so called, *qu.* σεπτὰς σεβασμοῦ ἄξιος worthy of veneration. **1797** *Monthly Mag.* III. 521 The heptad of wandering animals. **1850** J. BROWN *Disc. Our Lord* (1852) I. iv. 351 This prayer contains a sacred heptad of petitions.

b. *spec.* A group of seven days, a week; = HEBDOMAD.

1876 tr. *Keil & Delitzsch's Ezek.* II. 336 A feast of heptads of days or weeks of days. **1881** BLACKIE *Lay Serm.* ii. 83 The months are divided into heptads.

2. *Chem.* An atom or molecule whose equivalence is seven atoms of hydrogen, i.e. which can be combined with, substituted for, or replaced by seven atoms of hydrogen.

3. *Mus.* A scheme of seven tones in the duodenal system of analysis, containing all the notes from which consonant triads may be formed with the tonic.

1874 A. J. ELLIS in *Proc. R. Soc.* XXIII. 11 The *Harmonic Heptad* or *Unit of Chord-relationship*..The heptad also contains all triads, consisting of three tones, two of which are consonant with C but dissonant with each other.

heptadecad (hɛptə'dɛkəd). *Mus.* [f. HEPTA- + DECAD.] A scheme of twenty-four tones formed by the combination of seven decads, in the duodenal system of analysis.

1874 A. J. ELLIS in *Proc. R. Soc.* XXIII. 14 The *Harmonic Heptadecad* or *Unit of Modulation* (or *Decadation*) consists of seven interwoven decads, which are constructed on the seven tones of a heptad as tonics, and contains 24 tones.

'heptaglot, *a.* and *sb.* [f. Gr. ἑπτά HEPTA- + γλῶττα tongue, -γλωττος -tongued: cf. POLYGLOT.] **A.** *adj.* Using or written in seven languages. **B.** *sb.* A book in seven languages.

1684 N. S. *Crit. Enq. Edit. Bible* xxvii. 245 They are indeed much inferiour to the Parisian Heptaglots in the largeness and goodness of the Paper. **1885** *Encycl. Brit.* XIX. 417 It was in connexion with this polyglott that E. Castle produced his famous *Heptaglott Lexicon.*

So †**heptaglo'ttology**. *Obs.* (See quot.)

1618 E. RIVE (*title*) An Heptaglottologie, that is, a Treatise concerning Seven Languages.

heptagon ('hɛptəgən). [ad. Gr. ἑπτάγωνον, neut. of ἑπτάγωνος seven-cornered. Cf. F. *heptagone* (1542 in Hatz.-Darm.).]

1. *Geom.* A plane figure having seven angles and seven sides.

1570 BILLINGSLEY *Euclid* I. xxxii. 42 In an heptagon, from one angle may be drawne lines to foure opposite angles. **1660** BARROW *Euclid* IV. xi. Schol., The side of a Heptagone. **1885** LEUDESDORF *Cremona's Proj. Geom.* 187 Suppose it is required to inscribe in the conic a heptagon.

b. *Fortif.* A place strengthened with seven bastions for its defence.

1706 in PHILLIPS (ed. Kersey).

2. *attrib.* or *adj.* = HEPTAGONAL.

1775 R. PUTNAM in Romans *Florida* 335 It [a fort] was built of a heptagon figure, with one side fronting the river.

heptagonal (hɛp'tægənəl), *a.* (*sb.*) [f. HEPTAGON + -AL[1]: cf. F. *heptagonale* (1633 in Hatz.-Darm.).] Having seven angles and seven sides.

heptagonal numbers, the series of POLYGONAL numbers 1, 7, 18, 34, 55, 81, etc. formed by continuous summation of the arithmetical series 1, 6, 11, 16, 21, 26, etc.

1613 SELDEN in *Drayton's Poly-olb.* xi. (R.), In a circle describe an heptagonal and equilateral figure, from whose every side shall fall equilateral triangles. **1690** LEYBOURN *Curs. Math.* 279 It is called a Heptagonal Pyramide. **1796** HUTTON *Math. Dict.* s.v., One property..of these Heptagonal numbers is, that if any one of them be multiplied by 40, and to the product add 9, the sum will be a square number. **1828** STARK *Elem. Nat. Hist.* I. 398 Body heptagonal, yellowish brown, variegated with narrow transverse deep brown bars. **1853** RUSKIN *Stones Ven.* II. iii. §14. 37 We have therefore, externally a heptagonal apse.

b. *sb.* A heptagonal number.

1796 HUTTON *Math. Dict.* s.v., The Heptagonals are formed by adding continually the terms of the arithmeticals.

‖**heptagynia** (hɛptə'dʒɪnɪə). *Bot.* [mod.L. (Linnæus 1735), f. HEPTA- + Gr. γυνή woman, wife, female, taken in the sense of female organ, pistil.] An order in the Linnæan Sexual System, comprising plants having seven pistils. So **'heptagyn**, a plant of this order. **hepta'gynian**, **hepta'gynious** *adjs.*, of or pertaining to this order. **hep'tagynous** *a.*, having seven pistils.

1788 J. LEE *Introd. Bot.* (ed. 4) 103 Heptandria..Order IV. *Heptagynia*, containing such plants as have seven Styles. Of this Order there is but one Genus, viz. *Septas*. **1828** WEBSTER, *Heptagyn*, *Heptagynian*. **1854** MAYNE *Expos. Lex.*, *Heptagynious*. **1864** WEBSTER, *Heptagynous*.

heptahedron (-'hiːdrən, -'hɛdrən). Also heptaedron. [f. HEPTA- + Gr. ἕδρα seat, base.] A solid figure having seven faces. So **hepta'hedral**, †**hepta'hedrical** *adjs.*, seven-sided, seven-faced.

1658 PHILLIPS, *Heptahedrical*, having seven sides. **1696** *Ibid.*, *Heptaedrical Figure*, or *Heptaedron*. **1758** BORLASE *Cornwall* ii. §17. 141 A heptahedral cuspis of brass-coloured Mundic. **1804** WATT in *Phil. Trans.* XCIV. 310 *note*, Hexaedral and pentaedral prisms are most abundant; then the tetraedral, the triedral, heptaedral, and octaedral.

'heptal, *a.* [irreg. f. Gr. ἑπτά seven + -AL[1].] = HEBDOMADAL.

1857 DUNGLISON *Med. Dict.* 208 *Cycle, Hebdomadal or Heptal*. A period of seven days, or years, which according to some, either in its multiple or sub-multiple, governs an immense number of phenomena of animal life.

heptamerous (hɛp'tæmərəs), *a.* [f. HEPTA- + Gr. μέρος part + -OUS.] Consisting of seven members or parts. So **hep'tamerede** (see quot.).

a **1790** ADAM SMITH *Ess. Imitat. Arts* (T.), The heptamerede of M. Sauveur could express an interval so small as the seventh part of what is called a comma. **1864** WEBSTER (citing ASA GRAY), *Heptamerous*.

‖**hep'tandria**. *Bot.* [mod.L. (Linnæus 1735), f. Gr. type *ἑπτανδρος, mod.L. *heptandr-us*, f. HEPTA- + ἀνδρ- stem of ἀνήρ man, male: cf. DIANDRIA.] The seventh class in the Sexual System of Linnæus, containing plants having seven stamens. So **hep'tander**, a member of the class Heptandria (Webster 1828). **hep'tandrian** *a.*, of or belonging to Heptandria (Webster 1828). **hep'tandrous** *a.*, having seven stamens.

1753 CHAMBERS *Cycl. Supp.*, *Heptandria*..of this class are the horse-chesnut, etc. **1794** MARTYN *Rousseau's Bot.* ix. 88 The flowers of the class heptandria should have seven stamens. **1870** BENTLEY *Bot.* 246 A flower having seven stamens is Heptandrous.

heptane ('hɛptein). *Chem.* [f. HEPT(A- + -ANE, formative of the names of paraffins.] The paraffin of the heptacarbon series, having the formula C_7H_{16}. 'Of these hydrocarbons nine are possible and four are known' (*Fownes' Chem.* 1877).

1877 WATTS *Fownes' Chem.* (ed. 12) II. 49 *Normal heptane*, $CH_3-(CH_2)_5-CH_3$, is contained in Pennsylvanian petroleum, and in the light oils of Boghead and Cannel coal. **1880** *W. A. Miller's Elem. Chem.* (ed. 5) 196 Of the heptylene from normal heptane..somewhat less than one half combines with cold hydrochloric acid, producing a heptylic chloride.

So **heptene** ('hɛptiːn) [see -ENE], the olefine of the heptacarbon series (C_7H_{14}), also called **'heptylene**, homologous and polymeric with ethene (C_2H_4); it is known to exist in three isomeric forms; **heptine** ('hɛptaɪn) [see -INE], the hydrocarbon of the same series (C_7H_{12}), homologous with acetylene or ethine; **hep'toic** *a.*, applied to fatty acids, aldehydes, etc. belonging to the heptacarbon series, as ***heptoic acid***, $C_7H_{14}O_2$; **heptyl** ('hɛptɪl) [see -YL], the hydrocarbon radical (C_7H_{15}), of heptylic or œnanthylic alcohol and its derivatives; hence **hep'tylic** *a.*; **'heptyla,mine** (see AMINE). Hence **hepta'noic acid**, œnanthic acid, $CH_3{\cdot}(CH_2)_5{\cdot}COOH$; **hepte'noic acid**, any of several monocarboxylic acids, $C_6H_{11}COOH$, having one double bond.

1865–72 —— *Dict. Chem.* (1882) III. 144 Chloride of *heptyl ($C_7H_{15}Cl$) is a colourless liquid having an agreeable fruity odour, and burning with a smoky green-bordered flame. *Ibid.* 295 Of these acids, one only is accurately known. viz. *Normal* **Heptoic* or *Œnanthylic* acid. *Ibid.* 145 Preparation of *Heptylic alcohol from Castor-oil. *Ibid.* 147 When distilled with caustic potash, it yields **heptylamine* ($C_7H_{17}N$) as a light oily liquid, having an ammoniacal aromatic odour. *Ibid.* 148 *Heptylene is a colourless mobile liquid, having a peculiar alliaceous odour. **1873** *Fownes' Chem.* (ed. 11) 607 Another heptyl alcohol was separated from fusel oil. **1877** WATTS *Fownes' Chem.* (ed. 12) II. 59 **Heptene*, or *Heptylene*..also called *œnanthylene*..occurs in the light oils from Boghead and Cannel tar. **1877** WATTS *Fownes' Chem.* (ed. 12) II. 64 *Heptine, or œnanthidene, is formed by the action of potash on œnanthidene dibromide. **1880** *W. A. Miller's Elem. Chem.* (ed. 6) 196 When the isomeric paraffins, normal heptene, ethyl-isoamyl..are treated with chlorine, mono-chlorinated paraffins are produced. **1889** MUIR & MORLEY *Watts' Dict. Chem.* II. 676/1 Heptenoic acid $C_7H_{12}O_2$. **1928** *Chem. Abstr.* XXII. 5909 (*index*) Heptanoic acid. See Enanthic acid. **1948** A. W. RALSTON *Fatty Acids* ii. 86 None of the heptenoic acids has been identified in the naturally occurring fats and oils. **1964** N. G. CLARK *Mod. Org. Chem.* xvi. 317 By heating the heptonic acid with hydriodic acid and red phosphorus, (n-)heptanoic acid is produced.

Heptanesian (-'niːsɪən, -'niːʃən), *a.* [f. Gr. Ἑπτάνησος Heptanesus, lit. 'the Seven Isles', the Ionian Isles.] Of or pertaining to the Ionian Isles.

1881 *Encycl. Brit.* XIII. 205/2 Since 1863 the whole Heptanesian territory has been incorporated with the kingdom of Greece.

heptarch ('hɛptɑːk), *sb.* [f. HEPTA- + Gr. -αρχος ruling, ruler: cf. HEPTARCHY and *tetrarch.*] A ruler of one of seven divisions of a country; one of the rulers of the Heptarchy.

1822 *Blackw. Mag.* XII. 410 Ere yet the bloody Heptarch had controll'd, Or yet Northumbria knew the Saxon's power. **1853** LANDOR *Popery* xi. 33.

†**b.** A seventh king: with reference to Rev. xvii. 9–11. *Obs.*

1679 HARBY *Key Script.* II. 27 The Secular successive Heptarch of the Apostacy of Antichrist.

So **hep'tarchal**, **hep'tarchic**, **hep'tarchical** *adjs.*, of or pertaining to a heptarchy, esp. to the Anglo-Saxon Heptarchy. †**'heptarchist** = HEPTARCH.

1782 WARTON *Hist. Kiddington* (1783) 48 In 752, the Saxon heptarchists, Cuthred and Ethelbald, fought a desperate battle at Beorgford, or Burford. *Ibid.* 69 The Saxons practised this mode of fixing the several extents of their heptarchic empire. **1854** *Fraser's Mag.* XLIX. 152 We should return to the heptarchical regime of local self-government. **1859** C. BARKER *Assoc. Princ.* i. 7 Many of the heptarchal kings..exchanging the crown for the cowl. **1874** STUBBS *Const. Hist.* I. vii. 171 The heptarchic king was as much stronger than the tribal king, as the king of united England was stronger than the heptarchic king.

heptarch ('hɛptɑːk), *a.* *Bot.* [f. Gr. ἑπτά seven + ἀρχή beginning, origin: cf. DIARCH, MONARCH, OCTARCH, POLYARCH, TETRARCH, TRIARCH *adjs.*]

Arising from seven distinct points of origin, as the xylem of the root of some plants.

1884 [see DECARCH *a.*]. **1914** M. DRUMMOND tr. *Haberlandt's Physiol. Plant Anat.* vii. 353 (*caption*) The heptarch radial bundle [*sc.* stele] of an adventitious root. **1951** MCLEAN & IVIMEY-COOK *Textb. Theoretical Bot.* I. xx. 791 Dicotyledons usually have two..four..or five xylem groups, less frequently three (triarch) or seven (heptarch), and rarely more.

heptarchy ('hɛptɑːkɪ). [ad. mod.L. *heptarchia*, f. Gr. ἑπτά HEPTA- + -αρχία sovereignty, empire, after *tetrarchy.*] A government by seven rulers; an aggregate of seven districts or petty kingdoms, each under its own ruler; *spec.* the

seven kingdoms reckoned to have been established by the Angles and Saxons in Britain.

The term appears to have been introduced by 16th c. historians, in accordance with their notion that there were seven Angle and Saxon kingdoms so related that one of their rulers had always the supreme position of King of the Angle-kin (*Rex gentis Anglorum*), 'so that in the Heptarchy itself there seems always to have been a Monarchy' (Camden). The correctness and propriety of the designation have been often called in question, but its practical convenience has preserved it in use. See, besides the authors quoted, HALLAM *Middle Ages* (1878) II. viii. I. 270, 354–6; SIR J. MACKINTOSH *England* (1846) I. ii. 31; *Penny Cycl.* IX. 406; FREEMAN *Norm. Conq.* I. ii. 22; STUBBS *Const. Hist. Eng.* I. vii. 169; EDITH THOMPSON *Hist. Eng.* ii. §2.

1576 LAMBARDE *Peramb. Kent* 1 The exposition of this Map of the English *Heptarchie*, or seauen Kingdomes. *Ibid.* 5. [**1586** CAMDEN *Britannia* 48 (*marg.* Monarchia semper in Anglorum Heptarchia) Postquam enim in Britanniæ possessione pedem firmassent, in septem regna distribuerunt, Heptarchiamque constituerunt..tamen..ut Monarchiam in ipsa Heptarchia semper fuisse videatur. (See quot. 1610.)] **1592** STOW *Annales of Eng.* 63 Vntill the time that this *Heptarchie*, or Gouernement of seuen, was reduced to a Monarchie, or regiment of one. **1602** WARNER *Alb. Eng.* Epit. (1612) 360 The Saxon Heptarchia or their seuen Kingdomes. **1610** HOLLAND *Camden's Brit.* 135 After that these nations above said, had now gotten sure footing in the possession of Britain, they diuided it into seuen kingdomes, and established an Heptarchie. **1614** SELDEN *Titles Hon.* 30 In that Heptarchie of our Saxons, vsually six of the Kings were but as subiects to the supreme. **1638** SIR T. HERBERT *Trav.* (ed. 2) 308 Almeyda in despight of her united Heptarchy landed here [Ceylon] Anno Dom. 1506. **1641** MILTON *Reform.* II. (1851) 53 Hee ought to suspect a Hierarchy to bee as dangerous and derogatory from his Crown as a Tetrarchy or a Heptarchy. **1700** DRYDEN *Palamon & Arcite* III. 291 The next returning planetary hour Of Mars, who shared the heptarchy of power. **1774** WARTON *Hist. Eng. Poetry* (1775) I. 5 The inhabitants of Cornwall..remained partly in a state of independence during the Saxon heptarchy. **1799–1805** S. TURNER *Anglo-Sax.* (1836) I. III. v. 195 Ceawlin..changed the Saxon octarchy into a temporary heptarchy. **1812** CANNING *Sp. Ho. Comm.* 3 Feb. (Hansard ser. I. XXI. 530) Repeal the Union! Restore the Heptarchy as soon! the measure itself is simply impossible. **1834** PEEL *Ibid.* 25 Apr. (ser. III. XXIII. 69). **1851** KELLY tr. *Cambrensis Eversus* III. 301 In England there was a heptarchy, but in Ireland a pentarchy. **1885** *Pall Mall G.* 29 June 12 Australia is now only waiting for an Enabling Bill in order to form a Federal Council, the inevitable germ of an Australian heptarchy.

heptasyllabic (ˌhɛptəsɪˈlæbɪk), *a.* (*sb.*) [f. Gr. ἑπτασύλλαβ-ος of seven syllables (f. ἑπτά HEPTA- + συλλαβή SYLLABLE) + -IC.] Containing or consisting of seven syllables. **b.** *sb.* A verse or metrical line of seven syllables.

a **1771** GRAY *Corr.* (1843) 256 With Heptasyllabics mixed at pleasure. **1885** SIR P. PERRING *Hard Knots* 78 What is admitted in a decasyllabic line, must be admitted in a heptasyllabic. **1889** SWINBURNE *B. Jonson* 56 His use of the sweet and simple heptasyllabic metre.

So **hepta'syllable** (*rare*), a word or metrical line of seven syllables.

1758 BORLASE *Cornwall* 296 It is the Trochaic Heptasyllable, otherwise called the Trochaic Diameter Catalectic.

Heptateuch (ˈhɛptətjuːk). [ad. Gr. ἑπτάτευχος, f. ἑπτά seven + τεῦχος a book.] A volume consisting of seven books; a name sometimes given to the first seven books of the Bible, treated as a section having some historical unity; on the analogy of *Pentateuch*, the recognized name of the first five books.

1678 *Lively Orac.* IV. xxi. 291 Let her learn..the Heptateuch, or books of Moses, Joshua, and Judges. **1727–41** CHAMBERS *Cycl.*, *Heptateuch*, in matters of literature, a volume, or work consisting of seven books. **1798** W. TAYLOR in *Monthly Rev.* XXVII. 217 The Anglo-Saxon Heptateuch published by Thwaites, at Oxford, in 1698. **1819** SOUTHEY in *Q. Rev.* XXII. 71 Some one was to read aloud, from the Collations of Cassian, the lives of the Fathers, or some other edifying book, but not the Heptateuch, nor the other historical books of the Old Testament.

heptene, heptine, heptoic, heptyl, -ylic, etc. *Chem.*: see under HEPTANE.

heptode (ˈhɛptəʊd). *Radio.* [f. HEPT(A- + -ODE.] A valve with seven electrodes. Also *attrib.*

1932 *Post Office Electr. Engin. Jrnl.* XXIV. IV. 299/2 A complete electrode assembly of this type includes seven electrodes—hence the name 'Heptode' for the double-acting balanced thermionic valve. **1934** *Times* 11 Aug. 7/3 The days when one could speak simply of a screen-grid valve or a pentode are almost gone, for now there are in general use the double-diode-triode, the heptode, and many others with a double and even treble purpose. **1942** *Electronic Engin.* XIV. 629 The frequency changer follows normal practice..a separate triode with hexode or heptode comprising the local oscillator. **1943** *Gloss. Terms Telecomm.* (*B.S.I.*) 30 *Heptode*, a vacuum tube with seven electrodes normally comprising a hexode with an auxiliary anode between the first grid and the first screen grid or with a suppressor grid between the second screen grid and the (main) anode. **1945** *Electronic Engin.* XVII. 648 A circuit composing a heptode oscillator.

heptose: see HEPTA-.

heptoxide: see HEPTA-.

hep-tree: see HIP².

†**her, here,** *sb. poetic. Obs.* Forms: 1 **hearra, herra, hærra,** 3 **herre, hærre,** *north.* and *Sc.* 4–5 **her,** 5–6 **here,** (5 **heere, hery,** 6 **hair, heir, heyr**). [OE. *herra, hearra*, corresp. to OFris. *hêra*, OS. *hêrro* (MDu. *herre, hêr(r)e*, Du. *heer*), OHG. *hêrro* (MHG. *hêrre, herre*, Ger. *herr*), ON. *harri, herra* (Sw., Da. *herre*). In OHG. and OS., a subst. use of the comparative degree *hêr(o)ro* of the adj. *hêr* 'old', hence 'venerable, august', mod.Ger. *hehr* 'sublime, elevated, august, holy', identical with OE. *hár* hoary, grey, ON. *hárr*:—OTeut. **hairo-* prob. 'hoary with age, venerable'; supposed to have been first used as a form of address to superiors: cf. the Romanic use of L. *senior*, in It. *signore*, Sp. *señor*, F. *seigneur* 'lord', orig. 'older, elder'. Both in OE. and ON. adopted from OLG.; in OE. found orig. in the parts of the 'Cædmon' poems which are transliterated from an OS. original; also in later OE. and ME. poetry, and in Sc. to 16th c. Apparently only in poetical use.]

Lord, chief, master; man of high position or rank; sometimes more generally = Man.

a **1000** *Cædmon's Gen.* 521 Þe sende waldend god þin hearra þæs helpe of heofonrice. *Ibid.* 678 Nu hæbbe ic his her on handa, herra se goda; ȝife ic hit þe ȝeorne. *c* **1067** *Poem* in *O.E. Chron.* (MS. C.) an. 1066 Se in alle tid hyrde holdlice hærran sinum. *c* **1205** LAY. 5420 For þu ært ure hærre. **1297** R. GLOUC. (1724) 102 Þis lond ich habbe here so fre, þat to non herre y schal abuye. *a* **1400–50** *Alexander* 1920 All þe hathils & þe heris & þe hiȝe maistris. *c* **1400** *Destr. Troy* 10146 Antenour in angur angardly stroke, Vnhorset the here, hade hym to ground. *c* **1470** HENRY *Wallace* VII. 41 Arnwlff..Off South hantoun, that huge hie her and lord. **1500–20** DUNBAR *Poems* lxxxi. 29, I sa ane heir in bed oppressit ly. **1513** DOUGLAS *Æneis* V. vi. 8 Thiddir the heir [Æneas] with mony thowsand gan hy. *Ibid.* xii. 70 Ane of the eldest herys stude about, Clepit Nautes. **1530** LYNDESAY *Test. Pap.* 338 Thov arte bot kyng of bone, Frome tyme thyne hereis hartis bene from ye gone.

Hence †**here-man**, lord, master.

a **1400–50** *Alexander* 4938 A! A! happy haly here man.

†**her,** *poss. pron., 3rd pl. Obs.* Forms: see below. [OE. *hiera, hira*; *hyra, hiora, hiara, heora*, gen. pl., in all genders, of HE; cognate with OFris. *hiara, hira*, MDu. *hare* (*haerre, haer*), *hore, heur*, Du. *haar*; parallel in inflexion to OS. *iro, ira, ire, era*, OHG. *iro* (MHG. *ire, ir*, Ger. *ihr, ihrer*), Goth. *izê, izô*. In ME. (like the gen. sing. *his, hire*), treated as a possessive adj., though with fewer traces of inflexion than *his*. It also developed the absolute forms *heoren, heren*, HERN², and *hires, heres*, HERS² (now both *obs.*). Already in Ormin, the use of *heore, here*, was encroached upon by that of *þeȝȝre* from Old Norse, which, in the form *thair*, the northern texts of Cursor Mundi, Hampole, etc. have exclusively; Chaucer and other southern and south-midland writers retained *her*; Caxton, like Ormin, had both *her* and *their*; but *their* appears to have prevailed before 1500, and *her* has long disappeared even from the dialects which retain the cognate dat.-accus. *hem, 'em*.]

A. Forms.

α. 1 **hiera, hira, hiora, hiara, heara,** 1–2 **hyra, heora,** 2 **hera.**

c **855** *O.E. Chron.* (Parker MS.) an. 449 On hiera daȝum Hengest and Horsa..ȝesohton Bretene. *c* **898** *Ibid.* an. 894 Hiora cyning wæs ȝewundod. *Ibid.* an. 896 Þa Deniscan hæfdon hira wif befæst. *a* **950** *Durham Ritual* (Surtees) 48 In hiara ȝimersvnge ȝifeaiȝa. *c* **950** *Lindisf. Gosp.* Matt. vi. 5 Onfengon mearde heara [*Rushw.* heora lean, *Ags.* hyra mede, *Hatton* heore mede]. *c* **1000** *Ags. Gosp.* Matt. iv. 6 Hiȝ þe on hyra handum beron. *a* **1100** *O.E. Chron.* an. 1090 [Hi] aȝefon hera castelas him to hearme. *a* **1131** *Ibid.* an. 1125 Heora liman, þæt wæs here elces riht hand and heora stanen beneðan. *c* **1160** *Hatton Gosp.* Matt. iv. 6 On heora hande. *c* **1205** LAY. 420 He heora monredne mid monscipe onfeng.

β. 1–5 **heore, here,** 2–3 **hore,** 2–4 **hare,** 3–5 **hire, hure,** (3 **huere,** 4–5 **hyre**).

a **1100** *O.E. Chron.* (Laud MS.) an. 979 Heore rædas syndon nahtlice onȝean Godes ȝeþeaht. *a* **1131** *Ibid.* an. 1123 ¶2 Hi..wæron æfre toȝænes muneces and here reȝol. *a* **1175** *Cott. Hom.* 225 Þine þreo sunes..and hare þreo wif. *c* **1175** *Lamb. Hom.* 75 Hore loking, hore blawing, hore smelling, heore feling wes al iattret. *c* **1200** ORMIN Ded. 86 Acc nohht þurrh skill, acc all þurrh niþ, & all þurrh þeȝȝre sinne; & unnc birrþ biddenn Godd tatt he Forrȝife hemm here sinne. *Ibid.* 407, & shulenn habbenn heore læn Forr heore rihhtwisnesse. *c* **1200** *Trin. Coll. Hom.* 155 Hure riht time þenne man fasten shal. *c* **1205** LAY. 22843 Þa wifmen..kerueð of hire neose [*c* **1275** hure nose]. *a* **1225** *Ancr. R.* 70 Hit is hore meister. *a* **1300** *Geste K. Horn* 9 in Ritson *Metr. Rom.* II. 91 Huere sone hihte Horn. *a* **1300** *Assump. Virg.* (Camb. MS.) 713 Boþe here feet & here handes Where bounde with stronge bandes. **1340** *Ayenb.* 35 Ham þet habbeþ onworþ to lene of hire hand ac hi doþ lene hare sergons oþer oþre men of hire pans. **1362** LANGL. *P. Pl.* A. Prol. 41 Til heor Bagges and heore Balies weren bratful I-crommet. *c* **1380** *Sir Ferumb.* 2277 Hure helmes þay duden oppon hure hod. *c* **1385** CHAUCER *L.G.W.* 138 (Fairf.) This was hire [*v. rr.* here, her, hir, theyr, thair] song, 'the foweler we deffye'. **1387** TREVISA *Higden* (Morris *Spec. E.E.* 338) Chyldern in scoles..buþ compelled for to leve here oune longage, & for to construe here lessons & here þingis a Freynsch. *c* **1420** *Chron. Vilod.* 69 Ye Danys..chesen hure place Ryȝt at hure owne wyll. *Ibid.* 871 Ryȝt at hurre wyll. *Ibid.* 1059 Herre song þey lafton and songon nomore. **1426** AUDELAY *Poems* 17 The lust of hore lycam. *c* **1440** *Gesta Rom.* ii. 6 (Harl. MS.) Whenne the seruauntis hirde hire lord crye. **1482** *Monk of Evesham* (Arb.) 15 Lyke as they deserue here in this world by here lyuyng.

β. ². (?) Inflected forms. ? *a* **1123** *O.E. Chron.* an. 1101 For heoran aȝenan mycelan unȝetrywðan. *Ibid.* an. 1119 Þa tweȝen cyngas innan Normandiȝe mid heoran folcan coman toȝædere. *c* **1175** *Lamb. Hom.* 101 Heo setteð heoran handan ofer ifulȝ ede men.

γ. 2–4 **heor,** 2–5 **her, har,** (3 **ar**), 3–5 **hor, hur,** (5 **hurr**), 4–5 **hir, hyr.**

a **1154** *O.E. Chron.* an. 1135 Þa tocan þa oðre and helden her castles aȝenes him. *Ibid.* an. 1140 ¶7 [Hi] treuthes fæston ðæt her nouþer sculde besuiken other. *a* **1175** *Cott. Hom.* 227 Har non neste wat oðer cweð. *Ibid.*, þa..com se deofel to har anlicnesse. *c* **1200** *Trin. Coll. Hom.* 141 Hur eiðer alumð þe se. *c* **1250** *Meid Maregrete* xiii, Ðe sergaunz deden ar ernde. *c* **1275** *St. Patrick's Purg.* 168 in Horstm. *Altengl. Leg.* (1875) 3if þu wolt leue on hor lore. **1297** R. GLOUC. (1724) 398 Hii, þat myȝte ofscape, sone her red nome. *c* **1330** R. BRUNNE *Chron. Wace* (Rolls) 5046 He..loude ascried þem on har cry. *c* **1340** HAMPOLE *Prose Tr.* (1866) 24 Of hem silfe and of hir sugettis. **1362** LANGL. *P. Pl.* A. I. 97 Dauid..Dude hem swere on heor swerd to serue treuþe euere. *c* **1380** WYCLIF *Sel. Wks.* III. 153 To spoyle hor tenauntis and hor neghtboris. *c* **1386** CHAUCER *Prol.* 32, I was of hir [*v. rr.* here, her] felaweshipe anon. *c* **1420** *Chron. Vilod.* 12 To wex þe Bretones for hurr synne. *c* **1460** *Launfal* 232 Har kerteles wer of Inde sandel. **1480** CAXTON *Chron. Eng.* ccxli. (1482) 270 Hyr armure..and al was whyte hertes with crounes aboute hyr nekkes. **1485** —— *St. Wenefr.* 3 Her fader & moder cam & sawe how her doughter was biheded.

B. Signification and uses.

1. *Genitive case* of *Pers.* and *Refl. pron.*: Of them (L. *eorum*); of themselves. (In quot. *a* 1225 with *of.*)

c **825** *Vesp. Psalter* v. 10 [9] Forðon nis in muðe heara soðfestnis; heorte heara idel is. *a* **900** *O.E. Chron.* (Parker MS.) an. 875 Ælfred cyning..hiera an ȝefeng, ond þa oþru ȝefliemde. *Ibid.* an. 895 Þa burȝware hie ȝefliemdon, ond hira moniȝ hund ofsloȝon. *a* **1131** *Ibid.* an. 1123 ¶4 Þæh hit wære here unþancas. *c* **1200** ORMIN 471 Whillc here shollde serrfenn firrst. *c* **1200** *Trin. Coll. Hom.* 121 Ure drihten..lokede gif here ani understoden. *Ibid.* 213 Þesse wise biswikeð her aið er oðer. *a* **1225** *Ancr. R.* 176 3if nouðer of hore nere sec.

2. *Possessive adj. pron.* (orig. *possess. genitive*): Belonging to them; their; also *refl.* belonging to themselves, their own (L. *suus*).

917 *O.E. Chron.* (Parker MS.) an. 917 And ahreddon..eac hira horsa and hira wæpna micelne dæl. *a* **1100** *Ibid.* (Laud MS.) an. 1016 ¶9 Swa heora ȝewuna wæs. *a* **1121** *Ibid.* (Laud MS.) an. 1119 Maneȝa..mid heora castelan. *a* **1175** *Cott. Hom.* 221 Þat ece fer þe ham ȝearcod was fer hare prede. *c* **1200** *Trin. Coll. Hom.* 35 Ure helende com to helen men of heore symounden. **1382** WYCLIF *Matt.* vi. 5 Trewly y say to ȝou, thei han resseyued her meede. *c* **1386** CHAUCER *Prol.* 11 So priketh hem nature in hir corages. **1482** MARG. PASTON in *Paston Lett.* No. 865 III. 293 They withholde her catell and hem selfe bothe from the coorte.

b. Construction with *all*, *both*: *her aller*, *her bother*, *her beyre*, etc.: see ALL D. 4, BOTH 4 b, BO *a.* c.

3. After a *sb.*, as substitute for genitive inflexion.

c **893** K. ÆLFRED *Oros.* I. i. §4 Affrica and Asia hiera landȝemircu onginnað of Alexandria.

4. *Absolutely.* Afterwards expressed by HERS², and now by THEIRS. (F. *le leur*, Ger. *der ihrige*).

c **897** K. ÆLFRED *Greg. Past.* xliv. 319 Ða ðe hiera mildheortlice sellað. *c* **1000** *Ags. Gosp.* Matt. v. 10 Hyra [*Hatt.* heora] ys heofonan rice. *a* **1225** *Ancr. R.* 78 [He] foluwede ham, ase hore, hwuder so heo euer wolden. **1340** *Ayenb.* 144 Þe kingdom of heuene is hare.

her (hɜː(r), hə(r)), *pers. pron., 3rd sing. fem., dat.-accus.* Forms: 1–5 **hire,** (1 **hir**), 2–5 **hyre,** (3 **heore**), 3–5 **here,** (5 **heer**), 3–6 **hir,** 4–5 **hure,** 5 **hurre,** 5–6 **hyr,** 5–8 (*dial.*) **hur,** (6 **hare, harre**), 4– **her.** [OE. *hire*, dative case of *hio*, HEO 'she', cogn. with OFris. *hiri*, MDu. *hare, haer, hore*, Du. *haar*; cf. also the parallel OS. *iru*, OHG. *iru*, *iro* (mod.G. *ihr*), Goth. *izai*. The dative began in 10th c. to be used instead of the original accusative *híe, hí, híȝ, hý*, and now as indirect and direct objective represents both cases, as in 'we met *her* and gave *her* the book to take with *her*'.]

1. The female being in question: the objective case of SHE.

a. *Dative* or *indirect object.*

a **1000** *Elene* 963 (Z.) Gode þancode..þæs hire se willa ȝelamp. *c* **1000** *Ags. Gosp.* Matt. xiv. 7 Þa behet he mid aþe hyre [*Lindisf.* hir, *Rushw.* hire, *Hatton* hire] to syllenne. *a* **1154** *O.E. Chron.* an. 1140 ¶8 [Hi] brohten hire into Oxenford, and iauen hire þe burch. *a* **1175** *Cott. Hom.* 227 Se aengel cydde hyre þat godes sune sceolde been acenned of hire. *c* **1205** LAY. 3998 Þa deæde [sune] heore wæs leouere, þe quike here wes leoðere. **1297** R. GLOUC. (1724) 30 Þe fader..bad hire vnderstonde, To whom heo wolde y maried be. **1340–70** *Alex. & Dind.* 562 Hure was lecherie luf. **1362** LANGL. *P. Pl.* A. II. 1 Yit kneled I on my knees and cried hire of grace. *c* **1420** *Chron. Vilod.* 395 Hurre was lever to her' maytoynesse and masse. **1567** *Satir. Poems Reform.* iii. 74 Full weill was hir that day that sho was fre. **1642** ROGERS *Naaman* 498 To goe and doe as her listeth. **1712–14** POPE *Rape Lock* IV. 130 'Give her the hair'—he spoke, and rapp'd his box. **1847** TENNYSON *Princess* IV. 77 O Swallow..tell her, tell her, what I tell to thee. **1870** ROSSETTI *Blessed*

Damozel, Her seemed she scarce had been a day One of Gods choristers.

b. Governed by *preposition*.

c **1000** *Ags. Gosp.* John xx. 16 Da cwæð se hælend to hyre [*Lindisf.* hir, *Hatton* hire], maria. *a* **1075** *O.E. Chron.* (MS. C.) an. 1035 [He] let niman of hyre ealle þa betstan gærsuma ..þe Cnut cing ahte. *c* **1300** *Beket* 25 Of hire he hadde lute blisse. *c* **1330** R. BRUNNE *Chron.* (1810) 107 With hir went many a knyght. *c* **1400** *Rom. Rose* 2459 If thou myght Atteyne of hire to have a sight. *c* **1400** *Destr. Troy* 11006 When he neighed hur negh. **1556** *Chron. Gr. Friars* (Camden) 70 He had ij childerne by harre. *Ibid.* 72 The fayryst lady that she hade wyth hare..was stolne away from hare. **1634** MILTON *Comus* 264 I'll speak to her And she shall be my queen. **1712–14** POPE *Rape Lock* II. 6 But ev'ry eye was fix'd on her alone. **1864** TENNYSON *Enoch Arden* 474 And others laugh'd at her and Philip too.

c. *Accusative* or *direct object*.

c **975** *Rushw. Gosp.* Matt. i. 25 And ne groette hire [*Ags. G.* he ne grette hi]. *Ibid.* xxii. 28 Alle hæfdun hire [*Lindisf.* ða ilca, *Ags.* hiȝ, *Hatton* hy]. *a* **1131** *O.E. Chron.* an. 1127 He..sende hire siððen to Normandi; and mid hire ferde hire broðer Rotbert eorl of Gleucestre. *a* **1154** *Ibid.* an. 1140 ⁊ 8 þe king..besæt hire in þe tur; and me læt hire dun on niht of þe tur mid rapes. *c* **1275** LAY. 1146 þe deouel hire [*c* **1205** heo] louede. **1297** R. GLOUC. (1724) 12 Y ȝeue here þe to þi wyf. *c* **1400** *Apol. Loll.* 39 If ani of prestis..leuiþ not heer þat he holdiþ. *c* **1400** *Destr. Troy* 10976 He gird hir to ground, and greuit hir yll. **1556** *Chron. Gr. Friars* (Camden) 72 Dyvers lordes and ladys browte hare on hare way. **1621** QUARLES *Div. Poems, Esther* v, He observed her; He sent for ..dainty Myrrh. **1735** POPE *Ep. Lady* 137 Offend her, and she knows not to forgive; Oblige her, and she'll hate you while you live. **1842** TENNYSON *Day Dream, Arrival* iv, He stoops—to kiss her—on his knee.

2. For names of things grammatically feminine, or (in later use) feminine by personification.

c **825** *Vesp. Psalter* xxiii. 1 Earðe..and alle ða eardiað in hire. *c* **1000** ÆLFRIC *Manual of Astron.* (Wrt.) 18 þære lyfte ȝecynd is þæt heo sycð ælcne wætan up to hyre. *c* **1175** *Lamb. Hom.* 19 Al þet þe licome luueð, þet þa saule heteð, and wa is hire þer fore. *c* **1290** *S. Eng. Leg.* I. 312/449 Al so þe sonne, þat heo mouwe schyne a-boute eche on, For alle habbez liȝt of hire, and with-oute hire nouȝt on. *c* **1320** *Cast. Love* 96 þe corþe..And al þat euere in hire bi-lyþ. *c* **1394** *P. Pl. Crede* 668 And syþen þe sely soule slen & senden hyre to helle! *a* **1400–50** *Alexander* 1308 Bretens doun all þe bild..Drenches hire in þe hiȝ e see & drawis hire on hepis. **1538** STARKEY *England* I. iii. 78 Our mother the ground..wyl suffycyently nurysch..al bestys, fyschys, and foulys, wych are brede and brought vp apon hyr. **1598** W. PHILIPS *Linschoten* (1864) 187 They pray like-wise to the New Moone..and salute her with great Deuotion. **1738** POPE *Epil. Sat.* I. 143–4 Vice is undone, if she forgets her Birth ..'tis the Fall degrades her to a Whore; Let Greatness own her, and she's mean no more. **1827** KEBLE *Chr. Y., SS. Simon & Jude* i, The widowed Church is fain to rove.. Make haste and take her home.

b. Represented as used by Welsh or Gaelic speakers for *he, him*, or for the speaker himself.

1526 *Hundr. Merry T.* xcii. (1866) 150 By cottes blut and her nayle, quod the welchman, if her [a cock] be not ynough now her wyll be ynough anone for her hath a good fyre vnder her. **1657** H. CROWCH *Welsh Trav.* 3 Bid her, and other such like men. **1671** *Welsh Trav.* 31 in Hazl. *E.P.P.* IV. 332 Poor Taffie fell immediately into a great deep pit. Had not a shepherd stood his friend, and helpt hur quickly out, Hur surely there had made an end, Hur makes no other doubt. **1828** SCOTT *F.M. Perth* xxxiii, 'No offence meant', said the Highlander; 'but her own self comes to buy an armour.' 'Her own self's bare shanks may trot hence with her', answered Henry. **1893** STEVENSON *Catriona* 163 It will be made by a bogle and her wanting ta heid upon his body.

3. *Reflexive*: = herself; to herself. (Now *poetic*.)

c **1000** ÆLFRIC *Gen.* xxi. 16 Heo..sæt hire feorran. *Ibid.* xxxviii. 23 Hæbbe hire þæt heo hafaþ. *c* **1200** ORMIN 2655 ȝho ras hire upp. *c* **1200** *Trin. Coll. Hom.* 47 Hie brohte þat child mid hire in to þe temple. *c* **1220** *Bestiary* 241 Ðe mire ..resteð hire seldum. **1340** *Ayenb.* 260 Hy hyre ssewеþ ine alle þe oþre boȝes. *c* **1374** CHAUCER *Compl. Mars* 56 He preyede her to haste her for his sake. *c* **1420** *Chron. Vilod.* 765 And badde her heyȝe, and make hurr' all redy. **1611** BIBLE *Gen.* xxi. 16 She went and sate her downe ouer against him. **1662** GERBIER *Princ.* 8 She..had no time to shift her. **1666–7** DRYDEN *Ann. Mirab.* ccxcvi, Like some shepherdess ..Who sate to bathe her by a river's side. **1858** KINGSLEY *Sappho* 20 Then peevishly she flung her on her face.

4. For the *nominative*; esp. in *predicate* after *be*, etc. = she. (Considered incorrect: cf. HIM, ME.)

1698 VANBRUGH *Prov. Wife* IV. iv, But if it prove her, all that's Woman in me shall be imploy'd to destroy her. **1840–1** DICKENS *Humphrey's Clock*, 'There was him and her a sitting by the fire. *Mod. dial. and colloq.* I am sure it was her that told me. No! it could not be her. Which is her? Her with the hat. Is that her coming?

5. ***her one*** = Sc. *her lane*: see ONE, LONE.

6. quasi-*sb.*: cf. SHE.

1646 CRASHAW *Poems* 137 Now, if time knows That her, whose radiant brows Weave them a garland of my vows. **1860** WHITTIER in *Westm. Gaz.* (1895) 2 Jan. 8/2, 'I have lost him. But I can never lose a her; the women are more pertinacious than the men'.

her (hɜː(r), hə(r)), *poss. pron.*, *3rd sing. fem.* Forms: 1 **hiere, hyre, (hyra)**, 1–5 **hire**, 3–5 **hyre, hure, hyr, (3–4 yr)**, 4–5 **hur, (5 hurre, here)**, 4–6 **hir**, 6 **hare, (are)**, 4– **her**. [OE. *hiere, hire*, genitive of *hío*, HEO 'she', cognate with OFris. *hiri*, MDu. *hare*, Du. *haar*. (Analogous to OS. *ira, iro, iru, ire*; OHG. *ira, iro*, MHG. *ire, ir*, Ger. *ihr*; Goth. *izôs*.) In OE. used both as an objective and possessive genitive: the former use became obs. in ME., and *hire* remained a possessive genitive, indistinguishable in use from a possessive adj., and is thus included in the same class with *my, thy, his, our, your, their*. Like these, it has developed an absolute form HERS[1], for which HERN[1] was also used in late ME., and still exists in some dialects.]

1. as *gen. case of pers. pron.*: Of her; of the feminine being or thing in question.

a **900** *O.E. Chron.* (Parker MS.) an. 878 Him to com þær onȝen Sumor sæte alle..ond Hamtun scir se dæl se hiere behinon sæ was. *a* **1225** *St. Marher.* 2 Ha iherde on euch half hire, hu me droh to deaðe cristes icorne. *a* **1310** in Wright *Lyric P.* 113 Y wolde nemne hyre to day, ant y dorste hire munne.

2. *Poss. adj. pron.* (orig. *poss. gen.*): Of or belonging to her; that woman's, that female's; also *refl.* of or belonging to herself, her own.

a **900** *O.E. Chron.* (Parker MS.) an. 888 Hire lic liþ æt Pafian. *c* **1000** *Ibid.* (MS. D.) an. 917 þær wæron eac ofslæȝene hire þeȝna feower. *a* **1100** *Ibid.* (Laud MS.) an. 1036 þæt Ælfȝifu Hardacnutes modor sæte on Winceastre mid þæs cynges huscarlum hyra suna. *c* **1175** *Lamb. Hom.* 3 Heo nomen þe assa and hire colt. **1297** R. GLOUC. (1724) 370 Mold yr name was. **1362** LANGL. *P. Pl.* A. I. 10 Ich was a-ferd of hire Face. **1382** WYCLIF *Luke* ii. 51 His modir kepte to gidere alle these wordis, beringe to gidere in hir herte. *c* **1420** *Chron. Vilod.* 298 þis hard hayre he wered hurre body nexst. *c* **1440** *Gesta Rom.* i. 3 (Harl. MS.) My wif..wolle hyde his body by hire beddys syde. **1490** CAXTON *Eneydos* vi. 27 She drewe theym to her part. **1556** *Chron. Gr. Friars* (Camden) 72 Shee went hare wayes. *Ibid.* 86 The qwenes grace came..are owne persone, with hare cepter in hare honde. **1569** J. ROGERS *Gl. Godly Loue* 181 As ritch as hir husband. **1712–14** POPE *Rape Lock* I. 19 Belinda still her downy pillow prest Her guardian Sylph prolong'd the balmy rest. **1808** SCOTT *Marm.* II. iii, Her hopes, her fears, her joys, were all Bounded within the cloister wall. *Mod.* Her sister offered her services.

†**b.** Used of things whose names were grammatically feminine, e.g. sun, soul, book, shire, love. *Obs.* **c.** Of things personified or spoken of as female; esp. the earth, the moon, countries, cities, ships, the Church, a university, a school, the arts, sciences, passions, virtues, vices.

c **825** *Vesp. Psalter* ciii [i]. 19 Sunne oncneow setgong hire [*c* **1000** *Ags. Ps.* (Th.), Sunne hire setlgang sweotule healdeð]. **1382** etc. [see CHURCH *sb.* 8]. **1413** *Pilgr. Sowle* (Caxton 1483) IV. vii. 61 Thenne ganne this fayre grene appel tree to shaken hyr leues. *c* **1489** CAXTON *Sonnes of Aymon* i. 21 A ryver..I beleve verely that in al christendome is not her lyke. **1502** in *Arnolde's Chron.* (1811) 223 That the chartur aforsaid in alle & euerych her articles. **1534** TINDALE *Luke* xiv. 34 Salt is good but yf salt have loste hyr saltnes what shall be seasoned ther with? **1535** COVERDALE *2 Chron.* v. 7 The prestes broughte the Arke..vnto hir place. **1559** W. CUNNINGHAM *Cosmogr. Glasse* 142 In whose myndе knoweledge have once builded her Bowre. *Ibid.* 149 The moone is xviij. daies old, the time of hir shining is x. houres. *Ibid.* 205 Englande, and hir principall cities. **1586** T. B. *La Primaud. Fr. Acad.* I. (1589) 612 There is nothing more common than the Sun, which imparteth of hir light to all the celestiall bodies. **1611** SHAKS. *Wint. T.* III. iii. 93 The Shippe boaring the Moone with her maine Mast. **1649** BLITHE *Eng. Improv. Impr.* (1653) 9 The Earth..and the principall causes of her Barrenness. **1700** DRYDEN *Palamon & Arc.* II. 595 The ruined house that falls And intercepts her lord betwixt the walls. **1821** SHELLEY *Epipsych.* 376 The Moon will veil her horn In thy last smiles. **1895** *Pall Mall G.* 7 Oct. 1/3 England..has tried her best to head him off.

d. Of animals regarded as feminine, irrespectively of sex; e.g. a cat, hare, rabbit, mouse, etc.

c **1220** *Bestiary* 242 Ðe mire..fecheð hire fode. *c* **1386** CHAUCER *Knt.'s T.* 634 The bisy larke messager of day Salueth in hir song the morwe gray. *a* **1400–50** *Alexander* 412 [With] þe wose of þe wede hire wengis anoyntis. **1535** COVERDALE *Prov.* vi. 6 Go to the Emmet (thou slogarde) considre hir wayes. **1607** TOPSELL *Four-f. Beasts* (1658) 210 The Weasil..hangeth fast upon her throat, and will not lose her hold, run the Hare never so fast. *Ibid.* 398 If a male Mouse be flead all over, or her tail cut off; or if her leg be bound to a post in the house, or a bell be hung about her neck, and so turned going, she will drive away all her fellows. **1642** ROGERS *Naaman* 97 The Bezor..knowing by instinct what it is she is hunted for (not her skin, but her stone).

3. After a *sb.*, a substitute for the genitive inflexion. Cf. the similar use of HIS, THEIR.

c **893** K. ÆLFRED *Oros.* I. i. §9 Nilus seo ea hire æwielme is neh þæm clife. *c* **1435** *Chaucer's Wife's T.* (MS. Camb. Gg. 4. 27) *heading*, Here begynnyt[h] the wyf of bathe hire tale. **1546** *State Papers* (1830) I. 889 Elizabeth Holland her howse, newlie made in Suffolk. **1579** LYLY *Euphues* (Arb.) 94 Curio..haunted Lucilla hir company. **1655** FULLER *Ch. Hist.* VIII. i. §5 Presuming on the Queen her private practice. **1659** H. L'ESTRANGE *Alliance Div. Off.* 455 The Excellency of our Church her burial office. [**1873** F. HALL *Mod. Eng.* 355 *note*, In England, to this day, the vulgar write, in their Bibles, Prayer-books, and elsewhere, 'John Crane his book', 'Esther Hodges her book', etc.]

†**4.** *absol.* = HERS[1] (= Ger. *der, die, das ihrige*).

c **1200** *Trin. Coll. Hom.* 49 Duue..fedeð briddes þeh hie ne ben noht hire. *a* **1225** *Ancr. R.* 46 Al is hire þet holi chirche redeð oþer singeð.

her, obs. form of HAIR, HERE, ERE, HIGHER.

Heraclean (hɛrəˈkliːən), *a.* [f. L. *Hĕraclē-us*, also *-clīus*, a. Gr. Ἡράκλειος, f. Ἡρακλῆς (see HERCULES): see -AN.] Pertaining to Heracles. ***Heraclean stone*** (*lapis Heraclēus*, λίθος Ἡρακλεία): the magnet, so called from its great attractive power.

1883 G. CHRYSTAL in *Encycl. Brit.* XV. 219/1 This name [magnet] is said by Plato to have been given to it by Euripides, and he adds that most call it the Heraclean stone. **1885** RUSKIN *Pleas. Eng.* 157 All ordinary architectural lion sculpture is derived from the Heraclean.

Heracleid, -id (ˈhɛrəklaɪd, -ɪd). Also **Heraklide.** [ad. Gr. Ἡρακλείδης (pl. -αι), L. *Heraclīdēs* (pl. -æ), a descendant of Ἡρακλῆς or Hercules.]

a. One of the descendants of Heracles from whom the Dorian aristocracy of the Peloponnesus claimed descent. (Chiefly in *pl.*)

1835 THIRLWALL *Greece* vii. I. 273 *heading*, Return of the Heracleids. *a* **1873** LYTTON *Pausanias* 203 The heart of the Heracleid beats under the robe of the Mede. **1892** *Athenæum* 16 July 92/1 An ode composed by a Theban in honour of a Heracleid.

b. A 'strong man'. *humorous nonce-use.*

1871 M. COLLINS *Mrq. & Merch.* II. i. 17 The Heraklide showed symptoms of becoming confidential.

c. A poem describing the exploits of Heracles.

1725 [see *Theseid* s.v. THESEAN *a.*]. **1904** T. R. GLOVER *Stud. Virgil* iii. 75 Poets who have composed a Herakleid, a Theseid, or other poems of the kind.

Hence **Heraˈcleidan** *a.*, of or pertaining to a Heracleid.

1821 BYRON *Juan* III. *Isles of Greece* xiii, And there, perhaps, some seed is sown, The Heracleidan blood might own.

Heracleonite (hɛˈrækliːənaɪt). *Eccl. Hist.* Also **-akl-.** [f. pers. name *Heracleon* + -ITE.] One of a sect of Gnostics founded by Heracleon in the second century.

a **1555** PHILPOT *Exam. & Writ.* (1842) 424 They do follow the old superstition of the Heracleonites. **1727–51** CHAMBERS *Cycl.* s.v., The Heracleonites, after the example of their master, annulled all the antient prophecies; holding, that St. John was really the voice that proclaimed and pointed out the Messiah. **1882–3** SCHAFF *Encycl. Relig. Knowl.* I. 789 Irenaeus simply says that the Herakleonites, a Gnostic sect, anointed the dying with a mixture of oil and water.

heracleum (hɛˈrækliəm, hɛrəˈkliːəm). *Bot.* [mod.L. (C. Linnæus *Systema Naturæ* 1735), f. Gr. Ἡρακλεία, the plant named after Heracles.]

A plant of a genus of large herbs of this name, belonging to the family Umbelliferæ and native to northern temperate regions; COW-PARSNIP or HOGWEED.

1787 W. WITHERING *Bot. Arrangem. Brit. Plants* (ed. 2) I. 287 Heracleum. **1824** J. E. SMITH *Eng. Flora* II. 101 Heracleum. Cow-parsnep. **1847** H. C. WATSON *Cybele Britannica* I. 451 This [*Angelica sylvestris*] and the Heracleum are the two most widely distributed species of their order. **1864** D. OLIVER *Less. Elem. Bot.* II. 175 (*caption*) Vertical section of flower of Common Heracleum. **1894** W. ROBINSON *Wild Garden* (ed. 4) xiii. 133 Such plants as Heracleum, Willow Herb, and many others..should be planted only in outlying positions. **1951** *Dict. Gardening* (R. Hort. Soc.) II. 986/1 The Heracleums are sometimes grown in shrubberies or the rougher parts of the pleasure grounds.

Heraclitean (ˌhɛrəklaɪˈtiːən), *a.* (*sb.*) Also **Heracleitean.** [f. L. *Hēraclītē-us*, Gr. Ἡρακλείτειος, pertaining to Hēraclītus + -AN.]

a. Of, pertaining to, or of the style of Heraclitus of Ephesus, a Greek philosopher of the 5th century B.C. (called the 'weeping philosopher'), or his physical or other theories.

1791 W. ENFIELD *Hist. Philos.* I. 443 Plato himself, when he was young, learned the Heraclitean philosophy from Cratylus, and adopted that part which treated of the nature and motion of matter. **1864** *Reader* No. 105. 824/1 Full of their Heraclitean fire. **1875** JOWETT *Plato* (ed. 2) I. 426 Beginning with the mysteries and the Heracleitean alternation of opposites. **1955** J. K. BAXTER *Fire & Anvil* 65 A Heracleitean cosmos.

b. *sb.* A disciple of Heraclitus.

1882 R. ADAMSON in *Encycl. Brit.* XIV. 784/2 The extreme Heracliteans, as Cratylus, rejected the proposition, or combination of words, as expressing a unity and permanence not to be found in things.

Hence **Heracliˈteanism**; also **Heracleitean-ism.**

1885 PATER *Marius* I. 133 Heracliteanism had grown to be almost identical with the famous doctrine of the sophist Protagoras. **1932** *Times Lit. Suppl.* 21 July 531/1 Professor Laird yet finds it in him to relax his comity when dealing with the epistemological Heracleiteanism of Gentile.

Heraclitic (hɛrəˈklɪtɪk), *a.* and *sb.* [f. *Hēraclītus* (see prec.) + -IC.] **A.** *adj.* = HERACLITEAN. **B.** *sb.* A follower of Heraclitus. So **Heraˈclitical** *a.*; **ˈHeraclitism** = HERACLITEANISM.

1678 CUDWORTH *Intell. Syst.* I. iii. §28. 133 That even the Zenonian and Heraclitick Deity it self, was no other than such a plastick nature. *Ibid.* iv. §31. 387 Singular and Sensible Things, which, as the Heracliticks rightly affirmed, do indeed all flow. *a* **1688** —— *Etern. Morality* II. ii. §1 (1731) 45 The true meaning of the Heraclitical Philosophy was plainly this, That there is no other being in the World besides Individual Body or Matter. **1788** *Chambers' Cycl.*, *Heraclitism*..the philosophy of Heraclitus..The fundamental doctrine..was, that fire is the principle of all things. **1882** R. ADAMSON in *Encycl. Brit.* XIV. 784/2 The Eleatic doctrine that only unity has real being, the Heraclitic counter-doctrine that only in change, in the many, is truth to be found.

herald (ˈhɛrəld), *sb.* Forms: (3 **hyraudus**), 4–5 **heraud, -e, herowd, -e, herode**, (4 **herrod, herhaud**), 5 **herrowd, heroud, herewde, herrold, har(r)awd, -e, harood, -ud, -ott, -owed, harrote,**

harrold, 5-6 herawde, herrald(e, harralde, harhalde, 5-7 herault, harrot, 5-8 herauld, -e, 6 her(e)hault, herehaut, herehaught(e, haraude, -aulde, -ald, -rald, -olde, -rolde, -rould, harhodde, harad, -at, -et, -rat, -ratt, -otte, 6-7 harolde, heralde, 7 heralt, -aute, -old, haralt; (5-6) 7- herald. [ME. *heraud, herault*, etc., representing OF. *heraut, herault*, med.L. *haraldus, heraldus*, It. *araldo*, Sp. *haraldo, heraldo*, OSp. *faraute*; a word of uncertain origin, generally conjectured to be from Teutonic. Diez suggested as a possible source an OGer. **hariwald*, **heriwald*, 'wielder' or 'commander of an army', citing the proper names *Chariovaldus*, OS. *Hariolt*, ON. *Haraldr*; but this seems to fail to explain the sense. Others have suggested a possible derivation from OHG. *harên, herên* to cry, call, which suits the sense better, but involves other difficulties. See Markel, *German. elem. in französisch* (1887) 62.]

1. a. An officer having the special duty of making royal or state proclamations, and of bearing ceremonial messages between princes or sovereign powers. Also, **b.** employed in the tourney to make proclamations, convey challenges, and marshal the combatants. Hence, **c.** having the function of arranging public processions, funerals, and other state ceremonials; of regulating the use of armorial bearings (cf. DISCLAIM *v.* 7); of settling questions of precedence in processions or at court; and, in process of time, of recording the names and pedigrees of those entitled to armorial bearings: see *Heralds' College* in f.

a. 13.. *Guy Warw.* (A.) 3323 At an herhaud þan asked he, 'This armed folk, what may [þis] be?' **13..** *Coer de L.* 428 He comaunded hastely Herodes for to make cry, And every man for to wende Home. **1375** BARBOUR *Bruce* XII. 371 Throu-out the hoost..gert thai ga Herrodis for till mak ane crye. **c 1386** CHAUCER *Knt.'s T.* 1675 An herowd [*v. rr.* heraud(e, herald] on a skaffold made a hoo..And when he sawh þe pepul of noyse al stille Thus schewid he þe mighty dukes wille. **? a 1400** *Morte Arth.* 3013 An hawrawde hyes be·fore, the best of the lordes. **a 1400-50** *Alexander* 883 Heraudis [*Dubl.* Harraldes] on heȝe hors hendly a-rayed. **c 1465** *Eng. Chron.* (1856) 46 He..sente heroudis to the toun [Rouen] and bad thaym yelde it to the kyng of Englond. **c 1489** CAXTON *Sonnes of Aymon* ix. 203 Thus departed the herawde from the oost of Charlemagne. **1513** DOUGLAS *Æneis* v. v. 3 With ane harraldis lowde voce. **1565** in Turner *Select. Rec. Oxf.* 316 Wyne for the Quenes Haroldes. *Ibid.*, The Quenes harrodes. **1565-73** COOPER *Thesaurus*, *Caduceator*,..an ambassadour or harold sent to intreat of peace. **1570** LEVINS *Manip.* 15/46 An herald for peace, *caduceator*. **1599** SHAKS. *Hen. V*, IV. vii. 59 Take a Trumpet Herald, Ride thou vnto the Horsemen on yond hill. **1604** R. CAWDREY *Table Alph.*, *Herault*, kings messenger. **1656** BLOUNT *Glossogr.*, Harold, Heralt or Herald. **1667** MILTON *P.L.* II. 518 The sounding Alchymie By Haralds voice explain'd. **a 1674** CLARENDON *Hist. Reb.* XVI. §245 His Majesty..sent it likewise by Garter, Herauld and King at Armes. **1727-51** CHAMBERS *Cycl.* s.v., In the army, drums and trumpets have succeeded to the function of heralds, being sent by the generals on the same errands; and.. enjoying the same rights and privileges. **1838** THIRLWALL *Greece* xiii. II. 161 A herald came to demand an armistice. **1875** JOWETT *Plato* (ed. 2) III. 121 Need we hire the herald, or shall I proclaim the result?

b. 1377 LANGL. *P. Pl.* B. XVIII. 16 Faith..cryde *a! fili dauid!* As doth an Heraude of armes whan [auntrous] cometh to iustes. **c 1386** CHAUCER *Knt.'s T.* 159 By here Cote Armures and by hir gere The heraudes knewe hem best in special. **a 1440** *Sir Eglam.* 1109 At morne when day sprange, Gentyl men to haruds thrange. **a 1450** *Le Morte Arth.* 341 Heraudis he dyd go and Ride Another turnamente for to Crye. **1485** CAXTON *Paris & V.* (1868) 7 [He] sente his herraulds..to announce that the jousts shold be halden. **c 1560** A. SCOTT *Poems* (S.T.S.) ii. 63 The harraldes cryd, 'God schaw the rycht,' Syne bad thame go to-gidder. **1593** SHAKS. *Rich. II*, I. iii. 6 (Stage dir.) Enter King..and others. Then Mowbray in Armor, and Harrold. *Ibid.* 25 Tucket. Enter Hereford, and Harold. **1820** SCOTT *Ivanhoe* viii, The Prince..gave signal to the heralds to proclaim the laws of the tournament.

c. c 1384 CHAUCER *H. Fame* III. 321 Pursevantes and heraudes That crien ryche folkes laudes..Had on him throwen a vesture Whiche that men clepen a cote armure. **a 1500** *Sir Beues* (Pynson) 3453 Euery syde Armes were hanged fayre and wyde, Herodes gan the armes escrye. **1530** PALSGR. 456/2 He can blase armes as well as any herault..in Englande. **1562** LEIGH *Armorie* Pref. (1597) A ij, They..are named ancient Herehaughtes, who haue made distinction betweene the gentle and the vngentle. **1572** N. ROSCARROCKE *Prelim. Verses to Bossewell's Armorie*, Ye perfit skil Of Herehauts art. **1592** NASHE *P. Penilesse* (ed. 2) 27 a, Buying Armes of the Herald, who giues them the Lyon without tongue, tayle, or tallents. **1592** GREENE *Upst. Courtier* in *Harl. Misc.* (Malh.) II. 217 The herralde to blason their descente from an old house. **1598** B. JONSON *Ev. Man in Hum.* I. iii, The first red herring that was broil'd in Adam and Eve's kitchen, doe I fetch my pedigree from by the Harrots bookes. **1663** WOOD *Life* (O.H.S.) I. 480 (Burial of Archbp. Juxon) Persons that came to attend the corps, wherof Garter King at armes was one and four more heralds. **1687** DRYDEN *Hind. & P.* III. 156 Do you not know that for a little coin Heralds can foist a name into the line? **1766** ENTICK *London* IV. 26 The six heralds are Windsor, Chester, Lancaster, York, Richmond, and Somerset, who take place according to seniority in office. **1844** DISRAELI *Coningsby* IV. iv, The heralds they pay to paint their carriages.

†**d.** Formerly called, with reference to some functions of the office, *herald of (at) arms*.

1377 [see b]. **c 1435** *Torr. Portugal* 2465 Harroldys of armes cryed on hight, The prynce and that other knyght No more juste shall thay. **c 1530** LD. BERNERS *Arth. Lyt. Bryt.* (1814) 34 Than was it cried by an haraude of armes, yᵗ eche of them should do theyr best. **1556** *Chron. Gr. Friars* (Camden) 50 There was made a proclamacyon with dyvers harhoddes of armes and pursevanttes in their cote armeres. **1569** *Nottingham Rec.* IV. 134 Gevyn to the haret of armes ..xxs. **1646** BP. MAXWELL *Burd. Issach.* in *Phenix* (1708) II. 296 The Lords of the Council..sent a Gentleman..with an Herald at Arms, to..dissolve their Meeting. **1727-51** CHAMBERS *Cycl.* s.v., Heralds, or heralds at arms.

†**e.** ***King herald, Lyon herald***: ancient names of Garter king-of-arms and Lyon king-of-arms: see KING-OF-ARMS.

[**c 1276** in Spelman *Gloss.* (1664) s.v. *Heraldus*, Petrus Rex Hyraudorum citra aquam de Trent ex parte boreali. **13..** *Statuta Armorum* Stat. Realm (1810) I. 231 E qe nul Roy des Haraunz ne Menestrals portent privez armez.] **c 1460** J. RUSSELL *Bk. Nurture* 1035 A herrowd of Armes as gret a dygnyte has, Specially kynge harrawd must haue þe principalle place. **1596** DALRYMPLE tr. *Leslie's Hist. Scot.* VII. 140 The King of Scotis..in haist directes Lyon harrat King of armes to the Jnglis King. *Ibid.* 142 The king..his lettres delyuiris to lyon Harratt, wrytne in verie sour and proud wordes.

f. ***Heralds' College***, or *College of Arms*: a royal corporation, founded 1483, consisting of the Earl Marshal, kings-of-arms, heralds, and pursuivants, exercising jurisdiction in matters armorial, and now recording proved pedigrees, and granting armorial bearings. ***Heralds' Office***, the office of this corporation.

1588 THYNNE *Let. Ld. Burghley* in *Animadv.* Introd. 91 The whoole colledge of hereaudes. **a 1655** in Cotgrave *Treas. Wit & Lang., Her.* 126 He is at the Heralds Office yondir. What, Has he purchas'd Arms then? **a 1661** FULLER *Worthies* (1840) I. 153 If it was his assigned and not hereditary coat, it will be long enough ere therald's office grant another. **1709** STEELE *Tatler* No. 11 ¶4, I shall give you my Genealogy, as a Kinsman of ours has sent it me from the Heralds-Office. **1869** ROGERS *Hist. Gleanings* I. 32 A parvenu pays the Heralds' College for a pedigree.

2. *transf.* and *fig.* **a.** One who proclaims or announces the message of another; a messenger, envoy. Hence, a frequent title of newspapers, as *The Morning Herald, Glasgow Herald*, etc.

1377 LANGL. *P. Pl.* B. XVI. 247 þus haue I [Abraham] ben his heraude here and in helle. **1467** SIR J. PASTON in *Paston Lett.* No. 570 II. 301, I alweys schall be your herault bothe her, if sche com hydder, and at home when I kome hom. **1588** SHAKS. *L.L.L.* v. ii. 97 Their Herald is a pretty knauish Page: That well by heart hath con'd his embassage. **1615** J. STEPHENS *Satyr. Ess.* 201 His tongue, the Herald of his imagination, is a busie Officer. **1641** J. JACKSON *True Evang. T.* III. 230, I finde our very enemies Prophets to foretell, and Heraulds to declare it, for us. **1781** COWPER *Charity* 136 A herald of God's love to pagan lands. **1836** EMERSON *Nature, Beauty* Wks. (Bohn) II. 149 Beauty in nature is not ultimate. It is the herald of inward and eternal beauty.

b. A person (or thing) that precedes and announces the approach of another; a forerunner, precursor.

1592 SHAKS. *Rom. & Jul.* III. v. 6 It was the Larke the Herauld of the Morne. **c 1600** —— *Sonn.* i, Only herauld to the gaudy spring. **1759** DILWORTH *Pope* 76 One of the most active heralds to his rising fame. **1802** WORDSW. *To the small Celandine* viii, Herald of a mighty band, Of a joyous train ensuing. **1878** HUXLEY *Physiogr.* 197 Earthquakes are often the heralds of volcanic eruptions. **1894** H. DRUMMOND *Ascent Man* 295 The Flower, botanically, is the herald of the Fruit.

3. One skilled in heraldry; a heraldist.

1821 SCOTT *Kenilw.* xii, 'With neck reguardant,' said the herald. **1880** WARREN *Book-plates* xii. 126 A print-collector, an ex-librist, and a herald.

4. (In full, ***herald-moth***). Name of one of the noctuid moths, *Gonoptera libatrix*.

1832 J. RENNIE *Butterfl. & Moths* 82 The Herald.. appears in April and end of July. **1843** DUNCAN in *Nat. Libr.* XL. 231 The Herald-moth..is..found plentifully in October, whence Aurelians have called it the Herald, from an idea that its appearance gave indication of the approach of winter.

5. *attrib.* and *Comb.*, as ***herald angel, star***, etc.; ***herald-vouched*** adj.; **herald-crab** = *heraldic crab*; **herald-moth**: see sense 4; **herald-painter** (see quot. 1688); **herald-snake**, the southern African snake, *Crotaphopeltis hotambœia, hotambœia*, which has red or yellow lips and is also called the red-lipped snake.

1646 G. DANIEL *Poems* Wks. 1878 I. 45, I neither boast, nor Skorne, a faire discent, Noble, and Herald-vouched Ancient. **1671** MILTON *P.R.* II. 279 Now the herald lark Left his ground-nest, high towering to descry The Morn's approach. **1688** R. HOLME *Armoury* III. 147/2 A Herald Painter is such as Paints Coats of Arms on Escochions, Shields, Tables, Penons, Standarts, and such like. **1728** POPE *Dunc.* II. 18 The Queen, to glad her sons, proclaims By herald Hawkers, high heroic Games. **1753** WHITFIELD *Hymn*, Hark, the herald Angels sing, Glory to the new-born King. **1771** GRAY *Corr. N. Nicholls* (1843) 127 Jean Froissart, son of Thomas, by profession a herald painter. **1808** SCOTT *Marm.* IV. xiv, The Herald-bard [Sir David Lyndesay, Lyon-King and poet]. **1850** TENNYSON *In Mem.* xxxviii, The herald melodies of spring. **1878** B. TAYLOR *Deukalion* IV. i. 137 No herald star announced my birth. **1910** F. W. FITZSIMONS *Snakes S. Afr.* iii. 57/2 The Red-lipped or Herald Snake..is one of the best-known and most widespread snakes in Africa. **1947** J. STEVENSON-HAMILTON *Wild Life S. Afr.* xxxvi. 330 The red-lipped or herald snake (*Leptodira hotamboea*).—This is distinguished by its upper lip being of bright red colour; it carries large light-brown scales and a black headband. **1970** V. F. M. FITZSIMONS *Field Guide to Snakes S. Afr.* 118 Herald or Red-lipped Snake.., according to the prevailing colour on the upper lips, it is variously known as the White- or Yellow-lipped Snake.

Hence **'heraldess**, a female herald. †**'heraldet**, a petty herald. **'heraldship**, the office or dignity of a herald.

1881 J. M. RODWELL *Isa.* 98 Zion, heraldess of joy, get thee up into a high mountain. **1890** G. A. SMITH *Isaiah* II. v. 85 The verses from *Behold your God*, to the end of the Prologue are the song of the heraldess. **1625** B. JONSON *Staple of N.* IV. i, *Fit.* Her grace's herald? *Alm.* No herald yet, a heraldet. **1613** SELDEN *Illustr. Drayton's Poly-olb.* iii, [Woden], being by name president of ways, and by his office of heraldship Pacifex, i.e. Peacemaker.

'herald, *v.* Forms: see sb.; also 4-5 **hiraude, hyraude.** [a. OF. *herauder, heraulder, hirauder*, f. *heraut, hiraut* HERALD *sb.*]

1. *trans.* To proclaim, to announce, as at hand or drawing nigh; to usher *in*, introduce.

c 1384 CHAUCER *H. Fame* III. 486 His clarioun..With which he wonde is to hiraude [*v. rr.* herawde, heraude, hyraude] Hem that me list preised be. **1605** SHAKS. *Macb.* I. iii. 102 Wee are sent, To giue thee from our Royall Master thanks, Onely to harrold thee into his sight, Not pay thee. **1631** R. H. *Arraignm. Whole Creature* XV. §3. 261 She must be..Heralded, proclaimed, Trumpetted, as the onely Paragon of her Sexe. **1810** SOUTHEY *Kehama* VII. v, The Orient..Kindles as it receives the rising ray, And heralding his way, Proclaims the presence of the Power divine. **1855** LONGF. *Hiaw.* ix. 126 And the heron..Heralded the hero's coming. **1869** PHILLIPS *Vesuv.* iii. 46 Six months of continued earthquakes..heralded the eruption. **1886** F. W. ROBINSON *Courting Mary Smith* II. 292 The new young day which the chimes of Coalsby had heralded in a few minutes ago.

†**2.** *intr.* To act as herald. *Obs. rare*$^{-0}$.

1530 PALSGR. 583/1, I herawde, I expresse the offyce of an herawde, *je haraude*.

Hence **'heralding** *vbl. sb.* and *ppl. a.*

1814 CARY *Dante, Paradise* XXVI. 42 [St John] who chief proclaim'st E'en at the outset of thy heralding..the mystery of heaven. **1860** TYNDALL *Glac.* I. xxvii. 211 The tempest.. I heard its heralding roar in the gullies of the mountains.

herald, corrupt form of HARELD.

heraldic (hə'rældɪk), *a.* [f. HERALD *sb.*, prob. after F. *héraldique* (15th c. in Hatz.-Darm.).]

1. Of or pertaining to heraldry. Also *fig.*

1772 WARTON *Life Sir T. Pope* 199 (T.) Heraldic surcoats of arms. **1774** —— *Hist. Eng. Poetry* I. 336 The pompous circumstances of which these heraldic narratives consisted, and the minute prolixity with which they were displayed. **1847** *Gloss. Heraldry* 10 The distinction between the heraldic antelope and the natural. **1887** MISS BRADDON *Like & Unlike* i, Rich in the heraldic history of aristocratic alliances.

2. ***heraldic crab***: a Japanese crab, *Huenia heraldica*, one of the *Maiadæ*: see quot.

1863 WOOD *Nat. Hist.* III. 568 The Heraldic Crab, so called because the shape of its carapace presents a fanciful resemblance to the shield and mantle employed by heraldic painters in depicting coat armour.

he'raldical, *a.* [f. as prec. + -AL¹.] = HERALDIC.

1610 GUILLIM *Heraldry* III. xvi. (1660) 201 Whose great study and travell in this Heraldicall Art, hath..been sufficiently manifest. **1814** D'ISRAELI *Quarrels Auth.* (1867) 491 High notions of the importance of heraldical studies.

he'raldically, *adv.* [f. prec. + -LY².] In a heraldic manner; according to the rules of heraldry.

1807 G. CHALMERS *Caledonia* I. II. vi. 299 *note*, The armorial bearings of Scotland, most heraldically displayed. **1879** J. C. COX *Ch. Derbysh.* IV. 236 The church was heraldically visited..by Sir William Dugdale.

heraldist ('hɛrəldɪst). [f. HERALD *sb.* + -IST.] One who is versed in heraldry.

1814 D'ISRAELI *Quarrels Auth.* (1867) 492 [The] excesses of his pen..show the insensibility of the mere heraldist to the nobler genius of the historian. **1896** *Bookseller's Catal.*, The result of..most painstaking labour of the celebrated Heraldist and Archæologist.

†**'heraldize**, *v. Obs.* [f. HERALD *sb.* + -IZE.] *trans.* To emblazon.

1630 J. TAYLOR (Water P.) *Quarrel betw. Tower Hill & Tyburn*, These arms for thee my muse hath heraldized. **1760** STERNE *Serm.* III. 339 The opportunity..of raising a fortune, and heraldizing a name. **1784** *New Spectator* III. 5/1.

'herald-like, *a.* and *adv.* Like or after the manner of a herald.

c 1470 HENRY *Wallace* VIII. 1653 In Scotland sone he cummyn is onon, Bot harrold lyk he sekis his presens. **1625** K. LONG tr. *Barclay's Argenis* IV. ii. 238 A certaine souldier ..attired Herald-like. **1770** ARMSTRONG *Misc.* II. 179 (Jod.) According to nice heraldlike ceremony, the son..ought to take the wall of the father.

'heraldrist. *rare.* [f. HERALDRY + -IST: cf. *symmetrist*.] One who is versed in heraldry.

1875 M. A. LOWER *Eng. Surnames* (ed. 4) I. v. 89 The late celebrated heraldrist, Nicholas John Philipson of Newcastle-upon-Tyne.

heraldry ('hɛrəldrɪ). Forms: see HERALD. [f. HERALD *sb.* + -RY: cf. *poetry, pedantry*.]

1. The art or science of a herald; now, esp. the art or science of blazoning armorial bearings and of settling the right of persons to bear arms or certain bearings; in connexion with which it deals with the tracing and recording of pedigrees, and deciding of questions of precedence.

canting heraldry, that which deals with canting arms: see CANTING *ppl. a.*² 5.

1572 BOSSEWELL *Armorie* Ded., Such one was of late specially in this kinde of Herehaultry a very fruteful and worthy writer, master Gerard Leigh. **1663** GERBIER *Counsel* E viij a, The Antiquity and Origine of Herauldry. *a* **1668** DENHAM *Progr. Learn.* 183 'Twas no false heraldry when Madness drew Her pedigree from those who too much knew. **1769** *Junius Lett.* xii. 49 You may look back..to an illustrious pedigree, in which heraldry has not left a single good quality upon record. **1830** MACAULAY *Ess., Byron* (1887) 160 Is poetry, like heraldry, mere matter of arbitrary regulation? **1872** RUSKIN *Eagle's N.* §47 The most brilliant, and..most practically effective of the arts—Heraldry.

fig. **1641** 'SMECTYMNUUS' *Vind. Answ.* vi. 88 As for the Herauldry in blazoning Aerius for an heretick..We referre to former answeres. *a* **1652** J. SMITH *Sel. Disc.* iv. 70 All those discourses which have been written of the soul's heraldry, will not blazon it so well to us as itself will do. *Ibid.* ix. 410 Titles of worldly honour in heaven's heraldry are but only *tituli nominales*. **1823** in *Joanna Baillie's Collect. Poems* 263 Watt, who in heraldry of science ranks With those to whom men owe high meed of thanks.

†**b.** Heraldic practice or regulation. *Obs.*

1602 SHAKS. *Ham.* I. i. 87 Hamlet..Did slay this Fortinbras: who by a Seal'd Compact, Well ratified by Law, and Heraldrie, Did forfeite (with his life) all those his Lands.

†**c.** Heraldic title, rank, or precedence. Hence, 'An old and obsolete abuse of buying and selling precedence in the paper of causes for hearing' (*Wharton's Law Lex.* 1883). *Obs.*

1601 SHAKS. *All's Well* II. iii. 280 You are more sawcie with Lordes and honorable personages, then the Commission of your birth and vertue giues you Heraldry. *a* **1734** NORTH *Lives* I. 435 Nothing sat heavier upon his spirits than a great arrear of business..for he knew well that from thence there sprang up a trade in the register's office, called heraldry, that is, buying and selling precedence in the paper of causes.

2. A heraldic emblazonment or device; a collection of heraldic devices; armorial bearings; heraldic symbolism. Also *fig.*

1593 SHAKS. *Lucr.* 64 This Herauldry in Lucrece face was scene, Argued by Beauties red and Vertues white. **1602** — *Ham.* II. ii. 478 Pyrrhus..Hath now this dread and blacke Complexion smear'd With Heraldry more dismall. *c* **1708** SWIFT *Baucis & Philemon* 93 The ballads..high in order plac'd, describe The heraldry of ev'ry tribe. **1795** SOUTHEY *Joan of Arc* VIII. 37 Known by the buckler's blazon'd heraldry, Salisbury lay dead. **1870** F. R. WILSON *Ch. Lindisf.* 76 A series of panels filled alternately with heraldry and figures. **1889** *Century Mag.* Dec. 237/2 Nature soon covers the work of man in wood or stone with a carpet of moss and her own heraldry of lichens.

3. The office of herald or official messenger.

1594 HOOKER *Eccl. Pol.* I. xv. §1 The law of Heraldry in war is positive. **1834** LYTTON *Pilgr. Rhine* xix, Fulfilling the heraldry of God, to each Star he appointed the duty and the charge. **1835** — *Rienzi* III. i, I trust my next heraldry will be to a more friendly court.

4. The action of announcing and ushering in with pomp and ceremony; heraldic pomp.

1630 MILTON *Circumcision* 10 He who with all Heaven's heraldry whilere Entered the world, now bleeds to give us ease. **1800** COLERIDGE *Christabel* II, He would proclaim it far and wide, With trump and solemn heraldry. **1840** MILL *Diss. & Disc.* (1875) I. 427 A writer..announced, with all the pomp and heraldry of triumphant genius, a discovery.

†'**heraldy**. *Obs.* [f. HERALD *sb.* + -Y. With quots. 1390, 1747 cf. OF. *heraudie* cassock, long cloak.] = HERALDRY 1, 2.

1390 GOWER *Conf.* I. 173 (Fairf. MS.) Yet wole he [detraction] iangle noght forthi, As he which hath the heraldie Of hem that usen for to lye. **1615** J. STEPHENS *Satyr. Ess.* 355 He hath Heraldy enough to place every man by his Armes. **1651** CLEVELAND *Poems* 5 She Makes pearl and planets humble herauldy. **1738** STUART in *Phil. Trans.* XL. 51 Red, expressed by the lines thus |||| as in Heraldy. **1747** W. HORSLEY *Fool* No. 73 ¶7 With his Bib under his Chin, his motly Coat, like a Heraldy on his Shoulders.

heralt, obs. form of HERALD *sb.*

herand(e, obs. forms of ERRAND.

herapathite ('hɛrəpəθaɪt). *Chem.* [f. *Herapath*, an English analyst (1795–1868).] Iodo-sulphate of quinine in its crystalline form.

1865–72 WATTS *Dict. Chem.* III. 149. **1875** H. C. WOOD *Therap.* (1879) 61 Crystals of Herapathite separate, in the form of right-angled quadrate rhombic leaves. **1886** *Encycl. Brit.* XX. 185 Herapathite..possesses optical properties similar to those of tourmaline.

Herat (hɛ'rɑːt). The name of a city in north-western Afghanistan, used to designate a kind of carpet and rug made there, and the small, close design of leaf and rosette patterns characteristic of such rugs. Also **He'rati**.

1917 in R. Storrs *Orientations* (1937) x. 261 Some fine old carpets, including a brilliant Herât. **1931** A. U. DILLEY *Oriental Rugs & Carpets* Pl. 51 (*caption*) Herat rugs... Herat borders. *Ibid.* iv. 118 Herat, applied both to the 'Ispahan' weaving of the sixteenth century and to the blue Herati-patterned rug of the nineteenth century, is, rightly or wrongly, the outstanding name in rugs. **1957** *Encycl. Brit.* XIX. 622/1 (*caption*) The Herati pattern. *Ibid.* 628C/2 The Ferraghan [rugs], with their so-called Herati pattern—an all-over, rather dense design with a light green border on a mordant dye that leaves the pattern in relief. **1960** H. HAYWARD *Antique Coll.* 141/2 *Herat carpets*, fine quality Persian carpets... Knot: Ghiordes or Sehna. **1967** 'W. HAGGARD' *Conspirators* ix. 99 There was..fine old mahogany furniture and a Herati rug. **1969** — *Doubtful Discipline* xv. 166 The dealers call them Isfahans and most of the time they know they're Heratis. **1972** *Observer* 8 Oct. 14/1 (Advt.), A central panel leading to the reception panel shows the Herati pattern on a light red ground.

heraud, -aught, -ault, -aut, etc., obs. ff. HERALD, etc.

herb (hɜːb), *sb.* Forms: 3–6 **erbe**, 3–7 **herbe**, 4 **eerbe**, 6 **earbe**, **heerb**, *Sc.* **hairb**, 6–7 **hearbe**, 6– **herb**; also 5–6 **yerbe**, 9 *dial.* **yerb**, **yarb**, **yirb**. [In ME. usually *erbe*, a. OF. *erbe* (11th c. in Littré), mod.F. *herbe* (= It. *erba*, Sp. *yerba*, Pg. *herva*):—L. *herba* grass, green crops, herbage, herb. In OF. and ME. occasionally spelt with *h* after Lat.; regularly so since *c* 1475, but the *h* was mute until the 19th c., and is still so treated by many: see H (the letter).]

1. A plant of which the stem does not become woody and persistent (as in a *shrub* or a *tree*), but remains more or less soft and succulent, and dies down to the ground (or entirely) after flowering.

c **1290** *S. Eng. Leg.* I. 221/41 Of treon and herbes, þikke.. bi-set in eche side. *c* **1385** CHAUCER *L.G.W.* Prol. 109 To speke of gomme or erbe or tre. **1432–50** tr. *Higden* (Rolls) I. 257 Hilles and woodes..habundante in yerbes and pastures and mony wilde bestes. **1526** TINDALE *Matt.* xiii. 32 When it is growne it is the greatest amonge yerbes. *a* **1631** DONNE *Epigr.* (1652) 92 An Hearb thou [Tobacco] art, but useless. **1647** CLARENDON *Hist. Reb.* III. §64 Strewing Flowers and Herbs in the ways as they pass'd. **1880** GRAY *Struct. Bot.* iii. §3. 50 Herbs are plants in which the stem does not become woody and persistent, but dies annually or after flowering, down to the ground.

2. *spec.* Applied to plants of which the leaves, or stem and leaves, are used for food or medicine, or in some way for their scent or flavour.

c **1290** *S. Eng. Leg.* I. 18/598 A fair herbe, þat men cleopez letuse..In hire mouth heo pulte þarof a lef. *c* **1380** WYCLIF *Serm.* Sel. Wks. I. 28 Erbis of vertue þat growen in hem. *c* **1386** CHAUCER *Can. Yeom. Prol. & T.* 246 And herbes [*v.r.* erbis] koude I telle eek many oon As Egremoyne Valerian and lunarie And other swiche if that me liste tarie. *c* **1489** CAXTON *Sonnes of Aymon* xvi. 371 He toke an erbe, and robbed Charlemagnes noose & his lippes wyth it. **1577** B. GOOGE *Heresbach's Husb.* I. (1586) 38 b, Flaxe and Hempe.. be not to be received in the number of Corne nor Pulse, Fodder nor Hearbes. **1633** G. HERBERT *Temple, Sunday* vi, Those Who want herbs for their wound. **1725** WATTS *Logic* I. vi. §3 If the leaves are of chief use to us, we call them herbs: as sage, mint, thyme. **1802** *Med. Jrnl.* VIII. 530 Fumigations with aromatic substances, woods, herbs, and resins. **1839** E. D. CLARKE *Trav. Russia* 55/1 Broth, made with fish and wild herbs.

3. *collect.* Herbage. Also *fig.* (quot. 1677).

1382 WYCLIF *Heb.* vi. 7 The erthe drynkynge reyn..and bryngynge forth couenable eerbe. **1535** COVERDALE *Ps.* xxxvi[i]. 2 Cut downe like yᵉ grasse, and..wythered euen as yᵉ grene herbe. **1677** GALE *Crt. Gentiles* IV. 208 Rich men.. are deservedly stiled the Herbe of Drones, which they devour. **1725** POPE *Odyss.* v. 597 On the flow'ry herb..he lay. **1850** TENNYSON *In Mem.* xcv, Underfoot the herb was dry.

4. a. The leafy part of a (herbaceous) plant; esp. as distinct from the root.

1662 J. DAVIES tr. *Olearius' Voy. Ambass.* 314 The herb and seed of Werme. **1799** *Med. Jrnl.* I. 26 The herb and flowers of the arnica are..most conveniently given in simple infusion.

†**b.** ***in the herb***: green, not yet ripe. *Obs.* (Cf. in the blade, in leaf; F. *en herbe*).

1652 SPARKE *Prim. Devot.* (1663) 365 Since our haruest is but in the hearb.

†**5.** = HERBA, q.v. *Obs.*

6. General Combs., as ***herb-bed***, ***-eater***, ***-flower***, ***-garden***, ***-gatherer***, ***-juice***, ***-locust***, ***-lore***, ***-market***, ***-master***, ***-plot***, ***-seller***, etc.; ***herb-eating***, ***-like*** adjs.

1858 GLENNY *Gard. Every-day Bk.* 78/2 You get fine healthy young plants..to form a good *herb-bed. *c* **1515** *Cocke Lorell's B.* (Percy Soc.) 5 Patrycke peuysshe *heerbeter. **1651–3** JER. TAYLOR *Serm. for Year* II. x. (R.), His little garden made for..the feasting of a few Pythagorean herb-eaters. **1726** SWIFT *It cannot rain*, etc. Wks. 1755 III. I. 135 The new sect of herb-eaters [vegetarians]. **1731** ARBUTHNOT *Aliments* 215 *Herb-eating Animals. **1583** STANYHURST *Æneis* I. (Arb.) 40 Senting delicat *herbflowrs. **1535** COVERDALE *1 Kings* xxi. 2 Geue me thy vynyarde, I wyll make me an *herbgarden therof. **1570** LEVINS *Manip.* 34/11 *Herbe-garth, *herbarium, olearium*. **1552** HULOET, *Herbe gatherer, *herbarius*. **1885** TUER *Old Lond. Cries* 32 The simplers, or herb-gatherers.. supplied the herb-shops in Covent Garden. **1578** LYTE *Dodoens* III. xxvi. 351 Flowers..of a greene or *herbelike colour. **1658** ROWLAND *Moufet's Theat. Ins.* 997 Either the Bruchus, or the little *Herb-locust, Grashopper, or Kricket. **1955** J. R. R. TOLKIEN *Return of King* 145 A chance of talking *herb-lore with me. **1552** HULOET, *Herbe market, *lachanopolium*. **1715** LEONI *Palladio's Archit.* (1742) II. 82 The Herb-Market, now called *Montanara*. **1955** J. R. R. TOLKIEN *Return of King* 140, I will go and ask of the *herb-master. **1611** FLORIO, *Herbaio*..an *hearbe-plot where hearbes grow. **1530** PALSGR. 230/2 *Herbe sellar. **1782** S. PEGGE *Cur. Misc.* 45 At Coronations the ground is strewed with flowers by a person..called the *Herbstrewer.

7. Special Combs.: †**herb-bane**, name invented by Parkinson for the parasitic genus *Orobanche* or broom-rape; **herb beer**, a beverage prepared from herbs; **herb-doctor** *local U.S.*, one who treats or cures ailments by means of herbs; so **herb-doctress**; **herb-tea**, **herb-water**, a medicinal infusion of herbs. See also HERB-MAN, -WIFE, -WOMAN.

1640 PARKINSON *Theat. Bot.* 1362 *Orobanche*..Kill herbe or *herbe bane. **1891** *Daily News* 28 Nov. 5/5 The proprietor insists that his *herb beer is..a medicine..In the end 'herb beer' was declared to be a refreshment. **1854** THOREAU *Walden* 150 Hygeia, who was the daughter of that old *herb-doctor, Aesculapius. **1881** *Harper's Mag.* July 305/2 The herb-doctor was not so fortunate as another practitioner of his own class who came to England some years ago. **1891** *Ibid.* Jan. 220/1, I would say that Mr. Pettingill has behaved very strangely—sending for a herb doctor. *a* **1864** HAWTHORNE *S. Felton* (1871) 113 [Aunt Keziah was] a mixture of an Indian squaw and *herb doctress. **1744** BERKELEY *Siris* §75 When..*herb-teas shall be found to have little..effect. **1841** EMERSON *Lect., Conservative* Wks. (Bohn) II. 274 Swallowing pills and herb-tea. **1886** MRS. HUNGERFORD *Lady Branksmere* II. xxxiii. 230, I hope..you took the *herb-water I prescribed.

b. In various names of plants, as **herb St. Barbara** (†***herb St. Barbe***, ***herb Barbara***), a name for Winter-cress, *Barbarea*; **herb carpenter**, *Prunella vulgaris* = Carpenter's herb (CARPENTER *sb.* 5) (Britten & Holl.); **herb of the cross**, a name for Vervain, *Verbena officinalis* (see quot.); †**herb fluellin** = FLUELLIN; **herb frankincense**, an aromatic umbelliferous plant, *Laserpitium latifolium* (Miller *Plant-n.*); **herb of friendship**, a species of Stonecrop, *Sedum Anacampseros* (Miller); **herb Gerard**, Goutweed, *Ægopodium Podagraria*; **herb-Henry** [med.L. *malus Henricus*, Ger. *böser Heinrich*], Dog's Mercury; †**herb impious** [tr. L. *herba impia*], old name of *Filago germanica* (see quot.); **herb-lily**, a florist's name for plants of the genus *Alstrœmeria* (N.O. *Amaryllidaceæ*), natives of South America; **herb-Louisa**, the Lemon-scented Verbena, *Aloysia citriodora* (Miller); **herb Margaret**, 'the daisy, *Bellis perennis*' (Prior); **herb of St. Martin**, *Sauvagesia erecta*, a native of tropical America and the West Indies; **herb Mary**, **St. Mary's herb** = COSTMARY; †**herb paralysy**, an old name for the cowslip; †**herb Peter**, 'the cowslip, from its resemblance to St. Peter's badge, a bunch of keys' (Prior); **herb-royal** [F. *herbe royale*] southernwood; **herb Sophia**, a name for *Sisymbrium Sophia*; †**herb terrible**, an old name for the shrub *Daphne Tartonraira*; †**herb of vine**, an old name for Squinancywort, *Asperula cynanchica*; †**herb William**, a name for Bishop's-weed, *Ammi majus*; †**herb willow**, name given by Turner to the Yellow Loosestrife (*Lysimachia vulgaris*); extended by Gerarde to the Purple Loosestrife (*Lythrum Salicaria*), and various species of Willow-herb (*Epilobium*). See also *herb* ALOE, *h.* BENNET, *h.* BIFOIL, *h.* CHRISTOPHER, *h.* FIVELEAF, *h.* GIT, *h.* MASTIC, *h.* PATIENCE, *h. of* REPENTANCE, *h.* SQUINANTIC, *h.* TREFOIL, *h.* TRINITY, *h.* TRUELOVE, *h.* TWO-PENCE, under ALOE, etc.; also HERB-GRACE, HERB IVE, HERB JOHN, HERB PARIS, HERB ROBERT.

1578 LYTE *Dodoens* V. lxi. 626 *Herbe S. Barbe is a good herbe for salade. **1597** GERARDE *Herbal* II. viii. §5. 188 Winter Cresses, or herbe Saint Barbara. **1889** THISELTON DYER *Folklore Pl.* xix. 259 In Brittany, vervain is popularly termed the '*herb of the cross.' **1578** LYTE *Dodoens* I. xvii. 26 Paules Betony, *Herbe Fluellyn, or Speedewell. **1678** LITTLETON *Lat. Dict.*, *Herb-frankincense, *Libanotis*. **1578** LYTE *Dodoens* II. cix. 300 Now called *Herba Gerardi*..that is to say, *Herbe Gerarde. **1640** PARKINSON *Theat. Bot.* 943 Wee in English Goutewort or herbe Gerard after the Brabanders, and of some in our Land Aisweede, or Axeweede. **1827** T. FORSTER *Encycl. Nat. Phen.* 101 *Herb Gerard*..so called from St. Gerard, who is celebrated April 23d, and who used to be invoked against the gout. **1607** TOPSELL *Four-f. Beasts* (1658) 60 Black Hellebore, Aconitum, or Wolf-bane..*herb Henry, and others. **1597** GERARDE *Herbal* II. cxcv. §9. 518 Those flowers..that come after growe higher, as children seeking to..ouertop their parents..for which cause it hath beene called *Herba Impia*, that is, the Wicked Herbe, or *Herbe Impious. **1866** *Treas. Bot.* 1026/1 *S[auvagesia] erecta*, the *Herb of St. Martin.. has been used in Brazil for complaints in the eyes, in Peru for disorders of the bowels, and in the West Indies as a diuretic. **1882** J. SMITH *Dict. Econ. Plants, Herb of St. Martin*..Its leaves are..eaten as spinach. **1607** TOPSELL *Four-f. Beasts* (1658) 68 The priest..put thereunto frankincense, *herbmary, and fire. **1516** *Grete Herball* ccxii, *Herbe paralysy that some call artetyke..is principally good for palsy artetyke and gowty folke. **1552** COPLAND *Bk. Prop. Herbes*, Cristofer female..hath leues lyke *Herbe Peter, but they be nat in all so whyte. **1597** GERARDE *Herbal* (1633) Suppl., Herbe Peter, Cowslip. **1530** PALSGR. 230/2 *Herbe royall. **1597** GERARDE *Herbal* II. cxxxiii. §1. 408 *Herbe terrible is a small shrub two or three cubits high. **1668** WILKINS *Real Char.* 112 Smooth hard dry leaves; bearing a blew flower like that of Scabious..Herb terrible. **1529** *Grete Herball* ccx, *Herbe or grasse of vyne is other-wise called herbe squynantyke. **1597** GERARDE *Herbal* (1633) 1037 Of

some, *Herbe-William, Bull-wort, and Bishops-weed. **1614** MARKHAM *Cheap Husb.* I. Ameos, Comin royal, is a Herb of some called *Bulwort, Bishops-weed*, or *Herb-william.* **1548** TURNER *Names of Herbes* E ij, Lysimachia is of two sortes. The one..hath a yealowe floure..it may be called in englishe..*herbe Wylowe. **1601** HOLLAND *Pliny* II. 268 Herb Willow giueth the hair of the head a yellow colour.

herb, *v. rare.* [f. prec.] **a.** *to herb it*: to crop herbage, to graze. **b.** *intr.* To gather herbs.

1660 HOWELL *Parly of Beasts* 113, I [a boar] am going to herb it among that tuft of Trees. **1884** *Harper's Mag.* Oct. 788/2 Been herbin' again?

||**herba**. *Obs.* Also 6 yerua. [Ital. *herba*, Pg. *herva* grass. Called *panni d'herba* by the Venetian merchant Cesare Federici in 1563.] A sort of grass-cloth imported formerly from India.

1585 R. FITCH in Hakluyt *Voy.* II. 389 In this place [Orixa] is..great store of cloth which is made of grasse, which they call Yerua, it is like a silke. *a* **1692** SIR H. POLLEXFEN *Disc. Trade* (1697) 98 Muslins, Persian Silks, Herba Taffaties, Herba Longees, Japan Ware. **1701** *Lond. Gaz.* No. 3737/4 Stuffs mixed with Silk or Herba. **1727** A. HAMILTON *New Acc. E. Ind.* I. 397 Of Herba (a Sort of tough Grass) they make Ginghams, Pinascos, and several other goods for exportation. **1813** MILBURN *Orient. Comm.* II. 221 Piece-goods form the staple commodity of Bengal.. The following are the kinds imported..with the number of pieces allotted to a ton..Herba Taffaties 800.

herbaceous (hə'beɪʃəs), *a.* [f. L. *herbāce-us* grassy, f. *herba* HERB: see -ACEOUS. Cf. F. *herbacé* (16th c. in Hatz.-Darm.).]

1. Of the nature of a herb. **a.** Applied to plants which do not develop wood in the stem or branches, but die down every year, after flowering (opp. to *arborescent*); also to the soft succulent stems of such plants (opp. to *ligneous*).

1646 SIR T. BROWNE *Pseud. Ep.* II. vi. 97 Ginger is the root of neither tree nor shrub, but of an herbaceous plant. **1758** BORLASE *Nat. Hist. Cornwall* 254 The Alcyonium is of a middle nature betwixt the herbaceous and horny submarines. **1794** MARTYN *Rousseau's Bot.* xxv. 347 The stem is simple, herbaceous, and procumbent. **1859** DARWIN *Orig. Spec.* ix. (1878) 245 Two plants, one being woody and the other herbaceous. **1887** *Pall Mall G.* 6 Nov. 13/2 Horticulturists generally apply the term herbaceous in a more limited sense—that is, to those plants which die down annually, as the pæony and Michaelmas daisy.

b. Of the texture and colour of an ordinary leaf; applied esp. to green flowers or floral organs.

1794 MARTYN *Rousseau's Bot.* xv. 168 The flowers [of Lady's Mantle]..having no corolla..are only green, or what botanists call herbaceous. **1870** HOOKER *Stud. Flora* 307 Polygoneæ..sepals 3-6, petaloid or herbaceous.

†**2.** Composed of or containing herbs. *Obs. rare.*

1725 BRADLEY *Fam. Dict.* s.v. *Sallet*, One of the most agreeable of all the boil'd Herbaceous dishes.

†**3.** Feeding on herbs, herbivorous. *Obs. rare.*

1713 DERHAM *Phys.-Theol.* IV. xi.. (1786) I. 257 The herbaceous eaters, for instance, are many, and devour much. *Ibid.* (J.), Their teeth are fitted to their food..the herbaceous to gathering and comminution of vegetables.

4. ***herbaceous border***, a border filled with herbaceous perennial plants (so, as nonce-wd., ***herbaceous borderer***); ***herbaceous perennial***, a plant whose roots live for several years, although stem and leaves die down to the ground each year, after flowering.

[**1822** LOUDON *Encycl. Gard.* III. 993 (*heading*) Species and Varieties of..*Herbaceous Border-flowers. **1868** D. THOMSON *Handy Bk. of Flower Garden* 6 There is enough in a border of hardy herbaceous plants..to gratify the keenest sensibility.] **1881** T. MOORE *Epitome of Gardening* vi. 190 The herbaceous border should be a distinct compartment, and not less than 10 ft. in width. **1883** F. MILES in W. Robinson *Eng. Flower Garden* p. xl/2 What cannot be done with an herbaceous border edge when that edge is the green grass? **1909** H. G. WELLS *Tono-Bungay* III. ii. §1 An ardent rose grower and herbaceous borderer. **1931** C. ST. JOHN *Ellen Terry & Bernard Shaw* 132 Miss Audrey Campbell: an enthusiastic amateur actress, and a plant of 'vigorous habit' in Ellen Terry's herbaceous border of friends. **1968** R. HAY *Gardener's Round* 213 A friend, anxious to replant a fairly large herbaceous border, asked me to mark a catalogue for him. **1868** D. THOMSON *Handy Bk. Flower Garden* vi. 153 *Herbaceous perennials are a class of plants distinct in their nature. **1871** W. ROBINSON *Hardy Flowers* III. 277 (*heading*) A choice selection of the very finest herbaceous perennials. **1959** C. H. POTTER *Perennials in Garden* i. 8 The term perennial..refers to hardy herbaceous perennials which tend to live year after year without replanting.

Hence **her'baceously** *adv.*, in a herbaceous manner; in quot., With a flavouring of herbs.

1887 RUSKIN *Præterita* II. iv. 112 To have caught a chub in the Avon, and learned how to cook it spicily and herbaceously..would have been a better result.

herbagage, -gerie, -ry, var. HARBERGAGE, -GERY, *Obs.*

herbage ('hɜːbɪdʒ). Also 4-6 erbage, 5-6 (sense 3) arbage. [a. F. *herbage*, earlier *erbage* (12th c. in Littré), ad. med.L. *herbāticum* 'herba in pratis succisa', f. *herba* HERB: see -AGE.]

1. Herbs collectively; herbaceous growth or vegetation; usually applied to grass and other low-growing plants covering a large extent of ground, esp. as used for pasture.

1390 GOWER *Conf.* I. 326 She..let her wimpel falle Nigh to the wel upon therbage. **1419** *Surtees Misc.* (1888) 14 The whilke sall kytte the herbage that grewys apon the mote. **1555** EDEN *Decades* 188 To renewe the herbage for kyne and other beastes. **1651** HOBBES *Leviath.* I. xiv. 68 He that selleth Land, is understood to transferre the Herbage, and whatsoever growes upon it. **1727** A. HAMILTON *New Acc. E. Ind.* II. xxxiii. 11 A pretty good Garden, that furnishes the Governor's Table with Herbage and Fruits. **1845** DARWIN *Voy. Nat.* vi. (1879) 118 From a coarse herbage we passed on to a carpet of fine green verdure. **1856** SIR B. BRODIE *Psychol. Inq.* I. i. 4 Steep and lofty chalk hills, covered by a scanty herbage.

†**b.** *Cookery.* ? Herbs for garnishing a dish. *Obs.*

1494 FABYAN *Chron.* (1559) II. 402/2 Brawne and mustarde..Pyke in erbage.

2. The green succulent parts of herbaceous plants; the stem and leaves: = HERB 4.

1701 GREW *Cosmo. Sacra* IV. vii. (R.), Which comprehended, with the herbage of plants, their roots, and fruits. **1830** LINDLEY *Nat. Syst. Bot.* 17 A wholesome food; such as..the herbage of the Water-cress, the cabbage [etc.]. **1872** OLIVER *Elem. Bot.* II. 212 The herbage of Boragineæ is often very coarse and hispid.

3. *Law.* The natural herbage or pasture of any land as a species of property distinct from the land itself; hence 'a liberty that a man hath to feede his catell in another mans ground, as in the forest.' (Cowell *Interpr.* 1607.)

c **1450** in Arnolde *Chron.* (1811) 180 Graunts made..of estate of enheritaunce terme off lyf or terme of yeres or att wylle, of ony herbage or pannage. **1490** *Plumpton Corr.* (Camden) 94 Sir, afor the arbage, dout yt not; for sir Henry Wentforth, nor yet none other, can have it. **1535** *Act 27 Hen. VIII*, c. 6 §5 Tharbage of which parke..is common to the tenauntes, and inhabitantes of the towneshippes nexte adioynynge. **1611** COTGR., *Droict d'herbage*, herbage; or the libertie some haue to graze their cattell in other men's woods. **1647** HAWARD *Crown Rev.* 46 The Herbage and Pannage: Fee 11.0.0. **1778** *Phil. Surv. S. Irel.* 307 Herbage would have acted as a premium upon tillage, by being a tax upon pasturage. **1818** CRUISE *Digest* (ed. 2) I. 302 The herbage or vesture of land may be granted by copy. In a modern case it was resolved, that a person might hold the *prima tonsura* of land by copy, while another might have the soil, and every other beneficial enjoyment of it, as freehold.

4. *attrib.*, as ***herbage crop, plant.***

1826 LOUDON *Encycl. Agric.* (1831) Gloss. 1244 Herbage plants, forage plants, such as clover and other plants cultivated chiefly for the herb, to be used either green or made into hay. **1875** WILSON & THORNTON in *Encycl. Brit.* I. 370/2 Herbage and forage crops..grown expressly for the sake of the cattle food yielded by their leaves and stems.

Hence **'herbaged** *a.*, covered or overgrown with herbage; †**'herbager**, an animal that feeds on herbage; †**her'bagious** *a.* [= F. *herbageux* (Cotgr.)], abounding in herbage.

1727-46 THOMSON *Summer* 475 Or stream full-flowing, that his swelling sides Laves, as he floats along the herbaged brink. **1863** *Pilgrim. Prairies* I. 265 In the more thickly herbaged bottoms. **1599** NASHE *Lenten Stuffe* 25 What an aduantageable creature shee [the cow] is beyonde all the foure footed rablement of herbagers and grasse champers. **1632** LITHGOW *Trav.* 506 Now having seene..Herbagious fields.

herbal ('hɜːbəl), *sb.* [perh. repr. a med. or early mod.L. **herbāle* or **herbālis* (sc. *liber*), f. *herbālis* adj. (see next); cf. med.L. *nominale* name-book, *manuale* hand-book, also *diurnal, missal, ordinal, ritual*, etc., as names of books.]

1. A book containing the names and descriptions of herbs, or of plants in general, with their properties and virtues; a treatise on plants. *Obs.* exc. *Hist.*

1516 (*title*) The Grete Herbal. **1551** TURNER (*title*) A new Herball; wherin are conteyned the names of Herbes in Greke, Latin, Englysh, Duch, Frenche, and in the Potecaries and Herbaries Latin. **1578** LYTE *Dodoens* Ded., Hauing newly translated into English this Herball or Historie of Plantes. **1599** H. BUTTES *Dyets drie Dinner* F iij, Two kinds of Sage, not named in our Herbals. **1628** *Ann. Barber-Surg. Lond.* (1890) 540 To George Peren, Barber-Surgeon, my yearball knowne by the name of Gerard's yearball. **1799** *Med. Jrnl.* I. 211 *Herbarium Mauritianum.*—'The Mauritian Herbal': by P. R. Willemet..The herbal before us is the fruit of a journey to India. **1862** WRIGHT *Bacon's Ess.* Pref. 23 Consulting the old herbals of Lyte, Gerarde, and Parkinson.

†**2.** A collection of herbs or plants; *esp.* a collection of botanical specimens; = HERBARIUM 1.

1580 HOLLYBAND *Treas. Fr. Tong, Vn Herbier*, an Herball. **1594** PLAT *Jewell-ho.* II. 33 He may..lay it being drie in his herball. **1665** PEPYS *Diary* 5 Nov., Leaves..of several plants, kept dry; which preserve colour, however, and look very finely, better than any herball. **1712** STEELE *Spect.* No. 455 ¶2 To collect in voluminous Herbals all the several Leaves of some one Tree. **1847** EMERSON *Poems* (1857) 171 Who saw what ferns and palms were pressed..In the safe herbal of the coal?

†**b.** (See quot.) *nonce-use.*

1606 CHAPMAN *Gentl. Usher* Plays 1873 I. 278 These verdant herbals cleeped Broome Do pierce and enter euerie Ladies roome.

herbal ('hɜːbəl), *a.* [f. L. *herbāl-is* (in med.L.): cf. obs. F. *herbal* (opposed to *mineral*) Godef.]

1. Belonging to, consisting of, or made from herbs.

1612 tr. *Benvenuto's Passenger* (N.), Calling of me to that herball dinner and leane repast. **1766** G. CANNING *Anti-Lucretius* IV. 267 All the herbal fragrance of the Field. **1895** *Westm. Gaz.* 4 Sept. 5/1 A specific herbal remedy for the treatment of this disease.

†**2.** Of the nature of a herb, herbaceous. *Obs.*

a **1682** SIR T. BROWNE *Tracts* 68 The least of herbal Plants, which arise unto such a proportion.

†**'herbalism.** *Obs. rare.* [f. as next + -ISM.] The science of herbs or plants; botany.

1664 POWER *Exp. Philos.* 47 The old quarrel in Herbalism, which is the least of Seeds. **1716** M. DAVIES *Athen. Brit.* III. *Orig. Physick* 46 Those Pieces of Herbalism and Tillage, writ by Cato, Varro, Columella.

herbalist ('hɜːbəlɪst). [f. HERBAL *sb.* (or its source) + -IST.]

1. One versed in the knowledge of herbs or plants; a collector of or writer on plants; a botanist. Now used of the early botanical writers.

1594 DEE *Diary* (Camden) 50 Mr Gherardt, the chirurgeon and herbalist. **1601** CORNWALLYES *Ess.* II. lii. (1631) 331, I am no herbalist, not curious about flowers and weeds. **1672** *Mede's Wks.* Life 5 He was a curious Florist, an accurate Herbalist, thoroughly vers'd in the Book of Nature. **1758** BORLASE *Nat. Hist. Cornwall* 233 It is the *Eryngium marinum* of Herbalists. **1840** E. NEWMAN *Brit. Ferns* (1844) 291 We learn from the herbalists that this plant was much in vogue as a medicine.

2. A dealer in medicinal herbs or simples; one who prepares or administers herbal remedies.

1592 GREENE *Upst. Courtier* in *Harl. Misc.* (Malh.) II. 218, I thought them to be some herbalistes, or some apothecaries. **1611** FLORIO, *Herbaio*, a Simpler, an Herbalist. **1814** SCOTT *Wav.* lxv, He left an old man, a herbalist, who was supposed to understand a little of medicine, to attend Waverley. **1851** *Illustr. Catal. Gt. Exhib.* 197 These bunches are afterwards hung up in the herbalists' shops.

'herbalize, *v. arch.* [f. as prec. + -IZE.] *intr.* To collect (medicinal) herbs. Hence **'herbalizing** *vbl. sb.* and *ppl. a.*

1695 SIBBALD *Autobiog.* (1834) 131, I went and herbalized in the downes and woods with the gardner of the medicine garden. **1767** *Chron.* in *Ann. Reg.* 89/1 At the herbalizing feast of the company of apothecaries Mr. Latham recommended the Lamium Album or white nettle to the notice of his brethren. **1769** *Lloyd's Evening Post* 12-14 July 45 Yesterday the Apothecaries Company held their Herbalizing feast, at the Assembly-house on Blackheath. **1801** CHARLOTTE SMITH *Solit. Wand.* II. 93 Of the fruits of her herbalizing. **1835** *Gentl. Mag.* July 3 The Briseis of the tent, with her handmaids, was sent to herbalize on the banks of the river for some fresh and cooling diaphoretic.

herbar(e, obs. var. ARBOUR: see HERBER.

1590 SPENSER *F.Q.* II. ix. 46 The roofe hereof was arched over head, And deckt with flowers and herbars daintily.

†**her'barian.** *Obs.* [f. L. *herbāria* (sc. *ars*) botany, or *herbāri-us* botanist + -AN.] One skilled in the knowledge of herbs, a herbalist.

1577 HARRISON *England* III. ii. (1878) II. 14 As Pena the French herbarian hath also noted in the verie end of his herball. **1578** LYTE *Dodoens* Ded., This Herball..by the trauayle of sundry skylfull Herbarians into diuers other languages translated. **1578** BANISTER *Hist. Man* v. 82 A little pulse or grayne, called of the Herbarians Faseoli.

†**'herbarism.** *Obs.* [f. as next + -ISM.] The knowledge of herbs; = HERBALISM.

1597 GERARDE *Herbal* I. xxiv. §6 (1633) 35 Curious in herbarisme. **1640** PARKINSON *Theat. Bot.* 204 The professers of Herbarisme or Herbarists there. **1834** SOUTHEY *Doctor* I. 240 The very pith and marrow of herbarism.

†**herbarist.** *Obs.* Also 6-7 herberist. See also HERBORIST. [f. L. *herbāria* HERBARY, botany + -IST.] One skilled in herbs; a herbalist.

1577 HARRISON *England* II. xx. (1878) I. 329 Carolus Clusius, the noble herbarist. **1613** PURCHAS *Pilgrimage* (1614) 505 Gerard, with other Herbarists. **1640** (*title*) Theatrum Botanicum: The Theater of Plants,..by John Parkinson Apothecarye of London, and the Kings Herbarist. **1713** DERHAM *Phys.-Theol.* X. i. 454 Their seed hath been discovered by the industry of the ingenious Herbarist, Mr. Sam. Doody. **1794** MARTYN *Rousseau's Bot.* viii. 77 The science which distinguishes the true botanist from the mere herbarist or nomenclator.

herbarium (hə'bɛərɪəm). [Late L. (Cassiodorus *c* 550): the neuter of an adj., f. *herba* HERB, which gave also *herbārius* botanist, *herbāria* (sc. *ars*) botany, both in Pliny. See -ARIUM.] A collection of dried plants systematically arranged; a *hortus siccus*. Also, a book or case contrived for keeping such a collection; the room or building in which it is kept. Also *attrib.*

[**1700-19** TOURNEFORT *Instit. rei Herb.* I. 671 Herbarium sive Hortum siccum appellant collectionem plantarum exsiccatarum quæ in codicibus vel capsis asservantur. **1751** LINNÆUS *Philos. Botan.*, Herbarium præstat omni iconi, necessarium omni Botanico.] **1776** WITHERING *Brit. Plants* (1796) I. 35 An Approved Method of Preparing Plants for an Herbarium. **1794** MARTYN *Rousseau's Bot.* viii. 77 A *hortus siccus*, or *herbarium*, by which Latin terms we call a collection of dried plants. **1849** J. H. BALFOUR *Man. Bot.* 616 This [*sc.* the vasculum] should be of sufficient length to receive a plant of the full size of the herbarium paper. **1863** BERKELEY *Brit. Mosses* x. 41 No plants are so easy to prepare for the herbarium as Mosses. **1887** C. A. MOLONEY *Sk. Forestry W. Afr.* 319 He compared the available herbarium material of the two plants. **1898** B. TORREY in *Atlantic*

Monthly Apr. 461/2 A comparison with herbarium specimens. **1962** D. B. O. SAVILE *Coll. & Care Bot. Specimens* i. 50 (*heading*) Herbarium sequence. The operation of the phanerogamic herbarium of the Plant Research Institute may serve as an example of herbarium management. *Ibid.* 52 Ideally the herbarium units should be built like library stack rooms.
fig. **1870** LOWELL *Among my Bks.* Ser. I. (1873) 333 Relegated to that herbarium of Billingsgate gathered by the elder Disraeli. **1883** MRS. HOLMDEN tr. *Pressense's Study Orig.* 321 Language is a tissue of metaphors . . an herbarium in which the plants are withered.

'herbarize, *v. arch.* [f. as HERBARIST + -IZE: cf. *botanize*.] = HERBALIZE, HERBORIZE. Hence **'herbarizing, herbari'zation.**
1670 *Lex Talionis* 24 Having a laudable Custom once a Year . . to go a Herbarizing. **1734** J. SOAME *Anal. Hampstead Water* 27 (R.) The Apothecaries' Company very seldom miss coming to Hampstead every spring, and here have their herbarizing feast. **1768** MILLER *Gard. Dict.* (ed. 8), *Herbarize*, to go abroad in the fields in quest of different or new herbs or plants. **1794** MARTYN *Rousseau's Bot.* vi. 60 To enable you, after some months herbarization, to render the air, port, or habit of each plant familiar to you. **1845** A. WHITE in *Life Jas. Hamilton* (1870) 257 Excuse the familiarity of one who has herbarized.

Herbartian (hə'bɑːtɪən), *a.* and *sb.* [f. the name of J. F. *Herbart* (1776–1841), German philosopher + -IAN.] **A.** *adj.* Of or pertaining to Herbart, or to the system of psychology and teaching originated by him. **B.** *sb.* A disciple or follower of Herbart. Hence **Her'bartianism,** the doctrines of Herbart.
1884 W. JAMES *Coll. Ess. & Rev.* (1920) 267 The Herbartian psychologists have tried to distinguish feelings due to the *form* in which ideas may be arranged. **1886** *Encycl. Brit.* XX. 41/1 The whole Herbartian psychology. *Ibid.* 62/2 This difference between a conflict of presentations to enter consciousness . . and that opposition or incompatibility of presentations which is only possible when they are in consciousness has been strangely confused by the Herbartians. **1903** HAYWARD & THOMAS (*title*) The critics of Herbartianism. **1904** C. I. DODD (*title*) Introduction to the Herbartian principles of teaching. **1908** H. G. WELLS *New Worlds for Old* (1912) v. § 1. 91 This change in the circle of ideas (as the Herbartians put it) is the essence of the Socialist project. *Ibid.* x. § 1. 225 The majority of Socialists still fail to grasp completely the Herbartian truth. **1932** L. BLOOMFIELD in *Language* VIII. 225 Interpreting their methods in terms of Herbartian or Wundtian psychology. **1952** J. A. PASSMORE in G. F. Stout *God & Nature* p. xxix, The Herbartian ethnographic psychologists—Waitz, Lazarus, Steinthal—were at this time exerting a powerful influence upon him. **1971** *Language* XLVII. 980 The choice was between Herbartian and Wundtian doctrines.

herbarwe, -barow, etc., obs. ff. HARBOUR.

herbary ('hɜːbərɪ), *sb.* [Strictly, three different words: ad. L. *hebārius* botanist, herbalist; *herbārium*, in late L. sense 'collection of dried plants', F. *herbier*, and med.L. sense, 'collection of living herbs, place where herbs abound', OF. *erbier*; L. *herbāria* (OF. *herberie*, *erberie* 13th c. in Godef.) botany. See HERBARIUM.]
I. †**1.** One skilled in herbs, a herbalist. *Obs.*
1548 TURNER *Names of Herbes* 1 The commune names that Herbaries and Apotecaries use. **1565–73** COOPER *Thesaurus, Cucumis siluestris*, . . called of harbaries *Asininus.* **1568** TURNER *Herbal* III. 80 The Herbaries of oure time saye that they are hote and dry.
II. 2. A collection of dried plants, a herbarium.
1591 PERCIVALL *Sp. Dict.*, *Erbolario*, an herbarie, *herbarium.* **1810** E. D. CLARKE *Trav. Russia* (1839) 68/1 Books filled with plants for our herbary.
3. A place where herbs are grown; a garden of herbs or vegetables.
1634 JACKSON *Creed* VII. *Christ's Answ.* § 87 Wks. VI. 478 The sweetest flowers that grow either in the prophetical or evangelical herbary. **1774** WARTON *Hist. Eng. Poetry* xxviii. (1840) II. 413 *note*, An Herbary, for furnishing domestic medicines, always made a part of our ancient gardens. **1796** C. MARSHALL *Garden.* iii. (1813) 41 Let not pot herbs be forgot, but provide a general herbary in that part of the garden which is most contiguous to the kitchen.
4. A treatise on herbs; a herbal. (*nonce-use.*)
1897 DOWDEN *Fr. Lit.* I. iii. 40 The earliest versified Bestiary, which is also a Volucrary, a Herbary, and a Lapidary.
III. †**5.** The science of herbs; botany. *rare.*
1627 HAKEWILL *Apol.* III. viii. § 1 (1630) 246 The two legges of Physicke are Anatomie and Herbarie.

†**'herbary,** *a. Obs.* [ad. L. *herbāria* (*ars*): see HERBARIUM.] Relating to herbs; botanical. ***herbary art***, botany.
1657 W. COLES *Adam in Eden* To Rdr., This Herbary Art hath since groaned under the defects of many unworthy Authors.

herbegage, -gery, -ger(e, -geour: see HARBERGAGE, -GERY, HARBINGER.

herbegi, obs. or erron. f. *herberi*, HARBOURY.
a **1300** *Signs bef. Judgem.* 167 in *E.E Poems* (1862) 12 Louerd ȝif vs ur herbegi, aȝe to helle, let us neuer go.

†**herbelade.** *Cookery. Obs.* Also **hebolace, (h)erbeblade, hayrblad.** [cf. It. *herbolata* 'a kinde of tarte made of yoong herbes: greene sauce' (Florio) = OF. *herbolee* 'medicine prepared with herbes' (Godef.). Cf. also med.L. *herbolasta* 'panificium herbis fartum & conditum' (Du Cange).] A kind of pork-sausage mixed with herbs and baked in a crust.
? *c* **1390** *Form of Cury* 13 *Hebolace.* Take Oynons and erbes and hewe hem small and do þerto gode broth, and aray it as þu didest caboch. *c* **1430** *Two Cookery-bks.* 54 *Herbelade.* Take Buttes of Porke [etc.]. *c* **1450** *Ibid.* 76 Take a litul of þe broth þat þe porke was soden yn, and drawe hit þorgh a streynour, and caste to the erbeblade, and yef hit a boyle. **14..** *Noble Bk. Cookry* (1882) 58 To mak hairblad opyne.

herbengar, -er, obs. forms of HARBINGER.

herber(e, -eir, -our, common ME. forms of ARBOUR, esp. in its earlier senses, Green plot, herb- or flower-garden, orchard.

herber(e, -age, obs. ff. HARBOUR, -AGE.

herberewe, -reȝen, obs. ff. HARBOUR *sb.* and *v.*

herbergage: see HARBERGAGE.

herberger(e, -geour, -jour, etc., obs. ff. HARBINGER.

herbergery: see HARBERGERY.

herbergh, -berȝ, -berw(e, etc., ME. forms of HARBOUR *sb.*[1] and *v.*

herberi, -y(e, obs. var. HARBOURY *sb.*, HARBRY *v.*

†**herberie, erberie.** *Obs. rare.* [a. OF. *erberie*, *herberie*, a collection of herbs, a herb-market, 'herbes; increase, provision, or store of herbes' (Cotgr.), f. *herbe* HERB: see -ERY.] Herbs collectively, 'store' of herbs; herbage.
a **1400** *Pistill of Susan* 8 Of erbus and of erberi [*v.r.* erbage], so auenauntliche I-diht. *Ibid.* 11 Of Erberi and Alees, Of alle Maner of trees.

herberough, -rowe, -berrowe, -beruh: see HARBOUR *sb.* and *v.*

herbescent (hə'bɛsənt), *a.* [f. L. *herba* HERB + -ESCENT.] Growing like a herb; becoming or tending to become herbaceous.
1727 BAILEY vol. II, *Herbescent*, growing to an herb. **1886** *Syd. Soc. Lex.*, *Herbescent*, growing into a herb or in the form of one.

herb Eve: see HERB IVE.

herb-grace, herb of grace. Also **herb-a-grace,** and corruptly **herbgrass, herby-grass.** [app. of English origin: supposed to have arisen like the synonym, *herb of repentance*, out of the formal coincidence of the name *rue* with RUE *v.* and *sb.* repent, repentance. See quots. 1592–3, 1602. (But Parkinson, *Theatr. Bot.* 134 says 'from the many good properties wherunto it serveth'.)
Notwithstanding Turner, not known in French.]
1. An old name for the herb Rue, *Ruta graveolens.* (Now *Obs.* or *dial.*)
1548 TURNER *Names of Herbes, Ruta* is called . . in englishe and frenche, Rue and herbe grace, in dutch, Ruten. **1577** B. GOOGE *Heresbach's Husb.* III. (1586) 122b, Take of Gar-like heades, seven ounces, of hearbegrace three handfuls. **1592** GREENE *Upst. Courtier* (1871) 4 Some of them smiled and said 'rue was called herb *grace*' which though they scorned in their youth, they might wear in their age, and it was never too late to say *miserere.* **1593** SHAKS. *Rich. II*, III. iv. 105 Ile set a Banke of Rew, sowre Herbe of Grace: Rue, eu'n for ruth, heere shortly shall be seene, In the remembrance of a Weeping Queene. **1602** —— *Ham.* IV. v. 182 Ther's Rew for you, and heere's some for me. Wee may call it Herbe-Grace a Sundaies. *c* **1610** ROWLANDS *Terrible Battell* 24 *Angellica* is but a rotten root, Hearbe-grace in scorne, I trample vnder-foot. **1665** R. HOOKE *Microgr.* 141 The surface of Rue, or Herbgrass, is polish'd. **1679** G. R. tr. *Boyatuau's Theat. World* I. 27 Rue, or as we call it, Herb of Grace. **1701** C. WOLLEY *Jrnl. N. York* (1860) 44 The vertue of Rue or Herb-a-grace. **1865** *Cornh. Mag.* July 39 Shakespeare's 'herb o' grace' is sadly corrupted, and hardly recognizable under the form 'herby-grass'.
2. In general sense: a herb of virtue or valuable properties.
1866 *Treas. Bot.* s.v. *Verbena*, Vervein has ever been held to be 'an herb of grace', and so highly was it esteemed, [etc.].
3. (***herb of grace.***) *fig.*
1601 SHAKS. *All's Well* IV. v. 18 Indeed sir she was the sweete Margerom of the sallet, or rather the hearbe of grace. **1875** TENNYSON *Q. Mary* III. iv, Mercy, that herb-of-grace, Flowers now but seldom.

ˌherbicar'nivorous, *a.* [f. *herbi-*, combining f. L. *herba* HERB + *carnivorous.*] 'Living on both vegetable and animal food' (*Syd. Soc. Lex.*).

herbicide ('hɜːbɪsaɪd). [f. L. *herba* grass, green crops + -CIDE.] †**a.** Proprietary name for a preparation, prob. of sodium arsenite, used as a weed-killer. *Obs.* **b.** Any chemical agent that is toxic to some or all plants and is used to destroy unwanted vegetation. Hence **herbi'cidal** *a.*
1899 *Vermont Agric. Exper. Station Ann. Rep. 1898–99* 185 Carbolic acid is a valuable herbicide . . but . . the herbicidal action is of short duration. **1906** *U.S. Trade-mark 48,757* My [*sc.* W. J. Reade's] trade-mark consists of the coined word 'Herbicide'. The trade-mark has been continuously used in my business since 1894. **1915** *Chem. Abstr.* IX. 1973 (*caption*) Herbicides with arsenical base. **1942** W. W. ROBBINS et al. *Weed Control* xiii. 229 Studies of herbicides in soils show that the following factors determine the herbicidal effects of any chemical: (1) inherent toxicity of the chemical; (2) adsorption of the chemical by the soil; (3) decomposition . . tending to reduce toxicity; . . and (6) species tolerance. **1947** *New Biol.* II. 109 During recent years various organic compounds have been tested for their possible herbicidal value. **1954** *Sci. News* XXXI. 104 Weeds, therefore, could easily get life insurance were it not for the modern technique of chemical weed-killing, in particular by selective herbicides. **1959** *New Scientist* 5 Nov. 894/2 In abstracting and indexing the world's literature on weed control at Oxford [Department of Agriculture] we are constantly faced with difficulties caused by there being no agreement on what to call a herbicide. **1969** N. W. PIRIE *Food Resources* ii. 65 In Britain nearly all farms of more than 100 acres use herbicides on cereals. **1971** *Nature* 22 Jan. 224/1 Herbicidal attack appears to prevent the re-establishment of any new plant community . . for at least six years.

herbicolous (hə'bɪkələs), *a.* [f. L. *herba* grass + *-cola* inhabiting + -OUS.] Growing on herbaceous plants, as a fungus.
[**1863** BERKELEY *Outl. Brit. Fungology.* Gloss. *Herbicolæ.*] **1886** *Syd. Soc. Lex.*, *Herbicolous*, living on herbs.

herbid ('hɜːbɪd), *a. rare.* ? *Obs.* [ad. L. *herbid-us*, f. *herba*: see -ID. In obs. F. *herbide* (Godef.).] Grassy, grass-like.
1657 TOMLINSON *Renou's Disp.* 349 It beares an herbid and patulous umbell. **1727** BAILEY vol. II, *Herbid*, full of grass or herbs.

herbiferous (hə'bɪfərəs), *a.* [f. L. *herbifer* grass-bearing + -OUS.] Bearing or producing herbs.
1656 BLOUNT *Glossogr.*, *Herbiferous*, bringing forth hearbs or grass. **1731–52** in MILLER *Gard. Dict.* **1830** *Westm. Rev.* XIII. 208 Modern artists have none of the herbiferous taste of the Greeks.

herbigage, -bige, -binge, -binger: see HARBERGAGE, -BINGE, -BINGER.

†**'herbish,** *a. Obs.* [f. HERB + -ISH.] Resembling a herb; greenish.
1562 TURNER *Herbal* II. 70 b, Out of the which come furth floures, without of an herbishe color. **1578** LYTE *Dodoens* VI. xxiv. 688 Small white or yellowish knoppes, the whiche doo open into flowers of an herbish colour.

†**herbist.** *Obs.* [f. HERB + -IST, after F. *herbiste.*] = HERBALIST.
1611 COTGR., *Herbiste*, an Herbist, or Herballist . . that vnderstands the nature, and temper of hearbes. **1656** BLOUNT *Glossogr.*, *Herbalist* or *Herbist.*

†**'herbister.** *Sc. Obs.* [f. as prec. + -ER: cf. *barrister, chorister.*] = prec.
1623 *Kings of Scot.* in *Harl. Misc.* (Malh.) III. 463 A good medicinar and herbister.

†**herb Ive.** *Obs.* Also **herb Ivy, herb Eve.** [a. OF. *herbe ive*, f. *ive*, *Ajuga Chamæpitys*; supposed by Darmesteter to be a fem. deriv. of *if* yew.]
a. A name for Ground Pine, *Ajuga Chamæpitys.* **b.** Buck's-horn Plantain, *Plantago Coronopus.* **c.** Buck's-horn or Swine's Cress, *Senebiera Coronopus.*
[*c* **1265** *Voc. Plants* in Wr.-Wülcker 558/21 *Ostragium*, i. herbyue, i. liþewurt.] *c* **1386** CHAUCER *Nun's Pr. T.* 146 Of herbe yue growyng in oure yeerd ther mery is. *a* **1387** *Sinon. Barthol.* (Anecd. Oxon.) 17 *Cornu cervi*, i. herbive. **1548** TURNER *Names of Herbes, Coronopus* . . is called in Cambryge, herbe Iue . . it groweth muche aboute Shene aboue London. **1551** —— *Herbal* I. M ij, Coronopus . . is called in Englyshe herbe Iue or Crowfoote plant[ay]ne. **1578** LYTE *Dodoens* I. xviii. 28 Called in English . . Ground Pyne, Herbe Iue, Forget me not, and field Cypres. **1591** PERCIVALL *Sp. Dict.*, *Yva*, ground pine, herbe Iuie. **1597** GERARDE *Herbal* II. xcvi. § 2. 347 Buckes horne is called . . of many herbe Iuie, or herbe Eue. **1611** COTGR., *Ive arthritique*, Hearbe Iue, ground Pine, field Cyprues, Forget-me-not.

‖**Herbivora** (hə'bɪvərə), *sb. pl. Zool.* [neut. pl. (sc. *animalia*) of L. *herbivorus* herb-eating.] A general name for animals, esp. mammals, that feed on herbage or plants. *spec.* The name of a division of Marsupials, including the kangaroos; and of a division of Cetacea.
1830 LYELL *Princ. Geol.* I. 152 They serve to attest the contiguity of land inhabited by large *herbivora.* **1890** A. R. WALLACE *Darwinism* 18 There will also be carnivora destroying the herbivora.

herbivore ('hɜːbɪvɔə(r)). [a. F. *herbivore* (1748 in Hatz.-Darm.), ad. L. *herbivor-us* HERBIVOROUS.] A herbivorous animal; one of the Herbivora.
1854 OWEN *Skel. & Teeth* in *Circ. Sc.*, *Organ. Nat.* I. 254 The herbivore . . is, in Australia, a leaping animal. **1879** H. SPENCER *Data of Ethics* ii. 17 That the carnivore may live herbivores must die.

herbivority (hɜːbɪ'vɒrɪtɪ). *rare.* [f. mod.L. *herbivor-us* + -(I)TY.] Herbivorous nature.
1859 R. OWEN in *Encycl. Brit.* XVII. 159/2 The form of the molar teeth of one jaw is recognisable, but the herbivority of the fossil is not thereby determined.

herbivorous (hə'bɪvərəs), *a.* [f. mod.L. *herbivor-us* herb-eating + -OUS.] Herb-eating; applied to those animals that feed naturally on herbage or the leaves of plants.
1661 LOVELL *Hist. Anim. & Min.* Introd., Birds, which are..herbivorous, eating grasse or plants. **1794** HUNTER in *Phil. Trans.* LXXXIV. 409 If the bones were those of carnivorous animals and herbivorous. **1848** CARPENTER *Anim. Phys.* 33 The large herbivorous quadrupeds, such as the ox. **1860** tr. *Hartwig's Sea & Wond.* xiii. 240 The sea-snails are either predaceous or herbivorous.

†**herb John.** *Obs.* [transl. med.L. *herba Johannis*, F. *herbe de Saint-Jean*, in sense 1.]
1. St. John's-wort, *Hypericum perforatum.*
[*c* **1265** *Voc. Plants* in Wr.-Wülcker 557/18 *Ypis*, herbe Johan, uelderude.] *c* **1440** *Promp. Parv.* 140/2 Erbe Ion, or Seynt Ionys worte, *perforata, fuga demonum, ypericon.* *c* **1460** J. RUSSELL *Bk. Nurture* 992 Walle wort, herbe Iohn, Sentory, rybbewort, & camamelle.
2. App. a name for some tasteless herb of neutral qualities; hence applied, in proverbial phrases, to something inert or indifferent.
[Cotgrave has: *Herbe de S. Iean*, thin-leaued Mugwort; some also call Clarie so.]
1614 T. ADAMS *Devil's Banquet* 307 Balme, with the destitution of Gods blessing, doth as much good, as a branch of hearbe-Iohn in our Pottage. **1620** BP. HALL *Hon. Mar. Clergy* II. i, As for that parcell of the testimonie..it is a Herbe-Iohn in the pot to the purpose of my allegation. **1658** GURNALL *Chr. in Arm.* verse 14. ii. (1669) 12/1 Like Herb-John in the pot, that does neither much good nor hurt. **1679** *Hist. Jetzer* 33 The Bishop of Lausanne, being a Flegmatick and heavy piece, moved slowly, and was herb John in the whole proceeding.

herbless ('hɜːblɪs), *a.* [f. HERB *sb.* + -LESS.] Destitute of herbs or herbage.
1682 TATE *Abs. & Achit.* II. 1108 His bed the herbless ground. **1817** BYRON *Manfred* II. ii, Where the birds dare not build, nor insect's wing Flit o'er the herbless granite. **1847** MARY HOWITT *Ballads* 84 An herbless waste of stone.

herblet ('hɜːblɪt). [f. as prec. + -LET. Cf. obs. F. *herbelette.*] A little herb.
1611 SHAKS. *Cymb.* IV. ii. 287 You were as Flowres, now wither'd: euen so These Herbelets shall, which we vpon you strew. **1814** CARY *Dante Purg.* XXIX. 86 The flowers And the fresh herblets. **1842** G. TURNBULL in *Proc. Berw. Nat. Club* II. No. 10. 7 The forget-me-not, the ranunculus, and other semi-aquatic herblets.

†**'herbling.** *Obs.* [f. as prec. + -LING. Cf. *shrubling.*] = prec.
1562 TURNER *Herbal* II. 34 Lepidium yt Pliny describeth is no herblyng but a long and a great herbe.

herb-man. A man who deals in herbs.
1580 HOLLYBAND *Treas. Fr. Tong, Vn verdurier ou verduriére*, an hearbe man or woman which furnisheth a house with hearbes, bowes, and like greene things. **1598** FLORIO, *Herbaio*, an herbe man, a simpler, an herbarist.

herb of grace: see HERB-GRACE.

herbor(e, -bour(e, -borȝ, -borough, -borow, -borwe, etc., ME. ff. HARBOUR *sb.*[1], *v.*

herborgerie, -borgere, -borous, -bory: see HARBERGERY, -BINGER, -BOROUS, -BRY.

herborist ('hɜːbərɪst). [a. F. *herboriste* (1545 in Hatz.-Darm., who also cite *herboliste* 1530), 'derived from *herbe* by confusion with the radical of L. *arbor*' (Darmesteter): cf. the more etymological synonyms HERBALIST, HERBARIST, also the history of ARBOUR *sb.*] One skilled in herbs, a herbalist.
1578 LYTE *Dodoens* III. lvii. 398 Some Herboristes of Fraunce do cal it *Solanum lignosum.* **1601** CHESTER *Love's Mart., Dial.* lxxiv, For so our Herborists haue truly told. **1698** M. LISTER *Journ. Paris* (1699) 61 All the most curious Herborists in Europe. **1821** J. E. SMITH in *Mem.* (1832) I. 503 Some of our best herborists.

ˌ**herbori'zation.** [n. of action f. HERBORIZE: so F. *herborisation.*]
1. The action of herborizing; a botanizing excursion.
1698 *Phil. Trans.* XX. 385 The Book..is divided into Six Herborisations, each of which contains the Plants he met with in the Course of the Walk. **1816** J. SCOTT *Vis. Paris* (ed. 5) 302 Jussieu..announced excursions in the fields, or herborizations, and appointed his rendezvous near one of the barriers at eight o'clock. **1852** TH. ROSS *Humboldt's Trav.* I. xv. 490 We made a long herborization in a thick forest.
¶ 2. By confusion for ARBORIZATION.
1778 *Nat. Hist.* in *Ann. Reg.* 110/1 Agates and jaspers containing curious spots, shades, and herborizations. **1785** MATY in *New Review* Oct. 269 Mr. Daubenton gives an account of three different kinds of herborizations..amongst which are those found on agats.

herborize ('hɜːbəraɪz), *v.* [a. F. *herborise-r* (1611 in Cotgr.) 'derived from *herbe* by confusion with the radical of L. *arbor* tree: cf. *arboriser*' (Darmesteter). Cf. the more etymological *herbarize, herbalize.*]
1. *intr.* To tend herbs or plants; to garden. *rare.*
1664 URQUHART *Rabelais* I. xxiii. 109 Little Mattocks, Pickaxes..Pruning-knives, and other instruments requisite for herborising [**1653** gardning].
2. To gather herbs; to botanize.
1749 STACK in *Phil. Trans.* XLVI. 52 They herborized together in Catalonia. **1825** tr. *C'tess De Genlis' Mem.* V. 38, I went with my little companion to herborize in the woods. **1865** *Pall Mall G.* No. 134. 11/1 To herborize on the slopes of Parnassus.
Hence **'herborizer**, one who herborizes; **'herborizing** *vbl. sb.* and *ppl. a.*
1789 COXE *Trav. Switz.* I. ix. 91 Haller, whom he accompanied in his herborising excursions. **1853** *Fraser's Mag.* XLVII. 50 Herborizing never ceased..to be the scholar's chief delight. **1882** SALA in *Illustr. Lond. News* 16 Sept. 295, I am not as Jean Jaques was, a 'herboriser', I only study 'pot herbs'.

herborized, *ppl. a.* [see HERBORIZATION 2.] Used by confusion for *arborized*: see ARBORIZE.
1788 tr. *Fourcroy's Nat. Hist. & Chem.* I. 275 M. Daubenton has shewn..that herborized stones contain very fine mosses.

herbose (hɜː'bəʊs), *a.* [ad. L. *herbōs-us*, f. *herba*: see -OSE.] Abounding in herbs or herbage.
1721 BAILEY, *Herbose*, Grassy, full of Grass or Herbs. *a* **1763** BYROM *Crit. Rem., Hor. Odes* III. xviii. in Chalmers *Eng. Poets* XV. 239 Now in December, if we reason close, Are fields poetically call'd *herbose*? **1869** tr. *Pouchet's Universe* (1871) 42 In the Phoenician traditions, where they speak of a herbose or gelatinous sea, situated beyond the Pillars of Hercules.
Hence **her'bosity**, *rare.*
1731–52 MILLER *Gard. Dict., Herbosity*, grassiness, abundance of herbs.

herbour, obs. var. ARBOUR; see HERBER.

herbour, -bourgh, -bourough, -bowr(e, obs. ff. HARBOUR *sb.* and *v.*
1486 *Bk. St. Albans* F vij b, Ye shall say thus: An hert Herbourghith.

herbous ('hɜːbəs), *a.* [ad. L. *herbōs-us*: see prec. and cf. F. *herbeux, -euse.*] Belonging to or of the nature of a herb; herbaceous.
1712 *H. More's Enthus. Tri.* Schol. 52, I had usually sweet Herbous Scents in my Nostrils. **1725** BRADLEY *Fam. Dict.* s.v. *Jujube*, The Flowers are pale and herbous, consisting of five Leaves, standing Rosewise. **1893** *Scribner's Mag.* XIII. 324/1 Tall, herbous vegetation.

herb Paris. [ad. med.L. *herba paris*; in Fr. *herbe à Paris, parisette.* The origin of the name is obscure; some explain *paris* as the genitive of L. *par* 'equal, a mate, a pair', in reference to the regularity of its leaves and flowers (see quot. 1864); others refer it to the Trojan Paris.]
A general book-name for *Paris quadrifolia* (N.O. *Trilliaceæ*), also called True-love, a dictyogenous plant found in moist woods, bearing a single greenish flower at the top of the stem, and just beneath it four large ovate leaves in the form of a cross.
[**1558** MATTHIOLUS in *Dioscaridem* 539 Plantam quam herbariorum vulgus Herbam Paris appellat. **1568** TURNER *Herbal* I. 19 (not in ed. 1551) Ye same herbe is called of ye Barbarus writers *Herba paris.*]
1578 LYTE *Dodoens* III. lxxvii. 425 Herbe Paris hath a smoth round stalke..vppon the whiche growe foure leaues. **1597** GERARDE *Herbal* II. lxxxv. §7. 329 Herbe Paris..is proued to represse the force of poison. **1864** PRIOR *Plant-n.* (1870) 111 *Herb Paris*, incorrectly so spelt..being..*Herba paris*, Herb of a pair, of a betrothed couple, in reference to its four leaves being set upon the stalk like a trulove-knot, the emblem of an engagement, whence its synonym, *Herb Tru-love.* *a* **1888** MARY HOWITT *Autobiog.* (1889) I. 41 In other spots flourished..the rare four-leaved Herb Paris, bearing its berry-like flower at the central angles of its four leaves.

herbreoure, var. of HERBRYOUR, *Obs.*

herbri, var. HARBOURY *sb.* and HARBRY *v.*, *Obs.*

herb Robert. [ad. med.L. *herba Roberti.*
The name has been variously supposed to refer to Robert Duke of Normandy, to St. Robert, and to St. Rupert.]
The English name for a common wild species of Crane's-bill or Geranium (*G. Robertianum*), with divided leaves and light reddish purple flowers.
c **1265** *Voc. Plants* in Wr.-Wülcker 558/6 *Herba Roberti*, herbe Robert, chareuille. **1483** *Cath. Angl.* 183/2 Herbe Robert, *herba Roberti.* **1562** TURNER *Herbal* II. 136. **1578** LYTE *Dodoens* I. xxxii. 47 The fourth kinde [of Geranium] is called..in English Herbe Robert. **1579** LANGHAM *Gard. Health* (1633) 311 *Herbe Robert*..staunchet h bloud of greene wounds brused and applyed. **1747** WESLEY *Prim. Physic* (1762) 77 Drink Decoction of Herb Robert. **1826** K. DIGBY *Broadst. Hon.* (1846) II. 364 The herb Robert blooms about the 29th of April, the day of St. Robert founder of the Carthusians.

herbrough, obs. form of HARBOUR *sb.* and *v.*

herbry, var. HARBOURY *sb.* and HARBRY *v.*, *Obs.*

†**'herbryage.** *Sc. Obs.* [f. *herbry*, HARBOURY *sb.* or HARBRY *v.* + -AGE.] Entertainment, lodging.
c **1470** HENRY *Wallace* IV. 118 Bot he was than ȝeit still at herbryage.

†**herbryour.** *Sc. Obs.* Also herbre-, herbrey-, herbri-. [f. *herbry, herbery*, HARBOURY: cf. HARBINGER and HARBOURER.] One sent on before to secure lodgings for an army or company; in *pl.* an advance company sent to procure lodgings or a camping-ground; = *herberger*, HARBINGER 2.
1375 BARBOUR *Bruce* XVI. 465 The dowglass with thame ferd, That had thar herbreouris [*E.* herbryouris] all slayne. *Ibid.* XVIII. 334 Thai..saw thair herbreouris then Cum reboytit on that maneir.

†**'herbulent**, *a.* *Obs. rare*$^{-0}$. [f. L. *herba*: cf. *turbulentus*, f. *turba.*] = HERBOSE.
1656 BLOUNT *Glossogr.*, Herbulent (*herbulentus*), full of grass or hearbs.

herbure, -burgh(e, -burh(e, etc., obs. ff. HARBOUR *sb.*[1] and *v.*

herburgage, -burger: see HARBERGAGE, HARBINGER.

'herb-wife. = next.
1583 HOLLYBAND *Campo di Fior* 111 There is a certeine herbe-wife, Of whom if you do buye. **1631** *Act Com. Councell Lond.* 1 Oyster wiues, Herbe wiues, Tripe wiues, and the like. **1825** JAMIESON, *Yirb-wife*, an old woman, who pretends to be acquainted with the medicinal qualities of herbs. **1891** C. CREIGHTON *Epidemics Brit.* 483 Herb-wives and gardeners also prospered.

'herb-woman. A woman who sells herbs.
1608 SHAKS. *Per.* IV. vi. 92 Why, your herb-woman; she that sets seeds and roots of shame and iniquity. **1642** *Ordin. & Declar. Lords & Com., Lords Day* 5 Any Fruiterers or Hearbe-women. **1750** CHESTERF. *Lett.* (1792) III. ccxxix. 40 Even the herb-women at Athens were correct judges of it. **1853** HICKIE tr. *Aristoph.* (1872) II. 472 Euripides the son of the herb-woman.

herby ('hɜːbɪ), *a.* [f. HERB *sb.* + -Y.]
1. Full of or abounding in herbs; grassy.
1552 HULOET, Herby, or full of herbs, or hauynge herbes, *herbidus.* **1611** COTGR., *Herbageux*, grassie, herbie. *c* **1611** CHAPMAN *Iliad* V. 39 An herby seat on broad Scamander's shore. **1613** PURCHAS *Pilgrimage* (1614) 729 Columbus..After many dayes..incountred with that Herbie Sea. **1889** C. EDWARDES *Sardinia* 210 The herby slope.
2. Of the nature of a herb, herbaceous; pertaining to or characteristic of herbs.
1552 HULOET, Herby, or pertaynynge to herbes, *herbarius.* **1578** LYTE *Dodoens* III. xxxvi. 367 The flowers..of a white greene or herby colour. **1579** LANGHAM *Gard. Health* (1633) 189 Maudlinwort, or the herby part of the wilde Dasy. **1688** R. HOLME *Armoury* II. 73/2 The Bean Caper is an herby, not a wooddy stalk. **1784** TWAMLEY *Dairying* 114 The stem is herbaceous or of a herby nature. **1884** T. HARDY *Wessex Tales, Interlopers* (1889) 171 The herby breath of cows.

herbygage, -bynger, -byrȝe: see HARBERGAGE, -BINGER, -BOUR.

herc, herce, obs. forms of HARK, HEARSE.

hercogamy (hə'kɒgəmɪ). *Bot.* Also **herk-**. [f. Gr. ἕρκος fence, barrier + γάμος, -γαμια marriage.]
The prevention of self-fertilization in flowers by means of structural obstacles. So **herco'gamic, her'cogamous** *adjs.*, unable to be self-fertilized: see quot. 1880.
1880 GRAY *Struct. Bot.* (ed. 6) I. 414/2 *Hercogamous(-us)*, Said of hermaphrodite flowers when some structural obstacle prevents autogamy. **1883** D. W. THOMPSON tr. *Müller's Fertil. Flowers* 20 Axell considers that a further advance is shown in passing from dichogamic to herkogamic flowers. **1887** H. M. WARD tr. *Sachs' Phys. Plants* 799 All the marvellous adaptations of Dichogamy, Heterostylism, Herkogamy..may be looked upon in this sense.

†**hercotec'tonic**, *a.* *Obs. rare*$^{-1}$. [f. Gr. ἕρκος wall, barrier + τεκτονικός TECTONIC.] Of or pertaining to the construction of walls or fortifications.
1672 SIR S. MORLAND (*title*) The Count of Pagan's Method of Delineating..Fortifications..Reduced to English Measure, and converted into Hercotectonick-Lines.

†**Hercu'lanean**, *a.*[1] *Obs. rare.* [f. L. *Herculāne-us*, f. *Herculēs*: see -AN.] = HERCULEAN; in quot., *humorously*, 'very strong'.
1604 DEKKER *1st Pt. Honest Wh.* Wks. 1873 II. 28 Here's most Herculanian tobacco.

Herculanean (ˌhɜːkjuː'leɪnɪən), *a.*[2] [f. L. *Herculāne-us* belonging to *Herculāneum* + -AN.]
Of or pertaining to Herculaneum, a town in Campania, which was buried with Pompeii in the eruption of Vesuvius in 79 A.D., and has in modern times been partly excavated.
1780 COWPER *Progr. Err.* 398 Models of Herculanean pots and pans. **1819** WORDSW. *September* 1819, ix, O ye, who patiently explore The wreck of Herculanean lore.

Herculean (hə'kjuːlɪən), *a.* [f. L. *Hercule-us*, f. *Herculēs* (see below) + -AN. Cf. F. *Herculéen.*]
1. Of or pertaining to Hercules.
Herculean pillars, straits: see HERCULES 1 c.
1610 *Chester's Tri.* (Chetham Soc.) Particulars 2 Bearing Herculian Clubbes in their hands. **1613** PURCHAS *Pilgrimage* (1614) 233 The Arabike tongue..It is now the most universall in the world..from the Herculean Pillars to the Molluccas. *c* **1645** HOWELL *Lett.* xlviii. (1754) 354 You have knocked him down with a kind of Herculean Club. **1678** CUDWORTH *Intell. Syst.* I. iii. §33. 141 That the

Mediterranean Sea forced open that passage of the Herculean Straits. **1803** BEDDOES *Hygëia* ix. 17 It [epilepsy] was like-wise called the Herculean complaint, an appellation which medical etymologists are puzzled to explain.

2. Like Hercules, esp. in strength, courage, or labours; prodigiously powerful or vigorous; gigantic.

1596 NASHE *Saffron Walden* 116 The more than Herculean fury he was in. **1667** MILTON *P.L.* IX. 1060 The Danite strong, Herculean Samson. **1791** BOSWELL *Johnson* an. 1750 (1831) I. 201 Addison's style..though comparatively weak, when opposed to Johnson's Herculean vigour. **1814** BYRON *Corsair* I. ix, Robust but not Herculean —to the sight No giant frame sets forth his common height. **1891** *Spectator* 18 Sept., His labours in the cause of science were herculean.

b. *transf.* Of things: Strong, powerful, violent.

1602 MARSTON *Antonio's Rev.* II. iii. Wks. 1856 I. 100 Let mine out-woe me: mine's Hurculean woe. **1664** POWER *Exp. Philos.* 135 The first (which is the main and Herculean-Argument). **1747** WESLEY *Prim. Physic* (1762) p. xxv, The four Herculean Medicines, Opium, The Bark, Steel, and most of the Preparations of Quicksilver. Herculean indeed! Far too strong for common Men to grapple with.

3. Of a labour or task: Difficult or hard to accomplish as Hercules' labours were; requiring the strength of a Hercules; excessive, immense.

1617 MORYSON *Itin.* To Rdr. ¶v, The adding of these severall values in each daies journy, had been an Herculean labour. **1732** BERKELEY *Alciphr.* I. §1 Acquiring true knowledge, that Herculean labour. **1875** SCRIVENER *Lect. Text N. Test.* 13 An herculean task, to which not one life but many must needs be devoted.

Hercules (ˈhɜːkjuliːz). [L., ad. Gr. Ἡρακλῆς (-κλέης), f. Ἥρα, Hera, wife of Zeus + κλέος glory, renown, lit. 'having or showing the glory of Hera'.]

1. A celebrated hero of Greek and Roman mythology, who after death was ranked among the gods and received divine honours. He is represented as possessed of prodigious strength, whereby he was enabled to perform twelve extraordinary tasks or 'labours' imposed upon him by Hera, to which, and to his club, there are many allusions in literature. In Greek and Latin his name is used in exclamations and asseverations.

c **1369** CHAUCER *Dethe Blaunche* 1058 Thogh I had hadde ..al the strengthe of Ercules. **1551** T. WILSON *Logike* (1580) 74 b, A tale of one, whose carte stode fast in the mire, whiche man..cried to Hercules for helpe. **1581** PETTIE tr. *Guazzo's Civ. Conv.* I. (1586) 21 A travel and charge farre greater than the twelve labors of Hercules. *a* **1592** GREENE *George a Greene* Wks. (Rtldg.) 259/1 'Not Hercules against two' the proverb is. **1678** DRYDEN *All for Love* II. i, O Hercules! Why should a Man like this..Be all the care of heav'n? *Ibid.*, By Hercules, the Writing of Octavius!

b. A representation of Hercules or a strong man.

1638 F. JUNIUS *Paint. Ancients* 164 [He] was taken with nothing so much as with a little Hercules standing upon the table. **1753** HANWAY *Trav.* (1762) I. VII. xciii. 427 The arms of the house of Brandenburg, supported by two herculeses.

c. ***Pillars of Hercules, Hercules' Pillars***: the rocks Calpé (now Gibraltar) and Abyla (Ceuta), on either side of the Strait of Gibraltar, thought by the ancients to be the supports of the western boundary of the world, and to have been set up by Hercules; so ***Straits of Hercules***. Hence *fig.*, an ultimate limit, the *ne plus ultra*.

1387 TREVISA *Higden* (Rolls) I. 298 To þe see Gaditanus, þere Hercules his pileres stondeþ. **1581** PETTIE *Guazzo's Civ. Conv.* II. (1586) 87 We must laie before us the noble devise of Charles the fifth, to wit, the pillers of Hercules, and to dispose ourselves to goe beyond them. **1644** MILTON *Areop.* (Arb.) 64 A parochiall Minister, who has his reward, and is at his Hercules pillars in a warm benefice. **1855** MACAULAY *Hist. Eng.* xviii, The Mediterranean squadron.. was vainly struggling to pass the pillars of Hercules.

2. One who resembles Hercules in strength; a man of prodigious strength; a big man.

1567 *Triall Treas.* (1850) 11 Where is now that valiaunt Hercules? For all his bragges, he is nowe runne away. **1768–74** TUCKER *Lt. Nat.* (1852) II. 561 Others there are, who can be satisfied with nothing less than heroism in self-denial; they must be..Herculeses to subdue all monsters. **1858** GEN. P. THOMPSON *Audi Alt.* I. xlii. 163 The tea-kettle was brought in by a black Hercules.

3. A fanciful name given to powerful machines: **a.** A heavy weight used like the ram or 'monkey' in a pile-driving machine. **b.** A kind of machine for cleansing the streets.

1794 *Rigging & Seamanship* I. 80 The *Hercules* is used for setting straight the shank, welding..the arms to the shank, of large anchors. It consists of a weight of about 400 lb. faced with steel, and a long iron shank. **1880** *Encycl. Brit.* XI. 425/1 The 'Hercules', a ponderous mass of iron attached to a vertical guide rod, which was lifted originally by a gang of men with ropes, but afterwards by steam power, and allowed to fall by its own weight. **1890** *Daily News* 1 Feb. 3/3 This new contrivance is called the 'Hercules' machine—an apt name for the Augæan stable of London..This new Hercules can scrape thoroughly clean, in sixty minutes, half a mile in length by nearly thirty feet in width of the dirtiest street space in London.

4. *Entom.* (In full, ***Hercules beetle***). A gigantic lamellicorn beetle, *Dynastes* (or *Megasoma*) *Hercules*, about five inches in length.

1816 PRISC. WAKEFIELD *Nat. Hist. Insects* iv. 28 The largest of this genus is called the Hercules, and is a Native of South America. **1840** SWAINSON *Nat. Hist. Insects* 232 Turn to..the Hercules beetle..it cannot for a moment be doubted that this gigantic insect is completely arboreal.

5. *Bot.* = *Hercules' club.*

1756 P. BROWNE *Jamaica* (1789) 189 Zanthoxylum.. Prickly Yellow-wood, or yellow Hercules.

6. *Astron.* A name of one of the northern constellations, figured as a man kneeling on his right knee; known to the earlier Greek and Roman writers as ἐνγόνασι(ν, *genunixus, ingenic(u)lus*, the 'kneeler'.

1674 MOXON *Tutor Astron.* (ed. 3) 212 *Engonasis*..some will have it to be Hercules, that mighty Conqueror. **1727–41** CHAMBERS *Cycl.* s.v., The stars in the constellation Hercules, in Ptolemy's catalogue, are 29. **1838** *Penny Cycl.* XII. 148 *Hercules*, one of the old constellations, called ἐνγονασιν by Aratus, Hyginus, and Ptolemy, and described by the first as 'a figure like that of a man in sorrow'. [Hyginus *Poet. Astron.* (B.C. 10) *has* En Gonasin. Hunc Eratosthenes Herculem dicit.]

7. Comb. ***Hercules-like*** adj.; **Hercules' allheal**, a perennial umbelliferous plant, *Opopanax Chironium*; **Hercules braid** (see quot.); **Hercules knot**, a kind of knot, attributed to Hercules, very difficult to undo; **Hercules powder**, a powerful explosive used in mining operations.

1597 GERARDE *Herbal* 850 *Hercules Alheale or Woundwort. **1882** CAULFEILD & SAWARD *Dict. Needlework*, **Hercules Braid*, a thick corded worsted braid, which is employed for trimmings. **1601** HOLLAND *Pliny* II. 305 As for greene wounds, it is wonderfull how soon they will be healed, in case they be bound vp and tied with a *Hercules knot. **1646** SIR T. BROWNE *Pseud. Ep.* v. xxi. 265 The true lovers knot..had perhaps its originall from *Nodus Herculanus*, or that which was called Hercules his knot. **1593** *Bacchus' Bountie* in *Harl. Misc.* (1809) II. 304 All the other gods and goddesses, *Hercules-like, are cloyed with such cholericke clubbes. **1881** RAYMOND *Mining Gloss.*, **Hercules powder*. **1882** COPP *Amer. Mining Code* 101 The principal explosives used in mining are..rend-rock, Hercules..and other powders.

Hercules' club. [From the club which Hercules is represented as bearing; see prec., sense 1.] **a.** The name of a plant, *Xanthoxylon Clava-Herculis*; also, *Aralia spinosa* (*Syd. Soc. Lex.* 1886). **b.** A kind of firework. **c.** 'A stick of unusual size and formidable appearance' (Brewer).

1688 *Lond. Gaz.* No. 2362/3 Rockets..Reporters, Hercules Club..with all manner of other Fire-works were discharged. **1882** J. SMITH *Dict. Econ. Plants, Hercules' Club* ..of the Bean Caper family..Its wood is yellow, and is a useful timber.

herculite. [f. HERCUL-ES + -ITE.] A kind of explosive: see quot.

1892 *Pall Mall G.* 1 Sept. 7/1 Herculite, a new French explosive, is a yellowish-grey powder, composed of sawdust, camphor, nitrate of potash, and several substances that are kept secret.

hercynian (həˈsɪnɪən), *a.* [f. L. *Hercynia* (sc. *silva*) = Gr. Ἑρκύνιος δρυμός the Hercynian forest (see below and -AN).] **1.** Applied by and after the ancient writers to the wooded mountain-system of Middle Germany, or to portions of it.

1598 GRENEWEY *Tacitus' Descr. Germanie* iv. 266 The Hercynian forrest doth containe the Catti, and is the bounds of their territory. **1630** *R. Johnson's Kingd. & Commw.* 276 Bohemia..is incompassed with great Mountaines and the Hercynian woods. **1890** J. G. FRAZER *Golden Bough* I. i. 56 Down to the first century before our era the Hercynian forest stretched eastward from the Rhine for a distance at once vast and unknown. **1935** W. G. EAST *Hist. Geogr. Europe* ii. 51 The Hercynian forest, as Caesar described it, could be crossed in nine days by a fast runner.

2. In *Geol.* used by different writers in various senses, with allusion to the Harz Mountains.

The word was first used in geology as the G. *hercynisch* (according to Suess by von Buch) in sense c, and was adopted by several writers, chiefly German and French, in sense a; in 1887 Bertrand (*Bull. de la Soc. géol. de France* XV. 438) used it in sense b to replace the *variscisch und armoricanisch* of Suess, and this has become the usual sense in English.

a. Designating one of the Devonian formations of the Harz Mountains; so ***Hercynian fauna*** (after Kayser, 1879), ***gneiss*** (after Gümbel, 1868).

1880 J. D. DANA *Man. Geol.* (ed. 3) III. i. 151 In Europe, the Archæan system has been distinctly recognized in.. Bavaria (Hercynian and Bojie Gneiss). **1885** GEIKIE *Text Bk. Geol.* (ed. 2) 641 Grey gneiss, containing white or grey felspar, and abundant dark magnesia-mica..(termed the Hercynian gneiss). **1893** P. LAKE tr. *Kayser's Text Bk. Compar. Geol.* II. 101 First described by H. Römer and Giebel as Silurian, this Hercynian fauna of the Lower Harz has more recently been compared by E. Beyrich with the fauna of the Bohemian stages F, G, H of Barrande, and was afterwards described by Kayser..as Lower Devonian. **1895** J. D. DANA *Man. Geol.* (ed. 4) IV. ii. 570 Kayser concluded ..that the Lower Helderberg formation of America was Hercynian, that is, lowest Devonian. **1906** CHAMBERLIN & SALISBURY *Geology* II. viii. 450 The Hercynian fauna which characterizes this stage of the Devonian in southern Europe has much in common with the Helderberg fauna of America. **1955** G. G. WOODFORD tr. *Gignoux's Stratigr. Geol.* iv. 128 The Hercynian facies of the Lower Devonian appears in the Kellerwald.

b. Of, pertaining to, or contemporaneous with the mountain-building movements that occurred in Europe in late Carboniferous and early Permian times, or the mountains then formed; hence, late Palæozoic; = ARMORICAN *a.* 2.

1895 J. D. DANA *Man. Geol.* (ed. 4) IV. iii. 734 The 'Hercynian system' of Bertrand includes a long range of dislocated Devonian and Carboniferous rocks extending from Brittany to the Vosges and Ardennes, and beyond along the Black Forest, the Harz to Bohemia. **1926** *Publ. Carnegie Inst. Washington* No. 375. v. 69 The movements in late Stephanian and in Permian time can best be considered as the final effects of the Hercynian movement. **1935** E. B. BAILEY *Tectonic Ess.* i. 5 The Ardennes of Belgium and much of the Appalachians of America are alike members of the Hercynian System. *Ibid.* 8 Hercynian in Bertrand's sense has established itself apparently for all time in the literature of France, Switzerland, Britain, and America. **1948** R. L. SHERLOCK *Permo-Triassic Formations* iv. 40 Like the present Alps, the Hercynian Mountains were the result of the squeezing of the sediments deposited in a Mediterranean Sea, the Palaeozoic Tethys. **1967** D. H. RAYNER *Stratigr. Brit. Isles* i. 27 Extending down the centre of England..there are various Carboniferous outcrops whose structures are largely Hercynian in age but which follow older directions.

c. Applied (rarely in English) to those faults, folds, and other geological features in Europe with a predominantly north-western direction.

1904 H. B. SOLLAS tr. *Suess's Face of Earth* I. I. iii. 121 This..does not exclude the existence in Central Europe of two different directions, which have produced folds and mountain chains striking more to the north-east in the one case, in the other more to the north-west. The former is known as the direction of the Netherlands, the latter as the Hercynian direction. **1909** *Ibid.* IV. v. i. 2 The important point for L. von Buch, when he created the 'Hercynian system', was the (orographical) north-westerly direction, for Marcel Bertrand it was the tectonic age. *Ibid.* 33 These fractures..determine L. von Buch's 'Hercynian system', which embraces all the mountains striking to the north-west; many eminent German geologists still describe these long lines as Hercynian. **1935** E. B. BAILEY *Tectonic Ess.* i. 5 For von Buch, the Hercynian character was a west-north-westerly, or north-westerly, *trend*... Accordingly, among German-speaking tectonists, Hercynian is still commonly employed to group together a very important set of more or less north-westerly fractures and folds that characterize much of Czechoslovakia, Germany, and Scania.

hercynite (ˈhɜːsɪnaɪt). *Min.* Also hercin-, hyrcin-. [Named (1839) *Hercynit*, f. L. *Hercynia* (see HERCYNIAN *a.*).] Aluminate of iron, found in black octahedral crystals in the Bohemian Forest.

1849 J. NICOL *Min.* 251 Hercynite. **1887** DANA *Man. Min.* 215 *Hercynite*, a spinel affording on analysis alumina and iron protoxide, with only 2·9 per cent. of magnesia.

herd (hɜːd), *sb.*[1] Forms: 1 heord, hiord, 2–3 heorde, (3 hierde), 3– herd; also 3–5 hird, 4 hyrde, 4–6 herde, 5–6 heerd, 6–7 heard. [Com. Teut.: OE. *heord* str. fem. = OLG. **herda* (MLG. *herde*), OHG. *herta* (MHG. *hert(e*, Ger. *herde*), ON. *hjǫrð* (Sw., Da. *hjord*), Goth. *hairda*:—OTeut. **herdâ*- = pre-Teut. **kerdhâ*: cf. Skr. *çárdha-s* troop, OSlav. *črêda* herd, flock.]

1. a. A company of domestic animals of one kind, kept together under the charge of one or more persons. (The notion of a keeper is now little present, and the sense is scarcely distinct from 2.)

a **1000** *Ags. Voc.* in Wr.-Wülcker 274/18 *Arimentum*, hiord. *c* **1000** *Ags. Gosp.* Matt. xxvi. 31 Þurh þæs hyrdes slege byð seo heord todræfed. *c* **1000** ÆLFRIC *Exod.* iii. 1 He draf his heorde to inneweardum ðam westene. **1484** CAXTON *Fables of Æsop* III. vi, The wulf whiche is enemy of thy heerd. **1526** TINDALE *Mark* v. 11 Ther was there nye vnto the mountayns a greate heerd of swyne fedinge. **1577** B. GOOGE *Heresbach's Husb.* I. (1586) 3 b, My heardes of cattel lowing hard by me. *a* **1700** DRYDEN *Ovid's Met.* I. Wks. 1808 XII. 90 With this he did a herd of goats controul. **1750** GRAY *Elegy* i, The lowing herd winds slowly o'er the lea. **1865** H. H. DIXON *Field & Fern* vii. 134 A well-known breeder has a herd of shorthorns.

b. As contrasted with *flock* (see FLOCK *sb.*[1] 3), esp. in the phrase ***herds and flocks***, *herd* is restricted to cattle or bovine domestic animals.

1587 GOLDING *De Mornay* i. 5 But the tame..do naturally liue in flockes and heardes. **1596** BP. W. BARLOW *Three Serm.* i. 16 Heards and flockes of cattle and sheepe perish. **1611** BIBLE *Lev.* xxvii. 32 Concerning the tithe of the herd, or of the flock. **1740** C. PITT *Æneid* III. (R.), Our flocks to slaughter, and our herds destroy. **1873** C. ROBINSON *N.S. Wales* 29 Multitudinous as our flocks and herds have become.

†**c.** *fig.* A spiritual flock: cf. FLOCK *sb.*[1] 4. *Obs.*

c **1000** *Inst. Polity* in Thorpe *Anc. Laws* II. 304 þæt he sy ..rihtwis hyrde ofer cristene heorde. *c* **1175** *Lamb. Hom.* 95 Erest he scal hine seolfne wið sunnan isteoran and seoððan his heorde. **1612** *Two Noble K.* I. iv, The impartial gods, who from the mounted heavens View us their mortal herd, behold who err.

2. a. A company of animals of any kind, feeding or travelling in company; a school (of whales, porpoises, etc.).

c **1205** LAY. 305 Heo funden ane heorde of heorten. *c* **1250** *Gen. & Ex.* 2988 And gnattes hird ðor ðicke up-wond. *c* **1385** CHAUCER *L.G.W.* 1212 *Dido*, The hirde of hertis Is I-founde a-non. *c* **1440** *Promp. Parv.* 236/2 Heerde, or flok of beestys, what so euyr they be, *polia*. *c* **1470** in *Hors, Shepe & G.* etc. (Caxton 1479, Roxb. repr.) 30 An Herde of swannys, An Herde of cranys, An Herde of wrennys, An Herde of alle

dere. **1590** Spenser *F.Q.* iii. vii. 1 An Hynd forth singled from the heard. **1675** Teonge *Diary* (1825) 7 The porpuses com in heards on boath syds the ship. **1697** Dryden *Æneid* vii. 21 Herds of howling wolves that stun the sailors ears. **1735** Somerville *Chase* iii. 324 The grisly Boar is singled from his Herd. **1839** T. Beale *Sperm Whale* 20 The groups, herds, or 'schools', which are formed by the sperm whale, are of two kinds. *c* **1847** in *Knowledge* (1883) 188/2 Herds of the *Actinia bellis* in prime condition. **1860** Tyndall *Glac.* i. xvi. 118 We came upon the tracks of a herd of Chamois. **1875** Jowett *Plato* (ed. 2) III. 682 Herds of elephants. **1897** *Daily News* 15 July 5/5 We have ascertained that the seal herd is not in danger of extinction.

b. *to break herd*: to break away from or leave the herd; hence, to take an independent course.

1768 *Woman of Honor* I. 151 They dare not break herd, afraid of the ridicule of idiots for not resembling them.

3. a. A large company of people; a multitude, host. Now always in a disparaging sense: cf. b.

a **1400** *St. Alexius* (Vernon MS.) 182 Sittinge in a chirchezerde Among pore men an herde. **1486** *Bk. St. Albans* F vj, An Herde of harlottys. **1647** Clarendon *Hist. Reb.* vi. §7 He retir'd in the noonday, and in the face of that Rebellious Herd from Wells to Somerton. *a* **1700** Dryden (J.), Where one Cato shines, Count a degenerate herd of Catilines. **1818** Jas. Mill *Brit. India* II. iv. ix. 290 A herd of parasites and sycophants. *a* **1856** H. Miller *Cruise Betsey* ii. (1858) 247 Herds of ragged children playing in the lanes.

b. *the herd*: the multitude, the common people, the rabble. Often qualified by *common*, *vulgar*, etc.

1601 Shaks. *Jul. C.* i. ii. 266 When he perceiu'd the common Heard was glad he refus'd the Crowne. **1665** Glanvill *Scepsis Sci.* p. vii, For the good opinion of the rash and inconsiderate Herd of mankind. **1698** *Christ Exalted* 63 Will you now run with the Herd, and cry, God made Millions to damn them? **1807** Crabbe *Par. Reg.* i. 30 Fear, shame, and want the thoughtless herd pursue. **1835** Thirlwall *Greece* I. vi, The legitimate chief was distinguished from the vulgar herd.. by his robust frame. **1894** Gladstone tr. *Horace's Odes* iii. ii. 30 Neglected, Jove oft smites good men Mixed with the guilty herd.

c. Of things: A great number, a mass.

1618 J. Taylor (Water P.) *Wks.* (1872) Introd. 18 Seeing the herd of hireling coaches are more than the wherries on the Thames. **1751** Harris *Hermes* Wks. (1841) 143 We are now to descend to the common herd of attributives, such as *black* and *white*.

4. *attrib.* and *Comb.*, as ***herd-breed***, ***-bull***, ***-driver***, ***-flock***, ***-stall***, ***-swarm***; ***herd-abandoned*** adj.; **herd-testing** *vbl. sb.*, testing of the butterfat content of the milk from cows of a specified herd and their productivity; so **herd-tester**; **herd test**.

1821 Shelley *Adonais* xxxiii, A *herd-abandoned deer. **1607** Topsell *Four-f. Beasts* (1658) 183 To provide Goats for *herd-breed and profit. **1398** Trevisa *Barth. De P.R.* xviii. xiv. (1495) 774 The *hyrde dryuer rulyth the oxen to drawe euyn. **1583** Stanyhurst *Æneis* 35 From their region with prede too gather an *heard-flock. *a* **1839** Milman *Deborah's Hymn* Wks. 1839 II. 357 Why satt'st thou idle, Reuben, 'mid thy *herd-stalls? **1583** Stanyhurst *Æneis* i. (Arb.) 31 Clustred in *heerdswarme Feaze away thee droane bees with sting, from maunger or hiuecot. **1962** J. N. Winburne *Dict. Agric.* 374/2 **Herd test*, a type of semiofficial testing for milk production in which the whole herd of cows of milking age are included. **1960** B. Crump *Good Keen Man* 94 He told me.. all about one of his sisters who was training to be a *herd-tester. **1966** G. W. Turner *Eng. Lang. Austral. & N.Z.* vii. 149 A herd-tester is a man or woman who goes from farm to farm sampling milk to test cows for their productivity and the fat content of their milk. **1911** *Jrnl. Dept. Agric.* (N.Z.) 15 July 26 A striking case of the value of testing the individual members of a herd is reported from a district where a *herd-testing association has been established. **1956** Amess & Johnson *Dairying* (ed. 4) xv. 195 All herd-testing is now done by the New Zealand Herd Improvement Associations under direction from the Dairy Board.

b. *Psychol.* Denoting feelings, actions, thoughts, etc., common to a large company of people; esp. **herd instinct**, an instinctive tendency to think and act as one of a crowd. (Cf. sense 3.)

1908 W. Trotter in *Sociol. Rev.* I. 227 (*title*) Herd instinct and its bearing on the psychology of civilised man. **1908** *Westm. Gaz.* 22 Aug. 16/1 The fundamental assumptions of the Liberal and the Conservative are hostile, and are the outcome of herd tradition. **1912** J. London *Let.* 18 Jan. (1966) 359 There is a sort of herd psychology in this. **1914** G. B. Shaw *Androcles & Lion* (1916) 46 That herd instinct which makes men abhor all departures from custom. **1919** M. K. Bradby *Psychoanal.* 113 Not even abandonment to 'herd enthusiasm' could destroy the terrible loneliness of death. **1920** B. Russell *Pract. & Theory Bolshevism* I. 125 The Marxian assumes that a man's 'herd' from the point of view of herd-instinct, is his class. **1922** *Brit. Jrnl. Psychol.* Oct. 118 The love complex, the religion complex, the herd complex and many others. **1923** J. S. Huxley *Ess. Biologist* vii. 275 The herd ideas.. may be those of a nation or of a stratum within the nation. **1924** W. B. Selbie *Psychol. Relig.* 148 Man is a gregarious animal, and even in his civilized condition never quite loses his herd consciousness. **1927** N. P. Williams *Ideas of Fall & Orig. Sin* p. xxix, We therefore identify the 'inherited infirmity' of theology with 'inherited weakness of herd-complex'. **1927** M. Sadleir *Trollope* ii. 49 She was.. lacking in that pride of individuality which throws persons of a different type into automatic opposition to herd-bias. **1928** G. B. Shaw *Intell. Woman's Guide Socialism* v. 11 Our minds are mostly herd minds, with only a scrap of individual mind on top. **1932** Q. D. Leavis *Fiction & Reading Public* I. iii. 67 These writers are using the technique of Marie Corelli.. to work upon and solidify herd prejudice. **1939** J. Masefield *Live & Kicking Ned* 344 What saved us was the fact that Mimbo is an animal passion or herd-madness, which blinds each of the herd to all other things than the herd-enemy. **1942** R. A. Knox *In Soft Garments* xxi. 162 There is such a thing as herd-morality. You notice it especially in matters like divorce, where social considerations necessarily apply. **1960** C. Day Lewis *Buried Day* ii. 43 At the age of eight or nine the herd instinct begins to operate.

Hence **herdlike** *a.*; **herdwise** *adv.*, like a herd.

1871 B. Taylor *Faust* (1875) I. xxi. 189 Herd-wise hieing Through the moss and through the heather.

herd, *sb.*[2] Forms: 1–2 **hierde**, 1 **hiorde**, **hyrde**, 1–3 **heorde**, 1–6 **hirde**, 3–5 **hurde**, 3–6 **herde**, 4–5 **hyrde**, **heirde**, (**herthe**), 4–6 **heerde**; 4–6 **hyrd**, 4–6 (*Sc.* -9) **hird**, (4 **hered**, 5 **hirid**, **ȝerd**, 6 **hierd**, **heird**, **hurd**, **heard**); 4– **herd**. [Com. Teut.: OE. *hirde*, *hierde*, etc. = OS. *hirdi*, *herdi* (MDu. *hirde*, *herde*, MLG. *herde*), OHG. *hirti* (MHG. and mod.Ger. *hirte*), ON. *hirðir* (Sw. *herde*, Da. *hyrde*), Goth. *hairdeis*:—OTeut. **herdjo-z*, f. *herdâ*- herd *sb.*[1]]

1. A keeper of a herd or flock of domestic animals; a herdsman. Now usually with word prefixed, as *cowherd*, *swineherd*, but in Scotland and north of England still a common word for *shepherd*.

c **725** *Corpus Gloss.* 313 *Bobulcus*, hriðhiorde. *c* **897** K. Ælfred *Gregory's Past.* xvii. 109 Ure ealdan fædras wæron ceapes hierdas. *c* **1000** *Ags. Gosp.* Matt. xxv. 32 Swa swa se hyrde [*Lindisf.* & *Rushw.* hiorde; *Hatton* heorde] asyndraþ ða scep fram tyccenum. *c* **1175** *Lamb. Hom.* 97 Amos het a reoðer heorde. *c* **1200** *Trin. Coll. Hom.* 35 þe engel cudde þe herdes.. þat þe helende was þerinne iboren. *c* **1250** *Gen. & Ex.* 456 He was hirde wittere and wal. *a* **1300** *Cursor M.* 1059 (Cott.) þis abel was a hird for fee. *Ibid.* 19488 (Gött.) Sua dos þe heirdes þat er gode. *c* **1386** Chaucer *C.T. Prol.* 603 Ther nas baillif ne hierde [*v.r.* herde] nor oother hyne That he [ne] knew his sleighte and his couyne. **1393** Langl. *P. Pl.* C. x. 267 Hoow! herde! wher is þyn hounde? *c* **1460** *Towneley Myst.* (Surtees) 91 Herkyn, hyrdes, awake! **1491** Caxton *Vitas Patr.* (W. de W. 1495) ii. 227 b/2 He founde a heerde or keper of Camels. **1513** Douglas *Æneis* iii. Prol. 7 Hornyt Lady, paill Cynthia, nocht brycht.. That slepand kist the hird Endymione. **1563–87** Foxe *A. & M.* (1684) III. 571 Mr. Tyrels Servant.. being his Herd at a Farm of his. **1591** *Troub. Raigne K. John* ii. (1611) 90 As sheep without their heird. **1592** *Mem. St. Giles', Durh.* (Surtees) 17 Paid more to the hurd for mendinge certayn gapes in the more dyke. **1596** Spenser *F.Q.* vi. ix. 4 Whereas the Heardes were keeping of their neat. **1637–50** Row *Hist. Kirk* (1842) 451 When I was a young lad I wes a herd, and keeped the Sisters of the Sheines's sheep. **1755** *Mem. Capt. P. Drake* I. x. 74 The Herd sounding a Horn along the Streets, the Swine run from all Parts of the Town, to join and follow him. **1806** *Gazetteer Scotl.* (ed. 2) 384 They are obliged to employ herds to their cattle. **1825** Brockett, *Herd*, a keeper of cattle. **1876** L. Morris *Epic. Hades* (1878) 26 Unpolluted meads, where never herd Drives his white flock.

†**2.** *fig.* A spiritual shepherd, a pastor. In ME. often applied to Christ. *Obs.*

971 *Blickl. Hom.* 191 þanc ic do, Crist þu goda hyrde. *c* **1200** *Vices & Virtues* (1888) 43 Ðe gastliche hierdes, ðe sculen boðe lokin and stieren. *c* **1200** *Trin. Coll. Hom.* 41 Ure louerd ihesu crist is alre herdene herde. *c* **1200** Ormin 6841 Forr Crist iss.. Hirde, þatt uss fedeþþ. *a* **1300** *Cursor M.* 19384 þat hirdes war o crist scepe. *c* **1380** Wyclif *Sel. Wks.* III. 363 Crist was þe beste herd and so he puttide his lyf for his sheep. *c* **1440** *Gesta Rom.* xxiv. 92 (Harl. MS.) Neuertheles then þe hurde, *scil.* a prechour, comyth often tyme. **1549–62** Sternhold & H. *Ps.* lxxx, Thou Herde that Israell doost keepe.

†**3.** *transf.* A keeper, guardian. *Obs.*

Beowulf (Z.) 610 ȝehyrde on beowulfe folces hyrde fæstrædne ȝeþoht. **971** *Blickl. Hom.* 177 þa he bebyrȝed wæs, settan him hyrdas to. *a* **1000** *Cædmon's Genesis* 1007 (Gr.) Ne ic hyrde wæs broðer mines. *a* **1000** *Boeth. Metr.* xxi. 61 Hire aȝenes huses hirde. *Ibid.* xxvi. 16 þiodd aldor .. rices hirde. *c* **1000** Ælfric *Gloss.* in Wr.-Wülcker 163/42 *Paedagogus*, cilda hyrde *uel* lareow. *a* **1250** *Prov. Ælfred* in *O.E. Misc.* 102 Ealured englene hurde [*v.r.* herde] Englene durlyng. **1480** Caxton *Chron. Eng.* ccxxiii, Therle of Fyffe a fyers man and a sterne herd. **1570** *Satir. Poems Reform.* xxii. 61 Keip weill thy taill, gude Phillip, I am hird The to award from buffettis.

4. *Curling.* A guard-stone.

1789 Davidson *Seasons* 166 (Jam.) Gib o' the Glen, a noble herd Behind the winner laid. *Ibid.*, But miss'd his aim, and 'gainst the herd, Dang frae his clint a flaw.

5. *Comb.*, as †**herd-flock**, a company of shepherds; **herd-girl**, **-laddie**, **-lassie**, **-maid**, **-maiden**, a girl, etc. who assists, or acts as, a herd; **herd's purse** = shepherd's-purse; †**herd-work** (**-werch**), see quot. 1706. Also herd-boy, -man, etc.

c **1200** Ormin 3372 All þatt *hirdeflocc hemm sahh And herrde whatt teȝȝ sungenn. *a* **1856** H. Miller *Cruise Betsey* ii. viii. (1858) 352 Where she had plucked berries, a little *herd-girl, on the banks of the Auldgrande. **1865** H. H. Dixon *Field & Fern* vi. 174 He was with the Doctor at thirteen, and then became a *herd laddie. **1889** *Chambers' Encycl.* IV. 87/1 For many years James Wyllie (the 'herd-laddie') was the acknowledged [Draughts] Champion of the world. **1587** *Lyrics*, etc. in Arb. *Garner* II. 76, I sit and watch a *herd-maid gay. **1166** *Regist. Eccl. Christi Cant.* MS. (Cowell), Pro opere quod Anglice *Herdwerch dicitur. **1706** Phillips (ed. Kersey), *Herdwerch*, or *Heerdwerch* (Sax.), Herdsmen's Work or Labours, formerly done by Shepherds, Herdsmen, and other inferiour Tenants at the Will of their Lord.

herd (hɜːd), *v.*[1] Also (4 herdeye), 6–7 heard. [f. herd *sb.*[1]]

1. *intr.* To go in a herd; to form a herd or herds. Said also contemptuously of men: to congregate or live together as beasts. Constr. *together*, *with*.

1393 Langl. *P. Pl.* C. xiv. 148 Maules drowen hem to maules.. And femeles to femeles herdeyed [*v.r.r.* herdyede, herdeiede, herdyyng, herdede] and drow. **1580** Sidney *Arcadia* i. (1590) 31 They are but sheep which alwaies heard together. **1660** R. Coke *Justice Vind.* 12 Like swine feeding, eating and promiscuously herding together. **1662** J. Davies *Mandelslo's Trav.* 127 Females, which.. suffer themselves to be led up and down, till some of the wild Elephants herd with them. **1701** Rowe *Amb. Step-Moth.* ii. ii, Stoop to the meanest Arts which catch the Vulgar? Herd with 'em, fawn upon 'em, and caress 'em? **1774** Goldsm. *Nat. Hist.* (1776) III. 108 These animals are in general fond of herding and grazing in company. **1886** Emily Lawless *Hurrish* v. 57 It was a palace in comparison with the foul hovel in which he and his brother had herded together.

b. Of things: To come together, assemble; to be assembled or associated. *rare.*

1704 Swift *T. Tub* Wks. 1760 I. 100 All its properties and adjuncts will herd under this short definition. **1886** R. C. Leslie *Sea-painter's Log* 71 Away towards the north and west.. they [clouds] appear to be herding together.

2. To join oneself to any band or company; to become one of any faction or party; to associate as one of the 'common herd' or crowd, to go in company *with*.

?*a* **1400** *Morte Arth.* 1010 Ffor-thy hurdez he here, to owttraye hys pople. **1651** Davenant *Gondibert* ii. i. xvi, Here greedy Creditors their Debtors chace, Who scape by herding in th' indebted Throng. **1697** Dryden *Æneid* xi. 1188 The wretch.. spurring forward, herds among his Friends. **1715–20** Pope *Iliad* xi. 463 Hector.. Remounts his car, and herds amidst the crowd. **1789** Mad. D'Arblay *Diary* 13 Jan., 'Tis now a cause of humanity.. and I will not herd with those who think otherwise. **1855** Thackeray *Newcomes* I. 100 Ethel herded not with the children of her own age.

3. *trans.* To place in or among a herd; to associate. Also *fig.*

1592 *Nobody & Someb.* in Simpson *Sch. Shaks.* (1878) I. 310 The stag is hearded; come, my Lord, Shall we to horse, and single him againe? **1611** B. Jonson *Catiline* i. Wks. (Rtldg.) 276/1 The rest, However great we are, honest, and valiant, Are hearded with the vulgar. *a* **1631** Donne *Lett.* (1651) 43, I can allow myself to be.. appliable to my company, but not.. to herd myself in every troup. **1691** Swift *Athenian Soc.* 81 Wks. 1841 I. 599/2 Our good brethren.. Must e'en all herd us with their kindred fools.

4. To collect into a herd. Also *fig.* To amass.

1615 Tomkis *Albumazar* iii. v. in Hazl. *Dodsley* XI. 366 In all the years of my yeomanry, I could never yoke two crowns, and now I have herded ten fair twenty-shilling pieces. **1850** B. Taylor *Eldorado* xi. (1862) 106 Our mules had scattered far and wide.. and several hours elapsed before they could be herded and got into traveling order.

Hence ˈ**herded** *ppl. a.*, gathered or placed in a herd; ˈ**herding** *vbl. sb.*, association in herds, congregation; also *comb.*, as ***herding-place***; ˈ**herding** *ppl. a.*, gathering in herds, gregarious.

1666 Dryden *Ann. Mirab.* cclviii, The most in fields like herded beasts lie down. **1711** Shaftesb. *Charac.* (1737) I. 110 If eating and drinking be natural, herding is so too. *c* **1740** Fielding *Ess. Convers.* (R.), The tamer and gentler, the herding and flocking parts of the creation. **1805** Prisc. Wakefield *Dom. Recreat.* xiii. (1806) 195 Man, who is a herding, and not a solitary animal. **1847** Mary Howitt *Ballads* 235 Among the herded deer. **1860** *Merc. Marine Mag.* VII. 211 The herding places of vast numbers of amphibious animals.

herd, *v.*[2] Also 5–6 hurd, hird. [f. herd *sb.*[2]]

1. a. *trans.* To take care of or tend (sheep or cattle).

c **1400** *Apol. Loll.* 106 þe patriarkis.. herdid bestis. **1768** Ross *Helenore* 14 (Jam.) When they were able now to herd the ewes. **1816** Scott *Antiq.* iv, The very least boy that can herd a cow. **1892** E. Reeves *Homeward Bound* 283 Cattle, sheep, goats.. are all herded by boys or women.

fig. **1887** Swinburne *Locrine* iv. ii. 293 God, who herds the stars of heaven As sheep within his sheepfold.

b. *trans.* To lead or conduct as a shepherd. Also *transf.*, spec. (*U.S. slang*) to drive (a car, aircraft, etc.).

1883 *Eng. Illustr. Mag.* Nov. 72/1 It is also very picturesque to see.. the girls.. herding the geese and ducks homeward at sundown. **1895** Kipling *Second Jungle Book* 67 Who is Man that we should care for him..? I have followed him all day—at noon—in the white sunlight. I herded him as the wolves herd buck. **1927** W. Faulkner *Mosquitoes* 261 'Come on here, you men.' He named over his depleted watch and herded it forward. He herded it down to his cabin and nourished it with stimulants. **1954** —— *Fable* (1955) 100 He saw the two-seater.. the two S.E.'s above and behind it, herding it down. **1955** *Sunday Times* 25 Sept. 3/3 (*heading*) Herd that beast!.. I append an up-to-the-minute glossary of motoring terms.. *herd*, to drive a car. **1971** M. Tak *Truck Talk* 82 *Herd*, to drive a truck.

c. *intr.* To act as a herd, to tend cattle or sheep.

1768 Ross *Helenore* 31 (Jam.), I had na use to gang Unto the glen to herd this mony a lang. **1848** *Fraser's Mag.* XXXVIII. 315 It was long before I was hearted to herd again in the woods by myself.

†**2.** *fig.* (*trans.*) To keep safe, shelter, harbour.

a **1300** *E.E. Psalter* xlix. [l.] 19 þi tunge herded swikedomes ma. *Ibid.* lvii. 3 [lviii. 2] Un-rightwisnes herdes youre hand. **1535** Stewart *Cron. Scot.* III. 469 And [=if] he hurdit sic schrewis Within Ingland quhilk wes his mortall fa. *c* **1560** A. Scott *Poems* xv. 21 My lady, lord, thow gaif me for to hird, Within myne armes I nureiss on the nycht.

Hence ˈ**herding** *vbl. sb.*, the tending of sheep and cattle.

1733 P. Lindsay *Interest Scot.* 37 In the Summer we must be at the Expence of Herding, to save our Grass from being destroyed by our Neighbours Beasts. **1802** Finlater *Agric. Surv. Peebles* 195 (Jam.) The principles of herding are, to

allocate to each particular flock, separate walks upon the farm for each season of the year. **1871** *Daily News* 27 Feb., Single whales often broke away.. and required a good deal of herding to prevent their escape into the sound. **1883** GILMOUR *Mongols* xviii. 215 The Mongols have much solitary travelling and herding.

herd, obs. f. *heard*, pa. t. and pple. of HEAR *v.*

'herd-book. [f. HERD *sb.*[1] + BOOK.] A book containing the pedigree and other particulars of a breed of cattle or pigs: corresponding to the *stud-book* for horses, and the *flock-book* for sheep.

1822 COATES (*title*) The General Short-Horned Herd-Book, containing the Pedigrees of Short-Horned Bulls, Cows, etc. of the Improved Durham Breed. **1865** H. H. DIXON *Field & Fern* 86 In 1822, the very year that England began her Shorthorn Herd-Book. **1881** SHELDON *Dairy Farming* 3/1 Long and respectable pedigrees in their owners' herd-books.

herd-boy. [orig. f. HERD *sb.*[2] + BOY; but in later use app. understood as from HERD *sb.*[1], whence the bad form *herd's-boy*, and prob. sense 2. See HERDSMAN.]

1. A boy who acts as a herd or assists a herd.

1799 WORDSW. *Danish Boy* 19 Nor piping shepherd shall he be, Nor herd-boy of the wood. **1825** J. BANIM *Tales O'Hara Fam., Fetch*, The herdsboy's whistle faintly echoed. **1860** G. H. K. *Vac. Tour.* 162 Ossian began life as a herd-boy in Glen Shin.

2. A man or 'boy' engaged in tending a herd of cattle, a cow-boy. *U.S.*, *S. Afr.*, etc.

1878 J. MACDONALD *Food from Far West* vi. 45 The herd-boys—men on horseback—go through the ranges and gather the cattle into 'pens'. **1896** *Westm. Gaz.* 25 June 5/1 Cattle have been captured and fourteen herdboys killed. The defenders have formed a laager.

herdel(l, obs. form of HURDLE.

herden, variant of HARDEN, HURDEN.

herder ('hɜːdə(r)). Chiefly *U.S.* Also 7 hearder. [f. HERD *v.*[2] + -ER[1]. Cf. mod.Du. and LG. *herder*, also OFris. *herdere*:—OTeut. type **herdarjo-z*.] One who herds; a herdsman. Also *fig.*

1635 T. ODELL *Isaac's Pilgr.* title-p., The strife that Isaack had with his heard-men.. shadowing out the strife which Christ our Lord had with his hearders. **1846** WORCESTER cites *Monthly Rev.* **1877** BLACK *Green Past.* xiii, He was an imperious master with his herders. **1879** *Scribner's Mag.* XIX. 770/2 The herder, or 'cow-boy', dominates the town.

herderite ('hɜːdəraɪt). *Min.* [Named (1828) after Baron S. A. W. von Herder.] A fluo-phosphate of glucinum and calcium, found in brilliant transparent crystals.

1828 *Phil. Mag.* Ser. II. IV. 1, I propose the name of Herderite for the species. **1861** BRISTOW *Gloss. Min.*, *Herderite*, a very rare mineral, resembling Asparagus-stone.. Colour several shades of yellowish- and greenish-white.

herd(e)s, obs. forms of HARDS, HURDS.

herdess ('hɜːdɪs). [f. HERD *sb.*[2] + -ESS.] A female herd; a shepherdess.

c **1374** CHAUCER *Troylus* I. 653 An hierdesse, Whech that clepyde was senome Wrot in a compleynt of hire heuynesse. **1580** SIDNEY *Arcadia* lxix. 111 Poems 1873 II. 152 She is the heardesse faire that shines in darke. **1613–16** W. BROWNE *Brit. Past.* II. iii, The louely Heardesse of the Dell.

†**'herdful**, *a. Obs. rare.* [f. HERD *sb.*[1] + -FUL.] Rich in herds of cattle.

1618 CHAPMAN *Hesiod* I. 15 With Labour Men become Herd-full and rich.

herd-grass, herd's-grass. *U.S.* [f. HERD *sb.*[1] + GRASS.] A name for various grasses grown for hay or pasture; esp. Timothy, *Phleum pratense*, and Redtop, *Agrostis vulgaris*.

1747 FRANKLIN *Lett.* Wks. 1887 II. 81, I sowed nearly thirty acres with herd-grass and clover. **1787** M. CUTLER in *Life Jrnls. & Corr.* (1888) I. 288 They begin, however, to sow some quantity of herd's-grass seed, which they call Timothy. **1834** LOW *Pract. Agric.* (1847) 521 It [*Phleum pratense*] is called herd-grass in America, and is greatly valued there as an herbage and forage plant. **1856** OLMSTED *Slave States* 41 Herd's-grass (red-top), sometimes taking the place of the clover, or being grown with it for hay.

†**herd-groom.** *Obs.* [f. HERD *sb.*[2] + GROOM.] A shepherd-lad; a herdsman, shepherd.

c **1384** CHAUCER *H. Fame* III. 135 An han thise lytel herde gromes That kepen bestis in the bromes. *c* **1440** *Compleynt* 418 in *Temple Glas* (E.E.T.S.) 64 On bankys hy a-mong the bromys, Wher as these lytylle herdegromys Floutyn al the longe day. **1579** SPENSER *Sheph. Cal.* Feb. 35 So loytring liue you little heardgrommes, Keeping your beastes in the budded broomes. **1619** DRAYTON *Past.* ix. (R.), But he forsakes the herd-groom and his flocks, Nor of his bagpipe takes at all no keep. **1633** P. FLETCHER *Purple Isl.* VII. lxviii, Upon his shield that cruel herd-groom played.

herdic ('hɜːdɪk). *U.S.* Also **herdick**. [Named from the inventor, Peter Herdic of Pennsylvania.] A two- or sometimes four-wheeled cab or carriage having a low-hung body with the entrance at the back and seats at the sides. Also ***herdic-phaeton***.

1882 T. S. HUDSON *Scamper thro' Amer.* 74 Taking a herdick (small one-horse 'bus named after the inventor) we drove to the White House. **1883** E. M. BACON *Dict. Boston, Mass.* 207 The herdic-phaeton, or herdics as they are universally called.. of recent introduction (in 1881). **1884** *Boston Herald* 6 Oct. 1/6 Inquiry among the herdic drivers of this city yesterday failed to elicit any information.

herdle, obs. form of HURDLE.

'herdless, *a. rare.* [OE. *hierde-, hyrde-léas*, f. *hierde* HERD *sb.*[2] + *léas*, -LESS.] Without a herd or shepherd.

c **1000** ÆLFRIC *Hom.* I. 382 Ne beoð he hyrdelease þonne hi ðe habbað. *c* **1320** R. BRUNNE *Medit.* 452 þey renne aboute as herdles shepe. **1509** BARCLAY *Shyp of Folys* (1874) I. 46 As a herdles flocke strayth in Jepardy.

†**'herdman.** *Obs.* Forms: see HERD *sb.*[2] [f. HERD *sb.*[2] + MAN.] A man who herds cattle, sheep, or other animals; a herdsman.

c **1000** ÆLFRIC *Gen.* xiii. 7 Þurh þone intingan sacu betwux Abrames hyrdemannum and Lothes. *c* **1250** *Gen. & Ex.* 2395 He weren hirde-men. *a* **1300** *Cursor M.* 28396 Myn hird-men and als oþer maa Haf i þ aire seruis halden fra. *c* **1400** MAUNDEV. (Roxb.) xxiv. 110 Þai.. ware made hird-men and kepers of bestez. *c* **1440** *Promp. Parv.* 236/2 Heerd mann, *pastor, agaso*. **1523** FITZHERB. *Husb.* §123 The herdman wyll haue for euery beest .ii. d. a quarter. **1535** COVERDALE *Isa.* xl. 11 He shal fede his flock like an hirdman. **1559** W. CUNNINGHAM *Cosmogr. Glasse* 66 Plow-men, Heardmen, and Shepehards. **1611** BIBLE *Gen.* xiii. 7 There was a strife betweene the heardmen of Abrams cattell, and the heardmen of Lots cattell. **1635–56** COWLEY *Davideis* III. 217 In vain the Herdman calls him back.

b. *fig.* and *transf.* esp. A spiritual pastor.

c **1320** *Cast. Love* 587 Þenne nis þer such an herde-mon non Ne non so miȝtful lord as he is on. *c* **1477** CAXTON *Jason* 71 b, We wyll that thou be our pastour or herdman. **1553** *Primer* in *Liturg. & Doc. Edw. VI*, (1844) 457 Shepherd, and Herdman of our souls.

†**'herdness.** *Obs.* [OE. *hierd-, hyrdnys*, f. *hierde, hirde* HERD *sb.*[2] + -NESS.]

1. Guard, keeping, custody. Only OE.

c **1000** ÆLFRIC *Gen.* xlii. 17 He betæhte hiȝ þa þri daȝas to hirdnysse. —— *Exod.* xxii. 7 Ȝif hwa befæst his feoh to hyrdnysse.

2. A collective term for herds or flocks; 'stock'.

c **1250** *Gen. & Ex.* 1664 Laban bi-taȝte him, siðen to sen, His hirdenesse ðat it wel ben. *Ibid.* 2771 Moyses was numen an sel In ðe deserd depe sumdel, for te loken hirdnesse fare.

'herdship. *Obs.* or *dial.* [f. HERD *sb.*[2] + -SHIP.]

a. The office or charge of a keeper of cattle. **b.** The herd of beasts under his charge.

1601 DEACON & WALKER *Spirits & Divels* 19 Could the motions of men craue leaue, and enter into a whole heard-ship of Swine?

herdsman ('hɜːdzmən). [app. an alteration of the earlier HERDMAN (after *craftsman*, *kinsman*, etc.), intoduced when HERD[2] went out of English use, so that the word was referred to HERD[1], as = man of a herd. The word is not vernacular in the north, where HERD[2] remains in use.]

1. A keeper of domestic animals which go in herds, esp. of cattle.

1603 KNOLLES *Hist. Turks* (1621) 133 Who yet with their wives and children, as heardsmen.. wander up and downe the countrey. **1658** BRAMHALL *Consecr. Bps.* vii. 168 An heardsman in Turky hath as much right to order his heard, as an heardman in Christendome. **1784** COWPER *Task* I. 168 Our favourite elms, That screen the herdsman's solitary hut. **1845** MAURICE *Mor. & Met. Philos.* in *Encycl. Metrop.* 631/1 Plain simple herdsmen and warriors.

2. A name in Orkney for the Common Skua.

1885 SWAINSON *Brit. Birds* 210 Common Skua.. Herdsman (Orkney Isles): Because it is believed to protect the young lambs from the attacks of the eagle.

So **'herdsmaiden** (for *herd-maiden*), **'herdswoman**, a maiden or woman who tends cattle; **'herdsmanship**, the performance or occupation of a herdsman.

1818 SCOTT *Hrt. Midl.* xviii, Her juvenile exercise as a herdswoman had put 'life and mettle' in her heels. **1829** J. STERLING *Ess.* etc. (1848) I. 25 The popular prediction.. was now to be fulfilled by her daughter, the poor herdsmaiden. **1889** J. M. ROBERTSON *Christ & Krishna* xvi. 113 The theory of Krishna's herdsmanship being derived from the cloud-cows of the Vedas is new. **1896** *Westm. Gaz.* 24 Oct. 1/3 The home of the herdswomen, who.. tend the cattle in the heights. **1960** *Farmer & Stockbreeder* 8 Mar. 120 (*caption*) Good herdsmanship, prompt veterinary attention and close liaison between the herdsman and the farm staff are essential.

herdwick ('hɜːdwɪk). [f. HERD *sb.*[2] + WICK: cf. *bailiwick*, *bailiffwick*.]

†**1.** The tract of land under the charge of a 'herd' or shepherd employed by the owner or lord of the manor: see quot. 1537; a pasture-ground, a sheep-farm. *Obs.*

[*c* **1086** *Domesday*, *Gloc.* lf. 162 a, In Wales sunt iii hardvices Lamecare & poteschivet & Dinan.] ?*c* **1150** in Dugdale *Mon. Angl.* (1661) 39/2 (*Grant for foundation of a cell at Bredon*), Viginti solidos de Molendino de Crakemero ..et quadraginta solidos in soca de Stapelfordia; et unam Herdewicam in Hethcote, juxta Hertadona, in Pecco. **1537** *Certif. Reven. Furness Abbey* in Beck *Ann. Furnes.* (1884) App. 64 Pastures with Agistament and brusyng.. occupied to thuse of the said late Monastery for the sustentacyon of ther catell, and.. devyded into sundry herdwyks and shepe cots. *c* **1537** SIR J. LAMPLUGH *ibid.*, *note*, Erleghecote haythe always beyn a hyrdewyke or pasture ground for the schepe of thabbottes of Furnes.. and euer in theyr possessyon; and who soeuer inhabytyd therapone haythe always beyn the Abbottes hyrde, and remouable at theyr pleasures, and not tenauntes by ony custome. **1564** *Decree* in West *Antiq. Furness* (1744) App. ix, Those parcells following, that is to say, the herdwick called Waterside Parke.. the herdwick called Lawson Park.. the herdwick called Plumers.

2. (In full ***Herdwick sheep***): A hardy breed of mountain sheep in Cumberland and Westmorland.

Supposed to have originated on the herdwicks of the Abbey of Furness. They still usually belong to the landlord of a fell-side farm, along with which they are leased to the tenant.

1837 *Penny Cycl.* VIII. 223/2 A peculiar breed of sheep, called Herdwicks, from their being farmed out to herds at a yearly sum, is met with on the mountains, at the head of the Duddon and Esk rivers. **1868** A. CRAIG GIBSON *Joe & the Geologist* in *Folk-Sp. Cumbld.* (1880) 2 Yan wad ha' sworn he was summut akin tul a Herdwick tip. **1878** *Cumberland Gloss.*, *Herdwicks*, the mountain sheep of the west of Cumberland.. let out in herds or flocks with the farms. **1887** HALL CAINE *Son of Hagar* I. ii, Auld Mr. Ritson's, them herdwicks.

†**here**, *sb. Obs.* Forms: 1–5 here, 3 hære, 4 her, 4–5 heere. [Com. Teut.: OE. *here* masc., gen. *herȝes, heriȝes, heres* = OFris. *here, hiri*, OS. *heri* m. and n. (MDu. *hēre*, Du. *heir, heer* n., LG. *hêr* n.), OHG. *hari, heri* (MLG. *here*, Ger. *heer*) n., ON. *herr* m., gen. *herjar* (Sw. *här*, Da. *hær*), Goth. *harjis* m.:—OTeut. **harjo-z*, **harjo*[m] (in proper names of Roman age *chario-*) = OPruss. *karjis* host. App. a deriv. (adj.) from a radical *har-*, pre-Teut. *kar-*, *kor-*, in sense 'war': cf. OSlav. *kara* contention, strife, Lith. *kàras* war. Hence HARRY *v.*, HARBOUR, HERIOT *sbs.*]

An armed host, an army. Also, more generally: A host; a multitude, a great company.

In the *O.E. Chron.* the usual word applied to the 'host' of the Danish invaders.

c **855** *O.E. Chron.* (Parker MS.) an. 837 Þy ilcan ȝeare ȝefeaht Æþelhelm dux wiþ Deniscne here. *a* **890** *Ibid.* an. 872 Her for se here to Lunden byriȝ from Readingum. *c* **1000** *Ags. Gosp.* Matt. xxii. 7 Ða se cyning.. sende hys here. *c* **1200** ORMIN 3889 An here off Godess enngless. *c* **1205** LAY. 3830 Morgan ledde muchele hære. *c* **1300** *Cursor M.* 21840 (Edin.) Be ur scheld eke and ure spere Bituixin us and helles here [*Cott.* her, *other MSS.* here]. **13** .. *K. Alis.* 5265 Tygres, olyfaunz, and beres Comen flynge with grete heres. *a* **1400–50** *Alexander* 4800 So hard þai hampird oure heere & herid oure erles. **1450–70** *Golagros & Gaw.* 1147 The tothir knightis maid care of Arthuris here. [**1872** ROBERTSON *Hist. Ess.* 137 Over 35 men (or 3 × 12) constituted a *Here* by Ini's laws.]

b. *attrib.* and *Comb.*, as **here-burne**, a coat of mail; **here-dring**, a warrior; **here-feng**, booty; **here-gang**, an invasion by an army; **here-gume**, **here-kempe**, a warrior; **here-marke**, a standard, ensign; **here-scrud** (*-shroud*), **here-weeds**, armour, martial accoutrements; (all only OE. and early ME.). Also **herefare**, a military expedition (in 17th c. legal antiquaries). See also HEREGELD, HERETOGA, HEREYELD.

Beowulf (Z.) 1443 Scolde *here-byrne hondum ȝebroden. *c* **1205** LAY. 23966 Þe helm an his hæuede, and his hereburne. *Ibid.* 8601 Ȝif here is æi *heredring. *Ibid.* 11716 Heo funden *herre-feng inoh. **10**.. tr. *Bæda's Hist.* I. xi. [xiv.] (MS. B), To wiðscufanne swa reðum *heregange. *c* **1205** LAY. 18194 In þan hire-ȝeonge inne Walisc londe. *a* **1250** *Owl & Night.* 1191 Ich wot of hunger, of hergonge. *c* **1330** *Arth. & Merl.* 4094 Here is comand to this lond Gret hunger, and here gong. *c* **1205** LAY. 14534 Þus heo comen.. hæðene *here-gumen. *Ibid.* 28284 Sixti þusende *here-kempen harde. *Ibid.* 27469 Feollen *here-mærken [*c* **1275** hire markes]. *Ibid.* 28546 Heo.. heuen here-marken. *Ibid.* 5069 Leie a-dun þin *hære-scrud. *Beowulf* (Z.) 1897 Sæ-ȝeap naca hladen *here-wædum. *a* **1400–50** *Alexander* 1010 Al to heuy to be hildid in any here wedis.

1626 SPELMAN *Gloss.*, Herefare, *profectio militaris*. **1670** BLOUNT *Law Dict.*, Herefare. **1672** *Cowell's Interpr.* s.v. *Subsidy*, Burgbote, Brigbote, Herefare, Heregeld, etc.

†**here**, *a. Obs.* [OE. *héore, hýre*: cf. ON. *hyrr* sweet, smiling, mild; also OS. and OHG. *unhiuri* dreadful, MHG. *gehiure* gentle.] Gentle, mild, pleasant.

Beowulf (Z.) 1372 Nis þæt heoru stow. *a* **1000** *Cædmon's Gen.* (Gr.) 1467 Ið þæt heo [culufre] rumgal restestowe fæȝere funde and þa fotum stop on beam hyre. *c* **1205** LAY. 25867 Þa sæide þat wif here [*c* **1275** ore]. *c* **1420** *Sir Amadas* (Weber) 16 And how they were guode & here.

here (hɪə(r)), *adv.* Forms: 1 hér, 2–5 her, 4–7 heer(e, 2– here; also (1 hær, 2 heren, hur), 3–5 hier, 4 hir(e, *Kent.* hyer, 4–6 *Sc.* heyr, 4–7 *Sc.* heir(e, 5 hiere, 6–7 hear(e. [Com. Teut.: OE. *hér* = OFris. *hîr*, OS. *hêr, hîr* (MDu., Du. *hier*), OHG. *hiar, hear, hier* (MHG., mod.G. *hier*), ON. *hêr* (Sw. *här*, Da. *her*), Goth. *hêr*: app. from the pronominal stem *hi-* 'this' (see HE); the nature of the formation is obscure.]

A. *adv.* **1. a.** In this place; in the place (country, region, etc.) where the person speaking is, or places himself.

c **825** *Vesp. Psalter* cxxxi[i.] 14 Her eardung.. icȝeceas hie. *c* **950** *Lindisf. Gosp.* Matt. xiv. 17 Nabbas we her buta fif hlafum. *c* **1000** *Ags. Gosp.* Matt. xxviii. 6 Nys he her, he aras

..swa swa he sæde [1382 WYCLIF, He is not here, sothli he roos, as he seide]. c1175 *Lamb. Hom.* 83 Here he is and honen he nis. a1225 *Ancr. R.* 236 Ertu, cweð he, ʒet her? a1300 *Cursor M.* 3296 Mi hernes dun heir did i lai. 1382 WYCLIF *1 Kings* xix. 9 What dost thow here, Helyas? c1386 CHAUCER *Friar's T.* 272 Heere wynne I no thyng vp-on cariage. c1470 HENRY *Wallace* I. 305 Thi modyr and thow rycht heir with me sall bide. 1481 CAXTON *Reynard* (Arb.) 6, I here hier that reygnart is sore complayned on. 1581 PETTIE *Guazzo's Civ. Conv.* I. (1586) 1 b, Let him be heere for the space of sixe daies. 1617 MORYSON *Itin.* II. 186 We here in the Campe..have not had much to doe. 1662 CHAS. II in Julia Cartwright *Henrietta of Orleans* (1894) 121, I am doing all I can to gett him a rich wife heere. 1670 LADY M. BERTIE in *12th Rep. Hist. MSS. Comm.* App. v. 22 All heare are well. 1849 MACAULAY *Hist. Eng.* iii. I. 289 That load which pressed most heavily on..the great continental states was here scarcely felt.

b. With ellipsis of *I am* (or *we are*), in answer to a call or summons, or to attract attention; esp. in answer to a roll-call: = Present, *adsum.*

c970 ABBO *Hist. S. Eadmundi* in Surius *Vitæ SS.* (1618) IV. 443 Patria lingua dicens: Her, her, her; quod interpretatum Latinus sermo exprimit, Hîc, hîc, hîc. c1000 ÆLFRIC *Saints' Lives* (E.E.T.S.) II. 324 Hwær eart þu nu ʒefera? And him and-wyrde þæt heafod, Hêr, hêr, hêr. c1330 R. BRUNNE *Chron.* (1810) 22 Up and doune in þe felde þei souht it aboute..Tille þe hede him self said, here, here, here. c1485 *Digby Myst.* (1882) III. 726 Here, lord, here! qwat wol ʒe? 1590 SHAKS. *Mids. N.* I. ii. 45 *Quin.* Francis Flute the Bellowes-mender. *Flu.* Heere, Peter Quince. 1610 —— *Temp.* I. i. 2 *Master.* Bote-swaine. *Botes.* Heere, Master. 1837 DICKENS *Pickw.* xxxiv, 'Answer to your names, gentlemen, that you may be sworn', said the gentleman in black. 'Richard Upwitch'. 'Here', said the green-grocer.

c. Placed after the name of a person or thing to whose presence attention is called: = Who or which is here, whom you see here.

1596 SHAKS. *Merch. V.* III. iv. 29 Onely attended by Nerrissa heere. 1634 [see d]. 1673 DRYDEN *Amboyna* II. i, In the mean time, bear my worthy friend here company. 1751 tr. *Female Foundling* II. 4 My Daughter here wants Linen. *Mod.* 'My brother, here, is ready to give information.'

d. Used for the sake of emphasis after a sb. qualified by *this, these,* or after these demonstratives themselves when used absolutely; *dialectally* or *vulgarly* appended to *this, these,* when used adjectively. (Cf. F. *ce livre-ci, ceci, celui-ci.*)

c1460 *Towneley Myst.* (Surtees) 137 The best wyse that we may hast vs outt of this here. 1556 *Aurelio & Isab.* (1608) H viij, Now what experience will we have greter than this heare? 1609 HOLLAND *Amm. Marcell.* XXII. xv. 213 *note*, But this here seemeth to be venomous. 1634 MILTON *Comus* 672 And first behold this cordial julep here. 1762 FOOTE *Orators* II. Wks. 1799 I. 210, I should be glad to know how my client can be tried in this here manner. 1766 GOLDSM. *Vic. W.* xx, Are you, cried he, the bearer of this here letter? 1778 MISS BURNEY *Evelina* (1791) II. xxxvii. 243, I wou'dn't wish for better sport than to swing her round this here pond! 1838 DICKENS *O. Twist* xxxi, 'Now, with regard to this here robbery, master', said Blathers. 'What are the circumstances?' 1872 *Punch* 31 Aug. 92/2 'It is no use a trying on these here games with us'.

e. ***here today and gone tomorrow***: a catch-phrase indicating a constant change of events or someone (or something) remaining in a place for a short time.

1687 A. BEHN *Luckey Chance* iv. 47 Faith Sir, we are here to Day and gone to Morrow. 1776 H. NEWDIGATE *Let.* in A. E. Newdigate-Newdegate *Cheverels* (1898) i. 10 Going over for a day to Arbury to beat for Wood Cocks..as they are birds of passage, here today and gone tomorrow. 1895 KIPLING *Day's Work* (1898) 172 Here today and gone tomorrow. Didn't come to stay for ever. 1944 W. S. MAUGHAM *Razor's Edge* IV. iv. 132 Even in the old days you could never count on his being where you expected him to be. He was here today and gone tomorrow. 1972 *Listener* 23 Nov. 690/2 We [*sc.* the TUC] put forward proposals for a general rise in pensions—not a 'Christmas Box' that is here today and gone tomorrow.

2. a. In weakened sense, more or less directly indicating something present to the sight or the mind. Chiefly with verb *to be* (sometimes with ellipsis). *Here is* calls attention to what the speaker has, brings, offers, or discovers; = there is here, see or behold here. (F. *voici.*)

c1460 *Towneley Myst.* (Surtees) 66 And therto here my hand. 1596 SHAKS. *1 Hen. IV*, v. iii. 33 There's Honour for you: here's no vanity. 1603 —— *Meas. for M.* I. ii. 107 Heere's a change indeed in the Commonwealth. 1616 *Marlowe's Faustus* Wks. (Rtldg.) 126/2 What's here? an ambush to betray my life! 1632 MASSINGER *City Madam* I. i, Here's no gross flattery! Will she swallow this? 1741 RICHARDSON *Pamela* I. 136 O frightful, thought I; here's an account of the matter at once. 1884 W. C. SMITH *Kildrostan* 65 Here is half the summer past, and still I'm at the chimney nook. 1889 MRS. ALEXANDER *Crooked Path* vi, I says, 'here's your tea, sir', but he made no answer.

b. ***here's to*** (elliptical for *here's a health to*), ***here's hoping, how, looking (at you), luck,*** formulas used in drinking healths.

1592 SHAKS. *Rom. & Jul.* v. iii. 119 Heere's to my Loue. 1653 WALTON *Angler* xi. 209 Well then, here's to you Coridon; and now for my Song. 1738 SWIFT *Polite Convers.* 143 Come, Madam; here's a Health to our Friends, and hang the rest of our Kin. 1777 SHERIDAN *Sch. Scand.* III. (*Song*), Here's to the maiden of blushing fifteen, Now to the widow of fifty..Let the toast pass, drink to the lass. 1822 SCOTT *Pirate* xiv, Drink about, Master Yellowley..Here's to you, Master Yellowley. 1888 KIPLING *Soldiers Three* (1889) 51 He opened a bottle...'Here's luck!' 1896, etc. [see HOW *adv.* 18]. 1910 W. M. RAINE *B. O'Connor* iii. 40 'Here's hoping,' Bucky nodded gaily. 'I bet there will be a right lively wolf hunt.' 1933 M. LOWRY *Ultramarine* 164 Here's looking at you! 1938 E. HEMINGWAY *Fifth Column* (1939) 184 Here's looking at you... Here's how. 1973 E. LEMARCHAND *Let or Hindrance* xii. 142 Pollard..raised his glass to her. 'Here's hoping.'

3. Of a point or period of time: ***to be here***, to be present, to have arrived.

1891 E. PEACOCK *N. Brendon* I. 13 The Easter recess will be here in a day or two.

4. In this world; in this life; on earth. Also ***here below (†beneath, down).*** Cf. F. *ici bas.*

971 *Blickl. Hom.* 35 Þa hwile þe we lifʒaþ her on worlde. c1000 *Eccles. Inst.* in Thorpe *Anc. Laws* II. 394 Her ʒehyrð Drihten þa þe hine biddað. c1175 *Lamb. Hom.* 9 þet me her on þisse liue for his saule bidde. a1225 *Ancr. R.* 94. 1340 *Ayenb.* 232 Holy cherche þet is hier beneþe. 1382 WYCLIF *Heb.* xiii. 14 Sothli we han not here a citee dwellinge [TINDALE For here have we no continuynge citie]. 1393 LANGL. *P. Pl.* C. VII. 238 Thow wolt hongy heye þer-fore her oþer in helle. 1500–20 DUNBAR *Poems* lx. 7 Wnto wardlie prince heir downe. 1576 J. SANFORD *Gard. Pleas.* 138 Among us heere beneth. 1602 SHAKS. *Ham.* III. ii. 232 Both heere, and hence, pursue me lasting strife. 1632 J. HAYWARD tr. *Biondi's Eromena* 81 Experience teacheth us, that the influence of..planets are true..here below, which none can denie. 1766 GOLDSM. *Hermit* viii, Man wants but little here below, Nor wants that little long. 1824 MONTGOMERY *Hymn*, '*Friend after friend departs*', There is no union here of hearts, That finds not here an end.

5. a. At this point or period in action, speech, or thought; at this juncture; in this passage (of something written): freq. referring to what immediately precedes or follows.

871–89 *Charter of Ælfred* in *O.E. Texts* 452 Her sindon ðæra manna naman awritene ðe ðeosse wisan ʒeweoton sindon. a900 *O.E. Chron.* (Parker MS.) an. 871 Her cuom se here to Readingum. c1200 ORMIN 241 Her endenn twa Goddspelless þuss. a1300 *Cursor M.* 1627 *heading*, Her bigins at noe þe lele þe toþer werld right for to del. c1400 *Apol. Loll.* 52 An oþer poynt is her putt. 1551 T. WILSON *Logike* (1580) 79 b, Here Zenophon saied never a woorde. 1644 MILTON *Areop.* (Arb.) 33 Examples, which to set heer would be superfluous. 1662 *Bk. Com. Prayer, Morn. Pr.* Rubric, In Quires and Places where they sing, here followeth the Anthem. 1793 BEDDOES *Calculus*, etc. 212 Here are some experiments and reasons, upon which their theory of respiration is founded. 1875 JOWETT *Plato* (ed. 2) III. 296 Here Adeimantus interposed a question.

b. ***here's where***.., this is the point at which. *U.S. colloq.*

1923 R. D. PAINE *Comr. Rolling Ocean* xii. 203 'It makes me feel sick at my stomach', declared Briscoe. 'Here's where you feel sicker. Great Scott, look at that.' *Ibid.* xiv. 250 Here's where I slip it out to the old gink.

6. In the matter before us or in question; in this case; in this particular.

c1175 *Lamb. Hom.* 81 Her me ah to understonden for-whi hit seið alf quic and noht alf ded. c1386 CHAUCER *Merch. T.* 86 Heere may ye se and heer-by may ye preue That wyf is mannes helpe and his confort. 1586 YOUNG *Guazzo's Civ. Conv.* IV. 205 b, And here Ladie Caterine and Cavallero had the honour. 1592 SHAKS. *Rom. & Jul.* II. iii. 41 Here I hit it right. Our Romeo hath not beene in bed to night. 1614 BP. HALL *Recoll. Treat.* 1099 Here was his sin; An over-reaching of his commission. 1709 STEELE *Tatler* No. 76 ¶4 Here can then be no Injustice, where no one is injured. 1818 CRUISE *Digest* (ed. 2) V. 575 Certainly there is as much reason to adjudge the heir in by descent here, as there is to adjudge an heir in by descent where a recovery was had against the ancestor. 1878 MORLEY *Crit. Misc.* Ser. I. *Carlyle* 199 Here more than anywhere else you need to give the tools to him who can handle them.

7. a. With verbs of coming and bringing: To or towards this place; now, in ordinary use, taking the place of HITHER. ***look here***: see LOOK.

Beowulf (Z.) 376 Is his eaforan nu heard her cumen. c1175 *Lamb. Hom.* 5 He is iblesced þe þe her cumet on drihtenes nome. c1305 *St. Swithin* 9 in *E.E.P.* (1862) 43 Siþþe hit was þat seint berin her bi weste wende. 1508 DUNBAR *Flyting w. Kennedie* 218 Heir cumis our awin queir Clerk! 1583 HOLLYBAND *Campo di Fior* 127 See them, Looke here, Here they be. 1603 SHAKS. *Meas. for M.* v. i. 384 Returne him here againe. 1770 GOLDSM. *Des. Vill.* 96, I still had hopes..Here to return—and die at home at last. 1814 BYRON *Corsair* I. xvii, Call Pedro here! 1824 L. MURRAY *Eng. Gram.* (ed. 5) I. 292 The adverbs *here, there, where,* are often improperly applied to verbs signifying motion, instead of the adverbs *hither, thither, whither*: as 'He came *here* hastily'..should be, 'He came *hither*'. *Mod.* Bring them here at once.

b. Hence, by extension, after *belong* = to this place. *colloq.*

Mod. I'm a stranger, I don't belong here.

8. Used elliptically in calling an attendant, etc. (Cf. Goth. *hiri!* come here!) Hence, to call attention to or introduce a command: = Gr. ἄγε, L. *age*, F. *tiens, tenez.*

[1576 J. SANFORD *Gard. Pleas.* 52 She reaching him foorth to him, added moreover. Holde heere, for I will give him to thee.] 1632 J. HAYWARD tr. *Biondi's Eromena* 18 Here, take these hundred crownes. 1738 SWIFT *Polite Convers.* 211 Here, take away the Tea-table, and bring up Candles. 1873 BLACK *Pr. Thule* xi, Here, come out to the fresh air. *Mod.* John! here! quick.

9. here and there. a. In this place and in that; in various places; in some scattered places; at intervals of space: sometimes = *now and then.* Also, in same sense, with notion of constant or very frequent recurrence, ***every (†ever) here and there.*** (So, formerly, ***†here and yonder.***)

a1300 *Cursor M.* 13981 Iesus preched hir and þar. c1350 *Will. Palerne* 3821 But William as a wod man was euer here & þere. c1400 MAUNDEV. (1839) ix. 112 A lyttille Village, and Houses a brood here and there. 1412–20 LYDG. *Chron. Troy* III. xxvii, He shulde on peces hewen be a sonder Upon the playne dismembred here & yonder. 1513 MORE *Rich. III* (1883) 43 Yet began there, here and there about, some maner of muttering amonge the people. 1535 COVERDALE *1 Pet.* i. 1 Peter an Apostle of Iesu Christ, to them that dwell here and there as straungers thorow out Pontus, Galacia, Capadocia. 1587 R. HOVENDEN in *Collect.* (O.H.S.) I. 217 They be dispersed here and there in hedgerowis. 1602 SHAKS. *Ham.* I. i. 97 Young Fortinbras..Hath in the skirts of Norway, heere and there, Shark'd vp a List of Landlesse Resolutes. 1711 ADDISON *Spect.* No. 50 ¶6 Able to understand but here and there a Word of what they said. 1845 *Lond. Jrnl.* I. 189 Every here and there are seen dark pits and vaulted caverns. 1874 MICKLETHWAITE *Mod. Par. Churches* 326 A good picture may here and there be found in our churches. 1879 F. HALL in *Nation* (N.Y.) XXIX. 391/2 Her style is a curious medley, every here and there, of the ambitious and the slovenly.

b. To this place and to that: hither and thither; in various directions; to and fro.

1297 R. GLOUC. (1724) 378 Þe kyng hem sende her and þer aboute in Engelond. 1340 *Ayenb.* 66 Ase þe wyʒte þet ualþ ine hot weter, þet kest hyer and þer. 1500–20 DUNBAR *Poems* lxxii. 20 In yre thai hurlit him heir and thair. 1591 SPENSER *M. Hubberd* 1357 Th' Ape..Fled here and there, and euerie corner sought. 1646 F. HAWKINS *Youth's Behav.* (1663) 24 Be attentive, turning not thine eyes here and there. 1879 F. POLLOK *Sport Brit. Burmah* I. 78 The brute..was caught, and taken here and there for sale.

†c. This way and that way; with shifts or evasions. *Obs.* Also *attrib.* ? Shifting, evasive.

c1300 *Beket* 42 Tho Gilbert ihurde this; he stod in grete thoʒt, And feignede his word her and ther, and ne grantede noʒt. 1711 'J. DISTAFF' *Char. Don Sacheverellio* 11 Thou canting, whining, here and there Villain.

d. Hence **here-and-thereian** (*humorous nonce-wd.*), one who moves about from place to place.

1701 CIBBER *Love makes Man* IV. iv, I am a kind of a—what d'ye call 'um—a Sort of a Here-and-thereian; I am Stranger no where.

10. here...there. In one place...in another place; = L. *hic...illic, alibi...alibi.*

c1400 MAUNDEV. (Roxb.) xxii. 101 Þai er few, here a hare and þare a hare. 1535 COVERDALE *1 Kings* xviii. 4, I hyd an hundreth of the Lordes prophetes, here fiftye, and there fiftye in the caues. 1579 E. K. in *Spenser's Sheph. Cal.* Ep. Ded. §1 Borrowing here of the french, there of the Italian, euery where of the Latine. 1658 W. SANDERSON *Graphice* 12 Here, barrells flote, there packs, not yet through-wet.

11. here, there, and everywhere. In every place, indicated or not indicated. (Also formerly ***here and everywhere; here, there, all where.***)

c1590 MARLOWE *Faust.* iv. 67 That I may be here and there and everywhere. 1604 SHAKS. *Oth.* I. i. 138 An extrauagant, and wheeling Sranger, Of here, and euery where. 1606 —— *Tr. & Cr.* v. v. 26. 1632 LITHGOW *Trav.* 327 Like yong maides, and youths together, Run here and there, alwhere, and none know whether. 1790 J. B. MORETON *Mann. W. Ind.* 97 [He] must go round the corn field and cane pieces..he must be here and there and everywhere. 1879 F. POLLOK *Sport Brit. Burmah* I. 16 We were soon scattered here, there, and everywhere.

12. neither here nor there. Of no account either one way or the other; of no matter or consequence; unimportant.

1583 GOLDING *Calvin on Deut.* xcii. 570 True it is that our so dooing is neither here nor there (as they say) in respect of God. 1604 SHAKS. *Oth.* IV. iii. 59 'Tis neyther heere, nor there. 1749 FIELDING *Tom Jones* IX. vi, But if he does, that is neither here nor there. 1819 BYRON *Juan* I. li, But what I say is neither here nor there. 1844 DICKENS *Mart. Chuz.* xiv, You'll find him a little too much for your gravity. However, that's neither here nor there.

13. a. here goes! An exclamation declaring one's resolution or resignation to perform some act, usually of a bold or rash character. *colloq.*

1829 J. H. NEWMAN *Corr.* (1891) I. 209, I do not expect to finish this by post-time; but here goes. 1862 THACKERAY *Wks.* (1872) X. 218 Since it must be done, here goes! 1889 BROWNING *Asolando, Ponte dell' Angelo* xxi, Spare speech! I'm resigned: Here goes! roared the goblin.

b. here we go again: we are off on the same undesirable course, project, etc., as before. Also used as *attrib. phr.*

1954 R. BISSELL *High Water* (1955) xix. 161 'Time to get up, Mister Duke.' 'Oh, hell,' I thought. 'Here we go again.' 1958 B. MALAMUD *Magic Barrel* (1960) 72 'Ah, there I can't help you,' said the portiere. 'I haven't got the key.' 'Here we go again,' Carl muttered. 1962 J. BALDWIN *Another Country* (1963) II. iii. 270 'Oh, shit,' he said, 'here we go again.' 1969 *Listener* 12 June 836/1 One of William Glock's most difficult tasks in planning each year's series of Promenade Concerts is to write that desperate here-we-go-again introduction to the prospectus.

14. here we (you) are. Here is what we (you) want. *colloq.*

1850 SMEDLEY *F. Fairleigh* vi, Hum! ha! now let's see, here we are—the 'G-i-a-o-u-r'—that's a nice word to talk about.

15. *Here* was formerly often placed before vbl. sbs. and nouns of action. This is now rare.

c1200 *Trin. Coll. Hom.* 125 Þe erueðliche herbiwist and þe wunderliche heðen sið of ure louerd. *Ibid.* 185 Hure her wunenge is swiðe reulich. 1377 LANGL. *P. Pl.* B. XIV. 141 It semeth nouʒt þat ʒe shulle Haue heuene in ʒowre here beyng and heuene her after. 1586 A. DAY *Eng. Secretary* II. (1625) 60 To continue my here-being to some profitable purpose. 1605 SHAKS. *Macb.* IV. iii. 148 Which often since my heere remaine in England, I haue seene him do.

16. here- in combination with adverbs and prepositions.

[These originated, as in the other Teutonic langs., in the juxtaposition of *here* and another adv. qualifying the same verb. Thus, in HEREBEFORE, 1st quot. *hær beforan* = here (in this document), before (i.e. at an earlier place). Cf. *hereinbefore, hereinafter,* in which *herein* is similarly used. But as many advs. were identical in form with prepositions,

and there was little or no practical difference between 'here, at an earlier place ' and 'before or at an earlier place than this', the adv. came to be felt as a prep. governing *here* (= this place); and, on the analogy of this, new combinations were freely formed of *here* (*there, where*) with prepositions which had never been adverbs, as *herefor, hereto, hereon, herewith*.]

a. with adverbs: as ***here-above, here-beneath, here-within, here-without***; **hereforth**, forward in this direction or this way; **here-next**, next to this, immediately after this. Also HEREAWAY, HEREUNDER, etc. **b.** with prepositions = this, this place, this matter, etc.: as ***hereabove, here-among, here-beside, hereinto, here-within, here-without***; †**hereafore** = HEREBEFORE; †**herintil** (*Sc.*), herein; †**hermid**, herewith; †**hereover**, in addition to this; †**hertoȝeines**, against this, on the other hand. Also HEREABOUT, HEREWITH, etc., etc.

871–89 *Charter of Ælfred* in *O.E. Texts* 452 þas ȝewriotu þe *herbeufan awreotene stondað. **1646** F. Hawkins *Youth's Behav.* (1663) 32 As hath been said here above. **1892** C. E. Norton *Dante's Par.* xxviii. 185 He who saw it hereabove disclosed it to him. **1824** Southey *Bk. of Ch.* (1841) 224, I have told you *hereafore. **1640** E. Dacres tr. *Machiavel's Prince* 180 To the end hee might be able *here-among to undertake greater matters. *c* **1400** *Ywaine & Gaw.* 320 *Her bisyde es a well. **1530** Palsgr. 819/1 Here bysyde, *icy pres.* *c* **1305** *St. Christopher* 94 in *E.E.P.* (1862) 62 þat child him bad par charite þat he him ouer bere; Ȝe com *herforþ, quaþ Cristofre, y nuste wher þu were. *c* **1386** Chaucer *Wife's T.* 144 Heer forth ne lith no wey. **1489** *Sc. Acts Jas. IV*, c. 14 Officiaris þat beis necligent *herintill. *c* **1575** *Balfour's Practicks* (1754) 40 The Schiref..is on na wayis Judge competent heirintill. **1594** Hooker *Eccl. Pol.* I. i. §3 Our first entrance *hereinto. **1602** Carew *Cornwall* (1811) 188 A near friend..looked hereinto with an indifferent and unprejudicating eye. *c* **1205** Lay. 5355 *Her mid we sculled heom bicharren. *a* **1300** *Cursor M.* 141 (Gött.) *Here neist sal be siþen teld Hu Joseph was bath boght and seld. *Ibid.* 26138 (Cott.), I salle þe tel here nest to quam þou sal be shriue. **1398** Trevisa *Barth. De P.R.* II. ii. (1495) 27 *Here ouer angels kinde passyth a bodily kynde in subtilte of his essencia. *a* **1225** *Ancr. R.* 268 He eft seið riht *her to ȝeines—ne let tu..þine meiden no gult to ȝiues. *c* **1200** *Trin. Coll. Hom.* 115 Ȝie maisterlinges *her-wið-innen openeð ȝiure gaten. *a* **1533** Ld. Berners *Huon* clv. 593 We haue..chaumbers garnysshed and ordeyned as ye haue sene herewith-in. **1530** Palsgr. 819/1 *Here without, *icy dehors.*

B. as *sb.* = This place; also, the present; the present life. Freq. in phr. ***here and now***; also as *advb. phr.*; so ***here-and-nowness***. Also ***here and there*** sb. phr.

1605 Shaks. *Lear* I. i. 264 Thou loosest here a better where to finde. **1816** M. E. Bicknell *Let.* 26 Sept. in J. Constable *Corr.* (1964) II. 210, I know of no other plan but of my leaving here early on Monday. **1829** Carlyle *Misc.* (1857) II. 76 With Him it is a universal Here and Now. **1838** Dickens *O. Twist* II. xxxiv. 269, I—I—ought to have left here before. **1839** —— *Let.* *c* 24 July (1965) I. 567, I dine in town tomorrow and shall leave *for here* at 10 at night. **1855** Longf. *Hiaw.* Introd. 113 Full of all the tender pathos Of the Here and the Hereafter. **1857–8** Sears *Athan.* 19 [Motion] requires a here and a there. **1857** —— *Dorrit* II. xxxiv, You would rather not leave here till to-morrow morning. **1874** Geo. Eliot in *Macm. Mag.* XXXVIII. July 177 Widening his consciousness from Here and Now to larger wholes. **1887** Rider Haggard *A. Quatermain* xvi. 188 Here and now for thy dear sake I will forget my people and my father's house. **1922** W. S. Maugham *On Chinese Screen* xliii. 172 Your thoughts travel through time and space, far from the Here and Now. **1933** P. Godfrey *Back-Stage* xiv. 176 Its romantic appeal is an escape from here and now into an artificial world of somewhere else or some time past. *a* **1943** R. G. Collingwood *Idea of Hist.* (1946) 248 The detail of the here-and-now as given him in perception. **1957** C. Day Lewis *Pegasus* 56 The truant here-and-there of the Stour. **1959** *Listener* 26 Feb. 385/1 Whether Condorcet or Huxley is right is an undecidable question for us here and now. **1959** *Times Lit. Suppl.* 11 Sept. 522/3 All combine to form a subtle escape-route from the unwelcome here-and-now of the twentieth century. **1961** I. Murdoch *Severed Head* x. 85 She was all gentleness and filled with so genuine a concern to save me here and now from distress and anxiety. **1962** *Listener* 26 Apr. 717/2 Here and now Russia, while she does not want a war with us, is nevertheless our antagonist. **1963** *Times* 27 Feb. 13/1 They came, it seems, to a realization of the here-and-nowness of life. **1971** *New Scientist* 27 Apr. 263/1 Cocking's group have *their* minds firmly concentrated on the here-and-now.

here, obs. f. HAIR, HEAR, EAR; var. HAIRE, HER *sb.*, HER *pron. pers.* and *poss.*

hereabout (hɪərə'baʊt), *adv.* [f. HERE *adv.* 16 + ABOUT.]

†**1.** About or concerning this (thing, etc.). *Obs.*

a **1225** *Ancr. R.* 46 Scheaweð ofte ine scrifte ower ȝeme-leaste her abuten. *c* **1386** Chaucer *Miller's T.* 376 Go now thy wey and speed thee heer aboute. **1583** Hollyband *Campo di Fior* 343 We may remember that, which this maister hath tolde us hereabout. **1644** Hunton *Vind. Treat. Monarchy* vi. 49 Reade what I have said here-about.

2. About or near this place; somewhere in this neighbourhood.

a **1300** *K. Horn* 343 Ȝef horn were her abute..Wiþ him ȝe wolden pleie. *c* **1400** *Warres of Jewes* in Warton *Hist. Eng. Poetry* x. (1840) II. 106 Prophecie, they sayde, Which man her aboute [bolled] the laste. **1592** Shaks. *Rom. & Jul.* v. iii. 43 Ile hide me here about. **1653** Walton *Angler* ii. 47 There is not a likely place for a Trout here-about. **1856** R. A. Vaughan *Mystics* (1860) I. 234, I think it must lie somewhere hereabout. **1875** Tennyson *Q. Mary* III. v, There haunt some Papist ruffians hereabout.

b. About this point of action, time, etc.

1675 S. Sewall *Diary* 31 July I. 11 Herabout I waked.

herea'bouts, *adv.* [f. prec. + adverbial *-s*.]

1. = prec. 2.

1592 Shaks. *Rom. & Jul.* v. i. 38 And here abouts dwells. **1617** Moryson *Itin.* II. 130, I thinke it fittest to stay here-abouts a while. **1732** Fielding *Mock Doctor* IV. Wks. 1882 IX. 256 Is there no physician hereabouts famous for curing dumbness? **1862** Trollope *Orley F.* i, The land hereabouts ceases to be fertile.

†**2.** = prec. 1. *Obs. rare.*

1584 R. Scot *Discov. Witchcr.* XVI. iii. (1886) 400 He receiued some trouble himselfe hereabouts. **1649** Roberts *Clavis Bibl.* 381 The dissenting Opinions of learned writers heareabouts.

†**here a days**, *adv. Sc. Obs.* Nowadays.

1572 *Satir. Poems Reform.* xxx. 186 Quhilk will be found na fault now heir a dayis.

hereafter (hɪər'ɑːftə(r), -æ-), *adv.* (*a.*, *sb.*) [OE. *hérǽfter*, f. *hér* HERE *adv.* 16 + AFTER: cf. Da. *herefter*, Sw. *härefter*.]

1. After, in this writing, book, or place; in the sequel; after this in order or position; sometimes = next in order, immediately after.

c **900** tr. *Bæda's Hist.* III. xxii. [xxx.] (1890) 250 Swa swa we eft heræfter secȝaþ. *c* **1050** *Byrhtferth's Handboc* in *Anglia* VIII. 317/37 Heræfter we wyllað þisne circul amearkian. *a* **1225** *Ancr. R.* 112 Lo hwuch on asaumple her efter. *a* **1300** *Cursor M.* 27380, I sal þam recken siþen on rau, Wit þair springes her efter neist, Quen i ha tald þe office o preist. *c* **1315** Shoreham 164 Ase ich her after telle may. **1390** Gower *Conf.* III. 128 Of other sterres how they fare, I thenke here after to declare. **1508** Dunbar (*title*) The flyting of Dunbar and Kennedie heir efter followis. **1601** Chester *Love's Martyr* 165 (for 169) Hereafter folovv diverse Poeticall Essaies. **1818** Cruise *Digest* (ed. 2) V. 233 In consequence of the statute 32 Hen. VIII. c. 28 which will be stated hereafter.

2. After this in time; at a future time; in time to come.

1154 *O.E. Chron.* an. 1135 Men..sæden ð[at] micel þing sculde cumen her efter. *c* **1175** *Lamb. Hom.* 43 Herefter iseh paul hwer .iii. deoflen ledden an meiden. *a* **1300** *Cursor M.* 6568 (Gött.) Here efter it sal sare rew ȝou. **1388** Wyclif *Gal.* vi. 17 Heraftir no man be heuy to me, for Y bere in my bodi the tokenes of oure Lorde Jhesu Crist. *c* **1477** Caxton *Jason* 42, [I] wolde that I were there, where I shall be v honderd yere here after. **1483** *Vulgaria abs Terentio* 16b, I am so gladd that no thynge ereaftyr may make me sory. **1576** Fleming *Panopl. Epist.* 68 So would I have you thinke mee to be, at this present, and for ever hereafter to remaine. **1596** Shaks. *Merch. V.* II. vi. 20 More of this hereafter. **1712** Hearne *Collect.* (O.H.S.) III. 497, I shall send the rest hereafter. **1875** Jowett *Plato* (ed. 2) V. 180 We cannot.. anticipate the details which will hereafter be needed.

3. In a future state; in the world to come.

[**1340–70** *Alex. & Dind.* 363 We hopen haue þe lif þat come schal her aftur.] **1618** Bp. Hall *Serm.* vii. Wks. 1837 V. 102 To learn so to be happy here, that it [a Christian's heart] may be more happy hereafter. **1736** Butler *Anal.* I. ii. Wks. 1874 I. 40 The general doctrine of religion, that God will reward and punish men for their actions hereafter. **1858** Gladstone *Homer* III. 515 What we are as men here depends very much on our conception of what we are hereafter to be.

†**4.** After or in accordance with this. *Obs. rare.*

c **1380** Wyclif *Sel. Wks.* III. 358 Ȝif it were a trewe sentence, God myȝte move men hereafter.

B. as *adj.* To come, future. Now *rare.*

1591 Shaks. *1 Hen. VI*, II. ii. 10 That hereafter Ages may behold What ruine happened in reuenge of him. **1709** Mrs. Manley *Secret Mem.* (1736) 3 May his Hereafter Torments be never ending! **1799** Anna Seward *Lett.* (1811) V. 269 Claims..to hereafter compensation. **1881** F. E. Warren *Celtic Liturgy* 103 Requesting the prayers of their hereafter readers.

C. *sb.* **1.** Time to come: the future; futurity.

1546 J. Heywood *Prov.* (1867) 67 An auditour of a meane wit, Maie soone accompt, though hereafter come not yit. **1663** J. Spencer *Prodigies* (1665) 408 Distrustful fears in reference to hereafter. **1689** W. Sherlock *Death* iii. §6 (1731) 143 The Reason..will serve for all hereafters, but will never serve for any Time present. **1807–8** Syd. Smith *Plymley's Lett.* iii. Wks. 1859 II. 145/2 Leave hereafter to the spirit and the wisdom of hereafter. **1883** in J. G. Butler *Bible-Work* II. 768 To read the story of our own hereafter.

2. A future life; the world to come.

1702 Rowe *Tamerl.* I. i. 405 Wretches that are doubtful of Hereafter. **1713** Addison *Cato* v. i, 'Tis heaven it self, that points out an Hereafter. **1744** Wesley *Wks.* (1872) VIII. 26 What, if there be an hereafter, a judgment to come? **1855** Longf. *Hiaw.* VI. 65 For he sang of..life undying..In the land of the Hereafter.

†**here'afterward**, *adv. Obs.* Also **-wards**. [f. HERE *adv.* 16 + AFTERWARD *adv.*] Hereafter.

a **1300** *Cursor M.* 15375 Her efterward yeit sal yee se. *c* **1386** Chaucer *Friar's T.* 217 Thou shalt herafterwards my brother deere Come there thee nedeth nat of me to leere. **14..** *Voc.* in Wr.-Wülcker 589/12 *Imposterum*, hereafter-warde. **1530** Whytford *Werke for Househ.* D iij, Shal cause the persones..hereafterwarde to bless you & pray for you. **1674** N. Fairfax *Bulk & Selv.* 201 Not one age only, but ages time out of mind, and hereafterward.

†**here-again**, *adv. Obs.* [f. HERE *adv.* 16 + AGAIN *prep.* Cf. Ger. *hiergegen*.] = next.

c **1200** *Vices & Virtues* 105 Hier aȝean sæde ðe profiete [etc.]. *a* **1300** *Cursor M.* 798 Her egain [*v.rr.* here agayne, aȝeyn] mai naman sai. *Ibid.* 17034 And es naman..þat agh sai her again. *c* **1386** Chaucer *Knt.'s T.* 2181 (Harl.) And here agayn no creature..avayleþ for to stryue. **1393** Langl. *P. Pl.* C. xx. 109 If kynde witt carpe her-aȝen.

†**here-against**, *adv. Obs.* [f. HERE *adv.* 16 + AGAINST.] Against this; in opposition, contradistinction, or contrast to this; in comparison with this.

a **1225** *Ancr. R.* 94 Euerich worldlich gledunge is unwurð her aȝeines. *c* **1386** Chaucer *Knt.'s T.* 2181 (Ellesm.) And here agayns no creature on lyue Of no degree auailleth for to stryue. *c* **1430** *Pilgr. Lyf Manhode* I. lxxii. (1869) 42 The witt of heeringe oonliche enfoormeth the vnderstondinge more than thilke of taaste doth heer ayens. **1583** Golding *Calvin on Deut.* xcvi. 593 Now hereagainst a man might reply: I had leauer [etc.]. **1614** Raleigh *Hist. World* v. ii. §3 (1634) 587 Such as would speak here-against.

hereanent, *adv.* Chiefly *Sc. arch.* [f. HERE *adv.* 16 + ANENT *prep.*] Concerning this.

a **1225** *Juliana* 12 Nulich heronont buhen þe nawiht. *c* **1575** *Balfour's Practicks* (1754) 278 To compeir within ane schort day in the Kingis court, to answer heiranent. **1591** in De Foe *Mem. Ch. Scot.* Add. 58 The Lawes of the Realme ..and Constitution of our Kirk are clear hereanent. **1643** Drumm. of Hawth. *Declarat.*, etc. Wks. (1711) 211 The declaration of the commissioners of the general Assembly made hereanent.

hereat (hɪər'æt), *adv.* [f. HERE *adv.* 16 + AT *prep.*]

†**1.** At this place; here. *Obs.*

c **1400** *Destr. Troy* 8421 Lengys here at a litill, lystyn my wordes. **1647** N. Bacon *Disc. Govt. Eng.* I. xxv. (1739) 43 All Free-holders were bound to present themselves hereat. *a* **1650** *Turke & Gawin* 109 in Furniv. *Percy Folio* I. 94, I wold not longer be hereate.

2. At this; as a result of this.

a **1557** *Diurn. Occurr.* (Bannatyne) 11 Heirat was mony hurt with hagbuttis. **1586** Young *Guazzo's Civ. Conv.* IV. 204b, Heereat the Ladies objected. **1639** Fuller *Holy War* II. i. (1647) 44 All admired hereat. **1674** N. Cox *Gentl. Recreat.* (1677) 64 Hereat the young fly away for fear. **1860** Rawlinson & Wilkinson *Herodotus* IX. lxxvii. IV. 449 Greatly distressed hereat, they declared themselves to deserve a fine as laggards. **1877** Bryant *Poems, Sella* 149 Hereat broke in the mother.

hereaway ('hɪərəweɪ), *adv.* Now *dial.* and *U.S.* [f. HERE *adv.* 16 + AWAY *adv.*]

1. Away in this direction; in this quarter or neighbourhood, hereabouts.

14.. *Voc.* in Wr.-Wü lcker 590/41 *Istac*, herawey. **1483** *Cath. Angl.* 184/1 Heraway (*A.* hereaway), *hac, istac*. **1613** Purchas *Pilgrimage* (1864) 95 Minnagara, which Ortelius in his Map placeth here-away. *a* **1718** Penn in *Pa. Hist. Soc. Mem.* I. 203 The above was read..to the most eminent of Friends hereaway. **1855** Whittier *Lines on Fugit. Slave Act* vi, Hereaway The fell lycanthrope finds no prey. **1894** Crockett *Lilac Sunbonnet* 11 This is the first time you have been hereaway?

†**b.** In this present life. *Sc. Obs.*

a **1661** Rutherford *Lett.* (1765) II. ii. (Jam.), That light is not hereaway in any clay-body.

2. To this quarter or neighbourhood; hither. ***hereaway thereaway*** (*Sc.*), hither and thither, to and fro in every direction.

1549 Coverdale, etc. *Erasm. Par. Phil.* 2 The more they are holden vnder and turmoyled hereawaye and thereawaye, so muche more they come forwarde. **1598** R. Bernard tr. *Terence* 94 Follow me in this way, or hereaway. **1793** Burns *Wandering Willie*, Hereawa, thereawa, wandering Willie, Hereawa, thereawa, haud awa hame! *Mod. Sc.* They were all running hereaway thereaway.

'hereaways. Now *dial.* = prec.

1613 Purchas *Pilgrimage* II. x. (1614) 162 Here-awaies lived a people called 'Dogzijm', which others called Pagans. *Ibid.* v. xiv. 520 It should be sought here-a-waies, or found nowhere. **1869** in *Lonsdale Gloss.* **1877** *N.W. Linc. Gloss.* s.v., I hevn't seen him hereaways sin' June.

†**herebefore.** *Obs.* Forms: see BEFORE. [OE. *hér beforan*, f. *hér* HERE *adv.* 16 + BEFORE *adv.*: cf. MDu. *hierbevoren*, MLG. *hirbevoren*.]

1. Earlier in this document; herein before.

805–31 *Charter of Oswulf* in *O.E. Texts* 444 Deara saula ðe hær beforan hiora namon auuritene siondon. **1340** *Ayenb.* 59 Ase we zede hyerbeuore. **1395** *E.E. Wills* (1882) 8 That this be parfourned as hit is writen herbefore.

2. Before this time; before now; in time past.

c **1200** *Trin. Coll. Hom.* 63 Beten for þ at we hauen agilt her biforen. *c* **1320** *Cast. Love* 1329 Alle he ladde herbifore after his wille. *c* **1386** Chaucer *Knt's T.* 726 As I ful ofte haue seyd thee heer biforn. **1486** *Surtees Misc.* (1888) 53 Kinges herbefor resorting unto the citie. **1577** B. Googe *Heresbach's Husb.* I. (1586) 8 Our fathers herebefore observed the same. **1613** W. Browne *Sheph. Pipe* I. (R.), Some privy thing now causeth this richesse, As did the ring herebefore I gesse.

hereberȝe, -boroghe, etc., obs. ff. HARBOUR.

[**herebode, -bote**. Spurious forms (due to 17th century antiquaries) compounded of OE. *here* army, HERE *sb.*, and *boda* messenger, BODE *sb.*[1], confused with *bót* compensation, BOTE, BOOT *sb.*[1]

1671 Skinner *Etym. Ling. Angl.* Pppp 3b, *Herebode*, vox ant. For. AS. olim Edictum Regis quo Cives seu subditi ad Militiam evocabantur, ab AS. *Here*, Exercitus, & *Bode*, Nuncius, *Bodian*, Denunciare, Indicere. **1727** *Cowell's Interpr.*, *Herebote*, the King's Edict, commanding his Subjects into the Field: From the Saxon, *Here, exercitus*, and *Bode*, a Messenger. Hence *Herebote* in **1882** Ogilvie and *Cassell's Encycl. Dict.*, *Herebode* in *Century Dict.*]

hereby (hɪə'baɪ, 'hɪəbaɪ), *adv.* [f. HERE *adv.* + BY *prep.* Cf. MDu. *hierbi*, MLG. *hirbi*, Du. *hierbij*, MHG. *hierbî*, Ger. *hierbei*. The stress shifts

with the position of the word; cf. 'I 'hereby promise', 'I promise here'by'.]

†**1.** (*here'by*) By or near this place; in this neighbourhood; close by. *Obs.*

c **1250** *Gen. & Ex.* 3572 Quat Iosue to moysi, 'Ic wene he fiȝten dun her-bi'. *c* **1440** *York Myst.* xv. 13 Or he be borne in burgh hereby. *a* **1533** Ld. Berners *Huon* lxiii. 218 Sende fyrst to an abbay that is here by. **1588** Shaks. *L.L.L.* iv. i. 9 Hereby vpon the edge of yonder Coppice. **1631** Weever *Anc. Fun. Mon.* 588 Hereby was a religious House for preaching Friers. **1655** J. Jennings tr. *Elise* 30 A Tenants daughter of mine, a Gentleman here by.

†**b.** Past this place. *Obs.*

c **1400** *Rom. Rose* 6300, I wole nomore of this thing seyne, If I may passen me herby. *c* **1485** *Digby Myst.* (1882) iv. 277 The pepill that passis here-by.

†**2.** In connexion with this. *Obs.*

c **1230** *Hali Meid.* 23 Loke þenne her bi hwa se of hire meidenhad lihteð in to wedlac. *a* **1250** *Owl & Night.* 127 Her-bi men seggeþ a bispel.

3. By, through, or from this fact or circumstance; as a result of this; by this means.

c **1320** R. Brunne *Medit.* 67 Here by þou mayst lere þat of o dysshe þey etyn yn fere. *c* **1400** Maundev. (Roxb.) x. 39 Hereby schuld it seme þat haly writte ware noȝt trewe. **1526** Tindale *1 John* ii. 3 And herby we knowe that we have knowen him. **1594** Shaks. *Rich. III*, i. iv. 94, I will not reason what is meant heereby. **1665** Hooke *Microgr.* Table 247 A multitude of Phænomena explicable hereby. **1756** C. Lucas *Ess. Waters* III. 105 Hereby, we detect the errors of those who evaporate..waters. **1843** Bethune *Sc. Fireside Stor.* 11, I hereby promise to mend the whole in the most scientific manner. **1875** Jowett *Plato* (ed. 2) I. 157 Hereby you may know that I am right.

†**here'dation.** *Obs. rare*⁻¹. [f. L. type **hērēdāre* (f. *hērēd-em* heir): cf. *exhērēdāre* to disinherit.]

The action of inheriting; inheritance.

1606 Birnie *Kirk-Buriall* xix. (1833) F ij b, The Iewes doe comprise all titular rights vnder one of three: acquisition, like Abrahams (in the conqueis of the caue, Gen. 23) Heredation, like Isaacs (succeeding thereto) lucrifaction, like Iacobs.

heredipety (hɛrɪ'dɪpɪtɪ). [f. L. *hērēdipet-a* legacy-hunter (f. *hērēdium* legacy + *petere* to seek) + -y (as in *colloquy*, etc.).] Legacy-hunting.

1855 Milman *Lat. Chr.* I. ii. (1864) I. 91 Heredipety or legacy hunting is inveighed against, in the clergy especially, as by the older Satirists. *Ibid.* III. v. II. 29 Already heredipety, seeking inheritances by undue means, is branded as an ecclesiastical vice.

So **here'dipetous** *a.*, legacy-hunting.

1866 F. Hall in *Lyndesay's Monarche* 245 *marg.*, To the parrot came the magpie, heredipetous, and the raven and the kite, ready to help heavenward.

hereditability (hɪˌrɛdɪtə'bɪlɪtɪ). [f. next + -ity.]

= heritability.

a **1837** Sir E. Brydges (cited in Worcester, 1846). **1885** *Pop. Sci. Monthly* XXVI. 107 After the hereditability of the royal office has been accepted. **1895** *Ibid.* July 394 Teratological abnormities resemble neuropathies..in their origin and the characteristics of their hereditability.

hereditable (hɪ'rɛdɪtəb(ə)l), *a.* [a. obs. F. *héréditable*, ad. L. type **hērēditābilis*, f. *hērēditāre* to inherit, f. *hērēs*, *hērēd-em* heir.]

1. Of things: That may be inherited; subject to inheritance; heritable.

1494 Fabyan *Chron.* vii. 675 A prouerbe amonge the Frenshemen..(Principibus obsequi hereditarium non esse) the whiche is to meane, the seruyce of prynces is not heredytable. **1654** Gayton *Pleas. Notes* iv. v. 197 Dropsies, Gowts..and most diseases are as hæreditable from our Parents, as their estates. **1690** Locke *Govt.* i. ix. §103 Adam ..being neither monarch, nor his imaginary monarchy hereditable. **1841** Elphinstone *Hist. Ind.* I. 125 These people..are admitted..to have a hereditable and transferable interest in it. **1872** *Contemp. Rev.* XX. 399.

†**2.** Of persons: Capable of inheriting; having a right of inheritance; = heritable 3. *Obs.*

1643 Prynne *Sov. Power Parl.* i. (ed. 2) 97 Declaring some of his issues legitimate and hereditable to the Crowne, others not. **1655** M. Carter *Hon. Rediv.* (1660) 87 The making any men hereditable.

he'reditably, *adv.* [f. prec. + -ly².] By way of inheritance; heritably.

1495 *Act 11 Hen. VII*, c. 34 Preamble, The furst begoten sonnes of hym and of hys heires..in the realme of Englond hereditably to succede. *c* **1630** Risdon *Surv. Devon* (1714) II. 343 Which Land from that Family is Hereditably descended to Devia. *a* **1820** Tooke *Russ. Encycl.* (Webster 1828), The one-house-owners belong hereditably to no private persons.

†**he'redital,** *a. Obs.* [a. obs. F. *héréditał* (15th c. in Godefroi), ad. med.L. *hērēditāl-is*, f. *hērēditas* heredity.] = hereditary.

1490 Caxton *Eneydos* xix. 72 The successyon is vnto hym due of ryghte heredytalle and by veraye destynacy after my deth. **1574** J. Jones *Nat. Beginning Grow. Things* 13 As not only hereditall sicknesses doth shew, but also deformed persons doth proue.

hereditament (hɛrɪ'dɪtəmənt, hɪ'rɛdɪtə-). Also 7 hær-. [ad. med.L. *hērēditāmentum*, f. late L. *hērēditāre* to inherit, f. *hērēd-em* heir.]

1. *Law.* Any kind of property that can be inherited; any thing, corporeal or incorporeal, that in the absence of testamentary disposition descended to the heir at common law, and now (Act 60 & 61 Vict. c. 65) to the 'real representative'; real property.

1475 *Statute* in Campbell *Lives Chancellors* (1857) I. xxii. 320 The seid John [Fortescue] shuld..forfeit to you, soureyn lord and your heires, all the castelles, maneres.. seruices, fees, advousons, hereditamentes and possessions. **1483** *Plumpton Corr.* xci, Rents, services, reversions, & heredi[ta]ments. **1494** Fabyan *Chron.* vii. 650 [A] parlyament, at the whiche yᵉ duke of Alensone was iuged to lose his hede, & his heredytamentys to be forfaytyd vnto yᵉ Kynge. **1571** *Act 13 Eliz.* c. 10. §2 Tythes tenements or other hereditaments. **1628** Coke *On Litt.* 6 a, *Haereditament* is the largest word in all in that kind, for whatsoever may be inherited is an haereditament, be it corporeal or incorporeal, real or personal or mixt. **1765** Blackstone *Comm.* II. iii. 13 An incorporeal hereditament is a right issuing out of a thing corporate..or concerning, or annexed to, or exercisable within, the same. **1832** Austin *Jurispr.* (1879) I. xiii. 372 A corporeal hereditament is the thing itself which is the subject of the right, an incorporeal hereditament is not the subject of the right but the right itself. **1855** Macaulay *Hist. Eng.* xv. III. 540 The representation of Westmoreland was almost as much one of the hereditaments of the Lowther family as Lowther Hall.

fig. **1795** J. S. Hobart in *J. Jay's Corr.* (1893) IV. 196 This power ought to be exercised by the spiritual or the civil rulers solely: it is an hereditament of which they cannot be seized as tenants in common. **1847** Bushnell *Chr. Nurt.* vii. (1861) 178 A kind of hereditament in the family.

2. Heirship, inheritance.

1509–10 *Act 1 Hen. VIII*, c. 19 Preamble, The..Kyng.. restored and habled your said Suppliant..in name state degree blode and Hereditament. **1844** Mary Hennell *Social Syst.* 50 The natural head of the community was the family father; then the son; and this natural hereditament continued as long as the direct line was maintained.

†**he'reditance.** *Obs. rare*⁻¹. [f. late L. *hērēditāre* (see prec.) + -ance.] Inheritance, heirship.

1641 Earl Monm. tr. *Biondi's Hist. Civ. Warres Eng.* I. i.–v. 107 In successions, hereditance, and last wills and Testaments.

hereditarian (hɪrɛdɪ'tɛərɪən). [f. L. *hērēditāri-us* hereditary + -an.] One who holds the biological doctrine of heredity.

1881 J. Owen *Even. with Sceptics* I. v. 446 The modern hereditarian regards himself as the offspring, mentally as well as physically, of a long succession of ancestors going back as far as the anthropoid ape. **1896** E. A. Fay in *Amer. Ann. Deaf* June 233 Some of the most eminent hereditarians believe that acquired characteristics are never transmitted.

he'reditarily, *adv.* [f. hereditary *a.* + -ly².] In a hereditary manner; by way of (an) inheritance.

1603 Holland *Plutarch's Mor.* Ded. 2, With her Realmes and Dominions, the best parts and gifts that were in her be likewise hæreditarily descended upon your roiall person. **1638** T. Whitaker *Blood of Grape* 50 Children, which are hereditarily subject to the stone. **1796** Russell in *Phil. Trans.* LXXXVII. 26 The collyria they apply are secret compositions, which pass hereditarily from father to son. **1807** Knight *Ibid.* XCVII. 241 The acquired habits of the parents being transferred hereditarily to the offspring.

he'reditariness. [f. as prec. + -ness.] The quality of being hereditary; capability of being inherited, or transmitted from parent to offspring.

1640 Fuller *Joseph's Coat* vii. (1867) 181 First, for the hereditariness of it [a leprosy], it is a successive disease. **1683** *Brit. Spec.* 243 The unalterable Hereditariness of the Monarchy. **1861** Darwin in *Life & Lett.* (1887) II. 372 His paper about hereditariness beats everything. **1887** Smiles *Life & Lab.* 188 The hereditariness of family features appeared..in the configuration of the head.

†**heredi'tarious,** *a. Obs. rare.* [f. L. *hērēditāri-us* (see next) + -ous.] = hereditary.

1527 R. Thorne in *Hakluyt* (1589) 257 Some sicknesses are hereditarious, and comme from the father to the sonne.

hereditary (hɪ'rɛdɪtərɪ), *a.* (*sb.*) Also *erron.* 7 hær-. [ad. L. *hērēditāri-us*, f. *hērēditās* heredity. Cf. F. *héréditaire* (15–16th c.). The L. *hērēs*, *hērēd-em*, and its derivatives were till recently often written *hær-*, a spelling formerly also frequent in the English representatives of the family.]

A. *adj.* **1.** *Law* and *Hist.* Descending by inheritance from generation to generation; that has been or may be transmitted according to definite rules of descent; legally vesting, upon the death of the holder, in the person designated by the law as his heir.

hereditary countries (of the Austrian German emperors): those which were the original inheritance of the Archdukes of Austria, or were subsequently acquired by marriage, i.e. Upper and Lower Austria, Moravia, Styria, Carinthia, Carniola, Bohemia, Silesia.

1601 Dent *Pathw. Heaven* (1831) 4 [We] haue inherited his foul corruptions, as it were by hereditary right. *c* **1610** Sir J. Melvil *Mem.* (1735) 63 He lost the Kingdom of Denmark, pretending to make it hereditary, whereas it was elective. **1635–56** Cowley *Davideis* iii. *note* 33 There was always some haereditary Bowl with which they made their Libations to the Gods, and entertained Strangers. **1675** *Lond. Gaz.* No. 1049/2 From Vienna they write, that..great preparations were making in all the Hereditary Countreys. **1725** Pope *Odyss.* i. 242 To revisit your imperial dome, An old hereditary guest, I come. **1759** Robertson *Hist. Scot.* I. i. 42 All new grants of hereditary offices were prohibited. **1862** Stanley *Jew. Ch.* I. vii. 134 An hereditary priesthood ..in the family of Aaron.

2. Transmitted in a line of progeny; passing naturally from parents to offspring. **a.** esp. in *Biol.*, *Pathol.*, etc., of physical and mental characteristics, diseases, instincts, etc., that are or may be transmitted from generation to generation.

1597 Morley *Introd. Mus.* 163 The fault which like vnto a hereditarie lepresie in a mans bodie is uncurable. **1699** 'Misaurus' *Hon. of Gout* in *Harl. Misc.* (1809) II. 46, I have heard you confess that yours is an hereditary gout. **1826** Prichard *Phys. Hist. Mankind* (ed. 2) ix. i. §3 II. 537 All original or connate peculiarities of body are hereditary. *Ibid.* 544 Now it appears that such spontaneous tendencies are alone hereditary. **1833** *Destructive* 22 June 166/3 (*heading*) Absurdity of 'hereditary wisdom'. **1862** D. Wilson *Preh. Man* II. xxiii. 369 The hereditary instincts of forest life. **1875** Bennett & Dyer tr. *Sach's Bot.* 825 Two different sets of hereditary characters are combined in a hybrid, and there is hence a strong tendency towards the formation of new characters which may be more or less hereditary. **1899** W. James *Talks to Teachers* xiv. 164 The foreign terms 'déséquilibré', 'hereditary degenerate', and 'psychopathic' subject, have arisen in response to the same need. **1928** B. D. Jackson *Gloss. Bot. Terms* (ed. 4) 176/1 *Hereditary symbiosis*, the presence of mycobacteria in the tissues, including seeds. **1941** J. S. Huxley *Uniqueness of Man* ii. 48 The latter [*sc.* fraternal twins] will have hereditary outfits as different as those of members of the same family born at different times. **1967** Mahloudi & Pikielny in *Brain* XC. 672 With such divergence of opinion, it may be wise to drop the term paramyoclonus multiplex altogether. Instead we suggest the term *hereditary essential myoclonus*.

b. in *Theology.*

1577 tr. *Bullinger's Decades* (1592) 495 We shoulde seeme thereby to affirme, that sinne is *ex traduce* or hereditarie. **1592** Davies *Immort. Soul* viii. xvi, This Sin of Kind, not personal, But real, and hereditary was. **1615** G. Sandys *Trav.* 64 Branded..by God for..their owne wicked assuming of hereditary holinesse.

c. In general sense: Coming to one from one's precursors in national or physical life; identical with or similar to what was possessed by one's parents, so that it might be conceived as having been bequeathed by or inherited from them.

1601 R. Johnson *Kingd. & Commw.* (1603) 47 It hath been their hereditarie practise, to stande upon their guard, to prevent their enemies. **1644** Nye *Gunnery* Ded., The Patronage of Arts being hereditary to your noble Ancestors. **1752** Young *Brothers* i. i, Long burnt a fixt hereditary hate, Between the crowns of Macedon and Thrace. *a* **1856** H. Miller *Cruise Betsey* ii. xv. (1889) 483 His actual beliefs appeared to be very considerably at variance with his hereditary creed.

3. Of persons: Holding their position by inheritance.

1651 Hobbes *Leviath.* ii. xix. 98 If he have Right to appoint his Successor, he is no more Elective but Hereditary. **1697** Dryden *Æneid* Ded., That Romulus was no hereditary prince. **1812** Byron *Ch. Har.* ii. lxxvi, Hereditary bonds-men! know ye not Who would be free themselves must strike the blow? **1857** Buckle *Civiliz.* I. ix. 561 The great possessors of land were now being organized into an hereditary aristocracy.

4. Of, pertaining to, or relating to inheritance.

1790 Burke *Fr. Rev.* 30 It was still a line of hereditary descent; still an hereditary descent in the same blood, though an hereditary descent qualified with protestantism. **1848** W. H. Kelly tr. *L. Blanc's Hist. Ten Y.* I. 507 In whatever way the peerage be considered, said the enemies of the hereditary principle, the law of descent will be found to be useless. **1879** Khory *Princ. Med.* 4 Abnormal structures are the most obvious instances of hereditary transmission.

B. as *sb.* A hereditary ruler; in *pl.*, the House of Lords.

1836 *Radical* 13 Mar. 4/1 The debate, or rather debates in the House of Commons, on the question of justice to the Irish, are but a sad augury of its ever passing the 'Hereditaries' unemasculated. **1932** G. B. Shaw *Platform & Pulpit* (1962) 246 The hereditaries are brought up to exercise their personal power conventionally and leave the rest to their ministers.

hereditation (hɪrɛdɪ'teɪʃən). *Biol.* [n. of action f. late L. *hērēditāre* to inherit (in Vulgate), in med.L. also to invest with an inheritance: cf. 15th c. F. *(h)éréditation* succession, inheritance.] The action or operation of heredity.

1883 *Amer. Jrnl. Med. Sc.* Jan. 74 Hereditation as a cause may exist oftener than appears. **1885** P. Brooks *Myst. Iniq.*, etc. v. 87 It has its own despair already in itself, this hopeless struggle with hereditation, which..is..so literally a wrestling against flesh and blood. **1896** *Expositor* Dec. 416 We preserve hereditary good: we originate good hereditations.

hereditism (hɪ'rɛdɪtɪz(ə)m). [f. heredity + -ism.] The principle or doctrine of the hereditary transmission of characteristics, etc.

1884 *Edin. Rev.* July 229 Mr. Galton, the apostle of hereditism. **1890** *Nature* 9 Oct. 580 The doctrine of hereditism. **1897** *Genealog. Mag.* Oct. 341 Evidence that hereditism is not confined to flocks and herds.

So **he'reditist**, one who holds the doctrine that all individuality is determined by inheritance.

1895 *Daily News* 23 Jan. 6/5 The new theory of the hereditists, headed by Professor Lombroso, to the effect that genius is merely one of the manifestations of brain disease.

heredi'tivity. *Biol. rare.* [f. **hereditive* (f. heredity + -ive) + -ity.] (See quot.)

1876 Lankester tr. *Haeckel's Hist. Creat.* I. viii. 176 Hereditivity is the power of transmission, the capability of

organisms to transfer their peculiarities to their descendants by propagation.

heredity (hɪ'rɛdɪtɪ). [a. F. *hérédité* (11th c. in Littré) the quality of being heir, heritage, ad. L. *hērēditāt-em* heirship, inheritance, f. *hērēs, hērēd-em* heir: see -ITY.]

†**1.** Hereditary succession; inheritance; *concr.* that which is inherited; an inheritance. *Obs.*

c **1540** tr. *Pol. Verg. Eng. Hist.* (Camden) I. 252 This Richard was a manne.. well worthie the princelie hereditee of his father which hee soberlie governed. *Ibid.* 294 His promise.. made to the duke concerninge the hereditee of the kingdom.

2. *Law.* Hereditary character, quality, or condition; the fact of being hereditary or heritable.

1784 LAFAYETTE in Sparks *Corr. Amer. Rev.* (1853) IV. 61 If it is found that the heredity endangers the true principles of democracy, I am.. ready.. to renounce it. **1882** *Athenæum* 30 Dec. 896/2 The heredity and independence of the fiefs can be shown to have commenced in.. the tenth century.

3. *Biol.* The property of organic beings, in virtue of which offspring inherit the nature and characteristics of parents and ancestors generally; the tendency of like to beget like. (Often spoken of as a law of nature.)

1863 H. SPENCER *Princ. Biol.* §80 Some naturalists seem to entertain a vague belief, that the law of Heredity applies only to main characters of structure, and not to details. *Ibid.* §82 Some of the best illustrations of functional heredity are furnished by the mental characteristics of the human race. **1869** F. GALTON *Hered. Genius* 334, I was desirous of obtaining facts bearing on heredity from China. **1889** POULTON tr. *Weismann's Ess. Heredity* 72 The word heredity in its common acceptation, means that property of an organism by which its peculiar nature is transmitted to its descendants.

attrib. **1894** *Daily News* 12 July 6/2 Heredity philosophers should be interested in the portraits of Mr. Edison's parents.

here-dring, -fare, -feng: see HERE *sb.*

†**herefor, -fore,** *adv. Obs.* exc. *Sc.* [f. HERE *adv.* 16 + FOR *prep.*: cf. *therefore*; Du. *hiervoor*, Ger. *hierfür*, Da. *herfor.*]

1. For this: instead or in consideration of this, with a view to this. Still in occas. Sc. use, written *herefor*.

a **1300** *Cursor M.* 17506 (Gött.) þir guiftes her for [*Cott.* þar-for] giue we ȝu. *c* **1380** WYCLIF *Sel. Wks.* III. 343 He was tauȝt to strive not herfore. **1549** CHALONER *Erasmus on Folly* S ij a, Herefore haue I obteined the mercy of god. *Mod. Sc.* For the sum of twenty pounds, being the consideration herefor given.

†**2.** For this reason, on this account, therefore.

c **1200** *Vices & Virtues* 5 Hierfore ic am neðer and unmihti. *c* **1330** R. BRUNNE *Chron.* (1810) 149 Herfor kyng Richard wrathes him. **1380** *Lay Folks Catech.* (Lamb. MS.) 66 Here-fore þe gospel of Mathew seys þat crist bad vs pray thus. **1480** CAXTON *Chron. Eng.* li. 35 Saynt albone suffred his martirdome before that saynt edmond was martryd and herfor saynt albone is callyd the fyrst martir of Englond. **1581** PETTIE *Guazzo's Civ. Conv.* I. (1586) 2, I will not heerefore commende you so much. *c* **1620** A. HUME *Brit. Tongue* (1865) 13 Heerfoer, for distinctiones of both sound and symbol, I wald commend the symbol and name of i and u to the voual sound. **1697** DALLAS *Stiles* I. 84 Herefore I beseech your Lordships, that ye would.. ordain the said Director.. to grant.. Precepts.

Hereford ('hɛrɪfəd). The name of the county town of Herefordshire, a county in the west of England, used to designate a breed of cattle originating there, distinguished by their reddish-brown colour and white faces. Also '**Herefordshire**.

1789 W. MARSHALL *Rural Econ. Glouc.* II. 226 The Herefordshire breed of cattle.. may.. be deemed the finest breed of cattle in this island... In general appearance the Herefordshire cattle resemble very much those of Sussex. **1805** J. LAWRENCE *Gen. Treat. Cattle* 46 Are we to conjecture, that the Herefords owe their bald face to the smoky white faces of the red cattle of Montgomery? *Ibid.* 48 The distinguishing qualities of Hereford oxen. **1805** J. DUNCUMB *Agric. Hereford* 118 The Leicestershire cow.. will never breed a rival to the Herefordshire ox... There is an extraordinary difference between the weight of a Herefordshire cow and the ox bred from her. **1807** R. SOUTHEY *Lett. from Eng.* (1951) lxxi. 452 Here people will apply to.. a Herefordshire bull, the same epithets of praise ..which a sculptor would bestow upon the Venus de Medici. **1834** W. YOUATT *Cattle* iii. 31 The Herefordshire white-faced breed... The Hereford oxen are considerably larger than the North Devons... The old Herefords were brown or red-brown. **1836** *Penny Cycl.* VI. 379/2 The Herefordshire oxen are best suited to the rich pastures of their native county. **1844** H. STEPHENS *Bk. Farm* III. 1273 Another breed.. is the Hereford, which has long been famed for its excellent steers. **1862** J. C. MORTON *Farmer's Cal.* 578 The Herefords, another leading breed of cattle, characterized by red body and white or mottled face, come almost as early to maturity as the short-horn. **1875** *Encycl. Brit.* I. 388/1 The Hereford is the breed which in England contests most closely with the short-horns for the palm of excellence. **1889** R. WALLACE *Farm Live Stock* (ed. 2) vi. 74 *A Cross*, bred from a Galloway cow by a bull of one of the favourite or improved breeds, such as short-horn or Hereford, is usually an excellent butchers' animal... The Hereford crosses are.. polled, with a white head and a red or dark grey body. **1931** *Times Lit. Suppl.* 20 Aug. 625/3 The fat Herefords that graze lazily in English meadows. **1960** *Farmer & Stockbreeder* 15 Mar. 95 A yardful of well-finished Hereford-cross beef. **1973** *Country Life* 8 Mar. 654 Cattle Societies... The Hereford herd book society.

here'from, *adv.* Now *rare.* Also 6 *Sc.* heirfra. [f. as HEREFOR, -FORE *adv.* + FROM *prep.* Cf. Da. *herfra.*]

1. From this place; hence. Also, from this state or condition.

1596 DALRYMPLE tr. *Leslie's Hist. Scot.* I. 33 The boundes [L. *trajectus*] heirfra till Irland is only xvi. myles. **1679** J. BROWN *Life of Faith* (1824) II. viii. 222 Shall we never be redeemed herefrom? **1839** J. ROGERS *Antipopopr.* xii. §6. 278 Power to deliver hereto, and to deliver herefrom. **1870** MORRIS *Earthly Par.* IV. 247 Over the mountain-passes that men see Herefrom, a town there is.

2. From this thing, fact, or circumstance; from this source.

1594 T. B. *La Primaud. Fr. Acad.* II. Ep. to Rdr. 3 The profite and commodity that issueth herefrom is great. **1602** CAREW *Cornwall* II. (1811) 248 Others.. may (perhaps) take some light herefrom to do the like. **1762** *Phil. Trans.* LII. 472 Herefrom, possibly, the.. proportional distances of the fixed stars may be essayed at.

†**her'eft,** *adv. Sc. Obs.* [f. as prec. + EFT *adv.*] Hereafter.

c **1470** HENRY *Wallace* IX. 1007 Gud lordschip I sall gyff the hereft. *Ibid.* 1212 Tithandis off hym ye sall se son hereft.

heregeld ('hɛrɪgɛld). *Obs.* exc. *Hist.* Forms: 1 **hereʒield, -ʒild, -ʒyld, -ʒeld, -ʒeold,** 7– **heregeld, -gild.** [OE. *hęreʒield*, f. *hęre* host, the (Danish) army + *ʒield, ʒyld, ʒild* payment, tribute, tax = OS. *geld*, OHG. *gelt*, ON. *gjald*, Goth. *gild*, tribute, payment. The OE. word did not survive into ME. It was taken up by legal antiquaries and historical writers of the 17th century, who interpreted the Anglo-Saxon ʒ as *g*; the regular antiquarian form is, therefore, *heregeld, -gild* (cf. DANEGELD).]

O.E. Hist. The tribute paid to the Danish host; the tax collected to subsidize the Danes; Danegeld.

1018 *Charter of Cnut* in Thorpe *Dipl. Angl.* (1865) 307 Swa fela syðe swa menn ʒyldað hereʒyld oððe to scripʒylde [*Orig. Lat.* Ut quotiens populus universus persolvit censum Danis, vel ad naves.]. *c* **1050** *O.E. Chron.* (Laud MS.) anno 1040 Her wæs þet hereʒeold [*MS.F.* hereʒild] ʒelæst þæt wæron xxi þusend punda and xcix punda. *Ibid.* (MS.D.) an. 1052 On þan ylcan ʒeare alede Eadward cyng þæt hereʒyld þæt Æþelred cyng ær astealde.. þæt ʒyld ʒedrehte ealle Engla þeode on swa langum fyrste. **12..** *Charter Eadw. Conf.* (later copy) in Kemble *Cod. Dipl.* IV. 224 Ic kiðe ihu ..ðat seynt Eadmund inland is scotfre fram here-ʒeld and fram ilk oðer gouel.

1626 SPELMAN *Gloss.* 347 *Heregeld*, Pecunia, seu tributum alendo exercitui collatum. **1652** NEEDHAM tr. *Selden's Mare Cl.* 267 There intervened 39 years from the beginning of this Tribute (which they call *Heregild*, that is, a Military or Naval Tribute) to that abolishing of it by King Edward. **1672** *Cowell's Interpr.*, *Heregeld* is a Tribute or Tax levyed for the Maintenance of an Army. **1877** FREEMAN *Norm. Conq.* II. vii. 123 (ed. 3) The war-tax or *heregeld* was no longer exacted. *Ibid.* 124 *note*, The *heregeld* is a tax for the maintenance of the *here* or standing army as distinguished from the *fyrd* or militia.

herehau(gh)t(e, -hault, obs. ff. HERALD.

†**here-hence,** *adv. Obs.* or *dial.* Also 6, 9 *dial.* **herence.** [f. HERE *adv.* 16 + HENCE: cf. THEREHENCE, dial. *therence*; also Da. *herhen*, Ger. *hierhin* 'this way, in this direction'.]

1. From this source; from this fact or circumstance; as a result of this.

1526 TINDALE *Jas.* IV. 1 From whence commeth warre and fightynge amonge you? come they not here hence? even off youre volupteousnes. **1578** TIMME *Caluine on Gen.* 195 Herehence flow good works. **1591** R. TURNBULL *Expos. Jas.* 53 Herence is it that God saith by his Prophet, I will loue thee freely. **1695** KENNETT *Par. Antiq.* App. 693 Another observation I gather herehence.

2. From this point forward; from henceforth.

1594 KYD *Sp. Trag.* in Hazl. *Dodsley* V. 13 Here-hence the fight was eagerly renew'd. **1616** CHAPMAN *Hymne to Hermes* 59 But Hermes herehence having his content Cared for no more.

3. Away from here; hence.

1669 STURMY *Mariner's Mag.* I. 20 We will have him before we go here-hence. **1847** HALLIWELL, *Herence*, hence. *West.*

herein (hɪər'ɪn), *adv.* [orig. *hér inne*, f. *hér* HERE *adv.* 16 + *innan, inne*, adv., subseq. IN, *adv.* and *prep.* Cf. MDu. *hierinne, -in*, Du. *hierin*, MHG. *hier inne*, Ger. *hierinne, -in*, Du. *herind(e, heri*, Sw. *härinne, -in, häri.*]

1. Here within, in here; in this place; in this passage, book, etc.; also, into this place.

α. *c* **1000** ÆLFRIC *Hom.* II. 312 Se ylca is herinne ðe ʒiu ær ahredde ða ʒelyfedan cnihtas. *a* **1225** *Ancr. R.* 290 Ame dogge.. hwat wultu nu herinne? *c* **1450** *Merlin* 138 He resteth in my chamber here-ynne.

β. *c* **1200** *Trin. Coll. Hom.* 113 þe king of blisse wile faren herin. *a* **1300** *Cursor M.* 18434 Til adam.. Be comen wit his folk here-in. **1586** A. DAY *Eng. Secretary* I. (1625) 136 Of which this letter heerein inclosed shall beare sufficient testimony. **1673** RAY *Journ. Low C.* 286 Heerin were many vaulted or arched walks hewn out of the Rock. **1865** WOOD *Homes without H.* i. 20 The animal.. scoops out a burrow.. Herein it lies asleep all day.

2. In this thing, matter, or case; in this fact, circumstance, or condition; in this particular.

α. *a* **1225** *Ancr. R.* 12 Herinne is religiun, & nout iþe wide hod. *c* **1386** CHAUCER *Knt's T.* 2215 Wher moost sorwe is her Inne Ther wol we first amenden and bigynne.

β. *a* **1300** *Cursor M.* 21396 A titel sagh he [on þe cros] li, 'Her-in sal þou ha wictori'. **1514** BARCLAY *Cyt. & Uplondyshm.* (Percy Soc.) p. xlviii, Now judge, Coridon, if herein be pleasour. **1526** TINDALE *John* xv. 8 Heare in is my father glorified. **1590** SHAKS. *Com. Err.* III. i. 86 Heerein you warre against your reputation. **1710** BERKELEY *Princ. Hum. Knowl.* §59 Herein consists the knowledge of nature. **1897** LEADAM in *Eng. Hist. Rev.* Jan. 153 He insists strongly that the king can be sued, herein opposing Bracton.

†**3.** quasi-*sb.* This place. *Obs.*

c **1440** *Ipomydon* 1877, I am, he said, lorde of hereinne.

herein above, herein after, herein before = above, after, before, in this document, statute, etc. (cf. HERE *adv.* 16), are often written as one word.

1590 WEBBE *Trav.* (Arb.) 22 The city of Ierusalem, where part of the olde Temple is yet standing.. as herein after shall be shewed. **1687** *Pennsylv. Archives* I. 101 All and singular the premises hereinbefore mentioned. **1768–74** TUCKER *Lt. Nat.* (1852) II. 413 The illustrations hereinbefore attempted of several important scripture doctrines. **1802–12** BENTHAM *Ration. Judic. Evid.* (1827) III. 404 The several species of makeshift evidence hereinabove brought to view. **1863** KINGLAKE *Crimea* (1876) I. xv. 350 In the way hereinafter prescribed. **1875** POSTE *Gaius* II. §115 The requisitions hereinbefore explained.

hereintil, hereinto, heremid: see HERE *adv.* 16.

†**herely, heirly,** *a.* and *adv. Sc. Obs.* [perh. = OE. *herlíc, hérlíc* noble, ? praiseworthy, *Boeth. Metr.* ix. 18 (Gr.).] **A.** *adj.* ? Noble, stately. **B.** *adv.* ? Nobly, gloriously, splendidly.

c **1450** HOLLAND *Howlat* 411 Part of the feld Was siluer, set with ane hert, heirlie and hie. *Ibid.* 846 All thus thir hathillis in hall heirly remanit, With all welthis at wiss, and worshipe to vale. *Ibid.* 898 Thus was the Howlat in herde herely at hicht, Flour of all fowlis, throw fedderis so fair.

herem, var. CHEREM.

heremeit, -mit, -myt(e, obs. ff. HERMIT.

‖**herenach** ('hɛrənax). *Anglo-Irish.* Also 7 **herenagh, herinach,** 9 **erenach.** [Corruption of Irish *airchinneach*, OIr. *airchinnich* chief man, principal, prince, leader, f. *ar-, air-* over + *cenn, ceann* head; cogn. with Welsh *arbennig* (:—Proto-Celtic *(*p*)*arei-qennikos*, Stokes).]

In the ancient Irish Church, A lay superintendent of church lands; the hereditary warden of the church.

1607 DAVIES *1st Let. to Earl Salisb.* (1787) 250 For the Herinach, there are few parishes of any compass in extent, where there is not an Herinach. *Ibid.* 251 The founder gave the land to some clerk not being in orders, and to his heirs for ever, with this intent; that he should keep the church clean and well repaired, keep hospitality, and giue alms to the poor for the soul's health of the founder. This man and his heirs had the name of *Erenach*. **1609** in Reeves *Eccl. Antiq.* (1847) 209 The Corbe.. hath sometime under him severall herenaghes. **1727** *Cowell's Interpr.*, *Herenach*, an Archdeacon. **1848–51** O'DONOVAN *Four Masters* A.D. 601 *note*, Irish *Airchinneach*, i.e. the hereditary warden of the church, usually anglicised Erenach or Herenagh. **1864** MCLAUCHLAN *Early Scot. Ch.* xx. (1885) 292 The lands were usually farmed to a certain individual or family of the kin who were called herenachs.

Hence '**herenachy**, the office of a herenach.

1609 in Reeves *Eccl. Antiq.* (1847) 161 But hold their herenaghie free for ever.

hereness ('hɪənɪs). *rare.* [f. HERE *adv.* + -NESS.] The fact or condition of being here.

1674 N. FAIRFAX *Bulk & Selv.* 11 The herenesses and therenesses of ghosts. *Ibid.* 45 A thing is only there, to me, in behalf of my being here, and not there; for when I am there, the thing is clothed with hereness. **1891** E. B. BAX *Outlooks fr. New Standp.* iii. 167 But the thisness, the hereness and nowness is the illogical and irrational element in all Reality.

hereof (hɪər'ɒv). [f. HERE *adv.* 16 + OF *prep.*: cf. Da. *heraf*, Sw. *häraf.*]

1. Of this; concerning this.

c **1050** *Byrhtferth's Handboc* in *Anglia* VIII. 317/39 þehe sum þing herof underʒyte. *c* **1175** *Lamb. Hom.* 81 Her of seid seint Iohan.. in apocalipsi. *a* **1225** *Ancr. R.* 64 We schulen þauh sone her efter speken herof more. *c* **1386** CHAUCER *Frankl. T.* 691 What sholde I mo ensamples heer of sayn? **1398** TREVISA *Barth. De P.R.* III. viii. (1495) 54 To pursyewe the distynccyon herof. **1551** T. WILSON *Logike* Ep. (1580) A iij, The Printer hereof.. provoked me first hereunto. **1617** MORYSON *Itin.* II. 206 The Spaniards, departed.. on Tuesday the 16 hereof. *a* **1661** FULLER *Worthies, Cambridge* (1840) 223 The twigs hereof are physic [etc.]. **1711** STEELE *Spect.* No. 140 ⁋2 Upon the Receipt hereof. **1870** MYERS *Poems* (1875) 47 Thinking hereof I wot not.

†**2.** From this; from here. *Obs.*

c **1200** *Trin. Coll. Hom.* 131 Seint iohan.. com into þis wreche woreld.. her-offe at his ende wurþliche wende. **1297** R. GLOUC. (1724) 265 As þys kyng herof awoc. *c* **1380** WYCLIF *Sel. Wks.* III. 360 What preest shulde not be paied herof? **1489** CAXTON *Faytes of A.* III. vi. 177 A more harde questyon.. dependeth here of. **1568** GRAFTON *Chron.* II. 86 Hereof.. began the first occasion of the order of the Garter. **1587** GOLDING *De Mornay* Pref. 3 What will reasonablie insue hereof?

hereon (hɪər'ɒn), *adv.* Now *rare.* [f. HERE *adv.* 16 + ON *prep.* Cf. MDu. *hierane, -aen,* MHG. and Ger. *hieran.*]

†**1.** Herein. *Obs.*

c **1000** in *Cod. Dipl.* (Kemble) V. 248 Maneȝa oðre freolsas heron ȝewriten synd. **1481** CAXTON *Reynard* (Arb.) 6 Yf courtoys had ony parte hieron. **1565–73** COOPER *Thesaurus* s.v. *Cardo,* Hereon consisteth the whole matter.

2. a. Of position: On this place, etc. †**b.** Of motion; To this place (*obs.*).

c **1205** LAY. 1948 þis lond was ihaten Albion, þa Brutus cum her on. *c* **1315** SHOREHAM 3 This..laddre is charite.. Her-on Jhesus stawe uppe..for to teche ous steyȝe.

3. On this subject, matter, etc.; on this basis.

c **1175** *Lamb. Hom.* 23 Her on ic wille liggen a þet ic beo ealdre. *a* **1225** *Ancr. R.* 262 ȝif heo þencheð wel heron. *c* **1380** WYCLIF *Wks.* (1880) 438 þenke we heronne nyȝt & day. **1562** COOPER *Answ. Priv. Masse* (1850) 72 Hereon I conclude the priest is not bound to minister. **1664** POWER *Exp. Philos.* 61, I will not say, that our discourse hereon, shall pass for..authentick Truth. **1701** GREW *Cosm. Sacra* VI. viii. Index, With the Perfection of Will..And of Happiness grounded hereon.

4. On (the occurrence of) this; = HEREUPON 2.

1602 CAREW *Cornwall* (1811) 315 Hereon..our Foyens took heart at grass. **1855** SINGLETON *Virgil* I. 272 Hereon the Ithacan, with vast ado, Calchas the seer drags forth.

hereout (hɪər'aʊt), *adv.* In 3 herut, 4 here ute. [f. HERE *adv.* 16 + OUT *adv.* Cf. MDu. *hierute, -uut,* Du. *hieruit,* MLG. *hirût,* Ger. *hieraus, -auszen,* Da. *herud,* Sw. *härut.*]

1. Out of this place. (Of motion and position.)

a **1225** *Ancr. R.* 290 Ame dogge go herut. *a* **1300** *Cursor M.* 2033 (Cott.) þi fader slepand..Liggus here-oute, com se þou sall. *Ibid.* 2567 (Gött.) þu cum here vte. *c* **1425** *Seven Sag.* (P.) 1451 Here-out I hym herde, And cam out to clepyn hym inne. **1591** SPENSER *Vis. Bellay* 146 A Bird..Hereout ..did flie. **1599** A. M. tr. *Gabelhouer's Bk. Physicke* 49/1 Distille heerout a water. **1839** J. ROGERS *Antipopopr.* XII. iii. 273 The sinner..being in purgatory, or the priest.. bringing him hereout.

†**2.** From this source; hence. *Obs.*

1541 COVERDALE *Old Faith* ii. Wks. (Parker Soc.) I. 79 Hereout also bring they the doctrine of repentance. *a* **1568** —— *Hope Faithf.* xxv. (1574) 177 Hereout now it followeth, that the soules are passible.

here-'right, *adv. Obs.* exc. *dial.* In 5 her riȝt. [f. HERE *adv.* 16 + RIGHT *adv.*] Here on the spot; straightway, immediately.

c **1380** *Sir Ferumb.* 2738 Her riȝt ich þe diffye. **1633** FORD *'Tis Pity* II. vi, Pray read it me here-right. **1888** ELWORTHY *W. Somerset Word-bk.,* s.v. No! let's settle it here-right. **1893** *Wiltsh. Gloss., Here-right.* (1) Of time: on the spot, immediately..(2) Of place: this very spot.

Herero (hɛ'rɛərəʊ). One of a negroid people in South-West Africa, also called *Cattle Damara*; also their Bantu language, called *Otshi-Herero* by the Hereros themselves.

1862 W. H. I. BLEEK *Comp. Gram. S. Afr. Langs.* I. 8 The language of *Benguela*..is quite distinct..from the Herero species. *Ibid.* ii. 22 Kongo *bhobha* (to speak, talk) is Hereró *pópa* (to warn, persuade). **1868** F. W. KOLBE (*title*) A brief statement of the discovery of the laws of the vowels in Herero. **1880** *Encycl. Brit.* XI. 731/2 *Hereroland*..so called from the native race known to the Namaqua as Herero and to the Cape colonists as Damara. **1904** *Westm. Gaz.* 30 Jan. 2/2 The Kaffirs are joining the Hereros in attacking the Germans. **1952** L. G. GREEN *Lords of Last Frontier* (1953) ii. 18 Midway in the sixteenth century those forceful Bantu, the Hereros, reached the end of a long migration, and settled in the cattle country. *Ibid.* xv. 148 Hereros are tall people, especially the men... Features are almost European, with well-shaped noses, high foreheads and oval faces. **1961** L. VAN DER POST *Heart of Hunter* I. iii. 64 The black man, the Herero, the Bastaards, had kraals and lands of their own. **1972** *Cape Times* 10 Mar. 1/1 Mr. John Garvey Muundjua, a Herero who is the South West Africa National Union's 'Secretary for External Affairs'. **1973** *Times* 8 Mar. 6/2 Herero tribal leaders have rejected an invitation from the Government to appoint representatives to sit on the advisory council.

†**he'resian.** [f. as HERESY + AN.] A heretic.

1675–83 EVELYN *Hist. Relig.* (1850) II. 182 *note,* That grand heresian, Simon Magus.

heresiarch ('hɛrɪsɪˌɑːk, hɪ'riːsɪɑːk). Also 7 hær-. [ad. late L. *hæresiarcha,* ad. Gr. αἱρεσιάρχης leader of a school, chief of a sect, f. αἵρεσις HERESY + -αρχης ruler. Cf. F. *hérésiarque* (16th c. in Littré), perh. the immediate source.] A leader or founder of a heresy. Also *transf.*

1624 BP. HALL *Wks.* Ded. to Jas. I, It was a madde conceit of that old Heresiarch. **1640** —— *Chr. Moder.* (Ward) 29/1 It is one thing to be a heretic, another thing to be an hæresiarch. **1685** BOYLE *Enq. Notion Nat.* p. xiii, I was not ingag'd in this Controversie, by any Ambition of appearing in Print an Heresiarch in Philosophy, by being the Author of a strange Doctrine. **1762–71** H. WALPOLE *Vertue's Anecd. Paint.* (1786) III. 2 Jargon and austerities are the weapons that best serve the purposes of heresiarcs and innovators. **1868** MILMAN *St. Paul's* iv. 78 The later strife between Courtenay as Archbishop and Wycliffe as principal heresiarch.

So †**heresiarchy,** the founding of a heresy; in quot. erron. a chief or arch-heresy.

1638 SIR T. HERBERT *Trav.* (ed. 2.) 255 The rest of the Book consists of Heresiarchyes against our blessed Saviour.

†**heresi'astic,** *a. Obs. rare.* [irreg. f. HERESY (or its source), after *ecclesiastic, enthusiastic.*] Prone to heresy; heretical.

1663 GERBIER *Counsel* B iij b, I would go without being inrolled among Heresiastick Seekers.

he'resimach (-mæk). *rare.* [f. Gr. αἱρεσι-ς HERESY + -μαχος fighting: cf. Gr. αἱρεσιομάχος.] One who fights against heresy.

1824 THIRLWALL 29 Nov. in *Lett.* (1881) I. 81 More of the spirit of charity than commonly breathed through the disputations of the old Hæresimach [Tertullian].

heresiography (ˌhɛrɪsɪ'ɒgrəfɪ). [mod. f. Gr. αἵρεσις HERESY + -(O)GRAPHY; cf. *Christianography,* an earlier formation of Pagitt's. So mod.F. *hérésiographie.*] A description of, or treatise on, heresy or heresies. (The title of a work by E. Pagitt.) So **heresi'ographer,** one who treats of heresies.

1645 PAGITT (*title*) Heresiography: or A description of the Hereticks and Sectaries of these latter Times. *Ibid.* B iv b, These sad considerations made me..write an *Heresiography.* **1822** SOUTHEY in *Q. Rev.* XXVIII. 10 [Their] names have escaped the notice of our English heresiographers.

heresiologist (ˌhɛrɪsɪ'ɒlədʒɪst). [f. as prec. + -(O)LOGIST.] One who treats of heresy or heresies. So **heresi'ologer** in same sense; **heresi'ology,** the study of, or a treatise on, heresies.

1710 W. HUME *Sacr. Success.* 164 You may hear of his fame..from the antient Heresiologists. **1856** *Lit. Churchman* II. 47/1 Heresiologies..printed early in the sixteenth century. **1874** J. H. BLUNT *Dict. Sects* 184 For obtaining a complete acquaintance with heresiology. **1875** LIGHTFOOT *Comm. Col.* 285 Heresiologers distinguished four main forms of heresy in the pre-christian world. **1882–3** SCHAFF *Encycl. Relig. Knowl.* II. 976/1 The principal heresiologists of the early church are Justin Martyr.. Tertullian..Clement.

heresy ('hɛrɪsɪ). Forms: 3–5 eresie, 3–8 heresie, 4–5 eresye, 4–6 (h)erysy(e, herisie, heresye, (5 erreisye, 6 (h)eryse, er(r)ysse, -ee, -ye, hearesye, *Sc.* arrosie), 6–7 hæresie, 4– heresy. [a. OF. *eresie, heresie* (12th c.), mod.F. *hérésie,* ad. L. type **heresia* (whence also It. *eresia,* Pg. *heresia*), for L. *hæresis* school of thought, philosophical sect, in eccl. writers, theological heresy, a. Gr. αἵρεσις taking, choosing, choice, course taken, course of action or thought, 'school' of thought, philosophic principle or set of principles, philosophical or religious sect; f. αἱρεῖν to take, middle voice αἱρῖσθαι to take for oneself, choose.

The Gr. word occurs several times in N.T., viz. Acts. v. 17, xv. 5, xxiv. 5, xxvi. 5, xxviii. 22, where Eng. versions from Tindale render 'sect' (i.e. of the Sadducees, Pharisees, Nazarenes or Christians, considered as sects of the Jews); Acts xxiv. 14, where all versions from Wyclif to 1611 have 'heresy', R.V. 'a sect (*or* heresy)'; in 1 Cor. xi. 19 Wyclif, Genev., Rhem., and 1611 have 'heresies', Tind. and Cranm. 'sectes', R.V. 'heresies (*or* factions)'; in Gal. v. 20, Wycl., Tind., Cranm., Rhem. have 'sectes', Genev. and 1611 'heresies', R.V. 'heresies (*or* parties)'; in 2 Peter ii. 1 Wyclif, Tind., Cranm., Rhem. have 'sectes', Genev. and 1611 'heresies', R.V. 'heresies (*or* sects)'. The earlier sense-development from 'religious sect, party, or faction' to 'doctrine at variance with the catholic faith', lies outside English.]

1. a. Theological or religious opinion or doctrine maintained in opposition, or held to be contrary, to the 'catholic' or orthodox doctrine of the Christian Church, or, by extension, to that of any church, creed, or religious system, considered as orthodox.

a **1225** *Ancr. R.* 82 Eresie, God beo iðoncked, ne rixleð nout in Engelond. *c* **1290** *S. Eng. Leg.* I. 279/36 Swuch manere fals bi-leue: Men cleopenden heresie. *c* **1380** WYCLIF *Serm.* Sel. Wks. I. 35 Aȝens þis eresie shulde trewe preestis crye fast. **1388** —— *Acts* xxiv. 14 Aftir the secte which thei seien eresie, so y serue to God the fadir. **1494** FABYAN *Chron.* IV. lxix. 48 He fyll into the heresy called Aryannys heresy. **1535** STEWART *Cron. Scot.* II. 300 Fuill arrosie..That he leirit fra kirkmen of the Britis. **1583** WINȜET *Four Scoir Thre Quest.* Wks. 1888 I. 71 All hæresie that euir hes bene in the Kirk. **1596** DRAYTON *Leg.* iv. 909 What late was Truth, now turn'd to Heresie. **1689** tr. *Locke's 1st Let. on Toleration* 61 Use, which is the Supream Law in the matter of Language, has determined that Heresie relates to Errors in Faith, and Schism to those in Worship or Discipline. *a* **1694** TILLOTSON *Serm.* I. xxxiv. (R.), Deluded people! that do not consider that the greatest heresie in the world is a wicked life. **1855** MILMAN *Lat. Chr.* III. v. (1864) II. 2 Heresy, or dissent from the dominant religion..had been introduced into the criminal jurisdiction. **1862** STANLEY *Jew. Ch.* (1877) I. ix. 186 There are always theologians keen-sighted to see heresy in the simplest orthodoxy. **1885** *Catholic Dict.* s.v., Such Protestants as are in good faith and sincerely desirous of knowing the truth are not heretics in the formal sense..Their heresy is material only—*i.e.* their tenets are in themselves heretical, but they are not formal heretics: *i.e.* they do not incur the guilt of heresy.

b. with *a* and *pl.* An instance of this; a heretical opinion or doctrine. (For N.T. use, see note to etymology.)

1303 R. BRUNNE *Handl. Synne* 9671 þan ys a wykkede erysye. *c* **1340** HAMPOLE *Prose Tr.* (1866) 17 Errours and herysyes. **1479** *Eng. Gilds* (1870) 417 Heresies and errours, clepid openly lolladries. **1556** *Chron. Gr. Friars* (Camden) 20 Pecocke that was byshoppe of Chechester..was apeched of dyvers poynttes of eryses. **1557** N.T. (Genev.) *2 Pet.* ii. 1 There shalbe false teachers among you: which pryuely shal brynge in damnable heresies [WYCL. sectes of perdicioun, TIND., CRANM. damnable sectes, R.V. destructive heresies (*or* sects of perdition)], euen denying the Lord, that hath boght them. **1611** BIBLE *Transl. Pref.* 3 The Scripture..is.. a Physions-shop..of preseruatiues against poisoned heresies. **1852** MISS YONGE *Cameos* (1877) IV. xii. 143 Cardinal Farnese declared there were seven heresies in it.

2. By extension, Opinion or doctrine in philosophy, politics, science, art, etc., at variance with those generally accepted as authoritative. Also with *a* and *pl.*

c **1385** CHAUCER *L.G.W.* Prol. 330 (Fairf.) That is an heresye ageyns my lawe. **1559** W. CUNNINGHAM *Cosmogr. Glasse* 66 Bycause I will not have you to erre with Poëtes.. I will take the more diligence to drive this Heresie out of your heade. **1616** B. JONSON *Devil an Ass* II. i, Against the received heresy That England bears no dukes. **1711** SWIFT *Examiner* No. 40 ¶5 All the heresies in politics profusely scattered by the partizans of the late adminstration. **1843** MISS MITFORD in L'Estrange *Life* (1870) III. x. 176, I.. prefer Bristol to Bath..which I suppose, is a great heresy. **1877** E. R. CONDER *Bas. Faith* v. 209 The doctrines of Evolution..which it is intellectual heresy..to question.

3. In sense of Gr. αἵρεσις (see etym.): Opinion or doctrine characterizing particular individuals or parties; a school of thought; a sect.

1382 WYCLIF *1 Cor.* xi. 19 It bihoueth heresies for to be. **1387** TREVISA *Higden* (Rolls) III. 359 Aristotle gadrede meny disciples into his heresie [*in suam hæresim*]. **1611** BIBLE *1 Cor.* xi. 19 For there must bee also heresies [TINDALE, CRANMER, sectes; R.V. *margin,* factions] among you. **1679** HOBBES *Behemoth* (1840) 174 Heresy is a word which, when it is used without passion, signifies a private opinion. So the different sects of the old philosophers, Academians, Peripatetics, Epicureans, Stoics, &c., were called heresies. **1870** W. GRAHAM *Lect. Eph.* 230 The word heresies was the common name for the different philosophical sects, as the Stoics, the Epicureans [etc.].

4. *attrib.* and *Comb.,* as ***heresy-ferret, -hunt, -hunter, -hunting, -monger, mongering; heresy-stained*** adj.

1765 A. MACLAINE tr. *Mosheim's Eccl. Hist.* (1844) I. xiii. 344 This new set of heresy-hunters. **1814** W. TAYLOR in *Monthly Rev.* LXXIII. 533 Mad. Genlis, and other heresy ferrets, are here censured. **1831** CARLYLE in *Edin. Rev.* LIII. Mar. 168 Scenting out Infidelity with the nose of an ancient Heresy-hunter, though for opposite purposes. **1872** SPURGEON *Treas. Dav.* Ps. lxxiii. 15 If the consciences of heresy-mongers were not seared. **1882** J. PARKER *Apost. Life* I. 140 One of the earliest instances..of heresy-hunting. **1891** FROUDE *Divorce of Cath.* 186 More's chancellorship had been distinguished by heresy-prosecutions. **1894** *Westm. Gaz.* 2 Apr. 2/1 The heresy hunt of Mr. Smith..was one of the most protracted and determined of modern times. **1902** *Westm. Gaz.* 7 May 12/1 A proceeding quite in harmony with the usual methods of heresy-hunters. **1906** *Daily Chron.* 16 Oct. 3/3 The heresy-hunter made him his quarry.

heretable, -tage, obs. ff. HERITABLE, -TAGE.

†**here'through,** *adv. Obs.* [f. HERE *adv.* 16 + THROUGH *prep.*: cf. Du. *hierdoor,* Ger. *hierdurch.*] Through this; by this means; hereby.

c **1200** ORMIN 12710 Herþurrh maȝȝ mann sen full wel. *c* **1450** tr. *De Imitatione* III. lx. (1893) 141 Here þuruȝ it happeniþ þat..I se clerly what I owe to do. **1596** DALRYMPLE tr. *Leslie's Hist. Scot.* x. 287 Quha wan the gret Jre..of al the Douglasses heirthrouch. **1602** CAREW *Cornwall* 4 a, Her Highnesse shipping should heerethrough be defrauded of often supplies.

heretic ('hɛrɪtɪk), *sb.* (*a.*) Forms: 4 eretik(e, 4–6 heretyk(e, 4–7 -ike, 6–7 heretique, -icke, 6–8 -ick, 7– heretic; also 5 heretyc, eretyke, 5–6 herretyk, herytik(e, heretyck(e, erytyke, 6 eret-, erytycke, heretyque, herytyke, -ycke, hæretik, -ick(e, 7 -ique. [a. F. *hérétique* (14th c.) ad. eccl. L. *hæretic-us,* a. Gr. αἱρετικός able to choose, f. αἱρέ-εσθαι to choose; subseq. in eccl. writers (after αἵρεσις) heretical, heretic. OF. had the popularly formed *herege,* also *herite* (see EREGE, ERITE). To French derivation is due the position of the stress, as differing from words immed. from Gr. or L. such as *a'scetic, theo'retic*: cf. '*catholic.*]

1. One who maintains theological or religious opinions at variance with the 'catholic' or orthodox doctrine of the Christian Church, or, by extension, that of any church or religious system, considered as orthodox. Also *transf.* with reference to non-Christian religions.

c **1330** R. BRUNNE *Chron.* (1810) 320 þe kyng said & did crie, þe pape was heretike. *a* **1340** HAMPOLE *Psalter* x. 1 Heretikes & fals breþer. *c* **1400** MAUNDEV. (Roxb.) xvi. 73 If I be ane heretyc..þan es all heresy þat here es writen. **1556** *Chron. Gr. Friars* (Camden) 11 Thys yere was..an erytyke brentte in Smythfelde for eryse. **1563** WINȜET *Four Scoir Thre Quest.* Wks. 1888 I. 71 Gif ȝe heirfor haldis ws Catholikis to be hæretikis. **1611** BIBLE *Transl. Pref.* 8 Heretikes they call vs by the same right that they call themselues Catholikes, both being wrong. **1638** SIR T. HERBERT *Trav.* (ed. 2) 251 The Persian Religion at this day varies not from the Turks in any particle of the Alcoran; and yet they account one the other Hereticks. **1725** WATTS *Logic* I. iv. §8 When a papist uses the word heretics, he generally means the protestants. *a* **1856** H. MILLER *Test. Rocks* ix. (1857) 357 Every form of faith has its heretics. **1874** GREEN

Short Hist. vii. §8. 430 The League rejected Henry's claims as those of a heretic.

2. By extension, One who maintains opinions upon any subject at variance with those generally received or considered authoritative.

1599 SHAKS. *Much Ado* I. i. 236 Thou wast euer an obstinate heretique in the despight of Beautie. *c* **1620** A. HUME *Brit. Tongue* I. vii §8 My antagonist..began that I was becum an heretik, and the doctour spering how, ansuered that I denyed quho to be spelled with a w, but with qu.

3. *Comb.*, as ***heretic-burning***, ***-hunting***, ***-taker***.

1563–87 FOXE *A. & M.* (1861) VII. I. 47 Pashur was..the chief heretic-taker. **1895** J. J. RAVEN *Hist. Suffolk* 163 Gardiner and Bonner..were heretic-hunting and heretic-burning.

B. *attrib.* or *adj.* = HERETICAL. *rare.*

1382 WYCLIF *Titus* iii. 10 Schonye thou a man heretyk [**1388** eretik] aftir oon and the secunde coreccioun. **1606** *Proc. agst. Late Traitors* 2 That our said Sovereigne Lord the King..and whole Commonaltie of the realme of England..were heretique. **1682** DRYDEN *Relig. Laici* Pref. Wks. (Globe) 189 That they may be dispensed with in their obedience to an heretic prince. **1839** *Morn. Herald.* in *Spirit Metrop. Conserv. Press* (1840) II. 391 He must consider it heretic and sinful to 'search the Scriptures'. **1860** MOTLEY *Netherl.* x. II. 63 To deprive the heretic Queen..both of throne and life.

Hence †**hereticly** (**-ykely**) *adv.*, as a heretic.

1538 WRIOTHESLEY *Chron.* (1875) I. 90 Foure persons of the Anabaptistes heretykely bare fagottes the same daye at Paules Crosse.

heretical (hɪˈrɛtɪkəl), *a.* [ad. med.L. *hæreticāl-is*, f. *hæretic-us* HERETIC: see -AL[1].] Of or pertaining to heresy or heretics; of the nature of heresy.

1532 MORE *Confut. Tindale* Wks. 346/2 Al that in the while both bought and solde of those hereticall bokes. **1540** *Act 32 Hen. VIII*, c. 26 Diuerse heriticall erroniouse and dangerouse opinions and doctrines. **1566** in Peacock *Eng. Ch. Furniture* (1866) 104 Masse bookes..appertayninge to the hereticall service. **1602** FULBECKE *Pandectes* 40 They [the Turks] and the Persians, the one seeming hæreticall to the other, are in continuall warre. **1651** HOBBES *Leviath.* III. xlii. 318 To prove that Christians are not to tolerate..Hæretical Kings. **1702** C. MATHER *Magn. Chr.* IV. iv. (1852) 71 To bring heterodox, and it may be heretical persons into their communion. **1861** STANLEY *East. Ch.* vii. (1869) 246 No one likes to be called 'heretical', but neither is it a term of unmixed eulogy to be called 'orthodox'.

Hence **he'retically** *adv.*, in a heretical manner. **he'reticalness**, heretical quality or character.

1661 BAXTER *Mor. Prognost.* II. xxx. 54 If any Minister Preach or Pray..Heretically, to the Danger of the Peoples Souls. **1681** H. MORE *Exp. Dan.* App. ii. 291 Multitudes who, because of their supposed Hereticalness, lay dead, useless and unactive. **1701** STRYPE *Aylmer* (R.), He ignorantly and heretically held against the bishop, that the soul of man was of the substance of God.

†**hereti'caster.** *Obs. rare*[−1]. [f. HERETIC: see -ASTER.] A petty or contemptible heretic.

a **1711** KEN *Hymns Evang.* Poet. Wks. 1721 I. 10 A Remnant who the Gags of Schism shall close..Hereticasters anathematize.

hereticate (hɪˈrɛtɪkeɪt), *v.* [f. med.L. *hæreticāt-*, ppl. stem of *hæreticāre*, f. *hæretic-us* HERETIC.]

1. *trans.* To pronounce heretical.

1629 BP. HALL *Answ. Urban's Inurb.* 9 The Pope hath not power (that I may vse his owne word) to hereticate any Proposition. **1702** C. MATHER *Magn. Chr.* VII. iii. (1852) 512 Arbitrary and hereticating anathemas. **1873** F. HALL *Mod. Eng.* 19 *note*, Let no one be minded, on the score of my *neoterism*, to hereticate me, as threatening to abet some new-fangled form of religious heterodoxy.

2. To make a heretic of: applied (by opponents) to the ceremony of death-bed inauguration (*Consolamentum*) reported to have been practised by the Albigenses in the 12th c.

1731 S. CHANDLER tr. *Limborch's Hist. Inquis.* I. I. viii. 54 'Tis reported of Petrus Sancii, that being called to hereticate a certain sick Woman, she was not then hereticated; because he did not think it proper upon Account of her not being weak enough. And afterwards..Petrus Sancii did not hereticate her, because she recovered. **1832** S. R. MAITLAND *Albigenses & Wald.* XII. 459 Could Peter Auterius really believe that he saved the souls of those whom he hereticated? **1883** *Sat. Rev.* 31 Mar. 404/1.

Hence **hereti'cation** [med.L. *hæreticātio*], the action of hereticating (in both senses); esp. that attributed to the Albigenses. **he'reticator**, one who hereticates or denounces heresy.

1685 BAXTER *Paraphr. N.T.* Heb. i. Annot., The Hereticators will quarrel with it. **1731** S. CHANDLER tr. *Limborch's Hist. Inquis.* I. I. viii. 53 Others [Albigenses] only enter'd into a Covenant with these perfect ones..that at the End of Life they would be received into their Sect. This Reception is often called *Heretication*..This Admission..was called Spiritual Baptism, The Consolation, The Reception, and Good End. **1832** S. R. MAITLAND *Albigenses & Wald.* IX. 232 *note*, Their absolution was general, and performed by the imposition of hands, in the ceremony of *heretication*. **1880** *Guardian* 21 Apr. 520 The right of excommunication was instanced in the heretication of the Artemonites, a sort of premature Arians. **1883** *Sat. Rev.* 31 Mar. 404/1 They [Albigensians] adopted..a ceremony of imposition of hands, variously designated *consolamentum*, or 'heretication', followed by the *Endura* or fasting to death.

he'reticide. [erron. f. HERETIC + -CIDE 2.] The putting of a heretic to death.

1702 C. MATHER *Magn. Chr.* VII. iv. (1852) 525 Nor do I look upon hereticide as an evangelical way for the extinguishing of heresies.

he'reticize, *v.* [f. HERETIC + -IZE.] *trans.* To pronounce heretical.

1830 PUSEY *Hist. Enq.* II. 194 [It] was forthwith arbitrarily cried down, hereticized, and destroyed. *Ibid.* 310 The despised and hereticized Pietists.

here-till, *adv.* *Sc.* [f. HERE *adv.* 16 + TILL: cf. Da. *hertil*, Sw. *härtil.*] = HERETO.

1375 BARBOUR *Bruce* XIII. 241 Quhen her-till all assentit war. *Ibid.* xx. 144 Heir-till thair Athis can thai ma.

hereto (hɪəˈtuː), *adv.* [f. HERE *adv.* 16 + TO *prep.* Cf. MDu., Du. *hiertoe*, Ger. *hierzu.*]

†**1.** To this place, hither. *Obs.*

c **1205** LAY. 25321 Her to he wule leden kinges. **1598** R. BERNARD tr. *Terence, Andria* I. i. (1629) 9/2 Being hereto driuen through very pouerty.

2. To this matter, subject, etc.; with reference to or in regard to this point.

c **1175** *Lamb. Hom.* 33 Ne þenche ȝe herto. *a* **1225** *Ancr. R.* 388 Herto ualleð a tale. *c* **1386** CHAUCER *Melib.* ¶ 325 Heer-to accordeth Seint Paul the Apostle. *c* **1470** HENRY *Wallace* x. 1125 Will ye her to accord? **1526** TINDALE *2 Cor.* viii. 10 And I geve counsell hereto. **1682** NORRIS *Hierocles* 9 Agreeable hereto are the words of the Oracle.

3. (Annexed) to this document, etc.

1559 W. CUNNINGHAM *Cosmogr. Glasse* 152 An open sheet, whiche must here to be annexid. **1896** *Act 59–60 Vict.* c. 13 §1 The acts enumerated in the schedule hereto.

†**4.** In addition to this. *Obs.*

1577–87 HOLINSHED *Chron.* I. 45/2 Hauing no skill in warre-like discipline, and heerto being naked without furniture of armour.

†**5.** Up to this time, hitherto. *Obs.*

1559 W. CUNNINGHAM *Cosmogr. Glasse* 39 For the better understanding such thinges as herto are spoken. **1582** N. LICHEFIELD tr. *Castanheda's Conq. E. Ind.* lxxix. 159 b, Heereto he had bene a friend to the King of Calicut. **1607** SHAKS. *Cor.* II. ii. 64 If he remember a kinder value of the People, then he hath hereto priz'd them at.

†Hence ˌ**heretobe'fore**, *adv.* *Obs.* Heretofore.

1667 CHAMBERLAYNE *St. Gt. Brit.* I. Introd. (1684) 3 To endeavour the restauration of what was heretobefore better and the abolition of what is worse.

†ˈ**heretochy.** *Obs. rare.* [f. *heretoch* HERETOGA, after *county*, *duchy*, etc.] The territory ruled by a heretoga.

1577–87 HARRISON *England* I. vii. in *Holinshed* 16 Kent..was made an earledome or Heretochie..Athelstone his sonne, being the first Earle or Heretoch of the same. *Ibid.*, Northumberland..was onlie governed by earls as Heretoches, as an Heretochy.

heretofore (hɪətəˈfɔə(r)), *adv.* (*a.*, *sb.*) Also 4–5 heretoforn(e. [f. HERE *adv.* 16 + TOFORE, OE. *tóforan*; cf. MDu. *hiertevoren*, Ger. *hierzuvor.*]

A. *adv.* Before this time; before now; in time past; formerly.

c **1350** *Will. Palerne* 1816 For here-to-fore of hardnesse hadestow neuer. **1387–8** T. USK *Test. Love* III. viii. (Skeat) l. 113 Will of rightfulnesse is the ilke same rightfulnesse as here toforne is shewed. *c* **1430** *Hymns Virg.* 87 Where ben þese worþi þat were heere-to-forn? **1555** EDEN *Decades* 214 The lyke hath not heretofore byn knowen. *a* **1680** BUTLER *Rem.* (1759) I. 126 The Pagans heretofore Did their own Handyworks adore. **1732** BERKELEY *Alciphr.* II. §11 The political writings of such as have heretofore passed for wise men. **1860** TYNDALL *Glac.* II. iii. 244, I tried the methods heretofore pursued.

B. *adj.* Former, previous.

1491 *Act 7 Hen. VII*, c. 22 §3 Annuyties graunted..by..Piers Courteney somtyme Bisshoppe of Excestre or by any othre heretoforn Bisshoppe there. **1656–7** R. VENNING *Mercies Memorial* 17 Heretofore-mercies are grounds to look for hereafter-mercies. **1839** MRS. PAPENDIEK *Crt. & Priv. Life Q. Charlotte* (1887) II. xv. 94 But he felt the loss, for them, of his heretofore allowances. *a* **1864** HAWTHORNE *Amer. Note-Bks.* (1879) I. 22 In his heretofore voyages.

C. *sb.* Time past; the past.

1824 GALT *Rothelan* VI. vi, The same sort of being that he has been in the heretofore. **1876** J. MARTINEAU *Hours Th.* (1877) 230 The relation of his Now to a heretofore and a hereafter.

hereto'foretime, *adv.* *rare.* [f. prec. after *afore-*, *before-time.*] = prec.

1481 CAXTON *Reynard* (Arb.) 67, I haue yet here to fore tyme gyuen to you many a good counseyl and prouffytable. **1866** NEALE *Sequences & Hymns* 158 Though by the way we pass, we have not passed heretoforetime.

heretoga (ˈhɛrɪtəʊgə), **heretoch**, **-togh**. Forms: 1 **heretoȝa**, 2 **heretoche**, 3 **here-**, **hæretoȝe**, *Hist.* 6–9 **heretoch**, 8–9 **-togh**, **-toga**. [OE. *heretoȝa* = OFris. *hertoga*, *-tiga*, OS. *heritogo* (MDu. *hertoge*, *-toch*, *-tich*, Du. *hertog*), OHG. *herizogo* (MHG. *herzoge*, G. *herzog*), ON. *hertogi* (Sw. *hertig*, Da. *hertug*); f. *heri*, *here* HERE *sb.* army + OE. *-toȝa*, OLG. *-togo*, OHG. *-zogo* agent-noun, f. weak grade *tug-*, *tog-* of **teuhan*, OE. **téohan*, *téon* to lead: see TEE *v.* (cognate with L. *duc-ere*, *dux*). The Hist. forms *heretoch*, *-togh* represent med.L. *heretochius.*]

O.E. Hist. The leader of an army; the commander of the militia of a shire or district. As it was rendered by L. *dux*, and was the same word as Ger. *herzog*, it was taken by 17th and 18th c. writers as = Duke.

c **900** tr. *Bæda's Hist.* I. xii. [xv.] (1890) 52 Wæron ða ærest heora latteowas and heretoȝan tweȝen ȝebroðra Hengest and Horsa. *c* **1000** ÆLFRIC *Num.* xiii. 1 Moises se mæra heretoȝa. *a* **1175** *Cott. Hom.* 243 Se þe geð into fihte wið-ute heretoche. *c* **1205** LAY. 10268 Seuarus wes heora hæra-toȝe. **1577–87** [see HERETOCHY]. **1641** in *Harl. Misc.* (Malh.) V. 48 Lieutenants of counties (anciently known by the name of Heretoch). **1643** HERLE *Answer to Ferne* 24 The ancient Governours of the Militia of the Realme, both by sea and land cal'd Heretochs, which Lambard likens to the High Constables of France. **1761** HUME *Hist. Eng.* I. App. i. 92 *note*, The heretoghs or dukes, and the sheriffs, were chosen by the freeholders in the folkmote. **1765** BLACKSTONE *Comm.* I. 408 In the time of our Saxon ancestors..the military force of this kingdom was in the hands of the dukes or heretochs. **1848** LYTTON *Harold* VI. vi, If thou wert as frank in the grim land of thy heretogh. **1874** STUBBS *Const. Hist.* I. iv. 66 In A.D. 449, under two *heretogas*, Hengist and Horsa, the strangers came.

heretrix: see HERITRIX.

hereunder (hɪərˈʌndə(r)), *adv.* [f. HERE *adv.* 16 + UNDER *prep.* Cf. Du. *hieronder*, Ger. *hierunter*, Da. *herunder*, Sw. *härunder.*] Under this.

1. Subsequently (mentioned or set down) in this document, book, etc.

1425 *E.E. Wills* (1882) 65 þis here-vnder writen ys my last will. **1586** T. B. *La Primaud. Fr. Acad.* I. (1589) 101 The effects heerunder mentioned of this first vertue. **1693** *Vestry Bks.* (Surtees) 257 Wee whose names are hereunder written. **1893** CROCKETT *Stickit Minister* 241 The result is appended hereunder.

2. Under or beneath this surface or appearance.

1639 T. BRUGIS tr. *Camus' Mor. Relat.* 201 There must needs lie hereunder some falsity and deceipt.

3. Under this title, heading, etc.

1586 A DAY *Eng. Secretary* I. (1625) 95 Whatsoever containeth any speciall request, is hereundar included.

4. Under the authority of this (statute or the like).

1880 *Mississippi Code* §1114 No indictment hereunder shall be quashed for want of form.

hereunto (hɪərʌnˈtuː, -ˈʌntuː), *adv.* [f. HERE *adv.* 16 + UNTO *prep.*] Unto or to this place; to this thing, matter, subject, etc.; to this document.

1509 FISHER *Fun. Serm. C'tess Richmond* Wks. (1876) 299 Herevnto his ryghtwysnes also sholde enclyne hym. **1577** B. GOOGE *Heresbach's Husb.* I. (1586) 12 b, Hereunto is also ioyned my Larder. **1596** *Vestry Bks.* (Surtees) 40 In witnes whereof they have hearunto set their hands. **1630** WADSWORTH *Pilgr.* iii. 18 All the schooles are not admitted here vnto. **1711** ADDISON *Spect.* No. 126 ¶2 We whose Names are hereunto subscribed. **1803** *Med. Jrnl.* IX. 253 Adjoining hereunto on the east, is a ward, eighty feet front.

hereupon (hɪərəˈpɒn), *adv.* [f. HERE *adv.* 16 + UPON *prep.*]

1. Upon this thing, point, subject, or matter.

c **1175** *Lamb. Hom.* 49 Her uppon heo þencheð muchele mare þen uppon godalmihtin. **1591** SPENSER *M. Hubberd* 123 It behoues..to resolue first herevpon. *a* **1626** BACON *New Atl.* (1631) 2 Consulting hereupon amongst our Selves. **1651** HOBBES *Leviath.* III. xxxvi. 226 Hereupon a question may be asked.

2. Immediately following upon this (in time or consequence).

c **1340** *Cursor M.* 4945 (Fairf.) Her a-pon þai stale my þinge. *c* **1385** CHAUCER *L.G.W.* 1643 *Hypsip.*, And her-upon, at night they mette y-fere. **1568** GRAFTON *Chron.* II. 73 Hereupon the kinges messengers were put in prison. **1597** HOOKER *Eccl. Pol.* V. x. §1 What other effect could hereupon ensue. **1706** tr. *Dupin's Eccl. Hist. 16th C.* II. III. xviii. 261 Hereupon there was a great murmur. **1863** FR. A. KEMBLE *Resid. in Georgia* 34, I hereupon had to explain to them [etc.].

herewde, obs. form of HERALD.

herewith (hɪəˈwɪð), *adv.* and *a.* [f. HERE *adv.* 16 + WITH *prep.* Cf. Da. *herved.*]

A. *adv.* **1.** With this; along with or together with this.

1017–23 in Earle *Land Charters* 236 þis wæs ȝedon be þyssa witena ȝewytnessæ þe herwið nyð an awritene standað. *c* **1380** WYCLIF *Last Age Ch.* p. xxxii, Her wiþ acordiþ Carnosencis. **1528** GARDINER in Pocock *Rec. Ref.* I. xlviii. 93 The abstracts whereof we send unto your highness herewith. **1641** SIR E. NICHOLAS in *N. Papers* (Camden) 34 You shal receave hearewith a pacquett from his Majestie. **1755** G. WASHINGTON *Lett.* Writ. 1889 I. 145, I herewith send you a small map of the back country.

†**2.** At the same time with this; upon this; with these words, etc. *Obs.*

a **1300** *Cursor M.* 24479 (Cott.) Her-wit come me son succur. *c* **1340** *Ibid.* 11895 (Trin.) Herwiþ þei let þe heed doun And vp þe feet of þat feloun. **1546** J. HEYWOOD *Prov.* (1867) 61 Well (quoth she) till soone, fare ye well..Out at doores went she herewith.

3. By means of this; hereby.

1560 BIBLE (Genev.) *Mal.* iii. 10 Proue me now herewith, sayeth the Lord of hostes, if [etc.]. **1597** HOOKER *Eccl. Pol.* V. xxix. §5 The weak are offended herewith. **1893** M. S. TERRY in Barrows *Parl. Relig.* I. 698 Herewith we worship thee.

B. *adj.* Accompanying.

1917 'CONTACT' *Airman's Outings* p. xii, It was a squadron that possessed..the herewith testimonial.

herewithal (hɪəwɪˈðɔːl), *adv.* *arch.* [f. HERE *adv.* 16 + WITHAL.] = HEREWITH.

c **1384** CHAUCER *H. Fame* III. 516 Herwithal ther come anoon Another huge companye. **1501** *Plumpton Corr.* (Camden) 154, I copied them, as your worship shall see, & receive herewithall closed. **1585** ABP. SANDYS *Serm.* (Parker Soc.) 201 The eyes even of the wise are blinded herewithal. **1642** FULLER *Holy & Prof. St.* III. xiii. 184 Herewithall

Doctour Whitaker was much delighted. **1701** GREW *Cosm. Sacra* IV. (L.), Professing that herewithal he owed, and offered up himself body and soul, unto God.

†**'hereword.** *Obs.* [OE., f. stem of *hęrian* to praise + WORD.] Word of praise; praise, renown, glory.

a **1100** *O.E. Chron.* (MS. F.) an. 1009 (Earle) 142 *note*, Ða wold Brihtric ȝearnian him here word. *c* **1175** *Lamb. Hom.* 137 Þenne he biȝeteð hereword ðere mide. *c* **1205** LAY. 11917 Heo hæfde al þat hære-word [*c* **1275** here-word] of þan maidenen of þis ærd. *a* **1225** *Ancr. R.* 148 Þeo þet forleoseð & aspilleð al hore god þuruh wilnunge of hereword.

†**'hereworth,** *a. Obs.* In 3 **herewurð.** [See prec.] Worthy of praise; to be praised.

a **1225** *Juliana* 33 Herewurðe healent.

†**'hereyeld, herield.** *Old Sc. Law.* Forms: 6 **hereȝeld, -ȝeild,** (**herreȝelda**), **herield, hyrald, -eild,** 7 **herrezeld(e,** 9 **herezeld,** (*erron.* **herizeld**). [The same word as OE. *hereȝeld*, HEREGELD, used in Scotland in sense of HERIOT.]

The render to the superior of the best living animal of a deceased vassal; at an early date commuted for a fixed money payment, and now practically obsolete: see quot. 1861; corresponding to Eng. HERIOT.

a **1500** *Leg. Quat. Burg. Scot.* c. 17 In burgh sall nocht be herde bludewyt naȝit stokisdynt na merchet na hereȝelde [nec merchet nec herieth] na nane suilk maner of thyng. [**1508** in D. Black *Hist. Brechin* (1867) II. 31 A horse as the Herȝeld of..John Carnegy his father.] **1535** LYNDESAY *Satyre* 1986 Our gude gray meir was baittand on the feild And our Land's laird tuik hir, for his hyreild. *c* **1575** *Balfour's Practicks* (1754) 200 Na hereȝeld sould be paid. **1597** SKENE *De Verb. Sign.*, *Herreȝelda*, is the best aucht, oxe, kowe, or vther beast quhilk ane husband-man..hes in his possession, the time of his decease, quhilk aucht and suld be given to his Landis-lorde. **1693** STAIR *Inst.* (ed. 2) II. 111 §80 The Herezeld was found due to the La[dy] Liferenter, though the Defunct had the Room in Steelbow. **1861** W. BELL *Dict. Law Scotl.* s.v., This exaction has been long unknown in practice..Sometimes, in striking a composition, the value of the herezeld is stated against the vassal in money at a low conversion.

attrib. **1535** LYNDESAY *Satyre* 3904 From thine-furth thay sall want thair hyrald-hors. **1552** —— *Monarche* 4734 Than cumis the Landis Lorde, perfors, And cleiks tyll hym ane herield hors.

here'yesterday. *Sc.* ? *Obs.* [app. a corruption of *ereyesterday*, OE. **ǽrȝystrandæȝ*, f. ERE before + YESTERDAY: cf. Du. *eergisteren*, OHG. *êrgestern*, Ger. *ehegestern*, in same sense.] The day before yesterday.

a **1662** R. BAILLIE *Lett.* (1775) II. 73 (Jam.) Always here-yesterday, when we were at the very end of it.

herfest(e, obs. forms of HARVEST.

hergulutier, var. ARGOLETIER, HARGULATER.

herhaud, -hault, obs. ff. HERALD *sb.*

hericano, obs. form of HURRICANE.

†**'hericide.** *Obs. rare*$^{-1}$. [f. L. (*h*)*erus* master + -CIDE 2.] The murder of a lord or master.

1627–77 FELTHAM *Resolves* II. xlvi. 250 That punish Treachery, Perfidiousness, and Hericide with smart and ignominy.

herie, herier, heriful: see HERY *v. Obs.*, to praise.

herield, -iȝeld, var. HEREYELD, *Obs.*

herif, obs. form of HAIRIF.

†**'herigaut.** *Obs.* Also 4 **herygoud,** (8 **herigald**). [a. OF. *herigaut, hergaut, hargaut*, pl. *-gaus* (14th c. in Godefroi), med.L. *herigaldus*.] An upper garment or cloak worn by men and women in the 13th and 14th centuries.

1297 R. GLOUC. (Rolls) 11391 Mani on..hor armes awei caste & chaungede hom vor herigaus [*v.r.* hergaus]. *c* **1325** in *Pol. Songs* (Camden) 156 An heme in a herygoud with honginde sleven. **13..** *E.E. Allit. P.* B. 148 Hopez þou I be a harlot þi erigaut to prayse? [**1727** *Cowell's Interpr.*, *Herigalds*, a Sort of garment so called.]

herile ('hɛraɪl), *a. rare.* [ad. L. (*h*)*erīl-is*, f. (*h*)*erus* master.] Of or pertaining to a master.

1644 H. PARKER *Jus Pop.* 36 The power of Masters or Lords from the Greek we terme Despoticall, from the Latine Herile. **1656** STANLEY *Hist. Philos.* VI. (1701) 265/2 The Government of a Family..is partly Paternal, partly Nuptial, partly Herile, partly Acquisitive. [**1837–9** HALLAM *Hist. Lit.* (1855) IV. 177 In the sixth book we have disquisitions on matrimony..on paternal, and on herile power.]

So †**he'rility** [ad. med.L. (*h*)*erīlitās*], 'mastership' (Blount *Glossogr.* 1656).

herinacious, var. of ERINACEOUS.

1790 BRUCE *Trav.* V. 143 Long herinacious hairs which, like small thorns, grow about his back.

Hering ('hɛːrɪŋ, 'hɛ-). The name of Karl Ewald Konstantin *Hering* (1834–1918), German psychologist and physiologist, used *attrib.* or in the possessive to designate certain physiological effects observed, and principles enunciated, by him.

1891 M. FOSTER *Textbk. Physiol.* (ed. 5) IV. III. iii. 1232 Hering's theory attempts to reconcile..the various facts of colour vision with the supposition that we possess..six fundamental sensations. **1902** *Encycl. Brit.* XXI. 749/2 Hering's theory proceeds on the assumption of chemical changes in the retina under the influence of light. *Ibid.*, Hering's theory accounts satisfactorily for the formation of coloured after-images. **1911** GOULD *Pocket Med. Dict.* (ed. 6) 415 *Hering's Law*. The distinctness or purity of any sensation or conception depends upon the proportion existing between their intensity and the sum total of the intensities of all simultaneous sensations and conceptions. **1934** H. C. WARREN *Dict. Psychol.* 123/2 *Hering after-image*, the first positive after-image, or after-sensation, which occurs following a brief light-stimulus. *Ibid.*, *Hering illusion*, an illusion, or distorted perception of visual form, observed when a number of lines radiating from a point are crossed by two parallel lines on opposite sides of the point and equidistant from it; the parallel lines appear to bow outward, i.e. away from the central point. *Ibid.*, *Hering theory of vision*, the theory..according to which visual sensations are due to three pairs of antagonistic processes in the optic system. **1971** *Jrnl. Gen. Psychol.* LXXXIV. 164 The Zöllner and Hering illusions are examples of phenomena in which the overall pattern dominates the geometry and leads to the perceptual distortion of straight lines into curved lines.

hering, obs. form of HERRING.

heriot ('hɛrɪət). Forms: 1 **hereȝeatu, hereȝeatwa, -we,** 3–4 **heriet,** 6 **her(r)iotte, haryotte,** (**aryott**), 6–7 **har(r)iot,** 7 **herriott,** 7–8 **herriot,** 3–4, 7– **heriot.** [OE. *hereȝeatwa, -we*, f. *here* HERE *sb.* army, host + *ȝeatwa, ȝeatwe* trappings, equipments, ornaments, armour.]

†**1.** Military equipments. (Only in OE.)

c **888** K. ÆLFRED *Boeth.* xxxvii. §1 Mid gyldenum hylt sweordum, and mid maniȝfealdum hereȝeatwum ȝehyrste. *c* **993** *Battle of Maldon* 48 Hi willað eow to gafole garas syllan, ættrene ord and ealda swurd, ða hereȝeatu ðe eow æt hilde ne deah.

2. *Eng. Law.* A feudal service, originally consisting of weapons, horses, and other military equipments, restored to a lord on the death of his tenant; afterwards a render of the best live beast or dead chattel of a deceased tenant due by legal custom to the lord of whom he held; the corresponding payment in Sc. Law was the HEREYELD.

At an early period this render was commuted in many cases for a fixed money payment. The heriot is now an incident of manorial tenures only. In some exceptional cases, it is also due on a change of tenants, and even on the entry of a new lord. ***suit heriot***: see quot. 1882.

c **950** *Dipl. Angl. Ævi Sax.* (Th.) 499 And þam cinge minne hæreȝeatwa, feower sweord, and feower spæra, and feower scyldas. *a* **1035** *Laws of Cnut* II. c. 71 [72] (Schmid) And beon þa here-ȝeata [*v.rr.* hereȝeate, heriȝeata] swa hit mæðlic sy. Eorles..eahta hors, feower ȝesadelode and feower unȝesadelode, and feower helmas and feower byrnan and ehta spera and eall swa feala scylda and feower swurd and twa hund mancus goldes. *Ibid.* c. 78 [79] Se man þe on þam fyrdunge ætforan his hlaforde fealle..beon þa hereȝeata forȝyfene. *c* **1290** *S. Eng. Leg.* I. 445/480 On of is pouere Men wende of lif-dawe, And is beste best to heriet men brouȝte him, ase it was lawe. **1343** in Kennett *Par. Antiq.* (1818) II. 83 Juliana Hardy..diem clausit extremam, et accidit domino nova heriota ii. boves pret. xvi *s.* *c* **1500** in W. Denton *Eng. 15th Cent.* (1888) 319 *note*, Now yowr farmor takes in & lettes at hys wylle with owt fyne or aryott to yowe. **1523** FITZHERB. *Surv.* xii. (1539) 29 There be two maner of herriottes. **1611** COTGR. s.v. *Ample*, For a Heriot whereof the Landlord takes his deceased tenants best horse. **1641** BROME *Jovial Crew* I. Wks. 1873 III. 356 What Hariots have you tane from forlorne Widows? **1647** FULLER *Gd. Th. in Worse T.* (1841) 128 There accrueth to the land-lord a fine and heriot from his tenant taking a farther estate in his lease. **1767** BLACKSTONE *Comm.* II. vi. (1809) 97 Heriots..are a render of the best beast or other good (as the custom may be) to the lord on the death of the tenant. **1861** PEARSON *Early & Mid. Ages Eng.* 426 The heriot conveyed the acknowledgement of former vassalage, and, from analogy, one was claimed by the church at the death of every believer. **1874** STUBBS *Const. Hist.* I. ii. 24 *note*, The warhorse and spear were the gift of the *princeps* and the origin of the later heriot. *Ibid.* ix. 261 The change of the heriot to the relief implies a suspension of ownership, and carries with it the custom of livery of seisin. **1875** MAINE *Hist. Inst.* vi. 162 The Heriot of English Copyhold tenure..has been explained as an acknowledgment of the Lord's ownership of the cattle with which he anciently stocked the land of his villeins. **1882** A. BROWN *Scriven's Copyholds* vi. §1 (ed. 6) 213 A heriot reserved on lease, or *suit heriot*, partakes strictly of the nature of rent, so that the lord cannot seize, but must either distrain..or bring an action.

b. *transf.* Applied to analogous payments in other countries.

1642 FULLER *Holy & Prof. St.* v. xviii. 430 The petty-Land-lords of the times, to whom rich fines and heriots would accrue upon every exchange..took part with Andronicus. *c* **1645** HOWELL *Lett.* I. i. xxxviii, He is contented with a white Mule, and Purse of Pistols about the neck, which he receives evry yeer for a herriot or homage. **1705** BOSMAN *Guinea* 448 The eldest Son is sole Heir, but is obliged to present a Slave by way of Herriot to the King.

c. *fig.*

a **1670** HACKET *Abp. Williams* II. (1692) 228 His body was interred..in Llangeday, the heriot which every son of Adam must pay to the Lord of the Mannor of the whole Earth. **1680** CROWNE *Mis. Civ. War* II. 19 Cruelly sworn; But yet such oaths are heriots, which widows To custom always pay, when a life falls.

3. *attrib.* and *Comb.*, as ***heriot-land***; **heriot custom, heriot service** (see quot. 1767).

1002 in Earle *Land Charters* (1888) 220 Ðæt hereȝeatland æt Suttune. **1531** *Dial. on Laws Eng.* II. ix. (1638) 75 For heriot service the Lord shall distraine. *a* **1676** HALE *Anal. Law* xxvii. (1739) 71 This Acquisition by Act in Law may be ..4. By the Custom as in the Case of Heriot Custom. **1767** BLACKSTONE *Comm.* II. xxviii. (1799) 422 Heriot-service, and heriot-custom. The former are..due upon a special reservation in a grant or lease of lands, and therefore amount to little more than a mere rent: the latter arise upon no special reservation whatsoever, but depend merely upon immemorial usage and custom. **1896** *Daily News* 4 Nov. 6/6 In the Court of Appeal yesterday..Sir Thomas claimed that either by heriot custom or heriot service he was entitled to a heriot of the best beast of the deceased tenant.

Hence †**'heriotage** *Obs.* (see quot.).

1611 COTGR., *Droict de meilleur Cattel*, heriotage; the best chatell a tenant hath when he dies, due vnto his Land-lord.

heriotable ('hɛrɪətəb(ə)l), *a.* [See -ABLE.] Subject or liable to the payment of heriots.

1598 KITCHIN *Courts Leet* (1675) 269 The Husband and Wife and their Son purchase Lands joyntly Harriotable. **1607** NORDEN *Surv. Dial.* 102 It behoveth the Lord to know, who be the tenants..belonging to an heriotable tenement, because every part continueth heriotable. **1777** NICOLSON & BURN *Hist. Westm. & Cumb.* I. 174 The tenants are chiefly customary and heriotable. **1889** JESSOPP *Coming of Friars* v. 225 Richard..protested that his land was not heriotable.

herisipelas, obs. form of ERYSIPELAS.

herisson ('hɛrɪsən). [a. F. *hérisson*, OF. *heriçon, -ichon* (12th c. in Littré):—late L. **hericiōnem* URCHIN, augmentative of *hericius, ericius*.]

†**1.** A hedgehog, urchin. *Obs.*

1594 BLUNDEVIL *Exerc.* v. xii. (ed. 7) 555 He..hath the feet of a Herison. *c* **1600** BUREL *Pilgr.* in J. Watson *Coll. Poems* (1706) II. 26 (Jam.) The Houlet and the Herison Out of the airt Septentrion Come with ane feirfull voce.

‖**2.** *Fortif.* A barrier, consisting of a revolving beam, armed with iron spikes.

1704 in J. HARRIS *Lex. Techn.* **1727–41** CHAMBERS *Cycl.* s.v., Herissons are frequently placed before gates. **1853** STOCQUELER *Milit. Encycl.*, *Herisson*, a formidable hedge or chevaux-de-frise, made of one stout beam fenced by a number of iron spikes..which being fixed upon a pivot, revolves in every direction upon being touched, always presenting a front of pikes.

3. 'A sort of wooden horse set with spikes or points, formerly used as a military punishment, the culprit being mounted upon it' (*Cent. Dict.*).

herit, *v. rare.* Also 6 **heryt.** [a. OF. *heriter* (12th c. in Littré):—L. *hērēditāre*.] *trans.* To inherit.

a **1533** LD. BERNERS *Gold. Bk. M. Aurel.* (1546) Ffiij, He that lyueth, heryteth death. **1649** ROBERTS *Clavis Bibl.* 155 And make..them herit Glory's throne. **1876** 'INDIAN CHAPLAIN' *Mahabuleshwar Hills* 40 Each hallow'd spirit Hath gone the land of life and love to herit. **1922** JOYCE *Ulysses* 401 To herit the tradition of a proper breeding.

†**'herit,** *sb. Obs.* [? f. prec.] Inheritance.

c **1475** *Partenay* 38 In riches herite was not in þe best, But of good lyuyng was in-dede and set.

herita'bility. [f. next + -ITY.] The quality of being heritable, or capable of being inherited.

1832 *Fraser's Mag.* V. 45 This tax, thus securing the heritability of offices, was not perpetual. **1882** A. GRAY in *Proc. Amer. Acad. Arts* XVII. 449 The importance of heritability, which is an essential part of Darwinism, would seem to have had a significant illustration in the person of its great expounder. **1890** *Advance* (Chicago) 15 May, Did you ever think about the heritability of such qualities?

heritable ('hɛrɪtəb(ə)l), *a.* (*sb.*) Also 4–8 **here-.** [a. F. *héritable* (1206 in Godef.) f. *hériter*: see HERIT *v.*]

1. Capable of being inherited, inheritable; in *Sc.* and *Civil Law*, said esp. of property, or rights pertaining thereto, that pass by inheritance to heirs-at-law, as distinguished from *movable* property or rights, which do not so descend.

heritable jurisdictions, grants of criminal jurisdiction bestowed on some of the Scottish nobility with a view to the more easy and prompt administration of justice. Abolished 1747 by Act 20 Geo. II, c. 43.

c **1375** *Sc. Leg. Saints, Machor* 92 He gaf of heretable rycht To godis seruice al þat ton. **1523** LD. BERNERS *Froiss.* I. xiv. 14 The kyng..dyd gyue hym cccc. markis sterlyngis of rent heritable, to hold of hym in fee. **1632** LITHGOW *Trav.* 62 Ithaca..was the heretable Kingdome of the worthy Ulysses. **1687** *Royal Proclam.* in *Lond. Gaz.* No. 2221/4 No Law, Custom or Constitution..can..Restrain Us from conferring Heretable Rights and Priviledges upon them. **1689** *Proc. Convent. Est. Scotl.* in Somers *Tracts* II. 387 Imposing them where there were heritable Offices and Jurisdictions. **1746–7** *Act 20 Geo. II*, c. 43 §1 All Heretable Jurisdictions of Justiciary, and all Regalities and Heretable Baillieries..shall be..abrogated, taken away, and totally dissolved and extinguished. **1766** W. GORDON *Gen. Counting-ho.* 463 Inventory of the moveable and heretable estate. **1832** AUSTIN *Jurispr.* (1879) I. xiv. 392 The rights descendible to heirs as distinguished from those descendible to executors or administrators are in the law of Scotland denoted by the appropriate term heritable. **1848** MILL *Pol. Econ.* II. ii. §7 Other examples of property which ought not to have been created, are properties in public trusts; such as ..the heritable jurisdictions.

b. *Sc. Law.* Pertaining to or connected with heritable property.

heritable bond, a bond for a sum of money, to which is joined, for the creditor's further security, a conveyance of land or of heritage, to be held by the creditor in security of the debt. ***heritable security***, security either constituted by

infeftment in favour of the creditor, or depending on the force of a condition qualifying the right of property (Bell *Dict. Law Scotl.*).

c **1575** *Balfour's Practicks* (1754) 221 The executouris may not be callit.. to warrand ony heritabill infeftment or dispositioun maid be the deid befoir his deceis. **1801** *Hist. Europe* in *Ann. Reg.* 134/2 The value of what, in that part of the Island, is called heritable security. *Mod.* (Title of Company, Edin.), Heritable Securities and Mortgage Investment Association Limited.

2. Naturally transmissible or transmitted from parent to offspring; hereditary.

1570 BUCHANAN *Ane Admonit.* Wks. (1892) 32 Arrogance, crueltie, dissimulatioun, and heretabill tressoun. **1571** GOLDING *Calvin on Ps.* li. 7 Sinne floweth by infection intoo the offspring, and is as it were heritable. **1784** DE LOLME *Eng. Const.* I. iii. (ed. 4) 40 Heritable forms of devotions and creeds. **1879** *St. George's Hosp. Rep.* IX. 45 No heritable disease in the family.

3. Of persons: Capable of inheriting or taking by descent; succeeding by right of inheritance.

c **1575** *Balfour's Practicks* (1754) 289 The heritabill proprietar of the saidis landis. *a* **1661** FULLER *Worthies, Worc.* III. (1662) 171 His wife.. being a Double Inheritrix.. indented with Husband, that her Heritable Issue should assume her Surname. **1737** *J. Chamberlayne's St. Gt. Brit.* II. I. ii. 292 The Earl of Cassilis is Heritable Bailiff of Carrick. **1886** J. SMALL in *Encycl. Brit.* XXI. 496/1 Heritable officers who had fought against the prince were only suspended, not deposed.

B. *sb. pl.* (*Sc. Law*). Heritable possessions; lands and other property that passes to the heir-at-law.

1801 A. RANKEN *Hist. France* I. 278 The peaceable possession of.. heritables or immovables. **1888** J. WILLIAMS in *Encycl. Brit.* XXIV. 574/1 Except where there has been vitious intromission in movables, and in *gestio pro herede* and some other cases in heritables.

heritably (ˈhɛrɪtəblɪ), *adv.* [f. prec. + -LY^2.] By way of inheritance, by right of inheritance or succession; by heritable property.

1523 LD. BERNERS *Froiss.* I. cccxlviii, The erle of Flaunders shulde heretably haue the sayd profyte. **1577–95** *Descr. Isles Scotl.* in Skene *Celtic Scotl.* (1880) III. App. 434 It perteinis heretablie to ane Barron callit the Laird of Challow. **1619** SIR J. SEMPILL *Sacrilege Handl.* 37 An action heretably descended. **1737** *J. Chamberlayne's St. Gt. Brit.* II. II. iv. 376 This office of Chamberlainry was possessed heritably of late by the Dukes of Lenox. **1842** ALISON *Europe* (1849–50) XIV. xcv. §54. 132 The mass of mortgages or debts heritably secured in France on the land is eleven milliards of francs.

heritage (ˈhɛrɪtɪdʒ), *sb.* Also 3–5 eri-, 4–6 ery-, hery-, 5–6 heretage (4 hary-, 6 hæretage, heri-, heiritagie). [a. OF. *eritage, heritage* (= Pr. *heretatge*, OSp. *eredage*, It. *ereditaggio*, med.L. *hereditagium*), f. *hériter*: see HERIT *v.* and -AGE.]

1. That which has been or may be inherited; any property, and esp. land, which devolves by right of inheritance.

a **1225** *Leg. Kath.* 83, I þe heritage and i þe herd þæt com of hire burde. **1297** R. GLOUC. (1724) 523 Richard is brother Underueng the eritage, vor he nadde eir non other.. The erldom of Penbroc, & al is other eritage. **1382** WYCLIF *1 Kings* xxi. 3 Merciful be to me the Lord, that I ȝyue not the heritage of my fadres to thee. *c* **1440** *Generydes* 4642 My fader hath geve hym half his eritage. **1596** DALRYMPLE tr. *Leslie's Hist. Scot.* I. 17 In the same hæritage Ilke hes rychteouslie from age to age succeidet till vther. **1608** SHAKS. *Per* II. i. 129 (Globe) It was.. part of my heritage, Which my dead father did bequeath to me. **1810** SCOTT *Lady of L.* I. xxix, Lord of a barren heritage. **1841** W. SPALDING *Italy & It. Isl.* II. 134 In early life he attended his father in a duel about a heritage.

b. *spec. Sc. Law.* Land and similar property which devolves by law upon the heir and not on executors or administrators; heritable estate, realty.

As distinguished from *conquest*: land inherited and not purchased.

1508 DUNBAR *Tua mariit Wemen* 344 Mi euidentis of heritagis. *c* **1575** *Balfour's Practicks* (1754) 224 All conquest sould ascend anes, and thairefter may na mair ascend; bot sould descend as heritage. **1845** W. BURGE in *Encycl. Metrop.* 848/1 Where a middle brother or sister (or their issue) dies, leaving younger or elder brothers or uncles. The younger brother (or uncle) and his issue take the heritages; the elder and his issue, the conquest. **1874** *Act 37 & 38 Vict.* c. 94 §37 The distinction between fees of conquest and fees of heritage is hereby abolished.

c. *transf.* and *fig.* The 'portion' allotted to or reserved for any one; e.g. that of the righteous or the wicked in the world to come.

a **1225** *Ancr. R.* 302 To.. bruken buten ende þe eritage of heouene. *c* **1230** *Hali Meid.* 25 þu schuldest þin herte heouen þiderward as tin heritage is. *a* **1340** HAMPOLE *Psalter* xxiv. 14 It sall haf hale heritage in blisse. **1390** GOWER *Conf.* II. 364 Which hath his heritage in helle. **1738** WESLEY *Ps.* XLVII. iv, God our Heritage shall prove, Give us all a Lot of Love. *a* **1842** A. CUNNINGHAM *Wet Sheet & Flowing Sea*, The hollow oak our palace is, Our heritage the sea.

†**2.** The fact of inheriting; inheritance, hereditary succession. *Obs.*

a **1300** *Cursor M.* 609 [God] gaf it him als in heritage. *c* **1330** R. BRUNNE *Chron. Wace* (Rolls) 14203 He left hit til Iweyn in herytage. *c* **1375** *Sc. Leg. Saints, Clement* 640 þat Ihesu cristis patronag succed should be harytage. *c* **1400** MAUNDEV. (Roxb.) Pref. 2 þis es þe land þ at es hight til vs in heritage. **1483** CAXTON *Gold. Leg.* 242 b/2 These ben the thynges that I leue to yow to possede by ryghtfull herytage. **1556** *Aurelio & Isab.* (1603) K viij, This goode that they have lefte me be heritagie.

3. Anything given or received to be a proper and legally held possession.

c **1380** WYCLIF *Wks.* (1880) 348 If.. þi kynge.. worschipid þee myche & hiȝt þee greet eritage to be at hijs retenu & serue hym treuly. **1382** —— *Ps.* cxxvi[i.] 3 Lo! the eritage of the Lord the sones. **1611** BIBLE *ibid.*, Loe, children are an heritage of the Lord.

b. The people chosen by God as his peculiar possession; the ancient Israelites; the Church of God.

a **1340** HAMPOLE *Psalter* xxvii. 12 Make safe þi folke lord & blesse þin heritage. **1382** WYCLIF *Micah* vii. 18 That.. berist ouer the synne of the relikis of thin eritage. **1549** *Bk. Com. Prayer, Te Deum*, O Lorde.. blesse thyne heritage. **1611** BIBLE *1 Pet.* v. 3 Neither as being lords over God's heritage. **1612** T. TAYLOR *Comm. Titus* iii. 7 That people were more peculiarly called the lines and heritage of the Lord. **1881** N. T. *Eph.* i. 11 In whom also we were made a heritage.

4. That which comes from the circumstances of birth; an inherited lot or portion; the condition or state transmitted from ancestors.

a **1621** BEAUM. & FL. *Thierry & Theodoret* v. i, The people's charity was your heritage, and I would see which of you deserves his birthright. **1639** S. DU VERGER tr. *Camus' Admir. Events* 46 The only glory of obeying her as their mother was the fairest lot in their heritage. **1814** BYRON *Lara* I. ii, Lord of himself;—that heritage of woe. *a* **1872** MAURICE *Friendship Bks.* i. (1874) 22 To earn bread by the sweat of the brow is the common heritage of the sons of Adam.

†**5.** Heirs collectively; lineage. *Obs.*

1390 GOWER *Conf.* II. 74 They graunten him a lusty mede .. To him and to his heritage.

†**ˈheritage**, *v. Obs. rare.* [a. OF. *(h)eritagier, -ger* (in both senses), f. *(h)eritage*: see prec.]

1. *trans.* To inherit.

1382 WYCLIF *Ps.* xxxvi[i]. 11 The debonere forsothe shuln eritagen the erthe. —— *Ecclus.* iv. 14 Who holden it, shuln eritagen [**1388** enherite] lif.

2. To give for an inheritance.

1382 WYCLIF *Ecclus.* xvii. 9 The lawe of lif he eritagede them [**1388** He enheritide hem with the lawe of lijf].

†**heˈritagely**, *adv. Obs. rare*$^{-1}$. [f. HERITAGE *sb.* + -LY^2.] By inheritance, as a heritage.

c **1330** R. BRUNNE *Chron.* (1810) 251 þe whilk I hold, & salle þorgh right Clayme to hald, at alle my myght, Heritagelik of þe, & of þin heires þat after þe be.

heritance (ˈhɛrɪtəns). *arch.* [a. OF. *heritance*, f. *hériter* to inherit: see HERIT *v.*] Inheritance; heirship. Also *fig.*

1422 tr. *Secreta Secret., Priv. Priv.* (E.E.T.S.) 159 Esau, for a lytill Potage solde the ryght of his herytaunce. *c* **1489** CAXTON *Sonnes of Aymon* xix. 404 A prysoner, by whom I shall have peas, and all myn herytaunce agayne. **1566** DRANT *Wail. Hierem.* in Farr *S.P. Eliz.* (1845) II. 417 Our heritaunce is cut of quyte. *a* **1635** NAUNTON *Fragm. Reg.* (Arb.) 23 Our Common-Law, which is the heritance of the Kingdome. **1801** SOUTHEY *Thalaba* I. (D.), These were my heritance, O God! they gifts were these. **1896** MISS MACLEOD *Sin-Eater* Ded., The beauty of the world, the pathos of life, the gloom, the spiritual glamour.. the heritance of the Gael.

heritor (ˈhɛrɪtə(r)). Forms: 5 heriter, 5–6 heryter, 6 hery-, here-, heritour, 7–8 heretor, 6– heritor. [ME., a. AF. *heriter* = OF. *heritier*, earlier *eretier, eritier* = Pr. *(h)eretier*, Sp. *heredero*:—late L. *hērēditāri-um* (from *hērēditārius* adj. HEREDITARY), which took the place of *hērēd-em* heir. In 16th c. erroneously conformed to agent-nouns in *-our*, *-or*: cf. BACHELOR, and see -OR.]

1. One who inherits; an heir or heiress. **a.** by law.

1475 *Bk. Noblesse* (1860) 4 King Edward the thrid, first heriter to the said Royaume of Fraunce. **1525** LD. BERNERS *Froiss.* II. xxiv, Hys cosyn germaine, the vicount of Chateau Bein, who is the heryter. *Ibid.* xliii. (R.), They sholde take his doughter.. who was as then but fyue yeres of age, for herytoure of ye royalme of Portyngale. *c* **1575** *Balfour's Practicks* (1754) 230 The heritouris and airis may be followit at the ȝeiris end. **1879** T. P. O'CONNOR *Ld. Beaconsfield* 74 The heritor of the Duke's title and land.

b. by nature or acquisition.

c **1554** *Interl. Youth* in Hazl. *Dodsley* II. 8 And thou shalt be an heritor of bliss. **1823** *New Monthly Mag.* VII. 327 The fierce heritors of his renown. **1877** FARRAR *Days of Youth* xiii. 123 Our days are heritors of days gone by.

2. *Sc. Law.* The proprietor of a heritable subject; 'in connexion with parochial law, the term is confined to such proprietors of land or houses as are liable in payment of public burdens' (Bell *Dict. Law Scotl.*).

heritor's court, the court of a subject superior held within the bounds of his own fee and heritage.

1597 MONIPENNY *Chron.* in Somers *Tracts* (1816) III. 395 An iland, which is not divided by any haven or port of the sea, but by the severall lordships of the heritours thereof. **1637** RUTHERFORD *Lett.* (1862) I. 217 O that Christ were restored to be a freeholder and a landed heritor in Scotland. **1693** *Apol. Clergy Scot.* 17 Their Parliament lodged the power of Election in the Heretors and Elders of each Parish. **1697** DALLAS *Stiles* 736 A Heretor of Salmond-fishing within the Territory of the Burgh. **1746–7** *Act 20 Geo. II*, c. 50 §21 No tenant.. liable to perform any services whatsoever to his heretor or landlord. **1834** *Brit. Husb.* I. iv. 83 In Scotland no law exists by which repair [of a road] can be enforced; provided the heritors of a parish can show that their statute labour has been expended.

ˈheritress. [f. prec. + -ESS. (*Herytes* in 1533 prob. an error.)] An heiress, an inheritress.

a **1533** LD. BERNERS *Huon* clxiii. 642, I wyll neuer consent that a newe found damoysell should be herytes of suche a realme. **1847** *Blackw. Mag.* LXI. 752 She was the sole heritress of the father's thousands. **1889** *Univ. Rev.* Jan. 91 Stern rustic heritress Of Cato and Fabricius.

heritrix, heretrix (ˈhɛrɪtrɪks). Also 7 heretrice, (*erron.* heiretrice, heirtrix). [A fem. of HERITOR formed in imitation of feminines in L. *-trix* and F. *-trice*, from masculines in L. *-tor*, F. *-teur.*]

A female heir or heritor; an heiress.

c **1575** *Balfour's Practicks* (1754) 232 Ane heretrix being in ward and keiping of hir over-lord, may be disherishit, and foirfalt hir heritage. **1609** SKENE *Reg. Maj.* 38 The Warde and Mariage of Wemen Heretrices. *Ibid.*, Na woman being ane heretrice of land, may be lawfullie maried, without consent of her over-lord. **1611** SPEED *Hist. Gt. Brit.* IX. viii. §8 Isabell, Heiretrice of Ailmar Earle of Angoulisme. **1654** tr. *Scudery's Curia Pol.* Contents, Marriage of the Princess an Heretrix to the Crown. **1875** W. M^{c}ILWRAITH *Guide Wigtownshire* 90 Elizabeth Kennedy, heretrix of the said croft.

herk, herke, -ien, obs. forms of HARK *v.*

herken, -in, obs. forms of HEARKEN.

herl, *sb.* Also 4–6 herle. [Cognate with MLG. *herle, harle*, LG. *harl* fibre, filament, hair of flax or hemp: see HARL.]

†**1.** A fibre or filament; a hair. *Obs. rare.*

13.. *Gaw. & Gr. Knt.* 190 þe mane of þat mayn hors.. Ay a herle of þe here, an oþ er of golde.

2. A barb or fibre of the shaft of a feather, esp. of the peacock or ostrich, used in making artificial flies for angling. Also HARL, q.v.

a **1450** *Fysshynge w. angle* (1883) 35 The body of grene wull & lappyd abowte wyth the herle of the pecoks tayle. **1611** MARKHAM *Countr. Content.* I. xiii. (1668) 68 The herle of a Peacocks tayl. **1799** G. SMITH *Laboratory* II. 295 Peacock's herl alone, or interchanged with ostrich herl. **1867** F. FRANCIS *Angling* 269 Tie on peacock or ostrich herl at the same place. **1884** *Longm. Mag.* June 179.

b. An artificial fly, of which a peacock herl is the distinctive feature.

1799 G. SMITH *Laboratory* II. 301 Dark-blue-herl. The body, black rabbit's scut.

herle. *Sc.* A local name of the heron.

1508 DUNBAR *Tua mariit Wemen* 382, I thoght my self a papingay, and him a plukit herle. **1825–80** JAMIESON s.v., Herle is still the common name in Angus.

herling, hirling. *local.* The name, on the Scottish shore of the Solway Firth, for the fish *Salmo albus*.

1684 R. SIBBALD *Scotia Illustr.* III. vi. 24 Trachurus. Hunc esse suspicor, qui Dumfrisiensibus nostris *Hirling* dicitur. **1791** *Statist. Acc. Scot., Holywood* I. 19 (Jam.) The Cluden abounds in fine burn trouts, some salmon, some sea trout, and herlings. **1793** *Ibid., Dumfries* V. 132 (Jam.) The river Nith produces salmon, trouts, flounders, pike, eels, and a species somewhat larger than herrings, called hirlings. **1834** JARDINE in *Proc. Berw. Nat. Club* I. No. 2. 51 This fish I consider to be the *Salmo albus* of Fleming, the Herling or Hirling of the Scotch side of the Solway Frith, the Whiting of the English side. **1861** *Act 24 & 25 Vict.* c. 109 §4 All migratory fish of the genus salmon, whether known by the names.. yellow fin, sprod, herling, whiting.. or by any other local name. **1880–4** DAY *Brit. Fishes* II. 85.

b. *Comb.*, as ***herling-house***, ***-net***, etc.

1834 JARDINE in *Proc. Berw. Nat. Club* I. No. 2. 51 They are caught.. by the stake-nets of small mesh, or, as they are called, herling-houses. **1893** *Scot. Leader* 10 July 4 Ten men were arrested.. on a charge of poaching, herling and small-meshed herling nets being found in their possession.

herlot, obs. form of HARLOT.

herlys, obs. form of ARLES.

1487 *Churchw. Acc. Wigtoft, Linc.* (Nichols 1797) 87 Joh. Writh, on herlys for on worke xii^d.

‖**Herma** (ˈhɜːmə). Also 6–7 Herm. [L. *Herma*, pl. *-æ*, a latinized form of *Hermes*, a. Gr. *Ἑρμῆς* Mercury, applied also at Athens to 'any four-cornered pillar surmounted by a head or bust'.]

A statue composed of a head, usually that of the god Hermes, placed on the top of a quadrangular pillar, of the proportions of the human body: such statues were exceedingly numerous in ancient Athens, where they were used as boundary-marks, mile-stones, sign-posts, pillars, pilasters, etc.

1579–80 NORTH *Plutarch* (1676) 450 By throwing down and mangling of the Herms (to say, the images of Mercury). *Ibid.* (1631) 496 Three Hermes of stone (which are foure square pillars) vpon the tops of which they set vp heads of Mercurie. **1603** HOLLAND *Plutarch's Mor.* 401 (Stanf.) They portraied those Hermes, that is to say, the statues of Mercurie, in yeeres, without either hands or feet. **1638** F. JUNIUS *Paint. of Ancients* 165 Hermæ were stone statues of Mercury. **1796** HOLCROFT *Stolberg's Trav.* (1797) II. lvii. 332 Aspasia, as a Herma: which means only the head on a pillar, that, from its base, gradually extends itself. **1850** GROTE *Greece* VII. 227 The mutilation of the Hermæ, one of the most extraordinary events in all Grecian history. **1850** LEITCH *Müller's Anc. Art* §345. 412 The isolated statue was historically developed from the pillar; the Herma remained as an intermediate step, inasmuch as it placed a human head on a pillar having the proportions of the human form.

Hermæan (hə'miːən), *a.* [f. L. *Hermæ-us*, a. Gr. Ἑρμαῖος of or pertaining to Hermes + -AN.] Of Hermes; applied to ancient statues consisting of a block or pillar surmounted by a head: see prec.
1813 J. C. HOBHOUSE *Journ.* 663 It was a small many-breasted figure, hermæan in the lower extremities, or, with the legs and feet not cut out. **1816** J. DALLAWAY *Stat. & Sculpt.* 7 In a short time artists arose who ventured to engraft a head upon these blocks, and to distinguish by features the one from the other..that description of statue was called 'terminal', or 'Hermæan'.

Hermaic (hə'meɪɪk), *a.* (*sb.*) [ad. Gr. Ἑρμαϊκ-ός of or like HERMES.]
1. Of or belonging to Hermes Trismegistus; = HERMETIC *a.* 1.
1678 CUDWORTH *Intell. Syst.* I. iv. §18. 320 All the Hermaic or Trismegistic books that are now extant. **1744** BERKELEY *Siris* §287 Speculations contained in the Hermaic writings. **1872** W. MATHEWS *Getting on in World* ix. (1873) 132 To distinguish between the 'me' and the 'non-me' with more than Hermaic subtlety.
b. as *sb.* (*pl.*) The writings attributed to Hermes Trismegistus.
1678 CUDWORTH *Intell. Syst.* i. iv. §18. 325 Those Books which Porphyrius saith he met withal, (namely the Hermaicks, and those Writings of Chæremon).
2. = HERMÆAN.
1820 T. MITCHELL *Aristoph.* I. p. xxviii, He compared them to the Hermaic statues, so common in their streets. **1876** A. WILDER in R. P. Knight *Symbol. Lang. Anc. Art* 63 *note*, Four-square, like the Hermaic pillars.

Her'maical, *a.* [f. as prec. + -AL[1].] = prec. 1.
1678 CUDWORTH *Intell. Syst.* I. iv. §18. 319 The least part of the Hermaical Institutions. *Ibid.* 324 The Books called Hermes's or Hermaical.

‖**hermandad** (ɛrman'dad). [Sp. = brotherhood, fraternity, f. *hermano* brother: cf. L. *fraternitas*.] In Spain, originally the name of popular combinations formed chiefly to resist the exactions and robberies of the nobles, to which were subsequently given general police functions; in 1476 was formed the *Santa Hermandad* or Holy Brotherhood, a voluntary organization embracing the whole country, which was afterwards reorganized as a regular national police.
1760–72 tr. *Juan & Ulloa's Voy.* (ed. 3) I. 98 The officers and soldiers of the garrisons, the alcades in office and of the hermandad, and the town clerk. **1838** PRESCOTT *Ferd. & Is.* (1846) II. xiv. 40 To this end, the principal cities and communities of Aragon had recently adopted the institution of the hermandad. **1845** FORD *Handbk. Spain* I. 41 (Stanf.) The Miquelites are the modern 'Hermandad', the brotherhood which formed the rural police of Spain.

†**hermaphro'deity.** *Obs. rare*[−1]. [irreg. f. HERMAPHRODITE, after such words as *corporeity*.] The state of being hermaphrodite.
1610 B. JONSON *Alch.* II. iii, The one [sulphur].. Supplying the place of male, The other [mercury] of the female, in all mettalls. Some doe beleeue hermaphrodeitie That both doe act, and suffer.

hermaphrodism (hə'mæfrədɪz(ə)m). *Biol.* [a. F. *hermaphrodisme* (1781 in Hatz.-Darm.), irreg. f. *hermaphrodite*: see -ISM.]
= HERMAPHRODITISM.
1828 WEBSTER cites *Dict. Nat. Hist.* **1835–6** TODD *Cycl. Anat.* I. 700 The Conchifera..possess what has been called sufficient hermaphrodism. **1877** HUXLEY *Anat. Inv. Anim.* i. 67 There is some reason to suspect that hermaphrodism was the primitive condition of the sexual apparatus.

her'maphrodisy. *rare*[−1]. [ad. med.L. *hermaphrodisia* (obs. F. *hermaphrodisie*, *hermofrodisie*), f. Gr. ἑρμαφρόδῑτος, after ἀφροδίσια, deriv. of Ἀφροδίτη.] Hermaphrodite state or quality.
1807 SIR R. WILSON *Jrnl.* 8 July in *Life* (1862) II. viii. 295 The revolting hermaphrodisy of the 'blue stocking'.

hermaphrodital (-'daɪtəl), *a. rare.* [f. as next + -AL[1].] = HERMAPHRODITIC.
1823 *Examiner* 59/2 There is..in this popular artist's male figures a certain lack either of masculine proportion or energy, a look hermaphrodital. **1831** *Fraser's Mag.* IV. 367 The animal magnetists..supposed it possible to restore for a time man and woman to an hermaphrodital state.

hermaphrodite (hə'mæfrədaɪt), *sb.* and *a.* Also (*erron.*) 5–6 **hermofrodite.** [ad. L. *hermaphroditus*, a. Gr. ἑρμαφρόδῑτος, orig. proper name of Ἑρμαφρόδῑτος son of Hermes (Mercury) and Aphrodite (Venus), who, according to the myth, grew together with the nymph Salmacis, while bathing in her fountain, and thus combined male and female characters.]
A. *sb.* **1.** A human being, or one of the higher animals, in which parts characteristic of both sexes are to some extent (really or apparently) combined.
(Formerly supposed to occur normally in some races of men and beasts; but now regarded only as a monstrosity.)
[**1398** TREVISA *Barth. De P.R.* XVIII. li. (1495) 811 In harmofroditus is founde bothe sexus male and female: but alway vnperfyte.] *c* **1400** *Lanfranc's Cirurg.* 5 Cap. ix Of hermofrodite, þat is to seye, þat hath þe schappe of man & womman. **1576** GASCOIGNE *Steele Gl.* (Arb.) 50, I am in dede a dame, Or at the least, a right Hermaphrodite. **1600** HOLLAND *Livy* XXXI. xii. 780 Another likewise was found of sixteene yeeres of age, a very Hermaphrodite of doubtfull sex between both. **1628** COKE *On Litt.* 3 a, An hermaphrodite may purchase according to that sexe which prevaileth. **1667** *Phil. Trans.* II. 624 An Exact Narrative of an Hermaphrodite now in London. **1756** WESLEY *Wks.* (1872) IX. 474 Indeed, we are not told here, that angels are hermaphrodites. **1874** VAN BUREN *Dis. Genit. Org.* 38 The monstrosity known as hermaphrodite does exist, but is excessively rare.
b. An effeminate man or virile woman. **c.** A catamite.
1594 *Mirr. Policy* (1599) H iij, Sardanapalus..burnt himself, by which act he deliuered his subjects from a monstrous Hermophrodite who was neither true man, nor true woman, being in sexe a man, & in heart a woman. *a* **1649** DRUMM. OF HAWTH. *Jas. I*, Wks. (1711) 9 The womanish decking of the persons of some few hermaphrodites. **1716** ADDISON *Drummer* IV. i, He is one of your Hermaphrodites, as they call them.
2. *Zool.* An animal in which the male and female sexual organs are (normally) present in the same individual, as in various molluscs and worms.
1727–41 CHAMBERS *Cycl.* s.v., Divers of the insect and reptile kind are also hermaphrodites; particularly, worms, snails, etc. **1742** H. BAKER *Microsc.* II. xxi. 180 Lice are not Hermaphrodites, as has erroneously been imagined. **1859** DARWIN *Orig. Spec.* iv. 100 On the land there are some hermaphrodites, as land-mollusca and earth-worms. **1888** ROLLESTON & JACKSON *Anim. Life* Introd. 25 Some hermaphrodites, however, are self-impregnating, such as *Cestoda*, and *Trematoda*.
3. *Bot.* A plant or flower in which the stamens and pistils (or equivalent organs) are present in the same flower, as in the majority of flowering plants.
1727–41 CHAMBERS *Cycl.* s.v., The latest botanists..make a division of plants, which they call hermaphrodites; as having..the stamina and pistil in the same flower. **1806** J. GALPINE *Brit. Bot.* 365 *Tussilago*..female flowers numerous: hermaphrodites very few. **1862** DARWIN *Fertil. Orchids* Introd. 1 No Hermaphrodite fertilizes itself for a perpetuity of generations.
4. *fig.* A person or thing in which any two opposite attributes or qualities are combined.
1659 W. CHAMBERLAYNE *Pharonnida* I. i. (1820) 14 'Twas the short journey twixt the day and night, The calm fresh evening, time's hermaphrodite. **1687** *Good Advice* 38 Henry the Eighth, was a kind of Hermophrodite in Religion, or in the Language of the times, a Trimer. *a* **1711** KEN *Edmund* Poet. Wks. 1721 II. 116 He acts the Hermophradite of Good and Ill, But God detests his double Tongue and Will. **1784** *New Spectator* No. 4. 2/2 In the new comedy—I mean dramatic hermaphrodite—of *Reparation*. **1827** HARE *Guesses* Ser. I. (1873) 10 A race of moral hermaphrodites.
b. *Naut.* A sailing vessel that combines the characters of two kinds of craft; now esp. one that is square-rigged like a brig forward, and schooner-rigged aft. Also called *hermaphrodite brig*: see B. 4.
1794 *Rigging & Seamanship* I. 220 An *Hermaphrodite* is a vessel so constructed as to be, occasionally, a snow, and sometimes a brig. It has therefore two mainsails; a boom mainsail, when a brig; and a square mainsail when a snow. **1831** TRELAWNY *Adv. Younger Son* I. 177 She was rigged as a hermaphrodite. **1833** M. SCOTT *Tom Cringle* v. (1859) 109 A very taught-rigged hermaphrodite, or brig forward and schooner aft.
B. *adj.* **1.** Of men or beasts: Having parts belonging to both sexes (really or apparently) combined in the same individual.
1607 TOPSELL *Four-f. Beasts* (1658) 263 Nero did shew certain Hermaphrodite Mares, wherewithal his Chariot was drawn. **1774** GOLDSM. *Nat. Hist.* IV. 18 Their hermaphrodite natures. **1816** G. S. FABER *Orig. Pagan Idolatry* II. 487 That astronomical hermaphrodite deity.
2. *Zool.* **a.** Of an animal: Having the male and female generative organs present in the same individual. **b.** Applied to organs which combine the characters of both sexes.
1753 CHAMBERS *Cycl. Supp.* s.v., The common earth-worms easily shew their Hermaphrodite nature. **1797** M. BAILLIE *Morb. Anat.* (1807) 186 This worm is hermaphrodite. **1870** ROLLESTON *Anim. Life* Introd. 38 The generative glands of all Vertebrata appear to be hermaphrodite at certain periods of fœtal life. **1888** ROLLESTON & JACKSON *Anim. Life* 113 (Edible Snail) The hermaphrodite gland or ovotestis is lodged [etc.]. *Ibid.*, From the gland a convoluted hermaphrodite duct passes.
3. *Bot.* **a.** Of a flower: Containing both stamens and pistils. **b.** Of a plant: Bearing both stamens and pistils in every flower.
1769 E. BANCROFT *Guiana* 31 Numerous monopetalous hermaphrodite flowers. **1778** LIGHTFOOT *Flora Scot.* (1789) I. 460 Common Carline Thistle..the florets are all hermaphrodite. **1854** HOOKER *Himal. Jrnls.* I. vi. 157 This plant is occasionally hermaphrodite in Sikkim. **1877** DARWIN *Forms of Fl.* Introd. 1 Linnæus..divided them into hermaphrodite, monœcious, diœcious, and polygamous species.
4. *transf.* and *fig.* **a.** Consisting of, or combining the characteristics of, both sexes. **b.** More generally, combining two opposite qualities or attributes.
1593 NASHE *Strange Newes* B iv b, With these two Hermophrodite phrases, being halfe Latin and halfe English. **1613** PURCHAS *Pilgrimage* (1614) 602 What could that Hermaphrodite-armie doe, wherein were five and twenty thousand armed women? **1651** HOBBES *Govt. & Soc.* Pref., Hermaphrodite opinions of morall Philosophers, partly right and comely, partly brutall and wilde. *a* **1661** FULLER *Worthies, Linc.* II. (1662) 154 Epicœne, and Hermaphrodite Convents, wherein Monks and Nuns lived together. **1807–8** W. IRVING *Salmag.* (1824) 358, I beg of you..to discourage this hermaphrodite mode of dress. **1834** *Brit. Husb.* I. 158 The Hermaphrodite waggon is formed by uniting two carts, corresponding with the fore and hind parts of a waggon, by bolting them together. **1840** R. H. DANA *Bef. Mast* ix. 22 A small hermaphrodite brig. **1882** FARRAR *Early Chr.* II. 350 It was only by inventing elaborate series of hermaphrodite pairs of æons or emanations that they could imagine any communication of God's will to man.
Hence **her'maphrodited** *pa. pple.*, united in one person. (*nonce-wd.*)
c **1643** A. BROME *Death Jos. Shute* 47 Divinity and art were so united, As if in him both were hermaphrodited.

hermaphroditic (-'dɪtɪk), *a.* [mod. f. Gr. ἑρμαφρόδῑτ-ος HERMAPHRODITE + -IC.] Belonging to or of the nature of a hermaphrodite (*lit.* and *fig.*); combining male and female characteristics.
1625 B. JONSON *Staple of N.* I. i, Looke on me, and with all thine eyes, Male, female, yea hermaphroditicke eyes. **1761** STILES in *Phil. Trans.* LV. 264 If the flowers of these plants be hermaphroditic. **1862** *Intell. Observ.* No. 1. 31 Nearly all the flukes are hermaphroditic.
b. In a more general sense: Combining any two opposite attributes or qualities.
1881 SWINBURNE *Misc.* (1886) 222 The detestable as well as debateable land of pseudo-poetic rhapsody in hermaphroditic prose.

hermaphro'ditical, *a.* [f. as prec. + -AL[1].] = prec.
1605 TIMME *Quersit.* II. iii. 112 Ye have also seene in the aforesaid salt a hermaphroditicall nature—male and female, fixed and volatil. **1713** GAY *Guardian* No. 149 ¶15 The riding habit, which some have not injudiciously called the Hermaphroditical, by reason of its masculine and feminine composition. **1847–9** TODD *Cycl. Anat.* IV. 152/2 Every variety of so-called hermaphroditical malformation is referrible to an abnormal condition.
Hence **hermaphro'ditically** *adv.*
1682 SIR T. BROWNE *Chr. Mor.* I. §31 Unite not the Vices of both Sexes in one; be not..Hermaphroditically Vitious. **1836–9** TODD *Cycl. Anat.* II. 736/2 Both twins were hermaphroditically formed in their sexual organs.

her'maphroˌditish, *a. rare.* [f. HERMAPHRODITE + -ISH.] = HERMAPHRODITIC.
1764 T. BRYDGES *Homer Travest.* (1797) I. 325 To them the Amazons succeed, A strange hermaphroditish breed. **1858** CARLYLE *Fredk. Gt.* III. vi. I. 178 A monstrous, frightful, hermaphroditish, neither secular nor spiritual constitution.

hermaphroditism (hə'mæfrədaɪtɪz(ə)m). *Biol.* [f. HERMAPHRODITE + -ISM.] The condition of a hermaphrodite; coexistence or combination (real or apparent) of male and female organs in the same individual organism, or in the same flower.
1808 REECE *Med. Dict.* s.v. *Vagina* (Jod.), This appearance constitutes a species of hermaphroditism. **1828** STARK *Elem. Nat. Hist.* I. 381 Among the oviparous fishes, hermaphroditism was long considered as a rare and accidental circumstance. **1876** DARWIN *Cross-Fertil.* x. 410 The relationship between hermaphroditism and fertilisation by means of insects is likewise to a certain extent intelligible. **1888** ROLLESTON & JACKSON *Anim. Life* Introd. 25 The testis may ripen at a different time to the ovary, a phenomenon known as successive hermaphroditism.

her'maphrodiˌtize, *v. rare.* [f. as prec. + -IZE.] *trans.* To make a hermaphrodite of; *fig.* to render effeminate.
1598 E. GILPIN *Skial.* (1878) 4 Such as Hermaphroditize these poore times With wicked scald iests, extreame gullerie. **1620** E. BLOUNT *Horæ Subsec.* 426 These mens minds be truly Hermaphroditized.

her-mele: see *hair-meal* s.v. HAIR *sb.* 10.

hermeline, obs. form of ERMELIN.

hermeneut ('hɜːmɪnjuːt). *rare.* [mod. f. Gr. ἑρμηνευτής interpreter, agent-n. f. ἑρμηνεύ-ειν to interpret, f. ἑρμηνεύς interpreter, considered to be a derivative of Ἑρμῆς Hermes in his character of tutelary deity of speech, writing, and traffic.]
An interpreter; *spec.* one of those employed in the early Church to interpret the service to worshippers who used a different language.
1965 *Listener* 3 June 820/1 The word-event which once happened and in happening became the text..must become a word-event again through the interpretation of the 'hermeneut', who transposes it into the thought-mode of his own day. **1972** *Times Lit. Suppl.* 20 Oct. 1262/1 The quest for a hermeneutics.

hermeneutic (hɜːmɪ'njuːtɪk), *a.* [ad. Gr. ἑρμηνευτικός, f. ἑρμηνευτής: see prec.] Belonging to or concerned with interpretation; esp. as distinguished from exegesis or practical exposition.
1678 R. BURTHOGGE *Organum Vetus & Novum* 70 Ratiocination Speculative, is either Euretick or Hermeneutick, Inventive or Interpretative. **1807** W. TAYLOR in *Ann. Rev.* V. 507 In his apprenticeship to the hermeneutic muse. **1884** D. HUNTER tr. *Reuss' Hist. Canon* v. 90 The hermeneutic method of the profound and hidden meaning.

herme'neutical, *a.* [as prec. + -AL[1].] = prec.
1798 W. TAYLOR in *Monthly Rev.* XXVII. 510 Aggravated with uncandid hermeneutical dexterity. **1837** HALLAM *Hist. Lit.* ii. III. §67 The Lutherans extol Gerhard, and especially Glass, author of the Philologia Sacra, in hermeneutical theology. **1864** *Reader* 21 May 650 The edition [of Shakspere] being chiefly hermeneutical, the publishers are preparing an exegetical commentary as a companion to it. **1968** C. E. BRAATEN *History of Hermeneutics* vi. 138 Preaching today is the goal of exegesis and hermeneutical reflection.

Hence **herme'neutically** *adv.*, according to the principles of interpretation.
1828 WEBSTER cites M. STUART.

herme'neutics. [f. HERMENEUTIC *a.*: see -ICS. Also in form *hermeneutic*. Cf. Gr. *ἑρμηνευτική* (sc. *τέχνη*), L. *hermēneutica*, F. *l'herméneutique*.] The art or science of interpretation, esp. of Scripture. Commonly distinguished from *exegesis* or practical exposition.
1737 WATERLAND *Eucharist* (ed. 2) 315 Taking such liberties with sacred Writ, as are by no means allowable upon any known rules of just and sober hermeneuticks. **1839** LONGF. *Hyperion* IV. vii, Here.. I kept my papers and my great work on Biblical Hermeneutics. **1843** S. DAVIDSON *Sacr. Hermeneut.* i. (L.), The meaning of all language, written or spoken, is developed by the application of general laws, usually termed Hermeneutics. **1871** TYLOR *Prim. Cult.* I. 287 No legend.. is safe from the hermeneutics of a thorough-going mythologic theorist. **1967** J. MACQUARRIE *God-Talk* vii. 148 We could say that history is the hermeneutic of historical existence, or even that physics.. is the hermeneutic of nature.

herme'neutist. *rare.* [f. Gr. *ἑρμηνευτ-ής* HERMENEUT + -IST.] 'One versed in hermeneutics; an interpreter' (Ogilvie 1882).
1906 *Westm. Gaz.* 19 Jan. 4/2 More than could be expected from the most practical and most skilful hermeneutist.

Hermes ('hɜːmiːz). [L. *Hermēs*, Gr. *Ἑρμῆς*.]
1. In Greek mythology, a deity, the son of Zeus and Maia, represented as the messenger of the gods, the god of science, commerce, eloquence, and many of the arts of life; commonly figured as a youth, with the *caduceus* or rod, *petasus* or brimmed hat, and *talaria* or winged shoes. Identified by the Romans with Mercury. Hence **b.** A statue of Hermes = HERMA.
1727–41 CHAMBERS *Cycl.* s.v., Athens abounded more than any other place in hermes's.

†**2.** Used for the metal Mercury. *Obs.*
1667 MILTON *P.L.* III. 603 Though by thir powerful Art they binde Volatil Hermes, and call up unbound In various shapes old Proteus from the Sea.

3. ***Hermes Trismegistus*** (Gr. *Ἑρμῆς τρὶς μέγιστος*, L. *Hermes ter-maximus*, Hermes thrice-greatest), the name given by the Neo-platonists and the devotees of mysticism and alchemy to the Egyptian god Thoth, regarded as more or less identified with the Grecian Hermes, and as the author of all mysterious doctrines, and especially of the secrets of alchemy. Hence *hermetic*, *hermetically*, and the following expressions:

†**a.** ***Hermes' seal***: = Hermetic seal: see HERMETIC A. 2b. *Obs.*
1605 TIMME *Quersit.* III. 192 Hermes seale.. take the red hote tonges, and therewith wring or nippe the toppe close together; whereby it shall be so closed as if it had no vent before. **1641** FRENCH *Distill.* v. (1651) 119 Closed up.. in a glazen womb sealed with *Hermes* seales. **1662** J. CHANDLER *Van Helmont's Oriat.* 75 Let the neck be shut with a Hermes Seal, by the melting of the glasse in the same place. **1756** ROLT *Dict. Trade* s.v. *Hermetical Seal*, With a pair of pincers twisting it close together, which is called putting on Hermes's seal.

†**b.** ***Hermes' fire***: = CORPOSANT; also, a will-o'-the-wisp. Also ***St. Hermes' fire*** (? by confusion with *St. Elmo's fire*). *Obs.*
1611 COTGR., *Ardans*, S. Hermes fires; the flittering, or going fiers.. or flames, which be seen by night, and neere vnto waters. **1658** tr. *Bergerac's Satyr. Char.* xii. 45, I send St. Hermes fire (Jack in a lanthorn) to the marches. **1665** SIR T. HERBERT *Trav.* (1677) 11 The Greeks call'd them Castor and Pollux.. which some call Hermes fire; Saint Elmo others.

Hermesian (hə'miːsɪən), *a.* and *sb.* [f. proper name *Hermes* (see below) + -IAN.]
A. *adj.* Pertaining to Georg Hermes (1775–1831), a Roman Catholic priest, and professor of theology at Bonn, who propounded doctrines on the relation of reason to faith, which were afterwards condemned by the Pope. **B.** *sb.* A follower of Georg Hermes. Hence **Her'mesianism**, the doctrine of Georg Hermes.
1868 *Chambers' Encycl.* Supp. s.v. *Hermes*, The Hermesian method of investigation.. discards.. all principle of authority. **1882–3** SCHAFF *Encycl. Relig. Knowl.* II. 980 A strong re-action set in against the Hermesians.. In a short time the movement died out, or was suppressed. **1847** J. H. NEWMAN *Let.* 10 Jan. (1962) XII. 8, I dread Hermesianism. **1885** *Catholic Dict.* s.v., Hermesianism is now extinct.

hermet, -ett, obs. forms of HERMIT.

hermetic (hə'mɛtɪk), *a.* and *sb.* [ad. med. or mod.L. *hermetic-us*, irreg. f. *Hermes* (*Trismegistus*): see HERMES 3. (Apparently formed in imitation of *magnēs*, *magnētic-us*.)]
A. *adj.* **1.** (With capital initial.) Pertaining to Hermes Trismegistus, and the philosophical, theosophical, and other writings ascribed to him: see HERMES 3.
1676 NEWTON in Rigaud *Corr. Sci. Men* (1841) II. 397 If there should be any verity in the Hermetic writers. **1678** CUDWORTH *Intell. Syst.* I. iv. §18. 321 There may very well be some Hermetic or Trismegistic books genuine, though all of them be not such. **1792** T. TAYLOR *Proclus* II. 29 His familiarity with the Hermetic Pan.

2. *transf.* and *fig.* **a.** Hence, Relating to or dealing with occult science, esp. alchemy; magical; alchemical. ***hermetic art, philosophy, science***: names for alchemy or chemistry. Also, unaffected by external influences, recondite.
a **1637** B. JONSON *Underwoods* lxii. 77 With the Chimera of the Rosie Crosse, Their Charmes, their Characters, Hermetticke Rings. **1641** FRENCH *Distill.* v. (1651) 160, I extracted thence three drams of pure nitrous Hermetick Salt. **1651** BIGGS *New Disp.* ¶65 But warm'd at the Hermetick fire. **1652** ASHMOLE *Theat. Chem.* Prol. 5 A Particular account of the Hermetique Science. **1663** BUTLER *Hud.* I. ii. 225 By his side a pouch he wore, Replete with strange hermetic powder. **1712** STEELE *Spect.* No. 426 ¶2 Basilius Valentinus was a person who had arrived at the utmost Perfection in the Hermetick Art. **1790** BURKE *Fr. Rev.* 338 As the dream of the philosopher's stone induces dupes, under the more plausible delusion of the hermetic art, to neglect all rational means of improving their fortunes. **1839** *Fraser's Mag.* XIX. 447 The hermetic or philosophical fire.. is a perfectly invisible and universal essence. **1954** *Ann. Reg. 1953* 204 From the published texts [of the Spanish agreement with America] might be inferred the existence of certain secret clauses, guardedly described as 'hermetic'. **1965** *Listener* 2 Sept. 351/2 Poems ranging from the hermetic to the directly obscene. **1966** *Ibid.* 5 May 663/2 It is hermetic music and solely concerned with problems of formal design, structure, and instrumental texture. **1972** *Times Lit. Suppl.* 25 Aug. 984/3 The poetry which he had written between the wars was considered hermetic by some.

b. ***hermetic seal, sealing***: air tight closure of a vessel, esp. a glass vessel, by fusion, soldering, or welding; also applied in *Surg.* to a method of dressing wounds (see quot. 1886). Also *fig.* Hence *hermetic* for 'hermetically sealed'.
1663 JER. TAYLOR *Fun. Serm. Ld. Primate* Wks. 1831 IV. 53 Not nature, but grace and glory, with an hermetic seal, give us a new signature. **1705** C. PURSHALL *Mech. Macrocosm* 140 Boyle has observed Water to Dilate, and contract it self.. by an Hermetic Glass Bubble. **1825** BENTHAM *Indic. resp. Ld. Eldon* 47 The same hand.. has.. as if by an hermetic seal, closed all such crannies. **1886** *Syd. Soc. Lex.*, *Hermetic sealing*.. Also, a mode of treatment of penetrating wounds of the chest or abdomen by closing them externally with collodion and scraps of lint.

3. a. Pertaining to the god Hermes. **b.** Of or pertaining to a Herma: as ***hermetic column*** = HERMES 1 b.
a **1891** J. R. LOWELL *Old Eng. Dramatists* (1892) 17 They [*sc.* the Elizabethans] had the Hermetic gift of buckling wings to the feet of their verse. **1951** AUDEN *Nones* (1952) 60 In fake Hermetic uniforms. *Ibid.* 61 Keep well the Hermetic Decalogue.

¶ Erron. for HERMITIC, q.v.

B. *sb.* **1.** One skilled in hermetic art or science; an alchemist or chemist.
1684 tr. *Bonet's Merc. Compit.* IX. 319 Prepared Vitriol.. alone to several Hermeticks may seem sufficient to furnish an Apothecaries shop.

2. *pl.* Hermetic philosophy; alchemy.
1865 tr. *Hugo's Hunchback of Notre Dame* II. vii. 95 Hermetics, that sophia of all sophias.

her'metical, *a.* [f. as HERMETIC *a.* and *sb.* + -AL[1].]
1. = HERMETIC *a.* 1, 2.
1605 TIMME *Quersit.* I. xi. 46 The Hermeticall Philosophers deny that there is a quintessence, because there are not fower elements. **1659** HOWELL *Vocab.* To Rdr., Here he shall know the dark terms of Chymistry or the Hermetical Art. **1704** J. HARRIS *Lex. Techn.*, *Hermetical Physick*, is that Hypothesis.. which refers the Cause of all Diseases to Salt, Sulphur and Mercury. **1837** SIR F. PALGRAVE *Merch. & Friar* Ded. (1844) 11 He composed a treatise on Alchemical Science.. It has been thrice published.. by.. collectors of hermetical mysteries.

2. = HERMETIC *a.* 2b.
1664 BOYLE *Wks.* (1772) II. 489 (*title*) Discourse, containing some new Observations about the Deficiencies of Weather-Glasses, together with some Considerations touching the New or Hermetical Thermometers. **1727–41** CHAMBERS *Cycl.*, *Hermetical Seal*, a manner of stopping or closing glass vessels.. by heating the neck of the vessel.. and then, with a pair of pinchers twisting it close together. **1822–34** *Good's Study Med.* (ed. 4) II. 645 Air will here indeed find its way.. unless opposed by an hermetical seal. *Ibid.* III. 289 *note*, Sir David Barry recommends the hermetical sealing of the vessels.

¶ Erron. used for HERMITICAL, q.v.

hermetically (hə'mɛtɪkəlɪ), *adv.* [f. prec. + -LY[2].] In a hermetical manner.
1. Used to denote a method of sealing or closing a tube or vessel by fusing it at the opening, or by soldering or welding; hence, by any mode which renders it absolutely air-tight. See HERMETIC *a.* 2b.
1605 TIMME *Quersit.* II. v. 123 A smal cappe or cover, with his receiver, strongly and well luted, hermetically closed rounde about. **1692** BENTLEY *Boyle Lect.* iv. 134 When he suffer'd those things to putrefie in Hermetically sealed glasses.. no living thing was ever produced there. **1799** G. SMITH *Laboratory* I. 132 Hermetically closed up to prevent any water coming to them. **1877** W. THOMSON *Voy. Challenger* I. i. 24 The receiver is now hermetically sealed at the upper contraction.

b. *Surg.* Used of a method of dressing gunshot wounds; see HERMETIC *a.* 2b, quot. 1886.
1870 T. HOLMES *Syst. Surg.* (ed. 2) II. 203 A plan of treating gun-shot wounds of the chest by hermetically sealing their external orifices, was introduced during the late war in America.. The record of the results.. are sufficiently ample to warrant an unqualified condemnation of the practice.

c. *fig.* Closely, tightly; absolutely (closed).
1698 FRYER *Acc. E. India & P.* 40 Were not the Mouth of that Grand Imposter Hermetically sealed up, where Christianity is spread. **1780** COWPER *Let.* 2 July, If you trust me with a secret, I am hermetically sealed. **1855** PRESCOTT *Philip II*, Pref. (1857) 4 The Archives which have held the secrets of the Spanish monarchy hermetically sealed for ages. **1883** H. DRUMMOND *Nat. Law in Spir. W.* (ed. 2) 71 The passage from the Natural World to the Spiritual World is hermetically sealed on the Natural Side.

†**2.** By the method of alchemy. *Obs.*
1664 J. WILSON *Cheats* III. i, *Jol.* Pray, sir, proceed; and disclose this son of gold. *Mop.* Hermetically, I shall.

hermetico-, combining form of HERMETIC *a.* (sense 1), as in **hermetico-poetical** *a.*, dealing with hermetic philosophy in poetical form.
1678 (*title*) Ripley Reviv'd: or an Exposition upon Sir George Ripley's Hermetico-Poetical Works.

hermetism ('hɜːmɪtɪz(ə)m). [f. HERMET(IC *sb.* + -ISM.] Hermetic or theosophical philosophy; hermetics. So **herme'tologist**, a hermetist.
1894 G. S. HALL in *Forum* Aug. 719 (Cent. D. Suppl.), Its teachings.. make the doctrine of sin as vital as with the most ardent of the old hermetologists. **1898** H. C. BOLTON in *Smithsonian Rep. 1897* 213 Traditions of the kabala, the mysteries of hermetism, and the practice of transmutation. **1927** *Contemp. Rev.* July 59 M. Valéry's poetics have been accused of hermetism and of preciousness.

Hermetist ('hɜːmɪtɪst). [f. as HERMETIC + -IST.] A hermetic philosopher.
1827–48 HARE *Guesses* Ser. II. (1867) 467 The Cabbalists and Hermetists who assumed the Universality of Sensation. **1877** H. P. BLAVATSKY *Isis* Pref. 21 What the Hindu initiates and the Hermetists taught before him.

hermid, herewith: see HERE *adv.* 16.

hermin, -yn, obs. forms of ERMINE.

hermit ('hɜːmɪt), *sb.* Forms: *α.* 3 **armite**, 4–5 **ermyt(e**, 4–6 **armyte, armet**, 4–7 **ermite**, 7 **ermit**. *β.* 4–6 **hermyte**, 4–8 **-mite**, (5 **-mett**), 6– **hermit**. *γ.* 3–7 **heremite**, 4–5 **-myt(e**, 6 *Sc.* **-meit**, 6–7 **-mit**. See also EREMITE. [ME. *hermite*, *ermite*, a. OF. (*h*)*ermite*, L. *erēmīta* (med.L. also *herēmīta*), ad. Gr. *ἐρημίτης*, f. *ἐρημία* desert. Beside the forms immed. from French, ME. had *heremite* after med.L.; mod.Eng. has also EREMITE, q.v.]
1. a. One who from religious motives has retired into solitary life; esp. one of the early Christian recluses. See EREMITE 1.
α. *c* **1205** LAY. 18800 Sone þe armite [*c* **1275** heremite] com in. *a* **1300** *Cursor M.* 8135 (Gött.) An armyte [*v.rr.* heremite, ermyte] þar þai fand at hame In þat montayn, was halt and lame. *c* **1300** *St. Brandan* 610 The ermite that was so old aȝen hem com gon. *c* **1440** *Promp. Parv.* 141/2 Ermyte.. *heremita*. **1535** STEWART *Cron. Scot.* II. 704 Into that yle.. Ane halie armet duelland war tha dais. **1621** BURTON *Anat. Mel.* I. ii. I. ii, S. Hierome in the life of Paul the Ermite tells a story. **1651** JER. TAYLOR *Holy Dying* i. §3 (1727) 21 To be spent in the cottage of a frugal person, or to feed an Ermit.
β. *a* **1300** *Cursor M.* 17900 (Gött.) A man come þan widuten lite, þat semed wele haue bene hermite [*v. rr.* eremite, eremyte, Ermyte]. **1362** LANGL. *P. Pl.* A. Prol. 3 In Habite of an Hermite [*B.* Heremite, *C.* Ermite] vn-holy of werkes. *c* **1400** MAUNDEV. (Roxb.) vii. 24 A haly hermit mette.. a beste forschapen. **1481** CAXTON *Myrr.* I. v. 22 The other gaf it [their tresour] away and.. wente as hermytes. **1588** SHAKS. *L.L.L.* IV. iii. 242 A withered Hermite, fiuescore winters worne, Might shake off fiftie, looking in her eye. **1703** MAUNDRELL *Journ. Jerus.* (1732) 80 Hermits retiring hither for Penance and Mortification. **1847** EMERSON *Repr. Men, Goethe* Wks. I. 384 There is much to be said by the hermit or monk in defence of his life of thought and prayer.
γ. *c* **1275** LAY. 18804 Þan heremite he iseh come. *c* **1375** *Sc. Leg. Saints, Magdalena* 812 A preste.. þat fled þe warld as heremyt. **1497** BP. ALCOCK *Mons Perfect.* D iij b, An heremyte cam to saynt Anthony. **1500–20** DUNBAR *Poems* xxv. 9 O! ȝe heremeitis and hankersaidilis, That takis your pennance at your tablis. **1600** J. PORY tr. *Leo's Africa* II. 154 The rule of heremites, the professors.. whereof inhabite woods and solitarie places.

b. *transf.* A person living in solitude.
1799 CAMPBELL *Pleas. Hope* II. 38 The world was sad.. And man, the hermit, sigh'd—till woman smiled. **1841** EMERSON *Addr., Lit. Ethics* Wks. (Bohn) II. 213 The poets who have lived in cities have been hermits still. **1849** ROBERTSON *Serm.* Ser. I. viii. (1866) 138 A solitary man who.. led a hermit's life.. for hermit.. he was.

2. In senses immediately derived from 1. **a.** In the formal designation of certain monastic

orders: e.g. ***Hermits of St. Augustine***: see EREMITE 2.

1577-87 [see EREMITE]. **1706** tr. *Dupin's Eccl. Hist. 16th C.* II. IV. xi. 449 The Augustinians produced one [new branch] that of the Hermites of St. Augustin.

b. A quasi-religious mendicant; a vagabond; in Gypsy slang, a highwayman.

1495 *Act 11 Hen. VII*, c. 2 §3 Every vagaboundе heremyte or begger able to labre. **1568** GRAFTON *Chron.* II. 118 Peter Wakefielde..an Hermite, an idle gadder about, and a pratlyng marchant. **1840** LONGF. *Sp. Stud.* III. v, And you, by the pole with the hermit's head upon it.

†**c.** A beadsman. Also *fig.* *Obs.*

1588 SHAKS. *Tit. A.* III. ii. 41 As perfect As begging Hermits in their holy prayers. **1605** —— *Macb.* I. vi. 20 For those [honours] of old, and the late Dignities, Heap'd vp to them, we rest your Ermites. **1688** R. HOLME *Armoury* III. 190/2 Begging Heremits first began to propagate here in England.

3. Applied to various animals of solitary habits, as the hermit-crab, the hermit-bird; see 4b. In Austral. and N.Z. *spec.* of a sheep; also ***hermit sheep***.

1661 WALTON *Angler* i. (ed. 3) 33 There is a fish called a Hermit, that at a certain age gets into a dead fishes shell, and like a Hermite dwells there alone. **1677** N. COX *Gentl. Recreat.* IV. (ed. 2) 5. **1862** WOOD *Nat. Hist.* II. 239 All the Hermits build a very curious and beautiful nest. *Ibid.* (1865) III. 603 If two Hermits be removed from their houses, and put into a rock pool..the combats which take place..are as fierce and determined as any. **1874** A. BATHGATE *Colonial Experiences* xv. 212 A sheep which has been badly tutued and recovers, loses its gregarious habits, and becomes what the shepherds call a 'hermit'. **1917** E. GLEN *Six Little N.Zers* vii. 95 They brought in a 'hermit' sheep which lived by itself, and had been overlooked in the last muster. **1933** L. G. D. ACLAND in *Press* (Christchurch, N.Z.) 28 Oct. 15/7 *Hermit*, a single sheep which for some reason takes to living by himself, away from the mob. **1966** G. W. TURNER *Eng. Lang. Austral. & N.Z.* viii. 165 Sheep that recovered [from eating tutu] sometimes became hermit sheep, losing their gregarious habits.

4. *attrib.* and *Comb.*, as ***hermit-seat***; ***hermit-fancied***, ***-haunted*** adjs.; **hermit-like** *a.* and *adv.*, like a hermit.

c **1500** *Melusine* lvii. 336 He dide doo make many hermyte habytes. **1709** WATTS *Horæ Lyr.* II. *To Discontented*, Sylvia ..Flies to the woods; a hermit saint! **1727-46** THOMSON *Summer* 15 Come Inspiration! from thy hermit seat, By mortal seldom found. **1785** BURNS *Vision* I. xx, Near many a hermit-fancy'd cove. *a* **1800** COWPER *Snail*, Hermit-like, his life he leads. **1852** HAWTHORNE *Blithedale Rom.* xxiv, Within which lurked the hermit-frog. **1878** *Prodigal Son* IV. in Simpson *Sch. Shaks.* II. 109 Many other hermitlike fools.

b. In names of various animals of solitary habits: **hermit-bird**, (*a*) a humming-bird of genus *Phaëthornis*; (*b*) a South American Halcyonide bird of genus *Monasa*, a nun-bird; **hermit-crab**, †**hermit-fish**, **hermit-lobster**, a crab of the family *Paguridæ* which has the habit of taking up its abode in a cast-off molluscan shell for the sake of protecting its soft shell-less hinder parts; **hermit-crow**, a name of the chough; **hermit-thrush**, a migratory thrush, *Turdus solitarius*, common in most parts of North America, and celebrated for its song; **hermit-warbler**, the western warbler, *Dendrœca occidentalis*, of the Pacific slope of North America.

1837 SWAINSON *Nat. Hist. Birds* 154 The *hermit birds.. frequently rise up perpendicularly in the air, make a swoop, and return again to their former station. **1735** MORTIMER in *Phil. Trans.* XXXIX. 115 The *Hermit-Crabs are generally found in great Plenty under these Trees. **1863** WOOD *Nat. Hist.* III. 603 Like all its race, the Hermit-crab inhabits the shell of some mollusc. **1591** SYLVESTER *Du Bartas* I. v. 401 The *Hermit-fish..that builds him a defence 'Gainst Weather's rigour and Warr's insolence. **1850** JOHNSTON *Conchol.* 81 The other tribe are the soldier or *hermit lobsters (Paguri). **1840** SWAINSON *Nat. Hist. Insects* 106 *Hermit moths..extraordinary moths hitherto found only in New Holland. **1831** —— in *Fauna Bor. Amer.* II. 185 The food of the *Hermit Thrush consists chiefly of berries. **1884** ROE *Nat. Ser. Story* vii, The chief musician of the American forests, the hermit-thrush.

Hence **'hermit**, **'hermitize** *vbs. intr.*, to live as a hermit. **'hermitism**, **'hermitry**, the mode of life of a hermit.

1610 G. FLETCHER *Christ's Tri. after Death* xlvi, When with us hermiting in lowe degree, He wash't his flocks in Jordan's spotlesse tide. **1896** *Daily News* 25 Apr. 5/1 'Hermitism' is rule of life for the middle-aged in India. **1825** HONE *Every-day Bk.* I. 286 He starved and hermitized at Hessleborough. **1844** W. H. MAXWELL *Sports & Adv. Scotl.* xii. (1855) 117 On this isolated..isle, the..Duke was left to hermitize. **1882** H. C. MERIVALE *Faucit of B.* II. vi, Hermitry must be such a bore if persevered in, the essence of life being variety.

hermitage ('hɜːmɪtɪdʒ). Forms: 3-4 ermitage, 4-5 er-, her-, heremytage, 5 armitage, (6 heremet-, 7 heremitage), 4- hermitage. See also EREMITAGE. [a. OF. *hermitage* = Pr. *ermitatge*, It. *eremitaggio*, med.L. *(h)er(e)mitagium*, f. L. *erēmīta*, med.L. *herēmīta*: see prec. and -AGE.]

1. The habitation of a hermit.

c **1290** *S. Eng. Leg.* I. 138/1131 To þe Ermitage of Semplingham. *a* **1300** *Cursor M.* 8161 Right vnto þat hermitage, [*v. rr.* ermi-, ermy-, hermytage] þe king com to and his barnage. *c* **1330** R. BRUNNE *Chron. Wace* (Rolls) 13989 Til heremytages and til abbeyes, þer men holy bodies leyes. *c* **1400** MAUNDEV. (Roxb.) xi. 46 þare er also many kirkes and chapelles and hermytages. *a* **1500** *Chaucer's Dreme* 330 Ech seven yers mote of usage, Visite the hevenly armitage. **1585** T. WASHINGTON tr. *Nicholay's Voy.* III. xix. 106 They doe not dwell in Hermitages solitarily. **1632** MILTON *Penseroso* 168 May at last my weary age Find out the peaceful hermitage, The hairy gown and mossy cell. **1669** WOODHEAD *St. Teresa* II. xxxiii. 220 It being only an Heremitage. **1756** NUGENT *Gr. Tour* IV. 265 Near the city [Nants] is a famous hermitage, situated on a rock. **1832** G. DOWNES *Lett. Cont. Countries* I. 124 The other contains a habitation (formerly, I believe, a hermitage).

b. *transf.* A solitary or secluded dwelling-place.

1648 BOYLE *Seraph. Love* (1700) 159 My urgent Occasions..will recall me to morrow Morning to my own Western Hermitage. **1649** LOVELACE *Poems* (1864) 119 Mindes innocent and quiet take That [prison] for an hermitage. **1781** FLETCHER *Lett.* Wks. 1795 VII. 235, I am not without hope of seeing you in London before you see your future hermitage. **1827** POLLOK *Course T.* v, Vesper looked forth From out her western hermitage, and smiled.

c. The condition of a hermit. *rare.*

1582 N. T. (Rhem.) *Luke* xxi. 1 *marg.*, Solitarinesse or heremitage..is a goodly thing. **1893** P. WHITE *Hist. Clare* 10 [There he] lived his lonely life of hermitage.

2. Name of a French wine produced from vineyards on a hill near Valence: so called from a ruin on the summit supposed to have been a hermit's cell.

1680 SHADWELL *Woman Capt.* I. 5 (Stanf.) *Vin de Bon, Vin Celestine*, and *Hermitage*, and all the Wines upon the fruitful Rhone. **1709** ADDISON *Tatler* No. 131 ¶7 Two more [drops] of the same Kind heightened it into a perfect Languedoc: From thence it passed into a florid Hermitage. **1756** NUGENT *Gr. Tour* IV. 36 Hermitage for those who can bear a strong wine, at three livres a bottle. **1815** M. BIRKBECK *Journ. France* 43 We approach Tournon, from whence comes the famous Hermitage wine. **1822** *Magic Lantern* 9, I thought his white hermitage better than his claret.

hermitan, obs. form of HARMATTAN.

hermitary, *sb. rare.* [ad. med.L. *herēmītārium*, f. *(h)erēmīta* HERMIT: see -ARY[1] B. 2. (Cf. OF. *hermiterie.*)] A hermit's cell; a hermitage.

1754 *Howell's Lett.* II. lxxvii. 406 Monasteries, Hermitaries [*edd.* **1655**, **1713** Hermitages],..and other religious Houses.

hermitary, *a. rare.* [ad. med.L. *(h)erēmītārius*, f. *(h)erēmīta* HERMIT: see -ARY[1]. Also EREMITARY, q.v.] Of or pertaining to a hermit.

[**1491** *Heremytarye*: see EREMITARY.] **1633** *Costlie Whore* v. i. in Bullen *O. Pl.* IV, A hermetary life is better then a kingdome, So my Valentia beare me company.

hermitess ('hɜːmɪtɪs). A female hermit.

1633 A. H. *Parthen. Sacra* 38 The Violet is truly the Hermitesse of flowers. **1708** MOTTEUX *Rabelais* IV. lxiv, Spiritual Actresses, kind Hermitesses, Women that have a plaguy deal of Religion. **1797** COLERIDGE *Christabel* I. Concl., Like a youthful hermitess, Beauteous in a wilderness. **1836** MISS MITFORD in *Gd. Words* June (1895) 382 A young creature..living in London like a hermitess.

hermithood ('hɜːmɪthʊd). [f. HERMIT *sb.*: see -HOOD.] The state or condition of a hermit.

1915 C. C. MARTINDALE *In God's Army* I. ii. 62 Vocations to hermithood are few. **1938** *Times Lit. Suppl.* 19 Nov. 745/2 Sentenced to a compulsory hermithood in a hideous African desert, the convict contrives to be brought back to Constantinople.

Hermitian (hɜːˈmɪʃən), *a. Math.* Also herm-, -ean. [ad. F. *hermitien* sb. and adj. (L. Autonne 1902, in *Rendiconti d. Circolo matem.* XVI. 104), f. the name of C. *Hermite* (1822-1905), French mathematician: see -IAN.] Applied to a matrix in which pairs of elements symmetrically placed with respect to the principal diagonal are complex conjugates, and to other quantities (such as a self-adjoint operator of transformation, or a bilinear form) whose coefficients or elements form such a matrix; ***Hermitian conjugate***, the complex conjugate of the transpose of a matrix.

1927 *Proc. R. Soc.* A. CXIII. 628 If b commutes with H, the new matrix..will be a diagonal matrix, and if in addition the elements of the matrices b and b^{-1} satisfy the condition that $b(a'a'')$ and $b^{-1}(a''a')$ are conjugate imaginaries, each matrix G will be Hermitian when the corresponding matrix g is Hermitian. **1935** P. A. M. DIRAC *Princ. Quantum Mech.* (ed. 2) ii. 29 These are just the relations required for the matrix formed by the a_{rs} to be what is called a Hermitian matrix. A linear operator that satisfies this condition may conveniently be called a Hermitian operator. **1940** E. T. BELL *Devel. Math.* xiv. 285 From Hermite's arithmetical theory of these forms..evolved the extensive theory of Hermitian forms and matrices, which after 1925 became familiar to physicists through the revised quantum theory. **1951** J. A. SCHOUTEN *Tensor Analysis for Physicists* x. 241 For co- or contravariant hermitian tensors the following theorem holds. **1961** POWELL & CRASEMANN *Quantum Mech.* ix. 295 Other matrices related to $A = (a_{ij})$, which occur frequently in the theory, are the transpose of A,..and the Hermitian conjugate of A, $A^{\dagger} = (a^{*}_{ji})$. **1965** *Czech. Math. Jrnl.* XV. 37 Let A, H be n-by-n hermitian matrices. **1967** G. G. HALL *Appl. Group Theory* iii. 33 A less obvious example is that complex Hermitean 2 × 2 matrices form a four-dimensional real Euclidean space. **1969** T. F. JORDAN *Linear Operators Quantum Mech.* ii. 23 A Hermitian operator A is characterized by the equation $(\phi, A\psi) = (A\phi, \psi)$ or $(\phi, A\psi) = (\psi, A\phi)^{*}$ holding for all vectors ψ and ϕ. **1973** *Physics Bull.* July 449/2 The analogous results for hermitean matrices.

hermitic (həˈmɪtɪk), *a.* In 7-8 erron. **hermetic**. [Altered, after *hermit*, from earlier *(h)eremitic*, a. OF. *heremitique*: cf. EREMITIC.] = next.

[**1483** *Heremytyke*: see EREMITIC.] **1691** tr. *Emilianne's Obs. Journ. Naples* 228 The Heremetick State. **1790** W. WRIGHTE *Grotesque Archit.* 3 An hermetic retreat, to be composed of roots and irregular branches of trees. **1893** *Scribner's Mag.* XIII. 344/2 Mallarmé has withdrawn into a hermitic seclusion.

her'mitical, *a.* See also EREMITICAL. [f. as prec. + -AL[1].] Of or pertaining to a hermit.

1586 D. ROWLAND tr. *Jean de Luna's Lazarillo* (1672) U iv a, Some notion of the Hermiticall life. **1615** T. ADAMS *Black Devil* 26 The melancholly man..lives an Hermitical, solitary life. **1715** BENTLEY *Serm.* x. 350 Instead of the old Hermitical Poverty they had drain'd the Riches of Kingdoms. **1882-3** A. F. MITCHELL in Schaff *Encycl. Relig. Knowl.* I. 580 [The Culdees] seem at times [in 7th century] to have formed 'hermitical establishments'.

Hence **her'mitically** *adv.*

1842 J. MACKINTOSH *Let.* in *Life* (1854) 47 Hermitically inclined I fancied myself.

'hermitish, *a. rare.* [f. HERMIT *sb.* + -ISH: cf. EREMITISH.] Like, or like that of, a hermit.

1812 BENTHAM *Wks.* (1838-43) X. 471 A hermit's life, not much less hermitish than yours.

†**hermitress.** *Obs.* [a. obs. F. *hermitresse* (Godef., Cotgr.), irreg. f. *hermite* HERMIT, after words etymologically in *-tresse*.] = HERMITESS.

1611 COTGR., *Hermitresse*, an Hermitresse; a woman Hermite. **1616** DRUMM. OF HAWTH. *Sonn.* 50 Among these pines, Sweet hermitress, she did alone repair. **1823** *Blackw. Mag.* XIV. 221 He allows Hazlitt unrelentingly to parade such words as 'Heremitress'.

hermitship ('hɜːmɪt-ʃɪp). [f. HERMIT + -SHIP.] The condition or mode of life of a hermit.

1825 LYTTON *Falkland* 7 Your jests at my hermitship and hermitage. **1842** CARLYLE *Let.* 27 Oct. in *Pall Mall G.* (1891) 23 May 3/2 Emerson does not yet go into vegetables, into rural Hermitship; and we hope never will.

Hermo-, combining form of HERMES, as in **Hermo'glyphic**, **Her'moglyphist** [cf. Gr. ἑρμογλυφικός pertaining to a statuary, f. ἑρμογλυφεύς a carver of Hermæ, a statuary] (see quots.). **Hermokopid** [ad. Gr. ἑρμοκοπίδης], a mutilator of Hermæ: in quot. used *attrib.*

1623 COCKERAM, *Hermoglipchicke*, a grauer of Images. **1820** T. MITCHELL *Aristoph.* I. p. cxvi, Sophroniscus is somewhere mentioned by Lucian as an hermoglyphist; a person, whose business it was to engrave inscriptions on marble, or rather on the Hermaic statues. **1849** GROTE *Greece* II. lviii. (1862) V. 173 The facts disclosed indicated the band of Hermokopid conspirators to be numerous.

'hermodact, shortened form of next.

1678 SALMON *Lond. Disp.* 47/2 Colchicum..is of the nature of the Hermodact. **1693** —— *Bates' Disp.* (1713) 631/1 Pouder of Hermodacts compound.

hermodactyl (hɜːməʊˈdæktɪl). *Obs.* exc. *Hist.* Also 4 **ermodattile**, 5 **hermodactule**, 6 **-ill**, 6-8 **-il(e**, 8 **-yle**. [ad. med.L. *hermodactylus*, a. Gr. ἑρμοδάκτυλος lit. Hermes' finger.]

1. A bulbous root, probably that of a species of *Colchicum*, formerly imported from the East and used in medicine. Also, the plant itself.

c **1350** *Med. MS.* in *Archæol.* XXX. 380 Medelyd wᵗ rosalgere And ermodattilis of on ȝere. *c* **1400** *Lanfranc's Cirurg.* 236 Also take..hermodactulis wiþ sugre & coold watir. *c* **1550** LLOYD *Treas. Health* (1585) Q vi, A plaster made of the rote of walwort and Hermodactiles stampte wyth Hogges grese. **1616** J. BULLOKAR *Eng. Expos.*, *Hermodactiles*, little roots white, and round, solde by Apothecaries, etc. **1681** tr. *Willis' Rem. Med. Wks.* Vocab., *Hermodactils*, or mercuries finger, white and red. **1727** BRADLEY *Fam. Dict.* s.v. *Head ach*, [To clear the Brain] you may take two Drams of Hermodactil, with some Betony and Pimpernel-Leaves. **1847** E. J. SEYMOUR *Severe Dis.* I. 90 It was found..that this plant existed in Greek physic under the name of hermodactyls.

2. Applied by Lyte to the Meadow Saffron, *Colchicum autumnale*; and later to the Snake's-head Iris, *Iris tuberosa* (*Hermodactylus tuberosus*), which was supposed to be the source of the drug.

1578 LYTE *Dodoens* III. xxxv. 366 Of Hermodactil or Mede Saffron. **1664** EVELYN *Kal. Hort.* (1729) 199 March.. Flowers in Prime, or yet lasting, *Chelidonium* small with double Flowers, *Hermodactyls*, Tuberous Iris. **1768** MILLER *Gard. Dict.* (ed. 8), *Hermodactylus*,..by some botanic writers..supposed the true Hermodactyl, but what has been long used in Europe for that is the root of a Colchicum.

hermyn, obs. form of ERMINE.

hern, **hirn** (hɜːn), *sb.* Chiefly *Sc.* (in form *hirn*, *hyrn*) or *dial.* after 1500. Forms: 1-6, 9 *dial.* hyrne, 3-5 (also 9 *dial.*) hurne, herne, 3-6 hirne, (3 huyrne, 4 huir(e)ne, heorne, 5 hierne, hyerne, heerne, h(e)yron, heryn), 5-6 hyrn, 5-8 hirn. [OE. *hyrne* wk. fem. = OFris. *herne*, ON. *hyrna* (Da. *hjörne*) corner, angle, nook:—OTeut. **hurnjôn-*, f. stem of HORN *sb.*] A corner, nook, hiding-place.

c **897** K. ÆLFRED *Gregory's Past.* xxii. 168 Ahoh hie..on ðа feower hyrnan ðære earce. *c* **1000** *Ags. Gosp.* Matt. vi. 5 Standende on ȝe-somnungum and stræta hyrnum. *c* **1200** ORMIN 1677 Icc seȝȝde þatt itt [þatt waȝheriftt] wass þær

henngedd i þatt hirne. *c* **1290** *Beket* 691 in *S. Eng. Leg.* I. 126 Þo i-saiȝ he þis holi man In one huyrne [*v.r.* hurne] stonde. **1297** R. GLOUC. (Rolls) 7343 Þat he ne ssolde abbe..an herne to wite him Inne. *a* **1340** HAMPOLE *Psalter* cxvii. 21 Þe stane þat þe edifiand reprouyd here it is made in heuyd of hyrne. **1362** LANGL. *P. Pl.* A. II. 209 And alle fledden for fere and flowen in-to huirnes [C. III. 249 hernes]. *c* **1386** CHAUCER *Can. Yeom. Prol.* 105 Lurkynge in hernes [*v.r.* hirnes] and in lanes blynde. **1387** TREVISA *Higden* (Rolls) I. 9 Laborintus, Dedalus hous, haþ many halkes and hurnes. *c* **1400** *Destr. Troy* 8390 In foure hyernes of the house. *c* **1420** *Chron. Vilod.* l. 3577 Þe sexsten..sey hem in an hyron. *Ibid.* l. 3986 Stondyng in an heyron þere. *c* **1450** *Mirour Saluacioun* 2101 My teching was noght in hirnes nor pryuitie. *c* **1485** *E.E. Misc.* (Warton Club) 43 Ever I rene fro herne to herne. **1513** DOUGLAS *Æneis* III. iv. 8 Out of the quiet hyrnis the rowt wpstartis Of thai birdis. **1590** R. BRUCE *Serm. Sacram.* (1843) 109 The maist secret hirne of the conscience. *c* **1640** J. SMYTH *Lives Berkeleys* (1883) I. 33 The barrony..with all the hernesse, that is the Nookes and Corners thereof. **1776** C. KEITH *Farmer's Ha* in Chambers *Pop. Hum. Scot. Poems* (1862) 32 To ilka hirn he taks his route. **1895** *E. Anglian Gloss.*, *Hyrne*, a corner, the portion of the village situated in an angle or corner.

b. *Comb.* † **hirn-stone**, corner-stone.

c **1000** ÆLFRIC *Hom.* (Th.) I. 106 He is se hyrn-stan þe ȝefegð þa tweȝen weallas togædere. *c* **1200** ORMIN 13358 Crist iss ec þatt hirnestan þatt bindeþþ tweȝȝenn waȝhess.

hern, herne, *arch.* and *dial.* forms of HERON (q.v.), frequent in literary use.

hern, obs. pl. of EAR *sb.*^{1}

a **1300** *Cursor M.* 8080 Lang and side þair brues wern, And hinged all a-bout þair hern [*v.rr.* eres, ern, eren].

hern, *poss. pron.*^{1} *Obs.* exc. south and *midl. dial.* Also 4 **hiren,** 5 **huron.** [f. HER *poss. pron.*^{1}, apparently by form-association with the ME. pairs *mī*, *mīn*, *thī*, *thīn* (where the derivative form arose not by adding, but by dropping *n*). Cf. *hisn*, *ourn*, *yourn*, *theirn*.] = HERS.

1340 *Ayenb.* 111 Yblissed by þe guode wyfman þet of hiren þet flour þer to dede. *c* **1340** *Cursor M.* 20016 (Trin.) Þouȝe I be vnworþi mon, Hiren am I al þat I kon. **1388** WYCLIF *2 Kings* viii. 6 Restore thou to hir alle thingis þat ben hern [**1382** hyres]. *c* **1420** *Chron. Vilod.* l. 2628 Alle his clothus and huron weron wete also. **1599** CHAPMAN *Hum. Day's Mirth* Dram. Wks. 1873 I. 98 What shall I do at the sight of her and hern? *a* **1845** HOOD *Huggins & Duggins*, How often I should stand and turn, To get a pat from hands like hern. **1876** BESANT & RICE *Gold. Butterfly* xvi. 135 It won't fall on his head, but on hern.

† **hern,** *poss. pron.*^{2} *Obs.* Forms: 4 **heoren, heren, hiren,** 5 **hern.** [f. HER *poss. pron.*^{2}; formed as prec.] = THEIRS.

c **1340** *Ayenb.* 38 Hi..beþencheþ hou hi moȝe habbe of hiren. **13..** *Minor Poems fr. Vernon MS.* xxxii. 1145–9 Heoren is þe Ioye euerlastonde..'Blesset beo þe pore in spirit ay, ffor heoren is þe kyndom þer as dwelleþ God and Mon'. *c* **1340** *Cursor M.* 6155 (Trin.) Lafte þei not þat heren was Sheepe ne cow ox ne as. *c* **1449** PECOCK *Repr.* v. i. 479 The vnwisdom of hem schal be knowe to alle men, as hern was.

hernant ('hɜːnənt). (See quots.)

1858 SIMMONDS *Dict. Trade*, *Hernant-seeds*, a commercial name for the seeds of the *Hernandia ovigera*, imported into Liverpool from India for tanning purposes. **1866** *Treas. Bot.* 585/2 *Hernant seeds*..used for dyeing.

herne, obs. form of IRON.

herner, hernery: see HERONER, HERONRY.

hernesew(e, -shaw, obs. ff. HERONSEW.

† '**hernet.** *Obs. rare*$^{-1}$. [f. HERN, HERON + -ET^{1}.] A young heron.

1615 SIR R. BOYLE *Diary* (1886) I. 72 Paying me..2 cowple of fatt capons, 2 hernetts.

‖ **hernia** ('hɜːnɪə). *Path.* Pl. **herniæ, hernias.** Also 4–5 **hirnia, -ya, hyrnya,** 6 (*Anglicized*) **herny, -ie.** [L. = rupture. Cf. F. *hernie*.]

A tumour formed by the displacement and resulting protrusion of a part of an organ through an aperture, natural or accidental, in the walls of its containing cavity; rupture.

c **1386** CHAUCER *Pars. T.* ¶ 349 Horrible swollen membres that semeth lik the maladie of Hirnia. *c* **1400** *Lanfranc's Cirurg.* 273 If hernia be watri, þis is þe signe þerof. **1547** BOORDE *Brev. Health* clxxvi. 62 b, There be thre kindes named..a wateryshe herny, a wyndy hernye, a fleshely herny. **1578** LYTE *Dodoens* I. lx. 87 Hernies, Ruptures, or burstings. **1605** B. JONSON *Volpone* III. v, That I had Nestor's hernia thou wouldst think. **1727–51** CHAMBERS *Cycl.* s.v., Hernia's are often occasioned by blows, violent concussions, over-stretching in vomiting [etc.]. **1878** T. BRYANT *Pract. Surg.* I. 644 Abdominal hernia or rupture signifies the protrusion of any viscus through an opening in the parietes of the abdominal cavity.

b. *attrib.*, as ***hernia knife, truss.***

1878 T. BRYANT *Pract. Surg.* I. 663 With a hernia knife, ..or herniotome, the stricture should then be divided.

hernial ('hɜːnɪəl), *a.* [f. prec. + -AL^{1}.] Of or pertaining to hernia; chiefly in ***hernial sac.***

1736 AMYAND in *Phil. Trans.* XXXIX. 330 The Abscess formed in the Hernial Bag occasionally. **1811** HOOPER *Med. Dict.* s.v. *Hernia*, When the hernial contents..admit of being readily put back into the abdomen, it is termed a reducible hernia. **1878** T. BRYANT *Pract. Surg.* I. 645 A hernial tumour..is composed of a sac with its contents and the soft parts covering it.

herniary ('hɜːnɪərɪ), *a.* [f. as prec. + -ARY.] Of or pertaining to hernia or its surgical treatment.

1751 STACK in *Phil. Trans.* XLVII. 325 A rupture with a double herniary sack. **1770** *Monthly Rev.* 19 Mr. Arnaud may indeed be considered a herniary surgeon. **1876** BARTHOLOW *Mat. Med.* (1879) 313 Herniary protrusion and adhesion of the iris are prevented by dilating the pupil.

herniated ('hɜːnɪeɪtɪd), *a.* [f. HERNIA + -ATE^{3} + -ED^{1}.] Affected with hernia.

1879 *St. George's Hosp. Rep.* IX. 345 The herniated portion affected but a small part of the testis at its lower part. **1885** *Lancet* 26 Sept. 566 The herniated bowel.

herniation (hɜːnɪ'eɪʃən). *Path.* [f. HERNIA + -TION.] Protrusion as in a hernia.

1897 *Allbutt's Syst. Med.* III. 712 A series of herniations of the intestinal walls. **1962** *Lancet* 22 Dec. 1332/2 Powell and Johnstone have reported the case of a mother who had taken phenmetrazine during two of her pregnancies and produced both times an infant with a defect of the left diaphragm and herniation of abdominal organs into the thoracic cavity.

hernio-, comb. form of HERNIA, as in **herni'ology,** that part of pathology which treats of hernia, a treatise on hernia. **ˌherniolapa'rotomy** [Gr. λαπάρα the flank + -τομία cutting], 'the division of the abdominal walls in order to reach a strangulated hernia which has been returned *en masse*, so that the constricting part may be divided' (*Syd. Soc. Lex.*). **hernio'puncture,** 'the puncture of a hernia by means of a capillary trocar to diminish its size and so facilitate its reduction' (*ibid.*). **hernio'rrhaphy** *Surg.* [-RRHAPHY], the operation of repairing a hernia and suturing the opening.

1919 *Surg., Gynec. & Obstetr.* XXIX. 201 Treatment of the sac in herniorrhaphy... High ligation and amputation of the hernial sac is a point..on which most surgeons are agreed. **1962** *Lancet* 27 Jan. 221/1 This problem engaged our interest in 1959 when we reviewed 762 patients who had had herniorrhaphies performed in the previous ten years. **1963** *Ibid.* 19 Jan. 133/1 A man, aged 62, who had a large indirect inguinal hernia with an associated undescended testis, underwent right inguinal herniorrhaphy and orchidectomy.

herniotome ('hɜːnɪətəʊm). *Surg.* [f. HERNIO- + Gr. -τομος cutting.] A knife used in herniotomy.

1878 [see HERNIA b]. **1879** *St. George's Hosp. Rep.* IX. 368 The stricture having been divided with herniotome.

herniotomy (hɜːnɪ'ɒtəmɪ). *Surg.* [f. as prec. + Gr. -τομία cutting.] The operation of cutting for strangulated hernia. So **herni'otomist,** one who practises herniotomy.

1811 in HOOPER *Dict. Med.* **1878** T. BRYANT *Pract. Surg.* I. 670 Herniotomy or Kelotomy is to be performed. **1885** *Lancet* 26 Sept. 566 Herniotomy was performed, the sac being opened. **1897** W. ANDERSON *Jr. Arderne* 7 Lithotomists, herniotomists, oculists, and others.

† '**hernious,** *a. Obs.* [ad. med.L. *herniōsus*, f. *hernia*.] Affected with hernia.

1398 TREVISA *Barth. De P.R.* VII. lv. (1495) 270 Hernyous men that ben soo broke. **1623** COCKERAM, *Hernious*, a.. broken person. [*a* **1648** LD. HERBERT *Life* Wks. (1886) 192 He was burst in the body as we call it, or herniosus.]

hernsew, -shaw, -shew: see HERONSEW.

hero ('hɪərəʊ), *sb.* Pl. **heroes** ('hɪərəʊz). Forms: 6–7 **heros, heroë,** 6–8 **heroe,** 7– **hero;** *pl.* 4–7 **heroës,** 7– **heroes** (7 **hero's**). [Ultimately ad. L. *hērō-s*, pl. *hērō-ēs*, a. Gr. ἥρω-ς, pl. ἥρω-ες. In early use the L. or Gr. singular *hērōs* and pl. *hē'rō-ēs* appear unchanged (cf. F. *héros* sing. from 14th c.); beside them is also found a sing. '*hero-ë* like obs. F. *heroë* (Cotgr.), It. *eroe*, Sp. *heroe*; this became later *he-roe*, and finally *hero*. The pl. *heroes* is now disyllabic.]

1. *Antiq.* A name given (as in Homer) to men of superhuman strength, courage, or ability, favoured by the gods; at a later time regarded as intermediate between gods and men, and immortal.

The later notion included men of renown supposed to be deified on account of great and noble deeds, for which they were also venerated generally or locally; also demigods, said to be the offspring of a god or goddess and a human being; the two classes being to a great extent coincident.

verse of heroes, the hexameter.

1387 TREVISA *Higden* (Rolls) II. 401 [Sibylla Erythræa] wroot moche of Criste, and þat openliche, as in þis vers of heroes. **1555** EDEN *Decades* To Rdr. (Arb.) 49 Goddes made of men whom the antiquitie cauled Heroes. **1591** SPENSER *Virg. Gnat* 480 And you beside the honourable band Of great Heroës doo in order stand. *Ibid.* 593 Here manie other like Heroës bee. **1613–16** W. BROWNE *Brit. Past.* II. iv, So by Heröes were we led of yore. **1615** CHAPMAN *Odyss.* IV. 420 And what, my young Ulyssean heroë, Provoked thee on the broad back of the sea, To visit Lacedaemon the divine? **1621** BURTON *Anat. Mel.* I. ii. I. ii. (1651) 45 Plato..made nine kinds of [spirits]..4 Arch-Angels, 5 Angels, 6 Devils, 7 Heroes. **1621** G. SANDYS *Ovid's Met.* IV. (1626) 83 Whom when the Heros saw to hard rocks chaind..He would haue thought her marble. **1632** HEYWOOD *1st Pt. Iron Age* I. i. Wks. 1874 III. 266 Great Laomedon Denied the Heroe, both the meede propos'd. **1681** H. MORE *Exp. Dan.* ii. 57 The Vision of that Divine Heros on the white Horse. **1684** T. BURNET *Th. Earth* II. 220 Mighty men of old, or hero's. **1697** DRYDEN *Virg. Georg.* III. 56 Resembling Heroes, whose Etherial Root Is Jove himself. **1712** ADDISON *Spect.* No. 417 ¶ 6 Homer is in his Province, when he is describing ..a Heroe or a God. **1763** J. BROWN *Poetry & Mus.* iv. 42 A Chief sings some great Action of a God or Heroe. **1791** COWPER *Iliad* IV. 225 The Hero seeking earnest on all sides Machaon. **1840** THIRLWALL *Greece* VII. 199 He continued ..to receive marks of public reverence approaching to the worship of a hero.

2. A man distinguished by extraordinary valour and martial achievements; one who does brave or noble deeds; an illustrious warrior.

1586 WARNER *Alb. Eng.* III. xvi. 63 After silence short, The Brutaine Heros vailed, and did answere in this sort. **1600** W. WATSON *Decacordon* IX. v. (1602) 305 All the heroeces, nobles and gentles of these northern Isles. **1601** SHAKS. *All's Well* II. i. 40 Nobles, Heroes; my sword and yours are kinne. **1684** *Scanderbeg Rediv.* vi. 155 He is Master of all the Gallantry of Antient Hero's. **1727–46** THOMSON *Summer* 1501 Raleigh..whose breast with all The sage, the patriot, and the hero burn'd. **1747** MORELL *Joshua* Chorus, See, the conquering hero comes. **1862** *Sat. Rev.* 13 Sept. 302 The hero must, to give meaning to a meaningless phrase, fight for an idea..There is very little room for heroes in wars carried on to settle successions, to rectify frontiers, or to maintain the balance of power. **1885** EDNA LYALL *In Golden Days* I. v. 160 For already Sydney had become his hero of heroes.

3. A man who exhibits extraordinary bravery, firmness, fortitude, or greatness of soul, in any course of action, or in connexion with any pursuit, work, or enterprise; a man admired and venerated for his achievements and noble qualities.

1661 GLANVILL *Van. Dogmatizing* xxiv. 240 The sole Instances of those illustrious Heroes, Cartes, Gassendus, Galilæo, Tycho [etc.] will strike dead the opinion of the worlds decay. **1676** DRYDEN *Aurengz.* I. i, Who would not be the hero of an age? **1707** *Lond. Gaz.* No. 4343/1 Some other Protestant Hero like your Majesty. **1764** FOOTE *Patron* II. Wks. 1799 I. 340 No man is a hero to his *valet de chambre*. **1768** JOHNSON *Pref. to Shaks.* Wks. IX. 245 Shakespeare has no heroes; his scenes are occupied only by men, who act and speak as the reader thinks that he should himself have spoken or acted on the same occasion. **1853** MAURICE *Proph. & Kings* iii. 44 David no doubt became a hero in the eyes of the men and the virgins of Israel.

4. The man who forms the subject of an epic; the chief male personage in a poem, play, or story; he in whom the interest of the story or plot is centred.

1697 DRYDEN *Virg.*, *Life* (1721) I. 62 His Heroe falls into an..ill-tim'd Deliberation. **1711** STEELE *Spect.* No. 11 ¶ 5 The Youth, who is the Hero of my Story. **1770** *Junius Lett.* xxxviii. 188 The pomp of a mock tragedy, where..even the sufferings of the hero are calculated for derision. **1841** ELPHINSTONE *Hist. Ind.* I. iv. 175 The great Hindú heroic poem, the 'Mahá Bhárat', of which Crishna is, in fact, the hero. **1866** TROLLOPE *Claverings* xxviii, Perhaps no terms have been so injurious to the profession of the novelist as those two words, hero and heroine. In spite of the latitude which is allowed to the writer in putting his own interpretation upon these words, something heroic is still expected; whereas, if he attempt to paint from Nature, how little that is heroic should he describe!

5. *attrib.* and *Comb.* **a.** appositive, as ***hero-child, -horseman, -king, -leader, -martyr, -saint, -son, -soul, -woman***; **b.** attributive, as ***hero-air, -apartment, -cult, -dust, -fantasy, -figure, -form, -image, -race, -saga***; **c.** objective, as ***hero-nurser***; **d.** similative, as ***hero-like*** adj.; **e. hero-errant** [after *knight-errant*], a hero wandering in quest of adventures; **hero sandwich** *U.S. slang*, a very large sandwich; also *ellipt.* **hero.** Also HERO-WORSHIP *sb.*

1756–7 tr. *Keysler's Trav.* (1760) IV. 306 In the *hero-apartment, as it is called, besides the old Saxon warriors.. are to be seen the portraits of all the generals employed by king Augustus. **1871** TYLOR *Prim. Cult.* II. Index 417 *Hero-children suckled by beasts. **1945** KOESTLER *Yogi & Commissar* III. ii. 197 His famous speech on the 24th anniversary of the Soviet Revolution..which started the new *hero-cult. **1814** BYRON *Ode to Napoleon* xii, *Hero dust Is vile as vulgar clay. **1768–74** TUCKER *Lt. Nat.* (1852) II. 147 If Persia be subdued, our *hero-errant must seek adventures at the Ganges. **1960** C. DAY LEWIS *Buried Day* 22 Nor..did I indulge in the *hero-fantasies of the only child. **1958** *Punch* 23 July 102/3 But surely his agent..built up an image of this untalented scallywag as a top-line genius and *hero-figure for millions who little guessed? **1963** *Times Lit. Suppl.* 11 Jan. 29/3 The bodily posture adopted by Japanese hero-figures. **1776** MICKLE tr. *Camoens' Lusiad* 327 That *hero-form the Lusian standard rears. **1862** RAWLINSON *Anc. Mon.* I. iii. 68 The *hero-founder Nimrod. **1951** M. MCLUHAN *Mech. Bride* 63/1 Li'l Abner himself is a cluster of the swarming *hero images. **1840** ARNOLD *Hist. Rome* II. 266 Alexander's genuine successor, the *hero-king of the race of Achilles. **1670** DRYDEN *Grenada* (Jod.), Thence *herolike with torches by my side.. my love I'll guide. **1706** WATTS *Horæ Lyr.* II. *To W. Blackburn* v, But there's a heavenly art t' elude the grave, And with the *hero race immortal kindred claim. **1863** W. PHILLIPS *Speeches* xiii. 291, I thought I could hear our *hero-saint saying, 'I give my sword to the slave'. **1955** *Sat. Even. Post* 1 Jan. 16 When he got back to Brooklyn, the first thing he asked for was an Italian *hero sandwich.., two inches thick and eighteen inches long. **1957** *Britannica Bk. of Year* 512/1 *Hero-sandwich*, a sandwich made with a whole loaf of bread. **1959** R. CONDON *Manchurian Candidate* v. 91 She wiped her mouth with the back of her hand like a labourer who had just finished a hero sandwich and a bottle of beer. **1963** M. SCHERF *Death & Diplomat* (1964) v. 62

They have hot and cold heros next door. **1972** *New Yorker* 1 July 21/2 An office just above a hero-sandwich shop. **1870** BRYANT *Iliad* I. I. 6 Then the *hero-son of Atreus rose. **1860** GEO. ELIOT in *Life* (1885) II. 244 An almost unique presentation of a *hero-woman.

Hence (chiefly nonce-wds.), **hero** *v. trans.*, to make a hero of; to honour as a hero. **ˈheroarchy** [after *hierarchy*], rule or government of heroes. **ˈherohead, -hood, -ship**, the state, position, or character of a hero. **heˈrolatry** [after *idolatry*], hero-worship. **ˈheroless** *a.*, without a hero. **heroˈogony** [cf. *theogony*], generation of heroes. **herooˈlogical** *a.*, pertaining to the history of heroes. **heroˈologist**, one who writes or discourses of heroes. **heroˈology** (also ***heˈrology***), a history of or treatise on heroes. **heˈrotheism** [Gr. θέος god]: see quot.

1883 MRS. MITCHELL *Hist. Anc. Sculpt.* 212 Statues..not of gods, but *heroed mortals. **1840** CARLYLE *Heroes* i. (1858) 193 All dignities of rank, on which human association rests, are what we may call a *Heroarchy (Government of Heroes). **1895** *Athenæum* 31 Aug. 284/3 The dim past, before the Olympian divinities had come southwards to absorb their predecessors and degrade..their godhead to *herohead. **1843** CARLYLE *Past & Pr.* II. vii, All his *herohood and insight. **1864** SKEAT *Uhland's Poems* 71, I was not nourished For lofty hero-hood. **1806** *Edin. Rev.* VII. 487 The distinction between *herolatry and theolatry, or the sacred rites of heroes and the sacred rites of Gods, was perfectly well known in Greece. **1882** *Athenæum* 9 Sept. 329/3 The history of Ireland is also almost—if we may use the term —*heroless. **1880** J. DAVIES in *Encycl. Brit.* XI. 777/2 A brief and abruptly terminated *heroogony, or generation of heroes by immortal sires from mortal mothers. **1678** CUDWORTH *Intell. Syst.* I. iv. §32. 510 Eusebius..was of opinion that those poetick fables were at first only historical and *herological. **1774** WARTON *Hist. Eng. Poetry* xlvii. III. 195 Holland the *heroologist. **1678** CUDWORTH *Intell. Syst.* I. iv. §14. 257 A certain Mixture of Physiology and *Herology or History blended together. **1880** J. S. STALLYBRASS tr. *Grimm's Teut. Mythol.* xv. I. 366 We may conclude that all the Teutonic races had a pretty fully developed Heroology. **1784** COWPER *Task* iv. 644 His three years of *heroship expired. **1801** W. TAYLOR in *Monthly Mag.* XI. 646 *Herotheism, or the worship of deified men.

herocane, obs. form of HURRICANE.

herocism: see HEROISM.

Herodian (hɪˈrəʊdɪən), *a.* and *sb.*[1] [ad. L. *Hērōdiān-us*, a. Gr. Ἡρωδιαν-ός of or pertaining to Herod, *subst. pl.* followers of Herod: see -IAN.]

A. *adj.* 1. Of or pertaining to Herod, king of Judæa (B.C. 38–4), or to members of his family of the same name; built by Herod. ***Herodian disease***: phthiriasis or other loathsome skin disease, like that of which Herod Agrippa died (Acts xii. 23).

1633 EARL MANCH. *Al Mondo* (1636) 153 We may not wash our hands of crying, and from bloudy sins, and hug in our bosomes beloved, and Herodian sinnes, sinnes of higher tincture. **1650** WELDON *Crt. Jas. I*, 13 He dyed opportunely ..to leave a mark of ignominy on himselfe by that Herodian disease. **1861** *Sat. Rev.* 21 Dec. 644 For the Herodian period of Jerusalem the chief, or rather only, authority is Josephus.

2. Blustering, grandiose, magniloquent; after the style attributed to Herod in the miracle-plays. (Cf. OUT-HEROD.)

1886 F. YORK POWELL in *Academy* 15 May 337/2 The plain sensible style of this book is pleasantly in contrast with the Herodian vein of many local histories.

B. *sb. pl.* A Jewish party, mainly political, who were partisans of the Herodian or Idumæan dynasty (chiefly under Herod Antipas, B.C. 4–A.D. 39), and lax in their adherence to Judaism. Hence *transf.* as a term of reproach.

[*c* **1000** *Ags. Gosp.* Mark xii. 13 Sume of phariseum and herodianum.] **1382** WYCLIF *ibid.*, Summe of the Farisees and Erodians. *c* **1400** *Apol. Loll.* 56 Prelats not preching are raþer pilats than prelatis,..herodians of Heroud, not heyris of Crist. *a* **1592** H. SMITH *Serm.* 451 They jumpe with Caesar, like the Herodians. **1727–41** CHAMBERS *Cycl.* s.v., F. Hardouin will have the Herodians and Sadduces to have been the same thing. **1838** *Penny Cycl.* XII. 163/1 The Herodians are not mentioned either by Philo or by Josephus in his enumeration of the Jewish sects.

herodian (həˈrəʊdɪən), *sb.*[2] [In sense 1, irreg. f. Gr. ἐρωδι-ός heron, heronshaw + -AN. In sense 2, f. mod.L. *herōdi-us*, repr. Gr. ἐρωδιός.]

†1. A heron. *Obs.*

1609 BIBLE (Douay) *Lev.* xi. 19 The herodian, and the charadrion according to his kind.

2. *Ornith.* One of an order of birds, *Herodii* or *Herodiones*, comprising the herons, storks, ibises, and spoonbills.

Herodotean (hɪrɒdəˈtiːən), *a.* [f. the name of *Herodotus* (Gr. Ἡρόδοτος), Greek historian of the fifth century B.C.: see -AN.] Of, pertaining to, characteristic of, or mentioned by Herodotus.

1856 K. H. DIGBY *Lover's Seat* II. xiii. 67 They are remarkably Herodotean in their style of operation. **1857** DUFFERIN *Lett. High Lat.* 54 The Herodotean work of Sturleson. **1872** W. MINTO *Man. Eng. Prose Lit.* II. vi. 413 A Herodotean knack of giving numerical measures of extent. **1881** *Athenæum* 2 Apr. 456/2 Some of the reports which he received he recounts with Herodotean incredulity. **1883** *Macm. Mag.* May 67/2 This is what I mean by calling him Herodotean. Nothing was too small nor too apparently remote from the main studies of his life to escape him or be without interest for him.

†**ˈheroess.** *Obs.* Also 7 heroisse. [f. HERO + -ESS. Cf. rare Gr. ἡρώισσα.] = HEROINE.

1612 R. SHELDON *Serm. St. Martins* 48 That Heroisse [Q. Elizabeth] being departed. **1615** CHAPMAN *Odyss.* XI. 445 All th' heroesses in Pluto's house. **1694** tr. *Milton's Lett. State* 4 July an. 1654, A Heroess so matchless in all degrees of Praise and masculine Renown. **1715** tr. *C'tess D'Aunoy's Wks.* 6, I then forgot all that Romances had taught me concerning the Disdain and Pride of their Heroesses.

herohead, -hood: see HERO.

heroic (hɪˈrəʊɪk), *a.* and *sb.* [ad. L. *hērōic-us*, Gr. ἡρωϊκός pertaining to heroes, f. ἥρως HERO. Cf. F. *héroïque* (15th c. in Hatz.-Darm.).]

A. *adj.*

1. Of or pertaining to a hero or heroes; characteristic of, or suitable to the character of a hero; of a bravery, virtue, or nobleness of character, exalted above that of ordinary men.

a. Of actions, qualities, etc.

1549 *Compl. Scot.* 2 3our heroyque vertu is of mair admiratione, nor vas of valeria the dochtir of the prudent consul publicola. **1596** SPENSER *F.Q.* v. i. 1 But evermore some of the vertuous race Rose up, inspired with heroicke heat. **1634** SIR T. HERBERT *Trav.* 75 Requested..his death might be given him, by such a Heroicke hand as his, rather then perish by the rascall multitude. **1671** MILTON *Samson* 1711 Samson hath quit himself Like Samson, and heroicly hath finish'd A life heroic. **1713** STEELE *Guardian* No. 20 ¶4 There is something sublime and heroick in true meekness and humility. **1802** WORDSW. *Sonn.*, '*Milton! thou shouldst be living*', The heroic wealth of hall and bower. **1834** L. RITCHIE *Wand. by Seine* 153 The choir of the cathedral..is rich in heroic dust. **1849** MACAULAY *Hist. Eng.* ii. I. 167 The heroic death of his father.

b. Of persons, etc.: Of the nature of a hero.

1591 SHAKS. *1 Hen. VI*, II. v. 78 Whereas hee, From Iohn of Gaunt doth bring his Pedigree, Being but fourth of that Heroick Lyne. **1615** J. STEPHENS *Satyr. Ess.* 84 To exceed the patterne of heroicke Ancestry. **1638** SIR T. HERBERT *Trav.* (ed. 2) 67 The Decans turn back, leaving their heroick Captaine Godgee slaine in the field. **1657** R. LIGON *Barbadoes* 105 So noble and heroick a Bird. **1790** BURKE *Fr. Rev.* Wks. V. 36 This would be to act over again the scene of the criminals condemned to the gallies, and their heroick deliverer. **1878** MORLEY *Crit. Misc.* Ser. I. *Carlyle* 196 The distinction between the truly heroic ruler of the stamp of Cromwell, and the arbitrary enthusiast for external order, like Frederick.

2. Of or pertaining to the heroes of antiquity. ***heroic age*** or ***time***: that during which the ancient heroes existed; the period of Grecian history preceding the return from Troy; also *transf.*

1667 MILTON *P.L.* I. 577 The Giant brood Of Phlegra with th' Heroic Race..That fought at Theb's and Ilium. **1669** GALE *Crt. Gentiles* I. III. ii. 27 The ancient Mythologie, conteining fabulous narrations of the ancient Heroic times. **1697** DRYDEN *Æneid* VI. 881 Here found they Teucer's old heroic race. **1835** THIRLWALL *Greece* I. v. 123 The period included between the first appearance of the Hellenes in Thessaly, and the return of the Greeks from Troy, is commonly known by the name of the heroic age, or ages. **1850** LEITCH *Müller's Anc. Art* §410. 553 The heroic-ideal is expressed with highest force in Hercules..pre-eminently an Hellenic national hero. **1869** RAWLINSON *Anc. Hist.* 124 The simple hereditary monarchy of the heroic times. **1897** W. P. KER *Epic & Romance* i. 7 What the 'heroic age' of the modern nations really was, may be learned from what is left of their heroic literature, especially from three groups or classes,—the old Teutonic alliterative poems on native subjects; the French *Chansons de Geste*; and the Icelandic Sagas. **1912** H. M. CHADWICK *Heroic Age* v. 105 This carries us back..to what we may call the Russian Heroic Age. **1927** E. V. GORDON *Introd. Old Norse* p. xxix, The Germanic heroic age of the fourth to seventh centuries. **1928** W. W. LAWRENCE *Beowulf & Epic Trad.* 24 This was the usual procedure of a minstrel of the Heroic Age, who knew of all notable men about the circle of the seas. **1948** K. MALONE in *English Studies* XXIX. 170 All these passages serve to make our hero part and parcel of the heroic age of Germanic antiquity. **1965** K. SISAM *Struct. Beowulf* 7 The doors of Heorot opened into the Heroic Age.

3. a. Relating to or describing the deeds of heroes; of a poem or poetry = epic; so ***heroic poet***.

1581 SIDNEY *Apol. Poetrie* (Arb.) 28 The most notable [denominations of poesie] bee the Heroick, Lirick, Tragick [etc.]. **1589** PUTTENHAM *Eng. Poesie* I. xi. (Arb.) 40 Such therefore as gaue themselues to write long histories of the noble gests of kings and great Princes entermedling the dealings of the gods, halfe gods or Heroes..they called Poets Heroick, whereof Homer was chief and most auncient among the Greeks, Virgill among the Latines. **1667** MILTON *P.L.* IX. 25 This Subject for Heroic Song. **1693** DRYDEN *Juvenal* Ded. (1697) 26 An Heroique Poem is certainly the greatest Work of Human Nature. **1777** SIR W. JONES *Ess. Poetry E. Nations* 185 In comparing Homer with the heroick poets who have succeeded him. **1838** ARNOLD *Hist. Rome* (1846) I. vi. 100 The old heroic lays of Rome.

b. Of verse or metre: Used in heroic poetry. In Greek and Latin poetry it was the hexameter; in English, German, and Italian, the iambic of five feet or ten syllables; in French, the Alexandrine of twelve syllables.

1617 MORYSON *Itin.* I. 91 Andrew Morosini, who wrote the History of his time in Heroique Verse. **1693** DRYDEN *Juvenal* Ded. (1697) 88 The English Verse, which we call Heroique, consists of no more than Ten Syllables. **1817** COLERIDGE *Biog. Lit.* 267 In English we could commonly render one Greek heroic line in a line and a half of our common heroic metre. **1861** F. HALL in *Jrnl. Amer. Orient. Soc.* VII 23 The third hemistich of the heroic measure.

c. Of the style or language used in heroic poetry; magniloquent, grand; hence, high-flown, exaggerated.

1591 SPENSER *Teares Muses* 431 Whose living praises in heroick style, It is my chiefe profession to compyle. **1665** BOYLE *Occas. Refl.* Pref. (1845) 21 The Style of his Georgicks, as well Noble (if not strictly Heroick) as that of his Æneids. **1735** POPE *Prol. Sat.* 109 One dedicates in high heroic prose, And ridicules beyond a hundred foes. **1888** F. M. PEARD *His Cousin Betty* I. v. 106 John's prowess was painted in heroic colours. **1897** *Westm. Gaz.* 26 Aug. 3/1 We publish this..because it expresses in inflamed and heroic language a theory which..is becoming quite undeservedly popular among a certain class of politicians.

4. Having recourse to bold, daring, or extreme measures; boldly experimental; attempting great things.

1664 POWER *Exp. Philos.* 191 'Tis a Noble resolution to begin there where all the world has ended; and an Heroick attempt to solve those difficulties. **1836** GULLY *Magendie's Formul.* 117 Dr. Andrew Buchanan..has..shown how iodine may be given in most heroic doses without producing any of the disagreeable effects..on the digestive mucous membrane. **1880** MCCARTHY *Own Times* IV. lviii. 257 The country was in a temper to try heroic remedies. **1887** GOLDW. SMITH in *Times* (weekly ed.) 9 Dec. 7/2 Common-place reforms, which heroic legislation has overlooked.

5. In statuary: Of a size between life and colossal.

1794 T. TAYLOR *Pausanias* III. 76 But in Haliartus there is..an heroic monument of Cecrops, the son of Pandion.

6. *humorously*. Unusually large or powerful.

1850 L. HUNT *Autobiog.* II. xvii. 240 The men shaved themselves elaborately, cultivating heroic whiskers. **1875** HAMERTON *Intell. Life* I. iii. 20 His usual allowance was sixteen cups [of tea], all of heroic strength.

7. *Comb.* (parasynth.), as ***heroic-built, -minded*** adjs.

1667 MILTON *P.L.* IX. 485 Her Husband..of limb Heroic built, though of terrestrial mould. **1678** BUTLER *Hud.* III. i. 1372 Condemn'd to whipping, but declin'd it, By being more heroic-minded.

B. *sb.* †1. a. A man of heroic nature, a hero; *esp.* a personage of the heroic age, a demigod. b. Applied to a cavalier or royalist. *Obs.*

1613 JACKSON *Creed* I. xi. §3 Many other particular circumstances of his [Homer's] gods assisting the ancient heroics. **1625** *Ibid.* v. xxi. §4 Offering of sacrifices to the ancient heroics of Greece. **1667** WATERHOUSE *Fire Lond.* 143 O Lord..raise up the spirit of the Nehemiahs and such other Heroicks. **1682** MRS. BEHN *Round-heads* I. i, *Gill.* Heavens, Madam, I'll warrant they were Heroicks. *Lady L.* Heroicks! *Gill.* Cavaliers, Madam, of the Royal Party.

2. a. Heroic verse: chiefly in plural.

1596 NASHE *Saffron Walden* 4 When he was but yet a fresh-man in Cambridge, he..sent his accounts to his father in those ioulting Heroicks [Hexameters]. **1693** DRYDEN *Juvenal* Ded. (1697) 82, I wou'd prefer the Verse of Ten Syllables, which we call the English Heroique, to that of Eight. **1737** POPE *Hor. Epist.* II. ii. 82 When this Heroicks only deigns to praise, Sharp Satire that, and that Pindaric lays. **1779–81** JOHNSON *L.P., Pope* Wks. IV. 118 In heroicks, that may be admitted which ennobles, though it does not illustrate. **1807** SOUTHEY *Espriella's Lett.* I. 3 Some new Cervantes..to write a mock heroic. **1814** L. HUNT *Feast Poets*, etc. Pref. (1815) 14 The various and legitimate harmony of the English heroic.

b. *pl.* Sarcastically applied to high-flown or bombastic language, or sentiments thereby expressed.

1700 FARQUHAR *Const. Couple* v. i, This is the first whore in heroics that I have met with. **1754** RICHARDSON *Grandison* (1781) I. xiv. 82 Miss Barnevelt took a tilt in heroics. **1847** TENNYSON *Princ.* Concl. 64 In mock heroics stranger than our own. **1862** 'SHIRLEY' *Nugæ Crit.* vii. 308 Women, it is said, can write powerfully, but they cannot write moderately. They are always in hysterics or heroics. **1879** FROUDE *Cæsar* viii. 83 He [Cæsar] had no sentimental passion about him; no Byronic mock heroics.

†3. A heroic poet. *Obs.*

a **1680** BUTLER *Rem.* (1759) I. 172 Virgil..To whom th' Heroics ever since Have sworn Allegiance as their Prince.

Hence †**heˈroic** *v. nonce-wd.*, in ***to heroic it***, to write in heroic verse; **heˈroicism, heroˈicity, heˈroicness**, heroic character or quality = HEROISM; **heˈroicize** *v. trans.*, to make heroic; to exalt to the position of a hero; **heˈroicly** *adv.* = HEROICALLY.

1599 NASHE *Lenten Stuffe* 23 Homer of rats and frogs hath heroiqut it. **1648** W. MOUNTAGUE *Devout Ess.* I. xiv. §3. 190 There is more happynesse in the one, but more Heroicknesse in the other. **1648** EARL WESTMORELAND *Otia Sacra* (1879) 148 Things to whet, not try Thine own Heroicism by. **1671** MILTON *Samson* 1710 And heroicly hath finished A life heroic, on his enemies Fully revenged. **1673** *Rem. Humours Town* 59 You throw away your glorious Precepts, whilst you talk of Heroickness, to an impertinent and groveling Generation. **1847** FABER *Life St. Rose of Lima* p. xi, [A work] which treats of heroic virtue and what constitutes its heroicity. **1897** *Folk-Lore* Mar. 49 At times, as in the case of Arthur..it has become wholly heroicised, and the semi-divine child has to conform to the heroic standard.

heroical (hɪˈrəʊɪkəl), *a.* [f. as prec. + -AL[1].]

†1. = HEROIC *a.* 1. *Obs.* or *arch.*

1555 EDEN *Decades* To Rdr. (Arb.) 50 The heroicall factes of the Spaniardes of these days deserue so greate prayse. **1643** PRYNNE *Sov. Power Parl.* Ded. A ij b, One person of the exquisitest judgement, Heroicallest Spirit. **1700** DRYDEN *Fables* Ded. Wks. (Globe) 490 Though you have courage in a heroical degree. **1748** HARTLEY *Observ. Man* II. iii. 319 The Bulk of Mankind are at a Loss to believe the

Possibility of very heroical, generous, pious Actions. 1803 E. Hay *Insurr. Wexf.* Introd. 19 He manifested a most heroical disposition at the battles of Ross and Fooks's Mill. 1814 Mrs. J. West *Alicia de Lacy* I. 83 She would imitate such heroical subjection of personal desires.

†**b.** Of persons: = HEROIC *a.* 1 b. *Obs.* or *arch.*

1599 Shaks. *Hen. V*, II. iv. 59 His Mountaine Sire.. Saw his Heroicall Seed, and smil'd to see him Mangle the Worke of Nature. 1617 Moryson *Itin.* III. 16 That Heroicall Woman, Elizabeth late Queene of England. 1654 Trapp *Comm. Ps.* ii. 4 Luther, that Heroical Reformer, was Excommunicated by the Pope. 1743 in Entick *London* (1766) 417 To the memory of this most heroical person. 1824 Landor *Imag. Conv.* (1826) I. 390 Mezentius, the most heroical of all the characters in that poem.

†**c.** Grand, magnificent. *Obs.*

1577 Harrison *England* II. v. (1877) I. 116 Magnificent apparell both of stuffe and fashion exquisite and heroicall. 1604 R. Cawdrey *Table Alph., Heroicall*, beseeming a noble man, or magnificent. 1683 Evelyn *Diary* 16 June, Verrio's invention is admirable, his ordnance full and flowing, antique and heroical.

2. = HEROIC *a.* 2.

1553 Eden *Treat. Newe Ind.* Ded. (Arb.) 5 Howe excellently the Poet Homere had set forth his heroical factes. 1692 Washington tr. *Milton's Def. Pop.* M.'s Wks. 1738 I. 519 The fourth sort he makes of such as reigned in the Heroical days. 1859 Kingsley *Misc.* (1860) I. 1 When we read the history of heroical times and heroical men. 1871 R. Ellis *Catullus* lxviii. 92 Altar of heroes Troy, Troy of heroical acts.

3. = HEROIC *a.* 3.

1514 Barclay *Cyt. & Uplondyshm.* (Percy Soc.) p. lxvii, They count them poetes hye & heroicall. 1581 Sidney *Apol. Poetrie* (Arb.) 28 Xenophon.. made therein [in *Cyropædia*] an absolute heroicall Poem. 1863 Mrs. C. Clarke *Shaks. Char.* xvii. 416 This division of the play—the heroical—is conceived in the very highest spirit of chivalry.

†**b.** = HEROIC *a.* 3 b. *Obs.*

1546 Langley *Pol. Verg. De Invent.* I. viii. 17 a, Heroical meter is so called of the valiaunt dedes of armes of noble men that be contained in it. 1576 Fleming *Panopl. Epist.* 377 To write in heroicall Verses. 1599 Hakluyt *Voy.* II. I. 30 He.. handled the same Argument in Heroicall verse.

4. = HEROIC *a.* 5.

1770 J. Baretti *Journ. Lond. to Genoa* II. lv. 287 These statues are of that size that sculptors call heroical. 1840 Thackeray *Paris Sk.-bk.* (1872) 249 We have set up in our hearts a grand image of him endowed with wit.. and enormous heroical stature.

heroically (hɪˈrəʊɪkəlɪ), *adv.* [f. prec. + -LY².] **1.** In a heroic manner; after the way of heroes; with exalted bravery and fortitude.

a 1586 Sidney (J.), Not heroically in killing his tyrannical cousin. 1691–8 Norris *Pract. Disc.* (1711) III. 238 They represent it.. as something heroically excellent, the top and height of the Christian profession. 1743 H. Walpole *Lett. H. Mann* (1834) I. lxxxi. 285, I will bear this misfortune as heroically as I can. 1855 Macaulay *Hist. Eng.* xx. (1889) II. 445 The Jacobites.. represented him.. as a martyr who had heroically laid down his life for the banished King and the persecuted Church.

2. In the manner of heroic poetry.

1595 Spenser *Col. Clout* 447 Whose Muse.. Doth like himselfe Heroically sound. 1664 Dryden *Rival Ladies* Ded., Some.. if they were to write in blank verse, *Sir, I ask your pardon*, would think it sounded more heroically to write, *Sir, I your pardon ask.*

3. With 'heroic' medical or surgical treatment.

1889 J. M. Duncan *Lect. Dis. Wom.* xiii. (ed. 4) 94 She was the *protégée* of all the Ladies Bountiful in the neighbourhood, so that the doctors were afraid to treat her heroically.

heˈroicalness. [f. as prec. + -NESS.] Heroic character or quality.

a 1648 Digby (cited by Ogilvie). 1689 *Answ. 2 Papers* 38 The Heroicalness of his Temper, and Nobleness of his Soul. 1748 Richardson *Clarissa* (1811) V. viii. 121 In violent pain, that with all your heroicalness would make you mad.

heroi-ˈcomic, *a.* [f. Gr. ἥρω-ς HERO + COMIC.] That combines the heroic with the comic; of the nature of a burlesque on the heroic. So **heroi-comical** *a.*

1712–14 Pope (*title*) The Rape of the Lock. An Heroi-comical Poem. 1756 J. Warton *Ess. Pope* I. iv. 205 An heroi-comic poem may therefore be justly esteemed as the most excellent kind of satire. 1816 Singer *Hist. Cards* 241 The Heroi-comic Poem of *Il Malmantile Racquistato*. 1850 W. Irving *Goldsmith* x. 135 As to the heroi-comical poem.. it appears to have perished.

heroid (hɪˈrəʊɪd). [ad. L. *Hērōides*, the title of the Epistles of Ovid, according to Priscian, a. Gr. ἡρωΐδες, plur. of ἡρωΐς heroine.] A poem in epistolary form, expressive of the sentiments of some hero or heroine: from the *Heroïdes* of Ovid, which take the form of letters to heroes from their wives or sweethearts.

1795 W. Taylor in *Monthly Rev.* XVI. 166 The most important pieces in the first volume.. are Heroids, or heroic epistles; a form of composition probably invented by Ovid.

heroify (hɪˈrəʊɪfaɪ), *v.* [f. L. *hērō-em* HERO + -FY: cf. *deify*.] To make a hero of; to exalt to the position of a hero. Hence **heroified** *ppl. a.*

1812 L. Hunt in *Examiner* 14 Sept. 577/1 Lord Wellington was heroified in a similar manner. 1846 Grote *Greece* (1854) I. 552 Representing both gods and heroes as having been mere earthborn men.. deified or heroified after death as a recompense for services or striking exploits. 1882 Waldstein *Pythag. Rhegion* 13 That [statue] of a heroified pugilist, Euthymos.

heroin (ˈhɛrəʊɪn; formerly also hɪˈrəʊɪn). [a. G. *heroin*, f. Gr. ἥρως HERO; said to be so derived because of the inflation of the personality consequent upon taking the drug: see -INE⁵.] A white crystalline alkaloid prepared from morphine by acetylation, which is administered usu. in the form of its hydrochloride as a hypnotic and analgesic (though many countries prohibit this medical use), and which is illictly used as a powerful and addictive drug producing intense euphoric sensations. Also *attrib.*

1898 *Lancet* 3 Dec. 1511/1 A new hypnotic, to which the name of 'heroin' has been given, has been tried in the medical clinic of Professor Gerhardt in Berlin. According to a communication made by Dr. Strube to the *Berliner Klinische Wochenschrift* it is a product of the di-acetic ester of morphia, and it was discovered by Professor Dreser, chief of the chemical department of the Elberfeld Farben Fabriken. 1908 *Practitioner* Apr. 436 Subcutaneous injections of morphia or heroin locally. 1910 *Ibid.* Apr. 542 A sedative may be prescribed... Heroin hydrochloride is the best drug for this purpose. 1920 A. B. Baxter *Parts Men Play* xviii, She..took to opium cigarettes, and then to heroin. She disappeared one night. 1955 *Sci. News Let.* 2 Apr. 219/2 Morphine and heroin, for example, do not give normal persons the 'kick' and pleasant sensations they are supposed to give. 1962 K. Orvis *Damned & Destroyed* iv. 30 One would be compelled to rush wildly off in search of heroin-relief. *Ibid.* xi. 76 A heroin-party. 1968 *Lancet* 7 Dec. 1239/2 The cost of treating heroin addiction is particularly great. 1968 *Even. News* 11 Dec. 13/1 The 'erratic and unsatisfactory life' of a 19-year-old heroin addict ended when he took a barbiturate overdose. 1969 *Times* 9 July 2/3 (*headline*) Heroin 'black market' in West End. *Ibid.* 2/4 Scotland Yard's Drug Squad..have been raiding premises..for a gang of heroin 'pushers'. 1972 *Listener* 27 Jan. 125/3 The Marseilles-New York heroin traffic.

†**heroinal,** *a. Obs. rare.* [f. L. *hērōina* + -AL¹.] Of or pertaining to a heroine.

1652 Urquhart *Jewel* Wks. (1834) 242 Her mellifluent and heroinal breast.

heroine (ˈhɛrəʊɪn), *sb.* (*a.*) Also 7 heroina, 8 heroin. [ad. L. *hērōina*, *-inē*, a. Gr. ἡρωΐνη, fem. of ἥρως HERO: see -INE. Cf. F. *héroïne* (16th c.). The Lat. form was also in Eng. use in 17th c.] A female hero.

1. In ancient mythology, a female intermediate between a woman and a goddess; a demi-goddess.

a 1659 Cleveland *Mt. Ida* v, Next Pallas that brave Heroina came. 1725 Pope *Odyss.* XI. Argt., He sees the shades of the ancient heroines. 1835 Thirlwall *Greece* I. v. 149 Medea seems.. to have descended.. from the rank of a goddess into that of a heroine.

2. A woman distinguished by exalted courage, fortitude, or noble achievements.

1662 Evelyn *Chalcogr.* 61 A Sardonix which he cut, representing the head of that famous Heroine [Queen Elizabeth]. 1697 tr. *C'tess D'Aunoy's Trav.* (1706) 85 To distinguish herself from among the Heroina's of the most famous Ages. 1702 *Lond. Gaz.* No. 3796/12 Providence.. raised an English Heroine to dissipate the Designs of an Universal Monarchy. 1732 Lediard *Sethos* II. x. 475 The greatest heroins have but one life. 1859 Masson *Milton* I. 667 Over Scotland.. there were Presbyterian heroines very many, and Presbyterian furies not a few.

3. The principal female character in a poem, story, or play; the woman in whom the interest of the piece centres.

1715 J. Richardson *Ess. Paint.* 106 The other Saints have regard only to the Heroine of the Picture. 1782 V. Knox *Ess.* cxxi. (R.), They.. forget the hero and the heroine, the poet and the poem. 1847 Tennyson *Princ.* Prol. 217 'Take Lilia, then, for heroine' clamour'd he, 'And make her some great Princess, six feet high'.

4. *attrib.* or as *adj.* Heroine-like, heroic.

1702 *Lond. Gaz.* No. 3810/4 A Soul truly Great and Heroine.

5. *Comb.*, as ***heroine-worship***, ***-worshipper*** (cf. HERO-WORSHIP); ***heroine-like*** adj.

1804 *Something Odd* I. 168 Without screaming, or fainting, or practising any other of the heroine-like graces. 1900 *Westm. Gaz.* 1 May 4/2 Mrs. Cock has succeeded in giving a true and striking portraiture, without falling into mere heroine-worship. 1916 A. Bennett *Lion's Share* xxiii. 165 'Jenny!' Audrey protested, full of heroine-worship. 1943 Beerbohm *Lytton Strachey* 11 He was not a hero-worshipper, or even a very gallant heroine-worshipper. 1970 R. Rendell *Guilty Thing Surprised* ix. 111 It was a case of heroine worship on one side and a sort of flattered acceptance on the other.

Hence ˈ**heroine** *v. nonce-wd.*, in ***to heroine it***, to act or play the heroine; ˈ**heroineship**, ˈ**heroinism**, the condition or position of a heroine; ˈ**heroinize** *v. trans.*, to make into a heroine.

1759 Sterne *Tr. Shandy* (1802) I. xviii. 71 She could not heroine it into so violent.. an extreme as one in her situation might have wished. 1778 *Hist. Eliza Warwick* II. 29 A noble effort of heroinism. 1815 E. S. Barrett *Heroine* III. 174, I therefore heroinized and Heloised myself as much as possible. 1818 *Blackw. Mag.* III. 290 The heroineship of the book has passed to one of the daughters of Lady Juliana. 1887 *Graphic* 16 Apr. 414 Both qualifications for heroinism are combined by Rhona Lascelles. 1894 Mrs. H. Ward *Marcella* I. xi. 210 Her sense of heroineship.

heroism (ˈhɛrəʊɪz(ə)m). [ad. F. *héroïsme* (17th c.), f. *héros* HERO.] The action and qualities of a hero; exalted courage, intrepidity, or boldness; heroic conduct.

[1667 Waterhouse *Fire Lond.* 158 A staine to their Honour, and an abatement to their Herocisme.] 1717 Lady M. W. Montagu *Let. to Sarah Chiswell* 1 Apr., Admire the heroism in the heart of your friend. 1789 Bentham *Princ. Legisl.* xii. §27 *note*, Acts of heroism are in the very essence of them but rare: for if they were common they would not be acts of heroism. 1827 Hare *Guesses* (1859) 289 Heroism is active genius; genius, contemplative heroism. Heroism is the self-devotion of genius manifesting itself in action. 1875 Emerson *Lett. & Soc. Aims, Greatness* Wks. (Bohn) III. 270 No way has been found for making heroism easy, even for the scholar.

b. with *pl.* A heroic action or trait.

1859 Geo. Eliot *A. Bede* I. v. 94 To call forth many evil tempers from the selfish, and many heroisms from the sympathetic. 1891 *Daily News* 18 June 5/2 The Sepoy revolt, the history of which is rich in heroisms of women.

heroˈistic *a.* Of heroizing character.

1881 *Nation* (N.Y.) 18 Aug. 141 (Cent.) Agreeably.. to the heroistic account of her, not only was she not called Ursula, but [etc.].

heroize (ˈhɪərəʊaɪz), *v.* [f. HERO + -IZE.] **1.** *trans.* To make a hero of; to treat or represent as a hero.

1738 Weddell *Voy. up Thames* 52 He was glad to escape the Trouble of heroizing them. 1883 'H. A. Page' *Vers de Societé* 132 Did Mr. Elliott bear in mind how he was heroised in Edinburgh?

b. *spec.* To exalt into a mythological hero.

1891 W. M. Ramsay in *Athenæum* 15 Aug. 233/2 A heroized representation of the chief who was buried beneath the tumulus. 1894 *Q. Rev.* July 138 The deceased seated on thrones as heroised ancestors in Hades. 1897 *Edin. Rev.* Apr. 450 Ancestor worship.. regards the dead man as heroised or even deified.

2. To make or render heroic.

1886 *West. Daily Press* 15 Dec. 3 The Laureate should heroise the nation which he represents, and inspire it with noble and radiant thoughts.

3. *intr.* To play the hero.

1875 Browning *Aristoph. Apol.* 2369 Heroize And speechify and sing-song.

Hence ˈ**heroized** *ppl. a.*; ˈ**heroizing** *vbl. sb.* and *ppl. a.*; **heroiˈzation**, exaltation to the position of a hero.

1840 *Tait's Mag.* VII. 521 No.. heroization of a probably crazy or worthless individual. 1860 A. S. Windsor *Ethica* ii. 105 Heroizing is the radical vice of the day. 1891–7 [see HEROIZE *v.* 1 b].

herola (hɛˈrəʊlə). Also hirola. [Galla name.] A small, rare antelope, *Damaliscus hunteri*, native to Kenya and Somalia, and more frequently called Hunter's hartebeest.

1894 H. C. V. Hunter in Sclater & Thomas *Bk. Antelopes* I. 57 Their Galla name is 'Herola', not 'Horonta'. 1915 *Chambers's Jrnl.* Nov. 700/2 Then follows the curious Hunter's hartebeest or herola, having horns which somehow suggest a connecting link with the fleet and supremely graceful impala. 1957 *Encycl. Brit.* II. 22/2 In *Damaliscus*, the bastard hartebeeste,.. the horns arise directly from the head. The hirola or Hunter's hartebeeste (*D. hunteri*) has a white chevronlike marking on the forehead; it is found only on the north side of Tana valley in Jubaland, east Africa.

heroless, -logical, -logist: see under HERO.

heromancy, obs. form of AEROMANCY.

1546 Langley *Pol. Verg. De Invent.* I. xviii. 33 a, Heromancie that is a kinde of prophecyng by the Ayre.

heron, hern (ˈhɛrən, hɜːn). Forms: α. 4 heiroun, 4–5 heroun, 4–6 heyron, -one, -oun, -un(e, (5 haron), 6 heeron, (herron), 6–7 hearon, 4– heron. β. 4–7 herne, (5 heern), 5–7 hearne, 7 hearn, 5– hern. [ME. *heiroun*, *heyron*, a. OF. *hairon* (12th c. in Hatz.-Darm.), mod.F. *héron* = Pr. *aigron*, Fr. dial. *égron*, Sp. *airon*, It. *aghirone*:—late pop.L. **hāgirōn-em*, deriv. of **hāgir-us* (Sp. *agro*), ad. OHG. **haiger*, *heiger* a heron.

The form *hern* is *archaic*, *poet.*, and *dial.*; but the word is often so pronounced, even when spelt *heron*.

A diminutive from the Romanic form appears in F. *aigrette*. OHG. *heiger* appears to be a by-form of **hreiger* (MHG. *reiger*, Ger. *reiher*, MDu. *reigher*, Du. *reiger*) cogn. with OE. *hrágra* (:—**hraigron-*), heron.]

1. a. The name of a large natural group of long-necked long-legged wading birds, belonging to the genus *Ardea* or family *Ardeidæ*; especially and primarily, the Common or Grey Heron of Europe, *A. cinerea*.

a. 1302 *Regist. Whethamstede* (Rolls) II. App. D. 330 [Pro] heyruns et botors.. xxii.*s.* 1340 *Ayenb.* 193 Me ret of þe heyrone þet he drazþ uorþ his uader and his moder huanne hi byeþ ealde. *c* 1386 Chaucer *Frankl. T.* 469 Thise ffauconers.. That with hir haukes han the heron [*v.rr.* heyroun, herowne, heroun] slayn. *c* 1420 *Liber Cocorum* (1862) 29 Þo heroun is rosted.. And eton with gynger as his kynde is. 14.. *Nom.* in Wr.-Wülcker 702/33 *Hec ardia*, a haron. 1523 Ld. Berners *Froiss.* I. ccccvi. (R.), They toke their horses.. and went into the feldes and founde plentie of heerons to flye at. 1549 *Compl. Scot.* vi. 39 The herrons gaif ane vyild skrech. 1555 Eden *Decades* To Rdr. (Arb.) 53 Isopes frogges to whom.. Iupiter sent a hearon to picke them in the hedes. 1666 J. Davies *Hist. Caribby Isls* 87 A kind of Herons of an admirable whiteness, about the bigness of a Pigeon. 1789 Wordsw. *Even. Walk* 285 And heron, as resounds the trodden shore, Shoots upward, darting his

long neck before. **1839** STONEHOUSE *Axholme* 65 The common heron may still be seen standing motionless, near ditches and pools of water.

β. **13..** *Coer de L.* 2272 The pavylon with the golden herne. *c* **1440** *Anc. Cookery* in *Househ. Ord.* (1790) 439 Craunes and Herns shall be armed with larde. *c* **1440** *Promp. Parv.* 237/1 Heern, byrde [*v. rr.* heryn, herne], *ardea.* **1530** PALSGR. 231/1 Herne a foule, *heron.* **1604** DRAYTON *Owle* 71 The Herne, by soaring shewes tempestuous showres. **1621** BURTON *Anat. Mel.* III. iii. II. i. (1651) 609 As an Hearn when she fishes, still and prying on all sides. **1726–46** THOMSON *Winter* 146 Loud shrieks the soaring hern. **1850** TENNYSON *In Mem.* ci, The brook shall babble down the plain.. And flood the haunts of hern and crake. **1855** —— *Brook* 23, I come from haunts of coot and hern.

b. With defining epithet, applied to other species of the genus *Ardea* and allied genera.

1577 HOLINSHED *Chron., Scot.* vi. (1808) V. 10 A great store of soland geese (not vnlike to those which Plinie calleth water eagles, or (as we saie) sea herons). **1611** COTGR., *Aigrette*, a fowle very like a Heron, but White; a criell Heron, or dwarfe Heron. **1624** CAPT. SMITH *Virginia* v. 171 Many sorts of Fowles, as the gray and white Hearne. **1678** RAY *Willughby's Ornith.* 279 Lesser Ash-coloured Heron. A name for Night Heron, *Nycticorax Gardeni.* **1839** STONEHOUSE *Axholme* 65 The egret and the night heron are, I believe, entirely extinct. **1845** YARRELL *Hist. Birds* (ed. 2) II. 519 The Great White Heron (*Ardea alba*) can only be considered as an accidental visiter. *Ibid.* 531 The Squacco Heron feeds on small fishes, mollusca, and insects. **1893** NEWTON *Dict. Birds* 416 Schlegel retained all in the genus *Ardea*, dividing it into eight sections, the names of which may perhaps be Englished—Great Herons, Small Herons, Egrets, Semi-egrets, Rail-like Herons, Little Bitterns, Bitterns, and Night-Herons. *Ibid.* 418 Large as is the common Heron of Europe, it is exceeded in size by the Great Blue Heron of America, *Ardea herodias*.. The Purple Heron, *A. purpurea*, as a well-known European species.. also deserves mention here. *Ibid.* 419 *note*, *Ardea ralloides*.. is the 'Squacco-Heron' of modern British authors—the distinctive name, given 'Sguacco' by Willughby and Ray from Aldrovandus, having been misspelt by Latham.

2. *attrib.* and *Comb.*, as ***heron-crest, -pie, -plume; heron- (hern-)hawking; heron-billed, -built, -feathered, -haunted, -like, -topped*** adjs.; also **heron-bluter**, Sc. name of the snipe (Jam.); **heron- (hern)-dog**, a dog used in heron-hawking.

1932 W. B. YEATS *Words for Music* 12 The *heron-billed pale Cattle-birds. **1851** H. MELVILLE *Moby Dick* III. xxii. 153 Tall, *heron-built captains. **1817** MOORE *Lalla R., Veiled Proph.* iii, Chiefs of th' Uzbek race, Waving their *heron crests with martial grace. *a* **1613** OVERBURY *Newes, Countrey Newes* Wks. (1856) 174 That a courtier never attaines his selfe-knowledge, but by report. That his best embleme is a *heron-dog. **1935** C. DAY LEWIS *Time to Dance* 21 The *heron-feathered sky. **1903** *Daily Chron.* 10 Dec. 3/2 It [*sc.* a mist].. hid all the *heron-haunted flats and marshes. **1709** *Lond. Gaz.* No. 4539/1 Their Majesties came to this Place, to see the Diversion of *Hern-hawking. **1766** PENNANT *Zool.* (1776) I. 422 Heron-hawking being so favourite a diversion of our ancestors. **1611** COTGR., *Haironnier*, of or belonging to, a heron; also, *heron-like. **1895** *Pop. Sci. Monthly* Apr. 772 These heronlike falcons are distributed over the greater part of Africa. **1723** J. NOTT *Cook's & Confect. Dict.* 32 H, To make a *Hern Pye. **1963** V. CRONIN *Comp. Guide Paris* iv. 67 Where else but in Paris would a king raise a restaurateur to the nobility simply because he enjoyed his heron-pies? **1808** SCOTT *Marm.* IV. vii, His cap.. was graced With the proud *heron-plume.

† **'heroner.** *Obs.* Also 4 heroneer, 6 -eyr, hearoner, 7 herner. [a. F. *héronnier* (OF. also *haironnier*) adj., in *faucon héronnier*, f. *hairon, héron*, HERON. Treated in Eng. as a sb. in apposition to *falcon*, and thence used alone.] A falcon trained to fly at the heron; also, *falcon heroner.*

c **1374** CHAUCER *Troylus* IV. 385 (413) Ech for his vertu holden is for dere, Boþe heroner, and faukon for ryuere. *c* **1385** —— *L.G.W.* 1120 *Dido*, Ne gentil hawtein faucoun heroner. **1575** TURBERV. *Faulconrie* 29 The facon gentle.. is a very good hearoner. **1599** THYNNE *Animadv.* (1865) 39 But this 'heroner', is an especiall hawke.. of moore accompte then other hawkes are, because the flighte of the Herone ys moore daungerous then of other fowles. **1611** COTGR., *Faulcon haironnier*, a herner, a faulcon made onely to the heron.

heronry, hernery ('hɛrənrı, 'hɜːnərı). [f. HERON, HERN + -RY.] A place where herons breed.

α. **1616** SURFL. & MARKH. *Country Farme* 671 To prouide therefore for a Heronrie or place to breed herons in. **1622–3** in Simpkinson *Washingtons* (1860) App. 41 Cutting the greate tree in the heronrow. **1789** G. WHITE *Selborne* xxiii. (1853) 94 Send me word.. whether the heronry consists of a whole grove or wood, or only a few trees. **1872** JENKINSON *Guide Eng. Lakes* (1879) 25 It contains two or three wooded islets, upon one of which was a heronry.

β. **1603–4** *Act 1 Jas. I*, c. 27 §6 So that hee or they shall not shoote in anye.. Gunne, within sixe hundreth paces of any Hernerie. **1786** W. GILPIN *Lakes Cumbld.* (1808) II. xix. 76 The screams of a hernery (the wildest notes in nature).

heron's-bill. ? *Obs.* A book-name applied by Lyte to the British species of *Erodium* and *Geranium*; usually called Stork's-bill and Crane's-bill.

1578 LYTE *Dodoens* I. xxxii. 45 There is found in this contrey diuers sortes of herbes, whose seedes be long and sharpe like to a Hearons beake or byl, the which for the self same cause, are all comprehended under the name and kindes of Hearons bill. **1611** COTGR. s.v. *Aiguille*, Storkes bil, Cranes bill, Hearons bill, Pinkneedle. **1864** PRIOR *Plant-n.*, *Heron's Bill*, from the shape of the seed vessel.

'heronsew, -shew, -shaw. Now somewhat *arch.* or *dial.* Forms: α. 4–6, 9 *dial.* heronsew, -e (also 5 heroun-, heiroun-, heyroun-, heryn-sew(e, heronseu, 6 herensew, 8 herrensue, 8–9 heronsue, -seugh, *corrupt.* herrin-, herringsue). β. 5– hernsew, (5–6 hernesew, -e, 6 hearnsew, 7 hernseu, 9 *dial.* hernser, -sey, harnsa, -ser, -sey). γ. 6–9 heronshew, (6– hearonshew, 7 heronshoe, -showe, 9 *dial.* -sheugh, -shuf). δ. 5–7 hernshew, herneshewe, (6 hernshoe, hearnsheaw, 7 hearneshoe, 9 *dial.* herrinshouw). ε. 7– heronshaw. ζ. 6– hernshaw, (6 hearne-, 6–7 herne-, 7 hirnshaw(e). [ME. *heronsew*, etc., a. OF. *heronceau* (Palsgr.), earlier *heroncel*, pl. *-çaux* (Godef.), dim. of *heron.*

The ending *-sew* for F. *-ceau* has in some dialects come down as *-sue, -sey, -ser*; but it also passed in 16th c. into *-shew*, afterwards popularly made into *-shoe, -show*, and *-shaw.* In the last of these forms it was erroneously taken by Cotgr. for *shaw* = wood. In coast dialects *heron-* or *hern-* is now frequently corrupted to *herrin', herring*, the shoals of which fish are said to be followed by herons.]

lit. A little or young heron; but in current use = HERON.

α. *c* **1386** CHAUCER *Sqr.'s T.* 60, I wol nat tellen.. of hir swannes nor of hir heronsewes [*v.r.* heirounsewis]. **1409** *Durham MS. Cell. Roll*, In iij herounseus emp., xv *d.* **1542** BOORDE *Dyetary* xv. (1870) 270 A yonge herensew is lyghter of dygestyon than a crane. **1764** T. BRYDGES *Homer Travest.* (1797) II. 381 When to their view Appeared a long-legged heron-sue. **1785** HUTTON *Bran New Wark* 30 Nivver did hullet, herrensue, or miredrum, mak sic a noise before. **1796** W. MARSHALL *E. Yorksh.* (ed. 2) Gloss., *Herrinsew.* **1825** BROCKETT, *Heronsew, Heronseugh.* **1855** ROBINSON *Whitby Gloss.* s.v., 'As thin as a herring-sue', a tall lanky person. **1870** E. PEACOCK *Ralf Skirl.* II. 111 We got.. two butterbumps and a heronsew.

β. *c* **1440** *Anc. Cookery* in *Househ. Ord.* (1790) 450 Pygge rosted.. and hernesewes. **1567** MAPLET *Gr. Forest* 88 The heron or hearnsew is called Ardea for mounting aloft. **1635** SWAN *Spec. M.* viii. §2 (1643) 392 The Heron or Hernsew is a fowl that liveth about waters. *a* **1825** FORBY *Voc. E. Anglia, Harnsey*, a heron. **1885** SWAINSON *Names Birds* 144 Harnser (Suffolk).. Hernsew, Heronseugh (Yorkshire).

γ. **1563** B. GOOGE *Eglogs* viii. (Arb.) 68 The Hearonshew mountes aboue the clouds, Ye Crowes ech other do cry; All this showes rayn. **1613** MARKHAM *Eng. Husbandman* I. I. iii. (1635) 12 If Hernes or Heronshoes cry much in their flying. **1620** VENNER *Via Recta* iii. 64 The young Heronshowes are with some accounted a very dainty dish. **1805** SCOTT *Last Minstr.* VI. vi, Capon, heron-shew, and crane. **1893** *Northumbld. Gloss.*, Heronsheugh, heronseugh, heronshuf, heronsyueff, heerinseugh, a heron.

δ. **1575** E. HAKE *Newes out of Powles Churchyd.* D iij b, Both Capon, Swan, and Hernshoe good. **1575** LANEHAM *Let.* (1871) 8 Wyre cagez.. in them, liue Bitters, Curluz, Shoouelarz, Hear[n]sheawz.. and such like deinty Byrds. **1613–16** W. BROWNE *Brit. Past.* II. v, Upon whose tops the Herneshew bred her young.

ε. **1678** RAY *Willughby's Ornith.* 277 The common Heron or Heronshaw. Thence **1768** in PENNANT *Zool.* II. 339.

ζ. **1530** PALSGR. 187 *Heronceav*, an hernshawe. **1593** NASHE *Christ's T.* 91 a, A Hearneshaw (a whole afternoone together) sate on the top of S. Peters Church in Cornehill. **1596** SPENSER *F.Q.* VI. vii. 9 As when a cast of Faulcons make their flight At an Herneshaw, that lyes aloft on wing. **1617** MORYSON *Itin.* III. 146 The Ilands.. the English call Silly.. all abound with Conies, Cranes, Swannes, Hirnshawes, and other Sea birdes. **1867** CARLYLE *Remin.* (1881) II. 147 The only time I ever saw a hernshaw ('herrin'-shouw' the Annandalers call it) actually fishing.

† **b.** *criel-heronshaw* = CRYAL *heron*, the Egret or Lesser White Heron. *Obs.*

1655 MOUFET & BENNET *Health's Improv.* (1746) 176 All the Heronshaws, namely, the black, white, Criel-Heronshaw, and the Mire-dromble.

c. Phrase. ***to know a hawk from a heronshaw.***

Conjectural emendation of the Shakspearian 'I know a Hawke from a Handsaw', proposed by Hanmer (1744), who, being a Suffolk man, founded this on the East Anglian dialectal *harnsey, harnsa, harnser* (see β). Hence in later writers: see HANDSAW.

1766 PENNANT *Zool.* (1812) II. 11 Not to know the Hawk from the Heronshaw, was an old proverb taken originally from this diversion [heron-hawking]; but, in course of time, served to express great ignorance in any science. **1838** GEN. P. THOMPSON *Exerc.* (1842) IV. 315 What claim I have to your attention as one that knows a hawk from a herring-sue, it is for yourselves to settle. **1865** CARLYLE *Fredk. Gt.* XXI. v. X. 94 The clever Elliot, who knew a hawk from a hernshaw, never floundered into that platitude.

¶ Erroneously explained by Cotgr. from SHAW a wood; whence in Kersey and later Dictionaries; but app. never really so used.

1611 COTGR., *Haironniere*, a herons neast, or ayrie; a herneshaw, or shaw of wood, wherein herons breed. **1706** PHILLIPS (ed. Kersey), *Hern-shaw* or *hernery*, a Place where Herns breed. **1755** JOHNSON, *Heronry, Heronshaw*, a place where herons breed. **1826** J. THOMSON *Etymons Eng. Words*, *Hernshaw*, a heronry. [So in later Dicts.]

heroogony, -ologist, -ology, -ship, -theism: see under HERO.

heroon (hɪ'rəʊɒn). *Gr. Antiq.* Pl. -a. Also heröon, heroum. [L. *heroum*, a. Gr. ἡρῷον, f. ἡρώιος of a hero, f. ἥρως HERO.] A sepulchral monument in the form of a small temple; orig. a temple or sanctuary dedicated to a hero, often over his supposed tomb.

1775 R. CHANDLER *Trav. Asia Minor* 111 Searching about, we found.. an inscription, which has belonged to an heroum or sepulchre. **1820** T. S. HUGHES *Trav. Sicily* I. 298 The Heroa of Theseus and Pirithous. **1883** A. S. MURRAY *Hist. Greek Sculpture* II. 289 The heröon at Gjölbaschi in Lycia. **1904** T. R. GLOVER *Stud. Virgil* iv. 89 A hêrôon of Aeneas in Ambracia. **1950** *Antiquity* XXIV. 131 Dyggve himself has excavated such a Heroon at Kalydon.

heros, obs. f. HERO.

heroun, -e, obs. forms of HERON.

'hero-,worship, *sb.* The worship or adoration of heroes: **a.** of the deified heroes of antiquity and mythology; **b.** of heroic men generally.

1774 BURNEY *Hist. Mus.* I. 207 (Jod.) To the adoration of these [sun, moon, and stars] succeeded hero-worship in the deification of dead kings and legislators. **1796** W. TAYLOR in *Monthly Mag.* II. 778 Can it then be really true that hero-worship is a rational sort of idolatry? *c* **1820** S. ROGERS *Italy, Meillerie* 62 Records of the past That prompt to hero-worship. **1840** CARLYLE (*title*) On Heroes, Hero-worship and the heroic in History.

So **'hero-,worship** *v. trans.*, to worship as a hero; also **'hero-,worshipful** *a.*, **'hero-,worshipper.**

1857 HUGHES *Tom Brown* II. viii, He marched down to the School-house, a hero-worshipper, who would have satisfied the soul of Thomas Carlyle himself. **1865** MRS. CARLYLE *Lett.* III. 278, I have seldom seen a foolisher hero-worshipper. **1884** EDNA LYALL *We Two* xxii. (1889) 184 Tell him.. that you hero-worship Sir Michael Cunningham, the statesman of the age. **1914** G. B. SHAW *Pygmalion* (1916) 195 The weak may not be admired and hero-worshipped; but they are by no means disliked and shunned. **1918** BEERBOHM *And even Now* (1920) 203 The hero-worshipful gaze. **1936** N. MARSH *Death in Ecstasy* vii. 86 Maurice hero-worshipped Father Garnette. **1948** 'J. TEY' *Franchise Affair* xix. 224 The centre of an adoring family—secure, loved, hero-worshipped. **1960** C. DAY LEWIS *Buried Day* i. 21, I hero-worshipped him.

‖ **herpes** ('hɜːpiːz). Also 7 hirpes, 8 harpes. [L., a. Gr. ἕρπης (ἑρπητ-) shingles, lit. a creeping, f. ἕρπειν to creep.]

1. a. A disease of the skin (or sometimes of a mucous membrane) characterized by the appearance of patches of distinct vesicles. (Applied widely to a number of cutaneous affections.) Now recognized as a group of virus diseases, the chief of which are **herpes 'simplex**, ordinary or 'simple' herpes (as contrasted with *herpes zoster*), distinguished as ***herpes facialis, genitalis, labialis***, etc., according to the part of the body affected, and caused by *Herpesvirus hominis*; **herpes 'zoster**, shingles, caused by *H. varicellæ.*

1398 TREVISA *Barth. De P.R.* VII. lxi. (1495) 277 This euyll is callyd Herpes. *Ibid.* lxiii. 278 Suche a scabbe highte Herpes Cingula. **1562** TURNER *Herbal* II. 111 The herbe fyue leue.. stayeth and holdeth back crepinge sores called Herpetas. **1601** HOLLAND *Pliny* II. 391 Any sore that runneth on still and corrode as it goeth. [*margin*] Which also is called Herpes: as the shingles, wilde fire, and wolfe. **1643** J. STEER tr. *Exper. Chyrurg.* v. 14 Hirpes or wild fire had invaded his whole legge. **1771** MACKENZIE in *Phil. Trans.* LXII. 17 A gentleman's son.. with a herpes round the neck, which had proved extremely obstinate. **1807** MORRIS & KENDRICK *Edin. Med. & Physical Dict.* II, Herpes zoster. **1813** T. BATEMAN *Pract. Synopsis Cutaneous Dis.* vi. 233 The Herpes labialis.. occurs most frequently in the course of diseases of the viscera. **1842** T. H. BURGESS *Man. Dis. Skin* 81 The formation of vesicles in groups upon an inflamed base, is always sufficient to distinguish herpes from other vesicular affections. **1886** FAGGE & PYE-SMITH *Princ. & Pract. Med.* II. 670 His [*sc.* Willan's] species of herpes included (1) *Herpes zoster* or zona... (2) *Herpes circinatus*, which.. is now classed with *Tineæ.* **1907** *Jrnl. Amer. Med. Assoc.* 2 Mar. 746/2 (*heading*) The nature of herpes simplex. *Ibid.* 750/1 Herpes zoster and herpes simplex—both facial and genital varieties—while not clinically identical, are closely related. *Ibid.* 749/2 Another form of simple herpes.. is herpes genitalis. **1946** G. C. ANDREWS *Dis. Skin* (ed. 3) xx. 537 Certain types of herpes zoster have received descriptive terms, the more important of which is herpes zoster frontalis, which is an involvement of the area supplied by the upper branches of the trigeminal nerve. **1962** *Lancet* 13 Jan. 105/1, I have often been impressed by the frequent association of herpes zoster with stress and anxiety, especially in the elderly. **1967** A. C. ALLEN *Skin* (ed. 2) viii. 335/2 Herpes simplex (fever blisters, cold sores, herpes facialis, herpes labialis) is.. a mild, although recurrent, eruption.

b. ***herpes virus*** (also as one word), any of a group of related viruses that includes those causing shingles and chicken-pox, esp. *Herpesvirus hominis*, the cause of herpes simplex.

1925 *Amer. Jrnl. Path.* I. 337 (*heading*) Studies on filterable viruses... Cultivation of herpes virus. *Ibid.*, We have used herpes virus and a note on the cultivation of this virus is given below. **1955** *Sci. Amer.* May 33/1 The benign but recurrent lesions known as fever blisters or cold sores, caused by the herpes virus. **1968** A. ROOK et al. *Textbk. Dermatol.* I. xxiv. 763/2 The particles of herpesvirus are first found in the nucleus and later appear in the cytoplasm from which the virus is gradually released with destruction of the cell.

2. *Entom.* A genus of Coleoptera of the family *Curculionidæ* (weevils).

herpetic (hə'pɛtɪk), *a.*[1] [f. Gr. ἑρπητ- (see prec.) + -IC. Cf. F. *herpétique.*] Pertaining to or of the nature of herpes; affected with herpes.

1783 J. C. SMYTH in *Med. Commun.* I. 193 Herpetic spots and blotches. **1804** *Med. Jrnl.* XII. 97 Those herpetic affections which so frequently appear among the children of

the poor. **1865** Livingstone *Zambesi* xix. 375 We saw the herpetic eruptions round their mouths.

So **her'petical** *a.*, of the nature of herpes.

1767 A. Campbell *Lexiph.* (1774) 38 A pruriginous, herpetical, and incurable eruption of pustules.

her'petic, *a.*[2] *nonce-wd.* [f. Gr. ἑρπετ-όν reptile + -ic.] Crawling, reptilian.

1848 Lowell *Biglow P.* Ser. i. Poems 1890 II. 63 An abject and herpetic Public Opinion is the Pope, the Anti-Christ, for us to protest against.

herpetiform (hə'piːtɪfɔːm), *a. Path.* [ad. mod.L. *herpētiform-is*, f. *herpēs, herpēt-* herpes.] Presenting the form or appearance of herpes.

1854 in Mayne *Expos. Lex.* **1894** M. Morris *Dis. Skin* vi. 102 The vesicles are arranged in herpetiform groups.

herpetism ('hɜːpɪtɪz(ə)m). *Path.* [a. F. *herpétisme*, f. L. *herpēt-* herpes: see -ism.] A constitutional tendency to herpes or similar diseases.

1856 in Thomas *Med. Dict.* **1891** W. A. Jamieson *Dis. Skin* x. (ed. 3) 144 French authors speak much of herpetism.

herpetography[1] (hɜːpɪ'tɒgrəfɪ). [f. Gr. ἑρπετόν creeping thing, reptile, f. ἕρπειν to creep, crawl + -graphy.] (See quot.)

1736 Bailey (folio) Pref., *Herpetography*..a Description of creeping Things. **1886** in *Syd. Soc. Lex.*

herpe'tography[2]. [f. Gr. ἑρπητ- herpes + -graphy.] A description of the disease herpes.

1854 in Mayne *Expos. Lex.*

Hence **herpeto'graphical** *a.*

1854 Mayne *Expos. Lex.*, *Herpetographicus*..of or belonging to herpetography: herpetographical.

'herpetoid, *a. Zool.* [f. Gr. ἑρπετόν creeping thing, reptile + -oid.] Reptiliform; sauroid.

1889 *Cent. Dict.* s.v., The archæopteryx is a herpetoid bird.

herpetology[1] (hɜːpɪ'tɒlədʒɪ). [f. as herpetography[1]: see -logy. Cf. F. *herpétologie.*] That part of zoology which treats of reptiles.

1824 Watt *Bibl. Brit.* III. *Subjects, Herpetology.* **1828** Stark *Elem. Nat. Hist.* I. 333 *Reptiles*, This department of Natural History is frequently treated of under the general title of Herpetology. **1865** *Sat. Rev.* 7 Jan. 30/2 Indian reptiles..omitted in general works on Herpetology.

Hence ˌ**herpeto'logic**, ˌ**herpeto'logical** *adjs.*, pertaining to herpetology; ˌ**herpeto'logically** *adv.*, in relation to herpetology; **herpe'tologist**, one versed in herpetology.

1828 Webster, *Herpetologic, Herpetological, Herpetologist.* **1835** Kirby *Hab. & Inst. Anim.* II. xxiii. 442 The dragon of modern Herpetologists. **1850** H. Miller *Footpr. Creat.* v. (1874) 80 One of the links with the Saurians which establish its herpetological relationship. **1883** *Athenæum* 24 Feb. 250 The most distinguished herpetologist in this country. **1886** *Edin. Rev.* Apr. 320 Dr. Günther considers that herpetologically Egypt must be included in the Palæarctic region.

herpe'tology[2]. [f. as herpetography[2] + -logy.] That part of pathology which treats of herpes; a description of herpes.

1857 Dunglison *Med. Dict.* 460 *Herpetography*..a description of the different forms of herpes, as Herpetology, *Herpetologia*, is a treatise on the same. **1893** J. Hutchinson *Archives Surg.* V. No. 17. 88 No. clxviii [of Catechism of Surgery] (*title*) Herpetology.

herpe'totomy. [f. Gr. ἑρπετόν reptile + -τομία cutting.] The dissection of reptiles; the anatomy of reptiles. So **herpe'totomist**, a dissector of reptiles.

In mod. Dicts.

herple, variant of hirple *v.*

herpolhode ('hɜːpəlhəʊd). *Geom.* [f. Gr. ἕρπ-ειν to creep + πόλος pole + ὁδός way, path.] A plane curve described by the point of contact of an ellipsoid with a fixed plane, the centre of the ellipsoid being fixed while the ellipsoid rolls upon the plane.

1868 E. J. Routh *Rigid Dynam.* 329 The point of contact of the ellipsoid with the plane on which it rolls traces out two curves, one on the surface of the ellipsoid, and one on the plane..the second..is called the *herpolhode*.

Herr (hɛə(r), ‖hɛr). Pl. **Herren**. [G., master, lord; Mr. Cf. her, here *sb.*] The German equivalent of Mr.; a German gentleman.

1653 R. Creighton *Let.* 28 Jan. in M. M. Verney *Mem. Verney Fam.* (1894) III. iii. 81 Herr Skatt hath undertaken the cure. **1828** T. Carlyle *Let.* 16 Apr. (1887) 81 How is it that the Author of *Faust* and *Meister* can *tryste* himself with such characters, as 'Herr ——' (the simplest and stupidest man of his day, a Westmoreland Gerundgrinder and *Cleishbotham*)? **1849** Thackeray *Pendennis* I. xiv. 124 Herr Garbage's lions and tigers had drawn for a little time, until one of the animals had bitten a piece out of the Herr's shoulder. **1879** C. M. Yonge *Magnum Bonum* (1882) xxi. 294 He..was a decided favourite with Fräulein Rosalie, who would do anything for her dear young Herr. **1940** W. S. Churchill *Speech* 21 Oct. in *Second World War* (1949) II. xxvi. 452 But Herr Hitler is not thinking only of stealing other people's territories. **1954** 'M. Coles' *Not for Export* iii. 34 Life was difficult for the poor in Berlin, as the *Herr* would understand. **1959** *Times* 30 Jan. 11/2 The possibility that Herr Alfred Krupp may be allowed to retain his main holdings in coal, iron, and steel. **1967** 'G. Carr' *Lewker in Tirol* iii. 36 Your glass, *mein Herr. Ibid.* 53 It was in the corner of the big bar..the guides..meet their *Herren* there. **1971** W. Laqueur *Dict. Politics* 207 Brandt's attempts..incurred the wrath of Herr Ulbricht.

herrald(e, obs. forms of herald *sb.*

herre, obs. f. hair; var. harre, her *sb.*, *Obs.*

herreȝeld(a, -ȝelde, var. hereyeld, *Obs.*

‖**Herrenvolk** ('hɛrənfɔlk, -fəʊk). Also **h-**. [G., master-race.] The Nazi conception of the German people as born to mastery; also *transf.* as an appellation of other 'superior' groups. Also *attrib.* or as *adj.*

1940 *New Statesman* 17 Feb. 198/1 Show how German industry can enjoy prosperity without rearmament and no German worker will accept the starvation wages of a *Herrenvolk* pursuing the mirage of a closed imperialism. **1941** *Amer. Guardian* 15 Oct. 6/1 Hitler's race program was stolen from the White Trash Herrenvolk of Dixie. **1941** M. Treadgold *We couldn't leave Dinah* xii. 184 The representative of the Herrenvolk nodded. **1941** H. G. Wells *You can't be too Careful* v. ii. 245 A people..who were united in their dislike to the German *herrenvolk.* **1941** D. Wilson *Germany's 'New Order'* 22 A *Herrenvolk* to dominate other peoples. **1943** W. S. Churchill *End of Beginning* 103 Forms of warfare which, according to the German view, should be the strict monopoly of the *Herrenvolk.* **1944** G. B. Shaw *Everybody's Political What's What?* x. 82 Nations each of which regards itself as The Chosen Race or *Herrenvolk* appointed by God to own and rule all the others. **1944** H. G. Wells *'42 to '44* 187 The evil suggestion of inherently inferior peoples, predestined hewers of wood and drawers of the water for some imaginary *Herrenvolk.* **1947** *Penguin New Writing* XXXI. 157 He referred to them [*sc.* Sinhalese] in their presence as 'wogs'..and forced them to admit his herrenvolk creed. **1958** *Listener* 9 Oct. 566/2 The *Herrenvolk* ideas, against which so many of us..fought and suffered during the seven terrible years of the war. **1960** *Guardian* 28 June 10/5 A..Portuguese..cursing an African..in that unmistakable way which those who know Africa cannot fail to recognise—the herrenvolk attitude. **1964** *Punch* 1 July 31/3 Brutality and *herrenvolk* arrogance.

herrie, Sc. form of harry *v.*

'herriment. *Sc.* [f. *herry*, Sc. form of harry *v.* + -ment.] Harrying, ravaging, devastation.

1786 Burns *Brigs Ayr* 171 The herryment and ruin of the country. **1836** *Tait's Mag.* III. 426 It was..the scene of continual spreaths, liftings, reavings, and herriments.

herring ('hɛrɪŋ). Forms: *α.* 1 **hæring, -inc, -ingc, -incg**, 1–7 **hering**, 4–6 **heryng(e**, 5–6 **heeryng**, 6 **hearyng(e**, 6–7 (8–9 *dial.*) **hearing**, (5 **heirreng, hearrynge**, 6 **heyring**, 7 **heerring**); *β.* 5 **herryng(e**, 6–7 **herringe**, 6– **herring**. [OE. *hǽring, héring* = OFris. *hêreng*, EFris *häring, -ink*, MLG. *harink, herink*, LG. *hering*, MDu. *harinc, herinc*, Du. *haring*, OHG. *hâring*, MHG. *hærinc*, G. *häring, hering*. The Romanic names, F. *hareng*, It. *aringa*, etc. are from OHG.

(The ulterior derivation of the WGer. *hâring* is uncertain: one conjecture is, ad. L. *hālec*, changed by popular etymology (Diez). Kluge thinks the OHG. and MHG. variant with short vowel, *hęring*, was influenced by popular association with OHG. *hęri* 'host,' as if 'the fish that comes in hosts'; but the shortening of the *e* in later Eng. (rare before 16th c.) appears to be merely phonetic. The vowel is still long in various dialects.)]

1. a. A well-known sea fish, *Clupea harengus*, inhabiting the North Atlantic Ocean, and coming near the coast at certain seasons in enormous shoals to spawn. It is an important article of food, and is the object of extensive fisheries on the British, Dutch, and Norwegian coasts. Also applied to other species of *Clupea.*

Battle of (the) Herrings (F. *bataille des harengs*), popular name of the battle at Rouvrai, 12 Feb. 1429, fought in defence of a convoy of provisions: see quot. 1548.

α. *a* **700** *Epinal Gloss.* 910 *Sardinas*, heringas. *c* **1000** Ælfric *Colloquy* in Wr.-Wülcker 94/13 Hæringcgas and leaxas, mereswyn and stirian. *a* **1100** *Ags. Voc.* ibid. 319/13 *Taricus, uel allec*, hærinc. **12..** *Charter of Ælfwig* (dated 1060–66) in *Cod. Dipl.* IV. 172, vi. merswin and .xxx. þusenda hæryngys ælce eare. *c* **1300** *Havelok* 758 Keling he tok, and tumberel, Hering, and the makerel. *a* **1400** *Eng. Gilds* (1870) 354 Euerych sellere of herynge in þe lente. *c* **1440** *Promp. Parv.* 237/1 Heerynge, fisshe. **1477** in *Surtees Misc.* (1888) 27 Heirreng for iiij a penny. **1512** *Nottingham Rec.* III. 340 He sold his heyring at his plesure. **1535** *Act 27 Hen. VIII*, c. 3 Fisher men..vse commonly to conducte and conuey their hearing sprottes and other fyshe to..Kyngstone. **1548** Hall *Chron., Hen. VI*, 106 This conflict (because the most part of the cariage was heryng and lenten stuffe) the Frenchmen cal, the..battail of herynges. **1617** Moryson *Itin* ii. 206 Two hearings every fish day. **1624** Capt. Smith *Virginia* i. 10 All Herings in abundance. *c* **1790** Lady Nairne *Song 'Caller Herrin'*, Who'll buy my caller herrin' [*Sc.* hairin']? They're no brought here without brave darin' [*other rimes* farin', despairin']. **1828** *Craven Dial.*, *Heering, Hearing.*

β. **1398** Trevisa *Barth. De P.R.* xviii. xxi. (1495) 781 It is sayd that the camelion lyueth oonly by ayre..the herryng by water. **1472** *Surtees Misc.* (1888) 23 Feche & herrynge. **1570** Levins *Manip.* 136/19 Herring, *halec.* **1665** *Surv. Aff. Netherl.* 111 Our Fish, especially our Herring, being..of general use for food throughout Europe. **1720** De Foe *Capt. Singleton* xiii. (1840) 231 The majority..were for pickling up the poor Dutchmen among the herrings; in a word,..for throwing them all into the sea. **1880** Günther *Fishes* 659 *Clupea mirabilis.*—The Herring of the North Pacific.

b. With qualifications, expressing the condition of the fish, or the way in which it is cured.

black herring, a kind of cured herring. **fat herring**: see fat *a.* 2 f. **kippered h.**, = kipper, q.v. **mazy h.**, the highest brand of herring, which are full of roe. **red h.**, a herring having a red colour from being cured by smoking; also *fig.*: see red herring. **round shore-h.**, herring salted just as they come from the water. **split h.**, gutted herring cured and packed for the market. **white h.**, (*a*) fresh herring; (*b*) herring salted but not smoked. **white-salted h.**, herring cured according to the French method by gutting and packing in a thick brine, in which they stand until they are finally packed in fresh lime and salt. (See also bloated *ppl. a.*[1], corved, crux, full *a.* 1 e, green *a.*, shotten *a.*)

c **1420** *Liber Cocorum* (1862) 54 Cover þy white heryng..þen cover red heryng and set abufe. **1469** *Househ. Ord.* (1790) 102 White herringes a laste, that is to say xij barrelles. **1538** Bale *Thre Lawes* 1566 They loue no pese porrege nor yet reade hearynges in lent. **1605** Shaks. *Lear* iii. vi. 32 Hopdance cries in Tom's belly for two white herring. **1617** Moryson *Itin.* iii. 148 The English export into Italy great quantity of red Herrings. **1722** *Lond. Gaz.* No. 6040/1 Salt used in the curing and making of White-Herrings. **1831** Sir J. Sinclair *Corr.* II. 397, I begged him to give orders to send me some barrels of red herrings, caught and cured in Scotland. **1883** *Fisheries Exhib. Catal.* 72 Cured fish of various kinds—Black Herrings, Red Herrings, Kippers, Bloaters. **1888** *Argosy* 278 Fresh or white herrings, as they are called on the Norfolk coast, should be broiled.

c. Applied, with qualifications, to other fishes of the family *Clupeidæ*, or resembling them.

branch herring, the alewife, *Clupea vernalis.* **California h.**, a species inhabiting the North Pacific, *C. mirabilis.* **crake h.**, the scad. **fall h.**, *C. mediocris.* **freshwater h.**, the pollan, a variety of whitefish found in the loughs of Ireland, *Coregonus pollan.* **garvie-h.**: see garvie. **lake h.**, the cisco, *Coregonus hoyi*, which abounds in Lake Ontario. **Ohio h.**, the skipjack, *Clupea chrysochloris.* **rock h.**, a species of shad, *Alosa fixta.* **round h.**, *Etrumeus sadina.* **toothed h.**, the mooneye, *Hyodon clodalus.* Also **king of the herrings**, *Chimæra monstrosa*; also a species of ribbon-fish, *Regalecus glesne.* **mother** or **queen of the herrings**, the allise-shad, *Alosa vulgaris.*

1686 Ray & Willughby *Hist. Pisc.* ix. ix. §9 *Clupea..Angl.* A Shad, the Mother of the Herrings. **1836** Yarrell *Brit. Fishes* II. 364 Northern Chimæra. King of the Herrings..is generally taken when in pursuit of shoals of Herrings. **1861** Couch *Brit. Fishes* II. 138 Crake Herring, Scad (North of Ireland) *Trichurus vulgaris.* **1865** *Ibid.* IV. 292 An attempt to obtain examples of the Pollan in Ireland was met with the reply that no fish was known by that name, although..it was discovered that the Fresh-water Herring was familiarly known to every one.

2. Proverbial phrases. †***neither (no) barrel better herring, never a barrel the (a) better h.***: i.e. never one better than another, nothing to choose between them: see barrel 4. ***neither fish, flesh, nor good red h.***: see fish *sb.*[1] 4 c. ***dead as a h.***: see dead *a.* 32 b. ***I like not barrel or h.***: I dislike the whole of it. ***every h. should hang by its own head, gills, neck, tail***: every one should stand on his own merits (*local*). Also ***thick as herrings*** (i.e. in shoals); ***like herrings in a barrel; as thin as a herring.***

1546 J. Heywood *Prov.* (1867) 84 A foule olde riche widowe, whether wed would ye, Or a yonge fayre mayde, beyng poore as ye be? In neither barrell better hearyng (quoth hee). **1583** Stanyhurst *Æneis* ii. (Arb.) 45 For a ful reckning, I lyk not barrel or hearing. **1639** J. Clarke *Paroemiologia Anglo-Latina* 20 Every herring must hang by th' owne gill. **1672** W. Walker *Parœmiologia Anglo-Latina* 23/1 Every herring must hang by its own neck; gill. **1674** tr. *Martiniere's Voy. N. Countries* 127 There was never a Barrel better Herring, one as rich and ill favoured as the other. **1694** T. D'Urfey *Comical Hist. D. Quixote* I. iii. ii. 32 Let not the fault of the Ass be laid upon the Pack-Saddle, every Herring must hang by its own tail. **1721** J. Kelly *Compl. Coll. Scot. Prov.* 240 Let every Herring hing by its own Head. **1795** Wolcott (P. Pindar) *Pindariana* Wks. 1812 IV. 234 Virtues thick as Herrings in their souls. **1818** Scott *Rob Roy* xxvi, 'Na, na! let every herring hing by its ain head.' **1824** Carlyle in Froude *Life* (1882) I. 262 It is the law in Yarmouth that every herring hang by its own head. **1890** Hall Caine *Bondman* ii. ii, Adam, thinking as little of pride, said No, that every herring should hang by its own gills. **1891** N. Gould *Double Event* 117 (Farmer) People jammed inside like herrings in a barrel.

3. *attrib.* and *Comb.* **a.** General combs.: as ***herring-barrel, -boat, -curer, -fisher, -fishery, -fleet, -fry, -harvest, -lugger, -monger, -net, -pie, -scale, -season, spawn, -time, -tub***; ***herring-sized*** adj.

1420 *Inv.* in *Linc. Chapt. Acc. Bk.* A. 2. 30. lf. 69, 2d *herryngbarelles. **1613** Purchas *Pilgrimage* (1614) 466 And the Mast was one Cane as bigge as a Herring-Barrell. **1818** Scott *Rob Roy* xxvii, He wadna for a' the herring-barrels in Glasgow [etc.]. *a* **1856** H. Miller *Cruise Betsey* vi. (1858) 99 A fleet of *herring-boats lay moored beside them. **1615** E. S. *Brit. Buss* in Arb. *Garner* III. 625 The charge of one hundred Last of *herring casks or barrels. **1858** Simmonds *Dict. Trade*, **Herring-curer*, a gutter and salter of herrings. **1765** J. Brown *Chr. Jrnl.* (1814) 206 No *herring-drove, but a storm approacheth. **1704** *Lond. Gaz.* No. 4058/5 The Sorlings went off to the *Herring-Fishers. **1615** E. S. *Brit. Buss* in Arb. *Garner* III. 625 Upon conference with some experienced in this *herring fishery. **1838** *Penny Cycl.* X. 286/2 The principal herring-fishery off the coast of Norfolk and Suffolk commences in September and ends in the beginning of December. **1889** Edna Lyall *Hardy Norseman* iv. 39 We shall have the *herring-fleet back from Iceland before many days. **1591** Percivall *Sp. Dict.*, *Anchova*, *hering frie, *halecula.* **1865** H. H. Dixon *Field & Fern* iv. 65 Even the mild porpoise..is busy chasing the

herring-fry. **1599** NASHE *Lenten Stuffe* 54 Backe returned the Caterer..and powred downe the *herring merchant his hundred ducats. **1614** *Eng. way to Wealth* in *Harl. Misc.* (Malh.) III. 242 The *herring-mongers of Yarmouth. **1535** *Aberdeen Reg.* V. 15 (Jam.) Ane *harein nett. **1615** E. S. *Brit. Buss* in Arb. *Garner* III. 625 The particulars of her herring-nets, and of the warropes and other ropes, cords, and lines. **1599** NASHE *Lenten Stuffe* 71 Euery yeare about Lent-tide, the sherifes of Norwich take certayne *herring pies..and send them as a homage. **1778** *Eng. Gazetteer* (ed. 2) s.v. *Norwich*, The sheriffs are obliged by their charter to present the King with 12 herring-pies yearly. **1906** *Daily Colonist* (Victoria, B.C.) 11 Jan. 3/4 The practice of using *herring spawn..has been the habit of the Indians all over British Columbia for many years. **1972** *Guardian* 1 Apr. 7/8 Herring spawn is relatively vulnerable and relatively few survive. **1039** in Earle *Land-charters* 297 And hæfde hit him wel neh twelf monað and twegen *hæringc timan.

b. Special combs.: **herring-brook** = HERRING-POND; **herring choker** *slang*, (*a*) *Canad.* a nickname for a native or inhabitant of the Maritime Provinces; (*b*) *U.S.* a Scandinavian; **herring-cooper**: see quot.; **herring-drift**: see DRIFT 11 b; **herring-gull**, a species of gull, *Larus argentatus*, which follows herring-shoals and preys upon them; **herring-gutted** *a.*, having a narrow, thin body like a herring; †**herring-hang**, a building in which herrings are hung to cure; **herring-hog** (*dial.*), the grampus; **herring-king** = king of the herrings (see 1 c); **herring-man**, a man engaged in the herring-fishery; **herring-pike**, a fish of the group *Clupesoces*; **herring-salmon**, a name of N. American species of *Coregonus*; **herring-silver** (see quot.); **herring-wife**, a woman who sells herrings; **herring-work**, herring-bone work (Ogilvie).

1810 *Naval Chron.* XXIV. 451 Unknown on this side the *herring-brook. **1899** *Yarmouth Telegram* (Nova Scotia) 20 Oct. 1/1, I am down among the '*herring chokers' and 'blue noses' for a few weeks. *Ibid.*, Happy the wearied globe-trotter and denizen of the 'herring chokers' of Nova Scotia. **1944** H. WENTWORTH *Amer. Dial. Dict.* 290/1 *Herring-choker.* 1. A Prince-Edward-Islander, or native of any of the Provinces 'down east'. 2. A Scandinavian. **1954** *Fundy Fisherman* (Black's Harbour, N.B.) 3 Mar. 4/4 These Herring Choker senators point out that Duplessis has already peddled a lot of horse power to Ontario and indeed is selling plenty to Premier Frost et al. right now. **1968** *Word Study* Dec. 3/2 The Roman Catholic is frequently called a *fish*, short for *fish-eater*... Similar is the term *herring-choker*, another name for a Scandinavian. **1892** *Labour Commission Gloss.*, *Herring Coopers, who make the casks in which herrings are packed. **1851** *Illustr. Catal. Gt. Exhib.* II. 514 *Herring-drift, 18 feet deep, 11 fathoms long. **1857** *Chambers' Inform.* I. 709/1 Arctic gulls, whose plumage differs from that of the *herring-gull. **1892** *Daily News* 13 Dec. 4/8 The herring-gull—the pirate of the sea. **1726** ARBUTHNOT *Diss. Dumpling* 9 Meagre, *Herring-gutted Wretches. **1811** *Sporting Mag.* 38 Lank-jawed, herring-gutted plebeans. **1682** J. COLLINS *Salt & Fishery* 106 They are hanged up in the *Herring-Hangs, or Red-Herring Houses. *c* **1640** J. SMYTH *Hundred of Berkeley* (1885) 319 The Sturgeon, Porpoise, Thornpole..the *herringe hogge. **1674** JOSSELYN *Voy. New Eng.* 10 We saw many Grandpisces or Herring-hogs, hunting the scholes of Herrings. **1884** DAY in *Fisheries Exhib. Lit.* II. 165 The genus Chimæra..as it makes raids upon the Herrings, it is called the '*Herring King'. *a* **1568** ASCHAM *Scholem.* (Arb.) 152 Not much vnlike the fisher men of Rye, and *Hering men of Yarmouth. **1633** AMES *Agst. Cerem.* Pref. 28 Its a hard world, when hearing men revile fisher-men. **1836** RICHARDSON *Fishes* 180 The *Herring salmon forms its [the namaycush's] principal food in Lake Huron. **1706** PHILLIPS **Herring-silver*, Money formerly paid as an Equivalent for the Custom of giving a certain Quantity of Herrings for the Provision of a Religious House. **1611** COTGR., *Harengiere*, a *Herring-wife; a woman that cries, or sells Herrings.

Hence **herring** *v. trans.*, to manure with herring.

1880 GOODE & ATWATER *Hist. Menhaden* 249 (Cent.) In Maine they talk of land that has been herringed to death.

herring-bone, *sb.* (*a.*)

1. a. The bone of a herring.

1652 *Season. Exp. Netherl.* 8, I was pleased to hear so rich a Towne..could be Founded on Herring-Bones. **1857** *Chambers' Inform.* I. 709/2 The popular saying of being founded on herring-bones is as applicable to the thriving town of Wick, as Amsterdam.

b. *pl.* Small cirrocumulus clouds (cf. *mackerel sky*).

1905 *Westm. Gaz.* 22 Apr. 4/2 The sky was sunny, but mottled in the north-west with 'herring-bones', which prophesied wind.

c. *pl.* The herring-bone-line hatching used to represent mountains on a map.

1900 E. T. FOWLER *Farringdons* v, 'I see. And please what are the mountain-ranges that you are drawing now?' 'These,' replied Elisabeth, covering her map with herring-bones, 'are your scruples.'

d. *Furniture.* (See quot. 1952.)

1937 *Burlington Mag.* July 45/2 All the ornament required is to be found in the finely figured wood, the craftsmanship displayed in the herringbone and cross-banded borders. **1952** J. GLOAG *Short Dict. Furniture* 285 *Herringbone*, patterns in the form of a herring bone were used on the banding of drop fronts on early 18th century walnut furniture. **1960** H. HAYWARD *Antique Coll.* 142/1 *Herring-bone banding*, a decorative veneer border much used on walnut furniture of the late 17th and early 18th cent. consisting of two narrow strips of veneer laid together diagonally forming a pattern resembling a herring-bone or feather [etc.].

e. *Skiing.* (See quot. 1924.) Also *attrib.*

1904 E. C. RICHARDSON *Ski-Running* 35 A short, steep bit of slope may be overcome by the methods illustrated in Figs. 12 and 13, but both are fatiguing,..especially the 'herring bone'. **1924** *Tourist* Winter Sports No. 12/1 *Herring-bone*, a method of climbing without kick-turns which leaves tracks like the well-known stitch. **1972** M. YORKE *Silent Witness* iii. 58 [Her] muscles always screamed after..side-stepping or herring-bone climbing.

2. *attrib.* or *adj.* Resembling in appearance the bones of a herring.

a. *Sewing.* **herring-bone stitch**, a kind of stitch in which the threads are set obliquely at equal angles on opposite sides of a line, or crossing each other: hence ***herring-bone seam, thread.*** Also *absol.* = *herring-bone stitch*, etc.

1659 TORRIANO, *A-spina pesce*..the hearing-bone stitch. **1767** GOOCH *Treat. Wounds* I. 453 That kind of stitch called by sempstresses the herring-bone or a flat seam. **1866** R. CHAMBERS *Ess.* Ser. I. 198 Causes your clothes to be.. embroidered in the herring-bone fashion. **1880** *Plain Hints* 24 Herring-bone, called 'cat's teeth' in the West of England, is the name of the stitch used for flannel work.

b. *Arch.* Applied to a kind of masonry and of paving in which the stones or tiles are set obliquely in alternate rows so as to form a zigzag pattern: as ***herring-bone ashlar, balk, bond, work***, etc.

1703 MOXON *Mech. Exerc.* 238 They make a good Pavement, and..[it] looks handsomly, especially if laid Herring-bone fashion. **1836** PARKER *Gloss. Archit.* s.v., The interior, or backing, of Roman walls is often of irregular herring-bone work. **1848** *Rickman's Archit.* App. 36 Rude and wide jointed rag-work, with some herring-bone. **1853** *Archæol.* XXXV. 384 The walls to this room were 3 feet thick, with herring-bone masonry. **1865** LUBBOCK *Preh. Times* v. (1869) 157 Urns..decorated by..incised patterns in which the chevron or herring-bone constantly recurs.

c. *Weaving* and *Clothmaking.* Applied to stuffs in which a zigzag pattern (as in b) is worked: as ***herring-bone twill, -weaving.*** Also *absol.*, a stuff having a herring-bone pattern.

1860 *All Year Round* No. 53. 63 Barragons and fustians, herringbones, thicksets..dimities and velveteens, for which Bolton was famous. **1882** CAULFEILD & SAWARD *Dict. Needlework*, *Herringbone-twill*, a name by which a soft slight dress material is known. **1887** *Cassell's Fam. Mag.* Oct. 697/1 With an interwoven corded stripe, with chevron or herring-bone weaving between.

d. *Carpentry.* **herring-bone bridging**, so absol. *herring-bone*, 'strutting-pieces between thin joists, diagonally from the top of one to the bottom of another, to prevent lateral deflection' (Knight *Dict. Mech.* 1875).

e. ***herring-bone coralline*** (see quots.).

1755 J. ELLIS *Ess. towards Nat. Hist. Corallines* 17 Herring-bone Coralline. This Coralline is often found sticking to Oysters as they are brought to the London Market, during the Winter-season. **1850** A. PRATT *Common Things Sea-side* 258 The Herring-bone Coralline ('Halecium halecinum') which grows on stones and shells, in the deep parts of the sea. **1915** E. R. LANKESTER *Divers. Nat.* 97 Very minute jelly-fish,..[which] originate as buds from small branching polyps, one kind of which is common on oyster-shells, and is called 'the herring-bone coralline'.

f. Designating a type of milking parlour in which the stalls are arranged in a herring-bone pattern.

1957 *Farmer & Stockbreeder* 9 Apr. 45/1 The yard and parlour system obviously attracts those changing over to dairying and the main interest centred on the..herring-bone parlour design. **1963** *Ibid.* 5 Mar. 33/2 (Advt.), Gascoigne milking systems. Herringbone parlour for batch milking. **1970** *Times* 9 Mar. 13/5 Another innovation costs £120 a milking stall, or £600 for this item alone in the five-point herringbone parlour.

'herring-bone, *v.* [f. prec. sb.]

1. *trans.* To work with a herring-bone stitch. Also *absol.* or *intr.*

1787 MRS. TRIMMER *Econ. Charity* 79 Plain linen Caps, with binders herring-boned with coloured Cruel. **1873** MISS BROUGHTON *Nancy* II. 101 She has been teaching me how to herring-bone. **1880** *Plain Hints* 25 The raw edge should be herring-boned down about four or six threads deep.

2. *trans.* To mark with a herring-bone pattern.

1887 T. HARDY *Woodlanders* III. v. 101 A sanded floor, herring-boned with a broom. *Ibid.* xv. 307 The herring-boned sand of the floor.

3. To make (a wall, floor, etc.) of herring-bone work. Hence **'herring-boned** *ppl. a.*

1907 W. DE MORGAN *Alice-for-Short* ix, A 'erring-boned brick floor.

4. *Skiing.* (See HERRING-BONE *sb.* 1 e.) Hence **herring-boning** *vbl. sb.*

1904 E. C. RICHARDSON *Ski-Running* 35 (*caption*) Herring-boning. **1914** *Queen* 17 Jan. 128/2 He climbed very quickly, looking uncommonly like a monkey up a stick as he herring-boned in jerks up the slope. **1919** *Century Mag.* May 43/1 'You're herring-boning!' shouted Dean. 'Don't herring-bone! We'll come to that later.' **1946** H. CROOME *Faithless Mirror* 55 Half a dozen boys herringboning up from the road. *Ibid.* 67 Half a dozen skiers herringboned up the trail towards them.

herring-buss. *Obs.* exc. *Hist.* [a. Du. *haring-buis*: see BUSS *sb.*[1]] A two- or three-masted vessel used in the herring-fishery.

1615 E. S. *Brit. Buss* in Arb. *Garner* III. 636 To seek out the said Herring Busses, and to buy of them their herrings. **1691** *Lond. Gaz.* No. 2684/3, 7 or 8 French Frigats and Privateers..fell in with our Herring-Busses. **1776** ADAM SMITH *W.N.* IV. v. (1869) II. 93 The tonnage bounty upon the herring-buss fishery. **1831** CARLYLE *Sart. Res.* II. v, The common fleet of herring-busses and whalers.

†**herring-cob.** *Obs.* [See COB *sb.*[1] 8.] The head of a herring; *fig.* a stupid head: cf. CODS-HEAD. (In Dicts. from Littleton onward, erroneously given as 'a young herring'.)

1594, 1632 [see COB *sb.*[1] 8]. **1678** LITTLETON *Lat. Dict.* s.v. *Cob*, A herring-cob, *Halecula.* **1706** PHILLIPS (ed. Kersey), *Herring-cob*, a young Herring. **1719** D'URFEY *Pil to Purge Melanch.*, The rubbish and outcast of your herringcobs invention.

herringer ('hɛrɪŋə(r)). [f. HERRING + -ER.]

a. One who goes herring-fishing. **b.** A boat used in herring-fishing.

1857 KINGSLEY *Two Y. Ago* xiv, A lot of long-shore merchant-skippers and herringers, who went about calling themselves captains. **1887** *Pall Mall G.* 2 May 11/2 We are not going to ride to a mile and a half of netting, like a herringer of the Minch.

herring-pond. *humorous.* The sea or ocean, esp. the North Atlantic ocean.

1686 J. DUNTON *Lett. fr. New-Eng.* (1867) 19 I'le send an account of the wonders I meet on the Great Herring-Pond. **1689** in *Harl. Misc.* (1746) VIII. 603/1 My sometime Friends and Allies on the other Side of the Herring-pond. **1729** GAY *Polly* I. Wks. (1772) 146 How little are our Customs known on this side the herring pond. **1824** *New Monthly Mag.* X. 498 We hired a boat to cross the herring pond Which intersects great Britain and fair France. **1861** MRS. H. WOOD *E. Lynne* I. ii. (1888) 157 I'd send them over the herring-pond if I could.

‖**Herrnhuter** ('hɛrnhu:tər). Also 8 **Herren-, Hern-**, 8–9 **-hutter.** [f. *Herrnhut* (lit. the Lord's keeping), the name of their first German settlement on the estate of Count von Zinzendorf in Saxony. See quot. 1753.] One of the sect of 'United Brethren' or Moravians.

1748 *Whitehall Evening-Post* No. 449 An Edict is published against the Moravian Brethren, or.. Herrenhutters. [**1753** *Scots Mag.* May 212/1 Between this wood and the town or village is an hill called *Huthberg*, i.e. *Townguard Hill.* This gave occasion to the colonists to call themselves *Huth des Herrn*, and afterwards *Herrnhuth*, i.e. the guard or protection of the Lord.] **1834** MARY HOWITT *Sk. Nat. Hist.*, *Swallow* iv, Thou hast heard the lowing heifers On some good Herrnhuter's farm [in S. Africa]. **1879** BARING-GOULD *Germany* II. 189 His spiritual songs.. now stand in the hymn-book of the Herrnhuters.

Hence **'Herrnhutism, Herrn'hutenism, Herrn'hutianism**, Moravianism.

1753 *Scots Mag.* May 212/1 Herrnhutism does indeed.. appear to be..essentially evil. **1879** BARING-GOULD *Germany* II. 188 Pietism of mystic tendency culminated in Count..Zinzendorf..and Herrnhutenism. **1882–3** SCHAFF *Encycl. Relig. Knowl.* II. 1604 Mysticism entered into various combinations with Pietism, Herrnhutianism [etc.].

herrod, -old, -owd, obs. ff. HERALD *sb.*

herry, -ye, Sc. forms of HARRY *v.*

herrylle, obs. form of EARL.

hers (hɜːz), *poss. pron.*[1] Forms: 3–5 **hirs, hiris**, 4–5 **hires**, 5 **heres, -is, heerys, hyres**, 5–6 **hyrs**, 5– **hers.** [In form, a double possessive, f. poss. pron. *hire*, HER, thus *hires*, *her's*, *hers* (cf. *ours*, *yours*, *theirs*), app. by association with the possessive case in such phrases as 'a friend of *John's*', whence 'a friend of *her's*', formerly 'a friend of *her* (*hire*)'. Of northern origin; the midland and southern equivalent being HERN[1].]

a. The absolute form of the possessive pronoun HER, used when no noun follows: = Her one, her ones; that or those pertaining to her. (= F. *le sien, la sienne, les siens*, Ger. *der, die, das ihrige*.) See also HIS *absolute poss. pron.* b.

13.. *Cursor M.* 8608 (Gött) Fra hir fere scho stal hir barn, And laid bi hir hirs [*Trin.* And leide hiren þere] so for-farn. *Ibid.* 20016 (Cott.) Hirs [*v.rr.* hiris, hiren] am i wit all þat i can. **1382** WYCLIF *Job* xxxix. 16 She is maad hard to hir sones, as thoȝ thei be not hiris. *c* **1386** CHAUCER *Miller's T.* 221 Ffor this was his desir and hire [*Petw. MS.* hers] also. —— *Man of Law's T.* 129, I moot been hires [*v.rr.* hers, hirs], I may noon oother chese. *c* **1430** *Life St. Kath.* (1884) 1 To oure lordys wurschip and his holy moders and hyres. **1548** HALL *Chron., Edw. IV*, 219 [She] registered her selfe and hers, as persones there privileged. **1592** SHAKS. *Rom. & Jul.* II. iii. 59 As mine on hers, so hers is set on mine. **1621** LADY M. WROTH *Urania* 464 Shee was forced to confesse her's was the fault. **1841** MIALL in *Nonconf.* I. 257 They must be hers of her own right.

b. *of hers* = belonging to her.

1478 J. PASTON in *Paston Lett.* No. 812 III. 219 Aftyr the dyssease of a steppe modyr of hyrs. **1482** *Monk of Evesham* (Arb.) 70 A..neybur of herys [*printed* herns]. **1483** CAXTON *Gold. Leg.* 321 b/2 This lady..buryed them secretely in a felde of heerys. *c* **1630** RISDON *Surv. Devon* §293 (1810) 302 These her eleemosinary acts of hers are almost vanished. *Mod.* She mentioned the matter to a friend of hers.

†**c.** Formerly used for the first of two possessives followed by a substantive, as ***hers and my father***, now *her father and mine.*

1611 SHAKS. *Cymb.* V. v. 186 Hers and mine Adultery. **1707** in *Lond. Gaz.* No. 4356/2 Her Majesty..is very sensible of their Zeal for Her's and the Publick Service.

†**hers**, *poss. pron.*[2] *Obs.* Also 4 **heoris**, 4–5 **heres**, **heris**. [Formed in same way as prec. of HER 'their'; supplanted by THEIRS before 1500. A southern equivalent was HERN[2]. The earlier form was *here*, *hire*, etc.] = THEIRS.

c **1340** *Cursor M.* 2507 (Trin.) þei helde heres [*v.rr.* þairs, þaires] was þe lond, For þei hadde þe ouer hond. *Ibid.* 22578 And þo to hores [*v.r.* heris] vche a burne. *c* **1380** WYCLIF *Wks.* (1880) 300 Pore men..þat hauen greet neede for hem & heoris. *c* **1380** *Antecrist* in Todd *Three Treat. Wyclif* (1851) 133 Crist forsoke his wille; þei seken hers be it riȝt or wronge. *c* **1449** PECOCK *Repr.* 397 If Y..consente not for me and my Successours in my name and heris for to fulfille [etc.].

hers(e, Sc. forms of HOARSE.

hersale, obs. var. of HIRSEL, flock.

†**hersall**. *Obs. nonce-wd.* A Spenserian shortening of REHEARSAL. Cf. HERSING.

1590 SPENSER *F.Q.* III. xi. 18 With this sad hersall of his heavy stresse The warlike Damzell was empassiond sore.

Herschel ('hɜːʃəl). *Astron.* **1.** A name proposed (and to some extent used) for the planet now called Uranus, after its discoverer, Sir William Herschel in 1781.

1819 *Pantologia*, *Herschel*, the name by which several astronomers call the primary plant discovered by Dr. Herschell in March 1781. **1878** NEWCOMB *Pop. Astron.* 355 Herschel proposed to call the new planet Georgium Sidus.. Lalande thought the most appropriate name of the planet was that of its discoverer, and therefore proposed to call it Herschel.

2. Used *attrib.* or in the possessive to designate certain phenomena or principles discovered by or related to the work of Sir William or Sir John *Herschel* (see HERSCHELIAN *a.*), as ***Herschel('s) condition***, a condition that must be satisfied by a system of lenses if spherical aberration is to be absent in the images of two neighbouring objects; ***Herschel effect***, the partial destruction of the latent image on a photographic negative by the action of infra-red radiation; ***Herschel's fringes***, spectral fringes observed in a prism standing on a plane mirror at the line of separation between the brighter field, due to incident light internally reflected by the prism, and the darker field, due to light externally reflected by the mirror, first observed by Sir William Herschel.

1890 T. PRESTON *Theory of Light* viii. 153 (*heading*) Herschel's fringes. **1909** *Jrnl. Chem. Soc.* XCVI. II. 141 Warnerke's modification of the Herschel Effect and the Preparation of the Substance of the Latent Image. **1910** J. P. C. SOUTHALL *Princ. & Methods Geom. Optics* xii. 394 It has..been suggested that the other requirement should be the so-called Herschel-Condition; that is, that the function $\phi_1 Z_1 + \phi_2 Z_2$ should vanish not only for the particular value of x_1 but also for object-points on the axis very near to the point M_1 to which the value x_1 belongs. **1932** HARDY & PERRIN *Princ. Optics* vi. 98 The condition that $n \sin \frac{1}{2}\theta / n' \sin \frac{1}{2}\theta'$ = a constant must be satisfied for all values of θ. This is commonly called the Herschel condition although it had not been formulated mathematically when Herschel constructed his objective. *Ibid.* xi. 233 This Herschel effect has a very important significance in connection with theories of the latent image but has not been found very useful as a technique for infrared photography. **1957** R. S. LONGHURST *Geom. & Physical Optics* xiv. 280 Herschel's condition is the condition that must be satisfied if the system is to form, simultaneously, a good image of a neighbouring axial object point.

Herschelian (hə'ʃɛlıən), *a.* (*sb.*) [f. proper name *Herschel* + -IAN.]

Of or pertaining to the astronomer Sir William Herschel (1738–1822), or his son Sir John Herschel (1792–1871). ***Herschelian (telescope)***, a form of reflecting telescope having a concave mirror slightly inclined to the axis. ***Herschelian rays***, the ultra-red heat rays of the spectrum, the existence of which was first proved by Sir W. Herschel.

1792 *Phil. Trans.* LXXXII. 310, I looked at the planet with an Herschellean four and seven-feet reflector. **1837** GORING & PRITCHARD *Microgr.* 155 The Newtonian and Herschelian telescopes having very small angles of aperture, will admit of concave metals with spherical figures. **1838** *Proc. Amer. Phil. Soc.* I. 58 A seven feet Herschelian.

So **Her'schelic** *a.* = prec.

1874 FISKE *Cosmic Philos.* I. I. 19 Beyond the red..lie the so-called Herschellic rays, of least refrangibility.

herschelite ('hɜːʃəlaıt). *Min.* [Named 1825 after Sir John Herschel: see -ITE.] A hydrous silicate of aluminium, calcium, and sodium, now considered a variety of chabazite.

1825 T. THOMSON *Ann. Philos.* Ser. II. X. 262 Dr. Wollaston..has examined chemically a small quantity of Herschelite. **1868** DANA *Min.* (ed. 5) 437 Herschelite.. accompanies phillipsite in a lava at Aci Castello.

herse (hɜːs), *sb.* Also 5 **hierche**, 6 **hersse**, 6–7 **hearse**. [a. F. *herse* (12th c. in Littré) harrow:—L. *hirpex*, *hirpic-em*, large rake used as a harrow. The same word which, in a different group of senses, has now the form HEARSE.]

†**1.** A harrow, for agricultural use. Also **b.** A harrow used for a cheval-de-frise, and laid in the way or in breaches with the points upward to obstruct enemy. *Obs.*

[**1454** in Rogers *Agric. & Prices* III. 555/1, 2 new herciæ sive canill @ /8.] **1480** CAXTON *Ovid's Met.* XIII. xv, He kembyd his heer wᵗ an hierche in stede of a combe. **1727–41** CHAMBERS *Cycl.*, *Herse* is also a harrow, which the besieged, for want of *chevaux de frise*, lay either in the way, or in breaches, with the points up, to incommode the march as well of the horse, as the infantry.

c. A portcullis grated and spiked. *Hist.*

1704 J. HARRIS *Lex. Tech.*, *Herse*, in Fortification, is a Lattice in the form of a Harrow, and beset with many Iron Spikes. It is usually hung..that the herse may fall, and stop up the Passage..or other Entrance of a Fortress. **1841** *Archæologia* XXIX. 62 The..absence of the Herse is very unusual, and can only be explained, under the supposition that there was one at the porch of entrance, now fallen.

d. *Her.* A charge representing a portcullis or a harrow.

1525 LD. BERNERS *Froiss.* II. clxxi. [clxvii.] 501 The deuyse in yᵉ Standerde was a Herse golde, standyng on a bed goules.

†**2.** *Mil.* A form of battle array. Cf. HARROW *sb.*[1] 3. *Obs.*

The actual arrangement is much controverted.

1523 LD. BERNERS *Froiss.* I. cxxx. 156 The archers..stode in maner of a herse, and the men of armes in the botome of the batayle. *Ibid.* clx. 195 Men of armes afote and archers afore them, in maner of a herse. **1581** STYWARD *Mart. Discipl.* I. 92 To place the like number in an hearse or square Battaile. *Ibid.* 93 Sometime by reason of the ground it is necessarie to bring such a number into an hearse or twofolde battaile which maie be more auailable then the quadrant battaile. **1590** SIR J. SMYTH *Disc. conc. Weapons* 30–33. **1635** BARRIFFE *Mil. Discip.* xciv. (1643) 300 The Hearse Battell.. is when the depth doth manifold exceed the length, thrice at the least. **1884** R. F. BURTON *Bk. of the Sword* 245 The Phalanx or oblong herse was irresistible during the compact advance. **1897** *Eng. Hist. Rev.* July 432, etc.

3. A frame on which skins are dried: see quot.

1875 *Ure's Dict. Arts* III. 513 They [skins] must be set to dry in such a way as to prevent their puckering, and to render them easily worked. The small manufacturers make use of hoops for this purpose, but the greater employ a *herse*, or stout wooden frame.

Hence **hersed** *a.*, drawn up in the military formation called a herse.

1795 SOUTHEY *Joan of Arc* II. 88 From his hersed bowmen how the arrows flew Thick as the snow-flakes.

†**herse**, *v. Obs. rare.* [f. OE. type *hersian, related to *herian* HERY, as HALSE *v.*[1] is to HAIL *v.*[2]] *trans.* To glorify or extol.

a **1400–50** *Alexander* 2200 Mast hiȝe ȝe ere hersid & herid of ȝoure strenthe. *Ibid.* 2498 þe hiȝere I here him enhansed & hersude his name.

herself (hə'sɛlf), *pron.* [OE. *hire self*, *selfre*, f. *hire* HER, *dat.-acc. pers. pron.* + SELF. *Self* was in OE. an adj. which could be inflected in concord with any case of the pronoun; e.g. *héo self*, *hire selfre*, *hie selfe*; the dative form is the source of the modern use. For the history of the constructions see SELF.]

I. Emphatic use. = Very her, very she, that very woman, etc. = L. *ipsa*.

1. As dative and (later) general objective.

c **1200** *Trin. Coll. Hom.* 219 [Ysaie] nemnede hire cun to more and hire su[l]f to gerde. *a* **1400–50** *Alexander* 347 þan suld he say to hire-selfe sadly þire wordis. **1559** W. CUNNINGHAM *Cosmogr. Glasse* 1 Men did more earnestly.. seke Vertu for hir selfe. *Mod.* She was told that it was meant for herself.

2. Standing in apposition with the nominative pronoun, or with a sb. in nominative or objective.

c **1175** *Lamb. Hom.* 157 Heo werð hire solf waschen of hire fule sunnen. **1591** SHAKS. *Two Gent.* V. iv. 98 And Iulia her selfe did giue it me. **1697** DRYDEN *Virg. Georg.* III. 60 Envy her self at last..Shall give her Hands. **1762** GOLDSM. *Cit. W.* xviii. ⁋10 He..went in pursuit of Hansi herself. **1838** THIRLWALL *Greece* V. 43 Sparta herself forming the first. **1864** BRYCE *Holy Rom. Emp.* vi. (1875) 78 The Saracen wasted the Mediterranean coasts, and sacked Rome herself. *Mod.* I heard it from a lady who herself was present.

3. Taking the place of the nominative pronoun.

a **1300** *Cursor M.* 10822 (Gött.) Of þat ellde hir self was in [*Cott.* þat sco was in]. *a* **1400–50** *Alexander* 266 Sone as hire selfe it sawe. *c* **1400** *Destr. Troy* 4642 Hir seluyn is wrothe, And has wroght vs þis wedur. **1594** SHAKS. *Rich. III*, I. i. 81 The iealous ore-worne Widdow, and her selfe..Are mighty Gossips. **1808** T. JEFFERSON *Writ.* (1830) IV. 112 A determination..that herself and her allies will demand from Great Britain no renunciation of her maritime principles. **1814** BYRON *Lara* II. xxv, Herself would..seat her down upon some linden's root.

b. Used alone in predicate after *be*, *become*, etc., and in adverbial extensions = by herself. ***to be herself***: to be in her normal condition of mind and body, to be in full possession of her faculties: see SELF.

c **1320** R. BRUNNE *Medit.* 453 Oure lady wente here seluyn alone. *c* **1430** *Syr Tryam.* 408 There sche travaylyd of a chylde, Hyrselfe allone, withowtyn moo. **1636** MASSINGER *Gt. Dk. Flor.* IV. ii, Being herself, then, She must exceed his praise. *a* **1700** DRYDEN (J.), The more she looks, the more her fears increase At nearer sight; and she's herself the less.

c. By Welsh or Gaelic speakers (or in ridicule of their speech) ***herself***, ***her own self*** (***her nain sel'***) is used in the same way as HER *pers. pron.* 2 b.

c **1707** in *Scot. Antiq.* (1898) XII. 105 Her nane sell does not well farstand tese Nice Points. **1814** SCOTT *Wav.* xxix, It was either ta muckle Sunday hersell, or ta little government Sunday. **1828** [see HER *pers. pron.* 2 b].

II. Reflexive use. = L. *sibi*, *se*; Ger. *sich*.

4. Dative, and objective with preposition.

971 *Blickl. Hom.* 5 Heo hæfde hire sylfre ʒeworht þæt mæste wite. *c* **1230** *Hali Meid.* 5 Ha naueð nawt freo of hire seluen. *a* **1300** *Cursor M.* 19790 Bi hir self sco satt vpright. **1490** CAXTON *Eneydos* xvii. 67 As a woman disperate and from herselfe. **1531** TINDALE *Exp. 1 John* (1537) 7 The scripture abydeth pure in herselfe. **1690** *Lond. Gaz.* No. 2581/4 Much inclined to talk to her self. **1864** TENNYSON *Aylmer's F.* 304 Made her..Swerve from her duty to herself and us.

5. Accusative or direct object.

c **1374** CHAUCER *Boeth.* I. pr. i. 2 (Camb. MS.) She constreynede and shronk hyr seluen. **1390** GOWER *Conf.* II. 30 She about her white swere It did, and henge hir selven there. **1490** CAXTON *Eneydos* xvi. 62 She hath habandonned hersilfe..to receyue the false eneas. **1513** DOUGLAS *Æneis* IV. Prol. 256 Syne for disdene alace! her selfin slew. **1598** GRENEWEY *Tacitus' Ann.* I. xiv. (1622) 27 He had been taken by the enemy, if the first legion had not opposed her selfe. **1796** H. HUNTER tr. *St. Pierre's Stud. Nat.* (1799) III. 216 She supported herself..with a greatness of soul altogether incredible. **1864** TENNYSON *Aylmer's F.* 303 You have.. Perplext her, made her half forget herself.

III. From the 14th c. probably, as in the corresponding *his self*, there has been a tendency to treat *her* as the possessive pronoun, and *self* as sb., whence such expressions as ***her very self***, ***her own self***, ***her good***, ***dear***, ***sweet self***, and the like. See MYSELF, SELF.

(The formal identity of *her* personal pron. and *her* possessive (cf. *c* 1200 in 1) conceals the difference which is manifest in the parallel *himself*, *his very self*.)

hership ('hɜːʃıp). *Sc. arch.* or *Hist.* Forms: 4–7 **heir-**, 5–6 **her-**, 6 **hir-**, **hayr-**, **hear-** (**heirst-**), **heiri-**, **herry-**, 6–7 **hair-**, **-schip(e**, **-schyp(e**, (**-scheip**), 6– **hership**. [f. HERE army, host, or stem of OE. *herʒan*, ON. *herja*, to HARRY + -SHIP: cf. ON. *herskap-r* 'warfare, harrying,' which may be the actual source.]

1. Harrying, pillage, plundering, devastation; a warlike incursion, or foray; harrying of cattle.

1375 BARBOUR *Bruce* IX. 298 [The king] heryit thame on sic maneir, That..neir fifty ȝheir, Men menyt the heirschip of bouchane. *c* **1470** HENRY *Wallace* VIII. 942 On Inglismen full gret herschipe thai maid. **1549** *Compl. Scot.* i. 23 Maist extreme violent spulȝee ande hairschip of ther mouabil gudis. **1572** *Compl. Inhab. Elsdon* in *Northumb. Gloss.* s.v. *Har*, Night reffes and hearships by the thiefes of Easte and West Tividall. **1609** SKENE *Reg. Maj.*, *Stat. Robt. III*, 60 The paine of slavchter, reif, destructions and heirshippis.. It is statute that na man vse any..heirschippis, birning, Reif, slauchter, in time to come. **1814** SCOTT *Wav.* xv, The committing of divers thefts, reifs, and herships, upon the honest men of the Low Country. **1818** —— *Hrt. Midl.* xlii. *note*, Her'ship, a Scottish word which may be said to be now obsolete; because, fortunately, the practice of 'plundering by armed force', which is its meaning, does not require to be commonly spoken of.

2. A harried condition; hence, ruin, distress, famine, caused by robbery with violence or the like.

1536 BELLENDEN *Cron. Scot.* XI. xi. (Jam.), The landwart pepyll be thir waris war brocht to sic pouerte and heirschip, that thair land was left vnsawin and vnlabourit. **1556** LAUDER *Tractate* 109 Bryngand thame to pouertie, To hounger, hirscheip, and rewyne. **1609** SKENE *Reg. Maj.*, *Stat. Will.* 8 Trubland Gods people with skarsnes, povertie, and outer hairschip.

3. Booty, plunder; esp. cattle forcibly driven off.

1535 STEWART *Cron. Scot.* (1858) I. 117 All the heirschip, tane wes of befoir, To euerilk steid tha gart agane restoir. **1768** ROSS *Helenore* 46 (Jam.) The track at last he found, Of the ca'd hership on the mossy ground.

‖**hersillon**. *Obs.* [F. *hersillon*, f. *herse*.]

1704 J. HARRIS *Lex. Techn.*, *Hersillon*, in Fortification, is a Plank stuck with Iron Spikes, for the same use as the Herse. **1706** PHILLIPS (ed. Kersey), *Hersillon*, a Plank Ten or Twelve Foot long stuck full of Nails, with the points up.

hersing. *Obs.* Shortened f. REHEARSING.

a **1420** *Anturs of Arth.* li, With-outun any hersing [*other MSS.* more lettynge], There diȝte was thayre saȝtenyng.

†**hersoun**, *v. Obs. rare.* [app. for *hersen*, extended form of HERSE *v.*: cf. *halson*, HALSEN *v.* similarly formed.] *trans.* To glorify, do honour to.

a **1400–50** *Alexander* 1600 Bowes hym downe..And hersouns þat haly name þat he byheld written.

hersute, obs. form of HIRSUTE.

hert(e, obs. ff. HART, HEART, HURT.

hert, obs. f. *art*, inflection of BE *v.*

a **1300** *Cursor M.* 20219 Sun þou hert [*v.r.* ert] of heuen king.

herte-bren, obs. form of HEARTBURN.

†**herten**, *a. Obs.* [f. ME. *hert*, HART + -EN⁴.] Made of the skin of a hart.
13.. *Horn Childe* xxix. in Ritson *Metr. Rom.* (1802) III. 293 Therwith herten gloves to, Swiche was the maner tho.

Hertfordshire ('hɑːfədʃə(r), 'hɑːt-). Formerly Hart-. [Name of an Eng. county.] In phrase ***Hertfordshire kindness***: see quots.
a **1661** FULLER *Worthies* (1811) I. 427 'Hartfordshire kindness.' This is generally taken in a good and grateful sense, for the mutual return of favours received. *a* **1700** B. E. *Dict. Cant. Crew, Hartfordshire-kindness*, Drinking to the same Man again. **1738** SWIFT *Pol. Convers.* ii. *Lord Sm.* Tom, my service to you. *Nev.* My Lord, this moment I did myself the honour to drink to your Lordship. *Lord Sm.* Why, then, that's Hertfordshire kindness. **1787** GROSE *Prov. Gloss., Hartfordshire kindness.* That is, any one drinking back to his right-hand man; i.e. the person who immediately before drank to him.

herth(e, obs. ff. HEARTH, EARTH.

hertoȝeines, in opposition to this: see HERE *adv.* 16.

hertpeny, -ston, obs. ff. HEARTH-PENNY, -STONE.

Hertz (hɜːts, ‖hɛrts). **1.** The name of H. R. *Hertz* (1857–1894), German physicist, used *attrib.* to denote apparatus used or invented, phenomena discovered, or concepts elaborated by him.
1890 *Nature* Feb. 368 By separating the coats of the jar as far as possible we get a typical Hertz vibrator. **1892** O. LODGE *Mod. Views Electr.* 361 Hertz waves can get through deal doors and stone walls. **1898** *Science Siftings* XIV. 117/2 A Hertz-wave 'detector'. **1898** *Westm. Gaz.* 12 May 9/2 Experiments in Hertz-wave space telegraphy. **1902** *Encycl. Brit.* XXXIII. 230/2 This aerial being used as a Hertz oscillator or radiator. **1962** CORSON & LORRAIN *Introd. Electromagn. Fields* xiii. 488 The Hertz vector *Π* is defined by the equation $A = \epsilon\mu\frac{\partial\Pi}{\partial t}$.
2. *Physics.* (Usu. *hertz.*) A unit of frequency, equal to one cycle per second. Abbrev. Hz.
1928 *B.B.C. Handbk.* 270/1 *Hertz*, a term sometimes used to designate frequency, meaning one cycle per second. **1934** *Electr. Engin.* (U.S.) LIII. 403/2 It was proposed by the Italian committee that the name *hertz* be given to the unit of frequency—one cycle per second... The *hertz* is used almost universally in German technical literature. **1967** *Electronics* 6 Mar. 325/1 Markus continues to use 'cycles per second' instead of 'hertz'. **1967** *New Scientist* 5 Oct. 6/2 The frequency band between about 10 megahertz and 20 gigahertz is technically suitable for space communication.

Hertzian ('hɜːtsɪən), *a.* [f. the name *Hertz* (see prec.) + -IAN.] Of or pertaining to Hertz or to the phenomena discovered by him.
Hertzian telegraphy: wireless telegraphy. ***Hertzian waves*** (see WAVE *sb.* 5 a).
1890 A. E. BOSTWICK in *Appleton's Ann. Cycl.* 716/1 (Funk), Trouton..found that glass absorbs Hertzian vibrations with comparative rapidity. **1897** RUTHERFORD in *Phil. Trans. R. Soc.* A. CLXXXIX. 1 They were also found to be a sensitive means of detecting electrical radiation from Hertzian vibrators at long distances from the vibrator. *Ibid.* 8 A detector for electrical waves was devised, which proved to be a sensitive means of detecting Hertzian waves. **1898** *Daily News* 3 May 5/3 The General Post Office..is also carrying out experiments in wireless Hertzian telegraphy. **1900** *Jrnl. Soc. Arts* XLVIII. 788/1 The sensation created in 1897 by Mr. Marconi's application of Hertzian waves. **1900** J. J. FAHIE *Hist. Wireless Telegr.* 197 Sir William Crookes.. was..the first to distinctly foresee the applicability of Hertzian waves to practical telegraphy. **1907** J. ERSKINE-MURRAY *Handbk. Wireless Telegr.* 36 The transmitter consisted of a Hertzian oscillator placed in the focal line of a parabolic mirror. **1908** J. A. FLEMING *Elem. Man. Radiotelegr.* 132 An arrangement of two rods..with a spark gap in the centre constitutes the simplest form of linear radiator or Hertzian Oscillator for the production of damped electro-magnetic waves. **1914** R. STANLEY *Textbk. Wireless Telegr.* 91 Using a suitable length of spark gap the discharge of this Hertzian open circuit is oscillatory. **1922** A. N. WHITEHEAD *Princ. Relativ.* xiv. 117 Now consider the internal vibration of a molecule which radiates light of period *T*..as capable of being represented as the vibration of a variable electric Hertzian doublet with this period. **1940** *Chambers's Techn. Dict.* 412/2 *Hertzian waves*, electromagnetic waves having frequencies between zero and approximately ten thousand million cycles per second; especially those towards the upper limit of this range. **1971** *Gloss. Electrotechnical Power Terms* (*B.S.I.*) III. vii. 7 *Hertzian waves*, electromagnetic waves having frequencies below those of infra-red waves.

herumfrodite, var. HARUMFRODITE.

herust, heruest, -vist, obs. ff. HARVEST.

her-ward, originally *to her-ward*, towards her: see -WARD.
c **1477** CAXTON *Jason* 113 b, To redresse Jason and Argos to herward. **1580** SIDNEY *Arcadia* (1622) 68 But the Lion.. bent his race to her-ward. **1621** LADY M. WROTH *Urania* 108 Amphilanthus..was then looking from her-ward, carelesse of her.

†'**hery**, *v. Obs.* Forms: α. 1 hẹrian, hærian, hẹrȝan, 2–4 herien, 3 herien, heryhe, 3–5 herye, 4 heriȝe, (heyre), 4–6 herie, herry, 4–7 hery. β. [1 hereþ, herede], 3 hæren, huren, heoren, 4 here. [OE. *hẹrian, hærian*:—WGer. **harjan*, **hẹrjan*, Goth. *hazjan* to praise, glorify, extol: cf. OHG. *harên*, OS. *harôn* to cry, shout. In OE., *hẹrian* (*hẹrȝan, hẹriȝan*) was conjugated, pres. *herie* (*heriȝe, herȝe*), *herest, hereð, heriað*, pa. *herede*, pa. pple. *hered*; thence in ME. arose two types, *hery, heriest, herieþ, heriede*, etc., and *here, herest, hereþ, herede*, etc.; the latter coincided in form to some extent with HEAR, with which it was app. sometimes confused: see the quots. from Layamon.]
trans. To praise, glorify, exalt, honour, worship.
α. *c* **735** *Cædmon's Hymn* 1 in *O.E. Texts* 149 Nu scylun herȝan hefaenricaes uard [*later vers.* in *Bæda's Hist.* IV. xxv, Nu sculon heriȝean heofonrices weard]. *c* **825** *Vesp. Psalter* cl. 2 Hærȝað hine in mæhtum his. *c* **893** K. ÆLFRED *Oros.* III. vii. §8 Ic nat..for hwyȝe þa tida swelcra broca swa wel herȝeað. *c* **1000** ÆLFRIC *Hom.* II. 560 Ne hera ðu nænne man on his life. *c* **1175** *Lamb. Hom.* 97 Ðisses deiȝes hehnesse is to heriane. *c* **1205** LAY. 6234 We wulleð þine men beon þine mon-scipe herien. *a* **1300** *E.E. Psalter* cxlvii. 12 Heryhe þou þi God. **1382** WYCLIF *Wisd.* xi. 16 Summe errende herieden [**1388** worschipiden] doumbe edderes. *c* **1386** CHAUCER *Clerk's T.* 560 God they thanke and herye. **1388** WYCLIF *Ps.* cxlviii. 3 Sunne and moone, herie ȝe hym; alle sterris and liȝt, herie ȝe hym. *c* **1450** *Mirour Saluacioun* 3130 Nowe honoures it king and prince & heries the gloriouse name. **1579** SPENSER *Sheph. Cal.* Nov. 10 Nor Pan to herye, nor with love to playe. **1590** —— *F.Q.* II. xii. 13 For Apolloes temple highly herried. **1622** DRAYTON *Poly-olb.* xxiv. (1748) 364 And Thanet..even to this age doth hery Her Mildred.
β. *c* **897** K. ÆLFRED *Greg. Past.* xlviii. 373 Ðæt ðæt..mon hereð. **971** *Blick. Hom.* 13 Heo Drihten herede. *c* **1175** *Lamb. Hom.* 5 Þus ha hine hereden. *c* **1200** *Trin. Coll. Hom.* 167 He herede him ouer alle men. *c* **1205** LAY. 2389 He wolde..his godd hure [*c* **1275** herie]. *Ibid.* 13900 Þa we.. heoreð heom mid mihte. *Ibid.* 16281 God ich wulle hæren [*c* **1275** herie]. *c* **1250** *Hymn* in *Trin. Coll. Hom.* 258 Iherd ȝebeo þin holi nome. **13..** *Gaw. & Gr. Knt.* 1634 Þe lorde forto here. *c* **1400** *St. Alexius* (Trin.) 250 He herede god, and made him glad.
Hence †'**heried** (**hered**) *ppl. a.*, praised, glorified, exalted. Also †'**heryer** (OE. *hẹrȝere*), worshipper. †'**heryful** *a.*, praiseworthy.
a **950** *Durham Ritual* (Surtees) 124 þætte..ðv hæbbe herȝeras [*laudatores*]. *c* **1380** WYCLIF *Serm.* Sel. Wks. II. 94 If ony be heriere of God hem he heereþ. **1382** —— 2 *Kings* x. 19 That he distruye alle the heryeris [**1388** worschipers] of Baal. **1382** —— *Dan.* iii. 25 Blessid art thou, Lord God of our fadris, and heryful [**1388** worthi to be heried] or worthi to be preyside. *a* **1400-50** *Alexander* 1637 Þe hered haly name. **1583** STANYHURST *Æneis* II. (Arb.) 54 With Gods herried order kendled.

hery, obs. form of EERIE.

herycano, obs. form of HURRICANE.

†'**herying**, *vbl. sb. Obs.* Forms: α. 1 herung, -ing, 2 -unge, -inge. β. 2 heriȝinge, 3 heriung, 3–4 heriing, 4 herying(e, -yng, 4–5 heriyng(e, 5 hereynge. [OE. *hẹrung, hẹring*, f. *hẹrian* HERY *v.* + -ING¹.] Praising, praise; glorification. With *a* (and *pl.*) A song of praise.
α. *c* **897** K. ÆLFRED *Gregory's Past.* lvi. 435 On ðære heringe ðæs eadȝan weres. *c* **1000** ÆLFRIC *Hom.* I. 60 For manna herunge. *c* **1175** *Lamb. Hom.* 5 Biuoren him sungun þisne lofsong heliliche to heringe.
β. *c* **1175** *Lamb. Hom.* 5 Him to luue and heriȝinge. *a* **1225** *Ancr. R.* 148 A windes puf of wordes hereword; of monnes heriunge. **1382** WYCLIF *Matt.* xxvi. 30 An ympne, or heriynge, seid, thei wenten out in to the mount of Olyuete. *c* **1420** *Chron. Vilod.* st. 617 To monnes hele and his hereynge.

herytes, *Obs.*: see HERITRESS.

herywater, var. HARRY-WATER, *Obs.*

Herzegovinian (ˌhɜːtsəgə'vɪnɪən), *a.* and *sb.* Also Herzo-. [f. *Herzegovina*: see -IAN.] (Of or pertaining to) a native or inhabitant of Herzegovina, a region to the south of Bosnia, now forming part of Bosnia-Herzegovina, a constituent republic of Yugoslavia. So **Herz(e)govi'nese** *a.* and *sb.*
1876 *Fraser's Mag.* May 541/2 The Herzgovinese insurgents. **1880** *Encycl. Brit.* XI. 775/2 Much of the old Slavonic customs..still holds among the Herzegovinian Mussulmans. *Ibid.*, The Herzegovinians are tall, broad, and darker..than the Bosnians. **1900** tr. *Deniker's Races of Man* 345 The southern [Slav] group..comprises the Herzogovinians, Bosnians, Montenegrins. **1904** M. E. DURHAM *Through Lands of Serb* 6 These Herzegovinese migrated to Montenegro. **1918** R. J. KERNER *Jugo-Slav Movement* 4 The Herzegovinian Serbs of the Narenta. **1935** HUXLEY & HADDON *We Europeans* vii. 213 The Herzegovinian type has a broad head, and is rather tall and inclined to be fair.

hes, *pers. pron.* her, them: see HISE.

hes, var. ES *Obs.*, carrion; north. f. *has* (see HAVE *v.*); obs. f. *is* (see BE *v.*).
c **1300** *Cursor M.* 19422 (Edin.) 'Queþir hes þis..soþe oþir nan.'

Heshvan, var. HESVAN.

Hesiodic (hiːsɪ'ɒdɪk), *a.* [f. the name of *Hesiod* (Gr. Ἡσίοδος), Greek poet of about the eighth century B.C. + -IC.] Of, pertaining to, or resembling the poetical style of Hesiod, or the school of poetry which followed him. Also **Hesi'odian** *a.*
1838 *Penny Cycl.* XII. 186/2 Ulrici considers..the story of Prometheus and that of the Five Ages as much altered from their original Hesiodic form. **1847** J. LEITCH tr. *Müller's Anc. Art* §77 The Hesiodic bards come down to about the 40th Ol[ympiad]. **1873** J. DAVIES *Hesiod & Theognis* i. 19 Under one or other of these heads it is easy to group the Hesiodic poems. *Ibid.* ii. 23 The Hesiodian rhapsodists. **1908** A. W. MAIR *Hesiod* p. xi, The Hesiodic epic is the antithesis of the Homeric. **1970** G. E. EVANS *Where Beards wag All* xx. 223 In literature there was little beyond a Hesiodic theogony or some Orphic hymns to exhibit.

hesitance ('hɛzɪtəns). [f. L. *hæsitāntia* (see next and -ANCE).] Hesitation.
1601 BP. W. BARLOW *Defence* 44 Yet there may be, in faith,..haesitance and wavering. **1836** H. ROGERS *J. Howe* iii. (1863) 55, I know not how any could preach consistently, and without hesitance and regret. **1849** D. G. MITCHELL *Bath Summ.* (1852) 167.

hesitancy ('hɛzɪtənsɪ). Also 7 hæs-. [ad. L. *hæsitāntia* stammering, f. pres. ppl. of *hæsitāre* to HESITATE: see -ANCY.] The quality or condition of hesitating; indecision, vacillation; an instance of this.
1617 J. HALES *Serm.* 1 It brought..a preservation against all doubt and hesitancy. **1656** HEYLIN *Surv. France* 155 Without the least demure or haesitancie. **1768–74** TUCKER *Lt. Nat.* (1852) I. 69 Such hesitancies as these are weeds of the richest soils. **1886** MRS. LYNN LINTON *P. Carew* I. xii. 219 That perpetual hesitancy which belongs to people whose intelligence and temperament are at variance.

hesitant ('hɛzɪtənt), *a.* [ad. L. *hæsitānt-em*, pres. pple. of *hæsitāre* to HESITATE. Cf. F. *hésitant.*] Hesitating; irresolute, undecided; stammering.
1647 TRAPP *Comment.* 2 *Cor.* v. 6 Not haesitant, or halting, as Hadrian the Emperour was. **1651** BAXTER *Inf. Bapt.* 278 Are you not here hesitant also? **1683** KENNETT tr. *Erasm. on Folly* (1709) 16 The delivery of Achilles was rough, harsh, and hesitant. **1856** R. A. VAUGHAN *Mystics* (1860) I. III. i. 52 The hesitant and conflicting conjectures of Philo.

'**hesitantly**, *adv.* [f. prec. + -LY².] In a hesitant manner; hesitatingly.
1660 BOYLE *New Exp. Phys. Mech.* Pref. 4 Rather doubtfully, or hesitantly, then resolvedly. **1688** —— *Final Causes Nat. Things* ii. 78 We may rationally believe more, and speak less hesitantly. **1883** *Harper's Mag.* Nov. 953/1 He added, hesitantly: 'I'm afraid it bodes no good.'

hesitate ('hɛzɪteɪt), *v.* [f. L. *hæsitāt-*, ppl. stem of *hæsitāre* to stick fast, stammer in speech, be undecided, freq. of *hærēre* (pa. pple. *hæs-um*) to stick, adhere, hold fast. Cf. F. *hésiter.*]
1. *intr.* **a.** To hold back in doubt or indecision; to show, or speak with, indecision; to find difficulty in deciding; to scruple. Const. various preps.
1623 COCKERAM, *Hesitate*, to doubt. **1709** SHAFTESB. *Moralist* II. i. in *Charac.* (1711) II. 237 It must needs become a Sceptick above all Men to hesitate in Matters of Exchange. **1771** GOLDSM. *Hist. Eng.* II. 343 The citizens of London hesitated on the demand. **1839** THIRLWALL *Greece* VI. 149. **1848** RUSKIN *Mod. Paint.* II. III. II. iii. 179 *note*, He may pause, but he must not hesitate. *a* **1849** POE *Tales* (1884) I. 93 At the baptismal font I hesitated for a name. **1856** DE QUINCEY *Confess.* (1896) 216 This..surgeon saw no reason whatever in the simple practice of opium-eating for hesitating upon a life-insurance proposal. **1860** W. COLLINS *Woman in White* I. iv. 33, I hesitated about answering it. **1908** *Grand Mag.* Dec. 612/2 I'm only hesitating over the price.
b. with *infin.* or *clause.* (Rarely with *vbl. sb.*)
1755 WARBURTON *Serm.* xviii. Wks. 1811 X. 3 [They] could never hesitate a moment to conclude [etc.]. **1761** EARL HARCOURT in Ellis *Orig. Lett.* Ser. II. IV. 440 There was no room to hesitate one moment whether I was to accept such a..distinction. **1763** SCRAFTON *Indostan* iii. (1770) 69 Admiral Watson, apprehensive he might be reflected on.. hesitated signing. **1802** MILNE in *Med. Jrnl.* (1804) XII. 452, I have..never hesitated to inoculate every person that has been brought to me.
†**c.** To be uncertain, be in doubt *that. Obs.*
1807 T. THOMSON *Chem.* (ed. 3) II. 193 It was no longer possible to hesitate that this acid was composed of carbon and oxygen.
d. *spec.* in *Dancing* (see quot. 1919).
1914 V. CASTLE *Mod. Dancing* iv. 72 In my opinion it is much better to hesitate when the music hesitates. **1919** E. SCOTT *All about Latest Dances* 87 The term 'hesitate', as regards the waltz we are now considering, implies merely that you pause, or move in what appears a faltering manner at a given juncture.
e. To move in an indecisive, faltering manner.
1908 H. G. WELLS *War in Air* v. 168 He hesitated towards the door of the cabin. **1917** T. S. ELIOT *Prufrock* 27 Regard that woman Who hesitates toward you in the light of the door.
2. To stammer or falter in speech.
1706 PHILLIPS (ed. Kersey), To *Hesitate*, to stammer or falter, to hum and haw.
3. *trans.* **a.** To express or say with hesitation.
1735 POPE *Prol. Sat.* 204 Willing to wound, and yet afraid to strike, Just hint a fault, and hesitate dislike. **1794** GODWIN *Cal. Williams* i. 6, I hesitated a confused and irresolute answer. **1827** SCOTT *Napoleon* xxxviii, He humbly hesitated, that he could not safely honour it [a bill]. **1886** LOWELL *Orat. Harvard* 8 Nov. Wks. 1890 VI. 160, I choose rather to hesitate my opinion than to assert it roundly.

b. With sentence as quasi-obj.

1816 Scott *Tales my Landlord* II. xii. 311 'I am not sure,' hesitated Edith. **1881** C. E. L. Riddell *Sen. Partner* xvi, 'It looks awful like the stuff last night,' hesitated Mr. McCullagh.

'hesitater. Also -tor. [f. prec. + -ER[1]; the form in *-or* follows L. analogies.] One who hesitates, wavers, or is irresolute; a waverer.

1852 Lytton *My Novel* XII. xxv, 'Hear, hear', from the hundred and fifty hesitators. **1881** *Q. Rev.* July 8 Conscience made him not a coward but a hesitater.

hesitating ('hɛzɪteɪtɪŋ), *ppl. a.* [f. HESITATE *v.* + -ING[2].] That hesitates: see the verb.

1622 Bacon *Hen. VII*, Wks. 1825 III. 494 In speech he was slow, and in some measure hesitating. **1712** *Lond. Gaz.* No. 5001/3 Somewhat hesitating in his speech. **1849** Macaulay *Hist. Eng.* vii. II. 208 After this..James made his first hesitating and ungracious advances towards the Puritans. **1897** *Cavalry Tactics* xiv. 80 The bolder the better; hesitating cavalry are defeated cavalry.

Hence **'hesitatingly** *adv.*, in a hesitating manner; **'hesitatingness**, hesitating manner or quality.

1800 Mrs. Hervey *Mourtray Fam.* IV. 194 'Nothing serious is the matter, upon my honour', answered he, hesitatingly. **1890** *Spectator* 25 Jan., The hesitatingness of the one European, and the decisiveness of the other.

hesitation (hɛzɪ'teɪʃən). Also 7-8 hæs-. [ad. L. *hæsitātiōn-em*, n. of action f. *hæsitāre* to HESITATE. Cf. F. *hésitation* (*c* 1400 in Hatz.-Darm.).]

1. a. The action of hesitating; a pausing or delaying in deciding or acting, due to irresolution; the condition of doubt in relation to action.

1622 Bacon *Hen. VII*, Wks. 1825 III. 297 He did sadly and constantly, without hesitation or varying..stand to that he had said. **1683** Kennett tr. *Erasm. on Folly* 90 Without the least demur or haesitation. **1759** Robertson *Hist. Scot.* I. v. 378 She rejected it without hesitation. **1875** Jowett *Plato* (ed. 2) IV. 33 We have no hesitation in determining what is right and wrong.

b. with *pl.* An instance of this.

1695 Woodward *Nat. Hist. Earth* Pref., The Difficulties and Hæsitations of every one.

2. a. Embarrassed halting in utterance; stammering.

1709 Steele *Tatler* No. 5 ⁋2, I heard him send his Man of an Errand Yesterday without any Manner of Hæsitation. **1720** Swift *Wks.* (1778) X. 15 Many clergymen..write in so diminutive a manner..that they are hardly able to go on without perpetual hesitations or extemporary expletives.

b. ***hesitation-form***, a sound or form, e.g. (ɜː), used deliberately or accidentally when faltering or stammering in speech. So ***hesitation-vowel***, etc. (Cf. ER.)

1933 Bloomfield *Lang.* xii. 186 When a speaker hesitates, English and some other languages offer special parenthetic *hesitation-forms*, as [ə:] or [ɛ] in *Mr.—ah—Sniffen.* **1957** S. Potter *Mod. Ling.* v. 122 He may even inflict indeterminate *hesitation-forms* [ə:] or [ɑ:] upon his suffering hearers. **1965** *Canad. Jrnl. Ling.* XI. I. 36 This is often called the 'hesitation vowel' although it is not a vowel qua vowel at all.

3. In full ***hesitation waltz*** or ***valse***: a variety of waltz, characterized by the ***hesitation step*** (see quot. 1919). Also *fig.* So ***hesitation-valse*** (*nonce-wd.*) *v. intr.*

1914 V. Castle *Mod. Dancing* iv. 71 It is the Hesitation Waltz. **1918** J. M. Grider *Diary* 29 Jan. (1927) 71 It's a long jump from the Boston and the hesitation to the giant swing, but we had them all fox-trotting in no time. **1919** E. Scott *All about Latest Dances* 86 As you lift the left foot..from the floor, count a short one, two; and on three drag the other foot along the floor, bringing it over in front of the first foot, which is by this time on the floor... That is the hesitation step. **1920** A. M. Cree *Ball-Room Dancing* 41 The Hesitation Valse is a variety of the true valse that can very easily be performed once the valse is known. **1924** 'L. Malet' *Dogs of Want* v. §2 For over four hours a mixed multitude..had one-stepped, two-stepped, hesitation-valsed, and fox-trotted. **1927** *Daily Express* 31 Oct. 11/6 The foxtrot, tango, and the hesitation. **1959** *Chambers's Encycl.* IV. 364/1 During the first world war..the occasional waltzes..were danced with a slight hesitation movement. **1972** R. Mayne *Europeans* v. 136 Britain's slow hesitation waltz with European unity.

† **hesi'tatious,** *a. Obs. rare.* [f. as prec. + -OUS.] Characterized by hesitation.

1657 Earl Monm. tr. *Paruta's Polit. Disc.* 194 If a powerful and vain-glorious Prince..would make use of haesitatious counsels, [etc.].

hesitative ('hɛzɪteɪtɪv), *a.* [f. L. *hæsitāt-*, pa. ppl. stem of *hæsitāre* to HESITATE: see -IVE.]

Shewing, or given to, hesitation.

1795 *Montford Castle* II. 150 He stood hesitative and confused. **1865** Carlyle *Fredk. Gt.* XVIII. xiv. VIII. 86 For four days more, he hung about the place, minatory, hesitative; but attempted nothing feasible. **1882** Mozley *Remin. Oriel* I. 152 His hesitative manner of speaking.

Hence **'hesitatively** *adv.*, in a hesitating manner.

1881 R. A. King *Love the Debt* xix, 'I think I'd try giving her notice again, first', hesitatively suggested his feeble fellow-bachelor.

hesitatory ('hɛzɪteɪtərɪ), *a.* [f. as prec.: see -ORY.] = HESITATIVE.

a **1734** North *Exam.* (1740) 596 Being..cautelous, and not soon determined, but hesitatory at unusual Occurrences in his Office. **1849** Carlyle *Reminisc. Irish Journ.* 2 July (1882) 31 Voice thin, creaky, querulous-hesitatory.

† **'hesitude.** *Obs. rare*[−0]. In 7 hæs-. [f. L. *hæs-*, ppl. stem of *hærēre* to stick + -TUDE.]

1623 Cockeram II, Doubtfulnes, *Hæsitude.*

hesp, Sc. and north. form of HASP *sb.*

1824 Scott *Redgauntlet* Let. xi, A tangled hesp to wind.

hespe, obs. form of ASP[1].

c **1425** Wr.-Wülcker 646/36 *Hec tremulus*, a hespetre.

Hesped ('hɛspɛd). [Heb.] A funeral oration pronounced over the dead at a Jewish memorial service.

1650 E. Chilmead tr. *Leon Modena's Hist. Rites of Jews* v. ix. 242 If he were a Rabbine that is dead, or a person of quality, they then have Sermons, and Funeral Orations, which they call..*Hesped*, made for him. **1892** I. Zangwill *Childr. Ghetto* I. I. xiv. 295 Moses Ansell was at *Shool*, listening to a *Hesped* or funeral oration. **1970** L. M. Feinsilver *Taste of Yiddish* 131 *Hesped*, eulogy.

Hesper ('hɛspə(r)). *poet.* [ad. L. HESPER-US, q.v.] The evening star; = HESPERUS.

1623 Cockeram, *Hesper*, the euening starre. **1656** Stanley *Hist. Philos.* v. (1701) 178/1 A Phosphor 'mongst the Living, late wert thou, But Shin'st among the Dead a Hesper now. **1761** Beattie *Pastoral* x. 124 Lo beamy Hesper gilds the western sky. **1850** Tennyson *In Mem.* cxxi, Sad Hesper o'er the buried sun And ready, thou, to die with him.

hesper-, stem of HESPERUS, used in the same sense as HESPERID-, as the radical part of several chemical terms, as **he'speric, hespe'retic, hespe'rinic, hespe'risic** *adjs.*, denominating acids. **hespe'retin, -'etol**: see quots.

1881 Watts *Dict. Chem.* VIII. 1029 *Hesperetic acid*, $C_{10}H_{10}O_4$, is likewise formed by the action of alkalis on hesperidin. *Ibid.* 1028 *Hesperidin* is a glucoside, and is resolved by dilute acids into glucose and hesperetin $C_{16}H_{14}O_6$. **1886** *Syd. Soc. Lex.*, *Hesperetol* $C_9H_{10}O_2$, a yellowish oil that stiffens in a crystalline manner, obtained by the dry distillation of lime hesperetinate. *Ibid.*, *Hesperinic acid*, $C_6H_6O_3$,..obtained by the action of nitric acid on Hesperidene. **1889** Muir & Morley *Watts' Dict. Chem.* II. 684 *Hesperic acid*, $C_{22}H_{28}O_7$, an acid which may be extracted by alcohol from orange peel in water, a product of the decomposition of hesperidin.

Hesperian (hɛ'spɪərɪən), *a.* and *sb.* [f. L. *Hesperi-us*, Gr. *ἑσπέριος* of or situated towards the west, western, L. *Hesperi-a*, Gr. *Ἑσπερία* (poetical) the land of the west, applied by the Greeks to Italy, by the Romans to Spain or regions beyond; f. HESPERUS the evening star: see -AN.]

A. *adj.* **1.** Western, of or pertaining to the land of the west, or where the sun sets. *poet.*

a **1547** Surrey *Æneid* IV. 463 My dear son, Whom I defraud of the Hisperian crown. **1667** Milton *P.L.* I. 520 Who with Saturn old Fled over Adria to th' Hesperian Fields. **1679** *Establ. Test* 4 This Hesperian Garden of England. *a* **1708** J. Philips *Poems* (1776) 75 (Jod.) Th' utmost bound Hesperian, Calpe, by Alcides fixt. **1818** Shelley *Rev. Islam* VII. xiii, The gathering waves rent the Hesperian gate Of mountains. **1855** Milman *Lat. Chr.* IV. v. (1864) II. 285 When Ireland is described as a kind of Hesperian Elysium of peace and piety.

2. Of or pertaining to the HESPERIDES. *poet.*

1622 Massinger & Dekker *Virg. Mart.* IV. iii. D.'s Wks. 1873 IV. 73 Bury in Oblivion your fain'd Hesperian Orchards. **1634** Milton *Comus* 393 But Beauty like the fair Hesperian tree Laden with blooming gold, had need the guard Of dragon-watch. **1667** —— *P.L.* III. 568 Happy Iles, Like those Hesperian Gardens fam'd of old. **1708** J. Philips *Cyder* I. 33 (Jod.) Whose breath Nurtures the orange and the citron groves, Hesperian fruits. **1830** Macaulay *Moore's Byron* Ess. (1887) 159 The forests shining with Hesperian fruit and with the plumage of gorgeous birds.

3. *Entom.* Of or pertaining to the family of butterflies called *Hesperidæ* or Skippers.

1840 Swainson & Shuckard *Nat. Hist. Insects* 65 The enormous head of the Hesperian caterpillars. *Ibid.*, The Hesperian butterflies being the last of the *Papiliones*.

B. *sb.* **1.** An inhabitant of a western land.

1601 Holland *Pliny* I. 148 And fiue daies sailing from it, appeare the desarts of the Ethyopian Hesperians. *a* **1812** J. Barlow, cited in Webster (1828).

2. A Hesperian butterfly; a Skipper.

1869 *Rep. U.S. Commissioner Agric. 1868* 314 The family of skippers, Hesperians, are rather small, thick-bodied butterflies. **1881** *Papilio* I. 132 (*title*) Two new Hesperians.

hesperic: see HESPER-.

Hesperid ('hɛspərɪd). [ad. L. *Hesperid-es*: see below.] **1.** One of the HESPERIDES (nymphs).

1878 P. Robinson *In my Ind. Gard.* II. 105 The damsels of the land..stand about in a rural manner, much as did the Hesperids.

2. *Ent.* (Also **Hesperiid.**) One of the family Hesperidæ or Hesperiidæ of lepidopterous insects; a Hesperian butterfly; a skipper. Also *attrib.*

1889 in *Cent. Dict.* **1912** *Entomologist* XVL. 5 (*title*) A Supplementary Note on Hesperiid Classification. **1930–1** *Proc. Ent. Soc.* V. 88 Similar observations had been made on African Hesperiids. **1931** *Oxf. Univ. Gaz.* 17 June 704/1 The Hesperid butterfly *Parnara zelleri cinhara.* **1957** Richards & Davies *Imms's Gen. Textbk. Ent.* (ed. 9) III. 560 Its larvae and pupae exhibit definite Hesperiid characters.

hesperid-, Gr. *ἑσπεριδ-* stem of *Ἑσπερίδ-ες* Hesperides, forming technical terms of Botany and Chemistry, in the sense 'of or derived from the orange and its congeners': see HESPERIDES 2.

Hence: **a.** *Bot.* **he'speridate, hespe'rideous** *adjs.*, of the structure of the orange; of the orange kind. ‖**hespe'ridium**, a fruit of the structure of the orange, a many-celled superior indehiscent fruit, pulpy within and covered by a separable rind. **b.** *Chem.* **he'speridene, he'speridin, he'speridine**, chemical products obtained from the hesperideous fruits. See also HESPER-.

a. 1876 Harley *Mat. Med.* (ed. 6) 696 Fruit *hesperidate, with a hard rind. **1886** *Syd. Soc. Lex.*, **Hesperideous*, of, or belonging to, or having, an arrangement of parts, as in the orange. **1866** *Treas. Bot.* 586/1 **Hesperidium.* **1875** Bennett & Dyer tr. *Sachs' Bot.* 539 Closely resembling the berry is the fruit of the various species of Citrus, sometimes called Hesperidium, the pericarp of which consists of a leathery outer layer and a pithy inner layer. **1880** Gray *Struct. Bot.* vii. §2. 299 The *Hesperidium* (orange, lemon, and lime)..is a mere variety of the berry.

b. 1875 Watts *Dict. Chem.* VII. 644 **Hesperidene*, the terpene of essential oil of orange-peel. **1886** *Syd. Soc. Lex.*, *Hesperidene*, $C_{10}H_{16}$..the oil of Seville orange. **1838** T. Thomson *Chem. Org. Bodies* 764 Of **Hesperidin.* This substance was discovered by M. Lebreton, in 1828, in the unripe fruits of different species of orange and lemon trees. **1882** *Encycl. Brit.* XIV. 438/1 In the white portion of the peel [of lemon]..a bitter principle called **hesperidine* has been found.

‖**Hesperides** (hɛ'spɛrɪdiːz), *sb. pl.* [L. *Hesperidēs*, a. Gr. *Ἑσπερίδες*, pl. of *ἑσπερίς* 'western', 'a daughter of the west' or 'land of the sunset', f. *ἕσπερος* evening, the evening star: see HESPERUS.]

1. *Gr. Myth.* The nymphs (variously reckoned as three, four, and seven), daughters of Hesperus, who were fabled to guard, with the aid of a watchful dragon, the garden in which golden apples grew in the Isles of the Blest, at the western extremity of the earth.

1656 Blount *Glossogr.*, *Hesperides*, the daughters of Hesperus..They had Gardens, that bore golden fruit. **1671** Milton *P.R.* II. 357 Nymphs of Diana's train..And ladies of the Hesperides, that seem'd Fairer than feign'd of old. **1860** Ruskin *Mod. Paint.* V. IX. x. §8. 307 The Hesperides ..are four. Their names are, Æglé,—Brightness; Erytheia, —Blushing; Hestia,—the (spirit of the) Hearth; Arethusa, —the Ministering.

b. *transf.* (In quot. 1608 as *sing.*)

1608 Shaks. *Per.* I. i. 27 Before thee stands this fair Hesperides, With golden fruit, but dangerous to be touch'd. **1860** C. Sangster *Hesperus*, etc. 85 Some souls are the Hesperides Heaven sends to guard the golden age.

c. Hence, the garden watched by these nymphs; also, the 'Fortunate Islands' or 'Isles of the Blest' (*αἱ Μακάρων νῆσοι*), beyond the Pillars of Hercules, at the western extremity of the ancient world, in which the garden was supposed to be situated.

c **1590** Greene *Fr. Bacon* ix. 82 The fearful dragon held his seat That watch'd the garden call'd Hesperides. **1634** Sir T. Herbert *Trav.* 7 Iles of Cape de Verde..some thinke, these were the Hesperides, so famous for the Garden of golden Apples. **1826** J. Montgomery *Voy. round World* 53 The West Indies I behold, Like th' Hesperides of old, —Trees of life with fruits of gold!

2. *Bot.* The name given by Endlicher to one of his classes of plants, containing the orange family (*Aurantiaceæ*) and some related orders.

The name *Hesperideæ* was given by Linnæus to one of his natural orders, containing the genus Citrus and some others. Based on an identification of the orange, citron, etc. with the golden apples of the mythical Hesperides.

1857 Henfrey *Bot.* 211 Endlicher's System..Cl[ass] 51. Hesperides [containing] Humiriaceæ, Olacineæ, Aurantiaceæ, Meliaceæ, and Cedrelaceæ. **1866** *Treas. Bot.* 586/1.

Hespe'ridian, -ean, *a.* Of or pertaining to the gardens of the Hesperides.

1850 Leitch tr. *C.O. Müller's Anc. Art* (ed. 2) 621 A Hesperidian tree enwreathed by a serpent (symbol of a blessedness veiled in darkness and terrors). **1885** Pater *Marius* II. 52 Some vanished or delusive golden fleece, or Hesperidean fruit-trees.

hesperidin, -ine, -ium: see HESPERID-.

hesperinic, -isic: see HESPER-.

‖**Hesperis** ('hɛspərɪs). *Bot.* [L. *hesperis*, Gr. *ἑσπερίς* of evening or the west (see HESPERIDES); also as sb. 'the night-scented gilly-flower'.] A genus of cruciferous plants including the Rockets and Dame's Violet.

1664 Evelyn *Kal. Hort.* (1729) 205 May..Flowers in Prime, or yet lasting..Cowslips, Hesperis, Antirrhinum [etc.]. **1882** Ouida *Maremma* I. 115 The fragrant hesperis of the shore.

‖**Hesperornis** (hɛspəˈrɔːnɪs). *Palæont.* [f. Gr. ἑσπερ-ος western + ὄρνις bird.] The name of a genus of fossil birds of the western hemisphere.

1871 O. C. MARSH *Lett.* 29 Nov. in *Amer. Jrnl. Sci. & Art* (1872) Jan. 57, I shall fully describe this unique fossil under the name *Hesperornis regalis.* **1881** LUBBOCK in *Nature* No. 618. 406 The Hesperornis, described by Marsh in 1872 as a carnivorous swimming ostrich; provided with teeth; which he considers a character inherited from some reptilian ancestor. **1884** G. ALLEN in *Longm. Mag.* Jan. 290 Still more reptilian in some particulars is the hesperornis.

‖**Hesperus** (ˈhɛspərəs). [L. *hesperus*, a. Gr. ἕσπερος adj. of the evening, western; sb. the evening star.] The evening star.

c **1374** CHAUCER *Boeth.* I. metr. v. 22 (Camb. MS.) Þe eue sterre hesperus. *c* **1470** HENRYSON *Tale of Dog* 28 Quhen Hesperus to schaw his face began. **1559** W. CUNNINGHAM *Cosmogr. Glasse* 51 The Sonne is gone to rest, and Hesperus do shewe in the West verie bright. **1667** MILTON *P.L.* IX. 49 The Sun was sunk, and after him the Star Of Hesperus, whose Office is to bring Twilight upon the Earth. **1813** SHELLEY *Q. Mab* I. 259 Some shed a mild and silver beam Like Hesperus o'er the western sea.

hespine, var. form of ESPYNE *Obs.*

hess, Sc. f. *hoase*, HOARSE *a.*

Hessian (ˈhɛsɪən), *a.* and *sb.*[1] [f. *Hesse*, a grand duchy of Germany + -IAN.]

A. *adj.* Of or pertaining to Hesse in Germany.

Hessian bellows, a kind of bellows with the fan inside to furnish the blast; **Hessian bit**, 'a peculiar kind of jointed bit for bridles' (Ogilvie); **Hessian boot**, a kind of high boot, with tassels in front at the top, first worn by the Hessian troops, and fashionable early in the 19th century; **Hessian crucible** (see quot. 1874); **Hessian fly**, a fly or midge (*Cecidomyia destructor*), of which the larva is very destructive to wheat; so named, because it was erroneously supposed to have been carried into America by the Hessian troops, during the War of Independence.

1677 PLOT *Oxfordsh.* 250 He hath discovered also the mystery of the Hessian wares. **1705** *Phil. Trans.* XXV. 1992 A Furnace, to which the Hessian Bellows will be very useful. **1787** M. CUTLER in *Life Jrnls. & Corr.* (1888) I. 246 Here I saw the Hessian fly, as it is called, which has done immense injury to wheat. **1807** T. THOMSON *Chem.* (ed. 3) II. 92 Their method of proceeding was to apply a violent heat to the earths, which were surrounded with charcoal in a Hessian crucible. **1816** KIRBY & SP. *Entomol.* (1856) 26 In 1788 an alarm was excited in this country by the probability of importing, in cargoes of wheat from North America, the insect known by the name of the Hessian fly. **1833** MARRYAT *P. Simple* i. (1863) 5 A man..dressed in blue cotton-net pantaloons and Hessian boots. **1874** KNIGHT *Dict. Mech.* 652/1 Hessian crucibles are made of the best fire-clay and coarse sand..They are used in this country [United States] in all experiments where fluxes are needed. **1890** MISS ORMEROD *Injur. Insects* (ed. 2) 79 The year 1886 was memorable, agriculturally, for the appearance of the Hessian Fly as a pest of the Wheat and Barley in Great Britain. **1897** SIR A. WEST in *19th Cent.* Apr. 640 In the early days of Her Majesty's reign..Hessian boots were common: the last man to wear them was Mr. Stephenson, a Commmissioner of Excise..who wore them to the day of his death in 1858.

B. *sb.* **1.** A native of Hesse in Germany; a soldier of or from that country.

1729 A. IRWIN *Let.* 1 Feb. in *15th Rep. Hist. MSS. Commission* App. VI. (1897) 56 The House..voted 30,000 English and 12,000 Hessians, which is the same number I think we had last year. **1776** *Jrnls. Continental Congress* (1906) V. 640 The Hessians, and other foreigners, employed by the King of Great Britain. **1846** *Knickerbocker* XXVII. 559 A Montreal editor [noted] the demise at that city of an old Hessian who was in Burgoyne's army when he surrendered. **1872** C. GIBBON *For the King* xi, Everything depended on the whim of the dragoons and Hessians.

2. In U.S., A military or political hireling, a mercenary.

From the employment of Hessian troops by the British government in the American War of Independence. During the War of Secession, it was again used in the South as a term of obloquy for the Federal soldiers.

1877 in BARTLETT *Dict. Amer.*

3. (*hessians.*) Short for *Hessian boots* (see A).

1806 LAMB *Mr. H——* I. Wks. 578 Blank Dr. to Zedkiel Spanish for one pair of best hessians. **1888** *Daily Tel.* 1 June 5/1 Plain blue surtout, the buckskins and hessians..of Wellington at Waterloo.

4. A strong coarse cloth, made of a mixture of hemp and jute, employed for the packing of bales (*Dict. Needlework* 1882).

1881 YOUNG *Every Man his own Mechanic* 366 A piece of strong canvas or hessian should be tacked to the edges of the board. **1891** *Times* 28 Sept. 3/5 The demand for hessians has fallen off a little.

Hessian (ˈhɛsɪən), *sb.*[2] *Math.* [Named after Dr. Otto Hesse of Königsberg, who showed (in 1844) the importance of this covariant.] The Jacobian of the first derivatives of a function.

1856 CAYLEY in *Phil. Trans.* CXLVI. 636 The Hessian is the determinant formed with the second differential coefficients or derived functions of the quantic with respect to the several facients. **1880** R. F. SCOTT *Theory Determin.* 143 Jacobians and Hessians belong to that class of functions known as covariants. **1895** ELLIOTT *Algebra of Quantics* 14.

hessite (ˈhɛsaɪt). *Min.* [Named 1843, after G. H. Hess, of St. Petersburg: see -ITE.] Telluride of silver, occurring in grey, sectile masses.

1849 J. NICOL *Man. Min.* 477 Hessite..occurs massive and granular. **1868** DANA *Min.* (ed. 5) 51.

hessonite (ˈhɛsənaɪt). *Min.* Also **essonite**. [ad. F. *essonit* (R. J. Haüy *Traité Pierres Préc.* (1817) 51), f. Gr. ἥσσων less + -ITE[1]: so called because it is less hard and heavy than some minerals, such as hyacinth, which it resembles.] A variety of garnet containing calcium and aluminium. Also called *cinnamon-stone, grossularite.*

1820 R. JAMESON *Min.* I. 162 Cinnamon stone..Essonite. **1884** DANA *Min.* 266 Essonite [1892: more commonly hessonite] included a cinnamon-colored variety from Ceylon. **1895** *Amer. Jrnl. Sci.* L. 128 (*heading*) Apatite and hessonite in a pegmatite from Canaan, Ct. **1933** *Mineral. Abstr.* V. 281 The other [belt], from Ramona to Jacumba, is in granodiorite and the gem minerals in the pegmatites are mainly hessonite, beryl, and topaz. **1959** C. S. HURLBUT *Dana's Man. Min.* (ed. 17) v. 403 *Grossularite* (*Essonite, Cinnamon Stone*). Often contains ferrous iron replacing calcium and ferric iron replacing aluminium.

hest (hɛst), *sb. arch.* Forms: α. 1 hǽs, 2 hes, 2–3 hæs, 3 heas, 3–4 has. β. hesn. γ. 2–6 heste, 3– hest, (3 haste, 3, 5–7 heast, 4–5 heest(e, 5–6 heaste, 6 *Sc.* heist). [OE. *hǽs* fem. (inflected *hǽse*) was the regular repr. of OTeut. *hait-ti-, abstr. sb. from *haitan* 'to call upon by name', OE. *hátan*: see HIGHT *v.*; thence early ME. *hæs* (*has*), *heas*, *hes* (infl. *-e*), altered to *heste*, *hest*, by assimilation to sbs. in ME. *-te*:—OE. *-t*, as *ishefte*, *wiste*, OE. *ȝesceaft*, *wist*, from *sciеppan*, *wesan*. The early pl. of this was *hesten*. In 12th c., there was also a deriv. in *-n*, *hesn*, inflected *hesne*.]

1. Bidding, command, injunction, behest. *arch.*

α. *c* **1000** ÆLFRIC *Gram.* xxxiii. (Z.) 210 On ðisum and swylcum is ȝebed and na hæs. —— *Gen.* xxiv. 10 Be his hlafordes hæse. *a* **1200** *Moral Ode* 292 Nout of godes bode ne of godes hese [*v.r.* hease]. *Ibid.* 345 Þe narewei is godes hes [*v.r.* has]. *c* **1200** ORMIN 3537 Þurrh þatt Kaseress hæse. β. *c* **1175** *Lamb. Hom.* 139 To techen þe folke godes hesne to done, þe lewede godes hesne for to heren. *a* **1175** *Cott. Hom.* 229 He ȝestilde windes mid his hesne. γ. *c* **1175** *Lamb. Hom.* 9 Þa ilke þa haldet cristes heste. *a* **1225** *Ancr. R.* 8 Þeos..beoð Godes hesten. *a* **1225** *Leg. Kath.* 48 [He] sende heast & bode, se wide se þe lond was. **1377** LANGL. *P. Pl.* B. II. 82 Vnboxome and bolde to breke þe ten hestes. *c* **1449** PECOCK *Repr.* 465 Teching the doctrines and the heestis of men. **1609** SIR R. SHIRLEY in *Harl. Misc.* (Malh.) III. 93 Perform those heasts, which the great Persian..hath imposed upon thy integrity. **1610** SHAKS. *Temp.* III. i. 43 O my Father, I haue broke your hest to say so. **1633** T. ADAMS *Exp. 2 Peter* ii. 11 They stand round about the Lord..and execute his imposed hests like ready servants. **1818** SCOTT *Hrt. Midl.* xv, Christian or heathen, you shall swear to do my hest. **1858** CARLYLE *Fredk. Gt.* v. vi. II. 110 Standing like a hackney-coach..at the hest of a discerning public and its shilling.

†**2.** Vow, promise. Cf. BEHEST. *Obs.*

a **1200** *Moral Ode* 242 Þa þe gode biheten heste and nolden hit ileste. *c* **1330** R. BRUNNE *Chron. Wace* (Rolls) 6453 Þis ys þe heste [*v.r.* hete] þat y þe hight. *c* **1350** *Leg. Rood* (1871) 74 To þe land of hest þat ȝam was hight. *c* **1400** *Rom. Rose* 4477 Whanne heest and deede..varie, They doon a gret contrarie. *a* **1420** HOCCLEVE *De Reg. Princ.* 2243 Fy! what? a lorde breke his heste or bonde? **1513** DOUGLAS *Æneis* II. xi. [x.] 84 Thi moderis heist on na wis nedis the dout. **1567** TURBERV. tr. *Ovid's Ep.* (1576) 141 She thought it best To stand unto her former plighted hest. **1599** *Life Sir T. More* in Wordsw. *Eccl. Biog.* (1853) II. 46 To thee sweet Rose, by hest is this homage more than dewe.

†**3.** Will, purpose, determination. *Obs.*

(App. arising from an imperfect comprehension of sense 1.)

1500–20 DUNBAR *Poems* xxxii. 30 He..handlit hir as he had hest. **1583** STANYHURST *Æneis* II. (Arb.) 64 In one heast hee stieflye remayned. —— *Ps.* i. 2 (Arb.) 126 But in the sound law of the lord His mynd, or heast is resiaunt. **1845** CARLYLE *Cromwell* VIII. (1871) IV. 80 Swallowing in silence as his hest was.

†**hest**, *v. Obs.* [f. HEST *sb.* Cf. BEHEST *v.*]

1. *trans.* To promise.

14.. *Cast. Love* (Halliw.) 411 Tho thu to him thy hest hestyst [*earlier MS.* hiȝtest], Thorgh sothe then deth to him thou hettyst. *c* **1450** *Cov. Myst.* (Shaks. Soc.) 92 Ther hested I, as myn hert thought, To serve my God with hertyly love.

2. To bid, command.

1583 STANYHURST *Æneis* IV. (Arb.) 106 He persisting too doo what Iuppiter heasted, Sturd not an eye.

3. *catachr.* To grant (a wish).

1583 STANYHURST *Æneis*, IV. (Arb.) 98 Thy long wish is hested [*habes, tota quod mente petisti*].

Hence ˈ**hesting** *vbl. sb.*, purpose, design. (Cf. HEST *sb.* 3.)

1583 STANYHURST *Æneis* II. (Arb.) 45 This guest ful slylye did offer Hym self for captiue, thearby too coompas his heasting.

hest, obs. form of EAST.

c **1375** *Sc. Leg. Saints, Thomas* 441 In hest ynde.

†ˈ**hestcorn.** *Obs.* [f. HEST *sb.* + CORN.] (See quot. 1848.)

a **1537** in Dugdale *Monast. Angl.* (1661) II. 367/2 Quasdam avenas, vulgariter dictas Hestcorne, percipiendas de dominiis & Ecclesiis in illis partibus, quas Ministri dictæ Ecclesiæ, usque in præsens percipiunt pacifice & quiete. **1848** WHARTON *Law Lex.*, *Hest-corn*, vowed or devoted corn.

†ˈ**hestern**, *a. Obs.* [ad. L. *hestern-us.*] Of yesterday, yester-.

1577–87 HOLINSHED *Chron.*, *Irel.* H v/2 (N.) Exploytes that were enterprised but hestern day. **1708** MOTTEUX *Rabelais* (1737) V. 232 Those who supervis'd it noct Hestern.

hesternal (hɛˈstɜːnəl), *a.* [f. L. *hestern-us* (see prec.) + -AL[1].] Of yesterday; of yesterday's standing or date.

1649 BP. HALL *Confirm.* (1651) 67 Some hesternall teachers that refuse and disallow of it. **1789** M. MADAN tr. *Persius Sat.* iii. 106 (1795) 93 But him The hesternal Romans [*Quirites hesterni*], with cover'd head, sustained. **1827** LYTTON *Pelham* lvii (D.), In enervating slumbers from the hesternal dissipation or debauch.

hesthogenous (hɛsˈθɒdʒɪnəs), *a. Ornith.* [Badly formed from Gr. ἐσθής dress, clothing + -γενής born, produced + -OUS.] Of birds: Hatched with a clothing of down; ptilopædic: opposed to *gymnogenous.*

1850 NEWMAN in *Zoologist* VIII. 2780 Hesthogenous Birds. In these, immediately the shell is broken the chick makes its appearance in a state of adolescence rather than infancy. **1885** A. NEWTON in *Encycl. Brit.* XVIII. 31 Hesthogenous—a word so vicious in formation as to be incapable of amendment, but intended to signify those [birds] that were hatched with a clothing of down.

hestre, var. ESTRE, *Obs.*

hestunye, obs. form of ASTONY *v.*

c **1425** *Found. St. Bartholomew's* (E.E.T.S.) 21 The seruantes so yn soule he-stunyid and with grete feer affrayed.

Hesvan (ˈhɛsvən). Also **Chesvan, Heshvan,** etc. [Heb. *ḥešwān*, f. earlier *marḥešwān* (recorded in the Mishnah, 2nd cent. B.C.), ad. Akkadian *Araḫ samna* eighth month.] The eighth month of the Jewish ecclesiastical year and the second month of the civil year, corresponding to parts of October and November; also formerly called *Bûl.*

1833 H. NICOLAS *Chronol. Hist.* 167 Marchesvan, Chesvan, or Bul 29 or 30 [Days]. **1838** E. H. LINDO *Jewish Cal.* 5 The perfect [year] has 355 days, and is when the months of Hesvan and Kislev have each 30 days. **1876** *Encycl. Brit.* IV. 678/1 The signs + and − are respectively annexed to Hesvan and Kislev to indicate that the former of these months may sometimes require to have one day more, and the latter sometimes one day less, than the number of days shown in the table. **1903** M. JOSEPH *Judaism as Creed & Life* 310 The ordinary Jewish year consists of twelve months... Cheshvan or Marcheshvan (November). **1927** G. F. MOORE *Judaism* II. 67 If by the seventeenth of Marḥeshvan the autumn rains had not begun, the religious heads of the community began to fast in a mitigated fashion. **1956** PEARL & BROOKES *Guide Jewish Knowledge* 2 (*heading*) Cheshvan (Oct.-Nov.).

hesy, obs. form of EASY.

Hesychast (ˈhɛsɪkæst). *Eccl. Hist.* [ad. med.L. *hēsychasta*, ad. eccl. Gr. ἡσυχαστής quietist, hermit, f. ἡσυχάζειν to be still, keep quiet, f. ἥσυχος still, quiet.] One of a school of quietists which arose among the monks of Mount Athos in the 14th century. Also *attrib.* So **Hesychasm** (ˈhɛsɪkæz(ə)m), the doctrine or practice of Hesychasts.

1835 WADDINGTON *Hist. Church* (ed. 2) III. 214 These enthusiasts were orginally called Hesychasts, or, in Latin, Quietists. **1874** J. H. BLUNT *Dict. Sects* s.v., The well-known Light Theory of Dionysius was adopted by the Hesychasts..The Hesychast notion seems to have been a perversion of Dionysius' spiritual perception into a sensuous perception. **1880** *Encycl. Brit.* XI. 782 In the time of Justinian the word Hesychast was applied to monks in general simply as descriptive of the quiet and contemplative character of their pursuits. *Ibid.*, About the year 1337 this Hesychasm..attracted the attention of the learned and versatile Barlaam.

hesychastic (hɛsɪˈkæstɪk), *a.* [ad. Gr. ἡσυχαστικ-ός, f. ἡσυχάζειν or ἡσυχαστής (see prec.).]

1. Appeasing, quieting. In ancient Greek music applied to a style of melody which tends to appease the mind.

1694 W. HOLDER *Harmony* (1731) 151 The First of these [Keys] is call'd by the Greeks *Diastaltic*, Dilating; the Second, *Systaltic*, Contracting; the Last, *Hesychiastic*, Appeasing.

2. *Eccl. Hist.* Pertaining to the Hesychasts.

1880 *Encycl. Brit.* XI. 782/2 The supposed reward of Hesychastic contemplation.

het (hɛt), *ppl. a.* [In 1, pa. pple. of HEAT *v.* (cf. *lead*, *led*, etc.); in 2, app. the same word substituted for earlier Sc. *hait*, *hate*:—OE. *hát*, HOT. (But, possibly, shortened from *hate.*)]

1. *participle.* Heated. Also with *up* and *transf. colloq.* (orig. *dial.* and *U.S.*).

1375 BARBOUR *Bruce* IV. 113 He tuk a culter hat glowand That het wes in a fyre byrnand. *c* **1375** *Sc. Leg. Saints, Petrus* 693 For þai sa Increly ware hete. **1517** TORKINGTON *Pilgr.* (1884) 36 The watir was hett to wassh the ffete. **1570** LEVINS *Manip.* 86/17 Het, *calefactus.* **1862** LOWELL *Biglow P.* Poems 1890 II. 260 Don't you git het. [**1886** S. W. MITCHELL *R. Blake* ii. 17, I don't het up easy.] **1893** ZINCKE *Wherstead* 261 In East Anglia, an ironing-flat and a kettle of water are not heated, but '*het*'. **1894** KIPLING *Day's Work* (1898) 46 You look consider'ble het up. Guess you'd better ..cool off a piece. *a* **1898** *Mod. Sc.* 'Cauld kail het ower again'. **1902** G. H. LORIMER *Lett. Merchant* v. 59 But you mustn't get yourself all 'het up' before you take the plunge. **1930** W. DE LA MARE *On Edge* 244 You must have been

overdoing it. You look quite het up. **1932** C. WILLIAMS *Greater Trumps* x. 182 Yours is a remarkable family, Henry; you get all het up over your hobbies. **1945** L. A. G. STRONG *Othello's Occupation* ii. 43 The poor chap gets terrifically het up. **1967** *Listener* 20 Apr. 518/3 One thing that I think endears him to the normal young intellectual, is that he can get tremendously het-up about a cause.

2. *adj.* Hot. *Sc.* and *north dial.*

c **1375** *Sc. Leg. Saints, Bertholomeus* 35 Bundyne..With het chenȝeis, as fyre brynnand. **1513** DOUGLAS *Æneis* XII. v. 84 Of the hevy birding sa mait and het. **1535** STEWART *Cron. Scot.* (1858) I. 15 The hetter weir oft syis the sonner peis. **1597** MONTGOMERIE *Cherrie & Slae* 1253 He hit the yron quhyle it was het. **1786** BURNS *Earnest Cry* xx, But gie him 't het, my hearty cocks! **1814** SCOTT *Wav.* xxx, I'll put this het gad down her throat.

het: see HATE *sb.*[1], HEAT *sb.* and *v.*, HIGHT.

‖**hetæra** (hɪ'tɪərə), **hetaira** (hə'taɪrə). Pl. **hetæræ** (-riː), **hetairai** (-raɪ). [Gr. ἑταίρα, fem. of ἑταῖρος companion.] (In ancient Greece, and hence *transf.*) A female companion or paramour, a mistress, a concubine; a courtesan, harlot.

'In Attic mostly opposed to *a lawful wife*, and so with various shades of meaning, from *a concubine* (who might be a wife in all but the legal qualification of citizenship) down to *a courtesan*' (Liddell & Scott).

1820 W. TOOKE tr. *Lucian* I. 727 *note*, Finding no word in the dictionaries that completely answers to the greek hetære, as the term courtesan..I thought it, all things well considered, best to employ the word hetære as a grecian technical term. **1850** LEITCH tr. *C.O. Müller's Anc. Art* 363 A present to a hetaira. **1861** *Illustr. Times* 6 July 10 Certain naughty ones, who used to be called 'hetæræ', and are now known as 'horsebreakers'. **1868** TENNYSON *Lucretius* 52 Girls, Hetairai, curious in their art, Hired animalisms. **1874** MAHAFFY *Soc. Life Greece* vii. 200 There is no evidence of a society of cultivated hetairai at Athens in Pericles' day. **1885** E. PEACOCK in *Acad.* 31 Oct. 287/1 The *hetairae* about the court [of Chas. II]. **1888** LOWELL *Heartsease & Rue* 54 Mime and hetaera getting equal weight With him whose toils heroic saved the State.

Hence **he'tæric** *a.*, of or belonging to hetæræ.

1868 *Temple Bar Mag.* Nov. 568 Faithful to the lady of his original choice—usually of the hetæric class.

hetærism (hɪ'tɪərɪz(ə)m), **hetairism** (hɛ'taɪrɪz(ə)m). [a. Gr. ἑταιρισμός, f. ἑταιρίζειν to be a courtesan, f. ἑταίρα HETÆRA: see -ISM.]

1. Open concubinage.

1860 *Sat. Rev.* 4 Oct. 417/2 It is said that hetærism, with its Phrynes and Aspasias, is so far becoming a recognised institution. **1865** *Pall Mall G.* 9 Sept. 9/2 Beginning to recognize the existence of hetærism, not only as a fact, but as a thing to be talked about in drawing-rooms.

2. *Anthropol.* Applied by Sir J. Lubbock to a supposed primitive form of the sexual relations: communal marriage in a tribe.

1870 LUBBOCK *Orig. Civiliz.* iii. 67 The primitive condition of man socially was one of pure Hetairism..or, as we may for convenience call it, Communal marriage where every man and woman..were..equally married to one another. **1876** H. SPENCER *Princ. Sociol.* (1877) I. 662 Thought by several writers to imply that the primitive condition was one of unqualified hetairism.

Hence **hetairist, -istic** *a.*

1876 *Athenæum* 11 Nov. 627/1.

hetærocracy (hɛtɪə'rɒkrəsɪ), **hetair-**. [f. Gr. ἑταῖρος companion, fellow, or ἑταίρα HETÆRA + -CRACY.] **a.** The rule of fellows (of a college). **b.** The rule of courtesans.

1845 MOZLEY *B. White* Ess. 1878 II. 100 The 'hetairocracy' of Oriel Common Room stuck in his mind. **1860** HOOK *Lives Abps.* I. vi. 346 The government..had become what has been aptly styled an Hetaerocracy, and was in the hands of women, illustrious by their birth, but the licentiousness of whose lives surpasses belief.

hetærolite (hɛ'tɪərəʊlaɪt). *Min.* [f. Gr. ἑταῖρο-ς companion (see quot. 1877) + -LITE.] A black oxide of zinc and manganese, $ZnMn_2O_4$, isostructural with hausmannite and found in New Jersey associated with franklinite and with chalcophanite.

The mineral of quot. 1913 was later regarded as a separate species and named *hydrohetærolite*.

1877 G. E. MOORE in *Amer. Jrnl. Sci. & Arts* XIV. 423 From its invariable association with and close genetic relation to chalcophanite, I propose for the species the name *Hetærolite*. **1913** *Amer. Jrnl. Sci.* XXXV. 601 The herærolite from Leadville was found..about 700 feet below the surface. **1928** [see *hydrohetærolite* s.v. HYDRO-]. **1942** *Amer. Mineralogist* XXVII. 50 It was..proposed by Palache to adopt Moore's name hetaerolite for the anhydrous mineral, analogous to hausmannite,..since this was the sense of the original definition. The actual material of Moore..was separated under the name hydrohetaerolite as a distinct species. The hydrous mineral from Leadville.. also is to be classed as hydrohetaerolite.

hetæry (hɪ'tɪərɪ). *Gr. Hist.* [ad. Gr. ἑταιρεία, -ία, companionship.] An oligarchical club in ancient Athens for political and judicial purposes.

1849 GROTE *Greece* II. li. VI. 392 These clubs, or Hetæries, must without doubt have played a most important part in the practical working of Athenian politics. *Ibid.* 393 *note*, Having thus organised the hetæries, and brought them into cooperation for his revolutionary objects.

†**hetch.** *Obs.* *rare*$^{-0}$. Also **heach, heche.** A shortened form of *hetchel*, HATCHEL.

1598 FLORIO, *Pettine*,..a combe to dresse flaxe or hempe, called a hecke, or a hatchell. **1611** *Ibid.* (ed. 2), *Pettine*,..a hetch or hatchell to dresse flax. **1611** COTGR., *Seran*, a hatchell, or heach; the yron combe whereon flax is dressed.

hetch(e, obs. forms of HATCH *sb.*[1] and *v.*[1]

hetchel, var. HATCHEL *sb.* and *v.*

†**hetchill.** Obs. by-form of HUCKLE: perh. influenced by *aitch*-bone.

1601 HOLLAND *Pliny* II. 313 A suffumigation made with the fat taken from the hetchill peece or loines.

†**hete.** *Obs.* [By-form of HOTE, HIGHT *sb.*[1], conformed to the verbal inflexion *hete* of HIGHT *v.*: cf. BEHETE *sb.*] Command, promise.

a **1300** *Cursor M.* 6872 (Gött.) As godd had hight him in his hete. *Ibid.* 11897 Þai haf halden him þar hete [*Cott.* haite] Þar-in þai hang him be þe fete. **13..** *Gaw. & Gr. Knt.* 1525 Ȝe, þat ar so cortays & coynt of your hetes. *c* **1394** *P. Pl. Crede* 345 Lere me to som man..that..halt Godes hetes [*Royal MS.* hestys]. *c* **1420** *Sir Amadas* (Weber) 440 Weyte thou be large of pey and hete.

hete: see EAT, HATE, HEAT, HIGHT, HOT, HOTE.

†**hetefaste**, *adv.* *Obs.* Also 3 **heteueste, -feste.** [app. f. OE. *hęte* hatred, etc. (cf. *hętelice* violently, vehemently) + *fęste* firmly, FAST.] Firmly, securely, fast.

a **1225** *Juliana* 36 Bind him hetefeste [*v.r.* heteueste]. *a* **1225** *St. Marher.* 10 His twa honden to his..cneon heteueste ibunden. *a* **1225** *Ancr. R.* 34 (MS. Cott.) Haldeð him hetefeste. *Ibid.* 378 Ure Louerd was..ine a stonene þruh biclused heteueste.

hetelich, -like, obs. ff. HATELY, HOTLY *advs.*

†**heter, hetter**, *a.* *Obs.* Forms: 3–5 **heter, hetter, hatter,** 5 **hatir, hetire, hetur, hattir, hettur, hitter, hittur.** [Cf. MLG. *hetter*; app. a deriv. of *hatian* to HATE, cf. *hęte* sb. hate.] Rough; fierce, violent, cruel; severe; keen, eager.

13.. *E.E. Allit. P.* C. 373 Heter hayrez þay hent þat asperly bited. *c* **1380** WYCLIF *Sel. Wks.* II. 406 Þe sunne mai be derkkid heter bi fumes þat shal cleer þe erþe. *a* **1400–50** *Alexander* 520 And hent sall [he] a full hetire deth. *Ibid.* 702 Behald ouer þi hede and se my hatter werdis. **1674–91** RAY *N.C. Words, Hetter*, eager, earnest, keen.

heter-, the form of the combining element HETERO- used before vowels.

†**heteric** ('hɛtərɪk), *a.* *Obs.* [f. Gr. ἕτερ-ος other, different + -IC.] Applied by some phonetists to non-phonetic spelling, in which different symbols are used for the same sound, and different sounds expressed by the same symbol, as in current English. So **heterically** *adv.*, **hetericism, hetericist**.

1848 A. J. ELLIS *Plea Phonetic Spelling* (ed. 2), Hetericism is a bar to eduction. **1849** *Fraser's Mag.* XL. 418 This they call Phonetic spelling; the old system is branded as the Heteric. *Ibid.* 419 Mr. Ellis is particularly severe on such a piece of hetericism. *Ibid.* 423 The hetericist still faithful to his allegiance. *Ibid.* 424 Does Mr. Ellis intend that people should begin by writing one word in a thousand phonetically, and the rest heterically?

heterize ('hɛtəraɪz), *v.* *nonce-wd.* [f. Gr. ἕτερ-ος other, different + -IZE.] *trans.* To make different; to turn into another form. Hence **heteri'zation**, turning into a different form.

1865 J. H. STIRLING *Secr. Hegel* I. 126 The universe is but a materialisation, but an externalisation, but a heterisation of certain thoughts. *Ibid.* 128 Externalised, materialised, or, better, heterised thoughts (i.e.) thoughts in *another* form or mode. **1883** R. B. MUKHARJI tr. *Renan's Phil. Dial.* 79 *note*, Matter is the heterization of thought.

†'**heterly, 'hetterly**, *adv.* (*a.*) *Obs.* Forms: see HETER; also 5 **haterlynge**. [f. HETER + -LY[2], -LY[1].]

Roughly, fiercely, violently, cruelly, severely, sternly, keenly, eagerly.

a **1225** *Leg. Kath.* 2108 Þe king..Biheold hire heterliche, And bigon to þreatin hire. *a* **1225** *Ancr. R.* 290 Hot him ut hetterliche—þe fule kur dogge. *c* **1385** CHAUCER *L.G.W.* 638 *Cleopatra*, And heterly they hurtelyn al atonys. *c* **1400** *Destr. Troy* 5826 He hit hym so hetturly on hegh on the shild. *a* **1400–50** *Alexander* 5322 Hitterly on ilk side his heued he declines. *a* **1461** *How Gd. Wif taught hir Dau.* 28 in Hazl. *E.P.P.* I. 182 Mekely hym answere, and noght to haterlynge.

B. *adj.* = HETER. *rare.*

c **1400** *Destr. Troy* 5781 Nestor..hard hastid to helpe with heturly wille.

hetero, colloq. abbrev. of HETEROSEXUAL *a.* and *sb.*

1933 E. A. ROBERTSON *Ordinary Families* xiii. 272 The odd thing about me is that..I should be so purely 'hetero' in spite of lack of opportunity. **1957** J. OSBORNE *Look Back in Anger* II. i. 50 I'm tired of being hetero. **1960** I. JEFFERIES *Dignity & Purity* ii. 28 Is that really a fact about Proust being a secret hetero? **1968** J. R. ACKERLEY *My Father & Myself* xii. 117 Almost the first mischievous question he shot at me was 'Are you homo or hetero?' **1970** *Sunday Times* 6 Sept. 24 Talking..about homosexual life and letters..I meant to ask him..why homos found it so much easier to find sleeping partners than heteros.

hetero- (hɛtərəʊ), before a vowel **heter-**, combining form of Gr. ἕτερος the other of two, other, different; a formative of many scientific and other terms, often in opposition to *homo-*, sometimes to *auto-*, *homœo-*, *iso-*, *ortho-*, *syn-*. The more important of these, with their derivatives, will be found in their alphabetical places; others, of less importance or frequency, are entered here. **'heteracanth** (-əkænθ) *a.* *Ichth.* [Gr. ἄκανθα thorn, spine], having the spines of the dorsal and anal fins alternately broader on one side than the other; opp. to *homacanth*; **heteracmy** (-'ækmɪ) *Bot.* [Gr. ἀκμή point, culmination, ACME], the ripening of the stamens and pistils of a flower at different times, including *proterandry* and *proterogyny*; opp. to *synacmy*; **heteradenic** (-ə'dɛnɪk) *a.* *Anat.* [Gr. ἀδήν gland], of glandular structure, but occurring in a part normally devoid of glands (Ogilvie, 1882); **heterandrous** (-'ændrəs) *a.* *Bot.* [see -ANDROUS], having stamens or anthers of different forms (*Syd. Soc. Lex.* 1886); †'**heterarchy**, the rule of an alien; ˌ**heteraro'matic** *a.* = *heteroaromatic* adj.; **heteratomic** (-ə'tɒmɪk) *a.*, consisting of atoms of different kinds; opp. to *homatomic*; **heterauxesis** (-ɔːk'siːsɪs) [Gr. αὔξησις growth], (*a*) *Bot.*, growth at unequal rates, irregular or unsymmetrical growth; (*b*) hence applied to animals as well as plants, with a more specialized meaning (see quot. 1941); ˌ**hetero-aˌgglutina'bility**, the ability to undergo heteroagglutination; ˌ**hetero-aggluti'nation**, agglutination of cells due to the action of a hetero-agglutinin; so ˌ**hetero-a'gglutinating** *vbl. sb.*; ˌ**hetero-a'gglutinative** *a.*, producing heteroagglutination; ˌ**hetero-a'gglutinin**, an agglutinin that causes agglutination of foreign cells, esp. red blood cells of another group or from an animal of another species; ˌ**hetero'albumose** *Biochem.*, an albumose insoluble in water but soluble in solutions of sodium chloride; ˌ**heteroaro'matic** *a.* *Chem.*, heterocyclic and aromatic; also as *sb.*; '**hetero-atom** *Chem.*, an atom in the ring of a cyclic compound other than a carbon atom (also as two words); so ˌ**hetero-a'tomic** *a.*; ˌ**hetero-'axial** *a.* [a. G. *heteroaxial* (V. Goldschmidt *Index d. Krystallformen d. Mineralien* (1891) III. 136)], having a structure based on two axes or sets of axes; *spec.* of a geological feature: having an external symmetry that does not correspond with the symmetry of the individual components of the fabric; ˌ**heterobi'ography** *nonce-wd.*, biography written by another person; opp. to *autobiography*; so ˌ**heterobio'graphical** *a.*; **heteroblastic** (-'blæstɪk) *a.* *Biol.* [Gr. βλαστός germ], (*a*) arising from cells of a different kind; opp. to *homoblastic*; (*b*) *Bot.*, (characterized by) having a marked difference between the immature and adult forms; (*c*) *Petrol.*, composed of grains of two or more distinct sizes; opp. *homœoblastic*; ˌ**hetero'blastically** *adv.*, in a heteroblastic manner; **heterobranchiate** (-'bræŋkɪət) *a.* *Zool.* [Gr. βράγχια gills], having gills of diversified forms; applied in various classifications to a division of fishes, crustacea, gastropods, etc.; **hetero'carpian, -'carpous** *adjs.* *Bot.* [Gr. καρπός fruit], producing fruit of different kinds; so **hetero'carpism** (see quot.); **heterocellular** (-'sɛljʊlə(r)) *a.* *Biol.*, composed of cells of different kinds (as most organisms); opp. to *isocellular*; **heterocephalous** (-'sɛfələs) *a.* *Bot.* [Gr. κεφαλή head], applied to a composite plant bearing flower-heads of different kinds, male and female; '**heterocharge**, the charge on an electret that is polarized in the opposite direction to that of the original polarizing field; hence '**heterocharged** *a.*; **heterochiral** (-'kaɪərəl) *a.* [Gr. χείρ hand], of identical form but with lateral inversion, as the right and left hands; opp. to *homochiral*; hence **hetero'chirally** *adv.*; †**hetero'chresious** (erron. -cresious) *a.* *Obs.* [Gr. χρῆσις use], relating to different commodities or uses; opp. to *homochresious*; ˌ**heterochla'mydeous** *a.* *Bot.* [Gr. χλαμύς, χλαμυδ- cloak], having a perianth in which the calyx and corolla are of a different colour or texture; '**heterochrome** *a.* = HETEROCHROMATIC *a.* (sense 1); ˌ**hetero'chromia** (-'krəʊmɪə) *Med.*, a difference in colour between two organs (esp. the eyes), or between different parts of the same organ, that are usually the same colour; so ˌ**hetero'chromic** *a.*; ˌ**hetero'chromosome**

Cytol., a modified or differentiated chromosome, *esp.* a sex-chromosome; **heterochromous** (-ˈkrəʊməs) *a.* [Gr. χρῶμα colour], of different colours, as the florets of some *Compositæ*, e.g. the daisy and asters; **heterochthonous** (-ˈɒkθənəs) *a. Path.* [after AUTOCHTHONOUS *a.*], originating in or derived from another organism; **ˈheteroclin, -cline** *sb. Min.* [ad. G. *heteroklin* (A. Breithaupt 1840, in *Ann. Physik und Chem.* XLIX. 205), f. Gr. ἑτεροκλινής leaning to one side] = MARCELINE[2]; **heterocline** (-klaɪn) *a. Bot.* [Gr. κλίνη bed: cf. DICLINOUS], having male and female flower-heads or separate receptacles, heterocephalous; **ˌheteroˈcœlous** *a. Zool.* [Gr. κοῖλος hollow], applied to vertebrae in which the articular facets are saddle-shaped, as in certain birds; **ˈheterocyst** (-sɪst) *Biol.* [Gr. κύστις bladder, CYST], a cell of exceptional structure or form found in certain algæ and fungi; **ˌheteroˈcystous** (-ˈsɪstəs) *a. Biol.*, containing heterocysts; **heterodactyl** (-ˈdæktɪl), **-ˈdactylous** *adjs. Zool.* [Gr. δάκτυλος finger or toe], having the toes, or one of them, irregular or abnormal, as certain families of birds (Ogilvie, 1882); **heterodermatous** (-ˈdɜːmətəs) *a. Zool.* [Gr. δέρμα skin], having the skin or integument of different structure in different parts, as certain fishes and serpents; opp. to *homodermatous*; **heteroˈdesmic** *a. Chem.* [Gr. δεσμός bond], containing chemical bonds of more than one type; **heteroˈdogmatize** *v. nonce-wd.* [see DOGMATIZE], *intr.* to hold or pronounce an opinion different from that generally held; **heteroˈduplex** *a. Biochem.*, containing or consisting of polynucleotide strands derived from two different parent molecules; also as *sb.*, a heteroduplex molecule; **ˌheterodyˈnamic, -ˈdynamous** *adjs. Ent.* [ad. F. *hétérodyname* (E. Roubaud 1922, in *Bull. Biol. de la France et de la Belg.* LVI. 471)], (of an insect, its life cycle, etc.) characterized by having a continuous succession of generations only during the favourable part of the year; **heterœcious** (-ˈriːʃ(ɪ)əs) *a. Bot.* [Gr. οἰκία house, first formed as G. *heteröcisch* (A. de Bary 1866, in *Monatsber. d. K. Preuss. Akad. d. Wissensch. zu Berlin 1865* 32)], applied to fungi which at different stages of development are parasitic on different plants; opp. to *autœcious*; **heterœcism** (-ˈriːsɪz(ə)m), the condition of being heterœcious; hence **heterœˈcismal** *a.* = *heterœcious*; **heteroepy** (-ˈəʊɪpɪ) *nonce-wd.* [after *orthoepy*], pronunciation differing from the standard; so **heteroepic** (-əʊˈɛpɪk) *a.*, involving heteroepy; **heterogangliate** (-ˈgæŋglɪət) *a. Zool.*, having the ganglia of the nervous system unsymmetrically arranged, as most molluscs; opp. to *homogangliate*; **heterognathous** (-ˈɒgnəθəs) *a. Zool.* [Gr. γνάθος jaw], 'having differently-shaped jaws' (*Syd. Soc. Lex.*); **heterogynal** (-ˈɒdʒɪnəl), **heterogynous** (-ˈɒdʒɪnəs) *adjs. Zool.* [Gr. γυνή woman, female], applied to species of animals in which the females are of two kinds, perfect or fertile, and imperfect or 'neuter', as in bees, ants, etc.; **ˌhetero-iˈmmune** *a.*, immune to the cells or cell-products of an animal of a different species, or producing such immunity; **ˌhetero-inocuˈlation**, inoculation from another organism; also **ˌhetero-iˈnoculable** *a.*; **ˈheterojunction** *Electronics* [JUNCTION 2 b], an area of contact between different semiconducting materials; **ˌheterokiˈnesis** *Cytol.*, the division of a cell into cells having dissimilar hereditary tendencies; opp. *homœokinesis*; †**heteroˈkinesy** (also -chinesie) *Obs.* [ad. Gr. ἑτεροκινησία], motion caused by an external agent; opp. to *autokinesy*; **ˌheteroˈlecithal** (-ˈlɛsɪθəl) *a. Embryol.* [Gr. λέκιθος yolk of an egg], (of an egg cell) having the yolk unevenly distributed in the cytoplasm; **heterolobous** (-ˈɒləbəs) *a.* [Gr. λόβος lobe], having unequal lobes; **heteromalous** (-ˈɒmələs) *a. Bot.* [Gr. ὁμαλός even, level], applied to mosses which have the leaves or branches turned in different directions: opp. to *homomalous*; **heteromastigate** (-ˈmæstɪgət) *a. Biol.* [Gr. μάστιξ whip], having flagella of different kinds, as an infusorian: opp. to *isomastigate*; **heteromaton** (-ˈɒmətən) *nonce-wd.* [after AUTOMATON], a thing that is moved by something else; **heteronemeous** (-ˈniːmiːəs), **heteronemous** (-ˈniːməs) *adjs. Bot.* [Gr. νῆμα thread, filament] (see quots.); **ˌheteroˈnereid** *a.*, of, pertaining to, or of the character of a heteronereis; also as *sb.*, a heteronereis; **ˌheteroˈnereis** *Zool.*, a dimorphic sexual form of certain worms of the genus *Nereis*, so called because originally regarded as a distinct genus; also *attrib.*; **heteropetalous** (-ˈpɛtələs) *a. Bot.*, 'having dissimilar or unequal petals' (Mayne *Expos. Lex.*); **ˌheteroˈphoria** *Ophthalm.*, a latent tendency to squint; hence **heteroˈphoric** *a.*; **heterophˈthalmic** *a.*, characterized by heterophthalmy; **heterophthalmy** (-ɒfˈθælmɪ) [Gr. ὀφθαλμός eye], the condition in which the eyes are different in colour or direction; **heterophyadic** (-faɪˈædɪk) *a. Bot.* [late Gr. φυάς, φυαδ- shoot, sucker], producing two kinds of stems, one bearing the fructification, the other the vegetative branches, as in the genus *Equisetum*; **ˌheteropolymeriˈzation** *Chem.* [a. G. *heteropolymerisation* (T. Wagner-Jauregg 1930, in *Ber. d. Deut. Chem. Ges.* LXIII. 3213)], a reaction in which a polymer is formed from two or more different molecules, esp. such a reaction when one of the monomers will not polymerize by itself; so **ˌheteroˈpolymer**, a polymer so formed; **ˌheteropolyˈsaccharide** *Chem.*, any polysaccharide composed of molecules of two or more different monosaccharides; **heteroproral** (-ˈprɔərəl) *a. Zool.* [L. *prōra* prow], having unequal or dissimilar proræ, as a pterocymba in sponges; opp. to *homoproral*; **ˌheteroˈproteose** *Biochem.*, any of a class of proteoses that are insoluble in water but soluble in dilute salt solutions and are formed during gastric digestion; **heteropsychoˈlogical** *a.* (see quot.); **heteˈroptics** *nonce-wd.* [see OPTICS] (see quot.); **heterorhizal** (-ˈraɪzəl) *a. Bot.* [Gr. ῥίζα root], applied to the roots of cryptogamous plants (see quot.); **ˌheteroscеˈdastic** *a. Statistics* [Gr. σκεδαστ-ός capable of being scattered (σκεδάννυμι I scatter)], of unequal scatter or variation; having different variances; so **ˌheteroscedaˈsticity**; **heterosomatous** (-ˈsəʊmətəs) *a. Zool.* [Gr. σῶμα body], having a body deviating from the normal type; said esp. of flat fishes, which have the two sides of the body asymmetrical; so **ˈheterosome** (-səʊm), (*a*) a flat-fish; (*b*) *Cytol.*, a sex chromosome; **heteroˈsomous** *a.* = *heterosomatous*; **heterosoteric** (-səʊˈtɛrɪk) *a.* [Gr. σωτηρία salvation], relating to salvation by another; **heterospeˈcific** *a.*, (*a*) said of blood or serum of different blood groups; ***heterospecific pregnancy***, one in which the red blood cells of the fœtus would be agglutinated by the serum of the mother; (*b*) derived from an organism of a different species; **heteroˈsporic** *a.* = *heterosporous* adj.; **heterosporous** (-ˈɒspərəs) *a. Bot.* [Gr. σπόρος seed], producing two different kinds of spores; opp. to *homosporous* or *isosporous*; **heteˈrospory** *Bot.*, the condition of being heterosporous; **heterostaural** (-ˈstɔːrəl) *a.* [Gr. σταυρός cross], having an irregular polygon as the base of the pyramid; said of a heteropolar stauraxonial figure; opp. to *homostaural*; **heterostemonous** (-ˈstiːmənəs) *a. Bot.* [Gr. στήμων warp, thread, taken in sense 'stamen'], 'having dissimilar stamens' (Mayne *Expos. Lex.*); **ˌheterosuˈggestion** *Psychol.*, suggestion from another person, contrasted with AUTO-SUGGESTION; **ˌheterosyˈllabic** *a. Philol.*, belonging to a different syllable (opp. to *tautosyllabic*); **ˌheteroˈsyllis** *Zool.*, a breeding form of worms of the family Syllidæ; **ˌheteroˈtelic** *a.*, having or being an external end or purpose; **ˌheteroˈthallic** *a. Biol.*, (of a fungus) having an incompatibility system by which only genetically different strains can undergo nuclear fusion during sexual reproduction; so **ˌheteroˈthallism, -ˈthally**, the condition of being heterothallic; **heterothermal** (-ˈθɜːməl) *a. Biol.* [Gr. θερμός hot], having a temperature which varies with that of the surroundings, as plants and cold-blooded animals; opp. to *homœothermal* or *homothermous* (*Syd. Soc. Lex.* 1886); **heteˈrotonous** *a.* [Gr. τονός tone], having different or unlike tones; hence **heteˈrotonously** *adv.*; **ˈheterotope** *Physics* and *Chem.* [Gr. τόπος place], each of two or more elements the atoms of which have different atomic numbers and so occupy different positions in the periodic table; **heterotrichal** (-ˈɒtrɪkəl), **heteˈrotrichous** *adjs. Biol.* [Gr. θρίξ, τριχ- hair], belonging to the order *Heterotricha* of ciliate infusorians, in which the cilia of the oral region differ in size and arrangement from those of the rest of the body; also said of these cilia; **ˈheterotype, heteroˈtypic, heteroˈtypical** *adjs. Cytol.* [ad. G. *heterotypisch* (W. Flemming 1887, in *Arch. f. mikrosk. Anat.* XXIX. 400)], designating the first division of meiosis; **heteroˈxanthine** *Biochem.* [ad. G. *heteroxanthin* (G. Salomen 1885, in *Ber. d. Deut. Chem. Ges.* XVIII. 3407)], 7-methylxanthine, $C_6H_6O_2N_4$, a purine sometimes found in human urine; **heterozoœcium** (-zəʊˈiːsɪəm) *Zool.* [Gr. ζῷον animal + οἰκία house] = *heterozooid*; so **heterozoˈœcial** *a.*; **heterozonal** (-ˈzəʊnəl) *a. Cryst.*, said of faces (or poles) of a crystallographic system which lie in different zones (or zone-circles): opp. to *tautozonal*; **heteroˈzooid** (-ˈzəʊɔɪd) *Zool.*, any reduced or modified form of the typical bryozoan zooid, found chiefly in the class Gymnolæmata.

1880 GUNTHER *Fishes* 41 If the spines are asymmetrical, alternately broader on one side than on the other, the fish is called *heteracanth. **1870** *Nature* II. 482 The phenomena of Protandry and Protogyny forming together that of *Heteracmy. *a* **1656** BP. HALL *Serm. Christ & Cæsar* Wks. 1837 V. 281 Next to Anarchy is *Heterarchy. **1960** *Tetrahedron Lett.* XXIII. 8 (*heading*) New *heteraromatic compounds containing two boron atoms. **1886** VINES *Physiol. Plants* xvi. 376 Spontaneous variations in the relative rate of growth of opposite sides of the organ, or to express it in a single word.. spontaneous **heterauxesis*. **1940** NEEDHAM & LERNER in *Nature* 9 Nov. 618/1 We welcome a suggestion.. by Dr. Arthur L. Peck.. that for relative *growth*, in contradistinction to relative *proportions*, the word *heterauxesis* should be used... It is true that the terms auxesis, heterauxesis,.. etc., were formerly employed in plant physiology, but they have long been obsolete there. **1941** *Ibid.* 23 Aug. 225/1 *Heterauxesis* , the relation of the growth-rate of a part of a developing organism (whether morphological or chemical) to the growth-rate of the whole or of another part; a comparison between organisms of the same group, but of different ages and hence sizes. **1964** *Biol. Abstr.* XLV. 946/1 *Hetero-agglutinability of goat erythrocytes by zebu serum. **1913** *Jrnl. Exper. Zool.* XIV. 564 The iso-agglutinating action was noted as undiminished, whereas the *hetero-agglutinating action was entirely lost. *Ibid.* 561 (*heading*) *Hetero-agglutination and the question of specificity: reactions between Nereis and Arbacia. **1949** *Biol. Abstr.* XXIII. 156/2 Lecithin suppresses the auto-agglutination as well as heteroagglutination of rabbit erythrocytes by bovine plasma. **1938** BELDING & MARSTON *Textbk. Med. Bacteriol.* lx. 451 The demonstration of the M and N antigens in human cells requires the production of *heteroagglutinative immune sera by the injection of human cells into some experimental animal. **1906** DORLAND *Med. Dict.* (ed. 4) 332/1 *Hetero-agglutinin. **1913** *Jrnl. Exper. Zool.* XIV. 564 The egg-extract contained two agglutinating substances at least, namely: An iso-agglutinin and a hetero-agglutinin. **1945** *Biol. Bull.* LXXXIX. 193 Lobster-serum contains at least ten hetero-agglutinins for sperm or blood cells of various animals. **1956** *Nature* 18 Feb. 329/2 The injections caused no increase in the titre of natural heteroagglutinin against human red cells. **1884** KÜHNE & CHITTENDEN in *Amer. Chem. Jrnl.* VI. 33 We name.. No. II. *Heteroalbumose. *Ibid.* 103 Nothing characterises heteroalbumose more than its alteration by boiling and the properties of the coagulum thus formed. **1908** J. R. BRADFORD in Allbutt & Rolleston *Syst. Med.* (ed. 2) IV. I. 561 Albumoses, and especially hetero-albumoses, which are the kind commonly present in the urine, form a precipitate on the addition of nitric acid. **1958** A. ALBERT *Trends Heterocyclic Chem.* iv. 20 (*heading*) Addition to double-bonds in N-*heteroaromatic six-membered rings. **1958** *Jrnl. Chem. Soc.* 3076 A wide range of new heteroaromatic systems should exist, derived from normal aromatic compounds by replacing pairs of carbon atoms, one by boron and one by nitrogen. **1959** A. ALBERT *Heterocyclic Chem.* iii. 31 (*heading*) A general discussion on heteroaromatics. **1900** E. F. SMITH tr. *von Richter's Org. Chem.* (ed. 3) II. 435 The basal element of these rings is carbon, and accordingly the members not produced by C-atoms are designated as *hetero-atoms. **1949** G. B. BACHMAN *Org. Chem.* xxvii. 336 O-, S-, and NH-containing rings undergo substitution practically exclusively at the carbons holding the hetero atom. **1966** *McGraw-Hill Encycl. Sci. & Technol.* VI. 427/2 The number of heteroatoms in any one ring is commonly one or two, less commonly three or more. **1967** KATRITZKY & LAGOWSKI *Princ. Heterocyclic Chem.* v. 144 (*heading*) Four or five heteroatoms. Tetrazoles are formed by the action of nitrous acid on amidrazones, and pentazoles from the reaction of diazonium cations with azide anions. **1968** *New Scientist* 31 Oct. 268/3 Heterocyclic compounds containing nitrogen, sulphur and oxygen as the heteroatom. **1900** E. F. SMITH tr. *V. von Richter's Org. Chem.* (ed. 3) II. 435 *Hetero-atomic rings. **1926** *Mineral. Abstr.* III. 186 A study of the directions of optical extinction in the lamellae, the striations on the faces, and the etch figures on the basal plane, leads to the conclusion that the twinning is of the '*heteroaxial' type. **1938** E. B. KNOPF in *Mem. Geol. Soc. Amer.* VI. vi. 84 An example of heteroaxial orienting in two phases of the deformation is the fabric of certain pencil gneisses in which the symmetry of the grain fabric in the pencils does not conform with the fabric axes of the external form of the pencils. **1884** J. W. HALES *Notes & Ess. Shaks.* 7 We see no reason to take the words in any non-natural or *heterobiographical sense. **1825** *New Monthly Mag.* XIV. 78 That superior charm.. which autobiography possesses (if we must speak Greek) over *heterobiography. **1888** *Sat. Rev.* 20 Oct. 450/1 Heterobiography.. a word required for the process of having your biography written for you by some other person without your permission, and to your own amazement. **1888** H. GADOW in *Nature* 13 Dec. 150/2 This new cartilage is either homoblastic or *heteroblastic. **1894** S. H. VINES *Stud. Text-bk. Bot.* I. i. 14 In certain cases the embryo produced by the spore differs more or less widely from the adult form, and does not directly develope into it, but bears it as a lateral outgrowth; this mode of embryogeny is indirect or heteroblastic. **1932** A. HARKER *Metamorphism* xiii. 202 To rocks in which the essential constituents are of two distinct orders of magnitude Becke gave the name 'heteroblastic', in contradistinction to

'homoeoblastic'. 1954 R. L. Parker tr. Niggli's Rocks & Min. Deposits vi. 237 Crystalloblastic structures: homoeblastic, heteroblastic, porphyroblastic, with porphyroblasts or possibly crystalloid phenocrysts. 1963 Davis & Heywood Princ. Angiosperm Taxon. x. 342 Heteroblastic development results in the formation of adult and juvenile leaves. 1888 Nature 13 Dec. 151/1 Tenontogenous or desmogenous [sesamoids], like the patella, are formed *heteroblastically inside of a tendon. 1854 Mayne Expos. Lex., *Heterobranchiate. 1881 Lubbock in Proc. R. Inst. IX. 625 *Heterocarpism, if I may term it so, or the power of producing two kinds of reproductive bodies. 1880 Gray Bot. Text-bk. Gloss., *Heterocarpous, producing more than one kind of fruit. 1842 Brande Dict. Sci., etc., *Heterocephalous. 1935 A. Gemant in Philos. Mag. XX. 933 We observe both kinds of charges on electrets. One has the opposite sign to that of the adjacent polarizing electrode, and for the sake of shortness will be denoted as *heterocharge. 1965 New Scientist 27 May 590/2 Under a certain critical applied field the heterocharge decays to a constant value. 1965 Jrnl. Chem. Physics 1 Feb. 967 Both heterocharged and homocharged electrets have been made from common ice at reduced temperatures. 1879 Thomson & Tait Nat. Phil. I. i. §97 The similarity of a right-hand and a left-hand is called *heterochiral: that of two right-hands, homochiral. Any object and its image in a plane mirror are *heterochirally similar. 1895 S. H. Vines Stud. Text-bk. Bot. iii. 512 When the calyx and corolla clearly differ from each other in colour, texture, etc., the flower is said to be *heterochlamydeous. 1965 Bell & Coombe tr. Strasburger's Textbk. Bot. iii. 621 Perianths are of two kinds: (a) Homoiochlamydeous..or (b) heterochlamydeous, i.e. with dissimilar members, namely an outer, generally green calyx and an inner, mostly brightly coloured corolla. 1612 Sturtevant Metallica (1854) 69 *Heterocresious, are inuentions which produce different mechanick workes, warres and commodities. So milning and shipping are two Heterocresious inuentions, because the worke of the one is meale or flower, and the worke of the other is carriage or transportage. 1933 Nature 6 May 667/1 A solution of the problem of *heterochrome photometry of incandescent lamps. 1889 Ophthalmic Rev. July 205 Liability to disease on the part of the lighter eye in *heterochromia. 1964 F. C. Blodi in A. Sorsby Mod. Ophthalmol. III. iii. 375 There will be a gradual change in colour of the iris giving one of the varieties of heterochromia. 1911 Ophthalmoscope 1 July 501 Heterochromia iridium is found in two forms. In one the heterochromia is merely an anomaly, and in the other it is a symptom of a definite disease... This latter variety is best designated *heterochromic cyclitis. 1940 W. S. Duke-Elder Text-bk. Ophthalmol. III. xxxviii. 3229 Heterochromic cataract..is associated with an exceedingly slow and benign inflammation of the uveal tract. 1904 T. H. Montgomery in Biol. Bull. VI. 145 The *Heterochromosomes. I offer this name to include those peculiarly modified chromosomes to which have been given the names 'accessory chromosomes'.., 'small chromosomes'..and 'chromatin nucleoli'. 1926 Nature 9 Jan. 50/2 Cytological investigations in the Salicaceæ, undertaken to demonstrate the presence or absence of sex- or heterochromosomes in certain species of Salix. 1968 J. A. Serra Mod. Genetics III. xxiii. 552 In haploid organisms or the haploid phase the heterochromosomes are found separately in the mitoses of each sex. 1842 Brande Dict. Sci., etc., *Heterochromous. 1850 Hooker & Arnott Brit. Flora (ed. 5) 197 When the ray is of a different colour from the disk, they are heterochromous (as in Bellis). 1891 Foster Med. Dict. III, *Heterochthonous, originating from without the organism. 1921 Beattie & Dickson Textbk. Gen. Path. (ed. 2) ix. 273 Some have defined teratomata as heterochthonous tumours derived from the inclusion of another individual..or the ovum or germ-cell from which such twin would have been developed. 1950 G. P. Wright Introd. Path. xx. 374 Chorion carcinomas are not derived from the tissues of the mother, but from the tissues of a different, though at the same time fœtal, individual. For this reason such tumours are sometimes termed 'heterochthonous'. 1844 J. D. Dana Syst. Min. (ed. 2) vi. 443 *Heteroclin..was first instituted by Breithaupt, and named..in allusion to its oblique form of crystallization. 1898 E. S. Dana Textbk. Min. (ed. 2) iv. 343 Marceline (heterocline) from St. Marcel, Piedmont, is impure braunite. 1880 Gray Bot. Text-bk. Gloss., *Heterocline, nearly same as Heterocephalous, on separate receptacles. 1884 E. Coues N. Amer. Birds (ed. 2) 138 Both ends of each vertebra are saddle-shaped;..a condition which may be called *heterocœlous. 1933 H. F. Gadow Evol. Vertebral Column xxxv. 311 The embryonic vertebrae of all Birds are at first amphicoelous, then they change through opisthocoelous into the heterocoelous or saddle-shaped type, which..represents the highest stage of interaxial joint, allowing of most excursion. 1872 Q. Jrnl. Microsc. Sci. XII. 367 Its minute size calls to mind Nostoc minimum (Currey), but in it..the *heterocysts are large, whilst here..the heterocysts are but slightly wider, though longer than the ordinary cells. 1875 Bennett & Dyer Sachs' Bot. 215 Thus the whole unite into a single curved Nostoc-filament. Individual cells, apparently without any definite law, become heterocysts. 1882 Vines Sachs' Bot. 245 It is only in the higher forms that a few larger cells of a different colour—termed Heterocysts—are intercalated among the otherwise similar cells of a filament. 1887 Jrnl. R. Microsc. Soc. 793 (heading) *Heterocystous Nostocaceæ. 1951 Proc. Linnean Soc. Lond. CLXII. ii. 195 Heterocystous blue-green algae. 1854 Mayne Expos. Lex., Those in which the external toe is versatile: *heterodactylous. 1885 Kingsley Stand. Nat. Hist. IV. 369 While in the woodpeckers the first and fourth [toes] are directed backwards, in the trogons the first and second take that position; hence they are said to be heterodactylous. 1939 R. C. Evans Introd. Crystal Chem. i. 8 Crystals..in which two or more different types of bond are in operation between different parts of the structure are termed *heterodesmic. 1952 B. Mason Princ. Geochem. iv. 67 In heterodesmic structures the physical properties..are in general determined by the weakest bonds. 1651 Biggs New Disp. ⁋52 Physitians, who have *heterodogmatiz'd, and deviated from the ancient beaten path of clear reason and experience. 1963 A. H. Doerman in W. J. Burdette Methodol. Basic Genet. 34 The heterozygote is imagined to consist of a *heteroduplex molecule in which every genetic site is represented twice. 1966 Progress Nucleic Acid Res. V. 319 The exposed polynucleotide chains can be thought to anneal during the act of rejoining to produce a heteroduplex region lying between the two recombinant segments. 1968 Proc. Nat. Acad. Sci. LX. 243 Each heteroduplex should thus contain a single-stranded loop in the wild-type DNA strand at the point where the deletion occurs. 1968 Sci. Jrnl. Nov. 5/1 The mixture [of DNA] now contains some 'heteroduplex' molecules consisting of a wild-type and a mutant strand. 1931 Trans. Entomol. Soc. London LXXIX. 105 Essentially different is the *heterodynamic type, in which the annual cycle bears a more or less definite relation to the season. 1964 Borror & DeLong Introd. Study Insects (rev. ed.) iii. 44 Most insects in temperate regions have what is called a heterodynamic life cycle; that is, the adults appear for a limited time during a particular season, and some life stage passes the winter in a state of dormancy. 1929 *Heterodynamous [see homodynamous s.v. homo-]. 1882 Vines Sach's Bot. 332 In others the various reproductive forms are developed upon different hosts, for example, the æcidium-fruits of Æcidium Berberidis occur only on the leaves of Berberis vulgaris, whilst the uredospores and the teleutospores are formed only upon Grasses..Such forms as these are said to be *heterœcious (metœcious), to distinguish them from those..which inhabit the same host throughout their whole life (autœcious). 1875 Bennett & Dyer Sachs' Bot. 246 Puccinia graminis..shows..the *heterœcism which occurs also in some other Fungi. 1887 Athenæum 6 Aug. 184/3 De Bary discovered and demonstrated the wonderful fact of heterœcism, showing that a fungus on the wheat produces an entirely different fungus on the barberry. 1884 Ibid. 29 Mar. 414/1 He demonstrates it to be a true *heterœcismal uredine. 1873 M. Collins Sq. Silchester I. i. 21 The proper way to begin is to teach them a *heteroëpic abracadabra. 1838 Fraser's Mag. XVII. 742 His vile and barbarous Scotch orthoepy, or rather *heteroepy. 1839–47 Todd Cycl. Anat. III. 365/1 The *heterogangliate type of the nervous system..is established in the Mollusks. 1855 Owen Invertebr. Anim. (ed. 2) 470 The scattered centres of the nervous system, disposed according to the Heterogangliate type of that dominant system of organs. 1854 Mayne Expos. Lex., Heterogynus..*heterogynous. 1886 Syd. Soc. Lex., Heterogynous, applied to those insects, such as ants, in which each species comprises males, females, and neuters. 1903 Lancet 4 Apr. 944/2 The introduction of the *hetero-immune serum. 1967 C. W. H. Havard Lect. Med. vi. 147 Individuals respond immunologically to tissues of other species (hetero-immune) or to tissues of another individual of the same species (iso-immune). 1894 J. C. DaCosta Man. Mod. Surg. xv. 168 Primary syphilis is not auto-inoculable, but is *hetero-inoculable. 1888 E. L. Keyes Surg. Dis. Genito-Urinary Organs ii. ii. 44 Few at the present day can be found who..consider as gonorrhœa a urethral discharge producing syphilitic chancre by *hetero-inoculation. 1960 *Heterojunction [see homojunction s.v. homo-]. 1971 New Scientist 16 Sept. 628/1 The light produced in the active [region] travels into the n-type region between the two heterojunctions. 1893 *Heterokinesis [see homœokinesis s.v. homœo-]. 1896 E. B. Wilson Cell ix. 305 In the second case ('heterokinesis', qualitative or differential division), the daughter-cells receive different groups of chromatin-elements, and hence become differently modified. 1678 Cudworth Intell. Syst. i. i. §38. 47 Body hath no other Action belonging to it but that of Local Motion, which Local Motion as such, is Essentially *Heterokinesie. Ibid. i. v. 668 Plato rightly determined that cogitation, which is self-activity or autochinesie, was, in order of nature, before the local motion of body, which is heterochinesie. 1892 *Heterolecithal [see homolecithal s.v. homo-]. 1896 E. B. Wilson Cell 336 Heterolecithal..having unequally distributed deutoplasm (includes telolecithal and centrolecithal). 1854 Mayne Expos. Lex., Heterolobus, having unequal lobes..*heterolobous. 18.. Hare Guesses (1859) 182 Is not man the only automaton upon earth? The things usually called so are in fact *heteromatons. 1854 Mayne Expos. Lex., Heteronemeus (Bot.) applied by Fries to nemeous..vegetables in which the sporidia are lengthened by germination into filaments which unite to produce a heterogeneous body, as happens in the fungi and mosses: *heteronemeous. [Ibid., Heteronemus (Bot.), having unequal filaments, as those of the stamens of the Epacris heteronema.] 1886 Syd. Soc. Lex., *Heteronemous, applied to those plants the stamens of which are unequal in the length of their filaments. 1896 W. B. Benham in Cambr. Nat. Hist. II. x. 277 There are then three different kinds of males and of females in this one species [sc. Nereis], some being found at the bottom of the sea, as the large *Heteronereid form, while the small Heteronereid swims on the surface. 1963 R. P. Dales Annelids vi. 124 In heteronereids the parapodia are greatly increased in surface area and musculature. 1875 Encycl. Brit. II. 67/1 Another [sexual form] which becomes transformed into a *Heteronereis before the sexual elements are developed. 1880 F. M. Balfour Compar. Embryol. I. xii. 284 Claparède traced the passage of large asexual examples of the Nereis form into the large Heteronereis form. 1886 *Heterophoria [see exophoria s.v. exo-]. 1957 New Scientist 9 May 38/2 Treatment aims at restoring normal functioning of the eyes, especially in what is popularly known as 'lazy' eyes and squint, but also in the more common condition of heterophoria—a tendency to squint. 1894 Gould Dict. Med., *Heterophoric. 1970 Jrnl. Gen. Psychol. LXXXII. 109 The mean duration of lateral AM was not systemically affected by heterophoric change from zero to 28 prism diopters. 1924 Jrnl. Genetics XIV. 365 (heading) *Heterophthalmic cats. 1854 Mayne Expos. Lex., Heterophthalmia, term for the eyes being of different colour from each other: *heterophthalmy. 1886 Syd. Soc. Lex., Heterophthalmy, the condition in which the eyes are of a different colour, or are different in direction. 1931 Chem. Abstr. XXV. 2419 Benzalfluorene (IV) and I give in good yield in the fused mixt. at 130°..a white amorphous *heteropolymer. 1948 C. E. H. Bawn Chem. High Polymers iii. 85 The individual monomers undergoing copolymerization may not polymerize alone. A copolymer formed with the latter type of monomer is often called a heteropolymer. 1952 Jrnl. Polymer Sci. VIII. 260 It is..recommended that the word 'heteropolymer' not be used for a copolymer in which one of the units does not polymerize by itself. 1971 Nature 23 July 254/2 The requirements of the RNA-DNA reaction indicate that a heteropolymer is formed, for the omission of any one of the triphosphate substrates suppresses synthesis almost completely. 1931 Chem. Abstr. XXV. 2418, 2 unlike units of low mol. wt., each contg. a C:C union, can..be combined into a large mol. by polymerizing addn. The name additive *heteropolymerization is suggested for such a process. 1958 Van Nostrand's Sci. Encycl. 132/1 Heteropolymerization is an addition polymerization. 1948 W. Pigman Chem. Carbohydrates xii. 513 The second class (*heteropolysaccharides), which consists of polysaccharides giving after hydrolysis more than one monosaccharide type. 1970 Heteropolysaccharide [see homopolysaccharide s.v. homo-]. 1887 Sollas in Encycl. Brit. XXII. 418 (Sponges) The prows may be similar (homoproral) or dissimilar (*heteroproral). 1891 Jrnl. Physiol. XII. 21 There are at last three normal proteoses formed in gastric digestion. Of these, proto and *heteroproteose are first formed. 1916 A. P. Mathews Physiol. Chem. ix. 361 There are three divisions of the group: namely, the primary proteoses, including the proto-proteoses and hetero-proteoses, and the secondary, or deutero-proteoses. 1885 J. Martineau Types Eth. The. II. i. ii. 65 The chief *heteropsychological theories of ethics.. are all founded on an attempted identification of the moral sentiments with some other function of our nature. 1711 Spectator No. 250 ⁋7 This Irregularity in Vision..must be put in the Class of *Heteropticks. 1874 R. Brown Man. Bot. 135 In ferns and Equisetaceæ the root and stem are strikingly different..the root springs from any part of the spore, and hence to the roots of this great division has been given the name *Heterorhizal. 1905 *Heteroscedastic [see homoscedastic s.v. homo-]. 1937 Yule & Kendall Introd. Theory Statistics (ed. 11) xi. 214 Arrays in which the standard deviations are equal are sometimes said to be 'homoscedastic'; in the contrary case 'heteroscedastic'. 1965 M. G. Bulmer Princ. Statistics xii. 215 The variance of Y may not be constant but may depend on x; the regression is then said to be heteroscedastic. 1905 K. Pearson in Drapers' Company Res. Mem. (Biometric Ser.) ii. 23, I am thus inclined to speak of χ_1-1 and χ_2 as measures of *heteroscedasticity and heteroclisy. 1964 Johnson & Leone Statistics & Exper. Design II. xvii. 321 Replication at each vertex does provide some information on possible heteroscedasticity of the residual variation. 1854 Mayne Expos. Lex. s.v., Those [fishes] in which the right and the left sides of the body are dissimilar: *heterosomatous. 1938 A. F. Shull Heredity (ed. 3) x. 92 The spermatozoa of a mammal are of two kinds, half of them containing an X chromosome, half of them a Y (or no *heterosome at all in species in which Y has been lost). 1966 D. M. Kramsch tr. Grundmann's Gen. Cytol. ii. 102 Man has 22 autosomes and one heterosome in a haploid set. 1894 A. B. Bruce St. Paul's Concept. Christ. 403 The doctrine of Jesus was autosoteric, that of Paul was *hetero-soteric. 1929 R. R. Gates Heredity in Man ix. 191 In 12·5 per cent. of *heterospecific pregnancies an agglutinin passed from the mother's blood to that of the child. 1958 Stratton & Renton Pract. Blood Grouping i. 14 A mother of group O would have an incompatible or heterospecific pregnancy if the child were group A or group B. 1962 Lancet 5 May 965/1 Two of these components could agglutinate red cells in the presence of heterospecific serum by a mechanism previously unknown among viruses. 1969 Nature 6 Sept. 1021/2 The possible use of hybrids of tumour cells and heterospecific cells to stimulate an immune response. 1895 D. H. Campbell Struct. & Devel. Mosses & Ferns i. 6 In all of the *heterosporic Pteridophytes the reduction of the vegetative part of the gametophyte is very great. 1967 M. E. Hale Biol. Lichens iii. 46 The identity of this heterosporic mat. 1875 Bennett & Dyer Sach's Bot. 805 In Phanerogams the embryo-sac corresponds to the large, the pollen-grain to the small spore of *heterosporous Vascular Cryptograms. 1881 Nature XXIV. 474 Professor Williamson divides coals into Isosporous and Heterosporous coals. Ibid. 607 They further consider that some of his Calamariæ..were heterosporous. 1886 Athenæum 10 Apr. 491/2 Mr. Bennett has made use of the term Megasporangia in describing the heterosporous vascular cryptogams. 1898 Nat. Science June 375 Its independent appearance in distinct groups may be compared with the appearance of *heterospory. 1959 Chambers's Encycl. XI. 613/1 Heterospory..is well developed in the seed plants, where the microspores are the pollen grains. 1901 Baldwin Dict. Philos. I. 96/1 Wundt uses the term Fremdsuggestion for the contrasted and usual process of suggestion from another person. The analogous Greek formation would be *Heterosuggestion. 1921 Spectator 19 Mar. 364/2 A portion of the doctors and men of science..began to perceive that it was primarily not their suggestions, but the patient's own suggestions to his subconscious self, which produced the wonderful results... It was auto-suggestion, not hetero-suggestion. 1951 F. Hopkins in E. N. Chamberlain Text-bk. Med. ix. 660 The terms autosuggestion and heterosuggestion are used according as to whether the suggestion is made by oneself or others. 1913 J. M. Jones Welsh Gram. 72 In N. W[ales] the vowel is medium in aw, ew, iw before a vowel, that is the w is *heterosyllabic. 1896 Cambr. Nat. Hist. II. 278 In some genera [of the family Syllidae]..there occur changes quite similar to those characterising 'Heteronereis'—that is, the posterior segments in which the genital organs exist become altered, so that the worm consists of two distinct regions, and is termed a '*Heterosyllis'. 1967 H. W. & L. R. Levi tr. Kaestner's Invertebr. Zool. I. xix. 496 Reproduction is complicated by alternation of sexual and asexual generations... Syllis, 1–5 cm. change [sic] to heterosyllis. 1901 Baldwin Dict. Philos. I. 96/1 *Heterotelic, having or serving a foreign or external end. 1902 Ibid. II. 668/1 To the deist the world process is heterotelic;..to the thoroughgoing monistic idealist it is autotelic. 1904 A. F. Blakeslee in Science 3 June 865 According to their method of zygospore formation, the various species among the Mucorineæ may be divided into two main categories, which may be designated as homothallic and *heterothallic... In the heterothallic group..zygospores are developed from branches which necessarily belong to thalli or mycelia diverse in character, and can never be obtained from the sowing of a single spore. 1959 Chambers's Encycl. VI. 117/1 Sporodinia grandis is homothallic, and a single spore from a sporangium will give rise both to sporangia and to zygospores, whereas Mucor is heterothallic, and a single spore gives rise only to sporangia. 1906 *Heterothallism [see homothallism s.v. homo-]. 1952 New Biol. XIII. 107 The discovery of heterothallism proved to be of fundamental importance since it has now been shown to occur in a modified form in all the major groups of fungi. 1940 Bot. Rev. VI. 74 There has been progressive sexual differentiation beginning with the gametes..and extending outward from them to the gametangia and prothallia, as

indicated by the successive acquirement of heterogametangy and *heterothally. **1942** Heterothally [see *homothally* s.v. HOMO-]. **1822–34** *Good's Study Med.* (ed. 4) III. 194 The same sound..is consequently heard, not homotonously, or in like tones, but *heterotonously, or in separate and unlike. **1919** F. SODDY in *Jrnl. Chem. Soc.* CXV. 11 Boyle's practical definition of the element.. became replaced by a theoretical conception, to which..I propose to apply the term '*heterotope', meaning the occupant of a separate place in the periodic table of elements. **1959** L. W. H. HULL *Hist. & Philos. Sci.* viii. 267 It is now known that there are atoms of different weights having the same chemical properties. These are called isotopes. There are also 'isobaric heterotopes', which have the same weight but different chemical properties. **1885** E. R. LANKESTER in *Encycl. Brit.* XIX. 863/1 *Heterotrichal band circular. *Ibid.*, The *heterotrichous band. **1895** *Ann. Bot.* IX. 479 The indifference manifested in the second mitosis in animals..as to whether it be *heterotype or homotype, is of some theoretical interest. **1920** L. DONCASTER *Introd. Study Cytol.* vi. 89 When the heterotype chromosomes split longitudinally, part of one longitudinal half of one chromosome may exchange places with a similar part of the corresponding longitudinal half of the other. **1889** *Q. Jrnl. Microsc. Sci.* XXX. 203 In another deviation, which Flemming describes as the 'homöotypic Form' (that is to say, 'a form more like the usual one than the one just described, which he names "*heterotypic"'), it would appear..that longitudinal splitting may be entirely absent. **1931** W. SHUMWAY *Gen. Biol.* vi. 149 The first maturation division is sometimes called the heterotypic division because of its novel features of synapsis and tetrad-formation. **1969** Heterotypic [see *homœotypic* s.v. HOMŒO-]. **1888** *Heterotypical [see *homœotypical* s.v. HOMŒO-]. **1896** E. B. WILSON *Cell* ii. 60 (*caption*) Heterotypical mitosis in spermatocytes of the salamander. **1886** *Jrnl. Chem. Soc.* L. 266 These..researches have led to the isolation of another constituent of human urine, which it is proposed to call *heteroxanthine. **1943** *Thorpe's Dict. Appl. Chem.* (ed. 4) VI. 206/1 Heteroxanthine appears to be a product of the metabolism of theobromine and caffeine, for when these alkaloids are administered to rabbits, dogs or men, heteroxanthine appears in the urine. **1909** G. M. R. LEVINSEN *Cheilostomatous Bryozoa* 74 The same *heterozoœcium may appear in the same genus, even occasionally in the same species, sometimes as an avicularium, sometimes as a vibraculum... The genus *Microporella* as well as the genus *Escharina* may serve as examples of such a variable development of the two heterozoœcial forms. *Ibid.* 46 We can distinguish between four main forms of individuals (Bryozooids): ..*Heterozoœcia* (**Heterozooids*), which have no intestinal canal, and at most have a trace of a polypide in a small cell-body, furnished with a circle of fine bristles. The chamber contains a strong muscular apparatus for moving the operculum. **1959** L. H. HYMAN *Invertebrates* V. xx. 325 Other types of zooids are termed collectively heterozooids and are characterized by the reduction of the polypide, which loses its nutritive and reproductive function.

heteroauxin (ˌhɛtərəʊˈɔːksɪn). *Biochem.* [a. G. *hetero-auxin* (F. Kögl et al. 1934, in *Zeitschr. f. physiol. Chem.* CCXXVIII. 94), f. HETERO- + AUXIN.] A growth-promoting hormone, $(C_8H_6N)CH_2{\cdot}COOH$, that occurs in some plants and micro-organisms; also called *β-indolyl acetic acid*, *3-indoleacetic acid*.

1935 *Chem. Abstr.* XXIX. 195 Normal individuals excrete auxins and heteroauxin in the proportions of about 4:1. **1940** W. R. FEARON *Introd. Biochem.* (ed. 2) 446 It was found that urine was very rich in a growth-promoting factor, which on isolation proved to be chemically unrelated to auxin *a* or *b*, and was termed hetero-auxin. **1949** *New Biol.* VII. 69 Two principal plant hormones..have actually been isolated from plant tissues, viz. auxin and hetero-auxin. **1966** NOWAKOWSKI & CLARKE tr. *Kretovich's Princ. Plant Biochem.* v. 175 Heteroauxin is used for accelerating root formation in cuttings of various plants e.g. citrus.

heterocaryon, -caryosis, -caryotic: see HETEROKARYON, etc.

heterocerc (ˈhɛtərəʊsɜːk), *sb.* and *a.* *Ichthyol.* Also -cerque. [f. HETERO- + Gr. κέρκ-ος tail.] **A.** *sb.* A heterocercal fish. **B.** *adj.* = next.

1876 PAGE *Text-bk. Geol.* ix. 184 All the fishes of the palaeozoic periods being heterocercs. **1882** OGILVIE, *Heterocerc.*

heterocercal (-ˈsɜːkəl), *a.* [f. as prec. + -AL[1].] Having the lobes of the tail unequal. Opp. to *homocercal*.

1838 *Penny Cycl.* XII. 191/1 *Heterocercal*, the term chosen by M. Agassiz..to express a peculiar form of the tails of fishes..The tail is..unequally bilobate, as in the shark... The peculiarity of the Heterocercal fishes is that the vertebral column runs along the upper caudal lobe. **1851** RICHARDSON *Geol.* (1855) 133 The heterocercal character of the tail.

Hence **heterocerˈcality**, **ˈheterocercy** (-sɜːsɪ), the condition of being heterocercal.

1884 *Science* 3 Oct. 341/2 Whenever heterocercality manifests itself, there is degeneration of the caudal end of the chordal axis.

heterocerous (hɛtəˈrɒsərəs), *a.* *Entom.* [f. mod.L. *Heterocera* neut. pl., f. HETERO- + Gr. κέρας horn.] Belonging to the sub-order of lepidopterous insects *Heterocera* (Moths); so called from the diversified forms of the antennæ, which are not clubbed as in the *Rhopalocera* (Butterflies).

1881 *Athenæum* 19 Feb. 268/2 New Genera and Species of Heterocerous Lepidoptera from Japan.

heterochromatic (ˌhɛtərəʊkrəʊˈmætɪk), *a.* [f. HETERO- + CHROMATIC *a.* 1 in sense 1; in sense 2, f. next + -IC.] **1.** Relating to or possessing more than one colour; relating to light or other radiation of more than one wavelength. Also *fig.*

1895 F. W. OLIVER et al. tr. *Kerner's Nat. Hist. Plants* II. 569 Contrasting with these heterochromatic species are those with homochromatic flowers, which..invariably present the same colour and pattern. **1924** *Nature* 30 Aug. 329/2 The use of absorbing screens in heterochromatic photometry. **1932** W. S. DUKE-ELDER *Text-bk. Ophthalmol.* I. xxii. 861 The comparison of the luminosities of lights of different colours comprises the science of heterochromatic photometry. **1937** *Archit. Rev.* LXXXI. 198/2 Heterochromatic harmonies, or harmonies of different hue. **1969** *Nature* 11 Oct. 162/2 Along each heterochromatic channel there is..a positional as well as a wavelength variation which must be taken into account in the interpretation of line profiles.

2. *Cytol.* Of chromosome material: becoming heteropycnotic at some stage in the nuclear cycle.

1936 [see EUCHROMATIC *a.*]. **1942** *Nature* 17 Jan. 66/2 The two properties of inertness and abnormality of nucleic acid cycle are combined in the same genes or chromomeres... These are then said to be heterochromatic as opposed to the active or euchromatic genes. **1951** G. H. BOURNE *Cytol. & Cell Physiol.* (ed. 2) v. 195 On the one hand the heterochromatic regions may be thicker and more dark-staining than the euchromatic ones... On the other hand, a heterochromatic region or chromosome may appear thinner and stain more weakly than euchromatic regions in the same nucleus. **1956** *Nature* 10 Mar. 452/2 It usually appears as three dots arranged in a triangle, suggesting the presence of an under-stained ('heterochromatic') region close to the centromere. **1969** *Ibid.* 16 Aug. 684/2 In plants.. supernumerary heterochromatic chromosomes may make pollen grains undergo additional divisions and quicken cell division.

heterochromatin (ˌhɛtərəʊˈkrəʊmətɪn). *Cytol.* [a. G. *heterochromatin* (E. Heitz 1928, in *Jahrb. f. wissenschaftliche Bot.* LXIX. 764), f. HETERO- + CHROMATIN.] Heterochromatic chromosome material.

1932 [see EUCHROMATIN]. **1941** *Ann. Bot.* V. 203 Large distal segments which appear as heterochromatin in mitosis, that is to say they are overstained in resting nuclei and, after freezing, understained in metaphase. **1951** G. H. BOURNE *Cytol. & Cell Physiol.* (ed. 2) v. 196 Probably there are many varieties of heterochromatin and euchromatin, constituting a continuous 'spectrum', to the two ends of which the terms heterochromatin and euchromatin are somewhat arbitrarily applied. **1969** *Nature* 16 Aug. 683/1 The observations that heterochromatin formation is a variable property and represents cyclical physiological states of chromosome segments..led to a shift of emphasis from heterochromatin as a substance to heterochromatin as a state.

heterochromatization (ˌhɛtərəʊˌkrəʊmətaɪˈzeɪʃən). *Cytol.* Also **ˌheteroˌchromatiniˈzation**. [f. prec. + -IZATION.]

A change of state of chromosome material in which it becomes heterochromatic and the action of the genes is modified or suppressed; also, the extent to which such a change has occurred. So **ˌheteroˈchromat(in)ized** *ppl. a.*

1941 *Cold Spring Harb. Symp. Quant. Biol.* IX. 158/2 When extra heterochromatin..is added to a cell, the heterochromatization..is lessened. *Ibid.*, The euchromatic regions which have been transferred into the vicinity of heterochromatic ones are themselves partly ..'heterochromatized'. **1944** *Amer. Naturalist* LXXVIII. 207 Variable 'heterochromatinization' takes place not only in salivary gland cells but in other body cells as well. **1948** *Jrnl. Genetics* XLVIII. 80 The process of heterochromatization (heteropycnosis) is reversible. *Ibid.* 83 The active section is sometimes so highly heterochromatized that it becomes quite indistinguishable from the neighbouring inert region. **1957** C. P. SWANSON *Cytol. & Cytogenetics* xiv. 469 This proposes that heterochromatin is formed from euchromatin by a process of genic degeneration... The end point of such an evolutionary trend..would be heterochromatinization of the entire Y. **1964** *Science* 10 July 130/1 Tissue..in which the heterochromatized *X* is of paternal origin. **1969** *Nature* 16 Aug. 683/2 The *X* chromosome that forms the sex-chromatin mass of normal females..is clearly heterochromatic when it forms (by facultative heterochromatization) a distinct chromocentre in the interphase nucleus.

heterochronic (-ˈkrɒnɪk), *a.* *Biol.* and *Path.* [f. HETERO- + Gr. χρόνος time, χρονικός of or concerning time.] **a.** 'Occurring at different times; irregular; intermittent: applied to the pulse' (Mayne *Expos. Lex.* 1854). **b.** Occurring or developed at an abnormal time. So ‖**heterochronia** (-ˈkrəʊnɪə), **heterochronism** (-ˈɒkrənɪz(ə)m), **heteˈrochrony**, the occurrence of a process, or development of a tissue, organ, or organic form, at an abnormal time; also **heterochroˈnistic**.

1854 MAYNE, *Heterochronicus, Heterochronus*.. heterochronic: heterochronous: applied to the pulse. **1876** tr. *Wagner's Gen. Pathol.* 5 We may..designate the general morbid processes as Heterochronic and Heterotopic. *Ibid.* 355 They are developed at a time when their presence is an abnormality (Heterochronia). **1876** H. SPENCER *Princ. Sociol.* (1877) I. 502 Entire organs which, during the serial genesis of the type, came comparatively late, come in the evolving individual comparatively soon. This Prof. Haeckel has called heterochrony. **1879** tr. *Haeckel's Evol. Man* I. i. 13 Kenogenetic 'displacements in time', or 'Heterochronisms'. *Ibid.*, By heterotopy the sequence in position is vitiated; by heterochrony the sequence in time is vitiated.

heteˈrochronous, *a.* [f. as prec. + -OUS.]
a. *Path.* = HETEROCHRONIC *a.*

1854 [see HETEROCHRONIC *a.*].

b. *Palæont.* [ad. G. *heterochron* (E. Mojsisovics *Die Cephalopoden der Hallstätter Kalke* (1893) II. 5).] Originating or formed at different periods.

1895 [see HOMŒOMORPHY]. **1913** *Q. Jrnl. Geol. Soc.* LXIX. 166 Isochronous and heterochronous homœomorphy state whether the homœomorphous species lived in the same or at different times. **1952** R. C. MOORE et al. *Invert. Fossils* vi. 218 The other category includes two or more shells of different geologic age, in which one simulates the other. These are termed heterochronous homeomorphs.

†**heteˈroclital**, *a.* *Obs.* [f. L. *heteroclit-us* (see next) + -AL[1].] = next 2.

1592 G. HARVEY *Pierce's Super.* 75 As good forbear an irregular foole as beare a foole hetero-clitall. **1646** SIR T. BROWNE *Pseud. Ep.* VII. xix. 385 Sinnes heteroclitall, and such as want either name or president. **1673–4** GREW *Anat. Trunks* I. ii. §8 If there be any Heteroclital Plants, wherein they are found otherwise.

heteroclite (ˈhɛtərəʊklaɪt), *a.* and *sb.* [a. F. *hétéroclite* (16th c. in sense 2, 14th c. *etroclite*), a. L. *heteroclit-us*, a. Gr. ἑτερόκλιτος, irregularly inflected, f. ἑτερο- HETERO- + -κλιτος, verbal adj. from κλίν-ειν to bend, inflect.]

A. *adj.*

1. *Gram.* Irregularly or anomalously declined or inflected: chiefly of nouns.

1656 BLOUNT *Glossogr.*, *Heteroclite*, that is declined otherwise than common Nouns are. **1741** WATTS *Improv. Mind* I. vii. §1 The heteroclite nouns of the Latin tongue.

2. *fig.* Deviating from the ordinary rule or standard; irregular, exceptional, abnormal, anomalous, eccentric. Said of persons and things. (Very common in 17th and 18th centuries; now *rare*.)

1598 FLORIO, *Bischizzoso ceruello*, a fantasticall, heteroclite wit. **1600** *Hosp. Incur. Fooles* 94 Heteroclite, reuerse, thwart and headstrong Fooles. **1638** FEATLY *Strict in Lyndom.* I. 170 Who will not attribute more to the uniforme practise of the primitive Church, then to the heteroclyte practise of later Churches? **1688** BOYLE *Final Causes Nat. Things* IV. 194 This heteroclite animal [the bat]. *a* **1763** SHENSTONE *Wks. & Lett.* (1768) II. 225 Mortification ..may be given him by fools or heteroclite characters. **1867** *Chambers' Encycl.* IX. 265 From its peculiar characters, which led Pallas to call it *Tetrao paradoxus*, it has received the somewhat pedantic name of *Heteroclite Grouse*. **1893** F. HALL in *Nation* (N.Y.) LVII. 229/3 Nor need I dilate on the heteroclite *addression, fallacion, reminiscion*.

B. *sb.* [absol. use of A.]

1. *Gram.* A word irregularly inflected; *esp.* a noun which deviates from the regular declension.

1580 HOLLYBAND *Treas. Fr. Tong*, Examples of all the coniugations declyned at length through all moodes and tenses, with the Hiteroclites. **1612** BRINSLEY *Pos. Parts* (1669) 97 What mean you by *Heteroclits*? Nouns..declined otherwise than the ordinary manner. **1760** (*title*) Lily's Rules Construed; whereunto are added T. Robinson's Heteroclites. **1870** MARCH *Ags. Gram.* §100 Nouns..[that] vary in Case-endings (Heteroclites).

2. *fig.* A thing or person that deviates from the ordinary rule; an 'anomaly'. (Very common in 17th c.; now *rare* or *Obs.*)

1605 BACON *Adv. Learn.* II. i. §3. 8 A substantiall and seuere Collection of the Heteroclites, or Irregulars of Nature..I find not. *c* **1645** HOWELL *Lett.* IV. xxv. (1655) I. 83 Ther are strange Heteroclites in Religion now adaies. **1767** H. BROOKE *Fool of Qual.* (1792) II. xii. 189 Our Parliament would affect to be an heteroclite to all other parliaments. **1780** T. DAVIES *Life Garrick* II. xl. 141 The doctor was a perfect Heteroclite, an inexplicable existence in creation.

So †**heteroˈclitic(al)**, †**heteˈroclitous** *adjs.* = HETEROCLITE *a.*

1632 BURTON *Anat. Mel.* II. iv. I. iv. (ed. 4) 377 Loathsome and fulsome filthy potions, Heteroclitcall pills..horse medicines. **1648** PETTY *Adv. to Hartlib* 23 Parrot-like repeating heteroclitous nouns and verbs. **1656** EARL MONM. *Advt. fr. Parnass.* 449 Employing..for souldiers, those heteroclitick dispositions, who by reason of their restless natures, 'twas thought were likely to do worse. **1885** *Pall Mall G.* 13 Jan. 5/1 Every portion of Marlowe's work is stamped with mutiny and revolt, with love for unblessed speculation and interest in heteroclitical offence.

ˌheteroˈcyclic, *a.* and *sb.* [f. HETERO- + CYCLIC *a.*] **1.** *Bot.* = HETEROMEROUS *a.* 2b.

1895 S. H. VINES *Text-bk. Bot.* 500 When the whorls are heteromerous the flowers are said to be heterocyclic. **1924** HOLMAN & ROBBINS *Textbk. Gen. Bot.* vii. 228 The flowers of the great majority of plants are heterocyclic.

2. *Chem.* Pertaining to or containing a ring of atoms of more than one kind. Opp. to *homocyclic*, *isocyclic*. Also as *sb.*, a heterocyclic compound.

1899 E. F. SMITH tr. *V. von Richter's Org. Chem.* (ed. 3) I. 78 In the case of many heterocyclic compounds..the substances with open chains from which they may be theoretically deduced do not really exist. **1900** *Proc. Chem. Soc.* 6 Feb. 11 The action of bases on ethyl phenylpropiolate gives rise to heterocyclic compounds. **1936** L. J. DESHA *Org. Chem.* xxiv. 479 In the most typical heterocyclic compounds, the ring systems are extremely stable. **1956** *Nature* 16 June 1116/2 The oxygenated heterocyclics were discussed with emphasis on the biochemical aspects. **1966** *McGraw-Hill Encycl. Sci. & Technol.* VI. 427/2 Heterocyclic systems are encountered in many groups of

organic compounds, both synthetic and natural. **1968** *New Scientist* 31 Oct. 268/3 Classification of heterocyclics into suitable groups is somewhat of a problem.

Hence **'heterocycle**, a heterocyclic ring or compound.

1909 WEBSTER, *Heterocycle*, a heterocyclic compound. **1931** *Jrnl. Amer. Chem. Soc.* LIII. 806 Ethylene oxide, the simplest oxygen heterocycle. **1957** E. H. RODD *Chem. Carbon Compounds* IVA Introd. 1 Compounds containing these heterogeneous rings (heterocycles) are classed as heterocyclic.

heterodont ('hɛtərəʊdɒnt), *a.* and *sb.* *Zool.* [mod. f. HETER- + Gr. ὀδούς, ὀδοντ- tooth. In mod.F. *hétérodon.*]

A. *adj.* Having teeth of different kinds or forms (incisors, canines, and molars), as most mammals. Also said of the teeth. Opp. to *homodont.*

1877 TURNER in *Encycl. Brit.* VII. 232/2 In the majority of the Mammalia, the teeth in the same jaw vary in size, form, and structure, and they are therefore called Heterodont. **1886** *Athenæum* 9 Oct. 471/1 Existing toothed whales have what appears to be a homodont and not a heterodont dentition, but a heterodont dentition has been observed in the foetus of an existing whale.

B. *sb.* **1.** A heterodont animal.

2. A snake of the N. American genus *Heterodon.*

heterodox ('hɛtərədɒks), *a.* and *sb.* [ad. Gr. ἑτερόδοξ-ος of another opinion, holding opinions other than the right, f. ἑτερο- HETERO- + δόξα opinion.]

A. *adj.* **1.** Of doctrines, opinions, etc.: Not in accordance with established doctrines or opinions, or those generally recognized as right or 'orthodox': **a.** *orig.* in religion and theology.

1637–50 Row *Hist. Kirk* (1842) 354 Christ's locall descending to hell, and divers others heterodoxe doctrines. **1651** BAXTER *Inf. Bapt.* 294, I shall first shew you the Heterodox Opinion, And then that which I take to be the Orthodox. **1686** R. PARR *Life of Usher* 15 Articles.. Heterodox to the Doctrine and Articles of the Church of England. **1825** MACAULAY *Milton* Ess. (1887) 2 Some of the heterodox opinions which he avows..particularly his Arianism.

Hence **b.** *generally.*

1654 WHITLOCK *Zootomia* 210 That the name of any other Author, or Philosophy, seemeth Heterodoxe without examination. **1700** T. BROWN tr. *Fresny's Amusem. Ser. & Com.* 24 Some call it Over-witting those they deal with, but that's generally denied as a Heterodox Definition. **1859** W. COLLINS *Q. of Hearts* (1875) 6 The Major held some strangely heterodox opinions on the modern education of girls.

2. Of persons: Holding opinions not in accord with some acknowledged standard: **a.** in theology; **b.** in other matters of belief or opinion.

1657 G. STARKEY *Helmont's Vind.* 18 Whosoever should dare to swarve from these [Galen and Aristotle]..being looked upon as Heterodox, was the object of scorn and derision. **1723** J. ATKINS *Voy. Guinea* (1735) 20 The Eastern Sages..teach the Heterodox a Lesson of Humility. **1842** PUSEY *Crisis Eng. Ch.* 96 We cannot treat the Orthodox Greek Church, at once as orthodox and heterodox. **1875** STUBBS *Const. Hist.* III. xviii. 177 Admissions which recommended him to neither the orthodox nor the heterodox.

†**B.** *sb. Obs.* **1.** An opinion not in accord with that which is generally accepted as true or correct; a heterodox opinion.

1619 *Balcanqual's Let. fr. Syn. of Dort* in *Hales' Rem.* (1673) 524 Upon Tuesday..the Canons of the first and second Article..were approved, except the last of the second Article..and the second heterodox in that same Article. *Ibid.*, On Thursday morning..it was reasoned whether that last heterodox should be retained. **1646** SIR T. BROWNE *Pseud. Ep.* II. iii. 66 Not onely a simple Heterodox, but a very hard Paradox, it will seeme, and of great absurdity unto obstinate eares. **1691** W. NICHOLLS *Answ. Naked Gospel* 105 These and many more are the Heterodoxes of his Books.

2. A heterodox person. *rare.*

1647 TRAPP *Comm. Matt.* vii. 18 Heretics, then, and heterodoxes are not good honest men, as the vulgar counts them.

Hence **'heterodoxly** *adv.*, in a heterodox way; **'heterodoxness**, heterodox quality or character.

1664 H. MORE *Myst. Iniq., Apol.* 501 What Error or Heterodoxness in avowing it perfectly Celestial and Æthereal? *Ibid.* 523 The speaking of two persons thus in Christ..seemed to administer some scruple of Heterodoxness to some. **1674** C. ELLIS *Vanity of Scoffing* 9 A thing so heterodoxly yet so magisterially asserted. **1698** R. FERGUSON *View Eccles.* 10 These who have either unthinkingly, or Heterodoxly imbibed his notions.

†**'heterodoxal**, *a. Obs.* [f. as prec. + -AL[1].] Of heterodox character; heterodox.

c **1645** HOWELL *Lett.* IV. xv. (1754) 466 This new Piece of Philosophy..tho' heterodoxal and cross-grained to the old Philosophers. **1661** *Sir Harry Vane's Politicks* 11 Most of those Hearers..grew most Hetrodoxall Rabbies. **1674** HICKMAN *Quinquart. Hist.* (ed. 2) 217 Dr. Reynolds calls the Lambeth Articles Orthodoxal: no one intimated that they were Heterodoxal.

†**hetero'doxical**, *a. Obs.* = prec.

1651 BIGGS *New Disp.* ⁋214 Not only simply heterodoxicall, but a very rough-hewed paradoxicall asseveration. **1821** *Sporting Mag.* IX. 23 In..other parts.. similar heterodoxical passages may be found.

†**hetero'doxous**, *a. Obs.* = prec.

1650 B. *Discolliminium* 28, I could demonstrate it to be Heterogeneous, Heterodoxous, Incongrous.

heterodoxy ('hɛtərədɒksɪ). [ad. Gr. ἑτεροδοξία error of opinion, f. ἑτερόδοξ-ος HETERODOX.]

1. The quality or character of being heterodox; deviation from what is considered to be orthodox.

1659 J. ARROWSMITH *Chain Princ.* 317 That preamble, which the daring Heterodoxie of some modern writers put me upon. **1673** MARVELL *Reh. Transp.* II. 32 No Man's Shooe wrings him the more because of the Heterodoxy, or the tipling of his Shooe-maker. **1837** CARLYLE *Fr. Rev.* II. IV. ii, Does the reader inquire..what the difference between Orthodoxy or *My-doxy* and Heterodoxy or *Thy-doxy* might here be? **1869** RAWLINSON *Anc. Hist.* 519 The establishment of Christianity as the State Religion..turned the attention of the rulers..to minute questions of heterodoxy and orthodoxy.

2. With *a* and *pl.* An opinion or doctrine at variance with that generally received as true or right; a heterodox opinion.

1652–62 HEYLIN *Cosmogr.* To Rdr. (1674) Aijb/1 The Anarchy and licentiousness of Heterodoxies and confused Opinions. **1678** CUDWORTH *Intell. Syst.* I. i. §31. 39 Another heterodoxy of his, concerning the resurrection. **1755** CARTE *Hist. Eng.* IV. 201 Charging him with Popery, Arminianism, and other heterodoxies. **1870** L'ESTRANGE *Miss Mitford* I. vi. 197, I know that I have great poetical authorities against me in this heterodoxy.

heterodromous (hɛtə'rɒdrəməs), *a.* [f. mod.L. *heterodrom-us*, f. Gr. ἑτερο- HETERO- + -δρομος running + -OUS. In mod.F. *hétérodrome.*]

Running in different directions: opp. to *homodromous.* †**a.** *Mech.* Applied to levers of the first order, in which the power and the weight move in opposite directions (*obs.*). **b.** *Bot.* Turning in opposite directions on the main stem and on a branch, as the generating spiral of a phyllotaxis.

1710 J. HARRIS *Lex. Techn.* (ed. 2) II. s.v., The Wheel, Windlass, Capstand, Crane, &c. are perpetual Heterodromous Leavers. [**1727–51** CHAMBERS *Cycl.*, *Heterodromus Vectis*, in mechanics, a lever wherein the fulcrum, or point of suspension, is between the weight and the power.] **1870** BENTLEY *Bot.* (ed. 2) iii. §3. 140 The successive leaves form a spiral round the axis..In the majority of cases, the direction in both the stem and branches is the same, and it is then said to be *homodromous*; but instances..occur in which the direction is different, when it is called *heterodromous.* **1874** R. BROWN *Man. Bot.* 190.

So **hete'rodromy** *Bot.*, heterodromous condition.

1886 *Syd. Soc. Lex.*, *Heterodromy*, term applied..when the axial shoot of the stem coils from right to left, whilst that of the branch twists from left to right, or vice versâ.

heterodyne ('hɛtərəʊdaɪn), *a.* (and *sb.*) *Electr.* [f. HETERO- + -DYNE.] Pertaining to, involving, or designating the production of a beat frequency by the combination of two oscillations of slightly different frequency, esp. as a method of radio detection in which one oscillation is the incoming signal and the other is produced in the receiver. Also (now *rare*) as *sb.*, a heterodyne receiver or its local oscillator.

1908 J. ERSKINE-MURRAY tr. *Ruhmer's Wireless Teleph.* 201 One of the most interesting of Professor Fessenden's many inventions is what he has called the 'Heterodyne' receiver. **1915** W. H. ECCLES *Wireless Telegr.* 151 In receiving signals sent out by the spark sets..the heterodyne produced a telephone current variation averaging 4·65 times that due to the liquid barretter alone. **1919** *Wireless World* Mar. 663 (*heading*) Heterodyne reception. **1922** A. F. COLLINS *Bk. Wireless Telegraph* III. ii. 174 The oscillations set up by the incoming waves from the distant sending stations and those set up by the separate oscillator tube, or heterodyne..have a slightly different frequency. **1931** *B.B.C. Yearbk.* 442/2 *Heterodyne interference*, interference caused to broadcast reception by the carrier wave of an unwanted station beating with that of the wanted station. *Ibid.*, *Heterodyne reception*, a method of receiving C.W. wireless signals in which use is made of a local oscillator to 'beat' with or 'Heterodyne' the incoming C.W. **1946** *Nature* 6 July 33/1 The usual heterodyne methods of measuring a frequency..can be extended to the highest frequencies now in general use. **1957** W. FRASER *Telecommunications* xxii. 735 The heterodyne waveform when rectified produces a current which varies in amplitude at the beat frequency.

fig. **1930** *Musical Assoc. Proc.* 97 To write atonally in a harmonic form at present is to produce a thought 'heterodyne'.

Hence **'heterodyne** *v. trans.*, (*a*) to produce heterodyne interference with (a radio station) (*obs.*); (*b*) to change the frequency of (a signal) by a heterodyne process; *intr.*, to combine so as to produce beat oscillations or a different frequency; **'heterodyning** *vbl. sb.* and *ppl. a.*; **'heterodyned** *ppl. a.*

1923 *Glasgow Herald* 15 Oct. 6 A spark station previously heterodyned by a carrier. **1925** *Ibid.* 10 Nov. 8 Glasgow can be as effectively 'heterodyned' by a German station as Radio Paris can be by a Spanish one working on an almost identical wave-length. **1926** *Encycl. Brit.* III. 1044/2 If the signal current has a frequency of 10^5 cycles (3,000 metres), to give it an audible frequency of c″ – 512 the heterodyning current must have a frequency of 10^5 plus or minus 512. **1933** K. HENNEY *Radio Engin. Handbk.* x. 274 The frequencies in this selected range are made to heterodyne with an oscillator at a frequency of 42,000 cycles. **1934** *Proc. IRE* XXII. 1269 The oscillator operated at a higher frequency than the incoming carriers and heterodyned them to 6 and 7 megacycles. **1943** C. L. BOLTZ *Basic Radio* xiv. 223 This sound is called the heterodyne note, and the process is called heterodyning. **1965** WOZENCRAFT & JACOBS *Princ. Communication Engin.* vi. 493 At the receiver the signals are heterodyned back down from passband to baseband. **1967** *Electronics* 6 Mar. 288/3 In this coherent conversion system, heterodyning converts incoming reference and test signals to 45 Mhz and then to 1 kilohertz. *Ibid.* 291/1 A comparison is made between the phase of a heterodyned 1-khz test signal and the phase of a second 1-khz signal. **1972** *Science* 20 Oct. 252/2 It arises because the emission heterodynes with the collinear laser beam.

fig. **1931** T. H. PEAR *Voice & Personality* iv. 44 The rudeness..heterodynes the shyness. So, while an unselective receiver, or strange listener, perceives a jumbled mixture of both, the ear which is sensitised to rudeness hears it only, while you hear only shyness.

heterogamete (ˌhɛtərəʊ'gæmiːt). *Biol.* [f. HETERO- + GAMETE.] Either of a pair of conjugating gametes that differ in character or form.

1897 *Ann. Bot.* XI. 120 The stage of *Aphanochaete* is..the intermediate step between two motile heterogametes and the true sexuality realized in the higher types. **1949** B. B. MUNDKUR *Fungi & Plant Dis.* vi. 49 While the gametes are motile isogametes in *Synchytrium endobioticum*, they are non-motile heterogametes in *Olpidiopsis.*

heterogametic (ˌhɛtərəʊgə'miːtɪk), *a.* *Biol.* [f. HETERO- + GAMETIC *a.*] (Of a sex or its individual members) producing gametes that differ with respect to a sex chromosome. Opp. HOMOGAMETIC *a.* So **ˌhetero'gamety**, the state or condition of being heterogametic.

1910 E. WILSON in *Science Progress* IV. II. 572 If the two kinds of spermatozoa be designated as the 'X-class' and the 'Y-class', respectively, the eggs are all of the X-class. The male may, accordingly, be designated as the *heterogametic* sex, the female as the *homogametic.* **1932** SINNOTT & DUNN *Princ. Genet.* (ed. 2) x. 215 Two kinds of sperm (male heterogamety) are formed in equal numbers, half with X, and half with Y. **1966** *Amer. Naturalist* C. 122 The fact that heterogametic males do occur suggests..that *P. nubifer* is probably in the process of changing from male to female heterogamety. **1971** [see HOMOGAMETIC *a.*]. **1971** *Nature* 18 June 432/2 In animals with female heterogamety, many authors refer to the chromosome which is present only in females as *W* and the paired sex chromosomes of males as *ZZ.*

heterogamous (hɛtə'rɒgəməs), *a.* [f. Gr. ἑτερο- HETERO- + γάμ-ος marriage + -OUS: in mod.F. *hétérogame* (De Candolle).]

1. *Bot.* Variously applied to conditions in which stamens and pistils are not regularly present in each flower or floret.

Applied **a.** orig. by De Candolle to plants having flowers monœcious, diœcious, or polygamous; **b.** by Lessing to composites whose capitula or flower-heads contain florets differing in sex; **c.** by Trinius to grasses in which the arrangement of the sexes is different in different spikelets.

1839 J. LINDLEY *Introd. Bot.* (ed. 3) I. ii. 157 If all the flowers are hermaphrodite in the capitulum, it is homogamous; if the outer are neuter, or female, and the inner hermaphrodite, or male, it is heterogamous. **1842** in BRANDE. **1866** *Treas. Bot.*, *Heterogamous*, when in a capitulum the florets of the ray are either neuter or female, and those of the disk male. **1872** OLIVER *Elem. Bot.* II. 196 If all the florets of a flower-head (*capitulum*) be perfect, the flower-heads are *homogamous* (Dandelion); if part of them be imperfect, the heads are *heterogamous* (Daisy).

2. *Biol.* Characterized by the alternation of differently organized generations, as of a parthenogenetic and a sexual generation.

1897 ALLBUTT *Syst. Med.* II. 1031 Certain species [of Nemathelminthes] possess what is known as the 'free rhabditis form' and are heterogamous.

3. Of or pertaining to irregular marriage.

1862 M. HOPKINS *Hawaii* 159 Besides these he may have had other heterogamous connexions.

4. *Biol.* Involving, having the character of, or producing heterogametes.

1895 J. R. GREEN *Man. Bot.* I. I. ii. 215 The smaller are held..to be male, and the larger female. Plants with such gametes are called heterogamous. **1900** *Ann. Bot.* XIV. 662 The union of heterogamous walled aplanogametes. **1925** E. B. WILSON *Cell* (ed. 3) vii. 593 In true heterogamous forms the macrogamete becomes a large, non-motile cell. **1957** H. C. BOLD *Morphol. Plants* iii. 55 These plants are the male and female gametophytes which liberate the heterogamous gametes at maturity. **1969** G. W. PRESCOTT *Algae* i. 42 Sexual reproduction may include isogamous, anisogamous, or heterogamous methods, with or without special sex organs.

heterogamy (hɛtə'rɒgəmɪ). [f. as prec. + -Y.] The quality or condition of being heterogamous.

1. *Bot.* Mediate or indirect fertilization of plants.

1874 R. BROWN *Man. Bot.* ix. 418 These circuitous methods of fertilisation may be called *Heterogamy*, or 'crooked fertilisation,' in contradistinction to the typical and orthodox method, which may be styled Orthogamy, or direct ('straight') fertilisation.

2. *Biol.* The succession of differently organized generations of animals or plants, as where sexual generation alternates with parthenogenesis.

1884 A. SEDGWICK tr. *Claus' Zool.* I. 543 Chermes affords an example of heterogamy in that two different oviparous generations follow one another: a slender and winged

summer generation, and an apterous generation which is found in autumn and spring and lives through the winter. **1886** ROLLESTON & JACKSON *Anim. Life* Introd. 31 Alternation of Generations..whether in the form known as metagenesis, i.e. the alternation of asexual and sexual individuals, or as heterogamy, i.e. the alternation of parthenogenetic and sexual races. *Ibid.* 508 [In Insects] Alternation of Generations is coupled with parthenogenesis, and is known in this case as Heterogamy. **1889** GEDDES & THOMSON *Evol. Sex* xv. 207 A sexless fern-plant forms special reproductive cells (spores), which develop parthenogenetically into a sexual prothallus, from the fertilised egg-cell of which the fernplant arises..[this] is called by zoologists, in reference to flukes for instance, *heterogamy*.

3. *Biol.* **a.** The condition of having or producing heterogametes; reproduction involving heterogametes. **b.** Heterogamous reproduction.

1894 S. H. VINES *Text-bk. Bot.* III. 275 Heterogamy:—*a.* Oogamy: sexual cells, oospheres and undifferentiated male cells... *b.* Carpogamy: no differentiated female cell. **1897** *Ann. Bot.* XI. 106 Isogamy, heterogamy, and conjugation have been observed. *Ibid.* 118 The curious heterogamy of *Aphanochaete.* **1925** E. B. WILSON *Cell* (ed. 3) vii. 584 A third type is true heterogamy... The gametes are here widely different from each other. **1966** *McGraw-Hill Encycl. Sci. & Technol.* III. 83/2 Heterogamy is also characteristic of land plants and is regarded as the most advanced type of sexual reproduction.

Hence **hetero'gamic** *a.*, characterized by heterogamy (sense 3).

1904 *Science* 3 June 866/1 In the heterogamic subdivision of the homothallic group, a distinct and constant differentiation exists between the zygophoric hyphæ and the gametes derived from them. **1904** *Proc. Amer. Acad. Arts & Sci.* Aug. 210 Two genera of the homothallic group..are heterogamic in that their gametes show a certain constant inequality in size. **1927** GWYNNE-VAUGHAN & BARNES *Struct. & Devel. Fungi* 112 None of the heterothallic forms among the mucors is known to be heterogamic.

heterogene ('hɛtərədʒiːn), *a.* ? *Obs.* [ad. Gr. ἑτερογενής of different kinds, f. ἑτερο- HETERO- + γένος, γενε- kind: cf. F. *hétérogène* (17th c. in Hatz.-Darm.).] = HETEROGENEOUS.

1541 R. COPLAND *Guydon's Quest. Chirurg.*, Therfore they be called [he]therogenes that is to say of dyuers natures. **1610** B. JONSON *Alch.* II. v, Know you the sapor pontick? sapor stipstick? Or, what is homogene, or heterogene? **1663** BUTLER *Hud.* I. iii. 1318 A strange Chimera of Beasts and Men Made up of pieces Heterogene. **1709–29** V. MANDEY *Syst. Math., Geom.* 143 Homogene Figures, are of the same kind, as to the number of Sides: Heterogene the contrary. **1740** E. BAYNARD *Health* (ed. 6) 42 From a Het'rogen med'cine, The strife is intestine. **1822** *Blackw. Mag.* XI. 10 The diction, similes, and metaphors..are somewhat motley and heterogene. **1830** B'NESS BUNSEN in Hare *Life* I. ix. 394 A soil and nature foreign and heterogene.

heterogeneal (ˌhɛtərə'dʒiːniːəl), *a.* and *sb.* Now *rare.* Also 7 *erron.* -ial(l. [f. Scholastic L. *heterogene-us* (f. Gr. ἑτερογενής, ἑτερογενε-: see HETEROGENE) + -AL[1].]

A. *adj.* = HETEROGENEOUS.

1605 TIMME *Quersit.* I. xi. 48 Separated from the others, which are heterogeniall, or of another kinde. **1631** JORDEN *Nat. Bathes* ii. (1669) 9 Such water as is free from any heterogeneal mixture. **1660** R. COKE *Power & Subj.* 108 A Parliament is a politick body, compounded of heterogenial or dissimilar parts, viz. the King, the Lords, spiritual and temporal, in one distinct house, and of a house of Commons another distinct house. **1674** S. JEAKE *Arith.* (1696) 5 Numbers Heterogeneal are mixt Numbers of Whole and Broken, Abstract and Contract. **1704** J. HARRIS *Lex. Techn.*, *Heterogeneal Nouns* in Grammar, are such as have one Gender in the Singular..and another in the Plural. *Ibid.*, *Heterogeneal Surds*, are such as have different Radical Signs: As ∛aa: √bb **1805** E. DAYES *Wks.* 299 An heterogeneal color, orange, for instance.. viewed through a prism, will disappear, being resolved into the two homogeneal colors.. red and yellow. **1861** TULLOCH *Eng. Purit.* ii. 304 A system which admitted of such tyrannical action..was a heterogeneal thing.

B. *sb.* A heterogeneous person or substance.

1651 N. BACON *Disc. Govt. Eng.* II. iii. (1739) 16 By congregating Homogeneals, and severing Heterogeneals. *a* **1655** VINES *Lord's Supp.* (1677) 260 Whether this mixture of heterogeneals do not pollute the ordinances.

Hence **hetero'genealness**, heterogeneity.

†**hetero'genean**, *a. Obs.* [f. as prec. + -AN.] = HETEROGENEOUS.

a **1601** NASHE *Quaternio* (1632) 44 All the parts both homogenean and heterogenean of the dead corps. **1607** TOPSELL *Four-f. Beasts* (1658) 385 *Corpus heterogenes, in terra coalescens*: A Hetrogenean body encreasing in the earth. **1635** SWAN *Spec. M.* v. §2. (1643) 170 When they consist of Heterogenean parts, or parts of a divers kind.

heterogeneity (ˌhɛtərəʊdʒɪ'niːɪtɪ). [ad. med.L. *heterogeneitās* (*etherogeneitas* 14th c.), f. *heterogene-us*: see next and -ITY. Cf. F. *heterogeneité* (1641 in Hatz.-Darm.).] The quality or condition of being heterogeneous:

a. Difference or diversity in kind from other things; **b.** Composition from diverse elements or parts; multifarious composition.

1641 FRENCH *Distill.* v. (1651) 109 In the artificiall processe of manifesting the heterogeneity of water. **1674** JEAKE *Arith.* (1696) 304 To multiply Simple Surdes observe their Homogeniety or Heterogeniety. **1779** RAMSDEN in *Phil. Trans.* LXIX. 421 The advantage..of not being disturbed by the heterogeneity of light. **1784** HARTLEY *Observ. Man* II. ii. 111 As to the Chinese..its great Heterogeneity in respect of other Languages. **1862** H. SPENCER *First Princ.* II. xvii. §145 (1875) 396 Evolution is an integration of matter..during which the matter passes from an indefinite, incoherent homogeneity, to a definite, coherent heterogeneity. **1868** GLADSTONE *Juv. Mundi* vii. (1870) 194 In the members of the Olympian court itself we discern every kind of heterogeneity.

c. With *a* and *pl.* A heterogeneous element or constituent.

1651 BIGGS *New Disp.* ¶19 In their crudities, heterogenieties & impurities. **1796** KIRWAN *Elem. Min.* (ed. 2) I. 414 Mica, iron ore, and other heterogeneities are more frequent in it. **1837** CARLYLE *Fr. Rev.* I. IV. iv, So many heterogeneities cast together into the fermenting-vat.

d. *law of heterogeneity* (*Logic*): see quot.

1864 BOWEN *Logic* iv. 91 About the second principle, the Law of Heterogeneity, there is no dispute. According to this law, things the most similar must, in some respects, be dissimilar or heterogeneous; and, consequently, any Concept, however large its Intension may be, may still have that Intension increased, without thereby descending to individuals.

heterogeneous (hɛtərə'dʒiːniːəs), *a.* [f. Scholastic L. *heterogene-us* (see HETEROGENEAL) + -OUS.] The opposite of *homogeneous.*

The earlier word, and the more usual, esp. in technical expressions, till *c* 1725, was *heterogeneal.*

1. a. Of one body in respect of another, or of various bodies in respect of each other: Diverse in kind or nature, of completely different characters; incongruous; foreign.

1624 F. WHITE *Reply to Fisher* 243 The question..is heterrogeneous to this disputation. **1660** GOUGE Chr. Direct. ii. (1831) 21 Labour..to drive out all wandering heterogeneous thoughts that come to disturb thee. **1665** HOOKE *Microgr.* 25 Chusing two heterogeneous fluids, such as Water and Oyl. **1699** LD. TARBUT in *Pepys' Diary* (1879) VI. 195 Though it be heterogeneous from this subject. **1715** DESAGULIERS *Fires Impr.* 35 Its heat proceeds from a mixture of heterogeneous Bodies. **1743** *Lond. & Country Brew.* II. (ed. 2) 112 Which is perfectly heterogeneous to the true Management of the Hop. **1809–10** COLERIDGE *Friend* (1837) III. 199 Things utterly heterogeneous can have no intercommunion. **1850** J. H. NEWMAN *Diffic. Anglic.* 58 The National Church is absolutely heterogeneous to the Apostolical or Anglo-Catholic party of 1833. **1862** MILL *Utilit.* 16 Pain is always heterogeneous with pleasure. **1866** LIDDON *Bampton Lect.* ii. (1875) 44 A large collection of heterogeneous writings. **1876** MOZLEY *Univ. Serm.* viii. 180 We do not suppose that the two worlds, visible and invisible, are absolutely different and hetergeneous in fundamental structure.

b. *loosely.* Extraordinary, anomalous, abnormal.

1757 [see HETEROGENOUS I.]. **1768** W. DONALDSON *Life & Adv. Sir B. Sapskull* I. 58 Men of fashion are strange heterogeneous monsters. **1785** MRS. A. M. BENNETT *Juvenile Indiscret.* (1786) V. 242 Lady Belvoir and her two daughters are actual characters, however heterogeneous some people may think them.

2. Of a body in respect of its elements: Composed of diverse elements or constituents; consisting of parts of different kinds; not homogeneous.

1630 PRYNNE *Anti-Armin.* 182 The members of a haeterogenious body..are discrepant and various in themselues. **1639** FULLER *Holy War* v. xix. (1647) 261 The armie will be very heterogeneous, patched up of different people. **1649** A. ROSS *Life* in *Mahomet Alcoran* 405 He.. found at his doore an Heterogeneous Beast, called Elborach, half Asse, half Mule, but much swifter then either. **1701** DE FOE *True-born Eng.* I. 280 Thus from a Mixture of all Kinds began, That Het'rogeneous Thing, An Englishman. **1796** H. BROUGHAM in *Phil. Trans.* LXXXVI. 245 All sorts of light..simple and homogeneous, or heterogeneous and compounded. **1814** SCOTT *Wav.* li, This heterogeneous mass of wild and desperate men. **1865** GROTE *Plato* II. xxi. 52 Good is of a character exceedingly diversified and heterogeneous. **1867** RAWLINSON *Anc. Mon.* IV. vii. 419 In so vast and heterogeneous an Empire as the Persian.

3. *Math.* **a.** Of different kinds, so as to be incommensurable. **b.** Of different dimensions or degrees; non-homogeneous. ***heterogeneous surds***: see quot. 1796. (The later nomenclature is that of *like* and *unlike surds.*)

1656 HOBBES *Six Less.* Wks. 1845 VII. 199 Of these two sorts of angles the quantities are heterogeneous. **1660** BARROW *Euclid* v. xvi. Schol., Heterogeneous quantities are not compared together. **1727–41** CHAMBERS *Cycl.*, *Heterogeneous Surds.* **1796** HUTTON *Math. Dict.*, *Heterogeneous Quantities*..are those which cannot have proportion, or be compared together as to greater and less.. As lines, surfaces, and solids in geometry. *Heterogeneous Surds*, are such as have different radical signs; as $\sqrt{a}$ and $\sqrt[3]{b^2}$; or $\sqrt[3]{10}$ and $\sqrt[5]{20}$.

4. a. In various connexions:

heterogeneous attraction, attraction between atoms different in kind, chemical attraction; also that between the different kinds of electricity and magnetism. ***heterogeneous bodies***, 'such as have their parts of unequal density' (Hutton *Math. Dict.* 1796). ***heterogeneous nouns***, nouns of different genders in the singular and plural. ***heterogeneous numbers***, 'mixed numbers consisting of integers and fractions' (Hutton). ***heterogeneous reactor***, a nuclear reactor in which the fuel is not uniformly mixed with the moderator and/or coolant (opp. 'homogeneous reactor'); also ***heterogeneous pile***. Also in various other technical usages, as ***heterogeneous fusion, radiation, strain, stream.***

1727–41 CHAMBERS *Cycl.* s.v., Heterogeneous bodies are such, whose gravities in different parts are not proportionable to the bulk thereof. *Ibid.*, *Heterogeneous Nouns, Heterogeneous Numbers.* **1826–34** *Good's Bk. Nat.* (ed. 3) I. 93 The heterogeneous attraction, or that between the two different substances, is stronger than the common force of gravity. **1883** *Encycl. Brit.* XV. 693/1 Heterogeneous strain. **1902** *Ibid.* XXVIII. 567/2 In the case of crystalline fusion it is necessary to distinguish two cases, the Homogeneous and the Heterogeneous... In the second case, the solid and liquid phases differ in composition; that of the liquid phase changes continuously, and the temperature does not remain constant during the fusion. *Ibid.* XXIX. 257/1 The nuclear divisions are what Weismann calls 'differentiating' or heterogeneous divisions. In them the microcosms of the germ-plasm are not doubled, but slowly disintegrated. **1922** W. B. SCOTT *Physiogr.* vi. 154 Heterogeneous streams are those which have two or more different kinds of courses, and most rivers, including almost all the longer ones, are of this class. **1947** C. GOODMAN *Sci. & Engin. Nucl. Power* I. ix. 320 (*caption*) Heterogeneous reactor with circulating liquid fuel. **1949** M. L. OLIPHANT *Atomic Age* 23 The arrangement used is a so-called 'heterogeneous pile', consisting of some tens of tons of uranium rods or slugs disposed in a calculated 'lattice' throughout a mass of some hundreds of tons of graphite. **1958** O. R. FRISCH *Nucl. Handbk.* xii. 2 By far the largest number of reactors built to date have been thermal, heterogeneous reactors. **1958** *Chambers's Techn. Dict.* (ed. 3) 984/2 *Heterogeneous radiation*, that having particles of various energies and/or wavelengths.

b. Denoting the presence of more than one phase (solid, liquid, or gas) in a system or process.

1878 J. W. GIBBS in *Trans. Connecticut Acad. Arts & Sci.* III. 108 (*heading*) On the equilibrium of heterogeneous substances. **1895** *Jrnl. Chem. Soc.* LXVIII. II. 72 (*heading*) Graphical representation of heterogeneous systems. **1928** J. K. ROBERTS *Heat & Thermodynamics* xviii. 356 Heterogeneous reactions in which solids and vapours take part. **1950** *Sci. News* XV. 65 Much research had been carried out on heterogeneous catalysts, that is, catalysts at whose surfaces reactions between gases are brought about.

Hence **hetero'geneously** *adv.*, in a heterogeneous manner; **hetero'geneousness**, the quality or condition of being heterogeneous; heterogeneity.

1653 H. MORE *Conject. Cabbal.* (1662) 129 The Heterogeneousness of the Exposition of the First Day's Creation. **1768** JOHNSON *Gen. Obs. Shaks.*, *3 Hen. VI*, Dissimilitude of style, and heterogeneousness of sentiment, may sufficiently show that a work does not really belong to the reputed author. **1775** —— *Journ. to West. Isl.*, *Ostig in Sky* Wks. X. 439 The rooms are very heterogeneously filled. **1836–9** TODD *Cycl. Anat.* II. 105 The heterogeneousness of two fluids. **1864** PUSEY *Lect. Dan.* vii. 435 Unauthentic tradition is wont to connect things heterogeneously.

heterogenesis (ˌhɛtərəʊ'dʒɛnɪsɪs). *Biol.* [f. Gr. ἑτερο- HETERO- + γένεσις birth, generation.]

†**1.** Abnormal or irregular organic development: see quot. *Obs.* (So F. *hétérogénésie.*)

1854 MAYNE *Expos. Lex.*, *Heterogenesis*, name given by Breschet to a Class of organic deviations comprehending those in which there exists a relative anomaly, whether from the situation or from the colour of organs, the number or the situation of the fetuses belonging to the same gestation, the situation or the number of organs in particular.

†**2.** Applied to sexual reproduction from two different germs, male and female. *Obs.*

1858 CARPENTER *Veg. Phys.* §398 The process by which new individuals are produced is called *Heterogenesis.* In this process, two different cells are concerned..germ-cells and sperm-cells.

3. The birth or origination of a living being otherwise than from a parent of the same kind.

1864 *Q. Jrnl. Sc.* Jan. 17 Heterogenesis is a term employed to express the creation or birth of living beings in an abnormal manner. *Ibid.*, At present the evidence which we possess..is rather adverse to the doctrine of 'heterogenesis' in any form. **1870** HUXLEY in *Brit. Assoc. Rep.* p. lxxvii, The living parent was supposed to give rise to offspring which passed through a totally different series of states from those exhibited by the parent, and did not return into the cycle of the parent; this is what ought to be called *Heterogenesis*, the offspring being altogether, and permanently, unlike the parent.

b. *esp.* The generation of animals or vegetables of low organization from inorganic matter; abiogenesis; spontaneous generation.

1878 TYNDALL in *19th Cent.* III. 23 The notion of heterogenesis or spontaneous generation.

c. Alternation of generations.

1863 H. SPENCER *Biol.* I. II. vii. 211 Where propagation is carried on by heterogenesis, or is characterized by unlikeness of the successive generations, there is always asexual genesis with occasionally-recurring sexual genesis. **1875** tr. *Schmidt's Desc. & Darw.* 169 When the species is composed of a regular alternation of variously constituted generations and individuals. This particular sort of reversion is termed Alternate Generation, or Heterogenesis.

heteroge'netic, *a.* [f. prec.: cf. GENETIC *a.*]

1. *Biol.* Of or pertaining to, or characterized by, heterogenesis or heterogeny.

1872 *Proc. R. Soc.* XX. 264 The living units combine, they undergo molecular rearrangements, and the result of such a process of heterogenetic biocrasis is the appearance of larger and more complex organisms. **1874** *Contemp. Rev.* XXIII. 709 All the related heterogenetic phenomena. **1897** ALLBUTT *Syst. Med.* II. 1041 Giles holds that *A. duodenale* may become sexually mature while outside the body and in the free state; in other words, that it is heterogenetic.

2. a. *Philos.* Relating to external origination.

1887 WHITTAKER in *Mind* XII. 289 Prof. Wundt calls his own theory of the will 'the autogenetic theory', opposing it to 'the ordinary or heterogenetic theory'.

b. *Med.* Of a disease: produced by infection from outside the body.

1890 in BILLINGS *Med. Dict.*

3. *Path.* [ad. G. *heterogenetisch* (Friedberger & Schiff 1913, in *Berl. klin. Wochenschr.* 25 Aug. 1558/1).] = HETEROPHILE *a.* 1.

1918 C. H. BROWNING *Appl. Bacteriol.* x. 175 'Heterogenetic' antibodies (Friedberger). *Ibid.* 176 The capacity to produce a positive Wassermann reaction is probably a somewhat similar heterogenetic phenomenon. **1920** *Jrnl. Path. & Bacteriol.* XXIII. 364 The injection of organs of certain animals into rabbits leads to the development of 'heterogenetic' immune body for sheep's blood corpuscles. The tissues which act in this way are called 'heterogenetic antigens'. **1944** *Jrnl. Exper. Med.* LXXIX. 556 A heterogenetic antibody showing fixation of complement with human liver and agglutination of sheep erythrocytes was found in certain cases of acute infective hepatitis.

heterogenic (ˌhɛtərəʊˈdʒɛnɪk), *a.*[1] [f. Gr. ἑτερογεν-ής (see HETEROGENE *a.*) + -IC; in sense 2 prob. directly f. HETEROGENY 3 b.]

1. 'Occurring in the wrong sex, as a beard upon a woman' (Dorland, 1900).

2. *Biol.* Characterized by an alternation of generations; = HETEROGENETIC *a.* 1.

1901 *Jrnl. Exper. Med.* VI. 80 These various forms were but different phases in the cycle of a single heterogenic parasite.

3. *Med.* Derived from animals of a different species.

1911 *Jrnl. Exper. Med.* XIV. 245 Fetal tissues of the chicken grew extensively in human, rabbit, and dog plasma. In general, however, . . the development of the tissues is slighter . . in heterogenic than in autogenic and homogenic plasma. **1920** *Jrnl. Path. & Bacteriol.* XXIII. 366 There is established the existence of an apparently specific relationship between the lipoids of heterogenic organs and the heterogenetic antibody. **1922** *Jrnl. Exper. Med.* XXXV. 17 It would be of advantage to cultivate chicken tissue in heterogenic serum because it is much more difficult to keep alive *in vitro* permanently a strain of mammal fibroblasts than of chicken fibroblasts.

heterogenic (ˌhɛtərəʊˈdʒiːnɪk), *a.*[2] *Genetics.* [f. HETERO- + GEN(E + -IC.] Having more than one allele of a particular gene.

1947 D. LEWIS in *Heredity* I. 86 Pollen grains with such different alleles are described as heterogenic. *Ibid.* 88 Some types of heterogenic pollen were fully compatible on a style carrying only one of the alleles present in the pollen, but were incompatible on styles carrying the other allele only. **1967** *Hereditas* LVIII. 25 There is lack of interaction in all the twelve allelic pair constellations which are possible in the heterogenic pollen of the tetraploid.

heteˈrogenist. [f. HETEROGENY + -IST: cf. mod.F. *hétérogéniste.*] An upholder of the hypothesis of heterogeny or spontaneous generation.

1870 *Nature* 14 July 224/1 M. Pasteur's researches . . have . . strongly influenced the opinions of very many scientific men on the question of the truth or falsity of the doctrines of the heterogenists. **1871** TYNDALL *Fragm. Sc.* (1879) II. xiii. 304 The English heterogenist was far bolder. **1878** —— in *19th Cent.* Mar. 501 While no discovery of the age would bear comparison with this 'new birth of living particles', it is a mere commonplace occurrence to our fortunate heterogenist.

heterogenite (hɛtəˈrɒdʒɪnaɪt). *Min.* [ad. G. *heterogenit* (A. Frenzel 1872, in *Jrnl. f. prakt. Chem.* V. 404), f. Gr. ἑτερογεν-ής of different kinds, in allusion to the fact that the mineral differs in composition from some manganese oxides, which it outwardly resembles: see -ITE[1].] A name applied to various hydrous oxides of cobalt.

1872 *Jrnl. Chem. Soc.* XXV. 991 Heterogenite is a product of the decomposition of smaltine or tin-white cobalt (speiss-kobalt). **1922** *Amer. Mineralogist* VII. 195 It is therefore recommended that the prior name heterogenite be applied to *all cobalto-cobaltic hydroxides*, of varying purity. **1962** *Mineral. Mag.* XXXIII. 258 Of the many names proposed for natural cobaltic hydroxide, heterogenite has a clear priority over transvaalite, stainierite, mindigite, trieuite, and boodtite. Heubachite is a nickelian and schulzenite a cuprian heterogenite.

†**heteˈrogenize,** *v. Obs. rare.* [f. Gr. ἑτερογενής HETEROGENE + -IZE.] *intr.* To act in a manner heterogeneous or foreign to his own character.

1592 G. HARVEY *Pierce's Super.* 110 Never Artist so licentiously heterogenised or so extravagantly exceeded his prescribed limits as Ambition or Covetice.

heteˈrogenous, *a.* **1.** A less correct form of HETEROGENEOUS. (In mod. use prob. repr. the pronunc. (hɛtəˈrɒdʒɪnəs) given by some speakers to *heterogeneous*: cf. *homogenous* (HOMOGENEOUS *a.* ¶).)

1695 ALINGHAM *Geom. Epit.* 62 Heterogenous Quantities cannot be compared alternately. **1757** MRS. GRIFFITH *Lett. Henry & Frances* (1767) II. 260, I am afraid I shall carry but a very heterogenous dress along with me. **1812** *Examiner* 11 May 303/1 Of the most opposite and heterogenous kind. **1916** [see *club necktie* (CLUB *sb.* 19)]. **1961** WEBSTER, *Heterogenous* = Heterogeneous. **1971** *Nature* 20 Aug. 586/1 A very heterogenous collection of twenty articles discusses basic physiology of the small intestine. **1972** *Ibid.* 10 Mar. 78/1 A heterogenous population of schizophrenic patients.

2. *Surg.* [prob. directly f. Gr. γένος race.] Of transplanted tissue: †**a.** = HOMOGENOUS *a.* 2, HOMOPLASTIC *a.* 2. *Obs.*

1909 *Boston Med. & Surg. Jrnl.* 23 Dec. 916/1 Whether heterogenous grafts are taken from a living or from a dead subject, there is with them some likelihood of failure to form *permanent* skin.

b. = HETEROPLASTIC *a.* 3.

1939 S. FOMON *Surg. Injury & Plastic Repair* ii. 107 Failure of heterogenous transplants. **1949** EICHELBAUM & TURNER in M. Thorek *Mod. Surg. Technic* (ed. 2) II. xxix. 1149/1 The heterogenous graft . . has been abandoned in favor of the homogenous graft which as an autogenous graft is now in the widest use. **1965** *Jrnl. Amer. Med. Assoc.* 2 Aug. 380/1 Results with the processed heterogenous bone transplants closely parallel those with autogenous and homogenous bone transplants.

heterogeny (hɛtəˈrɒdʒɪnɪ). [mod. f. Gr. type *ἑτερογενεία, abstr. sb. from ἑτερογενής HETEROGENE; or, in 3, from HETERO- + -γενεια birth.]

†**I. 1.** Heterogeneousness. *Obs.*

1647 *Husbandman's Plea agst. Tithes* 67 There is no hetrogeny or disparitie in the matter.

2. *concr.* A heterogeneous assemblage.

1838 HAWTHORNE *Amer. Note-bks.* (1883) 158 Sometimes he would put up a heterogeny of articles in a lot . . and knock them all down, perhaps for ninepence. **1921** *S.P.E. Tract* v. 10 We find a heterogeny of words in use. **1927** *Sunday Express* 29 May 5/1 Every conceivable kind of article which forms the heterogeny of the shops patronised by women.

II. 3. *Biol.* **a.** Production of living beings from substances organic or inorganic without germs or ovules; spontaneous generation.

1863 DARWIN in *Life & Lett.* (1887) III. 20, I have written a letter . . to say, under the cloak of attacking Heterogeny, a word in my own defence. **1871** *Proc. Amer. Phil. Soc.* XII. 313 No better case has ever been made out for heterogeny than by Charlton Bastian. **1886** *Syd. Soc. Lex., Heterogeny,* . . also the production of a living being from the substance of a living being of some other kind; as in the supposed development of maggots from the substance of putrefying flesh.

b. Alternation of generations, *esp.* of a sexual and a parthenogenetic generation.

1886 W. E. HOYLE tr. *Leuckart's Parasites of Man* 25 The theory of the heterogeny of Entozoa. *Ibid.* 96, I have for some time been accustomed to call such an alternate succession of dimorphous sexual generations by the name 'Heterogeny'. **1889** E. B. POULTON et al. tr. *Weismann's Ess. Heredity* 325 In the *Daphnidae*, heterogeny may pass into pure parthenogenesis by the non-appearance of the sexual generations. **1931** BLACKLOCK & SOUTHWELL *Guide Human Parasitol.* xii. 105 Where one egg produces more than one adult, asexual multiplication has obviously followed the sexual multiplication, *i.e.* alternation of generations, or heterogeny, exists. **1946** B. DAWES *Trematoda* xiv. 501 Heterogeny, namely, the alternation of a parthenogenetic with a sexual generation.

heterogone (ˈhɛtərəgəʊn), *a. Bot.* [f. Gr. ἑτερο- HETERO- + γόν-ος offspring, race, -γονος generating.] = HETEROGONOUS 1.

1877 GRAY in *Amer. Jrnl. Sc.* Ser. III. XIII. 82, I propose the . . term of heterogone (or heterogonous) for these flowers. **1880** —— *Bot. Text-bk.* I. 235 The nature of heterogone dimorphism may well be understood from a single example. The most familiar one is that of Houstonia.

heterogonic (ˌhɛtərəʊˈgɒnɪk), *a.* [f. HETEROGON(Y + -IC; in sense 1 ad. F. *hétérogonique* (A. Pézard 1918, in *Bull. biol. de la France et de la Belg.* LII. 25).]

1. = ALLOMETRIC *a.*

1924 *Nature* 20 Dec. 895/1 Whereas in the male the ratio *abdomen-breadth* : *carapace-breadth* remained constant, in the female it increased continuously. . . Pézard (1918) has styled the growth of such an organ *heterogonic*. **1935** *Ibid.* 14 Sept. 433/2 Heterogonic growth clearly involves a regularly continuous change of proportions. **1964** H. W. MANNER *Elem. Compar. Embryol.* xi. 216 Differential growth is referred to as heterogonic growth.

2. Exhibiting heterogony (sense 1 b); applied to a life-cycle in which free-living organisms alternate with parasites, and to the free-living generation of such a cycle.

1926 J. H. SANDGROUND in *Amer. Jrnl. Hygiene* VI. 338 In the genus Strongyloides [of nematodes] heterogony may be involved in the life-cycle, but in many instances there is only one multiplicative generation and this mode of development has been called *direct* or, if we may introduce a new term to express this, homogonic in contradistinction to heterogonic or indirect. **1936** *Amer. Jrnl. Hygiene* XXIV. 83 No obvious necessity for the interpolation of a heterogonic generation in the reproductive cycle of *S. ratti* has manifested itself. **1951** L. H. HYMAN *Invert.* III. xiii. 304 The eggs . . may develop into free-living males and females, the offspring of which proceed to the parasitic phase so that the cycle is indirect or heterogonic.

So ˌ**heteroˈgonically** *adv.*

1932 J. S. HUXLEY *Probl. Rel. Growth* II. ii. 53 The trunk grows heterogonically with reference to the head.

heterogonous (-ˈɒgənəs), *a.* [f. as HETEROGONE *a.* + -OUS.]

1. *Bot.* Having incongruous reproductive organs; applied by Asa Gray to flowers in which cross-fertilization is secured by the stamens and pistils being dimorphic or trimorphic.

1877 [see HETEROGONE]. **1880** GRAY *Struct. Bot.* vi. §4. 225 They may be classed into those without and those with dimorphism of stamens and pistils, or, in other words, those with Homogonous and those with Heterogonous flowers. **1880** —— *Bot. Text-bk.* I. 236 Heterogonous trimorphism is known in certain species . . ; and the complication may have certain conceivable advantages over dimorphism.

2. *Biol.* Exhibiting irregular reproduction; producing offspring dissimilar to the parent.

1883 *Syd. Soc. Lex., Digenesis, heterogonous,* the form of digenesis in which the buds produce animals differing in appearance from their progenitors. **1886** *Ibid., Heterogonous,* being of, or produced by, irregular generation.

So **heteˈrogonism,** the condition of being heterogonous (in either sense).

1886 *Syd. Soc. Lex., Heterogonism,* the production of dissimilar offspring from similar parentage, as in Gymnoblasti where dissimilar gonosomes may arise from similar trophosomes.

heteˈrogony. [f. prec. + -Y[3].] **1. a.** *Bot.* and *Biol.* = HETEROGONISM.

1870 ROLLESTON *Anim. Life* Introd. 126 A series of phenomena . . which has been spoken of as 'Digenesis with Heterogony.'

b. *Biol.* Alternation of generations, *esp.* of a diœcious and a hermaphroditic generation.

1906 P. FALCKE tr. *Braun's Anim. Parasites Man* 273 In a number of Nematodes . . heterogony occurs. **1908** BEATTIE & DICKSON *Textbk. Gen. Path.* vi. 395 In other nematodes what is known as Heterogony occurs, in which there may be alteration [ed. 2, 1921, alternation] of fully developed sexual generations. **1936** *Nature* 9 May 780 Heterogony has been widely used to denote a certain type of reproductive cycle.

2. *Biol.* = ALLOMETRY.

1927 *Jrnl. Genetics* XVII. 309 (*heading*) Discontinuous variation and heterogony in Forficula. **1938** [see ALLOMETRY].

3. Phr. ***heterogony of ends***: a principle enunciated by Wundt (*Ethik* 1886), according to which the development of religion and of codes of moral and social behaviour produced results that are to be distinguished from the cause of the development and were not intended at its outset; e.g. moral customs are regarded as (unforeseen) outgrowths from religious ceremonial.

1887 *Mind* XII. 286 The most general results of the author's [*sc.* Wundt's] investigation are a 'law of three stages' of moral development and a 'law of the heterogony of ends'. **1897** J. H. GULLIVER et al. tr. *Wundt's Ethik* I. 330 The law of the *heterogony of ends*. We mean to express by this name what is a matter of universal experience: that manifestations of will, over the whole range of man's free voluntary actions, are always of such a character that the effects of the actions extend more or less widely beyond the original motives of volition, so that *new* motives are originated for future actions, and again, in their turn, produce new effects. **1911** *Encycl. Brit.* XVIII. 241/2 Each particular will is directed to particular ends, but . . beyond these ends effects follow as unexpected consequences, and . . this heterogony produces social effects which we call custom.

heterograft (ˈhɛtərəʊgrɑːft, -græft). *Med.* and *Biol.* [f. HETERO- + GRAFT *sb.*[1]] A graft taken from an individual of a species different from that of the recipient; a heterotransplant.

Quot. 1909 is in the sense of HOMOGRAFT.

1909 *Boston Med. & Surg. Jrnl.* 23 Dec. 918/2 Auto-grafts succeed better than hetero-grafts. **1923** STEDMAN *Med. Dict.* (ed. 7) 449/2 *Heterograft,* a graft taken from an animal—not from another person, *isograft,* or from another part of the same individual, *autograft.* **1927** H. T. KARSNER *Human Path.* xi. 313 The fact that chemical conditions must be nicely adjusted is indicated by the failure of heterografts and the relatively higher degree of success of autografts over homeografts. **1948** *Endeavour* VII. 165 In simpler organisms, such as *Hydra,* the graft can be of different species (heterograft). **1972** *Daily Colonist* (Victoria, B.C.) 12 Mar. 22/5 The Brooke research team looked to animals as a source of possible heterografts.

Hence ˈ**heterografted** *ppl. a.*; ˈ**heterografting** *vbl. sb.*

1927 H. T. KARSNER *Human Path.* xi. 312 Hetero-grafting . . would throw open a large field for transplantation of various tissues and organs which cannot be removed from human donors . . until death has occurred. **1961** *Biol. Abstr.* XXXVI. 2017/2 Regeneration of homografted and heterografted limbs in the stick insects. **1968** J. C. NORMAN et al. *Organ Perfusion & Preservation* xxviii. 382 Heterografted fox livers. *Ibid.* 383 The loss of perfusion immediately after heterografting.

heterography (-ˈɒgrəfɪ). [f. Gr. ἑτερο- HETERO- + -γραφία writing. Opposed to *orthography.*]

1. Spelling that differs from that which is correct according to current usage; 'incorrect' spelling.

1783 S. PARR *Wks.* (1828) VII. 390 Neoteric affectations of Archaism and Heterography. **1831** *Blackw. Mag.* XXX. 667 His orthography, or rather heterography, has been a subject of keen animadversion; and he has been charged with misspelling his own name. **1876** BLACKMORE *Cripps* xlv, I corrected his heterography. **1908** *Daily Chron.* 6 May 4/6 On the subject of 'howlers', we all make them at times, being victims of heterophasia (or heterography). **1920** W. PERRETT *Peetickay* 15 There is a pretty general consensus that unconventional spelling or heterography is bad spelling.

2. Irregular and inconsistent spelling (as the current spelling of English).

1847 DE QUINCEY in *Tait's Mag.* XIV. 162 All climates alike groan under heterography.

So **heteˈrographer,** one who practises heterography; **heteroˈgraphic** *a.*, pertaining to or characterized by heterography.

1864 *Realm* 20 Apr. 7 Mr. Landor . . records, in heterographic hexameters, Porson's opinion. **1865** H. B.

WHEATLEY in *Philol. Soc. Trans.* (*title*) Notes on some English Heterographers. **1883** H. P. SMITH *Gloss. Terms & Phrases, Heterographic*, using the same combinations of written letters to express different sounds, as English spelling does.

heteroideous (hɛtəˈrɔidiːəs), *a. rare.* [f. Gr. ἕτερο- HETERO- + εἶδος form + -OUS.] (See quot.)
  1866 *Treas. Bot.* 587/1 *Heteroideous*, diversified in form.

heterokaryotic (ˌhɛtərəʊkæriˈɒtɪk), *a. Bot.* Also -caryotic. [ad. G. *heterocaryotisch* (H. Burgeff 1913, in *Ber. d. Deut. Bot. Ges.* XXX. 680), f. HETERO- + KARY(O- + -OTIC.] Exhibiting or resulting from heterokaryosis. Hence ˌheteroˈkaryon (-ˈkæriən), a heterokaryotic cell, structure, or organism; ˌheterokaryˈosis (-kærɪˈəʊsɪs), the condition, prevalent among fungi, in which two or more genetically different nuclei are maintained in a common cytoplasm.
  1916 B. D. JACKSON *Gloss. Bot. Terms* (ed. 3) 178/1 *Heterokaryotic*,.. the character of spores in which both male and female nuclei exist (Burgeff); *Heterokaryosis* is the condition. **1932** *Phytopathology* XXII. 955 The term 'heterocaryosis' precisely describes the condition of a cell containing 2 or more genetically different nuclei. **1935** *Ibid.* XXV. 285 The very young spore already contains several nuclei; hence it is quite possible that each may carry different factors for cultural characters and pathogenicity. The organism may then be truly heterocaryotic. **1942** *Bull. Torrey Bot. Club* LXIX. 75 (*heading*) Heterocaryotic vigor in Neurospora. **1945** *Genetics* XXX. 13 The natural heterokaryon in *Neurospora crassa* generally contains both plus and minus nuclei. **1952** S. EMERSON in J. W. Gowan *Heterosis* xii. 200 (*caption*) Heterocaryon formation resulting from hyphal fusion. **1955** *New Biol.* XIX. 20 Heterokaryosis has this advantage over sex that a single organism can contain genes from more than two parents. **1969** *Nature* 30 Aug. 961/2 The diploid nuclei were produced by rare nuclear fusion in a balanced heterokaryon formed from two different uninucleate colour mutants.

†**heteˈrologal**, *a. Math. Obs.* [f. as HETEROLOGOUS *a.* + -AL¹.] Applied to those terms in two or more ratios or fractions which do not correspond, as the antecedent or numerator of one, and the consequent or denominator of the other: opp. to *homologal*.
  1674 JEAKE *Arith.* (1696) 48 The new Fraction.. will not be in its least terms, unless such Heterologal terms be first abbreviated to their lowest.

heterological (ˌhɛtərəʊˈlɒdʒɪkəl), *a.* [ad. G. *heterologisch* (Grelling & Nelson 1907, in *Abhandl. Fries'schen Schule* II. 307), f. HETERO- + Gr. λόγος word: see LOGOS.] Of an adjective or other predicate: not having the property it denotes. Hence ˌheterologiˈcality, the property of being heterological.
  1926, 1952 [see AUTOLOGICAL *a.*]. **1940** B. RUSSELL *Inquiry Meaning & Truth* v. 79 'Long' is heterological because it is not a long word, but 'short' is homological. **1950** *Analysis* X. 79 When one is asked, 'Is "heterological" heterological?' no answer need be given until the notion of heterologicality is further analyzed.

heterologous (-ˈɒləgəs), *a.* [f. Gr. ἕτερο- HETERO- + λόγ-ος ratio, relation, etc. + -OUS.] Having a different relation, or consisting of different elements; not corresponding: opp. to HOMOLOGOUS. *spec.* **a.** *Path.* Of a different formation from that of the normal tissue of the part.
  1822-34 *Good's Study Med.* (ed. 4) II. 578 *note*, One of the heterologous formations, as they are termed by Professor Carswell. **1864** W. T. Fox *Skin Dis.* 25 New formations are homologous (epidermic, pigmentary, dermic), or heterologous (pseudoplasms, neoplasms). **1878** T. BRYANT *Pract. Surg.* I. 96 The same kind of tumour may be, under certain circumstances, homologous, and under other circumstances heterologous.
  b. *Chem.* (See quot. 1886.)
  1880 *Libr. Univ. Knowl.* (N.Y.) VI. 609 His *Précis de Chimie Organique*, in which he [Gerhardt] sketches the idea of 'Homologous and Heterologous Series.' **1886** *Syd. Soc. Lex.*, *H[eterologous]* series, Gerhardt's term for bodies derived from each other by definite chemical metamorphoses, in contradistinction to *Homologous series.*
  c. (See quot. 1889.)
  1889 V. H. W. WINGRAVE *Dunman's Gloss. Anat. Terms*, *Heterologous stimuli*, stimuli which will excite a sensory nerve when applied either to its termination or in its continuity. **1913** *Amer. Jrnl. Physiol.* XXXII. 230 Aronsohn .. declared that substances in solution when poured into the nose, could be smelled... This conclusion was confirmed by Vaschide (1901), and by Veress (1903), though the latter showed that the solutions tested were rather in the nature of heterologous than homologous stimuli.
  d. *Path.* and *Bacteriol.* Deriving from, associated with, or belonging to another species or type of organism or an antigen or antibody of different constitution.
  1893 PARKER & RÖNNFELDT tr. *Weismann's Germ-Plasm* ix. 265 In the crosses between different species, the idioplasm of a cell in many stages will be composed of homologous as well as of heterologous ids. **1910** *Jrnl. Path. & Bacteriol.* XIV. 30 We have endeavoured to determine whether.. the inoculation of heterologous bacteria.. affects the production of specific agglutinins in animals previously immunised against the *Bacillus coli.* **1915** *Lancet* 3 Apr. 701/2 (*heading*) Heterologous transplantation: mouse tumours in rats. **1916** *Jrnl. Path. & Bacteriol.* XX. 214 Heterologous resistance as exemplified in the reactions of

the sera of animals immunised with transplanted new growths from alien species. **1933** W. W. C. TOPLEY *Outl. Immunity* vi. 91 A serum that agglutinates the same bacterium but has been produced by the inoculation of some other bacterium, differing in one or more of its antigenic components, is termed a heterologous serum. **1958** *Nature* 13 Dec. 1678/2 The multiplication of extraneous viruses in tumours grown in homologous and heterologous hosts depends on the host animal.

heterology (-ˈɒlədʒɪ). [f. as prec. + -Y; in sense 2, f. Gr. ἕτερο- + -λογια discourse.]
  1. The condition of being heterologous: opp. to HOMOLOGY.
  1854 in MAYNE *Expos. Lex.* **1871** T. H. GREEN *Introd. Pathol.* (1873) 105 Any deviation from the type of the parent tissue constitutes heterology. **1878** T. BRYANT *Pract. Surg.* (1879) I. 96 Tissues normal in themselves appear under the form of a tumour, sometimes in regions where this tissue normally exists, sometimes in places where it does not exist in the normal state of things. In the first case I speak of it as *homology*, in the second as *heterology.*
  2. *nonce-use.* Vocabulary of different names.
  1852 C. W. H[OSKINS] *Talpa* 28 Let the old drainer christen it, for my heterology is exhausted.

heterolysin (ˌhɛtərəʊˈlaɪsɪn). [a. G. *heterolysin* (Ehrlich & Morgenroth 1900, in *Berl. klin. Wochenschr.* XXXVII. 455/1), f. HETERO- + LYSIN.] A hæmolysin formed in the bloodstream of an animal when blood cells from one of a different species are introduced.
  1901 in DORLAND *Med. Dict.* (ed. 2). **1903** *Science* 3 July 9/1 Many observations upon the effects of iso- and heterolysins—as for kidney and liver cells—about which there is no reasonable doubt. **1934** ZINSSER & BAYNE-JONES *Textbk. Bacteriol.* (ed. 7) xvi. 212 The blood cells of one animal, injected into an animal of another species, give rise to a hemolytic substance in the blood serum of the second animal, which is strictly specific for the variety of cells injected. Such hemolysins.. are spoken of as *heterolysins.*

heterolysis (hɛtəˈrɒlɪsɪs). [f. HETERO- + -LYSIS.]
  1. a. The dissolution of blood cells by a heterolysin. **b.** The dissolution of cells of one kind by an enzyme of cells of another kind.
  1902 VAUGHAN & NOVY *Cellular Toxins* (ed. 4) vii. 129 Ehrlich suggests that the hemolytic action of the blood serum of one animal upon the corpuscles of another species be designated as 'heterolysis'. **1909** ALLBUTT & ROLLESTON *Syst. Med.* (ed. 2) VI. 783 The autolysis of bland infarcts is ..due to enzymes derived from the cytoplasm..and is a much slower process than the heterolysis due to the leucocytic invasion seen in infective infarcts. **1924** R. MUIR *Text-bk. Path.* i. 14 The term autolysis has been applied to the digestive softening of tissues produced by their own organisms. Such enzymes..may be produced by other cells, especially leucocytes—heterolysis. **1962** H. HANSON in A. Pirie *Lens Metabolism Rel. Cataract* 470 More significant for the specification of intracellular proteases are experiments on heterolysis, i.e. the action of cell proteases on proteins or peptides that are foreign to the cell.
  2. *Chem.* The splitting of a molecule into two oppositely charged ions.
  1938 C. K. INGOLD in *Trans. Faraday Soc.* XXXIV. 227, I would suggest that we may as well have two [new words] and be done with it: *viz.*, 'heterolysis' and 'homolysis', defined as follows: A:B→A + :B (*Heterolysis*) [and] A:B→A. + .B (*Homolysis*). Here the dots represent electrons. **1946** *Nature* 28 Sept. 448/2 A slow heterolysis of nitric acid cannot depend only on proton transfers. **1965** PHILLIPS & WILLIAMS *Inorg. Chem.* I. x. 344 Due to the high energy of production of A⁺A⁻, heterolysis..of homonuclear species is not very probable, except in the presence of catalysts.
  So **heteroˈlytic** *a.*, characterized by or of the nature of heterolysis (in either sense).
  1909 *Chem. Abstr.* III. 1766 Cancer tissue itself possesses no heterolytic properties. **1919** J. EWING *Neoplastic Dis.* iii. 67 A heterolytic action of tumor ferments has been actively claimed. **1941** *Trans. Faraday Soc.* XXXVII. 604 It is necessary to distinguish between two main types of bond-fission, *viz.*, symmetric or homolytic fission and dissymmetric or heterolytic fission, defined as follows (the dots representing electrons): R./.X (homolytic fission) [and] R/..X (heterolytic fission). *Ibid.* 608 The heterolytic substitutions under discussion are characterised by important electrical transferences in the reactant species. **1964** N. G. CLARKE *Mod. Org. Chem.* xxv. 514 This process is called heterolysis, and reactions involving it are termed heterolytic reactions.

heteˈromeran. *Entom.* [f. mod.L. *Heteromera* neut. pl. (Latreille, f. Gr. ἕτερο- HETERO- + μέρος part).] A beetle belonging to the *Heteromera*, a division of *Coleoptera* in which the two anterior pairs of legs have five tarsal joints, but the third pair only four.
  1842 BRANDE *Dict. Sci.*, etc., Heteromerans, Heteromera.

heteromerous (hɛtəˈrɒmərəs), *a.* [f. Gr. ἕτερο- HETERO- + μέρος part + -OUS.] Having or consisting of parts differing in character, number, or other respect.
  1. *Entom.* Having legs differing in the number of their tarsal joints; *spec.* belonging to the division *Heteromera* of coleopterous insects (see prec.).
  1826 KIRBY & SP. *Entomol.* III. 683 The term *heteromerous* properly belongs to all insects in which the different pairs of tarsi vary *inter se* in the number of their joints. **1845** DARWIN *Voy. Nat.* v. (1873) 98 Numerous Lamellicorn and Heteromerous insects.
  2. *Bot.* **a.** Applied to lichens in which the gonidia are arranged in one or more distinct

layers within the thallus; opp. to *homœomerous.*
  b. Applied to flowers in which the members differ in number in the different whorls: opp. to *isomerous.*
  1875 BENNETT & DYER *Sachs' Bot.* 265 The gonidia are crowded into one layer, by which the hyphal tissue is at the same time separated according to circumstances into an outer and inner or an upper and under layer; the thallus-tissue is then stratified, and such Lichens are termed Heteromerous. **1882** VINES *Sachs' Bot.* 601 When the number of members is the same in each whorl [of a flower] they are said to be *isomerous*, when this is not the case *heteromerous.*
  3. *Chem.* Unrelated as to chemical composition, as in certain cases of isomorphism.
  1864 in WEBSTER.

heteromorphic (hɛtərəʊˈmɔːfɪk), *a.* [f. Gr. ἕτερο- HETERO- + μορφή form + -IC.]
  1. Of different or dissimilar forms. *spec.*:
  a. *Entom.* Existing in different forms at different stages of life: said of insects which undergo complete metamorphosis (*Heteromorpha*). Hence in wider use in *Biol.*
  1864 in WEBSTER. **1874** LUBBOCK *Orig. & Met. Ins.* i. 6 The Homomorphic insects do not pass through such striking changes of form as the Heteromorphic. **1935** F. E. FRITSCH *Struct. & Reprod. Algae* I. 52 The last type of life-cycle..exhibits an alternation of a large sporophyte and a generally small gametophyte. This heteromorphic (antithetic) alternation is encountered solely among Phaeophyceae. **1967** ALEXOPOULOS & BOLD *Algae & Fungi* iv. 23 In heteromorphic alternation, the two sequential organisms differ morphologically.
  b. *Bot.* Applied to flowers or plants which occur in forms differing in the relative length of the stamens and pistils (including *dimorphic* and *trimorphic*).
  1874 in R. BROWN *Man. Bot. Gloss.* **1877** DARWIN *Forms of Fl.* i. 24, I formerly applied the term 'heteromorphic' to the legitimate unions; and 'homomorphic' to the illegitimate unions; but after discovering the existence of trimorphic plants..these two terms ceased to be applicable.
  c. *Cytology.* Applied to homologous chromosomes that differ in size or form.
  1917 E. E. CAROTHERS in *Jrnl. Morphology* XXVIII. 449 The unusual conditions of the chromosomes in this group have made advisable the introduction of four new terms... Heteromorphic—used to designate those tetrads made up of morphologically different homologues. **1925** E. B. WILSON *Cell* (ed. 3) vi. 571 The so-called heteromorphic chromosome-pairs in which the synaptic mates are visibly distinguishable by the eye by differences of size, form, mode of spindle-attachment or structure. **1955** *Jrnl. Genetics* LIII. 593 Symmetrical separation of the pair of heteromorphic X- and Y-chromosomes in the first anaphase of meiosis.
  d. *Min.* [tr. F. *hétéromorphe* (A. Lacroix 1917, in *Compt. Rend.* CLXV. 486).] (See quot. 1920.)
  1920 A. HOLMES *Nomencl. Petrol.* 117 *Heteromorphic*, a term applied to rocks of similar chemical composition, but of different mineral composition. **1921** —— *Petrogr. Methods* x. 410 Each of these rocks is a heteromorphic type of theralite.
  e. *Zool.* (See quots.)
  1931 W. C. ALLEE *Animal Aggregations* ii. 16 Heteromorphic colonies are formed when the divisions are unequal, as is the case with the strobila of the Scyphozoa, or during the processes of asexual reproduction of certain worms, such as *Autolytus. Ibid.* 23 Heteromorphic and polymorphic colonies are formed when there is a differentiation between the different members of the colony, as occurs in the hybrid Hydractinia, in which feeding, reproductive, and protective zoöids may be recognized.
  2. Deviating in form from the standard or type; of abnormal form: = HETEROMORPHOUS 1. In mod. Dicts.
  3. *Biol.* Resulting from heteromorphosis.
  1898 *Arch. f. Entwickelungsmech. d. Organismen* VII. 481 Neither the present nor other experiments indicate, that the influence of the organism as a whole upon the regenerating part is able to bring forth a heteromorphic structure..out of material which would normally produce something else. **1932** J. S. HUXLEY *Probl. Rel. Growth* vi. iii. 175 The regenerated heteromorphic appendage almost invariably is of a type which normally belongs to a more posterior segment—e.g. antenna regenerated instead of eye-stalk (Palaemon). **1966** E. D. HAY *Regeneration* ii. 75 The heteromorphic growths.. may result because an insufficient mass of cells is present for correct differentiation of the skeletal pattern.
  Hence ˌheteroˈmorphically *adv.*, by means of heteromorphosis.
  1959 *Jrnl. Biophysical & Biochem. Cytol.* V. 25 Cultures of subcutaneous areolar fibroblasts..are changed heteromorphically so as to resemble cultures of nervous tissue.

heteromorphism (-ˈmɔːfɪz(ə)m). [f. as prec. + -ISM.] **1.** The condition or property of being heteromorphic; diversity of form.
  1839 *Fraser's Mag.* XX. 699 The various portraits of her majesty astonish by their perplexing *poly-* or *heteromorphism.* **1865-72** WATTS *Dict. Chem.* III. 150 *Heteromorphism*, the property, sometimes observed in compounds, of crystallising in different forms, though containing equal numbers of atoms similarly grouped. **1874** LUBBOCK *Wild Flowers* ii. 36 Nor are these.. the only cases of Heteromorphism now known. **1881** *Jrnl. Bot.* X. 86 All we have to suppose is a peculiar heteromorphism.
  2. 'The property of replacing lost parts by new parts which are different from those that have

been lost' (*Cent. Dict.* Suppl. 1909); = HETEROMORPHOSIS b.

3. Also corresponding to other senses of HETEROMORPHIC *a.*

1895 F. W. OLIVER tr. *Kerner's Nat. Hist. Plants* II. 469 One branch of the colony is concerned in the acquiring of nutrition, another in reproduction... To this differentiation among equivalent members we may apply the term Heteromorphism. **1921** A. HOLMES *Petrogr. Methods* x. 407 (*heading*) Heteromorphism in igneous rocks. **1954** R. L. PARKER tr. *P. Niggli's Rocks & Min. Deposits* iv. 125 Variations in primary mineralogical composition..can result from the bulk chemical composition (heteromorphism).

heteromorphite (-'mɔːfaɪt). *Min.* [f. as prec. + -ITE.] A variety of JAMESONITE.

1865-72 WATTS *Dict. Chem.* III. 151 *Heteromorphite*, Feather ore, a sulphantimonite of lead..which occurs in capillary forms resembling a cobweb; also massive. **1868** DANA *Min.* (ed. 5) 91.

heteromorphosis (ˌhɛtərəʊ'mɔːfəsɪs, ˌhɛtərəʊmɔː'fəʊsɪs). [f. HETERO- + MORPHOSIS; in sense b ad. G. *heteromorphose* (J. Loeb *Untersuchungen z. physiol. Morphologie d. Thiere* (1891) I. i. 10), f. Gr. ἑτερο-ς different + μόρφωσ-ις formation.]

a. Abnormal tissue, or tissue formed at the wrong place; heteroplasia.

1891 FOSTER *Med. Dict.* III, *Heteromorphosis*, a malformation. The *heteromorphoses*..in Fuchs's classification of skin diseases are a genus..including nævus, ochthiasis, polytrichia, and polonychia. **1922** *Guy's Hosp. Rep.* LXXII. 200 Cells differing in structure from those characteristic of the part of the body are produced. Here we have a heteroplasia or heteromorphosis.

b. The regeneration of an organ or structure that is different from the one lost.

1894 *Jrnl. Morphology* IX. 418 To this phenomenon of the reproduction of an organ typically different from the one which had originally occupied that position, he [*sc.* Jacques Loeb] has given the name heteromorphosis. **1901** J. LOEB *Compar. Physiol. Brain* xiv. 203 The processes of heteromorphosis—that is, the transformation or substitution of one organ for a morphologically different one by means of certain external influences—force us to the same view. **1932** J. S. HUXLEY *Probl. Rel. Growth* vi. iii. 172 The production of axial heteromorphosis in regeneration, such as biaxial heads or tails, can also be satisfactorily interpreted in terms of the gradient hypothesis. **1940, 1966** [see HOMŒOSIS].

hetero'morphous, *a.* [f. as HETEROMORPHITE + -OUS.]

1. Of abnormal or irregular form.

1835-6 TODD *Cycl. Anat.* I. 139/2 Various animals..from exhibiting no uniform or regular shape, have been entitled ..heteromorphous. **1886** *Syd. Soc. Lex., Heteromorphous*, differing in form, shape, or external appearance, as compared with the normal.

2. *Entom.* = HETEROMORPHIC 1.

1855 OWEN *Invertebr. Anim.* 437 The differences of the larvæ which are distinguished by the entomological terms, Heteromorphous, Homomorphous, Capitate, &c., essentially depend upon their quitting the egg to enter into active life at different periods of development.

'hetero,morphy. [f. as prec. + -Y: after Gr. sbs. in -μορφία.] = HETEROMORPHISM 1.

1874 R. BROWN *Man. Bot.* 600 Deviations from ordinary forms, comprising..heteromorphy (deformities, polymorphy, alteration of colours).

heteronomic (-'nɒmɪk), *a.* [f. Gr. ἑτερο- HETERO- + νόμος law + -IC: cf. Gr. νομικός of or pertaining to law.] Showing a different law or mode of operation.

1. 'Of unlike or opposite polarity: applied to contact of parts of the human body in experiments on animal magnetism: opp. to *isonomic.*'

18.. *Amer. Jrnl. Psychol.* I. 502 (Cent.) Heteronomic [contact] is hyperæsthesic and increases it [muscular energy].

2. *Optics.* Affected by spherical aberration so as not to converge to one focus; divergent.

1889 *Anthony's Photogr. Bull.* II. 167 The diminution of the astigmatism of the heteronomic pencils.

heteronomous (-'ɒnəməs), *a.* [f. as prec. + -OUS.]

1. Subject to different laws, involving different principles.

1824 DE QUINCEY *Templars' Dial.* Wks. IV. 254 If two inconsistent principles of valuation be employed, then the table will be vicious because heteronomous [*erron.* -onymous].

2. *Biol.* Having different laws or modes of growth; applied to parts or members differentiated from the same primitive type.

1870 ROLLESTON *Anim. Life* Introd. 104 Arthropoda. Animals consisting of a series of more or less heteronomous segments. *Ibid.* 78 The development of wings and the differentiation of the body into three great heteronomous divisions, the head, the thorax, and the abdomen. **1878** BELL *Gegenbaur's Comp. Anat.* 238 The limitation of the number of the appendages..concurrently with the greater development of heteronomous metameres.

3. Subject to an external law: opp. to *autonomous.*

a **1871** G. GROTE *Eth. Fragm.* (1876) ii. 47 The will is..in a certain sense *autonomous*, not *heteronomous*. **1894** *Forum* (U.S.) July 572 Man has been..a thrall, owning obedience to a law conceived to be external..and other than the expression of his own nature. In a word he has been heteronomous. **1932** W. L. GRAFF *Lang.* vi. 221 These are *conditioned* sound changes, also called *dependent* or *heteronomous* because they appear to depend upon the extraneous influence of their phonetic surroundings.

Hence **hete'ronomously** *adv.*

1909 *Cent. Dict.* Suppl., *Heteronomously*, in a heteronomous manner. **1948** J. L. ADAMS tr. *Tillich's Protestant Era* iii. 46 Religion, if it acts heteronomously, has ceased to be the substance and life-blood of a culture and has become itself a section of it. **1966** J. A. SERRA *Mod. Genetics* II. xii. 118 In a few cases, however, the colour developed heteronomously; in such cases the host influenced the colour of the implanted eye.

heteronomy (-'ɒnəmɪ). [f. as prec. + -Y: after Gr. derivatives in -νομια.]

1. Presence of a different law or principle: see quot. 1824.

1824 DE QUINCEY *Templars' Dial.* Wks. IV. 205 He has certainly not vitiated the purity of this principle by the usual heteronomy (if you will allow me a learned word)—*i.e.*, by the introduction of the other and opposite law. **1828-30** W. TAYLOR *Hist. Surv. Germ. Poetry* III. 12 *note*, Heteroclitical phraseology is the first step to Heteronomy of apperception, —and insanity is nothing more.

2. *Moral Philos.* Subjection to the rule of another being or power (e.g. of the will to the passions); subjection to external law. Opp. to *autonomy.*

1798 WILLICH *Elem. Crit. Philos.* 160 Heteronomy, or a foreign legislation, is that, in which not the will itself, but something else determines us to act in a certain manner. **1855** MISS COBBE *Ess. Intuit. Mor.* 146 It would not be Free Self-legislation (autonomy), but (heteronomy) subservience of the Pure Will to a lower faculty. **1888** J. MARTINEAU *Study Relig.* II. III. ii. 282 So far as they obtain sway over him, he is under a heteronomy.

3. *Biol.* The condition of being heteronomous; differentiation from a common primitive type.

1870 ROLLESTON *Anim. Life* 115 The degree to which heteronomy or differentiation is carried out in the various regions of the body [in *Copepoda*].

heteronuclear (ˌhɛtərəʊ'njuːklɪə(r)), *a.* [f. HETERO- + NUCLEAR *a.*] **a.** *Chem.* Taking place on different rings in a polycyclic molecule.

1900 E. F. SMITH tr. *V. von Richter's Org. Chem.* (ed. 3) II. 390 It can first be ascertained whether the substituents are in the same nucleus (isonuclear) or in different nuclei (heteronuclear). **1951** I. L. FINAR *Org. Chem.* I. xxix. 586 When NO_2 or SO_3H is in the 1- or 2-position, heteronuclear substitution occurs in position 5 or 8.

b. *Physics* and *Chem.* Of a molecule: composed of atoms whose nuclei are unlike, i.e. atoms of different elements or of different isotopes of the same element.

1930 *Physical Rev.* XXXVI. 617 The words even and odd are applied..to the *complete* ψ function of any molecule, homonuclear or heteronuclear. **1940** *Ibid.* LVII. 684/2 The HD molecule is heteronuclear and there is no quantum number of total spin. **1950** J. W. T. SPINKS tr. *Herzberg's Molecular Spectra & Molecular Structure* (ed. 2) I. iii. 94 This agrees with the observed infrared spectrum of HCl.. and of other heteronuclear molecules.

heteronym ('hɛtərəʊnɪm). [f. as next, after *synonym.*]

1. A word having the same spelling as another, but a different sound and meaning: opp. to *homonym* and *synonym.*

1889 in *Cent. Dict.*

2. A name of a thing in one language which is a translation of the name in another language.

1885 B. G. WILDER *Jour. Nerv. Dis.* xii. (Cent.), Vernacular names which are more or less precise translations of Latin names, or of names in any other language, may be called heteronyms.

heteronymous (hɛtə'rɒnɪməs), *a.* [f. Gr. ἑτερώνυμος (f. HETERO- + ὄνομα name) + -OUS.]

1. Having different names, as a pair of correlatives, e.g. *husband, wife*: opp. to *synonymous.*

1734 WATTS *Ontology* vii, Synonymous Relatives or of the same Name..Heteronymous or of a different Name. **1829** JAS. MILL *Hum. Mind* (1869) II. xiv. 22 The second class [of relative terms] were called by the ancient logicians heteronymous; we may call them more intelligibly, double-worded relatives.

2. *Optics.* Applied to the two images of one object seen in looking at a point beyond it, when the left image is that seen by the right eye and *vice versâ*: opp. to *homonymous.*

1881 LE CONTE *Monoc. Vision* 95 When we look at the farther finger, the nearer one is so doubled that the left image belongs to the right eye and the right image to the left eye..the images are said to be *heteronymous*, i.e., of a different name. *Ibid.* 245 Phenomena illustrating the heteronymous Shifting of the two Fields of View.

3. 'Pertaining to, of the nature of, or having a heteronym' (*Cent. Dict.*).

Hence **hete'ronymously** *adv.* (see 2).

1881 LE CONTE *Monoc. Vision* 120 When we look at the farther finger, the nearer one is doubled heteronymously; when we look at the nearer finger, the farther one is doubled homonymously.

heteroousian, heterousian (ˌhɛtərəʊ'aʊsɪən, hɛtə'raʊsɪən, -'uːsɪən), *a.* and *sb.* *Theol.* Also 9 **heterusian.** [f. Gr. ἑτεροούσιος, ἑτερούσιος, f. ἑτερο- HETERO- + οὐσία essence, substance. Opp. to *homoousian* and *homoiousian.*]

A. *adj.* Of different essence or substance.

1678 CUDWORTH *Intell. Syst.* I. iv. §36. 612 The Homoousian Trinity of the orthodox went exactly in the middle, betwixt that Monoousian Trinity of Sabellius..and that other Heteroousian Trinity of Arius. **1790** PORSON *Lett. to Arch. Travis* ix. 221 The word *one* is applied, 1. to things homoüsian..2. to things heteroüsian, where there is a sameness of persons, but a difference of natures.

B. *sb.* One who held the Father and the Son to be different in essence or substance; an Arian.

1874 J. H. BLUNT *Dict. Sects, Heterousians*, a name given to the extreme Arians.

So **hetero'ousiast (hete'rousiast, hete'rusiast)** = B.; **hetero'ousious (hete'rousious)** *a.* = A.

1678 CUDWORTH *Intell. Syst.* I. iv. §36. 579 Neither a Trinity of Words only..nor yet a Jumbled Confusion of God and Creature (Things Heterousious) together. **1882-3** SCHAFF *Encycl. Relig. Knowl.* I. 33 Aetius..the apostle of a new Church, representing the widest going section of the Arian party..His adherents were called Anomœans, Heterusiasts, or Exukontians.

heteropathic (-'pæθɪk), *a.* [f. as next + -IC.]

1. *Med.* = ALLOPATHIC.

1830 *Edin. Rev.* L. 513 First stands the homöopathic.. Then the allopathic or heteropathic..the..method which hopes to cure disease by exciting some dissimilar affection.

2. Of different operation; differing in their effect.

1843 MILL *Logic* I. III. vi. 403 Though there be laws which, like those of chemistry and physiology, owe their existence to a breach of the principle of the Composition of Causes, it does not follow that those peculiar, or, as they might be termed, *heteropathic* laws, are not capable of composition with one another. **1870** JEVONS *Elem. Logic* xxix. 252 It is distinguished by Mr. Mill from cases of the heterogeneous or as he says the heteropathic intermixture of effects.

heteropathy (-'ɒpəθɪ). [f. Gr. ἑτερο- HETERO- + -παθεια, f. πάθος suffering.]

1. *Med.* = ALLOPATHY: opp. to *homœopathy.*

1847 CRAIG, *Heteropathy*, the method of attempting to remove one disease by inducing a different one.

2. *Path.* (See quot.)

1886 *Syd. Soc. Lex., Heteropathy*..Berthold's term for the form of idiosyncrasy in which the organic susceptibility behaves itself in a different fashion to the normal in the presence of any irritation.

3. Antipathy or aversion excited by suffering: opp. to *sympathy.* (*nonce-use.*)

1874 MISS COBBE in *Theol. Rev.* Jan. 74 At the sight of pain animals generally feel an impulse to destroy rather than to help. This emotion will be indicated by the term Heteropathy. **1881** —— *Duties Wom.* iv. 118 It is astonishing and horrible to witness how the deep-seated frightful human passion, which I have elsewhere named Heteropathy, develops itself in such circumstances.

‖**heterophasia** (-'feɪzɪə). *Path.* [f. Gr. ἑτερο- HETERO- + -φασια, f. φάσις speech.] = HETEROPHEMY (as a result of mental disease).

1877 GOULBURN *Bateman's Darwinism* 115 Perversion of language to which the name of Heterophasia has been given. **1882** tr. *Ribot's Dis. Mem.* 152 Sometimes the patient retains an extensive vocabulary of vocal..signs, but cannot use it correctly (cases of heterophasia).

Hence **hetero'phasiac**, 'one who is affected with heterophasia' (*Cent Dict.*).

'heterophemy (-fiːmɪ). [f. Gr. ἑτερο- HETERO- + -φημια, f. φήμη, φῆμις voice, speech.] The saying or writing of one word or phrase when another is meant.

1875 R. G. WHITE in *Galaxy* Nov. 693 The assertion made is most often not merely something that the speaker or writer does not mean to say, but its very reverse, or at least something notably at variance with his purpose. For this reason I have called it heterophemy, which means merely the speaking otherwise. **1885** —— *Stud. Shaks.* 33 As to the writing twice of Verona instead of Milan, it seems plainly a mere case of heterophemy. **1894** *Nation* (N.Y.) 22 Mar. 212/2 We are forced in charity to credit the bishop with a kind of 'heterophemy'.

So **hetero'phemism**, an instance or result of heterophemy. **hetero'phemist**, one who says something else than he means to say (whence **heterophe'mistic** *a.*). **hetero'phemize** *v. intr.*, to say something different from what one means to say.

1875 R. G. WHITE in *Galaxy* XX. 697 (Cent.) Henry Ward Beecher appears among the heterophemists..He heterophemizes in a very striking manner. *Ibid.* 698 (Cent.) Examples in which creditor is used for debtor—perhaps the most common of all heterophemisms.

heterophile ('hɛtərəʊfaɪl), *a.* and *sb.* Also **heterophil.** [a. G. *heterophil* (U. Friedemann 1917, in *Biochem. Zeitschr.* LXXX. 334), f. HETERO- + -PHIL(E).] A. *adj.* Able to react immunologically with sera, etc., from organisms of another species.

1920 *Jrnl. Path. & Bacteriol.* XXIII. 366 The term heterogenetic is not altogether appropriate in this connection, since the important character is not that the antibody is gererated by a different kind of antigen, but that it has an affinity for receptors of a species other than that in response to which it was developed, *heterophile* describes

this property better. **1929** TOPLEY & WILSON *Princ. Bacteriol. & Immunity* II. li. 748 It is now known that the so-called 'heterophile', or 'Forssman' antigen..is widely distributed among the animal species which have been examined, and in a curiously random fashion. **1935** *Arch. Path.* XIX. 841 Heterophile phenomena embrace those immunologic reactions in which the interaction of antigen and antibody is seemingly not specific in the strictly orthodox conception of the term. **1950** J. V. DACIE *Pract. Hæmatol.* xi. 150 The limits of the titre of heterophile antibodies present in health are ill-defined. **1960** I. A. STANTON *Dict. Med. Secretaries* 70/2 *Heterophile agglutination test*.., a method of testing for the presence of infectious mononucleosis. The blood of patients with this disease contains antibodies for the red blood cells of sheep.

B. *sb.* A polymorphonuclear leucocyte found in the blood of mammals and stained by both acidic and basic dyes; also *attrib.* or as *adj.*

1938 H. DOWNEY *Handbk. Hematol.* I. ii. 167 The special or 'heterophile' leucocytes of the animals commonly used in experimental research resemble the human neutrophile quite closely in size and morphology, but with slight variations in nuclei, and in the size and staining of the specific granules which make them distinctive. **1941** CALKINS & SUMMERS *Protozoa Biol. Research* xviii. 835 The heterophils are functional in immunity by virtue of their obvious phagocytic activities and probably because of their secretion of enzymes. **1965** P. D. STURKIE *Avian Physiol.* (ed. 2) i. 13 The heterophils in the blood of children are usually round and have a diameter of approximately 10 to 15 microns.

heterophilic (ˌhɛtərəʊˈfɪlɪk), *a.* [f. prec. + -IC.] = HETEROPHILE *a.*

1929 *Jrnl. Exper. Med.* XLIX. 497 Horse serum is known to contain a heterophilic antigen. **1966** *Jrnl. Cell Biol.* XXIX. 309 (*caption*) Thin section of heterophilic myelocyte found in rabbit bone marrow.

heterophony (hɛtəˈrɒfənɪ). [Gr. ἑτεροφωνία: see Plato *Leges* VII. 812D.] Simultaneous performance by two or more singers or instrumentalists of different versions of the same melody. Also **hetero'phonic**, **hete'rophonous** *adjs.*, different in sound.

1919 *Musical Q.* V. 599 Two forms of instrumental accompaniment were known to the Greeks, namely the homophonic and heterophonic. **1936** *Amer. Speech* XI. 299 Any phonic difference found between comparably situated sounds in heterophonous words in a given language constitutes a phonemic contrast. **1939** *Scrutiny* VII. 402 Ruth Crawford writes heterophonic music in which the various linear strands bear no relation to one another except that of proximity in time-space. **1945** *Times* 16 Mar. 6 The name for this simultaneous variation with its permitted dissonance is heterophony. **1962** *Listener* 21 June 1091/2 The pianos are brilliantly used as percussion instruments, sometimes in harp-like arpeggiated pentatonics, sometimes in wildly clashing heterophony. **1970** *Daily Tel.* 16 Nov. 9/4 Heterophony was..only just round the corner from the virelais, 'Se Ma Dame' and 'Comment qu'a moy', as treated here with instrumental doubling of the voice parts. **1971** *Guardian* 22 Feb. 8/4 The work was somewhat discursive, there being too few landmarks in the prevailing heterophonic texture to compel the listeners' attention throughout.

heterophyllous (-ˈfɪləs), *a.* [f. Gr. ἑτερο- HETERO- + φύλλ-ον leaf + -OUS. In F. *hétérophylle*.]

1. *Bot.* Bearing leaves of different forms upon the same plant.

1828 WEBSTER cites *Jrnl. Sci.* **1871-2** H. MACMILLAN *True Vine* iii. 110 Examples of heterophyllous and dimorphic plants, in which there is a very considerable difference in form in the same organs, not only at different times, but even simultaneously. **1882** VINES *Sachs' Bot.* 467 The leaves of the heterophyllous species which have them arranged in four rows, possess stomata on their inner surface.

2. *Zool.* Belonging to the group *Heterophylli* of cephalopods.

'hetero,phylly. *Bot.* [f. as prec. + -Y: in mod.F. *hétérophyllie*.] The condition of being heterophyllous.

1874 in R. BROWN *Man. Bot.* Gloss. **1886** *Encycl. Brit.* XX. 619/1 (*Rodriguez*) Variability of species and heterophylly are characteristic of the flora to quite an unusual degree.

‖**heteroplasia** (ˌhɛtərəˈpleɪzɪə). *Path.* Also anglicized as **heteroplasy** (-ˈɒpləsɪ). [f. Gr. ἑτερο- HETERO- + πλάσις moulding, formation: F. *hétéroplasie*.] The formation of a tissue different from the normal tissue of the part in which it occurs.

1854 MAYNE *Expos. Lex.*, *Heteroplasia*, *Heteroplasis*, terms for abnormal organic formation: heteroplasy. **1876** tr. *Wagner's Gen. Pathol.* 354 The so-called Heteroplasia, Heterologous new-formations, that is to say, tissues which bear little resemblance to normal tissues.

'heteroplasm. *Path.* [f. as prec. + Gr. πλάσμα anything moulded, a figure: F. *hétéroplasme*.] A tissue formed in a part where it does not normally occur.

1878 R. DRUITT *Surg. Vade M.* (ed. 11) 84 As Virchow showed, there is no such thing as heteroplasm. **1886** *Syd. Soc. Lex.*, *Heteroplasm*, Burdach's term for a morbid tissue foreign to the economy.

heteroplastic (-ˈplæstɪk), *a.* [f. as prec. + Gr. πλαστικός fit for moulding: F. *hétéroplastique*.]

1. *Path.* Of or belonging to heteroplasia; of the nature of a heteroplasm.

1854 in MAYNE *Expos. Lex.* **1876** tr. *Wagner's Gen. Pathol.* 270 Tubercle, carcinoma, and other heteroplastic new-formations.

2. *Biol.* Dissimilar in formation or structure, as the different tissues of the body.

3. *Surg.* Said of a graft between two individuals of different species.

[**1889**: see HOMOPLASTIC *a.* 2.] **1898** *Arch. f. Entwickelungsmech. d. Organismen* VII. 471 There were obtained a number of larvae of normal external form, but which were composed of parts derived from two distinct species... The general biological interest attaching to such heteroplastic combinations is naturally great. **1908** A. CARREL in *Jrnl. Amer. Med. Assoc.* 14 Nov. 1664/1 There are several varieties of heteroplastic transplantations according to the zoologic distance which separates the host and the owner of the transplanted tissue. **1909** [see HOMOPLASTIC *a.* 2]. **1917** *Brit. Jrnl. Surg.* V. 199 Heteroplastic grafts—i.e. bones transferred from one animal to another of a different species—..show neither vitality nor proliferative capacity. **1923** [see HETEROPLASTY 1 b]. **1924** *Proc. Nat. Acad. Sci.* X. 69 The heteroplastic transplantation of limbs. **1959** *Arkiv f. Zool.* XII. 183 Heteroplastic transplantation would be a most valuable means of demonstrating the role of movable cells during a regeneration, because the chromosome number and morphology reveals the origin of the cells.

So **hetero'plastically** *adv.*

1928 *Proc. Soc. Exper. Biol. & Med.* XXV. 686 (*heading*) Growth of heteroplastically transplanted eyes and limbs in Amblystoma. **1932** J. S. HUXLEY *Probl. Rel. Growth* II. ii. 53 Eyes and other organs when heteroplastically transplanted. **1960** B. I. BALINSKY *Introd. Embryol.* vi. 167 Hilde Mangold transplanted heteroplastically (from *Triturus cristatus* to *Triturus taeniatus*) a piece of the dorsal lip of the blastopore of an early gastrula.

heteroplastide (-ˈplæstaɪd). *Biol.* [f. as prec. + Gr. πλαστός moulded, formed + -IDE.] An organism composed of tissues of different kinds, as most animals and plants: opp. to *homoplastide*.

1889 VINES in *Nature* 24 Oct. 621 Death is..a characteristic feature of differentiated multicellular organisms (heteroplastides). *Ibid.* 622 How the mortal heteroplastides can have been evolved from the immortal monoplastides or homoplastides.

heteroplasty (ˈhɛtərəʊˌplæstɪ). [f. HETERO- + -PLASTY.] **1.** *Med.* and *Biol.* [ad. F. *étéroplastie* (P. F. Blandin *Autoplastie* (1836) 7).] The operation of grafting tissues between different individuals: **a.** Between two individuals of the same species.

1855 DUNGLISON *Dict. Med. Sci.* (ed. 12) 440/2 *Heteroplasty*, irregular plastic or formative operations, that do not admit of exact classification. **1874** *English Mechanic* 321 The name heteroplasty has been adopted for the operation of taking pieces of skin from amputated limbs, and using them to produce cicatrisation on the bodies of other subjects. **1901** A. G. GERSTER in R. Park *Treat. Surgery* liv. 1154 Heteroplasty..is the operation wherein living tissues foreign to the bearer of the defect are employed. The transfer of a skin-flap from one individual to another constitutes heteroplasty. **1909** *Boston Med. & Surg. Jrnl.* 23 Dec. 915/1 (*heading*) Heteroplasty. (Grafting from another person.)

b. Between two individuals of different species.

1923 H. NEUHOF *Transplantation of Tissues* i. 3 By heterotransplantation (heteroplasty, heteroplastic transplantation, zoöplasty) is meant the transference of a tissue from an individual of one species to an individual of a different species. **1929** *Ann. Surg.* XC. 929 In grafting skin derived from other animal species (heteroplasty), that of dogs, chickens or the internal pellicle of an egg may be used.

2. *Path.* = HETEROPLASIA.

1886 *Syd. Soc. Lex.*, Heteroplasty, same as Heteroplasia.

heteroploid (ˈhɛtərəʊplɔɪd), *a.* (and *sb.*) [a. G. *heteroploid* (H. Winkler 1916, in *Zeitschr. f. Bot.* VIII. 422), f. HETERO- + -PLOID.] Having a chromosome number that is neither the haploid nor the diploid number characteristic of the species; freq., in restricted sense, = ANEUPLOID *a.* (see quot. 1928); also as *sb.*, a heteroploid organism. Hence **'heteroploidy**, the condition of being heteroploid.

1926 T. H. MORGAN *Theory Gene* xii. 172 In so far as the addition of one or more chromosomes to, or loss from, a given group produces a new number, the word heteroploid has been used. *Ibid.* 176 In contrast to these triplo-types of Drosophila there is another heteroploid type..in which one of the small chromosomes is absent. *Ibid.* 188 The heteroploids are not so viable as the balanced types from which they arise. *Ibid.*, The occurrence of heteroploidy must be regarded as a significant genetic event. **1928** C. A. JØRGENSEN in *Jrnl. Genetics* XIX. 135 The term heteroploid was introduced by Winkler in 1916 to designate..not only the straight numbers $3n$, $4n$, $5n$, etc., but also $2n + 1$, $2n + 2$, $3n - 1$, etc. The heteroploid numbers were divided by Täckholm (1922) into euploid..and aneuploid... I prefer to restrict the term heteroploid to the series n, $3n$, $4n$, $5n$, etc. ..and to use the term *aploid* for the irregular numbers. **1934** *Nature* 3 Nov. 708/2 In the heteroploid series, all having 25 chromosomes, the anatomical differences..were due to the genic constitution of the extra chromosome. **1955** J. B. & H. D. HILL *Genetics & Human Heredity* xvii. 331 Although rare in animals, heteroploidy occurs frequently in plants. **1956** *Nature* 25 Feb. 384/2 It is of interest to try to find whether the heteroploid cells appear only in certain tissues or if they can arise anywhere in the young embryos.

heteropod (ˈhɛtərəpɒd), *a.* and *sb.* *Zool.* [f. next.] **A.** *adj.* Of or belonging to the *Heteropoda*. **B.** *sb.* One of the *Heteropoda*.

1835 KIRBY *Hab. & Inst. Anim.* I. ix. 301 The animal of the Heteropods having a proboscis and only two tentacles. **1882** GEIKIE *Text Bk. Geol.* (1885) 649 The heteropod genus so characteristic of Palæozoic time, *Bellerophon*.

‖**Heteropoda** (hɛtəˈrɒpədə), *sb. pl.* *Zool.* [mod.L., f. Gr. ἑτερο- HETERO- + πούς, ποδ- foot.] **a.** A group of Crustacea including forms with 14 feet, some of which are adapted for swimming. **b.** An order or subclass of Gastropods, having the foot modified into a swimming organ. **c.** A group of Echinoderms.

1835 *Penny Cycl.* III. 24/2. **1838** *Ibid.* XI. 92/2 Forskal places all the Heteropoda of Cuvier under his genus Pterotrachea. **1872** NICHOLSON *Palæont.* 245 Both families of the Heteropoda are represented by fossil forms. **1878** BELL *Gegenbaur's Comp. Anat.* 324 The foot of the Heteropoda is differentiated into a more independent organ.

Hence **hete'ropodan** = HETEROPOD *sb.*; **hete'ropodous** *a.* = HETEROPOD *a.*

1835 *Penny Cycl.* III. 24/2 A genus of the heteropodous mollusca of Lamarck.

heteropolar (ˌhɛtərəʊˈpəʊlə(r)), *a.* [f. HETERO- + POLAR *a.*] **1.** *Bot.* Having polar correspondence to something different from itself; having dissimilar poles, as in the figures called *Stauraxonia heteropola* (*Encyl. Brit.* XVI. 844).

2. *Electr.* Of an electric generator or its operation: using armature conductors that pass alternate north and south magnetic poles, so that the current generated is periodically reversed. Cf. HOMOPOLAR *a.* 2.

1896 S. P. THOMPSON *Dynamo-Electric Machinery* (ed. 5) 475 In cases where it [*sc.* a conductor] passes from being opposite a N-pole to being opposite a S-pole, the operation is said to be heteropolar. **1946** *Nature* 28 Sept. 455/1 For the majority of applications the modern heteropolar inductor alternator is the most suitable machine.

3. *Chem.* [a. G. *heteropolar* (R. Abegg 1906, in *Zeitschr. f. anorg. Chem.* L. 309).] Formed by ions of opposite sign, between which there is electrostatic attraction. Cf. HOMOPOLAR *a.* 3.

1922 [see *homœopolar* adj. s.v. HOMŒO-]. **1930** *Engineering* 5 Dec. 700/3 There were, further, different types of cohesive forces... (3) Ionic or heteropolar cohesion. In the rock-salt atom, for instance, the valency electron of the sodium migrated into the chlorine structure, giving rise to electrostatic action. **1964** J. W. LINNETT *Electronic Struct. Molecules* ix. 143 Values which bring the results for these heteropolar molecules to the same scale as that for homopolar molecules.

heteropter (hɛtəˈrɒptə(r)). *Entom.* One of the *Heteroptera*.

1864 in WEBSTER.

‖**Heteroptera** (hɛtəˈrɒptərə), *sb. pl.* *Entom.* [mod.L., f. Gr. ἑτερο- HETERO- + πτερόν wing.] A suborder of HEMIPTERA, comprising those insects whose wings consist of dissimilar parts, being coriaceous at the base and membranous at the tip; the true bugs. Opp. to HOMOPTERA.

1826 KIRBY & SP. *Entomol.* xlvii. (1828) IV. 385 He denominated the first of the sections Heteroptera. **1874** LUBBOCK *Orig. & Met. Ins.* i. 25 The Heteroptera cannot exactly be said either to sting or bite.

Hence **hete'ropteran** = HETEROPTER; **hete'ropterous** *a.*, belonging to or having the characters of the *Heteroptera*.

1842 BRANDE *Dict. Sci.* etc., *Heteropterans*, *Heteroptera*, the name of a section of Hemipterans, comprehending those in which the hemelytra terminate abruptly by a membranous appendage. **1895** *Naturalist* 213 Mr. Mason recorded 132 out of about 420 heteropterous hemiptera known to inhabit the British Islands.

heteropycnosis (ˌhɛtərəʊpɪkˈnəʊsɪs). *Cytol.* Also **-pyknosis**. [ad. G. *heteropyknose* (S. Gutherz 1907, in *Arch. f. mikrosk. Anat.* LXIX. 495), f. HETERO- + Gr. πυκν-ός thick, dense: see -OSIS.] The persistence of greater than average staining in chromosomal material; the character or condition, exhibited by some chromosomes or chromosomal regions in any particular nucleus, of being more (or, for negative heteropycnosis, less) condensed and hence appearing to take up more (or, less) stain than do the majority of chromosomes or chromosomal regions. Hence **heteropyc'notic** *a.*

1925 E. B. WILSON *Cell* (ed. 3) x. 759 In the greater number of cases heteropycnosis first takes place after the final spermatogonial division. **1934** *Genetics* XIX. 467 In the latter species [*sc.* *Drosophila melanogaster*] he finds that about half of the X chromosome is heteropycnotic in the interphase. **1952** G. H. BOURNE *Cytol. & Cell Physiol.* (ed. 2) v. 195 This property of heteropycnosis is especially characteristic of sex-chromosomes, such as the Y-chromosome of *Drosophila* species and the X-chromosomes of grasshoppers, but is also shown by many autosomal chromosome regions, and sometimes by whole autosomes. **1962** *Lancet* 19 May 1075/1 Once isopyknosis or

heteropyknosis of a given X chromosome has been established, it is irreversible. **1963** LEWIS & JOHN *Chromosome Marker* I. i. 18 This positive heteropycnosis is later reversed and by metaphase-I the X has become negatively heteropycnotic and stains faintly. **1968** H. HARRIS *Nucleus & Cytoplasm* iv. 75 It is probable that other highly condensed heterochromatic or heteropyknotic regions in interphase nuclei also synthesize very much less RNA than the euchromatic regions.

Heteroscian (hɛtəˈrɒʃɪən), *sb.* and *a.* [f. med.L. *heterosci-us* (usually in nom. pl. used subst.), a. Gr. ἑτερόσκιος diversely-shadowed (f. ἑτερο- HETERO- + σκιά shadow) + -AN.]

A. *sb.* A name applied to the people of the two temperate zones in reference to the fact that, in the two zones, noon-shadows always fall in opposite directions. (Cf. *Amphiscian, Periscian.*) Usually in *pl.*; the Lat. pl. *heteroscii* is also frequent.

'*Heteroscii*, in strictness, and according to the origin and reason of the word, is a term of relation, and denotes those inhabitants which, during the whole year, have their noon-tide shadows projected different ways from each other. Thus, we..are *heteroscii* with regard to those who inhabit the southern temperate zone: and they are *heteroscii* with respect to us.' (Chambers *Cycl.*)

[**1559** W. CUNNINGHAM *Cosmogr. Glasse* 68 Of the diversitie of shadowes, ther ar .iij. divers distinct habitations of people found,..Amphiscii, Heteroscii, Periscii, and we want apt English termes for them.] **1616** BULLOKAR *Eng. Expos.*, *Heteroscians*, any people dwelling vnder a temperate zone: so called because their shadowes at noone bend still but one way. **1652** URQUHART *Jewel* Wks. (1834) 259 Which to withhold from them, whether Periscians, Hetroscians, or Amphiscians, would prove very absurd. [**1796** HUTTON *Math. Dict.* I. 596 *Heteroscii*, in Geography, are such inhabitants of the earth as have their shadows at noon projected always the same way with regard to themselves, or always contrary ways with respect to each other.]

B. *adj.* Of, pertaining to, or of the nature of noon-shadows in the temperate zones.

a **1646** J. GREGORY *Posthuma, Terrest. Globe* (1650) 300 Of Oxford the Sign-Regent is Capricorn, the Noon-shadows are Heteroscian.

heterosexist (hɛtərəʊˈsɛksɪst), *a.* [See HETERO- and SEXIST *a.*] Of, pertaining to, or characteristic of discrimination by heterosexual persons against homosexuals.

1979 *Ms.* Jan. 4/1 At least one heterosexist assumption expressed in Signe Hammer's article should not pass unquestioned. There are some of us who as daughters competed with Daddy to possess Mommy. **1985** *Standard* 5 Feb. 13 A Council leader who blocked plans to send Town Hall workers on 'heterosexist awareness training' is being asked to apologise. **1986** *Times* 6 Dec. 17/2 Radical homosexual groups..place homosexuality and heterosexuality on an equal footing and denounce the church's traditional teaching as 'heterosexist'.

Also **heteroˈsexism**, prejudice and antagonism shown by heterosexual persons towards homosexuals; discrimination against homosexuals.

1979 J. PENELOPE *Articulation of Bias* (ERIC ED 179998) 1 Heterosexism designates, in particular, those central social structures which proscribe heterosexuality as the only 'natural' sexual interest. **1982** *Daily Tel.* 16 Feb. 16/3 The students' union at Warwick University..has invented.. a new term, 'heterosexism', to describe the attitude of so-called 'normal' people towards homosexuals. **1985** *Standard* 14 Feb. 13/4 Employers should make every effort to advertise job vacancies in the lesbian and gay press and 'heterosexism awareness' training should be given to all employees.

heterosexual (hɛtərəʊˈsɛksju:əl), *a.* and *sb.* [See HETERO- and SEXUAL.] A. *adj.* **1. a.** Characterized by a sexual interest in members of the opposite sex. **b.** Pertaining to sexual relations between people of opposite sex.

1892 C. G. CHADDOCK tr. *Krafft-Ebing's Psychopathia Sexualis* iii. 324 The object of post-hypnotic suggestion is to remove the impulse to masturbation and homosexual feelings and impulses, and to encourage heterosexual feelings with a sense of virility. **1927** *Scots Observer* 1 Oct. 15/3 A certain proportion of people..are as instinctively homosexual as the normal individual is heterosexual. **1935** *Discovery* Oct. 313/2 Homosexuality under the homosexual period of Greek life was not a sin, but it became so under heterosexual Christianity. **1969** *Daily Tel.* 21 Jan. 17/3 Co-educational schools probably tend to hasten heterosexual experimentation.

2. Pertaining to, characteristic of both sexes.

1918 *Genetics* III. 287 Studies..on ablation of the gonads in birds, combined with hetero-sexual transplantation, show that both the testes and ovary in birds produce substances that have a profound regulatory effect on growth. **1963** *Cytogenetics* II. 332 The corresponding ovaries, generally atrophied owing presumably to male testicular hormones, contained no heterosexual cells.

B. *sb.* A heterosexual person (see sense 1 above).

1920 J. RIVIERE et al. tr. *Freud's Coll. Papers* (1924) II. 207 To convert a fully developed homosexual into a heterosexual. **1966** K. WALKER *Sexual Behaviour* xxv. 222 Homosexuals vary as much in physique and in temperament as do heterosexuals. **1972** *Sat. Rev.* (U.S.) 12 Feb. 27/1 Homosexuals, like heterosexuals, should be treated as individual human beings.

Hence ˌ**heterosexuˈality**, the condition of being heterosexual; heterosexual characteristics.

1900 H. BLANCHAMP tr. *Féré's Sexual Instinct* viii. 183 Psycho-sexual hermaphroditism, in which there are traces of hetero-sexuality, though homo-sexuality predominates. **1965** *New Statesman* 30 Apr. 677/2 Many people are made unhappy by their heterosexuality, but I do not believe the psychotherapist exists who would try to cure that.

‖**heterosis** (hɛtəˈrəʊsɪs). [Late Gr. ἑτέρωσις alteration, f. ἕτερος different.] **1.** *Rhet.* 'A figure of speech by which one form of a noun, verb, or pronoun, and the like, is used for another' (Webster, 1864).

2. *Zool.* Segmentation in which the parts are different.

1902 E. R. LANKESTER in *Encycl. Brit.* XXV. 691/2 It becomes apparent from this enumeration that there are a good many important elements or 'meromeres' in an Arthropod metamere or somite which can become the subject of heteromerism or, to use a more apt word, of 'heterosis'. *Ibid.*, The Fourth Law of metamerism (auto-heterosis of the meromes).

3. *Genetics.* The tendency of cross-breeding to produce an animal or plant with a greater hardiness and capacity for growth than either of the parents; hybrid vigour.

1914 G. H. SHULL in *Zeitschr. f. induktive Abstammungsund Vererbungslehre* XII. 127, I suggest that instead of the phrases, 'stimulus of heterozygosis', 'heterozygotic stimulation', 'the stimulating effects of hybridity', 'stimulation due to differences in uniting gametes', etc...the word 'heterosis' be adopted. The corresponding adjective 'heterotic' may also be useful in such expressions as 'heterotic effects'. **1938** *Nature* 3 Dec. 1002/2 The expression of heterosis is much influenced by various external factors. **1959** *New Biol.* XXVIII. 75 Less severe departures from normal growth in hybrids may.. involve slower development and poorer growth coordination, or..higher growth rates and seemingly enhanced vigour—the latter the phenomenon of heterosis, or hybrid vigour.

heterosite (ˈhɛtərəʊsaɪt). *Min.* Formerly also **heteposite, heterozite.** [ad. F. *hétérosite, -zite* (named by F. Alluaud aîné: see L. N. Vauquelin 1825, in *Ann. de Chim. et de Phys.* XXX. 294, where the word is spelt *hétépozite*), irreg. f. Gr. ἕτερος different + -ITE[1].] A phosphate of iron and manganese, differing from purpurite in containing more iron.

1834 R. ALLAN *Man. Min.* 309 Heteposite. **1835** C. U. SHEPARD *Treat. Min.: Second Part* I. 258 Heterosite. (See Triplite). **1854** J. D. DANA *Syst. Min.* (ed. 4) II. 407 Heterosite, by Rammelsberg's analysis. **1858** J. NICOL *Elem. Min.* 241 Heterozite. **1951** C. PALACHE et al. in *Dana's Syst. Min.* (ed. 7) II. 676 Heterosite and purpurite are secondary minerals formed by oxidation of triphylite and lithiophilite.

heterostatic (-ˈstætɪk), *a. Electr.* [f. HETERO- + STATIC.] Applied to electrostatic instruments in which there is electrification independent of that to be tested.

1867 SIR W. THOMSON in *Rep. Brit. Assoc.* 501 The electric system here described is heterostatic, there being an independent electrification besides that whose difference of potential is to be measured. **1881** MAXWELL *Electr. & Magn.* I. 309 This method of using an auxiliary electrification besides the electrification to be measured is called the Heterostatic method in opposition to the Idiostatic method, in which the whole effect is produced by the electrification to be measured.

heterostrophic (-ˈstrɒfɪk), *a.* [f. Gr. ἑτερο- HETERO- + -στροφ-ος turning + -IC: cf. Gr. στροφικός.]

1. Turning or winding in another direction; *spec.* in *Conch.* applied to univalve shells in which the usual direction of the spire is reversed, as in a 'reversed' whelk.

2. *Gr.* and *Lat. Pros.* 'Consisting of two systems of different metrical form: as, a heterostrophic song or choric passage' (*Cent. Dict.*).

So **heteˈrostrophous** *a.* = prec. 1; **heteˈrostrophe, heteˈrostrophy**, the condition of being heterostrophic.

1854 MAYNE *Expos. Lex.*, *Heterostrophus* (*Conchol.*), applied to a spirivalve shell in which the terminal border is to the left side of the animal, as in the *Physa heterostropha*: heterostrophous. **1884** *Cassell's Encycl. Dict.*, *Heterostrophe*, the reversal of the direction in which the spire of a shell turns.

heterostyled (ˈhɛtərəʊstaɪld), *a. Bot.* [f. HETERO- + STYLE + -ED[2].] Having the styles or pistils of different individual plants of different lengths relatively to their stamens; the same as *heteromorphic* or *heterogonous*.

1876 DARWIN in *Life & Lett.* (1892) 311 The nature of heterostyled plants may be illustrated in the primrose. **1877** *Amer. Jrnl. Sc.* Ser. III. 82 Mr. Darwin's term [*dimorphism*] has the disadvantage of not indicating what parts of the blossom are *dimorphic*..This has been supplied by Hildebrand, in Germany, who has introduced [*Bot. Zeit.* 1871] the term *heterostyled* and the counterpart *homostyled*.

So **heteroˈstylism, ˈheterostyly**, the condition of having the styles of different lengths relatively to the stamens; heteromorphism, heterogony; **heteroˈstylous** *a.* = HETEROSTYLED.

1875 BENNETT & DYER *Sachs' Bot.* III. vi. 809 Another contrivance for the mutual fertilisation of different individuals of plants with hermaphrodite flowers,—Dimorphism (or Heterostylism)..In one individual the flowers all have a long style and short filaments, while in another individual all the flowers have a short style and long filaments. **1876** DARWIN in *Life & Lett.* (1892) 53 This account was published before I had discovered the meaning of heterostylism. **1887** WARD tr. *Sachs' Phys. Plants* 792 The same principle is also employed in the case of heterostylous flowers. **1887** GOEBEL *Morphol. Plants* 405 A further method for securing the mutual fertilisation of different plants of the same species is heterogony (heterostyly).

heterotactous (-ˈtæktəs), *a.* [f. Gr. ἑτερο- HETERO- + τακτ-ός ordered, arranged + -OUS.] Characterized by heterotaxy. **a.** *Anat.* and *Bot.* Having organs abnormally placed or arranged. **b.** *Geol.* Without regularity of stratification.

a **1889** G. K. GILBERT in *Worcester's Suppl.*, Heterotactous mountain mass.

heterotaxy (-tæksɪ). [f. Gr. ἑτερο- HETERO- + -ταξια, f. τάξις arrangement.]

1. *Anat.* and *Bot.* Aberrant or abnormal disposition of organs or parts.

1854 MAYNE *Expos. Lex.*, *Heterotaxia*, applied by Geoffroy Saint-Hilaire to those complex anomalies, which, while they are of anatomical importance, do not hinder the performance of any function, and are not apparent externally: heterotaxy. **1882** *Gard. Chron.* XVIII. 78, I believe this case might be reported..as partial heterotaxy. **1897** *Brit. Med. Jrnl.* 28 Aug. 34 The anomaly known as heterotaxy, or *transpositio viscerum totalis*.

2. *Geol.* Want of uniformity in stratification (Worcester *Suppl.* 1889).

heterotic (hɛtəˈrɒtɪk), *a.* [f. HETER(OSIS + -OTIC; in sense 1 f. directly on Gr. ἑτέρωσις alteration.]

1. Pertaining to the manipulation of differences (*nonce-use*).

1905 G. M. FISHER tr. *Höffding's Probl. Philos.* ii. 99 The advance of knowledge consists in a reduction of differences (to a 'heterotic minimum') and in an approximation to a pure description of a continuous process.

2. *Genetics.* Pertaining to or exhibiting heterosis (sense 3).

1914 *Zeitschr. f. induktive Abstammungs- und Vererbungslehre* XII. 127 A highly heterotic plant..because of its unusual vigor may develop branches from buds which in a weaker plant would remain dormant. **1944** *Bull. Torrey Bot. Club* May 267 (*heading*) Heterotic hybrids. **1967** *Amer. Naturalist* CI. 189 (*heading*) Opposite heterotic effects on male weights of reciprocal species hybrids.

heterotomic (-ˈtɒmɪk), *a. Bot.* [f. Gr. ἑτερο- HETERO- + -τομος cut + -IC: cf. Gr. τομικός of or for cutting.] = next, sense 1.

1886 *Syd. Soc. Lex.*, *Heterotomic*,..applied to a calyx or a corolla in which the alternate divisions are dissimilar.

heterotomous (-ˈɒtəməs), *a.* [as prec. + -OUS.]

1. *Bot.* Applied to a perianth having unequal or dissimilar divisions.

1847 in CRAIG.

2. *Min.* Having cleavage different from the ordinary.

1864 in WEBSTER.

heterotopy (hɛtəˈrɒtəpɪ). *Phys.* [ad. mod.L. *heterotopia* (also in Engl. use), f. Gr. ἑτερο- HETERO- + -τοπια, f. τόπος place.] Displacement in position, misplacement: **a.** *Path.* The occurrence of a tumour in a part where the elements of which it is composed do not normally exist. **b.** *Biol.* (See quot. 1879.)

1876 tr. *Wagner's Gen. Pathol.* 355 Tumors are abnormal only because they occur in a locality in which their elements do not normally exist (Heterotopia). **1879** tr. *Haeckel's Evol. Man* I. i. 12 The kenogenetic vitiations of the original palingenetic incidents of evolution depend in great measure on a gradually occurring displacement of the phenomena.. by adaptation to the changed conditions of embryonic existence.—This displacement may affect either the place or the time of the phenomena.—If the former, it is called Heterotopy; if the latter, Heterochrony. *Ibid.* 13 Displacement of position, or heterotopy, especially affects the cells or elementary parts which compose the organs; but it also affects the organs themselves.

Hence **heteroˈtopic, heteˈrotopous** *adjs.*, of, pertaining to, or of the nature of heterotopy; hence ˌ**heteroˈtopically** *adv.*, with the result of becoming heterotopic; **heteˈrotopism** = HETEROTOPY.

1878 BELL *Gegenbaur's Comp. Anat.* 45 The different position occupied by visual organs forbids us to suppose that they have had a common hereditary origin, and is in favour of these heterotopic organs having been independently differentiated from an indifferent apparatus. **1879** tr. *Haeckel's Evol. Man* I. i. 13 An analogous heterotopism affects the primitive kidneys in the higher Vertebrates. **1923** *Guy's Hosp. Rep.* LXXIII. 328 They re-acquired..the prospective fate of being differentiated heterotopically into squamous epithelium.

heterotransplant (ˌhɛtərəʊˈtrɑ:nsplɑ:nt, -træns-, -plænt), *sb. Med.* and *Biol.* [f. HETERO- + TRANSPLANT *sb.*] A piece of tissue or an organ taken from one individual and transplanted (or intended for transplantation) to another individual of a different species.

1918 *Jrnl. Med. Res.* XXXVII. 378 It is..improbable that the preponderance of lymphocytes in the heterotransplants ..was altogether due to the bacterial infection. **1935** *Amer. Jrnl. Cancer* XXIII. 284 One of the growing

heterotransplants of mouse sarcoma 37 was removed from a normal rat. **1959** *Ann. R. Coll. Surgeons* XXV. 45 So far with heterotransplants of human tissue the sex of the recipient has not appeared to influence the survival of the graft.

heterotransplant (ˌhɛtərəʊtrɑːnsplɑːnt, -træns-, -plænt), *v. Med.* and *Biol.* [f. prec. sb.] *trans.* To transplant from one individual to another of a different species. So ˌ**heterotrans'planted** *ppl. a.*

1920 *Jrnl. Exper. Med.* XXXI. 767 The greater part of the heterotransplanted thyroid suffered..through lack of suitability of the body fluids of the host. **1959** *Cancer Res.* XIX. 633 (*heading*) Heterotransplanted choriocarcinomas. **1962** *Ibid.* XXII. 563 Two choriocarcinomas..were successfully heterotransplanted to cortisone-treated hamsters.

heterotransplantable (ˌhɛtərəʊtrɑːns'plɑːnt-əb(ə)l, -træns-, -plænt-), *a. Med.* and *Biol.* [f. prec. vb., after *transplantable.*] Capable of being successfully transplanted from one individual to another of a different species. So ˌ**heterotransplanta'bility**.

1943 *Cancer Res.* III. 809/1 An interpretation of the significance of this demonstration necessitated a more accurate definition of the limits of heterotransplantability. **1947** Ackerman & del Regato *Cancer* iii. 70 Greene believes that failure in transplanting benign tumors suggests that heterotransplantability is a characteristic property of cancer. **1952** *Cancer Res.* V. 41/1 The heterotransplantable phase of the tumor's existence was of relatively short duration. **1971** *Nature* 16 Apr. 455/1 The newborn hamster treated with ALS seems to be more sensitive than the cortisone-treated adult for the purposes of testing heterotransplantability of cultured cells.

heterotransplantation (ˌhɛtərəʊtrɑːnsplɑːn-'teɪʃən, -træns-, -plænt-). *Med.* and *Biol.* [f. HETERO- + TRANSPLANTATION.] The operation of transplanting tissue from one individual to another of a different species.

1905 [see HOMOTRANSPLANTATION]. **1907** *Jrnl. Exper. Med.* IX. 226 These heterotransplantations were attempted with the aim of ascertaining whether the vessels, in spite of the toxic action of the cat's blood on the dog's tissue, could ..take over the function of the vessels removed. **1940** *Amer. Jrnl. Cancer* XXXIX. 170 The direct heterotransplantation of tissues is rarely, if ever, successful among higher mammals. **1971** [see HOMOTRANSPLANTATION].

heterotropal (-'ɒtrəpəl), *a. Bot.* [f. Gr. *ἑτερότροπ-ος* turning another way (f. *ἑτερο-* HETERO- + *-τροπος* turning) + -AL[1].] = HETEROTROPOUS.

1832 J. Lindley *Introd. Bot.* I. ii. 193 The radicle will point neither to the apex nor to the base of the seed, but the embryo will lie, as it were, across it, or be heterotropal, as is the case in the primrose. **1842** Brande *Dict. Sci.* etc., *Heterotropal*, a term applied to the embryo of a seed when the former lies across the latter; that is to say, neither pointing to its base nor apex. **1866** *Treas. Bot.* 588/1 *Heterotropal*, lying parallel with the hilum. A term applied only to the embryo.

heterotroph ('hɛtərəʊtrəʊf). *Biol.* Also **-trophe**. [f. HETERO- + Gr. *τροφός* feeder.] Any organism which requires an external supply of energy contained in complex organic compounds to maintain its existence.

1900 B. D. Jackson *Gloss. Bot. Terms* 311/1 *Heterotroph*, employed by Pfeffer to denote a pure saprophyte. **1959** *New Scientist* 7 May 1002/3 The evolutionary steps..were first, the formation of what he calls heterotrophes, organisms that absorbed as their nutrients organic substances dissolved in the seas in which they lived. **1971** Hawker & Linton *Micro-organisms* v. 145 Fungi, most protozoa, and many bacteria are heterotrophs.

heterotrophic (ˌhɛtərəʊ'trəʊfɪk), *a. Biol.* [f. HETERO- + Gr. *τροφικός* nursing.] Characterized by or exhibiting heterotrophy (in various senses: now only in the sense of HETEROTROPHY 1 c); living as a heterotroph. So ˌ**hetero'trophically** *adv.*

1893 *Jrnl. R. Microsc. Soc.* 665 According as lichens carry on their existence with or without these lodgers, the author [*sc.* Minks] places them respectively under the head of 'autotrophic' or 'heterotrophic' lichens. **1896** *Ibid.* 326 Prof. J. Wiesner proposes the general term *Trophy* for all unilateral excesses of growth in tissues or in organs which are dependent on the position of the organ in question, the term position being understood in a wide sense, as the relation in space of the heterotrophic organ to the horizon and to its parent-shoot. **1900** A. J. Ewart tr. *Pfeffer's Physiol. Plants* I. vii. 363 Plants which are unable to assimilate carbon dioxide must obtain all their organic food-materials from without (heterotrophic or allotrophic nutrition). **1935** W. H. Brown *Plant Kingdom* xvii. 378 Some of the autotrophic bacteria can live heterotrophically. **1969** *Ecology* L. 88/1 Eleven heterotrophic aerobic bacterial types were isolated from the microcosm. **1971** I. G. Gass et al. *Understanding Earth* ix. 139/1 Fox has been able to show that proteinoid microspheres will..come into existence spontaneously on innumerable occasions. If the correct foods are available, they can proliferate heterotrophically indefinitely.

heterotrophism (ˌhɛtərəʊ'trəʊfɪz(ə)m). *Biol.* [f. next: see -ISM.] = HETEROTROPHY 1 c.

1900 A. J. Ewart tr. *Pfeffer's Physiol. Plants* I. vii. 364 All stages of transition between pure autotrophism and heterotrophism are exhibited among obligate or facultative mixotrophic plants. **1936** W. Stiles *Introd. Princ. Plant Physiol.* xiii. 285 Some autotrophic plants..when kept in the dark and provided with such organic nutrients..exhibit a degree of heterotrophism. **1951** Werkman & Wilson *Bacterial Physiol.* 407 (*heading*) Carbon dioxide assimilation and concepts of autotrophism and heterotrophism.

heterotrophy ('hɛtərəʊˌtrəʊfɪ). [f. HETERO- + Gr. *τροφή* nourishment.] **1.** *Biol.* †**a.** [ad. G. *heterotrophie* (A. B. Frank 1885, in *Ber. d. Deut. Bot. Ges.* III. 143).] An abnormal mode of nutrition observed by Frank in some plants, as those of the N.O. *Cupuliferæ*, which have no root-hairs, their function being discharged by a fungus which closely surrounds the roots. *Obs. rare.*

1891 F. P. Foster *Med. Dict.* III. 1867/2 *Heterotrophy*, the quality of obtaining nutrition adventitiously by means of a Fungus whose mycelium takes the place of root-hairs.

†**b.** [ad. G. *heterotrophie* (A. Minks 1893, in *Verhandl. d. zool.-bot. Ges. in Wien* XLII. 402).] (See quot. 1900.) *Obs. rare.*

1900 B. D. Jackson *Gloss. Bot. Terms* 123/1 *Heterotrophy*, (1) used by Minks for those Lichens living symbiotically.

c. The state or quality of living as a heterotroph; heterotrophism.

1930 W. H. Lang tr. *Strasburger's Text-bk. Bot.* (ed. 6) 259 The heterotrophy is not always..complete... Some heterotrophic Phanerogams can construct their organic carbon-compounds in the normal fashion... The converse case is frequently met with. **1949** A. Nelson *Introd. Bot.* xxv. 387 There are degrees of morphological adaptation for heterotrophy.

†**2.** *Bot.* [ad. G. *heterotrophie* (J. Wiesner 1895, in *Ber. d. Deut. Bot. Ges.* XIII. 482).] (See quot. 1900.) *Obs. rare.*

1896 *Jrnl. R. Microsc. Soc.* 326 (*heading*) Heterotrophy and anisophylly. **1900** B. D. Jackson *Gloss. Bot. Terms* 123/1 *Heterotrophy*..(2) [used] by Wiesner for the compound position of a shoot with regard to the horizon and of the mother-shoot.

heterotropic (-'trɒpɪk), *a.* [f. as HETEROTROPAL *a.* + -IC: cf. Gr. *τροπικός* of or pertaining to turning.] **1.** *Physics.* = ANISOTROPIC, ÆOLOTROPIC.

1885 Watson & Burbury *Math. Th. Electr. & Magn.* I. 203 These ratios..have a determinate value at every point in a heterotropic medium, but may vary from point to point.

2. *Genetics.* Applied to chromosomes that are not paired at meiosis.

1905 E. B. Wilson in *Jrnl. Exper. Zool.* II. 508 Since there is no reason for considering the 'accessory chromosome' as in any sense accessory to the others,..I suggest that.. chromosomes of this type may provisionally be called *heterotropic* chromosomes (in allusion to the fact that they pass to one pole only of the spindle in one of the maturation-divisions). **1920** L. Doncaster *Introd. Study Cytol.* xi. 155 When..the heterotropic or *X*-chromosome passes undivided to one pole of the first spermatocyte division-figure, it divides equationally in the division of those secondary spermatocytes which contain it.

heterotropous (-'ɒtrəpəs), *a. Bot.* [f. as prec. + -OUS.] = HEMITROPOUS 2.

1830 Lindley *Nat. Syst. Bot.* 209 Embryo supposed by Von Martius to be heterotropous (that is, to have its radicle not turned towards the hilum). *Ibid.* 229 In Rhinanthaceæ it must be antitropous or heterotropous. **1857** Henfrey *Elem. Bot.* §240 Another condition [of the ovule] is more rarely met with, the *amphitropous* or *heterotropous* or *hemianatropous*, intermediate between orthotropous and anatropous.

heterousian, etc.: see HETEROOUSIAN.

heterozygote (ˌhɛtərəʊ'zaɪgəʊt). *Biol.* [f. HETERO- + ZYGOTE.] **1.** A diploid individual that has different alleles at one or more genetic loci. Also *attrib.* or as *adj.*, = *heterozygous.*

1902 Bateson & Saunders *Rep. Evol. Comm. R. Soc.* I. 126 The zygote formed by the union of a pair of opposite allelomorphic gametes, we shall call a heterozygote. **1902** W. Bateson *Mendel's Princ. Hered.* 23 This *Aa* is the hybrid or 'mule' form, or as I have elsewhere called it, the heterozygote, as distinguished from *AA* or *aa* the homozygotes. **1906** R. H. Lock *Variation, Heredity, & Evolution* vii. 186 *Plate*, Cobs borne by heterozygote plants pollinated with the recessive. **1930** R. A. Fisher *Genet. Theory Nat. Selection* 8 The heterozygote when mated to either kind of homozygote would produce both heterozygotes and homozygotes. **1949** Darlington & Mather *Elem. Genetics* v. 110 The original form of any heterozygote must be a mutation. **1971** J. Z. Young *Introd. Study Man* iii. 60 Apparently the heterozygotes have an increased resistance.

2. A bacteriophage that carries two different copies of some of its genetic information and produces two kinds of progeny when it infects a bacterial cell.

1952 Hershey & Chase in *Cold Spring Harbor Symp. Quant. Biol.* XVI. 474/1 Since there is adequate reason to call these markers allelic genes, the mottling particles are appropriately termed heterozygotes. **1968** D. S. Ray in Fraenkel-Conrat *Molec. Basis Virol.* ii. 247 The purified heterozygotes are twice the length of normal phage particles and apparently contain two DNA molecules.

Hence ˌ**heterozy'gosis** (-zaɪ'gəʊsɪs), the fusion of two genetically different gametes; the state or condition of being heterozygous; ˌ**heterozy'gosity** (-zaɪ'gɒsɪtɪ), the state or condition of being heterozygous; the degree or extent to which an individual is heterozygous with respect to its complement of genetic loci; ˌ**heterozy'gotic** *a.*, resulting from or pertaining to heterozygosis; ˌ**hetero'zygous** (-'zaɪgəs) *a.*, having different alleles at one or more genetic loci.

1902 Bateson & Saunders *Rep. Evol. Comm. R. Soc.* I. 130 The determination from statistical study of zygotes must be exceedingly difficult, seeing that both resulting forms may be heterozygous. **1905** *Rep. Brit. Assoc. 1904* 585 Appearances have been seen..suggesting at first sight that a heterozygosis between two gametes, *both* extracted, may give, *e.g.*, dominance. **1911** *Amer. Naturalist* XLV. 142 The surprises of heterozygotic 'constructions' or of new combinations in F_2 may..be responsible for the case of De Vries's buttercups. **1912** East & Hayes *Heterozygosis in Evol. & Plant Breeding* 37 Decrease in vigor due to inbreeding lessens with decrease in heterozygosity. **1914** Heterozygotic [see HETEROSIS 3]. **1949** Darlington & Mather *Elem. Genetics* xiii. 280 (*caption*) The potential variability existing in the differences between homozygotes ..must first be converted into heterozygotic potential by intercrossing. *Ibid.* xii. 261 It is only when a heterozygous species is crossed with another, heterozygous or homozygous, that its heterozygosity is shown by the mixture in the progeny. **1965** T. Dobzhansky *Heredity & Nature of Man* v. 156 Although persons who inherit this gene from both parents (homozygotes) die of fatal anemia, the heterozygous carriers may be said to show a hybrid vigor.. in malaria-ridden environments.

hetfull, obs. f. HEATFUL *a.*, passionate.

c **1470** Henry *Wallace* II. 91 A hetfull man the stwart was of blude.

heth(e, heþ, obs. forms of HEATH, HEIGHT.

†**hethe**, *v. Obs. rare.* Also 3 *Orm.* **hæþenn**. [a. ON. *hǽða* to mock, scoff at, f. *háð* scoffing, mocking.] To mock, scorn.

c **1200** Ormin 13682 And alle þa þatt..hæþenn upponn oþre menn þurrh here modiȝnesse. *a* **1310** in Wright *Lyric P.* x. 37 Y-here thou me nou, hendest in helde, Navy the none harmes to hethe.

†'**hethely**, *a.* and *adv. Obs.* Forms: 3 **hæþeliȝ, heythlik, hethli**, 4 **heþeliche, hetheli, -y**. [a. ON. *hǽðiligr* adj., ludicrous, contemptible, *hǽðiliga* scornfully, mockingly, f. *háð*: see prec.]

A. *adj.* Ludicrous, to be held in derision.

c **1350** *Sir Tristr.* 2897 To wiue on our kinde Heþeliche holdeþ he.

B. *adv.* Scornfully, derisively, contemptuously; esp. in early ME. phrase ***hetheli leten*** to think scornfully of, to scorn: see LET *v.*

c **1200** Ormin 7408 Þa þatt lætenn hæþeliȝ Off Godess hallȝhe lare. *Ibid.* 13272 Þatt he ne let nohht hæþeliȝ Hiss ȝunngre forr to follȝhenn. *a* **1300** *Cursor M.* 2606 (Cott.) Agar was..heythlik lete of hir lauedi. *Ibid.* 14669 (Gött.) Hethli [*Trin.* scornefuly] þai bihuted him. *c* **1325** *Metr. Hom.* 43 Forthi he schroudes his bodi And lates of pouer men hetheli. ? *a* **1400** *Morte Arth.* 268 His senatour has sommonde me, and said what hym lykyde, Hethely in my halle, wyth heynȝous wordes.

†**hethen**, *adv. Obs.* Forms: 3 **heðen**, 3–5 **heþen, hethen**, (3 **heoðen, heþenn**, 4 **heden, heiþen, -in, heythen, eþen, hiþen**, 4–5 **hethin, -yn, -ene**, 5 **hethinne, -un, hithinne**). [Early ME., a. ON. *heðan* (Sw. *häden*, Da. *heden*), f. root of HE *pron.*] = HENCE.

c **1200** *Trin. Coll. Hom.* 185 Heðen to fare to siker wunienge. *c* **1200** Ormin 15570 Gaþ till, and bereþþ heþenn ut Whattlike þise þingess. *c* **1250** *Gen. & Ex.* 1644 Hu fer ist heðen to laban? *a* **1300** *Cursor M.* 7578 (Cott.), I red betime þou hethen [*Fairf.* heythen] fle. **13..** *Ibid.* 8229 (Gött.) 'Sal nan', he said, 'þaim heden [*Cott.* heþen] stir'. *c* **1330** R. Brunne *Chron.* (1810) 26 After nyen and tuenty ȝere þe dede him hiþen nam. *c* **1394** *P. Pl. Crede* 408 'Fare well..for y mot heþen fonden.' *c* **1450** *St. Cuthbert* (Surtees) 2542 Þat sho was likly hethin to pas. ? *a* **1500** *Chester Pl.* (Shaks. Soc.) II. 56 Or I hethen wyn This cote shalbe myne.

b. With *from.*

a **1300** *E.E. Psalter* cxiii. [cxv.] 18 Fra hethen, and in to werld þat isse. *a* **1300** *Cursor M.* 22678 Right vn[t]o þe abime fra heþen. **1340** Hampole *Pr. Consc.* 6007 And swa sely may be alle þas, Þat fra hethen in charité gas.

Hence †**hethenforth, -forthward, -forward** *advs.* = HENCEFORTH, etc. †**hethensith**, departure, decease. †**hethenward** *adv.*, away from here, hence.

c **1200** *Trin. Coll. Hom.* 65 Doð giwer lichame heðenforð to hersumiende clennesse. *a* **1300** *E.E. Psalter* cxii[i]. 2 Fra heþen forth into werld þat isse. *c* **1340** *Cursor M.* 11695 (Fairf.) Fra now heyþen forwarde. *c* **1410** N. Love *Bonavent. Mirr.* I. 105 (Gibbs MS.), I schal neuer heþen forthwarde fele oght of hem.

c **1200** *Trin. Coll. Hom.* 125 Þe wunderliche heðen sið of ure louerd seint iohan baptiste. *Ibid.* 141 Hwu wunderlich was his hider-cume..and hwu siker his heðensið.

c **1200** Ormin 5490 Aȝȝ hemm langeþþ heþennwarrd, And upp till heoffness blisse. *a* **1400–50** *Alexander* 734 Hy þe hethen-ward [*Dubl.* hyneward], þou hathill.

hethen, heþen, heðen, obs. ff. HEATHEN.

hethenesse, heþenes, -inesse, obs. ff. HEATHENESSE.

hether, -most, obs. ff. HITHER, etc.

†**hether**, corrupt f. HELDER *adv.*, rather.

c **1550** Latimer *Serm.* (1562) 245 b, I will hether spend the time in exhorting you..then curiously to recite [etc.].

†**hething**, *vbl. sb. Obs.* Forms: 3 *Orm.* **hæþinng**, 3–4 **heþing**, 4 **-yng, hethinge, ethynge**, 3–6 **hething**, (*Sc.* 5 **heithing, -ding, heyden, -din, hathing**). [a. ON. *hǽðing* scoffing, mocking, derision, f. *hǽða* HETHE *v.*] Scoffing, derision, mockery; scorn, contempt; dishonour.

c **1200** ORMIN 240 þatt icc ne beo mang wimmannkinn Till hæþinng butenn chilldre. *a* **1300** *Cursor M.* 15881 þe feluns logh him til hething. *c* **1386** CHAUCER *Reeve's T.* 190 Allas, quod Iohn, the day that I was born; Now are we dryve til hethyng and til scorn. *c* **1450** HENRYSON *Mor. Fab.* 10 At the last shee saide halfe in hathing. *c* **1460** *Towneley Myst.* (Surtees) 236 Both on ernest and on hethyng. ? *a* **1500** *Pebles to Play* xi, Ane young man stert upon his feit, And he began to lauche For heydin. **1535** STEWART *Cron. Scot.* III. 265 The Scottis men..Bot scorne and hething send to him agane. *c* **1540** *Pilgr. T.* 388 in Thynne *Animadv.* 88 Abjuryd, and to hething scornyd.

b. An object or cause of scorn or derision.

a **1300** *Cursor M.* 15412 Hald yee it na hething. *a* **1340** HAMPOLE *Psalter* xxxvii. 7 Comm., Swa makis he me his hethynge. *c* **1460** *Towneley Myst.* (Surtees) 174 What, dewille, wille he be there? This hold I great hethyng.

Hence †'**hethingful** *a.*, scornful, contemptuous.

c **1400** *Destr. Troy* 3953 Bourdfull among buernes, blithe of his wordis, Hethyngfull to hathels, but it harmyt not.

hethinne, var. HETHEN *adv.*, *Obs.*

hethnes, -nesse, obs. ff. HEATHENESSE.

hethnical: see HEATHENIC.

hethon, -un, -yn, var. ff. HEATHEN, HETHEN.

hetien, heting, -ynge, obs. ff. HATE *v.*, HIGHT *v.*, -ING.

hetique, obs. f. HECTIC.

hetire, var. HETER *a.*, *Obs.*

‖**hetman** ('hɛtmən). Also 8 **hettman**, 9 **attaman**. [Polish *hetman* captain, commander = Boh. *hejtman*, Little Russ. *hetman* (Russ. *ataman*). Believed to be derived from Ger. *hauptmann* captain, app. through early mod.G. *heubtmann* and Boh. *heitman*.]

A captain or military commander in Poland and countries formerly united or subject to it; whence subsequently retained as a title among the Cossacks.

Under the suzerainty of Poland, 1592–1654, 'the hetman of the Cossacks' was a semi-independent prince or viceroy. His title and authority were at first continued after the acceptance of Russian suzerainty by the Cossacks in 1654; but the power and privileges of the office were gradually curtailed and abolished. In the late 19th c. the title 'Hetman (*ataman*) of all the Cossacks' was an appanage of the Cesarevitch, who was represented by a 'hetman by delegation', for each of the territorial divisions. Subordinate Cossack chiefs had also the title (*ataman*).

1710 WHITWORTH *Acc. Russia* (1758) 19 Every town is like a little common-wealth, and has its own *Hetman*, or Captain, chosen yearly. **1753** HANWAY *Trav.* (1762) I. VI. lxxxii. 374 His brother..is now Hetman of the Cossacks in the Ukraine ..This is a kind of vice-royalty, and is..the most lucrative of any employment in the empire. **1799** W. TOOKE *View Russian Emp.* I. 400 This submission [to Russia] took place in the year 1654 under the hetman Bogdan Chmelnitzki. *Ibid.* 403 The insignia of the hetman are, the truncheon, the national standard, the horse-tail, kettle-drums, and the national signet. **1818** BYRON *Mazeppa* iii, The Ukraine's hetman, calm and bold. **1837** *Penny Cycl.* VIII. 79/1 In 1592, Stephen Bathory, the king of [Poland]..appointed an Attaman or Hetman as chief over them [Cossacks]. **1894** *Daily News* 23 Oct. 5/3 The Czar's Body Regiment of Cossacks..received a congratulatory telegram from the Czar..'I drink with your hetman (the Cezarewitch) the health of the regiment'.

Hence '**hetmanate**, '**hetmanship**.

1879 *Encycl. Brit.* X. 6/1 During the hetmanate it had fortifications of which traces are still extant. **1881** *Athenæum* 30 July 147/1 Kostomarof..has completed an extensive monograph upon the Hetmanship of Mazeppa.

hett(e, obs. ff. HEAT *sb.*, HEAT *v.* (inf. and pa. t. and pple.), HET.

hetten: see HIGHT *v.*

hetter, hetur, var. HETER *a.*, *Obs.*

hettrand, -rent, -ret, obs. Sc. ff. HATRED.

heu, obs. form of HEW, HUE.

heuch, hooch (hu:x), *int. dial.* An exclamation of excitement; the cry of a dancer of the Highland fling. Hence **heuch** *v. intr.*, to utter this cry.

1871 C. GIBBON *Lack of Gold* xxx, They flung about with might and main, and deafening 'hoochs' that would have served for a war dance. **1896** J. LUMSDEN *Poems* 43 Lads and lasses lap and skirled Cried 'Heuch!' like warlocks driven Clean gyte. *Ibid.* 137 They danced, they snappit, an' heuched awa'.

heuch, var. of HEUGH, obs. Sc. pa. t. of HEW.

heuchera ('hɔɪkərə). *Bot.* [mod.L., f. the name of J. H. *Heucher* (1677–1747), German botanist (C. Linnæus *Hortus Cliffortianus* (1737) 82).] A plant of a large genus of perennial herbs, of the family Saxifragaceæ, native to North America. Hence **heuche'rella**, a member of a group of bigeneric hybrids between heuchera and tiarella.

1772 R. WESTON *Universal Botanist* III. 387 American Heuchera or Sanicle. **1829** *Bot. Reg.* XV. 1302 Small-flowered Heuchera. **1884** J. WOOD *Hardy Perennials* 143 The Heucheras bloom from May to August. **1924** R. WRIGHT *Pract. Bk. Outdoor Flowers* II. i. 99 The newer hybrid Heucheras. **1949** L. H. BAILEY *Man. Cultivated Plants* 481 Heucherella: from heuchera and tiarella. **1961** *Amateur Gardening* 23 Sept. 2/2 Hybrids, between heuchera and *Tiarella wherryi*, listed as heucherella. **1962** *Ibid.* 21 Apr. 4/2 Heucheras like open soil and an open position.

heue, obs. f. HEAVE, HEW, HIVE.

heued, obs. f. HEAD *sb.*[1]

heuene, obs. f. EVEN *adv.*, HEAVEN.

heufrasy, obs. f. EUPHRASY.

heug, obs. f. HUGE.

heu-'gase, *phrase.* The view-halloo in otter-hunting; used *interjectionally* and as *sb.*

1827 *Sporting Mag.* XX. 104 Mr. Treby's Harriers.. unhovered an otter. 'Heu gase! heu gase!' was vociferated from the lungs of many a tough one. **1828** *Ibid.* XXI. 306 The heugase, heugase (the view screech of the otter-hunter) is heard poured forth with joyful yell. [*Heu gase!* The cry is still used in North Wales and Shropshire..It is certainly the present customary cry with the Hawkstone Otter Hounds. F. T. Elworthy.]

heugh, heuch (hjux), *sb. Sc.* and *north. dial.* Forms: 4 **hogh**, 5 **hough**, 5–6 **hewch**, (5 **huwe**, 6 **hew, hewche, heuche, huche**), 5– **heuch**, 7– **heugh**, (9 *dial.* **heuf**). [Sc. (and north Eng.) repr. of ME. *hōgh*, OE. *hóh*, f. ablaut grade *hanh-* of HANG *v.* (cf. Goth. *faurahâh* curtain). Cf. HOE *sb.*[1], HOW *sb.*[2]; also, for form, CLEUCH, CLOUGH; and, for later phonology, Sc. *beuch*, *bew* = BOUGH.]

1. A precipitous or hanging descent; a craggy or rugged steep; a precipice, cliff, or scaur; most commonly, one overhanging a river or the sea.

a **1300** *Cursor M.* 15826 (Gött.) And rugged him vnrekinli bath ouer hil and hogh [*Cott.* ogh, *Fairf.* scogh, *Trin.* slowȝe; *rime* wogh]. *Ibid.* 22202 (Cott.) Ouer hogh to lepe his hals to brek [so *Gött.*, altered in others]. *c* **1425** WYNTOUN *Cron.* VII. iv. 93 The Kyng..Oure a Hewch gert cast hym downe, Doggis til ete his caryowne. *Ibid.* VIII. xxxviii. 92 Sum flede downe oure þe Hwe. *c* **1450** *St. Cuthbert* (Surtees) 5549 Him thoght þat abouen þat hough he and his men lay sure ynogh. **1513** DOUGLAS *Æneis* I. iv. 13 To se the hewis on ather hand is wondir. **1549** *Compl. Scot.* vi. 39 Vndir ane hingand heuch I herd mony hurlis of stannirs ande stanis that tumlit doune. **1597** MONTGOMERIE *Cherrie & Slae* 37 Euery blome on branche and bewch..hang their heidis out ouir the hewch. **1609** SKENE tr. *Quon. Attach.* c. 48 §10 (Jam.) Gif an wylde or head strang horse caries ane man..over ane craig, or heuch. *a* **1796** BURNS *Song, 'Simmer's a Pleasant Time'*, The water rins o'er the heugh. **1815** SCOTT *Guy M.* xxvi, From the top of a *heugh* or broken bank, [he] enjoyed the scene much more to his satisfaction. **1876** *Whitby Gloss.*, *Heuf*, or *Heugh*, a steep hill-side. **1894** CROCKETT *Raiders* 39 The most part of us were out on the heuchs, looking to seaward.

2. A glen or ravine with steep overhanging braes or sides; a cleuch.

c **1450** HENRYSON *Mor. Fab.* 27 Then was hee blyth, and in ane heuch him hid. **1549** *Compl. Scot.* vi. 40 Al..cryit.. as it hed bene ecco in ane hou heuch. **1753** *Stewart's Trial* 203 At the foot of the heugh (or deep hollow place) of Corrynakeigh in Koalifnacoan, he heard a whistle. **1801** LEYDEN *Gloss. to Compl. Scot.*

3. The steep face of a quarry or other excavation (***quarry heugh***); an excavation for coal, originally open; a coal-pit; *fig.* a pit.

1592 [see COAL-HEUGH]. **1592** *Early Rec. Min. Scot.* (1878) 65 That his gracis subjectis micht hawe a securitie to tak thair hewis. **1785** BURNS *Addr. to Deil* iii, Tho' yon lowin heugh's thy hame, Thou travels far. **1808–25** in JAMIESON.

4. *Comb.* **heughman**, a miner, collier.

1819 W. TENNANT *Papistry Storm'd* (1827) 11 The Dysart heughmen left their places O' darkness now, and wash't their faces.

heugh, *int.* Also 7 **heuk**. An exclamation of surprise; hollo! (Cf. HEWGH, WHEW.)

1668 ETHEREDGE *She Would if She Could* II. ii, Heuk! sly girl and madcap, to 'em, to 'em, to 'em, boys, alou! **1852** W. ANDERSON *Expos. Popery* (1878) 128 Heugh! Cardinal! revealed at last! **1890** W. A. WALLACE *Only a Sister?* 176 Heugh! What a fellow I am! I never asked her what she was doing here!

heui, heuid, heuine, obs. ff. HEAVY, HEAD *sb.*[1], HEAVEN.

heuk, var. HEUGH *int.*, HUKE *Obs.*

heulandite ('hju:ləndaɪt). *Min.* [Named 1822 after H. Heuland, an English mineralogist: see -ITE[1].] A mineral of the Zeolite group; a hydrated silicate of aluminium and calcium, found in crystals of various colours with pearly lustre.

1822 *Edin. Phil. Jrnl.* VI. 112 The Stilbite and the Heulandite. **1852** BROOKE & MILLER *Phillips' Min.* 439 Heulandite belongs to the anorthic system. **1868** DANA *Min.* (ed. 5) 445 Heulandite occurs principally in amygdaloidal rocks.

heumat, -met, -mont, obs. Sc. ff. HELMET.

heumite ('hju:maɪt). *Petrol.* [a. G. *heumite*, *heumit* (W. C. Brögger 1898, in *Skr. udg. af Videnskabsselsk. i Christiania* (*Math.-naturv. Klasse*) *1897* VI. 46), f. the name of *Heum* in southern Norway: see -ITE[1].] A brownish-black hypabyssal dike-rock containing alkali feldspars, biotite, and barkevikite, with nepheline, sodalite, and other rocks.

1901 *Jrnl. Chem. Soc.* LXXX. II. 169 Heumite is the name given to a dyke-rock from Heum, consisting of hornblende and felspar, with some biotite, and smaller amounts of nephelite, sodalite, diopside, &c. **1938** A. JOHANNSEN *Descr. Petrogr.* IV. 170 The heumite from Brathagen..contains essential soda-microcline and soda-orthoclase with a little andesine.

heureka, the proper spelling of EUREKA, 'I have found (it)', q.v.

1806 J. GRAHAME *Birds Scot.* 28 The Syracusan's voice did not exclaim The grand *Heureka* with more rapturous joy.

heuretic (hjʊ'rɛtɪk), *sb. rare.* [ad. Gr. εὑρετικός inventive, ingenious, f. εὑρίσκειν to find.] The branch of logic which treats of the art of discovery or invention.

1838 SIR W. HAMILTON *Logic* App. (1866) II. 230 That which treats of those conditions of knowledge which lie in the nature, not of thought itself, but of that which we think about..has been called *Heuretic*, in so far as it expounds the rules of Invention or Discovery.

‖**heurige** ('hɔɪrɪgə). Also (representing G. declined forms) **heurigen, heuriger**. [South G. and Austrian G., = (adj.) new, (sb.) new wine, from the latest harvest; vintner's establishment.] **1.** The wine from the latest harvest, produced in and near Vienna.

1935 SCHOONMAKER & MARVEL *Compl. Wine Bk.* vi. 152 Grinzing, now part of Vienna, is famous for its *vin nouveau* (*Heuriger*), served in picturesque rustic cafés to the music-loving population. **1941** 'R. WEST' *Black Lamb* (1942) II. 490 It is delightful to drink the heuriger wine in the gardens of Grinzing. **1964** F. BOWERS *Bibliogr. & Textual Crit.* I. 3 Experts..testify that a headache can be especially acute the morning after tasting *Heurige*, the new wine. **1967** A. LICHINE *Encycl. Wines* 115/2 The stinging new *heurige* wine served in their wine-garden is, for the tourists who flock there, the essence of Viennese gaiety.

2. An establishment or wine-garden where this wine is served.

1934 P. BOTTOME *Private Worlds* iii. 27 One hot summer night at a *Heurigen*, he had met a beautiful young dancer. **1939** N. MONSARRAT *This is Schoolroom* III. xvii. 400 We might..row across the lake to the tiny *Heuriger* and there drink a bottle of Niersteiner. **1965** *Daily Tel.* 23 Sept. 15/6 To be in Vienna and not visit a heuriger is like seeing Naples and not dying.

heurism ('hjʊərɪz(ə)m). [f. HEUR(ISTIC + -ISM.] The educational principle or practice of placing a pupil, as far as possible, in the position of a discoverer.

1919 *Times Educ. Suppl.* 17 Apr. 181/3 The whole trend of modern educational improvement is to give the pupils just the benefits that Professor Laurie demanded. Boy-scouting .., direct methods, heurism, and..'the play way'. **1920** T. P. NUNN *Education* 91 Dr. M. W. Keatinge,..a severe critic of heurism and of the general idea of freedom in education. **1925** C. FOX *Educ. Psychol.* 214 The second general principle of method [in teaching] is that known as heurism, i.e. the method of placing the pupil..in the position of the discoverer. This method had a great vogue a generation ago. **1959** *Chambers's Encycl.* VII. 80/2 All teaching is balanced between the poles of heurism and of didactic suggestion.

heuristic (hjʊ'rɪstɪk), *a.* (*sb.*) [irreg. f. Gr. εὑρίσκ-ειν (stem εὑρε-) to find, app. after words in *-istic* from vbs. in -ιζειν, -IZE; cf. Ger. *heuristik*, *-isch*.]

A. *adj.* **a.** Serving to find out or discover.

1821 COLERIDGE *Let.* 8 Jan. (1971) V. 133, I am..getting regularly on with my LOGIC—in 3 parts—..3. Organic or Heuristic (εὑριστικόν). **1853** *N. & Q.* 1. Ser. VII. 320 *Heuristic*,..as an English scholar would write it, or *Heuristisch*, as it would be written by a German. **1860** WHEWELL in *Todhunter's Acc. W.'s Wks.* (1876) II. 418 If you will not let me treat the Art of Discovery as a kind of Logic, I must take a new name for it, Heuristic, for example. **1877** E. CAIRD *Philos. Kant* II. xix. 662 The ideas of reason are heuristic not ostensive: they enable us to ask a question, not to give the answer. **1890** J. F. SMITH tr. *Pfleiderer's Devel. Theol.* IV. i. 321 Its proper place as an heuristic principle in practical sociology. **1955** *Sci. Amer.* July 72/3 Einstein's 1905 paper, for which (nominally) he had been awarded the Nobel prize, did not contain the word 'theory' in the title, but referred instead to considerations from a 'heuristic viewpoint'. **1967** *Listener* 28 Sept. 386/2 His [*sc.* M. McLuhan's] style is jargon-ridden—all this talk of 'heuristic probes', as if a probe could be anything but heuristic. **1973** *N.Y. Times* 2 May 36/2 The kind of criticism being written now is looser, more fluid, more ad hoc and heuristic.

b. *Educ.* (See quot. 1898.)

1848 [implied in HEURISTICAL *a.* below]. **1884** in *Spec. Rep. Educ.* II. 390 in *Parl. Papers 1898* (C. 8943) XXIV. 1 The heuristic method is the *only* method to be applied in the pure sciences; it is the best method in the teaching of the applied sciences. **1898** H. E. ARMSTRONG *Ibid.*, Heuristic methods of teaching are methods which involve our placing students as far as possible in the attitude of the discoverer—methods which involve their *finding out*, instead of merely being told about things. **1959** *Chambers's Encycl.* VII. 80/2 Science-

teaching should always be permeated by a heuristic bias (i.e. methods of investigation must be used whenever possible).

c. *Computers.* (See quot. 1964.)

1960 *Information Processing: Proc. Internat. Conf., 1959* (Unesco) 275/1 The technique of heuristic programming is under detailed investigation as a means to the end of applying large-scale digital computers to the solution of a difficult class of problems currently considered to be beyond their capabilities. **1964** T. W. McRae *Impact of Computers on Accounting* 297 Under an 'heuristic' programming procedure the computer searches through a number of possible solutions at each stage of the programme, it evaluates a 'good' solution for this stage and then proceeds to the next stage. Essentially heuristic programming is similar to the problem solving techniques by trial and error methods which we use in everyday life. **1969** P. B. Jordain *Condensed Computer Encycl.* 235 The heuristic program should be able to judge whether the problem is closer to solution after each attempt.

B. *sb.* **1. a.** = HEURETIC.

1860 Abp. Thomson *Laws Th.* §35 (ed. 5) 56 Logic may be regarded as Heuristic, or the Art of Discovering truth. **1945** G. Polya *How to solve It* p. vii, The subject of heuristic has manifold connections; mathematicians, logicians, psychologists, educationalists, even philosophers may claim various parts of it. *Ibid.* 102 The aim of heuristic is to study the methods and rules of discovery and invention. **1957** *Proc. Western Joint Computer Conf.* XV. 218 (*heading*) Empirical explorations of the logic theory machine. A case study of heuristic.

b. A heuristic process or method for attempting the solution of a problem; a rule or item of information used in such a process.

1957 A. Newell et al. in *Proc. Western Joint Computer Conf.* XV. 223 A process that *may* solve a given problem, but offers no guarantees of doing so, is called a heuristic for that problem. *Ibid,.* For conciseness, we will use 'heuristic' as a noun synonymous with 'heuristic process'. **1958** *IBM Jrnl. Res. & Devel.* II. 337/1 For the moment.. we shall consider that a heuristic method (or a heuristic, to use the noun form) is a procedure that may lead us by a short cut to the goal we seek or it may lead us down a blind alley. **1962** Ledley & Wilson *Programming & utilizing Digital Computers* viii. 349 Such criteria are called the heuristics of the problem. The field of heuristic programming is concerned with the investigation and understanding of various aspects of heuristics, such as how they are discovered, what kinds there are. **1967** A. Battersby *Network Analysis* (ed. 2) xii. 192 It would.. seem more reasonable to recalculate the float next time (6, 14) was a candidate for limited resources. Some heuristics do this.

2. *pl.* The study and use of heuristic techniques in data processing.

1963 *Times* 8 June 11/2 Whether every manager needs to know about cybernetics, econometrics, and heuristics is arguable, but cost analysis, market research, production control, and other developing subjects should be within his purview. **1967** *Observer* 9 Apr. 21/3 This branch of artificial intelligence—building machines to take short cuts to a solution—is known as 'heuristics' and is being actively pursued at the moment.

Hence **heu'ristical** *a.*; **heu'ristically**, in a heuristic manner; using heuristic processes.

1848 W. Ross *Teacher's Man.* v. 92 The Heuristical method. **1935** *Jrnl. Theol. Stud.* XXXVI. 314 The belief that the world's orderedness or knowability is an expression of mind, and that the category of purpose.. is applicable to it otherwise than heuristically. **1963** J. Lyons *Structural Semantics* ii. 17 What is not made clear is the purpose served by the semantic criterion (except heuristically) in the first place. **1965** *Language* XLI. 507 Nonlinguistic context may be heuristically useful in establishing lexical fields. **1965** N. Chomsky *Aspects of Theory of Syntax* i. 52 It is historically accurate as well as heuristically valuable to distinguish these two very different approaches to the problem of the acquisition of knowledge. **1968** P. A. P. Moran *Introd. Probability Theory* ix. 441 On solving this problem heuristically it is found that $u(t)$, also, is a random process.

heurt(e, var. HURT, roundel.

heurtleberry, variant of HURTLEBERRY.

heve, obs. inf. and pa. t. of HEAVE, obs. f. HIVE *sb.*

hevea ('hiːviːə). *Bot.* [mod.L., f. native name *hevé* (F. Aublet, *Histoire des Plantes de la Guiane Françoise* (1775) II. 871).] A South American tree of the genus so called, belonging to the family Euphorbiaceæ, and having milky sap which provides rubber.

1878 W. T. Thiselton-Dyer *Let.* 17 Apr. in *Indian Forester* (1879) IV. 42 The climate of Calcutta did not prove very favorable to the Heveas, which require the conditions of growth met with in hot and moist tropical forests. **1899** *Hooker's Icones Plantarum* XXVI. 2575 The seeds of *Hevea* are.. incorrectly described. **1909** J. C. Willis *Agric. in Tropics* xiii. 129 Hevea certainly forms 95% of all cultivated rubber. **1927** *Daily Tel.* 11 May 3/4 The rest would be dug up after the present season, and rubber planted in its stead, as the hevea trees remaining were widely spaced. **1935** *Nature* 16 Mar. 417/1 The exudation.. is known as hevea-latex, since *Hevea brasiliensis* is only one of some four hundred plant species which elaborate juices containing rubber. **1964** J. Hutchinson *Ess. Crop Plant Evol.* viii. 167 Such an evolutionary phenomenon as *Hevea* rubber, of which some individuals of the original domestication are said to be still alive.

heved, obs. pa. t. and pple. of HEAVE; obs. f. HEAD *sb.*[1]

heveëne ('hiːviːiːn). *Chem.* [f. *Hevea* name of the S. American genus of plants yielding caoutchouc + -ENE.] An oily hydrocarbon, C_4H_4, of amber-yellow colour; the least volatile product of the dry distillation of caoutchouc and gutta-percha.

1838 T. Thomson *Chem. Org. Bodies* 701 Heveëne is an oily body. **1855-7** W. A. Miller *Elem. Chem.* (1867) III. 656.

†**heveld-bed.** *Obs. rare.* [With *heveld* cf. MHG. *hevelte* vault of the sky, *hemelte* vault of an arch, vaulted roof, OHG. *himilizi, himilze*, ceiling, canopy.] ? A canopied bed, a tent-bed.

c **1230** *Hali Meid.* 21 þat wedlakes heueld bed nawt ham ne ihente.

†**heven**, *v.*[1] *Obs.* Forms: 1 hafenian, 4 heuenen. [OE. *hafenian* = OHG. *hębinôn, hęfenôn*, early MHG. *hebenôn*:—OTeut. type **habinôjan, habanôjan*, f. **habano-*, pa. pple. of **hafjan* to take, take up, lift: see HEAVE.] *trans.* To raise, lift up, exalt. *lit.* and *fig.*

Beowulf (Z.) 1574 Wæpen hafenade, heard be hiltum. **13..** *Gaw. & Gr. Knt.* 349 Such an askyng is heuened so hyȝe in your sale. **13..** *E.E. Allit. P.* B. 24 As he heuened aȝt happez & hyȝt hem her medez. *Ibid.* 506 Bot Noe.. heuened vp an auter & halȝed hit fayre. *Ibid.* 920 Owre fader hatz.. hiȝly heuened þi hele fro hem þat arn combred.

†**heven**, *v.*[2] *Obs.* Also 4 heuin, heyuen. [a. ON. *hefna* (Da. *hevne*, Sw. *hämna*).] **a.** *trans.* To avenge. **b.** *intr.* To take vengeance.

a **1300** *Cursor M.* 4326 Reu his res þan sal he sare, Or heuen [*v.r.* venge] his harm wit foli mare. *Ibid.* 11802 His wranges godd on him sal heuen. *c* **1400** *Destr. Troy* 2083 But þou put þe, priam, to so proude aunter, ffor to heuyn on þi harme in a hegh yre.

Hence †**hevening** [ON. *hefning*], vengeance, judgement, punishment.

1303 R. Brunne *Handl. Synne* 9763 But God, that forȝeteth noþyng, He sente þarfore grete heuenyng.

heven, -in, -yn, obs. ff. HEAVE *v.*, HAVEN, HEAVEN.

hevese, obs. f. EAVES.

hevi, -vy, obs. ff. HEAVY.

hevid, -od, obs. ff. HEAD *sb.*[1]

hevior, var. of HAVIER, gelded deer.

hew (hjuː), *v.* Pa. t. **hewed** (hjuːd); pa. pple. **hewn** (hjuːn), **hewed**. Forms: 1 **héawan**, 3 **hæuwen**, 3-5 **hewen**, (5 **-yn**), 3-6 **hewe**, (6-7 **heaw**), 4- **hew**. *Pa. t.* and *pple.*: see below. [A Com. Teut. vb.; originally reduplicated. OE. *héawan* = OFris. *hawa, howa*, OS. *hauuan, hauwan* (MLG. *houwen, howen, hoggen*, MDu. *hauwen, houwen*, Du. *houwen*); OHG. *houwan* (MHG. *houwen*, Ger. *hauen*), ON. *hǫggva* (Sw. *hugga*, Da. *hugge*), Goth. **haggwan* (not recorded); Pa. t., OE. *héow*, pl. *héowon* = OS. *heu*, pl. *heuwun* (MDu. *hieu(w)*, *(hau)*, *houwen*), OHG. *hio, hiu*, pl. *hiowun, hiuwen* (MHG. *hiu, hie*, pl. *hiuwen, hiewen*, Ger. *hieb, -en*), ON. *hjó*, pl. *hjoggum*; Pa. pple., OE. *(ȝe)héawen* = OS. *gihouwan* (MDu. *gehouwen*), OHG. *gihouwan* (MHG. *gehouwen*, Ger. *gehauen*), ON. *högg(v)inn*; OTeut. type **hauw-*, pa. t. *hehau-*, pple. *hauwan-*:—pre-Teut. **kou-*, **kow-*: cf. OSlav. *kovą, kovati*, to forge, Lith. *káuju* (*káuti*) to strike, forge, *kovà* battle. The original reduplicated pret. appeared in OE. as *héow*. In ME., this fell together with the pres. stem *héaw-*, under the form *hew*. But a weak pa. t. *hewede* appeared in the 14th c., and by 1500 superseded the strong form. A weak pa. pple. *hewed* also occurs from the 14th c., but has never been so common as the strong *hewen, hewn*. (The weak pa. t. and pple. found in MHG., MLG., and MDu. are from the parallel weak vb. OHG. *houwôn*: some refer the weak tenses in Eng. to a wk. OE. **heawian*.) Derivatives from the same root are HAG *v.*[1], HAG *sb.*[3], *sb.*[4], HAY *sb.*[1]]

A. Illustration of Forms of Pa. t. and Pa. pple.

1. *Pa. t.* **a.** *strong.* 1-3 **heow**, 3 **heuw, heou, heu**, 3-6 **hew, -e**, (4 **heew(e**, 4-5 **hewȝ, huȝ**, 5 **hue, heuch**).

a **900** *Judith* 304 Linde heowon. *c* **1205** Lay. 7480 Hardliche heo heowen. *Ibid.* 9796 Heo.. hardliche heuwen. *c* **1300** *Havelok* 2729 He grop þe swerd.. And hew on hauelok, ful god won. *a* **1330** *Otuel* 456 Eiþer huȝ on oþer faste. **1382** Wyclif *1 Sam.* xi. 7 Either oxe he hewȝ into gobetis. *c* **1400** *Destr. Troy* 7681 [He] hue hym to dethe. *c* **1420** *Anturs of Arth.* xlvi, On helmis thai heuen. **1430-40** Lydg. *Bochas* III. viii. (1554) 80 a, They his right [hand] hugh of by yᵉ wrist. **1470-85** Malory *Arthur* x. xxx, Thus they.. hewe on helmes and hawberkes.

β. weak. 4- **hewed**, (4 **heud, hewid(e**, 5-6 *Sc.* **hewit**, 6-8 **hewd**).

a **1300** *Cursor M.* 2497 (Gött.) Sua lang þai heud [*Cott.* heu, *Trin.* hew] on helm and schild. *c* **1400** *Ywaine & Gaw.* 641 (Mätz.) Al to peces thai hewed thair sheldes. *c* **1470** Henry *Wallace* v. 845 He.. Hewyt on hard with dyntis. **1535** Coverd. *Isa.* xxxviii. 12 He hewed me of. **1715** [see B. 4 c].

2. *Pa. pple.* **a.** *strong.* 1 **héawen**, 3-7 **hewen**, (3 *Orm.* **hæwenn, heuen, heun**, 4 **hewun, hewe**, 6 **heawen, hewin**, 6-7 **-yn**, 7 **hewghen**); 7- **hewn**.

c **1200** Ormin [see B. 4 b]. *a* **1310** in Wright *Lyric P.* xxxix. 110 He hath hewe.. a burthen of brere. **13..** *Gaw. & Gr. Knt.* 210 þe grayn.. of golde hewen. **1388** Wyclif *Gen.* vi. 14 Trees hewun and planed. *a* **1533** Ld. Berners *Huon* xlvi. 153, I had rather be hewyn al to peaces. **1615** W. Lawson *Orch. & Gard.* (1626) 10 This forme which I have.. rough hewen. **1756-7** tr. *Keysler's Trav.* (1760) III. 111 An oratory hewn out of the rock. **1853** [see B. 2].

β. weak. 4- **hewed**, (4-5 **hewyt**, 5-6 *Sc.* **-it**, 6-7 **hewde**, 7 **hued**).

1340 Hampole *Pr. Consc.* 371 Lymmes.. þat er hewed fra þe body. **1382** Wyclif *Gen.* xxii. 3 Whanne he had hewid his wode. **1563**, **1634** [see B. 7].

B. Signification.

I. *intr.* **1. a.** To strike, or deal blows, with a cutting weapon.

In later use often an absolute or elliptical use of some of the special trans. senses.

c **993** *Battle of Maldon* 324 Swa he on ðam folce fyrmest eode, heow and hynde oð ðæt he on hilde ȝecranc. *c* **1205** Lay. 28031 He bigon to hewene hardliche swiðe. *c* **1300** [see A. 1 *a*]. *c* **1380** *Sir Ferumb.* 3341 Ech on oþer gan to hewen. *c* **1400** Maundev. (Roxb.) xxi. 94 Men hewez with a hacchet aboute þe fote of þe tree. **1500-20** Dunbar *Poems* lxiii. 14 Masouns, lyand vpon the land, And schip-wrichtis hewand vpone the strand. **1605** Sylvester *Du Bartas* II. iii. I. 313 Then with their swords about them keenly heaw. **1607** Rowlands *Guy, Earl Warw.* 42 Guy hews upon him with his blade. **1697** Dryden *Æneid* II. 659 He hews apace: the double bars at length Yeild to his axe. **1828** Scott *F.M. Perth* xxxiv, The front lines, hewing at each other with their long swords. **1829** Southey *Sir T. More* I. 285 He hewed among the Moors to the right and left.

b. *fig.*

c **1430** Lydg. *Chichev. & Byc.* in Dodsley *O.P.* XII. 334 For alweys atte the countre taile Theyr tunge clappith & doth hewe. **1710** Addison *Whig Exam.* No. 2 ⁋9 Hacking and hewing in Satyr. *a* **1861** T. Winthrop *John Brent* (1883) xxviii. 298, I saw a vista in new life, hewed in and took in and took up a 'claim' which I have held good. **1891** *Harper's Mag.* Aug. 451/1 How closely they hewed to the line in this respect is attested by the dying remarks of one of the men hanged.

c. *Proverb.*

c **1330** R. Brunne *Chron.* (1810) 91 þat hewis ouer his heued, þe chip falles in his ine. **1387-8** T. Usk *Test. Love* I. ix. (Skeat) l. 20 He that heweth to hie, with chippes he maie lese his sight. **1546** J. Heywood *Prov.* (1867) 67 But this prouerbe precheth to men haute or hye, Hewe not to hye, lest the chips fall in thine iye. **1597** Montgomerie *Cherrie & Slae* 183 To late I knaw, quha hewis to hie, The spail sall fall into his eie.

II. *trans.* **2.** To strike forcibly with a cutting tool; to cut with swinging strokes of a sharp instrument, as an axe or sword; to chop, hack, gash.

975 *O.E. Chron.* (Parker MS.) an. 937 Ymbe Brunnan burh bord weal clufan, heowan heaþolinde hamora lafan. *c* **993** *Battle of Maldon* 181 Ða hine heowon hæðene scealcas. *c* **1000** Ælfric *On O. & N. Test.* (Gr.) 18/22 Iohannes þa heow þæt hors mid þam spuran. *c* **1205** Lay. 30406 Togadere gunnen resen þeines riche.. heouwen heȝe helmes, scænden þa brunies. **13..** *Guy Warw.* (A.) 305 He wald anon mine heued of smite.. Oþer hewe me wiþ swerdes kene. **1450-70** *Golagros & Gaw.* 702 Helmys of hard steill thai hatterit and heuch. **1576** Fleming *Panopl. Epist.* 159 To bee hackt and hewen in the fielde with the edged weapons. **1596** Spenser *F.Q.* VI. i. 37 They hew'd their helmes, and plates asunder brake. **1784** Cowper *Tirocinium* 303 The bench.. Though mangled, hacked, and hewed, not yet destroyed. **1853** Kingsley *Hypatia* xiii, His casque and armour.. were hewn and battered by a hundred blows.

3. To cut with blows so as to shape, smooth, trim, reduce in size, or the like; to shape with cutting blows of axe, hammer and chisel, etc. Now often with extension defining the result in shape or size. ***rough hew***: see ROUGH-HEW *v.*

c **900** tr. *Bæda's Hist.* IV. xiv. [xi.] (1890) 296 Ða heowon heo þone stan, swa swyðe swa heo meahton. *c* **1205** Lay. 16969 Men þat cuðen hæuwen stane. **1398** Trevisa *Barth. De P.R.* XVII. clxii. (MS. Bodl.), Tables & bordes.. araied and hewe and planed. **1526** *Pilgr. Perf.* (1531) 142 The free mason setteth his prentyse first longe tyme to lerne to hewe stones. **1573-80** Baret *Alv.* H 413 To cut out grossely: to hew rough. **1617** Moryson *Itin.* II. 297 His successours.. should pollish the stones which he had onely rough hewed. **1678** Cudworth *Intell. Syst.* I. i. §29. 36 When a rude and Unpolish'd Stone is hewen into a beautiful Statue. **1719** De Foe *Crusoe* I. iv, If I wanted a board, I had.. to cut down a tree.. and hew it flat on either side with my axe. **1825** J. Nicholson *Operat. Mechanic* 104 The breast is dressed smooth, and hewn to an exact arch of a circle. **1850** Prescott *Peru* II. 145 The mountain was hewn into steps. **1851** *Illustr. Catal. Gt. Exhib.* 964 On account of the great size.. they had to be hewn down considerably before they could be sawed. *Mod.* Masons hewing stones for the building.

4. a. To cut with an axe or the like so as to throw or bring down; to fell or cut wood either for destruction or use; to cut coal from the seam.

c **1000** *Laws of Ælfred* c. 12 (Schmid) Gif mon oðres wudu bærneð oððe heaweð unaliefedne. *a* **1310** [see A. 2 *a*]. *c* **1340** *Cursor M.* 1724 (Fairf.) Now.. sir noe.. hew þe timbre þat sulde þerto. **1388** Wyclif *Josh.* ix. 21 That thei hewe trees and bere watris in to the vsis of al the multitude. **1512** *Act 4 Hen. VIII.* c. 1 §4 To cutte and to hew heth in any mannes Grounde. **1611** Bible *1 Kings* v. 6 Command thou, that they hew me Cedar trees out of Lebanon. **1794** Mrs. Radcliffe *Myst. Udolpho* xv, Even the groves of mulberry-trees had been hewn by the enemy to light fires. **1845** S. Austin *Ranke's Hist. Ref.* II. 218 The liberty of the chase, of fishing, and of hewing wood. **1865** *Hurst Johnian* VII. 418 We each took a pick and hewed a small portion [of coal]. **1893**

Neasham *N.C. Sketches* 28 Seven men hewed 86 score at 13*d*. per score.

b. *esp*. with *down, to the ground*, and the like. Also ***to hew up***, to cut up by the root.

c **1200** Ormin 9285 Illc an treo.. Shall bi þe grund beon hæwenn upp. *c* **1290** *S. Eng. Leg.* I. 245/160 And hewe a-doun þat treo. *a* **1300** *Cursor M.* 8807 Son þe tre was heun [*Gött.* heuen, *Fairf.* hewen] dun. **1413** *Pilgr. Sowle* (Caxton 1483) IV. iii. 59 A grete tre was hewen doune for to be made a beme. **1526** Tindale *Luke* iii. 9 Euery tree therfore which bringeth not forth good frute shalbe hewen doune and caste in to the fyre. **1584** Powel *Lloyd's Cambria* 221 [He] caused the woodes to be hewen downe. **1862** Stanley *Jew. Ch.* (1877) I. xv. 301 Like a common woodcutter, he hewed down a bough, and threw it over his shoulder.

c. To cut *down* or bring *to the ground*, etc. (a man or beast) with blows of the sword or battleaxe; to slay with cutting blows.

c **1400** *Song Roland* 274, I shall bet hys men and hew hym to ground. *Ibid.* 748 He hewethe doun hethyn men full many. **1640** tr. *Verdere's Romant of Rom.* III. 214 The Gyants..cut and hewed down all before them. **1715–20** Pope *Iliad* VI. 10 And hewd the enormous giant to the ground. **1724** R. Falconer *Voy.* (1769) 25 You must..hew them [wild Hogs] down with your Cutlasses. **1847** Mrs. A. Kerr *Hist. Servia* 176 The defenders fled into the streets, where they were hewn down by the swords of their enemies.

5. To sever (a part from the whole) by a cutting blow; now with *away, off, out, from*, or similar extension.

c **1000** *Ags. Gosp.* Matt. xxi. 8 Sume heowun þæra treowa boȝas and strewodun on þone weȝ. *c* **1320** *Seuyn Sag.* (W.) 592 The gardiner..Hew awai the bough. **1340** [see A. 2 β]. *a* **1400–50** *Alexander* 3433 þan bad he bernes þaim to bynd ..& hewe of þaire hedis. *c* **1489** Caxton *Blanchardyn* xliii. 165 He smote & hewe bothe legges & armes from the bodyes. **1589** Warner *Alb. Eng.* v. xxvii. (1612) 137 Many Spurres hewen off the heeles. **1615** Crooke *Body of Man* 410 Hewen out of the deepe quarries. **1849** Freeman *Archit.* I. I. v. 91 The fragment of rock left when the rest is hewn away. **1855** Kingsley *Heroes, Theseus* II. 226 The man who..hews off their hands and feet.

fig. *c* **1440** *York Myst.* xxx. 209 þis harlott þat has hewed owre hartis fro oure brestis. **1526** Tindale *Rom.* xi. 22 Els thou shalt be hewen of.

6. a. To divide with cutting blows; to chop into pieces. *Obs.* exc. as in b.

1382 Wyclif *Job* xl. 25 Frendis shul hewen [*Vulg.* concident; **1388** kerue] hym, marchaundis shul deuyden hym? **1390** Gower *Conf.* II. 263 She..hew the flesshe, as doth a coke. *c* **1430** *Two Cookery-bks.* 6 Pyke owt þe bonys, an þan hewe it, an grynd it smal in a morter. **1483** Caxton *Gold. Leg.* 160 a/2 They hewe the cordes of the shyppe and anone the shyppe began to breke by the force of the see.

b. *esp.* with *asunder, in* or *to pieces, small*, or other extension, expressing the resulting state.

13.. *Coer de L.* 1305 The Duke Renaud was hewe smale Al to pesys. **1382** Wyclif *1 Sam.* xv. 33 Samuel hewide hym into gobbetis before the Lord. *c* **1400** Maundev. (Roxb.) xxxiv. 153 þe prestez..hewez þe body all in smale pecez. *c* **1400** *Melayne* 1332, I sall, by myghtfull god,..Hewe thi bakke in twoo. *c* **1470** Henry *Wallace* III. 391 Harnes and hedis he hew in sonderys fast. **1568** Grafton *Chron.* II. 339 They cut of his armes and legges, and then hewed his body all to peeces. **1611** Bible *1 Sam.* xi. 7 He tooke a yoke of oxen and hewed them in pieces. *a* **1661** Fuller *Worthies, Essex* (1840) I. 528 Thomas Barret..was from thense hayled forth, and lamentably hewyn a-pieces. **1773–83** Hoole *Orl. Fur.* xv. (R.), Him in a hundred parts Astolpho hews. **1841** James *Brigand* iv, They think that we are hewed into mince-meat.

7. To make, form, or produce by hewing (with obj. expressing the product).

to hew one's way, to make a way for oneself by hewing down obstacles. ***to hew out***, to excavate a hollow passage, etc. by hewing.

a **1100** *Gerefa* in *Anglia* IX. 262 Wingeard settan, dician, deorheȝe heawan. *a* **1300** *Cursor M.* 6643 (Cott.) 'Heu þe suilk tables', he said 'Als i þe forwit had puruaid'. **1377** Langl. *P. Pl.* B. xvii. 244 Ac hew fyre at a flynte. **1382** Wyclif *Isa.* xxii. 16 Thou heewe out to thee heer a sepulchre. **1481** Caxton *Reynard* (Arb.) 11 Theron was hewen in grete letters in this wyse [etc.]. **1563** *Homilies* II. *Agst. Per. Idol.* III. (1640) 46 Carved, graven, hewde or otherwise formed. **1634** Sir T. Herbert *Trav.* 25 Their Canoes or Boats are hued out of one tree. **1697** Dryden *Æneid* IX. 433 While I..hew a passage through the sleeping foe. **1705** Addison *Italy* Wks. 1811 II. 179 A long valley that seems hewn out on purpose to give its waters a passage. **1860** Tyndall *Glac.* I. xi. 78, I hewed sixty steps upon this slope. **1871** L. Stephen *Playgr. Eur.* xiii. (1894) 328 The ingenious natives have hewed a tunnel into the ice.

fig. **1586** T. B. *La Primaud. Fr. Acad.* I. Ep. Ded., This Platonical Academie and schoole of moral philosophy.. hewen out of the choicest timber of all countries. **1648** *Eikon Bas.* xiii. (1687) 674 Nor is it so proper to hew out religious Reformations by the Sword. **1822** R. G. Wallace *15 Yrs. India* 78 He determined to hew a way for himself to distinction through the ranks.

†**8.** Of a horse or man: To strike (one foot against the other): cf. cut *v.* 27. *Obs.* or *dial.*

1607 Topsell *Four-f. Beasts* (1658) 319 When a horse trots so narrow that he hews one leg upon another. **1617** Markham *Caval.* III. 74 You may make him ouerreach, or hew one foote ouer another. **1639** T. de Grey *Compl. Horsem.* 177 By hewing one legge against the other. **1828** *Craven Dial.*, *Hew*, to knock one ancle against another.

Hence **hewed** *ppl. a.*, cut or hacked; hewn or dressed, as stone; also (*U.S.*) ***hewed-log*** in attrib. use; **hewing** *ppl. a.*, that hews.

1551 Bible *1 Kings* vi. 36 (R.) Wyth thre rowes of hewed stone. *c* **1570** Turberv. *To Rayling Route Sycoph.* (R.), To yeelde his hewed head to bloes. **1576–1600** Edwardes *Paradise Dainty Devices* in *Brit. Bibl.* (1812) III. 19 Hewing axe yᵉ oke doth waste. **1632** Sherwood, Hewed or hewen, *haché*. **1793** in L. Collins *Hist. Sk. Kentucky* (1847) 517 Every purchaser or purchasers of lotts..shall build thereon a hued log house, with a brick or stone chimney. **1805** D. McClure *Diary* (1899) 14 There was a small church made of hewed logs. **1843** *Amer. Pioneer* II. 148 Two small hewed-log houses had been erected, and several cabins. **1849** *President's Mess. Congress* II. 1089 One hewed-log dwelling,..comfortably furnished cost $351. **1883** E. Eggleston *Hoosier School-boy* xvi. 106 There's the old hewed-log house..where we used to live.

†**hew**, *sb. Obs.* [f. hew *v.*] An act of hewing; a swinging stroke with an axe or other sharp-edged instrument; hacking, slaughter; a cut or gash produced by hewing.

1596 Spenser *F.Q.* VI. viii. 49 Of whom he makes such hauocke and such hew, That swarmes of damned soules to hell he sends. **1599** A. M. tr. *Gabelhouer's Bk. Physicke* Contents, All manner of woundes..ether through hewes or thrustes, throughe shottes, or falles. **1618** J. Taylor (Water P.) *Merry-Wherry-Ferry Voy.* Wks. (1872) 32 And if that King did strike so many blows, As hacks and hews upon one pillar shows.

hew, obs. form of ewe, hue, yew.

c **1475** *Pict. Voc.* in Wr.-Wülcker 758 *Hec verbica*, a hew ..*Hec erna*, a hewlambe.

hewable ('hjuːəb(ə)l), *a. rare.* [f. hew *v.* + -able.] Capable of being hewn.

1863 A. C. Ramsay *Phys. Geog.* 139 Building stones..of a hewable kind. *Ibid.* iv. (1878) 46 Quartz-rock, which is no longer hewable, like ordinary sandstone.

hewar, var. huer, *Obs*.

hewch, obs. f. heugh.

†**hewe.** *Obs.* Also 1 *pl.* **hiwan**, 2 *pl.* **hiwun**, 2–3 **heowe**, 4 **hewen**. [OE. *híwan* pl. (of **híwa*), members of a household, domestics, ME. *hiwen, heowen, hewen, heowes* and *hewes* pl.; also (later) *hewe* sing. = ON. *hjú, hjún*, OHG. *hîwun, hîun*, man and wife, members of the household, domestics, MDu. *huwen* domestics (OHG. sing. *hîwo* husband, *hîwa* wife); deriv. of *hîw-*, Goth. *heiwa-* household (in *heiwafrauja*, Mk. xiv. 14, οἰκοδεσπότης, master of the household, 'good-man of the house'. Cf. hewen, hide *sb.*², hind *sb.*², hird).

The Teut. *hiwa-* is thought by some to be coradicate with L. *civis* citizen.]

A domestic, a servant.

a **1000** *O.E. Chron.* (Laud MS.) an. 757 Hine of sloȝon his hiwan. *c* **1000** *Ags. Gosp.* Mark v. 19 Ga to þinum huse to þinum hiwum [*c* **1160** *Hatton G.* heowen]. *a* **1175** *Cott. Hom.* 225 Ga inn seðen mid þine hiwun. *a* **1310** in Wright *Lyric P.* xlii. 114 Mury hit ys in hyre tour, wyth hatheles ant wyth heowes. **1377** Langl. *P. Pl.* B. v. 559 He ne with-halt non hewe [A. vi. 42 non hyne] his hire þat he ne hath it at euen. *Ibid.* xiv. 3, I have an houswyf hewen and children. *c* **1386** Chaucer *Merch. T.* 541 O seruaunt tray-tour, false hoomly hewe. **1390** Gower *Conf.* I. 173 This fals envious hewe..torneth preising into blame.

hewe, obs. f. heave *v.*; erron. f. hove *v.*

hewel, -ell: see hickwall.

†**hewen.** *Obs.* In 1 **híwen**, 3 **hewenn**. [OE. *híwen* neut., deriv. of *híw-* family: see hewe.] Family, household.

c **1000** Ælfric *Gen.* xlii. 33 Nimað þa þing þe eowre hiwenu beþurfon. *c* **1200** Ormin 594. *Ibid.* 608 þatt hird wass i þatt time ȝehatenn Ytamaress hus, and Ytamaress hewenn.

hewer ('hjuːə(r)). [f. hew *v.* + -er¹.] One who hews. **a.** One who cuts wood or stone; *spec.* one who shapes and dresses stone for building. Cf. hardhewer. **b.** In *Lumbering*, 'One who uses a heavy broad-ax in squaring timber' (*Cent. Dict.*).

1382 Wyclif *1 Esdras* iii. 7 Thei ȝeue money to heweris of stonus, and to leieris. *c* **1440** *Promp. Parv.* 238/2 Hewar, *secator.* **1530** Palsgr. 231/1 Hewer of stones, *tailleur de pierres.* **1671** H. M. tr. *Colloq. Erasmus* 298 The hewers down of timber. **1789** Burns *To Capt. Riddel*, Our friends the Reviewers, those chippers and hewers. **1891** *Labour Commission* Gloss., *Hewers*, those who follow that branch of the masonry trade which consists in the cutting or dressing of the stone previous to its being placed on the walls.

c. In a colliery, the man who cuts the coal from the seam.

1708 J. C. *Compl. Collier* (1845) 35 To agree with your Hewers of Coals or Miners, by the Score of Corves. **1867** in W. W. Smyth *Coal & Coal-mining* 232 The hewer that keeps his safety lamp in the best order. **1885** *Law Times* LXXIX. 176/1 The plaintiff..a coal hewer or miner.

d. ***hewers of wood and drawers of water***: labourers of the lowest kind; drudges. (From *Joshua* ix. 21.)

[*c* **1000** Ælfric *Deut.* xxix. 11 Buton wuduheawerum and þam þe wæter beraþ. **1382** Wyclif *Deut.* xxix. 11 Out taak the hewers of trees, and hem that beren watris.] **1535** Coverdale *Josh.* ix. 21 Let them lyue, that they maye be hewers of wodd and bearers of water for the whole congregacion. **1755** *Man* No. 25. 2 Even hewers of wood and drawers of water are men in a lower degree. **1840** Dickens *Barn. Rudge* xxvi, Being but a hewer of wood and drawer of water, she is rheumatic.

hewer, variant of huer; obs. f. ewer².

? **1461** in *P. Lett.* No. 429 II. 75, ij. basanes and ij. hewers.

hewettite ('hjuːɪtaɪt). *Min.* [f. the name of Donnel Foster *Hewett* (1881–1971), American geologist: see -ite¹.] A deep red hydrated calcium vanadate, $CaV_6O_{16}\cdot 9H_2O$, occuring in nodules and as the coating of fibres or needles (see also quot. 1955).

1914 W. F. Hillebrand et al. in *Proc. Amer. Philos. Soc.* LIII. 31 The Peruvian mineral..we are pleased to name hewettite, after Mr. D. Foster Hewett, now of the U.S. Geological Survey, who has done so much to make the Minasragra occurrence known. **1955** *Amer. Mineralogist* XL. 691 There appear to be three types of material variously labelled 'hewettite' or 'metahewettite', namely, (I) hewettite, $CaO\cdot 3V_2O_5\cdot nH_2O$.., which exists in at least three hydrate forms,..(II) the unnamed sodium analogue of hewettite in the trihydrate form,..and (III) the material,.. possibly a mixed sodium-calcium variety of the sodium analogue, represented by specimen 4.

hewgag ('hjuːgæg). *U.S.* [Of uncertain origin.

It has been suggested that it is 'prob. based on *gewgaw*, a jew's harp'.]

A toy musical instrument for children, consisting of a wooden tube with a hole near one end, and the other closed by a piece of parchment, the vibration of which produces a wailing sound. (Humorously referred to as a sound of jubilation.)

1850 *California Courier* (San Francisco) 6 Sept. 2/3 Beat the hong-gong; sound the hew-gag! **1855** *Vermont Free Press* 8 June (Th.), The T.I.N. Horn-et Band, with Sackbut, Psaltery, Dulcimer,..and Hugag, marched next. **1858** S. Bowles in Merriam *Life* (1885) I. 295 To-day Hanscombe sends a letter 'all about it', setting it out with the accompanying 'sound of hew-gag'. **1889** *Voice* (N.Y.) 21 Nov., When a leading paper..sounds the hewgag, other papers..take up the cry, and repeat it. **1905** B. Tarkington *In Arena* 152 He had *all* the honours..; professors and students all kow-towed and sounded the hew-gag before him.

hewgh, *int.* An imitation of the sound of whistling; = heugh, whew.

1605 Shaks. *Lear* IV. vi. 93 O well flowne Bird: i' th' clout, i' th' clout: Hewgh. Giue the word.

hewhall, hew-hole: see hickwall.

hewin, obs. form of heaven *sb.*

hewing (hjuːɪŋ), *vbl. sb.* [f. hew *v.* + -ing¹.] The action of the verb hew, in various senses.

c **1440** *Promp. Parv.* 239/1 Hewynge (or hakkynge), *seccio*. **1497** *Naval Acc. Hen. VII* (1896) 324 For hewyng & sawyng of an Ankere Stoke—viijd. **1573** in Willis & Clark *Cambridge* (1886) I. 174 Item for hewing, marking, felling..and carriage. **1639** T. de Grey *Compl. Horseman* 41 How cometh the farcin..by enter-firing, and hewing, and lastly by spur-galling. **1670** Eachard *Cont. Clergy* 67 He falls to hacking and hewing, as if he would make all fly into shivers. **1863** Mary Howitt *F. Bremer's Greece* II. xii. 30 Blocks of marble in progress of hewing.

b. *Comb.*, as ***hewing-knife, -pick, -stone***, etc.

1404 *Durham MS. Sacr. Roll*, j hewyng knyffe. **1611** Cotgr., *Marteline*, a small hewing picke. **1854** H. Miller *Sch. & Schm.* (1858) 269 [He] brought his hewing stone.. from one of the quarries of Moray.

hewk(e, var. huke *Obs.*, a cloak.

hewles, obs. f. hueless.

hewmat, -met, -mond, -mont, obs. Sc. ff. helmet.

hewn (hjuːn), *ppl. a.* [pa. pple. of hew *v.*]

1. Fashioned by hewing with a chisel, axe, or other tool; made by or resulting from hewing.

13.. *Gaw. & Gr. Knt.* 789 Harde hewen ston. **1600** J. Pory tr. *Leo's Africa* II. 168 Made of smoothe and hewen stones. **1713** Berkeley *Guardian* No. 70 ¶2 Small inequalities in the surface of the hewn stone. **1854** Ronalds & Richardson *Chem. Technol.* (ed. 2) I. 63 The hewn logs are arranged with their sharp edges towards the stake. *a* **1856** H. Miller *Cruise Betsey* x. (1858) 165 Having seen similar markings on the hewn-work of ancient castles. **1864** Pusey *Lect. Daniel* viii. 485 From the hewn stump, which has vitality, a strong tree will shoot forth. **1869** 'Mark Twain' *Innoc. Abr.* xix. 196 A massive hewn-stone affair.

2. Excavated or hollowed out by hewing.

1382 Wyclif *Luke* xxiii. 53 He..puttide him in a graue hewun. **1526** Tindale *Ibid.*, He..layed it in an heawen toumbe.

†'**hewster**¹. *Obs.* [f. hew *v.* + -ster.] One who hews or hacks.

1587 Turberv. *Trag. T.* VIII. (1837) 214 Those hewsters drave the horses back.

†'**hewster**². *Obs.* [f. *hew*, hue *sb.*¹ + -ster.] A colourer, a dyer.

1600 *Chester Pl., Banes* (E.E.T.S.) 8 And then you, diers and hewsters, Antechrist bringe out.

†**hewt.** *Obs.* [prob.:—OE. *hiewet* hewing, cutting (*Gregory's Past.* xxxvi. 253), and thus corresponding in sense to OF. *copeiz*, copse.]

? A copse; a grove.

1575 Turberv. *Venerie* 75 He muste take good heede that he come not too earely into the springs and hewtes where he thinketh that the harte doth feed. [So **1677** in N. Cox *Gentl. Recreat.* 71; **1725** Bradley *Fam. Dict.* s.v. *Hart.*] *Ibid.* 82 Now the huntsman should go to seeke an harte in small groues or hewts. **1583** Stanyhurst *Æneis* II. (Arb.) 66 A tumb to Troytowne and mouldy tempil anceereth Vowd to

the godly Ceres; a ciper by the churche seat abydeth.. From diuerse corners to that hewt wee wyl make asemblye. **1616** BULLOKAR, *Hewte*, a little copse or groue. **1688** R. HOLME *Armoury* II. 188/1 Hewts, or Springs [are] the places where the Deer feeds; taken for the small Groves or Copyes; and the Springs the greater Groves.

hewy, obs. Sc. f. HEAVY.

hewyd, obs. f. HUED.

hewyn, obs. form of EVEN *sb.*

c **1475** *Pict. Voc.* in Wr.-Wülcker 801/14 *Hic esperes*, hewynsterre. *Ibid.* 42 *Hoc crepusculum*.. a hewyntyde. *Ibid.* 44 *Hoc vesperum*, a hewynsongtyde.

hewyn, -yne, -ynn, obs. forms of HEAVEN.

hex (hɛks), *v.* Chiefly *U.S.* [ad. Pennsylvanian G. *hexe*, f. G. *hexen.*] *intr.* To practise witchcraft. Also *trans.*, to bewitch, to cast a spell on.

1830 J. F. WATSON *Ann. Philad.* 232 A decent storekeeper once got him to hex for his wife, who had conceited that an old Mrs. Wiggand had bewitched her, and made her to swallow a piece of linseywoolsey. **1932** B. A. DE VOTO *Mark Twain's Amer.* iii. 74 The cat is hexen: it is approved by Mother Hawkins, a witch. **1935** *Language* XI. 147 Belief in witchcraft is fast disappearing and with it the word [hɛks] *to bewitch* or *a witch* or *wizard*. A countryman may still say: *My pigs are hext.* **1956** H. GOLD *Man who was not with it* (1965) xi. 97, I stood hexing the cars on Route One.

hex (hɛks), *sb.*[1] Chiefly *U.S.* Also **hexe**. [Pennsylvanian G., ad. G. *hexe*. Cf. HAG *sb.*[1]]

1. A witch. Also *transf.*, a witch-like female.

1856 G. HENDERSON *Pop. Rhymes* 43 'An old hexe', means an old witch, and is often applied, in a bad sense, to females of the present day. **1920** S. LEWIS *Main Street* xiii. 159, I couldn't talk to you without twenty old hexes watching, whispering. **1928** *Daily Express* 10 Dec. 11/1 York County's early settlers were Germans, and their present-day descendants still remain under the spell of medieval German necromancy. One of their sacred words is 'hex', said to be corrupt German for witch. **1935** *Amer. Speech* X. 170/1 *Hex*, a witch.. the *hex* trial at Lancaster.

2. A magic spell or curse.

1909 *Sat. Even. Post* 16 Jan. 7/1 'Old pal', agreed J. Rufus, 'the hex is sure on me'. **1942** D. POWELL *Time to be Born* (1943) xiii. 326 She could count on winning him... Unless Julian really could put a hex on her. **1951** M. LOWRY *Let.* Apr. or May (1967) 234 Everything from how to put the hex on your more troublesome pupils [etc.]. **1952** M. MCCARTHY *Groves of Academe* (1953) xii. 237 She hoped.. that the hex signs on the neighbouring barns would serve to ward off all evil influences from the vicinity and not, as the ignorant sometimes thought, to attract them or indicate their presence. **1958** *Times* 4 Oct. 8/7 If Ladan stayed Shehu would gather up his robes and depart, leaving a hex on us all. **1966** *Punch* 30 Mar. 458/3 'What?' says the young man, picking it up gingerly and nervously, half afraid she's put a hex on it. **1968** *Word Study* Oct. 6/1 Each of us carries around a set of shibboleths.. with.. totemic reverence..; meanwhile we trample blithely on spells and hexes we have never heard of.

hex (hɛks), *sb.*[2] Abbrev. of 'uranium hexafluoride'.

1956 S. GLASSTONE *Princ. Nuclear Reactor Engin.* viii. 449 For use in nuclear energy work, uranium is generally required either in the form of uranium metal, for fabrication into fuel elements, or as hexafluoride ('hex') to constitute the feed for the separation of the isotopes by the gaseous-diffusion method. **1964** M. GOWING *Britain & Atomic Energy* ii. 63 Secrecy in the project now and later was aided by the elaborate code systems used. These were different in different groups... Hexafluoride was known variously as 'VI', 'hex' and 'the working gas'. **1971** *New Scientist* 16 Sept. 617/2 Uranium hexafluoride ('hex' for short) is pumped through a cascade of.. thousands of membranes.

hex- (hɛks), Gr. ἕξ six, not used in comb. in Greek, exc. as standing for ἑξα- HEXA- before a vowel, but used as a combining element in modern formations, chiefly in *Chem.* (where HEXA- is more regular), in sense 'containing six atoms or molecules of the radical or substance'; as ***hexbenzoate***, ***hexbromide***, ***hexdecyl*** (= HEXADECYL), ***hexfluoride***, ***hexhydric*** adj. (containing six hydroxyl molecules).

1873 *Fownes' Chem.* (ed. 11) 500 Chromium forms a hexfluoride. *Ibid.* 561 A crystalline mass, consisting of quintone hexbromide. *Ibid.* 629 With benzoic acid, it forms a dibenzoate and hexbenzoate. *Ibid.* 803 Quinone treated with chlorine yields, as final product, hexchlorobenzene. **1877** *Ibid.* (ed. 12) II. 160 Hexdecyl or Cetyl Alcohol. **1878** KINGZETT *Anim. Chem.* 402 Hexhydric alcohol of the general formula $C_nH_{2n-4}(OH)_6$.

hexa- (hɛksə), before a vowel *hex-*, combining form of Gr. ἕξ six, freely used in Greek, and forming the initial element in various modern technical words, some adopted from Greek, others formed from Greek elements or on Greek analogies. In *Chem.* it indicates the presence of six atoms of some element, as in *hexacarbon*, *hexacompound* (see below), *hexabromide*, *hexachloride*, etc. **hexabasic** (-ˈbeɪsɪk) *a. Chem.*, having six atoms of a base, or of replaceable hydrogen; **ˈhexacanth**, **hexaˈcanthous** *adjs. Biol.* [Gr. ἄκανθα thorn], having six spines, rays, or hooks; **hexaˈcapsular** *a. Bot.*, having six capsules; **hexaˈcarbon** *a. Chem.*, containing six atoms of carbon: cf. HEXANE; ‖ **hexace** (ˈhɛksəsiː) *Cryst.* [Gr. ἀκή point], the summit of a polyhedron formed by the concurrence of six faces; **hexaceto-** *Chem.*, in combination, containing six molecules of acetic acid or acetyl; **ˌhexachlor(o)ˈbenzene**, C_6Cl_6, an agricultural fungicide used as a seed-dressing; **ˌhexachlor(o)cycloˈhexane** = *benzene hexachloride*; **ˌhexachlor(o)ˈethane** (-klɔərəʊˈiːθeɪn, -klɔərˈiːθeɪn), a toxic crystalline compound, $Cl_3C{\cdot}CCl_3$, having uses as an insecticide and anthelmintic and as an ingredient in smoke-producing mixtures; **hexaˈchlorophane, -phene**, a diphenylmethane derivative, $CH_2(C_6HCl_3OH)_2$, a white crystalline powder used as a disinfectant, esp. for the skin; **hexachætous** (hɛksəˈkiːtəs) *a. Entom.* [Gr. χαίτη long loose flowing hair], pertaining to the *Hexachætæ*, a division of the brachycerous Diptera, containing those two-winged flies which have a proboscis composed of six pieces; **heˈxachronous** *a. Pros.* [Gr. χρόνος time], consisting of six moræ; hexasemic; **hexaˈcolic** *a. Pros.* [Gr. κῶλον COLON[2]], consisting of six cola; **hexa-compound**, a chemical compound of the hexacarbon series: see HEXANE; **hexacoˈrallan, -ˈcoralline** *Zool. a.* [CORAL], pertaining to the *Hexacoralla*, a chief division of the *Coralligena* or corals in which the fundamental number of intermesenteric chambers of the body cavity and of the tentacles is six; *sb.*, one of these corals; **ˈhexact** *a.* and *sb.* = *hexactine*; **heˈxactinal, -acˈtinal** *a.* = *hexactine* adj.; **heˈxactine** *a. Zool.* [Gr. ἀκτίς, ἀκτῖν-ος ray], having six rays, as a sponge-spicule; also as *sb.*, a sponge-spicule having six rays; **hexactiˈnellidan** *a. Zool.* = HEXACTINELLID *a.*; **hexacˈtinian** *a. Zool.* [as prec.], pertaining to the *Hexactiniæ*, a group of *Actiniaria* having septa in pairs, in number six or a multiple of six; **hexaˈcyclic** *a. Bot.* [Gr. κύκλος circle], applied to flowers having six divisions of the floral cycle; **hexadacˈtylic** *a.*, **hexaˈdactylous** *a. Anat.* [Gr. δάκτυλ-ος finger, toe], having six fingers or six toes; so **hexaˈdactylism**, hexadactylous condition; **hexaˈdecanol** = *cetyl alcohol*; **ˌhexadeceˈnoic acid**, an unsaturated fatty acid, $C_{16}H_{30}O_2$, occurring naturally in several isomeric forms one of which is widespread in many animal and vegetable fats and oils; it has also been known as *palmitoleic*, *physetoleic*, and *zoomaric acid*; **ˈhexadrachm** *Numism.* [DRACHM], a coin of the value of six drachmas; **hexaˈethyl tetraˈphosphate** (hɛksəˈɛθɪl), a viscous brownish liquid capable of irreversibly inhibiting mammalian cholinesterase; orig. used to designate an insecticide later found to be a mixture of organic phosphates containing tetraethyl pyrophosphate as the chief active ingredient; **ˈhexafoil** [FOIL *sb.*[1]], a pattern having six leaf-like divisions or lobes; **ˈhexaglot** *a.* [Gr. γλῶττα tongue], written or composed in six languages; **hexaˈhydrate**, a hydrate that contains six molecules of water; so **hexahyˈdrated** *a.*; **hexaˈhydric** *a.*, containing six hydroxyl groups in a molecule; **hexa-ˈicosane** *Chem.*, one of the higher paraffins, $C_{26}H_{54}$; **heˈxaldehyde** *Chem.* = CAPROIC or HEXYL *aldehyde*, $C_6H_{12}O$; **heˈxalogy** [see -LOGY], a treatise on six subjects; **ˈhexamer** *Chem.* [-MER], a polymeric unit or molecule made up of six monomers; **hexaˈmeric** *a. Chem.*, consisting of a hexamer; **heˈxamerous** *a. Biol.* [Gr. μέρος part], having members in groups of six, or multiples of six; hence **heˈxamerism**; **ˌhexametaˈphosphate**, a phosphate regarded as being a salt of hexametaphosphoric acid, $(HPO_3)_6$; used loosely to designate a glassy, water-soluble sodium salt (also known as Graham's salt) having an approximate empirical formula $Na_2O{\cdot}P_2O_5$ and used industrially to soften water; **hexameˈthonium**, a quaternary ammonium ion, $[(CH_3)_3N(CH_2)_6N(CH_3)_3]^{++}$; also, any of the salts of this ion, some of which have been used as ganglionic blocking drugs in the treatment of severe hypertension; **hexaˈmethylene**, cyclohexane; **hexamethylenediamine** (-daɪˈæmiːn), a white crystalline solid, $H_2N(CH_2)_6NH_2$, used in the manufacture of nylon; **hexaˌmethyleneˈtetramine**, a colourless crystalline compound, $(CH_2)_6N_4$, having various industrial uses, esp. in the manufacture of phenol-formaldehyde resins and in many antiseptic preparations; **ˈhexamine** = *hexamethylenetetramine*; **hexaˈnemous** *a. Zool.* [Gr. νῆμα thread], having six threads (see quot.); **hexaˈpartite** *a.* [L. *partītus* divided], divided into six parts; **hexaˈpetaloid** *a. Bot.* [see PETAL *sb.* and -OID], having six divisions which have the appearance of petals; so **hexapetaˈloideous** *a.* (see quots.); **hexaˈpetalous** *a. Bot.* [PETAL], having six petals; **hexaˈphyllous** *a. Bot.* [Gr. φύλλον leaf], applied to a calyx having six sepals or to a leaf consisting of six leaflets; **hexaˈprostyle** *a. Arch.* [PROSTYLE], having a portico of six columns in front: cf. HEXASTYLE; **heˈxapterous** *a.* [Gr. πτερόν wing], provided with six wings or wing-like appendages; **ˈhexaptote** [Gr. πτωτός, from πτῶσις case], 'a noun declined with six cases' (Phillips 1658); **ˈhexarch** *a. Bot.*, having six rays, formed from six points of origin, as in some vascular bundles; **ˈhexarchy** [Gr. -αρχία rule], a group of six states; **hexasemic** (-ˈsiːmɪk) *a. Pros.* [Gr. ἑξάσημος], containing six units of time or moræ; **hexaˈsepalous** *a. Bot.* [SEPAL], having six sepals; **ˈhexasome** *Biol.*, a set of six homologous chromosomes; so **hexaˈsomic** *a.*, having six of one or more chromosomes in a nucleus that is not hexaploid; **hexaˈspermous** *a. Bot.* [Gr. σπέρμα seed], six-seeded (Mayne *Expos. Lex.* 1854); **hexaˈstemonous** *a. Bot.* [Gr. στήμων stamen], having six stamens (Mayne); **hexaster** (-ˈæstə(r)) *Zool.* [Gr. ἀστήρ star], in sponges, a star or stellate spicule with six (usually equal) rays; **hexasterophorous** (-æstəˈrɒfərəs) *a. Zool.* [Gr. -φορος bearing], provided with hexasters, as the tribe *Hexasterophora* of silicious sponges; **heˈxastichous** *a. Bot.* [cf. HEXASTICH], arranged in six rows (Mayne 1854); **hexastigm** [Gr. στίγμα prick, mark], a figure determined by six points: cf. HEXAGRAM; **hexasyˈllabic** *a.* [Gr. ἑξασύλλαβος: see SYLLABIC], consisting of six syllables; **hexatetraˈhedron** = HEXAKISTETRAHEDRON.

1878 KINGZETT *Anim. Chem.* 101 Stadeler.. constructed upon them the theory of bilirubin as a *hexabasic acid. **1880** *W. A. Miller's Elem. Chem.* III. i. (ed. 6) 300 The *hexabromide $C_6H_6Br_6$ can readily be obtained. **1870** ROLLESTON *Anim. Life* 251 The.. *hexacanth embryo.. has become greatly distended. **1897** ALLBUTT *Syst. Med.* II. 1008 The embryo of the cestodes is provided with six hooklets (hence the term 'hexacanth'). **1854** MAYNE *Expos. Lex.*, *Hexacanthus*.. having six rays.. six-rayed: *hexacanthous. **1775** ASH, **Hexacapsular*, having six seed vessels. **1866** ODLING *Anim. Chem.* 109 *Hexacarbon compounds such as amido-caproic acid or leucine. **1886** *Syd. Soc. Lex.*, **Hexacetodextrin*, a substance obtained when starch is heated to 160° C. with acetic anhydride. **1885** I. REMSEN *Introd. Org. Chem.* 253 As the final products, *hexa-chlor-benzene, C_6Cl_6, and hexa-brom-benzene C_6Br_6 are obtained. **1961** *Lancet* 22 July 176/2 Recently, several thousand cases of human porphyria have been seen in Turkey after the consumption of wheat containing 0·1–0·2% of hexachlorobenzene. **1908** *Chem. Abstr.* II. 793 *Hexachlorcyclohexanes.—On continuing the action of chlorine in the sunlight, a viscous liquid is obtained. **1945** R. E. SLADE *Gamma Isomer of Hexachlorocyclohexane* ('*Gammexane*') 11 The hexachlorocyclohexanes possess considerable chemical stability. **1898** *Jrnl. Chem. Soc.* LXXIV. I. 626 When a current of chlorine is passed into a mixture of pentachlorethane and aluminium chloride heated at 100°, *hexachlorethane is obtained. **1936** *Discovery* Aug. 255/2 A new way of killing mosquitoes.. involves the use of hexachloroethane. **1960** *Farmer & Stockbreeder* 16 Feb. 109 (Advt.), In the Nicholas Liver Fluke Drench, hexachloroethane particles are suspended in a free-flowing liquid and this ensures *accurate* dosing. Result: greater fluke kill than ever before! **1880** CLEMINSHAW *Wurtz' Atom. The.* 233 The *hexachloride of ruthenium is unknown. **1960** *Which?* Feb. 32/2 One can attempt to prevent the sweat from decomposing by using an antiseptic, such as **hexachlorophane*. **1948** *Jrnl. Amer. Med. Assoc.* 14 Feb. 471/2 The Council [on Pharmacy and Chemistry] considered the proposal of a pharmaceutical manufacturer for the use of the term *hexachlorophene as a generic designation for *bis*(2-hydroxy-3,5,6-trichlorophenyl) methane... The Council voted to recognize hexachlorophene as the generic, or common, designation. **1953** *Jrnl. Parasitol.* XXXIX. 79 Hexachlorophene.. is effective in removing *Raillietina cesticillus* from chickens. **1866** ODLING *Anim. Chem.* 66 *Hexa-compounds, including caproic acid, leucine, and grape sugar. **1877** HUXLEY *Anat. Inv. Anim.* 165 Another tabulate coral, *Pocillopora*, is a true *Hexacorallan. **1886** R. VON LENDENFELD in *Proc. Zool. Soc.* 590 The Recent Families of Sponges... With *hexact spicules and thimble-shaped chambers. **1887** tr. F. E. Schulze in *Challenger Rep., Zool.* XXI. 29 Regular Hexacts are all spicules in which the rays lie at right angles to one another, and are of equal length and similar form. **1940** L. H. HYMAN *Invertebrates* I. vi. 327 They [*sc.* triacts] may show their origin from a hexact by the presence near the middle of knobs or branches of the axial fibre. **1887** *Encycl. Brit.* XXII. 417 Modifications of the triaxon *hexactine type. **1900** E. A. MINCHIN in E. R. Lankester *Treat. Zool.* II. iii. 117 One or more rays of the *hexactine.. may become modified in various ways. **1940** L. H. HYMAN *Invertebrates* I. vi. 327 The basic regular hexactine consists of three axes crossing at right angles, forming six rays of approximately equal length. **1887** tr. F. E. Schulze in *Challenger Rep., Zool.* XXI. 37 Certain *Hexactinellidan families have typical and regular *Uncinata*, while in others they are absent. **1877** *Athenæum* 1 Dec. 703/1 Of *hexactinian corals. **1875** BENNETT & DYER *Sachs' Bot.* 554 Polycarpæ. Flowers pentacyclic or *hexacyclic. **1880** PROCTOR *Rough Ways* 213 The descendants of four grandparents of whom one only

was *hexadactylic. **1828** WEBSTER, **Hexadactylous*, having six toes. **1914** *Jrnl. Chem. Soc.* CV. II. 2251 Acetate of *l-γ-**Hexadecanol, $C_2H_5{\cdot}CH(O{\cdot}CO{\cdot}CH_3){\cdot}C_{13}H_{27}$. **1964** *Oceanogr. & Marine Biol.* II. 177 The higher aliphatic alcohols of the wax esters [found in fish lipids] usually contain hexadecanol (cetyl alcohol) and octadec-9-enol (oleyl alcohol) as main components. **1901** *Jrnl. Chem. Soc.* LXXX. I. 252 The product was found to yield a *hexadecenoic acid, $C_{16}H_{30}O_2$, melting at 36°, when fused with potassium hydroxide. **1948** A. W. RALSTON *Fatty Acids* ii. 98 The fats of fresh water fish contain somewhat less 9-hexadecenoic acid than those of marine origin. **1807** ROBINSON *Archæol. Græca* v. xxvi. 548 Pentadrachms and *hexadrachms. **1946** *Jrnl. Econ. Ent.* XXXIX. 812/1 *Hexaethyl tetraphosphate merits considerable attention as a commercial control for numerous insects causing serious damage to agricultural and garden crops. **1951** A. W. JOHNSON et al. in E. H. Rodd *Chem. Carbon Compounds* IA. iv. 342 A mixture of phosphates, known commercially as 'hexaethyl tetraphosphate', is formed when $POCl_3$ reacts with triethyl orthophosphate or with ethanol. **1965** A. & E. F. GROLLMAN *Pharmacol. & Therapeutics* (ed. 6) xxxi. 823 Hexaethyltetraphosphate.. is highly toxic, exerting a potent anticholinesterase action. **1862** *S. Kens. Spec. Exhib.* vi. 58 A vertical central stem rising from a wide *hexafoil-shaped base. **1895** *Athenæum* 13 Apr. 480/3 A small mediæval paten .. sunk in hexafoil. **1882–3** SCHAFF *Encycl. Relig. Knowl.* III. 2299 The *hexaglot edition of the Psalter published at Rostock, 1643. **1867** W. A. MILLER *Chem.* (ed. 4) III. 325 *Hexaglyceric bromhydrin. **1908** H. C. COOPER tr. *Holleman's Text-bk. Inorg. Chem.* (ed. 3) 487 Two *hexahydrates of chromic chloride, $CrCl_3{\cdot}6H_2O$, are known. **1951** C. PALACHE et al. *Dana's Syst. Min.* (ed. 7) II. 493 [Pentahydrite is] obtained in crystals together with the hexahydrate and tetrahydrate by evaporation.. of a solution of magnesium sulfate. **1880** G. LUNGE *Sulphuric Acid* II. III. i. 277 (*heading*) *Hexahydrated salt has been obtained by Mitscherlich from a solution of Na_2S in the air. **1951** C. PALACHE et al. *Dana's Syst. Min.* (ed. 7) II. 493 The minerals of this group.. are isostructural with the monoclinic artificial hexahydrated sulfates and selenates of Mg, Co, Ni, and Zn. **1885** *Jrnl. Chem. Soc.* XLVIII. II. 1046 (*heading*) Reduction in *hexahydric alcohols. **1964** N. G. CLARK *Mod. Org. Chem.* xvi. 315 The product, sorbitol, is a hexahydric alcohol (one of the 'sugar alcohols'), which occurs naturally in many fruits. **1889** *Watts' Dict. Chem.*, **Hexa-Icosane*.. a soft waxy substance found among the products of the distillation of cerotic acid. **1880** *Miller's Elem. Chem.* III. 751 Normal primary *hexaldehyde.. obtained by the distillation of a mixture of calcic normal hexylate and calcic formate. **1881** *Athenæum* 22 Jan. 134/3 Mr Scott's *hexalogy closes with what we may call a satiric chapter on cubic determinants. **1953** R. G. R. BACON in E. H. Rodd *Chem. Carbon Compounds* IIA. xi. 403 A mixture of polymers.. was separated, by means of a molecular still, into fractions ranging from trimers to *hexamers. **1969** *Nature* 1 Nov. 493/2 The insulin hexamer.. is a compact, oblate spheroid, formed by the coordination of three insulin dimers around the two zinc ions. **1940** *Jrnl. Chem. Soc.* 1169 The trimeric, tetrameric, and pentameric portions of the polymeride have been separated from one another by molecular distillation, leaving as residue a highly viscous liquid of mainly *hexameric complexity. **1903** *Science* 17 July 80/2 In some species [of corals] the *hexamerism becomes much obscured in later stages, while in others it is more or less distinctly preserved. **1877** T. H. HUXLEY *Man. Anat. Invertebr. Animals* iii. 159 The finally *hexamerous Anthozoon passes through a tetramerous and an octomerous stage. **1905** I. B. BALFOUR tr. *Goebel's Organogr. Plants* II. 538 The first flowers of some Caryophylleae are hexamerous. **1940** L. H. HYMAN *Invertebrates* I. vii. 579 In typical hexamerous anemones, the number of pairs of septa in the various cycles is then: 6 (primaries), 6, 12, 24, 48, etc. **1891** W. RAMSAY *Syst. Inorg. Chem.* xxiii. 370 **Hexametaphosphates.*—These are the salts prepared by the usual methods from ordinary metaphosphoric acid. **1892** *Jrnl. Chem. Soc.* LXII. II. 1050 The uncrystallisable hexametaphosphates, $Na_6(PO_3)_6$ and $Ag_6(PO_3)_6$, are obtained from Graham's soluble sodium metaphosphate.., which is a mixture of the foregoing sodium salt with several other hexametaphosphates. **1963** A. J. HALL *Textile Sci.* vi. 292 Important sequestering agents.. include sodium pyrophosphate $Na_4P_2O_7$, and especially hexametaphosphate $(NaPO_3)_6$. **1949** *Jrnl. Pharmacy & Pharmacol.* I. 603 An antidote exists for decamethonium iodide in *hexamethonium iodide.. and.. this substance has been suggested for use in hypertension and vascular diseases. **1964** S. DUKE-ELDER *Parsons' Dis. Eye* (ed. 14) xxi. 300 The operation is most conveniently done under basal anæsthesia, and the systemic administration of sympatholytic drugs such as hexamethonium may be of value in relieving congestion by lowering the general blood pressure. **1887** *Abstr. Proc. Chem. Soc.* III. 96 Hitherto all attempts to synthesise *hexamethylene-derivatives have been unsuccessful. **1909** C. A. KEANE *Mod. Org. Chem.* v. 64 The six carbon atom analogue of these alicyclic compounds is hexamethylene, C_6H_{12}. **1894** *Jrnl. Chem. Soc.* LXVI. I. 410 *Hexamethylenediamine nitrite. **1896** *Ibid.* LXX. I. 464 Hexamethylenediamine, $C_6H_{12}(NH_2)_2$, melts at 40° and boils at 192–195°. **1962** J. K. STILLE *Introd. Polymer Chem.* vi. 93 Nylon 66 is formed from the reaction of adipic acid (a six-carbon dibasic acid) and hexamethylenediamine (a six-carbon diamine). **1888** *Jrnl. Chem. Soc.* LIV. 1268 A well-cooled solution of *hexamethylenetetramine. **1940** *Thorpe's Dict. Appl. Chem.* (ed. 4) IV. 27/2 The inodorous solid product, hexamethylenetetramine, $C_6H_{12}N_4$ (hexamine, urotropine), is a serviceable antiseptic in cystic affections, and is administered to typhoid 'carriers' to destroy the bacilli of the disease in the urine. **1961** *Encycl. Brit.* IX. 524/1 Nitration of hexamethylenetetramine gives the explosive, RDX. **1914** *Brit. Pharmacopœia* 171 *Hexamine may be obtained by the interaction of ammonia with formic aldehyde. **1956** LD. AMULREE in A. Pryce-Jones *New Outl. Mod. Knowl.* 222 Others have used hexamine with glucose and vitamin B_1 but this treatment, again, does not seem to be generally applicable [in cases of senile dementia]. **1854** MAYNE *Expos. Lex.*, *Hexanemus*.. Having six threads.. six-armed: *hexanemous. **1819** *Pantologia*, **Hexapetaloid corol*, in botany, divided so near to the base as to have the appearance of a six-petalled corol, but in reality one-petalled, as in agapanthus. **1845** LINDLEY *Sch. Bot.* viii. (1858) 129 Flowers hexapetaloid, irregular. **1830** —— *Nat. Syst. Bot.* 252 Some of them have both the calyx and corolla equally formed, and coloured so as to be undistinguishable, unless by the manner in which those parts originate: these constitute the *hexapetaloideous form. **1707** H. SLOANE *Voy. Jamaica* I (Pref.), I have followed mostly the Method of Mr. Ray in his History of Plants, joining his Genera or Tribes together by the Method of Rivinus, or Number of the Petala or Leaves of the Flowers; As those which are Monopetalous first, those Dipetalous next, then the Tripetalous, Tetrapetalous, Pentapetalous, *Hexapetalous, and such as have no exact Numbers of Coloured Leaves in their Flowers. **1727** BAILEY vol. II, *Hexa-petalous*, composed of 6 leaves, as the *Filix*, *Pulsatilla*, etc. **1753** CHAMBERS *Cycl. Supp* s.v. *Hemerocallis*, The flower is hexapetalous. **1900** B. D. JACKSON *Gloss. Bot. Terms* 123/2 Hexarch. **1775** ASH, **Hexaphyllous.* **1875** *Encycl. Brit.* II. 411 The propylæum.. as applied to the Acropolis.. consists of a Doric *hexaprostyle portico internally. **1854** MAYNE *Expos. Lex.*, *Hexapterus* (*Bot.*), provided with six wings, as the capsule of the *Fritillaria imperialis*. (*Entomol.*), applied to the *Phalæna hexaptera*, because the male seems to have a third pair of small wings.. six-winged: *hexapterous. **1914** M. DRUMMOND tr. *Haberlandt's Physiol. Plant Anat.* vii. 352 It is customary to discriminate between diarch, tetrarch, pentarch, *hexarch and polyarch bundles. **1965** BELL & COOMBE tr. *Strasburger's Textbk. Bot.* I. iv. 170 Pentarch.. and hexarch roots also occur. **1799–1805** S. TURNER *Anglo-Sax.* (1836) I. III. vii. 206 [Ethelfrith] converted the Saxon States in England into an *hexarchy. **1888** F. H. HILL *G. Canning* xxiii. 217 The Concert of Europe.. a despotic hexarchy of States. **1870** BENTLEY *Bot.* 216 A poly-sepalous calyx may consist of two or more parts.. *hexa-sepalous of six. **1921** A. F. BLAKESLEE in *Amer. Naturalist* LV. 259 The following terms are suggested to designate sets with numbers of chromosomes from 1 to 12: monosome, disome, trisome, tetrasome, pentasome, *hexasome, heptasome, oktasome, enneasome, dekasome, hendekasome, dodekasome. **1922** *Genetics* VII. 527 If.. the chromosomes of a tetrasomic or *hexasomic set assort at random in an F_1 hybrid a 35:1 or 399:1 ratio will be found in the F_2. **1930** *Jrnl. Genetics* XXII. 146 Doubly and trebly hexasomic tetraploids are more likely to come from the derivatives of a tetraploid-hexaploid cross. **1955** J. B. & R. D. HILL *Genetics & Human Heredity* xviii. 363 Hexasomic tetraploid Globe: 4x + *21·22* + *21·22*. **1863** *Hexastigm [see HEXAGRAM 2]. **1896** *Academy* 28 Mar. 261/3 To render the Alcaic metre.. by two decasyllabic, one *hexasyllabic, and one octosyllabic line.

hexachord ('hɛksəkɔːd). *Mus.* [ad. late Gr. ἑξάχορδ-ος, f. ἑξα- HEXA- + χορδή string, CHORD. Cf. F. *hexacorde.*]

1. A diatonic series or scale of six notes, having a semitone between the third and fourth.

Adopted instead of the ancient TETRACHORD as the unit of analysis, in the scheme attributed to Guido d'Arezzo (11th c.), in which all recognized notes were distributed among seven hexachords; see GAMUT.

1730 PEPUSCH *Treat. Harmony* 76 It is by Canons and Fugues that we may be sensible of the Error of those, that reject the Hexachords as Useless. **1854** BUSHNAN in *Circ. Sc.* (*c* 1865) I. 289/2 A plaintive melody, consisting of an ascending and descending scale of the hexachord. **1880** W. S. ROCKSTRO in Grove *Dict. Mus.* I. 735 We look down upon his [Guido's] Hexachords from the perfection of the Octave. He looked up to them from the shortcomings of the Tetrachord.

†**2.** The interval of a sixth. *Obs.*

1694 W. HOLDER *Harmony* viii. (1731) 146 Hexachord, major and minor. **1727–41** CHAMBERS *Cycl.*, *Hexachord*, in the antient music, a concord commonly called, by the moderns, a *sixth*.. The hexachord is two-fold, greater and lesser.

3. 'A musical instrument with six strings' (Simmonds *Dict. Trade* 1858).

hexactinellid (ˌhɛksæktɪˈnɛlɪd), *a.* and *sb.* *Zool.* [f. mod.L. *Hexactinellidæ* (f. Gr. ἕξ six + ἀκτίς (ἀκτῖν-) ray + L. dim. *-ell-*): see -ID.]

A. *adj.* Of or belonging to the *Hexactinellidæ*, a family of siliceous sponges.

1865 DAWSON in *Relics Prim. Life* viii. (1897) 201 Spicules of sponges, some simple and others hexactinellid. **1879** NICHOLSON *Palæont.* (ed. 2) I. 147 At the present day we find an abundance of Hexactinellid sponges.

B. *sb.* A sponge of this family.

1879 NICHOLSON *Palæont.* I. 147 In the Tertiary period comparatively few hexactinellids make their appearance.

So **hexacti'nelline** *a.* = prec. A. (*Cent. D.*)

hexad ('hɛksæd). [ad. Gr. ἑξάς, -αδ- a group of six, f. ἕξ six.]

1. The number six (in the Pythagorean System); a series of six numbers.

1660 STANLEY *Hist. Philos.* IX. x. (1687) 528/1 The Pythagoreans held the number Six to be perfect.. The names of the Hexad are these.

2. A group of six.

1879 G. SALMON *Higher Plane Curves* vi. (ed. 3) 234 The following two groups of hexads of bitangents. *Ibid.*, These 1008 and 5040 hexads have been studied by Hesse as bitangents whose twelve points of contact lie on a proper cubic.

3. *Chem.* An element or radical that has the combining power of six units, i.e. of six atoms of hydrogen. Chiefly *attrib.* or *adj.*

1869 ROSCOE *Elem. Chem.* 187 Six molecules of water in which half of the hydrogen is replaced by a hexad group. **1877** *W. A. Miller's Elem. Chem.* I. (ed. 5) 34 Hexads or Elements, each atom of which in combining may represent six atoms of Hydrogen.

Hence **he'xadic** *a.*, of the nature of a hexad (sense 3).

1873 *Fownes' Chem.* (ed. 11) 251 Sulphur has.. lately been shown to form certain organic compounds in which it is tetradic, and others in which it appears to be hexadic.

hexadecane ('hɛksədɪkeɪn). *Chem.* [mod. f. Gr. ἑξα- HEXA- + δέκα ten (for Gr. ἑκκαίδεκα sixteen) + -ANE.] The paraffin of the 16-carbon series, also called CETANE. So **hexade'coic** *a.* **hexa'decyl**, the radical $C_{16}H_{33}$, also called CETYL.

1872 WATTS *Dict. Chem.* VI, *Hexadecyl.* **1880** *W. A. Miller's Elem. Chem.* III. i. (ed. 6) 163 Hexadecane Derivatives. **1889** *Watts' Dict. Chem.*, *Hexadecoic Acid.*

hexadecimal (hɛksə'dɛsɪməl), *a.* and *sb.* *Computing.* [f. HEXA- + DECIMAL *a.* and *sb.*]

A. *adj.* Pertaining to or being a system of numerical notation that employs 16 rather than 10 as the base.

1954 *Jrnl. Assoc. Computing Machinery* I. 52 Running time required for the same problem in hexadecimal notation is identical with that required by the decimal notation. **1964** *IBM Systems Jrnl.* III. 123 The fraction of a floating-point number is expressed in 4-bit hexadecimal (base 16) digits. **1978** *Pract. Computing* July–Aug. 43/3 The hexadecimal keypad is constructed from high-quality key mechanisms. **1985** *Inmac Catal.* Spring/Summer 40/1 Arithmetic is in octal (base 8) hexadecimal (base 16) and decimal (base 10) number systems.

B. *sb.* The hexadecimal system; hexadecimal notation.

1970 *Communications Assoc. Computing Machinery* XIII. 193/2 (*heading*) Another method of converting from hexadecimal to decimal. **1980** C. S. FRENCH *Computer Sci.* ii. 8 Conversions between Hexadecimal and Decimal follow the same pattern used for Binary and Octal.

Hence **hexa'decimally** *adv.*

1954 *Jrnl. Assoc. Computing Machinery* I. 52 One of the features of this revised MINIAC is that it may be operated hexa-decimally, yielding better than two additional decimal places. **1983** *Communications Assoc. Computing Machinery* XX. 110/1 The hexadecimally coded tones used for address, status, and control purposes are established by various national or international tone signalling standards.

‖**hexaëmeron** (hɛksə'iːmərɒn). Also **hexameron.** [Late L. *hexaēmeron* (the title of a work by Ambrose) = Gr. ἑξαήμερον, neut. of ἑξαήμερος of or in six days, f. ἕξ six + ἡμέρα day; ἡ ἑξαήμερος was the title of a work by Basil.] The six days of the creation; a history of the creation, as contained in Genesis; or a treatise thereon, as the works of Basil the Great and Ambrose.

a **1593** HARRISON *MS. Chronol.* II. *title* (in *Descr. Engl.* 1877 I. App. I. p. xlvii), The hexameron or worke done in those sixe daies wherein the worlde was created. **1651** BIGGS *New Disp.* Pref. 11 His hebdomadal work of the Hexameron Fabrick. **1696** WHISTON *Th. Earth* III. (1722) 259 In the first Constitution of the Expansum or Firmament on the 2nd Day of the Hexæmeron there would be Clouds. **1852** C. WORDSWORTH *Occas. Serm.* Ser. III. 19 Let us not allow our souls to dwell in a sabbath-less Hexameron of earthly care and toil. **1886** W. R. SMITH in *Encycl. Brit.* XXI. 125/2 The older account of the creation in Gen. ii.. does not recognize the hexaemeron, and it is doubtful whether the original sketch of Gen. i. distributed creation over six days.

Hence **hexaemeric** (hɛksəiː'mɛrɪk) *a.*, pertaining to the six days of the creation.

1895 *Athenæum* 19 Oct. 535/2 The hexaemeric work of creation.

hexagon ('hɛksəgən). [ad. late L. *hexagōn-um*, a. Gr. ἑξάγων-ον, neut. sing. of ἑξάγωνος six-cornered, f. ἕξ six + -γωνος, f. stem of γωνία angle. Cf. F. *hexagone.*]

1. *Geom.* A plane figure having six sides and six angles. (Loosely said of bodies of hexagonal section.)

1570 BILLINGSLEY *Euclid* IV. xvi. 124 We may in a Hexagon geuen either describe or circumscribe a circle. [**1571** DIGGES *Pantom.* III. viii. Rj a, By the rules giuen in Planimetra, yee shall finde the area of the lesser Hexagonum.] **1691** RAY *Creation* I. (R.), The space about any point may be filled up either by six equilateral triangles, or four squares, or three hexagons. **1788** REID *Act. Powers* III. ii. (R.), Bees.. make their cells regular hexagons. **1860** FARRAR *Orig. Lang.* i. 13 The waxen hexagon of the bee.

b. *attrib.* or *adj.* = HEXAGONAL.

1754 BP. POCOCKE *Trav.* (1889) II. 72 Two hexagon towers. **1851** *Illustr. Catal. Gt. Exhib.* 765 Hexagon and octagon Gothic fonts.

2. *Fortif.* A fort with six bastions.

1669 STURMY *Mariner's Mag.* 5 Let the Fort be an Hexagon, that is, of six Bastions. **1727–41** in CHAMBERS *Cycl.*

Hence '**hexagonize** *v.* [cf. Gr. ἑξαγωνίζ-ειν], *trans.* to make into a hexagon, to render hexagonal.

1885 J. M. COWPER *Our Parish Bks.* II. 42 Some.. church-warden.. seems to have endeavoured to 'hexagonise' the font by chipping off some of its corners.

hexagonal (hɛk'sægənəl), *a.* (*sb.*) Also 7 *erron.* **exagonal.** [f. HEXAGON + -AL[1].]

A. *adj.* **1. a.** Of or pertaining to a hexagon; of the shape of a hexagon; having six sides and six angles.

1571 DIGGES *Pantom.* IV. v. V iij b, The Diameter of the circle described within a Pentagonum is equall to the sides hexagonall and decagonall of the comprehending circle. **1664** POWER *Exp. Philos.* I. 49 Poppy Seeds.. are like an Hony-Comb on the Surface, with regular Sides and Angles, making all of them pentagonal and hexagonal areola's. **1862**

TYNDALL *Mountaineer*. viii. 67 Nature, prodigal of beauty, rains down her hexagonal ice-stars year by year.

b. ***hexagonal numbers***, the series of POLYGONAL numbers 1, 6, 15, 28, 45, 66, 91, etc., formed by continuous summation of the arithmetical series 1, 5, 9, 13, 17, 21, 25, etc.

(If any one of these be multiplied by 32 and 4 added to the product the result will be a square number.)

1727-41 CHAMBERS *Cycl.* s.v. *Polygonal number*. **1796** HUTTON *Math. Dict.* I. 468/2 If that common difference.. be 4, the series will be hexagonal numbers or hexagons.

2. Of solids: Whose section is a hexagon; constructed on a hexagon as base.

1646 SIR T. BROWNE *Pseud. Ep.* II. i. 53 As for the figure of crystall.. it is for the most part hexagonall or six cornerd. **1774** GOLDSM. *Nat. Hist.* (1776) VIII. 101 Each cell is like that of the bee, hexagonal. **1794** SULLIVAN *View Nat.* I. 447 Quartz.. When crystallized in hexagonal pyramids.. is called mountain crystal. **1871** TYNDALL *Fragm. Sc.* (1879) I. xii. 357 When silica crystallises, we have formed these hexagonal prisms capped at the ends by pyramids.

3. *Cryst.* Denominating one of the principal systems of crystallization, which is referred to three lateral axes, normally inclined to each other at 60°, and a vertical axis at right angles to these and differing from them in length. Also, Of or belonging to this system. ***hexagonal close-packed*** adj., applied to a type of crystal structure or lattice with hexagonal symmetry in which each ion or atom has twelve equidistant neighbours; so ***hexagonal close-packing*** (see quot. 1917); ***hexagonal symmetry***, the symmetry of a figure or body that coincides with its original position after rotation about an axis through an angle of 60° or any multiple of this.

1837 DANA *Min.* ii. (1844) 35 *Hexagonal System*. The vertical solid angles of the rhombohedron are formed by the meeting of three equal planes. **1878** GURNEY *Crystallogr.* 38 The line of intersection of six symmetral planes is an axis of hexagonal symmetry. **1895** STORY-MASKELYNE *Crystallogr.* Index, Hexagonal axes. **1917** *Physical Rev.* X. 678 The so-called hexagonal close-packing.. is one of the two alternative arrangements which the atoms would assume if they were hard spheres and were forced by pressure into the closest possible packing. **1920** *Science* 3 Sept. 228/1 The arrangement of atoms in zinc is like that in magnesium, namely: hexagonal close packed. **1966** L. G. BASSETT et al. *Princ. Chem.* iii. 171 The difference between hexagonal close packing and face-centered close packing arises from the two arrangements for atoms in the third layer.

B. *sb.* A hexagonal number.

1796 HUTTON *Math. Dict.* II. 258/2 The angles.. of the hexagonals [are] six.

Hence **he'xagonally** *adv.*, in a hexagonal manner; in the form of a hexagon; according to the hexagonal system of crystallization. **he'xagonalize** *v. trans.*, to form into hexagons.

1727 BAILEY vol. II, *Hexagonally*. **1794** G. ADAMS *Nat. & Exp. Philos.* II. xvi. 233 Its sides are flat, and from its base, hexagonally divided. **1837** DANA *Min.* (1844) 67 A hexagonally prismatic crystal of white lead. **1870** *Athenæum* 2 Apr. 454 With a small hexagonalized map in his pocket, the traveller.. could always tell his distance to a nicety.

†**hexa'gonial**, *a. Obs. rare.* [f. late L. *hexagōnium* HEXAGON + -AL[1].] = HEXAGONAL.

1609 C. BUTLER *Fem. Mon.* (1634) 104 Each hexagonial bottom of one side, answereth three third parts of the hexagonial Bases of three contiguous Cells on the other side. **1678** CUDWORTH *Intell. Syst.* I. iii. §37. 158 The Bees.. in framing their combs and hexagonial cells. **1775** ASH, *Exagonial*.

So †**hexa'gonian** *a. Obs.* = prec.

1598 R. HAYDOCK tr. *Lomazzo* I. 111 Their ouale.. temples; as also their circular, pentagonian, hexagonian, octogonian, square, and crosse ones.

†**hexa'gonical**, *a. Obs. rare.* [f. HEXAGON + -IC + -AL[1].] = HEXAGONAL.

1657 S. PURCHAS *Pol. Flying-Ins.* 71 Each hexagonical bottome of one side, answereth to three third parts of the hexagonical basis of three contiguous cells on the other side. **1679** M. RUSDEN *Disc. Bees* 9 Their several Combs, and hexagonical Cells.

hexagonous (hɛk'sægənəs), *a. Bot.* [f. HEXAGON + -OUS.] Having six edges; hexagonal in section. (Often written 6-*gonous*.)

1870 HOOKER *Stud. Flora* 350 Stratiotes aloides.. Fruit.. flagon-shaped, 6-gonous, green.

†**hexagony**. *Obs. rare*[−1]. [ad. late L. *hexagōnium* (Ambrose), by-form of *hexagōnum* HEXAGON.] A hexagonal structure, as the cell of a bee.

1655 BRAMHALL *Disc. agst. Hobbes* III. Wks. 1844 IV. 52 When I read in St. Ambrose of their [bees'] 'hexagonies' or sexangular cells.

hexagram ('hɛksəgræm). [f. HEXA- + Gr. γράμμα line, letter.]

1. A figure formed by two intersecting equilateral triangles, each side of the one being parallel to a side of the other, and the six angular points coinciding with those of a hexagon.

1871 B. TAYLOR *Faust* (1875) I. 256 Paracelsus ascribes a similar degree of virtue to the hexagram.

2. *Geom.* A figure of six lines.

The term is spec. applied to: (*a*) ***Pascal's mystic hexagram***, which is formed by lines joining six points on a conic, and has the property that the intersections of the first and fourth, the second and fifth, and the third and sixth of these lines lie on one straight line; (*b*) ***Brianchon's hexagram***, which is a six-sided figure circumscribed about a conic, and has the property that the three lines joining opposite angles intersect in one point.

1863 R. TOWNSEND *Mod. Geom.* I. 145 In a hexastigm or hexagram every triangle determined by three points or lines is said to be the opposite of that determined by the remaining three. **1885** *Encycl. Brit.* XVIII. 338 He [Pascal] established the famous theorem that the intersections of the three pairs of opposite sides of a hexagon inscribed in a conic are collinear. This proposition, which he called the mystic hexagram, he made the keystone of his theory.

3. In Chinese literature, one of the sixty-four figures, consisting each of six parallel (whole or divided) lines, which form the basis of the 'Yih-king' or 'book of changes'.

1882 R. K. DOUGLAS *China* xix. 359 Following each hexagram occur a few sentences of the original text. **1882** *Athenæum* 2 Sept. 296/3 The 'Yi King', or 'Book of Changes', consists of sixty-four hexagrams, the component parts of which are whole or divided lines, placed one over the other in a certain fanciful order, and called by a name which in its turn suggests an explanation found in the text.

‖**hexagynia** (hɛksə'dʒɪnɪə). *Bot.* [mod.Bot. L., f. HEXA- + Gr. γυνή woman, female, taken in sense of 'female organ, pistil'.] In the Sexual System of Linnæus, an order of plants having six pistils. Hence **'hexagyn**, a plant of this order. **hexa'gynian, hexa'gynious** *adjs.*, belonging to this order. **hexagynous** (hɛk'sædʒɪnəs) *a.*, having six pistils.

1778 LIGHTFOOT *Flora Scot.* 211 Enneandria, Hexagynia, *Butomus*. **1828** WEBSTER, Hexagyn.. Hexagynian. **1854** MAYNE *Expos. Lex.*, Hexagynious.

hexahedral (hɛksə'hiːdrəl, -'hɛdrəl), *a. Geom.* and *Cryst.* Also **hexaedral**. [f. next + -AL[1].] Of the form of a hexahedron; having six faces.

1800 tr. *Lagrange's Chem.* I. 381 A salt crystallized in long hexaedral laminæ. **1805-17** R. JAMESON *Char. Min.* (ed. 3) 206 Amphi-hexahedral [crystal], i.e. hexahedral in two senses, because by viewing the planes in two different directions, we obtain two six-sided surfaces. **1811** PINKERTON *Petral.* I. 325 Steatite, crystallised in hexahedral prisms. **1828** STARK *Elem. Nat. Hist.* II. 483 The Hexahedral or tessular form.

So †**hexa'hedrical** *a.* (in same sense).

1666 BOYLE *Orig. Formes & Qual.*, Like the Chrystals of Salt-petre.. long and Hexaedrical. **1669** —— *Contn. New Exp.* I. (1682) 103 If a Hexahedrical Bit be employed it will make the Cavity almost as cylindrical as can be desired.

hexahedron (hɛksə'hiːdrən, -'hɛdrən). *Geom.* and *Cryst.* Also 6-7 **hexaedron**, 7-8 **-um**. [neut. sing. of Gr. ἑξάεδρος, f. ἕξ six + ἕδρα seat, base. Cf. F. *hexaèdre*.] A solid figure having six faces; *esp.* the ***regular hexahedron*** or cube.

1571 DIGGES *Pantom.* IV. Def. xiv. T ij a, *Hexaedron* or *Cvbvs* is a solide figure, enclosed with sixe equall squares. **1677** PLOT *Oxfordsh.* 122 Sal Armoniac [shooting] into Hexaedrums. **1690** LEYBOURN *Curs. Math.* 299 The Side of the Hexaedron. **1895** STORY-MASKELYNE *Crystallogr.* §168 The square hexahedron or crystallographic cube.

hexahydrite (hɛksə'haɪdraɪt). *Min.* [f. *hexahydr(ate* + -ITE[1].] The hexahydrate of magnesium sulphate, $MgSO_4 \cdot 6H_2O$.

1911 R. A. A. JOHNSTON in *Sum. Rep. Geol. Surv. Br. Dept. Mines 1910* (Canada) 257 As this is the first instance in which this salt has been recorded as occurring in a state of nature, this substance is entitled to be regarded as a new mineral, and the name hexahydrite is proposed for it, in allusion to the six molecules of water which enter into its composition. **1959** BERRY & MASON *Mineralogy* xiii. 437 In dry air at ordinary temperatures epsomite loses up to $1H_2O$, changing to hexahydrite.

hexakis-, Gr. ἑξάκις six times, forming an initial element in some crystallographical terms. **ˌhexakisocta'hedron**, a solid figure contained by forty-eight scalene triangles. **ˌhexakistetra'hedron**, a solid figure contained by twenty-four scalene triangles, being the hemihedral form of the hexakisoctahedron.

1851 *Illustr. Catal. Gt. Exhib.* 121 Two trapezohedrons joined together produce the hexakisoctohedron. **1878** GURNEY *Crystallogr.* 90 This form may be called indifferently the hexakisoctahedron or the octakishexahedron. **1895** STORY-MASKELYNE *Crystallogr.* §187 The forty-eight scalenohedron or hexakisoctahedron occurs as a self-existent form only in the diamond. *Ibid.* §189 Of the hexakistetrahedron.. the minerals blende and fahlore offer the prominent examples.

he'xameral, *a.* [f. as next + -AL[1].] Consisting of six parts or divisions.

1879 NICHOLSON *Palæont.* (ed. 2) I. 182 A 'hexameral' arrangement of the septa.

hexamerous (hɛk'sæmərəs), *a.* [f. HEXA- + Gr. μέρ-ος part + -OUS.] **a.** *Bot.* Having the parts of the flower-whorl six in number. (Often written 6-*merous*.) **b.** *Zool.* Having the radiating parts or organs six in number, as an actinoid zoophyte.

1857 HENFREY *Elem. Bot.* 405 *Melanthaceæ*.. Herbs with.. regular 6-merous and 6-androus flowers. **1877** HUXLEY *Anat. Inv. Anim.* iii. 159 The finally hexamerous Anthozoon passes through a tetramerous and an octomerous stage. **1880** GRAY *Struct. Bot.* vi. §2. 176 In Monocotyledons, so-called hexamerous blossoms are really trimerous, the sixes being double sets of three.

hexameter (hɛk'sæmɪtə(r)), *a.* and *sb.* Also (4 **exametron(e, -oun, -ytron)**, 6-7 **hexametre, exameter**. [a. L. *hexameter* adj. and (sc. *versus*) sb., ad. Gr. ἑξάμετρ-ος, f. ἑξα- HEXA- + μέτρον measure, metre. Cf. F. *hexamètre* (1511).]

A. *adj.* (Now only as attrib. use of sb.)

1. *Pros.* Consisting of six metrical feet; *esp.* of the form of the dactylic hexameter.

1546 LANGLEY *Pol. Verg. De Invent.* I. viii. 16 a, A songe of Exameter Verses. **1601** HOLLAND *Pliny* I. 189 The heroick or hexametre verse we acknowledge to haue come first from the Oracle of Pythius Apollo. **1611** FLORIO, *Hesametro*, an exameter verse. **1727-41** CHAMBERS *Cycl.* s.v., Some of the French and English poets have attempted to compose in hexameter verses, but without success. **1756-82** J. WARTON *Ess. Pope* (Mason), In hexameter and pentameter verse.

b. Composing or writing hexameters.

1837 SYD. SMITH *Let. to Singleton* Wks. 1859 II. 289/1 A vast receptacle for hexameter and pentameter boys.

†**2.** *humorously* of an insect: Having six feet.

1652 J. TAYLOR (Water P.) *Journ. Wales* (1859) 11 Embrodered all over with such hexameter poudred ermins (or vermin) as are called lice in England.

B. *sb.* A 'verse' or line of six metrical feet; *esp.* the ***dactylic hexameter*** (*catalectic*), which in the typical form consists of five dactyls and a trochee, or (in Latin poets) more commonly a spondee; for any or all of the first four dactyls spondees may be substituted, but in the fifth foot a spondee is admitted only for special effect.

In English and German hexameters, stress is substituted for length in the first syllable of each foot; but it is often sought to combine with this an observance of quantity.

c **1386** CHAUCER *Monk's T.* 91 They ben versified communely Of vj. feet which men clepen Exametron [*v. rr.* exametroun, examytron, exametrone]. **1579** E. K. *Gloss. Spenser's Sheph. Cal.* May, Emblem, These Emblemes make one whole Hexametre. *c* **1645** HOWELL *Lett.* (1650) II. lv. 77 These 6 notes, Ut, Re, Mi, Fa, Sol, La,.. are all comprehended in this Exameter, '*Ut Relevet Miserum Fatum Solitosque Labores*'. **1751** JOHNSON *Rambler* No. 88 ¶10 We have already tried and rejected the hexameter of the ancients. *a* **1834** COLERIDGE *Ovidian Elegiac Metre* Wks. 1877 II. 344 In the hexameter rises the fountain's silvery column, In the pentameter aye falling in melody back. —— *Note* Poet. Wks. (1893) 614/2 The following verse from the Psalms is a rare instance of a perfect hexameter.. in the English language:—Gōd cāme | ūp wĭth ă | shōut : oūr | Lōrd wĭth thĕ | sōund ŏf ă | trūmpĕt. **1868** TENNYSON *Lucretius* 11 Fancy-borne perhaps upon the rise And long roll of the Hexameter. **1870** SWINBURNE *Ess. & Stud.* (1875) 272 The feeble and tuneless form of metre called hexameters in English.

b. *Comb.*

1599 NASHE *Lenten Stuffe* 4 Such a nigling Hexameter-founder as he [Homer] was.

he'xametral, *a.* [f. prec. + -AL[1].] Of or pertaining to the hexameter.

1818 J. C. HOBHOUSE *Hist. Illust.* (ed. 2) 376 He could not employ the hexametral structure. *Ibid.* 442 [Italian] heroic verses have not the advantage of the hexametral length.

hexametric (hɛksə'mɛtrɪk), *a.* [f. prec. + -IC.] Of or pertaining to a hexameter; consisting of six metrical feet; composed in hexameters.

1785 WARTON *Pref. to Milton's Smaller Poems* (T.), That Ovid among the Latin poets was Milton's favourite, appears not only from his elegiac but his hexametric poetry. **1867** SWINBURNE *Ess. & Stud.* (1875) 164 The verses are faultless, are English, are hexametric.

So **hexa'metrical** *a.* = prec.

1774 WARTON *Hist. Eng. Poetry* lix. (1840) III. 370 His version of Naogeorgus's hexametrical poem. **1861** *Sat. Rev.* 27 Apr. 423/1 The intricacies of the hexametrical cæsura.

hexametrist (hɛk'sæmɪtrɪst). [f. as prec. + -IST.] One who composes or writes hexameters.

1797 W. TAYLOR in *Monthly Mag.* III. 338 That the English dialect.. will be found inferior to the German for the purposes of the hexametrist. **1855** MILMAN *Lat. Chr.* VI. 434 Claudian, and even.. Merobaudes, stand higher in purity, as in life and poetry, than all the Christian hexametrists.

he'xametrize, *v.* [f. as prec. + -IZE.] **a.** *intr.* To compose or write hexameters. **b.** *trans.* To put in hexametrical form; to celebrate in hexameters.

1797 W. TAYLOR in *Monthly Mag.* III. 338 If.. to hexametrize should become an amusement of our poets. **1799** SOUTHEY in Robberds *Mem. W. Taylor* I. 301 A little practice has enabled me to hexametrize with facility. **1851** *Fraser's Mag.* XLIII. 249 The poet stands by hexameterizing his success.

hexametro-, stem of Gr. ἑξάμετρος HEXAMETER used as formative element and comb. form, as in **hexame'trographer** [see -GRAPHER], a writer of hexameters, a hexametrist; **hexametro'mania**, a mania for writing hexameters.

1865 *Lond. Rev.* 24 June 672/2 Homer is the quintain of most hexametrographers. **1865** *Sat. Rev.* 9 Dec. 736 Distaste for the new hexametro-mania had predisposed English instincts to enjoy a wholesome native metre, by way of antidote.

hexamitiasis (hɛksəmɪ'taɪəsɪs). *Med.* [f. the generic name *Hexamita*: see -IASIS.] A disease caused by protozoa of the genus *Hexamita*; *esp.*

an infectious catarrhal enteritis in turkeys often fatal to poults and caused by *H. meleagridis*.

1941 *Jrnl. Parasitol.* XXVII. 186 One essential difference in the pathology of hexamitiasis of pigeons [from that of turkeys] is the consistent catarrhal inflammation with a heavy mucous deposit in the rectum of young pigeons. **1966** T. DALLING *Internat. Encycl. Vet. Med.* III. 1432 In Great Britain, hexamitiasis appears to have been confined to a number of localized outbreaks and . . the disease at present is not of great economic importance.

‖**hexandria** (hɛk'sændrɪə). *Bot.* [mod.L. (Linnæus 1735), f. Gr. ἕξ six + ἀνδρ-, stem of ἀνήρ man, male, in sense of 'male organ, stamen'.] A class of plants in the Sexual System of Linnæus having six (equal) stamens.

1753 CHAMBERS *Cycl. Supp.*, *Hexandria*, in botany . . Plants of this class are garlic, hyacinth, etc. **1794** MARTYN *Rousseau's Bot.* ix. 88 The sixth class, hexandria, whose beautiful flowers have six stamens.

Hence **he'xander**, a plant of the class *Hexandria*. **he'xandrian, -ious** *adjs.*, of or pertaining to that class. **he'xandric, he'xandrous** *adjs.*, having six (equal) stamens.

1828 WEBSTER, *Hexander*, in botany, a plant having six stamens. *Hexandrian*, having six stamens. **1830** LINDLEY *Nat. Syst. Bot.* 228 There is a tendency . . to become pentandrous, or even hexandrous. **1854** MAYNE *Expos. Lex.*, Hexandrious, or hexandrous. **1872** OLIVER *Elem. Bot.* I. v. 51 Daffodil has . . stamens epiphyllous, hexandrous. **1886** *Syd. Soc. Lex.*, *Hexandric* . . *Hexandrious*.

hexane ('hɛksein). *Chem.* [f. Gr. ἕξ six + -ANE.] The paraffin of the hexacarbon series, C_6H_{14}; of this there are five forms. So **hexa'noic** *a.* = CAPROIC *a.*; **'hexanoyl** [-OYL], the radical $C_5H_{11}CO-$ of hexanoic acid; also called *caproyl*; **hexene** ('hɛksi:n), the olefine of the hexacarbon series (C_6H_{12}), also called *hexylene*, homologous and polymeric with ethene; it exists in numerous metameric forms; **hexine** ('hɛksaɪn), the hydrocarbon C_6H_{10} of the same series; **hexoic acid**, $C_6H_{12}O_2$, the same as caproic acid; **he'xoylene**, one of the isomeric forms of hexine.

1877 WATTS *Fownes' Chem.* (ed. 12) II. 48 Normal *Hexane or Dipropyl occurs in the light oils of Boghead and Cannel coal, and abundantly in Pennsylvanian petroleum. **1897** REMSON *Theoret. Chem.* (ed. 5) 208 Five hexanes are possible according to the theory, and all of them are known . . Normal hexane is formed when normal propyliodide is heated with sodium. **1926** *Chem. Abstr.* XX. 4598/1 **Hexanoic acid*, see *Caproic acid*. **1927** *Jrnl. Amer. Chem. Soc.* XLIX. 1828 (*heading*) Some bromine derivatives of pentanoic and hexanoic acids. **1949** *Union Internat. Chim. pure et appl.*, *Compt. Rend.* XV. 144 Rule 58.3. The Commission [of nomenclature of organic chemistry] . . recommends that the carboxyl carbon be always numbered as 1 whether the name be a Geneva name or a trivial name, but not when it is a 'carbonyl' name. *Examples of numbering*: *hexanoyl, caproyl [etc.]. **1952** *Ibid.* XVI. 101 Change: 'Caproyl' to 'Hexanoyl replacing caproyl' . . [rule] 58.3. **1967** *Canad. Jrnl. Chem.* XLV. 2600/2 When a cyclohexane solution of hexanoyl azide and acetophenone was irradiated with light of wavelength over 3000 Å, nitrogen was rapidly evolved. **1877** WATTS *Fownes' Chem.* (ed. 12) II. 59 **Hexene* or *Hexylene*, C_6H_{12}. Two hydrocarbons of this composition have been obtained, one from secondary, the other from tertiary, hexyl alcohol. *Ibid.* 177 Hexene Glycols, $C_6H_{12}(OH)_2$. *Ibid.* 64 *Hexines, C_6H_{10}. *Hexoylene.* **1886** *Syd. Soc. Lex.*, *Hexine* C_6H_{10} . . a mobile liquid obtained by Berthelot by acting on allyl iodide with sodium . . also called *Diallyl.* **1877** WATTS *Fownes' Chem.* (ed. 12) II. 294 *Hexoic or Caproic acids, $C_6H_{12}O_2$ . . There are eight possible forms of these acids, analogous to the eight pentyl alcohols. **1886** *Syd. Soc. Lex.*, **Hexoylene*, C_6H_{10}, Caventou's term for the hexine of petroleum oil formed in the preparation of hexylic alcohol.

† **'hexangle.** *Obs.* [A hybrid formation f. HEX(A- + ANGLE.] = HEXAGON. Also *attrib.* = HEXAGONAL.

1657 S. PURCHAS *Pol. Flying-Ins.* Ded. 3 The fabrick of her hexangle Combs. *Ibid.* 69 The wise Bee is not ignorant of Geometrical inventions, all her cells are hexangles.

hexangular (hɛk'sæŋgjʊlə(r)), *a.* [f. prec., after *angular*.] Having six angles; hexagonal.

1665 HOOKE *Microgr.* 88 Hexangular prismatical bodies. *a* **1711** KEN *Hymnarium* Poet. Wks. 1721 II. 120 The Bees who in their secret Hive, Mansions Hexangular contrive. **1871** TYNDALL *Fragm. Sc.* (1879) II. v. 66 In strict accordance with this hexangular type.

Hence **he'xangularly** *adv.*

1727 in BAILEY vol. II.

'hexaped. Also *erron.* **hexi-, hexoped.** [A hybrid formation f. HEX(A- + L. *pēs*, *ped-* foot.]

†**1.** A measure of six feet. *Obs. rare*$^{-0}$.

1623 COCKERAM, *Hexapede*, a fathome.

2. A creature with six feet, a hexapod. (In quot. 1865, *humorously*, a six-wheeled locomotive.)

1828 WEBSTER, *Hexaped*, an animal having six feet. (Ray, and Johnson after him, write this *hexapod*; but it is better to pursue uniformity, as in *quadruped*, *centiped*.) **1865** E. BURRITT *Walk Land's End* 7 The terrible hexiped of the fiery eyes.

‖**hexapla** ('hɛksəplə). Also anglicized **hexaple**. [a. Gr. (τὰ) ἑξαπλᾶ (the title of Origen's work), neut. pl. of ἑξαπλοῦς, -πλόος sixfold, f. ἕξ six (HEXA-) + -πλοος -fold.]

A sixfold text in parallel arrangement, as that made by Origen of the Old Testament, and that of the New published by Bagster.

[**1608** WILLET (*title*) Hexapla in Genesin: that is, sixfold commentarie vpon Genesis.] **1613** PURCHAS *Pilgrimage* (1614) 179 Of all these Origen compounded his Hexapla. **1684** N. S. *Crit. Enq. Edit. Bible* xviii. 178 He maintains that the Tetraples and Hexaples of Origen were not so call'd from the four or six Columns, but that they were call'd Tetraples, because they contain'd a fourfold Version; Hexaples because they comprehended six Versions. **1841** (*title*) The English Hexapla, exhibiting the six important English translations of the New Testament Scriptures. **1842** BRANDE *Dict. Sci.* etc., *Hexaple*, the combination of six versions of the Old Testament by Origen is so called: viz., the Septuagint, Aquila, Theodotion, Symmachus, one found at Jericho, and another at Nicopolis.

Hence **'hexaplar, hexa'plarian, hexa'plaric** *adjs.*, of the form or character of a hexapla.

1828 WEBSTER, *Hexaplar*, sextuple. **1845** S. DAVIDSON in *Kitto's Cycl. Bibl. Lit.* II. 733/1 His [Origen's] recension is called the Hexaplarian text. **1882–3** in Schaff *Encycl. Relig. Knowl.* III. 2286 The hexaplar version of sundry portions of the Old Testament, made by Paul of Telle, A.D. 616. **1894** *Athenæum* 26 May 681/2 The papyrus [of Ezekiel] . . contains Hexaplaric critical signs.

hexaploid ('hɛksəplɔɪd), *a.* and *sb.* *Biol.* [f. HEXA- + -PLOID.] **A.** *adj.* (Made up of somatic cells) containing six sets of chromosomes. **B.** *sb.* A hexaploid organism.

1920 G. TÄCKHOLM in *Svensk Bot. Tidskr.* XIV. 302 The diploid and tetraploid forms [of roses] of the types 1 and 2 are represented in about equal frequence in my material, the hexaploid (type 3) being rarely met with. **1921** *Ann. Bot.* XXXV. 185 The remainder of the tetraploids, the whole of the pentaploids and hexaploids, showed a partial reduction involving fourteen or twenty-eight chromosomes. **1952** *New Biol.* XIII. 32 The common bread-wheats which have 42 chromosomes, or 6 sets, are hexaploids. **1956** *Nature* 25 Feb. 384/2 Hexaploid cells in mouse blastocysts. **1970** *Watsonia* VIII. 130 Two other differences between the rhizome scales of the diploid and hexaploid were noticed.

Hence **'hexaploidy**, the state or condition of being hexaploid.

1922 *Genetics* VII. 540 There is evidence that does not support the view that tetraploidy and hexaploidy in wheat is actually due to chromosomal duplication. **1925** *Jrnl. Genetics* XV. 263 Tetraploidy and hexaploidy may play a part in the striking changes of the chromosome group from species to species.

hexapod ('hɛksəpɒd), *sb.* and *a.* [ad. Gr. ἑξαποδ- six-footed, f. ἕξ six (HEXA-) + πούς foot.]

A. *sb.* An animal having six feet, an insect; in early use, chiefly applied to insect larvæ.

1668 WILKINS *Real Char.* 125 Strait Beetle producing hexapod. **1691** RAY *Creation* II. (1704) 354 The Hexapods from which the greater sort of Beetles come. **1764** *Phil. Trans.* LIV. 65 Their first appearance is an hexapode (an ill-shapen grub) with six feet. **1816** KIRBY & SP. *Entomol.* (1843) I. 70 Larvæ which in this tribe are usually Hexapods. **1875** A. SWINBOURNE *Picture Logic* xiv. 94 A flea, madam, may be defined as an apterous hexapod.

B. *adj.* Having six feet; belonging to the class *Hexapoda* or *Insecta*, hexapodous.

1856–8 W. CLARK *Van der Hoeven's Zool.* I. 308 Diptera. —Hexapod Insects with two wings, and two poisers. **1880** BASTIAN *Brain* 100 The thoracic legs of hexapod Insects.

Hence **hexa'podal, he'xapodous** *adjs.*, having six feet, belonging to the class *Hexapoda*. **hexa'podan** *a.* and *sb.* = HEXAPOD *a.* and *sb.*

1830 R. KNOX *Béclard's Anat.* 24 The Insecta, or hexapodal articulate animals, have . . six articulated feet. **1836–9** TODD *Cycl. Anat.* II. 854/1 Insects . . may be characterized as a class of hexapodous . . animals.

hexapody (hɛk'sæpədɪ). *Pros.* [ad. Gr. type *ἑξαποδία, f. ἑξαποδ- of six feet, f. ἕξ six (HEXA-) + πούς, ποδ- foot. Cf. *dipody*, *monopody*.] A line or 'verse' consisting of six feet.

1844 BECK & FELTON tr. *Munk's Metres* 16 A series of one foot is called a monopody . . of six, a hexapody. **1868** JEBB *Ajax* Introd. 62 In Period I, each of the two verses is a hexapody. **1879** J. W. WHITE tr. *Schmidt's Rhythmic Class. Lang.* 64 The hexapody commonly called 'Alexandrine Verse', most used by the French in their tragedies. **1891** *Harper's Mag.* Mar. 570/2 Hundreds [of folk-songs] in Hungarian music consisting of dipodies, tetrapodies, tripodies, pentapodies, and hexapodies.

hexarch, erron. form of EXARCH *sb.*

hexastich ('hɛksəstɪk). Also 6–7 **hexastichon**, 7 **exasticke**, 7–8 **hexastick**. [ad. mod.L. *hexastichon*, a. Gr. ἑξάστιχον, neut. of ἑξάστιχος 'of six rows, of six verses', f. ἑξα- HEXA- + στίχος row, line of verse.] A group of six lines of verse.

1577–87 HOLINSHED *Chron.* III. 1237/1 As appeereth by this hexastichon, which I find among the said Iohn Lelands written epigrams. **1612** DRAYTON *Poly-olb.* i. Notes 19 His request to Diana in a Hexastich. **1662** J. BARGRAVE *Pope Alex. VII* (1867) 23 He gave me this insuing hexastichon. **1749** AMES *Typog. Antiq.* (1785) 301 Then follows a distich, and an hexastich by the expositor. **1800** MALONE *Dryden* (R.), Dryden . . furnished Tonson with a well-known hexastick, which has ever since generally accompanied the engraved portraits of Milton. **1891** [see *heptastich* s.v. HEPTA-].

Hence **hexa'stichic** *a.*, of six metrical lines.

1890 *Athenæum* 22 Nov. 700/3 There are hexastichic strophes throughout Prov. xxx.

hexastyle ('hɛksəstaɪl), *a.* and *sb.* Also 8 *erron.* **hectastyle.** [ad. Gr. ἑξάστυλ-ος, f. ἕξ six (HEXA-) + στῦλος pillar. Cf. F. *hexastyle.*]

A. *adj.* Having six columns; applied to a portico or to the façade of a temple.

1748 *De Foe's Tour Gt. Brit.* II. 301 (D.) One of the largest . . hectastyle porticoes in the kingdom. **1827** *Gentl. Mag.* XCVII. II. 607/1 The hexastyle temple at Pæstum. **1832** W. WILKINS in *Philol. Museum* I. 541 We have two examples of hexastyle peripteral temples.

B. *sb.* A portico or façade having six columns.

1704 J. HARRIS *Lex. Techn.* I, *Hexastyle*, an Ancient Building which had six Columns in the Face before, and six also behind. **1727–41** CHAMBERS *Cycl.* s.v., The temple of Honour and Virtue at Rome . . was a hexastyle. **1866** FELTON *Anc. & Mod. Gr.* II. viii. 140 Behind the Doric hexastyle was a magnificent hall 60 feet broad.

Hence **hexa'stylar** *a.* = HEXASTYLE *a.*

Hexateuch ('hɛksətju:k). [mod. f. Gr. ἕξ six (HEXA-) + τεῦχος book, after *pentateuch*. In Ger. (Wellhausen) 1876.] The first six books of the Old Testament, the Pentateuch with the book of Joshua.

1878 COLENSO (*title*) Wellhausen on the composition of the Hexateuch critically examined. **1882–3** SCHAFF *Encycl. Relig. Knowl.* II. 1149 A fabulous history of the events of the Hexateuch. **1885** *Athenæum* 14 Nov. 631/3 The Pentateuch, or rather the Hexateuch, now called the five books of Moses and the book of Joshua. **1891** DRIVER *Introd. Lit. O.T.* 109 Our analysis of the Hexateuch is completed.

Hence **Hexa'teuchal** *a.*, pertaining to the Hexateuch.

1889 *Yale Univ. Catal.* 108 Hexateuchal Analysis. **1892** HUXLEY in *Times* 11 Feb. 14/4 That component of the Hexateuchal compilation to which Genesis i–ii. 4 belongs.

hexatomic (hɛksə'tɒmɪk), *a.* *Chem.* [f. HEXA- + ATOMIC.] Containing or consisting of six atoms of some substance; having six replaceable hydrogen atoms; also = HEXAVALENT.

1873 J. P. COOKE *New Chem.* 290 No definite pentatomic hydrate is known, but of hexatomic hydrates there are several noteworthy examples. **1877** WATTS *Fownes' Chem.* (ed. 12) II. 187 Hexatomic Alcohols and Ethers: this class of compounds includes most of the saccharine substances found in plants. **1879** *Academy* 27 Dec. 467 Iron, manganese, chromium, and aluminium being regarded as hexatomic.

hexatone ('hɛksətəʊn). *Mus.* [f. HEXA- + TONE; cf. PENTATONE.] 'A gapped scale containing six notes within an octave' (Grove, 1954).

hexatonic (hɛksə'tɒnɪk), *a.* *Mus.* [f. prec. + -IC.] Characterized by hexatones.

1930 *Times Lit. Suppl.* 6 Feb. 95/1 Another good tune . . has additional sources of strength in being constituted as a ten bar sentence without any repetition of phrase, and being hexatonic in mode. **1946** R. BLESH *Shining Trumpets* (1949) ii. 44 The scalar concept scarcely enters into African music although it is constantly referred to as predominantly pentatonic and hexatonic, i.e., five and six-toned.

hexavalent (hɛk'sævələnt), *a.* *Chem.* [f. HEXA- + L. *valēnt-em* having power or value.] Combining with or capable of replacing six atoms of hydrogen or other univalent element or radical. (*Syd. Soc. Lex.* 1886.)

hexeity, obs. form of HÆCCEITY.

hexene, hexine, *Chem.*: see under HEXANE.

hexestrol, var. HEXŒSTROL.

hexiology (hɛksɪ'ɒlədʒɪ). *erron.* hexicology. [f. Gr. ἕξις habit + -(O)LOGY.] That branch of science which treats of the development and behaviour of a living creature as affected by its environment. Hence **hexio'logical** *a.*, of or pertaining to hexiology.

1880 MIVART in *Contemp. Rev.* Apr. 606 The inter-relations of living creatures, as enemies, as rivals, and as involuntary helpers, constitute a third department of Hexicology. **1881** —— *Cat* 494 The science of Hexicology is the study of all these more or less complex relations.

hexiradiate (hɛksɪ'reɪdɪət), *a.* [irreg. f. Gr. ἕξ six + L. *radiātus* rayed, RADIATE.] Having six rays, as the spicules of a glass-sponge; sexradiate.

1881 CARPENTER *Microsc.* xiii. (ed. 6) 608 Framework . . fundamentally consisting of an arrangement of six-rayed spicules . . hence the group is distinguished as *hexiradiate*.

hexist, obs. form of HIGHEST.

hexite ('hɛksaɪt). [See HEXA- and -ITE[1] 4.]

1. *Chem.* [ad. G. *hexit.*] = HEXITOL.

1899 E. F. SMITH tr. *V. von Richter's Org. Chem.* (ed. 3) I. 540 Certain hexites have been prepared by the reduction of the corresponding glucoses . . with sodium amalgam. **1938** G. H. RICHTER *Textbk. Org. Chem.* xx. 395 The relationship of the aldohexoses to the corresponding hexites and dicarboxylic acids.

2. A high explosive, hexanitrodiphenylamine, $[C_6H_2(NO_2)_3]_2NH$.

1931 J. F. NORRIS *Princ. Org. Chem.* (ed. 3) xxvi. 483 Hexite or hexil . . was the high explosive used in bombs which were dropped on London. **1944** *Jrnl. Amer. Med. Assoc.* 20 May 189/2 Hexite is now being made and used but not in as large quantities as trinitrotoluene. **1951** KIRK &

OTHMER *Encycl. Chem. Technol.* VI. 54 Hexite is only slightly less sensitive to impact than Tetryl, but is distinctly less sensitive to the impact of a rifle bullet.

hexitol (ˈhɛksɪtɒl). *Chem.* [f. HEX(OSE + -ITOL.] Any of a class of hexahydric alcohols that are closely related to the hexoses.

1894 *Jrnl. Chem. Soc.* LXVI. I. 395 According to theory, 10 stereoisomeric forms of hexitol should exist. **1913** T. H. POPE tr. *Molinari's Org. Chem.* II. 433 With hydrogen the hexoses form hexitols, which are not aldehydic but only alcoholic in character. **1959** A. WHITE et al. *Princ. Biochem.* (ed. 2) xviii. 423 The cyclic hexitol *myo*inositol.. occurs abundantly in nature, and is present chiefly in the form of polyphosphates in plants.

hexobarbital (hɛksəʊˈbɑːbɪtəl). *Pharm.* [f. as next: see BARBITAL.] The equivalent in the U.S. Pharmacopœia of HEXOBARBITONE.

1941 [see next]. **1943** WOOD & OSOL *Dispensatory of U.S.A.* (ed. 23) 511/2 Hexobarbitonum solubile... Soluble Hexobarbital; Soluble Evipal; Cyclural Sodium. **1957** T. SOLLMANN *Man. Pharmacol.* (ed. 8) 942/1 Hexobarbital sodium ('Evipal', 'Evipan') was introduced especially for intravenous anesthesia, as its action is brief.

hexobarbitone (hɛksəʊˈbɑːbɪtəʊn). *Pharm.* [f. HEX- (in *hexenyl*) + -O- + BARBITONE.] A short-acting barbiturate, $C_{12}H_{16}N_2O_3$, with hypnotic properties; also known by proprietary names, as *Evipal*, *Evipan*; *loosely*, = **hexobarbitone sodium**, the monosodium derivative of hexobarbitone, a very short-acting and soluble anæsthetic usu. given intravenously or intramuscularly; also called ***hexobarbitone soluble***.

1941 *Brit. Pharmacopœia 1932* (Add. 3) 8 (*heading*) Hexobarbitonum... Hexobarbitone. *Synonym.* Hexobarbital... Hexobarbitone is 5-*Δ*'-*cyclo* hexenyl-5-methyl-N-methyl-barbituric acid. **1943** *Brit. Med. Jrnl.* 5 June 714/2 Hexobarbitone given by mouth is an excellent hypnotic when there is no pain. *Ibid.* 20 Nov. 646/1 Cyanosis rapidly became extreme; 0·5 g. of hexobarbitone soluble (evipan sodium) was dissolved in 5 c.cm. of distilled water and administered intravenously. **1952** *Martindale's Extra Pharmacopœia* (ed. 23) I. 260 Hexobarbitone sodium has largely been superseded by thiopentone sodium which gives greater muscular relaxation. **1962** H. BURN *Drugs, Med. & Man* ix. 98 The substance hexobarbitone could be injected into a vein and the patient went to sleep with no more warning than he had when going to sleep in his own bed.

hexoctaˈhedron. *Geom.* and *Cryst.* [f. HEX(A)- + OCTAHEDRON.] †**a.** The critical form of the CUBO-*octahedron.* **b.** = HEXAKISOCTAHEDRON.

1570 BILLINGSLEY *Euclid* App. 459 An Exoctohedron is a solide figure contained of sixe equall squares, and eight equilater and equall triangles. **1837** DANA *Min.* i. (1844) 39 Hexoctahedron.. Here for each face of the octahedron, is substituted a low six-sided pyramid.

hexode (ˈhɛksəʊd), *a.* and *sb.* [f. Gr. ἕξ six + ὁδός way, path.] **A.** *adj. Electr. Telegr.* Of six ways: applied to a mode of multiplex telegraphy, whereby six messages can be transmitted simultaneously.

1886 W. H. PREECE in *Jrnl. Soc. Telegr.-Engin. & Electr.* XV. 231 A two-way mode of working, or a mode by which two messages are practically sent at the same time, will be diode working, three-way triode, four-way tetrode, five-way penthode, and-six way [*sic*] hexode. **1894** PREECE in *Times* 27 Jan. 4/3 The multiplex system of working of Mr. Delany, by which, with 'hexode' working, six messages could be transmitted simultaneously.

B. *sb. Radio.* [a. G. *hexode*]. A valve with six electrodes. Also *attrib.* or as *adj.*

1933 *Electronics* Mar. 76/2 The special tube which was selected.. is a hexode.. having a fourth grid and a redesign of all the grids. **1933** *Pract. Wireless* 27 May 358 (*caption*) Superhet circuit employing new Hexode single valve frequency changer. **1944** *Electronic Engin.* XVII. 60/1 In hexode valves the mutual conductance between the first grid potential and the anode current varies in a linear manner with the voltage applied to the third grid. **1955** J. THOMSON *Electronics* vi. 90 The simplest practical form of mixer valve, but one which is not much used nowadays is the hexode. *Ibid.* 91 The hexode may be regarded as a screen-grid tetrode with two control grids.

hexœstrol (hɛkˈsiːstrɒl). *Pharm.* Also **hexestrol**. [f. HEX(ANE + ŒSTR(US + -OL 2.] A synthetic œstrogen, $C_{18}H_{22}O_2$, related to stilbœstrol and used in hormone therapy.

1939 N. R. CAMPBELL et al. in *Lancet* 5 Aug. 312/1 The œstrogenic activity of the synthetic substance 4:4'-dihydroxy-γ:δ-diphenyl-*n*-hexane (hexœstrol) has been described. **1954** *Thorpe's Dict. Appl. Chem.* (ed. 4) XI. 370/2 Hexœstrol dipropionate is of particular value for inhibiting lactation, owing to its speed of action. **1960** *Farmer & Stockbreeder* 19 Jan. 62/3 Between the two most popular synthetic oestrogens—stilboestrol and hexoestrol—the latter was to be preferred as it was less toxic to man. **1971** *New Scientist* 8 Apr. 104/1 Potent drugs—for example the hormone hexoestrol.

hexogen (ˈhɛksədʒən). Also **hexogene**. [a. G. *hexogen.*] = CYCLONITE.

1923 *Chem. Abstr.* XVII. 2364 Nitrated hexamethylenetetramine (hexogen).. and mannitol hexanitrate occupy the highest places in the order of effectiveness. **1945** *Industr. & Engin. Chem.* XXXVII. 666/2 Increasing the weight of charge in a mercury fulminate detonator.. is not nearly so effective as substituting a composition having a higher rate of detonation, such as PETN or hexogen. **1960** *Guardian* 19 Aug. 10/4 Hexogen, he added, was a very powerful explosive used by the US Army.

hexoic acid, hexoylene: see under HEXANE.

hexokinase (hɛksəʊˈkaɪneɪs, -z). *Biochem.* [f. HEXO(SE + KINASE.] Any of various enzymes that catalyse the transfer of a phosphate group from adenosine triphosphate to glucose or other hexoses as the first step in glycolysis.

1930 O. MEYERHOF in *Lancet* 27 Dec. 1418/1 By itself this activator can do nothing, but its addition to the muscle extract induces hexoses to split even more rapidly than glycogen... I propose the name 'hexokinase' for it, since it acts just as other auxiliary enzymes designated as kinases. **1954** A. WHITE et al. *Princ. Biochem.* xvii. 404 There exists a hexokinase for fructose in yeast and bran apparently independent of the hexokinase for glucose. **1964** G. H. HAGGIS *Introd. Molecular Biol.* ii. 28 The breakdown of glucose to CO_2 and water involves a large number of enzymes, the first in the sequence being hexokinase.

hexone (ˈhɛksəʊn). *Chem.* Formerly also **hexon**. [See HEX- and -ONE; in sense 1, ad. G. *hexon, hexonbase* (A. Kossel 1898, in *Zeitschr. f. physiol. Chem.* XXV. 175).] **1.** In full, ***hexone base***: any of the three basic amino-acids arginine, histidine, and lysine.

Kossel distinguished between *hexon* and *hexonbase* (see quot. 1898[2]).

1898 *Jrnl. Chem. Soc.* LXXIV. I. 612 The substances.. are called protones; these are, by the prolonged action of pancreatic juice, partially broken up into hexones (lysine, histidine, arginine). *Ibid.* 715 By the further hydrolysis of the protamines the hexon bases, histidine, arginine, and lysine, are produced, the name hexon being retained for nitrogenous substances, and obtained by the decomposition of proteids containing six atoms of carbon. **1905** J. WADE *Introd. Org. Chem.* (ed. 2) lxxiii. 555 Histidine, the principal representative of the 'hexone' bases, is an important degradation product of proteïns. **1953** *Biochem. Jrnl.* LIII. 435/2 A new technique for the estimation and isolation of the hexone bases in protein hydrolysates.

2. The name for *methyl isobutyl ketone* as used industrially.

1938 T. H. DURRANS *Solvents* (ed. 4) II. iii. 126 Methyl isobutyl ketone, or 2-methyl pentanone 5, known industrially as hexone, is a medium boiling solvent for nitrocellulose. **1966** *McGraw-Hill Encycl. Sci. & Technol.* X. 423/1 In the industrial process employing hexone (the Redox process), the uranium fuel is dissolved in nitric acid.

hexose (ˈhɛksəʊs, -z). *Chem.* [f. HEX- + -OSE.] A monosaccharide that contains six carbon atoms; ***hexose phosphate***, a phosphate derivative of a hexose, as ***hexose monophosphate, diphosphate***, substances important as intermediates in many metabolic processes.

1892 E. F. SMITH tr. *V. von Richter's Org. Chem.* (ed. 2) 499 The hexoses occur frequently in plants, especially in ripe fruits. **1909** *Proc. R. Soc.* B. LXXXI. 528 (*heading*) The hexosephosphate formed by yeast-juice from hexose and phosphate. **1916** A. P. MATHEWS *Physiol. Chem.* iv. 169 All true nucleic acids, or polynucleotides, of animal origin.. have been found to contain a hexose group, or several of them. **1926** *Biochem. Jrnl.* XX. 854 Blood-plasma contains small amounts of a phosphatase similar to that found in bone. Like the latter it hydrolyses sodium glycerophosphate, hexosemonophosphate and hexosediphosphate. **1935** TIPSON & STILLER in Harrow & Sherwin *Textbk. Biochem.* ii. 63 The naturally occurring hexoses (*d*-glucose, *d*-mannose, *d*-galactose and *d*-fructose) are the only sugars which undergo fermentation by yeast. **1956** *Nature* 11 Feb. 274/1 In algae it is considered that the oxidative assimilation of hexose follows the same glycolytic pathway as in higher organisms. **1960** *McGraw-Hill Encycl. Sci. & Technol.* II. 460/1 The principal alternative pathways by which sugars are dissimilated.. are known as the hexose monophosphate pathways. **1965** *New Scientist* 17 June 761/1 Food sugars absorbed from the gut are hexoses.

So **heˈxonic** *a.* [-ONIC], designating an acid formed from an aldohexose by oxidation of the aldehyde group to a carboxyl group; **hexosamine** (hɛkˈsəʊsəmiːn) [AMINE], a derivative of a hexose in which a hydroxyl group is replaced by an amino group; so **hexosaˈminic** *a.*, designating the acid derived from hexosamine; **ˈhexosan** [-AN], a polysaccharide of which the constituent monosaccharides are hexoses.

1894 G. M'GOWAN tr. *Bernthsen's Org. Chem.* (ed. 2) ix. 236 By the conversion of the hexonic acids (through the hexoses) into the corresponding alcohols (mannite, etc.), the number of possible stereo-isomers is diminished. **1894** *Amer. Chem. Jrnl.* XVI. 227 If hexosans are gradually oxidized with chromic acid and afterwards distilled with acids, large amounts of furfurol are obtained. **1914** *Jrnl. Biol. Chem.* XVIII. 123 The hexosamine.. was obtained directly on concentration of the product of hydrolysis of chondroitin sulphuric acid. **1915** *Ibid.* XX. 441 (*heading*) Hexosaminic acid from ribose. **1921** A. L. SMITH *Lichens* v. 211 Besides these [carbohydrates], which rank as hexosans, Ulander found small quantities of pentosans and methyl pentosans. **1957** E. V. MILLER *Chem. Plants* i. 7 The hexosan cellulose is the fundamental constituent of the plant cell wall. **1958** FRUTON & SIMMONDS *Gen. Biochem.* (ed. 2) xxi. 536 The oxidation of D-galactose by *Pseudomonas saccharophila* also appears to involve the intermediate formation of hexonic acids. **1961** *New Scientist* 5 Jan. 15/1 In chronic brain diseases and manic psychoses the macromolecular hexosamine was elevated.

hexˈpartite, *a.* [Hybrid formation, f. Gr. ἕξ six + L. *partīt-us* divided.] Consisting of six divisions; sexpartite, sextipartite.

1842–76 GWILT *Archit.* §1499 ff. Hexpartite vaulting, where the ribs spring from the angles, and two others from a shaft placed in the middle of each long side, thus making six divisions.. Examples of hexpartite vaulting are scarce in England.

hex-radiate (hɛksˈreɪdɪət), *a.* [f. Gr. ἕξ six + L. *radiatus* rayed, RADIATE.] = HEXIRADIATE.

1883 W. S. KENT in A. J. Adderley *Fisheries Bahamas* 37 The glass-rope, birds'-nest, and hat sponges share.. the circumstance that the silicious spicules of which their skeletons are composed belong.. to what is known as the hex-radiate type.

hext, obs. form of HIGHEST.

hexuronic (hɛksjʊəˈrɒnɪk), *a.* [f. HEX(OSE + URONIC *a.*] ***hexuronic acid***, any of a class of uronic acids derived from hexose; *spec.* = *ascorbic acid.*

1928 A. SZENT-GYÖRGYI in *Biochem. Jrnl.* XXII. 1409 The substance is a hitherto unknown, highly reactive isomer of glycuronic acid, so that the substance is a hexuronic acid. *Ibid.*, The isolation of the hexuronic acid from oranges and cabbages is described. **1933** *Times Lit. Suppl.* 16 Nov. 798/3 They have discovered hexuronic acid to be identical with vitamin C. **1957** *Science News* XLV. 82 Monosaccharides include hexoses such as glucose,.. hexuronic acids such as glucuronic acid and galacturonic acid with the molecular formula $C_6H_{10}O_7$, and hexosamines. **1963** D. M. DOUGLAS *Wound Healing & Managem.* vi. 49 Szent-Györgi is credited with the chemical isolation of ascorbic acid, which he first called hexuronic acid... Szent-Györgi renamed hexuronic acid, ascorbic acid.

hexyl (ˈhɛksɪl). *Chem.* [f. Gr. ἕξ six + ὕλη, -YL, substance.] The hydrocarbon radical C_6H_{13}. It may exist in various forms, of which ***normal hexyl*** is also called *caproyl. attrib.* as in *hexyl alcohol, aldehyde*; *Comb.* as in **heˈxylamine**; **hexylreˈsorcinol** (also as two words), a crystalline derivative of resorcinol, $C_6H_3(OH)_2{\cdot}(CH_2)_5CH_3$, used as an anthelmintic and a urinary antiseptic.

1869 ROSCOE *Elem. Chem.* 333 Hexyl and heptyl alcohols are found in certain fermented liquors. **1886** *Syd. Soc. Lex.*, *Hexylamine* $C_6H_{13}NH_2$. An oily liquid obtained by treating hexyl chloride with an alcoholic solution of ammonia. **1924** *Jrnl. Amer. Med. Assoc.* 20 Dec. 2007/1 Unlike a great many antiseptics and germicides, hexyl resorcinol retains its bactericidal power when dissolved in urine of either acid or alkaline reaction. **1949** KRANTZ & CARR *Pharmacol. Princ. Med. Pract.* xviii. 247 Hexylresorcinol capsules are composed of a solution of the drug dissolved in olive oil. **1968** J. H. BURN *Lect. Notes Pharmacol.* (ed. 9) 125 Oil of chenopodium and hexylresorcinol (by mouth) are also used for ascaris infections.

Hence **ˈhexylene**, an earlier name of HEXENE. **heˈxylic** *a.*, of or pertaining to hexyl, as ***hexylic acid, aldehyde***, etc.

1873 *Fownes' Chem.* (ed. 11) 606 Hexylene hydrate is produced from mannite, a saccharine body. **1873** J. P. COOKE *New Chem.* (1875) 314 Our common kerosene is chiefly a mixture of hexylic and heptylic hydride. **1880** *Miller's Elem. Chem.* III. i. (ed. 6) 452 A mixture of this alcohol with primary hexylic alcohol is obtained from normal hexane.

hey (heɪ), *int.* (*sb.*) Forms: 3–4 **hei**, 4–8 **hay**, 7 **haye**, 5– **hey**. [ME. *hei*: cf. Du. and Ger. *hei*, Sw. *hej*, in sense 1. Cf. also HEIGH.]

1. a. A call to attract attention; also, an exclamation expressing exultation, incitement, surprise, etc.; sometimes used in the burden of a song with no definite meaning; sometimes as an interrogative (= *eh?*).

a **1225** *Leg. Kath.* 579 Hei! hwuch wis read of se icudd keiser! *c* **1305** *St. Kath.* 137 in *E.E.P.* (1862) 93 Hei traitours, quaþ þemperour, beo ȝe icome herto? **13..** *Gaw. & Gr. Knt.* 1445 Ande þay halowed hyghe ful hyȝe and hay! hay! cryed. **14..** *Christm. Carol* 3 (Mätz.) Hey, hey, hey, hey, The borrys hed is armyd gay. *a* **1529** SKELTON *E. Rummyng* 168 Hey, dogge, hay, Haue these hogges away! **1610** SHAKS. *Temp.* IV. i. 256 Hey *Mountaine*, hey. **1712** W. ROGERS *Voy.* 42 Our Musick play'd, *Hey Boys up go we!* and all manner of noisy paltry Tunes. *c* **1745** in Ritson *Scot. Songs* (1794) II. 84 (Jam.) Hey, Johny Coup, are ye waking yet? **1794** *Sheridan's Duenna* II. iii, Well, and you were astonished at her beauty, hey? **1802** MAR. EDGEWORTH *Moral T.* (1816) 232 Hey, Solomon, my friend? **1861** DICKENS *Gt. Expect.* xv, You are looking round for Estella? Hey?

b. *hey for* —— : an utterance of applause or exultant appreciation of some person or thing (cf. *hurrah for!*), or of some place which one resolves to reach.

1689 PRIOR *Ep. to F. Shepherd*, Then hey for praise and panegyric. **1837** LYTTON *E. Maltrav.* 30 We must make a dash at the spoons and forks, and then hey for the money. **1863** KINGSLEY *Water-Bab.* ii. (1864) 89 Then hey for boot and horse, lad, And round the world away. **1881** JAS. GRANT *Cameronians* I. iii. 42 Breakfast at nine, and then—hey for the covers!

c. as *sb.* A cry of 'hey!'

13.. *Gaw. & Gr. Knt.* 1158 Þe hindez were halden in, with hay & war. **1513** DOUGLAS *Æneis* III. viii. 36 And halsing gan the land with hey and haill. *a* **1627** MIDDLETON *Microcynicon* Wks. (Dyce) V. 489 With nailed shoes, and whip-staff in his hand, Who with a hey and ree the beasts command. **1790** A. WILSON *Wks.* (1876) II. 100 Our hechs an' heys are by.

2. a. In combination with various interjections or other words. (See also next and HEY-DAY.)

1519 *Four Elements* in Hazl. *Dodsley* I. 20 Sing, frisky jolly, with hey troly lolly, For I see well it is but a folly For to have a sad mind. *a* **1529** SKELTON *Agst. Comely Coystrowne* 30 Rumbyl downe, tumbyll downe, hey go, now, now! *a* **1546** COVERDALE *Goostly Psalmes*, Unto Christen Rdr., They shuld be better occupied, then with hey nony nony, hey troly loly, & soch lyke fantasies. *c* **1560** T. PRESTON *Cambyses* in Hazl. *Dodsley* IV. 236 They can play a new dance called *Hey-diddle-diddle*. **1562** PHAER *Æneid* IX. A a ij, Here is our enemy lo, heylagh, loud clamours than they throw. **1564** *Guid & Godly Ball.* 204 Hay trix, tryme go trix, vnder the grene wod tre. **1599** SHAKS. *Much Ado* II. iii. 71 Conuerting all your sounds of woe, Into hey nony nony. **1602** *Narcissus* (1893) 74 The world, hey dery diddle, goes round without a fiddle. **1606** *Choice, Chance* etc. (1881) 19 The ploughman..putting vp into..the market, with *haye Ree*, and *who* to his horse. **1641** BROME *Joviall Crew* III. Wks. 1873 III. 407 Then, hay tosse and laugh all night. **1672** VILLIERS (Dk. Buckhm.) *Rehearsal* v. (Arb.) 129 Hey down, dery down. **1695** CONGREVE *Love for L.* IV. xiii, Hey toss! What's the matter now? **1709** STEELE *Tatler* No. 2 ¶2 Hey! Hoop! d'ye hear my damn'd obstrep'rous Spouse? **1711** SWIFT *Wks.* (1778) XIII. 380 Hey dazy, will you never have done? **1867** JEAN INGELOW *Poems, Warblings of Blackbirds* iv, With a wild sweet cry of pleasure, And a 'Hey down derry, let's be merry! little girl and boy!'

3. In phrases, sometimes treated as words.

a. † **hey go-bet.** The int. *hey* followed by the phrase *go bet* (see BET *adv.*[2]), which was app., among other things, a call in hunting, and the name of a song and dance; used by Nashe as *sb.*, ? 'one to whom "hey go bet" is said', perh. a person ready at one's bidding. *Obs.*

c **1385** CHAUCER *L.G.W.* 1213 *Dido*, The heerde of hertes founden ys anoon With hay goo bet, prik thou, lat goon, lat goon. *a* **1550** *Frere & Boye* 300 in Hazl. *E.P.P.* III. 73 Ye hath made me daunce, maugre my hede Amonge the thornes, hey go bette. **1589** NASHE *Martins Months Minde* 11 Those whom he counteth his enemies (the worst better than the best of his hey gobetts). .... *Hunting Song* in *Halliwell*, But when my lips are very well wet, Then I can sing with the, Heigh, go bet!

b. hey-go-mad. A phrase expressive of boisterous excitement; sometimes used as adj. *dial.*

1759 STERNE *Tr. Shandy* I. 2 Away they go cluttering like hey-go mad. **1828** *Craven Dial.*, *Heigh-go-mad*, to be highly enraged. **1854** DICKENS *Hard T.* II. vi, Yo was hey-go-mad about her, but an hour sin. **1888** *Sheffield Gloss.*, *Heigh-go-mad*, said of a person who betrays excessively high spirits.

c. hey-pass. An exclamation of jugglers commanding an article to move: often joined with *repass*. Hence as a name for the command, and an appellation of a juggler. ? *Obs.*

c **1590** MARLOWE *Faust.* xi. 58 Do you hear? you heypass, where's your master? **1593** NASHE *Lenten Stuffe* 31 Whereof the onely Circes Heypasse and Repasse was that it drewe a thousand ships to Troy to fetch her backe with a pestilence. **1641** MILTON *Animadv.* (1851) 210 You wanted but *Hey-passe* to have made your transition like a mysticall man of Sturbridge. **1727** GAY *Fables* xlii. 35 (Jod.) Heigh! pass! 'tis gone. *a* **1834** LAMB *Lett.* xvii. To Wordsw. 161 Autumn hath foregone its moralities; they are 'hey-pass repass', as in a show-box.

d. hey presto. A phrase of command by conjurors and jugglers; hence *transf.* used to connote an instantaneous or magical transformation, or some surprisingly sudden performance; also *sb.* as a name for the command.

1731 FIELDING *Lottery* III. Wks. 1882 VIII. 481 The hammer goes down, Hey Presto! be gone! And up comes the twenty pound. **1761** GARRICK *Epil. to Hecuba*, Hey!—'Presto!—I'm in Greece a maiden slain—Now!—stranger still!—a maid, in Drury-Lane! **1873** MRS. ALEXANDER *Wooing o't* II. 55 Like some magician come to lift everyone out of the Slough of Despond, with a sort of 'Hey Presto!' **1877** SPURGEON *Serm.* XXIII. 677 Heigh, presto! the thing is done. **1891** A. LYNCH *Mod. Authors* 133 The melodramatic situations, the surprises, hi-prestos, climaxes.

e. hey, Rube! A rallying call or a cry for help used by circus people. As *sb.*, a fight between circus workers and the general public. *U.S. slang.* (Cf. REUB.)

1882 *Times* (Chicago) 3 Dec. Suppl. 12/4 A canvasman watching a tent is just like a man watching his home. He'll fight in a minute if the outsider cuts the canvas, and if a crowd comes to quarrel he will yell, 'Hey Rube!' That's the circus rallying cry, and look out for war when you hear it. **1935** *Amer. Mercury* XXXV. 229/2 Heyrube: general uprising of spectators. **1939** *Sat. Even. Post* 25 Mar. 75/2 The expression disappeared forty years ago, along with the old rallying cry, 'Hey, Rube!' **1956** H. GOLD *Man who was not with It* (1965) i. 6 We found ourselves with an old-fashioned hey-rube and obliged to move the show on that night. **1962** E. S. GARDNER *Case of Blonde Bonanza* (1967) xv. 182 And 'Hey Rube' is a rallying cry for the circus people to unite in a fight against the outsiders? **1973** *Daily Colonist* (Victoria, B.C.) 12 Oct. 2/2 There..could be a very interesting hey Rube between incumbent Frances Elford and Ald. Brian Smith.

hey, obs. form of EYE, HAY, HE *pron.*, HEO *pron.*, HI *pron.*, HIE, HIGH.

hey-day, heyday ('heɪdeɪ), *int.* Forms: 6–7 **heyda**, (6 **hoighdagh, hoy day**, 6–7 **hoyda, hoyday**, 7 **hoida**), 6–8 **hey day**, (7 **hay da, ha day**, 8 **heigh-day**), 7– **hey-day**, 8– **heyday**. See also HIGH-DAY. [app. a compound of HEY *int.*; the second element is of doubtful origin, but at length identified with *day*. The early *heyda* agrees in form, but less in sense, with Ger. *'heida, hei'da* = hey there!: cf. also Ger. *'heidi, hei'di*.] An exclamation denoting frolicsomeness, gaiety, surprise, wonder, etc.

1526 SKELTON *Magnyf.* 757 Courtly Abusyon, Rutty bully, ioly rutterkyn, heyda! **1552** HULOET, Heyda or hey, *euax*. *a* **1553** UDALL *Royster D.* III. iii. (Arb.) 48 Hoighdagh, if faire fine mistresse Custance sawe you now. **1598** B. JONSON *Ev. Man in Hum.* IV. ii, Hoyday, here is stuffe! **1607** HEYWOOD *Fayre Mayde* Wks. 1874 II. 11 Hoida; come up. **1622** B. JONSON *Masque Augures*, Hey-da! what Hans Flutterkin is this? what Dutchman doe's build or frame castles in the aire? **1672** VILLIERS (Dk. Buckhm.) *Rehearsal* II. iv. (Arb.) 61 Hey day, hey day! I know not what to do, nor what to say. **1709** STEELE *Tatler* No. 171 ¶3, I go no further than, Say you so, Sir? Indeed! Heyday! **1741** RICHARDSON *Pamela* (1824) I. 67 Hey-day, why so nimble, and whither so fast? said she. **1780** WESLEY *Wks.* (1872) X. 164 Heigh-day! What has this to do here? **1844** DICKENS *Mart. Chuz.* vii, Heyday! Pray, what does he want with me? **1855** KINGSLEY *Heroes, Theseus* II. (1856) 184 Hey-day, we are all masters here.

hey-day, heyday ('heɪdeɪ), *sb.* (*a.*) Also 6 **hayday**, 8 **hay day**. [Of uncertain origin; perh. connected with prec. The second element does not seem to have been the word *day*, though in later use often identified with it: see sense 2.]

1. State of exaltation or excitement of the spirits or passions.

c **1590** *Sir Thomas More* (1844) 41 To be greate..when the thred of hayday is once spoun, A bottom great woond vpp greatly vndoun. **1602** SHAKS. *Ham.* III. iv. 69 At your age, The hey-day in the blood is tame, it's humble. **1633** FORD *'Tis Pity* IV. iii, Must your hot itch and plurisy of lust, The heyday of your luxury, be fed Up to a surfeit? **1783** BURGOYNE *Ld. of Manor* I. i. (D.), A merry peal puts my spirits quite in a hey-day. **1794** SOUTHEY *Wat Tyler* I. i, Ay, we were young, No cares had quell'd the heyday of the blood. **1867** EMERSON *May-Day* etc. Wks. (Bohn) III. 423 Checked in these souls the turbulent heyday.

2. The stage or period when excited feeling is at its height; the height, zenith, or acme of anything which excites the feelings; the flush or full bloom, or stage of fullest vigour, of youth, enjoyment, prosperity, or the like. Often associated with *day*, and taken as the most flourishing or exalted time.

1751 SMOLLETT *Per. Pic.* (1779) II. lxviii. 221 Our imperious youth..was now in the heyday of his blood. **1768** STERNE *Sent. Journ.* (1775) 86 (*Hotel at Paris*), I was interrupted in the hey-day of this soliloquy, with a voice. *Ibid.* 135 (*Maria, Moulines*) To travel it through the sweetest part of France—in the hey-day of the vintage. **1807–8** W. IRVING *Salmag.* (1824) 143 In the good old times that saw my aunt in the hey-day of youth. **1824** SCOTT *St. Ronan's* iii, In his heyday he had a small estate, which he had spent like a gentleman. **1831** LYTTON *Godolphin* 38 In the flush and hey-day of youth, of gaiety, and loveliness. **1839** LONGF. *Hyperion* IV. ii, The heyday of life is over with him. **1873** SYMONDS *Grk. Poets* vii. 232 In the bloom and heyday of the young world's prime. **1877** MRS. OLIPHANT *Makers Flor.* xiv. 346 He was no more than thirty-six, in the hey-day of his powers.

b. *attrib.* Of or pertaining to the hey-day of youth; *erron.* belonging to a festive or gala day.

1739 CIBBER *Apol.* i. 14 All the hey-day expences of a modish Man of Fortune. **1792** *Fortn. Ramble* viii. 44 A man with his hayday dress..is passing over the bridge.

hey-day guise, hey-de-gay: see HAY *sb.*[4] 2.

‖**heyduck** ('haɪdʊk, 'heɪdʌk). Forms: 7 **heyduque**, 7– **-duke, -duck**, 9 **heyduc, heiduc, -duck, haiduk, hayduk**. [a. Boh., Pol., Serv., Roman. *hajduk*, Magyar *hajdú* pl. *hajdúk*, in Bulg. *hajdutin*, mod.Gr. *χαϊντούτης* = *chaidoutes*, Turkish *ḥaidūd* robber, brigand.]

A term app. meaning originally 'robber, marauder, brigand' (a sense still retained in Serbia and adjacent countries), which in Hungary became the name of a special body of foot-soldiers (to whom the rank of nobility and a territory were given in 1605), and in Poland of the liveried personal followers or attendants of the nobles.

1615 J. STEPHENS *Satyr. Ess.* 87 Like the Hungarian Heyducks their wrath is prone to mischief, and their amity is worth nothing. **1684** *Scanderbeg Rediv.* iv. 54 First Marched five Companies of Heyduques. **1685** *Lond. Gaz.* No. 2072/1 The Heydukes of Cattaro had made an incursion towards Goza, and had destroyed all that Country. **1729** *Brice's Weekly Jrnl.* (Exeter) 16 May 3 A Dwarf..is to attend on his Royal Highness in the Dress of a Heyduke. **1772** *Ann. Reg.* 82* Two Heyducks who were behind the coach, bravely exposed their lives to save the King [of Poland]. **1832** *Blackw. Mag.* XXXII. 13 The richly costumed heydukes and chasseurs of the Hungarian lords. **1847** MRS. A. KERR *Hist. Servia* 49 Such as refused to appear before the Kadi..fled into the forests and turned *Heyducs* or robbers. **1858** CARLYLE *Fredk. Gt.* VI. iii. II. 158 Carried by two shining particoloured creatures, heyducs so-called,..in a sublime sedan. **1889** *Athenæum* 15 June 768/1 One of that extinct species of servants, the heyducs, holds the horse of the fat monarch.

heye, obs. f. AWE, HIE.

heyer, -eer, var. HAIRE, *Obs.*

heyeth: see HEIGHT.

heyf, heyfar, -fer, etc., obs. ff. HEAVE, HEIFER.

heygh, heyȝ, obs. ff. HIGH.

heyghne, heyne, obs. ff. HAIN *v.*[2], to raise.

c **1475** *Crabhouse Reg.* (1889) 61 She heyned the stepul and new rofyd it. **1550** LEVER *Serm.* (Arb.) 34 By takyng of fynes, heyghnyng of rentes. **1635** RUTTER *Sheph. Holiday* (N.), And on the turfie table with the best Of lambs in all their flocke shall heyne the feast.

heygth, heyȝte, heyȝthe: see HEIGHT.

hey-ho, hey ho ('heɪ'həʊ), *int.* Forms: 5–6 **hay ho(e, hey(e how(e**, 6 **heigho**, 7 **heigh ho, heigh-ho, hi ho**, 6– **hey ho**. An utterance, app. of nautical origin, and marking the rhythm of movement in heaving or hauling (cf. HEAVE HO, *hale and how*, HALE *sb.*[4] 1); often used in the burdens of songs, with various emotional expression, according to intonation. In some later quots. blending with HEIGH-HO.

1471 RIPLEY *Comp. Alch.* in Ashm. (1652) 157 Hay hoe, careaway, lat the cup go rounde. ? *c* **1475** *Sqr. lowe Degre* in Ritson *Metr. Rom.* III. 179 Your maryners shall synge arowe Hey how and rumby lowe. **15..** *Peebles to Play* v, With hey and how rohumbelow, The young folk were full bauld. *a* **1550** *Frere & Boye* 50 in Hazl. *E.P.P.* III. 62 The lytell boye..Of no man had he no care, But sung, hey howe, awaye the mare, And made ioye ynough. **1579** SPENSER *Sheph. Cal.* Aug. 54 It fell vpon a holly eue, hey ho hollidaye. *Ibid.* 78 As the bonilasse passed bye, hey ho bonilasse. **1592** G. HARVEY *New Letter* 16 Let him be the Falanta downe diddle of Ryme, the Hay ho holliday of Prose. **1600** SHAKS. *A.Y.L.* II. vii. 180 Heigh ho, sing heigh ho, vnto the greene holly. **1605** —— *Lear* III. ii. 75 With heigh-ho, the Winde and the Raine. *a* **1614** *Eng. Helicon* in *Brit. Bibl.* (1812) III. 188, I knowe a simple countrie hinde, Heigh hoe, sillie swaine. **1659** *Pol. Ballads* (Percy Soc.) III. 147 Sing, hi ho, Wil. Lenthall, who shall our generall be? **1848** DICKENS *Dombey* v, [He] whistled 'With a hey ho chevy!' all through.

heyhoe: see HICKWALL.

heyhove, heyhte, heykylle, obs. ff. HAYHOVE, HEIGHT, HECKLE.

heyl, -e, obs. ff. AIL, HAIL, HEAL, HELE.

heylander, obs. f. HIGHLANDER.

heyld, obs. f. HIELD *v.*

heyler: see HILLER.

heylis, obs. f. HALSE *sb.*

heylle, var. HAIL *sb.*[2], *Obs.*

heyn(e, var. HAIN, HINE, HYNE, HOINE.

heynd, var. ENDE *Obs.*, a duck.

heynd, -e, var. HEND *a.*, *Obs.*

heyne: see HEYGHNE.

heynne, var. HYNE *adv. Obs.*, hence.

† **heyr.** *Obs.* (See quot.)

1669 WORLIDGE *Syst. Agric.* (1681) 327 *Heyrs*, young Timber-trees that are usually left for Standils in the felling of Copses. **1726** *Dict. Rust.* (ed. 3).

heyr, -e, obs. ff. HAIR, HAIRE, HEIR, HER *sb.*

† **'heyrat(t.** *Obs.* An American quadruped; app. the Kinkajou (*Cercoleptes caudivolvulus*).

1607 TOPSELL *Four-f. Beasts* (1658) 84 We may hereunto add the beast which is bred in America, called Heyratt, spoken of by Theuetus: which name signifieth a beast of Hony..for it will climb the trees, and coming to the caves of Bees..take out the Hony with their nails... It is about the bigness of a Cat, and of a Chesse-nut colour. **1677** G. CHARLETON *Exercit. Anim.* (ed. 2) 18 Heyrat. **1688** R. HOLME *Armoury* II. 183/1 The Heyrat a beast in America, as big as a Cat..a great climber of Trees.

heyron(e, -oun, -un(e, obs. ff. HERON.

heysoge, heysugge, obs. ff. HAYSUGGE.

heyt, obs. f. EAT, HAIT, HEAT, HEIGHT; obs. Sc. f. HATE, HOT.

heyte, obs. f. AIT[1].

heyth, obs. f. HEATH, HEIGHT.

heyþen, obs. f. HEATHEN; var. HETHEN.

heyty-titey, obs. var. HIGHTY-TIGHTY.

heyuen, obs. f. HEAVEN.

heyved, heywit, obs. pa. pple. of HEAVE.

heyward, obs. f. HAYWARD.

Hezbollah (hɛzbə'lɑː). Also **Hizbollah, -bullah**. [a. Pers. *ḥezbollāh*, Arab. *ḥizbullāh* Party of God, f. *ḥezb, ḥizb* party + *allāh* ALLAH.] The name of an extreme Shiite Muslim group, esp. in the Lebanon (see quot. 1986[2]). Also **Hezbo'llahi**, a member or adherent of this group.

1960 C. GEERTZ *Relig. Java* xi. 145 Hizbullah, a guerilla batallion [*sic*] of young men, grew out of a similarly named organization formed by the Japanese to give training in military drill to young Moslems.. Hizbullah was Indonesia-wide. **1981** *Times* 10 June 8/1 Large bands of 'Hesbollahis', or followers of the Party of God, charged at them with an assortment of weapons. **1985** *Listener* 2 May 3/3 Amal felt itself unable to side with Israel lest it be outflanked by its fast-growing and more extreme rival, the pro-Khomeini Hezbollah. **1985** *Guardian* 11 July 7/7 The radical Iranian-backed Hizbullah group. **1986** *Daily Tel.* 23 July 17/8 The southern suburbs [of Beirut]..remain exclusively controlled by the pro-Iranian Hizbollah (party of God) militia which is totally opposed to the Syrian move. **1986** *Lebanon News* 31 Oct. 5/1 One could trace the origins of Hezbollah to a meeting in the Iraqi city of Najef in 1969 where the idea of a Moslem revolution in Lebanon was first advanced.

†**hi, hy**, *pers. pron.*, *3rd sing. fem. acc. Obs.* Forms: 1 **hia, hea, hiæ, hiȝ,** (hio), 1–2 **hie,** 1–3 **heo,** 1–4 **hí, hý,** 2 **hye, hyo,** 2–3 **ha, hoe.** [OE. *hia, hie*, etc., acc. of *hiu, hio*, HEO, fem. of HE, corresp. to OFris. *hia*; cf. Goth. *ija*, the form corresp. to which was already lost in OHG. and OS., and supplied by *sia*, mod.Ger. *sie*, from stem *si-*, SE. In late OE. the originally distinct nom. and acc. began to be confounded under the forms *hie, hí, hiȝ, hio, heo*; and in later times, though *heo* was the typical nom. and *hi, hy* the acc., the two cases were hardly distinct. Following the example of *me, thee, us,* and *you*, and like the other OE. accusatives of the 3rd pers., *hia* began in the 10th c., in north-midl. dial., to be supplanted by the dative *hire*, HER. In the east-midl. dial. of the OE. Chronicle, this substitution was fully established by 1125; but the original acc. *hi, hy* remained longer in the west and south, being found in Layamon after 1200, and in Shoreham (Kentish) in the first quarter of the 14th c. During its obsolescence, another acc. form, *hes*, HIS, made its appearance in the south.]

= HER (acc.); also *refl.* herself. Used of females, and with nouns grammatically feminine: cf. HEO.

c **825** *Vesp. Psalter* xxxix. 15 Ða ðe soecað sawle mine ðæt hie afirren hie. **835** *Kentish Charter* in *O.E. Texts* 447 ȝif min wiif ðonne hia nylle mid clennisse swæ ȝehaldan. *a* **900** *Martyrology* Ibid. 178 Se casere hio heht ȝemartyrian. *c* **925** *O.E. Chron.* an. 919 [He] beȝet þa burȝ and him cirdon to mæst ealle þa burȝware þe hie ær budon. *c* **950** *Lindisf. Gosp.* Matt. i. 19, & nalde hea ȝebrenge..ah he walde deiȝlice forleitta hea [*c* **975** *Rushw. G.*, & ne walde hie..wolde deȝullice forleten hio]. *Ibid.* ix. 18 Onsett [þin] hond ofer hia ..þæt hiu lifiȝe [*Rushw.* ȝesette hond þin ofer heo, & heo leofaþ; *c* **1000** *Ags. G.*, Sete þine hand uppan hiȝ, and heo lyfað; *c* **1160** *Hatton G.*, Sete þine hand up on hyo, and hye lefeð]. *c* **950** *Lindisf. G.* Matt. xiv. 4 Ne is ȝelefed ðe to habbanne hia [*Rushw.* hire]. *Ibid.* xv. 23 Forlet hia, forðon [hiu] cliopas æfter usiȝ [*Rushw.* Forlet hiæ, forþon þe hiæ cæȝeþ æfter us]. *c* **1000** *Sax. Leechd.* I. 170 Gif he hy [*peoniam*] mid him hafað. *c* **1000** *Ags. Gosp.* Matt. xiv. 4 Nys þe alyfed hi [*v.r.* hiȝ] to wife to hæbbenne [*c* **1160** *Hatton G.*, hy to wife to hæbbenne]. *Ibid.* xv. 23 Forlæt hiȝ, forðam heo clypað æfter us [*c* **1160** *Hatton G.*, Forlæt hyo, forþan hyo clypað æfter us]. *a* **1050** *O.E. Chron.* (MS. C) an. 1037 Baldwine eorl hi [Ælfȝyfe] ðær wel underfeng, and hiȝ þær ȝeheold. *Ibid.* (Laud MS.) an. 1048 ⁊4 Se cyng..betæhte hy his swyster to Hwerwillon. *a* **1100** *Ibid.* (Laud MS.) an. 1075 Se cyng hi let bryngan to Westmynstre..and læȝde hi wið Eadward kyng hire hlaforde. *Ibid.* an. 1100 Se arcebiscop Anseälm hi him bewæddade and siððan to cwene ȝehalȝode. *a* **1175** *Cott. Hom.* 223 Adam hi nemnede eua. *c* **1175** *Lamb. Hom.* 3 Unbindeð hee [þe asse] and leadeð heo to me. *a* **1200** *Moral Ode* 215 Þa þe godes milce secheð he iwis mei ha ifinden. *c* **1205** LAY. 42 He hoe [þe boc] ȝef þare æðelen Ælienor. *Ibid.* 158 He heo wolde habben. *Ibid.* 3186 Ich heo [*c* **1275** hire, i.e. Cordelia] wulle þe biwiten & senden ha [*c* **1275** hire] þe in ane scipe. *a* **1250** *Owl & Night.* 29 Þe nihtegale hi iseȝ And hi biheold and overseȝ. *Ibid.* 939 And sat sum del and heo biþohte. *c* **1275** *Passion our Lord* 435 in *O.E. Misc.* 49 Þe rode..He ber heo on his schuldre. *c* **1315** SHOREHAM 102 Senne hys [*i.e.* is] swete and lyketh, Wanne a man hi deth. *Ibid.* 136 To healde hy [þe erthe] op hyt nys no ned.

†**hi, hy**, *pers. pron.*, *3rd pl. nom.* and *acc. Obs.* Forms: see below. [OE. *hiæ, hie*, etc., the original plural, nom. and acc., in all genders, of *hé, heo, hit* (see HE), corresp. to OFris. *hia*; cf. Goth. nom. pl. *eis*, **ijôs, ija*, acc. *ins, ijôs, ija*, the forms corresp. to which were already lost in OS. and OHG. and supplied by *sia*, and *sie, sio, siu*, mod.Ger. *sie*, from stem *si-*, SE. Since OE. times, a like fate has befallen this pronominal form in Eng. Already in 10th c. the northern dial. occasionally used, as equivalent to *hia*, the demonstrative *þá, tha*, plural of *the, that*; before 1200, the cognate form *þeȝȝ*, THEY, adopted from Norse, had quite superseded *hi, hia*, nominative, in north-midl. (Ormin); the corresponding northern form was *þai, thai*. By 1300, *þei, thei, they*, had become the standard Nominative form in midland English generally; though *her, hem*, were retained in the possessive and objective till the 15th c. Before 1400, *thei, thai* are seen side by side with *hi, hy*, even in s.w.; and before 1500, *hi*, already confounded in form with its sing. *he, hee*, disappeared from literature; although in the reduced form *ă* it still lingers in s.w. dialect. The Accusative *hi* was lost sooner than the nominative; in the 10th c., in north-midl. dial., it began, like the other accusatives *hine*, and *hí* sing. fem., and on the analogy of the original accusative pronouns of the first and second persons, to be supplanted by its own dative *heom, hem* (see HEM *pron.*); in the east-midl. dial. of the OE. Chronicle, *hem* had quite superseded *hi* before 1125; but in the west the acc. was used by Layamon after 1200, and in Kentish it was still Shoreham's form *c* 1315. When it disappeared in the south, it gave place, as in the fem. sing., to a form *hes*, HIS. q.v.; elsewhere it was succeeded by HEM, which itself in course of time was displaced by THEM. Thus, *they, them* are the present sense-equivalents of *hi* nom. and acc.]

I. 1. Nominative case. = THEY.

α. 1 **hiæ, hia, (hea), hie,** 2 **hye,** 2–3 **hie.**

805–31 *Kentish Charter* in *O.E. Texts* 444 Æc ic bebeode minum æfterfylȝendum..ðæt hiæ simle ymb xii monað ..ȝeȝeorwien ten hund hlafa. *c* **825** *Vesp. Psalter* xxi. 18 Hie soðlice sceawedun and ȝelocadon me. *c* **855** *O.E. Chron.* an. 755 Þa cuædon hie þæt hie hie þæs ne onmunden. *c* **897** K. ÆLFRED *Gregory's Past.* xlvi. 354 Ðonne hit tocymð ðæt hie hit sprecan sculon. *c* **950** *Lindisf. Gosp.* Matt. xxiii. 5 Þætte hia sie ȝesene [*c* **975** *Rushw. G.*, þæt hiæ siæ ȝesænæ]. *c* **975** *O.E. Chron.* an. 951 Þæt hie woldan eal þæt he wolde. *c* **1160** *Hatton G.* Matt. ix. 24 Hye teldan hine. *c* **1200** *Trin. Coll. Hom.* 51 Efter þan þe hie weren wuniende in ierusalem..þo hie forleten godes lore. *c* **1250** *Kent. Serm.* in *O.E. Misc.* 33 Hie answerden and seyde, Lord [etc.].

β. 1 **hio, heo,** 2 **hio, hyo,** 2–4 **heo.**

871–89 *Surrey Charter* in *O.E. Texts* 452 Þonne aȝeofen hio þa ilcan elmessan to cristes cirican. *a* **900** CYNEWULF *Elene* 166 (Gr.) Hio him andsware æniȝe ne meahton aȝifan. *c* **937** *O.E. Chron.* an. 937 Þæt heo [*MSS. A., B.* hie, *C., D.* hi] beaduweorca beteran wurdun. **971** *Blickl. Hom.* 199 Heo næfre swylc wundor ne ȝesawon. *Ibid.* 249 Hio wæron ȝefeonde mycle ȝefean. *c* **1000** ÆLFRIC *Gen.* iii. 7 Hiȝ oncneowon þa þæt hiȝ nacode wæron. *c* **1160** *Hatton Gosp.* Matt. x. 1 Þæt hyo adrifen hyo ut [*Ags. G.* hiȝ..hiȝ]. *a* **1175** *Cott. Hom.* 223 Nare hio blinde ȝescapene. *c* **1205** LAY. 183 He wes king and heo quen, & kine-lond heo welden. **1258** *Proclam. Hen. III*, Þe treowþe þæt heo vs oȝen. *a* **1375** *Joseph Arim.* 282 Þenne þei seȝen Ihesu crist in þat ilke foorme, þat heo seȝen him..whon heo furst comen.

γ. 1 **hi, hy, hiȝ,** 2–4 **hi (i, y),** 3–4 **hii,** 4 **hy.**

c **887** *O.E. Chron.* an. 887 And hi cuædon þæt hie þæt.. healdan sceoldan. **971** *Blickl. Hom.* 123 Þa hy þa up on þone heofon æfter urum Drihtne locodan. *c* **993** *Battle of Maldon* 19 Byrhtnoð..tæhte hu hi sceoldon standan. *a* **1000** *O.E. Chron.* an. 993 And hy þone ealdorman þær ofsloȝon. *c* **1000** *Ags. Gosp.* Matt. ix. 24 Hi [*v.r.* hiȝ] tældon hyne. *Ibid.* 32 Hiȝ brohton him dumbne man. **1154** *O.E. Chron.* an. 1137 Hi hadden him manred maked & athes suoren. *a* **1175** *Cott. Hom.* 219 To chiesen ȝief y wolden hare sceappinde lufie. *Ibid.* 223 I muȝon ȝecnowen eiȝðer god and euyl. *Ibid.* 225 Þa cweðen hi betwxe ham þat hi woldan wercen ane burch. *c* **1205** LAY. 2230, I funden [*c* **1275** hii funde] þa þreo maidenes. *c* **1275** *Ibid.* 3610 Hii [*c* **1205** heo] verde to one borwe. *Ibid.* 10314 Hii flowen forþ rihtes, þat i comen to þan Peutes. **1297** R. GLOUC. (1724) 369 Hii rerde abbeyes & prioryes vor her synnes. *c* **1315** SHOREHAM 47 Ere hy thys ordre have, Me schel hy wel assaye Of that hy redeth that hy wel Ham conne aneye. *a* **1327** *Pol. Songs* (Camden) 214 To the kyng Edward hii fasten huere fay. **1340** *Ayenb.* 16 Hi byeþ heaued of alle kueade..be hy dyadliche, be hy uenial. **1377** LANGL. *P. Pl.* B. I. 189 Aren no men auarouser þan hij Whan þei ben auaunced. *c* **1380** *Sir Ferumb.* 1014 Sory wer þey for hi ne miȝt hure pruwesse fulfille þore. *Ibid.* 2380 Y not how þay schul ascape þen, þat hy ne goþ to dede. *c* **1380** WYCLIF *Sel. Wks.* III. 110 Hy kepeþ here reule.

δ. 2–5 **he,** (4 **hey**), 5 **hee.**

a **1175** *Cott. Hom.* 219 Hi wolde mid modinesse beon betere þonne he ȝesceapen were. *c* **1175** *Lamb. Hom.* 91 Þa þet lond hefden he hit sealden. *c* **1200** *Trin. Coll. Hom.* 129 For þat þe he ne wuneð noht on hem, ne he on him. *c* **1220** *Bestiary* 351 Alle he [hertes] arn off one mode. **1297** R. GLOUC. (1724) 16 To wyte, weþer he [= they] wolde þes, oþer heo nolde non. *c* **1300** *Havelok* 152 He wrungen hondes, and wepen sore. *c* **1325** *Song Passion* 24 in *O.E. Misc.* 198 Ne cuþen hey him nout cnowe. *c* **1394** *P. Pl. Crede* 471 But oþer cures of Cristen þei coveten nouȝt to haue, But þere as wynnynge liþ he lokeþ none oþer. *c* **1410** *Chron. Eng.* (Ritson) 33 Schep he heden ase hors gret. *c* **1430** *Hymns Virg.* 59 To the child her seruice profren he [*rime* vanyte]. *c* **1450** LONELICH *Grail* xlii. 76 And whanne they syen he Wolde not so..Of here vyandes thanne ȝoven hee.

ε. 2–4 **ho.**

c **1175** *Lamb. Hom.* 79 A mon..fol imong þoues, ho him bireueden and ho him ferwundeden. *a* **1200** *Moral Ode* 98 Nabbeð hi naþing forȝeten of al þ et ho iseȝen. *Ibid.* 100 Al ho habbeð in hore write þet we misduden here. *Ibid.* 105 Hwi weren ho biȝeten, to whon were ho iborene? *a* **1250** *Owl & Night.* 66 And alle heo [*Cott. MS.* ho] þe driveþ heonne. *c* **1250** *Meid Maregrete* xx, Ho leiden honden hire upon. *c* **1275** *Sinners Beware* 136 *O.E. Misc.* 76 Þeos playdurs..Ho schule..In helle habben teone. ?*c* **1375** *Pol. Rel. & L. Poems* 239 For esye he comun al, esye ho ssuln wende.

ζ. 2–4 **ha,** 4 **a.**

c **1175** *Lamb. Hom.* 5 Þus ha hine hereden. *c* **1205** LAY. 5365 Ha [*c* **1275** hii] leopen on heore feire hors. *a* **1225** *Ancr. R.* 44 Ower graces..alse ha beoð iwriten ou. *c* **1325** *Poem Times Edw. II* (Percy) xliv, Loke that ha fare wel Hors & eke man. **1387** TREVISA *Higden* I. lix. (in Morris *Spec.* 340) Þe kynges of Engelond woneþ alwey fer fram þat contray..& ȝef a goþ to þe norþ contray, a goþ wiþ gret help & strengthe.

η. 3–4 **huy,** 4 **hui, hue.**

c **1290** *S. Eng. Leg.* I. 10/315 Þe croiz..deope under eorþe huy caste. *c* **1290** *St. Brandan* 669 in *S. Eng. Leg.* I. 238 An ester eue huy come. *a* **1300** *K. Horn* (Ritson) 1486 Hue gurden huem with suerde, Hue eoden..Towart the castele. *a* **1327** *Pol. Songs* (Camden) 214 That hue ne shulden aȝeyn him go. *a* **1350** *Childh. Jesus* 50 Ne dwelden huy nouȝt after ful longue Huy token with heom þat neod was. *c* **1375** *Pol. Rel. & L. Poems* (1866) 230 Þe ȝates of parais..Aȝein hui beoþ nouþe open.

II. 2. Accusative case. = THEM.

c **825** *Vesp. Psalter* xvi. 13 Aris, dryhten, forecym hie and forcer hie. *a* **855** *O.E. Chron.* an. 787 Se ȝerefa þærto rad, and hie wolde drifan to þæs cyninges tune. *c* **950** *Lindisf. Gosp.* Matt. x. 1 Þætte hia fordrife ða ilco and hea ȝeȝeme all un-hælo. *Ibid.* 26 Ne forðon ondredes ȝe hia *vel* ða. *c* **975** *Rushw. Gosp.* ibid., Ne forþon ondredaþ eow hiæ. *c* **975** *O.E. Chron.* an. 964 And [Eadgar cyng] sette hy mid munecan. *c* **1000** *Ags. Gosp.* Matt. xx. 25 Þa clypode se hælend hiȝ to him [*c* **1160** *Hatton G.*, þa clypede se hælend hyo to hym]. *Ibid.* xxiii. 5 Ealle heora weorc hiȝ doð þæt menn hi ȝeseon. *c* **1160** *Hatton G.* ibid., Ealle heore werc hyo doð þæt men hyo ȝeseon. *a* **1175** *Cott. Hom.* 227 He hi ledde ofer se mid dreie fote. *c* **1175** *Lamb. Hom.* 21 Þah ure an heofde idon eower alre sunne and he walde gan to scrifte and bi-reusien ha and forleten ha a mare. *Ibid.* 23 Þu scoldest heo biwiten al swa clenliche swa crist ha þe bitahte. *c* **1200** *Trin. Coll. Hom.* 51 Þe king..sende hie in to babilonie to þralshipe.. and þat lond folc hem ouersette mid felefelde pine. *c* **1205** LAY. 309 To his sune he heo [*c* **1275** ham] draf. *a* **1250** *Owl & Night* 1518 Overswithe þu hi herest. *c* **1250** *Kent. Serm.* in *O.E. Misc.* 33 Ha sente hi into his wyn-yarde. *c* **1315** *Shoreham* 14 He with-stent hi alle. *Ibid.* 16 The foend fondeth hy so.

3. *Reflexive* and *Reciprocal.* Themselves; each other.

c **825** *Vesp. Psalter* lxxii. 27 Ða afirrað hie from ðe forweorðað. *c* **855** *O.E. Chron.* an. 540 And steorran hie ætiewdon. *c* **1000** *Ibid.* (MS.D.) an. 925 Æþelstan..and Sihtric..heo ȝesamnodon æt Tame weorðþige. *c* **1000** ÆLFRIC *Exod.* xviii. 7 Hiȝ gretton hiȝ ȝesybsumum wordum. *c* **1000** *Ags. Gosp.* Matt. ii. 11 Hi [*v.r.* hiȝ] aðenedon hi [*v.r.* hiȝ], & hi to him ȝebædon. *c* **1160** *Hatton Gosp.* ibid., Hyo aþeneden hyo, & hyo to hym ȝebæden.

hi *pron.*, occasional variant of HE, HEO.

hi (haɪ), *int.* [A parallel form to HEY.] **1.** An exclamation used to call attention.

?*c* **1475** *Hunt. Hare* 136 Thei cryed, 'Hy, hy!' all at ones 'Kyll! kyll! for kockes bownes!' **1747** *Gentl. Mag.* 39 Hold, hold, 'tis a double; hark hey! bowler hye! If a thousand gainsay it, a thousand shall lye. **1847** ALB. SMITH *Chr. Tadpole* xxx. (1879) 267 'Hi!' cried the brigand, giving the mule a bang with the butt-end of his musket. 'Hi!' **1886** FENN *This Man's Wife* II. ii, It was not a thrilling word..it was only a summons—an arrest. Hi! **1894** —— *In Alpine Valley* I. 47 Here, hi! have a cigar? **1897** *Daily News* 2 Oct. 3/3 A good lunch, and then hi! for the Crystal Palace.

2. A word of greeting. *colloq.* (chiefly *N. Amer.*).

1862 M. D. COLT *Went to Kansas* ix. 143 When out on the prairie, up galloped an Indian on his pony with his saluting 'hi!' **1885** 'P. PERKINS' *Familiar Lett.* (1886) 33 We would have had to walk, I believe, if a *man* hadn't come along and let out the most satisfactory 'Hi, there!' you've ever heard, and stopped a car. **1920** F. SCOTT FITZGERALD *This Side of Paradise* (1921) II. i. 199 *Alec*: Hi, Amory! *Amory*: Hi, Alec! Tom said he'd meet you at the theatre. **1951** J. D. SALINGER *Catcher in Rye* iii. 26 He..came in the room. 'Hi,' he said.. like he was terrifically bored. **1953** H. CLEVELY *Public Enemy* xviii. 111 Tillic nodded to the uniformed commissionaire..and said: 'Hi, Charlie,' and they entered. **1959** I. & P. OPIE *Lore & Lang. Schoolch.* vii. 116 Hi, Roy Rogers! How about a date? **1963** H. GARNER in R. Weaver *Canad. Short Stories* 2nd Ser. (1968) 50 'Hi, Eric!' shouted Pete Adams..from where he was standing at the drinking fountain. **1972** WODEHOUSE *Pearls, Girls & Monty Bodkin* ii. 28 A musical voice in his left ear said 'Hi'. **1973** *Black Panther* 11 Aug. 2/2 (*letter to editor*), Hi, I've been following serialization of Operation Gemstone in the Panther Paper.

hi (haɪ), abbrev. of HIGH *a.*, freq. used in advertising and commercial slogans. (Cf. HI-FI.) Chiefly *U.S.*

1911 *T. Eaton & Co. Catal.* Spring & Summer 179/4 Hi-up battery. A very powerful cell for all forms of ignition work. **1930** *Engineering* 10 Jan. 63/3 This embodies the form of motor known as the Hicycle motor, that is, an alternating current induction motor, using a supply of a frequency of 180 cycles to 200 cycles. **1959** *Sears, Roebuck Catal.* Spring & Summer 87/4 Hi-Society—a glamorous new idea in lipstick! **1963** *Times* 12 Mar. p. xii/4 A new use for ball and chain. Known as the Hi-ball method, 100 acres of lightly timbered country can be cleared in a day. **1972** *Guardian* 3 Feb. 13/4 Kids prefer 'hi-riser' bicycles..with their apehanger handlebars and their drag style saddles.

hiacinth, obs. form of HYACINTH.

hiant ('haɪənt), *a. rare.* [ad. L. *hiānt-em*, pr. pple. of *hiā-re* to gape.] Gaping; having a wide aperture. (Chiefly in *Nat. Hist.*)

1800 HURDIS *Fav. Village* 17 E'er he pours into the distant deep, Through the wide fauces of yon hiant cliffs. **1848** HARDY in *Proc. Berw. Nat. Club* II. No. 6. 335 Maxillæ rather broad..the lobes hiant.

hiaqua ('haɪəkwə). Also **haiqua, haigua,** etc. [Chinook Jargon, f. Nootka.] An ornament or necklace composed of tooth-shells, formerly used as money by the Indians of the north Pacific coast of North America.

1824 G. SIMPSON *Jrnl.* in *Fur Trade* (1931) 96 The Ears are perforated all round and Beads or Hyaques suspended therefrom. *a* **1861** T. WINTHROP *Canoe & Saddle* (1883) vii. 95 Tribes..among whom hiaqua is plenty as salmon-berries are in the woods. **1862** *Nor' Wester* (Red River Settlement) 5 Mar. 4/3 Instead of the nose jewels being 'of tin' they were composed of the Hyaqua shells. **1881** E. B. TYLOR *Anthropol.* xi. 282 The Indians of British Columbia, whose strings of haiqua-shells..serve them..as currency. **1923** *Canad. Hist. Rev.* IV. 37 The shell *dentalium indianorum*,

commonly called hiquia, is much esteemed by the coast Indians, and amongst them has fulfilled some of the functions of money. **1953** E. E. CLARK *Indian Legends* 220 Hiaqua..—shell money and ornaments highly prized by the Indians of the Pacific Northwest Coast.

hiar, obs. form of HIGHER.

hiatal (haɪ'eɪtəl), *a.* [f. HIAT(US + -AL.] Of or pertaining to a hiatus.

1909 J. P. IDDINGS *Ign. Rocks* I. vi. 198 Hiatal fabrics being those in which variations in the sizes of crystals are not in continuous series, but in broken series with hiatuses, it follows that the most characteristic feature of such fabrics is the marked contrast between the sizes of some of the crystals. **1923** R. KNOX *Radiogr. & Radio-Ther.* (ed. 2) I. 319 Cardiospasm (Hiatal Oesophagismus). **1957** [see FIXATION 3 c]. **1961** *Lancet* 7 Oct. 810/1 In hiatus hernia, if the hiatal slit is small enough, the mucosal surfaces of the stomach may be adequately opposed.

hiate ('haɪeɪt), *v. rare.* [f. L. *hiāt-*, ppl. stem of *hiāre* to gape.] *intr.* To gape; to cause a hiatus. Hence **hi'ating** *ppl. a.* So **hi'ation**, gaping.

1646 SIR T. BROWNE *Pseud. Ep.* III. xxi. 162 The continuall hiation, or holding open its mouth [on the part of the chameleon], which men observing conceive the intention thereof to receive the aliment of air. **1876** R. ELLIS *Comm. Catullus* (1889) p. xiv, Latin..to which the hiating vowels *ē ī* are comparatively strange.

hiatus (haɪ'eɪtəs). Pl. hiatus, hiatuses. [a. L. *hiātus* gaping, gap, opening, f. *hiāre* to gape.]

1. a. A break in the continuity of a material object; a gaping chasm; an opening or aperture. Now *rare*.

1563 W. FULKE *Meteors* (1640) 17 b, These holes called *Hiatus*, differ from wide gapings, in nothing, but that they be lesse, and therefore seeme..deepe pits or holes, and not ..gaping. **1599** *Broughton's Let.* xiii. 44 Hades was below, and Abraham's bosome was aboue, and betweene them both a great huge Hiatus. **1675** R. BURTHOGGE *Causa Dei* 319 He saw two Openings or Hiatus in the Earth. **1695** WOODWARD *Nat. Hist. Earth* III. i. 117 The Water of this orb communicates with that of the Ocean, by means of certain Hiatus's or Chasmes passing betwixt it and the bottom of the Ocean. **1737** FRANKLIN *Lett.* Wks. 1840 VI. 5 Those hiatuses at the bottom of the sea, whereby the abyss below opens into it and communicates with it. **1885** *Manch. Exam.* 22 June 5/3 One side of the mountain was rent into a large hiatus about 200 yards square.

‖**b.** *Anat.* An opening or foramen. Also *attrib.*, as **hiatus hernia**, a hernia in which an organ, esp. the stomach, protrudes through the œsophageal opening in the diaphragm.

1886 *Syd. Soc. Lex.*, *Hiatus Fallopii*, a foramen situated on the upper surface of the petrous portion of the temporal bone leading to the aqueduct of Fallopius. **1928** *Acta Radiologica* IX. 301 Diaphragmatic hiatus-hernia and oesophageal diverticulum were roentgenologically diagnosed. **1934** *Jrnl. Amer. Med. Assoc.* 24 Feb. 586/1 A hiatus hernia should always be considered as a possible diagnosis when upper abdominal symptoms of doubtful origin occur chiefly or only at night. **1958** *Sunday Times* 28 Sept. 27/3 A condition known medically as hiatus hernia.. occurs when something goes wrong with the diaphragm. **1971** *Brit. Med. Bull.* XXVII. 34/1 Difficulty in swallowing is associated with..hiatus hernia.

c. *humorously.* A rent or hole in a garment.

1761 STERNE *Tr. Shandy* IV. xxvii, The hiatus in Phutatorius's breeches was sufficiently wide to receive the chesnut.

2. a. A gap or interruption of continuity in a chronological or other series; a lacuna which destroys the completeness of a sentence, account, writing, etc.; a missing link in a chain of events, etc.

1613 JACKSON *Creed* II. xix. §6 To forewarne the Reader of the *hiatus* in our aduersaries collections. **1655** FULLER *Ch. Hist.* II. iii. §17 A Dunce-Monk, being to make his Epitaph ..at Night left the Verse thus gaping, *Hic sunt in fossa Bedæ —— ossa*, till he had consulted with his Pillow, to fill up the *Hiatus*. **1676** W. HUBBARD *Happiness of P.* 57 When there are such Chasmaes and hiatus's in the superiour or inferiour parts of a state, they are sad Omens, portending ruine. **1797** *Monthly Mag.* III. 264 It was printed in the usual Greek characters, with all the *hiatus* filled up by conjecture. **1844** H. ROGERS *Ess.* I. ii. 59 In 1671..there is another hiatus in his correspondence. It extends over three years. **1874** CARPENTER *Ment. Phys.* I. i. §1 A Material Instrument, whose function it is to bridge over the hiatus between the individual Consciousness and the External World.

b. *Logic.* A step wanting in a chain of proof; a gap in reasoning or evidence.

a **1850** CALHOUN *Wks.* (1874) II. 269 Where is that hiatus ..between the premises and the conclusion?

3. *Gram.* and *Pros.* The break between two vowels coming together without an intervening consonant in successive words or syllables. Also *attrib.* and *Comb.*, as ***hiatus-consonant***, ***-filler***, ***-glide***; ***hiatus-filling*** adj.

The break or interval of silence is necessary in order that the two vowels may be separately heard, when there is no intervening consonant to mark the division between them.

1706 POPE *Let. to Walsh* 22 Oct., The *Hiatus* which has the worst effect, is, when one Word ends with the same Vowel that begins the following. **1875** LOWELL *Spenser* Prose Wks. 1890 IV. 309 *note*, He [Milton] also shuns a hiatus which does not seem to have been generally displeasing to Spenser's ear. *a* **1898** *Mod.* The article *an* has been reduced to *a*, except before vowels, where hiatus would result. **1945** *Mod. Lang. Notes* Dec. 550 The spelling *donmore* for *Dunmowe* may indicate the development of a hiatus-filling *r* in sandhi. **1948** D. DIRINGER *Alphabet* II. vi. 350 The letters..were also used as 'hiatus-consonants'. **1953** K. JACKSON *Lang. & Hist. Early Brit.* 278 The hiatus-glide with native *e* was..*i̯*. *Ibid.* 367 The hiatus-filler here is *u̯* rather than *i̯*. **1968** *Language* XLIV. 454 The general outlines of this 'hiatus diphthongization' have been known for more than three-quarters of a century.

‖**hibachi** ('hibatʃi, hɪ'bɑːtʃɪ). Also formerly **hebachi**. [Jap. *hibachi*, *hi-hachi*, f. *hi* fire + *hachi* bowl, pot.] A large earthenware pan or brazier in which charcoal is burnt esp. in order to warm the hands or heat a room.

1863 R. ALCOCK *Capital of Tycoon* II. xvi. 379 There were also some fifty *Hebachis*, or vessels for burning charcoal and warming the rooms, corresponding with the Spanish *Brazeiro*. **1874** *Trans. Asiatic Soc. Japan* II. 132 Boys and girls assemble around the *hibachi*. **1921** *Outward Bound* Apr. 22/1 The little *kimori* [sic, for *komori* nurse-maid] was bidden to join the family circle around the *hibachi*. **1959** R. KIRKBRIDGE *Tamiko* iv. 28 The small..mat room was bare except for..the hibachi, and a scattering of china on the shelf. **1965** *Austral. Women's Weekly* 20 Jan. 27/1 The other indispensable came from a prolonged stay in Yokohama, a small serviceable iron *hibachi*, the original of the Western barbecue grill, but portable.

†**hibber-gibber.** *Obs.* [Reduplicated derivative of GIBBER.] A confused repetition or babble of talking; gibberish.

1592 G. HARVEY *Pierce's Super.* 24 One madde knaue with his awke hibber-gibber is able to put down twenty of your smugged artificiall men that simper it so nicely.

hibernacle ('haɪbənək(ə)l). Also **hy-**. [ad. L. *hībernācul-um*: see below. So in mod.F.] A winter retreat; a hibernaculum.

1708 MOTTEUX *Rabelais* (1737) V. 231 The Legions on their Hybernacles think. **1791** E. DARWIN *Bot. Gard.* II. 17 *note*, What is in common language called a bulbous root, is by Linneus termed the Hybernacle or winter-lodge, of the young plant. **1822** *Blackw. Mag.* XI. 736 All the other snug and airless depositories and hybernacles of life in the city of cities.

hiber'nacular, *a.* [f. L. *hībernācul-um* (see next) = -AR.] Of or pertaining to a hibernacle.

1834 SELBY in *Proc. Berw. Nat. Club* I. No. 2. 35 Those insect tribes..had..quitted their hybernacular retreats.

‖**hibernaculum** (haɪbə'nækjuːləm). Also **hy-**. Pl. **-a**. [L. *hībernāculum* winter residence, usually in pl. *hībernācula* winter huts of soldiery, winter quarters, f. *hībern-us* wintry: see -CULE.]

†**1.** A greenhouse for wintering plants. *Obs.*

1699 EVELYN *Acetaria* Plan, Of Orangeries.. Hybernacula, Stoves, and Conservatories.

2. *Zool.* The winter quarters or place of retirement of a hibernating animal.

1789 G. WHITE *Selborne* xxvii. (1853) 108 Hedgehogs make a deep and warm hybernaculum with leaves and moss. **1816** KIRBY & SP. *Entomol.* (1843) II. 348 It shall seek out appropriate hybernacula or winter quarters and in them fall into a profound sleep. **1866** TATE *Brit. Mollusks* iv. 135 This it lines with leaves, retires to its hybernaculum and closes the aperture of the shell.

3. *Bot.* A part of a plant adapted to protect an embryonic organ during the winter, as a bulb or special bud.

1760 JAS. LEE *Introd. Bot.* (1788) Gloss. 418 *Hybernaculum*, Winter-lodge, the Part of a Plant that incloses and secures the Embryo from external Injuries. **1794** MARTYN *Rousseau's Bot.* i. 25 *note*, He [Linnæus] names them Hybernacula, winter germs or buds, into which the whole plant retires during the winter season. **1860** TYAS *Wild Fl.* 31 [Butterwort] There are formed small round leafy buds or hybernacula, about half an inch in diameter.

4. *Zool.* **a.** An encysted winter-bud of a polyzoan, which germinates in the following spring.

1885 E. R. LANKESTER in *Encycl. Brit.* XIX. 433/1 The only approach to a differentiation of the polypides in Paludicella is in the arrest of growth of some of the buds of a colony in autumn, which, instead of advancing to maturity, become conical and invested with a dark-coloured cuticle. They are termed *hybernacula*.

b. The epiphragm or false operculum of a snail.

1888 HUXLEY & MARTIN *Elem. Biol.* 273 It is no uncommon thing to find, during the warm season, individuals [snails] to the exterior of whose shells there adhere one or more (often a great number) of..hybernacula, cast off by their fellows on emerging from the dormant state. **1888** ROLLESTON & JACKSON *Anim. Life* 108 When the snail hibernates it closes the aperture of its shell by a whitish disc, the hibernaculum or epiphragma.

hibernal (haɪ'bɜːnəl), *a.* Also **hy-**. [ad. L. *hībernāl-is* wintry, f. *hībernus* wintry.]

1. Of, pertaining to, or proper to winter; appearing in winter.

1646 SIR T. BROWNE *Pseud. Ep.* IV. xiii. 225 [The dog-star] should rather manifest its warming power in the winter, when it remaines conjoyned with the Sun in its Hybernall conversion. **1799** *Spirit Pub. Jrnls.* (1800) III. 129 To sleep away the hibernal months. **1819** MONTGOMERY *Reign of Spring in Greenland*, etc. (ed. 2) 211 They meet the pale hybernal sun. **1870** HOOKER *Stud. Flora* 365 *Leucojum æstivum*; leaves hibernal.

2. *fig.* Pertaining to the winter of life; late.

a **1626** BP. ANDREWES *Serm.* (1856) I. 356 We have lost our regard so even of judgements and all, as neither vernal nor hibernal repentance we bring forth.

hibernant ('haɪbənənt), *a. Nat. Hist.* [ad. L. *hībernānt-em*, pr. pple. of *hībernāre* (see next). So in F.] Hibernating.

1836–9 TODD *Cycl. Anat.* II. 766/1 In the hibernant.. condition. **1842** M. HALL *Guist. Lect.* 15 The deep and long-continued sleep of the hibernant animal.

hibernate ('haɪbəneɪt), *v.* Also **hy-**. [f. L. *hībernāt-*, ppl. stem of *hībernā-re* to winter, f. *hīberna* winter quarters, *hībernus* wintry.]

1. *intr.* To winter; to spend the winter in some special state suited to resist it; said esp. of animals that pass the winter in a state of torpor. *transf.* Of persons: To winter in a milder locality.

a **1802** E. DARWIN cited in WEBSTER (1828). **1816** KIRBY & SP. *Entomol.* (1843) II. 349 It is probable that some insects of almost every order hybernate in the egg state. **1827** *Butterfly Collector's Vade-M.* 115 This species hybernates in the perfect state and sometimes survives the winter. **1865** *Pall Mall G.* 4 Oct. 10 There are now positively no places on the shores of the Mediterranean where invalids can hybernate cheaply and comfortably.

2. *fig.* **a.** Of persons: To remain in a torpid or inactive state. **b.** Of things: To lie dormant.

1829 SOUTHEY *Sir T. More* I. 39 Inclination would lead me to hibernate during half the year. **1862** M. HOPKINS *Hawaii* 305 The unsettled questions are hybernating, probably to bud and burgeon again at some future season. **1864** LOWELL *Fireside Trav.* 94 The public institution in which he hibernated (so to speak) during the other three hundred and sixty-four days of the year.

Hence **'hibernating** *vbl. sb.* and *ppl. a.*; **'hiber,nator**, an animal that hibernates.

1836–9 TODD *Cycl. Anat.* II. 766/2 In the sleep of the hibernating animal, the respiration is..impaired. **1870** HOOKER *Stud. Flora* 395 Propagated by budding from marginal clefts, and by autumnal hybernating bulbils. **1883** *Sunday Mag.* 674 The Faurde is really one of the hibernators, like our own hedgehog. **1888** ROLLESTON & JACKSON *Anim. Life* 262 'Hibernating gland', a gland found in many Rodentia, Chiroptera, and Insectivora.

hibernation (haɪbə'neɪʃən). Also **hy-**. [ad. L. *hībernātiōn-em*, n. of action f. *hībernāre*: see prec.]

1. The action of wintering, or passing the winter, esp. in some suitable place or condition.

1664 EVELYN *Kal. Hort.*, *New Conserv.* (R.), The several plants that were to pass their hybernation in the green-house. **1687–1700** SIR P. RYCAUT *Contn. Knolles' Hist. Turks* 1462 (L.) The next day..the vizier [marched] to Diarbechir, for his hybernation. **1808** SOUTHEY *Let.* 13 Sept. in C. C. Southey *Life & Corr.* III. xiv. 169, I am.. laying in health and exercise for the next season of hybernation. **1897** *Westm. Gaz.* 8 Apr. 1/3 My experiences may be of use next season to those who are in doubt about their next year's quarters for hibernation.

2. *Nat. Hist.* The dormant condition into which many animals and plants pass when the temperature falls below certain limits; esp. the winter sleep of some warm-blooded animals, as the dormouse, hedgehog, badger, bear, bat, etc.

a **1802** E. DARWIN cited in WEBSTER (1828). **1816** KIRBY & SP. *Entomol.* (1843) II. 349 Their hybernation in these circumstances has little or nothing analogous to that of larger animals. **1847** CARPENTER *Zool.* §221 This state of hybernation..is better displayed in the Dormouse, than in any other warm-blooded animal of our own country, except the Bats. **1856** DOVE *Logic Chr. Faith* IV. ii. §5. 221 [A plant] prepares itself for the period of hybernation. **1860** MAURY *Phys. Geog. Sea* vi. §325 The great serpents and reptiles have buried themselves for hibernation.

3. *fig.* Any condition or period of dormancy or suspended activity.

1829 DARWIN in *Life & Lett.* (1887) I. 176, I know scarcely any one that walks, and this..has reduced me to a sort of hybernation. **1865** *Pall Mall G.* 3 Aug. 1/1 With the revival of the Guild of Literature revive a number of questions which during its hybernation were put upon one side. **1879** *Cassell's Techn. Educ.* IV. 394/1 The long interval of half a century seems to be the period of hybernation during which the telescopic mind rests from its labours.

hibernatory (haɪ'bɜːnətərɪ). [f. L. *hībernāre* (see HIBERNATE): after *conservatory*.] A place for keeping plants in during the winter.

1852 *Beck's Florist* Oct. 225 This frame is to be employed for..propagating plants from cuttings, and lastly, to be used as a hybernatory.

Hibernian (haɪ'bɜːnɪən), *a.* and *sb.* Also **hy-**. [f. L. *Hibernia*, a corrupted form of *Iverna* (*Iuuerna*, *Iuverna*, *Iuberna*) = Gr. Ἰϝέρνη, Ἰέρνη = OCeltic **Iveriu* (acc. **Iverionem*, abl. **Iverione*), whence Ir. *Eriu*, acc. *Eirinn*, *Erinn* Erin, later MIr. nom. and acc. *Eri* (whence OE. *Yra-*, *Iraland*) Ireland. See -AN.]

A. *adj.* Of or belonging to Ireland; Irish.

1632 LITHGOW *Trav.* X. 436 The conscionable carriage of the Hybernian Clergy. **1711** POPE *Let. to J. C.* 15 June, What he observes at the Bottom of Page 20th..was objected to by yourself..'Tis right Hibernian, and I confess it what the English call a Bull in the Expression. **1773** BRYDONE *Sicily* xxiii. (1809) 227, I suppose your Hibernian squabbles ..would soon have an end. **1881** F. HALL in *Nation* (N.Y.) 19 The truly Hibernian predicament of being notoriously unknown. **1882** CAULFEILD & SAWARD *Dict. Needlework*, Hibernian embroidery..with Satin and Buttonhole Stitches upon velvet, silk, or net foundations, with coloured silks or filoselles.

B. *sb.* A native of Ireland; an Irishman.

1709 STEELE *Tatler* No. 35 ¶2 The Native Hibernians, who are reckoned not much unlike the ancient Bœotians. **1834** MEDWIN *Angler in Wales* II. 288 This was not lost on the shrewd quick-eared Hibernian.

Hence **Hi'bernianism**, Irish character or nationality; an Irish characteristic, trait, or idiom. **Hi'bernianly** *adv.*, in a Hibernian manner.

1833 *Fraser's Mag.* VIII. 620 He altered the family name from Macowen..to Owenson, and thereby destroyed its Hibernianism. **1873** *Harper's Mag.* 485 New scenes..new sea landscapes as Mrs. Trollope Hibernianly calls them. **1884** A. A. PUTNAM *10 Yrs. Police Judge* xii. 81 A prevailing disposition of the constabulary to let Hibernianism revel and rollic on the anniversary of its patron saint. **1894** F. HALL in *Nation* (N.Y.) LIX. 9/1 A colloquial Hibernianism.

Hibernically (haɪ'bɜːnɪkəlɪ), *adv.* [f. med. or mod.L. *Hibernic-us* Irish (f. *Hibernia*) + -AL[1] + -LY[2]: after L. *Hibernice.*] In an Irish manner; esp. in reference to speech: With something of an Irish bull, with an obvious contradiction or ludicrous inconsistency in terms.

1825 *Blackw. Mag.* XVIII. 727 Hibernically speaking, we have but one mode of complimentary reverence for the great. **1880** *Times* 28 Dec. 10/1 To make known to us something of what might be called, hibernically, solar geology.

Hibernican (haɪ'bɜːnɪkən), *a. rare*[−1]. [f. as prec. + -AN: after *Anglican.*] Of or pertaining to Ireland, or, esp., the Irish Church.

1885 R. W. DIXON *Hist. Ch. Eng.* III. 405 The other Hibernican prelates held their peace.

Hibernicism (haɪ'bɜːnɪsɪz(ə)m). [f. as prec. + -ISM: cf. *Anglicism, Scotticism*, etc.]

1. An idiom or expression characteristic of or currently attributed to Irish speech; esp. an Irish bull (see BULL *sb.*[4] 2).

1758 *Monthly Rev.* 342 As it stands, it reads somewhat like an Hibernicism. **1779** *Sylph* I. 240 That is the greatest trifle (to use a Hibernicism) of all. **1841** J. T. HEWLETT *Parish Clerk* I. 107 Mrs. Dowling had always, to use an Hibernicism, 'enjoyed' very delicate health. **1879** *Temple Bar Mag.* Jan. 5 They would, to use a Hibernicism, only have noticed it if it had left off.

2. The condition of being Irish; Irish nationality.

1807 SYD. SMITH *Wks.* (1859) I. 81/2 The defendant has pleaded that the deceased was an Irishman..and upon the proof of Hibernicism, acquittal followed of course.

Hibernicize (haɪ'bɜːnɪsaɪz), *v.* [f. as prec. + -IZE.] *trans.* To make or render Irish in form or character.

1812 H. & J. SMITH *Rej. Addr.* (1839) 40 *note*, This causes him..to..Hibernicise the rest of the poem. **1831** *Fraser's Mag.* III. 67 He has Hibernicized the whole realm of faëry. **1891** *Athenæum* 12 Sept. 350/2 Several of the Anglo-Norman families settled in Ireland became so thoroughly Hibernicized that they assumed surnames with the prefix *Mac*.

Hibernize ('haɪbənaɪz), *v. rare.* [f. L. type **Hibern-us* Irish (f. *Hibernia*) + -IZE.]

1. *trans.* = HIBERNICIZE.

1771 MACPHERSON *Introd. Hist. Gt. Brit.* 66 The proper terms..being Latin words hibernized. **1836** E. HOWARD *R. Reefer* xxxv, Not yet having sufficiently Hibernised my taste to luxuriate on Raleigh's root.

2. *intr.* To act as an Irishman.

1779 GIBBON *Misc. Wks.* (1814) II. 234 If you do not Hibernize, you might at least Bentinckize.

Hence **Hiberni'zation**, a making Irish.

1844 G. S. FABER *Eight Diss.* (1845) II. 268 This word likewise escapes Sir William's hibernisation. **1894** *Forum* (U.S.) Apr. 193 The usual Hibernization of the police force and the city departments promptly followed.

Hiberno-, formative element f. L. type **Hibern-us* Hibernian, Irish, as in **Hiberno-Celtic**, Celtic of Ireland.

1828 WEBSTER, *Hiberno-Celtic*, the native language of the Irish. **1907** *Daily Chron.* 6 Sept. 3/1 Hiberno-Egyptian. **1908** *Westm. Gaz.* 20 Aug. 5/2 A Hiberno-Romanesque church. **1939** *Burlington Mag.* Jan. 43/1 The brilliance and precocity of the Hiberno-Saxon arts. **1953** K. JACKSON *Lang. & Hist. Early Brit.* I. v. 175 This family of remote Hiberno-British princelings wished to make clear its claim to Roman status.

Hiber'nology. [f. L. type **Hibern-us* Irish + -(O)LOGY.] The study of Irish antiquities and history. Hence **Hiber'nologist**, a student of or authority on Hibernology.

a **1869** LD. STRANGFORD in *Lett. & Papers* (1878) 231 (D.) We may fairly contrast his Hibernology with that of the Hibernologists of the present generation.

Hi'bernophobe. *nonce-wd.* One who has a dread of or antipathy to the Irish.

1889 *Temple Bar Mag.* Dec. 533 It was long enough to demonstrate even to Protestant Hibernophobes that his system was the right one.

‖**hibiscus** (hɪ'bɪskəs). *Bot.* [Lat., a. Gr. ἰβίσκος some malvaceous plant (identified by Dioscorides with ἀλθαία).] A large genus of malvaceous plants (herbs, shrubs, and trees), mostly from tropical countries; the Rose-mallows.

1706 PHILLIPS (ed. Kersey), *Hibiscum* or *Hibiscus*, the Herb Marshmallows, of known Vertue against the Stone and Gravel. **1791** W. BARTRAM *Carolina* 104 The orange flowered Hibiscus is also conspicuously beautiful. **1857** LIVINGSTONE *Trav.* iii. 72 Nets made of the fine strong fibres of the hibiscus which grows abundantly in all moist places.

attrib. **1875** MISS BIRD *Hawaii* 134 Hats made from cane-tops, and trimmed with hibiscus blossoms.

hibrid(e, obs. forms of HYBRID.

hibschite ('hɪbʃaɪt). *Min.* [ad. G. *hibschit* (F. Cornu 1905, in *Tschermaks min. und petrogr. Mitt.* XXIV. 327), f. the name of J. E. *Hibsch* (1852–1940), Bohemian mineralogist: see -ITE[1].] A calcium aluminosilicate hydroxide, a member of the garnet family.

1907 *Mineral. Mag.* XIV. 400 Hibschite... Minute, octahedral, optically isotropic crystals of contact-metamorphic origin, occurring in enclosures of chalk-marl in phonolite at Aussig, Bohemia. **1942** *Amer. Mineralogist* XXVII. 783 *X*-ray powder patterns of hibschite from the type locality..closely resemble patterns of grossularite and plazolite. **1962** W. A. DEER et al. *Rock-Forming Min.* I. 79 Hibschite, $Ca_3Al_2Si_2(OH)_4O_8$, has a cell side of 12.16Å.. and eight molecules to the unit cell. **1966** [see *hydrogrossular* s.v. HYDRO-].

hic (hɪk), *int.* An imitation of the sound of a hiccup, esp. as an interruption in the speech of a drunken person.

1898 *Punch* 29 Jan. 41/2 What's (*hic*) Cuba to him, or he to (*hic*) Cuba?

‖**hicatee, hiccatee** (hɪkə'tiː). Also 7 **hecatee**. [app. ad. native name.] A fresh-water tortoise, *Chrysemis rugosa*, found in the Antilles.

1697 DAMPIER *Voy.* I. 102 There are 3 or 4 sorts of these Creatures in the West Indes. One is called by the Spaniards, Hecatee. **1756** P. BROWNE *Jamaica* (1789) 466 The Hicatee, or Land Turtle. This species is a native of the main-land, but frequently imported to Jamaica.

hiccius doccius ('hɪkʃɪəs 'dɒkʃɪəs). Also 7 **Hixius Doxius, Hictius Doctius, Hiccius-Docksius,** 8 **hiccius-doxius, hicksius doxius, hixious doxious, hiccius-doctius.** [Conjectured to be a corruption of the Lat. phrase *hicce est doctus* 'this or here is the learned man', if not merely a nonsense formula simulating Latin.]

A formula used by jugglers in performing their feats; hence, 'a cant word for a juggler; one that plays fast and loose' (J.). Also *attrib.* or as *adj.*

1676 SHADWELL *Virtuoso* II. 22, I shall stand here till one of 'em has whipt away my Mistris about business, with a *Hixius Doxius*. **1678** *Quacks Acad.* 5 All the use you are to make of such Terms, is the same Juglers do of *Hictius Doctius* and *Presto*. **1678** BUTLER *Hud.* III. iii. 580 An Old dull Sot; wh' had told the Clock..At Westminster, and Hickses Hall, And Hiccius-Docksius play'd in all. **1690** DRYDEN *Amphit.* v. i, Here is nothing, and here is nothing; and then hiccius doccius, and they are both here again. *a* **1734** NORTH *Exam.* I. iii. (1740) 211 The Author with his Hiccius-doxius Dexterity, can slur this on one Side, by a Word or two. **1794** *Sporting Mag.* III. 163 Our jugglers hixious doxious Shall distance all the Greeks.

hiccory, variant of HICKORY.

hiccough: see HICCUP.

hiccup ('hɪkʌp), *sb.* Forms: α. 6 **hicke up, hikup,** 6–7 **hickop,** 7 **hickhop, hecup,** 7–8 **hiccop,** 7–9 **hickup, hick-up,** 7– **hiccup;** β. 7– **hiccough.** See also HICKET, HICKOCK. [*Hickop, hiccup*, appears, from its date, to be a variation of the earlier *hickock*, HICKET q.v. *Hiccough* was a later spelling, app. under the erroneous impression that the second syllable was *cough*, which has not affected the received pronunciation, and ought to be abandoned as a mere error.]

a. An involuntary spasm of the respiratory organs, consisting in a quick inspiratory movement of the diaphragm checked suddenly by closure of the glottis, and accompanied by a characteristic sound. Also, the affection consisting in a succession of such spasms.

α. **1580** HOLLYBAND *Treas. Fr. Tong, Le hoquet*, the hickop, yexing. **1581** MULCASTER *Positions* x. (1887) 57 For the hikup. **1621** BURTON *Anat. Mel.* III. ii. VI. ii. (1651) 553 By some false accusation, as they do to such as have the hick-hop, to make them forget it. **1635** BRATHWAIT *Arcad. Pr.* 124 In the afternoone I am ever taken with a dry hecup. **1671** SALMON *Syn. Med.* III. xvii. 375 If the Hiccup come after taking it. **1727** BRADLEY *Fam. Dict.* s.v., You must in the very instant that the Hickup seizes the Party pull his Ring-Finger, and it will go off. **1893** BARING-GOULD *Cheap-Jack Z.* II. 190 Constitutional and chronic fits of hiccups.

β. **1626** BACON *Sylva* §686 It hath beene obserued by the Ancients, that Sneezing doth cease the Hiccough. **1744** BIRCH *Life Boyle* in *Boyle's Wks.* I. 83 (R.) Some are freed from the hiccough, by being told of some feigned ill news or even of some other things, that but excites a great attention of mind. **1794–6** E. DARWIN *Zoon.* I. 33 Seized with most violent convulsions of her limbs, with outrageous hiccough. **1876** FOSTER *Phys.* II. ii. (1879) 356 Hiccough.

†**b.** *transf.* A spasmodic affection of some other organ. *Obs.*

1634 HEYWOOD & BROME *Lanc. Witches* I. H's. Wks. 1874 IV. 184 O my hart has got the hickup, and all lookes greene about me.

c. *attrib.* **hiccup-nut** *S. Afr.*, the fruit of an ornamental shrub, *Combretum (Poivrea) bracteosum*, belonging to the family Combretaceæ; also, the plant itself; **hiccup strike** [It. *sciopero a singhiozzi*] *colloq.*, a strike normally of short duration which forms part of a series of similar and irregularly spaced strikes.

1862 HARVEY & SONDER *Flora Capensis* II. 512 *P[oivrea] bracteosa*... Fruit oval or slightly obovate, indistinctly 5-angled, glabrous, 1-seeded. Called '*Hiccup-nut' in the colony. **1868** J. CHAPMAN *Trav.* II. App. 447 The exquisite heads of scarlet flowers of the Hiccup-nut. **1899** WOOD & EVANS *Natal Plants* I. II. 63 The fruit is known locally as 'Hiccup Nut' and is palatable, but usually produces violent hiccough. **1951** *Dict. Gardening* (R. Hort. Soc.) II. 531/1 C. bracteosum. Hiccup-nut. **1950** *Times* 27 Jan., In the meantime the '*hiccup' strikes go on in the Paris region, where 12 'bus lines were out of action. **1962** *Daily Tel.* 28 June 26/3 Most are on what are known in Italy as 'hiccup strike', two-day stoppages at irregular intervals.

Hence **hiccupy** *a.*, marked by hiccups.

1853 LYTTON *My Novel* II. VII. x. 225 Long and loud talk recommenced, Burley's great voice predominant, Mr. Douce chiming in with hiccupy broken treble. **1895** DU MAURIER *Trilby* 165 He sang with a very cracked and hiccupy voice. **1911** J. C. LINCOLN *Cap'n Warren's Wards* i. 2 The train slowed down, in a jerky hiccoughy sort of way. **1968** *Listener* 11 July 55/2 Chopped-up, hiccupy sentences, often one word long. **1971** *Daily Tel.* 16 Oct. 7/6 The old Japanese anemone, mentioned in catalogues..as having the hiccupy name of Anemone hupehensis.

hiccup ('hɪkʌp), *v.* [f. prec. sb.]

1. *intr.* To make the sound of a hiccup; to be affected with hiccup.

α. **1580** HOLLYBAND *Treas. Fr. Tong, Hoqueter*, to hickop. **1684** tr. *Bonet's Merc. Compit.* XVI. 564 A Boy ten years old, Hickuped day and night for 8 dayes. **1798** ELLIS in *Anti-Jacobin* xiii. (1852) 58 He spoke; and to the left and right, Norfolk hiccupp'd with delight. **1852** R. S. SURTEES *Sponge's Sp. Tour* liv. 315 He hiccuped and spluttered at almost every word.

β. **1748** HARTLEY *Observ. Man* I. i. 97 Sneezing, Hiccoughing, Vomiting. **1844** DICKENS *Mart. Chuz.* xxv, As if a passing fairy had hiccoughed.

2. *trans.* To utter or bring *out* with interruption of hiccups, as a drunken person.

1788 DIBDIN *Musical Tour* vi. 20 Convivial lords..hiccup out *non nobis domine*. **1851** THACKERAY *Eng. Hum.* i. (1876) 155 [They] hiccupped Church and State with fervour. **1855** MACAULAY *Hist. Eng.* xix. IV. 222 An idle word hiccoughed out when they were drunk.

Hence **'hiccuping** *vbl. sb.* and *ppl. a.*

1748 [see 1 β]. **1803** BEDDOES *Hygëia* ix. 23 Sobbing and hiccuping..accompany epileptic fits. **1859** *Sat. Rev.* VII. 426/2 The dull apologies, the hiccuping excuses.

‖**hic et nunc** (hiːk ɛt nʊŋk), *phr.* [L., 'here and now'.] At the present time and place; in this particular situation; spatio-temporal nature of a phenomenon (see quot. 1948).

1935 *Studies in Hist. of Ideas* III. 469 One must distinguish between the *type* or *kind* of a sign, and its *hic et nunc* spatio-temporal exemplification. **1948** L. SPITZER *Linguistics & Lit. Hist.* 14 An explanation of the concrete *hic et nunc* of a historical phenomenon. **1950** I. SILONE in Koestler et al. *God that Failed* 103 A political revolution, *hic et nunc.* **1966** *Listener* 20 Oct. 580/1 The presence of God in the world, *hic et nunc*, at man's level.

hich, Sc. form of HIGH; obs. var. of HITCH.

†**hichcock.** *Obs.* [app. f. some sense of HITCH *v.* + COCK *sb.*; or related to HICK *sb.*[1]] 'A simpleton' (Nares).

1607 *Peele's Jests* Wks. (Rtldg.) 618/1 Among whom this hichcock missed his rapier; at which all the company were in a maze.

hichcoke, hichecock, var. HICKOCK *Obs.*

hichel(l, obs. ff. *hetchel*, var. HATCHEL.

hicht, obs. Sc. f. HEIGHT *sb.* and *a.*, HIGHT.

†**'hichty**, *a. Sc. Obs.* [app. f. *hicht* HEIGHT + -Y: cf. *mighty.*] High, lofty; *fig.* haughty.

1513 DOUGLAS *Æneis* VII. viii. 21 Wythin tha hychty boundis Turnus rycht Lay styll at rest amyddis the dirk nycht. **1535** STEWART *Cron. Scot.* III. 121 So hichtie than into his mynd wes he. **1596** DALRYMPLE tr. *Leslie's Hist. Scot.* IX. 214 Hichtie hardines and corageous spirit.

Hence †**'hichtiness**, haughtiness.

1596 DALRYMPLE tr. *Leslie's Hist. Scot.* I. 96 Of this cumis thair pryd and hichtines, and bosting of thair nobilitie.

‖**hic jacet** (hɪk 'dʒeɪsɛt). [Lat. = 'here lies'.] The first two words of a Latin epitaph; hence, an epitaph or monumental inscription.

1601 SHAKS. *All's Well* III. vi. 66, I would haue that drumme or another, or *hic iacet*. **1654** WHITLOCK *Zootomia* 416 Many..that, as to their dust, and Monuments, want a *hic jacet*. **1859** TENNYSON *Vivien* 751 Among the knightly brasses of the graves, And by the cold Hic Jacets of the dead. **1885** A. DOBSON *At Sign of Lyre* 55 (Stanf.) He let his human-nature rust—Write his *Hic Jacet* in the dust.

hick, *sb.*[1] [A familiar by-form of the personal name *Richard*: cf. *Dick*, and *Hob* = Robert,

Hodge = Roger.] **a.** An ignorant countryman; a silly fellow, booby. Now chiefly *U.S.*

1565 HARDING in Jewel *Def. Apol.* (1611) 529 Be it that Hicke, Hob, and Hans, of your Sects haue impudentlie accused him. *a***1700** B. E. *Dict. Cant. Crew, Hick*, any Person of whom any Prey can be made..; also a silly Country Fellow. **1702** STEELE *Grief A-la-Mode* IV. i, Richard Bumpkin! Ha! A perfect Country Hick. **1713** *Acad. Compl.* 204 (N. s.v. *Hycke-scorner*), That not one hick spares. *Ibid.*, That can bulk any hick. **1916** H. L. WILSON *Somewhere in Red Gap* iii. 113 So I yelled out back to an old hick of a gardener..and he comes running. **1923** R. D. PAINE *Comrades of Rolling Ocean* vi. 106, I come from a small town and that makes me a hick. My opinions aren't worth much. **1925** *Glasgow Herald* 16 Sept. 4 In the United States the 'Hicks' are still for the most part tenacious of that doctrine which assigns to speculations a 'bearish' or depressing influence on the markets. **1927** *Observer* 1 May 10/2 It is..much easier to write a good play about hicks, boobs, hayseeds, highbrows,..and sentimentalists than about decent English people. **1928** *World's Work* Apr. 628 Broadway humorists, only a few years ago, used to make fun of Long Islanders by calling them 'hicks'. **1929** A. CONAN DOYLE *Maracot Deep* 18 He could not make these country hicks understand. **1970** W. BURROUGHS JR. *Speed* ii. 39 The proprietor was a knobby, obliging old hick and he watched us all real close to make sure we didn't try to lift any fertilizer. **1970** J. HANSEN *Fadeout* (1972) ii. 10 He was killed... They just stopped playing him. As though we was such hicks we didn't know there's such a thing as tapes these days.

b. *attrib.* or as *adj.* Like a hick, unsophisticated, provincial. *colloq.* (chiefly *N. Amer.*).

1920 S. LEWIS *Main Street* xiv. 164 He graduated from a hick college in Pennsylvania. **1920** —— in *Sat. Even. Post* 11 Dec. 92/2 Why the plates turned over? That's hick-town stuff. **1921** H. C. WITWER *Leather Pushers* ix. 216 His.. features wasn't bad looking in a hick way. **1936** J. DOS PASSOS *Big Money* 256 Tad was sitting there hanging his head, his hick hands dangling between his knees. **1952** M. MCCARTHY *Groves of Academe* (1953) xii. 243 He..nodded triumphantly at his friend,..who had been trying to persuade him that science fantasy was hick. **1958** *Punch* 27 Aug. 283/3 Why stick with some depressing Yank writer who takes a cool six hundred pages to chronicle the twenty-four-hour doings of a single character in a hick town? **1967** *Listener* 17 Aug. 218/3 Telly was still rather a hick affair back in 1951.

hick, *sb.*[2] *rare.* Also hic. [See HICKET.]

1. a. A hiccup. **b.** A hesitation in speech.

1607 R. C. tr. *Estienne's World Wonders* I. xiv. 70 To pronounce them with their right accents..without either hicke or hem. **1796** PEGGE *Anonym.* (1809) 218 *Hiccup.*—The orthography of this word is very unsettled; some writing as here; others, *Hiccough, Hick, Hichoc*, and *Hicket*. **1825** JAMIESON *Hick*, the act of hiccuping. **1847** J. CRAWFORD in *Whistle-Binkie* (Scot. Songs) (1890) II. 237 Monie hicks an' hums Ye've war'd owre puirtith's antrin dauds.

2. *Comb.* †**hick-yex**, hiccup.

1628 HOBBES *Thucyd.* (1822) 99 Most of them had all the hickeyexe which brought with it a strong convulsion.

hick, *v. rare.* Also hic. [f. prec. sb.] *intr.* To hiccup. Hence '**hickingly** *adv.*, in the manner of a hiccup; with short spasmodic efforts.

1607 TOPSELL *Four-f. Beasts* (1658) 294 He would cough, and cannot but hickingly, as though he had eaten small bones. **1825** JAMIESON, *Hick*..to hiccup.

†**hickboo** ('hɪkbuː). *Air Force slang.* Also hickaboo. An air raid. *Obs.*

1919 *Athenæum* 23 May 360/2. **1925** FRASER & GIBBONS *Soldier & Sailor Words* 119 *Hickaboo*.., an Air Force term for an Air Raid.

hickell, obs. form of HECKLE *sb.*

hickery-pickery, vulgar perversion of HIERA PICRA.

1816 SCOTT *Old Mort.* viii, The leddy cured me wi' some hickery-pickery. **1887** J. SERVICE *Life Dr. Duguid* 280 How to use hykerie pykerie and rue.

†**hicket**, *sb. Obs.* Forms: 6 **hickot, hyckot**, 6–7 **hicket**, 7 **hi(c)quet, hickett, hycket**. [One of the earlier forms of *hiccup*, the other being *hickock*, both app. with a dim. formative *-et, -ock*. The echoic stem *hick* appears also in MDu. *hick*, Du. *hik*, LG. *hick*, Da. *hik*, Sw. *hicka* hiccup, MDu. *hicken*, Du. *hikken*, Da. *hicke*, Sw. *hicka* to hiccup; also Bret. *hok, hik* (Littré), F. *hoquet* (15th c.), Walloon *hikéte*, med.L. *hoquetus* (Du Cange), hiccup, F. *hoqueter* (12th c. in Hatz.-Darm.) to hiccup. The Eng. *hicket* corresponds in formation to the Fr., and is identical with the Walloon. Assuming this to be the earliest form, we have the series *hicket, hickot, hickock, hickop, hiccup* (*hiccough*).] Early form of HICCUP *sb.*

1544 PHAER *Regim. Lyfe* (1553) E viij a, It is good to cast colde water in the face of him that hath the hicket. **1545** RAYNOLD *Byrth Mankynde* III. iii. (1634) 173 Against Yexing or the Hyckot. **1584** R. SCOT *Discov. Witchcr.* XII. xiii. (1886) 195 The hickot is cured with sudden feare or strange newes. **1601** HOLLAND *Pliny* II. 442 Proceeding from excessiue yexing or hicquets. **1684** R. JOHNSON *Man. Physick* III. iv. 153 The causes of the Hicket are either internal or external.

b. = HICCUP *sb.* b.

1562 BULLEYN *Bk. Simples* 54 b, When the hart is weake or in a great hicket.

†**hicket**, *v. Obs.* Also 6 **hickot**. [f. prec. Cf. F. *hoqueter*, Walloon *hiketer*.] Early form of HICCUP *v.*

1584 R. SCOT *Discov. Witchcr.* XI. xv. (1886) 164 Some will hold fast their left thombe in their right hand when they hickot. **1634** T. JOHNSON *Parey's Chirurg.* XXII. xxxvii. (1678) 520 Repletion helps that hicketting that proceeds from inanition.

hickey ('hɪkɪ), *sb.* Chiefly *U.S.* Also **hickie**. [Origin unknown.] **1.** Any small gadget or device; something of little consequence; = DOOHICKEY.

Quot. 1909 is more specific than is warranted by the available evidence.

1909 WEBSTER, *Hickey* (a), a device for bending a conduit, consisting of an iron pipe used as a handle fitted at one end with a tee through which the conduit is passed; (b) a small fitting used in wiring for electric lights, a fixture piped for gas. **1913** in WENTWORTH *Amer. Dial. Dict.* 291/1 S.C. Rock Hill. Common. 'Hand me that hickey.' **1928** *Papers Michigan Acad. Sci. Arts & Lett.* X. 298 *Hickie*, a word applicable to anything whose name one does not remember; 'what's its name'. **1932** *Atlantic Monthly* CXLIX. 665 We have little hickeys beside our seats to regulate the amount of air admitted through a slot in each window. **1935** *Hearst's International* Oct. 24/2 The chances are the management will be putting hickeys in their keyholes. **1940** *Sat. Even. Post* 15 June 38/2 There was a violent distaste for the fraction-of-a-cent tokens, disks of aluminum with a hole in the center. These were variously called 'Chinese money', 'hickeys', 'monkey money' and 'agony money'.

2. A pimple; a love-bite. *U.S. dial.* or *colloq.*

Said by Wentworth and Flexner to be *c* 1915 but printed evidence is lacking.

1934 *Amer. Ballads & Folk Songs* (1960) 19 Godamighty made a 'gator wid hickies all over his Tail. **1937** *Ten-Story Love Mag.* May 2 (Advt.), Hickies spoil everything. I know. I had 'em until I began eating Fleischmann's yeast. **1946** *Publ. Amer. Dial Soc.* Nov. 17 *Hickey*, a small festered spot on the skin of a person. Salem. Reported 1942. **1956** H. GOLD *Man who was not with It* (1965) xviii. 158 A woman is not just soul and hickie-squeezing. *Ibid.* xxv. 235 Tall.. skinny, big blue hickie on the face.

3. *Printing.* (See quots.)

1940 *Correct English* (Chicago) Mar. 63/3 *Hickey*, printer's slang term for ornament. **1961** H. B. JACOBSON *Mass Communications Dict.* 163 *Hickey*. 1. Slang term for slight tears or rips in wet collodion or stripfilm negatives, or for small 'runs' or blemishes in sensitized coatings. 2. A speck on the printing area of an engraving that remains after the etch. Must be routed off. **1967** E. CHAMBERS *Photolitho-Offset* 273 *Hickeys*, faults in the printed result which show as irregular spots with white surrounding haloes, caused by dirt or hardened specks of ink.

4. See JIM-HICKEY.

hickey ('hɪkɪ), *a. slang.* [? f. HICK *v.*] Tipsy.

Recorded in dictionaries of slang: Grose (1788), Matsell (1859), Barrère & Leland (1889), Berrey & Van den Bark (1942), etc.

hickis taper, variant of HAG-TAPER.

hick-joint. *Masonry.* (See quot.)

1876 GWILT *Archit.* Gloss., *Hick-joint Pointing*, that species of pointing in which, after the joints are raked out, a portion of superior mortar is inserted between the courses, and made perfectly smooth with the surface.

hickle, dial. f. HECKLE; var. HICKWALL.

hicklety-picklety: see HIGGLEDY-PIGGLEDY.

†**hickock**, *sb. Obs.* Forms: α. 6 **hyckock**, 7 **hickock, hickcock, hic(c)ock, hick-hock, (hick-hoe)**. β. 6 **hitchcock, hytchcoke, (hitch cough), hichcoke, -koke, hichecock(e**. [A parallel form to HICKET, the difference being either that of two diminutive suffixes, or merely phonetic, as in the later *hickop, hiccup*. The explanation of the variant form in *hich-, hitch-*, is not clear; it is perh. to be sought in the dial. equivalence of *ch* and *k*.] An earlier form of HICCUP *sb.*

α. **1538** BALE *Thre Lawes* 524 Thre syppes are for the hyckock And vi more for the chyckock. **1612** WOODALL *Surg. Mate* Wks. (1653) 190 Against vomiting, and the Hickcock. **1660** HOWELL *Parly Beasts* 78 (D.) Go to the stomack, it hath..singultus or the hicock. **1670** COVEL *Diary* (Hakluyt Soc.) 140 A jerky motion like those who have a strong Hickock. **1678** HEXHAM *Dutch Dict.*, *Hick*, the Hick-hock.

β. **1551** TURNER *Herbal* I. C j, The brothe..dryueth awaye the hycthcoke. *Ibid.* C vj b, Dyll..swageth yᵉ hichkoke. **1562** *Ibid.* II. 54 Mynt..stancheth perbrekyng and the hitch cough. **1598** FLORIO, *Singhiozzi*, yeaxings, hichecocks.

†**hickock**, *v. Obs.* Forms: see prec. [f. prec.] An early form of HICCUP *v.*

1598 FLORIO, *Singhiozzare*, to sob, to throb..to yexe, to hichecocke. **1611** COTGR., *Sanglotter*, to yex or hickock.

hickol, dial. form of HICKWALL.

hickory ('hɪkərɪ). Forms: 7 **hiquery**, 7–9 **hickery**, 8 **-erie, -ary, heckarry**, 8– **hiccory, hickory**. [Shortened from *pohickery*, recorded as the native Virginian name in 17th c.]

1. a. A North American tree of the genus *Carya*, closely allied to the walnut, with tough heavy wood, and bearing drupes (mostly with a hard woody rind or husk) inclosing 'nuts', the kernels of which in several species are edible. Also **hickory-tree**.

There are about a dozen species, all natives of N. America, the commonest in the Eastern U.S. being the ***shell-bark***, ***scaly-bark***, or ***shag-bark h.*** (*C. alba*); others are the ***peccan*** or ***Illinois-nut h.*** (*C. olivæformis*), common in the Ohio and Mississippi valleys, the ***bitter-nut*** or ***swamp h.*** (*C. amara*), and the ***pig-nut, hog-nut***, or ***broom h.*** (*C. porcina*).

[**1653** J. FERRAR *Reformed Virginia Silk Worm* (Cent.), Popler, Plum, Crab, Oake, and Apple tree, Yea, Cherry, and tree called Pohickery.] **1682** T. A. *Carolina* 7 The Wild Wallnut, or Hiquery Tree. **1737** WESLEY *Wks.* (1872) I. 62 Many hickary-trees which bear a bad kind of walnut. **1748** *Phil. Trans.* XLV. 543 Hiccory, the most common Tree in their Woods. **1807** P. GASS *Jrnl.* 14 Here the soil is good, with cotton wood, sycamore, hickory, oak, and white walnut. **1849** BRYANT *Fountain* 23 The hoary trunks Of oak, and plane, and hickory, o'er thee held A mighty canopy. *Ibid.* 75 Indian maidens..That gather from the nestling heaps of leaves The hickory's white nuts.

b. In Australia, transf. to various trees whose wood is similarly used to that of the American tree; the native hickory of N.S. Wales is *Acacia leprosa* and *A. Melanoxylon*, of Tasmania *Eriostemon squameus* (Morris).

1884 BOLDREWOOD *Melb. Mem.* v. 35 The beautiful umbrageous blackwood [*Acacia Melanoxylon*], or native hickory, one of the handsomest trees in Australia.

2. a. The wood of the American hickory.

1676 T. GLOVER in *Phil. Trans.* XI. 628 There is also another sort of Timber called Hickery, that is harder than any Oak. **1771** SMOLLETT *Humph. Cl.* (1815) 234 Her earrings consisted of two pieces of hickory, of the size and shape of drumsticks. **1879** *Cassell's Techn. Educ.* IV. 160/1 Hickory is very tough and elastic.

b. A rod, stick, or the like, made of this wood.

1805 D. WEBSTER *Let.* 4 May in *Priv. Cor.* (1857) I. 206, I have only to take my hickory and walk. *a***1813** A. WILSON *Foresters* Poet. Wks. (1846) 220 Grant this, ye powers! to dominies distrest, Their sharp-tailed hickories will do the rest. **1857** WM. BOYD *Oakw. Old* 11, Let him sport his hound and hickory.

c. ***Old Hickory***, a nickname of Andrew Jackson, President of U.S. 1829–37.

1827 *Hallowell* (Maine) *Gaz.* 20 June 2/2 He was in favor of amending the Constitution, so as to let the people vote for Old Hickory. **1860** J. PARTON *Life A. Jackson* I. xxxiv. 381 It was on this homeward march that the nickname of 'Old Hickory' was bestowed on the General. **1907** *Springfield* (Mass.) *Republ.* 24 Oct. 8, I should not say that Old Hickory was faultless, but Andrew Jackson was as upright a patriot as ever any nation had. **1949** B. A. BOTKIN *Treas. S. Folklore* p. xx, In this land..men put daring above discipline and etiquette to give us heroes like the 'Swamp Fox', 'Old Hickory', [etc.]. **1967** *Oxf. Compan. Eng. Lit.* (ed. 4) 592/1 *Old Hickory*, a nickname of Andrew Jackson.

3. The nut of the American hickory.

1866 *Treas. Bot.* 228/2 These nuts [those of *Carya alba*] stand second in point of flavour among the hickories. **1882** *Garden* 11 Nov. 433/3 The Hickory is a fine nut.

4. *attrib.* and *Comb.* **a.** *simple attrib.* Adapted to the growth of hickory; made or consisting of the wood of hickory; resembling this wood, very hard or tough (also *fig.*). Also applied *fig.* to members of various religious sects.

1741 P. TAILFER, etc. *Narr. Georgia* 97 The Proportion of Pine Barren to either good Swamp or Oak and Hickory Land, is at least six to one. **1800** *Med. Jrnl.* III. 119 The sparks which were discharged from an hiccory fire. **1829** W. IRVING in *Life & Lett.* (1864) II. 369 As to the old general [Jackson], with all his hickory characteristics, I suspect he has good stuff in him [see 2 c]. **1831** *Boston* (Mass.) *Transcript* 12 Dec. 1/1 This assemblage of *Shaking* Quakers, for so many of them proved, who were only *hickory* ones till they joined the sett. **1850** LYELL *2nd Visit U.S.* II. 22 The soil of the 'hiccory grounds' is derived from the disintegration of granitic rocks. **1855** *Jrnl. Discourses* II. 322 If there are any Gentiles, or hickory 'Mormons'..write it down. **1859** BARTLETT *Dict. Amer.* s.v., A 'hickory Catholic'..is a flexible, yielding one. **1872** E. EGGLESTON *End of World* xxxix. 249 Any member of your class would do better to marry a good, faithful, honest New Light than to marry a hickory Methodist. **1940** *Sat. Even. Post* 30 Mar. 37/4 He is..referred to by the neighbors as a 'hickory Amish' because of some infraction not publicly mentioned, but most likely that of going to a movie.

b. *Comb.* **hickory-acacia** = native hickory of N.S. Wales, 1 b; **hickory-elm**, an American elm (*Ulmus racemosa*); **hickory-eucalyptus**, an Australian tree, *Eucalyptus punctata*, with very hard tough wood; **hickory-girdler** (also *hickory twig girdler*), a longicorn beetle, *Oncideres cingulatus*, of the United States; **hickory-horned** *a.*, having very tough or hard horns; applied to a kind of caterpillar (see quot.); **hickory-nut**, the nut of the hickory; **hickory-pine**, N. American species of pine, *Pinus Balfouriana*, var. *aristata*, and *P. pungens*; **hickory shad**, the gizzard-shad (*Dorosoma cepedianum*); also, the fall-herring; **hickory shirt** (*U.S.*), 'a coarse and durable shirt worn by laborers, made of heavy twilled cotton with a narrow blue stripe or a check' (*Cent. Dict.*); **hickory-tree** (see 1).

1816 KIRBY & SP. *Entomol.* xxi. (1828) II. 235 This caterpillar (*Ceracampa regalis*) is called in Virginia the *hickory-horned devil. **1683** PENN *Let.* 5 July in *Gentlem. Mag.* (1834) CIV. I. 42 Here is a *hickery nut tree, mighty large, and more tough then our ash. **1802** W. FORSYTH *Cult. Fruit Trees* xxi. (1824) 298 The Hickery Nut from North America. **1886** *Pop. Sci. Monthly* XXX. 71 (Cent.) The shell-barks, the hickory-nuts par excellence. **1800** B. HAWKINS *Sk. Creek Country* in *Georgia Hist. Soc. Colls.* (1848) III. 53 The fish taken here are, the *hickory shad, [etc.]. **1871** *Amer. Naturalist* V. 398 The 'Hickory Shad'..

were also filled with comminuted Crustacea. **1947** B. W. DALRYMPLE *Panfish* 341 Then suddenly a big buck Shad of four or five pounds, or a small Alewife or Hickory Shad. **1836** D. HARRIS in *Texas Hist. Assoc. Q.* (1900–1) IV. 160 Mother.. made two striped *hickory shirts and bags to carry provisions. **1850** L. H. GARRARD *Wah-To-Yah* xii. (1927) 58 Hickory shirts. *a* **1861** T. WINTHROP *Canoe & Saddle* (1883) iii. 33 Hickory shirts and woolen blankets are worn instead of skin raiment. **1889** FARMER *Dict. Amer.* s.v., Colloquially *hickory* has been employed as a nickname for persons and objects partaking of the qualities of the wood of this tree.. so *hickory shirts* for their strength. **1891** B. HARTE *Fam. Tasajara* I. 16 Fumbling in the breast pocket of his hickory shirt. **1882** *Garden* 27 May 370/2 The *Hickory twig girdler.. gnawing deep grooves round the shoots and small branches.

†**hick'scorner.** *Obs.* [See HICK *sb.*[1]] The name of a character in an allegorical interlude of the same title printed by Wynkyn de Worde, represented as a travelled libertine who scoffs at religion; hence, a scoffer in general.

c **1530** *Hickscorner* in Hazl. *Dodsley* I. 160 *Freewill.* Yea, but where is Hickscorner now? **1542** UDALL *Erasm. Apoph.* Pref. ***j, Zeno.. vsed to call Socrates the scoffer, or the Hicke scorner of the citee of Athenes. **1560–4** BECON *Supplic.* Prayers, etc. (Parker Soc.) 232 The papists deck themselves like hickscorner in game-players' garments. **1581** J. BELL *Haddon's Answ. Osor.* 12 b, Here you play hick-scorner concernyng the reformation of our maners. **1622** AILESBURY *Serm.* (1623) 49 Methinkes I foresee the Hic-scorners of this age knocking at Heauengate.

Hicksite ('hɪksaɪt). [f. proper name *Hicks* + -ITE.] A member of a seceding body of American Quakers, founded by Elias Hicks in 1827, and holding Socinian doctrines. Also *attrib.*

1839 MARRYAT *Diary Amer.* Ser. I. III. 95 The Friends.. have been separated into Orthodox and Hicksite. **1874** WHITTIER *Anti-Slavery Convent.* Prose Wks. 1889 III. 178 A few spectators, mostly of the Hicksite division of Friends, were present, in broad brims and plain bonnets.

hickup, obs. form of HICCUP.

hickwall ('hɪkwɔl). *local.* Forms: α. 5 **hyghwhele**, 6 **highwale**, **hucholl**, **hewhall**, 6–7 **hewel(l**, 7– **hew-hole**. β. 7 **highaw(e**, **heighaw**, **heyhoe**, **hiho**, 7–8 **high-hoe**, 9 **haihow**; 9 **heighhold**. (Cf. HIGH-HOLE, HECCO.) γ. 6 **hechewall**, 6– **hickwall**; also 6 **hicwaw**, 7 **hicway**, 7–8 **hickway**. (Cf. WITWALL.) δ. 9 **hickle**, **hickol**, **heckle**, **ickwell**, **ickle**, **eckle**, **eacle**, **eaqual**, **ecall**, **eikle**, **eekle**. (Cf. YUCKLE.) ϵ. 8 **hufil**, 9 **hefful**. (Cf. YAFFLE.) [A word of comparatively late appearance in writing, of which the original form and derivation are difficult to determine amid the variety of spellings in which it is found from the 16th c. onwards. It is probable that all these go back to imitations of the 'loud laughing note' of the bird, of which the early form *hygh-whele* (? = hyxwɛl) may be an imitation (already perhaps modified so as to make it articulate). Closely allied to this are the series *hueholl*, *hewhole*, and *heighaw*, *high-hoe*, *highhole*, accommodated by popular etymology to the habits of the bird. The series *hickwall*, *hicwaw*, *hickway* may easily have arisen from an earlier (hyxwɛl), by the hardening of *gh* to *k* (as in *heahfore*, *heyghfer*, *hekfer*, *heckfer* (HEIFER), and the words *hext*, *next*), although the second element takes the appearance of being = OE. *waȝ*, ME. *wagh*, and mod. *wall*, and the first has been explained as a derivative form of *hack* vb., quasi 'that which hacks walls'. From *hickwaw* Drayton's *hecco*, and the modern *hickle*, *ickle* series, are obvious phonetic descendants. Finally, *hefful*, *hufil*, show *f* for earlier *gh* (x), and thus attach themselves likewise to (hyxwɛl). There is perh. some attraction between some of these forms and the names YUCKLE, YAFFLE, which appear to represent an earlier **youchel*, **yawchel*, parallel to (hyxwɛl); and there may have been similar mutual influence between *hickwall* and WITWALL, the latter prob. orig. = ME. *wodewale*, WOODWALL.] The Green Woodpecker.

α. **14..** *MS. Arundel* 249 lf. 90 Hygh-whele, *picus.* *c* **1532** DEWES *Introd. Fr.* in *Palsgr.* 911 The high-wale, *lespec.* **1562** TURNER *Herbal* II. 25 Like vnto yᵉ ende of the tonge of an hueholl or wodspike. **1570** LEVINS *Manip.* 13/41 Hewhall, *vireo.* *Ibid.* 56/13 Hewell, bird, *vireo.* *a* **1678** MARVELL *Appleton House* 558 Yet that worm triumphs not long But serves to feed the hewel's young. **1678** RAY *Willughby's Ornith.* 135 The green Woodpecker, or Woodspite, called also the Rain-fowl, High-hoe, and Hew-hole. **1797–1804** BEWICK *Brit. Birds* (1847) I. 276 *heading*, The Green Woodpecker.. Hew-hole.

β. **1611** COTGR., *Epiche*, a Speight.. Wood-pecker, or Highaw. *Ibid.*, *Prinard*, a Heighaw, or Wood-pecker. **1674** RAY *Collect. Words* 84 (Halliw.) *Heyhoe*, the green wood-pecker. **1678** [see α]. **1688** R. HOLME *Armoury* II. xiii. 308/2 Woodspite, Hickwall, Witwall, Hiho, Red Sparrow. **1879** MISS JACKSON *Shropsh. Word-bk.*, *Haihow*,.. the Green Woodpecker.—Bridgnorth.

γ. **1546** LANGLEY *Pol. Verg. De Invent.* I. xvii. 30 b, The Hechewal, if a wedge be driuen into the whole of her nest.. compelleth it to fall out with an herbe that she knoweth. **1573–80** BARET *Alv.* H 416 An Hickwall, or witwall, *vireo.* **1580** HOLLYBAND *Treas. Fr. Tong*, *Pic*,.. a birde called a Speicht or Hicwaw. **1601** HOLLAND *Pliny* I. 351 The Wrinecke or Hickway, with some few others, haue two [toes] before and other two behind. **1611** FLORIO, *Picchio*,.. a bird called a wood hacker, a wood wall, a wood pecker, a tree iobber, a hickway. **1661** LOVELL *Hist. Anim. & Min.* Introd., The woodpecker.. nutjobber.. witwal, hickwall.. creeper. **1708** MOTTEUX *Rabelais* IV. lxii. (1737) 254 This same Herb your Hickways, alias Woodpeckers use. **1824** CARY tr. *Aristoph. Birds* III. i. 109 Those carpenter fowls, the hickwalls, Who with their beaks did hack the gates out workmanly. **1890** *Gloucestersh. Gloss.*, *Hickwall*, the green woodpecker.

δ. **1876** *S. Warwicksh. Gloss.*, *Hickle*, the green woodpecker. **1879** MISS JACKSON *Shropsh. Word-bk.*, *Ecall*, .. the Green Woodpecker. **1882** *W. Worcs. Gloss.*, *Eacle*, the Woodpecker. **1885** SWAINSON *Prov. Names Birds* 99 Green Woodpecker.. Eccle (Oxfordshire). Icwell (Northants). Eaqual or Ecall (Salop). Yuckel (Wilts). Yockel (Salop). **1890** *Gloucestersh. Gloss.*, *Heckle*, the green woodpecker (Heref.).

ϵ. **1788** W. MARSHALL *Yorks.* Gloss., *Hufil*,.. woodpecker. **1828** *Craven Dial.*, *Hefful*, a wood-pecker, a heigh-hold.

hi-coc(k)alorum, -olorum, occas. sp. of *high cockalorum*: see COCKALORUM 1 and 3.

hicra picra, vulgar perversion of HIERA PICRA.

1857 *Sat. Rev.* III. 239/2 A drug known by a familiar name, *hicra picra.*

hicwaw, hicway, var. of HICKWALL.

hid (hɪd), *ppl. a.* Forms: see under HIDE *v.* Hidden, concealed, secret.

a **1225** *Ancr. R.* 172 Semei bitocneð þe utwarde ancre—nout Hester þe ihudde. *c* **1380** WYCLIF *Wks.* (1880) 299 Pharisees.. þat ben hud monumentis. **1382** —— *1 Cor.* iv. 5 þe hid thingis of derknessis. **1500–20** DUNBAR *Poems* xxvi. 45 Hid malyce and dispyte. *a* **1598** ROLLOCK *Serm.* Wks. (Wodrow Soc.) I. 379 He will seirche.. to the hiddest hirnes of thy hart. **1608** DOD & CLEAVER *Expos. Prov.* ix. and x. 44 Such things as they can come by: which is called hid food. **1820** KEATS *Lamia* II. 54 Like the hid scent in an unbudded rose.

†**b.** In phr. *in hid* (*hiddis*), a literal transl. of L. *in occulto*, *in abscondito*. *Obs.*

a **1340** HAMPOLE *Psalter* xxvi. 9 He hild me.. in the hid [L. *in abscondito*] of his tabernakile. *c* **1380** WYCLIF *Serm.* Sel. Wks. II. 104 No man doiþ ouȝt in hiddis and ȝit he castiþ to be in apert. *c* **1400** *Apol. Loll.* 104 þingis þat þei don in hid.

hidage ('haɪdɪdʒ). *Obs.* exc. *Hist.* [ad. med.Anglo-L. *hīdāgium*, f. *hīda* HIDE *sb.*[2]: see -AGE.]

1. A tax payable to the royal exchequer, assessed at a certain quota for each hide of land.

a **1195** *Charter Hen. I.* in *Wetheral Reg.* (1897) 29 Terræ.. quiete de placitis.. et geldis et danegeldis et hidagiis et assisis. **1425** in Kennett *Par. Antiq.* II. 249 Cum hidagio hoc anno. **1480** CAXTON *Descr. Brit.* 21 Hidage, taillage for hydes of londe. **1607** COWELL *Interpr.*, *Hidage.* **1613–18** DANIEL *Coll. Hist. Eng.* 136 (D.) All the king's supplies made from the very beginning of his raigne.. Carucage, Hydage, Escuage, Escheates, Amercements, and such like. **1614** SELDEN *Titles Hon.* 270 The Aides taken in the infancie of the Norman State here was *Hydage.* **1765** BLACKSTONE *Comm.* I. viii. 310 Of the same nature with scutages upon knights-fees were the assessments of hydage upon all other lands, and of talliage upon cities and burghs.

2. The assessed value or measurement of lands, on which this tax was levied; cf. HIDATION.

1862 *Collect. Archæol.* I. 12 In many cases the manors are found to have retained their reputed hidage. **1883** F. SEEBOHM *Eng. Vill. Commun.* 38 The estimate thus given of the hidage of a manor.

‖**hidalgo** (hɪ'dælgəʊ). Also 7 **huydalgo**. [Sp. *hidalgo*, OSp. and Pg. *fidalgo*, formerly also *hijo dalgo* (pl. *hijos dalgo*), i.e. *hijo* (*filho*) *de algo*, son of something, 'the sonne of a man of some worth' (Minsheu). See Diez; and cf. FIDALGO.]

In Spain: One of the lower nobility; a gentleman by birth.

No one who was not a hidalgo was formerly entitled to the appellative *Don.*

1594 CAREW *Huarte's Exam. Wits* (1616) 220 These haue large liberties and exemptions, as in Spaine those Gentlemen who are called Hidalgos. **1630** *R. Johnson's Kingd. & Commw.* 267 The Dons of Spaine, the Monsiers of France.. the Hidalgos of Portugal.. and the younger Brethren in England, make a very poore company. **1638** SIR T. HERBERT *Trav.* (ed. 2) 116 Beaten off by fifty Huydalgoes. **1808** SCOTT *Let. to T. Scott* 20 June in *Lockhart*, There may be some hidalgo amongst the mountains of Asturias with all the spirit of the Cid. **1819** BYRON *Juan* I. ix, A true Hidalgo, free from every stain Of Moor or Hebrew blood. **1855** MILMAN *Lat. Chr.* IX. vii. (1864) V. 314 An outburst of reprobation.. from all the nobles and hidalgos of the kingdom.

b. *transf.* One like a hidalgo.

1826 H. N. COLERIDGE *West Indies* 81 In order to.. defeat those ingenious hidalgos the monkeys. **1867** MISS YONGE *Six Cushions* xi. 90 [He] was a ready-made hidalgo, as he well knew.

c. *attrib.*

1838 LYTTON *Calderon* vi, Those hidalgo titles of which your father is so proud. **1866** R. CHAMBERS *Ess.* Ser. II. 82 The old hidalgo idea.

Hence **hi'dalgoish** *a.*, resembling or characteristic of a hidalgo. **hi'dalgoism** (*hidalgism*), the practice or manners of a hidalgo.

1847 DISRAELI *Tancred* II. xvi, A hat a little too hidalgoish, but quite new. **1887** *Westm. Rev.* 1045 Petty princedom and effeminate hidalgoism. **1887** A. MOREL-FATIO in *Encycl. Brit.* XXII. 358/1 His [Cervantes'] main purpose was.. to show by an example pushed to absurdity the danger of hidalgism, of all those deplorable prejudices of pure blood and noble race.. which.. were destined to bring Spain to ruin.

'**hidated**, *ppl. a.* [f. med.L. type *hīdāt-us*, f. *hīda* HIDE[2].] Made or measured according to hides.

1889 *Athenæum* 28 Sept. 421/1 An elaborate hidated survey.. identified as belonging to the reign of Stephen. **1898** *Ibid.* 12 Feb. 211 The German hidated village is not a creation of the State.

hidation (haɪ'deɪʃən). The fixing of the number of hides; mensuration or assessment by hides.

1878 R. W. EYTON *Key to Domesday* 3 The older system [of mensuration in Domesday].. in that its basis was the Saxon hide, we may venture to call the System of Hidation. **1880** *Academy* 2 Oct. 234 There are frequent instances of a low hidation in Saxon times being increased.. by the Conqueror's officers.

Hidatsa (hɪ'dætsə). [Native name *hiratsa* willow wood lodge (Dr. Sturtevant).] A member of a group of N. American Indians; also, the language of this people. Also *attrib.*

1873 W. MATTHEWS *Gram. & Dict. Lang. Hidatsa* p. xvi, The origin of the word Hidatsa is obscure, yet it is the name by which these Indians now designate themselves... One of their villages on Knife River was named Hidatsa; and probably when they were reduced by smallpox the majority of survivors came from that village, which then lent its name to the whole Tribe... The name Hidatsa is said by some to mean 'willows'. **1890** J. G. FRAZER *Golden Bough* II. iv. 339 Some of the Hidatsa Indians explain the phenomena of gradual death.. by supposing that man has four souls. **1911** —— *Ibid.* (ed. 3) I. iii. 55 Similar practices are reported among the Illinois, the Mandano, and the Hidatsas of North America. **1964** E. BACH *Introd. Transformational Gram.* v. 89 Languages.. Arabic, Hidatsa. **1969** *Observer* (Colour Suppl.) 18 May 22/2 A special development in the warrior societies was found among the Mandan, Hidatsa,.. and Blackfoot, which had a hierarchy of societies.

hiddelles, var. HIDELS *Obs.*

hidden ('hɪd(ə)n), *ppl. a.* [See HIDE *v.*]

1. a. Concealed, secret, occult, etc.: see HIDE *v.*

a **1547** SURREY '*Good Ladies, ye that*' etc. in Tottel *Misc.* (Arb.) 19 That vnneath may I finde Some hidden place. **1582** N. T. (Rhem.) *1 Cor.* iv. 5 Who.. wil lighten the hidden things of darkenes. **1625–6** PURCHAS *Pilgrims* II. 1139 We entered into a very fair nook, and in the hidnest corner of it. **1712** W. ROGERS *Voy.* 179 Discovering part of the hidden Treasure. **1817** COLERIDGE *Sibyll. Leaves* Poems (1862) 87 A noise like of a hidden brook In the leafy month of June. **1875** JOWETT *Plato* (ed. 2) I. 267 Hidden meanings or remote allusions.

b. (*the*) ***hidden hand***, secret or occult influence, esp. of a malignant character.

1870 T. TAYLOR (*title*) The hidden hand. **1879** *Scribner's Monthly* July 326/2 Mr. Chaufrau played.. the negro Wool in a dramatization of Mrs. Southworth's '*Hidden Hand*'. **1932** *Ann. Reg.* *1931* II. 21 One Labour member attributed the appointment to the influence of a 'hidden hand' which was forcing the Labour Party to act against its principles. **1969** *Daily Tel.* 8 Mar. 20/3 Government action was being urgently considered against the 'hidden hand type of pressure' in public relations.

c. *Gram.* ***hidden quantity*** (see quot. 1898).

1898 G. M. LANE *Latin Gram.* §2459 A vowel which stands before two consonants, or a double consonant, belonging to the same word, so that its natural quantity cannot be determined from the scansion of the word, is said to possess Hidden Quantity. **1965** W. S. ALLEN *Vox Latina* 65 A long vowel in such a position is sometimes said to have 'hidden quantity'.

d. ***hidden reserve***: (*a*) in *Econ.* (see quot. 1965); (*b*) in general or transf. use, something kept in reserve in a concealed form.

1930 *Economist* 30 Aug. 408/1 Many of the assets in the balance sheet contain substantial hidden reserves. **1935** *Discovery* Oct. 290/2 It was not until the 'hidden reserve' of radioactivity was discovered that it was possible for the prolonged youth of the Earth to be explained. **1965** J. L. HANSON *Dict. Econ.* 213/1 If the assets of a firm have been deliberately undervalued, perhaps because the value of these assets has increased, the difference between their value as shown in the firm's balance sheet and their real value provides the firm with a 'hidden reserve', of which most shareholders will be unaware.

e. ***hidden persuaders***, a term used, orig. by the Amer. writer Vance Packard (b. 1914), to describe those involved in the organization and practice of advertising; hence ***hidden persuasion***.

1957 V. PACKARD (*title*) The hidden persuaders. **1959** *Daily Mail* 2 Apr. 1/4 This is the diet with the hidden persuader and the built-in will-power. **1960** *Guardian* 28 Dec. 8/4 The hidden persuasions. **1962** *Sunday Express* 30 Dec. 17/1 At sales time the hidden persuasion works harder —'15½ guineas slashed to £5'.

2. *Mus.* Applied to the consecutive fifths or octaves suggested between two parts when they move in similar motion to the interval of a fifth or octave.

1869 OUSELEY *Counterp.* ii. 8 These imaginary octaves or fifths are called 'hidden consecutives'. **1889** E. PROUT *Harmony* iv. §102 If two parts go by similar motion to octaves or perfect fifths, such progressions are called

'hidden' octaves or fifths... These octaves and fifths, being passed over, instead of sounded, are said to be hidden.

3. *Comb.*, as ***hidden-veined***, ***-working*** adjs.

1870 BENTLEY *Bot.* 144 In succulent plants, the leaves are termed hidden-veined.

hiddenite ('hɪdənaɪt). *Min.* [Named 1881, after W. E. *Hidden.*] A variety of spodumene, found in transparent emerald-green crystals, and sometimes cut as a gem.

1881 *Amer. Jrnl. Sc.* Ser. III. XXI. 130 **1881** *Athenæum* 16 Apr. 530/3 Dr. Lawrence Smith has proposed the name of 'Hiddenite' for the new mineral discovered by Dr. Hidden in North Carolina, which is known in the gem market as 'lithia-emerald'.

hiddenly ('hɪd(ə)nlɪ), *adv.* [f. HIDDEN *ppl. a.* + -LY².] In a hidden manner; so as not to be evident to the sight or understanding; secretly.

1580 HOLLYBAND *Treas. Fr. Tong*, *En cachette*, priuily, closely, hiddenly. **1642** T. GOODWIN *Heart of Christ in Heaven* 74 This marriage of Adam was ordained hiddenly, to represent and signifie Christs marriage with his Church. **1721** R. KEITH tr. *T. à Kempis' Solil. Soul* xiii. 207 Why therefore is it that thou withdrawest thy self sometimes so hiddenly from the Soul? **1846** TRENCH *Mirac.* vii. (1862) 197 *note*, The figure of all those who would do good hiddenly.

hiddenmost ('hɪd(ə)nməʊst), *a.* [f. as prec. + -MOST; after *inmost*, etc.] Most hidden or secret.

1892 E. C. STEDMAN in *Century Mag.* Apr., Describe, express, interpret, the hiddenmost nature of man.

hiddenness ('hɪd(ə)nnɪs). [f. as prec. + -NESS.] The condition or state of being hidden; secrecy.

c **1380** WYCLIF *Agst. Begging Friars* xliii. Sel. Wks. III. 397 He spake opunly to þo world, and in hyddenesse noþing. **1631** GOUGE *God's Arrows* IV. v. 380 The Philistines use it.. for the hiddennesse or secrecy of a cause. **1752** LAW *Spirit of Love* II. (1816) 27 Had not the Christ of God laid in a state of hiddeness in every son of man. **1885** PATER *Marius* I. 95 The hiddenness of perfect things.

hidder, -ir, var. of HEDER; Sc. ff. HITHER.

hiddill, -ils, var. HIDEL, -ELS.

hiddlin': see HIDLINGS.

hiddoues, -owus, obs. ff. HIDEOUS.

†**hiddy,** *a.* [? var. of HEADY *a.*] Lofty, towering.

1632 VICARS *Æneid* II. 39 The hiddie [*arduus*] horse standing within our town, Hath armed men disgorg'd.

hiddy-giddy ('hɪdɪ'gɪdɪ), *a.* and *adv.* *Sc.* [A riming jingle: cf. HEADY *a.* 2 b, and GIDDY.]

A. *adj.* Giddy, whirling. **B.** *adv.* In a giddy whirl; in confusion; topsy-turvy.

1450-70 HOLLAND *Howlat* 821 In came twa flyrand fulis.. and ȝeid hiddy giddy. **1535** LYNDESAY *Satyre* 4151 It gart my heid rin hiddie giddie. **1629** MAXWELL tr. *Herodian* (1635) 295 He fell to his hiddygiddy veneration of his country Deity.. with antique dances. **1819** W. TENNANT *Papistry Storm'd* (1827) 205 The Main-kirk rang wi' slaps and smites: Pell-mell, thwack! hiddie-giddie!

hide (haɪd), *sb.*¹ Forms: 1 hýd, 3 hude (*ü*), huide, 3-4 hid, 3-8 hyde, 4 hidd, 4-5 huyde, 4-6 hyd, 6 hydd, 4- hide. [OE. *hýd* str. fem. = OFris. *hûd*, OS. *hût* (MDu. *hut*, *huut* (*d*), Du. *huid*), OHG., MHG. *hût*, Ger. *haut*, ON. *húð*, Goth. **hûþs*:—OTeut. **hūði-z*:—pre-Teut. **kūti's*: cf. L. *cutis*, Gr. *κύτος*.]

1. a. The skin of an animal, raw or dressed: more particularly applied to the skins of the larger beasts and such as may be tanned into leather.

a **900** *O.E. Chron.* an. 891 Se bat wæs ȝeworht of þriddan healfre hyde þe hi on foron. *c* **1200** *Trin. Coll. Hom.* 199 þe neddre.. crieþeð nedlinge þureh nerewe hole, and bileueð hire hude baften hire. *c* **1220** *Bestiary* 144 Ðanne ðe neddre is of his hid naked. *c* **1230** *Hali Meid.* 37 Seoð þe cat at þe fliche & te hund at te huide. **1297** R. GLOUC. (1724) 116 þo carf he a bole hyde smale al to a þong. *c* **1400** *Rom. Rose* 7315 Teren the wolf out of his hide. **1467** in *Eng. Gilds* 396 That they do not shave flesh, skynnes, or huydes, but above the Brugge. **1495-7** *Nav. Acc. Hen. VII* (1896) 229 For halff an Oxe hyde all Redie coryed and Tanned. **1579** SPENSER *Sheph. Cal.* Sept. 223 Fast by the hyde the Wolfe Lowder caught. **1674** tr. *Scheffer's Lapland* 140 They put on a garment made of hides. **1727** SWIFT *Desire & Possess.* 57 Strip his Hyde, and pick his Bones, Regardless of his dying Groans. **1768** J. BYRON *Narr. Patagonia* (1778) 51 An ox's hide, used on board for sifting powder, and called a gunner's hide. **1853** C. MORFIT *Tanning*, etc. 146 Hides.. comprise the skins of oxen, horses, cows, bulls, and buffaloes, and are employed for thick sole leather.

b. In collocation with *hair*, esp. in phr. ***(in) hide and hair***: wholly, entirely; ***neither hide nor hair***: nothing whatever. (So Du. *huid en haar*.)

c **1330** [see 2]. *c* **1375** *Sc. Leg. Saints, Adrian* 514 Wnuemmyt in hyd ore hare. **1450-70** HOLLAND *Howlat* 950 This Howlat hidowis of hair and of hyde. *c* **1575** *Balfour's Practicks* (1754) 523 He sall exhibite the samin.. cattel, in hyde and hair, at ane certane day and place. **1857** HOLLAND *Bay Path* xxv. 303, I havn't seen hide nor hair of the piece ever since.

2. a. The human skin. (Since 17th c. contemptuous or jocular.)

a **1000** *Laws of Ælfred* c. 70 (Schmid) Gif mon oðrum rib forslea binnan ȝehalre hyde, ȝeselled x scill. to bote; ȝif sio hyd sie tobrocen.. ȝeselle xv scill. to bote. *a* **1300** *Cursor M.* 3661 þou wat mi hid es smith and bar, And esau es rugh wit har. *c* **1330** R. BRUNNE *Chron. Wace* (Rolls) 14904 He sey neuere er, So faire childre of huyde ne her. *c* **1460** *Towneley Myst.* (Surtees) 224 Alle rent is thi hyde. **1536** BELLENDEN *Cron. Scot.* (1821) I. p. lii, He wes fairer of visage and hide, than wes ony lady of the warld. **1645** MILTON *Colast.* Wks. (1851) 372 Who could have beleevd so much insolence durst vent it self from out the hide of a varlet? **1781** COWPER *Expost.* 486 He found thee savage.. Taught thee to clothe thy pink'd and painted hide. **1842** ORDERSON *Creol.* x. 106 One who.. tanned the hide of a poor pigmy. *a* **1873** LYTTON *Pausanias* 138 The poor fellow meant only to save his own hide.

†**b.** In alliterative collocation with *hue* (colour, complexion, countenance). *Obs.*

c **1330** *King of Tars* (Ritson) 752 Hit hedde bothe lymes and face.. Huyde and heuh, bon and fel, And everi lyme. *c* **1400** *Rowland & O.* 1230 Full fayre of hewe & hyde. *c* **1420** *Awntyrs off Arth.* 108 (Douce MS.) But on hide ne on huwe, no heling hit hadde. **1535** STEWART *Cron. Scot.* III. 305 His awin deir sone.. Of hyde and hew baith plesand wes and fair. *a* **1549** *Murning Maidin* xii. in *Laneham's Let.* (1871) Introd. 151 Ye ar so haill of hew and hyd. **1825-80** JAMIESON s.v. *Hyd*, 'It's sae dirty, it'll never come to hyd or hew.' *Loth.*

c. Impudence, effrontery, 'nerve'. (App. an elliptical use of 'thick hide'.)

Freq. in Australia and N.Z. but also occurs elsewhere.

1916 J. B. COOPER *Coo-oo-ee* xi. 150 Don't you think you have a hide to ask me? **1926** 'J. DOONE' *Timely Tips for New Australians*, *Hide*, a slang term denoting impudence. **1947** K. TENNANT *Lost Haven* ii. 37 He *might* have told me. Just springing it on me.. out of the blue... Like his hide! For two pins I'd tell him where to go. **1949** H. WADMAN *Life Sentence* 9 Talk about self-confidence... What a hide! **1959** P. H. JOHNSON *Unspeakable Skipton* v. 34 The beast has had the hide.. to dictate that to a secretary. **1961** *Coast to Coast 1959-60* 120 He wants to be a farmer. A farmer! Had the hide to try and tell *me* what farm life's like—me, born and bred on one.

3. As a material for clothing, shoes, etc.

a **1300** *Cursor M.* 935 God mad þam kyrtels þan of hide. *Ibid.* 2250 þar-for most þai þam hide Bath wit hors and camel hide. **1827** D. JOHNSON *Ind. Field Sports* 232 Pieces of cane bound round with.. slips of raw hide. **1860** LONGF. *Wayside Inn, K. Olaf* XIX. x, Eric severed the cables of hide. **1865** KINGSLEY *Herew.* x, They wore short jackets of hide.

4. A whip made of a beast's hide. Cf. COW-HIDE 3.

1851 MAYNE REID *Scalp Hunt.* xxiii, Pork and pipe-clay, accompanied with a too liberal allowance of the 'hide'.

5. *attrib.* and *Comb.*, as ***hide-beating***, ***-curing***, ***-dresser***, ***-dressing***, ***-factory***, ***-fair***, ***-knob***, ***-merchant***, ***-net***, ***-plate***, ***-seller***, ***-thong***, ***-whip***; **hide-blown** *a.*, bloated; **hide-drogher** [DROGHER], a coasting vessel trading in hides; the master of such a vessel; hence **hide-droghing**, trading with such a vessel; **hide-factor**, a dealer in hides who supplies tanners; **hide-handler**, a machine or vat in which hides are treated with the liquor used in tanning them; **hide-mill**, a machine for softening dried hides; **hide-money** (transl. of Gr. *δερματικόν*): see quot.; **hide-rope**, a rope made of plaited cowhide (Knight *Dict. Mech.*); **hide-scraper**, **-stretcher**, **-worker**, appliances used in preparing hides for leather.

1660 R. COKE *Power & Subj.* 150 Beat his hide, or make him to fear a *hide-beating. **1834** SIR H. TAYLOR *1st Pt. Artevelde* I. iii. (D.) Slothful, *hide-blown, gormandizing niggards. **1890** *Daily News* 24 Mar. 6/5 A Free Trade demonstration of the tanners and *hide-dressers.. in Paris.. A thousand men who used to be employed in tanning and *hide dressing. **1841** EMERSON *Lect.*, *Man the Reformer* Wks. (Bohn) II. 239 It is the sailor, the *hide-drogher, the butcher. **1882** *Harper's Mag.* Dec. 602 The beach where Dana once loaded his hides in his 'hide drogher'. **1840** R. H. DANA *Bef. Mast* xv. 41 A large ship.. as rusty and worn as two years' '*hide-droghing' could make her. **1894** *Daily News* 1 May 8/3 *Hide fairs were things common enough in many districts of rural England in old days. **1853** PRATT in C. Morfit *Tanning*, etc. 321 Three *hide-mills, for softening the dry Spanish hides. **1846** GROTE *Greece* II. vi. (1849) II. 475 *note*, The *hide-money (*δερματικόν*) arising from the numerous victims offered at public sacrifices at Athens, is accounted for as a special item of the public revenue. **1836-48** B. D. WALSH *Aristoph.*, *Knights* I. i, There succeeds a thievish, loud *hide-seller. **1851** MAYNE REID *Scalp Hunt.* li, Raw *hide-thongs were looped about our wrists and ankles. **1885** *Harper's Mag.* Jan. 274/2 A blunted piece of iron, known as a '*hide-worker'.. easily removes the hair after the hide is taken from the water where it was 'dumped' after the liming.

hide, *sb.*² *Obs.* exc. *Hist.* Forms: 1 hígid, hígd, híd, hýd, 1-9 hyde, 1- hide. [OE. *híd* str. fem., earlier *hígid*, app. from **híwid*, deriv. of *híw-*, *híg-*, household, family: cf. HEWE. The suffix is obscure.

In the Latin text of Beda, and elsewhere, expressed by *familia*, for which in the OE. transl. *híwisc* and *híwscipe*, derivatives of *híw-* family, interchange with *híd*.]

1. A measure of land in Old English times, continued also for some time after the Norman Conquest, varying in extent with the nature of the ground, etc.: primarily, the amount considered adequate for the support of one free family with its dependants; at an early date defined as being as much land as could be tilled with one plough in a year. See CARUCATE.

The question of the extent of the *hide* has been much controverted. The general conclusion appears to be that it was normally = 120 acres; but the size of the acre itself varied. See Maitland, *Domesday and Beyond*.

848 in Earle *Land Charters* (1888) 122 Ego berchtwulf cyning sile forðrede minum ðeȝne niȝen hiȝida lond in wudotune. **869** in Birch *Cartular. Sax.* (1885) 524 Eac wudulond all hit is ȝemæne þara fif & tuentiȝ hiȝda. *c* **900** tr. *Bæda's Hist.* IV. xviii. [xvi] (1890) 306 Is þæs ilcan ealondes ȝemet æfter Ongolcynnes eahte twelf hund hida [*Est autem mensura ejusdem insulæ* [*Vectæ*] *juxta æstimationem Anglorum, mille ducentarum familiarum*]. *a* **1000** *Laws of Æthelred* in Schmid *Gesetze* 242 And sceote man æȝhwilce hide pæniȝ oððe pæniȝes weorð, and bringe man þæt to cirican. *c* **1000** *Wergilde* c. 2 § 7 *Ibid.* App. vii. 396 Gif Wilisc man ȝeþeo, þæt he hæbbe hiwisc landes [*Laws of Ine* c. 32 Gif Wylisc mon hæbbe hide londes] and mæȝe cyninges gafol forðbringan, þonne bið his wer-gild cxx scill. And ȝif he ne ȝeþeo buton to healfre hide, þonne si his wer lxxx scill. **1086** *Domesday Bk.* in Kennett *Par. Antiq.* (1818) I. 88 Idem Rotbertus tenet Bernecestre.. Ibi sunt 15 hidæ et dim. Terra 22 car. *a* **1100** *O.E. Chron.* an. 1008 Her bebead se cyng þæt man sceolde ofer eall Angel cynn scypu feastlice wircean þæt is þonne [of] þrym hund hidum, and of .x. hidan ænne sceġð, and of .viii. hidum helm and byrnan. *Ibid.* an. 1086 Næs an hid landes innan Englæ lande þæt he nyste hwa heo hæfde. [*c* **1154** HENRY OF HUNTINGDON VI. 360 (Du Cange) Hida Anglice vocatur terra unius aratri culturæ sufficiens per annum. *c* **1175** *Dialog. de Scacc.* I. xvii, Quid Hida.. secundum vulgarem opinionem. Ruricolæ melius hoc norunt; verum sicut ab ipsis accepimus, hida a primitiva institutione ex centum acris constat.] *c* **1290** *S. Eng. Leg.* I. 52/185 An hondret hidene of guod lond with hire he ȝaf þer. **1297** R. GLOUC. (1724) 434 Of ech hyde of Engelond þre ssyllynges he nom þo. **13..** *K. Alis.* 458 Whan corne ripeþ in heruest tyde Mery it is in feld & hyde. **1494** FABYAN *Chron.* VII. ccxxii. 246 So an hyde of lande conteyneth .xx. acres. **1593** NORDEN *Spec. Brit.*, *M'sex* I. 5 The vsuall account of lande at this day in Englande is by acres, yardes, carewes, hydes, knightes fees, cantreds, baronies and counties. **1614** SELDEN *Titles Hon.* 273 By their account cxcii. acres made a Hyde. **1788** R. KELHAM *Domesday Bk.* (L.), The just value of a hide, that might fit the whole kingdom.. was ever of an uncertain quantity. **1895** POLLOCK & MAITLAND *Eng. Law* I. 347 In the north of England this unit appears as the carucate.. In the south the hide appears in place of the carucate, and the hide is generally regarded as made up of four, but it may well be of six virgates. **1897** MAITLAND *Domesday & Beyond* 510 They know but one tenemental unit. It is the *hiwisc*, the *terra unius familiæ*, the *terra unius manentis*, the manse, the hide.

b. ***hide and gaine*** [OF. *gaigne*, *gaingne* arable land, 'terre labourable' (Godefroy)].

These words appear to be given originally as synonyms of arable land. But later compilers took them as a phrase.

1347 in Fitzherb. *Abridg.* tit. *Admeasurement* ¶ 8 fol. 15 La terre a qe le comen est claim app[endant] fuit auncient terre hide & geign. **1628** COKE *On Litt.* 85 b, And the Common Law giueth errable land (which anciently is called Hyde & gaine) the preheminencie and precedencie before meadowes [etc.]. **1658** PHILLIPS, *Hide and Gain*, arable Land, or the same as gainage. **1708** *Termes de la Ley* 383 Hide and Gayne did anciently signifie arrable Land.

2. *nonce-use.* (Associated with HIDE *sb.*¹) As much land as could be measured by a thong cut out of a hide. (In quot. referring to the story of Dido's purchase of the site of Carthage, Virg. *Æn.* I. 368.)

1594 MARLOWE & NASHE *Dido* IV. ii, She crav'd a hide of ground to build a towne.

hide, *sb.*³ [f. HIDE *v.*¹]

†**I. 1.** (In ME. use.) The action or an act of hiding; concealment. *Obs.*

a **1300** *Cursor M.* 10771 Quen ioseph sagh na hide ne dught, Nedings forth his wand he broght. *Ibid.* 26115 O mans hert an opening wide, þat man can scheu wit-vten hide. *a* **1310** in Wright *Lyric P.* viii. 31 A stythye stunte hire sturne stryf, that ys in heovene hert in hyde.

II. 2. (In modern use.) A hiding-place; a cache. Also *attrib.*

1649 T. WODENOTE *Hermes Theol.* viii. 13 Hunted by an Orthodox Divine.. who can easily ferret them out of all their hides and holds. **1864** 'MANHATTAN' *Marion* I. 20 [He] would.. go early to his hide, and conceal himself, with the barrels of his duck gun loaded with buck-shot. **1884** *Public Opinion* 5 Sept. 301/1 A nice little 'hide', containing not only the articles he was in search of, but also other stolen property. **1920** *Nature* CV. 146/2 The cock bird discovered Mr. Brook leaving the 'hide'. **1934** *Brit. Birds* XXVIII. 97, I had just seen my companion into his hide tent.. when a small wader came off her nest at my feet. **1935** *Discovery* Aug. 228/1 We built our first hide.. four feet away from one nest. **1940** 'GUN BUSTER' *Return via Dunkirk* II. i. 85 The guns and vehicles went into a 'hide' in a large orchard. **1952** E. F. DAVIES *Illyrian Venture* xi. 220 The others had been sealed into a hide in the camp and were not discovered for four days. **1965** P. WAYRE *Wind in Reeds* iv. 43 He had already started work on the construction of permanent observation huts or hides built into the sea-wall itself, from which it was possible to watch the wild geese in comfort.

hide (haɪd), *v.*¹ Pa. t. hid; pa. pple. hid, hidden ('hɪd(ə)n). Forms: 1 hýdan, (*3rd sing.* hýt), hídan, 3-4 hude (*ü*), (*3rd sing.* hitt, hut, hit), 3-5 huide, huyde, 3- hide, (4-5 hid(d, hyd, 6 hyed). *Pa. t. α.* 1 hýdde, hídde, 2-4 hudde, 3-6 hidde, etc., (5 hude), 4- hid. *β.* 5 hidded, 5-7 hided. *Pa. pple. α.* 1 hýded, hídd, 2-4 ihud(de, 4-5 yhud(de, -hid(de, -hyd, (y)hed(de, i-hid, -hydd, hud, 4-6 hidd(e, etc., 4- hid. *β.* 6 hyden, 6- hidden. [OE. *hýdan* = MDu. *hûden* (*huyden*, *hueden*), MLG. *hûden* to hide, LG. (*ver*)*hüen*:—OTeut. **hûdjan*, variously referred to the root of OE. *hýd*, HIDE *sb.*¹, and to a pre-Teut. **keudh-*, *kudh-*, seen in Gr. *κεύθειν* to hide, cover up, conceal. The late

pa. pple. *hidden* is after strong vbs., e.g. *ride, ridden.*]

1. a. *trans.* To put or keep out of sight; to conceal intentionally from the view or notice of others; to conceal from discovery, to secrete. Freq. in phr. ***to hide away.*** Also const. *up.* (Cf. sense 2 b.)

c **897** K. ÆLFRED *Gregory's Past.* xxvi. 184 Swæ se læce hyt his isern wið ðone mon þe he sniðan wile. *c* **1132** *O.E. Chron.* an. 963 [He] fand þa hidde in þa ealde wealle writes þet Headda abb heafde ær ȝewriton. *a* **1200** *Moral Ode* 28 Al to muchel ich habbe ispent, to litel ihud in horde. *c* **1250** *Gen. & Ex.* 352 Ðo gunen he same sriden, And limes in leues hiden. *a* **1300** *Cursor M.* 3677 (Cott.) Wit a rugh skin sco hidd his hals. *c* **1340** *Ibid.* 910 (Trin.) þou wommon.. shalt haue euer þi heed hud. **1486** *Bk. St. Albans* E iv b, In moore or in moos he hidyth hem fast. **1490** CAXTON *Eneydos* xxiv. 89 She hidded the swerde. **1600** J. PORY tr. *Leo's Africa* II. 32, I had no leisure to hide away my coine from them. **1646** FULLER *Wounded Consc.* (1841) 339 Our English proverb saith, he that hath hid can find. **1770** *Junius Lett.* xxxvi. 177 Retire, then..and hide your blushes from the world. **1854** W. COLLINS *Hide & Seek* III. xxiii. 227, I shall find him! I don't care where he's hid away from me. *Ibid.* xxiv. 271 She..hid it away in her bosom. **1875** EMERSON *Lett. & Soc. Aims, Eloq.* Wks. (Bohn) III. 190 Mothers hid their sons, and wives their husbands..lest they should be led by his eloquence to join the monastery. **1884** 'MARK TWAIN' *Huck. Finn* xxiv. 241 It's reckoned he left three or four thousand in cash hid up som'ers. **1891** C. GRAVES *Field of Tares* 109 There was a fresh canvas upon the easel, the tattered one had been carefully hidden away. **1928** E. WALLACE *Flying Squad* xvi. 169 Bradley's fond of her. He hid her up once: why shouldn't he hide her up again? **1948** 'N. SHUTE' *No Highway* vi. 168 It was impossible to hide up evidence like that.

†**b.** To conceal so as to shield or protect. *Obs.*

a **1300** *E.E. Psalter* xxx. 21 [xxxi. 20] (Mätz.) þou salt am hide Fra fordrovinges of men. **1382** WYCLIF *Ps.* xxvi[i]. 5 He hidde me in his tabernacle in the day of euelis. **1535** COVERDALE *Ps.* lxiii[i]. 2 Hyde me from the gatheringe together of yᵉ frowarde. **1614** BP. HALL *Recoll. Treat.* 422 Many..having nothing but a cote of thatch to hide them from heauen.

c. ***to hide one's face***: (*a*) in Biblical language, to turn away or withdraw one's eyes, take no heed. (Also ***to hide one's ear, oneself.***) (*b*) = sense 1 d(*b*) below.

1382 WYCLIF *Job* xiii. 24 Whi thi face thou hidist, and demest me thin enemy? **1560** BIBLE (Genev.) *Ps.* xxx. 7 Thou didest hide thy face, and I was troubled. —— *Isa.* i. 15 When you shal stretch out your hands, I wil hide mine eyes from you. **1611** BIBLE *Lam.* iii. 56 Hide not thine ear at my breathing, at my cry. **1780** COWPER *Table T.* 422 When Avarice starves (and never hides his face) Two or three millions of the human race.

d. ***to hide one's head***: (*a*) to protect one's head, to shelter oneself, take shelter; (*b*) to keep out of sight, keep from shame or discomfiture.

c **1400** *Apol. Loll.* 40 Pore He was, for He had not were to hied His heuid. *a* **1529** SKELTON *Howe the douty Duke* 185 Crepe into your caues Your heedes for to hyde. **1563** W. FULKE *Meteors* (1640) 57 Some Rivers there be, that hide their heads under the Earth, and..far off, breake out againe. **1590** SPENSER *F.Q.* I. ii. 18 But yet I warne thee now..hide thy head. **1593** SHAKS. *Rich. II,* III. iii. 6 Richard, not farre from hence, hath hid his head. **1667, 1840** [see DIMINISHED 2]. **1778** A. HAMILTON *Wks.* (1886) VII. 539, I believe it [a faction] unmasked its batteries too soon, and begins to hide its head.

†**e.** ***all hid***: the signal cry in hide-and-seek; hence, an early name of the game itself. *Obs.*

1588 SHAKS. *L.L.L.* IV. iii. 78 All hid, all hid, an old infant play. **1602** DEKKER *Satirom.* (N.), Cries all hid, as boys do. **1607** TOURNEUR *Rev. Trag.* III. v. Wks. 1878 II. 82 A lady can At such all-hid beguile a wiser man. **1632** SHERWOOD, All hidde, *jeu, où vn se cache pour estre trouvé des autres.*

2. *refl.* and *intr.* **a.** *refl.* To put or keep oneself out of sight, or to conceal oneself.

c **897** K. ÆLFRED *Gregory's Past.* xv. 88 Ge fleoð, & hydað eow. *c* **1000** *Ags. Ps.* (Th.) ciii. 21 Hi on holum hydaþ hi georne. *c* **1200** ORMIN 13736 þeȝȝ baþe hemm hiddenn sone anan. *c* **1330** R. BRUNNE *Chron. Wace* (Rolls) 3410 þey nadde no tome for to fle, Ne place to huyden hem priue. *c* **1386** CHAUCER *Sqr.'s T.* 504 Right as a serpent hit hym vnder floures Til he may seen his tyme for to byte. **1489** CAXTON *Faytes of A.* II. iii. 94 They hided hem self within the thykke busshes. **1548** HALL *Chron., Hen. IV* 13 b, Lurkyng and hidyng him selfe in privy places. **1639** T. BRUGIS tr. *Camus' Mor. Relat.* 255 The blade hides it selfe in the handle. **1879** F. POLLOK *Sport Brit. Burmah* I. 116 Tigers have a wonderful knack of hiding themselves.

b. *intr.* To conceal oneself. Also with *up.*

hide fox and all after: a cry formerly uttered in the game of hide-and-seek, when one player hides and the rest seek him. Cf. 1 e.

c **1330** R. BRUNNE *Chron. Wace* (Rolls) 8864 On heþ and hilles to hyde in hulk. *c* **1340** *Cursor M.* 16742 (Trin.) þe liȝt bigan to hyde. *c* **1420** *Chron. Vilod.* st. 808 Where ever he satte, stode, or hude. **1602** SHAKS. *Ham.* IV. ii. 32 Hide Fox, and all after [cf. HIDE-AND-SEEK 1]. **1774** GOLDSM. *Nat. Hist.* (1776) VIII. 199 The recesses in which she ultimately hides. **1872** J. E. TAYLOR *Half Hours in Green Lanes* (1877) 108 The slightest sound would cause them to hide up.

c. ***to hide out***: to go into hiding; to hide from the authorities. *U.S.*

1884 J. C. HARRIS *Mingo* 124 The revenue fellers better not git too clost ter Hog Mountain, bekaze the hidin'-out bizness is done played. **1885** 'C. E. CRADDOCK' *Prophet Gt. Smoky Mts.* ii. 44 Loneliness had made his sensibilities tender and 'hiding out' affected his spirits more than dodging the officers. **1911** R. D. SAUNDERS *Col. Todhunter* i. 19 You got to hide out when that word is delivered, suh. **1924** F. R. BECHDOLT *Tales Old-Timers* 345 A man..could hide out and hold up his herd. **1969** C. F. BURKE *God is Beautiful, Man* (1970) 25 So he tries to find a pad where he can hide out.

3. *trans.* To keep (a fact or matter) from the knowledge or observation of others; to keep close or secret.

c **1200** *Trin. Coll. Hom.* 199 We hudeð liðere sinnen on us. *a* **1300** *Cursor M.* 1107 þis ded had euer i-wis ben hidd, If god him-self ne had it kydd. **1382** WYCLIF *Prov.* x. 14 Wise men hiden kunnyng. *c* **1430** *Life St. Kath.* (1884) 61 The place of hir sepulture was hydde from knowleche of cristen puple an hundert ȝeere and thrytty. *a* **1533** LD. BERNERS *Huon* lxxxiii. 261 He coude haue no power to hyde or couer the trouth. **1690** *Gt. Scanderbeg* 92 The Sultan..being defeated, hided Arianissa's condition. **1771** MRS. GRIFFITH tr. *Viaud's Shipwreck* 130 Protect my mother; hide from her the condition I am reduced to. **1837** CARLYLE *Fr. Rev.* II. IV. vii, He that has a secret should not only hide it, but hide that he has it to hide.

4. To keep from view (without implication of intention); to prevent from being seen; to obstruct the view of; to cover up.

c **1374** CHAUCER *Boeth.* III. metr. viii. 64 (Camb. MS.) The cauernes of the see I-hyd in flodes. **1398** TREVISA *Barth. De P.R.* v. ii. (1495) 103 Heer well dysposyd..hydyth and defendyth the hede. *c* **1420** *Pallad. on Husb.* IV. 487 Vndir cloude yhid the mone. **1577** B. GOOGE *Heresbach's Husb.* I. (1586) 45 Where the Grasse would so soone growe, as it woulde hide a staffe in a day. **1610** SHAKS. *Temp.* I. ii. 86 The Iuy which had hid my princely Trunck. **1709** BERKELEY *Th. Vision* §79 His thumb, with which he might hide a tower, or hinder its being seen. **1810** VINCE *Elem. Astron.* xxi. 229 A few seconds before the sun was totally hid. **1856** KANE *Arct. Expl.* I. v. 48 Littleton Island is before us, hiding Cape Hatherton.

hide, *v.*² [f. HIDE *sb.*¹]

1. *trans.* To remove the hide from; to flay. *rare.*

1757 W. THOMPSON *R.N. Advoc.* 41 They are neither sufficiently blooded, nor dressed in any tolerable manner more than hiding.

2. To beat the hide or skin of; to flog, thrash. (See also HIDING *vbl. sb.*²) *slang* or *colloq.*

1825 BROCKETT, *Hide,* to beat. 'I'll hide your jacket.' *a* **1825** FORBY *Voc. E. Anglia, Hide,* to thresh; to curry the hide. **1875** BUCKLAND *Log-bk.* 169 The cause of my being hided and flogged so often at school.

†**hide,** *v.*³ *Obs. rare.* [f. HIDE *sb.*²] *trans.* To fix the number of hides in (a piece of land).

1610 HOLLAND *Camden's Brit.* I. 400 The land belonging to this towne was never hided.

hide-all, *a.* That hides or covers up everything.

1837 COTTLE *Remin.* (1847) 48 [He] refused to wear the hide-all sable gown.

hide-and-coop. *U.S.* = HIDE-AND-SEEK.

1850 S. JUDD *R. Edney* 128 (Th.), As if religion were a game of hide and coop. **1909** *N. & Q.* 10th Ser. XII. 371/1 In 'hide and coop', each called out from his secret place a faint, long-drawn 'c-o-o-p'. **1910** S. E. WHITE *Rules of Game* III. xii. 258 The herders grinned as the rangers came in sight. They had been 'tagged' in this 'game of hide and coop'. **1923** K. D. WIGGIN *My Garden of Memory* 14 The board-piles afforded the best possible place for playing 'Hide and Coop'.

hide-and-peep. A child's game: hiding the face and peeping out again; bo-peep.

1832 W. STEPHENSON *Gateshead Local Poems* 27 Some children play'd at hide and peep, Beneath their mother's apron.

hide-and-seek. Also (chiefly *U.S.*) **hide-and-go-seek.**

1. A children's game, in which one or more of the players hide, and the rest, at a given signal, set out to find them.

The earlier name was *all hid*: see HIDE *v.*¹ 1 e; but *hide-and-seek* must have been well known before 1672: cf. 2.

1724 *Essex Inst. Hist. Coll.* XXXVI. 333 At night was at Madam Brownes playing hide and goe seek with Olive Parker, Wibird, &c. **1726–7** SWIFT *Gulliver* I. iii, The boys and girls would venture to come and play at hide-and-seek in my hair. **1735** PEGGE *Kenticisms, Hide-and-fox* [cf. HIDE *v.*¹ 2 b], hide-and-seek. **1821** J. F. COOPER *Spy* (1831) xxxvi. 405 Since when, we have been playing hide-and-go-seek with the ships. **1838** DICKENS *O. Twist* v, The ragged boys ..played a noisy game at hide-and-seek among the tombstones. **1861** HUGHES *Tom Brown at Oxf.* xvii, The children..play hide-and-seek, and look for nests in the gorse-bushes. **1908** T. ROOSEVELT *Lett. Children* 2 Jan. (1919), Do you recollect how we all used to play hide-and-go-seek in the White House? **1925** F. SCOTT FITZGERALD *Great Gatsby* v. 82 At first I thought it was another party, a wild rout that had resolved itself into 'hide-and-go-seek'. **1969** I. & P. OPIE *Children's Games* iv. 154 In Scotland it is often 'Hide and Go Seek'—as also in the United States. **1971** A. BAILEY *In Village* (1972) xx. 202 There are games of prisoner's base and hide-and-go-seek..with the parked cars providing a forest of hiding places.

2. *transf.* and *fig.* Applied to action in which one person or thing evades or appears to evade another. Also *attrib.*

1672 DRYDEN *Marr. à la Mode* III. ii, 'Sdeath, I begin to be weary of this hide and seek. **1706** FARQUHAR *Recruit. Officer* II. i, Our armies did nothing but play at prison bars, and hide and seek with the enemy. **1828** CHR. WORDSW. *K. Chas. I, Icôn Basilikè* 31 All these hide-and-seek devices, all this idle child's play. **1861** SALA *Dutch Pict.* xviii. 288 The treacherous sun..has been playing a game of hide-and-seek with me all day. **1870** MISS BRIDGMAN *R. Lynne* I. xvii. 298 Rose..could not have put her thoughts in any consecutive words—they seemed to be playing at hide-and-go-seek in her mind.

So **hide and seek** *v.*, to play at hide-and-seek.

1830 TENNYSON *Mermaid* iii, We would run to and fro, and hide and seek, On the broad sea-wolds in the crimson shells. **1847** —— *Princ.* II. 435 Some hid and sought In the orange thickets.

hideaway ('haɪdəweɪ), *sb.* and *a.*

A. *sb.* **1.** One who hides himself away; a fugitive. (Cf. *runaway, stowaway.*)

1871 *Echo* 5 Jan., The hideaways were soon killed or taken prisoners. **1883** G. ALLEN in *Col. Clout's Calendar* 33 Compelled the hide-aways to reveal themselves.

2. A small, quiet restaurant, etc., or a secluded place of entertainment.

1929 *World's Work* Nov. 40/2 The vaudeville performer on the two-a-day has played to punks in the hide-aways who turned his riot into an oil can. **1939** C. MORLEY *Kitty Foyle* xviii. 171 He took me to a French hideaway up on Pine Street. **1962** *Times* 9 May 7/1 Dozens of inexpensive hideaways where the entertainment ranges from progressive jazz quartets to the folk songs of the South and West. **1971** *New Yorker* 11 Sept. 99/2 (Advt.), We can take you on a tour of romantic little hideaways, golden beaches and the excitement of the bullring.

3. A place of concealment or retreat.

1930 'E. QUEEN' *French Powder Myst.* II. xiii. 104 This is also the conference room for directors' meetings, the Old Man's hideaway, et cetera. **1941** 'R. WEST' *Black Lamb* II. 12 A Bulgarian leader who was lying wounded in a hideaway. **1959** *Times Lit. Suppl.* 20 Nov. 680/5 They meet in his hideaway to discuss the state of the world.

B. *adj.* That hides or is hidden away.

1876 MRS. WHITNEY *Sights & Ins.* xvii. 177 Still little hideaway nooks. **1891** ATKINSON *Last Giant-Killers* 3 In those deep hide-away valleys or dales.

hidebind ('haɪdbaɪnd), *v.* [f. HIDE *sb.*¹ + BIND *v.*, after *hide-bound.*] *trans.* To render hidebound; to confine, constrict.

1642 ROGERS *Naaman* 149 Selfe hath hidebound thee and straited thee in thine owne bowells. **1840** DE QUINCEY *Style* I. Wks. XI. 177 Some scaly leprosy or elephantiasis, barking and hide-binding the fine natural pulses of the elastic flesh.

†**hidebinding.** *Obs.* [f. HIDE *sb.*¹ + BINDING *vbl. sb.* 2.] The disease HIDEBOUND: see next, B.

1748 tr. *Renatus' Distemp. Horses* 241 What the Country People call Hide-Binding is a mischievous Plague to Cattle of the Ox-kind.

hidebound ('haɪdbaʊnd), *a.* (*sb.*) [f. HIDE *sb.*¹ in locative relation + BOUND *ppl. a.*²: cf. *tongue-tied.*]

I. 1. Of cattle: Having the skin clinging closely to the back and ribs so that it cannot be loosened or raised with the fingers, as a result of bad feeding and consequent emaciation.

1559 [see B.]. **1600** HOLLAND *Livy* XXI. xl. 415 Their horses, no other than lame jades and poor hide-bound hildings. **1681** OTWAY *Soldier's Fort.* v. i, I had rather my Ox should graze in a Field of my own, than live hide-bound upon the common. **1876** T. HARDY *Ethelberta* (1877) 362 A hide-bound bull is going to be killed.

2. Of human beings: Having the skin tight and incapable of extension.

1599 *Broughton's Let.* v. 17 An *Archilochus* leane and hidebound with hart-fretting enuie. **1624** QUARLES *Div. Poems, Job* (1717) 196 My bones are hide-bound. **1708** MOTTEUX *Rabelais* IV. lii. (1737) 209 This did not make me ..Hide-bound and Costive. **1895** W. WRIGHT *Palmyra & Zenobia* iii. 21 They [the children] had not the hide-bound, hunger-pinched appearance of the children of Yabroud.

fig. *a* **1613** OVERBURY *A Wife* (1638) 113 And till he eat a schooleman, he is hide-bound. *a* **1641** SUCKLING *Poems* (1646) 8 His Muse was hydebound. **1863** MRS. GASKELL *Sylvia's L.* I. 55 Always ease an uneasy heart, and never let it get hidebound.

3. Of trees, etc.: Having the bark so closely adherent and unyielding as to impede growth.

1626 BACON *Sylva* §545 If Trees be Hide-bound, they wax lesse Fruitfull, and gather Mosse. **1727** POPE *Macer* 11 Like stunted hide-bound Trees, that just have got Sufficient sap at once to bear and rot. **1827** STEUART *Planter's G.* (1828) 27 No part of it appears stunted or hidebound.

fig. *a* **1661** FULLER *Worthies* (1840) III. 306 Hitherto the English pale had been hide-bound in the growth thereof, having not gained one foot of ground in more than two hundred years.

4. *transf.* and *fig.* Of persons, their minds, etc.: Restricted in view or scope; narrow; cramped; hence, bigoted, obstinately set in opinion.

1603 H. CROSSE *Vertues Commw.* (1878) 82 [To] intrinsicate into the maior of the matter, with such hide-bound reasons. **1644** MILTON *Areop.* (Arb.) 57 To blot or alter what precisely accords not with the hidebound humor which he calls his judgement. **1678** BUTLER *Hud.* III. i. 21 And still the harsher and hide-bounder The Damsels prove, become the fonder. **1724** R. WELTON *Subst. Chr. Faith.* 27 No narrow hide-bound mind that can only love and seek its own self. **1886** STEVENSON *Dr. Jekyll* iii. (ed. 2) 31 An excellent fellow..but a hide-bound pedant for all that.

†**b.** Close-fisted, stingy, niggardly. *Obs.*

1597–8 BP. HALL *Sat.* v. iv, The neighbours praisen Villio's hidebound son. **1616** BEAUM. & FL. *Scornf. Lady* III. ii, There's nothing in that hide-bound usurer. **1683** *Situation of Paradise* 73 (T.) Cares and sleepless nights tormented with continual lashings a hidebound miser.

II. 5. Having an edging or binding of hide.

1858 W. ELLIS 3 *Vis. Madagascar* xii. 336 The hard-wooded and hide-bound shields of the attacking party afforded no protection.

†**B.** *sb.* The diseases affecting cattle and trees, described above in 1, 3. *Obs.*

1559 COOPER *Thesaurus, Coriago,* the sickenesse of cattall when they are clounge, that their skynnes dooe cleve fast to their bodies, hyde bounde. **1607** TOPSELL *Four-f. Beasts*

(1658) 61 Oxen are also much troubled with a disease called the Hide-bound. **1639** T. DE GREY *Compl. Horsem.* 132. **1678** PHILLIPS (ed. 4), *Hide-bound*..is a disease whereunto Trees..by the cleaving of the Bark, are subject. **1727** BRADLEY *Fam. Dict.*, *Hide-Bound*, a Disease in Horses, when the Skin sticks so fast to their Backs and Ribs, that you cannot pull it from the Flesh with your Hands.

†**hidebounded**, *a.* *Obs.* = HIDEBOUND *a.* 4b.

1633 MASSINGER *Guardian* I. i, They are Hide-bounded money-mongers.

hided, ('haɪdɪd), *a.* [f. HIDE *sb.*[1] + -ED[2].]

1. Having a hide (esp. of a specified kind).

?*a* **1400** *Morte Arth.* 1001 He has a kyrtille one..It es hydede alle with hare. *c* **1440** *York Myst.* xxxi. 51, I am full tendirly hydid. **1576** NEWTON *Lemnie's Complex.* (1633) 99 Rough skinned, or thick leathery hided, such as..are the Bever and the Otter. **1830** *Blackw. Mag.* XXVIII. 237 These are flesh and blood, hided and hairy.

2. Made of twisted hide.

1807 *Naval Chron.* XXIII. 189 To which was fastened a hided rope.

†**hidegeld, -gild**[1]. *O.E. Law.* *Obs.* [OE. *hídȝield, -ȝeld* hide-payment: see HIDE *sb.*[2]] A tax paid on every hide of land; hidage.

a **1087** in *Dipl. Angl. Ævi Sax.* (Th.) 439 Wiðutan þam hidȝelde þe nan man wiðutan Gode anum atellan ne mæȝ. **1670** BLOUNT *Law Dict.* s.v. *Hidage*, That Tax which was also called Hyde-gyld. **1706** PHILLIPS (ed. Kersey), *Hidage* or *Hide-gild*.

†**hidegild**[2], **hydegild.** *O.E. Law.* *Obs.* [OE. *hýdȝield, -ȝyld*, f. *hýd* HIDE *sb.*[1], skin: see Schmid *Gesetze der Angels.*, Glossar 615.] A fine paid in lieu of a flogging.

a **1000** *Laws of Eadward & Guthrum* c. 7 §1 (Schmid) þeowman þolie his hyde oððe hyd-ȝyldes. **1708** *Termes de la Ley* 391 *Hydegild*, is a price or ransom to be paid for the saving of his Skin from being beaten.

hi-de-hi ('haɪdiː'haɪ), *int.* An exclamation, used chiefly by army instructors to greet, or attract the attention of, their troops. Also *transf.* and *attrib.*

1941 G. KERSH *They die with their Boots Clean* II. 67 'Now, when I say *Hi-de-Hi Squad*! you shout *Ho-de-Ho*!—and shout it loud! Now: *Hi-de-Hi Squad*!' We roar: 'Ho-de-Ho!' **1943** *N. & Q.* CLXXXV. 83/2 A reviewer in *The Listener* (27 May) writes:..the hi-de-hi qualities of Dr. I. A. Richards's latest book should..make our minds spring to attention with the appropriate ho-de-ho. **1944** *N. & Q.* CLXXXVI. 57/1 It was the C.O. of a training camp who instructed his officers on seeing their men in the street to come to attention and say hi-de-hi, whereupon the men came to attention and replied ho-de-ho. **1950** J. VEDEY *Band Leaders* iv. 29 He [*sc.* Harry Roy] made them sing Hi-de-hi at the May Fair.

hi-de-ho ('haɪdiː'həʊ), *int.* An exclamation of joy used chiefly by jazz and dance bands. Also *attrib.* and as *sb.*

1936 *Delineator* Nov. 10/6 They have not come here to dance and drink away an evening in the usual night-club hi-de-ho. **1946** MEZZROW & WOLFE *Really Blues* viii. 120 The hi-de-ho, vo-de-o-do and boop-boop-a-doo howlers that later sprouted up. **1949** L. FEATHER *Inside Be-Bop* iii. 23 There was plenty going on in the band besides hi-de-ho.

†'**hidel.** *Obs.* Forms: 4–7 **hidel**, 4 **hidil**, 5 **hydle, hydell, hedell**, 6 **hidelle, hidle, hydel, hiddill.** [f. HIDELS, *-s* being mistaken for the plural inflexion: cf. *burial, riddle.*] Hiding-place; = HIDELS. ***in hidel***, in concealment, in secret; ***but hidel***, without any concealment, openly.

a **1300** *E.E. Psalter* xxvi[i]. 5 He hiled me in hidel of his telde ai. *a* **1340** HAMPOLE *Psalter* Cant. 511 Him þat deuours þe pore in hidil. **1450–1530** *Myrr. our Ladye* 265 The same sowle..kepte close in the hydel of her deadely body. **1485** *Act 1 Hen. VII*, c. 6 §2 Beyng in sentwarie or in hedell for youre querell and title. **1503–4** *Act 19 Hen. VII*, c. 36 Preamble, Sir Edward kepith hym in such hidelles and other places fraunchesed. **1508** DUNBAR *Test. Kennedy* 53 I callit my Lord my heid, but hiddill. **1594** JAS. VI. *Let.* in J. Melvill *Diary* (Wodrow Soc.) 320 The retreat of our rebelles to corners and hiddilles. **1607** COWELL *Interpr.*, *Hidel* seemeth to signifie a place of protection, as a Sanctuarie.

hideland ('haɪdlænd). *Hist.* [f. HIDE *sb.*[2] + LAND.] = HIDE *sb.*[2] 1.

1577 HARRISON *England* II. xvii. (1877) I. 293 Etheldred made a law that everie man holding 310 hidelands, should find a ship. **1656** J. HARRINGTON *Oceana* (1700) 65 The proportion of a Hide Land, otherwise called *Caruca*, or a Plow Land, is difficult to be understood, because it was not certain. **1864** SIR F. PALGRAVE *Norm. & Eng.* IV. 61 A 'hyde land' or its synonyms being applied to sixty, eighty, an hundred, an hundred and twelve, or an hundred and fifty acres.

hideless ('haɪdlɪs), *a.* [f. HIDE *sb.*[1] + -LESS.] Without a hide or skin.

1854 H. H. WILSON tr. *Rig-veda* II. 109 From a hideless [cow] you have formed a living one.

hideling ('haɪdlɪŋ), *a.* and *sb.* *dial.* Also **hidling.** [In A. app. a derived use of HIDLINGS, the ending being confused with that of ppl. adjs. and vbl. sbs. in *-ing*. In B. the suffix is identified with that in *changeling*: see -LING.]

A. *adj.* Given to hiding or concealment.

1834 R. MUDIE *Feathered Tribes Brit. Isles* I. 327 The lesser white-throat is, however, a more hidling bird than the white-throat. **1839** W. MACGILLIVRAY *Hist. Brit. Birds* II. 334 So hideling are its habits that one seldom obtains a glimpse of it. **1864** *T. Bell's Brit. Quadrup.* 143 From their obscure and hideling habits, the Shrews are difficult of observation. **1867** DIMOCK in *Girald. Cambr.* (Rolls) V. 57 *margin*, Hares more hideling in their habits.

B. *sb.* A person or thing given to hiding itself.

1894 *Blackw. Mag.* Oct. 511/2 You would get a sight of that hideling the landrail.

†**hidel-like**, *adv.* *Obs.* [f. HIDEL + -LIKE = ON. *-liga*, advb. suffix.] Secretly.

c **1250** *Gen. & Ex.* 2882 Ðu art min ðral, ðat hidel-like min lond vt-stal.

†'**hidels.** *Obs.* Forms: 1 **hýdels**, 3 **hudles**, 4 **hyd-, hidd-, huydels, hiddils, hyddillis, hydlis**, 4–5 **hidles, -lis, -els, -ils**, 5 **hid-, hydeles**, 5–6 **hydles**, 6 **hiddelles.** [OE. *hýdels*, f. *hýd-an* to HIDE + -ELS: cf. RIDDLE.] Hiding-place.

c **975** *Rushw. Gosp.* Mark xi. 17 Cofa *vel* hydels ðeafana. *a* **1340** HAMPOLE *Psalter* ix. 30 He sittis in waitis with the riche in hidels that he sla the innocente. **1387** TREVISA *Higden* (Rolls) I. 199 Saturnus hid hymself in þat lond..and cleped þe lond Latium, þat is Saturnus huydels. *Ibid.* V. 117 [Herculeus] brak out of his hydels. *c* **1450** tr. *De Imitatione* III. xv. 83 Where is þe lurkynge hidels of glory & worship? [**1570** LEVINS *Manip.* 116/17 Hydles, *latebræ.*]

b. ***in hidels***, in a hiding-place; hence, in hiding, in secret.

a **1000** *Laws of Æthelstan* c. 4 §6 in Thorpe *Laws* I. 226 Gif hit on hydelse funden sy. *c* **1205** LAY. 1817 Heo..iþon wilderne an hudlese wuneden. *a* **1300** *Cursor M.* 7953 Þe sin þat þou in hidels did. **1382** WYCLIF *Matt.* vi. 4 That thi almes be in hidlis, and thi fadir that seeth in hidlis [**1388** hiddils], shal ȝelde to thee. **1481** CAXTON *Godefroy* cxxx. 194 Many..cam and solde it in the toun by nyght in hydles. **1517** in *Plead. Duchy Lancast.* (1896) I. 70, [60 others, who remained] in Hiddelles [near the said tenement].

†'**hide-money.** *Obs.* = HIDEGELD.

1563–87 FOXE *A. & M.* (1596) 186/2 The Kings officers gathered of euerie one hide monie through the realme.

hideosity (hɪdiː'ɒsɪtɪ). [f. HIDEOUS + -ITY, after *curiosity*, etc. ME. had *hidouste*, OF. *hideuseté.*] Hideousness; *concr.* an embodiment of hideousness, a very ugly object.

1807 C. WILMOT *Let.* 15 May in *Russ. Jrnls.* (1934) II. 245 Nothing before our eyes but Minerals & Fossils & Animals in every State of Hideosity. **1841** C. RIDLEY *Lett.* (1958) 69 Never in my life have I seen such frightful hideosities of beds as they are. **1856** *Illustr. Lond. News* 11 Oct. 359/1 Trafalgar-square, that place of monstrosities and hideosities. **1884** *Jaunt in Junk* xv. 243 Mere grotesque hideosity of carving. **1897** *United Serv. Mag.* 277 Laying bare, in spite of its repulsive hideosity..the whited sepulchre. **1970** *New Yorker* 12 Sept. 56/1 Don't speak to me of caravans... Such hideosities.

hideous ('hɪdɪəs), *a.* (*adv.*) Forms: 4–5 **hidous(e, (hid-, hyd-, -os(e, -ows(e, -owes, -oys, -us, -ws, hedous, -oes, -eows, hiddowus, hudous, idous, ydous,** *Sc.* **hid-, hyd-, -wis(e, -wys)s), hidowis, hydvouss)**, 4–6 **hydous(e**, 5–8 **hidious**, 6 **hiduous, hiddoues, hydeous, -ious, -youse, hedious, idyous,** *Sc.* **hiddows, -dowis, heiddyous**, 6– **hideous.** [ME. *hidous*, a. AF. *hidous* = OF. *hidos, -eus*, earlier (11th c.) *hisdos*, f. *hisde, hide* horror, fear. The alteration of *-ous* to *-eous* belongs to 16th c.: cf. *courteous, despiteous, piteous*, and see -OUS.

(As to origin of the Fr. word, see Diez, Littré, Brachet. Some think *hisdos* immediately represented L. **hispidōsus* (formerly attributed to Catullus), f. *hispidus* rough, shaggy, bristly, and that the sb. *hisde* was a back-formation from the adj. But this presents numerous difficulties.)]

1. Frightful, dreadful, terrible, horrible; hence, horribly ugly or unpleasing, repulsive, revolting. In the original sense the notion was that of 'causing dread or horror'; this has gradually passed into that of 'revolting to the senses or feelings'.

a **1300** [implied in HIDEOUSLY]. **1303** R. BRUNNE *Handl. Synne* 10216 Of þat syȝt he gan him grys, For þat syȝt was hydous And dreful and perylous. **1340** HAMPOLE *Pr. Consc.* 4772 It sal be hydus til mans heryng. *c* **1380** *Sir Ferumb.* 4435 Þe Sarsyn was an hudous man, By-twyne ys to browen was a span largeliche of brede. **1388** WYCLIF *Wisd.* x. 16 He stood aȝens hidouse [**1382** grisful] kyngis. *c* **1470** HENRY *Wallace* VI. 258 Aferd thai war with hidwis noyis and dyne. **1513** BRADSHAW *St. Werburge* II. 864 Wofully cruciat with peynes hiduous. **1667** MILTON *P.L.* I. 46 Hurld headlong.. With hideous ruine and combustion down To bottomless perdition. **1728** POPE *Dunc.* III. 166 Silence, ye Wolves! while Ralph to Cynthia howls, And makes Night hideous. **1774** GOLDSM. *Nat. Hist.* (1776) IV. 233 Resembling a baboon in size, strength of body, and an hideous wrinkled visage. **1783** WATSON *Philip III* (1839) 235 More than a hundred thousand men, women, and children, suffered death in its most hideous forms. **1853** KINGSLEY *Hypatia* ix, Lanes and alleys hideous with filth and poverty. **1896** DK. ARGYLE *Philos. Belief* Pref. 13 The hideous noises made by the rude machinery of the first steamboat.

b. Terrific on account of size; tremendously or monstrously large; huge, immense. ? *Obs.*

c **1330** R. BRUNNE *Chron.* (1810) 326 Þe kyng did mak right ȝare an hidous engyn. *c* **1440** *Gesta Rom.* xxx. 110 (Harl. MS.) He saw at the fote of the tree an hidowse pitte, ande ane orible dragone þere in. *c* **1440** *Promp. Parv.* 239/2 Hydows (*K.* hiddowus..), *immanis, immensus.* **1513** DOUGLAS *Æneis* III. vi. 137 Als grete, wele nere, As bene ane heiddyous huddoun, or a quhale. **1596** SPENSER *F.Q.* V. xii. 15 Of stature huge and hideous he was, Like to a Giant for his monstrous hight. **1634** SIR T. HERBERT *Trav.* 7 This hidious Cataract [waterspout], as I conceive, is exhaled by the Suns powerfull Attract. **1700** S. L. tr. *Fryke's Voy. E. Ind.* 105 The Elephant..tumbled down backwards into the River, with a most hideous plunge. **1796** MORSE *Amer. Geog.* II. 146 The great precipice below, which hangs over the sea, is so hideous.

2. Terrible, distressing, or revolting to the moral sense; abominable, detestable; odious.

c **1330** R. BRUNNE *Chron. Wace* (Rolls) 14268 Þerfore þe bataille was merueillous, & þe slaughter more hydous. **1382** WYCLIF *Jer.* xi. 15 Doth many hidous giltus [**1388** greet trespassis]. *c* **1475** MYRC 679 (Douce MS.) Thou shalt pronounce this idous thing With crosse & candell and bell knylling. **1605** SHAKS. *Lear* I. i. 153 In thy best consideration checke This hideous rashnesse. **1692** DRYDEN *St. Euremont's Ess.* 351 We shall find them composed of a hideous Melancholy that makes up all Man-haters. **1863** GEO. ELIOT *Romola* II. iv, Hard speech between those who have loved is hideous in the memory.

3. *absol.* A frightful person or object.

c **1420** *Awntyrs of Arth.* 131 Who þat myghte þat hedows see..How hir cholle chatirede, hyr chaftis and hir chynne!

†**B.** *adv.* = HIDEOUSLY. *Obs.*

1667 MILTON *P.L.* VI. 206 Nor less hideous joyn'd The horrid shock. **1705** BOSMAN *Guinea* 273 Here are..Snakes; some whereof are hideous great.

hideously ('hɪdɪəslɪ), *adv.* Forms: see prec. [f. prec. + -LY[2].] In a hideous manner: see the adj. The sense ranges from 'horribly, dreadfully, fearfully', in earlier use, to 'revoltingly' in later. It is sometimes misused as an intensive, intended to be stronger than 'awfully, terribly, dreadfully', when these have become too familiar.

a **1300** *Cursor M.* 16767 + 88 Ful hidously þen con it [þe erthe] quake. **1340** *Ayenb.* 2 Þe ilke þet zuereþ hidousliche be god oþer by his halȝen. **1382** WYCLIF *Num.* xxii. 27 The asse..felle down vndir the feet of the sitter, the which more hydowsly wrooth, bette with a staf the sides of hir. *c* **1386** CHAUCER *Knt.'s T.* 843 The brighte swerdes wente to and fro So hidously. *c* **1400** *Destr. Troy* 7522 Paris..Hurt hym so hidously, þat he his horse leuyt. *c* **1440** *Partonope* 2394 Alle aboute the lystes wyde He hym chased so hidously. **1591** SPENSER *Tears of Muses* 553 Heaps of huge words uphoorded hideously, With horrid sound though having little sence. **1634** SIR T. HERBERT *Trav.* 15 Both men and women hidiously cut and slash their flesh in sundry formes. **1650** FULLER *Pisgah* I. vi. 15 The word desert sounds hideously to English eares. **1796** MORSE *Amer. Geog.* I. 142 Those that are wounded show vast fury, roar hideously. **1882** MISS BRADDON *Mt. Royal* II. ix. 173 There is a calmness about your life which makes me hideously envious.

hideousness ('hɪdɪəsnɪs). [as prec. + -NESS.]

1. *objectively.* The quality of being hideous: dreadfulness; horrible repulsiveness. (See the adj.)

1340 HAMPOLE *Pr. Consc.* 9487 Þe hydusnes Of payne and sorrow þat in helle es. *c* **1380** WYCLIF *Wks.* (1880) 378 Warnyngis of hydousnes & perille of þis synne. **1530** PALSGR. 231/1 Hydiousnesse, *hideuseté*. **1599** SHAKS. *Much Ado* V. i. 96 Fashion-monging boyes, That..Goe antiquely, and show outward hidiousnesse. **1633** T. ADAMS *Exp. 2 Peter* ii. 10 He that hath wounded this lion at the heart, shall never fear the..hideousness of his roaring. **1796** MORSE *Amer. Geog.* II. 114 That natural wonder at Castleton, which is from its hideousness named the Devil's Arse. **1885** *Law Times* LXXIX. 132/2 Unsavory scandals..exhibited in all their native hideousness.

†**2.** *subjectively.* Horror, terror, dread. *Obs.*

1388 WYCLIF *Gen.* xv. 12 Whanne the sunne was gon doun, drede felde on Abram, and a greet hidousenesse [**1382** grisynes] and derk asaylide him. —— *Job* iv. 15 The heiris of my fleisch hadden hidousnesse. —— *Ezek.* xxxii. 10 The kyngis..shulen drede with greet hidousnesse on thee [**1382** with ful myche orrour shulen be agast vpon thee].

†'**hideousship.** *Obs.* [f. HIDEOUS + -SHIP: cf. *hardship, worship.*] Horror, dread.

c **1430** *Pilgr. Lyf Manhode* II. cxxix. (1869) 124 Gret hidousshipe and gret drede ye doon me.

hide-out ('haɪdaʊt). orig. *N. Amer.* Also **hideout.** A hiding-place. Also *attrib.*

1885 *Century Mag.* Mar. 684/2 They guv my place the name o' Hide-out, an' they didn't conscrip' me, nuther. **1913** A. B. EMERSON *R. Fielding at Snow Camp* 174 Meanwhile, the wind shrieked through the forest above their 'hideout'. **1920** B. CRONIN *Timber Wolves* 76 'In rough country like this a man could bury himself for years.'.. 'This coast is full of hide-outs, as they call them.' **1933** *Amer. Speech* VIII. 49/2 *Hide-out country*, any trackless wilderness. **1935** G. GORER *Africa Dances* III. iv. 225 Even if they are inspected by the local authorities..they have.. neighbouring hide-outs. **1940** *Economist* 11 May 848/1 The long coastline of Norway provides innumerable hide-outs for German submarines. **1958** *Listener* 25 Dec. 1074/2 The National Gallery pictures, tucked away in their air-conditioned, thermostatically controlled, war-time hideout in the Welsh mountains. **1963** *Daily Tel.* 14 Aug. 20/6 Special squads combed the hideout house. **1973** J. CLEARY *Ransom* iii. 71 She had made a mistake in choosing this place as their hide-out, but nowhere else had seemed better.

hider ('haɪdə(r)). [f. HIDE *v.*[1] + -ER[1].] One who hides (in various senses of the vb.).

c **1374** CHAUCER *Boeth.* V. pr. i. 117 (Camb. MS.) The hidere of the gold. **14..** *Voc.* in Wr.-Wülcker 575/19 *Contutator*, an hydere. **1540** COVERDALE *Confut. Standish* Wks. II. 366 An hider of the scriptures from the unlearned. **1631** *Star Chamb. Cases* (Camden) 86 Woe to hiders of corne. **1845** FORD *Handbk. Spain* I. 5 Many a treasure is thus lost from the accidental death of the hider. **1869** W. C. HAZLITT *Eng. Prov.* 204 Hiders are good finders.

hider, obs. form of HITHER.

hidey ('haɪdɪ), *int.* Chiefly *Austral.* and *U.S.* Also **hidy, highdey**. [Blend of HI and *howdey* (see HOW-DO-YE).] A word of greeting.

1941 BAKER *Dict. Austral. Slang* 35 *Hidey! Highdey!*, Hail!, How are you! **1959** I. JEFFERIES *13 Days* xi. 182 'Hidey,' I said. **1962** E. B. ATWOOD *Regional Vocab. Texas* iii. 70 *Hidy*, probably a blend of the old and new.

hiding ('haɪdɪŋ), *vbl. sb.*¹ [f. HIDE *v.*¹ + -ING¹.]

1. The action of the vb. HIDE¹, *lit.* and *fig.*; the condition of being hidden; concealment. (Often in phr. ***in hiding***, Sc. ***under hiding***.)

a **1225** *Ancr. R.* 174 Iþisse worde, Hester, beoð hudunge & heinesse boðe iueied togederes. *c* **1290** *Beket* 1355 in *S. Eng. Leg.* I. 145 In huydinge ase þei it were. *c* **1400** *Rom. Rose* 6712 Sothfastnesse wole none hidyngis. **1560** BIBLE (Genev.) *Hab.* iii. 4 There was the hiding of his power. **1656** BP. HALL *Occas. Medit.* (1851) 47 If our light be seen, it matters not for our hiding. **1814** SCOTT *Wav.* lxxii, A gentleman who was 'in hiding' after the battle of Culloden. **1834** H. MILLER *Scenes & Leg.* viii. (1857) 116 When under hiding, word was brought him that she lay sick of a fever. **1849** MACAULAY *Hist. Eng.* x. II. 612 The Popish priests, indeed, were in exile, in hiding, or in prison. **1890** BESANT *Demoniac* ii. 27 A man..who has to go away into hiding every month or so.

2. Something that hides; a means of concealment; a hiding-place.

1382 WYCLIF *Heb.* ix. 3 Aftir the veil, or hydyng, the secunde tabernacle. *c* **1430** *Pilgr. Lyf Manhode* III. xlvii. (1869) 160, I..seche hydinges and corneres. **1611** BIBLE *Deut.* xxxii. 38 Let them rise up..and be your protection [*marg.* an hiding for you]. **1859** G. W. DASENT *Tales fr. Norse* 94 Then he rode off with it to the hiding, where he kept the other two.

†**3.** Something hidden; *pl.* secrets. *Obs. rare.*

a **1325** *Prose Psalter* xliii. 23 [xliv. 21] He knewe þe hidynges of þe hert.

4. *attrib.* and *Comb.*, as ***hiding-hole***; †***hiding-cloth***, a curtain or veil; ***hiding power***, the capacity of paint or other colouring materials to obliterate certain surfaces. Also HIDING-PLACE.

c **1275** *Passion Our Lord* 480 in *O.E. Misc.* 50 Þat huding-cloþ to-delde in þe temple a to. **1611** COTGR., *Cache*,..a hiding hole, hidden corner. *c* **1731** SWIFT *Storm* 69 Else some hiding hole he seeks. **1852** MRS. STOWE *Uncle Tom's C.* xviii, The more drawers and closets there were, the more hiding-holes could Dinah make. **1951** R. MAYER *Artist's Handbk.* 433 *Hiding power*, degree of opacity in a paint or pigment; ability to mask or conceal an underpainting. The term *covering power* is sometimes confused with it. **1966** J. S. COX *Illustr. Dict. Hairdressing* 79/1 *Hiding power*, the power of an opaque dye or other colouring material, when applied to hair, to cover or hide its existing colour. **1967** *Gloss. Paper Ink Terms Letterpress Printing (B.S.I.)* 11 *Hiding power*, the capacity of an ink to obliterate the previously printed ink film.

'**hiding**, *vbl. sb.*² *slang* or *colloq.* [f. HIDE *v.*²]

1. A flogging, thrashing, beating.

1809 *Sporting Mag.* XXXIV. 95 As complete a hiding as the greatest glutton..would wish to take. **1817** SCOTT *Search after Happiness* xiii, Some tumours..Gave indication of a recent hiding. **1822** BEWICK *Mem.* 118 Giving him a severe beating, or, what was called, a 'hideing'.

2. In colloq. phr. ***to be on a hiding to nothing***, to be faced with a situation in which any outcome would be unfavourable or in which success is impossible, *spec.* (app. orig. in *Horse-racing*) that of being expected to win easily, so that one gains no credit from victory, and is disgraced by defeat. Cf. TO *prep.* 19a.

1905 A. M. BINSTEAD *Mop Fair* xi. 193 They will, like the man who was on a hiding to nothing the first time Tom Sayers saw him, 'take it lying down'. **1964** C. P. SNOW *Corridors of Power* ii. 17 He wanted to get out of his present job as soon as he had cleaned it up a little—'This is a hiding to nothing,' he said simply—and back to the Treasury. **1975** *Sunday Times* 8 June 28/2 The Indian batsmen were on a hiding to nothing. They could not win. **1977** *Times* 29 Jan. 10/7 Derby know they are on a hiding to nothing at Fourth Division Colchester, who have a reputation as giant-killers. **1980** *Spectator* 8 Mar. 3/1 Lord Soames would have been on a hiding to nothing in trying to exercise gubernatorial authority and viceregal judgment.

'**hiding**, *ppl. a.* [f. HIDE *v.*¹ + -ING².] That hides: see the verb.

1483 *Cath. Angl.* 185/2 Hydynge, *occultans, abscondens.* **1705** ELIZ. WEST *Mem.* (1865) 222 Not altogether a hiding God. **1874** J. P. HOPPS *Princ. Relig.* xiii. (1878) 42 Freed from most of these hiding veils.

Hence †'**hidingly** *adv.*, secretly, privily.

1382 WYCLIF *2 Sam.* xii. 12 Forsothe thou didist hidyngli. —— *Wisd.* xviii. 9 Hidendly [**1388** priueli] forsothe the riȝtwis childer of goode men sacrifieden.

hiding-place. [f. HIDING *vbl. sb.*¹] A place in which one hides or conceals oneself.

c **1440** *Promp. Parv.* 239/2 Hydynge place, *latibulum.. latebra.* **1560** BIBLE (Genev.) *Isa.* xxxii. 2 That man shalbe as an hiding place from the winde. **1611** —— *Ps.* cxix. 114 Thou art my hiding place and my shield. **1774** GOLDSM. *Nat. Hist.* (1790) VII. 278 (Jod.) They seldom therefore seek for hiding-places before the fall of the leaf. **1855** MACAULAY *Hist. Eng.* xvi. III. 641 The Protestants every where came forth from their hidingplaces.

hidir, obs. form of HITHER.

hidle, hidles, -is, var. HIDEL, HIDELS, *Obs.*

hidlings, *adv.* and *sb. Sc.* and *north. dial.* Also *erron.* **-lands** = **-lins**. [f. HID *ppl. a.* + -LING, -LINGS, adverbial formative: cf. *backling, -s*, etc.]

A. *adv.* In hidden wise, secretly.

a **1225** *Ancr. R.* 280 He mei hine unmunlunge aworpen [*v.r.* hodlinges casten]. **1808-18** in JAMIESON. *a* **1851** JOANNA BAILLIE (Ogilvie), An' she's to come to you here, hidlings, as it war. **1869** *Lonsdale Gloss.*, *Hidlands*, secretly.

b. More usually ***in hidlings*** (as if sb.): in secret, secretly.

1422 tr. *Secreta Secret., Priv. Priv.* (E.E.T.S.) 171 The hardy or the manfull in hidlynges he nendeynyth [= n'endeynyth] not any-thynge to do. **1563** WINȜET *Wks.* (1890) II. 33 It is a grete temptatioun..the samin man..suld inbring in hidlingis pestilent errouris. **1725** RAMSAY *Gentle Sheph.* II. i, And skulk in hidlings on the hether braes. **1801** in Ferguson & Nanson *Munic. Rec. Carlisle* (1887) 259 To sell in open market, or in hidlings. **1887** HALL CAINE *Deemster* xxiii. 146 It's been a quarrel and maybe a fight.. and he's been in hidlins.

B. app. taken as *sb. pl.* **a.** Hiding-places, secret places. **b.** Secret or clandestine operations.

1597 MONTGOMERIE *Cherrie & Slae* 764 Thair is no boundis, bot I haif bene, Nor hidlingis fra me hid. **1813** W. BEATTIE *Tales* 36 (Jam.) The hills look white, the woods look blue, Nae hiddlins for a hungry ewe, They're sae beset wi' drift. **1823** ELIZA LOGAN *St. Johnstoun* III. 19 (Jam.), I dinna ken what a' this hidlings is about. **1846-60** R. EG.-WARBURTON *Hunt. Songs* (1883) LIX. xiv. 166 One was shunted into hidlands, T'other laid upon the shelf.

hidlings, *a. Sc.* and *north. dial.* Also 9 **hiddlin'**. [The same word as prec. used as adj., and then often with final *-s* dropped: cf. DARKLING.] Hidden, secret, underhand, clandestine.

a **1810** TANNAHILL *Poems* (1846) 75 He ne'er kept up a hidlins plack, To spend ahint a comrade's back. **1818** MISS FERRIER *Marriage* II. 127, I wud nae count myself married i' the hiddlins way they gang aboot it noo. **1824** —— *Inher.* lxxxiv, Carrying on this hiddlin' coortship. **1887** J. SERVICE *Life Dr. Duguid* v. 31 His hiddlin' kind of ways.

†'**hidly**, *adv. Obs.* = HIDDENLY.

1382 WYCLIF *Jer.* xxxvii. 16 Sedechie..askide hym in his hous hidli [**1388** priuyli]. **1549** LATIMER *5th Serm. bef. Edw. VI* (Arb.) 151 It was..hidlye and couertly done.

†'**hidness.** *Obs.* [cf. OE. *ȝehýdnes* security.] Secrecy, HIDDENNESS.

c **1330** R. BRUNNE *Chron.* (1810) 77 Saynt Cutberte's clerkes in hidnes euer ȝede. *a* **1598** ROLLOCK *Serm.* Wks. 1849 I. 366 They use to be commended fra their secrecie and hidnes. *Ibid.* 373 This is ane mervellous hidnes.

hidos(e, hidous, etc., obs. ff. HIDEOUS.

†**hidour.** *Obs.* In 4 hidor, 4-5 hydour, 5 hydoure. [a. OF. *hideur, hidor*, in 12th c. *hisdur*, f. *hisde* horror, fear (see HIDEOUS) + *-eur*, L. *-ōrem*, as in *terreur, horreur*, and Eng. *dreadour*.]

a. Horror, terror, dread. **b.** Hideousness, terribleness.

c **1315** SHOREHAM 33 Thou aȝtest habbe more hydour Of thyne oȝene unryȝte. **13..** *E.E. Allit. P.* C. 367 Such a hidor hem hent and a hatel drede. **1422** tr. *Secreta Secret., Priv. Priv.* (E.E.T.S.) 216 Olyfantes..benne horribill hugely, and berryth grete hydoure. **1480** CAXTON *Chron. Eng.* clxxxvi, He opened his mouth toward Wales and made it quake thurgh the hydour of his mouth.

†**hidous**, *v. Obs. rare.* Also 4 **hydowse**. [f. *hidous* HIDEOUS. OF. had *hisder, hider* to feel terror; also *hidusable* frightful, terrible, as if from a vb. *hiduser*.] **a.** *intr.* To feel terror. **b.** *trans.* To feel terror at, dread, abhor.

c **1380** WYCLIF *Sel. Wks.* I. 269 A man kyndeli hidousiþ derknesse and is gladid bi liȝt. *Ibid.* III. 54 Þou, to take mankynde for to delyuere it, hidousist not þe virgyns wombe. **1382** —— *Dan.* vii. 15 My spirit hidouside.

†**hidousty.** *Obs.* [a. OF. **hidoseté, hideuseté* (Palsgr.), f. *hideux, -eus*: see -TY.] Hideousness.

c **1420** *Wyclif's 2 Macc.* vi. 12 (*Gloss to* dreden not) Nether haue hidoustee [11 *MSS.* either haue not hidouste].

hidro-: see HYDRO-.

hidrotic (hɪ'drɒtɪk), *a.* and *sb. Med.* [ad. med.L. *hidrōtic-us*, a. Gr. ἱδρωτικ-ός, f. ἱδρώς, -ῶτος sweat. Cf. F. *hidrotique*.]

A. *adj.* Of or pertaining to sweat; causing sweat; sudorific; diaphoretic.

1727-41 CHAMBERS *Cycl.* s.v., *Carduus benedictus.. angelica*, etc. are of the number of hidrotics, or hidrotic medicines. **1886** *Syd. Soc. Lex.*, *Hidrotic acid*..believed formerly to exist in sweat. *H. fever*, Blundell's term for those cases of puerperal fever in which profuse perspiration is a marked symptom.

B. *sb.* A medicinal agent causing perspiration.

1705 ARBUTHNOT *Coins* (T.), He seems to have been the first who divided purges into hydroticks and purgers of bile.

hidur, obs. form of HITHER.

hidus, hiduous, hidwis, etc., obs. ff. HIDEOUS.

†'**hidy**, *a. Obs. rare.* In 6 hydie. [f. HIDE *sb.*¹ + -Y.] Of or pertaining to hides.

1552 HULOET, Hydie, or of a hyde or skynne, *pelliceus.*

hidy-hole ('haɪdɪhəʊl). orig. *Sc.* Also **hidey-, hidie-**. [Alteration of *hiding-hole*: see HIDING *vbl. sb.*¹ 4.] A hiding-place.

1817 *Blackw. Mag.* Nov. 158/2 They're darned in some o' the queer hidy-holes about the rocks there. **1828** D. M. MOIR *Mansie Wauch* ix. 79 We got James..hauled out of his hidy-hole. **1870** R. CHAMBERS *Pop. Rhymes* 91 He had not been long in his hidy-hole, before the awful Etin came in. **1896** S. R. CROCKETT *Cleg Kelly* iii. 18 Tim Kelly's 'hidie holes', where he kept the weapons of his craft. **1920** *Glasgow Herald* 6 Dec. 10 The story of the Ballantrae smugglers' 'hidie-hole'. **1927** *Hutchinson's Myst. Story Mag.* IX. XLVIII. 50/2 So it's obvious that there may quite easily be another snug little hidy-hole which none of us knows of. **1934** D. L. SAYERS *Nine Tailors* 261 A nice little six-inch hidey-hole where nobody would ever dream of looking for it. **1955** J. THOMAS *No Banners* xxxiii. 330 There's a concrete hidey-hole underneath. **1959** P. H. JOHNSON *Humbler Creation* xlii. 286 So this was where he came,..into this snugness, this hidey-hole. **1969** I. & P. OPIE *Children's Games* iv. 157 Those who are still searching..rush to the places where they were last seen, thinking that they will be near the hidy-hole.

hie (haɪ), *v.*¹ Now *arch. or poet.* Pa. t. and pple. hied; pr. pple. hying. Forms: α. 1 **hiᵹian**, 2 **hihȝen**, *Orm.* **hiȝhenn**, 3 **hihe**, 3-5 **hiȝe**, **highe**, 4 **hiȝie**, (**heeȝe**), 4-5 **hyȝ(e**, **hyghe**, **heiȝ(e**, **heyȝe**, **heyghe**, **heȝe**, 4-7 **heighe**, 4-8 **high**, 5 **hyhe**, 5-6 **hygh**. β. 3-8 **hye**, 4 **hii**, 4-5 **hij**, (**heij**), 4-7 **hy**, 6 *Sc.* **he**, 3- **hie**. *Pa. t.* 1 **hiᵹode**, 3-4 **hiȝede**, etc. 3-5 **hiede**, **hyede**, 4- **hied**, (4-7 **hyde**, 5 **hiet**, **hide**, **hit**, etc.). [OE. *hiᵹian* (and ? *hīᵹian*) to strive, be intent or eager, pant; cf. MDu. *hîgen*, Du. *hijgen* to pant, breathe with difficulty, MLG. *hîgen, hîchen*, Ger. *heichen*.]

†**1.** *intr.* To strive, exert oneself, pant. *Obs.*

c **888** K. ÆLFRED *Boeth.* xxx. §1 Hiᵹaþ ealle mæᵹne ðæt he wold..ᵹefon. *c* **897** —— *Gregory's Past.* xxii. 169 He sceal simle hiᵹian ðæt he weorþe..ᵹeedniwad. **971** *Blickl. Hom.* 29 Þa þe he ᵹesyhþ to Gode hiᵹian. *c* **1200** ORMIN 2723 Forrþi birrþ uss hiȝhenn her To cwemenn Crist o life. *a* **1225** *Ancr. R.* 92 Ȝe schulen gostliche iseon þe blissen of heuene, uor to ontenden our heorte to hien touward heom.

2. To hasten, speed, go quickly.

c **1175** *Lamb. Hom.* 105 Þider we sculen hihȝen. *c* **1205** LAY. 2317 Alle heo hiȝeden to. **1297** R. GLOUC. (1724) 544 So quic so he miȝte hie. *a* **1300** *Cursor M.* 21278 Þe queles ar draun diuerse wise, þe first it gas, þe toþer it hise [*v.r.* hyes]. *c* **1320** R. BRUNNE *Medit.* 623 She ran þan þurgh hem, and hastyly hyde. **13..** *E.E. Allit. P.* B. 33 Hyȝ not to heuen in hatere to-torne. **1382** WYCLIF *Gen.* xviii. 6 Abraham hyede [**1388** hastide] into the tabernacle. *c* **1400** *Destr. Troy* 3893 [Was] neuer hatfull to hym to hygh into batell. *c* **1420** *Chron. Vilod.* st. 474 Aryse up my colour my frend, and heyȝe. *c* **1440** *Gesta Rom.* lxi. 254 (Harl. MS.) They sesyd of wepyng, and hijd to the castell. **1563** B. GOOGE *Eglogs*, etc. (Arb.) 115 Into the Hall with haste he hyes. **1592** SHAKS. *Rom. & Jul.* III. ii. 138 Hie to your Chamber, Ile find Romeo To comfort you. **1659** R. BROUGH *Pres. Schism* 519 We must hie away as we love our souls. **1667** MILTON *P.L.* II. 1055 Thither..Accurst, and in a cursed hour, he [Satan] hies. **1714** GAY *Sheph. Week* Prol. 37 I'le hye with Glee To Court. **1787** MAD. D'ARBLAY *Diary* 2 Feb., He shook his head at me ..and hied downstairs. **1840** DICKENS *Barn. Rudge* v, The locksmith..hied with all speed [to Southwark]. **1871** R. ELLIS *Catullus* lxiii. 19 Thither hie ye thither away To the Phrygian home.

†**b.** To hasten, make haste, use diligence or dispatch (*to do* something, or *that* something be done); to betake oneself quickly (*to* something).

c **1250** *Meid Maregrete* lxiii, To don ham to deþe he hiede bileue. **13..** *E.E. Allit. P.* B. 1584 To henge þe harlotes he heȝed ful ofte. *c* **1425** *Seven Sag.* (P.) 1916 Hye that thay were dyght. *c* **1450** MYRC 98 Teche the mydwyf that scho hye For to vndo hyre wyth a knyf. **1664** *Flodden F.* viii. 73 To handy stroaks they hyed apace.

†**c.** To advance or come on quickly, hasten on; to 'get on', make progress; to speed, prosper.

13.. *Sir Beues* (A.) 1485 Of þat feste nel ich namor telle, For to hiȝe wiþ our spelle. *c* **1340** *Cursor M.* 4700 (Trin.) So þe wo bigon vp hye. **1398** TREVISA *Barth. De P.R.* v. iii. (Tollem. MS.), He wexeþ feble..and elde hyeþ wel faste. *c* **1420** *Pallad. on Husb.* III. 1075 Whereof sum fruit wol targe and sum wol hie. *c* **1460** *Towneley Myst.* (Surtees) 95 Fayr falle thi growne, welle has thou hyde. **1581** SPENSER *Sheph. Cal.* (ed. 2) Aug. 195 The night higheth [**1579** nigheth] fast. **1608** TOURNEUR *Rev. Trag.* III. iii. Wks. 1878 II. 74 O sir destruction hies.

†**d.** *to hie it. Obs.*

1619 BP. J. WILLIAMS *Serm. Apparell* (1620) 11 To heighe it abroad, to visit and to see.

3. *refl.* = sense 2.

The refl. pron. was orig. a dative, as in OE. *hi eodon heom* they went them, *hi fleoþ him* they flee them, *heo sæt hire* she sat her.

c **1290** *S. Eng. Leg.* I. 258/59 Leoue sire, hiȝe þe hom. *c* **1300** *Cursor M.* 19771 (Edin.) And bad to þaim he suld him hii, Bot noȝt þai talde him resun qui. *c* **1400** *Destr. Troy* 3245 [Þai] hit hom into hauyn, as hom hap shope. **1587** GOLDING *De Mornay* xix. (1617) 335 We must hye vs thither. **1599** SHAKS. *Pass. Pilgr.* xii, O, sweet shepherd, hie thee, For methinks thou stay'st too long. **1641** MILTON *Reform.* II. (1851) 59 Certainly wee ought to hie us from evill like a torrent. **1713** WARDER *True Amazons* (ed. 2) 124 The Bees ..high them home as fast as they can. **1854** PATMORE *Angel in Ho.* I. II. ix. (1879) 225 The foolish hie them post haste through.

†**b.** = sense 2 b. *Obs.*

a **1300** *Cursor M.* 15772 Þat þou sal do, þar-to nu hij þou þe. *c* **1489** CAXTON *Sonnes of Aymon* xxvi. 559 Now, lordes, hyghe you of that ye have to doo. *c* **1586** C'TESS PEMBROKE *Ps.* LXX. i, Lord, hie thee, me to save. **1649** R. HODGES *Plain. Direct.* 10 Thou hyest thee about thy work.

†**c.** = sense 2 c. *Obs.*

1531 ELYOT *Gov.* I. viii, That I haue well hyed me, to make of a noble man a mason or peynter. **1583** GOLDING *Calvin on Deut.* cv. 704 When men come before a judge they thinke they haue hyed them well, if they may deceiue him.

†**4.** *trans.* To cause to hasten; to hasten, urge on, bring quickly; to drive *away*. *Obs.*

c **1320** R. BRUNNE *Medit.* 573 Þey hye hym, and ho goþ withoutyn any stryfe. **1382** WYCLIF *Esther* ii. 9 He shulde heȝen the wymmen enournyng. *c* **1430** *Syr Gener.* (Roxb.) 7326 Than gan he fast mercy crye, But [Clarionas] wold his deth hie. *c* **1430** LYDG. *Min. Poems* (Percy Soc.) 65 Anon they have hym hyed Unto the temple. **1563** WINȜET *Wks.* (1890) II. 76 That quhilk wes neulie inuentit, suld be explodit, and hyit away. **1575** J. STILL *Gamm. Gurton* II. iii. in Hazl. *Dodsley* III. 204 A man is well hied to trust to thee.

5. with advb. accusative; usually *to hie one's way*.

a **1300** *Cursor M.* 5000 (Cott.) And hijd þam þar wai [*Gött.* hied þaim in þair way] ful suith. **1810** SCOTT *Lady of L.* I. x, On the hunter hied his way. **1853** G. JOHNSTON *Nat. Hist. E. Bord.* I. 18 It hies its way down the valley.

†**hie, hy,** *sb. Obs.* Forms: 3 hih, hiȝ, 4 hi, hii, hij, hiȝe, hyȝe, hiy, (hey(e, hegh), 4–5 hie, high(e, 4–6 hy, hye, 5 hygh. [f. HIE *v.*[1]: cf. *haste* vb. and sb. Obs. in Eng. bef. 1500, in Sc. soon after 1600.] Haste, speed. Chiefly in phr. *in hie*, in haste, with haste, quickly, soon: often added merely for rime's sake.

c **1200** ORMIN 2686 Itt seȝȝþ þatt Sannte Marȝe for Wiþþ mikell hih þatt weȝȝe. *c* **1275** *XI Pains Hell* 269 in *O.E. Misc.* 230 Aftur schal Mihel lede him in hiȝ To paradys to oþur holi. *a* **1300** *Cursor M.* 1275 Quedir þat I sal haue it in hij [*v.rr.* hye, hey; *rime* merci]. *a* **1340** HAMPOLE *Psalter* i. 1 He ..þat has swa gret hegh on his way. *c* **1430** *Syr Gener.* (Roxb.) 9532 'Sir', he seid, 'I haue grete high, Toward Ynde I most nede'. *c* **1470** HARDING *Chron.* XXVII. i, Wherfore he wente vnto Ragan in hye. *c* **1475** *Rauf Coilȝear* 577 Of his harnes in hy he hynt. **1572** *Satir. Poems Reform.* xxxiii. 323 With speid thay ran in hy. *a* **1605** MONTGOMERIE *Misc. Poems* lii. 46 The quhilk but dowt wil be my deid In hy.

Hence †**hieful** *a.*, speedy, hasty, quick, prompt.

a **1225** *Ancr. R.* 302 Schrift schal beon..ofte imaked, hihful, edmod.

hie, high, *int. Sc.* and *north. dial.* [Cf. HI *int.*] The call to a horse to turn to the left: the opposite of *hup*.

1825 JAMIESON, *Hie Wo*, a phrase addressed to horses when the driver wishes them to incline to the left, *Roxb.* **1851** H. STEPHENS *Bk. Farm* (ed. 2) I. 160/1 (Language to horses) *To come towards you. Hie* is used in all the border counties of England and Scotland; *Hie here, come ather*, are common in the midland counties of Scotland. **1863** MORTON *Cycl. Agric.* Gloss. (E.D.S.) 148 To right, *Hupp*; To left, *Hie*.

Hence **hie** *v.*[2] *trans.*, to direct a horse to the left (by this call).

1851 H. STEPHENS *Bk. Farm* (ed. 2) I. 181/2 *Hupping* the horses constantly from you, until about half the division is ploughed, and then *hieing* them towards you. *Ibid.* I. 177/2 By *hieing* the horses towards him.

hie: see HE, HEO, HI *prons.*

hie, obs. f. HIGH *a.* and *v.*

hied, obs. f. HIDE *v.*

‖**hielaman** ('hi:ləmən). *Australia.* Also **hiele-, heela-, heelo-.** [Corruption of native Australian name *elimang, e-lee-mong, hīlaman.*] **a.** The narrow shield of the Australian aborigines, made of bark or wood (Morris *Austral Eng.*).

[**1798** D. COLLINS *Acc. N.S. Wales* 612 *E-lee-mong*, shield made of bark.] **1839** T. L. MITCHELL *3 Exp. E. Austral.* II. 349 There is much originality in the shield or hieleman of these people. **1848** H. W. HAYGARTH *Recoll. Bush Life Austral.* x. 113 The heeloman is a sort of shield, made of the toughest wood procurable, about three feet in length, and six inches in breadth at the centre, whence it gradually tapers off to a point at either extremity. **1852** MUNDY *Antipodes* iv. (1855) 102 The hieleman or shield is a piece of wood, about two and a half feet long, tapering to the ends, with a bevelled face not more than four inches wide at the broadest part. **1873** J. B. STEPHENS *Black Gin* etc. 26 No faint far hearing of the waddies banging, Of club and heelaman together clanging.

b. *Comb.* **hielaman tree**, the Bats-wing Coral, *Erythrina vespertilio*, used by the Australian aborigines for making their shields (Morris).

1884 A. NILSON *Timber Trees N.S.W.* 136 Heelaman tree. **1889** J. H. MAIDEN *Useful Native Plants Austral.* 426 *Heilaman tree.* The wood is soft, and used by the aborigines for making their 'heilamans' or shields.

hieland, obs. and Sc. var. HIGHLAND.

hield, heeld, heald (hi:ld), *v. Obs.* or *dial.* Forms: 1 hieldan, hyldan, heldan, (1–4 3rd s. hylt, helt), 2–5 helde(n, 3 healden, hælden, 4 heyld, (heill), 4–5 held, heelde, hilde, 4–6 heild, hield(e, hylde, 5–7 heeld, 9 *dial.* heald. See also HEEL *v.*[2], HELL *v.*[1] *Pa. t.* 1 hylde, 3 heolde, hæld(e, halde, 4 held(e, helte, hild(e, 5 (9 *Sc.*) helt; also held-, heilded(e, etc. *Pa. pple.* 1 hylded, 4 helded, held, etc. [OE. *hieldan*, late WS. *hyldan*, Kentish *heldan*, Angl. *hældan* = OS. *-heldian* (*af-heldian* to decline), MDu., MLG. *helden*, Du. *hellen* to slope, overhang, OHG. *heldan* (:—*haldjan*), MHG. *helden* to incline, lean:—OTeut. type **halþjan*, f. **halþo-*, OHG. *hald*, OE. *heald*, ON. *hallr* inclined, sloping, bent to one side.]

I. Intransitive uses.

1. To bend downwards or to one side; to lean, incline, slope. *Obs.* or *dial.* (See also HEEL *v.*[2] 1.)

c **888** K. ÆLFRED *Boeth.* xxxiii. §4 Heo ne helt on nane healfe. *c* **1205** LAY. 29642 Austin a cneowe heolde Adun to þere uolde. *a* **1300** *Cursor M.* 24407 Þan lete he dun his heued heild. *c* **1440** HYLTON *Scala Perf.* (W. de W. 1494) II. xxv, A cyte sette vpon an hylle heldinge to the southe. **1483** *Cath. Angl.* 180/2 *To Helde*..to bowe. **1501** DOUGLAS *Pal. Hon.* III. ix, This gudely carvell..Now sank scho low, now hie to heuin vpheildit. **1530** PALSGR. 585/1, I hylde, I leane on the one syde, as a bote or shyp or any other vessell. *Ibid.*, Sytte fast..for the bote begynneth to hylde. **1559** MORWYNG *Evonym.* 351 Let it be laid in a dish hielding toward the one syde. **1627** CAPT. SMITH *Seaman's Gram.* xi. 53 We say a Ship doth heeld on Starboord or Larboord, that is, to that side shee doth leane most. **1678** PHILLIPS (ed. 4), *Heeld* [so ed. **1696**; ed. Kersey **1706** *heel*], a term in Navigation, a Ship heelds..that is, leans most to that side. **1825** BROCKETT, *Heald*, to incline, to bend laterally.

†**b.** To bow, submit. *Obs.*

a **1300** *Cursor M.* 22235 All folk to rome suld heild, And truage als til hefd yeild. **13..** *Coer de L.* 791 If ever I stope or held, I hope never to be scheld! *a* **1400–50** *Alexander* 1622 Nouthire haylsid I him ne hildid him nouthire.

†**2.** To sink, droop, decline, fall; to come or go down (*lit.* and *fig.*). *Obs.*

c **1205** LAY. 3915 Suððen he adun halde. *Ibid.* 16478 Heo smiten a þan hæðene þæt heo adun helden. *a* **1300** *E.E. Psalter* ci. 12 [cii. 11] Mine daies als schadwe helded þai. *c* **1340** *Cursor M.* 6431 (Fairf.) Be þe sunne be-gan to helde Wiþ israel was left þe felde. *a* **1400–50** *Alexander* 3201 Doun he hildis all to-hewyn þaire handis be-twene. *c* **1430** *Syr Gener.* 4444 Ismael so Generides smet..That Generides began to helde; Welnigh he had goon to ground.

†**3.** To bend one's course, turn in a particular direction; to take one's way; to go or come. *Obs.*

c **1205** LAY. 6115 He to scipe wende And fram þan londe hælde. *Ibid.* 20186 Arður halde after Mid þritti þusend cnihten. **13..** *E.E. Allit. P.* B. 39 Þen þe harlot with haste helded to þe table. **13..** *Gaw. & Gr. Knt.* 1922 Þenne þay helden to home.

†**4.** To turn away or aside (*lit.* and *fig.*). *Obs.*

c **1205** LAY. 8878 A-weiward he halde, and nolde hit iheren. *a* **1300** *E.E. Psalter* xiii[i]. 3 Alle helded þai samen ai. *c* **1325** *Metr. Hom.* 83 Scho heldid sone to synfull layke. *a* **1340** HAMPOLE *Psalter* xiii. 4 All thai heldid, to gidere thai ere made vnprofitabile.

5. To incline *to*; to be of the party of, take up with, favour. *Obs.* or *dial.*

a **1300** *Cursor M.* 17462 All þat wit him heilded or held. *Ibid.* 19805 Þar was a man heldand to right, Cornelius to nam he hight. *c* **1325** *Metr. Hom.* 80 If thou will to my langynge helde. **1375** BARBOUR *Bruce* VI. 353 It [valour] wald till hardyment hald [*v.rr.* heyld, heill] haly, With-thi away war the foly. **1828** *Craven Dial.*, *Heald*, to be favourable to, 'he healds au to yan side'.

II. Transitive uses.

†**6.** To cause to take a downward or sloping position; to incline, bow, bend *down*. *Obs.*

Beowulf (Z.) 687 Hylde hine þa heaþo-deor. *c* **1000** *Ags. Gosp.* Luke xxiv. 5 Þa hiȝ adredon, and hyra andwlitan on eorþan hyldun. *a* **1300** *E.E. Psalter* xvi[i]. 6 Helde þine ere to me. *a* **1340** HAMPOLE *Psalter* xvii. 11 He heldid heuens and he lightid down. *c* **1440** *Promp. Parv.* 234/2 Heldyn, or bowyn, *inclino, flecto, deflecto.*

7. To pour out (liquor) by sloping or tilting the vessel that contains it; hence *gen.* to pour, shed (*lit.* and *fig.*). *Obs.* or *dial.* See also HELL *v.*[1]

c **1200** *Trin. Coll. Hom.* 213 To drinken..þat he sholde spelien wrecche men, oðer raðer helden hit ut þene men þermide fordrenchen. *a* **1225** *Ancr. R.* 428 Me schal helden eoli and win beoðe ine wunden. *a* **1340** HAMPOLE *Psalter* xxi. 13 As watere i am helt. **1382** WYCLIF *Lam.* ii. 4 [He] heeldide [**1388** schedde] out as fyr his indignacioun. *c* **1449** PECOCK *Repr.* III. viii. 323 In this dai venom is hildid into the chirche of God. **1674** RAY *N.C. Words* 24 *To Heald*, as when you pour out of a Pot. **1807** J. STAGG *Poems* 11 Some they helt it [drink] down sea fast, They suin cud hardly stan.

Hence '**hielded** *ppl. a.*, inclined, tilted; '**hielding** *vbl. sb.*, sloping, declension, pouring out; '**hielding** *ppl. a.*, leaning, inclining (*lit.* and *fig.*).

a **1300** *E.E. Psalter* lxi. 4 [lxii. 3] Als a heldeand wagh mai be, And a stane wall doune-put. *a* **1340** HAMPOLE *Psalter* xiii. 4 With that heldynge thai ere made vnprofitabile. *c* **1375** *Sc. Leg. Saints, Clemens* 397 Þe mone..In heldyne was of Martis house. *c* **1430** *Hymns Virg.* 23 Þat y be no þing hildande To loue uerrili þe worldis wele. *c* **1440** *Promp. Parv.* 234/2 Heldynge, or bowynge..*inclinacio.* **1627–47** FELTHAM *Resolves* II. xxxvi. 367 Pleasure..is at best but a hilded vessell.

†**hield, heeld, heald,** *sb. Obs.* Forms: 1–5 helde, 2 hulde (*ü*), 4–5 held, 6 heild, 9 heald. [OE. **hielde, hylde, helde*, wk. fem. f. *hieldan*: see HIELD *v.* But in later use perh. formed anew from the vb. stem.]

1. A slope, incline, declivity.

943 *Charter* in Kemble *Cod. Dipl.* III. 418 Ðonne andlang ðære dic oð ðæs clifes norð hyldan. *a* **1000** *Ags. Voc.* in Wr.-Wülcker 205/36 *Cliuium*, *i. discensum*, helde, burhsteal. *a* **1200** *Moral Ode* 343 Hi muwen lihtliche gon, mid ðere nuðer hulde..in-to ane bare felde. *c* **1250** *Hymn to God* 22 in *Trin. Coll. Hom.* App. 258 In heldes and in hulle. **13..** *Guy Warw.* (A.) 3442 Þe narwe paþe bi-tven the held. *c* **1420** *Pallad. on Husb.* VIII. 22 Neepis loueth heldis. **1513** DOUGLAS *Æneis* VII. Prol. 48 Montayne toppis sleikit wyth snaw our heildis.

b. *on held*: in a bent or stooping posture.

c **1460** *Towneley Myst.* (Surtees) 154 So I hobylle alle on held That unethes may I walk for eld.

2. *fig.* Inclination; declension, decline.

13.. *E.E. Allit. P.* B. 1520 As vchon hade hym in helde he haled of þe cuppe. **1599** NASHE *Lenten Stuffe* Ep. Ded. (1871) 14 His purse is on the heild.

3. *Naut.* = HEEL *sb.*[2]

1867 SMYTH *Sailor's Word-bk.*, *Heald*, the heel over of a grounded ship.

hield, obs. pa. t. of HOLD *v.*

hielding, see HIELD *v.*; var. HILDING.

hielmite ('hjɛlmaɪt). *Min.* [Named 1860 (*Hjelmit*), after the Swedish chemist P. J. Hjelm (1746–1813).] A black stanno-tantalate of iron and other bases, found as a massive mineral.

1861 *Amer. Jrnl. Sc.* Ser. III. XXXI. 362 Hjelmite..a new tantalate found at Kararfshol, in Sweden. **1868** DANA *Min.* (ed. 5) 519 Hielmite.

hiely, var. HEILY *a. Sc., Obs.*, haughty.

hiemal ('haɪməl), *a.* Now *rare*. Also **hy-**. [ad. L. *hiemālis*, f. *hiem-s* winter. Cf. F. *hiémal*.] Of or belonging to winter; winter-.

hiemal line (quot. 1635), the tropic of Capricorn, at which the sun arrives at the winter solstice.

c **1560** A. SCOTT *Poems* (S.T.S.) xiv. 18 Or sound of lark aboif þe revenous fowlis, And somersday the nichtis hiemaill. **1594** BLUNDEVIL *Exerc.* III. I. xi. (ed. 7) 296 Some [Signs are called] Hyemall or Brumall, as *Capricornus, Aquarius*, and *Pisces*. **1635** HEYWOOD *Hierarch.* III. 126 Betwixt th' Antarticke and the Hyemal lines. **1694** WESTMACOTT *Script. Herb.* 2 Awaking and germinating from their Hyemal repose. **1888** *Scot. Leader* 16 May 4 The first minister..delighted in the hyemal sport.

hiemate ('haɪmeɪt), *v. rare.* Also **hy-**. [f. L. *hiemāt-*, ppl. stem of *hiemāre* to winter, f. *hiem-s* winter.] *intr.* To winter, hibernate.

1623 COCKERAM, *Hyemate*, to winter at a place. *a* **1770** C. SMART *Hop Gard.* (R. Supp.), Whistling Eurus comes, With all his world of insects, in thy lands To hyemate. **1799** B. S. BARTON (cited in *Cent. Dict.*).

†**hie'matical,** *a. Obs. rare*[−1]. [irreg. f. L. *hiem-s* + -ATIC + -AL[1].] = HIEMAL.

1631 *Celestina* XIV. 159 O yee hyematicall and winterly months!

†**hie'mation.** *Obs. rare.* Also **hy-**. [ad. L. *hiemātiōn-em*, n. of action f. *hiemāre* to HIEMATE.] The spending of the winter, wintering.

1656 BLOUNT *Glossogr.*, *Hyemation*, a wintering. **1664** EVELYN *Sylva* xx. (1776) 413 Setting it in cases in our Conservatories of Hyemation. **1692** —— *Let. to Pepys* Aug. in *P.'s Diary* (1889) IX. 365, I hope, however, to get home ..about the end of October to my hyemation in Dover-street.

‖**hiems** ('haɪɛmz). *Obs.* Also 5 **yemps**, 6 **hiemps**. [L. = winter.] Winter; esp. in poet. personification.

c **1450** LYDG. *Secrees* 1456 Yemps endith the ende of Februarye. **1568** T. HOWELL *Arb. Amitie* (1879) 24 Now Hiemps heapes the dyke with snow and shewes her frostie face. **1605** *Tryall Chev.* II. ii. in Bullen *O. Pl.* III. 293 Where frosty Hyems with an ycie Mace Strikes dead all living things.

hien, hsien (hjɛn, ʃjɛn). Pl. uninflected. Also **heen**. [Chinese.] An administrative division of a fu or department, or of an independent chow or district; also, the seat of government of such a division. Also *attrib.*

1837 *Penny Cycl.* VII. 77/1 The subordinate cities and districts of each province in the three ranks of Foo, Chow, and Hien, are under the charge of their respective magistrates, who take their rank and titles from the cities they govern. **1901** *Westm. Gaz.* 23 Aug. 8/2 Among the candidates was a man who has the hsien B.A. degree. During the examination it was found that he had some books with him. The examiner at once ordered his expulsion from the hall, but the men from his hsien objected. **1909** *Ibid.* 24 May 8/2 A circular has been sent to all viceroys and governors by the Pekin Cabinet ordering that a stop be put to the old custom of levying benevolences on the governors of hien cities. **1938** *New Statesman* 15 Jan. 74/1 This means in practice control of the whole administrative machine down to the smallest units, the hsien. **1959** *Chambers's Encycl.* III. 439/2 The provincial health administration.. supervised the work of the *hsien* and municipal authorities. **1971** *N.Y. Times* 27 June 20 Each hsien [in China] has been given the target of becoming self-sufficient in food and light industrial products.

hiena, obs. form of HYAENA.

hiend, hienes(se, obs. ff. HIND, HIGHNESS.

hier, obs. form of HIRE *sb.* and *v.*

Hieracite ('haɪərəsaɪt). *Eccl. Hist.* [ad. med.L. *Hierācītæ* followers of Hierax (see below).] A follower of Hierax, an Egyptian ascetic (*c* 300 A.D.), who denied the resurrection of the body, and taught that celibacy is required for Christian perfection, etc.

1585–7 T. ROGERS *39 Art.* (1607) 154 The Hieracites, who have a phantasy, that no children departing this life before they come unto years of discretion and knowledge shall be saved. **1745** A. BUTLER *Lives Saints* (1836) I. 70 A subtle heretic of the sect of the Hieracites.

‖**Hieracium** (haɪə'reɪʃ(ɪ)əm), *Bot.* [Lat., a. Gr. ἱεράκιον name of a plant, f. ἱέραξ hawk.] A large genus of Composite plants, mostly with yellow flowers; called in Eng., Hawkweed.

1664 Evelyn *Kal. Hort.* (1729) 209 June..Flowers in Prime..Geranium..Hieracium. **1741** *Compl. Fam.-Piece* II. iii. 361 Columbines, and Hieraciums. *a* **1806** Charlotte Smith *Flora's Horologe* vi, See Hieracium's various tribe.

hie'raco-, combining form of Gr. ἱέραξ, -ᾱκος, hawk, as in **hieraco'sophic** *a.* [Gr. σοφία skill], pertaining to the management of hawks. **hieracosphinx** (haɪə'reɪkəʊsfɪŋks) *Egypt. Antiq.*, a hawk-headed sphinx.

1716 M. Davies *Athen. Brit.* III. *Diss. Physick* 2 Modern Practitioners..understand as little of them, as they do of the Geoponick, Hieracosophic, or Cynogetic Physicks.

‖**hiera picra** ('haɪərə 'pɪkrə). *Pharmacy.* [med.L., Gr. ἱερά (fem. of ἱερός sacred), a name given to many medicines in the Greek pharmacopœia + πικρά, fem. of πικρός bitter. The form in quot. 1400 is from OF. *gerapigre.*] A purgative drug composed of aloes and canella bark, sometimes mixed with honey and other ingredients. Also corruptly *hickery-pickery, hicra picra, higry-pigry*, which see.

1379–80 *Durh. MS. Burs. Roll*, In di. libr. de Gira pigra, xiid. *c* **1400** *Lanfranc's Cirurg.* 238 Ierapigre þat entriþ in pululas. **1616** Bullokar, *Hiera picra*,..often vsed in Phisicke to purge Choler out of the Stomacke. **1677** Wood *Life* (O.H.S.) II. 378, 6 pills of *Hiera picra*. **1754** Mrs. Delany *Life & Corr.* (1861) III. 268 He takes nervous draughts and *hiera picra*. **1896** *Daily News* 14 Dec. 6/6 Charged..with unlawfully conveying a packet of hiera picra, a powerful drug, into Holloway Gaol.

b. *fig.* (with allusion to the etymology).

a **1639** S. Ward *Serm.* (1862) 76 (D.) There is too much of this bitter zeal, of this Hierapicra in all our books of controversies.

hierarch ('haɪərɑːk), *a.* and *sb.* Also 5 ierarch. [ad. med.L. *hierarcha*, a. Gr. ἱεράρχης steward or president of sacred rites, high priest, f. ἱερός sacred + -αρχης, -αρχος, ruling, ruler.]

†**A.** *adj.* Having rule in holy things, or among the holy ones: applied to certain orders of angels. *Obs.* (Cf. hierarchy 1.)

1486 *Bk. St. Albans, Her.* A iv a, Of thorderis of angelis v. be ierarch and iiii. tron[ly].

B. *sb.* **1.** One who has rule or authority in holy things; an ecclesiastical ruler or potentate; a chief priest; a chief prelate, an archbishop.

1574 *Life 70th Abp. Canterb.* To Rdr. D ij b, The two Hierarches off Canterburie and Yorke. **1640** Bastwick *Lord Bps.* iii. C iij, And those Diverse, he makes to be Prelates, or Hierarchs. **1641** Milton *Ch. Govt.* v. (1851) 115 Their great Hierarch the Pope. **1841** G. Waddington *Hist. Ref.* III. xxxviii. 127 Nothing was farther from the thoughts of its hierarchs than any serious purpose of self-amendment. **1879** Farrar *St. Paul* I. 105 *note*, On the first summons of Peter and John before the Hierarchs.

2. Applied to an archangel; also to Christ, as commander of the celestial hierarchy.

1667 Milton *P.L.* v. 468 To whom the winged Hierarch [Raphael] repli'd. *Ibid.* xi. 220 The Princely Hierarch, In thir bright stand there left his Powers, to seise Possession of the Garden. **1855** Milman *Lat. Chr.* V. 233 Subject to the Hierarch of the Celestial Hierarchy.

hierarchal (haɪə'rɑːkəl), *a.* [f. prec. + -al¹.] Of or belonging to a hierarch or a hierarchy.

1641 'Smectymnuus' *Vind. Answ.* §13. 150 Enemies to the Hierarchall preeminency. **1773** J. Ross *Fratricide* I. 660 (MS.) Eve When first created..uprising from the sound Of hierarchal harmony! **1824** Southey *Bk. of Ch.* (1841) 171 An hierarchal government, like that of the Lamas, or the Dairis of Japan.

hierarchic (haɪə'rɑːkɪk), *a.* [ad. Gr. ἱεραρχικός, f. ἱεράρχης hierarch: see -ic. Cf. F. *hiérarchique.*] Of or belonging to a hierarchy.

1681 *Ess. Peace & Truth Ch.* 30 To enforce Humane Rites and Ceremonies, and stablish Hierarchick Policy in the Church. **1796** Morse *Amer. Geog.* II. 64 An empire, of which Upsala was for many centuries the political and hierarchic seat. **1853** *Tait's Mag.* XX. 388 All the hierarchic and aristocratic traditions and prejudices of Europe. **1879** Farrar *St. Paul* I. 106 The hierarchic clique, which..governed the body which still called itself the Sanhedrin.

hie'rarchical, *a.* [f. as prec. + -al¹.]

†**1.** Belonging to the angelic hierarchy. *Obs.*

1471 Ripley *Comp. Alch.* Pref. in Ashm. (1652) 121 Of Hierarchycall Jubylestes the gratulant gloryfycation.

2. Belonging to a priestly hierarchy, or body of ecclesiastical rulers.

1561 T. Norton *Calvin's Inst.* iv. vii. (1634) 548 In the Councell, where principally the image of the Hierarchicall order ought to be seene? **1692** Washington tr. *Milton's Def. Pop.* Pref. (1851) 16 An Hierarchical Tyranny, under a Cloak of Religion. **1735–8** Bolingbroke *On Parties* 14 The Excesses of Hierarchical and Monarchical Power..intirely occasion'd the Miseries, which follow'd. **1871** R. H. Hutton *Ess.* I. 393 The principle of Church development was exchanged for a principle of hierarchical encroachment.

3. Belonging or according to a regular gradation of orders, classes, or ranks: see hierarchy 4.

1832 tr. *Sismondi's Ital. Rep.* iii. 56 The nobles were not united by the hierarchical connection of the feudal system. **1864** H. Spencer *Illustr. Univ. Progr.* 180 The mutual influence of the sciences has been quite independent of any supposed hierarchical order. **1897** Capt. F. N. Maude *Volunt. v. Compuls. Service* 31 Kalkreuth..stood by..refusing to move, because he had received no orders from his hierarchical chief.

hie'rarchically, *adv.* [f. prec. + -ly².] In the manner of a hierarchy; from a hierarchical point of view; in a graduated order.

1624 Gataker *Transubst.* 97 Religiously and hierarchically (that is, as becommeth an Hierarch or a Bishop). **1831** Southey in *Q. Rev.* XLV. 441 To specialize particular banks, and to connect them hierarchically one with the other. **1882–3** Schaff *Encycl. Relig. Knowl.* III. 1874 Hierarchically the country [Portugal] is divided into four provinces.

'hierarchism. [f. hierarch (or hierarchy) + -ism.] Hierarchical practice and principles; hierarchical system.

1846 Worcester cites Kelly. **1852** Bunsen *Hippolytus* II. II. ii. (1854) II. 141 She establishes Catholic hierarchism without its hierarchical independence in reference to the State. **1855** Milman *Lat. Chr.* xiv. viii. VI. 565 The more dominant hierarchism of the West is manifest in the oppugnancy between Greek and Latin Church architecture.

hierarchist ('haɪərɑːkɪst). [f. as prec. + -ist.] An adherent or supporter of a hierarchy.

1640 Bp. Hall *Episc.* I. xi. 42 The Achillæan argument of the Hierarchists. **1644** Jessop *Angel of Eph.* 43 That argument which is used by our Hierarchists for the maintainance of their Episcopall Monarchie. **1882–3** Schaff *Encycl. Relig. Knowl.* I. 535 His little church at Norwich was persecuted by puritans as well as by hierarchists.

'hierarchize, *v.* [f. as prec. + -ize.] *trans.* To arrange in a hierarchy or gradation of orders. Hence **hierarchi'zation.**

1884 *Pall Mall G.* 1 Mar. 4/1 The millions of population that it contains seem to a Frenchman new to England so strangely hierarchised that he is at first bewildered. **1897** *Daily News* 23 Dec. 5/6 A rustic people that was never hierarchised. **1931** C. Williams *Place of Lion* ii. 26 These hierarchized celsitudes are but the last traces..of the ideas which Plato taught his disciples existed in the spiritual world. **1954** B. & R. North tr. *Duverger's Pol. Parties* II. iii. 405 Party hierarchization becomes more theoretical than practical. **1961** *New Left Rev.* May–June 34/2 Management ..is not so amalgamated or hierarchised. **1967** D. Cooper *Psychiatry & Anti-Psychiatry* v. 100 We have eliminated formal hierarchization to a point beyond which no similar experiment in the literature of the subject has gone. **1971** *Jrnl. Gen. Psychol.* LXXXIV. 202 By hierarchization Piaget means that there is a constant order of succession of different levels of functioning constituting a genetic sequence. **1971** G. Steiner *In Bluebeard's Castle* iv. 88 An explicit grammar is an acceptance of order: it is a hierarchization..of the forces and valuations prevailing in the body politic.

hierarchy ('haɪərɑːkɪ). Forms: α. 4–6 ierarchie, -y(e, gerarchie, -y(e, 5 iherarchye, 5–6 jerarchy(e, (6 *Sc.* cherarchy, ierarche). β. 6–7 hierarchie, 7– hierarchy. [ME., a. OF. *ier-, jerarchie* (14th c. in Hatz.-Darm.), *gerarchie* (15th c. in Littré) = It. *gerarchia*, ad. late L. *ierarchia* for *hierarchia*, a. Gr. ἱεραρχία the power or rule of a ἱεράρχης (hierarch), episcopate. The initial Gr. ι-, treated consonantally in late L., gave *j, g*, in the Romanic langs., and so in ME. The later β forms, like mod.F. *hiérarchie*, are directly ad. L. *hierarchia.*]

1. a. Each of the three divisions of angels, every one comprising three orders, in the system of Dionysius the Areopagite: see note s.v. cherub. Also, the collective body of angels, the angelic host.

α. *c* **1380** Wyclif *Serm.* Sel. Wks. II. 338 þer ben þree ierarchies. **1398** Trevisa *Barth. De P.R.* II. vii. (1495) 33 The hyghest Ierarchye of angels conteynyth thre ordres Seraphin, Cherubyn and Trones. **1483** Caxton *Gold. Leg.* 24 b/1 Saint denys in the booke of gerarchye of holy angellis in the vii chapytre saith. *Ibid.* 253 a/1 Me semed yᵗ all the Jerarchyes lyft her up. **1500–20** Dunbar *Poems* xlviii. 57 The blisfull sonne of cherarchy. **1528** Lyndesay *Dreme* 524 Thir ordouris nyne thay ar full plesandlye Deuydit in to Ierarcheis three.

β. **1531** Elyot *Gov.* I. i, Ministres, whom..he hath constituted to be in diuers degrees called hierarches. **1574** Newton *Health Mag.* Epist. 10 The Lord..conduct you to the ioyes of his glorious hierarchie. **1591** Greene *Maiden's Dr.* lii, I'll place his ghost among the hierarchies. *a* **1631** Donne *Poems* (1650) 255. **1667** Milton *P.L.* vii. 192 So sang the Hierarchies. *a* **1711** Ken *Hymnarium* Poet. Wks. 1721 II. 3 Thy Boundless Glories in Eternal Light, Angelick Hierarchies to Hymn excite. **1860** Pusey *Min. Proph.* 515 A subordinate order in the heavenly Hierarchy.

b. *transf.* of other beings: see quots.

1398 Trevisa *Barth. De P.R.* II. vii. (1495) 33 Saynt Denys spekyth of thre Iherarchyes, the fyrste is aboue heuen and stondeth in thre persones [i.e. the Trinity], the second in heuen and stondeth in holy angels. The thyrde vnder heuen and stondyth in prelates. **1450–1530** *Myrr. our Ladye* 274 *Trina celi*, the thre ierarchyes of heuen, the sonne, the starres, the mone. **1652** Bp. Hall *Invis. World* III. iii, [Lucifer]..ceaseth not still to oppose his hierarchy to the celestial. **1820** Keats *Ode to Psyche* 25 Loveliest vision far Of all Olympus' faded hierarchy!

2. a. Rule or dominion in holy things; priestly rule or government; a system of ecclesiastical rule.

1563–87 Foxe *A. & M.* (1684) III. 469 He speaketh of the Ecclesiastical Hierarchy or Regiment. **1581** J. Bell *Haddon's Answ. Osor.* 216 The principall stayes and proude pillers of this Ierarchy. **1654** Whitlock *Zootomia* 509 To reforme Hierarchy by Anarchy, a Remedy worse then the Disease. **1674** Hickman *Quinquart. Hist.* (ed. 2) 62 Vehement maintainers of Hierarchy and Ceremonies. **1841** Gallenga *Italy, Past & Pr.* (1848) I. 116 An unlimited centralisation of ecclesiastical hierarchy. **1851** Ht. Martineau *Hist. Peace* iv. x. (1877) III. 75 A scheme of a hierarchy which might easily become a despotism.

†**b.** *gen.* Rule, dominion. *Obs.*

1390 Gower *Conf.* III. 145 All the londe aboute, Which stant under his [the king's] gerarchie.

3. *concr.* The collective body of ecclesiastical rulers; an organized body of priests or clergy in successive orders or grades.

1619 Brent tr. *Sarpi's Counc. Trent* (1676) 553 Others placed this Hierarchy in Orders only, alledging Dionysius, who, in naming the Hierarchs, maketh mention of none but of Deacons, Priests, and Bishops. **1660** R. Coke *Power & Subj.* 148 The Pope and all the Hierarchy conspire with Stephen against Maud. **1738** Wesley *Psalms* lxxx. xiii, They once rever'd the Hierarchy, And bless'd the Mitre's sacred Power. **1856** Emerson *Eng. Traits, Relig.* Wks. (Bohn) II. 102 When the hierarchy is afraid of science, and education..there is nothing left but to quit.

4. A body of persons or things ranked in grades, orders, or classes, one above another; *spec.* in *Natural Science* and *Logic*, a system or series of terms of successive rank (as *classes, orders, genera, species*, etc.), used in classification.

1643 Milton *Divorce* viii. (1851) 41 There is a certain scale of duties, there is a certain Hierarchy of upper and lower commands. **1781** Gibbon *Decl. & F.* II. 36 Those who, in the Imperial hierarchy, were distinguished by the title of Respectable, formed an intermediate class between the illustrious præfects and the honourable magistrates of the provinces. **1864** Burton *Scot Abr.* I. ii. 96 All the world knows how difficult it is..to transfer any person from one social hierarchy into his exact place in another. **1864** Bowen *Logic* iv. 69 We have in each case a hierarchy of Concepts. **1875** Manning *Mission H. Ghost* xiii. 375 There is a Hierarchy of Being, and God is the Lord of all; and this Hierarchy of Being is also a Hierarchy of Intelligence. **1932** Von Wiese & Becker *Systematic Sociology* 355 Whenever persons join or otherwise enter into a plurality pattern they almost invariably take their places in an implicit or explicit hierarchy, and consciously or unconsciously expect the fact that there are ranks above and below them. **1947** *Soc. Research* XIV. 165 This hierarchy, like any other, is a social order in which human relations are determined by the degree of authority exercised by one group over another. **1961** G. G. Simpson *Princ. Animal Taxon.* i. 13 A hierarchy is a systematic framework for zoological classification with a sequence of classes (or sets) at different levels in which each class except the lowest includes one or more subordinate classes. **1963** Davis & Heywood *Princ. Angiosperm Taxon.* iii. 75 Before we go on to discuss the taxonomic hierarchy, it will be as well to list the ranks..which are accepted in the *International Code of Botanical Nomenclature.*

hieratic (haɪə'rætɪk), *a.* [ad. L. *hierātic-us*, a. Gr. ἱερᾱτικός priestly, sacerdotal, devoted to sacred purposes, f. *ἱερᾱτ-ος vbl. adj. from ἱεράομαι to be a priest.]

1. Pertaining to or used by the priestly class; used in connexion with sacred subjects. *spec.* **a.** Applied to a style of ancient Egyptian writing (called ἱερατικά by Clement of Alexandria, *c* A.D. 200), which consisted of abridged forms of hieroglyphics.

1669 Gale *Crt. Gentiles* I. I. xi. 64 Hieratic [letters], used by those who write of Sacreds. **1771** W. Jones *Zool. Eth.* 69 The next in order was the hieratic, or the writing used by the religious scribes and priests. **1850** Leitch tr. *C.O. Müller's Anc. Art* (ed. 2) §216 The hieratic character..seems to have arisen in the transference of hieroglyphics, particularly the phonetic portion of them, to papyrus, by the abbreviation and simplification of signs. **1850** Gladstone *Homer* II. ii. 165 Some other country having, like Egypt, an hieratic and also a demotic tongue. **1862** Rawlinson *Anc. Mon.* I. iv. 81 This mode of writing..has been called without much reason 'the hieratic'. **1883** Sayce *Fresh Light fr. Anc. Mon.* 86 It was from the hieratic forms of the Egyptian letters that the Phoenician letters were derived. **1886** Lowell *Orat. Harvard* 8 Nov. Wks. VI. 147 The teaching..of Hebrew, as the hieratic language.

b. ***hieratic paper***: = hieratica.

1656 [see hieratical]. **1855** *Househ. Words* XII. 67 The old hieratic paper soon lost its prestige.

c. Applied to a style of art (esp. Egyptian or Greek), in which earlier types or methods, fixed by religious tradition, are conventionally adhered to. Also *fig.*

1841 W. Spalding *Italy & It. Isl.* I. 176 Art in all its stages, from the rudest of the archaic or hieratic paintings to the finest design and finish of the Macedonian times. **1846** C. Maitland *Ch. Catacombs* 240 The intaglios of Kamai, almost the best hieratic work in existence. **1877** A. B. Edwards *Up Nile* xxii. 710 Sculptured in what is called the hieratic attitude; that is, with the left arm down and pressed close to the body.

d. Appropriate to sacred persons or duties.

1866 J. Martineau *Ess.* I. 14 It speaks..with hieratic grandeur. **1885** Pater *Marius* I. 32 A sort of hieratic beauty and orderliness in the conduct of life. **1893** *Nation* 9 Feb. 101/3 They have a sort of hieratic calm and peace.

2. *gen.* Priestly, sacerdotal.

1859 S. Sharpe *Hist. Egypt* xvi. §6 II. 199 Learned in the ten books, called hieratic, relating to the laws, the gods, the management of the temples, and the revenue. **1871** Morley *Crit. Misc.* 343 *note*, The essentially hieratic monarchies. **1885** W. H. Payne tr. *Compayre's Hist. Pedagogy* 15 It [education in the East] was administered by the hieratic class. **1893** in Barrows *Parl. Relig.* I. 663 The Law and the Prophets..constituted..the hieratic Hebrew books.

‖**hieratica** (haɪəˈrætɪkə). [L. *hierātica* (sc. *charta* or *papȳrus*), fem. of *hierāticus* (see prec.).] Papyrus of the finest quality, in ancient Egypt appropriated to sacred writings.

Now, a trade name of a special quality of paper.

1832 GELL *Pompeiana* II. 184 There was the *hieratica*.. and common waste paper.

hieˈratical, *a.* [f. as HIERATIC + -AL[1].] = HIERATIC.

1656 BLOUNT *Glossogr.*, *Hieratical*, sacred, holy, destined to things sacred. As Hieratick Paper, fine Paper, Dedicated onely to Religious Books. **1685** H. MORE *Illustr.* 324 The Hieratical power, riding this beast. **1859** W. H. GREGORY *Egypt* I. 206 Several hieratical papyri which we possess are dated from the Rameseum. **1884** *Harper's Mag.* May 836/1 Animals.. painted.. with a hieratical rigidity.

hieˈratico-, combining form of Gr. ἱερατικό-ς HIERATIC, as in **hieˌraticopoˈlitical** *a.*, combining priestly and political characters.

1685 H. MORE *Illustr.* 325 The secular or Civil part of the Hieraticopolitical Head of the Beast.

hieratite (ˈhaɪərətaɪt). *Min.* [a. It. *hieratite* (A. Cossa 1882, in *Atti d. R. Accad. dei Lincei* (*Trans.*) VI. 141), f. *Hiera*, ancient name of Vulcano, one of the Lipari Islands: see -ITE[1].] A colourless or greyish fluoride of potassium and silicon, K_2SiF_6, occurring in stalactitic concretions in the crater of Vulcano and on Vesuvius.

The abstract cited in quot. 1882 consistently spells the word *hieralite*, although Cossa's form was *-tite*.

1882 *Jrnl. Chem. Soc.* XLII. 705 For this natural fluosilicate he proposes the name *hieralite*, from *Hiera*, the Greek name for the island Vulcano. Hieralite is associated in the concretions with selensulphur, realgar, mirabilite, [etc.]. **1951** C. PALACHE et al. *Dana's Syst. Min.* (ed. 7) II. 104 Hieratite is isostructural with the corresponding salts of Rb, Cs, Tl, and NH_4.

hierce, hierche, obs. ff. HEARSE *sb.*, HERSE.

hierd(e, obs. f. HERD *sb.*[1] and [2].

hierer, hierling, obs. ff. HIRER, HIRELING.

hiero-, before a vowel **hier-**, combining form of Gr. ἱερός sacred, holy. See the following words.

hierocracy (haɪəˈrɒkrəsɪ). [See -CRACY.]

1. The rule of priests or religious dignitaries; government by priests or ecclesiastics: = HIERARCHY 2.

1794 W. TAYLOR in *Monthly Rev.* XV. 184 Under the hierocracy of Palestine, and in the feudal ages of Europe. **1801** T. JEFFERSON *Writ.* (1830) III. 469 Vermont will emerge next, because least.. under the yoke of hierocracy. **1852** GLADSTONE *Glean.* IV. viii. 146. **1892** A. B. BRUCE *Apologetics* II. viii. 280 The age of the hierocracy, when priests and scribes bore rule, not only failed to produce new prophets, but became incapable of appreciating the old ones.

2. *concr.* A body of ruling priests or ecclesiastics: = HIERARCHY 3.

1828 SOUTHEY in *Q. Rev.* XXXVIII. 579 It is this hierarchy, or hierocracy, who.. are to become the efficient and ruling instruments for tranquilizing Ireland.

hierocratic (haɪərəʊˈkrætɪk), *a.* [f. as prec.: see -IC.] Of or pertaining to a hierocracy.

1851 MRS. BROWNING *Casa Guidi Wind.* I. 994 By hierocratic empire, more or less Irresponsible to men. **1880** CONDER *Hand-bk. to Bible* I. vi. 126 The rule and government of the Hebrew people.. were.. hierocratic.

hieroˈcratical, *a.* [f. as prec. + -AL[1].] = prec.

1799 *Chron.* in *Ann. Reg.* 420 [Their] constitution was hierocratical.

hierodule (ˈhaɪərəʊdjuːl). *Gr. Antiq.*, etc. [ad. late L. *hierodūl-us*, a. Gr. ἱερόδουλος (masc. and fem.), f. ἱερόν (neut. of ἱερός used subst.) temple + δοῦλος slave. The L. pl. *hierodūli*, and a fem. pl. *hierodūlæ*, occur in Eng. writers.] A slave (of either sex) dwelling in a temple, and dedicated to the service of a god.

'Esp. applied to the public courtesans or votaries of Aphrodite at Corinth,' Liddell & Scott.

1835 THIRLWALL *Greece* I. v. 138 Sent to Delphi with a company of other *hierodules*. **1850** LEITCH tr. *C. O. Müller's Anc. Art* (ed. 2) §422 An ivory Aphrodite is celebrated by her hierodulæ in myrtle bowers. **1893** *Nation* (N.Y.) 27 Apr. 316/2 The Amazons—that is, the warrior priestesses, or hierodules, of the Cappadocian Hittites.

So **hieroˈdulic** *a.*, belonging to a hierodule.

1885 BLACK tr. *Wellhausen's Proleg. Hist. Israel* IV. i. 123 Captives were employed to do hierodulic services.

hierogamy (haɪəˈrɒgəmɪ). [f. HIERO- + Gr. -γαμια marriage.] A sacred marriage.

1882 MARY LOCKWOOD tr. *Lenormant's Begin. Hist.* App. I. iii. 550 The hierogamy of Zeus and Europa was annually celebrated at Gortyna in Crete.

hieroglyph (ˈhaɪərəʊglɪf), *sb.* Also 6 **gieroglife**. [Back-formation from HIEROGLYPHIC: cf. F. *hiéroglyphe* (1576 in Hatz.-Darm.). The Gr. ἱερογλύφος meant 'a carver of hieroglyphics': cf. sense 3. With the *gi-* form, cf. F. *gieroglifique* (Cotgr.) and It., and see HIERARCHY.]

1. A hieroglyphic character; a figure of some object, as a tree, animal, etc., standing for a word (or, afterwards, in some cases, a syllable or sound), and forming an element of a species of writing found on ancient Egyptian monuments and records; thence extended to such figures similarly used in the writing of other races. Also, a writing consisting of characters of this kind.

1598 FLORIO, *Geroglifico*, a gieroglife, mysticall or enigmaticall letters or cyfers vsed among the Egyptians. **1774** J. BRYANT *Mythol.* I. 375 The swan.. was certainly the hieroglyph of the country. **1831** *Fraser's Mag.* III. 12 These Hieroglyphs are a true Sacred Writing. **1859** GULLICK & TIMBS *Paint.* 35 The hieroglyphs were generally coloured on the great monuments. **1876** BIRCH *Egypt* 9 The hieroglyphs in the name of Ptolemy were fuller forms of the demotic signs used in the same name.

b. *attrib.* Inscribed with hieroglyphs.

1853 J. CUMMING *Scripture Read. Gen.* xli. 358 From hieroglyph monuments of Egypt.

2. *transf.* and *fig.* A figure, device, or sign having some hidden meaning; a secret or enigmatical symbol; an emblem.

1646 BUCK *Rich. III*, 115 (R.) A quaint device sent unto her in a rich jewel, fashioned much after the manner of the trivial hieroglyphs, used in France, called Rebus de Picardy. **1798** W. TAYLOR in *Monthly Mag.* VI. 552 Secret symbols and hieroglyphs, which described the concealed doctrines. **1871** SWINBURNE *Songs bef. Sunrise, Pilgrims* 27 For on your brows is written a mortal sentence, An hieroglyph of sorrow, a fiery sign. **1876** G. F. CHAMBERS *Astron.* 890 One of the signs or hieroglyphs in the centre of the Table.

b. *humorously.* A piece of writing difficult to decipher.

1875 L. MORRIS *Frederic* vi. in *Songs Two W.* Ser. III. (1878) 419 His writing Was so clear, and skilful, and fine, That I set him the task to decipher The hieroglyphs which are mine.

3. One who makes hieroglyphic inscriptions. *rare.*

1863 J. G. MURPHY *Comm. Gen.* xli. 8 The hieroglyphs, who belonged to the priestly caste, and whose primary business was to make hieroglyphic and other inscriptions.

ˈhieroglyph, *v.* [f. as prec.] *trans.* To represent by a hieroglyph; to write in hieroglyphs.

1622 MABBE tr. *Aleman's Guzman d'Alf.* I. 138 And therefore the Egyptians, when they would Hierogliffe a King, and by some mysticall Cyphers expresse his vigilancie, they did put a Scepter in his hand, with an eye on the top of it. **1867** DE MORGAN in *Athenæum* 20 July 71/1 The bricks are indeed alive, and the evidence is hieroglyphed upon them: but how are we to read it?

ˈhieroglyphed (-glɪft), *a.* [f. HIEROGLYPH *sb.* or *v.*] **a.** Written in hieroglyphs. **b.** Inscribed with hieroglyphs.

1877 A. B. EDWARDS *Up Nile* iv. 84 The first hieroglyphed sarcophagus we had yet seen. **1881** *Academy* No. 457. 104 *note*, These hieroglyphed names are phonetically spelled.

hieˈroglypher. *rare.* [? f. Gr. ἱερογλύφος carver of hieroglyphics + -ER.] One who writes in hieroglyphs.

1613 PURCHAS *Pilgrimage* (1614) 573 *note*, Christopher was first so painted of some Egyptian or Hieroglypher.

hieroglyphic (haɪərəʊˈglɪfɪk), *a.* and *sb.* Also 6–7 **hy-, -gli-, -f-, -i(c)que, -ik(e, -ick; 7 gie-**. [ad. F. *hiéroglyphique* (1529 in Hatz.-Darm.) or late L. *hieroglyphicus*, a. Gr. ἱερογλυφικός, f. ἱερός sacred + γλυφή carving (cf. γλυφικός). The adj. was used subst. by Plutarch, τὰ ἱερογλυφικά (*sc.* γράμματα) letters, writing, whence *hieroglyphics*.]

A. *adj.*

1. Of the nature of an Egyptian or similar hieroglyph (sense 1); written in or consisting of hieroglyphics.

1585 T. WASHINGTON tr. *Nicholay's Voy.* II. xvi. 50 A fair obelisquie.. 50 cubits high beset with letters Hieroglificque. **1662** STILLINGFL. *Orig. Sacr.* I. ii. §11 Translated into Hieroglyphick Characters. **1726** DE FOE *Hist. Devil* II. vi. (1840) 248 In the old writings of the Egyptians, I mean their hieroglyphic writing. **1857** MAX MÜLLER *Chips* (1880) I. x. 261 The Chinese.. was in its origin a hieroglyphic system. **1879** LUBBOCK *Addr. Pol. & Educ.* x. 186 The Rosetta stone ..containing an inscription in three characters, hieroglyphic, enchorial, and Greek.

2. *transf.* and *fig.* Of the nature of a hieroglyph (sense 2); having a hidden meaning; symbolical, emblematic.

1647 COWLEY *Mistr., Soul* iii, So that all fair Species be Hieroglyphick marks of Thee. **1706** PHILLIPS (ed. Kersey), *Hieroglyphick Marks* (in Palmestry), those winding Lines and Wrinkles in the Hand, by which the Professours of that vain Science pretend to foretell strange Things. **1878** C. STANFORD *Symb. Christ* vii. 175 It locked in hieroglyphic language the truth.

3. Containing or inscribed with hieroglyphs.

1663 COWLEY *Verses Sev. Occas., Complaint* i, A wondrous Hieroglyphick Robe she wore. **1675** COLES (*title*) Nolens Volens.. together with the Youths' Hieroglyphick Bible.

4. *humorously.* Difficult to decipher.

1856 OLMSTEAD *Slave States* 1 A hieroglyphic scrawl.

B. *sb.*

1. *orig.* in *pl.* = Gr. τὰ ἱερογλυφικά. The characters or mode of writing used by the ancient Egyptians (or by transference, other peoples), consisting of figures of objects directly or figuratively representing words (*picture-writing*), or, in certain circumstances, syllables or letters. The sing. is rarely used: see HIEROGLYPH.

1586 FERNE *Blaz. Gentrie* 149 The same that the auncient Hieroglyphiques weare with the Ægiptians. **1611** COTGR., *Gieroglifique*, gieroglifhicall; of, or belonging to, Gieroglifhickes. **1613** PURCHAS *Pilgramage* (1614) 811 The Indians of.. Mexico, shewed unto a Jesuit their Bookes.. which in figures and Hieroglyphickes represented things after their manner. **1638** SIR T. HERBERT *Trav.* (ed. 2) 338 They [Chinese] use not letters but Characters, or Hyerogliphicks, of which they have above 40000. **1712** W. ROGERS *Voy.* 319 The antient Mexicans.. in those pretended Histories, preserv'd by fanciful Hieroglyphicks. **1758** J. KENNEDY *Curios. Wilton. Ho.* 47 The Statue of Isis ..There are a great Multitude of Hieroglyphicks quite round the Bottom. **1845** MAURICE *Mor. & Met. Philos.* in *Encycl. Metrop.* II. 558/1 The invention of a system of hieroglyphics. **1851** LAYARD *Pop. Acc. Discov. Nineveh* x. 246 Between the figures is a cartouche, containing a name in hieroglyphics.

2. a. A picture standing for a word or notion, esp. one symbolizing something which it does not directly figure (like many of the Egyptian hieroglyphs); hence, a figure, device, or sign, having some hidden meaning; a secret or enigmatical symbol, an emblem; a hieroglyph.

1596 H. CLAPHAM *Briefe Bible* I. 19 Commending onely vnto them Hierogliphiks, or holy preaching signes. **1599** H. BUTTES *Dyets drie Dinner* E, Palme.. an Hieroglyphick or Embleme of victory and conquest. **1634** PEACHAM *Gentl. Exerc.* II. i. 107 Flax was the Hieroglyphicke of Fate among the Aegyptians. **1638** QUARLES (*title*) Hieroglyphikes of the Life of Man. **1638** SIR T. HERBERT *Trav.* (ed. 2) 45 A silken string circles both their bodies as the Hyerogliphic or bond of Wedlock. **1688** J. OGILVY tr. *Magaillan's Hist. China* 70 It is the nature of Hieroglyphicks not to be the natural figures of the things which they signifie, but only to represent them. **1758** JOHNSON *Idler* No. 34 ¶6 Water is the proper hieroglyphick of easy prattle. *a* **1806** HORSLEY *Serm.* (1811) 134 The Levitical rites were nothing less than the gospel itself in hieroglyphics. **1809** W. IRVING *Knickerb.* (1861) 262 He was the first to imprint New-year cakes with the mysterious hieroglyphics of the Cock and Breeches. **1891** WILSON in *Colleges Oxford* 245 The grotesque figures or 'hieroglyphics' in the Cloister Quadrangle [Magd. Coll.] were painted.. in honour of his coming.

b. pl. *humorously.* Characters or writing difficult to make out. Cf. HIEROGLYPH *sb.* 2 b.

a **1734** NORTH *Lives* I. 365 Petitions signed with numberless hands and frightful hieroglyphics. **1853** MRS. GASKELL *Cranford* xv. 296 About a year after Miss Matty set up shop, I received one of Martha's hieroglyphics, begging me to come to Cranford very soon. **1862** *Sat. Rev.* 8 Feb. 155 Inability to decipher the hieroglyphics of Bradshaw. **1874** L. STEPHEN *Hours in Library* (1892) I. ii. 64 Some ladies.. cross their writing till the page becomes a chequer-work of unintelligible hieroglyphics.

†**hieroˈglyphic**, *v.* *Obs.* [f. prec.]

1. *trans.* To represent by, or as by, a hieroglyphic; to symbolize.

1615 T. ADAMS *Blacke Devill* 36 Perhaps he meanes to hieroglyphicke unto us what wondrous engines silver tooles are in Rome. **1650** T. BAYLY *Herba Parietis* 15 By Cupid.. was hieroglyphict the love that was between her and her husband. **1653** E. CHISENHALE *Cath. Hist.* 125 It was made like a Nut, and did thereby Hieroglyphick its short continuance. **1715** M. DAVIES *Athen. Brit.* I. 282 As for Winefrid's Life being Hieroglyphick'd on the windows of Holywell Church.

2. To interpret or express, as a hieroglyphic.

1615 SIR E. HOBY *Curry-combe* iii. 112 He doth Hierogliphick my name of I. R. in English, Latin, and Hebrew, making mee in the one Lack Roague, in the other Iscarioth de Rubigine, and Ishmael Rabshacheh in the third.

hieroglyphical (haɪərəʊˈglɪfɪkəl), *a.* [f. as prec. + -AL[1].]

1. Of, pertaining to, or of the nature of hieroglyphics; like the Egyptian picture-writing.

1605 J. DOVE *Confut. Atheism* 50 These letters were but Hyeroglyphicall, like to the letters of the Egiptians, not Abcdarye letters, but shapes and Images of beastes. **1611** Gieroglíphicall [see HIEROGLYPHIC B. 1]. **1613** PURCHAS *Pilgrimage* (1614) 55 Obeliskes with hieroglíphicall inscriptions, carried from Hieropolis.. to Rome. **1748** HARTLEY *Observ. Man* I. iii. 307 Hieroglyphical Writing in all its Varieties. **1836** MACGILLIVRAY tr. *Humboldt's Trav.* xxiv. 360 The Aztec manuscripts or hieroglyphical pictures preserved in the house of the viceroys.

b. Relating to, or dealing with, hieroglyphics.

1811 LAMB *Guy Faux* Misc. Wks. (1871) 372 By the most hieroglyphical Egyptian. **1862** *Sat. Rev.* 8 Feb. 165 The hieroglyphical readings of Champollion and his successors.

2. Symbolical, emblematic; = HIEROGLYPHIC *a.* 2.

1581 MULCASTER *Positions* xxxix. (1887) 188 The nyne Muses.. painted vpon the wall.. would serue him for places of memorie, or for hieroglyphicall partitions. **1614** RALEIGH *Hist. World* III. v. §4 (R.) To this challenge the Scythian returned an hieroglyphical answer; sending a bird, a mouse, a frog, and five arrows. **1672** in Willis & Clark *Cambridge* (1886) II. 497 Gilding yᵉ diall.. and yᵉ Hieroglyphical Triangle. **1689** *Lond. Gaz.* No. 2501/3 (*Ld. Mayor's Shew*) The Rich Adornments of the Pageants, and Hieroglyphical Representations. **1711** ADDISON *Spect.* No. 64 ¶1 A good Courtier's Habit and Behaviour is hieroglyphical on these

Occasions. **1840** Hood *Kilmansegg, First Step* v, Cards like that hieroglyphical call To a geographical Fancy Ball On the recent [Mulready] Post Office covers.

3. Difficult to decipher or make sense of; cf. HIEROGLYPHIC *a.* 4.

1613-16 W. Browne *Brit. Past.* I. v, My blubbring pen her sable teares lets fall, In characters right Hyrogliphicall. **1767** Miss Dewes in *Mrs. Delany's Life & Corr.* Ser. II. (1862) I. 134 This was written in the dark, but you used to love hieroglyphical letters. **1851** Ruskin *Stones Ven.* (1874) I. xxi. 238 A particular method of handling..which has its effect at the intended distance, and is altogether hieroglyphical and unintelligible at any other. **1885** *Law Times* 11 Apr. 421/1 Notes often disjointed, sometimes hieroglyphical..as jotted down at the hearing.

hiero'glyphically, *adv.* [f. prec. + -LY².] In a hieroglyphical manner.

1. In, by, or with hieroglyphics or picture-writing.

1593 R. Harvey *Philad.* 57 They writ their Chronicle hieroglyphically. **1708** *Brit. Apollo* No. 88. 1/1 *Anubis* Hieroglyphically represented with a Head like a Dog's. **1775** Adair *Amer. Ind.* 319 Promise..to send the..snake's head, in the time appointed by our sticks hieroglyphically painted. **1882-3** Schaff *Encycl. Relig. Knowl.* I. 703 The native name was *Keme* represented heiroglyphically with the ideographic character of the crocodile-tail.

2. Symbolically, emblematically; metaphorically.

1624 Massinger *Parl. Love* v. i, That celestial fire Which hieroglyphically is described In this his bow, his quiver, and his torch. **1642** Cudworth *Serm. 1 Cor.* xv. 57 in *Disc. Lord's Supp.* (1670) 210 The Death of Christ.. Hieroglyphically instructed us that we ought to take up our Cross likewise, and follow our crucified Lord and Saviour. **1831** Carlyle *Sart. Res.* II. x, Receiving as literally authentic what was but hieroglyphically so.

hiero'glyphicize, *v. rare*⁻¹. [f. HIEROGLYPHIC + -IZE.] = HIEROGLYPHIZE.

1716 M. Davies *Athen. Brit.* III. *Dissert. Pallas Anglicana* 4 Under the name of Musick..is Hyeroglyphisiz'd the Protestant practical Harmony.

hieroglyphist (haɪəˈrɒglɪfɪst). [f. as HIEROGLYPH-ER + -IST.] A writer of hieroglyphs; one versed in hieroglyphs.

a **1829** Sir H. Davy cited in Worcester (1846). *a* **1857** Gliddon cited in Webster (1864). **1876** G. Meredith *Beauch. Career* II. ix. 152 Trying at condensation, as the hieroglyphists put an animal for a paragraph.

hie'roglyphize, *v. rare*⁻¹. [f. as prec. + -IZE.] *trans.* To write or express by hieroglyphics; = HIEROGLYPH *v.*

1662 Evelyn *Chalcogr.* iii. (1769) 42 Mexico..where they hieroglyphiz'd both their thoughts, histories, and inventions, to posterity, not much unlike to the Egyptians.

†**hie'roglyphy,** *v. Obs. rare.* [f. HIEROGLYPH: perh. associated with -FY.] = prec.

1762 Foote *Orators* I. i. (1767) 24 Not enigmatically hieroglyphied [**1799** -glyfied], but plainly..pourtray'd.

hierogram (ˈhaɪərəʊgræm). [f. HIERO- + -GRAM. Cf. F. *hiérogramme.*] A sacred symbol; a hieroglyph (*lit.* and *fig.*).

1656 Blount *Glossogr., Hierograms* (from the Gr.), sacred Letters or writings. **1831** Carlyle *Sart. Res.* II. x, Facts are engraved Hierograms for which the fewest have the key. **1873** L. Wallace *Fair God* I. vii. 33 In square marble panels ..were hierograms and sculptured pictures of men.

hiero'grammate, -at. [f. Gr. ἱερογραμματεύς sacred scribe, one of a lower order of the Egyptian priesthood, f. ἱερός sacred + γραμματεύς clerk, scribe.] A writer of sacred records, *spec.* of hieroglyphics.

[**1678** Cudworth *Intell. Syst.* I. iv. §18. 323 Then succeeds the Hierogrammateus or Sacred Scribe..to whom it belongeth to be thoroughly acquainted with the Hieroglyphicks.] **1864** *Athenæum* No. 1937. 785/3 The learned hierogrammates of the colleges of Thebes and Memphis. **1876** J. Ellis *Caesar in Egypt* 66 Well-versed In mystic records of Egyptus' land, And Hierogrammat of linguistic skill.

hierogra'mmatic, *a.* [f. HIEROGRAM on Gr. analogies: cf. *grammatic.*] Of the nature of a hierogram, relating to or consisting of hierograms. So **hierogra'mmatical** *a.*; **hiero'grammatist** = HIEROGRAMMATE.

a **1641** Bp. Mountagu *Acts & Mon.* 167 Symbolicall Philosophie, by figures and resemblances declaring their meaning, which is styled Hieroglyphicall, or Hierogrammaticall, and by Clemens, Mysticall Theologie. **1677** Gale *Crt. Gentiles* III. 66 Melampos, the Hierogrammatist. **1740** Warburton *Div. Legat.* IV. iv. Wks. 1811 IV. 143 The hierogrammatic, or sacerdotal..he [Porphyry] comprized..under the generic term of epistolic. *Ibid.* 157 Another alphabetic character for their sacred use.. called hierogrammatical. **1801** J. Hager *Babyl. Inscript.* 37 The Chaldeans..had a hierogrammatic or hieroglyphic writing. **1831** M. Russell *Hist. Egypt* v. (1853) 155 The Hierogrammatist or Sacred Scribe.

hierograph (ˈhaɪərəʊgrɑːf, -græf). [f. Gr. ἱερός sacred + -γραφος written (see -GRAPH). Cf. eccl. Gr. (τὰ) ἱερόγραφα representations of holy things.] A sacred inscription or symbol: a hieroglyph.

1835 *Blackw. Mag.* XXXVII. 860 We have deciphered their hierographs. **1854** J. D. Burns *Vis. Proph.* 116 He saw, in radiant signatures inscribed One hierograph.

So **hie'rographer** [eccl. Gr. ἱερογράφος], a sacred scribe; **hiero'graphic** [late L. *hierographicus*, Gr. ἱερογραφικός], **hiero'graphical** *adjs.*, of the nature of, or relating to, sacred writing or symbols; in quot. 1658 = hieratic.

1605 J. Dove *Confut. Atheism* 19 His name is engrauen there in in hierographicall letters. **1658** Owen *Consid. Walton's Biblia Polyglotta* 262 Clemens tells us of three sorts of Characters among the Ægyptians; one for things of common use, another, Hierographick, used by the Priests in their sacred Writings, and the other Hieroglyphick. **1730-6** Bailey (folio), *Hierographer*, a Writer of Divine Things. **1784** Astle *Orig. & Progr. Writ.* iii. (T.), Partly written in symbolic, and partly in these hierographic characters. *Ibid.*, These [characters] were properly what the ancients call hierographical.

hierography (haɪəˈrɒgrəfɪ). [ad. eccl. Gr. ἱερογραφία description of holy things, the Scriptures, f. ἱερός sacred + -γραφία writing, -GRAPHY.]

1. A description of sacred things; a description of religions.

1656 Blount *Glossogr., Hierographie*, a description or pourtrayting of divine things. **1877** J. E. Carpenter tr. *Tiele's Hist. Relig.* 1 The history of religion is not content with describing special religions (hierography).

†**2.** Sacred writing; writing by hierograms. *Obs.*

1731 *Hist. Litteraria* II. 551 They..lost the knowledge of their Hierography, or emblematical way of writing.

hie'rolatry. [See HIERO- and -LATRY.] Worship of holy beings or saints: hagiolatry.

c **1814** Coleridge in *Rem.* (1836) III. 71 To have traced the progress of the Christolatry..with the same historical distinctness..that the Protestants have that of hierolatry against the Romanists. **1861** *Macm. Mag.* V. 127 Mariolatry, hierolatry..amongst educated French Roman Catholics, of the male sex at least, may now be said to be nowhere.

hierology (haɪəˈrɒlədʒɪ). [f. HIERO + -LOGY. Cf. late Gr. ἱερολογία sacred or mystical language, benediction. In mod.L. *hierologia*, F. *hiérologie.*]

†**1.** 'A discourse on sacred things' (Webster 1828). *Obs.*

†**2.** Hieroglyphic lore; the study of Egyptian records. *Obs.*

a **1848** M. Russell *Hist. Egypt* xi. (1853) 452 The later discoveries in hierology. **1859** W. H. Gregory *Egypt* I. 36 It is the pride of modern hierology..to have brought to light some annals of a monarch [Sesortesen] whose existence and name were omitted by all historians.

3. Sacred literature or lore; the literature embodying the religious beliefs of a country or people; e.g. of the Egyptians, Greeks, Jews, etc.

1854 Emerson *Lett. & Soc. Aims, Quot. & Orig.* Wks. (Bohn) III. 214 The new researches..have opened to us the deep debt of the churches of Rome and England to the Egyptian hierology. **1862** Burton *Bk. Hunter* (1863) 352 Not to throw away the cosmogony and the hierology of Greece. **1879** *19th Cent.* Sept. 486 The conjectured relation between the *Nuk-pu-nuk* of Egyptian hierology and the 'I am that I am' of the Hebrew legislator.

4. The history of religions as a branch of study.

1883 *Contemp. Rev.* Aug. 204 Zoroastrianism..is of the highest value to hierology.

5. = HAGIOLOGY.

1890 E. Venables in *Rep. Linc. Archit. Soc.* 265 St. Edmund King and Martyr..the St. Sebastian of English hierology.

So **hiero'logic, hiero'logical** *adjs.*, belonging to hierology; **hie'rologist**, one versed in hierology.

1839 *Fraser's Mag.* XX. 204 Our living hierologists..have laboured conjecturally to fill up the vague outline of Herodotus. *a* **1848** M. Russell *Hist. Egypt* xiii. (1853) 504 Samuel Birch..one of the ablest of modern hierologists. **1864** Webster, *Hierologic, Hierological.*

†**hieromachy** (haɪəˈrɒməkɪ). *Obs. rare.* [f. Gr. ἱερό-ς sacred (HIERO-) + -μαχία fighting.] A conflict of ecclesiastics.

1574 *Life 70th Abp. Canterb.* To Rdr. Dijb, The ambitious and tragicall Hieromachie betwene the two Hierarches off Canterburye and Yorke for the papacie in England.

'hieromancy. [ad. mod.L. *hieromantīa* (a. mod.Gr. ἱερομαντεία), f. Gr. ἱερο- HIERO- + μαντεία divination: see -MANCY.]

1. Divination from the observation of objects offered in religious sacrifices, or from sacred things.

[**1753** Chambers *Cycl. Supp.*, Hieromantia.] **1775** Ash, *Hieromancy.*

2. Jugglery with sacred things. *nonce-use.*

1811 W. Taylor in *Monthly Rev.* LXIV. 168 He has known how to attach to his mystic hieromancy, both the unthinking and the designing erudition of the clerical order.

hiero'martyr. *Gr. Ch.* [f. HIERO- + MARTYR. Cf. Gr. ἱερομάρτυς.] In the Greek Calendar, a martyr who was in holy orders.

1864 Webster, *Hieromartyr*, a martyr who is also a priest.

‖**hieromnemon** (haɪərɒmˈniːmən). [Gr. ἱερομνήμων adj. ('mindful of sacred things') and sb., f. ἱερός sacred + μνήμων mindful.] A sacred recorder.

1. *Gr. Antiq.* The title of one of the two deputies sent by each constituent tribe to the Amphictyonic council, whose office was more particularly concerned with religious matters.

1753 Chambers *Cycl. Supp.* **1822** T. Mitchell *Aristoph.* II. 76

2. (See quot.)

1727-41 Chambers *Cycl., Hieromnemon*, an officer in the antient Greek church; whose principal function was, to stand behind the patriarch at the sacraments, ceremonies, etc. and shew him the prayers, psalms, etc. he was to rehearse.

hieromonach (haɪərəʊˈmɒnək). *Gr. Ch.* Also **hiero'monk.** [ad. Gr. ἱερομόναχος holy monk (see HIERO- and MONK).] A monk who is also a priest; a 'regular' as opposed to a 'secular' cleric.

[**1782** Burke *Penal Laws agst. Irish Cath.* Wks. VI. 285 Those who wish to address them [clergy of the Greek Ch.] with civility always call them *hieromonachi.*] **1882-3** Schaff *Encycl. Relig. Knowl.* III. 2082 One hieromonach (monk-priest), two secular priests. **1932** *Pax* Oct. 161 These are divided as follows: Maronite Antonians: 520 hieromonks, 221 monks. **1964** P. F. Anson *Bishops at Large* i. 37 Almost any alien calls himself..hieromonk..or any other Oriental ecclesiastical title.

Hieronymian (haɪərəʊˈnɪmɪən), *a.* and *sb.* [f. *Hieronymus* Jerome, a celebrated father of the Church in the 5th c.: see -IAN.] **A.** *adj.* Of or belonging to St. Jerome, the author of the Latin Vulgate translation of the Bible. **B.** *sb.* = HIERONYMITE *sb.*

1656 Blount *Glossogr., Hieronimians*, a Religious Order, that had their beginning of St. Hierome..There were also certain Hermites called Hieronimians of the foundation of one Charles Granel of Florence. **1884** *Athenæum* 19 Apr. 502/2 To determine..the basis of its readings, whether the old Latin or the Hieronymian Vulgate.

Hiero'nymic, *a.* [f. as prec. + -IC.] = prec. A.

1889 Hort in *Academy* 19 Jan. 42/1 Ceolfrid's Bible was to be Vulgate, Hieronymic in text, Augustinian in canon.

Hieronymite (haɪəˈrɒnɪmaɪt), *sb.* and *a. Eccl. Hist.* [f. as prec. + -ITE.] **A.** *sb.* A hermit of any of the various orders of St. Jerome. **B.** *adj.* Belonging to any of these orders.

1727-41 Chambers *Cycl., Hieronymites*, or Hermits of S. Jerom. **1843** Prescott *Mexico* II. i. (1864) 70 This extraordinary commission of three Hieronymite friars and an eminent jurist. *Ibid.* 74 He previously solicited authority for this from the Hieronymite commission in St. Domingo.

hieropathic (haɪərəʊˈpæθɪk), *a.* *nonce-wd.* [irreg. f. Gr. ἱερός sacred + πάθος feeling, emotion, affection + -IC.] Consisting in love of the clergy.

1844 Sir J. Stephen *Eccl. Biog., Hildebrand* (1875) 30 That hieropathic affection so familiarly known among ourselves, of which the female spirit is the seat, and the ministers of religion the objects.

hierophancy (ˈhaɪərəʊfænsɪ). [ad. Gr. ἱεροφαντία, f. ἱεροφάντης: see next and -ANCY.] The function of a hierophant; capacity of expounding sacred mysteries.

1851 S. Judd *Margaret* III. (1871) 379 The hierophancy that exists in all souls needed only to be awakened.

hierophant (ˈhaɪərəʊfænt). [ad. late L. *hierophantēs, -phanta*, a. Gr. ἱεροφάντης, f. ἱερός sacred + φαίνειν bring to light, make known, reveal. Cf. F. *hiérophante* (1535 in Hatz.-Darm.).]

1. *Antiq.* An official expounder of sacred mysteries or religious ceremonies, esp. in ancient Greece; an initiating or presiding priest.

1677 Hale *Prim. Orig. Man.* II. xii. 244 The Crafts of their Heathenish Priests and Hierophants. **1774** Burney *Hist. Mus.* (1789) I. 332 Eminent at Athens, as hierophant in the Eleusinian mysteries. **1776** R. Chandler *Trav., Greece* (1825) II. 223 The chief priest, hierophant, or mystagogue, was taken from the Eumolphidæ. **1882** Whittier *Quest. of Life* 5, I listen to the sibyl's chant, The voice of priest and hierophant.

2. *gen.* An expounder of sacred mysteries; the minister of any 'revelation'; the interpreter of any esoteric principle.

a **1822** Shelley *Def. Poetry* Pr. Wks. 1888 II. 38 Poets are the hierophants of an unapprehended inspiration. **1843** J. Martineau *Chr. Life* (1867) 105 The hierophant and interpreter of the godlike in the soul. **1856** R. A. Vaughan *Mystics* (1860) I. 6 A doubt as to whether 'able editors' were, after all, the great, divinely accredited hierophants of the species.

hiero'phantic, *a.* [ad. Gr. ἱεροφαντικός, f. ἱεροφάντης: see prec.] Of or belonging to a hierophant or hierophants; resembling or of the character of a hierophant.

1775 in Ash. **1816** *Edin. Rev.* XXVI. 182 The hierophantic race is not wholly extinct. **1849** Grote *Greece* II. xliii. V. 284 Gelo thus belonged to an ancient and distinguished hierophantic family. **1879** Mrs. Lynn Linton *Under which Lord?* III. xi. 254 He, grand, calm, handsome, hierophantic, solemnly exhorted all men to constancy and courage.

hierophobia (haɪərəʊˈfəʊbɪə). *nonce-wd.* [f. HIERO-, after *hydrophobia*.] Fear or horror of sacred things or persons.

1816 SOUTHEY in *Q. Rev.* XV. 310 Ali Bey has the hierophobia upon him, or philosophers' disease.

hieroscopy (haɪəˈrɒskəpɪ). [ad. Gr. *ἱεροσκοπία*, f. *ἱερά* sacrifices, victims + *-σκοπία* view (-SCOPY). Cf. F. *hiéroscopie* (Littré).] = HIEROMANCY 1.

1727–41 CHAMBERS *Cycl.*, *Hieroscopy*, a kind of divination, performed by considering the victim, and observing every thing that occurs during the course of the sacrifice.

Hierosolymitan (haɪərəʊˈsɒlɪmaɪtən), *a.* and *sb.* [ad. late L. *Hierosolymītān-us* (Augustine), f. *Hierosolyma* = Gr. *Ἱεροσόλυμα* the city of Jerusalem.] **A.** *adj.* Belonging to Jerusalem. **B.** *sb.* A native or inhabitant of Jerusalem.

1538 BALE *God's Promises* in Dodsley *O. Pl.* (1780) I. 32 Ten of the twelve trybes became Samarytanes. And the other two were Hierosolymytanes. **1721** BAILEY, *Hierosolomitan* [ed. **1731** *Hierosolomite*], belonging to Jerusalem. **1872** O. SHIPLEY *Gloss. Eccl. Terms* 44 The Armenian Liturgy is a division of the Caesarean family of liturgies, itself a branch of the Hierosolymitan.

So **Hierosolymite** (haɪərəʊˈsɒlɪmaɪt), *sb.* and *a.* [ad. Gr. *Ἱεροσολυμίτης* native of Jerusalem.] = prec.

c **1550** CHEKE *Mark* i. 5 Al yᵉ contree of Judai, and yᵉ hierosolymites cam vnto him. **1731** [see prec.]. **1863** *Reader* 18 July 53/3 All works of purely hierosolymite origin.

hierþe: see HEARTH *sb.*[2]

hierurgy (ˈhaɪərɜːdʒɪ). Also 8 -ourgy. [ad. Gr. *ἱερουργία* religious service, f. *ἱερουργός* sacrificing priest, f. *ἱερά* (neut. pl. of *ἱερός*) sacrifices + *-εργια* working, f. *ἔργ-ον* work: see -URGY.] A sacred performance; a religious observance or rite.

1678 CUDWORTH *Intell. Syst.* I. iv. §18. 342 Both in their Doctrine and their Priestly Hierurgies. *a* **1740** WATERLAND *Wks.* VIII. 333 (R.) All priests from him..consummating the spiritual hierourgy according to the laws of the church.

Hence **hieˈrurgical** *a*, relating to sacred rites.

1725–44 LEWIS *Pecocke* 268 The mystical and hierurgical rights of the priesthood.

hiet, obs. pa. t. of HIE *v.*[1]

hiew, obs. f. HUE.

hifalutin, var. HIGHFALUTIN.

hi-fi (ˈhaɪˈfaɪ). [colloq. abbrev. of HIGH FIDELITY.] That part of acoustics and electronics that deals with the design, construction, and use of equipment for the recording and reproduction of sound to a fairly high standard. Also *attrib.* or as *adj.*, esp. **hi-fi equipment, set, system**, equipment for the home designed to reproduce (and sometimes to record) sound to such a standard, consisting often of several distinct units. Also *ellipt.* for *hi-fi equipment*, etc.

1950 *Audio Engin.* Aug. 24 (*title*) Hi-fi at seven-and-a-half. **1952** *Time* 22 Dec. 62/2 Until last week, most 'hi-fi' sets, which reproduce music in the home with the clarity and realism of the concert hall, were custom-made from standard parts by small radio and phonograph shops at a cost of from $150 to $2,000. **1953** *House & Garden* Dec. 132 (*heading*) What do they mean when they talk about hi-fi? **1953** *Life* 15 June 146/1 The name most generally used for this new kind of sound reproduction is high fidelity or 'hi-fi'. **1958** *Observer* 20 Apr. 10/6 The choice of a loudspeaker system is quite the most important task confronting those in search of 'Hi-Fi'. **1958** *Gramophone* June 35/1 The latest hi-fi developments. **1959** E. FENWICK *Long Way Down* x. 93 They had spent the evening working on their hi-fi system: three speakers, at different points, and miles of wiring. **1959** C. MACINNES *Absolute Beginners* 26, I put a disc on to his hi-fi. **1959** *Spectator* 20 Nov. 708/1 As recordings, they may not command the velvety tone, sumptuous presence and richly defined detail of the best of modern hi-fi. **1962** A. NISBETT *Technique Sound Studio* iii. 69 The full hi-fi treatment (in the sense, that is, of extended frequency response). *Ibid.* iv. 76 Hi-fi (a term which covers any sound equipment from medium quality upwards). *Ibid.* v. 98 Wide-range hi-fi, demanding not only high-quality transmissions but also a wide dynamic range. **1963** *Which?* Jan. 3/2 People may also want to consider hi-fi equipment. **1971** *Ibid.* June 187/1 Look for discounts in tape and hi-fi magazines. **1971** *Daily Tel.* 27 Aug. 17/6 The study thinks there is a continuing swing to quality but the lack of standards of what constitutes Hi-Fi is felt to be a disadvantage.

higgis taper, var. HAG-TAPER.

higgle (ˈhɪg(ə)l), *v.* Also 8 **higle**. [app. related to HAGGLE, with the vowel-modification which often expresses less noisy or lighter action.]

1. *intr.* To cavil or dispute as to terms; to stickle; *esp.* to strive for petty advantages in bargaining; to chaffer. Cf. HAGGLE 2.

1633 T. ADAMS *Exp. 2 Peter* ii. 12 Either he higgles with some hollow reservation, or lispeth with some faltering equivocation. **1655** FULLER *Ch. Hist.* VI. i. 278 We will not higgle with so frank a chapman for a few months under or over. **1672** SHADWELL *Miser* I. Wks. 1720 III. 13 He has been higling with a fellow, above half an hour this morning, about five Coney-skins he sold him. **1800** MAR. EDGEWORTH *The Will* (1832) 99 He would not..stand to higgle with me for the price of a horse. **1875** JOWETT *Plato* (ed. 2) IV. 380 He is a disputant, and higgles over an argument.

2. To carry on the trade of a HIGGLER (sense 2); 'to go selling provisions from door to door' (J.).

1790, etc. [see HIGGLING *vbl. sb.* 2].

b. *trans.* To buy and fatten up for the market. *local.* (Cf. HIGGLER 2 b.)

a **1825** FORBY *Voc. E. Anglia* s.v., The poor often talk of 'higgling up a pig'; i.e. buying and fattening it up.

c. (See quot.)

1866 G. A. SALA in *N. & Q.* 3rd Ser. IX. 318/2 When *A* knowing or hoping that figs will be soon inquired for, buys up all the figs in the market he higgles; but when *A* keeps a grocer's shop and asks *B* eightpence for a pound of figs and *B* offers him sixpence, then *B* haggles.

higgle (ˈhɪg(ə)l), *sb.* [f. the vb.] The adjusting of prices so that demand and supply are equal.

1908 *Daily Chron.* 5 Dec. 4/6 If they were abolished altogether the 'higgle of the market' would level freights correspondingly down.

higgledy. Abbrev. of HIGGLEDY-PIGGLEDY.

a **1953** DYLAN THOMAS *Quite Early One Morning* (1954) 30 Neat and silly..they helped in the higgledy kitchen.

higgledy-piggledy (ˈhɪg(ə)ldɪˈpɪg(ə)ldɪ), *adv.*, *sb.*, and *a.* Forms: 6–8 **higle- -pigle-**, 7– **higgle- -piggle-**, **hickle- -pickle-**; 6 **-di**, **-die**, 6–7 **-de**, **-tee**, 7– **-dy**, 8 **-te**, 9 **-ty**. [A riming compound of obscure origin.

Mainly an example of 'vocal gesture', the odd conformation of the word answering to the thing described; whether founded on *pig*, with some reference to the disorderly and utterly irregular fashion in which a herd of these animals huddle together, is uncertain, though examples show that such an association has often been present to persons using it. If the collateral HIGLY-PIGLY were the original form, the sequence *pig*, *pigly*, *higly-pigly* would be not unlikely.]

A. *adv.* Without any order of position or direction; in huddled or jumbled confusion and disorder; with heads and tails in any or every direction. Usually *contemptuous.*

1598 FLORIO, *Alla rappa*, snatchingly, higledi-pigledie, shiftingly, nap and run. *Ibid.*, *Alla rinfusa*, pelmell, helterskelter, higledi-pigledie. **1674** tr. *Martiniere's Voy. N. Countries* 34 They ly higgledy piggledy, master, mistress, children, men and maid-servants alltogether. *c* **1682** HICKERINGILL *Black Non-Conf.* xvii. Wks. 1716 II. 137 Rashly, hand over-head, Hickletee-Pickletee. *a* **1700** B. E. *Dict. Cant. Crew*, *Higglede-piggledy*, all together, as Hoggs and Piggs lie. **1718** MOTTEUX *Quix.* (1733) III. 39 Not [to] set down at random, higgle-de-piggledy, whatever comes into his Noddle. **1792** GIBBON *Misc. Wks.* (1814) I. 366 The officers..lying higgledy piggledy on the ground with the common men. **1838** HAWTHORNE *Amer. Note-bks.* (1883) 187 Pigs, on a march, do not subject themselves to any leader among themselves, but pass on, higgledy-piggledy, without regard to age or sex. **1849** DARWIN in *Life & Lett.* (1887) I. 375 I will write higglety-pigglety just as subjects occur. **1883** STEVENSON *Silverado Sq.* (1886) 60 Our belongings, piled higgledy-piggledy, and upside down, about the floor.

B. *sb.* A confusion; a disorderly jumble.

1659 GAUDEN *Tears Ch. Eng.* 347 An higglede piggedle of Preachers. **1684** tr. *Agrippa's Van. Arts* lxii. 184 The Massie Body of which Higgle-de Piggle-de is joyn'd and soder'd together with a feign'd Sanctimony. **1859** DARWIN in *Life & Lett.* (1887) II. 241 Herschel says my book 'is the law of higgledy-piggledy'. **1880** E. THRING *Let. H. D. Harper* in *Daily News* (1897) 12 Feb. 6/3 Higgledy-piggledy has been solemnly dethroned.

C. *adj.* Void of order or regular plan; confused, jumbled; topsy-turvy.

1832 W. IRVING in *Life & Lett.* (1864) II. 483 Robert the Devil is brought out in a higgledy-piggledy manner at various theatres. **1866** *Sat. Rev.* 2 June 647/1 Our principle of arrangement was the great higgledy-piggledy plan. **1890** *Daily News* 8 Jan. 3/1 In a higgledy-piggledy world like this it is impossible to make very nice distinctions between good luck and good work.

Hence ˌ**higgledy-ˈpiggledyness**, the quality or condition of being higgledy-piggledy.

1854 *Punch* 18 Nov. 204/1 That structural higgledi-pigglediness. **1918** A. BENNETT *Roll-Call* I. i. 12 An agreeable and original higgledy-piggledyness!

higgle-haggle, *v.* [Reduplicated, combining HIGGLE and HAGGLE: cf. *gibble-gabble*, *tittle-tattle*, etc.] *intr.* To higgle or haggle with much alternation or 'coming and going'.

1839–41 S. WARREN *Ten Thousand a Year* II. vi. 145 After some little higgle-haggling he bought it. **1885** LOWE *Bismarck* I. ix. 633 This higgle-haggling was more than Bismarck could bear, and he lost his temper.

higgler (ˈhɪglə(r)). Also 7 **heglar**, (8 **hicklar**), 7–9 **higler**. [f. HIGGLE *v.* + -ER[1].]

1. One who higgles or chaffers in bargaining; = HAGGLER 2.

App. the source of sense 2, as in the corresponding senses of HAGGLER. See Pegge *Anecd. Eng. Lang.* 264.

2. a. An itinerant dealer; esp. a carrier or a huckster who buys up poultry and dairy produce, and supplies in exchange petty commodities from the shops in town; = HAGGLER 3, CADGER 1, 2.

1637 J. TAYLOR (Water P.) *Carriers' Cosmogr.* in Arb. *Garner* I. 237 There doth come from Great Marlow in Buckinghamshire some higglers or demi-carriers. **1647** LILLY *Chr. Astrol.* cxlix. 633 Hucksters, Heglars that buy and sell and forestall the Markets. **1722** DE FOE *Plague* (1756) 167 Higlers, and such People as went to and from London with Provisions. **1748** RICHARDSON *Clarissa* (1811) III. lx. 335 An honest higler..goes to town constantly on Mondays, Wednesdays, and Fridays. **1798** in *Strand Mag.* (1897) Aug. 216 Dressed in a drab jacket and had the appearance of being a hicklar. **1813** *Sporting Mag.* XLII. 214 A person keeping a higler's cart. **1891** T. HARDY *Tess* II. 262 He was a foot-higgler now, having been obliged to sell his..horse, and he travelled with a basket on his arm.

b. One who buys poultry to fatten for the market.

1840 *Penny Cycl.* XVIII. 476/2 Speckled colours are most generally seen with the higgler. **1846** J. BAXTER *Libr. Pract. Agric.* (ed. 4) II. 220 The following method of fattening fowls has been kindly furnished us by one of the first higglers in Sussex.

†**c.** A horse used by a higgler. *Obs.*

1719 D'URFEY *Pills* IV. 13 On Pads, Hawkers, Hunters, on Higlers and Racers.

d. (See quot.)

1930 M. CLARK *Home Trade* 176 The term 'higgler' is applied in the Covent Garden market to a dealer who buys his supplies of fruit with a view to selling what he buys at a profit to any buyer, either on that market or on any other; to wholesalers or to retailers.

higglery (ˈhɪglərɪ). [f. prec. + -Y.] A higgler's business or ware.

1769 *De Foe's Tour Gt. Brit.* (ed. 7) II. 149 The Butter-market, with all the Sorts of Higglery Goods.

ˈ**higgling**, *vbl. sb.* [f. HIGGLE *v.* + -ING[1].]

1. The action of the vb. HIGGLE; close bargaining, chaffering; stickling as to terms.

1700 T. BROWN tr. *Fresny's Amusem. Ser. & Com.* 78 There is much Higling and Wrangling for t'other Ten Pound. **1776** ADAM SMITH *W. N.* I. v. (1869) I. 32 It is adjusted by the higgling and bargaining of the market. **1860** MOTLEY *Netherl.* (1868) I. vi. 329 Saguntum was perishing while the higgling went on at Rome.

2. The occupation of a HIGGLER (senses 2, 2 b).

1790 J. B. MORETON *Mann. W. Ind.* 85 That sort of traffic called higling. **1832** *Boston Herald* 22 May 3/3 [One] who keeps what is called a higgling team. **1882** *Athenæum* 26 Aug. 271/2 Students of peculiar manners..will be glad to obtain the capital paper on Sussex higgling.

ˈ**higgling**, *ppl. a.* [f. as prec. + -ING[2].] That higgles; cavilling, wrangling.

1678 OTWAY *Friendship in F.* Epil. 21 For shame leave off this higling way of Wit, Railing abroad, and roaring in the Pit. **1691** SHADWELL *Scowrers* IV. i, This morning I beat twenty higling-women. **1815** *Sporting Mag.* XLV. 225 The higgling disposition of the French. **1830** in Cobbett *Rur. Rides* (1885) II. 308 A sort of higgling merchant.

†**high**, **hiȝ**, *sb.*[1] *Obs.* Forms: 1 **hyȝe**, 3 **huȝe**, **huiȝe**, **huie**, **hiȝe**, *Orm.* **hiȝ**. [OE. *hyȝe* = OS. *hugi* (MLG. *hoge*, *höge*, MDu. *hoge*, *hoghe*, *höghe*, Du. *heug*), OHG. *hugi*, *hugu* (MHG. *hüge*), ON. *hygr* (Sw. *håg*, Da. *hu*), Goth. *hugs*:—OTeut. **hugi-z* thought, understanding, mind; an important word in the older Teut. langs., but early obs. in ME.; also lost in mod.G.

To the Teutonic root *hug-* belong also HIGHT *sb.*[2] and *v.*[2], HIGHTLE *v.*, HIGHTLY, HO *v.*[3] to care, HOE *sb.*[3] care, HOW, HOWE *v.* and *sb.* care, with many words in the cognate langs.]

Thought, intention, determination, purpose.

a **1000** *Seafarer* 96 (Cod. Exon. 82 b) Ne mæȝ him þonne ..mid hyȝe þencan. *a* **1000** *Cædmon's Daniel* 117 Næs him bliðe hiȝe. *c* **1200** *Trin. Coll. Hom.* 119 Þat he haue milce of us and gife us hiȝe and mihte, to forleten and bireusen and beten ure sinnes. *c* **1200** ORMIN 2777 Aȝȝ..soþfasst hiȝ & hope onn himm. *c* **1205** LAY. 2337 Mid soðfasten huiȝe. *Ibid.* 3033 Cordoille..nom hire leaf fulne huie, þat heo liȝen nolden. *Ibid.* 4910 Mid soðfeste huȝe.

high (haɪ), *a.* and *sb.*[2] Compared HIGHER, HIGHEST, q.v. Forms: α. 1 **héah** (**héa-**, **héaȝ-**), **héh**, 2 **heah**, (**hah-**, **hach-**, **haȝ-**), 2–3 **heh**, 2–4 **heih**, 2–5 **heȝ**, 3 **hæh**, **hæȝ-**, **hæhȝ-**, *Orm.* **heȝh**, 3–4 **heiȝ**, 3–5 **hey**, **hei**, 4 **heyȝ**, **heiȝh**, **heeȝ**, **heij**, 4–5 **hegh**, **-e**, **heygh**, **heye**, 4–6 **heigh**, *Sc.* **heych**, **he**, **hee**, 5– *Sc.* **heich**, (6 **hech**). β. 3–5 **hyȝ**, **hiȝ**, 4 **hih**, **hi**, **hij**, 4–5 **hyh**, **hieȝ**, 4–6 **hygh**, **hy**, **hye**, **hie**, 5– **high** (5 **hyhe**, **yȝe**, 5–6 **hyghe**, **highe**, 6 **hiegh**, *Sc.* 6 **hiech**, **hyech**, 6– **hich**, 8– **hie**). [Com. Teut.: OE. *héah*, *héa-*, *héaȝ-* = OFris. *hâch*, *hâg* (WFries. *haeg*, *heag*, *heeg*), ODu. *hôh* (MDu. *hooch*, *hog-e*, Du. *hoog*), OS. *hôh* (MLG. *hoch*, *hog-e*, *ho*, LG. *hoog*), OHG. *hôh* (MHG., mod.G. *hoch*), ON. *há-r* (earlier *hǿ-r* from **hauhar*), (Sw. *hög*, Da. *høi*), Goth. *hauh-s*:—OTeut. **hauho-z*:—pre-Teut. **koukos*: cf. Lith. *kaukas* swelling, boil, *kaukaras* height, hill. OE. *héah*, *héh*, regularly gave ME. *hēgh*, *heygh* (heːx), whence later *hee* (still in Sc.); but in 14th c. this was narrowed to *hiȝ*, *high* (hiːx), whence *hie*, *hy*: cf. the parallel phonetic history of DIE *v.*, EYE. As with these words, Chaucer used both *heigh* (*hey*) riming with *seigh* saw, and *hy*, *hye* riming with *Emelye*, etc. The final guttural began to be lost in the 14th c., as shown by the spellings *he*, *hee*, *hey*, *hi*, *hii*, *hy*(*e*; mod.Eng. retains the late ME. spelling *high*, with the pronunciation (haɪ).]

A. *adj.* (Opposed, in most senses, to *low*.)

I. Literal senses.

1. a. Of great or considerable upward extent or magnitude; extending far upward; 'long upwards' (J.); lofty, tall.

c **825** *Vesp. Psalter* ciii[i]. 18 Muntas heæ. *c* **900** tr. *Bæda's Hist.* III. xii. [xiv.] (1890) 194 On bodie heah. **971** *Blickl. Hom.* 27 Upon swiþe hea dune. *c* **1000** ÆLFRIC *Hom.* I. 166 Uppan ðam scylfe þæs heaȝan temples. *c* **1175** *Lamb. Hom.* 93 Areran..anne stepel swa hehne. **1297** R. GLOUC. (1724) 174 þe heye hulle. *a* **1300** *Cursor M.* 11666 Scho bihild a tre was hei [*v.rr.* hey, hy, hegh]. *c* **1300** *Havelok* 1071 He was strong man and hey. **1382** WYCLIF *Matt.* iv. 8 A ful heeȝ hill. *c* **1386** CHAUCER *Frankl. T.* 463 Ther saugh he hertes with hir hornes hye [*v.rr.* highe, hihe, hyȝe, hee]. *c* **1394** *P. Pl. Crede* 208 Halles full hyȝe, and houses full noble. *a* **1400–50** *Alexander* 700 To þe hight of þe hye dyke. *Ibid.* 4863 He clynterand torres. *c* **1470** HENRY *Wallace* v. 300 In heich haddyr Wallace and thai can twyn. **1483** *Cath. Angl.* 180/1 Heghe, *sublimus.* **1535** COVERDALE *Deut.* ii. 10 Stronge people and hye of stature. **1590** SPENSER *F.Q.* I. i. 8 The trees so straight and hy. **1698** FRYER *Acc. E. India & P.* 150 Clad in Black Gowns..with high round Caps flat at top. **1821** SHELLEY *Epipsychid.* 396 The walls are high, the gates are strong.

b. Rising considerably from a surface. ***high relief***: see RELIEF.

c **1000** *Sax. Leechd.* II. 96 Gif þæs dolȝes ofras synd to hea. **1827** G. HIGGINS *Celtic Druids* 216 Worked in high-relief. **1859** JEPHSON *Brittany* viii. 122 The relief is not so high or bold.

c. Of clothes: high-necked.

1827 [see CANEZOU]. **1857** MRS. GASKELL *Let.* 13 & 14 Sept. (1966) 471 My grey carmelite, & black moiré, high, & next to no collars. **1875** L. TROUBRIDGE *Life amongst Troubridges* (1966) x. 102, I had a chemisette to make my gown high, and no ornaments. **1937** J. LAVER *Taste & Fashion* xiii. 185 In the early [eighteen-] sixties, it is interesting to note, there was less *décolletage* in good families in France than in England. The high dress was worn at dinner parties even of a formal kind. **1957** M. B. PICKEN *Fashion Dict.* 230/2 Boat-shaped neck-line..high in front and back, wide at sides.

d. *Typogr.* (See quots.)

1683–4 J. MOXON *Mech. Exerc. Printing* (1962) 37 Head sticks..are Quadrat high, straight, and of an equal thickness all the length. **1888** C. T. JACOBI *Printers' Vocab.* 59 *High spaces*, spaces specially cast nearly type-high. **1904** GOODCHILD & TWENEY *Technol. & Sci. Dict.* 287/2 *High*, a term applied to type or blocks which stand out in front of the rest of the type in the forme; *e.g.* new type stands higher than worn type. **1963** KENNEISON & SPILMAN *Dict. Printing* 92 *High quads* (or *spaces*), spaces cast to the height of the shoulder of type.

2. Having a (specified) upward dimension or extent.

a **1000** in *Shrine* (Cokayne) 88 Gyldenu onlicnes twelf elna heah. *a* **1175** *Cott. Hom.* 225 þritti fedme heah. *c* **1340** *Cursor M.* 1419 (Trin.) An ellen hyȝe þei wore. **1547** WRIOTHESLEY *Chron.* (1875) I. 181 A rych herse..of nyne stories heigh. **1596** DALRYMPLE tr. *Leslie's Hist. Scot.* I. 35 Sevin, or viii. cubites hich. **1597** SHAKS. *2 Hen IV*, III. ii. 34 When hee was a Crack, not thus high. **1633** T. JAMES *Voy.* 43 The snow was..halfe legge high. **1726** SWIFT *Gulliver* I. vi, The common size of the natives is somewhat under six inches high. **1858** HOGG *Veg. Kingd.* 747 The Cabbage Palm ..is..a lofty tree 170 to 200 feet high.

3. a. Situated far above the ground or some base; far up; having a lofty position. Formerly with names of countries, and still of districts, denoting the upper (or inland) part, as *High Asia*, *High Furness* (cf. *High* DUTCH, *High* GERMAN).

c **1000** ÆLFRIC *Hom.* I. 170 Seðe ȝebiȝde þone heaȝan heofenlican biȝels. *a* **1225** *Ancr. R.* 166 þe heouene is swuðe heih. **1340** HAMPOLE *Pr. Consc.* 3204 Hey Paradyse, þat blisful place. *c* **1400** MAUNDEV. Pref. (Roxb.) 3 Egipte þe hie and þe lawe. **1450–70** *Golagros & Gaw.* 252 Al thai that ar wrocht vndir the hie hevin. **1535** COVERDALE *Tobit* iii. 10 At this voyce wente Sara in to an hye chamber of hir house. **1700** S. L. tr. *Fryke's Voy. E. Ind.* 75 Their Sconces lying so high, that they had a great command of us. **1776** R. CHANDLER *Trav. Greece* (1825) II. 2 The sharp end is very often high in the air. **1789** BURNS '*Willie brew'd*', The moon .. That's blinkin' in the lift sae hie. **1836** A. & J. TAYLOR *Rhymes Nursery, The Star* i, Up above the world so high, Like a diamond in the sky. **1859** TENNYSON *Guinevere* 25 [He] Climb'd to the high top of the garden-wall. **1869** W. W. HUNTER (*title*) A Comparative Dictionary of the Non-Aryan Languages of India and High Asia.

b. Situated at a specified distance above some level; (so far) up.

1662 J. STRYPE in *Lett. Lit. Men* (Camden) 178 A very handsome [Chamber], and one pair of stairs high. **1722** DE FOE *Plague* (1884) 72 She lay in the Garret four Story high. **1839** R. S. ROBINSON *Naut. Steam Eng.* 5 The limit of atmospheric air, supposed to be forty-five miles high.

4. a. Of physical actions: Extending to or from a height; performed at a height. *spec.* in *Athletics*, as ***high hurdles***, ***jump***, etc. (Cf. sense 17 i.)

With noun of action, and akin to the adv., the stages of development being *to leap high, high leaping, a high leap.*

1596 SHAKS. *1 Hen. IV*, I. ii. 43 Now, in as low an ebb as the foot of the Ladder, and by and by in as high a flow as the ridge of the Gallowes. **1601** —— *All's Well* II. iii. 299 Which should sustaine the bound and high curuet Of Marses fierie steed. **1625** BACON *Ess., Dispatch* (Arb.) 243 It is not the large Stride, or High Lift, that makes the Speed. **1711** SHAFTESB. *Charac.* (1737) II. 381 You might well expect the fate of Icarus, for your high-soaring. **1891** H. S. CONSTABLE *Horses, Sport & War* 20 High action will cause splints, speedy-cuts, and other unsoundnesses. **1895** High hurdle, jump [see JUMP *sb.*[1] 1 b]. **1897** RANJITSINHJI *Cricket* iv. 156 It..enables the batsman to make a forcing-stroke along the ground instead of a risky high-drive. **1897** *Encycl. Sport* I. 50/2 High jumping may be..a gift. *Ibid.* 51/2 High kicking is very useful during the off-season. **1924** C. W. MASON *Chinese Confessions* xliv. 326 The high-jump and hurdles were my specialities. **1955** *Athletics* ('Know the Game' Series) 15 High jumping: Western roll; straddle; Eastern cut-off. **1964** M. WATMAN *Encycl. Athletics* 83/1 Britain possessed two world class high hurdlers in the 1930s.

b. Of a vowel-sound: Produced with the tongue or some part of it in a high or raised position. Hence in numerous adjectival *Combs.*, as ***high-back***, ***-central***, ***-front***, ***-mid***, ***-mixed***, ***-narrow***, ***-rising***.

1876 SWEET *Handbk. Phonetics* 11 The vertical movements of the tongue produce various degrees of 'height', or distance from the palate..From among the infinite degrees of height three are selected, 'high', 'mid', and 'low'. (*i*) is a high, (*æ*) a low vowel, while (*e*) as in 'say' is a mid vowel. **1888** —— *Hist. Eng. Sounds* i. 2 So we have altogether nine positions [of the tongue]: high-back..high-mixed..high-front [etc.]. **1924** H. E. PALMER *Gram. Spoken Eng.* I. 13 High-Rising. Nucleus-tone. **1934** J. J. HOGAN *Outl. Eng. Philol.* 15, *u*: high-back rounded, as in *wolf*. *Ibid.* 16, *oi*: mid-back rounded + high-front. **1934** WEBSTER I. xxviii/2 In English a high-central vowel is not usual. **1951** Z. S. HARRIS *Methods in Struct. Ling.* 57 High-rising [intonation] for impatient question. **1961** R. B. LONG *Sentence & its Parts* xix. 422 (*heading*) High-back /u/. **1962** *Amer. Speech* XXXVII. 169 This dipthong may be described as beginning at a somewhat retracted low-front position and terminating at an open, slightly rounded, high-central position. **1964** JAKOBSON & HALLE in D. Abercrombie *Daniel Jones* 98 The 'high-narrow' vowels are particularly short. **1964** *Language* XL. 100 The sounds..are high-mid. **1965** *Canad. Jrnl. Linguistics* Fall 65 In each case the checked high-front, high-back..and mid-back vowels are paired with phonically similar free vowels. **1966** *Publ. Amer. Dial. Soc.* XLVI. 32 Long, unrounded, high-mid front vowel.

c. ***high breast wheel*** (see quots.).

1880 *Encycl. Brit.* XII. 522/2 Overshot and High Breast Wheels. *Ibid.* 523/2 With greater variation of head-water level, a pitch-back or high breast wheel is better. **1888** *Lockwood's Dict. Mech. Engin.* s.v. *Breast wheel*, When the water flows in at a point above the horizontal line, the wheel is termed high breast, and when at a point below, low breast.

II. Figurative senses.

5. a. Of exalted rank, station, dignity, position, or estimation. (Of persons or their attributes; also, with emphatic force, in ***high God***, ***high heaven***.) Freq. in ***high life***, ***society***.

c **825** *Vesp. Psalter* lxxxviii. 28 [lxxxix. 27] Ic..settu hine heane fore cyningum eorðan. *Ibid.* xcviii[i]. 2 Dryhten in Sion micel and heh ofer alle folc. *c* **1175** *Lamb. Hom.* 19 He wes..heh ouer heouene and ouer eorða. *c* **1200** ORMIN 17393 þatt heȝhe maȝȝstre Nicodem. *c* **1205** LAY. 21972 And þus þer cleopede Howel hæhes cunnes. *a* **1300** *Cursor M.* 7945 (Cott.) Of he drightin stod þe nan au. *c* **1340** *Ibid.* 17300 (Trin.) Ouer þo iewes..As her prince an hy man. **1340** HAMPOLE *Pr. Consc.* 1465 Now er we heghe, now er we lawe. *c* **1380** WYCLIF *Sel. Wks.* III. 199 Grete richessis and heiȝe statis. *c* **1489** CAXTON *Sonnes of Aymon* Prol. 3 Princes and lordes of hie estate. **15..** in *Dunbar's Poems* (1893) 328 Befoir that hich grand Roy. **1581** MULCASTER *Positions* xxxvii. (1887) 153 In any either hie or low kinde of life. **1603** SHAKS. *Meas. for M.* II. ii. 121 Man, proud man, Drest in a little briefe authoritie..Plaies such phantastique tricks before high heauen, As makes the Angels weepe. **1613** MIDDLETON *Triumphs Truth* Wks. (Bullen) VII. 260 Like one of high blood that hath married base. **1713** STEELE *Englishm.* No. 54. 344 Sir Francis Walsingham was..high in the Queen's Favour. **1727** DE FOE *Protest. Monast.* 6 He had ..always liv'd in what we call high Life. **1759** TOWNLEY (*title*) High Life Below Stairs. **1801** M. EDGEWORTH *Belinda* I. ix. 277 He had merely considered her ladyship as an object of amusement, and an introduction to high life. **1853** MRS. GASKELL *Cranford* viii. 140 One would not have Lady Glenmire think we were quite ignorant of the etiquettes of high life in Cranford. **1859** TENNYSON *Guinevere* 560 Hereafter..We two may meet before high God. **1892** C. M. YONGE *That Stick* I. x. 106 Utterly inexperienced as she was, even in domestic, not to say high life. **1895** DOUGLAS in *Bookman* Oct. 22/2 The high position France had attained in 1684. **1920** D. PARKER (*title*) High society. **1955** 'E. C. R. LORAC' *Ask Policeman* iii. 28 Perhaps wealthy Australians were sent back to high-life schools in England in her day. **1971** 'D. HALLIDAY' *Dolly & Doctor Bird* xi. 155 The police ..would spoil the leisurely high-society image. Dirty little men running over the Begum's nice holiday island.

b. ***the Most High***: the Supreme Being; God.

1611 BIBLE *Ps.* lxxiii. 11 How doth God know? and is there knowledge in the most High? [**1382** WYCLIF in heiȝte; **1388** an heiȝe; **1535** COVERD. the most hyest]. **1667** MILTON *P.L.* VI. 906 A despite don against the most High. **1755** *Man* No. 28. 6 Revelation represents the Most-High to us as the most beneficent fountain of joy.

6. a. Of exalted quality, character, or style; of lofty, elevated, or superior kind; high-class. (Hence frequently in titles: see 20.) Freq. in ***high art***, ***comedy***, ***culture***.

c **897** K. ÆLFRED *Gregory's Past.* lvi. 433 Buton ðone hean foreðonc and ða ȝesceadwisnesse ðara godena monna. *Ibid.* lxiii. 459 Sio hea lar is betere maneȝum monnum to helanne. *c* **1175** *Lamb. Hom.* 17 þa ȝet he ȝef us ane heȝe ȝefe. *c* **1230** *Hali Meid.* 13 Iþe heȝe blisse of heuene. *c* **1380** WYCLIF *Serm.* Sel. Wks. I. 16 þei clepen it hey riȝt-wisnenesse. **1485** CAXTON *St. Wenefr.* 1 A man of hye merite. **1500–20** DUNBAR *Poems* lxxxviii. 3 Of high renoun, riches and royaltie. **1569** J. ROGERS *Gl. Godly Loue* 183 Surely it is an highe and pure love. **1715–20** POPE *Iliad* II. 404 Where now are all your high resolves at last? **1757** FOOTE *Author* I. Wks. 1799 I. 135 His peculiarities require infinite labour and high finishing. **1802** WORDSW. *Sonn.*, '*O Friend! I know not*,' Plain living and high thinking are no more. **1808** SCOTT *Marm.* III. xiii, High minds, of native pride and force, Most deeply feel thy pangs, Remorse! **1817** SHELLEY *Hymn Intell. Beauty* v, Hopes of high talk with the departed dead. **1817** B. HAYDON *Autobiogr.* (1926) I. xvii. 266, I had, by my public devotion to High Art, a claim on all the nobility and opulent in the kingdom. **1848** GEO. ELIOT *Let.* 11 Feb. (1954) I. 247, I cannot recognize the truth of all that is said about the necessity of religious fervour to high art. **1849** —— *Let.* 20 Sept. (1954) I. 308 She is a person of high culture according to the ordinary notions of what feminine culture should be. **1856** —— in *Westm. Rev.* IX. 3 High culture demands more complete harmony with its moral sympathies in humor than in wit. **1856** KINGSLEY *Plays & Purit.* 31 They railed in their ignorance..at high art and all art. **1870** BLAINE *Encycl. Rur. Sports* §460 The account given is not in unison with our notions of high play. **1883** 'V. LEE' in P. Gunn *Vernon Lee* (1964) vii. 88 A long pseudo-medieval ballad... It felt so completely high art. **1895** G. B. SHAW *Our Theatres in Nineties* (1932) I. 106 After the exasperatingly bad acting one constantly sees at the theatres where high comedy and 'drama' prevail, it is a relief to see even simple work creditably done. **1906** E. GARNETT in Defoe *Capt. Singleton* p. viii, Rembrandt's choice of beggars ..for his favourite subjects seemed a low and reprehensible taste in 'high art'. **1919** G. B. SHAW *Heartbreak House* p. viii, The only part of our society in which there was leisure for high culture. **1963** *Observer* 12 May 28/3 Miss Murdoch is one of the sharpest writers of high comedy at present active in the theatre. **1964** HALL & WHANNEL *Popular Arts* I. ii. 55 These popular arts..were not objects of contemplation like the works of high art, but communal artifacts. **1966** D. JENKINS *Educated Society* ii. 50 High culture..tries to be creative in relation to the future and responsible in relation to the past.

b. Of great consequence; important, weighty, grave, serious.

c **1200** ORMIN Ded. 66 Heh wikenn alls itt semeþþ. **13..** *Gaw. & Gr. Knt.* 1051 A heȝe ernde and a hasty me hade fro þo wonez. *c* **1500** *Three Kings' Sons* 81 Wise ynough to conduyte an hy matier. **1646** SIR T. BROWNE *Pseud. Ep.* I. ii. 5 A high and capitall errour. **1685–6** EARL SUNDERLAND 13 Feb. in Macaulay *Hist. Eng.* v. (1871) I. 320 *note*, Making a composition..for the high Misdemeanour they have been guilty of. **1699** BENTLEY *Phal.* 213 The accusation is a very high one. **1730** in *Swift's Lett.* (1768) IV. 249 Of very high consequence to the whole kingdom. **1815** SCOTT *Ld. of Isles* VI. iv, When tidings of high weight were borne To that lone island's shore. **1849** MACAULAY *Hist. Eng.* vi. II. 126 On pain of his high displeasure. **1863** H. COX *Instit.* I. vii. 81 Accused of high crimes and misdemeanours against the state.

c. Advanced, abstruse, difficult to comprehend (now only in particular collocations); †difficult to perform, arduous (*obs.*).

1382 WYCLIF *Prov.* xxiv. 7 Ful heeȝ to the fool is wisdam. **1471** RIPLEY *Comp. Alch.* I. xiii. in Ashm. (1652) 132 When they such hygh thyngs don take in hond. Whych they in noe wyse understonde. *a* **1533** LD. BERNERS *Gold. Bk. M. Aurel.* (1546) D ij, So high sentences, as he wrot. *a* **1568** ASCHAM *Scholem.* I. (Arb.) 32 Neuer passe farre forward in hie and hard sciences. **1611** BIBLE *Ps.* cxxxix. 6 Such knowledge is too wonderfull for me: it is high, I cannot attaine vnto it. **1667** MILTON *P.L.* IX. 602 Speculations high or deep. *Mod.* A branch of High Mathematics.

d. Having a highly developed or complex organization; spec. *Biol.*, phylogenetically advanced or developed; often in the comparative degree, as ***the higher apes***, ***the higher plants***.

[**1807** W. WOOD *Zoography* I. p. xii, If we ascend to a higher class of beings, and contemplate the extensive range of the animal creation.] **1848** J. LINDLEY *Introd. Bot.* (ed. 4) xvi. 323 Plants have no circulation of their fluids analogous to that of blood in the higher animals. **1867** H. SPENCER *Princ. Biol.* §364 Every type that is best adapted to its conditions, which on the average means every higher type, has a rate of multiplication that insures a tendency to predominate. **1875** *Encycl. Brit.* II. 168/1 As man is the highest animal. **1902** *Ibid.* XXVI. 366/1 The first is an amyloïn of a 'high', the second an amyloïn of a 'low' type. *Ibid.* XXVIII. 343/1 The gorilla and the chimpanzee, the highest members of the apes. *Ibid.*, The embryonic stages of higher forms. **1936** E. G. BOULENGER *Apes & Monkeys* 15 The apes and higher monkeys are quite as much reliant for their various needs upon the ground as among the tree-boughs. **1954** H. I. FEATHERLY *Taxon. Terminol. Higher Plants* 157 In the evolution of the higher plants, the greatest number of changes has come about in the reproductive organs. **1964** E. BECKER in I. L. Horowitz *New Sociol.* 114 Separation anxiety of the helpless higher-primate infant is the pivot for his early learning. **1966** R. & D. MORRIS *Men & Apes* vi. 165 This is the point at which we pass from the lower primates (the prosimians) to the higher primates (the anthropoids), and consider the evolution of monkeys, apes and man.

7. Chief, principal, main; special. (In OE. usually in combination, as ***héahburh*** chief town, ***héahsynn*** capital sin, etc.: see 19.) Now only in particular collocations: see HIGH ROAD, etc.

a **1300** *Cursor M.* 10428 For þair hei fest sake. *c* **1380** WYCLIF *Sel. Wks.* III. 341 He was not clepid..hiȝ disciple of Crist. *c* **1400** *Destr. Troy* 8738 Full solenly besyde the high aulter. **1490** CAXTON *Eneydos* xxii. 84 We wryte..the hyghe festes wyth rede lettres of coloure of purpre. *c* **1553** CHANCELOUR *Bk. Emp. Russia* in *Hakluyt* (1886) III. 40 A place..where the hie market is holden on Saint Nicholas day. **1622** CALLIS *Stat. Sewers* (1647) 88 There is no difference touching repairs of the High streams and the high-ways in my opinion. **1667** PRIMATT *City & C. Build.* 72 Houses which front high and Principal Streets.

8. a. Rich in flavour or quality; luxurious. (Of food or drink (*obs.*), or of feeding.)

c **1384** in *Wyclif's Wks.* (1880) 157 To drynke heiȝe wynes. **1597** SHAKS. *2 Hen. IV*, I. i. 10 Like a Horse Full of high Feeding. **1616** in J. Russell *Haigs* vi. (1881) 138 It was over high meat for my weak stomach to digest. **1626** BACON *Sylva* §48 Almonds that are not of so high a taste as Flesh. **1723** SWIFT *Stella at Wood-park* 21 Prouder than the devil With feeding high and treatment civil. **1732** LAW *Serious C.* vi. (ed. 2) 83 High eating and drinking, fine cloaths and fine houses. **1883** F. M. CRAWFORD *Mr. Isaacs* 2 Patient under blows and abstemious under high-feeding.

b. Of the condition of an animal or of soil: resulting from over-feeding or from too great an

application of manure. Also of a crop: produced by an over-manured soil.

1834 W. YOUATT *Cattle* xvi. 553 This occurs particularly in young cows after their first calving, and when they are in a somewhat too high condition. **1886** C. SCOTT *Sheep Farming* 116 Hill ewes are never in too high condition; the danger is all the other way. **1902** *Encycl. Brit.* XXVI. 361/1 It is better not to grow barley after roots fed off by sheep, as this rotation leaves the land.. in too 'high' a condition... By taking barley as a second corn crop, the latter following roots fed off, or a 'high' crop, [etc.].

9. a. Of meat, esp. game: Tending towards decomposition; slightly tainted; usually as a desirable condition.

c **1807** JANE AUSTEN *Watsons* (1954) 344 As the partridges were pretty high, Dr Richards would have them sent away to the other end of the Table. **1816** *Sporting Mag.* XLVIII. 258 The first place to ascertain if they [partridges] are beginning to be high, is the inside of their bills. **1825** C. M. WESTMACOTT *Eng. Spy* II. 112 The fish is rather high. **1879** F. POLLOK *Sport Brit. Burmah* I. 168 Alligators and crocodiles.. prefer their food very high.

fig. **1870** LOWELL *Study Wind.* 161 A jest or a proverb (if a little high he liked them none the worse).

b. Of tobacco: moist. *U.S.*

1850 *Rep. U.S. Comm. Patents, Agric. 1849* 322 Tobacco should not be too moist, or 'high' as it is termed, when put in the stalk-bulks. **1865** *Trans. Ill. Agric. Soc.* V. 669 Care must be taken that the tobacco does not imbibe too much moisture, or get too high in case before it is bulked.

10. a. Of qualities, conditions, and actions, physical or other: Of great amount, degree, force, or value; great, intense, extreme; strong, forcible, violent. ***high explosive***: see EXPLOSIVE *sb.* 2.

Often in reference to a vertical graduated scale on which the magnitude or intensity of some action records itself by upward extension, or is marked by the position of lines, etc.

13.. *E.E. Allit. P.* B. 976 Þe wenches.. folȝed.. Trynande ay a hyȝe trot þat torne neuer dorsten. *c* **1386** CHAUCER *Knt.'s T.* 940 Now looketh is nat that an heigh folye. *c* **1460** *Towneley Myst.* (Surtees) 84 When ryches is he, Then comys poverte. **1534** MORE *On the Passion* Introd. Wks. 1272/1 What state.. hath not high cause to tremble and quake? **1565–73** COOPER *Thesaurus, Ardentissimus color*.. a very high or glisteryng redde colour. **1601** R. JOHNSON *Kingd. & Commw.* (1603) 22 Where they are in high request. **1607** SHAKS. *Timon* IV. iii. 433 Till the high Feauor seeth your blood to froth. **1608** D. T. *Ess. Pol. & Mor.* 69 To sel their liues at as high a rate as possibly they can. **1634** SIR T. HERBERT *Trav.* 5 Wee had the winde high and large. **1674** MARTINIERE *Voy. N. Countries* 61 Even their Crowes are white, to as high a degree as our Swans. **1691** LOCKE *Lower. Interest* Wks. 1727 II. 72 The Exchange is High. **1693** WOOD *Life* (O.H.S.) III. 438 Earl of Westmorland also died, as 'tis reported, with high drinking. **1712** ADDISON *Spect.* No. 418 ¶8 Flowers with richer Scents and higher Colours. **1714** *Fr. Bk. of Rates* 3 When any high Duties were imposed upon the French Trade in England. **1722** DE FOE *Plague* (1884) 118 The Plague was so high, as that there dy'd 4000 a Week. **1789** M. MADAN *Persius* (1795) 44 *note*, Who think it a high joke. **1804** W. TENNANT *Ind. Recreat.* (ed. 2) I. 65 Rent in Calcutta still continues high. **1820** SCORESBY *Acc. Arctic Reg.* I. 350 *note*, The temperature in London was as high as 93°. 5. **1842** S. LOVER *Handy Andy* i. 9 Who.. had got the horse into a good high trot. **1897** ALLBUTT *Syst. Med.* II. 958 An essential constituent of several of the high explosives.

†**b.** Of the voice: Raised, elevated, loud. *Obs.*

c **1205**, *a* **1225** [see HIGHER A. 1 β, HIGHEST A. 1 β]. *c* **1250** *Gen. & Ex.* 2780 God sente an steuene, briȝt and heȝ; 'Moyses, moyses, do of ðin s[h]on'. **13..** *Gaw. & Gr. Knt.* 1165 Hunterez with hyȝe horne hasted hem after. *c* **1400** *Rowland & O.* 835 And vp he keste ane heghe cry. **1526** *Pilgr. Perf.* (W. de W. 1531) 92 b, With hygh & clamorous wordes or speche. **1565** in *Liturg. Serv. Q. Eliz.* (Parker Soc.) 521 After the Psalm the prayer following shall be said by the minister alone, with a high voice. **1646** F. HAWKINS *Youth's Behav.* I. (1663) 15 Shew no sign of choler, nor speak to him with too high an accent. **1776** *Trial of Nundoc.* 77/1 Nor did he read it in so high a voice, that I should hear it.

c. *Geog.* Of latitude: Denoted by a high number; at a great distance from the equator.

1748 *Anson's Voy.* II. v. 182 Very high latitudes not far from the polar circle. **1788** WESLEY *Wks.* (1872) VI. 282 Many other provinces in America, even as high as Newfoundland and Nova-Scotia. **1823** SCORESBY *Whale Fishery* 31 This kind of fog, peculiar to high latitudes. **1857** LD. DUFFERIN (*title*) Letters from High Latitudes.

†**d.** With defining words, denoting the proportion of precious metal to alloy: = FINE *a.* 2 b.

1594 PLAT *Jewell-ho* III. 85 The golde being 24 Carots high, & the siluer 12 ounces fine.

e. High-priced, expensive, costly, dear. Of money: lent out at a high rate of interest; dear.

1727 SWIFT *To Earl of Oxford* Wks. 1755 III. II. 47, I suppose now stocks are high. **1823** BYRON *Age of Bronze* xiv, But bread was high, the farmer paid his way. **1889** A. C. GUNTER *That Frenchman* xvii, This palace alone is worth a fortune, situated.. in the fashionable quarter of St. Petersburg, where land is very high. **1899** *Daily News* 31 Mar. 3/5 New York... Higher money.

f. Played for large stakes.

1828 SCOTT *F.M. Perth* xiii, You are playing a high game, look you play it fairly. **1889** *Law Rep.* Weekly Notes 21/2 A notice cautioning members against high play.

g. *Naut.* Near the wind: designating a vessel or its head when pointing close to the wind, as in the command ***no higher***.

a **1865** SMYTH *Sailor's Word-bk.* (1867), No Higher! **1948** R. DE KERCHOVE *Internat. Maritime Dict.*, No higher!

h. In card-playing: ***ace high*** (***king high***, etc.): having the ace (king, etc.) as highest card: said of the hand or suit, also *occas.* of the person. Cf. ACE 4.

1887 S. CUMBERLAND *Queen's Highway* 276 Had I a 'flush' with 'king high' some one would be sure to rake in the shekels with 'ace high'. **1964** N. SQUIRE *Bidding at Bridge* xxi. 172 You may rely upon two defensive tricks when your partner opens the bidding. These may not be in the actual suit he mentions, because it might, for example, be Knave high. **1973** D. WESTHEIMER *Going Public* v. 79 Margo drew the low hand, a nine-high nothing. 'Poker never was my game,' he said cheerfully.

11. a. Of time or a season: Well advanced; fully come, complete. (In ***high noon***, ***high day***, the notion that the sun is high in the heavens is often present.)

c **1275** *Passion Our Lord* 657 in *O.E. Misc.* 56 At þon heye vndarne.. þer hi were to-gadere. *a* **1300** *Floriz & Bl.* 151 Biþat hit was middai hiȝ Floriz was þe brigge niȝ. *c* **1350** *Will. Palerne* 2066, I seiȝ hire nouȝt seþ hieȝ midniȝt. **1362** LANGL. *P. Pl.* A. VII. 105 At heiȝ prime perkyn lette þe plouȝ stonde. **1393** *Ibid.* C. XIX. 139 Til *plenitudo temporis* hih tyme a-procheде. **1523** LD. BERNERS *Froiss.* I. cxxxii. 322 Tyle it was past hye none. **1546** J. HEYWOOD *Prov.* (1867) 41 We will dyne fyrst.. it is noone hy. **1581** LAMBARDE *Eiren.* I. vii. (1588) 36 It was.. high time to make a contrary law. **1611** BIBLE *Rom.* xiii. 11 Now it is high time to awake out of sleepe. **1655** H. VAUGHAN *Silex Scint.* I. *Regenerat.* i, It was high-spring, and all the way Primrosed, and hung with shade. **1693** G. POOLEY in *Phil. Trans.* XVII. 673 Sometimes the Courses, Seams or Rakes.. are perpendicular, which they call the High time of the Day, or Twelve a Clock. **1713** STEELE *Englishm.* No. 42. 273 It is high Time for every Englishman to exert himself in Behalf of his Country. **1828** J. R. BEST *Italy as it is* 228 The high bathing season of Leghorn. **1860** MISS MULOCK *Domestic Stories* (1862) 100 It was high summer, too, on the earth.

b. *spec.* Of a period of time: fully developed, at its peak.

1930 BAEDEKER *Northern Italy* (ed. 15) 622 The fine *Palazzo Larderel*.., formerly *Palazzo Giacomini*, in the High Renaissance style, by Giovanni Antonio Dosio (1558–80). **1934** *Burlington Mag.* Jan. 14/1 The usual technique of the high renaissance outside Venice. **1944** *Ibid.* Jan. 13/2 He was sufficiently adaptable to learn.. some later developments of the High Renaissance. **1956** K. CLARK *Nude* IX. 341 The root of high-renaissance taste. **1961** WEBSTER (s.v. *high* adj. 1 b), The high middle ages. **1962** *Listener* 18 Oct. 601/1 This happened during the mid-sixteenth century, in the aftermath of the High Renaissance. **1964** C. S. LEWIS *Discarded Image* vii. 182 Hence a modern finds those [chronicles] of the Dark Ages suspiciously epic and those of the High Middle Ages suspiciously romantic. **1965** K. CHARLTON *Educ. Renaissance Eng.* ii. 21 Such was the education of the High Middle Ages. **1972** *Country Life* 23 Mar. 696/3 The high Victorian Gothic style.

12. 'Far advanced into antiquity' (J.); of early date, ancient. In phr. ***high antiquity*** is blended the notion of ascending 'up the stream of time'.

1601 R. JOHNSON *Kingd. & Commw.* (1603) 28 Of no higher times, then when they first began. **1646** SIR T. BROWNE *Pseud. Ep.* V. xxii. 330 The nominal observation of the several dayes of the week.. is very high, and as old as the ancient Egyptians. **1774** WARTON *Hist. Eng. Poetry* (1775) I. 3 Poems of high antiquity. **1793** HELY tr. *O'Flaherty's Ogygia* Addr. 6 Too high a date. **1875** SCRIVENER *Lect. Text N. Test.* 17 A genuine semblance of high antiquity.

13. Of or in reference to musical sounds: Produced or characterized by relatively rapid vibrations; acute in pitch; shrill.

1390 GOWER *Conf.* III. 90 Now highe notes and now lowe, As by the gamme a man may knowe. **1573–80** BARET *Alv.* H 369 An Heigh, or shrill sound, *extentus sonus*. **1597** MORLEY *Introd. Mus.* 166 Songs which are made for the high key. **1674** PLAYFORD *Skill Mus.* II. 93 Raise your Treble or smallest string as high as conveniently it will bear without breaking. **1705** S. SEWALL *Diary* 28 Dec. (1879) II. 151, I.. went into a Key much too high. **1875** BLASERNA *Theory Sound* iv, Every ear.. distinguishes a high note from a low one.. The low notes are characterised by the small number, the high notes by the large number of their vibrations per second.

14. a. Showing pride, self-exaltation, resentment, or the like; haughty, pretentious, arrogant, overbearing; wrathful, angry. Of words, actions, feelings, etc.: hence (now only *dial.*) of persons. In *high words* now often blended with sense 10 b.

c **1205** LAY. 1503 Heȝe word he spekeð þæt alle heo wullet quellen Quic þat heo findeð. **1297** R. GLOUC. (1724) 442 Þoru som heye herte þer wax a lute stryf Bytuene þe Erl of Aungeo, & þe emperesse hys wyf. **1375** BARBOUR *Bruce* VI. 116 His hert, that wes stout and he, Consalit hym allane to byde. *c* **1450** tr. *De Imitatione* I. i. 2 High wordes makiþ not a man holy & riȝtwise. **1523** LD. BERNERS *Froiss.* I. ccxxxi. 313 A man of hye mynde, right cruell, and full of yuell condycions. *c* **1560** A. SCOTT *Poems* (S.T.S.) xxvii. 31 Quhen scho growis heich, I draw on dreich, To vesy and behald the end. **1647** CLARENDON *Hist. Reb.* VI. §166 The Soldiery.. grew very high, and would obey no Orders.. but of their own making. **1648** MILTON *Tenure Kings* (1650) 13 No Prince not drunk with high mind would arrogate so unreasonably above human condition. **1660–1** PEPYS *Diary* 20 Mar., Indeed the Bishops are so high, that very few do love them. **1710** STEELE *Tatler* No. 231 ¶2 [She] had from her Infancy discovered so imperious a Temper (usually called a High Spirit) that [etc.]. **1781** COWPER *Truth* 93 High in demand, though lowly in pretence. **1806** R. CUMBERLAND *Mem.* (1807) II. 156 The wild woman.. was at high words with the witches. **1849** MACAULAY *Hist. Eng.* ix. II. 404 Many who talked in high language about sacrificing their lives and fortunes for their country.

†**b.** Zealous, eager, 'keen'. *Obs.*

1662 J. BARGRAVE *Pope Alex. VII* (1867) 10 He is high for the House of Austria, and would be flayed alive for the King of Spain. **1692** LUTTRELL *Brief Rel.* (1857) III. 611 The house of lords were high on the lord Huntington and Marlboroughs commitment. **1704** [see HIGH-CHURCHMAN]. **1706–9** M. TINDALL *Rights of Christ. Ch.* iv. 144 Our first Reformers were as Low for Church, as they were High for Religion.

15. a. Extreme in opinion (esp. religious or political); carrying an opinion or doctrine to an extreme.

1675 BROOKS *Gold. Key* Wks. 1867 V. 14 To prove, against the Socinians and the high atheists of the day.. that there is a hell, a place of torment. **1829** I. TAYLOR *Enthus.* iv. (1867) 77 A.. plunge from the pinnacle of high belief, into the bottomless gulf of universal scepticism. **1885** H. O. WAKEMAN *Hist. Relig. Eng.* xi. 119 As men grasped high Sacramental doctrine more and more. *a* **1890** CHURCH *Oxford Movem.* xvi. (1891) 295 It was a high Anglican sermon. *Mod.* A high Calvinist, a high Ritualist, a high Tory.

b. *spec.* = HIGH CHURCH, A.

1706–9 M. TINDALL *Rights of Christ. Ch.* iv. 145 'Tis no wonder the Highfliers treat 'em [16th c. Reformers] so, since in all their Notions concerning the Power of Clergy, they are too High for the Reformation. **1710** ADDISON *Tatler* No. 220 ¶3 The present Constitution of our Church, as divided into High and Low. *a* **1734** NORTH *Exam.* II. v. §49 (1740) 345 Conformable Loyal Gentlemen, whom we will cry down for High Men, that is Adherents to Popery. **1827** WORDSW. *Sacheverel* 9 High and Low, Watch-words of Party, on all tongues are rife; As if a Church.. must owe To opposites and fierce extremes her life.

16. a. Emotionally exalted; elated, merry, hilarious: chiefly in phr. ***high spirits***, ***high*** (***old***) ***time***.

1738 SWIFT *Pol. Conversat.* 26 You would not have one be always on the high Grin. **1768** J. BYRON *Narr. Patagonia, Acc. Wager* (1778) 48 The men were in high spirits from the prospect they had of getting off in the long-boat. **1782** MAD. D'ARBLAY *Diary* 12 Aug., Daddy Crisp.. as usual, high in glee and kindness at the meeting. **1833** C. A. DAVIS *Lett. J. Downing* (1834) 177 Just after breakfast yesterday, I and the gineral had a high time [i.e. a heated argument] together. **1849** MACAULAY *Hist. Eng.* iv. I. 435 When his health was good and his spirits high, he was a scoffer. **1858** *Spirit of Times* 30 Jan. 345/1 Our friends.. are having a real 'high old time' generally, just now, in trotting on the ice. **1869** B. HARTE *Luck of Roaring Camp* (1871) 226 These are high old times, ain't they? **1870** D. J. KIRWAN *Palace & Hovel* xxxi. 470 That's a werry 'igh old game is the Canteen; sort of priveet like. **1873** J. H. BEADLE *Undevel. West* xxiii. 451 Santa Fe De San Francisco—so the old Spaniards named it—is a high old city. **1897** MAX PEMBERTON in *Windsor Mag.* Jan. 269/1 I've had a high old time hunting up six dozen of '53. **1899** R. WHITEING *No. 5 John St.* III. xxi. 215 'Ah, they was 'igh old times!' is his final word. **1941** E. BOWEN *Look at Roses* 255 Those two will be having a high old time, with the cat away. **1955** J. POTTS *Death of Stray Cat* ii. 11 You probably had a high old time chasing blondes. **1962** N. MARSH *Hand in Glove* vii. 235 We picked him up.. having a high old time with the boxer bitch.

b. Excited with drink, intoxicated. Phr. ***high as a kite***: very drunk. *slang.*

1627 MAY *Lucan* x. 496 He's high with wine. **1639** MASSINGER *Unnat. Combat* III. ii, When we are at the banquet, And high in our cups. **1846** J. TAYLOR *Upper Canada* 106, I met three gentlemen.. and they were all high. **1892** *Nation* (N.Y.) 28 July 66/3, I was told that Governor and legislators would get high on whiskey illegally sold on the evening of the very day when they had passed a stringent amendment to the [Maine] law. **1939** *Amer. Speech* XIV. 90/2 *High as a kite*, completely drunk. *a* **1966** M. ALLINGHAM *Cargo of Eagles* (1968) iv. 54 He.. gave them a champagne lunch in a marquee.. and held a sale. By then everyone was as high as a kite.

c. Under the influence of, stimulated by, a drug or drugs. Freq. const. *on*.

1932 *Evening Sun* (Baltimore) 9 Dec. 31/4 *High*, under the influence of a narcotic. **1940** *Amer. Speech* XV. 337/1 *To be high*, to be contented from the drug. **1951** *N.Y. Times* 13 June 24/5 We would go out together and get high. I used to sleep with him whenever we got high. **1951** *San Diego Even. Tribune* 28 June a-1/4 He'd been 'getting high' on heroin week-end after week-end. **1957** C. MACINNES *City of Spades* I. x. 72 Hamilton's acquaintances.. rocking high with charge. **1961** *Spectator* 17 Nov. 712 The momentary kick when the drug is taken, when you're 'high'. **1969** *New Scientist* 29 May 455/1 It is far safer to drive a car when high on marihuana than when drunk. **1970** 'D. SHANNON' *Unexpected Death* (1971) i. 9 He an his pal Roderick Drover had had some boyish fun last week sniping at an innocent driver—probably while high on something.

d. Highly interested in, keen *on*. *slang.*

1942 BERREY & VAN DEN BARK *Amer. Thes. Slang* §274/5 *Enthusiastic about*.. high on. **1966** L. DEIGHTON *Billion-Dollar Brain* xxii. 240 It's about Signe... She's high on you, you know. **1972** *Guardian* 30 Oct. 2/5 'I am not high on the Thieu brand of Government,' he [*sc.* McGovern] said, noting that 40,000 people had been executed.. by it.

III. 17. Phrases. **a.** ***high and dry***: said of a vessel cast or drawn up on the shore out of the water; hence *fig.* out of the current of events or progress, 'stranded' (sometimes with allusion to senses 5, 14, or 15, and to DRY *a.* sense 17). Also used in sense 'safe'.

high-and-dry church, a nickname for the old High Church party, as distinguished from that which originated with the 19th c. Oxford movement.

1822 R. G. WALLACE *15 Yrs. Ind.* 48 Another surf sent Ensign George True high and dry on the beach. **1838** DICKENS *Let.* 26 July (1965) I. 421, I no sooner get myself up, high and dry, to attack him [*sc.* Oliver Twist] manfully than up come the waves of each month's work. **1851** *Illustr. Catal. Gt. Exhib.* 359 Dry dock.. for laying up ships of war out of commission, or ships 'in ordinary', high and dry. **1853** BUNSEN *Let.* in *Life & Wks. Kingsley* (1901) II. 112 You know of the persecution of the Evangelicals, and High and dry against Maurice. **1857** TROLLOPE *Barchester T.* 39 (Hoppe) That party which is now scandalously called the high-and-dry church. **1864** J. H. NEWMAN *Apol.* 282

Principles..which went beyond that particular defence which high-and-dry men thought perfection. **1881** E. W. HAMILTON *Diary* 18 June (1972) I. 146 Meanwhile, Dr. Flood's successor had been appointed, and Dr. Flood was left high and dry without preferment owing to an undoubted breach of faith on the part of Duckworth. **1891** *Spectator* 10 Oct. 487 The high-and-dry aristocrats who looked on him as a tradesman. **1927** J. GALSWORTHY *Castles in Spain* 169 A true work of art remains beautiful and living, though an ebb tide of fashion may leave it for the moment high and dry on the beach. **1941** W. S. MAUGHAM *Writer's Notebk.* (1949) 305 The river has flowed on and left him high and dry on the bank. The writer has his little hour..but an hour is soon past. **1960** *Times* 30 Aug. 11/6 Cella's back-heel, so deceptive, so utterly unexpected, left Rossano high and dry.

b. ***with*** **(†*in, through*)** ***a high hand***: with imperious or absolute exercise of power; imperiously. So ***to take the high hand***, etc.

1382 WYCLIF *Num.* xxxiii. 3 Therfor thei goon forth..in an hiȝ hoond [**1535** COVERDALE, thorow an hye hande; **1611** with an high hand]. **1596** BP. W. BARLOW *Three Serm.* ii. 92 Much more will hee scourge them that sinne with an hie hand. **1622** MABBE tr. *Aleman's Guzman d'Alf.* II. 7 Carrying..all a kinde of high hand over their wiues. **1676** ALLEN *Address Nonconf.* 171 In truth he had with a high hand forbidden it. **1808** WELLINGTON in Gurw. *Desp.* IV. 96 An army that, to be successful and carry things with a high hand, ought to be able to move. **1837** CARLYLE *Fr. Rev.* III. IV. ii, The dominant party carrying it with a high hand. **1883** STEVENSON *Silverado Sq.* 71, I took the high hand in despair, said there must be no more talk of T. coming back.

c. ***on the high horse***: see HORSE.

d. ***high and low***: (people) of all conditions.

c **1200** *Moral Ode* 164 in *Trin. Coll. Hom.*, Þar sullen efninges ben to þe heie and to þe loȝe. ? *a* **1366** CHAUCER *Rom. Rose* 1252 Curtesye, That preised was of lowe & hye. **1535** COVERDALE *Ps.* xlviii[i]. 2 Hye & lowe, riche & poore, one with another. **1598** SHAKS. *Merry W.* II. i. 117 He wooes both high and low, both rich and poor, both yong and old. **1781** COWPER *Hope* 312 That all might mark—knight, menial, high, and low. **1894** GLADSTONE *Horace Odes* III. i. 15 One lot for high and low to draw.

†**e.** ***in high and low***: in all parts; in all points or respects; wholly, entirely. *Obs.*

a **1300** *Cursor M.* 27098 Alle þis werld on lagh and hei Es nackind forwit cristis ei. *c* **1386** CHAUCER *Prol.* 816 And we wol reuled been at his deuys In heigh and lough. **1428** *Surtees Misc.* (1888) 5 In hegh and lawe he submyt hym to yᵉ grace and awarde of yᵉ Mayr and Counsell.

f. ***high and mighty, high-and-mighty***: (*a*) formerly used as an epithet of dignity; (*b*) *colloq.* imperious, arrogant; affecting airs of superiority; also used *absol.* Hence ***high-and-mightiness***: the quality of being 'high and mighty'; also as a title of dignity or a mock title; also erron. for *high mightiness*: see MIGHTINESS.

1400 in Ellis *Orig. Lett.* Ser. II. I. 3 Right heigh and myghty Prynce, my goode and gracious Lorde. **1419** *Ibid.* 65 Most hy and moste myȝty Prynce. **1423** in *15th Rep. Hist. MSS. Comm.* App. VIII. 33 Ane he and mychty lord, George of Dunbare, Erl of the March. **1548** HALL *Chron., Edw. IV* 229 Right high and mightie prince, right puyssaunt and noble kyng. **1559** *Bk. Com. Prayer, Prayer Queen.* O Lord our heuenly father, high and mighty, King of Kynges. **1654** WHITLOCK *Zootomia* 83 Book-learned Physitians, against which they bring in their high and mighty word Experience. **1694** tr. *Milton's Lett. State* 1 Apr. an. 1656, Most High and Mighty Lords, our dearest Friends. **1804** M. WILMOT *Let.* 24 Apr. in *Russ. Jrnls.* (1934) I. 94 The High and Mighty then go into..another little room well heated. **1825** J. W. CROKER *Diary* Nov. in *C. Papers* (1884), Lord Grey, in his high and mighty way, was proceeding to make light of all this. **1852** C. M. YONGE *Two Guardians* xiii. 246 That touch of Edmund's, which had shown her how he regarded her 'high-and-mightiness', had made her..ashamed. **1855** THACKERAY *Newcomes* I. 229 Some of those bankers are as high and mighty as the oldest families. **1876** *Fam. Herald* 30 Dec. 129/2, I feel certain his serene high-and-mightiness has never ridden in a hay-waggon in his life. **1896** *Westm. Gaz.* 13 June 2/2 This high-and-mightiness is not calculated to endear the Under-Secretary to the Press in general. **1905** G. B. SHAW in *Grand Mag.* Feb. 116 Our high and mighties didn't exactly see the point. **1924** J. GALSWORTHY *White Monkey* II. ii, Mr. Mont's a gent..no high-and-mighty about *him.*

g. ***high priori***: a burlesque alteration of A PRIORI, connoting lofty or unfounded assumption.

1742 POPE *Dunc.* IV. 471 We nobly take the high Priori Road. **1851** MILL *Logic* iii. (ed. 3) I. 209, I am unable to see why we should be..constrained to travel the 'high priori road' by the arbitrary fiat of logicians.

h. ***on the high ropes*** (*colloq.*): in an elated, disdainful or enraged mood.

a **1700** B. E. *Dict. Cant. Crew* s.v. *Rope*, Upon the High-ropes, Cock-a-hoop. **1707** HEARNE *Collect.* 24 Feb. (O.H.S.) I. 336 Hei! day! What in the High-Rope! a high-Flyer & a Tantivi! **1708** MOTTEUX *Rabelais* v. xviii, He was upon the High-Rope and began to rail at them like mad. **1773** GOLDSM. *Stoops to Conq.* II. Wks. (Globe) 653/2 All upon the high rope! His uncle a colonel! **1838** DICKENS *Nich. Nick.* xxxi, I went there the night before last, but she was quite on the high ropes about something.

i. ***to be for the high jump***: see JUMP *sb.*¹ 7 and HIGH *a.* 4 a.

j. ***high, wide, and handsome*** (and similar phrases), in a carefree manner, in good style (see also quot. 1971). orig. *U.S.*

1907 S. E. WHITE *Arizona Nights* 35 Tim could talk high, wide, and handsome when he set out to. **1932** 'SPINDRIFT' *Yankee Slang* 21 *High, wide and handsome*, in good or great style. Common shout at a rodeo: 'Ride him, Cowboy, high, wide and handsome.' **1939** WODEHOUSE *Uncle Fred in Springtime* iii. 50 He has a nasty way of lugging Pongo out into the open and..proceeding to step high, wide and plentiful. **1958** L. VAN DER POST *Lost World of Kalahari* (1961) vii. 155 The day was riding high, wide and handsome into the deeps of the incredible blue sky. **1971** J. WAINWRIGHT *Last Buccaneer* II. 234 The cops 'll be high, wide and helpless. They won't know what in hell's hit 'em.

18. on high (rarely ***upon, of high***) [orig. *an high*, also reduced to A-HIGH: cf. *alow, aloud, afar, anear*; when the full form was retained, *an* was at length changed to *on*: see AN *prep.*].

a. In or to a height, above, aloft; *spec.* up to or in heaven.

c **1200** *Vices & Virtues* 95 Ðe faste hope hafð hire stede up an heih. *c* **1200** *Trin. Coll. Hom.* 111 Ure helende þe was þis dai heued on hegh. *a* **1300** *Cursor M.* 708 All thinges..On hei, on lau, on land, on see. *c* **1386** CHAUCER *Frankl. T.* 121 Hire to disporte vp on the bank an [*v.r.* on] heigh. **1480** CAXTON *Chron. Eng.* ccxliii. (1482) 284 There hyr heedes were set vpon high. **1535** COVERDALE *Isa.* xl. 25 Lift vp youre eyes an hie, and considre. **1611** BIBLE *Ps.* cxiii. 5 The Lord our God, who dwelleth on high. **1687** DRYDEN *Song St. Cecilia's Day* 61 The trumpet shall be heard on high, The dead shall live, the living die. **1834** MEDWIN *Angler in Wales* II. 305 From boats below, and roofs on high. **1870** L'ESTRANGE *Miss Mitford* I. 131 That heart-breathed sigh Which for thy life ascends on high.

†**b.** With a 'high' or raised voice; loudly; aloud. (Also *of high*.) *Obs.*

c **1290** *Beket* 1288 in *S. Eng. Leg.* I. 143 An bi-gan to telle is tale on heiȝ [*MS. Harl.* 2277 anheȝ]. *c* **1330** R. BRUNNE *Chron.* (1810) 139 Whan þis was set & stabled, & pes cried on hii. *a* **1450** *Knt. de la Tour* (1868) 40 He herde..iangle, and borde of highe. **1519** *Interl. 4 Elem.* in Hazl. *Dodsley* I. 23 If we call any thing on high, The taverner will answer. **1659** D. PELL *Impr. Sea* 313 Some of the prisoners have been heard to shout on high.

†**c.** *fig.* To an intense or high degree. †**d.** ? Openly, publicly. *Obs.*

1393 LANGL. *P. Pl.* C. VII. 124 Til ich, wratth, waxe an hyh and walke with hem bothe. *c* **1420** *Chron. Vilod.* 744 Suche on he was alle his leuyng.

e. ***from on high*** (rarely ***from high***): from a high place or position; *spec.* from heaven.

c **1380** *Sir Ferumb.* 2327 Þe Amyral þat was so riche, ys falle doun fram an heȝ. **1526** TINDALE *John* iii. 31 He that commeth from an hye is aboue all. **1531** —— *Exp. 1 John* (1537) 6 He which euer crepeth..can not fall from an hygh. **1611** BIBLE *Luke* i. 78 The dayspring from on high hath visited us. **1697** DRYDEN *Virg. Georg.* III. 681 Their Flock's Father (forc'd from high to leap) Swims down the Stream. **1742** GRAY *Eton Coll.* viii, Ambition this shall tempt to rise, Then whirl the wretch from high. **1819** HEBER *Hymn 'From Greenland's icy mountains'* iii, We, whose souls are lighted With wisdom from on high.

IV. Combinations and special collocations.

19. In OE. *héah* was very often combined with a subst. (= Skr. *karmadhāraya* compounds), instead of standing in grammatical concord with it; several of these combinations or compounds came into ME., where they were often written *divisim*, and were thus recognizable only by the uninflected form of the adj.; when adjective inflexions were lost, there was nothing to distinguish these from the ordinary use of the adj. before a sb. Among these may be mentioned the following:

a. in lit. sense 'lofty', as ***héah-beorȝ*** high mountain; ***héah-clif*** high cliff; ***héah-déor*** high deer, stag; ***héah-flód*** high flood, high tide, deluge; ***héah-lond*** HIGHLAND; ***héah-sǽ*** high or deep SEA; ***héah-setl*** (SETTLE) high seat, throne, seat of honour; ***héah-weofod*** high altar (WEVED): the last three passing into **b.** High in degree, rank, or dignity, excellent, main, chief, as ***héah-burh*** chief town; ***héah-cræft*** excellent art or skill; ***héah-freols*** high festival; ***héah-mæsse*** high MASS; ***héah-nama*** great or exalted name; ***héah-stræt*** HIGH STREET; ***héah-synn*** mortal sin, cardinal sin; ***héah-tíd*** HIGH TIDE.

c **888** K. ÆLFRED *Boeth.* i, Þær is Creca heah burȝ and heora cynestol. *a* **950** *Durham Ritual* (Surtees) 5 Gisæȝi folce minvm hehsynna hiara. *c* **950** *Lindisf. Gosp.* John xix. 13 Se groefa..ȝebrohte bute ðone hælend & sætt fore ðæm heh-sedle. *a* **1000** *Cædmon's Dan.* 699 To þære heah-byriȝ þæt hie Babilone abrecan mihton. *c* **1000** *Ecgberht's Confess.* Pref. in Thorpe *Ags. Laws* II. 132 (Bosw.) Bebeorh ðe wið ða eahta heahsynna. *a* **1100** *O.E. Chron.* (Laud MS.) an. 1086 Swa swiðe he lufode þa hea deor swilce he wære heora fæder. *c* **1200** *Trin. Coll. Hom.* 91 In his heorðliche heȝ settle. *c* **1200** ORMIN 4172 Itt iss aȝȝ heh messedaȝȝ.

c. *esp.* in names of offices and dignities, with sense 'chief, principal, highest, head, arch-', sometimes passing into the absolute sense, 'of high rank or dignity, exalted, lofty': e.g. ***héah-biscop*** high bishop, archbishop, pontiff; ***héah-boda*** (ME. *hehbode*) archangel; ***héah-cyning*** high king, chief king; ***héah-diacon*** archdeacon; ***héah-ealdor*** chief elder or ruler; ***héah-ealdormann*** chief alderman or ruler; ***héah-engel*** (ME. *heh-engel*) archangel; ***héahfæder*** (ME. *hehfader*) high father, great father, patriarch; ***héah-ȝeréfa*** high REEVE; ***héah-god*** high God, the Most High; ***héah-lǽce*** high leech, eminent physician; ***héah-sacerd*** chief priest; ***héah-þeȝen*** high thane, chief minister; etc.

Beowulf (Z.) 1039 Þæt wæs hilde-setl heah cyninges. **971** *Blickl. Hom.* 25 Mid heahfaderum & apostolum. *Ibid.* 147 Micahel se heahengel se wæs ealra engla ealderman. *c* **1000** *Laws of Wihtræd* Pref. (Schmid), Birhtwald Bretone heah-biscop. *c* **1000** *Laws of Æthelstan* Pref. (ibid.), Mid ȝeþeahte Wulfhelmes mines heh-bisceopes. *c* **1000** *Ags. Ps.* (Th.) lvi[i]. 2 Heonan ic cleopiȝe to heah Gode. *c* **1050** *Byrhtferth's Handboc* in *Anglia* VIII. 310/27 Se heah engel gabriel. *a* **1175** *Cott. Hom.* 219 Angeli (boden) arch-angeli (hahboden). **1200** *Ibid.* 239 Þer he sit..mid his apostlen mid þe haȝefaderen. *c* **1200** *Trin. Coll. Hom.* 125 Ure drihten sende his heȝ engel gabriel to..zacharie. *c* **1200** ORMIN 17107 Þatt kinedom þ att Godd Hehfaderr rixleþþ inne. **13..** *Sir Beues* (A.) 1873 Hiȝ dekne ich wile make þe. **1549** LATIMER *2nd Serm. bef. Edw. VI*, To Rdr. (Arb.) 46 The office of the high bishoppe. **1551** ROBINSON tr. *More's Utop.* Ep. to Giles (Arb.) 24 Sente thether by the hieghe Byshoppe. **1890** J. HEALY *Insula Sanctorum* 559 It was to this lonely but sweet retreat that Ireland's last High-king retired to die.

20. On the analogy of the preceding (19 c), frequently used with later official titles, implying the supreme officer or dignitary, or the officer who fulfils the function to the prince or state.

(Usually written as two words, but sometimes hyphened) e.g. *High Admiral, Bailiff, Chamberlain, Chancellor, Commissioner, Constable, Justice, Marshall, Master, Mightiness, Reeve, Sheriff, Steward, Treasurer*, etc. See these words.

a **1300** *Cursor M.* 4617 Stiward..Sal þou be made, and hei iustis. *Ibid.* 5008 Þar vs tok þe hei baili. *Ibid.* 10341 Ioseph ..Þat of egypti was hei stiward. **13..** *K. Alis.* 270 Oo madame, he seide, Olympyas, Heiȝe maister in Egipte j was. **1526** TINDALE *Acts* xxiii. 19 The hye captayne toke hym by the hond and went a parte with hym out of the waye. **1583** *N. Riding Rec.* (1894) 254 From the Quenes majestie or from her Lord Hye Admyrall. **1589** *Hay any Work* 27 The offices of our L. high Chancellor, high Treasurer, and high Steward of Englande. **1662** WOOD *Life* 10 Nov. (O.H.S.) I. 461 To be high-sherriff of Oxfordshire. **1747** *Gentl. Mag.* 510/1 Whereby his majesty's pacifick dispositions had been made manifest to their High Mightinesses. **1805** N. NICHOLLS *Corr. w. Gray* (1843) 33 The contest for the high stewardship at Cambridge, between Lord Hardwick and Lord Sandwich. **1824** WATT *Bibl. Brit.* II. 4 Civb, Townley, James..High Master of the Merchant-Taylor's School. **1845** S. AUSTIN *Ranke's Hist. Ref.* I. 497 The hands of the high chamberlain, William of Croi, Lord of Chievres.

21. a. In other collocations with specialized sense: **high camp**, 'camp' (CAMP *sb.*⁵) of a sophisticated kind (in quot. 1963 used adjectivally); also (with hyphen) *attrib.*; so ***high campery***; **high Change**, the time of greatest activity on 'Change, or the Exchange itself at such a time (cf. 11); **high command** (see COMMAND *sb.* 7 b); **high commission** (see COMMISSION *sb.*¹ 7); **high commissioner** (see COMMISSIONER 1 c); **high contrast** *Photogr.* (see quot. 1940); also (with hyphen) *attrib.*; **high country** *N.Z.*, hilly country that is difficult of access; freq. *attrib.*; *Canada* [tr. Canad. F. *haut pays*], the hinterland, the forests of N. and North-west Canada; hence **high countryman**; **high cross**, a cross set on a pedestal in a market-place or in the centre of a town or village; **high dilutionist** *Homœopathy*, an advocate of extreme dilution of medicine; **high farming**, the extensive use of fertilizers in land cultivation; **high finance**, finance concerned with large sums of money; **high forest**, a forest composed wholly or chiefly of trees raised from seed; also, in more general use, a forest of lofty trees (cf. G. *hochwald*); also *attrib.*; **high-fusing** *a.* (see quot. 1940); † **high game**, a form of cheating at cards; **high go** (*colloq.*), a bout of merriment, a frolic, a 'spree'; **high grinding** = *high milling* (MILLING *vbl. sb.* 1 a); † **high-head**, a high head-dress, such as those fashionable in England in the 18th c.; **high hook** *colloq.* or *slang*, the angler of a party who hooks the largest fish; **high-key** *Photogr.* (see quots.); **high kick** *Dancing*, a kick in the air, esp. one executed simultaneously by a row of female dancers and repeated by raising each leg in turn; also (with *high* used adverbially) **high-kick** *v.*, **high-kicking** *vbl. sb.* and *ppl. a.*; so ***high-kicker***; † **high-law** (*Thieves' Cant*), highway robbery; hence † **high-lawyer**, a highwayman; **high lead** *Forestry* (see quot. 1957); also (with hyphen) *attrib.*, as ***high-lead logging***; **high life**, a West African dance; also (with hyphen) *attrib.*; **high line**, (*a*) *Fishing* (*N. Amer. colloq.* or *slang*), the person who, or the boat which, has the best haul during a specified time; occas. a good catch; also *attrib.*; so **high liner**; (*b*) *Forestry*, an overhead cable attached to a spar tree in logging; so ***high-line logging***; **high-lining** *vbl. sb.*; **high-low bed** (see quot. 1964); † **high Mall**, the time of greatest resort in the Mall (cf. 11); **high mass** (see MASS *sb.*¹ 3 a, HIGH *a.* 19 b); **high milling** (see MILLING *vbl. sb.* 1 a); **high place**, in Scripture, a place of worship or sacrifice (usually idolatrous) on a hill or high ground; the altar and other appointments for such worship; also, in *pl.*, the upper echelon of any organization; **high polymer**, a polymer with a high molecular weight; also (with hyphen) *attrib.*; **high-rise** *a.*, of a building, tall, multi-storey; also *transf.*; as *sb.*, a tall building; also

occas. **hi-rise**; **high sign** *colloq.*, a surreptitious sign indicating that all is well or that the coast is clear; so **high-sign** *v.*; **high spot** (freq. in *pl.*) *slang*, the outstanding part or feature of something; ***to hit the high spots***, to go to excess or extremes; to rise to a very high level; to include or touch on the most important points or places; cf. HIGH LIGHT 2; **high step**, (*a*) a military step in which the feet and knees are raised high; also (with hyphen) *attrib.*; (*b*) in *pl.*, a step-ladder; **high stool**, a tall stool; **high table**, a table raised above the rest at a public dinner; *spec.* in colleges, the table at which the president and fellows sit; **high tea**, a tea at which meat is served; **high-tensile**, used *attrib.* of steel or other metals possessing great tensile strength; **high wine**, wine containing a high percentage of alcohol; **high wire**, a high tight-rope; **high yaller, yellow**, a half-caste of light yellow complexion; also as *adj. phr.*; **high-yield, -yielding**, designating something that furnishes or produces a large or valuable, etc., product or return.

1954 *High camp [see CAMP *a.* (and *sb.*[5])]. **1963** *Punch* 5 June 830/1 Gerda Charles..makes her young, with-it, high camp. **1964** *New Statesman* 6 Mar. 373/2 The..show starts depressingly, and the aura of high camp threatens to asphyxiate. **1968** *Listener* 27 June 843/2 The melodramatic trappings might have had a certain aesthetic high-camp value. **1967** *Spectator* 1 Dec. 690/3 Witness in this exhibition the *high campery of the Coldstream Guards in 1821. **1711** ADDISON *Spect.* No. 69 ¶ 1, I look upon *High-Change to be a great Council, in which all considerable Nations have their Representatives. **1851** MAYHEW *Lond. Labour* II. 45 (Hoppe) The Old Clothes Exchange, like other places known by the name..has its daily season of 'high Change'. **1940** A. L. M. SOWERBY *Dict. Photogr.* (ed. 15) 157 A negative is said to have *high contrast if tones but slightly different in the original subject show marked differences in the negative. **1961** G. MILLERSON *Technique Telev. Production* iii. 47 Subject contrast must be kept down, by preventing high-contrast surfaces appearing in the same shot. **1967** KARCH & BUBER *Offset Processes* iii. 64 High-contrast photography may be used. **1874** A. BATHGATE *Colonial Experiences* xv. 212 Squatters whose runs include *high country. **1903** S. E. WHITE *Forest* 278 The base-line ..was the only evidence of man we saw in the high country. **1930** L. G. D. ACLAND *Early Canterbury Runs* 1st Ser. i. 8 The severe snow storms..used up several years' profits of high country runholders. **1942** G. CAMPBELL *Thorn-Apple Tree* 152 Some time again we winter in the high country, maybe. **1947** D. MCELDOWNEY in D. M. Davin *N.Z. Short Stories* (1953) 379 The grass was sharp and scanty on the unfertilised high country soil. **1950** *N.Z. Jrnl. Agric.* Apr. 364/1 The merino..bred..for sale to high-country runs [in Canterbury]. **1972** P. NEWTON *Sheep Thief* xiv. 110 He was full of questions about the country and it was obvious that his one ambition was to become a high country musterer. **1922** C. G. TURNER *Happy Wanderer* 51 The *high-countryman may drink his cheque. **1596** *Hie crosse [see CROSS *sb.* 7 b]. **1609** in *Digby Myst.* (1882) p. xix, The pentice at y[e] highe crosse. **1697** *Lond. Gaz.* No. 3336/3 A great Bonfire at the High-Cross. **1847** *Brit. Jrnl. Homœopathy* V. 154 We can no more reject the conclusions of the *high dilutionists than we can despise those of their opponents. **1892** High dilutionist [see DILUTIONIST]. **1848** MILL *Pol. Econ.* I. 215 To apply the *high farming of Europe to any American lands. **1894** G. B. SHAW in *Fortn. Rev.* LXI. 480 High farming cannot increase the natural rent of an acre. **1931** C. S. ORWIN (*title*) High farming. **1966** *Listener* 1 Sept. 307/2 By 1939 British agriculture..had ceased to rely on the high farming we had developed in our own land. **1905** *McClure's Mag.* XXV. 48 In other words, we could eat our cake and have it, too—which is one secret of *high finance. **1934** L. MUMFORD in W. Frank *Amer. & Alfred Steglitz* ii. 50 Advertising, insurance, and high finance, the divine trinity that rules the world of industry. **1936** *Discovery* Sept. 280/2 It is not big guns nor even high finance that ultimately rules the world. **1879** *Encycl. Brit.* IX. 398/2 In..Germany..care is always taken that in *high forest there is a good stock of self-sown trees before the old crop is entirely removed. **1927** *Forestry* I. 1. 24 The three main forestry systems, High Forest, Coppice-with-Standards, and Coppice. **1938** C. P. ACKERS *Pract. Brit. Forestry* 9 High forest may be subdivided into..clear felling ..and..the selective system. **1953** *Brit. Commonw. Forest Terminol.* I. 151 *High Forest Systems*, crops normally of seedling origin, either natural or artificial or a combination of both. Rotation usually long. **1955** *Jrnl. Ecol.* XLIII. 572 It will be referred to in this paper simply as 'High Forest', the adjective 'high' being used in a double sense to indicate that both the trees themselves are lofty and in the more specialized sense of the forester, to indicate that they have grown uninterrupted by coppicing or pollarding. **1959** *Times* 2 June 12/6 Growing conifers as high forest. **1911** G. H. WILSON *Man. Dental Prosthetics* viii. 313 The *high fusing porcelains are practically insoluble. **1940** J. OSBORNE *Dental Mechanics* xxii. 412 Porcelains used in dentistry may be divided into two types according to their fusing temperatures: (1) *High fusing*, those whose fusing temperature is above the melting point of gold. (2) *Low fusing*, those whose fusing point is below 1065° C. **1956** J. N. ANDERSON *Appl. Dent. Mat.* xxiv. 330 For high-fusing porcelains, the furnace may be pre-heated. **1674** COTTON *Compl. Gamester* in Singer *Hist. Cards* (1816) 343 One most egregious piece of roguery..playing the *high-game at putt. **1825** *New Monthly Mag.* XVI. 355 Our volatile *high-go's were troublesome enough to every body. **1840** R. H. DANA *Bef. Mast* xxvii. 92 The last night they..were getting into a high-go, when the captain called us off. **1875** *Miller* May 55/1 (*title*) The Hungarian system of *high grinding. *Ibid.*, In such mills..the whole of the high-grinding system was carried out. *a* **1884** KNIGHT *Dict. Mech.* Suppl. 457/2 *High grinding*, a process of gradual reduction of the wheat by a succession of partial crushings, alternating with sifting and sorting the product. **1945** J. F. LOCKWOOD *Flour Milling* xvii. 283 The wheat could either be rapidly and roughly reduced to flour by setting the two stones very close together, a process called low grinding, or the reduction could be made slowly and carefully with the stones further apart; this was called high grinding. **1698** FARQUHAR *Love and Bottle* I. Wks. (Rtldg.) 488/1 She wore..a silk manteau and *high-head. **1791** WESLEY *Wks.* (1872) VIII. 307 Give no ticket to any that wear calashes, high-heads, or enormous bonnets. **1848** in *D.A.E.*, **High hook*, the one who catches the largest or the greatest quantity of fish. **1894** *Outing* (U.S.) XXIV. 259/2 F. was high hook with a five and a half pounder. **1918** *Photo-Miniature* XV. Mar. (Gloss.), **High-key*, a style of photographic print (portrait or landscape) consisting entirely of light tones, differing little from each other in depth. **1919** *Brit. Jrnl. Photogr. Alm.* 250 Photographs consisting almost entirely of light tones are said to be high-key. **1898** G. B. SHAW *Our Theatres in Nineties* (1932) III. 336 The four beauteous ladies who, though apparently competent dancers, persist in punctuating their evolutions with graceless *high kicks. **1906** E. DYSON *Fact'ry 'Ands* vii. 89 He came out on ther John's arm, 'igh kickin', 'n' singin' fit t' split. **1914** R. BROOKE *Let.* 3 Sept. (1968) 613 The play was too foolish for words... Not a high-kick or a wriggle or a ragtime song in the whole thing! **1933** P. GODFREY *Back-stage* xv. 194 Their white-washed legs..are doing energetic high-kicks and splits. *Ibid.* xviii. 224 They tap-dance, high-kick, turn cartwheels, and do the splits. **1962** A. HUXLEY *Island* xiii. 223 'What sort of dancing does he teach?' Mrs Narayan tried to describe it. No leaps, no high kicks, no running. **1966** 'J. HACKSTON' *Father clears Out* 92 He had high-kicked the boss at the..store for a fiver and had won by an ankle. **1896** W. STEVENS *Let.* 31 July (1967) 9 A plain little horse though a *high-kicker. **1897** KIPLING *Capt. Cour.* iv. 103 There's somethin' of a sea to-night... She *is* a high-kicker. **1897** G. B. SHAW *Our Theatres in Nineties* (1932) III. 12 Cancanist high-kickers. **1922** JOYCE *Ulysses* 359 Skirt-dancers and highkickers. **1895** *High-kicking [see SPLIT *sb.*[1] 4 b]. **1901** *Daily Chron.* 11 Dec. 6/5 Several dancers of the high-kicking and other schools. **1591** GREENE *Disc. Coosnage* (1859) 33 There be also other Lawes, as *High-Law, Sacking-Law, Figging Law, Cheting Lawe. *Ibid.* 41 *High Lawiers, Versers, Nips, Conny-catchers. **1967** E. CHAMBERS *Photolitho-offset* xi. 158 For high-key work, such as pencil sketches where delicate *high-light detail has to be retained in offset printing, the Sears method of making a continuous tone negative..is used. **1925** A. PHILIP *Crimson West* 144 He yawned sleepily. 'Got to fix a "spar-tree" for a "*high-lead" to-morrow, so I better hit the hay.' **1939** BEAULIEU & BARTON *Appl. Lumber Sci.* (ed. 2) 35 The High-Lead is the most common method of yarding by steam. **1951** W. F. HEALD *Scenic Guide to Oregon* 17 Modern 'high lead' and 'skidder' logging whisks tree sections. **1957** *N.Z. Timber Jrnl.* Aug. 59/1 *High lead*, extraction of timber by means of overhead cable attached to a high spar at hauler end. This gives the front end of logs sufficient lift to clear obstructions during haul. **1955** *Times* 23 Aug. 10/6 '*High lifes', marches, songs in the vernacular of dubious propriety. **1959** A. ABBS *Ashanti Boy* vi. 212 He has a big collection of high-life records. **1959** *Guardian* 22 Dec. 5/2 Man, I've got a.. West African band... They play high life. **1963** *Listener* 14 Mar. 456/1 A Ghanaian band was playing 'highlife' music for dancing. *Ibid.*, Highlife is as distinctively New African as the Kwela music played and danced to in Johannesburg at the other end of the continent. **1856** C. NORDHOFF *Whaling & Fishing* xviii. 354 Several had at different times been '*high line' from Harwich. **1864** *Harper's Mag.* Feb. 367/2 Captain Aleck was determined to fish for 'high line'. **1885** J. S. KINGSLEY *Stand. Nat. Hist.* III. 196 The emulation to be 'high-line' for the day and for the season is extreme. *Ibid.*, In a single day a high-line fisherman has caught from ten to fifteen barrels. **1890** *Grip* (Toronto) 5 Apr. 233/2 Always 'high line', he was always 'filled up' with the split mackerel of the North Bay. **1929** F. C. BOWEN *Sea Slang* 66 *High line*, on the Grand Banks a particularly good catch, also applied to the most successful fishing boat or clipper of the season. **1931** *Amer. Speech* VII. 49 The man who..attaches the 'high line' is called a 'skyrigger'. *Ibid.*, A 'high line', which is of one-inch steel, extends, often one-half mile, to either end of the 'set'. **1965** *Brit. Columbia Digest* Sept.–Oct. 19/1 Mobile spar trees, which are monstrous self-propelled cranes whose thick booms bear a multiplicity of sheaves and cables, are used in modern high-line logging to replace the spar trees used until recently as the focal point for the complicated system of cables and pulley-blocks. **1893** in *Funk's Stand. Dict.*, *High-liner. **1914** W. D. STEELE *Storm* 56 On the grounds he was a great 'killer', an unmerciful 'driver', and for three years running now the 'high liner' of the Old Harbor fleet. **1916** F. W. WALLACE *Shack Locker* 65, I ain't a highliner this season, but we've got one thing to brag about when it comes to fishin'. **1965** *Brit. Columbia Digest* Sept.–Oct. 20/1 But many [high-riggers] just disappeared, as did the giant trees they had topped, limbed and rigged for high-lining. **1964** G. D. CHERESCAVICH *Textbk. Nursing Assistants* vii. 52 **High-low bed*, an electrically or manually operated bed which can be raised to the height of the regular hospital bed and lowered to the height of the home bed. **1967** *Nursing Times* 18 Aug. 1088/2 There are many types of variable height beds (sometimes called high-low beds). **1676** ETHEREDGE *Man of Mode* III. iii, 'Tis now but *high Mall, madam. **1743** FIELDING *Wedding-Day* III. i. Wks. 1882 X. 368, I have seen him walking at high Mall. **1388** WYCLIF *Num.* xxii. 41 Balaach ledde Balaam to the *hiȝe placis [**1382** hye thingis] of Baal. **1611** BIBLE *Lev.* xxvi. 30, I will destroy your high places, and cut downe your images. **1662** STILLINGFL. *Orig. Sacr.* II. iv. §3 Naioth in Ramah, where was a high place whither the people came to sacrifice. **1918** L. STRACHEY *Eminent Victorians* 245 There were rumours of debaucheries in high places. **1922** G. M. TREVELYAN *Brit. Hist. 19th Cent.* iii. 54 Evangelicalism brought rectitude, unselfishness and humanity into high places. **1931** F. W. CROFTS *Myst. in Channel* xviii. 227 Persons in high places made comments. **1931** *Economist* 10 Oct. 656/1 Any talk at this moment in 'high places' of the abandonment of the gold standard would be quite likely to result in a stampede. **1938** *Archit. Rev.* LXXXIII. p. lvi, It is to be hoped that the contents..have percolated through to the authorities and those in 'high places' whose responsibility it is to plan ahead for the future of road transport in this country. **1971** G. HOUSEHOLD *Doom's Caravan* ii. 54 'It was her mother's correspondence which I feared might be of interest to enemy agents.' 'That has already been taken care of in high places.' **1946** *Nature* 27 July 122/1 The most important new dielectrics are usually of the *high-polymer type. *Ibid.* 19 Oct. 553/1 (*heading*) Effect of environment on the reactivity of high polymers. **1968** GREENWOOD & BANKS *Synthetic High Polymers* i. 3 A high polymer is simply a chemical substance which is made up of giant molecules. **1954** *Archit. Rev.* CXVI. 414/2 In general form—podium and *high-rise accommodation—this scheme follows the general pattern of current thought. **1958** *Listener* 20 Nov. 827/1 A point block of government offices is now going up at Wellington..and other high-rise slabs for offices and flats. **1961** *Observer* 7 Jan. 17/4 When one high-rise building is surrounded by many similar structures, height alone loses this special distinction. **1965** in *Amer. Speech* (1967) XLII. 159 Roosevelt Grier: the high-rise football star of the L.A. Rams. **1967** *Boston Sunday Herald* 26 Mar. I. 41/4 (Advt.), The convenience and prestige of a luxury high-rise. **1967** *Time* 20 Oct. 60 She likes the high-rise boots because 'they give my legs a sleek stocking look'. **1968** *Globe & Mail* (Toronto) 13 Jan. 45 (Advt.), Adult hi-rise building. *Ibid.* 17 Feb. 12 Block-heeled pump with high-rise vamp. **1903** R. L. MCCARDELL *Conversat. Chorus Girl* 111 When who should peek-a-boo in but my friend!.. I gave him the *high sign, but he passed me up. **1928** *Sunday Dispatch* 29 July 2 He gave the pawnbroker the high-sign. **1946** WODEHOUSE *Joy in Morning* xxv. 229 As soon as he is in a melting mood, you give me the high sign, and I carry on from there. **1957** *Amer. Ballads & Folk Songs* 135 She was pleadin' with him, her eyes all teary and dim, As I high-signed the barkeep for mine. **1962** L. DEIGHTON *Ipcress File* xii. 72 He gave us the high sign with thumb touching forefinger. **1962** K. ORVIS *Damned & Destroyed* xxv. 185, I high-signed him to follow. **1910** W. M. RAINE *B. O'Connor* 12 Here comes your train a-foggin'—also and likewise hittin' the *high spots. **1926** *Spectator* 11 Sept. 373/1 Chicago was the 'high-spot' of the trip. **1927** *Daily Express* 15 Sept. 9/5 The 'high spot' of the production—cinematic equivalent to the chariot-racing scenes in 'Ben-Hur'. **1928** *Sunday Dispatch* 22 July 23/4 It looks as though the standard of racing is going to hit the high spots. **1936** *Economist* 29 Feb. 483/1 The 'high-spot' was the 20 per cent. dividend (against 10 per cent.) announced by Associated Portland Cement. **1936** 'J. TEY' *Shilling for Candles* iv. 48 Two years of hitting the high spots must have educated you to something. **1961** J. CARTER *ABC for Book-Collectors* 111 'High spot' collecting is a sort of dictated eclecticism. **1964** *Publishers' Weekly* 28 Sept. 59 (*heading*), Religious books. Some Fall highspots, September through December. **1889** *Infantry Drill* I. 1. 32 The *High Step. **1894** MRS. ALEXANDER *Choice of Evils* II. viii. 199 He was exceedingly busy with hammer and nails, and the 'high steps', putting up fresh curtains. **1969** *Daily Tel.* (Colour Suppl.) 10 Jan. 32/1 The music [of the Celts] is the wail of the bagpipe, played to the jig and the fling and the high-step whirl. **1825** H. WILSON *Mem.* III. 76 The Duchess of Beaufort..appears never so happy nor so comfortable as when he is perched upon a *high stool by her side. **1837** DICKENS *Pickw.* l. 538 A high stool, four chairs, a table, and an old eight-day clock. **1892** C. M. YONGE *That Stick* I. xiii. 139 Whatever promise there may have been..must have been nipped upon the top of a high stool. **1935** G. GREENE *England made Me* I. 1 For half an hour she had sat on the same high stool, half turned from the counter. **1961** *Guardian* 14 Nov. 10/3 He sat on a high stool [at a bar]. **13.. ** *K. Alis.* 1084 Forth goth Alisaundre..Ryght to theo *heygh table. [**1431** cited from Oxford in Rogers *Agric. & Pr.* III. 550/3.] **1711** HEARNE *Collect.* (O.H.S.) III. 237 The Dean then went up to the Steps at the High-Table. **1886** WILLIS & CLARK *Cambridge* I. 116 A dais in parquet-work for the high table. *a* **1898** *Mod.* He dines at the High Table. **1831** F. A. KEMBLE *Rec. Girlhood* 14 June (1878) III. 49 We did not return home till near nine, and so, instead of dinner, all sat down to *high tea. **1856** E. G. K. BROWNE *Tractar. Movem.* (1861) 337 At one of the 'High Teas' of S. Barnabas. **1884** *Girl's Own Paper* May 427/2 For people who are not in the habit of giving dinner-parties..high tea is a capital institution. **1922** W. S. MAUGHAM *Chinese Screen* xlix. 193 He thought of the high tea to which he sat down when he came home from school..., a slice of cold meat, a great deal of bread and butter and plenty of milk in his tea. **1957** *London Mag.* Nov. 53 We ate high-tea made of fresh salmon, or mushrooms we'd risen at dawn to gather. **1923** *Man. Seamanship* (*H.M.S.O.*) II. 263 All material contributing to the longitudinal strength [of a ship's hull] is of *high tensile steel. **1932** *Discovery* May 146/2 High tensile irons, corrosion-resisting irons, and growth-resisting irons are now made in large quantities. **1937** *Archit. Rev.* LXXXI. 268 (*caption*) Right, a welded tubular bus frame seat, utilizing the strength of high-tensile alloy tube. *c* **1384** *Heiȝe wynes [see HIGH *a.* 8]. **1542** BOORDE *Dyetary* (1870) x. 254 Hyghe wynes, as malmyse, maye be kepte longe. **1871** *Trans. Ill. Agric. Soc.* VIII. 143 The necessity would still exist for converting..corn into beef and pork and highwines. *a* **1884** KNIGHT *Dict. Mech.* Suppl. 458/1 *High wines*, crude alcohol of higher proof than singlings. **1958** J. CAREW *Black Midas* vi. 112 They drank highwine and bush rum from half-pint tumblers. **1961** WEBSTER, *High wire. **1962** *Listener* 10 May 822/3 The bulk of the poems go all out for intellectual sophistication... He is not at his ease on the intellectual high wire. **1962** *Observer* 23 Sept. 26/5 A clown picking dust off his suit on the high wire. **1923** J. DOS PASSOS *Streets of Night* 133 Ought to see them *high yallers down there if you're stuck on girls. **1929** *Variety* 17 Apr. 51/3 She looks like a genuine high-yaller (that being her make-up in buxom mammy fashion). **1929** T. WOLFE *Look Homeward, Angel* (1930) II. xxii. 318 There's a High Yaller in here... You can have that if you want it. **1937** WYNDHAM LEWIS *Blasting & Bombardiering* IV. viii. 241 At present I should be living in a villa just outside Paris with a Japanese cook and a Zulu butler, with three highyaller kids getting ready to go to Eton. **1947** 'N. SHUTE' *Chequer Board* iii. 61 [He] had played and danced with various mulatto and 'high yaller' girls back home in Nashville. **1951** M. KENNEDY *Lucy Carmichael* I. iii. 25 She isn't exactly black... She's high yellow. **1969** 'J. MORRIS' *Fever Grass* xviii. 158 The big high yellow nodded at him with impersonal cordiality. **1957** *High yield [see *low-yield* adj. s.v. LOW *a.* 23]. **1958** *Times* 12 Sept. 10/1 A high yield nuclear device was successfully exploded. **1959** *Britannica Bk. of Year* 546/1 Another new term was *high-yield explosion*, an atomic explosion powerful enough to produce various widely felt and easily registered phenomena. **1960** *Farmer & Stockbreeder* 16 Feb. 66/3 He was no 'high-yield' merchant, but he would compare his profits..with any..breeder. **1970** *Daily Tel.* 16 Feb. 17

(Advt.), The aim of High-Yield Units is to give the highest return consistent with reasonable security of capital. **1946** *Nature* 12 Oct. 522/1 *High-yielding herds. **1956** *Ibid.* 3 Mar. 416/1 The cocoa trade has accepted the very high-yielding Upper Amazon selections.. as conforming to its quality requirements.

b. With agent-noun, denoting one who does (what is expressed) 'high' (see HIGH *adv.*): as ***high-attainer***, ***-bidder*** (see BIDDER 4 and HIGHEST A. 2), ***-feeder***, ***-jumper***; **high-liver**, (*a*) one who lives luxuriously; (*b*) one who professes a higher spiritual life than the ordinary; **high-ranker**, a person of high rank; **high-riser**, a type of child's small-wheeled, highly-manœuvrable bicycle with exaggeratedly raised handlebars; cf. CHOPPER 7 b. Also HIGH-BLOWER, etc.

1654 TRAPP *Comm. Job* iv. 13 So do the Enthusiasts, and *high-attainers. **1897** ALLBUTT *Syst. Med.* II. 860 When the patient has been a *high feeder. **1896** *Westm. Gaz.* 8 Apr. 8/1 A man became a mile-runner, a *high-jumper, a five-mile bicycle racer. **1881** J. W. BUEL *Border Outlaws* 166 All the band were known to be *high livers during their periods of plenty. **1883** *Century Mag.* XXVII. 211 None of our family have ever been high-livers. **1888** *Forum* (U.S.) Aug. 692 Among these high-livers and faith-curers. **1953** P. C. BERG *Dict. New Words* 93/1 **High-ranker*, a person of high rank, esp. in one of the Services. **1958** W. J. H. SPROTT *Human Groups* ix. 147 When he played against a gang high-ranker, he was seldom 'on form'. **1973** J. WAINWRIGHT *Pride of Pigs* 18 High-rankers and C.I.D. wallahs bobbing in and out. **1955** *Pop. Sci.* Aug. 110 Those bizarre-looking bikes with elevated saddles and exaggeratedly high handlebars are what the trade calls '*high risers'. **1971** *Time* 14 June 60 Demand rose to new heights in the mid-1960s with the introduction of high-risers—those small-wheeled children's bikes with elongated 'banana' seats, tall 'ape-hanger' handlebars, and moderate £30–£50 price tags. **1978** High-riser [see CHOPPER 7 b].

22. a. With nouns, forming *attrib.* phrases; unlimited in number: as ***high-action***, ***-caste***, ***-class***, ***-level***, ***-pressure***, ***-temperature***, etc.; **high-altitude**, occurring, working, or carried out at high altitudes; **high-angle** *Gunnery*, denoting the fire from guns, mortars, etc., at a high angle of elevation; hence ***high-angle gun***, etc.; also *transf.*, as of a camera; **high-board**, of or relating to diving from a high diving-board; **high-duty**, (*a*) subject to heavy customs duty; (*b*) designed to perform heavy tasks; = *heavy-duty* (HEAVY *a.*[1] 24 b); **high-fashion** (see FASHION *sb.* 9 c); **high-fibre**, containing a high proportion of dietary fibre; **high-flash**, denoting oil whose vapour ignites only at a relatively high temperature; **high-flux**, denoting (*a*) a high density of magnetic flux; (*b*) a large number of elementary particles per second; **high-humidity** *Forestry*, of the treatment of timber by exposing it to high humidity for a specified purpose; **high-level**, situated, built, etc., in, or carried out from, a high position; denoting talks, a meeting, etc., of an exalted status or grade; in the field of *Computers*, applied to a programming language that is largely independent of any particular kind of computer and bears some resemblance to an existing language (as English) or symbolism; **high-lift**, of something that is raised high or that lifts something up high; **high-pass** *Electr.*, denoting a filter that attenuates components with a frequency less that some cut-off frequency and passes components of higher frequency; **high-sea(s)**, operating or carried out on the high seas; ***High Sea Fleet*** = G. *Hochsee Flotte*; **high-velocity**, of high speed; *spec.* denoting a gun capable of discharging a projectile with great force and speed; also denoting the projectile so fired; **high-warp**, denoting a manner of weaving or tapestry in which the warp is vertical.

1958 *Listener* 13 Nov. 779/1 The manufacture of *high-accuracy gyroscopes. **1963** B. FOZARD *Instrumentation Nuclear Reactors* ix. 105 (*heading*) High-accuracy ratemeters. **1925** E. F. NORTON *Fight for Everest, 1924* 86 [They] were both suffering from very bad *high-altitude throat. *Ibid.* 106 This hateful duty of high-altitude cooking. **1955** E. HILLARY *High Adventure* 58 We signed on ten Sherpas to act as high-altitude porters. **1966** *Electronics* 3 Oct. 181 Also in the national space lineup is project '621', aimed at developing recoverable high-altitude sounding rockets. **1956** *Nature* 21 Jan. 121/1 *High-amplitude effects in reflexion amplifiers. **1879** *Man. Artill. Exerc.* I. v. 23 *High-angle fire from howitzers and mortars. **1890** G. S. CLARKE *Fortification* xiv. 205 Large numbers of high-angle guns which would prove most formidable to ships. **1915** *Pearson's Mag.* XXXIX. 66 High-angle trajectory. **1928** C. F. S. GAMBLE *N. Sea Air Station* ix. 122 The addition of some motor-cars equipped with machine-guns on 'high-angle mountings'. **1956** *Nature* 17 Mar. 502/2 (*caption*) High-angle photographs from a carbonized coking coal. **1963** *Listener* 28 Mar. 569/2 The mere novelty (for television drama) of the high-angle viewpoint gave the shot a sly edge. **1936** *Southern Counties' Amat. Swimming Assoc. Handbk.* 12 The positions in National championships are..C. D. Tomalin..*Highboard diving..1st. **1959** *Times* 22 Sept. 3/3 Phelps is the European and national highboard title-holder. **1937** *Discovery* May 156/1 *High carbon (hyper-eutectoid) steel. **1958** *Aspects of Translation* 84 The melting of the high-carbon cast iron. **1862** BEVERIDGE *Hist. India* VI. ii. II. 587 The *high-caste Brahmins. **1864** A. MCKAY *Hist. Kilmarnock* (1880) 168 Facilities for securing a *high-class education. **1909** *Proc. R. Soc.* A. LXXXII. 232 A small, adjustable, open, *high-conductivity, self-induction spiral. **1940** *Chambers's Techn. Dict.* 415/2 *High conductivity copper*, metal of high purity, having an electrical conductivity not much below that of the international standard. **1931** G. B. FORD *Building Height, Bulk & Form* Title-p., Uneconomic types of buildings on *high-cost land. **1964** *Ann. Reg. 1963* 259 German farmers were high-cost producers. **1703** *Art & Myst. Vintners* 69 There are *high-Countrey Wines. **1949** *Nature* 17 Sept. 485/2 (*heading*) *High-current betatron conditions. **1952** *Ann. Reg. 1951* 401 *High-density..central city areas. **1960** *Times* 28 Sept. 21/7 New plastics such as high-density polyethylene. **1962** *Listener* 15 Nov. 806/2 The high density life of the town. **1964** M. A. JOHNSON in *Oceanogr. & Marine Biol.* II. 33 The possibility of high-density turbidity currents in the ocean. **1973** *Times* 14 Aug. 2/5 Housewives doing their washing yesterday stopped the pumping of high density foam into the damaged Liberian tanker. **1920** *Ham's Yearbk.* I. *Customs* 173 In the case of *high-duty goods..the issuing officer will send an advice..to the Inspector-General of Waterguard. **1923** R. T. KENT *Kent's Mech. Engin. Handbk.* (ed. 10) ix. 692 (*heading*) Table 44.—Direct-connected, electrically-driven, two-stage compressors,.. Sea level high duty. Air pressure of 100–115 lb. **1937** *Times* 13 Apr. p. xxii/2 A high-duty lubricant has been introduced to deal with high tooth pressures now usual in rear axle mechanism. **1947** *Nature* CLIX. 51 The production of still stronger high-duty irons. **1962** SIMPSON & RICHARDS *Junction Transistors* ix. 202 A *high-efficiency hole injector. **1938** *Nature* 29 Oct. 781/1 Excitation..is..due..to the production of numbers of fairly *high-energy electrons. **1958** *Listener* 27 Nov. 871/1 Hoyle and Gold are convinced that the radio waves in these regions are emanating from high-energy particles moving in extensive magnetic fields. **1972** *Physics Bull.* Apr. 215/1 Bubble chambers are amongst the most widely used instruments in high energy physics for the detection of the tracks of ionizing particles. **1946** *Nature* 7 Sept. 350/1 A *high-fat diet. **1937** *Brit. Med. Jrnl.* 1 May 907/1, I have used diets with a *high-fibre content such as bran [in cases of constipation]. **1973** D. P. BURKITT in *Proc. Nutrition Soc.* XXXII. 148 Now that a low-fibre diet is known to be the cause of the disease, a high-fibre diet is becoming the standard treatment. **1981** N. BAWDEN *Walking Naked* I. 22 Drinking freshly squeezed orange juice and eating high fibre cereal. **1943** *Rep. Progress Physics* IX. 184 Thermionic emission under the Schottky *high-field condition. **1968** C. G. KUPER *Introd. Theory Superconductivity* vii. 130 Most of the Type II superconducting materials used for high-field magnets are rather 'dirty' metallurgically, and probably *do* contain normal inclusions. **1899** *Westm. Gaz.* 14 Feb. 4/3 A fourth *high-flash oil. **1904** GOODCHILD & TWENEY *Technol. & Sci. Dict.* 278/2 *High flash point*, oil whose vapour is only ignited at a high temperature. **1949** *Wireless World* Apr. 137/1 A *high-flux version (Type R22) of the single diaphragm T2 is now available with a density of 17,500 gauss in the 1⅜ in diameter gap. **1955** *Bull. Atomic Sci.* Mar. 93/2 A high-flux heavy water reactor primarily intended to investigate radiation damage in reactor building materials. **1971** *New Scientist* 3 June 579/1 The Franco-German high-flux reactor in Grenoble. **1936** *Nature* 11 July 87/1 The apparatus was designed to detect the presence of destructive insects in timber, and consists of a sound-proof chest, a sensitive microphone and a *high-gain amplifier. **1962** F. I. ORDWAY et al. *Basic Astronautics* v. 176 (*caption*) High-gain communications antenna. **1686** *Lond. Gaz.* No. 2140/4 White Stockings..*high-heel Shooes. **1925** H. L. HENDERSON in *Bull. N.Y. State College Forestry* XXV. XVI. 65 Another method is to use the *high humidity treatment. .. This process will balance up the moisture percentages in less than 24 hours. **1957** *N.Z. Timber Jrnl.* Aug. 59/1 *High humidity treatment*, temporarily raising the humidity of the circulating air in a kiln when drying wood requiring special treatment. **1893** *Outing* (U.S.) XXII, The following fall.. Harding was third in the *high-hurdle race. **1949** *Wireless World* Apr. 136/1 There seems to be a trend towards the use of *high-impedance windings in high-fidelity pickups. **1937** *Amer. Speech* XII. 315/2 His store..makes little attempt to attract a *high-income clientele. **1937** *Discovery* Feb. 45/1 For production of the screen image a *high intensity automatic arc is being used. **1962** F. I. ORDWAY et al. *Basic Astronautics* iii. 68 High-intensity solar ultraviolet radiation. **1960** *Encounter* XV. IV. 10 The average rate of profit..need not be lower in a *high-investment than a high-consumption economy. **1876** *Q. Jrnl. Geol. Soc.* XXXII. 185 The altitude of *high-level drift on the western slopes of the Pennine chain. *a* **1890** W. B. SCOTT *Autobiog. Notes* (1892) I. 197 The *High-Level Bridge..over the Tyne. **1936** *Discovery* May 132/2 The high-level gravels in which Harrison discovered those eoliths that gave proof of the oldest human culture in this island. **1943** *Aeronaut. Engin. Rev.* Apr. 59/3 The removal of objections against high-level daylight raids..[is] specified. **1951** *Ann. Reg. 1950* 45 It was the will that was lacking, and high-level meetings would not alter that. **1951** *Sci. Amer.* Sept. 42/1 Some, though they have obtained degrees, can hardly be classed as capable of high-level mental work. **1959** *Daily Tel.* 8 July 10/3 The proposed policy of continual high-level talks with Russia, extending over the next few years, has its opponents. **1964** *Jrnl. Assoc. Computing Machinery* XI. 21 Emphasis has been placed on simplicity and intuitiveness while maintaining so far as possible the inherent power of a high-level programming language. **1964** K. L. PIKE in D. Abercrombie *Daniel Jones* 425 High-level phonological units. **1965** N. CHROMSKY *Aspects of Theory of Syntax* iv. 153 Deviation from selectional rules involving high-level features is apparently more serious than deviation from sectional rules involving lower-level features. **1969** H. PERKIN *Key Profession* v. 209 A long-term high-level demand for university places. **1972** *Computer Jrnl.* XV. 195/1 The main purpose of a high-level language is to make programs and programming more intelligible to human beings. **1921** *Discovery* Apr. 96/2 *High-lift wings are, of course, those that give the highest lift-drift ratio. **1933** *Jrnl. R. Aeronaut. Soc.* XXXVII. 79 The Hall high-lift wing is an application of the same principle... Similar results are obtained, namely, a large increase in maximum lift and a shift backwards of the centre of pressure. **1958** *Times Rev. Industry* June 20/1 A new, high-lift boom machine. **1902** *Encycl. Brit.* XXV. 208/1 *High-nitrogen foods. **1960** *Farmer & Stockbreeder* 15 Mar. 113/1, 3 cwt per acre of the high-nitrogen compound in the seedbed should not affect it. **1932** *Chem. Abstr.* XXVI. 3097 Changes in design of cracking units to enable them to produce *high-octane gasoline. **1958** *Times* 6 Nov. 7/5 All high compression engines respond to high-octane, highly anti-knock fuel. **1972** M. GILBERT *Body of Girl* iv. 43 Filling the tank of an old Bentley with high-octane petrol. **1938** S. CHASE *Tyranny of Words* i. 6 We..allow our language forms or symbolic machinery to fashion a demonology of absolutes and *high-order abstractions. **1968** FOX & MAYERS *Computing Methods for Scientists & Engineers* vii. 134 Economization was effected just by removing successive high-order terms. **1960** *Farmer & Stockbreeder* 8 Mar. 48/2 (Advt.), The best *high-output combine in the world. **1963** *Listener* 14 Mar. 466/2 A living-room fire with a high-output back boiler. **1925** *Post Office Electr. Engin. Jrnl.* XVII. 311 Tests on *high pass filters of three sections. **1946** *Nature* 13 July 47/1 Figures 1, 2 and 3..were taken with a high-pass filter in the circuit which attenuated the low-frequency response of the micropone. **1940** *War Illustr.* 19 Jan. 620 (*caption*) The introduction into the Fleet Air Arm of *high-performance monoplanes like the Blackburn 'Skua'. **1966** T. WISDOM *High-Performance Driving* ii. 17 You need more skill for high-performance road-driving than you do for competitive motoring. **1930** *Wireless World* 21 May 538 (*heading*) *High permeability alloys. **1963** B. FOZARD *Instrumentation Nucl. Reactors* viii. 102 In general a tube must be placed..at least four inches away from another trochotron, a strong magnet, or a high-permeability screen. **1875** J. C. COX *Ch. Derbysh.* I. 195 The *high-pitch roof of the nave. **1944** *Mod. Lang. Notes* Dec. 515 *High-potency capsule. **1962** F. I. ORDWAY et al. *Basic Astronautics* xiii. 526 High-potency drugs such as the phenothiazines..could be incorporated. **1934** WEBSTER, *High-potential. **1954** *Essays in Criticism* IV. 313 The value of high-potential person-to-person situations. **1962** SIMPSON & RICHARDS *Junction Transistors* iv. 68 A particle such as an electron can pass through a high-potential barrier if the barrier is sufficiently thin. **1892** A. CONAN DOYLE *Adv. Sherlock Holmes* I. 2 A crack in one of his own *high-power lenses. **1898** *Westm. Gaz.* 28 May 2/1 Modern high-power guns. **1901** *Kynoch Jrnl.* June–July 108/2 Modern high-power smokeless propellants. **1934** *Discovery* Dec. 341/2 Here the microscope is set up vertically for high-power work. **1971** *Gloss. Electrotechnical, Power Terms* (*B.S.I.*) III. vii. 21 *High-power modulation*, modulation of the carrier of a radio transmitter. **1946** *Nature* 19 Oct. 537/2 For *high-precision measurements, as for observing wind-tunnel forces, the current is limited to 5 milliamp. **1960** *Times* 18 Nov. 4/6 The first essential..is a network of high-precision stations. **1824** R. STUART *Hist. Steam Engine* 67 To supersede the *high-pressure engines. **1846** MRS. GORE *Eng. Char.* (1852) 14 The high-pressure power of modern education. **1872** F. W. ROBINSON *Wrayford's Ward* III. 207 A high-class, high-priced, high-pressure seminary. **1891** *Daily News* 9 Feb. 2/7 About the middle of last week a large high-pressure system spread over the United Kingdom from the southward. **1907** *Westm. Gaz.* 15 Oct. 1/1 The high-pressure life which he led in London. **1928** D. BRUNT *Meteorol.* iv. 30 These high and low-pressure systems. **1933** *Archit. Rev.* LXXIV. 183/2 To launch a high-pressure salesmanship offensive. **1936** *Discovery* Feb. 38/2 Steam undergoes expansion in both high-pressure and low-pressure cylinders. **1940** *Topeka Jrnl.* 4 May 2 Photographers..hipressuring portrait sales. **1941** *Sat. Even. Post* 8 Feb. 54, I did not attempt to high-pressure the man too much. **1946** MEZZROW & WOLFE *Really Blues* viii. 128 He began to high-pressure us with a Chamber-of-Commerce spiel. **1958** J. CANNAN *And be a Villain* vii. 165, I get so confused by high-pressure salesmen. **1962** 'A. GARVE' *Prisoner's Friend* ii. 105 She didn't want to. Laurence high-pressured her into it. **1972** *Mod. Law Rev.* XXXV. I. 24 It is surely desirable to prevent abuses in marketing, particularly fraud, high pressure techniques, and the deliberate sale of defective goods. **1956** C. W. MILLS *Power Elite* xii. 282 *High-prestige organizations to which the elite usually belong. **1959** V. PACKARD *Status Seekers* (1960) vi. 84 A few old high-prestige neighbourhoods manage..to maintain their status. **1906** *Daily Chron.* 27 Sept. 3/6 The benefits of the *high-price policy which they choose to pursue. **1944** *Mod. Lang. Notes* Dec. 515 *High-protein foods. **1964** 'D. SHANNON' *Root of all Evil* (1966) v. 66 Sure, she gives me the high-protein diet, and I'm still learning to drink coffee without sugar. **1599** SHAKS. *Much Ado* v. i. 123 We are *high proofe melancholly. **1936** *Metals Handbk.* 925 (*heading*) Electrical properties of *high-purity annealed aluminium wire. **1910** *Westm. Gaz.* 21 Apr. 12/1 Until plenty of *high-quality beet is procurable. **1913** V. B. LEWES *Oil Fuel* 180 High-quality coal-gas. **1939** W. S. CHURCHILL *Into Battle* (1941) 85 High-quality war materials. **1948** *Wireless World* Jan. 2/1 Most high-quality radio receiver units will provide an output of well over 4 volts. **1880** WARREN *Book-plates* iii. 21 The prominent or *high relief portions. **1884** *High resistance [see RESISTANCE 6]. **1962** SIMPSON & RICHARDS *Junction Transistors* xi. 259 When feeding a high-resistance load from a relatively low-resistance source..the potentiometer should be connected as a voltage divider. **1946** *Nature* 19 Oct. 550/2 Using the *high-resolution system of the R.C.A. type E.M.U. microscope as a diffraction camera, we have attempted to find some feature of the diffraction by oxides of this type. **1970** G. K. WOODGATE *Elem. Atomic Struct.* 217 High-resolution optical spectroscopy. **1951** S. A. STOUFFER in Parsons & Shils *Toward General Theory Action* IV. v. 494 In a *high-risk cheating situation. **1963** *Economist* 14 Dec. 1175/2 All the 'high-risk' mothers. **1969** *Times* 3 Apr. 28/6 Many companies..had cancelled policies in high-risk areas such as the ghettoes. **1907** *Daily Chron.* 9 Oct. 4/6 The German *high-sea fleet. **1931** *Times Lit. Suppl.* 10 Sept. 673/3 A lack of familiarity with the naval idiom can alone account..for calling..the fleet under Cornwallis 'the high seas fleet'. **1961** A. J. MARDER *From Dreadnought to Scapa Flow* I. ix. 243 While the High Seas Fleet had concentrated .., the British Fleet was in a very different condition. **1949** *Wireless World* Mar. 16a (Advt.), *High stability capacitors. **1963** B. FOZARD *Instrumentation Nucl. Reactors* ix. 108 High-stability, close-tolerance components are required in the measuring circuits. **1959** V. PACKARD *Status Seekers* (1960) ix. 129 Some women said it made them 'feel good' just to go into a *high-status store. **1965** *Language* XLI. 295 An honored or high-status person. **1940** *Chambers's Techn. Dict.* 416/1 *High-strength brass. **1961** *Times* 13 Dec. 21/6 High-strength..paper bags. **1969** *Jane's Freight Containers 1968–69* 111/3 Aimed at providing a high-speed, high-

strength route for 'jumbo' freight cars. **1911** *Daily Colonist* (Victoria, B.C.) 11 Apr. 10/5 Harry Gillis..was killed and ten bricklayers narrowly escaped death today when Gillis came in contact with a 30,000 volt *high tension wire. **1970** *New Yorker* 10 Oct. 64/1 The denizens of the ocean, some of whom learned to produce high-tension electricity long before man. **1936** *Metals Handbk.* 439 The curves marked '*High Test' and 'Nickel' Irons in Fig. 21 were stressed to 10,000 psi. **1955** *Jrnl. Brit. Interplanetary Soc.* XIV. 159 Developments throughout the world have resulted in the production of hydrogen peroxide up to 90 per cent. strength, known as high-test peroxide or H.T.P. **1958** A. D. MERRIMAN *Dict. Metallurgy* 126/1 *High-test cast iron*, cast iron possessing a tensile strength not less than some arbitrary value, varying with different authorities. **1959** *Chambers's 20th Cent. Dict.* Suppl. 1378/2 *High-test*, (of petrol) boiling at comparatively low temperature and so of high performance. **1923** *Bull. Sch. Orient. & Afr. Stud.* III. I. 125 This significant tone of the future of all *high tone verbs need not be specially marked in broad transcriptions. **1964** J. CARNOCHAN in D. Abercrombie *Daniel Jones* 403 All these examples have a high-tone initial syllable. **1965** *Language* XLI. 347 A toneless base..to which I would add ..three affixes (the high-tone superfix, the suffix *-a*, and the mid-tone super fix) to produce the noun. **1692** *Let.* in *Select. fr. Harl. Misc.* (1793) 488 This was then thought consistent enough with the *high-tory loyalty. **1893** *Jrnl. Soc. Arts* 5 May 624/1 The phosphorescent glow of the novel high-frequency, high-voltage, *high-vacuum lamps. **1927** *Nature* 8 Oct. 510/1 We have made a further study of the phenomena exhibited by these high-vacuum tubes, with especial reference to the spectra of the discharge. **1971** *Gloss. Electrotechnical, Power Terms (B.S.I.)* II. ii. 8 High-vacuum diode. **1963** *Rep. Comm. Decimal Curr.* iii. 17 in *Parl. Papers 1962–3* (Cmnd. 2145) XI. 1 Because workable cent systems with *high-value major units are available..we preferred cent systems to mil ones. **1966** *Listener* 1 Sept. 307/2 High value perishable foods such as milk and meat and vegetables. **1892** F. IRWIN *Fortification* (ed. 2) 43 Modern *high-velocity guns. **1898** *Engineering Mag.* XVI. 112/2 These high-velocity bullets. **1934** *Discovery* June 155/2 The jet of high-velocity air is about 8 feet across, and an expenditure of energy at the rate of 400 horse-power is necessary to maintain it. **1946** *Nature* 28 Dec. 932/2 Anomalously short travel-time signifies the approach towards the surface, along the radius concerned, of a high-velocity medium. **1962** F. I. ORDWAY et al. *Basic Astronautics* viii. 334 The venturi principle is applied..in the aerodynamic wind tunnel to achieve high-velocity flow. **1964** CRYSTAL & QUIRK *Syst. Prosodic & Paralinguist. Features Eng.* iii. 38 Turbulent flow, with projection of high-velocity jet into pharynx. **1956** J. M. MOGEY *Family & Neighbourhood* 5 Before 1920 Oxford had not been a *high-wage town. **1964** S. M. MILLER in I. L. Horowitz *New Sociol.* 294 The high-wage..occupations. *a* **1877** KNIGHT *Dict. Mech.* II. 1103/1 **High-warp loom*, a tapestry loom in which the warp-frame is vertical and the weaver works standing. **1904** GOODCHILD & TWENEY *Technol. & Sci. Dict.* 287/2 *High warp*, tapestry in which the warp takes a vertical position, *e.g.* Gobelins tapestry. **1934** *Archit. Rev.* LXXV. *caption* facing 95 For instance, Burne-Jones drew cartoons for the revival of high-warp tapestry weaving which Morris initiated.

b. Parasynthetic combs., unlimited in number: as ***high-angled***, ***-arched***, ***-backed***, ***-bodiced***, ***-boned***, ***-browed***, ***-complexioned***, ***-couraged***, ***-crowned***, ***-fated***, ***-flavoured***, ***-foreheaded***, ***-horned***, ***-lineaged***, ***-motived***, ***-notioned***, ***-pooped***, ***-priced***, ***-principled***, ***-roofed***, ***-shouldered***, ***-souled***, ***-thoughted***, ***-towered***, ***-vaulted***, ***-walled***, ***-witted***, ***-zoned***, etc.; **high-blooded**, of high blood, race, or descent; **high-coloured**, (*a*) of a rich or luxuriant colour; (*b*) *fig.*, exaggerated, forced; as, *a **high-coloured description***; **high-geared**, having high gears; also *transf.*, fast-moving, active; **high-horsed**, mounted on the high horse: see HORSE; **high-kilted**, wearing the kilt or petticoat high, or tucked up; *fig.* indecorous; **high-lived**, pertaining to high life, frequenting high society; **high-necked**, having a high neck; *spec.* of a dress, high in the neck; **high-nosed**, having a high or long nose; *fig.* having a keen scent; †**high-palmed**, bearing the 'palms' of the antlers aloft; having lofty antlers; †**high-sighted**, having the sight directed aloft, supercilious. Also HIGH-HANDED, -HEARTED, etc.

1894 *Daily Chron.* 18 Aug. 5/1 Japan..has just paid great attention to *high-angled as well as direct fire. **1627** MAY *Lucan* x. (T.), *High-arch'd roofs. **1727** SOMERVILLE *Poems* 225 (Jod.) His high-arch'd neck he proudly rears. **1684** *Lond. Gaz.* No. 1949/4 A thick short Gelding somewhat *high Back'd. **1838** DICKENS *O. Twist* xxix, The high-backed oaken chair. **1899** *Daily News* 25 Dec. 5/2 A dangerous *high-banked river. **1632** MASSINGER & FIELD *Fatal Dowry* II. ii, Where heavenly virtue in *high-blooded veins Is lodged. **1826** MISS MITFORD *Village* Ser. II. (1863) 450 A high-blooded greyhound. **1900** *Westm. Gaz.* 26 Jan. 4/3 The broad-faced, *high-bosomed model is the palpable grandmother of many Rubenses. **1961** *Times* 25 Apr. 20/7 The white high-bosomed dress of Empire style. **1871** 'M. LEGRAND' *Cambr. Freshm.* 138 A Quixotic gentleman, of ancient lineage, in whose *high-bridged and defiant nose the Indian saw a resemblance to an eagle's beak. **1664** PEPYS *Diary* 28 Feb., His lady a very *high-carriaged, but comely big woman. **1907** *Daily Chron.* 30 July 4/4 It was a *high-ceilinged, sombre room. **1960** *Farmer & Stockbreeder* 9 Feb. Suppl. 3/2 A high-ceilinged, rather sunless sittingroom. **1551** T. WILSON *Logike* (1580) 52 b, A man maie be *high coloured..and yet not blacke. **1799** *Med. Jrnl.* I. 143 Urine high-coloured. **1925** F. M. FORD *No More Parades* 309 There were two girls who kept a tea-shop in Poperinghe... High coloured. **1612** DRAYTON *Poly-olb.* xiii. 221 The *high-complection'd Leame. **1599** MASSINGER, etc. *Old Law* v. i, Your hat is too *high-crowned. **1868** Q. VICTORIA *Life Highl.* 46 Welshwomen in their curious high-crowned..hats. **1748** MRS. DELANY *Life & Corr.* (1861) II. 491 The raspberries were particularly *high-flavoured. *a* **1635** NAUNTON *Fragm. Reg.* (Arb.) 28 Of a sweet aspect, but *high-foreheaded. **1899** *Daily News* 13 Feb. 5/3 Our *high-geared population. **1906** A. BENNETT *Whom God hath Joined* v. 169 Gater's high-geared bicycle. **1924** H. CRANE *Let.* 12 Jan. (1965) 169 Working at high speed as one does in such high geared agencies. **1562** PHAER *Æneid* IX. Cc iij, *Hyheaded..like two great okes by Padus banks. **1904** *Westm. Gaz.* 3 Aug. 2/3 In the shady *high-hedged garden. **1906** KIPLING in *Tribune* 15 Jan. 2/3 A high-hedged road. **1807** J. BARLOW *Columbiad* VI. 224 Gates in their van, on *high-hilled Bemus rose. **1896** A. E. HOUSMAN *Shropshire Lad* 83 Westward on the high-hilled plains Where for me the world began. **1613** T. MILLES tr. *Mexia's Treas. Anc. & Mod. Times* 714/1 Willing to be dismounted from their *high horsed frenzies. **1900** *Westm. Gaz.* 6 Feb. 3/2 To..ride off high-horsed on the theory that the battle had to be fought. **1928** *Observer* 22 Jan. 14/5 The high-horsed fanatics of universal Communism. **1824** SCOTT *Redgauntlet* Let. v, Who..had been carried home, in compassion, by some *high-kilted fishwife. *a* **1830** SCOTT in A. Cunningham *Burns* (1847) 184 In one or two passages of the 'Jolly Beggars', the Muse has slightly trespassed on decorum, where, in the language of Scottish song, 'High kilted was she As she gaed owre the lea'. **1840** HOOD *Kilmansegg*, *First Step*, iv, To dazzle the world with her precious limb,—Nay, to go a little high-kilted. **1762** GOLDSM. *Cit. W.* lxxi, All pretensions to high-life or *high-lived company. **1844** WILLIS *Lady Jane* I. 539 *High-neck'd gowns. **1870** BRYANT *Iliad* II. XVII. 185 To lead away the high-necked steeds. *a* **1635** NAUNTON *Fragm. Reg.* (Arb.) 15 Well-favoured, but *high nosed. **1658** OSBORN *Adv. Son* (1673) 218 Our high-nosed Hypocritical Zealots that pretent to smell ranck Idolatry in all Professions but their own. **1612** DRAYTON *Poly-olb.* vii. 108 The goodly Heards of *high-palm'd Harts. **1835** WILLIS *Pencillings* II. xxxix. 14 *High-peaked saddle. **1889** O. WILDE in *19th Cent.* Jan. 54 The *high-pooped galleys. **1921** W. DE LA MARE *Veil* 74 That midnight-stealing, high-pooped galliass, *Sleep*. **1947** *Horizon* XVI. 202 Muggleton was *high-pressured and loud. **1961** *Times* 15 Nov. 19/1 High-pressured modern life. **1749** FIELDING *Tom Jones* XII. ix, The honesty of this..boy was somewhat high—that is, somewhat *high-priced. **1791–1823** D'ISRAELI *Cur. Lit.*, *Libraries*, Rare and high-priced. **1962** *B.S.I. News* July 19/1 It was no use building a high-priced article for 20–30 years' service if it was to be outmoded by advancing techniques. **1714** SWIFT *Pres. St. Affairs* Wks. 1765 III. 293 The political creed of all the *high-principled men I have..met with. *a* **1633** AUSTIN *Medit.* (1635) 267 Like our Churches, *highroofed within but with a..low Gate. **1871** BRYANT *Odyss.* v. 54 His high-roofed palace. **1697** *Lond. Gaz.* No. 3313/4 A tall thin Man, *high Shoulder'd. **1837** THACKERAY *Ravenswing* vi, The little high-shouldered vulgar thing! **1960** *Farmer & Stockbreeder* 26 Jan. 65/3 Force the lacerated trimmings up a delivery chute into a *high-sided trailer. **1601** SHAKS. *Jul. C.* II. i. 118 Let *high-sighted Tyranny range on. **1741** RICHARDSON *Pamela* (1824) I. xv. 255 My *high-soul'd.. master. **1905** *Westm. Gaz.* 6 Dec. 5/2 There was no more high-souled, high-minded man than the man who was now Prime Minister. **1930** A. HUXLEY *Let.* 14 June (1969) 337 English reviews..have been rather snorty and high-souled about the book. **1596** B. GRIFFIN *Fidessa* i. (1815) 9 *High-thoughted (like to her) with bountie laden. **1860** MRS. BROWNING *V. Emanuel entering Florence*, High-thoughted souls. *a* **1631** DRAYTON *Wks.* III. 827 (Jod.) Amongst the *high-topt hills. *Ibid.* I. 24 (Jod.) *High-tow'red Harfleur. **1671** MILTON *P.R.* III. 260 Huge cities and high-towered. **1607** SHAKS. *Timon* IV. iii. 109 Some *high-Vic'd City. **1611** COTGR., *Haultmuré*, *high-walled. **1588** SHAKS. *Tit. A.* IV. iv. 35 *High witted Tamora. **1777–8** POTTER *Æschylus* (1779) II. 321 (Jod.) Hail Queen of Persia's *high-zon'd dames supreme!

B. *sb.* [Absolute uses of the adj.]

1. a. A high place or region; a height, eminence. *Obs.* exc. *Sc.* (chiefly in ***heighs*** (***hichs***) and ***howes***, heights and hollows).

13.. *Gaw. & Gr. Knt.* 1152 Hiȝed to þe hyȝe. **1382** WYCLIF *1 Sam.* x. 13 Forsothe he ceside to prophecie, and cam to the heiȝ [**1388** an hiȝ place; L. *ad excelsum*]. **1581** J. BELL *Haddon's Answ. Osor.* 416 b, There must be a thyrd place..in the highe betwixt heaven and hell I suppose. **1721** RAMSAY *To Ld. Dalhousie* 52 She..scours o'er heighs and hows a' day. *a* **1822** SIR A. BOSWELL *Sheldon Haughs* in Chambers *Pop. Hum. Scot. Poems* 168 Frae heighs and hows, frae hames and ha's. **1875** W. MCILWRAITH *Guide Wigtownshire* 24 We enter Kirkcoman parish among heighs and howes.

b. An area of high barometric pressure. Also *transf.*

1878 *Pop. Sci. Monthly* July 310 These high and low areas, or 'highs' and 'lows' as they are technically known, travel. **1901** *Yearbk. U.S. Dept. Agric.* *1900* 332 The hot wave..seemed to join forces with the permanent high over the ocean. **1958** 'N. SHUTE' *Rainbow & Rose* 290 A high had come along that the Met had not been able to forecast. **1966** *New Statesman* 27 May 759/1 There are..highs and lows of political intensity: right now, we are approaching a moderate high.

c. = the 'High Street' in Oxford.

1853 'C. BEDE' *Verdant Green* 1st Ser. x. 88 He at once sallied forth to 'do the High', and display his new purchases. **1912** A. QUILLER-COUCH in *Oxf. Bk. Victorian Verse* 860 Yet if at last not less her lover You in your hansom leave the High [etc.]. **1921** C. S. LEWIS *Let.* 10 May (1966) 59 It is still pleasant to see fewer foreign visitors pacing the High with guide books. **1955** *Times* 11 Aug. 7/6 A proposal..to close Magdalen Bridge,..preventing the High from being used as a motor thoroughfare.

d. = *high gear* (GEAR *sb.* 7 b).

1921 A. F. HALL *Handbk. Yosemite Nat. Park* 308 You may hear a driver boast that he made such and such a grade on 'high', but that is merely an admission of poor judgment. **1931** *Kansas City Star* 8 Aug., Now [all they talk about is] whether or not they were able to go up Pikes Peak on high. **1934** J. M. CAIN *Postman always rings Twice* ix. 89, I went into high. **1970** *Globe Mag.* (Toronto) 26 Sept. 7/1 Lewis moved into high, knowing, but really knowing that Walter would be in the race.

e. A record, a high level exceeding that previously attained.

1926 *Chicago Tribune* 23 Jan. II. 9/1 Wheeling and Lake Erie issues resumed their advance, the common toward a new high at 49⅝. **1928** *Weekly Dispatch* 3 June 7/2 When he buys, they buy; the lot of them can create..a new 'high' in any share in which Mr. Durant fancies. **1937** *Lit. Digest* 20 Mar. 3 (*heading*) Nazi epithets at U.S. set new high. **1939** [see *all-time* (ALL *a.* 13)]. **1951** W. STEVENS *Let.* 25 June (1967) 720 The whole thing has brought my morale up to an all-time high. **1953**, etc. [see LOW *sb.* 3 c]. **1959** *Encounter* Sept. 59/1 Beckett's stock has reached a steady high at Langham Place. **1964** R. D. HOPPER in I. L. Horowitz *New Sociol.* 317 The gross national product has reached an all-time high. **1968** *Listener* 22 Feb. 228/2 The series manifestly represented a new high in the adaptation of fiction to film.

f. = High School (SCHOOL *sb.*[1] 1 j). *N. Amer. colloq.*

1928 *Boston Even. Transcript* 30 Mar. 15/7 I'm hardly more than a schoolboy, not so very long out of Dorchester High. **1930** H. CRANE *Let.* 29 Nov. (1965) 359, I left East High without even a diploma—in my junior year. **1963** H. GARNER in R. Weaver *Canad. Short Stories* 2nd Ser. (1968) 49 He had graduated from technical high, and was going to university in the fall. **1968** *New Yorker* 18 May 56, I started playing drums in junior high.

g. *pl.* The higher range of audio-frequencies.

1940 in *Chambers's Techn. Dict.* 415/2. **1962** A. NISBETT *Technique Sound Studio* ii. 46 Such screens have the advantage of being dual purpose: used dead side to the microphone, they will damp down the highs: with the bright side forward, the highs will be emphasized.

h. A euphoric state induced by the taking of a drug or drugs. *slang.* (Cf. HIGH *a.* 16 c.)

1953 W. BURROUGHS *Junkie* (1972) xv. 149 Finally, the peyote came up solid like a ball of hair,..clogging my throat. As horrible a sensation as I ever stood still for. After that, the high came on slow. Peyote high is something like benzedrine high. **1956** H. GOLD *Man who was not with It* (1965) i. 6 Dreamy in my high, I floated down..to kick the smaller mark. **1967** *Listener* 3 Aug. 130/1 It is not easy..to describe the effect of a trip on LSD or a marijuana high. **1967** *Spectator* 4 Aug. 131/1, I was a drug addict..for two years. I was in an almost permanent state of high. **1969** *Times* 21 May 7/3 The two cigarettes smoked by each subject were intended to produce a 'normal social cannabis high'.

†**2.** Height, altitude; *fig.* highest pitch, acme.

c **1450** *Two Cookery-bks.* II. 75 Rered more þen an enche of hegh. **1557** PAYNEL *Barclay's Jugurth* A ij, Increased to the high of theyr perfection.

3. a. *Cards.* The ace or highest trump out. Also, the highest card in cutting for deal. ***high-low-jack*** (***and the game***): = ALL-FOURS 1. (See quots.)

[**1674** C. COTTON *Compl. Gamester* x. 111 This Game I conceive is called All-Fours from Highest, Lowest, Jack and Game, which is the Set as some play it. *Ibid.* 113 Sometimes you are highest, lowest, Jack, and Game.] **1814** C. JONES *Hoyle's Games Impr.* 170 All-fours..derives its name from the four chances therein, for each of which a point is scored, namely, *high*, the best trump out; *low*, the smallest trump dealt; *jack*, the knave of trumps; *game*, the majority of pips reckoned from such of the following cards as the respective players have in their tricks; viz. every ace is counted as 4; king 3; queen 2; knave 1; and ten for 10. **1818** TODD s.v. *All-fours*, The all-four are high, low, Jack, and the game. **1843** 'J. SLICK' *High Life N.Y.* II. 214 Under the table..was a hull squad of playin cards..as if somebody had got beat a playing high-low-jack and the game. **1895** *Funk's Stand. Dict.*, *High-low-jack*. Same as All-fours. **1898** B. KIRKBY *Lakeland Words* 72 *High-low*, a card game. High-low, Jack an' t' gam. **1911** R. F. FOSTER *Compl. Hoyle* 328 As High, Jack, and Game are always counted by the player holding those points at the end of the play, there can be no question about them: but serious disputes sometimes arise as to who played Low... It is even possible, if there is no other trump or counting card in play, for the Jack to be High, Low, Jack, and the Game. **1963** G. F. HERVEY *Handbk. Card Games* 16 The players then turn up their tricks and score for High, Low, Jack and Game.

b. Phr. ***how is that for high?***: an exclamation inviting admiration; in allusion to the card called the high in the game of high-low-jack. *U.S. colloq.*

1872 SCHELE DE VERE *Americanisms* 326 The phrase 'How is that for high?' borrowed from a low game known as Old Sledge, where the *high* depends, not on the card itself but on the adversary's hand. Hence the phrase means, What kind of an attempt is that at a great achievement? **1887** F. FRANCIS *Saddle & Mocassin* xviii. 315 'How's that for high, boys?' concluded the narrator, when he had told his tale. 'That's on top,' declared Black Jack; 'that takes the cake.' **1922** JOYCE *Ulysses* 122 What about that, Simon?..How's that for high?

high (haɪ), *adv.* Compared HIGHER, HIGHEST, q.v. Forms: 1 **héah**, **héaȝe**, 2–3 **heȝe**, **heȝhe**, **heie**, etc., 3– **hech**, etc.: see HIGH *a.* [OE. *héah*, later *héaȝe*, cf. OS. and OHG. *hôho*, MHG. *hôhe*, *hô*; thence early ME. *hêȝe*, by loss of final *-e*, *hêȝ*, blending in form with the adj.]

I. 1. a. At or to a great distance or extent upward; in or into a high position; far up; aloft.

c **1000** ÆLFRIC *Gram.* xxxviii. (Z.) 233 Heaȝe flyhþ se earn. *c* **1200** ORMIN 6057 Forr ærn maȝȝ fleȝhenn i þe lifft Full heȝhe towarrd heoffne. *a* **1225** *Ancr. R.* 130 Ant tauh heo vleon heie. *c* **1250** *Gen. & Ex.* 3380 He, and aaron, and hur ben gon, Heȝ up to a dune. *a* **1300** *Cursor M.* 2086 He sittes wit drightin hei o loft. *c* **1394** *P. Pl. Crede* 494 Wo worþe ȝou wyȝtes..þat þe toumbes of profetes tildeþ vp heiȝe. *c* **1470** HENRY *Wallace* IX. 996 To God a vow I mak beforn..to hyng the heych to morn. **1559** *Mirr. Mag.*, *O. Glendour* i, The fall of such as clymbe to hye. **1587** *Ibid.*, *Bladud* xxiii, Fly not so high for feare you fall so lowe. **1667** MILTON *P.L.*

II. I High on a Throne of Royal State.. Satan exalted sat. **1813** HOGG *Queen's Wake* 175 They seted her hiche on ane purpil swerde. **1860** TYNDALL *Glac.* I. xv. 100 Their direction changed high up the pass.

b. *Horsemanship.* With 'high action', lifting the feet far up from the ground.

1686 *Lond. Gaz.* No. 2164/4 Trots well, but gallops somewhat high. **1701** *Ibid.* No. 3703/4 Saddle-Nag.. trots high.

2. *fig.* **a.** In or to a high position, degree, estimation, amount, price, etc.; to a great extent, greatly; forcibly; strongly.

a **1225** *Ancr. R.* 352 Heie stod he þet spec of þisse wise! *c* **1340** *Cursor M.* 7304 (Trin.) For ȝoure richesse to heȝe ȝe rise. *a* **1400–50** *Alexander* 2200 Mast hiȝe ȝe ere hersid and herid of ȝoure strenthe. **1567** *Satir. Poems Reform.* vi. 24 Thocht he war neuer exalted so hie. **1641** FRENCH *Distill.* v. (1651) 113 Rectifie the Spirit as high as you can. **1652** SIR E. NICHOLAS in *N. Papers* (Camden) 284 [He] hath bid very high for it. **1667** MILTON *P.L.* III. 146 Both Heav'n and Earth shall high extoll Thy praises. **1691** tr. *Emilianne's Frauds Romish Monks* 407 Not in a condition to spend as high as others. **1724** DE FOE *Mem. Cavalier* (1840) 135 The king.. drove things too high. **1849** MACAULAY *Hist. Eng.* vi. II. 65 Lewis consented to go as high as twenty five thousand crowns. **1871** FREEMAN *Norm. Conq.* IV. xvii. 62 Every.. heart beat high with joy at the news.

†**b.** Loudly, aloud. *Obs.*

a **1225** *Ancr. R.* 152 A sopare.. remð and ȝeieð lude and heie þet he bereð. **1375** BARBOUR *Bruce* IV. 416 The cry raiss hydwisly and hee. *a* **1400–50** *Alexander* 948 Scho haldis out hire hede, and heȝe to him callis. *c* **1489** CAXTON *Sonnes of Aymon* iv. 121 [This] she sayd soo highe that her children vnderstode it. **1519** *Interl. 4 Elem.* in Hazl. *Dodsley* I. 33 What haste hast thou, That thou speakest so high? *a* **1648** LD. HERBERT *Life* (1886) 207 You must do me the honour to speak high, for I am deaf.

c. Richly, luxuriously; to excess.

1628 BP. J. WILLIAMS *Serm. at Westm. 6 Apr.* 8 It is a luscious kind of meate, and feedes very high. **1667** PEPYS *Diary* 29 July, Where it seems people do drink high. **1691** WOOD *Ath. Oxon.* II. 721 After his return he lived high.. without any visible income. **1697** DRYDEN *Virg. Georg.* III. 319 When once he's broken, feed him full and high. **1737** BRACKEN *Farriery Impr.* (1757) II. 103 If you feed a young Horse high, he should have Exercise. **1894** *Vermont Agric. Rep.* XIV. 102 Will a colt do well.. if fed high in winter? **1965** T. CAPOTE *In Cold Blood* (1966) iii. 135 Him and Carol lived too high, kept buying stuff they couldn't nohow afford. **1967** L. J. BRAUN *Cat who ate Danish Modern* xv. 137 David lived high, and he gave every thing away.

3. *Geog.* In or into a high latitude on the earth's surface; far from the equator.

1662 J. DAVIES tr. *Mandelslo's Trav.* 10 They put the Caspian Sea too high, and consequently allow Persia a greater breadth from North to South, than it really hath. **1720** DE FOE *Capt. Singleton* i. (1840) 11 Having been.. as high as the Cape of Good Hope. **1853** KANE *Grinnell Exp.* iii. (1856) 30 Our expedition met it as high as Storoë Island, in latitude 71°.

4. In reference to time: †**a.** Far on, late (*obs.*). **b.** Far back, early.

1523 LD. BERNERS *Froiss.* I. xc. 112 That yere [Easter] fell so hye that it was nere to thentring of May. **1613** PURCHAS *Pilgrimage* (1614) 266 The moneth Ramazan.. is their Lent; falling sometime high, sometime low. **1662** EVELYN *Chalcogr.* 26 For we shall not here ascend so high as Prometheus. **1724** A. COLLINS *Gr. Chr. Relig.* 208 Not the least ground to date the Samaritan Pentateuch so high as the times of Jeroboam. **1774** [see HIGHER B. 1 γ].

5. In reference to musical sounds: At or to a high pitch, shrilly.

1601 SHAKS. *Twel. N.* II. iii. 42 Your true loues coming, That can sing both high and low. *Mod.* The melody goes very high. I can't sing as high as that.

†**6.** Proudly, haughtily, overbearingly; arrogantly, presumptuously; with lofty ambition or profession; abstrusely (quot. 1667); with indignation or anger. *Obs.*

c **1400** *Destr. Troy* 1967, I shuld tere out þi tunge.. for chateryng so high. **1579** GOSSON *Sch. Abuse* (Arb.) 39 Nor the rich suffred to loke too hye. **1659** *Burton's Diary* (1828) III. 433 He.. did talk very high, how he would have a French cook, and a master of his horse. **1667** MILTON *P.L.* II. 558 Others.. reason'd high Of Providence, Foreknowledge, Will, and Fate. **1765** T. HUTCHINSON *Hist. Mass.* I. i. 105 The other threatened as high. **1844** WARDLAW *Lect. Prov.* (1869) I. 393 He resents it, as a reflection on his penetration. He takes it short and high.

II. Phrases.

7. ***high and low***: †**a.** Wholly, entirely (*obs.*): see HIGH *a.* 17 e; **b.** up and down, here and there; in every place or part.

1375 BARBOUR *Bruce* x. 471 He saw The castell tynt, bath hye and law. **1694** CONGREVE *Double Dealer* v. viii, Gadsbud, I can't find her high nor low. **1822** J. W. CROKER in *Diary* 11 Jan. (1884) He.. missed his snuff-box, and there was.. a search high and low. **1895** *Academy* 12 Oct. 294/2 Although the publishers have searched high and low, they have not [etc.].

8. ***to play high***: **a.** to play for stakes of a large amount; **b.** to play a card of high value.

1796 JANE AUSTEN *Pride & Prej.* viii. 31 Suspecting them to be playing high. **1885** PROCTOR *Whist* ii. 33 By playing high second hand you waste a good card.

9. a. ***to run high***: *lit.* said of the sea when there is a strong current with a high tide, or with high waves; hence *fig.* of feelings or conditions, manifesting themselves forcibly.

1711 ADDISON *Spect.* No. 125 ¶1 When the Feuds ran high between the Round-heads and Cavaliers. **1714** SWIFT *Pres. St. Affairs* Wks. 1755 II. I. 202 The tide runs high against the court and ministry. **1717** tr. *Frezier's Voy.* 14 The Sea ran too high to send Boats. **1763** WATSON in *Phil. Trans.* LIII. 11 At times.. her fever ran very high. **1836** MARRYAT *Midsh. Easy* xviii, The sea runs high, and the boat may be dashed to pieces on the rocks. **1849** MACAULAY *Hist. Eng.* ix. II. 416 The disputes.. had repeatedly run so high that bloodshed had seemed to be inevitable. **1893** EARL DUNMORE *Pamirs* II. 28 Party spirit ran high.

b. ***to live*** (or ***eat***) ***high off*** (or ***on***) ***the hog***: to live (etc.) in luxury. orig. *U.S.*

1946 *Call-Bulletin* (San Francisco) 27 May Edit. page, I have to do my shopping in the black market because we can't eat as high off the hog as Roosevelt and Ickes and Joe Davis and all those millionaire friends of the common man. **1946** *Time* 27 May 22/2 Eatin' on the Hog. In the years of political wars the Organization had grown and resistance diminished. **1956** 'E. S. AARONS' *Assignment Treason* (1967) ii. 27 He lives high off the hog. He needs money. **1966** A. PRIOR *Operators* vi. 69 That had been a good year, a year of living high off the hog. **1967** *Observer* 30 Apr. 11/5 Die.. for what? So that the Saigonese and other civilians can live high off the hog? **1967** K. GILES *Death in Diamonds* iii. 47, I hope these Uppings eat high on the hog. **1969** *New Scientist* 6 Mar. 511/1 A cod lives quite high on the hog—until he turns up on someone else's menu.

III. Combinations.

10. a. In syntactic comb. with pres. or pa. pple. of any verb which can be qualified in the active or passive by *high* or *highly*; e.g. *to aim high*, hence *high-aiming*; so ***high-aspiring, -bended, -blazing, -blest, -blown, -braced, -built, -climbing, -dressed, -dried*** (also as *sb.*), ***-embowed, -fed, -flushed, -gazing, -heaped, -judging, -laced, -lying, -mounted, -mounting, -perched, -piled, -placed, -prized, -raised, -reared, -seasoned, -seated, -soaring, -swelling, -swollen, -throned, -thundering, -towering, -tuned, -working***, etc.; †**high-cargued, -carved** *Naut.* (see CARGUED, CARVED); **high-descended**, of lofty or noble descent; **high-finished**, of high finish, highly elaborated; highly refined or accomplished; **high-grown**, (*a*) grown or increased to a height; (*b*) overgrown with tall vegetation; **high-keyed** *Mus.*, of a high pitch; also *fig.*; **high-sniffing** *colloq.*, contemptuous, disdainful; **high-strung**, strung to a high tension or pitch; *fig.* in a high state of vigour or of sensitiveness (now used esp. in the sense 'in a state of nervous tension').

1766 CRASHAW tr. *Marino* (T.), They *high-aim'd hopes. **1597–8** BP. HALL *Sat.* I. iii. (T.), Some upreard, *high-aspiring swain. **1645** RUTHERFORD *Tryal & Tri. Faith* vi. (1845) 71 Broken as a too *high-bended bow. **1667** MILTON *P.L.* XI. 145 God *high-blest. **1613** SHAKS. *Hen. VIII*, III. ii. 361 My *high-blowne Pride At length broke vnder me. **1671** MILTON *Samson* 1069 Haughty, as is his pile *high-built and proud. **1880** TENNYSON *Revenge* ix, Ship after ship.. their high-built galleons. **1530** TINDALE *Doctr. Treat.* (1848) 505 Here must a mark be set to those unquiet, busy, and *high-climbing spirits. **1667** MILTON *P.L.* III. 546 The brow of some high-climbing Hill. **1606** SYLVESTER *Du Bartas* II. iv. II. *Magnif.* 368 *High-descended Queen. **1779** POTTER *Æschylus* (ed. 2) I. 52 (Jod.) No prejudice of high-descended ancestry. **1756** FOOTE *Engl. fr. Paris* I. Wks. 1799 I. 98 Two pound of *high-dried Glasgow [snuff]. **1818** SCOTT *Heart of Midlothian* in *Tales of My Landlord* III. x. 265, I have always a chat with Mrs. Glass when I purchase my Scots high-dried. **1858** GEO. ELIOT *Scenes Clerical Life* I. 48 If Mr. Barton had shaken into that little box a small portion of Scotch high-dried, he might have.. [etc.]. **1632** MILTON *Penseroso* 157 To.. love the *high-embowed roof. **1628** FORD *Lover's Mel.* II. ii, Like *high-fed jaeds.. In antick trappings. **1770** LANGHORNE *Plutarch* (1879) I. 193/2 A *high-finished picture of Pericles. **1605** SHAKS. *Lear* IV. iv. 7 Search euery Acre in the *high-growne field. *Ibid.* II. iv. 231 *High-judging Ioue. **1893** *Funk's Stand. Dict.* I. 848/1 **High-keyed*, 1. *Mus.* high-pitched. 2. Sensitive, spirited; as, a *high-keyed* woman. **1906** *Daily Chron.* 18 June 6/3 Mr. P. Wilson Steer has several examples of his familiar high-keyed method, including a not too happy portrait of himself in a grey tweed suit. **1938** *Burlington Mag.* Feb. 75/2 Painted in thick and high-keyed colours. **1938** M. K. RAWLINGS *Yearling* xvi. 181 There was an excitement.. that made him nervous and high-keyed. **1851** J. G. WHITTIER *Works* (1898) 210 Madam in her *high-laced ruff. **1880** 'MARK TWAIN' *Tramp Abroad* II. xxxiv. 26 These were.. hob-nailed high-laced walking-shoes. *a* **1930** D. H. LAWRENCE *Phoenix II* (1968) 46 Even then, I lack high-laced boots and one stocking. **1877** BLACK *Green Past.* i, On the northern side of this *high-lying park. **1934** *Discovery* June 166/2 The more high-lying burials.. contained 'reserved slip' pottery. **1958** *Times* 19 Dec. 7/1 The difficulty is intonation in high-lying passages. **1969** *Daily Tel.* 12 Mar. 21/3 High-lying solos in the Mozart finale. **1863** LONGFELLOW *Tales Wayside Inn* 45 *High-perched upon the back of which there stood The image of a falcon carved in wood. **1906** *Westm. Gaz.* 16 June 12/2 Each high-perched farmhouse was changed by sunset glamour to a magic castle. **1945** W. S. CHURCHILL *Victory* (1946) 207 Flags from high-perched windows. **1862** W. C. BRYANT *Poet. Wks.* (1883) II. 312 Clouds, *High-piled. **1932** V. WOOLF *Common Reader* 2nd Ser. 226 Its high-piled metaphors. **1952** C. DAY LEWIS tr. *Virgil's Aeneid* XI. 257 Treading the high-piled embers as we perform your rites. **1605** SHAKS. *Macb.* IV. i. 98 *High plac'd Macbeth. **1725** POPE *Odyss.* x. 102 Cliffs, *high-pointing to the skies. **1645** QUARLES *Sol. Recant.* xii. 35 His *high priz'd benefits. **1610** HOLLAND *Camden's Brit.* I. 290 *High-raised mounts. **1594** SHAKS. *Rich. III*, v. iii. 242 *High rear'd Bulwarkes. **1896** A. E. HOUSMAN *Shropshire Lad* XXXVII. 53 The high-reared head of Clee. **1922** JOYCE *Ulysses* 422 The swancomb of the gondola, high-reared, forges on. **1588** SHAKS. *Tit. A.* IV. iv. 64 With a power Of *high resolued men. **1684** OTWAY *Atheist* III. i, The *high-season'd Dish. **1752** BERKELEY *Th. Tar-water* Wks. III. 504 High-seasoned food and strong liquors. **1667** MILTON *P.L.* VII. 585 Heav'n's *high-seated top. **1906** *Daily Chron.* 12 July 3/3 *High-sniffing pretenders.. affect to find in Mr. Meredith's poetry naught that is obscure. **1606** SHAKS. *Tr. & Cr.* IV. iv. 126 Farre *high soaring o're thy praises. **1398** TREVISA *Barth. De P.R.* XIV. xxxii. (1495) 479 The moost *hyghe strowtyng partyes of cragges ben callyd Scopuli. **1748** THOMSON *Cast. Indol.* II. lviii, *High-strung health. **1863** *Country Gentleman* 7 May 300/2 When the sire and the dam of a colt possess much spirit and are 'high strung'. **1868** W. JAMES in *North Amer. Rev.* CVII. 322 That high-strung attitude of vigilance, suspicion, and suspended judgment. **1872** J. G. MURPHY *Comm. Lev.* x. Introd., High-strung enthusiasm. **1902** A. BENNETT *Anna of Five Towns* xi. 283 You're so sensitive and high-strung. **1946** M. LOWRY *Let.* 15 Sept. (1967) 125 Writers often tend to be high-strung creatures. **1956** A. H. COMPTON *Atomic Quest* 125 He could keep a group of high-strung specialists working smoothly together. *c* **1590** GREENE *Fr. Bacon* ix. 190 Beauty's *high-swelling pride. **1594** SHAKS. *Rich. III*, II. ii. 117 Your *high-swolne hates. **1813** SCOTT *Trierm.* III. xiii, The water's high-swoln tide. **1875** LONGF. *Pandora* ii, Commissioned by *high-thundering Zeus. **1596** SPENSER *F.Q.* VI. ii. 32 Ne is there hauke.. Whether *high towring, or accoasting low.

b. With an adj. = Highly, to a great degree. (The hyphen shows that *high* qualifies the following adj., not the sb.)

1601 SHAKS. *Twel. N.* I. i. 15 So full of shapes is fancie, That it alone is high fantasticall. **1663** BOYLE *Colours* (J.), A high-red tincture. **1715–20** POPE *Iliad* XVIII. 433 High-eminent amid the works divine. **1865** *Union Rev.* III. 266 They use such high-learned words.

c. Occasionally hyphened to a verb to make the construction clear.

1632 SIR T. HAWKINS tr. *Mathieu's Unhappy Prosp.* 240 Shee stirred and high-reared her creast. **1788** COWPER *Morn. Dream* i, The billows high-lifed the boat.

†**high**, *v. Obs.* Forms: 1 **héan**, 3 **hæhȝen, hehen**, (*Orm.*) **heȝhenn**, 3–4 **hei(en**, 3–5 **heȝe(n**, 4–6 **hie, hegh(e, hey**, etc. (see HIGH *a.*), 4–7 **high.** [OE. *héan*, f. *héah* HIGH *a.*; cf. also Goth. *hauhjan*, OHG. *hôhjan, hôhen*, MHG. *hœhen* to raise, exalt. See also HAIN, HEYGHNE.]

1. *trans.* To make high or higher (*lit.* and *fig.*); to raise, lift up, elevate, exalt, extol.

c **900** tr. *Bæda's Hist.* II. iv. (1890) 106 He ongon hean and miclian [þa cirican]. *c* **1200** *Trin. Coll. Hom.* 25 Swo þat we on alle ure þanke þe heien. *Ibid.* 57 Heȝen his sete on heuene. *c* **1200** ORMIN 9204 Nu sket shall illc an dale been All heȝhedd upp and filledd. **1340** HAMPOLE *Pr. Consc.* 4125 He sal heghe himself to be Aboven þe haly trinite. *c* **1440** HYLTON *Scala Perf.* (W. de W. 1494) I. xviii, Who so hieth himself he shalbe lowed and who so lowyth himself he shalbe hyed. **1494** FABYAN *Chron.* an. 1465 (1553) 216 b, Syluer that.. was hyghed to xl. *d.* an vunce. **1523** FITZHERB. *Surv.* xi. (1539) 25 High no man for no hate.

2. *intr.* To become high or higher (*lit.* and *fig.*); to rise, mount up, ascend.

c **1200** ORMIN 6017 God man riseþþ aȝȝ uppwarrd.. annd heȝheþþ aȝȝ Biforenn Godess ehne. *a* **1225** *Ancr. R.* 72 Ase ȝe wulleð þat heo [þouhtes] climben & hien touward heouene. **1390** GOWER *Conf.* III. 295 Now it higheth, now it loweth, Now stant upright, now overthroweth. **1556** BURROUGH in Hakluyt *Voy.* (1886) III. 126 It.. hyeth two fadome and a halfe water. **1601** HOLLAND *Pliny* XVIII. xviii, The river Nilus higheth apace untill he be risen to his ful heigth. **1633** T. JAMES *Voy.* 35 The tydes doe high about some 6 Foot.

high, *int.* Variant of HEY, HI.

1800 WEEMS *Washington* ii. (1810) 15 'High! why not my son?' **1830** GALT *Lawrie T.* VI. iii. (1849) 260 She made no reply, but only a high-madam-ho signification that she recognised me.

high, obs. form of HIE.

high altar. [OE. *heah-altar.*] The principal altar of a church.

c **950** in T. Wright *Vol. Vocab.* (1873) II. 23 *Cibborium*, þæs heahalteres ofergeweorc. **13..** *Gaw. & Gr. Knt.* 592 So harnayst as he was he herknez his masse, Offred and honoured at þe heȝe auter. *c* **1460** *Oseney Reg.* 137 Reynolde, By the grace of god Bisshop of Clone,.. halowed the Chapell of Saunforde and the high auter. *c* **1553** in *Diary of H. Machyn* (1848) 399 The highe altar table. *a* **1700** EVELYN *Diary* 25 Oct. 1644, On the large high altar is a brazen vessel of admirable invention. *c* **1777** in *Cath. Rec. Soc. Publ.* VIII. 173 He lays buried in our Church at the foot of the High Altar. **1826** [see ALTAR 2]. **1894** C. M. CHURCH *Chapters Early Hist. Ch. Wells* App. W. 419 High altar dedicated to St. Andrew. **1927** W. CATHER *Death comes for Archbishop* IX. viii. 299 The next morning the old Archbishop lay before the high altar in the church he had built. **1954** *Oxf. Jun. Encycl.* XII. 8/2 Large churches often have subsidiary chapels with their own altars, and then the principal one is called the High Altar.

highaw(e: see HICKWALL.

highball, *sb.* Also high ball, high-ball.

1. A game, a species of poker, played with balls and a bottle-shaped receptacle.

1882 C. M. CHASE *Editor's Run in New Mexico* 134 Mexican monte, keno, faro, high ball, etc., are the prevailing games. **1894** J. N. MASKELYNE *Sharps & Flats* xi. 261–266. **1894** *Westm. Gaz.* 23 Apr. 3/1 Methods of cheating with dice, at highball, poker, roulette.

2. (In full ***highball signal.***) A signal to proceed given to a locomotive driver, formerly by hoisting a ball aloft. Also *gen.*, a signal to go ahead, a clear way, a straight course. *U.S.*

1897 *Chicago Record* 1 Mar. 6/1 'Milk trains'.. have 'rights' over the rails and get nothing but 'high balls'. **1909** *Sat. Even. Post* 26 June 9/1, I gave 'em the highball signal to go ahead. **1920** J. M. HUNTER *Trail Drivers of Texas* 68 We had a high ball trail from there on. *Ibid.* 354 Mr. Butler and I told them [*sc.* cowboys].. to strike a high ball to town. **1931** 'D. STIFF' *Milk & Honey Route* 207 *High ball*, signal for a train to pull out of town. **1938** A. E. PARKINS *South* 168 We

are informed that the signal the conductor waves to the engineer to go ahead is still known as the 'high ball' on most lines. **1940** *Sat. Even. Post* 16 Nov. 18 Picking up the highball as he drifted out of the freight yards, Engineer Joe De Nobel gave her the throttle. **1959** J. Thurber *Years with Ross* iv. 63 The parlance of railroading—deadhead, highball, whistle stop, gandy dancer.

3. A drink of whisky and soda or other mineral water served with ice in a tall glass. Also *attrib.* *U.S.*

1898 *N.Y. Jrnl.* 16 Sept. 4/2 Evening dress and khaki talked much sport and a little war over 'high balls' or chicken livers. **1899** Ade *Doc. Horne* ii. 11 Lush..drank two magnificent 'high balls'. **1909** Eaton & Underhill *Runaway Place* 128 The pleasant occupation of consuming three chocolate éclairs and a high ball. **1915** Wodehouse *Something Fresh* iii. 59 Beyond Baxter, a cigar in his mouth and a weak high-ball at his side, the Earl of Emsworth took his ease. **1925** H. L. Foster *Trop. Tramp Tourists* 109 The crowd from Ohio..celebrated by drinking several highballs. **1933** N. Coward *Design for Living* III. i Who'd like a highball? **1949** F. Maclean *Eastern Approaches* I. vii. 82 The crystal chandeliers shed a cheerful light on the silver trays of highballs and old-fashioneds. **1959** *Sears, Roebuck Catal.* Spring & Summer 1394/3 Highball glasses. **1965** *Amer. Speech* XL. 77 In sophisticated drinking circles the term *high-ball* has become practically archaic... The illuminati ask for 'whiskey and water' or 'Scotch and soda'. **1973** H. Nielsen *Severed Key* viii. 92 A soiled highball glass on the counter.

'highball, *v. U.S. slang.* [f. the sb.] **a.** *intr.* To give a locomotive driver a signal to proceed; also *transf.* **b.** To go or travel at speed (const. *it* or with *adv.*). **c.** *trans.* To drive (a locomotive or vehicle) at speed.

1912 *Railroad Man's Mag.* XVII. 493 The con high-balled, and the manifest freight Pulled out on the stem behind the mail. *Ibid.*, She whistled twice and high-balled out, They were off—down the Gila Monster Route. **1931** 'D. Stiff' *Milk & Honey Route* v. 53 Often they highball the cops and you get raided. **1935** Partridge *Slang To-Day* (ed. 2) 442 *Highball*, to travel swiftly; to depart, esp. hastily. **1941** *Amer. Speech* XVI. 233/1 *High ball*, to speed up operations. **1941** *Pop. Sci. Monthly* May 76 Its smooth power..is fully available, whether the giant is pulling away from a dead stop or highballing along at its maximum governed speed. **1943** S. K. Farrington *Railroading from Head End* 48 We highballed out at 5:05. No hurry, no lost motion, no excitement—just clocklike precision by every man jack of them. **1945** *This Week Mag.* 14 July 19/2 He highballed the big locomotive down the tracks. **1946** *Sat. Even. Post* 11 May 27/3 Everyone else had highballed..out of there. **1961** *Amer. Speech* XXXVI. 271 Imagine yourself on the seat of an enormous freighter, high-balling it down a West Coast highway. **1962** *Ibid.* XXXVII. 131 A logging train that is highballing or making a fast run. **1971** M. Tak *Truck Talk* 82 *Highball it*, to drive a tractor-trailer at or near its top speed.

'high-,binder. *U.S. slang.* [f. high *a.* 14: cf. bender 5, hellbender.]

1. A rowdy; one of a gang which commits outrages on persons and property.

1806 *Weekly Inspector* 27 Dec. last p., An association calling themselves 'High-Binders.' **1806** *N.Y. Evening Post* 26 Dec. 2 A desperate association of lawless and unprincipled vagabonds, calling themselves 'High-binders'..during the last winter, produced several riots. **1860** Bartlett *Dict. Amer.*, *High-binder*, a riotous fellow. New York slang.

2. One of a secret society or gang said to exist among the Chinese in California and other parts of the United States for the purpose of blackmailing and even of assassination.

1876 *San Francisco Call* 27 Mar. 1/7 Refined ladies could no longer submit to be jostled at the church door by the Mongolian *chiffonier* or high-binder. **1887** *Amer. Missionary* Aug. 235 The High-Binders were already on his track, and he scarcely feels safe even in Oakland. **1888** *Pub. Opinion* (N.Y.) 15 Dec. 193 The power of the Highbinder is the only one which the average Chinaman understands and fears, and his conduct is regulated by it to a greater extent than by the laws of the country in which he lives. **1892** *Boston* (Mass.) *Jrnl.* 10 Dec. 12/1 The Italian Mafia is a dangerous enemy to law and order, like the Chinese 'highbinders' of California.

3. *transf.* Used abusively to denote a swindler, esp. a fraudulent politician.

1890 C. L. Norton *Political Amer.*, *Highbinders*..applied ..to political conspirators and the like. **1903** A. H. Lewis *Boss* 136 He's goin' to take copies of th' accounts that show what th' Chief an' them other high-binders at the top o' Tammany have been doin'. **1908** G. H. Lorimer *J. Spurlock* xii. 324 That's what I do mean—it [*sc.* the railroad]'s been stolen by that Bonsall bunch of high-binders. **1916** H. L. Wilson *Somewhere in Red Gap* i. 21 So I left these two lady highbinders and went on into the retail side of the Family Liquor Store. **1952** in Wentworth & Flexner *Amer. Dict. Slang* (1960) 255/2 The winter meeting of the grand inner circle of high-binders at Miami Beach.

high-blower. A horse that makes a 'blowing' noise by flapping the nostrils at each expiration in galloping; also sometimes euphemistically applied to a 'roarer'. So **high-blowing** *vbl. sb.* and *ppl. a.*

1831 Youatt *Horse* xii. (1847) 254 Eclipse was a 'high-blower'. **1856** H. H. Dixon *Post & Paddock* ii. 35 The high-blowing Humphrey Clinker [race-horse so named]. *Ibid.* iii. 55 A roarer—or, politely speaking..'a high blower'. **1881** Sir F. Fitzwygram *Horses & Stables* III. xxiii. (ed. 2) 300 High Blowers. The noise, which some horses make by flapping the alæ of their nostrils, has occasionally been mistaken by inexperienced people for roaring. **1891** M. H. Hayes *Veterinary Notes* xi. (ed. 4) 304 Highblowing is not a disease, but is simply produced by the flapping of the horse's nostrils when he expels air quickly from his lungs.

'high-born, *a.* Born in a high rank of society; of noble birth.

a **1300** *Cursor M.* 14236 Lazar was a heie-born man. **1728** Pope *Dunc.* I. 297 High-born Howard, more majestic sire. **1780** E. Perronet *Hymn*, *'All hail the Power'* ii, Let high-born Seraphs tune the lyre. *a* **1859** Macaulay *Hist. Eng.* xxiii. V. 30 The posterity of a highborn beggar.

fig. **1871** J. Miller *Songs Italy* (1878) 13 The high-born beautiful snow came down.

high-borne, *a. rare.* [See borne.] Borne on high; exalted, lofty, of high bearing.

(But some take it in the example as = *high-born.*)

1588 Shaks. *L.L.L.* I. i. 173 This child of fancie, that Armado hight..shall relate In high-borne words, the worth of many a Knight From tawnie Spain.

high-boy.

†**1.** One who lives 'high'; a 'fast' man, libertine, gallant; cf. *roaring boy. Obs.*

1668 R. L'Estrange *Vis. Quev.* (1708) 104 Many Huffs and High-boys. *a* **1680** Brooks *Wks.* (1867) VI. 68 A high boy, or one that was strong to drink among others, or to drink down others!

†**2.** A partisan making high claims for his party; cf. high-flyer 3. *Obs.*

1648 Symmons *Vind. Chas. I* 117 These High-boyes say plainly that all such who are not of their opinion are perfect Malignants. **1715** Mrs. Centlivre *Gotham Election* Wks. 1760–1 I. 177 *Sir Rog.* I am amaz'd to find you in the Interest of the High-Boys.. *Ald.* Our Parson says that's only the Whig's Cant.

3. = tallboy 2. *U.S.*

1891 *Scribner's Mag.* X. 353 In the top drawer of a high chest of drawers, a 'high boy'. **1902** L. V. Lockwood *Col. Furnit. Amer.* 56 The common form of the flat-topped bandy-legged high-boy is made of cherry, maple or walnut. **1909** J. C. Lincoln *Keziah Coffin* i. 10 Removing towels, tablecloths, and the like from the drawers in a tall 'high-boy'. **1926** *Bulletin* 29 June 10/2 The..lady..belonged against a background of mahogany highboys, old china.. and an Adams' mantel. **1972** *Town & Country* Mar. 106/1 (*caption*) American William and Mary high-boy.

'high-bred, *a.*

1. Of high breed, stock, or descent; high-born.

1674 N. Fairfax *Bulk & Selv.* 50 The soul is too high bred to give us any rational accounts of the awarings of sense. **1760** R. Heber *Horse Matches* ix. 146 The high bred chesnut horse. **1820** Scott *Abbot* xxiv, The high-bred descendant of an ancient baron.

2. Of, pertaining to, or characteristic of high breeding or bringing-up; characterized by highly refined manners.

1796 Seward *Anecd.* II. 306 (Jod.) Prior was a very high-bred man, and made himself peculiarly agreeable to Louis XIV. by this talent. **1816** *Remarks Eng. Mann.* 103 A model of suavity and high-bred manners. **1875** Lowell *Wks.* (1890) IV. 309 He caught the grand manner and high-bred ways of the society he frequented.

highbrow, high-brow ('haɪbraʊ), *sb.* and *a. colloq.* orig. *U.S.* [Back-formation from high-browed *a.* 2.] **A.** *sb.* A person of superior intellectual attainments or interests: occas. with derisive implication of conscious superiority to ordinary human standards.

1908 *Sat. Even. Post* 29 Aug. 27/1 It takes all sorts of men to make a party, and Mr. Hearst apparently led in a few prize-fighters with the other high-brows and reformers he accumulated. **1911** H. S. Harrison *Queed* iv. 41 Who knew but what this little highbrow was the very man they were looking for? **1914** G. Atherton *Perch of Devil* I. 41 I'll be a real high-brow in less than no time. **1921** H. S. Walpole *Young Enchanted* III. vi. 301 There was the theatre (so much better than the highbrows asserted), there were concerts. **1922** D. H. Lawrence *Phoenix II* (1968) 240 Then the highbrows come and say: 'Poor Indian, dear Indian! why, *all* America ought to belong to him!' **1925** A. P. Herbert *Laughing Ann* 86 I'll be a high-brow, but I'll look hearty, And I won't laugh at the Liberal Party. **1934** S. R. Nelson *All about Jazz* i. 18 The strangely disreputable lady 'Jazz' —disreputable because she was not sponsored by the highbrows. **1955** *Times* 23 June 11/4 The highbrows in those parts all go up in smoke or mist if you confess to liking those among their native artists who seem most typically Scottish.

B. *adj.* Of, pertaining to, or characteristic of a highbrow; intellectually superior.

1884 L. Troubridge *Life amongst Troubridges* (1966) xii. 169 Mr. Hope had suggested that we would be at some highbrow part of the Exhibition—looking at pictures I think, but Jo had said firmly, 'If I know the Troubridges they will be at the Chocolate Stall', and we were! **1914** S. Lewis *Our Mr. Wrenn* 42 All them high brow sermons. **1916** S. Leacock in 'O. Henry' *Waifs & Strays* (1919) 161 Shakespeare, except as revived at twenty-five cents a seat with proper alterations in the text, is 'highbrow'. **1917** W. J. Locke *Red Planet* xxiv. 306 She'd die of culture in the mater's highbrow establishment. **1925** *Punch* 22 Apr. 437/2 'The programmes are too highbrow,' I maintained. 'They are hopelessly beyond the intelligence of the mass, at any rate.' **1931** R. Church *High Summer* 12 Mother insists on my being highbrow and visiting all the historical places. **1943** C. Gray *Contingencies* (1942) i. 41 The choice of programme was uncompromisingly what it is customary to describe as 'highbrow', but the house was packed on both occasions. **1963** Auden *Dyer's Hand* 408 All highbrow—lowbrow frontiers of taste.

So **'highbrowish** *a.*, fairly, or extremely, highbrow; **'highbrowism,** the condition of being highbrow, intellectual superiority.

1921 *Glasgow Herald* 22 Jan. 4/2 This doctrine is tainted with high-browism. **1923** A. Bennett *Things that have interested Me* II. 207 The audiences were artistic and earnest, with a dash of high-browism. **1926** Whiteman & McBride *Jazz* viii. 108 Does the very word 'classical' make you nervous because it sounds so high-browish? **1927** D. H. Lawrence *Let.* 19 May in E. & A. Brewster *Reminisc. & Corr.* (1934) 132, I can't stand high-browish..people any more. **1937** *John o' London's* 1 Jan. 585/1, I am incapable of 'highbrowism', I make no pretensions to be a literary critic. **1947** N. Cardus *Autobiogr.* I. 16 The..Bloomsbury-Chelsea highbrowism which does not understand that genius is a miracle to be revered. **1953** *Harper's Mag.* Mar. 48/2 Articles. Books. Highbrowish stories.

high-browed ('haɪbraʊd), *a.* [f. high *a.* + brow *sb.*[1] + -ed[2].]

1. Having a lofty forehead.

1848 'Geo. Eliot' *Let.* 23 Nov. (1954) I. 273 We have brought you [*sc.* Mother Nature] many gentle maidens and high-browed, brave men. **1875** *Brit. Q. Rev.* Apr. 500 One can conjure up a vision of them: the one fair, pale, high-browed. **1891** Flügel *Eng.-German Dict.*

2. = highbrow *a.* orig. *U.S.*

1906 'O. Henry' in Davis & Morris *Caliph of Bagdad* (1931) xiv. 238 That, in addition to the $150 that I screwed out of the high-browed and esteemed B. Merwin during your absence. **1908** R. W. Chambers *Firing Line* ix, You were very much amused, I suppose—to see me sitting bras-dessus-bras-dessous with the high-browed and precious. **1909** H. G. Wells *Ann Veronica* vii. 121 Their very furniture had mysteriously a high-browed quality. *Ibid.* viii. 144 Goopes, she was sure, was always high-browed and slow and Socratic. **1916** —— *Mr. Britling* II. iv. §10, I was too high-browed about this war business. **1923** A. Bennett *Things that have interested Me* II. 207 If artistic, earnest, and high-browed women only knew how to dress! **1927** *Daily Express* 3 May 3/7 Meeting a highbrowed friend.

high chair. [high *a.* 3.] A child's chair with high legs, usually fitted with a movable tray and footrest.

1848 Thackeray *Van. Fair* xliv. 400 Little Rawdon..was perched on a high chair by the baronet's side. **1853** C. Brontë *Villette* I. ii. 23 The demure little person..perched now on a high chair. *Ibid.* 25 She relinquished the high chair for a low stool. **1885** C. M. Yonge *Two Sides of Shield* II. i. 8 Mrs. Halfpenny [*sc.* the nanny] always put us on the high chair with our faces to the wall when we were jealous. **1913** C. Mackenzie *Sinister St.* I. i. 7 Stella was fitted into her high chair; the circular top was brought over from behind and thumped into its place with a click. **1943** C. McCullers *Heart is Lonely Hunter* II. ix. 214 Ralph banged his spoon on his high-chair tray. **1959** *Sunday Times* 25 Oct. 20/6 Spoon overboard: the tyrant in the high chair makes a point.

High Church, *a.* and *sb.* [app. deduced from *High Churchman* (see next) and used attrib. as in *High Church party*, and then substantively.]

A. *adj.* or *attrib. phrase.* Of, belonging to, or characteristic of High-Churchmen (see next); of or belonging to the principles and practices of High-Churchmen: see B.

1704 De Foe *Storm* xxiv, They say this was a High-Church Storm, Sent out the Nation to Reform. **1705** Hearne *Collect.* 4 July (O.H.S.) I. 1 The latter has promis'd to come over to the High Church Party. **1705–15** Burnet *Own Time* VI. (1823) IV. 249 Those men, who began now [anno 1704] to be called the high church party, had all along expressed a coldness, if not an opposition to the present settlement. **1710** *Let. to New Memb. Parlt.* in *Select. fr. Harl. Misc.* (1793) 565 Any manner of persons, either high-church, low, or no church. **1726** Amherst *Terræ Fil.* iii. 13 Maintaining the same principles with our jacobite high-church priests. **1730** Swift *Vind. Ld. Carteret* Wks. 1761 III. 194 Whether it contained any Tory or high-church principles. **1744** N. Tindal *Rapin's Hist. Eng.* III. 523 Those of the Clergy who began now [1700–2] to be called the High-Church party..set up a complaint all over England of the want of Convocations. **1814** Scott *Wav.* ii, Tory or High-Church predilections and prejudices. **1827** Hallam *Const. Hist.* (1876) III. xvi. 250 The nonjuring and high-church factions among the clergy produced few eminent men. **1830** W. Wilberforce *Private Papers* 31 Dec. (1897) 157 All my three Oxonians are strong friends to High Church and King doctrines. **1884** Mandell Creighton in *Dict. Eng. Hist.* 265/2 A movement which had its seat at Oxford, and was begun by Newman, Keble, Pusey, and Hurrell Froude, revived the old High Church party. **1890** T. F. Tout *Hist. Eng.* III. x. vi. 233 By the end of 1837 the High Church revival had become general. **1895** Oman *Hist. Eng.* xli. 679 To the new High-Church party we owe much good work in neglected parishes, and a restoration of decency and order in public worship. *Mod. colloq.* The women of the family are very High-Church.

B. *sb.* [orig. short for *H.C. party*, *H.C. principles.*] The party or principles of the High-Churchmen (see next).

1702 Lady Pye in *15th Rep. Hist. MSS. Comm.* App. IV. 26, I never saw so short a sorrow as was here [about King William's death]..and the High Church are elevated hereabouts. **1704** [C. Leslie] *Wolf Stript* 5 They [the Low-Church] profess themselves ready to joyn with the Dissenters in Confederacy against the High-Church. **1706–9** M. Tindall *Rights of Christ. Church* Pref., Nothing is more disputed at present than who is the best Churchman, both High and Low Church laying claim to it. **1709** *Refl. Sacheverell's Serm.* 24 This is the true Spirit of High-Church; they wou'd have the Mitre overtop the Crown. **1710** *Answ. Sacheverell's Serm.* 6 Several of the High Church are for a Union between the Church of England and the Church of Rome. **1710** Addison *Tatler* No. 220 ¶9 The Terms High-Church and Low-Church, as commonly used, do not so much denote a Principle, as they distinguish a Party. **1710** in Howell *State Trials* XV. 554 I'll lead you on, boys; huzza! high church and Sacheverell! **1726** Amherst *Terræ Fil.* Pref. 11 To convince the world how strenuous they were in the cause of high-church and the pretender.

1833 *Record* 24 Jan. 4/3 The order which resists Reformation is the High Church.

Hence **High-Church** *v. trans.* (*nonce-wd.*), to render High Church in doctrine and practice. **High-'Churchism, †High-'Churchship,** High Church principles, doctrine, or practice. **High-Churchist, -ite,** an adherent to High Church principles.

1720 GORDON & TRENCHARD *Indep. Whig* No. 42 ¶5 Italy ..(that Seat of High-Churchship). **1823** S. PARR *Wks.* (1828) VII. 272 An amusing..picture of generosity, whim, domination, and high churchism. **1846** MACFARLANE *Cabinet Hist. Eng.* XV. 128 The high-churchism of the Queen [Anne] naturally grew higher with sickness and danger. **1848** CLOUGH *Lett. & Rem.* (1865) 118 A—— belongs, I see, to the new High Churchites. **1863** OUIDA *Held in Bondage* (1870) 101 Stiltified County Queens, with daughters long on hand, had taken refuge in High-Churching their village. **1868** *Episcopalian* (N.Y.) 8 July, Another High-Churchist..used language inappropriate to be placed on record.

High-'Churchman. [orig. *high Churchman*: cf. *good Churchman*, *strict Churchman*, etc.]

A Churchman or member of the Church of England holding opinions which give a high place to the authority and claims of the Episcopate and the priesthood, the saving grace of the sacraments, and, generally, to those points of doctrine, discipline, and ritual, by which the Anglican Church is distinguished from the Calvinistic churches of the Continent, and the Protestant Nonconformist churches in England.

a. Originally applied in the 17th and early 18th c. to those who, holding a *de jure* Episcopacy, opposed a comprehension or toleration of differences in church polity, and demanded the strict enforcement of the laws against Dissenters, and the passing of such additional measures as the Occasional Conformity Bill. With these were then associated the doctrine of the divine right of kings (of the House of Stuart), and the duty of non-resistance on the part of subjects. The appellation was, in fact, practically synonymous with *Tory*, and was at first a hostile nickname, equivalent to the earlier *High-flyer*, *High-flying* or *High-flown* Churchman (q.v.); after the invention of the antithetic *Low-Churchman*, it began to be accepted as relatively appreciatory. **b.** In recent times, since 1833, the name has been increasingly appropriated to the adherents of the Oxford Movement led by John Henry Newman, and (afterwards) by Edward Bouverie Pusey. The ecclesiastical principles of these are more or less analogous to those of the 'old High-Churchmen', but exhibit (at least in their extreme form) a much closer approximation to those of the pre-Reformation Church. **c.** The name is occasionally applied to those who hold (except as to episcopacy) somewhat analogous opinions in the established Church of Scotland, and perhaps in some other religious communities.

1687 *Gd. Advice* 43 Against the will of the high Churchmen. **1702** *Reasons Addr. Maj. to invite Electress* etc. 9 Those..are particularly stil'd High-Flyers, High-Churchmen, a few of 'em Nonjurants, and all of 'em Torys. **1704** [C. LESLIE] (*title*) The Wolf Stript.. by one call'd an High Church-man. *Ibid.* 4, I venture, for it's a Venture at this Time, to own the name of an High-Church-Man. No man thinks it a Disparagement to be High, that is Zealous in any good thing. **1705** EVELYN *Diary* Oct. (1889) II. 389. **1708** (*title*) The Character of a High-Church-Man. *Ibid.* 7 A High-Church Clergyman is a Holy-man in his Conversation. **1709** SACHEVERELL *Serm. 5 Nov.* 19 Have they not lately Villainously Divided us with Knavish Distinctions of High, and Low-Church Men? **1741-3** WESLEY *Extract of Jrnl.* (1749) 99 Neither should I have wonder'd, if..the zealous high-churchmen had rose, and cut all that were call'd Methodists in pieces. **1791** BOSWELL *Johnson* I. 8 He was a zealous high-churchman and royalist, and retained his attachment to the unfortunate house of Stuart. **1835** HOOK *Ch. Dict., High Churchman.* This is the nickname given to those..who regard the Church, not as the creature and engine of State policy, but as the institution of our Lord. **1890** T. F. TOUT *Hist. Eng.* III. x. vi. 234 The Bennett judgment..in 1870 definitely permitted the teaching of the most distinctive doctrine of the new High Churchmen.

Hence **High-'Churchmanship,** the doctrine or practice of High-Churchmen, High-Churchism; adherence to the High Church party; also **High-'Churchmanism.**

1829 J. R. BEST *Pers. & Lit. Mem.* 198 High-churchmanism, a religion differing much more from low-churchmanism than from popery. **1874** GLADSTONE in *Contemp. Rev.* Oct. 672 It was thought to be like a sign of the double superlative in High Churchmanship. **1882** ABP. TAIT in *Macm. Mag.* XLVI. 417 So powerfully had the early teaching of Newman represented English High Churchmanship as the best barrier against the Church of Rome.

high cockalorum: see COCKALORUM.

high court. A supreme court; applied to various bodies having judicial functions, as *High Court of* CHANCERY, *High* COMMISSION *Court*, *H.C. of* JUSTICE, *H.C. of* PARLIAMENT: see these words. Without qualification *High Court* now means 'High Court of Justice'. (Also *attrib.*)

1450, etc. [see COURT *sb.* 10]. **1530** PALSGR. 231/1 Hye courte, *covr sovueraigne*. **1701** [see CHANCERY 2]. **1896** *Ch. Times* 13 Nov. 521/1 That the High Court would grant an injunction against the trustees. **1897** *Westm. Gaz.* 13 Apr. 2/1 It is difficult to grasp any plausible reason for the continued refusal..to give to County Courts equal jurisdiction to that enjoyed by the High Court. It is urged that the judges would not be equal to discharging the duties of a High Court judge.

high-crested, *a.* Having a high crest (in various senses); in quot. 1618 *fig.* Carrying the head high; elated; proud.

1618 BOLTON *Florus* IV. ix. 307 The miserable overthrow of Crassus made the Parthians higher crested. **1833** BROWNING *Pauline* 324 A high-crested chief, Sailing with troops of friends to Tenedos. **1861** L. L. NOBLE *Icebergs* 173 The rolling away of the high-crested seas.

†b. Having a high ridge. [See CREST *sb.*¹ 9.]

[**1545** ASCHAM *Toxoph.* (Arb.) 138 A certayne kynde of [arrow] heades whyche men call hie rigged, creased, or shouldred heades [*i.e.* high-ridged, -crested, or -shouldered].] **1678** PHILLIPS (ed. 4), *High-crested* [**1706** or *High-rigged*] (A Term in Archery). See Shoulder-head.

high day, 'high-day, 'highday, *sb.* [In I. from HIGH *a.*; in II. for *hey-day*.]

I. 1. A day of high celebration; a solemn or festal day.

c **1200** *Trin. Coll. Hom.* 215 Eche heȝe dai [þe hodede sholde] fede mid godes worde þe hungrie soule. *c* **1400** *Ywaine & Gaw.* 52 Thai saw tham never so On high dayes to chamber go. **1526** TINDALE *John* xix. 31 That saboth daye was an hye day. **1535** COVERDALE *Baruch* i. 14 Se that ye rede this boke..vpon the hye dayes, and at tyme conuenient. **1712** W. ROGERS *Voy.* 42 The Day kept for the Conception of the Virgin Mary, and a high Day of Procession. **1865** M. ARNOLD *Ess. Crit.* iii. 105 Here, the summer has, even on its highdays and holidays, something mournful. **1883** T. HARDY in *Longm. Mag.* I. 570 Never used but at high-days, holidays and family feasts.

†2. Full day, when the sun is high in the sky. Also *attrib.* as *high-day noon*. *Obs.*

1583 HOLLYBAND *Campo di Fior* 5, I will open both these windowes, that..ye may..see, that it is highe day. **1647** H. MORE *Song of Soul* I. III. xxvii, The Sun of righteousnesse at high-day noon.

II. 3. Perverted form of HEY-DAY *sb.* 2.

1771 SMOLLETT *Humph. Cl.* II. 50 (D.) In the high-day of youth and exultation. *a* **1791** WESLEY *Wks.* (1830) XIII. 221 I do nothing rashly—the highday of my blood is over. **1862** MERIVALE *Rom. Emp.* (1865) IV. xxxix. 398 The land-owners of Rome, in the highday of her insolent adolescence.

III. 4. *attrib.* **a.** Of or befitting a high day. **b.** Pertaining to the hey-day of youth.

1596 SHAKS. *Merch. V.* II. ix. 98 Thou spend'st such high-day wit in praising him. *a* **1625** FLETCHER *Mad Lover* I. i, Look to your wives, Your young trim wives, your high-day wives, Your marchpanes.

†high-day, *int. Obs.* Erroneous form of HEY-DAY, arising from confusion with prec.

1610 SHAKS. *Temp.* II. ii. 190 Freedome, high-day, high-day [*mod. ed.* hey-day] freedome. **1687** T. BROWN *Saints in Uproar* Wks. 1730 I. 80 High-day! who have we got here? **1708** MOTTEUX *Rabelais* v. xiv, High-day! Prithee,.. would'st thou have a man tell thee more than he knows?

highe, obs. form of HIE *v.*¹ and *sb.*

higher ('haɪə(r)), *a.* (*sb.*¹) and *adv.* Forms: α. 1 **hierra, híera, hír(r)a, hýr(r)a; héra; hérra, héarra,** 2-5 **herre,** 5 **heer, her, har,** 5-6 **harre.** β. 1 **híehra, héahra,** 2 **heahere,** 3 **hæhȝere,** (*Orm.*) **hehhre,** 3-4 **heȝer(e, heier,** 4 **hegher, -ur, heyer(e,** 4-6 *Sc.* **hear(e,** 5 **heiȝer, heȝare, heiar, heyar,** 6 *Sc.* **hecher.** γ. 4-6 **hier(e, hyer,** *Sc.* **hyear(e,** 5 **hiȝere, hiar,** 6 **hyar,** *Sc.* **hiear,** 6- **higher.** δ. *dial.* 9 **hicker.** [OE.: WS. *hierra, híera* (Anglian *héra, hérra*, whence ME. *herre, heer, her*, etc.), corresp. to OHG. *hôhiro*, Goth. *hauhiza*, f. *hauhs*, OE. *héah* HIGH *a.*; subseq. conformed to the positive, as *híehra, héahra*, whence ME. *heȝer, hegher*, later *higher*: see HIGH.]

A. *adj.* **1. a.** The comparative of HIGH *a.* in its various senses, q.v.

α. *c* **897** K. ÆLFRED *Gregory's Past.* Pref. 6 To hierran [*v.r.* hieran] hade. *Ibid.* lii. 409 Se mæȝðhad is hirra ðonne se ȝesinscipe. *c* **900** *O.E. Chron.* an. 897 Eac hieran [*MSS. B. & C.* hearran] þonne þa oðru. *a* **1000** *Cædmon's Dan.* 491 Wearð him hyrra hyȝe..þonne ȝemet wære. *c* **1000** *Phœnix* 28 in *Exeter Bk.*, Herra..þonne æniȝ þara beorȝa. *c* **1205** LAY. 22758 Þe an hine talde hæh, þe oðer muche herre. **13..** *Gaw. & Gr. Knt.* 333 Herre þen ani in þe hous by þe hede & more. *c* **1400** *Destr. Troy* 3924 Hoger of hert & of her wille. *c* **1450** MYRC 1527 The herre that a mon ys in degre.

β. *a* **1000** *Cædmon's Gen.* 274 Hu he him strenglicran stol ȝeworhte, heahran on heofonum. *a* **1175** *Cott. Hom.* 243 We scule bien..imeaded mid heahere mede. *c* **1200** *Vices & Virtues* 115 Ðat godes milce bie aure heier and more ðanne his rihte dom. *c* **1200** ORMIN 6297 All an oþerr lif Annd hehhre lif annd bettre. *c* **1205** LAY. 7740 Mid hæhȝere stefne. *a* **1300** *Cursor M.* 7331 Saul..was hegher [*v.rr.* heyer, heȝer] þan ani man. *c* **1375** *Sc. Leg. Saints, Marcus* 5 Þai ware of heare degre. *c* **1400** *Apol. Loll.* 8 Crist is..heiar wiþ out comparisoun þan ani pope. *a* **1400-50** *Alexander* 2097 Neuire þe heȝare of a hawe. **1581** *Satir. Poems Reform.* xliv. 269 Ane hear place.

γ. **13..** *Cursor M.* 15056 (Gött.) Comen of þat hei dauid kin, Of hier [*Cott.* heier] nane can neuen. **1375** BARBOUR *Bruce* I. 608 God of mycht Preserwyt him till hyer hycht. *c* **1400** MAUNDEV. (1839) viii. 92 Mount Syon..is a lytille hiere than the other syde of the cytee. **1508** KENNEDIE *Flyting w. Dunbar* 336 On Arthuris Sete, or on ane hyar hill. **1513** MORE in Grafton *Chron.* (1568) II. 758 His left shoulder much higher then his right. **1563-7** BUCHANAN *Reform. St. Andros* Wks. (1892) 15 Doctor..in the hyear faculteis. **1577** B. GOOGE *Heresbach's Husb.* II. (1586) 52 You must make the spaces betwixt hier. **1765** A. DICKSON *Treat. Agric.* (ed. 2) 135 Exposed to overflowings from higher ground. **1814** CHALMERS *Evid. Chr. Revel.* vii. 195 Geology gives a higher antiquity to the world. **1876** TAIT *Rec. Adv. Phys. Sc.* i. (ed. 2) 20 The energy of the universe is continually passing from higher to lower forms.

δ. **1876** *Whitby Gloss.*, *Hicker*, higher..'I want t'hicker yan o' them', the top one of the lot.

†b. Used in sense of *highest*. *Obs.*

1340 *Ayenb.* 122 Þri stages of uolke..huer-of þe on is heȝere, þe oþer men, þe þridde loȝest.

2. *spec.* Superior to the common or ordinary sort; passing or lying beyond the ordinary limits; as in ***the higher classes, the higher education of women, higher mathematics. higher criticism***: see CRITICISM 2 b. So ***higher critic***, one versed in higher criticism. ***Higher (School) Certificate***, an examination instituted in 1917 and replaced in 1951 by the Advanced level General Certificate of Education, taken by pupils of about 18. ***Higher Thought*** = NEW THOUGHT.

1836, etc. [see CRITICISM 2 b]. **1866** E. DAVIES (*title*) The higher education of women. **1868** *Rep. Sch. Inqu. Comm.* I. 115 in *Parl. Papers 1867–8* (C. 3966) XXVIII. 1, [Endowed] Schools have been regarded as the subjects of special trusts ..not as local contributions to the higher education of the country. **1877** *Encycl. Brit.* VII. 674/1 Every Jesuit college was divided into two parts, the one for higher the other for lower education. **1884** C. BIRD *Higher Educ. in Germany & England* i. 5 Few [*sc.* people] realise to what an extent we are surpassed by Germany..as regards the liberal provision made for higher education. **1896** *Spectator* 30 May 767/1 The great feature of the higher education should be a very well-marked revolt of the body against the mind. **1897** RENDEL HARRIS in *Contemp. Rev.* Sept. 342 He is a 'higher critic' occupied with the genesis of all Gospels out of their primitive deposit. **1909** CHESTERTON *Orthodoxy* v. 136 Of all conceivable forms of enlightenment the worst is..the Inner Light... Anyone who knows anyone from the Higher Thought Centre knows how it does work. **1909** H. G. WELLS *Ann Veronica* vi. 124 Jim is up to the neck in Mahatmas and Theosophy and Higher Thought and rot. **1918** *Univ. Cambridge Local Exam. Synd. Higher School Certificate Exam. List* 6 (*heading*) Exemption from the Previous examination by means of the higher school certificate examination. **1931** (*title*) Report of the Commission on Christian Higher Education in India. **1933** *Discovery* Sept. 271/2 He is best known for his researches on the Higher Thought Processes. **1945** *Guide Educ. Syst.* Gloss. 58 *Higher School certificate* (*higher certificate*), certificate awarded on results of the examination taken at about 18 by grammar school pupils. **1949** H. MCLENNAN *Cross-country* 169 So much for higher education in Canada. **1961** *Sunday Times* 26 Feb. 12/6 By 1970 there could be 140,000 children applying for the 70,000 places there will then be in higher education. **1963** BARNARD & LAUWERYS *Handbk. Brit. Educ. Terms* 106 The Higher School Certificate examination, which came into operation in 1917 and was conducted by certain university boards, was taken by pupils in grammar schools at about the age of 18. It was primarily intended to be a test of a two-years sixth form course of a somewhat specialised nature. **1968** *Listener* 6 June 723/1, I use the expression 'higher education' in the same sense as the Robbins Committee. Broadly, it covers courses for students of 18 and over which reach a standard above A-level in GCE and for which the normal entry qualifications are at least five O-level passes or the equivalent. Degree courses account for a big proportion of the field.

3. Phrases. **†a.** ***to have the higher hand***: to have the superiority; to gain the victory or mastery. **b.** ***with a higher hand***: see HIGH *a.* 17 b.

c **1250** *Gen. & Ex.* 3392 Israel Hadde heȝere hond. *c* **1386** CHAUCER *Prol.* 399 If þat he faught and hadde the hyer hond. *c* **1400** *Destr. Troy* 7075 That holly the herhond hade at his wille. **1563-87** FOXE *A. & M.* (1684) II. 425 It will shortly have the higher hand of all clouds. **1880** MRS. LYNN LINTON *Rebel of Fam.* ii, He..carried things with a higher hand than once she would have thought possible.

4. *Comb.*, forming comparatives to the combinations of HIGH *a.* (see HIGH *a.* IV).

1618 BOLTON *Florus* (1636) 307 Higher crested. **1876** GRANT *Burgh Sch. Scotl.* II. xiii. 348 *note*, On the rolls of the higher-class public schools. **1955** *Internat. Survey Programmes Social Devel.* (U.N.) 8 Training abroad on fellowships has made an important though necessarily limited contribution to the supply of higher-level technical and professional workers in some countries. **1958** B. ABEL-SMITH in N. Mackenzie *Conviction* 59 The middle classes.. participate with the higher income groups in special benefits from their employment. **1960** *Amer. Speech* XXXV. 230 English open internal juncture..is defined as the boundary point between two higher level phonological units (bounded sequences). **1962** CORSON & LORRAIN *Introd. Electromagn. Fields* i. 24 The sum of these four terms (neglecting higher-order differentials because we are interested in the limit S→—O) is equal to the right-hand side of Eq. *1–109*. **1964** CRYSTAL & QUIRK *Prosodic & Paralinguist. Features Eng.* iv. 52 One might set up the existence of higher-order patterns as a hypothesis. **1965** C. H. SPRINGER et al. *Adv. Methods & Models* iii. 76 We might as well finish the job by deriving formulas for these *higher-order* differences. **1967** *Computers & Automation* Feb. 30/1 The single most important tool is what has become known as a 'programming language', sometimes called a 'higher level language' (to distinguish it from the normal machine codes or assembly languages..). **1968** FOX & MAYERS *Computing Methods for Scientists & Engineers* iii. 32 It is..possible to start with a very accurate y_0 and use double or higher precision arithmetic, but this is lengthy.

5. quasi-*sb.* **a.** One higher; a superior, a better.

a **1225** *Ancr. R.* 198 Inobedience; þet is, þet child þet ne buhð nout his eldre..meiden, hire dame; euerich lowure his herre. **1840** MILL *Diss. & Disc.* (1875) I. 401 His reliance is upon reverence for a Higher above them.

†b. Superior position; the better (*of*). *Obs.*

a **1400-50** *Alexander* 2364 Alexander with his armee.. Has happend ȝit ai hedire-to þe herre [*v.r.* hyer] of his faes.

B. *adv.* **1.** The comparative of HIGH *adv.* in its various senses, q.v.

a. *c*900 tr. *Bæda's Hist.* III. vi. [viii.] (1890) 174 Heo wolden þone stan .. hear and ȝerisenlicor in þære ilcan stowe ȝesettan. *c*1350 *Will. Palerne* 529 Min hert is so hauteyn þat herre he wold. *c*1420 *Pallad. on Husb.* III. 445 Putte hit on ayein, And more a litel herre vppon hit wrote. ?*a*1500 *Chester Pl.* (E.E.T.S.) vii. 425 All heaven might not have gone har. 1589 R. ROBINSON *Gold. Mirr.* (Chetham Soc.) 48 How can Dame Fortune mount more harre?

β and *γ* *a*1300 *Cursor M.* 2232 A toure .. þat may reche heghur [*v.rr.* heier, heȝer] þan heuen. 1382 WYCLIF *Luke* xiv. 10 Frend, stiȝe hiȝere. 1398 TREVISA *Barth. De P.R.* III. xvii. (1495) 63 Suche foules fleen hyer in the ayre. 1508 DUNBAR *Tua Mariit Wemen* 160 With that sprang vp hir spreit be a span hecher. *a*1533 LD. BERNERS *Huon* lxxxiii. 262 Speke out hyer that ye may the better be herde. 1570 *Satir. Poems Reform.* xii. 128 Be Hanniballis, and heis ȝour hartis sum hear. 1715 LEONI *Palladio's Archit.* (1742) I. 84, I .. mention'd it a little higher. 1774 J. BRYANT *Mythol.* II. 93 Sesostris .. whose æra extends higher, than the Canon of Eusebius reaches. 1842 C. WHITEHEAD *R. Savage* (1845) II. ix. 298 He thought higher of human nature than he chose to acknowledge. 1860 TYNDALL *Glac.* I. xi. 74 Higher up the sky was violet.

2. *Comb.*, forming comparatives to the combinations of HIGH *adv.*

1598 GRENEWEY *Tacitus' Ann.* I. iv. 7 A higher aspiring mind. 1703 T. N. *City & C. Purchaser* 63 A Hall .. higher pitch'd. 1742 YOUNG *Nt. Th.* II. 54 Time higher aim'd, still nearer the great Mark. 1866 G. MACDONALD *Ann. Q. Neighb.* xxxiii. (1878) 586 She's higher-born than you. 1883 'MARK TWAIN' *Life on Mississippi* li. 502 Explosion followed explosion .. reports grew steadily sharper and higher-keyed. 1923 H. CRANE *Let.* 21 July (1965) 142 Being with the largest advertising agency in the world .. will get me higher-paid positions in other places after awhile. 1969 *Punch* 15 Jan. 91/3 Allied Breweries, the International Compressed Air Corporation or other proclaimed seekers of higher-educated manpower.

†**higher**, *sb.*[2] *Obs.* In 5 heyere. [f. HIGH *v.* + -ER[1].] One who raises or exalts.

1399 LANGL. *Rich. Redeles* II. 145 Þe hende Egle, þe heyere of hem all. *Ibid.* III. 74.

higher, *v. rare.* [f. prec. adj.: cf. *lower* vb.]

1. *trans.* To make higher, raise (*lit.* and *fig.*). The opposite of *to lower*.

*c*1715 in *N. & Q.* 7th Ser. (1889) VII. 57/2 The major .. desired him to higher all sails. 1831 *Blackw. Mag.* XXIX. 980 Our high opinion .. has not been lowered .. It has—pardon the expression—been highered. 1861 MAYHEW *Lond. Labour* III. 160 (Hoppe) When I highered the rope in my yard.

2. *intr.* To become higher, rise, mount, ascend.

1872 TENNYSON *Gareth* 20 To sweep In ever-highering eagle-circles up To the great Sun of Glory.

highermost ('haɪəməʊst), *a.* (*adv.*) *rare.* [f. HIGHER *a.* + -MOST: cf. *lowermost*, *uppermost*, *uttermost*, etc.] = HIGHEST.

1629 T. ADAMS *Shot* Wks. 245 The purest things are placed highermost. 1730 A. GORDON *Maffei's Amphith.* 315 Those highermost Rounds or Enclosures which appear no more. 1872 LONGF. *Div. Trag.* I. ii. 41 The bright triumphant host Of all the highermost Archangels.

higher-up. orig. *U.S.* [HIGH *a.* 5.] One occupying a superior position or post.

1911 *McClure's Mag.* Aug. 351 Resolved to get those dynamiters and to get the 'higher-ups', if there were any behind them. 1916 C. SANDBURG *Chicago Poems* 61 Higher-ups among the con men of Jerusalem. 1929 *Literary Digest* 12 Oct. 7/1 He is .. insists the New York Telegram—'only the henchman of higher-ups'. 1931 L. STEFFENS *Autobiogr.* II. x. 254 Other 'higher-ups' confessed. 1939 'G. ORWELL' *Coming Up for Air* II. viii. 145 The mysterious higher-ups who were running the war. 1953 K. TENNANT *Joyful Condemned* v. 47 She's in with all the higher-ups. 1960 H. L. LAWRENCE *Children of Light* iv. 63 Tell them the War Office is scared of a scandal and that the—er—higher-ups are willing to help them. 1970 K. GILES *Death in Church* ii. 38 The higher-ups were all chartered accountants from Krupps who did not like waste.

highest ('haɪɪst), *a.* (*sb.*) and *adv.* Forms: *α.* 1 **híehst, hýhst, héhst, hést, héahst,** 1–2 **híhst,** 2–3 **hehst,** 3 **heist, heest, hest, hæhst, hæxt, heixt,** 3–6 **hext,** 6 **hekst** (4 **hexist**). *β.* 1 **híȝest, héaȝest, -ost, héahest,** 2–4 **heiȝest,** 3 (*Orm.*) **heȝhesst, hehest,** 3–4 **heȝest, -ist,** 3–5 **heiest,** 4–5 **heghest, heyest,** 5 **heghist, heiȝest, heiast,** 5–6 *Sc.* **heast,** 6 **heighest,** *Sc.* **heychast, heest.** *γ.* 4–5 **hiȝest,** 4–6 **hiest, hyest,** (4–5 *Sc.* **hyeast**), 5 **hieghst,** 5–6 *Sc.* **hieast,** 6 **hyghest,** 6– **highest.** *δ.* 4–5 **heier(e)st, heirest,** 6 **hierest.** [OE. *híehst*, *hýhst*, *héhst*, and *héahst*, *héaȝost*, corresp. to OHG. *hôhist*, Goth. *hauhist-*, f. *hauh-*, OE. *héah* HIGH. From OE. *héhst*, *héahst*, by hardening of *h* before *s*, came ME. *hext* (like *next*), which survived to 16th c., but at length yielded to the disyllabic forms conformed to the positive, represented by OE. *héaȝest*, ME. *heȝest*, and mod. *highest*. The forms *heirest*, *hierest*, were formed on the comparative; cf. *nearest*, also *highermost*.]

A. *adj.* **1.** The superlative of HIGH *a.* in its various senses, q.v.

α. *c*825 *Vesp. Psalter* ix. 3[2] Ic .. singu noman ðinum ðu hehsta. *c*897 K. ÆLFRED *Gregory's Past.* xvi. 103 Ðeh ðe hi selfe wilnien ðæs heahstan. *c*950 *Lindisf. Gosp.* Matt. xxiii. 11 Se ðe heist is. —— Mark v. 7 Sunu godes ðæs heista [*Rushw.* hesta]. *a*1000 *Guthlac* 16 Se hyhsta ealra cyninga cyning. *c*1000 in *Narrat. Angl. Conscr.* (1861) 37 Seo is ealra duna mæst and hiȝest. *a*1050 *O.E. Chron.* (Parker MS.) an. 1031 Whenne þæt flod byþ ealra hehst. *a*1121 *Ibid.* (Laud MS.) an. 1101 Þis þa mid aðe ȝefestnodan .xii. þa hihste of æȝðre healfe. *c*1205 LAY. 2325 Þa hehste of þan hirde. *Ibid.* 13240 Þe hæhste mon of Brutlond. *Ibid.* 24587 Hæxt cniht on londe. *a*1225 *Juliana* 63 In to þe heste heouene. *a*1225 *Ancr. R.* 140 Wel neih heixt þinc wiðouten God one. *c*1230 *Hali Meid.* 41 Fram þe hehste heuene in to helle grunde. *c*1290 *Beket* 1314 in *S. Eng. Leg.* I. 144 Þe hexte of þe londe. *c*1305 *St. Christopher* 10 in *E.E.P.* (1862) 60 Þe hexiste þat an vrþe was. *c*1460 J. RUSSELL *Bk. Nurture* 32 When bale is hext þan bote is next. 1589 R. ROBINSON *Gold. Mirr.* (Chetham Soc.) 47 When raging floods of surging seas be hext .. The present fall, by Nature is the next.

β. *c*1000 *Ags. Ps.* (Th.) cxvii[i]. 21 [22] Se ȝeworden is hwommona heaȝost. *c*1200 *Vices & Virtues* 35 Karitas is heiȝest and betst of ðese þrie. *c*1200 *Trin. Coll. Hom.* 197 Mannes heued is heȝest lime. *c*1200 ORMIN 2146, I stall þær heȝhesst iss inn heoffne. *a*1225 *Juliana* 69 Wið heheste steuene. *a*1300 *Cursor M.* 1837 Þe heiest fell [*v.rr.* heyest, heȝest]. *c*1350 *Will. Palerne* 2907 Vp to þe heiȝest tour. *c*1380 WYCLIF *Serm.* Sel. Wks. I. 138 Þe heieste proprete. *c*1440 *Gesta Rom.* xci. 419 (Add. MS.) She is heghiste of all Criatures. *c*1470 HENRY *Wallace* VI. 588 He had the heast stait. 1530 LYNDESAY *Test. Papyngo* 164 On the heychast lytill tender twyste. 1553 GAU *Richt Vay* 39 The sone of the heest God.

γ. 13.. *Cursor M.* 10592 Sco was won to þe heist [*v.r.* hiest] stride. *c*1430 *Hymns Virg.* 92 This noon hete of þe someris day, Whanne þe sunne moost hiȝest is. 1559 *Mirr. Mag., Salisbury* xxxvi, Whan helth and welth is hyest. 1634 PEACHAM *Gentl. Exerc.* xxiii. 80 You must deepen your colours so that the Orpiment may be the highest. 1736 BUTLER *Anal.* II. vi. 309 Doubtful, in the highest supposable degree. 1818 SCOTT *Hrt. Midl.* xviii, Screaming at the highest pitch of her cracked and mistuned voice. 1860 TYNDALL *Glac.* I. xviii. 128 The highest point of the mountain. 1871 FREEMAN *Norm. Conq.* IV. xvii. 70 The results of this change have been of the highest moment.

δ. *c*1380 WYCLIF *Sel. Wks.* II. 265 (Bodley MS. 788) Preching and oþer speche is þe heirest dede of man, whan þat it is wel done. *Ibid.* II. 365 But whan he is heirest, as smoke þan he shal vanishe awey. *Ibid.* III. 341 Heierste viker of Crist. *Ibid.* II. 231, 281, etc. 1569 SIR T. HAWKINS in *Sir R. Hawkins' Voy.* (1878) 74 In the hierest place.

2. With agent-nouns: see HIGH *a.* 21 b.

1702 [see BIDDER 4]. 1706 ESTCOURT *Fair Examp.* I. 10 You may keep company with the highest Flyer of 'em all. 1717 tr. *Frezier's Voy.* 109 Sold to the highest Bidder.

B. *absol.* or as *sb.*

1. *absol.* ***the Highest*** (in some Bible versions, ***the Most Highest***): the Supreme Being, God.

*c*825 *Vesp. Psalter* xlv[i]. 7 [6] Salde stefne his se hesta. *c*900 tr. *Bæda's Hist.* IV. iii. (1891) 268 Se hehsta seleð his stefne. 971 *Blickl. Hom.* 7 Þæs Hehstan mægen þe ymbscineþ. *a*1340 HAMPOLE *Psalter* xvii. 15 Þe heghest gaf his voice. 1535 COVERDALE *Ps.* lxxii[i]. 11 Is there knowlege in the most hyest? —— *2 Esdras* vii. 62, I knowe Lorde, that the Hyest is mercyfull. *a*1628 SIR J. BEAUMONT *Epiphany* in Farr *S.P. Jas. I* (1848) 143 Since vnder this low roofe the Highest lay. 18.. WHITTIER *Ezekiel* iv, In sudden whirlwind .. The Spirit of the Highest came.

†**2.** The highest part, top, summit. (In quot. 1484, the deepest or innermost part, depth.) *Obs.*

1484 CAXTON *Fables of Æsop* III. i, He retorned ageyn in to the hyest of the woode. 1523 LD. BERNERS *Froiss.* I. lv. 76 He come to the hyest of the hyll. 1563 SHUTE *Archit.* D j b, Deuide the hanging line from the highest of the Abacus. 1634 SIR T. HERBERT *Trav.* 59 At the highest of this Palace, is cut .. the Images of a King.

3. Highest position or pitch: usually with *at*.

*a*1225 *St. Marher.* 14 From þe heste in heouene to þe laheste in helle. 1526 *Pilgr. Perf.* (W. de W. 1531) 73 b, Whan the sonne is in the hyest. 1577 B. GOOGE *Heresbach's Husb.* II. (1586) 59 After the Sunne hath beene at the highest. 1688 S. PENTON *Guardian's Instr.* A vj b, At this time, when Writing, both as to Substance .. and Ornament of Language, is at highest.

4. That which is highest (in *fig.* sense).

1861 TENNYSON *Guinevere* 654 We needs must love the highest when we see it. 1867 FROUDE *Short Stud.* (1876) I. 116 Such a man .. is decent and respectable, but the highest is not in him, and the highest will not come out of him.

b. ***in the highest***, in Biblical use, transl. L. *in excelsis*, Gr. ἐν ὑψίστοις = in the loftiest places, in the heavens; but in mod. use sometimes taken to mean 'in the highest degree'.

1526 TINDALE *Matt.* xxi. 9 Hosianna in the hyest. 1582 N. T. (Rhem.) *Luke* ii. 14 Glorie in the highest to God [WYCL., in the hiȝist thingis; TIND., an hye; CRANM., on hye; *Genev.* in the hye heauens]. 1611 BIBLE *ibid.*, Glory to God in the highest. 1897 *Sat. Rev.* 12 June 651/2 To praise in the highest 'The Cloister and the Hearth' is to echo Sir Walter Besant.

C. *adv.* **1.** The superlative of HIGH *adv.* in its various senses, q.v.

*c*1000 *Menologium* 110 On þam gim astihð on heofenas up hyhst. *a*1300 *Cursor M.* 439 He .. sette him heist [*v.r.* heyest] in his hall. *c*1375 *Sc. Leg. Saints, Johannes* 495 Þocht þe eyrne fle heyeste. *c*1400 *Rom. Rose* 4363 She canne .. whirle adown, and overturne Who sittith hieghst. 1530 PALSGR. Introd. 16 The frenche men judgyng a worde to be most parfaytly herde, whan his last end is sounded hyghest, use generally to gyve theyr accent upon the last syllable onely. 1570 *Satir. Poems Reform.* xxii. 46 Quha heichest clymmis the soner may thay slyde. 1657 R. LIGON *Barbadoes* (1673) 6 Trying which of them can leap highest. 1727 SWIFT *Gulliver* III. iii, The king when he is highest provoked. 1849 MACAULAY *Hist. Eng.* x. II. 645 At the very moment at which their disputes ran highest.

2. *Comb.*, forming superlatives to combinations of HIGH *adv.*

(Now usually expressed by *most*, as 'most high-sounding'.)

1588 SHAKS. *Tit. A.* II. i. 8 And ouer-lookes the highest piering hills.

highfalutin, -ing (haɪfə'luːtɪn), *sb.* and *a.* orig. *U.S. slang.* Also **-ten, hifalutin.** [f. HIGH *a.*: the origin of the second element is unknown; it was perh. a whimsical pronunciation of *fluting*, or a grandiose equivalent of *flying* or *flown*.]

A. *sb.* Absurdly pompous speech or writing; bombast.

1848 L. COOMBS *Sp. in New York* 29 Sept. (Bartlett), A regular built fourth-of-July .. Jefferson speech, making gestures to suit the highfalutens. 1864 LOWELL *Rebellion* Prose Wks. 1890 V. 133 It is a curious jumble of American sense and Southern highfaluting. 1885 *Century Mag.* Jan. 347/2 Nothing like short meter for taking the hifalutin out of stuff. 1889 *Times* 13 Apr. 11/2 'The misery of the Irish people' .. is merely a bit of high falutin.

B. *adj.* Absurdly pompous or bombastic in style.

1839 *Spirit of Times* 18 May 123/3 Them high-faluting chaps. 1857 T. H. GLADSTONE *Kansas* 43 (Bartlett) No highfaluten airs here, you know. 1862 B. TAYLOR *Home & Abr.* Ser. II. 396 Those who endeavour to be sublime are often simply highfalutin. 1870 LOWELL *Study Wind.* 36 A good human bit of writing .. not so highfaluting (let me dare the odious word!) as the modern style. 1941 *Coast to Coast 1941* 49 And then hear some announcer in his highfalutin voice, telling her summer was coming. 1948 *Manch. Guardian Weekly* 30 Sept. 9 When all the highfalutin and magical jargon of diplomacy is removed, you'll find the diplomats like a group of children aged about three or four. 1962 *New Statesman* 2 Mar. 308/2 This is .. a pleasing unsententious compilation, not really a lecture at all. Sir Compton is never highfalutin.

Hence **highfaluti'nation**, writing or speaking in a highfalutin style.

1894 HOLE *More Mem.* 178 Don't think me bumptious or given to hifalutination.

high fi'delity. [f. HIGH *a.* + FIDELITY 2 c.] In equipment used in the recording and reproduction of sound, the property of producing little distortion in the signal, so that the sound produced bears as close a resemblance as possible to the original. Also applied to the recording of electrical signals generally (quots. 1938, 1957). Also *attrib.* or as *adj.* So ***higher fidelity***. Cf. HI-FI.

1934 *Electronics* July 223/2 If the term 'high-fidelity' is to mean anything the predicated performance should be kept at a reasonably high level. 1934 *Wireless World* 19 Oct. 318/2 With the introduction of the 'high fidelity' receiver the broadcasters, who have repeatedly criticised the manufacturers for low-quality receivers which cut off the extreme notes, now make the admission that improvement is necessary in their own transmitters. 1937 *Time* 8 Mar. 62/1 (Advt.), Victor records: higher fidelity. 1938 *Jrnl. R. Aeronaut. Soc.* XLII. 1049 Present-day high fidelity 441-line television demands modulation frequencies as high as 4 megacycles. 1940 *Chambers's Techn. Dict.* 415/2 *High-fidelity*, an inexact term generally meaning sound reproduction of a superior, but undefined, quality. 1946 *Electronic Engin.* XVIII. 54 It has not been possible up to the present to obtain full advantage of the high fidelity of the moving coil pick-up. 1955 PRIESTLEY & HAWKES *Journey down Rainbow* 27 There was talk; there were high-fidelity records. 1957 *Times* 7 Oct. 8/3 The power of the transmitters guarantees high fidelity reception of the wireless signals. 1958 *Times* 17 May 9/5 This search for the elusive 'high fidelity' is pursued with an avidity only limited by the depth of his pocket. 1972 *Sci. Amer.* Sept. 100/3 If one wishes to transmit music with high fidelity, the required bandwidth is 15,000 hertz.

'**high-flown**, *a.* [f. HIGH *adv.* + FLOWN *pa. pple.* of FLY *v.*]

†**1.** Soaring high; carrying things to a high pitch; elevated; elated. In quot. *a*1656, Intoxicated, 'elevated'. *Obs.*

1647 N. BACON *Disc. Govt. Eng.* I. lii. (1739) 93 As yet oppression was not so high-flown. *a*1656 USSHER *Ann.* vi. (1658) 112 The king, being somewhat high flowen with drink. *a*1668 DENHAM *Prudence* 42 Nor high-flown hopes to Reason's lure descend. 1702 STEELE *Funeral* II. i. 35 We .. have nothing at all, of all this High-Flown Fury. 1842 C. BRONTE in Mrs. Gaskell *Life* xi. (1857) I. 257 In a high-flown humour, he forbade me to use either dictionary or grammar.

2. Of sentiments, language, style, etc.: Extravagant, hyperbolical; bombastic.

1665 SIR T. HERBERT *Trav.* (1677) 324 In his high-flown conceits. 1672–5 COMBER *Comp. Temple* (1702) 38 He is .. noted for his high flown style. 1781 GIBBON *Decl. & F.* III. 77 Such are the high-flown expressions of Prudentius. 1874 L. STEPHEN *Hours in Library* (1892) II. v. 156 Sentiments, which are occasionally too high-flown and overstrained. 1888 BRYCE *Amer. Commw.* I. xiv. 192 A piece of elaborate and highflown declamation.

†**3.** Of persons: Extreme in opinion or party feeling, esp. in support of claims of authority in church or state. Cf. HIGH-FLYER 3. *Obs.*

1672 WOOD *Life* (O.H.S.) I. 146 He was a high-flone Cavalier. 1681 LUTTRELL *Brief Rel.* (1857) I. 124 The former [party] are called by the latter, tories, tantivies .. high flown church-men, &c. 1705 HICKERINGILL *Priest-cr.* II. viii. 86 You see, old Highflown Beau! of whom they learnt.

'**high-flyer, -flier.** [f. HIGH *adv.* + FLYER.]

1. a. *lit.* One who or that which flies high, as a person, a bird, a balloon, or the like; also, a swing set in a frame.

1589 R. HARVEY *Pl. Perc.* (1590) 15 Men haue great desire to be compted high fliers and deepe swimmers. 1698 W. CHILCOT *Evil Thoughts* vi. (1851) 61 These highflyers, when they are in their altitudes, suddenly their waxen wings melt,

and down they fall headlong. **1855** BROWNING *Grammar. Funeral* 135 All ye highfliers of the feathered race, Swallows and curlews! **1886** T. HARDY *Mayor of Casterbr.* iii, Improvements..in the roundabouts and highfliers.

b. Popular name of the Purple Emperor butterfly, and of the genus *Ypsipetes* of moths.

1773 WILKES *Eng. Moths & Butterfl.* pl. 120 The Purple Highflier, or Emperor of the Woods. **1869** E. NEWMAN *Brit. Butterfl. & Moths* 152 Ruddy Highflyer. *Ibid.* 153 May Highflyer..July Highflyer.

c. A variety of walnut.

1822 *Trans. Lond. Hort. Soc.* IV. 517 The Highflyer Walnut. **1824** LOUDON *Encycl. Gardening* 742 Walnut... Highflyer of Thetford, the best variety known. **1866** LINDLEY & MOORE *Treas. Bot.* 640/2 A variety called the Highflyer Walnut, is considered the best English variety. **1880** *Encycl. Brit.* XII. 278/1.

2. One who soars high in his aims, ambitions, notions, etc.

1663 PEPYS *Diary* 27 May, He..would have me..to look him out a widow..A woman sober, and no high-flyer, as he calls it. **1694** CROWNE *Married Beau* II. Dram. Wks. 1874 IV. 278 Oh! pshaw, our hearts are seldom such high flyers. **1858** R. S. SURTEES *Ask Mamma* i. 1 He had all the airy dreaminess of an hereditary highflyer.

3. One who has lofty or 'high-flown' notions on some question of polity, esp. ecclesiastical. *spec.* **a.** In late 17th and early 18th c., One who made or supported lofty claims on behalf of the authority of the Church; a High-Churchman; a Tory. Cf. HIGH-FLOWN 3, HIGH-FLYING *a.* 3. **b.** In Scotland in end of 18th and beginning of 19th c., An Evangelical, as opposed to a Moderate.

1680 *Hon. Cavalier* 9 The honest Divines of the Church of England who for their Conscience and Obedience are Branded for High-flyers. **1699** H. CHANDLER *Effort agst. Bigotry* (1709) 19 The High-Flyers..talk and act as if they thought the Kingdom of God was nothing else but Circumstance and Ceremony. **1718** *Entertainer* A iij b, I am afraid St. Peter and St. Paul will scarce escape being censured for Tories and High-Flyers. **1730** SWIFT *Vind. Ld. Carteret* Wks. 1841 II. 113/1, I am told that she openly professes herself to be a highflyer. **1803** T. JEFFERSON *Writ.* (Ford) VIII. 222 A schism was taking place in Pennsylvania between the moderates and high-flyers. **1814** D'ISRAELI *Quarrels Auth.* (1867) 395 From a sullen sectarian [he] turned a flaming highflyer for the 'supreme dominion' of the Church. **1830** *Westm. Rev.* XIII. 78 The serious effusions of the clerical high-flyers. **1856** MASSON *Edinb. Sk.* (1892) 172 The small minority of Evangelicals, or 'High-fliers', as they were called, corresponded to the proscribed 'Liberals' in secular politics. **1897** *Q. Rev.* Oct. 486 When he [Sir W. Scott] wrote, the fierce ecclesiastical conflict between Moderates and 'high flyers' was still raging.

†**4.** A fast stage-coach. *Obs.*

1818 SCOTT *Hrt. Midl.* i, Mail-coach races against mail-coach, and high-flier against high-flier, through the most remote districts of Britain. **1868** DICKENS *Uncomm. Trav.* xxii. (Farmer), The old room on the ground floor where the passengers of the High-flyers used to dine.

5. *slang.* **a.** A pretentious or fashionable strumpet; a 'swell' beggar, one of the 'swell mob'; a begging-letter writer. †**b.** A frequenter of the gallery of a theatre (*obs.*). †**c.** An exaggerated statement; a 'cram' (*obs.*).

a **1700** B. E. *Dict. Cant. Crew, High Flyers*, Impudent, Forward, Loose, Light Women; also bold Adventurers. **1719** D'URFEY *Pills* V. 349 Bench-hoppers, High-Flyers, Pit-Plyers, be still. **1776** G. J. PRATT *Pupil of Pleas.* I. 168 If your Honour had heard the high-fliers he crammed my poor head with, all the while we were at it—the soft things he said [etc.]. **1821** EGAN *Tom & Jerry* v. (Farmer), As you have your high-flyers at Almack's. **1851** MAYHEW *Lond. Labour* I. 250 Pursuing the course of a 'high-flyer' (genteel beggar). **1859** *Autobiog. Beggar Boy* 17 The highflyer turns up his genteel proboscis at the common cadger.

d. = FLYER 5 b.

1961 in WEBSTER. **1964** *Economist* 22 Feb. 722/1 Stocks, variously called 'glamour' issues or 'high flyers'. **1969** *Daily Tel.* 8 Feb. 6/4 The other fund may have been lucky—or clever—enough to have a number of real 'high-fliers' in its portfolio and so has had to do comparatively little switching to achieve its 100 p.c. growth. **1969** *Times* 16 July 22/4 Another of last year's high flyers came unstuck yesterday when Qualitex Yarns revealed that it had missed its forecast.

high-flying, *sb.*

1. *lit.* Flying to a great height; lofty flight.

1653 H. COGAN tr. *Pinto's Trav.* xlv. 176 In the high flying of Falcons and Vultures.

2. Aiming high; lofty pretension.

1681 DRYDEN *Epil. to Lee's P'cess Cleves* 6 Never was man worse thought on for high-flying.

3. The principles of high-flyers (sense 3).

1730 SWIFT *Vind. Ld. Carteret* Wks. 1841 II. 115/1 To read pamphlets against religion and high-flying.

'high-flying, *a.*

1. *lit.* That flies high, as a bird.

1622 MABBE tr. *Aleman's Guzman d'Alf.* II. 39 Who wing their thoughts with such high-flying feathers. **1810** WORDSW. *Sonn.*, *'A Roman Master'*, Birds, high-flying in the element.

†**b.** *transf.* Swift. (Cf. HIGH-FLYER 4.) *Obs.*

c **1710** *Banbury Apes* (ed. 3) 3 A Messenger (on a High-flying Sorrel Horse).

2. Soaring high in notions, aims, ambitions, etc.

1581 SIDNEY *Apol. Poetrie* (Arb.) 23 That high flying liberty of conceit proper to the Poet. *a* **1649** DRUMM. OF HAWTH. *Hist. Jas. V*, Wks. (1711) 82 A man in the prime of his youth, of high-flying thoughts by his alliance with the king of England. **1692** tr. *Sallust* 245 With their lofty strains and high flying Language. **1793** BEDDOES *Calculus* p. vi, My hopes of the future improvement of medicine too high-flying. **1878** SPURGEON *Serm.* XXIV. 629 Little duties are almost too insignificant for such high-flying spiritual professors.

3. Making or upholding lofty claims for authority in church or state; holding the principles of the HIGH-FLYERS.

1695 *Enq. Anc. Const. Eng.* 32 Some high-flying Gentlemen, who if they could would make us all slaves to the King's absolute will. **1709** *Refl. Sacheverell's Serm.* 24 The High-flying Faction may call themselves Churchmen as long as they please. **1751** CARLYLE in Ramsay *Remin.* iii. (1870) 64 Webster, leader of the high-flying party. **1772** H. WALPOLE *Last Jrnls.* (1859) I. 40 Not indeed that high-flying Church under Bancroft and Laud, but the mild Church under Tillotson. **1792** T. JEFFERSON *Writ.* (1830) IV. 463 Gouverneur Morris, a high-flying monarchy man. **1897** A. BIRRELL in *Indep. & Nonconf.* Jubilee No., A great mortification to the high-flying Anglican who cannot bring himself to believe that there can be two Churches within the same realm at one and the same time.

b. Extreme; making high claims for something.

1876 DARWIN in *Life & Lett.* (1887) III. 186 How horrified some high-flying æsthetic men will be.

high 'frequency. [f. HIGH *a.* + FREQUENCY 4.]

1. a. A frequency (see FREQUENCY 4 b) having a relatively large number of cycles in a second. Applied esp. to an electric current or voltage, an electromagnetic wave or a sound wave. Abbrev. H.F., esp. in radio and telecommunications, where it also refers specifically to electromagnetic waves of 3–30 MHz. Often *attrib.*

1893 [see FREQUENCY 4 b]. **1923** *Nature* 7 July 12/2 The vibrations are of frequency 200,000 per second, such as are commonly used in wireless telegraphy and telephony. Such high frequencies are neither seen nor heard, but can be detected by special methods. **1934** S. G. B. STUBBS *Electr. Encycl.* II. 612/2 *High frequency* (*H.F.*), refers to alternating currents, the frequency of which is reckoned in thousands. There is no definite line of demarcation between high and low frequency, but in general an alternating current is reckoned as of high frequency when the number of periods is greater than 10,000 per second. **1960** H. CARTER *Dict. Electronics* 127 *High frequency.* (1) A general term used to distinguish signals of radio frequency from those of audio frequency. (2) A relative term used to describe frequencies at the upper end of a particular frequency band. (3) Term of specific application to radio waves in the frequency range between 3 and 30 Mc/s, i.e. of wavelengths from 100 m down to 10 m. **1962** A. NISBETT *Technique Sound Studio* iii. 79 High frequencies can be lost in a variety of ways. **1962** M. G. SAY *Newnes' Conc. Encycl. Electr. Engin.* 360/1 Fig. 1 (*b*) and (*c*) show that at high frequencies above 1,000 c/s there is an increasing tendency for the current to flow in a shallow surface layer of the conductor.

b. *transf.* A high rate of occurrence, in space or in time.

1935 HUXLEY & HADDON *We Europeans* ix. 267 Our picture of the human species will be like a contour-map, a region of high frequency for, say, round-headedness being separated from another similar peak by a 'valley' of low frequency. **1971** *Sci. Amer.* Oct. 21/1 A high frequency of kwashiorkor is now being found among the East Pakistan refugees in India.

2. *attrib.* (usu. with hyphen). **a.** In sense 1 a, implying an applicability to an oscillation with a high frequency, as ***high-frequency formula***, or an action or manner of working that involves such an oscillation.

1892 HEAVISIDE *Electr. Papers* II. 279 The high-frequency formulae are not so generally applicable as in the case of cores. **1893** *Jrnl. Soc. Arts* 5 May 624/1 The phosphorescent glow of the novel high-frequency, high-voltage, high-vacuum lamps. **1902** *Proc. R. Soc.* LXX. 341 The special manner in which a core or rod of iron or steel placed in a varying magnetic field is affected by high-frequency oscillations transmitted from considerable distances. **1903** *Daily Chron.* 14 Nov. 5/2 High-frequency apparatus and superb laboratories are beside the point compared with air and light. **1914** R. STANLEY *Text-bk. Wireless Telegr.* xii. 149 Do high and low frequency waves travel at the same speed? **1921** *Jrnl. Industrial & Engin. Chem.* July 639/2 High frequency voltage (10,000 to 20,000 cycles) is applied at the terminals of the coil. **1928** *Nature* 21 Apr. 623/1 High frequency sound waves of low intensity passed through these cells cause the protoplasm to rotate. **1955** F. E. TERMAN *Electronic Radio Engin.* (ed. 4) xxiv. 937 These requirements are usually more difficult to meet at the high-frequency end of the modulation range. **1960** R. W. MARKS *Dymaxion World of B. Fuller* 23/1 The high-frequency hiss of the surf. **1962** A. NISBETT *Technique Sound Studio* iv. 80 Another example of high-frequency attenuation will occur in recording if the tape is in imperfect contact with the head. *Ibid.*, Where the high frequency losses are progressive, measures may be taken to equalize for them. *Ibid.* 81 For a recording head the effect of high-frequency bias is to narrow the effective gap width.

b. In sense 1 b, meaning 'occurring often or involving a rapid succession of events'.

1957 D. L. BOLINGER in *Publ. Amer. Dialect Soc.* XXVIII. 89 Contrast the high-frequency *suppose* with the lower-frequency *suspect.* **1965** *English Studies* Feb. 75 It is hard to judge of the size of the corpus..but it seems to be adequate at least for high-frequency items.

3. *Comb.*, as ***high-frequency amplifier, choke, cinematography, condenser microphone, current, photography, response, transformer***; **high-frequency alternator**, any of several kinds of alternator designed to give an alternating current with a frequency greater than about 10 kHz; **high-frequency amplification**, the amplification of signals of high frequency; in *Radio* applied *spec.* to amplification at the carrier frequency in a radio receiver; **high-frequency heating**, the heating of a substance by placing it in an alternating electric field (dielectric heating) or magnetic field (induction heating) with a frequency above that of the mains electricity supply; **high-frequency induction furnace** (see quot. 1958); **high-frequency resistance**, (*a*) the increased electrical resistance of a conductor at high frequencies, owing to the *skin effect*; (*b*) a resistance for use at high frequencies; **high-frequency treatment**, (*a*) *Med.* (see quot. 1931); (*b*) *Metallurgy*, the hardening of metals by heating them inductively and quenching.

1901 *Proc. R. Soc.* LXVIII. 514 (*heading*) The *high frequency alternator. **1935** J. B. MOORE in K. Henney *Radio Engin. Handbk.* (ed. 2) 564 The high-frequency alternator is one of the most used types of transmitter for long-wave transoceanic code communication. **1919** *Wireless World* Nov. 448 An eight valve amplifier, comprising five stages of *high-frequency amplification, one stage of rectification, and two stages of audio-frequency amplification with transformer coupling. **1934** S. O. PEARSON in S. G. B. Stubbs *Electr. Encycl.* II. 612/1 The magnification of electrical variations at the signal—or radio—frequency of the received oscillations, that is, before they are applied to the detector of a wireless receiver, is termed high-frequency amplification. **1919** *Wireless World* Feb. 628 (*heading*) The use of impedance, capacity and resistance couplings in *high-frequency amplifiers. **1928** *High frequency choke [see CHOKE 6]. **1958** *Van Nostrand's Sci. Encycl.* (ed. 3) 812/1 High-frequency photography includes both still and motion-picture photography... In *high-frequency (slow-motion) cinematography the exposing rate may range from 32 to several thousand frames per sec. **1940** *Chambers's Techn. Dict.* 188/1 **High-frequency condenser microphone*, a condenser microphone in which the polarising voltage is alternating at a high radio-frequency, amplitude modulation of which is detected by a de-modulator and used for audio-frequency transmission. **1896** *McClure's Mag.* VI. 414/2 A *high frequency current. **1923** E. W. MARCHANT *Radio Telegr.* ii. 13 When we come to deal with the high-frequency currents that are employed in Radio, their behaviour is quite different. **1925** *Jrnl. Iron & Steel Inst.* CXII. 73 *High-frequency heating may be found useful in the forging and heat treatment of steel. **1967** A. K. OSBORNE *Encycl. Iron & Steel Ind.* (ed. 2) 218/1 The polarity of this field changes many times per second with the alternation of the current necessary for high frequency heating. **1920** *Trans. Amer. Electrochem. Soc.* XXXV. 158 Since the presentation of the above paper a development into commercial form of *high-frequency induction furnaces of the oscillatory current type has been actively continued. **1958** A. D. MERRIMAN *Dict. Metallurgy* 125/1 A high-frequency induction furnace is a melting furnace in which currents at a frequency above 500 c./sec. are used to induce eddy currents in the charge, which in turn generate heat in the material. **1958** *Van Nostrand's Sci. Encycl.* (ed. 3) 813/1 High-frequency photography which consists of a number of high-speed photographs made in rapid succession. **1892** HEAVISIDE *Electr. Papers* II. 193 The *high-frequency resistance is independent of the steady resistance, and must be much greater than it. **1951** A. HUND *High-Frequency Measurements* (ed. 2) ii. 96 Any amplitude differences are balanced out by properly chosen high-frequency resistances. *Ibid.* ix. 310 In *all* cases, the high-frequency resistance is that quantity which, when multiplied by the square of the effective value of the high-frequency current, gives the energy dissipated in the conductor. **1930** *Wireless World* 17 Dec. 686/2 (*heading*) *High frequency response. **1923** E. W. MARCHANT *Radio Telegr.* iv. 56 This change in voltage may be passed on..by means of a small *high-frequency transformer, to the grid of a second valve. **1931** S. R. ROGET *Dict. Electr. Terms* (ed. 2) 146/2 **High frequency treatment*, curative treatment involving the use of interrupted trains of damped high frequency oscillations. **1967** A. K. OSBORNE *Encycl. Iron & Steel Industry* (ed. 2) 202/2 High-frequency treatment.

†**'highful,** *a. Obs.* In 3 hey-, heiuol, heiȝful. [f. ME. *heȝ* HIGH + -FUL.] High; *fig.* haughty, proud.

1297 R. GLOUC. (Rolls) 4011 Þis wus a prout mandement & an heiuol dede. *Ibid.* 7729 Sturne he was þoru out al, & heiuol & prout.

high gate, 'high-gate. Now chiefly *Sc.* [See GATE *sb.*²] = HIGHWAY, HIGH STREET. Hence frequent in street- and place-names, esp. in the North.

c **1340** *Cursor M.* 16166 (Trin.) To heroudes þo he him sent: euen þe heȝe gate. **1375** BARBOUR *Bruce* VIII. 164 And saw the hye-gat lyand wass Apon a fair feld evin and dry. *c* **1489** CAXTON *Sonnes of Aymon* xxii. 486 Reynawde, that was vpon the hyghe gate of Ardeyn. **1533** BELLENDEN *Livy* v. (1822) 457 Than fled the hie gate to Rome. **1629** T. ADAMS *Soldier's Honour* Wks. (1630) 1084 Then should many worthy spirits get vp the High-gate of preferment. **1721** KELLY *Scot. Prov.* 273 (Jam.) Out the high-gate is ay fair play.

Highgate ('haɪgɪt). The name of a hill in London, used *attrib.* in ***Highgate resin***, a mineral resin similar to copal found in Highgate Hill. Also called *copalin(e), copalite, fossil copal.*

1813 T. THOMSON in *Ann. Philos.* II. 9 The colour of Highgate resin is of a dirty yellowish light brown. **1815** A. AIKIN *Man. Min.* (ed. 2) 64 Fossil Copal. Highgate Resin. Colour light yellowish dirty brown. **1839** *Phil. Mag.* XIV. 91 The Highgate resin has much resemblance to copal. **1898** E. S. DANA *Textbk. Min.* (rev. ed.) IV. 543 Copalite, or Highgate resin, is from the London blue clay. **1968** *Encycl. Brit.* VI. 462/2 *Copalite*.., also termed 'fossil resin' and

'Highgate resin', a naturally occurring organic substance found as irregular pieces of pale-yellow colour in the London clay at Highgate hill.

'high-grade, *a.* and *sb.* [HIGH *a.* 22 a.]

A. *adj.* Of a high grade or quality; *spec.*

a. (See quot. 1909.) **b.** Denoting ores rich in metal value; *spec.* in commercial use denoting those which, owing to convenience in situation and transport facilities, can be worked at a large profit.

1878 R. J. HINTON *Handbk. Arizona* 161 The Metallic Accident is a large lode of low-grade ore, with a number of high-grade feeders. **1880** 'MARK TWAIN' *Tramp Abroad* I. xxiv. 230 Only the few are educated up to a point where high-grade music gives pleasure. **1890** *Spectator* 7 June 787 Two or three high-grade schools. **1902** *Daily Chron.* 10 Apr. 7/2 Great Britain is becoming very short of high-grade ores. **1907** *Springfield Republ.* 13 May 3 (Advt.), Auction sale of high grade household furniture. **1909** *Cent. Dict.* Suppl., *High-grade*,.. specifically, having more than three quarters pure blood: applied by stockbreeders to animals. **1910** *Westm. Gaz.* 4 Jan. 5/2 The high-grade nature of the material and workmanship. **1919** *Empire Rev.* 79 Its products are high-grade steels. **1929** *Daily Express* 7 Nov. 8/4 The high-grade private car. **1932** *Discovery* Nov. 357/2 The institute conducts genetical studies leading to the breeding and selection of high-grade wheats. **1939** R. R. SNAPP *Beef Cattle* (ed. 3) xviii. 252 Their color indicates that they are high grade and purebred individuals of strictly beef type. **1940** *War Illustr.* 12 Apr. 360 A view of a Nazi petrol-substitute refinery where the raw material is converted into high-grade spirit suitable for use in the specially designed aeroplane engines. **1946** *Mind* LV. 114 Some human being in his right mind, that is to say, a human agent capable of relatively high-grade action. **1958** *Times Lit. Suppl.* 23 May 279/4 But, unlike other fellow-travellers, he was actually engaged in high-grade espionage.

B. *sb.* **a.** High-grade stock. **b.** (See quot. 1904 and cf. the vb.)

1882 *Rep. Maine Board Agric.* XXVI. 253 High-grades of either breed [Jersey or Guernsey]. **1904** *N.Y. Sun* 14 Aug. 11 One of the pests of gold mining in Colorado is the high grades, which is a polite term for the ore thief. The term high grades comes from the fact that they steal only high grade ore.

Hence **'high-grade** *v. intr.* and *trans.*, to steal high-grade ore.

1907 *Westm. Gaz.* 6 June 10/1, I had been 'high grading' in the Vindicator mine. **1923** 'B. M. BOWER' *Parowan Bonanza* vi. 73 He.. could not leave his claims and let Al Freeman.. 'high grade' his gold the minute his back was turned. **1927** *Blackw. Mag.* June 833/1 In Cobalt.. 'high-grading' was rigorously dealt with. **1963** *Time* (Canad. ed.) 18 Jan. 10/2 Some Timmins stores have been known to accept high-graded ore in payment for grocery bills.

'high-ˌhanded, *a.* Acting or done with a high hand (see HIGH *a.* 17 b), or in an overbearing or arbitrary manner.

1631 WEEVER *Anc. Fun. Mon.* 49 For this high-handed offence, their foresaid king is still plagued in hell. **1743** in Doran '*Mann*' & *Manners* (1876) I. vi. 164 Not.. any the worse for their high-handed proceedings. **1788** T. JEFFERSON *Writ.* (1859) II. 382 Some act of high-handed authority. **1870** FREEMAN *Norm. Conq.* (ed. 2) II. App. 548 An act of high-handed violence.

Hence **high-'handedness**, high-handed, overbearing, or arbitrary action or behaviour.

1874 MAHAFFY *Soc. Life Greece* v. 144 Thus he censures high-handedness even in the gods. **1891** *Leeds Mercury* 13 Aug. 4/5 Against wrong or highhandedness Lowell was ready to strike whenever or wherever he saw it.

high-'handedly, *adv.* [f. HIGH-HANDED *a.* + -LY[2].] In a high-handed manner.

1898 N. MUNRO *John Splendid* xxi. 206 Seven fugitives of the clan that had come so high-handedly through their neighbourhood. **1927** *Daily Express* 26 Oct. 1/2 High-handedly putting a pistol to the heads of his opponents. **1948** A. L. KROEBER *Anthropol.* (rev. ed.) 617 Freud.. treated the findings of psychology almost as high-handedly as he did those of prehistory and culture history.

high hat, 'high-hat. [HIGH *a.* 1.]

1. A tall hat; *fig.* a person of affected superiority. Also *attrib.* or as *adj.*, superior, lofty.

1889 in C. W. & P. Cunnington *Handbk. Eng. Costume 19th Cent.* (1959) 309 Is it not considered bad taste to wear anything else but a high hat with a Frock coat? **1899** A. H. QUINN *Pennsylvania Stories* 39 Houston.. was under strong suspicion of having worn a high hat out to college that morning. **1923** *N.Y. Times* 9 Sept. VII. 2/1 (Stage Gloss.), High Hat—swelled head. **1924** P. MARKS *Plastic Age* 149 Christmas Cove's a nice place; not so high-hat as Bar Harbor. *Ibid.* 196 We're a lot of low-brows pretending to be intellectual high-hats. **1927** *Cleveland Press* 29 Jan., We see no point in assuming a high hat attitude towards what one doesn't know. **1930** *Publishers' Weekly* 22 Mar. 1674 The shop is not 'high hat'. **1931** G. B. STERN *Shortest Night* xvi. 263 That hot-tempered young high-hat. **1932** E. WALLACE *When Gangs came to London* xxi. 186 Eddy was getting high-hat.. now this new and irritating situation had arisen. **1932** E. WILSON *Devil take Hindmost* xviii. 205 He gets high-hat and speaks with scorn of the Mexicans. **1953** R. LEHMANN *Echoing Grove* iii. 199 Forgive me if I sound high-hat—I don't think you can possibly understand it. **1969** in Halpert & Story *Christmas Mumming in Newfoundland* 197 They looked very smart in their trimmed pants, white shirts and high hat with ribbons and tassles.

2. *Photogr.* (See quot. 1930.)

1930 *Sel. Gloss. Motion Pict. Techn.* (*Acad. Motion Pict., Hollywood*) 16/1 *High hat*, a very low camera stand. **1953** *Time* 2 Nov. 35/2 *High-hat*, low camera support for 'worm's eye' pictures.

3. *Jazz.* A pair of cymbals worked by the foot. Also **hi-hat.**

1934 E. LITTLE *Mod. Rhythmic Drumming* I. xxii. 21 The 'High-Hat' pedal brings the cymbals within reach of the snare drum sticks. Rhythm can be played on them. **1948** *Metronome* Nov. 28 I'd rather use the high-hat as a back beat and break up the bass rhythms. **1949** L. FEATHER *Inside Be-bop* II. 58 In the old days the drummer frequently played high hat cymbal for the second and fourth beat accents. **1956** S. TRAILL *Play that Music* v. 56 Keep your hi-hat cymbals flat. **1956** M. STEARNS *Story of Jazz* (1957) xviii. 234 The left foot played the high-hat, and the right foot exploded the bass drum. **1966** *New Yorker* 11 June 153/1 Barbarin.. uses a high hat and ride cymbals to excellent effect. **1966** *Crescendo* Dec. 27/2 A tambourine on the hi-hat.. makes a jingle sound every time the hi-hat cymbals come down. **1968** *Ibid.* Apr. 29/1 An intriguing hi-hat backing from the excellent drummer.

'high-hat, *v.* Chiefly *U.S.* [f. prec.] *intr.* To wear a high hat; to assume a superior attitude. *trans.* To treat condescendingly. So **high-hatted** *a.*

1924 H. C. WITWER in *Cosmopolitan* Apr. 68/1 'Why high hat me?' he complains. 'I'm harmless and I may be able to do you a lot of good.' **1924** H. CRANE *Let.* 24 Jan. (1965) 171 It's become fashionable for the high-hatted uptowners now to buy Matisse's paintings. **1925** S. LEWIS *Martin Arrowsmith* xxxix. 455 If I blew in and old Mart high-hatted me, I'd just about come nigh unto letting him hear the straight truth. **1927** *Sat. Even. Post* 24 Dec. 22/3 What made me so sore.. was her thinkin' she could high-hat me. **1929** C. E. MERRIAM *Chicago* 292 Dever's dignity was mistaken by some for 'high-hatting'. **1941** N. COWARD *Australia Visited* III. 15 The true representative American.. is unpretentious... He dislikes being 'ritz'd' or 'high-hatted'. **1941** BELLOC *Silence of Sea* xxxi. 193 The Americans.. say of a proud man that 'he wears a high hat'... 'If you talk like that,' he was told, 'they will think you are high-hatting them.' **1965** *New Statesman* 7 May 730/2 Her ineffective efforts to make her sons 'high-hat the neighbours' and join the élite.

high-headed (stress variable), *a.* orig. *U.S.* [HIGH *a.* 22 b.] Carrying the head high; proud, arrogant.

1837 *Southern Lit. Messenger* III. 86 One of them high-headed Roanoke planters. **1903** W. B. YEATS *In Seven Woods* 43 And that high-headed even-walking queen. **1909** R. A. WASON *Happy Hawkins* i. 10 The most obstinate, high-headed, bull-intellected thin-skin 'at ever drew down top wages fer punchin' cows. **1955** W. W. DENLINGER *Compl. Boston* 112 A dog cannot display a high-headed style without well laid back shoulders.

'high-ˌhearted, *a.* Courageous, high-spirited; in early use sometimes, Haughty, arrogant.

1398 TREVISA *Barth. De P.R.* XV. lxviii. (1495) 514 In olde tyme men of Grecia were wroth and hyghe herted to men that wolde do wronge to theyr neyghbours. *a* **1450** *Knt. de la Tour* (1868) 19 The yongest is most curteys and humble, and is not so highe herted as that other. **1601** CHESTER *Love's Mart.* (1878) 65 His enemie, High-harted Lucius. **1650** STAPYLTON *Strada's Low C Warres* II. 47 The more high-hearted grew the Prince of Orange. **1856** LEVER *Martins of Cro' M.* 129 A fine, high-hearted, manly class they were.

Hence **high-'heartedness.**

1613 LADY ELIZ. CAREW *Mariam* IV. viii. Chorus, High hartednes doth sometimes teach to bow.

† **'highhede.** *Obs. rare.* In 3 **hiȝhede.** [f. HIGH *a.* + *-hede*, -HEAD.] Height, highness.

a **1300** *Floriz & Bl.* 327 Bihold of þe tur þe hiȝhede And wiþ þi fot met þe brede.

'high-heeled, *a.* Having high heels: used of boots or shoes; hence *transf.* of their wearers.

1642 HOWELL *For. Trav.* (Arb.) 31 The one goes high-heeled, the other low and flat. **1664** PEPYS *Diary* 15 Aug., He wears pretty high-heeled shoes, but not very high. **1878** BROWNING *Poets of Croisic* cxxxviii, Quick turn-about On high-heeled shoe. **1882** *Macm. Mag.* XLV. 395 Becurled and bewigged damsels, laced and high-heeled.

high-hoe: see HICKWALL.

'high-ˌholder. *U.S.* [Of same origin as next; altered by popular etymology.] = next.

1884 E. P. ROE in *Harper's Mag.* Mar. 622/1 The pigeon-hawk.. is about the size of our common flicker, or high-holder.

'high-hole. *U.S.* [A variant, due to popular etymology, of *hyghwhele*, *highwale*, *hewhole*, early forms of HICKWALL, q.v.; cf. Eng. dial. *hey-hoe*, *high-hoe*, etc.] The Golden-winged Woodpecker, or Flicker, of North America, *Colaptes auratus*.

1860 BARTLETT *Dict. Amer.* (ed. 3), *Clape*.. the Golden-winged Woodpecker.. elsewhere called High-hole, Yucker, Flicker, Wake-up, and Pigeon Woodpecker. **1884** *Century Mag.* Dec. 222/2 The high-hole appears to drum more promiscuously than does downy [woodpecker]. **1888** *Advance* 5 Apr. 209 The piercing note of the 'high-hole'.

† **'highing**, *vbl. sb. Obs.* [f. HIGH *v.* + -ING[1].] Raising aloft, exaltation, elevation.

a **1225** *Ancr. R.* 174 Hesteres nome & hire heiunge preoueð soð þet ich sigge. *c* **1380** WYCLIF *Serm.* Sel. Wks. I. 111 þe heyng of Crist. *c* **1449** PECOCK *Repr.* II. x. 201 In the Feeste of the Crossis Hiȝing.

highish ('haɪɪʃ), *a.* [f. HIGH *a.* + -ISH.] Somewhat high (in various senses).

1825 COBBETT *Rur. Rides* 472 Mounting a highish hill. **1828** LAMB *Lett.* (1888) II. 206 A friend nameless, but highish in office. **1884** Q. VICTORIA *More Leaves* 56 On a highish point called after me 'The Queen's View'.

high jinks: see JINK *sb.*[1] 3.

highland ('haɪlənd), *sb.* and *a.* Also 5–9 **hieland**, 6 **heland, hiland, -end, (helland, heleand)**, 7 **hyland, (hayelonde).** [f. HIGH *a.* + LAND.]

A. *sb.*

1. a. High or elevated land; a lofty headland or cliff. **b.** The mountainous or elevated part *of* any country; occas. also in the names of geographical districts, as the Hudson Highlands. (Perh. extended from 2.)

a **1000** *Cædmon's Exod.* 385 Heahlond stiȝon.. on Seone beorȝ. **1634** SIR T. HERBERT *Trav.* 186 Towards Sun-set wee see the Coast or high land of Brin John. *a* **1687** PETTY *Pol. Arith.* iv. (1691) 80 Wet Weather being propitious to High-lands, which drowneth the Low. **1726** SHELVOCKE *Voy. round World* (1757) 192 The Sierra, or highland of Motapa. **1748** *Anson's Voy.* II. v. 173 He was.. to cruise off the highland of Valparaiso. **1833** TENNYSON *Hesperides*, Beneath a highland leaning down a weight Of cliffs. **1839** THIRLWALL *Greece* lii. VI. 309 He then advanced toward the highlands of Nura. **1871** B. TAYLOR *Faust* I. ii. 44 Where over crags and piny highlands The poising eagle slowly soars.

2. *spec.* with capital initial. (Now always *pl.*, Sc. pronunc. ('hiːlənts).) The mountainous district of Scotland which lies north and west of a line drawn from the Firth of Clyde through Crieff to Blairgowrie and thence north and north-west to Nairn on the Moray Firth; the territory formerly occupied by the Celtic clans.

c **1425** [implied in HIGHLANDMAN]. **1529** LYNDESAY *Compl.* 384 And, in this realme, hes maid sic ordour, Baith throw the heland and the bordour. *a* **1687** PETTY *Pol. Arith.* iv. (1691) 70 The Land and Housing in Ireland, and the High-Lands of Scotland. *c* **1730** BURT *Lett. N. Scotl.* (1818) I. 37 The Kirk.. distinguishes the Lowlands from the Highlands by the language generally spoken. **1840** *Penny Cycl.* XVII. 507/2 Dunkeld.. by the beauty of its situation and its convenience as the point of entrance upon the Highlands. **1867** Q. VICTORIA (*title*) Leaves from the Journal of Our Life in the Highlands.

B. *attrib.* or *adj.* **1.** Of, pertaining to, or inhabiting high land or a mountainous district.

1595 DUNCAN *App. Etymol.* (E.D.S.), *Montannus*, hieland. **1637** *Boston Rec.* (1877) II. 19 The little marsh.. with a little hill of upland ground.. compast on three sydes with highland ground. **1781** GIBBON *Decl. & F.* III. lxv. 626 The highland robbers were subdued or extirpated. **1853** KANE *Grinnell Exp.* xxiv. (1856) 199 Merely the highland clouds over the mountains. **1861** MISS PRATT *Flower. Pl.* III. 274 Highland Cudweed. **1897** *Westm. Gaz.* 31 Aug. 7/1 The Fen agriculturists have stood the depression much better than their high-land neighbours.

2. a. *spec.* Of, belonging to, or characteristic of the Highlands of Scotland. ***Highland bonnet*** = SCOTCH CAP; ***Highland Boundary Fault***, a geological fault extending across Scotland from the Firth of Clyde on the west coast to Stonehaven on the east; also called ***Great Highland Fault***; (***West***) ***Highland cattle***, a breed of small cattle from the Highlands, characterized by thick, shaggy hair and long curved horns set wide apart; ***Highland dress***, the kilt and accompanying costume worn by the Highland clansmen and soldiers; ***Highland fling*** (see FLING *sb.* 4 a); ***Highland games*** (see GAME *sb.* 4 d); ***Highland honours*** (see quot. 1858); ***Highland kilt*** = KILT *sb.*; ***Highland pony***, one of a breed of ponies originating in the Highlands; ***Highland regiment***, in the British Army, a regiment originally composed of Highlanders, or raised in the Highlands, and retaining more or less of the Highland dress; ***Highland terrier***, a variety of terrier descended from the working terrier of the Scottish Highlands; also called ***West Highland white terrier***, ***White West Highlander***.

c **1425** [see HIGHLANDMAN]. **1500–20** DUNBAR *Poems* xxvi. 109 Than cryd Mahoun for a Heleand padȝane. **1610** HOLLAND *Camden's Brit.* I. 107 A number of hideous high-land Scots. **1648** MILTON *Observ. Art. Peace* Wks. 1738 I. 359 A generation of Highland Thieves and Red-shanks. **1760** *Aberdeen Jrnl.* 22 Jan., His Grace.. appears every Day in the Highland Dress, which becomes him extremely well. **1771** [see KILT *sb.*]. **1818** SCOTT *Rob Roy* II. xiv. 192 The Baillie, thus refreshed, was mounted on a small Highland poney. **1819** *Observer* 25 July 4/4 A parcel of these children dressed in the Highland kilt. **1819** *Edin. Even. Courant* 31 July 1 Lost, A Highland Terrier, that answers to the name of Brogach. **1821** *Edin. Star* 2 Feb., There is something so hearty and rapturous in the Highland honours which follow the toasts. **1822** D. WORDSWORTH *2nd Tour Scotl.* in *Jrnls.* (1941) II. 373 Boys dressed in their glossiest and best—little ones in Tartan with Highland bonnets. **1825** LOUDON *Encycl. Agric.* §6118 Along the eastern coast, north of the Firth of Forth, the Highland cattle are intermixed with various local breeds. **1828** SCOTT *F.M. Perth* iv, Two.. seemed to me.. to have Highland plaids about them. **1831** W. YOUATT *Horse* iv. 59 The Highland Pony is far inferior to the galloway. **1833** *Chambers's Edin. Jrnl.* II. 137/2 The popularity which Highland bonnets acquired from the glory of the Scottish regiments at Waterloo. **1834** W. YOUATT *Cattle* iii. 66 The striking peculiarities of the Highland cattle. **1844** H. STEPHENS *Bk. Farm* III. 1274 The West Highland has long been famed in Scotland as a superior breed of cattle. **1846** C. ST. JOHN *Short Sk. Highlands* xiv. 113 Why do Highland terriers so often run on three legs?..

I never had a Highland terrier who did not hop along constantly on three legs. **1853** J. E. Millais *Let.* ? 8 Oct. in M. Lutyens *Millais & Ruskins* (1967) 93 He comes out in the Highland kilt and cap. **1858** Q. Victoria *Let.* 1 Apr. in R. Fulford *Dearest Child* (1964) 83 Alfred and Arthur in Highland dress. **1858** *Illustr. News of World* 12 June 300/3 All the loyal toasts were proposed and drunk with 'Highland honours'—a kind of demonstration which the polite reader may think somewhat ludicrous.. since it consists of putting one leg on a chair and another on the table, elevating the right hand to its utmost stretch, and 'draining the wine cup to the very dregs'. **1875** *Encycl. Brit.* I. 389/1 The Kyloes or West Highland cattle. **1882** Pebody *Eng. Journalism* xxi. 158 Upon the shores of highland lochs. **1893** *Q. Jrnl. Geol. Soc.* XLIX. 354 The grey slate or phyllite, north of the Great Highland Fault. **1901** A. Geikie *Scenery Scotl.* (ed. 3) iii. 64 The line of the Highland boundary fault runs out to sea immediately to the north of Stonehaven. **1911** *Encycl. Brit.* VIII. 376/1 An application which was made (1900) by some of their admirers for separate classification was refused by the Kennel Club, but afterwards it was granted, the breed being classified as the West Highland white terrier. **1922** R. Leighton *Compl. Bk. Dog* xiv. 206 The Poltalloch, or White West Highlander. **1929** J. W. Gregory in Evans & Stubblefield *Handbk. Geol. Gt. Brit.* i. 10 The Middle Devonian age of the Highland Boundary Fault is shown near Loch Lomond. **1937** J. Macdonald *Highland Ponies* 39 For several years the Department of Agriculture for Scotland has been supplying Highland pony stallions for the use of the crofters. **1961** L. D. Stamp *Gloss. Geogr. Terms* 234/1 Geographically the 'Highlands of Scotland' is the name applied to the whole massif north of the Highland Boundary Faults. **1969** R. T. Wilcox *Dict. Costume* 305/2 *Scottish Highland dress*..: the kilt; a hill jacket..; the sporran. **1970** *New Yorker* 28 Feb. 44/2 Calvin was the little West Highland terrier she and Grandpa Nye had got on their wedding trip in Scotland in 1937. **1973** *Courier & Advertiser* (Dundee) 26 Feb. 1/1 (Advt.), Cattleman required for suckler herd and pedigree Highland cattle.

b. Resembling, having the characteristics of, or typical of the people of the Highlands of Scotland.

c **1780** J. R. (*song title*) The Highland character... No effeminate customs our sinews unbrace, No luxurious tables enervate our race. **1787** Burns in *Poems ascribed to Burns* (1801) 53 There's naething here but Highland pride, And Highland scab and hunger. **1792** —— *Poems & Songs* (1968) I. 358 In Heaven itself I'll ask no more Than just a Highland welcome. **1816** Scott *Antiquary* I. ix. 204 Rab Tull keepit a Highland heart, and bang'd out o' bed.. and he did follow the thing up stairs and down stairs. **1818** —— *Rob Roy* II. v. 54 Ay, he has a kind o' Hieland honesty—he's honest after a sort, as they say. **1829** *Blackw. Mag.* Sept. 400 Yet still the blood is strong, the heart is Highland, And we in dreams behold the Hebrides. **1871** L. W. M. Lockhart *Fair to See* (1872) I. ii. 58 I'm as Highland as—as—anything. **1897** R. M. Ferguson *Village Poet* 172 They'll not jew us—we're no' sae hieland.

highlander (ˈhaɪləndə(r)). [f. highland *sb.* and *a.* + -er[1] 1.]

1. An inhabitant of a high or mountainous land.

1632 Lithgow *Trav.* iii. 81 High-landers of Candy. **1681** Cotton *Wond. Peak* 45 More natural to your Peak Highlander. **1856** Stanley *Sinai & Pal.* ix. 329 The Israelite highlanders of the neighbouring heights.

2. a. *spec.* with capital initial. A native of the Highlands of Scotland. Also, a soldier of a Highland regiment.

1642 Howell *For. Trav.* (Arb.) 50 The Epirotiques in Greece, the Heylanders in Scotland. **1769** *De Foe's Tour Gt. Brit.* (ed. 7) IV. 236 The Natives of Inverness do not call themselves Highlanders, because they speak English. **1855** Macaulay *Hist. Eng.* xiii. III. 335 The Highlander.. was.. morally and physically well qualified for war. **1893** *Whitaker's Alm.* 205 Royal Highlanders. *Ibid.* 206 Seaforth Highlanders.

b. Highland cattle.

1771 *Caled. Mercury* 17 Aug., One Hundred Cows, mostly Highlanders, laid early on the grass in the spring to fatten. **1787** W. H. Marshall *Rural Econ. Norf.* (1795) II. 381 Highlanders, Scotch cattle of the Highland breed. **1825** Loudon *Encycl. Agric.* §6122 The other variety of Highland cattle is the Norlands, or North Highlanders. **1834** W. Youatt *Cattle* iii. 69 There is little or no variety of breeds of cattle in the Hebrides. They are pure West Highlanders. *Ibid.* 79 The character of the Highlander must still be, that he will pay better for his quantity of food than any other breed. **1875** *Encycl. Brit.* I. 389/1 They [*sc.* the Pembrokes] excel the West Highlanders in this respect, that they make good dairy cattle, the cows being peculiarly adapted for cottagers' purposes.

3. ***Highlanders***: playing cards of the third quality, so called from the device on the wrapper.

1842 *Bradshaw's Jrnl.* 16 Apr. in *Philol. Soc. Trans.* (1867) 63 The best cards are called Moguls, the others Harrys and Highlanders. **1866** in *Stationer & Fancy Trades Register* 1 Sept. *Ibid.*, The different qualities of cards are distinguished as Moguls, Harrys, Highlanders, and Merry Andrews.

4. A kind of artificial fly for fishing.

1867 F. Francis *Angling* x. (1880) 366 The Highlander may be found useful at times.

5. ***White West Highlander***: see *Highland terrier*.

ˈhighlandish, *a. rare.* [See -ish.] Of the nature of high land; like the Scottish Highlands.

1632 Lithgow *Trav.* x. 499 The high-landish mountaines overcled with Firre-trees. **1754** A. Drummond *Trav. Germany* etc. 10 (T.) The country round is altogether so high-landish.

ˈhighlandman. = highlander.

c **1425** Wyntoun *Cron.* ix. xiv. 1543 The Scottis Hielandmen, Ware neire the wattyr off Ile then. **1596** Dalrymple tr. *Leslie's Hist. Scot.* ix. 241 Quhen sum hilend men.. be brocht til obedience. **1609** Skene *Reg. Maj.* 134 *Hielandmen*, the inhabitants of the Hielands, & Jles of this Realme. *a* **1649** Drumm. of Hawth. *Hist. Jas. I*, Wks. (1711) 7 To defend the country against the incursions of these highlandmen. *a* **1835** Hogg *Song, 'Come o'er the stream, Charlie'* iii, A troop of our bold Highlandmen.

ˈHighlandry. [f. highland + -ry, as in *Irishry, Welshry*.] Highlanders collectively.

a **1771** Smollett cited in Ogilvie.

ˈhigh-life, -lifed, *a. U.S.* [high *a.* 16.] Full of life or spirit. (Cf. *high life* s.v. high *a.* 21.)

1861 *Trans. Ill. Agric. Soc.* IV. 376 A long narrow-headed high-lifed brainless animal. **1902** A. D. McFaul *Ike Glidden* ix. 70 Ike told him.. to always drive on the bit, because the colt was a high-life fellow. **1935** *Archit. Rev.* LXXVII. 64/2 He was busy building for 'high-life' America.

high light, ˈhigh-light. [high *a.* 10, light *sb.* 12.] **1. a.** In painting, photography, and cinematography, any of the brightest parts of a subject or a representation of it; often *pl.* Also *attrib.*

1658, 1859 [see light *sb.* 12]. **1892** A. Brothers *Photogr.* 335 In a portrait, if well lighted, there should be parts which are brighter than the rest of the face—on the forehead and nose, for instance; they are called *high lights*. **1903** A. Watkins *Photogr.* (ed. 2) 64 The tone D is called the 'high light', for although it is the blackest in the negative it represents white in the original. *Ibid.* 77 It may happen that there is no white part or high light in the subject you are developing. **1913** J. A. Sinclair *Handbk. Photogr.* (ed. 2) 226 To clear up high-lights or remove pressure marks from thick bromide papers. **1930** *Sel. Gloss. Motion Pict. Techn.* (*Acad. Motion Pict., Hollywood*), *High light*, object, scene, or picture having low color saturation, that is, containing a large proportion of white. **1931** Selden & Sellman *Stage Scenery* 158 In order to give interest to high lights and shadows. **1937** *Bell Telephone Q.* Apr. 110 The painter contributes highlight in the sense of accent. **1951** G. H. Sewell *Amateur Film-Making* (ed. 2) ii. 20 The high-light meter reads the intensity of the light falling upon the subject, instead of the light reflected from it. **1957** R. W. G. Hunt *Reprod. of Colour* vii. 73 A highlight mask is made by contact printing the transparency onto a very high contrast black and white negative material. **1968** *Gloss. Terms Offset Lithogr. Printing* (*B.S.I.*) 13 *Highlight stop*, a lens aperture used in half-tone photography which has a specific influence on the formation of highlight tones. *Ibid.* 17 *Highlight mask*, a mask used to retain or increase highlight contrast in the reproduction.

transf. **1929** K. H. Brown *Father* vi. 61 There were artless scarlet highlights cut from portions of the little boys' outgrown woolen underwear.

b. A bright tint in the hair; that portion of the hair that reflects the most light. Also *attrib.*

1941 *Hairdressers' Weekly Jrnl.* 1 Feb. 155/2 One can bring out high-lights on every shade of hair by the appropriate use of toning rinses. **1966** Cox *Illustr. Dict. Hairdressing* 79/2 *High-light cap*, a plastic head cap with holes in it used for drawing a strand or strands of hair through to bleach without bleaching the other hair.

2. *fig.* A 'bright', prominent, or outstanding feature or characteristic. Chiefly *pl.* Phr. ***to hit the high lights***, = *to hit the high spots* (s.v. high *a.* 21).

1855 *Knickerbocker* XLVI. 40 If we have chosen to speak of the shadows in the fair portrait, we have also neglected to point out the high lights. **1905** A. Adams *Outlet* 275 It was the recognized cattle centre of Montana.., but devoid of the high-lights which were a feature of the trail towns. **1922** A. Waugh *Public School Life* i. 16 It would be filled with high lights, with breathless escapades, with impossible heroics. **1923** *Weekly Dispatch* 21 Jan. 11 There is no 'hitting the high lights' when he is not in training. **1927** *Hutchinson's Myst. Story Mag.* Feb. 117 One by one, Dan and I met all the high lights of the town. **1931** *Times Lit. Suppl.* 15 Jan. 34/2 It is not readable in the sense that some modern biographies are readable; it has no 'high lights'. **1931** *Morning Post* 21 Aug. 11/7 These were the highlights of to-day's practice over the course. **1961** Baughman & Robinson *Secret Service Chief* (1963) ii. 23 Flipping the years like pages I see many interesting and instructive highlights—and some funny ones too. **1969** *Times* 10 Feb. 6/5 The highlight of the lunch will be a speech.. on the vital relationship between the industrial leader and his executive secretary. *Ibid.* 19 Feb. 17/2 Highlights from one of tonight's top soccer matches.

ˈhighlight, ˈhigh-light, *v.* [f. prec.] *trans.*

a. To bring into prominence, to 'feature', to draw attention to.

1934 M. Weseen *Dict. Amer. Slang* x. 143 *Highlight*, to give one a prominent place on a program or a leading part in a show. *Highlighted*, marked by; featured by. **1945** Nelson & Wright *Tomorrow's House* iv. 43/2 This seemingly minor problem.. highlights what should be the fundamental approach to planning. **1951** *Mind* LX. 23 The view is.. made more plausible by highlighting.. aspects of scientific procedure. **1952** Granville *Dict. Theatr. Terms* (ed. 2) 97 *Highlight*, to give prominence to an artiste in the billing or newspaper publicity matter, the build-up of a show, or of an individual artiste. **1955** Priestley & Hawkes *Journey down Rainbow* p. xi, Football games, night clubs, TV programmes, hotel festivities, can be ignored and certainly should not be high-lighted by the serious social critic. **1957** *Economist* 19 Oct. 192/1 The genuineness with which each holds the belief was highlit during last week's.. interview. **1958** *Listener* 2 Oct. 501/1 Statistics such as these are cold and dull and do little to highlight the tremendous importance of industrial organizations in modern society. **1965** *New Statesman* 30 Apr. 670/3 Thursday's polling is unlikely to highlight any notable national trends. **1967** Singha & Massey *Indian Dances* ii. 42 A tirmana is used to conclude a section of dance or highlight a portion in the middle.

b. *spec.* To tint or bleach portions of the hair in such a way that they catch and reflect the light. More widely in make-up: see quot. 1952. Also **ˈhighlighting** *vbl. sb.*

1942 D. Powell *Time to be Born* (1943) vi. 132 'You've had your hair dyed.'.. 'Not dyed. High-lighted is the new word,' said Vickey. **1952** Granville *Dict. Theatr. Terms* (ed. 2) 97 *Highlight*, in make-up, to accentuate cheekbones and other features and effectively contrast the shade, on the face. **1959** *Punch* 3 June 752/2 For grey hair there is a treatment.. which highlights the hair and dismisses yellow discoloration. **1972** *Vogue* 15 Mar. 3/2 New Pure Pearl-Light Everywhere Colour for highlighting round the eyes.

Hence **ˈhighlighter**, a marker pen which overlays a printed word, etc. with a transparent (usu. fluorescent) colour, leaving it legible and emphasized. (Also *Hi-liter*, proprietary in the U.S.)

1964 *Official Gaz.* (U.S. Patent Office) 26 May tm182 The Carter's Ink Company, Cambridge, Mass... Hi-liter for marking pens. First use June 1962. **1986** *Neat Ideas Catal.* Apr. 16/2 Stabilo Boss highlighters.

†**high-lone,** *adv. Obs.* [An alteration of *alone*, of obscure origin. *High* prob. expresses degree or intensity; cf. lone.] Quite alone, without support.

1597 Shaks. *Rom. & Jul.* i. iii. 37 (*Qo.*) Then she could not stand high lone. **1602** Marston *Antonio's Rev.* iv. iv, And when it [an infant] once goes high-lone, takes it back. **1602** Middleton *Burt* ii. ii, When I could not stand a' high lone without I held a thing. **1760** G. Washington *Diary* 13 Mar. (MS.), The Mares.. so poor were they, and so much abusd had they been.. that they were scarce able to go high-lone, much less to assist in the business of the Plantations.

high-low (ˈhaɪləʊ). [f. high *a.* + low *a.*; in contrast to 'top' boots and 'low' shoes respectively.] (Usually *pl.*) A boot laced or otherwise fastened up in front and reaching up over the ankle.

1801 Bloomfield *Rural T.* (1802) 8, I won the High-lows out and out. *a* **1825** Forby *Voc. E. Anglia, Highlows*, a covering for the foot and ancle, too *high* to be called a shoe, and too *low* for a boot. **1830** Cobbett *Rur. Rides* I. 73 From the sole six inches upwards is a high-low. **1851** *Ann. Reg.* 38 He was lacing up his high-lows in the washhouse.

attrib. **1836** Marryat *Japhet* xxxix, He was dressed in highlow boots, worsted stockings. **1858** O. W. Holmes *Aut. Breakf.-t.* 185 The dandies.. have split their waistbands and taken to high-low shoes.

Hence **ˈhigh-lowed** *a.*, wearing high-lows: cf. high-shod.

1839 *John Bull* 28 July in *Spirit Metrop. Conserv. Press* (1840) II. 251 The high-lowed ploughboy of Yorkshire.

†**highly,** *a. Obs.* Forms: 1 **héalíc**, 3 **hehliche**, 4 **heȝliche**, **hiȝlich**, *Sc.* **hyly**, 5 *Sc.* **hiely**. See also heily. [OE. *héalíc*, f. *héah* high *a.* + *-líc* = -ly[1].]

1. High, lofty, exalted.

(In quots., *a* 1400, 1450–70 perh. an adv.)

c **1000** Ælfric *Gen.* xiv. 20 Gebletsod sy se healica God. *c* **1000** *Hom.* II. 160 On healicum muntum. [*a* **1400** *Pistill of Susan* 6 (MS. I.) Halles and herbergages, hyly on hyht. **1450–70** *Golagros & Gaw.* 183 He had that heynd to ane hall, hiely on hight.]

2. Noble, splendid.

c **1000** Ælfric *Hom.* II. 86 Nan ȝereord nis swa healic saw Ebreisc. *c* **1000** *Saints' Lives, Oswald* (E.E.T.S.) 184 Leoht.. swilce healic sunnbeam. **13..** *Gaw. & Gr. Knt.* 183 Wyth his hiȝlich here, þat of his hed reches.

3. Of high degree; intense, profound.

c **1000** Ælfric *Hom.* II. 506 Mid healicum ȝedwylde. *c* **1205** Lay. 10291 þat Seuarus in his hirede Hæfde hehliche grið. **1340** *Ayenb.* 264 Yef þer by heȝliche chon.

highly, (ˈhaɪlɪ), *adv.* Forms: see high *a.* [OE. *héalíce*, f. *héah* high + *-líce* = -ly[2].]

1. *lit.* In a high place or situation; aloft, on high; so as to be high or lofty.

c **1000** Ælfric *Hom.* II. 254 [He] asette ðis ȝewrit.. bufon Cristes heafde, healice to tacne. *Ibid.* 318 Seðe on heofonum is healice sittende. *c* **1205** Lay. 8088 þe king hafde his kine-helm Hæhliche on hæfde. **13..** *Gaw. & Gr. Knt.* 983 þe lorde.. Hent heȝly of his hode, and on a spere henged. **1583** Stanyhurst *Æneis* i. (Arb.) 19 King Aeolus, highly In castel settled. **1597** A. M. tr. *Guillemeau's Fr. Chirurg.* 46 b/2 That the membre be collocated softlye, smoothly and highlye.

2. a. In or to a high position or rank.

c **900** tr. *Bæda's Hist.* v. xvii. [xix.] (1890) 458 Healice þa cyricean wæs reccende. *c* **1440** *Gesta Rom.* xxxii. 122 (Harl. MS.) He shulde wedde hir, & be hiliche avauncyd. **1548** Hall *Chron., Hen. V*, 34 b, Knowyng hym to be highly in the kynges favor. **1583** Golding *Calvin on Deut.* lxiii. 380 Yet the wickeddest sorte will needes be highliest exalted. **1704** Earl of Cromarty *Sp. Parl. Scotl.* 11 July, She is one of the Heads and highly situate. **1855** Macaulay *Hist. Eng.* xiv. III. 495 A much greater proportion of the opulent, of the highly descended, and of the highly educated.

†**b.** Supremely, principally; specially. *Obs.*

1340 *Ayenb.* 5 þe ilke þet deþ his hope heȝliche ine sseppe, zeneȝeþ dyadliche.

3. a. In or to a high degree, amount, extent, or condition; greatly, intensely, extremely, very, much.

With such verbs as *commend, esteem, extol, honour, praise, value*, the sense is coloured so as to run into 3 b or 4 b.

971 *Blickl. Hom.* 33 He wolde þæt his lof þe healicor weoxe. *c* **1200** *Trin. Coll. Hom.* 3 Here cumeð ure king, wule we.. him.. heiliche wurðie. **1375** Barbour *Bruce* i. 577 For his leawte.. rewardyt and that hely. *c* **1440** *Gesta Rom.* xvi.

54 (Harl. MS.) When the Emperoure herd this, he was hily meved in all his bowels. **1493** *Festivall* (W. de W. 1515) 49 Than this mayster . . thanked god hyghly. **1535** COVERDALE *Ps.* xlvii. 1 Greate is ye Lorde & hyelie to be praysed. **1648** BOYLE *Seraph. Love* (1660) 62 Rare Musick, which . . the knowingst Artists still do highliest value. **1711** ADDISON *Spect.* No. 106 ¶6 It renders his Conversation highly agreeable. **1726** SHELVOCKE *Voy. round World* (1757) 184 They would be highly to blame if they did not lay hold of this opportunity. **1826** DISRAELI *Viv. Grey* VI. i, It must be highly amusing.

b. At a high rate or price.

a **1225** *Leg. Kath.* 568 And wiþ kinewurðe ȝeoues ȝelden ou hehliche ower ȝong hider. *a* **1300** *Cursor M.* 15224 (Gött) His auen lauerd þaim for to selle, als heili als he might. **1362** LANGL. *P. Pl.* A. VII. 300 Bote he beo heihliche I-huret elles wol he chide. **1548** HALL *Chron., Hen. V*, 56 b, Other were sore fined and highly raunsomed. *Mod.* His services are perhaps too highly paid.

†**c.** With elevated voice; loudly, aloud. *Obs.*

c **1205** LAY. 822 Heihliche he cleopede. *c* **1375** *Sc. Leg. Saints, Laurentius* 708 Hely scho sa[i]d, þat al mycht heyre. ? *a* **1400** *Morte Arth.* 1286 They herde . . Hornez of olyfantez fulle helych blawene. *a* **1533** LD. BERNERS *Huon* lxxxiii. 262, I began to stryue with my brother so hyely that Gybouars myght here me.

4. a. With high quality of action; in high style; with stateliness or majesty; solemnly; nobly, excellently. ? *Obs.*

1154 *O.E. Chron.* an. 1137 §7 [Hi] bebyried him heȝlice in þe minstre. *a* **1225** *Juliana* 76 And don hire bodiþrin in stanene þruh hehliche. *a* **1300** *Cursor M.* 22767 þus heili, bot wel heiliker, Sal cume to deme þe demester. **13 . .** *Gaw. & Gr. Knt.* 755 Sum herber, þer heȝly I myȝt here masse. *c* **1477** CAXTON *Jason* 47 b, Ye haue seruid me hyely and well. *a* **1533** LD. BERNERS *Huon* clxxii. 684 The quene went forth hyely acompanyed. **1662** J. DAVIES tr. *Mandelslo's Trav.* 8 The Dutch entertain'd me very highly.

b. With honour, honourably; with high approval, appreciation, or praise: now chiefly with *think*, *speak*, or the like.

a **1225** *Ancr. R.* 190 Heie monnes messager, me schal heiliche underuongen. *c* **1350** *Will. Palerne* 1798 Hiȝliche þei heriede god of þat hap fallen. *c* **1477** CAXTON *Jason* 5 b, Hercules him self . . welcomed them hyely. **1548** HALL *Chron., Hen. V*, 34 b, These Ambassadours were highly received of the Emperor Sygismond. **1642** ROGERS *Naaman* 387 When we thinke the highliest of ourselves. **1657** BAXTER *Agst. Quakers* 10 Can they yet think highlier of themselves, or speak highlier of themselves, then this? **1849** MACAULAY *Hist. Eng.* vi. II. 119 He spoke highly of them to Barillon.

†**c.** Solemnly, seriously, earnestly. *Obs.*

c **1350** *Will. Palerne* 2336 Do now, god, þi grace, And late me haue al þe harm, heiȝeliche i beseche. *a* **1440** *Sir Degrev.* 1585 The stywarde heyle hath swornne. *c* **1440** *Gesta Rom.* i. 2 (Harl. MS.) Þer met wiþ him a clerke, the which hielie beheld him. **1513** MORE *Rich. III* (1883) 53 Euery man laughed . . to here it then so sodainly so highly taken.

d. To a high degree of artistic quality or finish; with perfect workmanship; elaborately.

1715 J. RICHARDSON *Theory Paint.* 156 'Twould be loss of Time to a Painter to finish such things highly. **1802** PALEY *Nat. Theol.* xxvii. (1819) 479 The hinges in the wings of an earwig . . are as highly wrought as if the Creator had nothing else to finish. **1842** MACAULAY *Let.* in Trevelyan *Life* (1876) II. ix. 110 They are not expected to be highly finished.

5. Proudly, haughtily, arrogantly; ambitiously; with indignation or anger. ? *Obs.*

a **1225** *Ancr. R.* 56 Nu comeð forð a feble mon, & halt him þauh heihliche. **1375** BARBOUR *Bruce* VIII. 143 Schir amer spak sa hely. *a* **1450** *Knt. de la Tour* (1868) 21 Whanne thei wille speke highely, lete hem be, and go from hem. **1513** MORE in Grafton *Chron.* (1568) II. 789 He tooke it so highly, that thereof ensued much trouble and great bloodshed. **1562** J. HEYWOOD *Prov. & Epigr.* (1867) 216 In thy walke, walke not to hyly. **1633** BP. HALL *Hard Texts* 128 Why shouldest thou take it so highly as to undertake a war hereupon? **1793** GOUV. MORRIS in Sparks *Life & Writ.* (1832) II. 272 The Council here talk so highly to Great Britain that you, who know mankind, will conclude them to be afraid.

6. Like other adverbs, *highly* is now generally hyphened to a ppl. adj., when this is used *attrib.*

1711 SHAFTESB. *Charac.* (1737) I. 259 The highly-rated burlesque poem. **1725** POPE *Odyss.* IV. 425 O highly-favoured delegate of Jove! **1831** J. S. MILL in *Examiner* 12 June 24 Indebted to men of highly-cultivated intellects. **1833** LYELL *Princ. Geol.* III. p. viii, The highly-inclined strata. **1836** J. S. MILL in *Lond. Rev.* II. 368 The feelings of a highly-educated and sensitive girl. **1860** RUSKIN *Mod. Paint.* V. VIII. ii. 171 A handsomer and highlier-furbished edifice. **1875** JOWETT *Plato* IV. 3 Two or three highly-wrought passages. **1910** *Busy Man's Mag.* July 88/1 He betrays a highly-strung temperament, which is seldom held in leash. **1964** S. DUKE-ELDER *Parsons' Dis. Eye* (ed. 14) xxiv. 362 Highly-strung people. **1969** *Jane's Freight Containers 1968–69* 143/1 There is considerable evidence of highly-integrated freight services being developed.

ˈhighman, high man. [f. HIGH *a.* + MAN: cf. also *low man.*] Usually *pl.* Dice loaded so as to turn up high numbers. Cf. HIGH-RUNNER.

1598 FLORIO, *Pise*, false dice, high men or low men. **1622** MABBE tr. *Aleman's Guzman d'Alf.* II. 341 There did I learne . . to make false Dice, as your High-men and your Low-men. *a* **1643** W. CARTWRIGHT *Ordinary* II. iii. in Hazl. *Dodsley* XII. 243 Your high And low men are but trifles; your pois'd dye, That's ballasted with quicksilver or gold. **1863** SALA *Capt. Dangerous* II. vii. 226 Gambling bullies . . throwing their Highmen.

ˈhigh-ˌmettled, *a.* Of high mettle; high-spirited, high-couraged.

a **1626** BACON *Q. Eliz.* Mor. & Hist. Wks. (1860) 488 In a military and high-mettled nation. **1667** DRYDEN *Sir Martin Mar-All* v. iii, Love's an high-mettled hawk that beats the air. **1714** SWIFT *Petit. to Parlt.* in *Davey's Catal.* (1895) 32 A chaise drawn by two high mettled horses. **1838** PRESCOTT *Ferd. & Is.* I. x, The high-mettled young cavaliers.

Hence **ˈhigh-mettle** *v.* to render high-mettled.

1837 CAMPBELL *Lines on Camp Hill* v, The captors of England's domains, That ennobled her breed And high-mettled the blood of her veins.

ˈhigh-ˌminded, *a.*

1. Having or characterized by a haughty, proud, or arrogant spirit. *arch.*

c **1503** in *Lett. & Papers Rich. III & Hen. VII* (1861–3) I. 239 The lady Luce was a proude hij myndyd woman, and lovyth not the kyngis grace. **1526** TINDALE *Rom.* xi. 20 Be not hye minded, but feare. **1530** PALSGR. 315/2 Hyemyneded, *orgueilleux, fiers.* **1535** COVERDALE *Ps.* cxxx[i]. 1 Lord, I am not hye mynded, I haue no proude lokes. **1623** BINGHAM *Xenophon* 110 To humble these high-minded men. *a* **1716** BLACKALL *Wks.* (1723) I. 9 Poor in Spirit may very properly denote one that is free from Pride, one that is not high-minded. **1865** KINGSLEY *Herew.* xv, Be not rash. Be not high-minded.

2. Having a morally lofty character; characterized by high principles; magnanimous.

1556 *Aurelio & Isab.* (1608) D iij, Eche of them confessede with a hey myndede courragie the faute to be his. *c* **1590** GREENE *Fr. Bacon* ix. 195 Martial Plantagenet, Henry's high-minded son. **1832** W. IRVING *Alhambra* I. 292 These cavaliers are evidently well-bred, and high-minded youths. **1881** H. MORLEY *Eng. Lit. Q. Vict.* iii. (Tauchn.) 77 What little there was of highminded statesmanship was often lost among lowthoughted cares of a political life.

Hence **highˈmindedly** *adv.*, **highˈmindedness.**

1571 GOLDING *Calvin on Ps.* lxiii. 12 His godly hyghmyndednesse is to bee noted. **1657** REEVE *God's Plea* 39 Oh beloved, let us abate of this high-mindednesse. **1824** CAMPBELL *Theodoric* 385 She bore her fate high-mindedly and well. **1884** W. S. LILLY in *Contemp. Rev.* Feb. 256 High-mindedness, he says, is the crown of all virtue, and the high-minded man occupies himself with honour, and lays claim to it, and takes pleasure in it.

ˈhighmost, *a. Obs.* or *dial.* [f. HIGH *a.*: see -MOST.] = HIGHEST.

1592 SHAKS. *Rom. & Jul.* II. v. 9 Now is the Sun vpon the highmost hill Of this daies iourney. **1688** R. HOLME *Armoury* III. 431/1 The first and highmost is an Instrument called a Spatha. **1828** *Craven Dial.*, *Heighmost*, highest.

high-muck-a-muck (ˈhaɪˌmʌkəmʌk). *N. Amer. colloq.* Also **high-you-muck-a-muck**. [app. ad. Chinook Jargon *hiu* plenty + *mucka-muck* food.] A self-important person, one who imagines he is more exalted than he is.

1856 *Democratic State Jrnl.* (Sacramento) 1 Nov. 3/1 The professors—the high 'Muck-a-Mucks'—tried fusion, and produced confusion. **1866** 'MARK TWAIN' *Lett. fr. Hawaii* (1967) 32 Not if I was High-You-Muck-a-Muck and King of Wawhoo. **1869** — *Sk. New & Old* (1875) 69 High Muck-a-mucks, the paleface from the land of the setting sun greets you! **1879** C. E. S. WOOD *Jrnl.* 13 Feb. in *Oreg. Hist. Q.* (1969) LXX. 144 Go to Thompsons 2 bit house, no deception there, hi you muck a muck and here's your bill of fare. **1920** S. LEWIS *Main Street* 117 He looks at me like he wants me to remember he's a highmuckamuck and worth two hundred thousand dollars. **1927** A. PHILIP *Painted Cliff* 14 J. B. Smith is the high muck-a-muck, the tyee of the mining business of British Columbia. **1947** *Chicago Tribune* 21 Dec. (Comics section) 8 They's a highmuckymuck in th'radio business vacationin' here, so we gotta be good. **1965** *Time* (Canad. ed.) 16 Apr. 14/3 Not all the Liberal high muckamucks were as warmly defended as Favreau.

highness (ˈhaɪnɪs), *sb.* Forms: see HIGH *a.* [OE. *héanes, -nis*; later *héahnes*, f. *héah* HIGH: see -NESS. OS. and OHG. *hôhnessa.*]

1. The quality or condition of being high; loftiness, tallness, altitude. Now *rare* in *lit.* sense, the usual word being HEIGHT.

c **897** K. ÆLFRED *Gregory's Past.* li. 397 Sio heanes ðonne ðara munta. *c* **1050** *Byrhtferth's Handboc* in *Anglia* VIII. 309/45 We ne maȝon hiȝ næfre ȝeseon for þære fyrlenan heahnysse. *a* **1225** *Ancr. R.* 372 Magdalene, þet speleð tures heinesse. *c* **1340** *Cursor M.* 11672 (Trin.) þe heȝenes of þis tre. **1398** TREVISA *Barth. De P.R.* v. xiii. (1495) 119 That it passe not dewe maner in lengthe, brede and hyghnesse. **1585** T. WASHINGTON tr. *Nicholay's Voy.* IV. xxiii. 139 A mount of great highnesse and sharpnesse. **1652** F. KIRKMAN *Clerio & Lozia* 108 Pattins, which render our highness and stature both alike. **1859** H. T. ELLIS *Hong Kong to Manilla* 124 They had all his highness of bone and lowness of flesh.

†**b.** *concr.* Something that is high; a high place, region, or part; a height; top, summit. *Obs.*

c **825** *Vesp. Psalter* cxlviii. 1 Herȝað dryhten of heofenum herȝað hine in heanissum. *c* **1000** *Ags. Gosp.* Matt. iv. 5 And asette hine ofer þæs temples heahnesse. *a* **1340** HAMPOLE *Psalter* xciv. 4 þe heghnessis of hilles ere his. **1450–1530** *Myrr. our Ladye* 190 Of whose sede, the hyenesse of goddes mounte flowreth with fayre blossomes. **1491** CAXTON *Vitas Patr.* II. (W. de W. 1495) 241 a/1 In the hyghenesse of heuen he had seen a douue.

2. Loftiness of rank, position, or character; high rank, condition, or quality; dignity, majesty.

c **1175** *Lamb. Hom.* 97 Disses deiȝes hehnesse is to heriane. **1297** R. GLOUC. (1724) 428 God hym ȝef þre þynges, as rychesse, And wysdom, & maystrye, & þys was gret heynesse. *c* **1380** WYCLIF *Serm.* Sel. Wks. I. 42 þus siche false presumpcioun of heynes of state. *c* **1485** *Digby Myst.* (1882) III. 2002 My lord of gret hynesse. **1553** GAU *Richt Vay* 49 He is set in greit power and henes. **1646** T. WHITAKER *Uzziah* 20 Uzziah . . doted upon his highnesse. *Mod.* The highness of his character atones for the lowness of his rank.

b. With possessive (e.g. the King's Highness; His, Her, Your Highness), as a title of dignity or honour given to princes. [Cf. GRACE, MAJESTY.]

'His, Her, Your, (etc.) Highness' was formerly the title of English kings and queens, varying with 'Grace', and later with 'Majesty'. In the Dedication of the Bible of 1611 to James I, 'Highness' and 'Majesty' are used indifferently, as they had been in reference to Queen Elizabeth; but in his reign 'Majesty' became the official style. 'Highness' was borne by the Lord Protector Cromwell and his wife. In present usage, 'all sons and daughters, brothers and sisters, uncles and aunts of the Sovereign are regarded as of the "Blood Royal", and designated "Royal Highness", which is bestowed also upon grandchildren, if they are the offspring of *sons*; but nephews, nieces, and cousins, in common with the children of *daughters*, are addressed as "Highness" only' (Whitaker, *Titled Persons* 1898). 'Highness' is also given to the chief Indian Feudatory Princes. 'Imperial' and 'Royal Highness' are applied to members of the Imperial and Royal families of other countries, 'Royal Highness' also to reigning Grand Dukes, 'Highness' and 'Serene Highness' to certain other princes (chiefly German); see SERENE.

[**1173** FOLIOT in *Mat. Hist. Becket* (Rolls) VII. 555 Vestræ, domine, celsitudini scribere tardavi.] **1402** PR. OF WALES *Let. to Hen. IV* (Nat. MSS. I. No. 36) More can I not write to yowr hynesse at this tyme. *c* **1460** FORTESCUE *Abs. & Lim. Mon.* vi. (1885) 118 His creauncers shul . . defame his highnes off mysgouernance. **1509** HAWES *Past. Pleas.* (Percy Soc.) 2 Your noble grace and excellent highnes For to accepte I beseche right humbly Thys lytle boke. **1529** WOLSEY in *Four C. Eng. Lett.* 11 This Kyndnes exibite from the Kyng's hyghnes. **1571** *Act 13 Eliz.* c. 29 §1 Within the Queenes Highnes Domynions. **1611** SHAKS. *Cymb.* I iii. 38 The Queene (Madam) Desires your Highnesse Company. **1611** BIBLE *Ded. to Jas. I* ¶6 The Lord of Heauen and earth blesse your Maiestie with many and happy dayes, that, as his Heauenly hand hath enriched your Highnesse with many singular, and extraordinary Graces; so [etc.]. **1653** *Weekly Intellig.* 14–21 Mar. in Ellis *Orig. Lett.* Ser. II. III. 367 The Privy Lodgings for his Highness the Lord Protector in Whitehall are now in readiness. **1714** SWIFT *Pres. St. Aff.* Wks. 1765 III. 296 His electoral highness should declare himself entirely satisfied. **1833** HT. MARTINEAU *Three Ages* I. 9 The King's Highness was not called upon to content himself with the homely fare of a farmhouse. **1848** W. H. KELLY tr. *L. Blanc's Hist. Ten Y.* II. 19 Her royal highness merely awaited an opportunity of getting rid of him. **1854** THACKERAY *Rose & Ring* vii, The first lord-in-waiting, entered and said, 'Royal Highnesses! Their Majesties expect you in the Pink Throne-room'.

†**3.** Haughtiness, pride; overbearingness. *Obs.*

c **1200** *Trin. Coll. Hom.* 143 Heinesse of oregel þe hie hadde. *a* **1340** HAMPOLE *Psalter* xxi. 21 Fra þe heghnes of iwes & all proud men. *c* **1394** *P. Pl. Crede* 542 Wiþ proude wordes . . Boþe wiþ 'þou leyest, and þou lext' in heynesse of sowle. **1553** GAU *Richt Vay* 95 Aganis al hienes and al oder sinnis. **1658** *Tradit. Mem. K. James* 131 [He] did by the highness of his hand bring it to the Counsell Table.

4. Greatness of degree, amount, force, etc.; high degree.

1659 B. HARRIS *Parival's Iron Age* 322 Through the highnesse of the wind, and strength of the stream. **1884** *Manch. Exam.* 10 July 5/1 Responsible for the highness of the rates.

Hence (*nonce-wds.*) **highness** *v. trans.*, to address with the title 'Highness'; **ˈhighnesshood, -ship** (*rare*), the rank or personality of one who has the title of Highness.

1658 COKAINE *Trappolin* III. i. Dram. Wks. (1874) 154 *Hora.* I will obey your Highness. *Tra.* Highness me no more! **1814** *Gonzanga* II. ii, My son wasn't grand enough for your Royal Highness-ship! **1818** J. W. CROKER *Jrnl.* 9 Dec. in *C. Papers* (1884) I. iv. 125 They don't quite *Highness* her [Mrs. Fitzherbert] in her domestic circle, but they *Madam* her prodigiously. **1844** *Blackw. Mag.* LV. 199 A king has descended from his throne, and a prince from royal highnesshood, to reward the virtues of the fair partners to whom they are unable to impart the rights of the blood-royal.

ˈhigh-pitched, *a.*

1. Of high pitch acoustically.

1748 J. MASON *Elocut.* 7 A Habit of reading in a high-pitched Key. **1889** 'J. S. WINTER' *Mrs. Bob* (1891) 10 Julia had a very high-pitched voice.

2. Of lofty tone or character.

1593 SHAKS. *Lucr.* 41 His high-pitch'd thoughts. **1875** McLAREN *Serm.* Ser. II. i. 2 The language . . seems much too emphatic and high-pitched, to be fully satisfied by a reference to anything in this life. **1897** DOWDEN *Fr. Lit.* III. i. 144 A relief from their fatigue of fine manners and high-pitched emotions.

3. Highly inclined to the horizon; steep.

1823 P. NICHOLSON *Pract. Build.* 427 After the decline of the Roman Empire, high-pitched roofs were very generally introduced. **1877** J. C. COX *Ch. Derbysh.* II. 81 Traces of the high-pitched roof.

ˈhigh-powered, *a.* [HIGH *a.* 22 b.] Having great power or drive (*lit.* and *fig.*); forceful, energetic; of good or high quality.

1903 *Daily Chron.* 1 Aug. 3/7 High-priced, high-powered cars. **1917** 'CONTACT' *Airman's Outings* p. xv, Modern two-seaters, high-powered, fast, and reliable. **1928** *Daily Mail* 16 Aug. 19/4 This class of fraud does not require so many high-powered salesmen as the old method of selling by personal canvas. **1934** T. S. ELIOT *Rock* ii. 51 Does the whole world stray in high-powered cars on a by-pass way? **1936** *Amer. Scholar* V. 83 The schools are failing, with all their high-powered modern pedagogy. **1944** *Living off Land* v. 114 High-powered microscopes. **1957** *Times Lit. Suppl.* 29 Nov. 724/2 American motor-cars that are always 'high-powered'. **1958** *Engineering* 14 Mar. 336/1 Automatic train control was developed . . early this century . . and, in 1920, a high-powered committee . . recommended its general adoption on all British railway lines. **1958** *Spectator* 25 July 138/1 High-powered promotion men. **1960** *News Chron.* 18 Mar. 6/4 The National Executive should . . set up a high-

powered inquiry into those industries which have already been nationalised. **1969** *Daily Tel.* 5 Feb. 15/1 The girl graduate, however high-powered her degree, is very often unemployable.

high priest, 'high-priest. [See HIGH *a.* 7.]

1. A chief priest; esp. the Jewish chief priest.

1382 WYCLIF *Sel. Wks.* III. 517 þe heyȝe prest Hely. **1526** TINDALE *John* xviii. 10 [He] smote the hye prestes servaunt. **1582** N. LICHEFIELD tr. *Castanheda's Conq. E. Ind.* xvii. 43 b, The kings high Priest. **1756–7** tr. *Keysler's Trav.* (1760) II. 399 The emperor Augustus Cæsar, high-priest, &c. having conquered Egypt, and united it to the Roman state, consecrated this obelisk to the sun. **1877** P. THOMPSON in *Queen's Printers' Aids to Bible* 148 To found and establish the Asmonæan dynasty of native high-priest-princes.

b. Applied to Christ as maker of the Atonement.

1526 TINDALE *Heb.* iv. 14 [v. 1] Seynge then thatt we have a grette hye prest whych hath entred heven..lett vs kepe oure profession. **1718** WATTS *Hymn*, With joy we meditate the grace Of our High Priest above. **1833** CRUSE *Eusebius* x. iv. 412 Our first and great High Priest.

2. *transf.* and *fig.* A hierophant; the head of any 'cult'.

1767 *Junius Lett.* ii. (1804) I. 17 Just indignation against this Junius, this high-priest of envy, malice, and all uncharitableness. **1831** BREWSTER *Newton* (1855) II. xvi. 118 The high priest of science found himself the inmate of a college. **1878** *N. Amer. Rev.* CXXVII. 106 Ricardo, the high-priest of the bullionists.

high-'priestess. A chief priestess. Also *fig.*

1645 PAGITT *Heresiogr.* (1647) 114 The high Priestesse of the new religion. **1647** R. STAPYLTON *Juvenal* 99 This grove's high-priestesse, heaven's true messenger. **1858** MISS MULOCK *Th. ab. Wom.* 244.

high-'priesthood. [f. HIGH PRIEST + -HOOD.] The office of high priest. Also *fig.*

1535 COVERDALE *1 Macc.* vii. 21 Thus Alcimus defended his hie presthode. **1640** BASTWICK *Lord Bps.* viii. I ij, He denyes Christs Highpriesthood in heaven. **1841–4** EMERSON *Ess.* Ser. I. xi. (1876) 272 The high-priesthood of the pure reason. **1885** *Athenæum* 21 Mar. 373/3 During the high-priesthood of John Hyrcanus.

high-'priestly, *a.* [f. as prec. + -LY[1].] Pertaining to or characteristic of a high priest.

1849 *Sidonia Sorc.* II. 183 Even in that glorious high-priestly prayer of His. **1874** H. R. REYNOLDS *John Bapt.* i. §5. 41 Authority..concentrated in high-priestly hands.

'high-ranking, *a.* orig. *U.S.* [RANKING *ppl. a.* s.v. RANK *v.*[1]] Of an officer: of high rank. Also more widely: senior, important.

1922 S. LEWIS *Babbitt* xviii. 232 He ought to have been a high-ranking officer, he had that natural ability to command. **1924** *Amer. Mercury* II. 173/1 Wary Wade, a high ranking student at Ohio State, has the right angle on boxing. **1936** *Time* 13 Jan. 26 To this dinner come high ranking members of both political parties in the Senate and House of Representatives. **1946** G. H. SEWARD *Sex & Social Order* x. 127 Such women relieved the ennui of wealthy high-ranking men. **1953** *Times* 6 Mar. 7/7 She left him..a son, Vassili, now a high ranking officer in the Soviet Air Force. **1957** H. ROOSENBERG *Walls came tumbling Down* 19 We were intended as exchanges against some high-ranking Nazis. **1960** P. H. REANEY *Orig. Eng. Place-Names* vii. 163 Holderness (ERY), 'headland of the hold', a high-ranking officer in the Danelaw. **1961** NEW ENG. BIBLE *Acts* xxv. 23 Accompanied by high-ranking officers and prominent citizens. **1964** *Observer* 16 Aug. 1/3 Six sets of the master-key..in a prison..would be available..to a limited number of high-ranking officers.

'high-,reaching, *a.* **a.** *lit.* That reaches high or aloft. **b.** *fig.* Aspiring, ambitious.

1594 SHAKS. *Rich. III*, IV. ii. 31 High-reaching Buckingham growes circumspect. [**1667** MILTON *P.L.* II. 644 At last appeer Hell bounds high reaching to the horrid Roof.] **1827** KEBLE *Chr. Y., Whitsun Monday* xii, Heroes and Kings, obey the charm, Withdraw the proud high-reaching arm. **1847** DISRAELI *Tancred* II. ix, A being formed for high-reaching exploits.

'high-ridged, *a.* Also 6–8 -rigged. Having a high ridge or ridges.

1545 ASCHAM *Toxoph.* (Arb.) 138 A certayne kynde of [arrow] heades whyche men call hie rigged, creased, or shouldred heades. **1706** PHILLIPS (ed. Kersey), *High-crested*, or *High-rigged*, a Term in Archery. **1747** tr. *Mem. Nutrebian Court* I. 13 A narrow, high-ridged nose.

'high-rigged, *a.* *Naut.* Having high rigging.

1795 J. PHILLIPS *Hist. Inland Navig.* 318 Detriment done to the locks and banks by high-rigged vessels.

high road, 'high-,road. [After HIGHWAY.] A chief or main road; a highway.

1709 STEELE *Tatler* No. 144 ¶2 [We] do not share alike in the Division of Her Majesty's High-Road. **1763** JOHNSON in *Boswell* 6 July, The noblest prospect which a Scotchman ever sees, is the high road that leads him to England. **1817** COLERIDGE *Biog. Lit.* 187 Words which he hears in the market, wake, high-road, or ploughfield. **1881** BESANT & RICE *Chapl. of Fleet* I. iii. The lane led on to the high-road.

b. *fig.*

1793 HOLCROFT *Lavater's Physiog.* III. xii. 64, I..will travel in the high-road of certainty, and confine myself to what is visible. **1839–40** THACKERAY *Catherine* v, I was on the high road to fortune.

'high-roller. *U.S. slang.* [HIGH *a.*, ? ROLLER *sb.*[1] 15.] One who spends extravagantly; one who gambles for high stakes.

1881 *Reinbeck* (Iowa) *Times* 15 Sept. 1/6 California's Speculators who invest large sums are called 'high rollers'. **1903** A. H. LEWIS *Boss* xiv. 184 I'd like to learn how you moral an' social high rollers reconcile yourselves to things. **1909** 'O. HENRY' *Roads of Destiny* xx. 340 There comes a party of these high-rollers that are always hunting up new places to eat in and poke fun at. **1927** K. NORRIS *Barberry Bush* vi. 156 'Say,' said Link, slightly drawling the last word, 'that girl is a high-roller, believe me. She's full of the Old Nick!' **1968** L. BLACK *Outbreak* ii. 20 He's a high roller... A big gambler. **1972** *Sunday Mail* (Brisbane) 2 July 19/5 The Hughes places had included some of the chief centres for the big-money gamblers, or 'high-rollers'.

†**'high-,runner.** *Obs.* A false die loaded so as to run on the high numbers; cf. HIGHMAN. So **'high-,running** *ppl. a.*

1668 DRYDEN *Evening's Love* III. i, The high-running dice. **1670** COTTON *Espernon* II. v. 235 False Dice..the high, and the low runners. **1721** J. DENNIS *Lett.* II. 407 (N.) The rhetorical author..makes use of his tropes and figures, which are his high and low runners, to cheat us.

high school: see SCHOOL *sb.*[1] 1 j.

'high-,set, *a.*

1. Set in a high or lofty position.

1382 WYCLIF *Job* xxxix. 28 In stones he dwellith, and in heȝe sett scarri flintis he bideth. **1765** A. DICKSON *Treat. Agric.* (ed. 2) 194 If the wrest is high set, the earth of the furrow will not touch the hinder part of the mold-board.

2. Set in a high key; high-pitched. Also *fig.*

a **1631** DRAYTON *Wks.* III. 1027 (Jod.) Thy high-set song. **1698** NORRIS *Pract. Disc.* IV. 54 His Spiritual and high-set Ear. **1742** RICHARDSON *Pamela* III. 335 Like well-tuned Instruments: But..too high-set for me. **1784** R. BAGE *Barham Downs* I. 54 Mr. and Mrs. Hunt seemed at present too high set for the dull conversation of business.

†**'highship.** *Obs.* In 3 **heih-, hehschipe.** [See -SHIP.] Elevation; high dignity; altitude.

a **1225** *Ancr. R.* 100 Vt of mine heihschipe. *c* **1230** *Hali Meid.* 5 þe hehschipe of meidenhad. *a* **1240** *Ureisun* in *Cott. Hom.* 189 þu hauest..ti muchele heh-schipe.

†**'high-shod, -shoed,** *a.* *Obs.* Wearing high shoes; hence, rustic, boorish. (See next.)

1656 J. HARRINGTON *Oceana* (1771) 152 (Jod.) Your high-shod prerogative and those same slouching fellows, your tribuns. **1693** DRYDEN *Persius* (1697) 478 The high-shoo'd Ploughman. *a* **1716** SOUTH *Serm.* (1717) IV. 497 Who..rejoice as much in their homely Dame, and ragged Children, together with their High-shoed Companions, as those who can..domineer over Kingdoms.

†**'high-shoe.** *Obs.*

1. One who wears high shoes, as rustics did in the 17th c.; hence, a rustic, countryman, plain man.

[**1603** BRETON *Packet Lett.* Wks. (1879) 49 (*Countryman's Let. to Sweetheart*) If my high shooes come home on Saturday, Ile see thee on Sunday.] **1650–66** WHARTON *Poems* Wks. (1683) 340 The Wary-High-Shooe, who so Idoliz'd The Covenant, that equally he priz'd It with his Bible. **1651** CLEVELAND *Rebel Scot* Poems 34 What all those wild Collegiates had cost The honest High-shoes. **1679** *Observ. last Dutch Wars* 4 Our Justices..in the more weighty points of the Law, would be baffled upon the Bench by every High-shooe. **1695** *Enq. Anc. Const. Eng.* 45 Whereby we of the high shoos, would be made as capable of judging..as the best gentleman of you all.

2. *pl.* **high shoon** used *attrib.* = Rustic, boorish. ***high-shoon-man***, a rustic, an agricultural labourer.

1654 WHITLOCK *Zootomia* 251 As if there were no medium between High-shoon Language, and that of the Buskin and Stage. **1664** EVELYN *Pomona* Pref. (1729) 50 This Improvement would be generally obstructed by the Tenant and High-shoon-men. **1676** MARVELL *Mr. Smirke* 52 He came with two Reprobates of his own Heresy into a little..Shire of Italy and..seduced three most simple high-shoon Bishops.

'high-,sounding, *a.*

1. Emitting a high or loud sound; highly sonorous.

1560 BIBLE (Genev.) *Ps.* cl. 5 Praise ye him with high sounding cymbals. **1717** FENTON *Poems* 212 (Jod.) When his highsounding lyre his valour rais'd. **1784** COWPER *Task* v. 681 Ah, tinkling cymbal and high-sounding brass, Smitten in vain!

2. Having an imposing or pretentious sound.

1784 DE LOLME *Eng. Const.* I. ii. (ed. 4) 33 Vested with more high-sounding prerogatives. *a* **1862** BUCKLE *Civiliz.* (1869) III. iii. 131 They had high-sounding titles. **1877** E. R. CONDER *Bas. Faith* iv. 145 What real meaning is there in the highsounding phrase, so often repeated, 'Knowledge of things in themselves'?

'high-speed, *a.* [HIGH *a.* 22 a.] **a.** Able or fitted to work or travel at high speed. **b.** Produced by swift processes or machinery. **c.** Produced or caused by, or during, high speed.

high-speed steel, an alloy steel of such toughness and hardness that it can be used for tools cutting so rapidly as to become red-hot.

1873 J. RICHARDS *Wood-working Factories* 63 High-speed loose pulleys. **1888** *Lockwood's Dict. Mech. Engin.* s.v., High-speed engines may be considered to embrace any engines making over 200 to 300 revolutions per minute... High-speed belting applies to belts for fans, wood-working machinery, centrifugal pumps, &c., in opposition to those for line and counter, and other slowly driving shafts. *High speed bearings*, bearings whose length exceeds their diameter by from four to six times. **1898** *Daily News* 1 Oct. 2/8 A high-speed destroyer. **1904** *Chambers's Jrnl.* 142/1 High-speed tool-steel lathes. **1908** *Daily Chron.* 6 Feb. 3/1 The crude truths that we look for only in the high-speed camera. **1909** *Westm. Gaz.* 11 Mar. 4/2 The high-speed flier of the future. **1912** *Chambers's Jrnl.* June 367/1 Their [*sc.* British makers'] introduction of high-speed steel in 1900. **1920** J. L. MYRES in H. G. Wells *Outl. Hist.* v. xxvii. 249/1 The bow..discharges a high-speed arrow with a twang. **1926** *Jrnl. Iron & Steel Inst.* CXIII. 307 High-speed steels are well known to be very complex alloys, a fact readily grasped when it is considered that even simple types contain elements such as tungsten, chromium, and vanadium, in addition to those usually found in plain steels. **1943** T. HORSLEY *Find, Fix & Strike* 20 He can concentrate on hitting his target..in the sure knowledge that he's virtually safe from a high-speed stall. **1943** *Sci. News* VII. 29 The dynamics of high-speed flow. **1950** *Gloss. Aeronaut. Terms (B.S.I.)* I. 29 High-speed wind tunnel. **1952** *This Week* 1 June 8/1 A second danger on the superhighways is something called 'high-speed hypnosis'—a trance-like state induced by mile after mile of effortless driving. **1954** WEBSTER Add. p. cxiii/2 *Skiing*, High-speed turn. **1956** A. H. COMPTON *Atomic Quest* 86 The action of high-speed neutrons moving through uranium 235 and plutonium. **1957** *Technology* Mar. 3/2 A complete set of all equipment likely to be of use in research from high-speed and time-lapse cameras down to X-ray cinematographic equipment for biological work. **1960** COOKE & MARKUS *Electronics & Nucleonics Dict.* 211/2 *High-speed carry*, a carry that bypasses the normal adding circuit in a computer. **1964** S. CRAWFORD *Basic Engin. Processes* iv. 104 High-speed steel, fully heat treated. An alloy steel containing tungsten.., with small percentages of chromium, vanadium and cobalt. **1967** *Technology Week* 23 Jan. 11/1 (Advt.), Sigma 5..does foreground real-time control..and high-speed input/output. **1969** *Times* 5 Feb. 13/6 The tracks are recorded by taking high-speed photographs. **1972** J. EASTWOOD *Henry in Silver Frame* ix. 95 The dentist's high-speed drill.

,high-'spirited, *a.* Possessing or marked by a lofty, courageous, or bold spirit; mettlesome.

a **1631** DRAYTON *Wks.* I. 113 (Jod.) A lady's sleeve high-spirited Hastings wore. **1660** MILTON *Free Commw.* Wks. (1851) 451 Of all Governments a Commonwealth aims most to make the People flourishing, vertuous, noble and high-spirited. **1777** ROBERTSON *Hist. Amer.* (1783) II. 216 Too high-spirited to be passive instruments in his hand. **1816** KEATINGE *Trav.* (1817) II. 13 Three hundred high-spirited stallions. **1887** JESSOPP *Arcady* iv. 110 She was an audacious, high-spirited little woman.

Hence **high'spiritedness.**

1647 TRAPP *Comm. 1 Cor.* xiv. 36 Take heed lest God for your arrogancy and high spiritedness lay you low enough.

'high-,stepper. A horse which lifts its feet high from the ground in walking and trotting; *transf.* a person of stately walk or bearing. So **'high-,stepping** *a.*

1848 THACKERAY *Van. Fair* li. 456 Splendid high-stepping carriage horses. **1860** MRS. RIDDELL *Too Much Alone* xxix, [The beauty] which makes a woman be called, when young and in good action, 'showy' and 'a high-stepper'. **1880** OUIDA *Moths* II. 54 She drove..very high-stepping English horses. **1886** 'MAXWELL GRAY' *Silence Dean Maitland* I. i. 9 A dog-cart, drawn by a high-stepping chestnut. *Ibid.* 10 Sending the high-stepper flying along the level down-road like the wind. **1973** D. RAMSAY *Deadly Discretion* 63 A millionaire..is pretty high stepping for a two-bit dancer.

†**'high-,stomached,** *a.* *Obs.* or *arch.* [See STOMACH.] Of high courage or spirit; high-spirited, haughty.

1548 HALL *Chron., Hen. VI*, 110 A man very wel borne..but no better borne then high stomacked. *a* **1592** H. SMITH *Wks.* (1867) II. 237 These nought-fearing fellows, these high-stomached men, which desire danger. **1593** SHAKS. *Rich II*, I. i. 18 High stomacked are they both, and full of ire. **1786** tr. *Beckford's Vathek* (1868) 103 In this deputation were some high-stomached sheiks, who..scrupled not to speak their opinion. **1894** CHARLES T. C. JAMES *Miss Precocity* II. ii. 24 He said she was 'high-stomached'. Very remarkable way of putting it..wasn't it?

'high-,strained, *a.* Highly strained; forced.

1659 D. PELL *Impr. Sea* Ded. A iij b, The Age wee live in is all for novelties, and high-strained Jigs of Musick. **1682** SIR T. BROWNE *Chr. Mor.* 109 The high strain'd paradoxes of old philosophy. **1748** HARTLEY *Observ. Man* I. iv. 449 The high-strained Encomiums..paid to Learning.

high street. [See STREET.] In OE., and often down to 17th c., A highway, a main road, whether in country or town; now, very generally, the proper name ('*High Street*') of that street of a town which is built upon a great highway, and is (or was originally) the principal one in the town.

In OE. times often applied to one of the Roman Roads or 'Streets'; it remains as the name of one of these, and of the mountain over which it passes in Westmorland.

? *c* **1000** *Charter of Oswald*, Kemble *Cod. Dipl.* III. 246 To ðære heahstræte. *c* **1200** *Trin. Coll. Hom.* 89 þat burh folc hihten þe heȝe strete. *a* **1300** *Cursor M.* 8071 (Gött.) þai went ham forth þe hie strett [*Cott.* þe mikel stret]. **1377** LANGL. *P. Pl.* B. XII. 105 Riȝt as syȝte serueth a man to se þe heighe strete. **1535** COVERDALE *Job* xxiii. 11 My fete kepe his path, his hye strete haue I holden. **1548** HALL *Chron. K. Edw. IV*, 210 Broughte..through the hygh streates of London, too the cathedrall church of sainct Paule. **1563** W. FULKE *Meteors* (1640) 38 b, The milke way..is the high street in Heaven that goeth streight to Jupiters palace. **1606** *N. Riding Rec.* (1883) I. 36 Yarme Bridge being a common and most necessarie passage..and being His Ma[ties] high streete. **1671** MILTON *Samson* 1599 The morning trumpets festival proclaimed Through each high street. **1726** LEONI *Alberti's Archit.* I. 69/2 High Streets..are designed for some certain purpose, especially any public one; as, for instance, those which lead to some Temple, or to the Course for Races, or to the Place of Justice. **1849** MACAULAY *Hist. Eng.* vii. II. 208 The Catholics were allowed..to carry the host in procession anywhere except in the high streets of royal burghs. **1896** *Oxford Sights & Scenes* 185 High Street

being called 'the High'. The usage is similar with other well-known streets in Oxford.

highstrikes ('haɪstraɪks). *jocular colloq.*, orig. *dial.* or *vulgar*. ¶ Perverted form of HYSTERICS.

1838 C. SELBY *Jacques Strop* ii. 4 Didn't I do the *high-strikes* famously? **1846** D. CORCORAN *Pickings* 149 She's one of the dreadfullest cases of the highstrikes I ever did see. **1899** *Pall Mall Mag.* Jan. 82 [Mrs.] Flounce fell into the highstrikes at traipsing the roads after four o'clock. **1914** G. ATHERTON *Perch of Devil* I. 204 If you don't get us out of this quick I'll have high-strikes. **1922** GALSWORTHY *Windows* I. 19 They say she 'ad the 'ighstrikes after. **1945** L. A. G. STRONG *Othello's Occupation* iv. 102 Maisie just cavorts along..till things get too much. Then she has the highstrikes. **1957** H. CROOME *Forgotten Place* xvi. 193 There I was, all in among the bicycles, having hysterics—yes, I mean it, genuine old-fashioned high strikes.

† **hight**, *sb.*[1] *Obs.* Forms: 3–4 **hiht**, 3–5 **hiȝt (-e)**, 3–6 **hight**, (4 **hit**); *Sc.* 4–5 **hicht** 4–6 **hecht**, (5 **heycht, height, heght**). [f. HIGHT *v.*[1]: a northern form (instead of the original OE. *hát*, ME. HOTE); after 15th c. only Sc. Cf. BEHIGHT *sb.*]

1. A command, order.

a **1300** *Cursor M.* 19330 (Edin.) We..ȝiu forbede þurȝ þe hiȝte of bissophede, þat ȝie in name of þat ihesu Be noȝte to preche sa bald. *c* **1375** *Sc. Leg. Saints, Petrus* 335 Cristis hecht for to fulfill, þan paul to Rome com petir till.

2. A promise; a vow.

a **1300** *Cursor M.* 785 þis hight..was ful fals and fikel. *c* **1375** *Sc. Leg. Saints, Machor* 1162 His hicht þat he mad to me. *c* **1400** *Apol. Loll.* 4 Aftir his hiȝt and couenaund. *c* **1425** WYNTOUN *Cron.* VIII. xviii. 12 In þat Heycht he wes noucht lele. *c* **1470** HARDING *Chron.* CLXXIV. xi, He hight the Kyng ..& held nothing his hight. **1535** STEWART *Cron. Scot.* III. 23 Oft syis fair hechtis makis fuillis fane. **1609** SKENE *Reg. Maj.* 30 Ane donation is vnderstand, to be ane hecht or bair promise, rather then ane trew or effectuall gift. **1808–25** JAMIESON, *Hecht, heycht*..this word is still used, *Lothian.* [**1862** HISLOP *Prov. Scotl.* 59 Fair hechts mak fools fain.]

† **hight, highth**, *sb.*[2] *Obs.* Forms: 1 **híȝð**, 3 **hihðe**, 4 **hihte, (hithte)**, 5 **hyȝt**. [OE. *híȝð*, f. *híȝian* to HIE, with suffix *-th* later *-t* after *gh*; cf. HEIGHT.] Exertion, impetuosity, haste.

c **1050** *Gloss.* in *Zsch. für deutsches Alterth.* XXXI. 14 *Acutis nisibus*, mid scearpum hiȝðum. *a* **1225** *Ancr. R.* 324 Schrift schal beon on hihðe imaked. *a* **1225** *Julianna* 77 þe reue..leup for hihðe wið lut men into a bat. *a* **1310** in Wright *Lyric P.* 110 For non hithte that he hath ne sytht me hym ner shake. *c* **1450** MYRC 559 Wheþer þe wordes were seyde a-ryȝt, And not turnet in þat hyȝt.

† **hight**, *sb.*[3] *Obs.* Forms: 1 **hyht**, (**hiht**), 2 **huht (-y-)**, 3 *Orm.* **hihht, hiȝt(e.** [OE. *hyht*:—OTeut. **huhti-* from root *hug-* of *hycgan* to think, hope. Cf. HIGH *sb.*[1]] Hope, glad expectation; gladness, joy.

971 *Blickl. Hom.* 165 Ðe bið þonne hyht and ȝefea. *c* **1000** *Agrs. Ps.* (Th.) cxiii. 20 [cxv. 11] Hio hyht heora habban on Drihten. *c* **1175** *Lamb. Hom.* 97 [He] ȝifð heom forȝifnesse and huht and heore ȝeomerinde mod iliðegað. *c* **1200** ORMIN 3816 Hihht & hope o Drihhtin God. *a* **1250** *Owl & Night.* 272 Hit is min hiȝte, hit is mi wune. *Ibid.* 1101 An hadde soþþe blisse and hiȝte.

hight, *sb.*[4] and *a.*, var. of HEIGHT *sb.* and *a.*

hight, *v.*[1] *arch.* Forms: see below. [A Com. Teut vb.; orig. reduplicated: OE. *hát-an*, pa. t. *heht*, contr. *hét*, pl. *hehton*, *héton*, pa. pple. *háten* = OFris. *hêta*, OS. *hêtan*, (MLG. *hêten*, MDu. *heeten*, *heiten*, Du. *heeten*), OHG. *heizzan*, (MHG. *heizen*, Ger. *heiszen*), ON. *heita* (Sw. *heta*, Da. *hede*), Goth. *haitan*, pa. t. *haihait*, pl. *-um*, pa. ppl. *haitans*, to call by name, to name, call to come or do something, bid, command. Of this vb. the Old Teutonic medio-passive voice, Goth. *haitada*, pl. *haitanda* (pres. t.), remained in OE. as *hátte*, pl. *hátton* (pres. and pa. t.), being the only trace of this voice in English. In the other Teutonic langs. the passive *form* had been lost, or rather blended with that of the active, but the *sense* remained, as one of the uses of the verb, which was thus both 'to call' and 'to be called'. In ME. the same fate befell the passive form, so that here also the active *hoten*, *hight*, came to be both 'to call' and 'to be called', the latter being the chief use in later times. In addition to this curious confusion, the active forms themselves suffered a remarkable series of changes, resulting finally in the entire loss of the present stem, and the substitution of that of the pa. t. The original pres. *háte* and pa. pple. *háten* regularly became in ME. *hôte*, *hôte(n* (to *c* 1456), northern *hāte*, *hāte(n*. The redupl. pa. t. *heht*. (Goth. *haihait* = **hehait*) gave ME. *heȝt*, *hiht*, *hight*; the contracted *hét* gave ME. *hēt*, *heet*, *hete* (to *c* 1470). Thus, the normal ME. inflexion was *hote*, *hēt* or *hight*, *hote(n*; but this was, from an early date, disturbed by the influence of 'levelling', and of various assumed analogies. From *c* 1200 the anomalous pa. t. *heht* often took, like the weak vbs., final *-e*, the loss of which, however, in 15th c., again made the form *hight*. About 1300, the pres. t. took (in midl. dial.) the vowel of the past, and became *hete*, *heet(e*, which survived to the 16th c. Farther north, the pres. assumed the form of the redupl. pa. t., and became *hight*, *hicht*, *hecht*, still extant in Sc. in sense 'promise'. Both forms of the pa. t. *hēt* and *hight* also passed over into the pa. pple., where *hight* is still a wellknown archaism. Dialectally, or by individual writers, this is extended as *highted*. There are various other anomalies; for which see the Forms below. The only parts of the vb. which remain in literary use are the pa. pple. *hight* 'called', and the kindred pa. t. *hight* 'was called', both conscious archaisms unknown to ordinary prose. In the dialects other forms and senses survive.]

A. Illustration of Forms.

1. Present stem. *α.* 1 **hát-**, 2–5 **hāt-**, 3–5 **hôt-**, (3 **hoat-**, 5 **hoot-**).

c **897** K. ÆLFRED *Gregory's Past.* Pret. 3 Ælfred kyning hateð gretan Wærferð biscep. *Ibid.* lviii. 443 Dryhten hwæt hætst ðu me don? *c* **1000** *Ags. Gosp.* Matt. xiv. 28 Hat me cuman to þe [*Lindisf. G.* haat meh ȝecumæ to ðe]. *c* **1050** *Byrhtferth's Handboc* in *Anglia* (1885) VIII. 303 þæt ȝer þe man hæt solaris. *c* **1175** *Lamb. Hom.* 15 God almihtin þe hat don þin god on-ȝein his uuel. *c* **1200** *Trin. Coll. Hom.* 201 Alle bileffulle ich hote þus waken. *a* **1225** *Ancr. R.* 186 So hat owr ueder ou. **1258** *Eng. Proclam. Hen. III*, I. 6 We willen and hoaten þæt alle vre treowe heom healden dead-liche ifcan. *c* **1320** R. BRUNNE *Medit.* 240 Thys y ȝow hote. **14..** *Wyclif's Deut.* xxiii. 23 *marg.*, Of him that hootith, and fulfillith it not. *c* **1440** *Promp. Parv.* 249/2 Hotyn or make beheste, *promitto*. *c* **1475** *Assembl. Ladies* 689 Now good, tell on, I hate you, by saynt Jame.

β. ? 3, 4–6 **hete**, 5–6 **heete**, (? 3, 4–5 **heit**).

a **1300** *Cursor M.* 5427 Heit [*Fairf.* hete] me truli, wit couenand. *c* **1330** R. BRUNNE *Chron.* (1810) 148 His help I ȝow hete. *c* **1386** CHAUCER *Man of Law's T.* 236 But oon auow to grete god I heete [*v.r.* hete]. *c* **1460** *Towneley Myst.* (Surtees) 72 Oylle of mercy I can hym heyt. *Ibid.* 74 A child to bere thou me hetys, How shuld it be? **1549–62** STERNHOLD & H. *Ps.* cxix. 76 As thou to me thy seruant hetest.

γ. 3–4 **hiht, hiȝt**, 4– **hight**, (4 **hite, hyte**, 4–5 **hyght**, 5 **hiȝte**); *Sc.* 4– **hicht, hecht**, (4–5 **hycht**, 5–6 **heght**, 6 **heycht**).

a **1300** *Cursor M.* 5431 (Cott.) Truli now i þe hight [*Gött.* hite]. *Ibid.* 24890 (Edin.) þu sal nu hiht and vow me her. *a* **1340** HAMPOLE *Psalter* Prol. 21 Hyghtand ioy til ryghtwismen. **1375** BARBOUR *Bruce* XII. 318, I hecht heir, in my lawte. *c* **1450** *St. Cuthbert* (Surtees) 5782 Here I hight amendement. *c* **1560** A. SCOTT *Poems* (S.T.S.) iii. 34 And hecht thame giftis, howbeid ȝe gif thame nocht. **1565** GOLDING *Ovid's Met.* VII. (1593) 169 And as for leach, was none that helpe could hight. **1674** RAY *N.C. Words* 25 *To Hight* (Cumb.), to promise or vow. **1789** BURNS 5 *Carlines* xi, He wadna hecht them courtly gifts..But he wad hecht an honest heart. **1872** BLACKIE *Lays Highl.* 3 Molaise..Hights me go, and I obey.

2. Past tense. *a. str.* 1 **heht**, 3 **hieȝt, (heitt)**, 4 **heȝt, heycht, hiȝt**, 4–5 **hight**; also *weak* 2–3 **hehte**, 3 **hæhte, hahte, hætte, heitte**, 3–4 **hihte**, 3–5 **hiȝte**, 4–5 **highte, hyghte**, 5 **heȝte, heghte**; *undetermined* 6– **hight, (hyght)**, *Sc.* **hecht, (heght)**.

a **1000** *Andreas* 365 (Gr.) He heht englas him to cuman. *c* **1175** *Lamb. Hom.* 121 Summe..hehten hine aredan. *a* **1200** *Moral Ode* 268 Al þet þe laþe gast hechte to. *c* **1250** *Meid. Maregrete* viii, E heitt hem aquelle. *Ibid.* lv, Olibrius heitte þe mai ut of prisun don. *c* **1250** *Gen. & Ex.* 218 And hieȝt him ded he sulde ben. *a* **1300** *Cursor M.* 15660 Has þou nu al forgeten þat þou hight. *c* **1300** *Harrow. Hell* 231 That I hihte the In the old lawe, thou dudest me. **1362** LANGL. *P. Pl.* A. III. 9 As þe kyng hihte. **1375** BARBOUR *Bruce* X. 262 He his man hecht for till be. *c* **1375** *Sc. Leg. Saints, Symon & Judas* 122 He heycht to mend his stat. *c* **1380** WYCLIF *Serm.* Sel. Wks. I. 101 þat he hiȝt hem graciously. *c* **1440** *York Myst.* xliv. 49 He highte vs fro harme for to hyde. *c* **1440** *Gesta Rom.* lxv. 284 þe porter hiȝte for to do it. *c* **1450** *St. Cuthbert* (Surtees) 8180 Wele he hight, bot euyl did he. **1460** CAPGRAVE *Chron.* 265 Notwithstanding that the kyng hite him this, he vas exiled. **1557** *Tottell's Misc.* (Arb.) 249 Hopefull youth that higth me health. **1578** *Ps. li.* in *Scot. Poems 16th C.* II. 114 Thou heght to Abraham anone, Isack his eldest son. **1793** BURNS *Meg o' the Mill* 9 The Miller he hecht her a heart leal and loving. [**1841** hight: see B. 5 *β* c.]

β. str. 1 **hét**, 2–4 **hēt**, 4–5 **heet, hett**; also 3 **heitt**, (? *weak*), 3 **heitte**, 4 **hete**, 4–5 **hette**.

c **900** tr. *Bæda's Hist.* III. xii. [xiv.] (1890) 194 þæs þe hine slean het. *a* **1000** *Cædmon's Gen.* 2613 (Gr.) He het his naman Adam. *c* **1175** *Lamb. Hom.* 7 þe witeȝa het þet we sculde makien his stiȝes. *c* **1290** *Beket* 806 in *S. Eng. Leg.* I. 129 Heo heten him don heom sikernesse. *c* **1330** R. BRUNNE *Chron.* (1810) 275 þre days trewe þe Inglis him hete. **13..** *Guy Warw.* (A.) 204 To him he cleped Gij, And him hete and comandi. **13..** *Gaw. & Gr. Knt.* 448 Loke, Gawan, þou be grayþe to go as þou hettez. **1377** LANGL. *P. Pl.* B. XX. 271 Enuye..heet freres to go to scole. **1393** *Ibid.* C. II. 17 He het þe elementes to helpe ȝow alle tymes. *c* **1430** *Syr Tryam.* 1043 When thou haste done that thou hett. **1460** *Lybeaus Disc.* 206 Kyng Artour.. Hette of the table rounde Four the beste knyghtes..Arme Lybeaus.

γ. erron. 6 **hote**.

1579 SPENSER *Sheph. Cal.* July 164 A shepheard trewe, yet not so true, as he that earst I hote.

3. Pa. pple. *a.* 1 **(ȝe)háten**, 2–3 **(ȝe-, i-)haten**, 3–4 **haten**, 4–5 **hate**; 2–6 **(ȝe-, y-, i-)hoten, (y-, i-)hote**.

c **888** K. ÆLFRED *Boeth.* i. §1 Ða wæs sum consul.. Boetius wæs haten. *c* **975** *Rushw. Gosp.* Matt. xxvii. 16 Monn se wæs haten barrabas [*Hatt. G.* ȝehaten]. **1154** *O.E. Chron.* an. 1132 An prior of St Neod, Martin was ȝehaten. *c* **1175** *Cott. Hom.* 219 Heo was ȝehoten leoht berinde. *c* **1175** *Lamb. Hom.* 97 He is ihate on grekisc paraclitus. *c* **1200** ORMIN 5200 He wass hatenn Helyseow. *c* **1205** LAY. 3156 þe kinge of Bruttaine þe Leir is haten. *c* **1250** *Meid. Maregrete* i, Ðe vie of one meidan was hoten Maregrete. **1297** R. GLOUC. (1724) 80 A lordyng of þe Romaynes, þat y hote was Galle. *a* **1300** *K. Horn* 201 Horn ihc am ihote. *a* **1300** *Cursor M.* 14503 His nam was haten caiphas. *Ibid.* 19465 þat ilk þat þan was hate saul. **1362** LANGL. *P. Pl.* A. I. 61 A wiht þat wrong is I-hote. *c* **1375** *Sc. Leg. Saints, Johannes* 65 þat hatine wes deme drusiane. *c* **1386** CHAUCER *Reeve's T.* 21 His name was hoote [*v.r.* hoten] deynous Symkyn. **1390** GOWER *Conf.* I. 55 A lord, whiche Phorceus Was hote. *c* **1400** *Solomon's Bk. Wisd.* 156 He was yhote Ionas. **1513** DOUGLAS *Æneis* III. i. 25 Our friendlie goddis, Penates hait [*rime* estait]. *a* **1643** W. CARTWRIGHT *Ordinary* III. i. in Hazl. *Dodsley* XII. 255 Aldersgate Is hoten so from one that Aldrick hight.

β. 3–5 **hatten (-in)**, 4–5 **hatte**. Chiefly *north.*

[? from the passive form *hatte*, or shortened from *hāten*.]

a **1300** *Cursor M.* 9545 (Cott.) þe toþer was hatten sothfastnes. **1375** BARBOUR *Bruce* XIV. 376 Thomas of dwn hattyn wess he. **1387** TREVISA *Higden* (Rolls) I. 97 þe tour is i-cleped and hatte Babel. *a* **1400** *Relig. Pieces fr. Thornton MS.* (1867) 11 The secunde dedely synne es hattene enuy. *c* **1450** *St. Cuthbert* 6827 His name was hattyn cuthrede.

γ. 4 **heiten, heit, hete, hett(e**, 4–5 (9 *dial.*) **het**.

a **1300** *Cursor M.* 1524 (Cott.) Sco was heiten [*v.r.* cald(e)] noema. *Ibid.* 14783 (Gött.) Ouþer es he prophete, Or crist himself to man es hete. *c* **1340** *Ibid.* 2658 (Trin.) As I bifore haue hette [*v.rr.* hight, heȝt, hith] to þe. *Ibid.* 12820 (Trin.) þat longe was hett [*v. rr.* hight, hiȝt] now comen es. *c* **1460** *Towneley Myst.* (Surtees) 39 So have I het. **1855** WAUGH *Lanc. Life* (1857) 65 A lawm, fause owd felly, het an elder.

δ. ? 3, 4— **hight**, (4 **heȝt, hiht, hith, hite**, 4–5 **hiȝt, -e, hyȝt, yhight, yhyȝt, ihight**, 4–6 **hyght**, 5 **height**, Sc. 4— **hicht, hecht**, 7 **heght**).

a **1300** *Cursor M.* 1276 (Cott.) þe oile me was hight [*v.rr.* heȝt, het]o merci. *Ibid.* 2590 (Gött.) As it was hite bifor þas dais. **1340** HAMPOLE *Pr. Consc.* 107 [God] has hight him yit þar to þe blise of heven. *c* **1374** CHAUCER *Troylus* v. 540 O hous of housses, whilom best yhight! *c* **1386** —— *Frankl. T.* 595 Wel ye woot what ye han hight [*v.rr.* hyȝt, hiȝt, hiht]. *a* **1400** *Pistill of Susan* 14 He hed a wif hiȝt Susan. *c* **1475** *Rauf Coilȝear* 449, I sall hald that I haue hecht. **1513** DOUGLAS *Æneis* I. i. 19 Thair was ane anciant ciete hecht Cartage. **1563** in *B. Googe's Eglogs* etc. (Arb.) 81 Happye (Googe) he maye be hyght. **1590** SPENSER *F.Q.* II. ix. 59 An auncient booke, hight Briton moniments. *a* **1605** MONTGOMERIE *Flyting* 451 Wee haue heght to Mahoun, for hand-sell, this hair. **1664** BUTLER *Hud.* II. iii. 106 A cunning man, hight Sidrophel. **1812** BYRON *Ch. Har.* I. iii, Childe Harold was he hight. **1863** BARING-GOULD *Iceland* 116 A glen which..has been hight the Vale of Shadows.

ε. 4 ***hehted, (hethede)**, 6–7 **highted**, *Sc.* 8–9 **hechted**.

c **1300** *Havelok* 551 Hwan þe swike him hauede hethede, þat he shulde him forth lede. **1583** STANYHURST *Æneis* III. (Arb.) 77 For those plats Strophades in languadge Greekish ar highted. **1602** FULBECKE *Pandectes* 83 So Arsaces..was.. highted a lawfull king. *a* **1833** J. BALLANTYNE in *Whistle-Binkie* (Scot. Songs) Ser. I. 33 Mony big loons hae hechted to wyle her awa.

4. Passive: see B. 5.

B. Signification.

I. *trans.* †**1.** To command, bid; to order, ordain. Constr. with person and thing, or pers. and *inf.* or *clause*; also with thing only, and *absol.* *Obs.*

a **900** *Charter* (Th.) 47 (Bosw.) [He] heht ðæt he cuome to him. *c* **1000** ÆLFRIC *Hom.* I. 394 We dydon swa swa ðu us hete. —— *Gram.* xxi. (Z.) 125 Mid ðam ȝemete we hatað oðre menn don sum ðing. *Ibid.*, Gehwa hæt oðerne, na hyne sylfne. *c* **1175** *Lamb. Hom.* 31 þenne þe preost hine hat aȝefen þa ehte. *c* **1200** *Trin. Coll. Hom.* 211 He ne wile don þat god him het..and doð þat þe deuel het. *c* **1275** LAY. 31552 We beoþ icome ase þou hauest i-hote. *a* **1300** *Vox & Wolf* 36 in Hazl. *E.P.P.* I. 59 Be stille, ich hote, a Godes nome! *c* **1300** *Beket* 2039 (Percy) We hoteþ þe ek in his half þat þu assoilli also þe Bischop [etc.]. *c* **1350** *Will. Palerne* 1082 [He] het hem alle hiȝe þider as harde as þei miȝt. **1362** LANGL. *P. Pl.* A. I. 17 He hihte þe eorþe to seruen ow vchone. *Ibid.* III. 9 Corteisliche þe Clerk þo as þe kyng hihte, Tok þe Mayden bi þe Middel. **1377** *Ibid.* B. II. 218 He was ..Ouer al yhowted and yhote trusse. **1387** TREVISA *Higden* (Rolls) I. 411 3if þe prince of þe lond hote, Briddes syngeþ wiþ mery note. **1447** BOKENHAM *Seyntys* Introd. (Roxb.) 5 Lete hem be hete Thedyr to bere and there to lete The same thyng. **14..** *Stac. Rome* 804 in *Pol. Rel. & L. Poems* 141 He hett also that men shoulde to chyrche goo. **1872** [see A. 1 *γ*].

†**b.** To bid come, call, summon. (Only in OE. and *arch.* in Spenser.) *Obs.*

a **1000** *Daniel* 532 Ða wæs to ðam dome Daniel haten. **1591** SPENSER *Daphn.* 11 Ne let the Sacred Sisters here be hight, Though they of sorrowe heavilie can sing.

2. To promise, to vow; to pledge oneself. (Constr. as in 1.) *Obs.* exc. *Sc.*

a **900** CYNEWULF *Juliana* 53 Gif þu to sæmran gode.. hætsð hæþen-weoh. *c* **1200** ORMIN 4922 þatt tatt icc het Drihhtin. *c* **1205** LAY. 23384 3et ich wulle haten mare. *c* **1250** *Gen. & Ex.* 4098 De lond hoten sal hem ben giuen. *a* **1300** *Cursor M.* 5429 (Gött.) Hite me treuli þu þi selue Sal me wid min eldris delue. *c* **1340** *Cursor M.* 3886 (Fairf.) þou sal haue rachel as I þe hiȝt. *c* **1375** *Sc. Leg. Saints, Baptista* 1022 Bath gold and fe Hechtand hyme in-to plente. *c* **1380** WYCLIF *Sel. Wks.* III. 30 We þat hoten grete avowis to voiden..siiknessis. *c* **1386** CHAUCER *Man of Law's T.* 236 Oon auow to grete god I heete. *c* **1400** MAUNDEV. Pref. (Roxb.) 2 þis es þe land þat es hight til vs in heritage. *c* **1460** *Towneley Myst.* (Surtees) 44 That he may fle Esaw, That us bothe hetes bale to brew. *c* **1470** HARDING *Chron.* CLXVIII. vi, Ever ye kyng Edward hight men greate hyre Hym for to take. **1577–87** HARRISON *England* I. vii. in *Holinshed* 15 He was so desperatelie wounded, that no man hight him life. **1724** RAMSAY *Tea-t. Misc.* (1733) II. 182 Rob my eem hecht me a stock. **1829** in Chambers *Scott. Songs* 40 Hope aye hechts his safe return.

†**3.** *parenthetical.* To assure (one that it is as one says): cf. 'I promise you.' *Obs.*

13.. *E.E. Allit. P.* A. 402 Maysterful mod & hyȝe pryde I hete þe arn heterly hated here. *c* **1350** *Will. Palerne* 1123 So harde þei hiȝed þan, i hote þe for soþe. **1375** BARBOUR *Bruce* VII. 156 The kyng, that hungry wes, I hicht. *c* **1420** *Pallad. on Husb.* III. 936 Also this y yow hete I preued haue. **1501** DOUGLAS *Pal. Hon.* I. xxxiii, Baith aixtree and quheillis of gold, I hote. **1515** *Scot. Field* 257 in *Chetham Misc.* (1856) II, I will wynde you to wreke, wees, I you heete.

4. To call, to name. (Now only in *pa. pple.*). *arch.*

c **893** K. ÆLFRED *Oros.* I. i. §17 Ða deor hi hataþ hranas. *c* **1175** *Lamb. Hom.* 77 þu scald..bere knaue child, and haten hit helend. *c* **1205** LAY. 2857 To hire he hefde loue, and læfdi heo hehte. *a* **1225** *Juliana* 55 Sathanas þat tu leuest upon & ti feader hatest. *c* **1350** *Will. Palerne* 405 þat menskful mayde Melior was hoten. *c* **1450** *St. Cuthbert* (Surtees) 477 A bischop hight Eugenius. *c* **1460** *Towneley Myst.* (Surtees) 145 Emanuelle is hete His name for to lere. **1580** SIDNEY *Ps.* XXIV. vi, Even He the King of glory hight. **1583** STANYHURST *Æneis* I. (Arb.) 26 Thee Romans of his owne name, Romulus, highting. **1605** VERSTEGAN *Dec. Intell.* (1634) 83 The nether Saxons are hight now Friesians. **1807–8** W. IRVING *Salmag.* (1824) 83 A little pest, hight Tommy Moore. **1845** HOOD *Recipe Civiliz.* 39 Look at the polish'd nations hight The civilized.

II. *intr.*: in origin *medio-passive.*

5. To call oneself, be called, have or bear the name. (Now only in the archaic pa. t. *hight.*)

a. Orig. in forms repr. the OTeut. passive, Goth. pres. t. *haitada, -anda.* Pres. and pa. t. 1 **hátte**, pl. **-on**, 2–5 **hatte**, pl. **-en**, 4–5 **hette, hatt, hat, hett.** The forms with *e* were prob. influenced by those in b (*b*).

c **897** K. ÆLFRED *Gregory's Past.* lviii. 445 On ðæm bocum ðe hatton Apocalipsin. *c* **1000** *Ags. Gosp.* Matt. xiii. 55 Hu ne hatte hys modor Maria? *c* **1200** *Trin. Coll. Hom.* 13 þe six werkes of brihtnesse hatten þus. *Ibid.* 89 Bethfage..hatte þe þrop. *a* **1300** *Cursor M.* 3948 'Tel me nam', he said, 'quat es þin?' 'Iacob i hatt' [*v.rr.* hate, het]. *Ibid.* 14218 Thomas þat hette didimus. *c* **1330** R. BRUNNE *Chron.* (1810) 22 Oxen hate þe toun, þer þe body felle. **1377** LANGL. *P. Pl.* B. XVI. 15 Herte hatte þe [h]erber þat it in groweth. **1398** TREVISA *Barth. De P.R.* III. i. (Tollem. MS.), A man hat [**1535** hight, **1582** is called] antrapos in Grew. *c* **1430** *Chev. Assigne* 232 Betryce she hette. *c* **1450** *St. Cuthbert* (Surtees) 377 Hardebrechins þe cite hatte. *c* **1460** *Towneley Myst.* (Surtees) 8 A good yoman my master hat.

(*b*) Extended to infinitive; and sometimes in indicative with person-endings.

c **1250** *Gen & Ex.* 813 Ðat burȝe..atteð cariatharbe. *a* **1300** *Cursor M.* 3948 (Cott.) Iacob ya, Sal þou na langer hetten [*v.rr.* hat, be cald] sua. *c* **1340** *Ibid.* 2650 (Trin.) And seide þou hettest now abrahame. *c* **1380** WYCLIF *Serm.* Sel. Wks. I. 365 Zacarie..tolde what þe child shulde hatte. *c* **1400** *Destr. Troy* 4257 Not Delphon but Doels sum demyt hit to het. *c* **1460** *Towneley Myst.* (Surtees) 74 Godes son shalle he hat [*rime* that].

b. Already in OE. the passive infinitive had to be supplied by the active **hátan**, ME. **hôten**, *north.* **hāte**; and from an early date in ME., the passive forms began to yield to the corresponding active ones: *α.* in Pres. t. 1 **hátan**, 3–5 **hôte(n**, *north.* 3–5 **hāte**, (4–6 **hait**). (By Spenser also erroneously in pa. t.) *β.* in Pa. t. **het, hete**; later also in pres. t. *γ.* in Pa. t. **highte** (etc.), later **hight** (the only part still in archaic use). *δ.* From 14th to 18th c. *hight* was extended to the pres. t. (sometimes with person-endings), and to the infinitive.

α. a **1000** *Cædmon's Gen.* 344 Se hehsta hatan sceolde Satan siððan. *c* **1200** *Trin. Coll. Hom.* 127 þis child shal hoten godes prophete. *a* **1300** *Cursor M.* 4752 (Cott.) In þe flum þat hait þe nile. *Ibid.* 2650 (Gött.) And said he suld hate [*v.rr.* hatte, hat] abraham. **1393** LANGL. *P. Pl.* C. III. 31 *Filius dei* he hoteþ. ? *a* **1400** *Arthur* 613 Now hyt hooteþ Glastyngbury. *c* **1511** *1st Eng. Bk. Amer.* (Arb.) Introd. 28/1 Oon aforemontayen and hooth caput viride. **1513** DOUGLAS *Æneis* I. Prol. 244 That in the text of Virgill..Hait Deiphebe. *Ibid.* ii. 58 Quhilkis, eist, south, and waist wyndis hait [*v.r.* hate] with ws. **1579** SPENSER *Sheph. Cal.* Sept. 194 Lowder (for so his dog hote). **1590** —— *F.Q.* I. xi. 29 It rightly hot The well of life.

β. a **1175** *Cott. Hom.* 227 His sune hete arfaxat. *a* **1300** *K. Horn* 9 Godhild het his quen. **1387** TREVISA *Higden* (Rolls) I. 115 In þat mount was þe litel strete of preostes, þat heet Be[th]phage. *c* **1425** *Eng. Conq. Irel.* (E.E.T.S.) 1 [An] heighe man in Irland, þat het dermond Macmorgh. **1470–85** MALORY *Arthur* VII. ii, What heteth your lady and where dwelleth she?

γ. a **1225** *Juliana* 5 Hire fleschliche feader affrican hehte. *c* **1290** *S. Eng. Leg.* I. 67/6 þat heiȝte Maximian. *a* **1300** *Cursor M.* 633 (Cott.) þar for hight [*v.r.* heȝt] sco virago. *a* **1300** *Ibid.* 2594 (Gött.) Sare..had..an hand womman þat agar hite. *c* **1330** R. BRUNNE *Chron. Wace* (Rolls) 9426 Sire Bertel þen hat þat on, þat oþer heyghte sire Iordan. *c* **1386** CHAUCER *Prol.* 719 At this gentil hostelrye That highte [*v.rr.* hyȝte, hiht] the Tabard. **1480** CAXTON *Descr. Brit.* 13 Bathe highte sommetyme Athamannus Cyte. **1513** BRADSHAW *St. Werburge* I. 314 The quene of eest-Englande saynt Heryswith she hyght. **1535** STEWART *Cron. Scot.* (1858) I. 6 In Grece..duelt ane king, the quhilk hecht Æalus. **1663** BUTLER *Hud.* I. i. 152 In School-Divinity as able As he that hight *Irrefragable*. **1714** GAY *Sheph. Week* II. 20 A Lass that Cic'ly hight, had won his Heart. **1841** LONGF. *Childr. Lord's Supper* 48 Father he hight and he was in the parish.

δ. c **1340** *Cursor M.* 3946 (Fairf.) Tel me man quat þou hiȝt. *c* **1385** CHAUCER *L.G.W.* Prol. 423 That highten Balades, Roundels, Virelayes. *c* **1386** —— *Knts. T.* 699 But ther as I was wont to highte Arcite, Now highte I Philostrate noght worth a myte. *c* **1430** *Syr. Gener.* 1665 'What dooth he hight', she seid, 'Madame?' *c* **1440** *York Myst.* xxvi. 225 What hytist thou? **1523** LD. BERNERS *Froiss.* I. clxiii. 201 Sir, sayde he, I hyght Iohan of Helenes, but what is your name? *a* **1536** *Calisto & Mel.* in Hazl. *Dodsley* I. 56 *Sem.* What hight she? *Cal.* Melibæa is her name. **1600** FAIRFAX *Tasso* I. Argt. 1 He sends them to the fort that Sion hights. *a* **1610** HEALEY *Cebes* (1636) 122 Shee that teareth her hayre, hight Sorrow. **1641** PRYNNE *Antip.* 154 Hightest thou Vrse? Have thou Gods curse. *a* **1643** W. CARTWRIGHT *Ordinary* II. ii. in Hazl. *Dodsley* XII. 241 How highteth she, say you?

¶ **III. 6.** Used by Spenser as a *pseudo-archaism* in various senses not otherwise exemplified:

a. to direct; **b.** to commit; **c.** to name, designate, mention; **d.** to mean, purport.

1579 SPENSER *Sheph. Cal.* July 164 A shepherd trewe, yet not so true As he that earst I hote. *Ibid.* Sept. 172 Say it out, Diggon, what euer it hight, For not but well mought him betight. **1590** —— *F.Q.* I. iv. 6 Yet charge of them was to a Porter hight. **1596** *Ibid.* IV. x. 38 An hundred brasen caudrons bright..Every of which was to a damzell hight. *Ibid.* V. xi. 8 But the sad steele seizd not, where it was hight, Uppon the childe, but somewhat short did fall. *Ibid.* VI. vii. 31 She could or save or spill whom she would hight.

Hence †'**highting (heting, hetting, hoting, hechting)**, *vbl. sb. Obs.*, bidding or promising; *concr.* a promise, a vow.

a **1300** *Cursor M.* 785 (Gött.) þis heting..was bath fals and fikil. *Ibid.* 792 (Gött.) Sum of þe hoting was gain sau. *a* **1340** HAMPOLE *Psalter* xxiv. 11 þai ere witnes of his hightynge. *c* **1380** WYCLIF *Sel. Wks.* III. 33 God is trewe in his heetynge. *c* **1440** *York Myst.* xlviii. 201 My hetyng haly schall I fulfille. *a* **1500** *Knt. & Wife* 47 in Hazl. *E.P.P.* II. 18 This knyȝt ..thouȝt to fulfyl his hettynge. *a* **1575** *Diurn. Occurr.* (1833) 300 He promittit in hechting to caus the toun men doe or die.

†**hight**, *v.*² *Obs.* In 1 **hyhtan**, 3 **hiȝten**. [OE. *hyhtan*, f. *hyht* HIGHT *sb.*³] *intr.* To hope, anticipate something with hope or joy; to rejoice, exult.

c **1000** *Ags. Ps.* (Th.) lxxxiii[i]. 2 Heorte min and flæsc hyhtað ȝeorne, on þone lifȝendan leofan Drihten. *Ibid.* xc[i]. 14 He hyhte to me. *a* **1250** *Owl & Night.* 437 Ech wiȝt is glad for mine þinge..And hiȝteþ aȝen mine kume.

†**hight**, *v.*³ *Obs.* Forms: 2–3 **hihten, huihten**, 4–5 **hiȝte(n**, 5 **hyght, heyghte**, 7 **hight.** [Early ME. *huihten, hihten*, of doubtful origin.

Perh., like prec., a deriv. of *hyht*, HIGHT *sb.*³, in sense 'to make joyous or delightful': cf. HIGHTLE *v.*, HIGHTLY.]

trans. To beautify, adorn, embellish, set off.

c **1200** *Trin. Coll. Hom.* 71 We shule..noht mid faire worde hihten þo ateliche sinnes. *Ibid.* 89 þat burh folc hihten þe heȝe strete and bihengen it mid palmes. *Ibid.* 195 Alle þos wennen huihten his wurðshipe. **1340–70** *Alex. & Dind.* 728 þe hauter of he[r]cules alle ȝe hihten. *c* **1374** CHAUCER *Boeth.* I. metr. ii. 4 (Camb. MS.) The lusty howres of the fyrst somer seson þat hyhteth [*v.r.* hiȝteþ] and aparaileth the Erthe with rosene flowres. **1387** TREVISA *Higden* (Rolls) I. 217 An hous i-made wel nyh al of gold and i-hiȝt wiþ precious stones. **1398** —— *Barth. De P.R.* II. v. (1495) 31 By theyr presence al that is in heuen and in erthe is wonderfully hyghted. **1633** T. ADAMS *Exp. 2 Peter* iii. 12 His land shall be husbanded, his house highted, his garments brushed.

Hence **highting** *vbl. sb.*; **highter**, an adorner or embellisher.

1387 TREVISA *Higden* (Rolls) I. 7 Faire florischers and hiȝteres of wordes and of metre. *Ibid.* II. 313 By cause of þe more hiȝtinge and fairenesse [*causa ornatus dignioris*].

hight *v.*⁴, obs. var. of HEIGHT *v.*

'hightail, 'high-tail, *v. colloq.* (orig. *U.S.*). [In allusion to the erect tails of animals in flight.] *intr.* To run (quickly) away, to move quickly. Freq. const. *it.*

1925 *Amer. Speech* I. 149/2 'I high-tailed out of there.' ..'High-tail' comes straight from the plains where a mustang, when startled, erects his tail in a sudden, quick gesture and runs like the wind. So to make a sudden departure is to 'high-tail'. **1928** L. R. FREEMAN *Nearing North* 157 A string of red-brown bodies hightailing it through the bush. **1930** *Detective Fiction Weekly* 19 Apr. 566/2 We high-tailed it for the hideout. **1953** M. LOWRY *Let.* Nov. (1967) 349, I hightailed it thither anyhow, fire-extinguisher in hand. **1958** P. DE VRIES *Mackerel Plaza* v. 62, I was only always high-tailing it after everything in skirts, that's all. **1959** C. WILLIAMS *Man in Motion* iii. 29, I ..high-tailed it in the other direction, and ducked into an alley. **1962** *Listener* 22 Mar. 524/2 The two of them high-tailed it for Oldham. **1971** *Nat. Geographic* May 721/2 Suddenly a Chinese goose, honking belligerently, high-tailed straight for me. **1973** *Caribbean Contact* Jan. 2/3 They get the point. Pronto. And high-tail it back home!

high-taper. [Altered from *higtaper* (Lyte, Gerarde, Cotgrave), earlier *higgis taper, hickis taper* (Turner).] = HAG-TAPER, q.v.

1605 TIMME *Quersit.* III. 179 Take of..hightaper, and of ferne, of each one pound and a halfe. **1861** MISS PRATT *Flower. Pl.* IV. 135.

highten, etc., obs. form of HEIGHTEN *v.*, etc.

highth, obs. or dial. var. of HEIGHT *sb.*, *a.*, *v.*; var. f. HIGHT *sb.*², *Obs.*, haste.

high-tide. [OE. *héahtíd*, f. HIGH *a.* + TIDE. Only in OE. and early ME.; in mod. Eng. ad. Ger. *hochzeit.*] A high time, high day, festival.

a **1000** *Laws of Æthelred* V. c. 14 (Schmid) To æghwilces apostoles heahtide. *c* **1250** *Gen. & Ex.* 1507 At heȝ tide and at gestning. **1837** CARLYLE *Fr. Rev.* II. I. x, A 'Feast of Pikes, *Fête des Piques*', notablest among the hightides of the year. **1870** MORRIS *Earthly Par.* II. III. 194 Unto the town, Where for the high-tide folk were dight. **1884** SYMONDS *Shaks. Predec.* viii. 315 To attend her high-tides, was the privilege and pleasure of a congregated nation.

high tide: see TIDE.

highting, *vbl. sb.*: see under HIGHT *v.*

†**hightle**, *v. Obs.* [deriv. of HIGHT *v.*³, with dim. and freq. suffix -LE.] *trans.* To adorn, ornament; = HIGHT *v.*³

13.. *E.E. Allit. P.* B. 1290 þe hous & þe anournementes he hyȝtled togeder. *a* **1400–50** *Alexander* 1541 (Ashm.) þan [he] him hiȝtild his hede & had on a Mitre. *Ibid.* 4540 He has a hatt on his hede hiȝtild o floures. *Ibid.* 4969 As it ware hiȝtild in þat hill with handis of aungels.

†**hightly**, *a.* and *adv. Obs.* Forms: 1 **hyhtlíc**, 2–3 **hihtlich**, 4 **hiȝtli.** [OE. *hyhtlíc* 'giving or having cause for hope or joy', f. *hyht* HIGHT *sb.*³]

A. *adj.* Joyous, exultant; delightful, pleasant; in OE., also, hopeful.

a **1000** *Andreas* 104 (Gr.) Hama hyhtlicost. *a* **1000** *Cædmon's Gen.* 146 Hyhtlic heofontimber. *Ibid.* 1605 Hyhtlic heorþwerod heafodmaga. *c* **1200** *Trin. Coll. Hom.* 213 þe lichame þe sholde ben þe soule hihtliche bure, makeð hire to ateliche quarterne.

B. *adv.* ? Pleasantly, becomingly.

13.. *Gaw. & Gr. Knt.* 1612 He..hatz out þe hastlettez, as hiȝtly bisemez.

'high-tone, *attrib.* or as *adj.* = next.

1897 E. W. BRODHEAD *Bound in Shallows* 105 They was high-tone lookin' fellers, and I'd like 'em to brag up the house. **1898** *Christian Herald* 19 Jan. 44/4 The infernal delusion that it was not high-tone for women to learn a profitable calling. **1925** F. SCOTT FITZGERALD *Let.* c. 27 Dec. (1964) 194 Saw Leslie also and went on some very high-tone parties. **1939** L. HELLMAN *Little Foxes* II. 66 Everybody going to be high-tone rich. Big rich.

'high-toned, *a.* [f. *high tone* + -ED².]

1. High in pitch (vocal or musical).

1779–81 JOHNSON *L.P.*, *Swift* Wks. III. 405 His voice was sharp and high-toned rather than harmonious.

2. High-strung, tense.

1804 ANNA SEWARD *Mem. Darwin* 49 His high-toned expectations. **1814** T. JEFFERSON *Writ.* (1830) IV. 236 His temper was naturally irritable and high-toned.

3. a. Having a high moral tone; high-principled; expressing lofty sentiments; having dignified or superior manners. Also, stylish, pretentious. Also *absol.* Cf. *high-tone* (HIGH *a.* 22 a).

1807 in *Western Pennsylvania Hist. Mag.* (1947) Mar.–June 56 The same editor also states that there were 'no Demo-Republicans in it, all high-toned gentlemen'. **1814** SCOTT *Ld. of Isles* II. viii, In whose high-toned impartial mind Degrees of mortal rank and state Seem objects of indifferent weight. **1829** *Virginia Herald* (Fredericksburg) 28 May 2/3 He might be President if he liked; but this high-toned eulogy, he thought highly objectionable. **1854** GEO. ELIOT in *Westm. Rev.* Oct. 453 That blending of the high-toned chivalry of Spain with the caustic wit and refined irony of Italy. **1856** EMERSON *Eng. Traits, Univ.* Wks. (Bohn) II. 92 It is contended..that the public sentiment within each of those schools is high-toned and manly. **1866** *Washoe* (Nevada) *Eastern Slope* 11 Aug. 2/2 It is [necessary] when the high toned meet..for the purpose of cutting off debate, that they should be ready to raise the previous question at any moment. **1876** 'MARK TWAIN' *Tom Sawyer* xxxvi. 272 A robber is more high-toned than what a pirate is..as a general thing. **1886** SWINBURNE in *19th Cent.* Jan. 150 The rough and ready hand of Rowley may be traced, not indeed in the more high-toned passages, but in many of the most animated scenes of *The Spanish Gipsy*. **1888** A. C. GUNTER *Mr. Potter* IV. xxiii. 278 The Democratic Party thought Sampson Potter a more high-toned name to run for Congress than Sammy Potts. **1912** BEERBOHM *Christmas Garland* p. v, Tripping off the pens of all higher-toned reviewers. **1956** AUDEN *Old Man's Road*, The smart crescent of a high-toned suburb. **1966** *Listener* 22 Sept. 426/1 The girls whose vicissitudes after graduating from a high-toned American college supply the film's story line.

b. *U.S. colloq.* Excellent, tasteful, of superior quality.

highty-tighty ('haɪtɪ'taɪtɪ), *int.*, *a.*, and *sb.* [A variant of HOITY-TOITY, q.v. app. sometimes associated in idea with *high*, *height*, or with *tight*, and modified in use accordingly. The pronunc. of *oi* as *i*, as in *ile, bile* = *oil, boil*, was formerly prevalent.]

A. *int.* An ejaculation expressing contemptuous surprise or anger: see HOITY-TOITY.

1747 W. HORSLEY *Fool* II. 168 Heyty titey, very fine truly. **1844** DICKENS *Mart. Chuz.* xlvi, 'Why, highty tighty, sir!' cried Mrs. Gamp, 'is these your manners?' **1866** *Cornh. Mag.* May 565 'Highty-tighty; what a much ado about nothing!' said the old lady.

B. *adj.* Petulant, huffy; supercilious.

1848 THACKERAY *Van. Fair* xviii, 'La, William, don't be so highty-tighty with us. We're not men. We can't fight you', Miss Jane said. **1855** —— *Newcomes* xlii, You know very well what I mean, sir! Don't try to turn me off in that highty-tighty way.

C. †*sb.* (See quots.) *Obs.* (or *dial.*)

a **1700** B. E. *Dict. Cant. Crew*, *Hightetity*, a Ramp or Rude Girl. **1725** in *New Cant. Dict.* **1785** GROSE *Dict. Vulg. T.*, *Heighty toity*, a hoyden, or romping girl. [**1877** *N.W. Linc. Gloss.*, *Highty-tighty*, a see-saw.]

'high-up, *a. colloq.*, orig. *dial.* [f. HIGH *a.* + UP *adv.*²] In a high or elevated position, high above the ground; also *fig.*, of high place or rank.

1868 J. C. ATKINSON *Gloss. Cleveland* s.v., He's some desput high-up chap. **1899** S. MACMANUS *In Chimney Corners* 155 There was a lot of high-up folk being entertained. **1899** *Westm. Gaz.* 12 June 1/3 The gilt-edged

lies of the high-up men. 1903 *Book Lover* May 3/1 In a high-up room in the Rue Lafayette. 1918 C. Wells *Vicky Van* ii. 23 A high-up Publican. 1920 J. M. Hunter *Trail Drivers of Texas* 219 Our 'high up' officers were..somewhere in town. 1934 E. Bowen *Cat Jumps* 74 The skies were disturbed by a high-up swift rustling sigh: the summer birds flying south. 1940 'G. Orwell' *Notebooks* 24 June in *World Review* (1950) June 27 High-up influences in England are preparing for a..sell-out. 1942 A. L. Rowse *Cornish Childhood* iv. 82 Myself sitting in the high-up baby's chair with the little tray attached in front. 1961 *Guardian* 27 May 3/7 His penetrating assessment of high-up American attitudes to Cuba.

Also *colloq.* as *sb.*, a person of high rank or status. Cf. HIGHER-UP.

1929 W. R. Burnett *Little Caesar* VII. vi. 299 Rico got in touch with some of the high-ups. 1939 *News Review* 30 Nov. 13/1 As time went on, the Nazi high-ups took Admiral Raeder's advice. 1946 J. Richardson *Phoney Phleet* 150 Two high-ups, lordly ones, or nobs. 1949 'M. Innes' *Journeying Boy* i. 6 Only the high-ups had their heads substantially above the soapsuds. 1969 Auden *City without Walls* 84 How golden-tongued was Socrates, Who always spoke the truth, But high-ups do not like to think. 1971 *Physics Bull.* Dec. 735/2 Whitten and Poppoff, both high-ups in NASA's Ames Research Center, have filled the gap admirably despite their lack of academic background.

highveld ('haɪfɛlt, 'haɪvɛlt). [Partial transl. of Afrikaans *hoëveld*, f. *hoog* high + VELD.] The inner plateau of the subcontinent of South Africa, which is from 5,000 to 6,000 feet above sea-level.

1878 A. Aylward *Transvaal To-day* 18 The High-veld... The large, bare, but healthy elevated plateau—the great watershed of the Transvaal. 1905 J. W. Gregory in *Rep. Brit. Assoc.* 399 The old rocks that form the foundation of the present high veldt of Rhodesia. 1906 Rider Haggard *Benita* v. 63 They were on the Transvaal high-veld. 1907 P. Fitzpatrick *Jock of Bushveld* 223 For perhaps a week the towering bulwarks of the Highveld were visible as we toiled along. 1954 D. D'Ewes *Mydorp* 51 Sirius and the Southern Cross..shining with the ecstatic brightness that only the high-veld sky can offer. 1961 L. van der Post *Heart of Hunter* I. ii. 45 My first memories are of the incomparable starlight of the high-veld of Southern Africa and the far sea-sound that goes with it. *Ibid.* III. xii. 161 The light of a high-veld sunset. 1971 *World Archaeol.* III. 178 The highveld reaches an altitude of 5,500 feet at Johannesburg. 1972 *Stand. Encycl. S. Afr.* V. 522/1 *Highveld*, Tvl. and O.F.S.... It lies about 1200 to 1800 metres above sea-level, more or less between 26° and 30° S.

high water. The state of the tide when the surface of the water is highest; the time when the tide is at the full.

1626 Capt. Smith *Accid. Yng. Seamen* 17 It flows quarter floud, high water, or a still water. 1656 tr. *Hobbes' Elem. Philos.* (1839) 439 In twenty-four hours and almost fifty-two minutes; which is..the time between the high-water of one day and the high-water of the day following. 1719 De Foe *Crusoe* II. xi, Put out to sea..at high-water. 1860 *All Year Round* No. 69. 449 High water is never so high, and low water is never so low, at quadratures as at syzygies.

Hence **high-'water mark.** (*a*) *lit.* The mark left by the tide at high water, the line or level then touched; *esp.* the highest line ever so touched. Also, by extension, the highest line touched by a flooded river or lake.

1553 Brende *Q. Curtius* F vj, The worcke did growe from the bottome of the Sea..but not yet broughte to the hyghe water marcke. 1626 Bacon *Sylva* §2 Betweene the Low water and High water Marke. 1748 *Anson's Voy.* II. viii. 219 They..lay their eggs..in the sand, just above the high-water mark. 1878 Huxley *Physiogr.* 180 The standard taken is neither high-water mark nor low-water mark, but the mean level between the two. 1892 J. D. Hood *Waterspouts Yorksh. Wolds* 48 Traces of the high-water-mark line apparent throughout the village.

(*b*) *fig.* The highest point of intensity, excellence, prosperity, or the like, attained.

1814 Earl of Dudley *Lett.* 13 June (1840) 43 The high-water mark of English faction is very much below the ebb of French violence. 1856 Emerson *Eng. Traits, Personal* Wks. (Bohn) II. 132 The Ode on Immortality is the high-water-mark which the intellect has reached in this age. 1890 *Spectator* 31 May 766 He [Defoe] nearly touches the high-water mark of English prose.

(*c*) *jocular colloq.* A dirty mark showing the limit to which a person has washed.

1886 in Baumann *Londinismen.* 1899 *Daily News* 31 Jan. 6/4 The high-water mark is plainly visible above a tattered scarf tied loosely round his neck.

highway ('haɪ,weɪ). Forms: see HIGH *a.* and WAY. [f. HIGH *a.* 7, 19 + WAY. In OE. a true compound; but in 15–17th c. often two words. Often antithetic to BY-WAY.]

1. a. A public road open to all passengers, a high road; esp. a main or principal road forming the direct or ordinary route between one town or city and another, as distinguished from a local, branch, or cross road, leading to smaller places off the main road, or connecting two main roads. ***the king's highway***: see quot. 1895.

859 in Earle *Land Chart.* 130 Circumcincta ab oriente cyniges heiweȝ a meritie stret to scufeling forde. *c*1200 *Trin. Coll. Hom.* 131 He nolde noht turnen ut of þe heȝeweie. *c*1325 *Poems times Edw. II* (Percy Soc.) lvii, Thei goth out of the hy-way. *c*1400 *Three Kings Cologne* (1886) 55 There was also bisyde þis hille a hiȝe-weye, and to þis hiȝeweye were .iij. weyes metyng to-gydir. 1450–1530 *Myrr. our Ladye* 140 There ys a dyfference bytwyxte an hyghe waye and a bypathe, for the hyghe waye ys large and commune to all. 1604 F. Hering *Modest Def.* 22 To make the Point as plaine as the Kings high-way. 1662 *Vestry Bks.* (Surtees) 109 Chosen Overseers for the hy wayes for this present yeare. 1796 Morse *Amer. Geog.* I. 452 The state [Connecticut] is chequered with innumerable roads or high ways crossing each other in every direction. 1813 *Examiner* 26 Apr. 260/1 The Coroner's Jury brought in a verdict of self-murder, and the poor creature's body was barbarously mangled by a stake, and buried in the highway. 1851 Helps *Comp. Solit.* i. (1874) 5 To make a road for himself..instead of using the King's highway. 1895 Pollock & Maitland *Hist. Eng. Law* I. 22 The two phrases ['the king's peace' and 'the king's highway'] are, indeed, intimately connected; they come from the time when the king's protection was not universal but particular, when the king's peace was not for all men or all places, and the king's highway was in a special manner protected by it.

b. ***to take (to) the highway***, to become a highwayman, footpad, etc.

1722 De Foe *Col. Jack* (1840) 71 We will take the highway like gentlemen. [1817 J. Evans *Excurs. Windsor* 31 Embarrassment..that had induced him to so rash a step as the highway.]

c. In allusion to Matt. xxii. 9, 10, Luke xiv. 23.

1843 H. Bonar *Hymn, 'Go labour on'* vii, Go forth into the world's highway, Compel the wanderer to come in. 1898 *Daily News* 6 Oct. 6/7 The South London officials of the Salvation Army have..been..gathering together of late from the highways and by-paths of Lambeth those who..are entitled to be ranked as 'Hooligans'. 1908 *Westm. Gaz.* 27 Jan. 1/3 It is highways and hedges work, and we shall need van for van and lecturer for lecturer. 1948 A. J. Toynbee *Civilization on Trial* vi. 111 The United States—who had previously not only welcomed European immigrants but whose employers of labour had sought them in the highways and hedges of Europe and compelled them to come in.

2. *transf.* **a.** The ordinary or main route, or line of communication followed, by land or water.

*c*1400 Maundev. (Roxb.) xv. 70 In þe desertes of Araby by þe hie way toward Egipte. 1684 *Roxb. Ball.* (1885) V. 464 From Westminster-Hall to the Temple each day The River of Thames 'twas made a High-way. 1837 W. Irving *Capt. Bonneville* I. 79 The Platte has become a highway for the fur traders. 1868 G. Duff *Pol. Surv.* 220 The great sea on the west, the natural highway of commerce.

b. Any track well-beaten or regularly traversed by animals or things.

1579 Tomson *Calvins Serm. Tim.* 253/2 Poore ignorant men runne thus like Cranes, and..goe the beastes high way, (as the prouerbe is). 1622 T. Scott *Belg. Pismire* 17 You may obserue the pathes and high-wayes betwixt one nest and another, is track't and beaten plaine with their little feet. 1855 Bain *Senses & Int.* II. i. §28 The Concurrence of Sensations in one common stream of consciousness,—in the same cerebral highway. 1866 B. Taylor *Poems, Passing the Sirens* 179 But mark the burning highway of the sun.

c. *Computers.* (See quot. 1962.)

1949 D. R. Hartree *Calculating Instruments & Machines* (1950) viii. 107 A number of source-gates..on the right, and a number of destination-gates on the left, are connected by a single bus labelled 'Highway'. In this bus there is a further gate, labelled 'transfer gate', which exercises the main control over transfer of words between the various sources and destinations. *Ibid.* 108 An instruction..opens the corresponding S-gate and D-gate through selecting circuits; then at the appropriate time the main transfer gate in the highway opens. 1962 *Gloss. Automatic Data Processing Terms (B.S.I.)* 87 *Highway*, a major path along which signals travel from one of several sources to one of several destinations. 1964 F. L. Westwater *Electronic Computers* i. 7 The number..can either be allowed to pass on to one of the so-called 'highways' in the computer or it can be obliterated. *Ibid.* 9 Numbers are driven out on to the highways serially by admitting electronic pulses to the registers.

3. *fig.* **a.** A course of conduct leading directly to some end or result.

1598 F. Meres tr. *Lewes' Sinner's Guide* Title-p., Brought into the Highway of Euerlasting Happinesse. 1625 Burges *Pers. Tithes* 36 This were the high way to become sonnes of Belial indeed. 1690 Child *Disc. Trade* Pref. (1694) 25 Trades that we have lost, and are in the highway to lose. 1875 Jowett *Plato* (ed. 2) V. 288 That state..I perceive to be on the highway to ruin.

b. The ordinary or direct course (of conduct, thought, speech, etc.).

*a*1637 B. Jonson *Discov., Otium Studiorum* Wks. (Rtldg.) 748/2 He never forced his language, nor went out of the highway of speaking, but for some great necessity or apparent profit. 1871 E. F. Burr *Ad Fidem* vi. 90 To march..in an orderly way, along the highways of thought.

4. *attrib.* and *Comb.* **a.** as ***Highway Board***, ***hedge***, ***passage***, ***side***, ***theory***; **b.** frequenting or plying one's trade on the highway, as ***highway robber***, ***stander***, ***thief***, ***woman***; **c.** used to run on the highway, as ***highway dog***, ***nag***, etc.; **d.** **Highway Code**, in Britain, an official publication containing the 'rules of the road', esp. for motor vehicles; first published in 1931, it has appeared subsequently in revised editions; also *transf.*; **highway rate, tax**, one imposed for the maintenance of highways; **highway robbery**, (freq. in trivial use of something that is exorbitantly expensive).

1930 *Act 20 & 21 Geo. V* c. 45 §1 The Minister shall..prepare a code (in this section referred to as the '*highway code') comprising such directions as appear to him to be proper for the guidance of persons using roads. 1935 *Archit. Rev.* LXXVIII. 110/3 The free issue of the Highway Code to all of his Majesty's lieges who have come (or are supposed to have come) to years of discretion is a portent. 1958 *Listener* 20 Nov. 835/1 The importance of reading the Highway Code. 1959 *Daily Tel.* 1 July 1/3 Highway Code revised for motorways. 1970 'A. Gilbert' *Death wears Mask* x. 166 And then there's the Highway Code. 1972 *Listener* 23 May 375/3 Here was a book that..had broken the Highway Code of conventional English culture. 1611 Markham *Countr. Content.* I. i. (1668) 10 A couple of good *high-way dogs, that is to say, Hounds..that..will hunt as well upon a dry, hard high-way as upon the freshest mould. 1680 Otway *Caius Marius* III. iii, Some Beggar's rotten Rags..left dangling on a *Highway Hedge. 1622 Mabbe tr. *Aleman's Guzman d'Alf.* II. 75 He bestowed his blessing vpon mee, and with it a good *high-way-Nag. 1621 Quarles *Div. Poems, Esther*, Making a *Highway-passage through the Main. 1840 Hood *Knt. & Dragon* viii, He collected..*Highway-rates on the roads. 1690 *Lond. Gaz.* No. 2607/2 Any *Highway Robbers, House-Breakers, or Murderers. 1904 Kipling *Traffics & Discov.* 330 The other six hundred [acres] are nearly all let to folk who knew my folk..but this Turpin is a new man—and a highway robber. 1778 J. Wedgwood *Let.* 19 Mar. (1965) 218 On Monday night last there was three *highway robberies between this place and Newcastle. 1853 Mrs. Gaskell *Cranford* x. 181 She indeed inclined to the idea that, in some way, the French were connected with..the burglaries and highway robberies. 1886 *Lantern* (New Orleans) 3 Nov. 2/3 Highway robbery is no name for it. 1920 A. Huxley *Limbo* 122 The organized highway robbery of Red Cross collectors. 1941 'R. Crompton' *William does his Bit* ii. 36 'I've heard people talk about highway robbery quite lately.' 'Yes, but they only mean people chargin' too much for meals,' explained Ginger, 'not the old sort.' 1967 J. B. Priestley *It's Old Country* ix. 107 Nothing on the wine list..under two-pound-ten. Highway robbery by candlelight. 1638 Sir T. Herbert *Trav.* (ed. 2) 87 Unexpected onsets of the Coolies and *high-way roagues. 1669 Worlidge *Syst. Agric.* (1681) 174 Any poor Cottager that lives by the *High-way-side. 1600 Rowlands *Lett. Humours Blood* xxviii. 34 Three *high-way standers, haueing cros-lesse cursse Did greete my friend with, Sir giue vs your pursse. 1897 *Daily News* 13 Sept. 7/5 The Colonial railway policy has been almost entirely dominated by what is called the *highway theory. 1618 Bolton *Florus* II. xvii. (1636) 146 From huntsman turning *highway theefe.

highwayman ('haɪ,weɪmən). [f. prec.: formerly as three words or two, without or with hyphens. In some districts with chief stress on *way*.]

1. One who frequents the highway for the purpose of robbing passengers; esp. one who does this on horseback, as distinguished from a *foot-pad.*

1649 *Thomasson Tracts* (Brit. Mus.) DXXXIII. xxxi. 20 This last session there suffered 28, most of them high way men. 1692 Bentley *Boyle Lect.* 34 'Tis like the friendship of pickpockets and highwaymen, that are said to observe strict justice among themselves. 1768–74 Tucker *Lt. Nat.* (1852) II. 553 The charms of riot and debauchery make highwaymen and housebreakers. 1782 Cowper *Gilpin* 237 They raised the hue and cry:—'Stop thief! stop thief!—a highwayman!' 1789–1840 [see FOOT-PAD]. 1849 Macaulay *Hist. Eng.* iii. I. 382 It was necessary to the success and even to the safety of the highwayman that he should be a bold and skilful rider.

fig. 1694 *Acc. Sev. Late Voy.* II. (1711) 25 We take..Guns and Lances, to resist the Highway-men the Bears.

2. *local.* A surveyor of highways. (In use in north Lincolnshire and elsewhere.)

1888 Freeman in W. R. W. Stephens *Life* (1895) II. 379 *Ex officio* guardians and highwaymen I count for a mistake.

3. Used *attrib.* or in the possessive designating a type of long loose coat or cape suggestive of the kind once worn by highwaymen.

1901 *Daily Chron.* 9 July 3/5 Sarah Bernhardt..looked very striking in a wonderful gown..half-concealed by a long paletot of white silk, made in the 'highwayman' shape, with a number of natty little capes. 1960 *Guardian* 29 July 7/1 A very dashing full length highwayman coat..with a huge cape collar. 1966 *Vogue* Nov. 88 (*caption*) Vogue's adventurers wear..highwaymen's coats.

Hence **,high'waymanhood**, the condition of a highwayman (see FOOTPADDERY quot. 1861).

highwood ('haɪwʊd). [f. HIGH *a.* + WOOD *sb.*[1]; cf. *high forest* (HIGH *a.* 21) and G. *hochwald.*] A forest of tall trees.

1900 J. Nisbet *Our Forests & Woodlands* iii. 105 Data are not yet available to indicate anything like definitely what rotation of oak in highwoods will prove most remunerative. 1904 G. A. B. Dewar *Glamour of Earth* v. 83 He turns bravely to the dripping highwood, to cut and lay in lands or rows the hazel and oak stems. 1905 J. Nisbet *Forester* I. II. ii. 346 Highwood..woods..are not cleared..until..maturity. 1959 E. Pound *Thrones* cvii. 110 High-wood is called saltus.

'high-wrought, *a.*

1. Agitated or excited to a high degree.

1604 Shaks. *Oth.* II. i. 2 It is a high wrought Flood. 1702 Rowe *Tamerl.* v. i, The high-wrought Tempest in my Soul. 1814 Scott *Wav.* xxvii, The present high-wrought state of his feelings.

2. Wrought with exquisite art or skill; 'accurately finished, nobly laboured' (J.).

1728 Pope *Dunc.* II. 187 Thou triumph'st, Victor of the high-wrought day, And the pleas'd dame, soft smiling, lead'st away. 1838 Lytton *Alice* v. vi, She understood not his high-wrought scruples.

higiene, obs. form of HYGIENE.

higle, etc., obs. form of HIGGLE, etc.

higlif (iglif). [Repr. Fr. pronunc. of 'high life' (HIGH *a.* 5).] High society.

1911 'I. Hay' *Safety Match* xiv. 222 That variegated cosmos which..Gallic students of British sociology term 'Le Higlif'. 1925 A. Huxley *Along Road* IV. 256 English *Higlif*, as seen through the eyes of an Italian touring company, was worth coming for. 1960 *Harper's Bazaar* Oct. 141/1 Token names which evoke romance or the longed-for

higlif. **1961** *John o' London's* 24 Aug. 235/2 It sees through this neurotic *hig-lif* caper to the fear and insecurity underneath.

higly-pigly, *adv.* = HIGGLEDY-PIGGLEDY.
1664 *Homer à la Mode* (N.), Just as neighbors higly piglie, Let their beasts graze, but then can quicklie.. Spy 'em from ev'ry one's i'th town. **1675** *F. Rous' Archæol. Atticæ* VI. II. ii. (ed. 8) 274 They sit higly pigly, and every one takes where he likes.

higra, higre, obs. forms of EAGRE.

higry pigry, vulg. perversion of HIERA PICRA.
1773 GRAVES *Spiritual Quixote* VIII. xix, Madam Wildgoose would send him some Higry pigry, which would stop it at once.

higt; see HIGHT *v.*

hig-taper, var. HAG-TAPER.

hih(e, obs. f. HIE *sb.* and *v.*

hi-hat, var. HIGH HAT 3.

hihful: see HIEFUL under HIE *sb.*

hiho: see HICKWALL.

hiht, hihþe, obs. ff. HEIGHT.

hii, obs. f. HI *pron.*, HIGH *a.*

hij, obs. f. HIE *v.*¹, HIGH *a.*

hijack ('haɪdʒæk), *v.* orig. *U.S. slang* (now passing into general use). Also **hi-jack**, (formerly) **highjack**. [Origin unknown.] *trans.* To steal (contraband or stolen goods) in transit, to rob (a bootlegger or smuggler) of his illicit goods; to hold up and commandeer (a vehicle and its load) in transit; to seize (an aeroplane) in flight and force the pilot to fly to a new destination. Also *transf.*
1923 *Lit. Digest* 4 Aug. 51/3 'I would have had $50,000,' said Jimmy, 'if I hadn't been hijacked.' **1927** 'J. BARBICAN' *Confess. Rum-Runner* xvii. 181 So we landed the cargo as quickly as we could, and took the chance of the cargo being seized or hijacked on shore. **1936** E. AMBLER *Dark Frontier* xi. 178, I still don't see how we're going to high-jack Groom's men. **1936** J. G. BRANDON *Pawnshop Murder* v. 47 Some one else has been on to this deal, given him the works and hi-jacked the stuff. **1959** A. W. SHERRING *Tip Off* i. 8 A stack of old banknotes leaves Central Post Office at three this afternoon. The van will be hijacked. **1961** *John o' London's* 12 Oct. 423/3 The plot concerns an attempt to hi-jack a million dollars. **1963** *Times* 4 Sept. 5/1 A lorry driver was beaten over the head and his load of cigarettes worth nearly £50,000 hi-jacked near Isleworth. **1968** *Daily Tel.* 7 Dec. 17/1 One of our planes with 35 on board was hi-jacked and flown to Cuba. **1970** *Daily Tel. Mag.* 16 Jan. 17/2 When a virus enters a cell it hijacks it, and makes it do what it wants.
So **'hijacking** *vbl. sb.* and *ppl. a.* Also **'hijack** *sb.*, an instance of hijacking; also *attrib.*
1923 *Lit. Digest* 4 Aug. 55/1 So much for hijacking on the high seas. **1924** *Daily Mail* 22 Dec. (N.Y. Corresp.), The duties of American coastguards are confined to seizing rum-ships; they cannot seize a Hi-Jacking ship unless it has pirated. **1927** *Observer* 16 Oct. 15/1 Play-goers here are not interested in the humours and results of Prohibition, boot-legging, and hi-jacking. **1928** *Hearst's International* Aug. 72/1 Some hi-jacking exploit. **1929** *Daily Express* 21 Jan. 2/7 A gang of 'hijack boot-leggers' who had forced a restaurant owner to pay them £1,000. **1966** *Times* 22 Sept. 1/2 A £7,000 reward has been offered by an insurance company for information about the hi-jacking of two lorries. **1967** *Listener* 10 Aug. 179/1 The aerial hijacking of Moise Tshombe was commissioned..by the Congolese Government. **1968** *Sun* 14 Nov. 5 Hi-jack figures released by Scotland Yard. **1968** *Daily Tel.* 7 Dec. 17/1 Our airline has been hit harder by hi-jacks than any other. **1972** *Guardian* 17 Nov. 14/1 The problems of becoming a hijack haven have made their mark.

'hijacker. Also **hi-jacker**, formerly occas. **highjacker**. [f. prec. + -ER¹.] One who hijacks (illicit liquor, a vehicle, an aeroplane, etc.).
1923 *Nation* 11 July 36 There was, of course, the rush of adventurers, oil promoters, highjackers (an oil-region term for murderous robbers). **1925** *Times* 26 Oct. 13/7 A shooting affray between bootleggers and 'hijackers' (men who prey on bootleggers) took place..in a lodging-house on the west side of New York. **1936** J. G. BRANDON *Pawnshop Murder* v. 43 Any lurking hi-jacker who might..have acquired an inkling of what he was carrying. **1969** *Guardian* 9 Sept. 8/1 The hijackers have put the lives of about 10,000 air passengers at risk.

‖**hijra, hijrah.** More accurate form of HEGIRA.

‖**hikayat** (hɪ'kaɪjæt). Also **Hikaiat, Hikayet.** [Malay, ad. Arab. *hikāya* story, narrative.] In classical Malay literature, a prose narrative combining romance and biography.
1808 *Asiatick Researches* X. iii. 177 The Cheritra or Hikaiat..is more generally written in prose, but frequently intermixed with verse. **1839** T. J. NEWBOLD *Straits of Malacca* II. xiv. 317 From Arabia and Persia, great part of that class of compositions termed Hikayet..are borrowed. **1887** H. N. VAN DER TUUK in *Misc. Papers relating to Indo-China* II. viii. 3 The Malay author says in the opening that his work..gives a great many beautiful tales in the beginning, and afterwards the tale named *Hikayat Pandawa Jaya.* **1894** N. B. DENNYS *Descr. Dict. Brit. Malaya* 152 There are several *Hikayats* extant. **1900** W. E. MAXWELL in W. W. Skeat *Malay Magic* ii. 16 This..Malay myth occurs in the 'Sri Rama', a Malay prose *hikayat.* **1964** M. TAIB BIN OSMAN in Wang Gungwu *Malaysia* III. xv. 211 In the written romances, we find princes and princesses bearing hindu and muslim names, hindu gods, muslim prophets and local heroes, indigenous beliefs, hindu ethics and muslim teachings: all blended together in the *hikayat* or story.

hike (haɪk), *v. colloq.* orig. *dial.* and *U.S.* Also †**hyke, heik.** [Of obscure origin. Cf. HOICK *v.*¹
A possible early example of this word may be seen in the following: **1736** *Applebee's Weekly-Jrnl.* 17 July 2/1 Gowing ..stood Centry 'till the Cargo amounted to as much as they could conveniently yike off with.]
1. *intr.* **a.** To walk or march vigorously or laboriously. **b.** To walk for pleasure; to go for a long walk, or walking tour, *spec.* in the country. Also, to travel by any means.
1809 S. WESLEY *Lett.* (1875) 32 Adieu for the present,—we must Contrive one more Pull at Surry before I hyke over to Staffordshire. **1825** J. JENNINGS *Observ. Dial. W. Eng.*, *To hike off*, to go away; to go off. Used generally in a bad sense. **1868** S. HALE *Lett.* (1919) 39 This day we moved over to the Thebes side and were to have done Karnak..but..I was really sick with heiking. *a* **1872** J. M. BAILEY *Folks at Danbury* (1877) 55 You've got to hike aroun', and fling some style inter the victuals. **1884** *Daily Tel.* 2 Feb. 3/1 (Farmer), We three, not having any regler homes..hike about for a living. **1886** S. HALE *Lett.* (1919) 157 You see the Churches can't do much, but Mr. Warner is wild to be heiking about. *a* **1902** *Scribner's Mag.* (Webster 1902), It's hike, hike, hike (march) till you stick in the mud, and then you hike back again a little slower than you went. **1904** *Chicago Evening Post* 23 Aug. 7 These girls had hiked up the dizzy trail along the face of Glacier to the summit. **1910** S. E. WHITE *Rules of Game* III. xii, 'I'm going to hike out before breakfast,' said he before turning in, 'so if you'll just show me where the lantern is, I won't bother you in the morning.' *Ibid.* v. viii, No animal in its senses would hike uphill and then down again. **1920** *Contemp. Rev.* Sept. 341 To take stick and pack, and 'hike' away from these cities for hundreds or thousands of miles. **1926** *Glasgow Herald* 25 Aug. 8 Guides in gay girlhood will hike through the hollow. **1927** A. CONAN DOYLE *Case-bk. S. Holmes* 149, I told him I was a busy man and could not spend my life hiking round the world in search of Garridebs. **1936** F. CLUNE *Roaming round Darling* xi. 101 Upon returning to Sydney I hiked out to Watson's Bay. **1937** *Amer. Speech* XII. 162/1 High school students have used *hike* to mean going to a play spot, either by automobile, by hayrack, or on foot. **1971** *Sci. Amer.* June 16/3, I occasionally take time off to hike in the mountains and ski.
2. *trans.* **a.** To force to move or go; to convey forcibly or laboriously; to pull *on, up, over*, etc.; to 'drag out'; to increase (a price, etc.). Also *fig.*
1867 S. HALE *Lett.* (1919) 32 Our side-saddles were *heiked* on to them. **1869** *Punch* 9 Jan. 8/2 If they finds any sitch thing as a jemmy about yer,..they'll hike yer off to be tried for intendin' to commit a felony. **1870** F. P. VERNEY *Lettice Lisle* xxiii, I'd like to hike out the whole boiling o' um. **1886** S. HALE *Lett.* (1919) 163 Tuesday he heiked us all forth early in the morning to the lake. **1899** *Strand Mag.* Apr. 454/1 We'll join hands end lay ourselves flat on the rock so thet you can hike your head over, and look all you want to. **1904** *Topeka Capital* 10 June 4 City Center kept the price of ice cream sodas at five cents until the State Sunday School convention struck town, and then the scale was hiked to ten cents. **1915** T. BURKE *Nights in Town* 119 Two bare-armed ladies, with skirts hiked up most indelicately behind them. **1921** *Chambers's Jrnl.* Dec. 835/2, I hiked him into a taxicab. **1927** *Blackw. Mag.* July 11/1 We flitted across the road like ghosts in the moonlight, hiking our equipage, and deposited same at the door of a wooden inn. **1929** W. P. RIDGE *Affect. Regards* 117 Saw where I was paying attention..and then barged in... And apparently managed to hike me out! **1969** C. IRVING *Fake!* (1970) xii. 147 To provide a testimonial which..was also so classy that it hiked the price to its limit, they hit on a scheme. **1973** *Observer* 22 July 13/1 The Bank of England hiked its minimum lending rate..to 9 per cent.
absol. *a* **1902** KIPLING (Webster 1902), If you persist in heaving and hiking like this.
b. *intr.* To work upwards out of place. Const. *up.*
c **1873** SCHELE DE VERE *MS. Notes* 488 (D.A.E.), What makes y[ou]r dress hike up so? **1890** *Amer. Dialect Notes* I. 61 The curtain hikes or hikes up. **1902** G. H. LORIMER *Lett. Merchant* ix. 119 We boys who couldn't walk across the floor without feeling that our pants had hiked up till they showed our feet to the knee,..didn't like him. **1948** *Sat. Even. Post* 4 Dec. 127/2 When I sit down, it hikes up.
Hence **hiker** ('haɪkə(r)), one who hikes or goes on a hike; **'hiking** *vbl. sb.* (also *attrib.*).
1901 *Princeton Alumni Weekly* 518/1 Here I got my first chance at 'hiking' in the Philippines. **1913** F. H. HARRIS *Dartmouth out o' Doors* 32 While building strong physiques for themselves, the cross-country 'hikers' are providing for happier possibilities for the generations to come. **1923** *T. Eaton & Co. Catal.* Spring & Summer 51 New styles for misses, including the hiking suit and costume skirt. **1926** *Daily Colonist* (Victoria, B.C.) 20 July 18/4 Women's Tweed Hiking Breeches..of good grade materials, smart fawn and grey mixtures; well tailored and buttoned at the knee. **1927** *Daily Express* 24 May 3/5 We [of the Camping Club] have 3,000 members... Most of these are solitary 'hikers', who carry all their kit with them. **1930** *Times Lit. Suppl.* 11 Sept. 710/4 A special kind of traveller, belonging to the class of 'hikers'. **1931** *Daily Tel.* 21 Jan. 8/6 'Hikers'' Hostels at 1s. a Night. **1931** *Times Lit. Suppl.* 7 May 368/1 The sturdy young 'heroes' who accompanied him on the hiking adventures. **1931** *Daily Tel.* 21 May 16/2 The widespread hiking movement in Germany and other Continental countries. **1959** M. SHADBOLT *New Zealanders* 71 He was used to hiking. **1972** *L. L. Bean, Inc. Catal.* (Freeport, Maine) Spring 8 *Sierra club cup* for hikers and campers. **1972** *Sci. Amer.* July 13/1, I enjoy cross-country skiing in the winter and hiking and bicycling the rest of the year.

hike (haɪk), *sb. colloq.* orig. *dial.* and *U.S.* Also †**heik.** [f. prec.] **1.** A vigorous or laborious walk; a tramp or march; a walking tour or expedition undertaken for exercise or pleasure. Also *fig.* **on hike**, on the tramp, hiking.
1865 S. HALE *Lett.* (1919) 15 I've been engaged this week in a pecunious *heik*; to wit, getting money from the ladies of the Parish to get a new gown for Dr. Hedge. **1868** *Ibid.* 45, *I* ascended the Grand Pyramid, Lucretia got half-way..and Susie didn't try. It is a fearful heik. *a* **1902** *Scribner's Mag.* (Webster 1902), With every hike there's a few laid out with their hands crossed. **1903** S. E. WHITE *Forest* ii. 18 All other utensils belong to permanent camps, or open-water cruises, —not to 'hikes' in the woods. **1907** R. W. SERVICE *Songs of Sourdough* (1908) 59 And I burrowed a hole in the glowing coal, and I stuffed in Sam McGee. Then I made a hike, for I didn't like to hear him sizzle so. **1907** R. BEACH *Barrier* (1908) iv. 53 He's the feller that killed the gold-commissioner. Of course that put him on the hike again. **1916** H. L. WILSON *Somewhere in Red Gap* ix. 369 What's the matter with him and Lon taking a swift hike down to New York? **1921** *Outward Bound* June 10/1 Chinese Boy Scouts..on 'hike' on the veldt of South Africa. **1921** *Blackw. Mag.* Aug. 262/1 Dempsey had passed the afternoon in a 'limbering-up hike'. **1932** *News Chron.* 28 Apr. 1/2 He then began a non-stop hike up and down the corridors of the hospital that had lasted till late this afternoon. **1970** H. D. CORBIN *Recreation Leadership* (ed. 3) xxiii. 333 The craving for adventure can be nurtured by a hike or an exploration perhaps more than by any other activity.
2. An increase (in prices, wages, etc.). Chiefly *N. Amer.*
1931 *Kansas City Star* 5 Aug., The hike was occasioned by the fact that cigarette butts..are now only a half inch. **1948** *Herald-Press* (St. Joseph, Mich.) 14 Aug. 3/1 There is enough unfilled demand for new cars to absorb a lot more price hikes. **1966** *Economist* 28 May 986/1 A wave of spending at the end of last year in anticipation of hikes in indirect taxes. **1968** *Observer* 28 Jan. 12/3 A 7.25 per cent price hike in two months. **1969** *Eugene* (Oreg.) *Register-Guard* 3 Dec. 1 A (*heading*) Senate votes hike in tax exemptions.

hil, obs. form of ILL, ISLE, HILL.

†**hilaire**, *a. Obs. rare.* In 6 **hylair.** [ad. L. *hilaris, hilarus* cheerful, merry. Cf. OF. *hilaire, hylaire*, prob. the proximate source.] Gay, cheerful.
1560 ROLLAND *Crt. Venus* I. 157 With hylair vult, and fassoun richt famous. *Ibid.* 357 To sum scho is hylair.

hilar ('haɪlə(r)), *a.* [f. HIL-UM + -AR¹. Cf. F. *hilaire.*] Of or pertaining to a HILUM (senses 2, 3).
1864 in WEBSTER. **1870** HOOKER *Stud. Flora* 239 Seeds.. with often a pencil of silky hairs at the hilar end.

†**'hilarate**, *v. Obs. rare*⁻⁰. [f. L. *hilarāt-* ppl. stem of *hilarāre*, f. *hilar-us, hilar-is*, cheerful, gay.] 'To make merry' (Cockeram 1623).

Hilaria (hɪ'lɛərɪə). [L., neut. pl. of *hilaris* HILARIOUS.] A festival in honour of Cybele, celebrated at the vernal equinox. (See quots.)
1738 CHAMBERS *Cycl.*, The *Hilaria* were solemnized with great pomp, and rejoicing. **1842** W. SMITH *Dict. Gr. & Roman Antiq.* 482/2 The hilaria were..either private or public. Among the former..the day on which a person married, and on which a son was born; among the latter, those days of public rejoicings appointed by a new emperor. **1907** L. R. FARNELL *Cults Gk. States* III. 301 The Attis-festival of the Hilaria. **1968** *Encycl. Brit.* II. 147/1 *April Fool's Day*..resembles the Hilaria of ancient Rome (March 25) and the Huli festival of India.

hilarious (hɪ'lɛərɪəs), *a.* [A recent formation, f. L. *hilari-s* + -OUS: cf. *capaci-ous, atroci-ous*, etc.]
1. Cheerful, cheery; gladsome.
1823 SCOTT *Peveril* xlvi, In answer to my hilarious exhortations to confidence. **1856** EMERSON *Eng. Traits, Univ.* Wks. (Bohn) II. 94 Cheery and hilarious tone. **1885** *N. Amer. Rev.* Apr. 335 As..hilarious as Anacreon.
2. Boisterously joyous or merry; rollicking.
1835–40 J. M. WILSON *Tales Bord.* (1857) I. 53 Neither cared the hilarious damsel for the reverend turrets of Innerkepple. **1871** L. STEPHEN *Playgr. Europe* viii. (1894) 186 They may take it for granted..that we were hilarious, excited [etc.]. **1875** H. C. WOOD *Therap.* (1879) 277 Others will become hilarious, erotic, or pugnacious.
Hence **hi'lariously** *adv.*; **hi'lariousness.**
1863 *Athenæum* 5 Dec., The conclusion was hilariously arrived at that the new Order should be named accordingly. **1866** MRS. STOWE *Lit. Foxes* 25 The holidays passed away hilariously. **1885** *Truth* 28 May 851/2 The fresh charm, hilariousness, and blush of spring.

hilarity (hɪ'lærɪtɪ). [ad. F. *hilarité* (14–15th c. in Hatz.-Darm.), ad. L. *hilaritās, -tāt-em*, f. *hilaris, -us* = Gr. ἱλαρός cheerful, gay: see -ITY.]
1. Cheerfulness, gladsomeness; calm joy.
1568 SKEYNE *The Pest* (1860) 25 Temperat hilaritie and blythnes are maist commendable. **1670** CLARENDON *Contempl. Ps.* Tracts (1727) 594 That joy..which extends the heart to such an hilarity in the eyes, and in the countenance..that it cannot be concealed. **1776** JOHNSON 12 Apr. in *Boswell*, No, Sir; wine gives not light, gay, ideal hilarity; but tumultuous, noisy, clamorous merriment. **1829** SOUTHEY *Sir T. More* II. 148 The pleasure which they partake conduces..to health and present hilarity.
2. Boisterous joy; merriment.
1840 THACKERAY *Paris Sk.-bk.* (1872) 30 The coarse and vulgar hilarity. **1853** DE QUINCEY *Autobiog. Sk.* Wks. I. 202 Festal music..is the most remote of any from vulgar hilarity. **1894** *Amer. Missionary* Nov. 378 The incomparable hilarity of the dusky cotton-pickers.

†'**hilarous**, *a. Obs. rare*⁻¹. [f. L. *hilar-us* (see prec.) + -OUS.] = HILARIOUS.

1659 D. PELL *Impr. Sea* 420 Archimedes..when hee found the resolution of the..question, which transported him into such an hilarious fit of mirthsomness.

Hilary ('hɪlərɪ). [f. *Hilarius*, name of a doctor of the church, bishop of Poitiers (died 367), whose festival in the English Calender is on Jan. 13.]

a. Name of a term or session of the High Court of Justice in England; and also of one of the university terms at Oxford and Dublin.

[**14..** *Customs of Malton* in *Surtees Misc.* (1888) 59 Yᵉ grett cowrtt next eftyr Sayntt Hyllare day.] **1577–87** HARRISON *England* I. ix. in Holinshed I. 181/2 Hilarie term beginneth the three and twentith daie of Januarie (if it be not sundaie) otherwise the next daie after, and is finished the twelfe of Februarie, it hath foure returnes. **1669** STURMY *Mariner's Mag.* II. 101 There are four times of the Year appointed for the Determining of Causes..Two of these Terms (viz.) Hillary Term, and Michaelmas Term, are at a constant time of the Year: but Easter Term and Trinity Term are sooner or later, as those Feasts happen. **1812** M. A. TAYLOR *Parl. Deb.* 6 May in *Examiner* 11 May 295/2 In Hilary Term, 1812, five decrees only were pronounced. **1875** *Act 38 & 39 Vict.* c. 77. Sched., O. lxi. r. 1 The Hilary sittings shall commence on the 11th of January and terminate on the Wednesday before Easter.

†**b.** *humorous. to keep Hilary term*: to maintain hilarity, be cheerful or merry. *Obs.*

1629 T. ADAMS *Heaven made sure* Wks. 905 When God speakes peace to the Soule..It giues end to all iarres..and makes a man keepe Hillary terme all his life.

Hence '**Hilary-mass**, the feast of Saint Hilary; '**Hilary-tide**, the time, term, or season immediately following this day.

c **1330** R. BRUNNE *Chron.* (1810) 284 At Saynt Hillarimesse at Westmynster salle be. **1875** STUBBS *Const. Hist.* II. xv. 262 These stated sessions were held by Edward I at Hilarytide, Easter, and Michaelmas.

hilasmic (hɪ'læzmɪk), *a. rare.* [f. Gr. ἱλασμός propitiation + -IC.] Propitiatory.

1893 *Ch. Q. Rev.* XXXVII. 186 Hilasmic rites for the purgation of sin.

hilch (hɪlʃ), *v. Sc. intr.* To limp, to halt. Hence **hilching** *ppl. a.*; **hilch** *sb.*, a limp.

1784 BURNS *Ep. to Davie* xi, My spaviet Pegasus will limp ..And then he'll hilch, and stilt, and jimp. **1785** —— *Halloween* xx, He swoor 'twas hilchin Jean McCraw. **1824** MACTAGGART *Gallovid. Encycl.*, *Hilch*, a singular halt.

†**hild**, *v. Obs.* Forms: 1 **hyldan**, 3–6 **hild-**, 4 **huld-(ü)**, 4–5 **hyld-**, 5 **held-**, (5 **hilt**). *Pa. t.* 1 **hylde**, 3–5 **hilde**, 4–5 **hildide**. *Pa. pple.* 3 **i-huld**, 4 **y-huld**, **huld**, **i-hylde**, 5 **y-hillid**, 5–6 **hylt(e)**, 6 **hild(e)**, **hylded**, 6–7 **hilded**, (7 **hileded**). [OE. *hyldan* (:—**huldjan*), f. *hold* carcase; cf. ON. *hylda* to slash (Vigfusson).] *trans.* **a.** To flay, skin. **b.** To strip off (the skin).

a **1000** *Gloss.* in Wr.-Wülcker 223/1 *Discoriat*, hyldeþ. *c* **1000** ÆLFRIC *Lev.* iii. 6 And hyldon þa offrunga and ceorfon to sticcon. *c* **1275** LAY. 20958 Þat folk hii a-slowe þe cherles hii hilden. [*c* **1205** uloȝen]. *c* **1290** *S. Eng. Leg.* I. 471/321 Ȝuyt hadde ich leouere ich were i-huld. *c* **1350** *Will. Palerne* 2587 Hastili hulde we þe hides of þise bestes. *c* **1380** *Sir Ferumb.* 1639 Al quike y rede þan let hem hylde þe glotouns alle & some. **1382** WYCLIF *Micah* iii. 3 Whiche eeten fleshe of my peple and hildiden the skyn of hem fro aboue. *c* **1440** *Anc. Cookery* in *Househ. Ord.* (1790) 458 Take conynges or hares, hilt and wassh hom. *c* **1440** *Gesta Rom.* xxxiv. 133 (Harl. MS.) To the secounde [tormentor] he comaundid to helde him qwyke. **1546** J. HEYWOOD *Prov.* (1867) 36, I will as soone be hylt, As waite againe for the mooneshine in the water. **1647** TRAPP *Comm. Matt.* vi. 2 Till half their hides be hilded off. **1654** —— *Comm. Job* xxxvii. 8 Till half hileded by the Countreymen.

Hence **hilding** *vbl. sb.*

1387 TREVISA *Higden* (Rolls) II. 359 Þe sleynge and þe hildynge of a leon. **1519** HORMAN *Vulg.* 80 b, Membraan, bycause it was pulled of by hyldynge.

hild, -e, obs. inf., pa. t. and pa. pple. of HIELD *v.*

hild, -e, obs. pa. t. and pa. pple. of HOLD *v.*

Hilde'brandic, *a.* [f. *Hildebrand* + -IC.] Of, pertaining to, or resembling the policy of Hildebrand, who as Gregory VII was Pope 1073–85, and was distinguished by his unbending assertion of the power of the papacy and hierarchy, and of the celibacy of the clergy. So '**Hilde,brandine** *a.*, '**Hildebrandism, -ist**.

1837 HALLAM *Hist. Lit.* ii. III. §8 Extravagances of *Hildebrandic principles. **1659** GAUDEN *Tears Ch. Eng.* 566 They sought by *Hildebrandine arts to exalt themselves above all that is called God in civil Magistracy. **1855** MILMAN *Lat. Chr.* VII. ii. (1864) IV. 63 The Hildebrandine decrees against lay investiture and the marriage of the clergy. *Ibid.* VI. iii. III. 450 Against the *Hildebrandism of Rome and the monasticism of Christendom. **1893** *Westm. Gaz.* 14 Apr. 7/2 Erastianism..is the control of the Church by the State; but an equal evil is Hildebrandism, the control of the State by the Church. **1680** G. HICKES *Spirit of Popery* Pref. 4 Our Covenanting *Hildebrandists..would set their feet on the Necks of Christian Princes.

†**hilden**, obs. form of *hill-den*, a mountain cave.

1583 STANYHURST *Æneis* I. (Arb.) 22 He [Æolus] maystreth monsterus hildens, Youre kennels, good syrs.

hilder, -or, obs. forms of ELDER *sb.*¹, the tree.

hilding ('hɪldɪŋ). *Obs.* or *arch.* Also 6 **held-**, **hield-**, 6–7 **hyld-**, 7 **hiled-**, 7–8 **heild-**. [A late word, of obscure etymology: perh. f. HIELD *hyld* vb., to bend downwards, bow, also to fall, sink, and to decline, turn waywardly aside + -ING. It is not clear whether the application was first to a horse or to a human being.]

†**1.** A worthless or vicious beast, esp. a horse; a sorry hack, a jade. *Obs.*

1589 R. HARVEY *Pl. Perc.* (1590) 18 Least standing long still in the open faire, they fall to downeright halting, and so be disclosed for arrant heldings. **1600** HOLLAND *Livy* XXI. xl. 415 Their horses, no other than lame jades and poor hidebound hildings. **1719** D'URFEY *Pills* IV. 16 A Runaway Beast that will not be held in..a very Heilding.

2. A contemptible, worthless person of either sex; a good-for-nothing. *arch.* **a.** Applied to a man.

1601 SHAKS. *All's Well* III. vi. 4 If your Lordshippe finde him not a Hilding, hold me no more in your respect. **1611** —— *Cymb.* II. iii. 128 A base Slaue, A Hilding for a Liuorie, a Squires Cloth. **1611** COTGR., *Caguemaille*, a filthie snudge, ..miserable scrape-good, couetous hylding. **1679** DRYDEN *Tr. & Cr.* III. ii, Away, away, you naughty hildings. **1843** LYTTON *Last Bar.* I. v, There's Master Sancroft, of the Oak, will not trust us a penny, the seely hilding.

b. Applied to a woman: A jade; a baggage.

1592 SHAKS. *Rom. & Jul.* III. v. 169 Out on her, Hilding. **1631** *Celestina* XII. 142 She is a crafty Hileding, and I will not give her time to invent some one villainous tricke or other. **1681** DRYDEN *Sp. Fryar* II. iii, How the Gipsey answers me! Oh, 'tis a most notorious Hilding! **1713** ROWE *J. Shore* IV. (1766) 135 This idle Toy, this Hilding [Jane Shore] scorns my power.

3. *attrib.* (in apposition) passing into *adj.*

1582 BRETON *Hunted Hart* in *Heliconia* (1815) I. 139 Shee then takes of those hylding curres agaıne. **1596** SPENSER *F.Q.* VI. v. 25 Thinking to take them from that hylding hound. **1597** SHAKS. *2 Hen. IV*, I. i. 57 Some hielding Fellow, that had stolne The Horse he rode on. **1613** MARKHAM *Eng. Husbandman* II. II. vii. (1635) 89 Those orts may be given to other heilding, and hungry Cattell. **1820** SCOTT *Ivanhoe* xxvii, Some hilding fellow he must be, who dared not stay to assert his claim.

hile, obs. f. HILL *v.*¹

hileded, erron. pa. t. HILD *v. Obs.*

hileg(e, variant of HYLEG, *Obs.*

†**hiler.** *Obs.* [f. HILL *v.*¹ + -ER¹.] A protector.

a **1340** HAMPOLE *Psalter* xvii. 3 My hilere and horn of my hele. *Ibid.* 33 Hilere he is of all hopand in him.

†**hilet.** *Obs.* [perh. f. root of HILL *v.*¹ to cover, etc.; but cf. HOLET.] A tent, a tabernacle.

1382 WYCLIF *1 Kings* xx. 12 Benadab..drank, and the kyngis, in hiletis [Vulg. *in umbraculis*; COVERD. in the pauylion]. *Ibid.* 16 Benadab forsothe drank drunken in his hilet [**1388** schadewyng place]. —— *Isa.* i. 8 Forsaken..as an hylet in a place of goordes [Vulg. *tugurium*; **1388** an hulke in a place where gourdis wexen]. —— *Ecclus.* xxxiv. 19 Coueryng of brennyng, and the hilet [**1388** a schadewyng place] of the mydday [Vulg. *umbraculum meridiani*].

hill (hɪl), *sb.* Forms: 1 **hyll**, 2–4 **hul**, 3–5 **hull(e**, 3–7 **hil**, 4–5 **hel(l**, 4–6 **hyl**, **hyll(e**, 4–7 **hille**, (6 **yll**), 3– **hill**. [OE. *hyll* str. masc. and fem. = LG. *hull*, Fris. *hel*, MDu. *hille*, *hil*, *hul*:—OTeut. **hulni-z*, pre-Teut. **kulní-s*; cf. Lith. *kilnus* high, *kalnas* hill, L. *collis* hill, *celsus* lofty, *culmen* top, from ablaut-stem *kel-*, *kol-*, *k'l-*.]

1. a. A natural elevation of the earth's surface rising more or less steeply above the level of the surrounding land. Formerly the general term, including what are now called mountains; after the introduction of the latter word, gradually restricted to heights of less elevation; but the discrimination is largely a matter of local usage, and of the more or less mountainous character of the district, heights which in one locality are called mountains being in another reckoned merely as hills. A more rounded and less rugged outline is also usually connoted by the name.

In Great Britain heights under 2,000 feet are generally called hills; 'mountain' being confined to the greater elevations of the Lake District, of North Wales, and of the Scottish Highlands; but, in India, ranges of 5,000 and even 10,000 feet are commonly called 'hills', in contrast with the Himalaya Mountains, many peaks of which rise beyond 20,000 feet. The pl. *hills* is often applied to a region of hills or highland; esp. to the highlands of northern and interior India.

c **1000** ÆLFRIC *Hom.* I. 576 Hi huntiað hi of ælcere dune and of ælcere hylle. *c* **1175** *Lamb. Hom.* 129 Uppan þan hulle synai. *c* **1200** ORMIN 12055 Þatt hill þatt wass swa wunnderr heh. *a* **1225** *Ancr. R.* 178 Euer so þe hul is more & herre, so þe wind is more þeron. *a* **1300** *Cursor M.* 13690 Mont oliuet it es an hill þat iesus hanted mikel till. **1340** *Ayenb.* 5 Ine þe helle of Synay. **13..** *E.E. Allit. P.* A. 787 On þe hyl of Syon. **1362** LANGL. *P. Pl.* A. Prol. 5 In a Mayes Morwnynge on Maluerne hulles Me bi-fel a ferly. *c* **1400** MAUNDEV. (1839) iii. 16 There is a grete Hille that men clepen Olympus. **1432–50** tr. *Higden* (Rolls) I. 423 There be hilles in Snawdonia of a grete altitude..whiche hilles men of that cuntre calle Eriri, that soundethe in Englishe the hilles of snawe. **1480** CAXTON *Chron. Eng.* lix. 43 Fast besyde salysbury upon an hull. **1559** W. CUNNINGHAM *Cosmogr. Glasse* 177 Aetna, the burning hil. **1630** *R. Johnson's Kingd. & Commw.* 69 Yea, in the ridge of their highest hils (mountaines indeed I cannot terme them) you shall find pooles. **1645** BOATE *Irel. Nat. Hist.* (1652) 81 Whereas..other Languages..have two severall words for to signifie those observable heights..The English language useth one and the same word for both, calling *hils* as well the one as the other..but that sometimes the word small or great is added. Now because this..would cause some confusion..that hath made us restrain it to one of the sorts, and to call hils only the lesser sort. **1784** COWPER *Task* II. 91 The hills move lightly, and the mountains smoke, For He has touched them. **1842** TENNYSON *Day Dream, Departure* i, O'er the hills, and far away Beyond their utmost purple rim. **1879** F. POLLOCK *Sport Brit. Burmah* I. 99 All inhabited hills varying from 1,500 ft. to 4,000. *Ibid.* II. 74 Men who came from the Nepaul hills, whose home was..at an elevation certainly not less than 10,000 feet. **1881** J. F. T. KEANE *Six Months Meccah* 1 The foot-hills of the approach to a range of mountains. **1888** R. KIPLING (*title*) Plain Tales from the Hills.

b. Often contrasted with *dale*, *plain*. (In this use *hill* occurs in the sing. without article.) ***hill and dale***: also, applied to any markings or groovings likened to hills and dales; *spec.* used *attrib.* to denote that manner of making gramophone records, or the records themselves, in which the undulations are cut in a vertical plane by the recording stylus. Also, applied to the alternating ridges and hollows of waste rock, etc., which are created by open-cast mining or ironstone working; also *attrib.*

c **1380** *Sir Ferumb.* 3997 Prykynge ouer hulle & pleyn, Til he cam to Charlemeyn. *c* **1440** *Gesta Rom.* xxxiv. 134 (Harl. MS.) Then the sonne..toke hir with him, and Ronne to-gedir ouer hillis and dalis, til tyme that thei come to the castell. *c* **1580** J. JEFFERE *Bugbears* III. iii. in *Archiv Stud. Neu. Spr.* (1897) XCVIII, Ylls, wodes and dales. **1590** SPENSER *F.Q.* I. ii. 8 But every hil and dale, each wood and plaine. **1630** *R. Johnson's Kingd. & Commw.* 639 When it is Summer in the Hils, it is Winter in the plaines. **1667** MILTON *P.L.* VIII. 262 About me round I saw Hill, Dale, and shadie Woods. **1850** TENNYSON *In Mem.* lxxix, And hill and wood and field did print The same sweet forms in either mind. **1918** in WEBSTER Add. **1929** WILSON & WEBB *Mod. Gramophones* ii. 34 This form of record has several advantages over the hill-and-dale cut. **1931** *News Chron.* 20 Mar. 15/2 A graph, whose hills and dales represent maximum and minimum velocity of each of a series of strokes. **1949** *Hansard, Commons* 6 Dec. 1835 The whole countryside is disfigured by deep cuttings and large tracts of what is known as hill and dale—impassable areas of heaped limestone. *Ibid.* 1844 We do not really know enough about hills and dales to be quite satisfied in all cases. **1964** A. NELSON *Dict. Mining* 218 *Hill-and-dale formation*.., a term applied to the ridges and hollows along the surface of dumped material (usually over-burden) at an opencast mine.

c. After *up*, *down*, used without the article: see DOWN, DOWNHILL, etc.

1667 MILTON *P.L.* IV. 777 Half way up Hill. **1879** F. POLLOK *Sport Brit. Burmah* II. 195 He had gone down hill. *Ibid.* II. 207, I followed..up hill and down dale, but never saw him more.

d. Proverbs and sayings. † ***to get the hill***, to get vantage-ground (*obs.*).

c **1305** *St. Lucy* 126 in *E.E.P.* (1862) 105 Euere heo lai stille as an hul. **1647** TRAPP *Comm. Rom.* vii. 19 Corruption, edg'd with a temptation, gets as it were the hill, and the winde, and, upon such advantages, too oft prevaileth. **1654** WHITLOCK *Zootomia* 292 A good Cause and Miscarriage meet oftner than Hills. **1819** *Metropolis* I. 58 Why, he's as old as the Hills. **1844** DICKENS *Mart. Chuz.* xxxv, All this time, Martin was cursing Mr. Pecksniff up hill and down dale. **1857** TRENCH *Proverbs* i. (ed. 4) 21 Do in hill as you would do in hall. **1892** BOWEN in *Law Times Rep.* LXVIII. 127/2 The law of estoppel by deed is as old as the hills.

e. ***over the hill***: having passed the prime in professional ability, physical beauty, etc. Chiefly *U.S.*

1950 *N.Y. Herald Tribune* 6 Dec. 35/2 He has lost his punch... He's a lot farther over the hill than I was when I hung up the gloves in 1927. **1952** M. R. RINEHART *Pool* xxxii. 259 The flawless skin goes, the lovely eyes fade, and she knows she is over the hill. **1957** I. CROSS *God Boy* (1958) xxiii. 197 As they say about boxers who are getting on in years, she is over the hill. **1962** *N.Y. Times Bk. Rev.* 17 June 20/3 Must you feel 'over the hill' after 40? **1972** H. KEMELMAN *Monday Rabbi took Off* ii. 24 When a rabbi gets to be around fifty, his chances of getting another job are not so good. He's like over the hill.

2. *fig.* Something of enormous mass; something not easily mounted or overcome.

c **1440** *Jacob's Well* (E.E.T.S.) 6 Ryȝt so, þis watyr & þis flood of þe gret curs flowyth hyȝe in-to þe hylles of prowde & ryche folk. **1644** MILTON *Sonn. to Virtuous Young Lady*, With those..That labour up the hill of heavenly Truth. **1738** WESLEY *Hymn*, '*The Voice of my Beloved*' i, O'er Hills of Guilt and Seas of Grief, He leaps. **1851** WILLMOTT *Pleas. Lit.* §21 (1857) 135 The hill of knowledge and fame was rapidly climbed.

3. a. A heap or mound of earth, sand, or other material, raised or formed by human or other agency. Cf. also ANT-, DUNG-, MOLE-HILL, etc.

1297 [see ANT-HILL 1]. *c* **1320** [see DUNG-HILL 1]. *c* **1340** *Cursor M.* 23221 (Fairf.) If a hille of fire ware made & þorou chaunce þou in hit slade. *c* **1450** *Merlin* xviii. 288 Ther was hilles of dede men and horse hem beforn. **1587** MASCALL *Govt. Cattle* (1662) 283 Moules..spoyle any faire meddow ..in casting up hils. *Ibid.* 289 Casting a great hill as big as two barrowfuls. **1590** SPENSER *F.Q.* II. vii. 6 He rose for to remove aside Those pretious hils [of gold] from straungers envious sight. **1654** WHITLOCK *Zootomia* 313 Looking down on the world as an Ant-hill. **1784** COWPER *Task* IV. 346 The wain..appears a moving hill of snow. **1834** H. MILLER *Scenes & Leg.* xix. (1857) 282 She clutched her hands into a hill of dried weed. **1887** *Kent Gloss.*, *Hill*, a heap of potatoes or mangold wurzel.

b. A heap formed round a plant by banking up or hoeing (see HILL *v.*² 2). Also, the cluster of plants on level ground. Cf. *a hill of beans* (BEAN *sb.* 6 e).

1572 MASCALL *Plant. & Graff.* (1592) 83 Then againe cast vp the earth about your hills, and cleansing them from all weedes..so let them rest till your Poles may be set therein. **1577** B. GOOGE *Heresbach's Husb.* II. (1586) 62 b, When the Hoppes..are cutte downe close to the grounde, and the hils being againe raised, are covered with doung. **1775** B. ROMANS *Nat. Hist. Florida* 120 A man ought to go through the field, and pull up those plants that look least promising leaving only three plants in each hill. **1799** G. WASHINGTON *Writ.* (1893) XIV. 232 No. 2..is to be..planted with potatoes; whether in Hills, or Drills, may be considered. *a* **1817** T. DWIGHT *Trav. New Eng.* etc. (1821) I. 108 The earth is raised to the height of from four to six inches, around the corn, and is denominated a hill; whence every planting is called a hill of corn. **1843** *Jrnl. R. Agric. Soc.* IX. II. 538 The general mode of planting hops is to place the hills at equal distances. **1854** *Trans. Pennsylvania State Agric. Soc.* 79 The best corn planter..marks the ground so as to keep the hills in rows in all directions. **1873** J. H. BEADLE *Undevel. West* 570 Each field..contained some three hundred hills of corn. **1884** H. BUTTERWORTH *Zigzag Journ. Western States* 42 Jerry was working like a beaver, and only three hills of potatoes to the square now. **1887** *Blackw. Mag.* June 815/2 In Virginia..a labourer is required for every 20,000 hills of tobacco. **1964** A. H. BURGESS *Hops* vi. 82 If rooted sets..are unobtainable, cuttings can be used for planting the [hop] garden. When this is done two or three cuttings should be planted at each hill.

c. The rising ground on which ruffs assemble at the breeding season; an assemblage of ruffs.

1768 PENNANT *Zool.* (1770) IV. 22 When a fowler discovers one of these hills, he places his net over night. **1859** FOLKARD *Wild-fowler* lix. (1875) 294 During the breeding season they [ruffs] frequent drier grounds, and assemble on small hillocks..An experienced fenman soon finds out their blood-stained hills. *Ibid.* 295 Frequently taking the whole hill at a single fold of the net. **1875** 'STONEHENGE' *Brit. Sports* I. ix. §1 A 'hill' of ruffs.

d. *Her.* A charge representing a hill, usually vert.

1828 in BERRY *Encycl. Her.* I. **1889** ELVIN *Dict. Her.* p. lii, Three Hills, as in the arms of Brinckman. **1966** SCOTT-GILES & BROOKE-LITTLE *Boutell's Heraldry* (rev. ed.) 301 *Hill, or Hillock*, a green mount.

e. A nitro-glycerine factory.

1897 *Pearson's Mag.* IV. 150/2 You have now reached the bottom of the 'hill'—all nitro-glycerine factories are called 'hills'. **1921** *Dict. Occup. Terms* (1927) §149 *Nitroglycerine hillman*, an explosive worker engaged on repetition work in nitroglycerine manufacture.

4. *attrib.* and *Comb.* **a.** Of or pertaining to a hill or hills, as ***hill-brow, -cop, -crest, -face, -foot, -ground, -line, -name, -pasture, -range, -ridge, -slope, -wash***. **b.** Of or pertaining to the hill-country of India, as ***hill-appointment, -station***, etc. **c.** For a hill or hill-country, as ***hill-chair, -gun***. Also, pertaining to the rearing and tending of sheep in hilly country. **d.** Inhabiting or frequenting hills, situated or held on a hill, as ***hill-bamboo, -convent, -culture, -fair, -fastness, -grass, -horse, -house, -kangaroo, -kid, -pony, -priest, -temple, -tent, -town, -tribe, -village***. Also HILL-FORT, etc.

1896 *Westm. Gaz.* 30 Dec. 3/2 There were only two *hill appointments possible at the time. **1827** D. JOHNSON *Ind. Field Sports* 232 The best kind of shafts are *hill bamboos which have no hollow. **1913** D. H. LAWRENCE *Love Poems* 40 The warm hay from The *hill-brow. **1954** J. R. R. TOLKIEN *Fellowship of Ring* 146 The north end of the hill-brow. **1861** in Hare *2 Noble Lives* (1893) III. 175 About eleven she set off again in her *hill-chair. **1878** SYMONDS *Many Moods, Riviera* 11 How well In this *hill-convent glides for them the day! **13..** *E.E. Allit. P.* A. 790 þe apostel hem segh..Arayed to þe weddyng in þat *hyl coppe. **1936** *Discovery* June 179/2 This midden culture, which we call Sotho, differs..in nearly every respect from our Shona or *Hill culture. **1950** WEBSTER Add., *Hillculture*, a system of agriculture utilizing erosion-preventing crops that are ecologically and economically best suited for sloping or hilly (often sub-marginal) land. **1886** C. SCOTT *Sheepfarming* 116 A successful hill lambing depends very much upon..the condition of the ewes at that period. *Hill ewes are never in too high condition. **1883** *Longm. Mag.* Nov. 71 The sportsman..has gone up the *hill-face. **1851** MAYHEW *Lond. Labour* I. 329 A *hill fair (that is where the fair is held upon a hill away from a town). **1841** THOREAU *Jrnl.* 13 Feb. (1962) I. 211/2 His *hill-farm is poor stuff. **1886** C. SCOTT *Sheepfarming* 101 Hill farms... Hill stocks should always be fixtures on the farm. **1946** *Act 9 & 10 Geo. VI* c. 73 §1 '*Hill farming land' means mountain, hill and heath land which is suitable for use for the maintenance of sheep of a hardy kind but not of sheep of other kinds, or which by improvement could be made suitable. *a* **1881** ROSSETTI *House of Life* v, Tender as dawn's first *hill-fire. **1650** TRAPP *Comm. Exod.* xx. 18 From the *hill-foot where they stood and trembled. **1891** S. C. SCRIVENER *Our Fields & Cities* 12 The river winds along the hill-foot. **1577** B. GOOGE *Heresbach's Husb.* I. (1586) 17 b, It is to be learned, what is best for the *hill ground, what for the valley. **1886** C. SCOTT *Sheepfarming* 123 The science of *hill-herding. **1799** J. ROBERTSON *Agric. Perth* 310 He keeps also fewer *hill-horses, a small species, of which at one time there were vast herds in the highlands. **1935** H. H. FINLAYSON *Red Centre* (1952) 40 The short-limbed, broad-chested, sturdy, *hill kangaroos or euros. **1944** *Living off Land* ii. 27 A number of men are required to capture the wallaby or the euro (hill kangaroo). **1816** SCOTT *Tales My Landlord* Introd., What resembled hares were in fact *hill-kids. **1873** W. CORY *Lett. & Jrnls.* (1897) 343 The crests of the *hill-line are crowned with the domes of the mosques. **1922** E. EKWALL *Place-Names Lancs.* 28 Very few *hill-names, apart from those which have given names to places, are found in early sources. **1962** *Coast to Coast 1961–62* 13 Nicholas wanted to..gambol as senselessly as the new lambs in the *hill paddocks. **1799** J. ROBERTSON *Agric. Perth* 525 All the tenants have a proportionable share of *hill-pasture. **1881** J. T. FOWLER in *Academy* 29 Oct. 334 The *hill-priests and the hedge-priests of the Northern diocese. **1844** MRS. BROWNING *Rhyme Duch. May* iv, I could see the low *hill-ranges. **1845** STOCQUELER *Handbk. Brit. India* (1854) 265 A promontory, or long *hill-ridge projecting into a basin. **1874** WHITTIER *Voices Freedom, Palestine* 29 Lo, Bethlehem's *hill-site before me is seen. **1749** H. PUREFOY in *Purefoy Lett. 1735–53* (1931) I. 162, I desire you will buy for mee ten ewes & lambs of the little short-legged horned *Hill Sheep. **1841** *Penny Cycl.* XXI. 358/1 The average weight of the fleece..is now at least 3 lbs. in the hill-sheep, and nearly 4 lbs. in the lowland-sheep. **1886** C. SCOTT *Sheepfarming* 103 Hill sheep farming. **1872** TENNYSON *Gareth & Lynette* 181 The damp *hill-slopes. **1908** *Daily Chron.* 14 May 5/4 On the north side of the valley the hill-slopes are fairly open. **1919** J. MASEFIELD *Reynard* 97 The hill-slope [seemed] steeper. **1879** F. POLLOK *Sport Brit. Burmah* I. 42 Now that European troops are being gradually concentrated on *hill stations. **1958** P. KEMP *No Colours or Crest* iv. 43 March-Phillipps had served in India ..where he had experienced..the glitter of social life in various hill stations. **1969** *Filmfare* (Bombay) 1 Aug. 31/4 Once, while shooting at a hill station, the entire R.K. unit was staying in a quaint hillside hotel. **1827** G. HIGGINS *Celtic Druids* 231 It may be correctly described as a *hill-temple. **1743** BULKELEY & CUMMINS *Voy. S. Seas* 89 The Carpenter went up to the *Hill Tent, so called from its situation. **1887** W. S. PRATT in W. Gladden *Parish Prob.* 433 Even the most humble, untaught player in a struggling *hill-town may fulfill..all the higher duties of his office. **1911** R. BROOKE *Poems* 24 Out of the white hill-town, High up I clamber. **1972** W. GARNER *Ditto, Brother Rat!* xxiii. 172 'Tell me about Vauban.'..'A dilapidated little hill town.' **1870** *Brewer's Dict. Phr. & Fable* 406/1 **Hill tribes*, the barbarous tribes dwelling in remote parts of the Deccan or plateau of Central India. **1946** *Nature* 6 July 35/1 Any hill-tribe tends to lead a more or less segregated life. **1972** *Nat. Geographic* Feb. 271/1 Although often labeled as a 'hill tribe', Thailand's Karens occupy both upland and lowland villages. **1905** *Daily Chron.* 9 Oct. 4/2 The picturesque little *hill-village of Moniaive [in Dumfriesshire]. **1947** *Geogr. Jrnl.* CX. 79 By no means all hill villages..are in the pastoral zone and many are associated with a fully-developed system of common arable fields. **1936** *Nature* 29 Aug. 357/2 A *hill-wash, some 11 ft. in thickness, contained large numbers of flint artefacts. **1958** F. E. ZEUNER *Dating Past* (ed. 4) 158 The Middle Older Loess of the section is a complex of loessic hillwash material derived from higher up the slope. **1963** *Times* 13 Feb. 14/7 Should lamb and *hill wool continue to be treated as special cases on social grounds?

e. Objective, instrumental, and locative, as ***hill-climber, -crowning; hill-born, -girdled, -girt, -surrounded*** adjs.; **hill-set** *a.* (after Matt. v. 14), 'set' or situated on a hill.

1911 E. POUND *Canzoni* 21 A swelling turbid sea *Hill-born and tumultuous. *a* **1963** C. S. LEWIS *Poems* (1964) 35 The hill-born, earthy spring,..The ripe peach from the southern wall still hot. **1897** *Daily News* 25 May 5/4 A gentleman..cyclist and champion *hill-climber. *a* **1758** DYER *Poems* (1761) 175 (Jod.) Whose *hill-crowning walls Shine, like the rising Moon thro' wat'ry mists. **1860** *All Year Round* No. 47. 492/2 A green, nestling, *hill-girt Devonshire valley. **1906** *Westm. Gaz.* 16 June 12/2 Brown-roofed, *hill-set villages. **1906** *Macm. Mag.* July 695 Ruler of his tiny hill-set principality. **1907** *Westm. Gaz.* 9 Aug. 2/4 Our hillset house of prayer. **1881** JEFFRIES *Wood Magic* II. vi. 152 The *hill-surrounded plain.

f. Spec. combs.: **hill-ant**, a species that forms ant-hills; **hill-berry**, the Deerberry or Wintergreen, *Gaultheria procumbens*, of N. America; **hill-bird**, (*a*) the fieldfare, *Turdus pilaris* (Swainson *Prov. Names Birds* 1885); (*b*) the upland plover or Bartramian sandpiper, *Bartramia longicauda*, of North America; †**hill-chapel**, a high-place for worship; **hill-climb**, the action of climbing hills, esp. as a test for motor vehicles; so **hill-climbing**, also *attrib.*; †**hill-digger**, one who digs into barrows or tumuli; so †**hill-digging**; **hill-engraver**, in map-making, one who makes the representations of elevations on an engraved plate; so **hill-engraving**; **hill-fever**, a kind of remittent fever prevalent in the hill country of India; **hill-folk, -people**, inhabitants or frequenters of the hills, hillmen; *spec.* (*a*) the Cameronians; (*b*) the elves or fairies of the hills; cf. HILLMAN; **hill-fox**, an Indian species of fox inhabiting the hills (*Canis Himalaicus*); **hill-gooseberry**, a Chinese myrtaceous plant (see quot.); **hill-king**, a king of the mountain-elves; **hill-map**, a map showing elevations; **hill-margosa, hill-mustard** (see quots.); **hill-oat**, a species of wild oat, *Avena strigosa*; **hill-partridge**, a gallinaceous bird of India, *Galloperdix lunulatus*; **hill-shading**, the lines of shading on a map to represent hills; **hill-spur** (see SPUR *sb.*¹ 11); **hill-star**, 'a humming-bird of the genus *Oreotrochilus*' (Cent. Dict.); **hill-stead**, a place on a hill; **hill-tit**, a bird of the family *Liotrichidæ*; **hill-wren**, a bird of the genus *Pnoepyga*.

1747 GOULD *Eng. Ants* 2 The *Hill Ants I so denominate from their usual Place of Residence, the sunny Banks or Sides of Hills. **1535** COVERDALE *Ezek.* vi. 4 The cities shalbe desolate, yᵉ *hillchapels layed waist: youre aulters destroyed. **1905** *Westm. Gaz.* 6 June 4/2 At the *hill-climb on May 27. **1907** *Ibid.* 26 Feb. 4/2 The club will organise competitions, hill-climbs, club-runs, and so on. **1971** I. WAGSTAFF in J. Walton *Castrol Guide Motoring Sport* x. 70 The object of a hill climb is for drivers..to reach the top of the hill in a shorter time than any other competitor. **1637** SHIRLEY *Hide Parke* IV. sig. G2, *Hill climbing white-rose, praise doth not lacke. **1861** MRS. NORTON *Lady La G.* II. 147 When wild hill-climbing wooed her spirit higher. **1900** [see CAR *sb.*¹ 1 c]. **1904** *Peel Guardian & Chron.* 23 Apr., The venue of the hill-climbing contest has not been fixed. **1908** *Westm. Gaz.* 19 Mar. 4/1 Its smooth and faultless running and wonderful hill-climbing abilities. **1931** [see DECOKE *v.*]. **1522** W. STAPLETON in Dawson Turner *Trial by Jury* etc. (1846) 54 Smith..examining the same Goodred upon *hill digging..If he wolde not confesse to them that he was an *hill-digger, he wold thrust his dagar throwe his chekes. **1847** *Norfolk Archæol.* I. 53–4. **1887** A. JESSOPP in *19th Cent.* Jan. 56 The hill diggers of the fifteenth century did their work most effectually. **1900** *Geogr. Jrnl.* June 589 The employment of *hill-engravers, who are, as already stated, so much required for the completion of the hill-engraving of the 1-inch map. *Ibid.* 578 Progress of the 1-inch Hill Map of the United Kingdom. **1804** C. B. BROWN tr. *Volney's View Soil U.S.* 234 In Bengal..there are woody eminences, infested..with what is there called the *hill fever. **1814** SCOTT *Wav.* xxxvi, He spared nobody but the scattered remnant of **hill-folk*, as he called them. **1816** —— *Old Mort.* iv, The stranger..being, in all probability, one of the hill-folk, or refractory presbyterians. **1838** *Penny Cycl.* X. 393/1 The *Canis Himalaicus*, *Hill Fox of the Europeans in the Doon, in Kumaon. **1859** LANG *Wand. India* 311 During this day's march we shot..a hill fox, a deer, and a wild dog. **1880** C. R. MARKHAM *Peruv. Bark* 292 The pretty pink-flowered *Rhodomyrtus tomentosa*, the berries of which are called '*hill-gooseberries'. **1884** CHILD *Ballads* II. xli. 361/2 The etin of the Scottish story is in Norse and German a dwarf-king, elf-king, *hill-king, or even a merman. **1866** *Treas. Bot.* 731/1 *M[elia] Azedarach*, vulgarly known as the Pride of India..Bead-tree, or *Hill Margosa, is widely diffused over the globe. **1895** *Oracle Encycl.* I. 539/1 Oriental Bunias, sometimes called '*hill-mustard', was introduced into Britain about one hundred years ago for the sake of its leaves, which are used for feeding cattle. *a* **1847** MRS. SHERWOOD *Lady of Manor* V. xxix. 65 Anecdotes told by the old Indians of the *hill-people. **1879** F. POLLOK *Sport Brit. Burmah* I. 3 Formerly gold was worked for by Shans and other hill people. **1878** HUXLEY *Physiogr.* 12 Commonly effected by a system of *hill-shading. **1871** W. MORRIS in Mackail *Life* (1899) I. 253, I went about looking for game about the *hill spurs. **1887** MEREDITH *Ballads & P.* 88 Down the hillspurs. **1637** *Boston Records* (1877) II. 18 James Pennyman shall have the *Hilsteade and the marsh ground under it. **1885** H. O. FORBES *Nat. Wand. E. Archip.* 207, I stalked a pretty little brown *hill-wren (*Pnoepyga pusilla*).

hill, *v.*¹ *Obs.* exc. *dial.* Forms: 3–4 **hule, hile**, 4–5 **hyl(e**, 4–6 **hil, hill(e**, 5–6 **hyll(e**, 4– **hill**. [ME. *hulen* (*ü*), *hilen, hyllen, hillen*, corresp. to an OE. type **hyllan*: cf. OS. *bi-hullean*, OHG. *hullan* (MHG., mod.G. *hüllen*), ON. *hylja*, (*hulda, hulit*, Da. *hylle*), Goth. *huljan*, f. *hul-*, weak grade of *helan*: see HELE *v.* It is probable that the ME. word was from Norse.]

1. *trans.* To cover, cover up; protect. Now *dial.*

a **1240** *Wohunge* in *Cott. Hom.* 279 Hwer wið þat blisfule blodi bodi þu mihtes hule and huide. *c* **1250** *Gen. & Ex.* 102 It mai ben hoten heuene-Rof; It hileð al ðis werldes drof. *a* **1300** *Cursor M.* 6802 (Cott.) He has noþer on bak ne bed Clath til hil [*v.rr.* hile, hule] him. *a* **1340** HAMPOLE *Psalter* xvi. 10 Vndire þe shadow of þi wenges hil me. **1362** LANGL. *P. Pl.* A. VI. 80 Alle þe houses beoþ I-hulet [*v. rr.* helid; *B.* hiled, ihyled, helied; *C.* heled]..Wiþ no led bote wiþ loue. **1496** *Dives & Paup.* (W. de W.) IV. xxiii. 189/2 Her here wexe soo moche that it hylled and hydde all her bodye. **1530** PALSGR. 585/1 You must hyll you wel nowe anyghtes. **1565** GOLDING *Ovid's Met.* I. (1593) 12 Go hil your heads. **1606** J. RAYNOLDS *Dolarney's Prim.* (1880) 88 So should the earth, his breathlesse body hill. *c* **1746** J. COLLIER (Tim Bobbin) *View Lanc. Dial.* Wks. (1862) 68 A floose of hay..quite hill'd us booath. **1854** MISS BAKER *Northampt. Gloss.* I. 323 Have you hilled the child up? **1868** B. BRIERLEY *Ab-o'-th' Yate on Times & Things* (1870) 121 Th' owd lad wur hillin' hissel up nicely.

b. *intr.* Of fish: To deposit or cover their spawn.

1758 *Descr. Thames* 29 A noted Place for Roach, Dace, and other small Fish, coming in Spawning Time to Hill, as it is called, otherwise laying their Spawn there in great Quantities.

c. See HILL *v.*² 2.

†**2.** To cover from sight; to hide, conceal. *Obs.*

a **1225** *Ancr. R.* 388 Herto ualleð a tale, and on iwrien [*v.r.* hulet] uorbisne. **1388** WYCLIF *Prov.* x. 12 Charite hilith alle synnes. *c* **1410** LOVE *Bonavent. Mirr.* xiv. (Pynson) E v, Our defautes and trespasses we hyll and hyde. *c* **1440** CAPGRAVE *Life St. Kath.* IV. 1379 Wype awey þat blyndenesse whiche hath hilled ȝour sight.

3. *Comb.* †**hilback**, the covering of the back, i.e. clothing (*obs.*).

1573 TUSSER *Husb.* x. (1878) 23 As interest or vsurie plaieth the dreuil, So hilback and filbellie biteth as euil.

Hence **hilled** *ppl. a.*, covered, armed.

c **1330** R. BRUNNE *Chron.* (1810) 224 He sped him þider in haste, with hilled hors of pris.

hill, *v.*² [f. HILL *sb.*]

I. *trans.* **1.** To form into a hill or heap; to heap up; *spec.* to throw up (soil) into a mound or ridge for planting purposes.

1581 *Act 23 Eliz.* c. 10 §4 Before..such Corn or Grain shall be shocked, cocked, hilled or copped. **1799** A. YOUNG *Agric. Linc.* xii. 266 Mr. Lloyd is much against hilling of manure. **1851** *Jrnl. R. Agric. Soc.* XII. II. 350 It [lime] is fetched from the chalk hills..and 'hilled' for 2 or 3 weeks before used, the heap being covered over with earth. **1884** *Chesh. Gloss.* s.v., I put some manure in and hilled the soil atop of it. **1887** *Blackw. Mag.* June 822/1 The tobacco-land is hilled up, but scarcely half of it as yet planted.

b. *fig.* To heap up, amass.

a **1618** SYLVESTER *Spectacles* xl, When hoord on hoord, when heap on heap he hilleth. **1627–47** FELTHAM *Resolves* I. xxxii. 109 When a man shall exhaust his very vitality for the hilling up of fatall gold. **1660** *Character Italy* 12 Another trick..that helpeth to hill up his fatal riches.

2. *Agric.* To cover and bank *up* the roots of (growing plants) with a heap of soil; to earth up. (Also *absol.*). [This seems to have been orig. a use of HILL *v.*[1] to cover (cf. HELE *v.*[2] 2 a), which has become associated with HILL *sb.* 3 b, and so with this verb, the forms being identical.]

1577 B. GOOGE *Heresbach's Husb.* II. (1586) 62 b, Set in grounde well covered with..moulde, and afterwarde hilled, and so suffered to remaine al Winter. **1601** HOLLAND *Pliny* I. 523 The skill and feat of baring the roots of trees, and also of hilling or banking them about. **1612** CAPT. SMITH *Map Virginia* 16 When it [corn] is growne midle high, they hill it about like a hop-yard. **1773** *Hist. Brit. Dom. N. Amer.* VI. iii. 123 The [tobacco] plants are set at three or four feet intervals or distances: they are hilled, and kept continually weeded. **1775** ROMANS *Florida* 175 The horse hoe..to do the laborious work of the hoe in hilling corn up. **1797** A. YOUNG *Agric. Suffolk* 89 At Midsummer they hill them [hops]. **1861** *Jrnl. R. Agric. Soc.* XXII. II. 305 Hilling, or earthing-up the plant.

3. To surround with hills.

1612 W. PARKES *Curtaine-Dr.* (1876) 25 Pleasant valleys hil'd on euery side.

4. To cover with hills or heaps.

1808 J. BARLOW *Columb.* VII. 750 Shocks, ranged in rows, hill high the burden'd lands.

II. *intr.* †**5.** To ascend, rise in or on a slope.

1538 LELAND *Itin.* I. 105 Cumming to highe ground and somewhat in sight by hilling I passid a Mile. *Ibid.* VII. 16 The Soyle of the Ground..is on mayne slaty Roke, and especially the parte of the Towne hilling toward the Castell.

6. To assemble on rising ground, as ruffs. See HILL *sb.* 3 c.

1768 PENNANT *Zool.* (1770) IV. 22 Soon after their arrival in the fens in spring, they [ruffs] begin to hill, i.e. to collect on some dry bank near a flash of water, in expectation of the Reeves, which resort to them. **1859** FOLKARD *Wildfowler* lix. (1875) 294 During spring, when the ruffs hill. *Ibid.* 295 Taking ruffs when not hilled.

hill, obs. form of ILL, ISLE.

†**hilla, hillir**, *int. Obs.* = HILLO.

a **1400–50** *Alexander* 1066 'A! hilla, haile', quod Alexander & him a narawe hent. **1513** DOUGLAS *Æneis* III. vi. 192 3a, thocht thi fallowis cry out, hillir haill!

hill-altar. An altar on a hill or height.

1539 BIBLE (Great) *2 Kings* xxiii. 5 Ministers of Baal..to burne incence in the hylaulters [**1611** high places]. **1585** ABP. SANDYS *Serm.* (Parker Soc.) 217 Sacrificing on their hill-altars. **1602** J. RHODES in Farr *S.P. Eliz.* (1845) II. 285 As he did [break] the hill-altars And groues of all idolaters.

'**hill-,billy.** Chiefly *U.S.* Also **hillbilly, hilly-billy, -billie.** [f. HILL *sb.* 4 + BILLY[1] 2.]

1. A person from a remote rural or mountainous area, *esp.* of the southeastern U.S. Also *attrib.* and *transf.*

1900 *N.Y. Jrnl.* 23 Apr. 2/5 In short, a Hill-Billie is a free and untrammelled white citizen of Alabama, who lives in the hills, has no means to speak of, dresses as he can, talks as he pleases, drinks whiskey when he gets it, and fires off his revolver as the fancy takes him. **1911** *N.Y. Sun* 10 Aug. (Funk), These two were farmers' boys and hillbillies and jayhawkers. **1932** E. WILSON *Devil take Hindmost* xxii. 236 A coarse-spoken frank humorous old hillbilly talking to neighbors. **1933** *Amer. Speech* VIII. III. 27/2 *Hill Billy*, a rube or uncouth and stupid fellow. **1952** *History Today* July 451/1 Most of his countrymen give him no grander name than 'hillbilly', a term as contemptuous as comic. **1957** *Daily Mail* 26 Sept. 8/2 At 47 the hillbilly who used to scratch a living as a dirt farmer at Greasy Creek in the Ozark Mountains has come a long way. **1966** D. STEWART in 'J. Hackston' *Father clears Out* p. x, As lively a collection of Australian hill-billies as I have ever seen. **1967** *Boston Sunday Herald* 2–8 Apr. 9/2 An Air Force man who wants a missile site, and the hill-billy fighting progress.

2. A type of American folk music. Also *attrib.*

1924 *Talking Machine World* XX. 207/1 Hill Billie Blues ..Banjo. **1925** *Ibid.* XXI. 186/2 The [rural] demand is largely for Blues, Coon songs, and Hilly-Billy numbers. **1932** *Daily Mirror* 1 July 10/3, I should not be surprised to hear that the hill-billy king and his suite visit the recording studio every morning of the week. **1953** A. MOOREHEAD *Rum Jungle* iv. 58 They wanted gramophones, and the music they liked best was hill-billy. **1955** L. FEATHER *Encycl. Jazz* (1956) 110 Piano with local hillbilly, Dixieland and swing bands from age 13. **1959** 'F. NEWTON' *Jazz Scene* x. 172 The full bag of hilly-billy melodies, or the like. **1971** M. BABSON *Cover-up Story* vi. 66 They may start out as Hillbilly, or Country and Western but they can be turned into Folk. **1972** *Jazz & Blues* Feb. 19/1 Fats Domino had done some real down home hillbilly-motown stuff.

'**hill-,country.** [HILL *sb.* 4.] A district composed of hills or elevated ground.

1582 N. T. (Rhem.) *Luke* i. 39 Marie..went vnto the hil countrie with speed. **1789** G. WHITE *Selborne* I. i. 2 The down..is a pleasing park-like spot..jutting out on the verge of the hill-country. **1816** U. BROWN *Jrnl.* in *Maryland Hist. Mag.* (1915) X. 283 A handsome hill country in a good state of cultivation. **1865** A. D. WHITNEY *Gayworthys* XV. 133 The slow, ponderous vehicle went..creaking on, up into the hill-country. **1875** W. MᶜILWRAITH *Guide Wigtownshire* 20 The church of Bargrennan is well attended by people from the hill-country around. **1903** *Westm. Gaz.* 14 Jan. 2/1 The Surrey hill-country.

hiller, -ern, -or, obs. ff. ELDER *sb.*[1], the tree.

'**hillet.** *rare.* [f. HILL *sb.* + -ET[1].] A hillock.

1538 LELAND *Itin.* II. 54 Conscending a Hillet even ther by. **1577** HARRISON *England* I. xxiv. (1881) III. 165 Neither will I speake of the little hillets seene in manie places of our Ile,..they are nothing else but Tumuli or graues of former times. **1695** *Phil. Trans.* XIX. 46 The three first Hillets, viz. the nearest to the Hole, are quite barren.

hill-fort. A fort constructed on a hill.

1833 M. SCOTT *Tom Cringle* xvi. (1859) 434 A sudden flash and a jet of white smoke puffed out from the hill fort above the town. **1862** BEVERIDGE *Hist. India* III. VII. iii. 84 The hill-fort of Wusota.

b. *esp.* A hill-top fortification of prehistoric age.

1851 D. WILSON *Preh. Ann.* (1863) II. III. iii. 90 The simple circular hill-forts wherein we trace the mere rudimentary efforts of a people in the infancy of the arts. **1871** FREEMAN *Hist. Ess.* Ser. I. viii. 219 That class of towns which, out of Gaulish hill-forts grew into Roman and mediæval cities.

hillibaloo, hilliebalow, var. of HULLABALOO.

hilliness ('hɪlɪnɪs). [f. HILLY *a.* + -NESS.] The quality or state of being hilly.

1629 MAXWELL tr. *Herodian* (1635) 332 By reason of the hillinesse and roughnesse of the countrie. **1649** BLITHE *Eng. Improv. Impr.* (1653) 121 Reducing the Hilliness to Plainess. **1887** HISSEY *Holiday on Road* 238 Some..may think that I have exaggerated the hilliness of Sussex.

'**hilling,** *vbl. sb.*[1] Now *dial.* [f. HILL *v.*[1] + -ING[1].]

1. Covering, hiding, protection.

a **1300** *E.E. Psalter* lx[i]. 5 [4] Be for-hild in hilinge of þi wenges I mon. **1388** WYCLIF *ibid.*, Keuered in the hilyng of thi wengis. *c* **1440** *Promp. Parv.* 240/1 Hyllynge, or happynge. **1580** LUPTON *Sivqila* 28 Caring for nothing, but for the hilling and filling of their owne backe and bellie.

2. *concr.* A covering; e.g. clothing, a bed-quilt, a roof, the cover of a book; cf. HELING 2. (In ME. freq. in phr. *food and hilling*.)

c **1325** *Gloss. W. de Biblesw.* in Wright *Voc.* 170 *Cele e tecte*, hiling of hous. *c* **1380** WYCLIF *Sel. Wks.* III. 427 When we haue fode and hyllynge [I. 203 hilinge]. **1388** —— *Prov.* xxi. 27 That thou take awei hilyng [**1382** couerynq] fro thi bed. *c* **1440** *Promp. Parv.* 229/2 Hatte, hed hillynge. **1496** *Dives & Paup.* (W. de W.) v. vii. 204/1 Hylynge lyfelode, and helpe of frendes. **1520** *Lanc. Wills* (1857) II. 9 My best bed hillinge of tapstre werke. **1601** HOLLAND *Pliny* I. 289 They [partridges] couer their egs with a soft carpet or hilling as it were of fine dust. **1657** TOMLINSON *Renou's Disp.* 55 The hillings from many seeds. **1888** *Sheffield Gloss., Hilling*, the quilt of a bed, a bed rug.

3. *Comb.* **hilling-stone**, stone used for roofing.

1660 *Act 12 Chas. II*, c. 4 Sched. II, Stones vocat' Hilling stone the thowsand iijs. iiijd. **1721** C. KING *Brit. Merch.* I. 355 Copperas, Bread, Hilling-stones and Calve-skins. **1811** *Self Instructor* 422 Slate and hilling stones.

'**hilling,** *vbl. sb.*[2] [f. HILL *v.*[2] + -ING[1].] The action of forming hills or heaps; *esp.* the earthing-up of plants; cf. HILL *v.*[2] 2.

1627–47 [see HILL *v.*[2] 1 b]. **1773** *Hist. Brit. Dom. N. Amer.* II. ii. 211 Horse-hoeings, as also hoeing and hilling by hand. **1796** J. ADAMS *Diary* 12 July Wks. 1851 III. 416 Ploughing for hilling among the corn. **1814** J. TAYLOR *Arator* 233 How often he had passed over the land..in fallowing, hilling, cutting off hills, planting, replantings. **1833** B. SILLIMAN *Man. Sugar Cane* 17 It is advisable not to plough deep, especially for the last hoeing or hilling. **1887** *Harper's Mag.* Jan. 306/1 There is a broad hilling up so as to have a slope inward toward the plants as well as away from them.

hillir: see HILLA.

†'**hillish,** *a. rare.* [f. HILL *sb.* + -ISH.] Of the nature of a hill, hill-like, hilly; pertaining to a hill.

1583 STANYHURST *Æneis* I. (Arb.) 19 Thee father almighty ..Mewed vp theese reuelers coupt in strong dungeon hillish [cf. HILDEN]. **1609** HEYWOOD *Brit. Troy* VI. xxv, The wounded Whale casts from his hillish Iawes Riuers of Waters, mixt with purple gore. **1631** MARKHAM *Weald of Kent* II. i. (1668) 6 It is not so hillish and sliding as the Weald.

hill-man, hillman.

1. Also **hillsman. a.** One who frequents the hills; *spec.* applied to the Scottish Covenanters (cf. CAMERONIAN and *hill-folk*). **b.** An inhabitant of a hill-country, a mountaineer: applied to the hill-tribes of India, etc.

c **1830** J. TRAIN in Scott *Old Mort.* Introd., The religious sect called Hill-men, or Cameronians. **1854** J. D. HOOKER *Himalayan Jrnls.* I. v. 136 Carriers and mountaineers... If they serve a good hills-man like themselves, they will follow him with alacrity, sleep on the cold, bleak mountain. **1859** LANG *Wand. India* 6 A sort of sedan-chair carried by four hill men. **1893** *Archæol.* LIV. 269 The pinch of poverty often drove the bravest of the hillmen to raid the cattle of the lowlands. **1897** *Daily News* 27 Nov. 5/7 The hillmen offered a stubborn resistance to the advance along its whole length. **1920** *London Mag.* Apr. 187/2 This rain would hold. He knew it with a hillsman's knowledge. **1938** V. MCNABB *Life of Our Lord* iii. 42 The hills-man from Galilee..had to pass through the country of Samaria.

2. One of the hill-folk (*b*); an elf or troll.

1882 CHILD *Ballads* I. vii. 90/2 A supernatural being, a demon or a hillman, seeks to entice away a mortal maid. **1884** *Ibid.* II. xli. 366/2 The hill-man, in several Norwegian copies, carries off the lady on horseback.

3. *spec.* **a.** (See quot. 1851). **b.** A miner, a slate quarryman [cf. Ger. *bergmann*]. **c.** A hill-climber.

1851 MAYHEW *Lond. Labour* (1861) II. 172 The labourers ..paid by the foreman or forewoman of the dust-heap, commonly called hill-man or hill-woman. **1865** J. T. F. TURNER *Slate Quarries* 13 The cleavers, or hillmen, build rough walls as a partial protection from the inclemency of the weather. *a* **1885** SHAIRP in W. Knight *Life* (1888) 74 Some of our party were very good hillmen. One day five or six set out on a race from our door..to the top of Fairfield.

hillo, hilloa ('hɪləʊ, hɪ'ləʊ), *int.* (*sb.*) [Cf. HALLO; see also HILLA.] A call used to hail a distant or occupied person; now, more often, to express surprise at an unexpected meeting.

1602 SHAKS. *Ham.* I. v. 115 *Hor.* Illo, ho, ho, my Lord! *Ham.* Hillo, ho, ho, boy; come bird, come. **1751** SMOLLETT *Per. Pic.* (1779) I. ii. 12 The publican..rebellowed in the same tone..'Hilloah'. **1826** DISRAELI *Viv. Grey* VI. ii, 'Hilloa, within!' shouted Essper. **1873** BLACK *Pr. Thule* xix, 'Hillo, Lavender!' he said, in a tone of surprise.

b. *sb.* As a name for this call.

1823 BYRON *Island* II. xviii, And then a pause, and then a hoarse 'Hillo!'

hillock ('hɪlək), *sb.* [f. HILL *sb.* + -OCK.]

1. A little hill.

1382 WYCLIF *Jer.* vi. 6 Delueth aboute Jerusalem an erthe hilloc. **1529** MORE *Comf. agst. Trib.* I. Wks. 1143/2 Where as with a verye fieble fayth & a faynte, we shall be scant hable to remoue a lyttle hillocke. **1665** MANLEY *Grotius' Low C. Warres* 521 The Ground easily swelling into little Hillocks. **1732** LEDIARD *Sethos* II. VII. 18 Upon..the plain..were a few verdant hillocks. **1884** Q. VICTORIA *More Leaves* 271 We got out and scrambled up a high hillock off the road.

2. A small mound or heap of earth, stones, or the like.

1382 WYCLIF *Gen.* xxxi. 51 Loo! this hillok [**1388** heep] and the stoon that I haue rerid bitwixe me and thee, witnes shal be; this hilloc and the stoon ben into witnessyng. **1538** LELAND *Itin.* III. 129 The Partition of the Shire a Mile and more by Northe West from Simon's Bathe at the Towres. These Towres be round Hillokkes of Yerth sette for Limites. **1791** W. BARTRAM *Carolina* 126, I beheld a great number of hillocks or small pyramids, resembling hay-cocks,..I knew them to be the nests of the crocodile. **1875** *Lyell's Princ. Geol.* (ed. 12) II. III. xlvii. 553 Just as the African sandwinds..raise a small hillock over the carcass of every dead camel exposed on the surface of the desert.

†**3.** A hump, bump, protuberance, or prominence on any surface. *Obs.*

c **1520** ANDREW *Noble Lyfe* dj, The Kamell is a lothly beste, and hathe an hyllocke vpon his backe. **1665** HOOKE *Microgr.* 35 At the upper part of the drop..there usually was made some one or more little Hillocks or Prominences. **1668** CULPEPPER & COLE *Barthol. Anat.* I. ii. 3 To tell mens Fortunes from the Lines and Hillocks in their Hands.

Hence '**hillock** *v. trans.*, to raise into a hillock, to heap up; **hillocked** ('hɪləkt) *ppl. a.*

1791 COWPER *Odyss.* v. 589 The suff'ring Chief.. occupying soon The middle space hillock'd it high with leaves. **1804** J. GRAHAME *Sabbath* (1839) 19/1 Fill up the furrows 'tween the hillock'd graves. **1867** F. M. LUDLOW *Little Brother* 91 On the pathless field of the hillocked sea.

hillocky ('hɪləkɪ), *a.* [f. prec. + -Y.] Abounding in or characterized by hillocks.

1727 BAILEY vol. II, *Hillocky*, full of Hillocks or little Hills. **1831** J. WILSON in *Blackw. Mag.* XXIX. 288. **1882** MISS BRADDON *Mt. Royal* II. x. 229 They crossed a bit of hillocky common.

†**hillous,** *a. Obs. rare.* [irreg. f. HILL *sb.* + -OUS.] Hilly.

1550 *Decree Chanc. Lancashire* in T. Baines *Hist. Lanc.* (1870) II. 46 The way..is very foul, painful and hillous.

hill-side. The lateral slope of a hill.

?*a* **1400** *Arthur* 369 He went ouer to þe hulle syde. **1509** HAWES *Past. Pleas.* XXVII. lxiv, We lyght adowne, under an hyll syde. **1644** MILTON *Educ.* Wks. (1847) 99/2, I shall.. conduct you to a hill-side, where I will point you out the right path of a virtuous and noble Education. **1810** SCOTT *Lady of L.* v. x, The next [breath of wind] but swept a lone hill-side Where heath and fern were waving wide.

attrib. **1859** W. COLLINS *Q. of Hearts* (1875) 4 Assembled together in our hill-side retreat. **1890** *Daily News* 20 Dec. 5/6 The name 'Hillside men'..applied to the Fenians.

Hence **hill'sider**.

1898 *Daily News* 22 Mar. 3/5 To object to any money being given to a poor hillsider.

hill-top. 1. The top or summit of a hill.

1530 PALSGR. 231/1 Hyll toppe, *crespe* or *creste de montaigne*. **1535** COVERDALE *Jer.* xxxi. 39 The hill toppe of Gareb. **1667** MILTON *P.L.* VIII. 520 The amorous Bird of Night Sung Spousal, and bid haste the Eevning Starr On his Hill top, to light the bridal Lamp. **1784** COWPER *Task* I. 222 'Tis perched upon the green hill top. **1875** JOWETT *Plato* (ed. 2) I. 497 The sun is still upon the hill-tops.

attrib. **1893** GRANT WHITE in *Westm. Gaz.* 7 June 2/1 The healthy antique principle of hill-top habitation. **1897** *Daily News* 3 June 5/6 The lighting of the hill-top bonfires.

2. Special Comb. **hill-top novel**, the name given by Grant Allen to those of his novels in which he expressed his views on moral and social questions, especially views not generally acceptable to his contemporaries; **hill-top surface** (see quot. 1961).

1895 G. ALLEN *British Barbarians* p. xi, I propose in future to add the words, 'A Hill-top Novel', to every one of my stories which I write of my own accord, simply and solely for the sake of embodying and enforcing my own opinions. *Ibid.* p. xvi, Why, once more, this particular name, 'A Hill-top Novel'? For something like this reason. I am

writing in my study on a heather-clad hill-top... Everything around is fresh and pure... But away below in the valley, as night draws on, a lurid glare..marks the spot where the great wen of London heaves and festers. **1896** *Pearson's Mag.* May 556/1 Latterly he [*sc.* Grant Allen] has doubled up his social philosophy with his fiction, producing what he calls 'Hill Top' novels. **1901** *Sketch* XXV. 256/2 The lady sports-woman is the Colonel's abomination; he regards her as a monstrous product of the divided skirt and the 'Hill-top' novel. **1930** J. Challinor in *Geography* Dec. 656 The object of the foregoing remarks is therefore to suggest that a hill-top surface, having a 'plateau quality' about it, need not necessarily be evidence of an uplifted peneplane. **1961** —— *Dict. Geol.* 100/1 *Hill-top surface*, an imaginary surface, as smooth as possible, touching the tops of the hills of a region.

'hillward, *adv.* and *a.* [f. hill *sb.* + -ward.]

A. *adv.* Towards the hill.

(In quot. 1570, phrase 'down the hill' with postposition.) [*c* **1570** *Pride & Lowl.* (1841) 9 Mee thought I had espied A thing come downe the hilward toward me.]

B. *adj.* That faces towards a hill.

1870 Morris *Earthly Par.* III. iv. 296 A house..whose hillward side Is midst the vines.

'hill-woman. A woman who lives on a hill or belongs to a hill-tribe; also, a forewoman in a dust-yard: cf. hill-man 1 a, 3 a.

1851 Mayhew *Lond. Labour* (1861) II. 173/2 The perquisites of the hill-man or hill-woman, are rags, bones, pieces of old metal, etc. **1895** Sir W. Hunter *Old Missionary* iv. 109 An aged grey-haired hillwoman.

†**'hillwort.** *Obs.* [f. hill *sb.* + wort.] An old name of Pennyroyal (or ? of Wild Thyme).

c **1000** Ælfric *Gloss.* in Wr.-Wülcker 133/34 *Samum*, hylwurt. *Ibid.* 137/2 *Pollegia*, hylwyrt. *c* **1265** *Voc. Plants* ibid. 555/1 *Pulegium*, puliol, hulwurt. **14..** *Voc.* ibid. 605/48 *Pulegium*, hullewort. **1528** Paynell *Salerne's Regim.* X iij, Hyll worte..taken with wyne purgeth blacke coler. **1597** Gerarde *Herbal* App., *Hilwort* is Puliol mountaine.

hilly ('hɪlɪ), *a.* [f. hill *sb.* + -y.]

1. Characterized by hills; abounding in hills.

1432-50 tr. *Higden* (Rolls) I. 333 Þe lond is..wiþ-ynne hilly and sondy. **1523** Fitzherb. *Husb.* §6 Oxen wyl plowe ..vpon hylly grounde, where as horses wyll stande still. **1625** N. Carpenter *Geog. Del.* ii. x. (1635) 173 Some plaine countries neere the..Pole may be colder then some hilly Regions neere the Æquatour. **1738** Wesley *Ps.* cxxv. ii, As round Jerusalem The Hilly Bulwarks rise. **1872** Black *Adv. Phaeton* xxx, The hillier regions of Dumfriesshire.

fig. **1635** J. Hayward tr. *Biondi's Banish'd Virg.* 22 Her dainty hands..delicately hilly, and lasciviously dimpled.

2. Of the nature of a hill; elevated; steep.

1390 Gower *Conf.* I. 25 The ston which fro the hully stage He syh doun falle on þat ymage. **1563** W. Fulke *Meteors* (1640) 57 b, Rivers..are swift..because they run downe from an hilly place. **1577-87** Harrison *England* i. xii. in *Holinshed* I. 60/1 First of all vpon the east side of the hauen a great hillie point called Downesend. **1622** Fletcher *Prophetess* v. ii, Better to have liv'd Poor and obscure, and never scal'd the top Of hilly empire. **1768** J. Byron *Acc. Wager* in *Narr. Patagonia* (1778) 23 A bay formed by hilly promontories.

b. Hill-like.

1658 Sir T. Browne *Hydriot.* Introd. 1 Graves of Giants under hilly and heavy coverings. **1697** Dryden *Virg. Georg.* ii. 481 A hilly Heap of Stones.

†3. Belonging to the hills; hill-dwelling. *Obs.*

1632 J. Hayward tr. *Biondi's Eromena* 168 Foure mountaine Swaines or hillie-men. **1698** Fryer *Acc. E. India & P.* 175 Though these Hilly People are of a rougher Temper.

hillyer, var. of hellier, tiler.

hilo[1] ('hiːləʊ). [Sp., = thread:—L. *fīlum.*] A thin vein of ore (see quot. 1908).

1848 *English & Foreign Mining Gloss.* 5/4 *Hilo*, a small vein or thread of ore in a lode. *hilo de la veta*, line or direction of the vein. *hilos altos*, threads or small veins of ore falling into or proceeding from the upper or hanging wall of a lode. *hilos baxos*, threads or small veins of ore proceeding from or falling into the lower wall of a lode. **1908** E. Halse *Dict. Spanish Mining Terms* 188 Hilo (thread), (1) *h. de la veta* or *h. del criadero*, direction of the vein or deposit..(2) small vein or thread of ore in a lode, *e.g., hilos altos*, threads falling into or proceeding from the hanging wall..; in the Cauca, the name is applied to small veins of gold-bearing quartz. *Ibid.* 186 *Hebra*, (1) a thread or yarn of a hempen or other rope..; several twisted together form the *hilo*.

Hilo[2] ('hiːləʊ). [Hawaiian.] *Hilo grass*, a large and coarse grass, *Paspalum conjugatum*.

1888 W. Hillebrand *Flora Hawaiian Islands* 493 The well known *Hilo grass*, which first appeared about 1840 in the district of Hilo and soon spread there,..is a native of tropical America..but is found now also in tropical Africa, the Galapagos Islands, Australia, and India. **1915** W. A. Bryan *Nat. Hist. Hawaii* 208 The well known and generally despised Hilo grass, occurs in moist, heavy soils in the lower zone. **1917** *Nature* 20 Sept. 57/2 In the moister portions of the islands large areas have been occupied by Hilo grass. **1929** W. T. Pope *Man. Wayside Plants Hawaii* 27 Vigorous cultivation of fields keeps Hilo grass in control.

‖**hilsa, hilsah** ('hɪlsə). *E. Ind.* [Hindī *hilsā.*] 'A rich and savoury fish of the shad kind (*Clupea ilisha*)' found in the Indian Seas, which ascends the Ganges and other rivers to spawn. (Yule.)

1810 T. Williamson *E. Ind. Vade M.* II. 154 (Y.) The hilsah (or sable-fish) seems to be midway between a mackerel and a salmon. **1879** F. Pollok *Sport Brit. Burmah* I. 4 The most delicious fish, such as the pomfret, hilsa, mango.

hilt (hɪlt), *sb.* Also 1 hilte, 1-5 hylt, 1-6 hylte, hilte, (3 *Lay.* heolte, helte), 4 hult, 5 *Sc.* helt. [OE. *hilt* str. n. and m., = MDu. *helt, hilt* m., ON. *hjalt* str. n.; also *hilte* wk. fem., corresp. to OS. *hilta* (MLG. *hilte*, MDu. *helte, hilte*) f., OHG. *helza* (MHG. *helze*) wk. f. The former appears to represent an OTeut. **heltoz—hiltiz*, neuter *s*-stem; the latter OTeut. **hiltjôn-*; of uncertain origin; not connected with *hold* vb. (Thence OF. *helt, helte*, later *heut, heu, heute*, It. *elso, elsa* hilt of sword or dagger.)]

1. a. The handle of a sword or dagger.

Beowulf (Z.) 1669 Ic þæt hilt þanan feondum ætferede. *c* **1000** Ælfric *Voc.* in Wr.-Wülcker 142/15 *Capulum*, hilte. *c* **1205** Lay. 1559 Þa brac þat sweord..Riht bi þere hilte. **13..** *Gaw. & Gr. Knt.* 1594 Hit hym vp to þe hult. **14..** *Sir Beues* (C.) 4313 Þe hylte was a charbocle ston. **1530** Palsgr. 531/2 Hylte of a swerde, *poignee.* **1590** Sir J. Smyth *Disc. Weapons* 4 Long heavie Daggers also, with great brauling Ale-house hilts. **1642** Fuller *Holy & Prof. St.* ii. xix. 127 He that hath the hilt in his hand in the morning, may have the point at his throat ere night. **1692** Sir W. Hope *Fencing Master* 2 The Hilt is divided into three parts, the Pomell, the Handle, and the Shell. **1847** James *J. Marston Hall* viii, The Duke..laid his hand upon the hilt of his sword.

†b. Formerly often in *plural*, with same sense.

Beowulf (Z.) 1615 Þa hilt somod since fage. *a* **1000** *Sal. & Sat.* 446 Ofer ða byrgena blicað ða hiltas. *c* **1000** Ælfric *Judg.* iii. 22 Þa hiltan eodon into þam innoþe. *c* **1400** *Melayne* 116 Gaffe hym þe hiltis in his hande. *c* **1450** *Merlin* 103 Arthur toke the swerde by the hiltes, and..yaf it to the Archebisshopp. **1599** Shaks. *Hen. V*, ii. i. 68 Ile run him vp to the hilts, as I am a soldier. **1632** J. Hayward tr. *Biondi's Eromena* 29 In whose belly, she..buried the Poyniard up to the hilts. **1753** L. M. tr. *Du Boscq's Accompl. Wom.* II. 205 The sword..bent to the very hilts.

†c. By extension, a sword-stick or foil. *Obs.*

1609 B. Jonson *Case is alt.* ii. iv, Let's to some exercise or other, my hearts. Fetch the hilts. Fellow Juniper, wilt thou play?

2. The handle or haft of any other weapon or tool.

1573-80 Baret *Alv.* H 454 The Hilt, or handle of any toole or weapon, *manubrium.* **1848** Lytton *Harold* ii. i, Before each guest was a knife, with the hilt adorned by precious stones. **1863** Kinglake *Crimea* (1876) I. xiv. 275 Unnecessary..to shew even the hilt of his pistol.

3. Phrases. †*by these hilts*: a form of asseveration. †*loose in the hilts*: unreliable, conjugally unfaithful. *up to the hilt* († *hilts*): completely, thoroughly, to the furthest degree possible; also *to the hilt.*

1596 Shaks. *1 Hen. IV*, ii. iv. 230 Seuen, by these Hilts, or I am a Villaine else. **1632** Chapman & Shirley *Ball* iv. iii, 'Tis not, I fear To fight with him, by these hilts! **1650** Howell *Cotgrave's Dict.* Ep. Ded., In French *Cocu* is taken for one whose wife is loose in the hilts. **1682** Villiers (Dk. Buckhm.) *Chances* Wks. (1714) 136 It's no matter, she's loose i' th' Hilts, by Heaven. **1687** R. L'Estrange *Answ. Diss.* 45 He is All, Politiques here, up to the Hilts. **1823** Byron *Juan* xi. lvii, A modern Ancient Pistol—by the hilts! **1862** *Lond. Rev.* 16 Aug. 135 The original statements..have been proved—if we may say so—up to the very hilt. **1883** J. Payn *Thicker than Water* iii. (1884) 18 The estate was mortgaged up to the hilt. **1950** J. D. Carr *Below Suspicion* x. 122 You may trust me to the hilt! **1965** *New Statesman* 16 Apr. 604/1 The Prime Minister..backs their decisions to the hilt. **1965** *Listener* 20 May 742/2 Every event I attended was subscribed to the hilt, and the house was full.

4. *Comb.* **hilt-guard**, the part which protects the hand when holding the hilt.

1874 Boutell *Arms & Arm.* v. 80 At the two extremities of its massive rectangular hilt-guard, the Roman sword commonly displays..the head of a lion or..an eagle.

Hence **'hiltless** *a.*, without a hilt.

c **1000** *Voc.* in Wr.-Wülcker 142/34 *Ensis*, hiltleas sweord.

hilt, *v.* [f. prec. sb.] *trans.* To furnish or fit with a hilt; to provide a hilt for.

1813 Scott *Trierm.* iii. xxvii, All the ore he deign'd to hoard Inlays his helm, and hilts his sword. **1822** —— *Nigel* xxvii, A long-bladed knife, hilted with buck's-horn. **1874** Boutell *Arms & Arm.* ii. 17 Not a very secure mode of hilting a sword.

Hence **'hilting** *vbl. sb., concr.* material for hilts.

1897 *Daily News* 25 Jan. 9/5 Prices of hilting are high, especially bone.

hilt, var. of hild *v. Obs.*, to flay; obs. or dial. f. *held*, pa. t. of hold *v.*

'hilted, *a.* [f. hilt *sb.* and *v.* + -ed.] Furnished with or possessing a hilt; in *Her.*, having a hilt of a different tincture from the blade.

Beowulf (Z.) 2987 Heard swyrd hilted. **1002** *Will of Wulfric* in Kemble *Cod. Dipl.* VI. 147 Twa seolfor hilted sweord. **1636** Davenant *Platon. Lovers* Wks. (1673) 410 A brace of massie hilted Rogues. **1766** Porny *Heraldry* (1787) 190 Ruby, two Swords in Saltier Pearl, pomeled and hilted Topaz. **1850** Blackie *Æschylus* I. 95, I can also hold a hilted dagger.

‖**hilum** ('haɪləm). [L. *hīlum* little thing, trifle; according to Festus, thought to have orig. meant 'that which adheres to a bean'; hence in mod. Bot. use (see 2).]

†1. Something very minute. *Obs.*

1659 D. Pell *Impr. Sea* 44 Unhewn Sailors, that have no more than a meer hilum of goodness in them.

2. *Bot.* The point of attachment of a seed to its seed-vessel; the scar on the ripe seed.

1753 Chambers *Cycl. Supp.*, *Hilum*, a word used by botanists to express the blackish spot in beans, commonly called by us the eye of the bean. **1830** Lindley *Nat. Syst. Bot.* 115 Seeds..with a smooth shining coat, and a broad pale hilum. **1880** Gray *Struct. Bot.* vi. §8. 277 In the simplest form of ovule, hilum and chalaza are one.

b. A similar mark on a starch-granule. c. 'The aperture in the extine of a pollen grain' (*Syd. Soc. Lex.*).

1867 J. Hogg *Microsc.* ii. i. 341 Most of the granules [of starch] have a circular spot, termed the hilum, around which a large number of curved lines arrange themselves.

3. a. *Anat.* = hilus. 'Applied also to certain small apertures and depressions' (*Syd. Soc. Lex.*).

b. *Path.* 'A term for a small flattened staphyloma of the iris from corneal perforation, in consequence of its likeness to the hilum of the garden bean' (*Syd. Soc. Lex.*).

c. A little opening in the statoblast of a sponge.

1887 Sollas in *Encycl. Brit.* XXII. 424 (*Sponges*) On one side of the capsule is a hilum which leads into the interior.

‖**hilus** ('haɪləs). *Anat.* [mod.Lat., altered from hilum.] The point at which any one of the viscera has its junction with the vascular system; a notch or fissure where a vessel enters an organ.

1840 G. V. Ellis *Anat.* 528 The spleen..is convex externally towards the ribs, and flat or slightly concave internally; and this surface, turned to the stomach, is marked by a fissure or hilus in which the vessels enter. **1881** Mivart *Cat* 233 This tube..emerges from a fissure in the concave surface, called the hilus of the kidney.

hilve, obs. f. helve.

hily, obs. f. highly.

him (hɪm, enclitic -ɪm), *pers. pron., 3rd sing. masc.* (and †*neut.*), *dat.-accus.* Forms: 1- him; also 1-6 hym (rarely 2-4 heom, 4-5 hem, hime, hom, 5 ham, 5-6 hyme). [OE. *him*, dat. sing., masc. and neuter, of he, it: cognate with OFris. *him* (MDu. *heme, hem, him*, Du. *hem*), and parallel in inflexion to OS. and OHG. *imu, imo* (MLG. *ime, eme*, MHG. *im(e*, Ger. *ihm*), Goth. *imma*. In 10th c. (as in the parallel *her, hem*), the dative appears to have begun to be used for the accus. *hine* in north-midl. dialect; by 1150 *him* had supplanted *hine* in north and midl., and before 1400 had become the general literary form, though some south-western writers of the 15th c. retained *hin, hen*, which, in the form *en, un, 'n*, is still current in southern dialect speech: see hin. (So in late OFris. *him* took the place of *hine, hin*; and in MDu., the dat. *heme, hem, him*, intruded upon the orig. accus. *hin, hen*; and mod.Du. has only the dat.-acc. *hem.*) But while *him* thus became both dative and accusative in the masculine, in the neuter the accusative *hit, it* survived, and at length superseded the dative, as in the modern 'give it a push'. Thus, from being originally dative masc. and neuter, *him* is now dat. and acc. masculine, having received extension in case, restriction in gender. Cf. the mod.Ger. restriciton of *ihm* to living beings.]

I. 1. As proper masculine pronoun of the third person sing., dative and accusative (objective indirect and direct) of he. Also as antecedent pron. followed by relative or prepositional phrase (cf. he 4). Used of persons and animals of male sex.

a. *Dative* or *indirect object* = to him. (= L. *ei, illi*, Ger. *ihm.*)

855 *O.E. Chron.*, Him þa Carl Francna cyning his dohtor geaf him to cuene. **971** *Blickl. Hom.* 111 Eall..þæt him.. wæs..leofost to agenne. *c* **1000** *Gosp. Nicod.* vi, Se Hælend hym and swarode and cwæþ. *a* **1175** *Cott. Hom.* 221 Uton wircan him gemace him to fultume. *c* **1205** Lay 143 Þe king heuede ane douter, þe him was swiþe deore. **1297** R. Glouc. (1724) 31 Þe kyng of France..bad hire fader graunt hym þe gode Cordeille. *a* **1300** *Cursor M.* 1360 (Gött.) Þis es þe oyle þat was hight hime [*v.r.* hyme]. *c* **1385** Chaucer *L.G.W.* Prol. 368 Him repenteth outrely of this. *c* **1400** *Destr. Troy* 1854 Iff ye send hom þat semly þat I sew fore. **1509** Barclay *Shyp of Folys.* (1874) I. 56 Wel is hym that wyth pacience can indure. **1577** B. Googe *Heresbach's Husb.* i. (1586) 8 b, [To] cary and transport such thinges as him listeth. **1671** Milton *P.R.* ii 266 Him thought, he by the brook of Cherith stood. **1768-74** Tucker *Lt. Nat.* (1852) II. 433 Ten acres of land which are worth him five pounds a year. **1852** Tennyson *Ode Wellington* vi. 13 O give him welcome, this is he Worthy of our gorgeous rites.

b. Governed by a preposition.

a **855** *O.E. Chron.* an. 838 Herebryht aldormon..ond monige mid him. *c* **1020** *Rule St. Benet* (Logeman) 29 þonne ic beo ungewemmed toforan heom. *a* **1175** *Cott. Hom.* 237 Þer cumeð þe hali engles him to. *c* **1300** *Cursor M.* 22498 (Edin.) Þoru dred of hem was don on rod. **1340** *Ayenb.* 62 He heþ zuich a lac ine him. **1362** Langl. *P. Pl.* A. i. 99 Holden with hem and with here [*B.* wiþ him & with hir]. *c* **1386** Chaucer *Man of Law's T.* 460 Fflemere of feendes out of hym and here. **1526** *Pilgr. Perf.* (W. de W. 1531) 3 And wolde not gyue to hym the due honour. **1552** Lyndesay *Monarche* 4734 The Landis Lord..cleiks tyll him ane herield hors. *c* **1645** Howell *Lett.* (1650) II. 116 From him whom I trust God defend me. **1710** Hearne *Collect.* 28 Mar. (O.H.S.) II. 368 We have..a folio Edition of him. **1856** *Sat.*

Rev. II. 274/1 We have little to add to the knowledge of him which readers . . already possess.

†**c.** *Absolute constr.* After L. ablative absolute: now expressed by nominative.

c **1000** *Ags. Gosp.* Mark v. 35 Him þa ȝyt sprecendum hi comon. *c* **1160** *Hatton Gosp.* ibid., Hym þa ȝyt spræcenden hio comen. **1377** LANGL. *P. Pl.* B. XIII. 280 Hym willynge þat alle men wende he were þat he is nouȝte. **1382** WYCLIF *John* viii. 30 Him spekinge thes thingis, many men bileueden in to him.

d. *Accusative* or *direct object.* (= L. *eum, illum,* Ger. *ihn,* OE. *hine.*)

(The 10th c. instances were probably felt as *dative.*)

[*c* **975** *Rushw. Gosp.* Matt. xvii. 5 Him ȝe ȝeheraδ [*Lindisf., Hatt.*, hine; *Ags. G.*, hyne]. *Ibid.* xviii. 32 þa ȝecæȝde him dryhten his [*L., H.*, hine; *Ags. G.*, hyne.] *c* **1132** *O.E. Chron.* (Laud MS.) an. 654 Him luuede al þeode. *Ibid.* an. 1114 þæt he sceolde him læden to Cantwarabyriȝ and blætson him to biscop. *c* **1154** *Ibid.* an. 1140 ℙ11 He helde him for fader and he him for sune. *c* **1175** *Lamb. Hom.* 59 þe lauerd þet him wrohte. *c* **1250** *Gen. & Ex.* 209 God bar him in-to paradis. **1375** BARBOUR *Bruce* IX. 465 He held euir agane the king, And hatit hyme atour all thing. *c* **1430** *Two Cookery-bks.* 18 Take a Capoun, and make hem clene, & sethe hym in Water. **1548** HALL *Chron., Edw. IV,* 222b, Shyppes, for to transport hym and hys over the sea into Fraunce. **1597** SHAKS. *2 Hen. IV,* II. iii. 32 And him, O wondrous! him, O Miracle of Men! Him did you leaue . . vn-seconded by you. **1852** MRS. STOWE *Uncle Tom's C.* v. 32 What has he done that mas'r should sell him?

†**e.** Redundant before sb. *Obs. rare.*

c **1386** CHAUCER *Knt.'s T.* 475 For Ialousie and fere of hym Arcite. —— *Merch. T.* 124 She goddes peple kept And slow hym Olofernus whil he slepte.

2. Formerly put also for other than male beings.

†**a.** *him* was in OE. the dative of the neuter *hit,* IT, as well as of HE. This use came down to the 17th c. esp. with a preposition; later use substitutes *it.*

c **1175** *Lamb. Hom.* 83 Oli haueδ huppen him lihtnesse and softnesse. **1297** R. GLOUC. (1724) 43 þe see goþ al abouten hym [Ireland] eke as ich vnderstonde. *Ibid.* 49 þer nes in al þe world swerd hym yliche. *c* **1325** *Lai le Freine* 210 A litel maiden-childe . . And a pel him about. *c* **1400** MAUNDEV. i. (Roxb.) 4 It takes in to him xl oþer ryuers. *c* **1425** *Craft Nombrynge* (E.E.T.S) 26 þou schalt write þe digitte ouer þe hede of þe neþer figure . . and sett þe articulle next hym toward þe lyft side. **1559** W. CUNNINGHAM *Cosmogr. Glasse* 41 The Fire conteyneth in him the Aëre. **1612** BRINSLEY *Lud. Lit.* viii. (1627) 93 Construe first the Nominative Case: and if there be an Adiectiue or Participle with him, then I must English them next.

b. *him* occurs also as accusative for things (in ME.) grammatically masculine, or (in later use) spoken of with the masc. pronoun. Still common in southern dial. In standard Eng. now only with things personified as masculine: cf. HE 2.

c **1420** *Chron. Vilod.* st. 486 Lord God! y betake my soule to þe; Bryng hym to þy joy. **1526** TINDALE *Matt.* xviii. 9 Yff . . thy fote geve the an occasion of evyll, cut hym of and cast hym from the. —— *1 Cor.* ix. 27, I tame my body and brynge hym into subieccion. **1545** ASCHAM *Toxoph.* (Arb.) 119 Take hede yat your bowe stande not to nere a stone wall, for that wyll make hym moyste and weke. **1558** WARDE tr. *Alexis' Secr.* (1568) 25 b, This herbe . . If you cannot get him alwayes greene, ye maye kepe him drie. **1639** in C. Kerry *Ch. St. Lawrence, Reading* (1883) 54 For mooving the pulpit and setting him lower. **1667** MILTON *P.L.* ix. 48 The Sun was sunk, and after him the Starr Of Hesperus. *Mod.* (*personif.*) Winter had wrapped his mantle about him. *Mod. dial.* (Gardener says of mowing-machine) 'He wants sharpening, sir; it's two years since he was done; I remember their putting him on the trolly just here, and taking him to the foundry'.

3. For the *nominative*: esp. after *than, as,* and in predicate after *be.*

Common in colloquial lang. from end of 16th c. Dialectally the use of *him* for *he* extends to all constructions in which French uses *lui* for *il.* The construction *than him* is sometimes a reminiscence of the Latin ablative.

c **1381** CHAUCER *Parl. Foules* 623 Hym that she chesith he shal hire han a swithe. *c* **1515** *Cocke Lorell's B.* 4 Here is gylys Iogeler of ayebery And hym sougelder of lothebery. **1605** SHAKS. *Macb.* v. viii. 34 And damn'd be him, that first cries hold, enough. **1610** —— *Temp.* v. i. 15 The King, His Brother, and yours, abide all three distracted . . but chiefly Him that you term'd Sir, the good old Lord Gonzallo. **1698** VANBRUGH *Prov. Wife* II. i, But sure it can't be him. **1759** JOHNSON *Dissert. Grk. Comedy* Wks. 1816 III. 20 No man had ever more discernment than him, in finding out the ridiculous. **1764** WESLEY *Jrnl.* 5 Feb., Why then does not Jacob speak as plain as him? **1768–74** TUCKER *Lt. Nat.* (1852) II. 137 What anybody else can do better or worse than him. **1797** BURKE *Regic. Peace* iii. Wks. VIII. 310 Is it him? **1840** BARHAM *Ingold. Leg., Jackdaw,* Heedless of grammar, they all cried, 'That's him!' **1893** *Northumbld. Gloss.* s.v., Him an' me's gannin'.

II. 4. *Reflexive* = himself, to himself. (= L. *sibi, se,* Ger. *sich.*)

a. *Dative* with trans. vb., or objective with prep. (Still in current use, when not ambiguous.)

c **855** *O.E. Chron.* an. 853 He . . hiene him to biscep suna nam. *c* **1000** ÆLFRIC *Gen.* vi. 2 Godes bearn . . namon him wif. *a* **1175** *Cott. Hom.* 227 He wolde of þise cynne him moder ȝeceosen. *c* **1205** LAY. 6356 þes Damus on his deie ane chiuese him ichæs. *c* **1250** *Gen. & Ex.* 437 He made him maniȝe fon. ? **1370** *Robt. Cicyle* 55 The aungelle before hym made hym to stande. **1605** SHAKS. *Macb.* v. iv. 4 Let euery Souldier hew him downe a Bough, And bear't before him. **1716** ADDISON *Freeholder* No. 41 (Seager) By this means he reconciled to him the minds of his subjects. *Mod.* He put the thought from him. He will take it with him in the carriage.

b. Formerly much used with intrans. verbs of motion or posture (including *be*), sometimes also with trans. verbs, app. in the sense 'for' or 'as to himself'; where, according to modern notions, it is superfluous. *Obs.* (or rare archaism.)

c **993** *Battle of Maldon* 11 Eac him wolde Eadric his ealdre ȝelæstan. *c* **1000** ÆLFRIC *Gen.* xviii. 8 Abraham stod him under þam treowe. —— *Deut.* xxiv. 5 Beo him æt ham. *c* **1175** *Lamb. Hom.* 27 þe unclene gast þe geδ him of þan sunfulle mon. *c* **1200** ORMIN 229 Zacariȝe for himm ham. *c* **1205** LAY. 532 þe king him com riden. *Ibid.* 25555 þa þe king him awoc. *a* **1225** *St. Marher.* 4 He . . ferde him soδδen into antioche. *a* **1300** *Cursor M.* 5235 (Gött.) Ioseph had him sonis tuin. *c* **1300** *Havelok* 286 Quanne the Erl godrich him herde Of þat mayden, hw wel she ferde. *c* **1340** *Cursor M.* 4055 (Fairf.) Ioseph him sagde a niȝt in squeuen. *Ibid.* 14333 (Fairf.) Ihesus him loked vn-to þe lift. *c* **1380** *Sir Ferumb.* 5045 þar as þat schryn hym was. *c* **1420** *Chron. Vilod.* st. 865 þis tempest obeyeth hym no more me to, Shipmon, þen hit dothe to þe. *c* **1630** MILTON *Passion* 21 Then lies him meekly down fast by his brethren's side.

c. *Accusative* or direct object. *arch.* and *poetic.*

c **1175** *Lamb. Hom.* 109 þe alde mei him witan iwis þone deδ. *c* **1275** LAY. 30574 Brian him [*c* **1205** hine] bi-þohte. *c* **1386** CHAUCER *Knt.'s T.* 551 He chaunged his array And cladde hym as a poure laborer. *c* **1450** LYDG. *Secrees* 1153 So shulde a kyng . . Shewe hym gracyous to hihe and lowe degre. *c* **1489** CAXTON *Sonnes of Aymon* xxii. 482 Richarde the duke of normandy . . recomendeth hym humbly to you. **1549** *Compl. Scot.* 118 Quhou he suld vse hym touart his maister. **1620** *Frier Rush* 6 Rush went forth to sport him. **1813** BYRON *Giaour* 68 He who hath bent him o'er the dead. **1820** KEATS *St. Agnes* xiii, He found him in a little moonlight room.

5. quasi-*sb.* Male person, man. Cf. HE 6.

1880 TROLLOPE *Duke's Childr.* (Tauchn.) I. 94 That other him is the person she loves. **1884** GILBERT *Orig. Plays* 129 'Mr. F. shall introduce him.' 'It ain't a him, it's a her.' **1898** *Daily News* 14 Mar. 4/7 The chances against her 'getting him', and her disinclination to wed any other 'him'.

6. ***him one, alone,*** by himself, alone: see ONE, ALONE. ***him self***: see HIMSELF, SELF.

Himalayan (hɪmə'leɪən, etymologically hɪ'mɑːləjən), *a.* [f. *Himālaya* (Skr. f. *hima* snow + *ālaya* dwelling, abode) + -AN. The second pronunciation, though etymologically correct, is now infrequent.]

1. Of or pertaining to the Himālayas, a system of mountains forming the northern boundary of India, and containing the highest summits in the world. Hence, in names of species of plants and animals native to this region.

Himalayan black bear, *Selenarctos thibetanus.* **H. pine,** or Neoza pine, *Pinus Gerardiana,* a pine of the N.W. Himalayas, each cone of which yields about 100 edible seeds or nuts; called also the Nepal nut-pine. **H. primrose,** *Primula sikkimensis.* **H. rhubarb,** *Rheum nobile,* and other species.

[**1858** *Proc. Zool. Soc.* 518 Black Bear of Europeans. . . The species is generally distributed over the lower ranges of the Western Himalayas.] **1866** *Treas. Bot.* 979/1 Himalayan Rhubarb. **1869** A. A. A. KINLOCH *Large Game Shooting* I. 49 The Himalayan Black Bear is pretty generally distributed throughout the Himalayas. **1878** R. N. CUST *Mod. Langs. E. Ind.* 119 At this point . . I leave the Western Himalayan branch and enter the Eastern. **1882** *Garden* 11 Mar. 171/1 This lovely Himalayan Primrose. **1925** G. BURRARD *Big Game Hunting* iv. 73 The Himalayan black bear is one of the most widely distributed game animals of the Himalayas. **1966** R. & D. MORRIS *Men & Pandas* viii. 177 The Himalayan, or Asiatic black bear (*Selenarctos thibetanus*).

2. *fig.* Like a vast mountain in weight and bulk; enormous, gigantic.

1878 *N. Amer. Rev.* CXXVI. 500 The North, as the wealthy section, would be called to bear this Himalayan debt.

Himalo- (hɪ'mɑːləʊ), used as combining form of the *Himalayas,* as in ***Himalo-Chinese*** adj.

1873 ELWES in *Proc. Zool. Soc.* 654 Himalayan or Himalo-Chinese Subregion. **1910** *Encycl. Brit.* III. 976/1 The Himalo-Chinese or Transgangetic province.

‖**Hi'mantopus.** *Ornith.* [L., a. Gr. ἱμαντόπους the stilt, f. ἱμάς, ἱμαντ-, thong, strap + πούς foot.] A genus of wading-birds; the stilts.

1753 CHAMBERS *Cycl. Supp., Himantopus* . . the name of a water bird, very remarkable for the length and slenderness of its legs. **1789** G. WHITE *Selborne* II. xlviii. (1853) 293 The flamingo . . bears no manner of proportion to the himantopus. **1875** DARWIN in *Life & Lett.* (1887) II. 97 The Himantopus . . is very variable in the length of its legs.

‖**himation** (hɪ'mætɪən). [Gr. ἱμάτιον.] The outer garment worn by the ancient Greeks: 'an oblong piece of cloth thrown over the left shoulder, and fastened either over or under the right' (Liddell & Scott).

1850 LEITCH tr. *C.O. Müller's Anc. Art* §301 (ed. 2) 339 Important passages in life . . reception of the manly himation, marriages, journeys. *Ibid.* §337 (ed. 2) 399 The *Himation* was a large square garment, generally drawn round from the left arm which held it fast, across the back, and then over the right arm, or else through beneath it towards the left arm. **1869** *W. Smith's Dict. Gr. & Rom. Antiq.* (ed. 2) 1173/1 It was the usual practice among the Greeks to wear an Himation, or outer garment, over the Chiton. **1879** GEO. ELIOT *Theo. Such* ii. 32 Clad in the majestic folds of the himation.

himme, himne, obs. ff. HEM *v.*², HYMN.

†**himp,** *v. Obs.* or *dial.* Also 6 hymp(e. [Found first in 16th c.; identical with Ger. dial. *humpen, hümpen, himpen,* Da. dial, *hompen* to hobble.] *intr.* To limp, to hobble.

1533 MORE *Confut. Barnes* VIII. Wks. 766/1 If . . the good wyfe of the bottell of Botolphs warfe, that . . halteth both in body and soule . . would hympe forth among them and say, by saint Halkin father Barns [etc.]. **1542** UDALL *Erasm. Apoph.* 180 Lame of one leg, and himping all his dayes. *Ibid.* 206 The deformitee and disfigure of hymping on the one legge . . did still remain. **1552** HULOET, *Hympe,* loke in *halt. a* **1825** FORBY *Voc. E. Anglia, Himp,* to limp.

Hence †**himp-halt** [cf. OE. *lemp halt* (Corpus Gl.), *laempihalt* (Epinal), 'lurdus'], one who walks with a limp. (In quot. as a nickname.)

1533 MORE *Confut. Barnes* VIII. Wks. 770/1 At that worde woulde hympe halt his hostes hoppe foorth againe, and say mary syr that it were in dede for me.

†**himple** ('hɪmp(ə)l), *v. Obs.* or *dial.* [In form a dim. or freq. of prec.: identical with MHG. *hümpelen, himpelen,* Ger. *humpeln, hümpeln,* mod.Du. *hompelen* to hobble, dial. Eng. *homple,* Sc. HUMPLE; cf. MDu. *humpelare* a limper.] = HIMP *v.*

1656 BLOUNT *Glossogr.*, To *Himple,* to halt, used in the North of England. **1658** PHILLIPS, *Himple,* an old Saxon word, signifying to halt, or go lame. **1721** in BAILEY.

himself (hɪm'sɛlf), *pron.* Forms: see SELF. [f. HIM *dat.-acc. pers. pron.* + SELF. *Self* was orig. an adj. which could be inflected in concord with any case of the pron. For the earlier constructions see SELF.]

I. Emphatic use. = Very him, very he, that very man, etc. = L. *ipse.*

1. As emphatic dative and (later) objective.

(The OE. accusative was *hine self(ne).*)

c **893** K. ÆLFRED *Oros.* v. xiii. §2 [Antonius] forlet Octauianuses swostor and him selfum onbead ȝewin & openne feondscipe. *c* **897** —— *Gregory's Past.* xvi. 100 He wæs on himselfum mid δæs halȝan gastes mæȝene swiδe healice up-abroȝden. **1535** COVERDALE *1 Macc.* viii. 7 They toke him self alyue.

2. Standing in apposition with the nominative pronoun, or with a sb. in nominative or objective.

(Originally *him* and *self* were unconnected syntactically, *self* being a nominative, in apposition to the subject, while *him* was a dative as in HIM 4b; but the juxtaposition of the two words resulted in the attraction of *self* to *him.*)

c **897** K. ÆLFRED *Gregory's Past.* xiv. 90 Đa scylde þe se him self ær nyste. *c* **1000** *Gospel Nicod.* xxxiv, Pilatus . . hym sylf awrat ealle þa þyng. *c* **1175** *Lamb. Hom.* 35 He heo dude him seolf. *c* **1200** ORMIN Ded. 195 He wollde ben himm sellf i waterr fullhtnedd. **1297** R. GLOUC. (1724) 377 He was ryche hym self. *a* **1300** *Cursor M.* 173 Iesu crist him selue [*v.rr.* him-self, him seluen] ches til him apostels tuelue. *c* **1300** *Beket* 274 And of the beste him silve he at, swithe scars and lute. *c* **1400** *Destr. Troy* 1236 The souerayn hym seluon was surly enarmyt. **1513** MORE in Grafton *Chron.* (1568) II. 758 Sanctified by saint Petter himselfe. *a* **1535** —— *Edw. V* (1641) 5 A proud appetite of the duke himselfe. **1581** PETTIE *Guazzo's Civ. Conv.* II. (1586) 74 They will make Heraclitus himselfe laugh at it. **1596** SHAKS. *Merch. V.* III. i. 82 A third cannot be matcht, vnlesse the diuell himselfe turne Iew. **1776** *Trial of Nundocomar* 36/2 Did your brother write his letters himself, or you for him? **1869** J. MARTINEAU *Ess.* I. 50 Not Wolsey himself could find more magnificent pleas.

3. a. With the nominative pronoun omitted, and *himself* taking its place. *arch.*

(= OE. *he self, he selfa.*)

c **1000** *Sec. Laws of Canute* c. 30 §3 (Schmid) Nime fife and beo he [*v.r.* him] sylfa syxta. *Ibid.* §7 Nime him fif . . and beo him sylf sixta. *c* **1200** *Trin. Coll. Hom.* 121 Alse him self seiδ. **1297** R. GLOUC. (1724) 12 Mony was þe gode body þat hym self slou þat day. **1388** WYCLIF *Hab.* i. 13 A more iust man than hymsilf [**1382** than hym]. **1535** STEWART *Cron. Scot.* (1858) I. 6 Siclike as him sell. **1619** *Crt. & Times Jas. I* (1849) II. 120 Sir Edward Villiers told him himself was the man. **1719** J. RICHARDSON *Art Critic.* 188 But Himself is seen throughout most apparently. **1864** TENNYSON *Aylmer's F.* 596 The dagger which himself Gave Edith.

b. Used alone in predicate after *be, become,* etc., and in adverbial extensions = by himself. ***to be himself***: to be in his normal condition of mind and body: see SELF.

1526 TINDALE *John* vi. 15 Therfore departed he agayne into a mountayne hym silfe a lone. **1591** SHAKS. *Two Gent.* II. iii. 24, I am the dogge: no, the dogge is himselfe, and I am the dogge: oh, the dogge is me, and I am my selfe. **1690** LOCKE *Hum. Und.* II. xxvii. (1695) 186 When we say such an one is not himself, or is besides himself . . as if . . the self same Person was no longer in that Man. **1700** CIBBER *Shaks.'s Rich. III,* v. iii, Richard's himself again. *a* **1716** SOUTH (J.), For one man to see another so much himself as to sigh his griefs, and groan his pains, so sing his joys [etc.]. **1837** CARLYLE *Fr. Rev.* I. IV. iv, He will not be Thou, but must and will be Himself. **1862** *Lond. Rev.* 50 Aug. 188 He would soon be himself again. **1866** LIDDON *Bampt. Lect.* i. §1 (1875) 5 His most startling revelation was Himself.

II. Reflexive use. = L. *sibi, se*; Ger. *sich.*

4. Dative, and objective with preposition. †***himselfward,*** toward himself (see -WARD).

c **1000** *Ags. Gosp.* Mark iii. 24 Gif his rice on him sylfum biδ to-dæled. *c* **1175** *Lamb. Hom.* 61 Efre mid him solue to wunen. *c* **1250** *Gen. & Ex.* 1338 God him δor bi him-seluen swor. *c* **1400** *Apol. Loll.* 60 God is al riȝtfulnes in himseluen. **1534** TINDALE *Luke* xv. 17 Then he came to him selfe and sayde [etc.]. **1549** COVERDALE, etc. *Erasm. Par. Rom.* 34 Let

no man idely liue to himselfwarde. **1562** J. Heywood *Prov. & Epigr.* (1867) 141 Euery man for him self, and god for vs all. **1607** Shaks. *Cor.* v. ii. 111 He that hath a will to die by himselfe, feares it not from another. **1700** S. L. tr. *Fryke's Voy. East Ind.* 10 If he designs to have it to himself again. **1795** Macneill *Will & Jean* ii. ix, Will.. Had some battles wi' himsel. **1809–10** Coleridge *Friend* (1865) 48 Charlemagne.. created for himself the means of which he availed himself. *Mod.* He gave himself a treat.

5. Accusative or direct object.

c **1175** *Lamb. Hom.* 75 Ne na mon nah him solue wernen henne. *c* **1200** *Vices & virtues* 111 Ðat he sceawede him selu. *a* **1225** *Ancr. R.* 56 Dauid.. forȝet him suluen. *a* **1300** *Cursor M.* 1608 Quen he to pin him-selfen did For his choslinges on rod-tre. *c* **1410** Love *Bonavent. Mirr.* xxxiv. 66 (Gibbs MS.) Makynge hym selfen god. **1582** N. Lichefield tr. *Castanheda's Conq. E. Ind.* vii. 17 b, Perswaded the Captaine generall, not to trouble himselfe with the want of the other Pilot. **1605** *Lond. Prodigal* i. i, The sea.. borrows of all the small currents in the world to increase himself. **1635** J. Hayward tr. *Biondi's Banish'd Virg.* 22 He could hardly.. beleeve himselfe; opening therefore his eyes better. *a* **1703** Burkitt *On N.T.* Mark xii. 34 Every man may, yea, ought to love himself. **1864** Tennyson *Aylmer's F.* 544 [He] bad him with good heart sustain himself.

III. 6. quasi-*sb.*

1622 Bacon *Hen. VII*, 89 Your King, whom he desires to make another Himselfe. **1816** Keatinge *Trav.* (1817) I. 320 Neither did he mix with the crowd of populace: indeed he had much the appearance of being a himself, at least to the aggregation about him.

IV. From the 14th c. there has been a tendency to treat *self* as a sb. (= person, personality), and substitute the possessive *his* for *him.* This is prevalent in the dialects, but in standard English has place only where an adj., etc. intervenes, as *his own, very, good, true, self.* See self. Also *hisself* as one word, representing a *colloq.* or *dial.* pronunciation of himself.

13.. *Cursor Mundi* 15626 (Gött.) His hali self all suett. *c* **1340** *Ibid.* 1726 (Fairf.) Noe.. wroȝt his-self [*Cott.* he self, *Gött.* himself] in þat labour. *c* **1340** *Ibid.* 3408 (Fairf.) þat we may wiþ his-seluen wone [*other texts* him-self, him seluen]. **1406** Hoccleve *La male regle* 435 Who.. his owne self forgetith. **1508** Fisher *7 Penit. Ps.* cii. Wks. (1876) 185 Also what domage his selfe sholde endure. **1562** Turner *Herbal* ii. 40 b, Matthiolus.. erreth.. much more hys selfe. **1601** Holland *Pliny* II. 573 A Summer parlour for pleasure, that Callistus.. built for his owne selfe. **1653** *Cloria & Narcissus* I. 111 Although he were on horseback and his selfe on foot. **1826** Disraeli *Viv. Grey* iv. i, 'Is not that Lord Lowersdale?' 'His very self.' **1832** W. Stephenson *Gateshead Local Poems* 48 He hang'd his-sel. **1838** Dickens *Nich. Nick.* xxxiv, Gorging his-self with vittles. *a* **1876** E. Leigh *Gloss. Words Dial. Cheshire* (1877) 103 'He is not hissell', *i.e.* 'He is out of his mind.' **1901** M. Franklin *My Brilliant Career* xxxii. 273 Pa is goin' to write a whole letter all by hisself. **1902** *Dialect Notes* II. 316 He has hurt *hisself* mighty bad. **1938** M. Richardson in B. A. Botkin *Treas. S. Folklore* (1949) iii. i. 443 He would chop a tree by hisself. **1945** A. Kober *Parm Me* 146 He sits and he *shuckles* hisself and is oney one thing he's saying all the time—nutting! **1965** T. Capote *In Cold Blood* (1966) iii. 166, I talked to the deputy. Then I told the warden hisself. **1969** Widdowson & Halpert in Halpert & Story *Christmas Mumming in Newfoundland* 149 A gentleman.. made hisself up with burnt cork. **1969** R. Pharr in A. Chapman *New Black Voices* (1972) 69 If he wants something for hisself, let him get out and work for it like we do. **1972** 'J. & E. Bonett' *No Time to Kill* x. 133 He's earned hisself a medal. **1973** *Black World* July 64/1 He can take care of hisself.

himward, -wards, orig. *to him-ward(s,* towards him: see -ward.

1563 *Ord. Pub. Fast* in *Liturg. Serv. Q. Eliz.* (Parker Soc.) 479 To turn his ire to himward, who had chiefly offended. **1577–87** Holinshed *Chron.* I. 113/2 God's high favour extended to himwards. **1888** Mrs. Lynn Linton *Long Night* II. ii. xii. 173 She was only dumbly conscious.. of Anthony Harford and her ever-increasing difficulties himward.

Himyarite ('hɪmjəraɪt), *sb.* Also **Ham-, Hhim-.** [f. name of *Himyar*, a traditional king of Yemen in Southern Arabia + -ite.] One of an ancient people of Southern Arabia (formerly called Homerites). Also *atttrib.* = **Himya'ritic** *a.*, of or pertaining to the Himyarites, their civilization, etc.; commonly applied to the language of this ancient people (a distinct dialect of Arabic akin to Ethiopic), and to its alphabet, and the inscriptions preserved in it. So **Him'yaric** *a.*

1842 [see Homerite]. **1843** J. Nicholson in *Kitto's Cycl. Bibl. Lit.* I. 668/2 The Himjarite alphabet. **1854** *Pop. Bibl. Educ.* I. 189/1 Although the old Hamyaritic characters had somewhat degenerated in form, yet they were still in use, in the first century of Christianity. **1864** E. Deutsch in *Reader* IV. 664/2 Osiander, the great Himyaritic scholar. **1864** Webster, *Himyaric.* **1881** *Athenæum* 29 Jan. 168/3 A paper 'On a Himyarite Tetradrachm of the Second Century b.c.'.

‖**hin** (hɪn), *sb.* Also 4 **hyn.** [ad. Heb. *hīn.*] A Hebrew measure of capacity for liquids, containing a little over a gallon.

1382 Wyclif *Exod.* xxx. 24 Oyle of the olyues, the mesure of hyn, that is, of two pownd. **1535** Coverdale *Ibid.*, An Hin of oyle olyue. —— *Lev.* xix. 36 A true Epha, a true Hin shalbe amonge you. **1660** Fuller *Mixt Contempl.* (1841) 177 Some have had a hin, others a homer, others an ephah of afflictions. **1864** R. S. Hawker *Quest Sangraal* 1 The Sangraal.. That held, like Christ's own heart, an Hin of blood! **1875** R. Conder in *Trans. Soc. Bibl. Arch.* IV. 122–3 The *log* or twelfth part of the *hin*, contains 24 cubic inches, the *hin*, 288 (or 1·0198 gallons).

†**hin, hine,** *pers. pron., 3rd sing. masc., accus. Obs.* exc. *dial.* Forms: 1 hiene, 1–2 hyne, 1–4 **hine,** 2–5 **hin,** 4–5 **hyn, hen;** 8–9 s.w. dial. **en, un, 'n.** [OE. *hine, hiene*, accusative of he; cognate w. OFris. *hine* (*hini, hin*), MDu. *hin, hen*; and parallel in inflexion to OS. and Goth. *ina*, OHG. *in, inan* (MLG. *ine, ene*, MHG. *in*, Ger. *ihn*). In English, as in Frisian and Dutch, this original accusative has been superseded by the dative *him.* Already before 1000, traces are found of the dative form used instead of the acc., and before 1150 *hine* was obsolete in the north and midlands. *Hine* was used in Kentish (beside *him*) in 1340, but appears rarely in literature after 1400, though still, in the reduced form *ĕn, ŭn, 'n* ((ə)n), the ordinary form of the accusative in s.w. dialects, as 'we zeed 'n gwayn', we saw him going. (See Barnes *Dorset Gram.* (1863) 20, Elworthy *W. Somerset Gram.* (1877) 36.)] = him, *direct objective.* Also *reflexive.*

c **855** *O.E. Chron.* (Parker MS.) an. 787 Hiene mon ofsloᵹ. **898** *Ibid.* an. 894 Hi hine ne mehton ferian. *c* **1000** *Gosp. Nicodemus* v, Gelæde hyne in to me. **1126** *O.E. Chron.* (Laud MS.), He sende him to Walingeforde.. and let hine don on harde bande. *c* **1175** *Lamb. Hom.* 19 We hine sculde luuian. *Ibid.* 23 Þa man þe beoð in þe castel and hin ȝemeð. *c* **1205** Lay. 584 Mid him he hine lædde. *Ibid.* 26371 Let hine halden France [*c* **1275** let him holde]. *a* **1225** *Ancr. R.* 86 Þe uorme.. preiseð hine biuoren himsulf, & makeð hine ..ȝet betere þen he beo. *c* **1250** *Gen. & Ex.* 3004 Fleȝes kin sal hin ouergon. *c* **1250** *O. Kent. Serm.* in *O.E. Misc.* 26 Hi wolden gon for to hyne anuri. *Ibid.* 27 Al swo hi hedden ifonden ure louerd, swo hin anurede. **1340** *Ayenb.* 16 Liȝtbere þe angel.. him wolde emni to god, þet hine zo uayr an zuo guod hedde y-mad. *c* **1450** Lonelich *Grail* xxxviii. 374, I saw hyn fyhten as I vndirstond. **1746** *Exmoor Scold.* (E.D.S.) 208 Whan tha hadst cort en by the heend Legs o'en. *Ibid.* 256 Tha wud'st ha' borst en to Shivers, nif chad net a-vung en. *a* **1754** Fielding *Fathers* iii. i, I would a brought un to town, but the dogs would not spare un. **1785** Sarah Fielding *Ophelia* II. iv, They called the dead halloo, and cried out—'To-un, boys, to-un!' **1856** *Punch* Jan. 37 Each feller I met, 'Didst thee zee un?' did cry.

b. Rarely (by confusion) for the dative.

1127 *O.E. Chron.* (Laud MS.), Se kyng of France.. iæf hine þone eorldom, and þet land folc him wið toc.

hina, obs. form of henna.

hina hina ('hina 'hina). *N.Z.* Also **hinihini.** [Maori.] = mahoe.

1867 J. D. Hooker *Handbk. N.Z. Flora* II. 765/1 Hina-hina, *Geolog. Surv. Melicytus ramiflorus.* **1868** J. Buchanan in *Trans. N.Z. Instit.* I. Essays iii. 37 Hinihini or Mahoe (*Melicytus ramiflorus*). A very variable tree in size of leaves and shape of trunk, the latter angled or round. **1921** H. Guthrie-Smith *Tutira* xxii. 206 The Kowhai and fuchsia and hina hina.. will have died out. **1946** J. C. Andersen in *Jrnl. Polynesian Soc.* June 151 *Hinahina*, alternative name for the tree mahoe.

hinaki ('hiːnakiː). *N.Z.* Pl. **hinaki.** [Maori.] A wicker eel-pot.

1845 E. J. Wakefield *Adv. N.Z.* I. viii. 252 They place eel-pots, called *hinaki*,.. at the lower extremity of funnels formed by series of upright poles driven into the bed of the river. **1905** W. B. *Where White Man Treads* 256 My father and his younger brother went to lift a 'hinaki' (eel basket) into the canoe. **1921** H. Guthrie-Smith *Tutira* x. 86 The huge *hinaki* or wicker-work pot, where eels required for immediate consumption were placed. **1952** *Landfall* VI. 288 It was a well-kept looking net.. and with fine meshes. It made me feel shy about my old hinaki. **1966** *Encycl. N.Z.* II. 441/1 Traps for eels and lampreys, termed hinaki, were made from the slim stems of the mangemange.

hinau ('hɪnaʊ). Also **hino(u), inau.** [Maori.] A New Zealand evergreen tree, *Elæocarpus dentatus*, yielding a black dye; the wood of this tree. Also *attrib.*

1832 G. Bennett in *London Med. Gaz.* X. 794/2 This tree, the Elæocarpus dicera of Forster, the Inau of the natives, is found abundant on the hills of New Zealand. **1835** W. Yate *Account N.Z.* (ed. 2) ii. 49 Hinau (*Dicera dentata*)—This tree.. grows to a height of sixty or seventy feet. **1845** E. J. Wakefield *Adv. N.Z.* II. 246 The *totara*, the *mai*, and the *hinau*, were found to work up into very handsome side-boards, tables, and book-shelves. **1859** A. S. Thomson *Story N.Z.* I. 156 The hinau berries are generally steeped for several days in a running stream... Hinau cakes are much esteemed. **1867** *Richmond-Atkinson Papers* (1960) II. 249 The board on the dead hinau tree announces that application for graves is to be made to E. Patten. **1883** J. Hector *Handbk. N.Z.* 130 (Morris), Hinau, a small tree about fifty feet high and eighteen inches thick in stem, with brown bark which yields a permanent blue-black dye, used for tanning. **1921** H. Guthrie-Smith *Tutira* xii. 99 Other large species in the mixed bush are hinau (*Elæocarpus dentatus*), tawa.. and maire. **1968** M. Johnson *N.Z. Flowering Plants* 61 *E. dentatus*, hinau, the larger of our two species, reaches about 50 feet.

Hinayana (hiːnə'jɑːnə). [Skr., f. *hīna* lesser, little + *yāna* vehicle.] The Lesser Vehicle, a name given to the system by the followers of the Mahāyāna, the Greater Vehicle; the Buddhism of Ceylon as distinguished from the northern or Mahāyāna Buddhism. Also *attrib.* Also **Hina'yanism, Hina'yanist; Hina'yanian** *a.*

Hīnayāna was the pristine form of the faith, while the Mahāyāna represents the general one, followed by the majority of followers.

1868 J. Fergusson *Tree & Serpent Worship* 65 Mahâyâna, or as M. Julien translates it, the 'Grand Véhicule', as opposed to Hînayâna or the 'Petit Véhicule'; the distinction between the two being in almost every respect identical with that which exists between Evangelical and Mediæval Christianity. **1877** T. W. Rhys Davids *Buddhism* viii. 200 The system of the *Little Vehicle* (*Hīnayāna*). **1882** *Encycl. Brit.* XIV. 229/1 These volumes [*sc.* the Kandjur] contain about a dozen works of the oldest school of Buddhism, the Hīnayāna. **1907** D. T. Suzuki *Outl. Mahayana Buddhism* 2 Buddhism was now split into two great systems, Mahâyânism and Hînayânism. *Ibid.* 8 The distinction of Mahâyânists and Hînayânists became definite. **1945** A. Huxley *Let.* 27 May (1969) 526 In later, Mahayana Buddhism much is said about the dangers of fixed, strained, rigid concentration of the attention (such as was practised by the Hinayanists). **1951** H. Zimmer *Philos. of India* 509 'The Big Ferryboat' (*mahāyāna*), the ferry in which all may ride, in contrast to 'The Little Ferryboat' (*hīnayāna*), the way of those lonely ones, 'lights unto themselves', who steer the difficult strait of individual release. **1956** A. Toynbee *Historian's Approach Relig.* 17 The Hinayanian Buddhist gospel of self-liberation through self-extinction. **1960** 'S. Harvester' *Chinese Hammer* xi. 110 The differences between Hinayana Buddhism, the original form, and the Mahayana version. **1973** *Times* 14 Apr. (Nepal Suppl.) p. ii/3 Buddhism in the Katmandu Valley subsequently forsook the ascetic path of Hīnayāna.

hinch, *v. Obs.* exc. *dial.* [Usually associated with *pinch*, or *crinch*, both implying compression, and perh. formed after them. Cf. also hunch *v.*]

1. As a riming synonym of pinch *v.*

a. *intr.*

1559 Aylmer *Harb. Faithf. Subj.* P j a, These Romaines.. being.. brought to the last cast by the long and daungerous warres of Hanibal and the Frenche, did.. bring in their mony and goodes, without hinching or pinching, to reliefe the charges of their common welth. **1600** Heywood *1st Pt. Edw. IV*, iv. iv. Wks. 1874 I. 73 What haue you saued now ..by your hinching and your pinching? not the worth of a blacke pudding. **1622** Mabbe tr. *Aleman's Guzman D'Alf.* I. 217 Stand not a hinching and a crinching with him. **1847** Halliwell, *Hinch*, to be miserly. *Linc.*

b. *trans.*

1590 Greene *Never too late* (1600) 102 A doubt whether it were Loue, or some other furie worse then Loue, that thus hincht him and pincht him.

2. *intr.* ? To spurn.

1626 W. Fenner *Hidden Manna* (1652) B v a, The more it is wilful; it hinches and winches, and snuffes against it. **1631** J. Speed *Love's Rev.* To Rdr., Whereat if any kick or hinch, Were he not gauld, he should not winch.

hinch, north. dial. f. haunch *sb.*[1], haunch *v.*[3]

hinch-boy, -man: see hench-boy, -man.

†**hinch-pinch.** *Obs.* or *dial.* [app. a modified reduplication of pinch, to express some kind of alternate action: see hinch. (App. unconnected with obs. Du. *hincke-pinck* lame, limping.)] The name of some rustic game.

1603 Harsnet *Pop. Impost.* 33 Fitting complement for Hynch pynch and Laugh not, Coale under Candlesticke: Frier Rush and Two-penny-hoe. *Ibid.* 134 The bowle of Curds and Creame.. set out for Robin Good-fellow, the Frier, and Sisie the Dairy-maide to meet at hinch-pinch and laugh not, when the Goodwife was abed. **1611** Cotgr., *Pinse morille*, the game called Hinch pinch and laugh not.

[Cf. the following: **1893** *Northumbld. Gloss.*, *Hinchy-pinchy*, a game in which the play is begun gently, and gradually increased in intensity. Boy: 'Aa'll play ye at hinchy-pinchy'. Strikes gently his companion, who returns the blow, until it becomes a fight. The term is also employed in games of leaping, where the first player gives an easy leap, and each succeeding player exceeds the leap of his predecessor. Dr. R. J. Lloyd says: 'Liverpool children have a rime, used in play, "Hinchy-binchy, barley straw, Forty pinches is the law"'.]

hinck, var. hink.

hincty ('hɪŋktɪ), *a. U.S. slang.* Also **hinkty.** [Origin unknown.] Conceited, snobbish, stuck-up.

Connection with clipped forms of 'handkerchief-head' (= an Uncle Tom Negro) has been suggested but the phonetic development is incapable of demonstration.

1924 in W. C. Handy *Treasury of Blues* (1949) 144 We'll I am hinkty and I'm low down too. **1936** *Esquire* (Chicago) May 192/3 '*She* couldn't be mixed up in no murder trial. She's too respectable.' 'A hinkty hussy!' said Sling. **1941** *Examiner* (San Francisco) 20 July PR 2 Jack, it ain't like me to be hincty so I'll be there with my boots laced tall. **1948** *Capitol News from Hollywood* Jan. 12/1 Patrons who dropped into the hincty, ultra-ultra Circus room of Santa Monica's lavish Hotel Ambassador. **1957** J. Kerouac *On Road* (1958) 86 Wetting their eyebrows with hincty fingertip. **1969** C. Himes *Blind Man with Pistol* vi. 72 All those hincty bitches fell on those whitey-babies like they was sugar candy.

hind (haɪnd), *sb.*[1] Forms: 1– hind; also 1–3 hynd, 3–7 hinde, 4–6 hynde, (5 hyynde). *β.* 6 hyne, hine. [OE. *hind* str. fem. = ON. *hind*: cf. OLG. **hinda* (MDu., Du. *hinde*), OHG. *hinta* (MHG., Ger. *hinde*), wk. fem., for which some suggest derivation from Goth. *hinþan* to catch; others would connect it with Gr. κεμάς young deer, pricket.]

1. The female of the deer, esp. of the red deer; *spec.* a female deer in and after its third year.

a **900** *Kent. Gloss.* in Wr.-Wülcker 59/15 *Dammula*, hind. *c* **1000** Ælfric *Gloss.* Ibid. 119/13 *Cerua*, hind. *c* **1090** *O.E.*

Chron. an. 1086 He lægde laʒa.. þæt swa hwa swa sloʒe heort oððe hinde þæt hine man sceolde blendian. *c* 1205 LAY. 30568 No mihten heo deor iwine Nouþer heort no hinde. *c* 1330 R. BRUNNE *Chron. Wace* (Rolls) 1365 He broughte a coppe wyþ milk & wyn þat milked was of a whit hynde. 1480 CAXTON *Chron. Eng.* cxiii. 94 He wold gone in to deuenshyre for to hunte for the hert & for the hynde. 1551 BIBLE 2 *Sam.* xxii. 34 God.. maketh my fete as swyfte as an hyndes. 1596 DALRYMPLE tr. *Leslie's Hist. Scot.* I. 39 Hart and hine, dae and Rae. 1687 DRYDEN *Hind & P.* I. 1 A milk-white Hind, immortal and unchang'd, Fed on the lawns. 1740 SOMERVILLE *Hobbinol* II. 122 Swift as the Hind, That, by the Huntsman's Voice alarm'd, had fled. 1871 R. ELLIS *Catullus* lxiii. 72 Be with hind that haunts the covert, or in hursts that house the boar.

2. (In full *hind-fish*.) One of various fishes of the family *Serranidæ* and genus *Epinephalus.*

1734 MORTIMER in *Phil. Trans.* XXXVIII. 317 The Hind .. is esteemed a good Fish to eat. 1885 LADY BRASSEY *The Trades* 408 The delicious little hind-fish (*Epinephalus guttatus*), spotted like a Japanese deer or a dappled fawn.

3. Comb., as *hind-hunting, hind-like, hind-spotted* adjs.; † **hind-fawn** = HIND-CALF; **hind's foot** (tr. F. *pied de biche*), a kind of crossbow; † **hind's tongue** = HART'S-TONGUE; † **hind-wolf**, ? a lynx.

1538 TURNER *Libellus* B ij, Hemionitis.. uidi et herbam.. quam uulgus appellabat Hyndes tonge. 1601 HOLLAND *Pliny* VIII. xix, The Hind-wolfe, which some call Chaüs, and the Gaules were wont to name Rhaphius (resembling in some sort a wolfe with leopard's spots), were showed first in the solemnitie of the games and plaies exhibited by Cn. Pompeius the Great. 1622 WITHER *Prayer Habak.* in Farr *S.P. Jas. I* (1848) 212 Who my feet so guides, that I, Hinde-like, pace my places high. 1647 W. BROWNE tr. *Gomberville's Polexander* II. iv. 206 A Hynde spotted Fawnes skin. 1648-60 HEXHAM *Dutch Dict.*, *Een Ree-kalf*, a Hinde-foane. 1874 BOUTELL *Arms & Armour* viii. 141 Of these cross-bows, or arblasts, there were three varieties, severally named —the hind's foot, the lever, and the rolling purchase.

hind (haind), *sb.*[2] Forms: α. *gen. pl.* 1 hína, (hiʒna), 3 hine; *nom. pl.* 1-4 hine, 3-4 hyne; 3 hinen, 4 hynen; *sing.* 3-7 (8-9 *dial.*) hine, hyne. β. 5 heynde, 6 hynd, (hijnde), 6-7 hynde, (7 hiend) 6- hind. [Early ME. *hine* sing., from earlier OE. (north midl.) and ME. *hine* pl.; app. developed from *hína, híʒna* genitive pl. of *híʒan, híwan,* in ONorthumb. *híʒu, híʒo,* 'members of a family or household, domestics' (see HEWE): cf. *híʒna fæder* (Lindisf. Gl.), *hína fæder, hine fæder, fæder híʒna, -híne* (Rushw. Gl.) = L. 'paterfamilias'. For the later change of *hine* to *hind,* cf. ASTOUND, SOUND.]

† 1. As *pl.* Household servants, domestics, servants. *Obs.*

c 975 *Rushw. Gosp.* Matt. x. 25 Nu hie fæder heora [*Lindisf. G.* fæder hiorades; *Ags. G.* hiredes fæder] belzebub nemdun hu micle mæ hiwæ *vel* hine [*Lindisf. G.* husa; *Ags. G.* ʒehusan] his. *c* 1200 Trin. Coll. Hom. 51 Hise wiðerfulle hine þo þen deules on helle. *c* 1300 *Havelok* 620 Louerd, we aren boþe þine, þine cherles, þine hine. *c* 1300 *Cursor M.* 29462 (Cott. Galba) If þou haue hine .. pai may þe serue to terme day. 13.. *E.E. Allit. P.* A. 1210 He gef vus to be his homly hyne. *c* 1380 Sir Ferumb. 5730 þat he.. to helle tok þo þe way And delyuerede þar is hyne.

2. As *sing.* A servant; *esp.,* in later use, a farm servant, an agricultural labourer.

† a. hine, *pl.* hinen, hines.

c 1205 LAY. 368 We habbeð seoue þusund.. wið outen wifmen.. children & hinen [*c* 1275 hine]. *c* 1230 Hali Meid. 7 Deð hire in to drecchunge to dihten hus & hinen. *a* 1240 *Ureisun* in Cott. Hom. 197 Ich am.. ðin owune hine. *c* 1250 Gen. & Ex. 3776 Wið wifes, and childre, and hines kin. *c* 1340 *Cursor M.* 23320 (Trin.) þe riʒtwis men shul se þo pynes Vpon oure lordes liþer hynes. *c* 1380 WYCLIF *Serm.* Sel. Wks. I. 140 He is an hyred hyne. *c* 1400 in *Eng. Gilds* (1870) 357 þat eueryich of hem habbe fowre hynen stalworthe. *c* 1460 *Towneley Myst.* xx. 386 Lord, shuld thou weshe feytt myne? Thou art my Lord, and I thy hyne. 1600 HOLLAND *Livy* XXVI. xxxv. 610 Their seruants and hines, such as should husband and till their grounds [*servos agri cultores*]. *c* 1650 WALLER *Answ. Suckling's Verses* 33, I need not plough, since what the stooping hine Gets of my pregnant land must all be mine.

β. hind, *pl.* hinds.

1520 *Test. Ebor.* (Surtees) V. 110 To every servaunte hynde and made viijᵈ. *c* 1550 CHEKE *Mark* i. 20 Zebedai yeer fayer in yᵉ boot with his hijndes, ỹ hired servants. 1594 PLAT *Jewell-ho.* I. 15 The labouring Hinde, when hee carryeth his dungue to the feelde. *a* 1639 T. CAREW *To Saxham* 42 Both from the Master, and the Hinde. 1703 ROWE *Ulyss.* II. i, The labours of the toiling hind. 1784 COWPER *Task* III. 747 Laborious hinds That had survived the father, served the son. 1849 MACAULAY *Hist. Eng.* iii. I. 375 It was necessary that a body of sturdy hinds should be on each side of his coach, in order to prop it.

b. *spec.* In Scotland and some parts of northern England: A married and skilled farm-workman, for whom a cottage is provided on the farm, and sometimes a cow; he has the charge of a pair of horses, and is responsible part in the working of the farm. An average-size farm has two hinds' houses besides the farm-house.

He bears to the farmer the same relation that a skilled journeyman holds to a master tradesman, and ranks above the farm-servants and labourers. In former times he furnished a fellow farm-worker from his own family, or by himself hiring one, to perform stated work: see BONDAGER. 1596 in H. Scott *Fasti* I. (1871) 277 [He had] two men and one woman servant and a hynd. 1744 HARRIS *Three Treat.* III. i. (1765) 151 A comfortable Cottage and Raiment

suitable to an industrious Hind. 1805 FORSYTH *Beauties Scotl.* I. 506 There are three different classes of servants employed in the husbandry of this county [Haddingtonshire], viz. the *hynd,* the *cottager,* and the *unmarried ploughman..* Of these the *hynd* holds the first rank. 1853 G. JOHNSTON *Nat. Hist. E. Bord.* I. 45 The wives of the hinds or married ploughmen. 1893 *Northumbld. Gloss.* s.v., A stipulation is often made.. that the hind must furnish a female field-worker at a stipulated price per day, with extra wage in harvest. This extra hand is called a 'bondager'.

c. A bailiff or steward on a farm (in some parts of England).

1495 *Act 11 Hen. VII,* c. 22 No chief Hyne or a Carter or chief Shepeherd above xxs. by the yere. 1585 *Vestry Bks.* (Surtees) 19 Given the same day to the hinde of Shadforthe for kepinge of twoe gimmers which we bought. 1771 SMOLLETT *Humph. Cl.* (1815) 41, I am persuaded, that my hind, Roger Williams, or any man of equal strength, would be able to push his foot through the strongest part of their walls. 1775 F. GREGOR tr. *Fortescue's De Laud. Leg.* xxix. 95 They don't want the attendance of the Hind. [*Note*] In some Parts of England he is called Bailiff. 1807 VANCOUVER *Agric. Devon* (1813) 85 Converted into the residence of the hind or bailiff of the estate. 1813 *Trewman's Exeter Flying-Post* 21 Oct. 4 Wants a Situation as Hind or Bailiff, a Young Man. 1869 *Lonsdale Gloss., Hind* (1) a farm bailiff.. (2) one entrusted with the charge of cattle. 1878 *Cumbld. Gloss., Hine,*.. a manager of an off-lying farm.

3. transf. A rustic, a boor.

c 1570 *Pride & Lowl.* (1841) 17 For of the hyndes or of the paysauntre I fear I should not have indifferents. 1599 B. JONSON *Ev. Man out of Hum.* I. ii, Why should such a prick-ear'd Hine as this, Be rich? 1645 MILTON *Colast.* Wks. (1851) 364 A Country Hinde somtimes ambitious to shew his betters that have no wit so simple as you take him. *c* 1750 SHENSTONE *Elegies* vii. 29, I bade low hinds the tow'ring ardour share. 1821 JOANNA BAILLIE *Metr. Leg., Malcolm's Heir* xvi, Like the son of a base-born hind.

† 4. A lad, boy, stripling; hence, more generally, Person, fellow, 'chap'. *Obs.*

1297 R. GLOUC. (1724) 485 Ther was mani a wilde hine, that prest was ther to, & wende in to the Gywerie, & woundede & to drowe. 13.. *Sir Beues* (A.) 497 3if 3e seþ schipes of painim londe, Selleþ to hem þis ilche hyne. 1375 BARBOUR *Bruce* XI. 217 Valtir, steward of scotland, syne, That than wes bot ane berdlass hyne. *c* 1386 CHAUCER *Pard. T.* 360 Bothe man and womman child and hyne and page. *c* 1450 *St. Cuthbert* (Surtees) 1420 He excused him, þat nobil heyn [= hyne] And saide his duellyng was ferr þeyn [= thyne]. 1513 DOUGLAS *Æneis* v. xiii. 1 All the peple, euery hyne. ? *a* 1550 *Frere & Boy* 12 in Ritson *Anc. Pop. Poetry* 35 A sone.. That was a good sturdy ladde, And a happy hyne.

5. Comb., as † **hine-folc; hind-boy, -man**, etc.

c 1250 Gen. & Ex. 3655 Here hine-folc ðe was hem mide. 1572 *Satir. Poems Reform.* xxxiii. 294 My Communis, with my hynd 3emen. 1581 *Ibid.* xliii. 190 The hirdis and hinde men in their labeis lay. 1603 FLORIO *Montaigne* (1634) 189 A certain swaine or hyne-boy of hers. 1615 MARKHAM *Eng. Housew.* (1660) 187 Brown bread.. for your hinde-servants.

hind (haind), *a.* (*sb.*[3]) Also *north.* 4- hint, 7 hin. [The OTeut. affinities of this word, and the related *hinder, hindmost, hindermore, hindermost, hindward,* are certain, but the particular history of the ME. words, and their mutual relations, are somewhat obscure. The older words were: (1) Gothic *hindana* prep. 'on that side of, beyond, behind' = OHG. *hintana,* Ger. *hinten,* adv. 'behind' = OE. *hindan* adv. 'from behind, at the back, in the rear'; (2) Goth. *hindar* prep. 'on that side of, beyond, behind' = OHG. *hintar,* Ger. *hinter* prep., in same senses = OE. *hinder* adv. 'on the further side, behind, back, down'; this is held to be the acc. neuter of a comparative adj. in -*dar* = Skr. -*taram,* Gr. -τερον, the root being *hin-,* prob. identical with that of HEN, HENNE, HENCE; OHG. had the adj. as a positive, *hintaro* (Ger. *hintere*) 'hind, hinder', compared *hintarôro, hintarôst,* Ger. *hinterst* 'hindmost'; ON. had *hindri* comp. (rare), *hinztr* superl.; this adj. was not in OE.; (3) Goth. *hindumists* superl. 'hindmost, uttermost', app. f. *hinduma* = OE. *hindema* (rare) 'hindmost'. OE. had also (4) *hindanweard* adv. 'towards the farther end', and *hindeweard* adj. 'turned backward'; also (5) the important adv. and prep. *behindan,* ME. *bi-hinden, bi-hinde,* BEHIND, the most permanent member of the OE. group, and (with the possible exception of 4) the only one whose survival into ME. is proved. In ME. there arose numerous new forms, viz. before 1300 *hinder* adj., before 1350 *hind* adj. and adv., *c* 1375-1400 *hindermore, hindermost, hindmost.* Since *hind-* was not an etymological element, it must have originated from the shortening of some form with a suffix, perh. from ME. *be-hind,* orig. *behind-an.* In that case, *hind-er* (if *hind* goes back before 1300) may have arisen as its normally-formed comparative; if, however, *hinder* was historically descended from OE. *hinder* adv. (of which there is no evidence and no strong probability), and taken as a comparative, *hind* might be inferred from it as its positive degree. *Hindermore, hindermost* were evidently formed on *hinder,* and *hindmost* on *hind*; the current

conjecture that the last was a double superlative formed on the long obsolete OE. *hindema* is historically untenable. In all these words the original short *i* is preserved in Sc. and north. Eng.: cf. Sc. *hint, ahint, hin'mest.*]

A. adj. a. Situated behind, in the rear, or at the back; posterior. Usually opposed to *fore,* in things existing in pairs front and back, as the limbs of quadrupeds, the wheels of a wagon, etc.

Often hyphened to its *sb.,* esp. when forming a specific name of a part, as in *hind-spring* of a carriage. See C. a.

13.. *Sir Beues* (A.) 3562 Wiþ his hint [*v. rr.* hynder, hinder] fot he [the horse] him smot. 1601 HOLLAND *Pliny* I. 350 In like sort, they that haue many feet: vnlesse it be the hin feet of all. 1601 *Househ. Ord.* (1790) 287 The hind knuckles.. of all the muttons and veales. 1670 NARBOROUGH *Jrnl.* in *Acc. Sev. Late Voy.* I. (1711) 31 The Male is smooth all over his hind parts. 1767 Byron's *Voy. r. World* (1776) 27 A negro butcher.. cuts the hamstrings of his hind legs. 1770 G. WHITE *Selborne* xxviii. 79 The fore-hoofs were upright and shapely, the hind flat and splayed. 1779 J. MOORE *View Soc. Fr.* (1789) I. xxxiv. 300 The lower and hind part of the body. 1822 IMISON *Sc. & Art* I. 103 [It] also presses the fore-wheels deeper into the ground than the hind wheels. 1849 MRS. CARLYLE *Lett.* II. 93 The infatuated little beast dances round him on its hind legs. 1881 FITZWYGRAM *Horses* (ed. 2) §879 If the fore legs be weak, they may suffer from excessive propulsion communicated to them by powerful hind quarters. 1891 C. T. C. JAMES *Rom. Rigmarole* 27 In the hind pocket of his tunic.

b. Hence, applied to the back part of (anything): = 'back of the——'. Cf. HIND-HEAD.

1870 ROLLESTON *Anim. Life* 114 He divides [the body] into a fore-body... a hind-body. 1894 R. B. SHARPE *Handbk. Birds Gt. Brit.* (1896) 10 The greyish shade which pervades the hind neck.

c. *to get on one's hind legs*: see LEG *sb.* 2 c. *to talk the hind leg(s) off a donkey,* etc.: see TALK *v.*

B. as *sb.* Short for *hind quarter, hind side* (see C. a), etc.

1892 *Daily News* 30 May 9/4 Refrigerated beef-quarters, of which there were 850 hinds.

C. Combinations. a. Of the adj.: see A.

1601 HOLLAND *Pliny* I. 217 One of their hin-feet. *a* 1652 BROME *Love-sick Court* v. ii. Wks. 1873 II. 158 Like burs or bryars Stuck in the hindlocks of our fleecy sheep. *a* 1687 COTTON *Poet. Wks.* (1765) 85 By Hindlock seizing fast Occasion. 1725 BRADLEY *Fam. Dict.* s.v. *Saddle,* The Saddle .. will be faulty if the Hind-Bow be not exactly the Shape and Circumference of the Body. 1797 *Sporting Mag.* X. 296 The hind-train [of a horse consists] of the rump, the tail, the haunches and the hind-legs. 1822 LAMB *Elia* Ser. I. *Dist. Corresp.,* They would show as fair a pair of hind-shifters as the expertest loco-motor in the colony. 1840 MARRYAT *Olla Podr.* (Rtldg.) 293 The hind-spring of your carriage. 1855 OWEN *Skel. & Teeth* 23 The 'ventral' [fins], answering to the hind-limbs. 1867 SMYTH *Sailor's Word-bk., Hind-castle,* a word formerly used for the poop, as being opposed to *fore-castle.* 1878 BELL *Gegenbaur's Comp. Anat.* p. xiv, The hind-gut of the Vertebrate is endodermal in origin. 1884 ROE *Nat. Ser. Story* ix, A hind-quarter of lamb. 1888 ROLLESTON & JACKSON *Anim. Life* 344 The hind-brain is constricted into two lobes—the cerebellum in front, and the medulla oblongata behind. 1894 G. ARMATAGE *Horse* ii. 14 The Spanish horse.. has the good head and neck of that breed [the Barb], but coupled with a weak and drooping hind-quarter. 1932 E. STEP *Bees, Wasps, Ants Brit. Isles* p. xxiv, In flight, the fore- and hind-wings of a side usually act as one.

b. Of the *sb.*: **hind-afore, hind-first, hind-side-foremost.**

1864 MRS. H. WOOD *Shadow Ashlyd.* (1878) 399 Her woollen shawl.. had turned hind-afore. 1881 *Oxfordsh. Gloss.* Suppl. s.v., Turn 'indfust, I tell tha.

c. quasi-*adv.* in comb.

1668 ETHEREGE *She would if she could* III. iii, Never hat took the fore-cock and the hindcock at one motion so naturally. 1871 *Figure Training* 102 No plan will ever.. give such elegance to the figure as the hind-lacing. 1872 J. G. MURPHY *Comm. Lev.* xiii. 40 Hind-bald.. in contradistinction to the baldness mentioned in the next verse [fore-bald].

† hind, *v. Obs.* In 5 hynde. [app. shortened from HINDER *v.*] *trans.* To hinder.

1426 AUDELAY *Poems* 32 Both the father and the moder hyndyd thay schal be. *c* 1460 G. ASHBY *Poems* (E.E.T.S.) 57/329 þat he hynde you nat by his greuance.

† hind, *adv. Obs. rare.* [app. short for *behind*: but cf. OE. *hindan.*] = BEHIND.

c 1340 *Cursor M.* 1846 (Fairf.) Grete perel was be-fore and hinde [*Cott. and other MSS.* bihind].

b. *hind and forth, hynt an(t)forth,* hind end foremost, backside foremost.

13.. *K. Alis.* (Bodley MS.) 4710 Hynt anforþ [*Weber* Hyndeforth] hij seten, saunz faile.. And hadden in her honde þe tail. *Ibid.* 5200 Hynd antforþ [*Weber* and forth] he tourneþ his pas When he gooþ on any cas.

'hindberry. *Obs. exc. north. dial.* Forms: see HIND *sb.*[1] and BERRY *sb.*[1] Also 8-9 hinebery. [OE. *hindberie,* corresp. to OHG. *hintperi* (MHG. *hintbere,* Ger. *himbeere*), Du. *hinnebesie* (Kilian), *hennebezie,* Da. *hindbær,* Sw. *hindbär*: see HIND *sb.*[1] and BERRY *sb.*[1] So called as growing in woods, and assumed to be eaten by hinds.] The raspberry.

a 700 *Epinal Gloss.* 69 *Acinum,* hind berie [*Erfurt* hinberʒen]. *c* 725 *Corpus Gloss.* 59 *Acinum,* hindberiae. *c* 1000 *Sax. Leechd.* II. 266 Genim hindheolopan leaf and hind berʒean. 1548 TURNER *Names of Herbes* F vij b,

Raspeses or hyndberies, in duch hyndberen. **1703** THORESBY *Let. to Ray* Gloss. (E.D.S.), *Hineberrys*, raspberrys. **1813** HOGG *Queen's Wake*, *Kilmeny* i, The scarlet hypp and the hindberrye. **1869** *Lonsdale Gloss.*, *Hindberry*, the wild raspberry. **1878** *Cumbld. Gloss.*, Raspberries or hine-berries.

hind-calf. [OE. *hindcealf* = OHG. *hintcalb*, MHG. *hintkalp*, MDu. *hindencalf*, *hindecalf* (Kilian): see HIND *sb.*[1] and CALF.] The young of a hind; a fawn.

a **900** *Kent. Gloss.* in Wr.-Wülcker 58/38 *Cerua carissima et gratissimus hinnulus*, eala ðu liofeste hind and ȝecwemest hindcealf. *c* **1000** ÆLFRIC *Gloss.* ibid. 119/17 *Hinnulus*, hindcealf. **1398** TREVISA *Barth. De P.R.* XVIII. xxiii. (1495) 781 Capriolus is lyke to an Enulus an hynde calfe. **1551** TURNER *Herbal* I. B ij a. **1598** MANWOOD *Lawes Forest* iv. §5 (1615) 42/1 The first yere, you shal cal him [the Hart] a Hind calfe or a calfe. **1601** HOLLAND *Pliny* II. 321 The rennet of a Fawne or Hind-calfe. **1774** GOLDSM. *Nat. Hist.* (1862) I. II. v. 324. **1891** C. WISE *Rockingham Cast.* 152.

hind-castle: see CASTLE 7, HIND *a.* C. a.

†**'hind-deck.** *Obs.* Also hindeck(e. [See HIND *a.*] The deck at the stern of early ships (see DECK *sb.*[1] 2); poop-deck, poop. (Cf. FORE-DECK.)

1600 HOLLAND *Livy* 614 (R.) To defend and keepe the poupe and hind-decke. *c* **1620** Z. BOYD *Zion's Flowers* (1855) 10 At foredeck some, at hindeck some must stand. **1637** GILLESPIE *Eng. Pop. Cerem.* Ep. B iij, The foredecke and hindecke of all our Opposities probations. **1697** POTTER *Antiq. Greece* III. xvi. (1715) 134 The Misen-sail, which.. hung in the Hind-deck.

hinde, var. HEND *a.*

Hindee: see HINDI.

Hindemithian (hɪndəˈmɪtɪən), *a.* and *sb.* [f. the name of Paul *Hindemith* (1895–1963), German musician + -IAN.] **A.** *adj.* Of, pertaining to, or characteristic of Hindemith, or his style of composition. **B.** *sb.* One who favours or imitates the style of Hindemith.

1941 A. COPLAND *Our New Mus.* 159 This last contains remarkable Hindemithian premonitions. **1954** *Encounter* June 60/1 How refreshing.. to meet a Hindemithian who does not think twelve-tone music a disease. **1958** *Listener* 18 Sept. 441/1 Reizenstein.. continues in a gravely Hindemithian style. **1962** *Ibid.* 21 June 1091/2 A gayer, more elastic Hindemithian counterpoint.

†**hinder**, *sb.* Chiefly *Sc. Obs.* [f. HINDER *v.*] Hindrance, obstruction, impediment, detriment.

c **1200** *Trin. Coll. Hom.* 213 þere teldeð þe werse þe grune of hindre þat is of bipeching. **1481** CAXTON *Reynard* (Arb.) 63 The moste hyndre that ye shal haue. **1568** MARY Q. SCOTS *Let.* Jan. in H. Campbell *Love-lett.* App. 31 Doing all the hinder and evill that ȝe may to the said rebellis. **1637–50** ROW *Hist. Kirk* (Wodrow Soc.) 167 A great hinder of the work of God.

hinder (ˈhaɪndə(r)), *a.*[1] and *sb.* Forms: 3– hinder, (3–4 hin-, hyndore, 4–5 hender, 4–6 hynder, -ir, 5 -ur, -yr). [See HIND *a.* (In Sc. and north. Eng. with short *i.*)]

A. *adj.*

1. Situated behind, at the back, or in the rear; posterior. (Notwithstanding its comparative form, it does not differ in sense from *hind*, but is more frequently used. Cf. *yon, yonder.*) ***hinder gate***, postern gate.

Formerly, like *hind*, often hyphened to its sb.: cf. 4.

c **1290** *St. Brandan* 642 in *S. Eng. Leg.* I. 237 So þat on is hindore [*Percy Soc.* 638 hynder] fet An Otur þare cam gon. Bi-twene is forþere fet he brouȝte a fuyr-Ire ant a ston. *c* **1380** *Sir Ferumb.* 3707 Now ne dar he noþyng drede Of þat hyndere falurede, þat comeþ after gon. *c* **1400** *Lanfranc's Cirurg.* 111 þat þe hyndere [*B.* hyndore] partie be pleyn. *c* **1400** *Rom. Rose* 5850 False-Semblant and Abstinaunce.. Shulle at the hynder gate assayle. **1535** COVERDALE *Josh.* viii. 12 He set them in the hynder watch betwene Bethel and Hai. **1590** SPENSER *F.Q.* III. vi. 32 Till they agayn returne backe by the hinder gate. **1616** SURFL. & MARKH. *Country Farme* 691 The Bore goeth wider with his hinder legs than the Sow, and commonly setteth his hinder steps vpon the edges of his foresteps on the out-side. **1712** ADDISON *Spect.* No. 265 ¶5 As I was standing in the hinder Part of the Box. **1875** H. C. WOOD *Therap.* (1879) 325 The fore feet lose their reflex activity before the hinder.

2. Of time. **a.** Last past, 'last'; as in ***this hinder day*** yesterday, ***this hinder night*** last night, yesternight. **b.** Last, as in HINDER END. *Sc.*

1375 BARBOUR *Bruce* x. 551 Quhen I wes ȝoung this hendir day. **1500–20** DUNBAR *Poems* lxxxi. 1 This hinder nycht halff-sleiping as I lay. *a* **1549** *Murning Maidin* 2 in *Laneham's Let.* (1871) Introd. 150 This hinder day I went alone. **1725** RAMSAY *Gent. Sheph.* I. i, I dream'd a dreary dream this hinder night. *a* **1774** FERGUSSON *Poems* (1789) II. 67 (Jam.) Quhilk happen'd on the hinder night.

†**3.** Latter (as opp. to *former*). *Obs.*

1551 T. WILSON *Logike* (1580) 20 b, When the former part (whereof any thing is rehearsed) and the hinder part (whiche is rehearsed of the former) are chaunged. **1669** BUNYAN *Holy Citie* 257 By the former Sea, the People of the Jews.. and by hinder Sea, the People of the Gentiles.

†**4.** *Comb.*: see I. **hinder-fallings**, excrements.

1530 PALSGR. 231/2 Hynderparte of the necke.. Hynderparte of the heed. *Ibid.*, Hynderwarde, *garde de derriere*. **1561** HOLLYBUSH *Hom. Apoth.* 38 b, Take the beanes or hinderfallinges of Goates. **1611** COTGR., *Les gardes d'un sanglier*, the deaw-clawes or hinder-clawes of a wild Bore. **1697** DAMPIER *Voy.* I. 89 [Seals] throw their bodies forward, drawing their hinder-parts after them. **1699** *Ibid.* II. I. 74 The hinderpart or Stern.

B. *sb.* (usu. *pl.*). Hindquarters, buttocks; hind legs.

1857 J. SCHOLES *Tim Gamwattle* 20 (E.D.D.), Thir is nah a barro e Smobruff uts big anouff fur iz hoindurs. **1880** J. F. S. GORDON *Bk. Chron. Keith* 55 Boasting of kissing, at their meetings, the Devil's 'hinder'. **1891** M. M. DOWIE *Girl in Karpathians* xiii. 173 The painter spread his coat upon the hinders of the second horse. **1892** J. LUMSDEN *Sheep-head & Trotters* 268 A pull that brought the pony in a moment back upon its hinders. **1948** F. BROWN *Dead Ringer* (1949) xi. 131 He stood up on his short little hinders and got himself a lawyer.

†**hinder**, *a.*[2] *Obs.* [app. deduced from OE. *hinder-* adv. (see HIND *a.*) in comb., as in *hinder-ȝéap* not straightforward, crafty, guileful, *hinder-hóc* snare, artifice, *hinder-scipe* knavery: cf. also MHG. *hinderlist*, Ger. *hinterlist* trickery behind any one's back to his injury. In *hinder-word*, perh. in comb.] Deceitful, crafty, insidious.

c **1200** *Trin. Coll. Hom.* 59 Mid his hinder worde bicherde him. *c* **1205** LAY. 10489 Carrais hine biðohte of ane hindere [*c* **1275** luþer] cræfte. *c* **1290** *St. Michael* 688 in *S. Eng. Leg.* I. 319 Hynderful [*altered* hinder] and of bost I-novȝ.

hinder (ˈhɪndə(r)), *v.* Forms: 1 hindrian, 3–6 hindre, 4–6 hyndre, hendre, hynder, 5 hindire, hunder, 5–6 hindur, hyndur, 5– hinder. [OE. *hindrian* = OLG. **hindarôn* (MDu., MLG. *hinderen*), OHG. *hintarôn* (Ger. *hindern*), ON. *hindra*:—OTeut. **hindarôjan*, f. **hindar* adv.: see HIND *a. lit.* To put or keep back: cf. the parallel FURTHER *v.* to put forward, also BACKEN *v.*]

†**1.** *trans.* To do harm to; to injure, impair, damage. *Obs.*

c **1000** *Inst. Polity* §2 in Thorpe *Laws* II. 306 (Bosw.) A he sceal hæðendom hindrian. *a* **1100** *O.E. Chron.* (Laud MS.) an. 1003 Ðonne se heretoȝa wacað þonne bið eall se here swiðe ȝehindred. *c* **1200** *Trin. Coll. Hom.* 193 þe man hindreð his aȝene soule. **1483** *Cath. Angl.* 186/1 To Hynder, *derogare, incommodare*. **1535** COVERDALE *Luke* xiii. 7 Cut it downe, why hyndreth it the grounde? **1561** HOLLYBUSH *Hom. Apoth.* 10 a, If any chylde weare Peony sede about hys body, no euell sprete can hinder him. **1639** in T. Lechford *Note-Bk.* (1885) 80 The Plaintiffe.. is otherwise hindred and damnifyed to the summe of twenty pounds.

†**b.** To speak to the injury of; to vilify, disparage, slander, belittle. *Obs.*

c **1375** *XI Pains of Hell* 102 in *O.E. Misc.* 226 Bacbyters of men, þat in word and dede.. Hyndren heor euen cristen þat þei may. *c* **1430** LYDG. *Compl. Bl. Knt.* xxx, Hindred.. to his lady grace With false tonges. **1555** W. WATREMAN *Fardle Facions* 333 To hindre and empaire the name, and memorialle of the deade. **1573–80** BARET *Alv.* H 462 To hinder ones good name, and speake ill of him.

2. To keep back, delay, or stop in action; to put obstacles in the way of; to impede, deter, obstruct, prevent.

c **1400** *Destr. Troy* 5612 [That] may hast vs to harme, & hindur our spede. **1413** *Pilgr. Sowle* (Caxton 1483) III. iv. 53 That was very wrong hyndering the trewe quarell and fortherynge the false. *c* **1450** *Merlin* 23 The prophetes hadden hyndred here purpos. **1526** *Pilgr. Perf.* (W. de W. 1531) 6 Not able.. to helpe hym any thynge in this his iourney.. but rather to hynder and let hym. **1614** BP. HALL *Recoll. Treat.*, *Holy Obs.* I. §31. 200 These are not qualities to hinder our love, but our familiaritie. **1715** DE FOE *Fam. Instruct.* I. i. (1841) I. 32 Thou shalt go to Church every day, and not be hindered. *a* **1804** W. GILPIN *Serm.* III. vii. (R.), The difficulty of the task should not hinder the attempt. **1874** GREEN *Short Hist.* i. §2. 15 Strife between these two kingdoms.. long hindered the full conquest of Northern Britain.

b. Const. ***to hinder*** a person ***from*** or ***in*** doing something; also (*obs.* or *rare*) **c.** *of, for, to do* a thing, *that, that not, but that* he should do a thing.

b. *c* **1440** *Gesta Rom.* xxiii. 75 (Harl. MS.) A clowde, so derk.. þat hit hundrid, & hit assundrid, & departid him fro all þe people. **1576** FLEMING *Panopl. Epist.* 279 Demaunding of me, what should hinder me.. from the use of such felicitie. **1666–7** PEPYS *Diary* 12 Feb., These pleasures do hinder me in my business. **1694** *Acc. Sev. Late Voy.* II. (1711) 131 This doth hinder the Ship very much in its sailing. **1769** *Junius Lett.* i. 6 Petitions have been hindered from reaching the throne. **1873** HOLLAND *A. Bonnic.* xii. 205 What's to hinder other people from liking one another?

c. *c* **1380** WYCLIF *Sel. Wks.* III. 431 It semeþ þat privat religiose ben hyndrid bi her ordris to kepe Cristis lawe. **1535** COVERDALE *Acts* viii. 36 What hyndereth me to be baptysed? **1568** GRAFTON *Chron.* II. 329 They hindered them nothing at all of their purpose. **1577–87** HOLINSHED *Scot. Chron.* (1805) II. 296 They would hinder.. that no great armie should be made out of France against them. **1600** HOLLAND *Livy* XXV. xxvii. 569 Marcellus.. determined to hinder Bomilcar for arriving at Saracose. **1611** in Picton *L'pool Munic. Rec.* (1883) I. 170 Mr. Rose did persyst.. in hindering the towne of a certen walle. **1690** LOCKE *Hum. Und.* III. iv. §15 That hinders not but that they are generally less doubtful. **1732** FIELDING *Miser* II. i. Wks. 1882 IX. 307 The death of my mother, whose jointure no one can hinder me of. **1741** MONRO *Anat. Nerves* (ed. 3) 31 Their Liquor will be hindred to flow. **1843** CARLYLE *Past & Pr.* I. ii, He does hinder that it become.. a part of it. **1862** F. HALL *Hindu Philos. Syst.* 144 Good works, they say, hinder the soul of emancipation.

†**d.** ***to hinder time***: to spend time, and so retard matters. *Obs. rare.*

1712 W. ROGERS *Voy.* 12 Not willing to hinder Time to carry her into any Harbour to examine.. we let her go.

3. *absol.* or *intr.* To delay or frustrate action; to be an obstacle or impediment.

c **1386** CHAUCER *Melib.* ¶230 Cassidorie seith that it is a manere sleighte to hyndre whan he sheweth to doon a thyng openly and werketh priuely the contrarie. **1450–70** *Golagros & Gaw.* 358 It hynderis neuer for to be heyndly of speche. **1612** BRINSLEY *Lud. Lit.* 82 They will doe them so falsly, as will oft more hinder then further. **1652** NEEDHAM tr. *Selden's Mare Cl.* 41 Nor doth it hinder at all, that in their Assignations or Distributions wee so often finde this Particle *usque ad Mare*. **1720** *Lett. fr. Lond. Jrnl.* (1721) 38 But Fate and all the Politicks of those Times hinder'd. **1828** CARLYLE *Misc.*, *Burns* (1872) II. 14 It is not the dark place that hinders, but the dim eye.

Hence **'hindered** *ppl. a.*

c **1440** *Promp. Parv.* 240/2 Hundryd, or harmyd, *dampnificatus*. **1644** DIGBY *Nat. Bodies* I. (1645) 366 A hindered water. **1876** T. HARDY *Ethelberta* (1890) 193 Amid the shouts of the hindered drivers.

hinder end, ˌhinder-ˈend. *Sc.* and *north. dial.* [f. HINDER *a.*[1] + END *sb.* In Sc. and north. dial. the two ends of a thing are spoken of as the *fore-end* and the *hinder-end* (with short *i*).]

1. The latter end; the opposite of the *fore-end* or beginning; *spec.* the end of life, *ultima dies.*

1523 FITZHERB. *Husb.* §148 Yf thou spende it in yᵉ begynnynge of the yere & shal want in yᵉ hynder ende. **1585** JAS. I *Ess. Poesie* (Arb.) 21 In the hinder end of this booke. **1598** D. FERGUSON *Coll. Scot. Prov.* (1785) 11 (Jam.) Falsehood made ne'er a fair hinder-end. **1723** DE FOE *Col. Jack* (1840) 124 The devil will have you at the hinder end of the bargain. **1877** *N.W. Linc. Gloss.* s.v., I was born at th' hinderend o' th' year. *Mod. Sc.* Poor man! he's near his hinder-end.

2. The rear or posterior end; the back of anything. (In Sc. usually *hint-end.*)

1816 SCOTT *Old Mort.* viii, Ye preached us.. out o' this new city o' refuge afore our hinder end was weel hafted in it. **1877** *N.W. Linc. Gloss.*, Th' pickin' furk's i' th' hinderend o' th' barn.

3. (Usually *pl.*) The part of anything (e.g. of corn) which remains after all selecting and sifting operations have been used; leavings. (Also *attrib.*, as ***hinder-end barley.***) Also *fig.*

1825 BROCKETT, *Hinder-ends*, refuse of corn—such as remains after it is winnowed. **1825–80** JAMIESON s.v., 5. *The hinder-end o' aw trade*, the worst business to which one can betake one's self. 6. *The hinder-end o' aw folk*, the worst of people. **1842** C. NEVILE *New Tariff* 15 Pigs.. fed upon hinder-end barley. **1877** *N.W. Linc. Gloss.* s.v., We send forends to market.. and chickens gets th' hinderends.

hinderer (ˈhɪndərə(r)), *sb.* [f. HINDER *v.* + -ER[1].] One who (or that which) hinders; †an injurer (*obs.*); an impeder, obstructor.

1387–8 T. USK *Test. Love* I. vi. (Skeat) I. 128 We.. oppression of these olde hinders shal againe surmounten. **1549** LATIMER *1st Serm. bef. Edw. VI* (Arb.) 40 These grasiers, inclosers, and rente-rearers are hinderers of the kings honour. **1602** *Life T. Cromwell* III. i. 97 I'll be no hinderer to so good an act. **1641** MILTON *Reform.* I. Wks. (1847) 4/2, I shall distinguish such as I esteem to be the hinderers of reformation into three sorts, Antiquitarians.. 2. Libertines. 3. Politicians. **1875** JOWETT *Plato* (ed. 2) I. 437 Is the body, if invited to share in the enquiry, a hinderer or a helper?

†**'hinderer**, *a.* *Obs.* In 4 hind(e)rere, 5 hynderour. [f. HINDER *a.*[1] + -ER[3]: cf. OHG. *hintarôro.*] = HINDER *a.* (In quot. 1340 as sb. (transl. L. *posteriora*) = hinder parts.)

a **1340** HAMPOLE *Psalter* lxxvii. 72 He smate his enmys in the hyndirere. **1388** WYCLIF *Gen.* xvi. 13 Y seiȝ the hyndere [**1382** the hyndirmore, Vulg. *posteriora*] thingis of him. —— *1 Kings* xxi. 21 Y schal kitte awey thin hyndrere thingis [**1382** hyndirmoris]. **14..** *Voc.* in Wr.-Wülcker 604/22 *Posterior*, hy[n]derour.

†**'hinderest**, *a.* *Obs.* [f. as prec. + -EST: cf. OHG. *hintarôst*, MHG., Ger. *hinterst*, MDu. *hinderste.*] Hindmost.

c **1385** CHAUCER *Prol.* 622 Euere he rood the hyndreste [*v.rr.* hyndeest, hinderest] of oure route. *c* **1450** *Merlin* xxiv. 446 Thei kepte hem-self all-ther hinderest for to diffende the other.. that myght no faster go.

†**'hinderful**, *a.* *Obs. rare.* [f. HINDER *a.*[2] + -FUL.] Iniquitous, impious.

Hence †**hinderfulliche** *adv.*, iniquitously, treacherously.

c **1200** *Trin. Coll. Hom.* 59 He.. forlet god.. and turnde on þe hinderfulle rede [*in consilio impiorum*]. *Ibid.* 83 Ac þis wiðerfulle mannisshe þe fondeð me hinderfulliche. *c* **1290** [see HINDER *a.*[2]]. **1569** *Cal. St. Papers, Foreign* (1874) 54 To purge the seas.. of such wicked and hinderful people.

†**'hinderhede.** *Obs.* In 4 hyndirhede. [f. HINDER *a.*[1] + *-hede*, -HEAD.] Posteriority.

c **1380** WYCLIF *Sel. Wks.* III. 78 þere ben two furþerhedis and two hyndirhedis also.

hindering (ˈhɪndərɪŋ), *vbl. sb.* [f. HINDER *v.* + -ING[1].] The action of the vb. HINDER:

†**a.** Detriment, damage, disparagement (*obs.*). **b.** Obstruction, impediment, hindrance.

c **1375** *Sc. Leg. Saints*, *Andrew* 973 þat mycht be hendringe to myn fame, And lattinge als to ȝore gud name. **1390** GOWER *Conf.* II. 64 Which shall be to the double shame, Most for the hindringe of thy name. *c* **1450** *Cov.*

Myst. (Shaks. Soc.) 234 ȝe do ȝourself ryght grett hyndrynge And short ȝoure lyff or ȝe beware. **1450–1530** *Myrr. our Ladye* 241 Leste the deceyte of the enmy . . had come vnto her to the hendrynge of her sowle.

'hindering, *ppl. a.* [f. as prec. + -ING².] That hinders, impedes, or obstructs. Hence **'hinderingly** *adv.*, so as to obstruct or prevent.

1390 GOWER *Conf.* I. 310 How hindring is a wofull peine To him, that love wold atteigne. **1646** H. LAWRENCE *Comm. Angels* 136 The objections . . are extreamely hindering. **1825** *Blackw. Mag.* XVIII. 295 Causes, which . . bear impulsively, or hinderingly, upon every action. **1868** GEO. ELIOT *Sp. Gipsy* 304 And slays all hindering men.

hinderland ('hɪndəlænd). [f. HINDER *a.*¹ + LAND. In sense 1, prob. from some locality.]

†**1.** A kind of cloth imported from some continental country: perh. from inland Germany. *Obs.*

1465 *Mann. & Househ. Exp.* (Roxb.) 316 My mastyr bout . . a pece of Hynderlond, prise the elle j. d. ob. **1812** J. SMYTH *Pract. of Customs* (1821) 134 Hinderlands, Brown, under 22½ inches in breadth, in a British-built Ship.

2. (*pl.*) = HINDERLING² 2 (for which *hinderlans* is a misprint in edd. of Scott).

1818 [see HINDERLING² 2]. **1891** STEVENSON & L. OSBOURNE *Wrecker* vi, 'Set down upon your hinderlands', cried my grandfather, almost savagely.

†**'hinderling¹.** *Obs.* [f. OE. *hinder* adv. (see HIND *a.*) or HINDER *a.*² + -LING]. A base, mean, degenerate person.

c **1200** ORMIN 486 And halde þe forr hinnderrlinng, And forr well swiþe unnwresste. **12..** *Laws Edw. Conf.* c. 35 §1 in Schmid *Gesetze* 516 Summa ira commotus, unus vocat alterum hinderling, i.e. ab omni honestate dejectum. **1387** TREVISA *Higden* (Rolls) VII. 109 Wherefore Westsexmen haveþ in proverbe of hiȝe despite hynderlyng whiche sowneþ i-cast doun fro honeste.

'hinderling². [f. HINDER *a.*¹ + -LING².]

†**1.** The backward direction: only in the OE. advb. phrase ***on hinderling*** backward. *Obs.*

c **1000** *Ags. Ps.* (Th.) lv. 8 [lvi. 9] þonne on hinderling hweorfað mine feondas fæcne. *Ibid.* lxix. [lxx.] 3 Hi on hinderlincg hweorfað and cyrrað.

2. *sb. pl.* (also *-lins*). Posteriors, buttocks. *Sc.*

1818 SCOTT *Rob Roy* xxiii, We downa bide the coercion of gude braid-claith about our hinderlins [so MS. and Standard ed. 1896; ed. 1 and subseq. edd. read *hinderlans*]. **1831** *Fraser's Mag.* III. 18 A jacket . . hung like a French coatee over his hinderlings. **1834** M. SCOTT *Cruise Midge* iv. (1863) 62 Wha will assure ye that they shall not kittle your hinderlins?

†**3.** (?) One who is behind or in the rear. *Obs.*

1619 W. SCLATER *Exp. 1 Thess.* (1630) 562 Our hinderlings haply may ouertake and out-strip vs in holy practice.

†**'hinderly,** *a.* (? *adv.*) *Obs.* [f. HINDER *a.*¹ + -LY².] Backward, behindhand.

1564 in *Camden Misc.* (1893–5) IX. 40 Wheras the cuntry is to miche hinderly in all good thinges perteining to religion. **1659** HAMMOND *On Ps.* cxii. 10 Paraphr. 572 Whilst themselves . . doe yet sensibly decay and grow hinderly.

'hindermate. *nonce-wd.* [f. HINDER *v.* + MATE, after *helpmate.*] A companion who is a hindrance.

a **1843** SOUTHEY *Comm.-pl. Bk.* IV. 441 There are hindermates as well as helpmates in marriage.

†**'hindermore,** *a.* (*sb.*) *Obs.* In 4 **hyndirmore,** *Sc.* **hendirmar.** [f. HINDER *a.*¹ + MORE *adv.*: see HIND *a.* Cf. *furthermore.*] More to the rear.

1375 BARBOUR *Bruce* VII. 599 Quhen thai that war hendirmar Saw that the formast left the stede, Thai turnit soyn the bak and fled.

b. as *sb.* The hinder part; the hind-quarters.

1382 WYCLIF *1 Kings* xvi. 3, I shal kitte of the hyndirmore of Baasa, and the hyndirmores of the hows of hym.

hindermost ('haɪndəməʊst), *a. arch.* [f. HINDER *a.*¹ + -MOST: see HIND *a.* Cf. *innermost, uppermost, uttermost.*] = HINDMOST.

1398 TREVISA *Barth. De P.R.* III. xxii. (1495) 70 The tresour of mynde is the hyndermest place of the brayne. *c* **1400** *Melayne* 1277 Oure Cristen knyghtis with þaire speres The Hyndirmaste fro þaire blonkes beres. *c* **1450** *Merlin* 286 These . . were hyndermeste in the route. **1541** R. COPLAND *Guydon's Quest. Chirurg.*, The formost is the byggest. The myddlemost the least, & the hyndermost is meane. **1719** DE FOE *Crusoe* II. xi, The stern of the hindermost boat. **1783** *Ainsworth's Lat. Dict.* (Morell) I. s.v., The hindermost dog may catch the hare. [**1814** W. TAYLOR in *Monthly Rev.* LXXIV. 305 It is not legitimate to combine both forms of inflection, and to say or to write *hindermost.*]

hindersome ('hɪndəsəm), *a.* Now *Sc.* and *north. dial.* [f. HINDER *v.* + -SOME.] Tending to hinder; †injurious, harmful (*obs.*); obstructive.

1580 HOLLYBAND *Treas. Fr. Tong, Injurieux*, hurtfull, hindersome. **1581** PETTIE *Guazzo's Civ. Conv.* II. (1586) 54 b, Toothsome to the taste, but hindersome to health. **1663** GERBIER *Counsel* 42 Needlesse and hindersome to the bording of a Roome. **1881** *Alloa Advertiser* No. 1617. 2/1 The weather continues as unsettled and as hindersome for farming operations as [etc.]. **1893** *Northumbld. Gloss.* s.v., The bad weather's very hindersome for the harvist.

†**hinderyeap,** *a. Obs.* In 1 -ȝéap, -ȝép, 3 -ȝæp. [OE. *hinderȝéap*, f. HINDER *a.*² + *ȝéap* crooked, deceitful.] Cunning, deceitful.

c **1000** ÆLFRIC *Colloq.* in Wr.-Wülcker 101 On spræcum glæwlice hinderȝepe, *in loquelis astuti, uersuti*. *c* **1050** *Supp. Ælfric's Voc.* ibid. 168/11 *Uersutus*, hinderȝeap. *c* **1200** ORMIN 6646 þatt mann iss fox and hinnderrȝæp and full off ille wiless.

'hind-head. *Obs.* or *arch.* [f. HIND *a.* + HEAD¹.] The back of the head; the occiput.

1666 *Despauterii Gramm. Inst.* I. (Jam.), *Sinciput*, the forehead. *Occiput*, the hindhead. **1689** BURNET *Tracts* I. 87 They christen . . pouring the Water on the Hind-head. **1826** KIRBY & SP. *Entomol.* III. 487 The occiput, or hind-head is that part of the face that either forms an angle with the vertex posteriorly or slopes downwards from it. **1865** KINGSLEY *Herew.* II. vii. 114 An angry savage smote him on the hind head full with a stone axe.

†**'hindheal.** *Obs.* [f. HIND *sb.*¹ + HEAL *sb.*; cf. OE. *hindhælepe.*] A plant: see quots.

[*c* **1050** *Nomina Herbarum* in Wr.-Wülcker 295/24 *Ambrosia*, hyndhæleþe. *Ibid.* 323/17 Hindheolað.] *c* **1265** *Voc. Plants* in Wr.-Wülcker 556/23 *Ambrosia* . . hindehele. *a* **1500** *Gl. Harl.* 3388 in *Sax. Leechd.* II. 393 *Eupatorium lilifagus, ambrosia maior*, wylde sauge, hyndhale. *a* **1500** *Gl. Sloane* 5 lf. 15 (*ibid.*) *Euperatorium*, ambrose, is an erbe that som men calliþ wilde sauge oþer wode merche oþer hyndale. **1597** GERARDE *Herbal* App., Hyndheele is Ambrosia.

‖**Hindi** ('hɪndiː), *a.* and *sb.* Also **Hindee.** [a. Urdū *hindī*, f. *hind*, India. The corresponding Persian is *hindwī, hinduī, hinduvī*, formerly used by Eng. writers in the same sense.]

A. *adj.* Of or belonging to Northern India or its language.

1825 W. T. ADAM *Stewart's Hist. Anecd.* (*heading*), Anglo-Hindawee. **1826** W. BOWLEY (*title*) The New Testament . . altered . . into the Hinduee language. **1851** F. HALL in *Benares Mag.* V. 22 *note*, The pandits draw no other distinction between the words *Hindí* and *Hindu'í* than that the first is used by the well-informed (who sometimes employ *Hindví*, also), and the second, by villagers. . . The form *Hindaví* is confined to the Muhammadans. **1878** R. N. CUST *Mod. Langs. E. Ind.* 49 The real and original Vernacular of the Hindi people.

B. *sb.* **1.** The great Aryan vernacular language of Northern India, spoken (with numerous dialects) from the frontiers of Bengal to those of the Panjāb and Sindh, and from the Himālaya Mountains to the Nerbudda.

It comes into contact on the N.W. and W. with Panjābī, Sindhī, and Gujarātī, on the S. with Marāthī, on the S.E. with Orīya, on the E. with Bengālī, sister Aryan languages, and on the N. with Nepālī (which some make merely a dialect of Hindī). Cf. HINDUSTANI.

1880 *Asiat. Ann. Reg., Acc. Bks.* 6/1 Even when they write in Hinduvi. **1801** COLEBROOKE in *Asiat. Res.* VII. 220 The language which forms the ground-work of modern Hindustáni, and . . is known by the appellation of Hindí or Hindeví. **1804** W. TENNANT *Ind. Recr.* II. 199 A manuscript in the Hindivi. **1807** W. T. ADAM (*title*) Arithmetic in Hindui. **1832** (*title*) Fables in Hinduwee. **1857** MONIER WILLIAMS *Sanskrit Gram.* Introd. 22 Out of them [patois modifications of Sanskrit] arose Hindí (termed Hindústání or Urdú, when mixed with Persian and Arabic words), Maráthí, and Gujaráthí. **1878** R. N. CUST *Mod. Langs. E. Ind.* 46 The Language-Field of Hindi is stated to comprise 248,000 square miles, and the number of the Hindi-speaking population . . cannot fall short of eighty millions. *Ibid.* 50 The result of this first attempt to take stock of the dialects of Hindi, represented actually by books or Vocabularies, is that there are . . in all fifty-eight varieties. **1886** YULE *Anglo-Ind. Gloss.* s.v. *Hindee*, The earliest literary work in Hindi is the great poem of Chand Bardai (c. 1200) which records the deeds of Prithirāja, the last Hindu sovereign of Delhi.

2. A native of Northern India. *rare.*

a **1853** ELLIOT *Hist. Ind.* (1867–77) III. 539 (Y.) Whatever live Hindú fell into the King's hands was pounded into bits under the feet of elephants. The Musalmáns, who were Hindís (country born), had their lives spared.

Hindki ('hɪndkiː). Also **Hindeki, Hindkee.** The name of a people, and of their language, of north-west India and Afghanistan.

1815 M. ELPHINSTONE *Acct. Kingdom of Caubul* II. xii. 309 It has been observed that there is scarcely any part of Afghaunistaun in which the whole population is Afghaun, and that the mixture is composed of Taujiks in the West, and of Hindkees in the East. **1875** *Encycl. Brit.* I. 235/2 *Hindkis*. This is the name given to people of Hindu descent scattered over Afghanistan. They are said to be of the *Kshatri* or military caste. **1886** YULE & BURNELL *Anglo-Indian Gloss.* 315/2 *Hindki* or *Hindeki*. This modification of the name is applied to people of Indian descent, but converted to Islam, on the Peshawar frontier, and scattered over other parts of Afghānistān. They do the banking business and hold a large part of the trade in their hands. **1911** *Encycl. Brit.* XVI. 80/2 The principal varieties of the northern group are Hindki (the same in meaning as Hindko) and Pōthwārī. **1919** G. A. GRIERSON *Ling. Surv. India* VIII. I. 333 The Lahndā of Deva Ghazi Khan goes by several names, such as Hindī, Hindkī, Jatkī, and Dērāwāl. . . I call it Hindkī in these pages. **1964** S. K. CHATTERJI in D. Abercrombie et al. *Daniel Jones* 409 Languages like . . Hindki (western Panjabi or Lahndi).

†**'hindlongs,** *adv. Obs. rare.* [for **hindlings*, f. HIND *a.* (*adv.*): cf. *headlings, headlong.*] In a backward direction.

1668 CULPEPPER & COLE *Barthol. Anat.* III. ix. 149 It goes hindlongs to the Ear.

†**'hindmore,** *a. Obs.* [f. HIND *a.* + MORE, under the influence of the earlier *hindmost.*] = HINDER *a.*¹

1632 HOLLAND tr. *Cyrupædia* I. viii. 48 Commanding the Caporalls to bring forward the hindmore band.

hindmost ('haɪndməʊst), *a.* Forms: 4–6 **hen-,** 5 **hynd-,** 6 **hyn-,** 6–9 **hin-,** 6– **hind-;** 4 **-mast,** 6 **-mest,** 9 *Sc.* **-maist,** 5– **-most.** [app. f. HIND *a.* + -MOST: see HIND *a.* The similarity to Goth. *hindumist*, and the analogy of ME. *formest*, FOREMOST, have given rise to the conjecture that this is a double superlative, f. OE. *hindema* + -EST; but the OE. word is known only once in Beowulf, and there is a chasm of 500 or 600 years between this and Barbour's *henmast*. Mod.Sc. uses *hinmest* of time and succession, *hintmest* of fixed position.]

1. Furthest behind or in the rear; last in position; last come to; most remote.

1375 BARBOUR *Bruce* VIII. 245 Gif the formast egirly Be met . . The henmast sall abasit be. *Ibid.* XII. 268 To meit thame that first sall assemmyll So stoutly that the henmast trymmyll. **1535** COVERDALE *1 Macc.* iv. 15 The hynmost of them were slayne. **1596** DALRYMPLE tr. *Leslie's Hist. Scot.* I. 43 This [Dunesbe] is the last and hindmest hil in Scotland. *a* **1635** CORBET *Iter Bor.* (R.), They curse the formost, we the hindmost. **1723** *Pres. St. Russia* I. 167 To the hindmost Recesses of Siberia. **1852** MISS YONGE *Cameos* II. iv. 43 The hindmost declared they would not stop till they were even with the front. **1860** TYNDALL *Glac.* I. vi. 42 The ridges . . have their hindmost angles wasted off.

b. Proverbial phrase, ***the devil*** (***Satan, hell***) ***take the hindmost.***

1611 BEAUM. & FL. *Philaster* V. iii, They run all away, and cry, 'the devil take the hindmost'. **1663** BUTLER *Hud.* I. ii. 633 Each Man swore to do his best . . And bid the Devil take the hinmost. **1728** POPE *Dunc.* II. 60 'So take the hindmost, Hell', (he said) 'and run'. **1811** BYRON *Hints fr. Hor.* 712 If Satan take the hindmost, who'd be last? **1890** *Spectator* 13 Sept. 331/1 A good example of the devil-take-the-hindmost attitude.

2. Last in order, succession, or time. (Chiefly *Sc.*)

? *a* **1500** (MS. 1592) *Chester Pl.* VII. 596 Though I come the hyndmoste [*MS.* 1607 hyndermost] of all. **15..** *Aberd. Reg.* (Jam.), To pa the henmest penny of the said fiftene £. **1526** TINDALE *1 Cor.* iv. 9 My thynketh that god hath shewed vs which are apostles for the hynmost off all. **1567** *Gude & Godlie B.* 186 We salbe cruellest on the hindmest day. **1593** SHAKS. *2 Hen. VI*, III. i. 2 'Tis not his wont to be the hindmost man. **1596** DALRYMPLE tr. *Leslie's Hist. Scot.* X. 326 Thair hindmest hand tha set not to the wark. **1889** BARRIE *Window in Thrums* 98 For the hinmost years o' his life. *Ibid.* 152 The henmost time I saw him.

Hindoo: see HINDU.

hindrance ('hɪndrəns), *sb.* Forms: 5–6 **hinderaunce,** 6 **hyndera(u)nce, hindraunce,** 6–9 **hinderance,** 6– **hindrance.** [f. HINDER *v.* + -ANCE, after words of F. origin such as *resistance.*] The action or fact of hindering.

†**1.** Injury, damage, hurt, disadvantage. *Obs.*

1436 *Libel Eng. Policy* in *Pol. Songs* (Rolls) II. 176 To oure losse and hinderaunce. *c* **1460** SIR R. ROS *La Belle Dame sans Mercie* 602 Thus hurtes ben of dyvers businesse Which love hath put to right gret hinderaunce. **1529** MORE *Comf. agst. Trib.* II. Wks. 1183/2 That he should neuer . . do any other beast anye harme or hynderaunce. **1590** SIR J. SMYTH in *Lett. Lit. Men* (Camden) 56 The book . . is now forbidden to be soulde, greatly to the hindrance of the pore printer. **1597** MORLEY *Introd. Mus.* 158 Nothing may be either added or taken away without great hinderance to the other parts.

2. Obstruction, prevention of progress or action.

1526 *Pilgr. Perf.* (W. de W. 1531) 47 b, Which ben great let & hynderaunce to the same. **1576** FLEMING *Panopl. Epist.* 49 Notwithstanding their impediments, provided for my hinderaunce. **1651** BAXTER *Inf. Bapt.* 248 Full liberty to speak without hinderance. **1690** LOCKE *Hum. Und.* III. xi. §4 Reason to doubt whether language . . has contributed more to the improvement or hinderance of knowledge. **1856** LEVER *Martins of Cro' M.* 193 To follow their own wayward fancies, without let or hinderance. **1879** F. POLLOK *Sport Brit. Burmah* II. 5 We went about freely; there was not the slightest hindrance.

b. with *a* and *pl.* An instance or cause of this; an impediment, obstacle.

1576 FLEMING *Panopl. Epist.* 288 Younge children, whose age is a hinderaunce. **1614** RALEIGH *Hist. World* III. (1634) 32 The Temple . . having received so many hinderances from the first foundation to the second of Darius. **1759** tr. *Duhamel's Husb.* III. xii. (1762) 405 With no hinderances or obstructions. **1877** SPARROW *Serm.* iv. 56 They become . . hindrances rather than helps in the matter of religion.

Hence †**'hindrance** *v. trans.*, to put a hindrance in the way of, to hinder. **'hindranceful** *a.*, full of hindrances or obstacles; obstructive.

1664 M. CASAUBON (*title* ed. 2) Of the Necessity of Reformation . . and what (visibly) hath most hindranced it. **1889** FR. A. KEMBLE *Far Away & Long Ago* iii. 31 The helpful or hindranceful damsel who condescended . . to endure the condition of servant.

hindside ('haɪndsaɪd). [f. HIND *a.* A.] The back part of anything. Also in quasi-combs., as ***hindside-foremost.***

1862 H. MARRYAT *Year in Sweden* II. 297 She set them hindside before. **1915** E. POUND *Lett.* (1951) 91 Objectivity and again objectivity, and expression: no hindside-beforeness. **1929** W. FAULKNER *Sartoris* (1932) IV. 270 Negro in a hind-side-before collar. **1931** E. WILSON *Axel's*

Castle iii. 88 His hindside-foremost presentations of thought. **1934** J. MARSTON *Andromeda* xiv. 194 That's crude sentimentality hindside up. **1942** *New Yorker* 10 Oct. 33 What's she doing out in this rain, shoving along the beach on her hindside?

hind-sight, 'hindsight.

1. a. (*hind-sight*) The backsight of a rifle.

1851 MAYNE REID *Scalp Hunt.* xxi, When you squint through her hind-sights. **1889** FARMER *Americanisms.*

b. ***to knock*** (or ***kick***) ***the hindsight out*** or ***off***: to dispose of or demolish completely. *U.S. colloq.*

1834 W. A. CARRUTHERS *Kentuckian in N.Y.* I. 21 As sure as you saw the fire at the muzzle of his gun, so sure he knocked the creter's hind sight out. **1850** L. H. GARRARD *Wah-To-Yah* (1927) xx. 248 They backed their ears preparatory to kicking the hindsights off the first man that struck them. **1872** E. EGGLESTON *Hoosier Schoolmaster* x. 58 Ef its rendered right, it'll knock the hind sights off of any rheumatiz you ever see. **1892** *Congress. Rec.* 1 Apr. 2843/1 The American producer..can knock the hindsights off the producer anywhere else on the face of the earth. **1954** in J. A. WEINGARTEN *Amer. Dict. Slang* 186/2.

2. (*'hindsight*) Seeing what has happened, and what ought to have been done, after the event; perception gained by looking backward: opp. to *foresight.*

1883 *Jrnl. Educ.* XVII. 264 That a school-man so preternaturally gifted with 'hind-sight' should have been so defective in 'fore-sight'. **1895** A. T. MAHAN in *Century Mag.* Aug. 631/2 Open to the proverbial retort that hindsight is always better than foresight.

†**'hindsome,** *a. Obs. rare.* [f. HIND *a.*[1] + -SOME.] Situated behind; hind-.

1634 T. JOHNSON *Parey's Chirurg.* III. viii. (1678) 60 The two hindsom-muscles serving for respiration.

Hindu, Hindoo ('hɪnduː, hɪn'duː), *sb.* and *a.* [a. Pers. *hindu*, Urdū *hindū*, adj. and sb., Indian; f. Pers. *hind*, India, Zend *hen̆du*, Achæmenian *hin̆d'u* = Skr. *sindhu* river, *spec.* the Indus, hence the region of the Indus, Sindh; gradually extended by Persians, Greeks, and Arabs, to northern India as a whole.]

A. *sb.* An Aryan of Northern India (Hindustan), who retains the native religion (Hinduism), as distinguished from those who have embraced Islam; hence, any one who professes Hinduism; applied by Europeans in a wider sense, in accordance with the wider application of *Hindustan.*

1662 J. DAVIES tr. *Mandelslo's Trav.* 74 The King of Cambaya, who was a Hindou, or Indian, that is, a Pagan. **1665** *Sir T. Roe's Voy. E. Ind.* in *P. della Valle's Trav. E. Ind.* 374 The Inhabitants in general of Indostan were all anciently Gentiles, called in general Hindoes. **1698** FRYER *Acc. E. India & P.* 113 At the House of an Hindu. **1804** W. TENNANT *Ind. Recreat.* (ed. 2) I. p. xviii, Intelligent natives of India, both Mussulmans and Hindoos. **1853** MAX MÜLLER *Chips* (1880) I. iii. 64 The Hindu was the last to leave the central home of the Aryan family.

B. *adj.* Of, pertaining to, or characteristic of the Hindus or their religion; Indian.

1698 FRYER *Acc. E. India & P.* 80 According to the Hindu Custom. **1799** COLEBROOKE in *Life* (1873) 432 In the vernacular dialects, or even in the Hindu language [i.e. Sanskrit]. **1804** W. TENNANT *Ind. Recreat.* (ed. 2) I. 36 They have in a great measure apostatised from the Hindoo system. **1858** J. B. NORTON *Topics* 30 All the Hindoo and Mahommedan troops in the king's army bound themselves by an oath to defend their sovereign.

Hence **Hinduic, Hindooic** (hɪn'duːɪk) *a.* = prec. B.

1889 R. B. ANDERSON tr. *Rydberg's Teut. Mythol.* 6 The Hindooic Aryans were possessors only of Kabulistan and Pendschab. **1893** *Mission. Herald* (Boston) May 199 A thing which..not all my pundit-ship or Hinduic sastraship can give.

Hinduism, Hindooism ('hɪnduːɪz(ə)m). [f. HINDU + -ISM.] The polytheistic religion of the Hindus, a development of the ancient Brahmanism with many later accretions.

1829 *Bengalee* 46 Almost a convert to their goodly habits and observances of Hindooism. **1858** MAX MÜLLER *Chips* (1880) II. xxvii. 304 Hinduism is a decrepit religion, and has not many years to live. **1878** A. BURNELL in *Academy* 604/2 The result of contact with foreigners has always been a revival of Hinduism.

Hinduize, Hindooize ('hɪnduːaɪz), *v.* [f. as prec. + -IZE.] *trans.* To render Hindu in character, customs, or religion. Hence **'Hinduized** *ppl. a.*

1857 *Sat. Rev.* IV. 460/1 He may become Hindooized himself. **1860** EDWARDES in *Mem. Sir H. B. Edwardes* (1886) II. 296 The Hindoos have Hindooised the Mahommedans in India. **1862** BEVERIDGE *Hist. India* II. IV. vi. 190 Extolled by hindooised Europeans. **1871** TYLOR *Prim. Cult.* I. 45 Lower in culture than some Hinduized nations who have retained their original Dravidian speech, the Tamils for instance.

Hindustani, Hindoostanee (hɪnduː'stɑːniː), *a.* and *sb.* Also Hindustanee, -sthani, Hindostanee, -stani, -staunee. [a. Urdū *hindūstānī*, Pers. *hindustānī* adj., of or pertaining to Hindustān, lit. 'the country of the Hindus' (f. *hindu* + *-stān* place, country): see HINDU.

To natives, *Hindustān* is 'India north of the Nerbudda, exclusive of Bengal and Behar', or, virtually, the region covered by *Hindī* and its dialects. But from early times, foreigners, Muslim and European, have extended it to include the whole of the peninsula 'from the Himālaya to the Bridge (i.e. Adam's Bridge)', and this is the general geographical use.]

A. *adj.* Of or pertaining to Hindustan (in the stricter sense), or its people or language, *esp.* the language described in B. 2.

1800 *Asiat. Ann. Reg., Suppl. Chron.* 111/1 Grammar and Dictionary of the Hindustanee language, the universal colloquial language throughout India. **1804** W. TENNANT *Ind. Recreat.* (ed. 2) I. 246 Trial by ordeal..still keeps its place in the Hindostanee code. *Ibid.* II. 392 The Hindoostanee and the Persian characters are both used. **1827** D. JOHNSON *Ind. Field Sports* 210 Fifty people were at a notch, or Hindostanee dance. **1879** F. POLLOK *Sport Brit. Burmah* I. 50 Even the Hindoostani mahout forgot about ha-lal-ing, and was glad to partake.

B. *sb.* **1.** A native of Hindustan; a Hindu or Muslim of Upper India.

1829 *Bengalee* 303 A desire to become half Hindoostanee and native himself. **1879** F. POLLOK *Sport Brit. Burmah* I. 49 He took the best Hindostani and a plucky Burmese Mahout with him.

2. The language of the Muslim conquerors of Hindustan, being a form of Hindi with a large admixture of Arabic, Persian, and other foreign elements; also called *Urdū*, i.e. *zabān-i-urdū* language of the camp, sc. of the Mogul conquerors. It later became a kind of *lingua franca* over all India, varying greatly in its vocabulary according to the locality and local language.

Formerly called *Indostan, Indostans* (cf. *Scots*). By earlier writers sometimes applied to Hindi itself.

[**1616** TERRY *Voy. E. Ind., Coryat* (Y.),[Coryate] got a great mastery in the Indostan or more vulgar language. **1772** HADLEY *Gramm. Indostan Lang.* Pref. 11 (Y.) A confused mixture of Persian, Indostans, and Bengals.] **1808** W. TENNANT *Ind. Recreat.* (ed. 2) III. 61 The Hindostanee, a kind of *lingua franka*..is the spoken language of India, and has become the key to all communication with the natives. **1815** ELPHINSTONE *Acc. Caubul* (1842) II. 85 The western tribes..understand Persian much more generally than the Eastern ones do Hindostaunee. **1878** R. N. CUST *Mod. Langs. E. Ind.* 47 Hindustáni or Urdu is not a territorial Dialect, but a Lingua-franca... It can scarcely be said correctly, that it is the common Language of any one District, though freely spoken by many classes.

So **Hindoo'stanish** *a.*

1811 SHELLEY *Let. to E. Hitchener* in *Life* I. 11 In the true style of Hindoostanish devotion.

hindward ('haɪndwəd), *a. rare.* [A recent formation from HIND *a.* + -WARD: cf. *foreward.* Cf. OE. *hinderweard* turned backward.]

1. Towards the rear; backward; posterior.

1797 COLERIDGE *Sonn. On Ruined House* 12 Thro' those brogues, still tatter'd and betorn, His hindward charms gleam an unearthly white.

2. Backward in development or progress.

1868 GLADSTONE *Juv. Mundi* viii. §5 (1869) 258 This inactive and hindward deity.

'hindward, *adv.* [cf. OE. *hindanweard* adv. 'toward the farther end'.] Backward; towards the rear or hinder part.

a **1300** *E.E. Psalter* xxxix. 15 [xl. 14] Þai torne hind-ward, and schoned þai be. **1382** WYCLIF *Ps.* lxix. 4 [lxx. 3] Be thei turned awei hindward, and waxe thei ashamed. *c* **1400** *Destr. Troy* 8553 He had hym of horse, hyndward anon. **18..** WALKER (Cent.), The thorax has two furrows, which converge slightly hindward.

†**'hindwin.** *Obs. rare.* [f. HIND *a.*: the rest uncertain.] The fundament or anus.

a **1300** *Cursor M.* 22395 All þe filthes of his maugh sal brist vte at his hindwin [*v.r.* fondament] for dred he sal haf.

hine, obs. or dial. form of HIND *sb.*[1] and [2]; var. of HIN *pron.*, HYNE *adv.*, hence.

†**'hinehede.** *Obs.* [f. *hine*, HIND *sb.*[2] + *-hede*, -HEAD (OE. type **hīȝna hád*).] **a.** Family, household; company. **b.** ? Service.

a **1300** *E.E. Psalter* xxi[i] 28 [27] All hinehedes [Vulg. *patriae*] of genge fol right. *Ibid.* ciii[i]. 14 Forth-ledand.. gresse to hinehede [Vulg. *servituti*] of men swa, þat þou oute-lede fra erthe brede. *Ibid.* cvi[i]. 40 [41] He set als schepe hine-hede [Vulg. *ut oves familias*].

hinene, var. HEN *adv.*, hence.

‖**hing** (hɪŋ). Also 6 hinge, 7 hingh. [Hindī *hīng*:—Skr. *hingu.*] The drug asafetida.

1586 R. FITCH in Hakluyt *Voy.* (1599) II. 252 One hundred and fourescore boates laden with Salt, Opium, Hinge, Lead, Carpets [etc.]. **1662** J. DAVIES *Mandelslo's Trav.* 84 The Hingh, which our Drugsters and Apothecaries call *Assa fœtida*, comes for the most part from Persia. **1698** FRYER *Acc. E. India & P.* 114 The Natives eat Hing, a sort of liquid *Assa Fœtida*, whereby they smell odiously. **1857** BELLEW *Jrnl. Pol. Mission* (1862) 270 (Y.) The assafœtida, called *hang* or *hing* by the natives, grows wild in the sandy.. plains..of Afghanistan.

hing, obs. and dial. f. HANG; obs. pa. t. of HANG; obs. f. HINGE.

hinge (hɪndʒ), *sb.* Forms: 4 heng, heeng, 4–8 hing, 5–6 henge, hyng, 6 ynge, 6–7 hindge, 7 hendge, 6– hinge. [ME. *heng, heeng*:—OE. type **hęncg*, a deriv. of HANG *v.*: cf. early mod.Du. *henghe, henghene*, 'hinge, handle (of a pot), hook' (Kilian), MLG. *henge*, LG. *henge, heng*, hinge of a door or the like. The palatalization of the *g* is not distinctly evidenced before 1590: but it appears to be now current in all dialects.]

I. 1. a. The movable joint or mechanism by which a gate or door is hung upon the side-post, so as to be opened or shut by being turned upon it.

c **1380** *Sir Ferumb.* 2181 So harde he bot..þat þe henges boþe barste, & þe stapel þar-with out sprong. **1382** WYCLIF *Prov.* xxvi. 14 As a dore is turned in his heeng; so a sloȝ man in his litle bed. **1466** *Mann. & Househ. Exp.* (Roxb.) 323 To the iren mongyr for neyles, hokes, and henges, iiij.*s.* viij.*d.* **1494–5** in Willis & Clark *Cambridge* II. 15 Gilbarto Smyth pro pare de hyngis et hukys xviij*d.* **1573–80** BARET *Alv.* H 464 The Hinge, or hingell of a gate: the hooke whereon a dore hangeth. **1592** GREENE *Art Conny Catch.* III. 12 He getteth the doore off the hindges. **1616** R. C. *Times' Whistle* etc. (1871) 120 Even as the hinges doe the dore vpholde. **1634** in *Harper's Mag.* (1884) Dec. 12/2 To flinge up alle doores out of hendges. **1762** FALCONER *Shipwr.* III. 229 On brazen hinges turn'd the silver doors. **1820** KEATS *St. Agnes* xli, The door upon its hinges groans.

b. The similar mechanism to provide for the turning or moving in a quarter or half revolution of a lid, valve, etc., or of two movable parts upon each other.

1562 *Child Marriages* 131 She had lost the key of a chest, & desired hym to pull out the nayles of the hindges. *a* **1602** W. PERKINS *Cases Consc.* (1619) 144 The frame of a great amphitheater, the two parts whereof were supported onely by two hinges. **1715** LADY M. W. MONTAGU *Bassette-Table* 43 This snuff-box—on the hinge see brilliants shine. **1825** J. NICHOLSON *Operat. Mechanic* 266 The hinge of the valve [of a pump]. **1874** BOUTELL *Arms & Arm.* iii. 45 Guards for the face..attached to the cap on each side by hinges to give free movement.

c. Of bellows: see quot.

1852 SEIDEL *Organ* 37 The other ends of the bellows (where they open widest), called the hinges, are provided with double or triple leathering.

d. In Philately: see quot. 1883.

1883 *Stamp-Collecting & Exchange* 8/2 There is only one really satisfactory process for mounting postage labels, viz., the now almost universal hinge-system. This consists of a piece of thin paper a little smaller than the stamp itself, and affixed to the album with a drop of gum, or, if the hinge be already prepared for adhesion,..no inconvenience or trouble will be experienced. **1892** *Stamp Collector* Apr. 33 In the earlier days of stamp collecting, before such things as gummed hinges were offered to the collecting public. **1967** *Exchange & Mart* 20 July 19/4 (Advt.), Stamps stay put without stamp hinges, in our brand new plastic stamp album. **1971** D. POTTER *Brit. Eliz. Stamps* xv. 163 At the turn of the century, hinges were monstrous things, designed for their sticking power.

2. A natural movable joint: *spec.* **a.** that of a bivalve shell; **b.** the *cardo* or basal part of the maxilla in insects.

1702 J. PETIVER in *Phil. Trans.* XXIII. 1566 This Shell is sometimes near 2 inches long, the hing of which is 1 and ¼. **1774** GOLDSM. *Nat. Hist.* (1776) VII. 12 The Bivalve, consisting of two pieces, united by a hinge, like an oyster. **1851** RICHARDSON *Geol.* viii. 242 The hinge is the point of the dorsal margin at which bivalve shells are united. **1862** DARWIN *Fertil. Orchids* iii. 99 So flexible..is the hinge that the weight of..a fly..depresses the distal portion.

3. *transf.* The axis of the earth; the two poles about which the earth revolves, and, by extension, the four cardinal points. (See CARDINAL *a.* 4.)

a **1300** *Cursor M.* 22754 He to brin sal se..bath land and see and all thinges, þat ani werlds hald wit hinges. *c* **1586** C'TESS PEMBROKE *Ps.* LXXXIX. iv, The heav'n, the earth.. The unseene hinge of North and South sustaineth. **1603** B. JONSON *Sejanus* v. vi, Shake off the loosned Glob from her long Hing. **1629** MILTON *Nativity* 122 The Creator..the well-balanced World on hinges hung. **1671** —— *P.R.* IV. 413 The winds..rushed abroad From the four hinges of the world. **1695** WOODWARD *Nat. Hist. Earth* I. (1723) 57 The prime Hinge whereon the whole Frame of Nature moves. **1697** CREECH *Manilius* II. xxxiii. 80 Observe the four fixt Hinges of the Sky.

4. *fig.* That on which something is conceived to hang or be supported and to turn; a pivot, prop. **a.** *generally.*

1604 SHAKS. *Oth.* III. iii. 365 That the probation beare no Hindge, nor Loope, To hange a doubt on. **1621** BURTON *Anat. Mel.* I. ii. III. i. (1651) 92 Perturbations..are..causes of Melancholy, turning it out of the hinges of his health. **1726** SWIFT *Gulliver* I. vi, We usually call reward and punishment the two hinges upon which all government turns. **1781** COWPER *Truth* 207 Say, on what hinge does his obedience move? **1884** GLADSTONE in *Standard* 29 Feb. 2/5 Because the borough franchise as it exists in England..is the hinge of the whole Bill.

b. The cardinal point of a discussion or controversy (cf. CARDINAL *a.* 1); the central principle of a thesis.

1638 CHILLINGW. *Relig. Prot.* I. iv. §53. 221 The hinge whereon your whole discourse turnes. **1687** R. L'ESTRANGE *Answ. Diss.* 8 The Roman Catholique-infallibility, and the Dissenters liberty are the Two Hinges of the Controversie here in Debate. **1769** *Junius Lett.* xvi. 71 This is not the hinge on which the debate turns. **1853** MARSDEN *Early Purit.* 224 The nature of the sacraments..was the hinge of the whole controversy with Rome.

c. A turning-point, critical point, crisis.

1727 in *Wodrow Corr.* (1843) III. 303 So it stands till tomorrow; when, may the Lord direct! for this is the very hinge of the present cause. **1775** BURKE *Corr.* (1844) II. 50 The hinge between war and peace is, indeed, a dangerous juncture to ministers. **1886** SPURGEON *Treas. Dav.* Ps. cxxix.

4 Here is the hinge of the condition; this makes the turning point of Israel's distress. **1887** Bowen *Virg. Æneid* I. 672, I tremble when Juno welcomes the guest; Ne'er, at the hinge of an hour so great, will she slumber or rest.

5. Phrase. ***off the hinges***, † ***out of*** (***the***) ***hinges***: unhinged; out of order; in (or into) disorder, physical or moral. Cf. *out of harre*, HARRE 3.

1611 Cotgr., *Hallebrené*, sad, crest-fallen, heauie-looking, drooping; off the hindges, cleane out of heart. **1630** Lennard tr. *Charron's Wisd.* I. xiv. §15 (1670) 58 The wildest and best Poets do love sometimes to play the fool, and to leap out of the hinges. *c* **1645** Howell *Lett.* (1650) III. 86 All businesses here are off the hinges. **1708** Motteux *Rabelais* IV. xix. (1737) 80 We are.. out of Tune, and off the Hinges. **1828** *Craven Dial.*, *Hinges*, 'To be off t' hinges.' To be out of health.

II. 6. *dial.* The 'pluck' (heart, liver, and lungs) of a beast. Also HENGE[1], *hange*.

1469 [see HENGE[1]]. **1787** Grose *Prov. Gloss.*, *Hinge*, the liver and pluck of a sheep for dog's meat. *West.* **1825** Britton *Beauties Wiltsh.* III. Gloss. (E.D.S.), *Hinge*, the heart, liver, and lungs of a sheep or pig. **1890** *Gloucestersh. Gloss.*, *Hinge*, or *Inge*. **1893** *Wiltsh. Gloss.*, *Hinge*, *Henge*.

III. 7. *attrib.* and *Comb.*, as ***hinge-band***, ***-maker***, ***-question***; ***hinge-like*** adj.; ***hinge-ways*** adv.; **hinge-area** (*Conch.*): see quot. 1872; **hinge-bound** *a.*, having the movement of the hinge obstructed; **hinge-joint** (*Anat.*), a joint whose movement can only be in one plane (e.g. that of the elbow or knee); a GINGLYMUS; ***double hinge-joint*** (see quot. 1886); **hinge-knife**, a clasp knife, opening and shutting with a hinge or joint; **hinge-ligament** (see quot. 1909); **hinge-line** (*Conch.*): see quot. 1888; **hinge-pin**, a pin or pintle which fastens together the parts of a hinge; **hinge-tooth** (*Conch.*), one of the teeth or projections on one valve of a bivalve mollusc which fit into corresponding indentations in the other valve.

1872 Nicholson *Palæont.* 200 The beaks of the dorsal and ventral valves are separated from one another by a narrower or wider space, which is termed the '*hinge-area'. **1842** *Mech. Mag.* XXXVI. 303 They [sluice doors] were frequently *hinge-bound and clogged up. **1802** Paley *Nat. Theol.* viii. (1830) 64 The head rests immediately upon the uppermost part of the vertebræ, and is united to it by a *hinge-joint; upon which joint the head plays freely forward and backward. **1886** *Syd. Soc. Lex.*, *Hinge-joint, double*, one in which the articulating surfaces of each bone are concave in one direction and convex in the direction at right angles, as in the carpo-metacarpal joint of the thumb. **1897** Mary Kingsley *W. Africa* 330 *Hinge-knives are apt to close on your own fingers. **1909** *Cent. Dict.* Suppl. 589/3 **Hinge-ligament*, in bivalve mollusks, a tough, uncalcified, elastic membrane which connects the two valves. **1945** E. Step *Shell Life* (rev. ed.) 56 The hinge-ligament exerts a pulling action which tends to separate the lower edges. *a* **1832** Bentham *Deontology* (1834) I. 141 But do they turn on these four *hinge-like virtues? **1849** Murchison *Siluria* ix. 192 The species have generally a roundish outline, with one valve convex.. and the *hinge-line straight. **1888** Rolleston & Jackson *Anim. Life* 124 Each valve [of the shell] presents a short straight margin, the hinge-line, along which it is united to its fellow. **1725** *Lond. Gaz.* No. 6388/7 Oliver Wolfe,.. *Hinge-maker. **1881** Greener *Gun* 215 The distance from the face of the breach-action to the *hinge-pin has been considerably shortened. **1858** *Princeton Rev.* Jan. 139 These are *hinge-questions upon which Mr. Brownson observes a prudent retinency. **1851–6** Woodward *Mollusca* 57 The genera of bivalves have been characterised by the number and position of their *hinge-teeth.

hinge, *v.* [f. HINGE *sb.*]

1. *trans.* To bend (anything) as a hinge.

1607 Shaks. *Timon* IV. iii. 211 Be thou a Flatterer now.. hindge thy knee. **1864** Sala in *Daily Tel.* 23 Nov., The wealthiest.. city in America bows the neck, and hinges the knee, and crooks to the control of this man.

2. To attach or hang with or as with a hinge.

1758–65 Goldsm. *Ess.*, *Eng. Clergy* Wks. (Globe) 293/2 The vulgar.. whose behaviour.. is totally hinged upon their hopes and fears. **1804** W. Taylor in *Ann. Rev.* II. 365 The laws, which hinge gaming transactions on a mere principle of honor. **1879** M. Pattison *Milton* vi. 70 Hooker's elaborate sentence.. is composed of parts so hinged.

3. *intr.* To hang and turn *on*, as a door on its post.

1719 Spotswood in W. S. Perry *Hist. Coll. Amer. Col. Ch.* I. 206 The law you hinge on. **1795** Burke *Corr.* (1844) IV. 317 Their adversaries endeavoured to give this colour to the contest, and to make it hinge on this principle. **1835** Thirlwall *Greece* I. iii. 75 The point on which the decision must finally hinge. **1886** *Bookseller* Jan. 4/1 The destinies of the Empire are found to hinge on some Asiatic question.

Hence **hinging** *vbl. sb.* (also *attrib.*).

1825 J. Nicholson *Operat. Mechanic* 591 Some information on the subject of hinging in general. **1846** Ruskin *Mod. Paint.* I. II. I. vii. §27 Peculiar and hinging points on which the rest are based.

hinged (hɪndʒd), *a.* [f. HINGE *sb.* + -ED[2].] Having a hinge or hinges; turning on hinges.

a **1672** Flatman *Poems, To Orinda* (1674) 2 Distinguish 't only from the common Croud, By an hing'd Coffin or a Holland Shroud. **1888** Rolleston & Jackson *Anim. Life* 159 *note*, In certain species of Micropteryx.. there is a hinged and toothed mandible.

hingeless ('hɪndʒlɪs), *a.* [f. HINGE *sb.* + -LESS.] Without a hinge or hinges.

1614 Sylvester *Litt. Bartas* 264 'Tis a wondrous thing to see that mighty Mound, Hingeless and Axless, turn so swiftly round. **1854** Woodward *Mollusca* II. 235 Craniadæ: shell orbicular, calcareous, hingeless. **1882** *Century Mag.* Apr. 912/2 Hingeless doors and shutters.

hinger, -ing, obs. Sc. ff. of HANGER, -ING.

hingle ('hɪŋg(ə)l), **hengle** ('hɛŋg(ə)l). *Obs.* exc. *dial.* Forms: 4 **heengle**, 4–6 **hengle**, 5 **hengel, -yl(l, -ylle**, 6 **hengil, hingil, hyngel, -yll**, 6–7 (9 *dial.*) **hingel**, 7 **-ell**, 9 *dial.* **hingle**; also *β.* 6 **hanggell**. [ME. *hengle*:—OE. type **hęngel*, corresp. to MDu., MLG., MHG. *hengel*, Ger. *hängel*:—**hangilo-*, agent-n. f. stem of HANG *v.*: cf. HINGE.]

A hinge: esp. that part of the hinge which is attached to the gate or door, and turns upon the crook or pintle fixed on the post.

Also *dial.* that part by which anything is hung.

c **1325** *Gloss. W. de Biblesw.* in Wright *Voc.* 170 *Verteveles*, hengles. **1382** Wyclif *Neh.* iii. 13 Thei.. setten his 3ate leuis, and lokis, and henglis. —— *Isa.* vi. 4 To-moued ben the thresholdes of the heenglis fro the vois of the criende. **1481–90** *Howard Househ. Bks.* (Roxb.) 211 A peyer of hokys, and the hengelis for a dore. **1487** *Churchw. Acc. Wigtoft* (Nichols 1797), Paid for hokes and hengles unto the skolehouse dore. **1553** Becon *Reliques of Rome* (1563) 258 The Apostolike See.. is the heade and the hanggell (*Cardo*) of all other sees. For as the doore is gouerned by the hanggell: so are all churches gouerned and ruled by the authoritye of that see. **1594** Blundevil *Exerc.* VIII. (ed. 7) 749 Upon which two Poles, otherwise called the hookes or hengils of the World, the heavens doe turne round about the earth. **1639** *MS. Acc. Stockton, Norfolk* (N.), Item, for the hingels of those doores. *a* **1825** Forby *Voc. E. Anglia*, *Hingle* (1) a small hinge, (2) a snare of wire; moving easily, and closing like a hinge. [**1886** *S.W. Linc. Gloss.*, *Hingle*, the handle of a pot or bucket, by which it hangs.]

hingle, dial. form of INGLE.

hinihini, var. HINA HINA.

‖**hinin** ('hinin). [Jap.] A member of an outcast group in Japan. Also *collect.* and *attrib.* Cf. ETA[3].

1884 tr. *J. J. Rein's Japan* II. i. 329 Geshas (female dancers and singers) and Jôrôs (prostitutes).. were despised, and considered.. socially below the level of the Hinin. **1891** A. M. Bacon *Jap. Girls & Women* ix. 228 The éta and hinin —outcasts who lived by begging, slaughtering animals, caring for dead bodies, tanning skins, and other employments which rendered them unclean. **1904** L. Hearn *Japan: Attempt at Interpretation* vi. 110 The banished man was most often doomed to become a *hinin* —one of that wretched class of wandering pariahs who were officially termed 'not-men'. **1970** J. W. Hall *Japan* x. 179 Tokugawa society.. was conceived of.. as falling into the following categories: the *kuge*, the samurai (including daimyo), priests, peasants, urban residents, and pariah (*hinin* and *eta*).

†**hink**, *sb.*[1] *Sc. Obs.* [prob. from HINK *v.*

Some would identify it with OE. *inca* doubt, question, scruple. But the prefixing of a non-etymological *h* is against Scottish practice.]

Faltering, hesitation, misgiving.

c **1614** J. Melvill *Autobiog.* (1842) 423 But the doing of it ..was a grait hink in my hart, and wrought sear remorse. **1668** M. Bruce *Serm.* in *Kirkton's Hist. Ch. Scot.* vii. (1817) 273, I have ay a hink in my heart about the Covenant. **1678** *Hist. Indulgence* Ep. in G. Hickes *Spirit of Popery* (1680) 74 They can.. hold up their face, and affirm, without hinck or hesitation, that [etc.]. **1709** M. Bruce *Soul-Confirm.* 8 (Jam.) He comes to.. a full assurance that he can say, We are sure we have not a hink in our hearts about it.

†**hink**, *sb.*[2] *Obs. local.* See quots.

1744–50 W. Ellis *Mod. Husbandm.* IV. III. 42 Here [Sandwich, Kent] they cut their drilled field-pease with what they call Hooks and Hincks. **1887** *Kent Gloss.*, *Hink*, a hook at the end of a stick, used for drawing and lifting back the peas, whilst they were being cut with the pea-hook. The pea-hook and hink always went together.

†**hink**, *v.* *Sc. Obs.* [perh. a. ONorse *hinka* to limp, hobble: cf. MHG., MLG., MDu. *hinken* to limp, halt.] *intr.* ? To halt; to falter.

c **1450** Henryson in *Bannatyne MS.* 133 (Jam.) Thy helth sall hynk, and tak a hurt but hone. **1697** Cleland *Poems* 105 (Jam.) Any that saw his strange deport, Perceiv'd his maw to hink and jarr.

hinkling, obs. var. of INKLING.

hinkty, var. HINCTY *a.*

hinmaist, -mest, dial. ff. HINDMOST.

hinna(h, var. HENNA.

hinne, var. HEN *adv.* *Obs.*

†'**hinniate**, *v.* *Obs. rare*$^{-0}$. [irreg. f. L. *hinnī-re* + -ATE.] 'To neigh' (Cockeram 1623).

hinnible ('hɪnɪb(ə)l), *a.* [f. late L. *hinnībilis*, f. *hinnīre* to neigh.] Able to neigh or whinny.

1656 Blount *Glossogr.*, *Hinnible*, that can neigh as a horse, apt to neigh. **1719** D'Urfey *Pills* (1872) III. 316 Achilles.. Was taught by the Centaur's rational parts the Hinnible to bestride. **1860** Mansel *Proleg. Log.* vi. 204 If he [the logician] is bound to know, as a matter of fact, that men are rational and horses hinnible.

hinny ('hɪnɪ), *sb.* [f. L. *hinnus* (in same sense): cf. Gr. ἴννος, γίννος.] The offspring of a she-ass by a stallion.

1688 R. Holme *Armoury* II. 155/2 An Hinnus is less than a Mule.. called also an Hinnulus or little Hinne. **1859** Darwin *Orig. Spec.* ix. (1873) 261 Both the mule and the hinny resemble more closely the ass than the horse. **1862** Huxley *Lect. Wrkg. Men* 91 It is a very rare thing to see a Hinny in this Country. **1890** O. Crawfurd *Round Calendar Portugal* 308 He loads a little swift-pacing ass or hinny mule with his wares.

hinny ('hɪnɪ), *v.* Also 5 **henny, hyney**, 6 **hynny**. [In 15th c. *henny*, ad. F. *hennir* to neigh; in current form conformed to L. *hinnīre*.] *intr.* To neigh as a horse, to whinny. Hence '**hinnying** *vbl. sb.* and *ppl. a.*

c **1400** tr. *Secreta Secret.*, *Gov. Lordsh.* (E.E.T.S.) 89 Alle þe hors of þyn ost shal noght cesse to henny to þou doo awey þe stoon. *Ibid.* 97 Hyneyinge of hors, chaterynge of bryddes. **1530** Palsgr. 585/1 Me thynketh this horse hynnyeth for yonder mare. **1684** tr. *Bonet's Merc. Compit.* XVI. 577 The Child loved a Foal.. the hinnying whereof when he heard [etc.]. **1880** *Macm. Mag.* Jan. 217/2 The sturdy colt that hinnied and snickered round its mother.

fig. **1614** B. Jonson *Barth. Fair* V. iii, Take no part with the wicked, young gallant; he neigheth and hinnieth; all is but hinnying sophistry.

hinny, hinnie, *Sc.* and *north.* form of HONEY.

‖**hinoki** (hi'noki). Also †**finoki**. [Jap.] A large conifer, *Chamæcyparis obtusa*, native to Japan, or the timber obtained from it.

1727 J. G. Scheuchzer tr. *Kæmpfer's Hist. Japan* I. I. 118 *Finoki* and *Suggi* are two sorts of Cypress-trees, yielding a beautiful light whitish wood. **1884** tr. *J. J. Rein's Japan* II. ii. 445 The pure and simple Shintô-temple.. is built of the white wood of the Hinoki. **1904** L. Hearn *Japan: Attempt at Interpretation* ix. 184 Such superior qualities of wood as *keyaki* or *hinoki*. **1964** *Illustr. Important Forest Trees Japan* (Japan Forest Technical Assoc.) 44/2 The hinoki cypress is abundantly found on ridges. **1965** J. Ohwi *Flora Japan* 117/1 *Chamaecyparis obtusa*... Hinoki... Much planted for timber. **1969** R. C. Bell *Board & Table Games* II. iii. 61 The best boards.. are also made of 'Gingko' (*Salisburia Adiantifolia*) and 'Hinoki' (*Thuya Obtusa*).

hino(u), varr. HINAU.

hint (hɪnt), *sb.* Also 7 **hent**. [app. a deriv. of HENT *v.* to lay hold of, seize, grasp; cf. HENT *sb.* The general notion appears to be something that is or may be seized or taken advantage of.]

†**1. a.** An occasion; an opportunity. (In quot. 1621, ? something to lay hold of, a 'handle'.) *Obs.*

1604 Shaks. *Oth.* I. iii. 142 Wherein of Antars vast, and Desarts idle.. It was my hint to speake. **1610** —— *Temp.* II. i. 3 Our hint of woe Is common. **1611** —— *Cymb.* V. v. 172 Hearing vs praise our Loues of Italy.. This Posthumus.. tooke his hint, And.. he began His Mistris picture. **1621** W. Sclater *Tythes* 199 Gaue euer man hent to his Argument from the matter of Abrahams Tithing? **1750** Johnson *Rambler* No. 14 ⁋15 To watch the hints which conversation offers for the display of their particular attainments. **1768** Ross *Helenore* 102 (Jam.) For fear I lost the hint. **1818** Scott *Hrt. Midl.* xviii, It is my hint to speak.

†**b.** Time, occasion (of action); moment (*Sc.*).

a **1670** Hacket *Abp. Williams* II. (1692) 57 What colour and tincture you give them in that hint, you shall know them by it for many years after. **1768** Ross *Helenore* 98 (Jam.) And in a hint he claspt her hard and fast.

2. a. A slight indication intended to be caught by the intelligent; a suggestion or implication conveyed in an indirect or covert manner.

1604 Shaks. *Oth.* I. iii. 166 Vpon this hint I spake. **1609** B. Jonson *Sil. Wom.* IV. i, The least hint given him of his wife now will make him raile desperatly. **1657** R. Ligon *Barbadoes* (1673) 82, I will give you some little hints of her shape and manner of growth. **1699** Burnet *39 Art.* xxxi. (1700) 352 Here are not general Words, ambiguous Expressions, or remote Hints, but a Thread of a full and clear Discourse. **1711** Addison *Spect.* No. 31 ⁋1 He had taken the Hint of it from several Performances which he had seen upon our Stage. **1759** Johnson *Idler* No. 46 ⁋4 She loves a sharp girl that can take a hint. **1849** Macaulay *Hist. Eng.* vi. II. 150 The king eagerly caught at the hint. **1850** Tennyson *In Mem.* xiv, And I perceived no touch of change, No hint of death in all his frame.

b. A small piece of practical information.

1777 P. Thicknesse *Year's Journey* II. 221 (*heading*) General hints to strangers who travel to France. **1807** R. Southey *Lett. fr. England* (1951) 348 The Monthly is more miscellaneous in its contents... All sorts of heretical opinions are started here, agricultural hints thrown out, and queries propounded of all kinds. **1830** Coleridge & Southey *Devil's Walk* 24 The Devil was charm'd, for it gave him a hint For improving the prisons of Hell. **1841** S. Ellis (*title*) Family secrets; or, Hints to those who would make home happy. **1872** *Young Englishwoman* Nov. 598 Household hints for young housewives. **1926** R. Macaulay *Crewe Train* II. x. 181 Audrey gave them household hints, about how to keep the kettle from furring, and the stove and the milk jar from smelling. **1972** *Guardian* 29 Mar. 11/5 Angela Kay's Household Hints.. has a pretty good selection of useful answers to some eight hundred possible problems.

3. *Comb.* (*nonce-wds.*)

1671 Glanvill *Disc. M. Stubbe* 34 Put these Passages into your Hint-box, or into your Snuff-box, if you think fit. *a* **1680** Butler *Rem.* (1759) II. 294 The Hint-Keeper of Gresham College is the only competent Judge to decide the Controversy.

hint (hɪnt), *v.* [f. HINT *sb.*, sense 2.]

1. *trans.* To give a hint of; to suggest or indicate slightly, so that one's meaning may be caught by the intelligent. **a.** with simple obj.

1648 *Hunting of Fox* 13 It will not be amisse to hint both unto you. **1655** J. JANE in *Nicholas Papers* (Camden) III. 228 The reason I formerly hinted to you. **1665** HOOKE *Microgr.* 209 Which.. may hint us the reason of that so much admired appearance.. in mother of Pearl-shells. **1725** DE FOE *Voy. round World* (1840) 241 The Doctor hinted it to me. **1790** PALEY *Horæ Paul.* Rom. i. 10 Nothing is yet said or hinted concerning the place. **1849** MACAULAY *Hist. Eng.* iii. I. 387 Oates.. had hinted a suspicion that the Jesuits were at the bottom of the scheme.

b. with obj. clause.

1665 HOOKE *Microgr.* 157 To hint that it is not safe to conclude any thing to be positively this or that. **1743** JOHNSON *Let. to Cave* Aug. in *Boswell*, As you hinted to me that you had many calls for money. **1832** G. DOWNES *Lett. Cont. Countries* I. 174 It was hinted to the elderly Frenchman that their nocturnal departure boded no good.

c. With direct speech as obj.

1843 DICKENS *Christmas Carol* iii. 107 'I'm sure he is very rich, Fred,' hinted Scrooge's niece. **1891** C. GRAVES *Field of Tares* 41 'I have been a stranger to the neighborhood,' returned the other, 'for years.' 'Many years?' hinted Mr. Brinnilow.

2. a. *intr.* ***hint at***: to make a slight, but intelligible suggestion of; = 1 a.

1697 ADDISON *Pref. Dryden's Georg.* (1721) 204 Agriculture ought to be some way hinted at throughout the whole Poem. **1735** LD. HARDWICKE in W. Selwyn *Law Nisi Prius* (1817) II. 986, I never heard such a justification in an action for a libel even hinted at. **1885** HAWTHORNE *Fr. & It. Jrnls.* II. 218 The spectator's imagination completes what the artist merely hints at.

b. With other constructions; also *absol.*

1865 *Punch* 21 Jan. 32 If I wos allowed to 'int, Ladies, I shud say, Torse Hup! **1891** HARDY *Group of Noble Dames* 77 Her husband's tutor was found to hint very strongly against such a step. **1894** G. DU MAURIER *Trilby* III. VII. 178 The night above was dark, but 'star-dials hinted of morn'.

†**c.** To give a hint to (a person). *Obs. rare.*

1658 SIR T. BROWNE *Hydriot.* Ep. Ded. A iij, We were hinted by the occasion, not catched the opportunity to write of old things, or intrude upon the Antiquary.

3. quasi-*trans.* (*nonce-uses.*) To send *off*, do *away*, by a hint.

1829 MARRYAT *F. Mildmay* ii, I was therefore 'hinted off'. **1830** *Fraser's Mag.* II. 182 He hints away every merit poor old Sherry could claim.

Hence **hinted** *ppl. a.* (whence **hintedly** *adv.*); **hinting** *vbl. sb.* and *ppl. a.* (whence **hintingly** *adv.*).

1820 L. HUNT *Indicator* No. 15 (1822) I. 115 The more obscure and awful hintings of the world unknown. *a* **1845** HOOD *Lamia* i. 55 If my brows, Or any hinting feature, show dislike. **1846** RUSKIN *Mod. Paint.* I. II. II. v. §10 She always tells a story, however hintedly and vaguely. **1851** THACKERAY *Eng. Hum.* iv. (1858) 191 There is a peculiar, hinted, pathetic sweetness and melody. **1892** *Cassell's Fam. Mag.* Aug. 536/1 '[It] might as well stand in my bedroom', Aston hintingly said.

hint: see HENT *v.* and *sb.*, HIND *a.*

hinter ('hɪntə(r)). [f. HINT *v.* + -ER¹.] One who or that which hints or gives a hint.

a **1659** CLEVELAND *Lond. Lady* 19 The hinter at each turn of Covent Garden.. the robust Church warden Of Lincoln's Inn back-corner. **1765** *Chron.* in *Ann. Reg.* 145/1 The hinter of it intitled to parliamentary reward. **1838** SOUTHEY *Lett.* (1856) IV. 544 Three poems, all designed as hinters.. Requiring them to mend their speed.

‖**hinterland** ('hɪntəlænd). [a. Ger. *hinterland*, f. *hinter-* behind + *land* land.] **1.** The district behind that lying along the coast (or along the shore of a river); the 'back country'. Also applied spec. to the area lying behind a port, and to the fringe areas of a town or city.

1890 *Spectator* 19 July, The delimitation of the Hinterland behind Tunis and Algiers. **1891** *Daily News* 12 June 5/2 Lord Salisbury even recognises.. the very modern doctrine of the Hinterland, which he expounds as meaning that 'those who possess the coast also possess the plain which is watered by the rivers that run to the coast'. **1897** MARY KINGSLEY *W. Africa* 408 The inhabitants of the shores and hinterland of Corisco Bay are.. savages. *a* **1910** in L. D. Stamp *Gloss. Geogr. Terms* (1961) 235 *Hinderland, Hinterland*, the region the seaborne trade of which belongs to a particular seaport or seaboard. **1922** *Geogr. Rev.* Apr. 260 The main factor which determined the selection of ports in prehistoric times was the presence of a populous hinterland of effective buyers. **1936** E. VAN CLEEF *Trade Centers & Trade Routes* iii. 34 The immediately contiguous territory within the continuous hinterland which in some instances contributes to the formation of the metropolitan city has been termed by the Germans, the 'Umland' or country about. **1938** A. J. SARGENT *Seaports & Hinterlands* 3 A port, essentially, is a transit area, a gateway through which goods and people move from and to the sea, by way of rail, inland waterway, or sometimes by road. The region to and from which this movement is directed is commonly and somewhat vaguely described as the hinterland. **1945** E. WAUGH *Brideshead Revisited* 7 Here the close, homogeneous territory of housing estates and cinemas ended and the hinterland began. **1950** *Geogr. Jrnl.* CXVI. 64 The approximate boundaries of urban spheres of influence or hinterlands. **1968** *Guardian* 23 Oct. 9 As Clydeside developed industrially so it attracted labour from its own hinterland and from famine-stricken Ireland.

2. *fig.* and *transf.*

1919 M. K. BRADBY *Psycho-Analysis* (1920) 75 Unexplored territories full of mystery and danger in the hinterland of their own minds. *Ibid.* 251 The individual who is introduced to the 'hinterland' of his own conscious being. *a* **1930** D. H. LAWRENCE *Last Poems* (1932) 182 We are mostly unexplored hinterland. **1965** *New Statesman* 23 Apr. 646/3 The council meets in that dour ecclesiastical hinterland of Westminster Abbey, where you can buy a second-hand cassock.

3. *Geol.* (See quot. 1961.)

1937 WOOLDRIDGE & MORGAN *Physical Basis Geogr.* vi. 76 The African 'hinterland' is believed to have moved northward towards the European 'foreland'. **1961** J. CHALLINOR *Dict. Geol.* 100/2 *Hinterland*, the moving block which compresses the sediments of a geosyncline and forces them towards the foreland.

hintzeite ('hɪntsaɪt). *Min.* [ad. G. *hintzeït* (L. Milch 1890, in *Zeitschr. f. Kryst. und Min.* XVIII. 480), f. the name of C.A.F. *Hintze* (1851–1916), German mineralogist: see -ITE¹.] = HEINTZITE.

1891, 1951 [see HEINTZITE].

hiortdahlite ('hjɔːtdɑːlaɪt). *Min.* [ad. G. *hiortdahlit* (W. C. Brögger 1888, in *Nyt Mag. f. Naturvidensk.* (1889) XXXI. III. 232), f. the name of Th. H. *Hiortdahl* (1839–1925), Norwegian chemist: see -ITE¹.] A rare mineral, essentially a fluoride-containing silicate of zirconium, sodium, and calcium, found in yellow triclinic crystals.

1892 E. S. DANA *Dana's Syst. Min.* (ed. 6) 377 (*heading*) Hiortdahlite. **1968** *Mineral. Abstr.* XVIII. 304/2 Hiortdahlite occurs as columnar crystals up to 3 and 4 cm long in pegmatite.. in the Korgeredaba pluton in southeastern Sangilen, Tuva.

hip (hɪp), *sb.*¹ Forms: 1 hype, 3 heppe, 3–4 hupe, 4–5 hepe, 4–7 hippe, 5 hype, 5–6 hyppe, 6–7 hyp, 4– hip. [OE. *hype* masc. = OLG. **hupi* (MDu. *höpe, hōpe, hēpe, huepe*, Du. *heup* fem.), OHG. *huf*, pl. *huffi* (MHG. *huf*, pl. *hüffe*, Ger. *hüfte* fem.), Goth. *hups*, pl. *hupeis*:—OTeut. **hupi-z*, pre-Teut. **kubis.*]

1. a. The projecting part of the body on each side formed by the lateral expansions of the pelvis and upper part of the thigh-bone, in men and quadrupeds; the haunch. Also used for the hip-joint.

971 *Blickl. Hom.* 11 Anra ȝehwylc hæfde sweord ofer his hype. *c* **1000** ÆLFRIC *Gloss.* in Wr.-Wülcker 159/43 *Clunes*, hypas. *a* **1225** *Ancr. R.* 280 He iseih hu ueole þe grimme wrastlare of helle breid up on his hupe. *c* **1325** *Poem Times Edw. II*, 134 in *Pol. Songs* (Camden) 329 A litel lettre In a box upon his hepe. **1382** WYCLIF *Gen.* xxiv. 3 Put thin hoond vndir myn hip [Vulg. *femur*]. *c* **1386** CHAUCER *Prol.* 472 A foot mantel aboute hir hipes [*v.rr.* hypes, hepis, hippes, hupes] large. *c* **1475** *Pict. Voc.* in Wr.-Wülcker 750/8 *Hic lumbus*, a hepe. *c* **1489** CAXTON *Sonnes of Aymon* x. 267 Wounded hym sore vpon his hippe. **1581** MULCASTER *Positions* vi. (1887) 48 Daunsing.. strengtheneth weake hippes, fainting legges. **1650** BULWER *Anthropomet.* xxi. 233 They were lame, and their Hyps contracted and crampt. **1753** HOGARTH *Anal. Beauty* x. 60 To be held fast to the outside of the hip. **1882** OUIDA *Maremma* I. 110 Her hands lightly resting on her hips.

fig. **1879** J. BURROUGHS *Locusts & W. Honey* 127 A little trout-lake which the mountain carried high on his hip.

†**b.** A projecting part of female dress, covering the hip. *Obs.*

1710 STEELE *Tatler* No. 245 ¶2 [She] carried off the following Goods.. Two Pair of Hips of the newest Fashion.

c. *Zool.* The first joint of the leg in the Arthropoda: = COXA 2.

1834 [see COXA 2]. **1834** MCMURTRIE *Cuvier's Anim. Kingd.* 307 Their legs.. are composed of seven joints, of which the two first form the hip, the third the thigh, the fourth and fifth the tibia, and the two others the tarsus.

2. Phrases. **a.** ***down in the hip***(***s***: said of a horse when the haunch-bone is injured; hence *fig.*, out of sorts, out of spirits. (Cf. also HIP *sb.*³)

1729 SWIFT *Grand Question Debated* 178 The Doctor was plaguily down in the hips. **1865** YOUATT *Horse* xvii. (1872) 382 The horse is then said to be down in the hip.

b. ***on*** or ***upon the hip*** (usually, *to take, get, have* one on the hip, phrases taken from wrestling): at a disadvantage; in a position in which one is likely to be overthrown or overcome.

c **1460** *Towneley Myst.* (Surtees) 90, I shrew you so smart, And me on my hyppys, bot if Igart Abate. **1587** GOLDING *De Mornay* i. 9 If these.. be but taken on the hip, they fall to quaking, they crie out vnto heauen. **1591** HARINGTON *Orl. Fur.* XLVI. cxvii. 4 To get the Pagan on the hippe: And hauing caught him right, he doth him lift, By nimble sleight. **1596** SHAKS. *Merch. V.* IV. i. 334 Now infidell I haue thee on the hip. **1602** WARNER *Alb. Eng.* x. lix. (1612) 260 When Dauid seem'd, in common sence, alreadie on the hip. **1655** GURNALL *Chr. in Arm.* i. §4 (1669) 63/2 Sometimes the Christain hath his Enemy on the hip, yea, on the ground. *a* **1700** B. E. *Dict. Cant. Crew*, s.v., *Upon the Hip*, at an Advantage, in Wrestling or Business. **1865** TROLLOPE *Belton Est.* xvii. 199 Feeling that she had the culprit on the hip. **1967** *Listener* 16 Nov. 628/3 You have me on the hip here a bit because I think.. that all these old ideas we had are as dead as the dodo.

†**c.** ***to fetch over the hips***: see quots. *Obs.*

1586 HOOKER *Girald. Irel.* in *Holinshed* II. 89/1 The lord Thomas being iustice or vicedeputie.. fetcht both the Alens so roundlie ouer the hips.. as they were the more egerlie spurd to compasse his confusion. **1624** SANDERSON 12 *Serm.* (1637) 184 Could any of you take it well at your neighbours hand, should hee.. fetch you over the hippe upon a branch of some blinde, uncouth, and pretermitted Statute?

d. ***hip and thigh***: with overwhelming blows or slaughter; unsparingly. Usually with *smite* or the like. (Of Biblical origin.)

1560 BIBLE (Genev.) *Judg.* xv. 8 He smote them hippe and thigh with a mighty plague. *a* **1641** BP. MOUNTAGU *Acts & Mon.* (1642) 115 Destroy all opposition whatsoever, Hip and Thigh.. Root and Branch. **1832** TENNYSON *Dream Fair Wom.* 238 Moreover it is written that my race Hew'd Ammon, hip and thigh, from Aroer On Arnon unto Minneth. **1863** WHYTE MELVILLE *Gladiators* I. 255 To smite the heathen hip-and-thigh with the edge of the sword.

attrib. **1832** SOUTHEY in *Q. Rev.* XLVII. 502 A hip-and-thigh reformer.. has replied to Lord Nugent.

3. *Arch.* **a.** A projecting inclined edge on a roof, extending from the ridge or apex to the eaves, and having a slope on each side; the rafter at this edge, the hip-rafter: see also attrib. uses in 4 c.

1690 LEYBOURN *Curs. Math.* 901 The Bricklayer sometimes will require to have running measure for Hyps and Valleys. **1703** MOXON *Mech. Exerc.* 240 Here at London, the Vallies are commonly tiled with Plain Tiles, and the Hips with Ridge.. Tiles. **1828** HUTTON *Course Math.* II. 87 When the angle bends inwards, it is called a valley; but when outwards, it is called a hip. **1887** *Homœop. World* 1 Nov. 511 The ridges, hips, and finials are of terra cotta.

b. A spandrel: see quot.

1726 LEONI *Alberti's Archit.* I. 55/2 The vacuities.. left between the back.. of the Arch, and the upright of the Wall it is turn'd from, call'd by Workmen, the Hips of the Arch.

4. *attrib.* and *Comb.* **a.** *attrib.* Reaching up to the hips, esp. as ***hip-boot.*** (See also *hip-bath* in b.)

1883 *Pall Mall G.* 6 Apr. 7/1 Two indiarubber hip fishing stockings. **1893** *Outing* (U.S.) XXII. 124/2 Gossamer hip-boots are good if of reliable stock. **1922** S. LEWIS *Babbitt* x. 138 He gloated on fly-rods and gorgeous rubber hip-boots. **1969** *Sears Catal.* Spring/Summer 709 Ted Williams hip boots have nylon added to latex for long-lasting strength and comfort.

b. *Comb.* in sense 1, as ***hip-ache, -deep, -swaying, -swinging*** adjs.; **hip-bath**, a bath in which a person can sit immersed up to the hips; **hip-belt**, antiquary's name for a belt worn diagonally about the left hip and the right side of the waist, a part of mediæval armour; **hip-disease**, a disease of the hip-joint, characterized by inflammation, fungous growth, and caries of the bones; †**hip-evil** = *hip-disease*; **hip-flask**, a flask for intoxicating liquor carried in a hip-pocket; †**hip-halt** *a.*, lame in the hip, limping; †**hip-hap**, a covering for the hips; **hip-hole**, a hollow dug in the ground to accommodate the hip (for greater comfort when sleeping on hard ground); **hip-huggers** *sb. pl.*, trousers that fit tightly to the hips; also **hip-hugger**, used *attrib.* of such trousers; **hip-hugging** *a.*, fitting closely to the hips; **hip-length** *a.*, denoting a garment which reaches down to the hips; **hip-line**, the outline or contour of the hips; **hip-lock**, in *Wrestling*, a close grip in which one contestant places a hip or leg in front of the other, and attempts to swing him over this to the ground; **hip-pain**, pain in the hip-joint, HIP-GOUT; **hip-pocket**, a pocket in a pair of trousers, just behind the hip; **hip-revolver**, one carried in the hip-pocket; **hip-strap**, a strap lying on the horse's hips, and supporting the breeching in a carriage-harness; **hip throw**, a throw in Judo; **hip-yoke**, in dressmaking, a shaped piece extending from the waist to the hips, designed to fit the figure closely without gathers. Also HIP-BONE, etc.

1822–34 *Good's Study Med.* (ed. 4) IV. 47 Even the *hip-bath, however, though it mitigates the pain, occasionally does nothing more. **1860** *Illustr. Lond. News* 26 May 503/1 Hip baths and sponge baths, of the best designs. **1874** BOUTELL *Arms & Arm.* x. 197 From the *hip-belt was suspended, on the left side, the long sword. *Ibid.* 203 In some few instances, however, the hip-belt appears worn over the taces. **1897** *Pall Mall Mag.* Dec. 507 My carriers.. were *hip-deep in the grass. **1879** *St. George's Hosp. Rep.* IX. 329 Her right lower limb was wasted and shortened from old *hip-disease. **1782** W. HEBERDEN *Comm.* xxi. (1806) 107 The *hip-evil evidently belongs to the scrofula. **1923** E. MARBURY *My Crystal Ball* lxxi. 352 Let these same people frequent ballrooms.. and they will find the *hip flasks in evidence and the consequent conditions a sorry spectacle. **1928** *Sunday Dispatch* 2 Sept. 7/1 [American *loq.*] We have become a people who think 'likker', talk it, and lead a hip-flask life! **1944** BRAHMS & SIMON *Titania has Mother* xiii. 145 Merry moujiks drinking from hip flasks and lolling in all directions. **1973** D. LEES *Rape of Quiet Town* ii. 33 A hip-flask full of brandy. **1390** GOWER *Conf.* II. 159 Therto he was *hippe-halt. *a* **1600** *Turn. Tottenham* 218 Some come hyp halt, and some trippand. *a* **1625** FLETCHER *Love's Cure* II. ii, A pox o' this filthy fardingale, this *hip-hape! **1936** F. CLUNE *Roaming round Darling* xxv. 271 Then we made a fire, boiled the billy, gouged out *hip-holes for ourselves, and camped till daylight. **1965** G. MCINNES *Road to Gundagai* x. 167, I tried digging a hip-hole. **1967** *Boston Sunday Herald* 26 Mar. (Advt.), Zowie prints and belted *hip-huggers.. striped and printed. **1967** *New Yorker* 26 Aug. 82 There are separates, too, such as long jackets, stovepipe hip-hugger trousers, [etc.]. **1973** *Houston* (Texas) *Chron. Mag. People, Places, Pleasures* 14 Oct. 24/5 Today the young women wear shorts and hip-huggers, the older sit in their traditional long black dresses. **1969** *Times* 7 Nov. 14/1 *Hip-hugging..

trousers. **1971** B. MALAMUD *Tenants* 43 Willie..was dolled up in hip-hugging yellow pants and two-tone brown-and-black shoes. **1921** *Hip length [see *gum-boots* s.v. GUM *sb.*^{2} 9]. **1931** *Daily Express* 18 Mar. 5/3 Hip-length coats. **1961** *Harper's Bazaar* Feb. 75 The hip-length cardigan. **1907** *Westm. Gaz.* 30 Mar. 14/1 It [*sc.* a skirt] blurs over the aggressive *hip-line. **1935** *Times* 2 Dec. 19/4 The coat just reaches the hipline. **1973** *Country Life* 8 Mar. 635/2 Dress in black-and-white-check wool with smooth hipline. **1888** *Century Mag.* July 373/2 The Tartar..caught him around the body, and, with a *hip-lock and a tremendous heave, threw him over his head. **1727** BRADLEY *Fam. Dict.* s.v. *Elm*, An admirable Remedy for the Sciatica, or *Hip-pain. **1880** *Cimarron News & Press* 22 July 3/2 Lee snatched Armstrong's revolver from his *hip pocket and pointed it at Armstrong. **1887** *Pall Mall G.* 16 July 7/1 Drawing his own six-shooter from his hip-pocket. **1922** S. LEWIS *Babbitt* xviii. 228 Drinking together from hip-pocket flasks. **1972** *Guardian* 27 Oct. 12/1 A general election..is one option in Mr Heath's hip pocket list. **1898** DOYLE *Trag. Korosko* iv. 109 I've got a little *hip revolver which they have not discovered. **1794** W. FELTON *Carriages* (1801) II. Gloss., **Hip Straps*, a part of the harness, which lies on the hips of the horse, and buckles to the breeching tugs, which it supports. **1920** *Glasgow Herald* 17 Apr. 6 The Hawaiian corps de ballet..began a..performance of rhythmical *hip-swaying dances. **1965** *Midnight* 12 July 3/1 The *hip-swinging wedding party was celebrated to the strains of the watusi and frug, pounded out by Christopher's group, the Wild Ones. **1966** *Word Study* Oct. 7/1 A hip-swinging, slender-bodied blonde. **1957** TAKAGAKI & SHARP *Techniques of Judo* II. iv. 50 Generally, when a *hip throw is employed, the opponent turns his back into you and pulls you to the right front corner by your right arm which is pulled tightly across his chest. **1960** *Oxf. Mail* 10 Mar. 8/2 He..went on to win the match with another ankle throw, with which he countered an attempted hip throw. **1931** *Daily Tel.* 21 May 6/4 Small gathers at each side of the *hip yoke in front.

c. *Comb.* in sense 3, as **hip-knob**, a knob or ornament surmounting the hip of a roof; **hip-mould, -moulding**, (*a*) the mould or templet by which the hip of a roof is set out; (*b*) the 'back' or outer angle of the hip (Chambers *Cycl.* 1727–41); **hip-pole**, a pole supporting the hip-rafter; **hip-rafter**, the rafter extending along the hip of a roof; **hip-tile**, a tile of special shape used at the hip of a roof; **hip-truss**, a combination of timbers supporting the hip-rafter. Also HIP-ROOF.

1849 *Ecclesiologist* IX. 71 A barge-board, having a cross, with sunken trefoiled panels for a *hip-knob. **1703** MOXON *Mech. Exerc.* 156 *Back* or **Hip-molding*, the backward Hips or Valley-Rafters in the way of an Angle for the back part of a Building. **1782** *Phil. Trans.* LXXII. 367 This *hip-pole was supported, at its proper distance from the *hip-rafter, by an iron-strap, or holdfast. **1703** MOXON *Mech. Exerc.* 240 *Hip Tiles, which are used sometimes for..Hips of Rooffs. **1842–76** GWILT *Archit.* §1836 Ridge roof and hip tiles are formed cylindrically, to cover the ridges of houses. **1879** *Cassell's Techn. Educ.* IV. 284/2 The true shape of the *hip-truss.

hip (hɪp), **hep** (hɛp), *sb.*^{2} Forms: *α.* 1 **héope, hiope**, 4–5 **hepe**, 4–6 **heppe**, 5 **heepe**, 7 **hepp**, 6– **hep.** *β.* 5 **hipe**, 6 **hipp**, 6– **hip.** [OE. *héope, hiope* wk. fem., from same root as OS. *hiopo*, OHG. *hiufo, hiafo*, MHG. *hiefe* wk. masc., thorn-bush, bramble:—OTeut. types **heupôn-*, **heupon-*. The regular mod. repr. of OE. *héope*, ME. *hēpe*, would be *hepe* or *heep*; *hep* and *hip* appear to be due respectively to ME. and mod.Eng. shortening of (eː).]

The fruit of the wild rose, or of roses in general.

α. *c* **725** *Corpus Gloss.* 1858 *Sicomoros*, heopan. *c* **1000** *Sax. Leechd.* II. 96 Genim brer þe hiopan on weaxaþ. *c* **1000** ÆLFRIC *Gloss.* in Wr.-Wülcker 133/36 *Butunus*, heope. **13..** *K. Alis.* 4983 Hawen, hepen, slon, and rabben. *c* **1350** *Will. Palerne* 1811 Hawes, hepus, & hakernes & þe hasel-notes. *c* **1386** CHAUCER *Sir Thopas* 36 Sweete as is the Brembul flour That bereth the rede hepe [*v.rr.* heepe, heppe, hipe]. **1483** *Cath. Angl.* 183/2 An Heppe, *cornum*. **1486** *Bk. St. Albans* E v a, Hawys and heeppes and other thyngs ynow. **1562** TURNER *Herbal* II. 119 Let them..take hede that make tartes of Heppes. **1565** GOLDING *Ovid's Met.* I. (1593) 4 Men themselves..Did live by respis, heps and haws. **1626** BACON *Sylva* §633 It may bee Heps and Brier-Berries would doe the like. **1648** SANDERSON *Serm.* II. 247 Hepps and haws grow in every hedge. **1794** MARTYN *Rousseau's Bot.* v. 52 The hep which is the fruit of it [rose]. **1861** S. THOMSON *Wild Fl.* III. (ed. 4) 265 Let us take the rose hep. **1883** *Century Mag.* XXVI. 354 Content to gather the heps and sow the seed.

β. **14..** [see *α* quot. *c* **1386**]. **1581** RICHE *Farew. Mil. Prof.* D iij, Hippes, Hawes, and Slowes. **1591** SPENSER *M. Hubberd* 948 Eating hipps, and drinking watry fome. **1601** HOLLAND *Pliny* I. 361 A red berry like to the hips of an Eglantine. **1711** ADDISON *Spect.* No. 69 ¶5 That no Fruit grows Originally among us, besides Hips and Haws, Acorns and Pig-Nuts. **1784** COWPER *Task* I. 120, I fed on scarlet hips and stony haws. **1840** HOOD *Kilmansegg, Courtship* xix, Pretty Cis..Who blushes as red as haws and hips. *a* **1861** MRS. BROWNING *De Profundis* ix, The little red hip on the tree.

b. *Comb.*, as ***hep-*** or ***hip-berry, -bramble, -briar, -rose, -stone, -thorn, -tree.***

c **1000** *Sax. Leechd.* II. 266 Heopbremles leaf. *a* **1387** *Sinon. Barth.* 36 *Rosa canina*..heppe-brer. *c* **1450** *Alphita* 157 s.v. *Rubus*, hepebrembel. **1483** *Cath. Angl.* 183/2 An Heppe tre [*A.* Hepe tre), *cornus*. **1513** DOUGLAS *Æneis* III. i. 46 Quhar hepthorne buskis on the top grew hie. **1770** WARING in *Phil. Trans.* LXI. 379 Almost as frequent as the common hep-tree. **1797** W. JOHNSON tr. *Beckmann's Invent.* I. 215 The wax almost resembles the hip-stone. **1829** GLOVER *Hist. Derby* I. 116 Red dog rose or hep tree.

hip (hɪp), *sb.*^{3} Also *pl.* **hipps.** [A variant of HYP, abbreviation of *hypochondria*. The spelling with *y* is more usual in the sb.; but *i* prevails in the vb. and derivatives.] Morbid depression of spirits; the 'blues'.

1710 *Tatler* No. 230 ¶5 Will Hazzard has got the Hipps, having lost to the Tune of Five Hundr'd Pound. **1725** BAILEY *Erasm. Colloq.* (1877) 130 (D.) When he is neither in a passion, nor in the hipps [*sollicitus*], nor in liquor. **1762** C. JOHNSTON *Reverie* (1763) I. 229 That..sentimental strain gives me the hip. *c* **1800** R. CUMBERLAND *John de Lancaster* (1809) I. 256 You have caught the hip of your hypochondriac wife.

hip, *sb.*^{4}: see HIP *int.*

† **hip**, *v.*^{1} *Obs.* or *dial.* Forms: 3–4 **huppe**, 4 **hupe**, (*pa. t.* 3 **hupte**, 4 **hipte**), 4–5 **hyppe, hippe**, 7– **hip.** [ME. *hüppe, hyppe*:—OE. type **hyppan* = OHG. **hupfen*, MHG. and Ger. *hüpfen*, Goth. type **huppjan*. This word is not found in the early stage of any of the langs.: cf. OE. *hoppian*, ON. *hoppa* to HOP.]

1. *intr.* To hop; now *north.* to hop on one foot.

A bird is said to 'hop' on two feet, a man to 'hip' on one.

a **1250** *Owl & Night.* 1636 þe nihtegale..hupte uppon on blowe ris. *c* **1300** *St. Brandan* 500 He hipte him amidde the see out of the schip biside. **1340** HAMPOLE *Pr. Consc.* 1539 Some gas hypand als a ka. **13..** *Gaw. & Gr. Knt.* 1459 þe hede hypped aȝayn, were-so-euer hit hitte. **1377** LANGL. *P. Pl.* B. xv. 557 þat hippe [*v.r.* huppe] aboute in Engelonde to halwe mennes auteres. *c* **1400** *Harl. MS.* 4196 lf. 93 (*Gloss. Hampole's Pr. Consc.* 301), It [þe foule] hipped bifore him in þe gate. **1825** BROCKETT, *Hip*, to hitch or hop on one foot. *Hip-step-and-jump*, a youthful gambol.

fig. *c* **1570** *Schort Somme 1st Bk. Discpl.* 75 Reideris sal..not hip from place to place.

†**2.** To walk lame, limp, hobble. *Obs.*

c **1430** *Pilgr. Lyf Manhode* III. xxx. (1869) 152 Boistows j am, and haltinge, and wronge. To the birly j go hippinge. *c* **1440** *Bone Flor.* 1993 He came thedur wyth an evyll, Hyppyng on two stavys. *c* **1440** *Promp. Parv.* 241/1 Hyppynge, or haltynge, *claudicacio*.

3. To pass over, miss, 'skip'; = OVERHIP. *dial.*

1804 TARRAS *Poems* 28 (Jam.) Rather let's ilk daintie sip; An' ev'ry adverse bliffert hip. **1828** *Craven Dial.*, *Hip*, to pass by, to skip over.

hip, *v.*^{2} [f. HIP *sb.*^{1}]

1. *trans.* To dislocate or injure the hip of; to lame in the hip. See HIPPED *a.*^{1} 3.

1610 MARKHAM *Masterp.* I. xii. 33 If a horse go stiffe, it is a signe either of wrinching, hipping, stifling or foundring either in body or legs.

2. To give a cross-buttock in wrestling; to throw one's adversary over the hip. Cf. HIPE.

1675 COTTON *Scoffer Scoft* 70 And a prime Wrestler as e're tript, Ere gave the Cornish Hug, or Hipt.

3. To form with a hip or sloping edge, as a roof. (See also HIPPED *a.*^{1} 2.)

1669 in Willis & Clark *Cambridge* (1886) II. 557 The roofe ..to be made after the best manner hipt of. **1776** G. SEMPLE *Building in Water* 13 The front of each Pier is hip'd of. **1851** TURNER *Dom. Archit.* I. vii. 346 A very steep tiled roof, hipped all ways.

4. To carry on the hip. *U.S.*

1818 H. C. KNIGHT *Lett. from South* 93 Some mothers here [*sc.* in Kentucky] hip their infants, as do the Sumatrans. **1843** 'R. CARLTON' *New Purchase* xx. 191 Still oftener each [log] is hipped and hipping is done by one man..who adroitly whips up the log on his hip.

hip, *v.*^{3} *colloq.* [f. HIP *sb.*^{3}: perh. back-formation from HIPPED *a.*^{2}] *trans.* To affect with hypochondria; to render low-spirited.

1842 MRS. BROWNING *Grk. Chr. Poets* etc. 94 Take courage! I rather would hearten than hip thee! **1843** LEFEVRE *Life Trav. Phys.* I. I. iii. 62 That my constant attendance upon my patient had hipped me. **1886** F. W. ROBINSON *Fair Maid* III. III. iii. 27 The place hips me to death.

hip, *v.*^{4}: see HIP *int.*

hip (hɪp), *v.*^{5} *slang* (orig. *U.S.*). [f. HIP *a.*] *trans.* To render 'hip'; to inform. (Freq. as pa. pple. in passive.) Hence **hipped** *ppl. a.* well-informed, 'with it'; (esp. with *on*) fond of, 'bitten with'.

1920 F. SCOTT FITZGERALD *This Side of Paradise* (1921) II. iii. 246 I'm hipped on Freud and all that. **1925** T. DREISER *Amer. Trag.* (1926) II. III. xv. 191 He is still hipped over this second girl. **1927** *Daily Express* 24 Oct. 8 'New York,' as the manager of one of the largest hotels remarked lately, 'is badly "hipped" on dining in public.' **1932** *Evening Sun* (Baltimore) 9 Dec. 31/4 *Hip*, to give information. **1938** *Amer. Speech* XIII. 314/1 *Hipped to the jive*, well informed on the latest slang expressions. **1944** D. BURLEY *Dan Burley's Orig. Handbk. Harlem Jive* 19 Uncle is hipping a whole lot of cats as to what to do when the action gets off the track. **1945** L. SHELLY *Jive Talk Dict.* 26 *Hipped spade*, smart Negro. **1947** *Esquire* Apr. 76 'Are there any squares in this outfit?' 'No, man, we're all hipped.' **1954** *Encounter* Feb. 55/1 If I admitted..to being a little bit hipped on the subject of Trotsky, I could sometimes gain an indulgent if flickering attention. **1958** J. KEROUAC *Subterraneans* 90 Sand must have hipped him quietly in a whisper somewhere what was happening with the lovers. **1962** *Spectator* 20 Apr. 511 Betjeman is absolutely hipped on his subject. **1973** *Black World* Jan. 64/2, I had just about decided to find some way to hip her to contraceptives.

hip, *int.* (*sb.*^{4}) Also **hep.**

1. 'An exclamation or calling to one; the same as the Latin *eho, heus!*' (J.).

1752 AINSWORTH *Lat. Dict.* **1768–74** TUCKER *Lt. Nat.* (1852) I. 34 Perhaps Dr. Hartley..may give me a hip, and call out, 'Prithee, friend, do not think to slip so easily by me'.

2. An exclamation used (usually repeated thrice) to introduce a united cheer: hence as *sb.*

1827 HONE *Every-day Bk.* 12 To toss off the glass, and huzza after the 'hip! hip! hip!' of the toast giver. *a* **1845** HOOD *Sniffing a Birthday* xiv, No flummery then from flowery lips, No three times three and hip-hip-hips! **1849** THACKERAY *Pendennis* xvi, 'Here's Mrs. Smirke's good health: hip, hip, hurray!'

Hence **hip** *v.*^{4} *intr.*, to shout 'hip'; *trans.*, to greet with 'hip'. Also **hip-(hip-)hurrah** *v.*

1818 MOORE *Mem.* (1853) II. 157 They hipped and hurraed me. **1832** *Examiner* 609/2 One set of men 'hip hurrah' and rattle decanter stoppers. **1871** CARLYLE in *Mrs. Carlyle's Lett.* I. 116 In the course of the installation dinner, at some high point of the hep-hep hurrahing.

hip (hɪp), *a.* *slang* (orig. *U.S.*). [Origin unknown.] = HEP *a.* Hence **'hip-cat** = HEP-CAT; **'hipness**, the condition or quality of being 'hip'.

1904 G. V. HOBART *Jim Hickey* i. 15 At this rate it'll take about 629 shows to get us to Jersey City, are you hip? **1926** *Detective Fiction Weekly* 16 Jan. 640/2, I sashayed for a legger an' run into a rube hip agent with a bottle and some jake which helped some. **1938** C. CALLOWAY *Hi De Ho* 16 *Hip*, wise, sophisticated, anyone with boots on. **1944** C. HIMES *Black on Black* (1973) 199 I'm a hipcat from way back. **1946** MEZZROW & WOLFE *Really Blues* xii. 226 Their hipness..bubbled up out of the brute scramble and sweat of living. **1951** *San Diego Even. Tribune* 28 June a-2/5 We did it because we thought it was 'hip' or smart. **1958** W. BRYANT *Jive in Hi-Fi* 13 The correct word is 'hip'. It comes from a story of a fisherman warning young fishermen never to wade in deep water without hip boots on because they could run into trouble. So, when you hear the words, 'I'm hip' or 'I'm booted' it's said to let you know they have no fear of trouble or that they understand what's shaking [i.e., happening]. **1957** J. KEROUAC *On Road* (1958) 10 Elmer Hassel, with that hip sneer. **1959** *Spectator* 31 July 134/2 He has a fast line of jive-patter and uses such hip endearments as 'angel-cake' and 'gorgeous'. *Ibid.* 7 Aug. 161/2 Audiences there are hip to the latest gossip. **1959** C. MACINNES *Absolute Beginners* 164 It was like getting a hip cat into a symphony concert, but I succeeded. **1959** *Observer* 4 Oct. 9/7 The only really *hip* Labour candidate. **1961** *New Left Rev.* May–June 47/1 The goofs of the second act did a lot to dispel the hipness of the first. **1961** *Listener* 9 Nov. 786/1 As Norman Mailer would say, it's 'hip' to use obscure terms and meaningless symbols. **1966** H. S. THOMPSON *Hell's Angels* (1967) 68 Frank was so completely hip that he went down to Hollywood and bought the blue-and-yellow striped sweatshirt that Lee Marvin wore in *The Wild One*. **1971** *Black Scholar* Jan. 22/2 As Cannonball Adderly has said 'Hipness is not a state of mind. It is a fact of life.' **1972** V. FERDINAND in A. Chapman *New Black Voices* 472 We sometimes..go in for that kind of living thinking it's hip.

hip-bone. [HIP *sb.*^{1}] The bone of the hip; i.e. either the *ilium*, or the *ischium*, or the *os innominatum* as a whole, or the upper part of the thigh-bone.

c **1400** *Lanfranc's Cirurg.* 23 þe schuldre boones & þe hipe boones [*B.* hepe bonys]. *c* **1475** *Pict. Voc.* in Wr.-Wülcker 750/10 *Clunis*, a hepebone. **1668** CULPEPPER & COLE *Barthol. Anat.* Man. IV. xvi. 351 Os Ischion or the Hip-bone is the third part. **1684** WOOD *Life* 24 Sept. (O.H.S.) III. 109 Bridge-bone..that bone that holds the two hipp-bones together at the bottom of the belly. **1695** BP. PATRICK *Comm. Gen.* 459 That Sinew (or Tendon) which fastens the Hip-bone in its socket.

hip-cat: see HIP *a.*

hipe (haɪp), *v.* *Wrestling.* [perh. a deriv. of HIP *sb.*^{1}: but the phonology is obscure.] To throw (an antagonist) in a particular manner: see quot. 1870. Hence **hipe** *sb.*, a throw of this kind; freq. with qualifying word, as ***left leg hipe, swinging hipe***, etc.; so **'hiper**, one who uses the hipe in wrestling.

18.. LITT *Wrestliana* in Blaine *Encycl. Rur. Sports* §463 Inside striking..is quite a different mode from what we have termed hipeing..To guard against an inside stroke, or hipe, the defendant should, if possible, keep himself on the ground. **1823** W. LITT *Wrestliana* 168 As a hiper, he is certainly the quickest and best on the list. **1870** BLAINE *Encycl. Rur. Sports* §462 Throwing, by lifting from the ground, and rapidly placing one of the knees between the thighs of the antagonist, is provincially called hipeing. **1883** *Standard* 24 Mar. 3/7 Wannop took the first fall by the outside hipe. *Ibid.*, Lowden hiped J. Wannop. **1888** *Encycl. Brit.* XXIV. 690/1 The 'left leg hipe'..consists in lifting and swinging him [*sc.* one's adversary] round to the right, then striking the inside of his right thigh with the outside of the left thigh, by which he gets off his balance and falls; the 'right leg hipe' is the same action *mutatis mutandis*. **1893** *Carlisle Patriot* 26 May 3/3 (Cumbld. Gloss.), In the third round S—— threw M—— after a tight bout with the inside hipe. In the next tussle J—— passed S—— by means of the outside hipe. **1893** ROBINSON & GILPIN *Wrestling* 56 Robley ..has been credited with being the first introducer of the swinging hype.

hipe (haɪp), *sb.*^{2} *Army slang.* [From the sound of the substitute commonly used for the word *arms* in such commands as 'Slope arms!'] A rifle.

1917 P. MACGILL *Brown Brethren* vi. 89 He seemed to have lost all interest in his best friend, his "ipe'. *Ibid.* xii. 173 'The sun's catchin' the sniper's 'ipe. **1927** D. B. W. LEWIS *On Straw* 59 Brass-Hats rich and ripe Clicked their heels together, Sloped the Army's hipe. **1942** 'N. SHUTE' *Pied Piper* 107 It was full of muckin' Jerries. All loosing off their hipes at Bert and me.

hipe, var. HYPE *v.*[1]

hiper-, obs. var. of HYPER-.

†**hip-frog**. *Obs. rare.* [f. HIP *v.*[1]] A frog that hops.

1611 CORYAT *Crudities* 357, I noted marveilous abundance of little hip-frogges.

hip-girdle. [HIP *sb.*[1]]
1. *Anat.* The pelvic girdle or arch, consisting of the ilium, ischium, and pubis.
2. = *hip-belt*: see HIP *sb.*[1] 4 b.

hip-gout. [f. HIP *sb.*[1] + GOUT.] = SCIATICA.

1598 SYLVESTER *Du Bartas* II. i. III. *Furies* 540 The Flix, the Hip-Gout, and the Watry-Tumour. **1657** W. COLES *Adam in Eden* xxxviii, The same easeth the pains of the Sciatica or Hipgout. **1891** A. RANKEN *Hist. France* I. 476 A remedy for the sciatica, or hip gout.

hip-hop, *adv.* [f. HIP *v.*[1] + HOP *v.*; or reduplication of *hop*, with alternation of lighter and heavier vowel: cf. *drip-drop*, *tip-top*: see DIB *v.*[2]] With hopping movement; with successive hops.

1672 VILLIERS (Dk. Buckhm.) *Rehearsal* III. ii. (Arb.) 87 To go off hip hop, hip hop, upon this occasion, is a thousand times better than any conclusion in the world, I gad. *a* **1729** CONGREVE (J.), Thus while he strives to please, he's forc'd to do't, Like Volscius hip-hop in a single boot. **1819** W. TENNANT *Papistry Storm'd* (1827) 182 Loupin' hip-hop frae spire to spire.

hipil, obs. form of HIPPLE, little heap.

hip-joint. [HIP *sb.*[1]] The joint of the hip, the articulation of the head of the thigh-bone with the ilium.

1794 E. FORD (*title*) Observations on the Disease of the Hip Joint. **1802** PALEY *Nat. Theol.* xxvii. (1830) 372 The ligament within the socket of the hip joint. **1842** E. WILSON *Anat. Vade M.* 123 The movements of the hip-joint are very extensive. **1879** F. POLLOK *Sport Brit. Burmah* I. 63 A young bull..got the shot..in the hip-joint, and fell.

b. hip-joint disease = *hip-disease* (HIP *sb.*[1] 4 b).

1854 MAYNE *Expos. Lex.*, *Hip-Joint Disease*, common term for the disease Coxalgia. **1876** *Clin. Soc. Trans.* IX. 159 She was the subject of hip-joint disease.

hipless ('hɪplɪs), *a. rare.* [f. HIP *sb.*[1] + -LESS.] Destitute of hips.

1870 MISS BROUGHTON *Red as Rose* I. vi. 122 Their little, bustless, waistless, hipless figures. **1897** *Westm. Gaz.* 25 June 10/1 You won't get efficient motherhood from these hipless, rushing women.

†'**hiplings**, *adv. Obs.* [f. HIP *sb.*[1] + -LINGS: cf. *headlings*.] With the hips foremost.

a **1649** WINTHROP *New Eng.* (1825) I. 261 It was a woman child, stillborn..it came hiplings till she turned it.

hipness: see HIP *a.*

hipo-: obs. spelling of HYPO-.

hipocras, obs. form of HIPPOCRAS.

hipparch ('hɪpɑːk). *Gr. Antiq.* [ad. Gr. ἵππαρχος, f. ἵππος horse + -αρχος ruling, ruler.] Commander of the horse; the title of officers appointed to command the cavalry in ancient Greece.

1656 BLOUNT *Glossogr.*, *Hipparch*, the Master of the horses. **1832** J. C. HARE in *Philol. Museum* I. 250 *note*, Callistratus, the son of Empedus, the hipparch. **1847** GROTE *Greece* II. xxxi. IV. 182 There were now created..two hipparchs, for the supreme command of the horsemen.

So **hipparchy** [ad. Gr. ἱππαρχία the office of a ἵππαρχος], the rule or control of horses.

1631 BRATHWAIT *Whimzies*, *Ostler* 70 He speakes in his ostrie (the chiefe seate of his hypparchie) like a frog in a well.

‖**Hipparion** (hɪ'pɛərɪən). *Palæont.* [mod.L., ad. Gr. ἱππάριον pony.] An extinct genus of quadrupeds of small size, of Miocene and Pliocene age, regarded as ancestrally related to the horse.

1859 DARWIN *Orig. Spec.* vii. (1878) 201 The differences between the extinct three-toed Hipparion and the horse. **1877** LE CONTE *Elem. Geology* III. (1879) 509 The Protohippus of the United States and allied Hipparion of Europe, an animal still more horse like..in structure and size.

hippeastrum (hɪpɪ'æstrəm). *Bot.* [mod.L. (see quot. 1821), f. Gr. ἱππεύς horseman, knight + ἄστρον star.] A member of the genus of South American bulbous plants so named, belonging to the family Amaryllidaceæ; the knight's star lily.

1821 W. HERBERT in *Bot. Reg.* VII. App. 7 Other points of agreement with Crinum separate them [*sc.* the plants] still more widely from the occidental bulbs which I have heretofore called Amaryllis, but in deference to the type of Linnæus, proposed now to call Hippeastrum or Knight's-star-lily. **1866** [see AMARYLLIS]. **1899** *Daily News* 16 Mar. 9/2 An immense stand of hippeastrums..carried off the palm in the shape of the society's gold medal. **1938** A. G. L. HELLYER *Your Garden Week by Week* 102 Start the remaining hippeastrum bulbs into growth now. **1961** *Amateur Gardening* 30 Sept. 6/2 Another plant to be rested is the hippeastrum—or, as many still prefer to call it, the amaryllis.

hipped, hipt (hɪpt), *a.*[1] [f. HIP *sb.*[1] and *v.*[2] + -ED.]

1. Having hips: esp. in comb., as ***large-hipped***.

1508 DUNBAR *Flyting w. Kennedie* 179 Hippit as ane horrow. **1597** A. M. tr. *Guillemeau's Fr. Chirurg.* 50 b/2 To be hipped and legged, or have a payere of goode and stedfast stiltes vnder them. **1611** COTGR., *Hanchu*,..great hipt. **1854** H. H. WILSON tr. *Rig-veda* II. 289 Wide-hipped Sinívālí..grant us, goddess, progeny.

2. *Arch.* Of a roof: Having hips (see HIP *sb.*[1] 3).

1823 P. NICHOLSON *Pract. Build.* 129 A hiped roof, over a rectangular plan. **1870** F. R. WILSON *Ch. Lindisf.* 50 The tower is covered with a hipped, slated roof.

3. Having the hip injured or dislocated; lamed in the hip; hip-shot.

1565-73 COOPER *Thesaurus*, *Delumbata quadrupide*, the beast being hipped. **1607** TOPSELL *Four-f. Beasts* (1658) 315 The Horse is said to be hipt, when the hip-bone is removed out of his right place..It cometh most commonly by some great stripe or strain. **1709** *Lond. Gaz.* No. 4601/4 All black, with his further Hip hipped. **1799** [see HIP-SHOT 1].

hipped (hɪpt), *a.*[2] *colloq.* Also 8 hip'd, hipt. [Altered spelling of HYPT, *hypp'd*, f. HIP *sb.*[3], orig. HYP.] Affected with hypochondria; morbidly depressed or low-spirited.

1710 [see HYPT]. **1712** STEELE *Spect.* No. 284 ¶4, I have been to the last Degree hipped since I saw you. **1833** LONGF. *Outre-mer* Prose Wks. 1886 I. 120 What with his bad habits and his domestic grievances, he became completely hipped. **1887** SMILES *Life & Labour* 446 When he..had nothing to do, he became hipped, then ill, and then was told that he was dying.

hipped, *ppl. a.*: see HIP *v.*[5]

hippelaph ('hɪpɪlæf). *Zool.* [ad. mod.L. *hippelaphus*, a. Gr. ἱππέλαφος (Aristotle), f. ἵππος horse + ἔλαφος deer.] A large kind of deer, the rusa deer of India (*Cervus* or *Rusa hippelaphus*).

1828 WEBSTER, *Hippelaph*, an animal of the deer kind.

hippen: see HIPPING.

hipper ('hɪpə(r)). *Austral.* [f. HIP *sb.*[1] + -ER[1].] (See quots.) Cf. *hip-hole* (HIP *sb.*[1] 4 b).

1934 *Bulletin* (Sydney) 26 Sept. 20/3 A tired man usually contents himself with a ground-sheet and blanket after digging himself a 'hipper'—a small cavity to accommodate his hips. **1945** BAKER *Austral. Lang.* 106 The hipper, something soft—such as a piece of possum skin or a stuffed strip of bagging—to put under the hip when lying on hard ground.

hipper, var. of HEPPER, a young salmon.

hippety ('hɪpɪtɪ). Also **-ity**. Jingling combination of HIP *v.*[1] and HOP *v.*, as in ***hippety-hop***, ***hippety-hoppety***.

1825 J. JENNINGS *Observ. Dial. W. Eng.* 45 *Hippety-hoppety*, *adv.*, in a limping and hobbling manner. **1880** *West Cornwall Gloss.* s.v., 'He goes hippety-hoppety' (walks unevenly). **1886** F. T. ELWORTHY *W. Somerset Word-bk.*, *Hippety-hop*, *hippety-hoppety*.., lame, limping in a very marked manner: applied to both man and beast. **1920** *Cornhill Mag.* Sept. 332 A row of children playing hippety-hop across a broad lawn. **1925** D. H. LAWRENCE *Refl. Death Porcupine* 186 'I am the captain of my soul!' Are you, old boy? Then why hippety-hop? **1950** J. DEMPSEY *Championship Fighting* 58 Under no circumstances take any little half-step or hippity-hop.

hippian, *a. rare.* [f. Gr. ἵππος horse + -IAN.] = HIPPIC.

1803 G. S. FABER *Myst. Cabiri* II. 303 *note*, Winged horses are assigned to Jupiter, as being an arkite or hippian deity.

hippiatric (hɪpɪ'ætrɪk), *a.* and *sb. rare.* [ad. Gr. ἱππιατρικός, f. ἱππιατρός veterinary surgeon, f. ἵππος horse + ἰατρός healer, physician.]

A. *adj.* Relating to the treatment of diseases of horses. **B.** *sb.* **a.** One who treats diseases of horses. **b.** *pl.* The treatment of diseases of horses, farriery; a treatise on this.

1646 SIR T. BROWNE *Pseud. Ep.* III. ii. 108 Absyrtus a Greek Author..who in his Hippiat[r]icks, obscurely assigneth the gall a place in the liver. **1674** JEAKE *Arith.* (1696) 63 The Weights among the Greeks are differently to be taken; as they are Attick, Physical, Hippiatrick, Indigenital, or Exotick. *Ibid.* 94 The Hippiatricks had a..Litra of 12 [Ounces]. **1829** *Sporting Mag.* XXIV. 154 This great master of hippiatrics..gives the preference to horses that turn out their toes.

So **hippi'atrical** *a.* = HIPPIATRIC A; **hi'ppiatrist**, one who practises, or writes on, hippiatry; **hi'ppiatry** (-eɪtrɪ) = HIPPIATRICS (see B. b above).

1653 URQUHART *Rabelais* I. xxxvi, (Which is a wonderful thing in Hippiatrie), the said horse was thoroughly cured of a ringbone which he had in that foot. **1674** JEAKE *Arith.* (1696) 93 Graecian Hippiatrical Measures. **1895** *19th Cent.* Mar. 444 Greek and Roman hippiatrists are equally divided on this point.

hippic ('hɪpɪk), *a. rare.* [ad. Gr. ἱππικός, f. ἵππος horse. Cf. F. *hippique*.] Pertaining to horses, esp. to horse-racing.

1846 H. TORRENS *Rem. Milit. Lit. & Hist.* I. 101 *note*, A curious instance of the enduring nature of the hippic principle among original nomads. **1871** *Daily News* 25 Aug., The hippic events of that cockney watering-place. **1885** *Soc. Lond.* 119 The other great hippic festivals of the year at Doncaster, at Stockbridge, and at Chester.

hippie, hippy ('hɪpɪ), *sb.* and *a. slang* (orig. *U.S.*). [f. HIP *a.* + -Y *suffix*[6].] **A.** *sb.* A hipster; a person, usually exotically dressed, who is, or is taken to be, given to the use of hallucinogenic drugs; a beatnik. **B.** *adj.* Of, pertaining to, or characteristic of hippies.

1953 D. WALLOP *Night Light* 157 Man, I really get a bellyful of these would be hippies. **1959** *Village Voice* 18 Nov. 13 Imagine coming on so jaded,..so hippie,..and fed up. **1965** *New Yorker* 24 July 27 All the hippies are leaving for the New World. **1967** *Daily Tel.* 21 Feb. 16/3 These people, 'writers, musicians, psychedelic popsters and hippies..' see London as a 'focal city for permissive experiments' in art and life. **1967** *Sunday Truth* (Brisbane) 2 Apr. 63/1 A hippie is the LSD Age's equivalent of a beatnik, and they turn on with marihuana, LSD, benzedrine or merely with the idea of turning-on. **1967** *Spectator* 7 July 32/3 Promises that in future they will live in accordance with the principles of love demanded by the hippies. **1967** *Guardian* 12 July 1/7 Have you ever been to the hippie district [of San Francisco]? **1967** *New Statesman* 27 Oct. 531/3 The [demonstration] marches cannot end the war, whether they are moderate and middle-class, insurrectionist, hippy or whatever. **1968** *Times* 16 Dec. 5/3 About 1,000 Hippies from several countries have set up a 'Hippy Republic' here [S. José, Costa Rica]. **1969** *Times* 27 Mar. 1/1 Without..losing her cool, as the hippy idiom would put it. **1969** *Daily Mail* 26 Sept. 7/1 The estimated number of full-time Hippies in London is 2,000,..and more than 60,000 part-timers in Britain alone. **1969** *Times* 5 Dec. 7/1 Religion, in one form or another, is frequently a straw to which the lost generation of hippies clings. *Ibid.*, The members of the hippy commune charged with the Sharon Tate killings are no more typical of America's long-haired 'make love, not war' youth than the soldiers involved in the alleged My Lai massacre are typical of the United States Army. **1972** *New Society* 30 Nov. 496/2 The word 'hippy' is now in current usage throughout Uganda, Tanzania and Kenya, and often just refers to anyone with long hair, almost always a European. **1973** *Friend* 13 July 839/1 'Hippie' is rather a general term applied quite often to anyone young and unkempt in appearance, who is considered to have dropped out of 'straight' society, and who in general puts little premium on the values of contemporary society which he has rebelled against.

Hence **'hippiedom**, the condition or fact of being a hippie; the domain of hippies; **'hippieland**, the domain of hippies; **'hippi(e)ness**, the quality or characteristics of a hippie or hippies.

1967 *N.Y. Times* 5 May 42 There are two philosophical trends in hippiedom. **1967** *Economist* 15 July 217/2 Some of the music is attracting attention outside of hippieland. **1968** *Blues Unlimited* Dec. 9, I guess California, and psychedelia, and hippieness have had the influence. **1969** *Listener* 20 Feb. 250/1 *One Step Away*..is the most comprehensive documentary I have seen so far about West Coast hippiedom. **1969** *Times* 5 Dec. 7/1 The west coast with its sunshine and sparkling surf, cut off by the desert on one side and the Pacific on the other, is the hot-house of America's hippiedom. **1970** K. PLATT *Pushbutton Butterfly* (1971) iv. 41 A lot of girls disappear in hippie-land. **1971** *Guardian* 17 June 9/4 A group like Exodus..with their veneer of Dutch hippiness. **1971** *Ibid.* 9 Sept 9/3 Descriptions of hippiedom by well-meaning admirers.

hipping[1] ('hɪpɪŋ). *north. dial.* Also **-in**, **-en**. [f. HIP *v.*[1] + -ING[1].] *pl.* Stepping-stones (by which one 'hips' or leaps across a stream).

1703 THORESBY *Let. to Ray* Gloss. (E.D.S.), *Hippins*, steppings; large stones set in a shallow water at a step's distance from each other, to pass over by. **1828** *Craven Dial.*, *Hippins*, stepping stones, over a river or brook.

b. So **hipping-stones**, stepping-stones.

1781 J. HUTTON *Tour to Caves* Gloss., *Hippen-stones*. **1850** *Tales of Kirkbeck* Ser. II. 120 The beck where they usually crossed by the hipping-stones.

hipping[2] ('hɪpɪŋ), **hippen** ('hɪp(ə)n). *Sc.* and *north. dial.* [f. HIP *sb.*[1] + -ING[1].] A napkin wrapt about the hips of an infant.

1768 ROSS *Helenore* 13 (Jam.) The first hippen to the green was flung. **1824** CARLYLE *Let. to Mrs. Carlyle* 12 Nov. in Froude *Life* (1882) I. xv. 256 His pap-spoons and his hippings. **1825** BROCKETT, *Hippings*, cloths for infants. **1893** *Northumbld. Gloss.*, *Hippin*, a napkin for the hips of an infant. Also often applied to the curtain of a theatre.

hippish ('hɪpɪʃ), *a. colloq.* [f. HIP *sb.*[3] + -ISH. More etymologically HYPPISH q.v.] Somewhat hypochondriacal; low-spirited.

1706 HEARNE *Collect.* (O.H.S.) I. 303 He is an Hippish Man, and of Low Church as to Principles. **1814** MAD. D'ARBLAY *Wanderer* III. 79 Staying within doors gives one a hippish turn. **1870** DISRAELI *Lothair* xxii.

Hence **hippishness** (Ash, 1775).

hipple ('hɪp(ə)l), *Obs.* exc. *dial.* Forms: 4 huple, hypil, hipil, -yll, heepil, 5 heple, hupple, 9 *dial.* hipple. [dim. of HEAP:—OE. type **hiepel*, **hȳpel*: cf. Ger. *häufel*, MHG. *hiufel*.] A little heap. †*hipyllmelum* = **hipplemeal*, in heaps, by heaps: see -MEAL.

1382 WYCLIF *2 Chron.* xxxi. 9 Why the heepils schulden so lyen. —— *Isa.* xvii. 1 Damasch shal..be as an hypil [**1388** heep] of stones. —— *Wisd.* xviii. 23 Whan forsothe now hipyllmelum thei hadden fallen dead, either vp on other. **1398** TREVISA *Barth. De P.R.* XVII. lxxii. (Tollem. MS.) [Hay is] gadered and made of heples into cockes. **1480** CAXTON *Descr. Brit.* I. xxii. (1527) 19 b, Hepes and hupples of stones and of grauell. **1788** W. MARSHALL *Yorksh.* Gloss. (E.D.S.), *Hipples*, cocklets, or small bundles of hay set up to dry.

hippo ('hɪpəʊ). Colloq. abbrev. HIPPOPOTAMUS.

1872 BAKER *Nile Tribut.* ii. 30 The hippo had been hauled to shore by ropes. **1893** SELOUS *Trav. S.E. Africa* 65 Our guide now wished me to remain here that I might look for the hippos.

b. *attrib.* and *Comb.*

1884 GORDON *Khartoum Jrnls.* 25 Sept. (1885) 98 Cassim gave him a wipe over the head with his Hippo whip. **1897** HINDE *Congo Arabs* 40 My first experience of hippo-shooting.

hippo, obs. f. HYPO, abbrev. of *hypochondria.*

hippo- (hɪpəʊ), before a vowel **hipp-**, combining form of Gr. ἱππο-ς horse, in words of Greek derivation, most of which will be found in their alphabetical places; the following are of rare occurrence, chiefly *nonce-wds.*: **hi'ppanthropy** [cf. *boanthropy*], a form of madness in which a man believes himself to be a horse; **hippodra'matic** *a.*, of dramatic nature or character in connexion with a circus; **hippoga'stronomy**, the art of cooking and eating horseflesh; **hi'ppogony** [Gr. -γονία a begetting; cf. *cosmogony*], 'pedigree or origin of a horse' (Davies); **hi'ppomachy** (-məkɪ) [Gr. -μαχία fighting], a fight on horseback; **hippo'mania** [-MANIA], excessive fondness for horses; so **hippo'maniac**, one affected by hippomania; **hippoma'niacally** *adv.*, like a mad horse; **hippo'manic** *a.*; **hi'pponomy** [after *economy*], the management of horses; **hippono'sology, hippopa'thology**, 'the doctrine of the diseases of the horse' (*Syd. Soc. Lex.*); hence **hipponoso'logical, hippopatho'logical** *adjs.*; **'hippophil(e** (-fɪl) [Gr. φίλος loving], a lover of horses; **hippo'phobia** [Gr. -φοβία fear, after *hydrophobia*, etc.], fear of or aversion to horses; **hippo-sandal** (see quots); **hipposte'ology**, the description of the bones of the horse; **hippo'tigrine** *a.*, pertaining to the striped members of the genus *Equus*, such as the zebra and the quagga; **hippo'tragine** *a.*, belonging to the sub-family Hippotraginæ of the family Bovidæ, a group of large African antelopes.

1854 MAYNE *Expos. Lex., Hippanthropia* ..*hippanthropy. **1886** *Syd. Soc. Lex., Hippanthropy.* **1811** KEEGAN (*title*) New Dialogues, in French and English.. with familiar conversations on..the Opera, Singing, *Hippodramatic Performances [etc.]. **1879** SALA *Paris herself Again* I. xvii. 291 The grandest of hippodramatic spectacles. **1860** *All Year Round* No. 74. 575 Our French friends' late experiments in *hippogastronomy. **1838** SOUTHEY *Doctor* cxliv. V. 88 There was nothing supernatural in Nobs. His *hippogony..would upon his theory have been in the course of nature. **1623** COCKERAM, **Hippomachie*, a iusting on horsebacke. **1658** PHILLIPS, *Hippomachie*, a fighting on hors-back. **1961** *Spectator* 9 June 853 The combination of *hippomania, secretarial-college chumship. **1963** *Daily Tel.* 8 Jan. 13/4 BBC television is to investigate present-day 'hippomania'... The word was apparently used by the Romans to describe excessive love by women for horses. **1940** V. WOOLF *Roger Fry* 126 He had been thrown riding 'with that *hippomaniac Goldie'. **1876** G. MEREDITH *Beauch. Career* III. xiv. 246 As if..an insane young chorister or canon were galloping straight on end *hippomaniacally through the Psalms. **1963** *Listener* 7 Feb. 260/3 The splendidly *hippomanic girl..who met her future husband after a toss in the hunting-field. **1618** M. BARET (*title*) An *Hipponomie, or the Vineyard of Horsemanship. **1854** MAYNE *Expos. Lex., Hipponosologicus*..*hipponosological. *Ibid., Hipponosologia*..*hipponosology. *Ibid., Hippopathologicus*..*hippopathological. **1834** W. PERCIVALL (*title*) *Hippopathology: a Systematic Treatise on the Disorders and Lameness of the Horse. **1852** *Fraser's Mag.* XLV. 535 That sympathy with the horses..felt..by the English *hippophile. **1841** LONGF. in *Life* (1891) I. 404 You know he has the *hippophobia. **1886** *Times* 1 Feb. 6/4 Known in society for his extraordinary hatred of horses. This aversion amounted to a real hippophobia. **1886** *Pall Mall G.* 5 Feb. 4/1 Major Brucy-Clarke introduced a *hippo-sandal—a sort of iron-soled boot to resist the wear and tear of civilized roads—which was fastened by straps and buckles on the outside of the hoof. **1897** *Archæol. Jrnl.* LIV. 309 Chancellor Ferguson, F.S.A., exhibited a hippo-sandal..showing it to be undoubtedly a horse-shoe, and probably used to protect a broken or injured hoof... Two other hippo-sandals of neo-archaic date were also exhibited ..Both are formed to enlarge the surface of the tread, so as to prevent the horse sinking into the soft mosses. **1847** CRAIG, **Hipposteology.* **1875** *Encycl. Brit.* I. 259/1 Of wild horses the asinine group is characteristic of Asia, and the *hippotigrine of Africa. **1947** J. STEVENSON-HAMILTON *Wild Life S. Afr.* vi. 51 The Cape mountain zebra (*Equus zebra*) is the smallest of the group of hippotigrine equines, standing some 4 feet at the shoulder. **1891** FLOWER & LYDEKKER *Introd. Mammals* 342 *Hippotragine Section. Includes very large African Antelopes, with long horns. **1910** H. F. OSBORN *Age of Mammals* v. 337 (*caption*) A recent hippotragine type of Africa, the sable antelope (*Hippotragus niger*).

hippoboscid (hɪpəʊ'bɒsɪd), *a.* and *sb.* [f. mod.L. *Hippoboscidæ*, f. HIPPO- + Gr. βόσκειν to feed: see -ID[2].] (Of or pertaining to) a member of the family Hippoboscidæ of blood-sucking flies, sometimes called louse-flies, parasitic on mammals and birds.

1891 *Insect Life* III. 357 Mr. Townsend read a paper on a remarkable new Hippoboscid..which had been taken on a bat. **1920** *Q. Rev.* July 91 Tsetse-flies..are the nearest living relations of the Hippoboscid family. **1962** W. R. HORSFALL *Med. Ent.* v. 171 Nycteribiidae and Streblidae..live in the manner of the hippoboscid flies. **1972** *Nature* 4 Feb. 249/1 Hippoboscids are at best poor fliers, with a strong tendency to wing degeneration.

hippocamp ('hɪpəʊkæmp). [ad. late L. *hippocampus* (see below).] = HIPPOCAMPUS 1.

1613–16 W. BROWNE *Brit. Past.* II. i. (R.), Fair silver-footed Thetis..Guiding from rockes her chariot's hyppocamps. **1851** C. NEWTON in Ruskin *Stones Ven.* I. App. xxi. 402 The sea-monsters who draw these chariots are called Hippocamps, composed of the tail of a fish and the fore-part of a horse.

hippocampal (hɪpəʊ'kæmpəl), *a. Anat.* [f. HIPPOCAMPUS + -AL[1].] Belonging to the hippocampus in the brain: see HIPPOCAMPUS 3.

1839–47 TODD *Cycl. Anat.* III. 294/2 The hippocampal commissure of the Wombat. **1881** MIVART *Cat* 269 The anterior end of the hippocampal gyrus.

hippocampus (hɪpəʊ'kæmpəs). Pl. -i. [a. late L. *hippocampus*, a. Gr. ἱππόκαμπος, f. ἵππο-ς horse + κάμπος sea-monster.]

1. *Mythol.* A sea-horse, having two fore-feet, and the body ending in a dolphin's or fish's tail, represented as drawing the car of Neptune and other sea-deities.

1606 DRUMM. OF HAWTH. *Let.* Wks. (1711) 232 Stately pageants..that of Cheapside was of Neptune on a hippocampus, with his Tritons and Næreides. **1840** HOOD *Kilmansegg, Marriage* xxviii, Hearty as hippocampus.

2. *Ichthyol.* A genus of small fishes, having a head shaped somewhat like that of a horse; the sea-horse.

1576 FLEMING *Panopl. Epist.* 353 The fishe called Hippocampus, is a present and sovereigne remedie, against the byting of a madde dogge. **1863** MISS SEWELL *Chr. Names* II. 279 The quaint little horny hippocampus.

3. *Anat.* Each of two elongated eminences (***hippocampus major*** and ***minor***) on the floor of each lateral ventricle of the brain; so called from their supposed resemblance to the fish (sense 2).

1706 PHILLIPS (ed. Kersey), *Hippocampa*..in Anatomy, the Processes of Channels of the upper or foremost Ventricles of the Brain. **1863** *Sat. Rev.* 606/2 A purely unscientific person..capable of going to his grave without the remotest notion whether he had a hippocampus or not, if Mr. Owen and Mr. Huxley had never discussed the subject.

hippocaust ('hɪpəʊkɔːst). [f. Gr. ἵππο-ς horse: after HOLOCAUST; rendering Skr. *açwamedha.*] The burning of a horse in sacrifice.

1858 F. HALL in *Jrnl. Asiat. Soc. Bengal* 249 Not..even by a hundred hippocausts. **1866** —— in *H. H. Wilson's tr. Vishṅu Puráṅa* III. 198 *note*, Or offers a hippocaust accompanied by remuneration, agreeably to rule.

hippocentaur (hɪpəʊ'sɛntɔː(r)). [ad. L. *hippocentaurus*, a. Gr. ἱπποκένταυρος (f. ἵππο-ς horse + κένταυρος CENTAUR), horse-centaur, opp. to ἰχθυοκένταυρος fish-centaur.] A fabulous creature combining the forms of a man and a horse; a centaur.

[**1398** TREVISA *Barth. De P.R.* XVIII. lxxix. (1495) 832 Ipocentaurus is a beest wonderly shape, in whom is acountyd the kynde of man and of an horse.] **1533** ELYOT *Cast. Helthe* (1539) 37 a, He affirmeth, that he did se an Hippocentaure. **1601** HOLLAND *Pliny* I. 157 In Thessalie there was borne a monster called an Hippocentaure. **1674** DRYDEN *State Innoc.* Apol., But how are poetical fictions, how are hippocentaurs and chimeras..to be imaged? **1880** MUIRHEAD *Gaius* III. §97 If one stipulate for something that can have no existence, such as a hippocentaur, the stipulation is equally useless.

Hence **hippocen'tauric** *a.*, of the nature of a hippocentaur.

1614 JACKSON *Creed* III. v. §15 A monstrous Hippocentaurique combination.

hippocras ('hɪpəʊkræs). *Obs.* exc. *Hist.* or *arch.* Forms: 4–6 **ypocras**, (5 **ypocrate**), 6–7 **ipocras, hipocras**, 6–7 (9 *arch.*) **ippocras, hypocras**, 7– **hippocras, -crass**, (6 **ypo-, ipo-, hypo-, -crass(e, -crase, -crace, -craze**, 7 **ippocrass(e, hyppocras**). [a. OF. *ipocras, ypocras* (*a* 1400), forms of the proper name *Hippocrates*; in sense 1, after the med.L. name, *vinum Hippocraticum* 'wine of Hippocrates', app. given to it because it was filtered through 'Hippocrates' sleeve' or 'bag': see next. See Skeat *Chaucer* V. 361.

c **1369** CHAUCER *Dethe Blaunche* 571 Ne hele me may noo physicien, Noght ypocras, ne Galyen.]

1. A cordial drink made of wine flavoured with spices, formerly much in vogue.

c **1386** CHAUCER *Merch. T.* 365 He drynketh Ypocras Clarree and Vernage Of spices hoote tencreessen his corage. **1466** *Mann. & Househ. Exp.* (Roxb.) 377 The same day my mastyr paid fore ypocras to the Ryalle x.*d.* **1513** DOUGLAS *Æneis* I. xi. 67 The quene..Bad fill it full of the riche Ypocras. **1570** LEVINS *Manip.* 7/23 *Hypocrace*, vinum myrrhatum. **1600** HEYWOOD *1st Pt. Edw. IV* Wks. 1874 I. 10 We'le take the tankards from the conduit-cocks To fill with ipocras and drinke carouse. **1613** in *Crt. & Times Jas. I* (1849) I. 285 The king and queen were both present, and tasted wafers and hippocrass, as at ordinary weddings. **1709** STRYPE *Ann. Ref.* I. xv. 196 After the christening were brought wafers, comfits..and hypocras and muscadine wine. **1843** LYTTON *Last Bar.* IV. vi, Now there appeared the attendants, with hippocras, syrups, and comfits.

†2. hippocras bag. A conical bag of cotton, linen, or flannel, used as a filter or strainer. *Obs.*

1601 HOLLAND *Pliny* II. 153 The wholesomest wines..be such as haue run through a strainer or Ipocras bag, and thereby lost some part of their strength. **1641** FRENCH *Distill.* v. (1651) 123 When you would have this or any other Liquor to be very clear, you may use the triple Hypocras bag. **1674** JOSSELYN *Voy. New Eng.* 190 Put them in an Hippocras bag and let it drain out of it self.

Hippocrates (hɪ'pɒkrətiːz). Name of a famous ancient Greek physician born about 460 B.C. **† Hippocrates' bag, Hippocrates' sleeve** [tr. L. *manica Hippocratis*] = prec. 2. *Obs.*

1626 BACON *Sylva* §6 Passing it [Ippocrasse] through a Wollen Bagge, which they call *Hippocrates Sleeue.* **1696** PHILLIPS (ed. 5), *Hippocrates Bag*, a Bag made of white Cotton, like a Sugar Loaf, pointed at Bottom. **1775** ROMANS *Florida* 137 It is then put into bags of the form of Hippocrates's sleave to drain it from all superfluous himidity.

Hippocratic (hɪpəʊ'krætɪk), *a.* [ad. med.L. *Hippocratic-us*, f. *Hippocrates*: see prec.]

1. Of or belonging to Hippocrates; following the method, or made according to the receipt of Hippocrates. ***Hippocratic oath***, an oath comprising the obligations and professional conduct of physicians, taken by those entering upon medical practice. **†*Hippocratic wine***, spiced wine, hippocras.

c **1620** BACON *Wks.* (1857) III. 831 Astringents.. Hippocratic wines. **1747** J. BARKER *Essay Anc. Mod. Physicians* Dedication p. v, By the Hippocratic Oath, a Physician is bound to honour the Master who has instructed him in his Art. **1869** E. A. PARKES *Pract. Hygiene* (ed. 3) 508 The Hippocratic rule, that the amount of food and exercise must be balanced. **1874** MAHAFFY *Soc. Life Greece* ix. 279 These enquiries belong to the history of medicine, and must be based on the Hippocratic writings. **1969** *Nature* 4 Jan. 2/1 The Hippocratic oath of the medical profession has excited the attention of several moralists.

2. Applied to the shrunken and livid aspect of the countenance immediately before death, or in a case of exhaustion threatening death: so called because described by Hippocrates.

1713 SPREGNELL *The Plague* in *Phil. Trans.* XXVIII. 120 Succeeded by..Lethargy, a dismal Hippocratic Face, staring Eyes. **1770** HANLY *Ibid.* LXI. 132 With a sharp pinched-up nose, hippocratic countenance. **1881** *Century Mag.* XXIII. 300/1 The lines of the face hippocratic.

fig. **1843** CARLYLE *Past & Pr.* III. viii, A terrible Hippocratic look reveals itself. **1880** *Internat. Rev.* VIII. 372 The absolutist régime there shows a Hippocratic visage.

So **Hippocratian** (-'kreɪʃən), **Hippo'cratical** *adjs.* = prec. **Hi'ppocratism**, the doctrine of Hippocrates. **Hi'ppocratize** *v. intr.*, to follow or imitate Hippocrates.

a **1849** POE *Loss Breath* Wks. 1864 IV. 307 The *Hippocratian pathology. **1876** W. STEPHENS *Mem. Chichester* 190 Half of the wine was to be hypocratian. **1625** HART *Anat. Ur.* I. ii. 32 With an *Hippocraticall face, deaths trustie messenger. **1799** *Med. Jrnl.* I. 363 A physician truly Hippocratical, and guided by observation. **1818** TODD, **Hippocratism* [cites Chambers]. **1869** tr. *Hugo's By King's Command* I. i. 3 He *Hippocratised and he Pindarised.

Hippocrene ('hɪpəʊkriːn). In 7 *erron.* **Hypo-**. [ad. L. *Hippocrēnē*, Gr. Ἱπποκρήνη for Ἵππου κρήνη 'fountain of the horse', so called because it was fabled to have been produced by a stroke of Pegasus' hoof. Cf. F. *Hippocrène* (16th c. in Littré).] Name of a fountain on Mount Helicon, sacred to the Muses; hence used allusively in reference to poetic or literary inspiration.

1634 HABINGTON *Castara* (Arb.) 64 My sacke will.. inspire so high a rage, That Hypocrene shall henceforth Poets lacke. **1638–48** G. DANIEL *Eclog* iii. 269 And Hypocrene it selfe is but a Tale To countenance dull Soules who drinke not Ale. **1693** CONGREVE in *Dryden's Persius* (1697) 400 This Hippocrene, which from a Rock did flow. **1820** KEATS *Ode to Nightingale* 16 O for a beaker..Full of the true, the blushful Hippocrene. **1841** LONGF. *Goblet of Life* ii, Maddening draughts of Hippocrene.

Hence **Hippo'crenian** *a.*, pertaining to Hippocrene.

a **1679** EARL OF ORRERY *Gusman* 1, There's no more Hypocrinian Moisture in my Brain.

hippocrepian (hɪpəʊ'kriːpɪən), *a.* (*sb.*) *Zool.* and *Bot.* [f. HIPPO- + Gr. κρηπίς shoe + -(I)AN.]

Resembling a horseshoe: *spec.* applied to the lophophore of certain polyzoans, and so to these polyzoans themselves. **b.** as *sb.* A hippocrepian polyzoan.

1877 HUXLEY *Anat. Inv. Anim.* viii. 461 The lophophore resembles that of the hippocrepian Phylactolaemata in being produced into two arms fringed with a double series of tentacula. **1888** DAWSON *Geol. Hist. Plants* iii. 94 Traces of the hippocrepian mark characteristic of *Protopteris.*

hippo'crepiform, *a. Bot.* [f. as prec. + -FORM.] Shaped like a horse-shoe.

1864 WEBSTER cites GRAY.

†**hippodame.** *Obs.* [ad. Gr. ἱππόδαμος horse-tamer, but in sense 1, app. confused with *hippotame*, HIPPOPOTAMUS.]

1. *erron.* used by Spenser for HIPPOCAMP.

1590 SPENSER *F.Q.* II. ix. 50 Infernall Hags, Centaurs, feendes, Hippodames. *Ibid.* III. xi. 40 His [Neptune's] swift charet.. Which foure great Hippodames did draw.

2. A horse-tamer.

1623 COCKERAM, *Hippodame*, a Horse breaker.

Hence **hi'ppodamist**, a horse-tamer; **hi'ppodamous** *a.*, horse-taming, horse-breaking.

1841 S. WARREN *Ten Thous. a Year* II. x. 293 The present famous hippodamist at Windsor, by touching a nerve in the mouth of a horse, reduces him to helpless docility. **1894** *Athenæum* 1 Sept. 284/3 The hippodamous gentry who receive more or less attention from him. [See HIPPOLOGICAL.]

hippodrome ('hɪpədrəʊm), *sb.* [a. F. *hippodrome* (13th c. in Hatz.-Darm., in form *ypodrome*), or ad. L. *hippodromos*, Gr. ἱππόδρομος race-course for chariots, f. ἵππο-ς horse + δρόμος race, course.]

1. In *Gr.* and *Rom. Antiq.* A course or circus for horse-races and chariot-races. Sometimes used as a high-sounding name for a modern circus.

[**1549** THOMAS *Hist. Italie* (1561) 36 b (Stanf.), There is a faire grene auncientl called *Hippodromus*.] **1585** T. WASHINGTON tr. *Nicholay's Voy.* II. xvi. 50 Of the noble antiquities.. found at Constantinople, are the Hippodrome. **1615** G. SANDYS *Trav.* 34 The swift hoofe beats the dustie Hippodrome. **1781** GIBBON *Decl. & F.* II. xli. 518 The glorious procession entered the gate of the hippodrome. **1855** MILMAN *Lat. Chr.* IV. viii. (1864) II. 380 Dragged amid the shouts of the rabble round the Hippodrome and then put to death. **1886** *Pall Mall G.* 14 Dec. 6/1 'Olympia' is to be open on Boxing Day, [with].. the famous Hippodrome which has just arrived from Paris.

2. *U.S. Sporting slang.* A fraudulent race, or other athletic contest, in which it is arranged beforehand which of the contestants shall win. (*Cent. Dict.*)

3. A theatre used for various stage entertainments.

1899 *Daily News* 10 July 8/1 Hippodromes, as such strictly, have not hitherto been greatly in fashion in London, and they have had but a fitful existence since Mr. Batty started the memorable one known by his name, at the time of the Great Exhibition of 1851. **1902** *Encycl. Brit.* XXXI. 49/1 London in 1902 had.. the 'Hippodrome' in Cranbourn Street. **1972** *Times* 8 Apr. 12/5 At the moment, 21 London theatres and halls are listed:.. they are the Duke of York's, Garrick, Her Majesty's, Coliseum, Hippodrome, Lyceum, [etc.].

Hence **'hippodrome** *v.* (*U.S. Sporting slang*), to conduct races or other contests in which the result is prearranged by collusion (see 2 above). **hippo'dromic**, and *erron.* **hippodro'matic** (confused with *hippodramatic*: see HIPPO-) *adjs.*, of or belonging to a hippodrome or circus. **'hippodroming**, *vbl. sb.* **hi'ppodromist**, a trainer or rider of a horse in a circus.

1840 MRS. SHELLEY in *Shelley's Ess.* I. Pref. 19 Well versed in nautical, *hippodromic, and other arts. **1893** *Nation* (N.Y.) 18 May 370/3 The 'Talisman' is to a painful extent melodramatic and hippodromic. *a* **1867** H. WOODRUFF *Trotting Horse* (1868) xxxv. 288 An arrangement was entered into by means of which the former and Lancet travelled together, to trot for purses and divide the profits. It was a new sort of thing, and was.. called '*Hippodroming'. **1946** *Chicago Tribune* 1 Feb. (Grafic Mag.) 13/1 Cynics argue there is a great deal of hippodroming [in ice hockey]. **1886** *Daily News* 14 Dec. 3/1 The *hippodromists confess that they have to get their clever ponies from Scotland and Wales.

hippo fly ('hɪpəʊ flaɪ). [prob. abbrev. of HIPPO(POTAMUS, in reference to the size of the fly.] A large blood-sucking fly of the family Tabanidæ, found in central Africa.

1901 *Geogr. Jrnl.* July 75 The large biting fly called the 'hippo' fly was a great annoyance. **1929** PATTON & EVANS *Insects, Ticks, Mites & Venomous Animals* I. 294 The Tabanidæ have received various local names such as horseflies, seroot flies, mangrove flies, hippo flies.

hippogriff, -gryph ('hɪpəʊgrɪf). [a. F. *hippogriffe* (16th c. in Hatz.-Darm.), ad. It. *ippogrifo* (Ariosto), f. Gr. ἵππο-ς horse + It. *grifo*, late L. *grȳphus* GRIFFIN.] A fabulous creature, like a griffin, but with body and hind-quarters resembling those of a horse.

1656 BLOUNT *Glossogr.*, *Hippogryph*, a kind of feigned beast, in part horse, in part Griffin. *a* **1659** CLEVELAND *Poems, Chym. Magic* 2 Tell us no more of Icarus, Of Hypogryph, or Pegasus. **1671** MILTON *P.R.* IV. 542 He caught him up, and without wing Of hippogrif, bore through the air sublime. **1790** GIBBON *Misc. Wks.* (1814) III. 487 The African magician.. sends him to wander through the air on a hippogrif. **1856** J. H. NEWMAN *Callista* 222 She thinks herself a Christian, when she is just as much a hippogriff, or a chimæra.

b. *transf.* and *fig.*

1837 CARLYLE *Fr. Rev.* I. IV. iv, Woe the day when they mounted thee.. on that wild Hippogryff of a Democracy; which.. no yet known Astolpho could have ridden! **1864** VAMBERY *Trav. Centr. Asia* 146, I was obliged, however, to tug a long time at the reins, before I could induce my long-eared hippogriff to change his headlong career.

Also †**hippo'griffic, -'griffin, -on, -'gryphon.**

1654 GAYTON *Pleas. Notes* III. xi. 147 Or Pacolets, or Bradamants, or Hippo-gryphon. **1656** EARL MONM. *Advt. fr. Parnass.* 368 Poets in their writings had mentioned Tritons,.. Sirins, Hypogriffiks, Phenixes. **1798** W. TAYLOR in *Monthly Rev.* XXVI. 247 Ariosto, whose hippogriffon so few have since been able to govern. **1848** C. C. CLIFFORD *Aristoph., Frogs* 31 Not hippogriffins, sir, nor yet stag-goats.

hippoid ('hɪpɔɪd). *Zool.* [f. Gr. ἵππο-ς horse + -OID: cf. *anthropoid*.] An animal resembling, or allied to, the horse.

1880 HUXLEY in *Times* 25 Dec. 4/1 A *primâ facie* probability that this primordial hippoid had a low form of brain.

hippolith ('hɪpəʊlɪθ). [ad. med.L. *hippolithus*, f. Gr. ἵππο-ς horse + λίθος stone: cf. F. *hippolithe*.] A concretion or calculus found in the stomach or intestines of a horse.

[**1661** LOVELL *Hist. Anim. & Min.* 81 The stone found in the stomack, called *hippolithus*.] **1828** WEBSTER cites QUINCY.

hippology (hɪ'pɒlədʒɪ). *rare.* [f. HIPPO- + -(O)LOGY.] The study of horses. So **hippo'logical** *a.*, relating to hippology; **hi'ppologist**, one versed in hippology.

1854 MAYNE *Expos. Lex.*, *Hippologia*.. hippology. **1885** tr. *Hehn's Wand. Pl. & Anim.* 424 The celebrated traveller and hippologist. **1887** F. H. HUTH (*title*) Bibliographical Record of Hippology, or Works on Horses and Equitation. **1894** *Athenæum* 1 Sept. 285/1 [Capt. Hayes] an author of renown in the field of hippodamous and hippological literature.

‖**hippomanes** (hɪ'pɒmənɪ:z). [Gr. ἱππομανές (see below), neut. of ἱππομανής, f. ἵππο-ς horse + μαν-, root of μαίνεσθαι to be mad. In mod.F. *hippomane*.] **a.** 'A small black fleshy substance said to occur on the forehead of a new-born foal'. **b.** 'A mucous humour that runs from mares a-horsing' (Liddell and Scott). (Both reputed aphrodisiacs.)

1601 HOLLAND *Pliny* I. 222 These foles verily, by report, haue growing on their forehead.. a little black thing of the bignesse of a fig, called *Hippomanes*. *a* **1661** HOLYDAY *Juvenal* 130 Cæsonia the wife of Caligula.. whom she drench'd with the love-cup made of the hippomanes, a tender peice of flesh taken from the brow of a young foal. **1697** DRYDEN *Virg. Georg.* III. 443. **1756** *Gentl. Mag.* XXVI. 170 The Hippomanes has been distinguished under two species; the one a liquor distilling from a mare, during the time of her heat. **1831** TYTLER *Hist. Scot.* (1864) IV. 201 Poison was compounded, according to the declaration of the wizard, of adders' skins, toads' skins, and the hippomanes in the head of a young foal.

hippomobile ('hɪpəʊməʊbi:l). (*Disused.*) [f. HIPPO- + MOBILE *a.*] A word used in the early days of motor vehicles for a horse-drawn vehicle. So **hippo'mobilism**, the use of a hippomobile.

1904 in A. B. F. Young *Compl. Motorist* xiii. 275 A hippomobile was despatched. **1904** *Westm. Gaz.* 15 Nov. 4/2 A motor-van.. would certainly do the journey more quickly.. and presumably such a vehicle will supersede the hippomobile in time. **1905** *Ibid.* 20 June 4/2 How much longer, motorists may be tempted to ask, is such a dangerous mode of locomotion as the hippomobile to be tolerated? **1908** *Daily Chron.* 16 Jan. 4/4 Hippomobilism was out of the question. **1963** BIRD & HUTTON-STOTT *Veteran Motor Car* 26 Even in 1899 this contrivance had an air of hippomobile antiquity.

†**hipponesse.** *Obs. rare.* A name of some fur-bearing animal.

1619 MIDDLETON *Love & Antiq.* 19 The names of those Beasts, bearing Furr, and now in vse.. Martin, Badger, Beare, Luzerne, Budge, Otter, Hipponesse, and Hare.

hippophagy (hɪ'pɒfədʒɪ). [f. Gr. ἵππο-ς + -φαγία eating.] The practice of eating horseflesh.

1828 WEBSTER cites *Q. Rev.* **1860** MRS. P. BYRNE *Undercurr. Overlooked* II. 115 [Denmark] is perhaps the only country where prisoners are condemned to hippophagy. **1892** *County Gentlem.* XXX. 103 Hippophagy has long been a recognized cult at Paris.

So **hi'ppophagism** = prec.; **hi'ppophagist**, an eater of horseflesh; **hippopha'gistical** *a.*, relating to hippophagy; **hi'ppophagous** *a.*, eating horseflesh.

1828 WEBSTER, *Hippophagous*, feeding on horses, as the Tartars. **1856** *Sat. Rev.* II. 485/2 It is.. of little use that historians and travellers tell of hippophagists. **1869** BARING-GOULD *Orig. Relig. Belief* 118 The hippophagism of the Tartar and ancient Norseman sprang up from the necessities of a nomad life. **1881** *Graphic* 10 Sept. 286 Sausage-makers of hippophagistical tendencies.

hippopotamic (ˌhɪpəʊpəʊ'tæmɪk, -'pɒtəmɪk), *a.* [f. HIPPOPOTAM-US + -IC.] Belonging to, like, or suggesting a hippopotamus; huge, unwieldly.

1785 J. DOUGLAS *Antiq. Earth* 9 These hippopotamic remains being discovered petrified. **1865** LIVINGSTONE *Zambesi* xvi. 326 They stare with peculiar stolid looks of hippopotamic surprise. **1884** *Punch* 15 Nov. 240/1 Rather hippopotamic in his humour.

So **hippopo'tamian, hippo'potamine** *adjs.* = prec.; **hippo'potamid** *Zool.*, an animal of the family *Hippopotamidæ*; **hippo'potamoid** *a.*, resembling a hippopotamus.

1864 *Realm* 6 Apr. 2 Ladies of such hippopotamian proportions. **1866** E. C. RYE *Brit. Beetles* 56 The heavy hippotamoid *Zabrus gibbus*. **1871** HUXLEY *Anat. Vert. Anim.* viii. 375 Merycopotamus.. appears to have been a Hippopotamid. **1883** *Nature* XXVII. 247 About thirty years is the extreme limit of Hippopotamine existence.

hippopotamus (hɪpəʊ'pɒtəməs). Pl. **-muses, -mi.** Forms: α. 4 **ypotame, -tamos, -tanos, -tanus,** 5 **ypotam, ipotayne,** (*pl.* **ypotamy**), 6–7 **hippotame,** (6 **hyppotame, hippotamon**). β. 6–7 **hippopotame,** (7 **hippopotum, -potamy, hyppopotamus**), 7– **hippopotamus,** (8–9 **-os**). [a. late L. *hippopotamus*, a. late Gr. ἱπποπόταμος (Galen), f. ἵππο-ς horse + ποταμός river. (The earlier Gr. writers used ὁ ἵππος ὁ ποτάμιος the riverine horse.) The earlier Eng. forms were a. OF. *ypotame* (13th c. in Hatz.-Darm.), ad. med.L. *ypotamus*, corruption of *hippopotamus*. The mod.Fr. is *hippopotame*.]

A pachydermatous quadruped, the African river-horse, *Hippopotamus amphibius*, a very large beast with a thick heavy hairless body, large muzzle and tusks, and short legs, inhabiting the African rivers, lakes, and estuaries.

α. **13..** *K. Alis.* 5166 Ypotamos comen flyngynge.. Grete bestes and griselich. *Ibid.* 5184 Ypotame a wonder beest is More than an olifaunt, I wis. *Ibid.* 6554 He sleth ypotanos, and kokadrill. **1340–70** *Alex. & Dind.* 157 Dredful dragonus.. Addrus and ypotamus, and oþure ille wormus. **1398** TREVISA *Barth. De P.R.* XIII. xxvi. (1495) 460 Some fysshe seke theyr meete oonly in water and some by nyghte vpon the londe, as Ypotanus, the water horse. *c* **1400** MAUNDEV. (1839) xxvi. 268 In that Contree ben many Ipotaynes [*Roxb.* ypotams]. **1563** HYLL *Art Garden.* (1593) 26 The hide of the riuer Horse, named Hippotamon. **1572** BOSSEWELL *Armorie* II. 65 b, The water Horsse of the Sea is called an Hyppotame. **1658** W. SANDERSON *Graphice* 22 Monsters, Chimeraes, Hippotames, and others such, which Heraulds undertake to bestow upon Gentlemens Buryings.

β. **1563** WARDE tr. *Alexis' Secr.* II. 28 b (Stanf.) A skin.. of a Hippopotame. **1600** J. PORY tr. *Leo's Africa* I. 39 The Hippopotamus or water-horse is somewhat tawnie. **1601** HOLLAND *Pliny* I. 91 (Stanf.) The river Bambotus full of Crocodiles and Hippopotames. **1605** DANIEL *Philotas* in Farr *S.P. Jas. I* (1848) 274 Me thought a mighty hippopotamus, From Nilus floting, thrusts into the maine. **1630** J. TAYLOR (Water P.) *Praise Hempseed* Wks. III. 63/1 The Ibis, Crocodile, a Cat, a Dog, The Hippopotamy, beetles, or a frog. **1774** GOLDSM. *Nat. Hist.* IV. x. 292 The hippopotamos is an animal as large, and not less formidable than the Rhinoceros. **1833** LYELL *Princ. Geol.* III. 221 The tusks of hippopotamuses often appear on the surface. **1865** LIVINGSTONE *Zambesi* iii. 81 A considerable body of bitter water containing leeches.. crocodiles and hippopotami.

attrib. **1875** MASKELL *Ivories* 14 The handle of a mirror in hippopotamus ivory. **1897** *Daily News* 6 Dec. 3/3 A hundred lashes with the hippopotamus hide whip.

hippotomy (hɪ'pɒtəmɪ). *rare.* [f. HIPPO- + Gr. -τομία cutting.] 'The anatomy or dissection of the horse' (Mayne *Expos. Lex.* 1854). So **hippo'tomical** *a.*, pertaining to hippotomy; **hi'ppotomist**, one versed in hippotomy.

1737 BRACKEN *Farriery Impr.* (1756) I. 203 Divided by two Necks (as they are termed by Hippotomists). **1847–9** TODD *Cycl. Anat.* IV. 716/1 Called by hippotomists the *os quadratum*. **1854** MAYNE *Expos. Lex.*, Hippotomical.

hippurate (hɪ'pjʊərət). *Chem.* [f. HIPPUR-IC + -ATE[4].] A salt of hippuric acid.

1854 in MAYNE *Expos. Lex.* **1857** G. BIRD *Urin. Deposits* (ed. 5) 206 Delicate feathers of hippurate of ammonia.

‖**hippuria** (hɪ'pjʊərɪə). *Path.* [mod.L., f. HIPPUR-IC, HIPPUR-ATE.] 'Bouchardat's term for the presence in excess of hippuric acid or hippurates in the urine' (*Syd. Soc. Lex.*).

1857 G. BIRD *Urin. Deposits* (ed. 5) 110 When an abnormally large proportion of this acid is present, as.. in hippuria.

hippuric (hɪ'pjʊərɪk), *a.* [f. Gr. ἵππ-ος horse + οὖρ-ον urine + -IC.] *Chem.* In ***hippuric acid***, an acid ($C_9H_9NO_3$) found in the urine of horses and other herbivora.

1838 T. THOMSON *Chem. Org. Bodies* 46 Of Hippuric Acid. Rouelle was the first person who discovered the existence of benzoic acid in the urine of the horse. **1846** G. E. DAY tr. *Simon's Anim. Chem.* II. 117 Hippuric acid is regarded by Liebig as an invariable constituent of ordinary human urine.

hippurid (hɪ'pjʊərɪd). *Bot.* [f. mod.L. *Hippūrideæ* (Link), f. *Hippūris* name of a genus of plants, a. Gr. ἵππουρις, f. ἵππο-ς horse + οὐρά tail.] A plant of N.O. *Hippurideæ* or *Haloragaceæ*, of which the typical genus is *Hippuris* or Mare's-tail.

hippurite ('hɪpjʊraɪt). *Palæont.* [ad. mod.L. *Hippūrītēs*, f. Gr. ἵππουρος horse-tailed (cf. prec.), subst., a sea-fish (*Coryphæna hippurus*), and a kind of insect.]

1. A fossil bivalve mollusc of the genus *Hippurites* or family *Hippuritidæ*.

[**1814** J. PARKINSON in *Geol. Trans.* II. 277 Observations on the Specimens of Hippurites from Sicily.] **1842** H. MILLER *O.R. Sandst.* viii. (ed. 2) 187 An entirely new field among the hippurites, sphærulites, and nummulites of the

same formations. **1851-6** WOODWARD *Mollusca* 40 The hippurite is distinguished by a cancellated texture.

b. *attrib.* or *adj.* = HIPPURITIC.

1863 LYELL *Antiq. Man* x. (ed. 3) 174 These caves are situated in rocks of hippurite limestone.

2. 'A kind of fossil cup-coral, *Cyathophyllum ceratites* of Goldfuss' (*Cent. Dict.*).

Hence **hippu'ritic** *a.*, pertaining to, or containing, hippurites (sense 1).

hippus ('hɪpəs). *Ophthalm.* [mod.L., f. Gr. ἵππος horse.] Tremor of the iris; *esp.* a rhythmic contraction and dilatation of the pupil independent of the light intensity; also, a complaint of the eyes, such that they are always winking.

1684 S. BLANCARD *Physical Dict.* 150 *Hippus* is an Affection of the Eyes, wherein they continually shake and tremble, and now and then twinkle. **1838** H. HOUSTON in S. Littell *Dis. Eye* 177 Oscillation of the iris is applied to the alternate contraction and expansion (hippus iridis), as well as to the trembling of the iris. **1904** L. W. FOX *Dis. Eye* xix. 428 Hippus is the term employed to designate a chronic spasm of the iris, as is seen in hysteria, neurasthenia,.. and various spinal diseases. **1932** W. S. DUKE-ELDER *Text-bk. Ophthalmol.* I. xii. 563 In the condition of hippus a rhythmic contraction and dilatation of the pupil occurs regularly a definite number of times per minute. **1968** J. L. SMITH *Neuro-Ophthalmol.* IV. iv. 60 No satisfactory explanation has been given for hippus as yet.

hippy, *a.*[1] *colloq.* [f. HIP *sb.*[3]] = HIPPISH.

1891 *Temple Bar Mag.* Aug. 478 [She] led him such an awful life, No wonder he was hippy.

hippy ('hɪpɪ), *a.*[2] [f. HIP *sb.*[1]] With large or prominent hips.

1919 F. HURST *Humoresque* 55, I seen you widening into a thirty-eight... You're getting hippy, girl. **1938** *Life* 5 Sept. 43 (*heading*) Hippy girls welcome the form-concealing flattery of hoopskirts. **1956** H. GOLD *Man who was not with It* (1965) xix. 172 She was getting a hippy and breasty look fast. **1969** 'M. FALLON' *Fine Night for Dying* ii. 21 A small hippy woman.

hippy, var. HIPPIE *sb.* and *a.*

hip-roof. *Arch.* [f. HIP *sb.*[1] 3.] A roof having hips or sloping edges (see HIP *sb.*[1] 3), the ends being inclined as well as the sides; a hipped roof.

1727-41 CHAMBERS *Cycl.* s.v., A hip-roof has rafters as long, and with the angles at the foot, etc., at the ends of buildings, as it has at the sides. **1772** *Phil. Trans.* LXIII. 43 A lofty building, with a pointed hip-roof. **1886** BYNNER *A. Surriage* xxvi. 291 A wooden structure..with a hip roof.

Hence **hip-roofed** *a.*, having a hip-roof.

a **1834** W. WIRT *Let.* in J. P. Kennedy *Life* (1860) II. vii. 116 A small, red, hip-roofed, one-storied old house.

hip-shot, *a.* (*sb.*) Also **hip-shotten.** [f. HIP *sb.*[1] + *shot*, pa. pple. of SHOOT *v.*]

1. Having a dislocated hip-joint; having the hip out of joint.

1639 T. DE GREY *Compl. Horsem.* 240 How doe you cure a horse that is hip-shot? **1799** *Sporting Mag.* XIV. 185 To be hipped or hipshot is to have one hip lower than the other. **1877** *Ohio State Jrnl.* 16 May, A hipshot, windbroken horse.

2. *fig.* Lame, clumsy; disabled, 'out of joint'.

1642 MILTON *Apol. Smect.* iv. 86 He has not spirit enough left him so far to look to his syntax, as to avoid nonsense.. This hipshot grammarian. **1661** NEEDHAM *Hist. Eng. Reb.* 70 Reformation, thou stalking horse of our hip-shotten state.

B. *sb.* Dislocation of the hip-joint.

c **1720** W. GIBSON *Farrier's Dispens.* xiv. (1734) 277 For a Hip-shot, or Dislocation. **1727** BRADLEY *Fam. Dict.*, *Hip-Shot*..befals these Animals many Ways, sometimes by the Wrench or Stroak of another Horse, and at other Times by a Slip, Strain, Sliding or Falling.

hipster[1] ('hɪpstə(r)). *slang* (orig. *U.S.*). [f. HIP *a.* + -STER.] One who is 'hip'; a hip- (or hep-)cat. Also *attrib.* Hence **'hipsterism**, the condition or fact of being a hipster; the characteristics of hipsters. Cf. HEPSTER.

1941 J. SMILEY *Hash House Lingo* 31 *Hipster*, a know-it-all. **1946** MEZZROW & WOLFE *Really Blues* 374 *Hipster*, man who's in the know, grasps everything, is alert. **1948** *Partisan Rev.* XV. 722 Carrying his language and his new philosophy like concealed weapons, the hipster set out to conquer the world. **1956** *Observer* 23 Sept. 2/5 'Hipster' is modern jazz parlance for 'hep-cat'. **1958** *Listener* 3 July 16/1 This whole vexed question of hipsterism, anger, French new realism, and so forth. **1958** *New Statesman* 6 Sept. 292/3 The anthology is valuable for a speculative essay by Norman Mailer on 'beat' or hipster culture. **1959** 'F. NEWTON' *Jazz Scene* 291 *Jive-talk* or hipster-talk is..an argot or cant designed to set the group apart from outsiders. **1959** N. MAILER *Advts. for Myself* (1961) 303 The exchange was called 'Reflections on Hipsterism', when it appeared in *Dissent*. I did not choose the title, and so I have altered the name of the piece. **1967** *Lancet* 15 July 150/2 The 'hipster' movement in California..seemed to be an outright rejection of accepted standards and values.

hipster[2] ('hɪpstə(r)). [f. HIP *sb.*[1] + -STER.] Used esp. *attrib.* of, or pertaining to, a garment, e.g. a skirt or trousers, that extends from the hips rather than the waist. In *pl.*, such a pair of trousers.

1962 *Sunday Express* 30 Dec. 16/4 Top girls are buying camel-hair hipsters with long matching braces. **1967** *Spectator* 14 July 53/3 A shop in the Chelsea Antique Market has neatly solved the male sartorial problem at a price level to fit any hipster pocket. **1968** J. IRONSIDE *Fashion Alphabet* 45 *Hipster*, a skirt which sits on the hips instead of the waist.

hipt, var. of HIPPED.

hipwort ('hɪpwɜːt). [f. HIP *sb.*[1]; so called from the resemblance of the hollow round leaf to the socket of the hip-joint; cf. COTYLEDON 2.] A name for Navelwort, *Cotyledon Umbilicus*.

1597 GERARDE *Herbal* II. cxliii. §3. 424 Nauelwoort is called..in English Pennywoort, Wall Pennywoort, Ladies nauell, and Hipwoort. **1706** PHILLIPS (ed. Kersey), *Hipwort*, a kind of Herb. **1863** PRIOR *Plant-n.*

hir, obs. ME. form of HER *pron.*

hirable: see HIREABLE.

Hirado (hɪ'rɑːdəʊ). Also **-ato.** The name of a small island off the west coast of the province of Hizen on the island of Kyushu in Japan, used *attrib.* to designate a rich elaborate (blue-and-) white porcelain.

The art was originally introduced from Korea about A.D. 1600.

1880 in A. W. Franks *Jap. Pottery* 96 The works were established..in accordance with the order of a prince of the Matsu-ura family residing at Hirato. Hence the articles made here are generally called Hirato ware. **1881** AUDSLEY & BOWES *Keramic Art Japan* 154 The productions of this kiln have commonly been called Hirado ware.

hiragana (hɪrə'gɑːnə). Also **firo-, -kana, -kanna.** [Jap., f. *hira* plain + *kana* (*kanna, kari-na*) borrowed letter(s).] The cursive form of the Japanese syllabary derived from the Tsau style of Chinese ideographs: intended for use by women. Cf. KATAKANA.

1822 F. SHOBERL tr. *Titsingh's Illustr. Japan* 122 These two kinds of poems are composed in *firokanna*, or women's writing. **1859** A. STEINMETZ *Japan & her People* I. vii. 305 The other style, called *hiragana*, employs at least six characters, radically different from each other, for each sound. **1861** G. SMITH *Ten Weeks in Japan* vi. 92 Sentences written in..the irregularly flowing easy current style of the Japanese Hiragana character, are to be met with in every direction. **1863** *Chambers's Encycl.* V. 687/1 The phonetic alphabet, invented about the year 810 A.D., is known as the Hiragana form of character. **1880** *Encycl. Brit.* XIII. 585/1 Each character may be written in either the *katakana* or the *hiragana* style. **1883** I. TAYLOR *Alphabet* I. 35 The Hirakana syllabary was derived from a cursive form of the Chinese writing called the Tsau or 'grass' character. **1928** G. B. SANSOM *Hist. Gram. Jap.* 45 At some period in the development of the script, probably about the time when the *hiragana* and *katakana* syllabaries were contrived. **1973** *Physics Bull.* May 280/3 We have also extended the process by including, in addition to the 881 Chinese characters, the 50 Japanese Kata-Kana and 50 Hira-Gana characters.

hiraude, obs. f. HERALD *v.*

hirawen, obs. f. IHRAM.

‖**hircarra, -ah, hurcaru** (hɜː'kɑːrə). *E. Ind.* Forms: 8 **ircara, hurcurrah, hircar, harcar,** 8–9 **hircarra(h, -cara,** 9 **harcar(r)ah, halcarrah, hurkorah, hurkaru.** [Hindī, Urdū, etc. *harkāra* messenger, courier.] An East Indian spy, messenger, or courier.

1747 *Exp. Paymaster Fort St. David* (MS.) Jan. (Y. Suppl.), Given to the Ircaras for bringing news of the Engagement..4. 3. 0. **1748** in J. Long *Unpub. Rec.* (1869) 4 (Y.) They were as far as Sundra Col, when first descried by their Hurcurrahs. **1757** in E. Ives *Voy. to India* (1773) 161 (Y.) Hircars or spies. **1761** M. WHITE in J. Long *Unpub. Rec.* (1869) 260 (Y.) The head harcar returned, and told me this as well as several other secrets very useful to me. **1773** *Gentl. Mag.* XLIII. 89/2 As the hircarrah came in a private manner, disguised, the President refused him an audience. **1803** WELLINGTON in Owen *Wellesley's Desp.* 786 We depended for our intelligence of the enemy's position on the common hircarrahs of the country. **1827** D. JOHNSON *Ind. Field Sports* (ed. 2) 37, I..took with me an Harcarrah, two guns..and a spear. **1834** *Baboo* I. vii. 118 (Stanf.) A Hurkaru announced Nuwab Yoosuf Ulee Khan Buhadoor. **1862** BEVERIDGE *Hist. India* II. VI. v. 690 Two friendly letters, the first brought by a camel-man, and the latter by hircarrahs.

hirchen, -on, -oun, obs. forms of URCHIN.

hircic ('hɜːsɪk), *a.* *Chem.* [f. L. *hirc-us* he-goat + -IC.] Of or pertaining to a goat. ***hircic acid***, a liquid fatty substance believed by its discoverer to be the odorous principle of mutton suet: now held to be a mixture of fatty acids.

1836-9 TODD *Cycl. Anat.* II. 233/1 A colourless volatile oil which..Chevreul terms..hircic acid. **1846** G. E. DAY tr. *Simon's Anim. Chem.* II. 65 Goat's milk is a very rich white fluid..with a peculiar disagreeable odour arising from the hircic acid which is present in the butter.

hircin ('hɜːsɪn). *Chem.* [f. as prec. + -IN.] A peculiar substance existing in the fat of the goat (and, in a less degree, in that of the sheep) on which its strong odour depends.

1836-9 TODD *Cycl. Anat.* II. 233/1 A distinct fatty matter ..which Chevreul has called hircin. **1842** BRANDE *Dict. Sci.* etc., *Hircine*..when saponified..produces hircic acid. *c* **1865** LETHEBY in *Circ. Sc.* I. 94/1 Tallow..contains a few other fats, as hircine, butyrine, etc.

hircine ('hɜːsaɪn), *a.* and *sb.* [ad. L. *hircīnus* (*hirquīnus*) of a goat; having a goatish smell.]

A. *adj.* Of, belonging to, or resembling a goat; *spec.* **b.** Having a goatish smell; **c.** Lustful.

1656 BLOUNT *Glossogr.*, *Hircine*, goatish, of a Goat. **1794** MARTYN *Rousseau's Bot.* xxiv. 338 The whole plant has a strong hircine smell. **1802** SIR J. E. SMITH in *Mem.* (1832) II. 152 *Orchis latifolia* has, occasionally, a very disagreeable hircine scent. **1822** SOUTHEY *Vis. Judgem.* v, And beyond the limits of ether Drove the hircine host obscene. **1859-63** WOOD *Illustr. Nat. Hist.* I. 656 Goat-like in aspect, and very hircine in many of its habits. **1881** RUSKIN in *19th Cent.* Oct. 520 Satyric or hircine conditions of thought.

B. *sb.* *Min.* A fossil amorphous resin which burns with a strong animal odour. Also called hircite (Dana *Min.* (1868) 747).

hircinous ('hɜːsɪnəs), *a.* *Bot.* and *Zool.* [f. L. *hircīn-us* + -OUS.] Having a hircine odour.

1866 *Treas. Bot.* 592/2 *Hircinous*, smelling like a goat.

‖**hircocervus** (hɜːkəʊ'sɜːvəs). [med.L., f. *hircus* he-goat + *cervus* stag: cf. F. *hircocerf.*] A fabulous creature, half goat, half stag.

1398 TREVISA *Barth. De P.R.* XVIII. c. (MS. Bodl.), Tragelaphus is icleped Ircoceruus also and haþ þat name tragelaphus of tragos þat is a gotte bucke & elephos þat is an herte. **1661** K. W. *Conf. Charac.*, *Informer* (1860) 47 Hees a clubfooted..large lugg'd eagle ey'd hircocervus [*printed* -rous], a meere chimera, one of the devils best boys. **1701** NORRIS *Ideal World* I. iii. 150 An Hirco-cervus or any other fictitious being is true and real with respect to the simple essences or natures. **1706** PHILLIPS (ed. Kersey). **1839-41** HOWITT *Vis. Rem. Places* (1882) 201 A large painting on the wall, a hircocervus or man animal.

†**hir'cose**, *a.* *Obs. rare.* [ad. L. *hircōs-us* goat-like, f. *hircus.*] 'Goatish, smelling like a goat, rammish' (Bailey, vol. II. 1727).

hircosity (hə'kɒsɪtɪ). [f. L. *hircōs-us* + -ITY.] Goatishness, lewdness.

1873 SYMONDS *Grk. Poets* viii. 245 About the audacious scene..there is no Aretine hircosity. It is merely comic.

†**hircu'lation.** *Obs. rare*[−0]. [? f. L. *hirculus* little goat.] (See quots.)

1656 BLOUNT *Glossogr.*, *Hirculation*, a disease in the Vine, when it bears no fruit at all. **1727** BAILEY vol. II, *Hirculation* (with Gardiners), a Disease in Vines, when they run out into Branches and Wood, and bear no Fruit.

†**hird, hired.** *Obs.* Forms: 1 **híred, híered, hýred, héored, héorod,** 2–3 **hired,** 2–4 **hird,** (3 (*Orm.*) also **hirrd**), 3–4 **hyrd,** 4 **hyrt,** 4–5 **herd(e.** [OE. *híred, hírd-es* household, family, shortened from **híwrǽd* (cf., in same sense, *híwrǽden* fem.) = OHG., MHG. *hîrât* marriage, setting up of a household (mod.Ger. *heirat*, also *heurat*), from **hîurât*, **hîwrât*, Goth. type **heiwarêds*; f. *hîwan* members of a household, Goth. *heiwa-* household- + *-rǽd*, condition, state, -RED.]

1. A household, family; a company of servants or retainers, a retinue; a king's court; also, a monastic household.

c **888** K. ÆLFRED *Boeth.* xxxvi. §1 On sumes cyninges hirede. *c* **893** —— *Oros.* VI. xxx. §7 Lucinius bebead þæt nan cristen mon ne come on his hierede. *c* **950** *Lindisf. Gosp.* Matt. xxiv. 45 Ðegn..ðone ȝesette hlaferd his ofer hiorod his. *c* **975** *Rushw. Gosp.* Matt. xiii. 27 Cumende..to fæder þas heoredes. *c* **1000** ÆLFRIC *Hom.* I. 314 Se halȝa hyred. *c* **1000** *Ags. Gosp.* Matt. x. 25 Gyf hi þæs hiredes fæder belzebub clypedon [*c* **1160** *Hatton G.*, þas hyrdes fæder]. **1045** *Will Thurstan* in Thorpe *Chart.* 574 Se hird on Seynt Eadmundsbiri. *a* **1100** *Ags. Voc.* in Wr.-Wülcker 308 *Familia*, hiwræden oððe hired. *a* **1100** *O.E. Chron.* an. 1085 Se cyng..heold þær his hired .v. dagas. *c* **1175** *Lamb. Hom.* 89 Ðat halie hired cristes apostles. *c* **1200** ORMIN 10926 þatt Cristess hirrd, Crisstene follc. *Ibid.* 15890 Hemm drifeþþ Crist ut off hiss hird. *c* **1205** LAY. 6152 Forði-wende þat hired swa þæ king hæhte. *c* **1250** *Gen. & Ex.* 1001 Of is hird euerilc wapman wurð circumcis. *c* **1350** *Will. Palerne* 1120 He..dede him on gate holly wiþ al his herde þat he a-sembled. *a* **1440** *Sir Degrev.* 1088 Ffolke frouschen in fere, In herd ys not to hyde.

2. *Comb.* (only in OE. and early ME.): **hired-child**, child of the house; **hirdcnave, hirdcniht, hirdswain**, a household attendant, retainer, menial; **hirdfolc**, household servants, followers; **hired-gome**, man of the court; **hirdifere**, attendants; **hiredplæie**, courtly amusement. Also HIRDMAN.

c **1205** LAY. 16553 þet þine *hired-childeren pleien mid þissen hunde. *Ibid.* 5664 Ne næuer nænne *hird-cnaue. *c* **1000** ÆLFRIC *Hom.* I. 374 Ðæs caseres ðeȝnas and *hired-cnihtas. *c* **1205** LAY. 4316 Anne hird-cniht he hauede. *Ibid.* 6463 þa hahte he al his *hird-folc faren to are burȝe. *Ibid.* 12289 Aure ælcne *hired-gume feire heo igrætten. *Ibid.* 6631 þer he hundede on comelan Wið his *hird-iferen. *Ibid.* 14481 Mid haueken & mid hunden *hired-plæie luuien. *Ibid.* 5662 þet he..neaue nenne *herd-swein.

hird, -e, obs. ff. HERD *sb.*[1] and [2], HERD *v.*[2], obs. pa. t. HIRE.

†**hirdman, hiredman.** *Obs.* Also 4 **hered-, hirde-.** [f. HIRD + MAN.] A member of a household; a domestic, a household servant; a retainer.

c **993** *Battle of Maldon* 261 Ongunnon ða hiredmenn heardlice feohtan. *c* **1000** ÆLFRIC *Gen.* l. 7 Pharaones yldestan hiredmen. *c* **1205** LAY. 2350 Ah he nom his enne

hired mon [*c* **1275** hired man] þe he wel trowede on. *c* **1230** *Hali Meid.* 31 Habbe monie under þe hirdmen in halle. *c* **1350** *Will. Palerne* 2139 Loke þat hirde-men wel kepe þe comune passage. **13..** *Gaw. & Gr. Knt.* 302 Alle þe heredmen in halle, þe hyȝ & þe loȝe. *c* **1425** *Thomas of Erceld.* (1875) 697 Of swilke an hird mane wolde j here þat couth me telle of swilke ferly.

hirds, obs. form of HARDS, HURDS.

'hirdum-'dirdum. *Sc.* and *north. dial.* [Redupl. of DIRDUM.] Uproar, tumultuous noise.

1724 *Muirland Willie* in Ramsay *Tea-t. Misc.* (1729) 18 Sick Hirdum, Dirdum, and sick Din Wi' he o'er her and she o'er him. **1869** *Lonsdale Gloss.*, *Hirdum-dirdum*, an uproar.

hirdy-girdy, *sb.* and *adv.* *Sc.* and *north. dial.* [Cf. prec., and HIDDY-GIDDY.]

†**A.** *sb.* Uproar, confusion, disorder. *Obs.*

a **1500** *Colkelbie Sow* I. 184 (Jam.) Wi sic a din and a dirdy, A garray and hirdy-girdy, The fulis all afferd wer. **1686** G. STUART *Joco-ser. Disc.* 44 What Hirdy-girdy this ye keep I canna get a wink of sleep. **1893** *Northumbld. Gloss.*, *Hirdy-girdy*, a disorderly noise, a disturbance. (Obs.)

B. *adv.* In or into disorder, in confusion.

16.. in Glanvill *Sadducismus* (1726) 399 They all ran hirdie-girdie. **1819** W. TENNANT *Papistry Storm'd* (1827) 50 Sae to the cross o' Anster ran Hirdie-girdie, woman and man. **1824** SCOTT *Redgauntlet* Let. xi, He ventured back into the parlour, where a' was gaun hirdie-girdie.

hire (haɪə(r)), *sb.* Forms: 1 **hýr, hír,** 3–4 **huire,** 3–5 **huyre, hure,** 4 **hir, hijre,** 4–5 **here,** 4–7 **hyre,** 5 **huyr, hyr,** 6 **hyire,** 6–7 **hier, hyer,** 3– **hire.** [OE. *hýr* str. fem., corresp. to OFris. *hêre* (WFris. *hiere*), OLG. **hûria* (MLG., MDu. *hûre*, LG. *hüre, hür*, Du. *huur*; Ger. *heuer*, Da. *hyre*, Sw. *hyra*, all from LG.):—OTeut. type **hûrjâ-*, not known in OHG., ON., or Gothic.]

1. Payment contracted to be made for the temporary use of anything. (In OE., esp. for money lent; usury, interest.) ***to be*** or ***have on hire, to let*** (†***put, set***) ***to hire***, i.e. at the service of another in consideration of payment made by him.

c **1000** ÆLFRIC *Deut.* xxiii. 19 Ne læne þine breþer nan þinȝ to hire. —— *Lev.* xxv. 37 Ne syle þu þin feoh to hyre. *c* **1000** *Ecgberht's Penit.* III. Proem. *a* **1300** *Cursor M.* 6778 Elles noght.. I lete to hire for ani mede. *c* **1386** CHAUCER *Prol.* 507 He sette nat his benefice to hyre [*v.rr.* hire, huyre]. **1413** *Pilgr. Sowle* (Caxton 1483) III. v. 53 Longe tyme haue ye putte youre tonges to hyre, ye witnessers of falshede. **1483** *Cath. Angl.* 186/2 To let to Hire, *locare.* **1495–7** *Naval Acc. Hen. VII* (1896) 186 Payed to Richard Yoksale of Portesmouth ffor the hyre of hys bote. **1497** *Ibid.* 250 Ffreight & hyre of a crayer. **1526** TINDALE *Mark* xii. 1 A certayne man planted a vyne yarde.. and lett it out to hyre to husbandemen. **1583** HOLLYBAND *Campo di Fior* 93 Of him that in.. streate keepeth horses to hier. **1587** F. JAMES in *Collect.* (O.H.S.) I. 199 Bote hyre from Lambeth. **1699** DAMPIER *Voy.* II. I. 13 The hire is pretty reasonable both for the Vessels, and the Men. **1717** tr. *Frezier's Voy.* 109 Paying him the King's Duty, and the Hire of the Mill. **1870** W. M. BAKER *New Timothy* 161 (Cent.) To keep one's conscience, too, on hire, as that drunken Isham.. at the livery-stable does a horse. *Mod.* Bicycles on hire.

2. Payment contracted to be made for personal service; wages.

a **1225** *Ancr. R.* 208 Etholden oðres hure, ouer his rihte terme, nis hit strong reflac? *c* **1290** *S. Eng. Leg.* I. 285/242 He scholde him paye is huyre. **13..** *Sir Beues* (A.) 2972 And of þe meistri icham sure, ȝif he wile ȝilde min hure. **1382** WYCLIF *Luke* x. 7 Forsothe a workman is worthi his hyre. **1483** CAXTON *Gold. Leg.* 283 a/2 They.. sayd they wold brynge hym thyder without ony freyght or huyr. **1502** *Priv. Purse Exp. Eliz. of York* (1830) 76 For the scole hyer of the same Edward.. every quarter viij d. **1583** HOLLYBAND *Campo di Fior* 61 What aske you for your hyer?.. I will contente myself with a small hier. **1796** MORSE *Amer. Geog.* I. 277 Their testimony against preaching for hire. **1882** OUIDA *Maremma* I. 4 They had other thoughts besides those of their hire and wages.

3. *fig.* Reward, recompense, payment (for work or service of any kind).

a **1225** *Ancr. R.* 428 Hore hure schal beon þe eche blisse of heouene. *a* **1300** *Cursor M.* 23192 Sathanas.. sal casten be.. in a stincand stang o fire; þar sal be yolden him his hire. **1382** WYCLIF *Rom.* vi. 22 Treuli the hyris of synne, deeth. **1481** CAXTON *Reynard* (Arb.) 30 Our lorde god shal ones rewarde them their hyre. *c* **1560** A. SCOTT *Poems* (S.T.S.) xxxii. 10 Schort plesour, lang displesour; Repentence is the hyre. **1608** D. T. *Ess. Pol. & Mor.* 2 b, Some.. that thinke the very disturbance of things established, a sufficient hyre to set them on worke. **1841** JAMES *Brigand* iv, And make her hand the hire of this Savoyard.

4. The action of hiring or fact of being hired.

1615 J. STEPHENS *Satyr. Ess.* 189 The dispersed hire of acquaintance to extoll things indifferent. **1835** LYTTON *Rienzi* I. iv, Ay, it is the duty of thy hire. **1863** MRS. C. CLARKE *Shaks. Char.* xiv. 357 A savage hire,—the wages he receives are as dispiteous. *Mod.* To arrange for the hire of a horse.

5. *attrib.* and *Comb.*, as ***hire-car***, ***-carriage***, ***hire-payer***, ***-wage***; **hire-system**, a system by which a hired article becomes, by virtue of a stipulated number of payments, the property of the hirer; so **hire-purchase**; used esp. *attrib.*; also as *vb.*, and **'hire-purchasing** *ppl. a.*; cf. *H.P.* (s.v. H III). Also HIREGANG, -MAN, -WOMAN.

1483 *Cath. Angl.* 186/2 An Hire payer, *mercedarius.* **1548** UDALL *Erasm. Par. Luke* xvi. 134 b, To digge in the field for hire wages from daie to daye. **1895** *Brit. Warehouseman* Feb. 30/2 The plaintiff let a piano to one Sullivan under an ordinary hire-purchase agreement. **1896** *Daily News* 24 Jan. 7/2 Mr. Moore.. was the inventor of the now widely adopted hire-purchase system. **1898** *Westm. Gaz.* 11 Jan. 2/1 Could not the hire-purchase system be worked? **1901** KIPLING *Kim* v. 122 The woman, she kept *kabarri* shop near where the hire-carriages are. **1909** *Chambers's Jrnl.* July 421/1 Not hire-purchased, you see; I'm not to be gulled by silly advertisements. No. I found my own shop and made my own choice. **1909** *Installation News* iii. 134/1 The hire and hire-purchase of cooking, heating, and other apparatus. **1923** 'BARTIMEUS' *Seaways* 36 If it wasn't for my daughter Annie bein' musical an' wantin' a pianner on the 'ire purchase, I wouldn't stop aboard 'er another night. **1930** *Economist* 25 Jan. 215/2 (Advt.), Bank of England and Hire Purchase. **1947** *E. Afr. Ann. 1946–7* 28/2 (Advt.), Largest fleet of hire cars in Kenya. **1960** *Author* Summer 64/2 All up-to-date readers are hire-purchasing electronic computers to read their library books for them. **1960** *Guardian* 9 May 6/7 The true-born, hire-purchasing Briton. **1964** R. BRADDON *Year Angry Rabbit* xi. 94 It was *her* hire car that rammed the car taking Dorfmann and Welch to the deportation ship. **1966** *Times* (Canada Suppl.) 28 Feb. p. ii, Planes and hire-cars whisk you to the magic. **1972** *Mod. Law Rev.* XXXV. I. 38 All three hire-purchase agreements were illegal.

hire (haɪə(r)), *v.* Forms: 1 **hýrian, hýran,** 3 **hure(n,** 3–4 **huyre,** 4–7 **hyre,** 6 **hiare, hyer,** 6–7 **hier,** 4– **hire.** [OE. *hýrian*, corresp. to OFris. *hêra*, OLG. **hûrian* (MLG., MDu. *hûren*, LG. *hüren*, Du. *huren*, Ger. *heuern*, Da. *hyre*, Sw. *hyra*, from LG.), f. the sb.: see HIRE *sb.*]

1. a. *trans.* To engage the service of (a person) for a stipulated reward; to employ for wages. Phr. ***hire and fire*** [FIRE *v.*[1] 16]; also as *sb.* and *attrib.*

c **1000** ÆLFRIC *Hom.* II. 72 Seðe.. wolde hyrian wyrhtan into his winȝearde. *c* **1000** *Ags. Gosp.* Matt. xx. 7 Us nan mann ne hyrode [*c* **1160** *Hatton G.* herde]. *a* **1225** *Ancr. R.* 126 Vorte huren mid ham, ase me deð mid garsume þeo þet wel vihteð. *c* **1330** R. BRUNNE *Chron.* (1810) 80 þe bisshop.. Hired ilk a man. *c* **1440** *Promp. Parv.* 241/2 Hyryn, *conduco.* **1535** COVERDALE *Prov.* xxvi. 10 Who so hyreth a foole, hyreth soch one as wyl take no hede. **1570** B. GOOGE *Pop. Kingd.* III. 43 b, They also hier folkes to say the Psalters speedily. **1663** COWLEY *Verses & Ess.*, *Ode on Harvey* iii, As if he hir'd the workers by the day. **1742** PITT *Sp. Ho. Com.* 10 Dec. in *Anecd. & Sp. Earl Chatham* (1797) I. v. 116 They have already been informed there was no necessity for hiring auxiliary troops. **1872** RAYMOND *Statist. Mines & Mining* 182 Chinamen are in the country and can be hired cheaply. **1958** *Listener* 23 Oct. 632/2 Men who can be hired and fired according to the current level of business. **1963** *Times* 6 Feb. 6/3 'Hire and fire' is no longer associated with the construction industries. *Ibid.* 24 Apr. 7/4 Sir Donald said a five-year building programme should be planned in the public sector to ensure continuity of work and stop the 'hire and fire' attitude. **1970** *Sci. Amer.* Mar. 35/3 The inability to hire and fire in order to vary the work force with fluctuations in the business cycle. **1973** *Advocate-News* (Barbados) 20 Feb. 4/2 The locals are in the 'hire and fire' positions.

b. *transf.* To engage or induce to do something by a payment or reward; to bribe.

c **1400** *Gamelyn* 786 He was fast aboute bothe day and other, For to hyre the quest to hangen his brother. **1529** MORE *Dyaloge* III. Wks. 246/1 A man could not hyre a Jewe to sit down vpon his byble of the olde testament. **1631** GOUGE *God's Arrows* III. xciii. 357 Cullin.. was hired by English runagates in the Low Countries to kill the Queene. **1697** DRYDEN *Virg. Æneid* II. 42 Thymœtes first ('tis doubtful whether hired, Or so the Trojan destiny required) Moved that the ramparts might be broken down. **1849** MACAULAY *Hist. Eng.* vi. II. 159 A popish priest was hired with the promise of the mitre of Waterford to preach at Saint James's against the Act of Settlement.

2. To procure the temporary use of (any thing) for stipulated payment.

c **1205** LAY. 30441 þa scipen heo gunnen hure mid ahten swiðe deore. *c* **1290** *Beket* 1161 in *S. Eng. Leg.* I. 139 [He] huyrde him a mere, For an Englichs peni, with an haltre, þis holi man to bere. *c* **1450** *Bk. Curtasye* 375 in *Babees Bk.* 310 For cariage þe porter hors schalle hyre. **1583** HOLLYBAND *Campo di Fior* 327 He had hired a house in Colme-streate. **1590** SHAKS. *Com. Err.* IV. i. 95 A ship you sent mee too, to hier waftage. **1718** LADY M. W. MONTAGU *Let. to Abbé Conti* 31 July, I hired an ass.. that I might go some miles into the country. **1863** MISS BRADDON *Eleanor's Vict.* (1878) I. iii. 24 He hired a villa by the Lake of Como.

3. a. To grant the temporary use of for stipulated payment; to let *out* on hire; to lease.

1382 WYCLIF *Mark* xii. 1 A man plauntide a vyneȝerd.. and hirede it to erthe tilieris. **1484** CAXTON *Fables of Alfonce* (1889) 3 [He] demaunded of the poure yong man that he wold hyre to hym a parte of his hows. **1589** G. FLETCHER in *Lett. Lit. Men* (Camden) 80 That no man should hier owt horse or boat to anie Englishman. **1611** BIBLE *1 Sam.* ii. 5 They that were full, haue hired out themselues for bread. **1662** WOOD *Life* (O.H.S.) I. 462 Having skill in gardning and manuring [he] hired himselfe to gent. there for that imployment. **1721** *Duxbury Rec.* (1893) 238 That the said money should be hired out at five pounds per cent. to such persons as shall give sufficient security for the same. **1842** TENNYSON *Dora* 36 He left his father's house, And hired himself to work within the fields.

b. *intr.* (for *refl.*) ***to hire out***, to engage oneself as a servant for payment. Chiefly *N. Amer.*

1776 S. CURWEN *Jrnl. & Lett.* (1864) 74 The inhabitants [of Sidmouth, Devon, England] chiefly hired out to the Newfoundland traders. **1833** C. A. DAVIS *Lett. J. Downing* (1834) 35, I had hired out here this summer. **1856** OLMSTED *Slave States* 83 Poor white girls never hired out to do servants' work. **1884** *Harper's Mag.* May 882/1 They hire out to.. farmers. **1969** in Halpert & Story *Christmas Mumming in Newfoundland* 26 They hired out as fishing servants.

hire, early form of HER *pron.*

hireable ('haɪərəb(ə)l), *a.* Also **hirable.** [f. HIRE *v.* + -ABLE.] Capable of being hired; obtainable for hire.

1864 CARLYLE *Fredk. Gt.* XII. xi. IV. 259 Four pretty Sovereignties. Three, or Two, of these hireable by gold, it is to be hoped. **1868** *Daily Tel.* 31 July 5/4 Prices of all purchasable or hirable things are high.

hired (haɪəd), *ppl. a.* [f. HIRE *v.* + -ED[1].] Engaged or employed for payment; let out on hire: mercenary. Also with adverbs, as ***hired out***.

c **1230** *Hali Meid.* 29 Eni driuel iþe hus oðer eni ihured hine. **1382** WYCLIF *Luke* xv. 19 Make me as oon of thi hyrid men [**1388** thin hirid men]. **1388** —— *John* x. 13 The hirid hyne fleeth, for he is an hirid hyne. *c* **1440** *Promp. Parv.* 241/2 Hyryd man, or servawnte, *conductius.* **1583** HOLLYBAND *Campo di Fior* 271, I have a hiered horse. **1597** DANIEL *Civ. Wars* VI. lix, With mercenarie breath And hyred tongue. **1711** STEELE *Spect.* No. 155 ¶1 Travelling together in the same hired Coach. **1789** GIBBON *Autobiog.* (1896) 127 An independent stranger in a hired lodging. **1808** SCOTT *Life Dryden* iv, To have recourse to hired bravoes to avenge his personal quarrel. **1863** KINGLAKE *Crimea* (1876) I. i. 9 He.. has a crowd of hired courtiers at his side.

b. ***hired man, woman, girl, people***: applied to free men or women engaged as servants (the latter word being formerly used to include slaves). *U.S.*

1639 *Plymouth Col. Rec.* (1855) I. 122 Roberte Eldred, the hyred servant of Nicholas Sympkins for the terme of three yeares. **1714** tr. *Joutel's La Salle's Jrnl.* 2 Hired People and Workmen of all Sorts, requisite for making of a Settlement. **1715** *Laws of Maryland* (1765) c. 44 §10 No Person whatsoever, shall trade.. with any Servant, whether hired, or indented, or Slave.. without Leave or License. **1737** *Plymouth* (Mass.) *Town Rec.* 18 May (1892) II. 321 A hired man with me on a fishing voyage. **1751** FRANKLIN *Obs. Increase Mankind* Wks. 1887 II. 227 Slaves may be kept as long as a man pleases.. while hired men are continually leaving their masters (often in the midst of his business). **1792** tr. *J. P. Brissot's New Trav. U.S.* 400 They [Quakers] have no slaves; they employ negroes as hired servants. **1818** J. FLINT *Lett. Amer.* (1822) 9 *Master* is not a word in the vocabulary of hired people. *Bos*, a Dutch one of similar import, is substituted. The former is used by Negroes, and is by free people considered as synonymous with slave-keeper. **1820** *Ibid.* 264 These I must call Americanisms.. Hired Girl for Servant Girl. Hired Man for Servant Man. **1842** J. F. WATSON *Ann. Philad.* (1857) I. 176 Now all hired girls appear abroad in the same style of dress as their ladies. **1877** BARTLETT *Dict. Amer.* (ed. 4), *Hired man*, a man-servant. *Hired woman*, a servant-girl. Many servants dislike to be called such, and think it more respectable to say 'help' or 'hired woman'. **1893** *Nation* (N.Y.) 19 Jan. 43/1 Where are the farms on which there is no place for the 'hired man' or 'hired girl'?

hired, hiredman: see HIRD, HIRDMAN.

hiree (haɪə'riː). [See -EE.] One who is hired.

1811 *Sporting Mag.* XXXVII. 75 Would.. either hirer or hiree disgrace themselves so much?

†**hiregang.** *Sc. Obs.* Also 6 **hyre-.** [f. HIRE *sb.* + GANG *sb.*] Hire, lease.

1513 DOUGLAS *Æneis* XII. ix. 50 His fader eyrit and sew ane peice of feild, That he in hyregang held to be his beild. **1535** *Reg. Mag. Sig. Scot.* 1513–1546. 324/1 Proficuum [xxvij libr.] a mense Julii 1515 per 17 annos, viz. cujuslibet bovis annuatim extenden. in le hiregang et laboribus ad 6 firlotas farine.

hireless ('haɪəlɪs), *a.* [f. HIRE *sb.* + -LESS.] Without hire or pay, unhired.

1651 DAVENANT *Gondibert* VI. lxvi, This fam'd Philosopher is Nature's Spie, And hireless gives th' intelligence to Art. **1796** COLERIDGE *Sonn. Erskine*, An hireless Priest before th' insulted shrine. **1817** —— *Biog. Lit.* 81 Preaching by the way in most of the great towns, as an hireless volunteer, in a blue coat and white waistcoat.

hireling ('haɪəlɪŋ), *sb.* and *a.* [OE. *hýrling* (rare), f. *hýr* HIRE + -LING. Not known in ME., and app. formed anew in 16th c.]

A. *sb.* **1.** One who serves for hire or wages; a hired servant; a mercenary (soldier). (Now usually somewhat contemptuous: cf. 2.)

c **1000** *Ags. Gosp.* Mark i. 20 Hi heora fæder zebedeo on scipe forleton mid hyrlingum [*c* **1160** *Hatton G.* hyrlingen]. **1535** COVERDALE *Tobit* v. 11 Axest thou after the kynred of an hyrelinge? **1547** J. HARRISON *Exhort. Scottes* G j b, To bee as common hirelynges to a forrein nacion. **1582** N. T. (Rhem.) *John* x. 13 The hireling fleeth because he is a hireling [WYCLIF hirid hyne; TINDALE heyred servaunt]. **1632** LITHGOW *Trav.* IX. 380, I dispatched my Dragoman, and the other Barbarian hireling. **1734** tr. *Rollin's Anc. Hist.*, The loss he had sustained by the robbery of his hireling. **1849** MACAULAY *Hist. Eng.* i. (1880) I. 57 Hirelings whom want and idleness had induced to enlist.

b. A hired horse. *nonce-use.*

1893 SIR G. CHESNEY *Lesters* III. II. xxi. 23 Lionel on his hireling was the only one up with the hounds at the last.

2. One who makes reward or material remuneration the motive of his actions; a mercenary. (Opprobrious.)

1574 tr. *Marlorat's Apocalips* 32 Least in sted of faithfull shepherds, they set hyrelings or rather wolues ouer the flocke of Christe. **1605** BACON *Adv. Learn.* I. ii. §5 As an hireling, that loves the work for the wages. **1667** MILTON *P.L.* IV. 193 So since into his Church lewd Hirelings climbe. **1721** POPE *Ep. to Earl of Oxford* 36 No hireling she, no prostitute to praise. **1821** BYRON *Sardan.* II. i, Baser Hirelings, who live by lies on good men's lives. **1849**

MACAULAY *Hist. Eng.* iv. I. 456 James..had now, in becoming King of England, become also a hireling and vassal of Lewis.

B. *adj.* Characteristic of or pertaining to a hireling; serving for hire or wages; to be had for hire; mercenary. (Usually opprobrious.)

1587 GOLDING *De Mornay* xxxii. 510 What find we in al the writings of the Heathen but a Hierling vertue? **1614** RALEIGH *Hist. World* I. ix. §1 (R.) The factious and hireling historians of all ages. **1681** DRYDEN *Abs. & Achit.* 922 The plot by hireling witnesses improv'd. **1720** *Lett. fr. Lond. Jrnl.* (1721) 47 Here are also hireling Chairs. **1738** JOHNSON *London* 213 Some hireling senators. **1843** MACAULAY *Ivry* iv, With all the hireling chivalry of Guelders and Almayne. **1894** *Law Times* XCVII. 384/1 [To] earn for itself the name of a profession of hireling subornees of perjury.

Hence **'hirelingship**, the condition of a hireling.

1827 POLLOK *Let.* in *Life* (1841) 357 Wherever you send him during the above specified hirelingship.

hireman ('haɪəmən). *Obs.* or *dial.* [OE. *hýrmann*, f. HIRE *sb.* + MAN.] A hired man, hired servant; retainer.

c **975** *Rushw. Gosp.* Mark i. 20 Forlet fæder his zebedeus in scipe mið þæm hyremonnum. *a* **1100** *Gerefa* in *Anglia* IX. 260 Symle he sceal his hyrmen scyrpan mid manunge. **12..** *Fragm. Ælfric's Gram.* in Wr.-Wülcker 552/20 *Mercennarius*, hurmon. *a* **1310** in Wright *Lyric P.* xv. 50 Alse ys hirmon halt in hous. **17..** *Hireman Chiel* in Child *Ballads* (1861) VIII. 234 He..has put on the hireman's coat, To keip him frae the cold. **1792** *Statist. Acc. Scotl., Forfars.* IV. 15 (Jam.) The wages of a hireman, that is, a man-servant hired for the half year..now are £3, or £3 10*s*.

†**Hiren** ('haɪərɪn). *Obs.* [A corruption of the female name *Irene*, F. *Irène*.] The name of a female character in Peele's play of 'The Turkish Mahamet and Hyrin the fair Greek' (*a* 1594); used allusively by Shakspere and early 17th century writers as meaning 'a seductive woman', a harlot.

1597 SHAKS. *2 Hen. IV*, II. iv. 173 Downe: downe Dogges, downe Fates: haue wee not Hiren here? **1598** SYLVESTER *Du Bartas* II. i. III. 35 Of charming Sin the deep inchaunting Syrens, The snares of vertue, valour-softning Hyrens. **1605** CHAPMAN, etc. *Eastw. Hoe* in *O. Pl.* IV. 218 (N.) 'Sfoot, lend me some money. Hast thou not Hyren here? **1615** T. ADAMS *Spir. Navigator* Wks. (1630) 402 There be Sirens in the sea of this world. Sirens? Hirens, as they are now called..What a number of these Sirens, Hirens, Cockatrices,..in plaine English, Harlots, swimme amongst vs.

hiren, obs. form of HERN, hers.

hirer ('haɪərə(r)). [f. HIRE *v.* + -ER[1].]

1. One who engages the services of a person or obtains the use of a thing for payment.

a **1500** in Arnolde *Chron.* (1811) 72 If the said hirer in gret duelle not in any parte therof but lete it out ageyn. **1592** WEST *1st Pt. Symbol.* I. §25 B, The lessee or hierer. **1767** BLACKSTONE *Comm.* II. xxx. 453 By this mutual contract the hirer, or borrower, gains a temporary property in the thing hired. **1885** *Law Rep.* 14 Q. Bench Div. 892 The relation..between hirers and letters of private carriages.

2. One who lets out something on hire. *Obs.* or *Sc.* (esp. in ***coach-hirer***, ***carriage-hirer***).

1591 PERCIVALL *Sp. Dict.*, *Arrendador*, a lettor, a hirer. **1598** FLORIO, *Nolatore*, a hyrer, a hackney man. **1755** JOHNSON, *Hirer* 2. In Scotland it denotes one who keeps small horses to let. **1766** BEATTIE *Ep. to Hon. C.B.* 27 'Tis wondrous hard, To act the Hirer, yet preserve the Bard.

†**'hire-woman.** *Sc.* ?*Obs.* [Cf. HIREMAN.] A hired woman, a woman-servant.

1552 ABP. HAMILTON *Catech.* (1884) 112 Thow sall nocht cowet thi nychtbouris house, nor his croft or his land, nor his servand, nor his hyir woman.

hirie-harie, variant of HIRRIE-HARRIE.

'hiring, *vbl. sb.* [f. HIRE *v.* + -ING[1].]

1. The action of the vb. HIRE; engaging a person or thing for hire; letting out on hire.

c **1400** *Three Kinges Cologne* 24 þe lordys of þe grounde haue..grete toll of hyryng of þes beestes. **1675** in Willis & Clark *Cambridge* (1886) III. 42 The hireing of workmen..may be intrusted..to the Vicechancellour. **1767** BLACKSTONE *Comm.* II. xxx. 453 Hiring is always for a price, or stipend, or additional recompence; borrowing is merely gratuitous. **1868** *Pall Mall G.* 12 Dec. 3 Hiring is an agreement for the continuous performance of certain tasks for current wages.

2. *local.* (See quot. 1825.) (Also ***statute hiring***.)

1825 BROCKETT, *Hiring*, a fair or market at which country servants are hired. **1826** in Hone *Every-day Bk.* II. 668 The 'hirings' for farmers' servants half yearly at Whitsuntide and Martinmas. **1885** R. BUCHANAN *Annan Water* v, A couple of female farm servants had come in to the spring 'hiring'.

3. *attrib.*, as ***hiring-agreement***, ***-time***, etc.; **hiring-fair** = 2; †**hiring man**, a man to be hired.

c **1425** *Eng. Conq. Irel.* 22 We come nat yn-to thys land as hyryng men. **1883** T. HARDY in *Longm. Mag.* July 257 Attending a wet hiring-fair at Candlemas, in search of a new master. **1892** *Antiquary* Jan. 14 The annual agricultural hiring-time in any district. **1897** *Daily News* 15 Oct. 8/7 The largest hiring fair in Berkshire was held at Newbury yesterday.

hi-rise, var. *high-rise* (HIGH *a.* 21).

hirk, hirkful, obs. ff. IRK, IRKFUL.

hirkle, obs. f. HURKLE *v.*

hirling, var. of HERLING.

Hirmologion (hɜːməʊ'ləʊdʒɪən). Also **Heirmologion, Hirmologium.** Pl **-ia.** [med. Gr. εἱρμολόγιον or f. εἱρμός (see HIRMOS) + λογ-, variant of λεγ- to say.] In the Eastern Church, a book containing eucharistic prayers, hirmoi, etc.

1850 in J. M. Neale *Eastern Church, Gen. Introd.* I. 890. **1952** *Monumenta Musicae Byzantinae* IV. 1 The final publication of the whole Byzantine Hirmologium is beyond the power of one man and must be based on a complete survey of all the sources. *Ibid* VI. 1. p. xxxiv, We have a better knowledge of old Hirmologia than of old Sticheraria. **1961** E. WELLESZ *Hist. Byzantine Mus.* (ed. 2) p. v, Some authors..prefer the Latin form *Hirmologium*, others the Greek spelling *Heirmologion* or *Hirmologion*.

hirmon, obs. f. HIREMAN.

hirmos ('hɜːmɒs). Also **heirmos, hirmus.** Pl. **-moi, -mi.** [Gr. εἱρμός series, connection.] In the hymnology of the Eastern Church, a model stanza forming a pattern for the other stanzas.

1850 J. M. NEALE *Eastern Church, Gen. Introd.* I. 830 There are a certain number of *Troparia*..called Hirmoi, on the model of which all other troparia, etc., are formed. *Ibid.* 835 Here we have the actual hirmos on which the third ode is arranged. **1863** R. F. LITTLEDALE *Offices East. Ch.* 214. **1880** *Encycl. Brit.* XII. 580/1 An *ode* is a song or hymn compounded of several similar 'troparia'... To these is always prefixed a typical or standard 'troparion', called the *hirmus*. **1959** *Chambers's Encycl.* VII. 348/2 A *contakion*, consisting (broadly speaking) of a *heirmos*, which set the pattern of what followed, succeeded by a series of *troparia*. **1961** E. WELLESZ *Hist. Byzantine Mus.* (ed. 2) 14 Dom Gaisser's article on the *Heirmoi*, the model strophes of the Easter Hymn, is the first detailed study of Byzantine hymnography.

hirn(e, obs. ff. HERN *sb.*, corner.

hirola, var. HEROLA.

hirondelle (hɪrɒn'dɛl). *Obs.* exc. in *Heraldry*. Forms: 7 **arrondell, arundell,** 8 **hyrondell,** 9 **hirondelle.** [a. F. *hirondelle*.] A swallow.

c **1600** *Burel's Pilgr.* in J. Watson *Coll. Poems* (1706) II. 62 (Jam.) The Arrondell, so swift of flight. **1661** MORGAN *Sph. Gentry* I. v. 58 More swift, than Bird hight Arundell. **1880** G. T. CLARK in *Encycl. Brit.* XI. 701/1 The Swallow, or hirondelle, forms the very early coat of the Arundells.

hirple ('hɜːp(ə)l), *v.* Chiefly *Sc.* and *north. dial.* [Origin unknown. (Its coincidence in sound and sense with Gr. ἕρπ-ειν is noticeable.)]

intr. To move with a gait between walking and crawling; to walk lamely, to drag a limb, to hobble. In early use said of the hare.

c **1450** HENRYSON *Mor. Fab.* 32 The hard-back Hurtchen, and the hirpland Hair. *a* **1605** MONTGOMERIE *Cherrie & Slae* (2nd version) 30 in *Poems* (1887) 286, I saw the hurcheon and the hare In hidlings hirpling heir and thair. **1768** ROSS *Helenore* 44 (Jam.) To Colin's house..He, tired and weary, hirpled down the brae. **1781** J. HUTTON *Tour to Caves* Gloss., *Hirple*, to limp in walking. **1821** CLARE *Vill. Minstr.* II. 117 Hirpling round from time to time. **1821** SCOTT *Pirate* vii, Neil Ronaldson, that canna walk a mile to hear the minister, but he will hirple ten if he hears of a ship embayed. **1866** J. PAYN *Mirk Abbey* II. 96 An old man and his wife..came hirpling out.

fig. **1792** BURNS *On Birth Posth. Child* ii, November hirples o'er the lea Chill on thy lovely form. **1893** CROCKETT *Stickit Minister* 17 It [the speech] ran or rather hirpled somewhat as follows.

Hence **hirpling** *ppl. a.*; **hirple** *sb.*, a crawling or limping gait.

1821 SCOTT *Pirate* xxxii, They will be waiting for him, hirpling, useless body. **1821-30** LD. COCKBURN *Mem.* ii (1856) 119 With a slow stealthy step—something between a walk and a hirple. **1830** GALT *Lawrie T.* VII. i. (1849) 363 Whose gallop was never better than a hirple.

†**hirpled, -ild,** *ppl. a. Obs.* Also 4 **harplid.** [Origin obscure: cf. ON. *herpa* cramp, contraction, *herpa-st* to be contracted as with cramp. See also the forms of HURKLE *v.*] Contracted, wrinkled.

a **1300** *Cursor M.* 8085 þair armes hari wit hirpild [*v.rr.* harplid, rungilt] hid.

†**hirqui'talliency.** *Obs. nonce-wd.* [f. L. *hirquitallīre* (of infants) to acquire a strong voice (f. *hircus* he-goat) + -ENCY.]

1652 URQUHART *Jewel* 125 To speak of her hirquitalliency.

hirrawem, obs. form of IHRAM.

hirrie-harrie ('hɪrɪ'hærɪ), *int.* (*sb.*) *Sc.* Also 6 **hiry hary,** 9 **hirie-harie.** An utterance expressive of rapid and tumultuous movement.

c **1520** in *Dunbar's Poems* (1893) 314 Hiry, hary, hubbilschow! Se ȝe not quha is cum now? **1808-80** JAMIESON, *Hirrie-harrie*, 1. An outcry after a thief. 2. A broil, a tumult. **1819** W. TENNANT *Papistry Storm'd* (1827) 86 Then, hirie-harie! folks did rusch.

hirrient ('hɪrɪənt), *a.* and *sb. rare.* [f. L. *hirrient-em*, pr. pple. of *hirrīre* to snarl.] **A.** *adj.* 'Snarling'; trilled. **B.** *sb.* A trilled sound. (Cf. *litera canina*, Lat. name for *r*.)

1832 J. K[ENRICK] in *Philol. Museum* I. 618 The peculiar barbarism of the Κᾶρες, which consisted in the frequent use of the hirrient ρ. **1860** FARRAR *Orig. Lang.* ii. 51 In the hirrients and the gutturals, the burr and roughness of the Northern tongues.

Hirschsprung ('hɪəʃprʊŋ). The name of Harald *Hirschsprung* (1830–1916), Danish physician, used in the possessive in ***Hirschsprung's disease***, congenital enlargement of the colon, occurring esp. in boys, *spec.* such enlargement due to the absence of the ganglion cells of a segment of the lower colon or rectum.

1900 DORLAND *Med. Dict.* 208/2 *Hirschsprung's d[isease]*, congenital hypertrophic dilatation of the colon. **1908** *Practitioner* Sept. 456 An example of idiopathic dilatation of the colon, or—as it is called in Germany—Hirschsprung's disease, is recorded by Wagner. **1949** *Lancet* 1 Jan. 10/2 A considerable proportion of cases of megacolon (not being Hirschsprung's disease) remain in the residual 'idiopathic' group. **1966** B. C. MORSON in Wright & Symmers *Syst. Path.* I. xvii. 549/1 Idiopathic megacolon..has to be distinguished from congenital megacolon Hirschsprung's disease), in which there is a characteristic underlying histological defect. **1968** F. A. JONES et al. *Clin. Gastroenterol.* (ed. 2) iv. 121 Confusion later arose because the term Hirschsprung's disease was applied to any megacolon.

†**hirse** (hɜːs). *Obs.* Also 6 *erron.* **hirst.** [a. Ger. *hirse*, MHG. *hirse*, *hirs*, OHG. *hirsi*, *hirso*; orig. a High German word, which in later times has spread into LG. and Scand. (Da. *hirse*, Sw. *hirs*), as well as Eng., where app. introduced by the 16th c. herbalists. See Kluge.] Millet.

[**1562** TURNER *Herbal* II. 57 Milium is named in Greke kegchros & piston, in Duche hirsz, in Frenche du Millet.] **1578** LYTE *Dodoens* IV. ix. 463 This plant [Milium] is called in..English Mill, Millet, and Hirse. **1579-80** NORTH *Plutarch* (1676) 77 A Vessell or Pan wherein they did fry millet or hirse. **1589** FLEMING *Virg. Georg.* I. 8 For Millet or for Hirst comes yearly care and paine. **1611** COTGR., *Millet*, Millet, Mill, Hirse. **1658** PHILLIPS, *Hyrse*, a kind of plant otherwise call'd Millet.

hirsel ('hɜːsəl), *sb. Sc.* and *north. dial.* Forms: 4 **hirsill, hyresel, hersale,** 5 **hyrsale,** 8– **hirsel,** (8 **hirdsell, hirsle,** 9 **her-, hirsell**). [ad. ON. *hirzla* from *hirðsla* custody, safe-keeping, f. *hirða* to herd, tend (sheep, etc.); but the north. Eng. and Sc. word has always been concrete, and intimately connected in sense with *hird*, HERD[2].]

1. a. The flock of sheep under the charge of a shepherd; the entire stock of sheep on one farm.

1366 *Durham Halm. Rolls* (Surtees) 55 Ordinatum est..quod quilibet eorum teneat hirsill' et quod custodiant porcos..citra..ne quis eorum teneat porcos absque hirsill'. **1378** *Ibid.* 148 Quilibet teneat hirsill cum porcis. **1728** RAMSAY *Robert Richy & S.* 4 Tenting his hirsle on the moorland green. **1737** —— *Sc. Prov.* (1776) 10 (Jam.) Ae scabbed sheep will smit the hale hirdsell. **1853** G. JOHNSTON *Nat. Hist. E. Bord.* I. 95 A hirsel of sheep animates the moor above. **1893** *Northumbld. Gloss.*, *Hirsel*, the general sheep stock belonging to a hill stock-farmer.

b. *fig.* A spiritual flock, a church.

c **1375** *Sc. Leg. Saints, Petrus* 670 Hyrde of goddis hersale all! *Ibid.*, *Jacobus Minor* 848 þat mene ine þis hale world sal se Bot a hyrde & a hyresel be. **1880** A. SOMERVILLE *Autobiog.* 26, I had an easy hirsel and never wearied.

c. The ground occupied by a flock of sheep.

1822 SCOTT *Fortunes of Nigel* III. ii. 50 Being in a strange country, like a poor lamb that has wandered from its own native hirsel. **1856** J. C. MORTON *Cycl. Agric.* II. 723/2. **1886** C. SCOTT *Sheep-Farming* 122 He will be able to divide the hill into 'hirsels', and the hirsel again into 'cuts'. **1922** *Glasgow Herald* 16 Dec. 4 There they are fed for days..till the hirsels are green again. **1944** G. HENDERSON *Farming Ladder* i. 28 A mountain sheep farm, or hirsel, is selected in such a manner that food and shelter can be obtained by the stock. **1965** *Punch* 3 Mar. 325/2 The Welsh fridd system, which keeps sheltered grazing fresh for lambing time, is so much better than the Scottish hirsel (where the flock grazes all the year round on one hill) that is rapidly winning popularity.

2. *transf.* A company or number to look after; a 'lot' of persons or things of one kind.

c **1425** WYNTOUN *Cron.* VIII. xi. 33 Thai thowcht for-thi mare honesté..to sla thame [prisoners] in mellé , Than swilke ane hyrsalle for till hald. **1808-80** JAMIESON s.v., It is common to speak of a hirsell of folk, a hirsell of bairns, etc. **1818** HOGG *Brownie of B.* I. 160 (Jam.) Ye're just telling a hirsel o'eendown lees. *a* **1845** *Hodgson MS.* in *Northumbld. Gloss.* s.v., A great hirsel of wood or of corn stacks.

Hence **hirsel** *v.* (*Sc.* and *north.*) *trans.* to arrange in hirsels, form a hirsel of.

1794-5 *Statist. Acc. Scotl., Dumfries* XIII. 573 (Jam.) In these [farms] there is room to hirsel or keep separate different kinds of sheep. **1802** C. FINLATER *Agric. Surv. Peebles* 195 (Jam.) The principles of hirseling are, to class into separate flocks such sheep as are endowed with different abilities. **1805** A. SCOTT *Poems* 14 (Jam.) When a' the rout gat hirsel'd right.

hirsle ('hɜːs(ə)l), *v. Sc.* and *north. dial.* Forms: 6 **hirsill, hirssill,** 8–9 **hirsle,** 9 **-sell, -sel.**

[Possibly from an earlier *hristle*; cf. ON. *hrista* to shake, Da. *ryste* to shake, stir, rustle.]

1. *intr.* To move or slide with grazing or friction. Also ***to hirstle one's way***.

1513 DOUGLAS *Æneis* III. x. 87 On blind stanis and rolkis hirssillit we. **1756** MRS. CALDERWOOD *Journey* (1842) 159 A very droll machine..just the body of a coach hirsleing on its

bare doup, and drawn by one horse yoked with ropes. **1815** SCOTT *Guy M.* xlv, So he sat himsell doun and hirselled doun into the glen. **1825–80** JAMIESON s.v., One hirsills doun a hill when..he to prevent giddiness, moves downwards sitting. **1893** *Northumbld. Gloss.*, s.v. 'Hirsel alang'—move along the seat. *Mod. Sc.* Hirsle yont!

2. *trans.* To move (something) with much friction or effort.

1711 RAMSAY *Elegy Maggy Johnstoun* 62, I hirsl'd up my dizzy pow, Frae 'mang the corn. **1895** CROCKETT *Men of Mosshags* 152 We are hirsled over moss and moor..as the devil drives.

†**hirst.** *Sc. Obs.* [Origin unknown.] A threshold; or perh., in early use, a hinge.

1513 DOUGLAS *Æneis* I. vii. 57 The brasin durris iargis on the marble hirst. *Ibid.* VI. ix. 87 Thai wareit portis, jargand on the hirst [*stridentes cardine*] Warpit wp braid. *Ibid.* VII. xi. 33 Wythin that girgand hirst [*stridentia limina*] also suld he Pronounce the new weyrs, battale, and melle. [**1819** HOGG *Lenachan's Farew.* ii. in *Jacob. Songs* (1887) 227 But if serf or Saxon came, He crossed Murich's hirst nae mair.]

hirst, obs. form of HURST.

hirsute (ˈhɜːsjuːt), *a.* Also 7 hersute. [ad. L. *hirsūtus* rough, shaggy, bristly, f. **hirsus*, by-form of *hirtus* in same sense. Cf. F. *hirsute.*]

1. Having rough or shaggy hair; hairy, shaggy.

1621 BURTON *Anat. Mel.* I. ii. III. xiv. (1651) 125 A rugged attire, hirsute head, horrid beard. **1681** H. MORE *Exp. Dan.* 80 That hirsute or long-haired Goat. **1825** SCOTT *Talism.* iii, The wild and hirsute appearance of the individual. **1855** MOTLEY *Dutch Rep.* III. vi. (1866) 463 Wearing his hair and beard unshorn..this hirsute and savage corsair seemed an embodiment of vengeance.

2. *Bot.* and *Zool.* Covered with long and stiffish hairs.

1626 BACON *Sylva* §616 There are..Bulbous Roots, Fibrous Roots, and Hirsute Roots. **1668** WILKINS *Real Char.* 125 Caterpillars..those that are hirsute..Palmer worm, Bear worm. **1776–96** WITHERING *Brit. Plants* (ed. 3) II. 424 The stems more or less hirsute. **1856–8** W. CLARK *Van der Hoeven's Zool.* I. 404 Caterpillars..sometimes pilose or hirsute. **1870** HOOKER *Stud. Flora* 122 Styles free or nearly so, hirsute.

3. Of or pertaining to hair; of the nature of or consisting of hair.

1823 BYRON *Juan* IX. liii, The usual hirsute seasons which destroy, With beard and whiskers.. the fond Parisian aspect which upset old Troy. **1840** H. AINSWORTH *Tower Lond.* (1864) 208 The giant clapped his hand to his chin—too late, however, to save a particle of his hirsute honours. **1882** MAY CROMMELIN *Brown-Eyes* xi. (1884) 92 A broad though kindly face, totally devoid of hirsute ornament.

4. *transf.* and *fig.* **a.** Rough, shaggy; untrimmed.

1621 BURTON *Anat. Mel.* III. ii. VI. iii. (1651) 558 Dressed in some old hirsute attires out of fashion. *a* **1849** H. COLERIDGE *Poems* (1850) II. 106 Garden-plots hirsute and weedy.

b. Of manners or style: Rough, unpolished.

1658 WOOD *Life* 5 Apr. (O.H.S.) I. 243 He look'd elderly and was cynical and hirsute in his behavior. **1854** GILFILLAN *Life Blair* B.'s. Wks. (1854) 1255 The tone and style of his poem..are somewhat hirsute and unpolished.

So **hirˈsuted** *a. rare* = prec. 2; **hirˈsutism**, an abnormal degree of hairiness.

1707 SLOANE *Jamaica* I. 113 Having neither hirsuted, spotted, nor undulated leaves. **1926** in *Index-Catal. Library Surg.-General's Office, U.S. Army* VI. 753/2. **1927** *Jrnl. Amer. Med. Assoc.* 19 Mar. 969 Hirsutism and suprarenal virilism. **1959** *New Biol.* XXVIII. 132 Other serious abnormalities occur in these diseases, but hirsutism in female patients is a particularly distressing result.

hirˈsuteness. [f. prec. + -NESS.] The state or quality of being hirsute; hairiness.

1621 BURTON *Anat. Mel.* I. iii. III. i. (1651) 208 Baldness comes from excess of driness, hirsuteness from a dry temperature. **1864** H. SPENCER *Illustr. Univ. Progr.* 62 Red republicanism has always been distinguished by its hirsuteness.

‖**hirsuties** (həˈsjuːtiiːz). [L., f. *hirsūt-us* HIRSUTE.] **a.** *Bot.* and *Entom.* Hairiness; a thick covering of hair. **b.** (See quot. 1854–67.)

1847 JOHNSTON in *Proc. Berw. Nat. Club* III. No. 5. 229 Body ovate..clothed with a white appressed hirsuties. **1854–67** C. A. HARRIS *Dict. Med. Terminol.*, *Hirsuties*, hairiness. The growth of hair in unusual situations, or in greater abundance than usual.

hirsuto- (həsjuːtəʊ-), comb. form of L. *hirsūtus* HIRSUTE, prefixed to adjs. of colour, etc., as ***hirsuto-atrous***, with black hairs; ***hirsuto-rufous***, etc.

hirt, obs. f. HEART *v.*, HURT *v.* and *sb.*

hirtle, hirtleberry, var. HURTLE, HURTLEBERRY.

hirudin (hɪˈruːdɪn). *Biochem.* [a. G. *her-, hirudin*, attributed to Jacobj (see F. Franz 1903, in *Arch. f. exper. Path. und Pharm.* XLIX. 362), f. L. *hirūdo* leech + -IN¹.] An anticoagulant protein produced by the salivary glands of leeches which acts by combining with thrombin in the blood.

1905 *Jrnl. Chem. Soc.* LXXXVIII. II. 339 The substance named hirudin separated from leech extract has a very variable activity. **1908** *Practitioner* Apr. 463 Coagulation is prevented by the use of 'hirudin'. **1963** R. P. DALES *Annelids* ii. 60 Leeches have one or more pairs of 'salivary' glands producing an anti-coagulant, 'hirudin', preventing the blood from clotting as it is ingested.

†**hirudinal** (hɪˈruːdɪnəl), *a. Obs.* [f. L. *hirūdo, hirūdin-em* leech + -AL¹.] Of or pertaining to a leech. So **hiˈrudinid**, a member of the *Hirudinidæ* or Leech family. **hiruˈdinean**, a member of the *Hirudinea* or order of annelids containing the leeches. **hiˌrudiniˈculture**, the artificial propagation of leeches. †**hiˈrudinous** *a.*, leech-like, blood-sucking (*fig.*).

1651 BIGGS *New Disp.* ⁋ 192 Exhausted by..hirudinall blood-suckings. **1654** GAYTON *Pleas. Notes* IV. ii. 181 Such an hirudinous and exacting Lady as Dulcinea. **1835** KIRBY *Hab. & Inst. Anim.* I. xii. 334 His fourth Order [of Invertebrate Animals] he names Hirudineans. **1861** HULME tr. *Moquin-Tandon* II. III. iv. 147 Hirudiniculture has for some years been an important branch of commerce. **1865** *Reader* 30 Sept. 368/1 Pisciculture, hirudi[ni]culture, pearlculture.

hirundine (hɪˈrʌndaɪn), *a.* [f. L. *hirundo* swallow + -INE.] Of or pertaining to a swallow.

1831 CARLYLE *Sart. Res.* II. ii, Swallows..swashing to and fro with..activity almost super-hirundine.

†**hiˈrundinous**, *a. Obs. rare*⁻⁰. [f. L. *hirundo, -inem* + -OUS.] Of or pertaining to a swallow (Blount *Glossogr.* 1656).

his (hɪz, -ɪz), *poss. pron.*, *3rd sing. masc.* and †*neut.* [OE. *his* (*hys*), genitive of personal pron. HE and *hit*, IT. The cognate langs. have only the parallel forms without *h*, Goth. and OS. *is*, OHG. *is*, *es*, in later stages supplanted by the originally reflexive *sîn*, *sein*, *zîn*, *zijn*. In OE., on the contrary, the refl. possessive *sín* was already obsolescent, and usually replaced by *his*, *hire*, *hira*. About the 11th c., the genitive *his* began, after the earlier analogy of *mín*, *ðín*, *úre*, *eower*, to be treated as an adj. (with pl. *hise*, occurring till the 15th c.). Like the other possessive pronouns also, *his* tended to develop absolute derivative forms, of which *hisis*, *hysen* (like *hiris*, *hiren*), occur in ME. The former did not take root (see next word), and the latter is only dialectal (see HISN).]

A. Forms.

1. *Sing.* 1– his; 1–6 hys, (2–7 is, 3 ys, hise, 3–4 hiss, hesse, 4 hes, heys, hisse, hijs, hus, 4–5 hese, 5 hyse, heis, 6 ys), 6–7 's.

a **855**– His [see B. *passim*]. *a* **1000** *Hymns* ii. 11 (Gr.) Se byð eadiȝ se..a hys willan wyrcð. *c* **1200** ORMIN 84 He sennde uss sone hiss word, hiss witt, Hiss Sune, hiss mahht, hiss kinde. *c* **1250** *Gen. & Ex.* 2713 A modi stiward he ðor fond Betende a man wid hise wond. *Ibid.* 2851 He bar hise ȝerde forð in is hond. **1297** R. GLOUC. (1724) 59 He let a moneþ of þe ȝer clepye aftur ys owne name. *a* **1300** *Christ on Cross* 5 in *E.E.P.* (1862) 20 Bihold to is brest nakid, and is blodi side. *a* **1300** *Cursor M.* 62 (Gött.) Hijs fal is neist at hand. *Ibid.* 12685 (Cott.) Hes knes war bolnd sua. *Ibid.* 17890 (Gött.) All-mighti godd es fader hiss. **13..** *E.E. Psalter* cxlviii. 8 (Mätz.) Blaste of stormes, þat makes worde hisse [*verbum ejus*]. *c* **1380** WYCLIF *Wks.* (1880) 347 He.. tristiþ not to hiss treuthe. *c* **1380** *Sir Ferumb.* 881 Attes nauel þe dent a-stod. **1393** LANGL. *P. Pl.* C. XIX. 267 Thus haue ich beo hus heraude. **1556** *Chron. Gr. Friars* (Camden) 68 He was dyschargyd ys byschopryge and all hys londes. *c* **1592** MARLOWE *Jew of Malta* IV. iii, Look how his brains drop out on 's nose. **1609** SIR R. SHIRLEY in *Harl. Misc.* (Malh.) III. 88 Man can receiue is birth but from one place. **1611** SHAKS. *Cymb.* v. v. 294, I cut off 's head. **1647** WARD *Simp. Cobler* 85 He..must lift up 's head.

†**2.** *Plural.* 2–5 hise, 5 hese. *Obs.*

a **1100** *O.E. Chron.* an. 1070 Abbot Turolde..wæs cumen ..mid ealle hise Francisce menn. *a* **1131** *Ibid.* an. 1123 Se kyng..bed hise biscopes, and hise abbates, and hise þeiȝnes ealle þet hi scolden cumen to his ȝewitene mot. *Ibid.* an. 1124 He sende..to hise casteles. *c* **1200** *Trin. Coll. Hom.* 93 þe holie procession þe he wile maken a domes dai mid hise chosene. *c* **1200** ORMIN 14343 To shæwenn hise mahhtess ..þurrh hiss goddcunnde kinde. *a* **1225** *Leg. Kath.* 406 An of hise [*v.r.* his] men. **1258** *Proclam. Hen. III*, Henr'..Send igretinge to alle hise holde ilærde and ileawede. *c* **1380** WYCLIF *Serm.* Sel. Wks. II. 1 Men shulden trowe bi hise wordis þat þei ben soþe. *c* **1400** *Destr. Troy* 6892 Henex, with hese men.

B. Signification.

†**1.** as *gen. case* of *pers. pron.*: **a.** *masc.* Of him; of the male being or thing in question, L. *ejus*; **b.** *neut.* of it; **c.** *refl.* of himself, of itself, L. *sui.*

c **897** K. ÆLFRED *Gregory's Past* lviii. 443 Hwæt maȝon we his nu don? *a* **1000** *Cædmon's Gen.* 616 (Gr.) Nu þu his [*i.e.* þæs leohtes] hrinan meaht. *c* **1000** *Sax. Leechd.* I. 74 Gedrinc his..þreo ful fulle. *a* **1300** *Cursor M.* 3874 Bisid lya al night he lai, His vnwitand. *Ibid.* 4305 And, maugre his, he dos him lute. *c* **1340** *Ibid.* 4373 (Fairf.) His hit ware no resoun Tille our lorde do suche tresoun. *c* **1400** MAUNDEV. (Roxb.) iv. 12 þe dragoun..bare him maugree his til a cragg of þe see.

2. *Poss. adj. pron. masc.* (orig. *poss. gen.*, and then, like L. *ejus*, often following its sb.).

a. Referring to a person: Of or belonging to him, that man's, the male being's; also *refl.* of or belonging to himself, his own (L. *suus*).

This includes the simple possessive relation as in 'his money, his lands', the subjective genitive as 'his defence of his doings', and the objective genitive as in 'his defeat, his murder, his murderer'. No special provision exists in the language for the distinction of the latter two, except by context (cf. 'his dismissal of the envoys was blamed; he received his (own) dismissal soon after'); but in some cases the objective genitive is expressed periphrastically by *of him* (e.g. 'his defence, I mean your defence of him, was well conducted'). But the periphrastic form occurs also for the possessive genitive, as 'for the life of him'.

a **855** *O.E. Chron.* an. 787 On his daȝum cuomon ærest .iii. scipu. *c* **1000** *Ags. Ps.* (Th.) xxxix. [xl.] 4 Se wer þe his to-hopa byð to swylcum Drihtne. *c* **1000** ÆLFRIC *Gen.* vii. 7 Hwæt þa Noe eode into þam arce and his þri suna and his wif and his suna wif. *a* **1123** *O.E. Chron.* an. 1101 Se cyng.. sende his broðer. *c* **1250** *Gen. & Ex.* 1737 Wið is wiues he takeð red. **1382** WYCLIF *Matt.* i. 25 He..clepide his name Jhesus. *c* **1440** *Promp. Parv.* 241/2 Hyse, or hys, *suus.* **1477** MARG. PASTON in *P. Lett.* No. 809 III. 215 The Holy Trenyte have yow in Hese kepyng. **1605** SHAKS. *Macb.* I. vii. 15 His Host, Who should against his Murtherer shut the doore. **1643** ANGIER *Lanc. Vall. Achor* 36 Which God forbid for his Christs sake. **1671** MILTON *P.R.* I. 92 Man he seems In all his lineaments, though in his face The glimpses of his Father's glory shine. **1714** ROWE *Jane Shore* III. i, His bold defence of me. **1832** TENNYSON *To J. S.* 49 His memory long will live alone In all our hearts. **1835–7** SOUTHEY in *Cowper's Wks.* III. 220 Cowper manifested no pleasure at his sight. **1847** GROTE *Greece* II. xlv. (1862) IV. 79 His friends retained his panoply.

b. Also used with objects which are not one's property, but which one ought to have, or has specially to deal with (e.g. to kill *his man*, to gain *his blue*), or which are the common possession of a class, in which every one is assumed to have his share (e.g. he knows *his Bible*, *his Homer*, *his Hudibras*, he has forgotten *his Greek*, *his arithmetic*, etc.).

1709 STEELE *Tatler* No. 39 ⁋ 36 A good Marks-man will be sure to hit his Man at 20 Yards Distance. **1827** LD. ELDON in S. Walpole *Hist. Eng.* I. 158 A sportsman was thought nothing of unless he could kill his thousand birds a day. **1863** KINGSLEY *Water-Bab.* iii. 132 He knows his Bewick. **1870** H. SMART *Race for Wife* vi, He'd like to see him well through 'his smalls', to begin with. **1882–4** [see BLUE *sb.* 9]. **1884** FREEMAN *Methods Hist. Study* (1886) 33 The historian of Teutonic nations..cannot afford wholly to shut up his Tacitus, his Strabo, and his Caesar.

c. In reference to inferior animals *his* (or *her*) now varies with *its*, according to the nominative pronoun used: see HE, IT.

c **1000** *Ags. Gosp.* Matt. xvii. 27 Nim þone ærestan fisc, and hys muþ ȝeopena [*Rushw.* Ontyn muð his]. *c* **1220** *Bestiary* 3 Ðe leun stant on hille, And he man hunten here, Oðer ðurȝ his nese smel. *Ibid.* 58 His [an eagle's] bec is al to-wrong. *a* **1250** *Owl & Night.* 779 Ne mai his [a horse's] strenthe hit ishilde. *c* **1380** *Sir Ferumb* 794 Set me be-for þe on is [the horse's] bak. **1535** COVERD. *Lev.* xi. 29 The Wesell, the Mouse, the Tode, euery one with his kynde. **1623** COCKERAM III. G vj, It hath cruell teeth and scaly back, with very sharpe clawes on his feete. **1653** WALTON *Angler* xi. 196 The Barbell is so called..from or by reason of his beard, or wattles at his mouth, his mouth being under his nose or chaps. **1697** DRYDEN *Virg. Georg.* III. 418 The fearful Stag dares for his Hind engage. **1733** POPE *Ess. Man* III. 32 Is it for thee the lark ascends and sings? Joy tunes his voice, joy elevates his wings. **1820** KEATS *St. Agnes* i, The owl, for all his feathers, was a-cold.

¶ Examples of *his* for *hir*, *her*, are app. errors, scribal or typographical.

c **1330** R. BRUNNE *Chron.* (1810) 248 That ilk ȝere the quene died in Lindseie, At Westminster, I wene, his [*i.e.* her] body did thei leie. **1577** HELLOWES tr. *Gueuara's Chron.* 115 Secretly he gaue poyson vnto his wife Sabina, whereby she finished his life.

3. Referring to neuter nouns or things inanimate.

Here are to be distinguished four groups: **a.** Names of inanimate things of *masculine* gender in OE. **b.** Nouns of *neuter* gender in OE. Both these had *his* in OE., resulting in ME. in **c.** a general use of *his* for all names of inanimate things, exc. in those instances where *her* was used, either traditionally from OE., or under the influence of translation (the sb. being fem. in Latin, etc.), or by personification. In this use, *his* was often exchanged for *thereof* in 16th c., and was gradually superseded by ITS from *c* 1600 onwards, though the historical *his* lingered in some writers till late in the 17th c. **d.** In modern use, esp. since 1700, the use of *his* with things implies personification.

a. *c* **1000** *Treat. Astron.* in *Sax. Leechd.* III. 248 þis is þæs monan ȝear, ac his monað is mare. *Ibid.* 274 Se þridda heafod wind hatte zephirus..þurh his blæð acuciað ealle eorðlice blædu.

b. *c* **1000** *Treat. Astron.* in *Sax. Leechd.* III. 246 Ælc ðæra twelf tacna hylt his monað. *c* **1000** ÆLFRIC *Gen.* i. 11 Æppelbære treow wæstm wircende æfter his cinne.

c. *c* **1250** *Gen. & Ex.* 327 Is fruit sired mannes mood, To witen boðen iwel and good. *c* **1325** *Prose Psalter* ciii[i]. 19 þe sonne knewe hys going doun. **1382** WYCLIF *Matt.* vi. 34 It sufficith to the day his malice. *c* **1386** CHAUCER *Prol.* 1 Aprille with hise shoures soote. *c* **1405** *Bidding Prayer* in *Lay Folks Mass Bk.* 65 That the erthe may bring forthe his fruyt. *c* **1449** PECOCK *Repr.* I. ii. 10 It longith not to Holi Scripture, neither it is his office. **1523** LD. BERNERS *Froiss.* I. ccx. 251 Euery batayle had his vawarde. **1526** TINDALE *John* iii. 8 And thou hearest his sounde [**1539** (Great Bible), the sounde therof]. **1561** DAUS tr. *Bullinger on Apoc.* (1573) 47 b, It seemeth to haue kept his olde wonte. **1563** *Homilies* II. *Whitsunday* I. (1859) 454 This feast hath his name, to be called Pentecost. **1611** BIBLE *Exod.* xxxix. 33 The tent, and all his furniture, his taches, his boards, his barres, and his pillars, and his sockets. **1612** BRINSLEY *Lud. Lit.* 93 The Preposition must be ioined with his case. **1634** W. WOOD *New Eng. Prosp.* (1865) 41 Boston is two miles North-east from Roxberry: His situation is very pleasant. **1644** NYE

Gunnery Contents, How to renew and make good any sort of Gun-powder that hath lost his strength. **1670** J. SMITH *Eng. Improv. Reviv'd* 225 Goutwort..easeth the pains of the Gout, and..had not his Name for nothing.

d. 1667 MILTON *P.L.* x. 652 The Sun Had first his precept so to move. **1725** POPE *Odyss.* XI. 195 The wide sea with all his billows raves. *Ibid.* XVII. 688 The sun obliquely shot his dewy ray. **1808** J. BARLOW *Columb.* I. 437 Saw proud Potosi lift his glittering head. **1818** JAS. MILL *Brit. India* II. v. v. 530 Famine now raged in all his horrors.

4. After a sb., used instead of the genitive inflexion. Cf. the similar use of HER, THEIR. Chiefly with proper nouns, but also with others.

Found already in OE., but most prevalent from *c* 1400 to 1750; sometimes identified with the genitive inflexion *-es, -is, -ys*, esp. in 16–17th c., when it was chiefly (but not exclusively) used with names ending in *-s*, or when the inflexional genitive would have been awkward. Archaically retained in Book-keeping and for some other technical purposes.

c **1000** *Ags. Ps.* (Th.) xcviii[i]. 6 þa Gode his naman neode cigdan. *c* **1000** ÆLFRIC *Num.* xiii. 29 We ʒesawon Enac his cynryn. *c* **1275** LAY. 29589 Amang þe king his cnihtes. *Ibid.* 11296 þo was in Norweie his erþ. *Ibid.* 19630 Ine Winchestre his toun. *c* **1380** *Sir Ferumb.* 3130 þay kemen atte laste to Amyral ys pauyloun. **1387** TREVISA *Higden* (Rolls) III. 203 To fore Noe is flood. *c* **1420** *Chron. Vilod.* 3944 To by-reue holy chirche his possessione. **1426** AUDELAY *Poems* 11 To forsake syr Sathanas his werkus everychon. *a* **1460** *Gregory's Chron.* in *Hist. Coll. Citizen Lond.* (Camden) 203 Beyng at Wynchester in Wycham ys college. **1551** ROBINSON tr. *More's Utop.* Ep., The twoo principall secretaries to the kyng his moste excellente maiestie. *c* **1555** HARPSFIELD *Divorce Hen. VIII* (Camden) 178 Since Christ his birth. **1568** R. FRANCK *North. Mem.* (1821) 31 Job's patience, Moses his meekness, Abraham's faith. **1579** E. K. *Gloss. Spenser's Sheph. Cal.* Jan. 60 Julia, themperor Augustus his daughter. **1583** STUBBES *Anat. Abus.* II. (1882) 3 When Pharao the king of Egypt his sinne was ripe. **1594** T. B. *La Primaud. Fr. Acad.* II. 425 Epicures and Atheists..who place Nature in God his stead. **1599** THYNNE *Animadv.* (1875) 64 Wordes are curteyled for the verse his cause. **1648** GAGE *West Ind.* i. (1655) 2 Fit mates for the Horseleech his two daughters, crying, Give, give. **1662** *Bk. Com. Prayer, Pr. for all Conditions of Men*, And this we beg for Jesus Christ his sake. **1667** PEPYS *Diary* 12 Aug., Do hear Mr. Cowly mightily lamented his death, by Dr. Ward..as the best poet of our nation. **1671** H. M. tr. *Colloq. Erasm.* 377 Whether of the two his death seemed to be more Christian? **1712** ADDISON *Spect.* No. 409 ¶7 In examining Æneas his Voyage by the Map. **1746** *Rep. Cond. Sir J. Cope* 13 The Orders contained in 'the Marquis his letter'. **1767** H. WALPOLE *Historic Doubts* etc. (1768) 66 King Edward the Fourth his death. **1843** CARLYLE *Past & Pr.* IV. i, It were better for you..to keep out of Pandarus his neighbourhood.

¶ Sometimes an erroneous expansion of *'s*.

1607 HARINGTON in Park *Nug. Antiq.* (1804) II. 238 Mrs. Sands his maid.

5. *his one*, Sc. *his lane*, for earlier *him one*: see ONE, LONE. *his own*: see OWN. *his self*: see HIMSELF IV. and SELF.

Hence **his** *v. trans. nonce-wd.*, to use *his* of, to qualify with *his*.

1621 BP. MOUNTAGU *Diatribæ* I. 167 Yet Colossus was no man nor woman that you His it. [Referring to Selden's 'upon a Colossus his backe'.]

his (hɪz), *absol. poss. pron.* [The 3rd pers. sing. masc. member of the series *mine, thine, his, hers, its, ours, yours, theirs*, formed or differentiated in various ways from the adjective possessives *my, thy, his, her, its, our, your, their*. In OE. and early ME., no such distinction existed; the simple possessive prons. *mín, þín, úre, éower*, and the genitive cases *hir, hire, hira* (with ME. *þeʒʒre*), were used in both constructions. The differentiation app. began about 1300, but was not complete till much later. In *min, þin* (*mine, thine*) the original forms remained when used absolutely; when followed by a sb., they were gradually reduced to *mi, thi*, now *my, thy*. In *her, our, your, their*, an absolute pron. was formed by the addition of *-is, -es, -'s, -s* (see HERS, etc.) In *his*, which already ended in *s*, although a form HISIS was tried in ME., the additional *-is, -es, -'s*, did not take root, and the absolute *his* (= *le sien, il suo, der seinige*), (although it may perhaps be considered as standing for *his's, his'*, as in possessives like *Jesus', Moses'*), remains identical in form with the simple or adjective possessive. The more recent *its*, also ending in *s*, has followed the example of *his*. For another type of the absolute pronoun see HISN.]

a. The absolute form of prec., used when no noun follows: = His one, his ones.

c **1000** *Ags. Ps.* (Th.) xcix. 2 [c. 3] We his syndon. *a* **1175** *Cott. Hom.* 231 þa cweð se hlaford to his. *a* **1225** *Leg. Kath.* 1392 As he het hise. **1297** R. GLOUC. (1724) 451 He..ladde ost gret ynou aʒe þe kyng & hys. *a* **1300** *Cursor M.* 1058 For-þi was he wit his for-lorn. *Ibid.* 6479 þi neghbur wijf ʒerne noght at haue, Ne aght of his. *c* **1300** *Beket* 1578 And strivede for holi churche aʒen the King and his. *c* **1330** R. BRUNNE *Chron.* (1810) 57 Edward him granted..þat neuer þe Dangilde for ne non of hise, Suld be chalenged for man of Danes lond. **1388** WYCLIF *Job* xxxix. 16 He [the ostriche] is maad hard to hise briddis, as if thei ben not hise [**1382** She..hir..hiris]. **1460** CAPGRAVE *Chron.* (Rolls) 146 Philip sold his prisoneres: Richard hung his. *a* **1533** LD. BERNERS *Huon* lv. 185 All yᵉ domages that thou hast done him & his. **1611** BIBLE *Song Sol.* ii. 16 My beloued is mine, and I am his.

1784 COWPER *Task* v. 343 He is ours..We are his. **1827** SCOTT *Napoleon* Introd. Wks. 1870 IX. 49 Blood..shed..without command of his. **1864** TENNYSON *En. Ard.* 756 [He] saw the babe, Hers, yet not his, upon the father's knee.

b. Used, normally in combination with or in opposition to *hers*, of an article, room (e.g. a W.C.), etc., intended for males. Occas. used before a following noun.

1949 *Good Housekeeping* June 26/2 With color contrasts in towels and washcloths, it's easy to distinguish 'his' from yours. **1950** *Charm* Apr. 82 Among your wedding gifts..may be a set of bath towels labelled with beautiful equity and foresight: 'His' and 'Hers'. **1953** *Imagination* June 115/1 Almost before Crae brought the car to a gravel-spraying stop..Ellena had the door open and was out and around the corner marked His and Hers. **1962** J. BLACKBURN *Gaunt Woman* x. 156 'His' was a gloomy little room, laid with dirty grey lino. **1964** *Guardian* 10 Oct. 5/2 We halve the available space..under the primitive his and hers law... There is usually a his chair and a her chair. **1965** *New Statesman* 21 May 790/3 What I call a His/Her double bedroom. **1967** *Guardian* 4 Jan. 7/4 *His and Hers.* J. R. L. Andersen reports on the Boat Show. Women's influence in the world of small boats is now almost dominant.

†**his, hise**, *pers. pron., 3rd sing. fem. acc. Obs.* Forms: 3 **hes, es**, 3–4 **his, is, as**, 4 **hys, ys, hise, hyse**. [This and the next are identical in form, and are intimately associated in their history, as well as in the obscurity of their origin. They appear together in south and s.e. of England before 1200, and continue in use there for about 200 years. They each take the place of an OE. *hí, hý* acc. (HI¹ and ²), when this was being displaced elsewhere by the dative (*hire* and *hem*); they each answer to OS. *sia, sea, sie*, OFris. *se*, MDu. *si, se*, MLG. *se*, OHG. *sia, sie*, MHG. *sie, si, sî*, Ger. *sie* 'her' and 'them', to which they appear to be in some way related. They are also enclitically combined as *-es, -s*, with a vb. or another pronoun: e.g. *dide-s, calde-s, sette-s, warp-es, he-s, me-s, we-s*.

Morsbach (*Anglia*, Mar. 1897, 331), founding on the fact that OFris. and MDu. *se* 'her, them', is an unemphatic form, often enclitic, and then in OFris. reduced to *-s* in combination with the vb., e.g. *bunden-s, bifuchten-s* (for *bunden + se*, etc.), suggests a like origin for these ME. pronouns. He would find the earliest extant form in the enclitic *-s* of *calde-s, sette-s, he-s, me-s*, etc., which he takes to represent, as in OFris., an earlier *se*, an unemphatic form from the pronominal base *se, séo*; this, after its origin was forgotten, is conjectured to have been expanded, as a separate word, to *es, is, hes, his*, on the analogy of such combinations as *madim* = *made him, torndem* = *tornde hem*. The form *hise* of the *Ayenbite* might be explained as similarly developed from the enclitic *-se*. But it is doubtful whether the chronology of the forms, as preserved to us, supports this development.]

= HER, it; *refl.* herself. (See also AS, ES *prons.*)

a **1200** *Moral Ode* 55 (Trin. Coll. Hom.) Se þe aihte wile holde wel þe while hes muʒe wealden ȝieue hes for godes luue þanne doð hes wel ihealden. *c* **1200** *Trin. Coll. Hom.* 159 An edie meiden..he hes fette hom. *c* **1200** *Vices & Virtues* 107 He is isali ðe hes [temperantia] halt. **1297** R. GLOUC. (Rolls) 6595 He..is kinges croune nom & sette is vpe þe rode heued. *a* **1300** *Fragm. Pop. Sc.* (Wright) 363 þulke soule nymeþ his in, and bileveþ i-wis In þe childes brayn and heʒ. *c* **1315** SHOREHAM 77 Thaʒ he by hyre ne ligge nouʒt Other halt hys ine hys house. *Ibid.* 136 The erthe hys hevy..Ho halt ys op. **1340** *Ayenb.* 179 Ase deþ þe cat mid þe mous þanne he his heþ ynome; and huanne he heþ mid hire longe yplayd, þanne he his etþ. *Ibid.* 191 þe prest his [i.e. a cow] nom bleþeliche, and hise zente to þe oþren.

†**his, hise**, *pers. pron., 3rd pl. acc. Obs.* Forms: 2–3 **hes**, 3 **es**, 2–4 **his**, 3–4 **is, hys, ys, as**, 4 **hise**. [See prec. This took the place of OE. *hí, hý* plural, and was equivalent in sense to ME. *hem.*] = THEM. (See also AS, ES *prons.*)

a **1175** *Cott. Hom.* 237 Eter gate me his scyft, and þer me hi to ʒesceodeð. *c* **1175** *Lamb. Hom.* 55 þa bodes he beodeð þer inne, Bute weo hes halden, we doð sunne, and uwilc mon hes undernim to halden wel. *c* **1200** *Vices & Virtues* 23 Nu ðurh godes grace þu hes hafst forsaken. *c* **1200** *Trin. Coll. Hom.* 145 Hie his fet lauede..and wipede his þer after mid hire faire here. *c* **1200** *Moral Ode* 259 *Ibid.* 228 þe waren swo lease men, þat mes ne mihte leuen. *c* **1220** *Bestiary* 786 Alle wes oʒen to hauen in mode. *c* **1250** *Gen. & Ex.* 135 He settes in ðe firmament. *Ibid.* 943 Vndelt hes leide quor-so hes tok. *Ibid.* 1700 Bala two childre bar bi him, Rachel caldes dan, neptalim. *Ibid.* 1702 Lia calde is Gad and asser. *Ibid.* 3025 Moyses askes up-nam, And warpes vt til heuene-ward. *c* **1250** *Old Kent. Serm.* in *O.E. Misc.* 34 þu his makest velaghes to us. **1297** R. GLOUC. (Rolls) 9163 þe bones hii bere..And yburede ys þere vayre ynou. *c* **1300** *Havelok* 1174 He ys hire yaf, and she as tok. *c* **1315** SHOREHAM 92 In ston ich wot that he hys wrot. **1340** *Ayenb.* 71 þe dyaþ hise heþ and neuremo his nele þe yelde. *Ibid.* 100 He his byat and his chasteþ. **13..** *K. Alis.* 4088 Darie hyght..Remuwe his tentis..And setten his bysyde Estrage.

his, obs. spelling of *is*: see BE *v.*

hish (hɪʃ), *v.*¹ *dial.* [Echoic: cf. HISS. With sense 2 cf. also MDu. *hissen, hisscen*, in Kilian also *hisschen*, to hound on a dog, to instigate, MLG. *hissen, hitsen*, Du. *hitsen.*]

1. *intr.* A by-form of HISS.

1388 WYCLIF *2 Chron* xxix. 8 [The Lord] gaf hem in to stiryng, and in to perischyng, and in to hisshing [**1382** whistlyng, *Vulg.* in sibilum]. **1398** TREVISA *Barth. De P.R.* XIII. xxvi. (1495) 458 The grekes tell that this fisshe..conceyuyth of the serpent, and therfore fisshars calle it wyth hysshynge and whystlyng. **1530** TINDALE *Num.* Prol. Wks. (Parker Soc.) I. 432 So manifestly proved that they cannot once hish against it.

2. To make a hissing noise to hound on a dog.

1860 GEO. ELIOT *Mill on Fl.* v. ii, I might hish at him by th'hour together, before he'd fly at a real gentlewoman like you.

hish, *sb.* [Echoic.] The rushing or whishing noise made by a scythe cutting grass, etc.

1893 M. GRAY *Last Sentence* III. III. xviii. 251 The hish of falling swathes. *Ibid.* 252 'Hish, hish!' went the scythes.

Hence **hish** *v.*² *intr.*, to make this sound.

1893 M. GRAY *Last Sentence* III. III. xiv. 188 The gardener's scythe hishing through the grass.

hisingerite ('hɪsɪŋgəraɪt). *Min.* [Named 1828 after W. Hisinger, a Swedish chemist: see -ITE. (The name had been previously proposed for *gillingite.*)] A hydrous silicate of iron of somewhat uncertain composition.

1823 H. J. BROOKE *Introd. Crystallogr.* 469 Hisingerit [= *gillingite*]. **1868** DANA *Min.* (ed. 5) 490 Cleve's analysis makes the scotiolite..essentially hisingerite.

†'**hisis**, *absolute poss. pron. Obs.* [f. HIS *poss. pron.*, in the same was as *hir-is, hir-es, hers, ouris, oures, ours*, etc. were formed from *her, our*, etc. As the simple possessive itself ended in *s*, it appears to have been generally felt to be unnecessary to add another *-is* or *'s*.] = HISN, HIS'N *absolute poss. pron.*

c **1380** WYCLIF *Three Treatises* (Todd 1851) I. 59 þat þe pope may do no symonye for alle beneficis ben hisis [*Bodley MS.* hise].

hislopite ('hɪzləpaɪt). *Min.* [f. the name of the Rev. Stephen Hislop (1817–63), Scottish missionary and naturalist: see -ITE¹.] An Indian variety of calcite coloured green by the presence of glauconite.

1859 S. HAUGHTON in *Phil. Mag.* XVII. 18, I propose to give the name of Hislopite to the remarkable combination of Calc-spar and Glauconite found by him [*sc.* Mr. Hislop] at Nágpur. **1893** *Rec. Geol. Surv. India* XXVI. 171 The name hislopite loses its specific value when the variation of the included so-called glauconite is..so great as the foregoing results show.

hisn, his'n ('hɪz(ə)n), *absolute poss. pron. dial.* Also 5 **hysene**, 6 **hizzen**, 20 **hissn**. [f. HIS *poss. pron.*, analogous to *hern, ourn, yourn, theirn*, apparently by form-association with *my, mine, thy, thine*, earlier *mí, mín, thí, thín*, in which the *-n* distinguishes the absolute from the adjective form. These forms in *-n* are midland and southern.] = HIS *absol. poss. pron.*

c **1410** LOVE *Bonavent. Mirr.* lxii. 119 (Gibbs MS.) Bote þat was oure ioye and noʒt hysene. **1575** LANEHAM *Lett.* (1871) 15 With humbl subiection of him and hizzen. **1748** RICHARDSON *Clarissa* xxxii. I. 219 [Anthony Harlow, a gentleman of family and fortune, writes] When you are hisn. *a* **1845** HOOD *Huggins & Duggins*, I often wish my lot was hisn. [*Provincial Adage*, 'Him as prigs what isn't hisn, When he's cotch'd he goes to prison.'] **1867** 'MARK TWAIN' *Celebr. Jumping Frog* 15 It always makes me feel sorry when I think of that last fight of his'n. **1910** C. E. MULFORD *Hopalong Cassidy* xx. 130 Taking the button and looking it over. 'Yep, its hissn, all right.' **1923** 'R. CROMPTON' *William Again* x. 179 Well it isn't his'n—it's stole stuff.

hisop, obs. form of HYSSOP.

hispa ('hɪspə). *Ent.* [mod.L. (C. Linnæus *Systema Naturæ* (ed. 12, 1767) II. 603), f. L. *hispidus* bristly, hairy.] A tropical leaf-beetle of the genus so named. Hence '**hispid**, '**hispine** *adjs.*, of or pertaining to the family Hispinæ, which has *Hispa* as its typical genus.

1794 P. A. NEMNICH *Allgemeines Polyglotten-Lexicon der Naturgeschichte* III. 165 *Hispa.* [*Entomol.*]... *Engl.* The hispa. **1835** *Boston Jrnl. Nat. Hist.* I. 147, I found full grown larvæ of a Hispa in the leaves. **1889** E. C. COTES *Further Notes Indian Insect Pests* 37 The Bengal Rice Hispa. **1922** D. SHARP in *Cambr. Nat. Hist.* VI. v. 282 *Hispa* is one of the most extensive of the numerous genera of Hispides. **1924** *Bull. Entomol. Res.* XIV. 245 (*title*) A new Hispid beetle. **1933** *Proc. Zool. Soc.* 669 (*title*) On the structure of larvae of Hispine beetles. **1962** R. WYNIGER *Pests of Crops in Warm Climates* III. 179 Sugar-cane hispid miner.

†**Hispanian** (hɪ'speɪnɪən), *a. Obs. rare.* [f. L. *Hispānia*, in 16th c. Eng. *Hispanie* Spain.] Of or belonging to Spain, Spanish.

[**1580** in Picton *L'pool Munic. Rec.* (1883) I. 42 Trading [to] Hispanie and Portingale.] **1656** BLOUNT *Glossogr.*, *Hispanian*, of or belonging to Spain, born in Spain.

Hispanic (hɪ'spænɪk), *a.* and *sb.* [f. L. *Hispānic-us* Spanish (f. *Hispānia*): see -IC.]

A. *adj.* **1.** Pertaining to Spain or its people; esp. pertaining to ancient Spain. So †**Hi'spanical** *a.* (*obs.*); **Hi'spanically** *adv.*, in the Spanish manner; **Hispanicism** (hɪ'spænɪsɪz(ə)m), a Spanish idiom or mode of expression; **Hi'spanicize** *v. trans.*, to render Spanish; '**Hispanism** = *Hispanicism*.

1584 R. SCOT *Discov. Witchcr.* III. vii. (1886) 38 *marg.*, Confession compulsorie; as by Hispanicall inquisition. **1632** LITHGOW *Trav.* I. 19 In this Hispanicall proverbe. **1831** *Fraser's Mag.* III. 613 A gentleman so Hispanically cognominated. **1836** MACAULAY *Ess.*, *Temple* (1887) 460 A

style..superficially deformed, indeed, by Gallicisms and Hispanicisms. **1878** H. A. WEBSTER in *Encycl. Brit.* VI. 155/2 Others [tribes] have been in large measure Hispanicized both in language and in habits. **1889** *Sat. Rev.* 12 Jan. 27/2 The Hispanicisms and generally uncultivated character of the style. **1949** S. DE MADARIAGA *Christopher Columbus* (ed. 2) 410 When he makes errors in Latin they are Hispanisms. **1964** Y. MALKIEL in *Archivum Linguisticum* XVI. 3 Differently developed Hispanisms in Arabic.

2. Spanish-speaking, esp. applied to someone of Latin-American descent living in the United States.

1974 *Econ. & Social Statistics for Spanish-Speaking Americans* (U.S. Congress. House Comm. Post Office & Civil Service) 166 For statistical or policy purposes Hispanic Americans do not presently exist in most agencies of the government. **1980** *Times* 29 Oct. 8 Hispanic children in Los Angeles are taught entirely in Spanish. **1986** *Washington Post* 6 Dec. A21 'Hispanic' means 'Spanish-speaking', nothing else.

B. *sb.* A Spanish-speaking person, esp. one of Latin-American descent, living in the U.S. Chiefly in *pl.*

1972 *N.Y. Times Mag.* 24 Sept. VI. 68/3 The fictional melting pot has become a pousse-café in which every layer is jealous of, or hostile to, every other layer; in a fever of ethnicism, Italians, Jews, Orientals, Blacks, Hispanics and others have withdrawn into themselves. **1976** *National Observer* (U.S.) 7 Aug. 1/2 The 1970 census found more Hispanics in New Jersey than in Arizona, more in Illinois than in New Mexico. Chicago has a quarter of a million Latinos, and Detroit has a *barrio* comprising almost 20 Spanish-speaking nationalities. **1979** *Times* 4 Dec. 6/7 How do we justify the United States..[saying] to Hispanics who are here legally that they have to wait nine years to bring their children to this country? **1984** *Miami Herald* 6 Apr. 7A/1 Spokesmen for Hispanics are seeking separate hearings on an alternative bill introduced by Rep. Edward Roybal, D-Calif.

Hispaniolate (hɪˈspænɪəleɪt), *v. rare.* [f. Sp. *españolar* to make Spanish, f. *español* Spanish, f. *España*:—L. *Hispānia* Spain: see -ATE³.] *trans.* To make Spanish, imbue with Spanish notions.

1860 MOTLEY *Netherl.* xxxiii. (1860) III. 454 The Hispaniolated counsellors of Duke John.

Hiˈspaniolize, *v.* [f. as prec. + -IZE.] = prec.

1583 STOCKER *Hist. Civ. Warres Lowe C.* I. a ij a, Certaine other Hispaniolized low Countrey men. **1600** O. E. *Repl. to Libel* Pref. 10 This reinged English, and Hispaniolized fugitiue. **1619** in *Crt. & Times Jas. I* (1849) II. 192 A privy councillor..wished that fenestration were the reward of such that had their tongues so Hispaniolised. **1823** SOUTHEY in *Q. Rev.* XXIX. 191 The favour with which he had been received at Madrid..had completely hispaniolized him.

Hispanist, hispanist (ˈhɪspənɪst). [f. HISPAN(IC *a.* + -IST.] A student of the literature, language, and civilization of Spain.

1934 WEBSTER, *Hispanist*, one versed in, or devoted to, the Spanish language or the study of Spanish. **1960** *Times* 17 Oct. 20/6 His untimely death is a grievous loss to hispanists in the University of London. **1964** *Archivum Linguisticum* XVI. 12 Such an approach predominates in the work of the contemporary Hispanist.

Hispanize (ˈhɪspənaɪz), *v.* [f. L. *Hispānus* Spanish, Spaniard + -IZE.] *trans.* = HISPANIOLIZE *v.*

1600 W. WATSON *Decacordon* (1602) 239, I was informed by an Hyspanized politicians meanes. **1612** T. JAMES *Jesuit's Downf.* 50 [Parsons] a Zoilus, a Timon, an hispanized Cameleon, like Proteus, wretched seed of Cain, and sonne of Beliall. **1824** *New Monthly Mag.* XI. 190 He selected..that only which was adapted for representation in Spain, hispanizing (if we may be allowed the term) whatever he found it convenient to transport with him.

Hiˈspano-, combining form of L. *Hispān-us* Spanish, prefixed to another adj. or suffix, which it either qualifies or is coupled with; as in **Hiˌspano-Aˈmerican**, Spanish and American; also as *sb.*; **Hiˌspano-ˈArab, -Aˈrabian, -ˈArabic**, Spanish and Arabian; **Hispano-Gallican**, belonging in common to Spain and Gaul (or France); so **Hispano-German, Hispano-Italian; Hiˌspano-ˈGothic**, Spanish and Gothic; **Hiˌspano-Mauˈresque, -Moˈresco, -Moˈresque**, Spanish and Moorish; **Hispano-Moresque**, belonging to the Moors of Spain, Spanish-Moorish; **Hiˈspanophil(e)**, a lover of Spain and Spanish culture.

1823 T. ROSS tr. *Bouterwek's Hist. Span. Lit.* 6 The nobles, who were of French or Hispano-Gothic origin. **1824** *Westm. Rev.* II. 449 Spain, Austria, the Hispano-Italian States. **1845** S. AUSTIN *Ranke's Hist. Ref.* III. 12 The Hispano-German army had conquered Rome. **1880** *N. & Q.* 16 Oct. 306/1 (*heading*) Hispano-Arabian poetesses. **1881** C. C. HARRISON *Woman's Handiwork* II. 104 A charm of Fortuny's studio was his Hispano-Moresco lustred pottery. **1897** *Westm. Gaz.* 24 Dec. 3/2 Hispano-Moresque [ware] is treated at greater length. **1904** W. H. HUDSON *Green Mansions* 4 The nervous olive-skinned Hispano-American of the tropics. [**1906** *Daily Chron.* 19 May 3/2 A Hispanofilo to the core.] **1909** *Ibid.* 18 Nov. 1/3 The eighteen-carat gold casket presented to the King of Portugal..is oblong in shape and in the Hispano Gothic style. **1910** *Ibid.* 4 Jan. 3/1 The true Hispanophil with the cult in his veins. **1920** *Glasgow Herald* 25 Nov. 6 All good British Hispanophils. **1933** *Archit. Rev.* LXXIII. 5/1 Most people would even be eager to concede that this hispano-arabian pastry was the reverse of a great art-form. *Ibid.*, And certainly nothing could be more unlike the structureless confections of the hispano-mauresque than the type of these Kasbahs. **1936** *Burlington Mag.* Apr. 198/2 The so-called mudéjar (Hispano-Moresque) style of the kingdoms of Aragon and Castile. **1942** *Ibid.* Feb. 41/1 The two pile carpets here reproduced ..provide a further link in the chain of Hispano-American art. **1959** *Listener* 12 Mar. 471/2 He belonged to a distinguished Hispano-Arab family. **1960** *John o' London's* 14 Apr. 432 Many an English Hispanophile. **1964** *Archivum Linguisticum* XVI. 3 *Plomo* may similarly have had a Hispano-Arabic predecessor. **1964** *Punch* 29 July 173/3 Recommended to all Hispanophiles. **1973** *Daily Tel.* 12 Jan. 29/1, I see happy Hispanophiles streaming from Greenock and Blackburn to the Costa del Sol.

Hisperic (hɪˈspɛrɪk), *a.* [ad. med.L. *Hisperica* (see def.). Cf. G. *hisperisch*.] Epithet of a variety of mediæval Latin, of which *Hisperica Famina* (probably of the 6th century) is a notable example, characterized by a highly artificial vocabulary of which the use of borrowed words of Hebrew, Greek, and other origin is a salient feature.

1904 W. P. KER *Dark Ages* 35 The 'Hisperic' vocabulary, which is that of Apuleius, Florus, Martianus Capella, exaggerated out of all measure. **1907** *Cambr. Hist. Eng. Lit.* I. 69 The hymn..known as **Altus prosator** contains very marked specimens of Hisperic Latinity. **1931** E. J. JONES *Hist. Educ. Wales* I. 179 Hisperic words are included in the Anglo-Saxon glossaries of the tenth century. **1948** E. S. DUCKETT *Anglo-Saxon Saints & Scholars* i. 75 Rhyming eight-syllabled lines, again filled with uncouth Hisperic words.

hispid (ˈhɪspɪd), *a.* [ad. L. *hispid-us* in same sense. Cf. F. *hispide* (14th c. in Hatz.-Darm.).] Rough with stiff hair or bristles; shaggy; bristly: in *Bot.* and *Invert. Zool.* Clothed with short stiff hairs or bristles; rough with minute spines.

1646 H. MORE in *J. Hall's Poems* To yng. Authour, John of the wilderness? the hairy child? The hispid Thisbite? or what satyr wild? **1648** HERRICK *Hesper., To J. Weare* 24 Sooner the in-side of thy hand shall grow Hisped, and hairie. **1753** CHAMBERS *Cycl. Supp.* s.v. *Leaf*, Hispid Leaf.. one whose surface is covered with more thick and rigid hairs than the pilose leaf. **1835** KIRBY *Hab. & Inst. Anim.* I. xi. 323 The Hispid Worms of Lamarck. **1872** OLIVER *Elem. Bot.* II. 212 The herbage of Boragineæ is often very coarse and hispid. **1877** COUES & ALLEN *N. Amer. Rodentia* 31 Pelage hispid, from abundance of large bristly hairs. *fig.* **1848** J. HAMILTON *Happy Home* ii. (1871) 37 The harsh and hispid law.

Hence **hiˈspidity**; **ˈhispidly** *adv.*

1660 H. MORE *Myst. Godl.* III. vi. §5 The hispidity, or hairiness of skin. **1854** MAYNE *Expos. Lex., Hispiditas*.. hispidity. **1870** HOOKER *Stud. Flora* 228 Sheep's-bit.. hispidly pubescent.

hiˈspidulate, *a.* [f. as next: see -ATE².] = next.

1854 in MAYNE *Expos. Lex.*

hispidulous (hɪˈspɪdjuːləs), *a.* [f. L. type **hispidul-us* (cf. *acidulus*) + -OUS.] Slightly hispid.

1854 in MAYNE *Expos. Lex.* **1870** HOOKER *Stud. Flora* 198 Leaves hispidulous lanceolate entire or distantly lobed.

hi-spy, var. HY-SPY.

hiss (hɪs), *v.* [A word imitating or exemplifying the sound to which it is applied; app. not recorded before the close of the 14th c., and not known in the earlier stage of any Teutonic lang. (An alleged OE. *hysian* is an error.) Kilian has in early mod. Flem. (1599) '*hisschen, hissen*, sibilare, Ang. *hisse*', but this word is not in MDu. nor in mod.Du., where 'to hiss' is *sissen*, Ger. *zischen*. Cf. HISH, HIZZ.]

1. *intr.* To make the sharp spirant sound emitted by certain animals, as geese and serpents, or caused (e.g.) by the escape of steam through a narrow aperture, or uttered in the pronunciation of '*s*'. (L. *sibilāre*.) Also in *Electricity* (cf. *hissing arc*).

1388 WYCLIF *Isa.* v.. 26 He schal hisse [**1382** whistlen] to hym fro the endis of erthe. *c* **1400** MAUNDEV. (1839) xviii. 196 þei speken nought, but þei hissen, as serpentes don. *c* **1440** *Jacob's Well* (E.E.T.S.) 107 As a chylde, þat dare noȝt passe, for þe goos hysseth at him. *c* **1532** DEWES *Introd. Fr.* in *Palsgr.* 917 The serpentes hysses. *a* **1637** B. JONSON *Eng. Gram.* Wks. (Rtldg.) 774/2 S is a most easy and gentle letter, and softly hisseth against the teeth in the prolation. **1656** BP. HALL *Occas. Medit.* (1851) 54 Hark how that iron, quenched in the water, hisseth. **1715–20** POPE *Iliad* I. 68 He twang'd his deadly bow, And hissing fly the feather'd fates below. **1843** LEVER *J. Hinton* xl, The little tea-kettle was hissing on the hob. **1872** BAKER *Nile Tribut.* xxi. 362 A few drops of water thrown on the surface will hiss and evaporate as though cast upon molten metal. **1961** J. THEWLIS *Encycl. Dict. Physics* III. 703/1 If the current passing through a carbon arc exceeds a certain value depending on the length of the arc, the latter begins to 'hiss'.

2. Of a person: To make this sound as an expression of disapproval or derision. (Usually const. *at*, with *indirect passive*.)

1388 WYCLIF *Jer.* xix. 8 Ech that passith bi it, schal wondre, and hisse [**1382** whistlen] on al the veniaunce thereof. **1535** COVERDALE *Lam.* ii. 15 Hissinge and wagginge their heades vpon the doughter Ierusalem. *c* **1566** J. ALDAY tr. *Boaystuau's Theat. World* I vj, Subject, as in a playe to be hissed at, and chased awaye with shame. **1649** JER. TAYLOR *Gt. Exemp.* III. Ad §15. 105 Thou art disgraced and hissed at. **1683** DRYDEN *Vind. Dk. of Guise* Wks. 1725 V. 329 To Clap and Hiss are the Privileges of a Free-born Subject in a Play-House. **1855** MACAULAY *Hist. Eng.* xiv, Those who had hissed when the subject was introduced.

3. *trans.* To express disapproval of (a person or thing) by making this sound.

1599 MARSTON *Sco. Villanie* I. iv. 190 Would not some freshman..Hisse and deride such blockish foolery? **1615** J. STEPHENS *Satyr. Ess.* 292 When hee heares his play hissed. **1720** PRIOR *Prol.* to '*The Orphan*' 4 Hireling actors..Whom you may clap or hiss for half-a-crown. **1833** LAMB *Elia* (1860) 274 They have hissed me.

4. To drive or send away with or by means of hissing. Chiefly with advbs., as *to hiss out, away, down*.

1519 HORMAN *Vulg.* 137 He was hyssed out of the place. **1548** UDALL *Erasm. Par. Luke* Pref. 12 The poetes doe hisse the olde goddes out of place. **1591** SYLVESTER *Du Bartas* I. iv. 459 He..Is to be hist from learned Disputations. **1642** FULLER *Holy & Prof. St.* IV. xi. 290 They had rather be hiss'd down then not come upon the stage. **1655** GURNALL *Chr. in Arm.* xix. (1669) 240/2 Thus faith hisseth Satan away with this his argument. **1779** JOHNSON *Lett. to Mrs. Thrale* 28 Oct., I always hissed away the charge. **1895** R. H. SHERARD in *Bookman* Oct. 17/2 The first performance of 'Faust', which was hissed off the stage on that occasion.

5. To utter or express by hissing or with a hiss, esp. as expressive of intense anger or hate.

1775 JOHNSON *Tax. no Tyr.* 78 One of the threats hissed out by the Congress. **1850** LYNCH *Theo. Trin.* vii. 135, I sat down to the piano whilst the kettle was hissing preparation. **1884** PAE *Eustace* 66 'You shall yet repent this', he hissed.

Hence **hissed** (hɪst) *ppl. a.*; **hisser**, one who hisses.

c **1440** *Gesta Rom.* xxxv. 137 (Harl. MS.) In that oþere side is an hisser or a siblatour, and he hissithe so swetlye. **1589** NASHE *Pref. to Greene's Menaphon* (Arb.) 13 Whose heroicall poetry..recalled to life what euer hissed [*ed.* **1616** histed] Barbarisme hath been buried this C. yeere. **1662** J. CHANDLER *Van Helmont's Oriat.* 164 He uncompelled, runs back to hissed-out elementary distemperatures. **1819** *Sporting Mag.* IV. 20 A rhapsody addressed to the clappers, hissers and damners, attending the theatres. *Mod.* 'S' is a hissed consonant.

hiss (hɪs), *sb.* Also 6 hys, hysse. [f. HISS *v.*]

1. a. A sharp continuous spirant sound such as is emitted by geese and serpents, and in the pronunciation of 's'.

1513 DOUGLAS *Æneis* XII. xiii. 176 Scho [an owl] soundis so with mony hys and how, And in hys scheild can with hyr wyngis smyte. **1598** BARRET *Theor. Warres* II. i. 17 The alarme..is sometimes done with a whistle or hysse, for not to disturbe the Campe. **1667** MILTON *P.L.* I. 768 Brusht with the hiss of russling wings. **1791** COWPER *Iliad* XVI. 435 The hiss of flying shafts. **1871** L. STEPHEN *Playgr. Europe* iii. (1894) 80 A layer [of snow]..slid smoothly down..with a low ominous hiss. **1887** BOWEN *Virg. Æneid* v. 278 Some snake..throat lifted to dart Hiss upon hiss.

b. *Phonetics.* A consonant pronounced with a hiss; a sibilant, esp. the sounds [s] and [z]. Also *attrib.*

1890 SWEET *Primer Spoken Eng.* 10 Buzzes (voiced hisses) when final begin with voice and end in whisper. **1892** —— *Short Hist. Eng. Grammar* §305 Words.. ending in a hiss-consonant. **1933** L. BLOOMFIELD *Language* vi. 100 Our gingival spirants [s, z] are hisses or sibilants. **1953** *Archivum Linguisticum* V. 68 The distinction between hiss- (Fr. *sifflantes*) and hush-sibilants (Fr. *chuintantes*).

2. This sound uttered in disapproval or scorn.

1602 DEKKER *Satiro-Mastix* To Rdr. A iv b, To beholde this short Comedy of Errors, and where the greatest enter, to giue them instead of a hisse, a gentle correction. **1667** MILTON *P.L.* x. 508 A dismal universal hiss, the sound Of public scorn. **1711** POPE *Temp. Fame* 405 Scornful hisses run thro' all the crowd. **1875** JOWETT *Plato* (ed. 2) III. 70 The applauses and hisses of the theatre.

†**hissa,** *int. Obs.* [Cf. *heisau*, under HEEZE *v.*, quot. 1549. Also Sp. *hiza*, 'hoise, as mariners hoise vp saile' (Minsheu); Pg. *iça* interj., a term used by seamen in hauling a rope: see HOISE.] A cry used on ship-board in hauling or hoisting.

c **1450** *Pilgr. Sea Voy* 13 in *Stac. Rome* etc. 37 With 'howe! hissa!' then they [the sailors] cry, 'What, howe, mate! thow stondyst to ny, Thy felow may nat hale the by'.

hissation, humorous for *hissing*: see -ATION.

his-self (dial. *hissel, hissen*): see HIMSELF IV.

hissiness (ˈhɪsɪnɪs). [f. HISSY *a.* (though recorded earlier) + -NESS.] Hissing manner or character.

1828 *Blackw. Mag.* XXIII. 398 Mr. Hunt..to the prating pertness of the parrot..adds the hissiness of the bill-pointing gander.

hissing (ˈhɪsɪŋ), *vbl. sb.* [f. HISS *v.* + -ING¹.]

1. The action of the verb HISS; the production of a sibilant sound; sibilation. With *a* and *pl.* An instance of this; a hiss.

1388 WYCLIF *Judges* v. 16 That thou here the hissyngis of flockis. **1535** COVERDALE *1 Kings* xix. 12 After the fyre came there a styll softe hyssinge [**1388** WYCLIF issyng]. **1656** tr. *Hobbes' Elem. Philos.* (1839) 489 The breath blown with violence from the mouth makes a hissing, because in going out it rakes the superficies of the lips, whose reaction against the force of the breath is not sensible. **1711** ADDISON *Spect.* No. 135 ¶7 That hissing in our Language, which is taken so much notice of by Foreigners. **1810** SHELLEY *Zastrozzi* xiii, The wind..whispered in low hissings among the withered shrubs.

2. The utterance of a hiss or hisses as a sign of disapproval or detestation.

1382 WYCLIF *Micah* vi. 16 Y shulde ȝeue thee in to perdicioun, and men dwellynge in it in to hissyng. **1597**

MIDDLETON *Wisdom of Solomon* vii. 15, I rather look for clapping than for hissing. *a* **1719** ADDISON *Playhouse* (R.), Thundering claps and dreadful hissings rise.

3. *concr.* An occasion or object of expressed opprobrium. *arch.*

1388 WYCLIF *Jer.* li. 37 Babiloyne schal be.. the dwellyng of dragouns, wondryng and hissyng [**1382** whistling]. **1560** BIBLE (Genev.) *Jer.* xix. 8, I wil make this citie desolate and an hissing. **1873** H. ROGERS *Orig. Bible* i. 51 That the Jews would at last become a hissing and a by-word among the nations.

4. *Comb.* **hissing-stock** (after *laughing-stock*), an object of expressed opprobrium or scorn.

1648 *Petit. Eastern Ass.* 4 To make our selves an hissing-stocke to Papists.

'hissing, *ppl. a.* [f. HISS *v.* + -ING[2].] **a.** That hisses (in the senses of the verb).

a **1547** SURREY *Æneid* II. (R.), Whoes waltring tongs did lick their hissing mouthes. **1590** SPENSER *F.Q.* I. ii. 9 For her he hated as the hissing snake. **1697** DRYDEN *Virg. Georg.* IV. 250 Others to quench the hissing Mass prepare. **1784** COWPER *Task* IV. 38 While the bubbling and loud-hissing urn Throws up a steamy column. **1834** *Blackw. Mag.* XXXVI. 484/2 The hissing iron became of a dull red. **1922** [see CLICK *sb.*[1] 1 b]. **1936** *Bell Syst. Techn. Jrnl.* XV. 197 If such a resistance element is in a current-carrying circuit associated with a telephone receiver or loud speaker.. a steady hissing noise which sounds like that due to shot effect or thermal agitation of electric charge is heard.

b. Of sounds: Sibilant, sibilated.

1697 DRYDEN *Æneid* XI. 820 He drowned One hissing letter in a softer sound. **1741** RICHARDSON *Pamela* (1824) I. xxix. 289 Methinks there is such a hissing sound in the word *sister*, that I cannot abide it. **1855** BAIN *Senses & Int.* II. ii. § 15 The hissing sound of *s*, the burring of the *r*, the hum of the *m*, are well marked modes of producing variety of effect.

c. *advb.* in phr. *hissing hot.*

1771 *Contemplative Man* I. 50 He sent them both hissing hot into the other World.

d. *Comb.* **hissing adder, sand-snake** (see quots.); **hissing arc**, an electric arc which emits a hissing sound.

1931 R. L. DITMARS *Snakes of World* vii. 72 *H[eterodon] contortrix* is the common eastern species [*sc.* of hognosed snake] found from Massachusetts to Florida and westward to Minnesota and Texas. It is known as the Flat-headed 'Adder', Hissing 'Adder', and other names in keeping with its antics. **1895** *Electrician* 18 Jan. 338/2 The potential difference for hissing arcs increases with length of arc, but appears to be fairly constant for a given length of arc... One talks of hissing, however, as if there were only one sort of hissing, whereas really there are at least two, with very different significations. **1941** J. D. COBINE *Gaseous Conductors* 293 The high-pressure carbon arc is seen to have two characteristics, one of hyperbolic shape for a silent arc, and the other, essentially linear, for a hissing arc. **1910** F. W. FITZSIMONS *Snakes S. Afr.* iii. 54/2 Psammophis sibilans. Hissing Sand Snake... Distribution: Tropical Africa and Egypt, Rhodesia, Transvaal, Zululand, Port Elizabeth. **1954** J. A. PRINGLE *Common Snakes* 20 Hissing Sand-Snake. *Psammophis sibilans*.. occurs in all the provinces of the Union [*sc.* of South Africa] except the Cape.

Hence **'hissingly** *adv.*

1611 COTGR., *Sifflantement*, hissingly, with a whistling sound.

hissy ('hɪsɪ), *a.* [f. HISS *sb.* + -Y[1].] Consisting of a hiss; of a sound, resembling that of a hiss.

1905 J. MASEFIELD *Tarpaulin Muster* (1907) 171 Snakes, ..laughing in a sort of hissy chuckle. **1948** I. BROWN *No Idle Words* 42 Cypress, though rather a 'hissy' word.

hist (hɪst), *int.* [A natural exclamation (also more exactly written *'st!*) enjoining silence (which seems to be suggested by the abrupt stoppage of the sibilant by the mute). Cf. IST, ST, WHISHT.]

1. A sibilant exclamation used to enjoin silence, or call on people to listen.

1617 MINSHEU *Ductor*, Hist, *nota silentij.* **1681** OTWAY *Soldier's Fort.* v. i, Didst thou hear nothing? Hist, hark! **1767–74** THORNTON tr. *Plautus' Discov.* (R.), Hist! silence! be of good heart. **1870** MORRIS *Earthly Par.* III. IV. 203 'Hist', said the old man, 'there he is'.

2. A similar sound made to urge on a dog or other animal. ***hist-a-boy***, an exclamation used to incite or urge on. *U.S.*

1841 EMERSON *Addr.*, *Conservative* Wks. (Bohn) II. 276 He must cry 'Hist-a-boy' and urge the game on. **1860** — *Cond. Life, Illusions* ibid. 443 To.. cry *Hist-a-boy!* to every good dog. [Cf. Sc. *hist-a-cat!*, *'st-a-cat!*, used in hounding a dog after a cat.]

hist (hɪst), *v.*[1] Now *poetic.* [f. HIST *int.*]

I. † **1.** *trans.* To summon with the exclamation 'hist!'; to summon in silence or without noise. *Obs.*

1632 MILTON *Penseroso* 55 The cherub Contemplation; And the mute Silence hist along, 'Less Philomel will deign a song. **1647** H. MORE *Song of Soul* I. II. lvii, Which he to me with earnest countenance show'd Histing me nearer. **1778** R. LOWTH *Transl. Isa.* v. 26 He will hist every one of them from the ends of the earth. *Ibid.* vii. 18 Jehovah shall hist the fly.. And the bee.. And they shall come.

2. *intr.* To be silent.

1867 J. CONINGTON *Virg. Æneid* I. 237 (ed. 2) Then should some man of worth appear Whose stainless virtue all revere, They hush, they hist [*ed.* 1 list]; his clear voice rules Their rebel wills, their anger cools.

II. 3. *trans.* To incite or urge on with the exclamation 'hist'; hence, generallly, to incite.

1604 MIDDLETON *Father Hubbard's Tales* Wks. 1886 VIII. 106 Lest they should be out, or faint, or cold, Their innocent clients hist them on with gold.

hist (haɪst), *v.*[2] Chiefly *U.S.* Also **h'ist, hyst.** [dial. form of HOIST *v.*; cf. HEIST.]

1. To provide the key for singing (a hymn, etc.). *rare.*

1857 *Harper's Mag.* Sept. 572/1 As they have no choir in the congregation, any one who considers himself qualified has authority to hist the hymns.

2. To raise aloft; = HOIST *v.* 1; also, to steal, hijack. Cf. HEIST *v.*, HOIST *v.* 6.

1867 'MARK TWAIN' *Celebr. Jumping Frog* 18 Dan'l give a heave, and hysted up his shoulders. **1872** 'AGRIKLER' *Rhymes* 17 Hev a fresh cask ready histed. **1919** H. L. MENCKEN *Amer. Lang.* iii. 91 They still cling, in their common speech, to such forms as *h'ist* for *hoist.* **1930** *Amer. Mercury* Dec. 456/1 *Hist*, to hold up; to hyjack. 'We hist the mutt's plant for fifty cases of skee.' **1936** M. MITCHELL *Gone with Wind* xxxiv. 569 You'd better hist up your skirts a little. **1938** D. RUNYON *Furthermore* xiv. 290 This is one of the very first cases of histing a truckload of legal beer that comes off in this country. **1938** M. K. RAWLINGS *Yearling* viii. 70, I h'isted him over old Caesar's rump and away we goed.

Hence **'histing** *vbl. sb.*

1935 J. T. FARRELL *Judgment Day* x. 213 There's been too many histing jobs pulled off lately in this neighborhood, and the sergeant has been hopping on my tail about them.

Histadrut ('hɪstədru:t). Also **Histadrud, Histadruth.** [mod.Heb. *ha-histadrūṯ* the federation: in full *ha-histadrûṯ ha-kᵉlālîṯ šel hā'-ôḇᵉḏîm bᵉ'eres yisrā'ēl* the general federation of workers in the land of Israel.] The General Federation of Labour in Israel, founded in 1920.

1923 P. GRAVES *Palestine* vii. 144 A young, idealistic party who work with the Ahaduth Ha-Avoda in the Histadrud Ha-Ovdim, or Workmen's Organization. **1925** L. STEIN *Zionism* v. 171 The *Histadruth* provides its members with evening classes, workmen's clubs, lectures, concerts, and travelling libraries. **1931** F. F. ANDREWS *Holy Land under Mandate* II. 26 The Histadruth has an active Press, its most influential paper being the daily, 'Davar', with a circulation of over four thousand. **1937** *Palestine Labour Studies* IV. 7 The Histadruth is—in aspiration and essence—an organization binding together the founders of a National Home, the builders of a country, the liberators of a people. **1952** S. SPENDER *Learning Laughter* xv. 196 The Histadrut (Trades Union Federation) is perhaps the most powerful Trades Union Organization in the world. **1972** *Times* 6 Apr. 15/7 He served in a number of senior posts in the Histadrut, the Israel Federation of Labour.

histamine ('hɪstəmi:n). *Biochem.* Formerly also **-in.** [f. HIST(IDINE + AMINE.] An amine formed from histidine by decarboxylation, widely found in both animal and plant tissues, and having a specific action as a stimulator of gastric secretion and as a dilator of the capillaries. Hence **'histaminase** [see -ASE], an enzyme which inhibits the action of histamine.

1913 DORLAND *Med. Dict.* (ed. 7), *Histamin*, betaimidazolylethylamin: used like pituitrin. **1913** *Jrnl. Chem. Soc.* CIV. I. 681 Histamine.. is a base which Barger and Dale separated from the intestinal mucous membrane. **1918** *Jrnl. Amer. Chem. Soc.* XL. 1723 The first 3 extracts were pale yellow in color and contained practically all the histamine. **1918** *Jrnl. Physiol.* LII. 110 In earlier papers P. P. Laidlaw and one of us [*sc.* H. H. Dale] referred to it by its chemical name, β-Iminazolylethylamine (abbreviated for conveinience to β-I.), being unwilling to coin a new name for a substance long known... Several later investigators of its action, however, have used for it the name 'histamine', which is so obviously appropriate for this amine derived from histidine, that we have adopted it here. **1920** *Nature* 4 Mar. 11/2 A compound of known chemical structure, called 'histamine',..which is able to produce a state of the circulation like that present in wound-shock. **1929** *Times* 28 Oct. 15/3 These products produce what is spoken of as 'histamine poisoning', the substance histamine being the principal toxic agent. **1930** BEST & MCHENRY in *Jrnl. Physiol.* LXX. 557 We suggest.. that the substance, or system, which produces a change in structure responsible for the loss of physiological activity of histamine be designated histaminase. **1951** WHITBY & HYNES *Med. Bacteriol.* (ed. 5) 90 The hypothesis that histamine-release is the immediate cause of the symptoms of anaphylactic shock formerly rested largely on the close similarity between the symptoms of histamine poisoning and of anaphylactic shock in different animals and *in vitro.* **1957** *New Biol.* XXIV. 54 Histamine belongs to a group of substances known chemically as amines and physiologically as vaso-dilators, i.e. they dilate the blood vessels. **1965** LEE & KNOWLES *Animal Hormones* viii. 119 Histaminase, which destroys histamine, does not affect the potency of the extract and gastrin appears to be a true hormone. **1968** J. H. BURN *Lect. Notes Pharmacol.* (ed. 9) 24 Histamine is an amine which can be formed by removing the –COOH group from the amino-acid histidine.

hister ('hɪstə(r)). [mod.L. (C. Linnæus *Systema Naturæ* (ed. 10, 1758) I. 358), f. L. *hister* = *histrio* actor.] A beetle of the genus so named of the family Histeridæ of clavicorn coleoptera. Also **'histerid** *a.*, belonging to this family; *sb.*, a beetle of this family.

1794 P. A. NEMNICH *Allgemeines Polyglotten-Lexicon der Naturgeschichte* III. 165 *Hister.* [Entoml. [*sic*]].. *Engl.* The hister. **1839** J. O. WESTWOOD *Introd. Class. Insects* I. 182 Cadet de Vaux, in his *History of the Mole*, observes that, almost as soon as it is dead, it is attacked by a number of Histers. **1874** J. G. WOOD *Insects Abroad* 89 The Giant Hister. **1915** W. A. BRYAN *Nat. Hist. Hawaii* 417 The histerid beetles. **1925** A. D. IMMS *Text-Bk. Entomol.* 483 Hister and its allies frequent dung and carrion. **1965** B. E. FREEMAN tr. *Vandel's Biospeleol.* xiii. 212 Patrizi.. has described another hypogeous histerid. **1966** C. SWEENEY *Scurrying Bush* iv. 52 Two adult histerid beetles, black, shiny and oval, occurred.

histic ('hɪstɪk), *a.* [f. Gr. ἱστός tissue + -IC.] Of or pertaining to tissues. (*Syd. Soc. Lex.* 1886.)

histidine ('hɪstɪdi:n, -ɪn). *Biochem.* Also **-in.** [ad. G. *histidin* (A. Kossel 1896, in *Zeitschr. f. physiol. Chem.* XXII. 176), f. Gr. ἱστ-ός web, tissue + -IDINE c.] An amino-acid; see quot. 1940.

1896 *Jrnl. Chem. Soc.* LXX. I. 582 The sulphate from.. sturgeon sperm has rather different solubilities in sodium chloride solutions, and the names *salmine* and *sturine* are suggested by the two protamines. By decomposing the latter base with sulphuric acid, a new crystalline base was prepared, which is called *histidine.* **1900** DORLAND *Med. Dict.* 301/2 *Histidin*, a substance, $C_6H_9N_3O_2$, obtainable from any protamin by the action of sulphuric acid and water. **1919** *Nature* CIV. 322/2 The diamino-acids lysin, histidin, and arginin. **1940** *Chambers's Techn. Dict.* 417/2 *Histidine*, α-amino-β-imidazole propionic acid, a protein derivative belonging to the group of hexone bases. **1963** H. BURN *Drugs, Med. & Man* (ed. 2) vii. 73 Protein is a structure rather like a house which is built from bricks, each of which is chemically an amino-acid. One of these bricks is an amino-acid called histidine.

'histin. [f. as HISTIC *a.* + -IN.] A name for fibrin.

1886 in *Syd. Soc. Lex.*

histiocyte ('hɪstɪəʊsaɪt). *Physiol.* [ad. G. *histiozyt* (Aschoff & Kiyono 1913, in *Folia Haematologica: Arch.* XV. 386), f. Gr. ἱστίο-ν web, dim. form of ἱστός web, tissue + -CYTE.] A large, highly phagocytic cell found in connective tissue and becoming motile when stimulated; also called *adventitious cell*, *clasmatocyte*, *macrophage*, *resting wandering cell.* So **histio'cytic** *a.*, of or pertaining to, of the nature of, histiocytes.

1924 *Jrnl. Infectious Dis.* XXXIV. 583 These resting wandering cells or histiocytes in all their modifications in the different organs and tissues.. are the most active elements in the various inflammatory processes and in particular in tuberculosis. *Ibid.*, It is natural that the lymphocytes should also play an active rôle in the same inflammatory processes and join the polyblasts of histiocytic origin. **1961** *Lancet* 2 Sept. 523/2 The dark red spleen.. was unremarkable microscopically except for an occasional large histiocyte in the red pulp with finely vacuolated cytoplasm. **1966** [see HISTIOCYTOSIS below].

Also **,histiocy'tosis** *Path.* [-OSIS], any condition characterized by a proliferation of histiocytes.

1925 W. BLOOM in *Amer. Jrnl. Path.* I. 623 For the want of a better name we would suggest 'lipoid-histiocytosis' as tending to convey the idea of a process involving the storing of lipoid material by the histiocytes throughout the body. **1953** L. LICHTENSTEIN in *A.M.A. Arch. Path.* LV. 102 The conditions previously designated eosinophilic granuloma of bone, 'Letter-Siwe disease' and 'Schüller-Christian disease' are interrelated manifestations of a single malady. The name 'histiocytosis X' is suggested as a provisional broad general description for this nosologic entity. **1966** *New Eng. Jrnl. Med.* 28 Apr. 929/1 The association of histiocytic proliferations with recurrent infections has been noted in histiocytosis X and in pigmented histiocytosis.

histioid ('hɪstɪɔɪd), *a.* *Phys.* and *Path.* [f. Gr. ἱστίον, dim. of ἱστός web, tissue + -OID.] = HISTOID.

1854 JONES & SIEV. *Pathol. Anat.* (1874) 134 Those new growths which resemble the simple tissues of the body may be called Simple Histioid Tumours. **1876** tr. *Wagner's Gen. Pathol.* 355 Virchow calls tumors which are composed of only one tissue, tissue-like, or Histioid.

histiology (hɪstɪ'ɒlədʒɪ). [f. as prec. + -LOGY. Cf. F. *histiologie.*] = HISTOLOGY.

1857 in DUNGLISON *Med. Lex.* **1886** *Syd. Soc. Lex.*, *Histiology*, Valentin's term for a description of the tissues.

Hence **histio'logical** *a.* = HISTOLOGICAL.

1857 in DUNGLISON *Med. Lex.*

histo-, combining form of Gr. ἱστό-ς web, tissue, occurring with sense 'tissue' in various biological terms, as **'histoblast** [Gr. βλαστός cell], the primary element or unit of a tissue (*Syd. Soc. Lex.* 1886); **histo'chemical** *a.*, relating to histochemistry; **histo'chemically** *adv.*, by histochemical means; **histo'chemistry**, the chemistry of organic tissues; **,histocompati'bility**, compatibility (sense 2 b) between a grafted tissue and the recipient; so **,histocom'patible** *a.*; **histodi'alysis** [see DIALYSIS], 'term for a resolution of an organic texture' (Mayne *Expos. Lex.* 1854); hence **histodia'lytic** *a.*, 'of or belonging to histodialysis' (*ibid.*); **hi'stogenous** *a.*, formed by tissue; **histo'graphic, -ical** *adjs.*, belonging to **hi'stography**, description of the tissues (Craig 1847); **histo'hæmatin** *Chem.* [see HÆMATIN], name for a kind of colouring matter occurring in animal tissues; **'histolyse** *v.*, to subject to histolysis; so ***histolysing*** ppl. adj.; **hi'stolysis** [Gr. λύσις loosening], disintegration or dissolution of organic tissue; hence **histo'lytic**

a., belonging to histolysis; **ˌhistometa'basis** *Palæont*, [METABASIS], a state of complete fossilization in which the minute markings of grain and texture are preserved; **ˌhistomorpho'logical** *a.*, relating to **histomor'phology**, the morphology of the tissues; **histomor'photic** *a.* [Gr. *μορφωτικός*, f. *μορφόειν* to form, shape], relating to the formation of tissue; **hi'stonomy** [Gr. *-νομία* arrangement], the subject of the formation and arrangement of organic tissues (Craig 1847); **ˌhistopatho'logic, -ical** *adjs.*, characterized by diseased tissues; of or pertaining to histopathology; **ˌhistopa'thologist**, one who specializes in histopathology; **ˌhistopa'thology**, (the study of) the tissue changes associated with a disease or disorder; **hi'stophyly** [Gr. *φυλή* tribe], the history of tissues within the limits of a particular tribe of organisms; **histo'physics**, the subject of physics as related to the tissues; **ˌhistophysio'logical** *a.*, relating to **histophysi'ology**, the physiology of the tissues (*Syd. Soc. Lex.* 1886); **histo'plasmin** [-IN[1]], a sterile preparation of a culture of the fungus *Histoplasma capsulatum*, used in skin tests for histoplasmosis; **ˌhistopla'smosis** [-OSIS], an infection due to the fungus *Histoplasma capsulatum*, endemic in parts of the United States and taking the form of either a benign transient infection of the lungs or, rarely, a disseminated, usu. fatal, disease of the reticulo-endothelial system; **hi'stotomy** [Gr. *-τομία* cutting], 'the dissection of the organic tissues' (Mayne 1854); **histo'trophic** *a.* [Gr. *τροφή* nourishment], relating to the formation and nourishment of the tissues; **'histozyme** [Gr. *ζύμη* leaven], Schmiedeberg's term for a substance that causes fermentation in the tissues.

1874 A. J. BARKER tr. *Frey's Histol. & Histochem.* §48 The chemical constitution of the animal cell . . a field of *histo-chemical inquiry of which little is known. **1955** *Brain* LXXVIII. 327 Lafora bodies (intracellular amyloid bodies) were encountered, and were examined *histochemically. **1971** *Jrnl. Insect Physiol.* XVII. 862 Approximately 10 per cent of the histochemically identifiable lysosomal phosphatase remains in tissue fragments attached to the silk. **1861** *N. Syd. Soc. Year-bk.* 1 Histology and *Histo-chemistry of man. **1948** G. D. SNELL in *Jrnl. Genetics* XLIX. 87 Genes of the type postulated in the genetic theory of tumour transplantation will be here referred to as *histocompatibility genes. The prefix 'histo' is used because the same genes which determine susceptibility or resistance to tumour transplants probably also determine susceptibility or resistance to tissue transplants in general. **1969** N. A. MITCHISON et al. *Organ Transplantation Today* 26 The genetic system controlling histocompatibility is not too complicated to defy analysis. **1964** *Transplantation* II. 656/1 An inbred strain is a *histocompatible donor to its F_1 offspring. **1907** *Practitioner* Sept. 455 The *Histogenous Cells which originate locally as the result of local tissue proliferation. **1946** *Nature* 3 Aug. 147/2 Histogenous demarcation of infected tissue (for example, abscission in shot-hole disease of peach and demarcation by cork layer in black root rot of tobacco). **1886** *Syd. Soc. Lex.*, **Histographic*, of or belonging to histography. **1854** MAYNE *Expos. Lex.*, *Histographicus*, *Histographical. **1885** C. A. MACMUNN in *Proc. R. Soc.* Nov. 248 Observations made on the spectra of the organs and tissues . . have brought to light the presence of a series of animal colouring matters. The name *histohæmatins is proposed for all these. **1963** R. P. DALES *Annelids* vi. 124 The muscles of the body wall are partly *histolysed and those of the parapodia augmented. **1946** *Nature* 14 Sept. 367/2 The cutis acts as a physico-chemical barrier, inhibiting the penetration of the *histolysing substances into the zone of amputation from the regenerating epithelium. **1857** DUNGLISON *Med. Lex.*, **Histolysis*. **1886** *Syd. Soc. Lex.*, *Histolysis* . . the retrograde metamorphosis of the tissues. **1868** J. H. BENNETT *Clin. Lect.* (ed. 5) 118 The successive formation of histogenetic and *histolytic molecules. **1885** W. ROBERTS *Treat. Urin. Dis.* III. iv. (ed. 4) 484 The blood and tissues are . . charged with the primary histolytic products. **1893** C. A. WHITE in *U.S. Nat. Mus. Ann. Rep. 1892* 264 The term *histometabasis is applied to that condition of fossilization in which an exchange of the original substance for another has occurred in such a manner as to retain or reproduce the minute and even the microscopic texture of the original. **1917** R. S. LULL *Org. Evol.* xxv. 412 The resultant fossil retains . . not only the external form but the histologic characters (histometabasis, . .) of the original structure as well. **1883** GOLGI in *Alien & Neurol.* July 387 Other *histo-morphological particulars. **1857** *Blackw. Mag.* LXXXII 16 Is . . there . . in albumen a mysterious *histomorphotic power in virtue of which it transmutes itself from the liquid into the solid condition? **1903** *Detroit Med. Jrnl.* Feb. 705/1 The *histopathologic states of the finer structures of the labyrinth. **1947** *Radiology* XLIX. 292/2 Histopathologic changes in organs and tissue may occur in the absence of or prior to observable changes in the blood or blood-forming tissue. **1934** WEBSTER, *Histopathological. **1940** E. VON HAAM in *Textbk. Clin. Path.* (ed. 2) xxii. 552 The histopathological change in the syphilitic lesion is a valuable addition to diagnostic methods. **1946** *Acta Med. Scand.* CXXIII. 445 Histopathological discoveries in amyotonia congenita. **1909** WEBSTER, *Histopathologist. **1961** *Lancet* 30 Sept. 770/2 London histopathologists. **1966** *Ibid.* 31 Dec. 1450/1 The wealth of photomicrographs is likely to appeal more to the practising histopathologist than to the physicians, dentists, and students. **1896** N. WALKER tr. P. G. Unna (*title*) The *histopathology of the diseases of the skin. **1908** *Practitioner* Jan. 27 The histo-pathology of the lesions. **1959** *Chambers's Encycl.* VI. 123/2 Fungi of this group cause systemic mycoses which may closely resemble tuberculosis in their symptomatology and histopathology. **1879** tr. *Haeckel's Evol. Man* I. i. 24 Tribal history of cells . . *histophyly. **1886** *Jrnl R. Microsc. Soc.* Apr. 365 On the *histophysics of the red blood-corpuscles. *Ibid.*, *Histophysiological researches on the extension of the nerves in the muscles. **1886** *Syd. Soc. Lex.*, **Histophysiology*. **1945** CHRISTIE & PETERSON in *Amer. Jrnl. Publ. Health* XXXV. 1135/2 *Histoplasmin is the term we used to designate the antigen we were using for skin testing. It is to be hoped that this natural term will be used for any antigen which may be found satisfactory for the purpose of skin testing in relation to histoplasmosis. **1964** B. D. FALLIS *Textbk. Path.* ix. 242/1 Skin tests using histoplasmin (the counterpart of tuberculin) suggest that in endemic areas histoplasmosis is a common disease, which is not usually clinically apparent. **1907** S. T. DARLING in *Maryland Med. Jrnl.* L. 125 (*heading*) Notes on *histoplasmosis—a fatal disorder met with in tropical America. **1955** *Sci. Amer.* Jan. 44/3 There has been a good deal of question about the mode of spread of histoplasmosis, a lung disease widely prevalent in the Middle West. **1973** *Daily Colonist* (Victoria, B.C.) 13 May 40/1 Pigeons on the roof are suspected as the source of an illness called histoplasmosis recently suffered by two law professors. *a* **1889** DUNGLISON *Med. Lex.* s.v. *Plastic*, Agents—hygienical or curative—which take part in such formations [of organized tissue], may be termed *histotrophic or constructive. **1876** *Med. News* (U.S.) LII. 542 That injections of *histozyme into the blood of dogs produced high fever.

histogenesis (hɪstəʊ'dʒɛnɪsɪs). *Biol.* [f. HISTO- + Gr. *γένεσις* birth, production.] The production or development of organic tissues.

1854 in MAYNE *Expos. Lex.* **1880** *Libr. Univ. Knowl.* VII. 554 Schwann is often called the founder of the science of histogenesis. **1881** *Athenæum* 29 Oct. 566/1 The histogenesis of man and the higher vertebrata.

histogenetic (-dʒɪ'nɛtɪk), *a.* [f. as prec.: see GENETIC.] Having the quality of producing tissue; relating to the formation of tissues.

1854 in MAYNE *Expos. Lex.* **1859** TODD *Cycl. Anat.* V. 139/1 Phenomena of a histogenetic nature. **1875** HUXLEY in *Encycl. Brit.* II. 50/1 Histogenetic elements; that is . . cells which by their metamorphoses, give rise to tissues.

Hence **histoge'netically** *adv.*, in relation to histogenesis; from a histogenetic point of view.

1885 *Encycl. Brit.* XVIII. 4002 Histogenetically, they [connective tissues] are the remains of that . . embryonic tissue from which the blood-channels themselves were made.

histogeny (hɪ'stɒdʒɪnɪ). [f. as prec. + -GENY.] = HISTOGENESIS.

1847 CRAIG, *Histogeny*, the formation of an organic tissue. **1854** in MAYNE *Expos. Lex.* **1879** tr. *Haeckel's Evol. Man* I. i. 24 Germ-history of the cells, etc. (Histogeny). *Ibid.* iii. 62 Histogeny, or the Science of the Evolution of Tissues, as first elaborated by Remak and by Kolliker.

histogram ('hɪstəʊgræm). *Statistics.* [f. Gr. *ἱστό-ς* mast, web + -GRAM.] A diagram consisting of a number of rectangles or lines drawn (usu. upwards) from a base line, their position along this line representing the value or range of one variable and their height the corresponding value of a second variable.

1891 in E. S. Pearson *Karl Pearson* (1938) 143 The geometrical representation of statistics. . . D. By Columns. *Histograms.* Optical advantage of vertical over horizontal columns. **1895** K. PEARSON in *Philos. Trans. R. Soc.* A. CLXXXVI. 399 The histogram shows, however, the amount of deviation at the extremes of the curve. [*Note.* The word 'histogram' was] introduced by the writer in his lectures on statistics as a term for a common form of graphical representation, *i.e.*, by columns marking as areas the frequency corresponding to the range of their base. **1903** *Nature* 17 Dec. 149/2 We should like to protest against any such crude process of determining goodness of fit as that of placing a normal curve down on seven or eight blocks forming a 'histogram' and judging the look of the fit. **1949** *Jrnl. R. Aeronaut. Soc.* LIII. 974/2 In Fig. 4 . . the best exponential curve has been fitted to the histogram of the lengths of over 1,300 conversations on the London Airport R/T channel of frequency 118·1 Mcs. **1969** *Nature* 15 Nov. 655/2 The 178 *z*-values analysed are collected in bins of 0·01*z* and are then marked off as a histogram on a *z*-scale.

histoid ('hɪstɔɪd), *a. Phys.* and *Path.* [f. Gr. *ἱστός* web + -OID.] Like or of the nature of tissue, esp. connective tissue: spec. said of tumours.

1872 PEASLEE *Ovar. Tumours* 25 A variety of histoid tumor.

histoire, early form of HISTORY.

histologic (-'lɒdʒɪk), *a.* = next.

1855 H. SPENCER *Princ. Psychol.* (1870) I. I. ii. 25 Nerve-tubes . . and nerve-cells . . are the histologic elements of which the nervous system is built up.

histo'logical, *a.* [f. HISTOLOGY + -IC + -AL[1].] Belonging to histology; relating to organic tissues.

1844-6 OWEN *Lect. Comp. Anat.* vi. 135 The cartilaginous or intermediate histological change between the primitive membranous and ultimate osseous stage. **1863** H. SPENCER *Princ. Biol.* §60 In the hydra the histological differentiation that has been established is extremely slight. **1879** *Cassell's Techn. Educ.* IV. 123/1 The skins, skeletons, spirit and histological preparations . . should be amalgamated into one series.

Hence **histo'logically** *adv.*, in relation to histology.

1859 TODD *Cycl. Anat.* V. 372/2 The matters thus excreted may be divided histologically into two chief constituents.

hi'stologist. [f. next + -IST.] One versed in histology.

1859 J. TOMES *Dental Surg.* 289 Few subjects have engaged the attention of histologists more frequently . . than the development of dentine. **1881** E. R. LANKESTER in *Nature* No. 628. 25 The medical histologist and physiologist has learnt that . . he must not confine himself . . to . . the chick.

histology (hɪ'stɒlədʒɪ). [f. Gr. *ἱστός* web + -LOGY. Cf. F. *histologie.*] The science of organic tissues; that branch of anatomy, or of biology, which is concerned with the minute structure of the tissues of animals and plants.

1847 CRAIG, *Histology*, the doctrine of the organic tissues. **1858** CARPENTER *Veg. Phys.* §39 These parts are called the tissues of plants, and a knowledge of their nature is called the science of vegetable histology. **1885** H. W. ACLAND in *Pall Mall G.* 9 Mar. 6/2 The assistant . . appointed . . for histology, that is to say, minute microscopical demonstrations.

histomap ('hɪstəʊmæp). [f. HISTO(RY + MAP.] (See quot. 1956.)

1945 *Amer. Speech* XX. 76/2 A 'Histomap of Religion' was sent to customers and friends at Christmas time, 1943, by the Kalamazoo Vegetable Parchment Company. **1956** R. REDFIELD *Peasant Soc. & Cult.* 72 A picture of their relationships would be something like those 'histo-maps' we sometimes see, those diagrams of the rise and change through time of religions and civilizations.

histone ('hɪstəʊn). *Biochem.* Formerly also **-on.** [ad. G. *histon* (A. Kossel 1884, in *Zeitschr. f. physiol. Chem.* VIII. 512), perh. f. Gr. *ἱστ-άναι* to arrest or *ἱστ-ός* HISTO-: see -ONE.] Any of a small class of simple, basic proteins which are soluble in water and dilute acids but insoluble in dilute ammonia and which are most commonly found in association with nucleic acids.

1885 *Jrnl. Chem. Soc.* XLVIII. I. 572 Extraction with dilute acid isolates a substance which belongs to the class of bodies called A-peptones by Meissner. . . The author names this substance *histon.* **1905** C. E. SIMON *Physiol. Chem.* (ed. 2) 194 The protamins are decomposed entirely like the albumoses and peptones, while the histons are only affected in part, which coincides with the position which the histons occupy midway between the protamins and the true albumins. **1952** *Sci. News* XXIV. 37 Histones . . are present in appreciable amounts in the nuclei of the tissue cells of all animal species examined. **1968** *New Scientist* 7 Nov. 319/3 What now seems much more possible is that the histones are simply the tool needed to shut down genes, and that they are instructed which particular gene . . to shut down by another, specific, molecule.

†**historial**, *a.* (*sb.*) *Obs.* [a. F. *historial* (1291 in Hatz.-Darm.), ad. late L. *historiālis* (Sidonius *c* 475), f. *historia* HISTORY.] Belonging to or of the nature of history; historical, historic.

1382 WYCLIF *Bible* Genl. Prol. Proph., The stories of Moises lawe . . and of othere historial bookis schulen be wel lokid. *c* **1386** CHAUCER *Doctor's T.* 156 This is no fable, But knowen for historial thyng notable. *c* **1449** PECOCK *Repr.* I. xiii. 66 The historial parties of the Oold Testament. **1598** HAKLUYT *Voy.* II. I. 72 To write and reduce in veritie Historiall, the great siege . . of Rhodes. **1649** ROBERTS *Clavis Bibl.* 382 Direct historiall Narrations.

B. *sb.* History, record.

1595 B. BARNES in Farr *S.P. Eliz.* (1845) I. 42 That historiall Of my sinnes numberlesse in deepe seas cast.

historian (hɪ'stɔərɪən), *sb.* (*a.*) Also 6 **-ien.** [a. F. *historien* (in OF. also adj.), f. L. *historia* HISTORY: see -AN.]

1. A writer or author of a history; esp. one who produces a work of history in the higher sense, as distinguished from the simple annalist or chronicler of events, or from the mere compiler of a historical narrative.

1531 ELYOT *Gov.* I. xxiv, Quintus Fabius for this qualitie is soueraignely extolled amonge historiens. **1581** SIDNEY *Apol. Poetrie* (Arb.) 25 The Historian [sayth] what men haue done. **1589** J. SANFORD tr. *Agrippa's Van. Artes* 15 There are . . other amonge the Historians, giltie of greater lies. **1663** COWLEY *Verses Sev. Occas., Royal Soc.* ix, And ne'r did Fortune better yet Th' Historian to the Story fit. **1769** *Junius Lett.* xii. 55 It is the Historian's office to punish, though he cannot correct. **1873** FREEMAN *Hist. Ess.* Ser. II. ix. 308 Gibbon is before all things the historian of the transition from the Roman world to the world of modern Europe. **1874** GREEN *Short Hist.* i. §4. 38 Baeda was at once the founder of mediaeval history and the first English historian. **1879** GAIRDNER *Early Chron. Eng.* ii. 77 He [William of Malmes.] is a genuine historian, not a dry compiler of annals like the writers who preceded him. **1884** FREEMAN *Methods Hist. Study* (1886) 33 The man [Polybios] who looked at his own age with the eyes of an historian of all ages.

†**2.** One who relates a narrative or tale; a story-teller; in quot. 1603 rendering Gr. *περιηγητής* 'local guide, cicerone'. *Obs.*

1586 YOUNG tr. *Guazzo's Civ. Conv.* IV. 202 b, You are but a simple Historian for ministring of mirth. **1603** HOLLAND *Plutarch's Mor.* 1194 Our discoursing Historians and expositours shewed us the place, where sometimes stood the obelisks of iron. **1667** MILTON *P.L.* VIII. 7 What thanks sufficient . . have I to render thee, Divine Hystorian.

3. One versed in history. *rare.*

c **1645** HOWELL *Lett.* (1655) IV. xi. 29 Not to be an Historian, that is, not to know what Forren Nations and our Forefathers did, '*Hoc est semper esse Puer*', as Cicero hath it. **1665** EVELYN *Corr.* 21 June, What your Lordship's curiosity will desire to dip into, to emerge a complete historian.

†**B.** *adj.* Relating to or founded on history; historical. *Obs. rare.*

1632 LITHGOW *Trav.* Author to Bk. B iv b, Go lively charg'd with stout Historian Faith, And trample downe base Crittickes in the Dust.

Hence **hi'storianess**, a female historian. *rare.*

1837 *New Monthly Mag.* XLIX. 597 Mrs. Macauley, the historianess, married his brother. *a* **1839** L. E. LANDON in L. Blanchard *Life* (1855) I. 48 She is a great historianess, a most charming delightful woman.

histori'aster. *rare.* [f. L. *historia* HISTORY + -ASTER.] A petty or contemptible historian.

1887 *Blackw. Mag.* Nov. 715 An 'historiaster' (as distinguished from an historian). **1894** *Westm. Gaz.* 23 Apr. 3/2 Our modern historiasters neglect this.

historiated (hɪ'stɔərɪeɪtɪd), *ppl. a.* [f. med. L. *historiāt-us*, pa. pple. of *historiāre* (see HISTORY *v.*) + -ED.] Decorated with figures of men or animals (or, sometimes, flowers: see FLORIATED), as illuminated or ornamental initial letters, etc.

1886 *Athenæum* 29 May 716/2 Ornamented with initial letters historiated with figures. **1895** M. R. JAMES *Abbey St. Edmund* 131 At Amiens four portions of a like historiated screen remain.

historic (hɪ'stɒrɪk), *a.* (*sb.*) [ad. L. *historic-us* adj. (and sb. 'historian'), a. Gr. ἱστορικ-ός, f. ἱστορία HISTORY. Cf. F. *historique* (1480 in Hatz.-Darm.), in OF. also 'historian'.]

A. *adj.* **1.** Of or belonging to history; of the nature of history; historical; esp. of the nature of history as opposed to fiction or legend.

1669 GALE *Crt. Gentiles* I. II. viii. 111 Evident from sacred Historic Observation. **1700** PRIOR *Carmen Seculare* 15 With equal Justice and Historic Care, Their Laws, their Toils, their Arms with his compare. **1847** TENNYSON *Princ.* Prol. 30 A hoard of tales that dealt with knights, Half-legend, half-historic. **1860** TYNDALL *Glac.* Pref., To make myself better acquainted..with the historic aspect of the question. **1871** FREEMAN *Hist. Ess.* Ser. I. i. 9 The sort of difficulty against which simple historic truth has to struggle. **1873** H. ROGERS *Orig. Bible* i. (1875) 36 The miracles imputed to the historic Christ. **1907** I. ZANGWILL *Ghetto Comedies* 391 'The unconditional historic necessity will carry us on of itself towards a better social state.' 'There you go with your Marx and your Hegel!' **1921** G. B. SHAW in *Nation* 19 Feb. 705/1 Mr. Hyndman falls back..on Historic Determinism, and declares that the Bolshevists must fail because the economic conditions are not ripe. **1940** 'G. ORWELL' *Inside Whale* 22 There is no perception here of what is now called historic necessity.

2. *esp.* Forming an important part or item of history; noted or celebrated in history; having an interest or importance due to connexion with historical events. (The prevailing current sense.)

a **1794** GIBBON *Autobiog. & Corr.* (1869) 22 My first introduction to the historic scenes, which have since engaged so many years of my life. **1851** D. WILSON *Preh. Ann.* (1863) II. IV. ii. 249 That historic ground and the moss-grown sculptures with which it is paved. **1876** FREEMAN *Norm. Conq.* (ed. 3) I. v. 321 A Norman castle and a Norman minster rose and fell on that historic spot.

3. Conveying or dealing with history; recording past events; = HISTORICAL (which is the usual prose equivalent).

1675 OGILBY *Brit.* 28 That Eminent Piece of Historick Poetry, Poly-olbion. **1725** POPE *Odyss.* I. 306 Then grateful Greece with streaming eyes wou'd raise Historic Marbles, to record his praise. **1762–71** H. WALPOLE *Vertue's Anecd. Paint.* (1786) III. 12 John Freeman, An historic painter, was a rival of Fuller. **1809** W. IRVING *Knickerb.* IV. i. (1849) 199 The true subjects for the historic pen. **1849** LINGARD *Hist. Eng.* Prelim. Notice (1855) 9 The stately and dignified march of the historic muse. **1871** FREEMAN *Hist. Ess.* Ser. I. xi. 314 The possession of real historic power.

4. Applied, in Latin and Greek Grammar, to those tenses of the verb which are used in narration of past events (opposed to *primary* or *principal*); also, in Latin, to the infinitive mood when used instead of the indicative; and, generally, to the present tense, when used instead of the past in vivid narration.

The term ***historic tenses*** has been variously used; they answer partly to the *secondary tenses* of some grammarians.

1845 JELF *Kühner's Greek Gr.* (1851) II. 52 The relative tenses are divided into Principal (Present, Perfect, and Future) and Historic Tenses (Imperfect, Pluperfect, and Future exactum). **1871** *Public Sch. Lat. Primer* §38 Tenses are Primary or Historic. The Present and Futures are Primary Tenses; the Imperfect and Pluperfect are Historic. The Perfect is Primary when Present-Past (*I have loved*), but Historic when Simple Past (*I loved*). *Ibid.* §117 *note*, The Inifinitive used predicatively for a Finite Verb, and called the Historic Infinitive. **1879** ROBY *Lat. Gram.* §1457 The Present tense expresses..An action in past time, but rhetorically assumed to be present. This is frequent in vivid narrations. (Historic present.)

B. *sb. rare.* †**1.** A historian. *Obs.*

1611 BROUGHTON *Require Agreem.* 25 Eusebius, being the common historique for the Church, telleth the common opinion for his time.

2. *ellipt.* A historic work, picture, subject, etc.

1830 H. ANGELO *Remin.* I. 203 He had tried all branches and attempted all styles; historics, landscape, familiar subjects.

historical (hɪ'stɒrɪkəl), *a.* (*sb.*) [f. L. *historic-us* (see prec.) + -AL[1].]

A. *adj.* **1. a.** Of or pertaining to history; of the nature or character of history, constituting history; following or in accordance with history.

1561 DAUS tr. *Bullinger on Apoc.* (1573) 101 b, The corporall [restoryng of Israel] may be called hystoricall, and was performed by Cyrus. **1597** HOOKER *Eccl. Pol.* v. lxviii. §2 Setting downe with historicall breuitie what was spoken. **1614** RALEIGH *Hist. World* III. ii. §3 (R.) The bulk and gross of his narration was founded upon mere historical truth. **1743** J. MORRIS *Serm.* iii. 86 Historical and moral evidence is not indeed of the same nature with mathematical demonstration. **1816** KEATINGE *Trav.* (1817) I. 300 It is not consistent with historical dignity..to notice such a trifle as a massacre of..unbelievers. **1884** (*title*) A New English Dictionary on Historical Principles. **1937** A. HUXLEY *Ends & Means* vii. 66 One word is common to all the dictatorial vocabularies and is used for purposes of justification and rationalization by Fascists, Nazis and Communists alike. That word is 'historical'. *Ibid.* 67 The dictatorship of the proletariat is an 'historical necessity'. The violence of Communists is justified because..it is being used to forward an ineluctable 'historical' process. **1964** S. BELLOW *Herzog* (1965) 99 You must sacrifice your poor, squawking, niggardly individuality..to historical necessity.

b. *spec.* Of, pertaining to, of the nature of history as opposed to fiction or legend.

1843 KNIGHT *Shaks.* I. x. 137 The notion..that nothing ought to be presented upon the stage but what was an historical fact. **1871** FREEMAN *Hist. Ess.* Ser. I. i. 29 The fact that his [Roland's] famous legendary death is a very easy perversion of his historical death. **1875** J. S. STUART-GLENNIE in *Encycl. Brit.* II. 651/2 The scepticism..as to the existence of an historical Arthur. **1877** DOWDEN *Primer Shaks.* vi. §15. 97 This historical Oldcastle is better known as Lord Cobham.

2. a. Relating to or concerned with history or historical events.

†***historical faith***: that concerned only with historical facts; intellectual belief or assent, as distinct from faith that is practically operative on conduct: cf. FAITH 3 b.

c **1513** *Bradshaw's St. Werburge* Ball. to Author 18 Sith thou gaue to vs a floure most riall Redolent in cronicles with historicall syght. *c* **1530** TINDALE *Wks.* 267 (R.) The historicall fayth hangeth of the truth and honestie of the teller, or of the common fame and consent of many. **1531** —— *Expos. 1 John* (1537) 12 The fyrst..is called an hystoricall fayth and belefe. *c* **1645** HOWELL *Lett.* (1655) II. x. 18. 339 The Prince of darknesse himself and all the cacodæmons by an historicall faith believe ther is a God. *a* **1699** W. BATES *Div. Medit.* ix. (R.), So many have an historical knowledge, yet because they are not united to Christ, they receive no benefit. **1865** MOZLEY *Mirac.* i. 2 By the historical imagination I mean the habit of realizing past time, of putting history before ourselves in such a light that the persons and events..are seen as once-living persons and once-present events.

†**b.** *transf.* Characterized by 'historical faith'.

1649 J. ECCLISTON tr. *Behmen's Ep.* 29 There may be many honest hearts among them; but many of them are onely Historicall, and Titular. *a* **1718** PENN *Life* Wks. 1726 I. 156 The Carnal, Fleshly, and Historical Christian of the Outward Courts.

c. ***historical method***, a method of investigation in which the history of the object is studied.

1843 MILL *Logic* II. VI. x. (1856) 498 Of the Inverse Deductive, or Historical Method. *Ibid.* 517 His [Comte's] work is hitherto the only known example of the study of social phenomena according to this conception of the Historical Method. **1889** FOWLER *Induct. Log.* (ed. 5) 204 A very important application of the Method of Concomitant Variations is what is now commonly known as the *Historical Method*. **1891** EDGEWORTH in *Econ. Jrnl.* I. 633 The historical method..defined by..Prof. Ashley as 'direct observation, and generalization from facts past or present'.

d. Related to or connected with history; considered from the historian's point of view; belonging to the past.

1881 E. A. FREEMAN *Hist. Geogr. Europe* I. i. 2 It is with political divisions that historical geography has to deal in the first place. **1894** G. A. SMITH (*title*) The historical geography of the Holy Land. **1923** L. D. STAMP *Introd. Stratigr.* i. 1 Stratigraphy is another name for Historical Geology. **1924** O. JESPERSEN *Philos. Gram.* ii. 31 Descriptive linguistics can never be rendered superfluous by historical linguistics. **1933** *Amer. Speech* VIII. III. 6/2 It is the paradox of linguistic geography that a method of research strictly limited to contemporary speech has proved to be the means of revitalizing the study of historical linguistics. **1964** R. H. ROBINS *Gen. Ling.* 5 Historical linguistics is the study of the developments in languages in the course of time.

3. a. Dealing with history, treating of history, as a ***historical treatise*** or ***writer***; using history as its basis, as a historical play, novel, etc.

1590 SPENSER *F.Q.* Pref., The Methode of a Poet historical is not such, as of an Historiographer. **1615** J. STEPHENS *Satyr. Ess.* 135 Considering our negligence of historicall Poems. **1780** VON TROIL *Iceland* p. viii, The grossest errors that ever disgraced the historical page. **1816** JANE AUSTEN *Let.* 1 Apr. (1952) 452, I am fully sensible that an historical romance, founded on the House of Saxe Cobourg, might be much more to the purpose of profit or popularity. **1826** *Blackw. Edin. Mag.* XX. 52/1 These historical novels may operate advantageously on the mind. **1827** LYTTON *Pelham* ii, She had read all the historical romances of the day. **1871** FROUDE in *Devon. Assoc. Trans.* IV. 38 The most perfect English history which exists is to be found..in the historical plays of Shakespeare. **1874** GEO. ELIOT *Legend of Jubal* 193 Imagination... Aiming at fiction called historical. **1876** STOPF. BROOKE *Primer Eng. Lit.* vii. §124. 130 In..such tales as *Kenilworth* and *Quentin Durward*, he [Scott] created the Historical Novel. *Ibid.* §125. 133 In our own day, a critical historical school has arisen, of which Mr. Freeman and Professor Stubbs are the leaders. **1881** *Athenæum* 30 July 147/1 The veteran historical writer Kostomarof. **1886** FREEMAN *Methods Hist. Study* Pref. 4 It is against this state of things..that a historical Professor at Oxford has to fight. *a* **1899** *Mod.* The author of numerous historical works. **1939** O. LANCASTER *Homes Sweet Homes* 18 The dashing cloak-flinging figure of historical fiction. **1951** *Observer* 28 Jan. 7/4 Philip Woodruff's *Colonel of Dragoons*..a very model of what historical fiction ought to be. **1972** *Guardian* 28 Mar. 12/5 The movie..is..a great deal more than a decently-handled historical pageant.

b. Of an artist or work of art: Representing history; depicting or describing historical events.

1658 W. SANDERSON *Graphice* 32 Three sorts of Painting; Prospective (or Landskip,) Historicall, and Life. **1715** J. RICHARDSON *Theory Paint.* 56 Every Historical Picture is a Representation of one single point of Time. **1768** W. GILPIN *Ess. Prints* 92 The best of his historical prints. **1872** RUSKIN *Eagle's N.* §210 The function of historical painting ..is to record of man what has been best in his acts and way of life, and fairest in his form.

4. Celebrated or noted in history; = HISTORIC 2 (which is now the usual word).

1834 MEDWIN *Angler in Wales* I. 25 It has become an historical fact..that 'Childe Harold' and the 'Bard of Memory' met at Pisa. **1845** M. PATTISON *Ess.* (1889) I. 10 It is the old historical lands of Europe that the lover of history longs to explore. **1857** MISS YONGE *Landmarks Hist., Mod.* v. III. (1865) 388 [Fleury] was seventy-three years old, feeble, and cautious, dreading, as he said, 'a historical administration'. **1858** LONGF. *M. Standish* Notes 132 This historical and gallant little ship [the May Flower] returned to England in the month of April, 1621.

5. *Gram.* = HISTORIC *a.* 4.

1867 W. SMITH tr. *Curtius' Gr. Gram.* (ed. 2) §225 Two classes of Tenses: A. Principal, viz.:—1. Present: 2. Perfect: 3. Future. B. Historical, viz.:—1. Imperfect: 2. Pluperfect: 3. Aorist. *Ibid.* §487 By a lively apprehension a past action may be represented as present, hence the use, very frequent in Greek, of the Historical Present, which frequently alternates with past tenses. **1965** *English Studies* Feb. 60 An interesting paper on 'Chaucer's Historical Present, its Meaning and Uses' by L. D. Benson.

6. *Biol.* Relating to the life-history of an organism or race of organisms.

1875 BENNETT & DYER tr. *Sachs' Bot.* III. iv. 695 The internal and external conditions of growth may therefore be distinguished as the historical and the physical; but those properties of a plant which have been obtained historically are generally termed hereditary. *Ibid.* 697 So far as the definition given above of historical properties concerns the inherited specific peculiarities of plants, the term is not metaphorical from the point of view of the Theory of Descent, but must be taken in its literal signification.

7. In *Comb.*, prefixed to an adj. to denote: **a.** 'historical and ...', as ***historical-comparative***, ***-economic***, ***-sociological***; **b.** 'historically, as applied to history', as ***historical-lexicographical***, ***-onomatological***, ***-typological***; also ***historical-minded*** adj., ***-mindedness***.

1933 L. BLOOMFIELD *Language* i. 19 These two streams of study, the historical-comparative and the philosophical-descriptive. **1948** J. TOWSTER *Political Power in U.S.S.R.* iv. 53 The historical-economic conditions of national movements. **1965** *Language* XLI. 138 Historical-lexicographical monographs. **1903** F. VON HÜGEL *Let.* 14 Mar. (1927) 117 Dr. Bigg, Dr. Bryce..are historical-minded also. **1964** *Language* XL. 115 Edgerton's linguistic work..historical-minded but not to the neglect of description. **1895** ACTON *Lect. Study History* 58 That influence for which the depressing names historicism and historical-mindedness have been devised. **1965** *Listener* 3 June 819/1 In one important aspect at least the change can be described as the growth of a new kind of historical-mindedness. **1960** *Amer. Speech* XXXV. 210 Four name maps described as a 'historical-onomatological record'. **1965** *English Studies* Feb. 73 The historical-sociological aspects of art. **1962** D. C. SWANSON in Householder & Saporta *Probl. Lexicogr.* 72 'Recent' refers to the other end of the (historical-typological) pole.

B. *sb.* (*ellipt.*) A historical statement, work, etc.

1666 WALLIS in *Phil. Trans.* I. 286 Granting his [Vossius'] Historicals to be all true. **1894** *Daily News* 28 Nov. 5/4 Historicals show signs of a rise, and politicals signs of a headlong fall. **1967** E. GRIERSON *Crime of one's Own* i. 7 The dreadful proliferation of Whodunnits and Historicals. **1967** H. HARRISON *Technicolor Time Machine* (1968) iv. 36 I've always been interested in doing a historical. **1971** 'A. BLAISDELL' *Practice to Deceive* iv. 55 Donaldson was yawning over a paper-back historical, when he was buzzed by the desk.

historically (hɪ'stɒrɪkəlɪ), *adv.* [f. prec. + -LY[2].] In a historical manner; in the way of history; according to, or in relation to, history.

1550 BALE *Apol.* 21 (R.) Now wyll I shewe hystorycallye the forme and fashyon of that popysh vowinge. **1591** HARINGTON *Orl. Fur.* (1634) 15 *note*, Rather in Fabulous and in Allegoricall sence, then plainelie and historicallie. **1673** O. WALKER *Educ.* (1677) 51 Let him every night at his going to bed recollect historically what he hath done and said that day. **1790** BURKE *Fr. Rev.* 187 The fact is so historically; and it agrees well with the speculation. **1878** GLADSTONE *Prim. Homer* 6 When we use the word Homer, we do not mean a person historically known to us, like Pope or Milton. **1937** A. HUXLEY *Ends & Means* vii. 67 No less 'historically' necessary and right are the brutalities of men in brown shirts. **1958** *Spectator* 27 June 849/1 Our undated and long-dated Government stocks are selling at historically low levels. **1959** *Brno Studies* I. 30 How rewarding the study of the written norm may be even for the historically-minded specialist. **1960** *Economist* 15 Oct. 285/3 The yields on copper shares are at historically high levels.

Comb. **1879** GAIRDNER *Early Chron. Eng.* vii. 319 The most historically-minded of English poets.

hi'storicalness. [f. as prec. + -NESS.] The quality of being historical; historical character.

1664 H. MORE *Myst. Iniq., Apol.* 489 Correspondent to the rest of the Historicalness of the Creation. **1882-3** SCHAFF *Encycl. Relig. Knowl.* II. 1294 Its historicalness was defended by De l'Isle.

histori'caster. [f. L. *historic-us* HISTORIC + -ASTER.] = HISTORIASTER.

1861 F. HALL in *Jrnl. Asiatic Soc. Bengal* 204 *note*, However reluctantly we receive the word of such as Ságaravarman, or his historicaster.

†**histo'rician.** *Obs.* [f. as HISTORIC + -IAN. Cf. *rhetorician*.] A writer of history, HISTORIAN.

1536 BELLENDEN *Cron. Scot.* (1821) I. p. xxii, The Romane historicianis and Ptolome..callit the hail ile, Britane. **1564** HAWARD *Eutropius* III. 25 As Fabius the historician dooth report. **1637** GILLESPIE *Eng. Pop. Cerem.* I. vi. 19 A learned Historician, observeth of the auncient Councels, that there were in them reasonings, colloquies, discussions.

historicism (hɪ'stɒrɪsɪz(ə)m). [f. HISTORIC *a.* + -ISM; tr. G. *historismus*.]

1. The attempt, found esp. among German historians since about 1850, to view all social and cultural phenomena, all categories, truths, and values, as relative and historically determined, and in consequence to be understood only by examining their historical context, in complete detachment from present-day attitudes.

1895 [see *historical-mindedness* s.v. HISTORICAL *a.* 7]. **1920** *Contemp. Rev.* Oct. 536 If we find in him..some acute historical observation, the merit must be attributed to the historicism of the century. **1938** *Mind* XLVII. 114 Historicism..acknowledges truth only as valid in a special epoch. **1946** A. L. ROWSE *Use Hist.* v. 140 Marxism..brings us up against the question of historical relativism, or historicism. **1949** WELLEK & WARREN *Theory of Lit.* iv. 32 We must..enter into the mind and attitudes of past periods and accept their standards, deliberately excluding the intrusions of our own preconceptions. This view, called 'historicism', was elaborated consistently in Germany during the nineteenth century. **1972** *Sci. Amer.* Dec. 89/1, I was surprised, however, to find an eminent scientist embracing historicism (the theory championed by Hegel and Marx holding that history is determined by immutable forces rather than by human agency) as an explanation for the evolution of science.

2. A tendency in philosophy to see historical development as the most fundamental aspect of human existence, and historical thinking as the most important type of thought, because of its interest in the concrete, unique, and individual.

1939 I. BERLIN *Karl Marx* iii. 49 Against the scientific empiricism of the French and English, the Germans put forward the metaphysical historicism of Herder and of Hegel. **1940** *Mind* XLIX. 120 Hegel is right in teaching..an 'absolute historicism'. **1964** C. S. LEWIS *Discarded Image* vii. 174 On this view the *differentia* of Christian historiography ought to be what I call Historicism; the belief that by studying the past we can learn not only historical but meta-historical or transcendental truth.

3. The belief that historical change occurs in accordance with laws, so that the course of history may be predicted but cannot be altered by human will; the resulting attitude to the social sciences, of regarding them as concerned mainly with historical prediction.

[**1901** C. S. PEIRCE *Coll. Papers* (1958) VIII. I. vii. 107 He may aim at hastening some result not otherwise known in advance than as that..to which some process seeming to him good must inevitably lead, such as..whatever the historical evolution of public sentiment may decree (*historicism*).] **1940** K. R. POPPER in *Mind* XLIX. 423 Marx's emphasis on historical method in sociology, a tendency which I may call 'historicism'. **1943** F. A. HAYEK in *Economica* X. 50 (*title*) Scientism and the study of society: the historicism of the scientistic approach. **1957** K. R. POPPER *Poverty of Historicism* 3, I mean by 'historicism' an approach to the social sciences which assumes that *historical prediction* is their principal aim, and..that this aim is attainable by discovering the 'rhythms'..that underlie the evolution of history. **1959** G. D. MITCHELL *Sociol.* i. 5 When we speak of historicism we refer to the attempt to discern a law governing social development.

4. Excessive regard for the institutions and values of the past; *spec.* in *Architecture*, the use of historical styles in design.

1939 *Archit. Rev.* LXXXVI. 55 If she has, in the New York Fair, done little more than to turn away from historicism to a new kind of pastiche, we can hope at least that with the new school of architects now springing up..the real reform will not be long delayed. **1942** *Ibid.* XCI. 52 In between there came a wave of European historicism, all the varieties of Victorian period imitation. **1966** *New Statesman* 25 Feb. 260/2 His [*sc.* I. J. Tengbom's] Högalids Church of 1916-23 and Concert Hall of 1920-26, both in Stockholm, are among the key monuments in Europe of the transition from historicism.

Hence **hi'storicist**, an adherent or proponent of historicism (in various senses); also, one who specializes in the historical branch of a subject; also *attrib.* or as *adj.* So **histori'cistic** *a.*

1937 J. ORR tr. *Iordan's Introd. Romance Ling.* iv. 298 His..field of research, namely, Indo-European philology, made him [*sc.* Meillet]..a historicist and comparatist. **1946** K. BURKE in W. S. Knickerbocker *XX. Cent. Eng.* 287 The modern historicist mode of thought. **1948** *Archit. Rev.* CIV. 226 Meldahl was the most important Danish historicist. **1949** *Mind* LVIII. 411 Guido de Ruggiero..avoided being committed to the amoralism inherent to any historicistic conception. **1954** *Word* X. ii. 123 A 'historicist' will be just as blind to the bundles of intimate connections which the synchronist points out between the different units of a language system. **1955** *Scott. Jrnl. Theol.* VIII. 181 The resurrection..cannot be proved by historicist methods, but it is an act. **1957** K. R. POPPER *Poverty of Historicism* ii. 41 Sociology, to the historicist, is theoretical history. **1959** G. D. MITCHELL *Sociol.* 5 The *historicist* tradition which we have seen in Comte. **1964** C. S. LEWIS *Discarded Image* vii. 175 The best medieval historians, like the best historians in other periods, are seldom Historicists.

historicity (hɪstə'rɪsɪtɪ). [f. L. *historic-us*, HISTORIC + -ITY.] Historic quality or character (opposed to legendary or fictitious: see HISTORIC 1).

1880 J. FENTON *Early Hebrew Life* 9 These stories are of doubtful historicity. **1884** FARRAR in *Contemp. Rev.* Mar. 446 Turning from the question of the genuineness of the gospel to its historicity.

historicize (hɪ'stɒrɪsaɪz), *v.* [f. as prec. + -IZE.]

1. *trans.* To make, or represent as, historic.

1846 GROTE *Greece* I. iv. (1862) I. 77 Here again he historicises various features of the old legend.

2. *intr.* To recount historical events. (*nonce-use*, after *moralize*.)

1887 *St. James's Gaz.* 24 Dec. 7/2 The author..moralizes and historicizes, so to say.

Hence **hi'storicizing** *vbl. sb.* and *ppl. a.*

1846 GROTE *Greece* I. v. (1869) I. 96 Another statement, formed in more historicising times. **1888** RHŶS *Hibbert Lect.* 651 The historicizing of the myth.

historicizer (hɪ'stɒrɪsaɪzə(r)). [f. HISTORICIZE *v.* + -ER[1].] One who historicizes.

1956 *Scott. Jrnl. Theol.* IX. 406 Mark really sees Jesus and the Church as the historicisers of the Jewish eschatological hope.

hi'storico-, combining form of Gr. ἱστορικό-ς HISTORIC, HISTORICAL: = historically..., historical and..., as in ***historico-cabbalistical, -critical, -dogmatic(al), -ethical, -geographical, -philosophical, -physical, -prophetic, -religious*** adjs. Also used to form sbs., as ***historico-novelese, -philology.***

a **1652** J. SMITH *Sel. Disc.* vi. 290 A historico-cabbalistical treatise of R. Abraham Ben Dior. **1738** tr. *Strahlenberg* (*title*) Historico-Geographical Description of the North and Eastern Parts of Europe and Asia. **1746** BERKELEY *Let. to Prior* 3 July Wks. 1871 IV. 309 Desiring that I would become a member of the Historico-physical Society. **1846** TRENCH *Mirac.* (1862) 81 The last assault upon the miracles is that which may be not unfitly termed the historico-critical. **1854** GEO. ELIOT tr. *Feuerbach's Essence Christ.* p. xli, This work is nothing but a faithful, rigid, historico-philosophical analysis of religion. **1864** J. H. NEWMAN *Apol.* 155 This historico-dogmatic work employed me for years. **1881** *Athenæum* 8 Oct. 465/3 Somewhat inclined to indulge in historico-philosophical thoughts, or, to use his own words, in historionomical ideas. **1900** W. A. ELLIS *Life Wagner* I. 225, I was wafted by the image of a great historico-political event. **1905** *Daily Chron.* 20 June 3/3 Pursuing his fascinating historico-biographic method, which gives to criticism the movement and charm of narrative. **1906** *Daily Chron.* 9 Oct. 3/3 'The King's Guerdon' is an historical romance, written in historico-novelese. **1926** *Year's Work in Eng. Stud. 1924* 58 The difficulties and toils of this historico-philology. **1929** S. HOOK in *Essays in Honor J. Dewey* 164 The historico-genetic method tends to minimize origins and beginnings, since it confessedly cannot explain them in terms of spatio-temporal continuity. **1931** *Times Lit. Suppl.* 26 Mar. 242/2 To study the Alsatian question from a historico-psychological standpoint. **1937** J. ORR tr. *Iordan's Introd. Romance Ling.* i. 48 Cases when the historico-comparative method may and must be dispensed with. *Ibid.* iii. 228 The whole applied from a historico-cultural angle. **1938** C. GRAY *Contingencies* (1947) 146 In..his invention of the historico-dramatic tableau he is the father of the Russian operatic composers.

historied ('hɪstərɪd), *a.* [f. HISTORY *sb.* and *v.* + -ED.]

1. Adorned with figures representing historical incidents: see HISTORY *v.* 2. *rare.*

1936 A. W. CLAPHAM *Romanesque Archit.* iii. 64 The historied capital, or capital carved with figure-subjects, appears first in minor features.

2. Having a history (esp. of a specified kind); recorded or celebrated in history, storied. Now *literary* and chiefly *poet.*

1818 TODD, *Historied*, recorded in history; containing history. See *Storied*. **1849** M. ARNOLD *Resignation*, He sees, in some great-historied land, A ruler of the people stand. *a* **1861** T. WINTHROP *Cecil D.* xvii. (Cent.), Richly historied Italy. **1889** W. B. YEATS *Wanderings of Oisin* 122 You move in another dominion And hang o'er the historied stone. **1896** BELLOC *Verses & Sonnets* 63 November is some historied Emperor, Conquered in age. **1934** R. GRAVES *Claudius the God* 333 It will be a matter for laughter to you..if your minds were ever dazzled by the historied glories of a remote past. **1943** S. SPENDER *Spiritual Exercises* 6 Within my shut skull flows a historied stream Of myths, fears, crimes.

†**hi'storier.** *Obs.* Also 6 -ar. [ad. OF. *historieur* (15th c. in Godef.), f. *historier* HISTORY *v.*] A historian.

c **1449** PECOCK *Repr.* III. xiii. 366 Sithen historiers dwelling in thilke same cuntre..kouthen knowe better the treuthe of the deede than othere men. **1490** CAXTON *Eneydos* vi. 24 Wrytynges and dyctes of olde and auncyente cronycles or historyers. **1523** SKELTON *Garl. Laurel* 351 Aulus Gellius, that noble historiar. **1581** MARBECK *Bk. of Notes* 924 Which al writers, Poets, historiers, cosmographers..do confesse.

‖**historiette** (hɪstɔərɪ'ɛt). Also 8 -etto. [F., f. *histoire* HISTORY + *-ette*, dim. suffix (after L. *historia*). Cf. It. *istorietta*.] A short history or story; an anecdote.

a **1704** T. BROWN *Wks.* (1760) II. 268 (D.) She thus continued her tragical historietto. **1786** MAD. D'ARBLAY *Let. to T. Twining* 10 July, My head is full of the charming little historiette in your father's letter. **1839** *New Monthly Mag.* LVII. 351, I..wrote..what I conceived was a very original and amusing historiette.

historify (hɪ'stɒrɪfaɪ), *v.* [f. L. *historia* HISTORY + -FY.]

1. *trans.* To relate the history of; to record or celebrate in history.

c **1586** C'TESS PEMBROKE *Ps.* LXXVI. ii, Thy conquest meete to be historified. **1646** SIR T. BROWNE *Pseud. Ep.* VI. vi. 295 The third time..wherein matters have been more truly historified, and may therefore be beleeved. **1823** LAMB *Elia* Ser. II. *Tombs in Abbey*, That Church which you have so worthily historified. **1884** A. A. PUTNAM *10 Years Police Judge* v. 28 In one of the years of the ten which this volume historifies.

2. *absol.* To write history; to narrate, relate.

1614 EARL STIRLING *Domes-day* II. (R.), I must historifie, and not divine. **1635** HEYWOOD *Hierarch.* II. 75 As th' author doth of him historifie. **1802** SOUTHEY *Lett.* (1856) I. 201, I have been historifying successfully.

†**3.** *trans.* To decorate with figures: cf. HISTORIATED. *Obs.*

1633 WOTTON in *Reliq. Wotton.* (1672) 465 Some fine historified Table Cloth for a Banquet.

historio-, combining form occurring in Greek (cf. Gr. ἱστοριογραφία HISTORIOGRAPHY) and now used to an increasing extent in English, as ***historio-cultural, -patriotic, -pœic*** adjs.

1958 W. STARK *Sociology of Knowledge* iv. 169 The historio-cultural sciences. **1967** *Listener* 16 Feb. 237/2 The story was tedious and repetitive as modern Russian historio-patriotic writing sometimes can be. **1953** *Antiquity* XXVII. 97 The abstract, age-long yearning of the Jewish nation in the Diaspora..found its historiopoeic expression in written history and poetry.

†**histori'ognomer.** *Obs. rare.* [f. Gr. ἱστορία HISTORY, app. after *physiognomer*.] One learned in history.

1593 R. HARVEY *Philad.* 13 In the best historicall Methode that I could make out of the best Historiognomers.

†**hi'storiograph.** *Obs.* [a. F. *historiographe* (14th c. in Littré), ad. late L. *historiographus*, a. Gr. ἱστοριογράφος, f. ἱστορία HISTORY + -γράφος writing, writer.] = next.

1474 CAXTON *Chesse* 23 Poule the historiagraph of the lombardes. **1535** JOYE *Apol. Tindale* 6 As wryteth that aunciaunt historiograph Josephus. **1664** EVELYN tr. *Freart's Archit.* II. i. 88 It was Architecture herself which was here the Historiograph..of this new kind of History. *a* **1734** NORTH *Exam.* II. v. §132 (1740) 397 One might expect from an Historiograph a plain, honest, and full Narration of the Fact.

Hence **histori'ographal** *a.*, of the nature of a historiograph, or historian; historical.

1841 G. S. FABER *Provinc. Lett.* (1844) I. 229 We may cite Mr. Palmer himself as our historiographal witness.

historiographer (hɪstɔərɪ'ɒgrəfə(r)). (Also 6 -graphier.) [f. prec. or late L. *historiograph-us* + -ER. Cf. OF. *historiographeur*.]

1. A writer or compiler of a history; a chronicler or historian.

1494 FABYAN *Chron.* VI. cxciv. 199 Henricus, the histo[rio]grapher, made of hym [the king] thyse verses. *c* **1540** tr. *Pol. Verg. Eng. Hist.* (Camden) I. 103 Thus..was this wall made..if we beleeve Gildas, a Brittyshe historiographer. **1542** UDALL *Erasm. Apoph.* 160 b, Valerius Maximus, and the other Historiographiers. **1669** GALE *Crt. Gentiles* I. Indrod. 7 Pieces of Mythologie..so commun among the ancient Poets, and Historiographers. **1728** MORGAN *Algiers* II. iv. 290 Why should these circumstances be mentioned by a Historiographer of such gravity? *a* **1834** LAMB *Ode to Treadmill* (L.), Inspire my spirit, spirit of Defoe..Historiographer of deathless Crusoe.

2. *spec.* An official historian appointed in connexion with a court, or some public institution.

1555 EDEN *Decades* 144 Iohannes Aiora is broker to..the kynges historiographer. **1691** WOOD *Ath. Oxon.* II. 265 James Howell..was made the Kings Historiographer, being the first in England that bore that title. **1796** MORSE *Amer. Geog.* II. 677 Rev. Dr. William Robertson..historiographer to his majesty for Scotland. **1862** *Fraser's Mag.* July 122-3 The reign of William and Mary, when the office of 'Historiographer' Royal was conferred on.. Thomas Rymer.

transf. **1865** M. ARNOLD *Ess. Crit.* v. (1875) 206 Scott became the historiographer royal of feudalism. **1871** L. STEPHEN *Playgr. Europe* viii. (1894) 173, I felt myself at liberty to accompany my friends in the humble character of historiographer.

3. One who describes or gives a systematic account of some natural object or objects (cf. HISTORY *sb.* 5); a writer of natural history.

1579-80 NORTH *Plutarch* (1676) 1 The Historiographers which do set forth the Description of the Earth in Figure. **1600** J. PORY tr. *Leo's Africa* II. 339 The Historiographers affirme, that this kinde of wilde horses ranging up and downe the Arabian deserts [etc.]. **1635** SWAN *Spec. M.* iv. §2 (1643) 67 Their tops are above the clouds..(as

Historiographers do report it). **1816** Kirby & Sp. *Entomol.* (1843) II. 41 The great historiographer of ants is M.P. Huber.

Hence **histori'ographership**, the office of historiographer.

1814 W. Taylor in Robberds *Mem.* II. 419, I am heartily glad you [Southey] got the laureateship, and wish you had also the historiographership. **1881** Saintsbury *Dryden* iii. 67 The late holder of the historiographership.

historiographic (hɪˌstɔərɪəʊ'græfɪk), *a.* [f. HISTORIOGRAPHY + -IC, after Gr. *ἱστοριογραφικός*.] Pertaining to the writing of history, or to the delineation of historic scenes.

1807 W. Taylor in *Ann. Rev.* V. 232 Worthy of historiographic sanction. **1883** H. M. Kennedy tr. *Ten Brink's E. Eng. Lit.* 112 The historiographic ascendency of this city [Winchester] was now past.

historio'graphical, *a.* [See -AL[1].] = prec.

1630 J. Taylor (Water P.) *Taylor's Trav.* Wks. III. 76 Dedicated—To the Cosmographicall, Geographicall.. Historiographicall, Calligraphicall Relater and Writer.. Sir Thomas Coriat. **1716** M. Davies *Athen. Brit.* II. 178 The t'other gentile English couple of Historiographical Scholars [Fuller and Strype]. **1891** Driver *Introd. Lit. O.T.* (1892) 18 *note*, Expressions such as might be used by any writer of the best historiographical style.

Hence **historio'graphically** *adv.*

1878 Besant & Rice *Celia's Arb.* III. i. 8 The historiographically gifted Ferdinand had found fresh and worthy subjects for his pen.

historiography (hɪstɔərɪ'ɒgrəfɪ). [ad. Gr. *ἱστοριογραφία*, f. *ἱστορία* HISTORY + *-γραφία* writing.] The writing of history; written history.

1569 J. Sanford tr. *Agrippa's Van. Artes* 14 b, Many, that impudently and shamefully auaunt themselves to profess Historiographie. **1597** Breton *Wit's Trenchmour* Wks. (1879) 13 (D.) Haue you not beene a little red in historiographie. **1797** *Monthly Mag.* III. 269 An important work.. beginning with the historiography of the first founders of the school of Florence. **1858** J. H. Newman *Hist. Sk.* (1873) III. IV. xi. 419 Monastic historiography.. proceeded from the motive of religious duty.

historiology (hɪstɔərɪ'ɒlədʒɪ). [f. as prec. + -LOGY.] The knowledge or study of history.

1616 Bullokar, *Historiology*, the knowledge and telling of old Histories. **1682** Bunyan *Holy War* Introd. lines, 'Tis strange to me that they.. that do excel Their equals in historiology Speak not of Mansoul's wars, but let them lie Dead like old Fables. **1813** W. Taylor in *Monthly Rev.* LXX. 285 Erudition has been divided by a German professor into glossology, bibliology, and historiology.

Hence **historio'logical** *a.*, pertaining to historiology.

1716 M. Davies *Athen. Brit.* II. 175 Where that eminent Prelate Umpires all Historiological Emulosities with amicable equity.

histori'onomer. *nonce-wd.* [f. Gr. *ἱστορία* HISTORY, after *astronomer*.] One versed in the principles which regulate the course of history. So **historio'nomical** *a.*

1854 Lowell *Jrnl. in Italy* Prose Wks. 1890 I. 191 By and by, perhaps,.. historionomers will have measured accurately the sidereal years of races. **1881** [see HISTORICO-].

†**hi'storious**, *a. Obs. rare.* [a. OF. *historieux*, ad. L. type **historiōsus*, f. *historia* HISTORY: see -OUS.] = HISTORICAL.

1523 Skelton *Garl. Laurel* 345 There Titus Lyvius hymselfe doth auaunce, With decades historious, whiche that he mengeth. *a* **1529** —— *P. Sparowe* 749 A thousand new and old Of these historious tales.

historize ('hɪstəraɪz), *v.* Now *rare* or *Obs.* [f. HISTOR-Y *sb.* + -IZE: cf. *botanize*, etc.]

1. *trans.* To tell the history of; to narrate or relate as history. ? *Obs.*

1599 Sandys *Europæ Spec.* (1632) 8 Euen those Legends of Saints and tales at which children.. smile, are there solemnly historized in their Cathedrall Pulpits. *c* **1645** Howell *Lett.* II. lxiii. (1655) 89 Sir W. Rawleigh.. whose Fame shall contend in longævity.. with that great World which he Historiseth so gallantly. **1657-83** Evelyn *Hist. Relig.* (1850) II. 220 *note*.

†**2.** To represent, display. *Obs. rare.*

1645 Evelyn *Dairy* 6 May, A long and spacious walk, full of fountaines, under which is historized the whole Ovidian Metamorphosis in rarely sculptur'd *mezzo relievo*.

3. *intr.* or *absol.* To compose history or narrative, to act the historian.

1632 [see HISTORIZING below]. **1640** Howell *Dodona's Gr.* Introd. Verses, While Druyd-like.. Under their blooming shade I historize. **1838** B. Corney *Controversy* 22 You have .. attempted to historize, to ratiocinate, to sentimentalize.

Hence '**historizing** *vbl. sb.* and *ppl. a.*

1632 J. Hayward tr. *Biondi's Eromena* To Rdr. A iv, I mean an historicall way of Poetizing, or Poeticall manner of historizing, or displaying of the fained.. adventures and actions of persons reall. **1647** Torshell *Design to Harmonize Bible* in *Phenix* (1721) I. 106 An Harmonious historizing of the Psalms. **1652** Gaule *Magastrom.* 103 In use among the historizing or exemplarizing atsrologers.

history ('hɪstərɪ), *sb.* Also 4 **histoire**, 5 **hystorye**, 5-6 **historye**, 6-7 **historie**. [ad. L. *historia* narrative of past events, account, tale, story, a. Gr. *ἱστορία* a learning or knowing by inquiry, an account of one's inquiries, narrative, history, f. *ἵστωρ*, *ἱστορ-* knowing, learned, wise man, judge :—**ϝίδτωρ*, f. *ϝιδ-*, *ἰδ-* to know. (The form *histoire* was from F.) Cf. STORY, an aphetic form of *history*.]

†**1.** A relation of incidents (in early use, either true or imaginary; later only of those professedly true); a narrative, tale, story. *Obs.* (exc. as applied to a story or tale so long and full of detail, as to resemble a history in sense 2.)

1390 Gower *Conf.* III. 48, I finde in a boke compiled To this matere an olde histoire, The which comth now to my memoire. **1484** Caxton *Fables of Æsop* VI. xiii, The carpenter told thystory to his felawes. **1551** T. Wilson *Logike* (1580) 77 Wee read a notable historie of a yong childe in Rome, called Papirius. **1563** W. Fulke *Meteors* (1640) 25 b, Which may be verified by an History that Plutarchus in the life of.. Flaminius reporteth. **1632** Lithgow *Trav.* VI. 248 Heere Dives the rich Glutton dwelt.. this I suspend .. for all hold it to bee a Parable, and not a History. **1700** T. Brown tr. *Fresny's Amusem. Ser. & Com.* 119 A Mountebank on the Stage.. gave them a History of his Cures. **1834** Medwin *Angler in Wales* II. 183 Byron had some excellent pairs of pistols, about most of which there were histories.

2. *spec.* A written narrative constituting a continuous methodical record, in order of time, of important or public events, esp. those connected with a particular country, people, individual, etc.

Chronicles, *annals*, are simpler or more rudimentary forms of history, in which the events of each year, or other limited period, are recorded before passing on to those of the next year or period, the year or period being the primary division; whereas in a *history*, strictly so called, each movement, action, or chain of events is dealt with as a whole, and pursued to its natural termination, or to a convenient halting-point, without regard to these divisions of time.

drum-and-trumpet history, a contemptuous term for a history that gives undue prominence to battles and wars.

1485 Caxton *Paris & V.* (1868) 206 The brave deeds which our ancestors accomplished. I have undertaken to draw the history for you. **1557** *More's Wks.* (*title*) The history of King Richard the thirde. **1563** Winȝet *Wks.* (1890) II. 49 Quhow worschipful wes he.. the historiis declaris, quhilkis schawis that the mother of Alexander the Empriour callit him in hir cumpanie. **1577** Holinshed (*title*) The Historie of Scotland; conteining the Beginning, Increase, Proceedings, Continuance, Acts, and Gouerment of the Scottish Nation, from the original thereof to the yeere 1571. **1685** Baxter *Paraphr. N.T.*, *Matt.* i. 1, I begin this History of Christ, with the Genealogy or Catalogue of his Ancestors. **1688** Shadwell *Sqr. Alsatia* II. Wks. 1720 IV. 44 How can there be a true History, when we see no Man living is able to write truly the History of the last Week? **1753** W. Smith *Thucyd.* I. (R.), Thucydides, an Athenian, hath compiled the history of the war between the Peloponnesians and the Athenians. **1803** *Med. Jrnl.* X. 517 Some important dates and circumstances towards the history of the Influenza. **1822** Miss R. Mangnall *Hist. & Misc. Quest.* Pref. 5 Opportunities of perusing the best English, Grecian, and Roman histories. **1823** Mrs. Markham [Eliz. Penrose] *Hist. Eng.* Advt. 3 In putting a History of England into the hands of their children. **1857** Buckle *Civiliz.* I. xiii. 711 Mezeray.. was also the first who saw that a history, to be of real value, must be a history, not only of kings, but of nations. *a* **1872** Maurice *Friendship Bks.* vi. (1874) 177 They profess to be Histories—that is, records of the actual growth and unfolding of a particular nation. **1874** Stubbs (*title*) The Constitutional History of England in its Origin and Development. **1874** Green *Short Hist.* Pref. 5 Whatever the worth of the present work may be, I have striven throughout that it should never sink into a 'drum and trumpet history'. **1928** *Daily Tel.* 14 Aug. 5/3 We have had enough of drum-and-trumpet history. **1967** *Listener* 16 Mar. 349/2 This is only one more step away from the older type of 'drum-and-trumpet' history.

3. (Without *a* or *pl.*) That branch of knowledge which deals with past events, as recorded in writings or otherwise ascertained; the formal record of the past, esp. of human affairs or actions; the study of the formation and growth of communities and nations.

In this sense often divided, for practical convenience, into *Ancient* and *Modern*, or *Ancient*, *Mediæval*, and *Modern History*. These have no very definite chronological limits; but Ancient History is usually reckoned as ending with the fall of the Western Roman Empire in A.D. 476. Mediæval, when separated from Modern History, is usually brought down to the period of the Oceanic discoveries in the 15th c. 'Ancient History' is also humorously used in the sense of 'matters which are out of date, or which no longer form part of practical politics', and *colloq.* of comparatively recent events which are regarded as nevertheless far back in a person's experience.

The ***Muse of History***, Clio, one of the Nine Muses, represented as the patroness of History; also often put for a personification of History.

1842 Caxton *Higden's Polychronicon* Proem, Some sothly techyth to lye, but historye representynge the thynges lyke unto the wordes embraceth al utylyte and prouffite. **1611** Shaks. *Cymb.* I. vi. 70 To think that man who knowes By History, Report, or his owne proofe What woman is.. will's free houres languish: For assured bondage? **1625** N. Carpenter *Geog. Del.* II. vii. (1635) 126 Where History is vncertaine, reasonable coniecture must challenge precedency. **1651** Hobbes *Leviath.* I. ix. 40 The Register of Knowledge of Fact is called History. **1735** Bolingbroke *Lett. Study Hist.* ii. (1752) 14, I have read somewhere.. that history is philosophy teaching by examples. **1798** Jane Austen *Northang. Abb.* (1870) I. xiv. 85, I can read poetry and plays.. But history, real solemn history, I cannot be interested in. **1816** Keatinge *Trav.* (1817) I. 241 We hardly find in classical history any parallel. **1828** Macaulay *Ess.*, *Hallam* ¶ 1 History, at least in its state of ideal perfection, is a compound of poetry and philosophy. **1837** Carlyle *Fr. Rev.* I. VII. v, If fame were not an accident, and History a distillation of Rumour. **1838** Macaulay *Ess.*, *Temple* (1865) II. 8/2 'There is a vile phrase of which bad historians are exceedingly fond, 'the dignity of history'. **1855** Bain *Senses & Int.* III. i. §76 The successions of events and transactions in human life, remembered and related, make History. **1865** M. Arnold *Ess. Crit.* ii. 75 The huge Mississippi of falsehood called history. **1876** Stopf. Brooke *Eng. Lit.* vii. 131 History.. was raised into the rank of literature in the latter half of the eighteenth century by three men [Hume, Robertson, Gibbon]. **1886** Freeman *Meth. Hist. Study* iii. 117, I should be most inclined.. to say that history is the science of man in his character as a political being.

b. **1595** Auncient Histories [see ANCIENT 3 b]. **1735** Bolingbroke *Lett. Study Hist.* ii. (1752) 36 Modern history shews the causes, when experience presents the effects alone: and ancient history enables us to guess at the effects, when experience presents the causes alone. **1773** Mrs. Chapone *Improv. Mind* x. (1827) 99, I only mean to warn you against mixing ancient history with modern. **1818** Hallam *Mid. Ages* (1878) I. Pref. 4 The subversion of the western empire is manifestly the natural termination of ancient history. **1853** Miss Yonge *Landmarks Hist. Mid. Ages* i. 1. (1868) 1 It is in effect impossible to draw any decided line between the periods of Ancient and Mediæval history. We have chosen to commence the latter from the Battle of Tours [A.D. 732]. **1884** Freeman *Meth. Hist. Study* (1886) 20, I need not tell you.. that I acknowledge no such distinction as that which is implied in the words 'ancient' and 'modern' history,.. I have never been able to find out by my own wit when ' ancient' history ends and when 'modern' history begins. *Ibid.* 12 Each time that I was appointed Examiner, I had to learn my trade afresh; my experience from the former time had already become a matter of ancient history. **1875** *Contemp. Rev.* XXVI. 870 The mutiny is now becoming an event of ancient history. **1908** *Busy Man's Mag.* Nov. 37/1 'Ancient history, governor,' said Woolford. 'We knew all that before.' **1910** Belloc *Pongo* v. 73 He reminded Dolly of the days when Consols were at 92... All that was ancient history. **1939** C. Day Lewis *Child of Misfortune* III. vi. 350 Already the crisis through which they had passed was beginning to seem ancient history. **1946** J. B. Priestley *Bright Day* x. 320 I'm going to risk telling you something... It's all ancient history, but.. we might as well get it straight. **1961** P. Spencer *Full Term* i. 15 You won't get anywhere by fretting about it... It's ancient history by now, anyway. People do odd things in drink.

c. **1768** Beattie *Minstr.* II. xxxiii, The Muse of History unrolls her page. **1848** Lowell *Fable for Critics* 916 Already for each I see History preparing the statue and niche. **1892** Edith Thompson *York & Lanc.* 137 History can hardly be said to know aught of the fate of his two young nephews.

4. *transf.* †**a.** A series of events (of which the story is or may be told). *Obs.*

1585 T. Washington tr. *Nicholay* (*title*) Nauigations, Peregrinations, and Voyages made into Turkie.. with diuers faire and memorable histories happened in our times. **1608** Topsell *Serpents* (1658) 601 As may appear by this succeeding discourse, of a true history done in England, in the house of a worshipful Gentleman. **1687** A. Lovell tr. *Thevenot's Trav.* I. 186 Many Figures in Bass Relief, representing several sacred Histories.

b. The whole train of events connected with a particular country, society, person, thing, etc., and forming the subject of his or its history (in sense 2); course of existence or life, career. Also in pregnant sense, An eventful career; a course of existence worthy of record. (See also LIFE-HISTORY.)

[**1608** Shaks. *Per.* V. i. 119 If I should tell my history, it would seem Like lies disdain'd in the reporting.] **1654** Whitlock *Zootomia* 200 For every one.. to turn over a new leafe in his own History, and amend his own Erratas. **1715** J. Richardson *Theory Paint.* 98 If there be any thing particular in the History of the Person which is proper to be Express'd. **1852** Lynch *Brief Medit.* in *Lett. to Scattered* etc. 255 Every man has a moral history. **1860** Geo. Eliot *Mill on Fl.* VI. iii, The happiest women, like the happiest nations, have no history. **1872** Yeats *Growth Comm.* 93 Travelling by sea was a task for which their previous history had not prepared them. **1875** Jowett *Plato* (ed. 2) IV. 272 Our idea of space, like our other ideas, has a history. **1895** 'Péronne' *Veil of Liberty* x. 209, I know what it is to love and to be parted. I, too, have a history.

c. (Without *a* or *pl.*) The aggregate of past events in general; the course of events or human affairs. ***to make history***: to influence or guide the course of history; also, to do something spectacular or worthy of remembrance (see *history-maker*, *-making*, sense 9).

1654 Whitlock *Zootomia* 306 Take a turn in the Temple of History, and there meet with instructive Lectures of Providence. **1845** Mill *Ess.* II. 221 It was Lessing by whom the course of history was styled 'the education of the human race'. **1862** *Chambers's Jrnl.* 1 Mar. 139/1 People engaged in public transactions are sometimes said to be making history, because they occasionally perform actions to which history condescends to impart perpetuity. **1871** Smiles *Charac.* i. 22 History.. is but continuous humanity influenced by men of character. **1874** Motley *Barneveld* I. vii. 311 The great tragi-comedy which we call human history. **1889** *Puck* XXV. 133/2 If the hero who thinks he 'makes history' could only wake from his sleep after three hundred years and read the works of half-a-dozen.. historians, he wouldn't know his own face on their pages. **1890** Wilde in *19th Century* July 137 Anybody can make history. Only a great man can write it. **1907** *Edin. Rev.* Jan. 4 The average man is of the Centre; and history in the long run is made by the average man. **1915** 'I. Hay' *First Hundred Thousand* xx. 311 We shall have a chance of making history over this, old man. **1959** N. Mailer *Advts. for Myself* (1961) 208, I had been ready to.. publish.. at my own expense, and try to make a kind of publishing history.

5. A systematic account (without reference to time) of a set of natural phenomena, as those connected with a country, some division of nature or group of natural objects, a species of animals or plants, etc. Now *rare*, exc. in NATURAL HISTORY.

[In this sense following the similar use of ἱστορία by Aristotle and other Greek writers, and of *historia* by Pliny.] **1567** J. MAPLET (*title*) A Greene Forest, or a naturall Historie, wherein may bee seene the most sufferaigne Vertues in all the whole kinde of Stones and Mettals; of Brute Beastes, Fowles, Fishes [etc.]. **1600** J. PORY tr. *Leo* (*title*) A Geographical Historie of Africa. **1608** TOPSELL (*title*) The History of Serpents. **1615** CROOKE *Body of Man* 270 Aristotle in his Bookes of the History and Generation of creatures, doth [etc.]. **1676** RAY *Corr.* (1848) 122 In the 'History of the Fero Islands' I find no more species of birds than what I have already inserted. **1774** GOLDSM. (*title*) History of the Earth and Animated Nature. **1790** BEILBY (*title*) General History of British Quadrupeds. **1797** —— (*title*) History of British Birds. **1834** MEDWIN *Angler in Wales* I. 30 The may-fly.. I am curious to know something of the history of this little creature.

6. †**a.** A story represented dramatically, a drama. *Obs.* **b.** *spec.* A drama representing historical events, a historical play.

1596 SHAKS. *Tam. Shr.* Induct. ii. 144 Your Honors Players.. Are come to play a pleasant Comedie.. It is a kinde of history. **1598** —— (*title*) The History of Henrie the Fovrth. **1600** —— *A. Y. L.* II. vii. 164 Last Scene of all, That ends this strange euentfull historie. **1602** —— *Ham.* II. ii. 416 The best Actors in the world, either for Tragedie, Comedie, Historie, Pastorall. **1623** (*title*) Mr. William Shakespeares Comedies, Histories, and Tragedies. **1864** KIRK *Chas. Bold* I. II. iii. 525 She was entertained with 'Histories'—a kind of dramatic representation. **1877** DOWDEN *Primer Shaks.* vi. §15. 97 Both parts of *Henry IV* consist of a comedy and a history fused together.

7. A pictorial representation of an event or series of incidents; in 18th c. a historical picture.

1514 BARCLAY *Cyt. & Uplondyshm.* (Percy Soc.) p. lxx, All the walles within of fynest golde, With olde historyes & pictures manifolde. **1585** T. WASHINGTON tr. *Nicholay's Voy.* II. xvi. 50 b, A great colomne, in ye which are carved by histories the things memorable, whiche have been done in this Hippodrome. **1670–98** LASSELS *Voy. Italy* I. 76 In the Sacristy we were shown.. the curious back of an altar of Ivory cut into Histories after a rare manner. **1715** J. RICHARDSON *Theory Paint.* 138 When a Painter intends to make a History. **1776** SIR J. REYNOLDS *Disc.* vii. (1876) 422 A landscape of Claude Lorraine may be preferred to a history by Luca Giordano. **1958** *Listener* 19 June 1024/3 It was a race that.. converted the classical 'history' into a kind of privileged leg show. **1963** *Ibid.* 28 Feb. 384/3 He [*sc.* Degas] remains.. even when he is no longer a painter of 'histories', a profoundly reactionary figure.

¶ **8.** *Eccl.* = L. *historia*, liturgically applied (*a*) to a series of lessons from Scripture, named from the first words of the Respond to the first lesson; (*b*) to the general order of a particular Office.

Misunderstood and erroneously explained in Rock *Ch. of Fathers* IV. xii. 124: see Proctor & Wordsworth *Sarum Breviary*, Index to Fasc. I, II.

9. *attrib.* and *Comb.*, as ***history-master***, ***-mill***, ***-monger***, ***paper***, ***-play***, ***-professor***, ***-wise***, ***writer***; †**history faith**, 'historical' faith (see HISTORICAL 2); **history-maker**, (*a*) a writer of a history; (*b*) one who 'makes history', i.e. performs important actions which shape the course of history; so **history-making** *a.* and *vbl. sb.*; **history-painter**, one who paints 'histories' (sense 7); so **history-painting**, **history-piece**.

1531 TINDALE *Expos. & Notes* (1849) 154 Let this therefore be an undoubted article of thy faith: not of a *history faith, as thou believest a gest of Alexander. **1895** LD. WOLSELEY *Decl. & F. Napoleon* i. 3 The sayings, doings, aspirations, even the villanies of this great *history-maker. **1898** 'MARK TWAIN' in *Harper's Mag.* Mar. 538/2 On Thanksgiving Day the sitting was a *history-making one. **1949** WYNDHAM LEWIS *Let.* Apr. 491 Excuse me for breaking in upon your as it were private, and partisan, history-making. **1963** AUDEN *Dyer's Hand* 278 Man is a history-making creature. **1891** W. J. GREENSTREET tr. *Guyau's Educ. & Heredity* iii. 128 The *history-master might have taken us to the National Library. **1889** 'MARK TWAIN' *Connecticut Yankee* iv. 39 Sir Kay.. began to fire up on his *history-mill, with me for fuel. **1963** *Times Lit. Suppl.* 11 Jan. 29/1 Grist to some history-mill. **1845** W. CORY *Lett. & Jrnls.* (1897) 37, I could get a sure living as a journeyman *history-monger. **1658** W. SANDERSON *Graphice* 18 Excellent *History Painters. **1711** SHAFTESB. *Charac.* (1737) III. 387 In a real history-painter, the same knowledg, the same study, and views, are requir'd, as in a real poet. **1686** AGLIONBY *Painting Illustr.* Explan. Terms, '*History-Painting is an Assembling of many Figures in one Piece, to Represent any Action of Life, whether True or Fabulous, accompanied with all its Ornaments of Land-skip and Perspective. **1713** BERKELEY *Guardian* No. 49 ¶8 As I can not go to the price of history painting, I have purchased at easy rates several beautifully designed pieces of landskip and perspective. **1857** J. A. SYMONDS *Let.* 8 Feb. (1967) I. 90, I was so amused yesterday with hearing the answers of some of the Sixth Form to our *History Paper. **1706** *Art of Painting* (1744) 345 He painted several *history-pieces. **1773** JOHNSON in Boswell 30 Apr., Robertson paints minds as Sir Joshua paints faces in a history-piece. **1957** N. FRYE *Anat. Criticism* iv. 283 The Elizabethan secular *auto* eventually became the *history-play. **1701** WALLIS in *Collect.* (O.H.S.) I. 329 An *history-professor. **1571** GOLDING *Calvin on Ps.* ix. 4 He sheweth in *historywise, that his enemies were overthrowen. **1587** —— *De Mornay* viii. 97 Iustine the *Historywriter witnesseth, that the Kings ..afore Ninus..were but particular Judges of Controuersies. **1770** ARMSTRONG *Misc.* II. 179 (Jod.) Superior in candour and impartiality to many at least of our modern history-writers.

†**history**, *v.* *Obs.* [ad. F. *historier* (14th c. in Hatz.-Darm.), ad. med.L. *historiāre* (in both senses), f. *historia* HISTORY.]

1. *trans.* To relate in a history or narrative; to record, narrate, recount.

1475 *Bk. Noblesse* (1860) 13 As in the .39. chapitre of the Actis of the said King Philip more plainly is historied. **1502** *Ord. Crysten Men* Epil. (W. de W. 1526) 426 Newely hystoryed and translated out of Frensshe into Englysshe. **1597** SHAKS. *2 Hen. IV*, IV. i. 203 And keepe no Tell-tale to his Memorie, That may repeat, and Historie his losse, To new remembrance.

2. To inscribe or adorn with 'histories' or historical scenes.

1585 T. WASHINGTON tr. *Nicholay's Voy.* II. xvi. 50 b, A great Colomne of Marble historied after the maner of those of Antonin and Adrian.. at Rome. **1670–98** LASSELS *Voy. Italy* I. 127 These doors are all of brass historied into figures containing the remarkable histories of both the Testaments. *Ibid.* 148 Its three brazen doors are historied with a fine basso relievo.

histotomy, -trophic, -zyme: see HISTO-.

‖**histrio** (ˈhɪstrɪəʊ). [a. L. *histrio, histriōn-em* stage-player. (In Holland only as L.)] = next.

[**1600** HOLLAND *Livy* 250 (R.) Heerevpon our owne countrie actors and artificiall professours of this feate were called *Histriones*, of *Hister*, a Tuscane word, which signifieth a player or dauncer.] **1658** PHILLIPS, *Histrio*, a Player of Farces, a Buffoon. **1850** CARLYLE *Latter-d. Pamph.* iv. 6 'Begone, ye imbecile hypocrites, histrios not heroes!' **1887** *Pall Mall G.* 6 July 1/2 A poor histrio, a stagey pedant.

histrion (ˈhɪstrɪən). Also 6 *erron.* **-an, -en.** [a. F. *histrion* (1570 in Hatz.-Darm.), ad. L. *histriōn-em*: see prec.] A stage-player, actor. (Now usually contemptuous.)

c **1566** J. ALDAY tr. *Boaystuau's Theat. World* S iv, Histrians that we have seene in our time flie on a rope in ye ayre. **1589** PUTTENHAM *Eng. Poesie* I. xiv. (Arb.) 48 Roscius ..the best Histrien or buffon that was in his dayes to be found. **1603** FLORIO *Montaigne* II. xxxvii. (1632) 426 Let her leave this care to Mimikes, to Histrions, and to Rhetoricke Masters. **1862** MERIVALE *Rom. Emp.* (1865) VI. lii. 295 It was found necessary to expel the histrions, or pantomimic dancers. **1889** *Evening News* 6 Nov. 2/6 When it is the fashion for histrions to air themselves in print.

†**histri'onian**, *a.* *Obs. rare.* [-IAN.] = next.

1609 R. BARNERD *Faithf. Sheph.* 85 This is a forewearing of the spirits, and too Histrionian like.

histrionic (hɪstrɪˈɒnɪk), *a.* and *sb.* [ad. late L. *histriōnic-us*, f. *histriōn-em*; cf. F. *histrionique* (1769 in Littré).]

A. *adj.* **1.** Of or belonging to stage-players, or to play-acting; theatrical; dramatic.

1759 DILWORTH *Pope* 91 The favourite passion of the histrionic tribe. **1774** WARTON *Hist. Eng. Poetry* lii. III. 285 In consequence of his love and his knowledge of the histrionick art, he taught the choristers over which he presided to act plays. **1867** *Cornh. Mag.* Jan. 31 He can also boast decent histrionic talents.

2. Theatrical in character or style, 'stagey'; also *fig.* 'acting a part', hypocritical, deceitful.

1648 J. BEAUMONT *Psyche* xx. (R.), The crisp'd, perfum'd, belac'd, befooled Wights, Jetting in histrionick pride I saw. **1679** HOBBES *Behemoth* (1840) 363 The Presbyterian preachers.. by a long practised histrionic faculty, preached up the rebellion powerfully. **1784** COWPER *Task* II. 563 Foppish airs And histrionic mumm'ry, that let down The pulpit to the level of the stage. **1889** *Globe* 7 Mar., Yesterday's histrionic proceedings.

3. *Path.* ***histrionic paralysis*** (see quot.). ***histrionic spasm***, spasm of the facial muscles.

1886 *Syd. Soc. Lex.*, *Histrionic spasm.* **1893** *Ibid.*, *Paralysis, histrionic*, Bell's facial palsy, so named because the power of facial expression is lost.

B. *sb.* **1.** A stage-player, actor. Also *fig.*

1859 SALA *Tw. round Clock* (1861) 256 Costumes.. ready for the histrionics who are to wear them. **1860** *All Year Rnd.* No. 75. 595 Commend me.. to this matchless histrionic!

2. *pl.* Play-acting, theatricals; theatrical arts; acting (of a part), pretence.

1864 *Sat. Rev.* XVII. 515/1 We have theatres in London ..not worse than the special Stratford histrionics. **1882** A. W. WARD *Dickens* i. 11 He loved the theatre and everything which savoured of histrionics. **1890** *Times* 10 Mar. 9/1 As a matter of common decorum or of satisfactory histrionics.

histri'onical, *a.* [f. as prec. + AL.]

1. = prec. adj. 1.

1609 HOLLAND *Amm. Marcell.* XVIII. vii. 117 In lieu of histrionicall actours and players. **1787** SIR J. HAWKINS *Life Johnson* 74 This supposed abuse of histrionical liberty. **1801** STRUTT *Sports & Past.* III. iii. §3 In the Saxon canons.. A.D. 960, it is ordered that no priest shall.. exercise the mimical or histrionical art.

2. = prec. adj. 2.

1560 BECON *New Catech.* Wks. 1844 II. 300 It was become deadly sin to minister the holy communion without these scenical, histrionical, and hickscorner-like garments. *a* **1626** BP. ANDREWES *Serm.* (1856) I. 414 This scenical, theatrical, histrionical godliness. *a* **1670** HACKET *Abp. Williams* I. (1692) 102 They [the Inquisition] are so histrionical in their ceremonies, as if they made a sport of barbarousness, that they cite the dead men three several days to appear.

histri'onically, *adv.* [f. prec. + -LY².] In a histrionic manner; in relation to, or in the style of, actors or acting; theatrically.

1647 TRAPP *Mellif. Theol.* in *Comm. Ep.* 637 They did all theatrically, histrionically, hypocritically. **1657** W. MORICE *Coena quasi Κοινή* Def. xix. 337 To translate the Stage into the Church, making some Histrionically to personate that which they are not. **1864** *Realm* 25 May 7 Signor Graziani ..is now a very fair Valentine considered histrionically.

histrionicism (hɪstrɪˈɒnɪsɪz(ə)m). [f. HISTRIONIC + -ISM.] Histrionic action; = next.

1870 *Daily News* 13 Dec., His vanity, his half-conscious histrionicism.. have been the subject of good-humoured laughter. **1873** BLACK *Pr. Thule* vi. 89 How could this girl have taught herself, in the solitude of a savage island, a species of histrionicism which women in London circles strove for years to acquire?

histrionism (ˈhɪstrɪənɪz(ə)m). [f. HISTRION or L. *histrio, -ōnem* + -ISM.] Theatrical practice, action, or style; 'acting'.

1682 SIR T. BROWNE *Chr. Mor.* III. §24 When personations shall cease, and Histrionism of happiness be over. **1835** *Fraser's Mag.* XII. 540 Something to wash down his lordship's dose of histrionism. **1862** CARLYLE *Fredk. Gt.* IX. iv. III. 113 The Cathedral Church,—where high Prince Bishops delivered *palliums*, did histrionisms.

'histrionize, *v.* *rare*⁻¹. [f. as prec. + -ISM.] *intr.* To act, as a stage-player; to play a part. (In quot., ***to histrionize it.***)

1652 URQUHART *Jewel* Wks. (1834) 229 During the five hours space that.. he was pleased to histrionize it, he shewed himself so natural a representative that [etc.].

hit (hɪt), *v.* Pa. t. and pa. pple. **hit.** Forms: 1 **hyttan**, 3–6 **hitte, hytte,** 4 **hutte, hete,** 4–5 **hyt,** 4–7 **hitt,** 5 (*3rd sing.*) **hit,** 4– **hit.** *Pa. t.* 1 **hytte,** 3–4 **hutte,** 3–5 **hitte,** (4 **hite**), 4– **hit,** (4–5 **hitt,** 5 **hyt(te,** 6–7 **hot,** 6–9 *Sc.* and *north.* **hat,** 7 **hatt**). *Pa. pple.* 4 **y-hyt,** 5 **hyt, yhytte,** 5–**hit,** (*dial.* 5 *Sc.* **hittin,** 6– **hitten, hutten,** 6 **hot**). [Late OE. *hyttan* = ON. *hitta* to hit upon, light upon, meet with, Sw. *hitta*, Da. *hitte* to hit, find.

App. from Norse: cf. Branch II; but the senses under I seem to have been developed at an early date in Eng. from the notion 'get at, reach'.]

I. To get at or reach with a blow, to strike.

1. a. *trans.* To reach or get at with a blow or a missile; to give a blow to (something aimed at); to strike with aim or intent. When the success of the actor is the prominent notion, its opposite is *to miss*; when the effect upon the object is prominent, the meaning tends to be 'to strike sensibly, so as to be felt'; cf. sense 8.

c **1205** LAY. 26060 Þe eotend smat after biliue & noht hine ne hutte. *Ibid.* 27680 He.. þene admiral hitte mid smærten ane dunte. **13..** *K. Alis.* 2155 Ac Alisaundre hutte him, certe, Thorugh livre, and longe, and heorte. *c* **1350** *Will. Palerne* 3621 No man þat he hit miȝth him withstonde. **1387** TREVISA *Higden* VI. xxix, Atte laste Harold was yhurt wyþ an arewe & loste hys on ye. **1413** *Pilgr. Sowle* (Caxton 1483) v. x. 101 Pacyence hitte Ire in the helme that it flewe a feld. **1460** *Lybeaus Disc.* 273 Was he never yhytte? **1484** CAXTON *Fables of Æsop* IV. ix, Thow shalt hytte hym with thy swerd and kylle hym. **1530** PALSGR. 585/2, I hytte a thyng that I throwe at. **1553** T. WILSON *Rhet.* (1580) 3 Phavorinus the Philosopher.. did hit a yong man over the Thumbes verie handsomely, for usyng.. over straunge woordes. *c* **1560** A. SCOTT *Poems* (S.T.S.) ii. 36 Sym said he sett nocht by hiss forss, Bot hecht he sowld be hittin. **1584** R. SCOT *Discov. Witchcr.* XII. xv. (1886) 206 A viper smitten or hot with a reed is astonied. **1601** SHAKS. *Twel. N.* II. v. 51 O for a stone-bow to hit him in the eye. *a* **1605** MONTGOMERIE *Misc. Poems* xxxiii. 17 He shot and hat me on the breist. **1743** *Broughton's Rules Boxing* in Blaine *Encycl. Rur. Sports* §1221 No person is to hit his adversary when he is down. **1828** *Craven Dial.*, *Hat*, præt. of hit. **1879** F. POLLOK *Sport Brit. Burmah* I. 193, I had hit the tigress hard as she sprang up. **1885** *Law Times* 9 May 29/2 The plaintiff.. fired at him, but did not hit him.

fig. **1611** MIDDLETON & D. *Roaring G.* Epil., Some dispraised The haire.. Some hit her o're the lippes, mislik'd their colour.

b. *Cricket.* (*a*) To strike (the ball) with the bat: hence with the bowler as object. (*b*) ***to hit off***, to make up (a number of runs) by hitting.

1857 HUGHES *Tom Brown* II. viii, When you or Raggles hit a ball hard away for six. **1865** F. LILLYWHITE *Guide to Cricketers* 86 Messrs. Tritton and Wright hit off 25 in 20 minutes. **1883** *Daily Tel.* 15 May 2/7 Dr. Grace hit Hill square for 4. **1884** *Pall Mall G.* 14 Aug. 9/1 Mr. Hornby hit each bowler twice for 4. **1888** *Daily News* 15 Sept. 3/4 The Englishmen had only 33 to get to win and this was hit off in twenty-five minutes for the loss of one wicket. **1892** *Ibid.* 1 Sept. 4/5 Yorkshire.. in the time remaining.. hit off 56 of these for the loss of two batsmen.

2. *absol.* or *intr.* To give a blow or blows; to strike with something in hand or with a missile.

? *a* **1400** *Morte Arth.* 1149 Arthur.. hittez ever in the hulke up to þe hiltez. **1581** MULCASTER *Positions* xxxviii. (1887) 178 Who so shootes at the like, in hope to hit, may sooner misse. **1669** STURMY *Mariner's Mag.* v. 57 Take aim to the Mark you would shoot to, and that is the way to hit. **1700** S. L. tr. *Fryke's Voy. E. Ind.* 25 Throw a Dart or long Stick, with which they'll hit within the compass of a farthing a mighty distance. **1850** S. G. OSBORNE *Gleanings* 112 There were.. lads.. hitting at stones with hammers. **1870** BLAINE *Encycl. Rur. Sports* §4038 (*Boxing*) He was.. an excellent 'stopper', hitting with his right and stopping with his left.

3. *trans.* Of a missile or moving body: To come upon with forcible impact; to strike.

c **1375** *Sc. Leg. Saints, Cristofore* 581 Sowne ane erow in þe ee hyme hit. **1628** DIGBY *Voy. Medit.* (1868) 77 He.. shott 7 peeces att my pinnace, all which hatt her. **1694** A. DE LA PRYME *Diary* (Surtees) 40 In at the window.. [it] was flung ..and had like to have hitten Mr. Walker on the head. **1700** S. L. tr. *Fryke's Voy. E. Ind.* 354 With an Elligar.. that sticks in the Fish it hits. **1828** SCOTT *F.M. Perth* xi, My pellet.. I trust, it did not hit your eye.

fig. **1513** DOUGLAS *Æneis* v. iii. 90 The meikle hillis Bemys agane, hit with the brute so schill is. **1847** TENNYSON *Princ.* v. 44 The sun, that now..hit the Northern hills.

4. *absol.* or *intr.* **a.** To come with forcible impact (*against*, *upon*, etc.).

c **1400** MAUNDEV. (Roxb.) xiii. 58 Þe whilk brand efterwardes hitt on þe erthe and stakk still þerin. **1530** PALSGR. 585/2, I went darkeling and dyd hytte agaynst a doore. **1659** B. HARRIS *Parival's Iron Age* 137 When we endeavour to shun one..Sand-bank, we hit against another. *a* **1704** LOCKE (J.), If bodies be extension alone, how can they move and hit one against another? **1860** TYNDALL *Glac.* I. xxv. 190 The little snow granules hit spitefully against the skin. *Mod.* The shot hit in front of the head high up.

b. To strike exactly or at the proper point. Usually in phr. ***to hit on*** so many ***cylinders***: (of an internal-combustion engine) to be running properly on so many cylinders; hence, ***to be hitting on all four*** or ***six*** (***cylinders***), to be running or working perfectly; *fig.* to be in good trim or form.

1912 [see CYLINDER *sb.* 6]. **1928** *Sat. Even Post* 10 Mar. 127/1 Modern science offers you a natural means to keep you 'hitting on all six'—every minute of the day.

5. *trans.* To deliver (a blow, stroke, etc.).

?*a* **1400** *Morte Arth.* 3687 Archers of Inglande..Hittis thourghe þe harde stele fulle hertly dynnttis. *c* **1400** *Destr. Troy* 5937 He..Hit on his hede a full hard dynt. **1460** *Lybeaus Disc.* 1631 Ayder yn other scheld hytte Strokes grymly greete. **1879** F. POLLOK *Sport Brit. B.* I. 122, I lifted the stick and pretended to hit at it a back-handed blow.

6. *With two objectives.* ***to hit any one a blow***: to strike him with a blow, to give him a blow.

1597 T. BEARD *Theatre God's Judgem.* I. xxi. (1631) 122 One of his seruants..hot him such a knock with a pistol that he killed him therewith. **1599** J. MINSHEU *Dial. Span. & Eng.* (1623) 18, I hit my selfe a blow..in this shin bone. **1763** C. JOHNSTON *Reverie* I. 135 Hitting him a plump in the bread-basket. **1858** HAWTHORNE *Fr. & It. Jrnls.* II. 23 Hitting the poor Venus another..blow.

7. *trans.* To knock (a part of the body) *against* or *on* something.

1639 T. BRUGIS tr. *Camus' Mor. Relat.* 249 [He] hit his nose so hard against the ground, that he lay quite stund with the fall. **1665** HOOKE *Microgr.* 178 It would swim to and fro ..but would often hit itself against the rocks or stones. *Mod.* In the dark he hit his foot against the step.

8. *fig.* **a.** To affect the conscience, feelings, comfort, prosperity, etc. of (any one) in a way analogous to physical hitting; to affect sensibly, painfully, or injuriously; to smite, wound, hurt. ***to hit home***: cf. HOME *adv.* 5.

c **1375** *Sc. Leg. Saints, George* 110 Sad sorow sa cane hyme hit. **1513** DOUGLAS *Æneis* IV. xi. 22 Now art thou hit with frawart weirdis vnkynd. **1553** T. WILSON *Rhet.* (1580) 138 A merie man can want no matter to hitte hym home. *c* **1565** LINDESAY (Pitscottie) *Chron. Scot.* (1728) 234 (Jam.) The chancellour..hearing the grose and ruid speach..thought he hat thame ovir near. **1620** SANDERSON *Serm.* (1681) I. 142 Christ hitteth him home, and presseth upon his particular corruption. **1678** R. BARCLAY *Apol. Quakers* x. §17. 307 This Objection hitteth not us at all. **1735** POPE *Donne Sat.* iv. 232 Dear Countess! you have charms all hearts to hit! **1861** BRIGHT *Sp. India* 19 Mar., The noble Lord felt himself hit. **1888** BRYCE *Amer. Commw.* II. xliii. 134 There is always a desire to hit companies. **1938** *Times* 30 Apr. 11/4 Mr. Roosevelt says that the one lesson in events abroad that has 'hit home' is that 'the liberty of a democracy is not safe if the people tolerate the growth of private power to a point where it becomes stronger than their democratic State itself'.

b. ***to be hard*** (sometimes ***heavily, badly***) ***hit***: to be severely or deeply affected by something; esp. to be seriously smitten by some adversity. (Cf. sense 1, quot. 1879.)

1854 LEVER *Dodd Fam. Abr.* xiv. 110, I got 'hit hard' at the Brussels races, lost twelve hundred at *écarté*. **1888** BRYCE *Amer. Commw.* III. xc. 229 Stocks had now fallen, and everybody was hard hit. **1891** N. GOULD *Doub. Event* 3 A friend of his had been hit heavily over a certain race. **1893** *L'pool Daily Post* 1 Jan., Liverpool was badly hit last year by the fall in cotton.

c. To criticize, make fun of or ridicule (a person or thing): sometimes const. *at*.

1843 *Punch* 23 Sept. 131/2 Instead of an outburst of enthusiasm at the line 'Confound their politics', the waltzer is supposed to execute a *pirouette*, which is supposed to hit at our wavering propensities. **1936** *S.P.E. Tract* XLV. 190 The member of a newspaper staff who is responsible for writing the headlines prefers..*hit*..to *criticize*. **1945** BAKER *Austral. Lang.* vi. 121 A man who has acquired a strong dislike of another person..hits or..criticizes him. **1969** *Pen* IX. 47 He could supply her with a list of synonyms for the verb 'savage', i.e...hit at.

d. To occur to (a person); to affect in a particular way, to appear to; to have an impact on.

1891 KIPLING *Light that Failed* v. 78 Look at their faces. It hits 'em. **1914** G. ATHERTON *Perch of Devil* I. xxx. 175 Lucky it hit him to buy the house and send that last five thousand. **1916** 'B. M. BOWER' *Phantom Herd* v. 68, I wanted to see how it would hit you. **1916** G. B. SHAW *Doctors' Delusions* (1932) 105 Their worthlessness would not hit us in the face as the worthlessness of Dr Saleeby's figures does. **1921** GALSWORTHY *To Let* II. xi. 212 Their manners now really quite hit you in the eye. **1937** *Even. News* 28 Jan. 7/1 (*headline*) Finding best colours for crossing that will 'hit the eye'. **1958** *Listener* 16 Oct. 600/2 This book..was published about two years ago, and it has not yet hit the architectural profession.

e. ***not to know*** (or ***to wonder***) ***what hit one***: to be killed; to be surprised or disconcerted.

1923 J. MINER *Jack Miner & Birds* viii. 27 He came to examine the decoys near me and while his attention was rivetted on them I raised up and fired, and he never knew what hit him. **1961** *Listener* 19 Oct. 589/1 Many of our less efficient firms would be hurt so hard that they could never quite know what had hit them. **1963** *Observer* 10 Feb. 24/3 They must have wondered what hit them in Paris last week, for almost every female member of the British Press made a dead set for the hosiery counter at Galeries Lafayette.

f. fig. ***to hit for six*** [cf. sense 1 b (*a*)]: to demolish an argument, scheme, etc., to vanquish; to deal a severe blow to.

1937 *Times Lit. Suppl.* 1 May 343/4 Lawrence..was chiefly concerned to hit swots and cads and foreigners for six. **1957** I. CROSS *God Boy* (1958) xiii. 109, I had really hit her for a six and made her change her tune properly. **1961** *Oxf. Mag.* 15 June 413/1 Mr. Sisam, the Secretary, hit most of the questioners for six. **1967** *Lancet* 1 July 41/1, I began to wonder if my massive and inexpert administration of chloroform had not hit his liver—perhaps not inappropriately—for six.

g. To give or administer a narcotic drug to (a person). Also *intr. slang* (orig. *U.S.*).

[**1949** N. ALGREN *Man with Golden Arm* 76 It [*sc.* a narcotic injection] hit all right. It hit the heart like a runaway locomotive, it hit like a falling wall.] **1953** W. BURROUGHS *Junkie* (1972) xiv. 144 'Hit me, will you, Ike?' Old Ike poked a gentle finger along the vein holding the dropper poised between thumb and fingers. **1959** —— *Naked Lunch* 67 The addict regards his body as an instrument to absorb the medium in which he lives, evaluates his tissue with the cold hands of a horse dealer. 'No use trying to hit there.' **1970** *N.Y. Times* 23 Feb. 26 How did he become an addict? 'You mean, who hit me first? My friend, Johnny.'

h. To kill; to rob. *slang* (orig. *U.S.*).

1955 *People* (Austral.) 19 Oct. 13/2 Dutch bellowed, 'Dewey's gotta go. He's gotta be hit.' **1968** N. GIOVANNI in A. Chapman *New Black Voices* (1972) 250, I have been robbed It looked like they knew That i was to be hit They took my tv My two rings. **1972** D. E. WESTLAKE *Cops & Robbers* (1973) xvi. 247 If they're cops, maybe it's not such a good idea to have them hit. **1973** *Publishers Weekly* 29 Jan. 229/2 A professional killer who has 'hit' 38 victims.

9. To cast, throw. *Obs.* exc. *dial.*

1362 LANGL. *P. Pl.* A. v. 172 Þenne Clement þe Cobelere caste of his cloke, And Hikke þe Ostiler hutte his hod aftur. **1862** H. KINGSLEY *Ravenshoe* xlii. (D.), Everthing past use was hit, as they say in Berkshire, out into the street.

10. *Backgammon.* To 'take up' (a man). ***to hit a blot***: to throw a number which enables the player to take up an unguarded man, that is, one left single and alone on any point in his adversary's tables. Hence *fig.* to discover a failing or a weak point. (See BLOT *sb.*[2])

1599 PORTER *Angry Wom. Abingd.* in Hazl. *Dodsley* VII. 276 *Mrs. Gour.* Look ye, mistress, now I hit ye. *Mrs. Bar.* Why, ay, you never use to miss a blot, Especially when it stands so fair to hit..I hot your man. **1691** T. H[ALE] *Acc. New Invent.* p. xxxviii, And he there hits a blot in the Papal Tenets that was never hit before. **1778** C. JONES *Hoyle's Games Impr.* 175 Suppose I leave two Blots, either of which cannot be hit but by double Dice. **1870** HARDY & WARE *Mod. Hoyle* 144 If you are obliged to leave a blot, by having recourse to the Calculations for hitting it, you will find the chances for and against you..Never fail spreading your men, either to take a new point in your table, or to hit a man your adversary may happen to enter. **1889** *Spectator* 14 Dec. 832 Mr. Morley has hit a blot in our policy.

II. To come upon, light upon, meet with, get at, attain to, reach one's aim, succeed, and the like.

This is the ON. sense; but with the exception of the single late OE. instance in 11, its exemplification in English as a whole is later.

11. *trans.* To come upon, light upon, meet with, get at, reach, find, esp. something aimed at. **a.** with material object. Freq. in modern (esp. U.S.) colloquial use, to arrive at; also, to go to (a place), go upon (a course). Phr. ***to hit the trail*** (less commonly ***the grit, pike, road***, etc.): to take the road, to get on the way, to go away.

a **1075** *OE. Chron.* (MS. D.) an. 1066 Ða com Harold..on unwær on þa Normenn, and hytte hi begeondan Eoforwic, æt Steinford-brygge. **1527** R. THORNE in Hakluyt *Voy.* (1589) 256 Sayling Northwarde..we shall hitte those Islandes. *c* **1532** DEWES *Introd. Fr.* in *Palsgr.* 908 To hitte or ouer-take, *attaindre*. **1621** T. WILLIAMSON tr. *Goulart's Wise Vieillard* 25 So farre out of the way..that they can hardly hit the right way againe to the..citie of God. **1704** ADDISON *Italy* (1733) 56 The Entrance is so difficult to hit. **1738** SWIFT *Pol. Conversat.* ii. 138 Egad, I can't hit the Joint. **1797** CAPT. TROUBRIDGE 25 July in Nicolas *Nelson's Disp.* (1845) II. 426 *note*, From the darkness of the night I did not immediately hit the Mole, the spot appointed to land at. **1852** MRS. CARLYLE *Lett.* II. 195 As soon as I knew where to hit you with a letter. **1873** W. F. BUTLER *Wild North Land* xviii. 208 In the morning 'Twa-poos', or the Three Thumbs, sets forth to look for a moose; he hits the trail and follows it. **1888** in *Amer. Speech* (1962) XXXVII. 76 *Hit the grit*, get going; get out of here. **1888** *Detroit Free Press* Oct. (Farmer), Professor Rose, who hit this town last spring, is around calling us a fugitive from justice. **1889** BARRÈRE & LELAND *Dict. Slang*, *Hit the flat, to* (cowboys), to go out on the prairies. **1893** P. H. EMERSON *On Eng. Lagoons* xii. 40, I have been hitting the road something to get here quick. **1896** ADE *Artie* xiv. 127 'A little more weather like this and we'll be hittin' the park,' he observed. **1897** *Outing* (U.S.) XXX. 374/1 Men can pass out the church door, shoulder their packs of general cussedness, and unconcernedly hit the trail to the lower [regions]. **1901** S. E. WHITE *Westerners* i. 7 Thought you wasn't no tenderfoot. Ever hit the trail? **1904** *Hartford Courant* 25 June 6 The..convention, whose delegates were so summarily ordered to hit the pike by the national committee-men. **1907** R. W. SERVICE *Songs of Sourdough* (1908) 65 It lies with thee—the choice is thine, is thine, To hit the ties or drive thy auto-car. **1918** C. E. MULFORD *Man fr. Bar-20* xiii. 131, I was a rich man until I hit town. **1925** WODEHOUSE *Carry on, Jeeves* v. 126 Jimmy Mundy..has come to save New York from itself; to force it —in his picturesque phrase—to hit the trail. **1925** Z. A. TILGHMAN *Dugout* 70, I must hit the road. **1931** 'D. STIFF' *Milk & Honey Route* 207 *Hitting the grit*, to be forced off a fast moving train. **1932** T. S. ELIOT *Sweeney Agonistes* 18 We hit this town last night for the first time. **1948** G. H. JOHNSTON *Death takes Small Bites* ii. 54 Go down this corridor, up the stairway at the end, straight on until you hit the second court. **1950** T. LONGSTAFF *This my Voyage* v. 97 So on May 31st Mumm and I hit the trail once more. **1973** *Christian Sci. Monitor* 14 Apr. B16/2 These two hit the road together, modern pilgrims making very little progress.

b. with immaterial object.

1555 EDEN *Decades* 309 To consyder howe they hytte the truthe sumtyme. **1581** PETTIE *Guazzo's Civ. Conv.* II. (1586) 68 You have hit my meaning right. **1685** LADY RUSSELL *Lett.* I. xxi. 57, I cannot hit the names of the rest. **1782** PRIESTLEY *Corrupt. Chr.* I. II. 272 Other persons..were able..to hit the happy medium. **1866** G. MACDONALD *Ann. Q. Neighb.* iii. (1878) 37, I never could hit his way of talking to his parishioners.

c. ***to hit the hay***, to go to bed. Also ***to hit the sack***. *slang* (orig. *U.S.*).

1912 *Dialect Notes* III. 578 *Hit the hay*, to go to bed. **1922** S. LEWIS *Babbitt* xix. 245 You probably want to hit the hay. **1930** 'SAPPER' *Finger of Fate* 184 On those two nights we all hit the hay before midnight. **1943** in J. J. Fahey *Pacific War Diary* (1963) i. 74, I hit the sack at 8 P.M. I slept under the stars on a steel ammunition box two feet wide. **1957** J. KEROUAC *On Road* (1958) 93 Terry and I..got ready to hit the sack. **1961** A. MILLER *Misfits* x. 98 Well, I don't know about you educated people, but us ignorant folks got to hit the sack.

d. ***to hit the bricks***: (*a*) (see quot. 1950); (*b*) to go on strike. *U.S. slang.*

1931 *Amer. Speech* VI. 439 *Hit the bricks, to*, to be released from prison. **1946** *Seafarers' Log* 1 Feb. 4/3 When you hit the bricks in those days you didn't expect to come back aboard real soon. *Ibid.* 17 May 6/4 The seamen responded almost unanimously to the strike call with organized and unorganized seamen alike tying up the ships and hitting the bricks. **1950** H. E. GOLDIN *Dict. Amer. Underworld Lingo* 97/2 *Hit the bricks*,..to be paroled, discharged, acquitted, or otherwise set free. 'Hawk's got a flat bit..so he's gotta hit the bricks.' **1964** *Time* 2 Oct. 111 The United Auto Workers hit the bricks against giant General Motors.

12. *intr.* With *upon, on* (†*of*), in same sense as 11. (With *indirect passive*.)

a **1300** *Cursor M.* 7152, I wat noght hu he on þam hitte. *c* **1375** *Sc. Leg. Saints, Clement* 836 Bot one þat place mycht nane of þame hyt. **1553** T. WILSON *Rhet.* (1580) 146 In readyng..he hit at length upon himself and the More. **1568** V. SKINNER tr. *Montanus' Inquis.* 17 a, So he can hit of the matter. **1609** B. JONSON *Sil. Wom.* IV. ii, No, but I could hit of some things that thou wilt miss. **1705** BOSMAN *Guinea* 34 The Means which they chiefly hit upon, and practised. **1715** VANBRUGH *Country Ho.* II. Wks. (Rtldg.) 464/1 Sure I shall hit of some way to get rid of this crew. **1764** REID *Inquiry* vi. §12 Like other facts, they are not to be hit upon by a happy conjecture. **1807** P. GASS *Jrnl.* 132 We..crossed a large mountain and hit on the creek and small valley, which were wished for by our guide. **1874** SAYCE *Compar. Philol.* ii. 69 Hypothesis after hypothesis, until the right one is at length hit upon.

†**13.** *intr.* To attain the object aimed at or end intended; to 'hit the mark'. Of events, etc.: To come to the desired end; to succeed; to come off as intended. *Obs.* or *dial.*

c **1400** *Destr. Troy* 2071 Thow se not þat sothely said ys of olde, And ofte happes to hit, qwo so hede tas. **1596** SHAKS. *Merch. V.* III. ii. 270 Hath all his ventures faild, what not one hit? **1668** SEDLEY *Mulb. Gard.* Prol., The cruel critic and malicious wit, Who think themselves undone if a play hit. **1744–50** W. ELLIS *Mod. Husbandm.* II. II. 127 (E.D.S.) This pirky wheat is often sown after turneps..and generally hits well. **1842** AKERMAN *Wilts. Gloss.* (E.D.S.) s.v., The apples hit well t'year.

14. *trans.* To attain to an exact imitation or representation of; to imitate exactly or to a nicety. Cf. *hit off* 25 c.

1602 *Narcissus* (1893) 484 Harke how Jumball hitts it [a cry] right. **1611** SHAKS. *Wint. T.* V. i. 127 Your Fathers Image is so hit in you. **1623** B. JONSON in *Shakspere's Wks.* To Rdr., O, could he but haue drawne his wit As well in brasse, as he hath hit His face. *c* **1633** MILTON *Arcades* 77 If my inferior hand or voice could hit Inimitable sounds. **1712** ADDISON *Spect.* No. 418 ¶3 It is pleasant to look on the Picture of any Face, where the Resemblance is hit. **1808** WOLCOTT (P. Pindar) *One more Peep at R. Acad.* Wks. 1812 V. 356 How dares thy hand, that cannot hit The features of a poor Tom tit, Attempt the Eagle's fury in its flight? **1842** MOTLEY *Corr.* (1889) I. iv. 119 One of the most difficult things in painting is to hit the exact colour of the human face.

15. To fall in with exactly; to suit, fit, be agreeable to.

c **1580** SIDNEY *Ps.* XL. iv, [I] sought with deedes thy will to hitt. **1601** HOLLAND *Pliny* I. 506 The dry marle, sorteth well with a moist soile; and the fatty, hitteth that which is dry and lean. **1632** MILTON *Penseroso* 14 Hail, divinest Melancholy, Whose saintly visage is too bright To hit the sense of human sight. **1692** BENTLEY *Boyle Lect.* ix. 327 All the Characters must hit and correspond one to another. **1766** GOLDSM. *Vic. W.* xvi, We did not immediately recollect an historical subject to hit us. **1850** TENNYSON *In Mem.* XLVII, What vaster dream can hit the mood Of Love on earth? **1884** CHURCH *Bacon* i. 20 In the hope..of hitting her taste on some lucky occasion.

†**16.** *intr.* To fall in suitably or exactly; to coincide; to square *with*, agree *with*. *Obs.*

1607 SHAKS. *Timon* III. i. 6 A Guift I warrant. Why this hits right: I dreampt of a Siluer Bason and Ewre to night. **1699** BENTLEY *Phal.* xi. 274 Plutarch..would never balk a good story though it did not exactly hit with Chronology. **1719** DE FOE *Crusoe* II. i, The Scheme hit so exactly with my Temper. **1722** —— *Col. Jack* (1840) 133 Was there nothing in his case that hit with your own?

17. *intr.* To agree together. *Obs.* or *dial.*

1605 SHAKS. *Lear* I. i. 308 Pray you let vs sit [*Qos.* hit] together. **1758** T. NEVILE *Imit. Hor. Ep.* I. xviii. 131 Believe me, contraries will never hit; The fop avoid the clown, the dunce the wit. **1828** *Craven Dial.*, *Hit*, to agree. **1876** *Whitby Gloss.*, s.v., 'We hit about it', agreed... 'Hae ye hitten on yet?', come to an agreement.

III. To aim, direct one's aim or course.

†**18.** *intr.* To aim, seek, strive. *Obs. rare.*

13.. *E.E. Allit. P.* A. 132 þe wyȝ..Hittez to haue ay more & more.

19. a. *intr.* To direct one's course, be directed; to pass, turn; to 'strike' *out*, *in*, in a particular direction. ? Now *dial.* and *U.S.*

13.. *E.E. Allit. P.* C. 380 Of a hepe of askes he hitte in þe myddez. *a* **1400–50** *Alexander* 445 He sall hit with his hede in-to þe heghe est. *c* **1400** *Destr. Troy* 4671 þai comyn to the cost..and þere hyt into hauyn. *Ibid.* 7242 Achilles also afterward rose, Hit on his horse, hurlit into fight. ? *a* **1500** *Chester Pl.* x. 275 Into Egypte till we hitte [*E.E.T.S.* hytt] The Angel will us leade. **1664** POWER *Exp. Philos.* 119 The Atoms of Fire, or Heat, which penetrate into the Bladder;.. Why could they not hit out, as well as in, through the same pores? **1713** POPE *Guardian* No. 40 *ad fin.*, Both Spenser and Philips have hit into the same road with this old West Country Bard of ours. **1895** T. HARDY in *Harper's Mag.* Mar. 568 I've seen her hit in and steer down the long slide on yonder pond. **1905** R. BEACH *Pardners* (1912) i. 24 We hit for camp on the run. *Ibid.* ii. 48 So me and 'Kink' Martin.. hit west. **1916** 'B. M. BOWER' *Phantom Herd* xiii. 218 When I hit for the land of orange blossoms and singing birds and sunshine.

b. *rare.* To go, pass. *U.S.*

1911 H. S. HARRISON *Queed* vii. 86 I've seen you hit by the window many's the time.

IV. Phrases.

20. *to hit it.* **a.** To hit the mark; to guess the right thing; to make a correct conjecture.

1588 SHAKS. *L.L.L.* IV. i. 127 Thou canst not hit it my good man. **1591** FLORIO *2nd Fruites* 25 *G.* That is stake-money under the line, is it not so? *T.* Yea sir, you hitt it right. **1738** SWIFT *Pol. Conversat.* iii. 199 Guess again... A Girl then... You have hit it. **1890** BOLDREWOOD *Col. Reformer* (1891) 134 You've just hit it there.

b. (Now usually *to hit it off*.) To agree. Also more widely, to become friendly, to be on good terms.

1634 STRAFFORD *Lett.* I. 299 Would to God our master could hit it with that crown! **1668** SEDLEY *Mulb. Gard.* I. i. Wks. 1722 II. 9 You and I shall never hit it. **1780** MAD. D'ARBLAY *Early Diary* (1889) II. 291 How do you and the great Mrs. Montague hit it off? **1844** ALB. SMITH *Adv. Mr. Ledbury* xxii. (1886) 66 The respective wives of these gentlemen never hit it exactly. **1861** HUGHES *Tom Brown at Oxf.* xi, Tom did not venture to inquire for a day or two how the two hit it off together. **1863** TROLLOPE *Rachel Ray* II. xiv. 297, I am so happy..that you and he have hit it off. **1954** T. S. ELIOT *Confid. Clerk* i. 16 Mr. Kaghan is prejudiced. He's never hit it off with Lady Elizabeth.

c. To attain exactly to the point wanted; to strike the scent in hunting (also *hit it off*).

1704 STEELE *Lying Lover* I. (1747) 16 Not ev'ry open-handed Fellow hits it neither. **1710** PRIDEAUX *Orig. Tithes* ii. 52 To look through every circumstance necessary to be considered in the adjusting of this point so as exactly to hit it. **18..** *Rec. N. Devon Staghounds* 65 (W. Som. Word-bk.) The hounds then hit it up the river. *Ibid.* 68 The hounds came to a check, and could never hit it off again.

d. To travel at speed. *U.S.*

1911 J. C. LINCOLN *Cap'n Warren's Wards* iii. 39 They nabbed us for speeding... Said we were hitting it at fifty an hour.

21. a. *to hit the mark, the nail, the needle, the pin, the nail upon the head*, usually *fig.*

c **1450** *Cov. Myst.* (Shaks. Soc.) 138 Now be myn trowthe ȝe hytte the pynne. **1530** *Proper Dyaloge* (1863) 15 Thou hyttest the nayle upon the head For that is the thinge that they dreed. **1580** SIDNEY *Arcadia* (1622) 305 Indeede she had hit the needle in that deuise. **1597** MORLEY *Introd. Mus.* 75 That we commonly call *hitting the eight on the face*, when we come to an eight, and skip vp from it agayne to another perfect concord. *a* **1613** OVERBURY *Charac.*, *Amorist* Wks. (1856) 57 To keep Cupid from hitting the blacke. **1680** H. MORE *Apocal. Apoc.* 54 This Bow-man hat the marke, when the Emperour Constantine turned Christian. **1866** MRS. GASKELL *Wives & Dau.* (Tauchn.) I. 69 He was rash.. hitting the nail on the head sometimes.

b. *to hit one in the teeth*: to reproach one (*with* a thing), throw it in one's teeth (see TOOTH).

22. a. *hit or miss*: Whether one hits or misses; at random, at haphazard, happy-go-lucky. (Cf. HITTY-MISSY.) Also *attrib.* and *subst.*

1606 SHAKS. *Tr. & Cr.* I. iii. 384 But hit or misse, Our proiects life this shape of sence assumes. **1654** WHITLOCK *Zootomia* 115 Whose practise in Physick is nothing but the Countrey dance, call'd Hit or Misse. **1705** HICKERINGILL *Priest-cr.* I. (1721) 14 Do we all march towards Heaven hit or miss, and by guess? **1848** in *Amer. Speech* (1935) X. 40/2 Hit-or-miss-carpet, a carpet woven from strips of old cloth sewed together. **1864** *Harper's Mag.* June 60/1 My husband is Colonel of the Third Regiment in the Hit-or-Miss Brigade, United States Cavalry. **1873** OUIDA *Pascarèl* II. 42 It is not the happy-go-lucky hit-or-miss sort of thing that you may fancy. **1927** J. ADAMS *Errors in School* 211 Hit-or-miss method. **1955** A. L. ROWSE *Expansion Eliz. Eng.* 399 They were impulsive, chancy, amateurish, very much hit-or-miss. **1959** P. BULL *I know Face* vii. 114 It was much a hit-or-miss part. **1967** KARCH & BUBER *Offset Processes* v. 168 Motor-driven lenses, or hit-or-miss methods involving tricky out-of-focus photographic and lighting techniques are used.

b. *hit and miss* = *hit or miss*. Also (with hyphens) *attrib.* and *spec.*, as **hit-and-miss governor**, a type of governor used in internal-combustion engines which causes the engine to miss one or more explosions when the speed is too great; **hit-and-miss ventilator** (see quots.).

1897 W. E. BARTON *Hero in Homespun* 377 They ripped up the new hit-an'-miss carpet for horse blankets. **1897** R. M. STUART *Simpkinsville* 156 Takin' 'em hit and miss, we wouldn't know the diff'rence hardly. **1902** A. C. HARMSWORTH et al. *Motors* viii. 162 Many of these engines have now the ordinary hit and miss exhaust governor as well. **1909** WEBSTER, *Hit-and-miss ventilator*, a window ventilator consisting of a perforated glass disk, lying flat against, and pivoted through its center to, a correspondingly perforated window. **1931** *Discovery* Sept. 298/1 [Without these criteria] the procedure would be unnecessarily hit-and-miss. **1940** *Chambers's Techn. Dict.* 417/2 *Hit-and-miss ventilator*, a ventilating device consisting of a slotted plate over which may be moved another slotted plate, so that the openings for access of air may be more or less restricted as required. **1955** W. W. DENLINGER *Compl. Boston* 156 Hit-and-miss, take-a-chance breedings are fewer. **1956** G. TAYLOR *Silver* iii. 53 A simple pattern, often seen on Communion Cups, consists of rows of 'hit and miss' ornament. **1970** *Morning Star* 11 July 2 The pedlars of such gifts are only worried about the wastage involved..and the general hit-and-miss aspect of the whole business.

23. Various phrases.

a. *to hit the pipe*: to smoke opium. Also *to hit the gong, gow, stuff*: to take drugs. So *to hit cigarettes*: to smoke heavily. *U.S. slang.*

1886 T. F. BYRNES *Profess. Criminals of Amer.* 385 Joe did not 'hit the pipe'. **1902** *Chicago Record Herald* 7 Sept. vi. 5/2 On each bunk two almond-eyed devotees of the drug may be seen 'hitting the pipe', as opium smoking is termed. **1933** *Amer. Speech* VIII. II. 27/1 When one has contracted the [drug] habit..he is..hitting the gow. *Ibid.* 27/2 When the opium addict is smoking he is said to be hitting the gong. **1936** *Ibid.* XI. 122/2 To hit the stuff, to be addicted to narcotics... The act of taking dope. **1939** *Ibid.* (1942) XVII. 206/1 Bill is hitting cigarets some.

b. *to hit the booze, bottle, jug, pot*: to drink excessively. *slang* (orig. and chiefly *U.S.*).

1889 *Oregonian* (Portland) 14 Oct. 3/1 If Dasher gets a dozen or more customers with his own appetite for hitting the booze he will have no trouble making it go. **1908** J. M. SULLIVAN *Crim. Slang* 13 *Hitting the pots*, excessive drinking. **1942** BERREY & VAN DEN BARK *Amer. Thes. Slang* §102.22 *Drink liquor, esp. intemperately*,..hit the booze,.. bottle. **1942** R. CHANDLER *High Window* (1943) x. 78 We were kind of hitting the bottle a little. **1946** MEZZROW & WOLFE *Really Blues* 374 *Hit the jug*, drink heavily, often from the bottle; have a drink. **1956** A. CHRISTIE *Dead Man's Folly* iii. 40 The most incredible shirts..covered with crawling turtles and things—made me think I'd been hitting the bottle. **1957** *Landfall* XI. 38 Everyone knew he'd turn out a flop... Hit the booze and got T.B. **1965** *Times Lit. Suppl.* 25 Nov. 1068/2 We are 'wild spiders crying together' ..who must crack or hit the bottle.

c. *to hit the ceiling*: see CEILING *vbl. sb.* 5 b.

d. *to hit the headlines*: see HEADLINE 2 c.

e. *to hit the deck*: (*a*) to go to bed; (*b*) to land an aircraft; (*c*) to fall to the ground; (*d*) to get up (from bed). *colloq.*

1918 *Sat. Even. Post* 21 Dec. 29 The sergeants and corporals emphasized the command to rise with sharp injunctions to 'Snap out of it!', 'Hit the deck!' **1935** W. DE LA MARE in *Proc. Brit. Acad.* 247 He hit the deck; he slung his hammock; he went to bed;..they all signify much the same thing. **1943** C. H. WARD-JACKSON *Piece of Cake* 36 *Hit the deck*, to land [an aircraft]. **1954** *Manch. Guardian Weekly* 4 Mar. 2/1 The whole House fell on its knees or went prone behind desks, as one Pacific veteran shouted out: 'Hit the deck, you damn fools!' **1956** *Amer. Speech* XXXI. 193 *Hit the deck!*, wake up; begin working; jump to the floor. **1958** F. C. AVIS *Boxing Ref. Dict.* 53 *Hit the deck*, a slang expression meaning to fall to the ring floor. **1961** F. H. BURGESS *Dict. Sailing* 115 *Hit the deck*, take an upper-deck siesta. **1966** 'J. HACKSTON' *Father clears Out* 52 I'm going to hit the deck now, and I'm going to turn the lamp out.

f. *to hit the silk*: see quot. 1941. *colloq.*

1941 *Amer. Speech* XVI. 166/2 *Hit the silk*, use a parachute. **1958** 'P. BRYANT' *Two Hours to Doom* 104 If it came to the worst, they could always drop altitude and hit the silk.

V. With adverbs in specialized senses.

24. hit in. †**a.** *trans.* To thrust in, push in with a stroke. *Obs.*

a **1400–50** *Alexander* 512 þan wendis þar-out a litill worm & wald it eft enter, And or scho hit in hire hede a hard deth suffirs.

b. *intr.* To strike in: see 19.

c. *Polo.* (See quot. 1963.)

1906 T. B. DRYBROUGH *Polo* (rev. ed.) xiv. 279 A ball once over the side-boards is out, although it rebounds in or is hit in by a player before it touches the ground. **1930** *Hurlingham Club Rules of Polo* (ed. 43) III. 60 (*heading*) Explanation of terms... 'Hit in' means 'to hit the ball into the field of play'. **1963** BLOODGOOD & SANTINI *Horseman's Dict.* 104 *Hit in*, in polo to hit the ball into the field of play; not to bowl it in under-hand.

25. hit off. a. *trans.* To produce or throw off with success.

1700 CONGREVE *Way of World* III. xiii, We hit off a little wit now and then, but no animosity. **1822** MARY A. KELTY *Osmond* I. 87 You used to be rather au fait at hitting off a sonnet.

b. To succeed in attaining or getting at or upon. (Said esp. of striking the scent in hunting.)

1678 DRYDEN *Limberham* IV. i, You have hit it off it seems. *a* **1698** TEMPLE (J.), What prince soever can hit off this great secret, need know no more. **1749** FIELDING *Tom Jones* x. vi, It happens to this sort of men, as to bad hounds, who never hit off a fault themselves. **1815** *Sporting Mag.* XLV. 299 The hounds again hit off the scent. **1879** F. POLLOK *Sport Brit. Burmah* I. 69 We started at daybreak..and soon hit off a trail.

c. To describe, represent, or reproduce successfully or to a nicety.

1737 WATERLAND *Eucharist* 81 He has very well hit off the Sense. **1831** MACAULAY in *Life & Lett.* (1883) I. 233, I never saw a character so thoroughly hit off. **1871** SMILES *Charac.* x. (1876) 275 Sometimes he hits off an individual trait by an anecdote.

d. See also senses 1 b and 20 b, c.

26. hit out. †**a.** *trans.* To knock out. *Obs.*

1393 LANGL. *P. Pl.* C. XXI. 386 And ho so hitteþ out a mannes eye oþer elles hus for-teþ. **1704** J. PITTS *Acc. Mahometans* 98, I have hit out the Devils Eyes already.

†**b.** To bring out, come out with. *Obs. rare.*

1579 E. K. *Ep. Ded. Spenser's Sheph. Cal.*, He mought needes in singing hit out some of theyr tunes.

c. To strike out, elicit.

1838 KEBLE *Occas. Pap. & Rev.* (1877) 31 [She] hit out the spark which has now become such an orb of poetical fame.

d. *intr.* To strike out with the fist. Also *fig.* to deal heavy blows *at*, to attack vigorously.

1856 READE *It is never too late* xv, No! give me a chap that hits out straight from the shoulder. **1873** *Punch* 10 May 190/1 Mr. Torrens hit out at Mr. Lowe. *a* **1895** LD. C. E. PAGET *Autobiog.* vi. (1896) 188 A member [of Parliament] should hit out seldom but hit hard.

27. hit up. a. To force up; to speed up. With *it*: to put on pressure; to make efforts in a certain direction.

1893 W. K. POST *Harvard Stories* 49, I could hear him objurgating Steve Hudson for hitting up the stroke. *Ibid.* 146 When you are doing better than three and a half [miles an hour], you are hitting it up pretty well. **1904** F. LYNDE *Grafters* xx. 257 Two days after the Universal's triumph in the Belmount field, the Argus began to 'hit it up' boldly toward the capital. **1912** MULFORD & CLAY *Buck Peters* iii. 49 Hit her up or you'll be late. **1918** in F. A. Pottle *Stretchers* (1930) 270 Back he went, while we waited. When he got back with his jam, we hit it up again. It seemed miles before we got anywhere.

b. To make or score (runs).

1895 [see UP *adv.*[1] 19 b]. **1899** *Daily News* 9 June 6/7 They were batting all day, and hit up 397 for the loss of seven wickets. **1928** *Evening News* 18 Aug. 10/5 Middlesex hit up 365 in the first day's play.

c. *to hit* (a person) *up for*: to ask (someone) for. *U.S.* and *N.Z. slang.*

1917 *Chrons. N.Z.E.F.* 5 Sept. 28/1 We hit him up for a loan for weeks afterwards and he always came to light too. **1935** C. W. THURLOW CRAIG *Paraguayan Interlude* xxv. 291, I..hit him up for a job, and here I am. **1936** J. STEINBECK *In Dubious Battle* 108 Don't hit 'im up for anything else but breakfast. **1957** I. CROSS *God Boy* (1958) xii. 98 'I'll have to hit my old man up for a new bike,' he said. **1972** M. J. BOSSE *Incident at Naha* iii. 135 She hit me up for bread.

VI. 28. *Comb.* **hit-wicket** (*Cricket*), the act of hitting the wicket with the bat or a part of the person, by which the batsman is 'out'.

1773 in *Q. Rev.* No. 316. 469 [We find] 'hit wicket' [scored for the first time in a match between Hambledon and England in 1773]. **1850** 'BAT' *Cricket Man.* 47 The hitter is given out as 'hit wicket'. **1897** RANJITSINHJI *Cricket* xix, The umpire at the bowler's end is the proper person to be appealed to..in all cases except those of stumping, hit-wicket, and run out.

hit, *sb.* Also 5 **hete**, 6–8 **hitt.** [f. HIT *v.*]

1. a. A blow given to something aimed at; a stroke (at cricket, billiards, etc.); the collision or impact of one body with another.

hit-in (in *Polo*), the hitting of the ball into the field of play. (Cf. HIT *v.* 24 c). *hit off* (in *Hockey*), the first stroke, which begins the game.

c **1450** *Cov. Myst.* (Shaks. Soc.) 185 To hym wyl I go, and ȝeve hym suche an hete That alle the lechis of the londe his lyf xul nevyr restore. **1598** FLORIO, *Colpo*, a blow, a stroke, a hit. **1602** SHAKS. *Ham.* V. ii. 292 A hit, a very palpable hit. **1681** COTTON *Wond. Peak* 32 How deep..By tumbling down stones..Till the first hit strikes the astonisht ear, Like Thunder under-ground. **1810** *Sporting Mag.* XXXVI. 195 The navigator could plant but few hits. **1811** *Ibid.* XXXVII. 92 He..can only be denied by a hit down. **1850** 'BAT' *Cricket Man.* 46 Whatever byes result from the hit, go to the hit. **1879** F. POLLOCK *Sport Brit. Burmah* I. 229 We..made some very disgraceful misses, and again some very pretty hits. **1893** *Westm. Gaz.* 22 Feb. 11/2 The annual encounter ..at hockey..Hit off will be at half-past two. **1930** *Hurlingham Club Rules of Polo* (ed. 43) III. 63 Penalty 2, *by the side fouled*—a hit in from behind by the other side..the defending side being free to place themselves where they choose. **1937** *Times* 16 July 5/5 Captain Morrison, after meeting a hit-in by Major Harrison put Adsdean further ahead with a stupendous shot under his pony's neck. **1959** *Times* 18 May 2/1 Lucas met a hit-in to score early in the second chukka.

b. A dose of a narcotic drug; the action of obtaining or administering such a dose. Also *attrib.*, as **hit-mark**, the scar from an injection of a drug. *slang* (orig. *U.S.*).

1951 *Nat. Educ. Assoc. U.S. Jrnl.* May 342/2 They are anxious to make a 'connection', 'score' or 'hit'. **1962** 'E. MCBAIN' *Like Love* (1964) ix. 119 A narcotics cop will insist on examining a prostitute's thighs for hit marks, even when he knows she couldn't possibly be a junkie. **1966** L. COHEN *Beautiful Losers* (1970) I. 106 They rustled among their veins for one that still carried blood, tapped the needles under the flesh, waited for the red signal of a 'hit', and then squirted the solution into circulation. **1970** *Daily Tel.* 27 Apr. 4/8 In San Francisco's Haight-Ashbury district, the hippie Mecca, the price of one 'hit' has dropped from 12s to 2s 6d. **1972** *Southerly* XXXII. 103 Somebody hands me a joint and I take a hit and hand it to Marlene who takes a hit. **1972** C. WESTON *Poor, Poor Ophelia* (1973) ii. 15 You're blind! You have to wait for a report to see the hit marks?

c. A killing; a robbery. Also *attrib.*, as **hit list**, (*a*) a list of persons to be assassinated; (*b*) *transf.*,

a list or group of persons, etc., against which some concerted action is intended; a list of objectives; **hit-man**, a hired murderer; **hit squad**, a group of esp. politically-motivated assassins or kidnappers; also *transf. slang* (orig. *U.S.*).

1970 *Sunday Truth* (Brisbane) 8 Mar. 32/5 The Mafia cringe at the way our boys carry out their hits. **1971** D. MACKENZIE *Sleep is for Rich* vi. 186, I got scared and called the whole thing off. Someone else must have made the hit. **1976** *Time* 5 Jan. 46/1 One intelligence official.. bitterly labeled *Counterspy*'s roster of CIA agents as nothing more or less than 'a *hit list'. **1977** *Time* 6 June 11/1 A particular sore point was Carter's original 'hit list' of 32 water projects. The President compromised and restored 14 of the originally doomed projects. **1978** *Guardian Weekly* 26 Nov. 7/1 ZANU, one of two Rhodesian nationalist guerrilla organisations, meanwhile issued a 'hit list' of supporters of the interim Government, describing them as 'priority military targets'. **1985** *Times Educ. Suppl.* 19 July 1/2 By the time talks resume.. the Government's 'hit list' of rate-capped authorities in 1986 to 1987 would be published. **1970** J. PHILIPS *Nightmare at Dawn* (1971) II. 97 He was.. a hired gun, a *hit-man. **1973** *Daily Tel.* 25 July 4/8 Bryant is alleged to have been a 'hit man' (assassin) for drug traffickers and to have carried out a 'contract' to kill Finley. **1976** *Times* 19 Apr. 6/5 Apart from the attempts to kill Major Muhayshi in Tunisia, a Libyan *hit squad sought him out in London in February. **1981** *Internat. Herald Tribune* 20 Nov. 6/4 Venezuelan democrats.. had to overthrow military dictatorships to gain power, and then defeat Castroite insurgents and rightist hit squads to keep it. **1985** T. LUNDBERG *Starting in Business* i. 14 The Government.. then has to.. set up Mr Tebbit's hit squads.

2. A stroke of sarcasm, censure, rebuke, etc.

c **1668** *Roxb. Ball.* (1892) VII. 381 'Tis Wit for Wit, and Hit for Hit. **1673** [R. LEIGH] *Transp. Reh.* 139 His snip-snap wit, hit for hit. **1800** *Sporting Mag.* XV. 265 We have received a number of hits about the soup or broth shops. **1873** HELPS *Anim. & Mast.* iv. (1875) 102 In Hudibras there is a sly hit at the sayings of the philosophers.

3. a. A stroke of good luck which one hits upon or meets with; a fortunate chance.

1666 PEPYS *Diary* 1 June, To lament the losse of the opportunity of the last yeare, which.. all might have been such a hit as will never come again in this age. **1684** T. BURNET *Th. Earth* I. 294 A lucky hit indeed, for chance to frame a world! **1704** CHURCHILL *Collect. Voy.* III. 9/1 One of these Hits is enough to Enrich a Family. **1875** WHITNEY *Life Lang.* vii. 120 Such words.. which only by a lucky hit gain life and a career.

b. *to look to* (or *mind*) *one's hits*: to look to one's chances.

1699 BENTLEY *Phal.* 190 He should have minded his hits better, when he was minded to act the Tyrant. *a* **1700** B. E. *Dict. Cant. Crew* s.v. *Eye*, To have an Eye to the main Chance, or look to your Hits. **1760** C. JOHNSTON *Chrysal* (1822) II. 248 If I mind my hits this trip, I shall be as rich as the best of them. **1840** MRS. F. TROLLOPE *Widow Married* xxiii, You had better mind your hits between mamma and me.

4. a. A successful stroke made in action or performance of any kind; esp. any popular success (a person, a play, a song, etc.) in public entertainment. Also *attrib.* and *Comb.*, as **hit parade**, a programme or grouping of 'hits'; **hit tune** (or **song**), a tune that proves popular.

1811 C. MATHEWS *Let.* 22 June (1838) II. 123 Maw-worm was a most unusual hit, I am told. **1815** W. H. IRELAND *Scribbleomania* 157 *note*, One of Mr. Lane's most fortunate hits. **1829** *Blackw. mag.* XXV. 399 Mr. Peel seems to have made a hit in the chief character of Shiel's play. **1835** DICKENS *Let.* 9 Dec. (1965) I. 103 The insertion of another Prison Paper would decidedly detract from the 'hit' of the first. **1847** ALB. SMITH *Chr. Tadpole* xxiv. (1879) 217 His general effect.. was pronounced to be a hit. **1908** *Sears, Roebuck Catal.* 199/1 Orchestra selections.. 'Broadway Hits'. **1918** *Talking Machine News & Jrnl. Amusements* Feb. 83 (Advt.), All the song-hits of the moment. *Ibid.* 89/2 (Advt.), When a title makes a hit, we are bound to have another something like it before long. *Ibid.* Mar. p. iv (Advt.), Always a hit!! A 'Record' in a Record. **1927** *Melody Maker* Aug. 800 (Advt.), The sensational hit. Sweeping the country like a cyclone. The Doll Dance. **1932** *Amer. Speech* Apr. 252 The motto of the song writers is.. 'A hit is not an aesthetic triumph, it is something that sells.' **1937** *Cinema Arts* June 22 (*caption*) The Hit Parade. **1937** W. S. MAUGHAM *Theatre* xxviii. 270 I'm very pleased with her. I think she'll make quite a hit. I've half a mind to give her a contract. **1942** BERREY & VAN DEN BARK *Amer. Thes. Slang* §580/2 A popular song which has stood the test of time; hit song or tune. **1947** R. DE TOLEDANO *Frontiers of Jazz* xvi. 172 Hit tunes of his own composition. **1948** *Manch. Guardian Weekly* 1 Jan. 13/4 The box-office of any hit-show on Broadway. **1948** F. BROWN *Murder can be Fun* (1951) i. 18 She had big blue eyes that would have been a hit on television. **1957** *Observer* 29 Sept. 13/1 It must first be said that Miss Storm has written a resounding, self-evident hit. **1957** *Times Lit. Suppl.* 4 Oct. 593/1 Hollywood now makes its smash hits out of American self-criticism. **1958** *Times* 26 May 7/6 The numbers listed in the hit parade all have a structure of professionalism. **1959** G. FREEMAN *Jack would be Gent.* vi. 129 The first dozen of you lucky kids.. will be presented with my latest hit disc. **1967** *Boston Sunday Globe* 23 Apr. A28/2 Lemons and peppermints have been 'hit items' from the very first fair, and so have rides on one of the Brookline Fire Department's engines. **1967** *Melody Maker* 29 July 7/3 I'm not chasing any hit records any more. **1968** *Brit. Med. Bull.* XXIV. 245/1 Fowler (1966), using a program in Elliot 803 Autocode, has explored the effect of combining models with varying distributions of hit numbers. **1969** *Punch* 29 Jan. p. v, Don Partridge, who shot from the pavement into the hit parade, is putting on a Buskers Concert.

b. A saying that goes to the point; a striking and effective expression; a telling phrase.

1836 T. HOOK *G. Gurney* (1850) I. i. 18 He suggested the introduction of two or three jokes—'hits', I recollect he called them—into the speeches of that personage. **1884** *Nonconf. & Indep.* 25 Sept. 929/2 The noble speaker had made the hit of the evening. **1885** *Law Times* LXXX. 10/1 One of his happiest hits is to brand wire pullers as the *chiffonniers* of politics.

c. A successful guess.

1852 GLADSTONE *Glean.* IV. i. 139 A knack of lucky conjecture.. resembling that which solves conundrums, often seems to be more successful in its hits than comprehensive mental grasp or the closest logical continuity.

d. *hit off*, the act of hitting off (HIT *v.* 25 c); a clever representation or imitation.

1830 J. BADCOCK in *Foote's Wks.* p. xi, The plaudits which would accompany a successful hit-off of the subject under treatment.

5. *Backgammon.* **a.** A game won by a player after his opponent has thrown off one or more men from the board, as distinguished from a *gammon* or a *backgammon*: see quot. 1888. **b.** The act of hitting a 'blot': see HIT *v.* 10.

1766 GOLDSM. *Vic. W.* ii, Backgammon, at which my old friend and I sometimes took a twopenny hit. **1778** C. JONES *Hoyle's Games Impr.* 171 Two of your Adversary's Men in your Tables are better, for a Hit, than any greater Number, provided your Game is forwardest. **1856** LEVER *Martins of Cro' M.* 18 A hardly-contested 'hit' of backgammon was being fought out. **1888** *Cassell's Bk. Sports & Past.* 385 There are three different kinds of wins, viz., the *hit*, the *gammon*, and the *backgammon*. The player who has played all his men round into his own inner table, and by fortunate throws of the dice has *borne* all his men, wins the *hit*.

6. An abundant crop of fruit (i.e. one that turns out a success). *west. dial.*

1800 *Trans. Soc. Arts* XVIII. 303 What in the Cider-countries is called a hitt. This.. superabundance of fruit, is very destructive to the trees; for so great a crop weakens them very much. **1890** *Gloucestersh. Gloss.*, *Hit*, an abundant crop of fruit.

hit, obs. f. HIGHT *v.*, HEIGHT; obs. and dial. f. IT.

hit and run. 1. *Baseball.* 'A play wherein a base runner starts with the pitcher's throw as the batter attempts a hit, a sacrifice hit' (*D.A.*).

1899 *Chicago Daily News* 2 May 7/1 A rare combination for the hit-and-run game. **1904** R. H. BARBOUR *Bk. Sch. & Coll. Sports* 188 *Team batting.* The best known example of this is what is called the sacrifice hit or 'hit and run'. *Ibid.* 191 The 'hit-and-run' play may also be used when there is a man on third and a run is badly needed. **1909** *Amer. Mag.* May 35/1 Evers and Kling analyzed and discovered every hit and run signal used by the Cincinnati club. **1957** *Encycl. Brit.* III. 164/1 Since the hit-and-run play involves two players, there is usually the exchange of a secret signal between them, or a signal to both of them by the manager or one of the coaches. **1967** [see BUNT *v.*[2] 2].

2. *Motoring.* The action of the driver of a motor vehicle who fails to stop after an accident for which he is responsible. Freq. *attrib.* Also **hit-run**.

1924 *Sci. Amer.* Sept. 181/1 With the bumper in circuit with the ignition, there would be no more 'hit-and-run' driving. **1926** *Amer. Speech* I. 460/1 The hit-and-run driver. **1933** *Bulletin* (Sydney) 11 Jan. 9 The power to inflict the death penalty on the hit-run driver who kills. **1944** E. S. GARDNER *Case of Careless Kitten* xxiv. 217 Lunk's dead, found at a road intersection a couple of blocks from his house, a hit-and-run car. **1949** 'M. INNES' *Journeying Boy* ix. 109 If Soapy had been a bit nearer the kerb, I'd have felt like a little hit and run. **1955** C. S. FORESTER *Good Shepherd* 24 He had been in trouble with the civil authorities for a hit-run automobile offence. **1965** 'L. EGAN' *Detective's Due* (1966) xii. 129 There had been a hit-run yesterday. **1972** *Times* 14 Dec. 4/8 Professor Christiaan Barnard.. will suffer no after-effects from injuries sustained when knocked down by a hit-and-run motorist.

3. Used *attrib.* to denote a raid, raider, etc., using swift action followed by an immediate withdrawal.

1940 *Hutchinson's Pict. Hist. War* 2 Oct.–26 Nov. 98 Two of the three trams blasted by bombs in a Nazi 'hit and run' raid on the morning of 25th October, 1940. **1941** *Ibid.* 14 May–8 July 71 The heavily armed raiding cruiser, or hit-and-run battleship. **1955** *Times* 20 Aug. 5/2 Some of them were indulging in violence and arson, adopting 'hit and run' tactics. **1957** L. F. R. WILLIAMS *State of Israel* 30 Arab forays, which often took the form of hit-and-run tactics. **1966** [see *fire-bombing* s.v. FIRE *sb.* B 5].

hitch (hɪtʃ), *v.* Forms: 5–6 **hyche, hytche, hich,** 6– **hitch.** [In *Promp. Parv.*, 1440, *hytche-n*; in 16–17th c. also without *h*, see ITCH *v.*[2]; app. identical in sense with early ME. ICCHE-N. If these are in origin the same word, it is equally difficult to explain the loss of *h* in the one, and its addition in the other form. In some uses *hitch* is equivalent in sense to Sc. and north. *hotch*, with which, if the *h* is original, it may be radically cognate. No related word appears in the cognate langs. The connexion of branches I and II is also uncertain.

(There does not appear to be any ground for connecting it with *hick-* in *hicket, hiccup*.)]

I. To move jerkily.

1. a. *trans.* To move (anything) as with a jerk, or in an abrupt or discontinuous manner; to shift (a thing) a little away or aside.

c **1440** *Promp. Parv.* 239/2 Hytchyn, or remevyn (*K.* hychyn, *P.* hytchen, *J.*, *W.* hythen), *amoveo, moveo, removeo.* *a* **1529** SKELTON *E. Rummyng* 401 Another than dyd hyche her, And brought a pottel pycher. **1639** FULLER *Holy War* I. xxiii. (1840) 38 Jerusalem.. hath somewhat altered her situation, having hitched herself more north-westward. **1674** N. FAIRFAX *Bulk & Selv.* 122 That the spring of the Watch.. should by its bear or elasticity hitch it forwards. **1849** C. BRONTE *Shirley* ix, Hitching his chair nearer the fire. **1884** GILMOUR *Mongols* 256 Hitching himself round.. looking at me.

b. *esp.* To raise or lift with a jerk. Usually with *up*. orig. *Naut.*

1833 MARRYAT *P. Simple* li, So saying, Swinburne hitched up his trowsers, and went down below. **1842** BARHAM *Ingol. Leg.* Ser. II. *Misadv. Margate* xix, And then he hitch'd his trousers up, as is, I'm told, their use. **1861** MISS TYTLER *Pap. Thoughtf. Girls* (1863) 38 Over-prominent shoulderblades, which she had not given over hitching awkwardly. **1865** DICKENS *Mut. Fr.* II. i, She hitched this chin up. **1869** BLACKMORE *Lorna D.* iii, She.. hitched her dress.

2. *fig.* **a.** To move or lift as by a jerk into some position; *spec.* to put (as by an effort) into a story, into verse, or the like; to insert or mention in a literary work, esp. by way of exposure or ridicule. Sometimes app. associated with sense 5.

1749 FIELDING *Tom Jones* VIII. i, Hitch him in distich. **1779** SHERIDAN *Critic* I. i, Now we must appear loving and affectionate, or Sneer will hitch us into a story. **1779** J. ADAMS in *Fam. Lett.* (1876) 355 If.. the letter should be caught and hitched into a newspaper, the world would say I was not to be trusted with a secret. **1788** V. KNOX *Winter Even.* I. II. xiii. 196 The most exalted persons.. cruelly hitched in a rhyme, and thrown out to the vulgar. **1805** W. TAYLOR in *Ann. Rev.* III. 58 Our endowed free schools.. keep down the price of education.. and they hitch into genteel life a number of young men, who are lost to industry. **1889** SERJ. ROBINSON *Bench & Bar* 305 A few words hitched in here regarding barristers' clerks may not be thought out of place.

b. *intr.* for *passive*.

1733 POPE *Hor. Sat.* II. i. 78 Whoe'er offends, at some unlucky time Slides into verse, and hitches in a rhyme, Sacred to Ridicule his whole life long. *a* **1797** MASON *Dean & Squire* (R.), I ask his pardon. At the time He chanc'd to hitch into my rhyme. **1805** FOSTER *Ess.* IV. v. 185 *note*, Names that may more commodiously hitch into verse.

3. a. *intr.* To shift one's position a little; to move with a jerk or succession of jerks.

1629 T. ADAMS *Serm. Rev.* vi. 16 Wks. 758 When.. the place of their hope became an Iland, loe now they hitch vp higher to the toppes of the tallest trees. **1655** FULLER *Ch. Hist.* II. ii. §52 To ease themselves a little, by hitching into another place. **18..** W. TAYLOR in *Ann. Rev.*, The Belgæ.. were hitching westward to make room for the Goths. **1865** CARLYLE *Fredk. Gt.* XVIII. xii. VIII. 35 Slow Fermor.. began hitching southward, southward gradually to Posen.

b. To jerk the body up and down; to HOTCH.

1510–20 *Compl. too late maryed* (1862) 8 Mo gallantes.. ren After a wentche, and lepe and hytche, Than dogges do about a faroweiye bytche. **1571** *Satir. Poems Reform.* xxix. 15 Quhat mervell than thochte chaist forett.. Hichit on þe hure so oppinly? **1868** H. WOODRUFF *Trotting Horse* iv. 59 When it was found that they began to hitch and hobble, a good let-up would do more to restore the stroke than anything else. **1889** *Century Mag.* 907/2, I do not know what would happen to a man who 'hitched' in his saddle.

4. a. To walk unevenly or lamely; to hobble; also (*dial.*) to hop.

1513 DOUGLAS *Æneis* IV. xi. 114 The tother.. Hichit on furth with slaw pace lyke ane trat. *a* **1605** MONTGOMERIE *Flyting w. Polwart* 395 Fra the how to the hight, some hobles, some hatches [? *error for* hitches; *rimes* 'witches', 'bitches']; With their mouthes to the moone, murgeons they maid. **1755** JOHNSON, *Hobble*, to walk lamely or awkwardly upon one leg more than the other; to hitch. **1787** GROSE *Prov. Gloss.*, *Hitch*, to move or walk. *Norf.* **1837** CARLYLE *Fr. Rev.* I. v. v, Surely also Punishment, this day, hitches (if she still hitch) after Crime, with frightful shoes-of-swiftness! **1868** ATKINSON *Cleveland Gloss.*, *Hitch*, to move a short distance in any direction; to hop. **1874** MRS. WHITNEY *We Girls* x. 214 She began to hitch along; for walk she wouldn't, and she didn't.

b. = HITCH-HIKE *v.* Also *trans.*, ***to hitch a lift***, etc.: to obtain a lift in a vehicle.

1931 'B. STARKE' *Touch & Go* ix. 133 She told me she had hitched her way down to New Orleans a week before. *Ibid.* xii. 192 Two lads spoke to me, and asked if I were hitching it by myself. **1948** PARTRIDGE *Dict. Forces' Slang* 94 Hitch a lift, or ride. **1959** 'G. CARR' *Swing Away, Climber* i. 17 We hitched—got lifts, you know—from Birmingham. **1960** *Sunday Express* 6 Nov. 7/5 The car in which he had hitched a lift crashed into a lorry. **1963** *Guardian* 4 Feb. 6/5 They hitch there and back.

II. To fasten by something that catches.

5. a. *trans.* To catch as with a loop, noose, or hook; to fasten, esp. in a temporary way (and against force acting in one direction). Also *fig.*

1627 CAPT. SMITH *Seaman's Gram.* vii. 30 Hitch, is to catch hold of any thing with a rope to hold it fast, or with a hooke, as hitch the fish-hooke to the Anchors flooke, or the Tackles into the Garnets of the Slings. **1726** LEONI *Alberti's Archit.* II. 14/1 Little knobs.. against which the ropes were hitched, to prevent their slipping. **1806–7** J. BERESFORD *Miseries Hum. Life* (1826) III. xxxiii, Hitching your knife in the gritty flaws of a black-lead pencil. **1824** MISS MITFORD *Village* Ser. I. (1863) 75 Hitching our shawls in a bramble. **1835** W. IRVING *Tour Prairies* xix. 162 The hunter.. hitches the running noose of the lariat over his [the wild horse's] head by means of the forked stick. **1844** *Regul. & Ord. Army* 351 The tackle is to be hitched on, and the horse run up quickly. **1852** OWEN *Invertebr. Anim.* xiv. (1855) 303 Sometimes the crab hitches one of its claws into some crack or fissure. **1864** RUSKIN *Arrows of Chace* (1880) I. 262 A stone under a glacier may be hitched or suspended in the ice itself for long spaces. **1870** GORDON *Bush Ball., Wolf & Hound* 35, I hitched my mare to a tree. **1872** ELLACOMBE *Ch. Bells Devon, Bells Ch.* ii. 217 Bells are sometimes chimed by

..hitching the rope round the flight or tail of the clapper. **1893** Q. [Couch] *Delect. Duchy* 286 He..hitched this hat upon a peg in the wall.

b. *fig.* To catch, arrest (attention, etc.). *rare.*

a **1764** Lloyd *Ruff. Poet* Wks. 1774 I. 171 As gaudy signs, which hang before The tavern or the alehouse door, Hitch every passer's observation. **1822** Hazlitt *Table-t.* Ser. II. xvi. (1869) 317 As if the mind were equally hitched in difficulties and distracted with doubts.

c. with *up*: To harness, yoke; *absol.* 'To harness a horse to a vehicle, make ready for driving' (*Cent. Dict.*). *U.S.* So ***hitch to.*** *Austral.*

1870 Emerson *Soc. & Solit., Civiliz.* ii. Wks. (Bohn) III. 11 Now that is the wisdom of a man..to hitch his waggon to a star. **1870** E. E. Hale *Ten Times One* iv. (Cent.), He would hitch up at once and drive over to Elyria. **1880** Earl Dunraven in *19th Cent.* Oct. 606 There was nothing for us to do but hitch up our teams and drive back to settlements. **1890** Boldrewood *Col. Reformer* (1891) 127 The three leaders was hitched to, and away we went.

d. ***to hitch horses together***, also short, ***to hitch***: to agree, get on well together, act in harmony. *U.S. colloq.*

1837–40 Haliburton *Clockm.* (1862) 117 They [man and wife] don't hitch their horses together well at all. **1842** Mrs. Clavers *Forest Life* I. 116 (Bartlett), I..have come to drive a spell for this old fellow, but I guess we shan't hitch long. *a* **1860** *McClintock Tales* (Bartlett), After he poked his fist in my face, one election, we never hitched horses together. **1862** Lowell *Biglow P.* Poems 1890 II. 283 An' so we fin'lly made it up, concluded to hitch horses.

e. *pass.* To be yoked; *fig.* to be married. *U.S.* Also ***to get hitched up***, to be married, to become married (chiefly *dial.* and *N.Z.*).

1857 Holland *Bay Path* xv. 172 Now and then a feller gets hitched to a hedge-hog [of a wife]. **1862** A. Ward *His Bk.* x, If you mean gettin hitched, I'm in! **1890** S. S. Buckman *John Darke's Sojourn in Cotteswolds* xxii, 'Twarn't long avor we got hitched up together. **1911** 'Kiwi' *On Swag* vii. 14 Elsie and I got 'hitched up'. **1944** J. H. Fullarton *Troop Target* iii. 24 That's the fifth o the old gang to get hitched up in five months.

6. *intr.* To become fastened or caught, esp. by hooking on; to be caught or stopped by some obstruction; to catch on something. Also fig.

1578 Lyte *Dodoens* IV. xxx. 487 The leaues..ende with clasping tendrelles, whereby it hitcheth fast and taketh sure hold. **1633** T. James *Voy.* 25 The Anker hitcht againe, and upon the chopping of a Sea, threw the men from the Capstang. **1793** Smeaton *Edystone L.* §167 *note*, We have had instances of the boat's gunnel hitching under a stone in the tackle. **1855** W. Irving *Tour Prairies* xx, The lariat hitched on one of his ears, and he shook it off. **1897** Mary Kingsley *W. Africa* 583 My descent being arrested by a collection of brush brushwood and rubbish..which had hitched far down in the shaft.

fig. **1781** Cowper *Conversation* 108 Set your opinion at whatever pitch, Knots and impediments make something hitch. **1828** Scott *Jrnl.* 18 Feb., Despatched all my sheriff processes, save one, which hitches for want of some papers. **1864** Bagehot in *Nat. Rev.* Nov. 31 Their traits were indistinct; we forgot them, for they hitched on to nothing, and we could not classify them. **1891** *Newcastle Daily Jrnl.* 23 Mar. 5/4 They want marriage..to be dissolved when one party tires of the other or desires to hitch on elsewhere.

7. Of a horse: To strike the feet together in going; to interfere. (Perh. related to 4. Cf. hitch *sb.* 3.)

1686 *Lond. Gaz.* No. 2128/4 Stolen..A brown Gelding..all his paces, and hitches a little in his pace. **1706** Phillips (ed. Kersey), *To Hitch*,..to knock the Legs in going as a Horse does.

Hence **hitching** *vbl. sb.* (also *attrib.* as in ***hitching-bar, -clamp, -post, -strap, -weight***, i.e. one used in tethering a horse); **hitching** *ppl. a.*

c **1440** *Promp. Parv.* 239/2 Hytchinge, or remevynge (*v.rr.* hichynge, hyhchynge), *amocio, remocio.* **1678** Bunyan *Welcome to Jesus* in *Pilgr.* (Virtue) 379 The desire of his mind is not to be judged by the slow pace of the dull beast he rides, as by his hitching, kicking, and spurring. **1832** *Examiner* 790/1 Nothing lets down a smart hit so lamentably as a hitching verse or hobbling rhyme. **1842** J. L. Scott *Jrnl. Missionary Tour Pennsylvania* (1843) vi. 68 When at the door they alighted, and he rode off to the '*hitching post*'. **1852** C. A. Bristed *Upper Ten Thousand* 67 [He] pulled a hitching-strap from under the seat, and fastened his off-horse very neatly to a lamp-post. **1871** Mrs. Stowe *Old Town Fireside Stories* 84 All the hitchin'-posts was full clean up to the tavern. **1882** Nares *Seamanship* (ed. 6) 130 The sail is..laced to the yard with hitching turns. **1884** *Harper's Mag.* Dec. 96/2 Every available hitching-post [for horses] in sight was taken. **1884** W. D. Howells *Silas Lapham* xviii. 336 He got the hitching-weight from under the buggy seat and made it fast to the mare's bit. **1920** J. Gregory *Man to Man* ix. 103 A dozen saddle-horses were tied at the hitching-rail. **1926** J. Black *You can't Win* ix. 108, I..limped outside where I had an old ' swift' tied to a hitching rack. **1963** *Guardian* 4 Feb. 6/3 At weekends hitching..is widely practised. **1963** J. N. Harris *Weird World Wes Beattie* (1964) xviii. 216 'Oh, Gargoyle, darling,' she said, sitting down on an old hitching block at the edge of the Rosedale pavement, 'isn't it too gorgeous?'

hitch (hɪtʃ), *sb.* [f. prec. vb.]

1. a. A sort abrupt movement, pull, or push; a jerk.

1674 N. Fairfax *Bulk & Selv.* 122 Some minute or minutes more to bear on towards a second hitch. **1835** Marryat *Jac. Faithf.* xii, Ben..gives his trousers one hitch, and calls for a quartern. **1847** Ansted *Anc. World* xvi. 401 One more great movement of elevation..acting by successive and repeated hitches, each of small amount. **1862** Carlyle *Fredk. Gt.* IX. xi. III. 186 Noailles..manœuvres him, hitch after hitch, out of Italy.

b. *colloq.* A little lift or push up; 'temporary assistance; help through a difficulty' (Ogilvie).

c. A catch in or a turn at wrestling.

1834 H. M. Brackenridge *Recoll.* ix. 94 I'll stan iny mon a hitch in Butler county, if so be he'll clear me o' the la'. **1880** *Harper's Mag.* Mar. 525 How with 'ducking' heads and muffled screams you..saw them scrambling for a 'hitch'.

2. *Mining.* A slight fault or dislocation of strata.

1708 J. C. *Compl. Collier* (1845) 39 Sometimes a Pit may happen to haue a Hitch or Dipping of the Thill or Bottom of the way. **1789** Brand *Hist. Newcastle* II. 679 *note*, A hitch is only a dike or fissure of a smaller degree. **1837** *Penny Cycl.* VII. 283/1 The dykes, if not large, are locally called troubles, slips, or hitches.

3. A limp, a hobble; an interference in a horse's pace. Cf. hitch *v.* 7.

1664 Etheredge *Com. Rev.* I. iii, I will as soon undertake to reclaim a horse from a hitch he has learned in his pace. **1682** *Lond. Gaz.* No. 1748/4 A bay Mare..and hath a hitch in her Pace. **1704** Steele *Lying Lover* I. i, With a pert Jirk forward, and little Hitch in my Gate like a Scholastick Beau. **1750** Chesterf. *Lett.* (1774) III. 42 There is still a considerable hitch or hobble in your enunciation.

4. a. *dial.* The act of hopping; a hop: cf. hop *sb.*[2] 3.

1799 J. Jefferson *Let. to J. Boucher* 24 Jan. (MS.), I remember, when a boy, the playing at 'hitch, step and jump'. **1807** J. Stagg *Poems* 11 Hitch step an' loup some try'd.

b. = *hitch-hike* sb. *colloq.*

1955 *Times* 27 Aug. 7/4 They are not asked in the middle of doing 200 miles in four hours for a half-mile 'hitch'. **1966** J. Philips *Wings of Madness* (1967) II. iv. 132, I came down by bus. I thought maybe you'd give me a hitch back.

5. a. The action of catching or fastening in a temporary way, as on a hook, etc.

1828 in Webster.

b. A mode of harnessing a horse or team; a vehicle with its horse or team. *U.S.*

1876 *Rep. Vermont Board Agric.* III. 143 If he can go best in one kind of a hitch, and, in that hitch, make the best time ever made by any horse. **1898** *Christian Herald* (N.Y.) 2 Mar. 167/2 Several hitches are a mule and steer together. **1905** *Springfield* (Mass.) *Weekly Republ.* 22 Sept. 12 There were also several other creditable displays, both single and double hitches. **1912** Mulford & Clay *Buck Peters* xxii. 201, I want a hitch of some kind,..something with speed and bottom, and the sooner the better.

6. a. A contrivance for fastening something, a catch.

1881 Raymond *Mining Gloss., Hitch*..2. A hole cut in the side-rock, when this is solid enough, to hold the cap of a set of timbers, permitting the leg to be dispensed with.

b. (Chiefly *Naut.*) Applied to a noose or knot of various kinds, by which a rope is caught round or temporarily made fast to some object. See clove-hitch, diamond *hitch*, half-hitch, etc.

1769 [see clove-hitch]. **1832** Marryat *N. Forster* xiii, The monkey of a boy who made her fast..had made a '*slippery hitch*', so away we went. *c* **1860** H. Stuart *Seaman's Catech.* 1 What is an admiralty hitch used for? For setting up lower rigging, or heaving turns taut with a marling spike. **1867** F. Francis *Angling* ii. (1880) 65 The float..is fastened on with two half hitches. **1888** *Century Mag.* XXXVI. 202/2 An expert packer, versed in the mysteries of the 'diamond hitch', the only arrangement of the ropes that will insure a load staying in its place. **1894** Phillipps-Wolley *Gold in Cariboo* 61 The diamond hitch had no mysteries for him, the loops flew out and settled to an inch where he wanted them to.

7. *fig.* An accidental or temporary stoppage, such as is caused by something suddenly getting caught or entangled; an impediment, obstruction.

1748 H. Walpole *Lett. H. Mann* (1834) II. clxxxvii. 229 There seems to be some hitch in Legge's Embassy. I believe we were overhasty. **1794** Ld. Malmesbury in *14th Rep. Hist. MSS. Comm.* App. v. 577 There was some hitch in the execution of our treaty. **1821** J. W. Croker *Diary* 3 June in *C. Papers* (1884), There may be some hitch in the arrangement. **1872** Bagehot *Physics & Pol.* (1876) 172 When any hitch has arisen in the moral system of the human world. **1885** *Manch. Exam.* 15 May 5/3 A hitch has occurred in regard to the Afghan boundary arrangement.

8. A period of service, e.g. in the armed forces. Chiefly *U.S. slang.*

1835 *Novascotian* (Halifax) 12 Nov. 332/2 At last he said, which way are you from, Mr. Slick, this hitch. **1913** *Army & Navy Jrnl. Philippines* 4 Oct. 15/1, I had to go or else re-up For seven long years hitch. **1955** C. S. Forester *Good Shepherd* 24 He was new to the ship, a transfer made when they were in Reykjavik, serving his second hitch. **1957** J. Kerouac *On Road* (1958) 257 Another hitch in prison and you'll be put away for life. **1959** *Listener* 15 Oct. 607/1 Newspapermen who did a hitch in Britain during the war. **1973** *Washington Post* 13 Jan. A3/2 In his work in intelligence, Pounder had many assignments, including a hitch as part of the White House security detail during President John F. Kennedy's Ireland trip.

9. *Comb.*: **hitch and kick, hitch-kick**, a form of high-kicking or long-jumping; **hitch-knot** = sense 6 b.

1898 *N.Y. Tribune* 6 Sept. 9/4 Michael Sweeney, the well-known jumper, broke a world's record in the hitch-and-kick by one inch. **1931** F. A. M. Webster *Athletes in Action* 155 Numerous men using the 'hitch-kick', or 'mid-air-running' style, have beaten 25 ft. **1957** Duncan & Bone *Oxf. Pkt. Bk. Athletic Training* (ed. 2) 71 Do not spend time on learning the hitchkick at the expense of developing speed, etc. **1847** T. Stoddart *Angler's Comp.* 69 In making large fly-hooks..I bring down the thread and fasten it, with a simple hitch-knot.

hitch-, in combs. = *hitching* vbl. sb. (see hitch *v.*). *U.S.*

1899 Ade *Doc. Horne* i. 7, I jumped off my horse and threw him one end of my hitch-rein and pulled him out. **1903** A. Adams *Log of Cowboy* xxi. 138 Tying our horses in a group to a hitch-rack in the rear of a saloon. **1906** H. D. Pittman *Belle of Bluegrass C.* xiii. 187 A slim-legged yellow girl..swinging by her arms from a hitch rail. **1922** *Blackw. Mag.* June 714/1 It needs many a coat of paint, clean, and hitch-up. **1935** C. Day Lewis *Time to Dance* 61 A coast-to-coast hitch-up. **1954** *Encounter* Oct. 3/1 The hitch-rail enclosing the county court-house.

Hitchcock (ˈhɪtʃkɒk). The name of L. H. *Hitchcock* (1795–1852) used *attrib.* to designate any one of various chairs made by him or produced in his chair factory at Barkhamsted, Conn.

c **1828** in M. R. Moore *Hitchcock Chairs* (1933) 5 Hitchcock chairs,..flag and wooden seats, warranted well manufactured. **1933** M. R. Moore *Ibid.* 3 The first Hitchcock chairs probably had the rush seat, but very soon were added the cane and solid wood seats. **1959** L. Boger *Compl. Guide Furnit. Styles* xxii. 373 The name Hitchcock is given to a particular type of painted American Empire open back chair. **1967** *Boston Sunday Herald* 30 Apr. I. 23/1 (Advt.), The charm of genuine Hitchcock Colonial chairs.

hitchcock, var. of hickock *Obs.*, hiccup.

hitchel, obs. and dial. form of hatchel.

hitcher (ˈhɪtʃə(r)), *sb.* [f. hitch *v.* + -er[1].] One who or that which hitches.

1. A hook for catching hold; a boat-hook.

1630 J. Taylor (Water P.) *Wks.* I. 64/2 One of them tooke a Hitcher or long Boate-hooke, and hitched in the sicke mans Breeches, drawing him backward. **1727** *Philip Quarll* (1816) 6 Having taken the hitcher of the boat, he groped along for sure footing. **1857** P. Colquhoun *Comp. Oarsman's Guide* 17 The boat should be brought in by the hitcher.

2. *Coal-mining.* A 'hanger-on'. (See quot. 1891.)

1890 *Daily News* 7 Feb. 5/6 It has surprised everybody to find that John Beard, the hitcher in the pit, should have escaped so marvellously. **1891** *Labour Commission* Gloss., *Hitchers*, the men who put the trams of coal on the carriage at the pit bottom.

3. One who hitch-hikes.

1960 *20th Cent.* Nov. 476 Do you often pick up hitchers? **1972** R. Quilty *Tenth Session* 19 When the road seemed to stretch endlessly..Bill always felt he was doing the company a service by picking up a hitcher. **1973** *Daily Colonist* (Victoria, B.C.) 1 July 4/2 The film company..advertised for hitchers to tell their stories of experiences good and bad.

hitch-hike (ˈhɪtʃhaɪk), *v.* orig. *U.S.* Also **hitchhike.** [f. hitch *v.* + hike *v.*] *intr.* To travel by means of lifts in vehicles. Also *fig.* Hence as *sb.*, such a journey. Also **ˈhitch-hiker**, one who hitch-hikes; **ˈhitch-hiking** *vbl. sb.*

1923 *Nation* 19 Sept. 297/2 Hitch-hiking is always done by twos and threes. **1927** *New Masses* June 15/1 Most young janes have their heads full of a trip to Paris, or a hitch-hike thru New England. **1927** *Glasgow Herald* 6 Sept. 10 There are apparently hitchhikers in the United States who boast they can travel 500 miles free of charge without walking more than 10. **1931** 'B. Starke' *Touch & Go* iv. 58, I..wondered how Dot would ever dare..tell the people there that she had hitch-hiked home. *Ibid.* 64 We may charge this wicked hitch-hiker the ten cents extra that she deserves for asking for a bath towel. **1940** A. Christie *Buckle my Shoe* 182 He told amusing stories of his hitch-hikes and tramps in wild places. **1941** Auden *New Year Let.* 68 Kids When their imagination bids Hitch-hike a thousand miles to find The Hesperides that's on their mind. **1945** *Daily Mirror* 27 Sept., Hitch-hiking by air from London to Manila, five British Red Cross welfare sisters arrived in Canberra, Australia. **1958** *Manch. Guardian* 26 Sept. 4/4 He decided to hitch-hike around the world. **1959** *Times* 1 Oct. 9/6 Hitch-hiking appears to have replaced old-fashioned walking and has obviously graduated into a recognized pursuit, ready perhaps to be nurtured and protected by an international organization empowered to negotiate with transport ministers and police chiefs. **1973** *Black World* Apr. 80/1 Walton sees the need for people to realize their own cultural heritage and not hitchhike on somebody else's.

ˈhitchlessly, *adv.* [hitch *sb.* 7.] Without a hitch.

1910 W. de la Mare *Private View* (1953) 26 Stealthily and hitchlessly the scenes clear, brighten, fade, and close. **1958** W. Stark *Sociology of Knowledge* viii. 325 It is thought which works in 'hitchlessly', as the Americans would say, with the established social pattern.

ˈhitch-pin. [f. hitch *v.* + pin.] In a pianoforte, The pin to which each string is attached at its fixed end, opposite to the *tuning-* or *wrest-pin.* Also *attrib.*, as ***hitchpin-block.***

1878 A. J. Hipkins in Grove *Dict. Mus.* I. 468 A hitchpin-block for the attachment of the other ends of the strings. **1881** *Ibid.* III. 194 The merit of Hans Ruckers..was his..boldly attaching the strings to hitchpins on the soundboard.

hitchy (ˈhɪtʃɪ), *a. rare.* [f. hitch *sb.* or *v.* + -y.] Characterized by hitches or hitching; jerky. Hence **hitchily** *adv.*, **hitchiness.**

1872 Howells *Wedd. Journ.* (1884) 46 Things go more hitchily the first year than ever they do afterwards. *Ibid.* 47 The great object is not to have any hitchiness.

hite: see HIGHT *v.*

hithe, hythe (haɪð). [OE. *hýð* fem.:—OTeut. type *hûþjâ-: not found in any of the other Teut. langs.] A port or haven; *esp.* a small haven or landing-place on a river. Now obsolete except in historical use, and in place-names, as *Hythe*, *Rotherhithe*, *Lambeth* (orig. *Lamb-hithe*), *Hythe Bridge* at Oxford, *Bablock Hithe* on the Thames above Oxford.

c **725** *Corpus Gloss.* 643 *Deconfugione, statione*, hyðae. *a* **1000** *Boeth. Metr.* xxi. 13 (Gr.) þæt is sio an hyð. *a* **1000** *Prose Life St. Guthlac* xi. (1848) 54 Comon þær þry men to þære hyðe. *c* **1000** *Ags. Ps.* cvi. 29 [cvii. 30] And he hi on hælo hyþe ȝelædde. *c* **1440** *Promp. Parv.* 242/1 Hyþe, where bootys ryve to londe, or stonde, *stacio.* **1538** BALE *Thre Lawes* 1345 In an oyster bote, a little beyonde quene hythe. **1723** *Banff Burgh Rec.* in Cramond *Ann. Banff* (1893) II. 219 [The shipmasters crave] ane further reparation to be made one Gutherie's Hyth. **1790** PENNANT *London* 473 (R.) When the hithe fell into the hands of King Stephen, he bestowed it on William de Ypres. **1853** M. ARNOLD *Scholar-Gipsy* viii. Crossing the stripling Thames at Bablock-hithe. **1886** WILLIS & CLARK *Cambridge* I. Introd. 11 The different hythes or landing-places along the river-bank. **1897** F. W. MAITLAND *Domesday & beyond* 189 Hythes outside the walls.

hiþen, var. HETHEN *adv. Obs.*, hence.

hither ('hɪðə(r)), *adv.* and *a.* Forms: α. 1–5 hider, 3–6 hyder, 4 huder, 4–5 hidir, -ur, 5 hydir, -ur, -yr, 4–6 hidder, -ir, hydder, -ir, -yr; 4 hiþer, 5–6 hyther, 5– hither. β. 3 hidere, 4–5 hidre. γ. 4–5 heder, -ir(e, -ur, -yr, 6 hedder; 4 heþer, 4–5 hethir, 5–7 hether. [OE. *hider* corresp. to ON. *heðra*, Goth. *hidrê*; f. demonstr. stem *hi-* (see HE, HERE) + suffix appearing also in L. *ci-trā* on this side. Not known in WGer. exc. in OE.; but it has been suggested that OS. *herod*, OHG. *herot*, in same sense, are of similar origin. For the later change of *d* to *th* (ð), cf. note to FATHER.] **A.** *adv.*

1. With verbs of motion (or cognate nouns): To or towards this place. (Now only literary; in ordinary speech supplanted by HERE q.v., sense 7).

c **725** *Corpus Gl.* 1158 *Istuc*, hider. *c* **825** *Vesp. Ps.* lxxii. 10. *c* **1000** ÆLFRIC *Gram.* xxxviii. (Z.) 223 *Huc*, hider. *a* **1123** *O.E. Chron.* an. 1101 þe mid unfriðe hider to lande fundode. *c* **1205** LAY. 26733 We beoð hidere [*c* **1275** hider] icumen. *a* **1300** *Cursor M.* 10315 Nu am i hidir to þe send. **1388** WYCLIF *John* xx. 27 Putte hider thin hond. *c* **1440** *Generydes* 168 Of my comyng heder. *c* **1450** *Merlin* 39 Bringe hethir the clerkes. **1550** CROWLEY *Last Trump.* 93 Come hither unto me. **1600** SHAKS. *A. Y. L.* II. v. 5 Vnder the greene wood tree, who loues to lye with mee.. Come hither, come hither, come hither. **1671** MILTON *Samson* 1445 My inducement hither. **1766** GRAY in *Corr. w. Nicholls* (1843) 63 Till my return hither yesterday. **1849** MACAULAY *Hist. Eng.* v. I. 557 Hither..came news that the frigates had forced a passage.

†**b.** (Of the direction of feeling.) *Obs. rare.*

1579 J. STUBBES *Gaping Gulf* E vj, That false Scot prelate Rosse, mortall enemy hether.

†**c.** With redundant *to* or *unto* (north. *till*). (Cf. *from hence.*) *Obs.*

1340 HAMPOLE *Pr. Consc.* 7746 Swa many myle, Fra heven tylle hyder. **1382** WYCLIF *Job* xxxviii. 11 Vnto hider thou shalt come, and no ferthere gon.

2. To or on this side (*of*). *rare.*

1864 CARLYLE *Fredk. Gt.* XII. ix. IV. 209 At Steinberg.. some twenty miles hither of Olmütz.

†**3.** Up to this point (of time, or of discourse, etc.); till now, thus far, hitherto. Also with redundant *to* (north. *till*). *Obs.*

a **1300** *Cursor M.* 581 Now haf i sceud yow til hider [*Gött.* hiþer] how [etc.]. *c* **1400** MAUNDEV. (1839) v. 44 From that tyme hidre, the Sowdan clepethe him self Calyffee. **1466** EDW. IV. in *Paston Lett.* No. 552 II. 282 Sithen the Conquest hither. **1607** TOPSELL *Four-f. Beasts* (1658) 267 Hither of causes and sickness in general. Now it is also meet, that we speak..of signes whereby sickness is known.

†**4.** To this end, aim, or result; to this subject, class, or category; hereto. *Obs.*

1538 STARKEY *England* I. i. 7 Hyther tendyth al prudence and pollycy. **1561** DAUS tr. *Bullinger on Apoc.* Pref. (1573) 12 S. John hath hyther borrowed all his thinges out of the Scriptures..to.. confirme his writinges by the scripture. **1608** D. T. *Ess. Pol. & Mor.* 118 Hither may that speech.. be well referred. *a* **1694** TILLOTSON *Serm.* (1743) I. v. 137 Hither belong all those texts which [etc.].

5. Phr. **hither and thither**. To this place and that, in this direction and in that (alternately); to and fro; in various directions. [In OE.; also with gen. endings *hidres ðidres.*] So ***hither and yon*** (***yond***). *dial.* and *U.S.*

c **725** *Corpus Gl.* 2148 *Ultroque citroque*, hider ond ðider [*MS.* hider]. *c* **888** K. ÆLFRED *Boeth.* xl. §5 Ac ic ondræde þæt ic þe læde hidres þidres on þa paþas of þinum wege. *c* **897** —— *Gregory's Past.* ix. 59 Ðæt scip..Drifen hider and ðider. *c* **900** tr. *Bæda's Hist.* v. xiii. [xii.] (1890) 428 Da ahof ic mine eagan upp & locade hider & ȝeond. *a* **1300** *Cursor M.* 16001 þai iesus ledd.. Bath hider & þider. **1413** *Pilgr. Sowle* (Caxton) v. i. (1859) 69, I sawe hym..fle hyder and thyder. **1621** G. SANDYS *Ovid's Met.* xv. (1626) 308 Hether and thether still the Spirit strayes. **1787** GROSE *Prov. Gloss.*, *Hither and yon*, here and there, backwards and forwards. *North.* **1821** GALT *Sir A. Wylie* II. 20 (Jam.) Noo that they're hither and yont frae ane anither. **1871** R. H. HUTTON *Ess.* (1877) I. 34 A Power..that moves us hither and thither through the ordinary Courses of our lives.

B. *adj.* Situated on this side, or in this direction; the nearer (of two things, or ends or parts of something). Also *fig.* of time. [Cf. L. *citer, citerior.*]

1387 TREVISA *Higden* (Rolls) I. 299 þere beeþ tweye Spaynes; þe hyder bygynneþ from þe pleynes and valeys of Pireneies..þe ȝonder Spayne conteyneþ þe west partye. **1577–87** HOLINSHED *Chron.* III. 942/2 On this hither side of the riuer. **1667** MILTON *P.L.* III. 722 That Globe, whose hither side With light..reflected, shines. **1703** MOXON *Mech. Exerc.* 53 Lay..the Mold flat upon the hither end of the using File. **1850** MERIVALE *Rom. Emp.* (1865) II. xix. 382 In the wildest districts of the Hither Province. **1863** HAWTHORNE *Our Old Home* 177 On the hither bank a fisherman was washing his boat. **1871** EARLE *Philol. Eng. Tongue* v. 219 A widening divergence separates them at their hither end.

b. *sup.* **hitherest**: nearest. *Obs.* exc. *dial.*

1462 *Mann. & Househ. Exp.* (Roxb.) 562 My master brake his hederest ponde at Sprottes. And..lete nat owte alle the water. **1876** *Whitby Gloss.*, *Hitherest*, the nearest.

'hither, *v.* [Elliptical use of adv. = *come hither.*] *intr.* To move or come hither; chiefly in phr. ***to hither and thither*** = to go to and fro; to move about in various directions.

1856 MRS. CARLYLE *Lett.* II. 275 Mr. C. always hithers and thithers in a weary interminable way. **1864** CARLYLE *Fredk. Gt.* XVI. xi. IV. 436 Confused hithering and thithering. **1876** *Whitby Gloss.* s.v., They come hithering frae all parts. **18..** *New Mirror* (N.Y.) III. 96 (Cent.) An old black trunk—a companion to our hithering and thithering for seven long years.

†**'hithercome.** *Obs.* Forms: see HITHER. [OE. *hidercyme*, f. *hider* HITHER + *cyme* COME *sb.*] The action of coming hither; advent, arrival.

c **900** tr. *Bæda's Hist.* I. iv. (1890) 32 Ða wæs fram Cristes hidercyme hundteontiȝ and fiftiȝ and six ȝear. *c* **1200** *Trin. Coll. Hom.* 141 Hwu wunderlich was his hider-cume. **13..** *Guy Warw.* (A.) 6216 Hou come þou hider, sir Gij? þine hider-com wil me harm. *c* **1440** *Bone Flor.* 515 God, and seynt Petur of Rome, Ylde yow yowre hedur-come.

†**'hithermore**, *a. Obs.* [f. HITHER *adv.* or *a.* + MORE: cf. next.] = HITHER *a.*

1609 HOLLAND tr. *Amm. Marcell.* XVII. xiv. 99 They came, therefore..to the hithermore banke of the river. **1610** —— *Camden's Brit.* I. 525 In the hithermore or South part. *Ibid.* 642 The hithermore is called Tullie..the farthermore is named Barry.

'hithermost, *a.* ? *Obs.* [f. HITHER *adv.* or *a.* + -MOST: cf. *hindermost, nethermost, uttermost*, etc.] Situated most in this direction; nearest.

1563 GOLDING *Cæsar* 80 (R.) The cities of the hythermost part of Spain. **1677** HALE *Prim. Orig. Man.* I. vi. 124 The hithermost and concluding extreme. **1712** W. ROGERS *Voy.* App. 56 The hithermost of the Rocks. **1864** CARLYLE *Fredk. Gt.* XII. ix, At Steinberg, his hithermost post.

'hither'side, hither-side. [Properly two words, *hither side*: see HITHER *a.* Cf. *inside, outside.*] This side; the nearer side.

1587 FLEMING *Contn. Holinshed* III. 1967/2 Ouertaking them three miles on the hitherside of Hardilo sands. **1670** MILTON *Hist. Eng.* IV. Wks. (1851) 147 Ail on the hitherside Humber. **1703** MOXON *Mech. Exerc.* 31 The Hither-side of the Anvil. **1751** JOHNSON *Rambler* No. 105 ¶8 On the hitherside of the lunar world. **1876** GEO. ELIOT *Dan. Der.* IV. lii. 52 With a dubious wink on the hither-side of him.

†**hithertill, -tills**, *adv. Sc.* and *north. dial. Obs.* Forms: see HITHER. [f. HITHER *adv.* + TILL *prep.* *Hithertills* has the adverbial genitive, like *toward-s*] = HITHERTO.

α. *a* **1300** *Cursor M.* 3605 þou has hidir-till Gladli don þi fader will. *c* **1340** *Ibid.* 10281 (Laud.), I haue no child heþer-tylle. **1567** *Ps. li.* in *Gude & G. Ballatis* (S.T.S.) 129 Mont Syone..In thrall is hiddertill.

β. **1513** DOUGLAS *Æneis* V. xi. 1 Thus, hiddirtillis, warryne derenys seir Exercit in wirschep of his fadir deir. **1603** *Philotus* xlvi, Father hithertils I trow, ȝe haue nane vther seine. **1637–50** ROW *Hist. Kirk* (1842) 460 Who hithertills had graciously..provyded for him.

hitherto (hɪðə'tuː, 'hɪðətuː), *adv.* (*a.*) Forms: see HITHER. [f. HITHER *adv.* + TO *prep.*]

A. *adv.* **1.** Up to this time, until now, as yet.

a **1225** *Leg. Kath.* 447 Hwucche men þu hauest ihaued hiderto to meistres. *a* **1300** *Cursor M.* 4554, I haf soght.. both farr and nerr..Bot hider-to moght i noght spede. **1482** *Monk of Evesham* (Arb.) 24 Verely wele y was hedir to but now..verely euyl y am and fele my selfe. **1526** TINDALE *John* ii. 10 Thou hast kept backe the goode wyne hetherto. **1651** HOBBES *Leviath.* II. xviii. 93 Except the vulgar be better taught than they have hetherto been. **1769** ROBERTSON *Chas. V*, VII. (1805) III. 259 The veil under which he had hitherto concealed his real sentiments. **1861** M. PATTISON *Ess.* (1889) I. 46 Objects hitherto unknown to Europe.

†**2.** Up to this point (in discourse, writing, argument, etc.); thus far. *Obs.* (or merged in 1).

a **1225** *Ancr. R.* 48 þis is nu ðe uorme dole, þet ich habbe ispeken hiderto. **1382** WYCLIF *Jer.* xlix. 1 Hyderto the domes of Moab. **1483** CAXTON *Gold. Leg.* 159 b/2 Hyderto endure the wordes of the sayd Sermon. **1526** *Pilgr. Perf.* (W. de W. 1531) 143 Thus hytherto we haue shewed [etc.]. **1602** SHAKS. *Ham.* III. ii. 216 Hitherto doth Loue on Fortune tend. **1762** KAMES *Elem. Crit.* xviii. (1833) 278 Hitherto of arranging single words.

3. To this place or point in space; thus far. *arch.*

1535 COVERDALE *Job* xxxviii. 11 Hither to shalt thou come, but no further. **1596** SHAKS. *1 Hen. IV*, III. i. 74 England, from Trent, and Seuerne, hitherto, By South and East, is to my part assign'd. **1694** S. JOHNSON *Notes Past. Let. Bp. Burnet* I. 64 Hitherto shall ye come and no further.

†**4.** To this end or purpose; to this subject or division; hereto; = HITHER 4. *Obs.*

1637 POCKLINGTON *Sunday no Sabb.* 2 Hitherto, if I can but hold me by my text, I hope not to fall into impertinences. **1656** RIDGLEY *Pract. Physick* 253 Hitherto belongeth mad love.

B. quasi-*adj.* [attrib. use of adv.: cf. *then.*]

1787 MAD. D'ARBLAY *Diary* (1842) III. 303 All his hitherto offences. **1874** J. H. NEWMAN *Tracts Theol. & Eccl.* 365 The hitherto editions. **1883** GREEN *Proleg. Ethics* III. ii. 207 The hitherto experience of men.

†**hithertoward, -towards**, *adv. Obs.* or *dial.* [f. prec. + -WARD, -WARDS.] = HITHERTO.

a **1400–50** *Alexander* 3517 As I ȝit haue hediretoward heried all my faes. **1483** *Cath. Angl.* 185/2 Hydirtoward ..*hucusque.* **1514** in Burton & Raine *Hemingbrough* 381 The custume..of our Monasterie hethertowardis usyd. *a* **1825** FORBY *Voc. E. Anglia*, *Hithertoward*, towards this time, or place.

hitherun'to, -'unto, *adv. arch.* [f. HITHER + UNTO *prep.*] = HITHERTO.

1505 F. MARSIN, etc., in *Mem. Hen. VII* (1858) 235, I have served the said queen many years, being her grace a little child hitherunto. **1579–80** NORTH *Plutarch* (1676) 595, I hitherunto haue done nothing worthy of my self. **1625** GILL *Sacr. Philos.* xii. 184 Hitherunto tend those words. **1657** CROMWELL *Sp.* 21 Apr. in *Carlyle*, To consider the Providence of God, how He hath led us hitherunto.

hitherward ('hɪðəwəd), *adv. arch.* Forms: see HITHER. [OE. *hiderweard*, f. *hider* HITHER + *-weard* -WARD. (In OE. also *adj.*)]

1. Towards this place; in this direction; hither.

†**b.** ***hitherward and thitherward***: see HITHER 5.

a **1100** *O.E. Chron* (Laud MS.) an. 1085 Menn..sædan þæt Cnut cyng of Den-mearcan..fundade hider-ward, and wolde ȝe-winnan þis land. *c* **1205** LAY. 30780 þe an hine putte hiderward And þe oþer hine putte ȝeondward. **1297** R. GLOUC. (1724) 516 Vor the baronie Vor loue him broȝte hiderward. **1398** TREVISA *Barth. De P.R.* XVI. i. (1495) 552 That reeryth partyes therof hitherwarde and thytherwarde. *c* **1450** tr. *De Imitatione* I. xiii. 14 A ship wiþoute gouernaunce is stired hiderwarde & þiderwarde. **1593** SHAKS. *3 Hen. VI*, V. i. 3 Marching hitherward. **1667** MILTON *P.L.* IV. 794 Some infernal Spirit see Hitherward bent. **1709** *Lond. Gaz.* No. 4561/3 They..could discern five or six Sail more plying hitherward. **1860** HAWTHORNE *Marb. Faun* I. xvi, It flows hitherward through old subterranean aqueducts.

attrib. **1831** LYTTON *Godolph.* lxi, Their hitherward career.

2. On this side (*of*). Also *fig.*

1864 LOWELL *Fireside Trav.* 51 Submerging them to the hair's-breadth hitherward of the drowning-point. **1864** CARLYLE *Fredk. Gt.* XV. xii. IV. 181 Hitherward of Sohr.

†**3.** Up to this time; until now; hitherto. *Obs.*

1297 R. GLOUC. (1724) 150 For Gyneman was for þe Stonhenge hiderward ȝet wroþ. *c* **1330** R. BRUNNE *Chron.* (1810) 21 A grete Daneis felde..þat euer siþen hiderward Kampedene men kalle. *a* **1450** *Knt. de la Tour* (1868) 136 The mischeef that is befalle sin hedirwarde. **1513** MORE in Grafton *Chron.* (1568) II. 768 From that time hetherward.

'hitherwards, *adv. arch.* [f. as prec. + -WARDS.] = prec.

c **1200** *Trin. Coll. Hom.* 55 Siðe mid winter com hiderwardes. *c* **1400** MAUNDEV. (1839) xiv. 154 Fro that tyme hiderwardes. **1596** SHAKS. *1 Hen. IV*, IV. i. 89 The Earle of Westmoreland..Is marching hither-wards. *a* **1626** BP. ANDREWES in Spurgeon *Treas. Dav.* Ps. lxxxv. 10 It is told here..that she [righteousness] but looked down hitherwards from heaven. **1896** SIR T. MARTIN *Virg. Æneid* VI. 236 'Twas thy sad image, That drove me hitherwards to make my way.

hithte, obs. form of HEIGHT.

Hitler ('hɪtlɛ(r)). [Name of Adolf *Hitler* (1889–1945), chancellor of the German Reich and leader of the National Socialist (NAZI) Party in Germany.] One who embodies the characteristics of Hitler; a dictatorial person. Also used in the possessive to designate the war of 1939–45; also *attrib.* and *Comb.*

1930 *Times* 27 Sept 10/1 The action of the Court was hailed in the Hitler camp as a great tactical success. **1931** WYNDHAM LEWIS *Hitler* I. i. 8 The Hitler Movement.. received so much advertisement in the English Press. **1932** *Times* 26 Mar. 9/5 General Groener has forbidden a rally of the Hitler Youth. **1934** E. WAUGH in *Ninety-Two Days* ii. 49 He was comic; huge feet and hands, huge mouth, and an absurd little Hitler moustache. **1934** J. SPENSER *Limey breaks In* v. 82 Sparkes wanted to be the Hitler of that kitchen. **1935** *Economist* 29 June 1478/1 Refusing to give the Hitler salute in his lecture-room. **1936** WODEHOUSE *Laughing Gas* xxiv. 257 The Hitlers and Mussolinis of the picture world. **1937** *Ann. Reg. 1936* II. 184 Membership of the Hitler Youth Movement became compulsory for all the young people of the country. **1939** *War Illustr.* 14 Oct. 138/3 Millions of leaflets warning the German people of the deadly consequences of 'Hitler's war' if it were prolonged. **1940** *Ibid.* 5 Jan. 574/3 This has been given public expression by Dr. Robert Ley..addressing the Hitler Youth. **1940** M. P. PRICE (*title*) Hitler's war and eastern Europe. **1962** J. MAYO *Season of Nerves* iv. 12 A tiny chin and a sandy Hitler moustache. **1963** N. FREELING *Because of Cats* vii. 108 The building..looks like nothing more than a Hitler-bunker. **1966** *Economist* 15 Oct. p. xii/1 The brief crop of 'Hitler babies', born in the 1930s..would soon be reaching working age—and the prospect was alarming.

So **Hitle'resque, Hitlerian** (-'lɪər-), **'Hitlerish** *adjs.*, of, pertaining to, characteristic of, or

(somewhat) resembling Hitler; **Hitleri'ana**, objects, etc., owned by or connected with Hitler; **'Hitlerism**, the political principles or policy of the Nazi party in Germany; **'Hitlerist**, **'Hitlerite**, a follower of Hitler; also (both words) *attrib.* or as *adj.*; **Hitle'ristic** *a.*; **'Hitlerize** *v.*, to make subject to Hitler, to make Hitlerite.

1930 *Times* 26 Sept. 13/2 These Hitlerite outbursts may disturb German Liberals and Socialists. *Ibid.* 27 Sept. 11/3 The most effective antidote to Hitlerism. **1930** *New Statesman* 1 Nov. 106/1 One may magnify or minimise the role of the Hitlerites, but [etc.]. **1931** WYNDHAM LEWIS *Hitler* 4 An exponent..of German National Socialism, or Hitlerism. *Ibid.* 32 The militant nationalism of the Hitlerist. **1931** *Times Lit. Suppl.* 16 Apr. 296/2 Hitlerite anti-Semitism. **1933** *Business Week* 24 May 23/1 (*heading*) Hitlerizing industry. **1934** A. HUXLEY *Beyond Mexique Bay* 113 Dislike and fear of Hitlerian Germany. **1935** N. MARSH *Enter Murderer* iv. 55 Sorry to be a bit Hitlerish, but it'll save time. **1940** *Ann. Reg.* *1939* 90 The cause they had undertaken till Hitlerism had been destroyed and a liberated Europe re-established. **1941** *Common Sense* (N.Y.) Jan. 30/1 For the Hitleristic reason of grabbing everything in sight. **1943** *Times* 27 Apr. 5/3 The inherent instability of its Hitlerized Europe publicly exposed by the defection of one of the members. **1944** J. S. HUXLEY *On Living in Revol.* xii. 131 In a totalitarian, Hitlerian way, or in a democratic, co-operative way. **1944** G. B. SHAW *Everybody's Political What's What?* xlii. 352 Political ignorance and idolatry will produce not only Hitleresque dictatorships but stampedes led by liars or lunatics. **1960** *News Chron.* 9 June 1/2 Mass crimes committed by Hitlerite agents. **1966** *New Statesman* 17 June 874/3 The collection of Hitleriana is small but fascinating. **1969** *Daily Tel.* (Colour Suppl.) 14 Feb. 12/3 The German ethos that produced Hitlerism. **1973** *Daily Tel.* 24 Apr. 18 Both men and women could be..detained indefinitely, without charge and without trial, during the Hitlerian war.

hittable ('hɪtəb(ə)l), *a.* [f. HIT *v.* + -ABLE.] Capable of being hit.

Mod. Cricket-Match Report, He lays on the wood with power when a hittable ball comes his way.

hitter ('hɪtə(r)). [f. HIT *v.* + -ER[1].] One who hits or strikes, as in boxing, cricket, etc. Also *fig.*

1813 *Sporting Mag.* XLI. 33 The advantage of being the more effective hitter. **1824** MISS MITFORD *Village* Ser. I. (1863) 172 Your blacksmiths are capital hitters. **1884** *Times* (weekly ed.) 7 Nov. 8/4 Writers..equally remarkable as 'good haters' and 'hard hitters'.

hitter, -ur, var. HETER *a. Obs.*, rough, fierce.

hitting ('hɪtɪŋ), *vbl. sb.* [f. HIT *v.* + -ING[1].] The action of HIT *v.* in various senses; striking, impact, collision; also *fig.*

c **1440** *Promp. Parv.* 242/1 Hyttynge, or towchynge, *tactus.* **1687** A. LOVELL tr. *Thevenot's Trav.* I. 283 There was no hitting of them. *a* **1742** BENTLEY *Serm.* ii. (R.), 'Tis the hitting and collision of them that must make them strike fire. **1891** J. MORLEY in *Daily News* 27 Oct. 6/3 A hitting below the belt, for which I will venture to say you won't find a parallel in the worst times of our political history.

hitting, *ppl. a.* That hits or strikes; striking (*lit.* and *fig.*).

1632 SHERWOOD, Violent hitting, *heurtant.* **1691** tr. *Emilianne's Frauds Romish Monks* 148 It was not any hitting or pinching Raillery. **1861** READE *Cloister & H.* I. 292 Men will shoot at their enemies with the hittingest arm.

hittique, obs. form of HECTIC.

1614 MARKHAM *Cheap Husb.* I. viii. (1668) 48 The Quartan, the Continual, the Hittique.

Hittite ('hɪtaɪt), *sb.* and *a.* [f. Heb. *Ḥitt(īm*, Hittite *Ḥatti* + -ITE[1]. The form *Hittite* occurs first in the Geneva version, 1560, of the Bible. The LXX has *Χέτταιοι* (identified as children of Heth (*Χέτ*), Heb. *benê Ḥêth*), the Vulgate *Hethæi*, whence *Ethei* in the Wycliffite versions, G. *Hethiter* (Luther), Eng. *Hethite* (Coverdale, etc.), F. *Héthéen*.] **A.** *sb.* **a.** In the Bible (Gen. xv. 20, etc.), one of a Canaanitic or Syrian tribe of greater or less extent, perh. an offshoot of the next. **b.** In modern archæology and philology, a member of a powerful and widespread ancient (non-Semitic) people, variously named *Khita* or *Kheta* in Egyptian, and *Khatti*, *Ḥatti* (see HATTIC *a.*) in Hittite and Assyrian, whose history can be traced from *c* 1900 to 700 B.C. in Asia Minor and northern Syria, or a member of a people conquered by the Hittite empire. **c.** The Indo-European language (written in cuneiform and hieroglyphs) of this people. **B.** *adj.* Of or pertaining to this people or their language.

1608 TOPSELL *Hist. Serpents* 93 Most fierce & cruell enemies, which should put & cast forth the Cananites, Hettites, and Cheuits. **1614** RALEIGH *Hist. World* I. viii. 162 The second sonne of Canaan was Heth or Cethus: of whom came the Hethites, or Hittites. **1871** tr. *Ewald's Hist. Israel* III. 262 Among the petty Hittite (i.e. generally Canaanite), and Aramean kings. **1879** *Academy* 16 Aug. 124/1 The sculpture accompanied by inscriptions in Hittite (or Hamathite) characters..discovered at Ibreez in Lycaonia..proves that the Hittites had penetrated through the eastern barrier of Asia Minor formed by the Taurus range. **1880** *Encycl. Brit.* XI. 808/2 The discovery of a new hieroglyphic character in the Hittite inscriptions. *Ibid.* XII. 26/2 Our knowledge of the Hittite language is confined to the proper names mentioned in the Egyptian and Assyrian inscriptions. **1880** [see HATTIC *a.*]. **1884** W. WRIGHT *Empire of Hittites* iv. 56 There can be little doubt that the Lycaonian *patois*, which continued to be the vernacular of the people till the days of Paul, was Hittite. **1884** A. H. SAYCE *Ibid.* xi. 170 The bilingual inscription of Tarkondêmos in cuneiform and Hittite. **1920** A. E. COWLEY *Hittites* i. 1 Until forty years ago, or less, the Hittites were still grouped with Hivites and Jebusites as an insignificant Syrian tribe unknown outside the Bible. **1926** *Year's Work in Eng. Stud.* *1924* 38 We have in Hittite..the earliest Indo-European language recorded. **1952** O. R. GURNEY *Hittites* vi. 130 The original home of Hieroglyphic Hittite seems on present evidence most likely to have been Kizzuwatna [1961 ed., Cilicia]. **1962** *Times* 31 Oct. 14/6 Stone stairway flanked by modern but Hittite-type lions. **1972** C. RAPHAEL *Feast of History* i. 15 All the peoples—Amorites, Moabites, Hittites, Horites, and of course the familiar Philistines..with whom the Hebrews dealt constantly in the Old Testament.

So **Hitti'tology**, the study of Hittite philology, archæology, or history; **Hitti'tologist**.

1948 D. DIRINGER *Alphabet* I. v. 89 Some Hittitologists accept the term *Nashili.* **1952** O. R. GURNEY *Hittites* 8 There developed an entirely German science of Hittitology devoted to the study of the cuneiform tablets. **1964** *Language* XL. 149, I am not a Hittitologist.

Hittorf ('hɪtɔːf). The name of Johann Wilhelm *Hittorf* (1824–1914), German scientist, used *attrib.* and occas. in the possessive to denote various phenomena, pieces of apparatus, techniques, and concepts observed or invented by him, as ***Hittorf dark space*** = *Crookes dark space*; ***Hittorf method***, a method of finding the transport numbers of ions in an electrolyte by measuring the change in concentration of the ions near the electrodes during electrolysis; ***Hittorf transport*** (or ***transference***) ***number***, a transport number as found by the Hittorf method.

1893 T. O'C. SLOANE *Stand. Electr. Dict.* 289 *Hittorf's solution*, a solution sometimes used as a resistance. It is a solution of cadmium iodide in amylic alcohol. *Ibid.* 466 *Hittorf's resistance*, a high resistance, often a megohm, composed of Hittorf's solution. **1897** M. M. P. MUIR tr. *Lüpke's Elem. Electro-Chem.* I. iii. 41 (*heading*) Hittorf's transport-numbers. **1909** *Jrnl. Amer. Chem. Soc.* XXXI. 351 (*heading*) The relation between the true transference number and the Hittorf transference number. *Ibid.*, The ordinary transference number (T_H) for concentrated solutions, as obtained by the Hittorf method, is erroneous in cases where the ions are hydrated, since it is calculated on the assumption that the water remains stationary during the passage of the current. **1916** F. B. PIDDUCK *Treat. Electr.* xii. 487 The negative glow and the Hittorf dark space expand continually as the pressure is reduced. **1941** J. D. COBINE *Gaseous Conductors* viii. 213 Following the cathode glow is another dark space variously called the cathode dark space, the Crookes dark space, the Hittorf dark space. **1942** GLASSTONE *Introd. Electrochem.* vi. 114 Although the Hittorf method is simple in principle, accurate results are difficult to obtain.

hitty-missy ('hɪtɪ 'mɪsɪ), *adv.* (*a.*) Also 6–7 hittie-missie, hit-I misse-I. [app. from *hit he*, *miss he*, or *hit I*, *miss I*: cf. WILLY-NILLY.] Hit or miss: see HIT *v.* 22; at random, at haphazard.

1553 T. WILSON *Rhet.* 47 b, Young boyes..which showte in the open and plaine feldes at all aventures hittie missie. **1565** GOLDING *Ovid's Met.* VIII. (1593) 195 The hand of prince Meleager Plaid hittiemissie. **1602** WARNER *Alb. Eng.* XIII. lxxvii. (1612) 319 Howbeit hit-I-misse-I, when was Speculation weake. **1611** COTGR., *Tombant levant*, well or ill, hittie missie; here or there, one way or other. **1705** HICKERINGILL *Priest-cr.* IV. (1721) 238 Hittee Missee, happy go lucky, as the blind Man kill'd the Crow. *a* **1825** FORBY *Voc. E. Anglia*, *Hitty-missy*, at random; hit or miss. **1897** F. HALL in *Nation* (N.Y.) LXIV. 357/3.

B. *adj.* Random, haphazard.

1885 *Pall Mall G.* 28 May 3 This hitty-missy, ready-go-lucky fashion. **1894** STEAD *If Christ came to Chicago* 338 The hitty-missy, hugger-mugger fashion.

hitwaw: see HICKWALL.

†**hity-tity.** *Obs.* [Cf. HIGHTY-TIGHTY: but there is no obvious connexion of sense.] Bo-peep.

1609 B. JONSON *Case is altered* IV. iv, If Rachel stand now, and play hity-tity through the keyhole, to behold the equipage of thy person?

hi'ulcity. *rare.* [ad. L. type **hiulcitās*, f. *hiulcus* gaping, split, cleft, f. *hiāre* to gape.] A gaping, opening, cleft.

a **1681** WHARTON *Eclipses* Wks. (1683) 103 That the Mountains of the Earth are not to be compared to the bigness thereof, the equal roundness of the Shadow tells us: Wherein we observe no Hiulcity or Cleft, by reason of the Vallies, nor yet any part..extended..because of the Mountains.

hive (haɪv), *sb.* Forms: 1 hýf, 2– hive, (4 huive, 4–7 hyve, heve, 5 hyfe). [OE. *hýf*:—OTeut. type **hûfi-z*; not preserved elsewhere in Teutonic; prob. related to ON. *húfr* hull of a ship, and to L. *cūpa* tub, cask. The form *hēve* is Kentish.]

1. An artificial receptacle for the habitation of a swarm of bees; a beehive.

Originally made, in a conical or dome-like form, of straw or the like, but now often a square box, constructed with movable compartments or other arrangements for the removal of the honey.

c **725** *Corpus Gloss.* 133 Alvearia, hyfi. *c* **1000** ÆLFRIC *Gloss.* in Wr.-Wülcker 123/16 *Canistrum, uel aluearium*, hyf. *c* **1000** *Sax. Leechd.* I. 98 Wiþ ðæt beon æt ne fleon, ȝenim þas ylcan wyrte..and ȝehoh hy to ðære hyfe. *a* **1132** *O.E. Chron.* an. 1127 He wunede eall riht swa drane doð on hiue. **13..** *Sir Beues* (A.) 1408 So faste hii gonne aboute him scheue Ase don ben aboute þe heue. *c* **1325** *Gloss. W. de Biblesw.* in Wright *Voc.* 172 *Rusche*, hyve [*Cambr. MS.* huive]. *c* **1440** *Jacob's Well* (E.E.T.S.) 142 þe bere delyteth myche in hony, and þer-fore he goth to an heve, to a swarm of been, & lycketh awey here hony. *c* **1460** *Towneley Myst.* (Surtees) 286 Honey takyn of a hyfe. **1577** B. GOOGE *Heresbach's Husb.* IV. (1586) 179 Some make their Hives of Lanterne horne, or Glasse..that they may viewe the maner of their working. **1605** CAMDEN *Rem.*, *Poems* 7 Out of the heues came swarmes of Bees. **1741** *Compl. Fam. Piece* III. 515 Any sort of Hive, whether of Straw, Board, or Glass. **1881** T. W. COWAN *Brit. Bee-kpr.'s Guide Bk.* ix. (1889) 46 No hive can be considered complete unless it has some arrangement for securing pure honey in the comb.

2. *fig.* A storehouse of sweet things.

1633 G. HERBERT *Temple*, *Home* iv, Must he leave that nest, That hive of sweetnesse. **1670** *Devout Commun.* (1688) 143 Whose bosom is the hive and centre of all goodness. **1798** S. ROGERS *Ep. to a Friend* 14 London hails thee to its splendid mart, Its hives of sweets, and cabinets of art.

3. *transf.* **a.** A place swarming with busy occupants.

1634 S. R. *Noble Soldier* v. iii. in Bullen *O. Pl.* I. 333 Religious houses are those hyves where Bees Make honey for mens soules. **1647** COWLEY *Mistr.*, *Wish* i, The Crowd, and Buz, and Murmurings Of this great Hive, the City. **1784** COWPER *Tiroc.* 458 Our public hives of puerile resort. **1849** MACAULAY *Hist. Eng.* ii. I. 200 A busy and populous hive, in which new wealth was every day created. **1863** P. BARRY *Dockyard Econ.* 2 A private shipyard is a hive of industry.

b. A place whence swarms of people issue; the nursery of a teeming race.

1788 PRIESTLEY *Lect. Hist.* v. lviii. 457 They no longer send forth those swarms of people..which made them be called the northern hive. **1818** CRUISE *Digest* (ed. 2) I. 2 Both the Danes and Saxons were undoubtedly swarms from the northern hive. **1835** THIRLWALL *Greece* I. ii. 54 The hive whence the Pelasgian people issued.

c. The abode of any gregarious domestic animal.

1641 BAKER *Chron.* (1660) 31 Hens, Peacocks, Geese, and Ducks bred in and accustomed to houses, forsook their wonted hives, and turned wilde. **1875** 'STONEHENGE' *Brit. Sports* I. I i. §3 The old hen of each hive or nide..is always anxious to retain her old nest.

d. *spec.* A breeding-place for oysters.

1882 *Daily Tel.* 18 Aug. 5/1 The ostriculturist has designed what is termed a 'hive' made of limed tiles, to which the spat can readily affix itself.

4. a. A hiveful of bees, a hived swarm.

c **1430** LYDG. *Min. Poems* (Percy Soc.) 154 Foo unto hevys and enemy is the drane. **1593** SHAKS. *2 Hen. VI*, III. ii. 125 The Commons like an angry Hiue of Bees That want their Leader, scatter vp and downe. **1711** SWIFT *Lett.* (1767) III. 219 [They] seemed to me to be just like a hive of bees working and labouring under huge weights of cares.

b. *transf.* A swarming or teeming multitude.

1832–4 DE QUINCEY *Cæsars* Wks. 1859 X. 168 Those Gothic, Vandal, and Frankish hives, who were as yet hidden behind a cloud of years. **1839** YEOWELL *Anc. Brit. Ch.* i. (1847) 2 It was here that the great hive of mankind was gathered together. **1864** TENNYSON *Boadicea* 19 There the hive of Roman liars worship a gluttonous emperor-idiot.

5. Something of the shape or structure of a beehive:

a. A head-covering of platted straw. **b.** A capsule or case containing many cells.

1597 SHAKS. *Lover's Compl.* 8 Upon her head a platted hive of straw. **1665** HOOKE *Microgr.* 155 Microscopical seeds..For first, though they grow in a Case or Hive oftentimes bigger then one of these..being not above $\frac{1}{32}$ part of an Inch in Diameter, whereas the Diameter of the Hive of them oftentimes exceeds two Inches. *Ibid.* 188 Whether the seed of certain Bees, sinking to the bottom, might there naturally form itself that vegetable hive, and take root. **1758** CH. LENNOX *Henrietta* (1761) I. 73 The shepherdess..with a straw hive on her head, and a tatter'd garment on.

†**6.** ? A contrivance of wickerwork, resembling a beehive, used for catching fish. *Obs.*

1533–4 *Act 25 Hen. VIII*, c. 7 No..person..shal..take..in..any..net..lepe, hiue, crele..or any other engine..the yonge frie..of any kinde of salmon. **1558** *Act 1 Eliz.* c. 17 §3 No..person..shall..take Fishe withe any maner of Nett, Tramell, Keppe, Wore, Hyvy, Crele, or by any other Engyne.

7. *attrib.* and *Comb.*, as **hive-bee**, the common honey-bee; **hive-bound** *a.*, confined to a hive; †**hive-cot**, a beehive; †**hive-dross**, bee-glue, propolis; **hive-evil**, a sickness to which bees are liable; **hive-honey**, honey from a hive; **hive-moth**, an alternative name for the wax-moth or honeycomb moth; **hive-nest**, a structure consisting of an aggregation of many nests constructed and occupied by a colony of birds, such as those of the republican grosbeak and republican swallow; **hive-vine**, 'the partridge-berry or squaw-vine, *Mitchella repens*' (*Cent. Dict.*).

1816 KIRBY & SP. *Entomol.* (1843) II. 103 The instincts that actuate the common *hive-bee. **1859** DARWIN *Orig. Spec.* xix. (1860) 411 The admirable architectural powers of the hive-bee. **1921** R. GRAVES *Pier-Glass* 30 A *hive-bound bee. **1945** W. DE LA MARE *Burning-Glass* 67 As passive as the hive-bound bees. **1583** STANYHURST *Æneis* I. (Arb.) 31 Lyke bees..Feaze away thee droane bees with sting, from maunger, or *hiuecot. **1658** ROWLAND *Moufet's Theat. Ins.* 916 Propolis the Arabians call Kur..the English, *Hive-dross. **1706** PHILLIPS (ed. Kersey), *Hive-dross* or *Bee-glue*, a kind of Wax which Bees make at the Mouth of their Hive, to

keep out the Cold. **1607** Topsell *Serpents* (1658) 650 If they be too many, they bring a sicknesse called the *Hive-evill. **1653** Walton *Angler* vi. 140 Take the stinking oil.. and *Hive-honey, and annoint your bait therewith. **1931** *Oxf. Univ. Gaz.* 17 June 703/1 *Hive-moth (*Galleria*) at Nairobi.

Hence **'hiveless** *a.*, destitute of a hive. **'hiveward** *adv.*, towards the hive.

1575 Gascoigne *Herbs, Fruit Reconciliation* Wks. II. 130 Like hiueless Bees they wander here and there. **1847** Tennyson *Princess* iv. 181, I..less from Indian craft Than beelike instinct hiveward, found at length The garden portals.

hive (haɪv), *v.* [f. hive *sb.*]

1. *trans.* To gather (bees) into a hive; to locate (a swarm) in a hive.

1611 Cotgr., *Rucher*, to hiue, make hiues. **1615** W. Lawson *Orch. & Gard.* (1626) 2 Your Gardner must.. watch his Bees, and hive them. **1796** Pegge *Anonym.* (1809) 265 Two swarms of Bees from different hives united, and were hived together. **1844** Gosse in *Zoologist* II. 607 A 'gum' or square box to hive the swarm for domestication.

2. *transf.* and *fig.* To shelter as in a hive; to afford shelter to, as a hive does; to house snugly.

c **1586** C'tess Pembroke *Ps.* lvii. i, Lord.. Hide me, hive me as thine owne Till those blasts be overblown. **1610** B. Jonson *Alch.* iii. ii, So hive him In the swan-skin coverlid, and cambric sheets, Till he work honey and wax. **1812** W. Taylor in *Monthly Rev.* LXVII. 529 The successive swarms of sharpers, which that city has hived, are notorious.

3. To hoard or store *up*, as honey, in the hive.

1580 Golding in *Baret's Alv.* To Rdr. A v a, Of fower Tungs the flowers hyued bee, In one sweete iuice to serue the turne of thee. *a* **1659** Cleveland (J.), He at Fuscara's sleeve arriv'd Where all delicious sweets are hiv'd. **1816** Byron *Ch. Har.* iii. cvii, The other, deep and slow, exhausting thought, And hiving wisdom with each studious year. **1821** —— *Sardan.* iv. i. 312 Happier than the bee, Which hives not but from wholesome flowers. **1868** G. Duff *Pol. Surv.* 7 It pleased M. Marc Monnier.. to hive up an enormous mass of information.

4. a. *intr.* To enter the hive, take to the hive, as bees. **b.** To live together as bees in a hive; also *transf.* to lodge together.

1596 Shaks. *Merch. V.* ii. v. 48 Drones hiue not with me, Therefore I part with him. **1655** H. Vaughan *Silex Scint.* i. *Man* (1858) 128 Where bees at night get home and hive. **1725** Pope *Let. to Blount* 13 Sept., We are.. forc'd to.. get into warmer houses and hive together in cities. **1871** J. Miller *Songs Italy* (1878) 81 Then I should hive within your hair, And I should bide in glory there.

5. *intr.* ***hive off***: To swarm off like bees. Now esp., to break away from, to separate from, a group. Also *trans.*, to remove from a group, a large unit, etc., to make separate.

a **1856** in Olmsted *Slave States* ii. (1861) 38 This way, gentlemen—this way!'..and the company immediately hived off to the second establishment. **1864** *Cornh. Mag.* Nov. 621 These emigrants are part of the swarm which annually hives off from the west. **1902** *Westm. Gaz.* 10 July 9/1 The Board is now hiving off to a mine with at least a promising name, the 'Baron Rothschild', in the Tati district. **1931** *Economist* 5 Dec. 1060/2 And even Syrai Proper has been made to hive off the autonomous Governments of the Jebel Druse and Alexandretta. **1937** *Nature* 16 Oct. 659/1 Experimental psychology..has hived off from physiology. **1951** *Engineering* 28 Sept. 403/2 The..firm..was 'hived off' from the parent company. **1957** *Economist* 30 Nov. 783/2 It will be remembered that, while part of the Moroccan Liberation Army..agreed to incorporation in the Royal Moroccan army, another part preferred to hive off and disappear into remote areas. **1959** Halas & Manvell *Technique Film Animation* xix. 257 Many animators with a flair for individual work have hived off from these studios. **1959** Duke of Bedford *Silver-Plated Spoon* x. 201 The trustees were slowly hiving off part of the family estates to meet the awful burden of taxation. **1961** T. Landau *Encycl. Librarianship* (ed. 2) 146/1 Large public library systems are increasingly 'hiving off' special sections dealing with foreign literature. **1963** *Times* 20 Apr. 7/6 The territorial wings of the U.F.P. in Northern and Southern Rhodesia and Nyasaland would now 'hive off' with 'full authority to act for themselves' under new names. **1969** *New Scientist* 1 May 262/2 The large machines are beginning to sprout small sideshoots on to which specialized tasks can be hived off. **1971** *Times* 21 Dec. 14/3 Strong opposition to the British Steel Corporation's plans to hive off part of the River Don works at Sheffield..is likely to be encountered.

Hence **hiving** *vbl. sb.* (also *attrib.*); **hiver**, one who hives (bees).

1577 B. Googe *Heresbach's Husb.* iv. (1586) 185 b, For commonly in the tenth yeere after their first hiving, the whole stocke dieth. **1627** W. Sclater *Exp. 2 Thess.* (1629) 265 The Church of no time may affoord hiuing for drones. **1707–12** Mortimer *Husb.* (J.), Let the hiver drink a cup of good beer, and wash his hands and face therewith. **1844** Tupper *Crock of G.* xxiii, With all her hiding and hiving propensities. **1876** Mrs. Whitney *Sights & Ins.* v. 25 All my hiving-up of what I am to gather.

hives (haɪvz), *sb. pl.* Also **hyves**. [Origin uncertain. Usually connected with heave *v.*, 'because hives appear above the skin' (Jamieson); but this derivation is difficult phonologically.] 'Any eruption on the skin, when the disorder is supposed to proceed from an internal cause' (Jam.); applied to red-gum or *Strophulus*, chicken-pox, nettle-rash; also, inflammation of the bowels or *Enteritis* (*bowel-hives*), and inflammation of the larynx, croup, or *Laryngitis*.

c **1500** *Roull's Cursing* 47 in Laing *Sel. Rem. Pop. Poetry Scot.*, Fflusix, hyvis, or huttit ill, Hoist, heidwark, or fawin ill. **1715** Bowel-hyve [see bowel *sb.* 6]. **1754–64** Smellie *Mid-wif.*, A child..struck out all over the body with small red eruptions: which in London the nurses call the red-gum, but in Scotland is termed the hives. **1825** Brockett, *Hives*, water-blebs, an eruption in the skin. **1886** *Syd. Soc. Lex.*, *Hives*, a popular name for the globular species of Varicella, or chicken-pox..also, any skin eruption; also, a synonym of Urticaria; also, a name for Croup. **1893** *Northumbld. Gloss.*, *Hive*, an inward feeling of enlargement. There are 'chest hives', 'bowel hives', etc., descriptive of an inward heaving or swelling. Hives are not usually outward eruptions, but when so they are commonly called het hives—hot heaves or hot spots.

b. hive-syrup *U.S.*, compound syrup of squills.

1839 *Southern Lit. Messenger* V. 65/2 There's nothing there but a few drops of peppermint,..and some of the patent hive-syrup. **1901** T. H. Sollmann *Text-bk. Pharmacol.* 612 *Syrupus Scillæ Compositus* (U.S.P.) (*Hive Syrup*)... Used especially in whooping-cough. **1936** Cook & LaWall *Remington's Pract. Pharm.* (ed. 8) 304 Syrupus Scillæ Compositus... Hive Syrup, Coxe's Hive Syrup.

† **hivie-skivy**, ? *adv. Obs. rare*⁻¹. ? = Hurry-scurry, helter-skelter. (Or ? *sb.*: see quot.)

1646 Butcher *Surv. Stamford* x. (1717) 76–7 The bull is turned out of the alderman's house; and then hivie-skivy, tag and rag, men, women, and children..with all the dogs in the town, promiscuously running after him with their bull-clubs.

hiya ('haɪjə), *int.* Also **hi-ya, hiyah**. [App. shortened from *how are you?* and influenced by hi *int.* 2.] A word of greeting.

1940 'N. Blake' *Malice in Wonderland* i. ii. 31 'Hi-ya, boys and girls,' he cried. 'Hi-ya, Teddy,' the cry went back. **1940** R. Chandler *Farewell, My Lovely* xxxix. 309 Hiya, babe. Long time no see. **1946** P. Quentin *Puzzle for Fiends* (1947) 190 'Hiyah, baby,' I said. **1959** *Elizabethan* May 35/1 Robin Fawcett turned the grin on Friday and me and said 'Hi-ya'.

Hizbollah, -bullah, var. Hezbollah.

Hizen (hiː'zɛn). Also † **Fisen, Fizen**. The name of a province in the north-west of Kyushu in Japan used *attrib.* and *ellipt.* to denote a class of porcelains characterized by rich decoration, delicate colouring, and fine workmanship, and including Hirado, Imari, and Nabeshima ware. Cf. Hirado.

1727 J. G. Scheuchzer tr. *Kæmpfer's Hist. Japan* II. App. 61 In *Fisen* they have a certain white clay, of which they make all sorts of Porcellane-ware. **1859** L. Oliphant *Narr. Elgin's Miss. China & Japan* II. iii. 52 The egg-shell China is..made principally in the provinces of Fizen and Satsuma. **1875–80** Audsley & Bowes *Keramic Art Japan* I. 26 The old red, blue and gold Hizen. *Ibid.*, Old Hizen ware..includes white porcelain. **1878** J. J. Young *Ceramic Art* ii. vii. 177 The rich beauty of the coloring of Hizen porcelain is indescribable. **1965** S. Jenyns *Jap. Porcelain* iii. 89 The early Hizen blue underglaze ware..was by far the most beautiful of all Japanese underglaze porcelains.

hizz (hɪz), *v.* Now *rare*. [Echoic: cf. *hiss*, *whizz*.] *intr.* To make a hissing or whizzing noise. Hence **'hizzing** *vbl. sb.* and *ppl. a.*

1583 Stanyhurst *Æneis* etc. (Arb.) 137 Three watrye clowds shymring toe the craft they rampyred hizing. **1598** Barret *Theor. Warres* v. v. 167 To passe amid the hizzing bullets. **1605** Shaks. *Lear* iii. vi. 17 To haue a thousand with red burning spits Come hizzing in vpon 'em. **1655–87** H. More *Antid. Ath.* App. (1712) 221 If we spit upon..metals ..heated.. they will make the spittle hizze and bubble. *a* **1716** South *Serm.* (1717) VI. 307 Hearing Bullets hizzing about his Ears. **1876** Smiles *Sc. Natur.* ix. (ed. 4) 110 The otter, polecat, stoat and weasel have a knack of blowing or hizzing when suddenly come upon.

† **hizzle**, *v. Obs.* In 6 **hizle**. [f. prec. with dim. suffix -le.] *intr.* = prec.

1583 Stanyhurst *Æneis* iii. 81 A prosperus hizling Of south blast, puffing on sayles dooth summon vs onward.

hizzy, Sc. and north. dial. form of hussy.

Hjelmslevian (hjɛlmz'lɛvɪən), *a.* [f. the name of Louis *Hjelmslev* (1899–1965), Danish linguist + -ian.] Of, pertaining to, or characteristic of the writings or theories of Hjelmslev.

1950 *Archivum Linguisticum* II. 96 'Form' is not used here in its Hjelmslevian sense. **1961** *Amer. Speech* XXXVI. 160 An elaborate and opaque Hjelmslevian terminology. **1963** *Ibid.* XXXVIII. 139 Levin, resorting to a Hjelmslevian concept, considers two forms as 'semantically equivalent insofar as they overlap in cutting up the general "thought-mass".' **1963** J. Lyons *Structural Semantics* vi. 113 The particular (Hjelmslevian) framework within which the analysis of the Greek system is presented.

hlonipa ('hlɒnɪpə), *v.* Also **hlonipha**. [a. Zulu, Xhosa *hlonipa* vb.] Among south-east African Bantu peoples of the Nguni group: to avoid in conversation the radical of the name of certain persons to whom such respect is due.

In English contexts often treated as a noun. In quot. 1850 *uku-* is the Xhosa infinitive prefix.

[**1850** J. W. Appleyard *Kafir Lang.* 70 The Kafir *women* have many words peculiar to themselves. This arises from a national custom, called *ukuhlonipa*.] **1913** Pettman *Africanderisms* 212 The word *hlonipa* means that they [*sc.* women] are too bashful or polite to use such names in common everyday speech. **1936** E. J. Krige *Social Syst. Zulus* ii. 30 The behaviour towards relatives-in-law is largely bound up with the custom of *hlonipha*. **1970** *Stand. Encycl. S. Afr.* II. 96/1 Among the Nguni peoples of South Africa the relationship [between parents-in-law and children-in-law] is clearly defined in a code of conduct known as *hlonipha*. A wife must *hlonipha* her in-laws, in other words she must act humbly and respectfully toward them and shun them.

h'm, hm, *int.* See hem *int.*, hum *int.*

1854 Thackeray *Rose & Ring* x, See it be done, or else, —h'm!—ha!—h'm! mind thine own eyes!

† **ho**, *sb.*[1] *Obs.* Also 1 **hóh**, pl. **hós**. [OE. *hóh*, *hó*:—**hanho-*, not found in the cognate langs., but recognized as the primitive of which *heel*:—**hâhil*:—**hanhil-* is a deriv.: see heel; also hoe *sb.*[1], heugh, hough *sbs.*] The heel.

c **1000** Ælfric *Gen.* iii. 15 Heo tobryt þin heafod and þu syrwst onȝean hyre ho. *c* **1000** *Ags. Ps.* (Spelm.) lv. 6 Hos mine [*Vesp. Ps.* helspuran mine, *Thorpe* hælun mine]. *c* **1000** *Ags. Gosp.* John xiii. 18 Se þe ytt hlaf myd me ahefþ hys ho [*Lind.* hel] onȝean me. *c* **1300** *St. Margarete* 160 He ȝenede & gan his ouere cheoke ouer hire heued do, & his nyþere cheoke byneþe at hire ho, & forsaulȝ so þis maide.

ho (həʊ), *int.*[1] and *sb.*[2] Also 4–6 **hoo**, (6 **hoe, hoha**), 6–7 **hoh**, 6–9 **hoa**. [A natural exclamation. Not recorded in OE.; cf. ON. *hó* 'int., also a shepherd's call'.] **A.** *int.*

1. An exclamation expressing, according to intonation, surprise, admiration, exultation (often ironical), triumph, taunting.

a **1300** *Cursor M.* 12129 'Ho!' [*Gött.* O ho!] all þan cun þai cri, 'Qua herd euer sua gret ferli'. **1599** Shaks. *Much Ado* ii. i. 205 Ho now you strike like the blindman. *a* **1623** —— *Epit. John Combes* in Aubrey *Lives*, 'Hoh!' quoth the Devill, ''Tis my John o Combe'. **1785** Burns *Jolly Beggars* Air iv, Sing, ho, my braw John Highland man! **1808** Scott *Marm.* ii. xxix, 'Ho! shifts she thus?' King Henry cried. **1830** Tennyson *Poems, Eng. War Song*, Shout for England! Ho! for England! George for England!

2. An exclamation to attract attention.

c **1430** Lydg. *Min. Poems* (Percy Soc.) 107 Then hyed I me to Belyngsgate; And one cryed, 'hoo! go we hence!' **1575** Gascoigne *Pr. Pleas. Kenilw.* Poems 1869 II. 97 Ho, Eccho; Eccho, ho, where art thou, Eccho, where? **1583** Hollyband *Campo di Fior* 327 Hoe boye, where is your maister? **1596** Shaks. *Merch. V.* ii. vi. 25 Hoa! who's within? **1611** Bible *Isa.* lv. 1 Ho, euery one that thirsteth, come ye to the waters. **1678** Bunyan *Pilgr.* i. 85 Then said Christian aloud, Ho, ho, So-ho; stay and I will be your Companion. At that Faithful looked behind him. **1788** Wesley *Wks.* (1872) VI. 303 Ho! Art thou one who readest these words? **1820** Shelley *Œdipus* ii. ii. 116 Hoa! hoa! tallyho! tallyho! ho! ho! Come, let us hunt these ugly badgers down. **1832** Macaulay *Armada* 28 Ho! gunners, fire a loud salute: ho! gallants, draw your blades. **1833** M. Scott *Tom Cringle* (1859) 44 'Ho, the ship, ahoy!' 'Hillo!' was the reply. **1864** Ballantyne *Lifeboat* (ed. 2) 99 Ho! comrades, look alive, here comes the lifeboat!

b. After the name of a thing or place to which attention is called: used by boatmen, etc., to call attention to the place for which they are starting; hence, generally, with a sense of destination.

1593 Peele *Chron. Edw. I*, Wks. (Rtldg.) 409/1 *A cry of* 'Westward, ho!' *Q. Elinor.* 'Woman, what noise is this I hear?' *Potter's Wife.* 'It is the watermen that call for passengers to go westward now.' **1595** Shaks. *John* iii. iii. 73 On toward Callice, hoa. **1601** —— *Twel. N.* iii. i. 146 Then Westward-hoe: Grace and good disposition attend your Ladyship. **1747** (*title*) A Race for Canterbury or Lambeth, Ho! **1855** Kingsley *Westw. Ho!* (1874) 9 Thou too shalt forth, and westward ho, beyond thy wildest dreams. **1881** Hindley *Cries Lond.* 141 Each night round Temple-Bar she plies, With Diddle Dumplings, ho!

3. As a call to animals, with various senses.

1878 *Cumbld. Gloss.*, *Ho*,..a word used in guiding horses to the left; come hither. *Ho Bye*,..stand out of the way. **1881** *Oxfordsh. Gloss.*, *Ho! ho*! a word used to call sheep to their food.

4. Repeated, ***ho! ho!*** or ***ho! ho! ho!***, it expresses derision or derisive laughter.

[*c* **1150** *Vita St. Godrici* (Surtees) 354 Quibus ille, Ho! Ho! Si in veritate tam pulchra fuisses, quam exterius appares.] **1552** Huloet, Ho, ho, a voice of wondringe or disdaininge, *hui*. **1575** J. Still *Gamm. Gurton* ii. iii. in Hazl. *Dodsley* III. 205 Did not the devil cry, ho, ho, ho? **1590** Shaks. *Mids. N.* iii. ii. 421 Ho, ho, ho; coward, why com'st thou not? **1627** Drayton *Nymphidia* Wks. 1753 II. 461 Hoh, hoh, quoth Hob, God save thy grace. **1763** Bickerstaff *Love in Village* i. vi, Serve the king, master! no, no, I pay the king, That's enough for me. Ho, ho, ho! **1820** Scott *Monast.* v, 'Ho! ho! ho!' and he shook his portly sides at his own jest. **1895** M. E. Francis *Daughter of Soil* 70 Ho! ho! ho! Twenty-two—did you ever hear o' sich a tale?

5. With other interjections.

See also gee-*ho!* heigh-ho! hey-ho! holla *ho!* hollo *ho!* o ho! oh ho! so ho! wa ho! what ho! wo ho! yo ho! etc.

1792 Ch. Smith *Desmond* II. 43 Hohoop, hohoop, Newminster, it is time to go, my lad—come, let us be off. **1821** *Blackw. Mag.* X. 35/1 *Ho, spy*! is chiefly a summer game. Some of the party of boys conceal themselves, and when in their hiding-places call out these words to their companions. **1879** Marzials *Song, Twickenham Ferry*, O-hoi-ye-ho, Ho-ye-ho, who's for the ferry? **1892** *Daily News* 26 May 3/2 Five more explosions followed. Each time the miner..uttered his warning, 'Ho—Ho—Ho—Hoy', and each time it felt as if the 1,200 acres of rock shook and trembled with each successive explosion.

¶ **6.** Cockney for *O*, *oh*.

1840 Dickens *Barn. Rudge* III. 405 'Ho master, ho mim!' cried Miggs..'Ho what a cutting thing it is'.

B. *sb.* A cry of 'ho', in any of the prec. senses.

(Some instances may belong to the next.)

c **1386** Chaucer *Knt.'s T.* 1675 An heraud on a Scaffold made an Oo [4 *MSS.* hoo] Til al the noyse of peple was ydo. *c* **1470** Henry *Wallace* ii. 265 Atour the wattir [they] led him with great hoo Till hyr awin hous with outyn ony hoo. *c* **1480** *Crt. of Love* 270 A messenger..from the king, which

let commaund anon, Through-out the court to make an ho and cry. **1533** Bellenden *Livy* I. (1822) 50 Quhen the serjandis had, with thair noyis and hohas, warnit the Albanis to here the kingis concioun. **1600** Shaks. *A.Y.L.* v. iii. 18 With a hey, and a ho, and a hey nonino.

ho, *int.*[2] and *sb.*[3] Also 4–6 hoo, 6 hoa, 6–7 hoe. [a. OF. *ho* halt! stop!]

†**A.** *int.* A call to stop or to cease what one is doing. ***to say*** or ***cry ho***: to stay, cease, check oneself. *Obs.* (It is often impossible to separate the interj. from the imperative of HO *v.*[2])

13.. *Gaw. & Gr. Knt.* 2330 þer-fore, hende, now hoo! *c* **1386** Chaucer *Knt.'s T.* 848 This duc..pulled out a swerd and cride hoo, Namoore vp on peyne of lesynge of youre heed. **1390** Gower *Conf.* II. 201 Of golde he shulde such plente Receive, till he saide ho. **1408** in Rymer *Fœdera* VIII. 540 Emisso per Nos Silentii Vocabulo consueto, scilicet, *Ho, Ho, Ho* (quod est) Cessate, Cessate, Cessate. *c* **1510** Barclay *Mirr. Gd. Manners* (1570) F ij b, The sacke without bottome which neuer can say hoo [*rime* gape for moo]. **1535** Coverdale *Prov.* xxx. 15 There be thre thinges that are neuer satisfied, and the fourth saieth neuer hoo. **1577** Stanyhurst *Descr. Irel.* in Holinshed (1587) II. 26/2 They would not crie hoa here, but sent in post some of their covent to Rome. **1631** R. H. *Arraignm. Whole Creature* xiii. §1. 175 To satisfie this all-devouring Minotaure, till it cry Hoe, or enough.

b. A call to an animal to stop or stand still.

1828 Webster, *Ho*, a word used by teamsters in stopping their teams..This word is pronounced also *whō*, or *hwō*. **1894** A. J. Stuart-Wortley *Grouse* 111 Many a one [dog] is spoilt by being so used to the sign and the ejaculation of 'Ho!' that he does not believe in the necessity of standing steady unless he hears it. *Ibid.* 112 The keeper..sees the dog drawing on birds, and immediately up goes his hand and 'Ho!' he shouts.

B. *sb.* Cessation, halt, pause, intermission; limit. ***withouten ho***, without stopping, straight on; ***no ho***, no cessation, end, or limit; ***out of all ho***, out of all bounds of moderation. *Obs.* or *dial.*

c **1374** Chaucer *Troylus* II. 1034 (1083) þan gan he telle his wo, But þat was endeles with-outen ho [*v.r.* hoo]. *c* **1470** Henry *Wallace* VI. 406 To the herrold [he] said syne with outyn ho. **1525** Ld. Berners *Froiss.* II. cxlii. 396 There is no hoo bytwene them as longe as speares, swordes, axes, or dagers wyll endure. *c* **1590** Greene *Fr. Bacon* xii. 73 He loued the faire maid of Fresingfield once out of all hoe. **1597** R. Bruce *Let.* in Wodrow *Life* (1843) 167 If they could have keeped any hoe or measure in their crooked course. **1684** Littleton *Lat. Dict.*, To have no ho, *modum tenere nullum*. *Ibid.*, Out of all ho, *immodicé*. **1711** Swift *Jrnl. to Stella* Lett. 1766–8 III. 135 When your tongue runs, there's no ho with you. **1818** Todd s.v., Mr. Malone [*d.* 1812] says, it is yet common in Ireland: as, there is no *ho* with him, i.e. he knows no bounds. **1828** *Craven Dial.*, s.v. There is 'no ho with him', he is not to be restrained.

Ho (həʊ), *sb.*[4] [Native name, said to be a contraction of *horo* man.] **a.** One of the principal dialects of central India, belonging to the Kolarian group. **b.** One who speaks this language. Also *attrib.* or as *adj.*

1840 S. R. Tickell in *Jrnl. Asiat. Soc.* IX. II. 997 The Ho language has no written character. **1860** F. Mason *Burmah* (ed. 2) 131 These Moondas now call themselves Hos. **1871** E. Balfour *Cycl. India* (ed. 2) II. 589/2 A Ho bridegroom buys his bride. **1905** P. Wagner tr. *Nottrott's Gram. Kol-Language* 4 The dialect of the Larka-Kols or Hos. **1906** G. A. Grierson *Linguistic Surv. India* IV. 116. **1908** H. H. Risley *People of India* 94 The Hos of Singhbhum. **1926** *Encycl. Brit.* XV. 891/2 The Hos, who are closely akin to the Mundas, also inhabit the Chota Nagpur division; in 1901 they numbered 386,000.

Ho (həʊ), *sb.*[5] [Native name, = a heap of dried peas.] Name of a tribe of the Ewe people living near the town of Ho in former Togoland, now part of Ghana.

1890 J. Frazer *Golden Bough* I. v. 265 The Ho tribe of German Togoland.

ho, *v.*[1] *rare.* [f. HO *int.*[1]: cf. ON. *hóa* 'to shout ho! or hoy!' (Vigf.)] *intr.* To cry 'ho'.

1377 Langl. *P. Pl.* B. x. 61 But hoen [*v.rr.* heon, howen howlen] on hym as an hounde and hoten hym go þennes. **1644** Quarles *Sheph. Orac.* iv, *N.* Ho, Shepheard, ho. *P.* I prithee leave thy hoing.

†**ho**, *v.*[2] *Obs.* Also 5–6 hoo. [f. HO *int.*[2], taken as the imperative of a vb.] *intr.* To cease, stop, pause.

1390 Gower *Conf.* III. 103 Till that men comen to the gates Of paradis, and there ho. *a* **1400–50** *Alexander* 2835 For-þi hoo with þi hautes & þine vnhemed wittis. **14..** in *Archæol.* LIV. I. 166/184 Here of herbys wul y ho. *c* **1430** *Pol. Rel. & L. Poems* 195 Whanne þou art tauȝt þat þou schuldist hoo Of sweering. *c* **1500** *Maid Emlyn* 411 in Hazl. *E.P.P.* IV. 96 Naye there do I ho.

ho (həʊ), *v.*[3] *dial.* [A recent spelling of the OE. vb. *hoȝian*, ME. *hoȝe*, *howe*: see HOW, HOWE *v.* Cf. HOE *sb.*[3]] *intr.* To care, be anxious, long.

1787 Grose *Prov. Gloss.*, *Ho.* To ho for anything, to long for any thing. *Berks.* **1847–78** Halliwell, *Ho*..to long for anything; to be careful and anxious. *West.* **1874** T. Hardy *Madding Crowd* II. 289 To ho and hanker after thik woman. **1881** *Isle of Wight Gloss.*, *Ho.* **1888** *Berksh. Gloss.*, *Ho*, to long for; to care greatly for.

ho, *int.*[3] A sailor's cry in heaving or hauling: see HEAVE HO; also HOW *int.*[1]

ho, obs. f. HE *pron.*, HOW, WHO; var. HEO, HI *prons. Obs.*, O *adv.*, ever; see also HOSE.

Hoabinhian (həʊəˈbɪnɪən), *a.* Also **Hoabinian**. [f. *Hoabinh*, the name of a village in Vietnam where the first major site was found + -IAN.] Of, pertaining to, or designating a Mesolithic or Neolithic culture found in parts of South-East Asia, particularly Vietnam, Laos, and Malaysia. Also *ellipt.* as *sb.*

1942 A. H. Brodrick *Little China* 63 Last of all..comes the Hoabinhian which may stretch back into the Old Stone Age, although nothing unquestionably Palaeolithic has been found. **1971** *Nat. Geographic* Mar. 339/1 The first domestication of plants in the world was done by people of the Hoabinhian culture, somewhere in South-east Asia. **1972** *Sci. Amer.* Apr. 36/2 Since the initial discovery, many other sites containing Hoabinhian artifacts have been found. *Ibid.* 39/3 Local cultures that were distinctly different from the late Hoabinhian evolved at the start of this period. **1972** M. Sheppard *Taman Indera* 3 The culture which these pre-historic cave dwellers followed probably preceded the end of the Ice Age. It has been named Hoabinhian, after a province in North Vietnam where this culture was first recognized.

‖**hoactzin, hoatzin** (həʊˈæktsɪn, həʊˈætsɪn). Also **hoazin**. [Said to be the native name, derived from the 'harsh grating hiss', which is the voice of the bird.] A remarkable bird, *Opisthocomus hoazin*, or *O. cristatus*, native of tropical America, considered to be the type and sole member of a group named by Huxley *Heteromorphæ*.

1661 Lovell *Hist. Anim. & Min.* Introd. 5 Birds, which are..exoticks, or outlandish, chiefely the American, and they are terrestriall; as..hoactzin..hoactli, heatototl. **1678** Ray *Willughby's Ornith.* 389 Its use in Physic recommends the bird Hoactzin, that utters a sound like its name. **1706** Phillips (ed. Kersey), *Hoactzin*, a Bird of the Bigness of a Hen, which feeds chiefly on Serpents, and is thence call'd by our Sea-men, the Snake-eater of America. **1889** *Athenæum* 2 Mar. 284/2 Mr. Sclater exhibited specimens of the eggs and chicks of the hoatzin..from..British Guiana. **1893** *Westm. Gaz.* 27 Nov. 7/1 Dr. Bowdler Sharpe..mentioned the hoatzin or reptilian bird, which builds its nest just above the water line, near lakes and rivers; the chicks have little claws or hooks on the end of their unfledged wings, with which they can climb up out of the flood if it threatens the security of the nest.

Hoadlyism (ˈhəʊdlɪɪz(ə)m). Also **Hoadleyism**. [f. name of Benjamin *Hoadly* (1676–1761), Bishop of Winchester + -ISM.] The opinions or policy characteristic of the latitudinarian clergy of whom Bishop Hoadly was typical. So **ˈHoadlyan** *a.*, **ˈHoadlyite**.

1800 J. Milner *Lett. to Prebendary* viii. 233 This doctrine ..is absurd in the highest degree on the principles of Hoadlyism. *Ibid.* 225, I know that the Hoadlyites deny the existence of such sacramental grace. *Ibid.* 238 The Hoadlyan system..incumbers it with a great number of perplexing consequences. **1863** J. S. Brewer *Eng. Studies* (1881) 300 He may write and preach as much Hoadleyism.. as he pleases. **1896** E. S. Purcell *Manning* I. 499 Its [*sc.* the Established Church's] Hoadleyism, if I may so speak, which prevailed before the Tractarian movement.

hoage, obs. f. *hoja*, KHOJA, a teacher.

hoagie (ˈhəʊgɪ). *U.S. local.* [Origin unknown.] A sandwich made with a French loaf split lengthways and filled with lettuce and a variety of cold meats and cheeses. Cf. *submarine roll*, *sandwich*.

1967 *Amer. Speech* XLII. 280 Temporary residents of Philadelphia attending Temple University..had some knowledge of the sandwich, locally known as a *hoagie*. **1973** *Home & Store News* (Ramsey, N.J.) Mar., *Hoagies* include ham, salami, provolone cheese and shredded lettuce all stuffed into a seven-inch submarine roll. A packet of salad dressing is included with each hoagie. **1973** *Welcomat* (Philadelphia) 10 Oct. 1/1 The Council for Social Development profited from the Pine Street Side-walk Fair, which is perhaps why five-inch 'hoagies' were sold for ninety cents.

Hoa Hao (ˌhəʊə ˈhaʊ). [Name of the village of birth of the founder, in Vietnam.] A form of nationalistic Buddhism, set up in 1939 in Indo-China by Huynh Phu So. Freq. *attrib.* Cf. CAODAISM.

1955 *Times* 2 May 12/2 The Hoa Hao commander-in-chief. **1969** *New Yorker* 20 Sept. 110/3 The scattered religious elements in the South—the Buddhists, the Catholics,..The Hoa Hao sect. **1971** I. M. Sacks in R. F. Spencer *Relig. & Change in Contemp. Asia* 54 The Hoa Hao religion was founded by the so-called 'mad monk', Huynh Phu So. The doctrines of Hoa Hao are..to honor one's parents; to love one's country; to respect Buddhism and its teachings; to love one's fellow man. ('Buddhism'..means.. the teachings of Huynh Phu So.)

hoaky, var. of HOCKEY[1], harvest-home.

hoald, dial. f. HOLD.

hoale, obs. f. HOLE, WHOLE.

hoam, dial. var. of HOME.

†**hoaming**, *ppl. a. Obs.* or *dial.* Origin and meaning uncertain.

The word in Dryden (though so in all the early edd. e.g. 1670, 1674, 1690, 1701, etc.) has been conjectured by many to be a misprint or error, and was altered by Scott in his 2nd. ed. (1821) to *foaming*; others conjecture *coaming* for *combing*. But *hoaming* is supported by the Echard quot. (unless the expression was merely taken from Dryden). Identity with the reputed Whitby use is for many reasons doubtful: cf. HOME *v.* Richardson understands it as 'a *humming* or *booming* sea'. Cf. also LOOM *v.* (to move).

1670 Dryden & Davenant *Tempest* I. i, *Vent.* What a Sea comes in. *Must.* A hoaming Sea! we shall have foul weather. **1694** Echard *Plautus, Rudens* 164 Now 'tis such a hoaming Sea, we've little hopes o' Sport; and except we light o' some Shell-Fish [etc.]. [Cf. **1876** *Whitby Gloss.* s.v., 'The tide comes hoaming in', flowing in. See *Heeaming* (*Heeaming* or *Yamming*, aiming homeward).]

hoan, -e, hoape, obs. ff. HONE *sb.* and *v.*, HOPE.

hoar (hɔə(r)), *a.* and *sb.* Forms: α. 1 hár, 3–5 hor, (3–4 heor, 4 hoer), 4–5 hoor, 4–7 hore, 6 *Sc.* hoir, 6–7 hoare, (whore), 6– hoar. β. *north.* and *Sc.* 4–6 har, hare, 5–6 hair, -e, 6 hayr. γ. 3 hær, 4–5 heer. [OE. *hár* = OHG. *hêr* 'old', hence 'venerable, august' (mod.G. *hehr* august, stately), ON. *hár-r* hoary, old:—OTeut. **hairo-z*, usually referred to an OTeut. **hai-*, pre-Teut. **koi-* to shine.]

A. *adj.* **1.** Grey-haired with age; venerable.

α. *Beowulf* (Z.) 1307 þa wæs frod cyning, har hilde-rinc, on hreon mode. *c* **1290** *St. Brandan* 265 in *S. Eng. Leg.* I. 226 A fair old man and swiþe hor. **1377** Langl. *P. Pl.* B. xvi. 173 þanne mette I with a man..As hore [*v.rr.* hoor, hoer, heor] as an hawethorne. *c* **1386** Chaucer *Merch. T.* 220, I feele me nowhere hoor but on myn heed. **1470–85** Malory *Arthur* II. xvii, An old hore gentylman. **1590** Spenser *F.Q.* I. x. 3 Through wisedome of a matrone grave and hoar. **1725** Pope *Odyss.* VIII. 112 A countless throng, Youth and hoar age. **1847** Longf. *Ev.* I. Prel. 4 The murmuring pines and the hemlocks..Stand like harpers hoar, with beards that rest on their bosoms. **1881** Jefferies *Wood Magic* II. iv. 108 A very old hare, quite hoar with age.

β. *a* **1400–50** *Alexander* 4996 'Behalds now', quod þis hare man. **1560** Rolland *Crt. Venus* IV. 661, I was sa auld ane man and hair.

2. Of colour: Grey, greyish white.

a. *esp.* Of the hair, head, or beard: Grey or white with age.

α. *c* **1290** *S. Eng. Leg.* I. 368/66 His berd is long and sid i-nouȝ, and sum-del hor a-mong. *c* **1380** *Sir Ferumb.* 1580 Al for elde ys hor þyn her. **1382** [see HOARHEAD]. **1398** Trevisa *Barth. De P.R.* v. iii. (1495) 108 Thei haue soone hoore heeres. **1482** *Monk of Evesham* (Arb.) 33 The heere of his hed was whore. **1583** Stubbes *Anat. Abus.* II. (1882) 43 Their old age, their hoare haires, their blindnesse. **1611** Bible *Isa.* xlvi. 4 Euen to hoare haires will I cary you. **1652** T. Hodges *Hoary Head Crowned* 23 His hoar head bring thou down to the grave with blood. **1798** Coleridge *Anc. Mar.* VII. xxiv, Whose beard with age is hoar. **1820** Keats *Isabella* xlviii, So she kneeled, with her locks all hoar.

β. *c* **1340** *Cursor M.* 5313 (Fairf.) His berde was side, his heued hare. **1513** Douglas *Æneis* IX. x. 52 The steyll helmys we thrist on hedis hayr.

b. Of the frost which feathers objects with white, and objects so whitened: see HOAR-FROST.

α. *a* **1000** *Andreas* 1260 (Gr.) Hrim and forst hare hild-stapan. **1477** Norton *Ord. Alch.* v. in Ashm. (1652) 55 As it sheweth in Ice and Frosts hore. **1583** Stanyhurst *Æneis* IV. (Arb.) 103 His beard with froast hoare is hardned. **1596** Spenser *F.Q.* IV. xi. 46 Like to the hore Congealed litle drops which doe the morne adore. **1785** Burns *Vision* II. xiv, When the North his fleecy store Drove thro' the sky, I saw grim Nature's visage hoar Struck thy young eye.

β. *c* **1450** Henryson *Mor. Fab.* 56 Both hill and holt hailled with frostes hair. **1513** Douglas *Æneis* VII. Prol. 42 With frostis haire ourfret the feildis standis.

c. Of colour simply.

a **900** Cynewulf *Judith* 328 Helmas and hupseax hare byrnan. *a* **1000** *Wanderer* 82 in *Exeter Bk.*, Sumne se hara wulf deaðe ȝedælde. *a* **1000** *Boeth. Metr.* v. 25 Of clife harum. **13..** *K. Alis.* 5031 Hi ben hore al so a wolf. **1552** Huloet, Hore, or whyte graye, *canus*. **1572** Bossewell *Armorie* II. 69 b, The Pellicane feruentlye loueth her byrdes, Yet when they bene haughtie, and beginne to waxe hore, they smite her in the face. **1727–46** Thomson *Summer* 1601 Island of bliss!..all assaults Baffling, as thy hoar cliffs the loud sea-wave. **1812** J. Wilson *Isle of Palms* III. 569 Folded up with blossoms hoar. **1890** R. Bridges *Shorter Poems* I. 9 Her leaves are glaucous green and hoar.

†**3.** Used frequently as an attribute of various objects named in ancient charters as marking a boundary line. *Obs.* Hence in many place-names. See also HOAR-STONE.

The meaning may have been 'grey' simply, or with lichen, and so 'grey with age', 'old, ancient'. Some have conjectured however (see *Archæologia* XXV. 33) that *hoar* 'by itself expresses a frontier or peninsular station'.

994 in Kemble *Cod. Dipl.* III. 279 Of ðam haran hæsle on earnhylle middewerde. **999** *Ibid.* 313 Of ðan haran stane on ðonne haran wiðiȝ. **1005** in Dugdale *Monast. Angl.* III. 11 Fram Egceanlæa to þam haran wiþie. *a* **1079** *O.E. Chron.* (MS. D) an. 1066 [He] com him to ȝenes æt þære haran apuldran. **1298** in *Archæol.* XXV. 35 Exinde usque ad Horeapeldre. [Cf. the place-names *Horethorne Down*, Somersetsh., *Hore Cross*, Staffordsh., *Hoar Grounds*, *Hoar Park*, Warwicksh., *Hormead*, Herts., *Horridge*, Gloucestersh., *Harestanes*, *Hartree*, *Harewood*, *Harwood*, Scotl., etc. See *Archæologia* XXV. 30–60.]

4. Of trees, woods, or the like: Grey from absence of foliage; showing the bare grey stems.

In later use a more or less traditional epithet, esp. in the alliterative phrase **holts hoar**, which referred perhaps to the grey lichen with which aged tree-trunks are clad, and thus combined the notion of old, ancient. When said of mountains the primary reference is to colour, which in later use is sometimes lost.

α. **13..** *Gaw. & Gr. Knt.* 743 Of hore okez ful hoge a hundreth to-geder. *a* **1400** *Isumbras* 167 The floures of the

thorne, Up-one those holtes hore. *c* **1430** LYDG. *Compl. Bl. Knt.* 119 In the parke, and in the holtes hore. **1555** EDEN *Decades* 132 The herbes waxe wythered.. and the medowes become hore. **1590** SPENSER *F.Q.* I. iii. 10 Under the steepe foot of a mountaine hore. **1632** MILTON *L'Allegro* 55 From the side of some hoar hill, Through the high wood echoing shrill. *a* **1650** *Flodden F.* 214 in *Percy Folio* I. 327 Underneath the holtes so whore.

β. *a* **1400** *Sir Perc.* 230 Fyftene wynter and mare He duellede in those holtes hare. *c* **1425** WYNTOUN *Cron.* VIII. xxvi. 228 Ðat semyd ane hare Wode for to be. **1513** DOUGLAS *Æneis* X. xiv. 142 This Troiane prynce.. Intil hys stalwart stelyt scheild, stikand out Lyke a hayr wod, the dartis bair about. *a* **1549** *Murning Maidin* 26 And walk among the holtis hair, Within the woddis wyld.

γ. *c* **1205** LAY. 16372 Swulc hit weoren an hær wude. *a* **1400-50** *Alexander* 776 þe holtez of þe heer wode.

b. Of things: Grey with age, venerable, ancient.

1590 SPENSER *F.Q.* II. vii. Argt., Guyon findes Mamon in a delve Sunning his threasure hore. *a* **1756** COLLINS *Pop. Superstit. Highlands* 142 To that hoar pile, which still its ruin shows. **1768** BEATTIE *Minstr.* I. xliii, Instructed by tradition hoar. **1856** H. C. ADAMS *First of June* (1862) 6 To trace legends back to yet more hoar antiquity.

5. White or grey with mould; mouldy, musty. Also *fig.* *Obs.* exc. *dial.*

1544 PHAER *Regim. Lyfe* (1560) Sj, Let them so stande, viii. dayes to putryfye tyll it be hoare, then fry them out. **1592** SHAKS. *Rom. & Jul.* II. iv. 141 An old Hare hoare, and an old Hare hoare is very good meat in Lent. But a Hare that is hoare is too much for a score, when it hoares ere it be spent. **1605** SYLVESTER *Du Bartas* II. iii. IV. *Captaines* 431 But the long Journey, we have gone, hath.. turn'd our victuals hoar. ['Still in use in Somerset' (Halliwell 1847-78).]

†**6.** From the use in *hoar frost* (sense 2 b) comes prob. that of 'Cold, nipping' (Jam.). *Sc. Obs.*

c **1450** HENRYSON in *Bannatyne Poems* 114 (Jam.) Fra hair weddir, and frostis, him to hap. **1513** DOUGLAS *Æneis* VI. vii. 79 By gousty placis, welsche savorit, mist, and hair. *Ibid.* VII. Prol. 130 The mornyng bla, wan and har.

†**b.** *fig.* 'Keen, biting, severe' (Jam.). *Sc. Obs.*

a **1605** MONTGOMERIE *Misc. Poems* iii. 61 Houbeit ȝe think my harrand something har.

†**7.** 'Harsh, ungrateful to the ear' (Jam.). *Sc.*

c **1450** HENRYSON *Test. Cres.* 338 Thy voice sa cleir unplesand hoir and hace. *Ibid.* 445 My cleir voice.. Is rawk as ruik, full hiddeous, hoir, and hace.

8. *Comb.*, chiefly parasynthetic, as ***hoar-haired, -locked***, HOAR-HEADED; also **hoar-leprosy**, white leprosy, elephantiasis; **hoar-rime** = HOAR-FROST; **hoar withy**, the White-beam, *Pyrus Aria*.

c **1205** LAY. 25845 Heor-lockede wif [*c* **1275** hor-ilocket]. **1549** *Compl. Scot.* vi. 59 The hayr ryim is ane cald deu, the quhilk fallis in mysty vapours, and syne it fresis on the eird. **1580** HOLLYBAND *Treas. Fr. Tong*, *Chenu*, horeheared, gray heared. **1607** SHAKS. *Timon* IV. iii. 35 This yellow Slaue, Will.. blesse th' accurst, Make the hoare Leprosie ador'd. **1879** BRITTEN & H. *Plant-n.*, Hoar Withy, *Pyrus Aria*, Hants., from the white under-surface of the leaves.

B. *sb.* †**1.** A grey-haired man. *Obs.*

Beowulf (Z.) 2989 Hares hyrste hige-lace bæron. **13..** *K. Alis.* 6752 Sey me now, ye olde hore! (Mony day is seothe ye weore bore).

2. Hoariness from age.

(But in first quot. perh. *for-hore*: see FOR- 10.)

[? *a* **1366** CHAUCER *Rom. Rose* 356 Hir heed for hoor [*Thynne* for hore] was whyt as flour.] **1500-20** DUNBAR *Poems* lxxxv. 59 Quhill store and hore, my ȝouth devore. **1796** BURKE *Let. Noble Ld.* 52 His grants are engrafted on the public law of Europe, covered with the awful hoar of innumerable ages. **1872** J. G. MURPHY *Com. Lev.* Introd., Now that it is touched with the hoar of a venerable antiquity.

3. A white or hoary coating or appearance; esp. hoar-frost, rime.

1567 TURBERV. *Epit. & Sonn.* Wks. (1837) 303 The hilles be ouerwhelmde with hoare. **1731** *Winter's Thought* in *Gentl. Mag.* (1732), The candy'd rhime and scattered hoar. **1732** *Gentlem. Guide to Cattle* (ed. 2) 9 Mornings when we perceive a white Hoar and Cobwebs upon the Grass. **1886** T. HARDY *Mayor Casterbridge* I. i, The thick hoar of dust which had accumulated on their shoes and garments.

†**b.** Canescent hairiness. *Obs.*

1551 TURNER *Herbal* I. B vij b, Most gentle, full of hore and softe, with whyte floures and whit sedes.

†**c.** Mould. *Obs.*

1548-67 THOMAS *Ital. Dict.*, *Muffa*, the hoare that is seene in stale breade. **1597-8** BP. HALL *Sat.* IV. i, His golden fleece o'ergrown with mouldy hoar. **1686** PLOT *Staffordsh.* 15 Interspersed with a white hoar or vinew much like that in mouldy bread.

d. A fog; a thick mist. (? Error for HAAR.)

1846 WORCESTER, *Hoar*.. (2) thick mist. *Loudon*.

†**hoar**, *v.* *Obs.* Forms: 1 **hárian**, 4-6 **hore**, 5 **hoore**, 6-8 **hoar**. [OE. *hárian*, f. *hár* HOAR *a.*]

1. *intr.* To become hoary or grey-haired.

a **1000** *Malchus* in *Shrine* (Cockayne) 39 þæt ic þa sceolde wesan ceorl on hariendum heafde. *c* **1000** ÆLFRIC *Gram.* xxvi. (Z.) 154 *Caneo*, ic harige. *a* **1310** in Wright *Lyric P.* 50 Help me, Lord, er then ich hore. **13..** *K. Alis.* 1597 His berd schal hore, his folk schal sterve. **1398** TREVISA *Barth. De P.R.* v. lxvi. (1495) 184 The heer of the temples hooryth sooner than the other heer.

b. *fig.* To grow old; to become inveterate.

a **1420** HOCCLEVE *De Reg. Princ.* 2808 Correcte it.. while that it is grene, For and it hore, this londe is but loste.

2. To become mouldy.

1573 *Art of Limning* 7 To have your ynke to continue longe, and not to hore, put therein baysalte. **1592** [see HOAR *a.* 5]. **1750** W. ELLIS *Country Housew.* 22 If Bread is kept in too moist a Place too long, it will rope, or hoar, or mould.

3. *trans.* To make hoary or white, to whiten. In quot. 1607, To smite with hoar-leprosy.

1591 SYLVESTER *Du Bartas* I. iii. 344 Hils hoar'd with eternall Snowes. **1598** *Ibid.* II. i. III. *Furies* 86 Heav'n.. hoars her head with Snowes. **1607** SHAKS. *Timon* IV. iii. 155 Hoare the Flamen, That scold'st against the quality of flesh. **1747** *Gentl. Mag.* 242 Hoar'd with stiff'ning frosts.

hoard (hɔəd), *sb.*[1] Forms: *α.* 1-4 **hord**, 4-6 **horde**, 5-7 (8 *Sc.*) **hoord**, 6 **hoorde**, 7- **hoard**; *β.* *north.* 4 *Sc.* **hwrde**, 4-5 (6 *Sc.*) **hurd**, 4-7 **hurde**, 7- *Sc.* **huird**. [OE. *hord* = OS. *hord* treasure, hidden inmost place, OHG., MHG. *hort*, ON. *hodd*, Goth. *huzd* treasure:—OTeut. **hozdom*, pre-Teut. **kuzdhó-*; perh. from **kudhto-* pple., concealed, hidden (Kluge). The usual 16-17th c. forms *hoord, hurde*, Sc. *huird*, imply an early lengthening of OE. *o* to *ō* as in *board, ford*; *hoard* is rare before 18th c.]

1. An accumulation or collection of anything valuable hidden away or laid by for preservation or future use; a stock, store, esp. of money; a treasure.

Beowulf (Z.) 2284 Ða wæs hord rasod onboren beaga hord. *Ibid.* 3012 Ac þær is maðma hord. **937** *Poem on Æthelstan* 10 in *O.E. Chron.*, Hi æt campe.. land ealgodon, hord and hamas. *c* **975** *Rushw. Gosp.* Matt. vi. 19 Ne hydeþ eow hord in corþe þær om and mohþa etaþ. *a* **1100** *Ags. Voc.* in Wr.-Wülcker 337/11 *Thesaurus*, hord. *c* **1200** ORMIN 6733 Rihht all swa summ hord off gold Mang menn iss horde deresst. *a* **1225** *Ancr. R.* 224 Heo gedereð hord. *a* **1300** *Cursor M.* 22179 For all þe hordes [*Gött.* hurdes] þar ar hid Sal hali in his time be kid. *c* **1375** *Sc. Leg. Saints, Laurentius* 178 Spere besyly Quhare are þe hurdis þat has he. *c* **1425** WYNTOUN *Cron.* VII. ix. 103 Na þai of þame made na hurde. *c* **1440** *Promp. Parv.* 246/2 Hoord, tresowre. **1590** SHAKS. *Mids. N.* IV. i. 40 A venturous Fairy, That shall seeke the Squirrels hoard. **1609** SKENE *Reg. Maj.* Table 65 b, The fraudfull conceling of ane huird, or thresour. **1695** WOODWARD *Nat. Hist. Earth* V. (1723) 265 This Hoord.. that was stowed in the Strata underneath. **1764** GOLDSM. *Trav.* 195 While his lov'd partner, boastful of her hoard, Displays her cleanly platter on the board. **1851** D. WILSON *Preh. Ann.* (1863) II. IV. iii. 262 A large hoard of coins was discovered. **1859** TENNYSON *Enid* 352 Our hoard is little, but our hearts are great.

b. *fig.* Said of intangible things treasured or valuable, things concealed or kept secret; now *esp.* an amassed stock (of facts, etc.).

a **900** CYNEWULF *Crist* 1055 in *Exeter-bk.*, Se mæra dæg hreðer-locena hord, heortan geþohtas ealle ætyweð. *a* **1000** *Cædmon's Gen.* 1602 Oð þæt breosta hord, gast,.. gangan sceolde to godes dome. *a* **1000** in Mone *Gl.* 417 *Arcana*, hordas, geryne. *a* **1000** *Psalm* (Cotton) I. 28 (Gr.) His synna hord selfa ontende. *c* **1200** ORMIN 12920 Soþfasstnessess hord þatt all mannkinn birrþ sekenn. *a* **1300** *Cursor M.* 19214 Vte o þair hali hertes hord Spedli þai speld godds word. **1340** *Ayenb.* 263 Hous.. in huychen þe uader of house woneþ, þe hord of uirtues gadereþ. *c* **1440** CAPGRAVE *Life St. Kath.* III. 1503 God sende vs alle, of vnyte þe hord. **1635** R. BOLTON *Comf. Affl. Consc.* iv. 20 A heavenly hoard of grace, good conscience, Gods favour. **1764** GOLDSM. *Trav.* 58 To see the hoard of human bliss so small. **1805** WORDSW. *Waggoner* IV. 179 A hoard of grievances. **1847-8** H. MILLER *First Impr.* xix. (1857) 339 He accumulates much larger hoards of facts.

†**2.** The place in which anything is hidden, hoarded, or stored up; a repository; a hiding-place, store; a treasury. Also *fig.* *Obs.*

In the phrase ***in*** (or ***on***) ***hoard***, the sense fluctuates between the deposit, the repository in which it is stored up, and the state or condition of being hoarded (sense 3).

a **1200** *Moral Ode* 259 þe wreche mon binom his ehte and leide his on horde. **1258** *Proclam. Hen. III*, We senden ȝew þis writ open iseined wiþ vre seel to halden a manges ȝew inehord [*v.r.* ine hord]. *c* **1375** *Sc. Leg. Saints, Johannes* 42 [He] prechit furth ay goddis word, þat he had plentiusly ine hurd. *c* **1380** WYCLIF *Wks.* (1880) 316 Widnesse of siche cloþis is an hord to hyde synnes. *c* **1386** CHAUCER *Pars. T.* ¶ 747 It is the deueles hoord, ther he hideth hym and resteth. *c* **1400** *Destr. Troy* 11539 All my gold.. þat I getyn haue, Kepid in hurd, holdyn full long. **1577** HELLOWES *Gueuara's Chron.* 297 He was the hoorde of al my profound secretts. **1611** COTGR., *Musse*, a secret corner, priuie hoord, hiding hole. **1663** GERBIER *Counsel* 22 If the building cannot suffer the Chimney to be made even with the upright of the wall, both sides may be made up to serve for hoards. [**1837** KEIGHTLEY *Hist. Eng.* I. 29 The Cambrian princes had.. to pay yearly twenty pounds weight of gold, and two hundred of silver into the hoard of treasury of the 'King of London'. **1876** FREEMAN *Norm. Conq.* V. xxiv. 383 The sums which went into, and which, when it was needed, came out of, the hoard of the English King. **1883** GREEN *Conq. Eng.* 403 *note*, The 'Hoard' (not yet the 'Exchequer') in Eadward's time was settled at Winchester.]

†**3.** Hoarding up. *Obs.*

c **1390** CHAUCER *Truth* 3 For horde haþe hate, and clymbyng tykelnesse.

4. *Comb.*, as **hoard-burg** (mod. archaism, for OE. *hordburg*), treasure city; †**hoard-house**, treasure-house, treasury (*obs.*); **hoard-ward** (for OE. *hordweard*), guardian of a hoard, treasurer.

c **1440** *Promp. Parv.* 502/1 Tresowrye, *erarium*.. an hoordhowse. **1892** STOPFORD BROOKE *E.E. Lit.* iii. 75 The hoard-ward knew the voice of a man. **1895** MORRIS *Beowulf* 17 The gem-rich hoard-burg of the heroes.

hoard, *sb.*[2] Now *rare* or *Obs.* Also 8 **hourd**, 9 **hord**. [app. a modern ad. AngloFr. *hurdis* (see HURDIS, HURDICE) mistaken for a plural of **hurd*: see the quot. from *Liber Albus*. But cf. also obs. F. *hourd* scaffold (Cotgr.), in OF. *hurt, hourt, hourd*, palisade, of which *hourdis*, HURDIS was a deriv.] = HOARDING *sb.*

[**1419** *Liber Albus* (1859) I. 477 Item, qe nulle hurdys, ne palys, nautre cloysure, soit fait devaunt nulle tenement en les hautes rewes ou venelles en la citee (*Riley's marg. note* Hoards or palings not to be erected before houses).] **1757** *Act 31 Geo. II*, c. 17 §7 No Builder or other Person, shall erect or set up.. in any of the public Streets.. any Hourd or Fence. **1810** *Hull Improv. Act* 51 Hords or fences to be erected where buildings are taken down. **1836** SMART, *Hoard*,.. a fence enclosing a house and materials while builders are at work. **1838** F. W. SIMMS *Pub. Wks. Gt. Brit.* 5 The hoard is to consist of uprights six inches by four inches scantling.

hoard (hɔəd), *v.* Forms: *α.* 1 **hordian**, 3 (*Orm.*) **hordenn**, 4 **horde**, 4-6 **hoorde**, (6 **whord**), 6-7 **hourd(e, (hord)**, 6-7 (8 *Sc.*) **hoord**, 7- **hoard**; *β.* *Sc.* and *north.* 6 **hurde**, 6- **hurd**. [OE. *hordian*, f. *hord* HOARD *sb.*[1] (Cf. Goth. *huzdjan*, OHG. *gihurten*, MHG. *gehürten*, MG. *gehorden*, which belong to a different conjugation.)]

1. *trans.* To amass and put away (anything valuable) for preservation, security, or future use; to treasure *up*: esp. money or wealth.

c **1000** ÆLFRIC *Hom.* II. 104 Hordiað eowerne goldhord on heofenum. *c* **1200** ORMIN 12281 Gredig̃liȝ to sammnenn all & hordenn þatt tu winnesst. **1526** *Pilgr. Perf.* (W. de W. 1531) 98 b, To helpe other with them, and not inordynately to hoorde & kepe them. **1530** PALSGR. 588/2, I hourde, *je amasse*. Declared in 'I hoorde'. **1535** COVERDALE *Prov.* xi. 26 Who so hoordeth vp his corne, shalbe cursed amonge the people. **1548** UDALL, etc. *Erasm. Par. Matt.* v. 36 Whorded and heaped up. ? *a* **1550** in *Dunbar's Poems* (1893) 306 Gif thow hes a benefice, Preiss nevir to hurde the kirkis gude. **1573** G. HARVEY *Letter-bk.* (Camden) 8 He did not wel to hord it up. **1583** STANYHURST *Æneis* II. (Arb.) 68 Theere Troian treasur is hurded. **1615** G. SANDYS *Trav.* 136 The Granaries of Joseph: wherein he hoorded corne. **1635** A. STAFFORD *Fem. Glory* (1869) 124 Whereof the Rich hide and hoard up their wealth. **1702** ADDISON *Dial. Medals* (1727) 25 Hoording up such pieces of money. **1840** HOOD *Kilmansegg, Moral*, Gold! Gold! Gold! Gold!.. Hoarded, barter'd, bought and sold. **1878** JEVONS *Prim. Pol. Econ.* 22 If the rich man actually hoards up his money in the form of gold or silver, he gets no advantage from it.

b. *absol.*

c **1000** ÆLFRIC *Hom.* I. 66 Seðe hordað, and nat hwam he hit gegadarað. *a* **1300** *E.E. Psalter* xxxviii. 7 [xxxix. 6] He hordes, and he wate noght To wham þat he samenes oght. **1590** SPENSER *F.Q.* I. x. 38 He.. Ne car'd to hoord for those whom he did breede. **1842** TENNYSON *Ulysses* 5 A savage race, That hoard, and sleep, and feed, and know not me. **1860** EMERSON *Cond. Life, Wealth* Wks. (Bohn) II. 349 They should own who can administer; not they who hoard and conceal.

2. *fig.* and *transf.* To keep in store, cherish, treasure up, conceal (e.g. in the heart).

1340 *Ayenb.* 182 þet greate lost þet god hordeþ and wyteþ to ham þet ouercomeþ þe aduersetes of þise wordle. *c* **1380** WYCLIF *Wks.* (1880) 321 Crist.. lokyng on þe citee.. wepte þer upon for greet synne þat it hoordede. **1596** SPENSER *F.Q.* IV. xi. 43 The goodly Barow which doth hoord Great heapes of salmons in his deepe bosome. **1699** DRYDEN *Ep. to J. Driden* 117 You hoard not health for your own private use; But on the public spend the rich produce. **1789** BURKE *Corr.* (1844) III. 119 Revenge will be smothered and hoarded. **1821** B. CORNWALL *Mirandola* IV. i, Half of the ills we hoard within our hearts Are ills because we hoard them. **1870** MORRIS *Earthly Par.* I. I. 370.

†**3.** *intr.* in reflexive or passive sense: To lie treasured up, lie hid. *Obs. rare.*

1567 TURBERV. *Epit. & Sonn.* Wks. (1837) 300 In common weales what beares a greater sway Than hidden hate that hoordes in haughtie brest?

hoarded ('hɔədɪd), *ppl. a.* [f. HOARD *v.* + -ED[1].] Stored up, treasured up: see the verb.

1596 SPENSER *F.Q.* IV. ix. 12 Great store of hoorded threasure. **1607** SHAKS. *Cor.* IV. ii. 11 Th' hoorded plague a' th' Gods requit your loue! **1693** S. HERVEY in *Dryden's Juvenal* (1697) 232 Say, Goat.. For whom thy hoorded Bags in silence sleep? **1751** GRAY *Ode on Spring* v, No hive hast thou of hoarded sweets. *a* **1859** MACAULAY *Hist. Eng.* xxv. V. 252 The hoarded ill-humour of six months was at liberty to explode. **1887** *Spectator* 21 May 684/1 Modern theories as to the hoarded wealth of India.

hoarded, *a.* [f. HOARD *sb.*[2] + -ED[2].] Provided with a hoard or hoarding.

1898 *Daily News* 29 Mar. 5/2 The large hoarded enclosure before the Royal Exchange.

hoarder ('hɔədə(r)). Forms: 1 **hordere**, 2 **-are**, 4 **hordyer**, 6 **horder**, *Sc.* **hurdar**, 6-7 **hoorder**, 7- **hoarder**. [f. HOARD *v.* + -ER[1].]

†**1.** The keeper of the hoard or treasure; a treasurer; a steward. Also *fig.* *Obs.*

944 in Kemble *Cod. Dipl.* IV. 280 Ðis forward was makid with Ordric hordere. *c* **1000** ÆLFRIC *Hom.* II. 178 Ða het he his hordere þæt glæsene fæt syllan ðam biddendan sub-diacone. **1131** *O.E. Chron.* an. 1131 Swa þæt he scolde setten þær prior of Clunni & circeweard, & hordere, & reil-þein. **1340** *Ayenb.* 121 þet is þe hordyer þet lokeþ þe herte. [**1876** FREEMAN *Norm. Conq.* V. xxiv. 434 The King's 'Hoarder' was as old as the King's 'hoard'.]

2. (in mod. use) One who hoards or stores up, esp. money. (Also with *up*.)

1500-20 DUNBAR *Poems* xxvi. 59 Hud-pykis, hurdaris, and gadderaris. *a* **1529** SKELTON *Image Hypocr.* Wks. 1843 II. 417/2 And yet ye be questors, And hoorders vppe of testers. **1552** HULOET, Horder of treasure, *abditor*. **1594** (*title*) in *N. & Q.* 3rd Ser. III. 1 God's justice shewed uppon a cruelle horder of corne. **1691** LOCKE *Lower. Interest* Wks. 1727 II. 80 Nobody else, but these Hoarders, can get a Farthing by this proposed change of our Coin. **1845** FORD

Handbk. Spain I. 66 Hoarders-up of unrevenged grievances. **1875** JOWETT *Plato* (ed. 2) III. 102 He is mean, saving..a skinflint, a hoarder.

hoarding ('hɔədɪŋ), *sb.* [f. HOARD *sb.*²]

1. A temporary fence made of boards inclosing a building while in course of erection or repair; often used for posting bills and advertisements; hence, any boarding on which bills are posted.

1823 P. NICHOLSON *Pract. Build.* 225 *Hoarding*, an inclosure of wood about a building, while erecting or repairing. **1860** W. COLLINS *Wom. White* III. xi. 413 A rough hoarding of boards had been knocked up before the vestry doorway. **1864** *Realm* 23 Mar. 6 He rents a hoarding, or a wall, or the side of a house; and woe to that man who, being unauthorised, sticks anything thereupon. **1878** *Print. Trades Jrnl.* No. 25. 14 A poster now to be seen on most of the London street hoardings.

2. *Mil.* See quot. 1875.

1865 KINGSLEY *Herew.* II. ix. 146 They had thrown up.. doubtless overhanging hoardings or scaffolds. **1875** PARKER *Gloss. Archit.*, *Hourd, Hoard, Hoarding*, boarding used for protection..A term in military architecture for the wooden gallery, protected by boarding in front, which was thrown out from the surface of the wall in time of war, to enable the defenders to protect the foot of the wall.

hoarding ('hɔədɪŋ), *vbl. sb.* [f. HOARD *v.*]

1. The action of the verb HOARD; esp. the accumulation and hiding of money. (Also with *up*.)

1593 SHAKS. *3 Hen. VI*, II. ii. 48 And happy alwayes was it for that Sonne Whose Father for his hoording went to hell. *a* **1639** W. WHATELEY *Prototypes* III. xxxix. (1640) 16 Such hoording is no oppression but good husbandry. **1845** FORD *Handbk. Spain* I. 5 In self defence they are much addicted to hoarding.

2. *concr.* (*pl.*) That which is hoarded; money laid up.

1715 SOUTH *Serm.* IV. 450 All a Man's Gettings and Hoardings up, during his Youth. **1870** SPURGEON *Treas. Dav.* Ps. xlix. 10 Their hoardings are no longer theirs.

hoarding, *ppl. a.* [f. HOARD *v.* + -ING².] That hoards: see the verb.

1595 SHAKS. *John* III. iii. 8 Shake the bags Of hoording Abbots. **1641** BROME *Joviall Crew* I. Wks. 1873 III. 356 The hoarding Usurer. **1827** HOOD *Hero & Leander* lxxii, And with concealing clay, Like hoarding Avarice locks up his eyes.

hoare, obs. form of WHORE.

†**hoared** (hɔəd), *ppl. a. Obs.* [f. HOAR *v.*]

1. Made or grown hoary.

1557 NORTH *Gueuara's Diall Pr.* 120 a/2 My whyte heares, and hored bearde. **1568** T. HOWELL *Arb. Amitie* (1879) 25 Now hored age with stealing steps creepes in. *a* **1643** W. CARTWRIGHT *Ordinary* III. i. in Hazl. *Dodsley* XII. 253, I no where hoart yfeel but on mine head [cf. HOAR *a.* 1, quot. 1386].

2. Grown mouldy.

1496 *Dives & Paup.* II. xx, They toke hored brede in theyr scryppes. **1551** BIBLE (Matthews) *Josh.* ix. 5 All their prouysyon of breade was dried vp and hored.

3. *Comb.*, as ***hoared-headed***, hoar-headed.

1590 SHAKS. *Mids. N.* II. i. 107 We see The seasons alter; hoared headed frosts Fall in the fresh lap of the crimson Rose.

'hoar-frost. Formerly, and still often, two words. [See HOAR *a.* and FROST *sb.* 2.] **a.** The white deposit formed by the freezing of dew, frozen dew, white frost. In scientific use now distinguished from rime.

Hoar-frost is a crystalline deposit of ice formed by the sublimation of water vapour; rime is a more amorphous deposit formed by the rapid freezing of supercooled droplets of water when they are brought by air currents into contact with a cold surface.

c **1290** *St. Michael* 617 in *S. Eng. Leg.* I. 317 Þe hore-forst [*v.r.* hor-forst] cometh ȝwane it is so cold þat it freoseth a-nyȝt, And þe Dev freose a-doneward. **1340** *Ayenb.* 108 The zonne..wasteþ þe cloudes and þe hore urostes bi þe morȝen. **1535** COVERDALE *Ps.* cxlvii. 16 He geueth snowe like woll, & scatereth yᵉ horefrost like ashes. **1644** Z. BOYD *Gard. Zion* 60 (Jam.) Sweet Mannah, round, small as the haire frost. **1730–46** THOMSON *Autumn* 1169 The rigid hoar-frost melts before his beam. **1880** MISS BRADDON *Just as I am* xii, All the trees were fairy-trees wreathed with hoar-frost. **1895** T. RUSSELL *Meteorol.* iii. 53 Hoar-frost is a name given to the curious, regular figures resembling ferns that form on objects, especially on the window-panes in houses... Rime is a thick, heavy frost forming on objects from frozen rain or mist. **1921** A. E. M. GEDDES *Meteorol.* vi. 182 An examination of these crystals shows that they have not been deposited first as water drops, for they are not frozen drops of water. A deposit of this form is called hoar frost. **1967** R. W. FAIRBRIDGE *Encycl. Atmos. Sci.* 402/1 'Frost' has several meanings, most commonly implying hoar-frost or white frost which occurs when the air has been damp, leading to direct sublimation and the building of interlocking ice crystals on exposed surfaces.

fig. **1852** BADGER *Nestorians* I. 243 The hoar-frost of care was prematurely sitting upon his locks.

attrib. **1804** ANNA SEWARD *Mem. Darwin* 323 A fine picture of an hoar-frost landscape.

b. hoar-frost curve or **line**: a line representing the conditions for equilibrium between the solid and the vapour phases of water in the absence of the liquid phase.

1879 *Encycl. Brit.* VIII. 731/2 At this point the steam line, ice line, and hoar-frost line intersect, and it has therefore been called the triple point. **1940** GLASSTONE *Text-bk. Physical Chem.* vi. 459 The vapor pressure curve of ice..is often called the hoar-frost curve.

Hence **'hoar-frosty** *a.*

1845 CARLYLE *Cromwell* (1871) I. 39 A cold hoarfrosty morning.

'hoarhead. [f. HOAR *a.* + HEAD *sb.*¹] A hoary head; hence, an old grey-haired man. Also *attrib.*

1382 WYCLIF *Lev.* xix. 32 Before the hoor heed aryse. **1560** BIBLE (Genev.) ibid., Thou shalt rise vp before the horehed. **1574** HELLOWES *Gueuara's Fam. Ep.* (1577) 125, I do not beleeue that the wisdome lyeth in horeheads, but in olde bookes. **1830** TENNYSON *Poems* 113 The hoarhead winter paving earth With sheeny white.

hoar-headed, *a.* [Parasynthetic f. *hoar head* + -ED².] Having the head hoary with age.

1561 T. HOBY tr. *Castiglione's Courtyer* II. M iv b, Hore-headed and toothlesse. *a* **1693** URQUHART *Rabelais* III. xxviii. 227, I see thee waxing a little hoar-headed. **1880** TENNYSON *Battle of Brunanburh* ix, Hoar-headed hero!

Hence **hoar-'headedness.**

1574 tr. *Marlorat's Apocalips* 22 Holy and reuerend Hore-headednesse pretendeth wisedome gotten by long experience.

hoarhound, another spelling of HOREHOUND.

'hoarily, *adv.* [f. HOARY *a.* + -LY².] With a hoary appearance; with a grey or whitish hue.

1890 W. C. RUSSELL *Ocean Trag.* II. xxi. 184 Clouds of foam..whirling hoarily under the black vapour.

hoariness ('hɔərɪnɪs). [f. HOARY *a.* + -NESS.] The quality or state of being hoary: see the adj.

1573–80 BARET *Alv.* H 492 Hoarinesse, whitenesse of haires, ancientie. *Ibid.* 494 Hoarienesse, vinewednesse, or mouldinesse, comming of moisture, for lacke of cleansing. **1599** MASSINGER, etc. *Old Law* III. ii, His white hairs, they'll betray his hoariness. **1647** TRAPP *Comm. Matt.* xxvii. 15 Custom without truth is but hoariness or mouldiness of error. **1705** C. PURSHALL *Mech. Macrocosm* 37 These Frosts seldom last long, that come with a Frozen Fog, or Hoariness. **1829** LOUDON *Encycl. Plants* 1001 The stem under the shelter of long grass, is covered with a white hoariness which is easily rubbed off. **1885** CLODD *Myths & Dr.* II. i. 144 Legends sacred with the hoariness of time.

†**hoarish** ('hɔərɪʃ), *a. Obs.* [f. HOAR *a.* + -ISH.] Somewhat hoary.

1398 TREVISA *Barth. De P.R.* XVII. xii. (1495) 610 That one wormode is grene, that other somdeale horisshe and lesse bytter. *a* **1547** SURREY in *Tottell's Misc.* (Arb.) 31 The white and horish heares, the messengers of age.

†**'hoarness.** *Obs.* [f. HOAR *a.* + -NESS.] The quality of being hoar or hoary; hoariness.

a **900** *Kent. Gloss.* in Wr.-Wülcker 76/21 *Canicies*, harnes. **1382** WYCLIF *Prov.* xx. 29 The dignete of olde men hornesse. **1398** TREVISA *Barth. De. P.R.* XIX. iv. (1495) 862 Thenne is whyte colour gendryd as it faryth in snowe in hoore froste and in horenes of heere. **14..** *Voc.* in Wr.-Wülcker 570/13 *Canicies*, hoorenesse. *c* **1450** *R. Gloucester's Chron.* (1724) 481/2 *note* (MS. Coll. Arms) A litelle harenesse hathe chaunged sumwhat his colour. **1562** BULLEYN *Def. agst. Sickness, Compounds* 17 a, It kepeth..the hedde from horenes. **1564** BECON *Dem. Holy Script.* Prayers, etc. (1844) 607 Having hoarness of manners, authority, gravity, and high knowledge. **1565–73** COOPER *Thesaurus*, *Mucor*,..hoarenesse, such as is on breade or meate long kept.

b. A close growth of white or grey hairs.

1578 LYTE *Dodoens* I. v. 10 The leaues..hauing a certaine fine horenesse upon them like veluet.

hoarse (hɔəs), *a.* Forms: α. 1 **hás**, 3–4 **hos**, 4–5 **hose, hoos, hoose,** (4 **hois**), 5 **hooce, hoce,** (**hoost**), 8–9 *dial.* **hoast**; *north.* and *Sc.* 4–5 **haase, hase,** 5 **hayse,** 5–6 *Sc.* **hace,** 6 **hays, hais,** (**hess**). β. 4–5 **hors, -e, hoors,** 5–6 **hoorse,** 6 **horce,** (**hourse**), 6–7 **hoarce,** (7 **hoars**), 6– **hoarse**; *Sc.* 8 **hers,** 8– **hearse,** 9 **herse, hairce, hairse,** *dial.* **hairsh, hearsh.** [A word of which the stem varies, not only in Eng., but in the other Teut. langs. The recorded OE. type was *hás* (ME. *hôs*, Sc. *hāse*), corresp. to OHG., MHG., OLG. *heis*, OS. *hês*, MDu. *hees*, LG. *hês*:—OTeut. **haiso-*. But beside this ME. had *hôrs, hoors*, now *hoarse*, Sc. *hairse, hairsh, hearsh*. Although written evidence for the *r* forms goes back only to *c* 1400, the correspondence of mod.Eng. *hoarse* and Sc. *hairse* implies the existence of an unrecorded OE. **hárs* beside *hás*.

The ON. normal repr. of OTeut. **haiso-z* would be **heiss*, instead of which ON. had *háss*, app. to be explained as for **hárs*:—**hairso-* (orig. *ai* before *r* gave *á* in ON.). The OFl. *heersch*, recorded by Kilian beside *heesch*, appears to go back similarly to an OLG. **heirs*. For these and other reasons it is now generally held that **hairso-* was the orig. OTeut. type, and that the *r* subseq. disappeared at different times in most of the dialects. The southern Scotch *hairsh, hearsh*, appears to exemplify a frequent Sc. interchange of *rs* and *rsh*, seen e.g. in *farce, farsch, scarce, scairsh, Erse, Ersch*, etc.]

1. Rough and deep-sounding, as the voice when affected with a cold, or the voice of a raven or frog; harsh and low in pitch; not clear and smooth like a pure musical note; husky, croaking, raucous. **a.** Of the voice (of persons or animals).

α. *c* **1000** ÆLFRIC *Gram.* xxx. (Z.) 190 *Raucus* and *rauca*, has. *a* **1250** *Owl & Night.* 504 Þu..pipest al so doþ a mose Mid cokeringe mid stefne hose. *c* **1374** CHAUCER *Troylus* IV. 1119 (1147) With brokyn vois, al hois [*Campsall MS.*, hoors; *MS. Gg.* 4. 27, hors] for shright. *c* **1440** *Promp. Parv.* 248/1 Hoos (*K.* hors, *P.* hoorse), *raucus*. *c* **1450** HENRYSON *Test. Cres.* 338 Thy voice..unplesand, hoir, and hace. **1468** *Medulla* in *Promp. Parv.* 248 *note*, *Raucus*, hoost. **1483** *Cath. Angl.* 177/1 Hase (*A.* Hayse), *raucus*. **1876** *Mid-Yorksh. Gloss.*, *Hôast*,..hoarse.

β. *c* **1400** *Lanfranc's Cirurg.* 59 A wood hound..if þat he.. berke, his vois is ful hors. *c* **1450** *Trevisa's Barth. De P.R.* XII. xviii. (MS. Bodl.), An henne..clokkinge wiþ an horse [*ed.* 1495 hoars] voice. **1584** R. SCOT *Discov. Witchcr.* I. ii. (1886) 5 His voice was hoarse and lowe. **1625** DONNE *Anat. World, Progr. Soul* (Song of Sorcerers), She feigns hoarse barkings, but she biteth not! **1762** BEATTIE *Bat. Pigmies & Cranes* 70 He [a frog]..mourns in hoarsest croaks his destiny. **1865** DICKENS *Mut. Fr.* I. iii, His voice was hoarse and coarse.

b. Of other sounds. (Chiefly *poetic.*)

1513 DOUGLAS *Æneis* IX. iii. 109 The ryver brayt with hais [*ed.* 1710 hers] sovnd. **1697** DRYDEN *Virg. Past.* IX. 52 The Tides with their hoarse Murmurs. **1699** GARTH *Dispens.* VI. 72 Where with hoars dinn imprison'd tempests rave. **1728** POPE *Dunc.* II. 233 This Drum, whose hoarse heroic bass Drowns the loud clarion of the braying Ass. **1883** OUIDA *Wanda* II. 40 The hoarse sound of the sea surging amongst the rocks.

2. *transf.* Having a hoarse voice or sound. **a.** Of persons and animals, or of the vocal organs.

α. *a* **1000** ÆLFRIC *Colloq.* in Wr.-Wülcker 90/40 Ic hæbbe sumne cnapan..þe eac swilce nu has ys for cylde and hreame. *c* **1330** *King of Tars* 599 Ofte he criyede, and ofte he ros, So longe that he wox al hos. *a* **1340** HAMPOLE *Psalter* lxviii. 4 Thai vndirstode me noght na mare than man may do a hase man. *c* **1400** *Ywaine & Gaw.* 3620 So was he hase and spak ful law. **1513** DOUGLAS *Æneis* III. Prol. 21 Chyde quhill thair heidis rife, and hals worth hais [*v.r.* hace, *rimes* place, face]. **1535** LYNDESAY *Satyre* 315 How-beit that I am hais [*v.r.* hess] I am content to beir a bais.

β. **1377** LANGL. *P. Pl.* B. XVII. 324 Til he be blere-nyed or blynde and hors [*v. rr.* hoos, hos] in þ e throte. **1538** BALE *Brefe Com. John Baptist* in *Harl. Misc.* (Malh.) I. 207, I oft haue bene horce Cryenge for custome. **1593** SHAKS. *2 Hen. VI*, v. ii. 7 Warwicke is hoarse with calling thee to armes. **1697** DRYDEN *Virg. Past.* I. 25 The hoarse Raven..croaking. **1728** POPE *Dunc.* I. 330 The hoarse nation croak'd, 'God save King Log!' **1786** BURNS *Earnest Cry* 7 Alas! my roupet Muse is hearse! **1826** MISS MITFORD in L'Estrange *Life* II. x. 231 Charles Kemble is at present as hoarse as a crow. **1887** J. SERVICE *Dr. Duguid* vii. 41 He..was now as hairse and roopit as a craw.

b. Of inanimate things. (Chiefly *poetic.*)

c **1369** CHAUCER *Dethe Blaunche* 347 Tassay hys horne, and for to knowe Whether hyt were clere, or horse of sovne. **1570** B. GOOGE *Pop. Kingd.* IV. (1880) 56 With Bagpipe hoarce he hath begon his Musicke fine. **1667** MILTON *P.L.* II. 661 The hoarce Trinacrian shore. **1765** BEATTIE *Judgem. Paris* cxxxiii, Raves the hoarse storm along the bellowing main. **1870** DICKENS *E. Drood* iii, Cloisterham, with its hoarse cathedral bell.

3. quasi-*adv.* = HOARSELY.

1709 *Tatler* No. 121 ¶ 1 He catched Cold, and..began to bark very hoarse. **1808** SCOTT *Marm.* I. Introd i, Now, murmuring hoarse..An angry brook, it sweeps the glade.

4. *Comb.* **a.** parasynthetic, as ***hoarse-throated, -voiced***; **b.** adverbial, as ***hoarse-resounding***, etc.

1598 FLORIO *Ital. Dict.* To Rdr. A vj b, An vnluckie, hoarce-voist..night-rauen. *a* **1729** CONGREVE *Hymn to Harmony* vi. (Jod.), Loud trumpets..And hoarse-resounding drums. *a* **1743** SAVAGE *Wks.* (1775) II. 75 (Jod.) Hoarse-echoing walls. **1791** COWPER *Iliad* II. 888 The hoarse-throated war. **1836–48** B. D. WALSH *Aristoph., Clouds* I. iv, The hoarse-roaring Ocean's fountains. **1887** BOWEN *Virg. Æneid* VI. 327 The hoarse-voiced torrents of doom.

Hence †**'hoarsehead**, hoarseness.

c **1440** *Promp. Parv.* 248/2 Hooshede, or hoosnesse (*K.* hoshed, *P.* hoorshede), *raucitas*.

hoarse, *v.* [f. prec.] **a.** *intr.* To be or become hoarse. **b.** *trans.* To make hoarse. *Obs.* exc. with *up* (*dial.* and *U.S.*).

c **1000** ÆLFRIC *Gram.* xxx. (Z.) 190 *Raucio*, ic hasiȝe, *rausi, rausum*. **1483** *Cath. Angl.* 177/2 Hase, *raucio*. **1629** T. ADAMS *Sinner's Passing Bell* Wks. 1861–2 I. 355 When his voice is hoarsed. **1877** BARTLETT *Dict. Amer.* (ed. 4) s.v., He's got a bad cold and is all hoarsed up. **1886** *S.W. Linc. Gloss.* s.v., I'm hoarst on my chest—hoarst up, a'most. **1897** *Voice* (N.Y.) 23 Dec. 5/1 My voice seems good when I begin, but I very soon 'hoarse up'.

hoarsely ('hɔəslɪ), *adv.* [f. HOARSE *a.* + -LY².] With a hoarse voice or sound.

a **1529** SKELTON *P. Sparowe* 419 The woodhacke, that syngeth chur Horsly, as he had the mur. **1580** SIDNEY *Arcadia* III. (1590) 280 His words..slowly and hoarcely pronounced. **1610** G. FLETCHER *Christ's Tri. over Death* lvii, The..waters hoarsely groan. *c* **1720** TICKELL *Imit. Proph. Nereus* 44 While hoarsely he demands the fight. **1821** SHELLEY *Prometh. Unb.* I. i. 715, I heard the thunder hoarsely laugh. **1883** MRS. OLIPHANT *Ladies Lindores* II. 300 'Sit down', he said, hoarsely, 'and I will tell you'.

hoarsen ('hɔəs(ə)n), *v.* [f. HOARSE *a.* + -EN⁵.]

1. *trans.* To make hoarse.

1748 RICHARDSON *Clarissa* (1811) V. vii. 79, I shall be obliged to hoarsen my voice, and roughen my character. **1881** PALGRAVE *Vis. Eng., Tower of Doom* ii, Hoarsening the cry Of those who watch'd. **1886** BARING-GOULD *Gold. Feather* i, The sore throat..hoarsened her voice.

2. *intr.* To become hoarse; to sound hoarsely.

1798 LANDOR *Gebir* VII. 148 The brazen clarion hoarsens. **1894** HALL CAINE *Manxman* 435 His voice had hoarsened.

Hence **'hoarsened** *ppl. a.*

1798 LANDOR *Gebir* I. 135 To tune afresh the hoarsened reed. **1876** GEO. ELIOT *Dan. Der.* v. xl, The last words had a perceptible irony in their hoarsened tone.

hoarseness ('hɔəsnɪs). [f. as prec. + -NESS.] The quality or condition of being hoarse.

α. *c* **1000** ÆLFRIC *Voc.* in Wr.-Wülcker 113/1 *Raucedo*, hasnys. **1387** TREVISA *Higden* I. vii. (Rolls) I. 11 My bareyn speche, hosnes and snochynge. *c* **1440** *Promp. Parv.* 248/2 Hooshede or hoosnesse [**1499** *Pynson*, hoorsnesse]. **1483** *Cath. Angl.* 177/2 An Hasenes, *raucedo, raucitas.*

β. **1495** *Trevisa's Barth. De P.R.* v. xxiv. 134 Hoorsnes of voyce. *Ibid.* VII. xxvii. 242 Horsnes and lettyng of the voyce. **1589** COGAN *Haven Health* ccxvii. (1636) 247 Red wine.. bindeth the belly and maketh hoarsenesse. **1648** *Hunting of Fox* 10 They (even to hoarsnesse) cried downe the Common-Prayer book. **1732** ARBUTHNOT *Rules of Diet* i. 247 Figs are useful in Hoarseness and Coughs. **1885** *Manch. Exam.* 22 Feb. 5/3 Mr. Reeves sang.. without the slightest trace of hoarseness.

hoar-stone. Forms: 1 hár stán, 3 hor ston, 6–8 hore-, 7 hoore-, 9 hoar-stone, *Sc.* hair-, hare stane. [In OE. two words: see HOAR *a.* and STONE.]

1. *lit.* A hoar, i.e. grey or ancient stone (? an ancient stone grey with lichen).

Beowulf (Z.) 887 He under harne stan, æþelinges bearn. *Ibid.* 2745 Nu ðu lungre geong hord sceawian under harne stan. **971** *Blickl. Hom.* 209 He þær ʒeseah ofer ðæm wætere sumne harne stan.

2. *spec.* **a.** A stone (ancient or grey with lichen), frequently mentioned in charters as marking a boundary line; an ancient boundary stone, merestone. (See HOAR *a.* 3.)

847 *Charter of Æthelwulf* in *O.E. Texts* 434 Đonon on ðone healdan weʒ wið huitan stanes, ðonon to ðæm beorʒe ðe mon hateð æt ðæm holne, ðonon an haran stan. *a* **1000** in *Heming's Chartulary* (1723) 348 Of ʒytinges æwylme on norðdene on þone grenan weʒ, þ[an] on þane haran stan, of ðam haran stane andlang grenan weʒes on scepe clif. ? *c* **1195** in *Archæol.* (1832) XXV. 55 Unam scilicet sub le Harestan. **1298** *Ibid.*, Et sic directe usque le Horeston in Twychenylde Grene. ? *a* **1300** *Ibid.* 58 Ad Haresteines et sic usque ad Depe-dale. **1503** in Hearne *Johannis Glastoniensis Chron.* (1726) 303 Inter Dominium de Andresey & Dominium de Stoke seu Dreycote, usque ad la Hore Stone. *a* **1831** W. HAMPER in *Archæol.* (1832) XXV. 30 The Hoar-stone is consequently nothing more than the stone of memorial or land-mark, describing the boundary of property. **1849** KEMBLE *Sax. in Eng.* I. 52 *note*, Artificial or natural stone posts are implied by the constantly recurring háran stánas, græʒan stánas, hoary or grey stones. **1851** D. WILSON *Preh. Ann.* (1863) II. iv. vii. 375 Hoare-stones, or landmarks of the fifth century.

b. An ancient stone associated with some event or tradition; a stone of memorial; a standing stone.

1666 in Hearne *R. Brunne's Chron.* (1810) 472 A stone of 8 foot high above ground.. It is now called, in the full of the mouth, hoore-stone, according to the dialect of Sommersett. **1808** SCOTT *Marm.* iv. xxv. *note*, The royal standard is traditionally said to have been displayed from the Hare Stane, a high stone, now built into the wall, on the left hand of the high-way leading towards Braid. **1812** *Archæol.* XVI. 361 The largest stone, at the east end, has been long known in that County, by the name of the Hoar Stone. *a* **1831** W. HAMPER in *Archæol.* (1832) XXV. 25 In many parts of Great Britain are to be seen upright rude Pillars or massive blocks of stone which in England are called *Hoar-Stones*.. in Scotland.. *Hare-Stane.* **1851** D. WILSON *Preh. Ann.* 92 The Hare Stane on the Borough Moor of Edinburgh. *Ibid.* (1863) I. v. 137 A hoare-stone or Stone of Memorial.

c. Hence very frequent as a place-name.

See a list in *Archæologia* (1832) XXV. 52.

† **'hoarsy,** *a. Obs. rare.* [f. HOARSE *a.* + -Y: cf. *hoary.*] = HOARSE.

1570 LEVINS *Manip.* 108/25 Horsy, *raucus.*

hoary ('hɔərɪ), *a.* Also 6–7 **hory,** (6 **hoory, horie, heorye**). [A late formation (16th c.) from HOAR *a.* or *sb.* + -Y: cf. *dusky, haughty, vasty.*]

1. a. Of the hair, head, or beard: Grey or white with age.

1530 PALSGR. 315/2 Hoory as a man or beestes heare is, *chaneu.* *a* **1547** SURREY *Carelesse man* in *Tottell's Misc.* (Arb.) 26 What will she do, when hory heares are powdred in her hedde? **1611** BIBLE *Lev.* xix. 32 Thou shalt rise vp before the hoary head. **1814** SCOTT *Ld. of Isles* iv. xix, Veterans.. Whose helmets press'd their hoary hair. **1885** R. BUCHANAN *Annan Water* i, With hoary bushy eyebrows.

b. Having white or grey hair, grey-haired.

1573–80 BARET *Alv.* H486 To waxe Hoarie, or white headed, *incanesco.* **1682** DRYDEN *Mac Fl.* 106 The hoary prince in majesty appeared. **1738** GLOVER *Leonidas* I. 55 Her sons, her matrons and her hoary sires. **1868** FREEMAN *Norm. Conq.* II. viii. 186 Men like the hoary sinner.. instinctively saw in him the destined enemy of his kind.

c. Ancient; venerable from age, time-honoured.

1609 DEKKER *Gull's Horne-bk.* (1812) 25 Venerable father of ancient, and therefore hoary customs. **1630** PRYNNE *Anti-Armin.* 238 Hoarie English Antiquities. **1781** COWPER *Expost.* 596 Windsor's hoary towers. **1852** ROBERTSON *Serm.* Ser. III. xviii. 232 A hoary and most remote antiquity. **1871** R. ELLIS *Catullus* lxiv. 1 Born on Pelion height, so legend hoary relateth.

2. Of colour: Grey, greyish white.

1573–80 BARET *Alv.* H493 A hoarie frost, *cana pruina.* **1579** SPENSER *Sheph. Cal.* Feb. 79 Clothed with cold, and hoary wyth frost. **1667** MILTON *P.L.* II. 891 The secrets of the hoarie deep. **1697** DRYDEN *Virg. Georg.* II. 168 With Ethiops hoary Trees and woolly Wood. **1784** COWPER *Task* III. 830 Winter's hoary wing. **1809** HEBER *Europe* 258 The hoary poplars wave. **1878** G. MACDONALD *Phantastes* i. 12 Below lay a sea, still as death and hoary in the moon.

† **3.** Mouldy, musty; corrupt. *Obs.*

Perh. in some instances confused with *hory*, filthy.

1530 PALSGR. 315/2 Hoory as meate that is kepte to longe, *fleury.* **1567** tr. *Ælfric's Let. to Bp. Wulsine* in Brady *Clavis Cal.* (1813) I. 280 Some pristes keepe the housell.. all the Yere for Syke Men,—But they do greatlye amysse, by cause it waxeth Heorye. **1603** KNOLLES *Hist. Turks* (1621) 624 Hoarie, moulded bread. **1693** EVELYN *De la Quint. Compl. Gard.* Dict., Musty, Mouldy, or Hoary Dung.

4. *Bot.* and *Entom.* Covered with short dense white or whitish hairs; canescent.

1597 GERARDE *Herbal* I. vii. §1. 8 Soft and downie, and somewhat hoarie. **1668** WILKINS *Real Char.* II. iv. §6. 112 That whose leaves are bigger, and hoary all over. **1796** WITHERING *Brit. Plants* (ed. 3) III. 725 Whole plant hoary with a dense cottony substance. **1870** HOOKER *Stud. Flora* 28 Perennial hoary herbs.

b. Hence used to designate species of plants and animals so clothed; often rendering L. *canus, incanus*, etc.: as ***hoary alder, creeper, mullein, stock***, etc.

1811 SHAW *Zool.* VIII. 261 Hoary Creeper, *Certhia canescens*.. bill stout and black. **1841** W. SPALDING *Italy & It. Isl.* III. 314 The white willow, and the common and hoary alder, form thickets.

c. In names of animals having a hoary appearance (see quots.).

1781 T. PENNANT *Hist. Quadrupeds* II. 398 Hoary M[armot] with the tip of the nose black.. hair universally rude and long; that on the back, sides and belly cinereous at the root, black in the middle, whitish at the tip, so that the animal has a hoary appearance. **1829** SIR J. RICHARDSON *Fauna Bor.-Amer.* I. 150 Hoary marmot, with long coarse fur, particularly on the chest and shoulders, where it is hoary. **1832** J. RENNIE *Butterfl. & Moths* 183 The Hoary Double Crescent.. frequents ash-trees. **1903** *Bull. Amer. Mus. Nat. Hist.* XIX. 539 Marmotta caligata (Eschscholtz). Hoary marmot. **1948** W. J. STOKOE *Caterp. Brit. Moths* I. 151 (*heading*) The Hoary Footman. **1954** O. J. MURIE *Field Guide to Animal Tracks* 136 The hoary marmot has also sought the high mountains. **1959** HALL & KELSON *Mammals N. Amer.* I. 192/1 The hoary bat is solitary and roosts in trees and shrubs.

5. *Comb.* **a.** parasynthetic, as ***hoary-dated, -feathered, -haired, -headed, -herbaged, -vested***, etc.; **b.** with another adj., as ***hoary-pubescent***, etc.

1598 B. JONSON *Ev. Man in Hum.* iv. viii, This hoarie-headed letcher, this old goat. **1771** WESLEY *Wks.* (1872) V. 61 When he is old and hoary-haired. **1797** T. PARK *Sonn.* 8 Classic Eton's hoary-vested towers. **1831** DON *Gard. Dict.* I. xvii, *Hoary-pubescent*, covered with white down which is pressed to the surface. *Ibid.*, *Hoary-villous*, covered with white villi. **1847** W. E. STEELE *Field Bot.* 53 Leaves hoary-white beneath. **1859** TENNYSON *Enid* 295 There musing sat the hoary-headed Earl. **1876** BLACKIE *Songs Relig. & Life* 11 A hoary-dated Patriarch pedigree.

hoase, obs. form of HOARSE, HOSE.

hoast (həʊst), *sb.* Chiefly *north. dial.* Forms: [1 **hwósta**], 4–9 **host,** 5, 9 *dial.* **hoost,** (6–9 **hoste, hoist**), 7– **hoast,** (**haust,** 9 **hoarst**). [The OE. *hwósta* is not known to have survived in ME.; the extant northern word (from 14th c.) was app. the cognate ON. *hóste* cough = OLG. **hôsto* (MLG. *hôste*, MDu. *hoeste, hoest*, LG. *hoost, hôst*, Du. *hoest*), OHG. *huosto* (MHG. *huoste*, Ger. *husten*):—OTeut. **hwôston-*, f. a root **hwôs-* (whence OE. *hwésan*:—**hwôsjan* to wheeze), pre-Teut. **kwōs-, kās-*; cf. Skr. *kās* to cough.

It is possible that OE. *hwósta* may have survived dialectally; some writers refer to a dial. form, *whoost*, which would be its representative; and this, as in *who, whoop*, might become *hoost*, whence mod. Shropshire *'oost.*]

A cough. In some Eng. dialects used only of cattle.

[*c* **1000** *Voc.* in Wr.-Wülcker 277/27 *Tussis*, hwosta.] *a* **1300** *Cursor M.* 534 Als aand with host in brest is spred. *c* **1440** *Promp. Parv.* 248/2 Hoose, or cowghe (*other MSS.* host.. hoost), *tussis.* **14..** *Nom.* in Wr.-Wülcker 708/2 *Hec tussis*, the host. *c* **1500** [see HIVES]. *a* **1510** DOUGLAS *K. Hart* II. 455 Heidwerk, Hoist, and Parlasy, maid grit pay. **1562** TURNER *Herbal* II. 34 Mastik is good.. for an old host or coughe. *a* **1605** MONTGOMERIE *Flyting w. Polwart* 302 The hunger, the hart-ill, and the hoist still thee hald. **1622** *Course Conformitie* 117 (Jam.) He that can swallow a camel.. without an hoast. *a* **1651** CALDERWOOD *Hist. Kirk* (1678) 60 (Jam.) From the thirteenth of November.. he became so feeble with a hoast. **1674** RAY *N.C. Words* 24 *An Haust or Hoste*, a Dry Cough. **1688** R. HOLME *Armoury* II. 172/1 The Cough, or Cold, and Shortness of Breath, or Hausts, an Inward Disease in Cows. **1773** *Epitaph* in *Spectator* (1884) 6 Sept. 1173 Of a cauld and a sair host, He died upon the Yorkshire coast. **1803** *Med. Jrnl.* X. 217 A great number of cats in Shrewsbury became seized with what is commonly called the *Hoost.* **1821** GALT *Ann. Parish* ii. (D.), I gave them a sign by a loud hoast. *a* **1825** FORBY *Voc. E. Anglia*, *Hoist*, a cough. **1863** MRS. GASKELL *Sylvia's L.* xxiv, I'll make him a treacle-posset; it's a famous thing for keeping off hoasts. **1879** MISS JACKSON *Shropsh. Word-bk.*, *Hoost* [oost], a cough: said of cattle. **1893** *Northumbld. Gloss.*, *Hoast*, *Hoist*, a cough.

hoast, *v.* Chiefly *north. dial.* Forms: [1 **hwóstan**], 5–9 **host,** (6 **hoyst,** 9 **hoist**), 8– **hoast,** (*dial.* **huist**). [OE. *hwóstan* = OLG. **hôstôn* (MLG. *hôsten*, MDu. *hoesten*), OHG. *huostôn* (MHG. *huosten*, Ger. *husten*), ON. *hósta* (Sw. *hosta*, Da. *hoste*), f. the sb.: see prec. The existing northern word (known only from 15th c.) appears to be the ON. word. Beside *hoast*, Sc. has also the form *huist*, going back to *hōst.*]

1. *intr.* To cough.

[*c* **1000** *Sax. Leechd.* II. 258, & hwostað [*MS.* hwosað] ʒelome.] *c* **1440** *Promp. Parv.* 249/1 Hostyn, or rowhyn, or cowghyn,.. *tussio.* **1483** *Cath. Angl.* 190/1 To Host, *tussire.* **1619** *Life & Death P. Simsone* (1845) 100 He hosted continually to his death. *c* **1750** in Ritson *Scot. Songs* (1794) II. 250 He hosts and he hirples the weary day lang. **1752** A. MACINNES in *Scots Mag.* (1753) July 342/2 Allan Breck came behind him, and hoasted. *a* **1825** FORBY *Voc. E. Anglia*, *Hoist*, to cough. **1885** *Queen* 31 Jan. 111 That hobbling 'hosting' old woman who asks for human charity.

2. *trans.* To cough *up* or *out*. Also *fig.*

1508 DUNBAR *Tua Mariit Wemen* 272 Ane hair hogeart, that hostit out flewme. **1513** DOUGLAS *Æneis* XIII. i. 10 The Latyn pepyll.. hostit owt full cleyr, Deip from thar brestis the hard sorow smart. **1583** *Leg. Bp. St. Androis* 146 in *Sat. Poems Ref.* xlv, He hosted thair a hude full fra him. **1786** BURNS *Willie Chalmers* v, And host up some palaver.

hoast, obs. form of HOST.

hoastman ('həʊstmən). Also 6 host-e, ost-, 7 oast-, 7–8 host-. [f. *host, oste*, in sense 'stranger, guest'; the seal of the corporation shows a member in his robes receiving a stranger with the words 'Welcome my oste'.]

A member of a corporation or merchant-guild in Newcastle-upon-Tyne, who had originally the functions of receiving strangers (called 'hosts' or 'oasts') who came to buy coal and certain other commodities, and of conducting their purchases, on which they levied a certain duty; in later times, they controlled the selling and exportation of coal; now, they merely form the premier civic corporation.

1518 *Merch. Adv. Newcastle* (Surtees) 51 The act for the ostmen that byes any merchaundyse of ther hosts, or it be presented to the Master of the Feloship. **1623–4** *Act 21 Jas. I*, c. 3 §12 Any.. Priviledge heretofore claymed.. by the auncient Fellowshipp Guild or Fraternitie commonlie called Hoastmen, for.. the selling, carrying, lading.. venting or trading of or for any Seacoles, Stonecoales or Pitcoales forth or out of the Haven and Ryver of Tyne. **1739** *Enq. Reasons Adv. Price Coals* 31 The Hostmen or Fitters at Newcastle are an incorporated Company. **1789** BRAND *Hist. Newcastle* II. 269 A society of ostmen or hostmen had existed as a guild or fraternity in the town of Newcastle upon Tyne from time immemorial. **1864** *Reader* 697 Jack Scott, the Newcastle hoastman's son, who ran away with Bessy Surtees, and who was afterwards known as Lord Eldon. **1893** *Northumbld. Gloss.* s.v., The term hoastman has long ceased to describe the profession of coal-shipper or 'engrosser' of the commodities enumerated in the charter of incorporation.. The Company of Hoastmen remains simply the premier Incorporated Company of Newcastle, and election to its membership is a much coveted honour.

hoastrie, var. of HOSTRY *Obs.*

hoat, obs. form of HOT.

hoatzin: see HOACTZIN.

hoax (həʊks), *v.* [Appears shortly before 1800; supposed to be a contracted form of HOCUS *v.*

This origin suits sense and form, but there is no direct evidence of connexion, and 18th c. quotations for HOCUS *v.* are wanting: see that word.]

trans. To deceive or take in by inducing to believe an amusing or mischievous fabrication or fiction; to play upon the credulity of.

1796 GROSE *Dict. Vulg. T.*, *Hoaxing*, bantering, ridiculing. Hoaxing a quiz; joking an odd fellow. University wit. **1800** *Gentl. Mag.* LXX. 947 *Hoax, Hoxe*, or *Goaxe*, a word much in vogue in political circles. It signifies to make any person the object of ridicule by a species of acclamation. The word is borrowed from the kennel. **1805** *Sporting Mag.* XXVI. 128 He would not be hoaxed any more. **1829** W. LEIGH *Let. to G. Townsend* 87 Either the statesman was hoaxing you, or the exile the statesman. **1869** TROLLOPE *He knew* etc. xviii. (1878) 100 The people who bring you news have probably hoaxed you.

absol. **1884** MRS. WALFORD *Baby's Grandmother* II. 119 My word! Bertha, you are hoaxing.

Hence **hoaxing** *vbl. sb.* and *ppl. a.*

1808 J. P. MALCOLM *Mann. & Cust. Lond.* 213 Contriving wonderful stories for the publick.. This waggery has recently received the elegant term of *hoaxing.* **1815** *Sixteen & Sixty* I. iii, Out of my presence, you hoaxing young rake-hell! **1834** LYTTON *Pilgr. Rhine* xii. 143 You know.. hoaxing is a fashionable amusement among the great.

hoax (həʊks), *sb.* [f. prec. vb.] An act of hoaxing; a humorous or mischievous deception, usually taking the form of a fabrication of something fictitious or erroneous, told in such a manner as to impose upon the credulity of the victim.

1808 *Sporting Mag.* XXXII. 104 The hoax was indeed most successful. **1814** *Stock Exch. Laid Open* 20 The day on which the hoax was practised on the Stock Exchange. **1815** *Sixteen & Sixty* II. iii, In spite of your hoax of the Bath Doctor. **1817** *Edin. Rev.* XXVIII. 382 Having amused himself with a mystification (or what is in England vulgarly called a *hoax*) on the Mayor. **1855** MACAULAY *Hist. Eng.* xxi. IV. 613 It is difficult to believe that a Prince.. would have been scared by so silly a hoax. **1876** HOLLAND *Sev. Oaks* xiv. 201 A paper which manufactured hoaxes and vended them for news.

b. *concretely.* One who is a deception, 'a fraud'.

1869 MRS. H. B. STOWE *Oldtown* xxiv. (1870) 263 After all, the beautiful little hoax had nothing for it but her attractive soul-case.

hoaxee (həʊk'siː). [f. HOAX *v.* + -EE.] One who is hoaxed; the victim of a hoax.

1840 *New Monthly Mag.* LIX. 277 Lynchpynne..was enjoying the miseries of the hoaxee immensely. **1860** *Macm. Mag.* I. 219 Perhaps a hoax must be a deception supported by evidence such as the hoaxee thinks he can appreciate, or wishes to appear to understand.

hoaxer ('həʊksə(r)). [f. HOAX *v.* + -ER[1].] One who hoaxes.

1814 *Stock Exch. Laid Open* 20 All the profit the hoaxers got. **1889** *Spectator* 16 Nov., Spite of his mercilessness as a hoaxer..Sothern was personally a very..kind-hearted man.

'hoaxical, *a.* [f. HOAX *sb.* + -IC + -AL[1].] Of the nature of a hoax.

1819 *Blackw. Mag.* IV. 564 Its want of unity, and therefore use..its hoaxical hodge-podging.

hoay, *int.*: see HOY.

hoazin: see HOACTZIN.

Hob (hɒb), *sb.*[1] Also 4-6 hobbe. [A familiar by-form of *Rob* = Robin, Robert: cf. the parallel *Hodge*, *Hick*, for Roger, Richard, with H for R; also *Dob*, *Dobbin*, and *Dick* with initial D.]

1. A familiar or rustic variation of the Christian name *Robert* or *Robin*. Hence formerly a generic name for: A rustic, a clown. Cf. HODGE.

c **1325** *Pol. Songs* (Camden) 216 Now Kyng Hobbe [= Sire Robert the Bruytz] in the mures ȝongeth, For te come to toune nout him ne longeth. **1399** LANGL. *Rich. Redeles* I. 90 Oþer hobbis ȝe hadden of hurlewaynis kynne. **1549** CHALONER *Erasm. on Folly* Dijb, The rudest hobbe that maie be piked from the plough. **1573** TUSSER *Husb.* ix. (1878) 17 To raise betimes the lubberlie, both snorting Hob and Margerie. **1607** SHAKS. *Cor.* II. iii. 123 To begge of Hob and Dicke, that does appeare Their needlesse Vouches. **1611** SPEED *Hist. Gt. Brit.* IX. xxii. (1632) 1115 Hob, Dic, and Hic (meaning the Rustickes). **1682** *New News fr. Bedlam* 11 More fitter for the Country Hobs. **1778** *Saints* 5 And Priests with Hob go Snacks and share the Field. **1825** BROCKETT, *Hob*..also a clown; contracted from Robin.

2. a. = Robin Goodfellow or Puck; a hobgoblin, sprite, elf. (See also HOB-THRUSH.)

c **1460** *Towneley Myst.* (E.E.T.S.) ii. 297 Whi, who is that hob ouer the wall? we! who was that that piped so small? **1559** *Mirr. Mag.*, *Owen Glendour* viii, Merlyn fathered by an Hob. *c* **1580** J. JEFFERE *Bugbears* III. iii. in *Archiv Stud. Neu. Spr.* (1897), Puckes, puckerels, hob howlard..and Robin Good-felow. *a* **1625** FLETCHER *Mons. Thomas* IV. vi, From elves, hobs, and fairies, That trouble our dairies..Defend us, good Heaven! **1627** DRAYTON *Nymphidia* Wks. (1753) 462 Yet much they doubted there to stay, Lest Hob should hap to find them. **1891** ATKINSON *Moorland Par.* 65 If there was a 'weight of work' craving to be done.. Hob would come unasked, unwarned to the rescue.

b. Phr. ***to play hob***: to 'play the devil', work mischief. Also ***to raise hob***. Chiefly *U.S.*

1838 *N.Y. Mirror* 2 June 387/1 They say it's playing *hob* with the fellers in these here parts. **1853** KANE *Grinnell Exp.* xxvi. (1856) 213, I need not say that the cold metal played hob with the tinkers. **1905** B. TARKINGTON *In Arena* 23, I believe that idiot's right, he won't lose votes by playing hob with *us*. **1911** J. C. LINCOLN *Cap'n Warren's Wards* vi. 88 Theoph's been raising hob because the Odd Fellows built on to their building. **1916** H. L. WILSON *Somewhere in Red Gap* iii. 120 He looked like one of them silly little critters that play hob with Rip Van Winkle..before he goes to sleep. **1927** P. MARKS *Lord of Himself* xvi. 244 Carl parked the car and stowed the flask in the door-pocket before speaking, and then he murmured sympathetically, 'It [*sc.* liquor] played hob with you, didn't it, old girl?' **1935** M. DE LA ROCHE *Young Renny* xxv. 219 It's the food you eat without enjoyment that plays hob with your stomach. **1940** D. A. LORD *Our Lady in Mod. World* iii. 141 The revolutionists who are playing hob with our generation are really masters of the obsolete. **1949** *Chicago Tribune* 14 June II. 1/1 The change in time on the new quiz programs is raising hob with getting the evening chores finished. **1967** *Electronics* 6 Mar. 352/2 The Chinese presumably could raise hob..with vlf transmission to submarines from the base at North West Cape.

3. A name for the male ferret. Also ***hob-ferret***.

1688 R. HOLME *Armoury* II. 136/1 The male..Ferret [is] the Hob. **1882** *W. Worc. Gloss.*, *Hob-ferret*, a male ferret. [In Staffordshire the male of a ferret is called 'the hob', the female 'the gill'.]

4. *attrib.* and *Comb.* †**hob-clunch**, a rustic, boor; **Hob Collingwood** (see quot.); **hob-ferret** (see 3); **hob-lantern** (also *hobby-lantern*), a Will-o'-the-wisp; **hob-like** *a.*, rustic, clownish, boorish: †**hoblob**, a rustic, clown: see LOB.

1578 WHETSTONE *2nd Pt. Promos & Cass.* III. ii, *Rapax.* What, bytest thou, *hobclunch? *John.* Yea, that chull and punch. **1829** BROCKETT, **Hob Collingwood*..the four of hearts at whist; considered by old ladies an unlucky card. **1825-80** JAMIESON, *Hob Collinwood*, the name given to the four of Hearts at whist. *Teviotd[ale]*. **1847-78** HALLIWELL, *Hobby-lanthorn*, an ignis fatuus. Also termed a *Hob-lantern. *Var. dial.* **1611** COTGR., *Rude*, rude..*hoblike, lumpish, loblike. **1583** STANYHURST *Æneis* IV. (Arb.) 99 Foorth with thee rustical *hoblobs. **1599** NASHE *Lenten Stuffe* 8 The draffe of the carterly Hoblobs.

hob, *sb.*[2] [Origin obscure: perhaps more words than one. Cf. HUB.]

1. a. (Formerly also *hub.*) In a fire-place, the part of the casing having a surface level with the top of the grate.

In its simplest form it appears to have been a boss or mass of clay behind the fire, the 'back of the chimney' or 'grate'; afterwards, the brick or stone back and sides of a grate; now, usually, the iron-plated sides of a small grate, on which things may be set to warm.

1511 *Nottingham Rec.* III. 332 Makyng of an hubbe in the ketchyn. **1600** SURFLET *Countrie Farme* I. xii. 54 Soot taken off from the hub of the chimney. **1674** RAY *N.C. Words* 26 *Hob*, the back of the Chimney. **1772** in Brand *Pop. Antiq.* (1813) II. 243 *note*, Ordering their cupfuls to be placed on the Hob of the Grate. **1801** *Trans. Soc. Arts* XIX. 325 The hobbs..project two inches and a half before the fire-grate. *a* **1825** FORBY *Voc. E. Anglia*, *Hob*, *Hub*..2. The flat ends of a kitchen range, or of a Bath-stove; not the back.. Saucepans, tea-kettles, etc. are set upon the hub. *a* **1839** PRAED *Poems* (1864) II. 201 If he puts up his feet on the hob. **1866** ROGERS *Agric. & Prices* I. xviii. 421 In the manor-houses..and still more in the cottages of the poor, the fire was made against a hob of clay.

b. One of the level supports on the top of a stove over which pots and pans, etc., are placed to be heated, etc.

1962 *Listener* 13 Sept. 411/2 The gas-cooker hobs have four self-lighting burners. *Ibid.* 411/3 Centre hob-grill. **1969-70** *Catal. Belling Electric Heating & Cooking* 59 No need to worry if anything boils over... No need to..take the pans off to lift the hob to get at the mess. Simply slide out the spillage tray from under the hob and clean it at the sink.

2. A (rounded) peg or pin used as a mark or target in games; *esp.* one of the iron pins used in quoits. Also, A game in which these are used.

1589 NASHE *Martins Months Minde* 20 Leauing the obscurer hobbs that first they began with, to shoote a maine for the vpshot, at the fairest markes of all. **1676** WYCHERLEY *Pl. Dealer* I. Wks. (Rtldg.) 105/2 To tell your honour the truth, we were at hob in the hall, and whilst my brother and I were quarrelling about a cast, he slunk by us. **1801** STRUTT *Sports & Past.* II. ii. 69 Stand at one of the iron marks and throw an equal number of quoits to the other, and the nearest of them to the hob are reckoned towards the game. **1847-78** HALLIWELL, *Hob*, a small piece of wood of a cylindrical form, used by boys to set up on end, to put half-pence on to chuck or pitch at with another half-penny. **1855** 'STONEHENGE' *Brit. Rur. Sports* (1859) 510 The Game [Quoits] is played by driving two hobs into the ground at the distance agreed upon [etc.]. **1883** *Almondbury Gloss.*, *Hob*, the name of a stone used in various games, such as 'cots and twys', for placing the stakes upon, or in 'duckstone'.

3. (Also *hub.*) 'A hardened, threaded spindle, by which a comb or chasing-tool may be cut' (Knight *Dict. Mech.*). Also, a master tap.

1873 C. P. B. SHELLEY *Workshop Appliances* iii. (1883) 100 Instruments, known as *hobs*, are also employed in forming the cutting ends of screw-chasing tools for use in the lathe. **1881** F. CAMPIN *Mech. Engin.* 49 The taps used for making screw tools and worm wheels are called hobs. *a* **1884** KNIGHT *Dict. Mech.* Suppl. 458/2 *Hob*, a hardened steel mandrel with a threaded portion which is fluted. **1888** *Lockwood's Dict. Mech. Engin.* 178 *Hob*, or *Hub*, a master tap.

4. The shoe of a sledge.

1788 W. MARSHALL *Yorksh.* Gloss. (E.D.S.), *Hob*, the shoe or soal [sole] of a sledge. **1852** G. H. ANDREWS *Agric. Engin.* III. 41 A long thick log of wood, which slides upon the ground as the hob or shoe of a sledge.

5. Short for HOBNAIL. Also dial. ***hob-prick***.

1828 *Craven Dial.*, *Hob-prick*, a wooden peg driven into the heels of shoes. **1874** T. HARDY *Madding Crowd* II. xix. 222 He now wears shining boots with hardly a hob in 'em.

6. *Comb.* **hob-grate**, a grate fitted with a hob or hobs.

1915 C. MACKENZIE *Guy & Pauline* i. 53 Guy sat by the small hob-grate. **1959** *Times* 27 Jan. 10/6 He sat erect in a tall wooden chair beside a hobgrate.

hob, *v.*[1] *local.* [Cf. HUB, sod, uneven spot of ground.] *trans.* To cut the high tufts of grass in a pasture, or those left or missed in ordinary mowing. See quots.

1799 A. YOUNG *Agric. Linc.* 196 Beasts are changed while hobbing is done; and the sooner it is hobbed the better. **1863** MORTON *Cycl. Agric.* II. Gloss. (E.D.S.), *Hobbing* (Linc.), mowing the high tufts of grass in a pasture. **1888** *Sheffield Gloss.*, *Hob*, to cut pieces of grass left untouched in hedge bottoms, etc., by a mowing machine, or by the ordinary scythe. A farmer will say..'Hob the hedge bottoms'.

hob, *v.*[2] *dial.* [Origin unknown.] *trans.* To bring *up* (a young animal) by hand.

1793 A. YOUNG *Agric. Sussex* 75 When they are a fortnight old, the calf is hobbed upon skim milk. **1875** PARISH *Sussex Gloss.* s.v., Two little pigs which she was hobbing-up.

b. *Comb.* **hob-lamb**, a lamb reared by hand.

1847 in HALLIWELL. **1875** PARISH *Sussex Gloss.*, *Hob-lamb*, a pet lamb, brought up by hand. **1893** in *Surrey Gloss.*

hob, *v.*[3] *dial.* [f. HOB *sb.*[2] 5.] *trans.* To furnish with hobnails. Hence **'hobber**, one employed in driving hobnails into boots; **'hobbing** *vbl. sb.*, the action of hobnailing boots and shoes; **hobbing boot** = *hobbing foot*; **hobbing foot** *local*, a shoemaker's last.

1866 R. HALLAM *Wadsley Jack* vii. 36 Thie fooit..weean't skar me—noa, not if it wor a hobbin fooit. **1874** T. HARDY *Madding Crowd* II. iv. 38, I went into Griffin's to have my boots hobbed. **1907** *Daily Chron.* 8 Jan. 6/2 The woman was struck on the head by a shoemaker's 'hobbing foot'. **1907** *Daily Chron.* 31 Jan. 6/7 He struck his wife on the head with an iron foot—a shoemaker's hobbing boot. **1921** *Dict. Occup. Terms* (1927) §429 *Hobber*..drives in hobnails round rims of soles of heavy boots, by hand with a hammer. **1922** G. BLAIR *Haunted Dominie* 43 There's some that skimp the hammerin' upon the hobbin'-feet. **1936** T. E. LAWRENCE *Mint* (1955) III. i. 166 Marching boots so hobbed that every pavement became a skating rink.

hob (hɒb), *v.*[4] [f. HOB *sb.*[2] 3.] *trans.* To cut or form by means of a hob or master tap. Hence **'hobbing** *vbl. sb.* Also ***hobbing machine***, a machine in which worm-wheels, spur and spiral gears are cut by means of a hob or master tap; ***hobbing cutter*** (see quot. 1940).

1892 *Lockwood's Dict. Mech. Engin.* App. 428. **1913** *Ibid.*, App. 439 *Hobbing Machines.* In these, spur and spiral gears as well as worm wheels are cut by a hob, the same hob serving for each type of gear by altering the angle of inclination of the thread. **1930** *Engineering* 17 Oct. 479/1 The defects of the present hobbing process of producing gear wheels. **1940** *Chambers's Techn. Dict.* 418/1 *Hobbing cutter*, a gear-cutting tool resembling a milling cutter or a worm gear, whose thread is interrupted by grooves so as to form cutting faces. **1943** *Jrnl. R. Aeronaut. Soc.* XLVII. 83 A hobbing machine with a properly designed solid master worm wheel will cut accurate and quiet-running gears. **1950** *Engineering* 18 Aug. 145/3 The majority of spur and helical gears are produced by hobbing.

hob, in the phrases *hob-a-nob*, *hob and nob*, *hob or nob*: see HOB-NOB; in *Hob Monday*, *Tuesday*, *-tide*, corrupt or erron. forms (perh. only scribal) of *hok-* or HOCK MONDAY, etc., cf. HOP-.

†**hoball**. *Obs.* Forms: 6 hoball, howball, hobbel, hobil, 9 hobbil, hob-hald. [perh. f. HOB *sb.*[1] 1; but this does not explain *howball*.] A clown, fool, idiot.

a **1553** UDALL *Royster D.* III. iii. (Arb.) 44 Ye are such a calfe, such an asse, such a blocke, Such a lilburne, such a hoball [*v.r.* hobil], such a lobcocke. **1570** LEVINS *Manip.* 55/34 A Cobbel, dullard, *hæbes*, *bardus*. An Hobbel, *idem*. *c* **1570** *Pride & Lowl.* (1841) 48 The worst of them no how-ball, ne no foole. **1828** *Craven Dial.*, *Hobbil*, a fool. **1847-78** HALLIWELL, *Hob-hald*, a foolish clown. *North.*

hobbadehoy, **hobbedehoy**, etc.: see HOBBLEDEHOY.

hobbed (hɒbd), *a. dial.* [? f. HOB *sb.*[2]] Having a hard inflamed lump.

a **1722** LISLE *Husb.* (1757) 352 Sometimes a cow's udder will be hobbed after she has calved.

hobber-nob, **-nobber**. [Corruption of *hob or nob*.] = HOB-NOB.

1800 in *Spirit Pub. Jrnls.* (1801) IV. 265 They never will go hobber-nob at the fount! **1829** D. CONWAY *Norway* 138 Such is the hobbernobbering—touching with yours the rim of the person's glass with whom you drink wine.

Hobbesian ('hɒbzɪən), *a.* [f. the name of Thomas Hobbes (1588-1679), an English philosopher: see -IAN.] Of or relating to Hobbes or his philosophy. Hence **Hobbesianism** = HOBBISM.

1776 G. CAMPBELL *Philos. Rhet.* (1801) I. I. ii. 76 Any admirer of the Hobbesian Philosophy. *a* **1866** J. GROTE *Exam. Utilit. Philos.* ix. (1870) 158 Mr. Mill tries to rise above his Hobbesianism. **1888** HUXLEY in *19th Cent.* XXIII. 165 The Hobbesian war of each against all was the normal state of existence.

hobbet, **-it**. *local.* [perh. a phonetic var. of HOPPET.]

1. A seed-basket: see HOPPET *sb.*[1] 1.

2. A local measure = $2\frac{1}{2}$ bushels.

1863 MORTON *Cycl. Agric. Gloss.* (E.D.S.), *Hobbet* (N. Wales) of wheat, weighs 168 lbs.; of beans, 180; of barley, 147; of oats, 105; being $2\frac{1}{4}$ bushels imperial. **1896** *Daily News* 8 Oct. 9/5 Potatoes are rotting in the ground and can be had for 3*s.* a hobbet.

hobbey, obs. form of HOBBY.

†**'Hobbian**, *a.* and *sb. Obs.* [f. *Hobb(es*: see HOBBESIAN *a.* and -IAN.] **A.** *adj.* = HOBBESIAN.

1687 *Death's Vis.* 214 Id'e make the Sceptic and the Hobbian Schools Recant their Maxims and Confound their Rules. **1696** J. EDWARDS *Demonstr. Exist. God* Ep. Ded. 4 The vanity and inconsistency of the Hobbian creed.

B. *sb.* = HOBBIST.

a **1691** BAXTER *Charac. Hale* in *Chambers' Cycl. Eng. Lit.*, The Hobbians and other infidels. **1754** *Connoisseur* No. 35 ¶13 Bob Booty was a strict Hobbian, and maintained, that men were in a natural state of war with each other. **1857** [see HOBBIST].

Hence **'Hobbianism** = HOBBISM.

c **1651** H. MORE in R. Ward *Life* (1710) 287 But the Error is..a kind of Theological Hobbianism. **1702** C. MATHER *Magn. Chr.* II. App. (1852) 218 Any governour that kens Hobbianism, can easily contrive ways enough to wreak a spite, where he owes it.

†**Hobbididance**, **Hoberdidance**. *Obs.* [The first element seems to be *Hobby* or *Hobert*, perh. in same sense as HOB *sb.*[1] 2, 4 (cf. *hobby-lantern*), but perh. associated with HOBBY-HORSE *sb.* 2; the rest seems to be F. *de danse* 'of the dance' sc. morris.] The name of a malevolent sprite or fiend, one of those introduced in the morris-dance.

1603 HARSNET *Pop. Impost.* x. 49 Fraterretto, Fliberdigibbet, Hoberdidance, Tocobatto were foure deuils of the round, or Morrice. **1605** SHAKS. *Lear* IV. i. 62 Five fiends have been in Poor Tom at once; of lust, as Obidicat; Hobbididence [*Qo.*[1] Hobbididence], prince of dumbness.. Flibbertigibbet of mopping and mowing.

†**hobbinoll**, **hobinoll**. *Obs.* Also hobbinol, -all, -old, hobinall, hobynoll, hobnol. [app. f. *Hob*, *Hobby*, or *Hobbin* (see prec.) app. with reference

to the sense 'rustic' of HOB *sb.*[1] + NOLL head, pate, noddle (or ? *Noll* = Oliver): cf. also HOBALL.] The name of a shepherd in Spenser's *Shepherd's Calendar*; hence, A countryman, rustic, boor.

[**1579** SPENSER *Sheph. Cal.* Apr. Argt., The speakers herein be Hobbinoll and Thenott, two shepheardes. **1579** E. K. *Gloss. Ibid.* Jan., *Hobbinol* is a fained country name, whereby . . seemeth to be hidden the person of some his very speciall and most familiar freend.] **1600** *Maides Metam.* IV. in Bullen *O. Pl.* I. 149 So Hobinoll the plowman calls his dame. **1636** HEYWOOD *Love's Mistris* II. Wks. 1874 V. 115 This hobinall, this rusticke, this base clowne. *a* **1652** BROME *Queen & Conc.* IV. v. Wks. 1873 II. 92 Indeed I do not like . . the countenances of these Hobnols. [**1880** *Encycl. Brit.* XI. 501/1 To the student of Spenser he [Gabriel Harvey] is familiar . . as the Hobbinol who wrote the poem prefixed to the 'Faerie Queen'.]

hobbish ('hɒbɪʃ), *a.*[1] *rare.* [f. HOB *sb.*[1] + -ISH.] Of the nature of a 'hob' or rustic; clownish.

1823 GR. KENNEDY *Anna Ross* (1837) 91 To associate with their rude hobbish boys.

†'**Hobbish**, *a.*[2] *Obs. rare.* [f. *Hobb(es* + -ISH.] = HOBBESIAN.

1704 E. WARD *Dissent. Hypocr.* 12 Their Notions Machiavilian, Hobbish, Draw Multitudes, because they're Mobbish.

Hobbism ('hɒbɪz(ə)m). [f. *Hobb(es*, (see HOBBESIAN) + -ISM.] The philosophy or principles of Thomas Hobbes.

1691 W. NICHOLLS *Answ. Naked Gospel* 90 A mixture of Platonism, Hobbism, and Sabellianism. **1706** HEARNE *Collect.* 26 Apr. (O.H.S.) I. 235 Y[e] . . Scheme savours of Hobbism. **1874** GREEN *Short Hist.* ix. §1. 602 'Hobbism' became, ere he [Thomas Hobbes] died, the popular synonym for irreligion and immorality.

So '**Hobbist**, an advocate or adherent of Hobbism, a disciple of Hobbes; *attrib.* = HOBBESIAN. **Ho'bbistical** *a.*, of, pertaining to, or according to the Hobbists. '**Hobbize** *v. intr.*, to philosophize in the way of Hobbes.

1681 BAXTER *Search Schism* ii. 19 Swearers and Atheists, *Hobbists and wicked men are members of their Church. **1756–82** J. WARTON *Ess. Pope* (1806) II. 47 With all the malignity of a discontented Hobbist. **1857** BUCKLE *Civiliz.* I. vii. 357 Every man who ventured to think for himself was stigmatized as a Hobbist, or as it was sometimes called a Hobbian. **1874** GREEN *Short Hist.* ix. §1. 602 The Hobbist philosophy. **1754** EDWARDS *Freed. Will* IV. vii. 238 He only acts by an *Hobbistical Fatality. **1696** J. EDWARDS *Demonstr. Exist. God* II. 109 We must not surmise that this great man began to *Hobbize.

hobbit ('hɒbɪt). [See below.] In the tales of J. R. R. Tolkein (1892–1973): one of an imaginary people, a small variety of the human race, that gave themselves this name (meaning 'hole-dweller') but were called by others *halflings*, since they were half the height of normal men. Also *attrib.* and *Comb.* Hence '**hobbitish** *a.*, resembling a hobbit, hobbit-like; '**hobbitomane**, a devotee of hobbits; '**hobbitry**, the cult of hobbits; hobbits collectively, or their qualities.

1937 J. R. R. TOLKEIN *Hobbit* i. 11 In a hole in the ground there lived a hobbit. **1947** C. S. LEWIS in *Ess. presented to C. Williams* 104 *The Hobbit* escapes the danger of degenerating into mere plot and excitement by a very curious shift of tone. As the humour and homeliness of the early chapters, the sheer 'Hobbitry', dies away we pass insensibly into the world of epic. **1954** J. R. R. TOLKIEN *Fellowship of Ring* 7 The memoirs of the renowned Hobbits, Bilbo and Frodo. *Ibid.* 11 A few notes . . are here collected from Hobbit-lore. *Ibid.* 20 The Thain was . . captain of the Shire-muster and the Hobbitry-in-arms. *Ibid.* 46 It was a tendency of hobbit-holes to get cluttered up. **1955** —— *Return of King* 416 *Hobbit* is an invention. In the Westron the word used, when this people was referred to at all, was *banakil* 'halfling'. But . . the folk of the Shire and of Bree used the word *kuduk*. . . It seems likely that *kaduk* was a worn-down form of *kûd-dûkan* [= 'hole-dweller']. The latter I have translated . . by *holbytla* ['hole-builder']; and *hobbit* provides a word that might well be a worn-down form of *holbytla*, if the name had occurred in our own ancient language. **1962** *Listener* 22 Nov. 881/3 The more ambitious hobbit saga, *The Lord of the Rings*. *Ibid.*, To those who are already hobbitomanes, this book is bound to be a delight. **1966** *New Statesman* 11 Nov. 701/2 The newest and richest site of hobbitry is the American campus, where students are said to greet each other with hobbitish salutations such as 'May your beard never grow less'. **1968** *Listener* 20 June 790/3 Professer Tolkien was thinking of the average, ambling Englishman when he wrote about his hobbits. **1970** H. PERRY *Human Be-In* i. 20 The consistently good people in the Tolkien books are Hobbits and they have the lowliest status of all the groups of characters in the books. The hippies thought of themselves as being or becoming Hobbits; from time to time as the winter wore on, a sign would appear in the window of one of their gathering places to this effect: Do not add to the street confusion this weekend. . . Be good little Hobbits and stay home.

hobbits, var. HOWITZ *Obs.*, a howitzer.

hobble ('hɒb(ə)l), *v.* Also 4 **hobelen**, 4–8 **hoble**, 5 **hobyll**, 6 **hobbil**, **-yll**. [Recorded from 14th c.: app. cognate with Du. *hobbelen* 'to toss, rock from side to side, ride on a hobby-horse, halt, stammer, stutter', which appears in *Teuthonista* 1475 as a synonym of *wyntelen*, 'hoblen, volutare, volvere', and is taken as dim. of *hobben* to toss or rock (as a boat on the billows): cf. sense 1.

Cf. also High Germ. dial. *hoppeln*, in Bavaria, to move up and down like a bad rider on a trotting horse, in Switz. to make clownish jumps, also, to jolt, as a cart over stones, iterative of *hoppen* to hop, referred by some to an original **hobbôn*, by-form of **hoppôn* to hop (Paul & Br. *Beitr.* IX. 163). But both form- and sense-history offer many obscurities; in particular, it may be doubted whether some of the trans. senses really belong to the same word.]

1. *intr.* To move unsteadily up and down in riding, floating, etc.; to rise and fall on the surge, as a boat; to rock from side to side, to wabble.

13.. *Sir Tristr.* 1161 Tristremes schip was ȝare . . þe hauen he gan outfare . . Niȝen woukes and mare He hobled vp and doun; A wind to wil him bare To . . an hauen in irland. **1375** BARBOUR *Bruce* IV. 447 Thai . . held thame thair so lang hobland, That of thre batis drownyt twa. **1545** ASCHAM *Toxoph.* (Arb.) 133 Yf the shafte be lyght, it wyl starte, if it be heuye, it wil hoble. *a* **1605** MONTGOMERIE *Flyting w. Polwart* 279 On Alhallow euen, When our good nighbours doe ryd . . Some hobland on ane hempstalke, hoveand to the hight. **1813–17** COGAN *Eth. Quest* Note B (R.), His hoop . . If it hobbles in its motion, upon perfectly level ground, it cannot be a perfect circle.

2. To walk with an unsteady rising and falling gait, as one whose limbs give way under him; to walk lamely and with difficulty; to limp.

1362 LANGL. *P. Pl.* A. I. 113 Out of heuene in-to helle hobleden faste. *c* **1394** *P. Pl. Crede* 106 We haunten none tauernes ne hobelen abouten; At marketts & myracles we medleþ vs nevere. *c* **1460** *Towneley Myst.* (E.E.T.S.) xvii. 6 Lo! so I hobyll all on held, That vnethes may I walk for eld. **1508** DUNBAR *Flyting w. Kennedie* 212 Upoun thy botingis hobland hard as horne. **1530** PALSGR. 586/1, I hoble, or halte, or lomber, as a horse dothe. **1601** ? MARSTON *Pasquil & Kath.* I. 136 Some old Beldame hobbling ore my graue. **1666** *Lond. Gaz.* 3 Sept., Many cripples were seen hobbling about not knowing which way to go. **1728** MORGAN *Algiers* I. iv. 99 In stony ways the poor creatures [camels] hobble very much. **1781** MAD. D'ARBLAY *Lett.* 15 May, I now hobble about the garden with a stick. **1871** L. STEPHEN *Playgr. Europe* xiii, The . . old gentleman . . now hobbles about on rheumatic joints.

b. To dance, to bob (with an implication of clumsiness or imperfection). Also *trans.*

[Cf. the Germ. dial. equivalents above.]

1535 LYNDESAY *Satyre* 5624 Menstrell, blaw vp ane brawll of France; Let se quha hobbils best. **1712** BUDGELL *Spect.* No. 301 ¶1 The same Folly . . makes Clodius, who was a celebrated Dancer at five and twenty, still love to hobble in a Minuet, tho' he is past Threescore. **1753** FOOTE *Eng. in Paris* II. Wks. 1799 I. 48 I'll just hobble over a minuet by way of exercise. **1762** GOLDSM. *Cit. W.* lxxviii, At sixty [she] shall hobble a rigadoon when she can scarcely hobble out without a crutch.

3. *fig.* To proceed irregularly and haltingly in action or speech; (of verse) to have an irregular or halting rhythm, to 'limp'. Also *trans.* to utter haltingly.

1522 SKELTON *Why nat to Court* 523 His Latyne tonge dothe hobbyll, He doth but cloute and cobbill In Tullis faculte. *a* **1568** ASCHAM *Scholem.* II. (Arb.) 146 Carmen Exametrum doth rather trotte & hoble, than runne smothly in our English tong. **1645** MILTON *Colast.* Wks. (1851) 351 His first Argument, all but what hobbles to no purpos is this. **1717** PRIOR *Alma* I. 162 While you Pindaric truths rehearse, She hobbles in alternate verse. *c* **1802** CANNING *Poet. Wks.* (1827) 45 When his speeches hobble vilely, What 'Hear hims' burst from brother Hiley. **1813** HOBHOUSE *Journ. Albania* (ed. 2) 1000 The Caimacam . . proceeded to speak to the Ambassador, but hobbled repeatedly, and was prompted . . by the Grand Signior. *Ibid.* 1001 The Caimacam . . began hobbling another speech.

4. *trans.* To embarrass, perplex, foil, nonplus: in Sc. *habble*.

1762 GOLDSM. *Cit. W.* cxix, I could give no account of myself (that was the thing that always hobbled me). *a* **1823** in Byron *Juan* XI. xix. *note*, You'll be hobbled in making a Clout. **1825** JAMIESON, *Habble*, to confuse, or reduce to a state of perplexity, *Roxb. To be habbled*, to be perplexed or nonplussed, to be foiled in any undertaking, ibid.

5. *slang.* To take into custody, 'nab'.

1812 J. H. VAUX *Flash Dict.*, *Hobbled*, taken up, or in custody.

6. To cause to hobble or limp. *lit.* and *fig.*

1870 LOWELL *Study Wind.*, *Chaucer* (1886) 243 Sometimes they thrust in a word or words that hobble the verse. **1897** MARY KINGSLEY *W. Africa* 109 On his feet are a pair of ammunition boots that fairly hobble him.

7. To tie or fasten together the legs of (a horse or other beast) to prevent it from straying, kicking, etc. [In this sense HOPPLE occurs earlier.]

1831 R. COX *Adv. Columb. Riv.* I. 155 *note*, Their two fore legs were tied together. This we called *hobbling*. **1835** W. IRVING *Crayon Misc.*, *Tour Prairies* xi. (1863) 61 The horses were now hobbled, that is to say, their fore legs were fettered with cords or leathern straps. **1835** J. P. KENNEDY *Horse Shoe R.* xvii. (1860) 206 The horses were hobbled, by a cord from the fore to the hind foot. **1892** E. REEVES *Homeward Bound* 211 Hundreds of cattle lying down, their fore legs hobbled with rope.

Hence **hobbled** *ppl. a.* (in sense 7).

1860 DICKENS *Uncomm. Trav.* xi, What tramp children do I see here . . making a toy of the hobbled old horse? **1878** MISS BRADDON *Open Verd.* xlv. 302 [She] had hung upon him like a log on a hobbled donkey.

hobble ('hɒb(ə)l), *sb.* [f. prec. vb.]

1. The action of hobbling; an uneven, clumsy, infirm gait, with sinking and rising of the body. Also *fig.* of utterance.

1727 SWIFT *Gulliver* I. iv, We can plainly discover one of his heels higher than the other; which gives him a hobble in his gait. **1750** CHESTERF. *Lett.* (1774) III. 42 There is still a considerable hitch or hobble in your enunciation. **1871** C. GIBBON *Lack of Gold* i, His pace was a species of hobble. **1874** WOOD *Nat. Hist.* 7 The walk of the Orangoutan is little better than an awkward hobble.

2. *fig.* An awkward or perplexing situation from which extrication is difficult. *dial.* and *colloq.* In Sc. *habble*, a difficulty, a perplexity.

1775 ASH, *Hobble*, . . a kind of blunder. **1776** FOOTE *Capuchin* II. Take care what you say! you see what a hobble we had like to have got into. **1799** G. WASHINGTON *Lett.* Writ. 1893 XIV. 193, I think you Wise men of the East, have got yourselves in a hobble. **1807** TANNAHILL *Poems* 41 (Jam.) Else, like the hero of our fable, We'll oft be plunged into a habble. **1820** BYRON *Blues* I. 64 Pray get out of this hobble as fast as you can. **1866** *Sat. Rev.* 10 Nov. 575 We had got into such a hobble, there really seemed no way out of it save by betaking ourselves to spiritual weapons.

3. A rope, strap, clog, or other apparatus used for hobbling a horse or other beast (see HOBBLE *v.* 7); *transf.* a fetter; = HOPPLE *sb.*[1] (Usually in *pl.*) Also (chiefly *Austral.*) ***hobble chain***.

1831 YOUATT *Horse* vii. (1847) 158 The Horse must be cast and secured, and the limb . . removed from the hobbles and extended. **1842–4** H. STEPHENS *Bk. of Farm* (1849) I. 525/1 The hobbles are then placed on the hind fetlocks [of the cow] to keep the heels down. **1850** SMEDLEY *F. Fairlegh* li. 449 A picturesque donkey, whose fore-feet being fastened together by . . 'hobbles', advanced by a series of jumps. **1901** 'M. FRANKLIN' *My Brilliant Career* (1966) ix. 52 The sound of camp-bells and jingle of hobble chains . . had come to these men. **1928** 'BRENT OF BIN BIN' *Up Country* xv. 272 He remembered the hobble-chains behind the old stable. **1959** *Listener* 15 Jan. 113/1 In a brawl, they're deadly. Anything goes—spurs, hobble chains, the lot.

4. In full ***hobble-skirt***. A close-fitting skirt usually confined by a wide band below the knees and above the ankles.

1911 *Smart Set* Mar. 40 A hobble skirt is an awful habit to get into. **1912** *Punch* 3 Apr. 255/1 The continued success of the hobble . . has . . restricted the use of textile material. **1918** *Wireless World* Oct. 372 A feminine atrocity in a cerise muslin sheath on 'hobble-skirt' lines. **1920** M. ASQUITH *Autobiog.* I. 221 From the hoop to the hobble is not a more violent change than from the riding-hats of 1894 to the riding-hats of 1917. **1921** C. TORR *Small Talk at Wreyland* ii. 69, I said, 'You don't go in for hobble-skirts, I see.' **1969** H. E. BATES *Vanished World* vii. 71 Ladies in flowered hats and hobble skirts.

'**hobble-bush**. The North American Wayfaring-tree, *Viburnum lantanoides*, a small shrub with cymes of white flowers and purple berries.

1842 LOUDON *Encycl. Trees & Shrubs* 520. **1858** THOREAU *Maine W.* ii. (1894) 116 The mountain-ash was now very handsome, as also the wayfarer's-tree or hobble-bush, with its ripe purple berries mixed with red.

hobbledehoy ('hɒb(ə)ldɪˌhɔɪ), **hobbadehoy** ('hɒbə-), **hobbedehoy** ('hɒbɪ-). *colloq.* Forms: α. 6 **hobledehoye**, 8–9 **hobble-de-hoy**, **hobblede-**, 9 **hobbledyhoy**; 8–9 **hob(b)letehoy**, **hobblety-hoy**. β. 6 **hobbard de hoy**, **habber de hoy**, 7 **hab(b)erdehoy**, **hoberdihoye**, **hobberdy-hoy**, **hober-de-hoy(e**, **hubber de hoy**, 9 **hobberdehoy**. γ. 7 **hobet-a-hoy**, **hobodyhoye**, 8 **hobedihoy**, **hobby de hoy**, 8–9 **hobbydehoy**, 9 **hobby-de-hoy**, **hobide-**, **hobada-**, **hobbydy-**, **hobbade-**, **hobbady-**, **hobbede-**, **hobbedyhoy**, **hobbety-**, **hobbity-hoy**. [A colloquial word of unsettled form and uncertain origin. One instance in *hoble-* occurs in 1540; otherwise *hober-*, *hobber-*, are the prevailing forms before 1700; these, with the forms in *hobe-*, *hobby-*, suggest that the word is analogous in structure to *Hoberdidance*, *Hobbididance*, and *hobidy-booby*, q.v.: cf. also HOBERD. Some of the variants are evidently due to the effort of popular etymology to put some sense into an odd and absurd-looking word. It is now perh. most frequently associated with *hobble*, and taken to have ludicrous reference to an awkward and clumsy gait.

The word has been often discussed: see Ray, Jamieson, Forby, Skeat (in *Philol. Trans.* 1885–6, 302). The form has naturally suggested a French origin. Jamieson held that '*hoberdehoy* has been undoubtedly borrowed from the French', and suggested, for first part, F. *hobereau*, *hobreau* hobby (the hawk), also 'petit gentilhomme campagnard' (Littré), according to *Dict. Trévoux*, 'also applied to those who are apprentices or novices in the world'. But no confirmatory evidence has been found in French or even in Anglo-French.]

1. A youth at the age between boyhood and manhood, a stripling; *esp.* a clumsy or awkward youth.

α. **1540** [see c. below]. **1723** STEELE *Consc. Lovers* III. i, I was then a Hobble-de-hoy, and you a pretty little tight Girl. **1738** SWIFT *Pol. Convers.* i. Wks. 1766 XI. 158 Why he's a mere hobbledehoy, neither a man nor a boy. **1821** *Blackw. Mag.* X. 571/1 The squire and his good lady . . followed by a dozen hoydens and hobbletehoys. **1841** L. HUNT *Seer* (1864) 11, I was then a little hobble-de-hoy. **1874** L. STEPHEN *Hours in Library* (1892) I. v. 172 Her awkward hobbledehoy of a son offends against the proprieties. **1891** *Pall Mall G.* 25 June 3/1 There is nowadays an immense public of hobbledehoys—of all ages—and there are even men of culture and critical capacity who take a perverse pleasure in affecting hobbledehoyhood.

β. **1573** TUSSER *Husb.* lx. (1878) 138 The first seuen yeers bring vp as a childe, The next to learning, for waxing too

wilde. The next keepe vnder sir hobbard de hoy, The next a man no longer a boy. **1611** J. Davies *Sco. Folly* Wks. 1878 II. 32/2 Peace lowing cow-babe, lubberly-hobberdy-hoy. **1637** Brian *Pisse-Proph.* (1679) 48 His Hubber de hoy, which is his man-boy, or half a man, and half a boy. **1648** Hexham *Dutch Dict.*, *Een jong manneken*, a young Boy, a Habberdehoy, or a Stripling.

γ. **1638** Ford *Fancies* iv. i. Wks. 1869 II. 293 This gelded hobet-a-hoy is a corrupted pander. **1750** W. Ellis *Mod. Husbandm.* VI. i. 149 What we call in the Country a *Hobby de Hoy*, between a Man and a Boy. *a* **1825** Forby *Voc. E. Anglia*, *Hobidehoy*, a lad approaching to manhood. **1828** *Craven Dial.*, Hobbity-Hoy. **1863** Miss Braddon *Eleanor's Vict.* I. x. 193 A gaunt, long-legged hobadahoy of eighteen.

b. *transf.* (In quot. 1702, ? a mongrel or nondescript affair.)

1678 T. Jones *Heart & Right Sov.* 118 Some ho-body hoyes, and no right sons of the one church or of the other. **1702** *Secret Mercury* 9 Sept. in Hone *Every-day Bk.* (1826) I. 1240 Enter a hobletehoy of a dance, and Dogget, in old woman's petticoats and red waistcoat. **1822** Lamb *Elia* Ser. i. *Roast Pig*, Things between pig and pork—those hobby de hoys. **1861** C. Boner *Forest Creatures* 12 They [young wild boars] are either the babes and sucklings of the present or the hobberdehoys of the last year.

c. *attrib.*

1540 Palsgrave tr. *Fullonius' Acolastus* i. i, Theyr hobledehoye tyme . . the yeres that one is neyther a man nor a boye. **1848** Thackeray *Bk. of Snobs* I, Mrs. Chuff's hobbadehoy footboy. **1886** Jerome *Idle Thoughts* (1889) 101 A man rarely carries his shyness past the hobbledehoy period.

2. Locally applied by children to a large clumsy top. (Cf. hobbler^2 2.)

1825 Brockett s.v., Children call a large unmanageable top, a hobblety-hoy.

Hence **hobblede'hoydom**, the condition of a hobbledehoy; also *concr.* hobbledehoys collectively. **hobblede'hoyhood**, the age or condition of a hobbledehoy, adolescence. **hobblede'hoyish** *a.*, like a hobbledehoy. **hobblede'hoyism**, the condition or character of a hobbledehoy.

1876 F. E. Trollope *Charming Fellow* I. vi. 69 The period of *hobbledehoydom. **1889** T. A. Guthrie *Pariah* iii. vii, The hobble-de-hoydom of that village . . had assembled. **1836** *Blackw. Mag.* XXXIX. 483 Enquiries into the exact period of Athenian *hobble-de-hoyhood. *a* **1863** Thackeray *Fatal Boots* iv, From boyhood until hobbadyhoyhood—from fourteen until seventeen. **1812** G. Colman *Poet. Vagaries* (1814) 12 When Master Daw full fourteen years had told, He grew as it is termed, *hobbedyhoy-ish. **1874** Burnand *My time* xxvi. 236 In a rude, shy, hobbledehoyish way. **1837** *New Monthly Mag.* L. 123 They feel themselves springing into *hobbledyhoyism. **1864** *Homeward Mail* 2 Aug. 665 It is an unfailing characteristic of hobbledehoyism to dress and to talk like a man, before thinking and acting as a man.

hobbler^1 ('hɒblə(r)). *Obs.* exc. *Hist.* Forms: 4–9 **hobler, hobeler, hobiler,** 4 **hoblur,** (4 **hobiner**), 5 **hobyler,** (*Hist.* 6 **hobellar, hobbiler,** 8 **hobelar,** 9 **hobbelar, hobiller, hobelour**), 9 **hobbler.** [In AngloFr. *hobeleor*, *-lour*, also *hobeler*, *hobler* (Godef.), in med.L. *hobellārius*, *hoberārius* (Du Cange), a deriv. of *hobi*, *hobin*, hobby *sb.*^{1}, app. of irregular formation.]

1. A retainer bound to maintain a hobby for military service; a soldier who rode a hobby, a light horseman. *Obs.* exc. *Hist.*

c **1308** *Pol. Songs* (Camden) 196 And thos hoblurs, namelich, That husbond benimeth eri of grund. [**1325** in *Calend. Rotul. Patent.* (1802) 96 De Hobelariis eligendis, apud Beaulieu 4° April.] **1375** Barbour *Bruce* xi. 110 And fifty thousand of archerys He had, forouten the hoblerys. **1480** Caxton *Chron. Eng.* cxcii. 169 The Englysshmen fled bytwene the hobylers and the grete hoost. **1577–87** Holinshed *Scot. Chron.* (1805) II. 20 Of such armed men as they called hoblers set forth by the borrowes and good townes twentie thousand. **1612** Davies *Why Ireland* etc. (1787) 25 Twenty hoblers, armed (the Irish horsemen were so called, because they served on hobbies). **1651** N. Bacon *Disc. Govt. Eng.* ii. xi. (1739) 59 By Hoblers, meaning those now called light Horse-men. **1736** Carte *Ormonde* II. 395 The Irish armies consisted of Hoblers which were their horse, and Kearnes which were their foot. **1872** E. W. Robertson *Hist. Ess.* Introd. 19 Richard de Burgh was ordered to forward from Ireland 300 Hobelers for service in the Scottish wars.

¶ Erron. used for *hobby*.

1828 Scott *F.M. Perth* viii, I guess him, by his trotting hobbler . . to be the follower of some of the southland lords. *Ibid.*, While he himself remounted his hobbler.

†**2.** (See quots.) *Obs.*

157. Lambarde in Strutt *Antiq. Eng.* (1775) II. 34 The hobbilers were aunciently suche men as in time of daunger rode in poste from place to place, to give notice thereof upon hobbyes, or nagges; whereof the name of hobbilers was given to them. **1659** E. Leigh *Eng. Descr.* 85 The whole Countrey [Isle of Wight] is divided into eleven parts, and every of them hath their . . Posts also or Runners, whom by an old name, grown almost out of use, they terme still Hoblers, who presently give intelligence of all occurrents to the Captain and Governour of the Isle.

3. *Comb.* **hobbler-archer**, an archer mounted on a light horse.

[**1364** *Chron. Will. Thorn* in Twysden *Scriptores Decem* (1652) 2140 Pro hoberariis sagittariis inveniendis et sustenandis. *Ibid.*, Prædictos hobilarios sagittarios.] **1786** Grose *Milit. Antiq.* (1801) I. 108 Sometimes archers were mounted on light horses, whence they were stiled hobiler archers.

hobbler^2 ('hɒblə(r)). [f. hobble *v.* + -er^1. (But sense 3 may be a distinct word.)]

1. A person that hobbles in his gait.

c **1665** *Roxb. Ball.* (1888) VI. 498 But now my resolve was never to trouble her, Or venture my carkis with such a blind hobbler.

†**2.** A child's top that wabbles or spins unsteadily. Hence (app.) ***hobler's hole***, ***hobler-hole***, ***hoblies hole***, ? a hole into which such a top was thrown, as a mark to be aimed at. *Obs.*

1594 Lyly *Moth. Bomb.* v. iii, Rather than I'le lead this life, I'le throw my fiddle into the leads for a hobler. **1609** Armin *Maids of More-Cl.* (1880) 87 Now Iohn, i'le cry first. And i'le cry lagge. I was in hoblies hole. **1633** B. Jonson *Tale Tub* iii. iv, I had whipp'd 'hem all, like tops In Lent, and hurl'd 'hem into Hoblers-hole; Or the next ditch. **1686** W. de Britaine *Hum. Prud.* xix. 85 Like a Top, which hath been for a long time scourged, and run well, yet at last to be lodged up for a Hobler. **1847–78** Halliwell, *Hobler-hole*, the hinder-hole at a boy's game.

b. *transf.* A person that vacillates or 'wabbles'.

1575 Gascoigne *Glasse Govt.* i. i. Poems 1870 II. 22 Shall I be cast vp for a hobler then? I am sure I was neuer yet vntrusty to any of you both.

3. a. An unlicensed pilot, on some parts of the coast of England: = hoveller 1. **b.** A man who undertakes the moving or transporting of vessels in and out of dock; a man employed in towing vessels by a rope on land. *local.* **c.** A casual labourer employed at quays, docks, etc. *local.*

1838 Holloway *Dict. Provinc.*, *Hobblers*, men employed in towing vessels by a rope on the land. *Somerset.* **1840** Marryat *Poor Jack* xxvi, Those pilots who ply in the Channel are called Hoblers. **1851** in *Illustr. Lond. News* (1854) 5 Aug. 118 Occupations of the people, Hobler, lumper. **1867** Smyth *Sailor's Word-bk.*, *Hobbler*, . . an unlicensed pilot . . Also, a man on land employed in towing a vessel by a rope. **1885** *Morn. Post* Aug., The men were all paid off, and four hobblers were engaged to perform the necessary work while the vessel remained in port. **1886** *Life H. S. Brown* i. (1887) 5 An Irishman, who was a hobbler on the quay.

hobbleshaw, -shew, -show: see hubbleshow.

hobbling ('hɒblɪŋ), *vbl. sb.* [f. hobble *v.* + -ing^1.] The action of the verb hobble, q.v.

1535 Lyndesay *Satyre* 4425 With hobling of ȝour hippis. **1754** Richardson *Grandison* VI. xxviii. 175 The hobbling it will cause in the reading will make it worse. **1867** Garfield in *Century Mag.* (1884) Jan. 417/2 That distressful hobbling which marks the mass of Parliamentary speakers.

hobbling, *ppl. a.*^{1} [f. as prec. + -ing^2.] That hobbles; characterized by hobbling: see the verb.

1545 Ascham *Toxoph.* ii. (Arb.) 126 That shafte whiche one yeare for a man is to lyghte and scuddinge, for the same selfe man the next yeare may chaunce be to heuy and hobblynge. **1615** Bedwell *Index Assurat.* O iv, A kind of rude Poeme, or hobbling kind of rythme. **1676** Wycherley *Pl. Dealer* ii. Wks. (Rtldg.) 118/1 Thou withered, hobbling, distorted cripple. **1717** Prior *Alma* iii. 144 In smooth-pac'd verse, or hobbling prose. **1777** Sheridan *Sch. Scand.* iv. i, Justice is an old, lame, hobling beldam. **1826** Scott *Woodst.* xxxviii, A stiff, rheumatic, hobbling gait.

Hence '**hobblingly** *adv.*, with a hobbling pace or movement; lamely.

1607 R. C. tr. *Estienne's World Wond.* 238 They neither cared for rime nor reason, neither regarded they how hoblingly they [their verses] ranne. **1668** H. More *Div. Dial.* II. 282, 347. **1833** *Fraser's Mag.* VIII. 64 He . . walks hobblingly upon three legs.

hobbling, *ppl. a.*^{2} [Related to hobbler^2 3.] In ***hobbling pilot*** = hobbler^2 3 a, hoveller 1. So ***hobbling boat*** = hoveller 2.

1891 *Labour Commission Gloss.*, *Hobbling Pilot*, a pilot who has the necessary marine knowledge but no licence from the Board of Trade. **1891** *Manch. Exam.* 24 Dec. 8/4 The officer . . hailed a hobbling boat and went ashore.

hobbly ('hɒblɪ), *a. dial.* [f. hobble *sb.* or *vb.* + -y. Cf. Du. *hobbelig* knobby, craggy, rugged, *een hobbelige weg* a rugged road.] Rough, uneven.

a **1825** Forby *Voc. E. Anglia*, *Hobbly*, rough; uneven; full of hobbles. **1825** Brockett s.v., A hobbly road.

hobby ('hɒbɪ), *sb.*^{1} Forms: 4 **hobyn,** 5–7 **hoby,** 6 **hobye, hobbie,** 7 **hobbey,** 6– **hobby.** [ME. *hobyn*, *hoby*, in OF. *hobin*, *hobi*, *haubby*, whence mod.F. *aubin*, It. *ubino*.

The OFr. was adopted from English, where the word is app. native. In all probability it is the by-name *Hobin*, *Hobby*, var. of *Robin*, *Robbie*: see Hob *sb.*^{1} According to Bp. Kennett (1695) *Gloss.* to *Paroch. Antiq.* s.v. *Hobelers*, 'Our ploughmen to some one of their cart-horses generally give the name of *Hobin*, the very word which Phil. Comines [*a* 1509] uses, *Hist.* vi. vii.' Another by-form of the same name, dobbin, has become a generic name for a cart-horse. Cf. also *dicky*, *donkey*, *neddy*, *cuddy*, names for the ass.]

1. A small or middle-sized horse; an ambling or pacing horse; a pony. Now *Hist.*, *arch.*, or *dial.*

In early times *hobbies* are chiefly referred to as of Irish breed; in later times, also, as Welsh or Scotch.

1375 Barbour *Bruce* xiv. 68 Hobynis, that war stekit thar, Rerit and flang . . And kest thame that apon thame raid. *c* **1400** *Rel. Ant.* II. 23 An Iyrysch man, Uppone his hoby. **1547** Boorde *Introd. Knowl.* iii. (1870) 131, I am an Iryshe man . . I can kepe a Hobby. **1602** *2nd Pt. Return fr. Parnass.* ii. iii. 647, I will . . buy an ambling hobby for my fayre. *Ibid.* v. 775 Hath the groome saddled my hunting hobby? **1611** Cotgr., *Hobin*, a Hobbie; a little ambling (and shorne-maned) horse. **1652–62** Heylin *Cosmogr.* i. (1682) 220 Hobbies . . afterwards became a common name for all Nags or Geldings. **1688** *Lond. Gaz.* No. 2340/4 Stolen . . a black Welsh Hobby, near 13 hand. *a* **1700** B. E. *Dict. Cant. Crew*, *Scotch-hobby*, a little sorry, scrubbed, low Horse of that Country. *c* **1730** Burt *Lett. N. Scotl.* (1760) II. xvi. 30 The little Highland Hobbies, when they find themselves bogged, will lie still. **1732** *Gentlem. Guide to Cattle* (ed. 2) 265 A Turk for the Sire, a Scotch Powny, or the Irish Hobby, for Dam. **1804** *Chron.* in *Ann. Reg.* 502/2 Sir William Kemp Bart. . . was riding on a hobby from which he fell and expired on the spot. **1852** Miss Yonge *Cameos* (1877) II. xviii. 193 The chiefs and cavalry, both Irish and Anglo-Irish, had small light horses called hobbies.

†**2.** = hobby-horse *sb.* 2. *Obs.* or *Hist.*

1760 Tollett in *Shaks. Plays* (1813) XI. 439 Our Hobby is a spirited horse of pasteboard, in which the master dances and displays tricks of legerdemain. **1820** Scott *Abbot* xv, Prance, hobby—hiss, dragon, and halloo boys!

3. = hobby-horse *sb.* 4. (In quot. 1860 with play on sense 5.)

1689 Prior *Ep. to F. Shepherd* 90 But leap *pro libitu*, and scout On horse called Hobby, or without. **1748** Shenstone *Ode Memory* viii, Bring the hobby I bestrode, When pleas'd, in many a sportive ring Around the room I jovial rode. **1860** *Punch* XXXIX. 95 *Master John Russel.* 'Please, Pam, find room for this'. *Master Pam* (the big boy of the school). 'No, certainly not. You must leave that old hobby of yours behind'.

†**4.** A kind of velocipede, introduced in 1818, on which the rider propelled himself by pushing the ground with the point of each foot alternately: = dandy-horse. *Obs.* exc. *Hist.*

1819 *Caricature* in *Miss Millard's Catal.* (1895) Jan. 19 The Newe Long Back'd Hobby made to carry three without Kicking. **1819** *Morning Chron.* 13 May *Advt.*, The Velocimanipede, or Ladies Hobby . . a Machine to carry One, Two, or Three Persons.

5. A favourite occupation or topic, pursued merely for the amusement or interest that it affords, and which is compared to the riding of a toy horse (sense 3); an individual pursuit to which a person is devoted (in the speaker's opinion) out of proportion to its real importance. Formerly hobby-horse *sb.* (sense 6).

1816 Scott *Antiq.* xi, I quarrel with no man's hobby. **1823** —— *Peveril* x, The pleasure of being allowed to ride one's hobby in peace and quiet. **1857** Hughes *Tom Brown* ii. ii, He's on one of his pet hobbies. **1874** Sayce *Compar. Philol.* viii. 312 Transgress the boundaries of scientific evidence, and incur the charge of riding a hobby too hard. **1880** L. Stephen *Pope* vi. 139 His [Lord Oxford's] famous library was one of his special hobbies.

6. *attrib.* and *Comb.*, as ***hobby farm***, ***farmer***, ***-groom***, ***-monger***, ***-rider***, ***-riding***, ***shop***, ***show***; †**hobby-headed** *a.*, explained by Weber 'shag-headed, as an Irish hobby'.

1960 *Hobby farm [see *golden handshake* s.v. golden *a.* 10 a]. **1968** *Globe & Mail* (Toronto) 15 Jan. 24/2 (Advt.), 50 acres . . ideal for retirement or hobby farm. **1961** *Ann. Reg.* *1960* 16 Loss relief for '*hobby farmers' was terminated. **1737** *List Govt. Officers* in *Chamberlayne's St. Gt. Brit.* ii. 241, 3 *Hobby Grooms. **1836** Mrs. Papendiek *Crt. Q. Charlotte* (1887) II. 194 The Hobby groom was . . sent off to London. **1613** Beaum. & Fl. *Coxcomb* ii. iii, Oh, you *hobby headed Raskal, I'le have you flead. **1866** Whipple *Char. & Charac. Men* 45 The *hobby-monger is the only perfect . . bore. **1883** *Times* 18 Aug. 9/2 The whole tribe of crotchet-mongers and *hobby-riders. **1945** *Time* 9 Apr. 82 Prison *hobby shops are not unusual. **1966** 'D. Shannon' *With a Vengeance* (1968) viii. 107 This is Mr. Seidenbaum from the hobby shop. **1967** 'W. Wright' *Shadows don't Bleed* i. 20 A girl friend of Bridget's who owns a hobby shop here in town. **1921** *Daily Colonist* (Victoria, B.C.) 9 Apr. 10/1 The first annual boys' *hobby show will be held at the Y.M.C.A. this afternoon and evening. . . The exhibition will consist of manual training work, working models of aeroplanes, boats, etc.

Hence '**hobbyism**, pursuit of or devotion to hobbies (see 5). '**hobbyist**, a person devoted to a hobby (sometimes used with a connotation of crankiness). '**hobbyless** *a.*, having no hobby.

1846 *Ecclesiologist* VI. 176 [Brass-rubbing] burdens Ecclesiology with the *hobbyism of an amusing trifle. **1871** Napheys *Prev. & Cure Dis.* iii. ix. 955 The pernicious counsel of some *hobbyist. **1892** *Daily News* 17 Feb. 3/1 The philatelists or collectors of postage-stamps, like nearly all other hobbyists, have long had their association. **1935** W. de la Mare *Early One Morning* 582 Of such kind are nascent cranks and hobbyists, and some of them attain at last to the rank . . of English 'characters'. **1937** Auden & Macneice *Lett. fr. Iceland* 105 A circle where one's known Of hobbyists and rivals. **1948** F. A. Staples *Water-Color Painting* 1 A non-technical manner suited to the hobbyist or art student. **1959** N. Mailer *Advts. for Myself* (1961) 137 'That's a nice Jap machine gun.' He looked at it with the professional curiosity of a hobbyist. **1971** *Guardian* 11 Aug. 10/4 The young hobbyist was encouraged to specialise. **1870** *Sat. Rev.* 4 June 730/2 How many *hobbyless wretches are still crawling about the world?

hobby ('hɒbɪ), *sb.*^{2} Forms: 5 **hobey(e,** 5–7 **hoby,** 6 **hobie,** 6–7 **hobbie, hobbey,** 5– **hobby.** [a. OF. *hobé*, *hobet*, med.L. *hobētus*, dim. of *hobe* the same bird; other diminutives were OF. *hobel*, *hobert*, *hoberet*, mod.F. *hobereau*. According to Darmesteter, perh. derived from OF. *hober* to move, stir, bestir oneself: cf. Du. *hobben* under hobble *v.*]

A small species of falcon, *Falco subbuteo*, formerly flown at larks and other small birds.

c **1440** *Promp. Parv.* 242/1 Hoby, hawke, *alaudarius, alietus.* **1486** *Bk. St. Albans* D iv a, Ther is an Hoby. And that hauke is for a yong man. **1588** GREENE *Pandosto* (1607) 28 No bastard Hawke must soare so high as the Hobby. **1642** *Fuller Answ. Ferne* To Rdr. 1 Be not like a Larke, dared into the net by a painted Hobby of pretended Conscience. **1678** MARVELL *Growth Popery* 10 As ridiculous..as for a Larke to dare the Hobby. **1828** SIR J. S. SEBRIGHT *Observ. Hawking* 45 The merlin and the hobby both breed in England.

b. *Comb.*, as ***hobby-like*** adj. or adv.; **hobby-bird** *dial.*, name for the wryneck (Swainson); **hobby-hawk**, same as *hobby*; **hobby-owl** *dial.*, name for the barn owl (Swainson).

1570 LEVINS *Manip.* 44/33 An Hobyhauke, *alaudarius.* **1628** WITHER *Brit. Rememb.* Pref. 123 She dares not onely, Hobby-like, make wing At Dorrs and Butterflyes.

†**hobby**, *v. Obs.* [f. HOBBY *sb.*[2]] *intr.* To hawk with a hobby.

c **1430** LYDG. *Min. Poems* (Percy Soc.) 203 On hobying whan she lyst to fare. **1526** SKELTON *Magnyf.* Wks. (Dyce) I. 276, I wolde hauke whylest my hede dyd warke, So I myght hobby for suche a lusty larke.

hobby-horse, *sb.* [f. HOBBY *sb.*[1] + HORSE.]

†**1.** A kind of horse: = HOBBY *sb.*[1] 1. *Obs.*

1598 FLORIO, *Vbino*, a hobbie horse, such as Ireland breedeth. **1609** DEKKER *Gvll's Horne-bk.* v. (1812) 130 At the doors, with their masters' hobby-horses, to ride to the new play. **1614** B. JONSON *Barth. Fair* III. iv. Wks. (Rtldg.) 321/1 A Carroch.. with four pyed hobbyhorses.

2. In the morris-dance, and on the stage (in burlesques, pantomimes, etc.), a figure of a horse, made of wickerwork, or other light material, furnished with a deep housing, and fastened about the waist of one of the performers, who executed various antics in imitation of the movements of a skittish or spirited horse; also, the name of this performer in a morris-dance. Hence, *to play (the) hobby-horse*: also *transf.* and *fig.*

1557 *Churchw. Acc. St. Mary's* in Coates *Hist. Reading* (1802) 130 Item, payed to the Mynstrels and the Hobby-horse on May Day 3*s.* **1569** *Nottingham Rec.* IV. 132 Gevyn to the mynstreles, and to them that did play with yᵉ hoby horse, xij*d.* **1583** STUBBES *Anat. Abus.* I. (1879) 147 Then haue they their Hobby-horses, dragons and other Antiques. **1599** B. JONSON *Ev. Man out of Hum.* II. i. Wks. (Rtldg.) 37/1 'Sblood! you shall see him turn morrice-dancer, he has got him bells, a good suit, and a hobby-horse. **1645** MILTON *Colast.* Wks. (1851) 365 The world Politician is not us'd to his maw, and therupon he plaies the most notorious hobbihors, jesting and frisking in the luxury of his nonsense. **1673** DRYDEN *Epil. Univ. Oxford* 14 Your delight Was there to see two hobby-horses fight. **1820** SCOTT *Abbot* xiv, He performed the celebrated part of the hobby-horse. **1821** —— *Kenilw.* xxxix, Captain Coxe..executed..a gambade, the like where-of had never been practised by two-legged hobbyhorse.

†**b.** Prov. ***the hobby-horse is forgot***: a phrase app. taken from some old ballad. *Obs.*

1588 SHAKS. *L.L.L.* III. i. 30 *Brag.* But O, but O. *Boy.* The Hobbie-horse is forgot. **1600** KEMP *Nine Daies Wond.* B ij b, With hey and ho, through thicke and thin, the hobby horse quite forgotten. **1602** SHAKS. *Ham.* III. ii. 142 Else shall he suffer not thinking on, with the Hoby-horsse, whose Epitaph is, For o, For o, the Hoby-horse is forgot. **1603** B. JONSON *Satyr* Wks. (Rtldg.) 538/2 But see, the hobby-horse is forgot. Fool, it must be your lot, To supply his want with faces, And some other buffoon graces. **1609** *Old Meg of Herefordsh. for a Mayd Marian* in Halliw. *Shaks. Wks.* 1855 IV. 286 But looke you, who here comes: John Hunt the hobby-horse, wanting but three of a hundred, 'twere time for him to forget himselfe, and sing, *but O*, nothing, *but O, the hobbie-horse is forgotten.* a **1625** FLETCHER *Women Pleased* IV. i, Shall the hobby-horse be forgot then? **1631** DRUE *Dutch. of Suff.* C iv b (N.), *Cl.* Answer me, hobbihorse, which way crost he..? *Jen.* Who do you speake to, sir? We have forgot the hobbihorse.

†**c.** A hobby-horse dance. *Obs.*

1670–98 LASSELS *Voy. Italy* I. 68 Women like those that danced anciently the Hobby-horse in Country Mummings. **1779** in Brand *Pop. Antiq.* (1870) I. 285 We are come over the Mire and Moss; We dance an Hobby Horse; A Dragon you shall see, And a wild Worm for to flee.

†**3.** *transf.* **a.** A person who plays ridiculous antics; a frivolous or foolish fellow, jester, buffoon. **b.** A lustful person; a loose woman, prostitute.

1588 SHAKS. *L.L.L.* III. i. 31 Cal'st thou my loue Hobbi-horse? **1599** —— *Much Ado* III. ii. 75, I haue studied eight or nine wise words to speake to you, which these hobby-horses must not heare. **1604** —— *Oth.* IV. i. 160. **1609** B. JONSON *Sil. Wom.* IV. ii. Wks. (Rtldg.) 225/1 What a neighing Hobby-horse is this! a **1616** BEAUM. & FL. *Little Fr. Lawyer* V. i, Make 'em tame fools and hobby-horses.

4. A stick with a horse's head which children bestride as a toy horse.

1589 PUTTENHAM *Eng. Poesie* III. xxiv. (Arb.) 286 King Agesilaus hauing a great sort of little children..tooke a little hobby horse of wood and bestrid it to keepe them in play. **1614** B. JONSON *Barth. Fair* I. Wks. (Rtldg.) 310/2 Did you all think..that I had changed it in the fair, for hobby-horses? **1632** SHERWOOD, A (childs) hobbie-horse, *baston, ou cheval de bois d'un enfant.* **1710** *Brit. Apollo* III. No. 115. 2/2 A Parcel of Hobby-Horses, Rattles and Penny-Fiddles. **1758** JOHNSON *Idler* No. 13 ¶3 She saw lady Fondle's eldest son ride over a carpet with his hobby-horse all mire. **1827** HONE *Table-Bk.* I. 685 A street seller of hobby-horses toys for the children of a hundred years ago.

b. A wooden horse fixed on a 'merry-go-round' at a fair. **c.** A rocking-horse for the nursery.

1741 GRAY *Let.* Poems (1775) 114 A Fair here is not a place where one eats gingerbread or rides upon hobby-horses. **1842** S. C. HALL *Ireland* II. 340 The merry-go-rounds and hobby-horses 'crammed'. **1894** T. HARDY *Life's Little Ironies* 91 The gyrating personages and hobby-horses.

†**5.** = HOBBY *sb.*[1] 4. *Obs.* exc. *Hist.*

1819 *Gentl. Mag.* Feb., A machine denominated the Pedestrian Hobby-horse, invented by a Baron von Drais.. has been introduced into this country by a tradesman in Long Acre. **1819** (17 Apr.) *Title of Plate* Johnson's Pedestrian Hobby-horse Riding School, at 377 Strand. **1819** *The Dandy & the Hobbyhorse* 10 For this good turn The sweep would ride The hobby horse And Dandy's pride. **1880** *Scribner's Mag.* Feb. 483 An old farmer..narrated how he had seen the low 'hobby-horses' of fifty-nine years ago driven on English roads by thrust of the toes on the ground. **1887** *Badm. Libr., Cycling* 59 The bicycle of the present day is a descendant in the right line of the 'dandy' or 'hobby horse' of 1819. **1892** [see DANDY-HORSE].

6. A favourite pursuit or pastime; = HOBBY *sb.*[1] 5. Now *rare.*

1676 HALE *Contempl.* I. 201 Almost every person hath some hobby horse or other wherein he prides himself. **1768** MAD. D'ARBLAY *Early Diary* 17 July, I never pretend to be ..above having and indulging a Hobby Horse. a **1791** WESLEY *Serm.* lxxxiii. II. 2 Wks. 1811 IX. 434 Every one has (to use the cant term of the day..) *his hobby-horse!* Something that pleases the great boy for a few hours. **1817** COLERIDGE *Biog. Lit.* 43 Metaphysics and psychology have long been my hobby-horse. **1867** DARWIN in *Life & Lett.* (1887) III. 134, I shall not make so much of my hobby-horse as I thought I could.

7. *attrib.* and *Comb.*, as **hobby-horse dance** (see sense 2); **hobby-horse man, 'hobbyhorseman**, (*a*) a man who sells hobby-horses; (*b*) a man who rode a 'hobby-horse' or dandy-horse (see 5); (*c*) a man who 'rides a hobby' (see 6).

1686 PLOT *Staffordsh.* 434 They had..a sort of sport.. call'd the *Hobby-horse dance, from a person that carryed the image of a horse between his leggs, made of thin boards. **1614** B. JONSON *Barth. Fair* IV. i, I cannot find my ginger-bread wife nor my *hobby-horse man, in all the Fair now. **1849** *Fraser's Mag.* XL. 417 Mr. Ellis really abuses these privileges of the hobbyhorseman. **1894** *Tablet* 27 Oct. 663 Taken up by small sectarians and hobbyhorsemen.

Hence **'hobby-horse** *v. intr.*, (*a*) to play the hobby-horse; (*b*) to move like a hobby-horse. **hobby-'horsical** *a.* (*humorous*), belonging or devoted to a 'hobby-horse' or hobby, crotchety, whimsical; whence **hobby-'horsically** *adv.* **hobby-'horsiness**, devotion to a 'hobby'.

1636 W. SAMPSON *Vow Breaker* I iij, Shall the Major put me besides the hobby-horse? let him *hobby-horse at home. **1819** KEATS *Let.* (1935) 315 He is not only reconcil'd to it but hobbyhorses upon it. **1830** J. SAVAGE *Hist. Carhampton* 583 A singular custom, called 'Hobby-horsing' prevails here [Minehead] on every first day of May. A number of young men..having..made some grotesque figures..rudely resembling men, and horses with long tails..perambulate the town.. performing a variety of antics. **1958** M. PUGH *Wilderness of Monkeys* ii. 22 A sheep started at his cursing and went hobby-horsing down the hill. **1965** *Sunday Tel.* 19 Sept. 24/7 She started to hobby-horse and at the third bounce in the height of the gust of about 30 knots in went her bows. **1967** *Daily Tel.* 30 Mar. 18/6 A continual hobby-horsing which stopped it dead about every third wave it hit. **1761** STERNE *Tr. Shandy* III. xxii, The generous (tho' *hobby-horsical) gallantry of my uncle. **1893** BLACKIE in *Westm. Gaz.* 15 Mar. 9/1 We quarrel a bit—he is so hobby-horsical, you can't avoid it. **1759** STERNE *Tr. Shandy* II. v, What he gained *Hobby-Horsically, as a body-servant. **1771** G. BURNS in *Burns' Wks.* (1845) 184 *note*, Having.. become most hobby-horsically attached to the study of medicine. **1881** *Nature* XXIV. 161 Practical, and altogether free from *hobby-horsiness.

hobbyism, -ist, -less: see after HOBBY *sb.*[1]

hobby-lantern = *hob-lantern*, HOB *sb.*[1] 4.

hobday ('hɒbdeɪ), *v.* [The name of F. T. *Hobday*, veterinary surgeon (1869–1939).] *trans.* To operate on (a horse) in order to improve its breathing. Chiefly as *vbl. sb.*, **'hobdaying**.

1938 F. T. G. HOBDAY *50 Yrs. Vet. Surgeon* iv. 55, I contributed considerably to the successful establishment of an operation now familiarly known..as being 'Hobdayed'. **1958** J. HISLOP *From Start to Finish* 171 *Hobdaying*, an operation to help the breathing of horses who are wrong in the wind, but not by putting a tube in their throat. **1963** *Times* 2 Mar. 3/4 A wind infirmity handicapped King of Saba last year and he has now been hobdayed.

hobeler, -beller, etc., obs. ff. HOBBLER[1].

†**hoberd.** [? a. OF. *hobert* hobby, hawk, or by-form of *Robert*: cf. HOB *sb.*[1]] A term or reproach.

c **1450** *Cov. Myst.* (Shaks. Soc.) 179 Do howlott howtyn hoberd and heyn. *Ibid.* 325 ȝour thrust, sere hoberd, for to slake, Eyzil and galle here I the take.

hoberdehoy, obs. var of HOBBLEDEHOY.

hobgoblin ('hɒbˌgɒblɪn), *sb.* (*a.*) Also 6–8 -gobling. [f. HOB *sb.*[1] 2 + GOBLIN[1].]

1. A mischievous, tricksy imp or sprite; another name for Puck or Robin Goodfellow; hence, a terrifying apparition, a bogy.

1530 PALSGR. 231/2 Hobgoblyng, *goblin mauffe.* **1567** DRANT *Horace, Art Poetry* (R.), An ould wyfes chat, or tale Of wiches, buggs, and hobgoblings. **1584** R. SCOT *Discov. Witchcr.* VII. ii. (1886) 105 Robin goodfellow and Hob gobblin were as terrible..as hags and witches be now. **1590** SHAKS. *Mids. N.* II. i. 40 Those that Hobgoblin call you, and sweet Pucke, You do their worke, and they shall haue good lucke. **1678** BUNYAN *Pilgr.* I. 81 Now he saw the Hobgoblins, and Satyrs, and Dragons of the Pit, but..after break of day they came not nigh. a **1704** T. BROWN *Praise Drunkenness* Wks. 1730 I. 34 No hobgobblings or dancing fairies. **1791** MRS. RADCLIFFE *Rom. Forest* vii, Stories of ghosts and hobgoblins have always been admired and cherished by the vulgar. **1850** W. IRVING *Goldsmith* i. 20 A huge misshapen hobgoblin used to bestride the house every evening with an immense pair of jack-boots.

2. *fig.* An object which inspires superstitious dread or apprehension; a bogy, bugbear.

1709 STEELE *Tatler* No. 118 ¶1 Some of the Deceased, who I thought had been laid quietly in their Graves are such Hobgoblins in publick Assemblies. **1823** BENTHAM *Not Paul* 277 Putting an extinguisher upon this hobgoblin may have the serious good effect, of calming a mass of disquietude. **1841–4** EMERSON *Ess., Self-rel.* Wks. (Bohn) I. 24 A foolish consistency is the hobgoblin of little minds.

3. *humorous.* An animal that causes terror.

1770 GRAY in *Corr. w. N. Nicholls* (1843) 113 Here is Mr. Foljambe, has got a flying hobgoblin from the East Indies.

4. *attrib.* and *adj.* Of, pertaining to, or connected with hobgoblins; like a hobgoblin.

1622 S. WARD *Life Faith Death* (1627) 72 Phylosophie.. hath taught them not to feare any such Hobgoblin spirits. **1628** WITHER *Brit. Rememb.* III. 737 Those hobgoblin terrors of the grave. **1679** DRYDEN *Troilus* Pref. B, His language is as hobgoblin as his person. **1801** MAR. EDGEWORTH *Gd. French Governess* (1832) 153 The sorrows of Werter, or some of our fashionable hobgoblin romances. **1875** JOWETT *Plato* (ed. 2) I. 386 Frightening us like children with hobgoblin terrors.

Hence (*nonce-wds.*) **hob'goblin** *v. trans.*, to terrify or pursue as a hobgoblin. **hob'goblinet**, a little hobgoblin. **hob'goblinism**, belief in hobgoblins. **hob'goblinry**, hobgoblin business.

1615 SIR E. HOBY *Currycombe* iv. 153 Agonies, the feare whereof the Popes pecuniarie Hobgoblinets..did afterwards rayse. **1713** DARRELL *Gentlem. Instr.* II. xii. (ed. 5) 222 We have been Hobgoblin'd too long into Religion. **1799** COLERIDGE *Lett.* (1895) 291 They believe that he hovers between heaven and earth, and at times hobgoblins his relations till they preform it for him. **1836** *Blackw. Mag.* XL. 159 The lower classes of Welsh were notorious for their faith in these local hobgoblinisms. **1843** BORROW *Bible in Spain* xlvii. 271 What do you mean by this foolish hobgoblinry? **1853** F. W. NEWMAN *Odes of Horace* 56 Some regard this as a piece of hobgoblinry.

hobhouchin. *Obs.* or *dial.* Also -howchin. [f. HOB *sb.*[1] + HOUCHIN.] An owl.

1682 N. O. *Boileau's Lutrin* III. 126 If poor Hobhowchin puts you in this fearing. **1750** W. ELLIS *Mod. Husbandm.* V. II. 100 With us the Owl is called Hobhouchin, and makes a great hooping Noise or cry, many times in the Night.

†**hobidy-booby.** *Obs. rare.* [f. *hobi-, hobbi-*, as in *hobbe-dehoy, Hobbi-didance*: see BOOBY.] ? A scarecrow.

1720 *Man's Treach. to Wom.* (N.), His legs are distorted so ..that he looks like a hobidy-booby, prop'd up with a couple of crooked billets.

hobie, obs. f. HOBBY.

hobiler, var. of HOBBLER[1].

hobinoll, var. HOBBINOLL *Obs.*

hobits, hobitzer, var. HOWITZ, HOWITZER.

'hob-job, *sb. dial.* and *slang.* [? f. HOB *sb.*[1] 1 + JOB.] *orig.* A clumsy unskilled job; hence app. a job of unskilled work, an odd job. Hence **hob-job** *v.*, **hob-jobber, hob-jobbing**.

1857 WRIGHT *Prov. Dict.*, *Hob-job*, a clumsy job. **1873** B. WAUGH *Gaol Cradle* 123 'Hob-jobbing', to use the vividly descriptive phrase of his class in life, through thirteen months the lad somehow managed to appease..the cravings of nature. *Ibid.*, Days came in which there was a hob-jobber's famine; no horses to hold, no parcels to carry. *Ibid.* 133 Every day not less than seventy thousand boys and girls are actually 'hob-jobbing about', utterly helpless, until they hob-job into gaols, penitentiaries, reformatories.

†**hoble**, *v. Obs. rare*[−1]. [? error for *hobie, hoby*, HOBBY *v.*] *intr.* To use a trammel-net.

1530 PALSGR. 586, I hoble, I tranell for larkes, *je tremaille.* [Cf. DARE *v.*[2] 5, quot. a 1556.]

hoble, obs. f. HOBBLE.

hobleshew, var. of HUBBLESHOW.

hoblies hole: see HOBBLER[2] 2.

†**hoblin.** *Obs. nonce-wd.* A factitious variant of *goblin, hobgoblin.*

1755 T. AMORY *Mem.* (1769) II. 61 Be they..hoblins or goblins, fairies or genii.

hoblob: see HOB *sb.*[1] 4.

†**'Hob-man.** *Obs.* In ***Hob-man blind***, the same as *hodman-* or HOODMAN-*blind*, blind-man's-buff.

1599 PORTER *Angry Wom. Abingd.* in Hazl. *Dodsley* VII. 364 'Tis Christmas sport of Hob-man-blind, all blind, all seek to catch, All miss. **1609** ARMIN *Ital. Taylor* (1880) 181 The Doctor now at hob-man blinde, Begins to cast about. **1638** HEYWOOD *Wise Wom. Hogsdon* III. Wks. 1874 V. 310 Why should I play at Hob-man blinde?

hobnail ('hɒbneɪl), *sb.* [f. HOB *sb.*[2] + NAIL.]

1. A nail with massive head and short tang, used for protecting the soles of heavy boots and shoes.

1594 *1st Pt. Contention* (1843) 64, I beseech God thou maist fall into some smiths hand and be turn'd to hobnailes. **1598** B. JONSON *Ev. Man in Hum.* I. iv. Wks. (Rtldg.) 6/2 All old iron, and rusty proverbs: a good commodity for some smith to make hob-nails of. **1607** HEYWOOD *Wom. kilde w. Kindn.* Wks. 1874 II. 95 They treade heavy where their Hob-nailes fall. *c* **1700** BP. KENNETT in *Lansd. MS.* 1033 lf. 184 [190] *Hob-nail*, small short nail, with a round head, used for the bottom of Plough-Men's shoes. **1804** ABERNETHY *Surg. Obs.* 50 The sensation as if he was lying on a number of hobnails.

2. *transf.* A man who wears hobnailed shoes; a rustic, clodhopper, clown. So ***Hobnails***, as generic proper name.

1645 MILTON *Colast.* Wks. (1851) 365 No antic hobnaile at a Morris, but is more hansomly facetious. **1684** OTWAY *Atheist* I. i, Thou unconscionable Hobnail. **1705** HICKERINGILL *Priest-cr.* I. (1721) 17 Then, replied *Hobnails*, how is it possible that there could be either Night or Day, when there was neither Sun, Moon, nor Stars? **1859** THACKERAY *Virgin.* I. 353 Troops of hobnails clumping to church.

3. *attrib.* or *adj.* Clownish, rustic, boorish.

1624 GEE *Foot out of Snare* in Somers *Tracts* (1810) III. 76 The first question that an hob-naile spectator made, before he would pay his penny..was, Whether there be a devil and a foole in the play? **1628** EARLE *Microcosm., Country Fellow* (Arb.) 50 Hee..has some thriftie Hobnayle Prouerbes to Clout his discourse. **1658** J. ROBINSON *Eudoxa* Pref. 3 Barbarous and hobnail phrases.

4. *attrib.* and *Comb.*, as ***hobnail shoe***; ***hobnail-proof*** adj.; **hobnail liver**: see quot.

1607 ROWLANDS *Dr. Merrie-man* (1609) 4 Their Shooes were Hob-naile proofe, soundly bepegg'd. **1847** BUCKSTONE *Rough Diamond* i, How I used to kick you in my hob-nail shoes! **1882** QUAIN *Dict. Med., Hobnail Liver*, a name given to a cirrhotic liver, when it presents small prominences on its surface resembling hobnails.

'hobnail, *v.* [f. prec. sb.]

1. *trans.* To furnish or set with hobnails.

1649 *Trag. Massenello* 62 I'le..hob-naile my shoos with a couple of old thorns.

2. To trample down, as with hobnailed shoes.

1875 TENNYSON *Q. Mary* II. ii, Your rights and charters hobnail'd into slush.

Hence **'hobnailer**, a machine for putting hobnails into the soles of boots (*Labour Commission Gloss.* 1892).

hobnailed ('hɒbneɪld), *a.* [f. as prec. + -ED.]

1. Furnished or set with hobnails; having the marks of hobnails.

1603 B. JONSON *Satyr* Wks. (Rtldg.) 538/2 Come on, clowns..bestir your hob-nail'd stumps. **1693** DRYDEN *Juvenal's Sat.* III. 399 Some rogue-soldier, with his hob-nail'd shoes, Indents his legs behind in bloody rows. **1871** L. STEPHEN *Playgr. Europe* viii. (1894) 175 The vocal music played on the planks by a pair of sturdy hobnailed boots.

b. ***hobnailed liver***: a cirrhotic liver, studded with projections like nail-heads.

1847–9 TODD *Cycl. Anat.* IV. 711 [The liver] presents what is termed a hobnailed appearance. **1886** *Standard* 19 Jan. 3/5 He found a large patch of cirrhosis, commonly known as hobnailed liver.

2. *transf.* Rustic, boorish, clownish.

1599 NASHE *Lenten Stuffe* 62 The hobnaylde houses of their carterly ancestrie. **1683** KENNETT *Erasm. on Folly* (Reeves) 33 The hob-nailed suiter prefers Joan the milkmaid before any of my lady's daughters. **1839** H. ROGERS *Ess.* II. iii. 135 Our national proverbs..the manual and vade-mecum of 'hobnailed' philosophy.

'hob-nob, *phrase* and *adv.* [In origin app. a variant of *hab nab*, *hab or nab*: see HAB *adv.*]

1. Phrase *hob, nob*: have or have not; used by Shakspere app. in the sense 'give or take'.

1601 SHAKS. *Twel. N.* III. iv. 262 His incensement..is so implacable, that satisfaction can be none, but by pangs of death and sepulcher: Hob, nob, is his word: giu't or take't.

2. *adv.* = *hab nab* (HAB *adv.* 1); hit or miss; however it may turn out; at random.

1660 FISHER *Rusticks Alarm* Wks. (1679) 505 [He] quotes as many of them, as he judges, as to number, may make a Jury, and so Hob-Nob, as they say, without mattering much what they are, so they Concord all in one in the bare naming of the Words. **1787** GROSE *Prov. Dict., Hob-nob* (sometimes pronounced hab-nab), at a venture, rashly. **1887** *S. Chesh. Gloss.* s.v., We'n go at it hob-nob at a venture.

3. hob or nob, hob a nob, hob and nob: (prob. = give or take, give and take) used by two persons drinking to each other. ***to drink hob or nob, hob a nob***, to drink to each other alternately, to take wine with each other with clinking of glasses.

1756 FOOTE *Eng. fr. Paris* I. Wks. 1799 I. 106 Then..they proceed to demolish the substantials, with, perhaps, an occasional interruption, of 'Here's to you friends', 'Hob or nob', 'Your love and mine'. **1762** GOLDSM. *Cit. W.* lviii, 'Hob and nob, Doctor; which do you choose, white or red?' **1772** GRAVES *Spir. Quix.* VIII. xxi. (1808) 366 Having drank hob-or-nob with a young lady in whose eyes he wished to appear a man of consequence. **1815** W. H. IRELAND *Scribbleomania* 213 With whig or with tory he'll drink hob a nob. **1861** DICKENS *Gt. Expect.* v, 'Have another glass!' 'With you. Hob and nob', returned the sergeant. 'The top of mine to the foot of yours—the foot of yours to the top of mine—Ring once, ring twice—the best tune on the Musical Glasses! Your health'.

b. quasi-*adj.* On intimate terms of good-fellowship, in close companionship.

1851 D. JERROLD *St. Giles* xv. 149 In those very good..old times, hob and nob with the housebreaker. **1859** THACKERAY *Virgin.* xlvi, I might be hob-and-nob with you now in your dungeon. **1871** *Daily News* 17 Nov., To make things pleasant..after a pleasant yet practical hob-and-nob fashion.

'hob-nob, *v.* [At first *hob or nob*, *hob-a-nob*, *hob and nob*, *hob-and-nob* (one or both vbs. inflected), from the adv. phrase: see prec. 3.]

1. *intr.* To drink to each other, drink together.

α. **1763** *Brit. Mag.* IV. 117 Do I go to hob or nob in white-wine, I am probably told red, is better for my nerves. **1794** WOLCOTT (P. Pindar) *Acad. Process.* Wks. 1812 III. 278 Deserts, for common serving-men, the room, And hobs or nobs with Ladies of the Broom. **1801** M. G. LEWIS *Tales Wond., Giles Jollup* i, A Doctor so prim and a sempstress so tight Hob-a-nobb'd in some right marasquin. **1805** *Sporting Mag.* XXVI. 148 Watch the eye of him who wishes to hob or nob. **1823** W. H. PYNE *Wine & Walnuts* (1824) II. x. 163 'Here's my hearty service to you, and let us hob and nob.' **1840** THACKERAY *Paris Sk.-bk.* (1869) 12 We hobbed and nobbed with..the celebrated bailiff of Chancery Lane. **1840** —— *Catherine* viii, The gallant Turpin might have hob-and-nobbed with Mrs. C. **1882** MISS BRADDON *Mt. Royal* I. vii. 201, I will hob and nob with her over one glass of toddy.

β. **1828** *Craven Dial.* s.v., I have frequently heard one gentleman, in company, say to another, will you hob-nob with me? When this challenge was accepted, the glasses were instantly filled, and then they made the glasses touch or kiss each other. This gentle striking of the drinking vessels I always supposed explained the term hob-nob. **1831** J. JEKYLL *Corr.* 27 Jan. (1894) 267 At a supper he hobnobbed with Lady Dudley Stuart. **1842** BARHAM *Ingol. Leg., Nell Cook* Moral, Don't..Hob-nob in Sack and Malvoisie. **1862** SALA *Acc. Addr.* 112 [She] insisted on the Captain hobnobbing with her.

2. To hold familiar intercourse, be on familiar terms *with*.

α. **1828** LADY GRANVILLE *Lett.* Mar. (1894) II. 17 It cannot be her interest to hob-and-nob with Lord Fitzwilliam. **1844** THACKERAY *Little Trav.* ii, An honest groom jokes and hobs-and-nobs..with the Kitchen maids. **1882** JESSOPP *Arcady* iii. (1887) 66 What a curious joy..to hob-a-nob for a season with the pigmies of the Meiocene. **1893** VIZETELLY *Glances Back* I. xvi. 303 The chairman..hobbed and nobbed unreservedly with his immediate neighbours.

β. **1866** *Sat. Rev.* 20 Jan. 86/1 Looking at the maid Clara, I found that she had seated herself at the table, and was prepared to *hobnob* it with me. **1871** DIXON *Tower* III. xviii. 191 Eliot, now hob-nobbing with the pirate in pretended friendship. **1879** G. MACDONALD *P. Faber* III. iii. 38 He..hob-nobbed with Death and Corruption.

Hence **ˌhob-'nobbing** *vbl. sb.*; also **'hob-ˌnobber**, one who hob-nobs; **'hob-ˌnobby** *a.*, characterized by or characteristic of hob-nobbing or familiar intercourse.

α. **1795** WOLCOTT (P. Pindar) *Sorrows Sunday* Wks. 1812 III. 370 May have her tea and rolls and hob and nobbing. **1812** *Examiner* 25 May 328/2 The joyous hobbing-a-nob of the lovers. **1830** *Westm. Rev.* XIII. 147 A little pleasant hobbing and nobbing. **1865** G. MEREDITH *R. Fleming* xxix. (1889) 244 The honour of hob-anobbing with a gentleman.

β. **1816** *Sporting Mag.* XLVII. 63 Young ladies..often left the solitary glass of wine which they took with the gentlemen hob-nobber half unfinished. **1853** W. JERDAN *Autobiog.* IV. xiii. 232 The toast was drunk with acclamation, and then followed hob-nobbing. **1888** E. M. MARSH *Saved as by Fire* viii, Diffusing a genial, hobnobby expression over the severest countenance. **1895** MISS DOWIE *Gallia* xi. 123 Upon an omnibus, too, that very hob-nobby and familiar vehicle.

'hob-nob, *sb.* [f. as prec. As a sb. more usual in the condensed form.]

†**1.** A 'sentiment' or phrase used in hob-nobbing.

1761 (*title*) The Masque: a new and select collection of the best English, Scotch, and Irish Songs..To which is added a complete collection of the various Toasts, Sentiments, and Hob-Nobs. **1770** (*title*) Toasts, Sentiments, Hob-nobs and Songs: The Company Keeper's Assistant.

2. A drinking to each other or together.

α. **1834** L. RITCHIE *Wand. by Seine* 71 At the end of the repast, a general 'choque', or *hob-or-nob* took place. **1888** J. RAMSAY *Scotl. 18th Cent.* II. viii. 132 When *hob or nob* was first introduced, on a young gentleman calling for wine a second time during dinner, George whispered him, 'Sir, you have had a glass already'.

β. **1825** FOSBROOKE *Encycl. Antiq.* 537 Pril and wril was an ancient form of hob nob.

3. A familiar conversation; a *tête-à-tête*.

1876 BLACK *Madcap V.* xviii, Sitting on a fence, having a quiet hobnob among themselves.

hobnol, var. HOBBINOLL *Obs.*

hobo ('həʊbəʊ). orig. *Western U.S.* 'An idle shiftless wandering workman, ranking scarcely above the tramp' (Funk).

1889 *Ellensburgh* (Wash.) *Capital* 28 Nov. 2/2 The tramp has changed his name, or rather had it changed for him, and now he is a 'Hobo'. **1891** J. FLYNT in *Contemp. Rev.* Aug., The tramp's name for himself and his fellows is Hobo, plural Hoboes. **1892** *Pall Mall G.* 28 Dec. 3/3 They will be vagrants on the streets and hobos of the night. **1896** *Pop. Sci. Jrnl.* L. 254 The tramp..can scarcely be distinguished from the dyed-in-the wool hoboe. **1896** *Atl. Monthly* Jan. 58 By the 'Ambulanter' it is called Gypsyland, by the tramp Hoboland. **1918** *Let.* in F. A. Pottle *Stretchers* (1929) x. 295 We had been so long separated from our organization that we had pretty thoroughly acquired a hobo frame of mind. **1925** J. BUCHAN *John Macnab* vii. 157 The gillies have..gathered in some wretched hobo they found looking at the river. **1928** *Punch* 15 Feb. 196/1 Few dramatic critics..could display so adequate a working knowledge of..the ways of hobos in the United States. **1959** I. & P. OPIE *Lore & Lang. Schoolch.* iii. 55 Gipsies, usually known as 'gyppoes' or 'hoboes'. **1963** H. GARNER in R. Weaver *Canad. Short Stories* 2nd Ser. (1968) 40 Harvest hands are like hobos, their friendships as casual as the mating of a pair of flies.

Hence **'hobo** *v. intr.* (and quasi-*trans.* with *way*), to act the hobo; to journey or travel as a tramp; also with *it*. Also **'hobodom, 'hoboism**, the realm or world of the hobo; **hobo'ette**, an occasional term for a female hobo.

1906 U. SINCLAIR *Jungle* xxv. 298 Then he explained how he had spent the last summer, 'hoboing it', as the phrase was. **1914** J. LONDON *Let.* 28 July (1966) 426 You can scarcely find a tramp today..who has not hoboed with me. **1918** *Dialect Notes* V. 5 Hoboettes of America. **1923** H. L. FOSTER *Beachcomber in Orient* ix. 183 Having hoboed my way thus far, I could afford to travel as a passenger the rest of the way. **1928** *Daily Mail* 9 Aug. 11/4, I sort of hoboed my way out to San Francisco. **1930** *Publishers' Weekly* 31 May 3736/2 Any hobo temporarily sober can find a publisher to place on the market with great éclat an epic of Hobodom, provided that there is sufficient of the hobo atmosphere. **1930** *19th Cent.* June 849 These were the high days of American hoboism. **1931** 'D. STIFF' *Milk & Honey Route* xv. 172 He can never understand why the hobos want to keep out the women, whom he labels..'the hoboettes'. **1949** *Landfall* III. 136 Have I..hoboed through fifteen of these United States only to be jailed like a common criminal? **1966** *Punch* 4 May 671/1 They give us a fleeting glimpse into their world of pop, incipient careers, hoboism and love. **1967** K. ALLSOP *Hard Travellin'* xvii. 206 Typical of this idiom is Benson's *Hoboes of America* pamphlet in which he loudly warns boys—and 'hoboettes' too. **1972** *Village Voice* (N.Y.) 1 June 78/3 He and his brother were hoboing it in Missouri.

hoboe, hoboy: see HAUTBOY.

hobohemia (həʊbəʊ'hiːmɪə). Chiefly *U.S.* [Blend of HOBO and BOHEMIA.] A community of hoboes, or the district in which they live; the life of the hobo. Also **hobo'hemian** *a.* and *sb.*

1923 N. ANDERSON *Hobo* i. 4 This four-part concept, Hobohemia, is Chicago to the down-and-out. **1931** 'D. STIFF' *Milk & Honey Route* p. v, I have a good deal to say..about Hobohemia, the habitat of hobos. *Ibid.* iii. 32 You will fall into your place in the Hobohemian pyramid of social status. **1936** F. CLUNE *Roaming round Darling* xx. 200 Nadbuck was a dinkum hobohemian. **1960** *Spectator* 2 Dec. 899 The New Lefties, the hobohemians, the *Encore* subscribers. **1973** *New Society* 3 May 257/3 An awareness of what aspects of hobohemia need consideration.

Hobson-Jobson ('hɒbsən 'dʒɒbsən). *Anglo-Ind.* Also 7 **Hosseen Gosseen, Hossy Gossy**; 8 **Hossein Jossen, Hassan Hassan**, etc. [Corruption by British soldiers in India of Arab. *Yā Ḥasan! Yā Ḥusayn!* = O Hasan! O Husain!] **1.** Anglicized form of the repeated wailings and cries of Muslims as they beat their breasts in the *Muharram* procession; hence this festal ceremony. Also *transf.*

Hasan and Husain, grandsons of Muhammad, were killed while fighting for the faith.

1634 T. HERBERT *Trav.* 167, I have seene them nine severall dayes..in the streets all together crying out *Hussan, Hussan.* **1698** J. FRYER *New Account E. India & Persia* 108 The Moors solemnize the Exequies of *Hosseen Gosseen. Ibid.* 357 That Liberty, which was chiefly used in their *Hossy Gossy.* **1773** E. IVES *Voy.* I. ii. 28 Their *Hassan Hassan*, in memory of the two sons of Ali by Fatima (Mahomet's daughter) being killed in one day fighting for the faith. **1817** T. S. RAFFLES *Hist. Java* II. 4 The ceremony of *húsen hásen*..here passes by almost without notice. **1829** *Oriental Sporting Mag.* (1873) I. 129/2 The folks makes sich a noise..shouting Hobson Jobson, Hobson Jobson. **1861** J. T. WHEELER *Madras* II. xxxii. 347 The Mussulman feast called '*Hossein Jossen*'. **1935** M. E. HOUTZAGER *Unconscious Sound- & Sense-Assimilations* ii. 52 Hobson-Jobson, suggestive of a proper name, is the name of a native festal excitement.

2. a. Used as the title of a famous collection of Anglo-Indian words.

1886 YULE & BURNELL (*title*) Hobson-Jobson, a glossary of colloquial Anglo-Indian words and phrases, and of kindred terms.

b. ***the law of Hobson-Jobson***: a phrase sometimes used of the process of adapting a foreign word to the sound-system of the adopting language. So **ˌHobson-'Jobsonism**.

1898 MORRIS *Austral Eng.* 287/2 The name of the shell is a corruption of this word, by the law of Hobson-Jobson. **1919** MENCKEN *Amer. Lang.* 41 Its variations show a familiar effort to bring a new and strange word into harmony with the language—an effort arising from what philologists call the law of Hobson-Jobson. **1934** *S.P.E. Tract* XLI. 21 There are the words ('Hobson-Jobsonisms') where the original [*sc.* Indian] form has been more or less modified in the process of Anglicization.

Hobson's choice: see CHOICE *sb.* 2 c.

hob-thrush, hob-thrust. *Obs.* exc. *dial.* Also 7– hob-thurst. [f. HOB *sb.*[1] + (perh.) THURSE, ON. *þurs* giant, goblin.]

1. A goblin: see quots. Now *dial.*

1590 TARLTON *News Purgat.* (Shaks. Soc.) 55 One of those *Familiares Lares*..as Hob Thrust, Robin Goodfellow and such like spirites..famozed in every olde wives chronicle for their mad merrye prankes. **1611** COTGR., *Loup-garou*,..also, a Hobgoblin, Hob-thrush, Robin-good-fellow. **1713** STEELE *Guardian* No. 30 ¶4 Our own rustical superstition of hob-thrushes, fairies, goblins, and witches. **1825** BROCKETT, *Hobthrust*, a local spirit, famous for whimsical pranks. **1867**

Murray's Handbk. Yorksh. 228 Hob Thrush, or 'Hob o' th' Hurst' was a woodland and mountain spirit. **1877** *Holderness Gloss., Hob-thrust*..a good-natured goblin who assists servant-maids in their early morning work, but in a state of nudity.

†**b.** ? Lycanthropy. *Obs.* (App. an erron. transl. of F. *loup-garou* lycanthrope, through a misunderstanding of Cotgrave's definition.)

1658 tr. *Bergerac's Satyr. Char.* xi. 47, I cure sick Persons of the Hob-thrush, by giving them a blow with a forke just between the two eyes.

c. Applied opprobriously to a rustic. *dial.*

1682 H. MORE *Annot. Glanvill's Lux O.* 91 That any ignorant rural Hobthurst should call the Spirit of Nature.. a prodigious Hobgoblin. **1854** BAMFORD *Dial. S. Lanc.* 188 (Lanc. Gloss.) 'Theau great hobthurst.'

2. (In full ***hob-thrush louse***). A wood-louse. *dial.*

1828 *Craven Dial., Hob-thrush-louse,* Millepes. **1873** *Swaledale Gloss., Hobthrush,* a wall-louse.

hobub, hoby, obs. forms of HUBBUB, HOBBY.

hoc, hock (hɒk), *sb. Obs.* exc. *Hist.* [a. F. *hoc* (1642 in Hatz.-Darm.), app. ad. L. *hoc* 'this'. (Not the same as It. *oca*, *F. hoca.*)] Name of an old card game, 'in which certain privileged cards give to the person who plays them the right of attributing to them whatever value he wishes' (Hatzfeld).

1730–6 BAILEY (folio), *Hock, Hoca,*..a Game at Cards. **1838** SOUTHEY *Doctor* cxlii. V. 46 The Game of Hoc, the Reverse, the Beast, the Cuckoo and the Comet. **1887** *All Year Round* 5 Feb. 66 Hoc was the favourite game of Cardinal Mazarin, which he introduced from Italy.

hoc, hoccamore, obs. ff. HOCK *sb.*⁴, HOOK, HOCKAMORE.

‖**hocco** ('hɒkəʊ). [Said to be the native name in Guiana. Used in French by Barrère 1745 and Brisson 1760.] A name given to several birds of the family *Cracidæ* or Curassows.

1834 MᶜMURTRIE *Cuvier's Anim. Kingd.* 140 The Hoccos are large gallinaceæ of America, which resemble turkeys with a broad, rounded tail, formed of large and stiff quills. **1852** TH. ROSS *Humboldt's Trav.* II. xviii. 154 The hocco, with its black plumage and tufted head, moves slowly along the sausos.

hoce, obs. f. HOARSE.

‖**hoc genus omne** (hɒk 'gɛnəs 'ɒmniː), phr. [L. (Horace, *Satires* I. ii. 2).] Usu. in phr. ***et*** (occas. ***and***) ***hoc genus omne***: and the whole of that class or group; and all that kind of thing (often as ornamental substitute for *et cetera*).

1748 CHESTERFIELD *Let.* 9 Mar. (1774) I. 271 All the shops, drolls, tumblers, rope-dancers, and *hoc genus omne.* **1834** C. C. F. GREVILLE *Mem.* (1874) III. xxiii. 95 He saw Newcastle, Winchelsea, Wetherell, and *hoc genus omne* as much the objects of idolatry as himself. **1867** ROSSETTI *Let.* 23 Oct. (1965) II. 641 When razzias occur on the part of organ-grinders, brass bands, *et hoc genus omne.* **1889** G. B. SHAW *Lond. Mus. 1888–89* (1937) 94 Handfuls of earls, a dean..half-a-dozen members of Parliament, *et hoc genus omne.* **1953** *Essays in Criticism* III. 2 The Herbert Warrens and the Sidney Lees, *et hoc genus omne.*

hoch (hoːx), *sb.* [a. G. *hoch*, short for *hoch lebe* long live.] An instance of the ejaculation *Hoch!*; an exclamation of loyal approval; a cheer, hurrah. Hence **hoch** *v. intr.*, to utter a *hoch* or *hochs*; *trans.* to cheer with cries of *Hoch!*

1867 J. PAGET *Let.* 20 Sept. (1901) 232 The regular German 'festive dinner'; with the speeches and songs between the courses; songs by the whole 400 of us; uproarious 'hochs'; clinking of glasses. **1870** E. G. E. WARD *Jrnl.* 23 Sept. in *Outside Paris* (1871) 18 The General was giving a dinner..to his officers, and we could hear their 'Hoch!' 'Hoch!' after the toasts. **1907** *Daily Chron.* 13 Sept. 6/6 On the whole it will be prudent for the average Englishman not to attempt a 'Hoch!' in welcoming the Kaiser to London to-day. **1909** *Ibid.* 2 June 5/6 They 'hoched' us on our way, and cheered when they got tired of 'hoching'. **1920** *Chambers's Jrnl.* June 374/2 If Britain had had a million Australian troops, they, the present gathering, would be 'hoch, hoching' in Berlin. **1921** A. S. M. HUTCHINSON *If Winter Comes* III. i. 148 The 25th anniversary of the Emperor William's accession was 'Hoch'd' throughout the German Empire. *Ibid.*, Such fervent and sincere 'Hochs!' never boomed across the seas of the world.

hoch, obs. Sc. f. HOUGH.

hoche, obs. f. HUTCH.

hochepot, hochpoch, -pot, obs. ff. HOTCHPOT, HOTCHPOTCH.

hocheur (ɔʃœr). [Fr., f. *hocher* to nod the head.] *Cercopithecus nictitans*, the white-nosed monkey or spot-nosed guenon, found in tropical Africa.

1840 tr. *Cuvier's Anim. Kingd.* 57 Next follows a group of smaller species..consisting of the Talapoin M[onkey]..the Moustache M[onkey]..the Vaulting M[onkey]..the Hocheur. **1883** *List Vert. Anim. Zool. Soc.* (ed. 8) 12 *Cercopithecus nictitans* (Linn.), Hocheur Monkey. **1905** *Westm. Gaz.* 6 Feb. 6/3 A specimen of the Hocheur monkey is among the new inmates of the Monkey House.

‖**hochgeboren** ('hoˈxgəˌboːrən), *a.* and *sb.* Also hochwohlgeboren. [Ger.] **A.** *adj.* = HIGH-BORN *a.* **B.** *sb.* A high-born person; such people collectively.

1905 M. A. VON ARNIM *Princess Priscilla's Fortnight* i. 7 Was she not a *hochgeboren*, a member of an ancient house? **1930** W. S. MAUGHAM *Cakes & Ale* iii. 38 She was a simple old lady..but she had not..forgotten that she was *hochwohlgeboren.* **1933** D. C. PEEL *Life's Enchanted Cup* xviii. 238 The German ladies..were convinced that we had forced Germany to go to war, and the Hochgeboren..felt bitter towards us. **1949** O. NASH *Versus* 139 Do not overlook the fact, *hoch-geboren* Bretheren and Sisteren. **1951** J. C. FENNESSY *Sonnet in Bottle* v. v. 173 He probably thinks he's as *hochgeboren* as the half-caste descendant of an English knight and a Peruvian D.P. **1972** 'J. MELVILLE' *Ironwood* v. 74, I am *hoch geboren*, as my stuffy German grandaunts still like to put it.

hochheimer: see HOCKAMORE.

†**hock** (hɒk), *sb.*¹ [OE. *hoc*: of unknown origin. (The pl. *hockes* has been adopted in Welsh as *hocys*, *hocos*.)] A general name for various malvaceous plants, esp. the Common and Marsh Mallow and the Hollyhock. *Obs.* (exc. in HOLLYHOCK).

c **725** *Corpus Gloss.* 1288 *Malva*, hocc, cottuc, *vel* ȝearwan leaf. *c* **1000** *Sax. Leechd.* II. 330 Hocces leaf wyl on ealoþ. *c* **1265** *Voc. Names Plants* in Wr.-Wülcker 559/3 *Malva*,.. hoc. **1398** TREVISA *Barth. De P.R.* XVII. cvii. (Tollem. MS.), Malua, þe hocke is a nesche herbe. **1578** LYTE *Dodoens* v. xxiii. 581 Flowers..in figure lyke to the common Mallowe or Hocke. **1611** COTGR., *Rose d'outre mer*, the garden Mallow, called Hocks, and Holyhocks.

hock (hɒk), *sb.*² [A southern by-form of *hoȝ*, *hoch*, HOUGH, which it has largely superseded.]

1. The joint in the hinder leg of a quadruped between the true knee and the fetlock, the angle of which points backward.

1540 *MS. Acc. St. John's Hosp., Canterb.*, For tar to ye cowse fote & mendyng a hocke *jd.* *c* **1720** W. GIBSON *Farrier's Guide* I. vi. (1738) 98 The bones of the Hock are in number the same with those in the Knee. **1854** R. OWEN *Skel. & Teeth* in *Circ. Sc., Organ. Nat.* I. 234 The heel-bone, 'calcaneum'..forms what is called the 'hock'. **1897** SIR E. WOOD *Achievem. Cavalry* v. 92 Your horses cannot charge in mud up to their hocks.

2. The knuckle end of a gammon of bacon, the hock-end.

1706 PHILLIPS (ed. Kersey), *Hock*, the small end of a Gammon of Bacon. **1815** *Sporting Mag.* XLVI. 13 A nice hock of ham which I made John leave for you.

3. *attrib.* and *Comb.*, as ***hock action, -bone, -end, -joint***, etc.; ***hock-deep*** adj.

1641 PRYNNE *Antip.* 2 Odo apprehends her the second time, and cuts off her sinewes at the hock bone. **1865** H. H. DIXON *Field & Fern* V. i. 7 Sir Walter had forgotten none of his beautiful hock action. **1868** OUIDA *Tricotrin* (1877) I. 75 The horses of the wagon..stood..hock-deep in grass and rushes. **1874** M. A. WARD *Outl. Zool.* 42 The hock-joint, containing six bones, viz., astragalus, os calcis, cuboid, and three cuneiform, corresponds to our ankle-joint.

†**hock,** *sb.*³ *Obs. rare.* [Etymology unknown.] A caterpillar.

c **1420** *Pallad. on Husb.* I. 882 Brenne heer and ther the heedles garlek stelis, The stynke of hit for hockis [*contra campas*] help and hele is. *Ibid.* 948 And other als seyn hockis [*campas*] forto lese Keste figtre aske on hem.

hock (hɒk), *sb.*⁴ Also 7 **hocke, hoc.** [Shortened from HOCKAMORE.] **a.** The wine called in German *Hochheimer*, produced at Hochheim on the Main; hence, commercially extended to other white German wines.

a **1625** FLETCHER *Chances* v. iii, *John*..What wine is it? *Fred.* Hock. **1676** D'URFEY *Mad. Fickle* I. i. (1677) 4 *Joll.* Here's a glass of excellent old Hock.. *Tilb.* Old Hock! what a Dickins is that?..Wine was never good since it has been corrupted with such barbarous notions. **1755** *Mem. Capt. P. Drake* II. iii. 156, I requested him to go and take a Whet of Old Hock before Dinner. **1864** I. TAYLOR *Words & Places* (1882) 282 It would be curious to trace the progress of the perversion whereby the wines which in the fifteenth century used to be correctly designated 'wines of Rhin' have come to be called Hocks. Hocheim..lies on the Main and not on the Rhein.

b. *attrib.*, as in **hock-bottle, hock-glass,** a bottle, or wine-glass, made of coloured glass, used for hock or other white wine; also **hock-cup.**

1851 *London at Table* III. 50 (*heading*) Champagne, Hock, or Chablis cup. **1892** BURTON *Mod. Photogr.* (ed. 10) 176 Hock bottles..from their deep red or orange colour, are useful for various parts of the work. **1899** *Daily News* 20 May 8/7 There is a wonderful hock-cup 'made in Germany', which the knowing ones partake of. **1958** A. L. SIMON *Dict. Wines* 66/2 *Hock cup.* To a bottle of Hock add 3 wine-glasses of Sherry, 1 lemon sliced, and some balm or borage.

hock, *sb.*⁵ [? shortened from *hōk*, HOOK.] A rod, stick, or chain, with a hook at the end.

1530 PALSGR. 231/2 Hocke, *crocq.* **1693** EVELYN *De la Quint. Orange Trees* xi, As to the Removing and Transporting Cases and Boxes of the Middle and smaller Size, every body knows 'tis done by..strong Coul-Staves, which with good Hocks take hold on the Bottom of the Cases at both sides. **1886** *Daily News* 16 Sept. 7/1 Passing a butcher's shop he caught up a 'hock', used for handing down joints of meat, and made several more blows at him.

hock, *sb.*⁶ [perh. related to HOC.] **a.** *U.S.* 'In the game of faro, the last card remaining in the box after all the others have been dealt' (*Cent. Dict.*).

1859 G. W. MATSELL *Vocabulum* 113 *Hock*, the last card in the box. **1913** C. E. MULFORD *Coming of Cassidy* vii. 118 In his agitation he exposed the hock card before he realized what he was doing. **1931** G. F. WILLISON *Here They dug Gold* 217 The last card, the 'hock',..likewise pays nothing.

b. ***from soda*** (***card***) ***to hock***: from the top card to the last in the dealing-box; hence, from beginning to end.

1902 H. L. WILSON *Spenders* v. 49 Young Bines played the deal from soda card to hock. **1918** C. E. MULFORD *Man fr. Bar-20* ii. 21 You got me beat from soda to hock. *Ibid.* xiii. 134 'Are you in?' 'Every d——d chip; from my hat to my worn-out boots; from soda to hock.' **1925** —— *Cottonwood Gulch* xvi. 219 You've got 'em all guessin', from soda to hock. Good for you! **1938** H. ASBURY *Sucker's Progress* 16 For many years a common expression was 'from soda to hock', meaning the whole thing, from soup to nuts.

hock (hɒk), *sb.*⁷ *U.S. slang.* [a. Du. *hok* hutch, hovel, prison, (*slang*) credit, debt.] **a.** Phr. ***in*** (occas. ***the***) ***hock***: (*a*) in the act (of gambling); (*b*) in prison; (*c*) in pawn; (*d*) in debt. So occas. ***out of hock.***

1859 G. W. MATSELL *Vocabulum* 113 When one gambler is caught by another, smarter than himself, and is beat, then he is in hock. Men are only caught, or put in hock, on the race-tracks, or on the steamboats down South... Among thieves a man is in hock, when he is in prison... 'If the cove should be caught in the hock he won't snickle,' if the fellow should be caught in the act, he would not tell. **1860** 'C. MARTEL' *Detective's Note-Bk.* 36 In about ten minutes from that time we had them 'in hock' (the cells). **1872** G. P. BURNHAM *Mem. U.S. Secret Service* p. vi, *In the hock*, in the act of commission; on the spot. **1883** H. C. LUKENS *Jets & Flashes* 146 We deeply regret that our india-rubber armor is in hock. **1896** ADE *Artie* xviii. 169 They go back home and leave all their stuff in hock. **1898** J. LONDON *Let.* 30 Nov. (1966) 7, I..got my watch out of hock. **1902** W. N. HARBEN *Abner Daniel* xxiii, I felt..ef they did git Jimmy out o' hock ..without me a-chippin' in, I'd never be able to look at 'em without remorse. **1903** A. H. LEWIS *Boss* 31 Well..even a crook has got to go somewhere. That is,..when he ain't in hock. **1908** G. H. LORIMER *J. Spurlock.* vii. 141 He made me feel that I was doing him a favour in consenting to have my evening clothes taken out of hock. **1911** C. E. MULFORD *Bar-20 Days* xiii. 141, I said pound, not pond. P-O-U-N-D; which means that it's pawned, in hock. **1913** —— *Coming of Cassidy* vii. 118 If the four lay under the Queen, Cassidy lost; if not, he either won or was in hock. **1926** J. BLACK *You can't Win* xxiv. 390, I was in hock to friends who saved me from a heavy sentence, provided me with work [etc.]. **1929** *Collier's* 5 Jan. 40/4 My cash was gone, and I was in hock for the next three years. **1956** B. HOLIDAY *Lady sings Blues* (1973) i. 1 She worked her way out of hock in the hospital and took me home to her folks. **1971** M. TAK *Truck Talk* 89 *In hock constantly,* humorous expression for the financial condition of any owner-operator who has a tractor manufactured by International Harvester Company.

b. *attrib.* and *Comb.*, as **hock-game** (see quot. 1859); **hock-shop,** a pawnshop.

1859 G. W. MATSELL *Vocabulum* 113 In a hock-game, if a man hits a card, he is obliged to let his money lie until it either wins or loses. **1871** *Sessions Papers* Apr. 485 That piece that I dropped in the *hock* shop. **1886** *Lantern* (New Orleans) 22 Sept. 2/3 Take the bed too, and run it into a hock shop. **1907** I. ZANGWILL *Ghetto Comedies* 296 The diamond necklace..stolen..and found afterwards..in a low 'hock-shop' in New Orleans. **1926** J. BLACK *You can't Win* xxi. 336 The average thief will walk by the hockshop and look in. The hockshop man..knows he has something 'hot', or crooked. **1969** C. IRVING *Fake!* (1970) xvi. 198 He had previously pawned one of the Matisse oils..to the Mont de Piété, the French national hockshop.

hock, *v.*¹ [f. HOCK *sb.*²: cf. HOUGH *v.*] *trans.* To disable by cutting the tendons of the ham or hock, in man or beast; to hough, hamstring.

1563–87 FOXE *A. & M.* (1596) 124/2 Those holie martyrs, whom the emperor Maximus had put out the right eie, and hockt their left legs. **1658** W. BURTON *Itin. Anton.* 16 His Son..to escape Severus..who pursued him, hockt all the Post horses he left behind him. **1730–6** BAILEY (folio), *To Hock*, to cut Beasts in the Hock or Hoof.

Hence '**hocking** *vbl. sb.*; '**hocker,** a hougher.

1892 R. KIPLING *Barrack-r. Ballads, Cleared* v, They only paid the Moonlighter his cattle-hocking price.

hock, *v.*² [f. *hock-* in HOCK-DAY.] **a.** *intr.* To observe Hocktide. **b.** *trans.* To bind or otherwise beset (persons) in the way practised at Hocktide.

1406 [see below]. **1727** *Cowell's Interpr.*, And in the Accounts of Magdalen College in Oxford there is yearly an allowance *pro Mulieribus Hockantibus*, in some manors of theirs in Hampshire, where the Men hock the Women on Monday, and e contra on Tuesday. **1843** *Fosbrooke's Encycl. Antiq.* 649 On Monday and Tuesday men and women reciprocally hocked each other, i.e. stopped the way with ropes, and pulled the passengers towards them desiring a donation.

Hence '**hocking** *vbl. sb.* Also in *comb.*, as **hocking-ale,** ale brewed for the festival at Hocktide; the festival itself, at which collections were made for parochial purposes.

1406 *Proclam.* in *Letterbk.* I. Guild Hall Lond., lf. xlix b [cf. Riley *Mem. Lond.* 562], Ista proclamatio facta fuit die Veneris proximo ante quindenam Pasche..Qe null persone di ceste Citee..teygne, ou constreyne ascun persone..deinz meason ou de hors pur hokkyng lundy ne marsdy proscheins appelles Hokkedayes. *Ibid.*, Darrestier tiel persone qi qe soyt fesaunt ou usaunt tiell hokkyng. **1466** *Mann. & Househ. Exp.* (Roxb.) 211 Item, the same day my mastyr gaffe the women to the hokkynge .xx.*d.* **1484** in Glasscock *Rec. St. Michael's, Bp. Stortford* (1882) 26 Item pd. for brewyng of the hokyng ale xvj*d.* **1618** in Brand *Pop. Antiq.* (1870) I. 159 Gained with hocking at Whitsuntide, £16 12*s.* 3*d.* **1854** TOULM. SMITH *Parish* (1857) 504 Then there was

the Hocking-Ale, one of great importance; and the thorough kindly Bid-Ale.

hock, *v.*³ *slang* (orig. *U.S.*). [f. HOCK *sb.*⁷] *trans.* To pawn.

1878 *San Francisco Trade Herald* Aug. 2/2 To soak—to hock—Yer upper benjamin at yer uncle's, to get the 'sugar' for a good square meal. **1902** H. L. WILSON *Spenders* xxxiii. 397 The only thing I'll do..is to hock a few blocks of the stock I bought outright. **1904** G. H. LORIMER *Old Gorgon Graham* 184 You can hock your overcoat before marriage to buy violets for a girl. **1922** H. L. FOSTER *Adv. Trop. Tramp* xx. 354 I've just hocked my camera, and all I've got is two dollars. **1945** G. MILLAR *Maquis* i. 23 You might be able to hock them if you run out of money. **1969** C. F. BURKE *God is Beautiful, Man* (1970) 65 Then he went and he took everything he had—his automobile—and he hocked them.

†**hock-ale.** *Obs.* = *hocking-ale*: see HOCK *v.*²

1484 in Glasscock *Rec. St. Michael's* (1882) 26 Item pd. for ix b. malte to the hoke ale vjs. iiijd.

†**hockamore** ('hɒkəmɔə(r)). *Obs.* Also 7 hoccamore. [Anglicized form of *Hochheimer*, from *Hochheim* on the Main.] = HOCK *sb.*⁴

1673 SHADWELL *Epsom Wells* III. 40 (Stanf.), I am very well, and drink much Hockamore. **1747** *Gentl. Mag.* 28 Suppose, by keeping cyder-royal too long, it should become unpleasant, and as unfit to bottle as old hockamore.

hock-cart. *Obs.* exc. *Hist.* [Cf. HOCKEY¹.] The cart or wagon which carried home the last load of the harvest.

1648 HERRICK *Hesper.* Argt., I sing of may-poles, hock-carts, wassails, wakes, Of bride-grooms, brides, and of their bridall cakes. *Ibid.*, *Hock-cart* 14 The Harvest Swaines, and Wenches bound For joy, to see the Hock-cart crown'd. **1648** EARL WESTMORELAND *Otia Sacra* (1879) 175 How the Hock-Cart with all its gear Should be trick'd up. **1864** *Chambers' Bk. of Days* II. 377/1 The grain last cut was brought home in its wagon, called the hock-cart, surmounted by a figure formed of a sheaf with gay dressings.

Hock-day. Now only *Hist.* Also (2 hocedei), 3 hokedey, 3-4 (7-9 *Hist.*) hoke-, hocke-, 4 hokke-, 4-6 hoc-, 5 hok-, -dai, -day. [Few words have received so much etymological and historical investigation as *Hock-day*, *Hocktide*, *Hock Tuesday*, *Hock Monday*. But the origin has not yet been ascertained. Early evidence shows that the first element was originally disyllabic, *hoke-*; but whether the *o* was long or short is not determined; it was evidently short when subsequently spelt *hocke-*, *hokke-*. *Hock-day*, which is the earliest of the group (*Hock Tuesday* appearing next), has not been found before the 12th c.; no trace of it appears in OE. or any Germanic lang. Skinner's conjecture that *Hock-tide* might be the MDu. *hogetide*, *hoochtide*, 'high time, festival, wedding', is out of the question, and Lambarde's explanation of *hock* as for OE. *hocor*, 'mockery, scorn, derision' (repeated by Speed, Blount, Phillips, Bailey, etc.), is on many grounds untenable. (H. Grotefend, *Handb. Hist. Chronol.* (1872) 87/2, cites from a Vienna document, 'der prieff ist geben dez mentags nach dem Goychkentag am newnten tag nach Ostern 1377', where *Goychkentag* coincides in date with *Hock-day*; but it is difficult to see any connexion between the names.)]

The second Tuesday after Easter Sunday; Hock Tuesday: in former times an important term-day, on which rents were paid, and the like, Hock-day and Michaelmas dividing the rural year into its summer and winter halves. It was also, from the 14th c., and probably earlier, a popular festival, signalized by the collection of money for parish purposes by roughly humorous methods: see HOCKTIDE, HOCK-MONEY. The plural, *Hock days*, includes also the preceding day, Hock Monday, which was similarly celebrated.

The date is sometimes given as the second Monday and Tuesday *after Easter week*; this appears to originate in different ways of reckoning the *quindena Paschæ* as the fortnight following Easter, or the two weeks before and after Easter. (Statements going back to the 15th or 16th c. assert that *Hock-day* commemorated either the massacre of the Danes on 13 Nov. 1002, or the death of Hardicnut on 8 June, 1042. From the dates of these events it is difficult to understand how either was associated with Hock-tide.)

c **1175** *Caen Cartulary* (*MS. Paris, Bibl. Nat., Lat.* 5650) lf. 54b (Du C.), Omnes bubulci..a hocedei usque ad Augustum habebunt de bidentibus lac mane diebus Dominicis. **1219** *Feet of Fines Michaelm. 3 Hen. III*, File III. No. 30 Quod ipsi homines veniant..bis in anno..semel ad Hokedey et iterum ad festum Sancti Martini. *a* **1252** *Rentalia Glaston.* (Som. Rec. Soc.) 10 A die lune prox. post hocke-dai. *a* **1259** MATT. PARIS *Chron. Maj.* anno 1255 (Rolls V. 493) De magno parlamento quod fuit in quindena Paschæ. Circa idem tempus scilicet in quindena Paschæ, quæ vulgariter Hokedai appellatur. *Ibid.* anno 1258 (V. 676) Et post diem Martis, quæ vulgariter *Hokedai* appellatur, factum est Parlamentum Londini. *c* **1260** *Deed Granting Messuage in Glastonbury* (*penes* Rev. W. E. Daniel), Octo denarios ad duos anni terminos, videlicet ad la Hokedaye quatuor denarios, et ad festum sci. Michaelis quatuor denarios. *c* **1330** *Annal. Lond.* an. 1269 in *Chron. Edw. I & II* (Rolls) I. 80 Die Martis, qui vocatur Hokkeday. **1369** in Madox *Formulare* (1702) 225 Die Martis proximo post quindenam Paschæ qui vocatur Hokeday. **1406** [see *hocking* under HOCK *v.*²]. **1450** in Leland *Collect.* 299 Sic monemus, ut ab hujusmodi ligationibus & ludis inhonestis diebus hactenus usitatis, vocatis communiter Hoc-dayes, ut prædicitur, cessent. **1467** in *Eng. Gilds* (1870) 385 At the lawday holdyn at hokday. **1512** *Yatton Churchw. Acc.* (Som. Rec. Soc.) 132 [Recd.] of I. Bek for his taverne of Ale at Hoc-day xxxvjˢ. viijᵈ. **1677** PLOT *Oxfordsh.* 202, I once thought they might anciently, as well as now, observe two Hock-days, one for the women and another for the men.. It is most certain that now we observe two of them here, on Monday for the women, which is much the more solemn, and Tuesday for the men, which is very inconsiderable. **1777** BRAND *Pop. Antiq.* (1849) I. 185 Hoke Day was..an annual festival, said to have been instituted in memory of the almost total destruction of the Danes in England by Ethelred in 1002. **1890** KITCHIN *Winchester* (1893) 166 There were usually two assemblies of the commonalty in each year, one on Hockaday (the Tuesday week after Easter), the other at Michaelmas.

hockelty. *U.S. slang.* Also **hocklety, hockley, hocly.** (See quots.) Cf. HOCK *sb.*⁶

1843 J. H. GREENE *Expos. Arts Gambling* 210 By hocklety and splitting, many men have experienced great disappointment on this same device of hocklety. *Ibid.* 166 *Hockley*, signifies the last card but one, the chance of which the banker claims, and may refuse to let any punter withdraw a card when eight or less remain to be dealt. **1867** *Bohn's Hand-bk. Games* 336 The last card but one is called hocly, and forms part of the banker's gain. **1895** MANSON *Sporting Dict.* 58 (Faro), *Hock* or *Hockelty card*, the last card remaining in the box, after the deal has been made.

hockelty-card. = HOCK *sb.*⁶ (*Cent. Dict.*).

hocker mocker, obs. f. HUGGER-MUGGER.

hockerye, var. of HUCKERY, *Obs.*

†**hocket.** *Obs.* Also 4-5 hoket, 7 hocquet. [a. F. *hoquet*, in OF. also *hocquet* shock, sudden interruption, hitch, hiccup: see Hatz.-Darm.]

1. Hitch, obstacle; interruption; chicane, trick.

[**1276** see HOCKETTOR.] **13..** *K. Alis.* 7000 Mony hoket is in amours; Stedfast seldom ben lechoures. *c* **1460** *Towneley Myst.* xxx. 233 Here I be gesse of many nyce hoket, Of care and of curstnes, hethyng and hoket. *Ibid.* 312 Hym thynke it no hoket his taylle when he Wryngys.

2. = HICKET, HICCUP.

1601 HOLLAND *Pliny* xx. xvii, The troublesome yex or hocquet. *Ibid.* II. 50 Against the Hocquet or Yex, there is a notable medicine made with it. **1617** MINSHEU *Ductor* s.v. *Hocke*, It is good to helpe the Hocket or Hicket.

3. *Mediæval Mus.* An interruption of a voice-part (usually of two or more parts alternately) by rests, so as to produce a broken or spasmodic effect; used as a contrapuntal device.

[**1326** ROBT. DE HANDLO *Regulæ* xii. §5 Hoketus.] **1776** HAWKINS *Hist. Mus.* liii. II. 195 De Handlo..says, that Hockets are formed by the combination of notes and pauses. **1875** STAINER & BARRETT *Dict. Mus. Terms*, *Hocket, Hoket, Ochetus*..was the same as *truncatio* (truncatio idem est quod hoket). **1880** GROVE *Dict. Mus.*, *Hocket*, a term which occurs in old English writers on music, beginning with De Handlo (1326), for passages which were truncated or mangled, or a combination of notes and pauses.

Hence †'**hockettor** *Obs.*, a tricker, a sharper.

[**1276** *Act 4 Edw. I, Stat. Rageman* in *Stat. Realm* I. 44/2 Par hoketours ou barettours [*v.r.* par hokettez ne par baretz].] **1672-1727** *Cowell's Interpr.*, *Hockettor* or *Hocqueteur*, is an old French word for a Knight of the Post, a decayed man, a Basket-carrier.

hockey¹ ('hɒkɪ), **hawkey** ('hɔːkɪ), **horkey.** Also 6 hocky, hooky, 7 hoacky, hoky, 8 hoaky, 9 hockay, hawkie. [Origin and etymological form unknown: cf. HOCK-CART.]

1. The old name in the eastern counties of England for the feast at harvest-home.

1555 [see 2]. **1600** NASHE *Summer's Last Will & Test.* in Hazl. *Dodsley* VIII. 49 Hooky, hooky, we have shorn, And we have bound; And we have brought Harvest Home to town. **1676** *Poor Robin's Alm.* Aug. in *N. & Q.* 1st Ser. (1850) I. 457/2 Hoacky is brought Home with hallowing Boys with plum-cake The Cart following. **1806** BLOOMFIELD *Horkey* Advt., The man who..goes foremost through the harvest with the scythe or the sickle, is honoured with the title of *Lord*, and at the Horkey, or harvest-home feast, collects what he can. **1812** E. D. CLARKE *Trav. Var. Countries* II. 229 *note*, At the Hawkie, as it is called, or Harvest-Home, I have seen a clown dressed in woman's clothes, having his face painted, his head decorated with ears of corn. **1822** J. GAGE *Hist. Hengrave* 6 The hockay, or harvest home..begins to fall into disuse. *a* **1825** FORBY *Voc. E. Anglia*, *Hawkey*, the feast at harvest home. **1826** G. H. I. in Hone *Every-day Bk.* II. 1168 This health-drinking.. finishes the horkey.

2. *attrib.* and *Comb.*, as ***hockey cry, load, night***; **hockey cake**, the seed cake distributed at a harvest-home; **hockey cart** = HOCK-CART.

1555 ABP. PARKER *Ps.* cxxvi. 376 He home returnes: wyth hocky cry, With sheaues full lade abundantly. **1602** WARNER *Alb. Eng.* XVI. ciii. 80 I'le duly keepe for thy delight Rock-Monday, and the Wake, Hawe Shrouings, Christmas-gambols, with the Hokie and Seed-cake. *a* **1613** OVERBURY *Charact.*, *Franklin* Wks. (1856) 150 Rocke Munday.. Christmas Eve, the hoky, or seed cake, these he yeerely keepes, yet holds them no reliques of popery. **1712** *Poor Robin* (N.), Harvest is done, therefore, wife, make For harvest men a hoaky cake. **1731** N. SALMON *New Surv. Eng.*, *Hertf.* II. 415 *Hockey Cake* is that which is distributed to the people at Harvest Home. The *Hockey Cart* is that which brings the last Corn, and the Children rejoycing with Boughs in their Hands, with which the Horses also are attired. **1806** BLOOMFIELD *Horkey* iv, 'Twas Farmer Cheerum's *Horkey night*. *Ibid.* xiii, Home came the jovial Horkey load, Last of the whole year's crop; And Grace amongst the green boughs rode Right plump upon the top. *Ibid.* xvi, Farmer Cheerum went..And broach'd the Horkey beer. *a* **1825** FORBY *Voc. E. Anglia*, *Hawkey-load*, the last load of the crop, which..was always led home on the evening of the hawkey, with much rustic pageantry. **1826** G. H. I. in Hone *Every-day Bk.* II. 1166 The last, or 'horkey load' (as it is here [Norfolk] called) is decorated with flags and streamers.

hockey² ('hɒkɪ). Also 6 -ie, 9 hawky, -key. [Origin uncertain; but the analogy of many other games makes it likely that the name originally belonged to the hooked stick. Of. *hoquet* 'shepherd's staff, crook', suits form and sense; but connecting links are wanting. The isolated occurrence of the word in 1527 is very remarkable. It is not certain that Cowper's 'sport' was the same.]

1. a. An outdoor game of ball played with sticks or clubs hooked or curved at one end, with which the players of each side drive the ball towards the goal at the other end of the ground. Also called *bandy* and *shinty*.

1527 *Galway Stat.* in *10th Rep. Hist. MSS. Comm.* App. v. 402 The horlinge of the litill balle with hockie stickes or staves. **1785** COWPER *Let.* 5 Nov., The boys at Olney have likewise a very entertaining sport, which commences annually upon this day [5th Nov.]: they call it Hockey; and it consists in dashing each other with mud, and the windows also. **1838** W. HOLLOWAY *Dict. Provinc.*, *Hawkey*, the name of a game played by several boys on each side with sticks, called hawkey-bats, and a ball.. *W. Sussex.* **1842** VIGNE *Trav. Kashmir* (1844) II. 289 At Shighur I first saw the game of the Chaughán..It is in fact hocky on horseback.. The ball is called in Tibiti, 'Pulu'. **1857** *Chambers' Inform.* II. 703 Shinty in Scotland, Hockey in England, and Hurling in Ireland seem to be very much the same out-of-door sport. **1865** LUBBOCK *Preh. Times* xiv. (1869) 498 Kane saw the children in Smith's Sound playing hockey on the ice.

b. In N. Amer. = *ice hockey*.

The older game is referred to as *field hockey*.

1895 *Rat Portage* (Ont.) *News* 11 Jan. 1/2 Hockey is the most popular winter sport in Canada, taking the place of lacrosse. **1906** *Daily Colonist* (Victoria, B.C.) 5 Jan. 2/1 The first hockey match of the season was played here between Rossland and Nelson teams. **1953** *Canad. Geogr. Jrnl.* XLVI. 138/2 The children maintain their own open air hockey rink on the ice of Green River. **1969** WIDDOWSON & HALPERT in Halpert & Story *Christmas Mumming in Newfoundland* 162, I dressed in a hockey suit.

2. (*U.S.*) The stick or club used in this game: cf. *bandy, shinty*.

1839 JACOB ABBOTT *Caleb in Town* ii. *The Hawkies* 38 Now, a hawkey is a small, round stick, about as long as a man's cane, with a crook in the lower end, so that a boy can hit balls and little stones with it, when lying upon the ground. A good hawky is a great prize to a Boston boy. **1866** *Harvard Mem. Biog.*, *J. Savage* I. 329, I remember him as yesterday, full of fun and courage, with his hockey in hand. **1868** MISS ALCOTT *Lit. Wom.* I. viii. 117 Laurie..lying flat [on the ice] held Amy up by his arm and hockey.

3. *attrib.* and *Comb.*, as ***hockey-ball, -bat, -club, -girl, -match, -playing, -set, -stick, -tournament, -type***.

1838 Hawkey-bat [see 1]. **1849** THACKERAY *Pendennis* iii, A little wretch whom he had cut over the back with a hockey-stick. **1884** *Bath Jrnl.* 16 Feb. 7/2 The festivities of the week include a hockey tournament. **1889** *John Bull* 2 Mar. 146/3 Hockey clubs now abound in the neighbourhood of London..while a Hockey Association has drawn up an admirable code of rules. **1906** *Daily Chron.* 4 Oct. 4/4 The 'hockey set' are as a rule some of the healthiest girls in college. **1909** *Ibid.* 5 May 9/2 'Dear me, no, Miss Bulliphant,' she replied in what I call the downright, hockey-girl manner. **1915** V. WOOLF *Voyage Out* xiv. 211 Hockey-playing young women in Wiltshire. **1936** 'R. WEST' *Thinking Reed* xii. 435 You look awfully well now, well to the point of hockey-playing. **1959** *Times* 16 Feb. 11/5 The models are all looking much better fed, and without yet suggesting hockey-girls they don't any longer look like haughty hunger-strikers. **1961** *Times* 18 May 17/1 Miss Sian Reynolds as a hockey-girl St. Joan. **1963** J. T. STORY *Something for Nothing* i. 17, I like the hockey type... I can't stand these sex-pots.

hockey³ ('(h)ɒkɪ). *Darts.* Now also oche. [Of uncertain origin.

A favourite explanation derives the word from the name of a supposed West Country brewery, S. Hockey and Sons, whose crates were allegedly lined up to measure the throwing distance. Other suggestions involve OF. *ochen* 'to cut a deep notch in' (see NOTCH *sb.*) and *hog-line* (HOG *sb.*¹ 13a) in Curling (see also Partridge s.v. (*h*)*oggins line*), but none is satisfactorily proven.]

The line behind which a player must stand when throwing darts at the board; the throwing-line.

1934 *Nat. Darts Assoc. Official Handbk.* 8 A Referee should be appointed to watch the 'hockey'. **1937** *Darts & Sports Weekly News* 4 Sept. 6/1 Even now a dart-player occasionally 'loses one' in the cross-beam between the hockey and the board. **1945** *Dart* 22 Sept. 1/1 My suggestion for the standard hockey that must one day be utilised for national and international competitions, is a raised one, placed 7′ 6″ from the face of the board. **1959** *Chambers's Encycl.* IV. 381/1 The 'hockey', or line behind which the player stands, should not be more than 9 ft from the board. **1980** *Observer* 10 Feb. 44/3 Lazarenko is on the 'oche'—the mark from which to throw. **1981** R. LEWIS *Seek for Justice* i. 18 The oche—the line behind which the [darts] thrower has to stand when he aims his arrows. **1984** *Sunday People* 15 Apr. 35/1 Eric Bristow had to fork out a quid before he could even step up to the oche.

'hockeyist. *Canad.* [f. HOCKEY[2] 1 b + -IST.] A person who plays ice hockey.

1895 *Athletic Life* Mar. 121 In his stead was elected.. an enthusiastic hockeyist and vice-president of the Victoria club. **1902** *Canadian Mag.* Mar. 435 The Montreal and Winnipeg Clubs for some years were acknowledged to excel all other hockeyists in Canada. **1963** *National Hockey Ann.* 36/2 Shack.. was actually a reluctant hockeyist and was thrust into the game by his father.

hocking: see HOCK *vbs.*[1] and [2].

†**hockle,** *v.*[1] *Obs.* [app. deriv. of HOCK *sb.*[2]; or iterative of HOCK *v.*[1], HOUGH *v.* But perhaps only an error of Skinner's perpetuated in Dictionaries.] To hough, to hamstring. Hence **hockler.**

1668-71 SKINNER *Etym. Ling. Angl.*, To Hockle, *Poplites seu Suffragines Succidere. Ibid.*, Hocklers of Horse, *qui equis suffragines succidunt.* **1678** LITTLETON *Lat. Dict.* **1721** BAILEY, *Hockle*, to hamstring, or cut the Joints towards the hough. **1755** in JOHNSON. Thence in mod. Dicts.

hockle, *v.*[2] *local.* ? *Obs.* To cut up (stubble).

1746 *Compl. Farmer* s.v. *Farm*, Hockling, or cutting up and raking haulm, 2s. 6d. per acre. **1785** in A. YOUNG *Ann. Agric.* IV. 108 We [near Hartlebury, Worcestersh.] pay about 4s. per acre for reaping wheat, and diet, if they set it up and hockle it.

hockle-bone, obs. form of HUCKLEBONE.

hockly ('hɒklı), *sb.* [Cf. HOCK *sb.*[6]] A term in the game of faro: see quot. 1850.

1805 *Sporting Mag.* XXVI. 203 The banker now claims the chance of hockly.. The advantage of hockly is relinquished by some bankers. **1850** *Bohn's Hand-bk. Games* 337 *Hockly*, a Certainty, signifies the last card but one, the chance of which the banker claims, and may refuse to let any punter withdraw a card when eight or less remain to be dealt.

†**'hockly,** *a. Obs. rare.* Cf. HUCKLE-BACKED.

1707 E. WARD *Hud. Rediv.* II. v. 22 Next to this hockly greasy Beast, Stood a young Beau, most nicely drest.

Hock Monday. *Obs.* exc. *Hist.* Also 5 **hoc, hok,** 6 **hoke, hocke.** [f. *hock* in HOCK-DAY + MONDAY.] The Monday in HOCKTIDE.

1481-90 *Howard-Househ. Bks.* (Roxb.) 202 Item. to women on Hoc Monday ijd. **1485** *Churchw. Acc. St. Mary Hill, Lond.* (Nichols 1797) 102 For bred and ale to the wyvys yn the parish that gathered on Hokmonday, 1s. 1d. **1516** in Lysons *Envir. Lond.* (1810) I. 1. 222 Recd. of the gaderynge of the churchwardens weyffes on Hoke Monday, 8s. 3d. **1555** W. WATREMAN *Fardle Facions* II. viii. 169 The kyng.. cometh to hunting.. accompaignied with a rable of women, in as good ordre as ours ware wonte to be vpon Hocke mondaie. **1578** *Churchw. Acc. Kingston-upon-Thames* in Lysons *Envir. Lond.* (1810) I. 1. 229 Recd. of the women upon Hoc Monday, 5s. 2d. **1677** PLOT *Oxfordsh.* 201. **1826** HONE *Ever-day Bk.* I. 476 Hock Monday was for the men, and Hock Tuesday for the women.

hock money. *Obs.* exc. *Hist.* Also 5 **hocke,** 5-6 **hok,** 6 **hoke, oke, hoxce.** [f. *hock-* in HOCK-DAY + MONEY.] The money collected by the men and the women at HOCKTIDE.

1484-5 *Churchw. Acc. St. Dunstan's, Canterb.*, Ress. by vs the seyde Wardeynes of Hockemoneye at Ester ixs. xd. **1499** in C. Coates *Antiq. Reading* 214 It. rec. of hok money gaderyd of women xxs. It. rec. of hok money gaderyd of men iiijs. **1515-6** in *Archæol.* VII. 251 Received of the men for oke money vs. viiid. Item of the wyffs of oke money xvs. id. **1556-7** *Ibid.* 252 For Hoxce money by them received to the use of the Church, xijs. **1826** HONE *Every-day Bk.* I. 476 At Hock-tide.. collections of Hock-money were made in various parishes.. until the Reformation.

hockorn, obs. form of ACORN.

hocks, var. of HOX *v. Obs.*

†**'hockshin.** *Obs.* or *dial.* In 4 **hokschyne,** 7 **huckson,** 8 **hucksheen.** [app. repr. OE. *hóhsinu*, pl. *hóhsina*, HOUGH-SINEW, with the *ó* shortened by position, and the second element associated with *shin.*] The under side of the thigh; the hough.

c **1394** *P. Pl. Crede* 426 His hosen ouerhongen his hokschynes on eueriche a side. **1648** HERRICK *Hesperides, Beggar to Mab*, Commend a crickets-hip, Or his huckson to my scrip. **1746** *Exmoor Scolding* 154 (E.D.S.) Thy Hozen muxy up zo vurs thy Gammerels to tha very Hucksheens o' tha. **1778** *Ibid.* Gloss., *The Hucksheens* the Legs up to the Hams, or Hocks. **1886** ELWORTHY *W. Somerset Word-bk.*, *Huckshins*, the hock-shins; under-side of the thighs just above the bend of the knee.

Hocktide. *Obs.* exc. *Hist.* Also 5 **hoke-,** 6 **hok-,** 6-7 **hoc-,** 7 **hocks-, hucx-, hocke-, huck-.** [f. *hock-* in HOCK-DAY + TIDE time, season.]

The time or season of the hock days: Hock Monday and Tuesday (the second Monday and Tuesday after Easter-day), on which in pre-Reformation times money was collected for church and parish purposes, with various festive and sportive customs; after the Reformation kept for some time as a festive season with various traditional customs, some of which survived into the 19th c.

The earlier custom seems to have been the seizing and binding (by women on Monday, and by men on Tuesday) of persons of the opposite sex, who released themselves by a small payment. After this was prohibited (see 1406 in HOCK *v.*[2], 1450 in HOCK-DAY), recourse was had to the plan of stretching ropes or chains across the streets and ways, to stop passers for the same purpose. (See 1777 in HOCK TUESDAY.)

1484 in Glasscock *Rec. St. Michael's Bp. Stortford* (1882) 26 Item pd. for bakyng of the brede at hoketyde vd. **1509** *Churchw. Acc. Kingston-upon-Thames* in Lysons *Envir. Lond.* (1810) I. 1. 168 Recd for the gaderyng at Hoc-tyde 0 14 0. **1510** *Churchw. Acc. St. Mary's* in Peshall *Hist. Oxford* 67 Recepts. Recd. atte Hoctyde of the wyfes gaderynge, xvs. ijd. **1546** *Churchw. Acc. St. Dunstan's, Canterb.*, Recevyd of the wyvys yt they did gether at Hoktyd iijs. ixd. **1611** SPEED *Hist. Gt. Brit.* VIII. v. §11. 392 The day of his [Hardicnut's] death is annually celebrated with open pastimes.. which time is now called Hoctide or Hucktide, signifying a time of scorning or contempt, which fell vpon the Danes by his death. **1625** PURCHAS *Pilgrims* III. 621 *margin*, Hocktide I haue seene kept with publike feasting in the street, the women also binding men, or compelling them to some ransome; the Tuesday fortnight after Easter. **1656** BLOUNT *Glossogr.*, *Hocktyde* or *Hockstyde*,.. in some parts of this Nation not yet out of memory, but observed the week after Easter. **1663** *Churchw. Acc. St. Peter's in East* in Peshall *Hist. Oxford* 83 Hocktide brought in this year £6. **1772-3** *Ibid.* 83 This parish of St. Peter in the East gained by the Hocktide and Whitsuntide, anno 1664, the sum of 14l. **1777** BRAND *Pop. Antiq.* (1849) I. 187. **1826** HONE *Every-day Bk.* I. 476. **1898** *L'pool Echo* 19 Apr. (2nd Tuesday after Easter) 4/3 'Kissing Day' at Hungerford.—Hungerford is once more celebrating Hock-tide, with all its quaint customs and ancient ceremonies.

b. *attrib.*, as ***Hocktide-festival, -money, -pastime.***

c **1505** *Churchw. Acc. St. Dunstan's, Canterb.*, Receyvid of Hocktyde money for iij yere xxiijs. viijd. **1613** WITHER *Abuses Stript* (1618) 232 Because that, for the Churches good, They in defence of Hocktide custome stood. **1636** J. TRUSSELL in *Ann. Dubrensia* (1877) 7 The Hocktide pastimes are Declin'd, if not diserted. **1884** SYMONDS *Shaks. Predecess.* iv. 176 They were acted.. at hock-tide festivals.

Hock Tuesday. *Obs.* exc. *Hist.* Also 5-6 **hok(e.** The Tuesday in HOCKTIDE; HOCK-DAY. Also called *binding-Tuesday* (*dies Martis ligatoria*): see BINDING *vbl. sb.* 6.

c **1250** *Reg. Salop Abbey* No. 179 Unum denarium coquinæ prænominati conventus die qui vulgariter dicitur Hoketysday persolvere. *Ibid.* No. 178 B, In die Hoketisday. **1480** CAXTON *Chron. Eng.* ccxliv. (1482) 301 On saynt Markes day that was that tyme hoketewysday, he toke his leue. **1575** LANEHAM *Let.* (1871) 26 *margin*, Hok Tuisday by the Couentree men. **1607** COWELL *Interpr.*, *Hoke-day*, otherwise called Hock-Tuesday. **1656** DUGDALE *Warwicksh.* (1730) 249/2 Hither came the Coventre men [in 1575], and acted the antient Play, long since used in that City, called Hocks tuesday, setting forth the destruction of the Danes in King Ethelred's time. **1777** BRAND *Pop. Antiq.* (1870) I. 105 *note*, Hoke Monday was for the men, and Hock Tuesday for the women. On both days the men and women, alternately, with great merriment intercepted the public roads with ropes, and pulled passengers to them, from whom they exacted money to be laid out in pious uses.

hocle-bone, obs. f. HUCKLEBONE.

hocour, -owre, var. HOKER *Obs.*

hocqueton, hocton, obs. var. HAQUETON, ACTON.

hocster, obs. f. HUCKSTER.

hocus ('həʊkəs), *sb.* Also 7 **hocas.** [Short for *hocus pocus*, HOCUS-POCUS.]

†**1.** A conjuror, juggler. *Obs.*

1640 G. H. *Witt's Recreat.* in *Facetiæ* (1817) II. 237 Epitaph.. On Hocas Pocas. Here Hocas lyes with his tricks and his knocks, Whom death hath made sure as his Juglers box. **1647** CLEVELAND *Poems, Rebell Scot* 36 Before a Scot can properly be curst, I must (like Hocus) swallow daggers first. **1675** *Coffee-Houses Vind.* in *Harl. Misc.* VI. 473 Our pamphlet-monger (that sputters out senseless characters faster, than any hocus can vomit inkle). **1694** R. L'ESTRANGE *Fables* xciv. (1714) 109 These Ordinary Hocusses.. have been made use of in all ages. **1699** —— *Colloq. Erasm.* (1711) 37 Running mad after Buffoons, Fortune-tellers and Hocus's.

†**b.** *transf.* A cheat, imposter, pretender. *Obs.*

c **1685** SOUTH *Serm. Will for Deed* Serm. (1715) 411 Just like that old formal Hocus, who denied a Beggar a Farthing, and put him off with his Blessing.

2. Jugglery, trickery, deception. *Obs.* or *arch.*

1652 GAULE *Magastrom.* 41, I must not believe there was any Hocas in this. **1693** R. GOULD *Corrupt. Times* 3 (Stanf.) A quick Eye may all their Hocus see. **1854** SYD. DOBELL *Balder* xxiv. 164 Here.. With neither gold nor tinsel, cap nor crown, Hocus nor title.. nor conjuring-rod nor sceptre.. To lie here thus.

3. Drugged liquor: cf. HOCUS *v.* 2.

In mod. Dicts.

4. *Comb.* as **hocus-trick,** juggling trick.

c **1680** *Roxb. Ball.* (1885) V. 595 Three Kingdoms now at stake do lie, And Rooks all Hocus-tricks do try, That ye may be undone. *a* **1683** OLDHAM *Poet. Wks.* (1686) 78 Such Holy Cheats, such Hocus Tricks, these, For Miracles amongst the Rabble pass.

hocus ('həʊkəs), *v.* [f. HOCUS *sb.*

Supposed to be the source of the later HOAX *v.*, though the want of instances for the 18th c. makes this less certain. Apparently revived in 19th c., perh. under the influence of *hoax.*]

1. *trans.* To play a trick upon, 'take in', hoax.

1675 R. HEAD *Proteus Rediv.* 322 The Mercer cries, Was ever Man so Hocuss'd? however, I have enough to maintain me here. *a* **1686** NALSON (T.), One of the greatest pieces of legerdemain, with which these jugglers hocus the vulgar and incautelous of the present age. **1847** DISRAELI *Tancred* VI. v, There is nothing.. I so revel in as hocussing Guizot and Aberdeen. **1883** LD. R. GOWER *My Remin.* I. 368 These people have been hocussed and cheated by the Government.

2. To stupefy with drugs, esp. for a criminal purpose; hence, to drug (liquor).

1831 in *Ann. Reg., Law Cases* (1832) 321/2 [A witness] saw May put some gin into Bishop's tea. He said, 'Are you going to hocus (or Burke) me?' **1837** DICKENS *Pickw.* xiii, 'What do you mean by "hocussing" brandy-and water?'.. 'Puttin' laud'num in it', replied Sam. **1848** THACKERAY *Van. Fair* lxiv, It was at her house at Lausanne that he was hocussed at supper and lost eight hundred pounds to Major Loader. **1885** JAS. GRANT *Royal Highlanders* (Rtldg.) 154 By unfair play he had rooked many: he had hocussed horses. **1887** BESANT *The World went* etc. xviii. 148 You shall hocus his drink and put him on board.

Hence **'hocussed** *ppl. a.*, **'hocussing** *vbl. sb.*; also **'hocusser,** one who hocusses.

1827-39 DE QUINCEY *Murder* Postscr. Wks. IV. 107 The landlord.. they intended to disable by a trick then newly introduced amongst robbers, and termed hocussing. **1862** MAYHEW *Lond. Labour* IV. 31 The 'Drummer' plunders by stupefaction; as the 'hocusser'. **1865** DICKENS *Mut. Fr.* II. xii, I will not say a hocussed wine. **1892** MIDDLETON *Rome* II. 53 The bribing of jockeys and the 'hocussing' of horses and their drivers were familiar to the ancient Romans.

hocus-pocus ('həʊkəs 'pəʊkəs), *sb.* (*a.*, *adv.*) Also 7 **hocas pocas, hokos pokos, hokus pokus.** [Appears early in 17th c., as the appellation of a juggler (and, apparently, as the assumed name of a particular conjuror) derived from the sham Latin formula employed by him: see below, and cf. Grimm, *Hokuspokus.*

The notion that *hocus pocus* was a parody of the Latin words used in the Eucharist, rests merely on a conjecture thrown out by Tillotson: see below.

1655 ADY *Candle in Dark* 29, I will speak of one man.. that went about in King James his time.. who called himself, The Kings Majesties most excellent Hocus Pocus, and so was called, because that at the playing of every Trick, he used to say, *Hocus pocus, tontus talontus, vade celeriter jubeo*, a dark composure of words, to blinde the eyes of the beholders, to make his Trick pass the more currantly without discovery. *a* **1694** TILLOTSON *Serm.* xxvi. (1742) II. 237 In all probability those common juggling words of *hocus pocus* are nothing else but a corruption of *hoc est corpus*, by way of ridiculous imitation of the priests of the Church of Rome in their trick of Transubstantiation.]

†**1.** A conjuror, juggler. (In 17th c. freq. as proper name or nickname of a conjuror.) Also *transf.* a trickster. *Obs.*

1624 GEE *New Shreds Old Snare* 21, I alwayes thought they had their rudiments from some iugling Hocas Pocas in a quart pot. **1625** B. JONSON *Staple of N.* II. Wks. (Rtldg.) 388/2 Iniquity came in like Hokos Pokos, in a Juglers ierkin, with false skirts. **1634** SIR T. HERBERT *Trav.* 55 A Persian Hocus-pocus.. performed rare trickes with hands and feet. **1648** C. WALKER *Relat. & Observ.* 12 This labyrinth into which these unpolitick *Hocas Pocasses* have brought us. **1650** H. MORE *Observ. Anima Magica* in *Enthus. Tri.* (1656) 117 He opens as Hokus Pokus do's his fists, where we see that here is nothing and there is nothing. **1680** HICKERINGILL *Meroz* 26 He shall now.. play as many tricks as Hocus Pocus at a fair. **17..** TOLLET in Johnson *Shaks. Plays, 1 Hen. IV*, v. v. (Jod.), I incline to call him hocus-pocus, or some juggler, or attendant upon the master of the hobbyhorse.

†**b.** ***to play hocus-pocus,*** to play the juggler, to juggle. *Obs.*

1659 *Lond. Chanticl.* ix. in Hazl. *Dodsley* XII. 343 Thou hast played hocus-pocus with me, I think. **1737** BENTLEY *Free Thinking* §12 (R.) Our author is playing hocus pocus in the very similitude he takes from that jugler.

2. Used as a formula of conjuring or magical incantation. (Sometimes with allusion to an assumed derivation from *hoc est corpus*: see etymology above.)

1632 RANDOLPH *Jealous Lov.* I. x, Hocus-pocus, here you shall have me, and there you shall have me! **1656** HOBBES *Lib. Necess. & Chance* (1841) 384 This term of *insufficient* cause.. is not intelligible, but a word devised like *hocus pocus*, to juggle a difficulty out of sight. **1772** FLETCHER *Logica Genev.* 201 The *hocus pocus* of a popish priest cannot turn bread into flesh. **1851** LONGF. *Gold. Leg.* I. *Court-yard*, The Priests.. began to mutter their *hocus-pocus.* **1886** MALLOCK *Old Order Changes* II. 47 This man, who only an hour ago was muttering hocus pocus, in the dress of a mediæval conjuror.

3. A juggler's trick; conjuring, jugglery; sleight of hand; a method of bringing something about as if by magic; trickery, deception.

1647 N. BACON *Disc. Govt. Eng.* I. lxiv. (1739) 135 Thus this Statute became like a Hocus Pocus, a thing to still the people for the present, and serve the King's turn. **1678** MARVELL *Growth Popery* 28 The same opportunities that others had of practising the Hocus Pocus of the Face, of Playing the French Scaramuccie. **1688** R. HOLME *Armoury* III. 447/1 The Art of Leger De Main or Jugling, otherwise called *Hocus Pocus.* **1774** *Westm. Mag.* II. 449 There hath been a mystery, a hocus-pocus, in all Religions, since the days of the Egyptians to those of the American Indians. **1842** DICKENS *Amer. Notes* xii, The vagabond arts of sleight-of-hand, and hocus-pocus. **1843** W. IRVING in *Life & Lett.* (1866) III. 300 These insurgent legions.. which, by the sudden hocus pocus of political affairs, are transformed into loyal soldiers.

†**4.** A bag or 'poke' used by jugglers. *Obs. rare.*

c **1640** [SHIRLEY] *Capt. Underwit* II. ii. in Bullen *O. Pl.* II. 342 His very fingers cryed 'give me the gold!' which.. he put in his hocas pocas, a little dormer under his right skirt.

B. 1. *attrib.* or *adj.* Juggling; cheating, tricky.

1668 R. L'ESTRANGE *Vis. Quev.* (1708) 117 Hocus Pocus Tricks are call'd Slight of Hand. **1698-1700** E. WARD *Lond. Spy* in Ashton *Soc. Life Q. Anne* (1882) II. 94 By virtue of this Hocus Pocus Stratagem he had conjur'd all the ill blood

out of my Body. **1773** MACKLIN *Love à la Mode* II. i, The law is a sort of hocus-pocus science. **1785** *Span. Rivals* 9 He looks rather hocus pocus, as a body may say. **1841** E. MIALL in *Nonconf.* I. 305 A sort of hocus-pocus use of the word 'church'.

2. as *adv.*

1815 W. H. IRELAND *Scribbleomania* 24 To joke us, Great Southey performs all his flights Hocus Pocus.

hocus-pocus, *v.* [f. prec.]

1. *intr.* To act the conjuror, juggle; to play tricks, practise deception.

1687 R. L'ESTRANGE *Answ. Diss.* 18, I never lov'd the Hocus-Pocussing of *Hoc est Corpus Meum.* *a* **1704** —— (J.), This gift of hocus pocussing, and of disguising matters, is surprizing. **1838** *Fraser's Mag.* XVIII. 157 So Talleyrand hocus-pocused in politics..nothing but political legerdemain. **1855** MISS MANNING *Old Chelsea Bun-ho.* xiii. 212, I..showed them some simple Hocus-pocussing.

2. *trans.* To play tricks upon; to transform as if by jugglery.

1774 *Westm. Mag.* II. 375 But, hocus'd-pocus'd All, with so much art! **1808** *Miss-led General* 30 Before Frederic was two years old..he was hocus-pocus'd, alias, metamorphosed, into a Bishop. **1892** *Nation* (N.Y.) 28 Apr. 317/1 So commonly is the law hocus-pocussed by the local boards before whom the new voters are made.

hocus-'pocusly, *adv.* [f. HOCUS-POCUS *a.* + -LY².] In a 'hocus-pocus' manner; by jugglery.

1791 LACKINGTON *Mem.* (1792) 107 Many of their hearers are not only methodistically convinced, or alarmed, but are also *hocus pocusly* converted.

hod (hɒd), *sb.* [Not in evidence before 16th c.: app. a modification of HOT *sb.*¹ in same sense: see esp. quot. 1300 there.]

1. An open receptacle for carrying mortar, and sometimes bricks or stones, to supply builders at work; also the quantity carried in it, a hodful.

Formerly a sort of tray; now, as in quot. 1688.

1573 TUSSER *Husb.* xvii. (1878) 37 A lath hammer, trowel, a hod, or a traie. **1611** COTGR., *Oiseau*..also, a Hodd; the Tray wherein Masons, &c. carrie their Mortar. **1636** *MS. Acc. St. John's Hosp., Canterb.*, For 4 hodes of lime and sand, j s. **1688** R. HOLME *Armoury* III. 395/2 The Hod is a kind of three square trough made up at one end and open at the other, haveing a staffe fixed to its bottom. **1800** B. RUSH in *Med. Jrnl.* III. 185, I have done but little more than carry the hod to assist in completing part of a fabric. **1848** MRS. JAMESON *Sacr. & Leg. Art* (1850) 297 Ascending a ladder with a hod full of bricks.

2. A receptacle for carrying or holding coal. Formerly *dial.* and *U.S.*, but now generally applied to a pail-shaped coal-scuttle, having one upper edge prolonged in a scoop-like form, for throwing coal on the fire.

1825, etc. Coal-hod [see COAL 16]. **1854** MISS BAKER *Northampt. Gloss.*, *Hod*, a trough or scope, made of wood or metal, for carrying coals or cinders. A coal-hod, or cinder-hod. **1870** MISS ALCOTT *Old-fash. Girl* ii. 26 Tom, resenting the insult, had forcibly seated her in the coal-hod. **1884** *Tradesman's Price List*, French 'Repousse' Coal Hod. Waterloo Coal Hods.

3. (See quot.)

1883 GRESLEY *Gloss. Coal-Mining*, *Hod*, a cart or sled for conveying coals in the stalls of thin seams.

4. *attrib.* and *Comb.* (from 1), as *hod bearing*, *-elevator*, *-work*; **hod-bearer**, **-carrier** = HODMAN q.v.; **hod-woman**, a woman acting as a hod-bearer; **hod-work**, unskilled labour, mere mechanical drudgery.

1831 CARLYLE *Sart. Res.* II. iii, Till the Hodman is discharged or reduced to *hod-bearing. **1771** SMOLLETT *Humph. Cl.* 29 May, The *hod-carrier, the low mechanic, the tapster, the publican. **1866** A. L. PERRY *Elem. Pol. Econ.* (1873) 95 Why class the brick-maker as a productive laborer, and refuse the epithet to the hod-carrier? **1875** KNIGHT *Dict. Mech.*, **Hod-elevator*, a hoisting device to raise hods loaded with bricks or mortar to the..building. **1891** R. H. BUSK in *N. & Q.* 31 Oct. 351/2 Hodmen and *hodwomen always display the former quality. **1837** CARLYLE *Mirabeau* in *Misc. Ess.* (1888) V. 211 To do *hodwork and even skilful handiwork.

Hence **'hodded** *a. nonce-wd.*, bearing a hod; **'hodful**, the quantity that a hod will contain.

1801 W. TAYLOR in *Monthly Mag.* XII. 588 With hodfuls of allusion to familiar national nature. **1812** H. & J. SMITH *Rej. Addr.* 78 Workmen in elder times would mount a ladder With hodded heads.

hod, *v. Sc.* [? Onomatopœic.] *intr.* To bob up and down in riding; to jog.

1785 BURNS *Holy Fair* vii, Here farmers gash, in ridin graith Gaed hoddin by their cotters. **1889** STEVENSON *Master of B.* 229 The smoking horses and the hodding post-boy.

hod, early ME. f. HAD, -HOOD, condition, etc.; dial. f. HOLD; obs. f. HOOD *sb.*¹ and *v.*

hodad ('həʊdæd). *Surfing slang.* [Origin obscure.] (See quots.)

1962 *Austral. Women's Weekly* Suppl. 24 Oct. 3/2 *Ho-dad*, anyone who annoys board-riders while they surf. **1963** *Pix* 28 Sept. 62/2 *Hodad*, non-surfing beach bum. **1965** *Daily Express* 16 Aug. 6/8, I could be a 'hodad' which means a man who talks big about his surfing exploits, but jibs at riding the big waves. **1965** *N.Z. Listener* 17 Dec. 4/5 Surfers..are..antagonistic towards..ill-mannered surf bums ('hodads'). **1971** *Studies in English* (Univ. Cape Town) Feb. 26 *Ho-dad* is a much misunderstood word. Basically, it is a double contraction from the American slang word *hood*, which in turn comes from *hoodlum*.

hodde, obs. form of HOOD *sb.*¹

hodden ('hɒd(ə)n). *Sc.* Also 8 **hoddan**, 8–9 **hoddin**, 9 **huddin**. [Origin unknown.]

1. Woollen cloth of a coarse quality such as used to be made by country weavers on their hand-looms.

1792 SINCLAIR in *Statist. Acc. Scotl.*, *Forfar* IV. 242 Of the wool..is manufactured almost every kind of cloth worn in the parish; hodden, which is most used for herds cloaks, and is sold at 1*s.* 8*d.* the yard; plaiding [etc.]. ? *a* **1800** *Bonnie Lizzie Lindsay* xxx. in Child *Ballads* VIII. ccxxvi. (1892) 262/2 And make us a bed o green rashes, And covert wi huddins sae grey. **1837** CARLYLE *Fr. Rev.* III. III. iv, Behold how their Peasants, in mere russet and hodden..dash at us like a dark whirlwind.

b. *attrib.* or *adj.* **c.** *Comb.*, as ***hodden-clad*** adj.

1812 W. TENNANT *Anster F.* II. xxi, Tenant and laird, and hedger hodden-clad. **1837** CARLYLE *Fr. Rev.* III. I. vi, The hodden or russet individuals are Uncustomary.

2. hodden grey. Grey hodden, made without dyeing, 'by mingling one black fleece with a dozen white ones' (*Gloss. to Burns*, Paterson, 1877). Applied to the 'cloth worn by the peasantry, which has the natural colour of the wool' (Jam.). Hence often taken as the typical garb of homely rusticity.

A poetic inversion of ***grey hodden***, used for rime's sake by Ramsay in a well-known passage, whence also in Burns, which has thence become a stock phrase, the two words being often hyphened, as if 'hodden' were a qualification of 'grey', or 'hodden-grey' were a colour.

1724 RAMSAY *Gent. Sheph.* V. ii, But Meg, poor Meg! maun with the shepherds stay, And tak what God will send in hodden grey. **1795** BURNS *A man's a man* 10 (*Scots Mag.* 1797, 611) What tho' on hamely fare we dine, Wear hoddan grey and a' that [*ed. Curry* 1800 though..hoddin]. **1816** SCOTT *Old Mort.* viii, An old woman..supported by a stout, stupid-looking fellow, in hodden-grey. **1837** R. NICOLL *Poems* (1843) 175 His coat is hame-spun hodden-gray. **1851** LONGF. *Gold. Leg.* I. *Court-yard*, He went..Clothed in a cloak of hodden grey.

attrib. **1820** SCOTT *Abbot* xvii, From the hodden-grey coat to the cloak of scarlet and gold. **1843** JAMES *Forest Days* I. ii, Plain hodden-grey cloth, of a coarse fabric.

b. *fig.*

1866 CHR. ROSSETTI *Prince's Progr.* etc. xvii, And heaven put off its hodden grey For mother-o'-pearl. *a* **1882** WHITTIER *Garris. Cape Ann* iv, Golden-threaded fancies weaving in a web of hodden gray.

'hodding-spade. *local.* (See quot.)

a **1825** FORBY *Voc. E. Anglia*, *Hodding-spade*, a sort of spade principally used in the fens, so shaped as to take up a considerable portion of earth entire, somewhat like a *hod.* **1863** MORTON *Cycl. Agric.* II. Gloss. (E.D.S.).

hoddy, hoddie ('hɒdɪ), *a. dial.* [? f. ME. *hôd*, *hode* state, condition: see HAD *sb.*] In good condition physically or mentally; healthy; in good spirits, pleasant, cheerful.

1664 J. WILSON *Cheats* V. v, O my Child, my Child—Thy father is prettie hoddie again, but this will break his heart quite. **1674** RAY *S. & E.C. Words* 68 *Hoddy*, well pleasant, in good tune or humour. *c* **1700** KENNETT in *Laud MS.* 1033 lf. 184 *Hoddy*, well, in good health. 'Pretty hoddy.' *Kent.* **1785** SARAH FIELDING *Ophelia* II. i, I love a hoddy girl. *a* **1825** FORBY *Voc. E. Anglia*, *Hoddy*, pretty well in health and spirits; in tolerably good case. **1890** *Gloucestersh. Gloss.*, *Hoddy pretty*, pretty well.

†**hoddy-dod, hoddidod.** *Obs.* [The element *dod* is evidently the same as in DODMAN a shell-snail; *hoddy-dod*, *hoddy-doddy*, *hodman-dod*, are perhaps in origin nursery reduplications; but the element *hoddy-* appears itself to have come to be associated with or to mean 'snail' (or ?horned), as in several words that follow.] A shell-snail.

1601 HOLLAND *Pliny* II. 368 So doth the ashes of shell-snailes or hoddidods. *Ibid.* 539 Hoddy-dods or shell-Snailes sticking hard therto and eating it. **1611** FLORIO, *Chiocciola* ..also a hoddydod, a shell-snaile, a perwinkle.

hoddy-doddy, *sb.* and *a. Obs.* exc. *dial.* [See prec. (In sense 3, with reference to the 'horns' of a cuckold; cf. sense 1.)]

A. *sb.* **1.** A small shell-snail. *dial.*

2. A short and dumpy person: cf. B.

Quot. *a* 1953 is perh. influenced by sense 3, noodle, 'dodderer'.

a **1553** UDALL *Royster D.* I. i. (Arb.) 11 Sometime I hang on Hankyn Hoddydodies sleeue. **1702** *Burlesque R. L'Estrange's Vis. Quev.* 76 Some thick and short like Hoddy Doddies. **1723** SWIFT *Cook Maid's Let.* 10 A personable man, and not a spindle-shank'd hoddy-doddy. **1877** E. LEAR *Laughable Lyrics*, You're such a Hoddy Doddy. *a* **1953** DYLAN THOMAS *Quite early one Morning* (1954) 64 Exhibitionists,..theological rhetoricians, historical hoddy-doddies, balletomanes,..windbags. **1969** R. J. WHITE *Women of Peasen Hall* v. 56 Gardiner always refers to him as 'Dids', or a 'Hoddy-doddy'—which is Suffolk for a diminutive person.

†**3.** A cuckold; a hen-pecked man; a noodle; a simpleton. *Obs.*

1598 B. JONSON *Ev. Man in Hum.* IV. viii. Wks. (Rtldg.) 25/1 You, That make your husband such a hoddie-doddie. **1656** S. HOLLAND *Zara* 162 Where shall I bath this vexed body, Tormented to a Hoddy-Doddy?

4. *dial.* (See quot.)

1847–78 HALLIWELL, *Hoddy-doddy*..a revolving light. *Devon.*

B. *adj.* **1.** Short and dumpy or clumsy.

1824 MISS FERRIER *Inher.* lxxviii, Shoals of hoddy-doddy, white-haired, blubbered boys and girls. **1854** MISS BAKER *Northampt. Gloss.* 329 *Hoddy-Doddy*, disproportionately stout. A short, lusty, squat looking person is said to be 'all hoddy-doddy'..with us it is restricted to females.

2. *dial.* Confused, in a whirl.

a **1809** J. PALMER *Like Master Like Man* (1811) I. 159, I gets up, all hoddy-doddy, and goes out to see what were matter.

hoddy-noddy. *rare.* [Reduplicated from NODDY.] A fool, simpleton, noodle.

1600 O. E. *Reply to Libel* I. vii. 181 If this hoddy Noddy thinke otherwise, let him..bring foorth his proofes. **1951** DYLAN THOMAS *Let.* 12 Apr. (1966) 356 No more of that beer-cheapened hoddy-noddy. **1970** 'M. HEBDEN' *Mask of Violence* (1971) xx. 183 They were..no end considerate. Shoved everybody out of the way. Damn near a punch-up with one lot of beer-cheapened hoddy-noddy.

†**'hoddypeak.** *Obs.* Forms: 6 **hody-**, **hodi-**, **hodie-**, **hoddy-**, **huddi-**, **-peke**, **-peeke**, **-peak(e**, **-peck**. [f. *hoddy* (see HODDY-DOD) + PEAK *sb.* or *v.*, but the sense is obscure.] A fool, simpleton, noodle, blockhead.

1500 in Furniv. *Ball. fr. MSS.* I. 254 Who dwelleth here, wyll no man speke? Is there no fole nor hody-peke? **1549** LATIMER *3rd Serm. bef. Edw. VI* (Arb.) 84 What ye brain-sycke fooles, ye hoddy peckes, ye doddye poulles, ye huddes, do ye beleue hym? are you seduced also? **1554** CHRISTOPHERSON *Exhort. agst. Rebel.* (N.), They counte peace to be cause of ydelnes, and that it maketh men hodipekes and cowardes. **1563–87** FOXE *A. & M.* (1684) II. 547 O most idiot huddipeaks and blockish condemners. **1589** NASHE *Anat. Absurd.* 13 A Paramour..vnder her husbands, that hoddy-peekes nose.

†**'hoddypoll.** *Obs.* In 6 **-poule**, **-peele**. [f. *hoddy* as in prec. + POLL head: cf. DODDYPOLL in same sense.] A fool, simpleton; a cuckold.

1522 SKELTON *Why not to Court* 670 Moche I wonder, How suche a hoddypoule So boldely dare controule. **1589** NASHE *Almond for Parrat* 4a, Learne of her..to make hodie-peeles of your husbandes, and leade them..vp and downe the streetes by the hornes.

†**hode**, *v.* [var. HADE *v.*¹] *Obs. trans.* To ordain, consecrate; in quot. 1275, to admit to a religious order.

[**900–1340** see HADE *v.*¹] *c* **1275** LAY. 28474 þare me hire hodede and munechene makede. *c* **1425** *Eng. Conq. Irel.* lv. 132 Ihon comyn [was]..of the clergye..by on accorde I-chose; & of the pope..theraftyr I-hodet & I-sacred.

hode, obs. form of HOOD *sb.*¹

Hodegetria (həʊdiː'giːtrɪə). [f. Gr. ὁδηγήτρια (see below).] An iconographical variant of the Virgin and Child in which the Child is depicted on the Virgin's left arm while she indicates Him with her right hand as 'The Indicator of the Way' (the meaning of the Greek word).

According to tradition the arrangement follows that of a painting originally attributed to St. Luke, but the earliest surviving example is probably to be assigned to the 7th century. The composition was frequently copied in Italy, the Byzantine world, and Russia. Sometimes, in the process of copying, the Child was transferred from the Virgin's left arm to the right and she indicates Him with her left hand, but there is no particular significance in this variant.

1880 E. VENABLES in Smith & Cheetham *Dict. Chr. Antiq.* II. 1152/2 The famous *Hodegetria*..which was for so many centuries regarded with the deepest reverence by the Greeks. **1911** L. GILLET in *Cath. Encycl.* XI. 397/2 Mention must be made of the numerous icons, the various types of the Madonna (Panagia, Nicopœia, Hodegetria). **1937** *Burlington Mag.* July 18/2 The Madonna Enthroned in the central field of the Antwerp altarpiece belongs to the Hodegetria type common in Italy in the thirteenth century. **1952** D. T. RICE *Eng. Art 871–1100* v. 116 The most usual type of Virgin was that known as the *Hodegetria* or Indicator of the Way, where the Virgin holds the Child on her left arm while she points to Him with her right hand; the Child's right hand is extended in blessing. **1959** C. CECCHELLI et al. *Rabbula Gospels* 49 The Madonna is a Hodegetria type, that is, inspired by a famous image venerated since the 5th century in the Church of the Guides at Constantinople.

ho-de-ho ('həʊdiː'həʊ), *int.* An exclamation, used as the appropriate response to HI-DE-HI *int.* Also *transf.*

1941, **1943**, **1944** [see HI-DE-HI *int.*].

†**hodelnesse.** *Obs. rare.* [perh. for *hodernesse*, or from the same root as HODER *v.*, *hoder-moder*.] Concealment, secrecy.

c **1475** *Partenay* 5961 His knyghtly entent Stilled ne put shold be in hodelnesse.

hode-man, obs. f. HOOD-MAN.

hoden ('uːdən), *a. Kentish dial.* Also **hooden**. [Origin uncertain: perh. from association with *wooden* from the wooden horse's head.] Of or pertaining to the horse with wooden head and clapping jaws featured in a masquerade which formerly took place, *spec.* in Kent, on Christmas Eve. **'hodener**, a performer in this masquerade; **'hodening**, the name of the performance; also *attrib.*

1807 *European Mag.* LI. 358 This [mumming] is called, *provincially*, a Hodening, and the figure above described a Hoden, or Woden horse. **1887** PARISH & SHAW *Dict. Kentish Dial.* 77 *Hoodening*.., the name formerly given to a mumming or masquerade. **1891** *Church Times* 2 Jan. 20/1

'Hodening' still goes on..at Deal and Walmer. **1909** P. MAYLAM *Hooden Horse* i. 2 Everyone springs up, saying, 'The hoodeners have come, let us go and see the fun.' *Ibid.* 7 A farm with more than one team would have a hooden horse to each team. *Ibid.* 9, I had intended to walk on to Deal and look for the hoodening parties there. **1966** G. E. EVANS *Pattern under Plough* xix. 193 The hobby-horses that appear in many countryside ceremonies and ritual dances, notably the *Hodening Horse*. **1971** *Country Life* 17 June 1533/1 The Hooden Horse, a mystic man-animal found only in East Kent, will be at large in Folkestone..June 19.

†**hoder**, *v. Obs.* Also 5 **hodur**. [ME. *hoder*, of which a modern form would be *hudder*, an iterative from same stem as *huddle*. Cf. LG. *hudern* to cherish, shelter, as a hen her chickens, iterative of MLG. *huden* to hide, conceal, cover up.]

1. *trans.* To huddle together.

c **1330** R. BRUNNE *Chron.* (1810) 273 Scatred er þi Scottis, & hodred in þer hottes, neuer þei ne the [*Pol. Songs* 286 Hodred in the hottes, *v.rr.* hodered, hodird, hoderd].

2. To cover or wrap up tenderly; to 'cuddle'.

c **1440** *Bone Flor.* 112 Sche schall me bothe hodur and happe, And in hur lovely armes me lappe.

hoder-moder: see HUDDER-MUDDER *adv. Obs.*

Hodge (hɒdʒ). Also 4 **Hogge**, 5 **Hoge**, 6 **Hodg**. [Abbreviated and altered from *Roger*, like *Hob* from *Robert*, *Hick* from *Richard*.]

1. A familiar by-form and abbreviation of the name *Roger*; used as a typical name for the English agricultural labourer or rustic.

c **1386** CHAUCER *Cook's Prol.* 12 Euer sippe I highte hogge of ware. [*Ibid.* 21 Oure host seyde I graunt it the, Now telle on, Roger.] **1483** *Cath. Angl.* 187/1 Hoge, *Rogerus*, nomen proprium. **1589** GREENE *Menaphon* (Arb.) 58 These Arcadians are giuen to take the benefit of euerie Hodge. *a* **1700** B. E. *Dict. Cant. Crew*, *Hodge*, a Country Clown, also *Roger*. **1794** WOLCOTT (P. Pindar) *Wks.* III. 350 No more shall Hodge's prong and shovel start. **1826** in Hone *Everyday Bk.* II. 1210 You seem to think that with the name I retain all the characteristics..of a *hodge*. **1885** *Observer* 13 Dec. 5/3 The conduct of Hodge in the recent election.

2. (See quots.) Cf. *haggis*.

1879 MISS JACKSON *Shropsh. Work-bk.*, *Hodge*, the large paunch in a pig. **1884** *Chesh. Gloss.*, *Hodge*, the stomach of a pig, cleaned out and eaten as tripe.

3. *Jolly Hodge* (also *Jolly Roger*), the pirate's flag bearing the Death's Head and Cross-bones.

1822 SCOTT *Pirate* xl, Up goes the Jolly Hodge, the old black flag, with the death's-head and hour-glass.

4. *Comb.*, as **Hodge-razor**, a razor made to sell to Hodge: see Peter Pindar's *Wks.* (1794) I. 151; hence, in Carlyle, anything made to sell; a sham.

1843 CARLYLE *Dr. Francia* in *Misc. Ess.* (1872) VII. 48 Hodge-razors, in all conceivable kinds, were openly marketed, 'which were never meant to shave, but only to be sold!'

hodgee, -gia, obs. ff. *hoja*, KHOJA, a teacher.

hodge-podge ('hɒdʒpɒdʒ), *sb.* Forms: 5 hogpoch, 6 hogepotche, 6–7 hodge-potch, 7 hodg-podge, -poge, (hogg-podg, hodge-bodge), 7–8 hodg-podg, 7– hodge-podge. [A corruption of HOTCHPOTCH; prob. assimilated to the familiar personal name HODGE.]

1. A dish made of a mixture of various kinds of meat, vegetables, etc., stewed together; a haricot; esp. in *Sc.* = HOTCHPOTCH 1.

1622 MABBE tr. *Aleman's Guzman d' Alf.* II. 275 A hodge-podge of boyled mutton, that was nothing but mammockes. **1641** *News fr. Hell, Rome, etc.* in *Harl. Misc.* (Malh.) IV. 398 This covered mess is a gallimawfry; or, as the Flemings calls it, a hodge-podge, wherein are sundry meats stewed together. **1658** PHILLIPS, A *Hodge-podge*, or *Hotch-pot*, a *Hachee*, or flesh cut to pieces, and sodden together with Herbs [**1706** (*ed.* Kersey) Also any kind of cold mixture of Things]. **1699** DAMPIER *Voy.* II. II. 38 The little Pieces of Beef were like Plums in our Hodg-podg. **1769** MRS. RAFFALD *Eng. Housekpr.* (1778) 141 A hodge-podge of Mutton. **1843** LEFEVRE *Life Trav. Phys.* III. III. xiv. 285 A basin of sour pea-soup, as thick as hodgepodge.

2. *contemptuous.* A clumsy mixture of ingredients.

1615 G. SANDYS *Trav.* I. 65 Hodgpodges made of flower, milke, and hony. **1673** *Charac. Coffee-Ho.* in *Harl. Misc.* (1810) VI. 467 As you have a hodge-podge of drinks, such too is your company. **1694** WESTMACOTT *Script. Herb.* 21 The Oyntment commonly sold in the shops..generally a sophisticated hodg-podge. **1803** *Med. Jrnl.* X. 265 Who place greater confidence in the unknown hodge podge of a stone-mason or a gingerbread-baker, than in the skill of an honest and able regular practitioner.

3. A heterogeneous mass or agglomeration; a medley, farrago, gallimaufrey.

[As to the origin of this sense cf. HOTCHPOT 3.]

1426 AUDELAY *Poems* 29 Cast ham in a hogpoch togedur fore to daunce. **1561** DAUS tr. *Bullinger on Apoc.* (1573) 58 Many at this day make an hogepotche of papistrie and the Gospell. **1579** E. K. *Ded. to Spenser's Sheph. Cal.*, They haue made our English tongue a gallimaufray or hodge-podge of al other speches. **1653** WALTON *Angler* xi. 216 'Tis a hodgepodge of business, And mony, and care. **1762** KAMES *Elem. Crit.* (1763) I. viii. 389 A perfect hodge-podge of chearful and melancholy representations. **1864** LOWELL *Fireside Trav.*, *Italy* 202 He [a horse] treated me to a hodge-podge of all his several gaits at once.

†**b.** See quot. and cf. *hodge-podge act* in 5. *Obs.*

1793 J. PEARSON *Polit. Dict.* 29 *Hodge-Podge*, the name of a bill passed at the end of the Session, to lick up every little thing forgot through the negligence of the Secretary of the Treasury, or the hurry of business.

4. quasi-*adv.* In confusion, promiscuously.

1848 LOWELL *Fab. Critics* 544 Roots, wood, bark, and leaves..clapt hodge-podge together, they don't make a tree.

5. *attrib.* or as *adj.* Of the composition of hodge-podge or a heterogeneous mixture; **hodge-podge act**, a name for a legislative act embracing a number of incongruous matters: cf. also 3 b.

1602 *Life T. Cromwell* I. ii. 80 Time who doth abuse the cheated world, And fills it full of hodge-podge bastardy. **1705** HICKERINGILL *Priest-cr.* II. v. 47 Take warning, that they make no more Hodge-podge Divinity. **1766** BARRINGTON *Observ. Stat.* (1796) 449 Thrown together in that very strange confusion which hath now obtained the name of a hodge-podge act. **1796** *Rep. Ho. Com.* (1803) XIV. 35 *note*, *Hodge Podge Acts*, these have been discontinued of late years, but the statute book abounds with them. **1842** *P. Parley's Ann.* III. 16 What is called a hodge-podge sea—that is, a sea which is met on the cross by a cross wind, with a cross tide, according to nautical explanation. **1861** *Macm. Mag.* May 31 The 23 Geo. III. c. 26 is quoted by the commissioners as a specimen of what is familiar to lawyers as a Hodge-Podge Act. **1878** S. WALPOLE *Hist. Eng.* II. 66 A hodge-podge committee on penal laws, prisons, Botany Bay, and forgery.

hodge-podge, *v.* [f. prec. sb.]

1. *trans.* To make a hodge-podge of; to mix up in disorder.

1769 MRS. RAFFALD *Eng. Housekpr.* (1778) 137 To hodge-podge a Hare. **1814** MAD. D'ARBLAY *Wanderer* I. 12 Lest it should..be hodge-podged into a conspiracy. **1883** *Sword & Trowel* Feb. 89/1 A collection of other writers' views mingled with scraps of hymns..hodge-podged together.

2. *intr.* To form a hodge-podge. Hence **hodge-podging** *ppl. a.*, heterogeneous.

1772 *Gentl. Mag.* XLII. 191/1 A hodge-podging habit, 'twixt fidler and beau.

†'**hodge-poker**. *Obs.* Also -pocher. [app. f. HODGE + POKER, bugbear, the devil.] A bug-bear or hobgoblin.

1598 FLORIO, *Fistolo*, a hobgoblin, a hag, a sprite, a robin-goodfellow, a hodge-pocher. *Ibid.*, *Folletto*,..a hobgoblin, a robin-goodfellowe, a hodgepoker, an elfe.

†'**hodgepot**. *Obs.* Also 5 **hogge pot, hogepotte**. [Corruption of HOTCHPOT: cf. HODGE-PODGE.]

1. *Cookery.* = HOTCHPOT 1, HODGE-PODGE 1.

c **1420** *Liber Cocorum* (1862) 32 Gose in a Hogge pot. *c* **1430** *Two Cookery-bks.* 18 A goos in hogepotte. **1550** J. COKE *Eng. & Fr. Heralds* §102 (1877) 89 The rest seke theyr lyvynges..of herbes, rotes, warmons, hodgepottes, fruyte, & such other beggery. **1616** BACON *Sp. agst. C'tess Somerset* (T.), As for mercury water, and other poisons, they might be fit for tarts, which is a kind of hodgepot. [**1897** *Chicago Rec.* 29 May, Samp cooked in Dutch fashion like a hutespot or hodgepot, with salt beef or pork and potatoes and other roots, such as carrots and turnips.]

2. *Law.* = HOTCHPOT 2.

1721 BAILEY, *Hodge-pot* (in *Law*), is the putting together of Lands of several Tenures, for the more equal dividing of them.

†**hodge-pudding**. *Obs. rare.* [cf. HODGE-PODGE.] A pudding made of a medley of ingredients. Also *fig.*

1598 SHAKS. *Merry W.* v. v. 159 *Ford.* What, a hodge-pudding? A bag of flax? *Mist. Page.* A puft man?

Hodgkin's disease. [So called from Dr. Thomas Hodgkin (1798–1866), who first described it.] A disease marked by enlargement of the lymphatic glands and spleen, with progressive anæmia: also called *lymphadenoma*.

1865 S. WILKS in *Guy's Hosp. Rep.* XI. 56 (*heading*) Cases of enlargement of the lymphatic glands and spleen (or, Hodgkin's disease). **1877** ROBERTS *Handbk. Med.* (ed. 3) II. 285 Simple Hypertrophy constitutes the prominent anatomical character of what is known as Hodgkin's disease.

hodid, obs. form of HOODED.

†**hodiern** ('həʊdɪɜːn), *a. Obs.* [ad. L. *hodiernus*, f. *hodiē* to-day.] = next.

1500–20 DUNBAR *Poems* lxxxv. 5 Hodiern, modern, sempitern, Angelicall regyne. **1666** BOYLE *Hydrost. Paradoxes* Wks. 1772 II. 754 Contrary to the common opinion..of divers hodiern mathematicians. *a* **1770** AKENSIDE *Virtuoso* vi, Hodiern and antique rarities.

hodiernal (həʊdɪ'ɜːnəl), *a.* [f. as prec. + -AL[1]: cf. *diurnal*.] Of or belonging to the present day.

1656 BLOUNT *Glossogr.*, *Hodiernal*, of to day, or at this time. **1715** M. DAVIES *Athen. Brit.* I. 191 Monks..of the more modern Accuracy, and hodiernal Improvement. *a* **1879** J. S. BREWER *Eng. Stud.* (1881) 267 The commonest events of hodiernal life.

hodja, var. KHOJA, a Turkish teacher.

hodman ('hɒdmən). [f. HOD *sb.*[1] 1 + MAN.]

1. A man who carries on his shoulder the hod supplying builders with mortar (which he also prepares), bricks, or stones; a 'bricklayer's labourer'. (Now very rarely used in the trade.)

1587 FLEMING *Contn. Holinshed* III. 1541/2 They were onlie good dikers and hodmen. **1706** PHILLIPS (ed. Kersey), *Hod-man*, a Labourer that bears a Hod. **1837** CARLYLE *Fr. Rev.* III. I. v, One of them..said, He was as weary as a hodman that had been beating plaster. **1848** MILL *Pol. Econ.* I. ii. §8 (1876) 26 The stupidest hodman, who repeats from day to day the mechanical act of climbing a ladder.

2. *fig.* **a.** One who more or less mechanically supplies material to a constructive worker. **b.** A mechanical worker in literature, a literary hack.

1829 CARLYLE in Froude *Life* (1882) II. 79 They [political economists] are the hodmen of the intellectual edifice, who have got upon the wall, and will insist on building as if they were the masons. **1849** MISS MULOCK *Ogilvies* xxv. (1875) 185 A sort of literary hodman. **1887** SIR J. D. HOOKER in *Darwin's Life & Lett.* I. 347 This generous appreciation of the hod-men of science, and their labours.

3. A term of contempt applied by undergraduates of Christ Church, Oxford, who were King's Scholars of Westminster School, to those who were not, and hence to men of other colleges.

1677 LITTLETON *Lat. Dict.*, *A Hodman*, in Christchurch at Oxford. Advena, alienigena (quippe quod Alumni Regii e Schola Westmonasteriensi eo adsciti se pro Indigenis habeant). **1721** AMHERST *Terræ Fil.* No. 1 The men [of Christ Church] gave themselves airs..those of other Colleges were 'squils' and 'hodmen'.

¶ Variously misexplained in dicts.: see quots.

1706 PHILLIPS (ed. Kersey), *Hodman*,..a young Scholar admitted from Westminster-School to be a Student in Christ's-Church College in Oxford. [Followed by Chambers (1727), Rees (1819), etc.] **1847–78** HALLIWELL, *Hodman*, a nickname for a canon of Christ Church, Oxford.

hod-man-blind, obs. f. HOODMAN-BLIND.

hodmandod ('hɒdmən,dɒd), *sb.* (*a.*). [A reduplicated variation of DODMAN, HODDY-DOD; app. influenced in form by *hodman*: it has the dial. variants *hodmadod*, *hodmedod*, *hodman Hob*, *hodmandon*.]

1. A shell-snail, a dodman.

1626 BACON *Sylva* §732 The Crab, the Crafish, the Hodmandod or Dodman, the Tortoise. *a* **1654** WEBSTER *Appius & Virg.* III. iv, I am an Ant, a Gnat, a worm..a Hodmandod amongst flies. **1674–91** RAY *S. & E.C. Words* 102 A *Hodmandod*, a shell-snail. **1766** [ANSTEY] *Bath Guide* vi. 27 As snug as a Hod'mandod rides in his Shell. **1858** SPURDENS *Suppl. Forby* in *E. Angl. Gloss.*, *Hodman Hob*, a snail-shell. **1893** *Wiltsh. Gloss.*, *Hodmedod*, a snail.

b. *fig.* Applied to a deformed person.

1663 KILLIGREW *Parson's Wed.* v. iv. in Hazl. *Dodsley* XIV. 525. **1807** *Flowers Lit.* 278 His head was thrice broader than his body, which..accident had made such a hodmandod one of the greatest philosophers of this age.

†**2.** An early corruption of the name HOTTENTOT.

1697 DAMPIER *Voy.* (1729) I. 536 The Natural Inhabitants of the Cape are the Hodmodods, as they are commonly called, which is a corruption of the word Hottantot. **1710** E. WARD *Vulgus Brit.* III. 40 So Hodmontots, because their Feasts Chiefly consist of Gutts of Beasts. **1729** *Cowley's Voy.* in *Collect. Voy.* IV. II. 35 The Hodmandods are born white, but make themselves black with Sut.

3. Any strange creature; a scarecrow. *dial.*

1881 *Isle of Wight Gloss.*, *Hodmandod*, any strange animal, a nondescript. **1888** *Berksh. Gloss.*, *Hodmedod*, a scarecrow; usually a figure with a hat on, holding a stick to represent a gun.

B. *adj.* Short and clumsy; = HODDY-DODDY B. 1.

1825 BRITTON *Beauties Wiltsh.* III. Gloss. (E.D.S.), *Hodmandod, hodmedod*, short and clumsy. **1893** *Wiltsh. Gloss.*

hodograph ('hɒdəʊgrɑːf, -æ-). [f. Gr. ὁδός way + -γραφος (-GRAPH), writing, writer.]

1. *Math.* A curve, invented by Sir W. R. Hamilton, of which the radius vector represents in magnitude and direction the velocity of a moving particle. Also *attrib.* Hence extended to curves in which the radius represents other vector quantities.

1846 *Proc. R. Irish Acad.* III. 347 The Newtonian law [of attraction] may be characterized as being the Law of the Circular Hodograph. **1879** THOMSON & TAIT *Nat. Phil.* I. I. §37 If from any fixed point, lines be drawn at every instant, representing in magnitude and direction the velocity of a point describing any path in any manner, the extremities of these lines form a curve which is called the Hodograph. **1883** A. S. HERSCHEL in *Nature* 15 Mar. 458 The square of the hodograph-radius signifies the square of the material point's velocity, or its directed actual energy. **1944** H. R. BYERS *Gen. Meteorol.* viii. 212 The details of the change of the geostrophic winds with height are studied by means of a hodograph. **1961** *Aero/Space Engin.* Feb. 24/2 (*title*) The hodograph and ballistic missile trajectory problems. **1966** *McGraw-Hill Encycl. Sci. & Technol.* XIII. 508/2 These [changes] are most readily described with the aid of a hodograph of the potential gradient vector... One vector only is shown..extending from the origin of coordinates to a point on the hodograph.

2. A machine invented by Prof. Marey, for registering the paces of a horse, etc. (Commonly, but unetymologically, spelt *odograph*.)

1883 *Mag. of Art* VI. 199 Some years ago one of the horses in Miss Thompson's 'Roll-Call' was severely attacked, and proved incorrect by scientific men, odograph in hand.

Hence **hodo'graphic** *a.*, of the nature of, or pertaining to, a hodograph; **hodo'graphically** *adv.*, by means of a hodograph.

1846 *Proc. R. Irish Acad.* III. 345 This hodographic curve. **1847** *Ibid.* 417 Note by Sir W. R. Hamilton, announcing a theorem of hodographic isochronism. *Ibid.*, The times of hodographically describing the intercepted arcs will be equal.

hodometer, occas. form of ODOMETER, q.v.

hodometrical (hɒdəʊ'mɛtrɪkəl), *a.* [f. Gr. ὁδός way + μετρικός METRIC + -AL[1].]

1. Relating to the measurement of a ship's 'way', i.e. the distance traversed by it.

1730–6 BAILEY (folio), *Hodometrical*.. is the Method of Computation of the Measure of the Way of a Ship between Place and Place.. and what Way she has made. **1753** in CHAMBERS *Cycl. Supp.* **1867** SMYTH *Sailor's Word-bk.*, *Hodometrical*, [applied to] a method of finding the longitude at sea by dead reckoning.

2. (Also *odometrical.*) Belonging to an odometer.

1847 CRAIG, *Odometrical*. **1882** OGILVIE, *Hodometrical*, 1. Pertaining to a hodometer. *Ibid.*, *Odometrical.*

ho'dometry, o'dometry. [f. as prec., after Gr. -μετρία -METRY.] Measurement, as by an odometer, of distances traversed.

1846 WORCESTER, *Odometry*, the measurement of distances.

hodone, obs. f. HUDDON, a kind of whale.

hodoscope ('hɒdəʊskəʊp). [f. Gr. ὁδό-ς way + -SCOPE.] **1.** *Microscopy.* (See quot.)

1915 J. W. EVANS in *Jrnl. Quekett Microsc. Club* XII. 613 It is frequently desirable to examine simultaneously the optical properties of a number of different directions in a mineral... For this purpose the microscope is.. converted into an optical instrument in which every point in the image corresponds not to a point in the object under examination, but to a direction along which light traverses that object in parallel paths. Such an instrument may be conveniently described as a *hodoscope* or path viewer, a term which is to be preferred to the word 'konoscope' employed by some authors.

2. *Physics.* An assembly of particle detectors used for observing the paths of cosmic-ray and other particles.

1950 *Physical Rev.* LXXVIII. 715/1 For the purpose of analyzing the shower phenomena in a hodoscope set it would appear desirable to use as large a number of narrow counters as possible. **1967** *Nuclear Instruments & Methods* LI. 1/1 An experiment on mu meson pair production was performed.. utilizing a 192 unit hodoscope. For each hodoscope counter only the detection or non-detection of a particle (and not pulse height) was recorded.

'hodsman, rare var. HODMAN; in quot. *fig.*

1863 BATES *Nat. Amazon* viii. (1864) 228 The little hodsmen soon have as much as they can carry.

hodur(e, var. HODER *v.*, *Obs.*; obs. f. ODOUR.

†**hodymoke.** *Obs. rare.* ? Concealment.

c **1450** MYRC 2031 Huyde hyt not in hodymoke, Lete other mo rede þys boke.

hoe (həʊ), *sb.*[1] *Obs.* exc. *dial.* Forms: 1 hóh, hó, (3–6 hogh), 5– howe, 7–8 haw(e, 5– hoe, hooe, hoo. [OE. *hóh*, *hó*, str. masc. (gen. *hós*, dat. *hóȝe*, *hó*, pl. *hós*) the same word as the northern HEUGH (and app. the same as HO *sb.*[1] heel):—OTeut. type **hanho-*, from ablaut stem of HANG *v.*]

'A projecting ridge of land, a promontory' (Sweet); 'originally a point of land, formed like a heel, and stretching into the plain, perhaps even into the sea' (Kemble); a height enduring abruptly or steeply: cf. HEUGH. Now only in the names of particular places, as *The Hoe* at Plymouth, *The Hooe* near Chipping Camden, *Hoo* in Kent, Bedfordshire, etc.; and frequent as a second element in place-names, as *Martinhoe*, *Morthoe*, *Pinhoe*, *Trentishoe*, in Devonshire, *Aynho*, *Ivinghoe*, *Stanhoe*, *Wyvenho*, elsewhere.

[OE. *hó* would normally give *hoo* (həʊ), which it has given in some of these cases. The *hoe* (huː) in other parts, may be derived from the OE. dative *hóȝe*, giving ME. *hoȝe*, *howe*, *how*, pronounced like *grow*, *stow*. Of this *hawe* may have been a dialectal form: cf. the phonology of HOE *sb.*[2], where we have also *howe*, *haw*, *hoe*. In the north of England, there is sometimes confusion between *-hoe* and *-how* from ON. *haugr*: see HOW *sb.*[2]]

?*c* **700** *Charter* (13–14th c. copy) in Kemble *Cod. Dipl.* I. 45, xl. terrae illius manentes ubi Hogh nuncupatur [= Hoo, co. Kent]. *c* **850** *Munster Glosses* (Kluge *Ags. Leseb.* 9) *Promontorium*, hooh. **972** *Charter* in Kemble III. 79 Of hrischeale to ðam ho. **988** *Ibid.* 236 Ðanon to Aelfriðe ho. *a* **1000** in Cockayne *Narrat. Angl. Conscr.* 24 Ða hean hos and dene and garsecg ðone æthiopia we ȝesawon. **14..** *Liber Sharbur.* in Spelman *Gloss.* s.v. *Hoga*, Edwinus inuenit quendam collem et hogum petrosum, & ibi incipiebat ædificare quandam villam, & vocauit illam Stanhoghiam, quæ postea vocabatur Stanhowe [Stanhoe]. **1590** SPENSER *F.Q.* II. x. 10 The westerne Hogh, besprincled with the gore Of mighty Goëmet. **1602** CAREW *Cornwall* (1811) 4 Upon the Hawe at Plymouth is cut out in the ground the portraiture of two men, with clubs in their hands, whom they term Gog and Magog. **1612** DRAYTON *Polyolb.* i. 13 That loftie place at Plimmouth call'd the Hoe [*rime* go]. **1797** POLWHELE *Hist. Devonsh.* I. 46 The hill between the town of Plymouth and the sea, that we call the Haw.

hoe (həʊ), *sb.*[2] Forms: 3–9 howe, 5 howwe, 6 houe, 7 haw, 7–8 haugh, 7–9 how, hough, 8– hoe. [a. F. *houe* (12th c. in Hatz.-Darm.: *houë* in Cotgr.):—OHG. *houwâ* (in MHG. *houwe*, mod.G. *haue*), hoe, mattock, pick-axe, f. *houwan* to HEW. The spelling *hoe* (due to the falling together of *-ōw*, *-oe*, in pronunciation, as in *flow*, *floe*) appeared in 18th c., and became the ordinary form *c* 1755. *How*, *hough*, are still dialectal; the Sc. is *howe* (hʌu, hou), riming with Sc. pron. of *grow*, *knowe*, etc.]

1. An agricultural and gardening tool, consisting of a thin iron blade fixed transversely at the end of a long handle; used for breaking up or loosening the surface of the ground, hoeing up weeds, covering plants with soil, and the like.

[*c* **1284** *Hist. et Cart. Mon. Gloucest.* (Rolls) III. 219 Quod sint in curia, becchiæ, howæ, civeræ, et alia minuta utensilia.] **1375** BARBOUR *Bruce* XVII. 344 The yngliss host Arme thame in hy.. With.. Pykis, howis, and ek staff-slyngis. *c* **1430** *Pilgr. Lyf Manhode* III. vi. (1869) 139 Of a bisshopes croos he made his howwe and his pikoyse. Pikoise was þe sharpe ende, and howwe was þe krookede ende. *c* **1440** *Jacob's Well* (E.E.T.S.) 265 Now schal I telle ȝow of þe howe or a pek-ex wherwyth ȝe muste stubbe out þe grauel. **1573** TUSSER *Husb.* xlvi. (1878) 98 A houe and a parer ..to pare away grasse and to raise vp the roote. **1606** BRYSKETT *Civ. Life* 66 Which to cut downe or roote vp, many sithes and howes would scarce suffice. **1664** EVELYN *Kal. Hort.* Apr. (R.), Remember to weed them.. and a little after to thin them with a small haugh. **1674** RAY *S. & E. C. Words* 68 A *How*: pronounced as mow and throw: a narrow iron rake without teeth, to cleanse Gardens from weeds. **1678** ANNE BRADSTREET *Poems* 6 Ye husband-men, your coulters made by me, Your houghs, your mattocks. **1694** WESTMACOTT *Script. Herb.* 182 It may be the better weeded with a Haw. **1722** DE FOE *Col. Jack* (1840) 132 With my haugh, or hoe, in my hand. **1753** HANWAY *Trav.* (1762) I. vi. lxxxiv. 382 A gardiner once threw a hough at him. **1764** GRAINGER *Sugar Cane* II. (R.), Let the hoe uproot Th' infected cane piece. **1884** PAE *Eustace* 70 Busy with hoe and rake amongst the flowers.

b. With qualifications, indicating the shape, the mode of use, etc. In respect of the latter, the chief distinction is that of ***draw-hoes*** (the original type) and ***thrust-hoes*** (as in the *Dutch hoe*). The name is also extended, as in ***horse-hoe***, to machines of various kinds which do the work of several hoes in stirring up the soil between plants, etc.

bayonet hoe, a form of draw-hoe, with the blade narrow and pointed much in the form of a trowel-bayonet (*Cent. Dict.*). **Dutch hoe**, **scuffle hoe**, kinds of thrust-hoes. **Spanish hoe**, **Vernon hoe**: see quot. 1855.

1744–46 [see HAND-HOE, HORSE-HOE]. **1744–50** W. ELLIS *Mod. Husbandm.* IV. I. 16 The *Beck-hough*, is an instrument differing from the common Pick-axe or Mattock, only by having its two Ends about four Inches broad. *Ibid.* 17 This common Hough (the hand-hough) with which we hough all our Turneps, etc., and.. the Dutch Hough, to hough between the close Rows of drilled Wheat, are of prodigious Value to the Farmer. *Ibid.* IV. 52 This Dutch Hoe is.. most conveniently fitted to hoe the Weeds up between the Drills of Wheat, Barley, etc. **1822** LOUDON *Encycl. Gard.* (1834) 519 Hoes are of two species, the draw-hoe and the thrust-hoe, of each of which there are several varieties.. The Spanish hoe.. Pronged hoes [etc.]. **1834** D. LOW *Elem. Pract. Agric.* (1843) 130 The mattock-hoe of the countries of the East. **1855** C. M'INTOSH *Bk. of Gard.* II. 38 The best hoe, when deep-stirring the soil between drilled crops is performed, is the Spanish hoe.. or the Vernon hoe.

2. A dentist's excavating instrument, shaped like a miniature hoe. (Knight *Dict. Mech.* 1875.)

3. *attrib.* and *Comb.*, as *hoe-handle*, *-helve*, *-work*; *hoe-armed* adj.; †**hoe-break** = HORSE-HOE. Also HOE-PLOUGH.

1744–50 W. ELLIS *Mod. Husbandm.* IV. I. 8 There are three Sorts of Hough Horse-breaks, actually in use. *Ibid.* 9 This Hough-break is light in itself. **1764** GRAINGER *Sugar Cane* I. 288 Might not the plough that rolls on rapid wheels, Save no small labour to the hoe-arm'd gang? **1817** SCOTT *Let. to Southey* 9 May, All sort of spade-work and hoe-work.

hoe, *sb.*[3] *Obs.* exc. *dial.* [Later form of OE. *hoȝu*, ME. *hoȝe*, *howe*, HOW *sb.*[1], q.v. Cf. HO *v.*[3]] Care, anxiety, trouble.

1567 TURBERV. tr. *Ovid's Ep.* 155 b, Though there bee a thousand cares that heape my hoe. **1798** CH. SMITH *Yng. Philos.* I. 195 Him that.. this gentlewoman is in such a hoe about. **1875** PARISH *Sussex Gloss.* s.v., I doänt see as you've any call to putt yourself in no such terrible gurt hoe over it.

hoe, *sb.*[4] *local.* [a. ON. *há-r* (Da. *haa*) dog-fish, shark.] The name, in Orkney and Shetland, of the Picked Dog-fish, *Squalus acanthias*.

a **1804** G. BARRY *Hist. Orkney Isl.* (1805) 296 The Piked Dog-Fish.. known by the name of the hoe, frequently visits our coasts. **1836** YARRELL *Brit. Fishes* II. 400 The Picked Dog-Fish.. among the Scotch islands.. is called Hoe.

b. *Comb.*, **hoe-mother** (contracted *homer*), the Basking Shark, *Selachus maximus*; **hoe-tusk**, the Smooth Houndfish, *Mustelus hinnulus*.

a **1804** G. BARRY *Hist. Orkney Isl.* (1805) 296 The Basking Shark.. has here got the name of the *hoe-mother*, or *homer*, that is the mother of the dog-fish. **1809** A. EDMONSTONE *View Zetland Isl.* II. 304 *Squalus Mustelus*.. Hoe-tusk, Smooth Hound.—Frequently met with in the bays.

hoe, *v.*[1] Forms: see HOE *sb.*[2] [f. HOE *sb.*[2]]

1. *intr.* To use a hoe; to work with a hoe.

c **1430** *Pilgr. Lyf Manhode* III. viii. (1869) 140 He sigh that folk howweden and doluen aboute the cherche. **1664** EVELYN *Kal. Hort.* (1729) 199 Weed and haugh betimes. **1832** MARRYAT *N. Forster* xiv, The slaves.. were at work hoeing. **1894** R. BRIDGES *Feast of Bacchus* I. 39 Here I find you, digging, hoeing.

2. *trans.* To weed (crops) with a hoe; to thin *out* (plants) with a hoe; to 'cultivate' with a hoe.

1693 EVELYN *De la Quint. Compl. Gard.* VI. II. 155 Asparagus.. must be carefully howed, or cleared of Weeds. **1748** *Anson's Voy.* III. ix. 393 Chinese, who had been hoeing rice in the neighbourhood. **1846** J. BAXTER *Libr. Pract. Agric.* (ed. 4) I. 243 Peas, properly drilled, and carefully hoed. **1858** GLENNY *Gard. Every-day Bk.* 81/1 Spinach.. is finer when hoed out to six-inch distances.

3. To break or stir up (the ground) with a hoe, so as to loosen the surface and destroy weeds; to dress with a hoe. See also ROW *sb.*[1] 6 b, c.

1712 J. JAMES tr. *Le Blond's Gardening* 44 Walks that.. would take up too much Time to hough and rake. *a* **1746** E. HOLDSWORTH *Rem. Virgil* 121 (Jod.) To hough the land in the spring time. **1858** GLENNY *Gard. Every-day Bk.* 133/2 Hoe the ground between the young evergreens and deciduous plants.

4. with adv. To dig *up*, raise *up*, take *away*, cut *down*, cover *in*, with a hoe.

1699 EVELYN *Kal. Hort.* (ed. 9) 56 Rake away what you pull or Haugh up. **1707** SLOANE *Jamaica* I. p. lxiv, When the Potatoes are full grown, they hough up the roots. **1788** *Trans. Soc. Arts* VI. 93, I.. hoed them in at the last hoeing about the middle of May. **1846** J. BAXTER *Libr. Pract. Agric.* (ed. 4) II. 339 Exposed to the frosts during the winter, from the earth being hoed away from them. **1885** *Gardening* 13 June 183 Dig them [sow thistles] in if you can, but in any case hoe them down. **1886** *Cassell's Fam. Mag.* May 337 This done, hoe up the soil between the rows.

Hence **hoed** (həʊd) *ppl. a.* Also **'hoeable** *a.*

1643 *New Plymouth Laws* 74 By ymproved lands are understood meddow land plowed land and howed lands. **1740** TULL *Horse-hoeing Husb.* xi. (1822) 138 The wheat.. may not be hoeable before the winter is past. **1744–50** W. ELLIS *Mod. Husbandm.* IV. III. 27 There is no such Necessity for deep Houghing, lest the houghed Turneps up-set and grow again. **1879** *Scribner's Monthly* Dec. 239/2 The owner has only to give it a year of ordinary cultivation, taking from it.. some profitable hoed crop.

hoe (həʊ), *v.*[2] *U.S.* [f. HOE-DOWN.] To dance or play a hoe-down.

1835 *Gent's Vade-Mecum* (Phila.) 21 Mar. 3/5 'Pooh!' replied his panting rib, hoeing it off like a regular Juba, 'don't be a nigger all the days of your life.' **1909** *Cent. Dict.* Suppl.

hoe, var. HEO, HI *prons.*, HO.

hoeboy, hoebuck, obs. var. of HAUTBOY, HAWBUCK.

hoecake ('həʊkeɪk). *U.S.* [Orig. cake baked on the broad thin blade of a cotton-field hoe (*Cent. Dict.*).] Coarse bread, made of Indian meal, water, and salt, and usually in the form of a thin cake.

1745 W. LOGAN *Jrnl.* 12 Oct. in *Pennsylvania Mag. Hist.* (1912) XXXVI. 12 Breakfasted on Tea & Hoe Cake Bread, which we have done in common. **1745** *Ibid.* 21 Oct. 162 Got Breakfast on Tea & Hoe Cake. **1774** P. V. FITHIAN *Jrnl.* 15 Jan. (1900) 93 Sup'd on chocolate, & hoe-Cake, so Called because baked on a Hoe before the fire. **1780** W. FLEMING in N. D. Mereness *Trav. Amer. Col.* (1916) 641, I had lived for a constancy on poor dried buffalo bull beef cured in the smook.. without any addition but a piece of Indian hoe-cake. **1793** J. BARLOW *Hasty Pudding* i, Some talk of Hoe-cakes, fair Virginia's pride. **1809** W. IRVING *Knickerb.* (1861) 138 Great roisters, much given to revel on hoe-cake and bacon. **1885** *Boston* (Mass.) *Jrnl.* 4 Sept. 2/4 Perhaps Americans will.. make international the power and elegance of hoe-cake and baked beans.

hoe-down. *U.S.* A noisy, riotous dance; = BREAKDOWN 2.

[**1807** W. IRVING *Salmagundi* 7 Mar. 98 As to dancing, no Long-Island negro could shuffle you 'double trouble', or 'hoe corn and dig potatoes' more scientifically.] **1841** *Picayune* (New Orleans 14 Jan. 2/1 He looks and walks the character to the life, and some of his touches are of the genuine 'hoe down', 'corn-field' order. **1849** T. T. JOHNSON *Sights Gold Region* iv. 38 One of our party commenced a regular hoe-down, knocking his shins with heavy boots. **1855** *Knickerbocker* XLVI. 227 Rude, high-legged reels and 'hoe-downs'. **1860** in BARTLETT *Dict. Amer.* (ed. 3). **1885** *Libr. Mag.* (N.Y.) July 1 They [negroes] danced their vigorous hoe-downs, jigs. **1919** T. K. HOLMES *Man fr. Tall Timber* vii. 84 A medley of old-time hoe-downs and jig music. **1961** *Times* 30 Mar. 6/7 The hoe-down sequence in *Seven Brides for Seven Brothers.* **1963** *Punch* 3 July 23/3, I was invited to the last hoe-down. **1967** 'J. MUNRO' *Money that Money can't Buy* ix. 114 Two more cowboys appeared. .. They played hoe-down music. **1969** *Guardian* 2 Sept. 8/2 The atmosphere was that of.. a hoedown in—well, perhaps in Hibbing, Minn.

hoeful ('həʊfʊl). [f. HOE *sb.*[2] + -FUL.] As much as can be lifted on a hoe.

1866 LIVINGSTONE *Last Jrnls.* (1873) I. v. 129 The final preparation is effected by men digging.. passing each hoe-ful into the left hand.

hoeing ('həʊɪŋ), *vbl. sb.* [f. HOE *v.*[1] + -ING[1].] The action of the vb. HOE; stirring up the ground, digging, weeding, etc. with a hoe.

1676 WORLIDGE *Cyder* (1691) 77 They require your care in hawing. **1699** EVELYN *Kal. Hort.* (ed. 9) 87 Begin the work of Haughing. **1787** WINTER *Syst. Husb.* 211 Hoeing is the breaking or dividing of the soil by plows or other instruments, while the corn or plants are growing thereon. **1842** BRAND *Dict. Sci.* etc. s.v., Hoeing is sometimes performed on surfaces which are without weeds, for the purpose of stirring the soil.

b. *Comb.*, as ***hoeing-instrument***, ***-machine***, ***-time***.

1744–50 W. ELLIS *Mod. Husbandm.* IV. III. 27 If the Ground is wettish at Houghing-time. **1875** KNIGHT *Dict. Mech.*, *Hoeing Machine*.. for tending drilled or dibbled crops.

'hoe-plough, *sb.* ? *Obs.* = HORSE-HOE.

1733 TULL *Horse-hoeing Husb.* xvi. 112 The Plow, which is almost the same with the Ho-Plow. **1775** ROMANS *Florida* 120 In a large field these hoeings are most commodiously performed by the hoe plough drawn by one horse.

Hence **hoe-plough** *v. trans.*, to hoe with a hoe-plough; **hoe-ploughing** *vbl. sb.*

1733 TULL *Horse-hoeing Husb.* x. 45 You may Ho-plow them. **1770-4** A. HUNTER *Georg. Ess.* (1803) I. 432 Hoe-ploughings necessary for completing the crop are three. **1790** CASTLES in *Phil. Trans.* LXXX. 356 The land should then be ploughed or hoe-ploughed twice.

hoer ('həʊə(r)). Also 8 hougher. [f. HOE *v.*[1] + -ER[1].] One who hoes or uses a hoe.

1744-50 W. ELLIS *Mod. Husbandm.* V. I. 86 Turnips may be houghed ill, if the hougher stubs them, as we call it, i.e. if he..only cut off the heads, and leave the roots in the ground. **1893** BARING-GOULD *Cheap-Jack Z.* II. 117 The wheat had to be hoed, and the hoers were women.

hœrnesite ('hɜːnɪzaɪt). *Min.* Also **hörnesite.** [ad. G. *hörnesit* (W. Haidinger, reported in *Jahrb. d. k.-k. geol. Reichsanstalt*: *Verhandl.* (1860) XI. 41), f. the name of M. *Hörnes* (1815-68), Austrian mineralogist: see -ITE[1].] A white hydrated arsenate of magnesium $Mg_3(AsO_4)_2.8H_2O$.

1868 J. D. DANA *Syst. Min.* (ed. 5) 817 Hœrnesite... First distinguished by Kenngott in minerals from the Bannat, Hungary. **1903** *Jrnl. Chem. Soc.* LXXXIV. II. 655 (*heading*) Crystallised magnesium phosphate and arsenate: artificial production of bobierrite and hœrnesite. **1968** I. KOSTOV *Mineralogy* 448 (*table*) Hörnesite. **1969** *Mineral. Abstr.* XX. 229/1 Hoernesite..is monoclinic.

‖**hoey.** [Chinese (Mandarin dial.) *hūy* (huːɪ), society, club, guild.] A society of Chinese: esp. a secret society formed by them in English-speaking countries or colonies.

1865 *Sat. Rev.* 25 Mar. 351 The people [Chinese] from every province form a secret society or 'hoey', bound together by solemn oaths, and imposing the most implicit obedience on its members. **1883** *Spectator* 24 Nov. 1504/2 The terrible law making entrance into a Hoey or Secret Society a crime punishable with death. **1885** *Cycl. India* (ed. 3) II. 91 *Hoe*, a secret society of the Chinese into which the members are initiated.

hof, early f. HOVE.

hof, hofen = *hove, hoven*, pa. t. and pple. of HEAVE *v.*

hofe, obs. f. HOOF.

hoff, obs. Sc. f. HOVE; dial. f. HOUGH *sb.* and *v.*

1825 BROCKETT, *Hoff*, hough, to throw any thing under the thigh. **1828** *Craven Dial.*, *Hoff*, the hock. In the plural *hoffs*, a ludicrous term for the feet.

Hoffmann ('hɒfmən). **1.** The name of Friedrich *Hoffmann* (1660-1742), German physician, used in the possessive in ***Hoffmann's anodyne*** (in full ***Hoffmann's mineral anodyne liquor***), compound spirit of ether, a mixture of alcohol and ether with ethereal oil.

1747 R. JAMES *New Univ. Eng. Dispensatory* 803/1 Liquor Mineralis Anodynus Hoffmanni. Frederic Hoffman's Anodyne Mineral Liquor. **1857** *Amer. Jrnl. Pharm.* May 200 For some years past the preparation sold under the name of Hoffman's anodyne has been forcibly dragged along by the materia medica list, supported alone by its unused formula and former character. **1878** W. B. WOODMAN tr. *von Ziemssen's Cycl. Pract. Med.* XVII. 442 The internal use of ether (Hoffmann's anodyne) may lead to poisoning. **1910** A. C. WOOTTON *Chron. Pharm.* I. xiii. 348 Hoffmann's 'Mineral Anodyne Liquor', the original of our Spiritus Ætheris Co., was a semi-secret preparation much prescribed by the famous inventor. **1945** D. GUTHRIE *Hist. Med.* xii. 217 One of his preparations, Hoffmann's anodyne (Spiritus Aetheris Co) still survives, although his extensive work..in nine volumes..has long since been forgotten.

2. The name of Friedrich *Hoffmann* (1818-1900), used *attrib.* and in the possessive to designate a form of continuous kiln consisting of a number of compartments with a common chimney, so arranged that the fire can be moved to each compartment in turn, with hot air from cooling bricks used for heating unburnt bricks.

1875 *Ure's Dict. Arts.* III. 20 (*heading*) Hoffmann's continuous kiln. **1879** *Notes on Building Construction* III. 101 Hoffmann's Kiln is used chiefly in brick-manufactories on a large scale, where a great number of bricks is required annually. **1960** M. BOWLEY *Innovat. Building Mat.* III. viii. 163 The majority of kilns in the industry are variations of the Hoffman kiln.

3. The name of Johann *Hoffmann* (1857-1919), German neurologist, used *attrib.* and in the possessive to designate various signs, etc., discovered or described by him, as ***Hoffmann('s) atrophy*** = *Werdnig-Hoffmann('s) atrophy*; ***Hoffmann('s) sign***: (*a*) increased sensitivity of the sensory nerves to mechanical stimulation; also called ***Hoffman('s) phenomenon, symptom***; (*b*) a type of reflex action of the fingers; also called *digital reflex*, ***Hoffmann('s) reflex***; also *ellipt.*

1900 DORLAND *Med. Dict.* 600/2 *Hoffmann's s[ign]*, increased mechanic irritability of the sensory nerves in tetany. **1908** A. GORDON *Dis. Nerv. Syst.* xxi. 399 Hoffmann's Sign.—Pressure upon sensory nerve produces marked pain. **1908** A. CHURCH *Dis. Nerv. Syst.* 916 (*heading*) Mechanical Hyperirritability (Chvostek's phenomenon, Hoffmann's phenomenon). **1910** OSLER & MACRAE *Syst. Med.* VII. 73 The sensory nerves may also be hypersensitive, and tapping at Valleix's points then calls forth abnormally intense sensations (Hoffmann's symptom). **1916** *Jrnl. Nervous & Mental Dis.* XLIV. 51 During a period spent at the Neurological Institute of New York, I was told of a reflex of the fingers which was designated by the term 'Hoffmann's Sign'. **1933** *Ibid.* LXXVII. 598 Of the 26 patients with the post-encephalitic Parkinson syndrome, the Hoffmann reflex was positive in 6 and the Babinski positive in 4. **1939** W. HAYMAKER tr. *Bing's Textbk. Nerv. Dis.* iv. 150 Increased galvanic irritability of sensory nerves, occurring at times in patients with tetany, is known as Hoffmann's phenomenon. **1950** R. N. DEJONG *Neurol. Exam.* xxxvi. 593 The Hoffmann is a positive sign of definite significance, even though it may occur on occasion in the absence of organic disease.

†**'hofles**, *a. Obs.* [f. ME. *hōf*, HOVE *sb.*[2] + *-les*, -LESS: cf. ON. *hóflauss* immoderate.] Immoderate, excessive; unreasonable; intemperate. ***att hofelæs*** (quot. 1200), immoderately.

c **1200** ORMIN 6224 Swa þatt ȝitt nohht att hofelæs Ne nede þeȝȝm to swinnkenn. *a* **1225** *Ancr. R.* 108 Muchel hofleas is þet cumen into anre huse..vorte sechen eise þerinne. *c* **1230** *Hali Meid.* 43 Sone so þu..þuncheð hofles & hoker of ewt þat mon seið þe oðer deð ȝette.

Hofmann ('hɒfmən). **1.** The name of August Wilhelm von *Hofmann* (1818-92), German chemist, used *attrib.* and in the possessive to designate dyestuffs discovered and chemical apparatus and procedures devised by him, as ***Hofmann('s) degradation***: (*a*) the elimination of a carbonyl group from an acid amide when it is heated in a sodium hypohalite solution, giving a primary amine; (*b*) the pyrolysis of a quaternary ammonium hydroxide to give a tertiary amine and an olefin; ***Hofmann('s) exhaustive methylation***: a method for determining the structure of amino compounds by methylation followed by pyrolysis, the resulting amine being subjected successively to the same procedure until trimethylamine and olefins are obtained; *loosely*, the Hofmann degradation (sense b); ***Hofmann('s) method***: (*a*) a method for finding the vapour density of a liquid (see quot. 1902[2]); (*b*) the preparation of amines by means of the Hofmann degradation of amides; ***Hofmann('s) reaction***: either of the Hofmann degradations; ***Hofmann('s) rearrangement***: the Hofmann degradation of amides; ***Hofmann('s) rule*** (see quot. 1954); ***Hofmann('s) violet*** (also ***Violet***): any of several basic dyes that are salts of ethyl and methyl derivatives of rosaniline and pararosaniline and were formerly used with wool, silk, and mordanted cotton.

1869 H. E. ROSCOE *Lessons Elem. Chem.* (new ed.) xxxix. 385 Triethylrosaniline, $C_{20}H_{16}(C_2H_5)_3N_3$, is manufactured for its splendid colour, and is known as Hofmann's violet. **1876** *Encycl. Brit.* V. 548/1 (*caption*) Hofmann's Vapour-Density Apparatus. *Ibid.*, Gay-Lussac and Hofmann's Methods. **1902** *Jrnl. Chem. Soc.* LXXXII. II. 663 Sodium hypochlorite is a more valuable reagent than the hypobromite in Hofmann's reaction. **1902** J. B. COHEN *Theoret. Org. Chem.* iii. 30 Victor Meyer's method and Hofmann's method consist in ascertaining the volume occupied by a given weight of the vaporised substance. *Ibid.* xiv. 195 If a primary amine is treated by Hofmann's method with an alkyl iodide in which the alkyl group is different from that present in the amine, a mixed amine is formed. **1902** *Encycl. Brit.* XXVII. 337/2 The basis of these methods consists in causing a swelling of the cell-wall..and subsequent staining with Hoffmann's blue. **1905** CAIN & THORPE *Synthetic Dyestuffs* xiv. 90 Hofmann's violet was the first violet dyestuff of this [rosaniline] series prepared, and is now merely of historical interest. **1910** *Chem. Abstr.* IV. 583 (*heading*) Acid properties of halogen amides. Hofmann's rearrangement. **1938** L. SMALL in H. Gilman *Org. Chem.* II. xii. 1024 The most generally applicable method for ascertaining structure is exhaustive methylation, also known as the Hofmann degradation. **1938** *Thorpe's Dict. Appl. Chem.* (ed. 4) II. 375/1 An important reaction of carboxylic acids is their conversion to amines by the Hofmann degradation, whereby the amide is treated with bromine and alkali. **1938** G. H. RICHTER *Textbk. Org. Chem.* xiv. 239 (*heading*) Hofmann's exhaustive methylation. *Ibid.* 241 The decomposition of these substances on heating to a high temperature has already been indicated in the Hofmann exhaustive methylation procedure. **1949** J. R. PARTINGTON *Adv. Treat. Physical Chem.* I. vii. 760 In Hofmann's method, a uniform glass tube about 1 m. long.. is supported in a glass jacket through which the vapour of a liquid, boiling in a separate vessel, is passed. *Ibid.* 761 A modified Hofmann apparatus for accurate vapour-density determinations. **1950** L. F. & M. FIESER *Org. Chem.* (ed. 2) xxxv. 865 The correct structure of the lobelia alkaloids.. was first deduced from the result of Hofmann degradation of the quaternary hydroxide. **1951** E. D. HUGHES in E. H. Rodd *Chem. Carbon Compounds* IA. 183 The Hofmann rule refers to the preferential formation of that ethylene which bears the smallest number of alkyl groups. **1952** K. VENKATARAMAN *Chem. Synthetic Dyes* I. i. 3 In 1866 Bardy oxidized a mixture of mono- and dimethylanilines to Methyl Violet, which soon eliminated the Hofmann Violets. **1954** *Van Nostrand Chem. Dict.* 356/2 *Hofmann rule*, in the decomposition of a quaternary ammonium hydroxide containing different primary alkyl radicals, the products are such that the ethylene formed will contain the least number of alkyl substituents. **1968** R. O. C. NORMAN *Princ. Org. Synthesis* xiv. 446 (*heading*) Hofmann rearrangement.

2. The name of Georg von *Hofmann*-Wellenhof (d. *c* 1890), Austrian bacteriologist, used *attrib.* and in the possessive in ***Hofmann('s) bacillus***, a non-pathogenic bacillus similar to the diphtheria bacillus and common in the nose and throat; variously known as *Corynebacterium pseudo-diphtheriticum*, *C. hofmanni*, etc.

[**1891** *Johns Hopkins Hosp. Bull.* II. 143/2 Kolisko and Paltauf..were able to find the pseudo-diphtheritic bacillus of von Hoffmann only very rarely.] **1897** *Jrnl. Path. & Bacteriol.* IV. 190 The cases affected with Hofmann's bacillus unassociated with diphtheria bacilli, which have come under my notice, have always recovered. **1897** *Trans. Brit. Inst. Prev. Med.* 12 Peters..does not seem to have noticed any difference of growth of the Klebs-Löffler and von Hoffmann bacilli on alkaline potato. **1959** F. S. STEWART *Bigger's Handbk. Bacteriol.* (ed. 7) xviii. 307 *C. pseudodiphtheriticum* (Hofmann's bacillus)..is often present in the nose and less frequently in the throat.

†**hofte.** *Obs.* [app. MDu. *hooft, hovet* HEAD *sb.*[1]]

1526 SKELTON *Magnyf.* 759 Decke your hofte and cower a lowce.

†**hoful**, *a. Obs.* [Late form of OE. *hogful*, ME. *hoȝful, hohful* HOWFUL: cf. HOE *sb.*[3]] Careful.

1565 T. STAPLETON *Fortr. Faith* 97 b, Euer hofull of his doings and behauiour.

Hence †**'hofully** *adv.*, carefully; †**'hofulness**, carefulness, care, solicitude.

1565 T. STAPLETON *Fortr. Faith* 86 b, The army..kepeth watche and warde hofullyer. *Ibid.* 119 b, Wemen seruing God hofully and chastly. **1566** —— *Ret. Untr. Jewel* IV. 64 The hofulnesse of all Churches.

hog (hɒg), *sb.*[1] Also 4(?)-6 hogge, 6- hogg. [First exemplified *c* 1340, but the derivative HOGGASTER occurs *c* 1175: origin unknown.

The word may possibly be contained in the OE. place-names *Hocgestán* (Hogston) and *Hocgetwistle*; but this is hardly likely. The conjecture that ME. *hog* represented Cornish *hoch*, Welsh *hwch*, swine, is improbable on phonetic and other grounds. The evidence afforded by the word itself and by its derivatives *hoggaster, hoggerel, hogget* (the first of which, applied to sheep, offers our earliest example of the word-group), makes it probable that the word originally had reference to the age or condition of the animal, rather than to either pig or sheep distinctively. Hence some have thought *hog* possibly related to HAG *v.*[1], with the notion of castration. But the notion of 'yearling' runs through most of the uses: cf. 2 b, 4, 4 b, 5, 13 b. In this uncertainty, the order of senses followed is merely one of practical convenience.]

I. 1. a. A swine reared for slaughter; *spec.* a castrated male swine, a barrow-pig or barrow-hog (see BARROW[2] 1 b); hence, a domestic swine generally. (Not used in Scotland.)

(The original application may either refer to the age, swine reared for the purpose of slaughter being seldom allowed to exceed much more than one year in age, or to the fact that the males intended for this purpose are usually castrated: see etym. note.)

1340 *Ayenb.* 89 Of hare moder þe erþe, þet berþ and noryssep azewel þe hogges, ase hy deþ þe kinges. **13..** *K. Alis.* 1885 Alisaunder & alle his kniȝttes Hem to pieces þai gonne talle, To bocher þat hog vpon his stalle. **1377** LANGL. *P. Pl.* B. VI. 183 'Suffre hem lyue' he sayde, 'and lete hem ete with hogges'. **1398** TREVISA *Barth. De P.R.* XVIII. lxxxvii. (1495) 837 Hogges bothe male and female haue lykynge to ete Akernes for it tempreth theyr flesshe. *c* **1440** *Promp. Parv.* 242/1 Hogge, swyne, *nefrendis, maialis.* **1474** CAXTON *Chesse* 83 Whan he wold haue buryed the body he founde hit an hogge or a swyne and not a man. **1483** *Cath. Angl.* 187/1 An Hogge, *maialis, est enim porcus carens testiculis.* **1530** PALSGR. 231/2 Hogge, *porc, porceau.* **1552** HULOET, Hogge called a barrow hogge or galt, *maias*... Hogge ungelt, *verres.* **1644** EVELYN *Diary* 30 Sept., A dish of trufles, an earth nut, found out by an hogg train'd to it. **1707** MORTIMER *Husb.* (1708) 186 The Males must be gelt, and the Sows spay'd; the spay'd Gelts..they esteem the most profitable, because of the great Quantity of Fat that they have upon their Inwards more than the Hogs. **1756-7** tr. *Keysler's Trav.* (1760) I. 433 It is remarkable, that in the Milanese all the hogs are black. **1846** J. BAXTER *Libr. Pract. Agric.* (ed. 4) II. 190 Hogs will thrive very fast when fed on it [parsnip], and will leave any other food to attack it.

b. ***bacon-hog***, a hog fattened for making bacon.

1612 J. TAYLOR (Water P.) *Trav.* Wks. (1872) 35 For most of them are as full of humanity as a bacon-hog. **1860** J. DONALDSON *Brit. Agric.* 490 Two lots of bacon hogs may be fattened during the curing season from October to April.

c. *U.S.* The flesh of the pig; pork; in alliterative phr. ***hog and hominy***, pork and Indian corn.

1776 W. HOOPER in *Lett. James Murray* (1901) 239 That I might enjoy in my own Cabin, eat my Hogg & Hominee without anything to make me afraid. **1816** *Mass. Spy* 10 Jan. (Th.), [If a man] can be content with hog and hommany, he can live easier in Ohio. *a* **1860** THORPE *Big Bear Arkansas* (Bartlett), I can give you plenty to eat; for, besides hog and hominy, you can have bar [bear] ham and bar sausages. **1870** *Daily News* 21 Oct., From abundant hog and hominy down to the last lean mule. **1888** *Century Mag.* XXXVI. 261/2 Corn-bread and bacon, or, in purer vernacular, 'hog and hominy'. **1948** E. N. DICK *Dixie Frontier* 290 The monotonous diet was often referred to as 'hog and hominy'.

2. a. Used as the name of the species, and so including the wild boar and sow: = SWINE. **b.** Formerly *spec.* a wild boar of the second year: cf. HOGGASTER.

c **1483** in Hall *Chron., Rich. III* (1548) 18 The Rat, the Catte and Lovell our dogge Rule al England vnder the hogge. [**1548** HALL *Comment*, Meanynge by the hogge, the

dreadfull wylde bore which was the kinges cognisaunce.] 1486 *Bk. St. Albans* E iij a, The boore .. is .. the secunde yere an hogge. 1660 HOWELL *Lexicon* 111, A wild Bore, the first year a Pigg, the 2. a Hogg, the 3. a Hoggsteer, the 4. a Bore, the 5. a Cingular. 1766 PENNANT *Zool.* (1768) I. 41 The hog is certainly the most impure and filthy of all quadrupeds. 1807 T. WILLIAMSON *Oriental Field Sports* (1808) I. 34 In grass covers a hog is often started, hunted, and killed, without being seen till he is dead. 1835 SWAINSON *Quadrup.* 224 It is generally supposed .. that the wild hog, or boar, is the origin of our domestic swine.

3. Applied, with distinguishing epithet, to different species of the family *Suidæ*. See also GROUND-, RIVER-, SEA-, WATER-HOG.

1732 *Gentlem. Guide to Cattle* (ed. 2) 109 The Bantam-Hogs, and the African Hogs from whence those of Hartfordshire are derived. 1781–5 W. SMELLIE tr. *Buffon's Nat. Hist.* (1791) VII. 58 The Babiroussa or Indian Hog. 1788 *Chambers' Cycl.* s.v., Of this genus are the common hog, the Guinea hog or *Porcus Guineensis*, the Mexican musk hog or *Tajacu*, the *hydrochæris* or Capybara, and the Babyroussa. 1856 KNIGHT *Cycl. Nat. Hist.* IV. 964 Aelian's Wart-Hog is a native of the North of Africa. 1860 *Chambers' Encycl.*, *Babyroussa* .. sometimes called the Horned Hog. *Ibid.* s.v., The Bush Hog of South Africa .. is about two feet six inches high, covered with long bristles.

II. 4. (Freq. in form **hogg**.) A name given to a sheep of a certain age. **a.** In Scotland and many parts of Engl. a young sheep from the time it ceases to be a lamb till its first shearing: see quot. 1842–4.

[1350 *Bp. Hatfield's Surv.* (Surtees) 226 Hogs et Jercs. Et de x hogs et jercs de remanentibus. Summa x.] c1460 *Towneley Myst.* xiii. 456 And of fefteyn hogys ffond I bot oone ewe. 1549 *Compl. Scot.* vi. 66 3ouis and lammis .. and mony herueist hog. 1606 *Choice, Chance* etc. (1881) 17 The Sheepheard he would .. talke of his Rammes and his Weathers, of his Ewes and his Lambs, his hogs and his sheerlings. 1674–91 RAY *N.C. Words* 38 *A Hog*, a Sheep of a year old; used also in Northampton and Leicester shires, where they also call it a Hoggrel. 1732 *Gentlem. Guide to Cattle* (ed. 2) 12, I have seen those of a year old .. which we call Hogs, or Hoggets, bring Lambs. 1842–4 H. STEPHENS *Bk. of Farm* (1851) 924 After a lamb has been weaned, until the first fleece is shorn from its back, it receives the name of *hogg*. 1867 *Gainsborough News* 23 Mar., 200 lambed and in-lamb ewes and gimmers, 200 he hogs, 140 she hogs. 1899 *Daily News* 21 Apr. 7/4 North hoggs and Yorkshire Wold hoggs are becoming scarce. 1963 *Times* 13 May 16/7 In six lamb crops, starting as a hogg, she has produced and reared 20 lambs.

b. With distinguishing epithets as ***chilver-*** or ***ewe-hog***, ***tup-hog***, ***wether-hog***, etc.

1607 TOPSELL *Four-f. Beasts* (1658) 495 The first year we call it in English a Lamb, the second year a Hog, Lam-hog, or Teg if it be a female, the third year Hoggrils and Theives. 1614 MARKHAM *Cheap Husb.* (1623) 106 The first year a male Lambe is called a weather-Hog and a female Lambe an Ewe-Hog. 1618–9 *N. Riding Rec.* II. 190 An old Malton man presented for stealing a gimmer hogge value 10*d.* 1794 T. DAVIS *Agric. Wilts* in *Archæol. Rev.* (1888) Mar., *Sheep*, .. wether-hogs, chilver-hogs from thence [Christmas] till shear-time. 1866 BRANDE & COX *Dict. Sci.* etc. II. 138 A lamb becomes a teg in its first winter, and afterwards a hogget; and on losing its coat a shearhog. 1882 *Somerset Co. Gaz.* 18 Mar., 12 good ewe and wether hogs, warranted sound.

c. Short for *hog-fleece*, *-wool*.

1854 MISS BAKER *Northampt. Gloss.*, *Hog*, a yearling sheep, which has only been shorn once .. Applied equally to the animal and to the fleece. 1879 *Cassell's Techn. Educ.* IV. 259/2 The fleeces shorn from sheep which have not previously been shorn as lambs, are called hogs or tegs .. 'hog' applies properly to the first shorn fleece of any long-stapled wool. 1884 *York Herald* 26 Aug. 7/3 The trade in wool remains firm .. all hog made from 11*s.* to 12*s.* 3*d.* per stone.

III. 5. Applied (chiefly in comb.) to various domestic animals of a year old. See *hog-bull*, *-colt*, in 13 b.

1775 ASH, *Hog*, a bullock of a year old. a1893 *Wilts. Arch. Mag.* XVII. 303 (Wilts. Gloss.) The word hog is now applied to any animal of a year old, such as a hog bull, a chilver hog sheep.

6. Short for *hog-fish*.

1623 WHITBOURNE *Newfoundland* 9 The Sea likewise all along that Coast, doe plentifully abound in other sorts of fish, as Whales .. Herring, Hogs, Porposes.

IV. 7. *fig.* Applied opprobriously to a person. **a.** A coarse, self-indulgent, gluttonous, or filthy person.

1436 *Libel* in *Pol. Poems* (Rolls) II. 171 Thus arn they hogges; and drynkyn wele ataunt; ffare wel, Flemynge! 1546 J. HEYWOOD *Prov.* (1867) 76 Ye haue bene so veraie a hog, To my freendis. 1594 SHAKS. *Rich. III*, I. iii. 228 Thou eluish mark'd, abortiue rooting Hogge. 1727 GAY *Molly Mog* viii, Who follows all ladies of pleasure, In pleasure is thought but a hog. 1890 BESANT *Demoniac* ii. 20, 'I am a hog! I am a hog!' he said .. 'I made no resistance; I drank because I was thirsty'.

b. A nickname for the members of St. John's College, Cambridge.

1690 DE LA PRYME *Diary* (Surtees) 20 For us Jonians are called abusively hoggs. 1795 *Gentl. Mag.* LXV. I. 22/1 The Johnian hogs were originally remarkable, on account of the squalid figures and low habits of the students. 1890 C. WHIBLEY *In Cap & Gown* xxvii, Perhaps .. Johnians were only called 'Hogs' because they were fond of good living.

c. A person who behaves in a rude mannerless fashion without respect for the safety or convenience of others; esp. in ROAD HOG *sb.*

1906 *Daily Chron.* 2 Feb. 7/3 Showing to the astounded heathens (save the word) the latest game of 'hog-amok'. 1928 *Daily Mail* 25 July 17/4 So far we have met no 'canal hogs'. 1942 *Topeka* (Kan.) *Capital* 16 May 7/2 The Office of Price Administration made things unpleasant for 'gas hogs' tonight.

8. *slang.* A shilling. In *U.S.*, a ten-cent piece.

1673 R. HEAD *Canting Acad.*, Shilling, *Bord* or *Hog.* 1725 *New Cant. Dict.* (Farmer), Half a Hog, Six-Pence. 1809 MAR. EDGEWORTH *Ennui* (1815) 74 'A hog to drink my health?' 'Ay, that is a thirteen, plase your honour; all as one as an English shilling.' 1859 MATSELL *Voc.*, *Hog*, a ten-cent piece. 1875 CRUIKSHANK *3 Courses & Dessert* 412 What's half a crown and a shilling? A bull and a hog.

9. A name given to various contrivances. **a.** A sort of broom or scrubbing-brush for cleaning a ship's bottom.

1769 FALCONER *Dict. Marine* (1789), *Goret* .. a hog, or large brush to scrub the ship's bottom under water. 1867 SMYTH *Sailor's Word-bk.*, *Hog*, a kind of rough, flat scrubbing broom, serving to scrape a ship's bottom under water.

b. *Paper-making.* A revolving stirrer in a chest of paper pulp which agitates the pulp so as to keep it of uniform consistence.

1807 *Specif. Cobb's Patent* No. 3084. 2 Agitators or hogs .. are placed in the said vats to keep the pulp duly suspended.

c. *Hop-drying* (see quot.)

1848 *Jrnl. R. Agric. Soc.* IX. II. 570 It is a very good precaution .. to have horses or hogs (as these plates, resting upon open brickwork, are called) over the fires, when there are three to the same space.

d. A railway locomotive used for hauling freight. *U.S. slang.*

1888 *Walla Walla* (Wash.) *Union* 24 Nov. 3/4 The 'hog' will haul nine loaded cars up the heavy Alto grade, while the ordinary road engine had a hard tussel to haul four or five. 1903 *Sci. Amer.* 23 May 392/2 In anthracite drifts steam locomotives of a small and peculiar type known as 'hogs' haul the trains. 1960 *Listener* 18 Aug. 250/2 A steam locomotive is a 'hog' or 'pig'.

e. *Forestry.* (See quots.)

1898 *Lumber Trade Jrnl.* 1 Jan. 31 (Advt.), The big slab grinding hog for grinding up slabs, edgings and mill refuse into fuel. 1904 *Dialect Notes* II. 398 *Hog*, a machine for grinding logs. 1913 WEBSTER, *Hog*, a machine with revolving knife cutters for grinding up edgings and slabs. 1957 *Brit. Commonw. Forest Terminol.* II. 93 *Hog*, a machine for reducing wood to coarse chips, usually for converting mill waste into fuel. 1969 *Timber Trades Jrnl.* 29 Nov. 57/3 Waste blocks .. are often chuted .. on to a conveyor which automatically takes them to a refuse hog.

f. A large, often old, car or motor-cycle. *U.S. slang.*

1967 W. MURRAY *Sweet Ride* vii. 112 The heat was on so bad we couldn't ride our bikes... Get on our hogs and them mothers'd pick us up. 1968–70 *Current Slang* (Univ. S. Dakota) III–IV. 68 *Hog*, .. an old, heavy Harley Davidson motor-cycle... 1956 or 1958 Cadillac; any large car which takes up all the road. 1971 *Black Scholar* Jan. 41/1 He bought him a 'Hog' with all the accessories on it. Man, this Cadillac had air horns, white-walls, [etc.]. 1971 P. L. CAVE *Chopper* v. 45 Pulling away, he swung the hog round in a wide U-turn and went after Ethel.

10. *Curling.* A stone which has not sufficient impetus to carry it over the hog-score or distance-line. Also, the distance-line itself, the hog-score.

a1772 GRAEME *Curling* 43 His opponent is glad, Yet fears a sim'lar fate, while ev'ry mouth Cries, Off the hog. 1824 J. MACTAGGART *Gallovid. Encycl.* 274 Sweeping is not allowed until the stone comes over the 'hogg', unless by the person who played it. 1853 W. WATSON *Poems* 63 Stan' back at the hog wi' a besom. 1856 'STONEHENGE' *Brit. Sports* (1859) 512 Every stone to be considered a hog which does not clear a square placed upon the score. 1897 *Encycl. Sport* I. 258 It [*sc.* a stone] must be over the Hog, but must not touch the Stone to be guarded.

V. 11. *Phrases* and *locutions.* Chiefly belonging to sense 1. ***like*** or ***as a hog on ice***, denoting independence, awkwardness, or insecurity (*U.S. colloq*).

1526 *Pilgr. Perf.* (W. de W. 1531) 24 Cast not your perles before hogges. 1546 J. HEYWOOD *Prov.* (1867) 38 Euery man basteth the fat hog we see, But the leane shall burne er he basted bee. 1587 MASCALL *Govt. Cattle* (1627) 270 Where-fore the common saying is, the hog is neuer good but when he is in the dish. 1638 CLARKE *Phraseol. Puer.* 76 *Triticum advexi & hordeum vendo* .. I have brought my hogges to a faire market. c1645 MILTON *Sonn.* xii, But this is got by casting pearls to hogs. 1660 HOWELL *Eng. Prov.* 5 You have spun a fair threed, you have brought your hogs to a fair market. Spoken in derision when a business hath sped ill. *Ibid.* 13 A great cry and little wool, quoth the Devil when he sheard the hogg. 1670 RAY *Prov.* (1768) 11 Better my hog dirty home than no hog at all. *Ibid.* 196 To make a hog or a dog of a thing. 1670–1705 [see HALFPENNYWORTH]. 1705 HICKERINGILL *Priest-cr.* I. (1721) 64 He truly setting the Tail on another Hog, affrighted the good King off the Bench. 1738 SWIFT *Pol. Conversat.* II. Wks. 1766 XI. 207 He .. snor'd so hard, that we thought he was driving his hogs to market. 1748 SMOLLETT *Rod. Rand.* xli, I should have remembered the old saying, Every hog his own apple. 1857 *San Francisco Call* 19 Apr. 2/3 He don't appear to care nothing for nobody—he's 'as independent as a hog on ice!' 1882 *Handbk. Prov.* 166 What can you expect of a hog but his bristles? 1894 *Vermont Agric. Rep.* XIV. 124 How would a Hackney look going around the track after old Highland Gray? 'Like a hog on ice.' 1922 C. SANDBURG *Slabs of Sunburnt West* 8 Chicago fished from its depths a text: Independent as a hog on ice. 1948 *Time* 9 Aug. 18/2 They like to think of themselves as independents—independent as a hog on ice.

b. ***to go the whole hog***: To go all the way, to do the thing thoroughly (*slang*); hence, in derivative uses.

[Many conjectural explanations have been offered. But cf. COWPER *Hypocrisy Detected* (1779) 12 [by J. Newton] But for one piece they thought it hard From the whole hog to be debarred; And set their wit at work to find What joint the prophet had in mind. *Ibid.* 22 Thus, Conscience freed from every clog, Mahometans eat up the hog.]

1828 in G. T. Curtis *Life D. Webster* (1870) I. 337 [Andrew Jackson] will either go with the party, as they say in New York, or go 'the whole hog', as it is phrased elsewhere. 1829 *Virginia Herald* (Fredericksburg) 28 Mar. 2/3 We all know that of late he has shown a disposition to become 'a whole hog man', but if he can swallow this, he can swallow anything. 1830 GALT *Lawrie T.* II. i. (1849) 43, I reckon Squire Lawrie may go the whole hog with her. 1835 H. C. TODD *Notes Canada & U.S.A.* 46 In Virginia originated *Go the whole hog*, a political phrase marking the democrat from a federalist. 1837–40 HALIBURTON *Clockm.* (1862) 21 We never fairly knew what goin the whole hog was till then. 1839 *Times* 11 Apr., If so, let him 'go the whole hog' in candour. 1840 *Boston Advert.* 30 June 3/3 Mr. Yorke would have been just the man for the Boston 'whole-hoggites'. 1852 *Household Words* 31 July 474/1 When a Virginian butcher kills a pig, he is said to ask his customers whether they will 'go the whole hog', as, in such case, he sells at a lower price than if they pick out the prime joints only. 1853 *Tait's Mag.* XX. 414 Stage morality, moreover, finds in Mr. Burke a whole-hogg defender. 1857 HUGHES *Tom Brown* II. ii, Yes, he's a whole-hog man is Tom. 1876 KINGSTON *Hist. Brit. Navy* 533 Russia has gone the whole hog, and has now produced two circular monitors. 1914 D. H. LAWRENCE *Prussian Officer* 207 Do you mean to say you used to go—the whole hogger? 1928 *Daily Chron.* 3 Nov. 4 The whole-hoggers argue that that statement leaves the position more ambiguous than before. 1929 S. ANDERSON in *Mercury Story Book* 234, I went the whole hog. 1964 R. H. GERHARD in D. Abercrombie et al. *Daniel Jones* 283 Bloomfield who first adopted it 'whole hog'. 1973 *Times* 28 Mar. 4/4 He does not go the whole hog with his father in his belief in the arcane and ancient mysteries of [bacon-]smoking.

c. ***to live high off*** (also ***on***) ***the hog***, etc.: see HIGH *adv.* 9 b.

VI. 12. General comb. **a.** attributive, as ***hog-butcher***, ***-farm***, ***-fat***, ***-grunt***, ***-hunt***, ***-market***, ***-merchant***, ***-spear***, ***-yard***, etc. Also, in sense 'Like that of a hog, hog-like', as ***hog rump***, ***shoulder***.

1707 A. VAN LEEUWENHOEK in *Phil. Trans.* XXVI. 114, I also caused a *Hog-Butcher to bring me divers Tongues of Hogs. 1699 DAMPIER *Voy.* II. 98 There are abundance of Crawls or *Hog-farms. 1749 FIELDING *Tom Jones* XVIII. vi, One would have thought that .. I had been the greatest *hog-merchant in England. 1679 *Lond. Gaz.* No. 1436/4 Also a bay Mare, with a *hog rump. 1807 T. WILLIAMSON *Oriental Field Sports* (1808) I. 40 They [bamboos] serve as shafts to mount *hog-spears. 1657 W. COLES *Adam in Eden* lviii, In such places as these cattle do commonly dung, abundance of this plant [henbane] groweth as in *Hog-yards.

b. objective and obj. genitive, as ***hog-driver***, ***-feeder***, ***-hunter***; ***hog-farming***, ***-feeding***, ***-hunting***, ***-raising***, ***-serving***, ***-shearing***.

a1704 T. BROWN in R. L'Estrange tr. *Erasm. Colloq.* (1711) 335 Let me die if I wou'd not sooner marry my daughter to .. a *hog-driver. 1552 HULOET, *Hogge feader, *porculator*. 1790 SIR M. HUNTER *Journ.* (1894) 79 At Wallajabad we had the finest *hog-hunting that ever was. 1661 K. W. *Conf. Charac.* (1860) 88 She to *hog-serving, to hackling, to spinning. 1662 MARTIN *Lett.* 95 [The] hideous cry of *Hoggshearing, where .. wee have a great deal of noise, and no Wool.

c. parasynthetic, as ***hog-buttocked***, ***-faced***, ***-necked*** adjs.; also HOG-BACKED.

1692 *Lond. Gaz.* No. 2730/4 A thin Horse, *Hog Buttock'd. 1640 (*title*) A certaine Relation of the *Hog-faced Gentlewoman called Mistris Tannakin Skinker. 1793 HOLCROFT *Lavater's Physiog.* xl. 212 Horses are divided into .. the swan-necked, the stag-necked and the *hog-necked.

d. The possessive case *hog's* is also largely used in quasi-combinations, as ***hog's bristle***, ***dung***, ***foot***, ***hair***, ***lard***, etc. (hyphened when attrib.).

1693 C. MATHER *Wond. Invis. World* (1862) 137 Several Poppets, made up of Rags and *Hogs-bristles. 1611 COTGR., *Onglons de pourceau*, *hogs-feet singed, then sodden vntill they be verie tender, then broyled [etc.]. 1819 REES *Cycl.* s.v. *Back-Painting*, With a *hog's-hair brush. 1688 BOYLE *Wks.* (1772) V. 372 Take rue .. with May or other unsalted butter, or else with fresh *hogs-lard. c1865 LETHEBY in *Circ. Sc.* I. 94/2 Hog's lard is fluid at 81°.

13. Special comb.: **a.** †**hog-babe**, a sucking-pig; **hog-cholera**, the swine-fever; **hog-cistern**, †**hog-loom**, a receptacle for pig-wash; **hog-constable** = HOG-REEVE; **hog-feast** (see quot.); **hog('s)-flesh**, pork; **hog('s)-grease**, the lard or fat of a hog; hence *hog-grease* vb., to smear with hog's grease; †**hog-grubber**, a mean or sneaking fellow; hence *hog-grubbing* adj.; **hog-head** *U.S. slang*, the driver of a locomotive; **hog-house**, a shed in which swine are kept; **hog-jobber**, a dealer in hogs; **hog-Latin**, bad, spurious, or mongrel Latin; **hog-line** *Curling*, the distance-line (= HOG-SCORE); **hog-loom** (see *hog-cistern* above); **hog-man**, a swineherd; **hog('s)-meat**, pork; **hog-plague**, the swine-fever; **hog-potato**, an inferior or small potato used to feed swine; **hog-pound**, a pigsty; **hog-ring**, a ring or bent wire put into the snout of a pig to prevent grubbing; **hog-ringer**, one who fastens rings in pigs' snouts; a kind of pincers used for the purpose; †**hog-rubber**, one who rubs hogs; hence, a term of opprobrium; †**hog's-face**, a person with a face like a hog's; a term of opprobrium; **hog-tight** *a.*, said of fences which are close enough to prevent swine from forcing their way through; **hog-wallow**, a

hollow or ditch in which pigs wallow; also, *spec.* in U.S., a natural depression having this appearance; **hog-ward**, a keeper of hogs; a swine-herd; **hog-wild** *a.*, wild in the manner of a hog; **hog('s)-yoke**, (*a*) a frame of wood put round a hog's neck to prevent its getting through hedges; (*b*) a quadrant.

1610 HEALEY *St. Aug. Citie of God* 170 Lette him bee Potina and suckle the *hog-babes. **1881** *Chicago Times* 16 Apr., Loss of..hogs in this state from so-called *hog cholera. **1865** *N. & Q.* 3rd Ser. VII. 295 The Huntingdonshire *hog-feast is the domestic rejoicing that follows upon that important event in a cottager's family—the killing of a pig. **1528** PAYNEL *Salerne's Regim.* E iv, The beste *hog fleshe. **1616** B. JONSON *Ev. Man in Hum.* I. i, Doe not conceiue that antipathy betweene vs, and Hogs-den; as was betweene Iewes, and hogs-flesh. **1825** SCOTT *Talism.* ii, Dried hog's-flesh, the abomination of the Moslemah. **1614** MARKHAM *Cheap Husb.* I. xlvii. 31 Take Waxe, *Hogges-grease and Turpentine. **1654** GAYTON *Pleas. Notes* III. ii. 71 Yet they did Hog-grease his body. **1676** *Lond. Gaz.* No. 1073/1, 4 Tierces of Hogsgreace. *a* **1700** B. E. *Dict. Cant. Crew* s.v. *Hog*, **Hog-grubber*, a close-fisted,..sneaking Fellow. **1907** *Sunset* XVIII. 290/2 The anxious gaze of the *hoghead (*Anglice*: engineer). **1931** *Illinois Central Mag.* June 30/2 To the initiated, a 'tallow-pit' is a locomotive fire-man and a 'hoghead' is the engineer. **1960** *Listener* 18 Aug. 250/2 Engineers are 'hogheads' or 'eagle-eyes'. **1806** FORSYTH *Beauties Scotl.* IV. 62 Having stables..milk-house, *hog-house, &c. **1896** *Westm. Gaz.* 26 Oct. 10/2 Chicago has just built for itself a new piggery..In the language of the West it is a '600,000 dollar hog-house'. **1723** *Lond. Gaz.* No. 6170/9 Thomas Greathead,..*Hogjobber. **1810** M. DWIGHT *Journey to Ohio* (1912) 53 He pass'd us on the road, singing & screaming, advising us to go back & learn *hog-latin—alias German—or dutch. **1834** C. A. DAVIS *Lett. J. Downing* 19 You shall give the address after all, only just let Seth stick a little Hog-latin into it here and there. **1930** *Daily Express* 8 Sept. 8/6 The millions now being wasted in teaching bewildered youngsters hog Latin and piano and bad Greek. **1904** *Westm. Gaz.* 13 May 3/1 There is no reason in the world why you should not mark out a '*hog' line with whitewash. **1963** *Times* 25 Feb. p. xvi/2 Briefly, the rule allows a curler to keep his grip on his rock until the first hog line is reached—a distance of 32 feet from the hack in which the toe is placed. **1732** *London Mag.* I. 278 He lov'd *hog-meat thorough done. **1886** *Syd. Soc. Lex.*, **Hog plague*, the same, according to Klein, as infectious pneumo-enteritis..Also called Swine fever. **1796** STEDMAN *Surinam* II. xxv. 224, I have here also found a kind of real potatoe..but they are only used by the negroes, being inferior to the *hog-potatoes in Great Britain. **1866** ROGERS *Agric. & Prices* I. xxi. 552, I find *hog-rings bought on two occasions in 1360 and 1374. **1692** in G. Sheldon *Hist. Deerfield, Mass.* (1895) I. 267 The *hogg ringers shall have 6*d.* per head for every hogg ya ring. **1802–25** SYD. SMITH *Ess.* (Beeton) 215 Because he has served the office of clerk, or sexton, or hog-ringer. **1614** B. JONSON *Barth. Fair* V. iii. Wks. (Rtldg.) 338/2 Yes good man *Hogrubber, of Pickthatch. **1621** BURTON *Anat. Mel.* III. ii. IV. i. (1638) 536 The very rusticks and hog-rubbers..if once they tast of this Loue liquor, are inspired in an instant. *c* **1630** *Trag. Rich. II*, (1870) 60 Heeres a fatt horson in his russet slops, And yett may spend 300[li] bith yeare, The third of which the *hoggsface owes the kinge. **1859** BARTLETT *Dict. Amer.* s.v., *Hog-tight and horse-high, always used together, of fences that are sufficient to restrain trespassing stock. Maryland. **1879** A. W. TOURGÉE *Fool's Errand* xxx. 194 The split-board paling..was 'horse-high, hog-tight, and bull-strong'. **1885** *Rep. Indian Affairs* 110 All of these tracts are enclosed with hog-tight fences. **1972** *Christian Sci. Monitor* 28 Sept. 16/4 The pioneers..tipped the stumps up with their roots in the air, and lined them along so they were, as the saying went, 'horse-high, hog-tight, and bull-strong'. **1840** *Amer. Jrnl. Sc.* XXXIX. 212 From the difference of surface, soil, and exposure, there arises a great diversity in the size, depth, and general appearance of the *hog-wallows. **1893** *N. & Q.* 8th Ser. IV. 406 Chapel Lane..was a hog-wallow, a fetid ditch, and open receptacle of sewerage and filth. **1883** GREEN *Conq. Eng.* 330 The *hog-ward who drove the swine to the denes in the wood-land paid his lord 15 pigs at the slaughter time. **1904** *Dialect Notes* II. 418, I never saw such an excitement over a little thing in Arkansas as there was over that debate. They went **hog wild.* **1938** J. RICE *Somers Inheritance* III. x. 178 The fact is they're eaten up with envy because they're not getting some of the money. They're hog-wild, that's it, hog-wild. **1940** C. MCCULLERS *Heart is Lonely Hunter* (1943) I. ii. 21 This here white man had just gone hog wild. He were butting his head against the side of this brick wall. **1969** *Eugene* (Oreg.) *Register-Guard* 3 Dec. 2D/1 Arkansas has gone hog wild over its second-ranked Razorbacks this week. **1577** TUSSER *Husb.* xvii. (1878) 38 *note*, *Hog yokes, and a twicher, and ringes for a hog. **1613** PURCHAS *Pilgrimage* (1614) 387 Weare a Yoke like a Hogs-yoke. **1707** MORTIMER *Husb.* (1708) 290 Hog-Yokes and Rings. **1841** F. A. OLMSTED *Incidents Whaling Voy.* vi. 83 A quadrant receives the very undignified and unphilosophical name of a 'hog-yoke'. *a* **1852** F. M. WHITCHER *Widow Bedott Papers* (1883) x. 35, I ain't so fond o' pork as to eat hog yokes. **1897** KIPLING *Capt. Cour.* v. 107 The old green-crusted quadrant that they called the 'hog-yolk'. **1929** F. BOWEN *Sea Slang* 67 *Hog yoke*, the old fashioned wooden quadrant in American ships and Grand Bankers, so-called from its likeness to the wooden yoke put over hogs to prevent them breaking through fences.

b. From senses 4 and 5: **hog-age** *U.S.*, adolescence (?*obs.*); **hog-bull**, a yearling bull; **hog-colt**, a yearling colt; **hog-fence**, pasture fenced off for feeding young sheep or 'hogs' during the winter; **hog-fleece**, the fleece obtained from a 'hog'; **hog-fold**, a fold for young sheep (Lisle *Husb.* *a* 1722); **hog-gap** (see quots.); so **hog-hole**; **hog-lamb**, a castrated wether lamb; **hog-pox** (see quot.); **hog-sheep** = sense 5; **hog-wool** = sense 5 c.

1848 J. MITCHELL in *Amer. Speech* (1935) X. 40 **Hog age*, between Boyhood & Manhood. **1893** FARMER & HENLEY *Slang*, *Hog-age*, the period between boyhood and manhood. **1794** T. DAVIS *Agric. Wilts* in *Archæol. Rev.* (1888) Mar., At this time it is used in a more extended sense for any animal of a year old, as a *hog bull, a chilver hog sheep. **1591** PERCIVALL *Sp. Dict.*, *Potrico*, a *hog colt. **1796** W. MARSHALL *W. Eng.* I. Gloss. (E.D.S.) *Hog-colts*, yearling colts. **1802** FINDLATER *Agric. Surv. Peebles* 192 Some better and lower lying pasture is saved..for them [lambs], for their Winter's provision; what is thus hained, is called the **hog fence.* **1865** H. H. DIXON *Field & Fern* IV. iv. 61 The weight of the *hogg fleeces depends so entirely on their keep. **1878** *Cumbld. Gloss.*, **Hog-gap*, a covered opening in a wall for sheep to pass through. **1818** SCOTT *Hrt. Midl.* xxviii, The bairns' rime says, the warst blast of the borrowing days couldna kill the three silly poor *hog-lambs. **1842–4** H. STEPHENS *Bk. of Farm* (1851) 923 When a male a tup-lamb, and this last is changed to hogg-lamb when it under-goes emasculation. **1749** W. ELLIS *Sheph. Guide* 324 This Disease, by many Farmers, is called the *Hog-Pox in Sheep, proceeding from Foulness of Blood, and as some think is somewhat of the Nature of the Small-Pox in the human Body. **1667** *Comenio's Dict.* 584 They did also pull off the fleeces of *hog-sheep (whom now a days we shear). **1807** VANCOUVER *Agric. Devon* (1813) 346 The ewes and lambs, with the preceding year's hog sheep, are brought down from the forests in the beginning of November. **1813** SIR J. CULLUM *Hist. Hawsted Suffolk* (ed. 2) 274 Their [Hoggets'] first fleece is called *Hog-wool.

c. In names of animals resembling the hog, or infesting swine, as **hog-ape** (also *hog-faced ape*), the mandrill baboon, *Simia porcaria*; †**hog-badger** (see quot. 1741); **hog-beetle**, a beetle of the family *Curculionidæ*; **hog-caterpillar**, 'the larva of a Sphinx-moth, *Darapsa myron*, so called from the swollen thoracic joints' (*Cent. Dict.*); **hog-choke, -choker**, *U.S.* (see quots. 1857, 1885); **hog-molly**, a name in U.S. of two fishes: (*a*) = *hog-sucker*; (*b*) = HOG-FISH 4; **hog-monkey** = *hog-ape*; **hog-mouse**, the shrew-mouse; **hog-mullet** = *hog-sucker*; **hog-perch**, the hog-fish, *Percina caprodes*; **hog-rabbit, hog-rat** (see quots.); **hog-sucker**, a North American fish, the Hammer-head, *Hypentelium nigricans*; **hog-tapir**, the Mexican tapir; **hog-tick**, a tick or louse parasitic on swine, *Hæmatopinus suis*.

1608 TOPSELL *Serpents* (1658) 675 The snout is like to the snout of a *Hog-ape, always gaping. **1793** PENNANT *Hist. Quadrup.* I. 187 Hog-faced Ape, *Simia Porcaria.* **1611** COTGR., *Taisson porchin*, the *hog Badger; is footed, and snowted like a swine. **1741** *Compl. Fam. Piece* II. i. 297 There are two Sorts of Badgers, viz. the Dog-Badger, as resembling the Dog in his Feet; and a Hog-Badger, as resembling a Hog in his cloven Hoofs. **1836–9** TODD *Cycl. Anat.* II. 895/1 A similar change in the form and relative size of parts of the head occurs in the *hog-beetles. **1857** *Harper's Mag.* XIV. 442 The refuse fish commonly taken (in North Carolina) are sturgeon..*hog-choke, or flounder, lampreys, and common eels. **1885** KINGSLEY *Stand. Nat. Hist.* III. 280 The nearest American relative of the sole ..*Achirus lineatus.* It is a worthless animal, as one of its popular names—*hogchoker—suggests. **1744–50** W. ELLIS *Mod. Husbandm.* III. ii. 36 But it happened, that good Part of his Bean-crop was spoiled by *Hog or Shrew-mice. **1845** *Encycl. Metrop.* XVI. 793 *Cœlogenus Paca*..They are sometimes called *Hog Rabbits, and are natives of Brazil. **1847** CARPENTER *Zool.* §147 Connecting the Rats with the Marmots is a curious animal of larger size, the Capromys or *Hog-rat, which inhabits Cuba. This is a climbing, not a burrowing species..and feeds entirely on vegetable matter. **1883** *Bull. U.S. Nat. Mus.* XXVII. 478 *Catostomus nigricans.* ..*Hog Sucker... United States from New York to Florida and westward to Alabama and Kansas; Great Lake region. **1888** GOODE *Amer. Fishes* 435 The..'Hog Sucker'.. abounds in most waters from the great lakes southward.

d. In names of plants devoured by, fit for, or left to hogs or swine, as **hog-apple** (see quot.); **hog-bed** (*U.S.*), the Ground Pine, *Lycopodium complanatum*; **hog('s)-grass**, Swine's Cress, *Senebiera Coronopus* (Britten & H.); **hog('s)-meat**, (*a*) *Aristolochia grandiflora*, (*b*) *Boerhaavia decumbens* of Jamaica; **hog-pea, -pease**, the commonfield-pea; **hog-peanut**, a twining plant of U.S., *Amphicarpæa monoica* (N.O. *Leguminosæ*), having purplish flowers and fleshy, pea-shaped fruits; **hog's bane**, Goosefoot or Sowbane; **hog's bread**, Sowbread, *Cyclamen*; also = *hog-meat* b (*Syd. Soc. Lex.* 1886); **hog's eye** (see quots.); **hog's garlic**, *Allium ursinum* (Miller *Plant-n.* 1884); **hog-slip** (see quot.); **hog's madder**, Ragwort, *Senecio Jacobæa*; †**hog's snout** (see quot.); **hog-succory**, a species of *Hyoseris*; **hog-wort**, *Heptalon graveolens* (N.O. *Euphorbiaceæ*) of U.S. (*Syd. Soc. Lex.* 1886).

1865 *Chambers' Encycl.* VII. 622 *Podophyllum peltatum*,.. is common in North America..and is known as May-Apple ..also as *Hog-apple. **1756** P. BROWNE *Jamaica* 329 The poisoned *Hog-meat. This plant is very common in St. Ann's. **1853** LINDLEY *Veg. Kingd.* (ed. 3) 507 According to Aublet the root of Boerhaavia decumbens (called Hog-meat in Jamaica), is emetic. **1744–50** W. ELLIS *Mod. Husbandm.* III. ii. 118 How another Farmer lost Crops of *Hog-peas, by the Slugs..he had sown his Hog-pea Seed in the random broad-cast way of sowing them. **1807** VANCOUVER *Agric. Devon* (1813) 183 A few *hog-pease and some beans, are occasionally cultivated. **1886** *Syd. Soc. Lex.*, *Hog's bane, the *Chenopodium murale.* **1607** TOPSELL *Four-f. Beasts* (1658) 73 The same gall with a little *Hogs-bread. **1854** MAYNE *Expos. Lex.*, **Hog's Eye*,..common name for the Hyophthalmus. **1886** *Syd. Soc. Lex.*, *Hyophthalmus*, the hog's eye plant, supposed to be the *Buphthalmum spinosum*, from the likeness of its flowers to a hog's eye. **1750** G. HUGHES *Barbadoes* 171 *Hog-slip, this is a trailing herbaceous vine, cloathed with sharp-pointed leaves. **1707** MORTIMER *Husb.* (1708) 188 For the Gargol in Hogs..Take Angelica, Rue, Staverwort, or *Hog's-Madder, and May-weed. **1834** M. G. LEWIS *Jrnl. W. Ind.* 168 The trees..were many of them entirely covered with the beautiful flowers of the *hog's-meat, and other creeping plants. **1559** MORWYNG *Evonym.* 367 The juice of Hamsig, Plantain,..Rostrum porcinum or *Hogges snout.

hog, *sb.*[2] *local.* [Origin obscure: it varies locally with *hod.*] A heap of potatoes or turnips covered with straw and soil; a 'clamp', 'pit'.

1790–1804 A. YOUNG *Ann. Agric.* XXXII. 213 The usual mode of preserving potatoes in this country is in hogs, as they are called. **1857** *Jrnl. R. Agric. Soc.* XVIII. I. 108 The potatoes are brought out of the 'hogs', or 'graves', or 'pits' —all of which are provincial terms for the same mode of covering them with straw and earth.

hog (hɒg), *v.*[1] [f. HOG *sb.*[1], in various senses unconnected with each other.]

I. 1. *trans.* **a.** To arch (the back) upward like that of a hog. Also *transf.* and *absol.*

1860 R. F. BURTON *Lake Regions Central Africa* I. 85 They [*sc.* asses] hog and buck till they burst their frail girths. **1956** *Archit. Rev.* CXIX. 143/2 Owing to the eccentric placing of the prestressing wires, which cannot be avoided, there is always the tendency for the units to 'hog', i.e., to assume a permanent deflection upwards during stressing.

b. To cause (a ship, her keel, a plank, etc.) to droop at the ends and rise in the centre, as the result of a strain.

1798 WOLCOTT (P. Pindar) *Tales of Hoy* Wks. 1812 IV. 417 A very bad world indeed in some parts—hogg'd the moment it was launch'd, a number of rotten timbers. **1802** *Naval Chron.* VIII. 257 The Mars..received some damage, which has hogged her a little. **1803** WELLINGTON *Let. to Lieut.-Gen. Stuart* in Gurw. *Desp.* (1837) II. 18 *note*, The.. draught bullocks always suffer by exposure. They stick in the mud, hog their backs, droop their heads and die. **1832** *Hull Newspaper*, The planks were hogged amidships.

2. *intr.* To rise arch-wise in the centre, as a ship when the ends droop or sink.

1803 *Deb. Congr. U.S.* 19 Jan. (1851) 407/1 He did not.. believe that there would be any more danger of the ship's hogging, when lowered down..than when on the stocks. **1818** R. SEPPINGS in *Phil. Trans.* 3 She hogged, or broke her sheer..one foot two inches. *c* **1850** *Rudim. Navig.* (Weale) 124. **1875** *Nat. Encycl.* XI. 662 In still water there is usually an excess of weight towards the ends, and an excess of buoyancy amidships, tending to make the ship hog, or arch upwards. *Ibid.*, In rough water, there is a tendency to hog and to sag alternately.

II. 3. *trans.* To cut (a horse's mane) short, so that it stands up like the bristles of a hog.

1769 *Dublin Mercury* 25 Sept. 1/3 A sorrel Horse..his mane hogged last May. **1880** W. DAY *Racehorse in Train.* vi. 42 Some, perhaps, would wish to plait or shave the tail and crimp or hog the mane to complete the picture.

III. 4. To make a 'hog' of (a lamb); to keep (a lamb) over winter for sale in the following year.

1853 *Jrnl. R. Agric. Soc.* XIV. II. 298 A good many of the lambs usually sold fat have been hogged, and kept on to be sold when fat. *Ibid.* 300 From the high rates of holding lambs, many farmers last season hogged the lambs. **1865** H. H. DIXON *Field & Fern* IV. ix. 183 Hundreds of acres are now let for hogging black-faces off the Grampians.

IV. 5. a. To appropriate greedily or selfishly. orig. *U.S. slang.*

1884 'MARK TWAIN' *Huck. Finn* xxvii. 275 S'pose somebody has hogged that bag on the sly? **1887** *Orange Jrnl.* 16 Apr. (Farmer *Amer.*), If the crook is obstinate enough to hog it all. **1888** *Daily Inter-Ocean* 13 Mar. (Farmer *Amer.*), To hog whatever there was in the business for themselves. **1896** *Columbus* (Ohio) *Disp.* 2 July, It would give them a chance to say I was hogging every-thing and giving no one else a chance. **1917** J. C. MCCORQUODALE *In Divers Moods* 16 What blinking luck!—Let's have a sup: Don't hog the lot. My Christ! it's cold. **1936** WODEHOUSE *Laughing Gas* xxii. 237 Maybe that will teach you not to go crawling to directors so that they will let you hog the camera! **1959** *Listener* 26 Mar. 566/1 He never hogs the limelight. **1960** *Woman* 9 Jan. 13/2 You've got a no-good wardrobe, piano, pram or bed, hogging precious space in the house. **1973** *Freedom* 7 July 1/4 The inquiry could go on without hogging the headlines from him.

b. *trans.* and *intr.* To behave as a road hog; to monopolize the road. Also as *vbl. sb.*

1897 KIPLING *Capt. Cour.* vi. 129 You..go hoggin' the road on the high seas with no blame consideration fer your neighbours. **1914** 'I. HAY' *Knight on Wheels* xx. 200 Now I will really hog it a bit: this is a lovely piece of road. **1925** R. J. B. SELLAR *Sporting Yarns* 135 As they were hogging it through the country-side with the speedometer hovering over the sixty mark. **1925** *Punch* 22 Apr. 432 'Frightful rate that bike we just passed was going, wasn't it?' 'Yes. They ought to have the man for "hogging".' **1926** *Chambers's Jrnl.* Dec. 875/1 Why don't you sound your hooter before hogging round corners? **1956** W. GRAHAM *Sleeping Partner* iv. 35, I hogged the road to Lewes cutting in and out among all the family 8-horse powers.

c. *trans.* To interfere with in wireless transmission, as by a more powerful instrument. So also *to hog the ether*.

1914 *Pears' Christmas Annual* 21/2 They should be hogged till doomsday..if a single ship was on fire! *Ibid.*, The operator heard. He started up as if he had been hogged himself. **1959** *News Chron.* 14 Dec. 4/6 The B.B.C., according to Mr. Collins, 'hog the ether to a shocking extent'.

d. *trans.* To eat (something) greedily.

1928 M. LOWRY *Lett.* (1967) 4 Sometime..wdst hog it over the way somewhere with me? **1932** D. H. LAWRENCE *Last Poems* (1933) 50 The only way to eat an apple is to hog

it down like a pig And taste nothing. **1946** B. MARSHALL *George Brown's Schooldays* v. 24 The Bruiser did not pause to observe it, hogging down the mashed up mess in front of him.

V. 6. To clean a ship's bottom with a 'hog'.

1769 FALCONER *Dict. Marine* (1789), *Goreter*, to hog a vessel; to apply the hog to her bottom. **1862** TOTTEN *Naval Text-bk.* 340 *To hog a vessel*, is to scrub her bottom.

VI. 7. (*Curling*) 'To play (a stone) with so little force, that it does not clear the hog-score' (Ogilvie). Also *fig.*

1822 *Blackw. Mag.* XII. 307 There's no a merchant amang us that's no hogged mair or less.

VII. 8. To carry on the back. *dial.*

1781 J. HUTTON *Tour to Caves* Gloss., *Hog*, to carry on the back.

VIII. 9. *trans.* To feed swine on (a crop or crop-covered land). Also with *down* or *off*. *U.S. colloq.*

1859 H. W. BEECHER *Pleasant Talk* 93 Some of the best farmers in this region hog their corn-lands. *Ibid.* 94 Land being hogged, will be free from cut-worms. **1863** *Rep. Comm. Agric. 1862* (U.S.) 82, I was forced to hog down my crop this year. **1937** *Amer. Speech* XII. 104 *To hog down corn* means to let hogs eat unharvested corn in the field. **1948** *Clarke Co. Democrat* (Grove Hill, Ala.) 19 Aug. 7/3 A good place to plant crimson clover and rye grass is where you hogged off peanuts.

Hence **'hogging** *vbl. sb.* and *ppl. a.*

1772–84 COOK *Voy.* (1790) V. 1726 Remaining part somewhat resembled the crest of their caps, or that which, in horses manes, is called hogging. **1812** *Q. Rev.* VIII. 49 The Tremendous..was launched without breaking or hogging, as it is sometimes called, the tenth part of an inch. **1852–61** *Archit. Publ. Soc. Dict.* IV. 64 *Hoggin* or *Hogging*, the term used by workmen for the curved form given to the cross section of a roadway to throw off the surface water. **1884** *Eng. Illustr. Mag.* Oct. 17/2 The 'hogging' of the mane.. varies in style from the Arab. **1891** *Athenæum* 22 Aug. 257/3 Longitudinal strains, or hogging, being..as often the cause of leakage in a long, heavily-timbered, carvel-built ship.

hog, *v.*² [f. HOG *sb.*²] *trans.* To store (potatoes, etc.) in a heap, covered with straw and earth.

1730 PARSON WALKER *Diary* 23 (Lanc. Gloss.), I put off at present, being throng hogging up some of my potatoes. **1884** *Cheshire Gloss.*, *Hog*, to earth up potatoes in a heap, or to throw compost into a heap.

hogan ('həʊgən). [Navajo.] The rude hut of Navajo and other American Indian peoples of the south-western United States.

1872 *Rep. Indian Affairs 1871* (U.S.) 379 When a member of a family dies, in most cases they immediately leave their hogan (or wigwam) with the dead body in it. **1904** *New York Even. Post* 2 July 2 The North American Indians in their primitive state, living in the tepees, hogans, sod-lodges and grass houses. **1927** W. CATHER *Death comes for Archbishop* VII. iii. 217 For his lodging the Bishop was given a solitary hogan. **1955** PRIESTLEY & HAWKES *Journey down Rainbow* 242 This lot have come in from their lonely hogans, the little round wooden huts with a corral or two for horses. **1973** *Times* 15 May 19/8 At night the doors to the Navajo's huts, or hogans, were often covered by a blanket.

Hogan Mogan, obs. form of HOGEN MOGEN.

Hogarthian (həʊ'gɑːθɪən), *a.* [f. name of William Hogarth, a satirical painter and caricaturist of the 18th c. + -IAN.] Of or pertaining to Hogarth, or characteristic of his style of painting.

1798 LAMB *Lett.* (1888) I. 93 Your old description of cruelty in hell, which was in the true Hogarthian style. **1828** *Ibid.* II. 203 'Tis true broad Hogarthian fun. **1837** CARLYLE *Mirabeau* in *Misc. Ess.* (1872) V. 230 In one point of view there is nothing more Hogarthian comic. **1886** SWINBURNE in *19th Cent.* Jan. 141 It [Michaelmas Term] is an excellent Hogarthian comedy, full of rapid and vivid incident, of pleasant or indignant humour.

'hogback, hog-back. Also (esp. in sense 2 a) hog's back.

1. a. A back like that of a hog.

1661 WALTON *Angler* I. iv. (ed. 3) 72 Note that a hog back and a little head to any fish, either Trout, Salmon or other fish, is a sign that that fish is in season. **1758** *Descr. Thames* 190 The Bream has a sharp Hogback.

b. The sunfish, a member of the genus *Lepomis*. *U.S.*

1832 *Coll. New H. Hist. Soc.* III. 86 The hogback or sunfish, as some call it, is a very attracting thing. It is about as large as the perch.

c. Any fish with a hog-like back.

1893 in *Funk's Stand. Dict.* **1923** *Chambers's Jrnl.* Dec. 791/2 Bill, said the latter, the hog-back run is come.

2. Something shaped like a hog's back. **a.** A sharply crested hill-ridge, steep on each side and sloping gradually at each end; a steep ridge of upheaval.

[Cf. The *Hog's-back*, a hill near Godalming.]

a **1840** J. P. KENNEDY *Quodlibet* 26 The farm where he now lives at the foot of the Hogback. **1847** in *31st Congress 1 Sess.* H.R. Ex. Doc. No. 5. II. 731 The banks [of a river] ..worn in some places into hog-backs. **1888** *Harper's Mag.* Nov. 860/1, I pushed forward across deep gulches, over high peaks and 'hog-backs'. **1896** *Advance* (Chicago) 1 Oct. 433 The dry knobs, or hog-backs, where the prairie breaks down to the streams.

β **1800** in *Vermont Hist. Soc. Proc. 1920–21* (1921) 168 Whats call'd the hogs back is a ridge of mountains on the north side (of the Onion river, Vt.). **1827** J. F. COOPER *Red Rover* i, The hog's back over which the water pitches. **1834** SIR W. NAPIER *Penins. War* XIII. ii. (Rtldg.) II. 209 A rugged hill..joined by a hog's-back ridge to the..mountain spine. **1862** H. MARRYAT *Year in Sweden* II. 388 Our way runs along a hogsback, till we reach the lake of Fur. **1863** G. T. LOWTH *Wand. in West. France* 216 There is a long elevated line of hill, a hog's-back, running from south to north. **1973** *Guardian* 23 Jan. 13/1 The Prime Minister..will be there, in his retreat on the hogs-back of the Delimara peninsula.

b. *Coal-mining.* (See quots.)

1867 W. W. SMYTH *Coal & Coal-mining* 27 Another sort of thinning is where the floor rises..sharply, in a 'hog-back' or saddle. **1883** GRESLEY *Gloss. Coal-mining*, *Hog-back*, sharply rising of the floor of a coal seam.

c. *N.Z.* (See quot. 1940.)

1933 *N.Z. Alpine Jrnl.* V. xx. 180 Dark clouds..a bevy of 'hog-backs'. *Ibid.* 235 A 'hog's back' warned that further storms were brewing. **1940** W. S. GILKISON *Peaks, Packs & Mountain Tracks* 24 He showed me a hogsback... Term applied to a particularly unwelcome cloud only too well-known to climbers, and almost invariably heralding a north-west storm.

3. A hog-backed tombstone.

1889 R. S. FERGUSON *Carlisle* iv. 54 The coped tombstones, commonly called Saxon hogbacks.

4. = HOG-FRAME.

1886 *Waterbury* (Conn.) *American* 2 Apr. (Cent.), The strength of her hull and the solidity of her hog-back.

'hog-backed, *a.* [f. prec. + -ED².]

1. Having a back like a hog.

1654 GAYTON *Pleas. Notes* IV. iii. 186 Being you were hog-backt, you must needs have more of them [bristles] about you. **1675** *Lond. Gaz.* No. 970/4 Likewise one light iron gray Gelding, with strong limbs, a little Hog-backed. **1758** *Descr. Thames* 183 The Pearch is Hog-backed. **1884** *West. Daily Press* 26 Jan. 3/2 This elephant is..hog-backed.

2. Having a rise in the middle like a hog's back.

1852–61 *Archit. Publ. Soc. Dict.* IV. 64 *Hog-backed*, the term used by common work-people for the rise purposely made in the centre of any very long line, such as the ridge of a barn roof. **1862** RAWLINSON *Anc. Mon.* I. i. 229 In form they [hills] are hog-backed. **1893** C. HODGES in *Reliquary* Jan. 11 The class of early grave covers, known as 'hog-backed' stones.

hog-boat, var. of HAG-BOAT.

1872 *Daily News* 24 Aug., On came the hog-boat full sail, and with the water spurting up at her bows.

hog-brace. = HOG-FRAME.

'hog-chain. A device serving the same purpose as a hog-frame; 'a chain in the nature of a tension-rod passing from stem to stern of a vessel, and over posts nearer amidships; designed to prevent the vessel from drooping at the ends'.

1875 KNIGHT *Dict. Mech.*

†**'hog-cote.** *Obs.* Also **hog's-cote.** A hog- or pigsty.

1401–2 *Durham MS. Terr. Roll*, Pro reparacione del Hogcote apud Holme, iiij *s.* viij *d.* *c* **1440** *Jacob's Well* (E.E.T.S.) 228, & haue made ȝoure herte an hoggys cote & a denne of theuys. **1573** TUSSER *Husb.* xvii. (1878) 38 A stie for a bore, and a hogscote for hog. **1707** MORTIMER *Husb.* (J.), Out of a small hogcote sixty or eighty load of dung hath been raised.

'hog-deer.

1. The common name of a small Indian deer, *Axis porcinus*. (Sometimes also used to include *A. maculatus*.)

1771 PENNANT *Synops. Quadrup.* 52 Porcine Deer.. called, from the thickness of their body, Hog Deer. **1843** SIR W. JARDINE *Natur. Libr.* XI. 170 **1893** R. LYDEKKER *Horns & Hoofs* 301 The hog-deer differs from the sambar by the absence of a mane on the neck and throat.

2. The Babiroussa or Indian hog.

1777 MILLER in *Phil. Trans.* LXVIII. 171 Porcupines, and the small hog-deer. **1835** KIRBY *Hab. & Inst. Anim.* (1853) II. 148 The *Babiroussa*, or *Babee rooso*, a name which signifies Hog-deer, given to this animal probably on account of its longer legs and slender form.

hoge, obs. f. HODGE.

hoge, hogge, obs. ff. HUGE *a.*

hoge-, hoggepotte, obs. forms of HODGEPOT.

†**hogen, hogan** ('həʊgən), *a.* and *sb.* *Obs.* [Abbreviation of HOGEN MOGEN.]

A. *adj.* **1.** High and mighty; superlatively fine.

a **1672** FLATMAN *Poems, Belly God* (1674) 119, 'Twas I set the world a gazing, When once they tasted of this Hogan Fish. **1733** *Revol. Politicks* III. 63 It was so predicted by a Renegado heretical Star-gazer in his *Hogan* Blast, call'd his Mene-Tekell.

2. Dutch.

1710 E. WARD *Brit. Hud.* xiii. 153 So the proud Hogen State we see.

B. *sb.* **1.** A Dutchman; *pl.* the Dutch, the States General.

a **1657** R. LOVEDAY *Lett.* (1663) 59 The Hogens, I confess, are anger'd into more animosity against us. **1672** W. DE BRITAINE *Dutch Usurp.* Ded. 1 The Hogans then my Muse's Pow'r should feel.

2. Strong drink: see HOGEN MOGEN B. 3.

1727 GAY *Molly Mog* xiii, Those who toast all the family royal, In bumpers of Hogan and Nog. **1737** GRAY *Let.* in Mason *Mem.* (1807) I. 158 For your reputation, we keep to ourselves your not hunting nor drinking hogan. **1905** in *Chambers's Eng. Dict.* **1963** *Punch* 20 Feb. 282/1 Hogan..is a strong Norfolk beer.

Hogen Mogen (ˌhəʊgən 'məʊgən), *sb.* and *a.* Forms: 7 Hoghan Moghan, (Hogin Mogin), 7–8 Hoghen-Moghen, 7–8 Hogan Mogan, Hogen Mogen. [A popular corruption or perversion of the Dutch *Hoogmogendheiden*, 'High Mightinesses', the title of the States-General. Obsolete in all senses, exc. perhaps A 2, B 1; and these are rare. In transf. senses sometimes with small initial letters.]

A. *sb.* †**1.** 'Their High Mightinesses', the States-General of the United Provinces of the Netherlands. Cf. MIGHTINESS. *Obs.*

c **1645** HOWELL *Lett.* (1655) II. xiv. 26 The Hoghen Moghen are very exact in their polemical government. **1657** —— *Londinop.* 390 The Hague subsists by the residence of the Hoghen-Moghen, the Council of State. **1678** BUTLER *Hud.* 1440, I have sent him for a Token To your Low-Country Hogen-Mogen. **1685** *Mischief Cabals* 4 The Hoghen-Moghen scorn'd to accept of any thing.

2. Hence, The Dutch; a Dutchman: contemptuous.

1672 W. DE BRITAINE *Dutch Usurp.* 25 The Hogan Mogans..did warm their hands at those unhappy flames. **1752** J. MACSPARRAN *Amer. Dissected* (1753) 19 King Charles the Second sent Sir Robert Carr..who soon subdued Hogan Mogan, and wrested this Country [New York] out of these Hollanders Hands. **1823** SCOTT *Peveril* xxii, I have seen thee wave thy whinyard at the throat of a Hogan-mogan—a Netherlandish weasand.

†**3.** *transf.* Any grandee or high and mighty person: used humorously or contemptuously of a person in power or who arrogates or affects authority.

1638 FORD *Lady's Trial* II. i, *Guy.* Here are lords too, we take it..*Ful.*..Tag, rag, or other, hogen-mogen, vanden, Skip-jacks, or choruses. **1649** C. WALKER *Hist. Independ.*, White-hall..where our Hogens Mogens or Councell of State sit. **1658–9** *Burton's Diary* (1828) IV. 222 [He] told Sir Arthur Haslerigge that it was he that endeavoured to make himself and Sir Henry Vane the great Hogen Mogens, to rule the Commonwealth. **1713** DARRELL *Gentlem. Instr.* III. iii. 394 The Temple and Gray's-Inn have declar'd me a publick Enemy to the Hoghen Moghen learn'd in the Law.

B. *attrib.* and *adj.* **1.** Dutch. (*contemptuous.*)

a **1658** CLEVELAND *Gen. Poems* etc. (1677) 99 A kind of Dutch Hotch-Potch, the Hogan Mogan Committee-man. *a* **1704** T. BROWN *Wks.* (1760) IV. 122 (D.) Are..our armies commanded by hogan-mogan generals that hate our nation? **1753** SMART in *Anderson's Poets* XI. 166 A snub-nos'd dog, to fat inclin'd, Of the true hogan-mogan kind. **1842** *United Service Mag.* I. 2 Their hogen-mogen admirers—*les braves Belges*.

†**2.** High and mighty. (Often *contemptuous.*)

1648 NEEDHAM *Mercurius Pragmat.* No. 7 G j b (Stanf.), Come creeping to the Hogan Mogan States of Westminster. **1676** BAKER in Rigaud *Corr. Sci. Men* (1841) II. 3 Yet dare I not arrogate..that Hogun Mogun title of Magnus Apollonius. **1705** HICKERINGILL *Priest-cr.* I. xii. (1721) 12 The Hogen Mogen States of Venice.

†**3.** Strong, heady (of drink): cf. HOGAN *sb.* 2. ***hogan mogan rug***, a strong drink: see RUG. *Obs.*

1653 J. TAYLOR (Water P.) *Cert. Trav. of Uncert. Journ.* Wks. (1872) 11 There was a high and mighty drink call'd Rug..Hogen Mogen Rugs, great influences To provoke sleep. **1663** DRYDEN *Wild Gallant* I. ii, I was drunk; damnably drunk with ale; great hogan-mogan bloody ale.

hogeous, obs. form of HUGEOUS *a.*

hog-fish. [f. HOG *sb.*¹ + FISH. Cf. Ger. *meerschwein*, obs. It. *pesce porco*, Sp. *puerco marino*, OF. *porpeis* (:—L. *porcum piscem*), PORPOISE.]

†**1.** The Porpoise, also called *sea-hog*. *Obs.*

1611 FLORIO, *Pesce porco*, the Molebout-fish, or Swine-fish, the Sea-swine, the Porpuis, Hog-fish or Sea-hog. **1686** J. DUNTON *Lett. fr. New-Eng.* (1867) 32 These Porpoises, or Hog-fish, are very swift in their motion. [**1850** L. HUNT *Autobiog.* I. ii. 55, I did not know that..porpoise meant hog-fish.]

†**2.** The West African Manatee. *Obs.*

1597 HARTWELL *Pigafetta's Lopez' Congo* I. iv. in Churchill *Voy.* (1752) VIII. 532 In the river [Congo] another kind of creature, that hath, as it were, two hands, and a tail like a target, which is called *ambize angulo*, that is to say, a hog-fish. **1613** PURCHAS *Pilgrimage* (1614) 697.

3. A fish of the genus *Scorpæna*, having bristles on the head, and cirri or tags on the head and body.

1608 TOPSELL *Serpents* 137 The Crocodiles doe also feare to meddle with the Sea-hogge or Hog-fish, because of his bristles all about his head. **1847** CARPENTER *Zool.* § 556 The *Scorpæna* or Hog-fish has the head flattened side-ways. **1863** BAIRD *Stud. Nat. Hist.* 494 *Scorpaena scrofa*, the hog-fish, a native of the European seas..is said to be very good eating.

4. Also applied to other kinds of fish, esp. the West Indian *Lachnolæmus maximus* or *suillus*, having 14 dorsal spines, and the hog-molly or log-perch, *Percina caprodes*, of North American rivers.

1734 MORTIMER in *Phil. Trans.* XXXVIII. 317 *Turdus flavus*, the Hog-Fish..*Suillus*, the great Hog-Fish. **1756** P. BROWNE *Jamaica* 445 The Hog-Fish. The two species are generally confounded under the same appellation in the markets. **1775** ROMANS *Florida* App. 52 We may with safety eat of all fish caught on the Florida shore, unless it should be of the hog-fish taken on the very outer reef. **1840–1** *Boston* (U.S.) *Jrnl. Nat. Hist.* III. 346 *Etheostoma*..The most common species found in the Ohio..called almost everywhere Hog-fish. **1843** *Zoologist* I. 191.

hog-frame. *Shipbuilding*, etc. A fore-and-aft frame, usually above deck and forming together with the frame of the vessel a truss to prevent hogging, used esp. in light-draught river steamers. Also called *hog-brace*, *hogging-frame*.

1864 in WEBSTER. **1875** KNIGHT *Dict. Mech.* 1108/1 The term 'hog-frame' has been adopted into carpentry and engineering in some forms of trusses for roofs and bridges.

hogg, var. HOG *sb.*[1] 4 a.

hoggard, obs. form of HOGHERD or ? *hogward.*
1655 tr. *De Parc's Francion* IV. 3 Our Regent (who had in him no more humanity than a Hoggard).

†**hoggaster.** *Obs.* Also 3–4 **hogaster;** 4 **hoggestere,** 6 **hogsteere,** 7 **hogsteare,** 9 **hogsteer** (all in sense 1); 9 **hogster** (in sense 2). [med.L. *hogaster*, dim. from Eng. *hog*; also in AFr. form *hogastre*. The forms *hogsteer*, etc., appear to be due to false etymology.]
1. A boar in its third year; cf. HOG *sb.*[1] 2 b.
c **1420** *Venery de Twety* in *Rel. Ant.* I. 151 The boor frist he is a pyg as long as he is with his dame.. the .iij. yere he is callyd an hoggaster. **1486** *Bk. St. Albans* E iij a, And an hoggestere when he is of yeris .iij. **1583** STANYHURST *Æneis* IV. (Arb.) 100 A sounder of hogsteers, Or thee brownye lion too stalck fro the mounten he wissheth. **1598** MANWOOD *Lawes Forest* iv. §5 (1615) 43 The third yeere he is a Hogsteare. **1831** in JOHNSON *Sportsman's Cycl.*
2. A young sheep, a hog or hogget.
[*c* **1175** *Caen Cartulary* (MS. Paris, Bibl. Nat., Lat. 5650) lf. 45 b, Septem viginti oves matres.. & 60. & 12. inter gerces & Hogastres, medietatem gerces & medietatem Hogastres. *c* **1290** *Fleta* II. lxxix, Tertium [ovile] pro hogastris annatis & juvenibus. **1332–3** in Rogers *Agric. & Prices* I. 679 Ewes.. Hoggasters.. Jercions.. Lambs.] **1706** PHILLIPS (ed. Kersey), *Hoggacius*, or *Hoggaster* (in old Latin Records), a young Sheep of the second Year. **1894** WYLIE *Eng. Hen. IV*, II. 478 The farmers threatened with distraint upon their beasts and hogsters.

hoggates, var. of HOWGATES *Obs.*, in what way?

hogged (hɒgd), *ppl. a.* [f. HOG *v.*[1] + -ED[1].]
1. a. Of a ship: Drooping at stem and stern; hog-backed. **b.** Of a road: Raised in the centre.
1769 FALCONER *Dict. Marine* (1789), *Arqué*, broken-backed or hogged; drooping at the stem and stern. **1867** SMYTH *Sailor's Word-bk.*, *Hogged*, a significant word derived from the animal; it implies that the two ends of a ship's decks droop lower than the midship part, consequently, that her keel and bottom are so strained as to curve upwards. The term is therefore in opposition to that of sagging. **1896** *Brit. Med. Jrnl.* 25 July, If the road be 'hogged'.. the wheel slides away from under him [a cyclist], and he falls sideways without the slightest warning.
2. Of a horse's mane: Cut off short.
1764 G. COLMAN *Prose on Sev. Occ.* (1787) II. 258 Hogged manes and hogged toupees, came in together. **1867** MISS BROUGHTON *Cometh up as a Flower* v. 44 A sedate cob, with a docked tail and hogged mane.

†**hoggener.** *Obs. local.* Also **hogner, -ener, -oner, hodgener.** App. the same as HOGGLER, q.v.
1558 *Churchw. Acc. St. Thomas, Launceston* in Peter *Hist. Launceston* etc. (1885) 371 Hoggeners monye. **1588** *Ibid.* 373 Hodgener bread. **1620** *Ibid.* 377 Hogner bread.

hogger ('hɒgə(r)). *Sc.* and *north. dial.* Also 7 **hoger,** 9 **hog(g)ar,** *Sc.* **hugger.** [Origin obscure.
Compare OF. *huguine* armour for the thighs and legs; but this would naturally give *hoggin* in Sc.]
1. A coarse stocking without the foot used as a gaiter. Cf. COCKER *sb.*[1] 2.
1681 GLANVILL *Sadducismus* II. 295 He observed.. that he [the Devil] had Hogers on his Legs without Shoes. **1768** ROSS *Helenore* 137 A pair of grey hoggers well clinked benew. **1829** BROCKETT, *Hoggers*, upper stockings without feet, used as gaiters—riding stockings. **1851** GREENWELL *Coal-trade Terms Northumb. & Durh.* 30 *Hoggers*, stockings without feet, chiefly used by the barrowmen.
2. A short piece of pipe of metal, indiarubber, etc. used as a connexion. Hence ***hogger-pipe, -pump.***
1851 GREENWELL *Coal-trade Terms Northumb. & Durh.* 30 *Hogger-pump*, the top pump of a set, with a short pipe cast on to it at right angles near the top. The hogger is attached to the short pipe. **1881** RAYMOND *Mining Gloss.*, *Hogger-pipe*, the upper terminal pipe of the mining pump. **1898** *Newcastle Correspt.*, The name 'hogger' is applied to rubber connexions for pneumatic brakes between carriages, as well as to the indiarubber pipe that connects the tender feed with the engine delivery pipe for feeding the boiler.

hoggerel, hogrel ('hɒgərəl, 'hɒgrəl). Forms: 6 **hogrell, -ele, hoggerell,** 6–8 **hogrel,** 7 **hoggril,** 8 **hoggeril,** 9 **-erel, -rel, hogerell.** [dim. of HOG *sb.*[1]: cf. *cockerel*.]
1. A young sheep of the second year (cf. HOG *sb.*[1] 4); with some, a sheep of the third year.
1530 PALSGR. 231/2 Hoggerell, a yong shepe. **1538** [see HOGGET 2]. *a* **1547** SURREY *Æneid* IV. 72 By sacrifice for grace, with Hogreles of two yeares [*bidentes*]. **1607** TOPSELL *Four-f. Beasts* (1658) 495 The first year we call it in English a Lamb, so the second year a Hog, Lam-hog, or Teg if it be a female, the third year Hoggrils and Theives. **1780** A. YOUNG *Tour Irel.* I. 364 Generally buy year-old wethers, hoggerils in May at 8*s.* to 10*s.* **1829** GLOVER *Hist. Derby* I. 214 Three ram hogerells.. were weighed.
†**2.** = HOGGET 1. (See quot. 1786.) *Obs.*

hoggery ('hɒgərɪ). [f. HOG *sb.*[1] + -ERY.]
1. A place where hogs are kept; a hog-yard.
1819 REES *Cycl.* s.v. *Hog Sty*, The building of a hoggery.
2. Hogs or swine collectively.
1856 MRS. BROWNING *Aur. Leigh* VII. 265 Crime and shame And all their hoggery trample your smooth world, Nor leave more footmarks than Apollo's kine.
3. Hoggishness, swinishness, brutishness. *rare.*
1864 in WEBSTER. **1933** J. CARY *Amer. Visitor* xx. 285 A dash of hoggery now and then may even improve and refine the artistic reactions.

hoggester(e, var. HOGGASTER; obs. f. HUCKSTER.

hogget ('hɒgɪt). Also **-it.** [f. HOG *sb.*[1] + -ET[1].]
1. A young boar of the second year. ? *Obs.*
[**1332–3** in Rogers *Agric. & Prices* I. 679 Sows.. Porci.. Hoggets. **1420** in *Annal. Præmonst.* II. 591 (Du C.) De porcis triginta tres, de Hogettis centum viginti sex, et porcellis octoginta novem.] **1786** *Chambers' Cycl.*, *Hogget*, or *Hogrel*, a young boar of the second year.
2. A yearling sheep; cf. HOG *sb.*[1] 4.
[**1370** *Mem. Ripon* (Surt.) II. 130 Equos.. vaccas.. hoggettes.. multon'.. oves matrices.. agnos.] **1538** ELYOT *Dict.*, *Bidentes*, shepe with ii. teth, called in some place hogrelles, or hogattes. **1706** PHILLIPS (ed. Kersey), *Hogget* or *Hogrel*, a Country-Word for such a Sheep [Hoggaster]. **1732** *Gentlem. Guide to Cattle* (ed. 2) 32, I have explained.. that at a Year old they are called Hogs, Hoggets or Hogarels. **1834** D. LOW *Elem. Pract. Agric.* (1843) 793 In ten days.. after shearing, the wether-hoggets, now dinmonts, and such of the ewe-hoggets, now gimmers, as are not to be retained on the farm for breeding, may be sold. *Ibid.* 794 From this time [weaning] forward the lambs, now termed hogs or hoggets, are kept separate from the breeding ewes. **1863** MORTON *Cycl. Agric.* II. Gloss. (E.D.S.), *Hogget* or *Lamb-hog*, a young sheep before the first shearing; a one-year-old sheep. **1884** F. J. LLOYD *Sci. Agric.*, Careful management should enable the hoggets to be sold when ten months old, weighing from 80 to 90 lbs. **1886** *Daily News* 14 June 2/8 (Norwich) Hoggetts in their wool brought 45*s.* to 55*s.*
3. A year-old colt. *dial.*
1787 GROSE *Prov. Gloss.*, *Hoggets*, hog-colts, colts of a year old. *Hants.*
4. *attrib.*
1841 *Penny Cycl.* XXI. 358/1 The hogget wool is.. finer than the other long wools, and is applicable to many new and valuable purposes. **1842** BISCHOFF *Woollen Manuf.* (1862) II. 154 When the lamb has not been shorn, the fleece taken off the succeeding summer is called hogget, or teg wool.

hoggett, var. *hoghead*, obs. f. HOGSHEAD.

hoggie, Sc. dim. of HOG; obs. f. *hoja*, KHOJA.

'**hoggin.** [perh. the same as *hogging* s.v. HOG *v.*[1] quot. 1852–61.] Screened or sifted gravel.
1852–61 *Archit. Publ. Soc. Dict.* iv. 64 Hoggin is the term applied to the siftings or screenings.. separated from the stones of rough pit gravel, and used for cushions, while the stone or 'ballast' is used for the carriage-ways. **1886** *Times* 22 Jan. 4 A coat of binding material, usually hoggin, is spread over the surface.. of road. **1892** *Pall Mall G.* 9 Sept. 2/1 There is [in a filter-bed] a foot of coarse gravel, six inches of fine hoggin, and three feet of sand.

hogging *vbl. sb.* and *ppl. a.*: see under HOG *v.*[1]

hogging-frame. The same as HOG-FRAME.
1864 in WEBSTER.

hoggish ('hɒgɪʃ), *a.* [f. HOG *sb.*[1] + -ISH.] Of, belonging to, or characteristic of a hog or pig; swinish, piggish; coarsely self-indulgent or gluttonous; filthy; mean, selfish.
1548 THOMAS *Ital. Dict.* (1567), *Ciacco*, an hoggysh or slouenly man. **1552** HULOET, Hoggish, or of a hogge, *porcarius, porcinus.* **1581** PETTIE tr. *Guazzo's Civ. Conv.* II. (1586) 109 b, Those shew themselves most hoggish and cruel to strangers. **1590** SPENSER *F.Q.* II. xii. 86 Grylle.. did him miscall That had from hoggish forme him brought to naturall. **1610** HOLLAND *Camden's Brit.* I. 375 Folke would say of one.. unmannerly after an Hoggish kind, that he was borne at Hocknorton. **1711** SHAFTESB. *Charac.* (1714) III. 228 Is not a hoggish Life the height of some Mens Wishes? **1842** TENNYSON *St. Sim. Styl.* 174 With colt like whinny and with hoggish whine They burst my prayer.
Hence '**hoggishly** *adv.*; '**hoggishness.**
1576 GASCOIGNE *Diet Droonkardes* (1789) 7 They are all eyther hoggishly dronke.. or else they become Asses. **1622** MABBE tr. *Aleman's Guzman d'Alf.* II. 90 This hoggishnesse of his, this his vncivill carriage.. did much trouble me. **1771** SMOLLETT *Humph. Cl.* Let. to Lewis 28 Apr., Well! there is no nation that drinks so hoggishly as the English. **1864** LOWELL *Fireside Trav.* 259 *Santo diavolo*! but what hoggishness!

'**hoggism.** *nonce-wd.* Hoggish condition.
1786 WOLCOTT (P. Pindar) *Bozzi & Piozzi* II. 63 At Corrachatachin's, in hoggism sunk, I got with punch, alas! confounded drunk.

†'**hoggler, hogler.** *Obs. local.* Of uncertain origin and meaning.
Occurs frequently in Churchwardens' Accts. in the s.w. of England. Bp. Hobhouse, Editor of the Croscombe Accts., in which the word occurs constantly, explains it as 'A field labourer of the lowest class'.
1465 *Churchw. Acc. Tintinhull* (Som. Rec. Soc.) 190 Et de Willelmo Warefull et Iohanne Trent de hogelers light hoc anno.. xxij*d.* **1474** *Churchw. Acc. Croscombe* (ibid.) 3 Comes the Webers and bryng in their stoke xij*d.*.. Comes tokers and bryngs in their stoke xij*d.*.. Comes Hoglers and bryngs in there stoke ij*s*, and more encrece x*d.* summa ij*s.* x*d.* **1476** *Ibid.* 4 Comes the Hogglers, and presents in of old and new .. iij*s.* x*d.*.. and they received ayen for a stoke.. ij*s.* Comes the maydens and bryng in of encres cler ix*d.* **1516** *Ibid.* 34 The maidens, young men, hoglers, tokers, and the pascale xxxvij*s.* j*d.*
So '**hoggling** (also **hokelyng**), the practice or action of the hogglers; also *attrib.* **hoggling-money**, the contribution of the hogglers to the parish chest; **hoggling-light**, app. a light (in the church) maintained by the hogglers: cf. quot. 1465 above.
1498 *Churchw. Acc. Pilton* (Som. Rec. Soc.) 65 Item receved of hoglyng money of our lady wardens vj*s.* **1510** *Ibid.* 57 Item for Issabell Man for hokelyng ly3ghte ij*d.* *Ibid.* 59 The Dettes that remayneth the said yere: Item Iohn Elyns for hokelyng a yere and a half. **1511** *Ibid.* 63 Item Iohn Elyns for hoggelyng lyght ij*s.* **1516** *Churchw. Acc. St. Michael's, Bath* (ibid.) 229 Venditio et incrementum forinsecum de la Hogeling. **1612** *Churchw. Acc. Cheddar* in *N. & Q.* 3rd Ser. III. 423 Received for the Hogling monie, ix*l.* xiij*s.* iiij*d.* **1626** *Churchw. Acc. Dursley, Gloucestersh.* in *Scott. Antiq.* (1890) June 40 For hoggling 19*s.* 5*d.*

hoggotton, obs. form of HAQUETON, ACTON.
1516 *Sc. Ld. High Treas. Accts.* in Pitcairn *Crim. Trials* I. 265* *note*, Blak vellous to be hoggottonnis.

hog gum. [f. HOG *sb.*[1] + GUM *sb.*] A kind of gum or resin obtained from various trees in the West Indies, etc. Hence **hog-gum tree.**
Among the trees said to yield the gum are *Moronobea coccinea*, *Rhus Metopium*, and *Clusia flava* of Jamaica, *Hedwigia balsamifera* of San Domingo, and, according to some, *Symphonia globulifera* of Guyana.
1756 P. BROWNE *Jamaica* 177 The Hog-gum tree. This tree is well known for its medicinal gum, to which the very hogs are said to have recourse when wounded in the woods. **1858** HOGG *Veg. Kingd.* 149 *Clusia flava*, the Yellow Balsam Tree, is a native of Jamaica.. This too yields a resinous juice, which is sometimes used among the negroes as a vulnerary, and was considered to be the Hog Gum. *Ibid.* 241 *R[hus] metopium* yields a great quantity of gummy resin.. and this it is which is considered by some the Doctor's Gum, or Hog gum of Jamaica. *Ibid.* 254 *Hedwigia balsamifera* is found in the woods and mountains of St. Domingo, and there called *Bois de cochon* or *Wild Boar's Tree*, because, it is said, these animals, when wounded, strip off the bark and heal their wounds by rubbing against the gum which exudes from it, and hence it may be regarded as another source of the Hog Gum. **1866** *Treas. Bot.*, *Moronobea coccinea*, the Hog Gum tree, is a lofty straight-stemmed tree.

hogh, -e, hoȝ, early ff. HEUGH, HOE *sb.*[1], HOUGH.

hoȝe, var. HOW *sb.* and *v.*, *Obs.*

hoghe, hoȝe, ME. form of HO *v.*[3], to care.

hoghefull, var. of HOFUL, careful. *Obs.*

†**hoghenhine, hogenhine, agenhine.**
Barbarous forms, handed down in the Law books, of early ME. *oȝen hine*, lit. own domestic (hind), member of one's own family (see HIND *sb.*[2] 2).
12.. *Laws of Edw. Conf.* c. 23 (Schmid) Habeat eum ad rectum tanquam de propria familia, quod Angli dicunt 'tuua nicte geste þe þirdde nicte aȝen hine' [*Holkham MS.* tuo niht gest þe þridde oȝen hine; *Hoveden*, Tvain nithes gest thrid nith hawan man, *Lambard*, Twa niȝht ȝest, þrid niȝht aȝen hine.] *c* **1250** BRACTON III. II. x, Prima nocte dici poterit *uncuth*, secunda vero *gust*, tertia nocte *hog-henehyne*. **1607** COWELL *Interpr.*, *Hoghenhine*, is he that commeth guestwise to a house, and lieth there the third night. After which time he is accounted of his familie in whose house he lieth. **1619** DALTON *Country Just.*, The 3rd night is called an *Hogenhine* or *Agenhine*.. and if he offend the King's Peace his Oast must be answerable for him. **1848** WHARTON *Law Lex.* 662/2 The third night, an agenhinde, a domestic.

†**hogherd** ('hɒghəd). *Obs.* [f. HOG *sb.*[1] + HERD *sb.*[2]] A swineherd.
c **1380** WYCLIF *Wks.* (1880) 149 To.. fle in-to an hogherdis office. **1382** *Pol. Poems* (Rolls) I. 269 As it were an hog- hyerd hyand to toun. **1562** J. HEYWOOD *Prov. & Epigr.* (1867) 214 Where hogis be parishioners, hogherd must be best. *a* **1704** T. BROWN *2 Oxford Schol.* Wks. 1730 I. 9 A wonderful encouragement indeed 'tis for a man to turn Country Parson! May I rather be a Hogherd.

'**hoghood.** The condition of a hog.
1837 CARLYLE *Fr. Rev.* III. I. vii, Many a Circe Island, with.. temporary conversion into beasthood and hoghood.

hogi, -gia, obs. ff. *hoja*, KHOJA, a teacher.

hog in armour.
1. An awkward or clumsy person, stiff and ill at ease in his attire. (Hence Thackeray's 'Count Hogginarmo' in *Rose and Ring* xiii.)
1660 HOWELL *Eng. Prov.* 19 He looketh like a Hogg in armour. **1774** *Westm. Mag.* II. 457, I never see Alderman —— on horseback, but he reminds me of an hog in armour; and yet a knowledge of dress is what this man has been all his life aiming to acquire. **1857** TROLLOPE *Three Clerks* (1860) 289 But he did not carry his finery like a hog in armour, as an Englishman so often does when an Englishman stoops to be fine.
b. An unwieldy iron-clad ship.
1865 *Examiner* 11 Mar. 146/2 If these vessels are made as proposed, to combine the greatest speed with the most efficient armament, they will be far superior to the slugs with iron skins, and the huge, unwieldy hogs-in-armour.
2. The nine-banded armadillo, *Dasypus* or *Tatusia novemcinctus*, of Central and N. America.
1729 *Collect. Voy.* IV. iv. 96 Here is.. a little Animal that is somewhat less than a Land-Turtle, having a jointed shell on his Back.. the Spaniards call it a *Hog in Armour*. **1834** *Blackw. Mag.* XXXVI. 40/2 Why, they have two monkeys on board, and a kangaroo, and a hog in armour.

'**hog-ˌkilling.** [HOG *sb.* 12 b.] The killing of a pig. ***hog-killing time*** U.S., the time when pigs are killed; a time of special enjoyment; also *absol.*

1817 in A. Royall *Lett. fr. Alabama* (1830) 36 It was hog-killing day at Wills. *a* **1883** G. W. BAGBY *Old Virginia Gentleman* (1910) 96 They are the fixtures used at hog-killing time. **1879** *Harper's Mag.* Nov. 812/1, I..was as big as a dog at hog-killing. **1903** A. ADAMS *Log of Cowboy* xiii. 83 According to their report the boys had had a hog-killing-time. **1927** H. A. VACHELL *Dew of Sea* etc. 259 When I ask my friends to have a hog-killing-time with me, I foot all bills. **1933** *Amer. Speech* VIII. 49/2 *Hog-killing*, any sort of hilarious celebration or jollification. We-all shore did have a hawg-killin' time over t' th' dance t'other night. **1951** *Publ. Amer. Dial. Soc.* XIV. 37 Hog killing time is a season of severe and lasting cold weather, required for the preserving of the meat; also a time of plenty and rejoicing.

'hog-like, *a.* Like or resembling a hog.

1800 G. SHAW *Zool.* I. 21 Short-tailed brown Baboon.. with black naked hog-like face. **1849** *Sk. Nat. Hist., Mammalia* III. 64 This animal is hog-like in its figure.

hogling ('hɒglɪŋ). [f. HOG *sb.*[1] + -LING.]

1. A young or little pig.

a **1440** *Sir Eglam.* 548 My lytylle spote hoglyn, Dere boght thy dethe schalle bee! **1549** CHALONER *Erasm. on Folly* B iv, Slicke and smothe skinned..lyke hoglyngs of Acarnania. **1583** STANYHURST *Æneis* III. (Arb.) 83 A strange sow..dug dieting her mylckwhit farroed hoglings.

2. A young hog (sheep), hoggerel, or hogget.

1890 *Scott. Antiq.* June 40 'Hogling' is a well-known term for a lamb, as 'hog' is for a young sheep.

3. 'An apple turn-over' (Halliwell 1847–78).

a **1825** FORBY *Hoglin*, a homely kind of pastry.

†**4.** *attrib.* or *adj.* (?) Hoggish, hog-like. *Obs.* (Perh. does not belong here.)

c **1645** HOWELL *Lett.* II. ix. (1655) I. 78 Yet I am sorry.. that..Marquis Spinola should in a hogling way, change his Master for the time.

'hog-louse [f. HOG *sb.*[1] (in reference to its shape) + LOUSE.] The woodlouse, *Oniscus asellus*.

1587 MASCALL *Govt. Cattle* (1627) 15 A small red worme, round, and full of legges, much like a hogge lowse. **1605** B. JONSON *Volpone* V. ii, He Will crumpe you, like a hog-louse, with the touch. **1743** T. LORD in *Phil. Trans.* XLII. 522 A few of one Sort, which rolled themselves up like Millepedes, or Hog-lice. **1805** PRISC. WAKEFIELD *Dom. Recreat.* I. (1806) 19 Hog-lice are used as medicine.

†**'hogmace.** *Obs.* A name given (at Sandwich, Kent) to the staff of office of that serjeant-at-mace, who was hog warden; also to the officer himself.

1792 W. BOYS *Hist. Sandwich* 689, 1559..The hogmace to have one yard [of cloth] for his coat. *Ibid.* 785 The hog-mace, or sergeant at brazen mace, is first mentioned in 1471. He bears a stout staff with a brazen head. **1881** JEWITT in *Art Jrnl.* 105 In 1452 an overseer of the streets was appointed 'who is to have a gown and a salary of 20s. a year; he is to bear the Hog Mace, to wait upon the mayor, &c.'

†**'hogman.** *Obs.* A name given in the Household Book of Edw. IV to the bread for the king's horses made from the bran of a bushel of flour.

a **1483** *Liber Niger* in *Househ. Ord.* (1790) 69 Office of Bakehouse hathe a Sergeaunt..yett myght there be made alweyes of a busshell xxix loves..The sergeaunt of thys office to make continually of every busshell xxvii loves.. Memorand', that the other twene loves be called under the name of Hogman, whiche mought be made according to service to be delyvered for the Kinges horses.

hogmanay ('hɒgməˈneɪ). *Sc.* and *north. Eng.* Forms: 7 **hogmynae,** 8 **hagmane, -menai,** 8–9 **hagmena, -menay, (hagman heigh), hogmanay,** (9 **hogmena, -menay, -maney, hanganay**). [Of obscure history, noted only from 17th c. App. of French origin: see note below.]

The name given in Scotland (and some parts of the north of England) to the last day of the year, also called 'Cake-day'; the gift of an oatmeal cake, or the like, which children expect, and in some parts systematically solicit, on that day; the word shouted by children calling at friends' houses and soliciting this customary gift.

c **1680** [see b]. **1693** *Scotch Presbyt. Eloq.* (1738) 120 It is ordinary among some Plebeians in the South of Scotland, to go about from Door to Door upon New-Year's Eve, crying Hagmane. **1790** *Gentl. Mag.* LX. I. 499/1 Concerning the origin of the expression 'Hagman Heigh'. *Ibid.*, In.. Scotland, and in the North of England, till very lately, it was customary for every body to make and receive presents amongst their friends on the eve of the new year, which present was called an *Hagmenay*. *Ibid.* II. 616/2 On the last night of the old year (peculiarly called *Hagmenai*). **1792** *Caledonian Mercury* 2 Jan. (Jam.), The cry of *Hogmanay Trololay* is of usage immemorial in this country. **1805** J. NICOL *Poems* I. 27 (Jam.) The cottar weanies, glad an' gay ..Sing at the doors for hogmanay. **1825** BROCKETT s.v. *Hagmena*, The poor children in Newcastle, in expectation of their hogmena, go about from house to house knocking at the doors, singing their carols, and [saying] 'Please will you give us wor hogmena'. **1826–41** R. CHAMBERS *Pop. Rhymes Scot.* (1858) 295 The children on coming to the door, cry 'Hogmanay!' which is in itself a sufficient announcement of their demands. *Ibid.* 296 Cries appropriate to the morning of Hogmanay..'Get up, goodwife, and shake your feathers, And dinna think that we are beggars; For we are bairns come out to play, Get up and gie's our hogmanay.' **1827** HONE *Table-Bk.* I. 7 The *Hagman Heigh* is an old custom observed in Yorkshire on new year's eve. **1830** SCOTT *Jrnl.* II. 360 We spent our Hogmanay pleasantly enough. **1884** *St. James's Gaz.* 27 Dec. 6/1 Seasonable mummery..was reserved for Hogmanay. **1890** *Scott. Antiq.* June 40 This is the sort of thing they used to sing as their 'Hagmena Song' in Yorkshire. **1893** HESLOP *Northumb. Gloss.* s.v., In North Northumberland the *hogmanay* is a small cake given to children on Old Year's Day; or the spice bread and cheese, with liquor, given away on the same day. **1897** E. W. B. NICHOLSON *Golspie* 100–108.

b. *attrib.* and *Comb.*, as ***hogmanay cake, day, night, concert, song,*** etc.

c **1680** in Law *Mem.* 191 *note* [Protest of the Gibbites] They solemnly renounce..Pasch-Sunday, Hallow-even, Hogmynae-night, Valentine's even [etc.]. **1826–41** R. CHAMBERS *Pop. Rhymes Scot.* (1858) 295 A particular individual..has frequently resolved two bolls of [oat]meal into hogmanay cakes. **1864** BURTON *Scot Abr.* I. v. 297 The eve that ushers in the new year is called in Scotland *Hogmanay* Night. **1897** *Westm. Gaz.* 21 Dec. 6/3 On New Year's Eve there is to be a grand Hogmanay concert for the special benefit of patriotic Scots in London.

[Note. *Hogmanay* corresponds exactly in sense and use to OF. *aguillanneuf* 'the last day of the year, new year's gift, the festival at which new year's gifts were given and asked with the shout of *aguillanneuf*.' Of this Godefroy gives many dialect variants and by-forms, as *ang- aguillenneu, aguilloneu, aguilanleu, haguilennef, haguirenleu, haguimenlo,* etc.; in mod.Fr. dialects it survives as *aiguilan, guilané, guilanneau,* in Normandy *hôguignettes, hoguinané,* in Guernsey *hoginono*; it is found in Sp. before 1600 as *aguilando*, now *aguinaldo*, handsel, Christmas-box. Copious examples are given by Godefroy of the phrases 'demander l'aguillanneuf', 'donner l'eguilanneu', 'petiz enffans qui demandoient aguillenleu le jour de l'an dernier', 'aller querant aguillenleu le dernier jour de decembre', 'comme jeunes gens ont accostumé a faire pour querir leur guillenleu', which require only to be translated, with the substitution of *hogmanay*, to be vernacular Sc. expressions. Although the phonetic difference between *aguillanneuf* and the Sc. word is great, the Norman form *hoguinané* is much closer to *hagmané, hogmanay*, and it cannot be doubted that both the custom and the term are from the French.

The French term is explained by Cotgrave, 1611, as '*au-guy-l'an-neuf* ["to the mistletoe the new year"] the voyce of country people begging small presents, or new-yeares-gifts, in Christmas: an ancient tearme of reioycing, deriued from the Druides, who were woont, the first of Ianuarie, to goe vnto the woods, where hauing sacrificed..they gathered Misletow', (etc.). And according to Souchet I. 16 (in Godefroy) 'With us (in la Beauce) people go on new year's day to their relatives' and friends' houses, to solicit gifts, vulgarly called *l'eguilanleu, pour le guy l'an neuf* [for the mistletoe the new year], for that on this day they distribute mistletoe for handsel and as a form of good augury.' But these explanations, with the reference to the *gui* or mistletoe, are now rejected by French scholars as merely 'popular etymology'. The alleged Fr. cry '*Au gui menez, tiri liri, mainte du blanc et point du bis*', cited second-hand in Jamieson, is not to be found in the French author from whom it professes to be quoted, and appears to be a figment.

Schuchardt (*Romania* IV. 253) suggests that Sp. *aguilando*, F. *aguilanleu, guilanlé*, etc., are corruptions of L. *calendæ*; see also Körting *Lateinisch-romanisches Wbch.* art. 324.]

hog mane. [See HOG *v.*[1] 3.] (See quots.) Hence **'hog-maned** *a.*

1804 CHARLOTTE SMITH *Conversations* I. 137 Your poney ..with his new bridle and his hog mane. **1823** CRABB *Technol. Dict.*, *Hogmane*, the mane of a horse when cut short. **1883** MISS BRADDON *Phantom Fort.* II. 201 A fine display of hog-maned ponies. **1884** *Times* (weekly ed.) 29 Aug. 14/2 The hog-maned, crop-tailed little Kerry nag. **1888** *Times* 22 Aug. 14/4, I did not bring the strawberry roan ..here; all I brought was one with a hog mane.

'hog-money. [From the figure of a hog borne on the obverse.] The coinage in circulation in the Somers Isles (now Bermudas) in the beginning of the 17th c. It consisted of copper pieces silvered, of the value of 2*d.*, 3*d.*, 6*d.*, and 1*s.*

[**1624** CAPT. SMITH *Virginia* v. 183 They had for a time a certaine kinde of brasse money with a hogge on the one side, in memory of the abundance of hogges was found at their first landing.] **1883** *Numism. Chron.* Ser. III. III. 117 The peculiar currency known as hog-money, struck for circulation in the plantation of the Somers Isles under the Charter granted to the Bermuda Company by James I in 1609. **1898** MISS RAWLINGS *Brit. Coin.* 204 It is..inferred that these pieces..date from some time between 1616 and 1624, and if this inference is correct the hog money has the honour of being the first coinage of the North American colonies.

†**hognel, hognall.** *Obs. local.* In ***hognel money***, of obscure origin and meaning: cf. *hoggling money*, under HOGGLER.

1546 *Inv. Ch. Goods Surrey* in *Surrey Archæol. Collect.* (1869) IV. 101 Recevid of the hognel money at the ffeast of the Nativitie of our lord God..viijli. xxiijs. vjd. **1784** in *N. & Q.* 4th Ser. II. 275 Mrs. Wright indebted to Richard Basset for keeping a mare four weeks for work, 5s. 6d., by the Hognall monney. **1857** *Ibid.* 2nd Ser. IV. 441 *Hognell*-money seems connected with *hock*-money.

'hog-nose. A name given to some N. American species of ugly but harmless snakes of the genus *Heterodon*. More fully ***hog-nose snake***.

1736 MORTIMER in *Phil. Trans.* XXXIX. 257 *Anguis capite Viperino*: The Hog-Nose Snake. **1796** MORSE *Amer. Geog.* I. 219 Bluish Green Snake with a stretched out triangular nose, or Hognose Snake, *Coluber mycterizans*. **1842** DE KAY *Zool. N. York* III. *Reptiles* 51–2 The Hog-nosed Snake, *Heterodon platyrhinos*. This well known species has a venomous aspect..It is also called..*Hog-nose*.

So **hog-nosed** *a.*, in ***hog-nosed boa, snake***.

1802 SHAW *Zoology* III. 361 Hog-nosed Boa. *Boa Contortrix*..a native of North America. **1842** [see above].

'hog-nut.

1. *U.S.* The fruit of the Broom Hickory, *Carya porcina*; also the tree.

1829 LOUDON *Encycl. Plants* 794 The Americans make very good and durable brooms by slitting into narrow slips the very tough wood of *Juglans glabra*, which is called pig or hog-nut, also broom hickory. **1866** *Treas. Bot.* 228/2 The Pig or Hog-nut, or Broom Hickory, *C[arya] porcina*, is a noble tree seventy or eighty feet high.

2. The Earth-nut or Pig-nut, *Bunium flexuosum*.

1771 WARNER *Plantæ Woodfordienses* 20 Hawk-nut, or rather Hog-nut. **1879** in PRIOR *Plant-n.*

hogo ('həʊgəʊ). *Obs.* Also 7 **hough goe, how go, hogow, hogou, huggo,** 7–8 **hogoe, hogoo.** See also HAUT-GOUT. [prop. *hogoo*, anglicized spelling of F. *haut goût* high savour or flavour.]

1. †**a.** A high or piquant flavour, a relish: = HAUT-GOUT 1. *Obs.*

1653 WALTON *Angler* vii. 159 To give the sawce a hogoe, let the dish (into which you let the Pike fall) be rubed with it [garlick]. **1657** R. LIGON *Barbadoes* (1673) 79 A greater Hough goe is not in the world. **1660** M. GRIFFITH *Fear of God & King* 76 (T.) The hogo of his delicious meats and drinks. **1688** R. HOLME *Armoury* III. 80/1 They..please the Pallet with a dellicate Ho-goo.

b. A 'high' or putrescent flavour; an offensive taste or smell; a taint; a stench, stink.

1654 GAYTON *Pleas. Notes* II. iii. 42 His Arme-pits..gave a stronger Hogo. **1669** W. SIMPSON *Hydrol. Chym.* 145 In sulphur are ferments, hogo's, smells. **1670** *Mod. Acc. Scotl.* in *Harl. Misc.* VI. 136 Their meat not affecting their distempered palates, without having a damnable hogoe. **1744–50** W. ELLIS *Mod. Husbandm.* IV. III. 36 It is mixed.. with fresh Oil to lessen its Hogo, or stinking Scent. *a* **1852** MOORE *Case Libel* iv, To keep the sulphurous hogo under. **1922** JOYCE *Ulysses* 368 Come near. Then get a hogo you could hang your hat on.

†**c.** *fig. Obs.*

1685 CROWNE *Sir C. Nice* IV. 33 Lock up the women till they'r musty, better they shou'd have a Hogo, than their reputations. **1719** D'URFEY *Pills* III. 177 That her Honesty sells for a Hogo of Honour.

†**2.** A highly flavoured dish: = HAUT-GOUT 3. *Obs.*

1649 C. WALKER *Hist. Independ.* II. To Rdr. 3 It must be a mixture, a Hogo of all Relishes. **1656** *Choyce Drollery* 34 (N.) Witnesse all who Have ever been at thy ho-go. **1730–6** BAILEY (folio), *Hogoe* (in Cookery), a Mess so called from its high savour or relish.

'hog-pen. *U.S.* [HOG *sb.* 13.] A pen or enclosure for swine.

1640 in *Maryland Hist. Mag.* (1910) V. 374 The Neck of Land called hog penn Neck. **1663** *Springfield* (Mass.) *Rec.* I. 312 There is granted to Rowland Thomas 6 acres of the low land on hog pen dingle below ye place where hog pen was. **1695** *Lond. Gaz.* No. 3048/4 A convenient Still-house ready fitted with Stills, Coppers, Hogpenns. **1769** in *Maryland Hist. Mag.* (1917) XII. 285 If the bounds of the Hog pen cannot be found. **1837** *Southern Lit. Messenger* III. 238 Cornwallis's cave is converted to a hog-pen. **1874** *Rep. Vermont Board Agric.* II. 512 In said basement I have my hog-pen. **1964** *Publ. Amer. Dial. Soc.* XLII. 21 All [pigs] may live in a *pigpen* or a *hogpen*.

attrib. **1850** *Rep. U.S. Comm. Patents, Agric. 1849* 122 Leached ashes, hen-house and hog-pen refuse are very valuable fertilizers.

'hog-plum. The fruit of species of *Spondias*, esp. *S. lutea*, found in the West Indies and Brazil, where it is a common food for hogs. Also the tree, more fully called ***hog-plum tree***.

1697 DAMPIER *Voy.* (1729) I. 123 They have abundance of large Hog-plumb Trees, growing about their Houses. **1725** SLOANE *Jamaica* II. 127 Hog plum.—The wood is soft and used for cork. **1756** P. BROWNE *Jamaica* 229 The Hog-Plumb Tree..The fruit..supplies the principal part of the food of the wild hogs in the season. **1858** HOGG *Veg. Kingd.* 247 The Hog-Plums (*Spondias*)..of the West Indies and South America..produce fruit which is eatable.

b. In North America applied to several other fruits and the trees that bear them, as the wild-lime of Florida (*Ximenia*), the Chickasaw plum (*Prunus angustifolia*), etc.

1889 FARMER *Americanisms, Hog plum* (*Ximenia*) a tall growing bush found in South Florida, the fruit of which is in size and shape like a plum, and pleasant to the palate.

hogpoch, -pot, obs. ff. HODGE-PODGE, -POT.

'hog-reeve. *U.S.* [f. HOG *sb.*[1] + REEVE.] An officer charged with the prevention or appraising of damages by stray swine; a field-driver. Formerly a town officer in New England; the office is now merely nominal.

1759 *Amherst Rec.* (1884) 21/1 Joseph Clark..John Petty sworn Hog Riffs. **1780** *Ibid.* 77/2 Voted—Israel Dickinson ..Benjamin Smith Hogreeves. **1837–40** HALIBURTON *Clockm* (1862) 138, I wonder, says he, if there's are a hogreave here, because if there be I require a turn of his office. **1888** BRYCE *Amer. Commw.* II. II. xlviii. 229 Hog reeves (now usually called field drivers).

hogrel, var. of HOGGEREL.

'hog-round. *U.S.* (See quot. 1899.)

1819 *Amer. Farmer* (Baltimore) I. 142 Bacon the hog round, 12 to 13 [dollars]. **1835** *Louisville Publ. Adv.* 14 Feb., 8000 lbs bulk pork, hog round..for sale. **1886** *Harper's Mag.* 206/2 Lard, made from hog-round. **1899** B. W. GREEN *Word Bk. Virginia* 189 Hams, shoulders and middlings have different prices, but when taken altogether at one price, it is so much hog-round.

hog's back, var. HOGBACK.

hog's bean, 'hog-bean. *Herb.* **a.** The Sea Starwort, *Aster Tripolium*. **b.** 'An old name for *Globularia*' (Miller *Plant-n.* 1884). **c.** A rendering of the word *Hyoscyamus*.

1597 GERARDE *Herbal* II. lxxxviii. 334 About Harwich it [*Aster Tripolium*] is called Hogs beanes, for that the swine doe greatly delight to feede thereon: as also for that the knobs about the rootes do somwhat resemble the Garden Beane. **1611** COTGR., *Turbit*,..sea Starrewort, blue Daisie or Camomill, Hogs-beanes. **1706** PHILLIPS (ed. Kersey), *Hogs-beans, Hogs-bread*, and *Hogs-fennel*, several sorts of Herbs. **1866** *Treas. Bot.*, *Hyoscyamus*, this name is the Latinised version of the ancient Greek name for the common Henbane, and literally signifies hog-bean.

hog-score. *Curling.* Also hog's score. [f. HOG *sb.*^{1} 10 + SCORE.] A distance-line drawn across the rink at about one-sixth of the rink's length from the tee, which a stone must cross in order to count in the game. Also *fig.*

1787 BURNS *Tam Samson* v, He was the king o' a' the core To guard, or draw, or wick a bore..But now he lags on death's hog-score, Tam Samson's dead. **1812** *Sporting Mag.* XL. 51. **1857** *Chambers's Inform.* II. 684/2 No sweeping to be allowed by any party till the stone has passed the hog's score.

hog's fennel. A name given to some weeds with fennel-like leaves: **a.** Sow-fennel, *Peucedanum officinale*: **b.** Mayweed, *Anthemis Cotula*.

1585 HIGINS tr. *Junius' Nomenclator* 129/2 *Libanotis*.. Hogs fenel, or beares roote. **1591** PERCIVALL *Sp. Dict.*, *Ervato*, maidenweede, hogfenell, *peucedanum*. **1608** TOPSELL *Serpents* (1658) 618 Of green hogs-fennel take the lowest branches. **1614** MARKHAM *Cheap Husb.* I. (1668) Table Hard Words, Mayth is a Weed that grows among corn, and is called of some Hogs-fennel. **1763** WATSON in *Phil. Trans.* LIII. 23 He..directs the patient..to be rubbed ..with the juice of *Peucedanum*, or hogs-fennel. **1822–34** *Good's Study Med.* (ed. 4) II. 590 A composition of arsenic, sulphur, hogs-fennel..and crows-foot.

hogshead ('hɒgzhɛd). Forms: 4–6 **hoggeshed**, (4 **hoogeshed**, 5 **hoggishede**, **hoggys hed**, **hogges heed**, **hoggesyde**), 6 **hoggesheed**, **hoggis heed**, **hogyshed**, 6–7 **hoggeshead**, 6– **hogshead**, (6 **hogs(h)ed**, **-heed**, 7 **hogs-head**, **hogs-hede**); also β. (6 **hoggett**), 7 **hoghead**, *Sc.* 6–7 **hogheid(d**, 7 **hodghead**. [f. *hog's* poss. of HOG *sb.*^{1} + HEAD^{1}. The reason of the name is uncertain.

The English word was taken later, in a disguised form, into most of the Teutonic languages, viz. early mod.Flem. and Du. *oxhooft* 'tonneau ou muid de France' (Plaintijn 1573), *hockshoot*, *ockshood*, *oghshood* 'dolium, *Angl.* hoggheshead' (Kilian 1599), mod.Du *okshoofd*, *oxhooft* (Hexham, 1678), MLG. *hukeshovet*, LG. *okshôfd*, Ger. *oxhoft*, Da. *oxehoved*, Sw. *oxhufvud*. In Sw. and Da. this is equivalent to 'ox-head', and the first element in Ger. also takes the form of 'ox'; but in LG. and Du. (where the word for 'ox' is *os*, formerly *osse*), *oxhooft* is meaningless as a native formation, while the early variants *hukeshovet*, *hockshoot*, *-hood*, more closely approach the English. The OF. *hoguette* 'petit tonneau,' cited by Godefroy from a charter of Henry V of Engl., has app. no standing or origin in Fr.: cf. the Eng. variant *hoghead*, Sc. *hoggit*, *huggit*, in *Suppl. to Jamieson*.]

1. A large cask for liquids, etc.; *spec.* one of a definite capacity, which varied for different liquids and commodities. See sense 2.

1390 *Earl Derby's Exp.* (Camden) 23 Clerico panetrie per manus Fyssher pro ij barellis et j hoogeshed vacuis per ipsum pro floure imponendo xviij *d.* **1392** *Ibid.* 156 Diuersis hominibus de Linne pro xiiij doliis vacantibus, ij pipes, v hoggeshedes..dolium ad ij *s.* ij *d.*, pipa ad xx *d.*, hoggeshedz ad xij *d.* **1423** *Rolls Parlt.* IV. 256/1 Tonnes, Pipes, Tertians, Hoggeshedes of wyn of Gascoign..shulden be of certein mesure..the Terciane IIII^{xx} IIII galons, the Hoggeshede III^{xx} III galons. *a* **1467** GREGORY *Chron.* 207 They fulle ungoodely smote owte the heddys of the pypys and hoggys hedys of wyne, that men wente wete-schode in wyne. **1578** in *10th Rep. Hist. MSS. Comm.* App. v. 428 Marchauntes shall not..marke any signe or signes upon anye pipe, bout, or hogsed. **1674** tr. *Scheffer's Lapland* x. 44 A garland.. about as big as the hoop of an hogshead. **1706** PHILLIPS (ed. Kersey) s.v., In Fortification Hogsheads fill'd with Earth serve to make Breast-works, to cover the Men. **1781** GIBBON *Decl. & F.* III. lxviii. 716 Innumerable fascines, and hogsheads, and trunks of trees, were heaped on each other. **1868** E. EDWARDS *Raleigh* I. vi. 97 Some of his trees were excellently fitted to make hogsheads.

β. **1577** in *Glasgow Burgh Rec.* (1832) 88 To ressave..ten hogheids, blawin and ticht, and to paye..twa schillingis for þe grathing of ilk ane þairof. **1644** Z. BOYD *Gard. Zion* in *Zion's Flowers* (1855) App. 10/1 Which..Blowes up the bung, or doth the Hodghead rent. **1687** WOOD *Life* 3 Sept. (O.H.S.) III. 228 The conduit..had a hoghead or vessell of clarret in it.

2. Hence, Such a caskful of liquor; a liquid measure containing 63 old wine-gallons (equal to 52½ imperial gallons). Abbreviated hhd.

This content was prescribed by a statute of 1423: see quot. in 1. The London hogshead of beer contained 54 gallons, that of ale 48 gallons; elsewhere the hogshead of ale or beer contained 51 gallons. ('Now seldom used of beer, but almost invariably of cider.' *Encycl. Dict.*)

1483 *Act 1 Rich. III*, c. 13 Euery hogshead to containe lxiij gallons. And euery barrell to containe xxxj gallons and an halfe. **1500** *Chron. Calais* (Camden) 50 Dyverse sortes of wyne, and ij hogshedys of ypocras. **1510** *H. Ld. Clifford's Househ. Bk.* (in *Craven Dial.* 1828), Itm payd at London.. to John Browne for a tonne of wyne, yᵗ ys to say v hogs-heeds of white and two of clared v. li. **1587** HARRISON *England* II. vi. (1877) I. 159 Hereof we make three hogges-heads of good beere. **1599** NASHE *Lenten Stuffe* 47 Hauing a drop or two of pitty left of the huge hogshead of teares they spent for Hero and Leander. **1713** STEELE *Englishm.* No. 8. 56, I sell it by the Gallon, as cheap as you can buy it any where by the Hogshead. **1749** REYNARDSON in *Phil. Trans.* XLVI. 65 The liquid Bushel is not 64, but 63 Pounds or Pints; eight whereof make the Hogshead equal to 63 Gallons. **1825** J. NICHOLSON *Operat. Mechanic* 54 By means of pumps a horse can raise 250 hogsheads of water, 10 feet high, in an hour. **1862** ANSTED *Channel Isl.* IV. App. A. (ed. 2) 566 The hogshead of cider in Jersey contains sixty gallons. **1897** *Whitaker's Alm.* 424 Of wines imported in casks the following are the usual measurements..Hogs-head of Claret 46; Port, 57; Sherry, 54; Madeira, 46 gallons.

β. **1499–1500** *Durham MS. Burs. Roll*, In v doliis et uno hoggett vini rubij. **1634** in *Glasgow Burgh Rec.* (Rec. Soc.) I. 23 Twa hogheidis of wine to the Bischope.

b. Of other commodities: A cask of capacity varying according to the contents and locality.

In later use varying from 100 to 140 gallons; the hogshead of molasses was in 1749 fixed at 100 gallons.

1491 *Vitas Patr.* (W. de W. 1495) I. cxxiv. 142bb, He sente..a thousande hogges heedes of beenes & peesen to make potage wyth. **1569** *Irish Act 11 Eliz.* Sess. III. c. 10 in Bolton *Stat. Irel.* (1621) 336 Shall pay..for every such hugshead of beafe fortie shilling sterling. **1745** *De Foe's Eng. Tradesman* iii. (1841) I. 20 Two carts loaded with about 12 hogsheads or casks of molasses. **1776** ADAM SMITH *W.N.* II. v. (1869) I. 378 About ninety-six thousand hogs-heads of tobacco are annually purchased in Virginia and Maryland. **1858** SIMMONDS *Dict. Trade* s.v., The hogshead is at present a large cask used for transporting various articles; for sugar ranging from 14 to 18 cwt. in weight.

β. **1588** in *Glasgow Burgh Rec.* (Rec. Soc.) I. 123 Ane hogheid of beiff.

fig. **1773** in Boswell *Tour to Hebrides* 21 Oct., This man is just a hogshead of sense.

3. Applied to a person with allusion to the animal. *couch a hogshead*: see COUCH *v.*^{1} 1 e.

c **1515** etc. [see COUCH *v.*^{1} 1 e]. **1586** A. DAY *Eng. Secretary* I. (1625) 110 If you delight in a Pigs-nie, you may by receiving of him be sure of a Hogs-head. **1619** R. HARRIS *Drunkard's Cup* 20 Their Parish Priests (as those hogs-heads terme him). **1645** MILTON *Colast.* Wks. (1851) 375 His jabberment in Law, the flashiest and the fustiest that ever corrupted in such an unswill'd hogshead.

4. Humorously applied to the head or lid of a pig-shaped vessel, used as a drinking cup.

1884 *Mag. of Art* Jan. 102 The vessel [a Sussex pig] is filled with liquor..and the head being taken off and filled, each guest is invited to 'drink a hog's-head of beer to the health of the bride'.

5. *attrib.*, as ***hogshead stave***; also **hogshead weight** (see quot.).

1600 HYLL *Arith.* xiii. 66, 112 Poundes weight maketh 1. hundred weight. 5. of those hundreds..1. Hogshead weight. **1772** *Ann. Reg.* 230 That a bounty of six pounds be allowed for every 1800 such hundred of hogshead staves.

'hogship. The personality of a hog.

1860 *Merc. Marine Mag.* VII. 295 Sacrifices were offered to his hogship [a half-hog deity].

hog-skin, hogskin.

1. The skin of a hog; leather made of this, pigskin; chiefly *attrib.*

1673 *Essex Inst. Hist. Coll.* L. 27 A meale trough..a hog-skin, a reele. **1705** *Lond. Gaz.* No. 4178/4 An Hogskin Saddle and curb Bridle. **1858** SIMMONDS *Dict. Trade*, *Hog-skin Saddle*, a superior kind of saddle made from tanned hogskin.

2. The skin of a hog used as a wine-bottle.

a **1700** B. E. *Dict. Cant. Crew*, *Boracho*, a But, a Drunkard, and a Hogskin. **1711** E. WARD *Quix.* I. 372 Till they had drank one Hogskin out.

hog's pudding. The entrail of a hog variously stuffed, according to locality, with a mixture of oatmeal, suet, tripe, etc., or of flour, currants, and spice.

1614 SELDEN *Titles Hon.* 72 As ridiculous a denomination, as Lucanica, signifying a kind of Hogs-pudding. **1712** ADDISON *Spect.* No. 269 ¶8 He had sent a string of Hogs-puddings..to every poor Family in the Parish. **1833** HT. MARTINEAU *Brooke Farm* vii. 87 Bacon in plenty..and hog's-puddings and lard for the children.

hog-stag. *Zool.* The male of the HOG-DEER (sense 1).

1781–5 W. SMELLIE tr. *Buffon's Nat. Hist.* (1791) IV. 111

hogsteer, -ster: see HOGGASTER.

'hogsty. Also **hog's sty**. A pigsty.

c **1475** *Pict. Voc.* in Wr.-Wülcker 803/44 *Hoc porcatorium*, a hogstye. *a* **1529** SKELTON *Merie T.* xiii. in *Shaks. Jest Bk.* (1864) II. 25 He wente & charged one of hys boyes, in an euenyng..to sette fyre in one of hys hogges sties. **1669** WOODHEAD *St. Teresa* II. xvii. 118 He replied, He would dwell not only there, but even in a Hog-stie. **1797** W. JOHNSTON tr. *Beckmann's Hist. Invent.* II. 41 Hog-sties were erected in the streets, sometimes even under the windows. **1821** *Blackw. Mag.* IX. 137 Loud was the grumph and grumble from hog-stye.

'hog-tie, *v.* orig. *U.S.* [HOG *sb.*^{1} 1.] *trans.* To secure by tying the four feet, or the hands and feet, together. Also *fig.*, to fetter.

1894 *Harper's Mag.* Feb. 356 A cow was soon caught.. thrown down, and hog-tied, which means all four feet together. **1903** A. ADAMS *Log Cowboy* xi. 75 We threw him, hog-tied him and rolled him into the water. **1905** A. H. LEWIS *Sunset Trail* i. 3 Something wherewith he might hogtie steers when in the course of duty he must rope and throw them. **1906** S. E. WHITE in *McClure's Mag.* Mar. 518/1 In time he got to be a fairly accurate and very quick shot. The same way with roping and hog-tying and all the rest. **1907** —— *Arizona Nights* III. xii. 300 With a short piece of hard rope the cow-boy always carries to 'hog-tie' cattle, he lashed her wrists together. **1910** W. M. RAINE *B. O'Connor* (1920) xx. 226 He's hogtied to the scenery long enough to do my business. **1924** C. E. MULFORD *Rustlers' Valley* xi. 136 However, just now we got to hog-tie our soarin' spirits. **1926** J. BLACK *You can't Win* xvii. 240 When I was caught in a burglary, overpowered, hog-tied, and waiting for the waggon. **1961** R. P. HOBSON *Rancher takes Wife* xv. 180 We hogtied the three..calves we were caring for and heaved them into the boat. **1968** *Word Study* Oct. 6/1 It often results in the present stupidly allowing itself to be hog-tied by the past. **1972** *Daily Tel.* 2 Nov. 19 Sir Stephen McAdden..said judges were hog-tied by stipulations banning sentences between six and 18 months on people under 21. **1973** J. ASHFORD *Double Run* xv. 132 They thought they'd got him hog-tied whereas in fact he was helping to play them for suckers.

'hog-tie, *sb.* *U.S.* [f. the vb.] The form of securing or fettering produced by 'hog-tying'; a secure hold.

1910 W. M. RAINE *B. O'Connor* (1920) vi. 78 They sure do hate to turn loose a gringo when they have got the hog-tie on him. **1940** E. T. SETON *Trail of Artist-Naturalist* 321 The two cowmen jerked loose the hog-ties, the broncos sprang to their feet, and of course ran away.

hogton(e, var. of *hocton*, *hocqueton*, ACTON.

1535 *Aberdeen Reg.* V. 15 (Jam.) Hat, bonet, gowne, hogton. **1538** *Ibid.* 16.

hog-trough ('hɒgtrɒf, -ɔː-). Also **hog's trough**. **a.** A trough for hogs to feed out of; a pig-trough.

1530 PALSGR. 231/2 Hogges troughe, *auge à pourceaux*. **1592** NASHE *P. Penilesse* (1842) 26 He falls like a hog's trough that is set on one end. **1679** OLDHAM *Sat. Jesuits* IV. 4 Once I was common Wood, a shapeless Log..The Workman yet in doubt, what course to take, Whether I'd best a Saint, or Hog-trough make. **1800** COLERIDGE *Lett.* (1895) 323 A Scotch Hog-trough. **1855** M. M. THOMSON *Doesticks* x. 83 After a long search [I] found him wrapped up in the colors, fast asleep with his head in a hog-trough. **1972** J. S. HALL *Sayings from Old Smoky* 87 Fifty years ago if a younger sister married first, folks would say the older sister 'had to dance in the hog trough'.

b. A trough-like hollow = *hog-wallow* (see HOG *sb.*^{1} 13 a).

1807 A. YOUNG *Agric. Essex* (1813) I. 200, I did not see one false furrow, or any tendency to a hog trough upon his whole farm.

hog-wash. Also **hog's wash**. [See WASH *sb.*] **a.** The swill of a brewery or kitchen given to hogs; pig's-wash.

c **1440** *Jacob's Well* (E.E.T.S.) 81 þey in þe kechyn, for iape, pouryd on here hefd hoggyswasch. **1611** COTGR., *Lavailles*, Swillings, Hogs-wash, washings for Swine. **1708** MOTTEUX *Rabelais* V. xv. (1737) 58 Ten Sows..could swill Hogwash. **1844** COL. HAWKER *Diary* (1893) II. 247 Wine little better than hogwash.

b. Contemptuously applied to weak inferior liquor or any worthless stuff. Esp. applied to inferior writings of any kind.

1712 ARBUTHNOT *John Bull* I. x, Your butler purloins your liquor, and the brewer sells you hogwash. **1773** GARRICK *Let.* 16 Nov. (1831) I. 583 The Fair Quaker, which we agreed to be *skimmed milk*, (nay, hogwash) whipped up into *syllabub*, and swallowed by a foolish audience as if substantial as *roast beef*. **1882** B. HARTE *Flip* ii, That's the sort of hog-wash the old man serves out to you. **1883** —— *In Carquinez Woods* 155 He had 'had enough of that sort of hog-wash ladled out to him for genuine liquor'. **1893** FARMER & HENLEY *Slang* III. 329/2 *Hogwash* ..(journalists').—Worthless newspaper matter. **1912** G. B. SHAW in *Daily News* 22 May 6/5 Exactly the same 'hogwash' ..would have been lavished on the veriest dastards as upon a crew of Grace Darlings. **1930** WYNDHAM LEWIS *Apes of God* v. 161 Yes, man alive, a lousy limited edition of an intellectually-fraudulent book that no one could sell, that no one would want!.. Not even as honest-to-goodness bookstall hogwash. **1939** L. DURRELL *Spirit of Place* (1969) 62 Only look at the faces of cabinet without reading their hogwash and you see that they are a pack of degenerates. **1955** A. HUXLEY *Genius & Goddess* 36 Tripe and hogwash dished out by the moulders of public opinion. **1965** *Spectator* 5 Mar. 293/1 The whole of the artistic world has been debauched by the hogwash of the do-it-yourself vogue.

'hogweed. *Herb.* A name given to various herbs of which hogs are fond, or which are thought fit only for hogs.

1. In England: cow-parsnip, *Heracleum Sphondylium*; knotgrass, *Polygonum aviculare*; sowthistle, *Sonchus*; coltsfoot, *Tussilago Farfara*; hedge parsley, *Torilis Anthriscus*.

1744–50 W. ELLIS *Mod. Husbandm.* III. I. 45 Hogweed, *Heracleum Sphondylium*. **1771** BURKE *Corr.* (1844) I. 260 My experiment of the cultivation of that species of the wild parsnip which they call *hog-weed*, did not answer. **1807** A. YOUNG *Agric. Essex* (1813) II. 87 Hogweed, *Polygonum aviculare*..this weed is a great plague on the bean stubbles. **1858** HOGG *Veg. Kingd.* 379 *Heracleum sphondylium* or Common Cow Parsnip..The whole plant is a wholesome and nourishing food for cattle, and is gathered in Sussex for fattening hogs, and hence called *Hog-weed*.

2. In the West Indies, species of *Boerhaavia*; in U.S. *Ambrosia artemisiæfolia*.

1707 SLOANE *Jamaica* I. 210 Hogweed. Hogs feed on this herb with much delight. **1756** P. BROWNE *Jamaica* 123 Hogweed..is frequently gathered for the hogs, and thought to be a very fattening and wholesome food for them. **1884** MILLER *Plant-n.*, Hog-weed, American, *Ambrosia artemisiæfolia*, *Boerhaavia erecta*, and other species.

3. ***poisonous hogweed***: see quot.

1858 HOGG *Veg. Kingd.* 643 *A*[*ristolochia*] *grandiflora*, a native of the West Indies..The roots are bitter..and are said to be destructive to swine..hence the plant is called Poisonous Hog-weed.

hoh, hoha, obs. ff. HO, *int.*[1] and *sb.*[2]

Hohenzollernism (ˌhəʊənt'sɒlənɪz(ə)m). [a. G. *Hohenzollern*, the name of a family originating from Hohenzollern in southern Germany which became successively electors of Brandenburg, kings of Prussia, and emperors of Germany (see PRUSSIAN B. *sb.* note) + -ISM.] The autocratic spirit or belligerent policies of the Hohenzollern dynasty. So ˌ**Hohen'zollernist** *a.*

1915 *Scotsman* 23 Jan. 12/2 The 'Prussianism' of to-day [is] merely 'Hohenzollernism' grafted on to a subject people. **1919** J. L. GARVIN *Econ. Found. Peace* xi. 252 Let us not think for a moment that such thoughts were associated only with Hohenzollernism, Junkerism, and militarism, and must disappear of themselves if Germany becomes an advanced democracy. **1919** G. B. SHAW *Peace Conference Hints* ii. 19 They were..far more determined to overthrow the Hohenzollernist Junkerdom than the Jingos. **1930** —— *What I Really wrote about War* (1931) 2, I did not want Hohenzollernism to win.

hohl-flute ('həʊlfluːt). [ad. Ger. *hohlflöte*, lit. hollow flute.] An open 8-ft. flute-stop on an organ, having a soft hollow tone resembling that of the Stopped Diapason.

1660 *Specif. Organ Banqueting Room, Whitehall* in Grove *Dict. Mus.* II. 591/1 Great Organ. 1. Open Diapason. 2. Holflute. **1852** SEIDEL *Organ* 21 In 1515..an organ in St. Mary's, at Danzic..contained..stop-diapason, flute..hohl-flute, gems-horn [etc.]. **1880** E. J. HOPKINS in Grove *Dict. Mus.* II. 591/1 'Hol-flute' was the name which Father Smith attached to a metal Stopped Diapason with chimneys.

hohmannite ('həʊmænaɪt). *Min.* [ad. G. *hohmannit* (A. Frenzel 1888, in *Min. und petrogr. Mittheil.* IX. 397), f. the name of Thomas *Hohmann*, mining engineer of Valparaiso, who discovered it: see -ITE[1].] A hydrous basic ferrous sulphate, $FeSO_4(OH).3H_2O$, occurring in triclinic crystals of a brownish red colour that rapidly dehydrate on exposure to air.

1888 *Jrnl. Chem. Soc.* LIV. 923 In a sample of copiapite, from Valparaiso, a new iron sulphate was found, to which the name Hohmannite has been given. **1900** E. S. DANA *Text-bk. Min.* 536 Amarantite. $Fe_2O_3.2SO_37H_2O$... Hohmannite is the same partially altered. **1938** *Amer. Mineralogist* XXIII. 745 On dehydration..hohmannite apparently loses the four loosely held molecules of water and forms what is here called metahohmannite. In this respect it differs from amarantite, which is much more stable under atmospheric conditions. **1968** I. KOSTOV *Mineral.* 499 Amarantite and hohmannite are triclinic-pinacoidal.

ho-ho (hoho). [Chin.] *ho-ho bird*, a mythical bird of pheasant-like appearance used frequently as an emblem of courage.

1901 C. MONKHOUSE *Hist. & Descr. Chinese Porc.* II. 158 It [*sc.* the phoenix] is referred to as the *fong-hoa* or *ho-ho* bird. **1927** W. B. HONEY *Guide Later Chinese Porcelain* 84 The phoenix (*fêng-huang*, the *ho-ho* bird of old catalogues) is apparently related to the sun-bird of Near Eastern and Indian mythology, and was an emblem of the empress. **1963** *Times* 7 May 7/2 A swordguard in silver formed as a Ho-ho bird and Kirin, undercut in the round with gilt details.

Hohokam (həʊhəʊ'kɑːm), *sb.* and *a.* [ad. Pima *hóhokam* those who have gone.] **A.** *sb.* **a.** An extinct people of North American Indians. **b.** The culture of this people, centred in Arizona and flourishing after *c* 450, characterized by irrigated agriculture and houses built in pits. **B.** *adj.* Of or pertaining to this people or culture.

1884 A. F. BANDELIER in *Archæol. Inst. Amer. Rep.* V. 80 The Casa Blanca and all the ruins of the Gila were the abode of the fore-fathers of the Pimas, designated by them as 'Vï-pï-sêt' (great-grandparents), or 'Ho-ho-qom' (the extinct ones). **1912** J. W. FEWKES *Casa Grande, Ariz.* 153 The Pima name Hohókam may be adopted to designate this ancestral stock, to whom may be ascribed the erection of the casas grandes on the Gila. **1937** *Southwestern Lore* Dec. 54 As a result of investigations conducted at Winona Village certain archaeological discoveries have definitely explained the affiliation with the Hohokam Culture. **1940** E. FERGUSSON *Our Southwest* 116 What happened to the early Hohokam people is still in dispute. **1948** A. L. KROEBER *Anthropol.* (ed. 2) xviii. 809 Parallel to the Anasazi development is the Hohokam one of lowland, desert, torrid southern Arizona. *Ibid.*, Ceremonial kivas did not develop among the Hohokam, but there were dugout courts for a ritual ball game.

ho-hum ('həʊhʌm), *int.* [f. HO *int.*[1] + HUM *int.*] = HUM *int.* (usu. as an expression of boredom). Also as *sb.* and *v.* As *adj.*, dull and routine.

1924 *Dialect Notes* V. 270 Oh ho hum (vex[ation] or dis[gust]). **1962** *Listener* 4 Oct. 536/3 Listing last week's dramas I find scarcely enough straw to make a useful brickbat:..the return, ho-hum, of *Maigret*. **1962** *John o' London's* 10 May 460/3 Mr. Ustinov sits there..blinking, double-talking and ho-humming. **1963** M. DUGGAN in C. K. Stead *N.Z. Short Stories* (1966) 101 His mouth served out its lying old hohums. **1969** *Daily Colonist* (Victoria, B.C.) 27 Sept. 2/3 People are pretty ho-hum on most parts of the [Vancouver] Island right now..but if anything does happen, they will be the first to cry for damages. **1973** *Jewish Chron.* 19 Jan. 14/1 So the Composers' Guild of Great Britain wants the Arts Council to twist the arms of orchestral managements to make them perform more works by British composers. Ho-hum.

hoi, *int.*: see HOY.

hoick (hɔɪk), *sb. colloq.* Also hoik. [See next.] **a.** *Rowing.* (See quot. 1898.) **b.** *Aeronaut.* A jerky pull (on the stick). (Cf. HOICK *v.*[1] 2.) **c.** *Cricket.* A jerky, hoisted shot.

1898 *Encycl. Sport* II. 297/1 *Hoick*, a jerk with the arms at the beginning or end of the stroke, which prevents a steady leg drive from the stretcher. **1907** *Daily Chron.* 8 Mar. 9/1 Cambridge sacrifice everything to a terrible hoick at the finish. **1946** A. PHELPS *I couldn't care Less* vi. 43 The Magister responded to my wild hoik on the stick and came off. **1954** A. G. MOYES *Austral. Batsmen* xii. 164 He..gets a lot of runs with a stroke which Cheetham called a 'hoik'. **1956** R. ALSTON *Test Commentary* ix. 60 Lindwall's one scoring stroke was an ungainly 'hoick' for six.

hoick (hɔɪk), *v.*[1] *slang* or *colloq.* Also hoik. [Perhaps orig. a local variant of HIKE *v.*]

1. *trans.* To lift up or hoist, often with a jerk or rapid movement. Also to haul or turn *out*. Also *transf.* and *fig.*

1898 G. NICKALLS in W. A. Morgan *'House' on Sport* 346 Until the finish, which, to be made really effective, must be honestly hoicked out. **1908** BELLOC *On Nothing* 136 Beneath him the sand sloped down until it met the sea... Every now and then Mahmoud would force a son or domestic of his to go down and hoick out a pearl. **1911** *Chambers's Jrnl.* Mar. 146/1 The patient Captain Croucher hoicked her from destruction in the nick of time. **1914** W. J. LOCKE *Fort. Youth* i. 20 He hoicked a bit of his shirt-tail from his breeches and proceeded to knot the cornelian heart secure therein. **1916** J. BUCHAN *Greenmantle* ii. 24, I had got myself adjusted to this trench business... And now you have hoicked me out. **1918** 'Q' *Foe-Farrell* vi, I dashed around to the rear of the cab, collared Farrell, and hoicked him inboard. **1930** BLUNDEN *De Bello Germanico* iii. 28 His cue to 'hoik out' the unwary scrimshankers. **1931** C. MACKENZIE *Buttercups & Daisies* v, Blackbirds and thrushes hoicking worms out of the moist ground. **1934** G. B. SHAW *Too True to be Good* II. 49 The noise stops; and the bicyclist, having hoiked his machine up on to its stand..comes past the pavilion. **1952** WODEHOUSE *Pigs have Wings* v. 99 'Mr. Galahad is in the amber drawing-room.'..'Then go and hoik him out of it.' **1954** W. FAULKNER *Fable* (1955) 66 No need for them to hunt down and hoick out and execute a mere thirteen men. **1962** M. MCLUHAN *Gutenberg Galaxy* 51 This process..hoicks societies of the world of 'sacred' or cosmic space and time into the detribalized or 'profane' space and time of civilized and pragmatic man. **1972** *Country Life* 9 Mar. 548/3 Is there anything conceivably related to the art of fly fishing in hoicking out trout that have had no chance to live a natural life?

2. To force (an aeroplane) to climb steeply to a higher level. Also *intr.*, to jerk oneself *out of*, etc.

a **1918** J. T. B. MCCUDDEN *Five Yrs. R.F.C.* (1919) 287 He..hoicked out of the dive with such vim that three wing-tips at once collapsed. **1919** *Glasgow Herald* 19 Dec. 10 The pilot yanks the joystick to hoick her up. **1928** *Daily Mail* 7 May 6/4 Hoiking.—Sweeping suddenly to avoid an obstacle or a dangerous approach to earth.

hoick, *v.*[2] [Prob. a dial. variant of HAWK *v.*[3]] = HAWK *v.*[3] Hence **'hoicking** *vbl. sb.*

1926 A. HUXLEY *Essays New & Old* 5 These frightful hoickings in the throat. **1926** —— *Jesting Pilate* I. 43 The holy man woke up and began to hoick and spit.

hoicks (hɔɪks), **hoick** (hɔɪk), *int.* (*sb.*) Also 8 hoics, 8- hoix; 8- hoic; 7 hoika. [Origin unknown: it has also the form YOICK, -S.] A call used in hunting to incite the hounds. Also *transf.*

1607 TOPSELL *Four-f. Beasts* (1658) 212 Speaking to his dogs by name, saying 'Now A!' then 'B!' 'Hoika C!' and such like words of art. **1756** FOOTE *Eng. fr. Paris* II. Wks. 1799 I. 110 Hoic a boy, hoic a boy..Hey boy, hoix, my little Buck. **1773** GOLDSM. *Stoops to Conq.* Epil. 13 Then hoiks to jigs and pastimes ev'ry night. **1859** *Art Taming Horses* xii. 199 Cover hoick! i.e. Hark into cover!..And to a particular hound—Hoick, Rector! Hoick, Bonny Lass!

b. *sb.* A cry of 'hoicks!'

1797 MRS. A. M. BENNETT *Beggar Girl* (1813) III. 52 A smacking of whips, coarse laughs, and loud hoic hoics, with shrill hollos.

Hence **hoicks** (hoick) *v.* **a.** *trans.* to incite or salute with 'hoicks!'; **b.** *intr.* to 'hark *back*'.

1762 SMOLLETT *Sir L. Greaves* Misc. Wks. 1806 V. 88 The fox-hunters..hoicksed the speaker, exclaiming,—'Well opened, Jowler—to 'un again, Sweetlips!' **1823** SCOTT *Fam. Lett.* 11 May (1894) II. 172 Come to Abbotsford with him, and we will hoicks back with you again to Rokeby. **1897** *Punch* CXIII. 121/2 Huntsman getting warm, and 'Hoicing'.

hoida, obs. form of HEY-DAY *int.*

hoiden, -on, var. spellings of HOYDEN.

hoie, hoigh. obs. forms of HOY *sb.*[1]

hoif, hoige, obs. forms of HOVE, HUGE.

†**hoigh.** *Obs.* [f. *hoigh*, HOY *int.*: cf. 'on the *qui vive*'.] Excitement; chiefly in phr. *on* (*o'*) *the hoigh*: eager, excited; excitedly, riotously.

1576 GOSSON *Spec. Humanum* iv. in *Sch. Abuse* (Arb.) Notes 77 To set our heartes on hoygh for aye. **1598** R. BERNARD tr. *Terence* (1607) 127 There comes running vpon the hoigh together to meete me, all the hucksters, fish-mongers, butchers. **1607** MIDDLETON *Fam. of Love* III. ii, Young wenches now are all o' the hoigh. **1641** BROME *Joviall Crew* I. Wks. 1873 III. 363, I left the merry Griggs..in such a Hoigh younder! such a frolic!

hoighce, obs. f. HOISE.

hoighdagh, obs. f. HEY-DAY *int.*

hoighty-toighty, var. HOITY-TOITY.

hoika: see HOICKS.

hoil(e, hoill, obs. Sc. ff. HOLE, HOLL *sb.*, WHOLE.

†**hoine, hoyne,** *v. Obs.* or *dial.* [a. OF. *hoigner*, *hogner* (13th c. in Hatz.-Darm.) to whine: cf. Palsgr. '*Je hoigne*, I whyne as a chylde dothe, or a dogge'.] *intr.* To whine; to grunt; to murmur, to mutter; = HONE *v.*[2]

c **1440** *York Myst.* xxx. 309 Yone lordyngis to lose þe Full longe haue thei hoyned [*printed* heyned; *rime* enioyned]. *a* **1529** SKELTON *Agst. Venom. Tongues* 4 Hoyning like hogges, that groynis and wrotes. **1847–78** HALLIWELL, *Hoine*,..to whine. *Linc.*

Hence †**hoinish** *a.*, grunting.

1633 T. ADAMS *Exp. 2 Peter* ii. 14 Worldlings are swine..insatiable in devouring, hoinish and grunting.

hoip, obs. Sc. spelling of HOPE.

‖**hoi polloi** (hɔɪ 'pɒlɔɪ; also pə'lɔɪ). [Gr. οἱ πολλοί, lit. 'the many'.] The majority; the masses. Also formerly in *Univ. slang*, candidates for a pass degree.

In English use normally preceded by the definite article even though *hoi* means 'the'.

[**1668** DRYDEN *Dram. Poesie* 65 If by the people you understand the multitude, the οἱ πολλοί. **1791** [see POLL *sb.*[3]]. *c* **1821–2** BYRON in *Lett.* (1830) I. 633 [We] put on masques, and went on the stage with the οἱ πολλοι.] **1837** J. F. COOPER *Europe* II. 94 After which the *oi polloi* are enrolled as they can find interest. **1855** *Read & Reflect* I. 60 The *hoi polloi* [of Mauritius], as we say at Oxford, are mindless—all blank. **1895** *Brewer's Dict. Phr. & Fable* (new ed.) 613/1 *Hoi Polloi* (*the*), the poll-men in our Universities, that is, those who take their degrees without 'honours'. **1905** *Daily Chron.* 29 Aug. 4/4 A couple of immense swells..staring stiffly at 'hoy-polloy'. **1932** F. L. WRIGHT *Autobiogr.* (1945) III. 256 Now it all ended in this triumph for them, hoi-polloi, rag, tag, and bobtail.

hoir, obs. form of HEIR, HOAR, WHORE.

hoise (hɔɪz), *v. Obs.* exc. *dial.* Pa. t. and pple. **hoised, hoist.** Forms: α. 5 **hysse,** 6 **hyce, hyse.** β. 5- **hoise** (6 **hoighce,** 6–7 **hoyse, hoisse,** 7 **hoiss**). [In 15–16th c. *hysse*, *hyce*, which corresponds with Icel. *hisa*, Norw., Sw. *hissa*, Da. *hisse*, LG. *hiesen*, *hissen* (Chyträus 1582, whence Ger. *hissen*), Du. *hijschen* (*het zeyl ophijsen* to hoise the sail, Hexham 1678); also F. *hisser* (16th c. *hinser*, *inser*, 1611 Cotgr. *yser*), It. *issare* (Diez), Sp. *izar* (1599 Minsheu *hiçar*), Pg. *içar*. It is not yet known in which language this nautical word arose; the English examples are earlier than any cited elsewhere. The β forms *hoighce*, *hoisse*, *hoise*, appear to arise from a broad pronunciation of *hyce*, *hysse*, *hyse* (the mod. repr. of which appears to be the northern HEEZE); they are earlier than the interchange of *oi*, *ī*, in *oil*, *īle*, *boil*, *bīle*, etc. Otherwise, Engl. *oi*, *oy*, is usually of foreign origin, French or Dutch: cf. *rejoice*, *boil*, *toy*, etc.

It is to be noticed that the word appears early as an interjection, being the actual cry of sailors in hauling: Eng. *hissa* (*c* 1450), Sc. *heisau* (*Compl. of Scot.* 1549), Sp. *hiza* (Minsheu 1599), now *iza*, Pg. *iça*, F. *inse! inse!* (Rabelais *c* 1530). These Romanic forms have the appearance of the imperative of the vb. *hizar*, *içar*, *inser*; but whether this is historically so, or whether the vb. was subseq. formed from the cry, is not clear.]

1. *trans.* To raise aloft by means of a rope or pulley and tackle, or by other mechanical appliance. **a.** Orig. *nautical*, and chiefly *to hoise sail*; often with *up*.

α. [*c* **1450** *Pilgr. Sea Voy.* 13 in *Stac. Rome* etc. 37 With 'howe! hissa!' then they [shipmen] cry, 'What howe, mate! thow stondyst to ny, Thy felow may nat hale [= haul] the by'. Cf. also *heisau* in HEEZE *v.* quot. 1549.] **1490** CAXTON *Eneydos* xxxi. 117 They made the saylles to be hyssed vppe. **1517** H. WATSON *Ship of Fools* A ij a, I tourne and hyse the cordes of the shyppe. **1530** PALSGR. 585/1, I hyse up the sayle, as shypmen do, *je haulce*. **1547** SALESBURY *Welsh Dict.*, *Kodi ancor i vyny*, hyce up an ancre. **1549**, etc. [see HEEZE].

β. **1509** HAWES *Past. Pleas.* (1555) 53 Hoyse up thy sayle. *Ibid.* 191 Then their anker they weyed in haste, And hoyst their sayle. *a* **1537** *Batayle Egyngecourte* (printed by J. Skot) A ij b, They hoysed their sayles sadly a lofte A goodly syght it was to se. **1589** GREENE *Menaphon* (Arb.) 58 Eurilochus..willed his men perforce to hoyse him a shipboord. **1610** SHAKS. *Temp.* I. ii. 148 They prepared A rotten carkasse of a Butt..There they hoyst vs To cry to th' Sea. **1615** G. SANDYS *Trav.* 207 We..hoissed sailes for Sidon. **1715–20** POPE *Iliad* I. 624 Then launch, and hoise the mast. **1791** COWPER *Odyss.* xv. 353 They..straining at the halyards, hoised the sail.

absol. **1685** *Roxb. Ball.* (1885) V. 544 We hoised and hast'ned up into the Straits.

†**b.** *to hoise out* (*forth*): to launch, lower (a boat). *Obs.*

1599 HAKLUYT *Voy.* II. 179 To hoise out their skiffe. **1628** *World Encomp. by Sir F. Drake* 18 A boat being therefore hoised forth. **1697–9** DAMPIER *Voy.* an. 1688 (R.) We hoysed out our boat, and took up some of them.

c. In other than nautical use.

1561 DAUS tr. *Bullinger on Apoc.* (1573) 148 b, Hoysing them horribly vp to a gibet. **1613** PURCHAS *Pilgrimage* IV. xvi. 370 Hoising them up and down by the armes with a cord. **1699** DAMPIER *Voy.* (1729) II. I. 48 There stands a Flag Staff, purposely for the hoysing up the English Colours. **1710** SWIFT *Baucis & Philemon* 57 The kettle to the top was hoist, And there stood fasten'd to a joist.

2. To raise aloft, lift up: usually with the notion of exertion; cf. HEEZE *v.*

1548 UDALL *Erasm. Par. Luke* xxiv. 175 Beyng hoighced vp vpon the crosse. **1570** B. GOOGE *Pop. Kingd.* I. 5 b, From the bottom deepe He hoyseth up the weeping soules, in blessed ioyes to sleepe. **1645** MILTON *Colast.* Wks. (1851) 374 The shame of all honest Atturneys, why doe they not hoiss him over the barre, and blanket him? **1690** W. WALKER *Idiomat. Anglo-Lat.* 36 Hoise this fellow on thy back, and carry him in. *a* **1763** SHENSTONE *Colemira* 59 When with nice airs she hoist the pancake round. **1830** J. WILSON *Noct. Ambr.* Wks. 1855 II. 349 Gin I could get a cleik o' the bane .. I might hoise it gently up .. and then pu' it out o' his mouth. **1842** S. LOVER *Handy Andy* xv. 142 'Remember, .. you won't tell we hoised you.'

b. ***hoist with his own petard*** (Shaks.): Blown into the air by his own bomb; hence, injured or destroyed by his own device for the ruin of others.

1604 SHAKS. *Ham.* III. iv. 207 (Qo. 2) Tis the sport to haue the enginer Hoist with his owne petar. **1826** SCOTT *Woodst.* xxxiii, 'Tis sport to have the engineer Hoist with his own petard, as our immortal Shakspeare has it. **1847** DE QUINCEY *Protestantism* Ess. (1858) 138 To see the cruel bibliolater, in Hamlet's words, 'hoist by his own petard'. **1866** GEO. ELIOT *F. Holt* ii. (1868) 30 They shall be hoist with their own petard. **1882** *Nature* XXVI. 146 The criticism of practical men .. was disarmed; these found them-selves hoist with their own petard.

†**3.** To raise in position, degree, or quality; to exalt, elevate; to raise in amount or price. *Obs.*

1581 W. STAFFORD *Exam. Compl.* III. (1876) 82 This rackynge and hoyssing vp of Rentes. **1583** STANYHURST *Æneis* I. (Arb.) 18 Shee pouts, that Ganymed by Ioue too skitop is hoysed. **1642** ROGERS *Naaman* 488 To bee hoysed up with such a spirit of freedom. **1679** CROWNE *Ambit. Statesm.* v. 80 I've torn my bowels out To hoyse my self into this Tyrant's favour. **1730** T. BOSTON *Mem.* vii. 100, I was somewhat hoised above it.

†**4.** To lift and move; to remove. *Obs.*

1593 SHAKS. *2 Hen. VI*, I. i. 169 Wee'l quickly hoyse Duke Humfrey from his seat. **1671** GREW *Anat. Plants* I. iii. App. §7 The Brushes of the Winds would injuriously hoise them to and fro. *c* **1750** *Rob Roy* ii. in Child *Ballads* VII. ccxxv. 248/1 He hoised her out among his crew, And rowd her in his plaidie.

†**5.** *intr.* (for *pass.*) To be raised, to rise. *Obs.*

1565 GOLDING *Ovid's Met.* II. (1593) 32 The waine for want of weight .. Did hoise aloft, and scaile, and reele as though it emptie were. **1570** B. GOOGE *Pop. Kingd.* 2 a, And with a worde he hoyseth up, into the starry raigne.

Hence **hoised** *ppl. a.*, **hoising** *vbl. sb.* and *ppl. a.*, '**hoiser**, one who or that which hoises. Also **hoise** *sb.*, a lift, HOIST I.

1568 T. HOWELL *Newe Sonets* (1879) 119 With hoysing waues and windes so hardly tost. **1576** GOSSON *Spec. Humanum* iii. in *Sch. Abuse* (Arb.) Notes 76 The prime of youth, whose greene vnmellowde yeares With hoysed head doth checke the loftie skies. **1611** COTGR., *Leveur*, a rayser .. hoyser, or heauer vp of. **1615** T. ADAMS *White Devill* 62 For the hoording of corne and hoysing of markets. **1632** SHERWOOD, A hoising instrument (to lift vp stones). **1786** BURNS *Ordination* xiii, They'll gie her on a rape a hoyse.

hoise, hois(s, obs. Sc. forms of HOSE.

†**hoisen,** *v. rare.* In 6 **hoysen.** = HOISE I.

1553 EDEN *Treat. Newe Ind.* (Arb.) 29 Hoyseninge vp his sayles.

hoist (hɔɪst), *v.* Also 6 **hoihst,** 6–7 **hoyst.** [orig. a corruption of *hoiss*, HOISE *v.*; perh. through taking the pa. t. and pple. as the stem: cf. *graff, graft*; also *amidst, whilst, wonst* = *once*.]

1. a. *trans.* To raise aloft; to set or put up; to place on high. (Also with *up*.)

1548 UDALL *Erasm. Par. Luke* xxiv. 181 b, His onely soonne they hoihsted vp and nayled on the crosse. **1573–80** BARET *Alv.* H 531 Hoist me this fellowe on thy backe Dromo and carrie him in. **1606** SHAKS. *Ant. & Cl.* IV. xii. 34 Let him take thee, And hoist thee vp to the shouting Plebeians. **1607** HEYWOOD *Wom. kilde w. Kindn.* Wks. 1874 II. 93 This marriage musicke hoists me from the ground. **1878** HUXLEY *Physiogr.* xii. 186 Beds of dead mussels were .. hoisted ten feet above high-water mark. **1883** MISS BRADDON *Phantom Fort.* III. 106 Lesbia mounted lightly to .. the box-seat; and Lady Kirkbank was hoisted up after her.

b. *esp.* A flag, colours, or the like. Here the sense is often the same as in 2.

1697 [see FLAG *sb.*[4] 2]. **1748** *Anson's Voy.* I. iv. 40 We saw the two forts hoist their colours. **1836** W. IRVING *Astoria* I. 201 The drums beat to arms, the colours were hoisted. **1874** GREEN *Short Hist.* vii. §6. 406 English vessels hoisted the flag of the States for a dash at the Spanish traders.

c. *spec.* To lift up on the back of another in order to receive a flogging. Cf. HOISTER b.

c **1719** *Lett. fr. Mist's Jrnl.* (1722) I. 183, I have been hoisted many a time for translating a Piece .. for him, while he had been hunting Bird-nests. **1835** MARRYAT *Jac. Faithf.* iv, He was hoisted: his nether garments descended, and then the birch descended with all the vigour of the Domine's muscular arm. **1862** MRS. H. WOOD *Channings* vii. 55 Seniors have been hoisted afore now.

d. *fig.*

1814 CARY *Dante, Par.* XXI. 124 Modern Shepherds [of the Church] need .. from behind, Others to hoist them. **1822** W. IRVING *Braceb. Hall* vii. 60 Having been hoisted to the rank of general.

2. To raise by means of tackle or other mechanical appliance. (Also with *up*.) ***to hoist down***: to lower. ***to hoist out*** (a boat): to launch, lower. See HOISE *v.* I.

1578 T. N. tr. *Conq. W. India* Pref. 9 But hoysted saile to search the golden vaine. **1594** tr. *Linschoten's Voy.* in Arb. *Garner* III. 20 They which hoist up the mainyard by a wheel. **1698** S. SEWALL *Diary* 14 Apr. (1878) I. 477 A Lad was kill'd by a hogshead of sugar falling on him as it was hoisting into a Boat. **1719** DE FOE *Crusoe* I. xviii, We saw them (by the help of my glasses) hoist another boat out. **1762** FALCONER *Shipwr.* II. 101 The boats then hoisted in are fix'd on board. **1794** *Rigging & Seamanship* I. 165 *Down-hauler*, a rope which hoists down the stay-sails. **1876** ROUTLEDGE *Discov.* 20 Engines of this kind .. are also much used by contractors, for hoisting stones.

†**3.** To lift and remove, to bear *away*. *Obs.*

c **1550** *Pryde & Ab. Wom.* 16 in Hazl. *E.P.P.* IV. 232 But theyr prayse and cloke wyll not serve, But hoyst them to the devyll of hell. **1599** NASHE *Lenten Stuffe* 47 She saw her mistris mounted a cock-horse, and hoysted away to hell or to heauen. **1762** MORE in *Phil. Trans.* LII. 452 The stream .. had hoisted us far out into the ocean.

†**4.** To overtax, surcharge. *Obs.*

1607 MIDDLETON *Michaelmas T.* IV. i. G iij b, Tis for your worships to haue land, that keepe great houses; I should be hoysted. **1611** COTGR., *Surtaux*, an ouer-cessing, ouer-rating, hoisting, surcharging, in the Subsidie booke. *Ibid.*, *Surtaxé*, ouer-sessed, hoisted, surcharged.

5. *intr.* (for *pass.*) To be raised, to rise aloft.

1647 H. MORE *Song of Soul* III. App. lvi, Thus dismist th' Assembly, bad Hoyst up into the Air, fly home through clammy shade. *c* **1860** H. STUART *Seaman's Catech.* 2 It will allow the yard to hoist close up to the block. **1892** *N.Y. Weekly Witn.* 13 Jan. 7/5 He .. marches .. toward hosannas that ever hoist and hallelujahs that ever roll.

6. *Criminals' slang.* To break into (a building) (? *obs.*); to steal, rob. Cf. HEIST.

1708, etc. [implied at HOISTER, HOISTING *vbl. sb.*]. **1796** GROSE *Dict. Vulgar T.* (ed. 2), *Hoist*, to go upon the hoist; to get into windows accidentally left open. **1931** *Amer. Speech* VII. 109 *Heist* (or *hoist*), to hold up a person, or to rob at the point of a gun. **1962** *Coast to Coast 1961–62* 21 'I know where we can hoist a car,' Mick said. 'We'll carry the stuff in it.'

Hence '**hoisted** *ppl. a.*; **hoister**, a housebreaker (? *obs.*); a shoplifter; a pickpocket; **hoisting** *vbl. sb.*, (esp.) shoplifting.

c **1611** CHAPMAN *Iliad* XVII. 256 Down fell Letheides, and .. the body's hoisted foot. **1708** J. HALL *Mem.* (ed. 4) 6 *Hoisters*, such as help one another upon their Backs in the Night-time to get into Windows. **1790** H. T. POTTER *New Dict. Cant & Flash Lang.* (1795) (ed. 2) 34 *Hoister*, a shoplifter. **1897** *Daily News* 21 Dec. 8/3 The hoisted board 'House Full' .. is a common occurrence. **1936** J. CURTIS *Gilt Kid* iv. 39 What did you get done for? Hoisting? **1938** F. D. SHARPE *Sharpe of Flying Squad* xiv. 154 Gangs of women shop-lifters or 'Hoisters' are to be found in Hoxton. **1960** *Observer* 25 Dec. 7/6 Various petty fiddles and con games to which Christmas trading lent itself, and of course hoisting —shoplifting. **1966** *New Statesman* 23 Dec. 934/2 You know Annie Ward, well she's on the hoisting racket. **1970** M. KENYON *100,000 Welcomes* ii. 10 That half-world of hustlers, hoisters, screwsmen, bogeys, bird, bent gear and tom. **1970** G. F. NEWMAN *Sir, You Bastard* ii. 45 The hoister was held under a guard a dozen strong. **1971** L. GRIBBLE *Alias the Victim* viii. 140 Cop slang. A hoister is a pick-pocket or shoplifter.

hoist, *sb.* [f. HOIST *v.*]

1. An act of hoisting; a lift; a shove up.

1654 GAYTON *Pleas. Notes* IV. xxv. 286 He is upon his second hoyst into the Cart. **1674** N. FAIRFAX *Bulk & Selv.* Ep. Ded., To be lifted up by the Hoist of breath. **1813** SCOTT *Fam. Lett.* 9 Mar. (1894) I. ix. 274, I wish you would give the raw author .. a hoist to notice, by speaking of him now and then. **1894** CROCKETT *Raiders* 231 As one gets to the edge of a wall when a comrade gives a hoist up.

2. Something hoisted; *Naut.* a number of flags hoisted together as a signal.

1805 W. PASCO in *Daily News* (1896) 21 Oct. 5/6 As the last hoist was handed down Nelson turned to Captain Blackwood .. with 'Now I can do no more'.

3. A thing by which something is hoisted; a machine for conveying persons and things from one level to another, in mines, factories, hotels, etc.; an elevator, a lift. Also preceded by a defining word.

1835 URE *Philos. Manuf.* 46 The teagle .. or hoist consists of three principal parts. **1852–61** *Archit. Publ. Soc. Dict.* IV. 64, *Hoist*, the name given to the machinery that has lately been introduced into building operations for the purpose of raising materials to the heights required in the construction. **1869** *Athenæum* 9 Oct. 466 Lifts and hoists are vulgar things in common hotels and warehouses for conveying ordinary people, sacks and casks to upper stories. *a* **1884** KNIGHT *Dict. Mech.* Suppl. 12/2 Pneumatic hoist. *Ibid.* 459/1 Builder's hoist. **1963** A. LUBBOCK *Austral. Roundabout* 195 Small bungalow homes with the sun-fresh washing blowing .. from the rotary hoists in their back gardens. **1967** *Nursing Times* 18 Aug. 1091/2 The Winchester hoist has also an important use in home nursing.

4. *Naut.* **a.** The middle part of a mast. **b.** The perpendicular height of a sail or a flag. **c.** The extent to which a sail or yard is hoisted (*Cent. Dict.*). **d.** The fore edge of a staysail.

1764 VEICHT in *Phil. Trans.* LIV. 288 Each of these parts of the mast are divided as to length, and have their proper names .. the middle part, which reaches from a little below the rigging, to that place, where the lowermost part begins .. is often called the hoist, or hoisting part. **1769** FALCONER *Dict. Marine* (1789), *Guindant*, .. the hoist or heighth of an ensign or flag. **1794** *Rigging & Seamanship* I. 89, *Stay-holes*, holes made through staysails, at certain distances along the hoist. **1841–62** TOTTEN *Naval Text Bk.* 340 The hoist of a sail or flag is its perpendicular height; applied to staysails or headsails, it means the foremost leeches. **1867** SMYTH *Sailor's Word-bk.* s.v. *Leeches*, The sails which are fixed obliquely on the masts have their leeches named from their situation with regard to the ship's length, as the hoist or luff, or fore-leech of the mizen, the after-leech of the jib, &c.

5. Housebreaking (? *obs.*); shoplifting. *Criminals' slang.*

1714 A. SMITH *Hist. Highwaymen* I. 143 He pursued his old Courses of going on the Top or Hoist, that is, breaking into a House in a dark Evening, by getting in at a Window one Story high, which they perform by one Thief standing on the Shoulders of another. *a* **1790** H. T. POTTER *New Dict. Cant & Flash Lang.* (1795) (ed. 2) 39 *Lift*, or *hoist*, shop-lifting, or robbing a shop. **1812** J. H. VAUX *Mem.* (1819) 180 *Hoist.* The game of shop-lifting is called the hoist; a person expert at this practice is said to be a good hoist. **1914** JACKSON & HELLYER *Vocab. Criminal Slang* 44 *Hoist*, the profession of shoplifting. **1938** F. D. SHARPE *Sharpe of Flying Squad* i. 15 Shoplifting as an art known as 'The Hoist', and its devotees are called 'Hoisters'. **1958** F. NORMAN *Bang to Rights* 72 My old woman's still out on the hoist now.

hoist-, in combination: **hoistaway** (*U.S.*), a mechanical lift or elevator; **hoist-bridge** (see quot.); **hoist-door** (see quot.); **hoist-hole**, an opening through which things are hoisted; **hoist-man** (see quot.); **hoist-rope**, a rope by which a sail, goods, etc. are hoisted; **hoist-way** (*U.S.*) = *hoist-hole*, the shaft of a lift or elevator.

1881 WORCESTER Suppl., *Elevator*, a mechanical contrivance for raising persons and goods from the lower story of a building to the higher stories .. called also lift and *hoist-away. **1875** KNIGHT *Dict. Mech.*, **Hoist-bridge*, a form of drawbridge, in which the leaf or platform is raised. **1881** *Harper's Mag.* Mar. 528/1 In the middle of the hall was the '*hoist-door', through which the wheat was hoisted up by a crane and stored in the loft. **1892** *Labour Commission* Gloss., **Hoist Men*, men attending the hydraulic cranes or steam winches used for hoisting the cargo from deck to quay .. men .. engaged in looking after the hoists or lifts in the yard. **1794** *Rigging & Seamanship* I. 128 The *hoist-rope is put through the holes in the head-stick. **1896** *Westm. Gaz.* 9 Oct. 5/1 Twelve sorters slid down a hoist rope through the flames.

hoist, pa.t. and pple. of HOISE; obs. Sc. form of HOST, var. HOAST.

hoister ('hɔɪstə(r)). [f. HOIST *v.* + -ER[1].] One who or that which hoists, raises, or elevates.

1862 GEN. P. THOMPSON in *Bradford Advert.* 1 Nov. 6/1 The hoister of the black flag. **1862** *Rep. to Ho. Repr. Prec. Met. U.S.* 408 New shaft house .. containing the 40-horse-power engine and hoister.

b. The person on whose back a pupil was hoisted to receive a flogging. (See HOIST *v.* I c.)

1836 E. HOWARD *R. Reefer* xiv, The two school men-servants came in, one .. being the obnoxious hoister.

hoisting ('hɔɪstɪŋ), *vbl. sb.* [f. as prec. + -ING[1].] The action of the verb HOIST: raising, lifting, elevation. *lit.* and *fig.*

1641 MILTON *Reform.* II. (1851) 40 He was the subversion and fall of that Monarchy which was the hoisting of him. **1796** BURKE *Regic. Peace* i. Wks. VIII. 189 The lowering or the hoisting of a sail. **1855** MILMAN *Lat. Chr.* V. 300 The criminal .. at a sign of the Judge was hauled up with a frightful wrench; and then violently let fall to the ground. This was called, in the common phrase, hoisting.

b. *attrib.* and *Comb.*, as ***hoisting-apparatus, -bridge, -crab, -engine, -jack, -line, -machine, -rope, -stage, -tackle***, etc.

1692 *Capt. Smith's Seaman's Gram.* I. xiv. 64 A hoistinglin for Pennant. **1751** LABELYE *Westm. Br.* 84 The Centers and hoisting Stage were compleated. **1852–61** *Archit. Publ. Soc. Dict.* IV. 63, *Hoisting bridge* .. lately employed in canal and railway works, where the platform is required to be raised so as to allow a barge or train to pass underneath. **1875** KNIGHT *Dict. Mech.*, *Hoisting-jack*, a contrivance by which hand-power is applied to lifting an object by working a screw or lever. **1876** *Engineering* XXI. 389 The hoisting rope is led to a drum on the second shaft, which we shall call the hoisting shaft. **1889** E. MATHESON *Aid Bk. Engin. Enterp.* (ed. 2) 725 An ordinary hoisting-crab or winch for working by hand.

hoistings, obs. form of HUSTINGS.

†**hoit,** *v. Obs.* or *dial.* Also **hoyt.** [Origin obscure: senses 1 and 2 are perh. unconnected. There seems to be connexion or association of sense with HOYDEN: see esp. *hoiting* ppl. a.]

1. *intr.* 'To indulge in riotous and noisy mirth' (Nares); to act the hoyden, to romp inelegantly.

c **1600** DAY *Begg. Bednall Gr.* II. i. (1881) 27 There you'll be hoyting and kissing the wenches you. **1611** BEAUM. & FL. *Knt. Burn. Pest.* I. iii, Hark my Husband he's singing and hoiting. *Ibid.* IV. iii, There he .. sings, and hoyts, and revels among his drunken companions. **1650** FULLER *Pisgah* II. IV. vi. 110 Let none condemn them [girls] for Rigs, because thus hoiting with boys. **1868** ATKINSON *Cleveland Gloss.*, *Hoit*, to play the fool .. to engage in some evident absurdity.

2. To move clumsily and with difficulty; to limp. *Sc.*

1786 BURNS *To Auld Mare* vii, Tho' now ye dow but hoyte and hoble An' wintle like a saumont-coble.

Hence (in sense 1) **hoiting** *vbl. sb.* and *ppl. a.* [with the latter, cf. HOYDEN *a.*]. Also **hoit** *sb.*, *north. dial.*, a spoilt child, a simpleton, an awkward silly girl, a hoyden.

1594 CAREW *Tasso* (1881) 87 Then would [I] hoyting wanton to a tribe Of loues my body haue abandoned. **1601** DONNE *Progr. Soul* xlvii, Us'd to wooe With hoiting gambols .. To make his Mistriss merry. **1612** tr. *Benvenuto's*

Passenger (N.), The court is not..a market-place for boyes, hoytings, and knaveries. **1649** DAVENANT *Love & Hon.* III. Dram. Wks. 1873 III. 141 Young enough, But given too much to hoyting, and to barley-break. **1676** LADY FANSHAWE in *Mem.* (1829) 33, I was that which we graver people call a hoyting girl. **1687** MRS. BEHN *Lucky Chance* II. ii, One of those hoiting Ladies that love nothing like fool and fiddle.

hoit, obs. Sc. f. HOT *a.*

hoity-toity ('hɔɪtɪ'tɔɪtɪ), *sb.*, *a.*, *adv.*, *int.* See also HIGHTY-TIGHTY. [app. a deriv. of HOIT *v.*, with reduplication; logically, the adj. ought to precede the sb. The sense seems in later times to have gradually been influenced by *high*, *height*, and their family; this becomes explicit in the spelling HIGHTY-TIGHTY.]

A. *sb.* **1.** Riotous or giddy behaviour; romping, frolic; disturbance, 'rumpus'; flightiness. Also, **b.** Assumption of superiority, 'airs', huffiness.

1668 R. L'ESTRANGE *Vis. Quev.* (1708) 100 The Widows I observ'd.. Chanting and Jigging to every Tune they heard, and all upon the Hoyty-Toyty, like mad Wenches of Fifteen. **1784** O'KEEFE *Fontainebleau* III. iii. (L.), My mother..was a fine lady, all upon the hoity-toities, and so, good for nothing. **1837** CARLYLE *Fr. Rev.* III. VI. ii, If this Danton were to burst your mesh-work!..what a hoitytoity were there, Justice and Culprit changing places. **1875** BROWNING *Aristoph. Apol.* 2374 After your three bouts At hoitytoity, great men with long words, And so forth.

2. A giddy or romping girl; a hoyden, romp. *dial.* Cf. HIGHTY-TIGHTY *sb.*

1719 D'URFEY *Pills* I. 255 The Frowzy Browzy, Hoyty Toyty, Covent-Garden Harridan. **1796** GROSE *Dict. Vulg. T.*, *Hoity-toity*, a hoity-toity wench; a giddy, thoughtless, romping girl.

B. *adj.* Frolicsome, romping, giddy, flighty. Also, **b.** Assuming, haughty, petulant, huffy.

1690 DRYDEN *Amphit.* II. ii, And that hoighty toighty business ought, in conscience, to be over. **1713** STEELE *Guardian* No. 10 ¶5 If any hoity-toity things make a fuss, they are sure to be taken to pieces the next visit. **1769** MRS. BROOKE *Emily Montague* (1784) I. iv. 16 There is generally a certain hoity-toity inelegance of form and manner at seventeen. **1820** KEATS *Cap & Bells* lxxix, See what hoity-toity airs she took. **1851** HELPS *Comp. Solit.* vii. (1874) 127 A good girl and not hoity-toity. **1896** SIR W. HARCOURT *Sp. Ho. Com.* 13 Feb., It is not to be got rid of by the use of, if I may use the phrase without offence, the hoity-toity language of the hon. and gallant member.

†C. *adv.* In a frolicsome or giddy manner. *Obs.*

1714 ARBUTHNOT *Harmony in Uproar* Misc. Wks. 1751 II. 31 All of a sudden we run as mad as ever; and hoity toity away went we. **1763** BICKERSTAFF *Love in Village* II. iii. 18th Air, Hoity, toity, Whisking, frisking.

D. *int.* An exclamation expressing surprise with some degree of contempt, esp. at words or actions considered to show flightiness or undue assumption.

1695 CONGREVE *Love for L.* III. x, Hoity toity, what have I to do with his Dreams or his Divination? **1749** FIELDING *Tom Jones* VII. viii, Hoity toity!..madam is in her airs, I protest. **1838** DICKENS *Nich. Nick.* xxix, 'Why he don't mean to say he's going! Hoity toity! Nonsense.' **1883** MRS. ALEXANDER *Executor* II. 91 'Hoity toity!' cried Mr. Harding, a little surprised. 'Well, you'll think better of it'.

Hence **hoity-'toityism**, **hoity-'toityness**, flightiness, huffiness, petulance. **hoity-toity** *v. intr.*, to act in a hoity-toity manner, to romp inelegantly, to hoyden.

1790 'TOBY TEACH 'EM' *Hist. Goody Goosecap* 23 Miss Sally Scramble..minded nothing but hoity-toitying about, and had nothing but play in her head. **1820** MISS MITFORD in L'Estrange *Life* (1870) II. 106 A person whose hoity-toityness is depressing beyond conception. **1881** T. WATTS in *Athenæum* 3 Sept. 308/2 The talk gets naturally upon 'lords' in general, gentility, nonsense, and 'hoity-toityism' as the canker at the heart of modern civilization.

hoix, var. spelling of HOICKS.

hoja(h, var. of KHOJA.

hok, hoke, obs. ff. HOCK, HOOK, OAK.

Hokan ('həʊkən). Name given to a group of languages of certain American Indian peoples inhabiting the west coast of the U.S. So **'Hokanist**, one who is versed in these languages. Also *Comb.*, as *Hokan-Siouan*.

1913 DIXON & KROEBER in *Science* 7 Feb. 225/2 The new larger [native Indian language] families..are..Hokan, comprising Shasta, Chimariko and Pomo, probably Karok, and possibly Yana. **1920** *Internat. Jrnl. Amer. Ling.* Dec. 280/2 It is difficult for me to suggest any alternative to the hypothesis of a common origin of the Hokan and Coahuiltecan languages. **1965** *Language* XLI. 303 Two Hokanists..have examined the Sapir (1929) subgrouping labelled Northern Hokan. **1965** *Canad. Jrnl. Ling.* Spring 83 These..families had been placed in the Hokan-Siouan superstock.

hoke (həʊk), *v.* [Back-formation from HOKUM.] On the stage or screen: to overplay (a part), to act (a part) in an insincere, sentimental, or melodramatic manner. Also *transf.* and with *up*.

1935 A. J. POLLOCK *Underworld Speaks* 57/1 *Hoke*, to string along; to jolly; to ridicule. **1938** M. MCCARTHY in *Partisan Rev.* Jan. 48 Actors who have been playing for a long time in the same play will..'hoke' their performances more and more. A giggle becomes a laugh; a catch in the throat, a sob. **1939** C. MORLEY *Kitty Foyle* xxv. 244 She had the guts to keep her stuff to exclusive outlets and hoke it up with all sorts of restrictions. **1940** S. LEWIS *Bethel Merriday* xxvii. 283 Mr. Nooks had..overplayed—'hoked' is the technical word—the role of the Apothecary. **1961** *Punch* 22 Feb. 331/2 The average moviegoer..is pleased to see pictorial evidence, a little hoked up for added amusement. **1971** M. BABSON *Cover-up Story* iii. 33 Just *try* it straight.. it's a mistake to hoke it up.

hoke, var. of HOLK, HOWK *v.*

hokeday, etc., early ff. HOCK-DAY, etc.

hokee-pokee. *rare*[−1]. [Cf. HOKEY-POKEY.] (See quot.)

1873 J. MILLER *Life amongst Modocs* (1876) xiii. 192 One man..danced a sort of a savage hokee-pokee, and sang.

†**hoker**, *sb. Obs.* Forms: 1 hocor, hocer, 2–4 hoker, 4–5 hokir, 5 hocowre, hocour. [OE. *hocor*, not found in the cognate langs.; the *o* is of doubtful length, but prob. short; possibly related to OE. *hux*, *husc* 'mockery', root *huc-*, *hoc-*. (Not related to OHG. *huoh*, MHG. *hûch*, *huoch* 'contempt, scorn, derision', in which the second *h* is Germanic, requiring OE. *h.*)] Mockery, derision; scorn, contempt; abuse, reviling.

1014 WULFSTAN *Serm. ad Anglos* in *Hom.* xxxiii. (1883) 164 To oft man mid hocere gode dæda hyrweð. *c* **1200** *Trin. Coll. Hom.* 163 Iuele word, hoker and scorn. *c* **1205** LAY. 29790 Bruttisce clerekes Him seiden hokeres. *c* **1386** CHAUCER *Reeve's T.* 45 She was as digne as water in a dich As ful of hoker and of bismare. **14..** *Cast. Love* (Halliw.) 211 Alle the fendes hadyn hocowre That mon shuld wonyn in the blessed honowre. **1421–2** HOCCLEVE *Dialog.* 741 My wyf mighte haue hokir & greet desdeyn.

b. *Comb.* **hoker-word**, mocking word; gibe.

1014 WULFSTAN *Serm. ad Anglos* in *Hom.* xxxiii. (1883) 164 Hocorwyrde dysiȝe. *c* **1205** LAY. 19595 [Hi] me atwiten mid heore hoker worden.

†**hoker**, *v. Obs.* [f. HOKER *sb.*] *trans.* To mock, scorn, revile.

a **1225** *Leg. Kath.* 458 þu..ure godes hokerest. *c* **1275** *Passion Our Lord* 456 in *O.E. Misc.* 50 He..gon him hokeri. *c* **1425** *Eng. Conq. Irel.* 140 Thay..weren shame-fully receyued, & lothly I-hokred.

b. *intr.* To pour scorn (*upon*).

c **1205** LAY. 14795 Ah nes hit nan..þat him ne hokerede on. *c* **1275** *Passion Our Lord* 449 in *O.E. Misc.* 50 þe princes and þet oþer volk hokerede him vp-on.

Hence **'hokering** *vbl. sb.*, mockery, scorn.

a **1225** *Ancr. R.* 188 þeo on hokerunge ȝeieden so lude. *a* **1240** *Wohunge* in *Cott. Hom.* 281 þe red ȝerde þat te was ..ȝiuen þe on hokerringe.

hokerere, var. of OCKERER *Obs.*, usurer.

†**'hokerful**, *a. Obs.* [f. HOKER *sb.* + -FUL.] Scornful. Hence **'hokerfully** *adv.*, scornfully.

a **1275** *Prov. Ælfred* 670 in *O.E. Misc.* 137 He wole liþen and hokerful ben. *c* **1325** *Lai le Freine* 61 A proude dame and an envieous, Hokerfulliche missegging.

†**'hokerly**, *adv. Obs.* [f. as prec. + -LY[2].]

1. Scornfully, mockingly, contemptuously.

c **1205** LAY. 19412 And lætten swiðe hokerliche of Lote þan eorle. **1297** R. GLOUC. (1724) 417 þe kyng..wel hokerlyche by held þe folc þat þere stod. *c* **1386** CHAUCER *Pars. T.* ¶510 Thanne wole he..answeren hokerly and angrily.

2. In a way worthy of scorn, contemptibly, ridiculously.

a **1225** *Ancr. R.* 140 þis is wunder ouer alle wundres, & hokerliche wunder. *c* **1230** *Hali Meid.* 15 Swa muchel þe hokerlucher him þuncheð to beon ouercumen.

hoker moker, obs. f. HUGGER-MUGGER.

hoket: see HOCKET.

hokey, hoaky ('həʊkɪ), *sb.* In *by hokey*, *by the hokey*, a petty oath, or asseveration. Also, *by the hokey fiddle*.

[*Hoakie*, in Ayrshire, according to Jamieson, means 'a fire that has been covered up with cinders, when all the fuel has become red'. This is hardly likely to be the source of the petty oath, which seems to be substituted for some other word.]

1825 JAMIESON s.v., Used also as a petty oath, *By the hoakie*. **1842** BARHAM *Ingol. Leg.* Ser. II. *Dead Drummer*, What sound mingles too?—by the hokey—a Drum! **1842** S. LOVER *Handy Andy* xi. 101 Hilloa, by the Hokey I have him! **1867** F. H. LUDLOW *Little Brother* 64 Then, by hokey, I'll like you very much indeed, old fellow! **1922** JOYCE *Ulysses* 513 By the hoky fiddle, thanks be to Jesus. **1958** *Engineering* 4 Apr. 426/1 It may be five years before it pays dividends but by the hokey fiddle it'll shake us.

hokey ('həʊkɪ), *a. slang* (orig. *U.S.*). Also hokie, hoky. [f. HOKE *v.*, HOKUM + -Y[1].] Characterized by hokum; sentimental, melodramatic, artificial.

1945 *N.Y. Times* 19 Aug. 3/8 Equally a part of America.. are the dull films, the tasteless, hoky confections that public taste ought to repudiate. **1968** *Surfer Mag.* Jan. 58/1 They know the films are hokie Hollywood products. **1969** *Northwest* (*Sunday Oregonian Mag.*) 14 Dec. 11/2 Not the 'hokey' set-ups I've been through a half dozen times, but a supervised transitional period. **1970** *New Yorker* 16 May 105/3 A funny and hokey reënactment of the pantomime pocket drama that Colette did in music halls all over France. **1971** *Rolling Stone* 24 June 31/4 A closing piece [on a record], 'Sometimes', is embarrassingly hokey.

hokey-cokey ('həʊkɪ'kəʊkɪ). [Cf. HOKEE-POKEE.] A kind of dance.

[**1943** *Dancing Times* Sept. 570/2, I found a party-dance that was quite new to me. Locally it was (inaccurately) called the 'Hokey Pokey'... The correct name is 'Cokey Cokey'... The chorus runs:..You do the Cokey Cokey and turn around That's what it's all about.] **1966** *Crescendo* Jan. 23/1 'The next dance will be a Veleta' is about my lot, and even then I'm likely to say 'Hokey-Cokey'. **1967** *Ibid.* May 10/3 Your bandleader must present all the ritual party dances including, of course, an ever popular Hokey Cokey. **1967** *Listener* 2 Nov. 587/1 It turned out to be a strong dose of barn-dance and hokey-cokey. **1972** *Sunday Express* 2 Jan. 15/1 (*heading*) Hokey-cokey at the club forces family to sleep in tent. *Ibid.* 15/4 It was 1.30 a.m. at the county council's staff social club and they were dancing the hokey-cokey.

hokey-pokey ('həʊkɪ'pəʊkɪ). *slang* or *colloq.* Also **hoky-poky**. [In sense 1, altered from *hocus-pocus*; in sense 2, perh. of distinct origin.]

1. (Cf. HOCUS-POCUS 2.) Deception, cheatery, underhand work.

1847–78 HALLIWELL, *Hoky-poky*, hocus-pocus. *North.* **1893** FARMER *Slang*, *Hokey-pokey*. 1. A cheat; a swindle; nonsense. (From *Hocus Pocus*.)

2. A cheap kind of ice-cream, sold by street vendors.

1884 *Sunday Mag.* Nov. 715/1 'Hokey-pokey, pokey ho!' ..a curiously compounded beverage. **1885** TUER *Old Lond. Cries* 58 Hokey Pokey is of a firmer make and probably stiffer material than the penny ice of the Italians. **1888** *Pall Mall G.* 25 Sept. 3/2 The correct origin of the term 'Hokey Pokey, a penny a lump'. [An incident is related as tending to identify the term with the It. *O che poco!* 'O how little!'] **1910** A. BENNETT *Clayhanger* II. 226 Three hokey-pokey ice-cream hand-carts, one after another, turned the corner of Trafalgar Road. **1955** *Times* 8 June 7/4 'Hokey-pokey', which, as children used to know, sold for a penny a lump and was (presumably because of its freezing touch on the tongue) the stuff to make you jump. **1970** J. BROWN *Unmelting Pot* i. 23 An Italian organ-grinder..who sold ice-cream or hokey-pokey at ½d a piece during the summer.

3. Cf. HOKEY *sb.*, and *pokey-hokey* in Spurdens *Supp. to Forby*.

1883 *Bread-Winners* 231 By the great hokey-pokey! they couldn't keep it up a minute when their wives came.

4. A toffee-like sweet. *N.Z.*

1939 'K. MANSFIELD' *Scrapbook* 3 We always gave him the same presents..three cakes of hoky-poky.

hokku: see HAIKU.

Hokonui ('hɒkənʊɪ). *N.Z.* [Maori place-name.] = MOONSHINE 4.

1947 D. M. DAVIN *Gorse blooms Pale* 29 The men outside ..tasting the jar of Hokonui that Tom MacDonald had brought. **1963** *Truth* (Wellington) 17 Sept., Today's distillers of Hokonui can use electricity, smokeless fuels, to keep their spasmodic industry out of sight.

hokster, hokester, obs. ff. HUCKSTER.

hokum ('həʊkəm). orig. *U.S. Theatrical slang.* Also **hocum**. [? A blending of HOCUS-POCUS and BUNKUM.] Speech, action, properties, etc., on the stage, designed to make a sentimental or melodramatic appeal to an audience. Also *transf.* Hence *gen.*, bunkum.

1917 *Sun* (N.Y.) 5 Aug. III. 3/7 'Jasbo' is a form of the word common in the varieties, meaning the same as 'hokum', or low comedy verging on vulgarity. **1922** C. SANDBURG *Slabs of Sunburnt West* 25 Hokum—they lap it up. **1926** *N.Y. Times* 29 Aug., This may be groundling comedy, but it is not pure hokum. **1926** *Ladies' Home Jrnl.* Apr. 38 'What they tell is..bold and defiant realism.' 'Bold and defiant hokum, I should call it.' **1927** *Sunday Express* 17 Apr. 4 Channing Pollock believed that in 'The Fool' he had written a work of genius. Even when other people said it was hokum he still went on. **1928** *Publishers' Weekly* 16 June 2440 It is pure hokum to suggest that all authors are always interesting. **1928** *Sunday Dispatch* 15 July 15/1 The Adelphi ..was occupied by a Mr. Sam Bernard with a musical play called 'The Belle of Bond Street'—what an outrage that 'Girl' and 'Belle' hokum must have become! **1930** *Publishers' Weekly* 15 Mar. 1559 In spite of the fact that the hokum of it all has been pointed out to them. **1937** *Daily Tel.* 26 Oct. 8/5 His story is what the film trade calls 'hokum', the recipe as before with inferior or stale ingredients. **1970** *New Yorker* 12 Dec. 125/1 Most people in Washington dismissed this statement as a piece of sentimental hokum. **1973** *Washington Post* 5 Jan. B7/4 *The Poseidon Adventure*.. strictly formula hokum but reasonably diverting.

hoky, variant of HOCKEY[1], harvest-home.

hol, see HOLE, HOLL, WHOLE.

hola, obs. f. HOLLA.

holacueur, obs. f. HALALCOR.

holagogue, etc.: see HOLO-.

holand, -er, obs. f. HOLLAND[1], -ER.

holarctic (həʊ'lɑːktɪk), *a.* [f. Gr. ὅλο-ς whole (HOLO-) + ARCTIC.] In the Geographical Distribution of Animals: Of or pertaining to the entire northern or arctic region, as the Holarctic region, or Holarctic family of birds.

Mr. P. Sclater divided the surface of the globe into six great zoological Regions, two of which, the *Palæarctic* and *Nearctic*, comprised the Old and the New World respectively north of the Tropic of Cancer (nearly). It has since been proposed to unite these into one region, to which

Prof. A. Newton has applied the term *Holarctic*. It corresponds essentially to Huxley's *Arctogæal*. **1883** A. HEILPRIN in *Nature* 26 Apr. 606 As regards the name 'Triarctic', by which I intended to designate the combined Neoarctic and Palæarctic regions.. I beg to state that at the suggestion of Prof. Alfred Newton.. it has been replaced by Holarctic. **1887** NEWTON in *Rep. Brit. Assoc.* 733 The great northern or 'Holarctic' fauna.

†**holard**[1]. *Obs.* [A by-form of HOLOUR, with suffix -ARD.] A whoremonger.

c **1460** *Towneley Myst.* (E.E.T.S.) xvi. 358 Haue at thy tabard, harlot and holard! Thou shalle not be sparde!

holard[2] ('hɒlɑːd). *Ecology.* [f. Gr. ὅλος whole + ἄρδειν to water.] The total water content of the soil.

1905 F. E. CLEMENTS *Res. Methods Ecol.* ii. 32 The total amount of water in the soil is divided into the available and the non-available water content. The terms suggested for these are respectively, holard.. chresard.. and echard. **1926** TANSLEY & CHIPP *Study of Vegetation* vii. 127 If the echard is subtracted from the holard (total amount of water in the fresh soil) the difference is called the chresard. **1929** WEAVER & CLEMENTS *Plant Ecol.* ix. 182 Of the total water content or holard (whole amount) the larger portion can be absorbed by the plant and is consequently termed available water.

holaspidean (hɒlæ'spɪdɪən), *a. Zool.* [f. mod.L. *Holaspideæ* (C. J. Sundevall *Methodi Naturalis Avium Disponendarum Tentamen* (1872) I. 53), f. Gr. ὅλος whole + ἀσπίς shield.] Pertaining to passerine birds that have a single series of large scutella on the posterior portion of the tarsus.

1885 J. S. KINGSLEY *Riverside Nat. Hist.* (1888) IV. 485 This peculiarity consists in the holaspidean tarsi, technically making them scutelliplantar, the hind surface of the tarsus being broken up into scutes similar to those covering the front part. **1907** R. RIDGWAY *Birds N. & Middle Amer.* IV. 329 In all Oscines except the Alaudidæ (in which the tarsus is holaspidean) [the tarsus] has the posterior margin contracted into a sharp or narrow ridge or edge. **1959** VAN TYNE & BERGER *Fund. Ornith.* ii. 48 Several types of passerine tarsal scutellation have been described... Holaspidean: With rear surface of tarsus covered by a single series of broad, rectangular scales.

holbard, -beard, -ber(d(e, -bert, obs. ff. HALBERD.

holbarder etc., obs. ff. HALBERDIER.

Holbein ('həʊlbaɪn, 'hɒl-). The name of the German painter Hans *Holbein* (1497–1543), used *attrib.* to designate embroidery, rugs, etc., embodying qualities or decoration characteristic of Holbein or his work. Hence **Holbei'nesque** *a.* [see -ESQUE], resembling the work of Holbein.

1881 C. C. HARRISON *Woman's Handiwork* I. 44 Holbein stitches appear the same on right and wrong sides of the material. **1882** CAULFEILD & SAWARD *Dict. Needlework* 252/2 *Holbein Stitch*, also known as Italian Stitch, and used in Holbein Embroidery to cover the outline patterns that form the work. *Ibid.* 253/1 *Holbein Work*.. consists of an outline Embroidery executed with great care and exactitude, so that the right and wrong side of the work are alike. **1895** J. A. GRAY *At Court of Ameer* xxxi, The most skilful of the artists gave an almost Holbeinesque look to his drawings. **1904** *Westm. Gaz.* 14 Nov. 4/2 His fine Holbeinesque drawings. **1931** A. U. DILLEY *Oriental Rugs & Carpets* vi. 146 The oldest group of rugs remaining to us of the weavings of the Ottoman Turks.. are the fifteenth-century products now handsomely called Holbein rugs in compliment to Hans Holbein the Younger. **1950** *Chambers's Encycl.* I. 612/2 The 'Holbein'.. and 'Landsknecht' types.. which are a German form of short dagger, the former so called from the sheaths being frequently decorated with Holbein's 'Dance of Death' in pierced and chased metal. **1960** *Times* 21 June 22/4 A Holbeinesque bracelet.

holcodont ('hɒlkəʊdɒnt), *a. Ornith.* [f. Gr. ὅλκος furrow + ὀδοντ- tooth.] 'Having teeth distinctly and separately socketed in a long continuous groove, as the *Odontolcæ*' (Cent. Dict.).

holcus ('hɒlkəs). *Bot.* [mod.L. (C. Linnæus *Hortus Cliffortianus* (1737) 468), f. Gr. ὁλκός a kind of grass.] A plant of a genus of annual or perennial grasses so called, native to Europe, Africa, and south-west Asia.

1771 P. MILLER *Abridgm. Gardeners Dict.* (ed. 6) s.v. *Holcus*.. Holcus with hairy chaff, and bearded seeds. *Ibid.*, Holcus with smooth husks. **1806** J. BARROW *Voy. Cochin China* 392 All the houses were enclosed by a fence made of strong reeds, of the straw of *holcus*, or twigs of wood. **1859** [see UNHUSKED *ppl. a.*']. **1915** L. H. BAILEY *Stand. Cyclop. Hort.* III. 1496/2 The name Holcus was accepted by some botanists. **1947** J. G. DICKSON *Dis. Field Crops* ix. 169 The holcus spot is characterized by tan red-bordered round to elliptical lesions on the leaves.

hold (həʊld), *v.* Pa. t. **held**; pa. pple. **held**, *arch.* **holden** ('həʊld(ə)n). Forms: see below. [A Com. Teut. redupl. str. vb. OE. *haldan, healdan*, pa. t. *heold*, pple. *halden, healden*, corresp. to OFris. *halda, helt, halden*, OS. *haldan, held, gihaldan* (MLG. *holden*, MDu. *houden*), OHG. *halten, hialt, gehaltan* (Ger. *halten, hielt, gehalten*), ON. *halda, helt, held-, haldenn*, Goth. *haldan, haihald, haldans*. The Anglian form *haldan* remained in the north as *hald, hauld, haud*, but regularly gave in midl. and general Eng. *hold*; the WSax. *healdan* gave in the south a pres. stem *heald, hæld, hyald, held* in ME. The 2nd and 3rd pers. sing. had often umlaut and contraction in OE. and early ME. The pa. t. OE. *heold* (:—redupl. **hehold*) became *heeld, held*, dial. *hield, hyld, huld* (-y-); rarely, with weak ending, *hulte, holdede*, in ME. The pa. pple. became *holden*, north. *halden* (*hauden, hadden*), south. *healden, helden*; also, with loss of suffix, *yhalde, yholde, holde*, etc.; in 16th c. *holden* began to be displaced by *held* from the pa. t., and is now archaic, but preserved by its use in legal and formal language; weak forms *holded, hoddit*, are frequent from 16th c. in dial. or individual use.]

A. Inflexional Forms.

1. a. Present stem. *α. Anglian* and *north.* 1–7 **hald**, (4–5 **ald**), 6–9 *Sc.* **hauld**, (6 **hawd**, 6– **haud**, **had**), 9 *north. Eng.* **hod**.

a **900** *O.E. Chron.* an. 874 Miercna rice to haldanne. *c* **950** *Lindisf. Gosp.* Mark v. 4 Nænig monn mæhte hine halda. *c* **1175** *Lamb. Hom.* 41 Haldeð broþerreddene eow bitwenen. *a* **1225** *Juliana* 47 Hu derst tu halde me? *a* **1300** *Cursor M.* 4034 Aiþer might þam ald. *Ibid.* 28353, I þat cuth na mesur hald. **1375** BARBOUR *Bruce* I. 514 To hald þat þai forspokyn haid. **1426** AUDELAY *Poems* 33 And ald houshold oponly. **1500–20** DUNBAR *Poems* xlix. 42 Micht non him hawd. *Ibid.* lxix. 27 Quhy wald thow hald that will away? **1535** STEWART *Cron. Scot.* II. 15 Ane pennyworth to had. **1724** RAMSAY *Tea-t. Misc.* (1733) I. 29 Twa good pocks.. The t'ane to had the grots The ither to had the meal. **1777–1836** J. MAYNE *Siller Gun* in Chambers *Pop. Hum. Scot. Poems* (1862) 122 Nought could hauld them. **1781** BURNS *My Nanie, O*, vii, I'm as blythe that hauds his pleugh.

β. 3– **hold**, (5 **hoold**, **old**, 5–7 **hould**).

c **1200** *Trin. Coll. Hom.* 161 Hie sullen weie holden. **1297** R. GLOUC. (1724) 460 Ych hym holde vaste. *c* **1400** *Destr. Troy* 11648 Hold hit onone! *c* **1460** FORTESCUE *Abs. & Lim. Mon.* v. (1885) 119 We most holde [*MS. Digby* 145 (1532) houlde] it for vndouted. **1546** J. HEYWOOD *Prov.* (1867) 62 Who maie holde that will awaie?

γ. WSax. and *south.* 1–4 **heald-**, 3 **hæld-**, 3–5 **held-**, (4 *Kent.* **hyald-**, **hye(a)ld-**).

971 *Blickl. Hom.* 13 We.. his bebodu healdan. *c* **1000** *Sax. Leechd.* I. 224 Heald hy mid þe. *c* **1200** *Trin. Coll. Hom.* 31 Heald þin cunde. *a* **1275** *Prov. Ælfred* 620 in *O.E. Misc.* 136 þenne miȝt þu þi lond mit frendchipe helden. *c* **1315** Healde [see B. 23 c]. **1340** *Ayenb.* 27 Zome þet me hyelde guode men. *Ibid.* 145 God of huam we hyealdeþ alle. *Ibid.* 220 [He] hyalde hit wyle þerhuyle hit ilest. **13..** *Coer de L.* 2340 Al my lond I will of him held.

b. 2nd sing. 1 ***hieltst, hyltst**, 2 **alst**, 3–4 **halst**, 4 *north.* **hald(e)s**, 3– **holdest**; 3rd sing. 1 **hielt, helt, hilt, hylt**, 2–4 **halt (alt)**, 4 **halth**, *north.* **hald(e)s**, 4–5 **holt**, 3– **holdeth**, 6– **holds**.

c **897** K. ÆLFRED *Gregory's Past.* xxxiii. 220 Se wisa hilt his spræce. **970** in Kemble *Cod. Dipl.* III. 466 Afene stream healt ðone norþ ende. *c* **1000** *Sax. Leechd.* II. 198 Sio.. helt þa lendenbrædan. *a* **1175** *Cott. Hom.* 233 Hlaford.. þe alste [= halst þe] hefenen þrimsettles. *c* **1250** *Gen. & Ex.* 924 Quo-so his alt him bi aȝt. *a* **1300** *Cursor M.* 2655 If þou halds mi techeyng. *c* **1300** *Beket* 1614 He halth me the meste wrecche. *c* **1315** SHOREHAM 90 ȝef thou hys [hestes] halst man. **1340** *Ayenb.* 259 Vor huo þet halt ald man uor child: he hine halt uor fol. *c* **1386** CHAUCER *Sqr.'s T.* 53 And halt [*v.r.* holte] his feeste so solempne. *c* **1400** MAUNDEV. (1839) xxvii. 270 Prestre Iohn holt fulle gret Lond.

2. *Pa. t.* *α.* 1 **hiold**, 1–4 **heold**, 1– **held**; 3 **hield**, (**hel**), 3–4 **huld**, 4 **heeld**, 4–5 **heild**, **helt**, 4–6 **hild**, **hyld**, 5 **hueld**, **hold**, **hyllde**.

c **897** K. ÆLFRED *Gregory's Past.* Pref. 4 Ure ieldran ða þe ðas stowa ær hioldon. *c* **1000** ÆLFRIC *Hom.* I. 46 Judei.. heoldon heora earan. *a* **1132** *O.E. Chron.* an. 1123 Fela oðre.. helden here castles him to ȝeanes. *c* **1200** *Trin. Coll. Hom.* 165 Ðu helde mi riht hond. *a* **1225** *Ancr. R.* 66 Eue heold.. longe tale mid te neddre. *c* **1290** *S. Eng. Leg.* I. 19/13 [The] taper.. þat heo huld in hire hond. *a* **1300** *Cursor M.* 408 þe seuend o werk he hild [*v.rr.* held, helde] him still. *Ibid.* 6038 Langer his forward heild he noght. *c* **1375** *Sc. Leg. Saints, Laurentius* 724 Mony feyndis hyld þare vay. **1382** WYCLIF *Eccl.* ii. 2 Laȝhing I heeld errour. *c* **1400** *St. Alexius* (Cott.) 315 He hyllde his hand so faste. *c* **1420** *Chron. Vilod.* st. 724 Seynt Wultrud hold hurr' ryȝt wel afrayde. *c* **1450** *Merlin* 64 Thus hilde the kynge that feeste. **1485** CAXTON *Chas. Gt.* 207 [An idol] helde in his ryght honde a grete keye. **1574** tr. *Marlorat's Apocalips* 40 He hilde himselfe still vnder his fathers obedience. **1601** SHAKS. *Jul. C.* v. v. 65, I held the Sword. **1841** LANE *Arab. Nts.* I. 93 A thing that thou heldest in thy hand.

β. 5 **hulte**. *γ.* 5 **holdede**.

c **1420** *Chron. Vilod.* st. 602 [He] hulte hym styll as he nouȝt rouȝt. *Ibid.* 937 His hond.. so hulte he. **1432–50** tr. *Higden* (Rolls) I. 89 The sonne of Mithridatis holdede that realme by xliij. yere.

3. *Pa. pple.* *α.* 1–2 **(ȝe)halden**, 2–3 **ihalden**, 4–5 **halden**, **-yn** (**alden**, etc.), 4–6 **haldin**, (6 *Sc.* **haldine**, **haulden**, 9 *Sc.* **hadden**, *north.* **hodden**).

c **950** *Lindisf. Gosp.* Matt. ix. 17 Æd-gædre biðon gehalden. *a* **1175** *Cott. Hom.* 229 þat naman ne mai bien ȝehalden. *a* **1300** *Cursor M.* 28470, I haue halden. **1413** *Pilgr. Sowle* (Caxton) v. xiv. (1859) 80 The feste.. is halden in this wyse. *a* **1557** *Diurn. Occurr.* (Bannatyne) 11 The Parliament to be haldin in Edinburgh. **1558** MAITLAND *Wynning of Calice* viii. in Sibbald *Chron. Scot. Poetry* (1802) III. 94 Be ilk man haulden in reverence. **1609** SKENE *Reg. Maj.* 37 Lands haldin be the heire. *Mod. Sc.* He's ower fou hadden.

β. 3–4 **y-**, **i-holden**, **-yn**, 3– **holden**, (4–5 **-in**, **-yn**, **-un**, **olden**).

a **1240** *Lofsong* in *Cott. Hom.* 205 Vuele i-holden treouðe. *c* **1250** *Gen. & Ex.* 2039 Holden harde in prisun. *c* **1320** *Cast. Love* 266 That never ȝet i-holdyn nes. **1377** LANGL. *P. Pl.* B. v. 281 Alle.. Ben holden.. to helpe þe to restitue. ? *a* **1400** *Praier Ploweman* in *Harl. Misc.* (1810) VI. 112 Ych am y-holden by charite to parte with hym of these goodes. **1411** *Rolls Parlt.* III. 650/1 At the last Parlement.. holden at Westm[inster]. **1868** LOWELL *Under Willows, Wind-Harp* 5 Only caught for the moment and holden.

γ. 1 **(ȝe)healden**, 3 **ihealden**, 4–6 **helden**.

c **1000** [see B. 6]. *a* **1300** *Cursor M.* 9504 He.. helden had þir laghes tuin.

δ. 4 **ihalde**, **yholde**, **yhealde**, **halde**, **halt**, 4–5 **holde**, **hold**, 6 *Sc.* **hald**.

c **1330** R. BRUNNE *Chron. Wace* (Rolls) 8242 þou hast halde þer lond wyþ wrong. **1340** *Ayenb.* 165 þe hestes.. huerto hi byeþ y-hyealde. *c* **1340** *Cursor M.* 10493 (Trin.), I out of chirche.. am don & for cursed holde. *c* **1386** CHAUCER *Wife's T.* 168 Seyde he had holde his day. **1393** LANGL. *P. Pl.* C. IV. 269 For a man yholde. *a* **1450** *Knt. de la Tour* (1868) 32 Ye are moche holde to youre God. **1513** DOUGLAS *Æneis* XII. iv. 9 Ane rych enornament Of cleyr Phebus, that was his grandschir hald.

ε. 6– **held**, 6 **helde**, **hild**.

1503 *Act 19 Hen. VII*, c. 24 The Shire-Court.. is held and kept in the City of Chichester. **1587** GOLDING *De Mornay* ix. 125 If he had hild himselfe to that which he saith. **1590** SHAKS. *Com. Err.* v. i. 44 How long hath this possession held the man. **1593** —— *Lucr.* 1257 O, let it not be hild [*rimes* kill'd, fulfill'd] Poor women's faults. **1621** BURTON *Anat. Mel.* II. iv. II. iii, To be held and chewed in the mouth. **1893** *Field* 11 Feb. 190/3 Their quarry got 'held' in a bit of bog.

ζ. 6–7 **holded**, 9 *dial.* **hoddit**.

1590 L. LLOYD *Dial Daies* Oct. 31 Which day amongst the antient Romans was holded a fortunate day for marriage. **1716** B. CHURCH *Hist. Philip's War* (1867) II. 71 A Court.. which was holded before I came home.

B. Signification.

In Gothic, *haldan* is recorded only in the sense 'to watch over, keep charge of, keep, herd, pasture (cattle)'. (Cf. the derivative BEHOLD = hold in observation.) This is generally accepted as the original sense in the Teutonic langs. (cf. Grimm, s.v. *Halten*, Verwijs & Verdam *Middelndl. Wbk.* s.v. *Houden*), whence have arisen the senses, 'to rule (people), guard, defend, keep from getting away or falling, preserve, reserve, keep possession of, possess, occupy, contain, detain, entertain, retain, maintain, sustain', in which it is now used. In some of these *hold* covers the same conceptual grounds as *keep* (which has superseded it in reference to cattle), in others it is a stronger synonym of *have*. But its typical current sense is 'to have or keep in one's grasp'; uses into which this notion does not enter, literally or figuratively, having mostly become obsolete. Hence it is the English equivalent of L. *tenēre*, F. *tenir*, and so of *contain, retain*, etc., as above. The verb had already a wide development of sense in OE., as far as we can go back; uses akin to the Gothic are here placed as sense 1.

I. Transitive senses.

†**1. a.** To keep watch over, keep in charge, herd, 'keep' (sheep, etc.); to rule (men). Only in OE. and early ME. *Obs.*

971 *Blickl. Hom.* 45 þære heorde þe hi ær Gode healdan sceoldan. *c* **1000** ÆLFRIC *Gen.* iv. 9 Sceolde ic minne broþor healdon? *Ibid.* xxxvii. 13 þine ȝebroþru healdaþ sceap on Sichima. *c* **1000** —— *Hom.* II. 230 Se ðe hylt Israhel. *Ibid.* 382 Ða weardas heoldon þæs cweartернes duru. *c* **1050** *Laws of Cnut* I. c. 20 (Schmid) þe he his men rihtlice healde. *a* **1100** *O.E. Chron.* an. 1014 Gif he hi rihtlicor healdan wolde. *a* **1175** *Cott. Hom.* 219 He halt mid his mihte hefene and eorðe.

†**b.** To guard, defend, preserve (from hurt).

c **1000** *Ags. Ps.* (Th.) cxx. 4 Se þe sceal healdan nu Israela folc utan wið feondum [*qui custodit Israel*]. **13..** *Guy Warw.* (A.) 7225 'God', he seyd, 'fader almiȝt, þat.. heldest Daniel fram þe lyoun, Saue me fram þis foule dragoun'.

2. a. To keep from getting away; to keep fast, grasp.

Often with advb. extension, as ***hold fast***; see also IV. ***to hold one's sides***: to press the hands against the sides, as in excessive laughter.

c **1000** ÆLFRIC *Hom.* I. 110 Iacob heold þone yldran broðer Esau be ðam fet. *c* **1205** LAY. 24752 Ælc mid his honde heold his iuere. **1398** TREVISA *Barth. De P.R.* v. xviii. (1495) 123 Joab helde the chynne of Amasa as though he wold kysse hym. **1550** LYNDESAY *Sqr. Meldrum* 378 Ane quaif of gold to hald his hair. **1578** LYTE *Dodoens* I. lviii. 85 The same decoction, holden and kept in the mouth. **1606** SHAKS. *Tr. & Cr.* v. iii. 59 Lay hold vpon him Priam, hold him fast. **1632** MILTON *L'Allegro* 32 Laughter holding both his sides. **1768** STERNE *Sent. Journ.* (1778) I. 43 (*In the Street*), I continued holding her hand. **1892** *Chamb. Jrnl.* 3 Sept. 561/2 A.. boy rushed up.. to hold the rector's horse.

b. *Cricket.* To catch (a ball): implying a difficult or skilful catch.

1744 *Laws* [of Cricket] in *New Dict. Arts & Sci.* (1755) IV. 3459/1 If the ball be held before she touches ground, though she be hugged to the body, it is out. **1868** *Baily's Monthly Mag.* July 127 Mr. Miles would have got ten wickets had there been any man in the field capable of holding a catch. **1882** *Daily Tel.* 24 June, Hornby drove Giffen hard to mid-on, where Bannerman held the ball cleverly. **1903** G. L. JESSOP in H. G. Hutchinson *Cricket* v. 130 'Dolly' catches are much more difficult to hold than those from hard drives.

c. *Sporting colloq.* To prove a match for, hold one's own against.

1883 *Times* 22 Oct. 10/2 It seems likely that she holds all the horses that ran in the Cesarewitch safe enough. **1891** *Sat. Rev.* 10 Oct. 412/1 On the more level slope he begins to hold his pursuer. **1893** *Sat. Rev.* 25 Mar. 323/1 Oxford rowed a slower stroke.. than their opponents, and yet appeared to hold them fairly easily from post to finish.

d. To keep back, detain, delay.

1891 F. H. SMITH *Col. Carter* 135 'Where did you get this?' he asked, aghast. 'From the carrier. It [*sc.* a letter] was held for postage.' **1904** *New York Times* 20 Aug. 1 The railroad has issued an order.. that trains shall not be held for the.. taking of baggage after the regular time scheduled for stops has expired. **1970** G. F. NEWMAN *Sir, You Bastard*

viii. 203 Sneed was greeted by Sergeant Waugh, who jumped back to try and hold the lift for him.

e. To detain in custody, keep under arrest. orig. *U.S.*

1903 *N.Y. Evening Post* 19 Aug., The men were held for felonious assault, and the woman as a witness. **1906** *Springfield* (Mass.) *Weekly Republican* 14 June 1 If the New York insurance officials cannot be held for larceny, they might evidently be held for forgery or perjury. **1922** H. Titus *Timber* iii. 32 'Why did he arrest you?' 'Oh, I dropped a cigarette out here in summer an' started a fire,..an' he held me under the fire law.' **1966** J. Bingham *Double Agent* xii. 183 He spoke to the Maltese police inspector. 'You would do me a personal favour if you would hold him for twenty-four hours.' **1972** J. Rathbone *Trip Trap* viii. 89 There were no convictions, but she had been held for questioning on three occasions.

f. *Boxing.* (See quot. 1954.)

1922 N. Clark *How to Box* xii. 191 It must be understood that it takes two to make a clinch, and unless both men are holding, the referee has not the power to call 'break-away'. **1923** T. C. Wignall *Story of Boxing* 318 The referee shall have power to disqualify for..holding, butting, shouldering, [etc.]. **1954** F. C. Avis *Boxing Ref. Dict.* 53 *Hold*, to grasp an opponent with the hands—not permitted. **1960** *Times* 28 Sept. 16/7 The referee had to speak to both men for holding. **1961** *Times* 8 Mar. 17/3 Spinks appeared to be palming and holding so flagrantly.

3. a. To keep from falling, to sustain or support in or with the hand, arms, etc.: applicable to any degree of exertion, from that involved in *holding up* (see sense 44) a heavy object, to that which does not differ from *having in the hand*, except by the mere implication of muscular action.

c **1000** Ælfric *Hom.* I. 538 Ealle..healdende palm-twigu on heora handum. [Cf. I. 90 Hæbbende heora palm-twigu on handa.] *c* **1290** *St. Dunstan* 13 in *S. Eng. Leg.* I. 19 Seint Dunstones moder taper..þat heo hald on hire hond. *a* **1300** *Floriz & Bl.* 746 His swerd fel of his hond..Ne miȝte he it holde. *c* **1320** *Seuyn Sag.* (W.) 2009 Another ymage That held a mirour in his hond. ? *a* **1366** Chaucer *Rom. Rose* 939 Ten brode arowis hilde he there. **1583** Hollyband *Campo di Fior* 25 Hold the basin high as you give water to ones handes. **1585** T. Washington tr. *Nicholay's Voy.* I. vi. 4 b, Holding in hys hande a long staffe of silver. **1613** Purchas *Pilgrimage* (1614) 371 Muttering their prayers, holding a bundle of small Tameriske-twigs. **1879** 'Cavendish' *Card Ess.* 191 My partner held good trumps. **1887** *Times* (weekly ed.) 2 Sept. 14/3 Holding a brief for the National League. **1887** Bowen *Virg. Æneid* II. 674 My wife..Holds our little Iulus before his father to see. *Mod.* Hold my book while I run back. The girl was holding the baby for her mother.

†**b.** *fig.* To uphold, support, maintain. *Obs.*

c **1000** *Laws Æthelred* v. c. 35 Utan ænne cyne-hlaford holdlice healdan. **1340** *Ayenb.* 35 Þe heȝe men..þet hyealdeþ and sosteneþ iewes and þe caorsins.

c. In pregnant sense: To hold so as to keep in position, guide, control, or manage, as *to hold the sceptre, the reins, the plough.*

1577 B. Googe *Heresbach's Husb.* I. (1586) 6 He customably used himselfe to hold the Plow. **1590** Spenser *F.Q.* I. iv. 41 Enraged wight, Whome great griefe made forgett the raines to hold Of reason's rule. **1621** T. Williamson tr. *Goulart's Wise Vieillard* 49 Even as wee see Pilots..holding the Rudder. **1631** Gouge *God's Arrows* v. xi. 421 More fit..to handle a mattocke then to hold a musket.

†**d.** To sustain, bear, endure, 'stand' (some treatment). *Obs.*

1592 Greene *Upst. Courtier* (1881) 237 The shoomaker cares not if his shooes hold the drawing on. **1606** W. Crawshaw *Romish Forgeries* A ij a, If the matter will not hold plea, and if my proofe be not substantiall. **1607** Shaks. *Cor.* III. ii. 80 Now humble as the ripest Mulberry, That will not hold the handling. **1664** Waller *Poems, To Sir T. Higgins*, Their small gallies may not hold compare With our tall ships.

4. To keep (the body, or a member) in a particular position or attitude; to 'carry', sustain, bear.

a **1300** *Cursor M.* 4196 Godd hald ouer him his holi hand! **1387** Trevisa *Higden* (Rolls) I. 229 A man sittynge þeron..halt his riȝt hond as þouȝ he spake to þe peple. **1545** Ascham *Toxoph.* II. (Arb.) 145 An other holdeth his necke a wrye. **1592** Shaks. *Rom. & Jul.* v. iii. 4 Holding thy eare close to the hollow ground. **1613** Beaum. & Fl. *Coxcomb* v. ii, Be not fearful, for I hold My hands before my mouth. **1885** Dora Russell *On Golden Hinges* II. xi. 165 She held herself like a queen. **1890** W. C. Russell *Ocean Trag.* I. iii. 52 She held her face averted. **1892** *Longm. Mag.* Jan. 230 She held her head as proudly as ever.

5. a. To have or keep within it; to retain (fluid, or the like), so that it does not run out; *esp.* to contain (with reference to amount or quantity); to be capable of containing, have capacity for.

c **1000** Ælfric *Hom.* II. 56 Ða wæter-fatu, sume heoldon twyfealde ȝemetu, sume þryfealde. *a* **1300** *Cursor M.* 5924 Ne was in hus na vessel fre þat watur hild, o stan ne tre. **1388** Wyclif *Jer.* ii. 13 Cisternes distried, that moun not holde watris. *c* **1400** Maundev. (1839) v. 54 That yle [Cycile] holt in compas about CCCL frensche myles. *c* **1480** *Lit. Childr. Lit. Bk.* 30 in *Babees Bk.* 18 Put not thy mete..In-to thy Seler that thy salte halte. **1531–2** *Act 23 Hen. VIII*, c. 4 §4 Euery barrell for bere shall conteine and holde .xxxvi. gallons. **1590** Shaks. *Mids. N.* v. i. 9 More diuels then vaste hell can hold. **1720** De Foe *Capt. Singleton* xii. (1840) 206 He stored the sloop as full as she could hold. **1736** Fielding *Pasquin* I. i, I'll make the house too hot to hold you. **1805** W. Saunders *Min. Waters* 225 The animal and vegetable matters which it holds in solution. **1847** *Jrnl. R. Agric. Soc.* VIII. I. 66 Peat holds water like a sponge. **1872** Black *Adv. Phaeton* xii, Cannot the phaeton hold five? *Mod.* This jug holds two pints.

b. *spec.* Of a theatre: to have capacity for (freq. with reference to the size of a theatre's seating capacity expressed in terms of the takings).

1740 C. Cibber *Apology for Life* xii. 240 Spectators, who may remember what Form the Drury-Lane Theatre stood in, about forty Years ago, before the old Patentee, to make it hold more Mony, took it in his Head to alter it. **1812** *Dramatic Censor 1811* Apr. 218 Which..will, at the old prices, hold as much money as the modern excessively large Theatres. **1894** G. B. Shaw *Let.* 20 Mar. (1965) 421 The Avenue [theatre] holds, when full, £200. **1946** —— *Matter with Ireland* (1962) 13 It [*sc.* the theatre] held more money per square foot of ground than the classical Royal.

6. a. To have or keep as one's own absolutely or temporarily; to own, have as property; to be the owner, possessor, or tenant of; to be in possession or enjoyment of.

to have and to hold: see Have *v.* 1 c.

a **855** *O.E. Chron.* an. 611 Her Cynegils feng to rice..and heold xxxi wintra. *c* **897** [see A. 2]. *c* **1000** *Ags. Ps.* (Th.) cxxii[i]. 1 Þu þe heofon-hamas healdest and wealdest [*habitas in cælo*]. *a* **1200** *Moral Ode* 55 in *Trin. Coll. Hom.* 221 Se þe aihte wile holde wel. *c* **1200** Ormin 2225 Þatt illke kinesæte þatt Daviþþ king hiss faderr held. *c* **1330** R. Brunne *Chron.* (1810) 14 If any Breton were fonden holdand lond. **1362** Langl. *P. Pl.* A. II. 38 Sir Simonye is of-sent to asseale þe Chartres, þat Fals oþur Fauuel by eny [fyn] heolden. *c* **1400** *Destr. Troy* 13697 Pirrus..Weddit þat worthi, & as wif held. *c* **1400** Maundev. (Roxb.) i. 4 Þe kyng..haldes grete and mykill land. For he haldes þe land of Hungary, Sauoy, Comany [etc.]. **1470–85** Malory *Arthur* xx. ii, Syr Launcelot holdeth your quene and hath done longe. **1574** tr. *Littleton's Tenures* 15 b, If an house be let to holde at will. **1651** Hobbes *Leviath.* II. xxvi. 148 By which he acquireth and holdeth a propriety in land, or goods. **1810** Scott *Lady of L.* II. xxxvii, My Sovereign holds in ward my land. **1844** *Jrnl. R. Agric. Soc.* V. I. 177 Farms are held on a variety of tenure. **1881** Gardiner & Mullinger *Study Eng. Hist.* I. vii. 135 No man who taught the contrary was to be allowed to hold a benefice.

b. To possess, have, occupy (a position, office, quality, etc.).

1340 Hampole *Pr. Consc.* 8129 If endlesnes any end moght hald, þan war it endlesnes unproperly cald. *c* **1400** *Apol. Loll.* 5 In dede þei hald not, ne do his office. *c* **1430** Lydg. *Min. Poems* (Percy Soc.) 174 Wheresoevere thou hoold residence. **1583** Stubbes *Anat. Abus.* II. (1882) 104 They may also lawfully hold superioritie ouer their brethren. **1631** Weever *Anc. Fun. Mon.* 242 He might well haue holden place with the worthiest. **1757** Beattie *Wolf & Sheph.* 10 One With whom wit holds the place of reason. **1809** Kendall *Trav.* I. v. 40 Their places, therefore, are practically holden during good behaviour. **1827** Scott *Surg. Dau.* i, Doctor Grey (he might hold the title by diploma for what I know). **1890** T. F. Tout *Hist. Eng. fr.* 1689. 137 Catholics could hold rank up to that of colonel.

c. Const. *of* or *from* (the superior from whom the title to an estate or office is derived). Also *fig.*

c **1205** Lay. 29377 And aȝef heom sone al þis ærd, of him to heoldenne. *c* **1290** *Beket* 2000 in *S. Eng. Leg.* I. 163 Þe baronie al-so, þat þou halst of him in chef. **1495** *Act 11 Hen. VII*, c. 48 §1 The same Castelles..be holden of your Highnes in Chief as of youre Crowne. **1604** Shaks. *Oth.* I. iii. 118 The Trust, the Office, I do hold of you. **1636** Massinger *Bashf. Lover* IV. iii, I hold my dukedom from you, as your vassal. **1703** Rowe *Ulyss.* IV. i, I have learnt to hold My Life from none, but from the Gods who gave it. **1818** Cruise *Digest* (ed. 2) I. 68 It has been contended that the word *feodum* signifies land holden of a superior lord, by military or other services.

d. *Mil.* To keep forcibly against an adversary, defend; to keep possession of, occupy.

1154 *O.E. Chron.* an. 1135 And [he] held Execestre aȝenes him. **1573** J. Sanford *Hours Recreat.* (1576) 173 They tooke and held the Citie with force. **1593** Shaks. *Rich. II*, II. iii. 164 To Bristow Castle, which they say is held By Bushie, Bagot, and their Complices. **1649** J. Taylor (Water P.) *West. Voy. to Mount* Wks. (1872) 18 The main Island is held for the Prince, by one Captain..called Sir John Grenville. **1667** Milton *P.L.* v. 723 With what Arms We mean to hold what anciently we claim Of Deitie or Empire. **1867** J. B. Rose tr. *Virgil's Æneid* 40 The foeman holds the wall. **1869** W. Longman *Hist. Edw. III*, I. xvii. 319 The bridge was held for some time..at last the French fled.

e. To occupy, be in (a place); also, in stronger sense, To remain in, retain possession or occupation of.

1297 R. Glouc. (Rolls) 7166 He ber þe croune & huld þe deis mid oþer atil also. **13..** *K. Alis.* 1154 Alisaundre heold the deys. *c* **1590** Greene *Fr. Bacon* ix. 124 As if science held her seat Between the circled arches of thy brows. **1634** Milton *Comus* 94 The star, that bids the shepherd fold, Now the top of heaven doth hold. **1704** J. Trapp *Abra-Mulé* II. i. 456 One who holds the very next Apartment. **1885** Mrs. Pirkis *Lady Lovelace* II. xxix. 123 For the nonce lighter questions held his brain. **1892** *Illustr. Lond. News* 7 May 559/3 His first piece..long held the boards.

f. *fig.* Of disease, error, etc.: To have in its power, possess, affect, occupy.

a **1300** *Cursor M.* 11829 Ydropsi held him sua in threst. **1420** *Proclam. Hen. V* in Rymer *Foedera* (1710) 917 Our sayd Father is holden wyth divers Sekeness. **1577** Hanmer *Anc. Eccl. Hist.* (1619) 241 The detestable heresie of Arius, which held their minds of a long time. **1610** Shaks. *Temp.* v. i. 116 Th' affliction of my minde amends, with which I feare a madnesse held me. **1711** Hearne *Collect.* (O.H.S.) III. 122 A Feaver that held him for about a Fortnight. **1886** Seeley *Short Hist. Napoleon I*, iv. §1. 118 The intoxication of the Marengo campaign still held him.

g. Phr. *to hold the stage* (or *house*): to command the attention of a theatre audience.

1889 Barrère & Leland *Dict. Slang*, *Hold the stage, to* (theatrical), is said of an experienced actor who is fully at home on the stage, and always commands the attention of the audience. **1893** Farmer & Henley *Slang*, *To hold the stage*, to have the chief place on the boards and the eye of the audience. **1916** *To-day* 22 July 368/1 You do not need to be a very experienced playgoer to know when an actress is holding a house. **1967** 'La Meri' *Sp. Dancing* (ed. 2) viii. 98 Many dancers assisted by only a pianist held the stage alone for the two hours of a complete evening's performance.

h. *to hold the line*: to maintain telephonic connection during a break in conversation. (Cf. 40 g.) Also *fig.*

1912 Beerbohm *Christmas Garland* 6 It was with a certain sense of his rashness in the matter, therefore, that he now, with an air of feverishly 'holding the line', said 'Oh, as to that.' **1915** *Punch* 10 Nov. 390/1 Such are some of the miseries of holding the line. **1931** Wodehouse *Big Money* i. 24 'Hold the line,' he said in a low, strained voice.

7. a. To keep, preserve, retain; not to lose, let go, part with, or emit; to detain; to arrest, rivet the attention of. Also *hold it!*: stay as you are; do not go on!; steady on!

c **1000** *Ags. Gosp.* Matt. ix. 17 Hiȝ doð niwe win on niwe bytta, and æȝðer byþ ȝe-healden [*Lindisf.* ȝehalden]. *c* **1020** *Rule St. Benet* (Logeman) 98 Him sylfum na healdende of eallum. *a* **1225** *Ancr. R.* 50 Þe blake cloð..halt his heou betere. **1258** *Proclam. Hen. III*, We senden ȝew þis writ..to halden a manges ȝew inehord. *a* **1300** *Cursor M.* 13409 'Quarfor', said he, 'þus has þou Halden þe god wine to now?' **1398** Trevisa *Barth. De P.R.* x. vii. (1495) 378 Cole rake in asshes holdeth and kepyth fyre. **1486** *Bk. St. Albans* C vij b, If she holde it past the secunde day after, she shall be hoole. **1577** B. Googe *Heresbach's Husb.* I. (1586) 7 b, But I holde you to long with commendation of that..I pray you let us goe to dinner. **1613** Purchas *Pilgrimage* (1614) 333 Might..dive in as long as they could hold their breath. **1861** *Temple Bar Mag.* III. 335 Constant changes of scene and method hold the attention. **1885** E. F. Byrrne *Entangled* II. I. xxiv. 130 She..found herself held by his eyes. **1926** A. Huxley *Jesting Pilate* IV. 262 That's good. Hold it. **1930** Auden *Poems* 23 Moisten the lips and start afresh. Hold it. **1948** M. Allingham *More Work for Undertaker* xiii. 160 Oh, I say, hold it... I don't think you ought to go as far as that. **1962** A. Christie *Mirror Crack'd* xv. 167 'That'll do. Hold it. We'll have one more... It looks smashing,' said the photographer. **1973** E. Berckman *Victorian Album* 20 'Let's go and talk to her quickly, quickly—.' 'Hold it, darling,' she interrupted.

b. With extension or complement: To keep in a specified place, state, condition, or relation; to oblige to adhere *to* (a promise or the like: cf. 10).

971 *Blickl. Hom.* 189 Þa heht Petrus and Paulus on bendum healdon. *c* **1200** *Trin. Coll. Hom.* 179 Heald me þe wrache. *c* **1205** Lay. 1044 Ȝe..haldeð me inne bende. *a* **1300** *Cursor M.* 3183 Abraham..hald still þin arm, And to þi sun do þou no harm. *Ibid.* 14405 Pharaon..þat þam in seruage held lang. *c* **1374** Chaucer *Anel. & Arc.* 339 Thus holdithe me my destenye a wrechche. *c* **1400** *Destr. Troy* 8083 To hold hym in hope & hert hym the bettur. **1482** *Monk of Evesham* (Arb.) 26 Beyng holde in a certeyn stupour and wondyr of mynde. **1545** Ascham *Toxoph.* I. (Arb.) 83 Suche a rable of shoters..as wolde holde vs talkyng whyles tomorowe. **1607** Shaks. *Cor.* II. iii. 202 His gracious Promise, which you might..haue held him to. **1754** Richardson *Grandison* (1820) II. 286 The captain is desirous to hold you to it. **1872** C. E. Maurice *Stephen Langton* iii. 213 John's army was held in check. **1892** *Temple Bar Mag.* Nov. 360 He was held at bay.

c. *refl.* To keep oneself; to adhere, remain, keep.

c **1230** *Hali Meid.* 25 Moni halt him til an make. **1297** R. Glouc. (1724) 379 'Þe kyng', he seyde, 'of Engelond halt hym to hys bedde'. *a* **1300** *Cursor M.* 6521 Moyses him hild awai. *Ibid.* 10413 Quen þat he heild him fra hame. **1377** Langl. *P. Pl.* B. xx. 245 Holdeþ ȝow in vnyte. *c* **1475** *Rauf Coilȝear* 373 For thy, hald ȝow fra the Court. *a* **1533** Ld. Berners *Huon* lv. 187 Euery man praysed gretely Huon that he helde hym selfe so fermely. **1535** Coverdale *Job* xxxvi. 2 Holde the still a litle. **1571** Campion *Hist. Irel.* II. vii. (1633) 98 Richard held himselfe in Ireland. **1861** *Temple Bar Mag.* I. 340 They held themselves aloof from the popular current.

†**d.** To continue to occupy; to remain in (a place); not to move from or leave; to 'keep'. *Obs.*

c **1386** Chaucer *Man of Law's T.* 623 She halt hire chambre. *a* **1450** *Knt. de la Tour* (1868) 64 Had they holde the highe waye. **1513** Douglas *Æneis* III. iii. 84 The schippis haldand the deip see. *a* **1547** Surrey *Æneid* II. Poems (1831) 131 Holding alway the chief street of the town. **1795** Osbaldiston *Brit. Sportsm.* 477 If it be rainy, then the hare will hold the highways more than at any other time.

e. *Hunting.* To keep going; to lead or drive (hounds). Cf. 24.

1891 *Field* 21 Nov. 792/2 We found Mark..holding the hounds up the common again. **1891** *Ibid.* 19 Dec. 954/2 Laurance..held his hounds across the valley.

f. *to hold the road*: to continue to occupy the road; to keep to the road without skidding, etc.

1926 T. E. Lawrence *Let.* 27 Sept. (1938) 500 The S.S. 100 holds the road extraordinarily. **1971** P. D. James *Shroud for Nightingale* ii. 43 [She] wondered whether her small car would hold the road.

8. a. To keep together, to keep in being, existence, or operation, to carry on; to convoke and preside over (a meeting, assembly, council, or the like); to go through formally, perform (any proceeding or function); to keep, observe, celebrate (a festival); to carry on, sustain, or have (communication, intelligence, conversation); to keep (company, silence, etc.); to use (language) habitually or constantly; = Have *v.* II.

a **1100** *O.E. Chron.* an. 1075 Hi ne dorstan nan ȝefeoht healdan wið Willelm cynge. *Ibid.* an. 1085 Her se cyng bær his corona and heold his hired. *c* **1200** *Trin. Coll. Hom.* 85 Sein[t] nicholas..þat wune heold to his liues ende. *c* **1205** Lay. 4766 Belin in Euerewic huld eorlene husting. *a* **1225** *Ancr. R.* 22 Vrom þet, efter Preciosa, holdeð silence. *a* **1300** *Cursor M.* 10215 A mikel fest..þat Iues held. *c* **1340** *Ibid.*

13363 (Trin.) A bridale was þere on I halde. **1375** BARBOUR *Bruce* I. 410 The king Eduuard.. Come to strevillyne. For till hald thar ane assemble. *c* **1450** *Merlin* 2 The fendes helden a gret conseill. **1485** CAXTON *Paris & V.* 8, I wyl holde you companye thyder. *a* **1535** MORE *Edw. V* (1641) 3 The Parliament holden the thirtieth yeere of King Henry the Sixth. **1579** SPENSER *Sheph. Cal.* July 29 To holden chat with seely shepherds swayne. **1654** tr. *Scudery's Curia Pol.* 41 Had he held intelligence with the King of Granada. **1726** SWIFT *Gulliver* I. v, [They] can hold conversation in both tongues. **1769** BLACKSTONE *Comm.* IV xix. 267 Any county, wherein the assises are held. **1814** CARY *Dante, Par.* XXVI. 93, I pray thee hold Converse with me. **1840** J. QUINCY *Hist. Harvard Univ.* I. 91 The first meeting of the Corporation.. was holden on the 13th of the ensuing July. **1849** MACAULAY *Hist. Eng.* vi. I. 667 Several opulent gentlemen were accused of holding conventicles.

b. *Mus.* †(*a*) To perform (a particular part in concerted music); = BEAR *v.*[1] 20. *Obs.* (*b*) To sustain (a note, esp. in one part while the other parts move).

1885 'RITA' *Like Dian's Kiss* xxiv. 180 The vocal thunder, having terminated in a prolonged holding of the low E, is followed by loud applause. **1889** E. PROUT *Harmony* xix. §501 A suspension may be very simply defined as a note of one chord held over another of which it forms no part. **1934** C. LAMBERT *Music Ho!* III. 205 When a guitar hung in every negro barber's shop, and a client who was waiting would vamp about on the instrument until at a lucky *trouvaile* everyone would shout 'Hold that chord'.

†**9.** To keep unbroken or inviolate; to observe, abide by (a command, vow, promise, faith, etc.); the opposite of *to break* or *violate*. *Obs.*

971 *Blickl. Hom.* 35 We sceolan þa ten bebodu healdan. *Ibid.* 45 Gif hi nellaþ healdan Godes æwe. *c* **1175** *Lamb. Hom.* 89 Ne we ne moten halden moyses e. **1258** *Proclam. Hen. III*, þæt heo stedefæstliche healden and swerien to healden.. þo isetnesses þæt beon imakede. *a* **1300** *Cursor M.* 10698 Hu Sco moght hir mari and hald hir vou. ?*a* **1366** CHAUCER *Rom. Rose* 266 Feith ne trouth holdith she To freend ne felawe, bad or good. *c* **1400** *Sowdone Bab.* 610, I aske nowe of the To holde covenaunte in this cas. *c* **1475** *Rauf Coilȝear* 449, I sall hald that I haue hecht. **1598** SHAKS. *Merry W.* v. v. 260 To Master Broome, you yet shall hold your word. *a* **1625** FLETCHER *Women Pleased* v. i. Wks. (Rtldg.) II. 200/1 'Tis fit you hold your word, sir.

10. †**a.** To oblige, bind, constrain; in later use, chiefly in pa. pple. ***holden***. *Obs.* or *arch.*

c **1205** LAY. 9459 þe to fehte heom scolde halden. **1382** WYCLIF *2 Kings* iv. 8 Ther was there a grete womman, that heelde hym, that he ete brede. *c* **1385** CHAUCER *L.G.W.* 1443 *Hypsip.*, Thanne were I holde to quyte thy laboure. ?*a* **1400** *Praier of Ploweman* in *Harl. Misc.* (1810) VI. 113 And thus ys my brother y-holde to done to me. **14..** HOCCLEVE *Compl. Virgin* 138 Thou art as moche, or more, holde him to hyde, Than Sem, þat helid his Fadir Noe. **1582–8** *Hist. James VI* (1804) 71 His brother should not be haldin to answere onie farder in that mater. **1794** S. WILLIAMS *Vermont* 253 They could not view themselves as holden.. to submit.

†**b.** ***to be holden***: to be obliged, under obligation *to* (any one), to be BEHOLDEN. *Obs.* or *arch.*

c **1350** *Will. Palerne* 317 To þis man & his meke wif most y am holde. **1390** GOWER *Conf.* III. 374 (MS. Harl. 3490) Whereof to him in speciall above all other I am most holde. **1485** CAXTON *Paris & V.* 34 We be moche holden to you. **1519** *Interl. Four Elements* in Hazl. *Dodsley* I. 15 Greatly am I now holden unto thee. **1666** PEPYS *Diary* 9 Apr., So we.. turned back, being holden to the gentleman.

c. ***to hold to bail***: to bind or constrain by bail; see BAIL *sb.*[1], esp. the note after sense 6.

1837 DICKENS *Pickw.* xxv, Pickwick and Tupman he had already held to bail. **1890** *Times* (weekly ed.) 28 Feb. 2/3 [He] was wrongfully held to bail to be of good behaviour.

11. a. To keep back from action, hinder, prevent, restrain; *refl.* to restrain oneself, refrain, forbear. *Obs.* or *arch.* exc. in special phrases; *spec.* **b.** To keep in, refrain from (speech, noise, etc.): see also *hold one's* TONGUE.

c **897** K. ÆLFRED *Gregory's Past.* xxxiii. 220 Ac se wisa hilt his spræce and bitt timan. **971** *Blickl. Hom.* 37 þæt we us healdan.. wiþ þa heafodlican leahtras. *a* **1300** *Cursor M.* 13647 He allan þat dos his will, And halds him fra dedis ill. **1382** WYCLIF *Luke* xxiv. 16 Sothli her yȝen weren holdun, lest thei knewen him. **1484** CAXTON *Fables of Æsop* III. iii, Who holdeth now me that wyth my foote I breke not thyn hede? **1542** UDALL *Erasm. Apoph.* 288 To suche poynte that thou maiest not hold vomityng. **1566** GASCOIGNE *Supposes* I. i, Holde thy talking, nourse, and harken to me. **1642–3** EARL OF NEWCASTLE *Declar.* in Rushw. *Hist. Coll.* (1721) V. 137 Let them call them what they will, so they would hold their Fingers from them. **1774** T. JEFFERSON *Autobiog.* App. Wks. 1859 I. 131 The only restraining motive which may hold the hand of a tyrant. **1844** DICKENS *Mart. Chuz.* xxv, I wish you'd hold your noise! **1891** *Graphic* Christm. No. 20/3 He had reluctantly held his fire, determined to wait till he could 'mak siccar'.

c. Phr. ***to hold one's horses***: used esp. in *imper.* (***hold your horses!***) = be patient, hold on! orig. *U.S.*

1844 *Picayune* (New Orleans) 16 Sept. 241/4 Oh, hold your hosses, Squire. There's no use gettin' riled, no how. **1847** J. S. ROBB *Streaks of Squatter Life* 24 Jest hold your hosses, boys—he'll come out directly. **1917** *Woman's Home Compan.* Nov. 58 Now Phebe.. you just hold your hosses and speak a little slower. **1939** *Chatelaine* Oct. 43/4 Hold your horses, dear. **1943** HUNT & PRINGLE *Service Slang* 39 *Hold your horses*, hold the job until further orders. (Comes from the Artillery.) **1945** S. LEWIS *Cass Timberlane* (1947) xl. 272 Hey, hold your horses, Cass. Don't get sore. **1967** N. FITZGERALD *Affairs of Death* vii. 119 'I'm going in to the station *now*,' he said. 'Hold your horses,' Marr said. 'The night's young.'

d. To keep (a person) from speaking; to prevent (a person) from being troublesome. *N. Amer. colloq.*

1901 ADE *Forty Modern Fables* 244 'And I guess that'll Hold you for a While,' added the Biggest Boy in the Room. **1922** S. LEWIS *Babbitt* v. 63 'I guess that'll hold you for a while, George!' said Finkelstein. **1935** N. L. MCCLUNG *Clearing in West* xvii. 136 Maybe that would hold Miss Adams! **1965** 'S. WOODS' *Though I know she Lies* xvi. 212 '*That* should hold him for a while,' said Derek with satisfaction.

e. ***hold everything!***: wait! take no action!

1930 in *Amer. Speech* VI. 92. **1948** C. DAY LEWIS *Otterbury Incident* viii. 93 Hold everything now, this is the big bang coming. **1951** L. HOBSON *Celebrity* (1953) xi. 155 Hold everything; let's see.

12. To have or keep in the mind, entertain: **a.** (a feeling, etc.) *Obs.* or *arch.*

a **1000** *Beowulf* (Z.) 1954 Hio.. heold heah-lufan wið hæleþa brego. *c* **1205** LAY. 30198 And for þere muchele luue þa heolde heore aldren. **1579** SPENSER *Sheph. Cal.* Jan. 64 She.. of my rurall musick holdeth scorne. **1591** SHAKS. *Two Gent.* III. ii. 17 Protheus, the good conceit I hold of thee. **1595** —— *John* III. iv. 90 You hold too heynous a respect of greefe. **1637** HEYLIN *Answ. Burton* Pref. C iv a, If they hold a Reverend esteeme of those who [etc.]. **1802** LEYDEN *Mermaid* xlv, That heart.. Can hold no sympathy with mine. **1846** H. TORRENS *Rem. Milit. Lit.* I. 39 The first.. who acknowledged the tactical theory and held great account of those who practised it.

b. (a belief, opinion, doctrine, etc.): To accept and entertain as true; to believe.

1340 *Ayenb.* 134 We þet þe riȝte byleaue hyealdeþ. **1485** CAXTON *Chas. Gt.* 224, I holde the cristen fayth. **1579** GOSSON *Sch. Abuse* (Arb.) 65 Let me holde the same proposition still. **1608** TOPSELL *Serpents* 134 All the Egyptians holde opinion, that the Crocodile is a Diuinatour. **1667** EARL OF CARDIGAN in *12th Rep. Hist. MSS. Comm.* App. v. 9 The Church of England holds the three creeds as well as we. **1678** CUDWORTH *Intell. Syst.* Contents I. iii. §36 It appears, that Aristotle also held the world's animation. **1890** T. F. TOUT *Hist. Eng. fr.* 1689. 102 Those who held most strongly the divine right of the people to choose their own ministers. **1892** *Monist* II. 162 Justified in holding this view.

c. With obj. clause: To be of opinion, think, consider, believe (*that*).

a **1300** *Sarmun* xiii. in *E.E.P.* (1862) 2 Ihc hold a fole þat he be. *c* **1340** *Cursor M.* 2507 (Trin.) þei helde heres was þe lond. **1413** *Pilgr. Sowle* (Caxton) I. v. (1859) 5, I holde nought that al be trewe that he seyth. **1535** COVERDALE *Matt.* xxii. 23 The Saduces which holde that there is no resurreccion. **1607** SHAKS. *Cor.* II. ii. 87 It is held, That Valour is the chiefest Vertue. **1771** JOHNSON *Lett. to Mrs. Thrale* 7 July, She holds that both Frank and his master are much improved. **1871** FREEMAN *Hist. Ess.* Ser. I. i. 15, I hold.. that the details.. are altogether unhistorical.

d. With obj. and complement or extension: To think, consider, esteem, regard as. Const. with simple compl. or (*arch.*) with *as*, *for*, or with infin.

c **1200** *Vices & Virtues* 63 And halt him seluen for ierðe. *c* **1205** LAY. 8082 Heo heolden hine for hæhne godd. *a* **1225** *Ancr. R.* 192 Holdeð hit alle blisse uorte uallen in misliche of þeos fondunges. *a* **1300** *Cursor M.* 27135 þou haldes þin aun gilt bot light. *c* **1386** CHAUCER *Prol.* 141 And to ben holden digne of reuerence. —— *Reeve's T.* 288 When this Iape is tald another day, I sal been halde a daf, a cokenay. *c* **1477** CAXTON *Jason* 63, I requyre yow that ye holde me for excused. *a* **1533** LD. BERNERS *Gold Bk. M. Aurel.* (1546) M viij b, They were holden and reputed as goddes after their death. **1641** J. JACKSON *True Evang. T.* III. 202, I hold mine own Religion so good, as it needs not fetch lustre from the disgrace of another. **1779** J. MOORE *View Soc. Fr.* (1789) I. xxiii. 179 The very idea of resistance.. they hold as absurd. **1849** MACAULAY *Hist. Eng.* viii. II. 364 For their absence the king was held responsible. **1855** *Ibid.* xii. III. 185 He held the lives of other men as cheap as his own. **1864** J. H. NEWMAN *Apol.* 419 If you would not scruple in holding Paley for an honest man.

e. Of a judge or court: To state as an authoritative opinion; to lay down as a point of law; to decide.

1642 tr. *Perkins' Prof. Bk.* v. §306. 135 It hath been holden in the time of King Henry the third that [etc.]. **1769** BLACKSTONE *Comm.* IV. iii. 49 It is clearly held, that one acquitted as principal may be indicted as an accessory after the fact. **1818** CRUISE *Digest* (ed. 2) III. 360 The Master of the Rolls held that the renewed lease was a new acquistion, which vested in the daughter as a purchaser. **1863** H. COX *Instit.* I. vi. 47 The Court.. held that the plea to its jurisdiction was insufficient.

f. To have in a specified relation to the mind or thought; to entertain a specified feeling towards; in such phrases as to ***hold in esteem***, ***contempt***, ***memory***, etc.

For these phrases, transitive verbs may usually be substituted; thus *to hold in esteem* = to esteem; *to hold in contempt* = to despise; *to hold in memory* = to remember.

a **1300** *Cursor M.* 2610 Yone lasce.. Als in despit sco haldes me. *Ibid.* 4245 Putifer.. held ioseph in mensk and are. *a* **1533** LD. BERNERS *Gold Bk. M. Aurel.* (1546) B iv b, In so hyghe estimation it holdeth the virtuous. **1585** T. WASHINGTON tr. *Nicholay's Voy.* III. xxi. 111 The temple of Solomon.. which they holde in great reverence. **1611** BIBLE *Phil.* ii. 29 Hold such in reputation. **1718** *Freethinker* No. 64 ¶7 Magna Charta.. with Us is justly held in the greatest Veneration. **1875** JOWETT *Plato* (ed. 2) III. 304 The wise and mighty one who is to be held in honour.

†**13. a.** To offer as a wager; to wager, bet, 'lay'.

c **1460** *Towneley Myst.* (E.E.T.S.) xvi. 328, I hold here a grote she lykys me not weyll. **1530** PALSGR. 691/2, I holde the a penye I tell the where this bell ryngeth. **1594** GREENE & LODGE *Looking Glasse* Wks. (Rtldg.) 126/1, I hold my cap to a noble that the Usurer hath given him some gold. **1698** VANBRUGH *Prov. Wife* II. i, *Const.* I'll hold you a guinea you don't make her tell it you. *Sir John.* I'll hold you a guinea I do. **1719** D'URFEY *Pills* II. 54 I'll hold ye five Guineas to four. **1768** GOLDSM. *Good-n Man* II. Wks. (Globe) 618/2 I'll hold you a guinea of that, my dear.

†**b.** To accept as a wager. *Obs.*

1530 PALSGR. 586/2 Lay downe your monaye, I holde it, *sus boutez vostre argent, je le tiens.* **1591** GREENE *Disc. Coosnage* (1592) 7 Saith the Connie, I durst laie xii. d. more. I hold it saith the barnacle. **1626** *Scogin's Jests* in *Shaks. Jest Bk.* (1864) II. 103 Yes.. and on that I will lay twenty pound. I hold it said the knight: lay downe the Money.

¶**14.** *Billiards.* = HOLE *v.*[1] 6. [A corruption of *hole*, by association of *holed* and *hold*: cf. 2, 5.]

1869 BLACKLEY *Word Gossip* 74 A player is continually said to have held a ball when he drives it into a pocket. **1877** BARTLETT *Dict. Amer.* (ed. 4) 283 Billiard players say, 'I held the ball', instead of I holed it.

II. Intransitive and absolute uses.

15. a. To do the act of holding; to keep hold; to maintain one's grasp; to cling. Also with *by* (†*upon*, *to*).

(App. *by* is intrumental: cf. 'he held the pig by the ears' with 'he held by the pig's ears'.)

c **1305** *St. Dunstan* 82 in *E.E.P.* (1862) 36 þe deuel wrickede her and þer: and he [Dunstan] huld euere faste. **1549** LATIMER *2nd Serm. bef. Edw. VI* (Arb.) 59 He toke sanctuary, and held by the hornes of the aultare. **1551** T. WILSON *Logike* (1580) 35 b, Some hold fast upon the saiyng of sainct Augustine, and build wonders upon that text. **1562** J. HEYWOOD *Prov. & Epigr.* (1867) 171 Holde fast when ye haue it. *a* **1654** SELDEN *Table-T.* (Arb.) 22 Do as if you were going over a Bridge.. hold fast by the Rail. **1796** C. MARSHALL *Garden.* xiv. (1813) 195 If the plants hold tight to the pots. **1842** TENNYSON *Epic* 21 There was no anchor, none, To hold by.

†**b.** In the imperative, used in offering or presenting; = Here! take it! [= F. *tiens*, Sc. *hae*.]

c **1489** CAXTON *Sonnes of Aymon* vi. 154 Holde here, worthy knyghte Reynawde, I gyve you my suster to your wyff and spouse. **1567** HARMAN *Caveat* 39 Holde, here is a couple of pence for thee. **1598** SHAKS. *Merry W.* I. iv. 166 Hold, there's money for thee. **1605** —— *Macb.* II. i. 4 Hold, take my Sword.

c. *Commerce.* To retain goods, etc.; not to sell.

1890 BOLDREWOOD *Col. Reformer* (1891) 149 What will you take for that cattle station..? No use holding, you know. **1892** *Standard* 7 Nov. 6/6 Spinners are holding tenaciously for full rates.

d. Of a female animal: To retain the seed; to conceive. Also *to hold to* (the male).

1614 MARKHAM *Cheap Husb.* I. iii. (1668) 34 To know whether your Mare hold to the Horse or no. **1617** —— *Caval.* I. 40 It is most infallible that she holdeth. **1851** *Jrnl. R. Agric. Soc.* XII. I. 64 A disposition in cows to conceive (or 'hold to the bull'). **1891** *Field* 28 Nov. 805/2 The chances are against the mare holding.

e. Only in pres. pple. *holding*: 'financial', in funds. *Austral.* and *N.Z. colloq.*

c **1926** 'MIXER' *Transport Workers' Song Bk.* 11 'What-ho, Jerry, how yer holding?'.. 'I haven't made enough this week For to pay the blooming rent.' **1930** *Bulletin* (Sydney) 29 Oct. 21/1 Whether a man was 'oldin' or whether a man was broke, Joe was a man you could bank on.

f. To be in possession of drugs for sale. *U.S. slang.*

1935 A. J. POLLOCK *Underworld Speaks* 3/2 *Are you holding?* Have you any dope to sell? **1953** W. BURROUGHS *Junkie* (1972) ii. 26 The connection was here about ten minutes ago. This character's holding, but he won't turn loose of any. **1961** R. RUSSELL *Sound* (1962) I. i. 15 Don't jump the light, baby, mother's holding, you know. *Ibid.* II. ix. 158 He was holding, just as Red had said. Santa had the sweets.

16. Of things: To maintain connexion; to remain fast or unbroken; not to give way or become loose.

c **1398** CHAUCER *Fortune* 38 Yit halt thin ancre and yit thow mayst aryue. *c* **1400** *Lanfranc's Cirurg.* 142 And þe nose were kutt al awey but þat it held faste at boþe þe eendis.. of þe wounde. **1506** GUYLFORDE *Pilgr.* (Camden) 65 They let fall the thyrde ancre, which, thankyd be Almyghty God, helde fast. **1611** SHAKS. *Wint. T.* IV. iii. 36 If the sprindge hold, the Cocke's mine. **1648** *Cornu-Copia* in *Harl. Misc.* (1810) VI. 33 To make glue for the joining of boards.. that shall hold faster than the boards themselves. **1795** OSBALDISTON *Brit. Sportsm.* 259 One of them will hold better than two of the common sort [of nails]. **1891** *Illustr. Lond. News* 31 Jan. 140/3 The helm was perfectly sound, and the lashings held bravely. **1893** *Longm. Mag.* Apr. 552 The lock held.

17. To maintain one's attachment; to remain faithful or attached; to adhere, keep, 'stick' *to*; to abide *by*. (Sometimes approaching sense 21.)

c **1200** *Trin. Coll. Hom.* 61 We.. biheten him festliche þat we wolden eure to him holden. *c* **1300** *Havelok* 1171 And þat she sholde til him holde. **1390** GOWER *Conf.* III. 355 For she.. Hath set me for a finall ende The point, wherto that I shall holde. **1611** BIBLE *Matt.* vi. 24 Hee will holde to the one, and despise the other. **1677** HALE *Prim. Orig. Man.* I. iii. 77 If they hold to their Principles. **1865** *Jrnl. R. Agric. Soc.* I. II. 323 Herefordshire has held stoutly by its native breed. **1879** MISS YONGE *Cameos* Ser. IV. xxviii. 299 The Queen.. held to her purpose.

18. To have capacity or contents; *spec.* in *Hunting*, said of a covert: To contain game.

1581 MULCASTER *Positions* xl. (1887) 230, I wishe the roome.. large to holde, and conuenient to holde handsomely. **1891** *Field* 21 Nov. 791/2 It [a covert] did not hold to-day, and we went on to.. Bourke's Gorse. **1893** *Ibid.* 11 Feb. 190/1 Leslie's Gorse did not hold.

19. a. To hold property by some tenure, to derive title to something (*of* or *from* a superior).

c **1275** *Luue Ron* 102 in *O.E. Misc.* 96 Henri king of engelonde, of hym he halt, and to hym buhþ. *c* **1330** R.

BRUNNE *Chron.* (1810) 42 He com vnto Gaynesburgh, of Suane forto halde. **1470–85** MALORY *Arthur* I. vii, He made alle lordes that helde of the croune to come in. **1550** CROWLEY *Last Trump.* 1234 As thou doest hold of thy kyng, so doth thy tenaunt holde of the. **1647** N. BACON *Disc. Govt. Eng.* I. lv. (1739) 98 A second sort of men that made the King uncapable to hold by Conquest, was the Clergy. **1734** tr. *Rollin's Anc. Hist.* (1827) I. Pref. 9 Not holding of a superior power. **1868** *Jrnl. R. Agric. Soc.* IV. II. 264 Mr. Sisman holds under a 21 years' lease. **1869** W. LONGMAN *Hist. Edw. III*, I xi. 206 Men holding by knight's service.

†**b.** Of a possession or right: To be held (*of* or *from*). *Obs.*

1648 CROMWELL in *Carlyle* (1871) II. 106 A Lease which holds of your College. *a* **1654** SELDEN *Table-T.* (Arb.) 64 *Allodium*..signifies Land that holds of nobody; we have no such Land in England. **1665** DRYDEN *Ind. Emp.* I. ii, My crown is absolute, and holds of none.

20. To depend; to belong or pertain. Const. *of*, †*on*, *at*. Now only as *fig.* from 19.

c **1430** *Pilgr. Lyf Manhode* III. lviii. (1869) 171 It holt not of hire but of yow; Helpeth me! *c* **1477** CAXTON *Jason* 23 What euyll woldest thou doo—if hit helde at no man but at the. **1485** —— *Paris & V.* 63 It holdeth not on me. **1589** PUTTENHAM *Eng. Poesie* III. xxiv. [xxv.] (Arb.) 294 Yet are generally all rare things and such as breede maruell and admiration somewhat holding of the vndecent. **1664** DRYDEN *Rival Ladies* v. iii, Julia goes first, Gonsalvo hangs on her, And Angelina holds upon Gonsalvo, as I on Angelina. **1889** W. S. LILLY *Century Revol.* 146 No wonder, for genius holds of the noumenal.

21. ***to hold with*** (arch. *of*, †*on*, *for*): to maintain allegiance to; to side with, be of the party of; *mod. colloq.* to agree with or approve of. (Cf. 17.)

1154 *O.E. Chron.* an. 1140 ⁊6 Ðat he neure ma mid te king his brother wolde halden. *c* **1300** *Havelok* 2308 He swore, þat he sholde with him halde Boþe ageynes stille and bolde. *c* **1385** CHAUCER *L.G.W.* Prol. 458 They aughte rathere with me for to holde. *c* **1460** *Towneley Myst.* (E.E.T.S.) xiv. 47 Any..That wyll not hold holly on me [Herod], And on mahowne. **1485** CAXTON *Chas. Gt.* 224, I am a paynym, & holde for my god Mahoun. **1549** COVERDALE, etc. *Erasm. Par. 1 Cor.* 1 Therof rose these sedicioguse wordes, I holde of Apollo, I holde of Cephas, I hold of Paule. **1577** HANMER *Anc. Eccl. Hist.* (1619) 115 Some there were, that held with both sides. **1786** tr. *Beckford's Vathek* (1868) 4 It was not with the orthodox that he usually held. **1837** CARLYLE *Fr. Rev.* I. I. i, These, and what holds of these may pray,—to Beelzebub, or whoever will hear them. **1895** *Cornh. Mag.* Nov. 502, I don't hold with him buying flowers when his children haven't got enough to eat.

22. To maintain one's position (against an adversary); of a place, to be held or occupied; to hold out: cf. 41 j.

a **1132** *O.E. Chron.* an 1123 ⁊7 Se kyng held stranglice hem to ȝeanes. *c* **1305** *St. Edmund* 493 in *E.E.P.* (1862) 84 Þe Couent ek of Canterbury aȝen seint Edmund hulde faste. **1340** HAMPOLE *Pr. Consc.* 4144 Alle..þat o-gaynes Goddes laghe will halde. **14..** *Songs & Carols 15th C.* (Percy Soc.) 27 Her husbondes agens hem durn not holde. **1523** in Halliwell *Lett. Kings Eng.* I. 279 As touching Berwick..it hath ere this holden against great puissance. **1606** SHAKS. *Ant. & Cl.* III. xiii. 170 Our force by Land Hath Nobly held. **1640** YORKE *Union Hon.* 40 Beating downe such holds as held against him. *a* **1713** ELLWOOD *Autobiog.* (1765) 3 [He] betook himself to London, that City then holding for the Parliament.

fig. **1776** *Maiden Aunt* I. 145 Do you not hold for congruity of soul in friendship, as well as love?

23. a. To continue, remain, or 'keep' in a state or course; to last, endure.

c **1200** ORMIN 3253 Uss birrþ beginnenn god to don, & haldenn a þæronne. **13..** *Coer de L.* 2419 To another town he went and held there. **1465** J. PASTON in *P. Lett.* No. 514 II. 209 If the werr hold. **1573** TUSSER *Husb.* xxiii. (1878) 62 The housing of cattel while winter doth hold. **1611** SHAKS. *Wint. T.* IV. iv. 36 Your resolution cannot hold. **1684** *Scanderbeg Rediv.* vi. 132 He entred into a Treaty with the Czar of Muscovy, which held a long time. **1719** DE FOE *Crusoe* II. iii. (1840) 61 The Battle, they said, held two Hours. **1754** RICHARDSON *Grandison* (1781) I. v. 18 The bloom of beauty holds but a very few years. **1856** KANE *Arct. Expl.* II. xxii. 219, I was only too glad, however, to see that their appetites held. **1888** 'FLOR. WARDEN' *Woman's Face* II. xiii. 55 The frost still held.

b. with *compl.* or *extension*.

c **1460** *Towneley Myst.* xxiii. 193 A, ha! hold still thore! **1535** COVERDALE *2 Kings* v. 9 So Naaman came..and helde still at the dore of Eliseus house. —— *Luke* vi. 42 Holde styll Brother, I wil plucke yᵉ moate out of thyne eye. **1599** SHAKS. *Much Ado* I. i. 91, I will hold friends with you Lady. **1703** T. N. *City & C. Purchaser* 242 Shingles seldom hold to be all 4 Inches broad. **1865** KINGSLEY *Herew.* i, Hold still, horse! **1873** BURTON *Hist. Scot.* V. lvii. 180 They held at him in this fashion to the very end. **1879** MINTO *Defoe* x. 161 Editors of journals held aloof from him. **1890** W. C. RUSSELL *Ocean Trag.* III. xxvii. 54 The weather held phenomenally silent.

c. To be or remain valid; to subsist; to be in force; to apply. Also *to hold good, to hold true.*

c **1315** SHOREHAM 64 That treuthynge darf naut healde. **1581** PETTIE *Guazzo's Civ. Conv.* III. (1586) 127 b, My rule holdeth not. **1594** SHAKS. *Rich. III*, II. iii. 7 Doth the newes hold of good king Edwards death? **1596** —— *1 Hen. IV*, I. ii. 34 Thou say'st well, and it holds well too. **1607** —— *Timon* v. i. 4 Does the Rumor hold for true, That hee's so full of Gold? **1674** PLAYFORD *Skill Mus.* III. 4 This Rule likewise holds, if the Notes descend a second. *c* **1680** BEVERIDGE *Serm.* (1729) I. 11 The same reason holds good also as to the sacrement of the Lord's supper. **1716** ADDISON *Freeholder* No. 31 The Logick will hold true of him which is applied to the great Judge of all the earth. **1818** SHELLEY *Let.* 30 Apr. (1964) II. 14 But this holds good, as I know, only to Milan. **1825** MCCULLOCH *Pol. Econ.* I. 15 It will hold good in nineteen out of twenty instances. **1841** *Jrnl. R. Agric. Soc.* II. II. 192 The same reason holds with regard to corn. **1871** SMILES *Charac.* ii. (1876) 33 The saying of the poet holds true in a large degree. **1892** H. R. MILL *Realm Nat.* vii. 101 This law does not hold for gases. **1937** *Discovery* May 139/1 His words of seven years ago hold good today.

d. To continue fine, to keep from raining. (Cf. 44 i.)

1893 *Chambers's Jrnl.* 10 June 355/2 If the weather holds, we'll both take a trip.

24. To continue to go, keep going, go on, move on, proceed, continue, or make one's way. Now esp. ***to hold on one's way*** or ***course.***

c **1450** HOLLAND *Howlat* 945 And ilk fowle tuke the flicht ..Held hame to thar hant, and thar herbery. **1450–70** *Golagros & Gaw.* 126 The heynd knight at his haist held to the tovne. **1576** GASCOIGNE *Philomene* (Arb.) 114 But if they hold on head, And scorne to bear my yoke. **1627** J. CARTER *Plaine & Compend. Expos.* 124 It lyeth us in hand to hold on our way. **1743** J. MORRIS *Serm.* vii. 183 He held on his way from the city. **1793** BURNS *Wandering Willie*, Here awa, there awa haud awa hame. **1850** R. G. CUMMING *Hunter's Life S. Afr.* (ed. 2) I. 242 We proceeded in a westerly course, and held up the lovely valley of Bakatla. **1889** DOYLE *Micah Clarke* xxxiv. 376 I've held on my course when better men than you have asked me to veil topsails. **1891** *Field* 24 Oct. 633/1 Instead of holding to Oakhill Wood, the pack bore to the right. **1892** *Ibid.* 30 Jan. 153/1 The merry chase held forward up the hill.

†**25.** To avail, profit, be of use: in interrogative or negative sentences. *Obs.*

c **1175** *Lamb. Hom.* 17 Hwet halt þe wredðe seodðan þus god almihtin hauet ihaten? *Ibid.* 33 Ne halt nawiht þat scrift. **1297** R. GLOUC. (1724) 105 Þo was þis lond kyngles, wat halt yt to telle longe? *c* **1320** *Sir Tristr.* 918 What halt it long to striue? Mi leue y take at te. *c* **1380** *Sir Ferumb.* 1602 What halt hit muche her-of to telle, to drecchen ous of our lay?

26. To take place, be held; to occur, prevail.

1461 *Paston Lett.* No. 420 II. 60 The gayle delyveryе holdeth not this daye. **1593** SHAKS. *Rich. II*, v. ii. 52 What newes from Oxford? Hold those Iusts & Triumphs? **1643** PRYNNE *Sov. Power Parl.* I. (ed. 2) 15 The Estates and Parliament generall of France..met and held but twice in the yeare only. **1892** *Field* 19 Mar. 404/1 Stormy weather again holds in north of Scotland.

27. (for *refl.*) To restrain oneself, refrain, forbear; to cease, stop, give over. Often in *imper.* as an exclamation: = Stop! *arch.*

1589 P. IVE tr. *Du Bellay's Instr. Warres* 265 If a third doe crie hould, to the intent to parte them. **1605** SHAKS. *Macb.* v. viii. 34 Lay on, Macduffe, And damn'd be him, that first cries hold, enough. *a* **1610** HEALEY *Theophrastus* (1636) 170 When he heareth any Fidlers, he cannot hold but he must keepe time. **1632** SIR T. HAWKINS tr. *Mathieu's Vnhappy Prosp.* 121 She could not hold from saying this. **1669** STURMY *Mariner's Mag.* VII. 19 Hold fast Gunner, do not fire till we hail them. **1672** VILLIERS (Dk. Buckhm.) *Rehearsal* v. i. (Arb.) 117 Well, I can hold no longer..there's no induring of him. **1775** SHERIDAN *Duenna* I. iv, Hold..a thought has struck me! **1818** SHELLEY *Rosalind* 297 'Hold, hold!' He cried,—'I tell thee 'tis her brother!'

28. In shooting: To take aim, to aim.

hold on, to aim directly at the game. ***hold ahead***, to aim ahead of it.

1881 GREENER *Gun* 485 It is a much disputed point amongst all who use the gun whether the shooter should 'hold on' or 'ahead'.

III. Phrases. (*to h. the plough, the reins, one's sides*, see 2 and 3 c; *to h. to bail*, see 10 c.; *to h. good, h. true*, see 23 c. *to h. at* BAY (*sb.*⁴ 3), *to h. one's* BREATH, *to h. a* CANDLE *to, to* HAVE *and to h.*, *to h. the* FIELD, *to h. one's* GROUND, *to h. with the* HARE *and run with the hounds*, *to h. one's* JAW, *to h. one's* NOSE, *to h. one's* PEACE, *to h.* (*in*) PLAY, *to h.* SHORT, *to h.* TACK, *to h. one's* TONGUE, etc.: see these words.)

29. hold (..) **hand.**

a. ***to hold one's hand***: to stay or arrest one's hand in the act of doing something; hence *gen.* to refrain, forbear.

c **1460** *Towneley Myst.* iv. 260, I byd the hold thi hand. **1535** COVERDALE *1 Chron.* xxi[i]. 15 It is ynough, holde now thy hande. **1602** *Narcissus* (1893) 654 Dorastus, hold thy handes, for I am slaine. **1699** DAMPIER *Voy.* II. III. 64 Called for an Axe to cut the Mizan Shrouds..He bad him hold his hand a little. **1768** ROSS *Helenore* 30 (Jam.) She hads her hand. **1889** J. S. WINTER *Mrs. Bob* I. vii. 118 She knew when to hold her hand and when to pile on all her strength.

†**b.** ***to hold hand***: (*a*) to bear a hand, to contribute help or support, co-operate, concur; (*b*) to be on an equality *with*, to match (quot. 1595). *Obs.*

1582–8 *Hist. Jas. VI* (1804) 237 The queene of England directit Sr. Johnne Forester, warden of the middle marches ..to mak sum incursiounes against the borderers on the syde of Scotland, and she should hald hand upoun hir syde that they should not escape butt captiuitye or punishment. **1595** SHAKS. *John* II. i. 494 She in beautie, education, blood, Holdes hand with any Princesse of the world. **1616** *Rich Cabinet* (N.), Curtesie and charitie doe commonly hold hands together. **1717** *Wodrow Corr.* (1843) II. 218, I hope you'll hold hand to this History of the Sufferings, since you have it so much at heart.

†**c.** ***to hold in hand***: to assure (one); to maintain (*that*...). To pay attention to; to keep in expectation or suspense (see HAND *sb.* 29 c, e). *Obs.*

1530 PALSGR. 587/1 He holdeth me in hande that he wyll ryde out of towne. **1658** W. BURTON *Itin. Anton.* 127 They ..who hold in hand that this Chester..was so named from a Gyant the builder thereof.

d. ***to hold someone's hand***, to give comfort or moral support to someone; to back someone up. *colloq.*

1935 C. ISHERWOOD *Mr. Norris changes Trains* vi. 90, I shall need your moral support. You must come and hold my hand. **1961** A. WILSON *Old Men at Zoo* iv. 220 Martha's been holding his hand in California. **1972** B. EVERITT *Cold Front* vii. 55, I 'held his hand' to the best of my ability with school-girl French and passable Italian.

30. hold..head.

a. ***to hold one's head high***: to behave proudly or arrogantly. **b.** ***to hold up one's head*** (fig.): to maintain one's dignity, self-respect, or cheerfulness.

1553 T. WILSON *Rhet.* (1580) 28 None can holde up their hedds, or dare shewe their faces..that are not thought honest. **1598** SHAKS. *Merry W.* I. iv. 30 Do's he not hold vp his head (as it were?) and strut in his gate? **1707** NORRIS *Treat. Humility* viii. 339 The proud man holds up his head too high to see his way. **1808** JANE AUSTEN *Let.* (1932) 205 Her Daughter..who says as little as ever, but holds up her head & smiles. **1849** MACAULAY *Hist. Eng.* x. II. 585 He had never held up his head since the Chancellor had been dragged into the justice room in the garb of a collier. **1859** LYTTON *What will he do with It?* I. II. v. 171 But they could never again hold up their heads with the noblemen and great squires in the county. **1867** TROLLOPE *Chron. Barset* II. lvi. 131, I have desired that they should be able to hold their heads high in the world. **1900** E. WHARTON *Gift from Grave* vi. 80 Why, you don't suppose if he were alive he could ever hold up his head again, with these letters being read by everybody? *a* **1953** E. O'NEILL *Touch of Poet* (1957) 33 *Nora.* You have the fine opinion av yourself! *Sara...* I've had need to have, to hold my head up, slaving as a waitress and chambermaid.

31. a. hold one's own. To maintain one's position against a competitor or an opposing force of any kind; to stand one's ground.

c **1330** R. BRUNNE *Chron.* (1810) 71 Sir Harald..Fulle wele his awen suld hald, if he had kept his treuth. **1526** *Pilgr. Perf.* (W. de W. 1531) 98 Neuer saye *Mea culpa*..but holde thyne owne. **1606** SHAKS. *Tr. & Cr.* IV. v. 114 Now Aiax hold thine owne. **1720** DE FOE *Capt. Singleton* xvi. (1840) 274 Our sheet anchor held its own. **1859** RUSKIN *Arrows of Chace* (1880) I. 194 Frightful superstitions still hold their own over two-thirds of the inhabited globe. **1885** TENNYSON *Charge Heavy Brigade* ii, But he..Sway'd his sabre, and held his own Like an Englishman there and then.

†**b.** To hold good. *Obs. rare.*

1632 ROWLEY *Wom. never vext* III. in *Contn. Dodsley's O. Pl.* (1816) V. 282 Does that news hold his own still, that our ships are..on the Downs with such a wealthy frautage?

32. hold water. a. To stop a boat by holding the blades of the oars flat against the boat's way.

a **1618** RALEIGH *Invent. Shipping* 10 The Pomerlanders.. used a kind of Boate, with the prowe at both ends, so as they need not to wend or hold water. **1626** CAPT. SMITH *Accid. Yng. Seamen* 30 To row a spell, hold-water, trim the boate. **1769** FALCONER *Dict. Marine* (1789) D dd, Pull the starboard oars, and hold water with the larboard oars! **1875** 'STONEHENGE' *Brit. Sports* II. VIII. ii. § 1. 648 Holding water is necessary when the boat is to be suddenly stopped.

b. To retain water, not to let water through or out (sense 5): hence, *fig.* To be sound, valid, or tenable; to bear a test or examination; to hold good when put to the test.

a **1300**, **1388** [see B. 5]. **1535** COVERDALE *Jer.* ii. 13 Vile and broken pittes, that holde no water. **1622** MABBE tr. *Aleman's Guzman d'Alf.* II. 79 This..will not hold water nor doe vs that good wee thought. **1652** FRENCH *Yorksh. Spa* ii. 32 Let them produce a more rational account of any other opinion, that will hold water..better than this of mine doth. **1755** SMOLLETT *Quix.* (1803) IV. 251 'Brothers', said he, 'the demand of Loggerhead will not hold water'. **1889** G. ALLEN *Tents of Shem* III. li. 251, I think these documents will hold water.

33. hold wind. *Naut.* To keep near the wind in sailing without making lee-way; to keep well to windward: usually ***to hold a good wind.***

1759 in A. DUNCAN *Mariner's Chron.* (1805) III. 360 To lie down in the fore-part of the boat, to bring her more by the head, in order to make her hold a better wind. **1769** FALCONER *Dict. Marine* (1789), *Sourdre au vent*, to hold a good wind; to claw or eat to windward. **1839** MARRYAT *Phant. Ship* viii, The vessels..could hold no wind. **1891** *Longm. Mag.* Oct. 587 The Duke..signalled to the whole fleet to brace round their yards and hold the wind between the two English divisions.

IV. With adverbs.

34. hold back. a. *trans.* To keep back; to restrain; to reserve from disclosure; to retain.

1535 COVERDALE *Job* xxvi. 9 He holdeth back his stole, that it can not be sene. **1597** SHAKS. *2 Hen. IV*, II. iii. 66 Many thousand Reasons hold me backe. **1665** DRYDEN *Ind. Emp.* IV. i, Sure thou bear'st some charm, Or some divinity holds back mine arm. **1841** R. OASTLER in *Fleet Papers* I. xlviii. 379 It is sinful to hold back the truth.

b. *intr.* (for *refl.*) To restrain oneself; to refrain; to hesitate.

1576 GASCOIGNE *Philomene* (Arb.) 117 Hold backe betime, for feare you catch a foyle. **1844** H. H. WILSON *Brit. India* III. 374 Holding back when the Native Government was anxious to advance. **1890** MRS. H. WOOD *House Halliwell* II. vii. 162, I have held back from asking you.

c. With *on*: to refrain from disclosing (something to someone).

1956 E. POUND tr. *Sophocles' Women of Trachis* 22 I'll tell the truth, I won't hold back on you.

35. hold down. a. *trans.* To keep down (*lit.* and *fig.*); to keep under, keep in subjection, repress, oppress.

1533 BELLENDEN *Livy* IV. (1822) 394 The fame and rumoure thareof was haldin doun amang the Veanis. **1606** MARSTON *Fawne* IV. Wks. 1856 II. 77 The more held down, they swel. **1840** MARRYAT *Poor Jack* xix, Confused, and holding down my head. **1881** N. T. (R. V.) *Rom.* i. 18 Men who hold down the truth in unrighteousness. **1883** *Daily News* 1 Feb. 5 Plump English folk, not at all starved or 'hadden doon', as his countrymen say.

b. *Mining* (*U.S.* and *Australia*). ***to hold down a claim*** (also absol. ***to hold down***): 'to reside on a section or tract of land long enough to establish a claim to ownership under the homestead law' (*C.D.*).

1888 *Harper's Mag.* July 236/1 A lone and unprotected female 'holding down a claim'. **1893** *Eng. Illustr. Mag.* X. 324/1 In mining slang Pilbarra did not 'hold down', and the place was ultimately almost deserted.

c. To remain in (a position or situation); to continue to occupy (a place or post) or succeed in discharging the duties of (one's employment). orig. *U.S. colloq.*

1891 C. Roberts *Adrift Amer.* 92 Jumping an east bound freight.., I managed to hold it down or keep on it till I got to Alameda. **1893** *Harper's Mag.* Dec. 80/2 If a man is to 'hold down' a big ranch in northern Mexico he has got to be 'all man'. **1896** Ade *Artie* xiv. 129 I'll bet that guy up in your place don't know nothin' on earth except how to hold down his measly job. **1902** G. H. Lorimer *Lett. Merchant* v. 60 The fellow who's got the right stuff in him is holding down his own place with one hand. **1910** S. E. White *Rules of Game* I. iii. 19, I didn't much think you could hold down a job here. You see there's too much doing here. **1913** F. H. Burnett *T. Tembarom* ii, I wonder, if I ever did get his job, if I could hold it down? **1931** G. D. H. Cole in W. Rose *Outl. Mod. Knowledge* xvi. 688 There are few pleasures in life equal to that of successfully holding down a difficult and responsible job. **1936** *Punch* 14 Oct. 439/2 He never could hold down a job. **1973** A. Behrend *Samarai Affair* i. 12 Captain Coldstream looked exactly what he was—an ex-sailor of quality now holding down an exacting shore job.

36. hold forth. †**a.** *trans.* To keep up, maintain, continue, go on with. *Obs.*

c **1250** *Gen. & Ex.* 165 Ðis fifte dai held forð his fliȝt. *c* **1400** *Ywaine & Gaw.* 2931 Thus thair wai forth gan thai hald. *a* **1420** Hoccleve *De Reg. Princ.* 317 He held forthe his oppynyoun dampnable. *a* **1547** Surrey *Æneid* II. 496 Hold fourth the way of health.

†**b.** *intr.* To continue one's course; to go on, proceed. *Obs.*

c **1200** *Trin. Coll. Hom.* 85 Iohan baptist.. bicom eremite and hield forð þerone. **1375** Barbour *Bruce* XIX. 249 Thai held furth soyn till Ingland. **1513** Douglas *Æneis* IX. vi. *heading*, Furth haldis Nysus and Eurillius baith tway.

†**c.** *trans.* To offer, proffer, propound, set forth, exhibit. ? *Obs.*

1560 Bible (Genev.) *Phil.* ii. 16 Holding forthe [ἐπέχοντες] the worde of life. **1648** *Eng. Way to Establ.* in *Harl. Misc.* (1810) VI. 42 Now Heaven holds forth power and opportunity far more liberally than ever heretofore. **1704** Swift *Mech. Operat. Spirit* Misc. (1711) 277 This Animal, by whom I take human Nature to be most admirably held forth in all its Qualities. **1736** Lediard *Life Marlborough* I. 63 A chappel.. where Mass was publickly held forth every Day. **1814** *Father & Son* II. i, The profligacy.. that impelled you to hold forth that language to me.

d. *intr.* [from Phil. ii. 16: see prec. sense.] To preach; to speak publicly, discourse, harangue. (Usually somewhat contemptuous.)

[**1694** J. Wallis *Def. Chr. Sabb.* II. 27 The Phrase of *Holding-forth* was taken up by Non conformists about the year 1642 or 1643, as I remember.. in contradistinction to the word *Preaching*.]

1667 Dryden *Maiden Queen* v. i, Lord! what a misfortune it was.. that the gentleman could not hold forth to you. **1693** Luttrell *Brief Rel.* (1857) III. 324 This week William Penn the quaker held forth at the Bull and Mouth in this citty. **1709** Steele *Tatler* No. 142 ⁋5 He is able to hold forth upon Canes longer than upon any one Subject in the World. **1881** Mrs. G. M. Craik *Sydney* II. ix. 262 Netty was holding forth with the utmost eloquence. **1889** Doyle *M. Clarke* xxii. 222 Nature is a silent preacher which holds forth upon week days as on Sabbaths.

37. hold hard. *intr.* (orig. a sporting phrase): To pull hard at the reins in order to stop the horse; hence *gen.* to 'pull up', halt, stop. Usually in *imper.* (*colloq.*)

1761 Colman *Jealous Wife* v. Wks. 1777 I. 130 (Farmer) Hold hard! hold hard! you are all on a wrong scent. **1829** *Sporting Mag.* XXIII. 280 But I must 'hold hard' here, as we say in the field. **1854** Wood *Sk. & Anecd. Anim. Life* (1855) 407 The 'Hold hard' of the conductor being sufficient to bring them [horses] to a stop. **1862** *Temple Bar Mag.* VI. 310 Hold hard, shipmates.

38. hold in. a. *trans.* To keep in, confine, retain; to restrain, keep in check.

a **1300** *Cursor M.* 5527 Wit herd werckes þai [Egyptians] heild þam in. *c* **1300** *Proverbs of Hending* x, Wis mon halt is wordes ynne. **1599** T. M[oufet] *Silkwormes* 73 Trie if thou canst hold in an outward smile. **1611** Bible *Ps.* xxxii. 9 As the horse, or as the mule.. whose mouth must be held in with bit and bridle. *a* **1745** Swift (J.), My nag.. became such a lover of liberty that I could scarce hold him in. **1888** E. Stuart *Joan Vellacot* I. x. 192 She held in the ponies, so that they recognized a strong hand.

b. *intr.* To 'keep in', continue in some position or condition understood or indicated by context; to restrain oneself, refrain, keep silence; to 'keep in' *with*.

c **1400** Maundev. (Roxb.) xxxi. 142 If a man.. couer þe coles þeroff with aschez, þai will hald in quikk a twelfmonth. **1596** Shaks. *1 Hen. IV*, II. i. 85 Such as can holde in. **1641** Trapp *Theol. Theol.* 229 To hold in with Princes and great ones. **1702** *Lond. Gaz.* No. 3838/1 [He] held in pretty near the French Town of Basse-Terre. **1849** J. A. Carlyle tr. *Dante's Inferno* 268 Alichino held in no longer, and in opposition to the others said [etc.].

39. hold off. a. *trans.* To keep off, away, or at a distance; to put off, delay.

c **1420** *Pallad. on Husb.* I. 98 An heir hil, that wynd that wold offende Let holde of. **1580** Lyly *Euphues* (Arb.) 387 Thou holdest me off with many delayes. **1602** Shaks. *Ham.* I. iv. 80 Hold off your hand. **1628** Earle *Microcosm.* (Arb.) 87 *A meere Complementall Man* is one to be held off still at the same distance you are now. **1725** Pope *Let. to Swift* 10 Dec., Absence does but hold off a Friend, to make one see him the more truly. **1867** Smyth *Sailor's Word-bk.*, *Hold off*, the keeping the hove-in part of a cable or hawser clear of the capstan.

b. *intr.* To keep oneself or remain off, away, or at a distance; to refrain from action; to delay.

1602 Shaks. *Ham.* II. ii. 302 If you loue me hold not off. **1790** T. Jefferson *Writ.* (1859) III. 133 Holding off, therefore, nearly three months. **1861** *Temple Bar Mag.* I. 339 The only person who at all held off from joining. **1887** *Spectator* 1 Oct. 1301 The storm may hold off. **1891** *Longm. Mag.* Oct. 592 The galleons.. had been observed to hold off. **1893** *Field* 15 Apr. 555/1 The rain 'holds off'.

c. *nonce-use* as *adj.* (***hold-off***). Given to holding off; distant.

1893 Stevenson *Catriona* 286, I saw I must be extremely hold-off in my relations.

40. hold on. a. *trans.* To keep (something) on; to retain in its place on something.

a **1529** Skelton *Agst. Garnesche* Wks. 1843 I. 118 Why holde ye on yer cap, syr, then? **1711** Hearne *Collect.* (O.H.S.) III. 106 Henry VIIIth's^ Charter to Stephen Tucker for holding on his Hat before the King. *Mod.* I can't keep on a bicycle unless somebody holds me on.

†**b.** To continue, keep up, carry on. *Obs.*

1500–20 Dunbar *Poems* xxxiv. 44 Hald on thy intent. **1656** Bp. Hall *Occas. Medit.* (1851) 70 Thus bountiful house-keepers hold on their set ordinary provision. **1757** Mrs. Griffith *Lett. Henry & Frances* (1767) II. 68, I.. am pleased to find that you still hold on a correspondence with her. *c* **1800** R. Cumberland *John de Lancaster* (1809) I. 150 In order to hold it [the harangue] on.

c. *intr.* To keep one's hold or grasp on something; to cling on; also *fig.* Also in jocular phrases.

1830 N. S. Wheaton *Jrnl.* 508 The rolling and tossing of the ship oblige us to 'hold on'. **1861** *Temple Bar Mag.* III. 509, I found myself holding on to a piece of plank. **1877** Spurgeon *Serm.* XXIII. 361 As though he held on by his teeth. **1930** 'Sapper' *Finger of Fate*, etc. 35 Having to hold on by one's eyebrows whenever one moves gets a bit monotonous after a time.

d. To maintain a course of action or movement; to keep on, continue, go on (rarely *refl.*).

a **1225** *Leg. Kath.* 434 He heold on to herien his heaðene maumez. **1405** *Bidding Prayer* ii. in *Lay Folks Mass Bk.* 65 For thaim that first began and langest haldis on. **1513** Douglas *Æneis* XI. iii. 41 Now haldis on. **1630** Sanderson *Serm.* II. 264 If we hold on as we do, in pampering every man his own flesh. **1667** Milton *P.L.* XI. 633 But still I see the tenor of Mans woe Holds on the same. **1725** De Foe *Voy. round World* (1840) 17 The gale held still on. *a* **1822** Shelley *There is no work* 7 O Man! hold thee on in courage of soul. **1889** Froude *2 Chiefs Dunboy* xv. 218 He held on till they were less than a mile apart.

e. *imper.* Stop! wait! (*colloq.*) Cf. 27, 37.

1846 C. M. Kirkland *Western Clearings* 45 'But hold on a little till I tell ye!' interposed Master George. **1848** Bartlett *Dict. Amer.* 198 'Hold on a minute', originally a sea phrase. **1867** Smyth *Sailor's Word-bk.*, *Hold on a minute*, wait or stop. **1883** *Bread-Winners* 62 'Hold on', he burst out; 'Don't talk to me that way.. I can't stand it'.

f. In shooting: see 28.

g. *Telephony.* To keep the line open.

1892 Kipling in *Times* 29 Nov. 8/1 A.. millionnaire,.. clawing wildly at the telephone.. 'Hello!.. I *told* you to hold on. What?.. No. Hold on.' **1919** V. Woolf *Night & Day* xxiv. 327 'I'll look at my engagements... Hold on.' She dropped the machine. **1920** *Punch* 1 Sept. 176/3 'What is your number, please?'.. 'Just hold on a minute while I look it up.' **1920** R. Macaulay *Potterism* III. i. 104 You mustn't ring off yet... Hold on while I tell daddy. **1949** J. B. Priestley *Home is Tomorrow* 38 (*into telephone*) Yes, I'll hold on. **1971** 'A. Cross' *Theban Mysteries* (1972) xi. 165 She did go to the phone, but she got the doctor's exchange, which said, 'Hold on,' and then went off the line.

41. hold out. a. *trans.* To stretch forth, extend (the hand or other limb, or something held in the hand).

1535 Coverdale *Esther* iv. 11 Excepte the kynge holde out the golden cepter vnto him. **1599** Shaks. *Hen. V*, II. i. 8, I dare not fight, but I will winke and holde out mine yron. **1761** Sterne *Tr. Shandy* III. xlii, We want a cavalier, said she, holding out both her hands, as if to offer them. **1848** Thackeray *Van. Fair* v, 'Hold out your hand, Sir!' Down came the stump with a heavy thump on the child's hand. **1879** McCarthy *Donna Quix.* xxxii, Throwing away the pitiful olive-branch of peace he had been pretending to hold out.

†**b.** To exhibit; to hold up (44c). *Obs.*

1613 Purchas *Pilgrimage* (1614) 160 They hold out to us the light of Scripture, themselves walking in darknesse. **1799** Mrs. Jane West *Tale of Times* III. 131 She felt the cruelty of thus holding her out to general ridicule.

c. *fig.* To offer, proffer, present.

a **1637** B. Jonson (J.), Fortune holds out these to you, as rewards. **1796** *Hist.* in *Ann. Reg.* 77 The French.. held out language promissory of equitable conditions. **1849** Macaulay *Hist. Eng.* v. I. 615 Hopes were held out to him that his life would be spared. **1890** T. F. Tout *Hist. Eng. fr.* 1689. 46 The inducement held out was the wonderful profits to be won.

d. To represent.

1829 Sir J. Parke in Barnew. & Cressw. *Rep.* X. 140 The defendant had held himself out to be a partner.. to the plaintiff. **1878** Sir N. Lindley *Partnership* (ed. 4) I. i. §2. 49 A person may hold himself out or permit himself to be held out as a partner, and yet conceal his name.

e. To keep out, exclude. Now *rare.* In *Cards*: see hold-out.

1583 Stubbes *Anat. Abus.* II. (1882) 37 Almost none of their leather will holde out water. **1592** Shaks. *Rom. & Jul.* II. ii. 67 Stony limits cannot hold Loue out. **1628** Rutherford *Lett.* (1862) I. 43 As an enemy holden out at the posts of our city. **1890** Ld. Lytton *Ring Amasis* vii. 147 He got [the boat] afloat, and found that it would hold out the water. **1894** [see hold-out].

f. To keep up, continue or maintain to the end.

1593 Shaks. *3 Hen. VI*, II. vi. 24 No way to flye, nor strength to hold out flight. **1599** Porter *Angry Wom. Abingd.* in Hazl. *Dodsley* VII. 338 'Tis not time of night to hold out chat With such a scold as thou art. **1618** Bolton *Florus* 330 Stiffer in holding out a rebellion. **1893** *Field* 11 Mar. 354/3 The way he holds his stroke out is very good.

†**g.** To bear or sustain to the end. *Obs.*

1595 Shaks. *John* IV. iii. 156 Now happy he, whose cloake and center can Hold out this tempest. **1736** Lediard *Life Marlborough* II. 456 The Place was ill-provided to hold out a Siege. **1771** Goldsm. *Hist. Eng.* II. 211.

h. To occupy or defend to the end (against an adversary).

1769 Goldsm. *Rom. Hist.* (1786) II. 13 He had.. conceived a resolution of holding out the town. **1826** Scott *Woodst.* ii, I will hold out the old house, and it will not be the first time I have held it against ten times the strength. **1879** Miss Yonge *Cameos* Ser. IV. xxxiii. 359 The burghers.. who had held out the city were put to death.

i. With *obj. clause*: To maintain. *rare.*

1848 Thackeray *Van. Fair* xiii, Holding out that the lady was a Duchess.

j. *intr.* To maintain resistance, remain unsubdued; to continue, endure, persist, last. (Also formerly †***to hold it out*** in same sense.)

1585 T. Washington tr. *Nicholay's Voy.* I. xix. 23 In despaire of succour, and not able to holde out any longer. **1595** Shaks. *John* v. i. 30 All Kent hath yeelded: nothing there holds out But Douer Castle. **1680** Burnet *Rochester* (1692) 150 He was not able to hold out long in discourse. **1707** Watts *Hymns* I. lxxxviii. i, And while the lamp holds out to burn The vilest sinner may return. **1728** Newton *Chronol. Amended* iv. 307 Babylon held out, and the next year was taken. **1802** H. Martin *Helen of Glenross* IV. 32 Miss Wansbro is so robust, she holds out to dance with all who ask her. **1802** *Med. Jrnl.* VIII. 212 Her constitution, shattered by the frequent attacks it endured, could not long hold out. **1855** Macaulay *Hist. Eng.* xii. III. 234 By no art could the provisions.. be made to hold out two days more.

1598 Shaks. *Merry W.* IV. ii. 141 Well said Brazon-face, hold it out. **1713** Addison *Cato* II. iii, We ought to hold it out 'till terms arrive. **1764** Garrick in *Colman's Posth. Lett.* (1820) 253, I cannot hold it out so long.

†**k.** To preach: = *hold forth* (36d). *Obs. rare.*

1689 Wood *Life* 28 Feb. III. 299 His old dancing school.. they have made a preaching place. Mr. Cornish holds out.

l. To keep back; to retain or detain; (also const. *on*) to withhold (information or the like). *colloq.* (orig. *U.S.*).

1907 E. S. Field *Six-Cylinder Courtship* 71 If it wasn't for Bellows and Rooker, we'd hold out on him every time. **1911** H. S. Harrison *Queed* v. 57 Surface, by clever juggling of his books had managed to 'hold out' a large sum of money in the enforced settlement of his affairs. **1916** H. L. Wilson *Somewhere in Red Gap* viii. 345, I wanted to send a postal card to the.. Dye Works at Red Gap, for some stuff they had been holding out on me a month. **1923** R. D. Paine *Comrades of Rolling Ocean* i. 13 He dumped his wages upon the sitting-room table, holding out only the price of a new pair of shoes. **1926** J. Black *You can't Win* ix. 112 The thief who holds out a lady's watch on his pal to give to his girl has no character. **1932** Wodehouse *Hot Water* i. 21 And me who had split Even Stephen with her on every deal, never chiselling, never holding out on her, no, not so much as a dime. **1944** L. A. G. Strong *All fall Down* 99 The thought came to me that maybe the old cuss was just holding out on me. **1945** J. B. Priestley *Three Men in New Suits* v. 88 'Boss,' said Markinch, who liked to be American too, 'he's holding out on us.' **1972** 'G. Black' *Bitter Tea* (1973) v. 81 If I find out that you've been holding out on me over this identification, I'll come down on you like a pile driver.

42. hold over. a. *intr.* (*Law*) To remain in occupation or in office beyond the regular term.

1647 N. Bacon *Disc. Govt. Eng.* I. lxii. (1739) 125 If the Lord fail, he loses his Tenure, and the Tenant might thenceforth disclaim, and hold over for ever. **1880** A. Brown *New Law Dict.* (ed. 2), *Holding over*, this is the phrase commonly used to denote that a tenant remains in possession of lands or houses after the determination of his term therein.

b. *trans.* To retain or reserve till a later time; to keep for future consideration or action; to postpone.

1852 Dickens *Bleak House* xxviii, I will hold the matter over with him for any reasonable time. **1861** *Temple Bar Mag.* III. 321 Comes down a telegraphic message to us to hold over all our warrants against him. **1865** Dickens *Mut. Fr.* I. vii, You needn't be afraid of my disposing of you. I'll hold you over. That's a promise. **1885** *Manch. Exam.* 8 July 5/1 The Sixpenny Telegrams Bill is to be held over till next year. **1891** *Illustr. Lond. News* 10 Jan. 54/1 Not to sell any sealskins.. but to hold them over till next winter.

c. *U.S. colloq.* (See quot. 1889.)

1872 'Mark Twain' *Innoc. at Home* 18 (Farmer), You ruther hold over me, pard. I reckon I can't call that hand. **1889** Farmer *Amer.*, *To hold over one* is to have an advantage in some way or other. This particular usage probably comes from poker phraseology. **1889** K. Munroe *Golden Days* xii. 127 Do we hold over Bowers?

43. hold together. a. *trans.* To keep together, retain in union or connexion. *lit.* and *fig.*

a **1225** *Leg. Kath.* 2268 Porphire & alle hise heolden ham togederes. **1573** J. Sanford *Hours Recreat.* Ep. Ded. (1576) A vij b, Her Grace, who is the best knot in this Garden, that holdeth Englishmen together. **1613** Purchas *Pilgrimage* (1614) 433 Two men.. held the ends together. **1784** Cowper *Task* II. 687 The sacred band That holds mankind together. **1850** Lyell *2nd Visit U.S.* II. 171 The roots also of trees.. were very effective formerly in holding the soil together.

b. *intr.* To continue in union or connexion; to remain entire; to cohere. *lit.* and *fig.*

c **1330** *Amis & Amil.* 151 That thai schuld frely fond, To hold togider at eueri nede. **1362** LANGL. *P. Pl.* A. I. 55 Husbondrie and he holden to-gedere. **1533** HEYWOOD *Johan & Tyb* B iv, The payle..is so rotten and olde, That it wyll not skant together holde. **1691** WOOD *Ath. Oxon.* II. 494 It was then commonly reported that if they hung him, his body would not hold together because of its rottenness. **1861** *Temple Bar Mag.* III. 509 There was hope that the ship would hold together.

44. hold up. a. *trans.* To keep raised or erect, keep from falling, support, sustain. (*to hold up one's head*: see 30 b.)

1297 R. GLOUC. (1724) 455 Ȝour ryȝt honden holdeþ vp to God..And byhoteþ hym to be stable. **1455** E. CLERE in *Four C. Eng. Lett.* 5 Then he hild up his hands and thankid God therof. **1558** TRAHERON *Answ. Priv. Papist* B iij (D.), I yield vnto you this noble victorie, and hold vp my handes. **1651** CLEVELAND *Poems* 45 Who name but Charles, he comes aloft for him, But holds up his Malignant leg at Pym. **1670–98** LASSELS *Voy. Italy* II. 97 Four great pillars of Jasper..hold up the back of this altar. **1854** *Jrnl. R. Agric. Soc.* XV. I. 49 The river..is held up in levels by 34 locks. **1894** *Daily News* 26 May 2/5 Four men..ordering the President..and the clerks to hold up their hands under threats of death, seized a sum of 2,500 dollars.

b. *fig.* To support, sustain, maintain, keep up.

c **1290** *Beket* 229 in *S. Eng. Leg.* I. 113 Swyþe wel bi-gan þis Ercedekne holi churche bi-lede, And stifliche heold op hire riȝte. **1389** in *Eng. Gilds* (1870) 6 To holde vp & meyntene þe poyntes. *c* **1465** *Paston Lett.* No. 536 II. 254 How that ever ye do, hold up your manship. **1590** SHAKS. *Mids. N.* III. ii. 239 Winke each at other, hold the sweete iest vp. **1667** PEPYS *Diary* 28 Jan., He tells me gold holds up its price still. **1890** T. F. TOUT *Hist. Eng. fr.* 1689. 147 Austria, whose arms alone held up the petty despots.

c. To offer or present to notice; to exhibit, display; to present in a particular aspect; to put up as a candidate (quot. 1813).

1602 SHAKS. *Ham.* III. ii. 24 To hold as 'twer the Mirrour vp to Nature. **1611** —— *Wint. T.* IV. iv. 567 What colour for my Visitation, shall I Hold vp before him? **1808** MRS. INCHBALD in *Brit. Theatre* XIV. 4 To hold up to detestation vices, now no longer to be tolerated. **1813** W. IRVING in *Life & Lett.* (1864) I. 293 William was held up for Congress, and ..lost his election. **1860** *Temple Bar Mag.* I. 30 Bacon..has been held up to opprobrium. **1892** *Sat. Rev.* 30 Apr. 497/1 [He] held up the Government..to hatred and contempt.

d. To let alone, resign, give up (quot. 1529); to keep back, withhold; in *Cards*, to keep in one's hand, refrain from playing.

a **1529** SKELTON *Bowge of Courte* 250 Holde vp the helme, loke vp, and lete God stere. **1535** COVERDALE *1 Esdras* v. 72 The Heithen in the londe..helde vp the buyldinge from them. **1807** T. JEFFERSON *Writ.* (1830) IV. 70 We..hold it up until we know the result of the instructions of February the 3rd. **1879** 'CAVENDISH' *Card Ess.* 111 You may make a trump by holding up. *Ibid.* 198 Prone to hold up ace, knave. **1889** *Kansas Times & Star* 4 Dec., Major Davenport is holding up the firemen's payroll for November owing to alleged irregularities. **1894** *Vermont Agric. Rep.* XIV. 70 When..a cow holds up her milk there is some disturbing element.

e. (*U.S.*) To stop by force and rob on the highway. (From the robbers' practice of commanding their victims to hold up their hands on pain of being shot; = Australian *to stick up.*) Also, to arrest the progress of, obstruct the passage of (*lit.* and *fig.*).

1887 A. A. HAYES *Jesuit's Ring* 228 Any man could hold up a wagon. **1894** *Times* 22 Oct. 5/4 At noon yesterday four unmasked men 'held up' a Texas Pacific train near that place. **1904** *Philadelphia Even. Telegr.* 15 Nov. 1 Out of the 900 steerage passengers that came over on the Merion, 135 failed to pass the immigration inspectors, and were held up. **1905** *N.Y. Evening Post* 16 Mar. 1 Another landslide has occurred..and nine passenger trains are held up in the mountains. **1906** *N.Y. Herald* 5 Mar. 5 It is thought the Senate Finance Committee will seek to devise new excuses for holding up the investigation of the State Banking Department, which it has succeeded in smothering for five weeks. **1909** H. N. CASSON *C. H. McCormick* 146 One bill for £15 was held up for a week because it was not properly drawn. **1972** *Daily Hampshire Gaz.* (Northampton, Mass.) 9 May 1/3 A passing motorist asked Witkos if he was 'going to let them hold up the traffic all day?'

f. *intr.* (for *refl.*) To keep up, not to fall: usually addressed to a horse.

1860 WHYTE MELVILLE *Holmby House* xviii. 266 'Hold up!' exclaimed Humphrey, as the sorrel cleared a high wall, with a drop into a sandy lane. **1890** DOYLE *Firm Girdlestone* xxxiii. 264 'Hold up, will ye!' The last remark was addressed to the horse, which had stumbled.

g. To maintain one's position or state; to endure, hold out; in *Hunting*, to keep up the pace.

1582 N. T. (Rhem.) *Acts* iv. *annot.*, Let no Catholike man be scandalized that this heresie holdeth vp for a time. *a* **1694** TILLOTSON (J.), Some few stout and obstinate minds, which, without the assistance of philosophy, could have held up pretty well of themselves. **1708** OCKLEY *Saracens* (1848) 219 The Saracens..made shift to hold up till night parted them. **1864** TENNYSON *Aylmer's F.* 733 'O pray God that he hold up', she thought, 'Or surely I shall shame myself and him'. **1888** MRS. NOTLEY *Power of Hand* I. xii. 144 If this wind holds up..we shall catch the coast..in six hours. **1892** *Field* 23 July 124/1 Having arrived at the starting point.. Prince is told to 'hold up'—an order which he obeys with alacrity.

h. To give in, submit, surrender (*obs.*); to check oneself, refrain, 'pull up' (*U.S. colloq.*).

1596 DALRYMPLE tr. *Leslie's Hist. Scot.* IX. 195 How lang thair lyfe was in, tha neuer held vp. **1843** MAURY in Mrs. Corbin *Life* (1888) 46 The doctor said I was destroying myself with over-much head-work, and..I have had to hold up somewhat. **1879** HOWELLS *L. Aroostook* (1882) I. xii. 170, I see your difficulty plainly enough, and I think you're quite right in proposing to hold up.

i. To keep from raining (when there is a threatening of rain); rarely, to cease raining, clear up. (Said of the weather, the day; also of the rain.)

1601 DEACON & WALKER *Spirits & Divels* 213 They may then cause it to hold vp, when it should raine, and to raine, when it should hold vp. **1700** S. SEWALL *Diary* 17 May (1879) II. 14 It rains hard. Holds up about 5 p.m. **1798** JANE AUSTEN *Northang. Abb.* (1833) I. xi. 63 Perhaps..it [the weather] may hold up. **1848** THACKERAY *Van. Fair* xxxiv. **1891** *Field* 21 Nov. 791/2 The day held up wonderfully, in spite of lowering clouds.

hold, *sb.*[1] Forms: 1 heald, 1–3 (4–8 *north.*) hald, 4–7 holde, 3– hold; also 4–5 *north.* halde, 4– *Sc.* and *north.* hauld, 6–7 hould(e, 9 *Sc.* haud, *dial.* hod. See also HOLT[2]. [f. HOLD *v.*; OE. had *heald* in senses 1 and 7, but in other senses the word is only ME. or later.]

I. The action or fact of holding.

1. †**a.** The action or fact of having in charge, keeping, guarding, possessing, etc.; keeping, occupation, possession; defence, protection, rule. *Obs.*

a **1100** *O.E. Chron.* an. 1036 Gecuron Harold to healdes ealles Engla landes. *c* **1200** ORMIN 5026 Forr all þin hellpe & all þin hald Iss uppo Godess are. *c* **1375** *Sc. Leg. Saints, Petrus* 730 He ȝalde þe spyrit, of god in-to þe halde. *c* **1450** *St. Cuthbert* (Surtees) 68 All' yreland rewme was in hys halde. **1487** *Act 4 Hen. VII*, c. 16 Many Dwelling-places.. have of late time been used to be taken in one Man's Hold and Hands. **1534** WHITINTON *Tullyes Offices* I. (1540) 10 Priuate by nature be no thynges, but eyther by olde occupyenge and holde..or els that be got by victorye. **1586** D. ROWLAND tr. *Lazar. de Tormes* (1672) U viij a, They gave me the hold and possession of the Hermitage.

b. Tenure. Cf. COPYHOLD, FREEHOLD, etc.

a **1645** HABINGTON *Surv. Worc.* in *Worc. Hist. Soc. Proc.* II. 185 For thys parishe..was as they saye of St. Peter's houlde. **1774** T. WEST *Antiq. Furness* (1805) 132 For the fyns and customs of the hold, as well of the said coppyholders as of the customary tenants. **1876** *Whitby Gloss.* s.v., 'He has his land under a good hod', on easy terms.

2. a. The action or an act of keeping in hand, or grasping by some physical means; grasp: esp. in *to catch, get, lay, lose, seize, take hold* (see also these verbs). Also, an opportunity of holding, sometimes almost *concr.*, something to hold by. (The main current sense.)

a **1300** *Cursor M.* 24451 To climb had i na hald. *a* **1350** *Childh. Jesus* 652 He tolde, How Jesues picher with outen holde Hangude on þe sonne bem. *a* **1400–50** *Alexander* 1440 And qua sa leddirs had nane..Wald gett þam hald with þair hend & on-loft clyme. **1537**, etc. [see CATCH *v.* 45]. **1585** T. WASHINGTON tr. *Nicholay's Voy.* III. x. 86 Wrestlers.. annointed with oyle..to the intent to giue or to take the lesse hold the one of the other. **1605** SHAKS. *Lear* II. iv. 73 Let go thy hold. **1613** PURCHAS *Pilgrimage* (1614) 32 Like men drowning, that get hold on every twig. **1653** WALTON *Angler* ii. 53 Leather-mouth'd fishes, of which a hook does scarce ever lose his hold. *a* **1684** LEIGHTON *Comm. 1 Pet.* ii. 1 As the stepping of children when they begin to go by hold. **1724** DE FOE *Mem. Cavalier* (1840) 157 The officers..were laid hold on. **1793** SMEATON *Edystone L.* §239 *note*, Every force exerted to drive the wad out..tends to make it take the stronger hold. **1816** SCOTT *Antiq.* vii, Take haud o' my arm, my winsome leddy! **1843** CARLYLE *Past & Pr.* II. xvi, The ..hand..suddenly quits hold. **1871** L. STEPHEN *Playgr. Europe* iv. (1894) 103 The hold was generally firm when the fissures were not filled with ice.

b. in *Wrestling, Boxing,* and *Judo. in holds,* at grips.

1713 SIR T. PARKYNS *Cornish-Hugg Wrestler* (1727) 14 A thorough-pac'd Wrestler, Perfect and Quick, in breaking and taking all Holds. *Ibid.* 43 Hand-Hold. *Ibid.* 46 Collar Hold. *Ibid.* 50 Under-Hold. *Ibid.* 56 Upper-Hold. **1870** BLAINE *Encycl. Rur. Sports* (ed. 3) §463 Some advantage.. such as catching his heel, mending his hold. **1891** *Sportsman* 8 July 6/3 Then they closed again, and were still in holds when time was called. **1954** E. DOMINY *Teach yourself Judo* iii. 39 Theoretically, a hold consists of nothing more than controlling your opponent's body with the weight of your own.

c. (*with*) *no holds barred,* (with) all restrictions relaxed. Also as *attrib. phr.*

1942 BERREY & VAN DEN BARK *Amer. Thes. Slang* §217/6. **1952** *Economist* 1 Nov. 313/1 An independent [broadcasting] agency..could talk back at the Russians with no holds barred. **1958** *Times* 28 Nov. 13/6 No holds were barred, so to speak, for the Prince's unorthodox education and his own reputedly emancipated views allowed almost every hypothesis. **1961** *Economist* 6 May 524/1 Waging..a sweaty, no-holds-barred tussle all around the world without benefit of parley. **1972** *Real Estate Rev.* Winter 29/1 This allows trust managers to compete on a no-holds-barred basis.

3. a. *fig.* A grasp which is not physical.

a **1300** *Cursor M.* 9350 It tok neuer in þer hertes hald. **1526** *Pilgr. Perf.* (W. de W. 1531) 241 How lytell hold or surety man hath by them. **1551** T. WILSON *Logike* (1580) 10 b, That constante holde of any thing whiche is in the mynde. **1596** SHAKS. *Merch. V.* IV. i. 347 Tarry Iew, The Law hath yet another hold on you. *a* **1628** PRESTON *Effect. Faith* (1631) 134 They are small things of no hold. **1667** MILTON *P.L.* x. 406 On your joynt vigor now My hold of this new Kingdom all depends. **1725** N. ROBINSON *Th. Physick* 292 When the Disease has taken any Hold of the Patient. **1829** LYTTON *Devereux* I. iv, The Abbé had obtained a wonderful hold over Aubrey. **1865** KINGSLEY *Herew.* xvii, It was there where he could most easily keep his hold on the country. **1894** J. T. FOWLER *Adamnan* Introd. 17 Their old religion had no great hold on the common people.

b. *Naut.* (See quots.)

1769 FALCONER *Dict. Marine, Hold*, in navigation, is generally understood to signify a particular situation of the ship with regard to the shore..Keep a good hold of the land ..implying to keep near, or in sight of the land. **1846** YOUNG & BRISBANE *Naut. Dict.* 177 *Keep a good hold of the land*, to keep as near it as can be done with safety.

4. Confinement, custody, imprisonment. Chiefly in phr. *in hold* (*† in holds, at, to hold*). *arch.*

a **1300** *Cursor M.* 17320–1 Þai..bad þam do him up at hald, In a hald in prisun state. *c* **1330** R. BRUNNE *Chron.* (1810) 120 Mald at þe last kyng Steuen scho toke, & led him to Bristow, & did him þer in hold. **1382** WYCLIF *Acts* xxii. 4 Byndinge to gidere and drawinge into holdis men and wymmen. *c* **1400** *Melayne* 583 We were taken in to holde. *c* **1511** *1st Eng. Bk. Amer.* (Arb.) Introd. 33/1 They hadde put in prysone or in holde the great kynge. **1577–87** HOLINSHED *Chron.* III. 1225/1 The said Storie hauing beene a while deteined in prison, at the last..brake foorth of hold. **1658** BRAMHALL *Consecr. Bps.* v. 129 Father Oldcorne being in hold for the powder treason. **1879** SALA in *Daily Tel.* 26 June, Where ear-cropt Prynne and Bastwick..lay in cruel hold for daring to assert the liberty of free writing.

5. †**a.** Retention; restraint. *Obs.*

a **1225** *Ancr. R.* 74 Þer is mest need hold hwon þe tunge is o rune. *c* **1430** *Syr. Gener.* 9240 There was noo hold but to go. **1508** KENNEDIE *Flyting w. Dunbar* 491 Na hald agayn, na hoo is at thy hips. **1680** H. MORE *Apocal. Apoc.* 225 And this is a good hold to the Church from relapsing into Heathenism again.

b. A delay, pause, postponement. Also *attrib.*

1961 *Observer* 28 May 4/2 The long countdowns, checks and 'holds' possible at Cape Canaveral would be suicide on the moon. **1968** *Time* 27 Dec. 13 The countdown schedule had been padded with enough precautionary hold time to enable technicians to replace the oxygen without delaying the launch. **1969** *New Scientist* 27 Feb. 439/1 Unless there has been a last-minute 'hold' at Cape Kennedy, the first of a pair of *Mariner* spacecraft should now be on its way. **1971** *Daily Tel.* 4 Jan. 2/4 Concorde, counting time for 'taxi-ing' and 'holds' could arrive in New York at 7 a.m. after taking off from Heathrow at eight. **1971** *Nature* 26 Nov. 181/2 Liquid-fueled rockets..could not be kept in the launching tower in a 'hold' status to await a transient event.

c. A facility offered by some telephone systems whereby an incoming connection is held open automatically until the person called is free to take or return to the call; freq. *attrib.* as *hold button*, etc. Usu. (of a caller) in advb. phr. *on hold*; also *fig.*, (in the state of being) postponed, delayed; awaiting action. orig. *U.S.*

1965 *Business Etiquette Handbk.* (Parker Publishing Co.) xv. 131 When your telephone has no 'hold' button..be discreet in your remarks while the caller is holding on... Don't put the second call on hold and just leave it there. **1971** D. E. WESTLAKE *I gave at Office* (1972) 19, I put him on hold and called Mr. Clarebridge. **1973** *Ottawa Jrnl.* 21 Feb. 54/4 Our sex life is on hold until after the 10 p.m. sportscast. **1976** *National Observer* (U.S.) 17 Apr. 10/5 To place the first caller on 'hold' and answer the second, I merely touch the handset button once and the new call is on the line. **1976** N. POSTMAN *Crazy Talk* 45 Everything goes on hold until the rules get straightened out. **1983** *Fortune* 14 Nov. 10/3 It offers conference calls, an office intercom system, and even that maddening canned music for callers put on hold. **1984** *Southern Rag* No. 22. 5/3 If you stay at home, you select your own artists, put them on hold if the baby cries, and move about freely in your own home. **1985** *Times* 5 June 16/6 (*heading*) Why auto is still on hold.

†**6.** Contention, struggle, pulling opposite ways; opposition, resistance; chiefly in *hard hold*, strong or tough struggle. *Obs.*

1523 in Ellis *Orig. Lett.* Ser. I. I. 220 Sithens the begynnyng of the Parliamente there hathe bene the grettiste and soreste hold in the lower Hous for the payemente of ijs. of the li. that ever was sene..in any parliamente. **1565** JEWEL *Repl. Harding* (1611) 273 As touching Plato, it seemeth there was hard hold, when a Naturall Philosopher must stand foorth, to prooue Christs Mysteries. **1577–87** HOLINSHED *Chron.* (1807–8) II. 331 There was hard hold about it in that court. **1580** LYLY *Euphues* (Arb.) 422 Great holde there hath beene who shoulde proue his loue best. **1600** HOLLAND *Livy* XLII. xxiii. 1128. **1618** BOLTON *Florus* II. xvii. (1636) 145 But the hardest hold of all was with the Lucitanians and Numantines. **1654** E. JOHNSON *Wond. wrkg. Provid.* 106 Great hold and keepe there was about choice of Magistrates this yeare.

II. *concr.* That which holds or is held.

†**7.** That which holds up or supports; a support, a defence. *Obs.*

1042 in Kemble *Cod. Dipl.* IV. 73 Wit synd ðisra landa hald and mund into ðam halȝan mynstre ða hwile ðe unker lif bið. *a* **1300** *Cursor M.* 23929 (Cott.) Leuedi..þat es nu mi hope be þan mi hald, Ogain þat brem þat es sa bald! *c* **1340** *Ibid.* 24095 (Fairf.) Allane he was my hope & halde.

†**8.** Property held; a possession, holding; *spec.* a tenement. Cf. COPYHOLD, FREEHOLD, HOUSEHOLD, LEASEHOLD, etc. *Obs.*

c **1250** *Gen. & Ex.* 1772 Yuel ist bi-toȝen Min swinc a-buten ðin holðe droȝen. **1303** R. BRUNNE *Handl. Synne* 7016 How he hadde lore a ryche holde, And for auaryce he hyt solde. *c* **1500** in Arnolde *Chron.* Index (1811) 2 That of ther londes and holdes they haue right. **1533–4** *Act 25 Hen. VIII*, c. 13 §14 No maner person..shal receiue or take in ferme.. aboue the numbre of two suche holdes or tenementes. **1581** W. STAFFORD *Exam. Compl.* ii. (1876) 35. *c* **1590** GREENE *Fr. Bacon* x. 11, I am the lands-lord, Keeper, of thy holds, By copy all thy living lies in me.

9. A place of refuge, shelter, or temporary abode; a lurking-place (of animals).

c **1205** LAY. 3861 Buten wuhlc wræcche swa cwic cuahte to holde. *c* **1320** *Sir Tristr.* 2807 Þe geaunt hem gan lede, Til

he fond an hald. *c* **1450** *St. Cuthbert* (Surtees) 7636 At Jarow stode walles alde, Whare some tyme was an abbot halde. **1513** DOUGLAS *Æneis* VIII. vi. 55 The auctoritie of god Apollyne, Hes me constrenyt to duell in this hald. **1611** SHAKS. *Cymb.* III. iii. 20 And often..shall we finde The sharded-Beetle, in a safer hold Then is the full-wing'd Eagle. **1688** R. HOLME *Armoury* II. 134/2 A Boare..when Lodged..Coucheth in his Den or Hold. **1787** BEST *Angling* (ed. 2) 37 His hold is usually under the roots of trees, and in hollow banks in the deepest parts of rivers. **1815** SCOTT *Guy M.* xii, Now they're out of house and hauld. **1867** F. FRANCIS *Angling* iv. (1880) 104 Reed or rush beds,..all of which are favourite holds.

10. A fortified place of defence; a fort or fortress; a STRONGHOLD. *arch.*

a **1300** *Cursor M.* 17342 þai ledd ioseph..To prisun in a stalworth hald [*Laud & Trin.* a strong holde]. *c* **1330** R. BRUNNE *Chron. Wace* (Rolls) 12773 þe wode þey tok, þat was bitwixt hem & Arthures hold. *c* **1400** *Destr. Troy* 9712 All his stid to distroy, and his stith holdis. **1461** *Paston Lett.* No. 416 II. 52 All the castelles and holdes in..Wales ar gyfen and yelden up into the Kynges hand. **1552** *Act 5 & 6 Edw. VI*, c. 11 §5 Castles, Fortresses, Fortilesses or Holds. **1605** VERSTEGAN *Dec. Intell.* v. (1628) 128 In seruice in the field, and in Garrisons in the holdes. **1691** WOOD *Ath. Oxon.* II. 291 He..did seemingly plot with them..to have the Tower, Windsore Castle, and other Holds delivered to them. **1800** STUART in Owen *Wellesley's Desp.* (1877) 572 When defeated there, it may be necessary to retire to the interior holds. **1848** LYTTON *Harold* VII. i, A rude fortress..out of the wrecks of some greater Roman hold.

11. a. Something which is laid hold of, or by or with which anything is grasped or laid hold of.

1578 BANISTER *Hist. Man* IV. 53 [The muscle] inserted by the stay of sinewy holdes, to all the ribbes. **1595** SHAKS. *John* III. iv. 138 He that stands vpon a slipp'ry place, Makes nice of no vilde hold to stay him vp. **1663** J. SPENCER *Prodigies* (1665) 366 To conclude it a falling Cause which catcheth at such weak and unfaithful holds. **1848** MARRYAT *Lit. Savage* xxxvi, Sharks..forming a semi-circle round me, watched with upturned eyes..the snapping of the frail hold that supported me upon the rock. **1876** *Whitby Gloss.*, *Hod*, a handle. 'A cannle-hod', a candle-stick.

b. A thing that holds something; as, a mortise, a lock in a river, a receptacle, etc.

1517 TORKINGTON *Pilgr.* (1884) 43 The very hold or morteys hevyn [= hewn] owt of the stone Rooke wherin the Crosse stode. **1677** PLOT *Oxfordsh.* ix. §46. 234 Locks, or Holds for water, made to let down flashes. **1885** *Manch. Exam.* 15 May 5/7 The first-class compartments are converted into 'boots' or holds only fit as receptacles for luggage.

†**12.** *Mus.* The sign now called a pause. *Obs.*

1674 PLAYFORD *Skill Mus.* I. xi. 36 A Hold..is placed over the Note which the Author intends should be held to a longer Measure than the Note contains. **1876** STAINER & BARRETT *Dict. Mus. Terms*, *Hold*, an old English name for the sign of a pause 𝄐.

13. A prison-cell: = HOLE *sb.* 2 b.

1717 *Hist. Press-Yard* 7, I was conducted to the door leading out of the lodge into the Condemn'd Hold. **1728** GAY *Begg. Op.* II. x. **1859** DICKENS *T. Two Cities* II. i, You were put into a species of Condemned Hold at the back.

14. *Cinemat.* (See quots.)

1918 H. CROY *How Motion Pictures are Made* vii. 179 If the story demands instantaneous materialization the effect is secured by a photographic means usually known as 'the hold'. It is so called by reason of the fact that all the other characters in such a scene must hold their positions while the trick character is made to materialize. **1940** *Chambers's Techn. Dict.* 418/2 *Hold*, the retention of an image on a screen longer than is natural.

hold (həʊld), *sb.*² Also 7 holt, hould, howld. [Corruption of earlier HOLL, HOLE, prob. by association with HOLD *sb.*¹ Cf. also MDu. and Du. *hol* (*a* 1500) in same sense.]

The interior cavity in a ship or vessel below the deck (or lower deck), where the cargo is stowed.

[**1470–1508** see HOLL *sb.* 2. **1483–1882** see HOLE *sb.* 6.] **1591** RALEIGH *Last Fight Rev.* (Arb.) 22 That the shippe had sixe foote water in hold. **1594** NASHE *Unfort. Trav.* 73 As a man falls in a shippe from the oreloope into the hold. **1597** SHAKS. *2 Hen. IV*, II. iv. 70 You haue not seene a Hulke better stufft in the Hold. *a* **1618** RALEIGH *Royal Navy* 25 If many had not been stricken downe into Holt in many voyages. **1627** CAPT. SMITH *Seaman's Gram.* ii. 12 The Cooke-roome..may bee placed..in the Hould. **1678** PHILLIPS (ed. 4), *The Howld* [1706 *hold*] *of a Ship*, the Room between the Keilson and lower Decks. **1726** SHELVOCKE *Voy. round World* 2 That I might have room to strike down some of my guns into the Hold. **1819** BYRON *Juan* II. xlii, Again blew A gale, and in the fore and after hold Water appear'd.

b. *Comb.* **hold-beam, -stanchion** (see quots. 1867); **hold-book**, a book containing an account of the cargo of a vessel; **hold-stringer**, a stringer or shelf piece for receiving the end of a hold-beam.

1800 *Asiat. Ann. Reg., Chron.* 67/1 The hold-beams had shrunk so considerably, that where there was room before to stand nearly upright, you could now only crawl on hands and knees. **1803** W. RAMSAY in *Naval Chron.* IX. 269 That a hold-book be kept to ascertain the stowage. **1867** SMYTH *Sailor's Word-bk.*, *Hold-beams*, the lowest range of beams in a merchantman. In a man-of-war they support the orlop-deck. *Ibid.*, *Hold-stanchions*, those which support the hold-beams amidships, and rest on the kelson. **1869** SIR E. REED *Shipbuild.* viii. 158 The heels of the stanchions are formed differently in different ships..to connect them with the keelsons or hold-stringers. **1874** THEARLE *Naval Archit.* 118 Hold stringers sometimes consist of plates and angle-irons, and at others, of angle-irons only.

hold, *sb.*³ Now only *Hist.* [a. ON. *hǫldr* (in early MSS. *haulðr*, *haulþr*), identified by Bugge with OE. *hæleð*, Ger. *held*, in Norse law 'a kind of higher yeoman, the owner of allodial land', *poet.* a 'man'.] In OE. times, the title of an officer of high rank in the Danelaw, corresponding to the High Reeve amongst the English.

c **910** *O.E. Chron.* an. 905 On ðara Deniscena healfe wearð ofslæȝen..Ysopa hold & Oscytel hold. *c* **1000** *Wergilds* c. 2 §4 in Schmid *Gesetze* 396 Holdes and cyninges heah-gerefan .IIII. þusend þrymsa. **1614** SELDEN *Titles Hon.* 225 Archbishops, Eorles, Bishops, Ealdormen, Holdes, Hehgerefas, Messethegnes, and Werldthegnes. **1717** *Blount's Law Dict.* (ed. 3), *Holdes*, Bailiffs of a Town or City. **1872** E. W. ROBERTSON *Hist. Ess.* 177 In later times, the Eorl and Hold seem to have answered amongst the Danish population of Northumbria, to the Ealderman and Heah-gerefa amongst the Angles.

†**hold**, *sb.*⁴ *Obs.* [OE. *hold*, cogn. with ON. *hold* (Da. *huld*, Sw. *hull*), flesh.] A carcase, dead body, corpse.

c **1000** *Ags. Gosp.* Matt. xxiv. 28 Swa hwær swa hold byð, þæder beoð earnas ȝegaderude. **11..** *Voc.* in Wr.-Wülcker 551/24 [*Cad*]*auer*, lic. *uel* hold. *c* **1200** *Trin. Coll. Hom.* 183 Aweilewei þu fule hold þat ich auere was to þe iteied.

†**hold, holde**, *sb.*⁵ *Obs.* [f. HOLD *a.*; OE. had *hyldo* in the same sense = OS., OHG. *huldí*, Ger. *huld*, n. of quality from HOLD *a.*] Allegiance, fidelity.

13.. *K. Alis.* 2912 Alle..swore heom holde, and lewte.

†**hold**, *a.* *Obs.* Also 3 heold, 4 hoild, huld, old. [OE. *hold* = OFris., OS. *hold* (MDu. *hout*, *houd-*, Du. *hou*), OHG. *holt* (MHG. *holt*, *hold-*, Ger. *hold*), ON. *hollr* (Da., Sw. *huld*), Goth. *hulþs*, favourably inclined, gracious, merciful: cf. Goth *wilja-halþei* benevolence, and **hilþan* to be inclined; prob. f. same root as HIELD *v.*]

1. Gracious, kind, friendly.

Beowulf (Z.) 267 þurh holdne hiȝe. *c* **893** K. ÆLFRED *Oros.* VI. xii, He wearð cristnum monnum..swiþe hold. *a* **1175** *Cott. Hom.* 231 To underȝeite wa an alle his cyne rice him were frend oðer fend, hold oðer fa. *c* **1250** *Gen. & Ex.* 1389 For kindes luue he was hire hold. *a* **1300** *Cursor M.* 13264 Leche to þam was he ful hold [*Gött.* hoild] He asked noþer siluer ne gold. *c* **1475** *Partenay* 2146 And of Ausoys the noble kyng hold.

2. Loyal, faithful, true. **a.** Of persons.

a **1000** *Oaths* c. 1 in Schmid *Gesetze* 404 Ic wille beon N. hold and ȝetriwe. *c* **1000** ÆLFRIC *Hom.* II. 552 Ðonne bið se holda ðeowa ȝeset ofer maneȝum godum. *c* **1200** ORMIN 10174 To winnenn ahhte to þe king, To beon himm holde & trowwe. *c* **1275** *Duty Christ* 20 in *O.E. Misc.* 141 He is vre beste king, we ouhte beon hym holde. *a* **1300** *Cursor M.* 20843 þat lijf, ne ded, ne wil, ne wa, Mai neuer turn mi hert þe fra, Bot hald it hold in þi seruis. *c* **1380** *Sir Ferumb.* 2592 For heo is trewe & holde.

b. Of things; esp. in *hold*(*e opes*, *opes holde*, late OE. *hold-áðas*, for earlier *hyld-áðas*, oaths of fealty.

In OE. *hyld-*, *hold-*, are in comb., but in later use *hold* is treated as adj.

[*a* **1000** *Oaths* c. 1 in Schmid *Gesetze* 404 þus man sceal swerigean hyldaðas.] *a* **1100** *O.E. Chron.* an. 1085² Ealle hi ..him hold aðas sworon. *a* **1122** *Ibid.* an. 1115 Ealle þa heafod men..dydon man-ræden and hold-aðas his sunu Willelme. *c* **1200** *Trin. Coll. Hom.* 163 On redinges and lorspelles, and on holde bedes. **1297** R. GLOUC. (1724) 383 Me suor hym holde oþes. *a* **1300** *Cursor M.* 21318 All war þair warkes old [*Gött.* hold]. *a* **1300** *K. Horn* 1249 Hi sworen oþes holde.

'holdable, *a.* [f. HOLD *v.* + -ABLE.] Capable of being held; tenable.

a **1649** DRUMM. OF HAWTH. *Fam. Ep.* Wks. (1711) 146 A fortress holdable and impregnable against the greatest assaults of his enemies.

'hold-all. [f. HOLD *v.* + ALL.] **1.** A portable case for holding clothes and miscellaneous articles required by soldiers, marines, travellers, etc.

1851 *Ord. & Regul. R. Engineers* xxiv. 119 The Knapsack is to contain the Great Coat, one Shirt, one pair of Stockings, Cloth and Shoe Brushes, Blacking, and Hold-all complete. **1859** F. A. GRIFFITHS *Artil. Man.* (1862) 164, 1 leather cartouch, 1 holdall. **1883** C. J. WILLS *Land of Lion & Sun* 55 An india-rubber soldier's hold-all. **1895** *Athenæum* 17 Aug. 220/1 To spend a fortnight attired in riding habits, ..with holdalls hanging like wallets over the saddles.

2. *fig.*, esp. with reference to books of the omnibus or encyclopædic kind.

1903 *Daily Chron.* 9 Nov. 3/3 There is a little of everything in the hold-all. **1904** M. DAVIES (*title*) The housewife's what's what: a hold-all of useful information for the house. **1964** [see CETERIS PARIBUS].

'hold-back. [f. *hold back*: see HOLD *v.* 34.]

1. Something that holds one back; a hindrance.

1581 PETTIE *Guazzo's Civ. Conv.* I. (1586) 9 To get the garland, by breaking in sunder those hookes, and hold-backs. **1640** HAMMOND *Serm., Poor man's Tithing* Wks. 1684 IV. 555 The only holdback is the affection and passionate love, that we bear to our wealth. **1863** MRS. WHITNEY *Faith Gartney* xix. (ed. 18) 179 Other families had similar holdbacks, that is the word, for they were not absolute insuperabilities.

2. The iron or strap on the shaft of a vehicle to which the breeching of the harness is attached. Also ***hold-back hook***.

1850 *N.H. Hist. Soc. Coll.* VI. 220 The hold-backs of his harness gave way, and precipitated his gig upon the horse. **1875** KNIGHT *Dict. Mech.*, *Hold-back Hook*, a projection on a carriage-shaft, to which the breeching-strap of a horse is connected, to enable the animal to hold back the vehicle.

3. The act of holding back. Also *attrib.*, unprogressive.

1852 *Trans. Mich. Agric. Soc.* III. 333 A few specimens of the hold-back and stand-still class. **1888** 'BUFFALO BILL' *Story of Wild West* 627 There was no brake on the wagon, and the horses were not much on the hold back.

'hold-down. [f. phr. *hold down* (HOLD *v.* 35).]

1. A device to prevent material or apparatus from shifting or shaking. Also *attrib.*

1888 *Lockwood's Dict. Mech. Engin.*, *Foundation Bolts*... Also termed hold-down bolts. **1962** J. GLENN in *Into Orbit* 188 Then the big hold-down clamps dropped away and I could feel us start to go. **1967** KARCH & BUBER *Offset Processes* x. 465 Set the rear pile hold-down..to hold the rear edge of the sheet to the pile.

2. A judo grip.

1954 E. DOMINY *Teach yourself Judo* iii. 39 In judo contests, there are three recognised methods of obtaining a point. The first is by means of a clean throw, the second by means of a 'Hold Down'. **1956** K. MASUDA tr. *Tomiki's Judo* iii. 91 In the practice of grappling, hold-downs, strangle-holds and bone-locks are connected with one another like the three sides of a triangle, the hold-downs being the base.

†**holde, hold**, *adv.* *Obs.* [OE. *holde*, f. HOLD *a.*] Graciously, kindly; loyally, faithfully.

c **1000** *Ags. Ps.* (Th.) lxxi[i]. 2 Heald þine þearfan holde mid dome. *c* **1250** *Gen. & Ex.* 3941 Ðoȝ balaac king me goue hold, His hus ful of siluer and of gold. **13..** *Gaw. & Gr. Knt.* 2129 Helde þou it neuer so holde.

holde, *v.*, abbreviated from BEHOLD.

1303 R. BRUNNE *Handl. Synne* 9390 As he [Belshazzar] þys hande began to holde Hys herte bygan to tremle and colde.

†**holdely**, *adv.* [OE. *holdlíce*, f. HOLD *a.* + -LY².] **a.** Graciously, kindly. **b.** Faithfully, loyally.

c **1000** ÆLFRIC *Hom.* II. 368 He cwæð eac swiðe holdlice be us. *c* **1050** *Suppl. Ælfric's Voc.* in Wr.-Wülcker 191/12 *Affectuose*, *uel deuote*, holdlice. *c* **1250** *Gen. & Ex.* 1546 He him bliscede holdelike and wel. **13..** *Gaw. & Gr. Knt.* 1875 Lays vp þe luf-lace, þe lady hym raȝt, Hid hit ful holdely, þer he hit eft fonde. *Ibid.* 2016 His oþer harnays, þat holdely watz keped.

holden, archaic pa. pple. of HOLD *v.*

holder¹ ('həʊldə(r)). [f. HOLD *v.* + -ER¹.]

I. One who or that which holds or takes hold.

1. a. One who holds or grasps.

14.. *Nom.* in Wr.-Wülcker 687/14 *Hic stinarius*, a halder. **1552** HULOET, Holder,..he that holdeth fast. **1610** W. FOLKINGHAM *Art of Survey* I. viii. 16 Rooks runne fluttering after the share at the verie heeles of the holder. **1756** T. HALE *Compl. Body Agric.* VI. lix. 331 The Holder may also make some alteration in the going of the Plow by the Handles. **1859** DICKENS *T. Two Cities* II. i, The holder of a horse at Tellson's door, who made off with it. **1863** A. J. HORWOOD *Yearbks. 30 & 31 Edw. I* Pref. 37 The rope broke not by reason of the holders moving or jerking it.

b. with *prep.*

1857 HUGHES *Tom Brown* I. vi, Bigoted holders by established forms and customs.

2. a. One who holds, occupies, possesses, or owns; a tenant, occupier, possessor, owner; a shareholder. Often in Comb., as *freeholder*, *householder*, *innholder*, *loanholder*, *shareholder*, etc.

c **1350** in *Eng. Gilds* 362 After þe deth of euerych haldere in ffee. *c* **1449** PECOCK *Repr.* (1860) I. 93 The holders of the ijᵉ opinioun. **1609** HOLLAND *Amm. Marcell.* XVIII. v. 111 Being now a landed man, and a holder of possessions there. **1838** DE MORGAN *Ess. Probab.* 218 Suppose that the holder of the policy wishes to sell his interest. **1848** J. J. RUSKIN *Let.* 22 Mar. in M. Lutyens *Effie in Venice* (1965) I. 17 A person of very sound Judgement on Railroad Shares... To Holders he says—if they have no other means of meeting Calls—sell. **1856** BOUVIER *Law Dict.* (ed. 6) I. 588 The holder of a bill of exchange is the person who is legally in the possession of it, either by endorsement or delivery, or both. **1869** ARBER *Latimer's Serm. bef. Edw. VI* Contents 3 The present holder of the farm.

b. *Sports.* The possessor for the time (as the winner) of a championship, cup, etc. which is open to competition.

1830 *Sporting Mag.* 2nd Ser. I. 337/1 The holder [of the sculls] shall row the best, or only, challenger, on the 10th of August. **1873** *Football Ann.* 54 Association Challenge Cup, 1872–73... Final Tie. Wanderers (holders) beat Oxford Association by two goals..to none. **1887** *Athletic Jrnl.* 9 Aug. 16 West Manchester (the winners and present holders of the Manchester Cup). **1900** *Field* 7 July 3/3 Hants County Public School Challenge Shield... This annual competition was held on the playgrounds of the holders, Churcher's College, Petersfield, on Thursday in last week. *Ibid.* 14 July 61/1 The holder of the challenge cup, Wadsley, was quite unable to do himself justice. **1928** *Daily Mail* 25 July 14/7 Middlesex, the holders, are..the only county to have won two matches in this group. **1955** *Times* 16 June 3/2 The effect on the players was clearly seen when L. Hoad, the holder, beat R. Bedard.

3. A contrivance for holding, containing, or supporting something. Often preceded by a word denoting what is held, as ***bouquet-***, ***cigar-***, ***gas-***, ***pen-***, ***whip-holder***, etc.: see the first element.

1833 J. HOLLAND *Manuf. Metal* II. 139 The tool for cutting, &c. is fixed in the two holders..by their screws.

1842–4 H. Stephens *Bk. Farm* (1871) I. 408 If she [the cow] is known to have a fractious temper, it is better to put a holder in her nose. 1846 R. Ford *Gatherings from Spain* xxiv. 338 A Spanish fore-finger and thumb are quite fire-browned and fire-proof, although some polished exquisites use silver holders. *c*1865 J. Wylde in *Circ. Sc.* I. 63/1 In using small holders, such should be.. emptied of all gas. 1876 G. Roslyn *Geo. Eliot in Derbysh.* 50 A small Quaker-shaped bonnet.. hung on a holder in the wall. 1884 *World* 29 Oct. 12 Long streamers of the brigade ribbon were tied round the bouquet-holders. 1916 E. F. Benson *David Blaize* vi. 111 A magnificent present of twenty-five cigarettes and a cherry-wood holder. 1957 J. Osborne *Entertainer* 16 He unwraps the cigarettes and takes out an ivory holder from his waistcoat.

4. a. A canine tooth.

1672 *Lond. Gaz.* No. 686/4 His [a dog's] Holders broak. 1854 Owen *Skel. & Teeth in Circ. Sc., Organ. Nat.* I. 279 Large conical teeth situated behind the incisors.. are called holders, tearers, laniaries, or more commonly, canine teeth.

b. A prehensile organ in some animals.

1774 Goldsm. *Nat. Hist.* (1862) I. xiv. 233 The insects have feelers; and the worms, holders. 1822–34 *Good's Study Med.* (ed. 4) I. 271 [Long tape-worm] with a terminal mouth surrounded by two rows of radiate hooks or holders.

5. With adverbs, as **holder-forth**, one who 'holds forth', a preacher, orator (somewhat *contemptuous*); **holder-on**, one who holds on (in quot. one who shoots direct at the game; see hold *v.* 28); **holder-out**, one who holds out: see hold *v.* 41 j; **holder-up**, one who holds up or sustains; a supporter, maintainer; *spec.* a workman who supports a rivet with a hand-anvil or sledge-hammer in riveting.

1661 *Trial J. James* in Howell *St. Trials* (1816) VI. 71 By this time John James was brought into the meeting-place, and the Lieutenant.. said to the women, What have you no better a *holder-forth than he? *a*1704 T. Brown *2 Oxf. Schol.* Wks. 1730 I. 2, I shall receive a call to be a Pastor or Holder-forth in some Congregation or other. *a*1754 Fielding *New Way to Keep Wife* i. ii, Thou art a fine promising holder forth.. and dost begin to preach in a most orthodox manner. 1881 Greener *Gun* 486 A bird crossing was fired at by one of the '*holders on'. 1643 E. Udall *Serm.* (1645) 21 Constant.. *holders out in righteousnesse to the end. *c*1374 Chaucer *Troylus* ii. 595 (644) Here comeþ.. his brother, *holdere vp of Troye! 1548 Udall *Erasm. Par. Luke* i. (1551) 225 The sturdy holders vp of their snoute, he hath cast downe. 1869 Sir E. Reed *Shipbuild.* xvii. 340 Each 'set' of riveters consists of two riveters, 'a holder-up', and one or two boys.

II. That of which hold is taken.

6. The strap by which a carriage window is drawn up; also, the strap on the back of a carriage by which footmen hold.

1794 W. Felton *Carriages* (1801) I. 137 By holders and strings are meant the lace.. for the purpose of holding by, or drawing up the glasses with. *Ibid.*, Every inside-holder takes a yard of lace, and every footman-holder a yard and a half. 1825 T. Cosnett *Footman's Direct.* 213 Hold fast with the holders on the left side with your left hand.

holder[2]. [f. hold *sb.*[2] + -er[1].] A workman employed in a ship's hold.

1495 *Act 11 Hen. VII*, c. 22 §1 An holder by the day ij[d] with mete and drinke. 1800 Colquhoun *Comm. Thames* iv. 179 Holders are persons who unstow the Cargo during the discharge. 1867 Smyth *Sailor's Word-bk.*, *Holders*, the people employed in the hold duties of a ship.

holderbat ('həʊldəbæt). [f. holder[1] + bat *sb.*[2]] A type of bracket for fastening a pipe to a wall or other surface, consisting of two semicircular parts that are clamped round the pipe and a projection on one of the parts that is built into the wall.

1914 Sage & Fretwell *Text-bk. Elem. Building Constr.* xi. 225 The best method, however, is to dispense with ears and use 'holderbats' built into the wall. 1955 N. W. Kay *Mod. Building Encycl.* 331/2 The holderbat has two portions, a circular ring, with a jointed or removable portion,.. and a tail which is cemented into the wall.

holdfast ('həʊldfɑːst, -æ-), *a.* and *sb.* [f. *hold fast*: see hold *v.* 2 + fast *adv.*] A. *adj.*

1. That holds fast, *lit.* and *fig.*; having a firm hold or grasp; persistent.

1567 Maplet *Gr. Forest* 57 The Pine tree is called hold-fast or pitchie tre. 1593 Shaks. *Lucr.* 555 In his hold-fast foot the weak mouse panteth. 1612 J. Davies *Muse's Sacr.* (1878) 12/2 With hold-fast armes of euerlasting loue. 1884 Tennyson *Becket* ii. ii, Only the golden Leopard printed in it Such hold-fast claws.

†2. Tenacious of what one has. *Obs.*

1560 Becon *New Catech.* Wks. 1844 II. 399 So hold fast and wedded to the world, that whatsoever they can get, they so hoard it up.

B. *sb.* 1. The action or fact of holding fast; firm or sure grasp. *lit.* and *fig.*

1578 Lyte *Dodoens* i. lviii. 84 The Strawberrie.. creepeth alongst the ground, and taketh roote and holdefast. 1628 Prynne *Love-lockes* 7 They serue.. but to giue the Deuill holdfast, to draw vs by them into Hell. 1691 T. H[ale] *Acc. New Invent.* 119 The Nature of Ground as to the hold-fast of Anchors. 1862 C. A. Johns *Brit. Birds* (1874) 29 Secure of its holdfast, it allows its victim no chance of escape.

2. Something to which one may hold fast or which affords a secure hold or support. (In some of the fig. uses perh. to be referred to sense 4.)

1566 T. Stapleton *Ret. Untr. Jewel* i. 8 We will trie farder what sure holdefast he hath to staie him self thereon. 1688 Boyle *Final Causes Nat. Things* iv. 187 Nature.. has furnished the several sorts of teeth with holdfasts, suitable to the stress.. they may be put to. 1793 Smeaton *Edystone L.* §121 We should then have lost the rock as a Holdfast, and Buttress against the great South-west seas. 1867 F. Francis *Angling* vi. (1880) 233 The sedge and alder being great holdfasts.

3. One that holds fast: †a. A stingy or hard-fisted person; a miser. *Obs.*

1576 Fleming *Panopl. Epist.* 320, I may sooner wring Hercules his clubbe perforce out of his fist, then get mine owne monie out of the hands of this injurious holdfast. 1660 tr. *Amyraldus' Treat. conc. Relig.* i. v. 60 A great Miser and hold-fast. 1706 Phillips (ed. Kersey), *Hold-fast*.. is also commonly taken for a griping covetous Wretch.

b. As name for a dog that holds tenaciously.

1599 Shaks. *Hen. V*, ii. iii. 54 Hold fast is the onely Dogge. 1752 Johnson *Rambler* No. 197 ⁋3 When I envied the finery of any of my neighbours, [my mother] told me that 'Brag was a good dog, but Holdfast was a better'. 1861 Dickens *Gt. Expect.* xviii.

4. a. Something that holds fast, binds, supports, or keeps together; *spec.* a staple, hook, clamp, or bolt securing a part of a building or other structure.

1576 Turberv. *Venerie* 196 You may take them out alive with your holdfasts and clampes. 1609 Holland *Amm. Marcell.* xiv. xi. 27 The insoluble bond and hold-fast of necessitie, binding the pride of mortall men. 1620–55 I. Jones *Stone-Heng* (1725) 46 They united.. the Stones together, by certain Ligatures or Holdfasts. 1703 Moxon *Mech. Exerc.* 64 The Hold-fast.. to keep the Work fast upon the Bench, while you either Saw, Tennant, Mortess, or sometimes Plain upon it. 1706 Phillips (ed. Kersey), *Hold-fast*, an Iron Hook in shape of the Letter S fix'd in a Wall to support it; also a Joyner's Tool. 1782 *Phil. Trans.* LXXII. 367 This hip-pole was supported.. by an iron-strap, or holdfast. 1803 *Trans. Soc. Arts* XXI. 349 The pole.. passes through the strong holdfasts in the braces. 1842–67 Gwilt *Archit.* Gloss., *Holdfast*, a long nail, with a flat short head for securing objects to a wall. 1877 W. Thomson *Voy. Challenger* I. i. 14 The Microscopes are secured to the table by brass holdfasts like those in common use on carpenters' benches.

b. *Bot.* An organ for superficial attachment developed by some algæ and fungi.

1841 W. H. Harvey *Man. Brit. Algæ* p. xiv, Most Algæ are, at some period of their growth, found attached to other substances by means of a root, or at least a hold-fast. 1895 G. Murray *Introd. Study Seaweeds* 23 The sculpturing of outward form reaches its highest point in the differentiation.. of a root-like holdfast. 1902 *Science* Jan. 59/2 Kelp hold-fasts, of which none grow in the immediate vicinity, were taken in abundance by the dredge. 1930 H. M. Fitzpatrick *Lower Fungi: Phycomycetes* iii. 45 In the typical epibiotic species (Rhizidiaceæ) the germ tube of the cytospore acts as a holdfast. 1931 L. Newton *Handbk. Brit. Seaweeds* p. vi, One of the main factors affecting the distribution of algæ is the securing of a suitable holdfast. 1962 C. J. Alexopoulos *Introd. Mycol.* (ed. 2) x. 213 The basal part of the hypha [of members of the order Eccrinales] is in the form of a disc-like holdfast by means of which the fungus is attached to the host. 1966 F. H. Brightman *Oxf. Bk. Flowerless Plants* 6/2 The holdfast is disc-shaped, but root-like structures also develop from the base of the stalk. 1971 *Where* July 202/2 They are the lovely coloured seaweeds or algae, with their interestingly-named parts: the 'holdfast' which forms the root, and the 'thallus' or fronds which make up the body.

Hence '**holdfastness**, tenacity, persistency.

1869 S. Bowles *Our New West* 466 A healthy copartnership of American enterprise and enthusiasm, and English solidity and holdfastness. 1897 *Harper's Mag.* Apr. 724 The Belgians.. combining the vivacity and quick wit of the Latin races with a sturdy energy and holdfastness.

holding ('həʊldɪŋ), *vbl. sb.* [f. hold *v.*]

I. 1. a. The action of hold *v.*, in various senses.

*a*1225 *Ancr. R.* 176 þet heo beo euer edmod.. mid louh holdunge of hire suluen. 1340 Hampole *Pr. Consc.* 5994 Alle wrang haldyngs of gudes sere. *c*1440 Hylton *Scala Perf.* (W. de W. 1494) i. lxxi, In the holdyng ne in þe kepyng. *c*1470 Henry *Wallace* viii. 1640 Thow werray help in haldyn off the rycht. 1545 Ascham *Toxoph.* ii. (Arb.) 149 Holdynge must not be longe, for it.. putteth a bowe in ieopardy. 1621 Lady M. Wroth *Urania* 451 They would almost in kindnesse hurt, with hard, but kindest holdings. *a*1774 W. Pearce *Serm.* (1778) IV. 31 This is the unity of the Christian Church, the holding of Christ for the head. 1855 Morton *Cycl. Agric.* I. 848 To obtain a holding, they are twisted round the stakes.

b. *spec.* The tenure or occupation of land.

1420 *Searchers Verdicts* in *Surtees Misc.* (1888) 16 A tenement of Sir John of Langton Knyght in the haldyng of John Rumby. 1480 Caxton *Chron. Eng.* clxii. 145 That he shold come to parlement for his lande and for his holdynge in walys. 1609 Skene *Reg. Maj.*, *Stat. Robt. III*, 59 To schaw his chartour (or maner of halding to his overlord). 1774 T. Jefferson *Autobiog.* App. Wks. 1859 I. 138 In the earlier ages of the Saxon settlement, feudal holdings were certainly unknown. 1818 Cruise *Digest* (ed. 2) I. 284 Such a holding now operated as a tenancy from year to year. 1875 Maine *Hist. Inst.* iv. 102 That the Irish holdings in 'rundale' are not forms of property, but modes of occupation.

†c. Consistency. *Obs. rare.* (Cf. *hold together*, hold *v.* 43 b.)

1601 Shaks. *All's Well* iv. ii. 27 This ha's no holding To sweare by him whom I protest to loue That I will worke against him.

d. With adverbs: see hold *v.* IV. *holding up* (see quot. 1888).

1581 Mulcaster *Positions* xv. (1887) 69 The holding in of the breath. 1606 Holland *Sueton.* 100 The cause of this holding of and delay. 1611 Bible *Jer.* vi. 11, I am weary with holding in. *a*1680 Butler *Rem.* (1759) I. 78 When.. a dull Sentence, and a moral Fable Do more, than all our Holdings-forth are able. 1689 Evelyn *Diary* 25 Aug., Londonderry reliev'd after a brave and wonderfull holding out. 1711 Mary Astell (*title*) Quaker's Sermon: or a Holding-Forth concerning Barabbas. 1888 *Lockwood's Dict. Mech. Engin.* 178 *Holding up*, the maintaining of a firm pressure against the heads of rivets while their closing up is being effected, a holding-up hammer being used for the purpose. 1908 J. G. Horner *Plating & Boiler-making* (ed. 2) xii. 214 Holding-up dollies were shown in Figs. 56 and 57... In girder work a rig-up like that shown in Fig. 235 is used. It consists of a heavy holding-up hammer a, on the end of a long elastic handle b.

e. *Association Football.* The obstruction of a player by taking hold of his jersey, etc.

1866 *Cassell's Illustr. Fam. Paper* 17 Mar. 509/2 'Holding' includes the obstruction of a player by the hands, arms, or body without kicking or throwing. 1967 *Association Football* ('Know the Game' Series) 33 Should the obstruction take the form of a personal foul, e.g., pushing, holding, charging unfairly or tripping, then the foul is penalised by a direct free kick.

2. That which holds or lays hold; an attachment; a means of laying hold or influencing.

1770 Burke *Pres. Discont.* Wks. 1842 I. 149 This is one of the principal holdings of that destructive system, which has endeavoured to unhinge all the virtuous, honourable, and useful connexions in the kingdom. *a*1797 —— *Wks.* (1842) I. Introd. 21 If I have assisted to loosen the foreign holdings of the citizen, and taught him to look for his protection to the laws of his country. 1806 R. Cumberland *Mem.* (1807) I. 242, I had a holding on Lord Halifax, founded on my father's merits. 1887 Mrs. L. Baxter *Tuscan Stud.* i. i. 40 The block in some manner slipped from the holdings and fell heavily into the river.

II. That which is held.

3. a. Land held by legal right, esp. of a superior; a tenement.

1640 W. Boswell *Let. to Laud* 12 June in Ussher *Proph.* (1687) 5 All evil Contrivances here and in France, and in other Protestant Holdings. *a*1810 Tannahill *Poem*, When John and me were married Our hading was but sma'. 1856 Froude *Hist. Eng.* (1858) I. i. 89 Capitalists were not allowed to drive the labourers from their holdings.

b. Property held, esp. stocks or shares.

1573 in Gross *Gild Merch.* (1890) II. 76 The sayde wardens.. shall have for their paynes double holdinges of all the bargaines. 1872 H. Spencer *Princ. Psychol.* (ed. 2) §515 II. 584 Documents representing holdings in foreign government debts. 1891 *Daily News* 28 Apr. 2/7 As the pressing sellers have disposed of their holdings, prices are now sound.

c. The cards held by a player.

1929 M. C. Work *Compl. Contract Bridge* iv. 38 With such holdings.. the rebid should be made. 1959 *Listener* 10 Dec. 1054/2 The high card holding is weak.

†4. An opinion held, a tenet. *Obs.*

*c*1449 Pecock *Repr.* i. i. 5 Thre trowingis holdingis or opinions. 1450–5 —— *Bk. of Faith* i. §2 (1688) 1 To followe the Determynations and the Holdingis of the Churche in mater of Feith. 1851 J. Hinton *Let.* in Miss Hopkins *Life* v. (1885) 84 A train of thought that has almost revolutionised my holdings.

†5. The burden of a song. *Obs.*

1598 *Servingman's Comf.* C, A song is to be song, the vndersong or holding whereof is, It is merrie in Haul, when Beardes wagges all. 1606 Shaks. *Ant. & Cl.* ii. vii. 117 Then the Boy shall sing. The holding euery man shall beare [*printed* beate] as loud, As his strong sides can volly.

III. 6. *attrib.* and *Comb.* a. Of or for holding.

1593 Shaks. *3 Hen. VI*, v. iv. 4 The Cable broke, the holding-Anchor lost. 1731 J. Tull *Horse-hoeing Husb.* xxii. (1733) 153 This Holding-Screw has a pretty broad Head. 1898 *Daily News* 15 Feb. 8/1 The car with its adjuncts was a marvel of holding capacity.

b. **holding ground**, (*a*) a bottom in which an anchor will hold, anchorage; also *fig.*; (*b*) a site for storing floating timber; **holding-note** (*Mus.*), 'a note sustained in one part while the others are in motion' (Stainer & Barrett); **holding operation**, an undertaking which prevents a situation from worsening, but can do little or nothing to improve it; **holding paddock** *Austral.* and *N.Z.*, a paddock where sheep or cattle are kept until required (for droving, shearing, etc.); similarly **holding pen, yard**.

1740 Woodroofe in Hanway *Trav.* (1762) I. iv. lix. 271 There is three fathoms water, and a good *holding ground. 1839 Marryat *Phant. Ship* xxiii, The anchor.. dragged, from.. bad holding-ground. 1849 Grote *Greece* ii. I. VI. 334 The assembly and the dikastery were Kleon's theatre and holding-ground. 1957 *Brit. Commonw. Forest Terminol.* 2 *Holding ground*, a boom site for storing timber. 1961 F. H. Burgess *Dict. Sailing* 116 *Holding ground*, the nature of the bottom and its holding quality for purposes of anchoring. 1774 Burney *Hist. Mus.* (1789) I. v. 58 Euclid tells us.. that sounds may be sustained in the same tone which we call a *holding-note. 1962 *Listener* 8 Mar. 400/1 Whether it [*sc.* a White Paper] will achieve its immediate object of persuading the unions to help the economy over its next stile by holding down labour costs, we must wait and see... As a *holding operation it may win some success. 1972 *Guardian* 9 Sept. 13/8 Mr Jenkins's last-minute scramble to satisfy the TUC.. was only a holding operation to keep him sweet with Congress. 1933 L. G. D. Acland in *Press* (Christchurch) 28 Oct. 17/7 **Holding paddock*, a small paddock, close to yards, wool-shed, or mustering hut, for holding (not feeding) sheep. 1934 *Bulletin* (Sydney) 16 May 38/4 At midday the cattle, mad with thirst, broke out of the holding paddock and vanished in a wild stampede over a high hillcrest into the vast unfenced wilderness of the hills beyond. 1941 *Coast to Coast 1941* 22 Wiggins said some steers had got out of his holding paddocks. 1950 *N.Z. Jrnl. Agric.* Oct. 35 Cattle in a holding paddock before being drafted. 1923 *Ibid.* 20 Mar. 144 The *holding-pens in the shed.. should never be too large. 1965 J. S. Gunn *Terminol. Shearing Industry* i. 32 *Holding pen*, one of the small pens or yards in which sheep are held, usually within the shed, under shelter, while awaiting shearing. 1950 *N.Z. Jrnl. Agric.* Apr. 377/2 For handling large herds [of cows] a crush yard is recommended, with the main *holding yard either in front or at one side. 1959 *Listener* 15 Jan. 115/1 There were

some good holding yards where we could put the cattle for the night.

c. *Aeronaut.* Used *attrib.*, of or pertaining to the process of 'stacking' aircraft in the air above a landing site before they come down to land.

1948 *Shell Aviation News* No. 116. 19/3 Holding procedures as an integral part of the traffic control system for jet transports should be completely eliminated. **1958** *Chambers's Techn. Dict.* 985/1 *Holding pattern*, a specified flight track..which an aircraft may be required to maintain about a holding point. *Holding point*, an identifiable point, such as a radio beacon, in the vicinity of which an aircraft under air traffic control may be instructed to remain. **1969** *Daily Tel.* 14 Nov. 1/7 Stacking over a 'holding area' while waiting a turn to land, is not uncommon, especially in poor weather conditions. **1972** *New Yorker* 16 Sept. 26/1 He turned on the plane's radio, in order to hear the traffic controller at the..airport talking to several airliners stacked in a holding pattern overhead.

holding, *ppl. a.* [f. as prec. + -ING².]

1. a. That holds, in various senses (see the verb); retentive; grasping; tenacious.

c **1400** tr. *Secreta Secret., Gov. Lordsh.* (E.E.T.S.) 70 Nedys þat he take first a holdynge mete yn þe ground of þe stomake. **1568** GRAFTON *Chron.* II. 49 He was free and liberall to straungers, and heard and holdyng from his familiers and servauntes. **1681** CHETHAM *Angler's Vade-m.* iv. §13 (1689) 42 It is..the most holding Bait of all other. **1891** *Field* 19 Dec. 957/1 Fetlock deep in holding clay. **1930** *Daily Express* 6 Nov. 16/1 The keen east wind dried up the course, which was inclined to be on the holding side. **1955** *Times* 19 May 4/4 In August last year the going was extremely holding.

b. ***holding company***: a trading company which possesses the whole of, or a controlling interest in, the share capital of one or more other companies.

1906 *Daily Colonist* (Victoria, B.C.) 18 Jan. 1/5 A bill to prohibit 'holding companies' such as have lately effected the merger of various corporations..was introduced in the legislature today. **1912** *Q. Rev.* Jan. 195 The Federal Steel Company, which is technically, like the Steel Corporation of to-day, a holding company. **1928** *Britain's Industr. Future* (*Liberal Ind. Inq.*) II. viii. 93 To treat trusts, cartels, combinations, holding companies, and trade associations as inexpedient abnormalities in the economic system. **1928** *Daily Mail* 7 Aug. 18/4 This conservative finance enables the Shell, as a holding company,..to maintain its dividends in times of depression. **1930** A. PALMER *Company Secretarial Pract.* xix. 255 The Act does not specifically define a holding company, but refers to it as a company holding shares, either directly or through a nominee, in a subsidiary company. **1958** *Times* 11 Aug. 11/2 Mrs. Roebling..is director or trustee of more than 16 organizations and president of a holding company. **1972** 'E. LATHEN' *Murder without Icing* (1973) xv. 131 Holland's other assets could take a long time to find. He's got everything wrapped up in holding companies.

2. *Farming.* Applied to animals 'held' or kept for breeding. Also *ellipt.* as sb. = *holding pig*, etc. [In origin, attrib. use of vbl. sb.]

1547 *Will of R. Meese* (Somerset Ho.), My blacke sowe with v holdinge pigges. **1615** MARKHAM *Eng. Housew.* (1660) 177 Holding Swine, which are onely to be preserved in good flesh. **1851** *Jrnl. R. Agric. Soc.* XII. II. 348 Pasture, which is grazed by the breeding cattle, or 'holding stock'. **1853** *Ibid.* XIV. II. 300 From the high rates of holding lambs, many farmers last season hogged the lambs.

3. ***holding-down bolt, pin, ring.***

1846 *Patent Jrnl.* I. 226/2 On each side of the holding down bolts..an upright pillar is erected. *a* **1877** KNIGHT *Dict. Mech.* II. 1112/2 *Holding-down Bolt*,..one of twelve or more strong bolts, which are passed from the outside of a steam-vessel through the floor-timbers, sleepers, foundation-plate of the engine, and the bosses on the cylinders, condensers, and side-frames, and are secured by strong nuts. **1892** W. W. GREENER *Breech-Loader* 19 Every gun provided with a holding-down bolt. *Ibid.* 260 Certain accessories.., such as cords, planks, and holding-down pins. **1899–1900** *Kynoch Jrnl.* Dec.–Jan. 29/2 The cones are secured to ships' decks by holding-down rings. **1930** *Engineering* 4 Apr. 440/2 Checking parts for fit and tightening holding-down and other bolts.

Hence 'holdingly** *adv. rare.*

c **1375** *Gloss.* in *Rel. Antiq.* I. 8 *Tenaciter*, holdynglyche. **1611** COTGR., *Tenacement*, fastly, cleauingly, holdingly.

holdless ('həʊldlɪs), *a. Mountaineering.* [f. HOLD *sb.*¹ + -LESS.] Affording no holds; having a smooth unbroken surface.

1922 E. R. EDDISON *Worm Ouroboros* xiii. 184 Cliffs smooth and holdless as a castle wall. **1933** [see ABSEIL]. **1971** *Country Life* 25 Feb. 410/1 Alastair solved problem after problem..making short work finally of the hardest obstacle, an awkward holdless entry to a chimney at the start of the last tower.

'hold-out. [See HOLD *v.* 41 e.] **a.** (See quot.)

1893 in FARMER *Slang.* **1894** MASKELYNE *Sharps & Flats* v. 73 The term 'Holdout' is the name given to a mechanical contrivance, constructed with the object of enabling the card-sharper to 'hold-out', or conceal one or more cards, until he finds that they will be useful to him.

b. The act of holding out; something that or someone who holds out; *spec.* (chiefly *U.S.*) a player, usu. in baseball, who refuses to play until he is promised higher pay.

1945 *Sun* (Baltimore) 17 Feb. 7/7 This is another year when any baseball holdouts will do their shouting in whispers. *Ibid.* (*heading*) Holdout is weapon. **1952** B. MALAMUD *Natural* (1963) 22 He was a holdout for £75,000 and was coming East to squeeze it out of his boss. **1964** *Amer. Speech* XXXIX. 91 Occasionally there was a hold-out, as in this lamentation: [etc.]. **1970** *Globe & Mail* (Toronto) 26 Sept. 35/1 Whatever became of another well-known holdout, Joe Kapp?.. Kapp keeps waiting for the Minnesota Vikings to pay him more money.

c. Of paint or ink (see quot. 1965).

1965 *Gloss. Paint Terms* (*B.S.I.*) 32 *Hold out*, the ability of a paint film to dry to its normal finish on a somewhat absorptive surface. **1971** *Timber Trades Jrnl.* 21 Aug. 29/1 Golden Royal hardboard..was already accepted as a good painting medium, but application of a seal..meant that.. certain properties, including paint hold-out, workabilty and strength, were improved. **1972** *Publishers Weekly* 4 Dec. 11 (Advt.), Its unique combination of high ink hold-out, high brightness, and high opacity.

'hold-over. [See HOLD *v.* 42.] **a.** An authorization granted by a bench of magistrates for the transfer of a publican's licence to another person for the unexpired term till the next annual licensing session. **b.** *U.S.* A cell for the retention of prisoners awaiting trial. **c.** One who continues to hold an office after his term has expired.

1888 *Wine, Sp. & Beer* 8 Mar. 174/1 The license became void, and being advised not to ask for a hold-over, the Company now applied to Special Sessions. **1888** *Missouri Republican* 24 Feb. (Farmer), Wilson was released from the hold over, where he has been held since Irwin's death. **1893** *Good Governm.* (N.Y.) 15 Aug., The obnoxious Republican hold-over still holds over.

d. Something left over; a remainder or survival. *U.S.*

1904 *Los Angeles Express* 11 Aug. 12 Doing the best it could on crackers and cheese and holdovers. **1909** 'O. HENRY' *Roads of Destiny* iv. 58 She was a hold-over from the Greek classics. **1929** *Atlantic Monthly* Mar. 298 The little village of Washington in Connecticut, one of the most charming holdovers of the past that state possesses. **1951** E. PAUL *Springtime in Paris* iii. 53 Like several other articles, it seemed to be a holdover from the previous tenant. **1969** *Times* 6 Mar. 23/1 Both the present assistant secretaries for international affairs in the Treasury..are Johnson hold-overs.

'hold-up. orig. *U.S. slang.* [See HOLD *v.* 44 e.]

1. a. One who robs by 'holding up' a traveller, train, etc.: see HOLD *v.* 44 e. **b.** An instance of 'holding up'; a robbery committed in this manner.

1878 F. M. A. ROE *Army Lett.* (1909) 206 The driver is their only protector, and the stage route is through miles and miles of wild forest, and in between huge boulders where a 'hold-up' could be so easily accomplished. **1885** *Harper's Mag.* Apr. 695/2 Darkness..into which one ventured with grave apprehensions lest a 'hold-up' might be in waiting for him. **1888** in Farmer *Dict. Amer.*, [He] was mortally shot by hold-ups, Tuesday night. **1896** *Boston* (Mass.) *Jrnl.* 29 Dec. 2/1 The prisoner confessed to a hold-up. **1897** *Ibid.* 16 Jan. 2/5 We are tired of reading in our papers nothing but hold-ups and killings. **1904** *Daily Chron.* 23 Dec. 4/5 There are epidemics of robberies, murders and hold-ups in all the large cities. **1928** *Daily Express* 15 June 7/5 The 'hold-up' of a steamer crowded with holiday-makers on Lake Windermere. **1968** *Globe & Mail* (Toronto) 17 Feb. 2/2 Police said they had recovered $3,991 from yesterday's holdup.

c. A stoppage or check in the passage or progress of a person or thing; a temporary stoppage of traffic; a cessation, stop. orig. *U.S.*

1837 *Knickerbocker* X. 439 The wheels of the coach are shod with the preparation of iron slippers, which are essential to a hold-up. **1882** in G. H. Putnam *Mem. Publisher* (1915) 289 We don't have hold-ups [*sc.* strikes] in Leadville. **1904** *N.Y. Tribune* 15 May 2 A vote of thanks to the Tribune for its efforts to end the hold-up of the Port Chester Railroad's application for a permit to cross streets in the Bronx. **1907** *Putnam's Monthly* July 482/1 He cursed the luck of the hold-up. **1913** A. B. EMERSON *R. Fielding at Snow Camp* 154 We got to sit down and wait for a hold-up [of the storm]. **1918** 'Q' *Foe-Farrell* vii. 125 There was a hold-up as we [in a taxi] neared the bridge. **1928** *Daily Express* 14 July 2/1 There had been two or three hold-ups with the points prior to my arrival at 4.50 p.m. **1964** *Ann. Reg. 1963* 224 In connexion with the various hold-ups of Allied military convoys on the autobahn..it was recalled that the D.D.R. had only temporarily handed over control of military traffic to the Soviet military. **1973** 'H. CARMICHAEL' *Too Late for Tears* xi. 131, I nearly didn't get here. Ran into a traffic hold-up and was stuck. **1973** E. LEMARCHAND *Let or Hindrance* viii. 93 The hold-up over the Fortnight film while Paul King finished editing the last part.

d. An instance of extortion. Chiefly *U.S.*

1908 L. MITCHELL *New York Idea* I. 15 The people insisted on electing a desperado to the presidential office —they must take the hold-up that follows. **1910** *Sat. Even. Post* 27 Aug. 6/3 Our house..cost twenty-five thousand dollars, exclusive of the plumber's little hold-up and the Oriental rugs. **1939** J. MULGAN *Man Alone* i. 14 It never was farming land. It's a hold-up, and God help the poor bastards who have to take it at that price.

e. *Bridge.* (See quot. 1959.) Cf. HOLD *v.* 44 d.

1945 PHILLIPS & REESE *How to play Bridge* III. 101 The principal device available to the declarer to prevent the establishment of an opponent's long suit is hold-up play. **1959** REESE & DORMER *Bridge Player's Dict.* 113 *Hold-up play.* A player is said to hold up when for tactical reasons he declines to play a winning card. Usually, his object is to destroy communication between the enemy hands, but there can be other and more subtle reasons for the hold-up. **1962** *Listener* 22 Mar. 534/1 This uncommon hold-up play will prevent the defence from bringing in the suit unless North has two entries.

f. (See quot.)

1945 H. D. SMYTH *Gen. Acct. Devel. Atomic Energy Mil. Purposes* ix. 94 The total amount of material tied up in a separation plant is called a 'hold-up'. The hold-up may be very large in a plant consisting of many stages.

2. *attrib.* = Engaged in, involving, or characterized by forcible stopping and robbing of a person.

1881 E. W. NYE *B. Nye & Boomerang* 192, I did give him the grand bounce, and now he hath joined a hold-up outfit on the overland stage route. **1899** *Chicago Tribune* 16 Jan., The holdup gang who shot and killed policeman..Wallner. **1930** [see BAIL *v.*³ 3]. **1959** *Times Lit. Suppl.* 20 Feb. 93/3 Unfortunately the stranger is not only a 'goy' and a drifter but he has been worse—a hold-up man, one of whose victims was once the grocer himself.

†holdur, erron. f. HELDER *adv.*, rather.

c **1400** *Destr. Troy* 2919 Holdur þen holynes happont so then.

hole (həʊl), *sb.* Forms: 1–5 **hol,** 4– **hole;** also 5–6 **hoole,** *Sc.* **hoill, hoil(e,** 6 **hooll(e, whole,** 6–7 **hoale,** 8–9 *Yorksh. dial.* **hoil.** [OE. *hol* neut., inflected *hol-e, hol-es, hol-u,* a hollow place = OFris. OS., OHG. (MHG., MLG., MDu., Du.) *hol* (Ger. *hohl*), orig. neuter of *hol,* HOLL *a.*, hollow. Also app. repr. OE. *holh,* HOLLOW *sb.*, in its inflected forms *hol-e, hol-es,* (?) *hol-u,* which fall together with the corresp. forms of *hol.* (The OE. *hole, holu, holum,* usually referred to *hol,* may equally well belong to *holh*: see Sievers *Ags. Gram.* (ed. 3) §242, Anm. 3, 4; and cf. inflexion of *healh, sealh, wealh.*)

The uninflected *hol* retained short *o* in ME., and was normally written HOLL (cf. OE. *sceal, smæl,* ME. *shall, small*); but in the inflected forms *ho-le, ho-les,* etc. (whether from *hol* or *holh*), the *o* in open syllable was normally lengthened, giving ME. and mod. *hōle, hōles.* (In mod.Eng., short *o* is further lengthened before *ll,* giving mod. dial. *hōll* (not distinguishable from *hōle*); in Sc. *-ōll* becomes *-ow, -owe,* giving *how,* HOWE, 'hollow'.) OE. *holh,* like other words in *-lh, -rh,* was susceptible of twofold inflexion, (1) with loss of *h, hole,* etc., (2) with consonant-ablaut, *holȝe, holwe,* etc. The former, as said above, fell together with the inflected forms of *hol*; the latter gave rise to ME. *holwe, holewe,* HOLLOW *sb.* and *a.* The development may be thus shown:

OE. *hol*	uninfl. *hol,*	ME.	*hŏll,*	mod.	(dial.) *hōll,* Sc. *how(e.*
	infl. *hol-e*	,,	*hole*	,,	*hole.*
,, *holh*	infl. *hol-e*				
	infl. *holw-e*	,,	*holwe,*	,,	*hollow.*

The senses, to a great extent, coincide or overlap; *holl* a. and sb., Sc. *how(e,* are, in use, the northern equivalents of *hollow*; *hole* sb. has all the senses of *holl* (*howe*) sb. and *hollow* sb., with a fuller development of its own. In the 15–16th c. Sc. spelling *hoill, oi* is merely the graphic form of *ō*; but in mod. Yorkshire *hoil,* the *oi* is diphthongal.]

I. A hollow place, cavity, excavation, etc.

1. a. A hollow place or cavity in a solid body; a pit, cave, den, hiding-place in the earth; a deep place in a stream, pond, etc.

946 *Charter Edmund* in Kemble *Cod. Dipl.* III. 423 To þam ealdan hole; of ðam hole. *a* **1000** *Boeth. Metr.* ii. 21 Me þas woruld sælða..on þis dimme hol dysine forlæddon. *c* **1000** *Ags. Ps.* (Th.) ix. 29 [x. 9] And settað his digollice, swa swa leo deð of his hole. *a* **1225** *St. Marher.* 10 He..weneð for to beoren me in to his balefule hole. *c* **1290** *S. Eng. Leg.* I. 85/75 In þe north-side of þe toun in one olde roche he was. He lai and darede out of is hole. **13..** *E.E. Allit. P.* C. 306 Out of þe hole þou me herde. *a* **1400–50** *Alexander* 4050 Haue ȝe na houses ne na hames, ne holis in to bery? *c* **1440** *Promp. Parv.* 243/1 Hoole, or pyt yn an hylle, or other lyke (*S.* hole, or eryth), *caverna.* **14..** *Nom.* in Wr.-Wülcker 722/35 *Hec crupta,* a hol in the erthe. **1548** HALL *Chron., Edw. IV.* 191 Whiche..hid themselfes and lurked in dennes and wholes. *Ibid., Hen. VIII,* 134b, With their swordes digged holes in the banke to clyme up. **1571** *Satir. Poems Reform.* xxvi. 23 Ȝour fais wist not in what hoil yame to hyde. *a* **1605** MONTGOMERIE *Sonn.* xxii. 11 Ȝe sall not haif ane hoill ȝour heids to hyde. **1653** WALTON *Angler* ii. 52 Go to the same hole, where..you will finde floting neer the top of the water, at least a dozen or twenty Chubs. **1657** R. LIGON *Barbadoes* (1673) 41 Great Rocks..so soft, as with your finger you may bore a hole into it. **1756** T. HALE *Compl. Body Husb.* III. xix. 122 Digging a Hole in the Ground. **1826** SCOTT *Woodst.* xxxiv, The head..dinted a hole in the soil of six inches in depth. **1883** J. G. WOOD in *Sunday Mag.* Nov. 676/2 All rivers have some portions deeper than others, 'holes' as we call them.

b. An excavation made in the ground for habitation by an animal, as the fox or badger; a burrow.

c **950** *Lindisf. Gosp.* Luke ix. 58 Foxas holas habbað [*Rushw. G.* Foxes holo habbas. *Ags. G.* Foxas habbað holu. *Hatt. G.* Foxas hæbbeð hole]. *c* **1200** *Vices & Virtues* 101 Hie [naddre] haueð hire hol. *c* **1220** *Bestiary* 248 Of corn and of gres [ðe mire] haleð to hire hole. **1375** BARBOUR *Bruce* XIX. 669 The fox..Lukit about sum hoill to se. **1481** CAXTON *Reynard* (Arb.) 12 Reynart..wente..in to his hole, for maleperduys was ful of hooles, hier one hool and there an other. **1697** DRYDEN *Virg. Georg.* III. 810 The Viper dead within her Hole is found. **1729** SWIFT *Let. to Bolingbroke* 21 Mar., To have done with the world..if I could get into a better..and not die here in a rage, like a poisoned rat in a hole. **1792** OSBALDISTON *Brit. Sportsm.* 40 If you intend to dig the badger out of his hole. **1885** *Leisure Hour* June 401 A snake-charmer's music inducing a large cobra to leave its hole.

c. A deep hollow or cavity in the surface of the body; e.g. an eye-socket. Cf. ARM-HOLE.

c **1300** *Havelok* 1813 þat þe rith eye Vt of þe hole made he fleye. **14..** *Voc.* in Wr.-Wülcker 598/4 *Nucha,* the hole of the polle. **1483** *Cath. Angl.* 187/2 An Hole in yᵉ nek, *frontinella.* *c* **1532** DEWES *Introd. Fr.* in *Palsgr.* 903 The holes under the armes, *les esselles.* **1638** SANDERSON *Serm.* (1681) II. 101 We might have waited till our eyes had sunk in their holes. **1758** J. S. *Le Dran's Observ. Surg.* (1771) 50 That Part vulgarly called the Hole of the Neck.

2. *transf.* †**a.** A secret place, a hiding-place; a secret room in which an unlawful occupation is pursued; a place where unlicensed printing was carried on.

1483 *Cath. Angl.* 187/2 An Hole, *latebra, latibulum.* **1660** PEPYS *Diary* 23 May, At a Catholique house, he was fain to lie in the priest's hole a good while. **1683** MOXON *Mech. Exerc.* 380 Many Printers for Lucre of Gain have gone into Holes, and then their chief care is to get a Hole Private, and Workmen Trusty and Cunning to conceal the Hole, and themselves. **1688** R. HOLME *Armoury* III. 122/1 *Holes*, in Printing dialect is a place where privat Printing is used, viz. the printing of unlicensed Books or other Men's Coppies.

b. A dungeon or prison-cell; *spec.* the name of one of the worst apartments in the Counter prison in Wood street, London. Cf. BLACK-HOLE. Now usu. the cell used for solitary confinement, and hence solitary confinement itself.

1535 LYNDESAY *Satyre* 1017 Wee haue gart bind him with ane poill, And send him to the theifis hoill. **1607** HEYWOOD *Woman killed with Kindn.* Wks. 1874 II. 125 He is deni'de the freedome of the prison, And in the hole is laide with men condemn'd. **1607** WENTW. SMITH *Puritan* III. F, But if ere wee clutch him againe, the Counter shall charm him. *Rav.* The hole shall rotte him. **1666** PEPYS *Diary* 2 July, He was clapped up in the Hole. **1678, 1722** Condemned hole [see CONDEMNED 3]. **1822** NARES s.v., We still hear of the *condemned hole* in Newgate. **1912** D. LOWRIE *My Life in Prison* iv. 39 'It's a case of spending the night at the springs if you're not at your cell for the count.' In answer to my hurried inquiry about 'the springs' he informed me that he referred to 'the hole'. **1927** *Amer. Speech* II. 282/1 *Hole*, dungeon or place for solitary confinement. **1935** N. ERSINE *Underworld & Prison Slang* 45 *Hole*,..the solitary confinement cells of a prison. 'Smitty just got tossed in the *hole.*' **1955** W. GADDIS *Recognitions* II. v. 488 He had..spent a fair amount of time in solitary confinement ('the hole', as it was called). **1970** G. JACKSON *Let.* 25 Mar. in *Soledad Brother* (1971) 197 They're out of the hole (isolation) already.

c. A small dingy lodging or abode; a small or mean habitation; an unpleasant place of abode; a term of contempt or depreciation for any place.

1616 W. HAIG *Let.* 2 Aug. in J. Russell *Haigs* vii. (1881) 156 Being innocent, it is a pity to smother me in this loathsome hole. *a* **1700** DRYDEN (J.), How much more happy thou, that art content To live within this little hole, than I Who after empire, that vain quarry, fly. **1726** LEONI *Designs* Pref. 1/2 You expect a stately Palace, where you find nothing but an ill-contrived Hole. **1836** T. HOOK *G. Gurney* III. 127 This house..to me the horridest hole I ever was in. **1876** GEO. ELIOT *Dan. Der.* III. xxv, Grandcourt..pronounced that resort of fashion a beastly hole, worse than Baden. **1889** J. S. WINTER *Mrs. Bob* (1891) 3 Two hundred a year for a little hole I could not get my piano into.

d. A shilling. *slang.*

1934 P. ALLINGHAM *Cheapjack* iv. 38 A penny is a 'clod', and 'sprasy' means sixpence. A shilling is also a 'hole', and a two-shilling piece is a 'two-ender'. **1939** [see BAR *sb.*[1] 3 c].

3. *fig.* A position from which it is difficult to escape; a fix, scrape, mess.

1760 C. JOHNSTON *Chrysal* (1764) I. II. vii. 132, I should take great pleasure in serving you, and getting you out of this hole. **1762** SMOLLETT *Sir L. Greaves* xvi, I should be in a deadly hole myself, if all my customers should take it in their heads to drink nothing but water-gruel. *a* **1825** FORBY *Voc. E. Anglia, Hole*, a scrape..A man gets himself into a hole by taking a wrong step. **1882** OUIDA *Under 2 Flags* i. (1890) 6 I'm in a hole—no end of a hole; and I thought you'd help me. **1925** WODEHOUSE *Carry on, Jeeves!* iv. 81 'Mr Bickersteth is in a hole, Jeeves,..and wants you to rally round.' 'Very good, sir.' **1937** A. CHRISTIE *Murder in Mews* 218 Lawyers, even the most respectable, have been known to embezzle their client's money when they themselves are in a hole. **1970** G. F. NEWMAN *Sir, You Bastard* v. 154 Too bad if he has, I'll be in a great big hole.

4. *technical.* **a.** A hemispherical cavity into which a ball or marbles are to be got in various games; esp. one of those into which the ball is driven at golf; hence, a point scored by the player who drives his ball from one hole to another with the fewest strokes. *spec.* one of the (usu. nine or eighteen) strips of land on a golf-course, consisting of a tee, fairway (and bordering rough), green and hole (sense 4 a), over which a golfer plays his ball; the play which takes place between teeing off and holing the ball; ***hole in one***, the driving of the ball from the tee into the hole with only one stroke. Also *fig.*

1583 HOLLYBAND *Campo di Fior* 129 We will playe at pit hole for nuttes. We will make a pitte hole, and there cast our nuttes. **1808–18** JAMIESON, *Golf, goff, gouf*, a game in Scotland, in which hooked clubs are used for striking balls, stuffed very hard with feathers, from one hole to another. **1874** J. BLACKWOOD *Let.* 4 Aug. in Geo. Eliot *Lett.* (1956) VI. 74 When we were a few holes out he exclaimed fervently, 'This is a great, glorious, and noble game.' **1887** J. L. STEWART *Golfiana Miscellanea* 100 The hole is won by the side holing at fewest strokes. **1890** HUTCHINSON *Golf* (Badm. Libr.) 43 You are playing a match of, say, eighteen holes, and have reached the putting-green of the last hole. **1891** H. G. HUTCHINSON *Famous Golf Links* 90 Point Garry is a long, hazardous hole. *Ibid.* 156 The third hole (135 yards) is an exact counterpart of the second. **1893** BARRIE & CONAN DOYLE *Jane Annie* II. 41, I gives in! You have my word of honour! It's your hole. **1896** PARK *Golf* 5 The size of the holes, as fixed by the laws of the game, is four and a quarter inches in diameter. **1908** J. BRAID *Advanced Golf* 252 Holes of about 360 to 380 yards. **1935** GRAVES & LONGHURST *Candid Caddies* 28 There are all kinds of variants on the 'hole in one' story where the player has achieved this feat with a club other than the one selected by the caddie. **1971** *Daily Tel.* 12 June 1/5 (*heading*) Golfer gets two holes in one. *Ibid.*, Successive holes in one have been done only twice before in Britain. **1972** I. STUART *Golf in Hertfordshire* 67 There are six par-three holes, all of them fair and only one over 200 yards. **1973** *Country Life* 17 May 1369/3 The final rounds of a 72-hole event.

b. *Billiards.* = POCKET.

1688 R. HOLME *Armoury* III. 262/2 The Holes in the four corners and sides of the..Billiard Table. **1725** *Cotton's Compl. Gamester* (ed. 5) 151 At the four Corners of the [Billiard] Table there are Holes, and at each side exactly in the Middle, one, which are called Hazards. **1778** C. JONES *Hoyle's Games Impr.* 191 He that stops either Ball, when running, loses one; and if near the Hole, loses two.

†**c.** The narrow closed part or bag at the lower end of a trawl-net or other fishing net: = COD *sb.*[1] 5.

1630 in *Descr. Thames* (1758) 72 The third Part, which is the Hole or Cod, Inch and Quarter wet and dry.

d. *Chess.* (See quots.)

1894 J. MASON *Princ. Chess* i. 24 *Hole*, a square on the third or fourth rank, neither commanded, nor liable to be commanded, by any friendly Pawn. **1895** H. E. BIRD *Chess Novelties* 115 KBP was followed by QP2, leaving at once a landing square (a nasty hole Steinitz would call it) for opponent's pieces. **1922** *Brit. Chess Mag.* Feb. 105/2 The net result of the two moves is to create a hole at White's Q Kt 4. **1955** *Chess* ('Know the Game' Series) 26/1 Another example of weakness in the pawn-formation is that of 'holes' or 'fore-posts' which may be occupied successfully by an opposing piece. **1968** O. HINDLE *Further Steps in Chess* iv. 49 Holes..are squares which the defender can no longer protect with his pawns. They are thus ideal posts for attacking pieces, which can settle on them without fear of being easily driven off.

e. *Eton Fives.* A small square portion of the floor enclosed by the pepper-box and step. Phr. ***to be in holes***; hence *attrib.* in ***holes innings***.

1897 *Encycl. Sport.* I 399 A, who begins serving, is bound to give C—who is said to be 'in holes'—the sort of service which he prefers. *Ibid.* 400 All alike differ from Eton Courts in having no pepper-box, hole, or step. *Ibid.* 402 In the first innings of a game A (who goes in first) is said to have 'holes innings', *i.e.*, when both A and B have been put out, A will be 'in holes'.

f. *Physics.* A position from which an electron is absent: orig. a concept in the theory of the positron, now esp. a position in a semiconductor which may be regarded as a mobile carrier of a positive charge. Also *attrib.* and *Comb.*

1930 P. A. M. DIRAC in *Proc. R. Soc.* A. CXXVI. 362 Only the small departures from exact uniformity, brought about by some of the negative-energy states being unoccupied, can we hope to observe. Let us examine the properties of the vacant states or 'holes'. **1933** *Ibid.* CXXXIX. 714 The few states which are unoccupied behave like ordinary particles with positive kinetic energy and with a positive charge. Dirac originally wished to identify these 'holes' with protons, but this had to be abandoned when it was found that the holes necessarily have the same mass as negative electrons. **1934** P. A. M. DIRAC in *Proc. Cambr. Phil. Soc.* XXX. 150 Any unoccupied negative-energy states would be observable to us, as holes in the distribution of negative-energy electrons, but these holes would appear as particles with positive kinetic energy... It seems reasonable ..to identify these holes with the recently discovered positrons. **1936** W. HEITLER *Quantum Theory of Radiation* 188 Thus..positive electrons are represented as holes in the distribution of electrons filling up the negative energy states. **1940** *Nature* 29 June 998/2 It is suggested..that in cuprous oxide the vacant lattice points and the points from which an electron is missing (positive holes) are dissociated. **1948** *Physical Rev.* LXXIV. 230/2 As a result, the current in the forward direction with respect to the block is composed in large part of holes, i.e., of carriers of sign opposite to those normally in excess in the body of the block. **1949** [see ACCEPTOR 3]. **1954** *Electronic Engin.* XXVI. 34 Positive charge carriers known as 'holes'... These holes are thought to have different mean life-times and mobilities in different diodes. **1957** *Ibid.* XXIX. 3 As all transistors have a finite base width all transistors must show hole storage effects due to the time taken for holes to cross the base from emitter to collector. **1962** SIMPSON & RICHARDS *Junction Transistors* ii. 32 Also, because impurities or defects that trap electrons may have characteristics quite different from those of their hole-trapping counterparts, the lifetime of minority carriers may be quite different in *p*-type and *n*-type materials of similar quality. **1966** *New Scientist* 11 Aug. 317/3 Travel is limited to the distance covered before electron and hole annihilate one another.

5. *local U.S.* **a.** An indentation or opening in the coast; a small bay, a cove.

1639 in *Virginia Hist. Mag.* (1895) III. 31 Yf the shipps be p'mitted to goe at pleasure and ride in every hole as is desired by them. **1748** H. ELLIS *Hudson's Bay* 149 This [flag] was to be raised at a good anchoring place called Five-Fathom Hole. **1807** C. W. JANSON *Stranger in Amer.* 390 Tobacco is..conveyed then down the river to Hobbs' Hole, where ships in the European trade lie ready to receive them.

b. A grassy valley surrounded by mountains.

6. = HOLL, HOLD (*sb.*[2]) of a ship.

1483 *Cath. Angl.* 187/2 An Hole,..*columbar est nauis.* **1678** MARVELL *Growth Popery* 11 The Hole of some Amsterdam Fly-boat. **1769** FALCONER *Dict. Marine* (1789) H iij b, The pointers..are..fixed across the hole diagonally. **1882** NARES *Seamanship* (ed. 6) 97 Abaft the main hole.

II. A perforation, and connected senses.

7. a. An aperture passing through anything; a perforation, opening.

c **725** *Corpus Gloss.* 1900 *Spiramentum*, hol. *c* **1200** *Trin. Coll. Hom.* 201 We..cumeð to þe stone, þe haueð fif hole narewe, þat is..his holie fif wunden. *c* **1290** *Beket* 1144 in *S. Eng. Leg.* I. 139 þoruȝ þe churche he made an hol. *c* **1375** *Sc. Leg. Saints, Ninian* 505 Ane alde coble þare he fand, þat mony hoilis in it had. *c* **1400** *Destr. Troy* 13501 Hit happit hym in hast the hoole for to fynd Of the cave. **14..** *Voc.* in Wr.-Wülcker 627/12 þe hoole of a prevay, *gumphus.* *a* **1529** SKELTON *Merrie T.* in *Shaks. Jest Bk.* (1864) II. 21 What shall those hoales serue for?..holes to look out to see thy enemyes. **1674** tr. *Martiniere's Voy. North. C.* 85 A top the House..there is a hole or window left for light to come in. **1687** *Lond. Gaz.* No. 2218/4 A new fashionable Suit..gold frost Buttons, and gold Holes. **1773** *Cook's Voy.* in Hawkesworth *Voy.* II. 332 A musket was fired..which fortunately struck the boat..and made two holes in her side. **1896** *Times* 16 Dec. 5/2 The service bullet was found to have drilled clean holes, and..the hole of exit was little, if any, larger than the hole of entry.

fig. **1611** BIBLE *Transl. Pref.* 1 If there be any hole left for cauill to enter.

b. ***hole in the wall***, (an originally disparaging term for) any small, obscure place; *spec.* in the U.S., a place where alcoholic drinks are sold illegally. Applied, esp. *attrib.*, to a business that is very small, mean, dingy, or the like, or to a person running such a business.

1822 W. HAZLITT in *New Monthly Mag.* IV. 102, I had heard Mr. James Simpkins..when the character of the *Hole in the Wall* was brought in question, observe—'The house is a very good house, and the company quite genteel.' **1856** *Iroquois Republican* (Middleport, Ill.) 25 Dec. 2/3 A 'grocery'—a 'doggery'—a 'hole-in-the-wall'—is an 'odious damned spot' in any community. **1870** DICKENS *E. Drood* xviii. 142 The Gate House, of which..the Verger's hole in the wall was an appanage or subsidiary part. **1887** *Minnesota Gen. Statutes Suppl.* (1888) 248 Whoever shall attempt to evade or violate any of the laws of this state..by means of the artifice or contrivance known as the 'Blind Pig', or 'Hole in the Wall'..shall..be punished. **1896** C. H. SHINN *Story of the Mine* 51 Many lived in 'dug-outs', which they called 'holes in the wall'. **1919** *Detective Story Mag.* 25 Nov. 129 He breakfasted at a hole-in-the-wall lunch room before starting out on his quest. **1923** D. SELLS *Brit. Trade Boards System* IV. ii. 259 The emphasis which reputable employers lay upon the benefit of Trade Boards in eliminating the 'hole in the wall' employer..from the field of industry, can hardly be overstated. **1940** F. RIESENBERG *Golden Gate* 212 Craft that could go into the 'holes in the wall' along the ragged Pacific Coast. **1945** E. S. GARDNER *Case of Gold-Digger's Purse* (1948) xiii. 153 It's just a little place—just a little lunch counter. Sort of a hole in the wall. **1945** 'L. LEWIS' *Birthday Murder* (1951) iii. 37 Sawn scorned..decadent play spots of the economically fortunate, and would insist on going to a hole in the wall infested by cockroaches, cocottes and cab drivers. **1951** C. W. MILLS *White Collar* I. ii. 30 The hole-in-the-wall business, also known as a Mom-and-Pop store. **1953** W. R. BURNETT *Vanity Row* viii. 60 A Bohemian section of the town..dotted with little..hole-in-the-wall cafés. **1958** *Time* 3 Feb. 23/1 To survive, most workers have to take second jobs, many of them in the innumerable hole-in-the-wall private enterprises that have sprung up. **1973** J. GOODFIELD *Courier to Peking* ix. 100 One of her favourite places was more a hole-in-the-wall than a shop.

c. ***in holes***: perforated with holes, worn into holes.

1851 MAYHEW *London Labour* II. 470/2, I can't abide this muckydam [*sc.* macadam] ..it's sloppy stuff, and goes so bad in holes. **1926** A. CHRISTIE *Murder R. Ackroyd* x. 127 He wouldn't even buy new face towels, though I told him the old ones were in holes.

d. Aeronautics. ***hole in the air***: an old name for an air-pocket (AIR *sb.*[1] III. 1).

1911 G. C. LOENING *Monoplanes & Biplanes* xiv. 305 The air is very variable, and even on a relatively calm day there are likely to be 'holes in the air'. **1916** H. BARBER *Aeroplane Speaks* 51 Now the Aeroplane is almost over the river, and the next instant it suddenly drops into a 'hole in the air'. **1917** C. C. TURNER *Aircraft of To-day* vi. 98 The terms 'air-pocket' and 'hole in the air' are frequently heard in flying circles.

e. colloq. ***hole in (the) heart***: a congenital malformation of the heart in which there is an abnormal communication between the right and left sides.

1958 *Hammersmith Post* 25 July 1/4 (*heading*) Mother reassured over 'hole in heart' operation. *Ibid.*, A seven-year-old boy..is due to have a 'hole in heart' operation. **1959** *Times Lit. Suppl.* 25 Sept. 549/5 The author describes the operation for a septal defect—the condition popularly known as a 'hole in the heart'. **1961** *Listener* 2 Nov. 693/1 The oxygenator took over the duties of heart and lung in the 'hole-in-the-heart' operation. **1966** *Guardian* 17 May 3/4 Oxygen 15..is being used..for the diagnosis of the hole-in-the-heart condition.

8. The orifice of any organ or part of the body. *spec.* (*slang*) The mouth, the anus, or the female external genital organs.

c **1340** *Cursor M.* 528 (Trin.) Seuen holes haþ mannes heed euen. *c* **1400** MAUNDEV. (Roxb.) xxii. 100 þai hafe in steed of paire mouth a lytill hole. *c* **1475** *Pict. Voc.* in Wr.-Wülcker 749/8 *Hec arteria*, the hole of the throt. **1486** *Bk. St. Albans* B j b, The Hoolis in the hawkes beke bene callede the Nares. **1530** PALSGR. 232/1 Hole that swete or heres cometh out at, *pore.* **1592** SHAKS. *Rom. & Jul.* II. iv. 94 This driveling Love is like a great Naturall, that runs lolling vp and downe to hid his bable in a hole. **1607** TOPSELL *Four-f. Beasts* (1658) 223 There are seven crosse ribs in his neck, and seven from his reins to his hole. **1615** CROOKE *Body of Man* 611 A Membrane where-with the hoale of the eare is stopped. **1687** A. LOVELL tr. *Thevenot's Trav.* I. 117 The hole of the Nostril full round. **1719** D'URFEY *Pills* IV. 72 It has a Head much like a Mole's, And yet it loves to creep in Holes: The Fairest She that e'er took Life, For love of this, became a Wife. *c* **1744** in *Oxf. Dict. Nursery Rhymes* (1951) 372 Little Robin red breast, Sitting on a pole, Niddle, Noddle, Went his head, And Poop went his Hole. **1922** JOYCE *Ulysses* 748 My hole is itching me. **1959** I. & P. OPIE *Lore & Lang. Schoolch.* iii. 49 Habitual grumblers in London's East End receive the poetic injunction: 'Oo, shut yer moanin' 'ole'. **1966** L. COHEN *Beautiful Losers* (1970) I. 9 Don't give me this all diamond shit, shove it up your occult hole.

9. *fig.* A flaw, fault, ground for blame. Usually in phr. ***to pick a hole*** or ***holes in*** something;

formerly also *to find* (*pick, make*) *a hole in a person's coat.*

1553 T. WILSON *Rhet.* (1580) 98 The Lawiers lacke no cases.. Is his Lease long.. Then (q^th he) let me alone with it, I will find a hole in it. **1599** SHAKS. *Hen. V*, III. vi. 88 If I finde a hole in his Coat, I will tell him my minde. **1648** NEEDHAM *Plea for King* 21 Every ambitious popular person would be ready to pick holes in their Coates, to bring them into disfavour of the People. **1682** WOOD *Life* 10 Feb. (O.H.S.) III. 4 If they did not appeare, there might some hole be picked in their charter. **1789** BURNS *Capt. Grose's Peregrin.* i, If there's a hole in a' your coats, I rede you tent it. **1871** MISS MULOCK *Fair France* i. 4 We do not go to visit a neighbour, in order to pick holes in him and his establishment. **1894** *Aspects Mod. Oxford* 93 Any one can pick holes in the University system of teaching and examination.

†**10. a.** An old game in which balls were rolled through little cavities or arches; called also *Pigeon-hole, Troll-madam, Trunks.* Cf. NINE-HOLES. **b.** An old game of cards.

1611 COTGR., *Trou Madame*, the Game called Trunkes, or the Hole. **1621** J. TAYLOR (Water P.) *Motto* Wks. (1630) 54/2 Ruffe, slam, Trump, noddy, whisk, hole, Sant, New-cut. **1816** *Sporting Mag.* XLVIII. 178 Another game called holes was occasionally played.

III. 11. Phrases. ***to be in the hole*** U.S.: to be in (usu. financial) difficulties (cf. 3). ***a hole in the head***, esp. in phr. ***to need*** (***something***) ***like a hole in the head*** (cf. Yiddish *ich darf es vi a loch in kop*): applied to something not desired at all or something useless. ***to make a hole*** (***in*** anything): to use up, or cause the loss of, a considerable amount of anything; to create a loss. ***to make a hole in the water***: see WATER *sb.* 6 f. ***a round peg*** (or ***man***) ***in a square hole*** (and *vice versa*): one whose situation does not fit his special aptitudes. ***to pick a hole*** or ***holes in***: see sense 9. ***to put in the hole*** (slang): to swindle, defraud. ***to take*** (something) ***a hole lower***: to take down, humiliate, humble; cf. BUTTON-HOLE 1 b.

1591 LYLY *Endym.* III. iii, He hath taken his thoughts a hole lower, and saith.. he will vaile bonet to beautie. **1611** COTGR., *Humilié*, humbled.. taken a hole lower. **1617** MORYSON *Itin.* II. 183 To lay five hundred of your best men on the earth, which losse will make a great hole in your Armie. **1625** BURGES *Pers. Tithes* 75 It will make a greater hole in thy conscience, then it can in thine estate by parting with it. **1706** MRS. RAY in *Lett. Lit. Men* (Camden) 208 Mr. Ray did not leave £40 a year.. out of which taxes, repairs, and quit-rent make a great hole. **1812** J. H. VAUX *Vocab. Flash Lang.* in *Mem.* (1964) 243 *To put a person in the hole*, to defraud him of his due share of the booty by embezzling a part of the property, or the money, it is fenced for; this phrase also applies generally to defrauding anyone with whom you are confidentially connected of what is justly his due. **1833** *Session Papers* 3 Jan. 115/1 Miller.. said they had *put him in the hole*, and he.. would say where they were; by *putting him in the hole*, I understand they did not take the property away as he expected. **1887** *Spectator* 26 Mar. 412/2 An average daily consumption of four glasses.. makes a hole in the income of the working class. **1890** *Centralia* (Wash.) *Chron.* 18 Sept. 3/2 His failure leaves a number of our local dealers in the hole for amounts ranging from £200 down. **1893** L. W. MOORE *His Own Story* xxi. 293 What was said at that time about his being 'put in the hole', I cannot say; but I do know he held me blameless, for none of the funds, except my own share, was ever in my possession. *a* **1895** LD. C. E. PAGET *Autobiog.* iii. (1896) 72 The Admiralty would not rescind their orders, so we were a round man in a square hole, and *vice versâ*. **1897** *Boston Jrnl.* 12 Mar. 10/1 The sporting-man was $40 in the hole. **1916** *Lit. Digest* 8 Jan. 87/1 The Wards were in the hole to the extent of close to $800,000. **1926** J. BLACK *You can't Win* ix. 104, I thought you put me in the hole for some coin, but I found out that the people lost just what you both said. **1939** WODEHOUSE *Uncle Fred in Springtime* iii. 45 How in the world did you manage to get in the hole for a sum like that? **1951** in M. McLuhan *Mech. Bride* 29/2 A smart operator needs a dame like he needs a hole in the head. **1951** J. D. SALINGER *Catcher in Rye* xiv. 91 The Disciples.. were about as much use to Him as a hole in the head. **1955** W. GADDIS *Recognitions* I. iii. 101, I need this drink like I need a hole in the head. **1971** D. CREED *Trial of Lobo Icheka* xiii. 133 He needed Petersen about as much as he needed a hole in the head.

IV. 12. *attrib.* and *Comb.*, as **a.** attrib. (sense 4 a) ***hole game, play***; **hole-card**, in stud poker, a card which has been dealt face down; also *fig.*; **hole-high** *a.* (see quots.); **hole-mouth(ed)** *Archæol.*, said of pottery vessels without a neck; **hole-nester**, a bird that nests in a hole; so **hole-nesting** *ppl. a.*; **hole-proof** *a.*, that will not wear into holes; **hole saw** = *crown-saw* (CROWN *sb.* 35); **b.** objective, as ***hole-cutter, -digger, -digging, -picking, -piercing, -punched, -puncher, -stopper***; **c.** locative, as ***hole-breeder, -builder, -creeping*** sb. and adj.; **d. hole-board** (see quot.); **hole-creeper**, a sneaking thief; **hole-man** (see quot.); **hole-stitch** (see quot.).

1874 KNIGHT *Dict. Mech., Compass-board*, the *hole-board of the loom for fancy weaving. It is an upright board of the loom through which pass the neck-twines. **1889** F. A. KNIGHT *By Leafy Ways* 155 The kingfisher, another *hole-breeder. **1891** *Daily News* 16 Feb. 5/1 Her eggs.. are white, like those of most *hole-builders. **1908** *Sat. Even. Post* 5 Dec. 19/2 Scarcely glancing at *his hole card Phelps let him take the pot, and it became Phelps' deal. **1926** C. E. MULFORD *Bar 20 rides Again* xxi. 282 Beginnin' with this hand I'm bettin' five hundred blind on th' hole-card, an' seein' if I can't bring this game to a finish. **1952** J. STEINBECK *East of Eden* ix. 79 The preacher turned over his hole-card, the sure-fire card. **1971** J. BALL *First Team* (1972) xxiii. 353 We may be playing with a bust hand; we don't know if our hole card has been stolen or not. **1462** in Scrope *Hist. Castle Combe* (1852) 323 Communis *holecreppar anserum et porcellorum tenentium. **1638** FORD *Fancies* III. iii, The page, that *hole-creeping page. **1852** SCROPE *Hist. Castle Combe* 235 He qualified himself.. by 'hole-creeping' after his neighbours' geese and pigs. **1897** *Westm. Gaz.* 9 Mar. 8/3 Drillers and *hole-cutters. **1876** PREECE & SIVEWRIGHT *Telegraphy* 188 To guide the *hole-diggers in the event of the marks.. having been removed. *Ibid.* 189 *Hole-digging.. for a telegraph pole. **1895** *Westm. Gaz.* 6 May 7/2 There is all the difference.. between the stroke and the *hole game [at golf], and at least a score of men have some chance. **1897** *Encycl. Sports* I. 472/2 A ball is said to be *hole high when it is played on to the putting green from a distance. **1961** J. S. SALAK *Dict. Amer. Sports* 228 *Hole-high* (golf), a point even with the hole but to one side or the other. **1851** MAYHEW *Lond. Labour* (1861) II. 447 The *holeman, who goes into the cesspool. **1909** *Cent. Dict.* Suppl., *Hole-mouthed vase. **1960** K. M. KENYON *Archæol. in Holy Land* v. 124 The type of jar, known as the hole-mouth jar, neckless with a simple in-curved rim, which was used for cooking and storage, may be as much as 3 feet in height. **1938** *Brit. Birds* XXXI. 242 In the present experiments three *hole-nesting species.. were selected. *Ibid.* XXXII. 31 In similar experiments with another hole-nester.. the male attacked the male mount but.. ignored the female mount. **1953** N. TINBERGEN *Herring Gull's World* x. 94 Territory in the Herring Gull most certainly has nothing to do with the reservation of a nesting site.. as it has in hole-nesting birds. **1801** C. GADSDEN in *J. Adams' Wks.* (1854) IX. 580 That his public actions may be judged of.. without any captious *hole-picking. **1889** LINSKILL *Golf* iii. (1895) 13 Besides '*hole play', which involves playing a succession of small matches from hole to hole round the links, there is also what is called 'score play'. **1913** *Work* 17 May 102 A.. cloth that will not tear—in fact, is *hole-proof. **1915** *Truth* LXXVIII. 848/1 Another customer tells me her experience in regard to some 'hole-proof' hose. **1962** *Economist* 2 June 897/1 Stockings.. to be ladderproof, although not holeproof. **1956** S. BELLOW *Seize Day* (1957) ii. 42 He put the *hole-punched cards in his pocket. **1961** *Lebende Sprachen* VI. 70/1 *Hole puncher. **1961** WEBSTER, *Hole saw. **1967** *Catal. Black & Decker Powertools*, A drill with power to spare... Will drive holesaws up to 1½" dia. **1882** CAULFEILD & SAWARD *Dict. Needlework* 253/2 **Hole Stitch*, a stitch used in Pillow Lace making, to form holes or small round spots in the centre of the thick parts of a pattern. **1794** WOLCOTT (P. Pindar) *Wks.* II. 85 A neighbouring town.. Begg'd him to be their tinker—their *hole-stopper.

hole (həʊl), *v.*¹ Forms: 1 holian, 3 holien, 4–5 hoole(n, 7 hoale, *Sc.* hoile (*oi* = *ō*), 4– hole. [OE. *holian* to hollow out, excavate = OHG. *holôn*, Goth. *hulôn*, f. *hol-*, HOLL *a.*]

I. To make a hole.

1. a. *trans.* To hollow out; to make a hole or cavity in; to perforate, pierce.

c **1000** ÆLFRIC *Hom.* II. 162 Ða ʒebroðra.. ʒemetton ðone clud ða iu swætende; and hi ða hwæthweʒa holodon. *c* **1330** R. BRUNNE *Chron. Wace* (Rolls) 6836 Þe wal þey holede. *c* **1440** *Promp. Parv.* 243/1 Holyn, or boryn (*P.* hoolen, or make hoolys), *cavo, perforo, terebro.* **1578** LYTE *Dodoens* VI. lviii. 746 Before they be holed or pearsed. **1648** MARKHAM *Housew. Gard.* III. x. (1668) 77, I use.. a piece of wood hoal'd. **1864** *Standard* 29 Nov. 3/3 She [the ship] has holed her bottom. **1890** *Times* 27 Dec. 9/1 Some 80 miles of the route already holed [for telegraph posts].

b. To make holes in (the earth) in agriculture; to dibble; to dig trenches for planting sugar-canes.

1756 P. BROWNE *Jamaica* 130 You begin to hole and continue to open the ground gradually. **1842** ORDERSON *Creol.* i. 5 Occasionally 'holing' his neighbours' fields. **1890** *Jrnl. Soc. Arts* 15 Aug. 827/2 Preliminary to the all-important progressive step in coffee culture, that of transplanting, is 'holing'.

c. To fire a bullet into.

1847 TROLLOPE *Macdermots* I. iv. 59 We'll hole him till there ar'nt a bit left in him to hole. *a* **1882** —— *Land-leaguers* (1883) I. ii. 34 Keep yourself from being holed as they holed Muster Bingham the other day.

2. To sink (a shaft), drive (a tunnel) through.

1708 J. C. *Compl. Collier* (1845) 13 We design to hole our Pit. **1816** *Chron.* in *Ann. Reg.* 129 The Tunnel.. was, after thirteen years' incessant labour, holed.. with great accuracy. **1870** *Daily News* 30 Nov., Next week this shaft will be holed to the 100 fathom level.

3. *Mining.* To undercut (the coal) in a seam so as to release it from the other strata.

1829 GLOVER *Hist. Derby* I. 58 A set of colliers, called holers, who begin in the right and hole or undermine all the bank or face of the coal. **1861** *Temple Bar Mag.* III. 137 The collier a hundred fathoms down.. holing under the coal. **1867** W. W. SMYTH *Coal & Coal-Mining*, In breaking down or getting the coal, the first operation is to bench, kirve, or hole it along the bottom of the seam.

4. *intr.* To make a hole or holes; to dig. Esp. in *Mining*: to make a hole *through* from one working to another.

a **1225** *Ancr. R.* 130 Þe mid hore lustes ne holieð nout aduneward, ase doð þe uoxes. **1303** R. BRUNNE *Handl. Synne* 10736 Þys mynur.. wroȝt on a day, and holed yn þe hyl. **1708** J. C. *Compl. Collier* (1845) 46 They frequently hole, or cut through from one Board to another. **1890** *Melbourne Argus* 29 May 9/8 From the bottom of the workings they sank 7 ft... and holed through to the crosscut.

II. To put or go into a hole.

5. *trans.* To put into a hole; to put in prison; to plant (sugar-canes) in holes or trenches.

1608 MIDDLETON *Mad World* IV. v, She could not endure the sight of a man, forsooth, but run and hole herself presently. **1618** J. TAYLOR (Water P.) *Waterman's Suit* Wks. (1872) 14 So their prodigal sons are holed in some loathsome jail. **1828** *Craven Dial.*, s.v., "To hole a person', to send him to gaol. **1866** *Morning Star* 27 Sept. 4/5 To work hard in holing canes or in throwing out trenches.

6. a. *spec.* in *Golf, Billiards, Bagatelle.* To drive (the ball) into a hole or pocket. Also *to hole out.*

1803 MARY CHARLTON *Wife & Mistress* I. 264 He contrived to hole both white and red ball at the next stroke. **1819** REES *Cycl.* s.v. *Billiards*, If the striker holes his adversary's ball, or forces it over the table, or on a cushion.. he loses two points. **1857** *Chambers' Inform.* II. 693/2 (*Golf*) The best club for holing out the ball. **1880** *Boy's Own Bk.* 633 Bagatelle.. The object.. is to 'hole' the balls. **1883** *Standard* 16 Nov. 5/2 The number of strokes he requires to take before 'holeing' the ball [at golf]. **1891** *Golf Rules* No. 35 in Linskill *Golf* (1895) 45 If the ball rest against the flag-stick when in the hole, the player shall be entitled to remove the stick, and, if the ball fall in, it shall be considered as holed out in the previous stroke.

b. absol. *Golf.* To drive the ball into a hole. ***to hole*** (***out***) ***in one***: to achieve a 'hole in one' (see HOLE *sb.* 4 a); also *fig.*

1867 *Cornh. Mag.* Apr. 492 The deadly accuracy with which they approach the hole, and 'hole out', as it is called. **1886** 'STONEHENGE' *Brit. Sports* 754/2 He who succeeds in holeing in fewer strokes than his opponent wins that hole. **1928** D. L. SAYERS *Unpleasantness at Bellona Club* xii. 141 'I say we shall find a long scratch on the paint,' said Parker... 'Holed it in one, Charles.' **1939** 'N. BLAKE' *Smiler with Knife* iii. 49 'Oh, E.B. The E.B. printed on the flag we found in that locker?' 'Holed out in one.' **1971** *Daily Tel.* 12 June 1/5 John Hudson made golfing history in the Martini tournament.. yesterday, holing in one at successive holes.

c. *Golf.* To drive the ball into (a hole).

1894 *Westm. Gaz.* 29 Sept. 7/1 Mr. W. T. Griffin holed the eighth hole of the.. links—100 yards—in one.

7. *intr.* To go into a hole. ***to hole up***, (*a*) to retire to a hole for hibernation; also, to seek shelter, to seek (temporary) quarters; (*b*) to lie in wait or in ambush, to hide (chiefly *U.S. slang*).

1614 B. JONSON *Barth. Fair* IV. iv, Let him hole there. **1625** —— *Staple of N.* v. i, Wi' your worming braine.. Which I shall see you hole with very shortly: A fine round head, when those two lugs are off, To trundle through a pillory. **1688** SHADWELL *Sqr. Alsatia* v. i, The rogue is hol'd some-where. **1828** *Craven Dial., Hole*, to earth as a fox. **1875** J. BURROUGHS *Winter Sunshine* 279 Only five days was I compelled to 'hole up' in my state-room. **1878** *Scribner's Mag.* XV. 303/1 The fox.. has run to earth, or, as we have it, 'has holed'. **1890** L. C. D'OYLE *Notches* 70 It was getting time for the bears to 'hole-up'. **1910** MRS. H. WARD *Canadian Born* ix. 181 I'm a poor old broken-down.. miner, who wants to hole-up somewhere, and get comfortable for his old age. **1912** MULFORD & CLAY *Buck Peters* xxvii. 235 Go slow, Tex; mebby he's holin' up on us, like he did on Buck. **1924** C. E. MULFORD *Rustlers' Valley* xii. 141 Now you'll mebby have to take to th' hills an' hole up just when I need you most. **1925** —— *Cottonwood Gulch* xvi. 218 It would have been only a matter of a few minutes before they would have forced him to abandon the horse and to hole up on the defensive, to make a losing fight. **1929** FAULKNER *Sartoris* IV. 282 Hole up here, you potlickin' fool. **1929** D. HAMMETT *Red Harvest* xviii. 179 You'll have to.. take a plant on Willson's... I hear whisper Thaler's holing-up there. **1939** R. CHANDLER *Big Sleep* xxvii. 240 That's the place where she's holed up. **1951** S. LEWIS *World so Wide* xii. 135 We've got to begin thinking about holing up for the night. **1952** WODEHOUSE *Pigs have Wings* ix. 178 The poltergeist, for such he assumed it to be, appeared to have holed up behind the door that led presumably to the kitchen. **1954** 'N. BLAKE' *Whisper in Gloom* II. xiv. 194, I bet you Elmer's holed up in Harwich, or somewhere near it. **1961** G. GREENE *Burnt-Out Case* II. iii. 37 Who would expect to find the Querry holed up in a leproserie? **1973** D. JORDAN *Nile Green* xlv. 234 We were holed up in the flat, drinking Gold Star beer.

†**III. 8.** *intr.* To become full of holes. *Obs.*

1611 COTGR., *Se Trouër*, to hole, to grow full of holes.

IV. 9. *trans.* To record by punching a hole in an allotted space in a card.

1911 *Chambers's Jrnl.* May 335/2 Not only are the old-time data, such as age,.. 'holed' into the card, but whether you are married or single. *Ibid.* 336/2 In this machine the data 'holed' in every tag can be all or partly recorded on another form.

†**hole**, *v.*² *Obs.* Forms: 1 hólian, 3 holen. [OE. *hólian*, cogn. with Goth. *hôlôn* to treat with violence; cf. OHG. *huolan* to deceive.]

a. *trans.* To oppress. **b.** *intr.* To commit oppression.

c **1000** *Lamb. Ps.* cxviii[i]. 121 (Bosw.) Ne sele ðu me holiendum me [Vulg. *calumniantibus me*]. *c* **1200** ORMIN 9319 Þatt holeþþ o þe laȝhe leod, & rippeþþ hemm & ræfeþþ.

hole: see HOLL *a.*, HELE *v.*¹, HULL.

hole, -ful, -ly, -some, etc., the common early (and etymological) spelling of WHOLE, etc.

holeable ('həʊləb(ə)l), *a. Golf.* Also **holable**. [f. HOLE *v.*¹ + -ABLE.] Of a stroke, esp. a putt: capable of sending the ball into the hole.

1909 *Westm. Gaz.* 30 Apr. 12/2 On the green Taylor failed at a holable putt for 5. *Ibid.* 10 June 12/3 Four holeable putts which he missed. **1927** *Sunday Express* 29 May 21/7 The short eleventh was halved in three, both players missing holeable putts. **1955** *Times* 1 June 4/1 Pattinson missed only one putt that looked holeable and holed a good number that were missable.

'**hole-and-'corner**, *adj. phr.* Done or happening in a 'hole and corner', or place which is not public; secret, private, clandestine, underhand. Contemptuously opposed to 'public' or 'open'.

1835 FONBLANQUE *Eng. under 7 Administ.* (1837) III. 205 Hole-and-corner meetings are got up to speak the voice of

the nation. **1839** STONEHOUSE *Axholme* 77 Any manufacturer of the hole and corner political petitions of the present day. **1862** H. KINGSLEY *Ravenshoe* III. 55 Tell me at once what this hole-and-corner work means. **1878** S. WALPOLE *Hist. Eng.* I. vi. 600 The Queen's friends declared that the King's supporters were 'hole-and-corner' men. **1883** BLACK *Shandon Bells* i.

Hence **hole-and-'cornerism**, hole-and-corner action; a system of secret procedure.

1873 *Daily News* 7 Nov. 5/4 The real..conduct of French politics at the present moment is by hole-and-cornerism.

holed (həʊld), *ppl. a.* [f. HOLE *v.*¹ or *sb.* + -ED.] Having a hole or holes; pierced, perforated.

c **1481** CAXTON *Dialogues* (E.E.T.S) 34/10 Everard the upholster can well stoppe a mantel hooled. **1548–77** VICARY *Anat.* ix. (1888) 74 Euery Spondel is holed on euery side. *c* **1611** CHAPMAN *Iliad* II. 686 His men yet pleased their hearts With throwing of the holed stone. **1645** RUTHERFORD *Tryal & Tri. Faith* (1845) 258 His dead, and holed, and torn body. **1885** *Garden* 10 Oct. 367/2 Holed peach leaves.

b. ***holed-stone***, a perforated stone considered to be a monument of prehistoric times.

1769 BORLASE *Antiq. Cornwall* (ed. 2) 178 The middle stone..has a large hole..whence it is called the Mên an Tol (in Cornish holed stone). **1861** BLIGHT *Week at Land's End* 19 Holed-stone near Bolleit. **1873** MISS A. W. BUCKLAND in *Jrnl. Anthrop. Instit.* IX. 153, I never heard of libations being poured through these Cornish holed-stones.

holeless ('həʊllɪs), *a.* [f. HOLE *sb.* + -LESS.] Without a hole or holes.

1887 *Bicycl. News* 17 Sept. 387/2 The week's washing.. hung in spotless but not holeless purity.

holely, erron. f. HOLEY *a.*

holer ('həʊlə(r)). [f. HOLE *v.*¹ + -ER¹.] One who makes a hole; *spec.* the collier who 'holes' or undercuts a coal-seam.

1829 [see HOLE *v.*¹ 3]. **1873** *Echo* 22 Sept. 2/2 The 'Holers', chiefly boys of about seventeen or eighteen, can earn from 5s. to 6s. per day. **1891** *Labour Commission* Gloss., *Holer's Day or Stint*, the measure of undercutting, undermining, or curving a length of seam.

holer, var. of HOLOUR *Obs.*

†**holet.** *Obs.* [f. HOLE *sb.* + -ET¹. Cf. OE. *gráfet* ? little grove, *þiccet* thicket.]

1. A little hole; a small cave.

c **1380** WYCLIF *Wks.* (1880) 322 Siche placis of newe ordris shulden be fled as fendis holetis. *a* **1440** *Pr. Life Alex.* (*MS. Lincoln A.* i. 17 lf. 30) (Halliw.) In thir holettez duelle we alwaye, and in thir caves. *c* **1491** *Chast. Goddes Chyld.* 93 O thou edder..tornynge hyder and thyder by a thousande holettes and halkes.

2. A hut, cot, tent, tabernacle; = HILET.

c **1380** WYCLIF *Serm.* Sel. Wks. II. 281 Bishopis of þe olde lawe..entriden..in to a litil holet þat was þe west part of þe tabernacle. *c* **1450** *St. Cuthbert* (Surtees) 1285 Hirdes holetts [*Pastorum tuguria* (Bede)] sowe he þare.

holethnic, holetrous: see HOLO-.

holewe, obs. form of HOLLOW.

holewort ('həʊlwɜːt). [Lyte's ad. Ger. *holwurz*.] = HOLLOWWORT; extended by Lyte to another species of *Corydalis*.

1578 LYTE *Dodoens* III. ii. 316 The roote whiche is holowe within is called in Germanie Holwurtz, that is to say in English Holowe roote, or Holewurt. **1863** [see HOLLOWWORT]. **1866** *Treas. Bot.*, Holewort, *Corydalis bulbosa*.

holey ('həʊlɪ), *a.* Forms: 4–7 **holy, hollie, -y**, 5–6 **hooly**, (6 *erron.* **holely**), 7– **holey**. [f. HOLE *sb.* + -Y. (The *e* is retained, to distinguish it to the eye from HOLY *a.*)] Full of holes.

1398 TREVISA *Barth. De P.R.* VIII. xxi. (Bodl. MS.), Thei [stars] beþ rounde in substaunce..nouȝt holouȝ noþer holly in þe vtter partie. **1551–2** *Act 5 & 6 Edw. VI*, c. 6 §6 Yf.. Clothe..happen..to be full of holes mylbrack or to be hollie [*Ruffhead* holely]. **1578** LYTE *Dodoens* II. xxv. 177 Leaues.. holy, as though they had bene eaten with Locustes, Paulmers or Snayles. **1637** RUTHERFORD *Let. to Ld. Lowdoun* 10 Sept., An old hollie and threed-bare garment. **1818** J. BROWN *Psyche* 127 'Tis just as holey as a crumpet. **1875** JOWETT *Plato, Gorgias* Introd. II. 287 Fools are supposed to be carrying water to this vessel in a holey sieve.

b. ***holey*** (erron. ***holy***) ***dollar***, a Spanish dollar out of which a dump had been punched (see DUMP *sb.*² b), formerly current in parts of Australia.

1857 D. BUNCE *Austral. Remin.* 59 Our first change for a pound consisted of two dumps, two holy dollars, one Spanish dollar, one French coin [etc.]. **1883** *Numism. Chron.* Ser. III. III. 119 These coins popularly called 'holey dollars' are extremely scarce.

holgh, holȝ, holh, obs. ff. HOLLOW.

holi, holie, obs. ff. HOLY *a.*

holi, var. HOOLEE.

holibut: see HALIBUT.

-holic: see -AHOLIC.

holick, obs. form of WHOLLY.

holidam(e, early form of HALIDOM, still used in edd. of Shakspere.

holiday ('hɒlɪdeɪ), *sb.* Forms: α. 1 **háliȝdæȝ, háli-dæiȝ**, 3 **halidei**, *pl.* **helidawes**, 4–5 **halidai, -daie, -day, -daye**, *pl.* **halydawes**, 4–6 **halyday** (5 **haleday**), 5–6 **hallidai, -day**. β. 4 **holidai**, 4– **holiday**; (also 5–9 **holyday**, 6 **holie, hollie daie, holydaie, holy daie, daye**, 6–7 **holliday, -e, hollyday, -daie, holy-day, holy day**, 7 **holedaye, holidaie**). [OE. *háliȝdæȝ* (dat. pl. *háliȝdaȝum*), found beside the uncompounded *háliȝ dæȝ* in two words (dat. pl. *hálȝum daȝum*). In the combined form OE. *á* instead of being rounded to ME. *ǒ*, was shortened to *a* (cf. HALLOW, HALLOWMAS, HALIBUT, HALIDOM), giving *halidai, halliday*, used till 16th c. But the uncombined form was in concurrent use, and became more frequent as the distinction in signification between sense 1 and sense 2 became more marked, until, in the 16th c., *holy day* or *holy-day* became the usual form in sense 1. About the same time *holiday* (*holliday*), with *o* short, being a later combination and shortening of *holy day*, rare in late ME., took the place of the earlier *haliday*, which however remained in the northern dialects, where also (esp. in Scotland) the uncombined form was *haly day*.

It is thus difficult to divide *holiday* and *holy-day* in sense 1. Under this article are included the combined forms *haliday, holiday*; the uncombined forms, as well as those in which the vocalization shows that the word was analyzed, are treated under HOLY-DAY. But the habits of mediæval scribes as to the combination or separation of the elements of compounds were so irregular, and the treatment of the matter by modern editors is so uncertain, that many ME. instances might be placed under either article.]

1. A consecrated day, a religious festival. Now usually written HOLY-DAY, q.v.

α. *c* **950** *Lindisf. Gosp.* Mark iii. 2 Hueðer on haliȝdaȝum ȝeȝemde [*Rushw. G.* ȝif he halȝes dæȝes ȝiȝemde]. *a* **1035** *Laws of Cnut* II. c. 45 (Schmid) Be hali-dæiȝes freolse. De die dominica et festis observandis. *a* **1225** *Ancr. R.* 18 ȝif hit is halidei..siggeð Pater Noster. *Ibid.* 24 Ine werkedawes, heihte & twenti Pater Nosters; ine helidawes, forti. *a* **1300** *Cursor M.* 6473 Hald þou wel þin halidai. **1362** LANGL. *P. Pl.* A. VIII. 22 þei holdeþ not heore haly-day [*B.* halidayes, *C.* halydaies] as holy churche [*B.* holi-cherche, *C.* holychurche] techeþ. *c* **1386** CHAUCER *Miller's T.* 154 This Absolon..Gooth with a Sencer on the haliday. **1426** AUDELAY *Poems* 6 In clannes kepe ȝour haleday. *c* **1440** *Promp. Parv.* 222/2 Halyday (*K.* halliday), *festivitas*. *c* **1450** MYRC 203 Aske the banns thre halydawes. **1481** CAXTON *Reynard* (Arb.) 28 Goo to chirche, faste and kepe your halydayes. **1530** PALSGR. 228/2 Halyday, *feste*.

β. *a* **1375** *Cursor M.* 11929 (Laud) Hyt fille vpon an holiday þat Sabot hight in Iewis lay. **1393** LANGL. *P. Pl.* C. VIII. 226 Hold wel þyn halyday [*MS. M.* 218 (*a* **1400**) halt þyn holidai]. *c* **1475** *Pict. Voc.* in Wr.-Wülcker 778/1 *Hoc festum*, a holyday. **1526** TINDALE *Acts* XX. 6 After the ester holidayes. **1551–2** *Act 5 & 6 Edw. VI*, c. 3 (*title*), An Acte for the keping of Hollie daies and Fastinge dayes. **1661** BP. NICHOLSON *Catech.* Pref. (1686) 8 Enjoined on the Lord's day, and every holiday to be done by every rector. **1782** PRIESTLEY *Corrupt. Chr.* I. IV. 336 Pagan festivals [were changed] into Christian holidays. **1844** LINGARD *Anglo-Sax. Ch.* (1858) I. vii. 288 The Sundays came round weekly; other holidays came yearly. **1873** SIR R. PHILLIMORE *Eccl. Law* 1037 Fish carriages..shall be allowed to pass on Sundays or holidays.

2. a. A day on which ordinary occupations (of an individual or a community) are suspended; a day of exemption or cessation from work; a day of festivity, recreation, or amusement. (In early use not separable from 1.)

α. *a* **1300** *Cursor M.* 12276 Iesus went him for to plai Wit childir on an halidai. **1478** W. PASTON, Jr. in *P. Lett.* No. 824 III. 237 One for the halydays..and a nothyr for the workyng days. **1495** *Act 11 Hen. VII*, c. 22 §3 That noe artificer..working but the half day take no wagis but for the half day, and nothing for yᵉ halyday.

β. **1540** HYRDE tr. *Vives' Instr. Chr. Wom.* I. v. (R.) On some working daies doe likewise,..specially if there bee any long space betweene the holly-daies. **1577** B. GOOGE *Heresbach's Husb.* III. (1586) 113 b, Doo you not knowe that it is holliday, a day to dance in, and make mery at the Ale house? **1601** CORNWALLYES *Ess.* II. xxvi. (1631) 3 Life being like a Prentises holy day. **1601** SHAKS. *Jul. C.* I. i. 2 Hence: home you idle Creatures, get you home: Is this a Holiday? **1782** COWPER *Gilpin* 8 Though wedded we have been These twice ten tedious years, yet we No holiday have seen. **1818** BYRON *Ch. Har.* IV. cxli, Butcher'd to make a Roman holiday. **1881** TROLLOPE *Ayala's Angel* III. 88 Glomax thought that Tony had been idle, and had made a holiday of the day from the first.

b. *collect. pl.* or *sing.* A time or period of cessation from work, or of festivity or recreation; a vacation. (See also BLIND MAN'S HOLIDAY.)

α. **13..** *Gaw. & Gr. Knt.* 1049 Er þe halidayez holly were halet out of toun. *c* **1420** *Pallad. on Husb.* I. 176 Necessite nath neuere halyday. **1573** G. HARVEY *Letter-bk.* 27 In the hallidais he tooke a iurni into the cuntri.

β. **1539** TAVERNER *Erasm. Prov.* (1552) 40 With sluggers or unhardye persons, it is always holy daye. **1546** J. HEYWOOD *Prov.* (1867) 83 Lightly he layde hir vp for hollie daies. **1647** CLARENDON *Hist. Reb.* IV. §119 The Christmas holidays giving more leave and license to all kinds of people. *a* **1652** BROME *Queene's Exch.* I. ii. Wks. 1873 III. 469 To make my rest of life all holidayes. **1806–7** J. BERESFORD *Miseries Hum. Life* (1826) III. v, My youngest boy, Tom, now at home for the holidays. **1825** SOUTHEY in *Life* (1849) I. 153 Blair spent one summer holidays with his mother Lady Mary, at Spa. **1863** MISS THACKERAY *Elizabeth* (1867) 166 Will Dampier ..went year by year to scramble his holiday away up and down mountain sides.

c. Cessation from work; festivity; recreation. ***to make holiday***, to cease from work, to take a day's recreation.

1526 *Pilgr. Perf.* (W. de W. 1531) 72 We shall..rest & make holyday for this tyme. **1592** WARNER *Alb. Eng.* VIII. xlii. (1612) 204 Ill therefore might it boode at her to make our Holly-day. **1600** DEKKER *Gent. Craft* Wks. 1873 I. 47 *Ham*...Lets play. *Jane.* I cannot liue by keeping holliday. **1714** ROWE *Jane Shore* (M.) When my approach has made a little holy-day. **1886** *Pall Mall G.* 13 Aug. 1/1 Men of business seat themselves in the railway carriages, bent on holiday.

†**d.** Phr. ***to speak holiday***, to use choice language, different from that of ordinary life. Cf. *holiday English, holiday terms* in 4. *Obs.*

1598 SHAKS. *Merry W.* III. ii. 69 He writes verses, hee speakes holliday, he smels April and May.

e. Euphemistically used for: imprisonment.

1901 *Pall Mall Mag.* Feb. 197 A sentence of a month or two..a little 'holiday' with food and shelter and warmth.

3. *colloq. Naut.* A spot carelessly left uncoated in tarring or painting; see also quot. 1882.

1785 GROSE *Dict. Vulg. T.* s.v., A holiday is any part of a ship's bottom, left uncovered in paying it. **1840** R. H. DANA *Bef. Mast* viii. 18 He only thinks of leaving no holidays (places not tarred). **1882** JAGO *Dial. Cornw.*, *Holidays*, parts left untouched in dusting. 'Don't leave any holidays.'

4. *attrib. and Comb.* **a.** *attrib.* or as *adj.* Of, belonging to, or used on, a holiday; befitting a holiday, festive, gay, sportive; superior to the ordinary workaday sort, as ***holiday centre, clothes, English, job, resort, terms***. Sometimes (esp. formerly of persons): Suited only to a holiday; not engaged in, or not fitted for, serious action; dainty; idle, trifling.

c **1440** *Jacob's Well* (E.E.T.S.) 136 Comoun strumpettes, hasardourys, & such oþere, & halyday-werkerys. *Ibid.* 196 þou þat hast getyn good be haly-day werkyng, haly-day chaffaryng, be false othys, be false dysceyȝtes. **1589** *Pappe w. Hatchet* (1844) 20 Put on your night cap, and your holiday English. **1594** GREENE & LODGE *Looking Glasse* Wks. (Rtldg.) 125/1 She will call me rascal, rogue, runagate [etc.] ..and these be but holliday-terms. **1598** SHAKS. *Merry W.* II. i. 2 What, haue scap'd Loue-letters in the holly-day-time of my beauty, and am I now a subiect for them? **1600** —— *A. Y. L.* I. iii. 14 They are but burs..throwne vpon thee in holiday-foolerie. **1610** —— *Temp.* II. ii. 30 Not a holiday-foole there but would giue a peece of siluer. **1676** WYCHERLEY *Pl. Dealer* III. i, Prithee, don't look like one of our Holyday Captains now-a-days. **1695** *Poor Robin's Alm.* in Brand *Pop. Antiq.* (1870) II. 353 A Holy-day Wife, all play and no work. **1701** ADDISON *Switzerland* Wks. 1721 II. 173 Their holy-day cloaths go from Father to Son, and are seldom worn out. **1765** FOOTE *Commissary* II. Wks. 1799 II. 29 Them holiday terms wou'd not pass in my shop. **1820** W. TOOKE tr. *Lucian* I. 558 Put on holiday-looks and pretend to be merry. **1836** EMERSON *Nature* i. Wks. (Bohn) II. 143 Nature is not always tricked in holiday attire. **1838** LYTTON *Alice* 13, I must give you a holiday task to learn while I am away. **1854** SHERWOOD & KELLY *Boys will be Boys* ii. 31 That part of the country..within the nearer reach of a holiday ramble. **1866** 'MARK TWAIN' *Lett. fr. Hawaii* (1967) 91 In Honolulu it is not a holiday job to ship a crew. **1900** *Captain* II. 375/1 When Mr. Soames asked the professor to come and be holiday tutor. *Ibid.*, Open to take a holiday tutorship. **1936** *Discovery* Sept. 263/1 A famous holiday-resort has been selected [as a meeting-place for the British Association]. **1944** J. S. HUXLEY *On Living in Rev.* I. iii. 6 The elaborate system of rest-houses and holiday centres and the equally elaborate arrangements for holiday transport. **1966** *Economist* 17 Sept. 1143/2 Very soon now a vast new 'holiday centre' will open in Aviemore itself, containing both accommodation of all kinds and prices and entertainments of a similarly wide variety. **1969** *Times* 14 June 18/4 (Advt.), Holiday job wanted..by 6th form girl.

b. objective, as ***holiday-keeper, -keeping, -maker, -making***; locative, as ***holiday-rejoicing*** adj.

1792 W. B. STEVENS *Jrnl.* 27 May (1965) 24 Set out in the afternoon, holiday-making to Birmingham. **1807–8** W. IRVING *Salmag.* (1824) 369 Holiday-loving rogues. **1836** DICKENS *Sk. 'Boz'* I. 323 The four clowns..may be all very well for the low-minded holiday makers. **1855** GEO. ELIOT in *Fraser's Mag.* LII. 60/1 The good people who come to take dinner..here, by way of holiday making. **1859** *Chambers's Bk. of Days* 16 May I. 643 The holyday-maker and his partner. **1890** *Daily News* 8 Apr. 6/2 The streets were thronged with holiday keepers. **1896** *Ibid.* 3 Feb. 8/4 To say nothing of the loss from holiday-keeping. **1969** *Daily Tel.* 4 Jan. 18/6 There is one valuable holiday-making aid to the Gulf and the Bay of Naples.

c. *Comb.* **holiday camp**, an informally run camp for a holiday; now esp. a complex of chalets, places of entertainment, etc., designed for family holidays; **holiday course** [= G. *ferienkurs*, F. *cours de vacances*, etc.], a series of lectures, classes, etc. which is held during a school or college vacation; **holiday home**, (*a*) a place where poor persons, or children whose parents cannot take charge of them, can be accommodated, sometimes at little or no cost to themselves, for a period of holiday; (*b*) a house where people spend their holidays; †**holidayman, -woman**, a man or woman taking a holiday, an idler or trifler; **holiday task**, homework to be done during the holidays.

1870 R. ST. J. CORBET (*title*) The *holiday camp: three days' picnic: story for boys and girls. **1927** *Cornh. Mag.* Feb. 225 Of the many thousands of children who were sent into the country..25% stayed for two weeks or more in the

Holiday Camps. These Camps are an interesting feature of the Copenhagen holiday system. *Ibid.* 226 Life in a Holiday Camp is always the simplest, and is spent, so far as possible, in the open air. *Ibid.* 231 The Danes do not regard the Holiday Camp system as an ideal system. **1940** *Manch. Guardian Weekly* 1 Nov. 320/1 Then there were the Holiday Camps, cheap, social, with every modern convenience and all the modern pleasures. Their official hosts and hostesses mapped out the day with a colossal time-table of delights. **1949** M. DICKENS *Flowers on Grass* vii. 181 I've got to go to a holiday camp to do some sketches of happy campers for publicity. **1958** *Times* 8 Sept. 6/1 A steel cabinet in the security block at Butlin's holiday camp at Ayr was forced at the weekend. **1906** *Teacher* 30 June 616/3 The Greifswald Holiday Course..the oldest of the German *holiday courses ..has now been in existence for fifteen years. **1887** *Girl's Own Paper* 22 Oct. 48/3 A lady who has a large house and grounds would give a lady of small means a '*holiday home'. **1931** *Geography* Sept. 219 The hostel..is more akin to the 'dak-bungalow' or the 'cold harbour' than to the rest-camp or holiday-home. **1937** *Discovery* June p. xlvi/2 (Advt.), Schools, coaching colleges, holiday homes. **1972** *Guardian* 1 Sept. 8/6 The 'white settlers' who buy croft houses for use as holiday homes. **1973** *Ibid.* 28 May 4/1 The Welsh Language Society is planning..to try to prevent the sale of houses as second or holiday homes. **1548** UDALL *Erasm. Par. Luke* x. 105 b, Although they seme as *holidayemenne, to repose theymselfes from all corporall businesse. **1600** SURFLET *Countrie Farme* 837 More fit for holidaie men, milke sops, and cowards. **1827** J. LEECH *Let.* in W. P. Frith *John Leech* (1891) I. i. 12, I think I shall get promoted when Dr Russell sees my *Holiday Task. **1899** KIPLING *Stalky & Co.* 180 They have a holiday task..which..none..will ever look at. **1912** E. W. HORNUNG *Fathers of Men* xi. 130 So they give you saying-lessons for holiday tasks at your school? *Ibid.* xii. 137 He'd no right to set us a holiday task of his own like that. **1930** C. MACKENZIE *April Fools* vii. 138 I'm reading 'Homes without Hands' for a holiday task.

Hence **holiday** *v. intr.*, to take a holiday; to go on a pleasure-excursion; whence **'holidayer**, a holiday-maker. **'holidayish** *a.*, of a character befitting a holiday, festive. **'holidayism**, the practice of making holiday, devotion to holidays.

1869 *Contemp. Rev.* XII. 629 The hero..meets an artist.. likewise *holidaying. **1871** CARLYLE in *Mrs. C.'s Lett.* II. 311 Craik from Belfast..was here holidaying. **1887** *Pall Mall G.* 29 Dec. 5 The prospective bridegroom holidays in Scotland for three weeks. **1886** *Birmingham Weekly Post* 7 Aug. 4/6 We hear..that many *holidayers spend their time in suburban public-houses. **1886** *Gd. Words* 247 Some more or less..*holidayish kind of work. **1886** LEWIS in *Pop. Sci. Monthly* XXIX. 708 Under the working of the civil law.. Sunday has tended and must tend to *holidayism.

holie, obs. form of HOLY, WHOLLY.

holier-than-thou: see HOLY *a.* 5 c.

†**holihede.** *Obs.* Forms: see HOLY *a.* [f. HOLY *a.* + *-hede*, -HEAD.] Holiness.

a **1300** *Cursor M.* 1439 No moght þan help na hali-heid [*v.rr.* hali-hede, halihede, holy hede]. *Ibid.* 2330 Fild of trout[h] and haly-hede. **1340** *Ayenb.* 247 Guode men þet ledeþ lif of angel an erþe be hire holyhede.

holihock, obs. form of HOLLYHOCK.

holily ('həʊlılı), *adv.* Forms: see HOLY *a.* [f. HOLY *a.* + -LY².]

1. In a holy manner; with sanctity or devoutness.

c **1200** ORMIN 15920 Forr all þatt tatt teȝȝ haliȝ & dafftiȝlike hemm ledenn. *Ibid.* 17282 To spellenn haliȝlike, and ec To wirrkenn hallȝhe tacness. **1340** *Ayenb.* 74 Þo þet..lokeþ holyliche hare herten. **1382** WYCLIF *1 Thess.* ii. 10 How hoolily, and iustli, and withouten querel..we weren. *c* **1386** CHAUCER *Merch. T.* 211 And lyue in chastitee ful holily. *c* **1450** *Mirour Saluacioun* 777 Hire sawle with-inne woke than fulle halily. **1526** *Pilgr. Perf.* (W. de W. 1531) 58 b, As longe as a persone is holyly occupyed, so longe he prayeth. **1605** SHAKS. *Macb.* I. v. 22 What thou would'st highly, That would'st thou holily. **1754** EDWARDS *Freed. Will* IV. vii. 236 To act holily and wisely in the highest possible Degree. **1894** *Athenæum* 3 Mar. 276/3 With an eloquent impulsiveness becoming their holily emotional themes.

2. Sacredly, scrupulously, inviolably; solemnly. Now *rare* or *Obs.*

c **1374** CHAUCER *Boeth.* III. pr. x. 70 (Camb. MS.) See now how þou mayst proeuen holyly and with-owte corupcion this þat I haue seyd. **1548** UDALL, etc. *Erasm. Par. Matt.* v. (R.), But I wil haue matrimony obserued more holyly & vndefyledly among them that professe the new lawe. **1577–87** HOLINSHED *Chron. Scotl.* (1805) II. 237 If the Scots would most holilie and handfastlie promise. **1651** *Life Father Sarpi* (1676) 41 And those that..had lived intimately with him, do most holily attest, that they were never able to observe any such defects in him.

holimonth ('hɒlımʌnθ). [Nonce-formation after *holiday*.] A month of recreation or abstinence from work; a month's holiday.

[(OE. had *háligmónað*, Holy-month, as the name of September (app. of heathen origin); but this did not survive.)]

1862 *Temple Bar Mag.* VI. 189 (*heading*), The Englishman's Holimonth. *Ibid.* 194 On every-days and on holidays, in working months and in Holimonths. **1896** *Advance* (Chicago) 4 June 822/2 A country holimonth with bicycle and kodak.

holin, obs. form of HOLLIN, holly.

holiness ('həʊlınıs). Forms: see HOLY *a.* [OE. *háliȝnes, -nys* (= OHG. *heilagnissa*), f. *háliȝ* HOLY + -NESS.]

1. The quality of being holy; spiritual perfection or purity; sanctity, saintliness; sacredness.

971 *Blickl. Hom.* 31 þa þe him þeowiaþ on rihtwisnesse & on haliȝnesse. *c* **1000** *Ags. Ps.* (Spelm.) xcv[i]. 6 (Bosw.) Haliȝnys on haliȝnysse. *c* **1175** *Lamb. Hom.* 99 Godes gast wissað efre to haliȝnesse. *c* **1230** *Hali Meid.* 31 Wið halinesse of heorte. **1297** R. GLOUC. (1724) 331 Þe betere hym were in holynesse to nyme hyr to wyue. *a* **1300** *E.E. Psalter* xcv[i]. 6 Helinesses and mikelhed in his helinesse. *c* **1386** CHAUCER *Man of Law's T.* 69 Hir herte is verray chambre of hoolynesse. *a* **1400** *Relig. Pieces fr. Thornton MS.* 23 Slouthe ..makes mane to yrke in prayere or halynes. *c* **1532** DEWES *Introd. Fr.* in *Palsgr.* 927 By my holynesse, *par ma saincteté*. **1651** HOBBES *Leviath.* III. xxxv. 220 Of Holinesse there be degrees. **1766** FORDYCE *Serm. Yng. Wom.* (1767) II. viii. 8 There rise up to view nameless beauties in holiness. **1850** LYNCH *Theo. Trin.* ii. 28 Holiness is innocence made perfect. **1885** F. TEMPLE *Relat. Relig. & Sc.* ii. 49 Holiness consists in the subjection of the whole being..to the authority of conscience. **1896** *Daily News* 13 Jan. 6/4 One of the most interesting of Mr. Granger's chapters is that in which he explains primitive 'holiness' as obedience to the public recognition of the rights of ghosts and gods.

2. With possessive, as a title of the Pope, and formerly of other high ecclesiastical dignitaries.

A transl. of L. *sanctitās*, given orig. to all bishops, then *c* 600 limited to patriarchs, and since the 14th c. to the Pope. The same title was also given to the Byzantine Emperors, and sometimes to other sovereigns; it was addressed by John of Salisbury to Henry II of England. (See Du Cange.)

[**1169** BECKET *Let. to Cdl. Hyacinth* in *Mat. Hist. Becket* (Rolls) VII. 125 Omnes ad sanctitatis vestræ confugiunt pedes. **1170** HEN. II *Let. to Pope Alexander* Ibid. 419 Si devotionis meæ, pater, erga sanctitatem vestram experimentum quæritis.] **1450** HOLLAND *Howlat* 75, I will appele to the Pape..For happin that his halynace Throw prayer may purchace To reforme my foule face. **1502** HEN. VII in Ellis *Orig. Lett.* Ser. I. I. 49 The Popes Holynesse hath named certeyn Legats to be sent to all Cristen Princis. **1579** FULKE *Confut. Sanders* 559 Your holines is heade of all holy churches. **1590** SHAKS. *Com. Err.* v. i. 110 Ill it doth beseeme your holinesse [a Lady Abbess] To separate the husband and the wife. **1689** *Let. fr. Pope to Pr. Orange* in *Harl. Misc.* (1808) I. 368 Great Prince, Although the semicircle of your Highness be..elevated above the full orb of my Holiness. **1756–7** tr. *Keysler's Trav.* (1760) III. 285 With the permission of his holiness Clement IX. **1858** CARLYLE *Fredk. Gt.* III. iv. I. 223, 'I could help you to repay it!' said his Holiness [Pope Leo].

†**3. a.** *concr.* A holy place, sanctuary; a holy thing, an object of religious devotion. *Obs.*

c **897** K. ÆLFRED *Gregory's Past.* xv. 93 Inngongende and utgongende beforan Gode to ðam haliȝnessum. **1014** WULFSTAN *Serm. ad Anglos* in *Hom.* xxxiii. (1883) 158 And haliȝnessa syndon to griðlease wide. *c* **1175** *Lamb. Hom.* 27 Þenne cumeð drihtenes engel and binimeð þa halinesse mid him toward heouene riche. *a* **1300** *E.E. Psalter* lxxxii[i]. 12 In eritage Goddes halines hagh we. [**1526** TINDALE *Heb.* ix. 1 And worldly holynes.]

†**b.** Holy rites; worship, devotion. *Obs.*

c **1205** LAY. 1820 Brutus & his duȝeðe makeden halinesse [*c* **1275** holynisse]. *Ibid.* 8049.

4. a. *attrib.*, as **holiness convention, meeting,** a gathering or meeting for the promotion of holiness (in some religious communities).

1892 *Daily News* 21 July 6/4 In the evening a holiness meeting was held.

b. (Usu. with capital initial) to denote any of various religious sects which emphasize sanctification, spiritual purity, and perfectionism, or members, churches, etc., of any of these sects. orig. and chiefly *U.S.*

1888 *California State Gaz.* 623/2 Pasadena..contains Methodist, Baptist,..Friends, and Holiness churches. **1913** H. KEPHART *Our Southern Highlanders* 271 In our day the same may be said of the Holy Rollers and Holiness People. **1928** *Amer. Mercury* Oct. 185/1 This..was first preached by the Straight Holiness sect in Kansas in the 1890's. **1940** J. B. HOLT in *Amer. Sociol. Rev.* V. 740 (*title*) Holiness religion: cultural shock and social re-organisation. **1947** J. WACH *Sociol. Relig.* II. v. 189 The Methodist and the Holiness movements are especially concerned with ethical perfection. **1957** J. M. YINGER *Relig., Soc. & Individual* I. x. 282 Any description of religious trends in the United States that did not refer to the strength of the 'holiness' sects..would be incomplete. **1958** M. ARGYLE *Relig. Behaviour* iv. 33 Many of these sects—the Pentecostal, Holiness, Nazarene churches and others—have increased enormously in proportion to their size during this period [*sc.* 1926–1953]. **1961** B. R. WILSON *Sects & Soc.* I. v. 98 Elim is in no way as extreme as some of the Holiness cults of Tennessee and North Carolina. *Ibid.* 105 In Britain it began..in such organisations as the Faith Mission, independent Holiness missions,..and among the Plymouth Brethren. **1968** W. PHILLIPS in P. Oliver *Screening Blues* ii. 63 Now the Holiness people, when they come in, They said, 'Boy we can make it by livin' above sin.'

holing ('həʊlıŋ), *vbl. sb.* [f. HOLE *v.* + -ING¹.]

1. a. The action of making a hole or holes. Also, the production of holes, e.g. in garments (cf. HOLE *v.*¹ 8).

1398 TREVISA *Barth. De P.R.* VIII. v. (1495) 303 The Ether ..neyther maye be departed by thyrlynge and hoolynge of a nother body. *c* **1440** *Gesta Rom.* iv. 10 (Harl. MS.) Some tyme is suche holiyng and perforacion goode. **1807** VANCOUVER *Agric. Devon* (1813) 126 The holeing, digging, gripping, ditching, hacking, and hand-beating. **1910** *Daily Chron.* 14 Mar. 6/4 The Stockings that are actually insured against holing.

attrib. **1846** J. BAXTER *Libr. Pract. Agric.* (ed. 4) II. 331 The slit or holing-in method of planting is used.

b. The action of undercutting a coal-seam.

1841 *Collieries & Coal Trade* (ed. 2) 249 When the workman has been for some time engaged in what is termed 'holing under'. **1877** *Encycl. Brit.* VI. 66/2 The process of holing in coal is one of the severest kinds of human labour.

c. *Golf.* The action of holing the ball; also *attrib.*, as ***holing distance, holing-out putt.***

1875 'STONEHENGE' *Brit. Sports* (ed. 12) 695/1 He who succeeds in holeing in fewer strokes than his opponent wins that hole. **1901** *Scotsman* 11 Sept. 10/1 A nicely-played mashie stroke took his ball within holing distance. **1906** *Westm. Gaz.* 10 Aug. 4/2 The longer holing-out putts. **1972** *Country Life* 7 Dec. 1600/3 As often as not, the ball would finish within likely holing distance.

2. *concr.* The stuff underlying a coal (or other) seam picked out to undermine it.

1882 *Nature* 27 July 299 The bottom bed—7 inches thick —together with a bed of soft shale 10 inches thick, serves as a holing. **1890** *Goldfields Victoria* 65 Soft black clay (holing) ..1 inch.

3. *attrib.*, as **holing-axe, -stuff** (see quots.).

1819 REES *Cycl., Holeing-stuff*,..the small earth or coals which is cut or picked out from under the coal in a pit. **1828** WEBSTER, *Holing-ax*, a narrow ax for cutting holes in posts. **1829** GLOVER *Hist. Derby* I. 58 Pecking out the holeing stuff with a light and sharp tool.

holinight ('hɒlınaıt). [f. HOLY *a.* + NIGHT.]

†**1.** (After HOLIDAY 1, HOLY-DAY.) A night that is kept holy, as the eve of a festival. *Obs.*

a **1225** *Ancr. R.* 22 Ȝif hit beo holiniht vor þe feste. *a* **1300** *Cursor M.* 27994 On fastin dai or hali night.

2. (*nonce-use*, after HOLIDAY 2.) A night of festivity or pleasure.

a **1821** KEATS *Day is Gone* 10 The dusk holiday or holinight Of fragrant-curtain'd love. **1884** *Century Mag.* XXVIII. 508 (*heading*), A Summer Holinight.

holioke, obs. form of HOLLYHOCK.

holiship: see HOLYSHIP.

holism ('hɒlız(ə)m, 'həʊlız(ə)m). [f. Gr. ὅλος whole + -ISM.] A term coined by Gen. J. C. Smuts (1870–1950) to designate the tendency in nature to produce wholes (*i.e.* bodies or organisms) from the ordered grouping of unit structures. So **holist**. Cf. HOLISTIC *a.*

1926 J. C. SMUTS *Holism & Evol.* 99 The whole-making, holistic tendency, or Holism, operating in and through particular wholes, is seen at all stages of existence. **1937** 'C. CAUDWELL' *Illusion & Reality* ix. 180 A large portion of reality will be conveniently removed to the sphere of religion, as among the vitalists, holists, entelechists and spiritualists generally. **1945** *Word* i. 109 Haldane suggested for this movement [in biology] the name 'holism'; others preferred to call it 'organicism'. To my mind, this new holism or organicism bears a close relationship to linguistic structuralism. **1952** C. P. BLACKER *Eugenics* x. 240 The principle of monism is much the same as that of General J. C. Smuts's holism. **1959** *Times* 11 Dec. 15/1 Holism has at last penetrated departments of nutrition, and a new school of nutrition has arisen which realizes that the integration of nutrition, health and disease is a problem that must be attacked on a wide front. **1964** *Listener* 21 May 825/1, I mentioned the unresolved conflict between the atomistic psychology of the Behaviourists and the somewhat schematic holism of the Gestalt school.

holistic, *a.* [f. as HOLISM + -ISTIC].

a. Of or pertaining to holism; characterized by the tendency to perceive or produce wholes. Cf. HOLISM.

1926 [see HOLISM]. **1927** *Brit. Weekly* 20 Jan. 418/4 The real entities of the material world must, like organisms, be creative, self-transcending, functional. They must be Holistic unities. **1931** SMUTS in *Times* 2 Sept. 7/7 Instead of the animistic, or the mechanistic, or the mathematical universe, we see the genetic, organic, holistic universe. **1964** *Punch* 20 May 736/1 If..we view a person as a large.. holistic, versatile, symbol processing system. **1970** *New Scientist* 9 July 96/1 Each level is equipped with its own 'laws of organization', 'intrinsic patterns' or whatever 'holistic' term you prefer to choose. **1971** *Nature* 13 Aug. 504/2 Professor J. S. Weiner has pioneered the modern holistic approach to the study of man. **1971** F. A. STAFLEU *Linnaeus & Linnaeans* ii. 39 'Canon' means here 'general rule or axiom' and has overtones of 'genuine and inspired', known instinctively by a holistic, not an analytical, approach to the phenomena of life.

b. ***holistic medicine***, a form of medical treatment that attempts to deal with the whole person and not merely with his or her physical condition.

1960 F. H. HOFFMAN et al. in *Psychosomatics* I. 249/2 Throughout the United States, concern with teaching about the whole man—'holistic' or comprehensive medicine—is a growing phenomenon in the medical school curriculum. **1976** *Ann. Internal Med.* LXXXIV. 603/1 The inability of physicians, psychiatrists included, to practice a genuinely holistic medicine that integrates knowledge of the body, the mind, and the environment is striking. **1980** *San Francisco Bay Guardian* 16–23 Oct. 11/2 Where traditional Western medicine identifies and attacks symptoms, holistic medicine seeks to identify the underlying conditions in the client's life that have caused the illness or allowed it to happen and then to alleviate them. **1984** *Sunday Tel.* 17 June 15/8 Priests and ministers are increasingly asked for services of healing and the laying-on of hands—by a public increasingly drawn to alternative and holistic medicine.

Hence **ho'listically** *adv.*

1926 J. C. SMUTS *Holism & Evol.* 127 There is a synthesis which makes the elements or parts act as one or holistically. **1961** J. WILSON *Reason & Morals* ii. 117 There may be sane people who do not 'appreciate' (i.e. respond holistically to) works of art or to nature.

†**holite.** *Obs. rare*⁻¹. [f. HOLY *a.* + -TY (if not an error for *iolite*, JOLLITY).] Holiness.

14.. *Passio Domini* in *MS. Cantab.* Ff. 5. 48. lf. 15 a, In heuon shal þai wone wᵗ me Wᵗouten pyne wᵗ holite.

†**holk**, *sb. Obs.* [OE. *holca* or ? *holc*, deriv. of *hol*, HOLL *a.*: cf. LG. *holke*, *hölke* small hole, Sw. *hålk*.] ? A hollow, cavity.

c **1000** *Sax. Leechd.* II. 148 On þam holcum þæs lichoman. *Ibid.* 160 On þam holcum þære lifre. *a* **1240** *Sawles Warde* 251 Ed ehnen, ant ed neauele, ant ed te breoste holke.

holk, howk (həʊk, haʊk), *v.* Now *dial.* Forms: 4–6 **holk(e**, 7–9 **hoke, huck**, *Sc.* 7–9 **howk**, 9 **houk**. [Northern ME. *holk*, cognate with MLG. *holken*, LG. *holken*, *hölken*, to hollow, Sw. *hålka*; f. root of HOLL *a.*, with dim. formative *-k*: cf. *talk*.]

1. *trans.* To hollow out by digging; to excavate; to dig out or up. With various spec. local senses: see quots.

13.. *E.E. Allit. P.* B. 1222, [He] holkked out his auen yȝen heterly boþe. **1483** *Cath. Angl.* 187/2 To Holke, *palare*. **1513** DOUGLAS *Æneis* I. vii. 18 ȝonder wther sum the new havin holkis. **1552** LYNDESAY *Monarche* 1702 Sum holkit claye, sum brynt the tylde. **1573** SEMPILL in *Satir. Poems Reform.* xxxix. 270 Hes scho not helpit to holk out ȝone Tod? **1686** G. STUART *Joco-ser. Disc.* 47 Who howks a hole for any other His sel' fau' in were he my brother. **1780** A. YOUNG *Tour Irel.* I. 261 They bring up their children to hoking potatoes. **1798** J. JEFFERSON *Let. to J. Boucher* 19 Mar. (MS.), *Huck*, to pick out any thing with an instrument, as to huck a thorn out of the finger. **1805** *Sporting Mag.* XXVI. 75 I'll away up to the kirk-yard, and howk a few graves. **1880** *Antrim & Down Gloss.*, *Hoke*, to hollow-out anything, such as a toy boat. A dog hokes out the earth from a rabbit hole. **1891** HALL CAINE *Scapegoat* xviii, To howk out her grave with his own hands. **1899** A. WERNER *Captain of Locusts* 160 They howked a grave near the kraal, and buried their chief *pro tem.* **1926** D. H. LAWRENCE *Let.* 28 Dec. (1932) 676 We shall stay here if not howked out. **1950** B. MARSHALL *Every Man a Penny* xlix. 229 Deep in their trenches the hairy men stood, howking out the brown earth. **1955** E. POUND *Classic Anthol.* II. 90 Howk 'em up with a landing scoop.

2. *intr.* To dig, make excavation, turn things up.

1513 DOUGLAS *Æneis* VI. ix. 139 Vndir his cost holkand in weill law. **1825** BROCKETT, *Howk*, to dig, to scoop. **1834** *Blackw. Mag.* XXXV. 874 He will lie upon his master's grave, and..howk wi' his paws. **1893** CROCKETT *Stickit Minister* 118 He was howkin' up in the garret twa afternoons last week. **1906** KIPLING *Puck of Pook's Hill* 69 Dan hiked and howked with a boat-hook (the brook was too narrow for sculls). **1950** *John o' London's* 24 Nov. 621/1 The solan goose ..starts howking and pecking at the rope which sustains the climber.

Hence **holked, -et, -it** *ppl. a.* (*a*) Excavated, dug out or up; †(*b*) Sunken, depressed, hollow. **holking** *vbl. sb.* and *ppl. a.*, excavating, burrowing.

c **1420** *Anturs of Arth.* 116 (Thornton) Hir eghne ware holkede fulle holle. *a* **1500** P. JOHNSTON *Thre Deid Powis* iii, Full laithly thus sall ly thy lusty heid Holkit and how. **1508** DUNBAR *Flyting w. Kennedie* 164 Ffor hiddowis, haw, and holkit is thyne ee. **1552** LYNDESAY *Monarche* 1528 Holkit Glennis, and hie montanis. **1785** BURNS *Addr. to Deil* ix, They..in kirk-yards renew their leagues, Owre howkit dead. **1850** W. ALLINGHAM *Poems* 116 In thy bed of clay the howking mole Bores no tunnel thorough.

holk, obs. form of HULK *sb.*

holks, *sb. pl. Sc.* and *north. dial.* Also 9 **howks**. [App. plural of HOLK *sb.*] A disease of the eyes or face.

1513 DOUGLAS *Æneis* III. Prol. 27 Suppose the holkis be all ourgrowin thi face. **1570** *Satir. Poems Reform.* xvi. 86, I thinke the holkis ouergangis ȝour ene. *a* **1843** SOUTHEY *Doctor* cxliii. (1848) 357/1 He [horse] had neither the howks, nor the haws. **1893** *Northumbld. Gloss.*, *Howks* or *Haaks*, a disease of the eye.

holl (həʊl), *a. Obs.* or *dial.* Forms: 1–5 **hol** (infl. **hole**), 4–9 **holl**, (5 **holle**, *dial.* 5–9 **hole**, 9 **howl(e)**: see also HOWE *a. Sc.* [OE. *hol* hollow = OFris., OS., OHG. (MLG., MDu., Du., MHG.) *hol* (Ger. *hohl*), ON. *holr* (Sw. *hol*, Da. *huul*) hollow, concave; cf. Goth. *hulundi* cave, *ushulōn* to hollow out; OTeut. stem **hulo-*, pre-Teut. **kulo-*; perh. related to *helan* to cover, HELE *v.*¹; or with suffixal *-l*, from root **ku-*, **kaw-*, of L. *cavus* hollow; cf. Gr. κύαρ hole, orifice. As shown under HOLE *sb.* (q.v.), OE. *hol* had *o* short, retained in ME., in which the *l* was normally doubled, while in *hōle*, which represents the inflected cases, the *o* was lengthened. Subsequently, short *o* before *ll* has also been lengthened (cf. *boll*, *roll*, *poll*), and in Sc. has become *-ow(e*, so that *holl* is in Sc. *how*, HOWE.]

1. Hollow, concave; having a void space within; empty.

c **1000** *Sax. Leechd.* I. 306 Ðas wyrte..on middan hol. *Ibid.* 316 Any hy beoð innan hole. *c* **1375** *Sc. Leg. Saints*, *VII Sleperis* 102 In a hol cowe [= cove] vndir a stane. *c* **1400** MAUNDEV. (Roxb.) ix. 35 þai failed in þaire hertes and become holle within. *c* **1440** *Promp. Parv.* 242/2 Hol, as pypys, or percyd thyngys [*v.rr.* hole, hollowe], *cavus*. **1483** *Cath. Angl.* 188/1 Holle, *cavus natura, concauus arte, cauatus vtroque intelligitur, inanis*. *a* **1500** *Deguileville's Pilgr.* 84 b (MS. St. John's, Camb.) in *Cath. Angl.* 188 *note*, Many a willowe is..hol with-in and fulle of wormys. **1513** DOUGLAS *Æneis* v. ii. 85 Of the holl grave law A gret eddir slydand gan furth thraw. *a* **1825** FORBY *Voc. E. Anglia*, *Holl*, adj. hollow. **1847–78** HALLIWELL, *Hole*..(5) Hollow; deep; concave. *North.* Metaphorically, hungry, cheerless, or comfortless. **1874** WAUGH *Jannock* iv. 30 (Lanc. Gloss.) 'He must be varra howle when he's hungry'... 'Howle!' said Adam, 'why he'll be like a two-legged drum, about t'middle o' t' forenoon'.

2. Deeply excavated or depressed, as a valley or ditch; lying in a hollow.

c **897** K. ÆLFRED *Gregory's Past.* xxxiii. 217 ȝif se weobud ufan hol nære. *a* **1000** *Charter of Æthelred* in Kemble *Cod. Dipl.* V. 124 On ðone holan weȝ. *a* **1000** *Martyrol.* 1 On anum holum stanscræfe. **1375** BARBOUR *Bruce* VI. 78 He saw the brayis hye standand, The vattir holl throu slike rynand. *Ibid.* VIII. 176 Sa holl & hye the dykis war. *c* **1420** *Anturs of Arth.* 116 (Douce) Withe eighen holked ful holle [*rimes* cholle, polle]. **1691** RAY *N.C. Words* 37 *Hole*, hollow, deep: an *hole dish*, opposed to shallow. **1828** *Craven Dial.* s.v. *Howl*, A howl dish, opposed to shallow. **1855** ROBINSON *Whitby Gloss.*, *Holl*, *Holl time* or *Hollow time*. 'The holl of winter', the depth of winter.

†**3.** In specific uses: **holbasin**, a deep basin; **holcress** (only OE. *hol cerse*), Field Gentian; **holrush** (*holrysche*), a bulrush; **holtile**, a concave tile such as those used for the ridges of a roof; **holleway**, hollow way, an excavated lane; **holwork**, the making of 'holtiles'; *concr.* a quantity of such tiles. Also HOLLEKE.

c **1000** *Sax. Leechd.* II. 34 Wiþ wenne on eaȝon, ȝenim þa holan cersan. **1323** in Rogers *Agric. & Prices* II. 436 Holwork. **1362** *Ibid.* 438 Holtiles. *c* **1440** *Promp. Parv.* 244/2 Holrysche, or bulrysche [*v.rr.* hool ryschyn, holryschyne], *papirus*. **1463** *Bury Wills* (Camden) 23, I wille she haue.. the grettere hol basyn of ij. smale basynes. **1471** *Ibid.* 242, j peluem laton voc' an holbasyn, j peluem laton voc' a flatbasyn. *c* **1475** *Pict. Voc.* in Wr.-Wülcker 798/20 *Hic traco*, a hollewey.

holl, *sb. Obs.* exc. *dial.* Forms: 1 **hol**, 1–9 **holl**, (5 **holle, houle**, 5–9 **howle**, 9 *dial.* **houl, howl**). [OE. *hol*, late OE. and ME. *holl*, neuter of prec. adj. used subst.; retained chiefly in the north (*pronounced* (həʊl, hɔʊl); in Sc., *holl* has regularly become *how*, HOWE *sb.*]

1. A hollow place; a cave, den; a HOLE.

c **1050** *Voc.* in Wr.-Wülcker 187/1 *Lustra*, wilddeora holl and denn. *c* **1205** LAY. 20864 [þe fox] i þan holle wendeð. *c* **1352** *Pol. Poems* (Rolls) I. 88 In holl gan thai it hide. *c* **1400** *Destr. Troy* 1362 Mony wyues..Hyd hom in houles and hyrnys aboute. *Ibid.* 11991 He..Hid hir in a howle vnder a hegh towre. *c* **1470** HENRY *Wallace* v. 1022 With a knyff he stekit him to dede; In a dyrk holl kest him doun in that sted. **1500–20** DUNBAR *Poems* xxxii. 47 All the hollis wes stoppit hard. *c* **1600** NORDEN *Spec. Brit.*, *Cornw.* (1728) 40 A holl or deepe vaute in the grounde, whereinto the sea floweth at high water.

b. A surface hollow, excavation, or deep depression in the ground; a ditch.

1701 *MS. relating to Suffolk Manors*, One little piece of ground extending beyond the holl of him the sᵈ. S.H. *a* **1825** FORBY *Voc. E. Anglia*, *Holl*, a ditch, particularly a dry one. **1825** BROCKETT, *Howl*, a hollow or low place. 'Wherever there's a hill, there's sure to be a howl.' **1855** ROBINSON *Whitby Gloss.*, *Holl*, a deep hollow valley. **1888** RIDER HAGGARD *Col. Quaritch* I. vi. 96 To be kicked through every holl on the place.

†**2.** The HOLD of a ship. Cf. HOLE *sb.* 6. *Obs.*

c **1470** HENRY *Wallace* IX. 122 Bathe schip maistir, and the ster man also, In the holl, but baid, he gert thaim go. *Ibid.* x. 836 Out off the holl thai tuk skynnys gud speid. *c* **1475** *Pict. Voc.* in Wr.-Wülcker 804/43 *Hec carina*, a holle. *Ibid.* 805/30 *Hoc columbar*, the holle of the schyp. *c* **1490** *Promp. Parv.* 243/1 (Pynson & MS. K) Holle [*c* **1440** hoole of a schyppe], *carina*. **1508** KENNEDIE *Flyting w. Dunbar* 458 Foul brow in holl thow preposit for to pas. **1627** CAPT. SMITH *Seaman's Gram.* vii. 33 When you let anything downe into the Howle, lowering it by degrees, they say, Amaine.

3. The middle or depth (of winter, night). *north.*

c **1375** BARBOUR *Troy-bk.* II. 1695 In-to þe holl of wyntir richt. **1828** *Craven Dial.*, *Hole*, *Houl*, middle. 'T' hole o' winter'. Sc. *how*, as 'how o' the nicht', midnight. **1868** ATKINSON *Cleveland Gloss.*, *Holl*,..the depth of winter; sometimes applied also to the 'dead time of night'.

holl, obs. form of HULL, WHOLE.

holla ('hɒlə, rarely hɒ'lɑː), *int.* and *sb.* Also 6–8 **hola**. [a. F. *holà* (15th c. in Littré) 'stop', 'cease', also a call to excite attention: 'hoe there, enough, soft soft, no more of that; also, heare you me, or come hither' (Cotgr.).]

†**1.** An exclamation meaning Stop! cease! Hence *to cry holla*; *to give the holla to*, to stop or check by this call. *Obs.*

1523 LD. BERNERS *Froiss.* I. ccclxv. 597 Than therle of Buckyngham sayd, hola, cease, for it is late. **1566** GASCOIGNE *Supposes* III. i, Holla! no more of this. **1600** SHAKS. *A. Y. L.* III. ii. 257 Cry holla, to the tongue, I prethee: it curuettes vnseasonably. **1622** J. TAYLOR (Water P.) *Farew. Tower Bottles* Wks. (1872) 11 But holla, holla, Muse come back, come back. **1630** LENNARD tr. *Charron's Wisd.* II. Pref. (1670) 207 No man stays us, or cryes hola unto it. **1675** HOBBES *Odyss.* XXIII. 259 Telemachus and the good servants two, When they had to the dancers said 'Hola!' Unto their beds within the palace go. **1681** COTTON *Wond. Peak* (ed. 4) 86, I must give my Muse the Hola, here.

2. A shout to excite attention: cf. HOLLO.

1588 SHAKS. *L. L. L.* v. ii. 900 Holla, approach. **1599** MINSHEU *Span. Dial.* 25/2 Hola Page, bring Cards, let vs passe away the time. **1668** R. L'ESTRANGE *Vis. Quev.* (1708) 63 Hola! Grannum, (quoth I, good lustily in her Ear..) what's your pleasure with me? **1756** FOOTE *Eng. fr. Paris* II. Wks. 1799 I. 111 Hola, Sir Toby, stole away! **1855** KINGSLEY *Heroes* iii. (1856) 170 Then Theseus shouted to him 'Holla, thou valiant pine-bender, hast thou two fir-trees left for me?'

3. A shout of exultation: cf. HOLLO.

1727 SWIFT *Wom. Mind* 64 So, holla, boys; God save the king. ? *a* **1800** in Hone *Every-day Bk.* I. 1431 Holla boys! holla boys! huzza-a-a!

4. Also *holla ho!* [F. *holà ho!*]

1596 SHAKS. *Tam. Shr.* IV. i. 12 Holla hoa, Curtis. **1796** SCOTT *Wild Huntsman* xlix, Behind him hound, and horse, and horn, And, 'Hark away, and holla, ho!' **1871** B. TAYLOR *Faust* (1875) I. v. 84 With open throat sing chorus, drink and roar! Up! Holla! Ho!

B. *sb.* A shout of *holla!*

1592 SHAKS. *Ven. & Ad.* 284 What recketh he his rider's angry stir, His flattering 'Holla', or his 'Stand, I say'? **1672** VILLIERS (DK. BUCKHM.) *Rehearsal* v. i. (Arb.) 115 He's here with a whoop, and gone with a holla [*ed.* **1714** holloe]. **1810** *Sporting Mag.* XXXV. 299 Reynard was unfortunately lost ..by a false holla from a man. **1833** M. SCOTT *Tom Cringle* (1859) 9 At the moment I thought I heard a holla.

holla, *v.*: see HOLLO *v.*

hollabaloo: see HULLABALOO.

Holland¹ ('hɒlənd). [Du. *Holland*, in earliest sources *Holtlant*, f. *holt* wood + *-lant* land; a name whereby was designated 'locus quidam silvis et paludibus inhabitabilis..ubi videlicet Mosa et Wal fluvius corrivantur', i.e. the district about Dordrecht, the nucleus of the original county of Holland.

This derivation, which, though it has been impugned, appears to be finally established (see W. F. Gombault in *Taal en Letteren* VIII. 197, April 1898), separates the name from that of Holland in South Lincolnshire, the physical conformation of which has often caused it to be associated with Dutch Holland. The English name seems to be f. *hol*, HOLL *a.*, sense 2 + LAND; but there is the difficulty that it appears in Domesday Book as *Hoiland*, a form not easy to account for.]

1. a. The name of a province of the Northern Netherlands, formerly a county or 'graafschap', *comitatus*, of the German Empire, now usually extended by Englishmen and other foreigners to the kingdom of the Netherlands.

? *a* **1400** *Morte Arth.* 35 Holaund and Henawde they helde of hyme bothe. **1436** *Libel* in *Pol. Poems* (Rolls) II. 180 But they of Holonde, at Caleyse byene oure felles And oure wolles. **1449** *Paston Lett.* No. 68. I. 86 The cheff schyppys of Duchelond, Holond, Selond, and Flaundrys. **1647** CLARENDON *Hist. Reb.* I. §143 He went ambassador into Holland to the States General. **1655** SIR W. LOWER tr. *De Cerizier's Innoc. Lord* 67 All those effeminates, whom the Cloth of Holland hurteth.

fig. **1866** HOWELLS *Venet. Life* 256 The vegetable and fruit market where whole Hollands of cabbage and Spains of onions opened on the view.

b. *attrib.* esp. in names of products received from Holland: see quots. **Holland-cloth**: see 2. **Holland sauce** = HOLLANDAISE. **Holland-toad**, a small Dutch herring-boat.

1577 B. GOOGE *Heresbach's Husb.* III. (1586) 147 Next are commended the Holland Cheese, the Cheese of Normandy, and the English Cheese. **1614** *Eng. Way to Wealth* in *Harl. Misc.* (Malh.) III. 237 Vessels of divers fashions..go..for herrings..and they are called..Holland-toads. **1684** tr. *Bonet's Merc. Compit.* 4 Lime mixed with Holland soap eats deep enough into the flesh. **1807** VANCOUVER *Agric. Devon* (1813) 58 A slate formerly taken up at East Alwington, and exported under the name of Holland blues. **1877** E. S. DALLAS *Kettner's Bk. of Table* 162 Dutch or Holland Sauce: Sauce Hollandaise. **1892** [see DUTCH *a.* 3 b].

2. a. A linen fabric, originally called, from the province of Holland in the Netherlands, ***Holland cloth***. When unbleached called ***brown Holland***.

1427 *Wills & Inv. N. C.* (Surtees 1835) 77 Unum superpellicium novum de holand-cloth. *c* **1450** *Cov. Myst.* (Shaks. Soc.) 241 A shert of feyn Holond. **1502** ARNOLDE *Chron.* (1811) 206 Item a pece Holland or ony other lynnen cloth. **1542** *Nottingham Rec.* III. 220 Thre elnes of Holand cloth. **1551–2** *Househ. Acc. P'cess Eliz.* in *Camden Misc.* II. 31 For vj. ellnes of hollande for towelles. **1596** SHAKS. *1 Hen. IV*, III. iii. 82 Holland of eight shillings an Ell. **1617** MORYSON *Itin.* III. 169 Women..cover their heads with a coyfe of fine holland linen cloth. **1661** in J. Russell *Haigs* (1881) 470 To bay holen..to make bands of. **1666** DRYDEN *Ann. Mirab.* ccvi, Some..For folded turbans finest holland bear. **1673–4** GREW *Anat. Trunks* II. vii. §13 All our fine Hollands are made of Flax. **1706** PHILLIPS (ed. Kersey), *Holland* or *Holland-Cloth*, a kind of Linnen Cloth made in that Country. **1848** DICKENS *Dombey* iii, Every chandelier or lustre, muffled in Holland. **1852** R. S. SURTEES *Sponge's Sp. Tour* (1893) 134 He had the house put away in brown Holland, the carpets rolled up, the pictures covered, the statues shrouded in muslin. **1884** *Times* (weekly ed.) 12 Sept. 7/1 Frocks of neat brown holland embroidered with scarlet.

b. *attrib.* or in *Comb.*: of Holland (cloth).

1554 *Bury Wills* (Camden) 146 Oon paier of holland shetes. **1660** in *Harl. Misc.* (1811) VII. 198 Six dozen of large fine Holland handkerchiefs. **1712** STEELE *Spect.* No. 518 ¶9 An open breast, with an audacious display of the Holland shirt. **1879** EDNA LYALL *Won by Waiting* xxvi, Looking cool and countrified in their brown holland suits.

3. *Comb.* (in sense 2), as *holland-weaver*; *holland-lined* adj.

1895 *Westm. Gaz.* 13 Sept. 3/1 Ancient holland-lined barouches.

Holland[2] ('hɒlənd). The name of J. P. *Holland* (1840–1914), the designer of a class of submarines adopted by the American navy, used as the proper name of the first submarine of this type and afterwards generically.

1899 *Westm. Gaz.* 7 Dec. 2/3 The President of the official Naval Board, and several of its members have signed a statement declaring that their 'Holland' has fulfilled all requirements in her trial trip. **1902** *Encycl. Brit.* XXXII. 576/2 The *Holland*, a smaller boat, having a length of about 59 ft., though begun after the *Plunger*, has already been completed. *Ibid.*, The latest Holland design is shown in Fig. 95. **1906** *Daily Chron.* 8 Sept. 5/3 The original Holland class of submarine.

Hollandaise ('hɒləndeɪz, ‖ɔlɑ̃dɛz). [Fr., fem. of *hollandais* Dutch, f. *Hollande* Holland.] ***Hollandaise sauce*** (see quot. 1907); ***à la Hollandaise***, served with Hollandaise sauce.

1841 THACKERAY in *Fraser's Mag.* XXIII. 719/1 Turbot with lobster-sauce is too much; turbot *à la Hollandaise* vulgar. **1861** MRS. BEETON *Bk. Househ. Managem.* 195 Green Dutch sauce, or Hollandaise verte. **1899** N. NEWNHAM-DAVIS *Dinners & Diners* iv. 26 Artichokes good, though we preferred plain vinegar as a dressing to the *hollandais* one. **1907** ESCOFFIER *Mod. Cookery* 22 Hollandaise Sauce... One and one-half lbs. of butter, the yolks of six eggs, one pinch of mignonette pepper and one-quarter oz. of salt, three tablespoonfuls of good vinegar. *Ibid.* 23 The consistence of sauces whose processes are identical with those of the Hollandaise may be varied at will. **1964** C. WILLOCK *Enormous Zoo* ix. 169 Nile perch with Hollandaise sauce.

'Hollander. [f. HOLLAND[1] + -ER[1].]

1. a. A native of Holland, a Dutchman; also a Dutch ship.

1547 BOORDE *Introd. Knowl.* ix. (1870) 148 And I am a Holander; good cloth I do make. **1604** SHAKS. *Oth.* II. iii. 80 Your Dane, your Germaine, and your swag-belly'd Hollander, (drinke hoa) are nothing to your English. **1708** J. CHAMBERLAYNE *St. Gt. Brit.* II. I. ii. (1737) 326 There has been at one Time in Brassay-Sound, 1500 Sail of Hollanders. **1777** FRANKLIN *Lett.* Wks. 1889 VI. 82 Those supplies were openly furnished by Hollanders at St. Eustatia. **1855** MACAULAY *Hist. Eng.* xvii. IV. 3 It was said ..Whenever the dignity of the English flag..was concerned, he forgot that he was a Hollander.

b. A South African colonist or immigrant of Dutch birth or descent. Also *attrib.*, or as *adj.*, and *Comb.*

1699 W. A. COWLEY *Voy.* in W. Hacke *Collect. Voy.* (1729) v. 34 The Village inhabited by the Hodmandods, so called by the Hollanders. **1897** in H. M. Stanley *Thro' S. Afr.* (1898) v. 75, I do not blame the Boers so much as I blame the Hollanders and our Jews here. **1899** *Westm. Gaz.* 16 Oct. 7/2 The Boers who have occupied Newcastle consist of both Transvaal and Free State commandos, with 400 Hollanders. **1899** *Daily News* 2 Nov. 5/2 It has not been he, but the 'Hollander', a most unfavourable specimen of the Dutch race, who has been concerned in all the doubtful intrigues..of the last few years. **1902** *Encycl. Brit.* XXXII. 721/1 The effect of this development was the production of a body of officials in the Transvaal, partly Hollander and German, partly Boer. **1903** G. W. T. OMOND *Boers in Eur.* 31 South Africa, big towns and seaports excepted, being Hollander-Boer to the core. **1934** [see AFRICAN *sb.* b]. **1971** *Rand Daily Mail* (Home Owner) 27 Mar. 16/1 Developer-builder Gard Duys, a Hollander with a soft spot for progressive architecture, is delighted with the result.

2. *Paper-making.* A beating-engine, invented in Holland, for the conversion of the bleached rags into paper-pulp. Also called ***Hollander-beater***.

1878 *Design & Work* 19 Jan. 88/3 About fifty years after the invention of the 'Hollander'..alkali began to be employed for boiling the rags. **1900** CROSS & BEVAN *Paper-Making* (ed. 2) 172 The ordinary form of beater is fitted with a single roll, and the general arrangement of its working parts is that..described..for a 'breaking' engine. This type of beater is known as the Hollander. **1902** *Encycl. Brit.* XXXI. 458/2 One of the various forms of beating engine or 'Hollander'. **1907** CROSS & BEVAN *Paper-Making* (ed. 3) 179 The Hollander consists of an oblong trough, with semi-circular ends, with a partition or mid-feather running down the centre so as to form a continuous channel round which the stuff can circulate. **1963** R. R. A. HIGHAM *Handbk. Papermaking* xiii. 266 In the middle of the eighteenth century, the development of the Hollander beater revolutionized stock preparation methods. This beater was invented in Holland—hence the name—and it replaced the old rag stampers.

3. A Dutch clinker.

1897 WEBSTER, *Hollander*. 2. A very hard, semi-glazed, green or dark brown brick, which will not absorb water;—called also Dutch clinker. Wagner.

4. (See quot.)

1879 *Encycl. Brit.* IX. 400/2 The largest spars [of timber] are called 'Hollander'.

'Hollandish, *a.* Now *rare.* [f. as prec. + -ISH.] Of or belonging to Holland (province or country); Dutch.

1611 CORYAT *Crudities* 652 The rest of the Zelandish and Hollandish cities. **1626** in *Crt. & Times Chas. I* (1848) I. 133 A Hollandish pirate..who in a short time hath taken 130 sail of ships. **1846** WORCESTER cites *Ann. Reg.*

hollandite ('hɒləndaɪt). *Min.* [f. the name of Sir Thomas Henry *Holland* (1868–1947), British geologist: see -ITE[1] 2 b.] An oxide of barium and manganese occurring as brittle silvery grey to black crystals having a metallic lustre.

1906 L. L. FERMOR in *Trans. Mining, Geol. & Metall. Inst. India* I. II. 77 For this new mineral I propose the name of *hollandite*, after Mr. T. H. Holland, F.R.S., Director of the Geological Survey of India, and President of this Institute. **1943** *Amer. Mineralogist* XXVIII. 505 Cryptomelane, hollandite, and coronadite are isostructural and form isomorphous mixtures to some extent. **1952** *Nature* 6 Dec. 974/1 The formula of hollandite, deduced from that of the psilomelane used in this investigation, is $Ba_{1\cdot01}(Mn,R)_8O_{16}$, in good agreement with that previously proposed by Byström and Byström, $Ba_{(2-x)}Mn_8O_{16}$, where *x* is approximately equal to one. It has been suggested that discrete water molecules may be present in hollandite as occupants of vacant sites of otherwise perfect sub-rows.

Hollands ('hɒləndz), *sb.* [ad. Du. *hollandsch* (*ch* mute), Hollandish, Dutch, in *hollandsch genever*, Hollands gin.] A grain spirit manufactured in Holland: more fully ***Hollands gin***, formerly ***Hollands geneva***.

[**1714** W. WAGSTAFFE *Let. fr. Bath* 27 By all Means, you must renounce Holland Geneva, and Brunswick Mum.] **1788** J. MAY *Jrnl. & Lett.* (1873) 26 A case-bottle..filled with Hollands, of which each of us took a sling. **1812** *Examiner* 23 Nov. 739/1 He..ordered a glass of Hollands and water. **1832** *Veg. Subst. Food* 53 The grain spirit.. known..as Hollands Geneva. **1862** *Chambers's Encycl.* IV. 755 The Dutch..call the Hollands-gin (which is their national spirit) *giniva*. **1894** CROCKETT *Raiders* (ed. 3) 138 A square bottle of Hollands.

'Hollantide, short for *All-hollantide*, All-hallowtide: see ALL-HALLOW(S.

1573 TUSSER *Husb.* xxi. (1878) 55 At Hallontide, slaughter time entereth in. **1580** R. HITCHCOCK *Politic Plat* in Arb. *Garner* II. 158 Continuing very good until Hollentide. **1607** MIDDLETON *Fam. of Love* IV. i, At what time wert thou bound, Club! at Guttide, Hollantide, or Candletide? **1731** SWIFT *Mem. Creichton* Wks. 1763 X. 195 The Hollantide after I arrived in Ireland. **1795** D. WALKER *Agric. Surv. Herts.* 28 From harvest to Hollandtide. **1870** *Dublin Even. Mail* 1 Nov., Great Hollantide Fair of Drogheda.

†**'hollbarowe.** *Obs.* [f. HOLL *a.* + BARROW *sb.*[3]] A barrow having a body of the form of a shallow box.

1453–4 *Durham MS. Hostill. Roll*, j Holl Barowe. **1480–1** *Durham MS. Cell. Roll*, Pro factura unius hollbarowe et ij stanebarowes, vj*d*.

holle, obs. form of HOLL, HULL, WHOLE.

†**'holleke.** *Obs.* [OE. *holléac*, f. *hol*, HOLL *a.* + *léac*, LEEK; cf. Ger. *hohllauch*.] A species of *Allium* or onion: according to 16th c. writers, the Chibol, Cibol, or Welsh onion, *Allium fistulosum*; earlier writers appear to apply it to the Scallion or Shallot (*A. ascalonicum*).

c **1000** *Voc.* in Wr.-Wülcker 270/29 *Duricorium*, holleac. **14..** *Nom.* Ibid. [710/28 *Hec hinnula*, a scalyone] 710/31 *Hec ascolonia*, a holleke. **1483** *Cath. Angl.* 187/2 An holleke, *hinula* [cf. John de Garlande (*c* 1225) *Dictionarius* (Wright *Vocab.* 136), inula Gallice dicitur *eschaloigne*]. **1548** TURNER *Names of Herbes* 25 s.v. *Cepa*, Hole leke. **1551** —— *Herbal* I. I ij b, Y^e herbe which is called of hym [Pliny] *cepa fissilis*.. is it that we call in englysh holleke, & the duche men call *Sere* or *Suer*, and in fresland *Suerley*. *Ibid.*, The onyons that we cal hollekes ar of this nature, that if one be set alone that their wil a greate sorte within a shorte space growe of that same roote. [**1611** COTGR., *Ciboule*, a Chiboll, or hollow Leeke.]

hollen, obs. form of HALLAN.

1674–91 RAY *N.C. Words* 135 The *Hollen*, is a wall about 2½ yards high, used in dwelling houses to secure the family from the blasts of wind, rushing in when the heck is open.

hollen, obs. f. HOLLIN, holly.

holler ('hɒlə(r)), *v. dial.* and *U.S.* Also **holer**, †**hollar**. [var. HOLLO *v.*] *intr.* To cry out loud, to shout; to complain. In a fight: to give up, to cry 'enough'. Also, to sing a 'holler' (see next). Occas. *trans.*

1699 in *Cal. Virginia State Papers* (1875) I. 67 We gott to the River side oppisett to the ffort, & theire hollerd & Immediately they answered. **1834** S. SMITH *Sel. Lett. J. Downing* 37 All hollering 'stooboy'. **1843** 'R. CARLTON' *New Purchase* I. xiv. 101 Provided you knew how 'to holler', within hearing of both. **1845** W. T. PORTER *Big Bear Arkansas* 41 Who hollered? Which gave up? **1852** *N. & Q.* 14 Feb. 148/2 The village boys..get some halfpence given them for their 'hollering'. **1859** *Atlantic Monthly* Aug. 239/2 Here is a boy that loves to..'holler' Fire! on slight evidence. **1883** BARING-GOULD *John Herring* I. i. 7 Cobbledick..said, 'If you holler, I'll smash your head'. **1898** C. M. YONGE *John Keble's Parishes* xv. 175 Curate. Have you heard the nightingale yet? Boy. Please, sir, I don't know how he hollers. Everything hollers, from a church bell to a mouse in a trap. **1901** MERWIN & WEBSTER *Calumet 'K'* viii. 155 I'll holler up to you, Max, when we're ready down below. **1904** 'No. 1500' *Life in Sing Sing* 249/2 *Hollar*, complain. **1926** J. BLACK *You can't Win* iv. 43 Holler before you're hurt; that's my motto. **1934** *Nat. Geographic* LXV. 624/2 Daybreak and sundown are favorite times for 'holerin''. It is an invariable accompaniment of driving the cattle home in the evening. **1936** J. A. & A. LOMAX *Negro Folk-Songs* II. iii. 113 He has hollered and moaned his troubles and his observations on the ways of the world. **1940** W. FAULKNER *Hamlet* IV. i. 343 And when I holler run, you run. You hear me? **1967** *Boston Globe* 30 Mar. 14/1 Everyone hollers about the damage to the children if the schools are shut one day because of a teacher-school committee disagreement. **1969** *Times* 22 July (Moon Report Suppl.) p. ii/3 When Colonel Aldrin jumped off the last step of the moon ladder..everyone in the Aldrin home was whooping and hollering. **1970** P. OLIVER *Savannah Syncopators* 66 (*caption*) Arthur Crudup 'hollers' with a high-pitched voice. **1973** J. THOMSON *Death Cap* xiii. 177 I'll holler you to come down.

holler ('hɒlə(r)), *sb.*[1] *dial.* and *U.S.* Also †**hollar**. [var. HOLLO *sb.*] = HOLLO *sb.*; also, a complaint, a cry of protest; *spec.* in the Southern States of America, a work-song.

1825 J. JENNINGS *Obs. Dial. W. Eng.*, Hollar. **1886** F. T. ELWORTHY *W. Somerset Word-Bk.* 346 *Holler*,..the cry given when the quarry is seen; the view-halloo. **1896** ADE *Artie* xvi. 147, I put up a holler right at the jump. **1901** 'J. FLYNT' *World of Graft* 133 Some gamblers were particularly loud in making their 'hollers', and threatened to bring about an investigation. **1908** J. M. SULLIVAN *Criminal Slang* 13 *Holler*, plaint of a victim. **1936** J. A. & A. LOMAX *Negro Folk-Songs* II. iii. 113 The holler is a way of singing—free, gliding from a sustained high note down to the lowest register. **1939** *Congress Rec.* 5 Aug. App. 3975/1 [Will Rogers] came across the American scene with..a hoot and a 'holler', and a laugh. **1940** J. W. WORK *Amer. Negro Songs* 34 Approaching his house or that of his sweetheart in the evening, or sometimes out of sheer lonesomeness, he would emit his 'holler'. *Ibid.* 35 In these 'hollers' the idiomatic material found in the blues is readily seen. **1956** M. STEARNS *Story of Jazz* (1957) i. 10 The street-cry and field-holler of the American Negro are earlier examples of the same tradition. **1958** P. GAMMOND *Decca Bk. Jazz* i. 20 Solo work-songs of field-hands..took the form of 'hollers' or 'arwhoolies'—long meandering cries that were half-sung thoughts and half yodels. **1959** R. CONDON *Manchurian Candidate* (1962) vii. 137 If you're ever around Wainwright, Alaska, you'll give me a holler. **1968** P. OLIVER *Screening Blues* 4 The more primitive examples of field cries, hollers and work songs, of children's game songs and unaccompanied blues were only heard on record in the rarest of instances.

holler ('hɒlə(r)), *sb.*[2] U.S. colloq. var. HOLLOW *sb.* 2.

1845 W. T. PORTER *Big Bear Arkansas* 151 [I] putt off emediately fur watur that I node waz klose down the holler. **1947** RANDOLPH & WILSON (*title*) Down in the holler: a gallery of Ozark folk speech. **1972** J. S. HALL *Sayings from Old Smoky* 8 Many of these stock boasts hinge on the steepness or wildness of the mountain country, the darkness of the 'hollers', even in midday, and the hardihood of the people.

Hollerith ('hɒlərɪθ). The name of Herman *Hollerith* (1860–1929), American inventor, used esp. *attrib.* in reference to the use of punched cards in accounting, statistics, etc. Hence as *sb.*, used *fig.* in reference to modern society viewed as a processing machine (see quot. 1957).

1890 *Jrnl. Franklin Inst.* XCIX. 306 The cost of compiling a census by the Hollerith system, would appear to be only one-third the cost of compiling the same census by the next best system. **1891** *Electrical Engineer* (U.S.) 11 Nov. 530/1 Not a little skill and judgment was necessary in perfecting the mechanical details of the Hollerith electric tabulating system. **1946** A. C. CLARKE in *Astounding Sci. Fiction* Sept. 24/1 That wonderful battery of almost human Hollerith analyzers. **1957** *London Mag.* June 61 The writer needs his partial disengagement from the social hollerith so as to free the one imcomparable tool that he can call his own. **1958** H. T. HIMMELWEIT et al. *Television & Child* 85 The number of Hollerith cards needed for each child. **1960** *Times* 31 Mar. 3/1 An internal Hollerith installation and external computing facilities are used extensively. **1970** *Computers & Humanities* V. 2 The first was the pre-computer phase of the 1950s, characterized by the use of Hollerith (IBM) cards and unit record equipment to sort and tally large bodies of information.

holli, holliche, obs. f. WHOLLY.

hollibut, obs. f. *holibut*, HALIBUT.

hollidam(e, -dome, obs. ff. HALIDOM.

hollie-, in comb. [= HOLY with shortened vowel: cf. *holiday*, etc.] In ***hollie point***, ***hollie stitch***: see quots.

1882 CAULFEILD & SAWARD *Dict. Needlework*, *Hollie Point*, a needle lace much worked in the Middle Ages. The word is a corruption of Holy Point and was used to denote Church Laces. *Ibid.*, *Hollie Stitch*, the Stitch used in making Hollie Point is a description of Buttonhole.

†**'holliglass.** *Obs.* Also 6 **holi-, holyglasse**. [A corruption of *howleglas*, *owliglasse*, OWLGLASS, f. Ger. *Eulenspiegel*.] An Owlglass, a buffoon.

1583 *Leg. Bp. St. Androis* 51 in *Satir. Poems Reform.* xlv, Now Holyglass, returning hame, To play the sophist thought no schame. **1596** BLAKE *Serm.* in G. Hickes *Spirit of Popery* (1680) 53 The Privy-Council were Holliglasses, Cormorants, and men of no Religion. *a* **1639** SPOTTISWOOD *Hist. Ch. Scotl.* VI. (1677) 425.

hollihocke, -oke, etc., obs. ff. HOLLYHOCK.

hollin, hollen ('hɒlɪn). Now *arch.* or *dial.* Forms: 1 holen, holeᵹn, 3–6 holin, -yn, 5 holing, holyng(e, 5–6 holyne, 6– hollen (6 holine, holene, hollynne, 7 hollyn, hollinge), 7–9 hollin. [OE. *holen*, *holeᵹn*, radically related to OHG. *hulis*, *huls*, Ger. and Du. *hulst* (also, from OHG., F. *houx*); the OE. form appears to be cognate with Welsh *celyn*, Corn. *celin*, Bret. *kelen*, Ir. *cuillean* holly.] = HOLLY. (Still a common form in Scotland.)

c **725** *Corpus Gloss.* 53 *Acrifolus*, holeᵹn. *c* **1000** ÆLFRIC *Gloss.* in Wr.-Wülcker 138/38 *Acrifolius*, holen. *c* **1325** *Gloss. W. de Biblesw.* in Wright *Voc.* 163 *La hous*, holyn.

c **1450** *Bk. Curtasye* 399 in *Babees Bk.* 311 þer browȝt schalle be a holyn kene, þat sett schalle be in erber grene. **1450** HOLLAND *Howlat* 48, I sawe ane Howlat..vndir ane holyne. **1501** *Presentm. Juries* in *Surtees Misc.* (1888) 30 Thomas Ternour..has pylled hollynnes in diverse places. *a* **1650** *Marr. Sir Gaw.* 55 in Furniv. *Percy Folio* I. 109 Betwixt an oke & a greene hollen. **1816** SCOTT *Antiq.* xxxiii, Make your merry men gather the thorn, and the brier, and the green hollin. **1858** KINGSLEY *Poems, Red King* 8, I saw thee lie under the hollins green.

b. *attrib.* and *Comb.* **hollin cock, hollin stick**: see quots.

c **1000** *Sax. Leechd.* II. 78 Wyl on wætere..holen rinde. *Ibid.* 356 ʒenim holen leafa. **13..** *Gaw. & Gr. Knt.* 206 In his on honde he hade a holyn bobbe. *c* **1325** *Gloss. W. de Biblesw.* in Wright *Voc.* 163 *La houce*, holin-tree. **1483** *Cath. Angl.* 187/2 An Holyn bery, *hussum.* **1560** ROLLAND *Crt. Venus* I. 88 His Spainȝe cloik was of the Holine hew. **1688** R. HOLME *Armoury* III. 349/2 Hollin Sticks used by Cordwainers, not that they are made of Hollin Wood, but a peculiar name so given them, with them they burnish and polish the upper Leather, and sides of the Sole Leather; also by the sharp ends they run Riggets, and score the Leather with what Devises they please. **1848** *Zoologist* VI. 2290 The missel thrush..a 'hollin cock'.

holliper, var. OLIVER[2].

† **'hollness, holness.** *Obs.* [f. HOLL *a.* + -NESS. Cf. HOWNESS.] Hollowness, cavity.

1483 *Cath. Angl.* 188/1 An Hollnes, *cauitas.* *c* **1490** *Promp. Parv.* 244/2 (MS. K) Holnes, *concavitas.*

hollo, hollow ('hɒlə), *int.* and *sb.* [Akin to *holla* and *hallo.*]

A. *int.* A call to excite attention, also a shout of encouragement or exultation: = HOLLA 2, 3.

1588 SHAKS. *Tit. A.* II. i. 25 Hollo, what storme is this? **1589** *Pappe w. Hatchet* C b, Hollow there, giue me the beard I wore yesterday. **1697** W. CLELAND *Poems, Hollow my Fancie* 79 Hollow my Fancie, hollow, Stay thou at home with me. **1710** *Acc. Last Distemp. T. Whigg* I. 10 Hollow, Hollow Boys, replied the staring Populace. **1761** STERNE *Tr. Shandy* VII. xiii, Hollo! Ho!—the whole world's asleep!—bring out the horses. **1796** SCOTT *William & Helen* i, Hollo! thou felon, follow here. **1815** *Savoyard* II. iii, Holo! there! (Enter Servant) Give me a goblet. **1885** BAILLIE-HAMILTON *Mr. Montenello* I. 176 Hollo! Thornton, is that you?

B. *sb.* A shout of *hollo!* a loud shout; *esp.* a cry in hunting; cf. HALLOO *sb.*, HALLOW *sb.*[2]

1598 TOFTE *Alba* (1880) 79 But when th' acquainted Hollow he doth heare..He leaues his flight, and backward turnes againe. **1670** *Caveat to Conventiclers* 4 He was no sooner seated, but he gave a lowd Hollow through the Air. **1697** tr. *C'tess D'Aunoy's Trav.* (1706) 9 They set forth lowder Hollows than before, and wished me a good Journey. **1798** COLERIDGE *Anc. Mar.* I. xviii, The Albatross..every day for food or play, Came to the Marinere's hollo! **1823** BYRON *Age Bronze* xiii, The hounds will gather to their huntsman's hollo.

attrib. **1766** GOLDSM. *Vic. W.* xxii, The deep-mouthed watch-dog, at hollow distance.

hollo, hollow ('hɒlə), **holla** ('hɒlə), *v.* Forms: 6–9 hollow, holla, 7–9 hollo, holloa (6 holow, 7 holo, holloe, 8 holloo. [Connected with HOLLA *int.*, HOLLO *int.*; also with HALLO *int.* and HALLOW *v.*[2]]

1. *intr.* To cry out loud, to shout, vociferate; to halloo. Cf. HOLLER *v.*

1542 BOORDE *Dyetary* xxxii. (1870) 295 Vocyferacyon, holowynge, cryeng. **1599** PORTER *Angry Wom. Abingd.* (Percy Soc.) 65 Why, hollow to me, and I will answere thee. **1642** FULLER *Holy & Prof. St.* II. xix. 122 'Tis madness to holloe in the ears of sleeping temptation. **1647** H. MORE *Song of Soul* II. App. lxvi, If one hollowed from highest Heaven aboven. **1654** H. L'ESTRANGE *Chas. I* (1655) 19 Houting and ho-lo-ing, not only to the disturbance of that duty, but scorn of our Religion. **1675** HOBBES *Odyss.* VI. 286 As far as one that Holla's heard can be. **1727** SWIFT *Gulliver* II. i, I was going to holla after them. **1737** FIELDING *Tumble Down Dick* iii. *Song*, Then to some hollow tree she flies, To hollow, hoot, and howl. **1748** F. SMITH *Voy. Disc.* I. 24 They Holloed at Times, as they approached. **1842** GEN. P. THOMPSON *Exerc.* I. 3 The more the boys holla'd [**1829** hallooed], and called out 'Whip behind'. **1865** KINGSLEY *Herew.* iii, Dont holla till you are out of the wood. **1885** BOMPAS *Life F. Buckland* 244 They all rushed after me shouting and holloing.

b. To call to the hounds in hunting.

1612 *Two Noble K.* II. ii, To our Theban hounds..No more now must we hollo. **1613** PURCHAS *Pilgrimage* (1614) 432 As we use here in England to hollow, whoope or shout at Houndes. **1674** N. COX *Gentl. Recreat.* I. (1677) 75 Blowing and hollowing until the Hounds are come in. **1735** SOMERVILLE *Chase* II. 63 He levels ev'ry Fence, Joins in the common Cry, and hollows loud. **1884** *Punch* 18 Oct., They hunted an' they hollo'd and they blew their horns also.

2. *trans.* **a.** with the thing shouted as object.

1593 SHAKS. *Rich. II*, IV. i. 54 As many lies As may be holloa'd in thy treacherous ear. **1596** —— *1 Hen. IV*, I. iii. 222 And in his eare, Ile holla Mortimer. **1654** GATAKER *Disc. Apol.* 85 The Independents may cry and hollow it up to the Pygmies on the tops of their Towres. **1701** ROWE *Amb. Step-Moth.* v. ii, I will pursue thee And hollow Vengeance in thy guilty Ears. **1788** V. KNOX *Winter Even.* xli. (R.), The hostlers..hollo to the three footmen..Who is it? who is it? **1855** BROWNING *Transcendentalism* 11 Speak prose and hollo it till Europe hears!

b. To call after (in hunting); to call or shout to.

1605 SHAKS. *Lear* III. i. 55 He that first lights on him, Holla the other. **1607** —— *Cor.* I. viii. 7 If I flye Martius, hollow me like a Hare. **1633** P. FLETCHER *Poet. Misc.* 59 Th' unlucky Parrat, and death-boding Owl..Hollow their mates.

3. With *adv.* **hollo away**, to drive away by holloing; **hollo in, off**, to call in or off (dogs, etc.) by shouting; **hollo out**, to shout out.

1602 *Narcissus* (1893) 478 Hollowe in the hind doggs. *a* **1621** BEAUM. & FL. *Thierry* II. ii, Let's to horse, And hollow in the troop. **1648** HERRICK *Hesper., Parson Beanes*, Six dayes he hollows so much breath away, That on the seaventh, he can nor preach, or pray. **1655** FULLER *Ch. Hist.* III. iv. §20 Such hounds are easier laid on, then either rated or hollowed off. **1683** KENNETT tr. *Erasm. on Folly* 111 They'l sometimes mutter their words inwardly and then of a sudden hollow them out. **1748** *Anson's Voy.* III. iii. 328 He hollowed out with great extasy, *The ship, the ship.*

Hence **'holloing** *vbl. sb.*; also *attrib.*

1596 SHAKS. *Merch. V.* v. i. 43 Leaue hollowing man, heere. **1601** HOLLAND *Pliny* I. 235 No voice, crie, hollaing and houting..affrighted this kind of fish. **1767** CARTERET in *Phil. Trans.* LX. 21 With a great hollowing noise. **1860** GEN. P. THOMPSON *Audi Alt.* III. cxix. 61 War, after all, is not settled by hollaing, any more than horse-racing.

holloa (hɒ'ləʊ), *int.*, *sb.*, *v.* A form of HOLLO leading on to HALLOA, q.v.

A. *int.* (See quots.)

[**1726** G. ROBERTS *Four Years Voy.* 30 So I answer'd him, Ho lo.] **1769** FALCONER *Dict. Marine, Holloa*,..an exclamation of answer, to any person, who calls to another to ask some question, or to give a particular order..The master..calls, Main-top, hoay! To which they answer, Holloa! **1866** CRAVEN *Meg's Diversion* II. 40 Holloa! Meg, frolicksome Meg, here! **1867** SMYTH *Sailor's Word-bk., Holloa*, or *holla*, an answer to any person calling from a distance, to show they hear. **1883** MRS. OLIPHANT *Ladies Lindores* I. 247 'Holloa!' he cried, 'Gone, are they!'

B. *sb.* A shout of 'holloa!'

1749 FIELDING *Tom Jones* VII. iii, The same holloa which attends the departure of a hare, when she is first started. **1861** HUGHES *Tom Brown at Oxf.* vi, It was an uncommon bad night for running by holloas.

C. *vb.* To call 'holloa!'; to shout so as to call attention, express surprise, etc.

1666 BUNYAN *Grace Ab.* ¶ 173 Then would the text cry..as if it did holloa after me. **1858** R. S. SURTEES *Ask Mamma* lxiv. 287 He holloaed out to the grooms. **1885** *Badm. Libr., Hunting* 144 The result of holloaing immediately a fox has crossed a ride often is to make him pop back again.

† **hollock.** *Obs.* Also **hallocke, hullock, -ok.** [a. Sp. *aloque* (in Minsheu *haloque*) adj., light red, sb., a species of wine of fine red colour, a. Arab. *ḥalūqi*, adj. from *ḥalūq*, an aromatic of clear red colour (Dozy). (Notwithstanding the identification by Florio, it is not related to It. *aigleuco*, L. *aigleucos*, Pliny.)] A Spanish wine of a fine red colour.

1576 GASCOIGNE *Diet Droonkardes* (1789) 18 We must have..Sack, Hollocke, Canaria wine. **1598** in *Aberdeen Burgh Rec.* (1844–8) II. 176 Thrie quartis of the best wyne, tovit, hullok, and wyne tent. **1599** MINSHEU *Span. Dial.* 18/2 Wines..Hallocke, claret, candie. **1611** FLORIO, *Aigléuco vino*, sweet hollocke wine. **1620** J. TAYLOR (Water P.) *Praise Hempseed* Wks. (1630) 65 Hollock and Tent would be of small repute. **1660** *Act 12 Chas. II*, c. 4 *Sched.*, Sackes, Canaryes, Malegaes, Maderaes, Romneys, Hollocks, Bastards, Tents & Allicants.

hollocore, obs. form of HALALCOR.

holloo, var. of HALLOO *int.* and *v.*

1671 EACHARD *Obs. Answ. Cont. Clergy* (1705) 4 Claps his Hands, and cries. Holloo to the Armies that are drawing up. **1709** STEELE *Tatler* No. 19 ¶ 2 To all that ride mad after Foxes, that holloo when they see an hare. **1735** SWIFT *Legion Club* 67 At the parsons, Tom, holloo, boy.

hollop, a sailor's corruption of ORLOP.

1751 SMOLLETT *Per. Pic.* lxxxvi, Several feet of underwater logging in her hold and hollop.

hollow ('hɒləʊ), *sb.* Forms: 1–2 holh, 3 holȝ, 6– holow, hollow. [OE. *holh* (cf. OHG. *huliwa, hulwa*, MHG. *hülwe*, pool, puddle, slough):—OTeut. **holhwo-*, app. radically related to OE. *hol*, HOLL *a.*, HOLE *sb.*, and *holc*, HOLK, cavity; but the nature of the formation is obscure. As shown under HOLE *sb.* (q.v.), *hollow* represents an inflexion of *holh*, **holw-e*, **holw-es*, etc., whence ME. *holwe, holewe, holowe*, while the inflexional type **hol-e*, **hol-es*, etc., fell together with HOLE *sb.*

OE. *holh* was only sb.; it was perh. from association with *hol*, which was both adj. and sb., that *holh* was also made an adj. in early ME.: see next word. But the history is peculiar, for while the sb. came down to 1205, in ME. only the adjective occurs; the sb. reappears *c* 1550, app. formed anew from the adj.; from which time both sb. and adj. have been in common use.]

1. A hollow or concave formation or place, which has been dug out, or has the form of having so been: †**a.** a hole, cave, den, burrow (*obs.*); †**b.** a hole running through the length or thickness of anything; a bore (*obs.*); **c.** a surface concavity, more or less deep, an excavation, a depression on any surface; **d.** an internal cavity (with or without an orifice); a void space; **e.** (see quot. 1940).

c **897** K. ÆLFRED *Gregory's Past.* xxxiii. 218 Holh wæs beboden ðæt sceolde beon on ðæm weobude uppan, forðæm ðæt wind ne meahte ða lac tostencean. *Ibid.* xxxv. 240 Ðær se iil hæfde his holh. *c* **1175** *Lamb. Hom.* 23 þah an castel beo wel bemoned mid monne and mid wepne, and þer beo analpi holh þat an mon mei crepan in. *c* **1205** LAY. 20848 [The fox] holȝes [*c* **1275** holes] him wurcheð.

β. *In modern English.*

1560 BIBLE (Genev.) *Gen.* xxxii. 25 He touched yͤ holow of his thigh, and the holow of Iaakobs thigh was losed. **1592** SHAKS. *Rom. & Jul.* III. v. 3 It was the Nightingale, and not the Larke, That pier'st the fearefull hollow of thine eare. **1605** —— *Lear* II. iii. 2 By the happy hollow of a Tree. **1611** BIBLE *Isa.* xl. 12 Who hath measured the waters in the hollow of his hand? **1613** PURCHAS *Pilgrimage* (1614) 774 The first Indians..had one, and some both of their teats bored thorow, in the hollow wherof..they wear a Reed. **1658** A. FOX *Wurtz' Surg.* III. viii. 240 If congealed bloud be in the body, and that within the hollow of it. **1687** A. LOVELL tr. *Thevenot's Trav.* I. 165 We rested in the hollow of a Rock, where we spent the Night. **1691** RAY *Creation* II. (1692) 62 The hollow of the Bones..serves to contain the Marrow. **1703** MOXON *Mech. Exerc.* 218 An Hollow on the Tooth [of a tool] makes a Round upon the Work; and a Round upon the Tooth, makes an Hollow on the Work. **1707** *Curios. in Husb. & Gard.* 253 A like Iron Pipe, whose hollow were very small. *c* **1850** *Rudim. Navig.* (Weale) 124 Sometimes the back sweep which forms the upper part of the top-timber is called the *top-timber hollow.* **1867** SMYTH *Sailor's Word-bk., Hollow*, the bore of a rocket. **1875** KNIGHT *Dict. Mech., Hollow*..the empty portion of a bastion... The depression in an anvil-face or fullering. **1884** A. R. PENNINGTON *Wiclif* ix. 296 Such places as the hollow of an oak. **1884** BOWER & SCOTT *De Bary's Phaner.* 201 Completely closed hollows or cavities. **1885** J. G. HORNER *Pattern Making* iii. 26 Many of the best wheels are made with hollows at the roots of the teeth, for here the action of leverage on the tooth induces the greatest stress. **1924** J. McC. WILSON *Pattern-Making* iv. 28 In finishing the pattern all the angled corners are filled in either with Angled or Hollowed Fillets... Hollows are used in well-finished work. **1940** *Chambers's Techn. Dict.* 418/2 *Hollows*, fillets, or curves of small radius, uniting two surfaces intersecting at an angle.

fig. **1853** ROBERTSON *Serm.* Ser. III. xxi. 271 The empty hollow of an unsatisfied heart.

2. *spec.* A depression on the earth's surface; a place or tract below the general level or surrounded by heights; a valley, a basin.

1553 BRENDE *Q. Curtius* 170 All the holowes and valeys there about rebounding with the voice of so many thousandes. **1601** HOLLAND *Pliny* I. 96 Within the inner compasse and hollow of Africke. **1649** *Providence* (R.I.) *Rec.* (1893) II. 9 His 6 acre Lot..runneth all along on the brow or top of that Hollow. **1725** DE FOE *Voy. round World* (1840) 258 A very narrow but deep hollow. **1846** H. BECKELY *Hist. Vermont* 55 The vallies and hollows interspersed among the mountains and hills are generally very fertile. **1878** HUXLEY *Physiogr.* 16 The river then does really occupy a hollow, inclosed on three sides by high ground. **1885** MISS THACKERAY *Mrs. Dymond* 18 Can you make out the sea, Susy? Look, there it is shining in the hollow.

3. The middle or depth (of night or of winter): = Sc. *howe.*

1865 CARLYLE *Fredk. Gt.* XV. ix. VI. 62 These were Friedrich's last general orders, given in the hollow of the night.

4. Short for *hollow meat, hollow moulding, hollow plane, hollow square*: see HOLLOW *a.* 7.

1726 NEVE *Builder's Dict., Hollow*, a Term in Architecture, by which is meant a Concave Molding, being about a Quadrant of a Circle; by some it is called a *Casement*, by others an *Abacus.* **1764** FOOTE *Mayor of G.* I. (1783) 13, I learnt to form lines, and hollows, and squares. **1823** EGAN *Grose's Dict. Vulg. T., Hollow*, among epicures, means poultry. Nothing but hollow for dinner. **1850** HOLTZAPPFFEL *Turning* II. 492 Concave and convex planes, called *hollows* and *rounds.*

5. *Bookbinding.* A strip of thick paper or pasteboard, cut to the height and thickness of the book for which the boards and cloth are intended, and which acts as a gauge for the guidance of the case-makers and as a stiffener for the cloth at the back of the book (*Ure's Dict. Arts* (1875) I. 421).

hollow ('hɒləʊ), *a.* and *adv.* Forms: 3 holh, holeh, holeuh, holu, 3–4 holȝ, holewe, 3–5 holw(e, 4 holou, -ouȝ, -ough, 4–5 holowȝ, 4–6 holow(e, 5 holgh, holuȝe, 6 hollowe, 6– hollow. [ME. *holȝ, holeh*, also *holu*, inflected *holwe, holewe*, identical in form with *holh, holȝ*, pl. *holȝes, holwes* sb.: see prec. The development of *-lw(e, -low* from *-lȝe, -lȝ*, is normal: cf. *follow, hallow, sallow*, etc.]

A. *adj.*

1. a. Having a hole or cavity inside; having an empty space in the interior; opp. to *solid.*

a **1250** *Owl & Night.* 1113 An holȝ [*v.r.* holeh] stoc hwar þu þe miht hude. *c* **1290** *S. Eng. Leg.* I. 202/96 In one holewe weie onder eorþe. **1297** R. GLOUC. (1724) 251 And made kynges fourme of bras al holu wyþinne. **13..** *Gaw. & Gr. Knt.* 2182 Al watz holȝ in-with, no-bot an olde caue. *c* **1350** *Will. Palerne* 295 Vnder an holw ok. **1387** TREVISA *Higden* (Rolls) III. 395 A ȝerde of fir holowȝ wiþ ynne as a pipe. **1398** —— *Barth. De P.R.* VIII. xxi. (1495) The sterres ben rounde..and ben sadde and sounde, not holough nother hooly in the vtter party. **1530** PALSGR. 232/1 Holowe spere, *bovrdon.* **1577** B. GOOGE *Heresbach's Husb.* IV. (1586) 190 b, The juice thrust into a hollow tooth, asswageth the paine. **1613** PURCHAS *Pilgrimage* (1614) 567 This was hollow, the other solid. *Ibid.* 833 Blow it thorow hollow canes. **1674** tr. *Scheffer's Lapland* 84 In trunks of trees made hollow either by fire or age. **1748** *Anson's Voy.* I. iii. 30 Orellana placed his hands hollow to his mouth, and bellowed out the war-cry used by those savages. **1817** J. BRADBURY *Trav. Amer.* 286 *note*, Although many species of trees are liable to become hollow, yet none are so perfectly hollowed as the gum tree. [**1848** LOWELL *Biglow P.* Ser. I. IV. 15 A marciful Providunce fashioned us holler, O' purpose thet we might our principles swaller.]

b. Having an empty or vacant space beneath.

1657 R. LIGON *Barbadoes* (1673) 43, I would raise my foundation..three foot above ground; leaving it hollow underneath for Ventiducts. **1687** A. LOVELL tr. *Thevenot's Trav.* I. 124 Alexandria is all hollow under, being an entire Cistern. **1703** T. N. *City & C. Purchaser* 136 They..dry and season their Boards..laying them..hollow for the Air to play between them. **1860** TYNDALL *Glac.* I. iii. 28 The floor..was snow, which I knew to be hollow beneath.

†**c.** Porous or open in texture or composition: the opposite of close, compact, or solid. *Obs.*

1398 TREVISA *Barth. De P.R.* III. xx. (1495) The tonge towchinge the complexion of the substaunce therof is holowe and full of holes. **1733** J. TULL *Horse-Hoeing Husb.* vi. 24 Roots and Plants, which otherwise require the lightest and hollowest Mould. *Ibid., note*, 'Tis easier..to imitate this Artificial Dust in hollow than in strong Land.

2. a. Having a hole, depression, or groove on the surface; depressed below the surrounding surface, sunken, indented; excavated, concave.

c **1205** LAY. 761 Wes þe wei holh & long. *a* **1250** *Owl & Night.* 643 Mi nest is holȝ [*v.r.* holeuh]. *a* **1385** CHAUCER *L.G.W.* 2193 *Ariadne*, The holwe rokkis answerden hire a-gayn. *c* **1440** *Promp. Parv.* 242/2 Holow, as vessellys ..*concavus.* **1577** B. GOOGE *Heresbach's Husb.* I. (1586) 44 Then must the grounde neither lye hollowe, nor in hilles. **1674** tr. *Scheffer's Lapland* 8 The snows..continue undissolv'd in hollow places between the hills. **1703** MOXON *Mech. Exerc.* 150 If any part of the Floor prove hollow, they lay a Chip..upon that hollow place, to bare up the Board. *Ibid.* 187 The hollow edge of the Hook. **1854** HAWTHORNE *Eng. Note-Bks.* (1879) I. 151 Our way to it was up a hollow lane.

b. Of the eyes, cheeks, etc.

13.. *E.E. Allit. P.* B. 1695 Holȝe were his yȝen. **1509** HAWES *Past. Pleas.* XXIX. (Percy) 135 Hys eyen holow, and his nose croked. **1577** B. GOOGE *Heresbach's Husb.* III. (1586) 117 A horse when he beginnes to be olde, his temples waxe hollowe. **1726** *Adv. Capt. R. Boyle* 114 With hollow Cheeks, and Eyes black. **1858** MRS. CARLYLE *Lett.* II. 358 Bess..was rather thinner, and her eyes hollower. **1873** LONGF. *Challenge* ix, Hollow and haggard faces Look into the lighted hall.

c. Of the sea: Having the troughs between the crests of the waves very deep.

1726 G. ROBERTS *4 Years Voy.* 19 With a very hard Gale of Wind..and a very deep hollow Sea. **1748** *Anson's Voy.* I. x. 104 The ship laboured very much in a hollow sea. **1805** *Naval Chron.* XIII. 469 The sea was running very hollow. **1867** SMYTH *Sailor's Word-bk., Hollow Sea*, the undulation of the waves after a gale; long hollow-jawed sea; ground-swell.

3. Empty, vacant, void; hence, having an empty stomach, hungry; lean, starved-looking.

1362 LANGL. *P. Pl.* A. v. 108 So hungri and so holewe. *c* **1386** CHAUCER *Prol.* 289 He nas nat right fat, I vndertake, But looked holwe and ther to sobrely. *c* **1460** *Towneley Myst.* ii. 310, I will fayre on feld ther oure bestis ar, To looke if thay be holgh or full. **1597** SHAKS. *2 Hen. IV*, I. iii. 75 His Coffers sound With hollow Pouerty, and Emptinesse. **1598** —— *Merry W.* IV. ii. 171 As iealous as Ford, that search'd a hollow Wall-nut for his wiues Lemman. **1858** CARLYLE *Fredk. Gt.* IV. ii. I. 392 That also is gone; and the hollow Eternities have swallowed it. **1878** B. TAYLOR *Deukalion* I. i. 21 The strains dissolve into the hollow air. *Mod.* It must be getting towards dinner-time; I'm feeling pretty hollow.

4. *transf.* Of sound: Wanting body; not full-toned; 'sepulchral'.

1563 SACKVILLE in *Mirr. Mag., Induct.* xliv, With broken and hollow playnt. **1583** EARL NORTHAMPTON *Defensative* Ep. Ded., Like young babies, they regarde... Rattles that can make a kind of hollow sound. **1633** T. JAMES *Voy.* 8 It made a hollow..noyse, like an ouer-fall of water. **1798** W. NARES in *Anti-Jacobin* xxii. (1852) 106 My voice as hollow as a ghost's. **1881** BROADHOUSE *Mus. Acoustics* 175 If only the uneven partials are present..the quality of tone is hollow. **1887** BOWEN *Virg. Æneid* II. 546 On the brass of the buckler it smote with a hollow ring.

5. *fig.* Of persons and things: Wanting soundness, solidity, or substance; empty, vain; not answering inwardly to outward appearance; insincere, false.

a **1529** SKELTON *Sp. Parrot* 595 So many holow hartes, and so dowbyll faces. **1579** LYLY *Euphues* (Arb.) 113 Too holy a profession, for so hollow a person. **1593** SHAKS. *2 Hen. VI*, III. ii. 66 It is knowne we were but hollow Friends. **1593** —— *Rich. II*, I. iv. 9. **1655** FULLER *Ch. Hist.* IV. iv. §14 The Kings Army was hollow at the heart. **1769** *Junius Lett.* xxix. 131 A false or hollow friendship. **1781** GIBBON *Decl. & F.* II. xlii. 562 Flattering and hollow words. **1832** LANDER *Adv. Niger* I. v. 209 The governor's pretensions are as hollow as they are improbable. **1855** MOTLEY *Dutch Rep.* V. iii. (1866) 696 The hollow truce with the Huguenots in France had.. been again succeeded by war.

6. [f. the adv.: cf. B. 2.] Complete, thorough, out-and-out. *colloq.*

1750 COVENTRY *Pompey Litt.* I. xvi. (1785) 41/1 It was quite a *hollow thing*; Goliah won the day. **1761** COLMAN *Jealous Wife* v. (D.), So, my lord, you and I are both distanced; a hollow thing, damme. **1852** DICKENS *Bleak Ho.* lxiv, Which, in the opinion of my friends, is a hollow bargain. **1894** *Times* 31 July 11/1 The Prince's cutter steadily left her opponent and gained a very hollow victory.

7. In various collocations, chiefly technical: ***hollow block, tile***; **hollow-adz, -auger**, tools with concave instead of flat face, for curved work (Knight *Dict. Mech.*); **hollow-bastion** (see quot.); **hollow fire** (see quot.); **hollow fowl, meat**, 'poultry, rabbits, etc., any meat not sold by butchers' (Halliwell); **hollow heart**, a disease of potatoes in which a cavity is formed in the centre of the tuber; **hollow-horn** *U.S.* (see quot. 1962); **hollow roll**: see ROLL *sb.*¹ 11 b; **hollow spar** [tr. Ger. *hohlspat*], a name for CHIASTOLITE (Ure *Dict. Chem.* 1823); **hollow-stock**, name of the plants *Leonotis nepetæfolia* and *Malvastrum spicatum* (Cent. Dict.); **hollow tower** (see quot.); **hollow-turner**, a mechanic who turns hollow or concave vessels, funnels, etc.; hence ***hollow-turnery***; †**hollow vein**, the *vena cava*; **hollow wall** = *cavity wall* (CAVITY 4); **hollow-way**, a way, road, or path, through a defile or cutting; also extended, as in quot. 1882. HOLLOW MONTH, MOULD, PLANE, SQUARE, -WARE: see these words.

1706 PHILLIPS (ed. Kersey) s.v. *Bastion*, **Hollow* or *Voided Bastion*, is that which has only a Rampart and a Parapet, ranging about its Flanks and Faces, so that a void Space is left towards the Center or Middle. **1964** J. S. SCOTT *Dict. Building* 167 **Hollow blocks* or *hollow tiles.* Concrete or burnt clay hollow building blocks are used for making partitions or external walls, or for forming reinforced concrete hollow-tile floors. Lightweight, thermally-insulating, hollow blocks are also made of foamed slag concrete, diatomite, gypsum, etc. **1881** RAYMOND *Mining Gloss.*, **Hollow-fire*, a kind of hearth with blast, used for reheating the stamps produced in the South Welsh process of fining, or the bars of blister-steel in the manufacture of shear-steel. **1885** T. MOZLEY *Remin. Towns*, etc. I. 89 People had then to be content with '*hollow fowl', as poultry, ducks, and rabbits were alike called. **1926** F. D. HEALD *Man. Plant Dis.* v. 94 *Hollow heart is most frequent in potatoes which have been stimulated to an excessive growth by abundant moisture. **1951** *Dict. Gardening* (R. Hort. Soc.) III. 1655/1 Hollow Heart is usually due to the tubers experiencing a dry period in which they mature and lose water so that when the rain comes the quick growth causes the inner tissues to split apart. **1805** R. PARKINSON *Tour Amer.* 87 There were a few half-starved cattle; in general standing shaking with cold, and many more complaining of what they call the *hollow-horn. **1825** J. LORAIN *Pract. Husb.* 455 The hollow horn, a disease which seldom fails to attack half-famished cattle. **1868** *Rep. Iowa Agric. Soc. 1867* 129 Cattle have few diseases in this locality except the 'buck eye' and 'hollow horn'. **1962** J. N. WINBURNE *Dict. Agric.* 382/1 *Hollow horn*, an imaginary disease arising from the erroneous belief that loss of appetite and listlessness in a cow was due to hollow horns. The remedy was supposed to be (a) boring a hole in each horn ..(b) filling the cavity with salt, sugar, and pepper, and (c) plugging the hole with a wooden peg. The belief was that if the cow had hollow horn this remedy would cure her, and if she did not have hollow horn, the remedy would prevent her getting it. **1828** *Craven Dial.*, **Hollow meat*, fowls. **1914** *Archit. Rec.* Feb. 142/2 Terra cotta *hollow tile was employed in the exterior and interior bearing walls. *Ibid.* 144/2 The floor construction used was the combination system of hollow tile and reinforced concrete. **1936** *Archit. Rev.* LXXX. 144/1 Floors and roofs throughout are hollow tile and concrete, and internal walls in the ward block are of hollow partition blocks. **1706** PHILLIPS (ed. Kersey) s.v. *Tower*, **Hollow Tower* (in *Fortif.*), a Rounding made of the remainder of two Brisures, to joyn the Courtin to the Orillon; where the Small-Shot are plac'd that they may not be too much expos'd to the Enemies View. **1887** T. HARDY *Woodlanders* II. 243 Peeping out she saw..the *hollow-turner..loading his wares—wooden bowls, dishes, spigots, spoons, cheese-vats, funnels and so on. *Ibid.* I. 56 A neighbour engaged in the *hollow-turnery trade. **1591** SYLVESTER *Du Bartas* I. vi. 719 Through branching pipes of the great *Hollow-vein. **1625** HART *Anat. Ur.* II. viii. 105 Through the mesaraicke veines into the great porter veine, and from thence into the great hollow veine. **1823** *New Pract. Builder & Workman's Compan.* 586/2 **Hollow-wall*, a wall built in two thicknesses, leaving a cavity between, which may be either for saving materials or for preserving an uniform temperature in apartments. **1891** *Notes on Building Construction* II. 10 The hollow wall is often arranged to begin on the damp-proof course. **1942** J. A. MULLIGAN *Handbk. Brick Masonry Construction* 362 The building code of the City of New York uses the term 'hollow wall' instead of cavity wall. **1761** STERNE *Tr. Shandy* (1802) III. 147 Acquainted intimately with every country..the..roads, and *hollow-ways which lead up to them. **1882** D. GARDNER *Quatre Bras*, etc. 182 *note*, The term 'hollow-way' is employed by English writers on this battle [Waterloo]..to designate any means of passage, from a footpath to a boulevard, which is enclosed on the sides to a considerable height, whether by walls, fences, hedges, houses, or embankments.

8. *Comb.* (parasynthetic), as ***hollow-backed, -billed, -cheeked, -chested, -footed, -horned, -jawed, -toned, -vaulted, -voiced*** adjs. **hollow-fronted, -nosed, -pointed** *adjs.*, said of a bullet with a hollow in the point to ensure expansion of the projectile on impact. Also HOLLOW-EYED, -HEARTED.

1523 FITZHERB. *Husb.* §78 The nyne propertyes of an asse ..the .vii. to be rounde foted, the .viii. to be holowe foted. **1598** FLORIO *Worlde of Wordes* 273/1 *Pettoruto*,..that is hollow chested. **1603** J. DAVIES *Microcosm.* Wks. 1878 I. 17/2 Breath'd out with grones, like hollow-voiced windes. **1791** COWPER *Yardley Oak* 4 A shattered veteran, hollow-trunked perhaps. **1831** YOUATT *Horse* 31 (U.K.S.) Some persons prefer a hollow-backed horse. **1851** H. MELVILLE *Moby Dick* III. xlv. 255 'Look!' replied the hollow-cheeked captain from his taffrail. **1854** OWEN *Skel. & Teeth* in *Circ. Sc., Organ. Nat.* I. 239 The ruminants.. called hollow-horned. **1886** W. B. YEATS *Mosada* 6 Bright-eyed, and hollow-cheeked From fasting. **1899** *Kynoch Jrnl.* Oct.–Nov. 14/2 If the ·577 pure lead hollow-fronted bullet hit a man he knew it at once. **1902** *Encycl. Brit.* XXXII. 244/1 The hollow-pointed expanding bullet with soft lead nose. **1902–3** *Kynoch Jrnl.* Dec.–Jan. 43/1 Without the mutilation so commonly caused by hollow pointed bullets. **1909** *Daily Chron.* 26 June 1/4 The other cartridges..being of nickle steel and hollow-nosed. **1920** G. BURRARD *Notes on Sporting Rifles* 40 A hollow-nosed bullet. **1963** V. NABOKOV *Gift* iv. 240 He listened to these hollow-chested verses.

B. *adv.*

1. In a hollow manner; with a hollow sound or voice; insincerely. *Obs.* exc. in comb. (see 3).

1601 SHAKS. *Twel. N.* III. iv. 101 Lo, how hollow the fiend speakes within him. **1607** TOPSELL *Four-f. Beasts* (1658) 291 Then he will cough more hollow.

2. Thoroughly, completely, out-and-out; also (*U.S.*) ***all hollow.*** *colloq.*

[The origin of this is obscure, and has excited conjecture from its first appearance in literature.]

1668–71 SKINNER *Etymol. Ling. Angl.* s.v., He carried it Hollow, *Luculenter Vicit vel Superavit*,..credo dictum quasi 'he carried it *wholy*'. **1762** FOOTE *Orators* I. Wks. 1799 I. 193 *Foote...* You succeeded? *Suds...* Yes, yes, I got it all hollow. **1767** CHESTERF. *Lett.* (1794) IV. cccxxi. 267 He set up for the County of Middlesex, and carried it hollow, as the jockeys say. **1786** WOLCOTT (P. Pindar) *Farew. Odes* xiv. Wks. 1794 I. 185 I'm greatly pleas'd..To see the foreigners beat hollow. **1824** W. IRVING *T. Trav.* II. 39 Her blood carried it all hollow. **1839** *Times* 19 Oct., In the article of hypocrisy..as in sheer impudence, Minto has it hollow. **1851** J. H. NEWMAN *Cath. in Eng.* 367 Local opinion would carry it hollow against popular opinion. **1859** GEO. ELIOT *A. Bede* 47 She beats us younger people hollow.

3. In Comb., qualifying ppl. adjs., to which *hollow* is hyphened; mostly in sense 'with a hollow sound', as ***hollow-bellowing, -blustering, -ringing, -sounding, -whispering***, etc.; also 'with a hollow foundation', as ***hollow-grounded***; **hollow-ground** *a.*, ground so as to have a concave surface; so ***hollow-grinding***.

1611 SYLVESTER *Du Bartas* II. iv. v. *Decay* 537 O feeble stay! O hollow grounded hope! **1726–46** THOMSON *Winter* 737 The hollow-sounding plain Shakes from afar. *Ibid.* 989 Muttering, the winds..Blow hollow-blust'ring from the south. **1728–46** —— *Spring* 918 The hollow-whispering breeze, the plaint of rills. **1864** TENNYSON *En. Ard.* 599 The hollower-bellowing ocean. **1885** *Army & Navy Co-op. Soc. Price List* 1048 The guaranteed razors. Cases containing 2 Hollow Ground. **1937** R. W. FAIRBROTHER *Text-bk. Med. Bacteriol.* ii. 10 In carrying out the examination by direct microscopy use is made of the hollow-ground slide, which is a slide with a hollow of approximately ½ in. ground out on one surface. **1951** R. H. HORDERN *Woodworking Industry Managem.* iv. 72 (*heading*) Hollow-grinding machine. *Ibid.* 73 This..will produce a hollow-ground bevel on the cutter. There are a number of reasons why hollow grinding is preferable to straight. **1968** *Gloss. Terms Mechanized & Hand Sheet Metal Work (B.S.I.)* 12 *Hollow grinding*, a method of grinding a tool to produce a concave face or faces behind a cutting edge.

hollow ('hɒləʊ), *v.*¹ [f. HOLLOW *a.*]

1. *trans.* To render hollow or concave; to make a hollow in; to excavate. Also with *out.*

c **1450** *R. Gloucester's Chron.* (1724) 415/1 *note* (MS. Coll. Arms) Suche a stroke cam doune..that hit holwed the stonene walle to a mannes gretnesse. *c* **1477** CAXTON *Jason* 20 b, How well the stone is myned and hollowed by continuell droppyng of water. **1577** B. GOOGE *Heresbach's Husb.* II. (1586) 55 b, Hollowing it cunninglie with an Aulle or a Bodking. **1727** *Philip Quarll* (1816) 46 A rock hollowed out like the entrance to a church. **1784** COWPER *Task* VI. 311 Some lonely elm That age or injury has hollowed deep. **1860** TYNDALL *Glaciers* I. xviii. 125 The wall of one [fissure].. was hollowed out longitudinally.

fig. **1842** TENNYSON *Love & Duty* 60 The want that hollow'd all the heart.

b. To bend into a hollow or concave shape.

1598 B. JONSON *Ev. Man in Hum.* I. iv, Hollow your body more sir, thus. **1832** TENNYSON *Pal. of Art* 109 Hollowing one hand against his ear, To list a foot-fall. **1889** *Macm. Mag.* Aug. 246/2, I hollowed my hands into the form of a binocular glass.

2. To form by making a hollow (*in* something); to excavate. Often with *out.*

1648 HERRICK *Hesper., The Cruell Maid*, Next, hollow out a tomb to cover Me. **1687** A. LOVELL tr. *Thevenot's Trav.* II. 19 Who led us into a Grotto hollowed in the Rock. **1796** H. HUNTER tr. *St. Pierre's Stud. Nat.* (1799) III. 338 Amphitrite..intreated the Nereids to hollow out that little bay. **1817** C. WOLFE *Burial Sir J. Moore* v, As we hollowed his narrow bed, And smoothed down his lonely pillow.

3. To make hollow in tone.

1772 NUGENT tr. *Hist. Fr. Gerund* I. 96 Hollowing his voice, and snuffling with much sedate confidence.

4. *intr.* To become hollow or concave.

c **1860** FABER *Hymn, The Length of Death* viii, How suddenly earth seems to hollow. **1892** *Harper's Mag.* 280/2 Her cheeks seemed to hollow in, and her chin shook.

Hence **hollowed** ('hɒləʊd), *ppl. a.*, made hollow, excavated; '**hollowing** *vbl. sb.*, a making hollow, excavation; also *attrib.*, as in ***hollowing-iron, -knife, -machine***, etc.

1607 MARKHAM *Caval.* VI. (1617) 64 Make it by a little hollowing to bear..from the false quarter. **1613** PURCHAS *Pilgrimage* (1614) 643 In boats made of a hollowed tree (like the Indian Canoas). **1641** in T. Lechford *Note-bk.* (1885) 428 One hollowing iron..one rabbetting iron. **1697** DRYDEN *Virg. Georg.* I. 207 Then first on Seas the hollow'd Alder swam. **1714** ADDISON *Spectator* No. 584 ¶6 The digging of Trenches, and the hollowing of Trees, for the better Distribution of Water. **1875** KNIGHT *Dict. Mech.*, *Hollowing-knife* (Coopering), a drawing-knife for working on concave surfaces. **1876** *Clin. Soc. Trans.* IX. 191 When the child was made to bend the body, this lumbar hollowing did not disappear. **1884** J. PAYN *Lit. Recoll.* 217 His hollowed hand and smiling attentive face. **1889** *Daily News* 12 Oct. 2/1 Wooden pipes and hollowed trunks of trees.

hollow, *v.*²: see HOLLO *v.*

holloware, var. HOLLOW-WARE.

Holloway ('hɒləʊweɪ). [f. the name of Thomas *Holloway* (1800–83), their inventor and manufacturer.] ***Holloway's pill***, a patent

medicine used principally for laxative purposes. Also *Holloway's ointment*.

1838 *Town* 16 June 440/1 (Advt.), Holloway's universal family ointment... Holloway's external disease pill. **1849** E. RUSKIN *Let.* 8 Nov. in M. Lutyens *Effie in Venice* (1965) I. 59, I get..a Holloway's Pill when I require such medicine. **1877** E. S. DALLAS *Kettner's Bk. of Table* 432 This is.. suggestive of the African tribes mentioned by Sir Samuel Baker, who believed in Holloway's Pills because of their rapid and irrepressible results. **1885** *Trade Marks Jrnl.* 18 Nov. 1084 Holloway's Pills... The firm trading as Thomas Holloway,..London; patent medicine vendors... Pills for human use. *Ibid.*, Holloway's Ointment... The firm trading as Thomas Holloway,..London; patent medicine vendors. .. Ointment. **1939–40** *Army & Navy Stores Catal.* 396/1 Holloway's Pills—box 1/3. **1951** *Chemist & Druggist Yearbk.* 196 Holloway's Pills, Ltd... King George's Avenue, Watford. *Ibid.* 457 (*heading*) Proprietary medicines advertised to the public. *Ibid.* 458/1 Holloway's ointment. Holloway's pills.

† **'hollowed**, *a. Obs.*: see quot.

a **1734** R. WODROW *Analecta* (1842) I. 104 Being of a hardy frolic temper, or a little hollowed, as we call it.

'hollow-'eyed, *a.* Having hollow eyes; having the eyes deep sunk in their orbits.

a **1529** SKELTON *Vppon Deedman's Hed* 11 No man may him hyde From Deth holow eyed. **1590** SHAKS. *Com. Err.* v. i. 240 A needy-hollow-ey'd-sharpe-looking-wretch. **1781** COWPER *Hope* 58 Hollow-eyed abstinence, and lean despair. **1870** P'CESS ALICE *Mem.* 31 Jan. (1884) 239 Victoria looks very hollow-eyed, pale and wretched.

'hollow-'hearted, *a.* Having a hollow heart; insincere, false.

1549 COVERDALE, etc. *Erasm. Par. Eph.* Prol. (R.), Holowe-herted flatterye and craftye deceauyng. **1648** GAGE *West Ind.* xii. (1655) 43 Inwardly false and hollow hearted. **1830** TENNYSON *Poems* 44 Hollowhearted apathy, The cruellest form of perfect scorn.

Hence **,hollow-'heartedness**, insincerity.

1549 COVERDALE, etc. *Erasm. Par. 1 John* 44 Except al holowhartednes be also plucked quite out of yᵉ mynde. **1678** J. BROWN *Life of Faith* (1824) I. ii. 44 The Lord discovereth the hollow-heartedness of many. **1816** SOUTHEY in *Q. Rev.* XV. 539 They are haughty toward strangers,..suspicious, and full of hollow-heartedness.

hollowly ('hɒləʊlɪ), *adv.* [f. HOLLOW *a.* + -LY².] In a hollow manner; with a hollow sound; insincerely.

a **1547** SURREY *Æneid* II. 70 Wherewith the caves gan hollowly resound. **1603** SHAKS. *Meas. for M.* II. iii. 23 Ile.. try your penitence, if it be sound, Or hollowly put on. **1607** MARKHAM *Caval.* VI. (1617) 63 It may couer all the hoofe hollowly that it may not touche the soale. **1814** *Mermaid* II. i, How strange and hollowly his accents sound! **1881** J. HAWTHORNE *Fort. Fool* I. v, The sound echoed hollowly through the house.

hollowness ('hɒləʊnɪs). [f. as prec. + -NESS.]

1. The quality or condition of being hollow; concavity; internal emptiness; sunken condition.

14.. *Voc.* in Wr.-Wülcker 571/32 *Cavitas*, holwnehse. *c* **1440** *Promp. Parv.* 244/1 Holownesse of a vesselle ..*concavitas*. **1545** RAYNOLD *Byrth Mankynde* 9 b, The.. matrix..a strong bladder, hauyng in it but one vniuersal holonesse. **1593** SHAKS. *Rich. II*, I. ii. 59 Greefe boundeth where it falls, Not with the emptie hollownes, but weight. **1664** EVELYN *Pomona* iii. (R.), Old trees (quite decayed with an inward hollowness). *a* **1822** SHELLEY *Mother & Son* iii. 9 Within her ghastly hollowness of eye.

†**2.** *concr.* and *semi-concr.* A hollow formation or place; a hollow, cavity, or concavity. *Obs.*

c **1374** CHAUCER *Troylus* v. 1809 His lighte gost ful blysfully is went Vp to þe holwghnesse of þe seuenþe spere. **1480** CAXTON *Descr. Brit.* 6 Atte cherdhoke there is a grete holownes vnder erthe. **1611** MARKHAM *Country Content.* I. xii. 65 The Perch..abideth most in Creeks and hollownesses, which are about the bank. **1715** MOLYNEUX in *Phil. Trans.* XXIX. 375 There are Nine of these Hollownesses and as many Eminences, undulated as they paint Sea Waves.

3. Of a sound or voice: see HOLLOW *a.* 4.

1398 TREVISA *Barth. De P.R.* VII. xxvii. (1495) 242 Yf holownesse comyth of drynesse, it is knowen by drye coughe. **1605** SHAKS. *Lear* I. i. 156 Whose low sounds Reuerbe no hollownesse. **1884** MRS. C. PRAED *Zero* II. 64 Helena was shocked at the hollowness of her voice.

4. Emptiness, vanity; insincerity, falseness.

1608–33 BP. HALL *Medit. & Vows* (1851) 202 Dissect this close heart of mine..and if thou findest any hollowness, fill it up. **1790** G. WALKER *Serm.* II. xxi. 118 A thorough man of the world, who knows it in all its hollownesses. **1886** *Manch. Exam.* 13 Jan. 5/7 The hollowness of his professions.

'hollow-root. *Herb.* [A 16th c. transl. of G. *holwurtz*, *hohlwurtz*, applied to *Aristolochia*, also to *Corydalis tuberosa*: see Grimm.]

a. A name for *Corydalis tuberosa* (*C. cava*), also called *hole-wort* and *hollowwort*); extended by Gerarde to other species of *Corydalis*. **b.** *erroneously*, A name for *Adoxa Moschatellina*.

1578 LYTE *Dodoens* III. ii. 316 (Of Holeworte) The roote whiche is holowe within is called in Germanie Holwurtz, that is to say in English Holowe roote, or Holewurt. **1597** GERARDE *Herbal* II. ccccxlvi. (1633) 1092. **1753** CHAMBERS *Cycl. Suppl.* App., *Hollow-root*..a name sometimes given to the..fumitory. **1788** *Chambers's Cycl.*, *Moschatellina*, hollow root, or tuberose moschatel..a little plant common under our hedges, in spring. **1884** MILLER *Plant-n.*, *Hole-wort*, Hollow-wort, or Hollow-root. *Corydalis tuberosa* and *Adoxa Moschatellina*.

'hollow-ware. Also **holloware**. Bowl- or tube-shaped ware of earthenware, wood, or metal: now especially the last.

1682 [see b]. **1703** T. N. *City & C. Purchaser* 274 All hollow Ware, (as they call Ridge-tyles, Corner, Gutter, and Dormar-tyles). **1744–50** W. ELLIS *Mod. Husbandm.* VII. II. 79 Maple..is approved of by the turner for making hollow-ware. **1880** *Statist. Manuf. U.S.* 1059 A coarse, greenish glass, often termed bottle-glass... It is called in this country hollow ware. **1891** *Daily News* 9 Feb. 2/4 Cast-iron hollow-ware is selling very slowly. **1959** *Sears, Roebuck Catal.* Spring & Summer 575/4 Melmac Dinner Sets..Holloware in solid color. **1963** *Times* 28 May 1/7 Domestic holloware made from aluminium. **1972** *Daily Tel.* 25 Apr. 15 Pans, or 'holloware' as they are called in the trade.

b. *attrib.* and *Comb.*, as ***hollow-ware maker***, ***making***, ***manufacturer***, †***pewterer***, ***trade***, ***utensil***.

1682 *Lond. Gaz.* No. 1717/8 Francis Scagood,..Hollow-Wear Pewterer, hath Molds and Stocks to Sell. **1881** *Porcelain Works, Worcester* 21 The manufacture of soup tureens, covered dishes, ewers and basins, &c. is called Hollow Ware Pressing. These objects are all made in moulds. **1888** A. N. PALMER *Hist. Old. Nonconf. Wrexham* 76 A hollow-ware manufacturer at Bewdley. **1962** *Engineering* 22 June 819/2 Aluminium sheet clad with stainless steel..is intended basically for the domestic holloware trade.

hollowwort ('hɒləʊwɜːt). = HOLLOW-ROOT *a.*

1863 PRIOR *Plant-n.*, Hollow-wort, or Hole-wort, from its hollow root, *Corydalis tuberosa*.

† **'hollowy, hol(o)wy**, deriv. or by-forms of HOLLOW *a.* and *adv.*

c **1400** *Lanfranc's Cirurg.* 78 (MS. B.), þere ben sixe manere of þese Vlcus..Venemy & holwy [*MS. A.* holowȝ]. *Ibid.* 93 þe Ulcus ys foule & stynkynge, þe lippes..alle aboute areryde & holwy [*MS. A.* holowe], & þis is þe dyfference bytwene cancre & a foule Ulcus & an hory. **1495** *Trevisa's Barth. De P.R.* v. xliii. 160 The reynes ben flesshly poores and holowy rounde and coueryd wyth fatnesse.

holluschickie ('hɒləstʃɪkɪ), *collect. pl.* Also **holloschickie**, **holluschuckie**. [ad. Russ. *kholostyakí* pl., bachelors.] Young males of the northern, Pribilof, or Alaska fur seal, *Callorhinus ursinus*; = BACHELOR 4 c.

1874, 1884 [see BACHELOR 4 c]. **1893** KIPLING *Seven Seas* (1896) 70 But he'll lie down on the killing-grounds where the holluschickie go. **1894** —— *Jungle Bk.* 97 They [*sc.* seals] were called the holluschickie—the bachelors. **1901** *Munsey's Mag.* XXV. 355/1 The holluschickie who have reached the age when they contemplate matrimony. **1929** *Encycl. Brit.* IX. 952/1 The young males or bachelors (*holloschickie*).

holly ('hɒlɪ). Forms: 2–5 **holi**, 3–6 **holie**, 4 **holiȝ**, 5 **hoolly**, 5–6 **holy**, 6 **holee**, 7– **holly**. [Shortened from OE. *holeȝn*, *holen*: see HOLLIN.]

1. A plant of the genus *Ilex*; *orig.* and *esp.* the common European holly, *I. Aquifolium*, an evergreen shrub or small tree with dark-green tough glossy leaves, having indented edges set with sharp stiff prickles at the points, and bearing clusters of small green flowers succeeded by bright red berries; much used for decorating houses and churches at Christmas. The American holly, *I. opaca*, is an evergreen tree similar to this, found in the United States from Massachusetts southward.

c **1150** *Voc.* in Wr.-Wülcker 545/23 *Ulcia*, holi. *a* **1225** *Ancr. R.* 418 Ne mid holie [*MS. T.* holin], ne mid breres ne ne biblodȝe hire sulf. **14..** *Songs & Carols 15th C.* (Percy Soc.) 84 Here commys holly, that is so gent. **1470–85** MALORY *Arthur* IV. xxvi, He sawe hym sytte vnder a tree of hoolly. **1545** ASCHAM *Toxoph.* II. (Arb.) 127 Peecynge of a shafte with brasell and holie, or other heauy woodes. **1562** *Ludlow Churchw. Acc.* (Camden) 108 Paid for holy and evy ..iiij d. **1610** GUILLIM *Heraldry* III. vii. (1611) 108 There is a kinde of Holly that is void of these prickles..and therefore called free holly. **1805–6** COLERIDGE *3 Graves* IV. xxiii, Lone hollies marked the spot. **1850** TENNYSON *In Mem.* xxx, With trembling fingers did we weave The holly round the Christmas hearth.

2. Applied, with or without defining word, to other plants (mostly shrubs) resembling the common holly; e.g. (in mod. Dicts.) to the holm-oak, *Quercus Ilex*; in Australia to species of *Hakea* and *Lomatia*. **Californian holly**, *Heteromeles arbutifolia* (Cent. Dict.); **Cape holly**, *Crocoxylon excelsum*; **ground holly**, *Chimaphila umbellata*; **mountain holly**, *Nemopanthes canadensis*; **New Zealand holly**, *Olearia ilicifolia* (*Treas. Bot.* and Miller *Plant-n.*). See also *box-holly* (BOX *sb.*¹ 3 b), KNEE-HOLLY, SEA-HOLLY.

1846 J. L. STOKES *Disc. Australia* II. iv. 132 Holly.. Hakea..Sandy Soil,—produces gum.

3. *attrib.* and *Comb.* **a.** Of or belonging to the holly, as *holly-bark*, *-berry*, *-bough*, *-bush*, *-leaf*, *-tree*, *-wood*; consisting or made of holly, or its wood, as *holly-hedge*, *-staff*, *-wand*. **b.** Special Combs.: **holly blue**, the azure blue butterfly *Celastrina argiolus*; **holly-boy**, an effigy of a boy made of holly, which (together with an *ivy-girl*) figured in certain village sports in East Kent on Shrove Tuesday; **holly-fern**, *Aspidium* (or *Polystichum*) *Lonchitis*, so named from its stiff prickly fronds; **holly-laurel**, 'the islay, *Prunus ilicifolia*, of California' (*Cent. Dict.*); **holly-leaved** *a.*, having leaves resembling those of the holly; **holly-oak**, the holm-oak or evergreen oak, *Quercus Ilex*; **holly-rose**, † (*a*) an old name for some species of *Cistus*; (*b*) a name for *Turnera ulmifolia*, a West Indian shrub with yellow flowers; **holly-set**, *a.* set with holly; *sb.* a hedge made of holly (cf. *quickset*).

1727–41 CHAMBERS *Cycl.* s.v. *Bird-lime*, Made from *holly-bark boiled ten or twelve hours. **1818** *La Belle Assemblée* XVII. 85/1 Cambridge hat..edged with *holly-berry red. **1853** F. O. MORRIS *Hist. Brit. Butterflies* 136 *Holly Blue. Azure Blue... This plain but neat species is to be found..in places where the holly abounds. **1905** *Daily Chron.* 6 Apr. 3/2 The holly-blue often flies on days when there is more hail than sun. **1927** [see CHALK *sb.* 7 b]. **1952** L. H. NEWMAN *Transformations of Butterflies & Moths* 46 Holly Blue caterpillars vary quite considerably, but the ground colour of the body is always a shade of green. **1970** *Times* 19 Aug. 9/6, I recently chased a Holly Blue around a holly tree for at least an hour before eventually retiring exhausted, with the total day's bag of one small butterfly. **1785** BURNS *Vision* I. ix, Green, slender, leaf-clad *holly-boughs. **1779** *Gentl. Mag.* XLIX. 137 The girls..were assembled in a crowd and burning an uncouth effigy, which they called an *Holly Boy, and which it seems they had stolen from the boys. **1664** EVELYN *Kal. Hort.* (1729) 218 Guard it with a Furse or *Holly branch. **1506** in Kerry *St. Lawrence, Reading* (1883) 52 It. payed for sysis to the *holy bush at Christmas ixd. **1594** PLAT *Jewell-ho.* III. 65 To take a Tauerne and get a Hollibush. **1861** MISS PRATT *Flower. Pl.* VI. 192 Rough Alpine Fern, or *Holly Fern. **1728–46** THOMSON *Spring* 635 Some to the *holly-hedge Nestling repair. **1601** HOLLAND *Pliny* I. 470 The *Holly leaues and all the kindes of Holme be set with sharpe prickes. **1777** COOK *2nd Voy.* IV. iii. (R.) The *holly-leaved barbary. **1597** GERARDE *Herbal* III. xxx. 1159 Holme Oke, Huluer Oke, or *Holly Oke. *Ibid.* III. iii. 1092 Of *Hollie Roses, or Cistus. **1700** tr. *Cowley's 6 Bks. Plants* IV. 90 Why Holly-Rose, dost thou, of slender frame, And without scent, assume a Rose's Name? **1664** EVELYN *Sylva* xxi. (1812) I. 274 Let every fifth or sixth be a *Holly-set; they will grow up infallibly with your Quick. **1787–9** WORDSW. *Even. Walk* 10 'Mid clustering isles, and *holly-sprinkled steeps. **1538** TURNER *Libellus* C j a, Angli an *holy tre, & an Huluar tre nominant. **1864** SYME *Eng. Bot.* (ed. 3) II. 222 There are records of Holly trees of great size growing in some of the counties of England. **1573** TUSSER *Husb.* lxxvii. (1878) 169 Let *holliewand threate, Let fisgig be beate. **1688** R. HOLME *Armoury* II. 41/2 The Hone is..*Hollywood converted into stone. **1864** SYME *Eng. Bot.* (ed. 3) II. 222 To the turner Holly wood is very valuable.

holly, obs. form of WHOLLY.

hollybut(t, -dame, obs. var. HALIBUT, -DOM.

hollyhock ('hɒlɪhɒk). Forms: 3 **holihoc**, 4–7 **holihocke**, 5 **holyhokke**, **holy hokke**, 6 **holioke**, **hollihoke**, **holyoke**, **-ocke**, **hollyhocke**, **hollyoke**, 6–7 **hollihocke**, **hollioke**, **holyhocke**, 7 **holliock**, **-oak**, **holyhock**, **hollyoak**, 7–8 **holyhock**, 8 **holyoak**, **holy-oak**, ? 9 **holly-oak**, 7– **holly-hock**, 8– **hollyhock**. [f. HOLY *a.* + HOCK *sb.*¹ mallow: evidently of hagiological origin; cf. the Welsh name *hocys bendigaid*, which appears to translate a med.L. **malva benedicta*. Another name was *caulis Sancti Cuthberti*, 'Seynt Cutberts-cole': see *Alphita* 61 s.v. *Euiscus*, 110 s.v. *Malua*.

The guess that 'the hollyhock was doubtless so called from being brought from the Holy Land' has been offered in ignorance of the history of the word.]

†**1.** *orig.* The Marsh Mallow, *Althæa officinalis* (in med.L. *ibiscum malva*, *bis malva*, OF. *vie mauve*, F. *guimauve*, Sp. *malvavisco*). *Obs.*

c **1265** *Voc. Names Plants* in Wr.-Wülcker 556/24 *Althea*, i. ymalue, i. holihoc. *a* **1387** *Sinon. Barthol.* (Anecd. Oxon.) 10 *Altea*, i. holihocke. *Ibid.* 43 *Wimave*, i. holi hocke. *c* **1400** *Lanfranc's Cirurg.* 56 Take malowe leues..& þe rote of holihocke [B. holy hokke]. *c* **1440** *Promp. Parv.* 243/2 Holy hokke, or wylde malowe.., *altea*, *malviscus*. *c* **1465** *Alphita* (Anecd. Oxon.) 4 *Alta malua..gall.* wymalue, *anglice* holyhokke. **1538** TURNER *Libellus* A ij a, Altheam, aliqui ebiscum, siue ibiscum nominant, officinæ maluam, bis maluam, nostrates Holy oke. **1610** MARKHAM *Masterp.* II. clxxiii. 489 An oyntment made of holy-hoxe, or sea-mallowes. **1614** —— *Cheap Husb.* II. xxv. 149 Annoint her feet with the juyce of the Hearb Holyhocke.

2. a. Now, The plant *Althæa rosea*, of the same genus as the prec., a native of China and southern Europe, having a very tall and stout stem bearing numerous large flowers on very short stalks; many varieties, with flowers of different tints of red, purple, yellow, and white, are cultivated in gardens.

1548 TURNER *Names of Herbes* s.v. *Malua*, Malua hortensis is of two kindes. The one is called alone in greeke Malache in englishe Holyoke, and of thys sort is the iagged mallowe. [He distinguishes it from 'Althea and Hibiscus.. in englishe marrishe Mallowe'.] **1551** —— *Herbal* I. B viij a, By thys description it is playne that our comon holyoke is not Althea. **1573** TUSSER *Husb.* xliii. (1878) 96 Holiokes, red, white and carnations. **1625** B. JONSON *Pan's Anniv.* 29 Bright crowne-imperiall, king's-speare holy-hocks. **1626** BACON *Sylva* §510 This Experiment of seuerall Colours, comming vp from one Seed, would be tried also in..Poppy and Hollyoke [**1677** Hollyoak]. **1641** *True Char. Untrue Bishop* 10 Who weareth..a fine holliock for the knot of his girdle. **1700** tr. *Cowley's 6 Bks. Plants* IV. 89 The Holihock disdains the common size Of Herbs, and like a Tree do's

proudly rise. **1741** *Compl. Fam.-Piece* II. iii. 357 Sow Pinks ..Holyoaks, annual Stocks. **1766** Anstey *Bath Guide* xi. 106 Like a Holy-Hock, noble, majestic, and tall. **1830** Tennyson *Song, 'A spirit haunts'*, Heavily hangs the hollyhock, Heavily hangs the tiger-lily.

fig. **1897** Violet Hunt *Unkist, Unkind!* ii. (ed. 2) 24 It takes a great bouncing hollyhock of a woman to look well here, not a white lily, as they call me in town.

b. *attrib.* and *Comb.*, as ***hollyhock blossom***, ***root***; **hollyhock disease**, = *hollyhock rust*; also, blight caused by the parasitic fungus *Colletotrichum malvarum*; **hollyhock fungus**, a fungus, *Puccinia malvacearum*, parasitic on the hollyhock; **hollyhock-rose**, an American species of club-moss, *Selaginella lepidophylla*, also called *resurrection-plant*; **hollyhock rust**, hollyhock fungus or the disease caused by this; **hollyhock-tree**, a malvaceous tree, *Hibiscus splendens*, found in Australia.

[**1865** *Gardeners' Chron.* 2 Sept. 817/2 We have received.. some information with respect to a Disease with which Hollyhocks are affected to such a degree as almost to preclude their cultivation.] **1898** W. Robinson *Eng. Flower Garden* (ed. 6) 389/1 Owing to the *Hollyhock disease it is often a better plan to abandon the named kinds increased from cuttings and resort to seedlings only for stock. **1951** *Dict. Gardening* (R. Hort. Soc.) II. 1006/1 Hollyhock disease is not seen in the neighbourhood of industrial towns. **1883** W. Robinson *Eng. Flower Garden* 13/2 The *Hollyhock Fungus (*Puccinia malvacearum*)..is.. destructive to the Hollyhock. **1616** Surfl. & Markh. *Country Farme* 145 The decoction of *hollihocke roots. **1899** G. Massee *Text-bk. Plant Dis.* 252 *Hollyhock rust. **1910** T. W. Sanders *Garden Foes* 227 Hollyhock Rust (Puccinia malvacearum). At one time this fungoid disease played great havoc with the hollyhock. **1951** *Dict. Gardening* (R. Hort. Soc.) II. 1005/2 The onset of Hollyhock rust..led to its almost complete disappearance as a florists' flower.

Hollywood ('hɒlɪwʊd). [A region near Los Angeles in California, the chief production centre of the U.S. cinema business.] Generally, the American type of moving picture, its characteristics and background. Also *attrib.* (or as *adj.*) and *Comb.*

1926 A. Huxley *Jesting Pilate* II. 198 What is this famous civilisation of the white man which Hollywood reveals? **1928** H. Crane *Let.* 27 Apr. (1965) 325 She ought to be a little different than the typical Hollywood hostess. **1929** E. Wallace *Red Aces.* i. 218 A high-class school at Brighton, where girls are taught to..use lipstick and adore the heroes of Hollywood. **1932** Kipling *Limits & Renewals* 143 The standardised Hollywood screech of a Producer. **1933** *Punch* 30 Aug. 225/1 An American producer says that if he had his way he could make Elstree into and English Hollywood. **1934** H. G. Wells *Exper. Autobiogr.* II. viii. 513 There was a vast editor's desk, marvellously equipped, like a desk out of Hollywood. **1935** R. Macaulay *Personal Pleasures* 137 It is not..for mechanically recorded voices, however Hollywood, to mimic this universal terrestrial passion [love]. **1937** *N. & Q.* 13 Mar. 181/2 Unlike the Japanese, they [*sc.* the Chinese] do not ape Hollywood. **1939** C. Morley *Kitty Foyle* 319 Those black and white yachting shoes..were definitely Hollywood. **1940** *Writer's Digest* June 13/2 It is at this point that the Hollywood ingenue goes Hollywood. **1942** T. Rattigan *Flare Path* I. 23 Face the music? How beautifully Hollywood! What was your idea? To get Teddy alone and say 'I love your wife'? **1959** *Listener* 10 Dec. 1048/3 A revolt against Hollywood-bourgeois values. **1970** G. Greer *Female Eunuch* 294 Her Hollywood-interior lodge.

Hence **Hollywoo'dese**, the style of language supposed to be characteristic of Hollywood films; **Hollywoo'desque** *a.*, characteristic of or resembling Hollywood films; **,Holly'woodian**, **-ean** *a.*, of, pertaining to, or characteristic of Hollywood or its films; **'Hollywoodish** *a.*, somewhat resembling Hollywood films; **'Hollywoodism**, characteristic style or idiom of Hollywood films; **'Hollywoodize** *v.*, to make typically Hollywoodian; so **'Hollywoo,dizing** *vbl. sb.*

1927 *Daily Express* 4 May 4 The cottage is so picturesque and Hollywoodesque that..it is more like a 'set' than a real house. **1928** *Ibid.* 4 May 10/2 Mr. Douglas Fairbanks..is meditating..a slap-up, original Hollywoodish sequel of his own devising. **1934** A. Huxley *Beyond Mexique Bay* 23 What frills, what flounces!..The cut was a Hollywoodian adaptation from the French. **1941** *Scrutiny* IX. 346 Puccini, that voice pervasively symbolic of the Hollywoodizing of human emotions. **1950** *John o' London's* 7 July 419/1 The modern kind of road-house which might adopt a Spanish wear with self-conscious Hollywoodism. **1951** F. Lawrence *Let.* 20 Jan. in *Mem. & Corr.* (1961) 298 We have a very 'Hollywoodean' place, not far from the Huxleys. **1957** *Essays in Crit.* VII. 209 One scarcely needs to pursue the poem through the Hollywoodese of 'our hearts go round'. **1959** *Encounter* July 53/2 Some deep Hollywoodean reason. **1960** *House & Garden* July 36 There is nothing Hollywoodian about Miss Caron's decorative indulgences. **1962** *Listener* 6 Sept. 342/2 Those brawny, masculine, sunburnt figures of my youth..were Hollywoodish figures. **1963** *Sunday Express* 24 Feb. 23/3 *Nine Hours to Rama* is a lamentable failure because it is permeated with Hollywoodisms. **1965** *New Statesman* 19 Mar. 462/1 So far, only the cosmopolitan and European [behaviour] has been permitted..and that, all too often, heavily Hollywoodised. **1967** *Guardian* 11 Apr. 5/1 Such incredible Hollywoodising of Malcolm X did much to create an atmosphere in which he could only be killed.

holm, holme[1] (həʊm). Also Sc. **howm.** [In sense 1, OE. *holm* sea, ocean, wave (only in poetic lang.); in sense 2, a. ON. *holmr* islet in a bay, creek, lake, or river, meadow on the shore; corresp. to OS., LG. *holm* hill.

These are generally held to be the same word; the sense 'hill' (not recorded in OE., though used by Layamon) being taken as the original (related to the stem of hill *sb.*, and so to L. *collis*, *culmen*); thence it is supposed arose the sense 'islet', and fig. that of 'billow', 'wave', 'sea'; but this last is obscure. (Med.L. *holmus*, *hulmus* are from Eng.)]

†**I. 1.** The sea, the wave. (Only in OE.)

a **1000** *Beowulf* (Z). 240 Hider ofer holmas. *Ibid.* 1593 þa ðe mid hroð-gare on holm wliton. [**1892** Stopf. Brooke *E.E. Lit.* iii. 59 The one who is killed swims in the holm.]

II. 2. A small island, an islet; esp. in a river, estuary, or lake, or near the mainland.

(Frequent in place-names, as *Steep Holme* in the Severn, *Priestholm* near Anglesea, *Rampsholm* and *Lingholm* in Derwentwater, *Willow Holm* near Carlisle; but, as a living word, applied only to the small grassy islets in Orkney and Shetland, and (as a foreign word) to those of Norway, Iceland, etc.)

?*c* **1050** *O.E. Chron.* (MS. C.) an. 902 þy ilcan ȝere wæs þæt ȝefeoht æt þam Holme Cantwara & þara Deniscra. *a* **1100** *Ibid.* (Laud. MS.) an. 1025 Her for Cnut cyng to Denmearcon mid scipon to þam holme æt ea þære halȝan. *c* **1440** *Promp. Parv.* 244/1 Holm, of a sonde yn the see (*K.* holme of sownde in þe see; *Harl.* holm or sond of the see), *bitalassum, vel hulmus.* **1556** W. Towrson in Hakluyt *Voy.* (1589) 112 The 13. daye we came betwext the flat Holmes and the steepe Holmes. **1693** J. Wallace *Orkney* 92 *Holm*, a little Isle for the most part desart, and only employed for pasturage. **1706** Maule *Hist. Picts* in *Misc. Scot.* (1818) I. 103 Some times they stand in little holms in the midst of lochs. **1839** Stonehouse *Axholme* 261 The monks of the Priory of Thornholmes..built a convenient house on a holme or small island between Owston and Gulnethorpe. **1846** McCulloch *Acc. Brit. Empire* (1854) I. 315 In Orkney ..Some of the islets, or holms, appear like gigantic pillars, rising perpendicularly from the sea: these are the resort of vast numbers of sea-fowl. **1886** Burton *Arab. Nts.* I. 126 An islet, a mere holm, girt on all sides by the sea.

‖**b.** (In Sw. and Da.) A dockyard, shipyard.

1654 Whitelocke *Jrnl. Swed. Emb.* (1772) II. 249 Whitelocke came to the holme where the ship was to be launched.

3. A piece of flat low-lying ground by a river or stream, submerged or surrounded in time of flood.

In living use in the south of Scotland (*howm*) and north of England, and extending far south in place-names; 'a flat pasture in Romney Marsh (Kent) is yet called *the Holmes*' (Way).

12.. *Newminster Cartul.* (Surtees) 229 Item in le Sutherholme, duas acras, in le Northerholme, tres rodas.. ab australi fine del holme usque ad aquilonalem finem ejusdem holmi. *c* **1440** *Promp. Parv.* 243/2 Holm, place.. be-syde a water, *hulmus.* **1531** *Nottingham Rec.* III. 369 For the holm bytwen the Grey Frere walle and Leen. **1799–1805** Wordsw. *Prelude* I. 275 O Derwent! winding among grassy holms. **1803** —— *Yarrow Unvis.* v, 'Oh! green,' said I, 'are Yarrow's holms'. **1806** *Gazetteer Scotl.* (ed. 2) s.v. *Dreghorn*, The holms on the banks of the rivers Annock and Irvine are a fine deep loam. **1864** Tennyson *North. Farmer* (*O.S.*) xiii, Wi 'auf the cows to cauve an' Thornaby holms to plow! **1865** Livingstone *Zambesi* xiii. 264 On these holmes herds of buffaloes and waterbucks daily graze.

†**III. 4.** A hill. *Obs. rare.*

c **1205** Lay. 20712 Into þan haȝe wude, in to þan hæȝe holme. *Ibid.* 20861 He [þe vox] ulih to þan holme, & his hol isecheð.

IV. 5. *attrib.* and *Comb.* (in sense 2 or 3).

1744 W. Stukeley in *Mem.* (Surtees) III. 173 The Roman money found here in great abundance; they call them Holm-pennys. **1865** H. H. Dixon *Field & Fern* V. 308 Half bred lambs are on the holme land near the river.

holm[2] (həʊm). Also 4– **holme**. [A phonetic corruption of *holn* from OE. *holen*, hollin, holly.]

1. The common holly. *Obs.* exc. *dial.*

c **1386** Chaucer *Knt.'s T.* 2063 Ook, firre, birch, Aspe, Alder, holm, popeler. *c* **1440** *Promp. Parv.* 244/1 Holme, or holy, *ulmus, hussus.* **1577** B. Googe *Heresbach's Husb.* II. (1586) 108 b, Holme, or Holly, is..continually greene. **1598** Stow *Surv.* xi. (1603) 98 Nayled full of Holme and Iuie. **1598** Florio, *Agrifoglio* [also *Aguifoglio*], the Holly, the Holme, or Huluer tree. **1601** Holland *Pliny* I. 470 All the kindes of Holme be set with sharpe prickes. **1774** Goldsm. *Nat. Hist.* (1862) I. II. v. 325 Feeding on holm, elder-trees, and brambles. **1859** *All Y. Round* No. 36. 225 Still called holme in Devonshire..in Norfolk it is called hulver. **1893** *Westm. Gaz.* 21 June 3/1 (New Forest) He 'rattles like a boar in a holme'..is still a familiar saying.

2. The holm-oak.

1552 Cooper *Elyot's Dict.* s.v. *Ilex*, A tree called of some Holme. **1577** B. Googe *Heresbach's Husb.* I. (1586) 4 Sometime I list to rest me under an old Holme. **1591** Spenser *Virg. Gnat* 215 The blacke Holme that loves the watrie vale; And the sweete Cypresse, signe of deadly bale. **1601** Holland *Pliny* I. 495 There is an Holme growing in the Vatican, elder than Rome it selfe. *a* **1701** Sedley *Virg. Past.* Wks. 1722 I. 262 Often from a hollow Holm the Crow Did on the left the coming Mischief show. **1726** Leoni *Alberti's Archit.* I. 25/2 The Holm, and all other Sorts of Oaks. **1814** Cary *Dante* (Chandos) 206 A sturdy holm, Rent from its fibres by a blast.

3. *Comb.*, as ***holm-berry*** (dial.), ***-dish*** (made of holly-wood), ***-wood***; **holm-cock**, **-screech**, **-thrush**, local names of the missel-thrush, from its feeding on holly-berries. See also holm-oak, -tree.

1601 Holland *Pliny* I. 267 Stakes and posts..of Holme wood. **1758** Borlase *Cornwall* 244 The..missel-bird.. which we call in Cornwall the holm-thrush. **1771** *Gentl. Mag.* XLI. 489 Holm dishes held our rustic cheer. **1885** Swainson *Prov. Names Birds* 1 Missel Thrush..Holm thrush, Holm cock, Holm screech (Cornwall, Devon, Dorset). **1891** T. Hardy *Tess* I. 102 Let me put one little kiss on those holmberry lips.

†**holme,** obs. form of hame[2], haulm.

c **1440** *Promp. Parv.* 244/1 Holme, or halm. **1523** Fitzherb. *Husb.* §15 They must have hombers or collers, holmes withed about theyr necks. **1552** Huloet, Thacke eryge, holme, or strawe, *stipula.* **1565–73** Cooper *Thesaurus* s.v. *Casa, Stramineæ casæ*, made of holme.

†**holmen,** *a. Obs.* [f. holm[2] + -en[4]; cf. *oaken.*] Of holm or holly; made of holly-wood.

13.. *K. Alis.* 4945 Her garnement..of holmen leues. *a* **1618** Sylvester *Mayden's Blush* 541 Hee makes a shift to cut an holmen pole. *Ibid.* 1782 The Lad here loads the Asse with Holmen sprayes.

†**holmes.** *Obs.* Also 5 **holmess**, 7 **hollmes.** [A corruption of Ulmes (Ulm.).] A fustian made at Ulm in Germany; more fully ***holmes fustian.***

1474 in Dauney *Anc. Scot. Melodies* (1838), Item, x. elnes of blak holmess fustian to the trumpatis doublats. **1547** Boorde *Introd. Knowl.* xiv. (1870) 161 A cyte called Ulmes, where fustyan vlmes is made, that we cal holmes. **1551** Ascham *Let.* Wks. 1865 I. II. 264 This city is enriched by making of fuschian called in England barburuslie holmes fuschian. **1624** *Naworth Househ. Bks.* (Surtees) 213, 3 yards of white hollmes, iijs. **1633** *Ibid.* 298, 9 yeardes of holmes fustian, xijs.

Holmesian ('həʊmzɪən), *a.* and *sb.* [f. Sherlock *Holmes*, name of the amateur detective who is the chief figure in the detective stories of A. Conan Doyle (1859–1931) + -ian.]

A. *adj.* Of, pertaining to, or in the manner of Sherlock Holmes. **B.** *sb.* A devotee of Sherlock Holmes.

1929 'G. Daviot' *Man in Queue* vi. 62 Grant disclaimed any such Holmesian qualities. **1934** J. Carter *New Paths in Book Collecting* 34 Mr. Desmond MacCarthy is a prominent Holmesian scholar. **1940** E. Bentley *Those Days* ix. 250 If the nature of the detective-story, as of other things, is to be found in its complete development, that was the Holmesian saga. **1947** C. Waugh *Comics* iii. 40 Hawkshaw's part is to uncover such fiendish plots with the aid of magnifying glass, pipe and Holmesian costume. **1958** *Times* 19 Feb. 10/4 In the belief no Holmesian had previously done so. **1972** *Times Lit. Suppl.* 7 Apr. 391/1 The great Holmesian game trundles along with unabated vigour.

‖**'holmgang.** [mod. ad. ON. *holmganga*, 'going to the holm' (or islet) on which a duel was fought.] A duel to the death.

1847 I. A. Blackwell in Mallett *North. Antiq.* 288 The question at issue was decided with sword and battle-axe by a holmgang. **1865** Kingsley *Herew.* I. iv. 145 Me happier the Valkyrs shall hail from the holmgang. **1891** Rider Haggard *Eric* xii. 115 The two who shall stand against me in holmgang.

Holmgren[1] ('həʊmgrən, 'həʊlmgrən). The name of A. F. *Holmgren* (1831–97), Swedish physiologist, used in the possessive in ***Holmgren's (wool) test***, a test for colour-blindness devised by Holmgren in which the subject is asked to match differently coloured pieces of wool; also ***Holmgren's wools***, †***worsteds.***

1879 B. J. Jeffries *Color-Blindness* xviii. 195 Dr. Magnus of Breslau has lately proposed a modification of Holmgren's test by letting the examined pick out from bundles of colored worsteds those which match the colors of the solar spectrum shown them at the same time. *Ibid.* xxii. 241 To further test railroad employés or others, after having decided on their color-blindness by Holmgren's worsteds, ..will be..of great value to examiners. **1890** Holmgren's wools [see green-blind *a.*]. **1932** S. Duke-Elder *Text-bk. Ophthalm.* I. xxv. 987 Holmgren's wool test, despite the strictures which have been passed upon it, is of great service. **1964** —— *Parsons' Dis. Eye* (ed. 14) xxiv. 364 Holmgren's Wools. These consist of a selection of skeins of coloured wools from which the candidate is required to make a series of colour-matches.

Holmgren[2] ('həʊmgrən, 'həʊlmgrən). The name of E. A. *Holmgren* (1866–1922), Swedish biologist, used *attrib.* to designate a system of canals discovered by him in the cytoplasm of some cells.

1921 *Anatomical Rec.* XXII. 78 Further work upon the Holmgren canals is required to clearly demonstrate the developmental stages. **1936** *Nature* 30 May 915/2 The relation of the vacuome system to the Golgi network or the Holmgren canals. **1952** G. H. Bourne *Cytol. & Cell Physiol.* (ed. 2) vi. 250 Evidence obtained from ultra-centrifugation of cells..shows that the Holmgren canals become stratified in a different position from the Golgi apparatus.

holmia ('həʊlmɪə). *Chem.* [mod.L., f. next after *erbia*, the oxide of erbium, *ceria*, the oxide of cerium, etc.; the oxide of holmium was not specifically named by either Cleve or Soret in their papers of 1879.] The sesquioxide of holmium, Ho_2O_3, a pale yellow basic compound.

The substance obtained by Cleve was later shown (by de Boisbaudran, 1886) to be a mixture of the oxides of holmium and of a new element, dysprosium.

1880 *Jrnl. Chem. Soc.* XXXVIII. 7 The author [*sc.* J. L. Soret] considers that the new earth, holmia, discovered by Clève, is identical with an earth..to which Delafontaine gave the name philippia. **1886** [see fractional *a.* b]. **1924** J.

W. Mellor *Inorg. & Theoret. Chem.* V. xxxviii. 697 The fractional crystallization of the ethyl sulphates enables holmia to be separated from erbia, thulia, etc., and to be partially separated from dysprosia. **1968** C. A. Hampel *Encycl. Chem. Elem.* 268/2 Holmia was not isolated into a reasonably pure compound until 1911.

holmium ('həʊlmɪəm). *Chem.* [mod.L. (P. T. Cleve 1879, in *Compt. Rend.* LXXXIX. 480), f. *Holmia* Stockholm (see quot. 1879) + -ium.] A silvery, relatively soft, metallic element of the lanthanide series which is present in monazite, gadolinite, and other rare-earth minerals and forms a series of strongly para-magnetic salts, mostly of a brown or yellow colour, in which it is trivalent. Atomic number 67; symbol Ho.

1879 P. T. Cleve in *Chem. News* 12 Sept. 126/2, I propose for this metal the name of Holmium, Ho, derived from the latinized name of Stockholm, in the neighbourhood of which so many minerals rich in yttria are to be found. **1886** [see dysprosium]. **1893** *Jrnl. Chem. Soc.* LXIV. ii. 467 The holmium oxides were obtained from strongly basic yttrium earths containing a large amount of yttrium oxide. **1924** J. W. Mellor *Inorg. & Theoret. Chem.* V. xxxviii. 696 The four rare earth elements—dysprosium, Dy; holmium, Ho; erbium, Er; and thulium, Tm—are considered as a family or sub-group of the yttrium elements. **1940** *Nature* 20 Apr. 633/1 The investigation of holmium with the mass-spectrograph has shown that the element is composed of one type of atom only, with a mass of 165. **1967** [see dysprosium].

holm-oak ('həʊməʊk). [f. holm² + oak.] The evergreen oak (*Quercus Ilex*), a native of Italy and other Mediterranean countries; so called from the resemblance of its dark evergreen foliage to that of the holly.

1597 Gerarde *Herbal* iii. xxx. 1159 The Ilex..might be called Holme Oke, Huluer Oke, or Holly Oke, for difference from the shrub or hedge tree *Agrifolium*, which is simply called Holme, Holly, and Huluer. **1599** Thynne *Animadv.* (1875) 47 The Cerrus, being the tree whiche we comonly call the 'holme oke' (as Cooper also expoundeth the Ilex to be that whiche wee call holme.) **1770** Langhorne *Plutarch* (1879) I. 8/1 Ægeus gave a scarlet sail dyed with the juice of the flower of a very flourishing holm-oak. **1837** Longf. *Frithiof's Homestead* 19 A table of holm-oak, Polished and white, as of steel.

attrib. **1830** tr. *Aristoph. Acharn.* 29 The sparks..leap aloft from the holm-oak embers.

holmquistite ('həʊmkwɪstaɪt, -kvɪst-). *Min.* [ad. G. *holmquistit* (A. Osann 1913, in *Sitzungsber. d. Heidelberger Akad. d. Wiss.* IVa. xxiii. 11), f. the name of P. J. *Holmquist*, Swedish mineralogist: see -ite¹.] A rare basic alumino-silicate of lithium, magnesium, and aluminium that is an orthorhombic member of the amphibole group and typically occurs in light blue to dark violet masses.

1914 *Chem. Abstr.* VIII. 1556 The formation of the holmquistite was no doubt a pneumatolytic process, connected with the intrusion of the well known Li-pegmatites of the region. **1930** *Amer. Mineralogist* XV. 292 Holmquistite from the North Carolina locality is composed largely of the lithia member of the amphibole group and a minor amount of a deficient silica member commonly found in basic rocks. **1966** W. A. Deer et al. *Introd. Rock-Forming Min.* ii. 159 Holmquistite typically occurs at the contact of lithium-rich pegmatites with country rocks.

holm-tree. [f. holm².]

1. The holly; = holm² 1. *Obs.* exc. *dial.*

c **1400** *Sowdone Bab.* 61 He rested him vndere an holme tre. **1576** Turberv. *Venerie* 89 Holtes of holme trees. **1778** *Eng. Gazetteer* (ed. 2) s.v. *Lydd*, Near the sea, is a place called Holmstone..which abounds..with holm-trees. **1887** T. Hardy *Woodlanders* III. 286 They had arranged that their meeting..should be at the holm-tree.

2. The holm-oak; = holm² 2.

1565 Cooper *Thesaurus* s.v. *Iligneus*, A branch of holme tree. **1606** Holland *Sueton.* 79 In the Iland Capreæ, the boughes of a very old holmetree..became fresh againe at his comming thither. **1802** *R. Brookes' Gazetteer* (ed. 12) s.v. *Landes*, The holm-tree, of the bark of which corks are made.

holn, pa. pple. of hele *v.*¹ *Obs.*

holnes, obs. form of wholeness.

holo- (hɒləʊ), before a vowel hol-, combining form of Gr. ὅλος 'whole, entire', occurring in various scientific and technical terms, for the more important of which see their alphabetical places; sometimes opposed to *hemi-* or *mero-*. In *Crystallography*, denoting that a crystal or crystalline form has the full number of faces (holohedral, holosymmetrical), or the full number of normals (holosystematic), belonging to its system.

† 'holagogue *Med. Obs.* [Gr. ἀγωγός leading], *sb.* a medicine reputed to expel all morbid humours; *adj.* having this property; **holar'thritic** *a.* [arthritic], affected with gout in all the joints; ‖**ho'lethnos** [Gr. ἔθνος nation, race], an undivided primitive stock or race; hence **ho'lethnic** *a.* (less correctly *holo-ethnic*), pertaining or relating to a holethnos; **holetrous** (-'iːtrəs) *a. Zool.* [Gr. ἦτρον abdomen], of or pertaining to the *Holetra*, a division of Arachnids in which the abdomen is closely joined to the thorax (Mayne *Expos. Lex.* 1854); **holoaxial** (hɒləʊ'æksɪəl) *a. Cryst.*, having or exhibiting all the axes of symmetry compatible with one another but no plane or centre of symmetry; also, more widely, having one or more axes of symmetry but no plane or centre of symmetry; **holo'baptist**, one who baptizes by immersion; **holoba'sidium** *Bot.*, = autobasidium; **holo'benthic** *a. Biol.* [Gr. βένθος depth of the sea], living in the depths of the sea at all stages of the life cycle; **holobranchiate** (-'bræŋkɪət), **-ious** (-ɪəs) *adjs. Ichthyol.* [Gr. βράγχια gills], having complete gills or branchial apparatus: opp. to *hemibranchiate*; **holo'carpic** *a. Bot.* [Gr. καρπός fruit, seed], designating or (of a fungus) possessing a thallus the whole of which becomes transformed into a reproductive structure at maturity; **holocephalan** (-'sɛfələn), **-ce'phalian** *sbs. Ichthyol.*, a fish of the sub-class Holocephali; *adjs.*, = *holocephalous* adj. (s.v. holo-); **holocephalous** (-'sɛfələs) *a.* [Gr. κεφαλή head], having an entire or undivided skull, as the group *Holocephali* of fishes, in which the hyomandibular bone is continuous with the cranium; so **holo'cephal**, a fish belonging to this group; **holochlamydate** (-'klæmɪdət), **-chlamydic** (-klə'mɪdɪk) *adjs. Zool.* [Gr. χλαμύς mantle], having the margin of the pallium entire, as the suborder *Holochlamyda* of gastropods; **'holochrone** (-krəʊn) *Math.* [Gr. χρόνος time], a curve such that the times of descent of a heavy particle through different portions of it are a given function of the arcs described; **'holocrine** (-kraɪn), *a. Physiol.* [ad. F. *olocrine* (L. Ranvier 1887, in *Jrnl. de Micrographie* XI. 9), f. Gr. κρίν-ειν to separate], of, pertaining to, or designating a gland in which the secretion is produced by the complete disintegration of its cells; **holocryptic** (-'krɪptɪk) *a.* [cryptic], wholly hidden or secret; *spec.* of a cipher incapable of being read except by those who have the key (Webster 1864); **holo'crystalline** *a.*, wholly crystalline in structure; opp. to *hemicrystalline*; **holodac'tylic** *a. Pros.*, consisting entirely of dactyls except the last foot, as a hexameter; **holo-enzyme** ('hɒləʊɛnzaɪm) *Biochem.* [a. F. *holoenzyme* (*Compt. Rend. XIIme Conf. Union Internat. de Chim.* 43)], the active form of an enzyme, consisting of the apo-enzyme combined with its co-enzyme; ‖**holo'gastrula** *Embryol.*, the gastrula of a holoblastic ovum (opp. to *merogastrula*); hence **holo'gastrular** *a.*, of the nature of a hologastrula; **holognathous** (həʊ'lɒgnəθəs) *a. Zool.* [Gr. γνάθος jaw], having the jaw in one piece, as the section *Holognatha* of gastropods; **holohemi'hedral** *a. Cryst.*, having the full number of planes in half the octants; sometimes said of the inclined hemihedral forms of the isometric system; **holohe'xagonal** *a. Cryst.*, having the full number of normals belonging to the hexagonal system; **holo'mictic** *a.* [ad. G. *holomiktisch* (I. Findenegg 1935, in *Internat. Rev. d. ges. Hydrobiol.* XXXII. 377), f. Gr. μικτός mixed], applied to a lake in which the full depth of water takes part in the circulation; **holo'morphosis** *Biol.*, the perfect regeneration of a lost member or part; **holo'nomic** *a. Mech.* [ad. G. *holonom* (H. Hertz *Ges. Werke* (1894) III. i. 91), f. Gr. νόμ-ος law], applied to a constrained system in which the equations defining the constraints are integrable or already free of differentials, so that each equation effectively reduces the number of coordinates by one; also applied to the constraints themselves; so **ho'lonomous** *a.*, in the same sense; **holo'parasite** *Biol.* [ad. G. *holoparasit* (F. Johow 1890, in *Verhandl. Deutsch. wissensch. Ver. Santiago* II. ii. 67)], an obligate parasite, unable to exist except in association with its host; so **ˌholopara'sitic** *a.*; **holo'parasitism**, the condition of being a holoparasite; **holophanerous** (-'fænərəs) *a. Entom.* [Gr. φανερός manifest], wholly discernible; applied after Latreille to the metamorphosis of insects when complete (Craig 1847); **holophytic** (-'fɪtɪk) *a. Biol.* [Gr. φυτόν plant], of, pertaining to, or designating a plant that is able to transform inorganic substances into food by photosynthesis, and so is neither parasitic nor saprophytic; **holo'plankton** *Biol.* [back-formation from the adj.], a collective term for aquatic organisms that are holoplanktonic; **ˌholoplank'tonic** *a.* [ad. G. *holoplanktonisch* (E. Haeckel *Plankton-Studien* (1890) iii. 25)], passing all stages of the life-cycle drifting or swimming weakly in the water; ‖**holo'plexia** *nonce-wd.* [as if mod.L., after *apoplexia* apoplexy], general or total paralysis (cf. hemiplegia); **holo'pneustic** *a. Ent.* [ad. G. *holopneustisch* (J. A. Palmén *Morphol. des Tracheensystems* (1877) vii. 78), f. Gr. πνευστικ-ός for breathing (πνεῖν to breathe)], having ten pairs of spiracles (in some cases eleven), all of which are functional; **ho'loptic** *a.* (see quot.); **holo'rhinal** *a. Ornith.* [Gr. ῥῑν- nose], having the nasal bones slightly or not at all cleft; **holo'saprophyte** *Bot.* [ad. G. *holosaprophyt* (F. Johow 1889, in *Jahrb. f. wissensch. Bot.* XX. 479)], an obligate saprophyte; so **ˌholosapro'phytic** *a.* **holosericeous** (-sə'rɪʃ(ɪ)əs) *a. Bot.* [L. *sēricum* silk], wholly covered with silky pubescence; **holosiderite** (-'sɪdəraɪt) [Gr. σίδηρος iron: see -ite], a meteorite consisting entirely or almost entirely of iron; **holosiphonate** (-'saɪfənət) *a. Zool.*, having a completely tubular siphon, as the order *Holosiphona* or *Dibranchiata* of cephalopods; **holospon'daic** *a. Pros.*, consisting wholly of spondees, as a hexameter; **holostean** (həʊ'lɒstɪən) [Gr. ὀστέον bone] *a.*, entirely bony; having a wholly osseous skeleton, as the group *Holostei* of ganoid fishes; *sb.* a fish belonging to this group; so **ho'losteous** *a.* = prec.; **holosteric** (-'stɛrɪk) *a.* [irreg. f. Gr. στερεός solid], wholly solid; applied to a barometric instrument in which no liquid is employed, as an aneroid; **holo'tesseral**, **holote'tragonal** *adjs. Cryst.*, having the full number of normals belonging to the tesseral, or the tetragonal, system; **holothecal** (-'θiːkəl) *a. Ornith.* [Gr. θήκη case, envelope], having the tarsal envelope entire or undivided; **holotrichous** (həʊ'lɒtrɪkəs) *a. Biol.* [Gr. θρίξ, τριχ- hair], belonging to the order *Holotricha* of infusorians, which have similar cilia all over the body; **holotrochous** (həʊ'lɒtrəkəs) *a. Biol.* [Gr. τροχός wheel], belonging to the division *Holotrocha* of Rotifers, which have one entire trochal disk; **holozoic** (-'zəʊɪk) *a. Biol.* [Gr. ζῷον animal], wholly like an animal in mode of nutrition: said of certain Protozoa, in opposition to *holophytic*.

1683 Salmon *Doron Med.* i. 38 *Holagogues, or Panchymagogues. **1854** Mayne *Expos. Lex.*, *Holagogus*,.. applied to medicines that evacuate or empty; holagogue. *Ibid.*, *Holarthriticus*, of or belonging to *Holarthritis*; *holarthritic. **1876** Douse *Grimm's L.* §7. 11 *note*, I shall venture, for brevity, to call the primitive undivided Indo-European people the 'Holethnos'..whence the adjective '*Holethnic' by correct derivation. **1890** *Athenæum* 7 June 733/1 The germ from which the Aryan 'holethnic' language was developed. **1902** H. A. Miers *Mineral.* i. i. 45 When an axis of *n*-fold symmetry is perpendicular to *n* digonal axes and there is no other element of symmetry, the crystal may be called '*holoaxial', since it possesses all the symmetry-axes compatible with each other, and only axes. **1903** H. Hilton *Math. Crystallogr.* v. 52 In this chapter we shall investigate those finite groups of the first sort—also called holoaxial groups—which contain only 2-al, 3-al, 4-al, and 6-al rotation-axes. **1961** Terpstra & Codd *Crystallometry* iv. 129 Crystals are divided according to their true symmetry into 32 crystal classes. Of these 32 classes, 11 have symmetry elements consisting exclusively of symmetry axes: these are called the eleven holoaxial classes. *a* **1641** Bp. Montagu *Acts & Mon.* (1642) 399 These hypocrites were not onely Hemerobaptists, but Horabaptists, and *Holobaptists, washing..almost every houre in the day, if not their whole body, yet some parts of the body. [**1900** B. D. Jackson *Gloss. Bot. Terms* 124/2 **Holobasid*, an undivided basidium in Basidiomycetes (Van Tieghem).] **1928** Holobasidium [see autobasidium]. **1970** J. Webster *Introd. Fungi* 279 In the toadstools and their allies the basidium is a single cylindrical cell, undivided by septa, typically bearing four basidiospores at its apex... Such basidia are termed holobasidia. **1902** *Encycl. Brit.* XXXIII. 935/2 Another hindrance to the extension of many deep-sea species is that they are *holobenthic. **1885** *Syd. Soc. Lex.*, **Holobranchiate*. **1854** Mayne *Expos. Lex.*, *Holobranchious. **1916** B. D. Jackson *Gloss. Bot. Terms* (ed. 3) 181/2 *Holocarpic. **1928** C. W. Dodge tr. *Gäumann's Compar. Morphol. Fungi* iii. 12 In the holocarpic forms, gametangial copulation naturally leads to the fusion of whole individuals. **1930** H. M. Fitzpatrick *Lower Fungi* ii. 24 In some of the lower families [of Phycomycetes] the entire thallus is transformed at maturity into a single reproductive organ (Olpidiaceae) or group (sorus) of them (Synchytriaceae). In such cases the organism is said to be holocarpic. **1970** J. Webster *Introd. Fungi* 62 In the Lagenidiales..the thallus is holocarpic. **1934** Webster, *Holocephalan *adj.* & *n.* **1942** L. H. Hyman *Compar. Vertebr. Anat.* (ed. 2) iv. 40 The chimaeras or holocephalans are peculiar-looking fish. **1934** Webster, *Holocephalian *adj.* & *n.* **1965** *Gen. & Compar. Endocrinol.* V. 434/2 The ratfish or chimera is a holocephalian. **1970** *Nature* 11 July 187/2 A holocephalian elasmobranch fish, *Hycholagus colliei*. **1886** *Athenæum* 12 June 782/2 *Callorhynchus*..is the southern representative of the northern '*holocephalous' *Chimæra*. **1905** Gould *Dict. New Med. Terms* 296/1 **Holocrine*, applied to a gland the cell of which, after having elaborated the material of secretion, falls into disuse and disappears. **1928** E. V. Cowdry *Special Cytol.* I. ii. 36 In the sebaceous glands the secretory products are elaborated by the fatty metamorphosis, destruction and discharge of the

cells themselves. These are the 'holocrine' glands of Ranvier. **1939** V. B. WIGGLESWORTH *Princ. Insect Physiol.* xi. 264 In Orthoptera, secretion is merocrine during continuous small meals, holocrine when a meal follows a period of fasting. **1949** *Gray's Anat.* (ed. 30) 1254 As the sebaceous glands produce their secretion by complete fatty degeneration of their central cells they are classed as holocrine glands. **1961** E. H. MERCER *Keratin & Keratinization* ii. 59 Some cutaneous holocrine glands of reptiles..are sac-like invaginations of the epidermis producing fatty materials. **1884** *Q. Jrnl. Geol. Soc.* XL. 446 The ground mass is *holocrystalline. **1891** *Athenæum* 19 Sept. 391/1 He..describes the principal igneous rocks in groups under the three heads, A. Holocrystalline, B. Hemicrystalline, and C. Highly Glassy Rocks. **1943** SUMNER & SOMERS *Chem. & Methods Enzymes* i. 32 A few examples of coenzymes and *holoenzymes are given in Table 11. **1950** Holoenzyme [see CO-ENZYME]. **1971** *Nature* 15 Oct. 478/2 The rate of production of active holoenzyme from apoenzyme is enhanced by tryptophan about ten-fold. **1895** STORY-MASKELYNE *Crystallogr.* §235 [Hexagonal system] Holo-systematic haplohedral forms; or *holohexagonal haplohedra. *Ibid.* §237 Holohexagonal merosymmetry. **1937** *Trans. Connecticut Acad. Arts & Sci.* XXXIII. 74 A normal (*holomictic) thermally stratified lake consists of an epilimnion and a hypolimnion. **1957** G. E. HUTCHINSON *Treat. Limnol.* I. viii. 537 Most of the lakes discussed herein are holomictic; that is to say, when they circulate, the circulation is complete to the bottom. **1901** T. H. MORGAN *Regeneration* i. 24 Under this heading [*sc.* homomorphosis] we may distinguish two cases, in one of which the entire lost part is at once, or later, replaced—*holomorphosis. **1904** E. T. WHITTAKER *Treat. Analyt. Dynamics* ii. 33 *Holonomic systems are therefore characterised by the fact that the number of degrees of freedom is equal to the number of independent coordinates required to specify the configuration of the system. **1954** R. A. BECKER *Introd. Theor. Mech.* xiii. 318 Simple examples of holonomic constraints involving a single particle are those where the motion is confined to a single curve or surface. **1899** D. E. JONES & WALLEY tr. *Hertz's Princ. Mech.* iv. 80 A material system between whose possible positions all conceivable continuous motions are also possible motions is callled a *holonomous system. **1911** A. & J. G. GRAY *Treat. Dynamics* x. 555 Systems are now called holonomous or not holonomous, according as the constraints are or are not defined by finite equations. **1891** *Jrnl. R. Microsc. Soc.* 70 Each of these classes, except the last, may be again divided into *Holoparasites and Hemiparasites. **1903** W. R. FISHER tr. *Schimper's Plant-Geogr.* 203 Holoparasites, which live entirely at the cost of the organic substance of their host, like holosaprophytes are devoid of chlorophyll. **1965** BELL & COOMBE tr. *Strasburger's Textbk. Bot.* I. iv. 197 While the semi-parasites can often at first glance hardly be distinguished from their green, wholly autotrophic relatives, the total or holo-parasites display a complete or almost complete loss of chlorophyll. **1902** *Encycl. Brit.* XXV. 439/2 Cytineæ, Balanophoreæ, Orobanchaceæ, Lennoaceæ, are families..which are characteristically *holoparasitic. **1927** W. MCDOUGALL *Plant Ecol.* ix. 125 The family Scrophulariaceæ contains representatives of all gradations from complete independence to *holoparasitism. **1885** *Holophytic [see HOLOZOIC *a.*]. **1888** ROLLESTON & JACKSON *Anim. Life* 820 In some instances where chlorophyl is present, nutrition appears to take place as in plants, in other words the Protozoon is holophytic. But the presence of chlorophyl need not necessarily lead to holophytic nutrition. **1900** *Ann. Bot.* XIV. 669 Thus either a saprophytic or holophytic nutrition can be maintained. **1964** PRIESTLEY & SCOTT *Introd. Bot.* (ed. 4) xxxvii. 593 It is usual for flowering plants to be autotrophic (holophytic). **1909** E. WARMING *Oecol. Plants* xxxviii. 161 These terms 'neritic' and 'pelagic' or 'oceanic' plankton approximately correspond to Haeckel's 'neroplankton' and '*holoplankton' respectively. **1942** H. U. SVERDRUP et al. *Oceans* xvii. 816 The holoplankton is composed of forms representing nearly every phylum of the animal kingdom. **1955** C. C. DAVIS *Marine & Fresh-water Plankton* i. 29 The life history is completed without the animals ever leaving their planktonic life. Animals of this type are classified as the holoplankton. **1893** G. W. FIELD tr. *Haeckel's Planktonic Stud.* in *Rep. U.S. Comm. Fisheries 1889–91* 583 Numerous organisms pass their whole life..hovering in the ocean, while with others this is not the case. The first group we call *holoplanktonic. **1963** J. E. G. RAYMONT *Plankton & Productivity in Oceans* xiv. 371 The holoplanktonic members are also subject to seasonal breeding. **1801** SYD. SMITH in *Mem.* (1855) I. 46 Why this *holoplexia on sacred occasions alone? Why call in the aid of paralysis to piety? **1892** J. A. THOMSON *Outl. Zool.* xiii. 266 In adult aërial life, the tracheæ of the body acquire stigmata, and the insect becomes '*holopneustic'. **1947** *Trans. R. Ent. Soc.* XCVIII. 459 Aquatic holometabolous larvae which are holopneustic do not appear to exist. **1960** RICHARDS & DAVIES *Imms's Textbk. Ent.* (ed. 9) I. 134 The Holopneustic Respiratory System.—This is the most primitive arrangement found in living insects, 10 pairs of functional spiracles being present. **1893** E. A. BUTLER *Household Ins.* ix. 186 The eyes of the males come completely into contact on the forehead..Flies whose eyes meet in this way are said to be '*holoptic' (whole-eyed). **1872** COUES *Key N. Amer. Birds* (1884) 165 A bird having the [nasal] bones..with moderate forking, so that the angle of the fork bounding the nostrils behind, does not reach so far back as the fronto-premaxillary suture, is termed **holorhinal*. **1892** GADOW *Classif. Birds* in *Proc. Zool. Soc.*, 5 *Œdicnemidæ*, Cosmopolitan, Holorhinal. No basipterygoid processes. **1890** *Jrnl. R. Microsc. Soc.* 205 Herr F. Johow describes the peculiarities of structure of the '*holosaprophytes', or saprophytes destitute of chlorophyll. **1902** *Encycl. Brit.* XXV. 439/1 Angiospermous holosaprophytes are not common. **1960** W. B. CROW *Synopsis Biol.* lxxxiv. 518 The completely saprophytic genera (holosaprophytes) in Britain are the orchids *Neottia* and *Corallorhiza* and the similar *Monotropa* which is allied to the heath family. **1895** *Ann. Bot.* IX. 327 A number of *holosaprophytic forms found in the tropics..constitute the Burmanniaceous genus *Thismia*. **1831** DON *Gard. Dict.* I. p. xvii, **Holosericeous*, covered all over with silky down. **1881** LUBBOCK *Pres. Addr. Brit. Assoc.* in *Nature* No. 618. 409 The whole class of meteorites, consisting of iron generally alloyed with nickel, which Daubrée terms *Holosiderites. **1870** ROLLESTON *Anim. Life* 264 *Holostean Ganoids. **1870** *N. & Q.* 4th Ser. VI. 414 **Holosteric*..has appeared of late years, as the distinguishing name of a particular form of barometer, resembling an aneroid. **1875** KNIGHT *Dict. Mech.* s.v., The *aneroid* of Vidi, and the bent tube of Bourdon, are examples of *holosteric* barometers. **1895** STORY-MASKELYNE *Crystallogr.* §176 Holo-systematic haplohedral forms; or *holo-tesseral hemihedra. *Ibid.* §207 Holosystematic haplohedral forms; *holotetragonal hemihedra. **1872** COUES *Key N. Amer. Birds* (1884) 125 A booted or *holothecal tarsus chiefly occurs in the higher *Oscines*. **1877** HUXLEY *Anat. Inv. Anim.* ii. 104 In the *holotrichous *Paramoecium*..there is a very distinct cortical layer. **1885** E. R. LANKESTER in *Encycl. Brit.* XIX. 861/2 All [the Ciliata] are *holozoic in their nutrition, though some are said to combine with this saprophytic and holophytic nutrition. **1888** ROLLESTON & JACKSON *Anim. Life* 820 The food-material consists..of living or dead animals or plants, and the Protozoon is then said to be holozoic.

holoblastic (hɒləʊ'blæstɪk), *a. Biol.* [f. HOLO- + Gr. *βλαστός* germ, -BLAST + -IC.] Of an ovum: Wholly germinal; undergoing total segmentation (as in most mammals). Opp. to *meroblastic*.

1872 COUES *Key N. Amer. Birds* (1884) 220 Supposing it already fertilized, the whole of its contents would develop into the body of the embryo. It would therefore be holoblastic. **1879** tr. *Haeckel's Evol. Man* I. 215 Such animal eggs have long been called holoblastic..by Remak, because in them the cleavage into cells extends to the whole mass.

So **'holoblast**, a holoblastic ovum (*Cent. Dict.*).

holocaine ('hɒləʊkeɪn). *Pharm.* Also † -cain. [a. G. *holocaïn*, after *cocaïn* (now *kokain*) COCAINE.] The proprietary name of a synthetic derivative, $C_{18}H_{22}N_2O_2$, of *p*-phenetidine which resembles cocaine in its action and is used (in the form of the hydrochloride) as a surface anæsthetic for the eye; phenacaine.

1897 *Lancet* 29 May 1466/1 A new alkaloid called holocaine..described as an effective anæsthetic for ophthalmic purposes. **1899** *Amer. Jrnl. Med. Sci.* CXVII. 121 The bactericidal power of holocain gives it the advantage that solutions..will keep themselves sterile. **1910** L. W. FOX *Pract. Treat. Ophthalm.* x. 287 The pain caused by this injection is very severe, and to mitigate this the eye should be thoroughly anaesthetized with holocain, cocain being insufficient. **1955** J. ADRIANI *Selection of Anesthesia* x. 98 Holocaine is prepared from para-ethoxy aniline (phenetidin). **1968** J. H. BURN *Lect. Notes Pharmacol.* (ed. 9) 62 Phenacaine (holocaine) is prompt in action and is used especially for the eye.

holocaust ('hɒləʊkɔːst), *sb.* [a. F. *holocauste* (12th c.), ad. late L. *holocaustum*, a. Gr. *ὁλόκαυστον* neut. of *ὁλόκαυστος* (by-form of *ὁλόκαυτος*), f. *ὅλο-ς* whole + *καυστός, καυτός* burnt.]

1. A sacrifice wholly consumed by fire; a whole burnt offering.

c **1250** *Gen. & Ex.* 1326 Ysaac was leid ðat auter on, So men sulden holocaust don. **1526** TINDALE *Mark* xii. 33 A greater thynge then all holocaustes and sacrifises. **1680** H. MORE *Apocal. Apoc.* 101 In the latter part thereof stands the altar of Holocausts. **1732** BERKELEY *Alciphr.* v. §3 Those Druids would have sacrificed many a holocaust of free-thinkers. **1847** GROTE *Greece* II. xxxii. (1862) III. 162 A holocaust of the most munificent character.

2. *transf.* and *fig.* **a.** A complete sacrifice or offering. **b.** A sacrifice on a large scale.

1497 BP. ALCOCK *Mons Perfect.* Ciij a, Very true obedyence is an holocauste of martyrdom made to Cryste. **1648** J. BEAUMONT *Psyche* XXIV. cxciv. (R.), The perfect holocaust of generous love. **1688** in *Lond. Gaz.* No. 2401/1 We..humbly offer our Lives and Fortunes..which is that true Holocaust which all true honest-hearted Scotsmen will give to so good..a Prince. *a* **1711** KEN *Anodynes* Poet. Wks. 1721 III. 477 While I thy Holocaust remain. **1868** M. PATTISON *Academ. Org.* v. 139 By another grand holocaust of fellowships we might perhaps purchase another respite.

c. Complete consumption by fire, or that which is so consumed; complete destruction, esp. of a large number of persons; a great slaughter or massacre.

1671 MILTON *Samson* 1702 Like that self-begotten bird In the Arabian woods embost, That no second knows nor third, And lay erewhile a Holocaust. *a* **1711** KEN *Christophil* Poet. Wks. 1721 I. 442 Shou'd gen'ral Flame this World consume .. An Holocaust for Fontal Sin. **1833** L. RITCHIE *Wand. by Loire* 104 Louis VII..once made a holocaust of thirteen hundred persons in a church. **1883** MRS. CROKER *Pretty Miss Neville* III. 124 When Major Percival has made a holocaust of your letters. **1940** *Hansard Commons* 6 Mar. 416 The general holocaust of civilised standards. **1944** H. F. RUBINSTEIN *Hated Servants* 167 The siege will take a heavy toll, and few who live to the end of it will survive the holocaust that must follow. **1987** *Sunday Tel.* 23 Nov. 15 (*heading*) Aids: the new holocaust.

d. ***the Holocaust***: the mass murder of the Jews by the Nazis in the war of 1939–1945. Also used *transf.*, of the similar fate of other groups; and *attrib.*

The specific application was introduced by historians during the 1950s, probably as an equivalent to Heb. *ḥurban* and *shoah* 'catastrophe' (used in the same sense); but it had been foreshadowed by contemporary references to the Nazi atrocities as a 'holocaust' (sense 2 c): see quots. 1942–49. The term is in common use among Jews, but seems to be otherwise relatively rare except among specialists.

[**1942** *News Chron.* 5 Dec. 2/2 Holocaust...Nothing else in Hitler's record is comparable to his treatment of the Jews. ..The word has gone forth that..the Jewish peoples are to be exterminated...The conscience of humanity stands aghast. **1943** *Hansard Lords* 23 Mar. 826 The Nazis go on killing..If this rule could be relaxed, some hundreds, and possibly a few thousands, might be enabled to escape from this holocaust. **1945** M. R. COHEN in S. Goldschmidt *Legal Claims against Germany* p.vi, Millions of surviving victims of the Nazi holocaust, Jews and non-Jews, will stand before us in the years to come. **1949** *Proc. Amer. Acad. for Jewish Research* XVIII. 193 Problems of Jewish Hurban research.] **1957** *Yad Washem Bull.* Apr. 35/2 (*heading*) Research on the Holocaust Period. **1958** *Ibid.* July 2/2 The catastrophe which overtook us...The Inquisition..is not the same as the Holocaust. **1962** B. GLANVILLE *Diamond* xviii. 296 The holocaust..was the inevitable end, the logical conclusion of the pogroms, the Mosley marches, the hatred. **1965** A. DONAT (*title*) The holocaust kingdom. **1967** N. COHN *Warrant for Genocide* ix. 208 By the autumn of 1944 the holocaust was nearing its conclusion. **1968** *Manch. Guardian Weekly* 25 Apr. 10/4 There is now within modern history a compartment of 'holocaust studies'—dealing with the wholesale destruction by the Nazis of European Jewry. **1972** F. FORSYTH *Odessa File* 306 The mausoleum of Yad Vashem,..the shrine to six million of his fellow Jews who died in the holocaust. **1980** *Jewish Chron.* 18 Apr. 9/3 A memorial service..to mark Holocaust Day.

transf. **1973** T. BIELECZKI & L. SZYMANSKI *Warsaw Aflame* 5 Genocide against the Polish as well as the Jewish sections of the population... *Warsaw Aflame* was..written by men who lived through the holocaust. **1981** N. DAVIES *God's Playground* II. xx. 454 From 1941, Poland became the home of humanity's Holocaust. **1981** F. RECTOR *Nazi Extermination of Homosexuals* vi. 115 The number of gay Holocaust victims is substantial. *Ibid.* 116 At least 500,000 gays died in the Holocaust. **1985** A. RAMATI *And Violins stopped playing* (1986) 7 The Germans don't even admit that there was a Gypsy holocaust..there are memorials in Auschwitz for all the nations whose people died there, except for the Gypsies!

Hence **'holocaust** *v. trans.*, to offer as a holocaust. **holo'caustal, holo'caustic** *adjs.*, belonging to or of the nature of a holocaust.

1651 CLEVELAND *Poems* 52 Where you might have seen His conscience holocausted to his spleen. **1828** *Blackw. Mag.* XXIV. 350 The retainers, ruggin' and rivin' at holocaustal sheep. **1871** R. B. VAUGHAN *St. Thomas of Aquin* II. 920 The first principles of holocaustic sacrifice.

holocellulose (hɒləʊ'sɛljʊləʊs, -z). *Chem.* [f. HOLO- + CELLULOSE *sb.*] A polysaccharide fraction obtained from plant material, esp. wood, by the removal of lignin and various extractives, and principally consisting of cellulose and hemicellulose.

1933 RITTER & KURTH in *Industr. & Engin. Chem.* XXV. 1250 The authors propose the word 'holocellulose' as preferable to *Skelettsubstanzen*, maintaining that the latter term does not describe the material correctly either from the physical or chemical point of view. **1946** *Nature* 14 Dec. 855/1 Holocellulose, now known to be a very important constituent of chemical pulps so far as their behaviour on beating is concerned. **1969** R. L. JANES in Macdonald & Franklin *Pulping of Wood* (ed. 2) I. ii. 52/2 In practice..all the holocellulose isolation procedures..leave behind traces of degraded lignin and/or adsorbed solvents.

Holocene ('hɒləʊsiːn), *a. Geol.* Also **holo-**. [ad. F. *holocène*, f. HOLO- + Gr. *καιν-ός* new, recent, after *Eocene*, etc.] Of, pertaining to, or designating the most recent geological epoch, which began approximately 10,000 years ago and still continues and which together with the Pleistocene epoch makes up the Quaternary period; also *absol.*

[**1867** P. GERVAIS *Recherches sur l'Ancienneté de l'Homme et la Période quaternaire* ii. 32 Les dépôts récents que j'avais proposé, il y a plusieurs années, de nommer *holocènes*.] **1897** *Q. Jrnl. Geol. Soc.* LIII. 434 Mollusca from the Holocene deposits of the Kennet Valley at Newbury. **1927** PEAKE & FLEURE *Apes & Men* 14 The Holocene is more often called the Recent Period. **1935** *Nature* 7 Sept. 353/1 The pauses in the contraction of the lake must be due to increased rainfall, but nothing like a 'pluvial period' is admitted in holocene times. **1963** R. CARRINGTON *Million Years of Man* xiii. 164 In this Holocene epoch..the hunters and food-gatherers of Upper Palaeolithic and Mesolithic times adopted an entirely new mode of existence. **1971** *Nature* 24 Sept. 281/1 A considerable isostatic rise in the land must have occurred in the late Pleistocene with continuation in the Holocene.

holochoanite (ˌhɒləʊ'kəʊənaɪt). *Palæont.* Also **Holo-**. [f. mod.L. *Holochoanites*, altered form of *Holochoanoida* (see next): see -ITE[1] 2 a.] A nautiloid cephalopod in which the septal necks extend from the septum in which they originate as far as the next septum towards the apex; also, a member of the obsolete sub-order Holochoanites, of which such necks were characteristic.

1898 A. HYATT in *Proc. Amer. Assoc. Advancem. Sci.* XLVII. 364 The suborders..are as follows: I. Holochoanites with the funnels of the siphuncle reaching entirely across each air chamber completely shutting off the interior of each chamber from the interior of the siphuncle. **1929** *Bull. Geol. Soc. China* VIII. 119 Stages in development of the primitive Holochoanite. **1944** E. O. ULRICH et al. *Ozarkian & Canadian Cephalopods* III. 28 Most of the Early Paleozoic holochoanites that have long straight conchs can be referred to the Endoceratidae, but a few..are being placed in the Suecoceratidae. **1952** R. C. MOORE et al. *Invertebr. Fossils* ix. 342/1 Thin-section studies indicate that the elongate septal necks which are supposed to distinguish the Holochoanites occur only in a minority of them.

Hence **ˌholochoa'nitic** *a.*, (having septal necks) characteristic of a holochoanite; (by some writers used to include MACROCHOANITIC *a.*).

1905 *Bull. N.Y. State Mus.* LXXX. 339 *Piloceras newtonwinchelli* Clarke is by the structure of its ectosiphuncle not a holochoanitic form..but an orthochoanitic form. **1950** *Jrnl. Paleontol.* XXIV. 604/1 Only a small part of Hyatt's Holochoanites is actually holochoanitic. **1964** C. TEICHERT in R. C. Moore *Treat. Invertebr. Paleont.* K. 164/2 Endoceratidae with holochoanitic, and even macrochoanitic, septal necks and complete endocone systems also appeared in the late Early Ordovician.

holochoanoidal (ˌhɒləʊkəʊə'nɔɪdəl), *a.* *Palæont.* [f. mod.L. *Holochoanoid-a* (A. Hyatt 1883, in *Proc. Boston Soc. Nat. Hist.* XXII. 260), f. HOLO- + Gr. χοάν-η funnel + *-oida* (see -OID): see -AL.] Originally, characteristic of the group Holochoanoida (now obsolete) of nautiloid cephalopods; hence, = HOLOCHOANITIC *a.*

1883 *Proc. Boston Soc. Nat. Hist.* XXII. 267 The first three genera appear to have holochoanoidal siphons. **1933** *Biol. Rev.* VIII. 443 There is no essential difference in the structure of the siphuncle, holochoanoidal (Foerste) or orthochoanoidal (Troedsson).

hologamy (həʊ'lɒgəmɪ). *Biol.* [ad. F. *hologamie* (P. A. Dangeard 1900, in *Botaniste* VII. v. 265), f. HOLO- + -GAMY.] **a.** A mode of reproduction found in certain protozoa and algæ, in which copulation consists in the fusion of whole organisms morphologically similar to the vegetative form.

1925 E. B. WILSON *Cell* (ed. 3) vii. 582 Hologamy or Macrogamy... This condition is seen in various flagellates, rhizopods, ciliates, diatoms, desmids and the Conjugatæ generally. **1940** L. H. HYMAN *Invertebrates* I. iii. 99 Sexual processes are absent except in *Scytomonas* where hologamy has been observed. **1965** V. A. DOGIEL *Gen. Protozool.* (ed. 2) vii. 308 Hologamy is characterized by an almost complete absence of the preparatory stage of gametocytes.

b. A mode of reproduction found in certain fungi, in which the entire thallus becomes a gametangium and fusion of two mature individuals occurs.

1928 C. W. DODGE tr. *Gäumann's Compar. Morphol. Fungi* iv. 12 This special case of gametangial copulation..is called hologamy. **1965** J. WILKINSON tr. *Langeron's Outl. Mycol.* (ed. 2) ix. 378 Hologamy is gametangial copulation of holocarps.

Hence **'hologamete**, a gamete that is morphologically similar to the vegetative cell and is not specially formed by fission; **holo'gamic, ho'logamous** *adjs.*

1925 E. B. WILSON *Cell* (ed. 3) vii. 583 Even when hologamous gametes are alike or closely similar in appearance they often display definite physiological differences that become evident at the time of conjugation. *Ibid.* 589 Gametes of the hologamic type. **1926** G. N. CALKINS *Biol. Protozoa* x. 498 In the case of *Scytomonas* (*Copromonas*) *subtilis*..the evidence appears to be fairly convincing that copulation of hologametes actually does occur. **1932** BORRADAILE & POTTS *Invertebrata* ii. 27 *Volvox*..and related forms have an anisogamy in which the female gamete is a hologamete. **1965** V. A. DOGIEL *Gen. Protozool.* (ed. 2) vii. 309 Hologamous copulation takes place also in some Phytomonadina belonging to the genus *Chlamydomonas*.

hologenesis (hɒləʊ'dʒɛnɪsɪs). [ad. It. *ologenesi*: see HOLO- and -GENESIS.] The name of a theory of evolution first propounded by D. Rosa (in *Ologenesi* (1918)), and later adopted by G. Montandon (in *L'Ologenèse humaine* (1928)) to account for the origin of human races.

[**1929** *Nature* 11 May 709/1 The theory of evolution which he [*i.e.* G. Montandon] applies is that formulated by Prof. Rosa of Modêna in 1918 and named by its originator 'ologenesi'.] **1931** *Ibid.* 12 Sept. 430/1 Having reached maturation, the germ plasm of the species undergoes a sudden change whereby the mother species suddenly gives rise to two daughter species... The daughter species then set out to unfold their determinants, and if the environment is favourable—for environment and selection play their part in the theory of hologenesis—then maturation stages are again reached and a further dichotomy with the production of a new species takes place. **1959** R. ALTEVOGT tr. *Rensch's Evol. above Species Level* iv. 58 Rosa advanced a theory of 'hologenesis' according to which dichotomic branchings necessarily proceed in predetermined directions. **1959** B. WALL tr. *Teilhard de Chardin's Phenomenon of Man* III. i. 187 Man, according to these authorities, must have started simultaneously in several regions on the 'anthropoid layer' of the Pliocene era... The idea involves 'hologenesis' and therefore polycentricity.

Hence **hologe'netic** *a.*

1936 *Nature* 27 June 1055/1 An exposition of the hologenetic point of view in the origin and distribution of races. **1948** A. L. KROEBER *Anthropol.* (ed. 2) iv. 170 The hologenetic theory makes a blanket assumption in advance instead of trying genuinely to investigate each case and then seeing whether there is a common principle in them all.

hologram ('hɒləʊgræm). *Physics.* [f. HOLO- + -GRAM.] A pattern produced when light (or other radiation) reflected, diffracted, or transmitted by an object placed in a coherent beam is allowed to interfere with an undiffracted background or reference beam related in phase to the first (or identical with it); a photographic plate or film containing such a pattern.

When suitably illuminated a photographic hologram causes a two- or three-dimensional image of the original (two- or three-dimensional) object to form in space.

1949 D. GABOR in *Proc. R. Soc.* A. CXCVII. 456 The name 'hologram' is not unjustified, as the photograph contains the total information required for reconstructing the object, which can be two-dimensional or three-dimensional. **1952** *Sci. News* XXVI. 40 In the taking of the hologram, the amplitude of the wave scattered by the object is much smaller than that of the primary wave coming from the source. **1956** *Nature* 31 Mar. 613/2 The resultant hologram..was put on to the optical bench. **1964** *Electronics Weekly* 16 Dec. 6/1 A recent demonstration..showed a toy train in accurate three-dimensional representation, using a hologram illuminated from behind by a gas laser. **1966** *Observer* 15 May 13 Every bit of a hologram contains information about the whole scene. So you can snip it into pieces, shine a laser at one of the pieces, and you will see the original scene, only somewhat fuzzier. **1967** *Applied Physics Lett.* XI. 294/2 An investigation here has shown the feasibility of using a deformable film on a solid substrate to record an ultrasonic hologram in a way similar to that in which photographic film records an optical hologram. **1968** *Ultrasonics* VI. 81/1 There may be several intermediary stages before the ultrasound hologram is in the form of a photographic transparency which can be used in the reconstruction process. **1968** *Times* 12 Dec. 15/3 Scientists at the Bell Telephone Laboratories..claim that as many as 1,000 different holograms..can be stored in a crystal of lithium niobate. **1971** R. J. COLLIER et al. *Optical Holography* x. 298 Holograms can be recorded in a thermoplastic film by causing its surface to deform in accordance with the light intensity variations of holographic interference patterns.

holograph ('hɒləʊgrɑːf, -græf), *a.* and *sb.* [a. F. *holographe* (also *olographe*) or ad. late L. *holograph-us*, a. Gr. ὁλόγραφ-ος, f. ὅλο-ς whole + -γραφος written.]

A. *adj.* Of a deed, letter, or document: Wholly written by the person in whose name it appears.

1753 *Stewart's Trial* 24 Principal holograph letter, by Allan Stewart..addressed to Duncan Stewart of Glenbucky. **1754** ERSKINE *Princ. Sc. Law* (1809) 298 Holograph deeds (written by the granter himself) are effectual without witnesses. **1897** *15th Rep. Hist. MSS. Comm.* App. VIII. 155 These letters are all holograph of the Duke. **1898** *Daily News* 26 Jan. 7/6 According to the law of Belgium, a man might make his testament in two or three different ways, and one of those was by a holograph will.

B. *sb.* **1.** A letter or other document written wholly by the person in whose name it appears.

1623 COCKERAM, *Holograph*, a Testament all written by the Testators hands. *a* **1834** LAMB *Let. to Manning* (L.), I have got your holograph. **1848** WHARTON *Law Lex.*, *Holograph*, a deed written entirely by the grantor himself, which..is held by the Scotch law valid without witnesses. **1856** MRS. BROWNING *Aur. Leigh* I. Poems 1890 VI. 32 A palimpsest, a prophet's holograph Defiled, erased and covered by a monk's.

2. *in holograph*: wholly in the author's handwriting.

c **1817** HOGG *Tales & Sk.* II. 255 Two short codicils in his own holograph. **1873** BROWNING *Red. Cott. Nt.-cap* IV. 650 Bequeathed..by testament In holograph.

holograph ('hɒləʊgrɑːf, -græf), *v.* [Back-formation from HOLOGRAPHY, after *photograph*, *telegraph* vbs.] *trans.* To record as a hologram, to make a holographic record of.

1968 *Ultrasonics* VI. 87/1 Although Greguss has demonstrated that ultrasound holograms can be visualized by this technique, he has not published results of any attempts to reconstruct images of the original objects holographed. **1970** *Sci. Jrnl.* Aug. 17/1 The light from a pulsed laser is split into two beams, one going direct to the metal film and the other going first to the object to be holographed and then to the metal film. **1970** *Physics Bull.* Nov. 493/2 In any sort of holography..the aim is to obtain an image of the object being 'holographed'.

holographic (hɒləʊ'græfɪk), *a.* [f. HOLOGRAPH or (sense 2) HOLOGRAPH(Y + -IC.] **1.** Of a deed, letter, or document: = HOLOGRAPH *a.*

1727–41 CHAMBERS *Cycl.* s.v. *Holographum*, The Romans did not approve of holographic testaments. **1895** *Columbus* (Ohio) *Disp.* 1 July 1 Heirs under the holographic will.

2. *Physics.* Of or pertaining to holography; produced by, involving, or used in holography.

1964 *Physics Lett.* XIII. 306 High resolutions did not heretofore appear attainable in comparable image-forming X-ray microscopy using..holographic wavefront reconstruction methods. **1966** *Nature* 5 Mar. 1015/1 Fig. 1 shows the experimental arrangement used to produce holographic recording[s] of a piece of steel channel- section girder, and to demonstrate interference effects on distorting it. **1967** *Proc. Inst. Electr. Engin.* LV. 570/1 The extension of holographic techniques to radio frequencies offers new possibilities. **1967** DEVELIS & REYNOLDS *Theory & Applic. Holography* i. 6 Holographic interferometry shows promise in the areas of vibration and stress analysis and turbulence studies. **1971** R. J. COLLIER et al. *Optical Holography* x. 294 We describe here a method of film preparation which can be easily followed in a photographic or holographic laboratory.

Hence **holo'graphical** *a.*; **holo'graphically** *adv.*, by means of holography; in a holographic manner.

1656 BLOUNT *Glossogr.*, *Holographical*, wholly written with his own hand, from whom it is sent. **1966** G. W. STROKE *Introd. Coherent Optics & Holography* v. 79 (*heading*) Optical filtering with holographically matched spatial filters. **1968** *Nature* 2 Nov. 474/2 Memory might behave holographically. **1968** *Physics Bull.* Dec. 423/1 An improved interferometer for comparing the shape of a diesel fuel injector cylinder against a holographically recorded master cylinder.

holography (hɒ'lɒgrəfɪ). [f. HOLOGRAPH or (sense 2) HOLO- + -GRAPHY.]

1. Writing wholly by one's own hand.

1802–12 BENTHAM *Ration. Judic. Evid.* (1827) II. 459 Autography or holography.

2. *Physics.* [f. after *photography*, *telegraphy*, etc., on the basis of HOLOGRAM.] The process or science of producing and using holograms.

1964 *Physics Lett.* XIII. 308 A well-resolved, magnified 'image' of the scattering object has been reproduced..without losing the general simplicity and speed which are characteristic of holography. **1965** *New Scientist* 19 Aug. 431 The technique, known as holography, relies on the fact that an optical description of an object can be stored as a diffraction pattern instead of as a photograph. **1967** *Contemporary Physics* VIII. 153 Leith and Upatnieks (1963, 1964) were the first to demonstrate the very striking three-dimensional imaging that could be obtained by holography. **1967** *Sunday Times* 12 Feb. 8/8 Holography is currently a fashionable topic in the scientific world. **1967** *Applied Physics Lett.* XI. 294/1 The advantage of using acoustic holography to visualize, in three-dimensional fashion, objects in optically opaque material has been intriguing to many investigators. **1969** H. M. SMITH *Princ. Holography* i. 6 Further work on x-ray holography is still awaiting a small, monochromatic source of x-rays. **1971** *Sci. Amer.* Dec. 39 In the past 10 years holography has been used to study how objects change shape under strain, to record high-speed events in gas dynamics and to store information with high density.

holohedral (hɒləʊ'hiːdrəl, -'hɛdrəl), *a.* *Cryst.* [f. HOLO- + Gr. ἕδρα seat, base + -AL[1].] Of a crystal: Having the full number of planes required by the highest degree of symmetry belonging to its system.

1837 DANA *Min.* i. (1844) 38 The holohedral and hemihedral forms may be separately considered. **1855** W. A. MILLER *Chem.* 103 Hemihedral forms..may be derived from a holohedral form, as the tetrahedron is from the octahedron.

So **holo'hedrism**, the condition or quality of being holohedral, crystallization in holohedral forms. **holo'hedron** [cf. F. *holoèdre*], a holohedral crystal or form.

(In mod. Dicts.)

holoku (həʊ'ləʊkuː). [Hawaiian.] A long gown with a train as worn in Hawaii.

1891 R. L. STEVENSON *Island Nights' Entertainments* (1893) 177 She..stood by the track-side in her red holoku. *Ibid.* 207 Kokua concealed the bottle under her holoku. **1923** C. CAMERON *Two Yrs. in Southern Seas* i. 20 Her gown was a 'holokus', the native robe of a long 'princess' style, loose and flowing with train of bright yellow. **1954** J. SHERIDAN in J. D. MacDonald *Lethal Sex* (1962) 155 A stately Hawaiian woman in a flowered *holoku*. **1960** *Guardian* 3 Nov. 10/4 Long-skirted dresses, called muumuus and holokus, that were adaptations of respectable female attire in Massachusetts. **1967** M. DAVIS *Strange Corner* (1968) xv. 111 He..dropped his eyes to the skin-tight white holoku and whistled.

‖**Holometabola** (ˌhɒləʊmɪ'tæbələ), *sb. pl.* *Entom.* [mod.L., neut. pl. (sc. *insecta*), f. Gr. ὁλο- HOLO- + μεταβόλος changeable.] The insects which undergo complete metamorphosis. (More usually called simply *Metabola*.) Hence **holometa'bolic**, **holome'tabolous** *adjs.*, undergoing complete metamorphosis. **holome'tabolism**, **holome'taboly**, complete metamorphosis.

1870 ROLLESTON *Anim. Life* Introd. 113 A period of quiescence as 'pupæ'..gives the Holometabolous orders of Insects an advantage as regards their distribution over the colder regions. **1875** BLAKE *Zool.* 281 In the 3rd or holometabolic sub-class, the insect passes through 3 stages.

holometer (həʊ'lɒmɪtə(r)). [f. HOLO- + -METER, Cf. F. *holomètre* (1690 Furetière), ad. mod.L. *holometrum*, f. Gr. ὁλο- HOLO- + μέτρον measure.] A mathematical instrument for making all kinds of measurements; a pantometer.

1696 PHILLIPS (ed. 5), *Holometer*, a Mathematical Instrument for the easie measuring of any thing whatever, invented by Abel Tull. **1727–41** CHAMBERS *Cycl.* s.v., The holometer is the same with what is otherwise denominated *pantometer*. **1830** *Mech. Mag.* XIV. 42 To determine how far the holometer be entitled to supersede the sector in point of expense, accuracy or expedition.

holomorphic (hɒləʊ'mɔːfɪk), *a.* [f. HOLO- + Gr. μορφ-ή shape, form + -IC.]

1. *Cryst.* The same as HOLOHEDRAL or HOLOSYMMETRICAL, esp. as distinguished from HEMIMORPHIC.

2. *Math.* Said of a function which is monogenic, uniform, and continuous.

1880 G. S. CARR *Synops. Math.* Index 886 Holomorphic functions. **1893** FORSYTH *Theory of Functions* 15 When a function is called holomorphic without any limitation, the usual implication is that the character is preserved over the whole of the plane which is not at infinity.

So **holo'morphically** *adv.*, in such a way as to be or remain holomorphic (in sense 2); **'holomorphy**, 'the character of being holomorphic' (*Cent. Dict.*).

1957 *Pacific Jrnl. Math.* VII. 812 There exist domains..such that all *G*-holomorphic functions can be continued *G*-holomorphically into a larger domain. *Ibid.* 820 If *D* is a

domain of holomorphy, then the set *C*..belongs to *D*. **1963** STANDRING & SHUTRICK tr. *Cartan's Elem. Theory of Analytic Functions* ii. 73 For functions of a complex variable, there is an equivalence between holomorphy and analyticity. **1966** *Mathematical Rev.* XXXI. 33/2 A closed holomorphic differential *p*-form in *x*, holomorphically varying with *y*.

Holophane ('hɒləʊfeɪn). Also **holophane**. [f. HOLO- + Gr. φαίνειν to shine, appear.] A proprietary name used *attrib.* or as *adj.* to designate a type of lamp-shade that encloses the bulb but is made of glass specially fluted to refract and reflect the light in the required manner with little loss; also applied to the glass itself.

1893 PSAROUDAKI & BLONDEL *Brit. Pat. 19,185*, Our invention has for object to replace the globes, shades, reflectors..in use, by others made of transparent or crystal glass giving the..following results:— 1st. They are shining on almost the whole of their visible surface and receive for this cause the name of 'holophane' (entirely shining). *Ibid.*, For making the globe appear 'holophane'. **1911** V. ZINGLER in L. Weaver *House & Equipment* 116 For general dispersed lighting, a bowl or hemisphere of holophane glass, mounted on the ceiling with the lamp inside, gives a soft and pleasing light. **1927** *Brit. Weekly* 14 Nov. 193/4 The modern electric lighting with soft light and clusters of Holophane globes is a marked improvement. **1956** L. E. JONES *Edwardian Youth* x. 245 An American inventor of a prismatic glass called 'Holophane' was looking for an assistant. **1964** S. DUKE-ELDER *Parsons' Dis. Eye* (ed. 14) xxxvii. 559 The distribution of light from artificial sources varies greatly. It can be modified by the use of reflectors and prismatic (holophane) globes.

holophote ('hɒləʊfəʊt). [f. HOLO- + Gr. φῶς, φωτ-ός light. (The adj. *holophotal* was first formed: see below.)] An optical apparatus, used in lighthouses, etc., by which the whole, or nearly the whole, of the light from a lamp or other source is made available for illumination by means of reflective or refractive media or both.

1859 T. STEVENSON *Lightho. Illumination* 25 The optical arrangement which produces this result may be termed a Holophote. **1862** *Rep. Juries Internat. Exhib.* XIII. 28 All rays coming from the back of the flame are directed through the holophote. **1882** *Athenæum* No. 2828. 21 Mr. J. H. A. Macdonald, Q.C., the late Solicitor-General for Scotland, has constructed an 'electric holophote course indicator'. **1884** *Globe* 8 July, It is the Holophote that reflects the red, white, and blue colours on the cascade, also the parti-colours on the fountains themselves.

So **holo'photal** *a.*, of the nature of or belonging to a holophote; reflecting or refracting all, or nearly all, the light. Hence **holo'photally** *adv.* **holopho'tometer**, an apparatus for measuring the whole light emitted from a source.

1850 T. STEVENSON in *Trans. Scott. Soc. Arts* IV. 5 Such a light I have called the 'holophotal', or light of maximum intensity. **1851** *Rep. Juries Gt. Exhib.* 531 An arrangement of apparatus has been suggested by Mr. Thomas Stevenson ..He has..termed it a holophotal system. **1871** R. L. STEVENSON in *Trans. Scott. Soc. Arts* VIII. 274 Another mode of holophotally producing the intermittent light. **1875** BEDFORD *Sailor's Pocket Bk.* v. (ed. 2) 132 The power of a reflector is much increased by what is termed the holophotal arrangement, where an annular lens is placed in front of the frame, while all the back rays of light, which are otherwise lost, are thrown back into the flame by a hemispherical mirror. **1888** *Times* (weekly ed.) 11 May 7/2 The holophotometer..is a marvellous apparatus, of great ingenuity, for measuring, by a careful adjustment of mirrors, the intensity of light all round.

holophrase ('hɒləʊfreɪz). *Philol.* [f. HOLO- + PHRASE *sb.*: cf. HOLOPHRASIS.] A single word used instead of a phrase, or to express a combination of ideas (e.g. *ungetatable*).

1899 E. J. PAYNE *Hist. New World* II. 201 This multiplication of elements denoting personality, in combination with more and more elements denoting Things, tends to the dissolution of the holophrase... The holophrase naturally follows the progression of the mind from point to point. **1914** W. R. M. LAMB *Clio Enthroned* 239 We can regard his periodic structures as a reversion..to the primitive holophrase. **1969** *Language* XLV. 325 *All gone* may be two words, or it may be a holophrase.

holophrasis (həʊ'lɒfrəsɪs). *Philol.* [f. HOLO- + Gr. φράσις speech, PHRASE.] The expression of a whole phrase or combination of ideas by one word.

1869 FARRAR *Fam. Speech* iv. (1873) 130 *Holophrasis*, is the reduction of whole sentences into words.

holophrastic (hɒləʊ'fræstɪk), *a.* *Philol.* [f. HOLO- + Gr. φραστικ-ός, f. φράζειν to indicate, tell, express. Cf. F. *holophrastique* (Littré).] Of the nature of holophrasis: expressing a whole phrase or combination of ideas by a single word. Hence (as a back-formation, after *spasm*, *spastic*, etc.) **'holophrasm** = HOLOPHRASE.

1860 FARRAR *Orig. Lang.* viii. 174 Many ancient languages are holophrastic. **1862** D. WILSON *Preh. Man.* I. i. 12 With their peculiar holophrastic power of inflecting complex word-sentences. **1862** D. WILSON *Preh. Man* II. xxv. 436 Holophrasms are common in all its [*sc.* the Algonquin] dialects. **1865** *Athenæum* No. 1960. 688/1 Holophrastic, polysynthetic languages. **1875** WHITNEY *Life Lang.* x. 209 The holophrastic utterances of a primitive time. **1900** *Amer. Anthropologist* II. 615 A word-sentence may be called a 'holophrasm'.

holorie: see under HOLOUR.

holostomatous (hɒləʊ'stɒmətəs), *a.* *Zool.* [f. HOLO- + Gr. στόμα, στοματ- mouth + -OUS.] Having the mouth entire; as the division *Holostomata* of gastropod molluscs, having shells of which the mouth is not notched or prolonged into a siphon; or the group *Holostomi* of eel-like fishes, which have all the bones of the mouth fully developed.

1872 NICHOLSON *Palæont.* 244 The shells in which the mouth has this form are termed 'holostomatous'. **1888** ROLLESTON & JACKSON *Anim. Life* 107 These two varieties of aperture are known respectively as 'holostomatous' and 'siphonostomatous'.

So **holostomate** (həʊ'lɒstəmət), **ho'lostomous** *adjs.* = prec. **holostome** ('hɒləʊstəʊm), one of the *Holostomata* or of the *Holostomi* (see above).

1864 WEBSTER, *Holostome*, a univalve mollusk having the aperture of the shell entire, or without a terminating canal. *Dana.* **1885** KINGSLEY *Stand. Nat. Hist.* I. 338 We will first consider the holostomate (entire mouthed) forms.

holosymmetry (hɒləʊ'sɪmɪtrɪ). *Cryst.* [f. HOLO- + SYMMETRY.] Same as HOLOHEDRISM; opp. to *merosymmetry*. So **holosy'mmetric**, **holosy'mme trical** *adjs.* = HOLOHEDRAL.

1895 STORY-MASKELYNE *Crystallogr.* §137 A holosymmetrical form in any system will be the term applied to a form in which all the faces required to complete the symmetry of the system are present, and are physically as well as geometrically similar. *Ibid.* §140 Holo-symmetry, where a form is at once holo-systematic and diplohedral. *Ibid.* §267 The holo-symmetrical type of the Hexagonal system.

holosystematic (hɒləʊsɪstɪ'mætɪk), *a.* *Cryst.* [f. HOLO- + SYSTEMATIC.] Having the full number of normals required by the complete symmetry of its system. Opp. to *merosystematic*.

1878 GURNEY *Crystallogr.* 54 A holosystematic form is one in which all the normals required by the Law of Symmetry are present. **1895** STORY-MASKELYNE *Crystallogr.* §139.

holothuria (hɒləʊ'θjʊərɪə). *Zool.* Pl. **-iæ**, **-ias**. = HOLOTHURIAN *sb.*

1792 M. RIDDELL *Voy. Madeira* 79 These holothuriae are singularly beautiful when floating on the surface of the water in a clear day. **1816** TUCKEY *Narr. Exped. R. Zaire* (1818) i. 11 The holothuria made its first appearance on the 4th instant. **1844** *Chambers's Edin. Jrnl.* 23 Nov. 323/2 It may be of small moment to you, who, mayhap, know nothing of holothurias. **1876** tr. *Beneden's Anim. Parasites* (1883) 5 Dr. Greef..found..a holothuria of a foot in length.

holothurian (hɒləʊ'θjʊərɪən), *a.* and *sb.* *Zool.* [f. mod.L. generic name *Holothūria*, f. *holothūria* (Pliny), a neuter pl. of Gr. ὁλοθούριον, a kind of zoophyte.]

A. *adj.* Of or pertaining to the genus *Holothuria* or division *Holothurioidea* of Echinoderms: see B.

1878 BELL *Gegenbaur's Comp. Anat.* 226 Organs..formed on the Holothurian type. **1886** *Athenæum* 21 Aug. 242/1 For two years a holothurian industry was maintained on the coast of Florida, but the export to China was not, apparently, very profitable.

B. *sb.* An animal belonging to the division of Echinoderms, of which *Holothuria* is the typical genus; they have an elongated form, a tough leathery integument, and a ring of tentacles around the mouth; a sea-slug, sea-cucumber, or trepang.

1842 BRANDE *Dict. Sci.* etc., *Holothurians.* **1872** NICHOLSON *Palæont.* 135 The last order..is that of the Holothurians or 'Sea-cucumbers'. **1893** *Nation* (N.Y.) 13 July 34/1 As soon as collected, the holothurians are boiled for a short time, split open, gutted, and smoked.

So **holothure** ('hɒləʊθjʊə(r)), a holothurian (Webster 1864). **holo'thurid**, **holo'thurioid**, *adjs.* belonging to the *Holothurida* or *Holothurioidea* among Echinoderms, holothurian; *sbs.* a holothurian.

1859 AGASSIZ *Ess. Classif.* 162 It was not until the present period, that the highest Echinoderms, the Holothuroids, assumed a prominent position in their class. **1877** HUXLEY *Anat. Inv. Anim.* ix. 552 The tentacula are developed around the mouth, the ciliated bands disappear, and the Holothurid Echinoderm is complete. **1887** *Athenæum* 5 Feb. 194/2 No naturalist doubts that the echinids, asterids, and holothurids have sprung from a common primitive form.

holotype ('hɒləʊtaɪp). *Biol.* [f. HOLO- + TYPE *sb.*¹ 8 e.] A specimen chosen as the basis of the first description of a new species.

1897 C. SCHUCHERT in *Science* 23 Apr. 637/2 A holotype in natural history is a particular individual deliberately selected by the author of a species, or it may be the only example of a species known at the time of original publication. **1946** *Nature* 23 Nov. 762/1 The holotype and only specimen of this was housed in the Bristol Museum. **1964** *Internat. Code Zool. Nomencl.* xvi. 77 If a nominal species is based on a single specimen, that specimen is the 'holotype'. **1966** *Internat. Code Bot. Nomencl.* ii. 18 As long as a holotype is extant, it automatically fixes the application of the name concerned.

holou(ȝ), **-ough**, **-ow**, **-owȝ**, obs. ff. HOLLOW.

†**holour.** *Obs.* Forms: 3 huler, 3–4 holer, 4 holyer, houlloure, 4–5 houlour(e, holour(e, 5 -or, hullour, -owre, -ur, -ar, hulour. [a. OF. *holier*, *holer*, *huler* (later also *houlleur*), var. of *horier*, *hourier*, *hurier*, ad. OHG. *huorari*, *huareri* (MHG. *huorer*, Ger. *hurer*), whorer, fornicator. The first *r* became *l* in OF. by dissimilation, as in *peregrinus*, *pelegrin*, PILGRIM.] A fornicator, whoremonger; a debauchee, ribald.

c **1230** *Hali Meid.* 31 [He] tukeð þe to bismere as huler his hore. **1297** R. GLOUC. (1724) 26 Ȝef alle luþer holers were y serued so, Me schulde fynde þe les such spouse bruche do. *c* **1340** *Ayenb.* 51 Þanne he becomþ ribaud holyer and þyef. *c* **1375** *Sc. Leg. Saints, Lucy* 226 Þe presydent gert hyme bryng Sere houlouris. *c* **1386** CHAUCER *Wife's Prol.* 254 Thou seyst that euery holour [*v.r.* hullur] wol hire haue. —— *Pars. T.* ¶783 Thise olde dotardes holours [*v.rr.* holors, houlours, hulours]. *c* **1440** *Promp. Parv.* 252/2 Hullowre, idem quod *Horel.* *c* **1460** *Towneley Myst.* xxiv. 373 Thise dysars and this hullars, Thise cokkers and thise bollars, And alle purscuttars.

Hence †**holoury** (*holorie*), fornication.

13.. *Minor Poems fr. Vernon MS.* xxxv. 391 Þe þridde is clept Holorie.

holp(e, **holpen**, pa. t. and pple. of HELP *v.* Also occas. used as pres. t. and infin. Now *U.S. dial.*

holrysche: see HOLL *a.*

hols (hɒlz), *sb. pl.* Colloq. (esp. school-children's) abbrev. of *holidays* (HOLIDAY *sb.* 2 b).

1905 H. A. VACHELL *Hill* vi. 137 The governor pointed that out last hols. **1921** S. THOMPSON *Rough Crossing* ii. 105, I may be staying in Oxford in the spring hols. **1931** *Church Times* 25 Sept. 344/4 After next 'hols' it will be a very different little boy who will take the train at Waterloo or Victoria. **1958** *Spectator* 30 May 677/1 The House broke up for the hols.

holscipe: see WHOLESHIP.

†**'holsom.** *Naut. Obs.* (See quot.)

1688 R. HOLME *Armoury* III. 164/1 *Howlsom*, is when a Ship will hull, try and ride well at Anchor, without rowling and tumbling and labouring much. Hence **1706** PHILLIPS (ed. Kersey), *Holsom.* **1727–41** in CHAMBERS *Cycl.* **1867** SMYTH *Sailor's Word-bk.*

holsom(e, obs. form of WHOLESOME.

†**holste.** An old name of some bird.

14.. *Pict. Voc.* in Wr.-Wülcker 762/25 *Hec talendiola*, a holste.

Holstein ('hɒlstaɪn, -stiːn). [Name of a region in N.W. Germany.] A breed of black-and-white dairy cattle, orig. raised in Friesland. Also *attrib.*

1865 *Rep. Comm. Agric. 1864* (U.S. Dept. Agric.) 161 Holstein cattle..[have] not received that appreciation in this country to which they are entitled. **1872** *Rep. Vermont Board Agric.* I. 176 The Dutch cattle, or as I believe it is settled they are to be called, the 'Holsteins'. **1876** *Trans. Ill. Dept. Agric.* XIV. 296 S. W. Kingsley spoke in favor of Holsteins for the dairy. **1971** *Farmers Weekly* 19 Mar. 77/3 The Dutch paraded six top-grade show cows, which were not for sale, while Canada exhibited 16 Holsteins from French herds.

holster ('həʊlstə(r)), *sb.* Also 7 **hulster**, 8 **houlster**. [Corresponds to mod.Du. *holster* (1678 in Hexham) in same sense: cf. also Icel. *husltr* case, sheath, Sw. *hölster*, Da. *hylster* sheath, holster, Goth. *hulistr* veil; also OE. *heolster* hiding-place, concealment; all from ablaut stem *hel-*, *hul-* to cover. The Ger. *holfter*, *hulfter* holster, MHG. *hulfter* quiver, OHG. *hul(u)ft* covering, appear to be from a different root. The history of mod. Eng. and Du. *holster*, before 17th c., does not appear.]

1. A leather case for a pistol fixed to the pommel of a horseman's saddle or worn on the belt.

1663 BUTLER *Hud.* I. i. 391 In th' Holsters, at his Saddle-bow Two aged Pistols he did stow. **1677** *Lond. Gaz.* No. 1163/4 His furniture was a green velvet Saddle with silver Lace, with a pair of Holsters answerable, and Horse Pistols. **1711** *Ibid.* No. 4897/3 A..Pad-Saddle, made fit for Houlsters. **1816** SCOTT *Antiq.* xxxiv, The arrival of a stranger..and a servant in black, which servant had holsters on his saddle-bow and a coronet upon the holsters. **1847** JAMES *J. Marston Hall* xi, I felt that my pistols were free in the holsters.

2. *attrib.* and *Comb.*, as ***holster-cap***, ***-case***, ***-pistol***; **hoster-gall**, a gall caused by the chafing of a holster; **holster-pipe**, 'that part of a holster which projects downward and receives the barrel of the pistol' (*Cent. Dict.*).

1688 *Lond. Gaz.* No. 2407/4 A blew Velvet Saddle with Silver Twist, and new *Holster-Caps of the same. **1846** *Hist. Rec. 3rd Light Dragoons* 39 The holster Caps and housings having a border of Royal lace. **1840** DICKENS *Barn. Rudge* i, A pair of pistols in a *holster-case. **1689** *Lond. Gaz.* No. 2509/4 A black Mare..with a *Holster Gall. **1679** *Lauderdale Papers* (Camden) III. xciv. 162 The Troop of Horse..all of yᵐ had *hulsterpistolls. **1858** CARLYLE *Fredk. Gt.* v. ii. I. 545 A pair of military boots or a holster-pistol of superior excellence.

Hence **'holstered** *a.*, bearing holsters.

1812 BYRON *Ch. Har.* I. li, The holster'd steed beneath the shed of thatch.

holster ('həʊlstə(r)), *v.* Chiefly *U.S.* [f. the sb.] *trans.* To put (a gun) into its holster. Hence **'holstered** *ppl. a.*

1930 *Argosy* 12 July 690/2 Both men had holstered rifles on their saddles. **1956** 'E. McBAIN' *Cop Hater* (1958) iv. 36 'We won't need these,' Bush said. He holstered his gun. **1972** B. F. CONNERS *Don't embarrass Bureau* (1973) II. 113 He holstered his weapon. **1973** R. HAYES *Hungarian Game* xvii. 108 The guard snatched at his holstered gun.

holt[1] (həʊlt). Also 4–7 holte, 5 halte, 6 *Sc.* hout, 6–7 hoult. [OE. *holt* = OFris., OS. *holt*, MDu., Du. *hout* wood (as material); OHG., MHG., Ger. *holz* wood, a wood, ON. *holt* wood, copse, now in Icel. 'a rough stony hill or ridge':—OTeut. ***hulto-**:—pre-Teut. ***kl̥dó-**: cf. OSlav. *klada* beam, rafter, stump, timber, Gr. κλάδος twig, OIr. *caill, coill* (-*ll* from -*ld*) wood.]

†**1.** Wood, timber. (OE. only, and doubtful.)

a **900** CYNEWULF *Juliana* 577 in *Exeter Bk.*, He læmen fæt biwyrcan het wundor-cræfte wiȝes womum and wudubeamum holte bi[h]lænan.

2. A wood; a copse. Now *poet.* and *dial.* (Occurs in many place-names and derived surnames.)

Beowulf (Z.) 2598 Hy on holt buȝon. *c* **1000** ÆLFRIC *Gram.* ix. (Z.) 59 *Nemus*, holt. *c* **1205** LAY. 20124 Þenne he cumeð of holte. *c* **1345** *Orpheo* 207 Now wol y be, And wonne there in holtys hore. *c* **1374** CHAUCER *Troylus* III. 302 (351) These holtes and these hayes That han in wynter ded ben and dreye. *a* **1450** *Le Morte Arth.* 3029 A chapelle he lette make By-twene two hye holtys hore. **1513** DOUGLAS *Æneis* VII. Prol. 66 Woddis, forestis, wyth nakyt bewis blout, Stud strypyt of thair weyd in every hout. **1600** FAIRFAX *Tasso* III. vi. 7 As the winde in hoults and shady greaues, A murmur makes, among the boughes and leaues. **1664** EVELYN *Sylva* (1776) 222 In the fresher bottoms and sides of hills, hoults, and in hedge rows. **1695** BP. PATRICK *Comm. Gen.* 241 A Holt or Grove of Oakes. **1796** SCOTT *Wild Huntsman* xxii, The timorous prey Scours moss and moor, and holt and hill. **1864** TENNYSON *En. Ard.* 676 Narrow breadth to left and right Of wither'd holt or tilth or pasturage. **1887** *Kent Gloss.*, *Holt*, a wood.

b. A plantation, esp. of osiers. *local.*

1611 COTGR., *Islaye*,.. a hoult, or plot wherein Oziers, or twig-withies grow. **1795** *Trans. Soc. Arts* XIII. 142 What has been done towards making these plantations or holts? **1813** T. MARTIN *Circle Mech. Arts, Basket-making* 67 In the fens, many holts (as they are provincially called), or plantations of osiers are raised. *a* **1825** FORBY *Voc. E. Anglia, Holt*, a small grove or plantation. We have gooseberry-holts, cherry-holts, nut-holts, osier-holts, &c.

3. A wooded hill.

[This sense may have arisen from a misunderstanding of 'holtis hie' in ME. poems; but cf. Icel. *holt* rough hill.]

1567 TURBERV. *Songs & Sonn.* (T.), Yee that frequent the hilles, And highest holtes of all. **1757** DYER *Fleece* II. 382 Whose rustic muse O'er heath and craggy holt her wing display'd. **1825** BROCKETT, *Holt*, a peaked hill covered with wood. **1848** LYTTON *Harold* VII. ii, Let his feet.. climb the green holts of England.

†**4.** (See quot.) *Obs.*

1611 COTGR., *Heulet*, a Hoult, or little Isle cut out of the land of purpose to be ouerflowed euerie tyde by the sea; that of the froth thereof.. salt may be made.

5. *Comb.*, as *holt side*; †**holt-felster**, i.e. holt-feller, a woodcutter; †**holt-wood**, a wood.

a **1000** *Phœnix* 171 in *Exeter Bk.*, Ðear he heanne beam on holt-wuda wunað. **13..** *Gaw. & Gr. Knt.* 742 Hiȝe hillez on vche a halue, & holt wodez vnder. *c* **1400** *Destr. Troy* 1350 The Troiens.. Fleddon in fere.. ouer hilles and hethes into holte woddes. *a* **1678** MARVELL *Appleton Ho.* 538 But most the hewel's wonders are, Who here has the holtfelster's care.

holt[2]. [An unexplained phonetic variant of HOLD *sb.*[1], which is still so pronounced in the midland (and some southern) counties and regionally in the United States.]

1. Hold, grasp, grip; support, sustenance. *dial.* and *U.S. colloq.* Cf. *a-holt* (s.v. A-HOLD *adv. phr.*).

c **1375** in *Pol. Rel. & L. Poems* 241 Alas! helle me hath in holt in ruyde; ȝe deuel in pine for worldes pride. *c* **1410** LOVE *Bonavent. Mirr.* lix. (Gibbs MS.) lf. 114 Þe.. strengeste holt and comforte þat þay myghten haue. **1619** R. HARRIS *Drunkard's Cup* 19 Yet would he not leaue his holte. **1825** J. NEAL *Bro. Jonathan* II. 60 [He cried] 'lay holt there; lay holt, every one o' you', throwing the reins behind him, into the carriage. **1848** BARTLETT *Dict. Amer., Holt*, for hold. Ex. 'Death has got holt of him.' **1881** *Leicester Gloss.* s.v., When they'n wanst took holt. *Mod. midl. dial.* Ketch 'olt on 'im! **1898** E. N. WESTCOTT *David Harum* xxii. 199 Of course you've heard the things that some folk say of him, an'.. they got some holt on your mind. **1909** R. A. WASON *Happy Hawkins* iv. 52 He'd 'a' been killed that trip if you hadn't taken holt when you did. **1930** *Amer. Speech* V. 151 *Catch holt of*, grab. 'Catch holt of my hand, quickly.' **1940** W. FAULKNER *Hamlet* iv. i. 313 'Grab a holt,' the Texan said. Eck grasped the wire also.

†**2.** A stronghold; = HOLD *sb.*[1] 10. *Obs.*

1586 J. HOOKER *Girald. Irel.* in *Holinshed* II. 11/1 Building a holt or castell vpon a certeine rockie hill. **1600** HOLLAND *Livy* XXXI. xxx. 791 Our ancestors inhabited those small holts [*castellis*]. *Ibid.* XL. xxii. 1075 They wasted and destroied their holts.

3. A place of refuge or abode; a lurking-place; an animal's lair or den, esp. that of an otter: = HOLD *sb.*[1] 9.

1590 SIR T. COCKAINE *Treat. Hunt.* D ij b, An Otter.. before he come to the holt where he lyeth. **1766** PENNANT *Zool.* (1812) I. 120 [The otter] forms before it reaches the top several holts, or lodges. **1885** *Badm. Libr., Hunting* 314 An old otter going for a strong holt. **1890** O. CRAWFURD *Round Calend. in Portugal* 24 The others.. frighten the trout from their 'holts' behind stones.

holus-bolus ('həʊləs'bəʊləs), *adv.* [Of dial. origin: app. a mock-latinization of 'whole bolus', or of an assumed Greek ὅλος βῶλος 'whole lump'.] All at a gulp; all in a lump; all at once.

1847–78 HALLIWELL, *Holus-bolus*, all at once. *Linc.* **1857** HUGHES *Tom Brown* I. i, As we say in the Vale, *holus-bolus* just as it comes. **1866** *Daily Tel.* 6 Feb. 3/3 One of the sails was rolled up in a lump and thrown into the hatchway holusbolus. **1868** W. COLLINS *Moonst.* (1889) 120 She.. making a sudden snatch at the heap of silver, put it back, holus-bolus, in her pocket. **1892** J. MORLEY *Speech* in *Pall Mall G.* 22 Aug. 6/3 Swallowing every proposal that is made holus bolus. **1897** *Sat. Rev.* 20 Mar. 282/2 Mr. Balfour simply decided that the Bill must go through holus bolus.

holvir, obs. form of HULVER, holly.

holw(e, obs. forms of HOLLOW.

†**holwort.** *Herb. Obs.* The name of a plant: cf. HOLLOWWORT, HULWORT.

1350 *Med. MS.* 1204 in *Archæol.* XXX. 386 Y^e lef is most like an hol worte plante.

holy ('həʊlɪ), *a.* (*sb.*) Forms: α. 1 **háliȝ, háleȝ,** 2–3 **haliȝ** (*def.* **halȝe**, *Orm.* **hallȝhe**), 2–4 (6 *Sc.*) **hali** (3 ali), 4 (5– *Sc.*) **haly**, (*Sc.* 5 **haily**, 5–6 **halye**, 6–7 **halie**). β. 3–4 **heli, hely**. γ. 2–5 **holi**, 3– **holy**, (3–6 **hole**, 3–7 **holie, holye**, 4 **hooli, hoely**, 4–6 **hooly**, 4–7 **holly**, 5 **oly**, 6 **wholy**). [OE. *háliȝ*, -*eȝ* (in inflexion contracted to *hálȝ*-), also Northumb. *hǽliȝ* (whence northern ME. *hely*), OFris. *hêlech*, OS. *hêlag*, -*eg* (MDu. *heilech*, -*egh*-, Du. *heilig*), OHG. *heilag* (MHG. *heilec*, Ger. *heilig*), ON. *heilagr* (Sw. *helig*, Da. *hellig*):—OTeut. type ***hailag-oz**, the sense of which is expressed in the Gothic of Ulfilas by *weihs* (but *hailag*, app. 'consecrated, dedicated', is read on a Runic inscription generally held to be Gothic). A deriv. of the adj. ***hailo-**, OE. *hál*, free from injury, whole, hale, or of the deriv. sb. ***hailoz-**, ***hailiz-**, in OHG. *heil*, ON. *heill* health, happiness, good luck, in ON. also omen, auspice: see -Y.

The sense-development from *hailo-* is not clear, because the primitive pre-Christian meaning is uncertain, although it is with some probablity assumed to have been 'inviolate, inviolable, that must be preserved *whole* or intact, that cannot be injured with impunity', a sense preserved in ON.; hence the adj. would naturally be applied to the gods, and all things specially pertaining to them; and, with the introduction of Christianity, it would be a ready word to render L. *sanctus, sacer*. But it might also start from *hail-* in the sense 'health, good luck, well-being', or be connected with the sense 'good omen, auspice, augury', as if 'of good augury': cf. OHG. *heilisôn*, OE. *hálsian*, to HALSE, augur, divine, exorcise, etc. The sense arrangement here is therefore merely provisional; we cannot in OE. get behind Christian senses in which *holy* is equated with L. *sanctus, sacer*.]

A. *adj.* **1.** Kept or regarded as inviolate from ordinary use, and appropriated or set apart for religious use or observance; consecrated, dedicated, sacred.

(This sense blends eventually with 3 b.)

c **1000** *Ags. Gosp.* Luke ii. 23 Ælc wæpned.. byð drihtne haliȝ ȝenemned. *c* **1050** *Bryhtferth's Handboc* in *Anglia* VIII. 310 He ys haliȝ sunna dæȝ. *c* **1175** *Lamb. Hom.* 87 Fram þan halie hester dei. **13..** *Cursor M.* 17288 + 83 Þe thrid day after.. Hald we hely pasche day. **1382** WYCLIF *Matt.* vii. 6 Nyl ȝe ȝeue holy thing to houndis. **1526** TINDALE *Heb.* ix. 2 The candlesticke, and the table, and the shewe breed, which is called wholy. **1549** COVERDALE, etc. *Erasm. Par. Tit.* 28 Neyther ought they to thynke any thinge that god hathe made to the vse of man to be holyar or vnholyar one than an other. **1559** W. CUNNINGHAM *Cosmogr. Glasse* 184 Helicon the holy Hill of the Musis. **1608** TOPSELL *Serpents* (1658) 633 The holy kinde of Asps they call *Thermusis*. **1613** PURCHAS *Pilgrimage* (1614) 542 What day they begin any great worke they after keepe holy. **1651** HOBBES *Leviath.* IV. xlv. 360 The word *Holy*.. implies a new Relation by Appropriation to God. **1713** ADDISON *Cato* I. ii, The pale trembling Vestal When she beholds the holy flame expiring. **1836** O. W. HOLMES *Poetry* III. 82 All is holy where devotion kneels.

2. As applied to deities, the development of meaning has probably been: Held in religious regard or veneration, kept reverently sacred from human profanation or defilement; hence, Of a character that evokes human veneration and reverence; and thus, in Christian use, Free from all contamination of sin and evil, morally and spiritually perfect and unsullied, possessing the infinite moral perfection which Christianity attributes to the Divine character. Cf. sense 4.

Its earlier application to heathen deities is found in ON., but app. not in OE.; in later use (see b) it renders Latin *sanctus, sacer*, so applied.

c **825** *Vesp. Psalter* xcviii[i]. 9 Haliȝ is dryhten god ur. *c* **950** *Lindisf. Gosp.* John xvii. 11 Ðu haliȝ fæder, ȝehald ða on ðinum noma þæt ðu sealdes me. *c* **1175** *Lamb. Hom.* 101 Alswa is þeo halȝe þreomnesse an god. **1382** WYCLIF *Lev.* xx. 26 ȝe shulen be holi to me, for Y the Lord am holy. —— *Acts* iv. 30 Signes and wondris for to be maad by the name of thin hooly sone Jhesu. —— *Rev.* iv. 8 Holy, holy, holy, the Lord God almiȝty. **1533** J. HEYWOOD *Pard. & Frere*, The holy Trynyte Preserve all that nowe here be. **1611** BIBLE *Ps.* xxii. 3 But thou art holy, O thou that inhabitest the praises of Israel. **1799** W. GILPIN *Serm.* I. xxi. (R.), The holy sufferer bowing his head, and crying, It is finished, gave up the ghost. **1827** HEBER *Hymn*, Only Thou art holy, there is none beside Thee [etc.]. **1857** BONAR *Hymn*, Holy Father! hear my cry; Holy Saviour! bend Thine ear; Holy Spirit! come Thou nigh.

b. 1606 SHAKS. *Ant. & Cl.* IV. viii. 29 Like holy Phœbus Carre. **1608** —— *Per.* III. iv. 7 Deliver'd, by the holy gods. **1850** BUCKLEY *Smart's Horace* 265 Swearing by holy Osiris.

3. Hence, **a.** Of persons: Specially belonging to, commissioned by, or devoted to God (or so regarded): e.g. angels, the Virgin Mary, prophets, apostles, martyrs, saints, popes, bishops, etc. ***the holy souls***, the souls of the faithful departed, the blessed dead.

c **950** *Lindisf. Gosp.* Mark viii. 38 [He] cymeð on wuldre fadores his mið englum halȝum. **971** *Blickling Homilies* (1880) vi. 67 Drihten.. helle bereafode, & þa halgan sauwla þonon alædde, & hie generede of deofles anwalde. *c* **1000** ÆLFRIC *Saints' Lives* (1890) II. 142 Nu cwæð se halȝa Beda. *c* **1200** *Trin. Coll. Hom.* 141 Þat holie maiden, ure helendes moder. **1340** *Ayenb.* 74 Vor al þet eure þoleden þe holy martires. **1357** JOHN DE THORESBY *Lay Folks Catechism* (1901) 2 This maner of knawying.. shuld we have had.. Noght so mikell als hali saules has now in heven, Bot mikel mare than man has now in erthe. *c* **1380** WYCLIF *Serm.* Sel. Wks. II. 229 Þe pope wole be clepid 'moost hooly fadir'. *c* **1425** *Hampole's Psalter* Metr. Pref. 21 A worthy holy man cald Rychard Hampole. **1591** SHAKS. *1 Hen. VI*, I. iv. 102 The Dolphin, with one Ioane de Puzel ioyn'd, A holy Prophetesse, new risen vp. **1626** T. H. *Caussin's Holy Crt.* 483 The holly Bishops.. began to declare the cause of theyr voyage. **1697** DRYDEN *Virg. Georg.* III. 737 The Victim Ox ..by the holy Butcher, if he fell, Th' inspected Entrails cou'd no Fates foretel. **1720** G. STANHOPE tr. *St. Augustine's Pious Breathings* (ed. 5) I. xxiii. 48 (*heading*) The Happiness of Holy Souls at their departure out of this World. **1781** GIBBON *Decl. & F.* III. 61 On the summit of a lofty mountain, the holy John had constructed, with his own hands, an humble cell. **1849** F. W. FABER *Jesus & Mary* 92 Pray for the Holy Souls that burn This hour amid the cleansing flames. **1885** MRS. MACQUOID *Louisa* III. vii. 115 Ah, may the Holy Virgin keep her from all evil! **1898** A. G. MORTIMER *Cath. Faith & Practice* II. xiv. 361 The Intermediate State, where the holy souls are waiting until their purification is accomplished. *Ibid.* 371 The joys and consolations of the holy souls in their preparation for Heaven. **1958** G. MONTAGUE *Probl. Liturgy* v. 305 It is clear ..that the Holy Souls could not be properly named as the titular of a church. The Souls in Purgatory are not an object of the public veneration of the church.

b. Of things: Pertaining to God or the Divine Persons; having their origin or sanction from God, or partaking of a Divine quality or character. ***the Holy Name***, the name of Jesus as an object of formal devotion among Catholics, as in the Litany of the Holy Name and the festival of the Holy Name of Jesus.

See also *M.E.D.* s.v. *holi* adj.[2] 2 a.

c **1000** *Ags. Ps.* (Th.) xix. [xx.] 6 He hine ȝehyrð of his þam halȝan heofone. *c* **1000** *Be Domes Dæȝe* D. 36 Haliȝe dreamas clænre stæfne. *c* **1175** *Lamb. Hom.* 119 Vre drihtnes halie passiun. *c* **1200** *Trin. Coll. Hom.* 143 Hali boc nemmeð þes woreld sæ. *c* **1250** *Gen. & Ex.* 51 Ðat heli luue, ðat wise wil. *c* **1315** SHOREHAM 53 Thourȝ hys holy dethe Of sennes he was leche. *c* **1400** MAUNDEV. (1839) xii. 139 Straungeres fro the holy and verry Beleeve. *c* **1440** *Thornton MS.* f. 192 Of the vertuz of the holy name of Ihesu. **1521** FISHER *Wks.* (1876) 313 This hooly gospel gracyously offereth vnto vs foure goodly instruccyons. **1526** [see NAME *sb.* 3]. **1534** ELYOT *Doctrinal Princes* 2 Any booke, holy scripture excepted. *a* **1700** DRYDEN tr. *Veni Creator* 9 Thrice holy fount, thrice holy fire, Our hearts with heavenly love inspire. **1720** T.M. tr. *Horstius' Paradise of Soul* (1771) 409 Great are the Honours and Priviledges of the Holy Name, Jesus. **1851** J. B. PAGANI *Life A. Gentili* III. xi. 196 Singing along the way the Litany of the Holy Name of Jesus. **1860** RAY PALMER *Hymn, 'Jesus, Thou joy of loving hearts'* v, Shed o'er the world Thy holy light! **1884** ADDIS & ARNOLD *Cath. Dict.* s.v. *Jesus*, An office of the Holy Name. **1901** G. TYRRELL *Autobiogr.* (1912) I. vii. 94 Two of the boys.. would bow their heads at the Holy Name at morning prayers. **1968** R. WOOLF *Eng. Relig. Lyric* v. 172 Both 'Luf es lyf' and 'My sange es in syhtyng' include verses expressing devotion to the Holy Name. *Ibid.* 173 In medieval spirituality.. the devotion to the Holy Name becomes a form of devotion to Christ in His humanity. **1970** R. W. PFAFF *New Liturgical Feasts Later Med. England* iv. 63 The quite historical indulgences connected with the Name of Jesus from the thirteenth century are concerned not with the mass but with pious ejaculations mentioning the Holy Name.

c. More generally: Of high and reverend excellence; formerly said of things highly esteemed for their qualities or 'virtues'.

1599 H. BUTTES *Dyets drie Dinner* F iij, Many do much extoll Sage, calling it an holy Hearbe, averring that it preventeth all abortument in women. **1634** SIR T. HERBERT *Trav.* 37 Paint their faces, and put Rice upon the paint, a holy remedy for each dayes chances. **1862** BURTON *Bk. Hunter* (1863) 399 There is a propensity to believe that whatever is old must have something holy and mysterious about it.

4. Conformed to the will of God, entirely devoted to God: in earlier times often connoting the practice of asceticism and religious observances; now usually: Morally and spiritually unstained; free from sinful affection; of godly character and life; sanctified, saintly; sinless. **a.** Of persons.

c **897** K. ÆLFRED *Gregory's Past.* xviii. 134 He wilniað ðæt hie mon hæbbe for ða betstan and ða halȝestan. *c* **950** *Lindisf. Gosp.* Mark vi. 20 Herodes.. wiste hine wer soðfæst & haliȝ. *c* **1200** ORMIN 5394 Rihht ædiȝnessess seoffne, þatt hallȝhe weress follȝhenn. *a* **1300** *Cursor M.* 10618 Þar was na mai of

nan oxspring Halier, noþer ald na ying. **1382** WYCLIF *Tit.* i. 8 Sobre, iust, hooly, contynent. **1426** AUDELAY *Poems* 15 Throȝ the prayere of a good prist, an hole and an hynd, that kepys his ordore. **1508** DUNBAR *Tua Mariit Wemen* 472 ȝit, am I haldin a haly wif our all the haill schyre. **1591** SHAKS. *Two Gent.* IV. ii. 41 Holy, faire, and wise is she. **1842** ARNOLD *Serm. Chr. Life* (1849) 29 For a moment it must overwhelm the mind of the holiest. **1875** MANNING *Mission H. Ghost* xvi. 436 A just man fulfils the law, and gives to every man his due; a holy man is specially united with God.

b. Of actions, feelings, etc.

c **1200** *Vices & Virtues* 13 And seðđen mid haliȝe wordes me wissede. *a* **1225** *Ancr. R.* 142 Heo owun to beon of so holi liue. *c* **1320** *Cast. Love* 814 Þe middel bayle.. Bi-toknep hire holy chastite. **1426** in *Surtees Misc.* (1888) 10 For the werke of the haly charite. **1548–9** (Mar.) *Bk. Com. Prayer, 2nd Collect at Evensong*, O God, from whom all holy desyres.. do procede. **1600** SHAKS. *A.Y.L.* III. v. 99 So holy, and so perfect is my loue. **1781** COWPER *Truth* 281 A demeanour holy and unspecked. **1813** HURN *Hymn, 'There is a river deep and broad'* iv, With holy joy their breast expands.

c. Used trivially: (*a*) with *horror* or the like (orig. *U.S.*), expressing intensity; (*b*) with unfavourable implication of piety or sanctimoniousness (*colloq.*); (*c*) used with a following word as an oath or expletive, as ***holy cow!***, ***holy Moses!***, ***holy smoke!***

holy Joe: see quots.; ***holy terror***: a person of exasperating habits or manners; ***holy Willie***: a hypocritically pious person.

[**1785** BURNS *Poems & Songs* (1968) I. 74 (*title*) Holy Willie's prayer. *Ibid.* 78 Here Holy Willie's sair worn clay Taks up its last abode.] **1837** *Southern Lit. Messenger* III. 668, I have a holy horror of gossips. **1855** [see MOSES 1 c]. **1860** S. MORDECAI *Virginia* xxxii. 317 The Virginia Legislature had such a holy horror of banks in 1803, that they refused a charter to the petitioners. **1874** HOTTEN *Slang Dict.* 193 *Holy Joe*, a sea-term for a parson. **1883** G. W. PECK *Mirth for Millions* p. viii, 'Have you read "Peck's Bad Boy"!' ..News agents on the Railroad cars found it almost impossible to meet the demand of those who yearned to become acquainted with this 'holy terror'. **1886** J. M. THOMPSON *Banker of Bankersville* 265 To get it by means of such a holy terror of exhortation. **1889** BARRÈRE & LELAND *Dict. Slang* I. 469/1 *Holy Joe* (prison and nautical), the chaplain or any religious person. **1892** KIPLING & BALESTIER *Naulahka* i. 4 By the holy smoke, some one has got to urge girls to stand by the old machine. **1893** *Strand Mag.* VI. 105/1 Not excepting even the Dwarf, and he's, generally speaking, a holy terror. **1916** 'TAFFRAIL' *Pincher Martin* iii. 34 Even the chaplain, the Reverend Stephen Holiman, set an example by shedding his clerical garments and trundling a barrow. The men loved seeing Holy Joe 'sweatin' himself', as they put it. **1916** G. B. SHAW *Androcles* p. xciv, The imitators of the apostles, whether they are called Holy Willies or Stigginses in derision, or, in admiration, Puritans or saints. **1917** *Dialect Notes* IV. 341 *Holy horrors*, a fright. 'It gave me the *holy horrors*.' **1920** 'SAPPER' *Bull-Dog Drummond* v. 125 'Holy smoke! laddie,' he murmured. **1921** N. H. THORP *Songs of Cowboys* (ed. 2) 73 Holy Moses and the Prophets how we split the Texas air. **1924** *Dialect Notes* V. 265 *Cow*: holy —— (vex[ation]: New York). **1933** J. MASEFIELD *Conway* 211 *Holy Joe*, one who is good at Scripture. **1934** J. A. LEE *Children of Poor* 130 The Holy Willies would throw a party. 'Come to our Sunday School?' **1941** BAKER *Dict. Austral. Slang* 35 *Holy Joes*, prudish, narrow-minded puritans. **1942** BERREY & VAN DEN BARK *Amer. Thes. Slang* §194/6 Holy cow! **1941** A. L. ROWSE *Tudor Cornwall* vi. 121 He must have been a holy terror to the neighbourhood. **1949** M. LOWRY *Let.* 26 Mar. (1967) 177 Holy great cow, what prose is this? **1951** J. CORNISH *Provincials* 40 Quit showing off. Holy cow! **1951** J. D. SALINGER *Catcher in Rye* xiv. 120 They all have these Holy Joe voices when they start giving their sermons. **1958** *Listener* 18 Sept. 429/3, I cannot find justification for Mr. McCallion's term 'holy voice'. **1959** 'J. ROSS' *Boy in Grey Overcoat* viii. 94 She said again, in that holy voice, [etc.]. **1960** I. CROSS *Backward Sex* 40 'Holy smoke,' he gasped, 'That's a funny face.' **1967** V. CANNING *Python Project* vii. 135, I said..'Holy Moses!' **1973** J. WAINWRIGHT *Pride of Pigs* 104 Holy cow! I forgot to switch the bloody immersion heater off.

5. a. In special collocations.

Holy Alliance: an alliance formed in 1815, after the fall of Napoleon, between the sovereigns of Russia, Austria, and Prussia, with the professed object of uniting their respective governments in a Christian brotherhood. † **Holy bone** [tr. L. *os sacrum*: cf. Ger. *das heilige bein*]: the SACRUM. **holy brotherhood** [tr. Sp. *Santa Hermandad*]: = HERMANDAD. **holy doors**: in the Greek Church, the doors in the screen which separates the altar and sanctuary from the main body of the church. **holy laugh** *U.S.*, a laugh by a person in a state of religious fervour. † **holy oak**: an oak marking a parish boundary, at which a stoppage was made for the reading of the Gospel for the day in the 'beating of the bounds' during the Rogation days; called also *gospel-oak*, *gospel-tree*. **Holy One**: a holy person; used as a title of God or Christ; one dedicated to or consecrated by God. **Holy Roller** (see ROLLER *sb.*[1] 17 b). **holy seed**: the seed of some species of *Artemisia*, also called Wormseed. Also *holy* CHURCH (sense 7), *H.* CITY (2 f), *H.* FAMILY (3), *H.* FATHER (6 d), *H.* GRAIL, *H.* INQUISITION, *H.* LEAGUE, *H.* OFFICE, *h.* OIL, *h.* ORDER, *H.* PASSION, *H.* ROOD, *H.* SATURDAY, *H.* SEE, *H.* SEPULCHRE, *H.* SPIRIT, *H.* SYNOD, *h.* TABLE, *H.* THURSDAY, *h.* WAR: see these words. See also main words below.

1823 T. MOORE (*title*) Fables of the *Holy Alliance. **1849** MACAULAY *Hist. Eng.* ii. I. 207 Apprehensions..resembling those which, in our age, induced the Holy Alliance to interfere in the internal troubles of Naples and Spain. **1615** CROOKE *Body of Men* 899 Ovt of the marrow concluded within the rackes of the *Holy-bone doe yssue sixe coniugations of Nerues. **1634** T. JOHNSON *Parey's Chirurg.* 574 The fracture of the Holy-bone. **1742** JARVIS *Quix.* xxii. (1897) 101 The fugitives would give notice of the fact to the *Holy Brotherhood, who..would sally out in quest of the delinquents. **1895** STANLEY WEYMAN *Minister of France* 49 You have been in the hands of the Holy Brotherhood? **1772** J. G. KING *Greek Ch.* 26 The *holy, royal, or beautiful doors. **1849** BERESF. HOPE in *Ecclesiologist* IX. 10 The chancel is separated from the nave by a rood screen of oak with holy-doors traceried in the head. **1829** *Western Monthly Rev.* II. 477 Dr. Roberts is very pointed in his testimony against the abominable practice of jumping, pointing, dancing, boreing... Might he not have added the '*holy laugh'? **1833** H. BARNARD *Let.* 27 Mar. in *Maryland Hist. Mag.* (1918) XIII. 328 The preacher in the midst of a fervent prayer, will all of a sudden burst out into a loud boisterous laugh... The most godly of his brethren join with him. This is called the 'Holy Laugh'. **1845** J. J. HOOPER *Some Adv. S. Suggs* x. 122 Near these last, stood a delicate woman in that hysterical condition in which the nerves are incontrollable, and which is vulgarly..termed the 'holy laugh'. **1948** E. N. DICK *Dixie Frontier* 198 When it got started in an audience, everybody would be seized with hearty natural laughter. It would last for hours sometimes. This was known as the 'holy laugh'. **1648** HERRICK *Hesper.*, *To Anthea*, Dearest, bury me Under that *holy-oke, or gospel-tree. **1535** COVERDALE *Jer.* li. 5 Of the Lorde of hoostes, of the *holyone of Israel. —— *Mark* i. 24, I knowe that thou art euen yᵉ holy one of God. **1560** BIBLE (Genev.) *Ps.* xvi. 10 Nether wilt thou suffer thine holie one to se corruption. **1667** MILTON *P.L.* XII. 248 He vouchsafes.. The holy One with mortal Men to dwell. **1860** T. H. GILL *Gold. Chain Praise* IV. ii, Holy One, who sin abhorrest.. Holy One, our sin who borest.. Holy One, who takest sorrow When we touch the thing abhorred! **1597** GERARDE *Herbal* II. ccccxxxv. 942 The seede is called euery where *Semen sanctum*, *Holie seede..in English, Wormseed.

b. In names of plants: **holy basil**, the common Indian species of basil, *Ocimum sanctum*. **holy grass**, a grass of genus *Hierochloe*, esp. ***northern h. g.***, *H. borealis* (quot. 1842); also, rarely = *holy-hay*; **holy hay**, Sainfoin; applied both to *Onobrychis sativa* and *Medicago sativa*: see LUCERNE, SAINFOIN; † **holy hemp**, 'an old name for *Galeopsis Ladanum*' (Miller); † **holy herb** [transl. Gr. ἱεροβοτάνη], a name in the Herbals for Vervain; † **holy rope**, an old name for Hemp-agrimony (*Eupatorium cannabinum*); **holy tree**, an Indian tree, *Melia Azedarach*, also called Pride of India; † **holy wood**, a name of the West Indian *Guaiacum sanctum*. See also HOLY GHOST, *holy* THISTLE.

1880 *Encycl. Brit.* XII. 720/2 The worship of the *tulsi* plant, or *holy basil, by the Hindus. **1894** A. K. NAIRNE *Flowering Plants W. India* 251 O[*cimum*] *sanctum*. Holy basil... Very commonly cultivated, particularly about temples and in Brahmins' gardens. **1906** T. COOKE *Flora of Presidency of Bombay* (1908) II. 440 The Holy Basil, the most sacred plant in the Hindu religion, very doubtfully indigenous. **1778** *Eng. Gazetteer* (ed. 2) s.v. *Cambridgeshire*, The dry and barren parts have been greatly improved by sowing that called saint-foin, and *holy-grass, from its having been first brought into Europe from Palestine. **1842** C. W. JOHNSON *Farmer's Encycl.* 636 Holy-Grass, Northern (*Hierochloe borealis*).. This grass is said to be used at high festivals, for strewing the churches in Prussia. **1872** SYME *Eng. Bot.* xi. (ed. 3) 16 Northern Holy Grass.. This grass, dedicated to the Virgin Mary on account of its sweetness, is strewn about Catholic churches on festival days. *a* **1661** FULLER *Worthies* (1840) II. 113 Saint-foin, or *Holy-hay. **1669** WORLIDGE *Syst. Agric.* (1681) 26 What annually yields its increase without a renovation of expence in Ploughing and Sowing; as we find in the Clover-grass or great Trefoyl, St. Foyn or Holy-Hay, La Lucern, Ray-grass, &c. **1884** MILLER *Plant-n.*, Holy Hay, *Medicago sativa*. **1567** MAPLET *Gr. Forest* 64 Veruen, of some after their language is called **Holy Herbe*. **1688** R. HOLME *Armoury* II. 114/1 Vervain of some called Holy Herb. *c* **1485** *MS. Bodl.* 536 in *Sax. Leechd.* III. Gloss. 332 *Holi roppe. **1597** GERARDE *Herbal* App., *Holy rope* is wild Hemp. **1866** *Treas. Bot.* 731/1 *M[elia] Azedarach*, vulgarly known as the Pride of India, False Sycamore, *Holy-tree. **1712** tr. *Pomet's Hist. Drugs* I. 65 *Holy-Wood grows plentifully in the West-Indies.

c. Compar. *holier* in colloq. phr. ***holier-than-thou***: characterized by an attitude of superior sanctity. (Cf. Isaiah lxv. 5.)

1912 T. DREISER *Financier* lxvi. 684 The 'holier than thou' attitude, intentional or otherwise, is quite the last and most deadly offense within prison walls. **1918** *Maclean's Mag.* Jan. 45/1 His holier-than-thou attitude irritates the officials. **1922** S. LEWIS *Babbitt* xix. 239 But I don't want you to think you can get away with any holier-than-thou stuff. **1928** F. HURST *President is Born* xiii. 155 If the whole holier-than-thou house of Schuyler has got to be protected from me, dammit, I'm not going to do the protecting. **1957** R. HOGGART *Uses of Literacy* vi. 169 They counter-accuse their accusers of being 'holier than thou', of smugness, of 'hypocrisy'. **1958** *Listener* 23 Oct. 660/1 She distrusted high flights of emotion, any parade of spiritual inclinations, any holier-than-thou attitudes. **1973** *Ibid.* 4 Jan. 9/3 The Mormons were not only holier-than-thou; they were thriftier.

B. *absol.* or as *sb.*

1. That which is holy; a holy thing.

c **950** *Lindisf. Gosp.* Matt. vii. 6 Nellas ȝe sella haliȝ hundum. **1548** UDALL, etc. *Erasm. Par. Acts* 45 a, That it was not lawfull to gyue to dogges the holy. **1613** PURCHAS *Pilgrimage* (1614) 827 The Friers went one day with their conjuring, and conjured holies, the Crosse, Stole, Holy-water. **1678** CUDWORTH *Intell. Syst.* I. iv. §16. 292 The only Inventor of the Natural Holy. **1831** CARLYLE *Sart. Res.* I. v, Clothes, a mystic grove-encircled shrine for the Holy in man.

† **2.** A holy place, sanctuary. *Obs.* (exc. as in 5).

1382 WYCLIF *Ps.* lxii[i]. 3 So in holi I aperede to thee.

† **3.** A holy person, a saint: = HALLOW *sb. Obs.*

1548 UDALL, etc. *Erasm. Par. Acts* 10 Neither wilte thou suffre thine holy, to see corrupcion. **1622** T. STOUGHTON *Chr. Sacrif.* ix. 114 So well pleasing are the Lords holies vnto him. **1648** HERRICK *Hesper.*, *To Mr. S. Soame*, Canonized here, Among which holies, be thou ever known.

† **4.** *pl.* Sacred rites, devotions. *Obs.*

1613 PURCHAS *Pilgrimage* (1614) 279 In their holies they most use the Arabike by reason of the Alcoran written in that language. *Ibid.* 542 Their Temples..to which they resort to say and doe their Holies.

5. **holy of holies**. [A Hebraism, *qōdesh haqqŏdāshīm*, rendered in Exod. xxvi. 34 'most holy place', but literally reproduced in LXX and Vulgate *τόν ἅγιον τῶν ἁγίων*, *sanctum sanctorum*, whence in Wyclif, etc.] **a.** The 'most holy place', the inner chamber of the sanctuary in the Jewish tabernacle and temple, separated by a veil from the outer chamber or 'holy place'. **b.** *transf.* The inner part of any temple; the sanctuary or bema of a Christian church, esp. in the Greek Church; a small recess containing a cross at the east end of a Nestorian church. **c.** *fig.* A place of special sacredness, an innermost shrine.

[**1382** WYCLIF *Exod.* xxvi. 34 The parti of the tabernacle that is clepid holi of halowes. *c* **1400** MAUNDEV. (1839) viii. 85 This Place the Iewes callen *Sancta Sanctorum*; that is to seye, holy of halewes.] **1641** MILTON *Ch. Govt.* I. v, The type of Christ in some one particular, as of entering yearly into the holy of holies..rested upon the high priest only. **1725** J. HENLEY tr. *Montfaucon's Antiq. Italy* (ed. 2) 56 A Priest..open'd the Doors of the Sanctuary , which the Greek call the Holy of Holies. **1778** *Eng. Gazetteer* (ed. 2) s.v. *Stonehenge*, The space within it has been called the *adytum*, or the Holy of Holies. **1876** OUIDA *Winter City* vi. 155 Self-engrossed, entirely shut in a Holy-of-Holies of culture and of criticism.

6. sup. *holiest*, used *absol.* **a.** As a title of God or Christ.

a **1300** *Cursor M.* 9337 Quen he þat haliest es cumen. **1866** J. H. NEWMAN *Hymn*, Praise to the Holiest in the height.

b. = holy of holies: see 5.

1611 BIBLE *Heb.* x. 19 Hauing therefore..boldnesse to enter into the holiest by the blood of Jesus.

C. *Comb.* **a.** adverbial, with other adjs., as ***holy-cruel***, ***-proud***, ***-wise***. **b.** parasynthetic, as ***holy-eyed***, ***-minded***, ***-rolling***, ***-tempered***, ***-thoughted*** adjs.; hence ***holy-mindedness***, etc. **c.** † **holy-maker**, sanctifier; also † **holy-making**, sanctification.

1601 SHAKS. *All's Well* IV. ii. 32 Be not so *holy-cruell: Loue is holie. **1922** JOYCE *Ulysses* 182 An ollav, *holyeyed. **1957** J. KEROUAC *On Road* (1958) 221 A thin..holy-eyed.. lost soul. *c* **1546** JOYE in Gardiner *Declar. Art. Joye* (1546) 14 b, The only rightwysnes, wisdome, *holy maker..and satisfaction sufficient for al that beleue in hym. **1535** COVERDALE *2 Esdras* viii 39, I wil remembre also the pilgramege, the *holymakynge and the rewarde. **1902** W. JAMES *Var. Relig. Exper.* xi. 296 The *holy-minded person finds..inner smoothness and cleanness. **1801** W. TAYLOR in *Monthly Mag.* XI. 43 Religion, or *holymindedness, may, with obvious advantage, be substituted. **1602** CAREW *Cornwall* (1811) 324 You neighbour-scorners, *holy-proud. Go people Roche's cell. **1965** *Punch* 20 Oct. 583/1 Sister Margaret, formidable pastor of one of those *holy-rolling Harlem churchlets. **1836** J. H. NEWMAN in *Lyra Apost.* (1849) 163 Like..*holy-tempered Nazarite. **1593** SHAKS. *Lucr.* 384 *Holy-thoughted Lucrece. *a* **1592** GREENE *Jas. IV*, II. ii, She's *holy-wise and too precise for me. *a* **1649** DRUMM. OF HAWTH. *Poems* Wks. (1711) 15 Goodness by thee The holy-wise is thought a fool to be.

† **'holy**, *v. Obs.* [f. HOLY *a.*, instead of the historical HALLOW *v.*] *trans.* To make holy, sanctify, consecrate; to make a saint of, canonize.

1578 *Almanack* in *Liturg. Serv. Q. Eliz.* (Parker Soc.) 446 The Temple of Jerusalem was finished and holied. **1584** R. SCOT *Discov. Witchcr.* IV. viii. (1886) 65 Written in virgine parchment, celebrated and holied by a popish priest. **1622** MASSINGER & DEKKER *Virg. Mart.* II. ii, On! I hug thee. *Theoph.* Both hug and holy me.

holy, var. HOLEY; obs. f. HOLLY, WHOLLY; early f. HOOLY *a.* and *adv.*

holyander, obs. f. OLEANDER.

holy bread. Forms: see HOLY; also 6–7 **hally-**, **halli-**, 7 **halle-**. The (ordinary leavened) bread which was blessed after the Eucharist and distributed to those who had not communicated: corresponding to the eulogia of the Greek Church and the French *pain bénit*. **b.** In post-Reformation times, The bread provided for the Eucharist.

a **1300** *Sat. People Kildare* x. in *E.E.P.* (1862) 154 Hail be ȝe, prestis..whan ȝe deliþ holibrede, ȝiue me botte a litil. **1303** R. BRUNNE *Handl. Synne* 838 Ete noght ar þou haue holy brede. *c* **1405** *Bidding Prayer* ii. in *Lay Folks Mass Bk.* 65 For thaim that halybred gaf to this kirk to day. **1548–9** (Mar.) *Bk. Com. Pr.*, *Communion* (Rubric), In suche Chapelles annexed where yᵉ people hath not bene accustomed to pay any holy bread, there they must..make ..prouision for the bering of the charges of the Communion. **1599** SANDYS *Europæ Spec.* (1632) 179 As in their Holy-bread on Sondayes for them that doe not communicate. **1600** SHAKS. *A.Y.L.* III. iv. 15 His kissing is as ful of sanctitie, As the touch of holy bread. **1619** *Vestry Bks.* (Surtees) 175 Pᵈ for holye brede for the whole yeare for the Communion, xviij*d.* **1782** PRIESTLY *Corrupt. Chr.* II. VI. 16 Some churches substituted what they called eulogies, or holy bread for the bread of the Lord's Supper. **1866** PEACOCK *Eng. Ch. Furniture* 86 *note*, The holy bread, holy loaf, or Eulogia, was ordinary leavened bread blessed by the priest after mass, cut up into small pieces and given to the people.

c. *attrib.* and *Comb.*, as ***holy bread cake***, ***cantle***, ***cloth***, ***loaf***, ***silver***, ***skep***.

1552 HULOET, Holy breade loofe, *strues.* **1575–6** *Durham Depos.* (Surtees) 278 The said inhabitors every 7 yere paid hally bread syllver, viz. 3*d.* for every Sonday in the hole yere. *Ibid.* 281 Hallybread caike. *Ibid.*, The said clerk cut off a part of the said caike, cauld the hally breid cantle, to gyve to ther next neighbour. **1640** *Vestry Bks.* (Surtees) 103 Item this yeere, 1640, the churchwardens receved of the parish for holly bread silver but only 3*s.* 6*d.*

† **holychurche, holicherche, halykirk,** etc., ME. ways of writing *holy church*, CHURCH 7.

1357 *Lay Folks Catech.* 29 The lawe and þe lare þat langes till halikirke. *c* **1450** *Merlin* 14 In the mercy and ordenaunce of god and holicherche.

Holy cross. a. The cross upon which Jesus Christ suffered death (see CROSS *sb.* 2 and *note*). Hence in derived senses (cf. CROSS *sb.* 3, 8, and 9).

c **1290**, *c* **1380**, **1548–9** [see CROSS *sb.* 2, 9, 3]. **13..** *Coer de L.* 1304 Thus, thorwgh tresoun of the Eerl Joys, Surry was lorn and the holy croys. **1470–85** MALORY *Arthur* XVII. x, Thenne he took her by the brydel and sayd, by the holy crosse ye shalle not escape me. **1583** HOLLYBAND *Campo di Fior* 51 Blesse thee with the signe of the holie crosse. **1826** HONE *Every-day Bk.* I. 1291 A Romish catholic festival in honour of the holy cross, or, as our ancestors called it, the holy rood.

b. In the titles of certain religious societies or communities.

[**1426** in *Eng. Gilds* (1870) 246 *note*, Willielmus Rydware, magister Gilde sancte Crucis de Bermyngeham.] **1547** *Rep. Commissioners* ibid. 248 The guilde of tholye Crosse in brymyncham. **1872** O. SHIPLEY *Gloss. Eccl. Terms*, *Holy Cross*, an order of Augustinian canons, suppressed in the 17th cent. **1884** *Cassell's Encycl. Dict.*, *Holy-cross*, a society consisting of clerical members of the ritualistic school of the English Church. It was founded in 1855.

c. *attrib.* **Holy Cross day**, the festival of the Exaltation of the Cross, September 14th; **holy cross toad**, a frog of New South Wales, *Notaden bennettii*, so called from a dark cross-shaped marking on the back.

1662 *Bk. Com. Prayer*, *Calendar*, Holy Cross Day. **1687** A. LOVELL tr. *Thevenot's Trav.* I. 232 And the four and twentieth, which is Holy-Cross-Day, according to the Calender of the Greeks. **1883** R. SINKER in *Prayer Bk. Comment.* (S.P.C.K) 34 'Holy Cross Day' in our Calendar, or, more strictly speaking, the 'Exaltation of the Cross' probably celebrates primarily the consecration of the Church of the Holy Sepulchre at Jerusalem in 335 A.D.; but its renown is specially due to the victory of Heraclius over the Persians and his restoration of the Cross to its shrine at Jerusalem. **1891** J. H. ROSE in *Proc. Linn. Soc. N.S.W.* 2nd Ser. VI. 265 *Notaden bennetti*, the Catholic frog, or as I have heard it called the 'Holy Cross toad'. **1969** M. BURTON *Animals of Australia* xiv. 120 The holy cross toad is unusual among Australian amphibians in that it comes out during the day to feed.

holydam, -dome, var. of HALIDOM.

holy-day ('həʊlɪdeɪ). Forms: see HOLIDAY. [OE. *háliʒ dæʒ*, two words, with the adj. subject to inflexion; ME. early and northern *haliʒ*, *haly day*, midland and southern *hooly day*, *holy day*, *holyday*. In early times, more usually a compound, OE. *háliʒdæʒ*. ME. *haliday*, later HOLIDAY, q.v. Since the 16th c. the habit has more and more prevailed to use the analytical form, whether written *holy day*, *holy-day*, or *holyday*, in the original sense, and to restrict *holiday* ('hɒlɪdeɪ) to the sense 'day of recreation' (although the spelling *holiday*, in the sense of *holy day*, has not become quite obsolete). See HOLIDAY I.]

A day consecrated or set apart for religious observance, usually in commemoration of some sacred person or event; a religious festival.

a **1000** *Laws of Æthelred* VI. c. 22 (Schmid) Woroldricra weorca on þam halʒan dæʒe ʒeswice man ʒeorne. *c* **1200** ORMIN 4350 Forr Saterrdaʒʒ wass haliʒ daʒʒ. **13..** *E.E. Allit. P.* B. 134 Hit watz not for a haly day honestly arayed. **1462** in Ellacombe *Ch. Bells Devon*, *Bells Ch.* ix. (1872) 469 Every Sonday and woly day. **1552** *Bk. Com. Prayer*, *Communion* (Rubric), Any holye dayes or fasting daies. **1603** KNOLLES *Hist. Turks* (J.), They kept that day as one of their solemn holydays for many years after. **1663** BUTLER *Hud.* I. i. 213 A Sect..That with more care keep Holy-day The wrong, than others the right way. **1844** LINGARD *Anglo-Sax. Ch.* (1858) II. App. A. 331 The days of St. Augustine and St. Boniface were ordered to be kept as holydays. **1871** *Daily News* 7 Apr., Of late years Good Friday has become.. a general holiday rather than a holy day. **1876** MISS G. CUMMING *In Hebrides* (1883) 2 We..soon found..that they were keeping holy-day or holiday, as the case might be.

attrib. **1549** LATIMER *5th Serm bef. Edw. VI* (Arb.) 141 It is a holy daye worcke to vyset the prisoners. **1552** HULOET, Holy daye euen, or halfe holy day, *profestus.* **1682** N. O. *Boileau's Lutrin* IV. 70 He calls..for's Holy-day Apparell!

holyer, var. of HOLOUR *Obs.*

holy fire. *arch.* [transl. L. *sacer ignis* 'sacred fire' (Celsus, Vergil); cf. Ger. *das heilige Feuer.*] Erysipelas, St. Anthony's fire: see FIRE *sb.* 12.

1398 TREVISA *Barth. De P.R.* XVII. xxii. (Bodl. MS.) Þe yuel þat hatte..Ignis saluaticus and sacer ignis the holy fuyre. **1607** TOPSELL *Four-f. Beasts* (1658) 201 The holy fire is a disease of Sheep almost incurable, because if any remedy do but touch them, they fall mad. *Ibid.* 476 Of the Holy fire which the Shepheards call the Pox, or the Blisters, or Saint Anthonies fire. **1813** T. BUSBY *Lucretius* VI. 764 Observe the Holy-Fire Eat as it creeps, and through the frame its dire, Its flamy virus lead!

Holy Ghost ('həʊlɪ 'gəʊst). [Properly two words (see HOLY *a.*, GHOST 6), and so always treated in OE., *se hálʒa gást*, *háliʒ gást*, but in ME. very generally as a combination, *haligast*, *holigost*; since 1500 again usually written as two words, but treated as a proper name or individual designation, and, as such, taken as a whole in the transferred and derivative uses.]

1. The Divine Spirit; the Third Person of the Godhead, the Holy Spirit.

a **900** *Halsuncge* in *Durh. Rit.* (Surtees) 114 Ic eow halsiʒe on fæder naman, and on suna naman..and on ðæs halʒan gastes. *c* **1000** *Ags. Gosp.* Matt. i. 20 Hyt ys of þam halʒan gaste. *c* **1160** *Hatton G.* Ibid., Hyt is of þan halʒen gaste. *c* **1175** *Lamb. Hom.* 101 Efter þes halʒa gastes to-cume. *c* **1200** *Trin. Coll. Hom.* 119 Þus hie seʒen þe holi gost on tungene euene. *a* **1225** *Juliana* 2 On his deorewurðe sunes nome, ant o þes haligastes. *c* **1250** *Gen. & Ex.* 2428 Quuor ali gast stille hadde seid.. Quuor iesu crist wulde ben boren. *a* **1300** *Cursor M.* 19349 Wit haligast he has us sent. *c* **1320** *Cast. Love* 562 Þorw God þe Holigostes miht. *a* **1340** HAMPOLE *Psalter* xvii. 13 Þe haly gast..þat is makere of haly writ. **1377** LANGL. *P. Pl.* B. XII. 141 For þe heihe holigoste [*v.r.* hye holygost] heuene shal to-cleue. *c* **1394** *P. Pl. Crede* 836 A man..þat myʒte wiþ his good lijf þat Holly Gost fongen. *c* **1450** tr. *De Imitatione* III. vi. 70 Þe holigost þe comfortour. **1483** *Cath. Angl.* 171/2 Þe Halygaste, *consolator*, *paraclitus.* **1535** JOYE *Apol. Tindale* (Arb.) 46 The holigost also before yᵗ declaring hym. **1548–9** *Bk. Com. Prayer*, *Ordering Priests*, Receiue the holy goste. **1621** BURTON *Anat. Mel.* III. i. I. ii. (1651) 416 The Holy Ghost is the love of the Father and the Son. **1627** J. COSIN tr. *9th c. Latin Hymn*, Come, Holy Ghost, our souls inspire. *a* **1699** STILLINGFL. *Serm.* III. v. (R.), He..bestowed these miraculous gifts of the Holy-Ghost on the Apostles. **1842** TENNYSON *St. Sim. Styl.* 216 For by the warning of the Holy Ghost, I prophesy that I shall die to-night. **1875** MANNING *Mission H. Ghost* i. 1 The Spirit of the Lord is God the Holy Ghost, and the Holy Ghost fills the whole world.

b. ***Order of the Holy Ghost***, a French order of Knighthood (*ordre du Saint-Esprit*), instituted by Henry III in 1578. So ***Knight of the Holy Ghost***; ***Cross of the Holy Ghost***: see quot. 1727–41.

1686 J. SERGEANT *Hist. Monast. Convent.* 98 The Order of the Holy Ghost in France was Instituted by Henry the Third, in memory of his Nativity, Election to the Polonian Kingdom, and his coming to..the Crown of France, all which hapned on Whitsunday. **1696** *Lond. Gaz.* No. 3241/3 Paris, Dec. 3... There is to be a Promotion of the Knights of the Holy Ghost very suddenly. **1727–41** CHAMBERS *Cycl.* s.v., Before they receive the order of the holy Ghost, that of S. Michael is conferred, as a necessary step; for which reason their arms are surrounded with a double collar. *Ibid.*, *Cross of the Holy Ghost*, consists of a circle in the middle, and on it the holy Ghost in figure of a dove: the four arms are drawn narrow from the centre, and widening to the ends.. This is the cross worn by the Knights of the order.

2. a. The figure of a dove as a symbol of the Holy Spirit. **b.** The cross of the Order of the Holy Ghost: see 1 b.

1520 *Mem. Ripon* (Surtees) III. 180 Pro nova factura cujusdam nebulæ pro lee Holy Goost. **1558** *Will of M. Ellys* (Somerset Ho.), Rynge of golde wᵗ a Holy goste in yᵗ. **1725** *Lond. Gaz.* No. 6404/1 His Star and Holy Ghost were of Diamonds.

3. (Also ***Holy Ghost's root.***) The plant Angelica, *Archangelica officinalis.* (Erroneously taken as *Angelica sylvestris.*)

1585 J. HIGINS tr. *Junius' Nomenclator* 136/2 *Sphondylium* ..the holye ghostes roote: Angelica. **1863** PRIOR *Plant-n.*, *Holy Ghost*, so called 'for the angel-like properties therein'. **1879** BRITTEN & HOLLAND *Plant-n.*, Holy Ghost, *Archangelica officinalis.*

4. *attrib.*, as in **Holy Ghost flower, -plant**, an orchid, *Peristeria elata*, also called *dove-plant*, from the resemblance of part of the flower to a dove; **Holy Ghost pear** = AVOCADO (from a mistaken rendering of this as 'advocate').

1866 *Treas. Bot.*, Holy Ghost Flower, *Peristeria elata.* **1882** *Garden* 10 June 401/3 The Dove plant..the beautiful Holy Ghost flower of the Spaniards. **1885** LADY BRASSEY *The Trades* 158 Specimens of the 'Holy Ghost' orchid, with the little dove brooding in the centre. **1889** *Cent. Dict.*, *Holy-Ghost pear.*

holyhock, holyoak, etc., obs. ff. HOLLYHOCK.

Holy Land. [transl. med.L. (11th c.) *terra sancta*, F. *terre sainte.*]

1. Western Palestine, or, more particularly, Judæa: so called as being the scene of the life and death of Jesus Christ, and (with reference to the Crusades) as containing the Holy Sepulchre; sometimes, in later use, as being the scene of the development of the Jewish and Christian religions.

1297 R. GLOUC. (1724) 392 Of so muche folc nyme þe croys, ne to þe holy londe go, Me ne sey no tyme byuore, ne suþþe naþemo. **1389** in *Eng. Gilds* (1870) 22 We shul preyen ..for ye holy londe and ye holy crosse, yat godd..bryng it oute of hethen power. *c* **1400** MAUNDEV. (Roxb.) Pref. 1 Þe land of repromission, þat men calles þe Haly Land. **1593** SHAKS. *Rich. II*, v. vi. 49 Ile make a voyage to the Holy-land. **1686** J. SERGEANT *Hist. Monast. Convent.* 98 To restore the Possessions of the Christians in the Holy Land. **1758** [see HOLY PLACE]. **1803** K. WHITE *Gondoline* v, And he was gone to the Holy Land To fight the Saracen.

2. *slang.* The parish of St. Giles's, London.

1821 *The Fancy* I. 250 (Farmer) The Holy-land, as St. Giles's has been termed, in compliment to the superior purity of its Irish population. **1891** *Licensed Vict. Gaz.* 3 Apr. 215/1 (ibid.) Whether the Irishmen of the Holy Land or the Hebrew scum of Petticoat Lane.

holy loaf. = HOLY BREAD. Also *attrib.* ***holy loaf money.***

1499 *Churchw. Acc. Croscombe* (Som. Rec. Soc.) 24 Paid.. for tynnyng of the lyght and the holy-lofe xvjᵈ. **1548–9** (Mar.) *Bk. Com. Prayer*, *Communion* (Rubric), The Parishioners of euerye Parishe shall offer euery Sonday, at the tyme of the Offertory, the iuste valour and price of the holy lofe..to the use of theyr Pastours and Curates. **1616** in T. D. Whitaker *Hist. Whalley* (1801) 149 The parishioners ..are accustomed to pay an ancient duty called 'Holy loaf money'. **1849** ROCK *Ch. of Fathers* I. 137 This holy loaf or eulogia was meant to be an emblem of..brotherly love.

holyn(e, holyng(e, obs. ff. HOLLIN, holly.

holy place. A place that is holy; a sanctuary. *spec.* **a.** The outer chamber of the sanctuary in the Jewish tabernacle and temple, separated by a veil from the 'most holy place' or 'holy of holies'. **b.** *pl.* (See quot. 1856.)

1526 TINDALE *Heb.* ix. 25 The hye prest entreth in to the holy place every yeare with straunge bloud. **1611** BIBLE *Exod.* xxvi. 33 The Vaile shall diuide vnto you, betweene the holy place and the most holy. **1758** (*title*) Travels through Egypt, Turkey, Syria, and the Holy Land; containing..A Description..4. Of the Holy Land, particularly of Jerusalem and the Holy Places. **1856** STANLEY *Sinai & Pal.* 431 What are technically called 'the Holy Places'. By this term are meant not the scenes of sacred events, taken generally, but such special localities as the Greek or Latin Church, or both cojointly, have selected as objects of pilgrimage.

† **'holyship.** *Obs.* = HOLINESS 2.

c **1680** HICKERINGILL *Wks.* I. 63 The King sent his Holiship all manner of Vessels belonging to a Chamber.

holy stone, holy-stone, *sb.* [Origin of name uncertain; in sense 2 perh. for *holey stone.*]

1. A soft sandstone used by sailors for scouring the decks of ships.

1823 in CRABB *Technol. Dict.* **1837** *Old Commodore* I. 64 A wet swab and a dry holy-stone will set all to rights. **1840** R. H. DANA *Bef. Mast* xxii. 66 The decks were..white as snow ..from constant use of holystones. **1867** SMYTH *Sailor's Word-bk.*, *Holy-stone*, a sandstone for scrubbing decks, so called from being originally used for Sunday cleaning, or obtained by plundering church-yards of their tombstones, or because the seamen have to go on their knees to use it. **1890** *Spectator* 5 Apr., I believe you will find the correct spelling to be 'holey', the stones used by preference being full of holes, like a sponge, and that any derivations of the name 'holy' were simply inventions to account for what sounded a remarkable name.

2. A stone with a natural hole in it, used as an amulet or charm.

1825 BROCKETT, *Holy-stones*, holed-stones, are hung over the heads of horses as a charm against diseases. **1855** ROBINSON *Whitby Gloss.*, *Holy-stone*, a flint or pebble in its natural state with a hole through it, numbers of which are found on our coast. They are also called 'lucky stones'.

'holystone, *v.* [f. prec. sb.] *trans.* To scour with a holystone.

1828 P. CUNNINGHAM *N.S. Wales* II. 217 Scrubbed, swabbed, scraped, or dry holystoned. **1830** MARRYAT *King's Own* li, No sails to set, and no holystoning the deck. **1840** R. H. DANA *Bef. Mast* iii. 6 Six days shalt thou labour and do all thou art able, And on the seventh—holystone the decks and scrape the cable. **1886** H. W. ELLIOTT *Arctic Prov.* 108 Floors scrubbed and sanded like a well holystoned ship's deck.

holy tide, holy-tide. A holy time or season; a day or season of religious observance.

a **1035** *Laws of Cnut* I. c. 17 §2 (Schmid) And beo þam halʒum tidum, eal swa hit riht is. *c* **1200** *Trin. Coll. Hom.* 3 Ðe holie tid þat me clepeð aduent. *a* **1300** *Cursor M.* 27210 In halitide or fastim dai. **1613** BP. CORBET *Journ. France* iii. Poems (1672) 129 Much like John Dory in the song, Upon a holy tide. **1810** SCOTT *Lady of L.* VI. iii, And now, by holytide and feast, From rules of discipline released.

attrib. **1828** SCOTT *F.M. Perth* ii, Now lay by thy work, lass, for it is holytide eve, and it becomes us to go to the evening service.

holy water. Forms: see HOLY and WATER; also 5–6 **hally, holli(e.** [OE. *háliʒwæter*, a true compound, whence in ME. *halywater*; subseq. analysed as two words.]

1. Water dedicated to holy uses and used for ritual purification of persons and things; water blessed by a priest and used in various rites and devotional acts.

c **900** tr. *Bæda's Hist.* v. iv. (1890) 396 Sumne dæl þæs haliʒ-wætres. *a* **1225** *Ancr. R.* 324 Confiteor, & haliwater, & beoden, & holie þouhtes. *c* **1380** WYCLIF *Sel. Wks.* III. 452 Waschen awey wiþ preieris of a Pater-noster, wiþ hali watir, wiþ pardon. **1382** —— *Num.* v. 17 He [the preest] shal take the holy watre in a britil vessel. *c* **1440** *Promp. Parv.* 223/1 Halywater, *aqua benedicta.* **1570** B. GOOGE *Pop. Kingd.* IV. 47 b, Then followeth good sir Blase, who doth a waxen Candell giue, And holy water to his men. **1602** FULBECKE *Pandectes* 77 The Pope's holiwater. *a* **1714** BURNET *Hist. Ref.* an. 1536 (R.) Jests about confession, praying to saints, holy-water, and the other ceremonies of the church. **1885** *Catholic Dict.* s.v., Before the High Mass on Sundays the celebrant sprinkles the people with holy water.

b. Prov. ***as the devil loves holy water***, i.e. not at all, or rather with violent dislike.

1570-6, 1738 [see DEVIL *sb.* 22 h]. ? *c* **1600** *Distracted Emp.* v. i. in Bullen *O. Pl.* III. 242 Faythe I love thee. Yes, as the devyll does freirs holye water.

†**c.** *fig.* in COURT HOLY WATER, gracious but empty promises, q.v.

2. *attrib.* and *Comb.*, as ***holy water basin, bearer, brush, can, casting, fat*** (FAT *sb.*[1]), ***font, fount, pot, stoup***; †**holy-water clerk**, one who carried the vessel containing holy water: often spoken of with contempt as holding a mean office; **holy-water sprinkle, sprinkler,** (*a*) a kind of brush used to sprinkle holy water, an aspergillum; (*b*) a kind of club armed on all sides with spikes; (*c*) a fox's 'brush'; †**holy-water stick** = *holy-water sprinkler* (*a*); †**holy-water stock,** a holy-water stoup or basin; †**holy-water stone,** a stone vessel for holding holy-water; †**holy-water strinkle,** (*a*) = *holy-water sprinkle* (*a*); (*b*) the plant Horsetail.

c **1440** *Promp. Parv.* 223/1 *Halywater berere, *aquabajulus.* *a* **1678** MARVELL *Appleton Ho.* 252 Another bolder, stands at push, With their old *holy-water brush. **1563-87** FOXE *A. & M.* (1861) VII. I. 47 *Holy-water-casting, procession-gadding, mattins-mumbling. **1303** R. BRUNNE *Handl. Synne* 11592 An *holywatyr clerk.. þat lytyl haþ lerned yn hys lyue, He ys ordeyned a prest to shryve. **1528** COWLEY in *State Papers* II. 141 A symple Irish preste, a vagabounde, without lernyng, maners, or good qualitye, not worthy to bee a hally-water clerc. **1660** HOWELL *Eng. Prov.* 10 The Parish-Priest forgetteth that ever he hath been Holy-water Clark. **1464** in *Ripon Ch. Acts* (Surtees) 222 Simul cum le *halywater fatt. **1566** in *Eng. Ch. Furniture* (Peacock) 37 An holiwater fat of Stone. **1513** in Glasscock *Rec. St. Michael's. Bp. Stortford* (1882) 33 Pd for mendyng of the *halywater potte iij *d.* *c* **1440** *Promp. Parv.* 223/1 *Haly water spryngelle.. *aspersorium.* **1614** T. ADAMS *Devil's Banquet* 17 The Priest must dash the graue with a holy-water-sprinkle. **1706** PHILLIPS (ed. Kersey), *Holy-Water sprinkle*, a Term us'd by Hunters for the Tail of a Fox. *a* **1887** JEFFERIES *Field & Hedgerow* (1889) 296 The spiked balls of a holywater sprinkle, such as once used in the wars. **1816** SCOTT *Antiq.* xxv, Another churchman in his vestments bore a *holy-water sprinkler. **1846** FAIRHOLT *Costume Eng.* 288 The Morning-star, a ball of wood, encircled by bands of iron in which spikes are inserted.. was sometimes termed jocularly a 'holy-water sprinkler', the way in which it scattered blood.. suggesting a similarity to the sprinkling of holy water. **1419** *Will of Maydeston* (Somerset Ho.), Vno *holiwaterstykke argent. **1552** HULOET, Holy water sticke or sprincle, *aspergillus.* **1530** PALSGR. 228/2 *Halywaterstocke, *benoistier.* **1566** in *Eng. Ch. Furniture* (Peacock) 34 One hallywater stock of stone broken in peces. *Ibid.* 52 One *hollie water stone—broken in peces and defacid. **1419** *Will of Maydeston* (Somerset Ho.), Vno vase argent vocat *holiwaterstop. **1483** *Act 1 Rich. III*, c. 12 §2 No Merchant Stranger.. shall bring into this Realm .. Candlesticks, Holy-water Stopps. **1872** O. SHIPLEY *Gloss. Eccl. Terms, Holy Water Stoup*, the stone, stoup, stock, vat ..or other receptacle for holy water, placed near the entrance of churches. *c* **1440** *Promp. Parv.* 223/1 *Haly water.. strencle.. *aspersorium.* **1538** TURNER *Libellus* B ij a, *Hippuris*,.. Hally water stryncle.

Hence **holy-watered** *a.*, sprinkled with holy water (in quot. *fig.*).

1608 TOURNEUR *Rev. Trag.* IV. iv. Wks. 1878 II. 124 Farewell, once dryed, now holy-watred Meade!

Holy Week. [After It. *la settimana santa*, F. *la semaine sainte.*] The week immediately preceding Easter Sunday, also called PASSION WEEK, q.v. (OE. *séo hálᵹe wucu* was used for Rogation Week.)

1710 *Lond. Gaz.* No. 4685/1 The Pope.. designs to officiate at some of the Functions of the Holy Week. **1727-41** CHAMBERS *Cycl.*, *Holy Week*, is the last week of Lent, called also *passion week.* **1812** BRADY *Clavis Cal.* (1815) I. 277 The week was called the '*Great Week*'.. the *Holy Week* from the extraordinary solemnities practiced throughout its continuance;—and *Passion Week.* **1884** W. E. ADDIS & T. ARNOLD *Catholic Dictionary* (1897) 445/1 We have said that in Holy Week the Church commemorates Christ's Passion.

holy well. [See WELL *sb.* A combined form, as in *holiday*, is represented in the proper names *Holywell, Hollywell* ('hɒlɪwɛl), *Halliwell.*] A well or spring reputed to possess miraculous healing properties, as being a channel of divine influence.

854 *Charter* in Kemble *Cod. Dipl.* V. 100 Donne upp on Beaddingbroc on halgan welle. **1672** PETTY *Pol. Anat.* 364 They [the Irish] have a great opinion of holy-well's, rocks, and caves. **1793** in *Archæol.* XI. 127 The bath near one end of the church of East Dereham in Norfolk.. was more likely to have been a holy well. **1846** R. HART *Eccl. Rec.* (ed. 2) 224 Holy wells are occasionally found in churchyards. **1871** TYLOR *Prim. Cult.* II. 195 Cornish-folk still drop into the old holy wells offerings of pins, nails, and rags.

holyworkfolk: see HALIWERFOLK.

Holy Writ. [See HOLY *a.* and WRIT.] Holy writings collectively; *spec.* the Bible or Holy Scriptures. In earlier times, sometimes including other writings dealing with sacred subjects.

c **900** tr. *Bæda's Hist.* II. xvi. [xx.] (1890) 152 Æfter þon þe halige writu sprecað. *c* **1200** *Vices & Virtues* 15 We findeð on hali write. *a* **1225** *Ancr. R.* 98 Ase holi writ seið, 'hore speche spret ase cauncre'. *c* **1305** *St. Kenelm* 258 in *E.E.P.* (1862) 54 Þe pope nam þis holi writ. *a* **1375** *Lay Folks Mass Bk.* App. iv. 90 Wiþ-outen witnesse of holi writ Wisdam weore hit non. *c* **1400** MAUNDEV. (1839) xii. 136 Thei han Gospelles and the Prophecyes and the Byble writen in here Langage, Wherfore thei conne meche of Holy Wrytt. **1604** SHAKS. *Oth.* III. iii. 324 Confirmations strong, As proofes of holy Writ. **1700** DRYDEN *Cock & Fox* 380 Of Daniel you may read in holy writ. **1714** POPE *Wife of Bath* 346 And close the sermon, as beseem'd his wit, With some grave sentence out of holy writ. **1805** COLEBROOKE in *Asiat. Res.* (1808) VIII. 483 Writers on ethics sometimes draw from the Vedas illustrations of moral maxims, and quote from their holy writ passages at full length, in support of ethical precepts. **1817** COLERIDGE *Sibyl. Leaves* (1862) 245 To Nature and to Holy Writ Alone did God the boy commit.

‖**hom** (həʊm). Also **homa.** [Pers. *hōm*, Zend. *haoma*, = Skr. *sōma.*] The sacred plant of the ancient Persians and Parsees; also its juice: originally the same as the SOMA of the Vedas.

1855 BAILEY *Mystic* 35 And hom sweet herblet of immortal life Sipped till transmute he stood. **1862** F. HALL in *Parthenon* 1 Nov. 844/1 Under the name of *homa*, the part which this liquid [the juice of the *soma*, or acid asclepias] plays in the offerings of the Parsees is almost equally conspicuous. **1870** ROCK *Text. Fabr.* 238 The tree-like ornament.. seems the traditionary form of the Persians' 'hom'. **1878** MRS. PALLISER tr. *Jacquemart's Hist. Furniture* 468 Hom or sacred palm depicted upon Persian textiles. **1886** *Edin. Rev.* July 151 A shrub of homa on an enamelled gold vase.

b. *attrib.* and *Comb.*

1882 E. W. WEST *Pahlavi Texts* II. 165 *note*, This twig a small fragment of which is pounded with the Hôm-twigs when preparing the Hôm-juice.

hom, obs. f. HOME; var. HEM *pron.*, *Obs.*, them.

homacanth: see HOMO-.

homage ('hɒmɪdʒ), *sb.* Also 3–5 **omage**, 5–6 **hommage**, (5 *erron.* **homoge, umage, ymage**). [a. OF. *ommage, homage, humage* (12th c.), mod.F. *hommage* (formerly *omnage* = Pr. *homenatge*, Sp. *homenage*):—late L. *homināticum* (in Du Cange), f. *homo, homin-* man: see -AGE. The (late) OE. equivalent was *mann-rǽden*: see MANRED.]

1. In *Feudal Law*, Formal and public acknowledgement of allegiance, wherein a tenant or vassal declared himself the man of the king or the lord of whom he held, and bound himself to his service.

Phrases. ***to do*** (†***make***), ***render homage; to resign homage***, formally to renounce allegiance.

c **1290** *Beket* 600 in *S. Eng. Leg.* I. 123 Homage he scholde don to him. **1297** R. GLOUC. (Rolls) 7987 So þat þis Macolom.. Dude king willam omage, & bicom is man al out. **13..** *Guy Warw.* (A.) 1294 Mine men ȝe beþ & to me swore, Omage ȝe schul me þer-fore. *c* **1400** *Ywaine & Gaw.* 1952 And evermar to be hir frende, Umage made he to that hende. *c* **1470** HENRY *Wallace* I. 116 King Eduuard.. thar he gat ymage of Scotland swne. **1548** HALL *Chron., Hen. IV* 8 To resigne to hym all the homages and fealties dewe to him as kyng. **1597** SKENE *De Verb. Sign.* s.v., Weemen makis na homage, bot onely fidelitie.. Homage concernis service specially in weirfare, to the quhilk weemen ar nocht subject. **1670** MILTON *Hist. Eng.* I. (1851) 23 He.. gave them that Iland to hold of him as in Homage. **1843** CARLYLE *Past & Pr.* II. xi, Coming to do homage for his Father's land. **1867** FREEMAN *Norm. Conq.* I. iii. 99 Homage was there; for the relation of every man to his Lord was a relation of homage.

b. ***homage ancestral*** (see quot. 1595). ***homage feudal, liege*** (see quot. 1856.). ***new homage***, homage by an alienee or his successors, as distinguished from homage ancestral. ***plain homage*** (see quot. 1727–41). ***simple homage*** = feudal homage.

[*a* **1481** LITTLETON *Ten.* II. vii. (1516) B iv, Tenure per homage auncestrell.] **1595** *Rastell's Expos.*, *Homage auncestrell*, is where a man and his ancestours of time out of mind, did hold their land of their lord by homage. **1628** COKE *On Litt.* 100 b, I think there is little or no land at all at this day holden by homage auncestrel. **1727-41** CHAMBERS *Cycl.* s.v., *Plain Homage*, or homage of a fee, where no oath of fidelity is taken. **1851** BURRILL *Law Dict.* 575 Simple homage; that kind of homage which was merely an acknowledgment of tenure, with a saving of the rights of other lords. **1856** *Bouvier's Law Dict.* (ed. 6) I. 588 Homage was liege and feudal. The former was paid to the king, the latter to the lord.

c. An act of homage; a render or money payment made as an acknowledgement of vassalage.

[**1432-50** tr. *Higden* (Rolls) II. 89 Tenauntes were wonte to yelde theire wepens for an homage in the firste commenge of newe lordes.] **1599** NASHE *Lenten Stuffe* 71 Euery yeare about Lent-tide, the sherifes of Norwich take certayne herring pies.. and send them as a homage. *c* **1645** HOWELL *Lett.* xxxviii. (1726) 68 He is contented with a white Mule, and Purse of Pistoles about the Neck, which he receives every year for a Herriot or Homage. **1661** in Tighe & Davis *Ann. Windsor* (1858) II. 302 To indeavour to take off the some of 36*li* 6*s.* charged as a homage dew to his Matie. **1774** T. WEST *Antiq. Furness* (1805) 109 Rents, services, homages.

2. A body of persons owning allegiance; *spec.* in *Eng. Law*, the body of tenants attending a manorial court, or the jury at such a court.

a **1300** *K. Horn* 1497 Þe king and his homage ȝeuen Arnoldin trewage. *a* **1577** SIR T. SMITH *Commw. Eng.* II. xvii. 65 [In a manor] his tennantes being sworne make a Iurie which is not called the enquest, but the homage. **1620** J. WILKINSON *Courts Baron* 143 You shall sweare that you as Foreman of this Homage.. shall duely inquire and true presentment make. *Ibid.*, Then call the rest of the Homage and sweare them. **1804** *Occurr.* in *Ann. Reg.* 84 Court of Piedpoudre. Before the steward of Bartholomew fair and a special homage. *Ibid.*, The homage returned a verdict for the plaintiff. **1865** *Spectator* 7 June 9/2 With the consent of the 'homage', i.e., of his copyholders.

3. *fig.* Acknowledgement of superiority in respect of rank, worth, beauty, etc.; reverence, dutiful respect, or honour shown.

1390 GOWER *Conf.* I. 249 The yonge ladie was forth fet, To whome the lordes done homage. **1450-70** *Golagros & Gaw.* 283 Thair gat he nane homage For all his hie parage. **1526** *Pilgr. Perf.* (W. de W. 1531) 25 b, To do homage and honour to almyghty god. **1590** SHAKS. *Com. Err.* III. ii. 43 Your weeping sister is no wife of mine, Nor to her bed no homage doe I owe. **1671** MILTON *P.R.* II. 376 All these are Spirits of air, and woods, and springs, Thy gentle ministers, who come to pay Thee homage, and acknowledge Thee their Lord. **1785** BURNS *Cottar's Sat. Nt.* xviii, The parent-pair their secret homage pay. **1803** MACKINTOSH *Def. Peltier* Wks. 1846 III. 272 They are compelled to pay a reluctant homage to the justice of English principles. **1823** CHALMERS *Serm.* I. 417, I offer them the homage of my respectful Congratulations. **1856** EMERSON *Eng. Traits, Wealth* Wks. (Bohn) II. 68 There is no country in which so absolute a homage is paid to wealth.

4. *attrib.* and *Comb.*, as ***homage-breaker, -fee, -gift, -penny; homage-doing*** adj.; **homage-jury**, the jury at a manorial court.

c **1586** C'TESS PEMBROKE *Ps.* LXXII. iv, The kinges of Tharsis homage guifts shall send. **1623** LISLE *Ælfric on O. & N. Test.* Ded. xiv, If after him.. Be under thee such homage-breakers found. **1650** TRAPP *Comm. Numb.* xv. 20 Ye shall offer up a cake, As an homage-peny, as acknowledging God, the chief Lord of all. **1686** in Tighe & Davis *Ann. Windsor* (1858) II 421 Paid to Sr Thomas Duppa the homage fee 16 06 8. **1729** JACOB *Law Dict.*, *Homage Jury*, is a Jury in a Court Baron, consisting of Tenants that do Homage to the Lord of the Fee. **1864** BURTON *Scot. Abr.* I. i. 19 [He] called this homage-doing King his vassal.

'**homage**, *v.* [f. prec. sb., or ad. F. *hommager* (Cotgr.), f. *hommage* (see prec.).]

†**1.** *trans.* To render or pay as a token of homage. *Obs.*

a **1592** H. SMITH *Wks.* (1866) I. 112 Every man must homage his heart. **1662** COWLEY *Civ. War* 63 To her great Neptune homag'd all his streams, And all the wide-stretch'd ocean was her Thames.

†**2.** *intr.* To pay homage. *Obs.*

1592 *Nobody & Someb.* 240 in Simpson *Sch. Shaks.* (1878) I. 286 Servants homaging And crying *Ave.* **1636** HEYWOOD *Love's Mistris* II. Wks. 1874 V. 115 To whom Jove some-times bends.. Mars homageth, and Phebus will submit.

3. *trans.* To do homage or allegiance to.

1632 LITHGOW *Trav.* IX. 380 To Court I came, and homag'd Royall James. **1677** GILPIN *Demonol.* (1867) 178 How he was homaged by fowls and fishes. **1773** J. ROSS *Fratricide* II. 100 (MS.) For him the Universe.. and all Creation ought To homage without ceasing. **1862** CARLYLE *Fredk. Gt.* IX. ix. III. 146 Don Carlos.. styles himself 'King of the two Sicilies'.. whom Naples.. willingly homages as such.

†**homageable**, *a.* *Obs.* [f. HOMAGE *sb.* + -ABLE. Cf. obs. F. *hommageable.*] Bound to render homage.

c **1645** HOWELL *Lett.* I. II. xv. (1655) 85 He of Holland being homegeable to none.. was the more potent. *Ibid.* I. VI. xii. 254 The Dutchy of Bar; for which he is hommageable to the Crown of France, as he is to the Emperor for Lorain. **1764** *Antiq.* in *Ann. Reg.* 169/1 Great and small homageable fiefs.

†'**homagely**, *adv.* *Obs.* *rare*$^{-1}$. In 5 **homage-liche.** [f. as prec. + -LY[2].] By way of homage.

c **1420** *Chron. Vilod.* st. 210 And b[t] homagelyche to hym þey dedon so abeyȝe.

homager ('hɒmɪdʒə(r)). Also 5 **omager(e, homegere, homyger,** 6 **homagier.** [a. OF. *hommager, -ier*, f. *hommage* HOMAGE: see -ER[2].]

One who owes homage or fealty; one who holds lands by homage.

crown homager, the crown of a vassal king. ***liege homager***: cf. HOMAGE *sb.* 1 b.

? *a* **1400** *Arthur* 133 Kynges.. þat were to hym Omager. *a* **1529** SKELTON *Agst. the Scottes* 122 Pardy, ye were his homager And suter to his parlement. **1601** HOLLAND *Pliny* I. 69 The Camuni.. did seruice as homagers to them. **1608** D. T. *Ess. Pol. & Mor.* 71 They would acknowledge themselves.. liege-homagers for it to the Crowne of France. **1610** GUILLIM *Heraldry* IV. i. (1660) 269 This Kind of Crown.. some have given it the name of a Crown Homager. **1769** *De Foe's Tour Gt. Brit.* (ed. 7) IV. 293 The Isle of Man.. for several Generations, has belonged to Families, who have been Homagers to the Crown of England for it. **1867** FREEMAN *Norm. Conq.* I. iv. 231 Before long we find him again the faithful homager of King Lewis.

b. *spec.* in *Eng. Law*, A manorial tenant.

1598 KITCHIN *Courts Leet* (1675) 7 Homagers of Court ought to enquire in this Court. *c* **1640** J. SMYTH *Lives Berkeleys* (1883) I. 282 All of them homagers to the Castle of Berkeley. **1714** SCROGGS *Courts-leet* (ed. 3) 159 The Oath of a Stranger in the Lord's Court to the Homagers. **1889** JESSOPP *Coming of Friars* v. 225 The homagers were afraid to give a verdict against the steward.

c. *fig.* Cf. HOMAGE *sb.* 3.

c **1400** *Rom. Rose* 3288 Whanne thou were maad the omager Of God of Love to hastily. **1606** SHAKS. *Ant. & Cl.* I. i. 31 Thou blushest Anthony, and that blood of thine Is Cæsars homager. **1673** *Lady's Call.* I. v. §34. 43 Interest.. should render her an homager to that omnipotent power. **1877** MRS. CHAPMAN in *Ht. Martineau's Autobiog.* III. 101 The newspapers were zealous heralds and homagers.

†**homagy**. *Obs. rare*⁻¹. [ad. med.L. *homāgium*, f. F. *hommage* HOMAGE.] Allegiance; rendering of homage.

1610 HOLLAND *Camden's Brit.* II. Irel. 72 We have given also unto him for his homagy and service, the Cantred.

homalogonatous (ˌhɒmələʊˈgɒnətəs), *a. Ornith.* [f. mod.L. *Homalogonatæ* (see below), f. Gr. ὁμαλός even, level, ordinary + γόνυ, γονατ- knee: see -OUS.] Belonging to Garrod's division *Homalogonatæ* of birds, comprising those which have a *rectus femoris* or *ambiens* muscle in the leg.

1872 COUES *Key N. Amer. Birds* (1884) 195 Passeres have no ambiens.. Birds having it are homalogonatous or 'normally-kneed'.

homalographic (ˌhɒmələʊˈgræfɪk), *a.* (*erron.* homolo-, though usual in sense 1.) [f. Gr. ὁμαλός (see prec.) + GRAPHIC: cf. F. *homalographique*.] **1.** *Geog.* Delineating in equal proportion; applied to a method of projection in which equal areas on the earth's surface are represented by equal areas on the map or chart.

1864 WEBSTER, *Homolographic projection.* **1866** PROCTOR *Handbk. Stars* 22 The problem proposed by Babinet, and solved by Cauchy, of the homolographic (or, as I prefer to call it, the equigraphic) projection of maps; that is of the construction of maps in which all areas shall be correctly given. —— in *Intell. Observ.* No. 54. 429 The homolographic projection of the globe. **1921** *Times Lit. Suppl.* 6 Oct. 646/3 This map of the Pacific, on Mollweide's homolographic projection. **1937** *Geogr. Jrnl.* XC. 569 Equal-area projections being desirable for distribution maps, a modification of Goode's Homolographic projection—called by the compilers the 'Interrupted Mollweide's Homolographic'—is employed.

2. *Anat.* (See quot. 1886.)

1886 *Syd. Soc. Lex., Homalographic method,* Le Gendre's name for a mode of exhibiting or representing the anatomical structures by making plane sections, if possible, on a frozen body. **1889** J. M. DUNCAN *Lect. Dis. Wom.* xxx. (ed. 4) 250 He has shewn it in a homalographic section made on a woman recently delivered.

Hence ˌ**homaloˈgraphically** *adv.*

1969 N. R. HANSON *Perception & Discov.* xix. 325 We never see it sinusoidally, orthogonally, or homolographically, we just represent that world this way.

ˈ**homaloid.** *Geom.* [f. Gr. ὁμαλός (see above) + -OID.] A homaloidal space of any number of dimensions; a 'flat'.

1876 CLIFFORD in *Proc. Lond. Math. Soc.* VII. 67 On the free motion under no forces of a rigid system in an *n*-fold homaloid.

homaloidal (hɒməˈlɔɪdəl), *a. Geom.* [f. as prec. + -AL¹.] Of the nature of a plane; flat: see quots.

1875 PROCTOR *Fam. Sci. Stud.* (1882) 21, I personally have often found relief from the dreary infinities of Homaloidal space (that is space where straight lines are straight and planes plane..) in the consoling thought that, after all, this other may be the true state of things. **1885** C. L. MORGAN *Springs of Conduct* II. iii. 79 The space that we know is practically homaloidal. It is possible that it may not be theoretically homaloidal—that is to say, it is possible that the shortest path between two points may not be an absolutely straight line, but a very, very little curved.

‖**Homaloptera** (hɒməˈlɒptərə), *sb. pl. Entom.* [mod.L., f. Gr. ὁμαλός (see above) + πτερόν wing.] A division of dipterous insects, in Leach's classification. Hence **homaˈlopterous** *a.*, belonging to the *Homaloptera*.

1817 LEACH *Zool. Misc.* III. 60 Order 16 Omaloptera. **1835** KIRBY *Hab. & Inst. Anim.* II. xx. 317 The *Homaloptera* (Forest-fly, etc.) called also *Pupipara*. **1874** *Chambers' Encycl.* s.v., All the Homaloptera are parasites.

ˌ**homaloˈsternal**, *a. Ornith.* [f. as prec. + L. *stern-um* breast-bone; + -AL¹.] Having a flat keelless sternum or breast-bone; ratite.

homarine (ˈhɒmərain), *a.* and *sb.* [f. mod.L. *Homarus*, generic name of the lobster; f. F. *homard* (formerly *homar*, a. ON. *humarr*, Da. *hummer*) lobster.] **A.** *adj.* Related to or having the characteristics of a lobster. **B.** *sb.* A crustacean of the genus *Homarus*: a lobster.

1880 HUXLEY *Crayfish* 316 Whether a given crustacean belonged to the Astacine, or to the closely allied Homarine group. *Ibid.*, Whether the crustacean in question was a marine Astacine, or a true Homarine.

homatomic, homaxonial: see HOMO-.

homatropine (həʊˈmætrəpiːn). *Pharm.* Also †-in. [ad. G. *homatropin* (A. Ladenburg 1880, in *Ber. d. Deut. Chem. Ges.* XIII. 107), f. HOM(O- b + ATROPINE.] A synthetic alkaloid, $C_{16}H_{21}NO_3$, the tropine ester of mandelic acid, which is used chiefly as the hydrobromide in ophthalmology to dilate the pupil of the eye.

1880 *Jrnl. Chem. Soc.* XXXVIII. 410 Homatropine aurochloride.. forms first as an oil, which becomes crystalline on standing. **1901** T. SOLLMANN *Text-bk. Pharmacol.* xi. 261 For ophthalmologic examinations the preference should be given to homatropin, since its effects set in and disappear more quickly. **1951** A. GROLLMAN *Pharmacol. & Therapeutics* xiv. 271 Homatropine methylbromide.. was introduced as a substitute for atropine in the treatment of gastro-intestinal spasm. **1970** DUKE-ELDER & ABRAMS in S. Duke-Elder *Syst. Ophthalm.* V. ix. 388 Homatropine is weaker than atropine but has the advantage of wearing off more quickly.

homber, obs. var. HAMBARGH.

1411 *Nottingham Rec.* II. 88 Ad faciendum hombers. *Ibid.*, Ad artem de hombermaker. **1523** [see HOLME].

homblock, obs. form of HEMLOCK *sb.*

1578 LYTE *Dodoens* II. lxix. 238 It is good for them that haue taken excessiuely of the iuyce of Homblocke.

hombre (ˈɒmbreɪ). Chiefly *U.S.* [Sp.; cf. OMBRE.] A man of Spanish descent; by extension, a man.

1846 S. S. MAGOFFIN *Down Santa Fé Trail* (1926) 93 Not only the children, but.. *hombres* (men) swarmed around me like bees. **1851** N. KINGSLEY *Diary* 2 Feb. (1914) 172 [I] had a fine sing in the evening with three or four other 'hombres'. **1918** C. E. MULFORD *Man fr. Bar-20* viii. 79 'Friend of this hombre?' 'Yes; sort of.' **1930** [see FIX *sb.* 5]. **1930** *London Mercury* Feb. 324 'Look here,' said Clytemnestra.. 'is this *hombre* worth it?' 'If you don't think so, leave him to me.' **1940** *Amer. Speech* XV. 220/2 Cowboys living a rough and hardy existence occasionally develop into 'tough hombres'. **1957** *Times Lit. Suppl.* 25 Oct. 646/4 This book describes the doings of the bad hombre. **1972** P. CLEIFE *Slick & Dead* xxx 250, I had to find a tough hombre with enough guts and initiative to act on his own.

hombre, var. OMBRE.

Homburg (ˈhɒmbɜːg). [Name of a town near Wiesbaden, Germany.] In full ***Homburg hat***. A soft felt hat with a curled brim and a dented crown, first worn at Homburg, once a fashionable health-resort.

1894 *Country Gentlemen's Catal.* 155/1 'The Homburg Hat', as worn by H. R. H. Prince of Wales—10/6. **1901** *Sketch* 4 Sept. 254/1 The quiet gentleman in dark clothes and a Homburg hat. **1904** *To-Day* 29 June 256/1 At one time any man who wore a 'Homburg' was popularly supposed to be either an actor or an artist. **1922** E. WALLACE *Valley of Ghosts* xv. 142 He.. put his Homburg hat on the table. **1940, 1958** [see ANTHONY EDEN]. **1972** WODEHOUSE *Pearls, Girls & Monty Bodkin* v. 68 Characters.. who kept getting locked up in cellars under the river by sinister men in Homburg hats and raincoats.

home (həʊm), *sb.*¹ and *a.* Forms: 1-2 **hám**, 3-5 (7) **hom**, (3-4 **hoom**, 4-5 **hoome**), 4- **home**, 5-7 **whome**, 6 **whom**); *north.* and *Sc.* 3-5 **ham**, 4- **hame**, (5 **hem**, 5-7 **hayme**, 6 **heme**, 6, 9 **heame**, 7 **haim**, 9 **haam**). [Com. Teut.: OE. *hám* = OFris. *hém*, OS. *hêm* (MDu., Du. *heem*), OHG. *heim* (MHG., Ger. *heim*), ON. *heimr* dwelling, world, (Sw. *hem*, Da. *hjem*), Goth. *háims* fem., village. Cf. Lith *kēmas*, *kaímas*, village, homestead, OPruss. *caymis* village; Skr. *kšēmas* safe dwelling, f. **ksi* to dwell secure.

In the earlier stages of Teutonic, the acc. case was used without a preposition (accusative of direction) like L. *domum*, with the sense 'to one's house, to home'; and the dat. (= locative), OHG. *heimi*, *heime*, MHG. *heime*, OS. *hême*, in the sense 'at home', L. *domī*. The former usage survives in 'go home', where HOME is now treated as an *adv*.]

A. *sb.* †**1. a.** (Only in OE. and early ME.) A village or town, a collection of dwellings; a vill with its cottages. *Obs.*

c **900** tr. *Bæda* II. xiv. [xvi.] (1890) 146 He rad betweoh his hamum oðþe be tunum. **901** *O.E. Chron.* an. 901 Æþelwald sæt binnan þæm ham mid þæm monnum þe him to ʒebuʒon. *c* **1205** LAY. 19455 þa wes Verolam a swiðe kinewurðe hom.

†**b.** An estate, a possession. *Obs.*

c **950** *Lindisf. Gosp.* Matt. xix. 22 Wæs forðon hæbbend moniʒra homas *vel* æhta [*possessiones*]. *c* **1000** ÆLFRIC *Gen.* xlvii. 20 þa hiʒ ciptun ealle hira hamas for þæs hungres micelnyssa. *c* **1205** LAY. 19537 Ne læten ʒe næuere þas hæðene, bruken eoure hames.

2. a. A dwelling-place, house, abode; the fixed residence of a family or household; the seat of domestic life and interests; one's own house; the dwelling in which one habitually lives, or which one regards as one's proper abode. Sometimes including the members of a family collectively; the home-circle or household. In N. America and Australasia (and increasingly elsewhere), freq. used to designate a private house or residence merely as a building.

c **950** *Lindisf. Gosp.* John xiv. 2 In hus fadores mines hamas meniʒa sint [*Ags. G.* maneʒa eardungstowa; *Vulg.* mansiones]. **971** *Blickl. Hom.* 25 Se ham is ʒefylled mid heofonlicum gastum. *c* **1000** *Laws of Æthelbirht* c. 3 (Schmid) Gif cyning æt mannes ham drincæð. *c* **1175** *Lamb. Hom.* 49 Riche men.. þe habbeð feire huses and feire hames. *c* **1275** in *O.E. Misc.* 170 Al hit wolle agon. His lond and his hus and his hom. *a* **1300** *Cursor M.* 5619 Noght fer fra þe kinges hame. **1393** LANGL. *P. Pl.* C. XII. 46 God is nat in þat hom. *c* **1440** *Promp. Parv.* 244/2 Hoome.. *mancio.* *c* **1489** CAXTON *Sonnes of Aymon* xxviii. 588 All the sike.. retourne to theyr home in goode helthe. **1605** SHAKS. *Lear* II. i. 126, I best thought it fit To answere from our home. *a* **1667** COWLEY *Elegy* in *Eng. Poets* (1810) VII. 61 There banish'd Ovid had a lasting home. *a* **1835** MRS. HEMANS *Homes of Eng.* i, The stately homes of England! How beautiful they stand. **1849** MACAULAY *Hist. Eng.* iii. I. 351 That attachment which every man naturally feels for his home. **1871** FREEMAN *Norm. Conq.* IV. xvii. 81 [He] returned to the home which, almost alone among princely homes, supplied a model for lowlier homes to follow. **1879** M. J. LAMB (*title*) The homes of America. **1882** *Harper's Mag.* Dec. 58/1 A lovely drive.. is bordered with homes, many of which make pretensions to much more than comfort. **1889** *Kansas Times & Star* 6 July, A fine stone-front home at Twenty-seventh and Troost. *Ibid.* 5 Dec., For rent, a fine home at 1223 Broadway. **1894** H. DRUMMOND *Ascent Man* 390 Sacred and happy homes.. are the surest guarantees for the moral progress of a nation. **1929** *Publishers' Weekly* 7 Dec. 2661/1 Then out to see the new Ranh Brauch, a stunning private home turned over to the library. **1930** *San Antonio* (Texas) *Light* 31 Jan., Wilson wounded Elliott and his wife in a dispute Wednesday at the Elliott home in Mendota. **1955** A. ROSS *Australia 55* 37 More houses (or 'homes' as a house is kindly called here) are needed. **1968** *Globe & Mail* (Toronto) 17 Feb. 1/1 Her three.. sons were shot to death in their home. **1971** *Timber Trades Jrnl.* 14 Aug. 21/1 The June figures showed more private homes completed than in any month since December 1968. **1973** *Guardian* 18 May 1/6 Motorway schemes.. often wipe out considerable numbers of reasonable homes in accessible areas. **1973** *Ibid.* 20 Oct. 11/6 In Beverly Hills and Bel Air, we saw the homes (never called houses) of Jane Withers, Greer Garson, and Barbra Streisand.

b. *transf.* Applied to the dwelling- or resting-place of animals or things.

1774 GOLDSM. *Nat. Hist.* II. v. i. (*Squirrel*), It continues for some hours at a distance from home, until the alarm be past away. **1821** BYRON *Heaven & Earth* I. i. 155 Foam, Which the leviathan hath lash'd From his unfathomable home. **1864** WOOD (*title*) Homes without Hands, being a Description of the Habitations of Animals. **1893** SIR R. BALL *Story of Sun* 295 To rend this stone from the home where it was originally placed. **1936** C. F. M. SWYNNERTON in *Trans. R. Ent. Soc.* LXXXIV. 520 *Home*.. that portion of the tsetse-habitat used by the tsetse.. for both resting and breeding.

c. The usual contents of a house; a houseful.

1887 *Charity Organis. Rev.* III. No. 34. 369 The creditor relies.. on the power of selling up the 'home'. **1888** *Times* 16 Oct. 3/2 He emigrated to America, leaving his wife and children with a home of furniture.

3. (Without qualifying word or plural.) The place of one's dwelling or nurturing, with the conditions, circumstances, and feelings which naturally and properly attach to it, and are associated with it. ***a home from home***, a place away from home which provides home-like accommodation or amenities; also (outside Britain), ***a home away from home***.

The absence of the article is prob. connected historically with the constructions *at home, to go home* (both in OE.), *from home* (*c* 1300); but it appears also to be connected with the generalized or partly abstract sense, which includes not merely 'place' but also 'state', and is thus construed like *youth, wedlock, health*, and other nouns of state.

c **1460** *Towneley Myst.* xiv. 212 In euery place he shall haue hame. **1546** J. HEYWOOD *Prov.* (1867) 9 Home is homely, though it be poore in syght. **1611** COTGR. s.v. *Pouvoir*, When all is done home's homelie. **1616** S. WARD *Coale fr. Altar* (1627), True zeale loues to keepe home. **1813** BYRON *Corsair* III. xviii, Oh ! what can sanctify the joys of home? **1822** J. H. PAYNE *Song, Home, Sweet Home*, Be it ever so humble, there's no place like home. **1858** HAWTHORNE *Fr. & It. Jrnls.* (1872) I. 51 This life of wandering makes a three days' residence in one place seem like home. **1872** in S. Walker *Whistling Commercial* (Advt.), The real comforts of a home from home. **1882** A. W. WARD *Dickens* vii. 223 He was most English in that love of home to which he was never weary of testifying. **1906** *Morning Post* 1 Feb. 7/2 To provide them with a 'home from home' while engaged in the studies which fitted them for the positions in life they were destined to fill. **1907** *Daily Chron.* 30 Nov. 3/3 The British man is a clubbable animal, and doesn't mind paying handsomely for his 'home from home'. *c* **1926** 'MIXER' *Transport Workers' Song Bk.* 21 It's like a home-away-from-home. **1961** *Times* 26 May 9/6 Durrants Hotel in George Street, for years the home-from-home of English County families. **1961** M. BEADLE *These Ruins are Inhabited* (1963) xii. 165 The delicatessen that is the foreigners' home-away-from-home in Oxford. **1962** *Guardian* 6 Oct. 12/4 The idea is to provide a 'home from home' atmosphere for boys between 16 and 19.

4. *fig.* In various connexions, referring to the grave, or future state: the 'long' or 'last' home.

1303 R. BRUNNE *Handl. Synne* 9195 To þy long home shalt þou wende. *c* **1375** *Sc. Leg. Saints* Prol. 32 Quhene he sal cume til his lang hame. **1535** COVERDALE *Eccl.* xii. 5 Man goeth to his longe home. **1588** SHAKS. *Tit. A.* I. i. 83 These that I bring vnto their latest home. **1638** SIR T. HERBERT *Trav.* (ed. 2) 204 A deadly flux.. brought that religious Gentleman.. in the vigour of his age, to an immortall home. **1722** WOLLASTON *Relig. Nat.* ix. 218 Preparing for our removal hence to our long home. **1833** I. TAYLOR *Fanat.* iii. 70 Whatever is spurious is marked already for oblivion, and moves on to its home.

5. A place, region, or state to which one properly belongs, in which one's affections centre, or where one finds refuge, rest, or satisfaction.

1548 HALL *Chron., Hen. V.* 38 b, He subdewed Wales.. and broughte that unruly parte to his olde home and aunciente degree. **1567** THROCKMORTON *Let. to Eliz.* 9 Aug. in Tytler *Hist. Scot.* (1864) III. 270 They [the Hamiltons] account but the little king betwixt them and home, who may die. **1589** WARNER *Alb. Eng.* VI. xxxii. (1612) 160 His Brothers twaine, his Nephewes twain, and Neeces three did stand Betwix himselfe and home. **1596** SHAKS. *1 Hen. IV*, IV. i. 57 A Randeuous, a Home to flye vnto. **1667** MILTON *P.L.* x. 1085 Till we end In dust, our final rest and native home. **1873** LYTTON *Kenelm Chillingly* II. xv, Wherever woman has a tongue, there Mrs. Grundy has a home. **1884** *Contemp. Rev.* Mar. 315 In the Church of England he found a satisfying home.

6. One's own country, one's native land. Used by Britons abroad, by inhabitants of (former) British colonies and territories, and † by those of British descent in the U.S., for Great Britain = the mother-country, the 'old country'. (Cf. *at home*: II b.)

1595 SHAKS. *John* II. i. 31 Till then faire boy Will I not thinke of home, but follow Armes. **1601** —— *All's Well* II.

v. 71 That presently you take your way for home. **1755** WASHINGTON *Let. to Aug. Washington* Apr. (Bartlett), My command was reduced, under a pretence of an order from home. **1817** BROUGHAM in *Parl. Deb.* I. 545 Whether in consequence of orders from home, or of the views entertained by the local governments. **1837** *Lett. fr. Madras* (1843) 92 Home always means England; nobody calls India home. **1842** *N.Z. Govt. Gaz.* Suppl. II. 40 In accordance with instructions from home. **1886** FROUDE *Oceana* (ed. 2) 78 The Controller..had many questions to ask about 'home' and what was going there.

7. The seat, centre, or native habitat; the place or region where a thing is native, indigenous, or most common.

1706 PRIOR *Ode to Queen* 315 Flandria, by plenty made the home of War. **1871** FREEMAN *Norm. Conq.* IV. xviii. 125 The return of the Conqueror was ushered in by the destruction of the ecclesiastical home of the nation. **1874** GREEN *Short Hist.* vii. §5. 386 The South and the West still remained..the great homes of mining and manufacturing activity. **1886** POSNETT *Comp. Lit.* IV. ii. 258 Sicily, then, was the real home of bucolic poetry.

8. An institution providing refuge or rest for the destitute, the afflicted, the infirm, etc., or for those who either have no home of their own, or are obliged by their vocation to live at a distance from the home of their family.

1851–61 MAYHEW *Lond. Labour* II. 81 (Hoppe) These birds are not admitted into the Sailors' Home. **1863** S. LOW *Charit. Lond.* 31 The Home for Confirmed Invalids. *Ibid.* Index 312 Home for Aged Annuitants. **1897** *Whitaker's Alm.* 282 Dr. Barnardo's Homes for Orphan Waifs. *Ibid.* 285 Homes for Working Girls in London.

9. a. In games: The place in which one is free from attack; the point which one tries to reach; the goal.

1854 DICKENS *Let.* 12 July (1938) II. 566 The keeping up of a 'home' at rounders. **1855** —— *Dorrit* vii. 50 The prison children..whooped and ran, and played at hide and seek, and made the bars of the inner gateway 'Home'. **1870** HARDY & WARE *Mod. Hoyle, Backgammon* 141 The object of the game is to bring the men round to your own 'home', or inner table. **1897** *Daily News* 18 June 2/3 All the time Watts kept Persimmon in waiting, and not till the line for home did he let the great horse go.

b. *Lacrosse.* Each of the three players stationed nearest their opponents' goal.

1869 W. G. BEERS *Lacrosse* (1875) xii. 191 It is essential that Goal-keeper,..and Home should be special men accustomed to those positions. *Ibid.* 195 *Home.* Should stand within eight or ten feet of the opposing goal. *Ibid.* App. 254 The players of each side shall be designated as follows:..'Home', nearest opponent's goal. **1892** *Lippincott's Mag.* XLIX. 746 Outside home, and inside home. *Ibid.* 748 To secure the ball in the 'draw-off'..and pass it to the home or attack men. **1897** *Encycl. Sport* I. 607/1 The three *Homes* must be adepts in taking short and hard catches with absolute certainty. **1964** *Lacrosse* ('Know the Game' Series) 35 First Home should make moves to as far away as Third Home level, to the goal, and round it. **1973** *Sunday Tel.* 4 Mar. 38/6 First home, Janet Roberts, with her dynamic underarm flick, deserved more than the two she obtained.

10. The accusative retains its original use after a verb of motion, as in *to go* or *come home* (= L. *ire, venire domum*); but as this construction is otherwise obsolete in the language, *home* so used is treated practically as an adverb, and has developed purely adverbial uses. See HOME *adv.*

11. at home. a. At or in one's own house, or place of abode. (In OE. often = 'in the house', as distinct from outside.)

805–31 *Charter* in *O.E. Texts* 444 Of hiȝna ȝemenum godum ðaer aet ham. *c* **1000** *Ags. Gosp.* Mark ix. 33 þa hi æt ham [*Lindisf.* æt huse] wæron. —— Luke ix. 61 Læt me æryst hit cyþan þam ðe æt ham [*Lindisf.* æd ham; *Rushw.* æt huse] synt. *c* **1205** LAY. 2436 þa wæs Guendoleine at hame. **13..** *Coer de L.* 256 At home ne dwellyd never none, On forfeyture on lyff and londe. **1484** CAXTON *Fables of Alfonce* (1889) 11 A lytyl catte which she hadde at home. **1504** ATKYNSON tr. *De Imitatione* I. xx. (1893) 168 To byde at whome. **1573** J. SANFORD *Hours Recreat.* (1576) 220 When the Catte is not at home, the Myce daunce. **1616–1798** [see CHARITY 9]. *a* **1631** DONNE *Lett.* (1651) 44 Naturall and inborn charity, beginning at home. **1712** STEELE *Spect.* No. 431 ¶3, I had not been long at home with him. **1820** W. IRVING *Sketch Bk.* I. 39 There is still a little world of love at home, of which he is the monarch.

fig. *c* **1440** *York Myst.* xlviii. 360 3e herde þem noght, youre eris ȝe hidde, Youre helpe to þame was noȝt at hame. **1796** BURNEY *Mem. Metastasio* I. 70 A sure sign that your head is at home.

b. In one's own neighbourhood, town, country, etc.; in one's native land. (Opp. to *abroad.*) In the mother-country, in England. (Cf. sense 6.)

The application has gradually widened from uses in which it is hardly distinguishable from the prec.

c **1386** CHAUCER *Prol.* 512 He..dwelleth at hoom, and kepeth wel his folde. *c* **1400** *Destr. Troy* 9337 Oure buernes ..þat might haue leuet in hor lond, as lordes at hame. **1548** HALL *Chron., Edw. IV* 195 b, That he then myght do at his pleasure, bothe at home and in outward parties. **1678** WANLEY *Wond. Lit. World* v. i. §93. 467/2 Unfortunate in his Wars at home and abroad. **1751** in J. F. Hageman *Hist. Princeton* (1879) I. 59 The administration of his Excellency ..has been disadvantageously represented to the ministry at home. **1861** T. GILBERT *N.Z. Settlers & Soldiers* 33 The.. cliffs of Mokau..call to mind the chalk cliffs of dear old England—Beachy Head, and other favourite localities at 'home'. **1873** C. ROBINSON *N.S. Wales* 105 To all who are struggling to get on at home and yet can hardly keep their heads above the water..we say..come out to this Land of Plenty. **1908** E. J. BANFIELD *Confessions of Beachcomber* I. ii. 77 Australians cannot with justice complain when the good old folks at home blunder..the while..so much local misapprehension prevails.

c. At one's ease, as if in one's own home; in one's element. Hence, Unconstrained, unembarrassed; familiar or conversant *with*, well versed *in*.

1513 MORE in Grafton *Chron.* (1568) II. 811 In his custodie, where he might recon himselfe at home. **1528** TINDALE *Answ. Sir T. More* 57 The mayde was at home also in heuenly pleasures. **1787** 'G. GAMBADO' *Acad. Horsemen* (1809) 45 Supposing you are now at home enough on horseback, to ride out alone. **1816** KEATINGE *Trav.* (1817) I. 23 The complete manner in which they appear to be at home at the table. **1860** W. GORDON *Dearest Mamma* 11 Pray make yourselves at home, gentlemen. **1878** BOSW. SMITH *Carthage* 376 In politics he does not seem to have been at home. **1886** RUSKIN *Præterita* I. v. 171 More at home on the hills than in the counting-house.

Hence ***at-homeish, at-homeness***: see AT HOME *advb. phr.*

d. Conventionally understood as = Accessible to callers; prepared to receive visitors. Hence, used as a formula inviting company to an informal reception. See also AT HOME *sb.*

1601 SHAKS. *Twel. N.* I. v. 117 If it be a suit from the Count, I am sicke, or not at home. What you will, to dismisse it. **1710–13** SWIFT *Jrnl. to Stella* (K.O.), The Minister is not at home, which I knew to be a lie. **1760** C. JOHNSTON *Chrysal* II. I. i. 7 Turning to the footman, 'I thought, sirrah (said she), that I was not to be at home this evening!' *Ibid.* ii. 10 You know your company is always welcome. I am always at home to you! **1782** COWPER *Progr. Err.* 167 Their answer to the call is—*Not at home.* **1849** THACKERAY *Pendennis* xli, The Marchioness of Steyne would be at home to Mr. Arthur Pendennis upon a given day. **1896** *Westm. Gaz.* 7 Sept. 3/2 Mrs. S. is 'At home' first and third Mondays. **1898** *Card,* Mrs. M——. At Home, Randolph Assembly Rooms, Monday, February 21st, 9 to 11 o'clock. R.S.V.P. *Notice,* Owing to a recent bereavement Mrs. —— will not be at home on Thursdays at present.

Hence '***not-at-home***', the intimation or arrangement that one is not accessible to visitors.

1874 T. HARDY *Madding Crowd* I. ix. 123 Not-at-homes were hardly naturalized in Weatherbury farm-houses.

e. *Cribbage.* (See quot. 1877.)

1796 C. JONES *Hoyle's Games Improved* 294 By attending to the above Calculation any Player may judge whether he is at Home or not. **1877** *Encycl. Brit.* VI. 577/1 (*Cribbage*) Each player ought to reckon slightly over six in hand and play and five in crib, or seventeen and a half in two deals to be *at home.* A player who scores more than the average and leaves his adversary six or seven points in arrear is *safe at home.* When at home it is best to play off; when the adversary is safe at home it is best to play on.

f. Used in colloq. phrases expressing (freq. scornful) doubt or a query about the identity of a person or thing, *e.g.* 'Who is he when he's at home?'

1887 KIPLING *Plain Tales fr. Hills* (1888) 99 You.. dimonstrate to *my* frind here, where *your* frinds are whan they're at home? **1914** E. PUGH *Cockney at Home* 118 Who is Popkins when he's at home? **1930** J. B. PRIESTLEY *Angel Pavement* ii. 64 'And we can't all look like Mr. Ronald Mawlborough either.' 'Who's he when he's at home?' Mr. Smeeth inquired. **1957** M. KENNEDY *Heroes of Clone* III. ii. 165 'And what's existentialist, when it's at home?' she asked. **1960** R. COLLIER *House called Memory* viii. 112 *Peachy*? I have no idea what you mean. What's that when it's at home? **1972** A. ROSS *London Assignment* 20 'Farrow?' I said. 'Who's he when he's at home?'

g. Used of a match when the team referred to is playing on its own ground. (Cf. AWAY *adv.* 11.)

1898 *Football Telegraph* (Kettering) 1 Jan. 3/2 Last season,..a splendid victory was achieved at home, the locals winning by 2 goals to 0. **1930** *Daily Tel.* 5 Dec. 20/3 Clapton Orient, 'at home' to Luton Town at Highbury. **1967** *Listener* 17 Aug. 223/1 They had just lost three matches at home.

12. from home. Away from one's house or place of abode; not at home; abroad. †*fig.* Ill at ease, out of one's element. (See also quot. 1573.)

a **1300** *Cursor M.* 3350 Ysaac was not fra hame. **1573** J. SANFORD *Hours Recreat.* (1576) 223, I come from home, that is, I neither winne nor lose. **1618** J. TAYLOR (Water P.) *Penniless Pilgr.* (1883) 27 Her husband being from home. **1737** BRACKEN *Farriery Impr.* (1757) II. 77 You are never from Home, if you have such a Horse under you. **1738** JOHNSON *London* 225 Sign your will, before you sup from home. **1886** MRS. HUNGERFORD *Green Pleasure & Grey Grief* III. vi. 113 Having run away from home.

13. nearer home. a. *lit.* Nearer one's own dwelling-place or country. **b.** *fig.* In or into closer relation or connexion with oneself; so that one is more closely touched or intimately affected.

1577 HARRISON *England* III. ii. (1878) II. 13 Peradventure we might haue found the same neerer home. **1709** *Refl. Sacheverell's Serm.* 22 The Dr. ought to look nearer home. **1712** ADDISON *Spect.* No. 415 ¶10 In..China, as in Countries nearer home. **1863** QUEEN VICTORIA *Let.* 5 Aug. in R. Fulford *Dearest Mama* (1968) 254 No one saw the correspondence. I think the King should look nearer home for such things. **1875** JOWETT *Plato* (ed. 2) III. 167 There are whole countries too, such as India, or, nearer home, Ireland. **1886** C. M. YONGE *Chantry House* II. xiv. 138 'I meant something nearer home,' said Clarence, and proceeded to ask if I did not think Lawrence Frith..smitten with Emily. **1969** *Listener* 2 Jan. 22/2 It seemed thus to be about something both larger and nearer home than Cohn-Bendit's subject.

14. to home. *dial.* (also *U.S.*) = At home.

1795 B. DEARBORN *Columbian Gram.* 139 Improprieties, commonly called Vulgarisms..[include] To home for At home. **1833** J. NEAL *Down-Easters* I. 62 When he's to home ..he's match for gab with anybody 't ever you come across. **1839** *Knickerbocker* XIV. 153, I used to be quite good at reckoning, when I was to home, in the state of New Hampshire. **1868** LADY VERNEY *Stone Edge* ii, I'm main sorry Master Broom ain't to home. **1873** 'S. COOLIDGE' *What Katy Did* xii, 'Tain't every girl would know how to take care of a fat old woman, and make her feel to home. **1910** *Dialect Notes* III. 450 (Western New York) Is your father to home? **1935** Z. N. HURSTON *Mules & Men* (1970) I. ix. 192 Come on, Big Sweet, we got to go to home. **1972** J. GORES *Dead Skip* (1973) viii. 52 White meat don't turn me on. I got Maybelle and four cute kids to home.

15. *attrib.* and *Comb.* **a.** Simple attrib., appositive, etc., as ***home-address, -breeding, -haven, -island, -lesson, -name, -tree, -woe*** (tr. Ger. *heimweh*), ***-worship, -wreck.*** Also, in sense To, for, or towards home, homeward, as ***home-breeze, -correspondent, -letter, -longing, -wind***: cf. HOME *adv.* 8 a.

1886 MRS. HUNGERFORD *Lady Valworth's Diamonds* xxiii. (1888) 156 If you will give me his *home address. **1865** H. H. DIXON *Field & Fern* IV. v. 90 There is no *home breeding to any great extent. **1825** EMILY TAILOR *Vis. Las Casas* 10 Her full sails catch the *home-breeze joyfully. **1887** ERROLL *Ugly Duckling* III. ix. 143 Something like *home-comfortableness. **1840** LONGF. in *Life* (1891) I. 359, I hope I shall be a better *home-correspondent than I have been hithertofore. **1852** SUSAN WARNER *Queechy* (1853) I. 219 Without one softening or home-like touch from any *home-feeling within. *a* **1618** SYLVESTER *Paradox agst. Libertie* 725 As hee sees his ship her *home-haven enter safe. **1887** *World* 21 Sept. 15/2 Miss P...has opened a *home-hospital in Weymouth Street. **1887** *Spectator* 10 Sept. 1220/2 *Home lessons, also, are longer and more exacting than with us. **1894** H. NISBET *Bush Girl's Rom.* 212 Have you got your *home-letter ready? **1822–34** *Good's Study Med.* (ed. 4) II. 507 *Home-longing, when at a remote distance from one's friends and country. **1886** *Illustr. Lond. News* 27 Nov. 569 Her *home name is 'the Princess Mary'. **1649** G. DANIEL *Trinarch., Hen. V*, cxvii, Soe farre Devided ..as hee shall not heare *Home-whineinges. **1855** LONGF. *Hiaw.* iv. 234 Ruler shall you be..Of the *home-wind. **1892** R. KIPLING *Barrack-r. Ballads, Eng. Flag* x, The East Wind roared..Me men call the Home-Wind, for I bring the English home. **1879** F. W. ROBINSON *Coward Conscience* I. iii, A *home-wreck and a soul cut adrift.

b. In relation to domestic economy: ***home art(s), care, circle, daughter, education, girl***, etc.; **home-bird, homebody** orig. *U.S.*, a person, etc., who prefers staying at home to going out or travelling; **home boarder**, a day-boarder, day-boy; **home computer**, a small computer designed for use in the home, esp. for recreational or educational purposes; **homecraft**, an art or craft pursued in the home; also, the household arts; **home loan**, a loan granted to someone to assist in the purchase of a house, flat, etc., to live in; **home unit** *Austral.*, a flat or apartment, normally one owned by the occupant. (Nowadays indistinguishable from B 1, since present-day hyphening cannot be assumed to be a reliable guide to grammatical function.)

1597 DANIEL *Civ. Wars* VII. lii, Th' ayde, home-disobedience would afford. **1602** CAREW *Cornwall* II. (1811) 234 Afflictions by home-neighbours. **1621–31** LAUD *Sev. Serm.* (1847) 86 He may have leisure from home-cares. **1641** BROME *Joviall Crew* II. Wks. 1873 III. 381 Such was his love to keep me a home-Man. **1740** J. CLARKE *Educ. Youth* (ed. 3) 204 This is an objection..against a Home-Education. **1802** *Edin. Rev.* I. 80 The home-group, in which his infancy was spent. **1821** J. F. COOPER *Spy* I. xi. 175 Marry him I don't think I will —— unless he becomes steadier and more of a homebody. **1841** DICKENS *Let.* 16 Mar. (1969) II. 238 With love *to* all your home circle and *from* all mine. **1850** C. KINGSLEY *Alton Locke* vi. 97 To..live a life of sneaking and lying under petticoat government, as all home-birds were sure to do in the long-run. **1853** MRS. GASKELL *Ruth* III. viii. 230 Leonard's remaining such a home-bird..with such a mother..will do him no harm. **1853** MISS SHEPPARD *Ch. Auchester* I. 7 A domestic presence of purity, kindliness, and home-heartedness. **1855** —— *Let. c* 20 Oct. (1966) 873 Thank you for your kind message to my home circle. **1857** A. J. SYMONDS *Let.* 24 May (1967) I. 110 There were two brothers homeboarders but belonging to the School. **1870** MORRIS *Earthly Par.* II. III. 78 All folk unto the homestead draw, And noted how a homeman there Turned round unto the hillside bare. **1878** *N. Amer. Rev.* CXXVII. 354 Some features of home-life in France. **1881** C. M. YONGE *More Bywords* (1890) 125 An excellent plan..for bringing the whole family together round our dear old mother and her home daughter. **1883** *Evang. Mag.* Aug. 349 The dictating of a letter to the home-circle. **1886** F. W. ROBINSON *Courting Mary Smith* II. xx. 101, I was too much of a home-bird to be satisfied with the change. **1902** *Encycl. Brit.* XXV. 686/1 The Home Arts and Industries Association. **1905** H. A. VACHELL *Hill* xi. 228 He wished to educate his only son at Harrow as a 'Home-Boarder', or day-boy. **1914** M. HILL (*title*) Homecraft in the classroom. **1924** WODEHOUSE *Bill the Conqueror* ii. 32 He said this girl was one of those domestic girls, a little home-body, and might be leaving the party any moment now. **1927** PEAKE & FLEURE *Hunters & Artists* 79 *Art mobilier*, which has been translated 'mobiliary art', 'portable art', or 'home art'. **1927** *Daily Express* 26 Feb. 5/2 Women who seek a pleasant paying homecraft. *Ibid.* 23 Mar. 5 Modern Homecraft Notions. **1934** T. WILDER *Heaven's My Destination* 53 Snappiest little home-girl in Oklahoma. **1941** *Brit. Jrnl. Psychol.* Apr. 306 Finally she had to leave her University post... 'I could no longer keep it and be a home daughter.' **1944** J. S. HUXLEY *On Living in Rev.* iii. 28 Ma Ferguson, pictured as a very motherly sort of home-body. **1959** S. GIBBONS *Pink Front Door* iv. 52 The daughter at home, 'the home bird'. **1959** *News Chronicle* 12

Aug. 6/8 She liked to be a homebody and . . lie with her head on her master's foot. **1961** R. B. LONG *Sentence & its Parts* ii. 54 She isn't a home girl. **1961** *Spectator* 17 Mar. 352 The great increase of home-care cases that must follow the demolition of the mental hospitals. **1962** *Southerly* XXII. II. 92 By 'standard words' is implied those which soberly indicate what they have to indicate (like home-unit and bombora). **1966** AUDEN *About House* 24 A cellar never takes umbrage; It takes us as we are, explorers, homebodies. **1966** *Times* 7 Apr. 12/1 The ban on home loans by local authorities has been lifted. **1967** *Guardian* 16 May 8/4 The one school with 'home boarders'—where some boys live in the town and take 'bed and breakfast' at home. **1967** *Canad. Ann. Rev. 1966* 92 Government support to develop a complex of services, including hospital-based home care programs. **1967** E. HUNT *Danger Game* viii. 151, I know Mrs. Dell lived in a home unit in Coogee. **1969** T. PARKER *Twisting Lane* 48, I was a great home-bird myself. **1969** *West Australian* 5 July 48/2 (Advt.), Prestige loc[ality] . . suitable flats or home units. *Ibid.*, Home unit Scarborough open for inspection... This spotless apartment.. compr[ises] 2 good bedrms. [etc.]. **1972** *P.O. Telephone Directory* Sect. 102 (London Postal Area E-K) 513/3 Homecraft Supplies. **1972** *Publishers Weekly* 30 Oct. 33/2 A country of home-bodies with the concerns of homebodies is quite different from an outgoing one. **1973** *Times* 27 June 23/1 (*headline*) Tempers fray in tussle between home loan chiefs and Government. **1973** *Sun-Herald* (Sydney) 26 Aug. 11/2 (*heading*) A bolt of lightning damaged a block of home units at Vaucluse. **1976** *Computers: Next 5 Yrs.* (12th IEEE Computer Soc. Internat. Conf.) 218/1 A distinction must be drawn between a hobby computer and a home computer... The home computer must be designed for the person whose interests lie in the results produced by the machine, rather than in the machine itself. **1978** *Times* 16 Sept. 17/6 London's next home computer show . . takes place at the West Centre Hotel next Thursday. **1985** *Listener* 31 Jan. 33/1 The phoney war in the home-computer market has become a real price war.

c. In same sense as B 2.

1745 W. ELLIS *Mod. Husb.* VI. I. 33 My Rows of broad Beans in my Home-close. **1774** *Garton Inclos. Act* 3 All the home-steads, home-closes, and ancient inclosures. **1853** C. W. ADAMS *Spring in Canterbury Settlement* vii. 69 The home-station was situated at the mouth of the river Motunau. **1870** MORRIS *Earthly Par.* II. III. 486 Over the homefield toward the wall they drew. **1884** W. SHEPHERD *Prairie Experiences* 205 Stock are always restless at first on a drive, and are striving to get back on their home-ranges. **1890** BOLDREWOOD *Col. Reformer* (1891) 353 They were fairly on the sandy home-station track. **1902** *N.Z. Illustr. Mag.* VII. 117/2 We'll keep the home-block. **1903** 'T. COLLINS' *Such is Life* 170 In two seconds more, Cleopatra was stretching away . . towards Yoongoolee home-station, distant about sixteen miles. **1904** 'G. B. LANCASTER' *Sons o' Men* 3 Lane's out-station was twelve rough miles from the home-block. **1915** D. H. LAWRENCE *Rainbow* i. 6 A confusion of sheds spread into the home-close. **1933** C. DAY LEWIS *Dick Willoughby* 9 The cowman and his herd moving into the home-meadow.

d. In same sense as B 3.

1597 DANIEL *Civ. Wars* Wks. (1717) 200 The glory lost, which Home-Broils hinder might. **1601** HOLLAND *Pliny* II. 137 Ech region is furnished sufficiently with home-physicke of their owne. **1622** BACON *Hen. VII* 76 To set prices by Statute . . vpon our Home-Commodities. **1713** in *Lond. Gaz.* No. 5130/6 Neither do we . . fear any Foreign Rivalship to our Home-Manufactures. **1766** W. GORDON *Gen. Counting-ho.* 365 Whether foreigner or home-trader. **1797** NELSON *Let.* Apr. (1845) II. 374 Had there been no Fleet in the Channel, the French might have come up the Mediterranean and taken us all; therefore the Home Fleet certainly took care of us and covered us. **1799** J. ROBERTSON *Agric. Perth* 351 The home-market price was raised. **1804** EARL LAUDERD. *Pub. Wealth* (1819) 153 In the home-trade. **1867** SMYTH *Sailor's Word-bk.*, *Home-Service*, the Channel service; any force . . stationed in and about the United Kingdom. **1883** *Peel City Guardian* 15 Sept., Our harbour is once more almost empty, as the Home Fleet are fishing off Douglas. **1889** *Spectator* 2 Nov., What may be called the home-missionary spirit. **1903** *Westm. Gaz.* 30 Mar. 2/2 What military stations abroad are now reckoned as Home stations. **1904** *To-Day* 14 Dec. 162/1 The Present Home Fleet is to be called the Channel Fleet. **1906** *Daily Chron.* 24 Oct. 7/4 A distinct fleet will be constituted from the ships in commission in reserve, to be called the 'Home Fleet'. **1915** KIPLING *Fringes of Fleet* 35 From the peace of the German side he had entered our hectic home-waters. **1927** W. DEEPING *Kitty* i. 10 A home-service job with one of the home-service battalions. **1941** *Ann. Reg. 1940* 55 Small bodies of highly mobile and strongly armed troops, known as 'Ironsides', after the first Commander-in-Chief of the Home Forces. **1972** *Whitaker's Almanack 1973* 461/1 Sir Andrew Lewis K.C.B. (Commander-in-Chief Naval Home Command).

e. In same sense as B 4, q.v.

f. In same sense as B 5.

1638 FORD *Fancies* I. i, Speak a home-word For my old bachelor lord. **1694** CROWNE *Married Beau* Ep., A more blunt expression . . when they wou'd make a home-proof of such a transgression. **1723** M'WARD *Earnest Contend.* 196 (Jam.) Your great confidence makes plain and home-dealing with you . . necessary. [**1711**, **1881** Home-truth: see B 5.]

†**g.** Of, pertaining to, or concerning oneself; intimate, private, personal. *Obs.*

1711 SHAFTESB. *Charac.* (1737) I. 170 Such confidence they had in this home-dialect of soliloquy. **1726** BUTLER *Serm. Rolls* x. 195 If this sincere Self-Enjoyment and Home-Satisfaction be thought desirable.

h. objective and obj. gen., as ***home-breaker***, ***-breaking***, ***-builder***, ***-buyer***, ***-lover***, ***-owner*** (so ***-ownership***), ***-seeker***, HOME-KEEPER, -KEEPING, -MAKER; ***home influence***, ***news***; ***home-building***, ***-loving*** adjs.

1928 *Sunday Dispatch* 2 Sept. 17/1 As a *home-breaker woman is . . as good as a man. **1936** N. COWARD *To-night at 8.30* II. 74 You mean you'd prefer to be implicated with a professional homebreaker as opposed to an amateur one? **1907** *Daily Chron.* 18 June 3/6 *Home-breaking is a more serious offence against society than house-breaking. **1884** J. HALL *Chr. Home* 82 The recollection . . will prevent the young *home-builders from being paralyzed with surprise. **1825** COLERIDGE *Aids Refl.* Aph. xxxvi. (1848) I. 86 The *home-building, wedded, and divorceless swallow. **1969** *Times* 20 May 28/3 (*headline*) S[elective] E[mployment] T[ax] hits *home buyer. **1973** *Times* 6 Oct. 1/1 A plan to help young home-buyers is likely to be announced within the next week. **1847** G. AQUILAR (*title*) *Home influence. **1852** C. M. YONGE *Two Guardians* xiv. 255 Marian had . . weakened the only home influence . . which held Caroline to the right. **1966** D. JENKINS *Educated Society* v. 208 Home influence . . [is] a major factor in determining whether people will be able to take advantage of educational opportunities. **1856** EMERSON *Eng. Traits, Result* Wks. (Bohn) II. 133 Truth in private life, untruth in public, marks these *home-loving men. **1876** STOPF. BROOKE *Eng. Lit.* 8 A home-loving people. **1852** MRS. GASKELL *Let.* 2 Mar. (1966) 181, I don't think there is much *home news. Last week was very quiet; and very busy with writing. **1936** *Punch* 5 Aug. 144/3 It is one of our principles that our students should *earn while they learn*, and for this reason our first practical efforts will be in the realms of the easiest department of Romantic Journalism, namely Home News. **1945** NELSON & WRIGHT *Tomorrow's House* xvii. 203/1 There are almost 35,000,000 dwellings in the United States. Maybe you own one of them... To the *homeowner who is intrigued by . . tomorrow's house, several possibilities are open besides . . selling the roof over his head. **1956** J. H. GREENBERG in Saporta & Bastian *Psycholinguistics* (1961) 474/1 Homeowners must pay real estate taxes. **1960** *Times* 21 Nov. (Canadian Suppl.) p. v/6, Canadians are the greatest home-owners in the world. **1960** *Times* 24 Oct. (Financial Rev.) p. xi/5, Thrift and *home-ownership. **1972** *Guardian* 6 July 24/7 Home ownership in cities averaged 42 per cent. **1889** *Advance* (Chicago) 7 Mar. 191 The *home-seekers of the 19th Century Pilgrim Fathers. **1911** *Daily Colonist* (Victoria, B.C.) 1 Apr. 12/1 (Advt.), Pandora Avenue Homeseekers. We have the finest residential buy in Victoria today. **1937** *Sunday Dispatch* 14 Feb. 18/4 The scope for the homeseeker is, in fact, extremely wide. **1963** *Times* 12 Feb. 8/1 *A Homeseeker*. Once you have found the house you are looking for, talk . . about a loan to help you buy.

i. locative, in sense 'at home', with ppl. adjs., vbl. sbs., nouns of action, agent-nouns, as ***home-baked***, ***-based***, ***-built***, ***-consumed***, ***-cooked***, ***-cured***, ***-fed***, ***-formed***, ***-grown***, ***-killed***, ***-left***, ***-produced***, ***-raised***, ***-reared***, ***-woven***, HOME-BREWED, -MADE, -SPUN; ***home-abiding***, ***-cooking***, ***-curing***, ***-dressmaking***, ***-growing***, ***-nursing***, ***-sewing***, ***-sitting***, ***-staying***, ***-touring***, ***-washing***; ***home-duty***, ***-execution***, ***-growth***, ***nurse***, ***-stay***; HOME HELP; ***home-baker***, ***-brewer***, ***-dressmaker***, ***-dweller***, ***-grower***, ***-patient***, ***-sewer***, ***-stayer***, ***-tarrier***, etc.

1886 MARY HOWITT in *Gd. Words* 545 The *home-abiding poet Whittier. **1766** H. BROOKE *Fool of Quality* (1870) I. 99 Nurse went upstairs with a most bountiful cut of *home-baked bread and butter. **1816** JANE AUSTEN *Emma* II. ix. 186 The finest looking home-baked apples I ever saw in my life. **1870** LOWELL *Study Wind.* 251 The home-baked Saxon loaf. **1490** *Canterb. City Rec.*, Robertus Dehytyngton, *homebaker. **1944** *Ann. Reg. 1943* 8 British and American *home-based bombers made . . day or night raids. **1956** *Nature* 25 Feb. 366/2 Six . . schemes, applicable to the tropics, which were for home-based work . . were added. *a* **1631** DRAYTON *Wks.* II. 586 (Jod.) *Home-begotten hate. **1676** *Rep. Fr. Capers* 4 Aug. in Marvell *Growth Popery* (1678) 59 With their own *home-built Ships. **1904** *Westm. Gaz.* 27 Dec. 4/3 A considerable proportion of export tonnage besides *home-consumed manufactures . . is conveyed by horse-drawn vehicles. **1923** H. CRANE *Let.* 12 Oct. (1965) 150 A very fine *home-cooked chicken dinner. **1968** M. KANE *Walk of Devil* iii. 27, I know what you need... A nice home-cooked dinner in pleasant surroundings. **1934** *Amer. Speech* IX. 113/2 The tourist who enjoys strange foods . . will rarely escape the *home-cooking and the home-made pies that emerge from tin cans and factory-like bakeries. **1937** 'M. HILLIS' *Orchids on Budget* (1938) vi. 94 Steaks and roasts are so well prepared in the best restaurants that you might . . turn up your nose at them for home cooking. **1968** O. WYND *Sumatra Seven Zero* i. 5 The other patrons . . all came often to get away from home cooking. **1973** H. NIELSEN *Severed Key* i. 6 Didn't I ever tell you how much I hate home cooking? **1863** MRS. GASKELL *Cousin Phillis* in *Cornh. Mag.* Nov. 619, I handled and weighed in my fancy the *home-cured ham. **1959** R. POSTGATE *Good Food Guide* 236 Breakfast was home-cured ham, thick, well grilled, with eggs and tomato. **1960** *Farmer & Stockbreeder* 16 Feb. Suppl. 8/1 When Denmark entered the trade at the end of the nineteenth century, bacon was still being produced from the whole sides in an adaptation of the traditional *home-curing method. **1960** *Sunday Express* 11 Sept. 15/6 The ideal fabric for the home *dress-maker. **1971** *Guardian* 10 Aug. 9/2 These costly fabrics (up to £50 a yard) are . . being displayed . . as temptations to home dressmakers. **1896** *Woman's Life* 4 July 138/1 Many people put up with faults in *home dressmaking which they would rate in a regular dressmaker. **1966** H. YOXALL *Fashion of Life* viii. 68 When I first joined *Vogue* the early demise of home-dressmaking was predicted. **1850** MRS. GASKELL *Let.* 14 May (1966) 117 Girls, having . . the *home-duties of parents dependent upon them. **1593** Q. ELIZ. tr. *Boeth.* IV. pr. i. 76 *Home-dweller in thy country. **1549** COVERDALE, etc. *Erasm. Par. Eph.* Prol., By foreigne, or *homedwelling enemies. **1573** TUSSER *Husb.* xxxiii. (1878) 72 Fat *home fed souse, is good in a house. **1825** J. S. MILL in *Westm. Rev.* III. 418 The *home-grower is subject to many taxes, from which foreign corn is exempt. **1827** —— *Ibid.* VII. 173 They consume **home-grown* corn. **1846** J. BAXTER *Libr. Pract. Agric.* (ed. 4) II. p. xxxviii, The independent production of home-grown wool. **1895** *Cricket Handbk.* 31 It is sincerely to be hoped that the means may yet be found of recruiting the eleven from home-grown cricketers. **1935** *Discovery* June 162/1 The Great War undoubtedly had a great influence in fostering the canning of home-grown foods. **1959** *Times* 31 Mar. 11/1 Yet there was nothing unprofessional about the timing, staging, or lighting of even these most home-grown numbers. **1966** *Times* 28 Feb. (Canada Suppl.) p. xiii/3, Last summer, with a home-grown production of a musical . . it played a six weeks season. **1973** J. THOMSON *Death Cap* iv. 56 A board . . announcing in crude, hand-painted letters: 'For Sale. Home-grown Produce. Flowers. Fruit. Vegetables. Eggs.' **1825** J. S. MILL in *Westm. Rev.* III. 413 If the new material . . be of *home growth, the production of that material would open a new channel for the profitable employment of agricultural capital. **1873** E. E. ESTCOURT *Question of Anglican Ordinations* ii. 15 All the preceding seems to have been the direct home-growth of Lollardism or of Wicliffe's teaching. **1906** *Daily Chron.* 20 Sept. 6/1 Not even an expert could tell the difference between home-bred and *home-killed meat unless he were on the spot. **1602** WARNER *Alb. Eng.* XII. lxxvi, Why you Should *home-left love forget. **1958** *Home nurse [see HOME HELP]. **1963** *Times* 24 May 8/5 All the old public assistance buildings replaced by pleasant old people's homes, with sufficient home nurses or home helps. **1905** *Daily Chron.* 25 Oct. 7/4 Instruction of . . future mothers . . in . . *home-nursing. **1959** *Sears, Roebuck Catal.* Spring & Summer 831/3 Illustrated family handbook of home nursing and medical care. **1801** *Med. Jrnl.* V. 5 A *home-patient of the Manchester Infirmary. **1827** *Lincoln Cabinet* 59 Persons residing in Lincoln . . unable to attend at the dispensary, shall be deemed home-patients. **1905** *Westm. Gaz.* 21 Aug. 2/1 Out of deference to the agrarian interest, prohibitive Customs and 'sanitary' restrictions keep out the food which is ready on the frontiers, while the prices of *home-produced flesh rise to a height hitherto unknown. **1966** *Times* 28 Mar. (Austral. Suppl.) p. v/6, Home-produced crude oil. **1866** *Rachel's Secr.* I. 103 Everything was either home-made or *home-raised. **1886** *Badminton Libr., Shooting* I. 3 *Home reared birds. **1630** LORD *Banian* Ep. Ded., Informe the *home-residers with the Manners and Customes of the People. **1964** *McCall's Sewing* ii. 19/2 Whether you are a beginner or an experienced *home-sewer, every pattern should be carefully studied. **1908** *Westm. Gaz.* 13 June 13/2 Every *home-sewing room should include . . a skirt-board [etc.]. **1964** *McCall's Sewing* ii. 15 Without patterns, home-sewing would probably be a lost art. **1728** SAVAGE *Bastard* 76 The guilt of *homeshed blood. **1649** G. DANIEL *Trinarch., Hen. V*, ccxciii, Enflame *home-sitters by long Pedigrees Of their Atcheivments. **1655** GURNALL *Chr. in Arm.* Ded., To have their Will ready made, and their worldly interests set at *home stay. **1655** E. WATERHOUSE in E. Terry *Voy. to E. India* A vij a, To the gain of homestayes. **1854** THOREAU *Walden* 170, I the *home-staying, laborious native. **1905** *Daily Chron.* 9 June 8/5 The home-staying Englishman. **1579–80** NORTH *Plutarch* 190 The *home-tarriers and house-doves that kept Rome still. **1898** *Westm. Gaz.* 7 Apr. 3/2 A recipe . . for the *home-washing of lace. **1888** *Century Mag.* XXXVI. 769/1 *Home-woven hats, or knitted caps.

j. dative, instrumental and other relations, as ***home-bound***, ***-fraught***, ***-sheltered***, ***-tied*** adjs. **k.** similative, as ***home-sweet*** adj.

1882 MAY CROMMELIN *Brown-Eyes* vi. (1884) 69 Why should the Marken men be so *homebound? **1853** TALFOURD *Castilian* IV. iii, We'll ensure one hour of *home-fraught comfort. **1823** MOORE *Fables Holy Alliance*, etc. 104 Calm, wedded affection, that *home-rooted plant. **1882** H. S. HOLLAND *Life & Logic* (1885) 216 Its dear shores and *home-sweet hills. **1897** *Daily News* 30 Mar. 8/2 Work amongst the *home-tied and crippled children of London.

B. *attrib.* passing into *adj.*

These uses do not differ essentially from those treated under 15; but *home*, being here written separately, functions as an adjective used attributively; in sense 5 it is even used predicatively, and qualified by adverbs *more*, *most*, *so*, etc., like an ordinary adjective. In sense 1, the use is nowadays indistinguishable from 15.

1. Of, relating to, or connected with home or one's home; reared, fostered, or carried on at home; proceeding from home; domestic, 'family'. Freq. as ***home comfort***.

[*c* **1000** *Sax. Leechd.* II. 244 Ham [and] wilda hænna.] **1552** HULOET, Home supper, *domicœnium*. **1573** TUSSER *Husb.* lvi. (1878) 127 Home wants to supplie. **1641** BROME *Joviall Crew* II. Wks. 1873 III. 380 Home came I In my home Cloaths again. **1849** THACKERAY *Pendennis* (1871) 624 But this was only a home pastime, and the young school-boy was not fond of home sports. *a* **1855** C. BRONTË *Professor* (1857) II. xxv. 223 To sit on a foot-stool at the fire-side—to enjoy home-comforts. **1883** E. BLACKWELL *Booth, of Blue Ribbon Movem.* viii. 91 Home comforts [had gone] to make way for home necessities. **1883** MRS. CUDLIP *Mod. Housew.* 84 A room that . . had the real genuine 'home look' about it. **1886** W. J. TUCKER *E. Europe* 308 The entire garments worn are home manufacture and home tailoring. **1922** JOYCE *Ulysses* 296 Their abodes were equipped with every modern home comfort. **1942** *R.A.F. Jrnl.* 13 June 15 Some have heard about the living-out system, and dream of feather beds and home comforts. **1973** 'B. MATHER' *Snowline* xix. 225 The place where we're staying—all home comforts and no questions asked.

2. a. In the neighbourhood of or surrounding one's home, or the mansion on an estate. Hence, belonging to head-quarters, principal; as ***home station***.

1662 *Providence* (R.I.) *Rec.* (1893) III. 17 The high way . . where John Steere his howse standeth and his home share of Land. **1699** *Boston Rec.* (1881) VII. 236 A great White Oake standing neer by Mr. Benja White's home meadow. **1815** JANE AUSTEN *Emma* I. xii, Keeping in hand the home farm at Donwell. **1857** R. B. PAUL *Lett. fr. Canterbury, N.Z.* 89 If you have not decided on the site of your home station on a previous visit to the run, the first step will be to ride well over it. **1864** TROLLOPE *Small Ho. Allington* (1879) I. 7 An inner gate, leading from the home paddock, through the gardens. **1865** M. A. BARKER *Station Life in N.Z.* (1870) v. 31 By the time we reached the Home Station we were ready for luncheon. **1886** *World* 17 Dec. 11 The home covers were shot on Friday. **1887** *Spectator* 9 Apr. 495/1 The two home farms brought in a gross revenue of £250. **1930** L. G. D. ACLAND *Early Canterbury Runs* v. 113 He arranged that his executors should bury him in one of the home paddocks at Cracroft. **1939** P. A. ROLLINS *Gone Haywire* 62 The ol' man's bin steadily enlargin' his home range till now it

includes mos' all the head-waters o' Elk Prairie Crick. **1946** F. D. DAVISON *Dusty* ix. 95 The sheep were approaching the home paddock. **1966** *Te Reo* IX. 54 The home paddock and the night paddock which . . must in the early years have been the same piece of land.

b. ***Home Counties***, the counties nearest to London, namely Surrey, Kent, Essex (and formerly Middlesex); sometimes with the addition of Hertfordshire, Buckinghamshire, Berkshire, and occasionally Sussex. ***Home Circuit***: the assize circuit which has London as its centre: its area has been repeatedly changed; at present (1898) it includes the counties of Hertford, Essex, Sussex, Kent, Surrey, Huntingdon, Cambridge, Norfolk, and Suffolk. (See CIRCUIT *sb.* 5.)

1737 *J. Chamberlayne's St. Gt. Brit.* II. *List Offices* 262 Clerk of the Assize of the Home-Circuit. **1837** *Penny Cycl.* VII. 195/1 The Home Circuit comprehends the counties of Hertford, Essex, Kent, Sussex, and Surrey. **1862** TROLLOPE *Orley F.* (1868) 67 Mr. Furnival practised at the common law bar, and early in life had attached himself to the home circuit. **1883** H. P. SMITH *Gloss. Terms* etc. 253 *Home Circuit*, or *South Eastern Circuit*, Norfolk, Suffolk, Essex, Herts, Surrey, Kent, Sussex. **1898** *Mddx. & Herts. N. & Q.* IV. 153 The publication, . . will . . relate not only to London, Middlesex and Hertfordshire, but also to Essex, Buckinghamshire, Berkshire, Surrey and Kent; that is, to the Home Counties. **1959** I. & P. OPIE *Lore & Lang. Schoolch.* xii. 233 In London and the Home Counties the police now chase off the streets even the simple waits singing Christmas carols. **1966** *Listener* 11 Aug. 218/1 The chances are . . small that a writer setting his play in outer suburbia or inner Home County will make of it more than a painful banality. **1972** J. BLACKBURN *For Fear of Little Men* ii. 29 Her accent clashed dramatically with the jargon of Home Counties suburbia.

c. Belonging to the county or locality in which a sporting contest or match takes place. ***home-and-home***: applied to two matches, one of which is played at the home or locality of each side.

1800 *Spokane Falls* (Wash.) *Globe* 26 July 1/3 Six hundred baseball cranks witnessed . . one of the prettiest exhibitions of ball playing that ever took place on the home grounds. **1802** *Sporting Mag.* XIX. 219/2 They were willing to run a match with a leash of greyhounds . . or six brace belonging to each county, running home and home, for a sum to be agreed on. *Ibid.* 221/2 He has refused to run you *home* and *home*, or in any *central county* between the two. **1886** *Times* 21 June 10/5 (Cricket, Gentlemen of England *v.* Australians) The home fielding did not realize expectation. **1886** *World* No. 632. 9/1 The home crew jumped away with the lead, but the visitors speedily joined company with them again. **1887** F. GALE *Game of Cricket* 51 The principal innkeeper and a few good local players inaugurated occasionally good out and home matches, in the same season. **1888** *Observer* 1 July 2/4 A draw, greatly in favour of the home team. **1890** *Daily News* 10 Dec. 2/4 Somersetshire . . have arranged home-and-home matches with Surrey, Lancashire, Yorkshire, Kent [etc.]. **1889** *Seattle Post-Intelligencer* 3 July 1/8 The home team played an up hill game. **1916** E. F. BENSON *David Blaize* iv. 60 The home team took the visitors off to the dormitories to put on their flannels. *Ibid.* 62 The field was cleared for the match; the home side won the toss. **1930** H. G. WELLS *Autocr. Mr. Parham* II. iii. 109 That complete lack of information about the visitors attributed to the home team. **1955** L. A. G. STRONG *Dr. Quicksilver* 25 The creator of Zeal-of-the-Land Busy was on his home ground in the last two lines. **1962** *Listener* 4 Jan. 41/1 Three generations on my home ground were equally disgruntled. **1969** *Ibid.* 3 Apr. 473/3 The factual conclusion is that if Arsenal had fouled more in these two home games (amongst others), they might have won them. **1972** *Oxford Mail* 15 Feb. 12/6 Carlisle dropped an unexpected home point last weekend.

d. ***home signal***: on railways, a stop signal marking the end of a block section, and controlling entry either to station limits or the block section ahead. (Cf. DISTANT *a.* 3 d.)

1874, 1889 Home signal [see DISTANT *a.* 3 d]. **1923** W. G. CHAPMAN *10.30 Limited* x. 79 The home signal is the second signal reached and is usually near a signal box. It is a stop signal and must not be passed at 'Danger'. **1940** A. E. TATTERSALL *Railway Signalling* i. 16 Home and starting signals only for each direction at stations on single lines which are staff or electric token posts will be necessary. **1963** KICHENSIDE & WILLIAMS *Brit. Railway Signalling* ii. 16 Stop signals are . . divided into two types: 'home' signals, usually placed on the approach side of a signal box, and 'starting' signals, placed beyond or in advance of a signal box. . . Before a signalman can accept a train from the previous signal box, the line must usually be clear for ¼-mile beyond his home signal. **1968** L. T. C. ROLT *Railway Engin.* vi. 93 By exhibiting three, or in some cases four, 'aspects' they [*sc.* colour light signals] combine the function of home and distant signals.

e. ***Home Service***, one of the programme services broadcast by the B.B.C. (see quot. 1966). Also ***Home programme*** and *ellipt.*, ***the Home***. (On 30 Sept. 1967 the name was changed to 'Radio 4'.)

1939 *Radio Times* 8 Sept. 3/1 In addition to the Home Service . . two other British programmes are going out every day. One is a short-wave service to the whole world, . . the other a short-wave service meant primarily for Europe. **1947** 'G. ORWELL' *Let.* 25 Jan. (1968) IV. 276 It was done on the Eastern and African services, but in those days I wasn't well-connected enough to crash the Home. **1948** [see BREAK *v.* 51 g]. **1960** *B.B.C. Handbk.* 238, 1939 . . Home Service replaced National and Regional Services. **1965** G. MELLY *Owning-Up* vi. 64 Loudspeakers in every bedroom with a control swith marked 'Light. Home. Room Service'. **1966** *B.B.C. Handbk.* 44 The Home Service serves the broad middle section of the community. . . It is the main vehicle for news and for the daily reporting of Parliamentary proceedings.

3. a. Relating to, fostered, produced, or carried on in, or proceeding from, one's own country or nation; domestic: opp. to *foreign*.

[**1577–87** HOLINSHED *Chron.* I. 4/1 Diuers other, both forraine and home-writers.] **1591** SHAKS. *Two Gent.* II. iv. 119 Ile leaue you to confer of home affaires. **1634** SIR T. HERBERT *Trav.* 150 They are not very inquisitive about foreigne affaires, they are content with home occurrents. **1765** J. WEDGWOOD *Let.* 2 Mar. (1965) 29 Our home consumption is very trifleing in comparison to what are sent abroad. **1765** in *Amer. Hist. Rev.* (1921) XXVI. 743 The planters . . reside Mostely on the Borders of James and York rivers which is the best soil for tobaco Especially the Sweet sented which is so much Esteemed in England, where they keep it for their own use, or what they Call home Consumption. **1825** J. S. MILL in *Westm. Rev.* III. 418 A protecting duty, in that case, would be a premium on home production, and, therefore, injurious. **1842** *Niles' Reg.* 12 Feb. 384/2 A state convention is to be held . . at Hartford, Connecticut, to adopt measures for laying before congress the claims of home industry. **1842** BISCHOFF *Woollen Manuf.* (1862) II. 171, I consider the home trade the safest . . but I think the foreign trade . . the most extensive. **1844** MILL *Ess. Pol. Econ.* i. 14 It would be for the interest . . of Germany herself, to keep her linen a little below the value at which it could be produced in England, in order to keep herself from being supplanted by the home producer. **1848** —— *Pol. Econ.* II. III. xviii. 122 The value . . of a foreign commodity, depends on the quantity of home produce which must be given to the foreign country in exchange for it. *Ibid.* v. iv. 400 It would seem that . . taxes on exports . . fall entirely on foreigners, taxes on imports wholly on the home consumer. **1866** A. L. PERRY *Elem. Pol. Econ.* (1873) 518 A duty . . laid on foreign hats to encourage the home manufacture. **1876** C. M. YONGE *Womankind* xiii. 97 Factories or small home industries, such as glove or lace making. **1885** *Manch. Exam.* 29 June 5/1 We have reached a crisis in our home politics. **1886** *Globe* 25 Mar. 2/4 The home producer complained of foreign goods being carried at a cheaper rate than his home produce. **1926** A. HUXLEY *Jesting Pilate* I. 87 We shipped the best part of a thousand lacquered kettle-drums—for home consumption, I suppose. **1937** E. SNOW *Red Star over China* vii. 253 The bulk of manufacturing . . was by handicraft and home industry. **1940** *Time* 1 Jan. 29/3 Entente Cordiale . . was probably intended as French propaganda for home consumption on the present Anglo-French alliance.

b. Treating of domestic affairs; dealing with matters concerning one's own country, as contrasted with foreign countries, or to the mother-country as distinguished from the colonies. ***Home Office***: in Great Britain, the department of the 'Secretary of State for Home Affairs' (abbrev. ***Home Secretary***); the building in which its business is carried on.

1797 *Jacob's Law Dict.* s.v. *Secretary*, Secretaries of State: for the Home Department; for Foreign Affairs; the Colonies, etc. **1818** SCOTT *Rob Roy* vii, The Secretary of State for the Home Department. **1828** *Home Missionary Mag.* May 1 The design of the American Home Missionary Society [founded 1819] is to promote . . the religious benefit of a great and growing nation. **1836** *Ibid.* Sept. 37/1 Endeavour to engage Ministers . . to promote the great cause of Home Missions. **1836** [*title*] Home and Colonial School Association. **1842** *Ainsworth's Mag.* I. 232, I had occasion to accompany a home missionary into a few of the dens of London. **1844** *Ibid.* VI. 113 The manœuvres by which certain county members manage to obtain audiences of the home secretary, or the colonial secretary. **1855** MRS. GASKELL *Let.* 27 July (1966) 363 Papa . . finished up his Home Mission with an address to the Students in the Chapel. **1844** H. H. WILSON *Brit. India* II. 514 The Home authorities earnestly recommended to the Indian Governments the immediate [etc.]. **1863** S. LOW *Charit. Lond.* 255 The societies . . may . . be classed either under Home Missionary or Foreign Missionary. **1865** DICKENS *Mut. Fr.* I. iii, A recommendation to the Home Office to offer a reward for the solution of the mystery. **1881** E. W. HAMILTON *Diary* 25 Dec. (1972) I. 204 An office established to register the decrees of the Home Secretary and other Ministers. **1886** H. C. E. CHILDERS *Let.* 11 Nov. in S. Childers *Life* (1901) II. 245 The prerogative of mercy inherent in the Crown is dispensed . . by the Home Secretary. **1938** M. C. BOATRIGHT in B. A. Botkin *Treas. S. Folklore* (1949) I. iv. 96 A Presbyterian home missionary came to a cabin and engaged a woman in conversation. **1958** S. HYLAND *Who goes Hang?* viii. 44 Home Secretary. A question to the Home Sec. **1966** *Listener* 17 Mar. 373/1 The Ministry of Defence is classified as a 'home' rather than an 'overseas' department.

4. In games: Of, pertaining to, or situated at or near 'home': see A 9; reaching or enabling a player to reach 'home'. Also *transf.* (Also hyphened.)

1856 *Spirit of Times* 4 Oct. 86/1 He was headed off and put out on the home base. *Ibid.*, An injudicious attempt . . to get a home run. **1857** *Chambers' Inform.* II. 689/2 Keep on your ground, and smother these balls by the home-block, rather than risk your wicket by stepping in to hit them. **1867** H. CHADWICK *Base Ball Player's Bk. Reference* 138 Standing at the home base. **1886** MRS. BURNETT *Ld. Fauntleroy* vi. (1888) 122 But Mr. Hobbs took me several times to see base-ball . . Here is the first base and that's the second, and that's the third, and that's the home-base. *Ibid.*, Once round the field is a home run and counts one. **1895** *Pall Mall G.* 15 Oct. 9/1 (Golf) In the new order of things this first hole has become the last or home hole. **1920** S. LEWIS *Main St.* 300 He invariably decided that coming confinement-cases or land-deals would prevent his 'getting away from home-base for very long this year'. **1926** *Daily Colonist* (Victoria, B.C.) 22 July 12/3 Thirteen hurlers appeared. There were ten home runs, seven two-baggers and four triples. **1962** *Listener* 22 Feb. 337/2 In a big hit, what the Americans call a 'home run', the wood of which the bat is made is called upon to sustain stress several times bigger than would be required to break it in two, if maintained for a longer time. **1966** *Ibid.* 3 Nov. 644/1 The correspondent who never gets to home base comes to believe he is identifying himself with the ordinary sensible Briton.

5. a. That strikes home; that comes home to one; searching, poignant, pointed; effective, appropriate; to the point, close, direct. Now chiefly in ***home question***, ***home truth***, which are often hyphened: see also HOME-THRUST.

Home was here originally adverbial (*home-speaking* = speaking home, *home-thrust* a thrust home): see HOME *adv.* 4, 5; separation from the vbl. sb. has led to its treatment as an adj., and its extension to other sbs. as in *home truth*.

a **1625** FLETCHER *Faithf. Shepherdess* IV. iv, But why Do I resolve to grieve, and not to die? Happy had been the stroke thou gavest, if home. **1625** BP. MONTAGU *App. Cæsar.* 34 This is plaine and home enough. **1642** JER. TAYLOR *Episc.* (1647) 132 An instance may be given, full, and home to this purpose. **1643** HERLE *Answ. Ferne* 14 The full and home testimony of Forteskue. **1654** H. L'ESTRANGE *Chas. I* (1655) 45 The Earl of Bristow . . returned so home an answer, as the House was amply satisfied with it. **1709** STEELE *Tatler* No. 31 ¶9 The other, with a sly serious one, says home Things enough. **1711** SHAFTESB. *Charac.* (1737) III. 328 If he has indirectly spoken some home-truth. **1783** MAD. D'ARBLAY *Diary* 9 Dec., This was rather a home stroke to be sure. **1785** *Ibid.* 16 Dec., It is, I own, a very home question. **1788** H. WALPOLE *Remin.* in *Lett.* (1857) I. ix. p. cxlii, That negociation not succeeding, the Duchess made a more home push. **1843** LEFEVRE *Life Trav. Phys.* II. I. xiii. 16 People who pique themselves upon telling home truths. **1844** ALB. SMITH *Adv. Mr. Ledbury* xxv. (1886) 78 This was a very home question. **1881** MARY A. LEWIS *2 Pretty Girls* III. 267 What a nice word 'home' is, and everything connected with it . . All except home-truths. **1897** SIR H. GOUGH *Old Mem.* ii. 95 That curious feeling of victory already won seems to be the prevailing sentiment in a good home charge.

b. ***home key***: in *Mus.*, the basic key in which a work is written.

1959 D. COOKE *Lang. Mus.* v. 269 'They finally decide on E minor, which is, after all, the home key.' It is obvious that a modern composer need not be concerned about ending in the 'home key', after the 'progressive tonality of Mahler, Nielsen and others'. **1968** *Listener* 22 Aug. 250/1 The 'home' key of Weill's original score . . is C.

home, *sb.*[2] *rare.* = HOMELYN.

1836 YARRELL *Brit. Fishes* II. 429 *The Homelyn Ray*, . . The Home, Sand Ray, and Spotted Ray.

home (həʊm), *adv.* Forms: see HOME *sb.*[1] [Originally the accusative case of HOME *sb.*, in its primary sense as the case of destination after a verb of motion: cf. L. *īre domum* to go home. But at length treated as a simple adv., and, in senses 4, 5, formerly compared *homer*, *homest*.]

1. a. To one's home, house, or abode; to one's dwelling-place, own district, or country.

c **1000** *Ags. Gosp.* John vii. 53 And hiȝ cyrdon ealle ham. *c* **1070** *O.E. Chron.* (MS. C.) an. 1049 Se cing lyfde eallon Myrceon ham. *c* **1200** *Trin. Coll. Hom.* 53 King chirus . . let hem . . faren hom in to ierusalem. *c* **1330** R. BRUNNE *Chron.* (1810) 69 Now gos he home. *c* **1450** *Cov. Myst.* 30, I krepe hem to my stynkyng stalle. *c* **1450** *How Gd. Wif taught hir Dought.* 165 in Hazl. *E.P.P.* I. 191 Borowed thinge wole home, my leue childe. **1578** *Nottingham Rec.* IV. 181 Or fetche anne wayre whome vpon the Sabothe Daye. **1651** CLEVELAND *Poems* 35 God would have chang'd his doom, Not forc'd him wander, but confin'd him home. **1719** DE FOE *Crusoe* I. xiii, I lugged the money home. **1802** MAR. EDGEWORTH *Moral T.* (1816) I. vi. 37 In their way home. **1831** SIR J. SINCLAIR *Corr.* II. 208 The value of the ship and cargo, going out and coming home. **1849** KINGSLEY *Poems*, *Sands of Dee*, O Mary, go and call the cattle home. **1885** W. C. SMITH *Kildrostan* 50 I'll see Miss Ina home.

fig. **1581** W. CHARKE in *Confer.* IV. (1584) A a ij, Howsoeuer you labour to auoyde the direct course of disputation . . I must call you home by and by. **1629** H. BURTON *Babel no Bethel* 31 This comes home to my stating of the question. **1686** W. DE BRITAINE *Hum. Prud.* Ep. Ded., If the World would spend that time in active Phylosophy . . and come home to business. **1872** ELLACOMBE *Ch. Bells Devon.*, *Bells Ch.* iii. 225 This is continued till the end of the peal, when the bells are brought 'home' to their regular places.

b. To the home- or mother-country from a colony or foreign possession.

1613 PURCHAS *Pilgrimage* (1614) 523 *note*, A letter which was brought home by the last Indian Fleet. **1762** in B. Peirce *Hist. Harvard* (1833) 278 The persons who sued for it will make application home for another [Charter]. **1874** GAIRDNER *Lancaster & York* vii. (1875) 133 The Regent Bedford . . wrote home to the government in England. **1954** *Ann. Reg. 1953* 286 Americans were the target of propaganda of the 'Go Home, Yank!' type. **1973** *Guardian* 9 June 13/7 Vauxhall car workers . . were . . shouting, 'Yankees Go home! Bloody Americans!'

c. To the place of final rest, to the 'long home'; to the grave; to 'the place appointed for all living'. ***to go home***: to die (common dialectally).

1528 *Will of J. Buckingham*, My wiffe to bryng me home and to pay my dettes. **1816** SCOTT *Antiq.* xxxii, But ye are sure your mother, the Lady Countess, is gane hame? *c* **1855** HARRIET PARR *Hymn*, '*Hear my prayer, O heavenly Father*' v, Guide and guard me with Thy blessing, Till Thine angels bid me home.

d. With ellipsis of *go*, *drive*, esp. in ***home, James*** (***and don't spare the horses***)*!*

1583 STOCKER *Hist. Civ. Warres Lowe C.* I. 112 a, The fugitiues . . had . . made their reckoning, that they should home to their houses. **1859** G. MEREDITH *R. Feverel* xxi, 'Shall we home?' Adrian inquired. **1927** E. WALLACE *Mixer* viii. 114 'All right, Paul,' returned Mr. Sparkes. . . 'Home, James.' 'James' grinned in the darkness, and the car moved forward. **1934** F. HILLEBRAND (*song title*) Home James, and don't spare the horses. **1964** WODEHOUSE *Frozen Assets* xi.

213 Okay, Watson, drive on. Home, James, and don't spare the horses.

2. a. It sometimes expresses the result of motion (which is not expressed by the verb). = Come home, arrived at home, at home after absence.

1587 HARRISON *England* II. xvii. (1877) I. 293 They [ships] will be there in thirtie or fortie daies, and home againe in Cornewall in other eight weekes. **1726** *Adv. Capt. R. Boyle* 349 The Secretary would have me home with him. **1848** EMILY DICKINSON *Lett.* (1894) I. 72 Only twenty-two weeks more, and then home again you will be to stay. **1870** E. PEACOCK *Ralf Skirl.* I. 273 My son will be home soon. **1885** HOWELLS *S. Lapham* II. i. 20 Like people who have been home from Europe three years.

b. *transf.* Safely or successfully at the end of (usually something arduous). Esp. in phr. ***home and dry***.

Baker also records ***home and dried*** (***on the pig's back***) from Australia.

1930 V. PALMER *Passage* I. x. 86 You've done it this time, Lew! Home and dry on the pig's back! **1938** 'N. SHUTE' *Ruined City* ii. 26 'That's the Finnish business, then,' he said. 'We're practically home on that.' **1951** L. G. D. ACLAND *Early Canterbury Runs* 382 *Home and dry*, out of trouble. **1958** *Times* 21 Apr. 5/4 It was a most exciting finish, for apart from Miss Willcox, who, bar accidents, was 'home and dry', any one of six could easily have come second. **1962** J. BRAINE *Life at Top* iii. 46, I was in. I was home and dry. I'd got the order. **1963** *Guardian* 8 Feb. 1/1 Labour members felt after the ballot that Mr. Wilson was 'home and dry'. **1965** M. WEST *Ambassadors* xi. 253 We're home and dry... Small casualties. A new Government.

3. Technical. **a.** *Naut.* Towards or into the ship. Hence, of an anchor, away from its hold, so as to drag: cf. ANCHOR *sb.* 6 e.

1603 KNOLLES *Hist. Turks* (1621) 724 Her ankars came home, and she driven upon the flats, was cast away. **1711** W. SUTHERLAND *Shipbuild. Assist.* 165 Tumbling home. **1748** *Anson's Voy.* III. v. 334 A sudden gust of wind brought home our anchor. **1813** *Sporting Mag.* XLII. 238 He was sorry to inform him that the anchors came home. **1833** T. RICHARDSON *Merc. Mar. Archit.* 13 Giving only six inches tumble home of the topside. **1874** THEARLE *Naval Archit.* 40 There is a considerable 'fall home' to the ship's side.

b. In games, sport, etc.: To the 'home' or goal; arrived at the 'home': see HOME *sb.* 9. Also in sense shown in 4.

1778 C. JONES *Hoyle's Games Impr.* 185 In order to prevent *B* from getting his Man home. **1812** *Sporting Mag.* XXXIX. 184 The ball did not reach half home. **1855** SMEDLEY *H. Coverdale* xliv, I..beg to enter a horse of mine ..in order to discover whether Broth-of-a-boy can show him the way home. **1897** *Whitaker's Alm.* 634/1 G. Martin, Essex Beagles, was the first man home. **1903** J. A. T. BRAMSTON in Benson & Miles *Bk. Golf* 114 Be content merely to return to the fair course, and to get 'home' with the next shot. **1920** H. S. BROWNING *How to play Cards* 110 When each has dealt once, they [*sc.* the players of cribbage] should stand abreast at seventeen to eighteen, and so on throughout the game. The player who has maintained this average is said to be 'home'. **1934** W. J. LEWIS *Lang. Cricket* 130 *Home*, in various terms and phrases with reference to the batsman's ground, i.e. within the popping crease, as *to get home* in completing a run; [etc.]. **1954** F. C. AVIS *Boxing Reference Dict.* 47 *Get home*, to hit an opponent with the blow intended. **1955** *Times* 30 June 4/1 Nielsen's strength, his power of service, but not least his tactical skill in attacking Rosewall's service at all costs, just and only just got him home, when the whole issue was in doubt until the very last point. **1973** *Country Life* 17 May 1369/3 No man has won or lost until he has played home from the 14th tee.

4. a. Of physical actions: To the point or mark aimed at; to its ultimate position, as far as it will go; so as to reach, touch, or penetrate effectually; into or in close contact; closely, directly.

1548 BRADFORD *Let. to Traves* 12 May in Foxe *A. & M.* (1838) VII. 281 You hit me home, and give me that I look for. **1586** A. DAY *Eng. Secretary* I. 137 God when he striketh, smiteth home. **1603** KNOLLES *Hist. Turks* (1621) 8 Resolutely charging them home, put them to flight. **1627–77** FELTHAM *Resolves* I. xlv. 72 An arrow, aimed right, is not the worse for being drawn home. **1669** STURMY *Mariner's Mag.* 16 Hawl home the Top-sail Sheets. **1677** EARL OF ORRERY *Art of War* 17 Those will charge the homest, who find they are strongest, at the grapple. **1686** GOAD *Celest. Bodies* III. ii. 403 Strike the Nail homer yet. **1692** *Capt. Smith's Seaman's Gram.* II. xxi. 134 Put the Cartredge home with the Rammer. **1769** FALCONER *Dict. Marine* s.v., In the stowage of the hold, &c., a cask, bale, or case is said to be *home*, when it bears against, or lies close to some other object, without leaving any interval between. **1801** NELSON in Nicolas *Disp.* (1846) VII. p. cciv, Time is precious,..strike quick and home. **1863** WHYTE MELVILLE *Gladiators* xii. (1864) 83 She could see that her thrust had pierced home. **1872–6** VOYLE *Mil. Dict.* (ed. 3) s.v., Is the shot well home? **1897** SIR E. WOOD *Achievem. Cavalry* xii. 226 That the squadrons should ride home on the enemy as far as possible.

b. *Naut.* Full in (from the sea), full to the shore.

1793 SMEATON *Edystone L.* 193 Nothing to hinder the Ground Swells..from coming home upon the Edystone Rocks uncontrouled. **1794** LD. HOOD 5 Aug. in Nicolas *Disp. Nelson* (1845) I. 476 *note*, The wind not blowing home to the shore with so much violence. **1894** *Daily News* 6 Sept. 3/1 It is one of those harbours which, as the sailing book says, 'a swell is apt to come home'—especially with a north-easterly wind.

5. *fig.* **a.** To the very heart or root of a matter; into close and effective contact; so as to touch, reach, or affect intimately; closely, directly, effectively, thoroughly, out and out. *to bring a charge home to* (a person): to fix it upon him, convict him of it.

1542 UDALL *Erasm. Apoph.* 218 To be pared home ieste for ieste. *c* **1586** C'TESS PEMBROKE *Ps.* LIV, Lord..pay them home, who thus against me fight. **1588** J. UDALL *Diotrephes* (Arb.) 25 If they happen to speake home now and then. **1611** SHAKS. *Cymb.* III. v. 92 No farther halting: satisfie me home, What is become of her? **1641** M. FRANK *Serm., Christm.* i. (1672) 49 To drive that lesson homer. **1650** T. B. *Worcester's Apoph.* 43 To bring the similitude a little homer. **1682** LUTTRELL *Brief Rel.* (1857) I. 200 He putt the case very home to the court. **1697** F. SMITH in *Lett. Lit. Men* (Camden) 255 Wicked enough..to forge..old writings.. and to charge this home upon the Monks. **1722** DE FOE *Moll Flanders* (1840) 309 The witnesses swear so home against you. *a* **1825** FORBY *Voc. E. Anglia* s.v., The meat is home done. **1858** HAWTHORNE *Fr. & It. Jrnls.* II. 13 One who cannot get closely home to his sorrow. **1869** FREEMAN *Norm. Conq.* (1876) III. xii. 208 The charge is..not brought home to William. **1895** F. HALL *Two Trifles* 10 He professes to bring home to me what amounts to portentous folly.

b. esp. *to come* (*get, go*) *home to*: to touch, affect, or move intimately.

1625 BACON *Ess.* Ded. Dk. Buckhm. (Arb.) 498, I doe now publish my Essayes; which, of all my other workes, haue beene most Currant: For that, as it seemes, they come home, to Mens Businesse, and Bosomes. **1660** BOYLE *New Exp. Phys. Mech.* Pref. 16 He has already provided, that this piece shall..be done into Latine, that so it may come home to divers worthy Persons. **1713** STEELE *Englishm.* No. 48. 313 Applause must never come quite home to them. **1769** *Junius Lett.* xvi. 71 There is no precedent, in all the proceedings.. which comes entirely home to the present case. **1823** *New Monthly Mag.* IX. 106/2 It..comes home to the heart with a refreshing and harmonizing power. **1864** CARLYLE *Fredk. Gt.* XII. xii. IV. 274 That Walpole will probably be lost, goes much home to the Royal bosom. **1871** FREEMAN *Norm. Conq.* (1876) IV. xviii. 211 Whose tale..comes more deeply home to us than anything else in the local history. **1931** *Punch* 4 Nov. 496/1 Yet we have to admit that these songs 'get home' on us: that, singing them, we become as little children. **1958** *Church Times* 29 Aug. 3/4, I know that a lot of this will not get home among those who do not want to resolve discord.

6. To 'oneself'; hence, †to one's normal condition; to consciousness, sense, self-control, self-possession (*obs.*).

1526 *Pilgr. Perf.* (W. de W. 1531) 269 Whiche may not longe..beare such eleuacyons of the soule, but anone calleth it home. **1576** FLEMING *Panopl. Epist.* Ep. Ded. ¶iij b, Having called home my wandering witts. **1614** BP. HALL *Recoll. Treat., Heaven upon Earth* §21. 131 That great King ..now comming home to himselfe..complaines, that [etc.]. **1660** FULLER *Mixt Contempl.* (1841) 244 Manasseh..came home to himself, and destroyed the profane altars he had erected. **1645** QUARLES *Sol. Recant.* vii. 43 Call home thy selfe: Inspect thy selfe anew.

7. Phrases. **a.** *to bring oneself home, to be brought home, come, get home*: to recover oneself (financially), recoup oneself, regain one's position.

1760 C. JOHNSTON *Chrysal* II. I. ii. 9 Her patroness.. having lost every rubber; and, what was still worse, several by-bets which she made to bring herself home. **1782** MISS BURNEY *Cecilia* VIII. viii, He has taken a very good road to bring himself home again. **1806** R. CUMBERLAND *Mem.* (1807) I. 256, I believe he got home pretty well upon the sale of it. **1831** SCOTT *Abbot* Introd., The book-seller..is at once, to use a technical phrase, 'brought home', all his outlay being repaid. **1886** *So English* (N.Y.) 14 They..determined to let this particular race be their getting-home stakes. **1895** MISS BRADDON in *Westm. Gaz.* 6 Nov. 1/3 The publisher.. has to consider whether he can 'come home' upon the publication of a book by a new writer.

b. *to call home*: to publish the banns of marriage of; to 'ask in church'. *dial.*

1891 T. HARDY *Tess* (1892) 267 You was not called home this morning. **1892** E. SLOW *Wiltsh. Gloss.*

†**c.** *to come short home*: to fail to reach home (as the aim or goal of effort); to come to grief; so *to come home by misfortune*, etc. *Obs.*

1548 HALL *Chron., Hen. VI* 175 b, The erle of Warwicke had come to short home to tel these Tidynges, if the duke.. might have had his awne will. **1596** HARINGTON *Metam. Ajax* (1814) 36 An hundred thousand of them came home by weeping-cross. **1600** HOLLAND *Livy* XXXIV. xiii. 861 Many of his enemies were caught up and came short home. *a* **1610** HEALEY *Cebes* (1636) 154 He that either refuseth it or misapplyeth it, comes home by misfortune and ruine. **1655** STANLEY *Hist. Philos.* III. (1701) 87/2 Take heed your Herd come not short home. **1722** DE FOE *Col. Jack* (1840) 230 They very often came short home, for the Germans had the better of them.

d. *to write home about*: to boast of, to 'make a song about'. Usu. in negative contexts.

1914 'I. HAY' *Knight on Wheels* xxix. 291 'Anything doing at present?' 'Nothing to write home about, thanks.' **1925** A. HUXLEY *Those Barren Leaves* II. 96 There is nothing in these virtues *à la* Dickens to 'write home about'. **1930** M. KENNEDY *Fool of Family* xix, I know Bach had twenty sons, but they weren't anything to write home about. **1950** A. BARON *There's no Home* 11 Oh, this is something to write home about, all right. **1958** *Times* 3 Nov. 3/6 But for much of the day there was little to write home about as M.C.C.'s last eight wickets fell for 125 runs. **1959** *Times* 10 Aug. 6/1 Student nurses..dismiss their share of the award as not worth writing home about. **1967** V. CANNING *Python Project* ii. 25 He has a small place in the country... Don't run away with the idea of anything worth writing home about when I say 'place'. It's a crumby little cottage.

8. *Comb.* **a.** In sense 'to one's home, homewards', with nouns of action (esp. vbl. sbs.), agent-nouns, verbs, and participles; as *home-arrival, -bringing, -calling, -farer, -goer, -going* (also as *adj.*), *-march, -return, -sailing, -writing*; *home-bring, -deliver, -revoke* vbs.; *home-borne, -bound, -brought, -come, -faring, -speeding, -taking* adjs. Also HOME-COME, -COMING.

a **1000** in Mone *Gloss.* 357 (Bosw.) Ne hi beoþ hambroht ne ȝeæwnode. **1493** *Sc. Acts Jas. IV* (8 May) §11 (1814) 234 For the honorabill hamebringing of a Quene. **1586** WARNER *Alb. Eng.* IV. xxii. 109 To winne and weare the home-brought Spoyles. **1590** SHAKS. *Com. Err.* I. i. 60 My wife.. Made daily motions for our home returne. **1591** SYLVESTER *Du Bartas* I. iii. 974 Weening to home-revoake him With a love-potion. **1615** CHAPMAN *Odyss.* XVI. 200 T'attend the home-turne of my neerer kind. *a* **1625** FLETCHER *Mad Lover* Prol. 14 Our home-bound voyage. *a* **1670** SPALDING *Troub. Chas. I* (1829) 81 The committee..would come and visit their College in their home-going. **1820** SCOTT *Abbot* xv, The home-driven poniard of Roland Græme. **1838** MISS PARDOE *River & Desert* II. 52 The salutation of the home-speeding mariner. **1849** MRS. OLIPHANT *Marg. Maitland* xxii, The sorting of my things for our homegoing. **1870** W. BINNIE in Spurgeon *Treas. Dav.* Ps. xlv. Introd., The home-bringing of Christ's elect. **1891** MORRIS *News fr. Nowhere* i. 9 As the homefarer caught sight of it. **1908** *Westm. Gaz.* 12 Dec. 6/3 Who holds up to her home-come soldier's lips The babe he hath not seen. **1910** *Daily Chron.* 21 Jan. 6/6 The newsboy..handing them out to the sleepy home-goers. **1918** W. J. LOCKE *Rough Road* xix, The home-come warrior. **1937** J. JOYCE *Let.* 1 Nov. (1966) III. 408 We are sorry to hear you had such a stormy homegoing. **1958** *Time* 8 Dec. 42/2 To home-deliver fully 85% of the Sunday papers. **1967** K. GILES *Death & Mr. Prettyman* viii. 146 With a small van we could home-deliver so they don't have to leave the telly. **1973** D. CRAIG *Bolthole* i. 9 They were beginning to reach thick home-going traffic.

b. In senses 4 and 5: with ppl. adjs., as ***home-charged, -directed, -driven, -hunted, -set, -thrusted***; with nouns of action, as ***home-charge, -push, -speaking***.

1609 R. BARNERD *Faithf. Sheph.* 71 This home-speaking is the sharpe edge of the sword. **1611** BP. HALL *Serm.* xxxiv. Wks. 1837 V. 462 The Canon is fully and home-charged. *a* **1657** LOVELACE *Poems* (1864) 203 Like a glorious general, With one home-charge lets fly at all. *a* **1683** OLDHAM *Poet. Wks.* (1685) 4 That its each home-set thrust their blood may draw. **1748** RICHARDSON *Clarissa* (1811) II. 202 My aunt was displeased at this home-push. **1755** J. N. SCOTT *Ess. transl. Homer* 16 Struck brave Agènor with home-thrusted Spear. **1814** *Sporting Mag.* XLIV. 147 The most ingenious, home-directed..cuts.

c. In senses 'in or at one's home', 'in one's home country', as ***home-living*** ppl. adj. and vbl. sb.

1881 W. D. HAY *300 Years Hence* i. 48 The disabilities under which the home-living population laboured. **1963** F. F. LAIDLER *Gloss. Home Econ. Educ.* 42 *Home living*, life within the home and family.

home (həʊm), *v.* [f. HOME *sb.*[1]]

1. *intr.* To go home. (Cf. elliptical use of HOME *adv.* 1 d.)

1765 [see HOMING *vbl. sb.* 2]. **1862** [see HOMING *ppl. a.*]. **1889** *Pall Mall G.* 24 Aug. 6 One bird [swallow] homed from Paris in ninety minutes. **1893** *Nat. Observer* 14 Oct. 559/1 Your tourist is homing from abroad.

2. To have one's home or dwelling-place, dwell.

1832 J. BREE *St. Herbert's Isle* etc. 160 He homed where man had immortal grown. **1890** R. BRIDGES *Shorter Poems* III. 13 Dost thou..home in our creations?

3. *trans.* To establish in or furnish with a home.

1802 SOUTHEY in C. C. Southey *Life* (1850) I. 195 When I am housed and homed. **1839** BAILEY *Festus* (1854) 174 Homed and heavened within the embrace of God. **1864** *Gd. Words* 792/2 As colonists or as settlers [they] have homed themselves all the world over.

4. a. *intr.* Of a homing pigeon: to fly back to its 'home' or loft after being released at a distant point; to arrive at the loft at the end of such a flight. Hence of any animal: to return to some specific territory or spot after being removed by an external agent or leaving it of its own accord. Freq. const. *to*.

1875 *Live Stock Jrnl.* 23 Apr. 57/3 Pigeons home by sight and instinct. **1895** *Cambr. Nat. Hist.* III. ii. 35 Snails and slugs possess to a considerable extent the faculty of 'homing', or returning to the same hiding-place day after day, after their night excursions in search of food. **1899** *Westm. Gaz.* 12 Apr. 9/1 The first [pigeon] homed at nine o'clock. **1904** *Daily Chron.* 25 July 9/2 Out of this vast army of birds not one homed on the day of release. **1934** E. S. RUSSELL *Behaviour of Animals* iv. 71 Arey and Crozier.. relate of *Chiton tuberculatus*..that it keeps to one limited area and does not wander very far, though it does not appear to 'home' to a particular spot as does the limpet. **1956** W. H. THORPE *Learning & Instinct in Animals* xvi. 412 In one case a dog homed a 'bee-line' distance of 6 kilometres. **1958** *Observer* 26 Jan. 18/2 Migrating birds, and birds that can 'home' over great distances. **1966** R. ARDREY *Territorial Imperative* (1967) iv. 134 No random hunting or zigzag uncertainties marred the voyages. Sunfish truly home, and home to territories. **1971** *Nature* 17 Sept. 218/2 Visual recognition of their external surroundings..was used to resettle birds to 'home' to new loft-sites in place of old ones.

b. *trans.* To train (a carrier-pigeon) to fly home.

1928 *Sunday Dispatch* 29 July 22 Leatham (Downpatrick) has achieved what many thought impossible—viz., homing a bird from San Sebastian (Spain), distance over 800 miles, to the Emerald Isle, 300 miles of which, supposing the bird crossed from the northern coast of France, is over water.

5. *intr.* Of a vessel, aircraft, missile, etc.: to be set, or guided, to its target or destination, by use of a landmark or by means of a radio beam, etc. Also *fig.* Freq. const. *on* or *in on*.

1920 *Wireless World* Mar. 728/2 The pilot can detect instantly from the signals, especially if 'homing' towards a beacon. **1940** *Jrnl. R. Aeronaut. Soc.* XLIV. 569 The tanker must be equipped with D.F. gear, so that the two aircraft may 'home' on each other if visibility is poor. **1947** CROWTHER & WHIDDINGTON *Science at War* 119 Torpedoes and bombs that follow or 'home' on to their targets. **1948** [see *A.D.F.* s.v. A III]. **1948** *Ann. Reg. 1947* 458 The equipment [for automatic take-off and control of an aircraft], which can be fitted to a standard aircraft, homes on a beam sent out by a radio beacon. **1955** C. M. KORNBLUTH *Mindworm* 53 That was near. He crossed the street and it was nearer. He homed on the thought. **1956** *Amer. Speech* XXXI. 228 A good officer could even 'home in on a bottle of whisky' placed on the landing field. **1958** 'P. BRYANT' *Two Hours to Doom* 58 Infra-red missiles which homed on the radiations given off from jet engines. **1962** F. I. ORDWAY et al. *Basic Astronautics* ix. 386 The guided vehicle then homes on the reflected signals as in the active case. **1971** *Daily Tel.* 23 Aug. 1/5 The other helicopter located the dinghy by homing in on the bleeping of the emergency distress [call]. **1971** *New Scientist* 16 Sept. 629/1 Mexico's Professor S. F. Beltran homed in on education as a critical need. **1972** *Daily Tel.* 7 June 2/8 A killer satellite is one which can home in on other objects in earth orbit and destroy them.

'home-along, *adv. dial.* Homewards.

1874 HARDY *Far fr. Madding Crowd* I. iv. 44 So I'll take myself home-along. **1905** E. PHILPOTTS *Secret Woman* II. vi. 154 I'll take Salome home-along presently. **1912** C. MACKENZIE *Carnival* xxxiii. 343 Well, I'm going home-along myself in November month.

home-born, *a.* Born or produced at home; of domestic or native origin; native.

1587 HARRISON *England* II. xx. (1877) I. 329 Homeborne and forren simples. **1598** *Ord. Prayer* in *Liturg. Serv. Q. Eliz.* (Parker Soc.) 687 Foreign..rebels, and homeborn unloyal and discontented runagates. **1611** SPEED *Hist. Gt. Brit.* v. iii. §15 Gildas our ancientest home-borne writer. **1734** WATTS *Reliq. Juv.* (1789) 106 This wicked pride is a home-born and domestic enemy. **1871** EARLE *Philol. Eng. Tongue* §142 Even in the home-born words.

†**b.** *fig.* Homely, uncultured; = next 2. *Obs.*

1589 NASHE *Ded. to Greene's Menaphon* (Arb.) 10 Though their home-born mediocritie be such in this matter.

home boy. Also **home-boy.** [f. HOME *sb.* + BOY *sb.*] **a.** A boy who is fond of staying at home. **b.** *Canad.* A boy who has been brought up in an orphanage or institution. (See HOME *sb.*^{1} A 8.) **c.** *U.S.* (See quot. 1970.)

1886 RUSKIN *Præterita* I. xi. 371 Both despised me, as a home-boy, to begin with. **1913** S. A. FRANCIS *Canadian Home Boy* iii, The Canadian reader will need no explanation of the title 'Home Boy', but to the British reader this term will convey little meaning... It denotes a boy who has been brought up in some charitable 'Home', and from whom little that is good is expected. **1932** N. M. JAMIESON *Cattle in Stall* 192 [A] lonesome little English home boy [was] playing his mouth organ softly in the dusk. **1967** *Amer. Speech* XLII. 238 *Home boy* is a slang expression particularly in vogue among students at Southern Negro colleges... *Home boy* and similar forms, such as *home girl* and *home people*, denote individuals who come from the same hometown as the speaker. **1970** C. MAJOR *Dict. Afro-Amer. Slang* 66 *Homeboy*, person from one's home town.

home-bred, *a.* [HOME *sb.* 15 i.]

1. Bred or reared at home; often synonymous with *home-born*: native, indigenous; domestic.

1587 HARRISON *England* II. vi. (1877) I. 148 Conserues of old fruits, forren and home-bred. **1592** SHAKS. *Ven. & Ad.* 764 A mischief worse than civil home-bred strife. **1609** BIBLE (Douay) *Gen.* xvii. 12 As wel the homebred shal he circumcised, as the bought servant. **1662** STILLINGFL. *Orig. Sacr.* III. ii. §2 The native and home-bred Greeks, such as Aristotle and Epicurus. **1791** NEWTE *Tour Eng. & Scot.* 237 There are no home-bred agues. **1869** FREEMAN *Norm. Conq.* (1876) III. xiii. 308 Foreign invaders or home-bred rebels.

2. Of homely breeding; lacking breadth of culture and experience; unpolished; unsophisticated.

1602 CAREW *Cornwall* (1811) 172 Not only the homebred multitude..but even persons of the better calling. **1691** NORRIS *Pract. Disc.* 340 The young Home-bred Heir that thinks his Father's Mannour a considerable part of the World, is sent abroad to see more of it. **1758** JOHNSON *Idler* No. 49 ¶2 A story..which will strike a home-bred citizen. **1827–48** HARE *Guesses* Ser. II. (1873) 520 Home-bred wits are like home-made wines, sweet, luscious, spiritless, without body, and ill to keep.

home-brew. [f. HOME *sb.* + BREW *sb.*^{1}]

1. Home-brewed ale, beer, or other beverage. Also *fig.*

1853 KANE *Grinnell Exp.* xlvi. (1856) 429 A strong and manly home-brew of the best language in the world. **1874** LOWELL *Agassiz* Poet. Wks. 1890 IV. 110 The cider of the Judge's wit (Ripe-hearted homebrew). **1886** T. HARDY *Mayor Casterbr.* I. 119 You can have some home-brew if you want to, you know.

2. *Canad. Sport.* A player, *spec.* of professional football, who is native to the country, town, etc., which he or his team represents. Also *attrib.*

1957 *Star Weekly* (Toronto) 17 Aug. 9/1 The Leos still are short of homebrews and are plagued by a problem at quarterback they have never succeeded in solving. **1958** *Edmonton* (Alberta) *Jrnl.* 18 June 12/3 To make room for import talent en route from the States, Edmonton Eskimos announced the release of 16-year-old home-brew third sacker Gene Kinesewich today. **1964** *Winnipeg Free Press* 19 June 36/4 The chief economic factor is that American players, whether Canadianized or not, still draw more salary than homebrews. **1970** *Toronto Daily Star* 24 Sept. 18/2 So what has become of Mike Wadsworth..and Walt Balasuk, another homebrew tackle?

home-brewed, *a.* [f. HOME *sb.* 15 i.] Brewed at home or for home consumption. *absol.* Home-brewed ale, etc. Also *fig.*

1754 *Connoisseur* No. 26 ¶4 Every hedge ale-house that promises good home-brewed. **1771** SMOLLETT *Humph. Cl.* 8 June, The sparkling beverage home-brewed from malt of my own making. **1815** SCOTT *Guy M.* xxiv, Home-brewed ale of excellent quality. **1883** J. PARKER *Tyne Ch.* 107 What he called 'real old English home-brewed'.

fig. **1808** 'C. HOGG' [E. S. BARRETT] *Miss-led General* 182 One Whitepot, a very good sort of a home-brewed general. **1894** *Law Times* XCVII. 387/2 Sir Richard Malins.. dispensed a home-brewed equity of his own.

home center. *U.S.* [f. HOME *sb.*^{1} 2 + CENTRE 6 a.] A shop which sells building, hardware, and decorating materials for the home. Also *attrib.*

1966 *Building Materials Merchandiser* Dec. 59/2 Small towns everywhere can provide a good base for a modern, one-stop Home Center where hardware, paints and related items are sold together with lumber and building materials. **1971** *Hardware Retailer* June 41 Today's Home Center is a hardware store. **1972** *Hardware Retailing* May 298/2 That these products are hot sellers is borne out by the experience of thousands of home centers. **1972** *Home Center* June 14 Handyman, the Home Center chain with 26 stores in California, the northwest and Scottsdale, Ariz., will move into Texas this year. *Ibid.* 53 Today's Home Center *is* much more than a lumberyard, but building materials and hardware are the heart of every Home Center operation.

†**home-come.** *Obs.* = HOME-COMING *sb.*

c **1000** ÆLFRIC *Hom.* I. 80 Æfter ðæs wælhreowan ham-cyme. *c* **1230** *Hali Meid.* 31 [þu] hauest aȝain his ham cume sar care & eie. *c* **1375** *Sc. Leg. Saints, Johannes* 64 þe quhilk ..[scho] ȝarnyt his hame-com in þe land. *c* **1440** *Bone Flor.* 1744 Tythandes..of my lordys home come. **1513** DOUGLAS *Æneis* XI. i. 122 This is our hamecom thou desyrit lang.

'home-,comer. [HOME *adv.* 8 a.] One who comes home. Also in more recent use with special reference to the Isle of Man.

1540 PALSGRAVE tr. *Acolastus* sig. C 1, The father reioyseth the sonne to be a safe home commer vnto hym. **1637** RUTHERFORD *Let. to Mistress Stuart* Lett. (1671) 353 My blessing..be on the home-comer. **1927** *Peel City Guardian* 27 May, The Homecomers will arrive at Montreal during the afternoon of June 2nd. **1930** *Ibid.* 21 June 6/1 The White Star liner, 'Doric', will anchor in Douglas Bay..with 279 'homecomers' on board. **1947** *Chicago Tribune* 1 Nov. 19/5 Illinois' embattled players..adjourned to the Champaign Country club..to escape a horde of homecomers who are flooding this university community.

'home-coming, *sb.* [f. HOME *adv.* 8 a.] A coming home, arrival at home. Also *attrib.*, and with special reference to the Isle of Man.

c **1374** CHAUCER *Troylus* v. 503 þat may fynde at myn homcomyng, Crisseide comyn! **1586** A. DAY *Eng. Secretary* II. (1625) 72 Let them rest untill my home comming. **1772** MACKENZIE *Man of World* II. ix. (1823) 475 The maid sat up to wait their home coming. **1820** SCOTT *Abbot* iii, First to welcome my home-coming. **1894** *Daily News* 12 Nov. 5/7 The homecoming of the Marquis of Hamilton and his bride to the ancestral home of the Abercorn family. **1903** *Westm. Gaz.* 11 Sept. 4/2 The only greens..that there is any reasonable chance of getting on to at St. Andrews are the greens of the home-coming holes. **1926** *Peel City Guardian* 26 June 2/2 The Mayor of Douglas intends to do what he can ..to promote a big home-coming of Manx people and their descendants for June of next year. **1927** *Ibid.* 7 May, A meeting of the Executive Committee in connection with the Manx Homecoming movement. **1935** *Chronicle-News* (Trinidad, Colo.) 16 Oct., A 'Homecoming Dance' at the Trinidad high school will be held Saturday evening following the Trinidad-Salida football game. **1947** R. ALLEN *Home made Banners* iii. 17 In the crowded beer parlors they tended to herd together, like old grads on the eve of a homecoming game.

'home-coming, *a.* [f. HOME *adv.* 5, 8 b.]

a. That comes home to one; effective; impressive.

1867 A. THOMSON *Sk. Script. Char.* 33 The most valuable and homecoming of all evidences.

b. That comes, or is coming, home.

1898 *Month* Nov. 487 The lowing of the home-coming cattle.

'home-croft. = CROFT *sb.*^{1} 2. In accordance with a housing scheme for industrial workers, a detached cottage, with land and outbuildings for poultry and other small livestock. Also *attrib.* Hence **'homecrofter, 'home-crofting** *vbl. sb.*

1859 GEO. ELIOT *A. Bede* I. vi, The calves are bleating from the home-croft. **1925** *Public Opinion* 7 Aug. 121/1 The industrial workers to spread out and become home-crofters as well as workers. **1925** *Spectator* 5 Dec. 1018/1 Dr. Hilda Clark, whose work in Vienna was of such immense importance, has also sent us a terse but comprehensive account of the work and its objects. We note the interesting fact that she now calls these Land Settlements 'Homecroft Holdings'. *Ibid.*, We do not think that the word 'homecrofting' had been heard of in Vienna three years ago. **1926** *Ibid.* 24 July 130/1 The land and buildings shall be used in perpetuity as 'home-crofts'. **1927** *Daily Express* 21 Nov. 3/1 Earl Beauchamp opened the first six cottages of a 'home-crofting' experiment.

home-de'fence. [HOME *sb.*^{1} 15 d.] The defence of one's native or home country; an armed force designed for this. Also *attrib.*

1642 CHAS. I *Answ. Declar. both Houses* 1 July 51 For home-defence of the Kingdome. **1671** J. OGILBY *America* II. 29 Lest if Carthage should be invaded by a foraign Enemy, it should want People for a Home-defence. **1885** *Marine Engineer* 1 July 89/2 With such a fleet..we could dispense with the Channel Squadrons, for home defence. **1904** *Rep. R. Comm. Militia & Volunteers* in *Parl. Papers* XXX. 16 A home-defence army. **1917** 'CONTACT' *Airman's Outings* 189 Mention must also be made of the Home Defence groups, but for which wholesale Zeppelin raids on the country would be of common occurrence. **1922** *Encycl. Brit.* XXXI. 83/2 On the War Office taking over the responsibility for anti-aircraft defence from the Admiralty in Feb. 1916, a definite Home Defence organization was adopted. *Ibid.*, In June the Home Defence wing was formed to include all Home Defence units. **1934** S. BALDWIN in *Hansard Commons* 19 July 1275 Of these 41 squadrons, 33 will be allotted to Home Defence, raising the existing 42 squadrons at home to a total of 75 squadrons. **1939** *War Illustr.* 4 Nov. 237/1 Further openings for the older men will be given in two new directions..Home Defence Battalions..and an Auxiliary Pioneer Corps which will take over military pioneer work, both overseas and here. **1964** E. H. POWELL in I. L. Horowitz *New Sociol.* 342 The home-defense brigades partially filled this need.

home eco'nomics. orig. *U.S.* [HOME *sb.*^{1} B. 1.] The art or science of domestic economy. Hence **home e'conomist.**

1899 (*title*) Lake Placid conference on home economics proceedings. **1926** *Chicago Drovers' Jrnl.* 5 May 3/3 Here all of the home economics work..will be housed. **1943** M. LYON *And so to Bedlam* 262 The young woman..was a graduate home economist. **1960** A. E. BENDER *Dict. Nutrition* p. v, Medical practitioners,..home economists,.. all, from time to time, step into the food field. **1963** *Weekly News* (Auckland) 27 Mar. 11/1 Miss Elsa Haglund, of Sweden, home economics officer of the [United Nations] Food and Agriculture Organisation, with headquarters in Rome. *Ibid.* 11/2 It is the job of the home economist to study ..the..living patterns in any district. **1969** *Daily Nation* (Nairobi) 7 Nov. 32/1 A thorough knowledge of hygiene, nutrition and home economics is essential and applicants must be in possession of a valid driving licence. **1970** *Globe & Mail* (Toronto) 25 Sept. B 6/4 (Advt.), Applicants should have a diploma or a degree in Home Economics or Food Science and experience in the formulaton of foods. **1973** *Jrnl. Genetic Psychol.* CXXII. 309 A home economics class composed of 28 eighth-grade girls.

home-felt, *a.* [f. HOME *adv.* 5.] Felt 'at home', intimately, or in one's heart.

1634 MILTON *Comus* 262 A sacred and home-felt delight. **1718** POPE *Chorus Youths & Virg.* 34 What home-felt raptures move. **1822** W. IRVING *Braceb. Hall* (1845) 275 Whatever is most homefelt and delightful in rustic life. **1860** I. TAYLOR *Spir. Heb. Poetry* (1873) 139 Worship..homefelt —national—near to the heart of..the worshippers.

home-fire. Used, like *hearth*, as symbolic of the home and family life, and especially popular during the war of 1914–18 in phr. ***to keep the home-fires burning***: to keep the home going, to 'carry on' at home.

1892 I. ZANGWILL *Childr. Ghetto* I. I. xiii. 288 Happy fathers of happy children, men who warmed their hands at the home-fire of life. **1914** IVOR NOVELLO *Song*, Keep the home-fires burning, While your hearts are yearning. **1928** D. L. SAYERS *Unpleasantness at Bellona Club* iii. 29 Health gone—no money—heroic wife keeping the home fires burning. **1931** P. WILLIAMS *Word of To-Morrow* IV. i, When they were holding the line in France, and he and all the other old gollywogs were keeping the home fires burning, snug and comfortable. **1972** *Listener* 6 July 13/2 Famine, rapine, rape... All keep the home fires burning, spread good cheer.

'home-folk, -folks. *colloq.* (chiefly *U.S.*). [HOME *sb.*^{1} 15 i.] The people from or near one's home, *i.e.* one's friends, relatives, or neighbours.

1884 'C. E. CRADDOCK' *In Tenn. Mts.* 288 All the home-folks, an' everybody that kems hyar to sot an' talk. **1900** J. W. RILEY (*title*) Home-folks. **1907** *Westm. Gaz.* 21 Sept. 6/2 They wander from the home-folks' ken. **1909** *Ibid.* 2 Dec. 2/3 Of home-folk caught by crumbling walls. **1915** H. L. WILSON *Ruggles of Red Gap* (1917) v. 99 Then we tried his home-folks in Boston. **1955** E. POUND *Classic Anthol.* I. 19 when I come in from being out My home-folk don't want me about. **1964** MRS. L. B. JOHNSON *White House Diary* 7 Jan. (1970) 33, I greeted L. F. McCollum of Continental Oil of Houston as homefolks.

home front: see FRONT *sb.* 5 f.

'home-guard, Home Guard. [HOME *sb.*^{1} 15 a.] **a.** A member of a local volunteer force. *U.S.* **b.** *Hist.* In England, the Territorial Forces.

1861 *Richmond* (Va.) *Examiner* 6 Sept. 2/4 The Secessionists..attacked the..Home Guards. **1862** O. W. NORTON *Army Lett.* (1903) 123 Nothing would make me ready to fight sooner than to hear some home guard abuse McClellan. **1873** 'MARK TWAIN' & WARNER *Gilded Age* xviii. 170 He was captain of the home-guards in Hawkeye. **1891** *Century Mag.* Jan. 409 An unexpected musketry fire was opened from the Indiana side by a party of home-guards. **1896** *Congress. Rec.* 25 Apr., App. 298 Before Gen. Burnside came, the mountain men of East Tennessee organized themselves into companies called 'Home Guards'. **1909** *Westm. Gaz.* 7 Jan. 7/3 A movement has been set on foot which has for its object the presentation of colours to the 'Home Guard', as we call the Territorials. **1919** F. HURST *Humoresque* 245, I know half a dozen who have got in the home guard..and have saved themselves by volunteering from being sent to France. **1969** E. W. MORSE *Fur Trade Canoe Routes* I. ii. 15 With the Hudson's Bay Company it was the 'Home Guard' Indians, the Swampy Crees, who served as middlemen.

c. One who lives or works continuously in the same place; *spec.* (*a*) a resident logger; (*b*) a non-migrant beggar, hobo, or thief. Also *collect. N. Amer. colloq.*

1919 *Camp Worker* (Vancouver) 19 Sept. 8/3 Camp poorly organized; too many home guards. **1923** N. ANDERSON *Hobo* i. 7 The vagabond who has settled and retired, the 'home guard' as they are rather contemptuously referred to by the tribe of younger and more adventurous men who still choose to take the road. *Ibid.* vii. 96 The home guard, like the hobo, is a casual laborer, but he works, often only by the day, now at one and again at another of the multitude of unskilled jobs in the city. **1926** J. BLACK *You can't Win* xvi. 219 The gangs [of thieves] are made up of natives and 'home guards'. **1931** 'D. STIFF' *Milk & Honey Route* iii. 37 At the other extreme from the ramblers we find a large variety of home guards who keep pretty much to one locality. **1942** R. E. SWANSON *Rhymes of Western Logger* 35 You talk of your drums! you home-guard bums should have seen the size of her 'main'! **1955** *Publ. Amer. Dial. Soc.* XXIV. 98 They will say about home guards, they'll say, 'Pay no attention to him..he's just a local character.'

d. In form ***Home Guard***. The military force organized in 1940 for the defence of Great Britain and Northern Ireland against possible invasion, orig. called Local Defence Volunteers. Also a member of this force. (Disbanded 31 July 1957.) Similarly in other countries.

1940 W. S. CHURCHILL *Into Battle* (1941) 251 Behind the regular Army we have more than a million of the Local Defence Volunteers, or, as they are much better called, the 'Home Guard'. **1942** *Ann. Reg. 1941* 45 On May 14 the Home Guard celebrated its first anniversary. **1943** *N. & Q.* 10 Apr. 220/1 A company of a Home Guard battalion. **1945** *Daily Mirror* 15 Aug. 3/1 When an eighteen-year-old Home Guard decided to impersonate his brother and take his place in the Army he ran into trouble right away. **1970** *Daily Tel.* 21 Mar. 4/7 Lebanon is to establish a 'home guard' to police the border areas with Israel, where tension between Palestinian guerrillas and the Lebanese Army has been high. **1970** *New Yorker* 19 Sept. 34/1 At the entrance to the hospital [in Israel], a Home Guard..sucked furiously on his unlit pipe.

home help. [HOME *sb.*[1] 15 b.] A domestic worker; *spec.* a woman made available by local authorities, etc., for help in the home.

1900 *Daily News* 13 June 8/6 The West Central Jewish Girls' Club... Its objects are educational, recreational, and religious. There are 221 members..home-helps, 17. **1939** M. SPRING RICE *Working-class Wives* 14 While women..go into hospital..trained home helps can be provided to look after the father and children. **1958** *Times* 24 Feb. 11/1 One obvious solution to the problem is for local authorities to provide a better service of home helps and home nurses. **1958** P. TOWNSEND in N. Mackenzie *Conviction* 117 There is the nucleus of a home help service. **1973** *Times* 17 Jan. 4/2 Their response epitomizes some of the misconceptions about home helps which Mrs Clark..rebuts.

homeish: see HOMISH.

ˈ**home-keeping,** *a.* [HOME *sb.* 15 h and i.] That keeps or takes care of a home; that keeps or remains at home, home-staying.

1591 SHAKS. *Two Gent.* I. i. 2 Home-keeping-youth, haue euer homely wits. **1826** MISS MITFORD *Village* Ser. II. (1863) 258 An eldest sister..a home-keeping Martha North. **1888** *Daily News* 26 Sept. 6/1 The sun of an Indian summer —no home-keeping Englishman knows what that means.

So ˈ**home-keeping** *sb.*; ˈ**home-keeper,** the keeper or guardian of a home.

1598 FLORIO, *Mansionaro*, a homekeeper, a housling. **1846** GROTE *Greece* I. i. (1862) I. 47 We find ascribed to her ..attributes of industry and home-keeping. **1898** *Pop. Sci. Monthly* LII. 534 Oikology, from its Greek derivation, includes also family life or homekeeping. **1898** *Chicago Advance* 20 Jan. 75/1 A living homekeeper's thoughtful care.

homeland (ˈhəʊmlænd). **a.** The land which is one's home or where one's home is; one's native land. In earliest use *attrib.* = HOME *sb.* 15 d.

1670 BLOME *Treat. Trav. & Traff.* 53 Another sort of Merchants, which may be termed Homeland-Traders.. who drive a trade to Scotland and Ireland. **1833** I. TAYLOR *Fanat.* v. 139 A homeland densely peopled. **1874** GREEN *Short Hist.* i. §1. 4 The gods whom our English fathers worshipped in their English home-land. **1887** *Home Missionary* (N.Y.) Feb. 385 [Nebraska] was the native home-land of the buffalo. **1941** W. S. CHURCHILL in *Second World War* (1950) III. 583 We should therefore face now the problems..of driving Japan back to her homelands and regaining undisputed mastery in the Pacific. **1963** *Ann. Reg. 1962* 314 A series of 'independent' Bantu 'homelands', where each ethnic group would have a vote. **1968** G. JONES *Hist. Vikings* III. i. 145 The political and dynastic history of the Scandinavian homelands. **1970** *Caribbean Studies* July 90 With such chronological spacing for Homeland English ..it is not surprising that..English usage in colonised places also had its period of graduation before being lexicographically chronicled, and..that such chronicles should be..modest imitations of the recognised Homeland product. **1970** *Nature* 24 Oct. 311/2 One of the regions of South Africa now set aside as a 'homeland' for the native population.

b. = HOME *sb.*[1] 6.

c **1892** C. BINGHAM *Song*, The Dear Home-Land. **1899** *Daily News* 26 Oct. 7/1 Looking..at the old Home-land through the eyes of Young Australia. **1905** *Daily Chron.* 22 June 6/6 We are here to-night..a body of Canadian business men, chiefly in order that we may learn to know the people of the homeland. **1907** SCOTT & WALLAS (*title*) The call of the Homeland: a collection of English verse.

home language. [HOME *sb.*[1] B. 1 and 3.] The language spoken in one's home; one's native language; the mother-tongue.

1926 M. WEST *Bilingualism* I. i. 14 The Magh has Magh as his Home language. **1933** L. BLOOMFIELD *Language* iii. 56 Ordinarily one language is the *home language*, while the other serves a wider range. **1934** *Cape Argus* 3 May 9/6 The only thing to do, therefore, is to define the words 'home language' as the language best known and understood by the child. **1957** R. MACNAB *Emergence of Afrikaans* 4/1 Some of the descendants of those great Scottish churchmen now have Afrikaans as their home language, while their cousins have English. **1958** *Sunday Times* (Johannesburg) 21 Sept. 25/2 Applicants must be bilingual and preference will be given to those whose home language is Afrikaans.

ˈ**home-leave.** [HOME *sb.*[1] 6.] Leave, often of fairly lengthy duration, granted to officials and others serving overseas.

1923 KIPLING *Irish Guards in Gt. War* I. p. viii, Their short home-leaves gave them sudden changes to the tense home atmosphere. **1946** *Nature* 7 Sept. 320/2 Home-leave at regular intervals and free, or at least assisted, passages for themselves and their families..should be provided for officers whose homes are not in the Colony in which they serve. **1962** *Times* 6 Aug. 9/6 The parents' frequent home-leaves. **1973** *Guardian* 30 May 15 Lieutenant Mark Phillips ..was hurried off to Germany to join his regiment... Within the fortnight he was back again on weekend leave, prompting Mr. Arthur Lewis to ask a Parliamentary question..about whether officers of the Queen's Dragoon Guards got special privileges for home leave.

homeless (ˈhəʊmlɪs), *a.* [f. HOME *sb.* + -LESS.] **1.** Having no home or permanent abode. Usually of persons; hence *transf.* of their condition, etc. (In quot. 1615 quasi-adv. in comb.)

1615 CHAPMAN *Odyss.* I. 94 His daughter 'tis, who holds this homeless-driuen, Still mourning with her. **1782** V. KNOX *Ess.* cxlv. (R.), Friendless, homeless, unbeloved, unregarded. **1793** COWPER *A Tale* 28 Or was the merchant charged to bring The homeless birds a nest? **1802** WORDSW. *Sonn.*, '*Jones! as from Calais*', A homeless sound of joy was in the sky. **1871** R. ELLIS *Catullus* lxiii. 58 Shall a homeless Attis hie him to the groves uninhabited?

2. Affording no home or dwelling-place.

1797 MRS. RADCLIFFE *Italian* vi, Going forth into a new and homeless world. **1812** J. WILSON *Isle of Palms* II. 455 Thus left by herself on the homeless sea.

Hence ˈ**homelessly** *adv.*, in a homeless condition, without a home. ˈ**homelessness,** homeless condition.

1829 *Blackw. Mag.* XXVI. 286 Who o'er this scene of clay Once wandered homelessly. **1848** DICKENS *Dombey* xlviii, Forgetful of her homelessness. **1862** R. VAUGHAN *Eng. Nonconf.* 41 His life of poverty and homelessness.

homelet (ˈhəʊmlɪt). [f. HOME *sb.* + -LET.] A tiny or diminutive home.

1855 WAUGH *Lanc. Life* (1857) 192 In the hilly parts.. many tiny homelets of past ages still stand.

ˈ**home-life.** [HOME *sb.*[1] 15 b.] Life at home or in domestic surroundings.

1846 QUEEN VICTORIA *Jrnl.* 8 June in E. Longford *Victoria R.I.* (1964) I. xiii. 184 When one is so happy and blessed in one's home life, as I am, Politics..must take only a 2nd. place. **1859** C. FOX *Jrnl.* 5 Jan. (1882) xxv. 344 Settled once more into dear, beautiful home-life. **1867** 'T. LACKLAND' *Homespun* I. 39 The sincerest pleasures of the home-life are woven closely in with those of the garden. **1871** SMILES *Charac.* i. (1876) 29 Its citizens had no true family or home life. **1879** *Rep. Indian Affairs* 32 The absence of the example of the better home-life of our own people. **1898** T. N. PAGE *Red Rock* vii. 64 These men were thoroughly enjoying home life. **1906** J. LONDON *Let.* 8 Apr. (1966) 199 In addition to home-life articles..I could furnish you other descriptive articles suitable for your pages. **1933** *Punch* 31 May 608/2 The kind of thing that might quite easily wreck one's home-life altogether. **1973** E. LEMARCHAND *Let or Hindrance* xii. 148 Most of my women are married, and one doesn't want to disrupt what home life they have.

†ˈ**homelihede.** In 5 homlyhed. [f. HOMELY *a.* + -*hed*(*e*, -HEAD.] Homeliness, familiarity.

c **1440** *Jacob's Well* (E.E.T.S.) 246 Loue þe companye of poore folk, & holde here manerys in homlyhed.

ˈ**homelike,** *a.* [f. HOME *sb.* + LIKE *a.*] Like or resembling home; suggestive of home; homely. Hence ˈ**homelikeness.**

1817 COLERIDGE *Biogr. Lit.* 98 A more home-like acquaintance with the language. **1858** MRS. OLIPHANT *Laird of Norlaw* II. 209 An unexplainable something of familiarity and homelikeness. **1886** MRS. ALEXANDER *By Wom. Wit* I. ii. 61 It is..not too fine for use, and supremely home-like. **1887** EDNA LYALL *Knight-Errant* II. ix. 215 Its air of comfort and homelikeness.

homelily (ˈhəʊmlɪlɪ), *adv.* [f. as next + -LY[2].] In a homely manner.

1489 *Barbour's Bruce* XVII. 4 (MS. E) He resauit thame hamlyly [*MS. C* richt gladly, *ed.* 1616 tenderly]. **1556** J. HEYWOOD *Spider & F.* xxxv. 7 To talke trewly and homlily. **1687** SHADWELL *Juvenal* 53 A People who lived plainly, homelily, and virtuously. **1755** JOHNSON, *Homelily*, rudely, inelegantly.

homeliness (ˈhəʊmlɪnɪs). [f. HOMELY *a.* + -NESS.] The quality or condition of being homely; †familiarity, intimacy (*obs.*); †kindness, kindliness (*obs.*); simplicity, plainness; lack of beauty.

a **1340** HAMPOLE *Psalter* Prol., Fosterand barnes wiþ hamlynes. *c* **1380** WYCLIF *Wks.* (1880) 462 Crist bicliptide ȝonge and pore in tokene of his homelynesse. *c* **1386** CHAUCER *Melib.* ¶720 Ouer greet hoomlynesse engendreth dispreisynge. *c* **1449** PECOCK *Repr.* 244 Forto cleue to a thing ..and ȝit for to haue noon homelynes with the same thing were an vnchereful thing. **1576** FLEMING *Panopl. Epist.* 304 With homelines of style and basenesse of phrase. **1656** BP. HALL *Occas. Medit.* (1851) 55 Homeliness makes less shew, and hath less danger. **1764** HURD *Dial. Uses of For. Trav.* (R.), I have never heard that the loveliness of her form is impaired, or even disgraced, by the homeliness of her habitation. **1837** HOWITT *Rur. Life* II. iii. (1862) 107 Life in the country..presenting a picture of simplicity, homeliness, and quiet. **1849** MACAULAY *Hist. Eng.* vi. II. 69 She well knew that she was not handsome, and jested freely on her own homeliness.

†ˈ**homeling.** *Obs.* [f. HOME *sb.* + -LING.] A home-born inhabitant; a native. **b.** *attrib.* or *adj.* = Indigenous, native.

1577 HARRISON *England* II. ix. (1877) I. 189 So long as our homelings had the dominion of this Ile. **1609** HOLLAND *Amm. Marcell.* XXII. viii. 200 The homeling inhabitants cal it Achileos-dromon. *a* **1649** DRUMM. OF HAWTH. *Poems* Wks. (1711) 37 Which (homelings) from this little world we name.

home-lot. *U.S.* = HOUSE-LOT, HOMESTEAD 3.

1638 *Dedham* (U.S.) *Rec.* (1892) III. 51 Abraham Shawe selleth..one portion of Grownd called an hill or Iland as it lyeth to his home lott. **1714** in Temple and Sheldon *Hist. Northfield, Mass.* (1875) 134 The rear of said home-lots' fence shall have one-half of said fence to be accounted as Public Fence. **1875** TEMPLE & S. *Ibid.* 13 Every engager for the First and Second Settlements received, in addition to a home-lot, a share of these interval lands. **1895** J. WINSOR *Mississ. Basin* 293 Twelve families were soon picking out their home lots along its banks.

homelty-jomelty: see HUMBLETY-.

homely (ˈhəʊmlɪ), *a.* Forms: see HOME. [f. HOME *sb.* + -LY[1]. Not recorded in OE., but the cognate word exists in OFris. *hêmelîk*, OHG. *heim*(*e*)*lîch*, ON. *heimiligr* (Da. *hemmelig*).]

†**1.** Of or belonging to the home or household; domestic, 'family'. *Obs.*

13.. *E.E. Allit. P.* A. 1210 He gef vus to be his homly hyne. *a* **1366** CHAUCER *Rom. Rose* 1373 Many hoomly trees ther were, That peches, coynes, and apples bere. **1388** WYCLIF *Gal.* vi. 10 To alle men; but most to hem that ben homliche of the feith. **1483** *Cath. Angl.* 172/2 To make Hamely, *domesticare*. **1552** LATIMER *Serm. & Rem.* (1845) 40, I heard say, that there were some homely thieves, some pickers in this worshipful house. **1577** HARRISON *England* III. vii. (1878) II. 44 Dogs of the homelie kind, are either shepheards, curs, or mastiffes.

2. Become as one of the household; familiar, intimate; at home *with*. Now *rare* or *arch.*

c **1375** *Sc. Leg. Saints, Ninian* 853 þis mane, þat vas hamely Vith hyme. *c* **1380** WYCLIF *Serm.* Sel. Wks. I. 13 To be more homely wiþ him þan þei weren before. **1460** CAPGRAVE *Chron.* (1858) 201 That he [Mortimer] was ovyr homeli with the qweén. *a* **1533** LD. BERNERS *Gold. Bk. M. Aurel.* (1546) Hij, This goode emperoure was..homely with euery man. **1636** RUTHERFORD *Let. to Earlestown* 6 July, Ye see your father is homely with you.

b. Familiar, that one is 'at home' with. *rare.*

1889 RIDER HAGGARD *Cleopatra* i, When the matter [she had heard] had become homely in her mind, and her fear had fallen from her, she spoke of the prophecy.

3. Characteristic of home as the place where one receives kind treatment; kind, kindly. Now *rare* or *Obs.*

c **1375** BARBOUR *Troy-bk.* I. 331 And with suete wordys hambly Reconfortit thame rytht hertly. *c* **1470** HENRY *Wallace* VIII. 1660 He agayn, with humyll hamly cher, Resauit him. **1867** G. MACDONALD *Poems* 20 Whom gentler, homelier feelings stir.

4. Such as belongs to home or is produced or practised at home (esp. a humble home); unsophisticated, simple; plain, unadorned, not fine; everyday, commonplace; unpolished, rough, rude. (Sometimes approbative, as connoting the absence of artificial embellishment; but often apologetic, depreciative, or even as a euphemism for 'wanting refinement, polish, or grace'.)

a. Of things.

c **1386** CHAUCER *Sompn. T.* 135 Thanne hadde I with yow hoomly suffisaunce I am a man of litel sustenaunce. *c* **1475** *Rauf Coilȝear* 112 Heir is bot hamelie fair. **1490** CAXTON *Eneydos* 1 Some gentylmen..desired me to vse olde and homely termes in my translacyons. **1553** T. WILSON *Rhet.* (1580) 164 Who can tell if suche men are worthe a groate, when their apparell is so homely? **1573** TUSSER *Husb.* lxxiii. (1878) 164 Though home be but homely, yet..home hath no fellow. **1634** SIR T. HERBERT *Trav.* 96 The Buzzar in this Towne is but homely. **1711** ADDISON *Spect.* No. 119 ¶5 The Clown..clothed his Ideas in those plain homely Terms that are the most obvious and natural. **1795** *Gentl. Mag.* 607/2 The unfortunate King of Poland..lives in a very homely manner. **1813** BYRON *Corsair* I. ii, Earth's coarsest bread, the garden's homeliest roots.

b. Of persons.

1399 LANGL. *Rich. Redeles* II. 43 Ȝe myssed ten schore Of homeliche hertis. **1426** AUDELAY *Poems* 13 Hou homle hosbondmen here hertys thai aryse. **1504** ATKYNSON tr. *De Imitatione* I. ii. (1893) 154 A pore homely laborynge man. **1549** LATIMER *5th Serm. bef. Edw. VI* (Arb.) 134 In his persuasiones he is very whomlye. **1605** SHAKS. *Macb.* IV. ii. 68 If you will take a homely mans aduice, Be not found heere. **1704-5** I. MORRIS in *Pa. Hist. Soc. Mem.* IX. 371, I beg excuse for being thus homely and plain. **1863** MRS. CARLYLE *Lett.* III. 155 A dear little homely woman.

5. Of persons, etc.: Of commonplace appearance or features; not beautiful, 'plain', uncomely. (Said also of the features themselves.)

1590 SHAKS. *Com. Err.* II. i. 89 Hath homelie age th'alluring beauty tooke From my poore cheeke? *a* **1619** FOTHERBY *Atheom.* II. xii. §1 (1622) 332 Some parts of Man

be..comely, some homely. **1634** MILTON *Comus* 748 It is for homely features to keep home. **1669** PENN *No Cross* xi. §10 Nothing is Homely in God's Sight but Sin. **1706** PHILLIPS, *Homely*, ugly, disagreeable, course, mean. *a* **1797** H. WALPOLE *Mem. Geo. II* (1847) III. viii. 211 She..was extremely deformed and homely. **1873** OUIDA *Pascarel* II. 161 To bethink themselves of homelier and humbler charms. **1886** MRS. LYNN LINTON *P. Carew* viii, The homely vein running through her own four daughters, of whom not one was really pretty and some were really plain.

6. *Comb.*, as ***homely-featured***, ***-looking*** adjs.; also †**homely-man**, †**homely-woman**, a domestic.

c **1490** *Promp. Parv.* 245/1 (MS. K) Homliman, or woman, *domesticus*, *domestica*. **1784** COWPER *Task* IV. 252 Like homely-featured Night. **1864** A. MCKAY *Hist. Kilmarnock* 99 Our farmers were then more homely-looking individuals than at present.

†**homely**, *adv.* *Obs.* [f. HOME *sb.* + -LY[2]: cf. MHG. *heim(e)lîche*.]

1. Familiarly, intimately.

13.. *Seuyn Sag.* (W.) 3228 Down he broght hir til his hows, Hamely als sho war his spows. *a* **1340** HAMPOLE *Psalter* iv. 1 Hamly he spekis til him. **1387** TREVISA *Higden* (Rolls) I. 371 His briddes..comeþ homeliche to manis honde. *c* **1440** *Promp. Parv.* 245/1 Homly, or yn homly maner, *domestice, familiariter*. *a* **1553** UDALL *Royster D.* I. iv. (Arb.) 27 What..A nourse talke so homely with one of your worship? **1650** TRAPP *Comm. Gen.* xxxi. 34 Presumptuous sinners deal as homely with the dear mercies of Almighty God.

2. Kindly.

1375 BARBOUR *Bruce* XVIII. 546 His frendis thus gat curtasly He couth ressawe, and hamely. **1508** DUNBAR *Tua Mariit Wemen* 230, I..him behaldis hamely, with hertly smyling. **1596** SPENSER *F.Q.* VI. ix. 17 There he was welcom'd of that honest syre, And of his aged beldame homely well.

3. Plainly, simply, unpretentiously; without adornment or polish; without refinement; rudely, roughly.

c **1386** CHAUCER *Prol.* 328 He rood but hoomly in a medlee cote. **1549** LATIMER *2nd Serm. bef. Edw. VI* (Arb.) 66 Homlyes..they maye be well called, for they are homely handeled. **1552** HULOET, Homely, or after a rude fashion, *agreste*. **1563** FOXE *A. & M.* 1077/1 Of these yeomen of the garde..the fourth (whose name was Homes), used him very homely, unkindly, and churlishelie. **1599** H. BUTTES *Dyets drie Dinner* B v, It was very homely and rudely distilled,.. not in a limbeck. **1697** DRYDEN *Æneid* VII. 928 Thus.. homely drest, He strides into the hall.

4. Without reserve or circumlocution; directly 'home'; straight to the point; plainly.

c **1374** CHAUCER *Troylus* II. 1510 (1559) Sche nolde feyne But as his sustir homeli soþ to seyne. **1465** *Paston Lett.* No. 501 II. 183 For yeve me that I wryte thus boldly and homly to you. **1621** ELSING *Debates Ho. Lords* (Camden) 107 Yf he can accuse, lett him doe y[t] homely. **1688** H. CARE *King's Right Indulg.* 28 They..spoke homely of the Clergy, who assisted the Pope's proceedings, crying out upon these shrivled Ribbaulds.

homelyn ('həʊmlɪn). Also **hommelin**, **homlin**, **homerling**. [Origin unascertained: there is no allied name in the cognate langs.

(The suggestion of Jamieson that it is a deriv. of ON. *hamla*, OE. *hamelian* to HAMBLE, mutilate, appears to have no basis other than the similarity of sound.)]

A fish, the Spotted Ray, *Raia maculata*.

1666 MERRETT *Pinax Rerum Nat. Brit.* (1667) 185 *Raia lævis*, a Homelyn..in Cornubia, a Guilt head. **1808** E. DONOVAN *Brit. Fishes* V. ciii, It perfectly agrees with the Homerling Ray. **1810** P. NEILL *List. Fishes* 28 (Jam.) *Raia rubus*, Rough ray: Hommelin. **1836** YARRELL *Brit. Fishes* II. 431 The Homelyn and the Thornback..are the two species most common in the London market.

home-made, *a.* [f. HOME *sb.* 15 b and *adv.* 8 b.]

1. Made at home or for home consumption; of domestic manufacture. Also *absol.*, and *ellipt.* as *sb.*

a **1659** CLEVELAND *Poems, Sanbourn* 35 Loaves of Home-made Bread. **1768** BOSWELL *Corsica* iii. (ed. 2) 193 None but the very peasants wear home-made cloth. **1823** J. F. COOPER *Pioneer* xi. (1869) 47 The thick coat of brown 'home-made'. **1886** LOWELL *Wks.* (1890) VI. 173 An over-weening confidence in itself and its home-made methods. **1898** *Westm. Gaz.* 17 Nov. 7/1 There are two fogs familiar to the Londoner—the 'home-made fog', still, cold, anticyclonic, [etc.]. **1932** BLUNDEN *Face of Eng.* 110 A box or two of popcorn and 'home-mades' in the front window of a cottage. **1934** H. G. WELLS *Exper. Autobiogr.* II. ix. 808 He [*sc.* Stalin]..preferred that it [*sc.* criticism] should be home-made by the party. **1946** A. HUXLEY *Let.* 19 June (1969) 547 Whether there are powers of evil other than our own home-made devils is an open question. **1955** [see FARM-HOUSE b]. **1959** *Brno Studies* I. 24 The most important of such home-made digraphs is obviously *gh*, which replaced the old grapheme *h* in medial and word-final positions.

†**2.** Sent home, home-delivered. *Obs. rare.*

1663 BUTLER *Hud.* I. iii. 852 Seconding With home-made thrust the heavy swing, She laid him flat upon his side.

'**home-maker**. [HOME *sb.*[1] 15 h.] A housewife, esp. one in charge of the domestic arrangements (as opp. to a paid housekeeper); also, one who manages a household. So '**home-making** *sb.* and *a.*

1876 C. M. YONGE *Womankind* xxx. 266 Home-making is ..her paramount earthly duty. **1886** *Pall Mall G.* 26 Oct. 5/2 Teaching girls how to become good housekeepers and home-makers. **1890** W. BOOTH *In Darkest Eng.* I. viii. 66 The general shiftlessness from the home-making point of view. **1895** J. R. MILLER (*title*) Home-making, or the ideal family life. **1905** *Daily Chron.* 10 May 4/5 There could not be a greater boon to the many distressed home-makers of Canada than the advent of..domestic servants from the British Isles. **1934** *G.K.'s Weekly* 11 Jan. 306/1 The breathless never-can-we-catch-up feeling..is essential to the happiness of the true homemaker. **1954** J. STEINBECK *Sweet Thursday* 88 It was real nice. She was a home-maker. **1963** A. HERON *Towards Quaker View of Sex* ii. 19 Home-making is a satisfying outlet for young women. **1968** *Ideal Home* Nov. 42/1 Homemaking for young marrieds. **1973** *N.Y. Law Jrnl.* 31 Aug. 1/2 These services might include specialized centers which can provide extensive supervision and education during the day, twenty-four-hour home-maker services, and counselling.

home market. [HOME *sb.*[1] B. 3.] The market for goods or produce in the place or country of production.

1758 HUME *Ess.* II. vi. 188 A great number of commodities are raised and perfected for the home-market. **1776** ADAM SMITH *Wealth of Nations* I. I. xi. 243 The bounty..may.. have occasioned..a greater cheapness of corn in the home-market than what would otherwise have taken place there. **1794** T. COXE *View U.S.* 382 To extend the home market for our agricultural products. **1813** *Niles' Reg.* IV. 274/1 Then shall the home market still the rage for foreign export. **1843** *Amer. Pioneer* II. 214 Money became plenty, and a cash home-market was established. **1847** C. LANMAN *Summer in Wilderness* i. 14 This city is the home market for all the natural productions of a wilderness country. **1892** *Rep. Vermont Board Agric.* XII. 132 Furnishing a home market for their products. **1972** D. G. RHYS *Motor Industry* ii. 40 The immediate post-war concentration on export markets had repercussions on the home market.

home movie. [HOME *sb.*[1] B. 1.] A home-made movie; a film made of the activities of one's own circle. Also *attrib.*

1939–40 *Army & Navy Stores Catal.* 910 Home movie camera. **1941** *Time* 16 June 33/1 Once 'expense' might have been a reason for doing without home movies. **1967** *Listener* 27 July 123/2 Some home movies of a retired politician. **1968** M. RICHLER *Cocksure* x. 53 The usual home movie stuff. Mortimer mowing the lawn. **1969** *Listener* 1 May 594/1 Old newsreels, live film (as distinct from reconstructions) of men and events—home movies, for that matter—are primary sources.

'**homeness**. [f. HOME *sb.* + -NESS.] The quality or condition associated with home.

1840 MALCOLM *Trav.* 6/1 The cold emotions of wonder.. now give place to a sense of exhilaration and homeness. **1879** G. MACDONALD *P. Faber* III. viii. 128 Not the less was the air around them the air of homeness.

homeo-: see HOMŒO-.

home perm. [HOME *sb.*[1] B. 1.] A permanent wave in the hair produced by equipment designed for use in the home (as opp. to one prepared professionally in a hairdressing establishment). So **home-perm** *v.*, **home-permed** *ppl. a.*

1949 *Women's Own* 29 Sept. 3/3 (Advt.), Give yourself a Toni Home Perm today! **1954** M. ALLINGHAM *No Love Lost* i. 129, I..bought..one of those cheap home perm outfits. **1955** G. FREEMAN *Liberty Man* III. vi. 173 The rows of industrious home-permed heads over the desks. **1959** [see APPLICATOR]. **1959** *News Chron.* 11 Aug. 6/2 Home perms are now being used on many children. **1969** J. FREDMAN *Fourth Agency* i. 8 Her iron-grey hair had been home-permed.

'**home place**. *U.S.* [HOME *sb.*[1] 15 a.] The place or piece of ground where one's home is situated.

1736 in *N.H. Probate Rec.* II. 625, I give & bequeath..my Dwelling and Devise to my Son..all my land..Known by the name of my home place. **1885** *Weekly New Mexican* 12 Feb. 4/3 They are connecting D.D.'s outlying ranches with the home place. **1931** *Amer. Speech* VII. 93 *Home-place*, the part of a farm on which the house and out-buildings are located. **1946** G. FOREMAN *Last Trek of Indians* 91 They continued in their attachment to the old home place. **1973** *Amer. Folklore Newslet.* Spring 2/2, I enjoy going back to the old home place, now deserted, and the double-log cabin falling into decay.

home plate. *Baseball.* [HOME *sb.*[1] B. 4.] The plate at the apex of the diamond at which the batter stands, and which must be touched by the base runner before a run is scored.

1875 *Chicago Tribune* 3 Aug. 7 He stole third..and reached the home-plate. **1889** 'MARK TWAIN' *Yankee* xxii. 245 No fault of hers that she couldn't fetch the home-plate. **1891** N. CRANE *Baseball* 79 *Ball*, a pitched ball, which does not pass over the home plate [etc.]. **1957** *Encycl. Brit.* III. 160/2 The outfielders are called right fielder, centre fielder and left fielder with relation to a man standing on home plate. **1970** *Globe & Mail* (Toronto) 26 Sept. 51/5 Let's appoint the umpires... Porky, you take homeplate.

homer[1] ('həʊmə(r)). [f. HOME *sb.* and *v.* + -ER[1].]

1. [HOME *v.* 4.] A homing pigeon.

1880 *Times* 24 Nov. 10 The homer bird is sometimes called the Antwerp. **1888** *Pall Mall G.* 1 Aug. 2/2 Country doctors often employ homers to return with prescriptions to their surgeries in special cases. **1892** *Cassell's Sat. Jrnl.* 13 Aug. 1124/1 During Mr. Gladstone's Midlothian campaign ..by means of homers, the reporters despatched messages from mining villages to Edinburgh.

2. [HOME *sb.*[1] B. 4.] In *Baseball*, a home run. So **homer** *v.*, to hit a home run.

1868 *New Eng. Base Ballist* 6 Aug. 3/1 The second inning saw a change as the Champions went out for two runs, one of these a 'homer'. **1951** in WENTWORTH & FLEXNER *Dict. Amer. Slang* (1960) 265/1 Bobby Thomson, who homered.. and Monte Irwin, who also homered. **1961** *Listener* 19 Oct. 594/2 A homer is a mighty hit at baseball: into the stands or out of the ground—the equivalent of a six at cricket. *Ibid.*, Babe Ruth hit his sixty homers in a season of 154 games. **1967** *Boston Herald* 8 May 16/2 Fregosi homered in the fifth and Knoop in the sixth off reliever Bob Humphreys for the only Angel extra-base hits. **1972** *N.Y. Times* 4 June v. 1/8 Johnny Bench had homered in the seventh.

3. [HOME *sb.*[1] 6.] (See quot. 1945.) *Austral.* and *N.Z. slang.*

1945 BAKER *Austral. Lang.* viii. 156 *Homer*, a wound sufficiently serious to cause a man to be sent home. **1949** E. DE MAUNY *Huntsman in Career* 180 'Don't say you've got a "homer" already, mate.' He pointed to Peter's bandaged hand. **1950** G. WILSON *Brave Company* xi. 173, I nearly did get a homer that time.

4. [HOME *v.* 5.] A homing device.

1958 *Chambers's Techn. Dict.* Add. 985/1 *Homer*, any arrangement which provides signals or fields which can be used to guide a vehicle to a specific location, usually determined by a homer transmitter. **1959** *Daily Tel.* 1 June 9/3 Thunderbird is what is known as 'a semi-active homer'. It receives the echoes of the illuminating radar's beam in a set in its own nose and homes on to the target accordingly. **1959** 'J. WYNDHAM' & PARKES *Outward Urge* i. 29 Fix up one of the dispatch homers on it, and let it jet itself along.

‖**homer**[2] ('həʊmə(r)). Also **chomer**. [ad. Heb. *χōmer*, lit. 'heap'.] A Hebrew measure of capacity, the same that in later times was called the COR, containing 10 ephahs, or 10 baths (liquid measure). Its content has been very variously calculated, but was probably about 80 gallons.

(Not to be confounded with the omer *ʿōmer*, = $\frac{1}{10}$th of an ephah.)

1535 COVERDALE *Ezek.* xlv. 14 Ten Battes make one Homer. **1611** BIBLE *Isa.* v. 10 The seed of an Homer shall yeeld an Ephah. **1778** LOWTH *Transl. Isa.* v. 10 A chomer of seed shall produce an ephah. **1876** *Helps Study Bible* 241, 10 ephahs = 1 kor, or homer.

¶ Also erroneously used for OMER, q.v.

homer, contr. of *hoe-mother*: see HOE *sb.*[4]

Homerian (həʊ'mɪərɪən), *a.* [f. L. *Homēri-us*, f. *Homērus* Homer + -AN.] = HOMERIC.

1796 BURNEY *Mem. Metastasio* II. 419 The Homerian imitation of Alcides extricating himself from Cimmeria. **1814** J. GILCHRIST *Reason True Arbiter Lang.* 46 The true Homerian and Virgilian strain.

home-ribbed, *a.* [f. HOME *adv.* 8 b.] Well ribbed up: see quot. 1720.

1688 *Lond. Gaz.* No. 2312/4 A grey Nag..his Ears cropt close, home rib'd. **1720** W. GIBSON *Diet Horses* i. (1731) 16 When the short Ribs advance pretty near the Haunch Bone, a Horse is then said to be home-ribbed [*printed* -rid] and well coupled. **1815** *Sporting Mag.* 114 We do not quite agree ..as to the preference due to the home-ribbed racer.

Homeric (həʊ'mɛrɪk), *a.* [ad. L. *Homēric-us*, a. Gr. Ὁμηρικός, f. Ὅμηρος Homer, the traditional name of the author of the two Greek epic poems, the *Iliad* and the *Odyssey*. In F. *Homérique*.]

Of, pertaining to, or characteristic of Homer, the poems ascribed to him, or the age with which they deal; like, or of the style of, Homer.

the Homeric question: the question of the authorship, date, and construction of the Homeric poems.

a **1771** R. WOOD *Ess. Homer* 215 (Jod.) The whole Homerick history. **1835** THIRLWALL *Greece* I. 159 The Homeric world..is at once poetical and real. **1838** *Penny Cycl.* XII. 277/1 The Hymn to Apollo..The Hymn to Hermes..The Hymn to Aphrodite and that to Demeter.. are the principal of the Homeric hymns..These, with the 'Battle of the Frogs and Mice', make up the sum of the Homeric poems, genuine and spurious. **1858** GLADSTONE (*title*) Studies in Homer and the Homeric age. **1889** *Pall Mall G.* 14 Mar. 7/2 A great Homeric laugh showed that the joke had gone home.

†**Ho'merical**, *a.* *Obs.* [f. as prec. + -AL[1].] = HOMERIC. ***Homerical medicines***: see quot. 1584.

1578 in Nichols *Progr. Q. Eliz.* (1823) II. 172 The Homericall Jupiter. **1584** R. SCOT *Discov. Witchcr.* XII. xiii. (1886) 195 Of these Homericall medicines he saith there are foure sorts, whereof amulets, characters, and charmes are three..the fourth..he saith, consisteth in illusions, which he more properlie calleth stratagems [*Ibid.* xii, Ferrarius.. saith that this is called *Homerica medicatio*, bicause Homer discovered the bloud of the word suppressed, and the infections healed by or in mysteries]. **1779–81** JOHNSON *L.P.*, *Pope* Wks. IV. 126 It has been objected by some..that Pope's version of Homer is not Homerical.

Homerically (həʊ'mɛrɪkəlɪ), *adv.* [f. HOMERIC + -AL[1] + -LY[2].] In a Homeric manner; in the style of Homer or the Homeric poems.

1841 D'ISRAELI *Amen. Lit.* (1867) 522 Chapman often caught the ideas of Homer, and went on writing Homerically. **1892** *Athenæum* 19 Nov. 696/2 The more Homerically the great fundamental passions of man's nature are treated..the more powerful is the effect.

†**Ho'merican**, *a.* *Obs.* [f. as HOMERIC + -AN.] = HOMERIC.

1678 CUDWORTH *Intell. Syst.* I. iv. §16. 290 The Third in the Persian Trinity..as it was in the Homerican. **1749** FIELDING *Tom Jones* Contents, A battle sung by the muse in the Homerican style. **1820** W. TOOKE tr. *Lucian* I. 1. 501 *note*, Parody of an homerican verse.

Homerid ('həʊmərɪd). [ad. Gr. Ὁμηρίδ-ης, usu. in pl. Ὁμηρίδαι, Lat. *Homēridæ*, a guild of poets in Chios who claimed descent from Homer and a

hereditary property in the Homeric poems, which they recited publicly. In F. *Homéride*.]

1. One of the *Homeridæ* (see above); a Homeric rhapsodist.

1846 GROTE *Greece* II. 177 The Homerids were still conspicuous in the days of Akusilaus, Pindar..and Plato.

2. A Homeric scholar.

1866 BLACKIE *Homer & Iliad* I. 141 The greatest modern Homerid, Wolf.

Hence **Homeridian** (həʊmə'rɪdɪən) *a.*, of or pertaining to the Homerids.

1852 BRISTED *Eng. Univ.* 315 The Homeridian Hymns.

Homerist ('həʊmərɪst). [ad. L. *Homērista*, a. Gr. *Ὁμηριστής*.] **a.** An imitator of Homer. **b.** A Homeric rhapsodist. **c.** A Homeric scholar.

1599 *Broughton's Let.* iv. 15 You will be the Homerist of our time. *a* **1711** KEN *Hymnotheo* Poet. Wks. 1721 III. 292 The Homerists sat singing to bare walls. **1886** *Athenæum* 11 Sept. 331/2 The copious literature..poured forth by the new school of Homerists.

So '**Homerize** *v.* [cf. late Gr. *Ὁμηρίζειν*] *intr.*, to practise the style of Homer.

1764 *Acc. Bks.* in *Ann. Reg.* 272/2 Phidias and Apelles may be said..to have homerized.

Homerite ('həʊməraɪt). [a. Gr. *Ὁμηρῖται pl.*] = HIMYARITE.

1613 PURCHAS *Pilgrimage* (1614) 665 This Hellisthæus had warred against the Homerites for quarrell of Religion. **1708** OCKLEY *Saracens* (1848) 136 Homerites, a warlike tribe of the Arabs. **1842** PRICHARD *Nat. Hist. Man* 143 The dialect of the Hhimyarite Arabs, the *Homerites* of the Greeks.

Hence **Home'ritic** *a.*, Himyaritic.

1801 J. HAGER *Babylon, Inscr.* 18 The Homeritic alphabet, the oldest which the Arabians possessed.

†**homerkin.** *Obs.* [Cf. *firkin*, *kilderkin*.] A liquid measure.

1662-3 in H. F. Swayne *Churchw. Acc. St. Thomas, Sarum* (1896) 335 One Homerkin of Beere 12*s*.

Homerology (həʊmə'rɒlədʒɪ). [f. *Homer* (see HOMERIC) + -(O)LOGY.] The study of Homer and of the Homeric poems, their authorship, date, etc.

1876 GLADSTONE *Homeric Synchr.* 8 It is pleasant to see that in Germany, and even in this country..Homerology does not cease to flourish. **1878** —— *Prim. Homer* i. 1 To rescue this circle of studies from inadequate conceptions, and to lay the ground for a true idea of them I have proposed to term them Homerology. **1887** *Athenæum* 17 Sept. 357/1 Orthodox homerology.

Hence **Home'rologist**, one versed in Homerology.

1890 *Athenæum* 29 Nov. 729/1 Among those whom Mr. Gladstone calls Homerologists.

'**homeroom.** *U.S.* [HOME *sb.*¹ 5.] (See quot. 1961.)

1915 *Ann. Rep. Comm. Educ. 1914* (U.S. Office of Educ.) I. iii. 45 The regular or home-room teacher feels a definite responsibility for the class wherever it may be. **1928** *Bull. Nat. Assoc. Secondary-School Principals* XIX. 16 The foundations of all guidance within the school are found in the homeroom organization. Efficiency in secondary school administration is demanding that every teacher shall be a 'homeroom' teacher. **1930** *School Rev.* Apr. 300 The homeroom organization..in Detroit may be defined as a large number of one-room schools..gathered together under one roof with a central office to facilitate their proper functioning. *Ibid.*, The home room is the unit of organization of the school and is the center of the pupil's school activities. **1961** WEBSTER, *Homeroom*. 1. A schoolroom where pupils of the same class or grade but often with different academic programs report at the opening of school and meet informally under the guidance of a teacher to conduct class business, plan and organize group activities, and discuss individual and group problems. 2. A group of pupils assigned to the same homeroom. **1966** BEREITER & ENGELMANN *Teaching Disadvantaged Children* iv. 71 The homeroom should have at least 400 square feet of floor space, and should be equipped with a piano and (like the other rooms) a chalkboard. **1968** 'R. MACDONALD' *Instant Enemy* i. 8, I got in touch with her homeroom teacher and found she'd been playing hookey all day.

Home Rule. [HOME *sb.* B. 3.] Government of a country, colony, province, etc., by its own citizens; the political principle or theory, according to which a country or province manages its own affairs; used *spec.* in British politics with reference to the movement, begun about 1870, to obtain for Ireland self-government through the agency of a national parliament.

The phrase 'Home Rule' had been used incidentally in 1860. But at the meeting for the local autonomy of Ireland held on 19 May, 1870, the phrase 'Home Government' was adopted, though 'Home Rule' is said to have been suggested, and became almost immediately the popular phrase.

1860 A. M. SULLIVAN in *Nation* (Dublin) 28 July, (Heading of National Petition to the Queen) The National Petition taking England at her word. The Vote for Home Rule. [**1870** in O'Connor *Parnell Movem.* (1886) 225 On May 19, 1870..A new organisation was founded..'The Home Government Association of Ireland'..Ireland to be exclusively mistress of Irish affairs.] **1871** BRODRICK in *Macm. Mag.* May 42 Beyond this I am not prepared to go in the direction of what is called 'home-rule' in Ireland. **1871** J. F. MAGUIRE *Sp. Ho. Com.* 26 June in Hansard CCVII. 634 There is at present a wonderful amount of misconception in the minds of Englishmen with respect to what is termed 'Home Rule'. I am myself a Nationalist, and in favour of Home Rule, but at the same time I am a loyal subject of Her Majesty. **1871** *Punch* 29 July 41/2 What used to be called 'Repeal' is now denominated 'Home Rule'. **1871** *Times* 9 Oct. 5/5 Home Rule is still the topic of the day. The country rings with the cry. **1886** *Observer* 28 Feb. 4/4 Home Rule for London, then, rather than police reform, ought to have been the chief question. **1890** *Echo* 6 Dec. 1/4 Prof. Galbraith was present at the first meeting..which was held at Bilton's Hotel, Dublin, on the 19th May, 1870, and was chosen one of the hon. secretaries. He it was who coined the expression Home Rule.

b. *attrib.* (also **home-rule**).

1871 *Times* 9 Oct. 5/6 Home Rule Association. **1880** MCCARTHY *Own Times* lxii. IV. 380 Home Rule agitation. **1886** *Morn. Post* 17 Apr. 5/3 The Home Rule members speak confidently as to the prospect of legislation. **1886** CARNEGIE *Triumph. Democr.* 16 The Republic has solved the problem..by adopting the federal, or home-rule system. **1893** TENNYSON in A. Tennyson *Mem.* (1897) II. 462, I love Gladstone, but I hate his Home-rule policy.

Hence **Home-'Ruler**, one who advocates or practises Home Rule. Also **Home-'Rule** *v. trans.*, to govern by Home Rule. **Home-'Ruling** *ppl. a.*, advocating or practising Home Rule.

1880 MCCARTHY *Own Times* lxii. IV. 382 Several Irish elections..were fought out on the question for or against Home Rule; and the Home Rulers were successful. **1886** *Pall Mall G.* 2 June 2/1 To detach from Home-Ruled Ireland..the counties of Down and Antrim. **1891** SIR C. G. DUFFY *Ibid.* 7 Apr. 2/1 An eminent English Home Ruler last year said to an Irish friend that the greatest impediment to Home Rule was the Home Rulers. **1894** *Westm. Gaz.* 11 June 1/2 'We have changed all that now', the Home Ruling Liberals will say.

home science. [HOME *sb.*¹ B. 1.] The art or science of domestic economy.

Term not used in Britain.

1912 *Calendar Univ. Otago* 79 The Home Science Department (opened in April, 1911) has been housed for the present in part of the old Mining School. **1943** J. H. MURDOCH *High Schools N.Z.* vi. 362 Home science students may substitute arithmetic for mathematics. **1963** F. F. LAIDLER *Gloss. Home Econ. Educ.* 46 The term 'Home Science' as used in New Zealand is, in general, comparable with the terms 'Domestic Science' in the U.K. and 'Home Economics' in the U.S.A. **1969** *Australian* 24 May 31/5 (Advt.), Home Science Teacher required immediately for second term, Woodstock Presbyterian Girls' School. **1969** *Hindu* 3 Aug. 2/2 (Advt.), Good academic record..preferably a B.Sc. degree in Home Science.

†'**homeself**, *a. Obs. rare.* [Cf. HOME *adv.* 6.] Carried on with oneself; private.

1650 W. BROUGH *Sacr. Princ.* (1656) 364 Wholsome Home-self Conferences.

home-sick, homesick ('həʊmsɪk), *a.* [f. HOME *sb.* 15j + SICK *a.*: after next.] Depressed in consequence of a longing for home during absence from it; affected with homesickness.

c **1798** [see HOMESICKNESS]. **1827** KEBLE *Chr. Y.* Prayer at Sea iii, The homesick seaman. *a* **1859** MACAULAY *Hist. Eng.* xxv. V. 287 A servant of the true God..banished, homesick, and living on the bounty of strangers. **1867** TROLLOPE *Chron. Barset* II. lix. 168, I am homesick. I'm not accustomed to be away from mamma for so long.

'**home-sickness, homesickness.** [f. HOME *sb.* + SICKNESS: app. at first a rendering of Ger. (Swiss) *heimweh*.] A depressed state of mind and body caused by a longing for home during absence from it; nostalgia.

1756 tr. *Keysler's Trav.* (1760) I. 174 The *heimweh*, i.e. 'homesickness' with which those of Bern are especially afflicted. **1775-83** THACHER *Mil. Journ.* (1826) 242 Cases of indisposition caused by absence from home, called by Dr. Cullen Nostalgia or home-sickness. *c* **1798** COLERIDGE *Home-Sick* iv, (Written in Germany) Home-sickness is a wasting pang. **1805** W. TAYLOR in *Ann. Rev.* III. 235 A cat is as subject as a mountaineer to the home-sickness. **18..** KINGSLEY in *Life* I. 3 (D.), I have..continually the true 'heimweh' home-sickness of the Swiss and Highlanders. **1871** L. STEPHEN *Playgr. Eur.* i. (1894) 1 Symptomatic of the proverbial homesickness of mountaineers.

'**homesite.** *N. Amer.* [HOME *sb.*¹ 2.] = HOUSELOT.

1911 *Daily Colonist* (Victoria, B.C.) 2 Apr. 12/2 Saanich Waterfront... Magnificent homesites of nearly two acres from $450. **1968** *Globe & Mail* (Toronto) 17 Feb. 46/6 (Advt.), Landscaped, fenced homesite.

homesoken, rare form of HAMESUCKEN.

homespun ('həʊmspʌn), *a.*, *sb.* [HOME *sb.* 15 i.]

A. *adj.* **1.** Spun at home; of home manufacture; made of the material mentioned in B. 1.

1591 FLORIO *2nd Fruites* A iv, One being onely clad in home-spunn cloth. **1616** R. C. *Times' Whistle* II. 718 Thy syre..kept his wife in a course homespun gowne. **1796** MORSE *Amer. Geog.* I. 451 The farmers..are mostly clothed in plain, decent, homespun cloth. **1842** BISCHOFF *Woollen Manuf.* II. 304 In the form of iplik, or homespun thread.

2. *fig.* Of domestic origin or quality; simple, unsophisticated, unvarnished; plain, homely; unpolished, rude.

1600 DEKKER *Fortunatus* Wks. 1873 I. 130 His wooing is plaine home-spun stuffe. **1618** J. TAYLOR (Water P.) *Penniless Pilgr.* Wks. (1883) 62 Yet this plain home-spun fellow keeps..thirty, forty, fifty servants. **1766** FORDYCE *Serm. Yng. Wom.* (1767) I. iv. 123 Sobriety is..void of show; substantial, home-spun, and hardy. **1874** MAHAFFY *Soc. Life Greece* iv. 79 The plainest homespun morality. **1874** L. STEPHEN *Hours in Library* (1892) II. ii. 40 Crabbe was one of those simple, homespun characters.

B. *sb.* **1.** Cloth made of yarn spun at home; hodden; also, a coarse and loosely-woven material made in imitation of home-made cloth.

1607 ROWLANDS *Guy, Earl Warw.* 59 Homely Countery-gray, Such as the poor plain people term home-spun. *a* **1667** WITHER in Southey *Comm.-pl. Bk.* Ser. II. (1849) 306 Clad in home-spun gray. **1796** MORSE *Amer. Geog.* I. 520 Most of the families..are clothed in strong, decent home-spun. **1858** LONGF. *M. Standish* iii. 53 She, the Puritan girl..Making the humble house and the modest apparel of homespun Beautiful with her beauty. **1883** *Cassell's Fam. Mag.* Oct. 697/1 Homespuns are still much worn.

b. Anything of plain, homely, or rude texture.

1845 *Athenæum* 4 Jan. 17 The edifice is of uniform texture, instead of being..of superfine quality in one part, and arrant home-spun in another. **1887** HALL CAINE *Deemster* vii. 44 The young rogue, who spoke the home-spun to the life. **1889** *Pall Mall G.* 21 Dec. 3/1 Nor is the style..comparable in any way with the classic homespun of Cellini.

2. *transf.* One who wears homespun; hence, a rustic, a clown.

1590 SHAKS. *Mids. N.* III. i. 79 What hempen home-spuns haue we swaggering here? **1604** *Fr. Bacon's Proph.* in Hazl. *E.P.P.* IV. 281 Sheepes Russet to home spunne.

3. *Comb.*, as ***homespun-clad, -hooded*** adjs.

1860 O. W. HOLMES *Elsie V.* (1886) 4 Some of our most illustrious public men have come direct from the homespun-clad class. **1897** *Westm. Gaz.* 27 Mar. 5/2 Peasants, dressed in coarse, woollen homespun-hooded garments.

homestall ('həʊmstɔːl). [OE. *hámsteall* homestead, f. *hám* HOME + *steall* position, place.]

†**1.** = HOMESTEAD. *Obs.*

990 in Kemble *Cod. Dipl.* III. 255 Ane hide on Cumtune on his hamstealle. **12..** *Ibid.* IV. 133 Ðet he uðe Christe into Christes cheriche ðane homstal ðet he on set. *c* **1277** *Charter* in Cowell *Interpr.* (1701), De uno itinere..quod..ducit versus Homstale. **1598** KITCHIN *Courts Leet* (1675) 244 If a Cottage or a House is decayed, it is called a Home-stall. **1655** *New Eng. Hist. & Gen. Reg.* (1865) XIX. 42 A Home-stall of 6 acres, with a dwelling house, barne..and orchard vppon it, £35. **1701** *Providence* (R.I.) *Rec.* (1893) IV. 237 John Whipple..shall have the home stall, or to say the Dwelling house. **1767** BLACKSTONE *Comm.* II. 4 A property was soon established in every man's house and home-stall; which seem to have been originally mere temporary huts or moveable cabins.

2. A farm-yard. *dial.*

1661 WOOD *Life* 5 Nov. (O.H.S.) I. 419 This house hath a fair homestall and six yard land belonging to it. **1677** PLOT *Oxfordsh.* 239 Manure..from the Home-stall, or from the Mixen in the field. **1735** SOMERVILLE *Chase* III. 154 Thro' ev'ry Homestall, and thro' ev'ry Yard, His Midnight walks, panting, forlorn, he flies. **1845** ALB. SMITH *Fort. Scatterg. Fam.* xi. (1887) 40 At one of the gates belonging to the homestall at the back of the house.

Hence **homestalled** *a.*, having a homestall.

1815 LAMB *Lett.* (1837) II. 18 Our rosycheeked, homestalled divines.

homestead ('həʊmstɪd), *sb.* [OE. *hámstede*, f. *hám* HOME + *stede* place, STEAD. Cf. OFris. *hêmsted*, ON. *heimstöð*.]

1. *gen.* The place of one's dwelling or home: †**a.** The place (town, village, etc.) in which one's dwelling is. *Obs.* **b.** A home or dwelling.

972 in Kemble *Cod. Dipl.* III. 77 Of hamstede on ropleah ȝeat. **1612-15** BP. HALL *Contempl.*, *N.T.* II. iii, I do not see thee led into..thy homestead of Nazareth, but into the vast wilderness. **1799** W. TOOKE *View Russian Emp.* I. 435 The Orenburg-Kozaks..At present they have their homestead about the Samara. **1853** KANE *Grinnell Exp.* iii. (1856) 25 The cabin, which made the homestead of four human beings. *a* **1859** MACAULAY *Hist. Eng.* xxiii. V. 9 To play the men for their own homesteads.

2. a. A house with its dependent buildings and offices; esp. a farm-stead.

a **1700** DRYDEN (J.), Both house and homestead into seas are borne. **1818** COBBETT *Pol. Reg.* XXXIII. 412 A most beautiful country, studded..with farm-houses, barns and homesteads. **1834** *Brit. Husb.* I. 99 We now present a collective plan of a homestead, or farm-steading, upon a compact and very moderate scale. **1839** STONEHOUSE *Axholme* 285 After the fire..many of the old homesteads were never rebuilt. **1847** LONGF. *Ev.* I. ii. 26 Twilight descending Brought back..the herds to the homestead.

b. Freq. in Australia and N.Z.: the residence of the owner of a sheep or cattle station; in later use also = STATION *sb.* 14 (quot. 1898).

1849 *Handbk. Suburban & Rural Districts Otago Settlement* 7 Sheep or cattle owners, who, establishing their temporary homesteads, or stations, near or in the bush, might run their flocks or herds amongst the hills. **1851** E. SHORTLAND *Southern Districts N.Z.* xiv. 263 Farmers and stock-keepers, however, who have their homesteads on the plain. **1853** C. W. ADAMS *Spring in Canterbury Settlement* vii. 70 This homestead much resembles a small English farm-house, save that the sleeping loft had seldom fewer than ten occupants. **1891** R. PRICE *Through Uriwera Country* 61 As an out-station is to the homestead of a sheep-run, so is this little fort to Te Teko. **1901** M. FRANKLIN *My Brilliant Career* (1966) viii. 39 Home to..the dear old homestead I love so well. **1911** C. E. W. BEAN '*Dreadnought' of Darling* i. 4 Most homesteads are apt to consider themselves pretty well on the outskirts of things if they get only one mail a week. At this particular station they get two mails a year. **1930** L. G. D. ACLAND *Early Canterbury Runs* 1st Ser. i. 8 'Station' is being driven out of use in its original sense of 'a place from which to work a run' by 'homestead'. ..When an old fashioned squatter or station hand used the

word 'homestead' he used it to signify the owner's residence as opposed to the men's quarters and other station buildings. **1933** —— in *Press* (Christchurch) 28 Oct. 15/7 *Homestead.* In the old days, the owner's residence, but only if it was some distance from the rest of the station buildings. .. When the Government began cutting up the runs in the 'nineties, they or their surveyors adopted the word to signify what had been formerly called *the station*, and the new settlers followed them, so that the new sense of the word is now widely used. **1941** I. L. IDRIESS *Great Boomerang* ii. 10 Fifty miles from the homestead, on the New South Wales-South Australian border. **1946** F. DAVISON *Dusty* ix. 97 People came from all over the settlement, camping in and around the old homestead. **1961** B. CRUMP *Hang on a Minute* 73 They arrived at the Paranui homestead in the late afternoon.

3. *U.S.* A lot of land adequate for the residence and maintenance of a family; 'a farm occupied by the owner and his family'; esp. the lot of 160 acres granted to a settler by the Homestead Act of Congress, 1862.

Hence ***homestead grant, law, policy***, etc.; ***homestead exemption***, 'the exemption by law from forced sale under execution for general debts of a certain amount of real estate occupied by the owner as a homestead' (Funk).

1693 *Providence* (R.I.) *Rec.* (1893) IV. 92 We..have..sold..all the remaining part of our home stead or house lott. **1706** *Prop. Rec. Cambr., Mass.* (1896) 227 The said piece of Land be and shall be from time to time improved by him..for a house Lott or home Stead to Build upon. **1876** *Johnson's New Univ. Cycl.* II. 971 A home and shelter for a family under the name of a homestead, which was to be held exempt from the ordinary incidents of ownership. **1879** *Constit. California* c. 17 §1 The Legislature shall protect, by law, from forced sale, a certain portion of the homestead and other property of all heads of families. **1884** MULHALL *Dict. Statist.* 231 *Homestead Grants.* In 1862 the United States law was passed to encourage settlers from Europe, whereby lots of ¼ square miles or 160 acres are given to immigrants, on condition of 5 years' occupation. **1886** *Times* 9 Oct. 10/1 The Canadian homestead policy is a more favourable one than that of the United States.

4. *attrib.* (see also 3).

1845 R. W. HAMILTON *Pop. Educ.* viii. (ed. 2) 185 The scattered population, in which homestead virtues were once supposed to find their favourite abode.

Hence **'homesteadless** *a.*, without a homestead.

1887 W. G. PALGRAVE *Ulysses* 301 Left houseless and homesteadless on a desolated land.

'homestead, *v. N. Amer.* [f. prec. sb.] *trans.* To take up and occupy as a homestead (sense 3). Also *absol.*

1872 *Newton Kansan* 12 Sept. 3/3 [He] had homesteaded the south-east quarter of sec. 14. **1877** H. RUEDE *Sod-House Days* (1937) 123 If he homesteads, you would have to be here inside of 6 months. **1879** *Congress. Rec.* 26 Apr. 952/1 To prove their right to pre-empt or 'homestead' their lands. **1884** *Pall Mall G.* 26 Aug. 5/1 Can a man, if he chooses, homestead a hundred and sixty acres of land, free of purchase-money? **1888** *Ibid.* 20 Mar. 3/1 He homesteaded his 160 acres. **1888** *Chicago Advance* 5 Apr. 216 The farmers who homesteaded on a Nebraska prairie twenty years ago. **1912** J. SANDILANDS *West Canadian Dict.* 23 Any person who is the sole head of a family, or any male over 18.., may homestead a quarter-section of..land in Manitoba, [etc.]. **1952** J. STEINBECK *East of Eden* 6 There was still marginal land to be homesteaded. **1959** *Times Lit. Suppl.* 6 Nov. p. xii/4 Yoknapatawpha County is William Faulkner's just as much as if he had homesteaded there and proved his claim. **1972** *New York* 12 June 15/3 A couple who leave Lima to homestead in the jungle.

homesteader ('həʊmˌstɛdə(r)). [f. HOMESTEAD *sb.* + -ER¹.] The holder of a homestead; *spec.* in *U.S.*, one who holds lands acquired under the Homestead Act of Congress.

1872 J. H. TICE *Over Plains* 80 As far as the eye can reach the plain is dotted with new shanties of the homesteaders and pre-emptioners. **1879** *Scribner's Mag.* Nov. 136/1 The random cabins of the 'homesteaders'. **1882** *Brandon Daily Mail* (Manitoba) 23 Dec. 4/3 Some of the neighbors found the old homesteader near his tent dead. **1888** *Pall Mall G.* 14 Jan. 7/1 He..has four grown sons, all homesteaders, who have four houses, one on each homestead, to comply with Government regulations. **1906** *Daily Colonist* (Victoria, B.C.) 6 Jan. 5/5 Each route north was lined this summer and fall with homesteaders, timber cruisers and miners. **1909** *Daily Chron.* 30 June 4/4 For these homesteaders of the ultimate [*sc.* Canadian] wheat-lands..the main ordeal will be..loneliness and monotony. **1928** W. BAUCKE *Where White Man Treads* (ed. 2) 307 The nation composed of a large salting of freehold homesteaders will be the staunchest and strongest. **1950** J. JENKS *From Ground Up* xix. 204 Those who have the qualities and the desire to become homesteaders.

'homesteading. 1. A homestead, a farm-stead.

1850 JAMES *Old Oak Chest* III. 80 A small house with a very tolerable homesteading.

2. The granting of land according to the Homestead Act of Congress, 1862 (see HOMESTEAD *sb.* 3). *U.S.* Also, a similar settlement in Canada.

1891 *Grip* (Toronto) 13 June 377/1 Mr. Dabin moved that certain settlers in the North-West be granted the privilege of second homesteading. **1906** *Daily Chron.* 1 Oct. 4/4 There is no more homesteading—viz., free grants of land—it has to be bought. **1925** *Glasgow Herald* 10 Aug. 4 Homesteading has been a great factor in the agricultural development of Western Canada. **1936** *Scrutiny* IV. iv. 441 *Honey in the Horn* is a detailed account of life in the state of Oregon during the homesteading period (1906–8).

homester ('həʊmstə(r)). [f. HOME *sb.* + -STER.] A contestant in a sporting match who belongs to the locality; one of the home team.

1891 *Lock to Lock Times* 24 Oct. 16/2 In the second half the homesters were seen to much better advantage, but the defence of the visitors was so good that nothing definite was scored. **1893** *Westm. Gaz.* 16 June 5/3 The homesters winning the toss put together the capital score of 305, whilst the Australians before the call of time lost three good wickets for 41 runs.

'home-stretch. *U.S.* [HOME *sb.*¹ B 4, STRETCH *sb.* 8.] The return stretch of a course; *esp.* the stretch of a racecourse on which a race finishes. Also *fig.*

1841 *Picayune* (New Orleans) 19 Jan. 1/6 At the head of the home stretch Cowboy overtook him and..beat him out by a length. **1860** [see BEEF *v.* 2]. **1861** *Trans. Ill. Agric. Soc.* IV. 38 On the last home stretch the steam [of the plough] became so low that it required some minutes to get up sufficient to run the furrow through. **1864** *Congress. Globe* 12 Mar. 1069/3 Already we see the slave States..on the home-stretch to become free. **1868** W. WOODRUFF *Trotting Horse* xxiv. 207, I passed first one and then the other, and came on the home-stretch with a clear lead. **1878** *Trans. Ill. Dept. Agric.* XIV. 146 Still, a fleet horse who gathers up handsomely on the home-stretch, is not to be sneezed at by any one. **1897** *Boston* (Mass.) *Jrnl.* 6 Jan. 10/1 The horses had thundered down the home stretch with a finish so close as to cause the judges to wrangle among themselves. **1903** [see BREAK *sb.*¹ 8 b]. **1968** *Daily Tel.* 4 Nov. 17/1 It was a furious home-stretch spurt that will last until he reaches his home in Minnesota at five a.m. on Tuesday, election day.

'home-thrust, *sb.* [f. HOME *adv.* 4, 5.] *Fencing.* A thrust which goes home to the party against whom it is directed; hence *fig.* and *transf.*

1622 MABBE tr. *Aleman's Guzman d'Alf.* I. 136 To giue..a slash on the arme, and to receiue a home-thrust, and full *Stocada* in his owne bosome. **1774** WESLEY *Wks.* (1872) XIII. 406 This is a home-thrust at the Mosaic law. **1862** BEVERIDGE *Hist. India* VIII. vi. III. 479 This home-thrust his lordship appears to have had some difficulty in parrying.

So **'homethrust** *a.*, that is thrust home, that reaches its mark. **'homethrust** *v.*, to thrust home, to deliver a homethrust. **'homethruster,** one who thrusts home.

c **1680** HICKERINGILL *Wks.* (1716) I. 165 God bless me from you, you are Home Thrusters. **1836** J. HALLEY in Arnot *Life* (1842) 75 A weak and rather impudent effort at homethrusting. **1856** R. A. VAUGHAN *Mystics* (1860) I. 168 His plain, homethrust speech had wrought the multitude to what he would.

'home-town. orig. *U.S.* [HOME *sb.*¹ 15 a.] The town in which one's home is, or was originally; one's native town. Also *attrib.*

1912 *Top-Notch Mag.* (U.S.) 1 Aug. 64/2 He was killed in a pool-room row in my home town up the State. **1919** H. L. WILSON *Ma Pettengill* xi. 307 Having got the thanks of the French nation and his home-town paper. **1935** R. FROST *Let.* 21 Aug. (1964) 262 The sordidness..of home-town society all over Russia. **1938** *Times Lit. Suppl.* 6 Aug. 514/4 'Home-town' mixture, Scandinavian, Italian,..all, whatever the race, nationality, class or occupation, end..by being good fellows. **1948** *Oakhillian* Summer 12 The other dignitaries returned to their various hometowns. **1953** [see FAKE *sb.*² 3]. **1971** *Nat. Geogr. Mag.* Oct. 551/2 They [*sc.* boats] hold about a dozen people each and introduce the visitor to some of the more interesting of the hometown folk.

home video. Also home-video. [HOME *sb.*¹ B. 1.]

I. *attrib.* **1.** Of or pertaining to video and video equipment for use in the home.

1968 [see VIDEO *sb.* 6]. **1977** *Washington Post* 20 Feb. K6 The home-video idea..is making one of its periodic bids for attention. **1979** *Ibid.* 11 Feb. L5/2 To imagine how large the home-video market may become, think of the record industry. **1980** *Christian Science Monitor* (Midwestern ed.) 4 Dec. 19/1 The road out of the red will be long, bumpy, and paved with home-video sales. **1982** *N.Y. Times* 30 Mar. C12 Hollywood is worried these days about..the unknown impact of new home-video technologies.

II. *absol.* or as *sb.* **2. a.** The production or use of video recordings intended to be watched at home.

1977 *Economist* 14 May 117/3 Home video looks like being the next major consumer electronics market. **1983** *N.Y. Times* 27 June 1 Only six years ago, the business that Hollywood calls 'home video'..did not exist. **1985** *Music Week* 2 Feb. 40/4 CBS will be giving its all to convincing record retailers to take on home video.

b. A video recorder or video recording marketed for home use; also, a home-made video recording (cf. HOME MOVIE).

1983 *Listener* 21 Apr. 29/2 The ladies who feature with her on her home-video were such that 'a man would be lucky to get out of them alive' (hysterical laughter). **1984** *N.Y. Times* 5 July C14 'Blacks laugh at different things' when they see home videos of his show.

homeward ('həʊmwəd), *adv.* and *a.* Forms: see HOME *sb.* [OE. *hámweard* (= OHG. *heimwart*), f. *hám*, HOME *sb.*¹ + *-weard*, -WARD. In OE. a true comb., hence in ME. the *a* of the first syllable remained (shortened) in some southern dialects; in others the comb. was analysed as *hômward*, or with the ME. shortening *homward.*]

A. *adv.* Towards home; in the direction of one's home, dwelling-place, or native land.

855 *O.E. Chron.*, Æþelwulf..þa him ham weard for. *a* **1100** *Ibid.* an. 1048 And ȝewende þa hamweard. *c* **1205** LAY. 16941 Ælc uærde heomward. *c* **1250** *Gen. & Ex.* 2376 He..bad hem rapen hem homward swiðe. *c* **1375** *Sc. Leg. Sts., Machor* 1327 His wayag hamewart tuk in hy. *c* **1385** CHAUCER *L.G.W.* 2162 *Ariadne*, Homward saylyth he. *c* **1420** *Chron. Vilod.* st. 762 So sore wepyng boskede hem hamarde to go. *c* **1450** MYRC 1176 That thou myȝtes hamward wende. **1474** CAXTON *Chesse* 156 Retournyng agayn homeward. **1526** *Pilgr. Perf.* (W. de W. 1531) 20 To drawe homewarde towarde dethe. *c* **1560** A. SCOTT *Poems* (S.T.S.) xxv. 1 Returne the, hairt, hamewart agane. **1583** STANYHURST *Æneis* II. (Arb.) 67 Thence dyd I trudge hoamward. **1750** GRAY *Elegy* i, The ploughman homeward plods his weary way. **1784** COWPER *Task* I. 522 The mariner Bound homeward, and in hope already there.

b. *Comb.*, as ***homeward-going, -veering, -wending*** adjs. Also HOMEWARD-BOUND.

1813 BYRON *Giaour* 4 The homeward-veering skiff. **1898** *Westm. Gaz.* 31 Jan. 2/1 The homeward-going teams.

B. *adj.* Directed or going homeward; leading home. Primarily with such sbs. as *march, way*; hence of things moving home.

1566 DRANT *Horace, Sat.* II. i. (R.), Which in their extreame dayes Will part from lyfe..to goe theyr homewarde wayes. **1696** TATE & BRADY *Ps.* cxix. 176 Till I despair to find my home-ward way. **1799** WORDSW. *Ruth* xli, At evening in his homeward walk. **1816** J. WILSON *City of Plague* I. i. 153 Upon our homeward voyage. **1817** W. SELWYN *Law Nisi Prius* (ed. 4) II. 937 Surinam, where she had taken in her homeward cargo.

homeward-bound, *a.* [See BOUND *ppl. a.*¹] Bound homeward; preparing to go home; directing one's course homeward. Said esp. of a ship returning home from a foreign port.

1602 CAREW *Cornwall* (1811) 9 When either outward or homeward bound they are checked by an east..wind. **1702** *Lond. Gaz.* No. 3826/3 With 6 homeward-bound Merchant Ships. **1832** MARRYAT *N. Forster* xxiii, The crew..were picked up by a homeward-bound vessel.

absol. **1887** *Pall Mall G.* 6 July 5/1 There is no precaution taken against outward-bounds meeting homeward-bounds?

Hence **'homeward-'bounder** *colloq.*, a homeward-bound vessel.

1867 SMYTH *Sailor's Word-bk.*, *Homeward-Bounder*, a ship on her course home. **1897** *Daily News* 2 June 8/6 What time the homeward bounders were heading..for the white cliffs of opposite Albion.

'homewardly, *adv. rare.* [f. HOMEWARD *a.* + -LY².] In a homeward direction.

1797 SOUTHEY *Poems, Hannah* 13 It was eve When homewardly I went.

homewards ('həʊmwədz), *adv.* Forms: see HOME *sb.* [OE. *hámweardes*, f. *hámweard*, with adverbial genitive: = OHG. *heimwartes*, Ger. *heimwärts*: see -WARDS.] = HOMEWARD *adv.*

898 *O.E. Chron.* an. 894 ⁊ Sio oþeru fierd wæs ham weardes. **1375** BARBOUR *Bruce* VII. 492 Than hamvardis buskit he to fair. **1481** *Churchw. Acc. Yatton* (Som. Rec. Soc.) 114 For custom of yᵉ bell att Redclyff hyll, utwardys and whomwardys. **1586** WARNER *Alb. Eng.* III. xiii. (R.), The Grecians homewards drewe. **1638** SIR T. HERBERT *Trav.* (ed. 2) 341 Tis high time to look homewards. **1860** TYNDALL *Glac.* I. xv. 102 We..turned our faces homewards.

'homework. [HOME *sb.*¹ 15 b.]

1. Work done at home, esp. as distinguished from work done in a shop or factory. Also *attrib.*

a **1683** B. WHICHCOTE *Sel. Serm.* (1698) 402 Wherefore let every Man, in the first place, look after his Homework; what he hath to do at Home. **1856** KANE *Arct. Expl.* II. viii. 85 Bonsall and Kane took the entire home-work on themselves today. **1861** G. MOORE *Lost Tribes* xviii. 364 One [apartment] more open and larger is reserved for visitors, or ..is used for spinning or other home-work. **1901** *Act 1 Edw. VII.* c. 22 §110 Prohibition of home work in places where there is infectious disease. **1907** *Rep. Sel. Comm. Home Work* in *Parl. Papers* VI. 61/1 Any instance of sweating in home work in connection with such things as ladies' jackets. **1908** *Franco-Brit. Exhib., Women's Section* 64 Frame of Quilting and Embroidery, lent by Home Work Co-operative Society. **1935** *Times Lit. Suppl.* 21 Dec. 882/1 The particularly mean swindlers who prey on the unemployed, either by 'homework' or by salaried jobs..are duly pilloried.

b. Phr. ***to do one's homework***: to do the preparatory work for a meeting, discussion, etc.

1934 R. STOUT *Fer-de-lance* iii. 40 There's three things I want to know. Or am I supposed to go up front and do my home work? **1959** *Listener* 6 Aug. 200/2 The Soviet reporter had been 'doing his homework' to some effect. **1966** M. CATTO *Bird on Wing* ii. 36, I have taken the trouble to do my homework on him. I know more about him than he thinks! **1971** *Guardian* 25 Feb. 15/2 The Government, says the report, appears not to have done its homework in considering how local radio should be financed.

2. Lessons and exercises to be done by a school-child at home.

1889 A. E. FLETCHER *Sonnenschein's Cycl. Educ.* (ed. 2) 155/1 Written home-work. **1897** C. DUKES in P. A. Barrett *Teaching & Organisation* 366 The large amount of homework which is assigned to pupils for preparation alone in the evening. **1905** *Westm. Gaz.* 28 Jan. 5/2, I think it is a wrong principle altogether to help a child with his home-work. **1970** C. LACEY *Hightown Gram.* viii. 168 I've just caught two boys in the quad, copying homework.

3. *slang.* Petting; also concr., a girl-friend: used esp. in phr. ***a bit*** (or ***piece***) ***of homework.***

1942 BERREY & VAN DEN BARK *Amer. Thes. Slang* §847/3 'Petting', 'Necking'..homework. **1945** L. LANE *How to become a Comedian* vii. 75 Bert Errol [a female impersonator], when on the stage, looks a ravishing and beautiful bit of home-work. **1948** PARTRIDGE *Dict. Forces' Slang* 95 *Homework*; *a piece of homework*,..one's sweetheart or temporary girl friend. **1953** E. AMBLER *Schirmer*

Inheritance 177 'And that little bit of homework you've got with you?' 'Miss Kolin, you mean? She's an interpreter.' **1968** J. SYMONS *Man whose Dreams came True* III. v. 171 He produced a dog-eared snap of a girl in a bikini. 'How's that for a piece of homework?'

Hence **'home-worker, -working.**

1902 A. BALLANTYNE in T. Oliver *Dangerous Trades* vii. 98 The home-worker..has been left outside the protecting pale of the Factory Acts. **1907** *Rep. Sel. Comm. Home Work* in *Parl. Papers* VI. 19/1 The duty of seeing to the sanitary condition of the home workers' premises. **1907** *Daily Chron.* 11 Feb. 4/4 The success of this home-working experiment under leasehold conditions. **1973** *Guardian* 17 Oct. 15/8 Most home workers are women..a classic case of powerless employees... They need..the flexibility of working hours that home work allows... The unions, understandably, are completely opposed to home working.

'homewort. *Herb. rare.* [OE. *hámwyrt*, f. *hám* HOME *sb.*[1] + *wyrt* WORT.] The house-leek.

c **1000** *Sax. Leechd.* II. 105 Wiþ poc adle onred hamwyrt. **1884** MILLER *Plant-n., Sempervivum tectorum*,..Common House-leek, 'Fuet', Home-wort.

homey, homie ('həʊmɪ). *N.Z. slang.* [HOME *sb.*[1] 6.] An Englishman; a British immigrant, esp. one newly arrived.

1927 J. DEVANNY *Old Savage* 170 The crowd at the house were mostly 'homies'. **1939** A. E. BROWN *Farmer's Wife* III. v. 161 My fishman has a pleasant slow drawl that betrays the 'Homie'. **1939** J. MULGAN *Man Alone* 28 That Saturday night I met you and our homey here. **1953** M. SCOTT *Breakfast at Six* viii. 67 These Homies with money, they stick together. **1970** D. M. DAVIN *Not Here, Not Now* IV. i. 217 An English accent. How hard it was to remember that it was as natural to a homey as your own accent was to you.

homey, variant of HOMY *a.*

homichlin ('hɒmɪklɪn). *Min.* [mod. (Breithaupt 1858) f. Gr. ὁμίχλη mist, dimness (in reference to the tarnishing of the surface) + -IN.] A sulphide of copper and iron, akin to Barnhardite.

1859 *Amer. Jrnl. Sc.* Ser. II. XXVIII. 132 Under the name Homichlin, Breithaupt has described an ore from Plauen. **1865-72** WATTS *Dict. Chem.* III. 163.

homicidal (hɒmɪ'saɪdəl), *a.* [f. HOMICIDE + -AL[1]. Late L. had *homicīdālis*.] Of, pertaining to, or characterized by homicide; tending to or resulting in homicide; man-slaying; murderous. (Of persons and their acts, or of things personified.) ***homicidal insanity, mania***: see quot. 1883.

1725 POPE *Odyss.* IV. 718 The troop forth-issuing from the dark recess, With homicidal rage the king oppress. **1791** COWPER *Odyss.* VIII. 139 In aspect dread as homicidal Mars. **1847** TENNYSON *Princ.* Prol. 219 Some great Princess, six feet high, Grand, epic, homicidal. **1851** LONGF. in *Life* (1891) II. 225 The firing of those homicidal guns. **1862** LYTTON *Str. Story* II. 8 No unfrequent illusion of homicidal maniacs. **1883** A. S. TAYLOR *Princ. Med. Jurispr.* (ed. 3) II. 551 Homicidal mania or monomania is commonly defined to be a state of partial insanity, accompanied by an impulse to the perpetration of murder; hence it is sometimes called impulsive or paroxysmal mania.

Hence **homi'cidally** *adv.*, in a homicidal manner.

1893 *Daily News* 29 Nov. 4/8 A verdict that the wound.. was homicidally inflicted was returned.

homicide ('hɒmɪsaɪd), *sb.*[1] [a. F. *homicide* (12th c.), ad. L. *homicīda*, f. shortened stem of *homo, homini-s* man + *cædĕre, -cīdĕre* to kill: see -CIDE I.] One who kills a human being; a man-slayer; in earlier use often = murderer.

c **1375** *Sc. Leg. Saints, Mathou* 563 Of dauit, homycyde & auster bath. **1421-2** HOCCLEVE *Dialog* 64 Had I be for an homysede yknowe, or an extorcioner or a robbowr. **1591** SHAKS. *1 Hen. VI*, I. ii. 25 Salisbury is a desperate Homicide, He fighteth as one weary of his life. **1632** MASSINGER & FIELD *Fatal Dowry* V. ii, I have lost a son,..I require his blood From his accursed homicide. **1791** COWPER *Iliad* V. 38 Gore-tainted homicide, town-battering Mars! **1821** BYRON *Sardan.* IV. i. 180 And her, the homicide and husband-killer. *fig.* **1635** [GLAPTHORNE] *Lady Mother* V. i. in Bullen *O. Pl.* II. 184 O, dispaire, Grimme homicide of soules.

†**b.** ***self-homicide***, a suicide. *Obs.*

1681 NEVILE *Plato Rediv.* 212 So that for the Parliament to seek to take from him such Authority, were to be *felo de se*, as we call a self-Homicide.

c. *attrib.* Man-killing, homicidal.

1382 WYCLIF *Acts* iii. 14 ȝe..axiden a man homeside, or mansleer, for to be ȝouun to ȝou. **1796** BURKE *Regic. Peace* i. Wks. VIII. 119 This regicide and homicide Government. **1825** T. JEFFERSON *Autobiog.* Wks. 1859 I. 94 Their unholy and homicide alliance.

'homicide, *sb.*[2] [a. F. *homicide* (12th c.), ad. L. *homicīdium*: see prec. and -CIDE 2.] The action, by a human being, of killing a human being.

In *Law*, usually classed as *justifiable, excusable*, or *felonious*. ***justifiable homicide***, the killing of a man in obedience to law, or by unavoidable necessity, or for the prevention of an atrocious crime. ***excusable homicide***, homicide committed by misadventure, also in cases of self-defence, where the assailant did not originally intend murder, rape, or robbery: but the distinction between *justifiable* and *excusable* homicide is merely verbal in modern Eng. law. ***felonious homicide*** comprehends the wilful killing of a man through malice aforethought (murder); the unlawful killing of a man without such malice, either in a sudden heat, or involuntarily while committing an unlawful action not amounting to felony (manslaughter, in Scots Law called *culpable homicide*); also, the destroying of one's own life, self-murder, suicide. The degrees of culpable homicide have been defined by statute in divers colonial and American jurisdictions, as part of a systematic criminal code or otherwise. See ***manslaughter, murder***.

c **1386** CHAUCER *Pars. T.* ¶498 Another homycide is that is doon for necessitee as whan o man sleeth another in his defendaunt. **1484** CAXTON *Fables Alfonce* (1889) 1 This man dyd not the homycyde. *c* **1560** A. SCOTT *Poems* (S.T.S.) xxxvi. 58 Lord God, deliuer me, and gyd Frome schedding blude, and homicyd. *a* **1612** DONNE *Βιαθανατος* (1644) 90 It [suicide] is not onely Homicide, but Murder. **1769** BLACKSTONE *Comm.* IV. 179 In some cases homicide is justifiable, rather by the permission, than by the absolute command of the law. **1809-10** COLERIDGE *Friend* (1865) 44 [He] is acquitted of murder—the act was manslaughter only, or it was justifiable homicide. **1856** EMERSON *Eng. Traits, Race* Wks. (Bohn) II. 26 These Norsemen are excellent persons in the main..But they have a singular turn for homicide.

†**b.** ***self-homicide***, self-murder, suicide. *Obs.*

a **1612** DONNE *Βιαθανατος* (1644) 26 Of such condition is this Self-Homicide. **1650** *Vind. Hammond's Addr.* §32. 12 Self-homicide is evill, and forbidden by God.

'homicide, *v.* (Also pa. pple. in 5 homycied.) [f. HOMICIDE *sb.*[2]] *trans.* To kill or murder.

c **1470** HARDING *Chron.* LXXXI. v, That place..Wher that gyaunt and she were homycied. **1858** CARLYLE *Fredk. Gt.* II. xi, Her ancestor was Husband to an Aunt of that homicided Duke.

homicidial (hɒmɪ'sɪdɪəl), *a. rare.* [f. as next + -AL[1].] = HOMICIDAL.

1808 HELEN ST. VICTOR *Ruins Rigonda* III. 168 The wretched end of her homicidial father.

homicidious (hɒmɪ'sɪdɪəs), *a. rare.* [f. L. *homicīdi-um* HOMICIDE *sb.*[2] + -OUS.] = HOMICIDAL.

1632 LITHGOW *Trav.* IX. 407 An inhumane and homicidious Pope. **1689** *Def. Liberty agst. Tyrants* 162 The Cruel and Homocidious Directors and Appointers of these Bloody Sports. **1808** J. BARLOW *Columb.* III. 585 Dread Zamor leads the homicidious train.

†**homicidy, -ie.** *Obs.* [ad. L. *homicīdi-um* HOMICIDE *sb.*[2]] = HOMICIDE *sb.*[2]

c **1386** CHAUCER *Pars. T.* ¶490 (Harl. MS.) Vnderstonde wel þat homicidie þat is man-slaughter is in diuers wise. **1440** J. SHIRLEY *Dethe K. James* (1818) 20 This abhominable..homycidie, and false treason of this cruell murdur.

homiculture ('hɒmɪkʌltjʊə(r)). Erron. **homo-**. [f. L. *homo, homi(ni)-* man + CULTURE.] The physical cultivation or development of mankind.

1886 *Aberdeen Free Press* 4 Sept. 4/3 All honour therefore to Sir George Campbell for grappling so boldly at the British Association with the question of 'Homi-Culture'. **1888** *Pub. Opinion* 29 Sept., Marriages..made on bases which, if not those that the laws of homiculture would lay down, are at least not diametrically opposed to them.

homiform, erroneous f. HOMINIFORM.

homilete ('hɒmɪliːt). [ad. Gr. ὁμιλητής disciple, scholar, f. ὁμιλέειν to hold converse with, to attend the lectures of.] A preacher, a HOMILIST.

1875 *Presbyt. Quarterly* Jan. 120 (Cent.) The pulpit wants above all else enthusiastic homiletes. **1891** J. H. THAYER in *Class. Rev.* V. 22/1 After all it holds true that the province of the exegete is distinct from that of the homilete.

homiletic (hɒmɪ'lɛtɪk), *a.* and *sb.* Also 7 homilitick. [ad. Gr. ὁμιλητικός affable, conversable, f. ὁμιλητός, vbl. adj. of ὁμιλέειν to consort with, hold converse with, f. ὅμιλος assembled crowd, throng. Cf. F. *homilétique*.]

A. *adj.* Of the nature of or characteristic of a homily; by way of a homily. ***homiletic divinity*** or ***theology*** = Homiletics: see B. 1.

1644 SIR E. DERING *Prop. Sacr.* C iv, Polemick and Homilitick Divinity. **1846** TRENCH *Mirac.* xxx. (1862) 432 Many admirable homiletic applications of this portion of the history have been made. **1884** D. HUNTER tr. *Reuss's Hist. Canon* v. 76 The homiletic use of the apostles' writings.

B. *sb.* usually in *pl.* **homiletics** [see -ICS, and cf. Gr. ἡ ὁμιλητική the art of conversation; also Ger. *homiletik*].

1. The art of preaching; sacred rhetoric.

1830 PUSEY *Histor. Enq.* II. 126 If..the teaching of Homiletic were confined to the multiplication of methods for laying out a discourse [etc.]. **1846** WORCESTER cites *Brit. Crit.* for *Homiletics*. **1858** *Sat. Rev.* V. 288/1 We proceed to an analysis of this remarkable specimen of Christian homiletics. **1865** D. P. KIDDER *(title)* Treatise on Homiletics. Designed to illustrate the true Theory and Practice of Preaching the Gospel. **1882-3** SCHAFF *Encycl. Relig. Knowl.* 1013 His [Hyperius'] work *De Formandis Concionibus Sacris*..distinguishes him..as the founder of the science of homiletics.

2. *pl.* Homiletical works; homilies. *rare.*

1850 CARLYLE *Latter-d. Pamph.* vii. (1872) 221 Reading its liturgies, homiletics, and excellent old moral horn-books.

homi'letical, *a.* [f. as prec. + -AL[1].]

†**1.** Of or pertaining to familiar intercourse or discourse; conversable, sociable. *Obs.*

1668 WILKINS *Real Char.* II. viii. 206 Conversations, or the right Demeanour of our selves considered as Members of Society, in our converse with others; the due managing of the common Affairs and Businesses of life..These are commonly called Homiletical Vertues. **1687** ATTERBURY *Luther* (R.), His virtues active chiefly and homiletical: not those lazy sullen ones of the cloister. **1691** NORRIS *Pract. Disc.* 92 To yield some compliance and conformity with the Humours and Dispositions of those with whom we Converse; for this is a necessary part of Homilitical Vertue.

2. = HOMILETIC *a.*

1838-9 HALLAM *Hist. Lit.* IV. IV. iv. § 7. 155 A less homiletical form, and a comparative absence of Scriptural quotation, are the chief distinctions. **1849** SIR J. STEPHEN *Eccl. Biog.* (1850) II. 74 Whitfield's homiletical labours, during each of his next five and thirty years.

Hence **homi'letically** *adv.*, after the manner of a homily or sermon.

1867 DEUTSCH *Talmud* in *Q. Rev.* Oct. 427 Tho' it might be explained homiletically or otherwise in innumerable new ways.

†**ho'milian.** *Obs. rare.* [f. Gr. ὁμιλία homily + -AN.] = HOMILIST.

a **1641** BP. MOUNTAGU *Acts & Mon.* (1642) 509 Hippolytus and other Homilians.

homiliary (hɒ'mɪlɪərɪ). [ad. med.L. *homīliārium, homīliāri-us (liber)*, f. *homīlia* HOMILY: see -ARY.] A collection of homilies or sermons to be used in Church-service; a book of homilies.

1844 S. R. MAITLAND *Dark Ages* 64 *note*, I cannot help thinking that the Codex might be that service-book which was then more properly and strictly, and commonly too, (if not exclusively) called a Homiliary. **1882-3** SCHAFF *Encycl. Relig. Knowl.* III. 1733 A kind of homiliary..destined to be used at the celebration of the respective saints' days.

homilist ('hɒmɪlɪst). [f. HOMILY + -IST.] One who writes or delivers homilies, or hortatory sermons; a preacher.

1616 BEAUM. & FL. *Scornf. Lady* IV. i, To this good homilist I have been ever stubborn, which God forgive me for and mend my manners. **1642** HALES *Schism* 7 What if the Homilist have Preached, or delivered any Doctrine, of the Truth of which we are not well perswaded? **1849** ROCK *Ch. of Fathers* I. i. 22 We have the testimony of the homilist Ælfric. **1882** FARRAR in *Contemp. Rev.* XLII. 807 Among the classic homilists of the English Church.

Hence **homi'listical** *a.*, characteristic of a homilist.

1659 GAUDEN *Tears Ch. Eng.* 621 Armed..onely for the preaching or Homilisticall flourishes of a Pulpit.

homilite ('hɒmɪlaɪt). *Min.* [f. Gr. ὁμιλία association, ὁμιλέειν to be in company + -ITE.] A borosilicate of iron and calcium, allied to datolite.

1881 *Watts' Dict. Chem.* VIII. 1038 *Homilite*, a mineral occurring, together with erdmannite and melinophane, at Stockoe near Brevig in Norway.

homilize ('hɒmɪlaɪz), *v.* [f. HOMILY + -IZE.] *intr.* To discourse, to preach, sermonize. (In quot. 1857 perh. *trans.* To preach to.)

1624 BP. MOUNTAGU *Immed. Addresse* 169 Basil..excelled in that popular kind of Homilizing. *a* **1662** HEYLIN *Laud* (1668) 9 Not cloying them with continual Preaching, or Homilizing. **1683** O. U. *Parish Ch. no Conventicles* 21 Must the Parochial Ministers be bound to preach or homilize every Holy-Day? **1857** *Fraser's Mag.* LVI. 496 The stones at our feet can homilize and humanize us.

homill, obs. Sc. f. HUMMEL.

homily ('hɒmɪlɪ). Forms: 4-6 **omelie, -y(e**, 5 **homilye**, 6 **omylie, omilie**, 6-7 **homely**, 6- **homily**. [a. F. *omelie* (12th c. in Hatz.-Darm.), mod.F. *homélie*, ad. eccl. L. *homīlia*, a. Gr. ὁμιλία intercourse, converse, discourse, (eccl.) sermon, homily, f. ὅμιλος crowd, throng, f. ὁμοῦ together + ἴλη crowd, band, troop.]

A religious discourse addressed to a congregation; a sermon; esp. a practical discourse with a view to the spiritual edification of the hearers, rather than for the development of a doctrine or theme: see quot. 1883. In the Church of England spec. applied to the discourses contained in the *Books of Homilies* published in 1547 and 1563 for use in parish churches.

c **1386** CHAUCER *Pars. T.* ¶1014 Of..Omelies and moralitee and of deuocion. **1390** GOWER *Conf.* II. 191 Gregoire upon his Omelie Ayein the slouthe of prelacie Compleigneth him. *c* **1440** *Gesta Rom.* ix. 25 (Add. MS.) Seynte Austyn seithe in an Omelie. **1534** MORE *On the Passion* Wks. 1307/1 The omely or lecture vpon the seconde chapiter. **1548-9** (Mar.) *Bk. Com. Prayer, Commun.* Rubric, After the Crede ended, shall folowe the Sermon or Homely, or some porcion of one of the Homelyes, as thei shalbe herafter deuided. **1562** *Homilies* Pref. (1859) 4 [The Queen] hath..caused a Book of Homilies, which heretofore was set forth by her most loving brother..to be printed anew. **1649** JER. TAYLOR *Gt. Exemp.* I. Ad §8. 115 The good example of the Preacher is alwayes the most prevailing Homily; his life is his best Sermon. **1844** *(title)* The Homilies of the Anglo-Saxon Church. Part I. The Homilies of Ælfric. **1883** SCHAFF *Encycl. Relig. Knowl.* 1611 In the Western Church the terms 'sermon' and 'homily' were at first used interchangeably; but in time each came to designate a special kind of discourse. The sermon was a discourse developing a definite theme..The homily pursued the analytical method, and expounded a paragraph or verse of Scripture. **1886** HALL CAINE *Son of Hagar* II. xvi, The service was soon done, and then the parson delivered a homily.

b. *transf.* A serious admonition, exhortation or counsel; a lecture; a tedious moralizing discourse.

1600 Shaks. *A.Y.L.* iii. ii. 164 O most gentle Iupiter, what tedious homilie of Loue haue you wearied your parishioners withall. **1824** W. Irving *T. Trav.* I. 252 There are homilies in nature's works worth all the wisdom of the schools. **1838** James *Robber* vi, I vow and protest you have read them a homily as fair as any in the book. **1848** Lytton *Harold* v. i, Edith, after a long homily from the King, returned to Hilda.

hominal ('hɒmɪnəl), *a.* [a. F. *hominal*, f. L. *homo, homin-em*, man: see -AL[1].] Of or relating to man (in Natural History); human.

1861 Hulme tr. *Moquin-Tandon* I. vi. 35 Voltaire seems to have been the first who looked upon Man as constituting a separate kingdom.. Most naturalists and ethnologists of the present day have adopted this moral, human, or hominal kingdom.. Amongst living beings, or in the organic world, there are therefore three kingdoms: the vegetable, the animal, and the hominal. **1892** *Daily News* 14 Jan. 5/3 The most remarkable studies of M. Quatrefages were on marine animals and on the human or 'hominal' kingdom.

†**homi'neity.** *Obs.* [f. L. *homo, homin-em*, man, after *deity*.] The essential quality of mankind; that which constitutes man.

1659 Stanley *Hist. Philos.* xi. (1701) 448/1 Many Individual Men are such by participation of the Idæa of Man, (as if we should say Homineity). *Ibid.* 449/1.

hominess: see under HOMY *a.*

homing ('həʊmɪŋ), *vbl. sb.* [f. HOME *v.*]

†**1.** *Naut.* (with *in*) The curving inwards of the sides of a vessel above its extreme breadth; 'falling' or 'tumbling home'. *Obs.*

1622 R. Hawkins *Voy. S. Sea* (1847) 220 This race building, first came in by overmuch homing in of our shippes.

2. The action of going home; return home; the faculty possessed by animals (e.g. pigeons, turtles, etc.) of returning home from a distance. Freq. *attrib.*

1765 *Treat. Dom. Pigeons* 88 When they come to be trained for the homing part. **1875** *Live Stock Jrnl.* 16 Apr. 35/2, I have always admired the homing faculty in the pigeon. **1886** E. S. Starr in *Century Mag.* XXXII. 375 The much discussed question of the homing of the pigeon, or, as the French term it, *orientation.* **1894** A. Morrison *Mean Streets* 249 At his regular homing-time he appeared. **1901** *Camb. Nat. Hist.* VIII. ix. 387 The same homing instinct has been observed in some females of the Green Turtle. **1907** G. B. Shaw *John Bull's Other Island* i. 16 *Broadbent:* Here you are, belonging to a nation with the..most inveterate homing instinct in the world! and you pretend youd rather go anywhere than back to Ireland. **1922** Flattely & Walton *Biol. Sea-Shore* viii. 178 There is evidence of a 'homing sense' in the common limpet and its relatives. **1939** *Copeia* iii. 127 Most grown turtles (89·5 per cent) showed some homing instinct or tendency to return to territory from which they were moved. **1956** W. H. Thorpe *Learning & Instinct in Animals* xvi. 412 Experiments on the homing of dogs. *Ibid.*, The homing performances of bats. **1967** Gardiner & Flemister *Princ. Gen. Biol.* (ed. 2) xiv. 248 Insects respond to polarized light, and..this capacity is used in orientation and homing behavior.

3. (In sense of HOME *v.* 5); also *attrib.*, esp. in ***homing device***, an automatic device for guiding aircraft, missiles, etc.

1923 *Jrnl. Inst. Electr. Engin.* 803/2 As this method seriously affects the compass and takes a machine off its course, wing coils are only used for 'homing', i.e. flying along a radius towards a transmitting station, thus enabling the aircraft to return to its base. **1933** *Bureau of Standards Jrnl. Res.* XI. 740 In these tests the direction finder was used as a homing device. **1940** *Illustr. London News* CXCVII. 567 (*caption*) Direction-finding radio compass for work in connection with loop aerial and 'homing' beam. **1947** Crowther & Whiddington *Science at War* iv. 178 Another ..success was gained against the acoustic homing torpedo. **1951** *Gloss. Aeronaut. Terms (B.S.I.)* iii. 27 *Homing aids*, systems designed to guide an aircraft to an aerodrome or carrier. **1955** *Times* 28 June 8/6 There are..other means of detecting a camouflaged operations centre, such as high altitude vertical photography and 'homing' on to radio transmissions. **1957** *Oxford Mail* 20 Aug. 1/4 After launching, the weapon is guided to the target by a special homing head which picks up the ground radar beams reflected back from the enemy. **1962** *Gloss. Aeronaut. Terms (B.S.I.)* vi. 4 *Homing guidance*, a system wherein devices built into a missile enable it to detect and steer itself towards, or to intercept, a target.

homing, *ppl. a.* [f. HOME *v.* + -ING[2].] That goes home; *spec.* applied to pigeons that are trained to fly home from a distance.

1862 Huxley *Lect. Wrkg. Men* 105 The so called 'homing' birds having enormous flying powers. **1886** *Daily Tel.* 7 Sept., Nowadays, the 'homing pigeon'..is so much better understood than of yore..that no other agency than electricity would be capable of outstripping him.

hominid ('hɒmɪnɪd), *sb.* and *a.* [ad. mod.L. *Hominid-æ*, a family of mammals represented by the single genus *Homo* (man), f. L. *homo, homin-em*, man: see -ID. Cf. F. pl. *hominides.*]

A. *sb.* A member of the mammal family Hominidæ (J. E. Gray 1825, in *Ann. Philos.* XXVI. 338), of which *Homo sapiens*, man, is the only surviving species.

1889 *Cent. Dict.*, *Hominid*, one of the *Hominidæ*; a man. **1916** *Bull. Amer. Mus. Nat. Hist.* XXXV. 347 Some day.. one will discover a hominid of small stature, and almost erect posture. **1925** *Glasgow Herald* 25 July 4 That the human race, with all its tentative as well as more or less realised Hominids, arose from an ancestral stock common to it and the Anthropoids. **1957** *Observer* 1 Sept. 11/1 This glittering..exhibition is..the latest in toyfairs for spoilt hominids. **1969** *Times* 17 Jan. 13/6 A fragment of the upper part of a thigh bone from a hominid which lived at least three million years ago has now been recovered from the Olduvai Gorge, in Tanzania.

B. *adj.* Of, belonging to, or characteristic of a hominid or the Hominidæ.

1916 *Bull Amer. Mus. Nat. Hist.* XXXV. 347 The divergence of the Hominid branch occurred..from the anthropoid stem after the separation of the gibbons. **1939** C. S. Coon *Races of Europe* ii. 51 During the Middle Pleistocene..a mixture took place between early white dolichocephals and one or more non-*sapiens* hominid species, including *Homo neanderthalensis.* **1971** J. Z. Young *Introd. Study of Man* xxxii. 444 Hominid creatures existed a good deal earlier than had previously been supposed. **1971** *Nature* 30 July 308/1 So few identifiable parts were visible that it is remarkable it was recognized as hominid.

†**'hominiform,** *a. Obs.* [f. L. *homin-em* man + -FORM.] Of human shape.

1678 Cudworth *Intell. Syst.* i. v. 673 Monstrous shapes ..mixtly Boviform and Hominiform.

hominify ('hɒmɪnɪfaɪ), *v.* [f. as prec. + -FY.] *trans.* To make a man of; to render human.

1579 J. Jones *Preserv. Bodie & Soule* i. xli. 91 Damnably teaching, that they in God are Deified, and God in them Hominified. **1633** T. Adams *Exp. 2 Peter* i. 16 Mankind had not been redeemed, unless the Word of God had been hominified. **1890** F. Hall in *Nation* (N.Y.) II. 380/3 A work of the celebrated historian Abulfazl being, thus, hominified and accorded royal rank.

hominine ('hɒmɪnaɪn, -iːn), *a.* and *sb.* [f. L. *homin-em* man + -INE. Cf. *asinine.*] **A.** *adj.* **1.** Of or belonging to man zoologically; of the human species.

1883 *American* V. 204 If the footprints are really those of a hominine species. *Ibid.* 267 The most distinctively simian, and consequently least hominine, characteristic.

2. Of, belonging to, or characteristic of a hominine or Homininæ.

1959 *Cold Spring Harbor Symp. Quant. Biol.* XXIV. 244/1 The earlier forms are the more hominine... This suggests the probability that the known Australopithecines represent a somewhat specialized offshoot from the mainline of hominine evolution.

B. *sb.* [f. mod.L. *Homininæ* (G. Heberer 1949, in *Die Umschau* 1 May 258/1), the sub-family including man.] A member of the sub-family Homininæ, which is sometimes used as a division of the family Hominidæ to comprise large-brained hominids, in contrast to the small-brained ones of the sub-family Australopithecinæ.

1961 K. P. Oakley in *Times* 5 Sept. 13/5 Three main points of emergence in man's evolution—the first tool-makers, the first hominines, and the first men of our own species. **1963** G. G. Simpson in S. L. Washburn *Classification & Human Evol.* (1964) i. 29 In the Hominidae, I see no sufficient reason for having two subfamilies, especially as each has only one known genus as I and, I believe, most others now define the genera. 'Australopithecine' and 'hominine' may still be used as strictly vernacular terms for structural level. **1971** *Nature* 6 Aug. 383/1 The bones throw some light on the structure and function of the lower limb skeleton of Middle Pleistocene hominines in East Africa.

ˌhomini'section. *rare.* [f. L. *homin-em* man + SECTION.] Human anatomy.

1888 Coues in *Auk* V. 105 If the author is correct in identifying the muscle..with the myon of that name in hominisection.

hominist ('hɒmɪnɪst). *rare.* [f. L. *homo, homin-em* man + -IST.] One who advocates for men the rights and privileges conventionally accorded to women. Also *attrib.* or as *adj.*

1903 G. B. Shaw *Man & Superman* p. xviii, The wildest hominist or feminist farce is insipid after the most commonplace 'slice of life'. **1914** R. Brooke *Let.* 10 June (1968) 592 If feminists are 'women' trying to be men, I suppose 'men' trying to be women are hominists.

hominivorous (hɒmɪ'nɪvərəs), *a.* [f. L. *homin-em* man + *-vor-us* devouring + -OUS.] Devouring or feeding upon human beings.

1859–63 Wood *Illustr. Nat. Hist.* (1876) 224 There are man-eaters among the Hyænas, and these hominivorous animals are greatly dreaded. **1861** Hulme tr. *Moquin-Tandon* ii. iv. i. 237 The Hominivorous fly..inhabits Cayenne. **1868** P. M. Duncan tr. *Figuier's Insect World* ii. 72 Let us..observe that this hominivorous fly is not, properly speaking, a parasite of man.

hominization (hɒmɪnaɪ'zeɪʃən). [a. F. *hominisation* (P. Teilhard de Chardin *Le Phénomène Humain* (1948) iii. i. 199), f. L. *homo, homin-* man + -IZATION.] The evolutionary development of characteristics, esp. mental or spiritual ones, that are held to distingush man from other animals.

1953 J. S. Huxley *Evol. in Action* vi. 136 The original stock of pre-human apes differentiated into many species, all showing a trend towards what has been called hominization —the acquisition of more human characters. **1959** B. Wall tr. *Teilhard de Chardin's Phenomenon of Man* iii. i. 180 Hominisation can be accepted in the first place as the individual and instantaneous leap from instinct to thought, but it is also..the progressive phyletic spiritualisation in human civilisation of all the forces contained in the animal world. **1962** W. Howells *Ideas on Human Evol.* 295 (*heading*) The hominization of the masticatory apparatus, and modifications of diet.

Also **'hominized** *ppl. a.*

1959 B. Wall tr. *Teilhard de Chardin's Phenomenon of Man* iii. iii. 223 Are not the artificial, the moral and the juridical simply the hominised versions of the natural, the physical and the organic? **1973** *Times Lit. Suppl.* 27 Apr. 479/3 To supersede Rudolph Otto's notion of the holy as the numinous..and to do this for a hominized, secularized world.

hominoid ('hɒmɪnɔɪd), *a.* and *sb.* [f. L. *homo, homin-* man + -OID.] **A.** *adj.* **a.** Of human form; man-like (rather than ape-like). Cf. HUMANOID *a.* and *sb.*

1927 *Glasgow Herald* 3 Sept. 4/2 The divergence of the Hominoid and the Anthropoid branches. **1937** *Discovery* Feb. 62/1 He fixes the habitat for the first hominoid being as central Asia.

b. [ad. mod.L. *Hominoidea* (G. G. Simpson 1931, in *Bull. Amer. Mus. Nat. Hist.* LIX. 272).] Of, belonging to, or characteristic of a hominoid or the Hominoidea.

1950 *Q. Jrnl. Geol. Soc.* CV. 238 In all the hominoid species of Miocene and Pliocene age so far known..the canine is in the form of a strong pointed tooth. **1959** *Cold Spring Harbor Symp. Quant. Biol.* XXIV. 238/1 In 1949, Hürseler in Basel re-evaluated the..*Oreopithecus* material from the 19th century, and recognized it as being hominoid. **1973** *Nature* 3 Aug. 313/1 Species of *Ramapithecus* are among the few hominoid species currently considered as possibly close to the direct line of human ancestry.

B. *sb.* **a.** An animal resembling man.

1927 *Glasgow Herald* 3 Sept. 4/2 The early hominoids.

b. *spec.* [ad. mod.L. *Hominoidea* (see above)]: a member of the superfamily Hominoidea, which includes man and the anthropoid apes.

1949 W. E. Le Gros Clark *Hist. Primates* 74 The earliest fossil records or *true* Man, that is, of hominoids which definitely come within the family of the Hominidae, have been found in the Far East. **1950** *Q. Jrnl Geol. Soc.* CV. 231 A great many specimens of fossil hominoids..were collected. **1963** R. Carrington *Million Years of Man* iii. 26 The smallest and most primitive of all living hominoids are the gibbons. **1967** W. E. Le Gros Clark *Man-Apes or Ape-Men?* i. 2 The human and anthropoid ape families are now usually included in a common group, a superfamily called the Hominoidea (or, colloquially, hominoids).

hominy ('hɒmɪnɪ). Forms: 7 **homini, homminey, omine,** 7–8 **hominne,** 7–9 **hom(m)on(e)y,** 8 **hommany, -iny,** 8– **hominy.** [Of American Indian origin: see the early quots.

The actual origin seems unsettled. J. H. Trumbull, in Note to Roger Williams's *Key into Lang. of America* (1643), Narragansett Club ed., 1866, has '*Appuminnéonash*, "parched corn". From *appωn, apwóon*, "he bakes or roasts", and *min* pl. *minneash*, "fruit, grain, berry". In this and other compounds of *minneash* we discover the origin of the much-corrupted modern name *hominy*'. But see a different suggestion in *Trans. American Philol. Assoc.* 1872.]

a. Maize or Indian corn hulled and ground more or less coarsely and prepared for food by being boiled with water or milk.

1629 Capt. Smith *Contn. Hist. Virginia* (1630) 43 Their servants commonly feed upon Milke Homini, which is bruized Indian corne pounded, and boiled thicke, and milke for the sauce. **1634** *Relat. Ld. Baltimore's Plantat.* (1865) 17 Their ordinary diet is Poane and Omine, both made of Corne. **1672** Josselyn *New Eng. Rarities* 101 They beat the corn in a mortar and sift the flower out of it: the remainder they call *Homminey.* **1683** Penn *Wks.* (1782) IV. 306 Their diet is maize..sometimes beaten and boiled with water, which they call homine. **1699** J. Dickenson *Jrnl. Trav.* 70 Our chief Dyet was Hommoney. **1751** J. Bartram *Observ. Trav. Pennsylv.* etc. 60 Kettles of Indian corn soop, or thin homony. **1771** Smollett *Humph. Cl.* 10 June Let. i, Our entertainer..made him own that a plate of hominy was the best rice-pudding he had ever eat. **1827** J. F. Cooper *Prairie* I. ii. 30 The delicious hommony prepared by his skilful.. spouse. **1836** Whittier *Mogg Megone* i. 326 Or offering up, at eve, to thee, Thy birchen dish of hominy. **1860** S. Mordecai *Virginia* xxxi. 314 Slow as the process of 'beating hominy' is, it was a great resource, as was the eating of it for lack of hoecake. **1888** *Rep. Vermont Board Agric.* X. 30 The refuse of white corn after what is termed the 'hominy' has been removed, is more valuable as a feed for stock than yellow corn. **1922** W. G. R. Francillon *Good Cookery* (ed. 2) xiv. 251 Wash and soak the hominy in water, overnight. Boil gently for half-hour or more. Stir frequently, and serve as oatmeal porridge. **1926–7** *Army & Navy Stores Catal.* 21/2 *Hominy*, finest pearl—bag about 5 lb. ¼. **1959** E. Tunis *Indians* 43/1 Wherever corn was raised in the East, hominy was an important food. **1963** R. I. McDavid in Mencken *Amer. Lang.* 699 In South Carolina I was taught that hominy designated what the less fortunate called grits.

b. *attrib.* and *Comb.*

1687 J. Clayton in *Phil. Trans.* XLI. 159 At all Hours of the Night, whenever they awake, they go to the Hominy-pot. **1711** in *Col. Rec. N. Carolina* (1886) I. 765 The planter here..dare not allow himself to partake of his own creatures except it be the corn of the country in hominy bread. **1775** Adair *Amer. Ind.* 407 The second sort is yellow and flinty, which they call 'hommony-corn'. **1827** J. F. Cooper *Prairie* ii, Others [were engaged] in plying the heavy pestle of a moveable hominy-mortar. *Ibid.* xvi, Giving her a morsel of venison, now and then, or a spoon around his hominy-dish. **1843** 'R. Carlton' *New Purchase* I. xv. 111 Here were all the vulgar pots, kettles, frying-pans, homminy-block, and the like. **1875** Knight *Dict. Mech.*, *Hominy-mill*, a machine in which shelled corn is subjected to a grating or beating action which removes the cuticle and the germ. **1876** M. N. Henderson *Pract. Cooking* 71 When the milk is salted and

boiling, stir in the hominy grits, and boil twenty minutes. **1961** *Listener* 17 Aug. 234/2 In Dixie you are offered some strange dishes; one is called 'hominy grits'—..it tastes like a cross between porridge and tapioca.

homish ('həʊmɪʃ), *a.* Also homeish. [f. HOME *sb.*[1] + -ISH.]

† **1.** Belonging to or suited for home; domestic.

1561 HOLLYBUSH (*title*) A most Excellent and Perfecte Homish Apothecarye; or Homely Physick Booke. **1577** DEE *Gen. & rare Mem.* 10 Nor homish Subject, or wauering vassal..durst..privily muster to Rebellion.

2. Resembling or suggestive of home; homelike.

1789 MRS. PIOZZI *Journ. France* I. 327 The gardens have a homeish and Bath-like look. **1838** PRESCOTT in Ticknor *Life* (1864) 114 The complexion of Anna's sentiments looked rather homeish.

Hence '**homishness**, homish quality.

1835 *New Monthly Mag.* XLIII. 15 [Pictures] add a 'homeishness' to the rooms. **1889** *Spectator* 14 Sept., As for the squalor of the streets, they cease in a short time to perceive it, or even derive from it a sense of homishness.

hommack, var. HUMMOCK.

hommage, obs. f. HOMAGE.

hommany, -iny, etc., var. HOMINY.

‖**homme** (ɔm). [Fr., man.] In Fr. combinations: **homme d'affaires** (ɔm dafɛr), a business man, an agent, a lawyer; **homme fatal**, used jocularly as the masculine equivalent of a *femme fatale*; **homme moyen** (ɔm mwajɛ̃), used in various phrases with defining adjective, esp. **homme sensuel moyen**, average sensual man (cf. AVERAGE *a.* 2b); also **homme moyen sensuel**.

1717 M. W. MONTAGU *Let.* 17 May (1837) I. 410 Every pashá has his Jew, who is his *homme d'affaires*. **1815** SCOTT *Guy M.* II. xviii. [*sic* = xvii.] 305 Dinmont..stood poking his large round face over the shoulder of the *homme d'affaires*. **1851** E. RUSKIN *Let.* 20 Dec. in M. Lutyens *Effie in Venice* (1965) II. 235 It would cost him nothing farther than a letter to his homme-d'affairs at Vienna to arrange. **1882** [see SENSUAL *a.* 4a]. **1894** G. DU MAURIER *Trilby* III. VIII. 103 The good Taffy had constituted himself Trilby's secretary and *homme d'affaires*. **1922** C. E. MONTAGUE *Disenchantment* v. 66 Church parades, a ministration of which the average private, *l'homme moyen sensuel* of Matthew Arnold, had taken a long and glad farewell. **1928** A. HUXLEY *Point Counter Point* xiv. 266 Scientific eyes, economic eyes, *homme moyen sensuel* eyes. **1932** *N. & Q.* 8 Oct. 269/1 They represent the opinion of the *homme lettré moyen* of our day rather than give us examples of brilliant criticism. **1935** *Times Lit. Suppl.* 9 Nov. 724/4 She intrigues to interest Edward Hudson, an *homme fatal*, in her friend. **1936** C. S. LEWIS *Allegory of Love* iv. 173 Even so, long after the original reasons for the tradition have been forgotten, the *homme sensuel moyen* with his fair, large ears appears in the *Midsummer Night's Dream*. **1958** *Spectator* 7 Feb. 166/1, I find it difficult to imagine anything more nicely calculated to convince *l'homme moyen cynique* that the Parker Tribunal was an elaborate white-washing operation fixed up by the Government. **1959** *Encounter* XII. II. 32 Humbert Humbert, her *homme fatal*. **1959** *Times* 22 Sept. 11/3 A good family solicitor..is very much the *homme d'affaires*. **1961** *Guardian* 16 Feb. 10/4 Camus finds his 'homme moyen sensuel' in Dr Rieux, who is not interested in the salvation of men but wishes to cure them. **1972** *Listener* 22 June 840/3 He works much too hard at being mysterious, at playing *l'homme fatal*.

homme, obs. f. HAM.

hommel, obs. f. HUMBLE, HUMMEL.

‖**homo** ('həʊməʊ, 'hɒməʊ), *sb.*[1] The Latin word for *man*. **a.** From its use in Latin works on logic, frequently employed, in quasi-logical or scholastic language, in the sense 'human being'. **b.** *Zool.* The genus of which Man is the single living species, having many geographical races and varieties. Many other species of the genus *Homo* have been proposed, to include various fossils of extinct hominids (as *Homo neanderthalensis*, *H. erectus*, *H. habilis*, etc.). ***Homo sapiens*** ('seɪpɪɛnz, 'sæpɪɛnz) [mod.L. (Linnæus *Systema Naturæ* (ed. 10, 1758) I. 20), f. L. *sapiens* wise]: the human species; the form of man represented by the surviving races and varieties.

1596 SHAKS. *1 Hen. IV*, II. i. 104 *Homo* is a common name to all men. **1649** *Moderate Intelligencer* No. 213. 10 Fijb (Stanf.), You have made the word Malignant of that latitude, that it almost comprehends all, that is a *homo*. **1797** *Encycl. Brit.* X. 507/2 In the *Systema Naturæ*, Man (*Homo*) is ranked as a distinct genus of the order *Primates*. **1802** W. TURTON tr. *Linnæus's Gen. Syst. Nature* I. 9 Homo. *Sapiens*. Diurnal; varying by education and situation. *a* **1843** SOUTHEY *Comm.-pl. Bk.* (1849) IV. 419 One of these homo's had 800 head of game in his larder. **1861** THACKERAY *Philip* Wks. 1887 I. v. 155 But, being *homo*, and liable to err. **1864** *Rep. Brit. Assoc. 1863* II. 82 The author [*sc.* W. King] is led to regard the Neanderthal skull as belonging to a creature cranially and psychically different from man; and he proposes to distinguish the species by the name of *Homo Neanderthalensis*. **1886** BESANT *Childr. Gibeon* II. iii. I. 285 A Homo in the abstract, male or female. **1896** KIRKALDY & POLLARD tr. *Boas' Text-bk. Zool.* 536 All Men are usually regarded as one species, *Homo sapiens*, divided into a number of races. **1924** G. ELLIOT SMITH *Evol. Man* ii. 76 The Rhodesian species was the most primitive member of the genus *Homo* at present known. **1940** *Nature* 17 Feb. 261/1 Many anthropologists, disregarding the rules of nomenclature, relegate all forms of Homo that do not differ structurally from what they loosely term 'modern man' to the sole species *Homo sapiens*. **1964** L. S. B. LEAKEY et al. *Ibid.* 4 Apr. 8/1 Genus *Homo* Linnæus. Species *habilis* sp. nov. (Note: The specific name is taken from the Latin, meaning 'able, handy, mentally skilful, vigorous'. We are indebted to Prof. Raymond Dart for the suggestion that *habilis* would be a suitable name for the new species.) **1969** LEAKEY & GOODALL *Unveiling Man's Origins* (1970) p. xiv, The word *Homo* is the scientific name for the genus of man, and includes the species *sapiens*, which is man as we know him today, and other species such as *erectus* and *habilis*. Many other species names, in this genus, have been proposed from time to time (such as *heidelbergensis* and *neanderthalensis*) but these are not now generally recognized. **1971** J. Z. YOUNG *Introd. Study Man* xxxi. 444 Most of the characteristics of *Homo* seem to have evolved well within the Pleistocene. **1971** *Sci. Amer.* Dec. 42 In a heavy brow ridge and a low forehead, the Pyrenees fossils more closely resemble *Homo erectus*, the 500,000-year-old fossil man of Java and China.

c. Used with L. or mock-L. adjs. in names imitating *Homo sapiens*, etc., and intended to personify some aspect of human life or behaviour (indicated by the adj.). ***Homo faber*** ('feɪbə(r)) [H. Bergson *L'Evolution Créatrice* (1907) ii. 151], a term used to designate man as a maker of tools.

1911 A. MITCHELL tr. *Bergson's Creative Evolution* ii. 146 We should say perhaps not *Homo sapiens*, but *Homo faber*. **1934** A. TOYNBEE *Study Hist.* III. 229 As *Homo Belligerans*, he focuses his convergent beams upon a single point on an aerial plane that is determined by the momentary presence of a hostile piece of aircraft. **1944** H. G. WELLS *'42 to '44* II. 100 Since poor rambling *Homo insipiens* began to put facts together and ask questions about them, he has been accumulating a vast disorder of answers. **1946** M. L. ANDISON tr. *Bergson's Creative Mind* ii. 99, I believe that it is of man's essence to create materially and morally, to fabricate things and to fabricate himself. Homo faber is the definition I propose. **1948** *Education* (Boston) Oct. 80/2 The range of possible noises that homo loquens can produce is ultimately conditioned by the structure of the human vocal apparatus and hearing apparatus. **1956** A. HUXLEY *Adonis & Alphabet* 10 There are many anthropologists who prefer to think of man as *homo faber*—the smith, the maker of tools. **1959** *Encounter* July 46/1 The Stoic philosophers..seem to have made much of these emblems of moral dangers, turning..Odysseus into the ideal *homo viator*. **1960** E. DELAVENAY *Introd. Machine Transl.* 1 We can therefore rely on the inventiveness of *homo faber*. **1961** *Times* 25 Apr. 15/7 Symbolizing..this concept of *homo turisticus*, the new Hilton hotel..will have 500 rooms—all with a view of the Parthenon. **1962** *Daily Tel.* 7 Apr. 13 The bustling homo-sapiens was becoming homo-sedentarius, a quiet animal who sat and used his intelligence to push buttons and pull switches. **1962** M. MCLUHAN *Gutenberg Galaxy* 70 As long as *homo sedens* avoids the more potent kinds of optical conditioning..the mere shades of sacral life, as between nomadic and sedentary man, do not faze Eliade. **1963** AUDEN *Dyer's Hand* II. 88 Something managers need to be reminded of, namely, that the managed are people with faces,..that *Homo Laborans* is also *Homo Ludens*. **1964** *English Studies* XLV. (Suppl.) 244 An arraignment of Walter Pater in his quality as homo aestheticus. **1972** *N.Y. Times Bk. Rev.* 26 Nov. 22/3 *Homo lexicographicus* is a chalcenterous subspecies of mankind. **1973** HOLT & MARJORAM *Maths. in Changing World* ii. 21 On a more sophisticated level of appreciation, there seems to be evidence for an evolution of intelligence from *Homo faber*, the tool-user, to *Homo sapiens*, the wise one.

homo ('həʊməʊ), *sb.*[2] and *a.* A colloq. abbrev. of HOMOSEXUAL *a.* and *sb.*

A. *sb.*

1929 M. LIEF *Hangover* vi. 100 Do you think Will Hays will let that play get by—with all those homos and everything? **1933** C. MACKENZIE *Water on Brain* iv. 44 There's a nasty old homo at the next table trying to catch your eye. **1967** *Listener* 21 Sept. 381/2 Sally's breathless confession to Dr Dale about hubby being a homo must have caused many a benighted bigot's heart to stop. **1973** A. S. NEILL *Neill! Neill! Orange Peel!* (rev. ed.) II. 216, I never had any symptoms of homosexuality but I wonder if some homos could date their condition to some early incident that made a girl, and subsequently all girls, taboo.

B. *adj.*

1933 E. A. ROBERTSON *Ordinary Families* xiii. 271 Round about six, fifteen and twenty are the recognized 'homo' ages in women. **1957** F. KING *Man on Rock* iv. 120 Sometimes they muttered to each other that he was 'homo'.

Hence '**homoism** (*nonce-wd.*), homosexuality; homosexual practices.

1949 WYNDHAM LEWIS *Let.* 3 Mar. (1963) 480 Homoism died down in the 'thirties, but is so prevalent now as to be the [word] among the student or intellectual young.

homo-, before a vowel **hom-**. **a.** combining form of Gr. ὁμός same; a formative of many scientific and other terms, often in opposition to *hetero-*. The more important of these, with their derivatives, will be found in their alphabetical places; others, of less importance or frequency, follow here.

The pronunciation of the first syllable, with primary or secondary stress, varies; etymologically the *o* is short (ɒ) and is so usually pronounced by scholars (cf. HOLO-); but popularly it is often (əʊ); when stressless it is (əʊ) (though some make it (ɒ)).

homacanth ('hɒməkænθ) *a.* *Ichth.* [Gr. ἄκανθα thorn, spine], having the spines of the dorsal and anal fins symmetrical; opp. to *heteracanth*; **homatomic** (hɒmə'tɒmɪk) *a.*, consisting of like atoms; opp. to *heteratomic*; **homaxonial** (-æk'səʊnɪəl), **homaxonic** (-æk'sɒnɪk) *adjs.*, in *Morphology*, having all the axes equal; **homobaric** (-'bærɪk) *a.* [Gr. βάρος weight], of uniform weight; **homoblastic** (hɒməʊ'blæstɪk) *a.* *Biol.* [Gr. βλαστός germ], arising from cells of the same kind; opp. to *heteroblastic*; **homobranchiate** (-'bræŋkɪət) *a.* *Zool.* [Gr. βράγχια gills], having gills of uniform structure: applied to decapod crustaceans; opp. to *heterobranchiate*; **homocarpous** (-'kɑːpəs) *a.* *Bot.* [Gr. καρπός fruit], applied to composite plants in which all the fruits arising from a flower-head are alike; opp. to *heterocarpous*; **homocategoric** (ˌhɒməʊkætɪ'gɒrɪk) *a.* [see CATEGORIC], belonging to the same category; '**homocharge**, the charge on an electret polarized in the same direction as the original polarizing field; **homochiral** (hɒməʊ'kaɪərəl) *a.* [Gr. χείρ hand], of identical form and turned in the same direction, as two right or two left hands; opp. to *heterochiral*; hence **homo'chirally** *adv.*; **homochla'mydeous** *a.* *Bot.* [Gr. χλαμύς cloak], having the outer and inner layers of the perianth alike, not differentiated into sepals and petals; † **homo'chresious** (erron. -cresious) *a.* *Obs.* [Gr. χρῆσις use], relating to the same commodity or use; opp. to *heterochresious*; **homochromic** (-'krəʊmɪk), **-chromous** (-'krəʊməs) *adjs.* [Gr. χρῶμα colour], of the same colour, as the florets of most *Compositæ*; opp. to *heterochromous*; see also quot. 1876; **ho'mochromy** *Zool.*, cryptic colouring (of an animal); **homochronous** (həʊ'mɒkrənəs) *a.* [Gr. χρόνος time], occurring at the same time, or at corresponding times (cf. HETEROCHRONOUS); **homo'cyclic** *a.* *Chem.*, containing or designating a ring formed of atoms of a single element; **homodemic** (-'dɛmɪk) *a.* [Gr. δῆμος people, tribe] = *homophylic*; **homodermatous** (-'dɜːmətəs), **-dermous** (-'dɜːməs) *adjs.* *Zool.* [Gr. δέρμα skin], having the skin or integument of uniform structure, as certain serpents; opp. to *heterodermatous*; **homo'dermic** *a.* *Biol.* [as prec.], derived from, or relating to derivation from, the same primary blastoderm (endoderm, mesoderm, or ectoderm) of the embryo; **homo'desmic** *a.* *Chem.* [Gr. δεσμ-ός bond], containing only a single kind of chemical bond; **homody'namic** *a.* *Ent.* [ad. F. *homodyname* (E. Roubaud 1922, in *Bull. Biol. de la France et de la Belg.* LVI. 470)], (of an insect, its life cycle, etc.) characterized by a continuous succession of generations throughout the year, so long as reasonably favourable conditions prevail; **homodynamous** (hɒməʊ'dɪnəməs) *a.* *Comp. Anat.* [Gr. δύναμις power, force], (*a*) having the same force or value; applied (after Gegenbaur) to parts serially homologous; (*b*) = *homodynamic* adj.; so **homodynamy** (-'dɪnəmɪ), the condition of being homodynamous; '**homodyne** [after HETERODYNE], a name given to a radio receiver and a method of detection which employs a local oscillator tuned to the carrier frequency of the detected signal; **homogangliate** (-'gæŋglɪət) *a.* *Zool.*, having the ganglia of the nervous system symmetrically arranged, as in the *Articulata*; opp. to *heterogangliate*; **homoglot** ('hɒməglɒt) *a.* [Gr. -γλωττος -tongued; cf. *polyglot*], having the same language; **homo'hedral** *a.* [Gr. ἕδρα seat, base], (properly) having like or corresponding faces; but used by Miller as = HOLOHEDRAL; '**homojunction** *Electronics* [JUNCTION 2b], an area of contact between different conductivity types of a single semiconducting material; **homo'lateral** *a.*, on or affecting the same side of the body; **homo'lecithal** *a.* *Embryol.* [Gr. λέκιθος yolk of an egg], (of an egg cell) having the yolk uniformly distributed throughout the cytoplasm; **homomalous** (həʊ'mɒmələs) *a.* *Bot.* [Gr. ὁμαλός even, level], applied to leaves or branches (esp. of mosses) which turn in the same direction: opp. to *heteromalous*; **ho'momeral, -'omerous** *adjs.* [Gr. μέρος part], having like or corresponding parts (*Cent. Dict.*); **homo'metrical** *a.*, in the same metre; hence **homo'metrically** *adv.*; **homo'morphosis** *Biol.*, the regeneration of an organ or part similar to the one lost; **homonemeous** (-'niːmɪəs) *a.* *Bot.* [Gr. νῆμα thread, filament], applied (after Fries) to algæ and fungi in which the filaments in germination produce a homogeneous body; opp. to *heteronemeous* (Mayne *Expos. Lex.* 1854); **homo-organ** *Biol.* = HOMOPLAST 2; **homopathy** (həʊ'mɒpəθɪ) [Gr. ὁμοπάθεια, f. πάθος suffering], sameness of feeling, sympathy (cf.

HETEROPATHY); **homoperiˈodic** *a.*, agreeing in having the same periods; **homopetalous** (-ˈpɛtələs) *a. Bot.*, having the petals alike; opp. to *heteropetalous* (Mayne 1854); **homophyadic** (-faɪˈædɪk) *a. Bot.* [late Gr. φυάς, φυαδ- shoot, sucker], producing only one kind of stem, as some species of *Equisetum*; opp. to *heterophyadic*; **homophylic** (-ˈfɪlɪk) *a. Biol.* [cf. Gr. ὁμόφυλος of the same race or stock], belonging to the same race; relating to homophyly; **homophyllous** (hɒməʊˈfɪləs) *a. Bot.* [Gr. φύλλον leaf], 'having leaves or leaflets all alike' (Mayne 1854); opp. to *heterophyllous*; **homophyly** (həʊˈmɒfɪlɪ) [Gr. ὁμοφυλία], the condition of being of the same race; **homoˈpolymer** *Chem.*, a polymer formed from only one kind of monomer; so **ˌhomopolyˈmeric** *a.*; **ˌhomopolymeriˈzation** *Chem.* [a. G. *homopolymerisation* (T. Wagner-Jauregg 1930, in *Ber. d. Deut. Chem. Ges.* LXIII. 3213)], a reaction in which identical molecules become joined, forming a homopolymer; so **homoˈpolymerize** *v. trans.* and *intr.*, to form a homopolymer (of); **ˌhomopolyˈsaccharide** *Chem.*, any polysaccharide composed of molecules of a single monosaccharide; **homoproral** (-ˈprɔərəl) *a. Zool.* [L. *prōra* prow], having equal or similar proræ, as a pterocymba in sponges; opp. to *heteroproral*; **hoˈmorgan** *Biol.* = *homo-organ*; **ˌhomosceˈdastic** *a. Statistics* [Gr. σκεδαστ-ός capable of being scattered (σκεδάννῡμι to scatter)], of equal scatter or variation; having equal variances; so **ˌhomoscedaˈsticity**; **homoseismal** (-ˈsaɪzməl) *a.* and *sb.*, **homoˈseismic** *a.* [Gr. σεισμός earthquake], proposed substitutes for COSEISMAL, COSEISMIC; **homosporous** (həʊˈmɒspərəs) *a. Bot.* [Gr. σπόρος seed], producing only one kind of spores; opp. to *heterosporous*; **homoˈstatic** *a. Med.* and *Biol.*, applied to transplant tissue which is inert and not actively growing in the donor's body; opp. *homovital* adj.; **homostaural** (-ˈstɔːrəl) *a.* [Gr. σταυρός cross], having a regular polygon as the base of the pyramid; said of a homopolar, stauraxonial figure; opp. to *heterostaural*; **homosystemic** (-sɪˈstɛmɪk) *a.*, belonging to the same system; **homotatic** (-ˈtætɪk) *a. Dynamics* [Gr. τατός vbl. adj. of τείνειν to stretch; τάσις stretching, tension], 'pertaining to a homogeneous stress' (*Cent. Dict.*); **homoteleutic** (-tɪˈljuːtɪk) *a.* [cf. HOMŒOTELEUTIC], having the same ending; **homoˈthallic** *a. Biol.*, (of a fungus) having no genetically controlled incompatibility system; not heterothallic; so **homoˈthallism**, **-ˈthally**, the condition of being homothallic; **ˈhomotherm** *Zool.* = *homœotherm* (s.v. HOMŒOTHERMIC *a.*); **homoˈthermic** *a. Zool.* = HOMŒOTHERMIC *a.*; **homothermous** (-ˈθɜːməs) *a. Biol.* [Gr. θερμός hot], having a uniform temperature, which does not vary with that of the surroundings, as warm-blooded animals; opp. to *heterothermal*; **homothetic** (-ˈθɛtɪk) *a. Geom.* [Gr. θετικός, f. τιθέναι to place], similar and similarly placed; also extended to any figures in homology with reference to the line at infinity as axis of homology; †**homoˈtimous** *a. Obs.* [Gr. ὁμότῑμος, f. τῑμή honour], held in equal honour; **homotonous** (həʊˈmɒtənəs) *a.* [Gr. τόνος tone], having the same tone or sound; hence **hoˈmotonously** *adv.*; so **hoˈmotony**, sameness of tone; **homoˈvital** *a. Med.* and *Biol.*, applied to transplant tissue which in the donor's body contains actively multiplying cells; opp. *homostatic* adj.

1880 GÜNTHER *Fishes* 41 If in the depressed position the spines cover one another completely, their points lying in the same line, the fish is called *homacanth. **1883** P. GEDDES in *Encycl. Brit.* XVI. 845/1 Questions of symmetry, for which Haeckel's nomenclature of **homaxonial, homopolic*, etc. is distinctly preferable. **1885** E. R. LANKESTER *Ibid.* XIX. 849/2 A spherical (*homaxonic)..perforated shell of membranous consistence. *a* **1889** *N.Y. Herald* (Worcester Suppl.), A *homobaric cargo. **1888** *Homoblastic [see *heteroblastic* s.v. HETERO-]. **1854** MAYNE *Expos. Lex.* s.v. *Homobranchiatus, Crustacea*, including such as have gills pyramidal and composed of layers piled one upon another: *homobranchiate. *Ibid.*, *Homocarpus*,..*homocarpous. **1866** *Treas. Bot.*, *Homocarpous*, having all the fruits of a flower-head exactly alike. **1883** P. GEDDES in *Encycl. Brit.* XVI. 845/1 Whether two organisms..are of the same category of individuality..are *homocategoric. **1935** A. GEMANT in *Phil. Mag.* XX. 933 We observe both kinds of charges on electrets. One has the opposite sign to that of the adjacent polarizing electrode,..the other has the same sign as the adjacent polarizing electrode, and will be denoted as *homocharge. **1965** *New Scientist* 27 May 590/2 Under a certain critical applied field the heterocharge decays to a constant value and a homocharge does not appear. **1879** *Homochiral [see *heterochiral* s.v. HETERO-]. **1889** SIR W. THOMSON *Math. & Phys. Papers* (1890) III. 410 *note*, Two men of exactly equal and similar external figures would be ..*homochirally similar if each holds out his right hand, or each his left. **1893** —— in *Academy* (1894) 1 Sept. 150/2 Two equal and similar right-hands are homochirally similar. **1895** S. H. VINES *Students' Text-bk. Bot.* II. 512 When the perianth-leaves are all alike, the flower is said to be *homochlamydeous. **1876** tr. *Haeckel's Hist. Creat.* I. xi. 263 Darwin's *homochromic selection of animals, or the so-called 'sympathetic selection of colours'. **1842** BRANDE *Dict. Sci.* etc., **Homochromous.* **1850** HOOKER & ARNOTT *Brit. Flora* (ed. 6) 199 *Tanacetum.* Heads discoid, homochromous. **1899** *Natural Sci.* Dec. 396 *Homochromy and other protective adaptations. **1967** *Oceanogr. & Marine Biol.* V. 470 The chiton *Middendorfia caprearum* shows a conspicuous homochromy with the substratum. **1876** tr. *Haeckel's Hist. Creat.* I. 217 The law of contemporaneous or *homochronous transmission, which Darwin calls the law of 'transmission in corresponding periods of life'. **1612** STURTEVANT *Metallica* (1854) 70 *Homocresious inuentions are such which produce..emporeuticall workes for the same use. So a horse-milne, a water-milne, a wind-milne are Homocresious, because they all grinde flower. **1903** *Nature* 17 Sept. 475/1 The rings may be either *homocyclic or heterocyclic without the character of the spectra being altered. **1932** H. G. RULE tr. *Schmidt's Text-bk. Org. Chem.* (ed. 2) II. i. 347 These [*sc.* carbocyclic compounds] are sometimes called homocyclic or isocyclic compounds. **1961** G. M. BADGER *Chem. Heterocyclic Compounds* i. 10 The systematic method for naming dicyclic and polycyclic compounds follows that used for homocyclic compounds. **1883** P. GEDDES in *Encycl. Brit.* XVI. 845/1 The parts and units thus recognized by ontogenetic research, respectively or successively homodermic, homosystemic, and *homodemic, may..be termed..either 'specially homologous', 'homogenous', 'homophylic', or 'homogenetic' in the language of phylogenetic theory. **1854** MAYNE *Expos. Lex.*, *Homodermatous. **1883** *Homodermic [see *homodemic*]. **1886** VINES in *Encycl. Brit.* XX. 421/1 This correspondence, which is of high..importance in determining homologies, may be termed homodermic. **1886** *Syd. Soc. Lex.*, **Homodermous*,..applied to those snakes which have the scales equal in size over the body. **1939** R. C. EVANS *Introd. Crystal Chem.* i. 8 Crystals..in which only one type of force occurs, are said to be *homodesmic. **1957** H. D. MEGAW *Ferroelectr. in Crystals* 205 In a homodesmic structure it is incorrect to speak of 'molecule' or 'molecular weight', since the molecule is coextensive with the crystal. **1931** *Trans. Entomol. Soc.* LXXIX. 105 The outstanding characteristic of this *homodynamic..type of development is the absence of a definite annual life-cycle, the number of generations in a year depending on the actual weather conditions. **1964** BORROR & DELONG *Introd. Study Insects* (rev. ed.) iii. 44 Many insects, particularly those living in the tropics, have a homodynamic life cycle; that is, development is continuous and there is no regular period of dormancy. **1878** BELL *Gegenbaur's Comp. Anat.* 415 They appear to be *homodynamous organs, which gradually get to vary greatly in form in correlation with their great variety of function. *Ibid.* 446 Nerves..homodynamous with the spinal nerves. **1929** V. E. SHELFORD *Lab. & Field Ecol.* vi. 160 Roubaud separates the higher Diptera into two categories, homodynamous and heterodynamous. **1878** BELL *Gegenbaur's Comp. Anat.* 64 *Homodynamy..subsists between parts of the body which are affected by a general morphological phænomenon serially expressed in the organism. **1928** STERLING & KRUSE *Radio Man.* iv. 149 If the local generated frequency is tuned to exactly the same frequency as the received signals..the condition of 'zero beat' is said to exist. This means of receiving has also been termed '*homodyne' method. **1965** *New Scientist* 11 Feb. 344/1 The approach adopted..is to stabilise the laser at a single frequency, using an 'optical homodyne' receiver. The system uses a helium-neon laser stabilised at 6328 angstroms as both transmitter and local oscillator. **1835–6** TODD *Cycl. Anat.* I. 245/1 This *homo-gangliate disposition of the nervous system. **1841–71** T. R. JONES *Anim. Kingd.* (ed. 4) 291 The jointed legs developed in more highly organized forms of homogangliate beings. **1859** *Life E. Henderson* 123 The inhabitants of Scania and those of Zealand may have been *homoglot. **1877** W. A. MILLER *Elem. Chem.* (ed. 6) I. §82. 143 **Homohedral* or *Holohedral* forms, are those which..possess the highest degree of symmetry of which the system admits. **1960** R. L. ANDERSON in *IBM Jrnl. Res. & Devel.* IV. 287 Junctions between two dissimilar semiconductors will be referred to as heterojunctions and those in the same semiconductor with different doping as *homojunctions. **1966** *New Scientist* 11 Aug. 316/3 On bringing two conductivity types of the same material..into contact, in a homojunction, considerable border disturbances take place between the hordes of electrons and holes confronting each other. **1971** *Sci. Amer.* July 39/2 The structure therefore has a *p-n* junction in gallium arsenide (a homojunction). **1910** *Practitioner* July 98 Should the lesion be in or close to the red nucleus, the tremor will be on the opposite side of the body, while if any other part of the system be affected the tremor will be *homolateral. **1919** *Jrnl. Exper. Zool.* XXIX. 255 At the sides of the body, those parts innervated by the pallial strands are conspicuously homolateral in their responses. **1956** *Nature* 17 Mar. 529/2 These thoracic responses also remained when the major portion of the homolateral corpora pedunculata was removed. **1892** E. L. MARK tr. *Hertwig's Text-bk. Embryol.* i. 28 The translator has been accustomed for several years to use the word *homolecithal instead of alecithal, heterolecithal being employed as a coördinate term to embrace telolecithal and centrolecithal eggs. **1914** W. E. KELLICOTT *Textbk. Gen. Embryol.* iii. 93 It is often difficult to distinguish the telolecithal egg from the homolecithal type. **1958** B. M. PATTEN *Found. Embryol.* iv. 78 In the egg of *Amphioxus* the yolk is relatively meager in amount and fairly uniformly distributed throughout the cell. An ovum with such a yolk distribution is termed isolecithal (homolecithal). **1854** MAYNE *Expos. Lex.*, *Homomallus*,..*homomallous. **1864** WEBSTER, *Homomalous.* **1881** WEST in *Jrnl. Bot.* X. No. 220. 115 In *Timmia austriaca*..they [the leaves] seem to have a homomallous tendency. **1854** MAYNE *Expos. Lex.*, *Homomeris*,..those in which the rings of the body are like each other: *homomerous. **1877** C. B. CAYLEY (*title*) The Iliad of Homer, *Homometrically translated. **1901** T. H. MORGAN *Regeneration* 23 When the new part is like that removed, or like a part of that removed, as when a leg or a tail is regenerated in a newt, the process is one of '*homomorphosis'. **1967** GARDINER & FLEMISTER *Princ. Gen. Biol.* (ed. 2) xxii. 464/1 The conditions of homo- and heteromorphosis make it apparent that in the construction of a new part the old exerts some kind of influence. **1883** P. GEDDES in *Encycl. Brit.* XVI. 842/2 The idorgan..is.. defined as a morphological unit consisting of two or more plastids, which does not possess the positive character of the person or stock. These are distinguished into *homoplasts* or **homo-organs* and *alloplasts* or *alloeorgans*. **1678** CUDWORTH *Intell. Syst.* I. v. 826 That Συμπάθεια, or Ομοπάθεια, That Sympathy, or *Homopathy, which is in all Animals..It being One and the Same thing in them, which Perceives Pain, in the most distant Extremities of the Body..and which moves one Part to succour and relieve another labouring under it. **1893** FORSYTH *Th. Functions* §116. 224 Two functions which are doubly-periodic in the same period..*Note.* Such functions will be called *homoperiodic. *Ibid.* 226 Homoperiodic functions of the same class are equivalent to one another if they have the same infinities. **1889** BENNETT & MURRAY *Cryptog. Bot.* 113 The classification of the species into two distinct groups of '*homophyadic' and 'heterophyadic' is not a natural one. **1883** *Homophylic [see *homodemic*]. **1883** P. GEDDES in *Encycl. Brit.* XVI. 845/1 Haeckel proposed to term **homophyly* the truly phylogenetic homology in opposition to *homomorphy*, to which genealogic basis is wanting. **1946** A. M. Ross in Richardson & Wilson *Fund. Plastics* ix. 146 Neither the vinyl chloride-vinyl acetate copolymers nor the vinylidene chloride-vinyl chloride copolymers can be fractionated so as to yield either pure *homopolymer. **1970** *New Scientist* 30 Apr. 230/3 Teflon homopolymers are good reinforcing fillers. **1971** *Nature* 26 Nov. 197/1 Combinations of synthetic primer oligomers with *homopolymeric templates..allow one to distinguish the viral enzyme from other DNA polymerases. **1931** *Chem. Abstr.* XXV. 2419 The hydrocarbons which are well adapted to heteropolymerization show no marked tendency to *homopolymerization. **1937** R. S. MORRELL et al. *Synthetic Resins* x. 251 Products..not easily obtained by homopolymerization. **1963** A. J. HALL *Textile Sci.* ii. 88 It [*sc.* acrylonitrile] very readily undergoes polymerisation by itself (homopolymerisation) and with other polymerisable compounds (copolymerisation). **1952** C. E. SCHILDKNECHT *Vinyl & Related Polymers* iii. 173, 2-Isopropenyl thiophenes would not *homopolymerize on heating with peroxide catalyst, but..copolymerized with butadiene. **1957** *Ann. N.Y. Acad. Sci.* LXIX. 334 Some amino acids.. do not homopolymerize to linear peptides under the thermal conditions that were employed. **1970** *Nature* 3 Jan. 60/1 *Bis*-(betachloroethyl) vinyl phosphonate is difficult to homopolymerize by a free radical mechanism to high molecular weight polymers. **1948** W. W. PIGMAN *Chem. Carbohydrates* xii. 513 Members of the first class (*homopolysaccharides) give only one monosaccharide type when completely hydrolyzed. **1970** G. O. ASPINALL *Polysaccharides* i. 5 The first broad division in the classification of polysaccharides is between homopolysaccharides..and heteropolysaccharides. **1887** *Homoproral [see *heteroproral* s.v. HETERO-]. **1905** K. PEARSON in *Drapers' Company Res. Mem.* (Biometric Ser.) II. 22 If..all arrays are equally scattered about their means, I shall speak of the system as a *homoscedastic system, otherwise it is a heteroscedastic system. **1934** *Brit. Jrnl. Psychol.* XXIV. 337 It is essential for factor studies that the correlation surfaces of the pairs of variables should be comparable. This is the case when each is homoscedastic, homoclitic, with rectilinear regression lines. **1970** *Nature* 12 Dec. 1098/1 Although the compared sample groups appear to be homoscedastic (F test) and results from the t test are significant ($P < 0{\cdot}001$), the size of the sample population is so small that we have relied on the non-parametric Mann-Whitney U test. **1905** *Drapers' Company Res. Mem.* (Biometric Ser.) II. 22, $\chi_1 = 1$ is a necessary result of *homoscedasticity. **1957** DIXON & MASSEY *Introd. Statistical Analysis* (ed. 2) xi. 199 The regression curve of Y on X and the regression curve of X on Y are both straight lines with homoscedasticity (constant variance) for both X and Y variables. **1887** GOEBEL *Morphol. Plants* 228 The heterosporous [family]..Salvineaceae comes very near to the *homosporous Ferns. **1952** W. P. LONGMIRE in *Jrnl. Nat. Cancer Inst.* XIV. 669 The term **homostatic graft* might be applied to inert tissues such as bone and cartilage when transferred from one individual to another of the same species; and the term *homovital graft* might be used in reference to grafts whose cells must continue to grow and reproduce for the graft to be effective after similar transplantation. **1971** BILLINGHAM & SILVERS *Immunobiol. Transplantation* vi. 93 The long-term preservation of homostatic grafts is relatively simple. **1883** *Homosystemic [see *homodemic*]. **1821** *Blackw. Mag.* X. 384 They are merely *homoteleutic, and..do not rhyme any more than *correct* with *direct*. **1904, 1959** *Homothallic [see *heterothallic* adj. s.v. HETERO-]. **1967** M. E. HALE *Biol. Lichens* iii. 42 There is good reason..to suppose that lichens are homothallic. **1906** A. F. BLAKESLEE in *Science* 27 July 120/2 *Homothallism and heterothallism therefore seem to be fixed conditions in the forms in which the sexual character has been determined. **1966** J. R. RAPER *Genetics of Sexuality in Higher Fungi* iii. 40 Three types of homothallism are found among self-fertile species. **1942** *Nature* 10 Jan. 56/1 It is also possible that such behaviour exists as a stage in the transit between full *homothally and full heterothally. **1949** DARLINGTON & MATHER *Elem. Genetics* xii. 240 In some fungi..two cells of a single haploid hypha fuse in sexual reproduction. This is called homothally. **1934** WEBSTER, *Homotherm. **1960** K. SCHMIDT-NIELSEN *Animal Physiol.* iii. 42 As an example of temperature regulation in a homotherm, let us look at the situation in man. **1971** *Language* XLVII. 417 Homotherms—that is, warm-blooded vertebrates, such as birds and mammals. **1890** BILLINGS *Med. Dict.* I, *Homothermic. **1901** *Proc. R. Soc.* LXVIII. 353 Variation in production of heat is the ancestral method of homothermic adjustment. **1960** K. SCHMIDT-NIELSEN *Anim. Physiol.* iii. 38 Homothermic animals maintain a constant body temperature. **1881** I. C. ROSSE *Cruise Corwin* 12 Such *homothermous animals as whales, seals, walrus [etc.]. **1880** G. S. CARR *Synops. Math.* Index, *Homothetic conics. **1892** ROUTH *Analyt. Statics* II. §182 A shell bounded by two similar and similarly situated surfaces has been called a *homothetic shell* by Chasles (1837). This is a convenient term when the surfaces are either not

concentric or not ellipsoids. **1658** J. ROBINSON *Eudoxa* v. 36 We speak of *Homotimous persons, level in the same degree of honour. **1775** ASH, **Homotonous.* **1785** COWPER in *Life & Wks.* (1835–7) II. 195 To discover homotonous words in a language abounding with them like ours, is a task that would puzzle no man competently acquainted with it. **1855** BAGEHOT *Lit. Stud.* (1895) I. 141 Closing every couplet with sounds homotonous. **1822–34** *Homotonously [see *heterotonously* s.v. HETERO-]. **1763** LANGHORNE *Effus. Friendsh.* (L.), Thomson has often fallen into the *homotony of the couplet. **1952** *Homovital [see *homostatic* above]. **1959** P. B. MEDAWAR in L. A. Peer *Transplantation of Tissues* II. ii. 41 Homovital grafts start alive and.. remain so, but homostatic grafts are progressively revitalized by the tissues of their hosts.

b. In *Chemistry*, denoting a compound homologous with that whose name follows (see HOMOLOGOUS 3), as in ***homatropine***, ***homocuminic***, ***homolactic***, ***homosalycilic acids***, ***homocinchonine***, ***homofluoresceine***, ***homopyrocatechin***, ***homoquinine***.

1865–72 WATTS *Dict. Chem.* III. 163 *Homocuminic Acid*, an acid homologous with cuminic acid. *Ibid.*, *Homolactic Acid*,..name..given by Cloez..to an acid, isomeric if not identical, with glycollic acid. **1880** *W. A. Miller's Chem.* (ed. 6) III. I. 684 Creosol or Homocatechol Monomethylin. **1881** *Athenæum* 15 Jan. 99/3 Homo-fluoresceine, a new Colouring Matter from Orcine and its Derivatives. *Ibid.* 24 Dec. 856/3 The authors have extracted from the bark of the China Cupræa an alkaloid closely resembling quinine in its general properties.. They have named it homoquinine.

homocaryon, -caryosis, -caryotic: see HOMOKARYOTIC *a.*

homocentric (hɒməʊˈsɛntrɪk), *a.* and *sb.* [ad. mod.L. *homocentric-us* (1535 Fracastoro *Homocentricorum*), f. Gr. ὁμο- HOMO- + κεντρικ-ός CENTRIC; cf. F. *homocentrique* (1690 Furetière), *homocentricalement* (*a* 1553 Rabelais).]

A. *adj.* **1.** Having the same centre, concentric.

1696 in PHILLIPS (ed. 5). **1834** *Nat. Philos., Hist. Astron.* vi. 30/1 (U.K.S.) A circle homocentric with the ecliptic. **1952** G. SARTON *Hist. Sci.* I. xx. 510 The main achievement of the astronomers of this period, if not of Aristotle himself, was the completion of the theory of homocentric spheres.

2. Of rays of light or a beam of particles: diverging from or converging to a single focal point (or appearing to do so when produced).

1886 C. M. CULVER tr. *Landolt's Refraction & Accommodation of Eye* i. 13 In order that the homocentric rays may remain homocentric, the surface must have such a form that the angles of incidence shall be everywhere the same. **1949** *Proc. R. Soc.* A. CXCVII. 456 An electron gun, combined with a suitable aperture and electron lens system, produces a coherent illuminating beam, as nearly homocentric as possible. **1969** G. A. FRY *Geom. Optics* vi. 41 As long as the wave fronts are spherical and concentric, the rays all converge at the center of curvature of the wave front and constitute a homocentric bundle of rays.

†**B.** *sb.* (In old Astronomy.) A sphere or circle concentric with another or with the earth: opp. to ECCENTRIC B. 1. *Obs.*

1621 BURTON *Anat. Mel.* II. ii. III. (1651) 251 Maginus makes eleven Heavens.. Fracastorius 72 Homocentricks.

So †**ˈhomocentre** = B.; †**homoˈcentrical** *a.* = A.; hence **homocenˈtricity**, the condition of being homocentric; **homoˈcentrically** *adv.*

1686 GOAD *Celest. Bodies* II. i. 124 The Luminaries..[are] far from being Homocentrical, as possible the Infancy of the World, with Fracastorius since might imagine. **1690** LEYBOURN *Curs. Math.* 735, I call that Circle an Homocentre, which has the same Centre that the Earth has. *a* **1693** URQUHART *Rabelais* III. xxii. 178 Homocentrically poysed. **1959** BORN & WOLF *Princ. Optics* iv. 168 In general, the homocentricity of a pencil is destroyed on refraction or reflection.

homocerc (ˈhɒməʊsɜːk), *sb.* and *a.* *Ichthyol.* Also -cerque. [f. HOMO- + Gr. κέρκ-ος tail.]

A. *sb.* A homocercal fish. **B.** *adj.* = next.

1876 PAGE *Adv. Text-bk. Geol.* xvii. 308 The homocerque or equally-lobed, and the undivided tails become the .. normal forms.

homocercal (hɒməʊˈsɜːkəl), *a.* *Ichthyol.* [f. as prec. + -AL[1].] Having the lobes of the tail equal; having a symmetrical tail. Also said of the tail. Opp. to *heterocercal*.

1838 *Penny Cycl.* XII. 191/1 In and above that [oolitic] system Homocercal forms appear. **1849** MURCHISON *Siluria* xiii. 342 All other species now living..have homocercal tails. **1880** *Nature* XXI. 430 The diphycercal tail is a more primitive.. form than the heterocercal, of which the modern homocercal is a further specialisation.

So **ˈhomocercy** (-sɜːsɪ), homocercal condition.

1881 in WORCESTER Suppl.

homock, obs. var. HUMMOCK.

homoclime (ˈhɒməʊklaɪm). *Geogr.* [f. HOMO- + Gr. κλίμα (see CLIMATE) or Eng. CLIME.] A region or place that has a similar climate to some given region.

Orig. defined more narrowly: see quot. 1916.

1916 T. G. TAYLOR *Control of Settlement* (Commonwealth Bur. Meteorol. Bull. XIV) 23 Those regions in which climate, topography, and industries, &c., are similar I call 'homoclimes'. *Ibid.*, Homo-climes are British Isles, North France, much of the German Empire, [etc.]. **1931** A. A. MILLER *Climatology* ii. 14 Stations having similar climographs are described as 'homoclimes'. Alice Springs is the homoclime of Biskra (Algeria), Perth of Cape Town, Brisbane of Durban, etc. **1950** *New Biol.* VIII. 68 The first work to do..is to define the climate where the insects must be established, and to locate its homoclimes (i.e. areas of similar climate).

homocline (ˈhɒməʊklaɪn). *Geol.* [f. HOMO- + *cline*, as in *anticline*, *syncline*, etc.] A set of strata dipping throughout in the same general direction; *esp.* one over which the angle of dip is more or less uniform.

1915 R. A. DALY in *Geol. Survey Canada Mem.* LXVIII. 53 For convenience the word 'homocline' will here be used as a general name for any block of bedded rocks all dipping in the same direction... A 'homocline' may be a monocline, an isocline, a tilted fault-block, or one limb of anticline or syncline. **1942** M. P. BILLINGS *Struct. Geol.* iii. 42 The term homocline..may be applied to strata that dip in one direction at a uniform angle. Although many homoclines are, if large areas are considered, limbs of folds, the term is useful to refer to the structure within the limits of a small area. **1965** G. J. WILLIAMS *Econ. Geol. N.Z.* xix. 344/1 The dominant structure of the Tertiary beds of the Taranaki region is that of a gently (about 4°) south or south-south-east dipping homocline.

Hence **homoˈclinal** *a.*, of, pertaining to, or associated with a homocline.

1916 R. A. DALY in *Bull. Geol. Soc. Amer.* XXVII. 92 The broad, useful concept denoted by the 'monoclinal' of W. B. and H. D. Rogers needs a new name... They intended to name a body of strata showing throughout dip in the *same* direction and for that 'homocline' (or 'homoclinal'; adjective, 'homoclinal') is the appropriate word. **1922** C. A. COTTON *Geomorphol. N.Z.* I. viii. 98 A striking effect of homoclinal drifting is seen where a stream crosses the strike diagonally. **1941** —— *Landscape* x. 91 Moderately inclined strata now outcrop as homoclinal ridges. **1954** W. D. THORNBURY *Princ. Geomorphol.* ix. 225 Homoclinal ridges develop upon the dipping beds on the flanks of anticlines and synclines.

homocysteine (hɒməʊˈsɪstiːn, -ˈsɪstiːɪn). *Chem.* [f. HOMO- b + CYSTEINE.] An amino-acid, $HS{\cdot}CH_2{\cdot}CH_2{\cdot}CH(NH_2){\cdot}COOH$, which is important as an intermediate in the metabolism of methionine and cysteine.

1932 *Jrnl. Biol. Chem.* XCIX. 137 If the hydrolysis, however, should take place between the methyl group and the sulfur then methyl alcohol and homocysteine would result. **1935** *Ibid.* CXII. 149 (*heading*) The isolation of homocysteine and its conversion to a thiolactone. **1962** *Biochem. & Biophys. Res. Comm.* IX. 493 The normal pathway for the metabolism of methionine involves demethylation to homocysteine which in turn combines with serine to form cystathionine, an intermediate along the pathway to cysteine and cystine.

homocystine (hɒməʊˈsɪstiːn). *Chem.* [f. HOMO- b + CYSTINE.] An amino-acid $({-}S{\cdot}CH_2{\cdot}CH_2{\cdot}CH(NH_2){\cdot}COOH)_2$, which is the oxidized form of homocysteine.

1932 *Jrnl. Biol. Chem.* XCIX. 136 We have drawn the conclusion that the compound is bis-(γ-amino-γ-carboxy-propyl) disulphide, the next higher symmetrical homologue of cystine. Because of this relationship we wish to suggest the name of homocystine for the compound. **1962** *Biochem. & Biophys. Res. Comm.* IX. 493 (heading) The identification of homocystine in the urine.

Hence **ˌhomocystiˈnuria** [-URIA], a rare condition, caused by a hereditary enzyme deficiency, in which homocystine is present in the urine.

1962 CARSON & NEILL in *Arch. Dis. Childhood* XXXVII. 512/2 The following abnormalities were discovered... A so far undescribed abnormality in cystine metabolism, homocystinuria. **1969** *New Scientist* 3 July 10/1 Prevention of postnatal brain damage by dietary treatment has been reported in a number of other inborn errors of metabolism. Examples include galactosaemia, tyrosinosis, maple syrup urine disease and possibly homocystinuria.

homodont (ˈhɒməʊdɒnt), *a.* and *sb.* *Zool.* [mod. f. HOM(O- + Gr. ὀδούς, ὀδοντ- tooth.]

A. *adj.* Having teeth all of the same kind. Also said of the teeth. Opp. to *heterodont*. **B.** *sb.* A homodont animal.

1877 TURNER in *Encycl. Brit.* VII. 232/1 A few mammals, as the toothed whales, have the teeth uniform in size, shape, and structure, and are named Homodont. **1888** ROLLESTON & JACKSON *Anim. Life* 363 In homodont dentitions..the number [of teeth] is often great, e.g. 100 in *Priodon*.

†**homodox** (ˈhɒməʊdɒks), *a.* *Obs.* [ad. Gr. ὁμόδοξ-ος of the same opinion, f. ὁμο- HOMO- + δόξα opinion: cf. HETERODOX.] Of the same opinion. So †**homoˈdoxian** *a.* = prec.; *sb.* a person of the same opinion.

1656 BLOUNT *Glossogr.*, *Homodox*, that is of the same opinion with another. **1716** M. DAVIES *Athen. Brit.* II. To Rdr. 14 The Homodox Idolatry of the Cacodox Arians and Socinians. *Ibid.* 244 The Orthodox..Territories and Hereditaments of Homodox Antiquity. *Ibid.* II. 238 Homodoxian Witnesses to the Arian Law.

homodromous (həʊˈmɒdrəməs), *a.* [f. mod.L. *homodrom-us*, f. Gr. ὁμο- HOMO- + -δρομος running + -OUS. In mod.F. *homodrome*.] Running in the same direction: opp. to *heterodromous*. †**a.** *Mech.* Applied to levers of the second and third orders, in which the power and the weight move in the same direction. **b.** *Bot.* Turning in the same direction, as two generating spirals of a phyllotaxis (e.g. on the main stem and on a branch).

1710 J. HARRIS *Lex. Techn.* II. s.v. *Homodromus*, Of this Homodrom[o]us kind of Leavers, are the Rudders and Oars of Ships and Boats. **1870** [see HETERODROMOUS]. **1878** MASTERS *Henfrey's Bot.* 273 An inflorescence homodromous with the principal axis.

So **hoˈmodromal**, **ˈhomodrome** *adjs.* = prec. b.; **hoˈmodromy**, homodromous condition.

1849 J. H. WILSON tr. *Jussieu's Elem. Bot.* 192 This series of axes is either homodrome or heterodrome. **1866** *Treas. Bot.*, *Homodromal*, having all the spires turned the same way. **1875** BENNETT & DYER *Sachs' Bot.* 171 Two spirals are constructed..the two are homodromal, running in the same direction round the stem. **1880** GRAY *Struct. Bot.* (ed. 6) 415/2 Homodromy.

Homœan (hɒˈmiːən), *a.* and *sb.* *Theol.* Also **Homoian** (hɒˈmɔɪən). [f. mod.L. *homœ-us*, f. Gr. ὅμοιος like, similar + -AN.] **A.** *adj.* Of or pertaining to the Homœans.

1833 J. H. NEWMAN *Arians* IV. iv. 362 Furthering their splitting into the Homœan and Homœusian factions. **1888** *Encycl. Brit.* XXIII. 720/1 He appears to have joined the Homoian party, which took shape and acquired influence before the council of Constantinople in 360. *Ibid.*, The Homoian formula, 'filium similem esse patri suo'. **1950** J. N. D. KELLY *Early Chr. Creeds* ix. 290 It gave expression to the new 'Homœan' formula of compromise..—*like in all respects*—and strictly avoided technical terms.

B. *sb.* One of a group of Arians that developed *c* 355 and repudiated both the Homoousion and the Homoiousion, maintaining simply that in the Trinity the Son is 'like' the Father.

1896 G. P. FISHER *Hist. Chr. Doctrine* 142 The 'Homœans' would not go a step beyond the affirmation of a 'likeness',—meaning a likeness in will and active energy. **1912** *Eng. Hist. Rev.* Oct. 761 It was of course the Homoeusians, not the Homoeans, who inclined towards the Nicenes. **1957** *Oxf. Dict. Chr. Ch.* 81/1 The middle party, called 'Homoeans'.., aimed at avoiding dogmatic precision as far as possible. **1966** P. R. COLEMAN-NORTON *Roman State & Chr. Ch.* II. 420 Probably the Homoeans, moderate Arians, are meant.

homœo-, combining form of Gr. ὅμοιος of the same kind, like, similar (also occasionally written **homoio-**, and, in fully anglicized words, esp. in U.S., **homeo-**); occurring in various terms, chiefly scientific or technical, sometimes in opposition to *hetero-*. For many of the more important of these, see in their alphabetical places as main entries.

The etymological pronunciation would be (hɒˈmiːəʊ), as in (hɒˈmɔɪəʊ); but usage favours (ˈhɒmɪəʊ), or in popular use (ˈhəʊmɪəʊ); the last esp. in *homœopathy* and its family (the only really popular members of the group).

homœarchon (hɒmɪˈɑːkɒn), **homœoˈarchon** = *homœoarchy*; **homœoarchy** (hɒˈmiːəʊɑːkɪ) [Gr. ἀρχή beginning], similarity of the beginnings of two words occurring near each other, as a cause of mistakes in copying (distinguished from *homœotel*); **homœoˈblastic** *a.* *Petrol.* [ad. G. *homoeoblastisch* (F. Becke 1904, in *Compt. Rend. IX. Session Congr. géol. internat.* II. 570)], composed of grains of equal size; **homœocephalic** (hɒˌmiːəʊ-, ˌhɒmiːəʊsɪˈfælɪk) *a.* [Gr. κεφαλή head], pertaining to skulls of similar form and structure; **ˌhomœochlaˈmydeous** *a.* *Bot.* = *homochlamydeous* adj. s.v. HOMO-; **homœoˈcrystalline** *a.* (see quot.); **hoˈmœodont** *a.* (see quot.); **homœogeneous** (ˌhɒmiːəʊˈdʒiːnɪəs) *a.* [after *homogeneous*], of a similar kind; **homœogenesis** (ˌhɒmiːəʊˈdʒɛnɪsɪs) *Biol.* [Gr. γένεσις generation], degree of relationship or similarity of the races from which individuals are descended; **ˈhomœograft** *Med.* and *Biol.* = HOMOGRAFT; so **ˈhomœografted** *ppl. a.*, **-grafting** *vbl. sb.*; **ˌhomœokiˈnesis** *Cytol.*, the division of a cell into cells having similar hereditary tendencies; **ˌhomœo-osˈmotic**, **homœosˈmotic** *adjs.* *Physiol.* [OSMOTIC *a.*], (of an animal) maintaining a more or less constant concentration of solute in its body fluids regardless of fluctuations of the concentration in the surrounding medium; usu. spelt *homoi(o)-*; so **ˌhomœo-osˈmosis**, **homœosˈmosis**; **homœophony** (ˌhɒmiːˈɒfənɪ) [Gr. φωνή voice, sound], similarity of sound; **homœoˈpolar** *a.* *Chem.* [ad. G.: see HOMOPOLAR *a.* 3] = HOMOPOLAR *a.* 3; **homœosemant** (-ˈsiːmænt) [Gr. σημαντός adj., f. σημαίνειν to signify], a word of similar meaning; **homœotel** (hɒˈmiːəʊtɛl) [Gr. τέλος end], the similar ending of two words or clauses near each other, as a cause of a mistake in copying = HOMŒOTELEUTON 2; **homœotopy** (hɒmɪˈɒtəʊpɪ) [Gr. τόπος place], similarity of words or parts of words, as a cause of mistakes in copying; **ˈhomœotype** *Taxon.* = HOMOTYPE 2; **homœoˈtypic**, **-ˈtypical** *adjs.* *Cytol.* [ad. G. *homöotypisch* (W. Flemming 1887, in *Arch. f. mikrosk. Anat.* XXIX. 400)], designating the second division of meiosis; **homœozoic**

(ˌhɒmiːəʊˈzəʊɪk) *a.* [Gr. ζωή life], containing similar forms of life.

1896 W. M. LINDSAY *Lat. Textual Emend.* 50 The homœoteleuton and *homœarchon of these lines has led to omission. **1942** *Jrnl. Theol. Stud.* XLIII. 86 In ver. 39 it seems clear that ℵ* omitted was θεριαμος..οι δε (by homoeoarchon [*printed* homoeoarcton]). **1883** A. WATTS in *Expositor* Jan. 68 This is another term which I have ventured to coin..homœotel..is a confusion of the word or letter with which, upon turning from copy to transcript, the copyist actually broke off; *homœarchy is a mistaking of the one which, upon thus breaking off, he accidentally observed to follow next. **1920** A. HOLMES *Nomencl. Petrol.* 118 **Homœoblastic*, a term used instead of equigranular and applied to metamorphic rocks to indicate that the texture so described is due to recrystallisation. **1932**, **1954** Homœoblastic [see *heteroblastic* s.v. HETERO-]. **1866** J. A. MEIGS *Obs. Cranial Forms Amer. Aborig.* 18 In the *homoiocephalic comparison of the old and new worlds, these Arickaree skulls may be fairly regarded as the American representatives of the Swedish crania. **1900** B. D. JACKSON *Gloss. Bot. Terms* 125/1 **Homoiochlamydeous*, used by Engler and Prantl when the perianth is uniform. **1965** Homoiochlamydeous [see *heterochlamydeous* adj. s.v. HETERO-]. **1888** TEALL *Brit. Petrogr.* Gloss. 434 **Homœocrystalline*, a term applied by some authors to a granitic structure when the minerals are developed in equal proportions. **1888** *Amer. Naturalist* 834 He [Rütimeyer] divides the molar teeth of Mammalia into three categories, the simply conic '*Homœodont'; the vertically plicate 'Elasmodont'; and the cross-crested by junction of four tubercles, the 'Zygodont'. **1890** J. MARTINEAU *Seat Author. Relig.* IV. ii. 394 The imitation being not homogeneous but *homœogeneous with the original. **1864** *Reader* No. 94. 477/1 The lowest degree of human hybridity, in which the *homœogenesis is so feeble as to render the fecundity of the first crossing uncertain. **1913** *Arch. f. Entwicklungsmech. d. Organismen* XXXVII. 263 Desquamation is approximately equally marked in both auto and *homöo grafts. **1915** *Jrnl. Exper. Med.* XXI. 174 In..the first 4 to 5 days after transplantation, there is no noticeable difference between the auto- and homeograft. **1952** *Cancer Res.* XII. 379/1 Tumor homoiografts between mice of unrelated inbred strains. **1920** *Jrnl. Exper. Med.* XXXII. 115 In a few instances..well established blood supply, and evidence of growth were found. This is observed generally with *homeografted tissues. **1930** *Physiol. Rev.* X. 582 It has been maintained..that the result of *homoiografting of skin largely depends upon whether donor and host do or do not belong to the same blood group. **1893** PARKER & RÖNNFELDT tr. *Weismann's Germ-Plasm* 34 These kinds of division we may speak of as *homœokinesis and heterokinesis, that is, as a division into parts similar or dissimilar to each other with regard to the hereditary tendencies they contain. **1896** E. B. WILSON *Cell* ix. 305 Mitotic division is conceived [by Weismann] as an apparatus which may distribute the elements of the chromatin to the daughter nuclei either equally or unequally. In the former case ('homœokinesis', integral or quantitative division), the resulting nuclei remain precisely equivalent. **1939** A. KROGH *Osmotic Regulation in Aquatic Animals* 240 *Homoiosmosis. **1964** *Oceanogr. & Marine Biol.* II. 307 Osmo-regulators exhibit an appreciable tendency towards homeo-osmosis. **1905** *Biol. Bull.* VIII. 266 Only a slight..change is induced by a change in the osmotic pressure of the external medium. The animals are '*homoiosmotic'. **1931** *Biol. Rev.* VI. 473 In contrast with these are the 'homoiosmotic' organisms which include typically estuarine animals such as *Carcinus maenas*. **1939** A. KROGH *Osmotic Regulation in Aquatic Animals* 8 When animals maintain a total concentration of their body fluids different from that of the surrounding water they can be termed 'homoiosmotic'. **1953** E. PALMER tr. *Ekman's Zoogeogr. Sea* vi. 118 Bony fishes and fresh-water animals in general are homoio-osmotic. **1967** G. E. HUTCHINSON *Treat. Limnol.* II. xviii. 153 Such animals have thus become at least to some extent osmotically independent of their environment; they are at least partly homoiosmotic. **1827** HARE *Guesses* Ser. I. (1873) 105 In such expressions as my father and myself..we are misled by *homœophony. **1922** A. D. UDDEN tr. *Bohr's Theory of Spectra* III. iii. 93 The latter kind of compounds, to which the greater number of simple inorganic compounds belong, is frequently called 'heteropolar' and possesses a far more typical character than the first compounds which are called '*homoeopolar'. **1923** E. N. DA C. ANDRADE *Struct. Atom* xii. 232 We shall also make use of Abegg's terminology of homœopolar and heteropolar compounds. **1873** F. HALL *Mod. Eng.* 172 What we have long and loosely called synonyms. *Note*, The exact technicality is **homœosemants*. **1883** A. WATTS in *Expositor* Jan. 67–8 There is a most unmistakeable mental effect of *homœotel which operates..in leading the copyist..to think that he has reached a certain word when he has only reached another that resembles it. **1883** A. WATTS in *Expositor* Jan. 67 **Homœotopy*..the way in which two like places in the copy may..affect the copyist..whether they are like words, like terminations, like prefixes [etc.]. *Ibid.* 68 It very frequently happens that in printing *homœotopy* occasions a double instead of an omission. **1905** SCHUCHERT & BUCKMAN in *Science* 9 June 900/2 *Homoeotype.. homotype... A specimen identified by a specialist after comparison with the holotype or lectotype. **1939** *Ann. Entomol. Soc. Amer.* XXXII. 694 Homoeotype: A specimen named by another than the author upon comparison with the type. The value of a homeotype is apparent. **1967** [see HOMOTYPE 2]. **1889** *Homœotypic [see *heterotypic* s.v. HETERO-]. **1925** E. B. WILSON *Cell* (ed. 3) vi. 532 (*heading*) The inter-kinesis and the homeotypic division. **1969** BROWN & BERTKE *Textbk. Cytol.* xx. 436 Previously, meiosis I was called the heterotypic mitosis, implying that it is an atypical mitosis, which it certainly is; and meiosis II was called the homeotypic mitosis, implying that it is a fairly typical mitotic division, which it is. **1888** *Jrnl. R. Microsc. Soc.* 553 He [*sc.* Flemming] finds that these cells [*sc.* spermatocytes] exhibit a remarkable dimorphism of mitosis; in the heterotypical form the chromatic formations exhibit metakinesis. The two forms, the other of which may be called *homœotypical, are sometimes found together. **1852** E. FORBES in *Trans. Brit. Assoc.* 73 On a New Map of the Geological Distribution of Marine Life, and on the *Homoiozoic Belts. **1866** BRANDE & COX *Dict. Sci.* etc., *Homœozoic Belts*.

homœoid (ˈhɒmiːɔɪd). *Math.* [f. Gr. ὅμοι-ος like + -OID.] A shell bounded by two surfaces similar and similarly situated with regard to each other, a homothetic shell; sometimes restricted to such a shell bounded by concentric ellipsoids. Hence **homœˈoidal** *a.*, belonging to a homœoid.

1883 THOMSON & TAIT *Nat. Phil.* (new ed.) I. II. §494 g. 42 In every case the thickness of the homoeoid is directly proportional to the perpendicular from the centre to the tangent plane at any point. *Ibid.*, The one point which is situated similarly relative to the two similar surfaces of a homoeoid is called the homoeoidal centre.

homœomeral (hɒmiːˈɒmərəl), *a.* *Pros.* [f. HOMŒO- + Gr. μέρ-ος part + -AL[1].] Consisting of (metrically) similar parts.

homœomerian (hɒmiːəʊˈmɛrɪən). [f. L. *homœomerīa*, Gr. ὁμοιομέρεια HOMŒOMERY + -AN.] A holder of the theory of homœomery. Hence **homœoˈmerianism**.

1847 LEWES *Hist. Philos.* (1867) I. 101 Atomism is homœomerianism stripped of qualities. It is therefore the system of Anaxagoras greatly improved.

homœomeric (hɒmiːəʊˈmɛrɪk), *a.* [f. HOMŒO- + Gr. μέρος + -IC.] **a.** Relating to homœomery; of the nature of homœomeries. **b.** Consisting of similar parts, homogeneous.

1836 in SMART. **1865** GROTE *Plato* I. i. 53 The Homœomeric particles congregated together, each to its like. **1884** *Penn. Sch. Jrnl.* XXXII. 267 This homœomeric work, so deep and so broad in its results.

So **homœoˈmerical** *a.* = prec. a.

1706 PHILLIPS (ed. Kersey), *Homoeomerical Principles*, certain Principles which, according to Anaxagoras, are in all mix'd Bodies. So that when they become Parts of the Body of a living Creature, they there make such Masses and Combinations as are agreeable to their Nature.

†**homœoˈmerious**, *a. Obs. rare.* In 7 erron. homio-. = HOMŒOMEROUS 2.

1656 STANLEY *Hist. Philos.* VI. (1701) 255/1 From these are thus denominated, Homiomerious mixt Bodies, as Metals, Gold, Brass, Silver, Stone and the like.

homœomerous (hɒmiːˈɒmərəs), *a.* [f. Gr. ὅμοιος like + μέρος part + -OUS.] Having or consisting of similar parts.

1. *Bot.* Applied to lichens in which the gonidia and hyphæ are distributed uniformly through the thallus: opp. to *heteromerous*.

1875 BENNETT & DYER *Sachs' Bot.* 265. **1882** VINES *Sachs' Bot.* 320 The disposition of the gonidia and hyphæ in a thallus may be such that these two structures appear about equally mingled..and the thallus is in this case called *homoiomerous*.

2. = HOMŒOMERIC a.

1892 *Athenæum* 30 July 154/2 In the chapter on Anaxagoras Mr. Burnet..understands the 'everything in everything' to refer to the opposite qualities hot and cold, and so forth, not to the 'homœomerous' seeds of things.

homœomery (hɒmiːˈɒmərɪ). Also homoio-, and in L. form **homœomeria**. [ad. L. *homœomerīa* (Lucretius), ad. Gr. ὁμοιομέρεια, n. of quality f. ὁμοιομερής consisting of like parts, f. ὅμοιος like + μέρος part.] **a.** The theory (propounded by Anaxagoras) that the ultimate particles of matter are homogeneous or of the same kind. **b.** *pl.* The ultimate particles of matter, regarded, according to this theory, as homogeneous.

1660 STANLEY *Hist. Philos.* IX. (1701) 403/1 They who assert Homoiomeria's, and bulks, and leasts, and indivisibles, to be elements, conceive their substance eternal. **1678** CUDWORTH *Intell. Syst.* I. v. §20. 380 Anaxagoras..supposed Two Substantial Self-existent Principles of the Universe, one an Infinite Mind or God, the other an Infinite Homoiomery of Matter, or Infinite Atoms. *Ibid.* v. 741 [see ATOMOLOGY]. **1766** G. CANNING *Anti-Lucretius* III. 266 Of Anaxagoras why the scheme reject, And flaws in Homœomery detect? **1865** GROTE *Plato* I. i. 51 Particles of the same sort he [Anaxagoras] called Homœomeries: the aggregates of which formed bodies of like parts.

homœomorph (ˈhɒmiːəʊmɔːf). Also homeo-. [f. HOMŒO- + Gr. μορφ-ή form.] Something that is homœomorphous or homœomorphic.

a. *Cryst.* 'A substance exhibiting homœomorphism' (*Cent. Dict.*).

b. *Palæont.* One of two or more homœomorphous fossils or fossil species.

1898 S. S. BUCKMAN in *Q. Jrnl. Geol. Soc.* LIV. 453 The compressed species of the Arietidan Epoch, which are generally classed as *Oxynotoceras*, are, as their septal details show, certainly polygenetic homœomorphs. **1920** A. M. DAVIES *Introd. Palæont.* i. 29 The failure to discriminate between homoeomorphs has frequently led to mistakes in the correlation of strata. **1952** R. C. MOORE et al. *Invertebr. Fossils* i. 34 Two convergent species, so similar as hardly to be distinguished on superficial characters, are called homeomorphs.

c. (Usu. *homeo-*.) *Math.* A figure or a topological space that is homœomorphic to some other one.

1926 *Trans. Amer. Math. Soc.* XXVIII. 3 Such a C_n is he homeomorph of an *n*-dimensional polyhedron..whose faces are all simplicial cells. **1951** M. H. A. NEWMAN *Topology of Plane Sets of Points* (ed. 2) iii. 61 Homeomorphism is an equivalence relation, and a space and its homeomorphs have all their topological properties in common. **1965** S. BARR *Exper. Topology* vi. 70 Perhaps it is a Moebius in disguise—the homoeomorph of one?

homœomorphic (hɒmiːəʊˈmɔːfɪk), *a.* Also homeo-. [f. as next + -IC.] **1.** *gen.* Of the same kind or form.

1902 *Buck's Handbk. Med. Sci.* (rev. ed.) IV. 660/1 In a remarkable proportion of cases of mental and other nervous disturbances we find a history of antecedent nervous conditions, either homoeomorphic, i.e. of the same order, or heteromorphic, of different type.

b. *Palæont.* = HOMŒOMORPHOUS *a.* c.

1923 H. H. SWINNERTON *Outl. Palæont.* x. 214 These forms presented homeomorphic resemblances to *Amaltheus*.

2. (Usu. *homeo-*.) *Math.* [ad. F. *homéomorphe* (H. Poincaré 1895, in *Jrnl. de l'École polytechn.* I. 9).] Related by a homœomorphism, topologically equivalent *to* a complex, figure, or topological space; that is a homœomorphism.

1918 O. VEBLEN *Analysis Situs* (Cambridge Colloq. Lect., Vol. 5, Pt. 2) i. 3 Two complexes related by a homeomorphism are said to be homeomorphic. **1926** *Trans. Amer. Math. Soc.* XXVIII. 4 The manifold condition is equivalent to demanding that all these complexes be homeomorphic to cell boundaries. **1932** *Ann. Math.* XXXIII. 550 The isomorphism..induces a homeomorphic (i.e., a one-one bi-continuous) correspondence between the points of the two group spaces. **1956** E. M. PATTERSON *Topology* i. 6 Topologically, the Möbius band is a different surface from the cylinder, which means that the two surfaces are not homeomorphic. **1967** F. HARARY *Seminar on Graph Theory* ii. 15 A subdivision of a graph *G* is any graph obtainable from *G* by replacing some line *uv* of *G* by a new point *w* and two new lines *uw* and *wv*. Two graphs are homeomorphic if there is a third graph which can be obtained from each by a sequence of subdivisions. **1967** D. W. BLACKETT *Elem. Topology* i. 13 Any two circles are homeomorphic and..any circle is homeomorphic to any square. On the other hand, a circle and a figure eight are not homeomorphic.

Hence **homœoˈmorphically** *adv.* *Math.*, in a way that preserves all topological properties.

1927 *Trans. Amer. Math. Soc.* XXIX. 438 Two *h*-cells can be homeomorphically transformed into one another in such manner that two (*h*−1)-cells of their boundaries are similarly transformed. **1965** S. BARR *Exper. Topology* i. 6 If we draw a triangle on a lump of Plasticine, it is conceivably possible to distort it homoeomorphically so as to get rid of the three angles and make it into a circle.

homœomorphism (hɒmiːəʊˈmɔːfɪz(ə)m). Also homeo-. [f. HOMŒO- + Gr. μορφ-ή shape + -ISM.] **1.** *Cryst.* Homœomorphous constitution.

1854 DANA in *Amer. Jrnl. Sc.* XVIII. 35 (*title*) On the Homœomorphism of the Mineral Species of the Trimetric System. **1865–72** WATTS *Dict. Chem.* III. 432 An interesting example of homœomorphism is afforded by nitrate of potassium, which is dimorphous, having a rhombohedral form similar to that of calcspar, and a trimetric form like that of arragonite.

2. (Usu. *homeo-*.) *Math.* [ad. F. *homéomorphisme* (H. Poincaré 1895, in *Jrnl. de l'École polytechn.* I. 7).] A one-to-one transformation of one complex or topological space on to another that is continuous and has a continuous inverse; a topological transformation; a topological equivalence between two figures.

1918 O. VEBLEN *Analysis Situs* (Cambridge Colloq. Lect., Vol. 5, Pt. 2) i. 3 A (1–1) continuous transformation of a complex into itself or another complex is called, following Poincaré, a homeomorphism. **1929** *Fundamenta Math.* XIV. 94 Let I_1 be the interval from (0, 1) to (0, 0) in a plane E_2, and let Φ be a homeomorphism between the arc x_1y_1 and the interval I_1. **1956** E. M. PATTERSON *Topology* i. 2 The fundamental type of equivalence in topology is called topological equivalence or homeomorphism. **1961** S. S. CAIRNS *Introd. Topology* iii. 54 Topology is the study of those properties of spaces which are preserved by homeomorphisms. **1965** S. BARR *Exper. Topology* vi. 77 There is one crossing of the edge with itself at *C*, which cannot be removed by distortion, or even the cutting and re-joining allowed by homoeomorphism. **1969** LUNDELL & WEINGRAM *Topology CW Complexes* ii. 46 Since each cell σ of *X* is compact and *Y* is Hausdorff, $f|\sigma$ is a homeomorphism onto its image cell $\tau \subset Y$.

homœomorphous (hɒmiːəʊˈmɔːfəs), *a.* [f. HOMŒO- + Gr. μορφή shape + -OUS. Cf. F. *homéomorphe*.] Of similar form or structure: *spec.* **a.** *Cryst.* Having similar crystalline forms: said esp. of substances differing in chemical composition or atomic proportions. **b.** *Path.* (See quot. 1854.)

1832 JOHNSTON in *Rep. Brit. Assoc.* 429 The differences under discussion have given rise in Germany to another term, *homoiomorphous*..It groups together crystalline forms differing widely in their angles, provided they belong to the same system of crystallization. **1854** MAYNE *Expos. Lex.*, *Homœomorphus*,..homeomorphous. Applied to tumours containing those elements which are found in a normal state of the organism. **1865–72** WATTS *Dict. Chem.* III. 431 Many substances commonly regarded as isomorphous are in reality only homœomorphous, inasmuch as their atomic volumes differ considerably.

c. *Palæont.* Exhibiting or characteristic of homœomorphy; similar in general aspect but dissimilar in detail.

1895 S. S. BUCKMAN in *Q. Jrnl. Geol. Soc.* LI. 456 Biplicate *Terebratulæ* are, at any rate in the Jurassic rocks, independent, or heterogenetic, homœomorphous derivatives of non-plicate forms. **1913** —— *Ibid.* LXIX. 167

The two species..look like enough to be confused (are homœomorphous) until they are analysed ontogenetically. **1962** *Proc. Geologists' Assoc.* LXXIII. 12 It requires only sufficient skill and discernment..to see repeatedly, in one guise or another, homoeomorphous resemblances in many groups of organisms.

homœomorphy (ˈhɒmiːəʊmɔːfɪ). *Palæont.* Also **homeo-**. [f. HOMŒO- + Gr. μορφ-ή shape + -Y³.] A superficial resemblance between two fossils or two fossil species sufficient to suggest a taxonomic identity that close examination shows not to exist; esp. a resemblance that is due to convergent evolution.

1895 S. S. BUCKMAN in *Q. Jrnl. Geol. Soc.* LI. 457 Mojsisovics has called such cases, between non-contemporaneous ammonites, 'heterochronous convergence'. I would rather apply the term 'heterochronous homœomorphy' to the phenomenon; and the term 'isochronous homœomorphy' would describe the resemblance between the contemporaneous *Buckmani* with its derivatives. **1952** R. C. MOORE et al. *Invertebr. Fossils* vi. 219 In spite of their resemblance, these two shells could hardly be farther apart in classification. They constitute remarkable examples of homeomorphy. **1969** *Nature* 4 Jan. 15/1 The problem of homoeomorphy—the production of similar morphologies in distantly related stocks either more or less contemporaneously or at different geological times.

homœopath (ˈhɒm-, ˈhəʊmiːəʊpæθ). Also **homeo-**. [Mod. (= Ger. *homöopath* 1824, F. *homéopathe*, 1827 in Hatz.-Darm.), f. HOMŒOPATHY. Cf. ALLOPATH.] One who practises or advocates homœopathy.

1830 *Edin. Rev.* L. 513 Over a great part of the continent ..the dispensers of health and longevity are now known as Homöopaths or Allopaths. **1861** BUMSTEAD *Ven. Dis.* (1879) 817 According to the homœopaths, gold is of great value in many tertiary lesions. **1883** *Nation* (N.Y.) XXXVI. 540 The case needed surgical care, which the allopath could give, and the homoeopath could not.

homœopathic (hɒm-, həʊmiːəʊˈpæθɪk), *a.* (*sb.*) [f. HOMŒOPATHY + -IC. Cf. F. *homéopathique* (1827) and Ger. *homöopathisch* (1824).]

1. Belonging to or of the nature of homœopathy; practising or advocating homœopathy.

[**1824** HAHNEMANN *Organon der Heilkunst* (ed. 3) 1 Diesen homöopathischen Heilweg lehrte bisher niemand.] **1830** *Edin Rev.* L. 513 First stands the homöopathic..then the allopathic or heteropathic [method]. *a* **1845** HOOD *To Hahnemann* iii, Thanks to that soothing homœopathic balm. **1876** B'NESS BUNSEN in Hare *Life* (1879) II. viii. 467, I am resolutely homœopathic.

2. *fig.* Very small or minute, like the doses usually given in homœopathy. (Often *humorous.*)

1838 DICKENS *O. Twist* xlii, Mr. Claypole taking cold beef from the dish, and porter from the pot, and administering homœopathic doses of both to Charlotte. **1841** MOTLEY *Corr.* (1889) I. iv. 70 Prussia is a mild despotism to be sure. 'Tis the homœopathic tyranny—small doses, constantly administered, and strict diet and regimen. **1876** C. M. DAVIES *Unorth. Lond.* 307 The chapel was homœopathic in its dimensions.

B. *sb.* A homœopathic drug or medicine.

1854 W. IRVING in *Life & Lett.* (1864) IV. 179 You ask me whether the homœopathics still keep me quite well.

homœoˈpathically, *adv.* [f. prec. + -AL¹ + -LY².] In a homœopathic manner; in accordance with homœopathy. Also *fig.*

1837 T. HOOK *Jack Brag* xx, The application of a remedy homœopathically. **1842-1865** [see ALLOPATHICALLY]. **1855** LD. HOUGHTON in *Life* (1891) I. xi. 505 The Burns anniversary acted on me homœopathically; I went to it with a bad headache, and have none this morning.

homœopathicity (-ˈɪsɪtɪ). [f. as prec. + -ITY.] Homœopathic quality or character.

1842 F. BLACK *Homœop.* i. 2 Ordinary practice owes much of its success to the homœopathicity of the means. **1887** *Homeop. World* 1 Nov. 495 The homeopathicity of the cure of the child.

homœˈopathism. *rare.* = HOMŒOPATHY.

1834 MOTLEY *Corr.* (1889) I. 36 He spoke of Cooper, Irving..steamboats, homoeopathism, himself, elocution, with Shakespeare and the musical glasses.

homœopathist (hɒm-, həʊmiːˈɒpəθɪst). [f. HOMŒOPATHY + -IST.] = HOMŒOPATH.

1830 *Edin. Rev.* L. 507 Shakspeare, who was so many things without suspecting it, was, among the rest, a Homöopathist. **1881** *Scribner's Mag.* XXII. 305 The allopathist calls the homeopathist a 'quack', and the latter regards the former as a 'butcher'.

homœopathy (hɒm-, həʊmiːˈɒpəθɪ). Also **homeo-**, and formerly erron. **homöo-**. [Mod. (first used in Ger. (*homöopathie*) by Hahnemann), f. ὅμοιος like + -πάθεια, f. πάθος suffering. (Gr. ὁμοιοπάθεια meant 'sympathy, (also) likeness of affection or condition, homogeneousness'). Cf. F. *homéopathie* (1827 in H.-D.) and ALLOPATHY.]

A system of medical practice founded by Hahnemann of Leipsic about 1796, according to which diseases are treated by the administration (usually in very small doses) of drugs which would produce in a healthy person symptoms closely resembling those of the disease treated.

The fundamental doctrine of homœopathy is expressed in the Latin adage 'Similia similibus curantur', 'likes are cured by likes'.

1826 *Lancet* 14 Oct. 55 A new medical doctrine..had sprung up in the German universities..It originated with a Dr. Hahnemann, a physician of Leipzig, about 30 years ago, and is called Homœopathia. **1830** *Edin. Rev.* L. 505 *Homöopathie*, which for the last twenty years, has caused no little sensation among our Teutonic neighbours, though its very name has as yet scarcely penetrated into our insular regions. **1838** *Penny Cycl.* XII. 277/2 *Homœopathy.* **1847** CRAIG, *Homeopathy.* **1849** LEWIS *Infl. Author. Matt. Opin.* iii. §12. 51 Mesmerism, homœopathy, and phrenology, have now been before the world a sufficient time to be fairly and fully examined by competent judges.

homœoplastic (hɒmiːəʊˈplæstɪk), *a.* [f. Gr. ὅμοιος like + πλαστικός PLASTIC.] **1.** *Path.* Said of a tumour or growth similar in structure to the tissue in which it occurs: opp. to *heteroplastic*.

1876 tr. *Wagner's Gen. Pathol.* 363 Transformation of.. homœoplastic into heteroplastic formations, so-called Degeneration. **1878** T. BRYANT *Pract. Surg.* I. 95 Lobstein ..naming those tumours homœoplastic which were similar in structure to the natural constituents of the body.

2. (Also *homoio-*.) *Med.* and *Biol.* = HOMOPLASTIC *a.* 2.

1913 *Arch. f. Entwicklungsmech. d. Organismen* XXXVII. 249 Loeb did not at that time distinguish between the results of auto- and homoeoplastic transplantation. Later he found a marked difference in the results obtained after auto- and homoeotransplantation in the case of tumors. *Ibid.* 250 The homoeoplastic transplants acted quite differently. **1938** *Amer. Jrnl. Physiol.* CXXI. 650 (*heading*) Homeoplastic transplantation of adrenal glands in rats of inbred strains. **1952** G. R. CAMERON *Path. Cell* xxvii. 527 Homoioplastic transplantation succeeds with some tissues, but it is doubtful whether success is prolonged or permanent.

Hence **homœoˈplastically** *adv.*; **ˈhomœoplasty** = HOMOPLASTY.

1915 *Jrnl. Exper. Med.* XXI. 164 The difference in the growth of auto- and homeoplastically transplanted thyroid tissue. **1929** *Ann. Surg.* XC. 926 Homoplasty, homeoplasty and isoplasty mean tissue transplantation from one individual to another of the same species.

‖**homœoptoton** (həʊmiːɒpˈtəʊtɒn). Also **homoio-**. [Late L., a. Gr. ὁμοιόπτωτον (sc. ῥῆμα), f. ὅμοιο-ς like + πτωτός, vbl. adj. of πίπτειν to fall, decline (cf. πτῶσις fall, inflexion, case).] A rhetorical figure consisting in the use of a series of words in the same case or with the same inflexion.

1678 in PHILLIPS (ed. 4). **1721** in BAILEY. **1883** H. P. SMITH *Gloss. Terms* etc. 253.

homœosis (hɒmiːˈəʊsɪs). *Biol.* Also **homeosis**. Pl. **homœoses**. [mod.L., ad. Gr. ὁμοίωσις a becoming like, f. ὅμοιος like.] The replacement in a metamerically segmented animal, esp. in the course of regeneration, of a structure forming part of one segment by a structure characteristic of another segment; also used of an analogous process in plants (e.g. the replacement of stamens by petals). So **homœˈotic** *a.*, exhibiting or characterized by homœosis; **homœˈotically** *adv.*

1894 W. BATESON *Study of Variation* i. 85 For the word 'Metamorphy' I therefore propose to substitute the term Homœosis. *Ibid.*, The distinction between Homœotic Variation and strictly Meristic Variation is sufficiently obvious. **1913** —— *Mendel's Princ. Heredity* (ed. 2) xi. 198 A simple homœosis of the stamens and carpels. **1913** —— *Prob. Genetics* iii. 68 When a lumbar vertebra varies homoeotically into the likeness of the last dorsal and bears a rib. *Ibid.*, The consequences of such homoeoses are sometimes very extensive. **1940** R. GOLDSCHMIDT *Material Basis Evol.* 326 For a long time the phenomenon of homoeosis (called heteromorphosis by some authors) has been known as an occasional monstrosity in arthropods... The classical example is the regeneration of an antenna after removal of the eyestalk in Decapods. **1962** D. J. MERRELL *Evol. & Genetics* x. 101 The homeotic mutants cause one of a series of parts to assume the character of another member of the series. **1966** E. D. HAY *Regeneration* i. 34 A unique kind of heteromorphosis called homeosis occurs occasionally in arthropod regeneration.

homœostasis (hɒmiːˈɒstəsɪs, hɒmiːəʊˈsteɪsɪs). Also **homeo-**. [mod.L., f. HOMŒO- + Gr. στάσις standing still, stationariness.] The maintenance of a dynamically stable state within a system by means of internal regulatory processes that tend to counteract any disturbance of the stability by external forces or influences; the state of stability so maintained; *spec.* in *Physiol.*, the maintenance of relatively constant conditions in the body (e.g. as regards blood temperature) by physiological processes that act to counter any departure from the normal.

1926 W. B. CANNON in A. Pettit *À Charles Richet* 91 The steady states of the fluid matrix of the body are commonly preserved by physiological reactions...Special designations are therefore appropriate:—'homeostasis' to designate stability of the organism; 'homeostatic conditions' to indicate details of the stability; [etc.]. **1941** —— in *Science* 3 Jan. 8/1 The functioning of the human brain has made social homeostasis differ markedly from physiological homeostasis... An upset of constancy necessarily results. Railways replace canals, automobiles crowd out the horse and buggy, [etc.]. **1949** KOESTLER *Insight & Outlook* xx. 279 The chemical balance of the body fluids (homeostasis). **1955** L. R. DICE *Man's Nature* ix. 113 The individual organism, to maintain its homeostasis (state of balance), will throw away not only water and salts, but even sugar if necessary. **1962** *Lancet* 6 Jan. 31/1 These clinical indications of defective renal homœostasis suggest the need for a more thorough exploration of renal function. **1962** V. C. WYNNE-EDWARDS *Animal Dispersion* xxiii. 561 The general concept of homeostasis in aquatic populations through growth-inhibitory substances..is complicated by the fact that, in some of the very same species, growth-*promoting* metabolites have also been discovered. **1964** M. MCLUHAN *Understanding Media* (1967) II. x. 109 The city, as a form of the body politic, responds to new pressures and irritations by resourceful new extensions—always in the effort to exert staying power, constancy, equilibrium, and homeostasis. **1964** N. WIENER *God & Golem* vi. 86 Science is an important contribution to the homeostasis of the community. **1971** *Nature* 20 Aug. 562/2 Drinking is essential for the homeostasis of body fluids.

homœostasy (hɒmiːˈɒstəsɪ), anglicized form of prec.

1945 S. BRODY *Bioenergetics & Growth* x. 250 A calcium hexose monophosphate is the important intermediary in.. calcium homeostasy. **1959** *Times Rev. Industry* Jan. 42/1 The human body contains a vast hierarchy of controls which help to maintain a constant and stable state. The American physiologist W. B. Cannon termed this condition homeostasy. **1971** D. WATTS *Princ. Biogeogr.* v. 223 This notion has also been criticized by Lack on the grounds that ..the stability produced from homeostacy [*sic*] could equally well result from the density-dependent factors already described.

homœostat (ˈhɒmiːəʊstæt). Also **homeo-**. [Back-formation from HOMŒOSTATIC *a.*, after words like *thermostat* (see -STAT).] A homœostatic apparatus or system; something that adapts itself (within limits) to changes in its environment in such a way as to preserve a state of internal stability.

1948 W. R. ASHBY in *Electronic Engin.* XX. 382 The homeostat will adapt not only to random changes in hand settings but to *any* change in the dynamic nature of the machine. **1959** S. BEER *Cybernetics & Management* iii. 23 In a homeostat a critical variable is held at a desirable level by a self-regulatory mechanism. **1960** *20th Cent.* Mar. 269 Something goes wrong with our lives; this puts our homeostat out of order; as a result we may be unable to digest properly (and so we get stomach ulcers). **1964** J. Z. YOUNG *Model of Brain* i. 3 When we say that living things have 'needs' we emphasize that they are self-maintaining systems; 'homeostats' in modern terminology. **1971** *Nature* 22 Jan. 233/2 Beer and others have shown how a large industrial company can usefully be considered as a homeostat.

homœostatic (hɒmiːəʊˈstætɪk), *a.* Also **homeo-**. [f. HOMŒOSTASIS, after *stasis, static*.]

Maintained by, involving, or effecting homœostasis; of or pertaining to homœostasis.

1926 [see HOMŒOSTASIS]. **1929** *Physiol. Rev.* IX. 401 The adjectival form, *homeostatic*, would apply to the physiological reactions or agencies or to the circumstances which relate to steady states in the organism. *Ibid.* 417 (*heading*) The homeostatic functions of hunger and thirst. **1955** J. Z. YOUNG in B. I. Evans *Studies in Communication* 93 Since man's special homeostatic machinery is mainly social, medicine may often be called upon to assist in correcting some social incapacity. **1959** S. DUKE-ELDER *Parsons' Dis. Eye* (ed. 13) ii. 22 The pressure within the eye is maintained at its homeostatic level despite considerable variations in the other factors which tend to alter it. **1961** *Lancet* 2 Sept. 551/1 A general disturbance of the homœostatic mechanisms regulating immune tolerance. **1963** R. P. DALES *Annelids* viii. 167 We are not yet certain about the nature of these homeostatic mechanisms which maintain the annelid body as a whole. **1964** A. RAPOPORT in I. L. Horowitz *New Sociol.* vi. 99 Man as a physico-chemical system in homeostatic equilibrium with the environment. **1964** N. WIENER *God & Golem* vi. 87 The difficulties of establishing a really homeostatic regulation of society are not to be overcome by replacing one set pattern..by an equal and opposed set pattern of the same sort. **1971** D. WATTS *Princ. Biogeogr.* v. 230 Many populations have homeostatic mechanisms within them which are designed to maintain stability through reducing the number of species which are overspecialized.

Hence **homœoˈstatically** *adv.*

1959 S. BEER *Cybernetics & Management* xv. 140 These two systems are linked homeostatically as mutually vetoing systems against the two managerial criteria. **1962** J. C. WYNNE-EDWARDS *Animal Dispersion* xv. 363 It is social integration that supplies the means of controlling population-density homeostatically. **1971** *Nature* 22 Jan. 233/2 With the health sciences system and its environment homeostatically related.

‖**homœoteleuton** (həʊˌmiːəʊtɪˈl(j)uːtɒn). Also **homoio-**. [Late L., a. Gr. ὁμοιοτέλευτον (sc. ῥῆμα), f. ὅμοιο-ς like + τελευτή end, ending.]

1. A rhetorical figure consisting in the use of a series of words with the same or similar endings.

1586 A. DAY *Eng. Secretary* II. (1625) 86 *Omoioteliton*.. when words and sentences in one sort doe finish together, as thus; Weeping, wailing, and her hands wringing, she moved all..to pittie. **1678** in PHILLIPS. **1721** in BAILEY.

2. The occurrence of similar endings in two neighbouring words, clauses, or lines of writing, as a source of error in copying.

1861 SCRIVENER *Crit. N.T.* (1883) 9 Or a genuine clause is lost by means of what is technically called Homœoteleuton ..when the clause ends in the same word as closed the preceding sentence, and the transcriber's eye has wandered from the one to the other, to the entire omission of the whole

passage lying between them. **1896** *Eng. Hist. Rev.* Apr. 952 It [a clause] fell out..owing to one of the commonest causes of such omissions in manuscripts, a homoioteleuton.

So †**ho'mœoteleft** (for *-teleut*), a word having a similar ending to another (*obs.*). ˌ**homœote'leutic** *a.*, (*a*) having similar endings; (*b*) resulting, as an error, from homœoteleuton.

1652 Urquhart *Jewel* Wks. (1834) 211 Would wish presbytery were of as empty a sound, as its homœoteleft Blitery. **1880** Muirhead *Ulpian* xxiv. §24 *note*, Most eds... agree that the *non*..should be deleted. Hu. retains it by assuming a homeoteleutic omission. **1890** *Athenæum* 2 Aug. 161/3 A half-mythical rhyming history of the Norman dukes, written in homœoteleutic lines.

homœothermic (hɒmiːəʊ'θɜːmɪk), *a.* *Zool.* Usu. **homoio-**; also **homeo-**. [ad. G. *homöotherm* (C. Bergmann 1847, in *Göttinger Studien* I. 613): see HOMŒO- and THERMIC *a.*] Maintaining an almost constant body temperature; warm-blooded; homothermous. Also **homœo'thermal** *a.*, in the same sense.

1870 Rolleston *Anim. Life* Introd. 49 The warm-bloodedness or homoeothermal character of Birds. **1885** W. Stirling tr. *Landois' Text-bk. Human Physiol.* I. vi. 426 Bergmann introduced the word homoiothermal animals for the warm-blooded animals. **1889** V. H. W. Wingrave *T. Dunman's Gloss. Anat. Terms* App. 175 *Homœothermic*,..of even temperature: applied to warm-blooded animals which maintain the same temperature, irrespective of that of the surrounding medium. **1891** *Ann. Rep. Smithsonian Inst. 1890* 407 Man, mammals, and birds are called creatures of equable temperature, homeothermic. **1903** *Phil. Trans. R. Soc.* B. CXCV. 37 Variation in production of heat is the ancestral method of homœothermic adjustment. **1928** Pearse & Hall *Homoiothermism* v. 31 Homoiothermal animals. *Ibid.* 33 Homoiothermic marine animals. **1965** B. E. Freeman tr. *Vandel's Biospeleol.* xiv. 237 Not one true cavernicole is known among the homoiothermic vertebrates, that is to say the birds and mammals. **1966** *New Statesman* 11 Nov. 697/1 Man is a homoiothermic animal... When it is cold the body attempts to reduce heat loss.

Hence **'homœotherm**, a homœothermic animal.

1891 *Ann. Rep. Smithsonian Inst. 1890* 411 These phenomena, which are numerous and active in animals of the higher class (homeotherms), are much less so in cold-blooded animals. **1968** D. W. Wood *Princ. Animal Physiol.* viii. 123 In contrast to poikilotherms, homeotherms maintain their body temperature at a more or less constant level, irrespective of the environmental temperature.

homœothermism (hɒmiːəʊ'θɜːmɪz(ə)m). *Zool.* Usu. **homoio-**; also **homeo-**. [f. prec. + -ISM.] The maintenance or possession of an almost constant body temperature. Also **'homœothermy**, in the same sense.

1903 *Phil. Trans. R. Soc.* B. CXCV. 36 During the cold weather Echidna abandons all attempts at homœothermism and hibernates for four months. **1928** Pearse & Hall *Homoiothermism* xii. 91 Homoiothermism apparently had its origin at the time when the great dinosaurs were becoming extinct. **1961** Webster, Homoiothermy, homeothermy. **1966** W. S. Hoar *Gen. & Compar. Physiol.* x. 321 Increasing complexity of organization (especially behavioral organization) makes homeothermy a necessity. **1972** *Sci. Amer.* June 71/2 Maintaining homeothermy is energetically expensive.

homœotransplant (hɒmiːəʊ'trɑːnsplɑːnt, -træns-, -plænt), *sb.* *Med.* and *Biol.* Usu. **homoio-**; also **homeo-**. [f. HOMŒO- + TRANSPLANT *sb.*] = HOMOTRANSPLANT *sb.*

1914 *Jrnl. Med. Res.* XXX. 115 A second piece [of the thyroid] was placed into the left ear of the second or control animal as a homeo-transplant. **1930** *Physiol. Rev.* X. 551 Regenerative processes are, as a rule, more extensive in autotransplants than in homoiotransplants. **1952** *Jrnl. Nat. Cancer Inst.* XIV. 692 Tumor homoiotransplants, i.e. tumors transplanted within the species but outside the strain of origin, fail to grow, or grow temporarily and then regress.

homœotransplant (ˌhɒmiːəʊtrɑːns'plɑːnt, -træns-, -plænt), *v.* *Med.* and *Biol.* Usu **homoio-**; also **homeo-**. [f. prec. sb.] *trans.* = HOMOTRANSPLANT *v.*

1926 *Amer. Jrnl. Path.* II. 117 Bone and bone marrow adjoining the xiphoid cartilage were homoiotransplanted together with the cartilage. **1930** *Physiol. Rev.* X. 561 Tumours differ from normal tissues in that they can be homoiotransplanted as well as autotransplanted.

So **homœotrans'planted** *ppl. a.*; also ˌ**homœotransplanta'bility**.

1915 *Jrnl. Amer. Med. Assoc.* 27 Feb. 727/2 In the homoiotransplanted tissue the fibroblasts very soon form dense fibrous material. **1930** *Physiol. Rev.* X. 551 Directly around the homoiotransplanted cartilage there forms..a thick layer of fibrous tissue. **1954** *Cancer Res.* XIV. 1 (*heading*) The cytotoxicity of serum for mouse mammary cancer cells. I. The effects of admixture *in vivo* upon homoiotransplantability.

ˌ**homœotransplan'tation**. *Med.* and *Biol.* Usu. **homoio-**; also **homeo-**. [f. HOMŒO- + TRANSPLANTATION.] = HOMOTRANSPLANTATION.

1913 [see HOMŒOPLASTIC *a.* 2]. **1928** D. Marine in E. V. Cowdry *Special Cytol.* I. xvii. 564 In man, by transplanting within the same blood group, it is probable that the average life of homeografts might be prolonged, but homeotransplantation at present has no permanent value. **1953** G. D. Snell in Homburger & Fishman *Physiopath. Cancer* xiv. 355 It is more plausible to expect..serial transfer of normal tissue to occur in isotransplantation than in homoiotransplantation.

homo-erotic (hɒməʊɪ'rɒtɪk), *a.* and *sb.* *Psychiatry.* Also **homoerotic**. [f. HOMO- + EROTIC *a.* and *sb.*] **A.** *adj.* Pertaining to or characterized by a tendency for erotic emotions to be centred on a person of the same sex; of or pertaining to a homo-erotic person. Freq. a synonym of *homosexual*.

1916 E. Jones tr. *Ferenczi's Contrib. Psycho-Analysis* xii. 268 The development of a homo-erotic obsessional neurosis. **1917** C. R. Payne tr. *Pfister's Psychoanalytic Method* ix. 178 After the damming up of the homoerotic instinctive activity, a physical symptom appeared. **1936** W. S. Sadler *Theory & Pract. Psychiatry* xxxviii. 626 Many notable individuals in history have been homoerotic, among them Alexander the Great and Michelangelo. *Ibid.* 627 On getting into the case, I found that she was homoerotic—homosexual. **1959** *Jrnl. Analytical Psychol.* IV. 11. 120 From his dreams in particular the repressed homo-erotic aspect of these clearly emerged. **1961** *Encounter* Mar. 75 The only enduring friendships are 'homo-erotic'. **1969** *Listener* 20 Feb. 250/3 A slick, unreal, wise-cracking comedy about New York homo-erotic life. **1971** M. Altschuler in Marshall & Suggs *Human Sexual Behavior* ii. 48 One may see, in various houses, boys and young men..wrapped in each other's arms... This behavior is not specifically homosexual, but it may be called homoerotic. It is noticed only during fiestas.

B. *sb.* A homo-erotic person.

1936 W. S. Sadler *Theory & Pract. Psychiatry* xxxviii. 626 The congenital, full-fledged homoerotic is never really cured.

Hence **homo-e'roticism, -'erotism**, the concentration of erotic impulses on a person of the same sex.

1916 E. Jones tr. *Ferenczi's Contrib. Psycho-Analysis* xii. 253 Even superficial observation of these two kinds of homo-erotism shews that they belong..to quite different syndromes. **1936** W. S. Sadler *Theory & Pract. Psychiatry* xxxviii. 628 The well-known tendency toward a certain degree of homoeroticism in the Army and Navy. **1950** E. Jones tr. *Ferenczi's Sex in Psychoanalysis* xii. 299 Homo-erotism... The word..is in my opinion preferable to the ambiguous expression homosexuality, since it makes prominent the psychical aspect of the impulse in contradistinction to the biological term 'sexuality'.

homogametic (hɒməʊgə'miːtɪk), *a.* *Biol.* [f. HOMO- + GAMETIC *a.*] (Of a sex or its individual members) producing gametes that all have the same kind of sex chromosome. Opp. HETEROGAMETIC *a.*

1910 [see HETEROGAMETIC *a.*]. **1971** *Nature* 18 June 432/1 In the Lepidoptera, males are homogametic and females heterogametic.

Hence **homoga'mety**, the state or condition of being homogametic.

1939 C. H. Waddington *Introd. Mod. Genetics* iii. 81 In a type with female homogamety, *Drosophila* for example, the non-disjunctional *XX* eggs with the extra chromosome when fertilized by *X* sperm give super-females. **1961** A. Müntzing *Genetic Res.* xiii. 98/2 The occurrence of homo- and hetero-gamety in dioecious plant species was first demonstrated by Correns in *Bryonia dioica*.

homogamous (həʊ'mɒgəməs), *a.* *Bot.* [f. Gr. ὁμο- HOMO- + -γαμος married, γάμ-ος marriage + -OUS.] **a.** Having all the florets (of a spikelet or capitulum) hermaphrodite, or all of the same sex: said of certain grasses and composites: opp. to HETEROGAMOUS 1 b, c.

1842 in Brande *Dict. Sci.* etc. **1850** Hooker & Arnott *Brit. Flora* (ed. 6) 229 Heads homogamous (all the florets perfect and fertile). **1872** Oliver *Elem. Bot.* II. 196 If all the florets of a flower-head..be perfect, the flower-heads are homogamous (Dandelion).

b. Applied to flowers in which the stamens and pistils ripen together.

1854 Mayne *Expos. Lex.*, *Homogamius*, *Homogamus*,.. applied by Sprengel (*Homogamia*) to the case in which the male and female organs of a plant arrive together at maturity: homogamious: homogamous. **1881** Müller in *Nature* XXIII. 337 The hermaphrodite flowers are homogamous and short-styled, like *Syringa vulgaris*.

c. *Evolution.* Of or pertaining to homogamy (sense b).

1903 *Biometrika* II. 481 The whole range of effect from pure random matings to perfectly homogamous unions within a population is almost but not quite as important as the difference between self and cross fertilization in plants.

So **ho'mogamy**, (*a*) homogamous condition; fertilization of a flower by its own pollen or by that of another flower on the same plant (cf. b above); (*b*) *Evolution*, preferential breeding between individuals similar in some characteristic; inbreeding; also **homo'gamic** *a.*, = HOMOGAMOUS *a.* c.

1874 R. Brown *Man. Bot.* 432 Sprengel's term *Homogamy*..has a prior claim over Bennett's *Synacmy*. **1897** G. J. Romanes *Darwin, & after Darwin* III. i. 5 For the sake..of securing more descriptive terms, I will coin the words Apogamy and Homogamy... Homogamy..answers to discriminate isolation, or segregate breeding: only individuals belonging to the same variety or kind are allowed to propagate. **1903** *Biometrika* II. 481 If the male class of a given character tends to mate with a female class with generally like character, we have a tendency to homogamy. **1907** *Fabian News* XVII. 55/2 Professor Pearson's theory of homogamic mating. **1947** *Evolution* I. 270/2 The concept of homogamy or associative mating states that within a population the most similar individuals will mate with each other. **1970** T. Dobzhansky *Genetics Evol. Process* iv. 100 There may, however, be assortative mating, such as some preference for mating of like (homogamy). *Ibid.* x. 328 If eggs of the two species of sea urchins..are exposed to mixtures of sperm of both species, homogamic fertilizations greatly outnumber heterogamic ones.

homogen ('hɒmədʒɛn). [f. HOMO- + -GEN.]

†**1.** *Bot.* (See quot.) *Obs.*

1866 *Treas. Bot.*, *Homogens*, a name given by Lindley to a division of Exogens characterised by the wood being arranged in the form of wedges, and not in concentric circles.

2. *Biol.* A part or organ homogenetic with another: see HOMOGENETIC 1.

1870 Ray Lankester in *Ann. Nat. Hist.* VI. 43 The hœmochyle or blood-lymph system of Vertebrates has no homogen, or but a very rudimentary one, in the other groups of animals. **1875** *Contemp. Rev.* XXVI. 946.

b. A race of organized beings descended from a common ancestor.

1888 *Pop. Sci. Monthly* Dec. 179 We can consider the different men as forming a relative homogen—a species, as M. de Quatrefages contends.

homogenate (hə'mɒdʒɪneɪt). [f. HOMOGEN(IZE *v.* + *-ate*, after *condensate*, *filtrate*, etc.] The suspension of cell fragments and cell constituents that is obtained when tissue is homogenized.

1941 V. R. Potter in *Jrnl. Biol. Chem.* CXLI. 775 Rat liver which had been freshly homogenized and diluted..was used unless otherwise indicated. This material will be referred to as a 'homogenate'. **1948** *Biochem. Jrnl.* XLII. 205/2 Stained smears of such homogenates consisted merely of amorphous material quite unrecognizable as belonging to the organ in question. **1962** *Lancet* 27 Jan. 191/2 Samples of lung were homogenised in 10 volumes of 0·85% saline, and the homogenate was allowed to stand for three hours. **1970** *Nature* 28 Mar. 1252/1 After homogenizing for 30 s in a chilled, loose-fitting, mechanically driven glass homogenizer, the homogenate was centrifuged at 3,000 r.p.m.

homogene ('hɒmədʒiːn), *a.* and *sb.* Now *rare* or *Obs.* [ad. Gr. ὁμογενής, ὁμογενε-, of the same kind, f. ὁμο- HOMO- + γένος, γενε(σ)- kind. Cf. F. *homogène*.] **A.** *adj.* = HOMOGENEOUS.

1607 *Schol. Disc. agst. Antichr.* I. ii. 102 Homogene to the bread and to the wine. **1610, 1709** [see HETEROGENE]. **1794** Sullivan *View Nat.* II. 95 An uniform and homogene liquor.

B. *sb.* That which is homogeneous.

1725 Swift *Let. to Sheridan* 25 Jan., I affirm..that cold and rain congregate homogenes; for they gather together you and your crew, at whist, punch, and claret. **1874** Geo. Eliot *Coll. Breakf. P.* in *Jubal* etc. 227 Making their absolute and homogene A loaded relative.

homogeneal (hɒməʊ'dʒiːnɪəl), *a.* and *sb.* Now *rare.* Also 7–8 *erron.* **-ial**(l. [f. Scholastic L. *homogene-us* (f. Gr. ὁμογενε-: see prec.) + -AL¹.]

A. *adj.* = HOMOGENEOUS.

homogeneal surds: see quot. 1706; now called *like surds*.

1603 Sir C. Heydon *Jud. Astrol.* vi. 163 That which was conceiued..liueth after the same manner, an Homogeneall kinde of life..annexed vnto her [the mother], as a part of her selfe. **1625** N. Carpenter *Geog. Del.* I. ii. (1635) 40 The water is an vniforme and homogeneall body. **1662** Gurnall *Chr. in Arm.* verse 17. II. xxiv. §5 (1669) 318/2 Truth is one; it is Homogenial. **1706** Phillips (ed. Kersey), *Homogeneal Surds*, such as have one common Radical Sign. **1805** [see HETEROGENEAL]. **1877** W. Bruce *Comm. Rev.* 313 Goodness and truth are homogeneal and congenial to each other.

B. *sb.* A homogeneous substance or person.

1651 [see HETEROGENEAL B.]. **1686** Goad *Celest. Bodies* 429 There may be Communication between Homogeneals.

Hence **homo'genealness**, homogeneity.

1755 in Johnson.

†**homo'genean**, *a.* *Obs.* = HOMOGENEOUS.

a **1601** [see HETEROGENEAN].

homo'geneate, *v.* *rare.* [f. as prec. + -ATE³.] *trans.* To make homogeneous, to unite into one body of uniform composition.

a **1648** Digby *Closet Open.* (1677) 130 Care..that the rise or barley be well homogeneated with the Milk. **1652** Urquhart *Jewel* Wks. (1834) 283 Homogeneated by naturalization. **1848** G. Chalmers *Allan Ramsay's Wks.* III. App. VII. 313 Nor was society, in any part..so homogeneated.

homogeneity (hɒməʊdʒɪ'niːɪtɪ). [ad. Scholastic L. *homogeneitās*, f. *homogene-us* (see next and -ITY). Cf. F. *homogénéité* (16th c.).] The quality or condition of being homogeneous: **a.** Identity of kind with something else; **b.** Composition from parts or elements of the same kind; uniformity of composition or nature.

1625 N. Carpenter *Geog. Del.* I. iv. (1635) 88 A Harmony and Communion..a Homogenity of the Forme and Nature. **1664** H. More *Myst. Iniq.*, *Apol.* 494 The Homogeneity and Unorganizedness of the Heavenly Body. **1674** [see HETEROGENEITY]. **1779** *Phil. Trans.* LXIX. 493 The homogeneity of the air. **1854** *Fraser's Mag.* XLIX. 23 There is no homogeneity between the men or the subjects of their communications. **1862** [see HETEROGENEITY].

c. *concr.* Something homogeneous.

1638 Rawley tr. *Bacon's Life & Death* (1651) 58 All things in the Body do dissolve, and return to their Homogeneities, or..Elements. **1887** F. Robinson *New Relig. Medici* 79 He is regarded..as a homogeneity.

d. ***law of homogeneity*** (*Logic*): see quot.

1864 BOWEN *Logic* iv. 90 The Law of Homogeneity affirms that things the most dissimilar must, in some respects, be similar or homogeneous; and consequently, any two Concepts, how unlike soever, may still both be subordinated under some higher Concept.

homogeneous (hɒməʊ'dʒiːnɪəs), *a.* Also *erron.* genous. [f. Scholastic L. *homogene-us* (see HOMOGENEAL) + -OUS.] The opposite of *heterogeneous.*

In early use *homogeneal* was more frequent, esp. in technical expressions.

1. a. Of one thing in respect of another, or of various things in respect of each other: Of the same kind, nature, or character; alike, similar, congruous.

1641 MILTON *Ch. Govt.* I. vi, Of such a councell..every parochiall Consistory is a right homogeneous and constituting part. **1664** H. MORE *Myst. Iniq., Apol.* 485 It may be..homogeneous enough to the natural Scope of our first Rule. **1779–81** JOHNSON *L.P., Pope* Wks. IV. 14 Of all homogeneous truths, at least of all truths respecting the general end. **1855** BAIN *Senses & Int.* III. i. §38 Between the world and mind there is no comparison, the things are not homogeneous. **1879** TOURGEE *Fool's Err.* xxiv. 147 To secure a development homogeneous with that of the North.

†**b.** *loosely.* Congruous, befitting. *Obs.*

1708 S. SEWALL *Diary* 20 Aug. (1879) II. 230 They..solicited me to Pray; I was loth, and advis'd them to send for Mr. Williams, as most natural, homogeneous.

2. a. Of a thing in respect of its constitution: Consisting of parts or elements all of the same kind; of uniform nature or character throughout.

c **1645** HOWELL *Lett.* (1655) II. lx. 84 Som do hold that this Island was tied to France..for if one..observe the rocks of the one, and the cliffes of the other, he will judge them to be one homogeneous piece. **1646** SIR T. BROWNE *Pseud. Ep.* II. i. 52 Ice is a similary body, and homogeneous concretion. **1782** PRIESTLEY *Corrupt. Chr.* I. v. 425 Man is an homogeneous being. **1796** PEARSON in *Phil. Trans.* LXXXVI. 421 It was of a perfectly homogeneous texture. **1863** KIRK *Chas. Bold* I. II. i. 444 Here the population was homogeneous..without any foreign intermixture. **1869** TYNDALL *Notes Lect. Light* 23 In the air this shifting of the rays..is often a source of grievous annoyance to the astronomer who needs a homogeneous atmosphere.

b. *Physics.* Of light: not decomposable into light of other colours. Hence of radiation generally: monochromatic.

[**1671** NEWTON in *Phil. Trans. R. Soc.* VI. 3081 Light is not similar, or homogeneal, but consists of difform Rays, some of which are more refrangible than others.] **1783** *Phil. Trans. R. Soc.* LXXIII. 97 An oblique pencil of homogeneous rays. **1863** E. ATKINSON tr. *Ganot's Physics* VII. iv. 406 In optical researches it is frequently of great importance to procure homogeneous or monochromatic light. **1897** NICHOLS & FRANKLIN *Elem. Physics* III. vii. 73 Homogeneous light is sometimes called monochromatic light. **1913** *Proc. R. Soc.* A. LXXXIX. 246 The wave-length of a homogeneous beam of X-rays. **1942** W. B. BOAST *Illum. Engin.* i. 3 Radiant energy from a gaseous-discharge source, such as mercury vapor,..consists of..one or more homogeneous component radiations.

c. *Physical Chem.* Consisting of, occurring in, or involving a single phase.

1874 *Proc. R. Soc.* XXII. 30 The body may be either homogeneous throughout, as a continuous solid, or liquid, or gas; or it may be heterogeneous, as a mass of water and aqueous vapour (*i.e.* steam). **1878** J. W. GIBBS in *Trans. Connecticut Acad. Arts & Sci.* III. 116 By *homogeneous* is meant that the part in question is uniform throughout, not only in chemical composition, but also in physical state. **1930** W. T. HALL *Textbk. Quantitative Analysis* xi. 135 A mixture of two solid substances is not homogeneous. A solution, on the other hand, is homogeneous when it is thoroughly mixed. **1940** C. N. HINSHELWOOD *Kinetics Chem. Change* iv. 70 A reaction may be partly homogeneous and partly heterogeneous. **1947** S. GLASSTONE *Elem. Physical Chem.* xviii. 587 Homogeneous reactions..take place entirely in one phase, either gas or solution. **1966** *McGraw-Hill Encycl. Sci. & Technol.* II. 547/1 If the catalyst is in the same phase as the reactants, the process is homogeneous catalysis... A homogeneous catalyst is molecularly dispersed (dissolved) in the reactants which are, most commonly, in the liquid state.

d. *Nuclear Science.* Of a nuclear reactor: having the fuel intimately and uniformly mixed with the moderator (which if liquid may also serve as the coolant).

1947 C. GOODMAN *Sci. & Engin. Nuclear Power* I. ix. 273 The reactors are considered to be of two classes: heterogeneous and homogeneous. In the latter, the fissionable material is uniformly distributed throughout the active portion of the reactor. **1955** *Times* 10 Aug. 8/4 The so-called 'homogeneous reactor', in which the nuclear fuel is circulated in solution. **1964** M. GOWING *Britain & Atomic Energy* x. 273 The possibilities of a homogeneous heavy water pile..were it is true not promising.

3. *Math.* **a.** Of the same kind, so as to be commensurable. **b.** Of the same degree or dimensions; consisting of terms of the same dimensions.

1695 ALINGHAM *Geom. Epit.* 14 All Homogenious Magnitudes i.e. Magnitudes of the same kind, have a Proportion or Relation one to another. **1815** HUTTON *Math. Dict.* (ed. 2), *Homogeneous Equations*..in which the sum of the dimensions of *x* and *y*..rise to the same degree in all the terms. **1859** BARN. SMITH *Algebra* (ed. 6) 201 The terms..are said to be of the Same Dimensions or Homogeneous, when the sum of the indices in each term is the same.

c. ***homogeneous co-ordinates***, a system in which the ratios of the co-ordinates (one more than necessary) are substituted for the co-ordinates themselves, making the equations (all except one) homogeneous.

1879 *Encycl. Brit.* X. 408/1 For the proper development of the science [of analytical geometry] homogeneous coordinates..are required. **1934** D. M. Y. SOMMERVILLE *Analyt. Geom. Three Dimensions* ii. 18 If [*X, Y, Z*] are the ordinary non-homogeneous coordinates..let $X = x/w$, $Y = y/w$, $Z = z/w$, then [*x, y, z, w*] are called the homogeneous cartesian coordinates. **1965** H. EVES *Surv. Geom.* II. x. 71 Homogeneous coordinates enable us to establish the important principle of duality of plane projective geometry.

¶ The spelling **homogenous** is less common than the pronunc. (hə'mɒdʒɪnəs), which perh. owes its currency partly to the influence of the vb. *homogenize* and its derivs.

1956 J. N. ANDERSON *Appl. Dent. Mat.* xx. 243 Thorough mixing of the dry ingredients..and vigorous spatulation..help to produce a homogenous mix. **1961** WEBSTER, *Homogenous* = Homogeneous. **1964** E. PALMER tr. *Martinet's Elem. Gen. Ling.* ii. 39 No linguistic community of any great size is homogenous. **1970** *Times* 2 June (Container Suppl.) p. i/6, As general cargo is homogenized into standard boxes, it will inevitably follow in the path of the homogenous bulk trades such as oil and ore. **1971** *Nature* 17 Sept. 203/1 Fractions which were homogenous by thin-layer chromatography..were used. **1972** *Ibid.* 21 Jan. 138/2 A procedure for purification has been described that gives a product which appears homogenous.

Hence **homo'geneously** *adv.*, in a homogeneous manner. **homo'geneousness**, the quality or condition of being homogeneous, homogeneity.

1651 BIGGS *New Disp.* ¶ 154 Which cannot..be wholly homogeneously resolved. **1658** J. ROBINSON *Eudoxa* 66 An Homogeneousness in the derivation of the matter. **1835–6** TODD *Cycl. Anat.* I. 81/2 Homogeneousness of substance is ..an indication of low organization. **1854** J. SCOFFERN *Chem.* in *Orr's Circ. Sc.* 26 The cooling mass does not cohere homogeneously. **1875** BENNETT & DYER *Sachs' Bot.* 40 Dilute solution of potash..dissolves protoplasm..and makes it homogeneously transparent.

homogenesis (hɒməʊ'dʒɛnɪsɪs). *Biol.* [f. HOMO- + -GENESIS.]

†**1.** Applied to asexual reproduction: see quot. (Opp. to HETEROGENESIS 2.) *Obs.*

1858 CARPENTER *Veg. Phys.* §395 This kind of multiplication of the same parts by a simple process of growth..which..may be called homogenesis.

2. The ordinary form of sexual reproduction, in which the offspring resembles the parent and passes through the same course of development. (Opp. to HETEROGENESIS 3.)

homogenetic (-dʒɪ'nɛtɪk), *a. Biol.* [f. HOMO- + GENETIC.]

1. Having a common descent or origin; applied by Ray Lankester to organs or parts of different organisms which, however variously modified, show a correspondence of structure due to derivation from a common ancestor. Nearly synonymous with HOMOLOGOUS 2, and opp. to HOMOPLASTIC.

1870 RAY LANKESTER in *Ann. Nat. Hist.* VI. 38 We surely are not to understand that these muscles are homogenetic, that the common ancestor of Mammalia and Sauropseda possessed all these muscles. **1874** *Blackie's Pop. Encycl.* s.v. *Homology*, It has..been proposed to distinguish those homologies where community of descent is obvious as homogenetic.

2. Relating to ordinary reproduction or HOMOGENESIS (sense 2).

1889 in *Cent. Dict.*

So **homoge'netical** *a.*, of, relating to, or having reference to, homogeny or community of descent.

1870 RAY LANKESTER in *Ann. Nat. Hist.* VI. 37 The homogenetical agreement can be one of no greater detail than is indicated by the condition of this region in the supposed common ancestor of Mammalia and Sauropsida.

homogenic (hɒməʊ'dʒɛnɪk), *a.*[1] *Med.* [f. Gr. ὁμογενής of the same kind + -IC.] Obtained from an animal, or from animals, of the same species.

1911 *Jrnl. Exper. Med.* XIV. 244 Autogenic and homogenic plasma constitute the best media, but heterogenic plasma can also be used. **1922** *Ibid.* XXXV. 18 The action of different dilutions of homogenic and heterogenic sera on the rate of growth of chicken fibroblasts.

homogenic (hɒməʊ'dʒiːnɪk), *a.*[2] *Genetics.* [f. HOMO- + GEN(E + -IC.] Having only one allele of a particular gene; of or pertaining to organisms that have identical alleles of some gene.

1947 D. LEWIS in *Heredity* I. 101 Heterogenic (S4.6) pollen grains in a style carrying S6 and not S4 should have the same incompatibility reaction as the homogenic (S6.6) pollen grain in a style carrying both these alleles. **1966** J. R. RAPER *Genetics of Sexuality in Higher Fungi* i. 3 Homogenic incompatibility, in which mating is prevented between strains having the same factor(s). *Ibid.* 4 Outbreeding is enhanced by homogenic incompatibility. **1973** *Nature* 3 Aug. 305/1 Which reacted according to the tetrapolar mechanism of the homogenic incompatibility system in the same way as known in other Basidiomycetes.

homogenist (həʊ'mɒdʒɪnɪst). [f. HOMOGENY + -IST.] One who maintains the theory of a common descent.

1874 SAYCE *Compar. Philol.* iii. 109 To overthrow the arguments of the homogenists.

homogenization (hə,mɒdʒɪnaɪ'zeɪʃən). [f. HOMOGENIZ(E *v.* + -ATION.] **1.** The process of making or becoming homogeneous; the action of homogenizing. Also *fig.*

1908 *Practitioner* June 830 Methods for concentrating the bacilli..depend mainly on the homogenisation of the sputum by means of dilute alkalies or of enzymes. **1915** *Jrnl. Physical Chem.* XIX. 225 The stability of an emulsion is tremendously enhanced by homogenization. **1936** W. L. DAVIES *Chem. Milk* xii. 256 The homogenisation of cream, especially coffee cream, is widely practised. **1962** *Lancet* 22 Dec. 1330/2 Tissues were similarly extracted by fourfold homogenisations at 0°C in perchloric acid. **1963** *Times* 30 May 13/2 This homogenization of political discourse presents the Labour Party with some difficulties. **1964** M. MCLUHAN *Understanding Media* (1967) II. xxxi. 345 America long ago achieved its Common Market by mechanical and literate homogenization of social organization. **1965** P. G. SHEWMON in R. W. Cahn *Physical Metall.* viii. 370 Rates of homogenization are of interest in many metallurgical problems.

2. The state produced in something that has been homogenized; uniformity of composition.

1938 D. K. BULLENS *Steel & its Heat Treatment* (ed. 4) I. v. 131 When the more rapid cooling is to be used..it is desirable to attain homogenization of the austenite. **1955** P. BECHER *Princ. Emulsion Technol.* v. 76 In order to achieve complete homogenization of milk..it is often necessary to employ a two-stage machine. **1962** A. G. GUY *Physical Metall.* (1963) viii. 253 At a moderate temperature the rapid diffusion of zinc in copper produces effective homogenization of cast brasses.

homogenize (həʊ'mɒdʒɪnaɪz), *v.* [f. HOMOGENE + -IZE.] **1. a.** *trans.* To render homogeneous; to unite or incorporate into a single whole of uniform composition; to make uniform or similar. Also *fig.*

1886 *Fortn. Rev.* XL. 201 The whole island [Ireland] would have become homogenized by the action of strong centripetal forces. **1908** *Practitioner* June 831 Nebel homogenises the sputum with lime-water. **1957** W. H. WHYTE *Organization Man* xxiv. 323 In the new middle-class rhythm of life obligations are homogenized, for the overriding aim is to have oneself precommitted to regular, unvarying monthly payments on all the major items. **1964** M. MCLUHAN *Understanding Media* (1967) II. x. 101 The new centralist power always takes action to homogenize as many marginal areas as possible. *Ibid.* xxiii. 244 Any community that wants to..maximize the exchange of goods ..has simply got to homogenize its social life. **1965** *Times Lit. Suppl.* 25 Nov. 1063/3 To omit the commas..is in a sense to denature or homogenize the lines.

b. To subject (milk or another emulsion) to a process by which the suspended globules or droplets are broken up into smaller ones and distributed throughout the liquid, so that they have no tendency to collect into a cream.

1904 *Sci. Amer.* 16 Apr. 315/2 To the many methods of purifying, modifying, and preserving milk must now be added a process for homogenizing it so that it will keep almost indefinitely. **1913** *Pharmaceutical Jrnl.* 24 May 734/1 It has become the practice of the emulsion manufacturer to perfect his emulsions by the use of..the apparatus constructed for the dairyman and used..for homogenising milk. **1936** W. L. DAVIES *Chem. Milk* xii. 256 Gaulin..first conceived the idea of homogenising already existing emulsions, such as milk, so as to obtain greater stability. **1949** KIRK & OTHMER *Encycl. Chem. Technol.* IV. 823 The purpose of homogenizing evaporated milk is to prevent fat separation in the manufactured product. **1971** *Nature* 29 Oct. 617/2 Machines with triple-piston pumps..are used extensively in..the dairy industry, for homogenizing milk, cream, ice-cream mix and other products.

c. To make (an alloy) more uniform in chemical composition by holding it at a high temperature for a period and then allowing it to cool slowly.

1924 [see *homogenizing* vbl. sb. and ppl. adj. below]. **1948** *Metals Handbk.* (Amer. Soc. Metals) 977/1 The [magnesium] alloys that contain aluminum may be homogenized in cast form. **1955** E. JOHNSON in W. C. Newell *Casting of Steel* x. 448 The practice of homogenizing alloy castings at 850°C to 950°C for one hour per inch of heaviest section is common. **1965** P. G. SHEWMON in R. W. Cahn *Physical Metall.* viii. 372 This also indicates one reason why a wrought product is more easily homogenized ..than a cast product.

d. To prepare a suspension of cell fragments and cell constituents from (tissue) by physical treatment in a liquid medium.

1936 *Jrnl. Biol. Chem.* XXXVI. 504 A new method for the study of tissue respiration is described in which the tissues are homogenized in a buffer medium by a high speed glass pestle. **1959** *Sci. News* LIII. 51 They killed the guinea-pig, rapidly dissected out its liver, and homogenized it in sugar solution in a Waring blendor. **1964** G. H. HAGGIS et al. *Introd. Molecular Biol.* ii. 31 The tissue is first homogenized, the cells being disrupted by the shearing forces of the homogenizer. **1971** *Nature* 10 Sept. 127/1 The brains were homogenized in cold distilled water (6 ml./brain) at 850 r.p.m. using a 'Teflon' pestle.

2. *intr.* To become homogeneous; to respond to homogenization.

1938 D. K. BULLENS *Steel & its Heat Treatment* (ed. 4) I. v. 131 The same procedure of air cooling may be used even upon steels that would readily homogenize at ordinary annealing temperatures. **1949** BRICK & PHILLIPS *Structure & Properties of Alloys* (ed. 2) xi. 323 Small castings usually

consist of very fine dendrites that homogenize quite readily with respect to C and Mn.

So **ho'mogenizing** *vbl. sb.* and *ppl. a.*

1913 *Pharmaceutical Jrnl.* 24 May 734/1 The actual homogenising section of the machine is a valve formed by an agate cone which is pressed into a gun-metal seating. **1924** JEFFRIES & ARCHER *Sci. of Metals* x. 353 The effect of a homogenizing treatment on the properties of an alloy. **1963** *Times* 14 Feb. 12/7 The curious homogenizing process of reaching a consensus. **1964** M. MCLUHAN *Understanding Media* (1967) II. xxxi. 344 The homogenizing power of the literate process had gone further in America by 1800 than anywhere in Europe.

homogenized (hə'mɒdʒɪnaɪzd), *ppl. a.* [f. HOMOGENIZ(E *v.* + -ED[1].] **1.** Rendered uniform throughout in composition or character; *loosely*, = HOMOGENEOUS *a.* 2.

1935 G. E. DOAN *Princ. Physical Metall.* iv. 140 The true solidus line of alloys of this kind is..determined..by reheating specimens of a completely homogenized alloy. **1959** *Observer* 29 Mar. 15/4 As for his [*sc.* the novelist's] 1980s these are just a little more prefabricated and homogenised than our time. **1964** M. MCLUHAN *Understanding Media* (1967) I. v. 60 The fragmented man creates the homogenized Western world, while oral societies are made up of people differentiated..by their unique emotional mixes. **1967** *N.Y. Times* (Internat. ed.) 11–12 Feb. 4/7 The time for studying people in different environments is running out. The world is becoming homogenized.

b. *esp.* of milk, cream, etc.: having the globules of fat reduced in size and distributed throughout the liquid; also of other emulsions (see HOMOGENIZE *v.* 1 b).

1904 *Sci. Amer.* 16 Apr. 315 Homogenized milk, a trade-name for milk which has been heated to 185°F. and forced by heavy pressure through a number of very fine openings. **1913** *Pharmaceutical Jrnl.* 24 May 734/1 Homogenised oil emulsions are permanent for an almost indefinite time. **1923** W. CLAYTON *Theory Emulsions* viii. 123 In America homogenised cream is extensively used in the manufacture of ice-cream, where a smooth texture is demanded. **1951** *Good Housek. Home Encycl.* 509/1 Homogenised milk is considered more quickly digestible on account of the fineness of the fat globules. **1963** *Observer* 5 May 9/5 A sales drive by dairymen to popularise homogenised milk and collect an extra halfpenny a pint is gathering momentum. **1969** *Daily Colonist* (Victoria, B.C.) 24 Sept. 9/3 (Advt.), Empress pure peanut butter. Homogenized, regular or chunk style.

2. Of various things in respect of each other: not readily differentiated; similar in nature, meaning, etc. (Used when an expected or desirable difference is not found.)

1958 *Vogue* Oct. 153 Beside this deeply particular tragedy, Mr Eliot's homogenized characters seem insufficient. **1959** N. MAILER *Advts. for Myself* (1961) 210 Each reference to yourself as individual as a carloading of homogenized words. **1970** *New York* 16 Nov. 50/2 Even these words have become murky, homogenized.

homogenizer (hə'mɒdʒɪnaɪzə(r)). [f. HOMOGENIZ(E + -ER[1].] A machine or apparatus designed to homogenize some kind of material (as milk or tissue). Also *fig.*

1886 *Sci. Amer.* 11 Dec. 371 The mixture is thoroughly amalgamated and ground together in an apparatus called by the inventors a 'homogenizer'. **1908** *N.Y. Produce Rev. & Amer. Creamery* 11 Nov. 92/2 (*heading*) A new homogenizer. **1910** *Ibid.* 9 Feb. 600/1 A machine of much interest to the dairy trade..is the Gaulin Homogenizer. **1936** *Jrnl. Biol. Chem.* XXXVI. 496 To prepare tissue for study, a measured volume of the desired buffer is placed in the homogenizer tube, which is then weighed. **1955** P. BECHER *Princ. Emulsion Technol.* v. 74 A homogenizer is a device in which dispersion is effected by forcing the mixture to be emulsified through a small orifice under very high pressure. **1956** *Nature* 4 Feb. 233/2 Disintegration of spleen cells (grinding in a homogenizer at high speed) destroys their protective effect on antibody formation. **1969** J. G. BRENNAN et al. *Food Engin. Operations* v. 93 The many applications for ultrasonic homogenizers..include: the manufacture of salad creams, ice-cream mixes,..and baby foods. **1973** *Daily Tel.* 24 Mar. 14/4 The social and aesthetic attitudes have been passed through the homogeniser of the bureaucratic hive-mind.

homogenous (həʊ'mɒdʒɪnəs), *a.* [f. HOMO- + Gr. γένος race + -OUS.] **1.** *Biol.* = HOMOGENETIC 1.

1870 RAY LANKESTER in *Ann. Nat. Hist.* VI. 36 Structures which are genetically related, in so far as they have a single representative in a common ancestor, may be called *homogenous*. We may trace an *homogeny* between them, and speak of one as the *homogen* of the other. Thus the fore limbs of Mammalia, Sauropsida, Batrachia, and Fishes, may be called..*homogenous*, but only so far as relates to general structure. **1872** DARWIN *Orig. Spec.* (ed. 6) xiv. 385.

2. *Surg.* Of transplanted tisssue: = HOMOPLASTIC *a.* 2.

1919 *Ann. Surg.* LXIX. 123 It is possible that further experiments with homogenous transplants from young to old and from old to young animals would answer this question. **1939** S. FOMON *Surg. Injury & Plastic Repair* ii. 107 Homogenous transplants..are usually taken from members of the same family. **1964** R. BATTLE *Plastic Surg.* ii. 37 Any graft, either autogenous or homogenous, that is not immediately required can be stored for use at a later date.

homogenous, var. HOMOGENEOUS *a.*

homogentisic (hɒməʊdʒɛn'tɪsɪk), *a.* [tr. G. *homogentisinsäure* homogentisic acid (Wolkow & Baumann 1891, in *Zeitschr. f. physiol. Chem.* XV. 245), f. HOMO- b + GENTISIC *a.*] ***homogentisic acid***: a crystalline compound, $C_8H_8O_4$, which oxidizes to a black compound in air, is an intermediate in the metabolism of aromatic amino-acids, and is excreted in large amounts by persons with alkaptonuria; alkapton, 2,5-dihydroxyphenylacetic acid. So **homo'gentisate**, a salt or ester of this acid.

1891 *Jrnl. Chem. Soc.* LX. 1129 These [crystals] consisted of a substance very similar to, but not identical with, Kirk's uroleucic acid, and the name homogentisic acid is given to it. *Ibid.*, Lead homogentisate, $(C_8H_7O_4)_2Pb + 3H_2O$, crystallises in colourless, brilliant, transparent needles and prisms. **1942** *Jrnl. Amer. Med. Assoc.* 11 July 882/1 Homogentisic acid isolated from one of the positive urines itself gave a strongly positive reaction. **1961** *Lancet* 5 Aug. 320/1 The homogentisate level in body fluids and urine. **1969** *Listener* 16 Jan. 74/3 It's now known that not only do one's genes decide whether one is to have red hair, double-jointed thumbs or a Hapsburg lip, but they also decide whether one is going to excrete homogentisic acid or not. **1970** C. N. GRAYMORE *Biochem. Eye* vii. 478 Phenylalanine and tyrosine are converted through quinone intermediates to homogentisic acid.

homogeny (həʊ'mɒdʒɪnɪ). [Ultimately, ad. Gr. ὁμογένεια community of origin, f. ὁμογενε- of the same race or same kind: see HOMOGENE.]

†**1.** Uniformity of nature, homogeneity. *Obs.*

1626 BACON *Sylva* §333 The Exhaling, or..Driuing backe of the principall Spirits, which preserue the Consistence of the Body; So that when their Gouernment is Dissolued euery Part returneth to his Nature or Homogeny.

2. *Biol.* The quality of being homogenous; correspondence of structure due to common descent.

1870 RAY LANKESTER in *Ann. Nat. Hist.* VI. 36 If, however, we compare the fore limb of Sauropsida and Mammalia, it is possible to go a step further with the homogeny. **1872** NICHOLSON *Biol.* 49 Mr. Ray Lankester has recently proposed to supersede the term 'homology', and to substitute for it the two terms 'homogeny' and 'homoplasy'.

homogone ('hɒməgəʊn), *a. Bot.* [f. HOMO- + Gr. -γονος generating.] = HOMOGONOUS 1.

1877 GRAY in *Amer. Jrnl. Sc.* Ser. III. XIII. 82 The counter-part homogone (or homogonous) would designate the absence of this kind of differentiation.

homogonic (hɒməʊ'gɒnɪk), *a. Biol.* [f. HOMO- + Gr. -γονος generating, γόνος offspring + -IC.] Applied to a life cycle of certain nematodes in which the offspring of a parasitic generation themselves develop into parasites, without the intervention of a free-living generation; also applied to organisms reproducing by such a cycle. Opp. HETEROGONIC *a.* 2.

1926 [see HETEROGONIC *a.* 2]. **1939** *Amer. Jrnl. Hygiene* XXX. D. 15 In those *Strongyloides* infections where both modes of larval development are commonly encountered, there is little constancy in the daily yields of heterogonic, i.e., indirect or free-living adult, in contrast to homogonic, or direct, progeny. **1951** L. H. HYMAN *Invertebrates* III. xiii. 307 It is probable that any species of *Rhabdias* may employ either the homogonic or heterogonic type of life cycle. **1968** N. D. LEVINE *Nematode Parasites* ii. 75/1 Absence of food, too, led to homogonic development.

Hence **homo'gonically** *adv.*, by means of a homogonic life cycle.

1938 *Amer. Jrnl. Hygiene* XXVIII. 224 The production of these two types of progeny was related to the age of the single, homogonically derived parasite. **1968** N. D. LEVINE *Nematode Parasites* ii. 75/1 In a loam soil..40% of the larvae developed into females, 40% into males and 20% homogonically into infective larvae.

homogonous (həʊ'mɒgənəs), *a.* [f. HOMO- + Gr. -γονος generating or γόνος offspring + -OUS.]

1. *Bot.* Having similar reproductive organs; applied by Asa Gray to flowers in which there is no difference of length in the stamens and pistils of different individuals; opp. to HETEROGONOUS 1.

1877 [see HOMOGONE]. **1880** GRAY *Struct. Bot.* vi. §4. 225 Those..with Homogonous and those with Heterogonous flowers.

2. *Biol.* Exhibiting ordinary reproduction; producing offspring similar to the parent; opp. to HETEROGONOUS 2.

1883 *Syd. Soc. Lex.*, *Homogonous digenesis*, that form of digenesis in which, as in Annelides, the buds produce animals similar to those from which they spring. **1886** *Ibid.*, *Homogonous*, having like offspring.

homograft ('hɒməʊgrɑːft, -græft). *Med.* and *Biol.* [f. HOMO- (in *homogenous*, *homologous*, and *homoplastic*) + GRAFT *sb.*[1]] A graft taken from another individual of the same species as the recipient; a homotransplant; ***homograft reaction***, the immunological reaction that causes a homograft to be rejected by the recipient's body.

1923 H. NEUHOF *Transplantation of Tissues* ii. 32 Autografts of skin have a degree of permanency in both animal and clinical surgery whereas..occasional successes with homografts of skin have been more than counter-balanced by the frequent failures. **1944** *Jrnl. Anat.* LXXVIII. 182/2 The time-relations of the homograft reaction vary from one pair of animals—donor and recipient—to another. **1955** *Sci. News* XXXV. 105 Blood vessel homografts are now being used on an ever increasing scale. **1960** *News Chron.* 22 June 6/4 Within a decade, the homograft barrier will be penetrated and human 'spare-part' surgery will be a reality. **1961** *New Scientist* 15 June 632/3 Only identical twins can accept organ and tissue grafts from one another without exciting the homograft reaction. **1962** *Lancet* 27 Jan. 193/2 A woman who had received a homograft of bone-marrow from her brother. **1968** D. LONGMORE *Spare-Part Surg.* vi. 161 For the past three years my colleagues and I have been transplanting heart-lung homografts experimentally in animals.

Hence **'homografted** *ppl. a.*; **'homografting** *vbl. sb.* = HOMOTRANSPLANTATION.

1923 H. NEUHOF *Transplantation of Tissues* i. 3 Homotransplantation (homoplasty, isoplasty, homografting, homoiotransplantation, homoplastic transplantation, isoplastic transplantation) is the transference of a tissue from one to another individual of the same species. **1937** *Surgery* I. 558 (*heading*) Homografting of skin: with report of success in identical twins. **1952** *Jrnl. Nat. Cancer Inst.* XIV. 669 Many surgeons..have found the results of grafting with autogenous tissues..superior to the results obtained by the use of similar homografted material. **1953** *Proc. Soc. Exper. Biol. & Med.* LXXXII. 523/2 Skin homograftings have been permanently successful only between identical twins..or between members of the same family.

homograph ('hɒməgrɑːf, -græf). [f. HOMO- + Gr. -γραφος written, -GRAPH.]

†**1.** (See quot. 1823.) *Obs.*

1810 J. SPRATT in *Nicholson's Jrnl.* XXV. 325 (*title*) Invention of a Homograph, or Method of Communication by Signals, on Sea or Land. **1823** CRABB *Technol. Dict.*, *Homograph* (*Mil.*), a sort of telegraphic signals performed by means of a white pocket handkerchief.

2. *Philol.* A word of the same spelling as another, but of different origin and meaning.

1873 F. HALL *Mod. Eng.* 170 Homographs, identical to the eye; as *base*, *bore*, *dun*, *fair*..in their various senses.

homographic (hɒməʊ'græfɪk), *a.* [mod. f. Gr. ὁμο- HOMO- + γραφικός GRAPHIC: cf. F. *homographique* (Chasles).]

1. *Geom.* Having the same anharmonic ratio or system of anharmonic ratios, as two figures of the same thing in different perspective; belonging or relating to such figures: see quot. ***homographic substitution***: see SUBSTITUTION.

1859 CAYLEY *Sixth Mem. Quantics* in *Phil. Trans.* CXLIX. 77 Any figure..in the first plane gives rise to a corresponding figure in the second plane, and the two figures are said to be homographic to each other. To a point of the first figure there corresponds in the second figure a point, to a line a line, to a range of points or pencil of lines, a homographic range of points or pencil of lines. **1866** BRANDE & COX *Dict. Sci.*, etc., *Homographic*, a term of modern geometry, introduced by Chasles.

2. *Gram.* Said of spelling in which each sound is always represented by the same character, which stands for that sound and no other; strictly phonetic; opp. to *heterographic*.

1864 in WEBSTER. **1870** COLANGE tr. *Zell's Pop. Encycl.* I. 1160.

3. *Philol.* Of, belonging to, or consisting of homographs.

1880 *Direct. Sub-Editors N.E. Dict.* 4 Your slips are now in homographic groups, i.e. groups of words identical in spelling, but perhaps really consisting of several distinct parts of speech, or even of words having no connexion.

homographically (hɒməʊ'græfɪkəlɪ), *adv. Math.* [f. HOMOGRAPHIC *a.*: see -ICALLY.] In a homographic manner.

1860 *Phil. Trans. R. Soc.* CXLIX. 67 Four or more tetrads of points in a line may be homographically related to the same number of tetrads in another line. **1947** HODGE & PEDOE *Methods Algebraic Geom.* I. vi. 217 A one-to-one correspondence..is set up between the ranges,..and we say that these ranges are projectively, or homographically, related.

homography (həʊ'mɒgrəfɪ). [f. HOMO- + Gr. -γραφια writing, -GRAPHY.]

1. *Geom.* The relation between homographic figures; = HOMOLOGY 4.

1859 CAYLEY *Sixth Mem. Quantics* in *Phil. Trans.* CXLIX. 77 The theory of homography in geometry of two dimensions may be made to depend upon..the homography of ranges or pencils. **1959** E. M. PATTERSON *Topology* (ed. 2) ii. 21 Congruence and similarity in Euclidean geometry and homography in projective geometry are all equivalence relations. **1965** H. EVES *Surv. Geom.* II. xii. 203 A transformation of the form $z' = (az + b)/(cz + d)$, $ad - bc \neq 0$, is called a homography (or bilinear substitution).

2. *Gram.* 'That method of spelling in which every sound is expressed by a single character, which represents that sound and no other' (Webster 1864).

Homoian, var. HOMŒAN *a.* and *sb.*

homoio-: see HOMŒO-.

homoiousian (hɒmɔɪ'aʊsɪən, -'uːsɪən), *a.* and *sb. Theol.* [f. Gr. ὁμοιούσι-ος of like essence (f. ὅμοιος like, similar + οὐσία essence) + -AN.]

A. *adj.* **a.** Of like essence or substance. **b.** Relating to or maintaining likeness (as distinct from *identity* and from *difference*) of substance between the Father and the Son: see B.

(Distinguished from *heteroousian* and *homoousian*.)

1683 W. CAVE *Ecclesiastici* 167 The Synod was divided into two principal Factions, the one of the Semiarian or Homoiousian Party,..the other of the Heterousians. **1854** BADHAM *Halieut.* 175 As important and difficult as the homoousian and homoiousian controversy. **1866** FELTON *Anc. & Mod. Gr.* II. II. iv. 320 The questions..whether the Son was homoöusian with the Father; whether he was homoiousian [etc.]

B. *sb.* (With capital initial.) One who held the Father and the Son, in the Godhead, to be of like, but not the same, essence or substance; a Semi-Arian.

1732 BERKELEY *Alciphr.* VII. §12 What was the Intention of those venerable Fathers the Homoousians and the Homoiousians? **1776** [see HOMOOUSIAN B.]. **1876** C. M. DAVIES *Unorth. Lond.* 333 Probably since the era of the homöousian and the homoiousian so great a difference has not turned on a single syllable.

Homoiousion (hɒmɔɪ'aʊzɪɒn, -'aʊsɪɒn, -'uː-). *Theol.* [eccl. Gr. ὁμοιούσιον, neuter form of ὁμοιούσιος: see HOMOIOUSIAN *a.* and *sb.* and cf. HOMOOUSION *sb.* and *a.*] ***the Homoiousion***, the term used to express the doctrine put forward by the Semi-Arians, that the Son is 'of like substance' with the Father; the doctrine itself: opposed to the term ὁμοούσιον (see HOMOOUSION *sb.* and *a.*). The masc. form **Homoiousios** is also used.

[**1683** W. CAVE *Ecclesiastici* 164 They rejected both the ὁμοούσιον and the ὁμοίουσιον [*sic*], as Expressions unknown to Scripture.] **1833** J. H. NEWMAN *Arians* iv. 369 Acacius.. proposed a creed in which the Homoousion and Homoiousion, were condemned..and his own Homoion adopted. **1873** W. BRIGHT *Orations of St. Athanasius against Arians* p. lxvii, The Semi-arians..insisted on their own formula of the 'Homoiousion'. **1969** A. RICHARDSON *Dict. Chr. Theol.* 347/2 In their manifesto of 358 they rejected the *Homoousios*..and proposed the *Homoiousios*.

homokaryotic (ˌhɒməʊkærɪ'ɒtɪk), *a. Bot.* Also **-caryotic.** [ad. G. *homocaryotisch* (H. Burgeff 1913, in *Ber. d. Deut. Bot. Ges.* XXX. 680), f. HOMO- + KARY(O- + -OTIC.] Exhibiting homokaryosis. Hence **homokaryon** (-'kærɪən), a homokaryotic cell, structure, or organism; **homokaryosis** (-kærɪ'əʊsɪs), the condition, prevalent among fungi, in which two or more genetically identical nuclei are maintained in a common cytoplasm.

1916 B. D. JACKSON *Gloss. Bot. Terms* (ed. 3) 183/2 Homokaryotic. **1921** *Phil. Trans. R. Soc.* B. CCX. 111 The contamination may be purely cytoplasmic, and the progeny of such a cell will therefore still be homocaryotic. **1928** B. D. JACKSON *Gloss. Bot. Terms* (ed. 4) 443/1 Homocaryosis. **1939** *Mycologia* XXXI. 226 Although the conidia and ascospores of *B[otryosphaeria] Ribis* are multi-nucleate, all of the nuclei of a single conidium or ascospore have the same origin and hence are homocaryotic or genetically similar. **1949** H. W. FLOREY et al. *Antibiotics* II. xvi. 673 Heterokaryons are, in general, more vigorous than the homokaryons from which they originate. **1951** D. G. CATCHESIDE *Genetics of Micro-Organisms* iv. 72 Not too much reliance must be placed in the homocaryosis of a strain maintained for some time by vegetative transfers. **1955** G. M. SMITH *Cryptogamic Bot.* (ed. 2) I. xi. 414 Multi-nucleate mycelia of Mucorales and of other fungi may be homokaryotic..or they may be heterokaryotic. **1969** G. SERMONTI *Genetics Antibiotic-Producing Microorganisms* ii. 38 In such cases a balanced combination of two (or more) genotypes enjoys a selective advantage over either homokaryon. *Ibid.* v. 165 They often continue to segregate even after homokaryosis has been established.

†**ho'mologal**, *a. Math. Obs.* [f. med.L. *homolog-us*, a. Gr. ὁμόλογος agreeing, HOMOLOGOUS + -AL[1].] Corresponding, as the two antecedents or the two consequents in a proportion: = HOMOLOGOUS 1. (Opp. to *heterologal*.)

1570 DEE *Math. Pref.* 32 After the proportion of the Pyramidal or Conik homologall lines. **1656** tr. *Hobbes' Elem. Philos.* (1839) 202 Like figures are alike placed, when in both of them the homologal strait lines..are parallel. **1674** JEAKE *Arith.* (1696) 48 Multiplication..of these new Homologal terms.

homologate (həʊ'mɒləgeɪt), *v.* Chiefly *Sc.* [f. med.L. *homologāre* (1268 in Du Cange), after Gr. ὁμολογεῖν to confess, acknowledge + -ATE[3]. Cf. F. *homologuer* (1539 in H. Estienne).]

1. *trans.* To express agreement with or approval of; to assent to, acknowledge; to countenance; to ratify, confirm.

1644 BP. MAXWELL *Prerog. Chr. Kings* viii. 92 Saint Paul homologates this doctrine. *a* **1715** BURNET *Own Time* (1766) I. 347 To accuse a minister before a Bishop was an acknowledging his jurisdiction..or, to use a hard word much in use among them, it was homologating his power. **1819** SCOTT *Leg. Montrose* ii, Whilk I was altogether unwilling to homologate by my presence. **1876** GRANT *Burgh Sch. Scotl.* II. ii. 105 Sometimes one body of patrons elected the teacher, the others afterwards homologating the appointment. **1879** M. PATTISON *Milton* xiii. 190 It could hardly but be that one or two of the incidents which Milton has supplied, the popular imagination has been unable to homologate.

b. *spec.* in *Sc. Law.* To ratify or render valid (a deed in itself defective or informal) by some subsequent act which expresses or implies assent to it.

a **1765** ERSKINE *Inst. Law Scot.* (1773) 465 A marriage contract, though defective in the legal solemnities, is held.. to be homologated by the subsequent marriage of the parties. **1790** in Dallas *Amer. Law Rep.* (1798) I. 366 The agreement being homologated, that is to say recorded and confirmed by the Court of Parliament, became obligatory.

2. *intr.* or *absol.* To agree, accord; to express agreement or assent.

a **1649** DRUMM. OF HAWTH. *Skiamachia* Wks. (1711) 191 It did homologate both in the end and means with their commission, and the matter of their present deliberations. **1678** R. BARCLAY *Apol. Quakers* v. §26. 189 The Apostle clearly homologates, or confesses to the sentence of Peter.

3. *trans.* To represent as agreeing (*with* something else); to identify. *rare.*

1794 J. HUTTON *Philos. Light* etc. 51 While it homologates this irradiated substance or modification of matter with that of light, it also excludes it from being any species of heat.

homologation (həʊmɒlə'geɪʃən). Chiefly *Sc.* [ad. med.L. *homologātiōn-em*, n. of action f. *homologāre* (see prec.). Cf. F. *homologation* (16th c.).]

The action of homologating; assent, ratification, confirmation. Mostly in legal use; *spec.* in *Sc. Law* (see prec. 1 b).

1656 BLOUNT *Glossogr.*, *Homologation*, an admission, allowance, or approbation, a consent unto. **1754** ERSKINE *Princ. Sc. Law* (1809) 318 One's subscribing as witness to a deed, does not infer homologation. **1818** COLEBROOKE *Treat. Obligat.* I. 128 A *recognition*, confirming and ratifying an obligation, to which an exception might be opposed, or for the rescission of which an action might be sustained, is termed *homologation*. It is *approval*, or *assent-subsequent*. **1849** *Tait's Mag.* XVI. 422 A distinct categorical homologation of our principle. **1861** W. BELL *Dict. Law Scotl.*, *Homologation*, is a technical expression, signifying an act by which a person approves of a deed; the effect of such approbatory act, being to render that deed, though itself defective, binding upon the person by whom it is homologated. All deeds, informal or defective, may be homologated.

homologen (həʊ'mɒlədʒɛn). *Chem.* [f. HOMOLO(GOUS + -GEN.] A proposed name for the group of atoms by which each of the compounds in a homologous series differs from the preceding: e.g. the group H_2C in the hydrocarbons of formula $Cn\ H_{2n} + {}_2$, etc. So **homolo'genic** *a.*, said of the molecule or group to which the 'homologen' is successively added.

1876 *Johnson's New Univ. Cycl.* II. 979.

homologic (hɒmə'lɒdʒɪk), *a.* [f. HOMOLOGY (or its source) + -IC. In F. *homologique.*] = next.

1880 *Nature* XXI. 313 The civilised philosopher classifies by essential affinities—homologic characteristics.

homological (hɒmə'lɒdʒɪkəl), *a.* [f. as prec. + -AL[1].] **1.** Involving or characterized by homology, homologous; relating to homology.

1849 OWEN *Disc. Nat. Limbs* 72 Whatever higher homological proposition may be demonstrated of the one must apply to the other. **1850** H. MILLER *Footpr. Creat.* viii. (1874) 154 What may be termed homological symmetry of organization. **1854** OWEN *Skel. & Teeth* in *Circ. Sc.*, *Organ. Nat.* I. 211 The homological characters of bones. **1885** LEUDESDORF *Cremona's Proj. Geom.* 11 Consider two homological figures..let *O* be their centre, *s* their axis of homology.

2. *Philos.* = AUTOLOGICAL *a.*

1940 [see HETEROLOGICAL *a.*]. **1952** *Mind* LXI. 88 A homological predicate, genuinely predicable of itself.

Hence **homologi'cality** *Philos.*, the property of being homological; **homo'logically** *adv.*, (*a*) in a homological manner; in relation to homology; (*b*) *Philos.*, by virtue of being homological.

1864 WEBSTER cites DANA. **1866** DK. ARGYLL *Reign Law* iv. (1867) 208 Limbs which are homologically the same are put to the most diverse..uses. **1866** ODLING *Anim. Chem.* 137 The most oxidised of known 2-carbon uric acid products are homologically the representatives of the least oxidised 3-carbon products. **1952** *Mind* LXI. 85 Neither is the word *short*, simply because its meaning is predicable of its own verbal sign, homologically predicable of itself. *Ibid.* 86 This anomalous distinction between two such comparable predicates seems to be incompatible with genuine heterologicality and homologicality.

homologist (həʊ'mɒlədʒɪst). *rare.* [f. HOMOLOGY + -IST.] One versed in homologies.

1849 OWEN *Disc. Nat. Limbs* 68 Which the homologist is ready to give to the determination of the special character of the parts. **1894** *Athenæum* 18 Aug. 226/3 Those poor laboratory homologists from whom his tolerant contempt is so thinly veiled.

homologize (həʊ'mɒlədʒaɪz), *v.* [f. as prec. + -IZE.]

1. *intr.* To be homologous, to correspond.

1733 CHEYNE *Eng. Malady* I. x. §4 (1734) 94 The Self-motive, Self-active, and living Principle concurs with, and homologises to Mechanism in the animal Functions. **1886** *Nature* 4 Feb. 333/1 Two ventricles..which homologise with the lateral ventricles in the cerebrum of Mammalia.

2. *trans.* To make, or show to be, homologous.

1811 T. JEFFERSON *Writ.* (1830) IV. 156 To homologize our constitution with that of England. **1880** *Nature* XXI. 9 This neuration is in some cases..difficult to homologise with that of existing forms.

Hence **ho'mologizer**, one who homologizes.

1716 M. DAVIES *Athen. Brit.* III. *Diss. Pallas Anglicana* 10 What Thorndike, Heylin, Hicks..with all our present Saxon Homologizers do unanimously maintain.

‖**homologon** (həʊ'mɒləgən). [Gr., neut. of ὁμόλογος agreeing, consonant, f. ὁμός same + λόγος ratio, proportion, analogy.] A thing corresponding to another; a homologue.

1871 J. F. CLARKE *10 Gt. Relig.* I. iv. §1. 145 One of the curious homologons of history is this repetition in Europe of the course of events in Asia.

homologous (həʊ'mɒləgəs), *a.* [f. med.L. *homo-log-us* or Gr. ὁμόλογ-ος agreeing (see prec.) + -OUS.] Having the same relation, proportion, relative position, etc.; corresponding. Specifically:

1. a. *Math.* Having the same ratio or relative value as the two antecedents or the two consequents in a proportion, or the corresponding sides in similar figures.

1660 BARROW *Euclid* v. def. 11, *B* and *D* are homologous or magnitudes of a like ratio. **1750** *Phil. Trans.* XLVII. iv. 23 Comparing the homologous terms. **1855** H. SPENCER *Princ. Psychol.* (1872) II. VI. ix. 118 The quantitative relation between any two sides of the one, is equal to that between the homologous sides of the other.

b. *Mod. Geom.* Having a relation of homology, as two plane figures; homological; homographic and in the same plane. (See HOMOLOGY 4.)

1879 SALMON *Conics* 59 Two triangles are said to be homologous, when the intersections of the corresponding sides lie on the same right line called the axis of homology; prove that the lines joining corresponding vertices meet in a point.

2. a. *Biol.* Having the same relation to an original or fundamental type; corresponding in type of structure (but not necessarily in function); said of parts or organs in different animals or plants, or of different parts or organs in the same animal or plant. (Distinguished from *analogous*: see quot. 1854 s.v. ANALOGOUS 1 b.)

1846 OWEN in *Rep. Brit. Assoc.* 174 There exists doubtless a close general resemblance in the mode of development of homologous parts. **1868** DARWIN *Anim. & Pl.* II. 322 In the vertebrata the front and hind limbs are homologous. **1880** GRAY *Struct. Bot.* i. 6 The name of leaves has been.. extended..from the green expansions which constitute foliage to other forms under which such appendages occur ..The latter are homologous with leaves or the homologues of leaves.

b. *Path.* Of the same formation as the normal tissue of the part: said of morbid growths. (Opp. to HETEROLOGOUS.)

1871 T. H. GREEN *Introd. Pathol.* (1873) 106 A growth primarily homologous may subsequently become heterologous. **1878** T. BRYANT *Pract. Surg.* I. 97 The cartilaginous tumour is homologous..if it springs from cartilage.

3. *Chem.* Applied to series of compounds differing in composition successively by a constant amount of certain constituents, and showing a gradation of chemical and physical properties; *esp.* to series of organic compounds differing by multiples of CH_2, as the alcohols, aldehydes, ethers, etc.

1850 DAUBENY *Atom. The.* viii. (ed. 2) 252 Four classes of homologous bodies, to adopt the term which Gerhardt has proposed, namely, alcohols, ethers, aldehydes, and acids. **1869** ROSCOE *Elem. Chem.* 292 These homologous series of mono-, di-, tri-, and higher carbon groups. **1876** FOSTER *Phys.* (1879) App. 677 The Acetic Acid Series..one of the most complete homologous series of organic chemistry.

4. a. In other applications: = Corresponding.

1837 BREWSTER *Magnet.* 22 Making the homologous poles of two magnetized wires repel each other. **1855** H. SPENCER *Princ. Psychol.* (1872) II. VI. xiii. 173 A symmetrical figure is one in which the homologous parts on opposite sides are equal in magnitude. **1895** STORY-MASKELYNE *Crystallogr.* §82 Two poles or planes thus symmetrically disposed in regard to an origin-plane will be termed homologous to each other in respect to that plane of symmetry.

b. *Cytol.* Of chromosomes: pairing at meiosis, and normally (except in the case of the sex chromosomes of some species) identical in morphology and in arrangement of genetic loci.

1903 W. S. SUTTON in *Biol. Bull.* IV. 238 The double basis of hybrid characters is to be found in the pairs of homologous chromosomes of the presynaptic germ-cells. **1920** W. E. AGAR *Cytol.* v. 125 It was found that there were in each diploid nucleus two chromosomes of each size... In the meiotic prophase the two chromosomes of each type, usually called homologous chromosomes, pair together to form the bivalents. **1970** AMBROSE & EASTY *Cell Biol.* x. 327 The nature of the forces responsible for the pairing of homologous chromosomes in the early stages of prophase I, and for their separation at the diplotene stage, is not yet understood.

c. *Med.* Derived from or involving an organism or organisms of the same species; also, involving or containing antibodies or antigens that react specifically with one another, as when an antibody has been produced by injection of an antigen.

1915 *Jrnl. Path. & Bacteriol.* XX. 76 Heterologous immunity, in which cancer cells from one species are used as antigens to immunise animals of strange species, is.. different in many ways from homologous immunity. **1928** BUCHANAN & FULMER *Physiol. & Biochem. Bacteria* I. iii.

361 By the use of ox serum and complement he could secure marked agglutination of bacteria in a dilution of the homologous antiserum by itself too weak to produce any trace of agglutination. **1933** W. W. C. TOPLEY *Outl. Immunity* vi. 91 The antiserum that is produced by the inoculation into a suitable animal of a particular bacterium is frequently referred to as a homologous serum. **1946** K. LANDSTEINER *Specificity Serol. Reactions* (rev. ed.) i. 8 Reactions of an antibody with the corresponding antigen are said to be homologous, while heterologous reactions.. are those taking place with substances other than the inciting antigen. **1958** *Immunology* I. 111 Morgan (1947) injected rhesus monkeys with homologous brain and cord in water-in-oil emulsion containing killed *Mycobacterium tuberculosis.* **1961** *Lancet* 29 July 245/1 Serum-autoantibodies against, for example, thyroid or brain can be readily elicited in rabbits or guineapigs by immunisation with the relevant homologous or, indeed autologous, tissue. **1968** J. C. NORMAN et al. *Organ Perfusion & Preservation* xxvii. 375 The feasibility of heterologous or homologous intermediate hosts for human resuscitative storage is untried.

homolographic: see HOMALOGRAPHIC.

homologue ('hɒməlɒg). [a. F. *homologue*, ad. Gr. ὁμόλογον (HOMOLOGON).] That which is homologous; a homologous organ, etc.: see prec.

1848 OWEN *Homol. Vertebr. Skel.* 5 Homologues.. used.. by geometricians as signifying 'the sides of similar figures which are opposite to equal and corresponding angles', or to parts having the same proportions. **1857** *Chambers' Inform.* I. Index 802 The arms of a man, the pectoral fin of a fish, and the wings of a bird, are homologues of one another. **1871** H. MACMILLAN *True Vine* iii. (1872) 109 Every Christian.. is a homologue of the Great Archetype.

homology (həʊ'mɒlədʒɪ). [ad. late L. *homologia*, a. Gr. ὁμολογία agreement, assent, f. ὁμόλογος HOMOLOGOUS. Cf. F. *homologie.*] Homologous quality or condition; sameness of relation; correspondence.

1. In general sense. (Before 19th c. only in Dicts.)

1656 BLOUNT *Glossogr., Homology*, an agreement. **1721** BAILEY, *Homology*, Proportion, Agreeableness. **1871** DARWIN *Desc. Man* I. ii. 59 We find in distinct languages striking homologies due to community of descent. **1875** O. W. HOLMES *Crime & Autom.* in *Old Vol. Life* (1891) 325 The plain law of homology, which declares that like must be compared with like.

2. *Biol.* Correspondence in type of structure (of parts or organs); see HOMOLOGOUS 2. (Distinguished from ANALOGY 9.) Also, that branch of Biology or Comparative Anatomy which deals with such correspondences.

general homology, the relation of an organ or organism to the general type. ***lateral homology***, the relation of corresponding parts on the two sides of the body. ***serial homology***, the relation of corresponding parts forming a series in the same organism (e.g. legs, vertebræ, leaves). ***special homology***, the correspondence of a part or organ in one organism with the homologous part in another (e.g. of a horse's 'knee' with the human wrist).

1835-6 TODD *Cycl. Anat.* I. 525/2 The cephalic processes .. have no real homology with the locomotive extremities of the Vertebrata. **1846** OWEN in *Rep. Brit. Assoc.* 175 The correspondency of a part or organ.. with a part or organ in a different animal.. (i.e.) special homology. *Ibid.*, A higher relation of homology is that in which a part.. stands to the fundamental or general type.. (i.e.) general homology. **1855** BAIN *Senses & Int.* III. ii. §28 The homologies of the skeleton imply a wide range of similarities. **1859** DARWIN in *Life & Lett.* (1887) II. 240 Homology and Embryology. **1871** H. MACMILLAN *True Vine* 99 From the leaf.. all the floral organs are developed, and to it.. all parts are reducible by homology. **1872** NICHOLSON *Biol.* 42 Lateral homology consists in the structural identity of the parts on the two sides of the body. **1878** BELL *Gegenbaur's Comp. Anat.* 63 We distinguish, accordingly, physiological likeness, or Analogy, from morphological likeness, or Homology.

b. *Path.* Of a morbid growth: see HOMOLOGOUS 2 b.

1871 T. H. GREEN *Introd. Pathol.* (1873) 106 A knowledge of the homology or heterology of a growth. **1878** [see HETEROLOGY].

3. *Chem.* The relation of the compounds forming a homologous series: see HOMOLOGOUS 3.

1876 *Johnson's New Univ. Cycl.* II. 979 *Homology*, a term expressing a principle in the chemistry of organic compounds.. first introduced by the illustrious Gerhardt.

4. *Mod. Geom.* The relation of two figures in the same plane, such that every point in each corresponds to a point in the other, and collinear points in one correspond to collinear points in the other; every straight line joining a pair of corresponding points passes through a fixed point called the ***centre of homology***, and every pair of corresponding straight lines in the two figures intersect on a fixed straight line called the ***axis of homology***.

1879 [see HOMOLOGOUS 1 b]. **1885** LEUDESDORF *Cremona's Proj. Geom.* 11 Two corresponding straight lines therefore always intersect on a fixed straight line, which we may call *s*; thus the given figures are in homology, *O* being the centre, and *s* the axis, of homology.

homolysis (hə'mɒlɪsɪs). *Chem.* [f. HOMO- + -LYSIS.] The splitting of a molecule into two neutral atoms or radicals.

1938 [see HETEROLYSIS 2]. **1966** W. A. PRYOR *Free Radicals* ix. 119 Molecule-induced homolysis is postulated to occur when radicals are formed at an anomalously rapid rate from the interaction of nonradical species.

Hence **homo'lytic** *a.*, of the nature of or involving homolysis; **homo'lytically** *adv.*, by homolysis.

1941 Homolytic [see *heterolytic* after HETEROLYSIS]. **1952** *Sci. News* XXVI. 57 A covalent bond may.. break by homolytic fission, each of the electrons separating with one of the atoms, giving two free atoms, e.g.: H–Cl→H– + Cl–. **1964** N. G. CLARK *Mod. Org. Chem.* xxv. 515 Heat and/or illumination first causes a molecule of chlorine to break homolytically into two chlorine atoms.

homomorph ('hɒməʊmɔːf). [f. Gr. ὁμο- HOMO- + μορφή form.] A thing of the same form as another; applied to letters or characters having the same form (as Russian H = *n*, Greek *H* = *ē*, Roman H), and to different words having the same spelling.

1886 G. MALLERY *Photogr. N.A. Ind.* 239 Characters substantially the same, or homomorphs, made by one set of people, have a different signification among others. **1895** HOFFMAN *Begin. Writing* 176 Writing by such a method demands.. a thorough command of the language, its homomorphs and homophones.

homomorphic (hɒməʊ'mɔːfɪk), *a.* [f. as prec. + -IC.] **1.** Of the same or similar form. *spec.* **a.** *Entom.* Said of insects in which the larva more or less resembles the imago (*Homomorpha*); hemimetabolous or ametabolous. **b.** *Bot.* Applied to flowers or plants in which there is no difference in the relative length of the stamens and pistils; also to the self-fertilization of such flowers. **c.** *Biol.* Applied to organs or organisms showing an external resemblance, but not really related in structure or origin. **d.** *Zool.* Applied to a colony in which all the constituent individuals are alike. **e.** *Cytol.* Applied to homologous chromosomes that do not differ in size or form. (In all senses but c. opp. to *heteromorphic*; in sense c. to *homologous.*)

1872 NICHOLSON *Biol.* 50–1 Many examples are known, both in the animal and the vegetable kingdom, in which families widely removed from one another in their fundamental structure, nevertheless present a.. close resemblance. For this phenomenon the term 'homomorphism' has been proposed, and such forms are said to be 'homomorphic'. **1873** HOOKER tr. *Syst. Bot.* 154 Heteromorphic unions produce considerably more capsules and good seeds than homomorphic unions. **1874**, **1877** [see HETEROMORPHIC]. **1875** BLAKE *Zool.* 372 The nutritive zooids all resemble each other, or they are homomorphic. **1891** T. J. PARKER *Lessons Elem. Biol.* xii. 137 There are no special reproductive individuals, so that the colony is *homomorphic*. **1896** HENSLOW *Wild Flowers* 86 Every flower had become homomorphic and self-fertilizing. **1917** E. E. CAROTHERS in *Jrnl. Morphol.* XXVIII. 449 The unusual conditions of the chromosomes in this group have made advisable the introduction of four new terms. 1. Homomorphic—used to designate those tetrads made up of morphologically similar homologues. **1925** E. B. WILSON *Cell* (ed. 3) xii. 937 Twenty-eight male offspring have thus been examined from five matings with especial reference to three chromosome-pairs.. which may be either heteromorphic or homomorphic. **1931** W. C. ALLEE *Animal Aggregations* ii. 23 Homomorphic colonies have all the individuals morphologically similar and may be found among sponges and at certain times among hydroids and bryozoans. **1968** J. A. SERRA *Mod. Genetics* III. xxiii. 533 These bodies are homomorphic sex chromosomes.. not heterochromosomes.

2. *Math.* Related or produced by a homomorphism; giving rise *to* a second set under a homomorphism; that is a homomorphism.

1935 *Proc. Nat. Acad. Sci.* XXI. 482 We define a continuous homomorphic mapping π_m of $\mathfrak{H}p^{m+1}(\mathfrak{G})$ into $\mathfrak{H}p^{m}(\mathfrak{G})$. **1939** *Amer. Jrnl. Math.* LXI. 783 Two homomorphic rings. **1941** BIRKHOFF & MACLANE *Surv. Mod. Algebra* xiii. 350 This device for getting a field as a homomorphic image of a polynomial ring is important in the discussion of algebraic numbers. **1966** *Mathematical Rev.* XXXI. 15/2 It is homomorphic to (i.e., can be contracted into, by identification of sets of connected vertices) the complete graph of order *k*. **1968** I. ADLER *Groups in New Math.* xiii. 230 If there is a homomorphism that matches the members of one group with the members of another, we say that the first group is homomorphic to the second, and that the second group is a homomorphic image of the first group.

transf. **1959** S. BEER *Cybernetics & Management* vi. 49 A black Box is homomorphic with a cybernetic system, because the latter has undergone a many-one simplifying transformation (which makes it tractable) without losing its key characteristic (of indefinability).

Hence **homo'morphically** *adv. Math.*, by a homomorphism.

1941 BIRKHOFF & MACLANE *Surv. Mod. Algebra* xiii. 350 The direct sum $A + B$ of two rings *A* and *B* may be mapped homomorphically on the summand *B* by the correspondence $(a, b) \to b$. **1952** EILENBERG & STEENROD *Found. Algebraic Topology* i. 7 If *G* and *H* are groups, the notation $\phi: G \to H$ means that ϕ maps *G* homomorphically into *H*. **1971** M. HERZOG in Powell & Higman *Finite Simple Groups* v. 200 *G* is *p*-solvable if and only if it can be mapped homomorphically on $N_G(P)/W$.

homomorphism (hɒməʊ'mɔːfɪz(ə)m). [f. HOMO- + Gr. μορφ-ή form + -ISM.] **1.** The condition of being homomorphic; resemblance of form, *esp.* without real structural affinity; also **'homo,morphy.**

1869 NICHOLSON *Zool.* 233 Homomorphism subsists between the Polyzoa and the Hydroida. **1872** [see HOMOMORPHIC *a.* 1 a.] **1874** R. BROWN *Man. Bot.* Gloss., *Homomorphy*. **1883** Homomorphy [see *homophyly* s.v. HOMO-].

2. *Math.* [See -MORPHISM.] A many-to-one (or one-to-one) transformation of one set into another that preserves in the second set the operations or relations between the elements of the first.

1935 *Duke Math. Jrnl.* I. 2 There exists an operation *F* defined topologically for all the chains and such that $F\{c_p\}$ is a homomorphism of $\{c_p\}$ into $\{c_{p-1}\}$, and of $\{c_0\}$ into the identity. **1941** BIRKHOFF & MACLANE *Surv. Mod. Algebra* vi. 155 Under any homomorphism $G \to G'$, the identity *e* of *G* goes into the identity of *G'*, and inverses into inverses. **1959** E. M. PATTERSON *Topology* (ed. 2) iv. 82 In fact, there is a homomorphism between the groups (not to be confused with homeomorphism). **1965** PATTERSON & RUTHERFORD *Elem. Abstract Algebra* iii. 79 A mapping *f* of a ring R_1 into a ring R_2 is called a homomorphism if $f(x + y) = f(x) + f(y)$, $f(xy) = f(x)f(y)$ for all $x, y \in R_1$. **1969** F. HARARY *Graph Theory* xii. 143 If *G'* is the graph resulting from a homomorphism ϕ of *G* we can consider ϕ as a function from *V* onto *V'* such that if *u* and *v* are adjacent in *G*, then ϕu and ϕv are adjacent in *G'*.

transf. **1966** S. BEER *Decision & Control* vi. 113 A scientific model is a homomorphism on to which two different situations are mapped, and which actually defines the extent to which they are structurally identical.

homo'morphous, *a.* [f. as HOMOMORPHIC *a.* + -OUS.] Of the same form; = HOMOMORPHIC *a.*

1854 MAYNE *Expos. Lex., Homomorphus, Bot.*, having the same form: homomorphous. **1855** [see HETEROMORPHOUS]. **1864** *Reader* 2 Apr. 434/1 A step higher than the simple homomorphous organization of Amœba. **1874** LUBBOCK *Orig. & Met. Ins.* iii. 43 The Orthoptera and other Homomorphous insects. **1884** BOWER & SCOTT *De Bary's Phaner.* 283 [It] has homomorphous leaves in many rows.

homonomous (həʊ'mɒnəməs), *a.* [f. Gr. ὁμό-νομ-ος (f. ὁμός same + νόμος law) + -OUS.] Subject to the same or a constant law; *spec.* in *Biol.*, having the same law or mode of growth: said of homologous parts or organs (opp. to *heteronomous*).

1854 in MAYNE *Expos. Lex.* **1870** ROLLESTON *Anim. Life* 112 The great number of homonomous segments.. in Myriapoda. **1878** BELL *Gegenbaur's Comp. Anat.* 64 The individual fingers and toes.. are homonomous structures.

homonomy (-'ɒnəmɪ). [f. as prec. + -Y: after Gr. derivatives in -νομια.] Homonomous condition. *spec.* in *Biol.* (see prec.).

a **1682** SIR T. BROWNE *Tracts* (1684) 127 The key hereof is the homonomy of the Greek made use of in the Latin words. **1870** ROLLESTON *Anim. Life* Introd. 114 In the homonomy and number of their segments and appendages, the Myriopoda resemble certain of the Crustacea. **1878** BELL *Gegenbaur's Comp. Anat.* 64 Homonomy.. describes the relation to one another of those parts which are arranged along a transverse axis of the body. **1888** ROLLESTON & JACKSON *Anim. Life* 147 The larva.. has a somewhat vermiform appearance owing to the great homonomy or similarity of the remaining somites.

homonuclear (hɒməʊ'njuːklɪə(r)), *a.* [f. HOMO- + NUCLEAR *a.*] **a.** *Physics* and *Chem.* Of a molecule: composed of atoms whose nuclei are alike, i.e. atoms of the same element or (more strictly) the same isotope.

1930 *Physical Rev.* XXXVI. 617 In the case of homonuclear molecules (molecules composed of atoms whose nuclei are identical in charge and mass), any electron state may be either 'odd' or 'even'. **1970** *Nature* 25 Apr. 354/1 Vibrational levels of N^{+}_{2}, like those of N_2, are metastable because both molecules are homonuclear.

b. *Chem.* Taking place on the same ring in a molecule.

1938 G. H. RICHTER *Textbk. Org. Chem.* xxix. 596 In discussing the reactions of naphthalene it is customary to speak of homonuclear substitution if the groups are entering the same ring, and heteronuclear substitution if the radicals are entering different rings. **1951** I. L. FINAR *Org. Chem.* xxix. 586 Substitution products of naphthalene... When OH.. or $NH{\cdot}CO{\cdot}CH_3$ is in the 2-position, homonuclear substitution usually takes place in the 1-position.

homony, obs. form of HOMINY.

homonym ('hɒmənɪm). Also **homonyme**. [ad. late L. *homōnym-um* (Quintilian), a. Gr. ὁμώνυμ-ον, neut. of ὁμώνυμος HOMONYMOUS. Cf. F. *homonyme* 'an equiuocation, or word of diuers significations' (Cotgr.).]

1. a. The same name or word used to denote different things. **b.** *Philol.* Applied to words having the same sound, but differing in meaning: opp. to *heteronym* and *synonym*.

1697 tr. *Burgersdicius his Logic* I. xxv. 100 Those [words] that differ not in termination; as grammatica, the art of grammar, and grammatica, a woman, are not conjugates, but homonyms. **1851** SIR F. PALGRAVE *Norm. & Eng.* I. 350 During the later periods of the Empire there are so many homonyms as to confuse the most attentive investigator. **1876** DOUSE *Grimm's L.* §17. 34 A monosyllabic language, indeed, like the Chinese, is but, as it were, a cluster of homonyms.

c. *Taxonomy.* A generic name or a binomial that duplicates a name attached to a different plant or animal.

1892 *Bull. Torrey Bot. Club* XIX. 290 Homonyms.—The publication of a generic name or a binomial invalidates the use of the same name for any subsequently published genus or species respectively. **1920** *Jrnl. Bot.* LIX. 156 Specific names should be rejected when they are homonyms. **1951** G. H. M. LAWRENCE *Taxon. Vascular Plants* ix. 213 A name of a taxon is illegitimate and must be rejected if it is a later homonym, that is, if it duplicates a name previously and validly published for a taxon of the same rank based on a different type. **1967** R. E. BLACKWELDER *Taxonomy* xxii. 463 Priority determines which homonym can be retained as an acceptable name. **1972** W. T. STEARN *A. W. Smith's Gardener's Dict. Plant Names* (rev. ed.) 13 Similar names applied to different plants are called homonyms. The rejection of later homonyms has caused a number of unavoidable but regrettable name changes.

2. A person or thing having the same name as another; a 'namesake'.

1851 F. HALL in *Benares Mag.* V. 27 It is to this Mushtáq that Mannú Lála..alludes, and not to his titular homonym of Azímábád, as our author imagines. **1864** SIR F. PALGRAVE *Norm. & Eng.* III. 118 He bestowed the Duchy upon his Father's homonym Robert the Younger. **1865** W. G. PALGRAVE *Arabia* II. 138 The locust of Arabia is..twice or three times the size of its northern homonym.

Hence †**ho'monymal** *a.*, agreeing in name.

1641 H. L'ESTRANGE *God's Sabbath* 102 For Island..their dayes are homonymall with ours in England..as derived from the same idoles.

homo'nymic, *a.* [f. as next + -IC.] Of or relating to homonyms or homonymy. So **homo'nymical** *a.* (in mod. Dicts.).

1862 F. HALL in *Jrnl. Asiatic Soc. Bengal* 10 The *Viśwaprakáśa*, an homonymic lexicon..written in the year 1111. **1867** WHITNEY *Stud. Lang.* xii. (1870) 454 The homonymic designation of a thing by something which called to the mind the sounds of which its name was composed.

homonymous (həʊ'mɒnɪməs), *a.* [f. late L. *homōnym-us*, a. Gr. ὁμώνυμ-ος of the same name, sb. a namesake, pl. τὰ ὁμώνυμα (Aristotle) equivocal nouns, ambiguous words; f. ὁμός same + ὄνομα (Æolic ὄνυμα) name: see -OUS.]

1. a. Denoting different things by the same name (said of the same word used in different senses in *Taxonomy*, etc.); equivocal, ambiguous.

1621 W. SCLATER *Tythes* (1623) 115 Your Minor is euery whit homonymous. **1656** STANLEY *Hist. Philos.* VI. (1701) 244/2 Terms are of three kinds, *Homonymous*, *Synonymous*, and *Paronymous*. *Homonymous*, whose name only is common, their Essence divers. *a* **1661** FULLER *Worthies, Lanc.*, [John Smith] became Fellow and Proctor of the University [of Cambridge] when past Sixty years of age, when the Prevaricators gave him this Homony[m]ous Salute Ave Pater. **1725** WATTS *Logic* I. iv. §6 Equivocal words, or those which signify several things, are called homonymous, or ambiguous. **1801** COLEBROOKE in *Asiatic Res.* (1803) VII. 216 A list of homonymous indeclinables is subjoined. **1896** WALSINGHAM & DURRANT *Rules for Nomencl.* 9 Invalid names considered merely as words are of three classes:—(1) Homonymous (*i.e.* the same name applied to different conceptions). **1964** *Internat. Code Zool. Nomencl.* 55 Homonymy does not exist between two identical species-group names originally or subsequently placed in different genera that bear homonymous names.

b. *Philol.* Of the nature of homonyms: said of words identical in sound but different in sense.

1876 DOUSE *Grimm's L.* §17. 34 The meanings of the several primitives are in general so widely different that the homonymous derivatives remain to all time clearly distinguished in use.

2. a. Having, or called by, the same name.

1658 PHILLIPS, *Homonymous*, things of several kindes, having the same denomination, a Term in Logick. **1748** HARTLEY *Observ. Man* I. i. 99 The homonymous nerves of the right and left Sides. **1881** *Athenæum* 26 Feb. 305/2 There seems to have been..a single capital, homonymous with the island.

b. *Optics.* Applied to the two images of one object seen in looking at a point nearer than the object, when the right image is that seen by the right eye and the left by the left: opp. to HETERONYMOUS 2. Also applied to diplopia in which images are doubled in this way. Of hemianopia: characterized by the loss of vision in the same half (left or right) of the visual field of each eye.

1881 LE CONTE *Sight* II. i. 95 When we look at the farther finger, the nearer one is so doubled that the left image belongs to the right eye and the right image to the left eye..; when we look at the nearer finger, the farther one is so doubled that the right image belongs to the right eye and the left image to the left eye. In the former case, the images are said to be *heteronymous*, i.e. of different name, and in the latter case they are said to be *homonymous*, i.e. of the same name, as the eye. **1882** Homonymous hemianopia [see HEMIANOPIA]. **1884** H. E. JULER *Handbk. Ophthalmic Sci.* v. 383 This projection of the object to o' is on the same side as the deviating eye L, and the diplopia is therefore called homonymous. **1966** S. LERMAN *Basic Ophthalmol.* viii. 467 If the left eye deviates inward..the patient will suffer from a homonymous (uncrossed) diplopia.

Hence **ho'monymously** *adv.*

1751 HARRIS *Hermes* III. iii. (1786) 342 One Word may be not homonymously but truly and essentially common to many Particulars past, present and future. **1881** [see HETERONYMOUSLY].

homonymy (həʊ'mɒnɪmɪ). Also 7 erron. **-imie**, **-omie**. [ad. late L. *homōnymia*, a. Gr. ὁμωνυμία, f. ὁμώνυμος (see prec.). Cf. F. *homonymie* (1606 in Hatz.-Darm.).] The quality of being homonymous; the use of the same name for different things, as in *Taxonomy*, etc.; †equivocation, ambiguity (*obs.*); sameness of name with difference of sense.

[**1551** T. WILSON *Logike* (1580) 65 *Homonymia*, whiche maie be called in Englishe, the doubtfulnesse of one woorde, when it signifieth diversly.] **1597** MORLEY *Introd. Mus.* 150 You play upon the Homonymie of the word Loue. **1616** BULLOKAR, *Homonymie*, a terme in Logicke, when one word signifieth diuers things: as Hart: signifying a beast, and a principall member of the body. **1751** HARRIS *Hermes* (1841) 181 Proper names..often fall into homonymie, that is, different persons often go by the same name. **1847** GROTE *Greece* I. xviii. (1849) II. 24 There existed certain homonymies and certain affinities of religious worship, between parts of Bœotia and parts of Thessaly. **1896** WALSINGHAM & DURRANT *Rules for Nomencl.* 9 A name homophonous with a valid name is invalid in accordance with the rule governing homonymy. **1964** [see HOMONYMOUS *a.* 1].

homo-organic, var. HOMORGANIC *a.*

†**homo'ousial**, *a. Obs. rare.* = HOMOOUSIAN *a.*

1695 HOWE *Wks.* (1834) 163/1 Those three Divine Persons..all homoousial, or consubstantial to one another. *a* **1834** COLERIDGE *Lit. Rem.* (1836–9) IV. 234 Why not..retain the same term in all languages? Why not *usia* and *homoüsial*, as well as *hypostasis*..and the like?

homoousian, **homousian** (ˌhɒməʊ'aʊsɪən, həʊ'maʊsɪən, -'uːsɪən), *a.* and *sb. Theol.* [ad. med.L. *homoūsiān-us*, f. *homoūsius* (Jerome), a. Gr. ὁμοούσιος, ὁμούσιος, f. ὁμός same + οὐσία essence, substance: see -AN. In mod.F. *homousien*. Opp. to *heteroousian* and *homoiousian*.

The form *homoūsian* is normal, according to the regular equivalence of Roman ū to Gr. ου; but Engl. writers have mostly thought of the Gr. letters.]

A. *adj.* **a.** Of the same essence or substance; co-essential, consubstantial. **b.** Relating to or maintaining the consubstantiality of the persons of the Trinity: see B.

1678 CUDWORTH *Intell. Syst.* I. iv. §36. 597 The Genuine Platonists would doubtless acknowledge also, all the Three Hypostases of their Trinity to be Homo-ousian, Co-Essential or Con-Substantial. **1716** M. DAVIES *Athen. Brit.* III. *Crit. Hist.* 48 The first Father of the Homousian Orthodoxy. **1744** LARDNER *Credib. Gosp. Hist.* I. l. §2. V. 134 The council of Nice established the homousian or consubstantial doctrine. **1864** LOWELL *Fireside Trav.* 38 So homoousian both in look and soul, So indiscernibly a single whole. **1866** [see HOMOIOUSIAN A.].

B. *sb. Eccl. Hist.* (With capital initial.) One who holds the three persons of the Trinity to be of the same essence or substance; an orthodox Trinitarian.

1565 T. STAPLETON *Fortr. Faith* 17 b, The Arrians called the Catholikes Homoousians. **1678** CUDWORTH *Intell. Syst.* I. iv. §36. 610 The Arians call us Homoousians, because..we defend the Father, Son and Holy Ghost, to be in the language of the Greeks Homoousious, that is of One and the Same Substance. **1748** LARDNER *Credib. Gosp. Hist.* I. lxx. §7. VII. 429 These measures incommoded by turns the Homoüsians and the Arians. **1776** GIBBON *Decl. & F.* (1848) I. 475 The profane of every age have derided the furious contests which the difference of a single diphthong excited between the Homoousians and the Homoiousians. **1885** E. S. FFOULKES *Prim. Consecr.* v. 162 The Acacians, long afterwards, condemned the Homoousians, the Homoiousians and the Anomeans in one lot.

Hence **homo'ousianism**, the doctrine of the Homoousians. **homo'ousianist** = HOMOOUSIAN B. So also **homo'ousiast** = HOMOOUSIAN B. **homo'ousious** *a.*, consubstantial. **homousie** [cf. Gr. (τὸ) ὁμοούσιον, neut. of ὁμοούσιος, used subst.], consubstantiality.

1869 O. W. HOLMES *Cind. fr. Ashes* in *Old Vol. Life* (1891) 244 A very worthy professor..but thought by certain experts to be a little questionable in the matter of *homoousianism. **1716** M. DAVIES *Athen. Brit.* III. *Crit. Hist.* 37 The term Homousian or *Homousianist, nick-names invented by the Blaspheming Arians. **1626** BP. MOUNTAGU in *Cosin's Corr.* (1869) I. 99 For the *Homousiasts, they rest all upon God and neclected means. **1835** *Penny Cycl.* III. 3/1 Gregory of Cappadocia..committed many acts of violence against the Homoousiasts. **1678** CUDWORTH *Intell. Syst.* I. iv. §36. 606 It is full of divine things, by reason of its being cognate or congenerous, and *homoousious with them. *Ibid.* 610 [see HOMOOUSIAN B.]. **1886** *Westm. Rev.* Oct. 475 As a substitute for the absent *homousie or identity of being with God.

Homoousion (hɒməʊ'aʊzɪɒn, -'aʊsɪɒn, -'uː-), *sb.* and *a. Theol.* [eccl. Gr. ὁμοούσιον, neut. of ὁμοούσιος: see HOMOOUSIAN *a.* and *sb.*]

A. *sb. the Homoousion* (τὸ ὁμοούσιον): the term ὁμοούσιος as used, e.g. in the formula promulgated by the Council of Nicæa in A.D. 325, to express the doctrine that the Son is 'of one substance' with the Father (τῷ πατρί); the doctrine itself: opposed to the term ὁμοιούσιος (see HOMOIOUSION). The masc. form Homoousios is also used.

[**1683**: see HOMOIOUSION.] **1781** GIBBON *Decl. & F.* II. xxi. 251 Their [*sc.* the Arians'] patron, Eusebius of Nicomedia,..confessed, that the admission of the *Homoousion*, or Consubstantial..was incompatible with the principles of their theological system. *Ibid.* 252 The mysterious *Homoousion*, which either party was free to interpret according to their peculiar tenets. **1833** J. H. NEWMAN *Arians* iv. 333 The Novatians, as maintaining the Homoousion, were included in the persecution. **1875** *Encycl. Brit.* II. 538/2 At length the tenet of the *Homoiousion* was substituted for that of the *Homoousion* at the Council of Rimini (Ariminum) in 360. **1921** C. H. TURNER *Catholic & Apostolic* (1931) 129 The very existence of Christianity in any full sense of the term was at stake over the Homoousion. **1969** C. D. DARLINGTON *Evol. Man & Society* xiv. 311 Why not agree, he asked, to the *homoousion* or consubstantiality of the Father and Son? **1971** *Cath. Dict. Theol.* III. 39/2 What Nicaea had done with the homoousios to overcome Arianism, Trent was to do with transubstantiation to overcome other heresies.

B. *adj.* (Usu. in form *homoousios.*) Of the same essence or substance: = HOMOOUSIAN *a.* a.

1834 *Penny Cycl.* II. 317/1 In the western part of the Roman empire, all adversaries of the doctrine of Athanasius, that the Son was *homoousios*, or of the *same* essence with the Father, were called Arians; although some of these opponents taught..that the Son was *homoiousios*, or of *similar* essence. **1936** G. L. PRESTIGE *God in Patristic Thought* x. 197 According to the Valentinians..the abortive and degenerate fruit of the final aeon in the divine Absolute (pleroma), was homoousios with angelic ('spiritual') beings. *Ibid.* 198 A piece of marble closely resembling Mr. Gladstone..is made of different stuff from that of which Mr. Gladstone himself consisted: it is in the image of Mr. Gladstone, but not homoousios with him. **1969** A. RICHARDSON *Dict. Chr. Theol.* 347/2 The Lord and Lifegiver could not be Homoousios with those to whom he gives life.

homophene ('hɒməʊfiːn). [irreg. f. HOMO- + Gr. φαίν-ειν to show, to appear. (The Gr. formation would be *ὁμοφανής, giving Eng. *homophane*.)] A word having the same form to the eye as another; used esp. in reference to the reading of deaf-mutes, who recognize words only by sight. Hence **homo'phenous** (more correctly **-phanous**), *a.*

1883 A. G. BELL in *Ann. Deaf & Dumb* (1884) Jan. 44 Homophenous words, or words that have the same appearance to the eye. *Ibid.* 59 A knowledge of homophenes, that is..of those words that present the same appearance to the eye. **1884** A. J. ELLIS in *Athenæum* 12 Jan. 55/3 The word *homophenes* (similarly appearing), on the model of *homophones* (similarly sounding), was suggested to Prof. Graham Bell some years ago by Mr. Homer, late Principal of the Providence (Rhode Island) School for Deaf-Mutes, and has now been permanently adopted. *Ibid.*, Here every word in the sentence is homophenous with the corresponding word in the list.

homophile ('hɒməʊfaɪl), *sb.* (and *a.*) [f. HOMO- + -PHIL, -PHILE.] A term for a homosexual (regarded as a person belonging to a particular social group rather than as someone who is sexually abnormal). Also *attrib.* or as *adj.*

1960 G. WESTWOOD *Minority* v. 71 The so-called homophile organizations on the Continent provide wider facilities. In Amsterdam the 'Cultuur-en-Ontspannings-centrum' (C.O.C.) maintains clubrooms..and regular lectures are arranged on homosexuality. **1960** *News Chron.* 13 Oct. 4/6 Nor do Danes frown much on sex abnormalities. Danish 'homophiles' have their own monthly magazine. **1961** *Encounter* May 75 The relationships between homophiles seem to approximate very closely to the relationships between adult heterosexual men and women. **1963** CORY & LE ROY *Homosexual & his Society* xx. 245 The great bulk of publicity about the existence of homophile organizations—as they are usually called, somewhat euphemistically—has been, of necessity, by word of mouth. *Ibid.* 247 The participants and sympathizers in the homophile movement. **1965** *Guardian* 23 Apr. 11/5 The Dutch Society of Homophiles, set up 18 years ago as a private club for homosexuals. **1971** *Daily Colonist* (Victoria, B.C.) 15 Oct. 20/8 Homosexuals want legal marriage for tax reasons and to foil the designs of relatives, George Hyslop, founder of a Toronto homophile organization, told the Canadian Mental Health Association.

homophone ('hɒməʊfəʊn), *a.* and *sb.* Also **-phon**. [ad. Gr. ὁμόφωνος of the same sound, f. ὁμο- HOMO- + φωνή sound. Cf. F. *homophone.*]

A. *adj.* Having the same sound. *rare.*

1623 COCKERAM, *Homophon*, of one sound. **1880** *Encycl. Brit.* XI. 796 Ten homophone letters were added.

B. *sb.* **1.** *Philol.* (Usually in *pl.*) Applied to words having the same sound, but differing in meaning or derivation; also to different symbols denoting the same sound or group of sounds.

1843 GLIDDON *Anc. Egypt* (1850) 6/2 An alphabet composed of 16 distinct articulations, for each of which there was a number more or less great of homophones—i.e. symbols differing in figure, though identical in sound. **1866** FELTON *Anc. & Mod. Gr.* I. i. iii. 45 Each syllable or word [in Chinese] has..a considerable number of characters, made up originally of different elements..Practically each of these homophones may be used for the word, in whatever sense that word may be employed. **1873** F. HALL *Mod. Eng.* 170 *note*, Homophones, identical to the ear only; as *ail* and *ale*. **1883** I. Taylor *Alphabet* I. 29 We have in English the four homophones *rite*, *write*, *right*, and *wright*. By the aid of the variant spelling a child readily learns that these homophones are really four different words.

2. *Mus.* = HOMOPHONY 1. *rare.*

1879 GROVE *Dict. Mus.* I. 746 *Homophone*..voices or instruments sounding alike—unison..sometimes applied to music written in what was formerly called the Monodic style..now ordinarily employed for music in plain harmony..as opposed to the Polyphonic treatment.

homophonic (hɒməʊ'fɒnɪk), *a.* *Mus.* [f. as prec. + -IC.] **1.** Producing, or consisting of, sounds of the same pitch; unisonous, in unison. Said of ancient music; opp. to *antiphonic.*

1881 BROADHOUSE *Mus. Acoustics* 342 Helmholtz in his chapter on 'The Tonality of Homophonic Music' enumerates five scales which differ more or less from our modern major scale.

2. *loosely.* Said of music characterized by the predominance of one part or melody, to which the rest merely furnish harmonies; more correctly called *monophonic* or *monodic*. Opp. to *polyphonic.*

1879 E. PROUT in Grove *Dict. Mus.* I. 55 The homophonic rather than the polyphonic style predominates in the music [allemande], which frequently consists of a highly figurate melody, with a comparatively simple accompaniment. **1885** *Athenæum* 7 Mar. 319/2 [Bach's] compositions are polyphonic rather than homophonic.

3. *Philol.* = HOMOPHONOUS *a.* 2.

1942 [see BIMORPHEMIC *a.*].

homophonous (həʊ'mɒfənəs), *a.* [f. as prec. + -OUS.] **1.** *Mus.* = HOMOPHONIC 1.

1753 in CHAMBERS *Cycl. Supp.* **1872** F. HÜFFER in *Fortn. Rev.* Mar. 271 The homophonous innocence of the Doric and Mixolydic scales.

2. Having the same sound; of the character of homophones (see HOMOPHONE B. 1).

1826 *Edin. Rev.* XLV. 145 Each sound..may be represented by several homophonous signs. **1892** *Athenæum* 16 Apr. 501/1 The 'Scott Library' is sure to be confounded with the 'Stott Library', so homophonous are they.

homophony (həʊ'mɒfənɪ). [ad. Gr. ὁμοφωνία unison, f. ὁμόφωνος (see HOMOPHONE).]

1. *Mus.* Homophonic music or style. **a.** Unison, or music performed in unison: opp. to *antiphony*. **b.** *loosely*. Monophony, monody: opp. to *polyphony*. (See HOMOPHONIC.)

1776 BURNEY *Hist. Mus.* I. 137 Antiphony is more agreeable than homophony. **1879** *Grove's Dict. Mus.* I. 111 The leading feature in..the 17th century is..the development of homophony with its melodious character and its richness of harmony, in contradistinction to the old strict polyphony.

2. *Philol.* The quality of being homophonous; identity of sound (of words or characters).

1842 BRANDE *Dict. Sci.* etc. s.v., In French, which is peculiarly a dialect of Latin abounding in contractions, homophonies are numerous. **1892** *Spectator* 13 Aug. 233/2 Evident corruptions of the texts..specially favoured by the homophonies of the characters.

'homoplasmy. = HOMOPLASY.

1874 R. BROWN *Man. Bot.* 558 Cases of homoplasmy in plants are referable to two distinct classes..resemblances in general habit, and resemblances of particular organs.

homoplast ('hɒməʊplæst). *Biol.* [f. as prec. + Gr. πλαστός moulded: cf. *bioplast.*]

1. An organ or part homoplastic with another (see next); opp. to HOMOGEN 2.

1870 RAY LANKESTER in *Ann. Nat. Hist.* VI. 39 Such details of agreement..we must set down to the fact that they are to a great degree homoplasts, similar forces or requirements operating on similar materials in the two stocks..having produced results in the way of structure which have a certain agreement.

2. An aggregate or fusion of plastids all of the same structure: opp. to *alloplast.*

1883 [see *homo-organ* s.v. HOMO-].

homoplastic (-'plæstɪk), *a.* [f. as prec. + Gr. πλαστικός fit for moulding.] **1.** *Biol.* Having a similarity of structure without community of origin: said of parts or organs of different animals or plants. Opp. to HOMOGENETIC.

Nearly synonymous with HOMOMORPHIC 1 c, and with ANALOGOUS 1 b; but implying that the similarities are due to similarity of environment.

1870 RAY LANKESTER in *Ann. Nat. Hist.* VI. 40 The right ventricle of the bird's heart is not homogenous with the right ventricle of the mammal's heart, nor the left with the left; but the two cavities in each case are homoplastic. **1872** DARWIN *Orig. Spec.* (ed. 6) xiv. 386 Homoplastic structures are the same with those which I have classed..as analogous modifications or resemblances.

2. *Med.* and *Biol.* Of transplantation: involving the transfer of tissue from one individual to another of the same species. Of transplanted tissue: obtained from another individual of the same species as the recipient.

[**1889** L. OLLIER in *Arch. de Physiol. normale et path.* I. 168 Nous divisons les greffes en trois catégories: Les greffes autoplastiques... Les greffes homoplastiques, c'est-à-dire empruntées à un autre individu, mais à un sujet de la même espèce. Les greffes hétéroplastiques.] **1909** *Jrnl. Med. Res.* XXI. 320 He [*sc.* Carrel] also distinguishes an autoplastic transplantation, when the segment is taken from the same animal; a homoplastic, when the segment is taken from another animal of the same species; and a heteroplastic, when the segment is taken from an animal of another species. **1912** *Ann. Surg.* LVI. 381 Autoplastic bony pieces are in respect to regeneration much to be preferred to homoplastic. **1935** *Jrnl. Amer. Med. Assoc.* 8 June 2076/1 These homoplastic grafts all sloughed, while autoplastic grafts were highly successful on the same patient. **1958** *Immunology* I. 1 The homoplastic transplantation of the cortex of the adrenal gland in mice.

So **homo'plastically** *adv.*, between individuals of the same species; **'homoplasty**, homoplastic transplantation, homotransplantation.

1912 *Ann. Surg.* LVI. 378 The best material for free bony grafts is living, periosteum covered bone, if possible from the same individual himself (autoplasy [*sic*]). Or in case this is impossible, from another individual (homoplasty). **1923** H. NEUHOF *Transplantation of Tissues* ii. 31 The results have seemed to indicate that blood relationship has a bearing on the success of homoplasty. **1926** *Jrnl. Exper. Zool.* XLV. 52 Fore-limb buds of R. palustris tadpoles were transplanted homoplastically beneath the integument of the back. **1929** *Ann. Surg.* XC. 929 The lower the organism in the phylogenetic scale, the better the results obtained with homoplasty. **1942** *Univ. Calif. Publ. Zoöl.* LI. 43 Gastrular anlagen were implanted homoplastically into tadpoles.

homoplastide (-'plæstaɪd). *Biol.* [f. as prec. + Gr. πλαστός moulded + -IDE.] An organism consisting of a number of cells all of the same kind. Opp. to *heteroplastide* and *monoplastide.*

1889 VINES in *Nature* 24 Oct. 621 The body of unicellular organisms (monoplastides), as also that of undifferentiated multicellular organisms (homoplastides). *Ibid.* 622 [see HETEROPLASTIDE].

homoplasy (həʊ'mɒpləsɪ). *Biol.* [f. as prec. + Gr. -πλασια, f. πλάσις moulding, formation.] Homoplastic condition; similarity of structure produced independently by the operation of similar external circumstances. Opp. to HOMOGENY 2.

1870 RAY LANKESTER in *Ann. Nat. Hist.* VI. 39 When identical or nearly similar forces, or environments, act on two or more parts of an organism which are exactly or nearly alike..[or] on parts in two organisms, which parts are exactly or nearly alike and sometimes homogenetic, the resulting correspondences called forth in the several parts in the two organisms will be nearly or exactly alike..I propose to call this kind of agreement *homoplasis* or *homoplasy*. *Ibid.* 40 What, exactly, is to be ascribed to homogeny, and what to homoplasy, in the relations of this series of structures, is a matter for careful consideration. **1886** *Syd. Soc. Lex.*, *Homoplasy*, the assumption by organisms..of externally similar forms when exposed to similar external conditions. A good example is seen in the similarity of the American aloe, which is an Agave, to the true aloe.

homopolar (hɒməʊ'pəʊlə(r)), *a.* [f. HOMO- + POLAR *a.*] **1.** *Bot.* Having equal poles, as in the figures called *Stauraxonia homopola* (1883 *Encycl. Brit.* XVI. 844).

2. *Electr.* Of an electric generator or its operation: having or involving such an arrangement of magnets that the direction of the flux does not alternate with relation to the motion of the armature conductor(s), so that a direct current is generated without the use of commutators.

1896 S. P. THOMPSON *Dyn.-Electr. Machinery* (ed. 5) 475 (*heading*) Homopolar ('unipolar') dynamos. *Ibid.*, Where the motion is such that the conductor moves continuously past poles of one kind only, the inductive operation is said to be homopolar. **1938** MEARES & NEALE *Electr. Engin. Pract.* I. iv. 233 A homopolar dynamo is essentially a low voltage, heavy-current machine, but..it is generally more satisfactory to employ a motor generator driven from the ordinary supply mains. **1962** [see *Faraday('s) disc*].

3. *Chem.* [ad. G. *homöopolar* (R. Abegg 1906, in *Zeitschr. f. anorg. Chem.* L. 309); cf. *homœopolar* s.v. HOMŒO-.] Formed by or arising out of the sharing of electrons between neutral atoms, without ionization; covalent.

1922 C. H. DESCH *Metallography* (ed. 3) xv. 341 In all probability the new theory of valency based on the distribution of electrons in the molecule, will provide a satisfactory explanation of the formulæ of compounds of electrically similar ('homopolar') elements. **1930** G. THOMSON *Atom* 219 In such compounds the two atoms are on an equal footing and the compounds are called homopolar. **1940** MOTT & GURNEY *Electronic Processes in Ionic Crystals* i. 9 The transition from polar to homopolar binding. **1972** M. H. BATTEY *Min. for Students* i. 9/1 The covalent (or homopolar) bond is formed when two atoms.. share a pair of electrons, one electron being supplied by each atom.

Also **homopolic** (-'pɒlɪk) *a.* = sense 1 above.

1883 Homopolic [see *homaxonial*].

||**Homoptera** (həʊ'mɒptərə), *sb. pl.* *Entom.* [mod.L. (Latreille 1817), f. Gr. ὁμο- HOMO- + πτερόν wing: cf. Gr. ὁμόπτερος with the same plumage.] A suborder of HEMIPTERA, comprising insects of very various forms, with wings of uniform texture: contrasted with HETEROPTERA.

1826 KIRBY & SP. *Entomol.* xlvii. (1828) IV. 385 He denominated the last of these suborders Homoptera. **1835** KIRBY *Hab. & Inst. Anim.* II. xx. 319 The Homoptera have four deflexed wings often of a substance between coriaceous and membranous. **1874** LUBBOCK *Orig. & Met. Ins.* i. 25 The Homoptera agree with the Heteroptera in the structure of the mouth, and in the metamorphoses.

Hence **ho'mopter** [F. *homoptère*, Latreille], **ho'mopteran**, a member of the *Homoptera*; **ho'mopterous** *a.*, belonging to or having the characters of the *Homoptera*.

1826 KIRBY & SP. *Entomol.* xlvii. (1828) IV. 385 Very considerable differences take place in the economy of Homopterous insects. **1842** BRANDE *Dict. Sci.* etc., *Homopterans, Homoptera*, the name of an order of insects, dismembered from the *Hemiptera* of Linnæus, including those in which the wing-covers are of an uniform semimembranous consistency. **1864** WEBSTER, *Homopter.*

homorganic (hɒmɔː'gænɪk), *a.* Also occas. **homo-organic.** [f. HOMO- + ORGANIC *a.*]

1. *Bot.* 'Having the same, or a uniform, organization; applied to plants' (*Syd. Soc. Lex.*). Now *rare* or *Obs.*

1854 MAYNE *Expos. Lex.*, *Homorganus*,..homorganic: homorganous.

2. *Phonetics.* Produced by the same vocal organ or organs; sharing a specific type of articulation.

1864 MAX MÜLLER *Sc. Lang.* Ser. II. iii. (1868) 148 The hard aspirates are the hard letters, *k, t, p*, together with the corresponding winds or homorganic winds. **1880** SAYCE *Introd. Sc. Lang.* I. 289 Wherever homorganic sounds are produced, the vocal organs pass at once from the position required for the first to that required for the second. **1958** PRIEBSCH & COLLINSON *German Lang.* (ed. 4) II. i. 113 An affricate is a combination of a stop..with its homorganic spirant. **1959** M. SCHLAUCH *Eng. Lang. Mod. Times* 9 A liquid or a nasal plus a homorganic voiced stop. **1960** Z. S. HARRIS *Struct. Ling.* 532 These occur only after voiced or voiceless consonants homo-organic with their own. **1972** *Archivum Linguisticum* III. 39 A preceding alveolar is lost, and a homorganic nasal intervenes following a bilabial or velar stop.

homosexual (həʊməʊ-, hɒməʊ'sɛksjuːəl), *a.* and *sb.* [Irreg. f. HOMO- + SEXUAL *a.*]

A. *adj.* Involving, related to, or characterized by a sexual propensity for one's own sex; of or involving sexual activity with a member of one's own sex, or between individuals of the same sex.

1892 C. G. CHADDOCK tr. *Krafft-Ebing's Psychopathia Sexualis* III. 255 He had been free from homo-sexual inclinations. *Ibid.* 256 The homo-sexual woman offers the same manifestations, *mutatis mutandis.* **1897** H. ELLIS *Stud. Psychol. Sex* I. i. 2 Among animals in a domesticated or confined state it is easy to find evidence of homosexual attraction, due merely to the absence of the other sex. **1914** G. B. SHAW in *New Statesman* 14 Nov. 21/2 The forty tolerated homosexual brothels of Berlin. **1921** E. J. KEMPF *Psychopath.* xiii. 645 Her social interests were decidedly homosexual. **1921** *Blackw. Mag.* Jan. 134/2 What the nature of the friendship was we cannot say; it may have been homosexual, a love which was common among the later Greeks. **1929** R. GRAVES *Good-Bye to all That* iii. 40 In English preparatory and public schools romance is necessarily homosexual. **1942** *Jrnl. Compar. Psychol.* XXXIII. 160 Homosexual mountings are characteristic of the male Rhesus monkey, particularly during adolescence. **1948** A. C. KINSEY et al. *Sexual Behav. Hum. Male* xxi. 610 A considerable portion of the population..has at least some homosexual experience between adolescence and old age. **1961** E. WAUGH *Unconditional Surrender* II. vii. 173 'I'm sure you aren't a pansy.' 'Pansy?' 'You're not homosexual?' Even this did not disconcert Uncle Peregrine... 'Good gracious, no. Besides the "o" is short. It comes from the Greek not the Latin.' **1963** A. HERON *Towards Quaker View of Sex* iii. 24 Not all effeminate men are homosexual, and few homosexual men can be really described as effeminate. **1965** ROSEN & GREGORY *Abnormal Psychol.* xviii. 381 Homosexual behavior in human females, also known as lesbianism or sapphism,..is less likely to arouse social censure than male homosexuality. **1973** *Daily Tel.* 5 Apr. 9/8 For the first time at a National Union of Students conference homosexual and lesbian students spoke out openly.

B. *sb.* A person who has a sexual propensity for his or her own sex; *esp.* one whose sexual desires are directed wholly or largely towards people of the same sex.

In non-technical contexts it is often taken to mean a male homosexual, a female one being termed a lesbian.

1912 E. PAUL tr. *A. Moll's Sexual Life of Child* v. 127 An adult homosexual who as a child once did some needlework for a joke. **1932** S. GIBBONS *Cold Comfort Farm* xi. 153 There were many homosexuals to be seen in Hyde Park. **1954** W. MAYER-GROSS et al. *Clin. Psychiatry* iv. 179 Male homosexuals are frequently classified into the active and the passive type; female homosexuals into the masculine and feminine. **1955** *Sci. News Let.* 21 May 334/3 The idea that homosexuals are necessarily bad security risks is debunked in a report..before the American Psychiatric Association. **1969** A. GLYN *Dragon Variation* vii. 198 Uses quite a lot of cologne, doesn't he? Is he a homosexual? **1973** *Daily Tel.* 10 July 6/3 Homosexuals and lesbians make up a sizeable minority of the population.

Hence **homo'sexualist**, a homosexual.

1931 A. EILOART tr. *Heyer's Hypnosis* xiii. 204 It should be considered that a homosexualist thus suggestively transformed for weeks or even months, marries..within that time. **1933** H. WILLIAMSON *Gold Falcon* i. 19 His book ..proving..that Hamlet should be played as a homosexualist in vain love with Horatio had just been published. **1961** —— *Innocent Moon* v. 100 Even Jesus.. according to Nordau..was a homosexualist and should have been locked up. **1971** *Southerly* XXXI. 84 He consigned me to the lavatory-cleaning brigade together with a group of homosexualists.

homosexuality (,həʊməʊ-, ,hɒməʊ sɛksjuː'ælɪtɪ). [f. prec. + -ITY.] The quality of being homosexual, homosexual character or nature; also, homosexual behaviour or activity.

1892 C. G. CHADDOCK tr. *Krafft-Ebing's Psychopathia Sexualis* III. 185 (*heading*) Great diminution or complete absence of sexual feeling for the opposite sex, with substitution of sexual feeling and instinct for the same sex. (Homo-sexuality, or contrary sexual instinct.) **1892** J. A. SYMONDS *Let.* 21 Oct. in P. Grosskurth *J. A. Symonds* (1964) 269 There is an inborn bias toward homosexuality. **1897** H. ELLIS *Stud. Psychol. Sex* I. iv. 101 Bourneville believes that 75 per cent. of the inmates of the Parisian venereal hospitals have practised homosexuality. **1948** A. C.

KINSEY et al. *Sexual Behav. Hum. Male* xxi. 615 Among many clinicians this work has been taken to mean that the sex hormones control the heterosexuality or homosexuality of an individual's behavior. **1959** B. WOOTTON *Social Sci. & Social Path.* 15 Many citizens..prefer to look on adult homosexuality as a matter of private taste. **1965** ROSEN & GREGORY *Abnormal Psychol.* xviii. 381 All persons..have a greater or lesser tendency to homosexuality as well as heterosexuality. **1972** *Daily Tel.* 11 Mar. 3/2 'Gay Cambridge', the Cambridge branch of the Campaign for Homosexual Equality,..claimed that sex education at school did not adequately cover homosexuality.

homo'sexually, *adv.* [f. as prec. + -LY².] In a homosexual manner; with respect to homosexual activities or homosexuality.
1921 J. C. FLÜGEL *Psycho-anal. Stud. of Family* ii. 16 Homosexually disposed parents would..tend to bring up homosexual children. **1921** E. J. KEMPF *Psychopath.* ii. 95 One of our patients..has been fighting strong cravings to become homosexually submissive. **1933** *Jrnl. Mental Sci.* LXXIX. 144 One was homosexually assaulted at the age of 12. **1948** A. C. KINSEY et al. *Sexual Behav. Hum. Male* xxi. 632 A homosexually experienced male could undoubtedly find a larger number of sexual partners among males than a heterosexually experienced male could find among females. **1963** A. HERON *Towards Quaker View of Sex* iii. 25 It is seldom that a public figure feels he can afford to disclose that he is in fact homosexually inclined. **1973** P. EVANS *Bodyguard Man* xxiii. 145, I thought you might be homosexually attracted to each other.

homostyled ('hɒməʊstaɪld), *a. Bot.* [f. HOMO- + STYLE + -ED².] Having the styles or pistils (in different individual plants) of the same length relatively to the stamens (= HOMOGONOUS 1, HOMOMORPHIC 1 b): opp. to *heterostyled.* Also **homostylic** (hɒməʊ'staɪlɪk), **homostylous** (-'staɪləs), *adjs.* in same sense; **homostyly** ('hɒməʊstaɪlɪ), the condition of being homostyled.
1877 [see HETEROSTYLED]. **1883** THOMPSON tr. *Müller's Fertil. Flowers* 20 Homostylic plants with irregular flowers. **1886** *Syd. Soc. Lex., Homostylous.* **1887** GOEBEL *Morphol. Plants* 481 *Homostyly*, same as homogony.

homotaxial (-'tæksɪəl), *a. Geol.* [f. HOMO- + Gr. -ταξια (f. τάξις) arrangement + -AL¹.] Applied to strata in different regions, having the same relative position with respect to those underlying and overlying them, but not necessarily contemporaneous: cf. HOMOTAXIS; also to the fossil remains (usually of similar character) found in such strata.
1870 HUXLEY *Anniv. Addr. Geol. Soc.* in *Q. Jrnl.* XXVI. p. xlii, Certain forms of life in one locality occur in the same general order of succession as, or are *homotaxial* with, similar forms in the other locality. **1888** J. PRESTWICH *Geol.* II. 4 The homotaxial relations of the groups.
Hence **homo'taxially** *adv.*, in the way of or in relation to homotaxy. Also **homo'taxeous**, **homo'taxic** *adjs.* = HOMOTAXIAL.
1866 *Intell. Observ.* No. 56. 97 As homotaxeous, and not as contemporaneous. **1872** NICHOLSON *Palæont.* (1879) I. 42 The Silurian rocks of Europe, North America, South America, Australia, &c., contain very similar fossils, and are undoubtedly 'homotaxeous'. **1877** HUXLEY *Anat. Inv. Anim.* Introd. 22 The species which constitute the corresponding or homotaxic terms in the series, in different localities, are not identical. **1880** DAWKINS *Early Man* 22 *note*, If..we look at them, homotaxially, from the point of view offered by the European Meiocenes, they are Meiocene.

homotaxis (-'tæksɪs). *Geol.* [irreg. f. Gr. ὁμο- HOMO- + τάξις arrangement. The Gr. formation would be *ὁμοταξία homotaxy.] The condition of being homotaxial; the relation of strata having the same relative position in the geologic series, or of the similar forms of life occurring in such strata.
1862 HUXLEY *Anniv. Addr. Geol. Soc.* in *Q. Jrnl.* XVIII. p. xlii, For Geology (which after all is only the anatomy and physiology of the earth) it might be well to invent some single word (such as 'homotaxis', similarity of order), in order to express an essentially similar idea [i.e. to 'homology' in anatomy]. *Ibid.* p. xlvi, The mischief of confounding that 'homotaxis' or 'similarity of arrangement' which can be demonstrated, with 'synchrony' or identity of date, for which there is not a shadow of a proof, under the one common term of 'contemporaneity'. **1870** *Ibid.* XXVI. p. xliii, The use of the term 'homotaxis' instead of 'synchronism' has not, so far as I know, found much favour in the eyes of geologists. **1883** *Nature* 18 Jan. 262 It cautions the student against the confusion of geological synchrony with stratigraphical homotaxis.

homotaxy (-tæksɪ). Etymol. regular f. for prec.
1873 F. HALL *Mod. Eng.* 295 *note*, *Homotaxis* is impossible ..*homotaxia, homotaxy*, is the eligible form. **1889** in *Cent. Dict.*

homotopic (hɒməʊ'tɒpɪk), *a.* [f. HOMO- + Gr. τοπικ-ός in respect to place (see TOPIC *a.* and *sb.*).]
1. Relating to the same place or part, or corresponding places or parts.
1876 tr. *Haeckel's Hist. Creat.* I. 217 The laws of homotopic transmission..which might be called the law of transmission in corresponding parts of the body.
2. *Math.* [ad. G. *homotop* (Dehn & Heegaard *Analysis Situs* in *Encykl. d. math. Wiss.* (1907) III. I. I. 165).] Related by a homotopy *to* another complex or path, or the mapping of which it is an image; that is a homotopy.
1918, 1930 [see HOMOTOPY]. **1956** E. M. PATTERSON *Topology* i. 11 A curve which can be deformed continuously into another is said to be homotopic to it. **1961** HOCKING & YOUNG *Topology* iv. 149 We may view homotopic mappings as being members of a one-parameter family of mappings with a continuous parameter. **1967** W. S. MASSEY *Algebraic Topology* ii. 64 Two continuous maps ϕ_0, ϕ_1: $X \to Y$ are homotopic if and only if there exists a continuous map ϕ: $X \times I \to Y$ such that, for $x \in X$, $\phi(x, 0) = \phi_0(x)$, $\phi(x, 1) = \phi_1(x)$.
Hence **homo'topically** *adv.*, by a homotopy; as regards homotopy.
1930 S. LEFSCHETZ *Topology* ii. 77 We will say that *A* and *A'* are homotopically deformable, or simply deformable, into one another, over *G.* **1952** F. BAGEMIHL et al. tr. *Pontryagin's Found. Combinatorial Topology* iii. 83 The mappings ϕ and θ are said to be homotopically inverse to one another. **1968** H. F. CULLEN *Introd. Gen. Topology* vii. 368 The usual space E^1 of real numbers is homotopically equivalent to the trivial space consisting of 0 alone, say.

homotopy ('hɒməʊtɒpɪ, hə'mɒtəpɪ). *Math.* [ad. G. *homotopie* (Dehn & Heegaard *Analysis Situs* in *Encykl. d. math. Wiss.* (1907) III. I. I. 164): see prec. and -Y³.] **a.** A mapping that deforms one path continuously into another in such a way that all the intermediate paths lie within the topological space of which the two given paths are subspaces (see quot. 1970). **b.** The property of being homotopic.
1918 O. VEBLEN *Analysis Situs* (Cambridge Colloq. Lect., Vol. 5, Pt. 2) v. 126 The term *homotopy* will be used to designate a deformation in the general sense..and two generalized complexes..will be said to be homotopic if one can be carried into the other by means of a homotopy. **1930** S. LEFSCHETZ *Topology* ii. 77 The singular translation of *A* into *A'* just described is called a homotopic deformation, or homotopy, or simply deformation. **1951** M. H. A. NEWMAN *Topology of Plane Sets of Points* (ed. 2) vii. 179 It is homotopies..and not identities between paths that are interesting. **1956** E. M. PATTERSON *Topology* i. 11 Homotopy plays an important part in modern topology. **1961** HOCKING & YOUNG *Topology* iv. 151 Theorems about homotopy are but special cases of more general theorems on the extension of mappings. **1970** C. R. F. MAUNDER *Algebraic Topology* ii. 25 Two continuous maps f, g: $X \to Y$ are homotopic (or '*f* is homotopic to *g*') if there exists a continuous map F: $X \times I \to Y$, such that $F(x, 0) = f(x)$ and $F(x, 1) = g(x)$, for all $x \in X$. The map *F* is said to be a homotopy, and we write $f \simeq g$ for '*f* is homotopic to *g*'.

homotransplant (hɒməʊ'trɑːnsplɑːnt, -træns-, -plænt), *sb. Med.* and *Biol.* [f. HOMO- + TRANSPLANT *sb.*] **a.** A piece of tissue or an organ taken from one individual and transplanted (or intended for transplantation) to another individual of the same species.
1929 *Ann. Surg.* XC. 934 Eight days after operation, the homotransplant appeared well fixed. **1947** *Jrnl. Bone & Joint Surg.* I. 621 In order that homotransplants of bone may be available for use, methods of storing and preservation must be considered. **1963** R. Y. CALNE *Renal Transplantation* iii. 33 Experimental renal homotransplants initially have the appearance and behaviour of autotransplants.
b. A homotransplantation operation.
1955 *Jrnl. Clin. Invest.* XXXIV. 329/1 Dederer.. performed a homotransplant of a kidney from one puppy to another of the same litter.

homotransplant (ˌhɒməʊtrɑːns'plɑːnt, -træns-, -plænt), *v. Med.* and *Biol.* [f. prec. sb.] *trans.* To transplant from one individual to another of the same species.
1953 *Brit. Jrnl. Surg.* XL. 447/1 Attempts at homotransplanting kidneys in humans in France have had no more success than the animal experiments of the past fifty years. **1955** *Proc. R. Soc.* B. CXLIII. 560 When ovary and skin are homotransplanted concomitantly, the ovary may survive while the skin is destroyed. **1961** *New Scientist* 7 Sept. 593/1 The natural history of a kidney homotransplanted between genetically dissimilar people.
So **homotrans'planted** *ppl. a.*
1939 *Proc. Soc. Exper. Biol. & Med.* XLI. 474 (*heading*) Persistence of medullary tissue in homotransplanted adrenals. **1961** *New Scientist* 7 Sept. 593/1 A homotransplanted kidney starts to function within fifteen minutes of establishing the new circulation of blood.

homotransplantable (ˌhɒməʊtrɑːns'plɑːnt-əb(ə)l, -træns-, -plænt-), *a. Med.* and *Biol.* [f. prec. vb., after *transplantable.*] Capable of being successfully transplanted from one individual to another of the same species.
1957 *Jrnl. Nat. Cancer Inst.* XVIII. 529 It has been suggested..that chromosomal imbalance in homotransplantable tumors produces a simplified antigenic composition of the tumor cells. **1962** FELDMAN & YAFFE in Wolstenholme & Cameron *Transplantation* (Ciba Foundation symposia) 170 Further serial transfers through 3–4 transplant generations established homotransplantable tumour lines.
Hence ˌ**homotransplanta'bility**.
1957 *Jrnl. Nat. Cancer Inst.* XVIII. 529 The only nonmalignant tissue reported as showing some degree of homotransplantability is the ovary of the rat. **1967** W. ANDERSON *Boyd's Path. Surgeon* (ed. 8) ix. 107 In the past it was possible to transplant a tumor only to another member of the same species (homotransplantability).

homotransplantation (ˌhɒməʊtrɑːnsplɑːn-'teɪʃən, -træns-, -plænt-). *Med.* and *Biol.* [f. HOMO- + TRANSPLANTATION.] The operation of transplanting tissue from one individual to another of the same species.
1905 A. CARREL in *Jrnl. Amer. Med. Assoc.* 25 Nov. 1645/2 If the organ is replaced in the same animal from which it was removed, the operation is called an autotransplantation. If it is placed in another animal of the same species it is called a homotransplantation, while if it is placed in an animal of a different species, the operation is called a heterotransplantation. **1915** *Ibid.* 4 Dec. 1966/2 Homotransplantations between related and non-related rabbits. **1917** *Ann. Surg.* LXV. 702 Autotransplantation and homotransplantation of segments of veins and arteries are perfectly feasible. **1953** *Brit. Jrnl. Surgery* XL. 447/1 It is in the chronic group of cases that homotransplantation of kidneys would be necessarily first applied. **1971** *Nature* 22 Jan. 270/1 Minced skeletal muscle regenerates with autotransplantation and homotransplantation in the rat, and with heterotransplantation in the mouse.

homotropal (həʊ'mɒtrəpəl), *a. Bot.* [f. as next + -AL¹.] = next.
1844 in HOBLYN *Dict. Med.* (ed. 2) 148. **1855** BALFOUR *Bot.* (ed. 3) 302 In an anatropal seed, where the micropyle is close to the hilum, and the chalaza at the opposite extremity, the embryo is erect or homotropal.

homotropous (-'ɒtrəpəs), *a. Bot.* [f. Gr. ὁμο- HOMO- + -τροπος turning + -OUS (after F. *homotrope*, A. Richard 1819): cf. Gr. ὁμότροπος of like disposition.] Of the embryo of a seed: Having the radicle directed towards the hilum. Opp. to *antitropous* or *heterotropous.*
1829 P. CLINTON tr. *Richard's Elem. Bot.* (ed. 4) 398 The embryo is said to be homotropous when it has the same direction with the seed, that is to say, when its radicle corresponds to the hilum. **1870** BENTLEY *Bot.* (ed. 2) 342 The embryo is said to be *erect* or *homotropous.*

homotype ('hɒməʊtaɪp), *sb.* [f. Gr. ὁμο- HOMO- + τύπος TYPE.] **1.** *Biol.* A part or organ having the same type of structure as another, a homologue; applied *esp.* to serially or laterally homologous parts in the same organism.
1840 T. A. G. BALFOUR *Typ. Char. Nat.* (1860) 64 A general likeness is sufficient in nature to constitute, in the eyes of naturalists, a type, and hence they speak of such as homologies or homotypes. **1849** OWEN *Nat. Limbs* 19 The femur, the homotype of the humerus. **1854** —— *Skel. & Teeth* in *Circ. Sc., Organ. Nat.* I. 170 So far as each segment ..is a repetition or 'homotype' of every other segment. **1872** MIVART *Elem. Anat.* 215 The successive vertebræ..are serial homologues, or homotypes. **1939** *Ann. Ent. Soc. Amer.* XXXII. 695 Homotype: 1. That which is constructed on the same plan or type—as metameres of the body. *Not* a nomenclatural term.
2. *Taxonomy.* A specimen identified as a type by someone other than the author of the original description, after comparison with the holotype.
1896 WALSINGHAM & DURRANT *Rules for regulating Nomencl.* 13 A specimen named by another than the author, after comparison with the type, is called a Homotype... We have added the term *Homotype* to those proposed by Mr. Oldfield Thomas. **1939** *Ann. Ent. Soc. Amer.* XXXII. 695 Homotype:... 2. Equals Homoeotype. **1967** R. E. BLACKWELDER *Taxonomy* xxix. 591 Specimens identified as to time or person of identification. Metatypes, homotypes (homoeotypes), and so on.
Hence **homotypal** ('hɒməʊtaɪpəl) *a.* = HOMOTYPIC *a.* 1. **homotypy** ('hɒməʊtaɪpi, həʊ'mɒtipi), relation of homotypes; homology; *esp.* serial or lateral homology.
1849 OWEN *Nat. Limbs* 29 To discern their *homotypal relations and their classification. **1871** H. MACMILLAN *True Vine* iii. (1872) 102 The vine presents a repetition both of homotypal parts and of homotypal arrangement of parts. **1874** *Pop. Encycl.* s.v., **Homotypy*, another term for serial homology. **1878** BELL *Gegenbaur's Comp. Anat.* 64 Homotypical organs..are often so changed that their homotypy cannot be recognised, and has to be worked out.

homotype ('hɒməʊtaɪp), *a. Cytol.* [f. HOMO- + Gr. τύπος TYPE *sb.*¹] = HOMOTYPIC *a.* 2.
1895 [see *heterotype* s.v. HETERO-]. **1907** C. E. WALKER *Essent. Cytol.* v. 46 The first division following the meiotic is very commonly given a special name—the 'homotype' division. **1920** L. DONCASTER *Introd. Study Cytol.* v. 67 This second division is therefore spoken of as a homotype mitosis.

homotypic (hɒməʊ'tɪpɪk), *a.* [f. HOMOTYP(E + -IC.]
1. Of the character of, or relating to, a homotype; homologous.
1886 *Syd. Soc. Lex., Homotypic.*
2. *Cytol.* = *homœotypic* adj. (s.v. HOMŒO-).
1904 *Amer. Naturalist* XXXVIII. 741 This mitosis differs from that of the 'typical' mitoses of cells and is called 'homotypic'. **1965** J. WILKINSON tr. *Langeron's Outl. Mycol.* ix. 378 Interkinesis is very short and the two daughter-nuclei very rapidly enter the prophase for the second meiotic (homotypic) division. **1972** *Nature* 21 Apr. 375/1 He did not believe that cancer should be thought of as a disease of cells nor of homotypic collections of cells.
3. *Ecol.* Consisting of individuals of a single species.
1930 W. M. WHEELER in E. V. Cowdry *Human Biol.* 141 Many species often assemble to form aggregations on the same tree or flower, or under the same stone, and these aggregations may be either homotypic, i.e. consisting of members of the same species, or heterotypic, when individuals of more than one species assemble.
Also **homo'typical** *a.*
1870 ROLLESTON *Anim. Life* 93 The large pincers of the scorpion are homotypical..with the large pincers of the crayfish. **1916** BAINBRIDGE & MENZIES *Essent. Physiol.* (ed. 2) xv. 456 In the second division each chromosome splits

longitudinally in the ordinary way (homotypical mitosis). **1931** J. E. Frazer *Man. Embryol.* i. 3 In the second maturation division each cell with its reduced chromosome number divides into two cells containing like numbers... Hence this division is an ordinary or 'homotypical' one. **1931** W. C. Allee *Animal Aggregations* i. 15 Homotypical associations consist of members of the same species which have arisen either sexually or asexually, which may have remained together because they are the offspring of the same parent, or which may have become accidentally associated together although of different parentage.

homousian: see HOMOOUSIAN.

homozygote (hɒməʊ'zaɪgəʊt). *Biol.* [f. HOMO- + ZYGOTE.] A diploid individual that has identical alleles at one or more genetic loci. Also *attrib.* or as *adj.*, homozygous.

1902 Bateson & Saunders *Rep. Evol. Comm. R. Soc.* I. 126 Similarly, the zygote formed by the union of gametes having similar allelomorphs, may be spoken of as a homozygote. **1902** W. Bateson *Mendel's Princ. Heredity* 23 This *Aa* is the hybrid, or 'mule' form, or as I have elsewhere called it, the heterozygote, as distinguished from *AA* or *aa* the homozygotes. **1903** —— in *Nature* 19 Mar. 463/1 The homozygotes will all have pink eyes. **1909** R. H. Lock *Rec. Progress in Study of Variation* (ed. 2) vii. 185 Let the F_1 plants, arising from the smooth yellow heterozygote grains, be crossed with the wrinkled white parent. **1927** Haldane & Huxley *Animal Biol.* ii. 67 Homozygote parents. **1930** R. A. Fisher *Genet. Theory Nat. Selection* i. 8 The heterozygote when mated to either kind of homozygote would produce both heterozygotes and homozygotes. **1949** Darlington & Mather *Elem. Genetics* xiii. 276 If we breed a homozygote, or a group of like homozygotes, the offspring will be genetically.. identical both with their parents and with one another. **1965** T. Dobzhansky *Heredity & Nature of Man* v. 156 Persons who inherit this gene from both parents (homozygotes) die of fatal anemia.

Hence ˌ**homozy'gosis**, the fusion of two genetically identical gametes; the state or condition of being homozygous; ˌ**homozy'gosity**, the state or condition of being homozygous; the degree or extent to which an individual is homozygous with respect to its complement of genetic loci; ˌ**homozy'gotic** *a.*, of or pertaining to homozygosis; homozygous; ˌ**homozy'gotically** *adv.*; **homo'zygous** *a.*, having identical alleles at one or more genetic loci.

1902 Bateson & Saunders *Rep. Evol. Comm. R. Soc.* I. 152 The various homo- and hetero-zygous combinations. **1905** W. Bateson in *Rep. Brit. Assoc. 1904* 348 The other possibility is that this phenomenon is due to simultaneous homozygosis of independent allelomorphs. **1916** *Mem. N.Y. Bot. Gard.* VI. 349 Such a condition might also arise from inbreeding in which what is called 'homozygosity' might develop, giving similarity to the hereditary complex. **1925** D. F. Jones *Genetics Plant & Animal Improvement* xv. 503 Only by bringing sexually reproducing organisms to a fairly high degree of homozygosity can there be any possibility of successfully predicting the outcome in particular matings. **1927** *Hereditas* VIII. 77 Both *V. tricolor* and *V. arvensis* are homozygotic in respect of the modifying gene. *Ibid.* 147 One gene.., when homozygotically present, turns the full yellow to a yellowish white. **1942** *Nature* 10 Jan. 54/2 Such self-mating gives immediate homozygosis. **1949** Darlington & Mather *Elem. Genetics* xiii. 279 The homozygotic potential will remain as such so long as cross-breeding is absent or at least restricted to like homozygotes. **1957** C. H. Waddington *Strategy of Genes* ii. 48 Further, gene-fixation and the passage to homozygosity, will be still more delayed if the environment does not remain perfectly uniform. **1969** *Sci. Jrnl.* Dec. 86/2 Various disorders due to homozygosity for rare recessive genes..are much commoner in such inbred populations than in outbred populations. **1970** Ambrose & Easty *Cell Biol.* x. 335 White-eyed females would only be observed if they were homozygous for this recessive gene.

†**homple.** *Obs.* ? Some kind of linen fabric.

c **1450** in *Rel. Ant.* I. 27 Loke well your lawne, your homple, and your lake..Ye washe cleyn. [**1847–78** Halliwell, *Hompel*, a kind of jacket. *North.*]

homple, var. of HUMPLE *v.*

homrai ('həʊmraɪ). [Nepal.] A large black-and-white hornbill, *Buceros bicornis*, which is found from India to Sumatra.

1832 B. H. Hodgson in *Jrnl. Asiatic Soc. Bengal* I. 251 The Homrâi reaches its full size in four and [*sic*] five years; it is gregarious and sedate. **1882** D. G. Elliot *Monogr. Bucerotidæ* [s.v. *Dichoceros bicornis*] (*heading*) The Homrai. *Ibid.* 3 The Nepaulese name for this species, 'Homrai', is derived from the notes it is accustomed to utter. **1905** *Pall Mall Gaz.* 24 Apr. 6/3 This curious bird (*Dichoceros bicornis*) is also known as 'Homrai'. **1939** F. N. Chasen *Birds of Malay Peninsula* IV. 90 (*heading*) The Great or Homrai Hornbill.

‖**homuncio** (həʊ'mʌnsɪəʊ). [L. dim. of *homo, homin-*, man.] = HOMUNCULE.

1643 Prynne *Sov. Power Parl.* App. 153 An hundred Homuncioes more or lesse. **1650** Bulwer *Anthropomet.* 253 Such an Homencio was Mr. Jefferies the late Queens Dwarfe. **1753** *Ess. Celibacy* 64 Producing an homuncio by the laws of matter and motion. **1802** Bentham *Wks.* (1838–43) XI. 129 But it is something for an Homuncio like myself to put all these potentates into jeopardy.

homuncule, -uncle (həʊ'mʌŋkjuːl, -'ʌŋk(ə)l). [ad. L. *homunculus*, (also in Eng. use) dim. of *homo* man. Cf. F. *homuncule* (18th c. in Littré).]

A little or diminutive man; a mannikin.

1656 H. More *Enthus. Tri.* 46 That there is an artificiall way of making an Homunculus, and that the Fairies of the woods, Nymphs and Giants themselves had some such originall. **1696** J. Edwards *Demonstr. Exist. God* II. 124 Parcelsus's artificial homuncle. **1759** Sterne *Tr. Shandy* I. ii, Homunculus. **1839** *New Monthly Mag.* LVI. 25 The door opened suddenly, and admitted an homuncule, of about four feet three.

Hence **ho'muncular** *a.*, diminutive, pigmy.

1822–34 *Good's Study Med.* (ed. 4) IV. 13 Delappius..not only saw these homuncular tadpoles, but pretended to trace one of them bursting through the tunic by which it was swaddled.

homy, homey ('həʊmɪ), *a. colloq.* [f. HOME *sb.* + -Y. For analogical spelling, cf. *bony, limy.*] Resembling or suggestive of home; home-like; having the feeling of home; homish.

1856 Kingsley in *Life* (1877) I. 488, I like to..feel 'homey' wherever I be. **1864** *Ibid.* II. 194, I saw..plenty of our dear English 'lady's smock' in the wet meadows near here [Bayonne], which looked very homy. **1874** Mrs. Whitney *We Girls* ix. 181 'What a beautiful old homey house it is!' 'And what a homey family!'

Hence '**hominess**, homy quality or character, homelikeness.

1885 Roe *Driven back to Eden* 69 A sense of rest, quiet, comfort, and hominess. **1888** *Pall Mall G.* 30 Apr. 11/2 The 'Hominess' of the French Character.

homyger, obs. form of HOMAGER.

homynable, shortened form of ABHOMINABLE.

1489 Caxton *Faytes of A.* III. xvii. 208 It is an homynable horreur.

hon.[1] (ɒn), abbrev. of HONOURABLE, HONORABLE.

1721 in D. Wilkins *Leges Anglo-Saxonicæ* List of Subscribers, The Hon. Henry Booth of the Middle Temple, Esq. **1777** *Jrnls. Continental Congress* (U.S.) X. 10 The following Gentlemen were chosen, viz. Hon. John Hancock, Samuel Adams, [etc.]. **1861** T. Hughes *Tom Brown at Oxf.* I. iii. 39 The fourth man of the breakfast-club, the Hon. Piers St. Cloud, was in his third year. **1873** 'Mark Twain' & Warner *Gilded Age* (1874) xxxiii. 304 Mr. O'Riley, still bearing the legislative 'Hon.' attached to his name. **1914** W. S. Churchill in *World Crisis* (1923) I. viii. 186 Why cannot the right hon. and learned Gentleman (Sir Edward Carson) say boldly, [etc.]. **1922** Joyce *Ulysses* 379 Over against the Rt. Hon. Mr. Justice Fitzgibbon's door. **1925** T. Dreiser *Amer. Trag.* III. xiv. 182 One Hon. Alvin Belknap, of Belknap and Jephson, of this same city. **1938** N. Marsh *Artists in Crime* ii. 13 He's an Hon., you know, and old Lord Pilgrim is doddering to the grave. **1945** N. Mitford *Pursuit of Love* ii. 14, I was a Hon, since my father, like theirs, was a lord. **1962** 'M. Innes' *Connoisseur's Case* v. 54 So old Mrs. Coulson..was an Hon?

hon.[2] (ɒn), abbrev. of HONORARY *a.*

1840 *Wiltshire Topographical Soc. Laws & Regulations*, Members of the Wiltshire Topographical Society... Geo. Alexander, Esq. Architect, London, *Hon. Sec.* **1876** *Monthly Packet* Feb. notices p. [5] Your correspondent could obtain further information from the Hon. Sec. **1957** R. W. Zandvoort *Handbk. Eng. Gram.* I. ii. 34 Members wishing to resign..are requested to notify the hon. secretary before January 1st. **1966** J. Betjeman *High & Low* 44 (*title*) The Hon. Sec.

hon[3] (hʌn), colloq. abbrev. of HONEY *sb.* (sense 5).

1906 *Dialect Notes* III. 141 *Hon'*, sweetheart, darling, baby. 'Going to school, hon'?' Very common in addressing children of a tender age. *a* **1911** D. G. Phillips *Susan Lenox* (1917) I. ix. 155 'Never mind, hon,' he said... 'My, but you're purty!' **1953** *Fortune* July 158/2 She saw I was reading. 'What you got there, hon?' she asked me. **1954** P. Highsmith *Blunderer* (1956) xxviii. 201 'Let's go, hon.' Bill often proposed leaving before his wife did. **1959** [see DARL].

Honan (həʊ'nɑːn). The name of a province of N. China, used to designate: **a.** a variety of silk manufactured there; **b.** ceramics of the Sung dynasty, probably manufactured there.

[**1878** J. J. Young *Ceramic Art* II. v. 149 The aubergine, or purple egg-plant violet, was also made under Sung, and is one of the celebrated productions of Kiun, in the province of Ho-nan.] **1923** *Daily Mail* 24 Apr. 1 Fine quality real Silk Honans, beautifully printed. **1923** Hobson & Hetherington *Art Chinese Potter* Pl. XCVIII, Bowl of conical form with rounded sides and pointed base;.. Probably Honan ware. Sung dynasty. **1960** H. Hayward *Antique Coll.* 144/2 *Honan wares*, black- and brown-glazed Chinese porcelain wares of the Sung dynasty, probably made in Honan province. **1968** J. Ironside *Fashion Alphabet* 250 *Honan.* This is a silk pongee cloth from the Honan area of China, which has a particularly uniform colour. **1972** *Times* 30 May 11/2 (Advt.), A large Honan deep bowl.

honcho ('hɒntʃəʊ). *slang* (chiefly *U.S.*). Also **hancho**. [ad. Jap. *han'chō* group leader.] Originally, the leader of a small group or squad; hence, anyone in charge in any situation; the 'boss'. Hence as *v. trans.*, to oversee; to be in charge of.

1947 J. Bertram *Shadow of War* VII. i. 212 But here comes the *hancho*. This boat must be finished to-night. **1955** *Amer. Speech* XXX. 118 *Honcho.* 1. *n.* A man in charge. (This is a Japanese word translated roughly as 'Chief officer', brought back from Japan by fliers stationed there during the occupation and during the Korean fighting...) 2. *v.* To direct a detail or operation. **1964** *Sat. Rev.* (U.S.) 10 Oct. 82/2 Jack Bullock, who *honchoes* the Curaçao casino. **1967** *N.Y. Times* 4 June IV. 1 Mr. Komer expects to be able to name these 45 key provincial *honchos*, and he hopes to place civilians in at least a quarter of the posts. **1972** C. Weston *Poor, poor Ophelia* (1973) xiii. 77 It's out of our territory, but I'll call Pete Springer. He's honcho in that division. **1973** *New Yorker* 30 July 24/1, I was the first employee who was not one of the honchos.

hond, -e, obs. ff. HAND, HOUND.

honda ('hɒndə). *Western U.S.* Also **hondo, -oo, ou, -u.** [Sp. *honda* sling.] The eye at the end of a lasso through which the rope passes to form a loop (see also quot. 1958). Also *fig.*

1887 *Scribner's Mag.* II. 508/2 The common [cowboy] terms are..*heel*, to lariat an animal by the hind leg, *hondou* (derivation unknown, though probably from the Spanish *honda*, the eye of a needle), the slip-knot of the lariat. **1894** *Dialect Notes* I. 324 *Hondoo, hondou*, the slip-knot of a reata. **1895** *Montgomery Ward Catal.* 338/1 Lariat Hondas... Hondas for lariats; firmly pressed rawhide. **1933** *Amer. Speech* Feb. 28/2 *Hondo*, a small loop made of metal or rawhide to prevent the rope from burning or cutting the hands and to hold the loop open. **1958** *Ibid.* Dec. 270 *Hondoo*, the loop plaited in the end of a rope to make a running noose. Also the metal grommet or thimble inserted in that loop. **1964** 'F. O'Rourke' *Mule for Marquesa* xi. 177 He tied the lead lines to a slip rope, dropped the loop over a rock, wedged the honda.

hondel, hondle, obs. ff. HANDLE *v.*

honderyd, -yth, hondre, -ed, -eth, obs. ff. HUNDRED, -EDTH.

hondhabend, -habbing, var. HAND-HABEND.

Honduran, Hondurean (hɒn'djʊərən, -riːən), *a.* and *sb.* [f. next: see -AN.] **A.** *adj.* Of, pertaining to, or characteristic of Honduras. **B.** *sb.* A native or inhabitant of Honduras or British Honduras. So **Hondu'ranean, -'anian** *adjs.* and *sbs.*

1895 Savage & Gunter *His Cuban Sweetheart* II. xii. 166 The Honduranean magnates. *Ibid.* III. xiii. 184 The sunburned neck of the average Honduranean. **1902** R. H. Davis *Capt. Macklin* iii. 105 The Honduranian consul. **1911** D. Folkmar *Dict. Races or Peoples* 77 Honduran (see *Spanish American*). **1918** D. G. Munro *Five Republics Central Amer.* vi. 131 It must not be supposed, however, that the Honduraneans are necessarily inferior, intellectually or physically, to the inhabitants of the other republics. **1926** *Glasgow Herald* 17 June 10 The Honduran steamer Olancho. **1927** *Blackw. Mag.* Aug. 186/1 Living under Honduranian laws..these people, once British, are gradually being forced to give up their birthright. **1934** A. Huxley *Beyond Mexique Bay* 27 They are true-born Panamanians, Nicaraguans, Hondureans, or whatever it may be. **1941** P. E. James *Latin America* xxiii. 691 From it [*sc.* the banana world] Honduras derives financial profit through taxation but it cannot be considered to form a coherent part of the Honduran state. **1950** *Caribbean Q.* II. II. 3 The poetry and painting of contemporary British Hondurans. **1959** W. S. Stokes *Latin American Politics* ix. 194 Even with such liberal land laws..which has permitted practically all Hondurans..to own land, Honduras has not been able to achieve democratic government. **1972** *Guardian* 29 Jan. 1/1 Some major move up to the Honduran frontier.

Honduras (hɒn'djʊərəs, hɒndjʊ'ræs). The name of a Central American republic and of the nearby British Honduras (now Belize), used *attrib.* to designate various plants native to the area, as **Honduras bark**, the dried bark of the tree *Picramnia antidesma*, also called *cascara amarga*, and formerly used to treat dysentery, syphilis, and other diseases; **Honduras cedar**, a local species of *Cedrela*, esp. *C. odorata*; **Honduras mahogany**, *Swietenia macrophylla*; **Honduras rosewood**, a species of *Dalbergia*, esp. *D. stevensonii*; **Honduras sarsaparilla**, the dried root of *Smilax ornata*, used in various medical preparations or as a flavouring.

1887 *Colonial & Indian Exhib., Rep. Col. Sect.* 256 'Majoe bitter'..has been lately introduced into medicine in the United States under the name of 'Honduras bark' or 'Casc[ar]a amarga'. **1931** M. Grieve *Mod. Herbal* I. 166 Cascara amarga... Synonyms. Mountain Damson Bark. Simaruba. Honduras Bark. **1875** T. Laslett *Timber & Timber Trees* xxxii. 266 The Cuba, Honduras, and Mexican Cedars are varieties of the *Cedrela odorata*. **1919** W. Winn *Timbers* i. 95 Cedar, *Cedrela odorata*, also known as.. Honduras Cedar. **1950** C. W. Bond *Colonial Timbers* 73 Honduras cedar is of considerable value for decoration. **1962** R. J. Streets *Exotic Forest Trees Brit. Commonwealth* 221 'Honduras Cedar', 'West Indian Cedar'. A native of the continent of tropical America and several of the West Indies. **1803** T. Sheraton *Cabinet Dict.* 254 From this province [*sc.* Honduras] is imported the principal kind of mahogany in use amongst cabinet-makers, which generally bears the name of Honduras mahogany. **1851** Chaloner & Fleming *Mahogany Tree* v. 48 Honduras Mahogany is found to work as freely and bend as readily as English Oak. **1902** G. S. Boulger *Wood* II. 237 Honduras mahogany, reaching 50 ft. at its first branch and 3 ft. in diam., yields logs 25–40 ft. long and 12–24 in. square, or even larger. **1969** T. H. Everett *Living Trees of World* 212/1 The Honduras mahogany is native from southern Mexico and Central America to Peru, Bolivia and Brazil. **1904** H. Stone *Timbers of Commerce* 64 Rosewood. Dalbergia sp... Alternative Names. Honduras Rosewood. **1956** *Handbk. Hardwoods* (Forest Prod. Res. Lab.) 205 Honduras rosewood grows to a height of 50–100 ft. **1830** G. Spratt *Flora Medica* II. 212 The Honduras Sarsaparilla has a whitish or dirty brown cuticle. **1840** [see SARSAPARILLA 1 b]. **1950** R. C. Wren *Potter's Cycl. Bot. Drugs* (ed. 6) 308 Honduras Sarsaparilla is generally imported in long thin bundles with few rootlets attached.

hone (həʊn), *sb.*¹ Forms: 1 hán, 4 honne, 5 hoone, 7 hoan(e, 5– hone. [OE. *hán* str. fem. = ON. *hein* str. fem. (Sw. dial. *hen*, Da. *heen*).]

†**1.** A stone, a rock. (OE.) *Obs.*

Frequently applied to a stone serving as a landmark.

939 in Birch *Cartul. Sax.* II. 458 þonne norþ fram setle to netles stede to þære hane. **966** *Ibid.* III. 435 Of þære græȝan hane and lang hearpdene. **12..** *Ibid.* II. 481 þonon on þa readan hane, of þære hane on þone herpaþ.

2. A whetstone used for giving a fine edge to cutting tools, esp. razors.

c **1325** *Poem Times Edw. II*, 86 in *Pol. Songs* (Camden) 327 He put in his pautener an honne and a komb. *c* **1440** *Promp. Parv.* 245/1 Hoone, barbarys instrument, *cos.* **1545** Raynold *Byrth Mankynde* II. vi. 127 Rub it on a Barbers Whetstone, called a Hone. **1612** Woodall *Surg. Mate* Wks. (1653) 2 Take in his Chest a good Hoane. **1746** Simon in *Phil. Trans.* XLIV. 323 The Whetstones or Hones..sold for Lough-Neagh Stones, are none of these, but of a soft gritty kind, and found near Drogheda. **1807** P. Gass *Jrnl.* 79 Part of a log quite petrified..of which good whet-stones or hones could be made. **1881** Young *Every Man his own Mechanic* §358 After a few hours set it on a hone.

3. Stone of which such whetstones are made; hone-stone. (Several kinds of stone varying greatly in mineral composition are used for this purpose.)

1793 Hely tr. *O'Flaherty's Ogygia* II. 178 Lough-Neach ..which most assuredly converts holly into hones. **1806** *Gazetteer Scotl.* (ed. 2) 163/2 In the parish of Ratho is found a species of whetstone or hone, of the finest substance. **1875** Knight *Dict. Mech.* s.v., Various kinds, differing greatly in texture and hardness, are employed. Norway ragstone, water-of-Ayr, bluestone, German-hone, and many other varieties.

4. *attrib.* and *Comb.* **hone-pavement**: see quot. 1788; **hone-stone**, = senses 2 and 3; *spec.* a very siliceous clay slate having a conchoidal fracture across the grain of the rock; also called *novaculite*.

1788 *Chambers' Cycl.* s.v., Bed of hones, or hone-pavement, one of the tools used in the operation of grinding specula for telescopes; formed of pieces of the finest blue hone or whetstone. *c* **1790** Imison *Sch. Art* II. 108 The hone pavement has uniformly taken out all the emery strokes. **1855** tr. *Labarte's Arts Mid. Ages* i. 25 Hone-stone, a compact, fine-grained magnesian limestone. **1882** Geikie *Text-bk. Geol.* II. II. §6. 122 Whet-slate, novaculite, hone-stone, an exceedingly hard fine grained siliceous rock.

hone, *sb.*² *north. dial.* Also 4 hon, howne, 4–5 hoyn(e, 4–9 hune. [ME. *hōn*, app. derived from hone *v.*¹] Delay, tarrying: in the phrases ***but, without hone***, often a convenient metrical tag.

a **1300** *Cursor M.* 5795 Siþen sal þou wit-outen hon Wend to king pharaon. *Ibid.* 8413 Curtaisli, wit-vten hone, He yatte hir freli al hir bone. *c* **1375** *Sc. Leg. Saints, Paulus* 804 Bad þame..Set fyre at anis but ony howne. *c* **1400** *Rowland & O.* 341 Send owte Rowlande withowtten hone [*rime* tone]. *c* **1460** *Towneley Myst.* xxii. 228 Withoutt any hoyne [*rime* soyne = soon]. **1535** Stewart *Cron. Scot.* III. 434 For to devyiss without[in] ony hune, Richt wyslie than quhat best wes to be done. **1560** Rolland *Crt. Venus* IV. 629 That thay suld pas but hone. **1820** *Edin. Mag.* May 422/2 The trauchl't stag i' the wan waves lap, But huliness or hune.

†**hone**, *sb.*³ *Obs. dial.* A swelling or tumour.

[See honewort, quot. 1633, the sole authority for this.]

hone, *v.*¹ *north. dial.* Forms: 4 hon(e, 5–6 hoyne. [Goes with hone *sb.*² (the vb. being app. the source): origin obscure. The rimes show that it had ME. close *ō*, giving Sc. (ø, y); its mod. Eng. form would be *oo* (uː), and it is thus distinct from hone *v.*² The *oy* in some texts is northern spelling of *ō*.] *intr.* To delay, tarry, hesitate.

a **1300** *Cursor M.* 6088 Yee be alle belted, wit staf in hand, Hones noght quils yee ar etand. *Ibid.* 19867 Petre þan bigan til hon. *c* **1400** *Melayne* 819 In no place wolde he hone [*rime* done]. *c* **1460** *Towneley Myst.* iii. 319 It shall be done full sone brether, help to bere..ffull long shall I not hoyne to do my devere. *Ibid.* viii. 363 It may not help to huyer ne hone [*rime* bone = boon]. **1570** Levins *Manip.* 215/20 To Hoyne, *hærere.*

hone, *v.*² *dial.* and *U.S.* Also 8 hoan, hoon. [a. OF. *hogner, hoigner*, Norman dial. *honer*, (13th c. in Littré) 'to grumble, mutter, murmure; to repine; also, to whyne as a child, or dog' (Cotgr.), app. f. *hon*, a cry of discontent (cf. '*Hoigner*, ou *hogner*, faire hon hon, et criailler comme font les enfants quand ils voudraient bien avoir quelque chose', Duez *Dict.* 1664, in Godef.).] *intr.* To grumble, murmur, whine, moan.

1621 Burton *Anat. Mel.* III. ii. III. 614 Admiring and commending her still, and lamenting, honing [1638, 1651, etc. moaning], wishing himselfe any thing for her sake. **1657** G. Starkey *Helmont's Vind.* 243, I know that the Galenical Tribe will whine and hone pitifully, rather than lose to be reputed Chymists. **1825** Lamb *Elia* Ser. II. *Convalescent*, He lies pitying himself, honing and moaning to himself. **1828** Scott *F.M. Perth* v, Thou awakest to hone, and pine, and moan, as if she had drawn a hot iron across thy lips. **1955** D. Niland *Shiralee* 36 Macauley felt her scrabbling over the blanket, and then sitting beside his bulk, hooning to herself.

b. To whine or pine *for*; to hanker *after*.

1600 Holland *Livy* I. vii. 6 Some of the Oxen..missed their fellowes behind, and honing after them, bellowed as their nature is. **1708** *Brit. Apollo* No. 36. 3/1 When in Wezon 'tis gone, For another I hoan. *a* **1713** Ellwood *Autobiog.* (1714) 64, I had no Money..nor ever honed after it. **1754** Richardson *Grandison* xxxv. (1812) I. 264 She brought a servant up with her..who hones after the country. **1883** C. F. Smith in *Trans. Amer. Philol. Soc.* 50 *Hone*, 'to pine *or* long for anything', is not yet obsolete in the South, though perhaps rare. **1884** *Harper's Mag.* Oct. 800/1 'I'm just honin' after food', is another example of the Tennessee patois.

Hence **ˈhoning** *vbl. sb.* and *ppl. a.*

1802 Lamb *Cur. Fragm.* iv. Poems, Plays, etc. (1884) 203 What weeping, sighing, sorrowing, honing..friends, relatives. **1837** J. Hogg *Tales by Ettrick Shepherd* II. 235, I heard a kind o' hooning sound. **1878** Seeley *Stein* II. 505 When I had heard his honing and moaning about Moscow.

hone, *v.*³ [f. hone *sb.*¹] *trans.* To sharpen on a hone. Hence **honed** *ppl. a.*, **honer**.

1826 Carlyle *Early Lett.* (1886) II. 349 Without aid from any grinder or honer whatever. **1828** Webster s.v., To hone a razor. **1837** *Fraser's Mag.* XV. 576 A well-honed knife. **1856** *Leisure Hour* V. 13/1 Honing and strapping his stock of razors.

hone in *O hone*: see ohone, alas!

honement, obs. form of ointment, ointment.

honer, honerable, obs. ff. honour, -able.

honest (ˈɒnɪst), *a.* Also 4–5 onest(e, 4–6 honeste. [a. OF. *honeste* (12th c. in Littré), mod.F. *honnête* (= It. *onesto*, Sp., Pg. *honesto*), ad. L. *honestus* honourable, respectable, decent, fine, handsome, f. *honos, -or, honōr-*, honour.]

†**1. a.** Of persons: Held in honour; holding an honourable position; respectable. *Obs.*

c **1325** *Metr. Hom.* 160 A widou..com this Candelmesse feste, And scho wald haf als wif honeste Hir messe. **13..** *K. Alis.* 158 Olimpias..Wolde make a riche feste Of knyghtis and ladies honeste. **1388** Wyclif *Ecclus.* xi. 23 It is esy in the iȝen of God, sudeynli to make onest a pore man. *c* **1400** *Destr. Troy* 1471 A woman..Onest & abill, & Ecuba she hight. **1548** Hall *Chron., Hen. VIII* 46 b, The honest and sustanciall persons arrested or indited. **1624** Capt. Smith *Virginia* IV. 111 Houses, wherein liue the honester sort of people, as Farmers in England. **1687** A. Lovell tr. *Thevenot's Trav.* III. 57 He told me That that Country is pleasant enough, and full of good honest People. **1692** *Lond. Gaz.* No. 2735/4 The Purchaser to take 2 honest Men, and the Seller 2 more, for all such Goods.

b. ***to make an honest woman*** (*of*): to marry (a woman) after seduction; also without depreciatory reference, to marry. *dial.* and *colloq.* (The sense may have been associated with 3 b 'chaste'.)

1629 Earle *Microcosm., Servingman* (Arb.) 84 The best worke he does is his marrying, for it makes an honest woman. **1749** Fielding *Tom Jones* XV. viii, Miss Nancy was, in vulgar language, soon made an honest woman. **1818** Scott *Hrt. Midl.* in *Tales my Landlord* 2nd Ser. IV. ix. 201 Effie was married—made, according to the common phrase, an honest woman. **1824** —— *St. Ronan's* xxv, My right honourable father nourished some thoughts of making an honest woman of Marie de Martigny. **1825** Jamieson s.v., If he..marries her, he is said to 'make an honest woman of her', i.e. he does all in his power to cover her ignominy, and to restore her to her place in society. **1887** Miss Braddon *Like & Unlike* III. v. 64, I wish he had been free to make your sister an honest woman. **1927** W. E. Collinson *Contemp. Eng.* 108 The old phrase to make an honest woman (of a girl in trouble) is often used in jest in innocent contexts. **1968** R. Harris *Nice Girl's Story* v. 38 When are you going to be made an honest woman?

c. As a vague epithet of appreciation or praise, esp. as used in a patronizing way to an inferior. (Cf. *worthy*.)

1551 T. Wilson *Logike* (1580) 83, I had good chere in suche a mannes house. *Ergo*, he is an honest man. **1583** Hollyband *Campo di Fior* 309 Honest man, is this the way to Bolonia? **1590** Shaks. *Mids. N.* III. i. 187 Your name honest Gentleman? **1681** Dryden *Abs. & Achit.* 508 These were for laying honest David by, On principles of pure good husbandry. **1709** *Tatler* No. 45 ¶7 Let Mr. Bickerstaff alone (says one of the Honest Fellows), when he's in a good Humour, he's as good Company as any Man in England. **1815** Scott *Guy M.* ix, Cannot he sing his sang..like Collector Snail, honest man, that never fashes ony body? **1846** Brockett (ed. 3) s.v., A Northern baronet..chairman of quarter sessions, was accustomed, when he sentenced a prisoner, to begin, 'Now, my honest man, you have been convicted of felony'.

†**2.** Of things, conditions, actions, etc. *Obs.*

a. Worthy of honour, honourable, commendable; bringing honour, creditable.

13.. *Coer de L.* 1773 Christmas is a time full honest; Kyng Richard it honoured with gret feste. **1340** *Ayenb.* 222 Þet stat of spoushod is zuo holy and suo honeste. *c* **1386** Chaucer *Merch. T.* 780 In honeste wyse as longeth to a knyght. **1477** Earl Rivers (Caxton) *Dictes* 2 Alle vertuouse and honest thynges. **1526** Tindale *Rom.* xii. 17 Prouyde afore honde thynges honest in the sight of all men. **1533** Bellenden *Livy* II. 153 Thare wes na batall mair honest, than this last rehersit. **1548** Hall *Chron., Edw. IV*, 223 b, Kyng Henry..founded a solempne schoole at Eton..an honest Colege of sad Priestes, with a greate nombre of children. **1621** Burton *Anat. Mel.* I. i. II. xi. (1651) 29 That respects onely things delectable and pleasant, this honest. **1700** Dryden tr. *Ovid's Met.* XIII. 408 Many a manly wound All honest, all before. **1715–20** Pope *Iliad* v. 312 Know, 'tis not honest in my soul to fear, Nor was Tydides born to tremble here.

b. Free from disgrace or reproach; respectable, decent, seemly, befitting, becoming.

1340 *Ayenb.* 229 Loke þe uram uoule wordes þet ne byeþ naȝt honeste. *c* **1350** *Leg. Rood* (1871) 76 To plant þa wandes in honest place, Forto be keped honestly, And wirschipd als þai war worthy. *c* **1440** *Gesta Rom.* xvii. 60 (Add. MS.) It were more honest that I shuld have such a wyf, and my felaw to have suche a wyf as I have. **1514** *Test. Ebor.* (Surtees) V. 52, I will that, the day of my buryall, she maik an honest dynner to my frendes and neybours. **1633** Earl Manch. *Al Mondo* (1636) 37 Honest sepulture is a blessing. **1653** Walton *Angler* ii. 44 Now lets go to an honest Alehouse and sing Old Rose. **1674** Playford *Skill Mus.* I. 61 Corants, Sarabands, and Jigs, used for honest mirth and delight at Feasts.

c. Decent or respectable in appearance; without blemish; comely, 'fair'; neat, tidy.

a **1300** *Cursor M.* 19850 (Cott.) All maner crepand beist, Þaa þat er noght tald honest. *c* **1340** *Ibid.* 6067 (Trin.) A clene lomb þat is honest. **1388** Wyclif *Ruth* iii. 3 Be thou waischun and anoyntid, and be thou clothid with onestere clothis. **1493** *Festivall* (W. de W. 1515) 31 The people wolde ..clyppe theyr berdes & polle theyr heedes & so make them honest ayenst eester day. **1526** Tindale *1 Cor.* xii. 23 Apon those members of the body Which we thynke lest honest put we most honestie on. *c* **1566** J. Alday tr. *Boaystuau's Theat. World* R iv, [He] hath created the chin..after so honest a forme, and hath enriched it with a bearde.

3. Of persons: Having honourable motives or principles; marked by uprightness or probity.

†**a.** In early use in a wide sense: Of good moral character; virtuous, upright, well-disposed.

1390 Gower *Conf.* I. 110 A king wise and honest in alle thing. *Ibid.* III. 136 So shulde he be the more honest To whom god yaf so worthy a yifte. **1535** Coverdale *1 Kings* i. 52 Yf he wil be an honest man, there shall not one heer fall from him vpon the earth. **1585** T. Washington tr. *Nicholay's Voy.* I. xxii. 28 Beyng a good Pilot and a very honest man. **1613** Purchas *Pilgrimage* (1614) 393 For the credit of this honest and loyall..societie. **1672** Cave *Prim. Chr.* I. i. (1673) 10 The honester and severer Romans were ashamed on 't. **1702** Rowe *Tamerl.* Ded., It were to be wish'd..that the World were honest to such a degree, and that there were not that scandalous defect of common morality.

b. *spec.* Chaste, 'virtuous'; usually of a woman. *arch.*

c **1400** *Cato's Mor.* 57 in *Cursor M.* App. iv. 1670 Fle to take wife..bot ho be honest..ne halde hir for na druri if ho be vnchest. **1428** *E.E. Wills* (1882) 79 The mariage of onest and poure maidens. **1535** Coverdale *2 Esdras* xvi. 49 Like as an whore enuyeth an honest woman. **1598** Shaks. *Merry W.* IV. ii. 103 Wives may be merry, and yet honest too. **1661** Pepys *Diary* 11 Aug., Colonel Dillon..comes to church with them, which makes me think they are not honest. **1669** Shadwell *R. Shepherdess* I. i, You marry'd me to keep me honest, did you? **1711** Steele *Spect.* No. 118 ¶2 The Maid is honest, and the Man dares not be otherwise.

c. That deals fairly and uprightly in speech and act; sincere, truthful, candid; that will not lie, cheat, or steal. (The prevailing modern sense, the 'honest man' being the 'good citizen', the law-abiding man, as opposed to the rogue, thief, or enemy of society.)

c **1400** *Destr. Troy* 48 Ouyde and othir þat onest were ay.. Thes dampnet his dedys. *c* **1500** *Doctr. Gd. Servaunts* in *Anc. Poet. Tracts* (Percy Soc.) 8 Ye seruauntes..Be ye honest and dylygent. **1581** Pettie *Guazzo's Civ. Conv.* I. (1586) 42 He, which plainly telleth the truth, sheweth him-selfe to be an honest man. **1674** Brevint *Saul at Endor* 282 The honestest Monks we know are sometimes tempted to say strange things. **1734** Pope *Ess. Man* IV. 248 An honest man's the noblest work of God. **1751** Johnson *Rambler* No. 189 ¶12 She..was at last convinced that she had been flattered, and that her glass was honester than her maid. **1791** 'G. Gambado' *Ann. Horsem.* iv. (1809) 83 A dealer in Moorfields (who..is no honester than he ought to be). **1849** Macaulay *Hist. Eng.* vii. II. 177 Though often misled by prejudice and passion, he was emphatically an honest man. **1897** W. Raleigh *Style* 125 The pillory and the stocks are hardly educational agents, but they make it easier for honest men to enjoy their own. *Proverb*, 'When thieves [or rogues] fall out, honest men come by their own.'

d. Ingenuous; without disguise, open, frank, not concealing one's real character (good or bad).

1634 Ford *P. Warbeck* II. i, Bless the young man! Our nation would be laugh'd at For honest souls through Christendom. **1680** Otway *Orphan* II. v, I am a doating honest Slave. **1701** Rowe *Amb. Step-Moth.* I. i. 171 Dull heavy things! Whom Nature has left honest In meer frugality. **1849** Macaulay *Hist. Eng.* iv. I. 437 The honest monk was so illiterate that he did not know what he ought to say on an occasion of such importance. **1866** Howells *Venet. Life* ii. 23 He beheld the honest swindling countenance of a hotel *portier*.

e. ***honest broker***: a sobriquet (tr. G. *ehrlicher makler*) for the German statesman Bismarck; more generally, a representative of a country attempting to mediate diplomatically between two opposing nations, states, etc.; also *transf.*, any such mediator in industrial or other disputes.

[**1878** *Times* 21 Feb. 5/1 To my [*sc.* Bismarck's] mind, it is rather the mediation of an honourable broker who really wishes to carry on business.] **1884** W. Beatty-Kingston tr. *Busch's Our Chancellor* II. ii. 130, I [*sc.* Bismarck] don't picture to myself a peace-mediator playing the part of an arbitrator..; but a more modest one [*sc.* rôle], something like that of an honest broker, who really wants to transact business. **1884** in J. R. Ware *Passing Eng.* (1909) 154/1 *Honest broker*, matrimonial agent. 'Marriages are not all made in heaven; some of them are made by marriage brokers ..though the "honest broker" does not seem to find the trade very remunerative.' **1926** Fowler *Mod. Eng. Usage* 548/1 *Honest broker*, Bismarck. **1934** *S.P.E. Tract* XLII. 88 *Honest broker*, coined by Bismarck as *ehrlicher Mäkler* 1878. **1967** *Guardian* 4 Feb. 9/3 (*heading*) 'Honest broker' role still possible for Britain. *Ibid.* 9/4 An 'honest broker' must have something special to offer, Britain has..immense diplomatic experience and Anglo-Saxon commonsense. **1968** G. Jones *Hist. Vikings* IV. ii. 371 A compromise was reached whereby Edmund should have Wessex and Knut

the rest of the country. Among the honest brokers was Eadric Streona. **1970** *Times* 31 Mar. (Australian Suppl.) p. ii/3 On another corner of the Asian board Australia acted the comparatively successful honest broker between the United States and the kingdom of Cambodia representing Cambodia in Saigon and the United States in Phnom Penh. **1973** *Times* 9 Feb. 1/6 As Rhodesia and Zambia were not on speaking terms an intermediary or 'honest broker' had to be found.

f. ***Honest Injun***: see INJUN b.

g. ***Honest John***: (*a*) *colloq.* an honest man; (*b*) an American type of missile designed to carry a nuclear warhead.

1935 *Amer. Speech* X. 20/1 Any honest citizen; a hard-working fellow... *honest John.* **1954** *Birmingham* (Ala.) *News* 7 Mar. A24/5 The Army is stockpiling the plane-killing Nike units, and semi-guided field artillery rockets designated as the 'Honest John'. **1957** P. FRANK *Seven Days to Never* iii. 95 The atomic cannon and Honest John rockets . . began to arrive in Europe. **1973** 'H. HOWARD' *Highway to Murder* v. 57 One thing for sure was that she trusted me to play Honest John. **1973** *Guardian* 7 June 1/5 Britain, West Germany and Belgium are to buy the American Lance battlefield nuclear missile—to replace the obsolescent Honest John.

4. a. Of actions, feelings, etc.: Showing uprightness or sincerity of character or intention; fair, straightforward; free from fraud.

a **1300** *Cursor M.* 22914 Sant gregor gaf ansuer honest. **13 . .** *K. Alis.* 4011 He no dude no treson, His dede n'as bote honest. **1508** DUNBAR *Gold. Targe* 166 Leuefell Company, and Honest Besynes. **1568** GRAFTON *Chron.* II. 382 Their honest and reasonable excuses could not be heard. **1617** MORYSON *Itin.* II. 268 A quiet harvest that might arise out of their own honest labour. **1658** BRAMHALL *Consecr. Bps.* ix. 218 It is none of the honestest Pleas, Negare factum, to deny such publick Acts as these. *a* **1732** GAY *Fables* II. vi. 10 Unbrib'd, unaw'd, he dares impart The honest dictates of his heart. **1848** THACKERAY *Van. Fair* lii, The very best and honestest feelings of the man came out in these artless outpourings of paternal feeling. **1883** *Law Times* 20 Oct. 408/1 The object of a bankruptcy law . . should be the economical and honest distribution of a bankrupt's estate.

b. Of money, gain, etc.: Gained or earned by fair means, without cheating or stealing; legitimate.

[**1676** WYCHERLEY *Pl. Dealer* III. Wks. (Rtldg.) 125/2 You must call usury and extortion God's blessing, or the honest turning of the penny.] **1700** T. BROWN tr. *Fresny's Amusem. Ser. & Com.* 25 Some call Trade, Honest Gain, and . . have lacker'd it with the Name of Godliness. **1825** MRS. CAMERON *Houlston Tracts* I. 10 (*title*) An Honest Penny is worth a Silver Shilling. **1873** *Slang Dict.* 194 Instructions to earn an honest shilling. **1887** JESSOPP *Arcady* vii. 216 He turns an honest penny by horse hire.

c. Of a thing: Not seeming other than it is; genuine, unadulterated, unsophisticated.

1598 SHAKS. *Merry W.* IV. ii. 126 Behold what honest cloathes you send forth to bleaching. **1674** tr. *Martiniere's Voy. N. Countries* 31 We were glad to betake ourselves to the provisions we had brought . . which was honest Bisket and salt Beef. **1812** CRABBE *T. in Verse* xiv, His Conscience never checks him when he swears The fat he sells is honest fat of bears. **1838** *Penny Cycl.* XII. 307/2 The honest mouth of a three-year old horse should be thus formed [etc.]. **1884** CHILD *Ballads* II. xxxvii. 322/2 Bringing some honest bread and wine with her.

d. ***honest-to-God***, ***honest-to-goodness***: genuine(ly, real(ly. *colloq.* (orig. *U.S.*).

1913 J. LONDON *Valley of Moon* I. x, Honest to God, Saxon, he don't like all his horses as much as I like the last hair on the last tail of the scrubbiest of the bunch. **1916** 'B. M. BOWER' *Phantom Herd* iii. 45 The real honest-to-goodness-twelve-months-in-the-year West. **1916** JOYCE *Portrait of Artist* v. 212 Oh, honest to God, if the crook of it caught him that time he was done for. **1918** B. HALL *Diary* in Hall & Niles *One Man's War* (1929) xxxiv. 352 The only honest-to-God aviator the Americans have ever produced —Raoul Lufbery! **1921** GALSWORTHY *To Let* III. v, She was . . 'honest to God' indifferent to it all. **1924** W. M. RAINE *Troubled Waters* xiii. 144 Few will believe it, but it's an honest-to-goodness fact. **1929** W. H. THOMSON *That Terrier 'Brick'* xiii. 69 Honest-to-goodness, I didn't know that I was doing anything wrong. **1933** E. CALDWELL *God's Little Acre* i. 11 'A real honest-to-God albino?' Shaw asked. 'As real as the day is long.' **1937** [see COPPER-BOTTOMED *a.*]. **1937** J. B. PRIESTLEY *Two Time Plays* p. xi, It was not until I substituted for him an honest-to-goodness exiled German professor that the play began to look right. **1945** *Tee Emm* (Air Ministry) V. 40 Plain honest-to-God engine failure. **1952** S. KAUFFMANN *Philanderer* (1953) iii. 50, I don't see a glimmer nowadays. Or if I do, I honest-to-goodness think it's a disappearing glimmer. *Ibid.* v. 80 The fact that we honest to God really dislike each other is thundering out loud now that the entertainment has stopped. **1959** 'J. WELCOME' *Lady is Tramp* viii. 125 I'm just pure honest-to-God terrified. **1960** *Farmer & Stockbreeder* 5 Jan. (Suppl.) 4 Like all good meals, there'll be bread and butter with it —not just a substitute for butter, but the real thing, the honest-to-goodness dairy product. **1963** *Times* 4 Mar. 11/6 One recalls a very distinguished industrialist (an individualist himself) who said he preferred 'honest to God engineers and creative designers'. **1963** J. A. T. ROBINSON (*title*) Honest to God. **1973** J. THOMSON *Death Cap* vii. 107 It's an honest-to-God mushroom and . . I'd have it for tea to prove it.

5. a. as *adv.* = Honestly; or (*poet.*) in comb. with another adj., expressing union of the two qualities denoted.

a **1592** GREENE *Jas. IV*, II. i, Yet would I, might I choose, be honest-poor. **1596** SHAKS. *Merch. V.* III. iv. 46 As I have euer found thee honest true. **1654** GAYTON *Pleas. Notes* IV. i. 176 And why slay him, if that he honest meant? **1671** F. PHILLIPS *Reg. Necess.* 330 Wares and Commodities, honester made.

b. Used to emphasize the truth of a statement. *colloq.* (orig. *U.S.*).

1876 'MARK TWAIN' *Tom Sawyer* ix. 100 Tell me, Joe, —*honest*, now, old feller—did I do it, Joe? **1901** MERWIN & WEBSTER *Calumet 'K'* viii. 160 Max . . said to his sister: 'Honest, Hilda, I don't see how he does it.' **1913** A. BENNETT *Regent* II. viii. 236 'But I'm not sarcastic!' he protested. 'Honest?' . . 'Honest!' he solemnly insisted. **1923** R. D. PAINE *Comr. Rolling Ocean* vi. 105 He is not so bad as he sounds, honest, Jud. **1928** F. B. YOUNG *My Brother Jonathan* II. iv, If it weren't for the life at Prince's I don't think I could stick it . . honest! **1972** 'J. & E. BONETT' *No Time to Kill* viii. 103 Of course I don't know a thing, but, honest, I can't see anyone here doing these people in.

6. *Comb.*, as ***honest-hearted***, ***-looking***, ***-minded***, ***-natured*** adjs.

1599 SANDYS *Europæ Spec.* (1637) 206 An honest-hearted desire, but no probable dessein. **1600** HAKLUYT *Voy.* III. 174 (R.) Worshipful, honest-minded, and well disposed merchants. **1607** SHAKS. *Timon* V. i. 89 My honest Natur'd friends. **1783** BURNS *Song, 'My father was a farmer'* ix, A cheerful honest-hearted clown. **1895** J. SMITH *Perman. Mess. Exod.* xix. 304 Jethro brings in his honest-heartedness. **1897** *Mag. of Art* Sept. 251 Honest-looking enough.

†**honest**, *v.* *Obs.* [ad. L. *honest-āre* to honour, dignify, adorn, embellish, f. *honest-us* HONEST. Cf. obs. F. *honester*.]

1. *trans.* To confer honour upon; to honour.

1382 WYCLIF *Ecclus.* xi. 23 Li3t is forsothe in the e3en of God, sodeynly to honesten [**1388** to make onest; Vulg. *honestare*] the pore. *a* **1575** ABP. PARKER *Corr.* (Parker Soc.) 411 For his more estimation I have honested him with a room in the arches. **1609** B. JONSON *Sil. Wom.* I. iv, You have very much honested my lodging with your presence. *a* **1613** OVERBURY *A Wife* (1638) 279 To honest it with the tittle of clemency.

2. To cause to appear honest or honourable; to justify, defend, excuse.

1602 WARNER *Alb. Eng.* Epit. (1612) 396 It stood him vpon to honest his actions. **1651** CHARLETON *Eph. & Cimm. Matrons* II. Pref., That learned and pious Divine; who was willing to honest the poor womans lapse. **1654** H. L'ESTRANGE *Chas. I* (1655) 186 Specious pretences they wanted not to honest, to justifie the enterprize.

3. To 'make an honest woman of': see HONEST *a.* 1 b.

1611 SPEED *Hist. Gt. Brit.* IX. xii. (1632) 717 Honested by lawfull matrimony. *a* **1652** BROME *Cov. Gard.* V. iii, I ask no further satisfaction of you, then to be honested by marriage.

¶ **4.** *nonce-use*, from the adj.

1669 SHADWELL *R. Shepherdess* I. i, You marry'd me to keep me honest, did you? I'll honest you; I will go instantly and meet 'em all three.

†**'honestate**, *v.* *Obs.* *rare*$^{-0}$. [f. L. *honestāt-*, ppl. stem of *honestāre*: see prec.] 'To honour' (Cockeram 1623).

†**hone'station.** *Obs.* *rare*$^{-1}$. [f. L. type **honestātiōn-em*, f. *honest-āre* to HONEST.] The action of making honourable; something that does honour to one; an honourable quality or attribute.

1648 W. MONTAGUE *Devout Ess.* I. x. §6. 118 By which virtuous qualities and honestations they have been more happy than others in their applications to move the mindes of men.

†**ho'nestete.** *Obs.* Also **onestete(e.** [a. OF. *honestete* (mod.F. *honnêteté*, = Pr. *honestetat*, Sp. *honestidad*, Pg. *honestidade*):—Com. Rom. type **honestitāt-em*, for L. *honestāt-em*.] = HONESTY.

c **1315** SHOREHAM 69 3et scholdy nau3t Honestete so 3wene. **1340** *Ayenb.* 53 Þe uerste libbeþ be þe ulesse, þe oþer be his ioliuete . . þe uerþe be his onestete. **1377** LANGL. *P. Pl.* B. xv. 90 As holynesse and honestete [*v.r.* honeste] oute of holicherche spredeth. *c* **1386** CHAUCER *Clerk's T.* 366 Wedded with fortunat honestetee.

†**ho'nestify**, *v.* *Obs.* *nonce-wd.* [f. L. *honestus* HONEST + -FY.] *trans.* = HONEST *v.* 3.

a **1652** BROME *Mad Couple* V. ii, I'le marry, and honestifie her.

honestly ('ɒnɪstlɪ), *adv.* [f. HONEST *a.* + -LY[2].] In an honest manner.

†**1.** In an honourable or respectful manner, honourably, worthily, respectably; in a seemly or becoming manner; decently. *Obs.*

1340 *Ayenb.* 47 Ofte hy sseaweþ and di3teþ ham þe more quaynteliche and þe more honesteliche. *c* **1386** CHAUCER *Merch. T.* 782 His housynge, his array, as honestly To his degree was maked as a kynges. *c* **1400** MAUNDEV. (Roxb.) vi. 20 He gers þam be keped honestly and wirschipfully. **1504** *Bury Wills* (Camden) 104 Yf yt be so yt I . . fall to pouerte, and may not leue honestly. **1559** *Ibid.* 153 To bringe my bodie honestly to the grounde. **1645** USSHER *Body Div.* (1647) 275 Friends and Neighbours should see that his body be honestly buried, and Funerals decently performed.

2. a. With honourable or upright conduct; esp. without fraud or falsehood; with honest intention or by honest means; sincerely, fairly, frankly, without disguise.

1390 GOWER *Conf.* III. 342 For he hath first his love founded Honestelich as for to wedde. **1428** *E.E. Wills* (1882) 78 That he gouerne hym goodly and onestly. **1526** *Pilgr. Perf.* (W. de W. 1531) 48 b, A man that hath a good crafte wherby he myght lyue honestly. **1597** MORLEY *Introd. Mus.* Ded., A nomber of honest poore men, who liue (and that honestly) vpon teaching. **1625** HART *Anat. Ur.* II. ix. 110 He dealt honestlier then the Parson. **1735** BERKELEY *Reasons not repl. to Walton* §7, I can honestly say, the more he explains, the more I am puzzled. **1738** SWIFT *Pol. Conversat.* 185, I came honestly by it. **1788** V. KNOX *Winter Even.* lxxvi. (R.), The stripling is often sent . . to the banks of the Ganges, there to heap up enormous riches, honestly if he can; but at all events to fulfil the ultimate end of his mission. **1875** JOWETT *Plato* (ed. 2) I. 99 He does not like honestly to confess that he is talking nonsense.

b. Used parenthetically or as an exclamation, either to emphasize the honesty of one's intentions, statements, etc., or as an expression of exasperation.

1898 G. B. SHAW *Mrs. Warren's Profession* III. 204 Honestly, dear Praddy, do you like seeing them together? **1921** —— *Back to Methuselah* III. 129 *Mrs. Lutestring.* You were kind enough to say that I frighten you. *Burge-Lubin.* Honestly, you do. **1929** E. O'NEILL *Dynamo* I. ii. 32 Honestly, I think you've got a nerve to——. **1957** N. MARSH *Off with his Head* iii. 56 No, honestly, this is just *too* mummerset. **1970** 'D. SHANNON' *Unexpected Death* (1971) ii. 24 Angel said, 'Honestly! *More* rain. I'll be going stir-crazy . . cooped up in here.' **1973** *Courier & Advertiser* (Dundee) 21 Feb. 13/5 Honestly, some of these drivers should have their heads seen to!

†**3.** Chastely, 'virtuously'. *Obs.*

13 . . *E.E. Allit. P.* B. 705 Ellez þay mo3t honestly ayþer oþer welde. **1613** PURCHAS *Pilgrimage* (1614) 824 The married Women live honestly. **1691** WOOD *Ath. Oxon.* II. 56 Whether the Females lived honestly, 'tis not for me to dispute it.

'honestness. *rare.* [f. as prec. + -NESS.] The quality of being honest. †**a.** Comeliness; ornament. *Obs.* **b.** Virtuousness; honesty.

c **1420** *Chron. Vilod.* st. 569 Abou3t þe tombe for honestnas, Hit was y-sowed. **1556** J. HEYWOOD *Spider & F.* xxxix. 16 Honestnes is vertousnes, and woorshipfulnes.

honesty ('ɒnɪstɪ). Forms: 4-5 **oneste, -ty**, 4-6 **honeste**, 5-6 **-tee**, 5-7 **-tie**, 6 **-tye**, 6- **honesty.** [a. OF. (*h*)*oneste* (12th c. in Littré, earlier (*h*)*onestet* = It. *onestà*, Sp. *honestad*, Pg. *honestat*), ad. L. *honestās, -ātem*, n. of quality f. *honestus* HONEST, or ? *honos* honour.]

I. The quality of being honest.

†**1.** Honourable position or estate; high rank; respectability. *Obs.*

1509 FISHER *Fun. Serm. C'tess Richmond* Wks. (1876) 296 The straungers of honeste whiche . . resorteth for to vysyte the souerayne must be consydered. **1520** *Caxton's Chron. Eng.* III. 19/2 He [Daniel] . . was made a man of greate honeste.

†**b.** Honour conferred or done; respect. *Obs.*

c **1330** R. BRUNNE *Chron.* (1810) 151 He sent his sister Jone with mykelle honeste. **1382** WYCLIF *1 Cor.* xii. 23 The membris that ben vnhonest, han more honeste. *c* **1400** *Destr. Troy* 2861 Þe lell gentils, þat Venus the worthy worshippit for god, And most honouret of other with oneste þere. **1531** ELYOT *Gov.* I. xx, Refuse nat to doe me that honestie in your presence. *a* **1553** UDALL *Royster D.* IV. iii. (Arb.) 63 More shame and harme . . Then all thy life days thou canst do me honestie. **1613** J. DUNSTER in Spurgeon *Treas. Dav.* Ps. lxxiv. 2 There is an honesty which belongeth to the dead body of a man.

†**c.** Honour gained by action or conduct; reputation, credit, good name. *Obs.*

1382 WYCLIF *Wisd.* vii. 11 Vnnoumbrable honeste [is] by the hondis of it. **1513** MORE *Rich. III* (1883) 56 Doctour Shaa by his sermon loste hys honestie, and sone after his life. **1526** *Pilgr. Perf.* (W. de W. 1531) 173 b, He hath sclaundred me before many, & so I haue lost myne honesty. **1548** UDALL *Erasm. Par.* (?) Pref. 15 Defence of their owne poore honesties.

†**d.** *concr.* (*collect.*) Honourable or respectable people. (Cf. *the quality.*) *Obs. rare.*

1563 ABP. PARKER *Articles*, That vseth . . delay to make any accompte in the presence of the honestye in the parish. **1575** J. STILL *Gamm. Gurton* IV. ii. in Hazl. *Dodsley* III. 228 If such a toy be used oft among the honesty, It may [not] beseem a simple man of your and my degree.

†**2.** The quality of what is becoming or befitting; decency, decorum; comeliness. *Obs.*

1375 BARBOUR *Bruce* I. 548 Hys Eyn with his hand closit he, For to dey with mar honeste. *c* **1400** MAUNDEV. (1839) xx. 221 The ordynance . . ne the honestee ne the clennesse is not so arrayed there, as it is here. **1538** STARKEY *England* I. i. 2 [They] lyuyd lyke wylde bestys in the woodys, wythout lawys and rulys of honesty. **1547** *Homilies* I. *Gd. Wks.* III. (1859) 59 How their profession of chastity was kept, it is more honesty to pass over in silence. **1652** NEEDHAM tr. *Selden's Mare Cl.* 36 For honestie sake, and for the friendship which the Republick had with the hous of Austria.

3. Honourable character.

†**a.** Formerly in a wide general sense, including all kinds of moral excellence worthy of honour.

1340 HAMPOLE *Pr. Consc.* 5829 'A gude castelle' he says 'kepes he þat his body kepes in honeste'. **1390** GOWER *Conf.* III. 272 Nought only upon chastete, But upon alle honeste. *c* **1430** *Syr Gener.* (Roxb.) 1856, I shal be glad him forto see, Mi worship to kepe with honestie. **1548** UDALL, etc. *Erasm. Par. Matt.* ii. 26 Encreased in all kynde of honestie, and heauenlye giftes. **1611** B. JONSON *Catiline* III. ii, Let not . . wicked friendship force What honesty and vertue cannot work.

†**b.** *spec.* Chastity; the honour or virtue of a woman. *Obs.*

c **1385** CHAUCER *L.G.W.* 1673 *Hypsip.*, Why lyked me thy yelow heer to see More then the boundes of myn honestee. *c* **1400** *Destr. Troy* 2965 Hit were sittyng for sothe, & seemly for wemen . . ouer all, þere onesty attell to saue. **1573** J. SANFORD *Hours Recreat.* (1576) 158 A poore manne proude, a woman without honestie. **1621** BURTON *Anat. Mel.* III. iii. II. i. (1651) 612 It was commonly practised in Diana's temple, for women to go barefoot over hot coals to try their

honesties. **1634** SIR T. HERBERT *Trav.* 52 A Venus (like in honestie, though not in beautie).

†**c.** Generosity, liberality, hospitality. *Obs.*

c **1400** *Cato's Mor.* 152 in *Cursor M.* App. iv. 1671 þat þou has gitin to þe, vse hit in honeste & be noȝt calde niþing. **1551** RECORDE *Cast. Knowl.* (1556) 138 A manne not onlye of greate learning, but also of as great honesty in seekinge to profite all men by his trauaill. **1607** SHAKS. *Timon* III. i. 29 A Noble Gentleman 'tis, if he would not keep so good a house..euery man has his fault, and honesty is his.

d. Uprightness of disposition and conduct; integrity, truthfulness, straightforwardness: the quality opposed to lying, cheating, or stealing. (The prevailing modern sense.)

1579 LYLY *Euphues* (Arb.) 197 Yet hath he shown himself as farre from honestie, as he is from age, and as full of craft, as he is of courage. **1599** SANDYS *Europæ Spec.* (1632) 102 Our grosse conceipts, who think honestie the best policie. **1601** SHAKS. *Jul. C.* II. i. 127 What other Oath, Then Honesty to Honesty ingag'd, That this shall be, or we will fall for it. **1657** R. LIGON *Barbadoes* (1673) 121 The Saylers will as certainly take it, as you trust it to their honesties. **1727** DE FOE *Syst. Magic* I. i. (1840) 18 Honesty shall be praised and starved..to be high and great, is to be wise and good. **1849** MACAULAY *Hist. Eng.* vii. II. 221 Either of the two suppositions was fatal to the King's character for honesty.

e. *transf.* of things: cf. HONEST *a.* 4 c.

1842 BISCHOFF *Woollen Manuf.* (1862) II. 95 The German, or rather the Polish cloth, cannot be depended upon for honesty, in either the breadth or the length of the cloth.

II. 4. a. The popular name of *Lunaria biennis*, a cruciferous plant with large purple (sometimes white) flowers and flat round semi-transparent pods (whence the name), commonly cultivated in gardens. Also applied to other species of *Lunaria*.

1597 GERARDE *Herbal* II. cxvii. 378 We cal this herb in English Pennie flower..in Northfolk, Sattin, and white Sattin, and among our women it is called Honestie. **1794** MARTYN *Rousseau's Bot.* ii. 31 The second class contains those whose seed vessel is a silicle..as..honesty. **1868** G. MACDONALD *R. Falconer* II. 44 Purple-black heartseases, and thin-filmed silver pods of honesty. **1884** MILLER *Plant-n., Lunaria biennis*, Bolbonac, Common Honesty.

b. (In full, ***maiden's honesty***.) A local name of wild Clematis or Virgin's Bower (*C. Vitalba*).

1640 PARKINSON *Theat. Bot.* 384 The Italians call it *Vitalba*..and in English of most country people where it groweth Honestie. *a* **1697** AUBREY *Wilts.* (R. Soc. MS.) 120 (Britten & H.) About Michaelmass all the hedges about Thickwood..are as it were hung with maydens honesty: which looks very fine. **1888** *Berks. Gloss., Honesty*, the wild clematis is always so called.

†**c.** ***small honesty***: an old name for various species of Pink (*Dianthus*). *Obs.*

1578 LYTE *Dodoens* II. vii. 156 Called in Englishe by diuers names, as Pynkes, Soppes in wine, feathered Gillofers, and small Honesties. **1597** GERARDE *Herbal* II. clxxiii. 478.

honewort ('həʊnwɜːt). [See quot. 1633.] A name for Corn Parsley (*Petroselinum segetum*); also erroneously extended to other umbelliferous plants, as *Sison Amomum*, *Trinia vulgaris*, and *Cryptotænia canadensis*.

1633 JOHNSON *Gerarde's Herbal* 1018 Of Corne Parsley or Honewort..About the yeere 1625, I saw Mistriss Ursula Leigh..gather it in the wheate ershes about Mapledurham ..who told me it was called Honewort, and that her Mother ..taught her to use it..for a swelling which shee had in her left cheeke..This swelling her Mother called by the name of a Hone; but asking whether such tumors were in the said Isle [of Wight—where the mother lived]..usually called Hones she could not tell. **1711** J. PETIVER in *Phil. Trans.* XXVII. 382 Its lower Leaves like Hone-wort, but deeper cut. **1879** BRITTEN & HOLLAND *Plant-n.*

honey ('hʌnɪ), *sb.* (*a.*) Forms: α. 1 huniȝ, hunæȝ, 3 huniȝ, 3–4 huni, (uni), 4–5 huny, (4 houny, 5 *Sc.* hwnie, -ny), 6–7 hunny. β. 4–7 honi, (5 ony, hoony), 4–8 hony, 5–6 honye, 5– honey, (6–7 honie, honnie, honny). γ. *Sc.* and *north.* 7– hinny, -ie, -ey. [OE. *huniȝ* = OFris. *hunig* (mod. Fris. dial. *hunig, -ing, huynig, hönning, -ig*), OS. *honeg, -ig* (MDu. *honich, -inc*, Du. *honig, -ing*, MLG. *honnich*, LG. *honnig*), OHG. *honag, honang* (MHG. *honec, -ic, -ich*, G. *honig*), ON. *hunang* (OSw. *hunagh, honag*, Sw. *honung*, Da. *honning*):—OTeut. **huna(n)gom* neut., not recorded in Gothic, which has instead *miliþ* = Gr. μελιτ-. The β forms are mainly graphic, in accordance with the usual ME. writing of *o* instead of *u* before *n*; but there may have been a northern form **hōni*, to which mod.Sc. *hinnie* goes back (like *brither, mither*) through *ü, ö*, to *ō*.]

A. *sb.* **1. a.** A sweet viscid fluid, of various shades from nearly white to deep golden, being the nectar of flowers collected and worked up for food by certain insects, esp. the honey-bee.

c **825** *Vesp. Psalter* xviii. 11 [xix. 10] Swoetran ofer huniȝ and biobread. *c* **893** K. ÆLFRED *Oros.* I. i. §23 þær [Estland] bið swyðe mycel huniȝ & fisc[n]að. *c* **1200** ORMIN 9225 Itt wass huniȝ off þe feld. *c* **1230** *Hali Meid.* 9 Ha lickeð huni of þornes. **1297** R. GLOUC. (1724) 43 Hony & mylk þer ys muche. *a* **1300** *Cursor M.* 21296 þe stile o matheu, water it was..And john honi suet als suilk. *c* **1394** *P. Pl. Crede* 726 Dranes doþ nouȝt but drynkeþ vp þe huny. **1422** tr. *Secreta Secret., Priv. Priv.* (E.E.T.S.) **247** Hote drynke makyd wyth Hoony. **1483** *Cath. Angl.* 192/1 To make Huny, *mellifacere.* **1508** FISHER 7 *Penit. Ps.* cxxx. Wks. (1876) 227 O swete wordes, more sweter than hony and suger. **1563** WINȜET *Wks.* (1890) II. 48 Quhais speche wes..nocht wordis sa mekle as certane hwnie. **1582** T. WATSON *Centurie of Love* xii. Poems (Arb.) 48 Hunny mixt with gall. **1590** SPENSER *F.Q.* II. iii. 24 Sweete wordes, like dropping honny, she did shed. **1611** BIBLE *Exod.* iii. 8 A lande flowing with milke and hony. **1626** BACON *Sylva* § 612 There be three things in vse for Sweetnesse, Sugar, Honey, Manna. **1794** BURNS *My Tocher's the Jewel*, It's a' for the hiney he'll cherish the bee. **1838** THIRLWALL *Greece* xxxvii. V. 21 His body, immersed in honey, was carried home for a royal burial.

b. With qualifications.

honey of borax, borax h., a mixture of clarified honey and borax, used as a remedy in aphthous diseases (Hoblyn *Dict. Med. Terms*, 1844). †**corn h.**, **stone h.** (see quot. 1609). **clarified h.**, honey melted in a waterbath and freed from scum. **clover h.**, **heather h.**, that gathered from these flowers respectively. †**live h.**, (see quot. 1609). **unripe h.** (see quot. 1884). **virgin h.**, **white h.**, honey that flows from the cells spontaneously without pressure, being that made by bees that have not swarmed. **wild h.**, †**wood h.**, that made by wild bees.

c **1000** *Ags. Gosp.* Matt. iii. 4 Hys mete wæs..wudu-huniȝ. *c* **1200** *Trin. Coll. Hom.* 139 Moren and wilde uni was his mete. *c* **1430** *Two Cookery-bks.* 29 Do þer-to hwyte Hony or Sugre. *Ibid.* 35 Take wyne & pouder Gyngere, Canelle, & a lytil claryfyid hony. **1526** TINDALE *Matt.* iii. 4 Hys meate was..wylde hony. **1607** TOPSELL *Four-f. Beasts* (1658) 165 This powder with Hony-Attick, taketh away the spots in the face. **1609** C. BUTLER *Fem. Mon.* (1634) 108 While it continueth liquid, and will run of it self, it is called Live-honey: when it is turned white and hard..it is called Corn-honey, or Stone-honey. *a* **1648** DIGBY *Closet Open.* (1677) 4 It is of three sorts, Virgin-honey, Life-honey, and Stock-honey. **1727–41** CHAMBERS *Cycl.* s.v., We have two kinds of honey, white and yellow.——The white, *mel album*, called also virgin honey, trickles out spontaneously from the comb, by turning it up. **1884** PHIN *Dict. Apicult.* 73 *Unripe Honey*, honey from which the water has not been sufficiently evaporated.

2. Applied to products of the nature of, or resembling honey: esp. **a.** the nectar of flowers; **b.** a preparation consisting of the expressed juice of dates or other fruit of palm trees.

1732 POPE *Ess. Man* II. 90 Taste the honey, and not wound the flow'r. **1737** WHISTON *Josephus, Wars Jews* IV. viii. §3 The better sort of them [palm trees], when they are pressed, yield an excellent kind of honey. **1836** MACGILLIVRAY tr. *Humboldt's Trav.* xxv. 387 This juice or honey has an agreeable acid taste. **1855** TENNYSON *Maud* I. IV. x, The honey of poison-flowers. **1883** V. STUART *Egypt* 271 The treacle which drains from the sugar is called black honey, and is much used by the natives. **1885** GRAY *Bot. Text-bk.* II. 451 The nectar..is the sweetish liquid commonly called the 'honey' of the flower, secreted by certain specialized organs known as nectar-glands.

3. (? Short for *honey-cake*.) ***singing hinny***, a currant cake baked on a girdle. *north.*

1832 W. STEPHENSON *Local Poems* 27 Ma canny bairns come get your tea, I've made a singing hinny. **1855** J. R. LEIFCHILD *Cornwall* 283 The Cornish cottage has no 'singing hinnies', or rich girdle cakes.

4. *fig.* **a.** Sweetness.

1592 SHAKS. *Rom. & Jul.* v. iii. 92 Death that hath suckt the honey of thy breath. **1613** —— *Hen. VIII*, III. ii. 22 Matter..that for euer marres The Hony of his Language. **1738** POPE *Epil. Sat.* I. 67 The Honey dropping from Favonio's tongue. **1855** THACKERAY *Newcomes* I. 216 Mrs. Mack was not all honey. **1893** STEVENSON *Catriona* 365 He said it with a serious heat of admiration that was honey to the girl.

b. A colour resembling that of honey. Also *attrib.* and *Comb.* (see sense 6 c).

1814 P. SYME *Werner's Nomencl. Colours* 34 Honey Yellow, is sulphur yellow mixed with chestnut brown. **1838** T. THOMSON *Chem. Org. Bodies* 524 It is honey-yellow, transparent, brittle. **1888** C. T. WHITMELL *Colour* XII. 183 Yellows may be distinguished as..honey..gold, [etc.]. **1923** *Daily Mail* 8 May 14 In Reseda,..Champagne, Honey, Copper. **1958** *Times* 16 Aug. 4/7 The Leccesi were fortunate in having close by an inexhaustible supply of honey-gold limestone. **1959** A. K. LANG in H. Q. Masur *Murder Most Foul* (1973) 76 A confection of honey blonde hair. **1973** G. BEARE *Snake on Grave* iv. 23 Her skin was deeply tanned, a smooth honey gold.

5. a. A term of endearment: Sweet one, sweetheart, darling. (Formerly chiefly Irish and, in form *hinnie, hinny*, Sc. and Northumbr. Now also common in N. Amer., whence also in Britain and elsewhere.)

c **1350** *Will. Palerne* 1655 William..seide, 'mi hony, mi hert al hol þou me makest'. *c* **1386** CHAUCER *Miller's T.* 431 Alisoun his hony deere. **1500–20** DUNBAR *Poems* lxxv. 3 My hwny [*v.r.* hunny], my hart, my hoip, my heill. *c* **1600** *Timon* II. i. (Shaks. Soc.) 24 My sparrow, my hony, my duck, my cony. **1607** TOURNEUR *Rev. Trag.* II. ii, Hunny, how's this? **1712** ARBUTHNOT *John Bull* III. vi, Our affairs, Honey, are in a bad condition. **1749** FIELDING *Tom Jones* VII. vi, Follow her, boy, follow her; run in, run in, that's it, honeys. **1809–12** MAR. EDGEWORTH *Ennui* viii. Wks. 1832–3 VI. 74 Have done being wild, honey-dear, and be a credit to your family. **1818** SCOTT *Hrt. Midl.* xvi, Where did he change his clothes again, hinny? *a* **1825** *Song* in Brockett s.v. *Hinney*, Where hest thou been, maw canny hinny? **1832** MRS. TROLLOPE *Dom. Mann. Amer.* (1894) I. 140 My children.. she always addressed by their Christian names, excepting when she substituted the word 'honey'. **1859** MRS. STOWE *Minister's Wooing* xxiii. 215 Come to ole Candace!..Honey, darlin', ye a'n't right—dar's a drefful mistake somewhar'. **1919** C. H. DARLING *Jargon Bk.* 17 *Honey*, sweetheart. **1929** M. CONNELLY *Green Pastures* (1930) I. v. 55 Come on, honey, an' meet de folks. **1939** [see CHIN *sb.*[1] 1 d]. **1952** *Manch. Guardian Weekly* 20 Mar. 3 She doesn't have a thing that you haven't got, honey, but she has it over here. **1952** S. KAUFFMAN *Philanderer* (1953) i. 15 'I think you know I really understand it. But, honey I ——.' A little pause here. **1961** J. HELLER *Catch-22* (1962) xviii. 178 'Be thankful you've got me,' she insisted. 'I am, honey.' **1962** J. LUDWIG in R. Weaver *First Five Years* 22 'Honey,' he said to the girl, 'let your *babbe* stay out here with the baby.' **1964** L. NKOSI *Rhythm of Violence* 27 Men are monsters!..Especially black men, honey. **1968** *New Society* 29 Aug. 305/1 'Honey' as an endearment, now rediscovered by southern Englishmen via Hollywood.

b. Anyone or anything good of its kind. *slang* (orig. *U.S.*[5]).

1888 *Missouri Republican* 24 Feb., Dave is a honey. **1933** *Amer. Speech* VIII. III. 35/1 [Pugilist slang] *Bear-cat*, an excellent fighter, a *honey*. **1934** H. N. ROSE *Thesaurus of Slang* ii. 3/1 Anything pleasing or attractive: *a honey*. **1935** [see DILLY *sb.*[5]]. **1939** *Evening News* 7 Nov. 4/5 A shot you are pleased with is a 'honey' or a 'peach' or an 'eagle'. **1946** G. GIBSON *Enemy Coast Ahead* xiii. 185 On the controls she [*sc.* an aeroplane] was as light as could be. This ship was certainly a honey. **1949** *N.Y. Times* 2 Oct. 1 It is a honey of a taut melodrama. **1958** M. ALLINGHAM *Hide my Eyes* xvi. 160 It had been a honey of an evening. **1959** *Vogue* Nov. 119 The Mini-Minor is a honey for parking. **1968** *Globe & Mail* (Toronto) 3 Feb. 38/1 (Advt.), A real honey, automatic power steering, power brakes, radio.

c. (See quot. 1960.) *U.S. slang.*

1934 L. HELLMAN *Children's Hour* I. 27 *Martha*:..has she always been like this? *Cardin*: She's always been a honey. Aunt Amelia's spoiling hasn't helped any, either. **1960** WENTWORTH & FLEXNER *Dict. Amer. Slang* 265/1 *Honey*, a person who is difficult to please; a difficult problem or task.

6. *attrib.* and *Comb.* **a.** Of, for, pertaining to, or connected with honey; as ***honey bike, brake*** (see BRAKE *sb.*[6] 1), ***-cake, colour, -crock, -cup, drink, -harvest, -knife, -mead, -pore, -scale, -shop, -time, wine***, etc.

c **1460** *Towneley Myst.* v. 4 The smell of my son is lyke To a feld with flouris, or *hony bike. **1542** UDALL tr. *Erasm. Apoph.* 118 *bis* [119] Fair and smoothe speakyng..Diogenes customably vsed to call an *hony brake, or a snare of honey. **1710** ADDISON *Tatler* No. 255 ¶ 2 It was usual for the Priest ..to feast upon the Sacrifice, nay the *Honey-Cake. **1853** HICKIE tr. *Aristoph.* (1872) II. 418, I will now knead you a honey-cake. **1611** FLORIO, *Melichlorone*, a stone partly yellow and partly of an *hony colour. **1596** SPENSER *F.Q.* v. ii. 33 Like foolish flies about an *hony-crocke. **1833** TENNYSON *Poems* 70 Like to the dainty bird..Draining the *honeycups. *a* **1648** DIGBY *Closet Open.* (1669) 97 To make *Honey drink. To two quarts of water take one pound of Honey. *a* **1700** DRYDEN *Ovid* (T.), Bees..bring Their *honey-harvest home. **1843** *Zoologist* I. 28 An abundant honey-harvest. **1884** PHIN *Dict. Apicult.*, **Honey-knife*, 1. A long thin knife used for separating the combs from the sides of a box-hive. 2. A knife..used for cutting-off the caps of the honey-cells. *a* **1735** ARBUTHNOT *Congress of Bees* Misc. Wks. 1751 II. 141 The first Foundation of their Work the skilful *Honey-Masters call *Commosis*. **1845** LINDLEY *Sch. Bot.* iv. (1858) 26 Petals numerous, small, with a *honey-pore at the back. **1831** DON *Gard. Dict.* Gloss., **Honey-scales*, the scales in flowers which secrete honey. **1658** ROWLAND *Moufet's Theat. Ins.* 906 The Bees do frequently resort thither..their nest or *Honey-shop is not far off. **1552** HULOET, *Hony tyme when it is rypely gathered.

b. objective and obj. gen., as ***honey-dresser, -farmer, -gatherer, -hunter, -maker, -worker; honey-bearing, -dropping, -eating, -gathering, -making, -secreting, -storing, -yielding***, etc., sbs. and adjs. Also HONEY-EATER.

1611 FLORIO, *Melifero*,..*honie-bearing. **1552** HULOET, *Hony dressers, *mellisones*. **1596** FITZ-GEFFRAY *Sir F. Drake* (1881) 82 *Honie-dropping Aganippes fount. **1679** M. RUSDEN *Further Discov. Bees* 53 *Hony-gathering being past, the Bees have no more need of them [drones]. **1853** LYNCH *Self-Improv.* ii. 40 The continued honey-gathering of the bee. **1608** TOPSELL *Serpents* 68 There are none Idle, although they be not all *Honny-makers. **1881** *Encycl. Brit.* XII. 136/1 *Honey-secreting glands are to be met with on the leaves.

c. parasynthetic, as ***honey-coloured, -hearted***, etc., adjs. Also HONEY-LIPPED, -MOUTHED, etc. **d.** similative, etc., as ***honey-brown, -dun, -pale, -tasting, -yellow; honey-like*** adjs. Also HONEY-SWEET. **e.** instrumental, as ***honey-bubbling, -flowing, -heavy, -laden, -loaded, -steeped, -stored***, etc., adjs.

1596 FITZ-GEFFRAY *Sir F. Drake* (1881) 89 Aganippes *hony-bubling fountaine. **1879** BROWNING *Ivan Ivanov.* 62 The bush of *honey-coloured beard. *a* **1000** *Guthlac* 1276 in *Exeter Bk.*, Wyrta ȝeblowene *huniȝ-flowende. **1580** SIDNEY *Arcadia* I. Wks. 1725 I. 3 The honey-flowing speech that breath doth carry. **1884** MISS GORDON-CUMMING in *Cent. Mag.* XXVII. 920 *Honey-laden blossoms. **1698** J. PETIVER in *Phil. Trans.* XX. 323 The bottom of each Flower contains a *Hony-like Liquor. **1611** FLORIO, *Melino*, honie-sweete, *honie-tasting.

7. a. Special Combinations: **honey ant** = HONEY-POT 4; †**honey-apple**, (*a*) in OE., a lozenge or pastille containing honey; (*b*) tr. L. *melimēlum*, Gr. μελίμηλον, 'a sweet-apple, an apple grafted on a quince' (Liddell and Sc.); **honey-baby** *colloq.* = HONEY *sb.* 5; **honey-badger** = HONEY-RATEL; **honey-bag**, the enlargement of the alimentary canal in which the bee carries its honey; **honey-basket**, the corbiculum of the bee: cf. quot. s.v. BASKET *sb.* 7; **honey-bearer**, a honey-ant which stores up in its distensible abdomen the honey collected by the workers; †**honey-beer**, ? mead; **honey-bucket** *N. Amer. slang*, a container for excrement; **honey-bun, honey-bunch** *colloq.* = HONEY *sb.* 5; **honey-cell**, a cell of a honeycomb; **honey chile** chiefly *Southern U.S.* (esp. *Black*)

colloq., = HONEY *sb.* 5; **honey-creeper**, a South American bird of the sub-family Cœrebinæ or a Hawaiian bird of the family Drepanididæ; **honey-extractor** (see quots.); **honey-fall** = HONEY-DEW 1; also *fig.*; **honey-flow**, the secretion of honey or nectar by flowers; † **honey-fly** = HONEY-BEE; **honey-gate** (see quot.); **honey-gilding**, (*a*) a dull gilding made from gold-leaf and honey, and used to decorate porcelain; (*b*) the process of applying such a solution; **honey-gland**, a gland secreting honey, a nectary; **honey-gold**, = *honey-gilding* (*a*); **honey-holder** = *honey-bearer*; † **honey-kite** = HONEY-BUZZARD; **honey-man**, a man who sells honey or has charge of bees; **honey-mark** = *honey-spot*; **honey-moth**, the honeycomb moth; **honey-mouse** = *honey possum*; † **honey-people**, fancifully applied to honey-bees; **honey possum**, a small West Australian marsupial, *Tarsipes spenseræ*; † **honey-rore** = HONEY-DEW 2; **honey-soap** (see quot.); † **honey-sop**, a sop made with honey; also, a term of endearment; † **honey-spot**, a mole on the flesh; **honey-stomach** = *honey-bag*; **honey-sucker**, one that sucks honey; *spec.* applied to birds of the family *Meliphagidæ*, and popularly to various other small birds, as the *Cœrebidæ*, *Nectariniidæ* (sun-birds), etc.: cf. HONEY-EATER; † **honey-tear** (OE. *huniȝtéar*, ME. *hunitiar*, *-ter*), virgin honey, nectar; sweet wine; **honey-tube**, one of the two setiform tubes on the upper side of the abdomen of an aphis, which secrete a sweet fluid; **honey-water**, water with honey dissolved in it; **honey-week** (*nonce-wd.*), a honeymoon lasting only a week; † **honey-wooled** *a.*, having wool of a honey colour; **honey-words**, words of sweetness, honeyed words: cf. B.

1868 *Amer. Naturalist* II. 382 A species of '*Honey-ant' is also found in Texas. **1874** *Ibid.* VIII. 366 The average weight of a non-producing ant is two milligrammes, that of a full honey-ant two hundred and forty milligrammes, a contrast simply immense. **1882** PROCTOR *Nature Stud.* 27 The honey-ants are a nocturnal species. **1882** H. C. MCCOOK (*title*) The honey ants of the Garden of the Gods. **1894** *Westm. Gaz.* 27 Feb. 1/3 Our human specialists are never quite so utterly sacrificed to their kind as the honey-ants. **1910** W. M. WHEELER *Ants* xx. 362 Honey ants have been reported from North America, South Africa and Australia. **1923** *Jrnl. Proc. R. Soc. W. Austral.* IX. 47 The geographical distribution of the various honey ants seems to point to drought as one of the most important factors in their development. **1944** *Living off Land* ii. 25 The bushman who finds honey ants can consider himself in champion class. *a* **700** *Epinal Gloss.* 830 *Pastellas*, *hunaeȝaepl. *a* **1000** *Ags. Voc.* in Wr.-Wülcker 279/25 *Passtellus*, huniȝæppel. **1678** LITTLETON *Lat. Dict.*, A honey-apple, *melimelum*. **1948** E. WAUGH *Loved One* 134 She was my *honey-baby. **1959** *Times* 20 June 7/6 Most people know..what is meant by..'a honey-baby'. **1884** J. S. KINGSLEY *Stand. Nat. Hist.* V. 392 The ratels or *honey badgers..surpass the skunk in burrowing activity. **1590** SHAKS. *Mids. N.* III. i. 171 The *honie-bags steale from the humble Bees. **1774** GOLDSM. *Nat. Hist.* (1862) II. IV. xi. 518 The..honey-bag..when filled, appears like an oblong bladder. **1882** PROCTOR *Nature Stud.* 26 This species [honey-ants]..possesses, apparently at least, a fourth caste, that of the *honey-bearers, whose abdomen is distended till it is almost spherical. **1731** MEDLEY *Kolben's Cape G. Hope* II. 57 They owe not their healths a little to the simplicity of their drink, which is only water, milk, and *honey-beer. **1931** BROPHY & PARTRIDGE *Songs & Slang 1914–18* 318 **Honey-bucket*, latrine receptacle for excreta. *Canadian.* **1962** F. G. VALLEE *Kabloona & Eskimo in Central Keewatin* 48 And where do they get the money? From emptying honey buckets for the Whites and mostly sitting on their butts. **1963** *Observer* 22 Dec. 13/3 The plumbing is definitely un-American. We were warned that the 'honey-buckets' would be a draughty experience. **1969** *Beaver* (Winnipeg, Man.) Summer 6/2 A woman taxi driver tells me most houses have honey-buckets, and galvanized [bath] tubs filled by hand. **1911** *Dialect Notes* III. 544 *Honey-bun. **1913** *Maclean's Mag.* Mar. 58/2 'Come, honey-bun,' she enticed. **1949** *Horizon* XIX. 239 Now, honey-bun, let's talk it over. **1957** M. SUMMERTON *Sunset Hour* iii. 46 'You might have warned me you were coming!' 'No time, honey bun.' **1969** R. TASHKENT *Ambiguous Man* iii. 34 I'm sorry, honeybun—sorry. Guess I'm a little upset. **1904** G. H. LORIMER *Old Gorgon Graham* 150 Honey, Honey, Funny *Honey-bunch. **1912** *Collier's* 5 Oct. 34/2 Why, can't you see, Honey-bunch, can't you see? **1937** A. REID in *Famous Plays* (Gollancz) 721 Jenny..control yourself! *Jenny*: Very well, honey bunch! I'll try for the present. **1942** WODEHOUSE *Money in Bank* (1946) xiv. 122 But where does that get us, honeybunch? **1949** F. SARGESON *I saw in my Dream* 144 Honeybunch..what's it like sleeping all on your lonesome? **1926** T. S. STRIBLING *Teeftallow* viii. 67 Stan up fo yo' baby... Thah you ah, *honey chile, lookin' yo' baby in de eye. **1948** MENCKEN *Amer. Lang.* Suppl. II. vii. 125 Southern speech has suffered cruelly on the stage and in talkies, where kittenish actresses from the domain of General American think that they have imitated it sufficiently when they have thrown in a few *you-alls* and *honey-chiles*. **1957** O. NASH *You can't get there from Here* 96, I early abandoned the hopeless fight against honey-chile and you-all. **1957** TRAGER & SMITH *Outl. Eng. Struct.* 82 There are current in popular literature allusions to 'Brooklynese' or 'honey-chile' accents. **1971** J. YARDLEY *Kiss a Day* viii. 153 Honey chile may well be talking through the back of her gorgeous neck. **1973** *Listener* 5 July 21/3 They [*sc.* the speakers] [were not] supposed to be rendering Deep South 'honey-chile' drawls. [**1822** J. LATHAM *Gen. Hist. Birds* IV. 207 Some few, indeed, of the Creepers have the tongue divided at the end and such no doubt are capable of licking honey from flowers.] **1872** COUES *N. Amer. Birds* 91 The Cærebidæ, or *honey-creepers of the tropics. **1885** J. S. KINGSLEY *Stand. Nat. Hist.* IV. 540 The honey-creepers in the New World 'represent' the sun-birds. **1912** BRABOURNE & CHUBB *Birds S. Amer.* I. 395 Turquoise Honey-Creeper. **1944** G. C. MUNRO *Birds of Hawaii* 89 (*heading*) Hawaiian Honey-creepers. Drepanididae. Hawaiian Honey-creeper Family. **1970** R. MEYER DE SCHAUENSEE *Guide Birds S. Amer.* 368 Honeycreepers form a composite family of groups of birds much unlike each other... They share the habit of feeding on the pollen and nectar of flowers, as well as on berries, small seeds and insects. **1884** PHIN *Dict. Apicult.*, **Honey-extractor*, a machine by means of which the honey is thrown out of the cells by centrifugal force. **1597–8** BP. HALL *Sat.* III. i. 16 They lickt oake leaues besprint with *hony fall. **1855** *Whitby Gloss.*, *Honeyfall*, a befalment of good things. 'They have had a brave honeyfall lately.' **1893** S. SIMMINS *Mod. Bee-Farm* (rev. ed.) 255 Frequent rainfalls destroy all chance of a good *honey flow. **1894** *Farm, Field & Fireside* 13 July 352/3 There is no reason why a swarm hived towards the end of the honey-flow should not at once have its energies directed to storing surplus. **1955** E. HILLARY *High Adventure* i. 14 All through the exciting months of the honey-flow, the dream of a bumper crop would drive us on. **1958** *Irish Beekeeper's Manual* (Stationery Office, Dublin) xvi. 53 One or more crates of sections may be removed at any time during the honey flow, after the sections in a crate have been completely sealed. **1972** *Country Life* 3 Feb. 253/1 The worker bee at the height of the honey flow, as it is called by beekeepers, works so hard that it wears itself out and dies in a short time. **1483** CAXTON *Cato* D ij b, The poure man had in hys gardyn many *hony flees or bees. **1591** SYLVESTER *Du Bartas* I. vii. 591 Prince and People, rise, And run to School among the Hony-Flies. *a* **1700** in Palgrave *Gold. Treas.* (1863) 73 The care-burthen'd honey-fly. **1884** PHIN *Dict. Apicult.* 44 Since thick honey does not flow freely through the ordinary faucet, beekeepers have adopted the 'molasses-gate' as it is called. When used for honey it is properly called a *honey-gate. **1958** M. WYKES-JOYCE *7000 Yrs. Pott. & Porc.* 271/2 *Honey gilding. **1960** R. G. HAGGAR *Conc. Encycl. Cont. Pott. & Porc.* 207/1 Honey-gilding was a more satisfactory process. **1960** H. HAYWARD *Antique Coll.* 129/1 Honey gilding was used at the Chelsea and Worcester porcelain factories. **1971** *Country Life* 10 June 1416/3 When heavily laid on in broad masses, honey gilding could be further enriched with light and shade patterns by chasing with a finely pointed agate. **1874** LUBBOCK *Wild Flowers* iii. 54 The *honey-glands are..situated in pairs at the base of the petals. **1954** G. SAVAGE *Porcelain* viii. 220 Gilding was often lavish, but of the brassy mercuric variety, whereas, for much of the eighteenth century, *honey gold was sparingly and tastefully applied. **1965** FINER & SAVAGE in *Lett. of J. Wedgwood* 8 The porcelain manufacturers used, first honey-gold..and later, mercuric gilding. **1894** *Westm. Gaz.* 27 Feb. 1/3 The specialised *honey-holders are fed by the workers till they can contain no more without danger of an explosion. **1883** *Cassell's Nat. Hist.* III. 290 The *Honey-Kite inhabits..the greater part of Europe. **1552** HULOET, *Hony man, or seller of hony, *mellarius*. **1836–48** B. D. WALSH *Aristoph.*, *Knights* II. iv, Honeymen besides, Prepared to join his banners. *a* **1803** *Young Benjie* xii. in Child *Ballads* (1886) lxxxvi. II. 282/2 'O how shall we her ken?'..'There's a *honey-mark on her chin.' **1832** J. RENNIE *Butterfl. & Moths* 211 Tineidæ..Galleria..The *Honey [moth] (*G. alveria*). **1855** MRS. GATTY *Parables fr. Nat.* Ser. I. (1869) 23 The mischievous honey moth has laid her eggs in our combs. **1923** *Austral. Zoologist* III. 148 The *Tarsipes* are known throughout the district as '*Honey Mice', which is such an excellent vernacular name, when one considers the habits detailed later on, that I venture to submit it for general use. **1965** Honey-mouse [see *honey possum*]. **1598** SYLVESTER *Du Bartas* II. i. III. *Furies* 336 Never did the..king Of *hony-people..Lead to the field.. More busie buzzers. **1941** E. TROUGHTON *Furred Animals of Australia* 80 The *Honey Possum is readily distinguished by having three well-marked dark brown stripes along the back. **1965** *Austral. Encycl.* VII. 234/1 Honey-possum (*Tarsipes spenserae*). Restricted to the south of Western Australia, this species (which is also known as the honey-mouse), feeds on nectar, pollen, and small insects, gathered from blossoms. **1632** VICARS tr. *Virgil* (N.), He..felt loves *honey-rore Soak in. **1878** H. BEASLEY *Druggist's Receipt Bk.* (ed. 8) 239 The *honey soap usually sold, consists of fine yellow soap perfumed with oil of citronella. **1500–20** DUNBAR *Poems* lxxv. 30 My *hwny soppis, my sweit possodie. **1591** PERCIVALL *Sp. Dict.*, *Cahinas*, hony sops made of bread, hony and water. **1606** *Wily Beguiled* in Hazl. *Dodsley* IX. 269 Ha, my sweet honey-sops! how dost thou? **1547** SALESBURY *Welsh Dict.*, *Man geni*, Mole, *hony spotte. *c* **1050** *Gloss.* in Wr.-Wülcker 370/37 *Carene*, cerenes, oððe *huniȝteares. *a* **1175** *Cott. Hom.* 217 Ælc word of him swete, al swa an huni tiar felle upe ȝuire hierte. *a* **1240** *Ureisun* Ibid. 183 Ihesu swete..mi leof..Min huniter. **1884** SEDGWICK tr. *Claus' Zool.* 569 Many of them [*Aphidæ*] possess, on the dorsal surface of the antepenultimate segment, two '*honey tubes', from which is secreted a sweet fluid—the honey dew—which is eagerly sought for by ants. **1597** A. M. TR. *Guillemeau's Fr. Chirurg.* 23 b/2 He must washe his mouthe with *honye-water, to the purifyinge of the dissease. **1792** NELSON 5 Feb. in Nicolas *Disp.* (1845) I. 292 To tell her where honey-water is sold in Norwich. **1833** T. HOOK *Widow & Marquess* x. (1842) 143 The happy couple left town..to pass the *honey week—for they had not time to make a moon of it. **1607** TOPSELL *Four-f. Beasts* 598 Their best sheep..near the Alpes, they are gray or *hony-wolled. **1595** BARNFIELD *Cassandra* xxi. in *Poems* (Arb.) 70 Scarce were these *honywords breath'd from her lips. **1818** KEATS *Endym.* III. 420 Tears, and smiles, and honey-words.

b. In names of plants and fruits: **honey agaric** = *honey fungus*; **honey-apple** (see 7); **honey-balm**, a labiate plant, *Melittis Melissophyllum*; **honey banana**, a West Indian name for a diploid variety of *Musa acuminata*, bearing small, sweet, thin-skinned fruit; also ellipt. *honey*; **honey-berry**, the sweet berry of a West Indian tree, *Melicocca bijuga*; also, that of the Nettle-tree of Southern Europe, *Celtis australis*; **honey-blob** (**hinny-**) *Sc.*, a sweet yellow gooseberry; **honey-bloom**, the Fly-trap of North America, *Apocynum androsæmifolium*; **honey-bottle** (*local*), the bloom of *Erica Tetralix*; **honey-bread**, the Carob (*Ceratonia Siliqua*); **honey-cherry**, a sweet variety of cherry; **honey fungus**, a fungus, *Armillaria mellea*, which causes a root disease in trees and shrubs, indicated by honey-coloured toadstools around affected plants and black threads like bootlaces attached to their roots; **honey-garlic**, a name of *Allium siculum* (*Nectaroscordum*); **honey-locust**, name of the thorny leguminous trees of the North American genus *Gleditschia*, esp. *G. triacanthos*; also applied to the mesquit, *Prosopis juliflora*, a similar tree found in the South-western States; **honey-lotus**, a local name of the White Melilot, *Melilotus alba*; † **honey-meal** [tr. L. *melimēlum*] = *honey-apple* b. (see 7); **honey-mesquit**, *Prosopis juliflora* (see *honey-locust*); **honey mushroom** *U.S.* = *honey fungus*; **honey-pear**, a sweet variety of pear; **honey-plant**, a plant yielding nectar; 'the genus *Hoya*' (Miller); '*Melianthus*' (*Treas. Bot.*); in Tasmania, *Richea scoparia* (Morris *Austral Eng.*); **honey-pod** = *honey-mesquit* (Cent. Dict.); **honey-stalks** *sb. pl.*, applied by Shakespere to the stalks or flowers of clover; **honey-ware** = BADDERLOCKS; **honey-wood**, the Tasmanian tree *Bedfordia salicina* (Morris). See also HONEYSUCKLE, HONEYWORT.

1894 W. SOMERVILLE tr. *Hartig's Text-bk. Dis. Trees* I. 207 *Agaricus melleus*. The *Honey Agaric. This fungus belongs to the most widely distributed and destructive of parasites. **1909** E. W. SWANTON *Fungi* II. 176 *A*[*rmillaria*] *mellea* ..'Honey Agaric'. **1945** M. C. RAYNER *Trees & Toadstools* ii. 35 The Honey Agaric forms its sporophores only after the tissues in which it grows have been killed. **1938** *Jrnl. Jamaica Agric. Soc.* XLII. 460 The Red banana, *Honey, Apple and Fillbasket eventually found their way here. *Ibid.* 464 (*heading*) Honey [banana]. This variety is..also known by the names Sucrier and Lady's Finger... The skin is very thin and ripens to a deep yellow. The flavour of the fruit is very sweet and gives the variety its name. **1959** N. W. SIMMONDS *Bananas* v. 76 Notes on the principal clones. AA group. (a) 'Sucrier'. Principal synonyms..'Honey'..(West Indies). **1961** [see FIG *sb.*[1] 1 c]. **1882** J. SMITH *Dict. Econ. Pl.*, *Honey-berry of Guiana..where it forms large forests. **1746** H. WALPOLE *Lett.* (1820) I. 144 He stopped..to buy *honey-blobs, as the Scotch call gooseberries. **1855** THACKERAY *Newcomes* xxiii, Confessing..that she preferred it to the rasps and hinnyblobs in her grandmama's garden. **1880** JEFFERIES *Gt. Estate* 6 Wild moor-like lands, beautiful with heaths and *honey-bottle. **1757** A. COOPER *Distiller* III. lii. (1760) 221 The black Heart Cherry, the common red Cherry, the black Cherry, the Merry or *Honey Cherry. **1895** W. SCHLICH *Man. Forestry* IV. iii. 382 The *honey fungus (*Agaricus melleus*, L.)..causes a well-known disease amongst conifers. **1919** W. E. HILEY *Fungal Dis. Common Larch* viii. 153 (*heading*) The effects of the honey fungus on its hosts. **1962** *Amateur Gardening* 27 Jan. 25/1 The honey fungus, Armillaria mellea, produces thick black threads or rhizomorphs somewhat similar to black leather laces. **1971** *Homes & Gardens* Sept. 97/2 Honey fungus or armillaria.. sometimes attacks and kills the roots of trees and shrubs. **1884** MILLER *Plant-n.*, *Nectaroscordum*, *Honey-Garlic. **1743** J. F. GRONOVIUS *Flora Virginica* 194 *Gleditsia*, ..*Honey-locust. **1759** P. MILLER *Gardeners Dict.* (ed. 7) I, s.v. Gleditsia. The first sort [of *Gleditsia*] is very common in most parts of North America, where it is known by the Title of Honey Locust. **1788** *Chambers' Cycl.*, Honey-locust. **1812** BRACKENRIDGE *Views Louisiana* (1814) 104 Beautiful woods of tall oak, walnut, mulberry, sassafras, honey locust. **1819** A. L. HILLHOUSE tr. *Michaux's N. Amer. Sylva* II. 137 In different parts of the United States, this species [sc. *Gleditsia triacanthos*] is called indifferently Sweet Locust and Honey Locust. **1838** [see GLEDITSCHIA]. **1863** [see *sweet locust* (SWEET *a.* and *adv.* C. 1 b)]. **1869** [see LOCUST *sb.* 5]. **1968** N. TAYLOR *Guide to Garden Shrubs & Trees* 135 Honey-Locust (*Gleditsia triacanthos*). A spiny-trunked native tree [*i.e.* native to U.S.A.] with small, numerous leaflets, greenish-yellow flowers, and a twisted, persistent pod. **1611** COTGR., *Pomme de paradis*, an excellent sweet apple..some also call so our *Honnymeale, or S. Johns apple. **1664** EVELYN *Kal. Hort.* (1729) 220 Apples.. Pearmain, Pear-apple, Honey-meal. **1938** J. S. BOYCE *Forest Pathology* vi. 110 *Armillaria mellea*..known as the *honey mushroom, causes this disease. **1845** *Statist. Acc. Scotl.* IV. 60 The..*honey pears which were produced in the orchard. **1880** JEFFERIES *Gt. Estate* ii. 25 She watched the bees busy at the sweet-scented '*honey-plant'. **1588** SHAKS. *Tit. A.* IV. iv. 91 Words more sweet, and yet more dangerous Then baites to fish, or *hony stalkes to sheepe. **1849** D. LANDSBOROUGH *Pop. Hist. Brit. Seaweeds* 111 In Scotland in the Lowlands, it is by some called badder-locks, and hen-ware, which may be a contraction of *honey-ware, the name given to it in the Orkney Islands. **1933** J. GRAY *Lowrie* 34 He never said onything aboot tangles, hinniwirs, an' dills.

B. *adj.* [from the attrib. use in 7, and fig. senses 4 and 5.]

1. Resembling, or of the nature of, honey; sweet, honeyed; lovable, dear. *lit.* and *fig.*

c **1450** LYDG. *Secrees* 378 Omerus with the hony mouth. *c* **1572** GASCOIGNE *Fruites Warre* (1831) 210 Rethorike that hoonnie harmelesse arte. **1592** SHAKS. *Ven. & Ad.* 16 A thousand honie secrets shalt thou know. **1596** —— *1 Hen. IV*, I. ii. 179 My good sweet Hony Lord, ride with vs to morrow. **1609** B. JONSON *Case is altered* v. iv, My most honey gold! **1631** WEEVER *Anc. Fun. Mon.* 20 And to bring you this honie example. *a* **1700** DRYDEN (J.), Why, honey bird, I bought him on purpose for thee. *c* **1822** BEDDOES *Poems, Pygmalion* 162 As if sweet music's honiest heart did break!

2. *Comb.* (*parasynthetic*): see A. 6 c.

honey, *v. arch.* [f. prec. sb.]

†**1.** *trans.* To make sweet with or as with honey; to sweeten, dulcify. *lit.* and *fig. Obs.*

13.. *Augustin* 496 in Horstmann *Alteng. Leg.* (1878) I. 70 Wiþ hony of heuene ihonied swete. *c* **1450** LYDG. *Secrees* 882 Sugryd galle honyed with Collusyoun. **1622** T. SCOTT *Belg. Pismire* 49 The brimme whereof shee hath cunningly hunnied with faire pretences of seeming pietie. **1645** RUTHERFORD *Tryal & Tri. Faith* xv. (1845) 164 The law of God, honeyed with the love of Christ.

†**2.** To address as 'honey', to use endearing terms to. *Obs.*

1602 MARSTON *Antonio's Rev.* I. i. Wks. 1856 I. 75 Canst thou not hony me with fluent speach? **1631** CHETTLE *Hoffman* (N.), If he be no worse; that is doe worse, And honey me in my death-stinging thoughts.

b. *absol.* or *intr.* To use honeyed or endearing words; to talk fondly or sweetly. *arch.* and *U.S.*

1602 SHAKS. *Ham.* III. iv. 93 Honying and making loue Ouer the nasty Stye. **1847** TENNYSON *Princess* Prol. 115 One Discuss'd his tutor, rough to common men But honeying at the whisper of a lord. **1884** —— *Becket* Prol., The King came honeying about her.

†**3.** *trans.* To coax, flatter, tickle, delight. *Obs.*

1604 MARSTON & WEBSTER *Malcontent* III. ii, O unpeerable! invention! rare! Thou god of policy! it honeys me. **1605** CHAPMAN, etc. *Eastw. Hoe* III. ii. D iv b, Was euer Rascall honnied so with poison? **1622** FLETCHER *Sp. Curate* IV. ii, I am honyed with the project.

honey-bear.

1. A small quadruped, somewhat larger than a polecat, the potto or kinkajou, *Cercoleptes caudivolvulus*, a native of tropical America.

1838 SWAINSON *Anim. in Menag.* 77 Baron Humboldt affirms that it [the Potto] makes use of its long tongue to suck honey, and hence is a great destroyer of the nests of bees: this habit has procured for it.. the name of the Honey Bear. **1883** LADY BRASSEY *The Trades* 452 From Colon one of the officers had brought back a honey-bear—an intelligent brute, about the size of a mongoose.

2. The sloth-bear, *Melursus labiatus*, of India.

1875 *Encycl. Brit.* III. 462/1 There is but one species, the Sloth or Honey Bear.. It inhabits the mountainous regions of India. **1880** A. R. WALLACE *Isl. Life* iii. 44 The great features of the Oriental region are, the long-armed apes, the orang-utans, the tiger, the sun-bears and honey-bears.

honey-bee. A bee that gathers and stores honey, esp. the common hive-bee.

c **1566** J. ALDAY tr. *Boaystuau's Theat. World* N iv b, Arthenor writeth that honie Bees and other flies chased out of a towne all the inhabitantes thereof. **1614** RALEIGH *Hist. World* I. (1634) 75 Some affirme that hee (Jupiter) was fed by Honi-Bees. **1663** GERBIER *Counsel* F v b, Your Honey-bee-like disposition. **1835** W. IRVING *Tour Prairies* 62 Some of the ancient settlers.. pretend to give the very year when the honey bee first crossed the Mississippi.

'honey-bird.

†**1.** A fanciful name for a bee. *Obs.*

1605 SYLVESTER *Du Bartas* II. iii. IV. *Captaines* 1143 Quails [have] but One Chief, the Hony-birds but One, One Master-Bee.

2. A bird that feeds on honey or the nectar of flowers, as those of the family *Meliphagidæ*. Cf. HONEY-EATER, -SUCKER.

1870 WILSON *Austral. Songs* 99 Honey-birds loitered to suck at the wattle. **1898** MORRIS *Austral Eng.* s.v. *Honey-eater*, The whole series are sometimes called Honey-birds.

3. = HONEY-GUIDE I.

1850 R. G. CUMMING *Hunter's Life S. Afr.* (ed. 2) I. 41, I saw to-day for the first time the honey-bird. This extraordinary little bird.. will invariably lead a person following it to a wild-bees' nest. **1893** SELOUS *Trav. S.E. Afr.* 455 Two of our Kafirs.. had gone in pursuit of a honey-bird.

honey-buzzard. A bird of prey of the genus *Pernis*, esp. the European species *P. apivorus*, which feeds chiefly on the contents of bees' and wasps' nests.

1674 RAY *Words, Eng. Birds* 82 The Honey-Buzzard: *Buteo apivorus.* **1766** PENNANT *Zool.* (1768) I. 146 As he [Mr. Willughby] found the combs of wasps in the nest, he gave this species the name of the honey buzzard. **1825** P. J. SELBY *Illustr. Brit. Ornith.* I. 23 The Honey Buzzard preys upon moles, mice, and small birds. **1883** *Cassell's Nat. Hist.* III. 289 Crows and Rooks mob the Honey-Buzzard with almost the same eagerness as they chase the Eagle-Owl. **1971** *Country Life* 25 Mar. 705/2 Seven species breed regularly within the city limits [*sc.* West Berlin].. honey-buzzard (4–5 pairs).

honeycomb ('hʌnɪkəʊm), *sb.* Forms: see HONEY and COMB. [OE. *huniȝcamb*, f. *huniȝ* HONEY + *camb* COMB *sb.*[1] (sense 8).]

1. A structure of wax containing two series of hexagonal cells separated by thin partitions, formed by bees for the reception of honey and their eggs.

The shape and arrangement of the cells secures the greatest possible economy at once of space and of material.

a **1050** *Liber Scintil.* x. (1889) 50 Sawl ȝefylled trytt huniȝcamb [*fauum*]. *c* **1275** *Pass. Our Lord* 616 in *O.E. Misc.* 54 Hi hym.. brouhten of one visse ibred And ek enne huny-comb. *a* **1340** HAMPOLE *Psalter* xviii. 11 Swetter abouen huny and huny kambe. *c* **1440** *Promp. Parv.* 245/1 Hony coom,..*favus.* **1500–20** DUNBAR *Poems* lxxxii. 39 Merchandis.. hamperit in ane hony came. **1577** B. GOOGE *Heresbach's Husb.* IV. (1586) 191 b, Blewe knoppes, or tuftes, like Honicoames. **1651** HOBBES *Leviath.* III. xxxvi. 230 The fault that Ionathan had committed, in eating a honey-comb. **1774** GOLDSM. *Nat. Hist.* (1776) VIII. 100 The honeycomb of the bee is edgeways with respect to the hive. **1857** MRS. CARLYLE *Lett.* II. 314 Tea, eggs, brown bread and honey-comb.

fig. c **1386** CHAUCER *Melib.* ¶ 147 He seith that wordes þat been spoken discreetly by ordinaunce been honycombes, for they yeuen swetnesse to the soule. **1642** J. EATON (*title*) The Honey-combe of Free Justification by Christ alone. **1842** TENNYSON *E. Morris* 26 Was he not A full-cell'd honeycomb of eloquence Stored from all flowers?

†**2.** A term of endearment. Cf. HONEY 5. *Obs.*

c **1386** CHAUCER *Miller's T.* 512 What do ye, hony comb, sweete Alisoun? **1552** HULOET, Darlynge, a wanton terme.. as be these: honycombe, pyggisnye, swetehert, trueloue.

3. A cavernous flaw in metal work, esp. in guns.

1530 PALSGR. 232/1 Honny combe, *marcq.* **1588** LUCAR *Colloq. Arte Shooting* App. 2 Whether or no any hony-combes flawes or crackes are in the peece. **1706** PHILLIPS (ed. Kersey), *Honey-comb*, a Flaw in the Metal of a Piece of Ordnance. **1763** DEL PINO *Sp. Dict.*, *Escarabajos*,.. what gunners call honey-comb, that is, holes in the metal. **1828** J. M. SPEARMAN *Brit. Gunner* (ed. 2) 339 Efforts to force the water through any honey-combs or flaws which there may be in the bore. **1881** GREENER *Gun* 146 A scratch or spot of honey-comb in the grooves renders the rifle completely useless for match-shooting.

4. The reticulum or second stomach of ruminants, so called from the appearance of its inner surface.

1727–41 CHAMBERS *Cycl.* s.v. *Ruminant*, The reticulum, which we call the hony-comb. **1774** GOLDSMITH *Nat. Hist.* II. II. i. **1859** TODD *Cycl. Anat.* V. 302/2 The second cavity, the honeycomb.. is so called from the appearance of its mucous membrane.

5. a. Honeycomb work (see 6).

1838 H. G. KNIGHT *Norm. in Sicily* 276 The vault is ornamented with the Moorish honeycomb. **1882** *Daily Tel.* 23 Nov., A large white quilt, real honeycomb.

b. *Textiles.* Used *attrib.* of a fabric in which the warp and weft threads form ridges and indentations, producing a cell-like appearance.

1879 T. R. ASHENHURST *Weaving & designing Textile Fabrics* 250 Another cloth which may be mentioned is one known as the honeycomb cloth, which presents to the eye a series of ridges and cavities. **1913** *T. Eaton & Co. Catal.* Fall & Winter 113/3 Full Bleached English Honeycomb Quilts ..fringed all round..for single beds. **1921** *Daily Colonist* (Victoria, B.C.) 5 Apr. 18/4 (Advt.), Honeycomb Towels at, each, 15c. **1929** WOODHOUSE & BRAND *Towels & Towelling* ix. 99 The unbroken diamond in the first unit.. is filled in with the 8-thread honeycomb weave. **1968** 'A. GILBERT' *Night Encounter* iii. 41 High bed with a honeycomb quilt.

c. A structure consisting of numerous intersecting surfaces designed to reduce turbulence and straighten the air flow in a wind tunnel.

1912 *Sci. Amer.* 14 Sept. 220/1 The usual method of eliminating swirls and irregularities of speed is to pass the air through a sheet metal 'honeycomb' at the front end [of the tunnel]. **1918** COWLEY & LEVY *Aeronautics* i. 8 At both ends of the channel proper there are placed two metal honeycombs. **1947** A. POPE *Wind-Tunnel Testing* ii. 60 If the contraction ratio of the tunnel is large, and a good honeycomb is installed, the turbulence can be low indeed. **1966** OWER & PANKHURST *Measurem. Air Flow* (ed. 4) vii. 200 The resistance coefficient of a honeycomb or a gauze is conveniently expressed in term of the loss of pressure.. suffered by the air in passing through it.

d. A material consisting of a regular network of parallel, open-ended cells formed out of many bent or moulded strips (e.g. of metal or plastic) bonded together; it is usually used faced on both sides with sheeting, forming a ***honeycomb sandwich.*** Freq. *attrib.*

1937 *Jrnl. Franklin Inst.* CCXXIV. 282 Barkley-Grow Aircraft Corp... has fabricated an all metal honeycomb structure of great strength and lightness. **1946** *Mod. Plastics* Sept. 130/2 Standard thicknesses of honeycomb have been selected. *Ibid.*, Fire resistance may be obtained with stainless steel or laminated asbestos paper skins on asbestos honeycomb core. **1949** *Aircraft Engin.* XXI. 12/1 This flooring material is a honeycomb sandwich of aluminium alloy. **1964** OLEESKY & MOHR *Handbk. Reinforced Plastics* IX. 492 Honeycomb sandwich flooring is currently being used in large computer room applications. **1966** *New Scientist* 26 May 523/3 Temperature-resistant honeycomb has been used in heat-sensitive areas of many aircraft.

6. *attrib.* and *Comb.* Of or pertaining to a honeycomb; like, or arranged in the form of, a honeycomb; having a surface hexagonally marked; as ***honeycomb cell, decoration, flannel, ground, limestone, ornament, pattern, sponge, work***; **honeycomb bag** = sense 4; **honeycomb coil** *Electronics*, an inductance coil in which the turns cross one another obliquely and adjacent ones are separated, giving a criss-cross pattern; **honeycomb coral**, a coral of the genus FAVOSITES; **honeycomb moth**, a tineid moth of the genus *Galleria* which infests beehives; **honeycomb radiator**, a radiator for an internal-combustion engine that is pierced by numerous short tubes running from front to back through which the air passes, the ends of which give it a honeycombed appearance; **honeycomb ringworm, scall**, species of the disease FAVUS; **honeycomb stitch** (see quot.); **honeycomb stomach** = sense 4; so **honeycomb tripe**; **honeycomb-stone**, fossil honeycomb coral; **honeycomb wall**, a (brick) wall containing numerous small openings close together at regular intervals.

1865 *Chambers' Encycl.* VIII. 367 The stomach.. consists of four distinct bags or cavities.. The second cavity is the *Honeycomb bag. **1922** *Wireless World* 30 Dec. p. xiv (Advt.), Gimbal type *Honeycomb coil. **1959** K. HENNEY *Radio Engin. Handbk.* (ed. 5) iii. 9 Honeycomb coils were a type of universal winding with relatively few, widely spaced turns per layer giving a typical 'honeycomb' appearance. **1873** DAWSON *Earth & Man* v. 91 The Favosites or *honeycomb coral, presenting regular hexagonal cells with transverse floors or tabulæ. **1884** *Advt.*, *Honeycomb Flannel.. for Petticoats and Skirts. **1721** MRS. BRADSHAW in *Lett. C'tess Suffolk* I. 75 There is one [edging], of a *honeycomb ground. **1813** BAKEWELL *Introd. Geol.* (1815) 463 *Honeycomb lime-stone, a name which conveys a tolerably correct idea of its appearance. **1840** J. & M. LOUDON tr. *Köllar's Treat. Insects* I. 75 This enemy is the caterpillar of a moth, called the..*honeycomb-moth. **1864–5** WOOD *Homes without H.* viii. (1868) 192 The last of our burrowers is the Honey-comb Moth belonging to the genus Galleria. **1838** H. G. KNIGHT *Norm. in Sicily* 272 *note*, The *honeycomb ornament is common in the alcoves, and vaulted apartments of the Arabians. **1882** CAULFIELD & SAWARD *Dict. Needlework*, **Honeycomb Pattern*, cast on any number of stitches that divide by six. First row——Knit. Second row—— Purl [etc.]. This completes one Honeycomb. **1904** A. B. F. YOUNG *Compl. Motorist* iii. 55 The front of the car consists of a water-tank pierced like a honeycomb throughout its whole surface with apertures of equal dimensions; this is known as a '*honeycomb radiator'. **1919** *Jane's All the World's Aircraft* 16 b A 'V' type honeycomb radiator is fitted directly behind the airscrew. **1946** A. W. JUDGE *Mod. Petrol Engines* vii. 261 The honeycomb radiator, which has been so widely used in automobile and aircraft work, consists of a series of thin brass tubes expanded at their ends and joined together at these ends by a soldering process. **1867** J. HOGG *Microsc.* II. i. 296 The Favus fungus.. is commonly called the cupped ringworm or *honycomb scall. **1874** *J. Pereira's Mat. Med.* 1015 *Turkey Sponge*,..the common variety is called *honeycomb sponge. **1882** CAULFIELD & SAWARD *Dict. Needlework*, **Honeycomb Stitch*, this stitch is used to draw together in an ornamental pattern the gathers upon the neck and sleeves of smock frocks, and also for all kinds of decorative gathering. **1861** HULME tr. *Moquin-Tandon* II. I. 43 The reticulum or *honey-comb stomach. **1753** CHAMBERS *Cycl. Supp.*, **Honeycomb-Stone.* **1894** J. P. ALLEN *Pract. Building Constr.* (Index), *Honeycomb walls. **1913** G. G. SAMSON *Every Man his own Builder* iii. 108 Some people build them [*sc.* sleeper walls] as 'honeycomb' walls. **1969** *New Yorker* 5 Apr. 99/1 A honeycomb wall turns into an entrance to whatever place they imagine. **1874** T. HARDY *Far fr. Madding Crowd* I. ix. 127 Snow-white smock-frocks ..marked on the wrists, breasts, backs, and sleeves with *honeycomb-work. **1895** *Jrnl. R. Inst. Brit. Archit.* 14 Mar. 348 A richly fretted ceiling of Arabian honeycomb-work.

honeycomb, *v.* [f. prec. sb.]

1. a. *trans.* To fill like a honeycomb with cells, cavities, or perforations; to render cavernous, hollow, or insubstantial in this way; to undermine.

1774 GOLDSM. *Nat. Hist.* (1776) VII. 67 If it had been honey-combed by worms in the quarry. **1834** MEDWIN *Angler in Wales* I. 163, I have known tents.. completely honeycombed in a very few weeks. **1860** *All Year Round* No. 78. 30 The drains may honeycomb the basement and not remove the refuse passed into them.

b. *intr.* for *pass.* To become cavernous.

1851 *Jrnl. R. Agric. Soc.* XII. II. 382 Peat land is subject to 'honey-comb', or contract when dried by frost.

2. *fig.* **a.** To penetrate through and through so as to render hollow, rotten, etc.; to undermine.

1855 H. ROGERS *Ess.* II. vii. 331 This great empire is rotten; honey-combed as it were. **1875** MᶜLAREN *Serm.* Ser. II. vii. 113 The small continuous vices, which root underground and honeycomb the soul. **1878** BAYNE *Purit. Rev.* xi. 477 His theory is here again honeycombed by his own averments of fact.

b. *absol.*, and *intr.* for *pass.*

1868 LORD STRANGFORD *Sel. Writings* (1869) I. 338 The very same man who has been honeycombing away at the.. cranky old Ottoman empire. **1879** BARING-GOULD *Germany* II. 179 Floating dogmas.. all imperceptibly, yet certainly, honeycombing and melting away.

3. *trans.* To mark with a honeycomb pattern.

1888 *Daily News* 28 Nov. 7/6 Velveteens, plain, shaded, and honeycombed, in light shades. **1889** *Ibid.* 21 Nov. 6/1 The bodices.. are honeycombed, after the most approved fashion, across the chest and shoulders.

4. *Building.* To build as a honeycomb wall.

1908 C. F. MITCHELL *Brickwork & Masonry* (ed. 2) ii. 103 To facilitate the circulation of air beneath the basement floors, these walls are usually honeycombed. **1964** E. C. ADAMS *Sci. in Building* I. v. 170 This [*sc.* ventilation] can be done.. by 'honeycombing' sleeper walls.

honeycombed ('hʌnɪkəʊmd), *a.* [f. prec. vb. or sb. + -ED[1] or [2].] **1. a.** Having perforations, excavations, or cavernous parts, like a honeycomb; esp. abounding in little cells, as cast metal when not sound. **b.** Marked with a honeycomb-like pattern.

1627 CAPT. SMITH *Seaman's Gram.* xiv. 65 Honicombed, is when shee is ill cast or ouermuch worne shee will bee rugged within. **1676** WISEMAN *Surg.* (J.), A mariner having discharged his gun, which was honeycombed, and loading it suddenly again, the powder took fire. **1802** *Med. Jrnl.* VIII. 471 The head of the tibia.. quite spongy or honey-combed in its texture. **1806** *Gazetteer Scotl.* (ed. 2) s.v. *Greenock*, Coarse-grained basaltic whin, intermixed with honey-combed lava. **1897** ALLBUTT *Syst. Med.* III. 16 Its free surface, owing to the movements of the heart, becomes roughened in a peculiar manner, presenting a shaggy or honey-combed appearance.

2. Of, pertaining to, or having the defect of 'honeycombing' in wood.

1919 S. J. RECORD *Identification Economic Woods U.S.* (ed. 2) I. 58 When the interior finally dries, the internal strains frequently become so great that large checks open up, producing a honeycombed condition.

ˈhoneycombing, *vbl. sb.* [f. HONEYCOMB *v.* + -ING¹.] **1.** The action of the vb., esp. marking with a honeycomb pattern; an instance of this.

1889 *Daily News* 21 Nov. 6/1 Liberty frocks, with their many folds upon the chest, held in by honeycombing.

2. (See quot. 1945). See also HONEYCOMBED *a.* 2.

1938 H. E. DESCH *Timber* xi. 133 When the interior dries below the fibre saturation point it..is restrained from shrinking, and interior checks may result. This condition is known as honeycombing. **1945** D. J. SCHWARTZ et al. *Fund. Shopwork* 458 *Honeycombing*, a form of defective separation in wood which usually occurs in the interior and follows the medullary rays. It is caused by improper seasoning. **1966** A. W. LEWIS *Gloss. Woodworking Terms* 14 *Check*, small seasoning cracks or shakes, invisible from the outside of the wood; also called 'honeycombing'.

Also as *ppl a.*

1893 E. H. BARKER *Wand. by South. Waters* 277 The honey-combing action of water.

ˈhoney-dew.

1. A sweet sticky substance found on the leaves and stems of trees and plants, held to be excreted by aphides: formerly imagined to be in origin akin to dew.

1577 B. GOOGE *Heresbach's Husb.* IV. (1586) 180b, The leaves..bedewed with Hony..In the morning, our common people call it Manna, or Hony dewe, cleaving to the leaves before the rising of the sunne. **1588** SHAKS. *Tit. A.* III. i. 112 Fresh teares Stood on her cheekes, as doth the honydew Vpon a gathred Lillie almost withered. **1657** S. PURCHAS *Pol. Flying-Ins.* 133 Pliny affirmed the Hony-dew to bee either the sweat of the heaven, or the slaver or spittle of the stars, or the moisture of the aire purging it self. **1789** G. WHITE *Selborne* lxiv. (1875) 309 In the sultry season of 1783 honeydews were so frequent as to deface and destroy the beauties of my garden. **1883** J. G. WOOD in *Gd. Words* Dec. 763/1 The sweet juice which is exuded by the aphis..is popularly known as 'honey-dew'.

2. An ideally sweet or luscious substance; often, like dew, represented as falling; sometimes applied to the nectar of flowers or to honey itself.

1608 TOPSELL *Serpents* 65 Their stomach..wherein they [bees]..keepe their Honny dew which they haue gathered. **1646** G. DANIEL *Poems* Wks. 1878 I. 52 Sweet, as the Hony-deaw, which Hybla hath. **1695** BLACKMORE *Pr. Arth.* II. 347 Hony-Dews fall in delicious Showers. **1797** COLERIDGE *Kubla Khan* 53. **1798** —— *Anc. Mar.* v. xxvi, The other was a softer voice, As soft as honey-dew. **1871** B. TAYLOR *Faust* (1875) I. xxii. 197 Little step and lofty leap Through honey-dew and fragrance.

fig. *a* **1835** MRS. HEMANS *Poems, Fount. Obliv.*, The cool honey-dews of dreamless rest. **1878** SYMONDS *Sonn. M. Angelo* 2 On bitter honey-dews of tears.

3. A kind of tobacco sweetened with molasses.

1843 J. LUMSDEN *Let.* 15 May in *Amer. Memoranda* (1844) 14 The manufacturing of the nigger-head,..pigtail, honey-dew, and other varieties of the stimulating and soothing herb. **1857** KINGSLEY *Two Y. Ago* viii, I say, how do you sell honeydew? **1894** *Daily News* 12 Mar. 6/2, I took up a paper containing 2 oz. of sunflaked honeydew.

4. A colour resembling that of a honeydew melon.

1921 *Daily Colonist* (Victoria, B.C.) 19 Oct. 5/6 (Advt.), Combination dark tones and lighter hues, such as algonquin, honeydew, jade. **1949** *Brit. Colour Council Dict. Colours Int. Decoration* III. 13 *Honeydew*, a colour name.. adopted here as a more attractive name for B.C.C. standard Carrot.

5. honeydew melon, a cultivar of the musk melon, *Cucumis melo*, which has a smooth ivory or pale yellow skin and sweet greenish flesh.

1916 *Country Gentleman* 2 Sept. 1615/1 (*heading*) The honey dew melon. *Ibid.*, A new melon has recently been introduced... It has been christened Honey Dew... The Honey Dew is the result of crossing the Rocky Ford cantaloupe with a South African melon somewhat resembling a Casaba. It was propagated by John E. Gauger, of Colorado. **1923** A. WARD *Encycl. Food* 314 The Honey Dew has a smooth, somewhat warted, creamy-white to greyish skin. **1959** P. ROTH *Goodbye, Columbus* (1969) iii. 46 And there were melons—cantaloupes and honey dews. **1962** WHITAKER & DAVIS *Cucurbits* ix. 189 All 'Honey Dew' melons should have an adequate ethylene treatment. *Ibid.* x. 207 The cultivars 'Hales's Best' and 'Honey Dew' were.. low in soluble solids.

So **ˈhoney-dewed** *a.*, (*a*) bedewed with honey; (*b*) covered with honey-dew.

1596 R. L[INCHE] *Diella* (1877) 34 Thy hony-dewed tongue exceedes hir far in sweete discourse. **1798** SOUTHEY *Poems, Oak of Fathers*, The bees o'er its honey-dew'd foliage play'd. **1868** DARWIN *Anim. & Pl.* II. xxv. 337 Horses.. injured by eating mildewed and honeydewed vetches.

ˈhoney-drop.

1. A drop of honey: sometimes taken as a type of what is sweet and delicious. Cf. *honey-dew* 2.

1600 FAIRFAX *Tasso* XV. xxxvi, The honeydrops from hollow oaks distill. **1610** SHAKS. *Temp.* IV. i. 79. **1641** TRAPPE *Theologia Theologiæ* 359 The Promises are the hony-drops of Christs mouth. *a* **1711** KEN *Preparat.* Poet. Wks. 1721 IV. 97 Jonathan from his pointed Spear Suck'd Honey-drops, and his Eyesight Grew quick and bright. **1852** JAMES *Agnes Sorrel* (1860) I. 116 To sweeten the cup of pain with the wild honey-drops of pleasure.

2. A mole on the skin. Cf. *honey-mark, -spot*, s.v. HONEY *sb.* 7.

? *a* **1800** *Bondsey & Maisry* v. in Child *Ballads* IV. lxxxvi. (1886) 283/1 Here she is, my sister Maisry, Wi' the hinny-draps on her chin.

ˈhoney-ˌeater. a. An animal that feeds on honey; = HONEYSUCKER. (In quot. 1731 = HONEY-GUIDE 1.)

1731 MEDLEY *Kolben's Cape G. Hope* II. 155 These Gnat-snappers, or Honey-eaters are a sort of guides to the Hottentots in the search of honey. **1882** PROCTOR *Nature Stud.* 26 Like many other ants, these little honey-eaters are divided into different castes or classes. **1884** J. S. KINGSLEY *Stand. Nat. Hist.* V. 392 The ratels belong to the genus Mellivora, the Honey Eaters.

b. An Australasian bird of the family Meliphagidæ.

In Morris *Austral English*, 56 Australian species of Honey-eaters are named, e.g. *banded, black, bridled, brown honey-eater*, etc.

1822 J. LATHAM *Gen. Hist. Birds* IV. 208 None of them, although the tongue be cloven into two filaments, are at all fringed at the edges, as is the case with very many of the honey-eaters. **1845** J. GILBERT in J. Gould *Mammals of Australia* I. tab. 5 It [sc. *Tarsipes rostratus*] inserted its long tongue precisely in the way in which the Honey-eaters among birds do theirs into the flower-cups for honey. **1862** WOOD *Illustr. Nat. Hist.* II. 212 The true Honey-Eaters form a very numerous group of birds. **1864–5** —— *Homes without H.* xxv. (1868) 470 In Australia there is a large group of rather pretty birds, popularly called Honey-eaters, because they feed largely on the sweet juices of many flowers. **1901** A. J. CAMPBELL *Nests & Eggs Austral. Birds* I. 354 The range of the splendid little Black Honeyeater extends across the southern part of Australia. **1936** [see COACH-WHIP 1 b]. **1964** A. L. THOMSON *New Dict. Birds* 375/2 The diet of the majority of honeyeaters consists of a mixture of nectar, pollen, and insects.

honeyed, honied (ˈhʌnɪd), *a.* Forms as in HONEY *sb.*; also 5 hownyd. [f. HONEY *sb.* + -ED².]

1. Abounding in or laden with honey; sweetened as with honey; consisting of or containing honey.

c **1374** CHAUCER *Boeth.* III. metr. ii. 54 (Camb. MS.) Al thowh þat the pleynynge bysynesse of men yeueth hem honyede drynkes and large metes. **1551** TURNER *Herbal* I. H vj b, Wyne lyke vnto honyed wyne. **1601** HOLLAND *Pliny* I. 422 Of Hydromel and Oxymel (i. Honied water, and Honied vinegar). **1657** W. COLES *Adam in Eden* lviii, The remedy is to drink honyed water. **1791** COWPER *Odyss.* VII. 139 The honied fig, and unctuous olive smooth. **1801** *Med. Jrnl.* V. 61 Diabetic urine..marked by a saccharine or honied taste. **1812** BYRON *Ch. Har.* II. lxxxvii, Still his honied wealth Hymettus yields. **1841–71** T. R. JONES *Anim. Kingd.* (ed. 4) 329 Honeyed fluids from the flowers.

2. *fig.* Sweet; sweet-sounding, dulcet, mellifluous.

1435 MISYN *Fire of Love* II. v. 79 Þe sweitt honyd mynde of Ihesu. **1500–20** DUNBAR *Poems* lxvii. 17 With gall in hart, and hwnyt hals. **1599** SHAKS. *Hen. V*, I. i. 50 His sweet and honyed Sentences. **1639** T. BRUGIS tr. *Camus' Mor. Relat.* 244 Whom we will call by the name of Mela, for the honeyed sweetnesse of her disposition. *a* **1839** PRAED *Poems* (1864) II. 351 Conviction hung On soft Persuasion's honied tongue. **1852** M. ARNOLD *Tristr. & Iseult* II. 47 Silken courtiers whispering honied nothings.

Hence **ˈhoneyedly** *adv.*, sweetly, in dulcet tones. **ˈhoneyedness**, sweetness as of honey.

1611 COTGR., *Emmielleure*, sweetnesse, honiednesse. **1849** CLOUGH *Dipsychus* II. vi. 46, I too..Can speak, not honiedly, of love and beauty, But sternly of a something much like duty. **1887** MRS. C. READE *Maid o' Mill* I. xix. 286 'I'll be your chaperon, if I may', honeyedly.

ˈhoney-flower.

1. a. A flowering shrub of the Cape of Good Hope, of the genus *Melianthus*.

1712 J. PETIVER in *Phil. Trans.* XXVII. 421 Great Cape Honey-Flower. **1731** MEDLEY *Kolben's Cape G. Hope* II. 243 These Honey-flowers contain a great deal of sweet juice. **1882** J. SMITH *Dict. Econ. Pl.*, *Honey-flower*,..a soft-wooded shrub..The flowers are of a dark brown colour.

b. An Australian flower, *Lambertia formosa*.

1802 BARRINGTON *Hist. N.S. Wales* iv. 101 They returned ..dreadfully exhausted, having existed chiefly by sucking the wild honey-flower and shrubs. **1889** J. H. MAIDEN *Useful Native Pl. Austral.* 37 'Honey-flower' or 'honey-suckle'. This plant is as well known to small boys about Sydney as to birds and insects. [Named] on account of the large quantity of a clear honey-like liquid the flowers contain.

c. A local name of the Bee Orchis.

1879 BRITTEN & HOLLAND *Plant-n.*, Honey-flower (Kent).

2. *gen.* A flower yielding honey.

1887 J. SERVICE *Dr. Duguid* vi. 36 All sorts of honey-flowers, marigolds, pansies, roses, clover.

ˈhoney-ˌfuggle, -ˌfugle, *v.* *U.S. colloq.* Also -fackle, -fogle. [app. f. HONEY *sb.* + FUGLE *v.*¹, perh. after dial. *connyfogle* (E.D.D.).]

1. *trans.* **a.** To dupe, deceive, swindle.

1829 *Virginia Literary Museum* I. 458 *Honeyfuggle*, to quiz, to cozen. **1856** *Knickerbocker* XLVIII. 286 They go cavorting out, honey-fuggling their consciences. **1888** *Century Mag.* XXXVI. 81/2 A-tryin' to honey-fugle the varmint to git 'im to come underneath. **1902** W. N. HARBEN *Abner Daniel* xix, He's been tryin' to honey-fuggle the old man into a trade. **1906** *Dialect Notes* III. 141 He can't honey-fuggle him.

b. To obtain by duplicity or wheedling.

1905 D. G. PHILLIPS *Plum Tree* xxiii, Whatever terms he could honeyfuggle out of my conciliation-mad candidate. **1942** BERREY & VAN DEN BARK *Amer. Thes. Slang* §223/7 Coax; wheedle..honeyfogle.

2. *intr.* To act in an underhand or indirect way, in order to deceive or to obtain by duplicity.

1856 *Congress. Globe* 22 July, App. 965 Pardon me for using the word, but Sharp 'honey-fuggled' around me. **1888** *Missouri Republican* 20 Jan. (Farmer), Noonan's companion objected to this honey-fugling by knocking the demonstrative stranger down. **1906** *Nation* (N.Y.) 22 Feb. 149 'Don't honey-fugle,' he advised the committee, 'but go to the bottom in any way possible.' **1941** *Time* 26 May 16/3 Things which..Baruch had to wangle by what he called 'buttering & honey-fuggling'. **1952** T. PYLES *Words & Ways Amer. Eng.* vi. 129 Even today some of these 'tall' words, words like..*to honeyfogle*..are popularly regarded as picturesque and admirably American.

†**ˈhoneyful,** *a. Obs.* [f. HONEY *sb.* + -FUL.] Full of or abounding in honey or sweetness.

c **1340** HAMPOLE *Prose Tr.* 1 This name es..in my mouthe honyfull swetnes. **1610** HEALEY *St. Aug. Citie of God* 685 Hony-full Calydna.

honey-guide.

1. (Also ***honey-guide cuckoo.***) A small tropical bird of the predominantly African family Indicatoridæ, which feeds on insects, honey, and beeswax, a habit which makes some species useful as guides to bees' nests.

1777 A. SPARRMAN in *Phil. Trans. R. Soc.* LXVII. 43 The Dutch settlers thereabouts have given this bird the name of *Honig-wyzer*, or Honey-guide, from its quality of discovering wild honey to travellers. **1786** *Chambers' Cycl.*, *Cuculus indicator*, a species of cuckow found in the interior parts of Africa..called by the Dutch settlers *honig-wyzer* or *honey-guide*. **1798** *Sporting Mag.* XII. 89 A remarkable bird called the Honeyguide. **1843** *Penny Cycl.* XXVI. 59/2 The Honey-Guide Cuckoo. **1865** LIVINGSTONE *Zambesi* x. 209 The honey guide is an extraordinary bird; how is it that every member of its family has learned, that all men, white or black, are fond of honey? **1900** *Ibis* 7th Ser. VI. 691 Having heard the story of the Honey-guide before, I was much interested. **1955** *Bull. U.S. Nat. Mus.* CCVIII. 1 The honey-guides are a small family of picarian birds related to the barbets, the woodpeckers, and the toucans. **1966** E. PALMER *Plains of Camdeboo* xii. 215 It is not only the honey-guides..that use other birds' nests.

2. A marking in a flower, which serves to insects as a guide to the position of the honey.

1879 LUBBOCK *Sci. Lect.* 6 The lines and bands by which so many flowers are ornamented have reference to the position of the honey;..these honey-guides are absent in night flowers, where they of course would not show.

ˈhoneyish, *a. rare.* [f. HONEY *sb.* + -ISH.] Somewhat honey-like.

1657 W. COLES *Adam in Eden* lxvi, A sweet honeyish moisture. **1693** BRANCARD *Phys. Dict.* 138/1 A honyish kind of Substance. **1969** P. DICKINSON *Pride of Heroes* 40 There is honeyish Mrs Singleton in her dottily beautiful car.

honeyless (ˈhʌnɪlɪs), *a.* Destitute of honey.

1601 SHAKS. *Jul. C.* V. i. 35 Your words, they rob the Hibla Bees, And leaue them Hony-lesse. **1609** C. BUTLER *Fem. Mon.* (1634) 134 Many Hives are left Honniless. **1874** LUBBOCK *Wild Flowers* iii. 68 The inner, honeyless stamens.

honey-lipped (-lɪpt), *a.* = HONEY-MOUTHED.

1828 *Blackw. Mag.* XXIV. 705 He is..as honey-lipped as a bee-hive in spring. **1855** I. TAYLOR *Restor. Belief* (1856) 301 Honey-lipped gentlemen..who would gladly keep entire a Theism—patched with borrowings from the Gospels.

†**honey-month.** *Obs.* [After HONEYMOON.] The first month after marriage; the honeymoon.

1696 C. LESLIE *Snake in Grass* (1697) 31 In their Haste, and in their Honey-Month while they were New-fangl'd. **1710** STEELE *Tatler* No. 192 ¶2 Sometimes the Parties.. grow cool in the very Honey Month.

honeymoon (ˈhʌnɪˌmuːn), *sb.* **1. a.** 'The first month after marriage, when there is nothing but tenderness and pleasure' (Johnson); originally having no reference to the period of a month, but comparing the mutual affection of newly-married persons to the changing moon which is no sooner full than it begins to wane; now, usually, the holiday spent together by a newly-married couple, before settling down at home.

1546 J. HEYWOOD *Prov.* (1867) 14 It was yet but hony moone. **1552** HULOET, Hony mone, a terme prouerbially applied to such as be newe maried, whiche wyll not fall out at the fyrste, but thone loueth the other at the beginnynge excedyngly, the likelyhode of theyr exceadynge loue appearing to aswage, yᵉ which time the vulgar people cal the hony mone, *Aphrodisia, feriæ, hymenæ.* **1612** BRETON *Cornucopia* (T.), And now their honey-moon, that late was clear, Doth pale, obscure, and tenebrous appear. **1651** N. BACON *Disc. Govt. Eng.* II. xxxv. (1739) 161 The first year of her Marriage was Honey-moon with her; she thought nothing too dear for the King. **1656** BLOUNT *Glossogr.*, *Hony-moon*, applyed to those marryed persons that love well at first, and decline in affection afterwards; it is hony now, but it will change as the Moon. [**1693** *Oxford Act* 3 Brisk and Bonny, As Bridegroom's self, in Moon-call'd-Hony.] **1801** MAR. EDGEWORTH *Out of Debt* i. Wks. 1832–3 IV. 196 Mr. and Mrs. Ludgate went down in the hoy to Margate, to spend the honeymoon in style. **1880** DIXON *Windsor* III. ix. 89 They kept their honey-moon for a year.

b. *transf.* The first warmth of newly established friendly relations.

1580 LYLY *Euphues* (Arb.) 268 It being now but Honnie Moone, I endeauoured to courte it with a grace. **1655** FULLER *Ch. Hist.* IV. ii. §8 Kingdoms have their honey-moon, when new Princes are married unto them. **1735–8** BOLINGBROKE *On Parties* 120 In the Honey-moon of his Accession. **1795** BURKE *Regic. Peace* iv. Wks. IX. 87 Spain, in the honey-moon of her new servitude. **1867** GOLDW. SMITH *Three Eng. Statesmen* (1882) 7 The brief honeymoon of the new king and his parliament. **1969** *Daily Tel.* 9 Sept. 1/2 MPs fear that the honeymoon between the troops and the civilians might be over. *Ibid.* 13 Sept. 3 It is an open secret that the honeymoon between Xerox and Rank Organisation is over. **1971** *Guardian* 15 Jan. 12/1 The Government has had its honeymoon, free from captious criticism, as Mr Wilson promised.

c. ***second honeymoon***, a holiday or trip, resembling a honeymoon, taken by a couple who have been married for some time.

1872 PRINCESS OF WALES *Let.* 31 Jan. in G. Battiscombe *Queen Alexandra* (1969) viii. 118 This quiet time we two have spent here together now has been the happiest days of my life... It has been our second honeymoon. **1894** G. DU MAURIER *Trilby* III. VIII. 152 So Taffy and his wife have come for their second honeymoon, their Indian-summer honeymoon, alone. **1910** *Nat. Police Gaz.* 16 July 3/4 They acted as if they were on their second honeymoon. **1967** 'M. HUNTER' *Cambridgeshire Disaster* xxi. 137 They began what he called an extended second honeymoon, driving where she liked.

2. *attrib.* and *Comb.*, as ***honeymoon couple, period, trip***, etc.; **honeymoon suite** = *bridal suite*.

1904 *Daily Chron.* 31 Mar. 6/6 The young honeymoon couple were heard of at Newport, Mon. **1970** W. J. BURLEY *To kill a Cat* v. 81 A honeymoon couple stood close, arms round each other. **1953** E. SIMON *Past Masters* II. i. 69 The Labour Government's honeymoon period looks like having come to an end. **1970** *Guardian* 9 Dec. 11/1 This Government's honeymoon period has been significantly shorter than previous in-coming Governments'... The package of..increased charges announced by the Chancellor on October 27 was the chief single cause of a rapid deterioration in the Government's popularity. **1881** E. W. HAMILTON *Diary* 26 Dec. (1972) I. 205 Lord Lyons says that Gambetta has got very well through his first short (honeymoon) session, and has displayed great vigour and tact as a parliamentary leader. **1956** 'E. MCBAIN' *Cop Hater* (1958) ix. 80 The cafe still served as a sort of no-man's-land between the respectable workaday world..and the sinful.. brothels... Jenny's served the same purpose as the shower stall does in a honeymoon suite. **1967** C. O. SKINNER *Madame Sarah* viii. 163 Bernhardt enjoyed Chicago. Her quarters at the Palmer House roused in her continual.. mirth, for she occupied the 'honeymoon suite'. **1968** B. NORMAN *Hounds of Sparta* xxvii. 183 'The *honeymoon* suite, for God's sake.'.. 'I knew nothing about that, believe me.' **1865** TROLLOPE *Belton Est.* xxxii. 391 After their honeymoon trip. **1882** MISS BRADDON *Mt. Royal* II. vii. 134 It was a dreary departure for a honeymoon tour.

Hence (*nonce-wds.*, chiefly *humorous*) **'honey-'moonish** *a.*; **'honey-'moonlight, -'moonshine; 'honey-'moon-struck** *a.*

1741 H. WALPOLE *Lett. H. Mann* (1833) I. vii. 21 Quite bridal together, quite honey-moonish. **1869** F. LOCKER-LAMPSON in Ld. Tennyson *Tennyson* (1897) II. iii. 76 Lovers..steeped in honeymoonshine. **1872** HOWELLS *Wedd. Journ.* (1884) 8 There was not a suspicion of honey-moonshine about us. *Ibid.* 197, I wanted to know..whether you seemed honey-moon-struck. **1888** *Chicago Advance* 16 May 371 The effects..are ascribed..to the peculiar refractive power of honey-moonlight.

'honey,moon, *v.* [f. prec. sb.] *intr.* To spend the honeymoon.

1821 MISS MITFORD in L'Estrange *Life* (1870) II. 135 How did I know but you were tourifying or honeymooning? **1828** J. JEKYLL *Corr.* 15 Dec. (1894) 190 The Speaker and his bride..are honeymooning at Hastings. **1891** MRS. CLIFFORD *Love Lett. Worldly Wom.* 244 Some one offered us a country seat to honeymoon in, but we declined.

Hence **'honey,mooner; 'honey,mooning** *vbl. sb.* and *ppl. a.*

1845 W. G. S. CAVENDISH *Handbk. Chatsworth & Hardwick* 196 Other honeymooners here [*sc.* at Hardwick]. **1861** HUGHES *Tom Brown at Oxf.* xlvii, As soon as I can get his discharge, and he has done honeymooning, we shall start. **1873** *Daily News* 25 Aug., Some miserable honeymooner..glad to get a reasonable being to talk to. **1873** M. COLLINS *Miranda* III. 227 A honeymooning couple. **1968** *Punch* 18 Sept. 398/1 Hawker-Siddeley have dramatised for us the folly of paying a man £15,000 a year to sit around in an airport lounge with a lot of delayed honeymooners.

'honey-mouthed, *a.* Sweet or soft in speech: often implying insincerity. (Cf. *mealy-mouthed.*)

1539 LATIMER *Serm. & Rem.* (Parker Soc.) 413, I like not these honey-mouthed men, when I do see no acts nor deeds according to their words. **1611** SHAKS. *Wint. T.* II. ii. 33 If I proue hony-mouth'd, let my tongue blister.

'honey-pot.

1. a. A pot in which honey is stored. **b.** A receptacle, of wax or other substance, in which many species of wild bees store their honey. (*Cent. Dict.*)

1483 *Cath. Angl.* 192/1 An Huny pot or hony wesselle, *mellarium*. **1589** *Pappe w. Hatchet* Bijb, The Martin-mongers swarmd to a lecture, like beares to a honnie pot. **1694** DRYDEN *Love Triumph.* IV. i, Mind to have a lick at the honey-pot yourself.

2. a. *pl.* A children's game. Also *attrib.* in reference to the posture.

One of the players, called a honey-pot, sits with his hands locked under his hams, while the 'honey-merchants' lift him by the arm-pits as handles, pretend to carry him to market, and shake him, with the aim of making him let go his hold. Also called in Scotland *honey-pigs*.

1821 *Blackw. Mag.* X. 36/2 Common games..as the Skipping-rope, and Honey-pots. **1854** H. MILLER *Sch. & Schm.* (1858) 52 A game at marbles, or honey-pots, or hy-spy. **1860** LADY CANNING in Hare *2 Noble Lives* (1893) III. 110 It was an easy pass..I could not resist a 'honey-pot' descent. **1886** *Daily Tel.* 10 Apr. 5/2 To squat low down on his haunches, like a political 'honey-pot'.

b. ? orig. *Austral.* Term applied to the action of jumping into a swimming-pool, etc., with one's hands clasped round one's drawn-up legs.

1941 in BAKER *Dict. Austral. Slang.* **1951** J. FRAME *Lagoon* 16 She would dive backwards and do a honey-pot into the water.

3. The female pudenda. *slang.*

1719 T. D'URFEY *Pills* III. 342 For when you have possession got, Of Venus Mark, or Hony-pot. **1970** G. GREER *Female Eunuch* 265 If a woman is food, her sex organ is for consumption also, in the form of *honey-pot*.

4. In full ***honey-pot ant***. An ant belonging to one of several North American, Australian, or South African genera in which some of the workers become distended with surplus food, which is regurgitated when it is needed by the rest of the colony.

1880 *Jrnl. Linn. Soc. Zool.* XV. 185 Certain individuals in each nest serve as animated honey-pots. **1927** HALDANE & HUXLEY *Animal Biol.* xii. 291 (*caption*) A store-chamber of the honey-pot ant. **1934** A. RUSSELL *Tramp-Royal in Wild Australia* xxxviii. 253 Worker ants and honey-pot ants. *Ibid.*, The honey-pot stores the honey in its abdomen. **1968** P. P. & M. W. LARSON *Lives of Social Insects* xxi. 157 Honeypots, or repletes..serve their nest mates simply as receptacles for the colony's extra food supplies. *Ibid.* (*caption*) Honeypot ants represent an adaptation of some ant species to dry and inhospitable environments. **1970** BROWN & TAYLOR in *Insects of Australia* (C.S.I.R.O.) xxxvii. 956/1 Some formicine ants in arid areas..store regurgitated honey-dew and nectar in the enormously distended crops of special large 'honeypot' workers.

5. Something very attractive or tempting, *spec.* an attractive girl or young woman, one who invites or attracts attention. Also *attrib.*

1929 H. A. VACHELL *Virgin* iii. 58 What a honeypot she was, whether in or out of breeches and boots. **1945** A. L. ROWSE *West-Country Stories* 4 His honey-pot young wife. **1972** *Daily Tel.* 7 Jan. 11/2 This mother, who is a tart, decides to set the girl up as a photographer's model, and a great honey-pot she turns out to be for the local talent who come in droves to photograph her splendid features. **1972** *Guardian* 15 Aug. 16/1 The hordes of eager students that descend on London..present too tempting a honey-pot for the smart operators to stay away from. **1973** *Times* 29 May 14/5 Concentrating facilities at centres of attraction, so-called 'honeypot' areas, and discouraging motorists from heading towards 'quiet' areas.

honeypot: see HANEPOOT.

honey-ratel ('hʌnɪˌreɪtəl). A name of the ratel, from its fondness for honey.

1816 KIRBY & SP. *Entomol.* (1843) I. 238 The honey-ratel ..has a particular instinct enabling it to discover bees. **1835** KIRBY *Hab. & Inst.* II. xxiii. 463 Bee cuckows..indicating to the honey-ratel..the subterranean nests of certain bees.

'honeysome, *a. rare.* [f. HONEY *sb.* + -SOME.] Sweet, like honey.

1593 NASHE *Christ's T.* 64 Marke how sweete and honny-some they are. **1877** BLACKMORE *Cripps* (1887) 348 He should rather speak honeysome words.

'honey-stone.

†1. A stone said to have a sweet smell or taste.

1567 MAPLET *Gr. Forest* 15 The Melanite is a Stone, which distilleth..that iuice which is verie sweete and honie like; wherfore it may well be called Melanite, as you would say Honistone. **1659** TORRIANO, *Melite*, a kind of yellow stone, which, broken and put into water, smelleth of honey, called the sweet or Honey-stone.

2. A synonym of MELLITE, called by Werner, 1789, *honigstein*, from its colour.

1795 SCHMEISSER *Min.* I. 299 Honey stone..was first discovered by Mr. Werner. **1884** BAUERMAN *Min.* 393 Honey stone..is a mellitate of aluminium.

'honey-suck. Now only *local.* Forms: 1 **huniȝsuge, hunisuge, -suce, 4–5 honysouke, 7– honey-suck.** [OE. *huniȝsúge, -súce*, f. *huniȝ* honey + *súgan, súcan* to suck; the ME. form represents the second of these.]

1. An earlier equivalent of the name HONEYSUCKLE (senses 1 and 2): used with the same laxity of application.

*c***725** *Corpus Gloss.* 1214 *Ligustrum*, huniȝsuge. *a***1100** *Ags. Voc.* in Wr.-Wülcker 298/23 *Lugustrum*, hunisuce. **14**.. *Voc.* Ibid. 572/12 *Cerifolium*, honysouke. *Ibid.* 611/30 *Serpillum*, peletur *vel* honysouke. **1597** GERARDE *Herbal* II. ccccclxxvii. 1018 Medow Trefoile is called..of some Suckles, and Honisuckes. **1879** BRITTEN & HOLLAND *Plant-n.*, Honey-suck. (1) Flowers of *Trifolium pratense*... (2) *Lonicera Periclymenum*.

†b. = HONEYSUCKLE 1 b. *Obs.*

1388 WYCLIF *Matt.* iii. 4 His mete was honysoukis, and hony of the wode. **14**.. *Voc.* in Wr.-Wülcker 593/24 *Locusta*, a honysouke.

†2. Honey 'sucked' or gathered by bees. *Obs.*

1608 TOPSELL *Serpents* (1658) 645 Then they [Bees] flye not far from their own homes, but sustain themselves with their own Honey-suck already provided.

'honey,sucker. An animal that feeds on honey; *spec.* applied to numerous small birds that feed on honey and the nectar of flowers, esp. the *Meliphagidæ*, also the *Nectariniidæ, Cœrebidæ*, etc.; a nectar-bird; a HONEY-EATER.

1772–84 COOK *Voy.* (1790) VI. 2034 There are four species that seem to belong to the trochili, or honey-suckers of Linnæus. **1837** SWAINSON *Birds* II. 144 The *Meliphagidæ*, or honeysuckers, are distinguished..by their notched bill. **1883** G. ALLEN in *Longm. Mag.* July 308 Butterflies..sail further up mountain heights than the bees and other meadow honeysuckers.

honeysuckle ('hʌnɪsʌk(ə)l). [ME. *hunisuccle, -soukil*, app. extended from *hunisuce, honysouke*: see HONEY-SUCK.]

1. A name for the flowers of clover, esp. the common red clover; also applied to other flowers yielding honey. *Obs.* exc. *dial.*

*c***1265** *Voc. Names Pl.* in Wr.-Wülcker 558/15 *Ligustrum, i.* triffoil, *i.* hunisuccles. **1387–8** T. USK *Test. Love* III. vi. (Skeat) l. 6 If thou shalt haue Honie soukels, thou leauest the fruict of the soure Docke. *c***1440** *Promp. Parv.* 245/1 Hony socle, *apiago.* **1530** PALSGR. 232/1 Honnysuckell, *lait Nostre Dame.* **1603** OWEN *Pembrokesh.* (1891) 72 Fine grasse full of the hearbe called *Trifolium*..and of the Countrie people honie suckles both white and red. **1626** BACON *Sylva* §496 Flowers that haue deepe Sockets, doe gather in the Bottome a kinde of Honey; As Honey-Suckles (both the Woodbine and the Trifoile). **1697** DRYDEN *Virg. Georg.* IV. 87 Then Melfoil beat, and Honey-suckles pound, With these alluring Savours strew the Ground. **1879** BRITTEN & HOLLAND *Plant-n.*, Honeysuckle..(2) *Lotus corniculatus*. Ches... (4) *Trifolium pratense*... Mr. Elworthy says that in *Som.* the name is restricted to the flowers of *T. pratense.* (5) *Rhinanthus Crista-galli.*

†b. A rendering of L. *locusta* taken as the name of some plant; hence used by confusion where the real sense was 'locust' (the insect). *Obs.*

*c***1380** WYCLIF *Serm.* Sel. Wks. II. 5 Sum men seien þat locusta is a litil beest good to ete. Sum men seien it is an herbe þat gederiþ hony upon him; but it is licli þat it is an herbe þat mai nurishe men, þat þei clepen hony soukil. **1387** TREVISA *Higden* (Rolls) I. 159 Som leueþ onliche by honysoukels [*solis locustis vivunt*] i-dryed wiþ smoke oþer wiþ þe sonne. **1430–40** LYDG. *Bochas* VII. (1554) 172b, Honisocles his moderate feedyng..This blessed Baptist. **1483** CAXTON *Gold. Leg.* 370 b/1 Takyng onelye for her refeccion honysocles and locustes. **1493** *Festivall* (W. de W. 1515) 106 [Iohn the Baptist] sucked hony of floures that be called honysocles that poore people gadereth and frye theym in oyle to theyr mete.

2. The common name of *Lonicera Periclymenum*, also called Woodbine, a climbing shrub with fragrant yellowish trumpet-shaped flowers, frequent in woods; thence extended to the whole genus. ***fly-honeysuckle***, the species *L. Xylosteum* and *L. ciliata*: see also 3. ***trumpet*** or ***coral honeysuckle***, a North American species, *L. sempervirens*, with evergreen foliage and scarlet flowers.

1548 [see 4]. **1562** TURNER *Herbal* II. 82a, Wodbynde or Honysuckle..windeth it self about busshes. **1590** SHAKS. *Mids. N.* IV. i. 47 So doth the woodbine, the sweet Honisuckle, Gently entwist. *a***1711** KEN *Hymnotheo* Poet. Wks. 1721 III. 10 Sweet Honeysuckles round the Branches twin'd. **1753** CHAMBERS *Cycl. Supp.* s.v., The Virginian scarlet honey-suckle, called the trumpet honey-suckle. **1796** WITHERING *Brit. Pl.* (ed. 3) II. 247 *Lonicera periclymenum*, ..Common Honeysuckle, Woodbine Honeysuckle. *L. Xylosteum*,..Upright Honeysuckle. **1890** *Chambers' Encycl.* V. 763 The Fly Honeysuckle, *Lonicera Xylosteum*, is an erect shrub..common in shrubberies.

b. The flower of the woodbine.

1573–80 BARET *Alv.* W 368 Woodbin that beareth the Honiesuckle. **1640** *Sicily & Naples* (T.), A honey-suckle The amorous woodbine's offspring.

3. Applied, with or without qualifying word, to various shrubs or plants of other genera, in some way resembling the common honeysuckle.

a. Applied in Australia to species of *Banksia*, the flowers of which contain a sweet honey-like liquid, eagerly sucked out by the aborigines; also in N.S. Wales to the HONEYFLOWER, q.v.; in New Zealand to *Knightia excelsa*; in New England to species of Columbine, esp. the native species *Aquilegia canadensis*; in Jamaica to *Passiflora laurifolia*.

b. bush-honeysuckle, name for the shrubs of the genus *Diervilla*, nearly allied to the common honeysuckle, natives of N. America and Japan. **dwarf honeysuckle**, a species of Cornel, *Cornus suecica*, having berries like those of the honeysuckle. **false honeysuckle**, 'the genus *Azalea*' (Miller *Plant-n.*). **fly-honeysuckle**, a South African shrub of the genus *Halleria* (N.O. *Scrophulariaceæ*); see also 2, and FLY *sb.*[1] 11 b. **French honeysuckle**, name given to *Hedysarum coronarium*, a native of Italy, a leguminous plant, with flowers resembling those of the red clover (cf. 1). **ground honeysuckle**, a name for Bird's-foot Trefoil, *Lotus corniculatus*. **purple honeysuckle**, a name for *Rhododendron nudiflorum* (*Azalea nudiflora*). **red honeysuckle** = *French h.*; also a name for red clover (see 1). **Virgin Mary's honeysuckle**, the Common Lungwort, *Pulmonaria officinalis*. **West Indian honeysuckle**, *Tecoma* (*Tecomaria*) *capensis* and various species of *Desmodium*. **white honeysuckle**, *Rhododendron viscosum* (*Azalea viscosa*); also white clover (see 1).

1592 GREENE *Upst. Courtier* Bij, A little dapper flowre, like a grounde Hunnisuckle, called thrift. **1629** PARKINSON *Paradisus* (1656) 340 The red Sattin flower, although some foolishly call it, the red or French Honysuckle. **1756** P. BROWNE *Jamaica* 327 *Passiflora foliis ovatis*..*The Honey-suckle*..cultivated in many parts of America for the sake of its fruit: it is a climber. **1788** *Chambers' Cycl.*, *Halleria*..is called by some gardeners the African fly-honeysuckle, from its resemblance to the upright or fly-honeysuckle. **1794** MARTYN *Rousseau's Bot.* xxv. 366 French Honeysuckle

which is distinguished..by its jointed, prickly, naked, straight legumes; its pinnate leaves. **1796** WITHERING *Brit. Pl.* (ed. 3) II. 201 *Cornus herbacea*, dwarf honeysuckle, dwarf cornel. **1834** Ross *Van Diemen's L. Ann.* 125 (Morris *Austral Eng.*) Some scattered honeysuckles, as they are called. **1861** MRS. MEREDITH *Over the Straits* III. 78 A very singular and handsome species of Banksia (colonially termed Honeysuckle). **1873** *Gard. Chron.* 26 Apr. 579/3 Virgin Mary's Honeysuckle.

4. A figure or ornament somewhat resembling a sprig or flower of honeysuckle: *esp.* in *Arch.*

1548 HALL *Chron., Hen. VIII* 58b, The apparell..was blacke velvet, covered all over with braunches of hony suckels of fyne flat gold. **1849** LAYARD *Nineveh* II. 294 We have..in the earliest monuments of Nineveh, that graceful ornament, commonly called the honeysuckle, which was so extensively used in Greece. **1852–61** *Archit. Publ. Soc. Dict.* VI. 27 *Palmette*... In England, by some authors and most workmen, the name Honeysuckle is given to it... It is a small ornament, one of those called running ornaments, and appears to be a diminutive of the Palm.

5. The colour of the flowers of the common honeysuckle: see quot.

1890 *Daily News* 20 Nov. 2/1 A rich, soft silk of the colour known as 'honeysuckle', being a combination of pale pink and even paler yellow.

†**6.** *fig.* Applied to a person, as a term of praise or endearment. (Cf. HONEY *sb.* 5.) *Obs.*

1598 E. GILPIN *Skial.* (1878) 36 Who would not thinke him perfect curtesie? Or the honny-suckle of humilitie? **1638** FORD *Fancies* II. ii, Yes, honeysuckle, and do as much for them one day.

†**7.** Honey 'sucked' or gathered by bees; = HONEY-SUCK 2. *Obs. rare*⁻¹.

1607 WALKINGTON *Opt. Glass* vii. (1664) 81 Like an industrious Bee..can gather such Honey-suckle from the sweetest flowers.

8. *attrib.* and *Comb.*, as ***honeysuckle arbour, colour***; **honeysuckle-apple**, in New England, a fungus, *Exobasidium Azaleæ*, occurring on the branches of *Rhododendron nudiflorum* (*Azalea nudiflora*), and eaten by children (*Cent. Dict.*); **honeysuckle clover, honeysuckle grass**, names for white clover (Britten and H.); **honeysuckle ornament** = sense 4; **honeysuckle-tree**, (*a*) the common honeysuckle; (*b*) name for various Australian trees and shrubs of the genus *Banksia*; **honeysuckle-trefoil**, name for red clover.

1796 WITHERING *Brit. Pl.* (ed. 3) III. 652 Purple Trefoil, Honeysuckle Trefoil, Cow Clover. **1852** MRS. MEREDITH *Home in Tasmania* I. 164 (Morris) The honeysuckle-tree (*Banksia latifolia*)..the blossoms form cones..the size and shape of a large English teazel, and are of a greenish yellow. ..The honeysuckle trees grow to about thirty feet in height. **1862** *Chambers' Encycl.* V. 621 The Honeysuckle ornament, so much used in Ionic architecture, is one of the features which indicate its eastern origin. **1892** *Daily News* 29 Sept. 6/2 Brocade of honeysuckle colours. **1893** *Ibid.* 14 Feb. 8/7 A Louis XIII dress in English-made honeysuckle brocade.

honeysuckled ('hʌnɪsʌk(ə)ld), *a.* [f. prec. + -ED².] Overgrown, or scented, with honeysuckle.

c **1645** HOWELL *Lett.* (1655) I. xxiv. 36 Those Beams that irradiat only, and guild your Honey-suckled fields. **1822** W. IRVING *Braceb. Hall* (1823) II. 167 Divided by honey-suckled hedges into sheltered fields. **1825** R. P. WARD *Tremaine* III. v. 26 Having slept in a pure honey-suckled air.

'**honey-,sweet**, *a.* (*sb.*) **A.** *adj.* Sweet as honey: often a term of endearment.

c **1000** in Thorpe *Anal. Anglo-Sax.* 45 (Bosw.) Mid hunig-swettre þrotan. *c* **1386** CHAUCER *Merch. T.* 152 The lusty lyf ..That is in mariage hony sweete. **1575** G. HARVEY *Letter-bk.* (Camden) 91 Not sick After so hoonysweete a licke. **1599** SHAKS. *Hen. V*, II. iii. 1 Honey sweet Husband. **1633** FORD *'Tis Pity* II. iv, Most dainty and honey-sweet mistress. **1865** M. ARNOLD *Ess. Crit.* vi. (1875) 238 Oh, honey-sweet Proserpine.

B. *sb.* Local name for the Meadowsweet (Elworthy *W. Somerset Word-bk.*).

'**honey-tongued**, *a.* Speaking sweetly, softly, or winningly; mellifluous; using honeyed discourses.

1588 SHAKS. *L.L.L.* v. ii. 334 Pay him the dutie of honie-tongued Boyet. **1598** F. MERES *Pallad. Tamia* II. 281 b, The sweete wittie soule of Ouid liues in mellifluous and hony-tongued Shakespeare. **1861** J. RUFFINI *Dr. Antonio* vi, I hate honey-tongued people.

honeywort ('hʌnɪwɜːt). [See WORT.]

1. The English name of the genus *Cerinthe* of boraginaceous plants, cultivated in gardens, and much frequented by bees for their honey.

1597 GERARDE *Herbal* II. cxlix. §1. 431 Cerinthe or Honie woort, riseth foorth of the grounde after the sowing of his seede. **1668** WILKINS *Real Char.* II. iv. §3. 80. **1855** SINGLETON *Virgil* I. 188 Bruised balm, and honeywort's humble herb. **1866** *Treas. Bot.* 257/1 Honeywort, an appellation due to the abundance of honey secreted by their blossoms, which are much resorted to by bees.

2. Locally applied to Crosswort (*Galium cruciatum*), from its strong sweet scent.

1863 MARG. PLUES *Rambles Search Wild Fl.* (1892) 158.

3. *attrib.*, as in **honeywort hawkweed**, a bookname for *Hieracium cerinthoides*.

1861 MISS PRATT *Flower. Pl.* III. 215. **1884** MILLER *Plant-n.*, Honey-wort Hawkweed.

‖**hong** (hɒŋ). Also 8 **haung**. [ad. Chinese *hang* row, rank.] In China, a series of rooms or buildings used as a warehouse, factory, etc.; *spec.* (*a*) one of the foreign factories formerly maintained at Canton; (*b*) the corporation of Chinese merchants at Canton who (before the treaty of Nanking in 1842) had the monopoly of trade with Europeans; (*c*) a foreign trading establishment in China or Japan.

1726 SHELVOCKE *Voy. round World* 458 The English have no settled Factory at Canton, and are only permitted to hire large Hongs, or Houses, near the water side. **1727** A. HAMILTON *New Acc. E. Ind.* II. 227 (Y.) When I arrived at Canton the Hapoa ordered me lodgings..in a Haung or Inn belonging to one of his Merchants. **1797** SIR G. STAUNTON *Embassy China* II. 565 (Y.) A Society of Hong, or united merchants, who are answerable for one another, both to the Government and to the foreign nations. **1836** J. F. DAVIS *Chinese* I. iii. 87 (Stanf.) Some Hong merchants. **1844** H. H. WILSON *Brit. India* I. viii. I. 512 The Chinese Government ..confined the trade..to a certain number of native merchants of Canton incorporated under the designation of Hong. **1888** A. J. LITTLE *Thro' Yangste Gorges* 210 A hong ..consists of a series of lofty one-storied buildings, situated one behind the other, and separated by intervening courtyards.

hong(e, obs. inf. and pa. t. and pple. of HANG *v.*

honger, -ir, -ur, etc., obs. ff. HUNGER.

‖**hongi** ('hɒŋɪ). *N.Z.* [Maori.] The pressing of noses together as a form of salutation. Hence as *v. intr.*

1843 E. DIEFFENBACH *Trav. N.Z.* I. I. ii. 61 Leaving him to indulge his natural feeling in hongi..or nose-rubbing. **1862** *Richmond-Atkinson Papers* (1960) I. xiii. 791 A great many of them hongi'd with Parris and seemed very glad to see him. **1882** T. H. POTTS *Out in Open* 23 The hongi, a method of salutation by rubbing noses together, we saw frequently performed. **1905** W. B. *Where White Man Treads* 63 Our chief..as is our custom, presented his nose for the 'hongi', which the stranger, not understanding, ignored. **1941** BAKER *N.Z. Slang* ii. 21 We have to thank our original inhabitants for specifying, inaccurately as might be expected, the expression *to rub noses* as the equivalent of the Maori ceremony known as *hongi*. (The nose is pressed, not rubbed.) **1949** P. BUCK *Coming of Maori* (1950) III. vi. 418 The visiting party..pressed noses with the chief mourners. The nose pressing (*hongi*) process sometimes occupied much time. **1952** R. FINLAYSON *Schooner came to Atia* xvi. 83 The Maori people in New Zealand greet friends with the hongi. **1959** TINDALE & LINDSAY *Rangatira* xvi. 149 He greeted..Rona-Nui by gripping both her hands and pressing his nose and forehead against hers in the hongi salutation.

Hong Kong (hɒŋ kɒŋ). [Name of a British crown colony in the South China Sea.]

1. *Croquet.* (See quot. 1863.)

1863 M. REID *Croquet* 10 A ball croque'd beyond the boundaries is sent to 'Hong Kong', or 'up the country'. **1897** *Encycl. Sport* I. 253/2 *Hong Kong, Off to*——. The old term for the driving of an opponent's ball from the croquet to the extreme corner of the ground. **1957** V. NABOKOV *Pnin* v. 131 Madam Shpolyanski insisted it was perfectly acceptable and said that when she was a child her English governess used to call it a Hong Kong.

b. Colloq. phr. *to go to Hong Kong*, to go away, to 'go to hell'.

1880 R. JEFFERIES *Hodge & M.* I. ii. 40 The excitement of the day was a pleasurable sensation, and as for his master he might go to Kansas or Hong-Kong. **1921** A. BRAZIL *Fortunate Term* xii. 160 Opal Earnshaw may go to Hong-Kong if she likes. I don't care about her and her meannesses.

2. Used *attrib.*, *spec.* to designate a strain of the influenza virus discovered in Hong Kong in 1968, and influenza caused by it.

1911 *Encycl. Brit.* XIII. 659/1 The only legal tender is the Mexican dollar, and the British and Hong-Kong dollar, or other silver dollars of equivalent value duly authorized by the governor. **1968** *Weekly Epidemiological Rec.* 16 Aug. 411 (*table*) Influenza... A2/Hong Kong/1/68. *Ibid.* 23 Aug. 421/2 Preliminary tests of paired sera..have shown very poor results against the new Hong Kong variant. *Ibid.* 30 Aug. 448/2 The Hong Kong strains should be classified as viruses A2. **1968** *Jrnl. Amer. Med. Assoc.* 16 Sept. 23/1 (*heading*) Experts attend Hong Kong flu talk in Atlanta. **1968** *Times* 23 Dec. 6/2 He was not feeling his best and had what scientists felt could be the symptoms of Hongkong influenza. **1970** *New Scientist* 8 Jan. 45/2 It made sad listening for those abed with Hongkong 'flu. **1973** J. GOODFIELD *Courier to Peking* viii. 101 When she finally got to the Hong Kong and Shanghai Bank, she..withdrew fifty Hong Kong dollars.

honied: see HONEYED.

†'**honily**, *a. Obs. rare.* [f. ME. *honi*, HONEY *sb.* + -LY¹.] Like honey; as of honey. Hence **honily-like** *adv.*

1435 MISYN *Fire of Love* I. xxv. 55 With swettyst sound of heuyn honily lyke þa synge. *Ibid.* xxviii. 60 Honily swetnes.

honily ('hʌnɪlɪ), *adv. rare.* Like or as honey.

1871 R. ELLIS *Catullus* xcix. 2 Dear one, a kiss I stole.. Sweet ambrosia, love, never as honily sweet.

†**honish**, *v. Obs.* Forms: 4 **honyse, honessche, hunysche, honysh**; 5 *pa. pple.* **honest**. [f. OF. *honiss-*, extended stem of *honir* (mod.F. *honnir*), ad. OHG. *hônen* (mod.Ger. *höhnen*) to scoff at, scorn.] *trans.* To bring to disgrace or ruin; to dishonour, insult; to destroy, put an end to.

13.. *E.E. Allit. P.* B. 596 He..harde honysez þise oþer & of his erde flemez. **1362** LANGL. *P. Pl.* A. XI. 48 Honesschen him as an hound, and hoten him go þennes! *a* **1400–50** *Alexander* 3004 Hys hors it honyshyd for euer. *Ibid.* 3791 Sum in þaire harnais for hete was honest for euire.

‖**honi soit qui mal y pense** (ɔni swa ki mal i pɑ̃s). [Fr.] 'Shame on him who thinks evil of it'; a proverb, orig. used as the motto for the Order of the Garter. (See GARTER *sb.* 2.)

13.. *Gaw. & Gr. Knt.* (ad fin.), Hony soyt qui mal pence. **1589** PUTTENHAM *Eng. Poesie* II. 116 King *Eduuarde* the thirde, her Maiesties most noble progenitour, first founder of the famous order of the Garter, gaue this posie with it. *Hony soit qui mal y pense*, commonly thus Englished, Ill be to him that thinketh ill. **1716** [see GARTER *sb.* 8]. **1776** H. WALPOLE *Let.* 22 Aug. (1857) VI. 370, I will prevent all clamour, by adopting St. George's motto,—'*Honi soit qui mal y pense*'. **1887** *Athenæum* 5 Nov. 600/1 The maxim 'Honi soit qui mal y pense' is one which needs to be frequently invoked by the friendly narrator and critic of Samoan manners. *a* **1930** D. H. LAWRENCE in Lawrence & Gelder *Young Lorenzo* (1931) 262 So Tolstoi says that all nude study is bad art—Honi soit qui mal y pense. **1959** *Chamber's Encycl.* III. 510/2 The reason for the adoption of the garter and the motto *Honi soit qui mal y pense* as the emblem and motto of the order is also unknown.

Honiton ('hʌnɪtən, 'hɒn-). The name of a town in Devonshire used *attrib.* to designate a type of pillow lace which is made there, consisting of floral sprigs either hand-sewn on to fine net, or joined by bars of other lace-work, as ***Honiton guipure, lace, sprig***. Also *absol.* = *Honiton lace.*

1831 M. EDGEWORTH *Let.* 11 June (1971) 548, I..made myself very comfortable finishing sewing the Honiton edge on my frill. **1840** *Observer* 16 Feb. 8/2 Her Majesty the Queen wore on her head a wreath of orange blossoms and a veil of Honiton lace. **1851** *Illustr. Catal. Gt. Exhib.* III. III. 559/1 Honiton guipure mantle. Bridal scarf and rich flounce in Honiton lace. *Ibid.* 560/1 Specimen of lace net..for the application of Brussels and Honiton sprigs. *Ibid.*, Tamboured lace scarf, imitation of Honiton, manufactured in London. **1858** SIMMONDS *Dict. Trade, Honiton lace*, a pillow, or cushion, lace made in Devonshire, remarkable for the beauty of its figures and sprigs, which are sewed on to net by the needle. **1865** F. B. PALLISER *Hist. Lace* xxxii. 382 Queen Adelaide..gave the order for a dress to be made of Honiton sprigs. **1882** *Encycl. Brit.* XIV. 188/2 Honiton pillow lace resembles Brussels lace. **1895** *Army & Navy Co-op. Soc. Price List* 15 Sept. 1126 Real Lace Handkerchiefs. Honiton. **1963** *Times* 8 Mar. 14/7 Her..crinolined profusion of Honiton lace and orange blossom under a train of silver moiré.

honk (hɒŋk), *v.* [Echoic: see the sb.] **1.** *intr.* Of a wild goose: to utter a deep, harsh cry or 'honk'. orig. *N. Amer.*

1854 THOREAU *Walden* xv. (1886) 271 Their commodore honking all the while with a regular beat.

2. orig. *U.S.* **a.** *intr.* Of a motor-horn or vehicle: to emit the harsh sound of a motor-horn. Also with driver as subj. and *transf.*

1895 F. REMINGTON *Pony Tracks* 256 The irrepressible Dan begins to 'honk' on his horn. **1911** R. W. CHAMBERS *Common Law* x. 312 Where now the lonely taxi honks. **1911** H. S. HARRISON *Queed* i. 6 Now and then a chauffeur honked by. **1915** *Literary Digest* 4 Sept. 467/1 Nearly a dozen autos may be always seen 'honking' their way through Nome's busy thoroughfares. **1928** *Observer* 22 Jan. 10/7 'Sunstar'.. is feeling fit again and proposes to honk off to Doncaster tonight. **1929** *Times* 2 Jan. 15/5 The car had been honking underneath my office window for some time.

b. *trans.* To utter with such a sound; to cause to make the sound 'honk'; to remove or drive away by the honking of motor vehicles.

1906 'O. HENRY' *Four Million* 51 She would honk loudly the word 'Clara'. **1914** R. & E. SHACKLETON *Four on Tour* 83 The [motor] horn was honked suddenly. **1926** [see BEAT *v.*¹ 3c]. **1927** *Observer* 28 Aug. 10 In the shadiest lanes we were honked and hooted out of the way. *Ibid.* 18 Sept. 8/3 The leisured stroller..is being 'honked' off the highway. **1958** [see BLEEP *sb.*].

Hence '**honking** *vbl. sb.* and *ppl. a.*

1854 THOREAU *Walden* xv. 271, I was startled by the loud honking of a goose. **1924** *Glasgow Herald* 18 Aug. 8 The thundering and purring and swishing and honk-ing of the road traffic. **1931** G. ATHERTON *Sophisticates* III. v. 295 The narrow thoroughfare was crowded with honking cars and taxis. **1955** *Times* 11 May 4/1 Much honking of horns from the cars round the ground. **1969** *New Yorker* 29 Mar. 27/1 There was little honking; and our driver..was relaxed and cheerful. **1973** C. EGLETON *Seven Days to Killing* ix. 99 Dodging through the honking traffic.

honk (hɒŋk), *sb.* [Echoic.] **1.** The cry of the wild goose. orig. *U.S.* and *Canada.*

1854 THOREAU *Walden* xiii. (1886) 247 The faint honk or quack of their leader.

2. The harsh sound of a motor-horn. orig. *U.S.*

1910 'O. HENRY' *Strictly Business* (1917) v. 57 The honk of the returned motor car at the door.

'**honker**. [f. HONK *v.* + -ER¹.]

1. A name for a wild goose.

1888 TRUMBULL *Bird Names* (U.S.) 1 *Branta canadensis*, ..[termed] Honker or Old Honker in recognition of its hoarse notes or 'honking'.

2. *transf.* **a.** One who 'honks' (in various senses).

1891 *Outing* (U.S.) Oct. 43/1 Though a fair 'honker', I cannot successfully imitate the constantly varying note of the snow goose. **1965** *New Statesman* 6 Aug. 183/3 The honker and the light-flasher drew up alongside. **1972** *Jazz*

& Blues Sept. 12/1 Others in the R & B field..are just dismissed as 'honkers'.

b. The horn of a motor vehicle.

1928 *Funk's Stand. Dict.*, *Honker*, the warning horn of a motor-car.

c. *slang.* A nose.

1948 R. PARK *Harp in South* xxi. 267 It's yer own fault for having such a God-forgotten honker [*sc.* a large nose].

honkers ('hɒŋkəz), *a. slang.* [Etym. unknown.] Drunk.

1957 R. LONGRIGG *Switchboard* v. 191 He stumbled out on to the lawn... 'Honkers.' 'Poor man. Pushed.' **1958** *News Chron.* 22 May 4/5 You drink wallop, sludge, or plasma (it's all ale or beer). If you get drunk you are honkers, plastered,..blotto. Or just plain paralytic. **1970** C. WOOD *Terrible Hard* xii. 167 Roll on Wednesday week and we'll all get honkers on champers.

honk-honk, reduplication of HONK *sb.* b.

1908 H. G. WELLS *War in Air* ii. 43 A curious, amusing, wheezing sound had got into his 'honk, honk'. *Ibid.* 58 Honk-honking and emitting weird cries. **1909** S. FORD (*title*) Honk, honk!! Shorty McCabe at the wheel. **1915** T. BURKE *Nights in Town* 210 The honk-honk of motors. **1917** *Ideas* 23 Mar. 23/2 With a wild 'honk-honk!'..the motor rounded the corner. **1935** WODEHOUSE *Blandings Castle* ii. 44 'Good-bye.' 'Honk-honk!' said Freddie moodily.

honky ('hɒŋkɪ, 'hʌŋkɪ). *U.S. Black slang.* Also **honkey, honkie.** [Etym. unknown; perh. a var. of *hunky* (see HUNK *sb.*[3]).] A white man; white men collectively. Also *attrib.* or as *adj.*

Disparaging in all applications.

[**1946** MEZZROW & WOLFE *Really the Blues* xii. 216 First Cat: Hey there Poppa Mezz, is you anywhere? Me: Man I'm down with it, stickin' like a honky. *Ibid.* 374/2 *Honky*, factory hand.] **1967** *Newsweek* 24 Apr. 16/1 'Go for the honkies'... The chemistry in tranquil Nashville, Tenn., spelled riot... Stokely Carmichael..exhorted: 'You have to go for the honkies..who are keeping you in the ghettos... Victims should never, ever apologize for their use of violence.' **1967** *Guardian* 29 Aug. 7/5 'Honky' (the white man) was using weapons like the Vietnam war. **1969** 'J. MORRIS' *Fever Grass* xxv. 248, I killed for the same thing you want. You're not like the rest of these honkeys. **1970** *Peace News* 17 Apr. 8/4 It is the pacifist who must declare, out of his own values, that there are neither Panthers nor Pigs, neither Niggers nor Honkies but only human beings. **1971** *Black Scholar* 35/1 You screamed on me 'bout that honky gunsel upstairs. **1971** *Black World* Mar. 69/2 Blacks should 'beware of honkies bearing gifts'. **1971** *Guardian* 1 May 9/1 Many blacks..came to see it [*sc.* the African-American Institute] as a 'honky' (white) conservative force. **1971** *It* 9–23 Sept. 8/3 The phoniness of news, TV, rich honky pop stars, etc. **1971** B. MALAMUD *Tenants* 46 Mary forcefully shoved him away. 'Split, honky, you smell.' *Ibid.* 133 'Now you leave this honky to me,' said Bill. 'He is my guest.'

honky-tonk ('hɒŋkɪtɒŋk). *colloq.* (orig. *U.S.*). Also **honkatonk, honkey-tonk.** [Etym. unknown.] **1.** A tawdry drinking-saloon, dance-hall, or gambling-house; a cheap night-club. Also in somewhat extended uses, and *attrib.* or as *adj.*

1894 *Daily Ardmoreite* (Ardmore, Okla.) 24 Feb. 1/4 The honk-a-tonk last night was well attended by ball-heads, bachelors and leading citizens. **1924** *Étude* Sept. 595/3 These dance resorts were known as 'Honky-Tonks'—a name, which in itself suggests some of the rhythms of Jazz. **1927** C. SANDBURG *Songbag* 232 It was moaned by resonant moaners in honky tonks of the southwest. **1928** M. C. SHARPE *Chicago May* 287 *Honky-tonk*, gaudy saloon with back-room hangout. **1930** C. E. MULFORD *Deputy Sheriff* xiii. 168 'This place ain't no damn' honkatonk, stranger,' reproved the bar-tender... 'Folks get throwed outa here sometimes.' **1935** A. J. POLLOCK *Underworld Speaks* 57/1 *Honkey tonk*, an underworld dance hall in which female entertainers are employed. **1936** *Delineator* Nov. 48/2 The inner room of a honky-tonk on a back street..New Orleans. **1940** W. FAULKNER *Hamlet* IV. ii. 387 Its master whose anonymous dust lay with that of his blood and of the progenitors of saxophone players in Harlem honky-tonks. **1945** J. STEINBECK *Cannery Row* i Honky-tonks, restaurants and whore-houses. **1950** A. LOMAX *Mr. Jelly Roll* 54 These honkey-tonks ran wide open twenty-four hours a day... Their attendance was some of the lowest caliber women in the world and their intake was the revenue from the little, pitiful gambling games they operated. **1955** A. ROSS *Australia 55* 108 The town itself, a little honky-tonk in character, boasts many saloons. **1957** G. LASCELLES in S. Traill *Concerning Jazz* 77 Others of possibly less talent were doing stalwart work as accompanists to the blues singers in the honky-tonks of New Orleans and St. Louis. **1962** *Daily Tel.* 31 May 19/4 A Parliamentary Bill would have to be promoted if the Norfolk Broads were to be saved from further 'honky-tonk development of the very worst type'. **1969** I. & P. OPIE *Children's Games* 15 It is not only Battersea Park (the enchanted garden of our childhood) that has been turned into a honky-tonk.

2. Rag-time music or jazz of a type played in honky-tonks, esp. on the piano. Freq. *attrib.*, passing into *adj.*, as **honky-tonk piano**, an out-of-tune or tinny-sounding piano. Cf. BARREL-HOUSE 2.

1933 *Fortune* Aug. 90/2 Sometimes they spent weeks in preparation for a single recording date, yet they never sacrificed the informal, honky-tonk spirit. **1936** *Swing Music* Autumn 62/2 Superficially, 'Honky Tonk' is the musical interpretation of a train journey; fundamentally it is a twelve-bar blues. **1942** BERREY & VAN DEN BARK *Amer. Thes. Slang* §579/4 *Honkytonk*, primal 'swing' of the style played in the bordels of New Orleans, Memphis and St. Louis, in which a free rein is given to improvising. **1946** R. BLESH *Shining Trumpets* (1949) ix. 202 Among them were masters of the blues and barrel-house piano (or, as Morton calls it 'Honky Tonk music'). **1953** *Observer* 27 Dec., The barrelhouse piano, also known as the..honkytonk piano. **1964** *Amer. Folk Music Occasional* I. 45 They didn't play for no white folks, because the white folks didn't want that kind of music, they called it honky-tonk. **1972** *Drive* Spring 78/2 Happy, beery men thumping honky-tonk pianos.

honne, obs. f. HONE; var. of HEN *adv.* hence.

‖**honnête homme** (ɔnɛtɔm). [Fr.] An honest, decent man; a gentleman.

1666 W. TEMPLE *Let.* 1 Apr. in *Wks.* (1720) II. 18 Confessor is honneste Homme. **1709** SWIFT *Let.* 13 Nov. in *Lett. Lit. Men* (Camden, 1843) 341, I ever thought it a mighty oversight in Courts to let the *honnete homme*, the *homme d'esprit*, and *homme de bien*, gain ground among them. **1923** OGDEN & RICHARDS *Meaning of Meaning* i. 21 The *honnête homme* may be unprepared for the lengths to which verbal ingenuity can be carried. **1931** T. S. ELIOT *Charles Whibley* 10 Whibley had this discretion, that of the *honnête homme* as critic, to select subjects suited to his own temperament. **1937** A. HUXLEY *Ends & Means* i. 2 The *honnête homme* makes his appearance as the ideal of seventeenth-century gentlemen. **1960** J. BAYLEY *Characters of Love* iii. 131 Iago..is in many ways a terrible parody of the Augustan *honnête homme.* **1970** *Times* 12 May 11/1 His opening speech on tobacco, far from being a declaration on behalf of the *honnête homme*, is a means of forcing his will.

honor, honorable, etc.: see HONOUR, etc.

†**honorance.** *Obs.* Also 4 honur-, 7 honour-. [a. OF. *honorance, -urance*, f. *honorer, honurer* to HONOUR: see -ANCE.] The action of honouring or doing homage; honour. Chiefly in phr. *in (the) honorance of.*

a **1300** *Cursor M.* 8896 Þis ilk tre..þat man mad til sli honurance. *c* **1330** *Assump. Virg.* (B.M. MS.) 1 In honorance of ihesu cryst. **13..** *Coer de L.* 5870 In sygnifyaunce, Off Jesu Crystys honoraunce. **1367–89** in *Eng. Gilds* 89 In ye honurance of ihesu crist of heuene. *a* **1716** SOUTH *Serm.* (1744) VIII. 244 As honour is in honourance, in him that honours rather than in him that is honoured.

honorand ('ɒnərænd). [ad. L. *honōrand-us*, gerundive of *honōrāre* HONOUR *v.*]. Someone to be honoured, *spec.* with an academic honorary degree.

1950 A. P. HERBERT *Independent Member* lxxxiii. 478 The Honorands, the eight or nine distinguished persons who are to be voted Honorary Doctors. **1961** M. BEADLE *These Ruins are Inhabited* (1963) xii. 170 The American honorand at *this* June's Encaenia. **1966** *New Statesman* 10 June 849/1 A kind of *festschrift* without an honorand. **1971** *Oxford Times* 25 June 30/1 There was brilliant sunshine for the Encaenia... For the first time for eight years there was no woman in the procession of honorands.

†**honorant.** *Her. Obs.* [a. F. *honorant*, pr. pple. of *honorer* to HONOUR: see -ANT.] **a.** One who honours. **b.** See quots.

1602 SEGAR *Honour Mil. & Ciuil* IV. xxi. 236–7 These diuers degrees were in the Emperiall Court called *Administrantes, Vacantes*, and *Honorarij*..The same course is to be kept among the Honorants or seruants extraordinary. —— *L'Envoy* in Guillim *Heraldry*, Made Honour only by the Honorant. **1661** MORGAN *Sph. Gentry* IV. ix. 115 Among the Honorants or servants extraordinary.

honorarily ('ɒnərərɪlɪ), *adv.* [f. HONORARY + -LY[2].] In an honorary manner; by way of honour.

1842 A. J. CHRISTIE in tr. *Fleury's Eccl. Hist.* I. 203 *note*, St. Cyril of Alexandria ascribes προσκύνησις to the martyrs, but..relatively and honorarily.

honorarium (hɒn-, ɒnə'rɛərɪəm). Pl. **-ums, -a.** [Late L. *honōrārium* gift made on being admitted to a post of honour, douceur, fee, neut. sing. of *honōrārius* HONORARY. In F. *honoraire.*] An honorary reward; a fee for services rendered, esp. by a professional person.

1658 EVELYN *Corr.* 8 Nov., What equipage and *honorarium* my Lord dos allow? **1669** *Boston Rec.* (1881) VII. 151 The said John Woodmansey doth hereby binde and engage himself..to pay..one pepper corne..for ever as an honorarium to the towne of Bostone. **1727–41** CHAMBERS *Cycl.*, *Honourary, Honorarium*, is also used substantively, for a lawyers fee; or a salary given to public professors of any art or science. **1852** W. JERDAN *Autobiog.* II. xi. 122, I am afraid..the architect of the monument..never received the proposed honorarium. **1895** W. MUNK *Sir H. Halford* 42 The emoluments and honoraria of physicians.

honorary ('ɒnərərɪ), *sb.* Now *rare* or *Obs.* [ad. L. *honōrārium*: see prec.] = prec.; also, a gift; an honouring distinction.

1615 CHAPMAN *Odyss.* XIII. 15 An honorary given to age. **1650** TRAPP *Comment. Numb.* iii. 9 The ministers of the Gospell are called gifts, Eph. 4. 8. 11, honouraries, such as Christ bestowed upon his Church. **1776** ADAM SMITH *W.N.* v. i. III. (1869) II. 345 In some universities, the salary makes but..a small part of the emoluments of the teacher, of which the greater part arises from the honoraries or fees of his pupils. **1845** LD. CAMPBELL *Chancellors* (1857) III. liv. 68 The usual amount of honoraries to counsel.

honorary ('ɒnərərɪ), *a.* Also 8–9 **honourary.** [ad. L. *honōrāri-us*, f. *honor* HONOUR: see -ARY. In F. *honoraire.*]

1. Denoting or bringing honour; conferred or rendered in honour.

1614 SELDEN *Titles Hon.* 22 Hee caused that Honorary title to bee scratcht out of the letters. **1698** FRYER *Acc. E. India & P.* 287 The wonderful Works of the Creation should be brought as Honorary Presents. **1705** ADDISON *Italy* (J.), Honorary arches erected to emperors. **1774** J. BRYANT *Mythol.* I. 319 It was an honorary term...It signified a lord or prince. **1841** ELPHINSTONE *Hist. India* II. 477 Without..receiving the honorary dress usual on such occasions. **1847** GROTE *Greece* II. xxviii. (1862) III. 48 The simple crown of olive, an honorary reward.

2. *spec.* Conferred or rendered merely for the sake of honour, without the usual requirements, functions, privileges, or other adjuncts.

1661 BRAMHALL *Just. Vind.* ix. 258 Some few honorary priviledges..which signifie not much. **1732** LEDIARD *Sethos* II. x. 409 The vivacity of this young prince..had already chang'd this honorary title into a real one. **1813** J. THOMSON *Lect. Inflam.* 27 The precise period at which the different universities in Europe first began to confer honorary titles or degrees is not well ascertained. **1897** *Westm. Gaz.* 14 Dec. 6/2 The honorary colonelcy.

b. *honorary monument*, a cenotaph.

1658 SIR T. BROWNE *Hydriot.* iii. 41 Beside their real Tombs, many have found honorary and empty Sepulchres. *a* **1782** W. COLE in Willis & Clark *Cambridge* (1886) I. 86 There is but one Monument..w[ch] is only an Honorary one or Cenotaph. **1850** P. CUNNINGHAM *Handbk. Lond.* 538/1 Honorary monument to Shakspeare. *Note*, The word honorary, as here used, is meant to imply that the person to whom the monument is erected is buried elsewhere.

3. Holding a title or position conferred as an honour, without emolument, or without the usual duties, obligations, privileges, etc.; titulary. Also, giving services (as secretary, treasurer, etc.) without emolument.

1705 HEARNE *Collect.* 17 Nov. (O.H.S.) I. 81 Ag[t] Honorary Freemen having Right to vote. **1727–41** CHAMBERS *Cycl.* s.v., In the college of physicians, London, are honourary fellows. **1873** *Daily News* 22 Sept. 3/1 The Emperor intends to appoint the King honorary colonel of the 13th Infantry Regiment. **1878** BOSW. SMITH *Carthage* 21 The Suffetes had gradually become little more than an honorary magistracy.

4. Depending on honour; said of an obligation which one is bound by honour to discharge, but which cannot be formally or legally enforced.

1794 GOUV. MORRIS in Sparks *Life & Writ.* (1832) II. 405 The United States will be under a kind of honorary obligation to discharge the debt. **1848** ARNOULD *Mar. Insur.* I. iv. (1866) I. 152 Merely an honorary engagement, of which the Courts will take no notice.

5. *Law. honorary feud, service*: see quots.

1670 BLOUNT *Law Dict.*, *Honorary Services*..are such as are incident to the Tenure of Grand Serjeanty, and annexed commonly to some Honor or Grand Seigniory. **1767** BLACKSTONE *Comm.* II. xiv. 214 The emperors began to create honorary feuds or titles of nobility. **1809** TOMLINS *Law Dict.*, *Honourary..Feuds*, are titles of nobility, descendible to the eldest son. **1849** MACAULAY *Hist. Eng.* ii. (1866) I. 121 Those honorary services which are still, at a coronation, rendered to the person of the sovereign by some lords of manors.

[**honorate**, erron. form of ONERATE *v.*]

†**hono'ration.** *Obs. rare*[−1]. [ad. L. *honōrātiōn-em*, n. of action f. *honōrāre* to honour.] The action of honouring.

1496 *Dives & Paup.* (W. de W.) I. xiii. 46/1 Worshyp that is called honoracyon, & veneracyon.

honorial (ɒ'nɔərɪəl), *a.* [f. HONOUR, HONOR *sb.* + -IAL.] Of or relating to titles of honour, or persons of title or rank; of or pertaining to an honour (sense 7).

1810 EVANS & BRITTON in J. Britton *Beauties Eng. Wales* XI. Norfolk 53 (*heading*) Civil, political, and honorial history. **1828** T. ALLEN *Hist. County York* I. II. vi. 327 (*heading*) Ecclesiastical and civil government, honorial history. **1943** F. M. STENTON *Anglo-Saxon Eng.* xvii. 628 On every great honour..there appear tenants holding considerable estates... The honorial barons, as tenants of this class may conveniently be called, have received less attention..than is their due. *Ibid.*, In the honorial court..the lord's baronial tenants played a leading part. **1962** H. R. LOYN *Anglo-Saxon Eng.* viii. 329 Honorial courts dealt primarily with military feudal questions.

honorific (ɒnə'rɪfɪk), *a.* (*sb.*) [ad. L. *honōrific-us*, f. *honor* HONOUR *sb.* + *-ficus* making, -FIC. Cf. F. *honorifique* (1507 in Hatz.-Darm.).]

A. *adj.* Doing or conferring honour; importing honour or respect; *spec.* applied to phrases, words, or forms of speech, used, esp. in certain Oriental languages, to express respect, *e.g.* certain adjectives meaning 'august', 'eminent', 'venerable', etc., substituted in Chinese and Japanese for the possessive pronouns of the second and third person; forms of the verb used in respectful address, etc.

1650 BULWER *Anthropomet.* vii. 83 They had no other Nurses lesse honorifique than Eunuchs. **1816** KEATINGE *Trav.* (1817) I. 239 The epithet Abu, father, is honorific. *a* **1846** LANDOR *Wks.* (1868) I. 396/1 Generous to the robber, honorific to the poisoner and assassin. **1861** F. HALL in *Jrnl. Asiat. Soc. Bengal* 204 *note*, The S'ri is to be regarded as honorific. **1879** CUST in *Trans. Philol. Soc.* 617 The verb [in Korean] has a simple affirmative form, a conditional, an interrogatory, an honorific, a causative, and several others. **1888** *Times* 8 Oct. 5/2 A solemn proposal..that the honorific title of 'Worshipful' should be bestowed by the government on its president.

B. *sb.* An honorific phrase or word: see above.

1879 BAILEY in H. Spencer *Princ. Sociol.* §398 II. 153 They use none of the honorifics so profusely common in Singhalese; the pronoun *to*, thou, being alone used. **1889** *Athenæum* 2 Mar. 273/1 Where these honorifics occur [in Japanese] the sentence can always be easily turned so as to

give their significance, which is often of a merely pronominal character, the honorific indicating a reference to the person addressed or forming the subject of the thought.

So †**hono'rifical** *a.* = HONORIFIC a.; hence **hono'rifically** *adv.*, in an honorific manner.

1656 Blount *Glossogr.*, *Honorifical*, that brings or causeth honor. **1816** Keatinge *Trav.* (1817) I. 344 A very brave people, honorifically, or nic-named by the Moors, The Sons of Lions. *c* **1878** Birch *Anc. Hist. fr. Mon.* Introd. 20 (S.P.C.K.) Queens were honourifically styled wives or handmaids of the God Amen.

†**honorificabilitu'dinity.** *Obs. rare*$^{-0}$. [ad. med.L. *honōrificābilitūdinitās* (Mussatus *c* 1300 in Du Cange), a grandiose extension of *honōrificābilitūdo* honourableness (in a charter of 1187, Du Cange), f. *honōrificābilis* honourable. Cf. *Complaynt of Scotland* (1548–9), Prolog. lf. 14 b, Shaks. *L.L.L.* v. i. 44, and Marston *Dutch Courtezan* v. (1605) H, where the L. abl. pl. *honōrificābilitūdinitātibus* is cited as a typical long word, as *honōrificābilitūdinitāte* had been previously by Dante *De Vulg. Eloq.* II. vii.] Honourableness.

[**1599** Nashe *Lenten Stuffe* 24 Physitions deafen our eares with the Honorificabilitudinitatibus of their heauenly Panachæa, their soueraigne Guiacum.] **1656** Blount *Glossogr.*, *Honorificabilitudinity*. Hence in Bailey, Ash, etc. **1800** *Spirit Pub. Jrnls.* (1801) IV. 147 The two longest monosyllables in our language are strength and straight, and the very longest word, honorificabilitudinity.

†**hono'rificence.** *Obs. rare.* [ad. L. *honōrificentia*, f. *honōrificent-*, collateral stem of *honorific-us* HONORIFIC: see -ENCE. Cf. obs. F. *honorificence*.] A doing of honour. So †**hono'rificent** *a.* = HONORIFIC.

1640 Bp. Hall *Episc.* III. iv. 238 There is *Honorificentia ætatis*, the honorificence of age. **1681** H. More *Exp. Dan.* IV. Notes 118 That honorificent Title . . prefixt to it.

†**ho'norify**, *v. Obs. rare*$^{-1}$. [ad. eccl. L. *honōrificāre*, f. *honōr-* HONOUR: see -FY. Cf. obs. F. *honorifier*.] *trans.* To do honour to, to honour.

1606 Ford *Fame's Memor.* xcvii, Making large statues to honorifie Thy name.

‖**honoris causa** (ɒ'nɔərɪs 'kɔːzeɪ, 'kaʊzɑː). [L.: lit., for the sake of honour.] In order to honour or out of respect for a person mentioned; now used chiefly as a description of such university degrees as are conferred upon persons in recognition of certain distinctions or achievements without the customary academic examination or thesis.

1611 Coryat *Crudities* 240, I wil once more speake of our most worthy Ambassadour Sr Henry Wotton, *honoris causâ*. **1626–7** in T. Birch *Crt. & Times Chas. I* (1848) I. 193 His colleagues shall be the Earl of Salisbury, *honoris causâ*, and Sir Richard Western. **1882** *Standard* 19 Dec. 2 (Stanford), Receiving the degree of D.D., *honoris causa*, from the late Dr. Sumner, Archbishop of Canterbury in 1857. **1935** *Discovery* Nov. 325/2 Uvarov was honoured by the University of Madrid with the degree of Doctor *honoris causa*. **1955** *Times* 26 May 12/5 He was instructor to the Oxford University Air Squadron and was given the degree of M.A. *honoris causa* at the end of his term of duty. **1963** [see ACADEMICIAN 1].

†'**honorous, honourous**, *a. Obs.* [a. OF. type **honoros, -eus*, AF. *-ous*:—L. type **honōrōsus*, f. HONOUR: see -OUS.] Honourable.

c **1475** *Partenay* 1321 Hyr honorous fader. *Ibid.* 3236 We will, lord honourous. *a* **1562** Cavendish *Wolsey* (1825) I. 2 Of his ascending and descending from honorous estate.

honour, honor ('ɒnə(r)), *sb.* Forms: 3–4 onur, honur(e, 4 onour(e, 4–6 honoure, -owre, (5 onnere, 5–6 honnour(e, 6 honnor), 3– honour, 4– honor. [a. OF. *onor, -ur, honor, -ur* (11th c.), AF. (*h*)*onour*, mod.F. *honneur* (= It. *onore*, Sp., Pg. *honor*):—L. *honōr-em* repute, esteem, official dignity, honorary gift, ornament, grace, beauty.

The oldest Fr. forms were *onor*, *onur*, later and AF. *onour* (Latin *h* having disappeared in Romanic, and *o*, *u*, *ou* being successive symbols for the OFr. vowel, derived from L. *ō*, which passed through a very close *ō* to *ū*); these varied with *enor*, *anor*, *-ur*, *-our*, whence the early ME. *anur*, *anour* (see ANOUR, ANOURE); but the influence of L. spelling brought back into Fr. at an early date the non-phonetic *h*, giving *honor*, *honur*, *honour*, which were also prevalent ME. spellings. *Honor* and *honour* continued to be equally frequent down to the 17th c. In the Shakspere Folio of 1623 *honor* is about twice as frequent as *honour*. The two forms appear indiscriminately in the early 17th c. dictionaries, but *honour* was favoured by Phillips, Kersey, Bailey, Johnson. Ash, 1775, adopted '*Honor* (a modern but correct spelling)', and this is said to have been fashionable at the time (see quots.). Nevertheless *honour* carried the majority of English suffrages eventually, while *honor* was (under the lead of Noah Webster) generally accepted in U.S. As to derivatives, Bailey, 1731, considered *honorable*, *honorary*, 'the best spelling', but referred them to *honourable*, *honourary*, as the more usual. Phillips, in his various edd., had *honorary*, Kersey (1706) *honourary* or *honorary*, Chambers (1727–41) *honourary*. Johnson, 1755, has *honour*, *honourable*, *honorary*.

1758 L. Temple *Sketches* (ed. 2) 19 Our Reformers in the Art of Spelling . . at present . . write Honor, Favor, Labor. *a* **1791** Wesley *Wks.* (1872) VIII. 317 Avoid the fashionable impropriety of leaving out the *u* in many words, as *honor*, *vigor*, etc. This is mere childish affectation. **1871** R. F. Weymouth *Euph.* 6 The clause 'they hang that are in honour' suggests the suspicion that Lilie would aspirate the *h* in *honour* and its congeners; a suspicion confirmed by our finding elsewhere *unwholesome* balanced against *unhonest*, and *hue* against *honesty*.]

1. High respect, esteem, or reverence, accorded to exalted worth or rank; deferential admiration or approbation. **a.** As felt or entertained in the mind for some person or thing.

c **1375** *Leg. Rood* 123 Men suld hald þat haly tre In honore. *c* **1450** *St. Cuthbert* (Surtees) 6957 Gude men him in honour had. **1611** Shaks. *Wint. T.* v. i. 51 Good Paulina, Who hast the memorie of Hermione I know in honor. **1664** Marvell *Corr.* Wks. 1872–5 II. 164 Desirous of shewing . . the great honour She retains and cherishes for Your Majesty. **1713** Steele *Guardian* No. 1 ¶3 To shew my honour for them. **1809–10** Coleridge *Friend* (1837) III. 76 Honor implies a reverence for the invisible and super-sensual in our nature. **1857** Ruskin *Pol. Econ. Art* 2 True wealth I hold in great honour.

b. As rendered or shown: The expression of high estimation. (See also 9 c, e.)

c **1275** Lay. 6085 Hii . . leide hine mid honure Heȝe in þan toure. *a* **1300** *Cursor M.* 23586 Heuen and erth als creature Sal ber þam wirscip and honur. *c* **1400** *Ywaine & Gaw.* 720, I aw the honor and servyse. **1535** Coverdale *2 Kings* Contents xxiii, How Iosias . . setteth vp the true honoure of God againe. **1653** H. Cogan tr. *Pinto's Trav.* xxxix. 154 The Prince was exceedingly pleased with this honour done unto him. **1759** Robertson *Hist. Scot.* I. III. 174 He received the queen herself with the utmost honour and respect. **1875** Stubbs *Const. Hist.* II. xv. 304 Let then the honour be given where it is due.

c. As received, gained, held, or enjoyed: Glory, renown, fame; credit, reputation, good name. The opposite of *dishonour*, *disgrace*.

c **1200** *Trin. Coll. Hom.* 83 Hie giuen here elmesse . . oðer for onur to hauen, oðer ne mai elles for shame. **1297** R. Glouc. (Rolls) 8176 Deie we raþer wiþ onour. **1475** *Bk. Noblesse* (1860) 26 The hope and trust of recovering on another day . . onnere and fortune. **1548** Hall *Chron.*, *Hen. VI* 134 The duchesse of Bedford . . myndyng also to marye, rather for pleasure then for honour. **1593** Shaks. *3 Hen. VI*, I. i. 246 But thou preferr'st thy Life before thine Honor. **1617** F. Moryson *Itin.* II. 164 Wounds are badges of honour, yet may befall the coward assoone as the valiant man. **1765** Blackstone *Comm.* I. xviii. 467 The honour of originally inventing these political constitutions entirely belongs to the Romans. **1820** G. W. Featherstonehaugh in *Sir J. Sinclair's Corr.* (1831) II. 73, I have the honour to forward to you . . a pamphlet [etc.]. **1822** Southey *Vis. Judgem.* III, Peace is obtain'd then at last, with safety and honour! **1878** Edith Thompson *Hist. Eng.* xv. §3. 82 To their honour, the patriot nobles did not take thought for themselves alone. **1896** J. Bryce in *Daily News* 20 July 7/4 A country feels that its honour is affected when it yields to threats, seems to give way on any disputed point through fear, and incurs the imputation of cowardice.

2. a. Personal title to high respect or esteem; honourableness; elevation of character; 'nobleness of mind, scorn of meanness, magnanimity' (J.); a fine sense of and strict allegiance to what is due or right (also, to what is due according to some conventional or fashionable standard of conduct).

1548 Hall *Chron.*, *Edw. IV*, 233 b, The king of England had so great trust . . in the honor and promise of the French kyng. **1649** Lovelace *Poems* (1864) 27, I could not love thee, dear, so much, Lov'd I not Honour more. *a* **1677** Barrow *Theol. Wks.* (1830) I. 89 A man of honour, surely is the best man next to a man of conscience. **1687** A. Lovell tr. *Thevenot's Trav.* III. 111 The Japanese make it a point of honour to breed Merchants. **1705** Stanhope *Paraphr.* II. 94 What is Honour, but a greatness of mind which scorns to descend to an ill and base thing? **1764–7** Ld. G. Lyttelton *Hen. II*, III. 178 The idea of honor . . as something distinct from mere probity, and which supposes in gentlemen a stronger abhorrence of perfidy, falsehood, or cowardice, and a more elevated and delicate sense of the dignity of virtue, than are usually found in vulgar minds. **1809** Wordsw. *Sonn.*, Say, what is Honour? 'Tis the finest sense Of justice which the human mind can frame. **1824** Scott *Redgauntlet* ch. ix, Honour is sometimes found among thieves. **1880** W. Cory *Lett. & Jrnls.* (1897) 460 The sentiment of Honour is a lay thing; it is a rival of the sentiment of saintliness.

b. A statement or promise made on one's honour; word of honour. *arch.*

1658–9 *Burton's Diary* (1828) IV. 6 You took the honour of a Lord the other day. You may well take the word of a gentleman now. **1708** Mrs. Centlivre *Busie Body* I. (1749) 21 He had given her his Honour, that he never would . . Endeavour to know her till she gave him leave. **1825** Moore in *Mem.* (1853) IV. 309 Having first made the prince and all the rest give their honours that they would not [etc.].

3. a. (Of a woman) Chastity, purity, as a virtue of the highest consideration; reputation for this virtue, good name.

1390 Gower *Conf.* III. 24 So as she may . . Her honour and her name save. **1596** Spenser *F.Q.* IV. i. 6 Nathlesse her honor, dearer then her life, She sought to save, as thing reserv'd from stealth. **1610** Shaks. *Temp.* I. ii. 348 Till thou didst seeke to violate The honor of my childe. **1675** Wycherley *Country Wife* II. Wks. (Rtldg.) 77/2 To neglect her own honour, and defame her own noble person with little inconsiderable fellows. **1747** Hoadley *Susp. Husb.* I. ii, And yet I'll answer for her Honour. **1856** Bouvier *Law Dict.* I. 589 To deprive a woman of her honor is, in some cases, punished as a public wrong.

†**b.** *concretely*: cf. Ger. *die scham. Obs.*

1688 R. Holme *Armoury* III. 94/2 These Buskes . . if to keep the Belly down, then it reacheth to the Honor. **1724** *Weekly Jrnl.* No. 276 Her What, in Heroicks, we call Honour.

4. a. Exalted rank or position; dignity, distinction.

a **1300** *Cursor M.* 487 And þus he [Lucifer] leses his gret honur. *Ibid.* 24713 Chamburlain o grett honure. *a* **1440** *Sir Degrev.* 283 Knyghtus . . Lordus off honore. **1534** More *On the Passion* Wks. 1286/2 Gyuing to a poore man . . landes . . with the honour of a dukedome also. **1568** Grafton *Chron.* II. 350 They would not . . disgrade him from the honor of Knighthood. **1595** Shaks. *John* I. i. 182 A foot of Honor better then I was, But many a many foot of Land the worse. **1632** J. Hayward tr. *Biondi's Eromena* 185 The affect of honour being somewhat a-kin to that of gold, whereof the more one hath the more he covets. **1765** Blackstone *Comm.* I. vii. (1809) 271 The king is likewise the fountain of honour. **1857** Miss Mulock *Nothing, Fam. in Love*, It is the apex of feminine honour to be a bride.

b. With possessive pronoun, = 'honourable personality': formerly (and still in rustic speech) given to any person of rank or quality; now a formal title for the holders of certain offices, esp. County Court judges.

1553 Gresham in Burgon *Life* (1839) I. 98, I received your honnor's letter of the 24th of this present. **1577** J. Langley in Ellis *Orig. Lett.* Ser. II. III. 51 My dutie humblye remembred to your Honor [Lord Burghley]. **1607** Shaks. *Timon* I. ii. 183, I beseech your Honor, vouchsafe me a word. *a* **1612** Harington *Let. to Lady Russell* in *Metam. Ajax* (1813) p. xv, Your honors most bownde John Harington. **1647** Ward *Simp. Cobler* 29 What greater honour can your Honors desire? **1723** Steele *Consc. Lovers* IV. i, Ah! says I, Sir, your Honour is pleas'd to joke with me. **1755** Johnson, *Honour*, . . 3 The title of a man of rank. Not now used. **1785** Burns *Earnest Cry* xxiv, God bless your honours a' your days. **1796** G. M. Woodward *Eccent. Excurs.* 83 Indeed the title of Your Honor is bandied about and indiscriminately used. **1827** Jarman *Powell's Devises* II. 179 That part of his honor's decision which gave the estate to the trustees. **1832** Ht. Martineau *Weal or W.* iv. 38 Indeed, but they have, your honour. **1833** Marryat *P. Simple* xiii, (Irishman) Plase your honour, it's all an idea of mine. **1885** Tennyson *Tomorrow*. **1896** *Law Times* 11 July 261/2 At Bow County Court on the 6th inst., before Judge French, Mr. Sharman . . applied to his Honour to direct [etc.]. *Mod.* (*Beggar*). Has your honour a copper to spare for a poor man?

5. a. (Usually in *pl.*) Something conferred or done as a token of respect or distinction; a mark or manifestation of high regard; *esp.* a position or title of rank, a degree of nobility, a dignity.

13.. *K. Alis.* 1388 [1391] He . . ȝaf vche lordyng gret honoure, And parted wiþ hem his fader tresoure. *c* **1440** *Gesta Rom.* xlv. 176 (Harl. MS.) He yede forthe to bataile, and had þe victorye; and after took boþe honoures and dolours, as is seide befor. **1599** Shaks. *Hen. V*, IV. viii. 63 Keepe it fellow, And weare it for an Honor in thy Cappe. **1634** Sir T. Herbert *Trav.* 48 The English Agents receive custome of all strangers, that honour being granted them from the Persian King. **1663** Marvell *Corr.* Wks. 1872–5 II. 91 A clause to be entered against buying and selling of honours. **1701** W. Wotton *Hist. Rome*, *Marcus* iv. 56 Divine Honors were payd him. **1806** Wordsw. *Char. Happy Warrior* 44 Who . . does not stoop, nor lie in wait For wealth, or honours, or for worldly state. **1849** Macaulay *Hist. Eng.* vi. II. 126 Papists were admitted in crowds to offices and honors.

†**b.** An obeisance; a bow or curtsy. *Obs.*

1531 Elyot *Gov.* I. xxii, The first meuyng in euery daunse is called honour, whiche is a reuerent inclination or curtaisie, with a longe deliberation or pause. **1605** Chapman *All Fooles* Plays 1873 I. 136, I . . plant my selfe of one legg Draw backe the tother with a deep fetcht honor. **1719** D'Urfey *Pills* (1872) II. 171 Make your Honour Miss, Now to me Child. **1741** Richardson *Pamela* II. 360 They . . made their Honours very prettily, as they pass'd by us. **1805** E. de Acton *Nuns of Desert* I. 113 He walked onward, without deigning to make a departing honour.

c. *pl.* Civilities or courtesies rendered, as at an entertainment: in phr. ***to do the honours***.

1659 B. Harris *Parival's Iron Age* 177 Received with respect . . at Amsterdam, where that illustrious Magistracy performed the honours of the Republick. **1715** Vanbrugh *Country Ho.* I. Wks. (Rtldg.) 462/1 This son of a whore does the honours of my house to a miracle. **1737** Pope *Hor. Epist.* I. vi. 100 Then hire a Slave, or (if you will) a Lord, To do the Honours, and to give the Word. **1768** in *Priv. Lett. Ld. Malmesbury* I. 168 The Duchesse . . did the honours of the table, or rather received them, as ladies here never interfere with carving. **1826** Disraeli *Viv. Grey* VI. iii, The Prince did the honours of the castle to Vivian with great courtesy. **1857** Dickens *Lett.* 15 Sept., The mayor called this morning to do the honours of the town.

d. ***last, funeral honours***: the observances of respect usual at the burial of the dead. ***military honours***: the external marks of respect paid by troops to royalty, high military or civil officials, at the burial of an officer, etc. ***honours of war***: the privileges granted by a victorious commander to a capitulating force, as of marching out under arms with colours flying and drums beating; also formerly = military honours.

1513 More *Rich. III* (1883) 1 This noble Prince . . with greate funerall honoure . . was entered at Windesor. **1674** tr. *Martiniere's Voy. N. Countries* 57 Doing him his last honour. **1727–41** Chambers *Cycl.*, *Funeral honours*, are the ceremonies performed at the interments of great men; as hangings, hearses, funeral harangues, etc. **1756–7** [see FUNERAL A. 1]. **1790** Bruce *Trav.* II. IV. 401 As soon as the prince Facilidas had paid the last honours to his father. **1813** in Gurw. *Wellington's Desp.* XI. 101 *note*, The French troops shall file out tomorrow . . with all the honors of war, with arms and baggage, and drums beating, to the outside, where they will lay down their arms. **1853** Stocqueler *Mil. Dict.* s.v., In another sense, the 'honours of war' signifyeth compliments which are paid to great personages, military characters, etc., when they appear before any armed body of men; or such as are given to the remains of a deceased officer.

—*Military Honours*, are salutations to crowned heads and officers of rank, by dropping colours and standards, officers saluting, bands playing, artillery discharging salvoes, etc. **1855** TROLLOPE *Warden* xi, She capitulated, or rather marched out with the honours of war.

e. *pl.* Special distinction gained, in a University or other examination, for proficiency in scholarship beyond that required to pass the examination. Now, in many universities, a course of study or a series of examinations in a subject or group of subjects of a higher or more specialized character than is required for a pass or ordinary degree. (Cf. *honours degree, school* in 10.)

1782 V. KNOX *Ess.* in C. Wordsw. *Schol. Acad.* 232 If he aspires at higher honours. **1790** GOOCH *Ibid.* 321 Peacock kept a very capital Act indeed, and had a very splendid Honor. **1802–6** COX *Recoll. Oxford* 49 Several shy men of first-rate scholarship shrunk from 'challenging the Honours' (as the phrase was). *a* **1819** *Oxford Spy* (ed. 4) xxi, A man, who gains the highest honours. **1846** MCCULLOCH *Acc. Brit. Empire* (1854) II. 341 A private tutor's fee, an expense which is seldom incurred except by those who are preparing for honours. **1847** JAMES *Convict* i, You had taken high honours at this university. **1856** LEVER *Martins of Cro' M.* 86 There were clever men reading for honours. **1880** TROLLOPE *Duke's Childr.* I. iii. 33 He..had gone out in honours, having been a second class man. **1883** (*title*) The Honours Register of the University of Oxford. A Record of University Honours and Distinctions.

6. a. A person, thing, action, or attribute that confers honour; a source or cause of honour; one who or that which does honour or credit (*to*).

[*a* **1330** *Otuel* 473 It hadde be more honour to þe, For soþe to habbe i-smite me. *c* **1450** *Merlin* 580 So that it myght be savacion to theire soules..and honour to theire bodyes.] *a* **1568** ASCHAM *Scholem.* I. (Arb.) 62 Erasmus the honor of learning of all oure time. **1611** TOURNEUR *Ath. Trag.* I. i. Wks. 1878 I. 9 Nephew, you are the honour of our bloud. **1798** FERRIAR *Illustr. Sterne* vi. 176 It is an honour to think like great men. **1894** IAN MACLAREN *Bonnie Brier Bush* VII. ii. 265 You are an honour to our profession.

b. (Usually in *pl.*) An adjunct or part of anything which gives it distinction; a decoration, adornment, ornament. (*poetic.*)

1613 SHAKS. *Hen. VIII*, III. ii. 354 He..beares his blushing Honors thicke vpon him. **1625** FLETCHER *Noble Gent.* v. Wks. (Rtldg.) II. 278/2 With the whisking of my sword about, I take thy honours off. **1725** POPE *Odyss.* XI. 235 The autumn..The leafy honours scattering on the ground. *Ibid.* XVIII. 182 He shook the graceful honours of his head. **1784** COWPER *Task* I. 321 The woods, in scarlet honors bright.

7. *Law.* A seigniory of several manors held under one baron or lord paramount.

1439 *Rolls Parlt.* V. 16/1 Tenauntz of oure Lorde the Kynge, as of his Castell and Honure of Tutbury, parcell of his Duchie of Lancaster. **1523** FITZHERB. *Surv.* x. (1539) 15 The lorde of the honour or manour. **1641** *Termes de la Ley, Honour*..is used specially for the most noble sort of Lordships, whereof other inferiour Lordships or Manors doe depend by performance of customes and services. **1655** DIGGES *Compl. Ambass.* 17 Given under our signet at our Honour of Hampton Court. **1708** *Lond. Gaz.* No. 4424/4 The Humble Address of the Honour and Borough of Cockermouth, in the County of Cumberland. **1845** STEPHEN *Comm. Laws Eng.* (1874) I. 215 If several of these manors were held..under one great baron or lord paramount, his seigniory over them was termed an *honor*.

8. a. *Cards.* (Chiefly *pl.*) In Whist, The four highest trumps (ace, king, queen, and knave): the relative proportion in which they are held by the two sides being an element in counting the points in some forms of the game: cf. CAN YOU?; EASY *a.* 18. In Ombre and Quadrille, The aces of spades and clubs, and the lowest card of the trump suit. Also at Bridge (see quots. 1909 and 1936). Phr. ***honours are even***: often used fig. to denote equality in a contest (real or imaginary).

1674 COTTON *Compl. Gamester* x. (1680) 82 The four Honours are the Ace, King, Queen, and Knave. **1741** RICHARDSON *Pamela* II. 259 We cast in, and..I had all four Honours the first time. **1778** C. JONES *Hoyle's Games Impr.* 47 It being 5 to 4 that your Partner has an Honour in that Suit. *a* **1839** PRAED *Poems* (1864) II. 63 Well—four by honours, and the trick! **1878** H. H. GIBBS *Ombre* 12 The Ace of Clubs called *Basto* both in English and Spanish, is the Third Honour even though another suit may be trumps. *Ibid.* 14 The Matadores when united in the same hand may be called Honours. **1886** *Biritch, or Russian Whist* 4 There are five honours, viz.:—Ace, King, Queen, Knave and Ten, if trumps are declared. **1896** MAITLAND in *Eng. Hist. Rev.* Oct. 643 The honours were divided; but the state, as by this time its habit was, took the odd trick. **1909** W. DALTON *'Saturday' Bridge* 5 Honours consist of ace, king, queen, knave, and ten of the trump suit. When there are no trumps they consist of the four aces. **1920** B. CRONIN *Timber Wolves* iii. 62, 'I don't know your name?'..'But then I don't know yours, do I? That makes the honours even, don't you think?' **1927** W. E. COLLINSON *Contemp. Eng.* 31 The card-expressions now most prevalent in a figurative application are drawn in the main from bridge, e.g. to call one's hand (or one's bluff), to finesse, Honours are even, After you, partner, etc. **1936** E. CULBERTSON *Contract Bridge Complete* xxxviii. 421 An honour-card is technically a ten or higher card. **1939** N. DE V. HART *Bridge Players' Bedside Bk.* 22, I got home by playing for split honours. **1947** S. HARRIS *Fund. Princ. Contract Bridge* II. i. 43 South should remember to lead a top honour from the hand which contains double honours in sequence. **1967** P. ANDERTON *Play Bridge* vii. 49 You drop 100 points on going down but get 100 for honours.

b. *Golf.* (See quot.)

1896 PARK *Game of Golf* 6 This privilege of playing first from the Tee is called 'the honour'.

9. Phrases. **a.** *Comm.* ***for*** (***the***) ***honour*** (***of***...): said of the acceptance or payment of a bill of exchange (which has been refused by the drawee and duly protested) by a third party, with the object of preserving the mercantile honour or credit of the drawer or indorser. ***act of honour***, an instrument drawn by a notary public by which such payment or acceptance is formally agreed upon.

1832–52 MCCULLOCH *Commerc. Dict.* 583 When the drawee refuses to accept [a bill of exchange], any third party, after protesting, may accept for the honour of the bill generally, or for the drawee, or for the indorser. **1882** *Act 45 & 46 Vict.* c. 61 §65 Where an acceptance for honour does not expressly state for whose honour it is made, it is deemed to be an acceptance for the honour of the drawer.

b. ***in honour***: in allegiance to the moral principles which are imperative in one's position, or to some conventional standard of conduct (see 2); as a moral bounden duty: sometimes implying that there is no legal obligation (cf. *debt of honour*).

1597 SHAKS. *Lover's Compl.* 150 Finding myself in honour so forbid. **1654** tr. *Scudery's Curia Pol.* 40 His Master esteemed himselfe obliged in honour to requite the injury. **1738** SWIFT *Pol. Conversat.* xxxvi, Young Ladies under twenty..being in Honour obliged to blush. **1883** *Wharton's Law Lex.* 388/2 Honorary Trustees..are bound, in honour only, to decide on the most proper and prudential course.

c. ***in honour of*** (†***in*** or ***to the honour of, in honour to***): as an expression of respect or reverence for; for the sake of honouring; in celebration of.

c **1300** *St. Margarete* 279 If eni man in honour of me eni chapel doþ rere. *c* **1385** CHAUCER *L.G.W.* Prol. 81 Ye see I do yt in the honour Of love. **1526** *Pilgr. Perf.* (W. de W. 1531) 1 Diuyded in to thre bokes, in the honour of the Trinite. **1613** PURCHAS *Pilgrimage* (1614) 834 The Divel..in honour of whom they sacrifice their Captives. **1635** PAGITT *Christianogr.* (1646) I. 37 A goodly Temple erected to the honor of St. Thomas the Apostle. **1788** CLARA REEVE *Exiles* II. 158 To..keep every thing in good repair, in honour to the memory of the noble benefactors. **1897** HALL CAINE *Christian* x, I believe this rout to-night is expressly in honour of the event.

d. *on* or ***upon one's honour***: a phrase by which the speaker stakes his personal title to credit and estimation on the truth of his statement; used formally by members of the House of Lords in their judicial capacity; hence, an expression of strong assurance: cf. 2b. ***to be upon*** (***his***) ***honour, to put*** a person ***upon his honour***, i.e. under honourable obligation.

a **1460** *Gregory's Chron.* in *Hist. Coll. Lond. Cit.* (Camden) 119 The for sayde captaynys have sworne a-pon hyr honowre that [etc.]. **1485** *Rolls Parlt.* VI. 288/1 Yee shall swere, that [etc.]..upon youre Honour and Worship. **1548** HALL *Chron., Hen. IV* 17 Assuryng hym on his honour that if [etc.]. **1656–7** *Burton's Diary* 10 Jan. (1828) I. 335 Promising, upon her honour, to return within six weeks. **1765** BLACKSTONE *Comm.* I. xii. (1800) 402 A peer sitting in judgment, gives not his verdict upon oath, like an ordinary juryman, but upon his honour: he answers also to bills in chancery upon his honour. **1856** BOUVIER *Law Dict.* I. 589 In courts of equity, peers, peeresses and lords of parliament, answer on their honor only. **1862** THACKERAY *Wks.* (1872) X. 194 This I declare upon my honour. *Mod.* They were upon their honour not to tell.

e. *to do honour to*: (*a*) to treat with honour, show or pay due respect to, confer honour upon, to honour; (*b*) to do credit to, bring respect to.

c **1320** R. BRUNNE *Medit.* 1131 We onely hym þanke and do hym onoure. *c* **1400** *Destr. Troy* 4659 Agamynon..To Diana full derely did his honowre. *c* **1425** *Seven Sag.* (P.) 531 Thow doost thy selfe lytil honour, For to suffyre thy sone by slawe. **1548** HALL *Chron., Hen. V* 75 To se his estate and dooe hym honor. *a* **1691** BOYLE *Hist. Air* (1692) 189 His late Majesty..doing me one day the honour to discourse about several marine observations. **1738** SWIFT *Pol. Conversat.* lxxxii, Mr. Colly Cibber, who does too much Honour to the Laurel Crown he deservedly wears. **1898** E. E. HALE in *Chr. World* 19 May 7/4 He did me the honour to say that this was precisely true.

f. *to do the honours*, ***last honours***, etc.: see 5c, d.

g. ***honour bright*** (*colloq.*): used as a protestation of (or interrogatively as an appeal to) one's honour or sincerity.

1819 MOORE *Tom Crib* 36 (Farmer) At morning meet, and—honour bright,—Agree to share the blunt and tatters. **1840** DICKENS *Barn. Rudge* viii, 'I do', said the 'prentice, 'Honour bright. No chaff, you know'. **1852** GEO. ELIOT in Cross *Life* (1885) I. 293 Is it not so, honour bright? **1856** EMERSON *Eng. Traits* vii. Wks. (Bohn) II. 52 The phrase of the lowest of the people is 'honour-bright', and their vulgar praise 'his word is as good as his bond'.

h. *code* or ***law of honour***: the set of rules and customs which regulate the conduct of some particular class of person according to a conventional standard of honour: see 2.

1785 PALEY *Mor. Philos.* I. ii. (1830) 2 The Law of Honour is a system of rules constructed by people of fashion, and calculated to facilitate their intercourse with one another; and for no other purpose. **1843** LEVER *J. Hinton* xviii. (1878) 126 They know how imperative is the code of honour as regards a bet. **1887** FOWLER *Princ. Mor.* II. iv, Similarly, lawyers, doctors, clergymen, bankers are said to have a code of honour, or, what amounts to the same thing, to observe certain rules of professional etiquette.

i. ***court of honour***: a court or tribunal for determining questions concerning the laws or principles of honour, as the courts of chivalry which formerly existed in Europe.

1687 LUTTRELL *Brief Rel.* (1857) I. 413 His majestie haveing required the duke of Norfolk, earl marshall of England, to hold..a court of honour, his grace hath appointed the 5th of Octob. next to keep it. **1768** BLACKSTONE *Comm.* III. vii. (1800) 104 This court of chivalry..As a court of honour, it is to give satisfaction to all such as are aggrieved in that point. **1801** *Med. Jrnl.* V. 4 Your valuable Journal serves, among other useful purposes, as a Court of Honour, to which any Member of the Faculty may appeal, respecting the misconduct of another.

For other phrases, as AFFAIR, BED, DEBT, LEGION, MAID, POINT, WORD *of honour*, etc., see these words.

10. *Comb.*, as ***honour-giver, -seeker***; ***honour-fired, -flawed, -giving, -owing, -splitted, -thirsty, -worthy*** adjs.; also **honour(s) board**, a board at a school or college on which are inscribed the names of members who have gained honours; **honour-court**, a court held within an honour or seigniory (sense 7); **honours degree**, an academic degree with honours or obtained in an honour school; similarly ***honours examination***; **honour(s) list**, (*a*) a class list of candidates who have been successful in an examination for honours; (*b*) a list of honours conferred by the Sovereign, as at the New Year; also *fig.*; **honour-man** (also ***honours-man***), one who has taken, or is studying for, academical honours (sense 5 e); **honour-point** (*Her.*), the point just above the fess-point of an escutcheon; **honour-policy**: see quot.; **honour-roll**, a roll of honour; **honour(s) school**, a course of study designed for those who aim at an honours (as distinguished from a pass) degree (at Oxford University, 'qui honorem ambiunt'); similarly ***honour moderations***, *colloq.* ***honour mods.***; **honour system**, a system in which examinations are completed, services paid for, etc., without, or with only a minimum of, supervision; **honour-trick** *Bridge*, a combination of cards which may be expected to win a trick.

1931 E. WAUGH *Remote People* 211 They have *honour boards, on which the name of one boy is inscribed every year. **1960** C. DAY LEWIS *Buried Day* vi. 129 My name was never inscribed on the University Honours Board in the Big School. **1670** BLOUNT *Law Dict.*, **Honor Courts*, are Courts held within the Honors aforesaid. **1851** *Oxf. Univ. Cal.* 127 A reference will be made in the lists of *Honours and ordinary Degrees, to the distinctions awarded by the Moderators. **1904** *Daily Chron.* 31 Oct. 4/4, I cannot deal here with the wholly false and mischievous qualification of an 'Honours Degree' that the rich women are answerable for. **1969** *Oxf. Univ. Handbk.* 159 About one third of the students at Oxford are working for honours degrees in mathematics or natural science. [**1852** *Oxf. Univ. Commission Rep.* III. 62 With regard to the Examination for Honours, the course of classical reading seems to have become more and more limited.] **1885** *Oxf. Univ. Cal.* p. iii, *Honours Examinations for Women. **1927** C. E. MALLET *Hist. Univ. Oxf.* III. xxiii. 168 The Honours Examination at Oxford was established. *Ibid.* 170 In 1830, a Fourth Class in Honours was provided, and the Honours examination was separated from the examination for the ordinary Pass degree. **1972** *Univ. Oxf. Exam. Decrees* 33 No person whose name shall be placed in any Class List issued by the Moderators shall be admitted again as a candidate in the same Honours Examination. **1611** SHAKS. *Wint. T.* II. i. 143 Be she *honor-flaw'd. **1595** —— *John* I. i. 53 The *Honor-giuing-hand Of Cordelion. **1849** THACKERAY *Pendennis* I. xix. 179 A man may be famous in the *Honours-lists and entirely unknown to the undergraduates. **1862** *Oxf. Univ. Cal.* 273 Honours Lists issued by Moderators. **1910** H. G. WELLS *New Machiavelli* (1911) III. i. 304 The New Year and Birthday honours lists are always very sagely and exhaustively considered. **1923** J. M. MURRY *Pencillings* 272 It will dawn upon me when I read my own name in capitals at the top of the Honours List, created Baron for my services to literature. **1929** *Melody Maker* Dec. 1169/1 This disc goes right into the honours list. **1964** *Granta* 2 Nov., He hoped as it was Coronation year to do rather better than usual in the New Year's honours list. **1839** J. ROMILLY *Diary* 12 Jan. (1967) 161 This year we have allowed our Lecture rooms to the *Honor-men. **1880** *Times* 12 Nov. 8 It represents to the honour-man, whose attainments are not classical, the goal of his studies in that direction. **1891** *Daily News* 26 Sept. 7/5 A Cambridge honoursman will..read with pupils. **1911** *Rep. Brit. Assoc.* 219 It has been suggested that if students are not encouraged to come to the university younger the better men should be allowed to enter for *Honour Mods. after six months. **1913** Honour mods. [see DIVVERS]. **1922** *Rep. R. Comm. Oxf. & Camb.* 29 The marked vitality of *Honour Classical Moderations bears witness to the interest still awakened by the classical languages and literatures. **1965** W. R. WARD *Victorian Oxford* x. 213 Scholarship was now examined at Honour Moderations and the final school was left unencumbered for the examination of history and philosophy. **1970** *Oxf. Univ. Cal.* 195 The prizes are awarded each year by the Moderators for Honour Moderations in English Language and Literature. **1610** GUILLIM *Heraldry* I. vii. (1660) 41 The *Honour Point. **1661** MORGAN *Sph. Gentry* I. i. 2 The middle point of an escotcheon is called the Honour-point. **1895** SIR W. R. KENNEDY in *Law Times Rep.* LXXII. 861/1 All these 'disbursements' policies were p. p. i. or '*honour' policies—policies, that is to say, wherein it was stipulated that the policy should be deemed sufficient proof of interest. **1909** *Daily Chron.* 7 Apr. 3/3 Such is the *honour-roll of these sturdy spirits. **1949** Honor roll [see BULLETIN 4]. **1902** *Encycl. Brit.* XXXIII. 603/2 At Oxford there are now the following '*Final Honour Schools'. **1923** *Granta* 2 Mar., At

Oxford the Honours School of English claims that its 'first' is harder to win than a 'first' in any other School there. **1965** W. R. Ward *Victorian Oxford* x. 220 Rawlinson alleged that the standard in the non-classical honour schools would be less than the proposed mixed degree. **1970** *Oxf. Univ. Cal.* 194 Candidates must be members of the University reading for a Final Honour School. *a* **1871** Grote *Eth. Fragm.* v. (1876) 141 Aristotle admits (into his catalogue of pleasurable pursuits) the life of the *honour-seeker. **1904** *Pittsburgh Gaz.* 3 Dec. 4 The most successful plan of combating the tendency of college students to cheat in examinations has been some form of an '*honor system' by which the pupil is implicitly trusted and his statement accepted that he used no dishonest aids. **1934** H. G. Wells *Exper. Autobiogr.* I. vi. 323 He had in operation an honour system of discipline that was far in advance of the times. **1936** *S.P.E. Tract* xlv. 181 *Honor system* denotes the practice, adopted at certain institutions, of conducting written examinations without supervision, the candidates being put upon their honour to use no illegitimate aids. **1958** *Sunday Times* 16 Mar. 22/5 Self-service stores must run on the honour system. **1966** *Listener* 24 Feb. 266/2 On the buses and trams an 'honour' system: you throw your money into a coin box..and tear off your own ticket. **1969** 'E. Lathen' *Come to Dust* xiv. 140 Two young women had been discovered..in circumstances all too clearly proscribed by the parietal rules and Brunswick's honor system. **1580** Sidney *Arcadia* vi. (1590) 486 *Honour-thirstie minds. **1931** E. Culbertson *Contract Bridge at Glance* 6 A defensive *honour-trick is a card, or combination of cards, which may be expected to win even if the opponents play the hand at a trump. **1959** Reese & Dormer *Bridge Player's Dict.* 116 The Culbertson system, which first popularized the honor-trick method of valuation, uses the following table for counting honor-tricks. **1535** Coverdale *Song 3 Child.* 22 That thou only art the Lorde God, & *honoure worthy thorow out all the worlde. **1609** J. Rawlinson *Fishermen Fishers of Men* Ep. Ded., Your most honoured and honour-worthy Father.

honour, honor ('ɒnə(r)), *v.* Forms: 3–4 onure(n, honure(n, onoure(n, 3–6 honoure, honore, (honire), 4–5 oner, 5 honnoure, honer, (*pa. t.* honret), 5–6 honowre, 4– honour, 6– honor. See also anoure, an early by-form. [a. OF. (*h*)*onorer*, *-urer*, *-ourer*, etc. (mod. F. *honorer*) = Pr. *honorar*, (*h*)*onrar*, Sp. *honrar*, It. *onorare*:—L. *honōrāre*, f. *honōr-em*, honour.]

†**1.** *trans.* To do honour to, pay worthy respect to (by some outward action); to worship, perform one's devotions to; to do obeisance or homage to; to celebrate. *Obs.* (or merged in 2 or 3.)

c **1290** *Beket* 2423 in *S. Eng. Leg.* I. 176 For-to honouri þis holi man þere cam folk i-novȝ. *a* **1300** *Cursor M.* 2709 Bot an allan he honired o þaa. *c* **1300** *St. Margarete* 82 Such a fals god to onoure. **1382** Wyclif *Gen.* xxiv. 26 The man bowide hym silf and onouryde [**1388** worschipide; Vulg. *adoravit*] the Lord. **1393** Langl. *P. Pl.* C. vi. 105 To þe kirke gan ich go god to honourie. *c* **1400** *Destr. Troy* 3001 Þere honestly sho offert, honourt hir goddes. **1559** W. Cunningham *Cosmogr. Glasse* 201 They do honour the Sonne, Mone, and Sterres. **1593** Shaks. *Ven. & Ad.* Ded., Till I haue honoured you with some grauer labour. **1613** Purchas *Pilgrimage* (1614) 458 Heere also they beginne to honor the Crosse. **1697** Dryden *Virg. Georg.* iv. 544 They..honour with full Bowls their friendly Guest.

b. To address with 'your honour'. *nonce-use.*

1726 *Adv. Capt. R. Boyle* 25 To convince your Honour of the Truth (for I honour'd him much) here's the Letter.

2. To hold in honour, respect highly; to reverence, worship; to regard or treat with honour or respect.

a **1300** *Cursor M.* 14336 (Cott.) Honurd be þou fader, euer and oft, Wit angels þine þar vp oloft. *c* **1300** *Ibid.* 25230 (Cott. Galba) þat we tak neuer þi name in vayn..bot honore it als es worthy. **1382** Wyclif *Exod.* xx. 12 Honour thi fader and thi moder. *c* **1440** *York Myst.* xx. 147 To honnoure god ouere all thing. **1538** Starkey *England* i. iv. 139 Only for theyr vertue they [priests] schold be honowryd. **1548–9** (Mar.) *Bk. Com. Prayer, Matrimony*, Wilt thou loue her, coumforte her, honor, and kepe her in sickenesse and in health? **1589** R. Harvey *Pl. Perc.* 13 Honor gray heares. **1651** Hobbes *Leviath.* i. x. 43 To honour those another honours, is to Honour him. **1713** Steele *Englishm.* No. 4. 26 There is no Man whom I so highly honour as the Merchant. **1743** J. Morris *Serm.* vii. 205 We should love and honor our parents. *a* **1873** Lytton *Pausanias* 35 Yes, I honour Sparta, but I love Athens.

3. To confer honour or dignity upon; to do honour or credit to; to grace.

a **1340** Hampole *Psalter* xxiv. 2 Þai sall be honurd with aungels. **1382** Wyclif *Esther* vi. 9 Thus shal ben honoured, whom euere the king wile honoure. *c* **1400** *Destr. Troy* 12944 Þan honered hym þat od kyng with ordur of knight. **1596** Shaks. *Merch. V.* iii. ii. 214 Our feast shall be much honored in your marriage. **1602** —— *Ham.* i. iv. 16 It is a Custome More honour'd in the breach, then the obseruance. **1677** Lady Chaworth in *12th Rep. Hist. MSS. Comm.* App. v. 36, I beg to know if your Lordship intends to honour my poore house with being heere. **1730** Pulteney *Let. to Swift* 9 Feb. S.'s Lett. 1766 II. 121 None gave me greater pleasure, than the kind letter you honoured me with. **1756–7** tr. *Keysler's Trav.* (1760) IV. 413 Such persons..as he honours with the title of Excellency. **1838** Thirlwall *Greece* xliii. V. 291 Charidemus..had been honoured with a crown, and other marks of popular favour. **1859** Max Müller *Chips* (1885) III. iv. 76 A nation honours herself by honouring her sons.

†**b.** To decorate, adorn, ornament, embellish. [Cf. anoure.] *Obs.*

1528 in Willis & Clark *Cambridge* (1886) I. 486 The new churche..which I have honored att myne owne propre costes and charge. **1613** Purchas *Pilgrimage* (1614) 83 The continuance of this Daphnæan grove, honored with Buildings and spectacles.

4. *Comm.* To accept or pay (a bill of exchange, etc.) when due. Also *fig.*

1706 Phillips (ed. Kersey), *To Honour a Bill of Exchange* (among Bankers), to pay it in due time. **1709** Steele *Tatler* No. 57 ¶2 They jest by the Pound, and make Answers as they honour Bills. **1779** Franklin *Lett.* Wks. 1889 VI. 444, I shall pay it all in honoring their drafts and supporting their credit. **1809** R. Langford *Introd. Trade* 19 The utmost punctuality should be observed in honouring Bills. **1838** D. Jerrold *Men of Character* I. ix. 109 'With great pleasure'—and Saffron honoured a challenge to wine. **1859** Thackeray *Virgin.* xxi, Nature has written a letter of credit upon some men's faces, which is honoured almost wherever presented.

honourability, honor- (ɒnərə'bɪlɪtɪ). *rare.* In 5 honourablyte, honurabilite. [a. OF. *honorablete* (13th c.) from *honorable*: subseq. conformed in Fr. and Eng. to the ordinary type of sbs. from L. *-bilitās*: see -ability.] The quality of being honourable, honourableness; *pl.* things that are honourable, honours.

c **1400** tr. *Secreta Secret., Gov. Lordsh.* (E.E.T.S.) 103 Þat he be of greet corage yn purpos, and louynge honurabilite. *Ibid.* 107 Wys and willynge, honourablyte vnderstondynge, lele, and eschewand oþer fleand all velanye and blame. **1708** Motteux *Rabelais* (1737) V. 233 What tho' Honorabilities it offers. **1895** *Pall Mall Mag.* VII. 272 To appreciate Lowe's ..'profound honourability', as Dr. Richard Congreve calls it.

honourable, honorable ('ɒnərəb(ə)l), *a.* (*sb.*, *adv.*) Also 4–6 onour-, oner-, honur-, honer-, honner-, -abil(l, -abyll. [a. OF. *honorable*, *honurable* = Pr., Sp. *honorable*, It. *onorabile*; ad. L. *honōrābil-is*, f. *honōrāre* to honour: see -ble.]

A. *adj.* **1.** Worthy of being honoured; entitled to honour, respect, esteem, or reverence.

a. Of persons.

a **1340** Hampole *Psalter* viii. 6 He [Crist] is honurabile till all. **1382** Wyclif *Dan.* xiii. 4 [Susanna 4] Jewis camen to gidre to hym, for that he was more honorable of alle. *c* **1397** Chaucer *Lack Stedf.* 22 O prince desire for to beo honourable. **1540** Hyrde tr. *Vives' Instr. Chr. Wom.* i. vi. (R.), Three thinges made Pallas honorable; virginitie, strength, and wisedome. **1589** R. Harvey *Pl. Perc.* (1590) 13 Men..honorable..for their calling. *a* **1673** Swinnock in Spurgeon *Treas. Dav.* Ps. lxxxix. 6 The ancientest, the honourablest house of the creation. **1675** tr. *Machiavelli's Prince* vi. (1883) 41 They remain..honourable and happy.

b. Of things.

1390 Gower *Conf.* III. 225 His name is good and honourable. *c* **1566** J. Alday tr. *Boaystuau's Theat. World* R v, Who..hath made yᵉ most honorablest members to sight, and the foule..placed out of sight. *a* **1619** Fotherby *Atheom.* ii. xiv. § 1 (1622) 354 The very name of Philosophie, is both honourable, and holy. **1631** *High Commission Cases* (Camden) 233 There is noe tyme fitter for it then this honourable day [the Saboth day]. **1738** Swift *Pol. Conversat.* 83 Marriage is honourable, but House-keeping is a Shrew. **1875** Jowett *Plato* (ed. 2) V. 73 The soul which came from heaven is more honourable than the body which is earth-born.

†**c.** Respectable in quality or amount; considerable; decent. *Obs.*

c **1330** R. Brunne *Chron.* (1810) 324 Þei wilde biseke Edward þat he mot him ȝelde tille him in a forward þat were honorable to kepe wod or beste. **1588** Shaks. *L.L.L.* v. ii. 327 Monsieur the nice, That when he plaies at Tables, chides the Dice In honorable tearmes. **1590** Sir J. Smyth *Disc. Weapons* 7 b, To reduce all the great and honorable bands aforesaid, into little bands of 150 or 200. **1666** Evelyn *Diary* 24 May, Dined with Lord Cornbury..who kept a very honorable table.

2. a. Holding a position of honour; of distinguished rank; noble, illustrious.

a **1340** Hampole *Psalter* lxxxviii. 27 He honorabilest of all and highe bifore kyngis. *c* **1400** *Destr. Troy* 3973 Ecuba, the onest & onerable qwene. **14..** tr. *Alain Chartier's Quadril.* (MS. Univ. Coll. 85) 1 The right honeurable magnificence of nobles. *c* **1450** *St. Cuthbert* (Surtees) 2609 Elfled, þat honorabil abbas. **1513** More *Rich. III* (1883) 13 Manye of them far more honorable part of kin then his mothers side. **1596** Shaks. *Merch. V.* iii. iv. 70 Tell quaint lyes How honourable Ladies sought my loue. **1849** Macaulay *Hist. Eng.* vi. II. 61 This man, named Edward Petre, was descended from an honorable family.

b. Applied as an official or courtesy title of honour or distinction.

The prefix 'Honourable' (Hon.) is given to sons of peers below the rank of Marquess and to daughters of peers below the rank of Earl, to Maids of Honour, all Justices of the High Court (not being *Lords* Justices nor Lords of Appeal), to Lords of Session, the Lord Provost of Glasgow (during office), and especially to members of Governments or of Executive Councils in India and the Colonies. (Whitaker *Titled Persons.*) In the U.S. it is given to members of both Houses of Congress, and of State legislatures, to judges, justices, etc. *Honourable* is also applied to the House of Commons collectively; 'honourable member' or 'gentleman' is applied to members individually; also formerly to the East India Company, etc.

Most Honourable is applied to Marquesses; also to the Order of the Bath and H.M. Privy Council (collectively).

Right Honourable is applied to peers below the rank of Marquess, to Privy Councillors, and to certain civil functionaries, as the Lord-Mayors of London, York, and Belfast, and the Lord Provosts of Edinburgh and Glasgow; sometimes, also, in courtesy, to the sons and daughters of peers holding courtesy titles. (See further, Whitaker *Titled Persons* (1898) 44.)

a **1450** *Paston Lett.* No. 75 I. 96 To my right honorabull and right wurshipful Lord, my Lord Viscont Beaument. *c* **1490** *Ibid.* No. 918 III. 364 Onerabyll and well be lovyd Knythe. **1538** Starkey *Will* in *Lett.* (1878) 8 *note*, Item I geve to the veray honnerable and my singulier good lorde, my lorde Montague. **1538** in Ellis *Orig. Lett.* Ser. i. II. 90 Mooste humbly besechith your honorable Lordship. **1583** Stubbes *Anat. Abus.* ii. (1882) 8 Hir royall Maiestie and hir most honorable Councel. **1593** Shaks. *Ven. & Ad.* Ded., To the Right Honorable Henrie Wriothesley, Earle of Southampton, and Baron of Titchfield. **1612** T. Ryves in Ellis *Orig. Lett.* Ser. iii. IV. 172 Honourable Sir, Yow have beene pleased. **1643** *Let. from Irish Council* 28 Oct. in Clarendon *Hist. Reb.* vii. § 344 To our very good lord, the lord Speaker of the right honourable the Lords' House of Parliament..and to our very loving friend, William Lenthall, esq., Speaker of the honourable Commons House in Parliament. **1674** Grew *Anat. Plants, Lect. Mixture* i. iv. (1682) 229 Agreeable to the Doctrine of the Honourable Mr. Boyle. **1698** Fryer *Acc. E. India & P.* 38 In pay for the Honourable East India Company. **1709** Pope *Ess. Crit.* 588 Fear most to tax an Honourable fool, Whose right it is, uncensur'd, to be dull. **1727** Pope, etc. *Art of Sinking* 122 The honourable the directors of the academy. **1744** (*title*) A Treaty Held in the Town of Lancaster, Pennsylvania, by the Honourable the Lieutenant-Governor of the Province, and the Honourable the Commissioners for the Provinces of Virginia and Maryland, with the Indians of the Six Nations. **1783** Sheridan *Sp. Ho. Com.* in Moore *Life* (1825) xi. I. 508 An Honourable friend of mine, who is now, I believe, near me..that Honourable gentleman has told you that [etc]. **1817** *Parl. Deb.* 731 The Chancellor of the Exchequer expressed his anxiety to consult the wishes of honourable gentlemen on the subject. **1820** in Bischoff *Woollen Manuf.* (1862) II. 9 Your petitioners humbly pray that they may be heard by their counsel at the bar of your Honourable House. **1872–6** Voyle & Stevenson *Milit. Dict.* (ed. 3), *Honourable Artillery Company*, a volunteer force and the oldest military body in England.

3. a. Of things: Characterized by or accompanied with honour; bringing or fraught with honour to the possessor. ***honourable mention***: see mention *sb.* 2 e.

c **1374** Chaucer *Boeth.* iv. pr. vi. 109 (Camb. MS.) Many oothre folk han bowht honourable renoun of this world by the prys of the gloryous deth. **1540** *Act 32 Hen. VIII*, c. 48 The castell of Douer..is..a very honorable strong & defencible fortresse. **1548** Hall *Chron., Hen. V* 51 It is more honorable to bee praised of his enemies then to be extolled of his frendes. **1581** Savile *Tacitus' Hist.* i. lxxxvii. (1591) 50 Good hope of honourabler seruice here-after. **1591** Shaks. *Two Gent.* iii. i. 64 Sure the Match Were rich and honourable. **1642** Milton *Apol. Smect.* (1851) 270 A composition and patterne of the best and honourablest things. **1839** Thirlwall *Greece* VI. 27 Areopagus.. deprived Æschines of his honourable office. **1866** *Lond. Gaz.* 26 June 3646/1 Grand prizes and money awards of the total value of 250,000 francs (£10,000), 100 Gold Medals,.. 5000 Honourable Mentions. **1869** *Bradshaw's Railway Manual* XXI. App. 99 Honourable mention.—International Exhibition, 1862.

b. Consistent with honour or reputation.

1548 Hall *Chron., Edw. IV* 232 The Frenche kynge.. offered me..bothe honorable and honest overtures of peace. **1632** J. Hayward tr. *Biondi's Eromena* 186 To yeeld it up upon honorable conditions. **1697** Dryden *Virg. Georg.* iii. 176 Such is the Love of Praise, an Honourable Thirst. **1791** Mrs. Radcliffe *Rom. Forest* i, And withheld him from honourable retreat while it was yet in his power. **1829** Lytton *Devereux* ii. iv, Let us effect an honourable peace. **1855** Macaulay *Hist. Eng.* xii. III. 149 To capitulate on honourable and advantageous terms.

4. Showing or doing honour; honouring.

a **1340** Hampole *Psalter, Cant.* 508 Trouth and luf..hild apostils and haly men as honurabil clathynge. **1390** Gower *Conf.* I. 208 He wolde an honourable feste Make. *c* **1500** *Doctr. Gd. Servaunts* in *Anc. Poet. Tracts* (Percy Soc.) 4 Seruauntes ought to be honourable..To all men seruysable. **1568** Grafton *Chron.* II. 252 She made him honourable chere. *a* **1592** H. Smith *Wks.* (1866–7) I. 441 There be many names of honour, but this is the honourablest name. **1595** Shaks. *John* i. i. 29 An honourable conduct let him haue. **1743** Pococke *Descr. East* I. 57 The Cashif..shew'd me great civility; which was more honourable than if I had placed myself lower at the table. **1791** Boswell *Johnson* Advt., An honourable monument to his memory.

5. Characterized by principles of honour, probity, or rectitude; upright, honest: the reverse of base. **a.** Of persons.

1601 Shaks. *Jul. C.* iii. ii. 87–8 For Brutus is an Honourable man, So are they all; all Honourable men. **1601** —— *All's Well* v. iii. 239 So please your Maiesty, my master hath bin an honourable Gentleman. **1784** Cowper *Tiroc.* 738 A wretch, whom..The world accounts an honourable man. **1838** James *Robber* iv, I have always found you honourable and generous.

b. Of things.

1592 Shaks. *Rom. & Jul.* ii. ii. 143 If that thy bent of Loue be Honourable, Thy purpose marriage, send me word to morrow. **1614** Raleigh *Hist. World* II. v. iii. § 15. 442 This was thought the best, and most honourable course. **1769** *Junius Lett.* xxxv. 157 On your part we are satisfied that every thing was honourable and sincere. **1825** Lytton *Zicci* 24 Honourable and generous love may even now work out your happiness.

B. *sb.* **a.** An honourable or distinguished person. **b.** One who has the title of Honourable. So ***Right Honourable***. (*colloq.*)

c **1400** *Destr. Troy* 6708 Ector full onestly þat onerable þanket. **1695** Congreve *Love for L.* i. xiii, *Tat.* Won't a baronet's lady pass? *Scan.* No, nothing under a right honourable. **1800** Mrs. Hervey *Mourtray Fam.* I. 229 My poor brain..never can remember all the forms required by your Honourables and Right Honourables. **1880** Warren *Book-plates* viii. 95 Six bear courtesy titles or are Honourables.

†**C.** *adv.* Honourably. *Obs. rare.* [Perh. only misprints.]

1593 Shaks. *3 Hen. VI*, iii. ii. 123 Widow goe you along: Lords vse her honourable. **1654** tr. *Scudery's Curia Pol.* 71, I have not done lesse honorable.

Hence '**honourable** *v. trans.*, †(*a*) to honour; (*b*) to address with the title 'Honourable'.

1455 *Paston Lett.* No. 239 I. 328 Plese it your hyghe Majeste..to be honorabled and worsshepyt as most ryghtful Kyng and oure governour. **1877** LOWELL *Lett.* (1894) II. viii. 220 It is altogether a bore to be honorabled at every turn.

'honourableness, honor-. [f. prec. adj. + -NESS.] The state or quality of being honourable (in various senses: see the adj.).

1553 T. WILSON *Rhet.* (1580) 35 Fortitude..Of this vertue there are fower braunches, Honourablenesse, Stoutnesse, Sufferaunce, Continuaunce. **1639** FULLER *Holy War* I. viii. (1647) 11 The equitie and honourablenesse of the cause. **1748** RICHARDSON *Clarissa* (1811) III. xvii. 107 The honourableness of my intentions to your dear self. **1872** *Cassell's Mag.* 13 Jan. 309 The payment and receipt of wages, so far from detracting from the honourableness of the relation, places both master and servant on a footing of plain justice.

'honourableship. *nonce-wd.* The rank of one who has the title 'Honourable'; used with *poss. pron.* as a mock title.

1825 KNAPP & BALDW. *Newgate Cal.* IV. 290/1 To be cozened by their Honourableships. **1859** *Tait's Mag.* XXVI. 36 The Honourable takes the lead of course in deference to his honorableship.

honourably, honorably ('ɒnərəblɪ), *adv.* [f. as prec. + -LY².] In an honourable manner; with honour or respect; consistently with honour; creditably, reputably: see the adj.

1303 R. BRUNNE *Handl. Synne* 10594 Onourablye he dyd hyt graue Yn hys cherche. **1377** LANGL. *P. Pl.* B. XII. 155 Clerkes..comen..And deden her homage honourablely to hym. *a* **1400** *Relig. Pieces fr. Thornton MS.* 15 To lyffe perfitly..þat es to lyffe honourabilly mekely and lufe-somly. **1588** SHAKS. *L.L.L.* v. ii. 448 The Noble Lord Most honorably doth vphold his word. *a* **1619** BEAUM. & FL. *Valentin.* IV. iv, When I am dead speak honourably of me. **1710** in C. Wordsw. *Schol. Acad.* 305 He took his degree very honourably, and I believe will have an *optime.* **1780** BURKE *Sp. Bristol prev. to Elect.* Wks. III. 355, I had served the city of Bristol honourably. **1882** FROUDE *Short Stud.* (1883) IV. v. 339 The fitting and peaceful close of a life honourably spent.

honoured, honored ('ɒnəd), *ppl. a.* [f. HONOUR *v.* + -ED¹.] Held in honour, highly respected; dignified; celebrated: see the verb.

1601 SHAKS. *All's Well* I. iii. 162, I am from humble, he from honored name. **1644** SIR S. LUKE in Ellis *Orig. Lett.* Ser. III. IV. 222 Honoured Sir, Give mee leave to beg your favour. **1809-10** COLERIDGE *Friend* (1865) 131 Have I then endeavoured to connect public odium with his honoured name? **1855** MACAULAY *Hist. Eng.* xvii. IV. 40 There Ken passed a happy and honoured old age.

†**b.** *Her.* The same as *crowned. Obs.*

1688 R. HOLMES *Armory* II. vii. 138/2. **1828-40** WM. BERRY *Encycl. Herald., Honoured* or *Crowned,* the former term is sometimes used in old blazon when any animal, &c. is borne crowned.

honourer, honorer ('ɒnərə(r)). [f. HONOUR *v.* + -ER¹.] One who honours; †a worshipper (*obs.*).

a **1340** HAMPOLE *Psalter* cxxxiv. 15 Honurrers of maw-metis. *Ibid., Cant.* 500 Honurers of riche men. **1563** *Homilies* II. *Idolatry* I. (1859) 172 The Prophet curseth the image honourers in divers places. **1603** B. JONSON *Sejanus* Ded., Your Lordship's most faithful honorer, Ben Jonson. **1710** R. WARD *Life H. More* 165 He was a sincere Honourer and Approver of it. **1845** TRENCH *Huls. Lect.* I. iv. 64 The honourers and sanctifiers of these relations.

honouring, honoring ('ɒnərɪŋ), *vbl. sb.* [f. HONOUR *v.* + -ING¹.] The action of the verb HONOUR; honour. (Now chiefly as gerund.)

c **1375** *Sc. Leg. Saints, Baptista* 1149 ȝet of sancte Iohnne in honoryng I ma eke to a ferly thing. **1500-20** DUNBAR *Poems* xliv. 3 Thay [wemen] suld haif wirschep and grit honoring Off men. **1535** COVERDALE *Wisd.* xiv. 27 The honouringe of abhominable ymages. **1667** MILTON *P.L.* VIII. 569 An outside? fair no doubt, and worthy well Thy cherishing, thy honouring, and thy love.

'honouring, 'honoring, *ppl. a.* [f. as prec. + -ING².] That honours; see the verb. Hence **'honouringly** *adv.*

1845 R. W. HAMILTON *Pop. Educ.* iii. (ed. 2) 45 We honouringly contrast its patience, its contentment, its cheerfulness with its treatment. **1854** EMERSON *Lett. & Soc. Aims, Quot. & Orig.* Wks. (Bohn) III. 223 A phrase or a single word is adduced, with honouring emphasis, from Pindar.

honourless ('ɒnəlɪs), *a.* [f. HONOUR *sb.* + -LESS.] Destitute of honour; unhonoured, or unworthy of honour.

1560 PHAER *Æneid* x. (1562) Ffiij b, Unfamous free from wars, and honourlesse lead out his age. **1618** BOLTON *Florus* II. viii. (1636) 117 To draw the Romans into an honourlesse league with him against the Macedonians. **1870** MORRIS *Earthly Par.* III. IV. 284 And honourless did all things seem and vain. **1873** *Argosy* XV. 192 The would-be honourable, but, in this case, truly honourless, gentleman.

b. *nonce-use.* That has not 'taken honours' at the University: see HONOUR *sb.* 5 e.

1872 J. C. JEAFFRESON *Wom. in Spite of Herself* I. I. vii. 117 An ordinary honourless Oxford or Cambridge M.A.

†**honourment.** *Obs.* [a. OF. (*h*)*onorement,* f. *honorer* to HONOUR + -MENT. Cf. ANOUREMENT adornment.] The action of 'honouring' or embellishing; adornment, decoration.

1440 in *Lincolnsh. Ch. Goods,* With all the honourments for the sepulchre. **1486** *Surtees Misc.* (1888) 55 The stretes ..furnishede wᵗ clothis of the best..for the honourment of the same. **1521** in *Archæol.* (1792) X. 98 [The wife of Christopher Sunlay] gave to the honourement of the ferture of 1 crucifix of silver and gylt.

hont, etc., obs. form of HUNT, etc.

†**'hontous,** *a. Obs.* Also 5 **hountouse, hounteous.** [a. OF. *hontos, -us, -ous, -eus,* mod.F. *honteux,* f. *honte* (from Teutonic: cf. Goth. *hauniþa,* OHG. *hônida, hônda*) shame, disgrace.] Full of shame; ashamed; shameful.

c **1477** CAXTON *Jason* 35 b, Ye haue sent him from you all hountouse and shamed. *Ibid.* 42, I am ashamed and hontouse to lyue. *c* **1500** *Melusine* xxxiv. 238 Whan the noble pucelle Eglantyne vnderstode the kyng her vncle, she was shamfull & hontous.

So †**hontage, hountage** [a. OF. *hontage, hountage*], shame, disgrace. †**hountee,** shame.

The connexion and meaning of the first quot. is doubtful.

13.. *Minor Poems fr. Vernon MS.* 528 In his askyng he geteþ hountage. *c* **1430** *Pilgr. Lyf Manhode* IV. xviii. (1869) 184 Þe skyn of whiche j make my barmfell j clepe Hountee and confusioun.

Honved ('hɒnveɪd). [Hungarian, = *hon* home + *véd* defence.] The name given to the Hungarian second-line formation during the revolutionary war of 1848-9; later also used of the militia reserve. Also, a member of either force.

1854 E.O.S. *Hungary & its Revolutions* 429 The new army,..namely, the Honveds, National Guards, and Volunteers. **1875** *Encycl. Brit.* II. 604/2 The Hungarian militia or 'honveds', as they are called. **1913** *Times* 7 May 7/3 It [*sc.* an ordnance factory] will supply the needs of the Honved troops and of the Hungarian quota of the joint army and navy. **1931** F. ECKHART *Short Hist. Hungarian People* vii. 192 At his [*sc.* Kossuth's] impassioned speeches, the *Honvéds* (Defenders of the Fatherland] assembled..round the standards of the King of Hungary. **1956** C. A. MACARTNEY *October Fifteenth* I. i. 15 The Magyars did not mind taking commissions in the Honvéd, which, however, was a body not much more serious than our own militia of the day. **1959** D. SINOR *Hist. Hungary* xxix. 267 Some 152,000 Hungarian *honvéd* (as the soldiers of this war were called)..had to face the 1,200 guns of an enemy some 370,000 strong. **1962** C. A. MACARTNEY *Hungary* vii. 163 The rank and file of the *Honvéd* were as a rule conscripted into the Imperial forces and sent to foreign stations.

honyock, honyocker, varr. HUNYAK.

hoo (huː), *int.* and *sb.* A natural exclamation, used to express various feelings, as a call to attract attention, etc. Also, imitative of the sound of an owl, the wind, etc. (See also WHOO.)

1606 SHAKS. *Ant. & Cl.* II. vii. 141 Hoo, saies a, there's my Cap. **1607** —— *Cor.* II. i. 116 Take my Cappe, Iupiter and I thanke thee; hoo, Martius comming home? **1883** BRINSLEY-RICHARDS *7 Years Eton* 116, I heard a cry of Hoo! tug! and..had just time to see the wretched little colleger clattering down the staircase.

b. Often doubled, or otherwise extended.

1607 SHAKS. *Cor.* III. iii. 137 Our enemy is banish'd, he is gone: Hoo, oo. **1851** CARLYLE *Sterling* II. v. (1872) 127 A dreary pulpit or even conventicle manner; that flattest moaning hoo-hoo of predetermined pathos. **1855** THACKERAY *Rose & Ring* x, I'm hungry for his blood. Hoo —oo, aw! **1884** *Daily News* 27 Feb. 5/6 One could distinguish the hoo-hoo-oo, the strange war-cry of the [Soudanese] rebels. **1911** T. E. LAWRENCE *Home Lett.* (1954) 154 With a mighty firing of guns & pistols, and the hu-hu-hu and violent tahleel of the women [*sc.* native women in Syria].

hoo (huː), *v.* Also *Sc.* **hou.** [f. prec.; see also WHOO *v.* and cf. HUE *v.*²] *intr.* To make the sound 'hoo!' Hence **'hooing** *vbl. sb.* and *ppl. a.*

? *a* **1800** in Cromek *Rem. Nithsd. & Gal. Song* (1810) 276 When the gray Howlet has three times hoo'd. **1820** *Edin. Mag.* May 422/2 The houlet hou't through the riftit rock. **1842** MRS. CARLYLE *Lett.* I. 157 The hooing and squealing of a child..to keep off the crows. **1865** *Cornh. Mag.* July 37 The West-countryman says the wind 'hoois', and the North-countryman that 'it soughs'. **1880** MARK TWAIN *Tramp Abroad* I. 328 The clamorous hoo-hooing of its cuckoo clock.

hoo, ME. spelling of HO *int.* and *v.*; obs. and dial. f. HEO *pron.,* she; Sc. f. HOW; obs. f. WHO.

hooboobe, -bub, etc., obs. ff. HUBBUB.

hooce, obs. form of HOARSE.

hooch (huːtʃ). *colloq.* (orig. and chiefly *N. Amer.*). Also **hootch.** [Abbrev. of HOOCHINOO.]

a. = HOOCHINOO 2. **b.** In more general use, alcoholic liquor, spirits, esp. of low quality or illegal provenance.

1897 M. H. E. HAYNE *Pioneers of Klondyke* 91 The manufacture of 'hooch', which is undertaken by the saloon-keepers themselves, is weirdly horrible. **1903** *N.Y. Even. Post* 25 Sept. 3 In this bottle was some of the native spirits called 'hooch', distilled from sugar and graham flour. **1904** E. ROBINS *Magnetic North* ix. 161 Apart from the question of drinking raised again by the 'hootch',..they were ready to eat the more. **1907** R. W. SERVICE *Songs of Sourdough* (1908) 18 A broken wreck with a craze for 'hooch', and never a cent to my name. **1922** G. C. F. PRINGLE *Tillicums of Trail* 41 I've cut out the hootch. It was getting me at White Horse. **1923** C. J. DUTTON *Shadow on Glass* 200, I thought of our modern 'hooch ships' that were doing the same thing. **1927** *Punch* 20 Apr. 428/3 He knows what the poor want in the great black city of Chicago. They want cash. He knows what the thirsty want. They want hooch. **1927** *Amer. Speech* III. 167/2 *Hootch,* bad whiskey. **1953** M. SCOTT *Breakfast at Six* xii. 99 He's sure to have lots of hootch outside, and he'll get more expansive as the evening goes on. **1960** *Times* 5 Feb. 9/5 He apparently received consignments of empty whisky bottles from Madrid, which were filled with the 'hooch'. **1964** *Globe & Mail* (Toronto) 15 Dec. 31/8 The least the authorities could do when they make a raid would be to pack the confiscated hootch and ship to some underprivileged country. **1969** *New Yorker* 5 Apr. 97/1 The people of the city were prepared to swallow any old hootch under the rule of some wild thirst. **1970** *Times* 15 Oct. 30/3 The distilled spirits industry..wages an expensive propaganda campaign against..hooch.

hooch, hootch: see HOOCHIE.

hoochie ('huːtʃɪ). *Mil. slang.* Also **hooch, hoochy, hootch.** [? ad. Jap. *uchi* dwelling.] A shelter or dwelling (esp. one that is insubstantial or temporary).

1952 *San Francisco Examiner* 26 Oct. 18/4 The 'hoochie' is a GI term for a bunker or a prepared defensive position. **1954** *Britannica Bk. of Year* 637/2 In its final stages, the war in Korea yielded a number of new terms, among them the British soldier's name for a dugout—a Hoochie. **1960** *Amer. Speech* XXXV. 264 Cinderella-san lived in hootchie with sisters. **1960** (*citing an Army weekly newspaper in Korea*) in *Sat. Rev.* (1968) 26 Oct. 35/3 All through our hootch, Not a creature was stirring. **1964** *N.Y. Times* 4 Sept., *Hooches,* the huts woven from banana leaves and roofed with straw or corrugated tin that are the standard housing for Vietnamese outside the cities. Some Americans have appropriated the term for their own quonset-styled barracks. **1966** *Flying* Dec. 54/2 A hootch (a house or a hut is known as a hootch in Vietnam). **1968** *N.Y. Rev. Books* 4 Jan. 4/1 Such targets as hooch lines (rows of houses along a road or canal). **1968** *TV Times* (Austral.) 6 Mar. 11/1, I was lying in a little scrap of a tent the Australians call a hoochie. **1969** I. KEMP *Brit. G.I. in Vietnam* iv. 75 Around us were scattered the makeshift 'hooches' of the A.R.V.N. soldiers, built of bamboo, wattle and mud; rectangular in shape with sloping, thatched roofs, they were..small. **1969** *Time* 5 Dec. 18/3 Calley's men in less than 20 minutes ignited 'hootches' and chased all the villagers..into groups, and shot everyone. **1971** *Fremdsprachen* XV. 207 A stereo set was blaring in an enlisted men's hootch shortly after midnight.

Hoochinoo ('huːtʃɪnuː). Also **Hootsenoo,** etc. [ad. Tlingit *Hutsnuwu,* lit. 'grizzly bear fort'.]

1. A member of a small Indian people found in Admiralty Island, Alaska. Also *attrib.* or as *adj.* In *pl.* the tribe.

1878 DENNIS in W. G. Morris *Rep. Customs Dist. Alaska* (1879) 122 On top of this there came a fight among the Hootzenoo Indians here. **1890** M. BALLOU *New Eldorado* (ed. 5) 321 We pass the Indian village of Kootznahoo, occupied by a tribe of the same name, a people who have always proved to be restless and aggressive. **1915** J. MUIR *Trav. Alaska* (1917) 211 They were about to set out on an expedition to the Hootsenoos to collect blankets as indemnity or blood-money for the death of a Chilcat woman from drinking whiskey furnished by one of the Hootsenoo tribe.

2. (Usu. with lower-case initial.) An alcoholic liquor made by Alaskan Indians, esp. the Hoochinoo people; also any inferior alcoholic drink (esp. whisky) in Alaska and the Canadian north-west.

1877 *Puget Sound Argus* (Pt. Townsend, Wash.) 23 Nov., I have frequently seen soldiers go to the Indian ranch for their morning drink of kootznehoo. *c* **1898** in P. Berton *Centennial Food Guide* (1966) 58/2 Whenever whisky runs short the Yukoner falls back upon a villanous decoction.. known as 'hootchinoo', or 'hootch'. **1899** *Boston Jrnl.* 11 Jan. 4/5 Recently the House gave its official sanction to the word by enacting that no whisky, beer or 'hoochinoo' shall be sold in Alaska. **1937** C. L. ANDREWS *Wrangell & Gold of Cassiar* 49 A discharged soldier named Doyle..went to Hootznahoo, showed them how to distill a villainous compound from molasses, yeast, berries, sugar, or other compounds. It was first so called from the village, 'Hootznahoo' paraphrased as 'Hoochinoo'. **1958** P. BERTON *Klondike Fever* 27 Another was to collect the excise duty on all locally made hootchinoo.

b. In full *hoochinoo still.* A still for the manufacture of hoochinoo.

1879 *Chicago Tribune* 14 May 6/3 We accidentally dropped upon a hootchenoo still in full operation. **1883** J. WRIGHT *Among Alaskans* 150 Mr. Dennis had appointed the most reliable Indians as policemen, giving them authority, under United States revenue customs laws, to seize and destroy the hoochinoos or whisky-stills.

hoochy-coochy: see HOOTCHY-KOOTCHY.

hood (hʊd), *sb.*¹ Forms: 1 hód, (hood), 3-5 hod, 4-6 hode, hoode, *north.* hud(e, 4- hood, (5 houd, hoyd, 6 hodde, whod(e, whode, whodde, *mod.Sc.* huid, hude(ü)). [OE. *hód* str. masc. = OFris. *hôd,* MDu. *hoet*(*d-*), Du. *hoed,* MLG. *hôt, hût,* OHG., MHG. *huot* (Ger. *hut* hat):—OTeut. *hôdo-z,* f. *hôd-,* in ablaut relation with **hattus* (:—**hadnús*) HAT, q.v.]

1. a. A covering for the head and neck (sometimes extending to the shoulders) of soft or flexible material, either forming part of a larger garment (as the hood of a cowl or cloak) or separate; in the former case, it can usually be thrown back so as to hang from the shoulders

down the back; in the latter sense it was applied in 14–16th c. to a soft covering for the head worn by men under the hat.

*a*700 *Epinal Gloss.* 239 *Capitium*, hood. *a*1000 *Ags. Voc.* in Wr.-Wülcker 199/18 *Capitium*, hod. *c*1205 LAY. 13109 þe hod hongede adun. *c*1290 *S. Eng. Leg.* I. 284/209 þis þeues with þis wide hodes. *c*1325 *Poem Times Edw. II* 187 in *Pol. Songs* (Camden) 332 Als ich evere brouke min hod under min hat. *c*1375 *Sc. Leg. Saints, VII Sleperis* 269 He .. Kist his hud done oure his face. *c*1386 CHAUCER *Prol.* 103 He was clad in cote and hood of grene. *c*1400 MAUNDEV. (Roxb.) xxvi. 121 Hudes vsez þai nane. 1410 *E.E. Wills* (1882) 16 A grene Gowne and a hoyd percyd with Ray. *c*1460 in *Babees Bk.* 13 Holde of þy cappe & þy hood also. 1535 STEWART *Cron. Scot.* II. 266 Vpoun his heid come nother hat nor hude. 1548 HALL *Chron., Hen. VIII* (1809) 619 He had on his head a whode. *a*1592 GREENE *Jas. IV*, III. ii, A fool may dance in a hood, as well as a wise man in a bare frock. 1600 J. PORY tr. *Leo's Africa* II. 222 Certaine jackets of leather with hoods upon them, such as travellers use in Italie. 1667 MILTON *P.L.* III. 490 Then might ye see Cawles, Hoods, and Habits with thir wearers tost And flutterd into Raggs. 1739 GRAY *Let.* in *Poems* (1775) 62 We are .. as well armed as possible against the cold, with muffs, hoods, and masks of bever. 1865 DICKENS *Mut. Fr.* I. i, The girl pulled the hood of a cloak she wore, over her head and over her face.

b. A separate article of apparel for the head worn by women; also, the close-fitting head-covering of an infant. ***French hood***, a form of hood worn by women in the 16th and 17th centuries, having the front band depressed over the forehead and raised in folds or loops over the temples.

*c*1430 LYDG. *Min. Poems* 201 For to kepe hire froom the heete, She weryth a daggyd hood of grene. *c*1532 DEWES *Introd. Fr.* in *Palsgr.* 906/3 The frenche hode, *le chapperon a plis.* 1533 HEYWOOD *Pard. & Frere* in Hazl. *Dodsley* I. 203 Her bongrace which she ware, with her French hood. 1541–1636 [see FRENCH HOOD]. 1556 *Chron. Gr. Friars* (Camden) 17 The comyn strompettes that ware takene in London ware raye hoddes. 1610 B. JONSON *Alch.* II. vi, Sh' is not in fashion, yet; she weares A hood: but 't stands a cop. 1667 PEPYS *Diary* 27 Mar., To put myself and wife .. in mourning and my two under-mayds, to give them hoods, and scarfs, and gloves. 1712 ADDISON *Spect.* No. 271 ¶4, I was .. in an Assembly of Ladies, where there were Thirteen different coloured Hoods. 1792 S. ROGERS *Pleas. Mem.* I. 110 Her tattered mantle and her hood of straw. 1897 *Civ. Serv. Supply Assoc. List*, Infant's Silk Hoods, Cashmere Hoods, White Knitted Hoods.

†**c.** ***by my hood***: an asseveration. *Obs.* (Actual reference uncertain.)

*c*1374 CHAUCER *Troylus* V. 1151, I commende hire wisdom by myn hod! 1546 J. HEYWOOD *Prov.* (1867) 84 Onely for both I wed not, by my hood. 1596 SHAKS. *Merch. V.* II. vi. 51 Now by my hood, a gentle, and no Iew.

d. *fig.* A cap of foam, mist, or cloud.

1814 SCOTT *Ld. of Isles* III. xvi, Corrywrekin's whirlpool rude, When dons the Hag her whiten'd hood. 1841 in *Chambers's Pop. Rhymes Scotl.* 149 When Ruberslaw puts on his cowl, The Dunion on his hood, Then a' the wives o' Teviotside Ken there will be a flood. [These are two hills.]

2. a. As a mark of official, or professional dignity, worn by ecclesiastics, physicians, civic officials, etc.; now *spec.*, the badge, varying in material, colour, and shape, worn over the gown (or surplice) by university graduates as indicating their degrees. (Cf. AMICE[2].)

1362 LANGL. *P. Pl.* A. VII. 256 þat Fisyk schal his Forred hode for his [foode] sulle, And eke his cloke of Calabre. 1377 *Ibid.* B. XX. 175 A Fisicien with a forred hode. *c*1489 CAXTON *Sonnes of Aymon* xi. 282 The kynge .. was cladde wyth the abbyt of religyon and the hode vpon his hede. 1548–9 (Mar.) *Bk. Com. Prayer, Offices* etc. 37 Such hoodes as pertaineth to their seueral degrees. 1598 STOW *Surv.* x. (1603) 87 Whoodes of Budge for Clearks. 1603 *Constit. & Canons Eccles.* §58 Such Hoods as by the orders of the Universities are agreeable to their degrees. 1688 R. HOLME *Armoury* III. 19/2 About the beginning of Queen Elizabeths Reign [Masters and Stewards of Incorporated Societies] cast them [Hoods] off their heads, and hung them on their shoulders. 1714 BYROM *Jrnl. & Lit. Rem.* (1854) I. I. 26 To treat all our white-hoods, or Masters of Arts of two or three years standing. 1868 MARRIOTT *Vest. Chr.* 228. 1895 RASHDALL *Univ. Mid. Ages* II. 640 At Paris [*c* 1500] the Rectors wore violet or purple, the Masters scarlet, with tippets and hoods of fur. The hood was not originally restricted to Masters, being part of the ordinary clerical dress of the period, and was not even exclusively clerical. Bachelors of all Faculties wore hoods of lamb's wool or rabbit's fur. *Ibid.* note, At Oxford, undergraduates lost their hoods altogether in 1489.

b. The ornamental piece attached to the back of a cope, orig. shaped like and used as a hood.

*a*1225 *Ancr. R.* 56 Ȝif he haueð enne widne hod & one ilokene cope. 1509 *Bury Wills* (Camden) 112, I wole have in the whod theroff [a cope] the salutacion off our Lady. 1885 *Catholic Dict.* (ed. 3), *Cope* .. a wide vestment .. open in front and fastened by a clasp, and with a hood at the back. 1890 *Lippincott's Mag.* July 73 A gorgeous cope of crimson silk and gold-thread damask .. the coronation of the Virgin was figured in colored silks on the hood.

†**3.** The part of a suit of armour that covers the head; applied to the helmet itself, or to a flexible head-covering inside the helmet. *Obs.*

*c*1205 LAY. 27630 [He] smat þane king a þene helm .. and æc þere burne-hod. *c*1400 *Destr. Troy* 10297 þai hurlit of his helme .. Harmyt the hode, þat was of hard maile. 1860 FAIRHOLT *Costume* 126 The hood of chain-mail drawn over and enveloping the head. 1874 BOUTELL *Arms & Arm.* vii. 110 This hauberk .. had a hood or coif, of the same fabric with itself ..; and over this hood, as a second defence for the head, the close-fitting iron helm was worn.

4. A covering of leather put over the head of a hawk to blind her when not pursuing game.

*c*1575 *Perf. Bk. Kepinge Sparhawkes* (1886) 15 Put on an easy hoode in the dark .. be suer the hode be esy. 1629 *Leather* 10 Sheath makers. Hawkes-Hood-makers. Scabberd-makers. 1826 SIR J. S. SEBRIGHT *Obs. Hawking* (1828) 9. 1852 R. F. BURTON *Falconry Valley Indus* iv. 47 *note*, The use of the hood at home is to keep the hawk quiet. .. In the field the hood prevents the hawk fluttering upon the fist every time that a bird rises.

5. Applied to various things serving for a covering, capping, or protection, or resembling a hood in shape or use.

a. The straw covering of a beehive. **b.** A roof-like and often curved projection, e.g. over a window, door, bed, passage, etc.; the head or cover of a carriage; the cover of a pump; *Naut.* 'a covering for a companion-hatch, skylight, etc.' (Smyth *Sailor's Word-bk.* 1867). **c.** 'A dome-shaped projection or canopy over a discharging or receiving orifice in a structure, as of a fireplace, chimney, or ventilator' (Knight *Dict. Mech.*); the 'cowl' of a chimney. **d.** *Hydraulics.* 'The capping of the piles of a starling' (ibid.). **e.** 'The leathern shield in front of a wooden stirrup, which serves to protect the foot of the rider' (ibid.). **f.** *Shipbuilding* (*pl.*). The foremost and aftermost planks, within and without, of a ship's bottom. **g.** In plants, any hood-like part serving as a covering, esp. the vaulted upper part of the corolla or calyx in some flowers. **h.** In animals, a conformation of parts (as in the cobra and the hooded seal), or arrangement of colour about the head or neck, resembling or suggesting a hood. **i.** = *hood-sheaf* (see 8).

1658 EVELYN *Fr. Gard.* (1675) 68 You shall make the hood with fine earth and hay. 1686 PLOT *Staffordsh.* 387 A straw hood .. to keep the wax and hony from melting in the Summer. 1750 BLANCKLEY *Naval Expos., Hood* .. to go on the Top of the Chimney .. and to shift as the Wind does, that it [the smoke] may always fly out to leeward. 1765 *Treat. Pigeons* 115 [In the jacobine] the upper part of this range of feathers is called the hood. 1790 W. MARSHALL *Midland Co.* Gloss. (E.D.S.), *Hoods*, the covering sheaves of shucks; hood-sheaves. 1803 R. PERCIVAL *Acc. Ceylon* in *Penny Cycl.* (1840) XVI. 62/1 [The Cobra Capello] distends from its head a membrane in the form of a hood, from which it receives its name... When the hood is erected it completely alters the appearance of the head. 1815 W. BURNEY *Univ. Dict. Marine* s.v., *Naval Hoods*, or *Hawse-Bolsters*, .. large pieces of plank, or thick stuff, wrought above and below the hawse-holes. 1821 CLARE *Vill. Minstr.* II. 201 Cuckoo-flowers just creeping from their hoods. 1826 in Hone *Every-Day Bk.* II. 683 The hood of the chaise struck against the projecting branch of a tree. 1828 STARK *Elem. Nat. Hist.* I. 363 Reptiles .. Naia .. hind head furnished with a hood; poisonous fangs in the upper jaw. 1831 J. HOLLAND *Manuf. Metal* I. 311 This operation .. must be performed under the hood of a smith's forge-hearth. 1841 *Penny Cycl.* XXI. 164/2 (Seals) That the connection of the nostrils with this hood .. indicate[s] its importance as ancillary to the sense of smelling. *c*1850 *Rudim. Navig.* (Weale) 124 *Hood*, .. a covering to shelter the mortar in bomb-vessels. In merchant ships it is the berthing round the ladder-way. 1859 JEPHSON *Brittany* vii. 87 Tiers of slated hoods protecting the windows. *c*1860 H. STUART *Seaman's Catech.* 65 What is the rabbet in the stem for? To receive the ends of the outside planks, which are called 'fore hoods'. 1862 DARWIN *Fertil. Orchids* i. 29 The upper sepal and two upper petals form a hood. 1867 SMYTH *Sailor's Word-bk.*, *Hood of a pump*, a frame covering the upper wheel of a chain-pump. 1874 THEARLE *Naval Archit.* 15 Inner posts .. for securing the after ends, or hoods, of the outside plank. 1883 W. H. FLOWER in *Encycl. Brit.* XV. 444/1 *Cystophora* .. Beneath the skin over the face of the male .. is a sac capable of inflation, when it forms a kind of hood covering the upper part of the head. 1887 *S. Chesh. Gloss.* s.v., The two end sheaves of the hattock are used as hoods for the remaining six. 1887 HALL CAINE *Deemster* xii. 77 There was no hood above the bed. 1897 MARY KINGSLEY *W. Africa* 32 He took me .. to two newly dug graves, each covered with wooden hoods in a most business-like way.

j. A waterproof folding top or cover of a perambulator, motor vehicle, charabanc, etc.; the movable cover of a typewriter or other machine.

1866 *Leisure Hour* XV. 349/1 Children are likely to be exposed for longer times to the scorching sun or the piercing wind in a perambulator (if without hood or sunshade) than when carried in arms. 1895 *Army & Navy Co-op. Soc. Price List* 15 Sept. 1172 Perambulators .. with .. reversible jointed hood. 1904 A. B. F. YOUNG *Compl. Motorist* (ed. 2) viii. 198 It is a fine-weather vehicle, but a hood can be supplied for use in wet weather. 1912 *Motor Man.* (ed. 14) iii. 101 Complete protection can be obtained with a hood by fitting side curtains, which can be let down. 1942 *Short Guide Gt. Brit.* (U.S. War Dept.) 26 The top of the car is the hood. 1967 R. MOLLON *Nursery Handbk.* (1968) i. 37 Be sure that the pram .. has a good waterproof hood. 1969 C. CAMPBELL *Sports Car* (ed. 3) ix. 226 An open cockpit and an erect windscreen completely spoil the airflow pattern over a sports car and a higher maximum speed is always given with the hood erect. 1971 *Daily Tel.* 24 Nov. 11/4 The weather during the test was too unpleasant to try the MGB as it should really be driven, with the hood down.

k. In various animals, esp. *Nautilus macromphalus* (see quots.).

1883 *Encycl. Brit.* XVI. 674/1 This part of the external annular lobe of the fore-foot [of *Nautilus*] is called the 'hood'. 1888 ROLLESTON & JACKSON *Anim. Life* 456 In *Nautilus* .. the fore-foot is divisible into an outer and inner portion. The outer portion .. is thickened dorsally where it abuts against the coil of the shell and forms the hood. 1902 *Encycl. Brit.* XXV. 543/2 Movable (hinged) sclerite (so-called hood) [of *Cryptostemma karschii*] over-hanging the first pair of appendages. 1932 BORRADAILE & POTTS *Invertebrata* xvi. 527 When the animal [sc. *Nautilus*] is retracted into the living chamber the hood acts as an operculum. 1967 H. W. & L. R. LEVI tr. *Kaestner's Invertebr. Zool.* I. xv. 418 The sheaths of the dorsal (anterior) tentacles are fused into a hood that is used in *Nautilus* to cover most of the aperture when the body is withdrawn.

l. A covering for the head of a horse.

*a*1884 KNIGHT *Dict. Mech.* Suppl. 461/1 *Hood*, that part of a horse blanket which covers the horse's head and neck. 1963 BLOODGOOD & SANTINI *Horseman's Dict.* 105 *Hood*, horse's head covering with eyeholes (with or without ear coverings) of serge, wool or rubber.

m. *Photogr.* (See quot. 1918.) In full, ***lens hood***.

1892 [see FINDER 3 d]. 1892 *Photogr. Ann.* II. 41 Have two caps for each lens, one to fit the hood and one to fit the other end of the mount. 1918 *Photo-Miniature* Mar. 25 *Lens hood*, the detachable rim of a lens-tube somewhat larger in diameter and carrying the lens-cap. Also any separate device of tubular box- or bellows-form fitted to the lens-tube, to screen the lens from strong light. 1939–50 *Army & Navy Stores Catal.* 906/2 Voightländer cameras... Fitted with a large brilliant view finder and deep hood. 1961 G. MILLERSON *Technique Television Production* iii. 28 (*caption*) Interchangeable camera lenses with lens hoods.

n. A protecting cover, also sometimes acting as a reflector, placed over a lamp.

1907 *Yesterday's Shopping* (1969) 260/3 Candle reading lamp. Telescopic corrugated hood. 1913 J. B. BISHOP *Panama Gateway* v. vi. 382 The reflecting hood is provided with shading skirts, which prevent the glare of the lamp filament from penetrating into distance along the axis of the canal. 1939–40 *Army & Navy Stores Catal.* 277/3 The Reader. Chrome-plated with specially designed hood to shade light.

o. The bonnet of a motor vehicle. orig. and chiefly *U.S.*

1929 W. FAULKNER *Sartoris* II. vi. 145 He lifted the hood and removed the cap from the breather-pipe. 1942 *Short Guide Gt. Brit.* (U.S. War Dept.) 26 What we call the hood (of the engine) is a bonnet. 1960 *Times* 14 Sept. 12/6 You .. discover that not only does the engine wear a hood instead of a bonnet but [etc.]. 1970 *Globe & Mail* (Toronto) 26 Sept. 29/5 (Advt.), A Rolls Royce whose hood was draped in white damask set with candelabra and plates.

p. A roughly shaped hat of felt, straw, or similar material for the hatter to shape by blocking or stitching.

1932 D. C. MINTER *Mod. Needlecraft* 159/1 Felt or felted hoods and hats are beaten, steamed, and moulded from the flat. 1963 P. MOYES *Murder à la Mode* vii. 122 The shapeless felt 'hoods' which would eventually be steamed and seamed into smart hats.

6. The hooded seal; = HOOD-CAP 2.

1854 *Chamb. Jrnl.* I. 76 Four varieties of seal .. the young *harp* and young *hood*, the old *harp* and the *bedlamer*, or old *hood*.

7. Proverbs and proverbial phrases. (See also APE *sb.* 4, BONE *sb.* 9.)

[*c*1400 *Rom. Rose* 7388 With so gret devotion They made her confession, That they had ofte, for the nones, Two hedes in one hood at ones.] *c*1430 *Pilgr. Lyf Manhode* IV. xix. (1869) 185 Alle þilke .. þat hauen here hoodes wrong turned, and þat prosperitee hath blindfelled. *c*1475–1580 [*Two faces under one hood*: see FACE *sb.* 2]. *c*1510 *Robin Hood* VII. in Child *Ballads* (1888) v. cxvii, That he ne shall lese his hede, That is the best ball in his hode. 1550 LEVER *Serm.* (Arb.) 99 These Flatterers be wonders perilous felowes, hauynge two faces vnder one hoode. 1580 H. GIFFORD *Gilloflowers* (1875) 71 Fortune's flattering vowes, Who in one hoode a double face doth beare. 1613 SHAKS. *Hen. VIII*, III. i. 23 All Hoods make not Monkes. *a*1700 B. E. *Dict. Cant. Crew* s.v., *Two Faces under one Hood*, a Double Dealer.

8. *attrib.* and *Comb.*, as ***hood-box***, ***-fillet***, ***-hole***, ***-maker***; ***hood-like*** adj.; **hood-cover, hood-fend**, a protecting covering over a carriage, an opening, etc.: see sense 5; **hood dryer** (see quot. 1966); **hood-end** (*Shipbuilding*): see quot.; **hood-gastrula**, a form of secondary gastrula resulting from unequal segmentation, an amphigastrula; **hood-jelly**, one of the *Hydromedusæ* or acalephs proper; **hood-sheaf**, each of two sheaves placed slantwise on the top of a shock of corn so as to carry off the rain; **hood-shy** *a.* (see quot.); † **hood-skull** = sense 3.

1604 MIDDLETON *Father Hubburd's T.* Wks. (Bullen) VIII. 102 All my pack contained in less than a little *hood-box. 1962 *Guardian* 5 Dec. 6/4 Hairdryer, brush, comb and *hood dryer. 1966 J. S. COX *Illustr. Dict. Hairdressing* 80/2 *Hood dryer*, a hair dryer in the form of a hood secured to a pedestal. 1867 SMYTH *Sailor's Word-bk.*, **Hood-ends*, the ends of the planks which fit into the rabbets of the stem and stern posts. 1804 *Naval Chron.* XII. 474 Several of the *hood-fends opened. 1894 H. SPEIGHT *Nidderdale* 208 The *hood-fillet is plain. 1879 tr. *Haeckel's Evol. Man* I. viii. 201 In common with Mammals, these animals exhibit unequal cleavage, and form a *Hood-gastrula. 1647 WARD *Simp. Cobler* 27 Women .. peering out of their *hood-holes. 1861 J. R. GREENE *Man. Anim. Kingd., Cœlent.* 124 A *hood-like, crescentic fold of the ectoderm. 1530 PALSGR. 231/2 *Hode maker, *faiseur de chaperons*. 1799 J. ROBERTSON *Agric. Perth* 159 The two *hood sheaves are .. laid on in opposite directions, as a covering. 1848 *Jrnl. R. Agric. Soc.* IX. II. 501 The wheat is invariably covered with 'hood-sheaves'. 1886 SALVIN & BRODRICK *Falconry Brit. Isles* Gloss. 151 **Hood-shy*, a term used for Hawks that have been spoilt to the hood. 1537 *Ld. Treas. Acc. Scotl.* in Pitcairn *Crim. Trials* I. *288 To the Kingis grace, ane Pissane of Mailye and ane *Hudskule.

hood (hʊd), *sb.*[2] Abbrev. of HOODLUM.

1930 *Amer. Mercury* Dec. 456/1 None of those St. Louie hoods are going to cut in here, see? **1934** J. T. FARRELL *Young Manhood* xiv. 218 Jim Doyle stood by the kitchen sink, a cigar pasted in his round, jolly face, and he greeted them, calling them hoods. **1959** *Manch. Guardian* 5 Aug. 1/1 The 'News' suggests 'a special committee to greet the Kremlin's No. 1 Hood at the Washington Airport'. **1966** WODEHOUSE *Plum Pie* vii. 177 The hood was beating the tar out of me.

hood (hʊd), *v.* Also 6 hudde. [f. HOOD *sb.*[1]] *trans.* To cover with or as with a hood: sometimes with the intention of protection or concealment.

c **1420** *Pallad. on Husb.* III. 717 With cley & mosse here hedys hode & hyde. *c* **1440** *Promp. Parv.* 242/1 Hoodyn, *capucio.* **1579–80** NORTH *Plutarch* (1676) 84 Valerius and his company..hudded them with their gowns over their heads. **1593** BILSON *Govt. Christ's Ch.* 90 This is a shift that hoodeth some mens eies. *a* **1693** URQUHART *Rabelais* III. xvii. 141 She began to hood her self with her Apron. **1810** CRABBE *Borough* i, Their head the gown has hooded. **1826** SEBRIGHT *Obs. Hawking* (1828) 9 To hood a hawk, requires a degree of manual dexterity that is not easily acquired. **1852** WOOD *Nat. Hist.* (1874) 43 When a Chetah is taken out for the purpose of hunting game, he is hooded.

b. To cap a shock of corn with two hood-sheaves (see HOOD *sb.*[1] 8).

1825–80 in JAMIESON. **1856** *Jrnl. R. Agric. Soc.* XVII. II. 480 Hooding or capping the sheaves is common in some parts.

hood: see also HUD.

-hood (hʊd), *suffix.* [ME. *-hod* (*-hode*):—OE. *-hád* = OS. *-hêd*, OHG. *-heit.*] Orig. a distinct sb., meaning 'person, personality, sex, condition, quality, rank' (see HAD *sb.*), which being freely combined with nouns, as in OE. *cild-hád* child-condition, *mæȝð-hád* virgin state, *pápan hád* papal dignity, ceased at length to be used as a separate word, and survived as a mere suffix, and is thus noteworthy as a late example of the process by which suffixes arose. The ME. form was regularly *-hôd* with open *ô*, as still in Chaucer; but in the 15th c. it had become close *ō* (riming in Bokenham's *Seyntys* with *gōd* 'good'), and this duly gave mod.Eng. *hood.* A parallel suffix, from same root and in same sense, is -HEAD, ME. *-hed, -hede*, Sc. *-heid.*

A considerable number of derivatives in *-hood* go back to OE. *-hád*, e.g. *bishophood, childhood, priesthood*; many are of later origin, either with *-hood* substituted for the cognate *-hede, -head*, e.g. *falsehood, lustihood*, or as analogical formations, in some of which *-hood* has displaced earlier suffixes. Being a living suffix, *-hood* can be affixed at will to almost any word denoting a person or concrete thing, and to many adjectives, to express condition or state, so that the number of these derivatives is indefinite. Nonce-formations are numerous:

1599 NASHE *Lenten Stuffe* 46 Their heauenly hoods in theyr synode thus decreede. *a* **1639** W. WHATELY *Prototypes* I. iv. (1640) 45 It is not man-hood, it is dog-hood, or I may terme it beare-hood. **1662** SPARROW tr. *Behme's Rem. Wks.*, *Apol. conc. Perf.* 117 Man in his self-hood and I-hood. **1876** W. BATHGATE *Deep Things of God* ii. 19 Acquainted with the great reality of their Soulhood. **1883** *Daily News* 3 Oct. 2/2 Believing in the white Aylesburys..as the final expression of duckhood.

hood-cap (ˈhʊdkæp). [f. HOOD *sb.*[1] + CAP *sb.*]

1. A close cap or bonnet covering the sides of the face, worn by women in the early part of the 16th c.

1842 AGNES STRICKLAND *Queens Eng.* IV. 116 The oil painting [of Katherine of Arragon] at Versailles... The hood cap of five corners is bordered with rich gems.

2. The hooded or bladder-nosed seal, *Cystophora cristata*; so called from having a piece of loose skin over its head, which it inflates when menaced.

1864 in WEBSTER.

hooded (ˈhʊdɪd), *a.* [f. HOOD *sb.*[1] and *v.*]

1. a. Wearing or covered with a hood, having a hood on.

c **1440** *Promp. Parv.* 242/1 Hodyd, *capiciatus.* **1603** HOLLAND *Plutarch's Mor.* 358 (R.) He went hooded, as it were with his robe cast over his head. *a* **1621** BEAUM. & FL. *Thierry & Theod.* v. ii, He can sleep no more Than a hooded hawk. **1687** DRYDEN *Hind & P.* III. 1024 And sister Partlet with her hooded head, Was hooted hence. **1734** POPE *Ess. Man* IV. 198 The friar hooded, and the monarch crown'd. **1873** OUIDA *Pascarèl* I. 146 A little laughing group of sightseers, cloaked and hooded.

†**b.** *hooded man*: (*a*) A Lollard: see quot. 1460; (*b*) a native Irishman: see quot. 1596. *Obs.*

1460 CAPGRAVE *Chron.* (Rolls) 244 Hodid men were cleped then thoo Lolardis, that wold nevir avale here hood in presens of the Sacrament. [**1596** SPENSER *State Irel.* Wks. (Globe) 631/2 For a theif it [the Irish mantle] is soe handsome..he can in his mantell pass through any toune or company, being close hooded over his head..from knowledge of any to whom he is endaungered.] **1621** BOLTON *Stat. Irel.* 5 (Act 18 Hen. VI) That no Lord..shall bring or lead..Hoblors, kearnes, or hooded men. **1641** *Relat. Answ. Earl Strafford* 29 The Kings owne Souldiers..could in no construction bee called Irish-Rebells, English-Enemies, or Hooded-men.

c. Of a garment: Having a hood attached to or forming part of it.

1590 MARLOWE *Edw. II*, I. iv, He wears a short Italian hooded cloak. **1816** WORDSW. *French Army in Russia* 5 Humanity..Hath painted Winter..In hooded mantle, limping o'er the plain. **1866–7** J. THOMSON *Poems, Naked Goddess* 115 Vestal sister's hooded gown.

2. Of animals: Having a conformation of parts or an arrangement of colour resembling or suggesting a hood; **hooded crow**, *Corvus Cornix* (see also quot. 1893); **hooded seal**, see HOOD-CAP 2; **hooded serpent** or **snake**, a snake of the family *Elapidæ* or *Najidæ*, having the power of distending the elastic skin of the neck, so as to resemble a hood or cowl: esp. the Indian cobra, *Naja tripudians.*

1500–20 DUNBAR *Poems* xxxiii. 71 The hudit crawis his hair furth ruggit. **1549** *Compl. Scot.* vi. 39 The huddit crauis cryit varrok varrok. **1638** SIR T. HERBERT *Trav.* (ed. 2) 347 The Dodo..her head is variously drest, the one halfe hooded with downy blackish feathers; the other, perfectly naked. **1774** GOLDSM. *Nat. Hist.* IV. 126 The cobra di capello or hooded serpent. **1785** LATHAM *Gen. Syn. Birds* III. II. 426 Hooded M[erganser]... Size nearly that of a Wigeon. **1802** BINGLEY *Anim. Biog.* (1813) II. 461 The Hooded or Spectacle Snake. When it is irritated or preparing to bite, this animal..seems, as it were, hooded by the expanded skin of the neck: hence its name of *Cobra di Capello*, or Hooded Serpent. **1820** SCORESBY *Acc. Arctic Reg.* I. 511 The Hooded Seal is common near Spitzbergen. **1840** *Penny Cycl.* XVI. 62/2 We owe to Dr. Cantor..the introduction of a new genus of hooded snakes, *Hamadryas.* **1875** *Encycl. Brit.* III. 421/1 The Mitred Basilisk occurs in Guiana, the Hooded Basilisk in Amboyna. **1890** LD. LUGARD *Diary* 15 Mar. (1959) I. 144, I saw here [*sc.* in East Africa] the large hooded raven. **1893** NEWTON *Dict. Birds* 117 The so-called 'Hooded Crow' of India, *C*[*orvus*] *splendens*, is not very nearly allied to its European namesake. **1938** *Brit. Jrnl. Psychol.* XXVIII. 334 Of the progeny of the hooded rats..I took at random six females. **1942** C. BARRETT *On Wallaby* iv. 78 Hooded crows were on parade long before reveille. **1954** M. K. WILSON tr. *Lorenz's Man meets Dog* x. 107 Our hooded capuchin, Gloria,..was rather larger than a cat. **1955** *Arctic Terms* 40/1 *Hooded seal*, a large seal, *Cystophora cristata*, of the North Atlantic, dark in color with a unique inflatable muscular bag on its nose. Also called 'bladder-nose'. **1961** *Coast to Coast 1959–60* 62 I've heard that there is a place hereabouts which is a haunt of the hooded robin. **1972** *Country Life* 17 Feb. 381/1 The hooded crow, or hoodie, as it is commonly called in Scotland where the grey-mantled bird is seen as often as..the ordinary..crow.

3. Of a corolla or other part: Hood-shaped, cucullate; hence, of a flower or plant: Having a hood-shaped corolla, calyx, etc., as ***hooded matweed, hooded willow-herb***, etc.

1597 GERARDE *Herbal* I. xxviii. §2. 38 Hooded Mat weede. **1665** HOOKE *Microgr.* 128 Round and uniform heads, very much resembling the form of hooded Mushroms. **1668** WILKINS *Real Char.* 96 Having Hooded flowers. **1834** MARY HOWITT *Sk. Nat. Hist.* (1851) 83 Here too the spotted Arum green, A hooded mystery, is seen. **1861** MISS PRATT *Flower. Pl.* IV. 205 Common Skull-cap..is also called Hooded Willow-herb.

4. Having a hood or protective covering.

1847 DISRAELI *Tancred* II. xi, The porter rose from his hooded chair. **1859** REEVE *Brittany* 236 A curious hooded house. **1868** HOLME LEE *B. Godfrey* iv. 19 The Cheap Jack's hooded cart.

5. *transf.* and *fig.* **a.** Covered, enveloped. **b.** Blindfolded, hoodwinked. **c.** Covered up, concealed.

1652 PEYTON *Catastr. Ho. Stuarts* (1731) 36 We are hooded, and cannot see that God hath done miraculous Works. *a* **1653** G. DANIEL *Idyll* iii. 90 The Lust of Tyrants (over-banded still By hooded Law) carnalls the world at Will. **1695** SIBBALD *Autobiog.* (1834) 127, I..came into the world hooded (as they call it) with the after birth upon my head. **1866** B. TAYLOR *Poems, The Neighbor*, Beneath the cloaked and hooded sky.

hooden, var. HODEN.

hood-end: see HOOD *sb.*[1] 8 and HUD *sb.*[2] 3.

hooder (ˈhʊdə(r)). *local.* [f. HOOD *v.* + -ER[1].] A hood-sheaf: see HOOD *sb.*[1] 8.

1805 R. W. DICKSON *Pract. Agric.* (1807) II. 280 These top sheaves, from the manner in which they cover the others, are termed *hooders.* **1862** *Jrnl. R. Agric. Soc.* XXIII. 216. **1886** *Chesh. Gloss.*, *Hudders.*

ˈhoodful. [f. HOOD *sb.*[1] + -FUL.] As much as a hood will hold.

c **1500** *Maid Emlyn* in *Anc. Poet. Tracts* (Percy Soc.) 13 She wold make theyr berdes whether they wold or no, and gyve them to were a praty hoodefull of belles. **1583** *Leg. Bp. St. Androis* 146 in *Satir. Poems Reform.* xlv, He hosted thair a hude full fra him.

hoodie, hoody (ˈhʊdɪ). Also 8 *Sc.* hoddy, huddie. [f. as HOODED 2, with denominative *-ie*, -Y: cf. HAWKEY.] The Hooded or Royston Crow, *Corvus Cornix.* Also **hoodie-crow**.

1789 DAVIDSON *Seasons* 4 (Jam.) Upon an ash above the lin A hoody has her nest. **1797** *Statist. Acc. Scotl., Perths.* XIX. 498 There are also carrion crows (hoddies, as they are called here). **1816** SCOTT *Antiq.* viii, They are sitting..like hoodie-craws in a mist. **1863** KINGSLEY *Water-Bab.* vii. (1886) 296 On the rabbit burrows on the shore there gathered hundreds and hundreds of hoodie-crows, such as you see in Cambridgeshire. *Ibid.* 298 But they are true republicans, these hoodies, who do every one just what he likes.

hooding (ˈhʊdɪŋ). [f. HOOD *v.* or *sb.*[1] + -ING[1].]

1. The wearing or putting on of a hood.

c **1575** *Perf. Bk. Kepinge Sparhawkes* (1886) 14 Hoding is a singuler poynt in hawking.

†**2.** The making of, or material for, hoods. *Obs.*

c **1450** *Stratford MSS.* (Wright *Prov. Dict.*), Also the maystir schalle every yere ordeyn cloth for hodynge.

3. *Naut.* (*pl.*) = HOOD *sb.*[1] 5 f.

1627 CAPT. SMITH *Seaman's Gram.* ii. 4 Those plankes that are fastened into the ships stem are called whoodings. **1867** SMYTH *Sailor's Word-bk.*, *Hoods*, or *Hoodings*, the foremost and aftermost planks of the bottom, within and without.

4. *attrib.* **hooding-end** = *hood-end*; **hooding-sheaf** = *hood-sheaf*: see HOOD *sb.*[1] 8.

1711 W. SUTHERLAND *Shipbuild. Assist.* 161 Hooding-ends; the But-ends in the Rabbits of the Stem and Sternpost, which are more hid by the Rabbits than the other But-ends are. **1802** ACERBI *Trav.* I. 30 The sheaves of corn..are..covered with one hooding-sheaf expanded at the end, for warding off the rain.

hoodless (ˈhʊdlɪs), *a.* [f. HOOD *sb.*[1] + -LESS.] Without a hood; not having or wearing a hood.

13.. *E.E. Allit. P.* B. 643 Abraham, al hodlez with armez vp-folden, Mynystred mete byfore þo men. *c* **1369** CHAUCER *Dethe Blaunche* 1038 That he Go hoodlesse into the drie see. **1894** *Thinker* VI. 335 A Eucharistic vestment..which is practically a hoodless cope.

hoodlum (ˈhuːdləm). *slang* (orig. *U.S.*). [The name originated in San Francisco about 1870–72, and began to excite attention elsewhere in the U.S. about 1877, by which time its origin was lost, and many fictitious stories, concocted to account for it, were current in the newspapers. See a selection of these in *Manchester* (N. H.) *N. & Q.* Sept. 1883.]

A youthful street rowdy; 'a loafing youth of mischievous proclivities'; a dangerous rough. Also in more general use.

1871 *Cincinnati Commercial* 6 Sept. (Suppl.) 2/5 Surely he is far enough away here in this hideous wild of swamp, to escape the bullying of the San Francisco 'hoodlums'. **1872** *Sacramento Weekly Union* 24 Feb. 2 (Farmer) All the boys to be trained as scriveners..clerks, pettifoggers, polite loafers, street-hounds, hoodlums, and bummers. **1877** *Boston Jrnl.* Aug. (Cent.), You at the East have but little idea of the hoodlums of this city [San Francisco]. They compose a class of criminals of both sexes..travel in gangs; and are ready at any moment for the perpetration of any crime. **1882** *Chicago Advance* 6 Apr. 221 Let our Legislature pass a law to take away the hoodlum's pistol..and he will become harmless. **1886** *Pall Mall G.* 8 Feb. 8 A miscellaneous assortment of hoodlums and corner men, anxious to profit by the excitement generated in Trafalgar-square. **1888** BRYCE *Amer. Commw.* III. v. xc. 236 *note*, The term 'hoodlums' denotes those who are called in Australia 'larrikins', loafing youths of mischievous proclivities. **1929** F. A. POTTLE *Stretchers* (1930) iv. 64 Then we were a mob of unorganized, distrustful, sick, and unshaved hoodlums, whose one burning desire was to escape from the army and go back home. **1935** A. SQUIRE *Sing Sing Doctor* iv. 43 The hoodlums of the neighbourhood..flattered him, and he ran along with the gang. **1952** R. FINLAYSON *Schooner came to Atia* 4 He's not one of that gang of hoodlums. **1959** [see BELSEN]. **1970** G. F. NEWMAN *Sir, You Bastard* viii. 208 The man is a vicious hoodlum.

2. hoodlum wagon *U.S.* (see quot. 1920).

1908 *Sat. Even. Post* 31 Oct. 39/2 The jolting of the hoodlum-wagon now focused the herd's attention. **1919** H. L. WILSON *Ma Pettengill* iii. 79 The hoodlum wagon going back next morning to see what could be salvaged. **1920** J. M. HUNTER *Trail Drivers of Texas* 299 A second wagon for carrying the extra beds and bringing wood and water into camps... This equipage is called the hoodlum wagon. **1968** R. F. ADAMS *Western Words* (ed. 2) 152/1 *Hoodlum wagon*, a cowboy's name for the bed wagon.

Hence **ˈhoodluming** *vbl. sb.*, **ˈhoodlumish** *a.*, **ˈhoodlumism.**

1872 *Newton Kansan* 14 Nov. 4/1 The Rev. Dr. Cunningham in a recent sermon traced the history of 'Hoodlumism'. **1883** *Jrnl. Educ.* XVIII. 297 There is nothing that is sweeter nuts to a half-grown hoodlumish pupil..than to annoy and baffle the teacher. **1885** *Pall Mall G.* 29 Aug. 6/1 Children are brought up in the school of 'hoodlumism' and utterly lost. **1892** *Chicago Advance* 31 Mar., It is too near hoodluming to be worthy of notice. **1920** [see *group-behaviour* (GROUP *sb.* 6 b)]. **1970** G. GREER *Female Eunuch* 271 A new all-time low in political scurviness, hoodlumism.

†**ˈhoodman.** *Obs.* A hooded man; the blindfolded player in the game of HOODMAN-BLIND.

1565–73 [implied in next]. **1601** SHAKS. *All's Well* IV. iii. 136 *Ber.* A plague vpon him muffeld; he can say nothing of me: hush, hush. *Cap. G.* Hoodman comes.

ˈhoodman-ˈblind. An old name for BLIND-MAN'S-BUFF.

1565–73 COOPER *Thesaurus*, *Mya*..a childish play called hoodman blind. **1602** SHAKS. *Ham.* III. iv. 77 What diuell was't That thus hath cousen'd you at hoodman-blinde? **1609** ARMIN *Maids of More-Cl.* (1880) 104 Was I bewitcht, That thus at hud-man blind I dallied? **1611** COTGR., *Clignemusset*, the childish play called Hodman blind, Harrie-racket, or, are you all hid. **1790** PORSON *Lett. to Travis* 172. **1822** W. IRVING *Sketch Bk., Christm. Eve*, Here were kept up the old games of hoodman blind, shoe the wild mare [etc.]. **1850** TENNYSON *In Mem.* lxxviii, Again our ancient games had place..And dance and song and hoodman-blind.

hood-mould. A moulding over the head of a window, door, etc.; a label or dripstone; cf. HOOD *sb.*[1] 5 b. So **hood-moulding.**

1842–76 GWILT *Archit.* III. iii. §8. 939 In most cases, especially to windows, a string course forms a real drip or

weathering..thus becoming what is termed a hood moulding. **1849–50** WEALE *Dict. Terms, Hood-mould*, a band or string over the head of a door, window, or other moulding, in an ancient building; so called from its enclosing, as within a hood, the inferior mouldings and the opening itself. **1878** McVITTIE *Christ Church Cathedral* 59 A hood-mould over the arch of each bay terminating in masks.

hoodoo ('huːduː), *sb.* and *a.* Chiefly *U.S.* [App. an alteration of VOODOO.]

A. *sb.* **1.** One who practises voodoo.

1875 L. HEARN *Amer. Miscellany* (1924) I. 127 Supposing you fall in love with a girl and can't get her, and that you go to one of these hoodoos, he will do something awful to her with charms. *Ibid.*, She would die..unless she could get some other hoodoo doctor to take the charm away by a counter charm. **1881** *Harper's Mag.* Apr. 738/2 Suddenly she..rushed forward with an African yell and joined in the dance as wild as any Hoodoo among them. **1885** STEVENSON *Dynamiter* xi. 148 [A mulatto sorceress] exercising among her ancient mates, the slaves of Cuba, an influence as unbounded as its reason is mysterious. Horrible rites, it is supposed, cement her empire: the rites of Hoodoo. *Ibid.* 175 To swear to them, on the authority of Hoodoo or whatever his name may be. **1946** R. TALLANT *Voodoo in New Orleans* 16, I heard people say hoodoos was cannibals and used to eat babies. *Ibid.* 195, I got Adele to a good hoodoo woman and she uncrossed her.

2. An occult cause of bad luck; a person or thing whose presence is supposed to bring bad luck.

1882 J. H. BEADLE *Western Wilds* (ed. 2) xxxiv. 558 If you can find an Indian tradition to match it, your hoodoo is complete. **1889** *N.Y. Sun* 20 Mar. (Cent. Dict.), The prospect of pleasing his party and at the same time escaping a hoodoo must be irresistibly attractive. **1892** *Pall Mall G.* 28 Dec. 3/3 This year I am a tramp, a dead-beat, a hoodoo! **1894** *Columbus* (Ohio) *Disp.* 18 Sept., Superstitious persons are likely to think that T. J. starts in his race against B. with a heavy handicap, or 'hoodoo', in the language of the street. **1896** *Montreal Gazetteer* 21 Nov. 12/4 The Hoodooed Texas..Means to exorcise the hoodoo which makes so much trouble for the battle-ship Texas. **1916** H. CRANE *Let.* 26 Jan. (1965) 3 Examination time is on... Latin and Geometry are due tomorrow. They are my hoodoos. **1945** E. WAUGH *Brideshead Revisited* vii. 177 So you see things never looked like going right. There was a hoodoo on us from the start. **1958** L. VAN DER POST *Lost World of Kalahari* viii. 195 By nightfall everyone..seemed convinced there was a permanent hoodoo on us.

3. A fantastic rock pinnacle or column of rock formed by erosion or other natural agency; an earth-pillar. Also *attrib.* orig. *U.S.*

1879 W. WHITMAN *Specimen Days & Collect.* (1882) 148, I had wanted to go to the Yellowstone river region—wanted specially to see..the 'hoodoo' or goblin land of that country. **1884** H. BUTTERWORTH *Zigzag Journ. Western States* 54 There is a region there called Goblin Land, full of lofty stone monuments, the remnants of erosion, called hoodoos. **1921** *Chambers's Jrnl.* June 373/2 Strange, isolated pillars, the 'hoodoos' stood like vedettes on the heights. **1940** *Canad. Geogr. Jrnl.* Feb. 84/2 The presence in Jasper Park of..earth pillars or 'hoodoos' similar to those at Banff. **1941** C. A. COTTON *Landscape* iii. 15 The picturesque minor surface-relief forms termed hoodoo columns and earth pillars are slender residual columns of unconsolidated sediment. **1968** R. W. FAIRBRIDGE *Encycl. Geomorphol.* 46/1 Occasionally, denudation of badland slopes can produce interesting features such as earth pillars and hoodoos with an overhanging 'hat'.

B. *adj.* Unlucky, bringing bad luck.

1889 *Kansas Times & Star* 17 Sept., Joe Bracken took sick Friday, September 13, but says that hoodoo date doesn't discourage him. **1904** *New York Globe* 2 Apr. 1 It is hard to find a crew for a 'hoodoo' ship. **1909** 'O. HENRY' *Roads of Destiny* vii. 110 He's the hoodoo planet of the heavens. **1922** *Blackw. Mag.* Sept. 321/1 My name is Armstrong—Hoodoo Armstrong. **1926** *Scots Observer* 30 Oct. 21/2 That particular service was hoodoo.

Hence **hoodoo** *v. trans.*, to exercise occult influence over; to bewitch; to bring bad luck to.

1886 *Harper's Weekly* 25 Dec., The surest way to provide against being 'hoodooed', as American residents call it, is to open one's pillow from time to time. **1888** *Judge* (U.S.) 21 July 239/2 A Washington paper..drops into the following poetry, which is sufficient to hoodoo the organization for the balance of the season. **1895** *Chicago Advance* 25 July 117/1 Like the Mississippi, it [the St. Laurence] hoodoos whoever once touches it. You return again and again, and go away regretfully. **1896** *Watertown* (Wis.) *Daily Times* 9 Nov. 2/1 The coterie of democrats that hoodooed the Wilson bill. **1902** KIPLING *Traffics & Discov.* (1904) 7, I wasn't going to deadhead along o' *that* crowd... 'T'would have hoodooed my gun for all time. **1914** V. LINDSAY *Congo* 5 Mumbo-Jumbo will hoo-doo you.

'**hoodooism**. [f. HOODOO *sb.*] **a.** The practice of hoodoo rites. **b.** The faculty of attracting misfortune.

1881 *Harpe's Mag.* Apr. 737/1 What *is* Hoodooism, anyhow? **1921** *Double Dealer* July 22/1 The white folks gaze at the negro with incredulous eye and wonder what amazing story of hoodooism will come from his lips. **1966** *Listener* 14 Apr. 542/3 Hoodoo-ism is not confined to steam locomotives. I have known a hoodoo diesel rail car.

† **hood-pick**. *Sc. Obs.* Also 6 **huid-, hude-, hud-, hudipyk**. [app. f. HOOD *sb.*[1] + PICK *v.*; but the analysis is not clear.] A miser, a skinflint.

1500–20 DUNBAR *Poems* xvi. 23 Sum gevis to littill full wretchitly, That his giftis ar not set by, And for a huidpyk [*v. rr.* hudipyk, hudepyk] haldin is hie. *Ibid.* xxvi. 59 Hudpykis, hurdaris and gadderaris, All with that warlo went. *a* **1605** POLWART *Flyting w. Montgomerie* 213 Alace! poore hood-piks hunger-bitten.

hoodwink ('hʊdwɪŋk), *v.* [f. HOOD *sb.*[1] + WINK *v.*]

1. *trans.* To cover the eyes with a hood or other covering so as to prevent vision; to blindfold.

1562 *Apol. Priv. Masse* (1850) 10 Will you enforce women to hoodwink themselves in the church? **1631** *Star Chamb. Cases* (Camden) 62 Hawthorne's face was hoodwinked with a cloake or coate. **1690** W. EDMUNDSON *Jrnl.* (1715) 127 Then they hood-winkt my Sons to hang them. *a* **1691** FLAVEL *Sea-Deliv.* (1754) 157 The fog hoodwinked our eyes. **1752** CARTE *Hist. Eng.* III. 342 Several gentlemen..were taken up and carried to the Tower, hoodwinked and muffled that they might not be known. **1801** STRUTT *Sports & Past.* I. ii. 28 When the hawk was not flying at her game she was usually hood-winked with a cap or hood provided for that purpose. **1836** W. IRVING *Astoria* II. 302 One of the savages attempted to hoodwink him with his buffalo robe with one hand, and to stab him with the other.

2. *fig.* To cover up from sight.

a **1600** HOOKER *Eccl. Pol.* VI. vi. §10 Had it pleased him not to hoodwink his own knowledge, I nothing doubt but he fully saw how to answer himself. **1610** SHAKS. *Temp.* IV. i. 206 For the prize Ile bring thee too Shall hudwinke this mischance. **1674** R. GODFREY *Inj. & Ab. Physic* 187 The Necessary..Ingredients, are so hood-winkt by the Adjuncts, that they are unable to peep out of the mixture.

3. *fig.* To blindfold mentally; to prevent (any one) from seeing the truth or fact; to 'throw dust in the eyes' of, deceive, humbug.

1610 HEALEY *St. Aug. Citie of God* 848 Let not the faithlesse therefore hood-winck them-selves in the knowledge of nature. *a* **1619** FOTHERBY *Atheom.* I. xii. §5 (1622) 134 Some men..may so hoodwinke their conscience. **1756** C. LUCAS *Ess. Waters* III. 246 The public..is easily hood-winked. **1852** DICKENS *Bleak Ho.* II. viii. 115 A man of business who is not to be hoodwinked. **1874** L. STEPHEN *Hours in Library* (1892) II. vi. 180 A professor..trying to hoodwink me by a bit of technical platitude.

†**4.** *intr.* To shut one's eyes, to wink. *Obs. rare.*

1641 MILTON *Animadv.* Wks. (1851) 198 Wherfore have you sat still, and comply'd and hoodwinkt, till the generall complaints of the Land have squeez'd you to a..hollow-hearted confession.

Hence '**hoodwinking** *vbl. sb.* Also '**hood,winkable** *a.*, capable of being hoodwinked; '**hoodwinker**, one who hoodwinks.

1609 HOLLAND *Amm. Marcell.* XIV. vii. 17 There was nothing so rife as the hangman, sequestring of pillage, hood-wincking [*obductio capitum*]. **1858** GREENER *Gunnery* 383 The 'hoodwinking' of the public by not disclosing the fact. **1884** *Harper's Mag.* Dec. 93/1 Hypocrisy..the hoodwinker of communities. **1889** *Poet Lore* Aug. 387 The hoodwinkable stupidity of the public.

'**hoodwink**, *sb.* [f. prec. vb.]

†**1.** The act of hoodwinking; the game of hoodman-blind or blind-man's-buff. *Obs.*

1573–80 BARET *Alv.* H 597 The Hoodwinke play, or hoodmanblinde, in some places called the blindmanbuf. **1622** DRAYTON *Poly-olb.* XXX. 134 By Moone-shine..giue each other chase, At Hood-winke, Barley-breake [etc.].

2. A concealment from view; a blind.

1583 STANYHURST *Æneis* IV. (Arb.) 100 Too mask her Phansye with hudwinck. **1586** J. HOOKER *Girald. Irel.* in *Holinshed* II. 86/1 Where are the tokens of my wilfull hudwinke? **1732** GAY *Distr. Wife* I, Flattery, fondness and tears ..hood-winks that wives have ready. **1894** BLACKMORE *Perlycross* 417 Hood-winks of nature, when she does not wish man to know everything about her.

†**3.** One who hoodwinks; a deceiver. *Obs.*

1638 in Maidment *Bk. Scot. Pasquils* (1868) 66 These hoodwinks now ar stolne Lyke thieves to court.

†'**hoodwink**, *a.* *Obs.* [? for *hoodwinkt.*] = HOODWINKED; blindfold.

1580 SIDNEY *Ps.* X. vi, God sleepes..His farr-of sight now hud winck is. **1647** H. MORE *Song of Soul* II. i. I. x, Some uncouth might them hoodwink hither drave. **1652** EARL MONM. tr. *Bentivoglio's Hist. Relat.* 106 What hoodwink and untimely wisdome is it?

hoodwinked ('hʊdwɪŋkt), *ppl. a.* [f. HOODWINK *v.* + -ED[1].] Blindfolded, blinded. *lit.* and *fig.*

1640 BP. HALL *Chr. Moder.* (Ward) 26/2 If an hood-winked man had reeled upon him heedlessly in his way. *a* **1643** W. CARTWRIGHT *Lady Errant* I. iii, Wear the day out in a hoodwinkt room. **1643** MILTON *Soveraigne Salve* 1 To unblind the hoodwinkt world. **1837** *Morisoniana* 100 The hood-winked person at the play of 'blind-man's buff'.

hoodwort ('hʊdwɜːt). [f. HOOD *sb.*[1] + WORT.] An American species of *Scutellaria* or Skull-cap, *S. laterifolia*.

hoody: see HOODIE.

hooer ('huːə(r)). *Austral.* and *N.Z.* [Representation (in various spellings) of a vulgar or colloq. pronunciation of *whore*.]

a. = WHORE 1. **b.** A strong term of abuse (of a man or woman).

1937 in PARTRIDGE *Dict. Slang* 401/2. **1969** D. NILAND *Dead Men Running* iii. 86 The cheek of that hooer, I thought; a dirty-looking stranger. **1971** *N.Z. Listener* 22 Mar. 12/3 The dirty hua didn't even take a shower before he shot through.

hooey ('huːɪ). *slang* (orig. *U.S.*). [Orig. unknown.] Humbug, nonsense.

1924 P. MARKS *Plastic Age* 100 My prof's full of hooey. He doesn't know a C theme from an A one. *Ibid.* 160 'Bunk!' he exclaimed. 'Hooey!' **1931** E. LINKLATER *Juan in Amer.* III. v. 247 *We'll* be on Broadway if you don't talk hooey like that 'worth while' crack. **1932** WODEHOUSE *Hot Water* xiii. 223 Well, of all the hooey! **1934** *Discovery* Jan. 4/2 The United States of America, whose capacity for new words passes all belief, is responsible for hooey. **1935** *Punch* 10 Apr. 400/1 You have been misled, Hubert. I see it all. Somebody has been telling you the old, old story... Hooey, Hubert. Boloney. **1935** L. MACNEICE *Poems* 21 Ireland is hooey, Ireland is A gallery of fake tapestries. **1948** V. PALMER *Golconda* xxv. 210 All this political hooey..doesn't affect me. **1952** PARTRIDGE *From Sanskrit to Brazil* 94 These charges of anachronism are, to put it courteously, sheer 'hooey'. **1966** AUDEN *About House* 21 Lip-smacking Imps of mawk and hooey Write with us what they will. **1970** G. GREER *Female Eunuch* 81 The horse between a girl's legs is supposed to be a gigantic penis. What hooey!

hoof (huːf), *sb.* Pl. **hoofs**, sometimes **hooves**. Forms: 1 **hóf**, 4 **houf**, 4–6 *north.* **hufe**, (5 **huyfe**); 5–7 **hoofe**, (5 **howue**), 6– **hoof**, (6 **hofe, houfe, houe**, 7 **hoove, hooff, huff(e)**. [Com. Teut.: OE. *hóf* = OFris., OS. *hôf* (MLG., LG. *hôf*, MDu., Du. *hoef*), OHG., MHG. *huof* (Ger. *huf*), ON. *hófr* (Sw. *hof*, Da. *hov*), Goth. not recorded:—OTeut. type **hôfo-z*:—pre-Teut. **kō-pos*.]

1. a. The massive horny growth which sheathes the ends of the digits or incases the foot of quadrupeds forming the order *Ungulata*, primarily that of the horse and other equine animals: it corresponds to the nails or claws of other quadrupeds.

false or ***spurious hoof***: see quot. 1854. ***on the hoof***, alive; also *transf.* and *fig.* ***cloven hoof***: see CLOVEN 1 c.

c **1000** *Rune Poem* xix. (Gr.), Hors hofum wlanc. *a* **1100** *Ags. Voc.* Ibid. 307 in Wr.-Wülcker *Ungula*, hof, oððe clawu. **1340** HAMPOLE *Pr. Consc.* 4179 þe nedder..sal byte þe hors by þe hufe harde. **1382** WYCLIF *2 Kings* ix. 33 The hors houes [**1388** howues] that treden hyre. **1398** TREVISA *Barth. De P.R.* XIII. xii. (MS. Bodl.), Hooues and clees of beestes. **1531** ELYOT *Gov.* I. xvii, Discrepant in figure from other horsis, hauing his fore hoeues like to the feete of a man. **1535** COVERDALE *Lev.* xi. 3 What so euer hath hoffe]WYCLIF clee] and deuydeth it in to two clawes. **1553** EDEN *Treat. Newe Ind.* (Arb.) 16 Theyr fete..hauing fyue toes like hoeues vndeuided. **1570** LEVINS *Manip.* 157/20 Ye Hoof of a foote, *vngula*. **1621** QUARLES *Argalus & P.* (1678) 64 His proud Steed removes The hopeful fallows with his horned hoves. **1635** J. HAYWARD tr. *Biondi's Banish'd Virg.* 20 A short pasterne with a hard, high, concavous, and round huffe. **1686** PLOT *Staffordsh.* 372 The hooves, and horns of Cattle. **1747** *Gentl. Mag.* 208 He [the rhinoceros] has three hoofs on each foot forwards. **1818** H. B. FEARON *Sk. Amer.* 220 Cattle..are sold in this State, on the hoof, for about 3 dollars per hundred weight. **1832** TENNYSON *Dream Fair Wom.* 21 Clattering flints batter'd with clanging hoofs. **1854** OWEN *Skel. & Teeth* in *Circ. Sc., Organ. Nat.* II. 244 In the horse the rudiments of the two stunted toes were their upper ends or metatarsal bones; in the ox they consist of their lower ends or phalanges; these form the 'spurious hoofs', and are parts of the second..and fifth..toes. **1881** STEVENSON *Virg. Puerisque* (1895) 265 The hooves of many horses, beating the wide pastures in alarm. **1902** *Encycl. Brit.* XXV. 186/1 The estimated dead weight of the sheep imported on the hoof for slaughter. *a* **1936** KIPLING *Something of Myself* (1937) iii. 71 Why buy Bret Harte, I asked, when I was prepared to supply home-grown fiction on the hoof? **1957** WODEHOUSE *Over Seventy* iv. 53 An august figure, weighing seventeen stone or so on the hoof. **1971** *Farmer's Weekly* 19 Mar. 67/3 You can't grade hoggets on the hoof.

b. In allusion to the cloven hoof attributed to the Devil: cf. CLOVEN 1 c; also, to the hoof of 'the Beast', i.e. Antichrist.

1638 A. CANT *Serm.* in Kerr *Coven. & Covenanters* (1895) 77 In their [the English] reformation something of the beast was reserved: in ours not so much as a hoof. **1658** WOOD *Life* 24 July (O.H.S.) I. 257 Wilson..did, after his humoursome way, stoop downe to Baltzar's feet, to see whether he had a huff on, that is to say, to see, whether he was a devil, or not, because he acted beyond the parts of man. **1788** T. JEFFERSON *Wks.* (1859) II. 485 Here the cloven hoof begins to appear. **1863** MRS. C. CLARKE *Shaks. Char.* vii. 171 He has nowhere given to virtue the hoof of a fiend. **1885** J. PAYN *Luck of Darrells* xxxi, [It] had caused him to show the cloven hoof too soon.

2. a. *transf.* Hard or callous skin on the hands (cf. *horny-handed*). *dial.* **b.** *fig.* A callous sheath or covering, as insensible as a hoof.

1647 TRAPP *Comm. Matt.* xx. 7 Such an hoof they have over their hearts, that scarce any thing will affect them. *Ibid.*, *Acts* xxviii. 27 It is a heavy case when men have got a kind of hoof over their hearts. **1888** *Sheffield Gloss.*, *Hoof* or *Hoove*, hard skin on the hands made by working.

3. a. In certain phrases, put for a hoofed animal, as the smallest unit of a herd or drove.

1535 COVERDALE *Exod.* x. 26 There shal not one hooffe be left behynde. *a* **1592** GREENE *George a Greene* Wks. (Rtldg.) 254 Sirrah, you get no victuals here, Not if a hoof of beef would save your lives. *a* **1799** WASHINGTON (Webster 1828), He had not a single hoof of any kind to slaughter. **1851** MAYNE REID *Scalp Hunt.* xxxii, We should lose every hoof of them [the buffaloes]. **1859** TENNYSON *Enid* 1334 'Horse and man', he said, 'All of one mind,..Not a hoof left'.

†**b.** *fig.* A fragment or particle. *Obs.*

1655 FULLER *Ch. Hist.* I. i. §10 Yet we will not willingly leave an hoofe of the British Honour behind.

4. a. Applied humorously or derogatively to the human foot: esp. in phrases ***to plod away on*** (obs.), ***beat, pad, be upon the hoof***; to go on foot, to be on the move. ***to see a person's hoof in anything***, to trace or detect his influence or interference in a matter.

1598 SHAKS. *Merry W.* I. iii. 92 Goe, Trudge; plod away ith' hoofe: seeke shelter, packe. *c* **1645** HOWELL *Lett.* I. i. xvii. (1655) I. 25 A mischance befell the horse..insomuch that the Secretary was put to beat the hoof himself, and Foot

it home. *a* **1687** COTTON *Epistles* vi. Poems (Chalmers) 736 (Farmer) Being then on foot away I go And bang the hoof incognito. **1687** T. BROWN *Saints in Uproar* Wks. 1730 I. 78 We beat the hoof as pilgrims. **1713** DARRELL *Gentlem. Instr.* (ed. 5) II. vii. 167 A Man that is thus upon the Hoof can scarce find leasure for Diversion. **1750** WARBURTON *Doctr. Grace* xii. Wks. 1811 VIII. 399 The good man was.. forced to beat it on the hoof as far as Hernhuth in Germany. **1794** J. WOLCOTT (P. Pindar) *Poor Sold. Tilbury* Wks. 1812 III. 241 Thus Poverty and Merit beat the hoof. **1834** M. SCOTT *Cruise Midge* (1859) 300 Contriving.. to tread heavily on my toes with his own hoofs. **1838** DICKENS *O. Twist* ix, Charley Bates expressed his opinion that it was time to pad the hoof. **1860** THACKERAY *Round. Papers, Screens Dining-Rooms* (1863) 87, I once said to a literary gentleman,..'Ah! I thought I recognized your hoof in it'.

b. ***under the hoof***: trampled, downtrodden, under the oppression *of*.

1841 GEN. P. THOMPSON *Exerc.* (1842) VI. 25 He taunted the unfortunate Canadians while they were under the hoof. **1852** MRS. STOWE *Uncle Tom's C.* xxxv. 312 'I'd rather ten thousand times', said the woman, 'live in the dirtiest hole at the quarters than be under your hoof!' 'But you are under my hoof, for all that', said he.

5. *attrib.* and *Comb.* **a.** Simple attrib., as ***hoof-beat, -clang, -fall, -hold, -mark, -print, -stroke, -track, -tramp, -tread***; **b.** locative, as ***hoof-brittle, -cast, -loosened*** adjs.; instrumental, as ***hoof-pitted, -plod, -ploughed, -printed*** adjs.; similative, as ***hoof-button***; ***hoof-footed, -shaped*** adjs.; also ***hoof-like*** adj.

1847 LONGF. *Ev.* II. ii. 43 The *hoof-beats of fate. **1881** *Century Mag.* XXIII. 937/1 The hoofbeats came nearer.. over the sandy road. **1727** BRADLEY *Fam. Dict.* s.v., The Horse will at last grow to be Hoof bound, which dis-temper in the Hoofs as well as *Hoof brittle, *Hoof cast, malt Hug, &c., you may consult under their respective heads. **1705** *Lond. Gaz.* No. 4179/4 A great Coat..with black *Hoof Buttons. **1808** SCOTT *Marm.* II. Introd. 50 *Hoof-clang, hound, and hunters' cry. **1910** J. FARNOL *Broad Highway* II. xlvii, Nodding sleepily with every plodding *hoof-fall. **1923** H. SUTCLIFFE *Wrack o' Doom* ii, The broken lands that gave no *hoof-hold. **1802** BINGLEY *Anim. Biog.* (1813) I. 119 *note*, Their feet are armed with strong, blunt, and *hoof-like nails. **1727–41** CHAMBERS *Cycl.*, **Hoof-loosened*, is a dissolution or dividing of the horn or coffin of a horse's hoof from the flesh, at the setting on of the coronet. **1812** BYRON *Ch. Har.* I. xlix, Wide scatter'd *hoof-marks dint the wounded ground. **1821** CLARE *Vill. Minstr.* I. 204 Narrow *hoof-plod lanes. **1612** DRAYTON *Poly-olb.* xv. 243 In sacred Tempe..about the *hoofe-plow'd Spring. **1804** J. GRAHAME *Sabbath* 636 *Hoof-prints fill'd with gore. **1818** SCOTT *Hrt. Midl.* xxix, Avoid the soft ground, my lad; leave no *hoof-track behind you.

c. Special comb.: **hoof-and-mouth disease** = *foot-and-mouth disease*; **hoof and tongue sickness** = *foot-and-mouth disease* (*s.v.* FOOT *sb.* 35); **hoof-binding** = HOOF-BOUND *sb.*; **hoof-cushion** = *hoof-pad*; **hoof-footed** *a.*, having hoofs on the feet; **hoof-pad**, a pad or cushion to prevent a horse's foot or shoe from striking or cutting the fellow foot; **hoof-paring knife**, a farrier's knife with a recurved blade, for paring the hoofs of horses; **hoof-pick**, a hooked instrument for picking stones out of a horse's hoof; **hoof-rot** = *foot-rot* (*s.v.* FOOT *sb.* 35); **hoof-spreader** (see quot.); **hoof stick**, an instrument for manicuring the nails.

1887 LOWELL *Democr.* 11 Would it account for the phylloxera, and *hoof and-mouth disease, and bad harvests ..and the German bands? **1867** *Queenstown Free Press* 22 Jan. (Pettman), We have had a great deal of *hoof and tongue sickness amongst our cattle. **1727–41** CHAMBERS *Cycl.* s.v. *Horse-shoe*, Ponton, or Pantable shoe, which opens the heels, and helps *hoof-binding. **1721** BRADLEY *Philos. Acc. Wks. Nat.* 88 The general Heads..are, the Tallon-footed, the Claw-footed, the *Hoof-footed, and the double Hoof or Cloven-footed. **1890** *19th Cent.* Nov. 845 His comrades will borrow the tools of daily use, such as brushes, *hoof-picks, dusters. **1863** H. S. RANDALL *Pract. Shepherd* ii. 25 Scab and *hoof-rot, those dire scourges of the ovine race. **1893** W. B. E. MILLER et al. *Dis. Live Stock* v. 355 (*heading*) Hoof rot—foot rot. **1875** KNIGHT *Dict. Mech.*, **Hoof-spreader*, a device for expanding mechanically the hoof of a horse suffering from contraction of the foot. **1960** *Woman* 30 Jan. 15/2 First she lifts her cuticles gently with a *hoof stick. **1970** *Observer* 8 Feb. 36/7 Keep the cuticle free from the nail with a rubber hoof stick.

Hence ˈ**hoofish** *a.*, resembling that of a hoof, hoof-like; ˈ**hoofless** *a.*, without a hoof or hoofs.

1728 MORGAN *Algiers* I. iv. 99 After a Rain..their [Camels'] soft hoofless Feet being extremely apt to slip. **1862** MRS. CROSLAND *Mrs. Blake* II. 245 Beneath the hard, brute heel Whose hoofish tread yet leaves you leal. **1897** *Naturalist* 206 The hoofless reindeer with a prodigality of horn.

hoof (hu:f), *v.* [f. HOOF *sb.*]

1. a. *intr.* (Also *to hoof it.*) To go on foot; to foot it.

1641 [see *hoofing*, below]. **1685** CROWNE *Sir C. Nice* II. Dram. Wks. 1874 III. 283, I am growing a woman's ass.. and I must hoof it away with her load of folly upon my back. **1728** MORGAN *Algiers* I. iv. 98 Neither are their women and children (many of which hoof it over those Desarts..) very apt to lag behind. *a* **1852** MOORE *Case of Libel* v, And so my gentleman [the devil] hoofed about. **1877** J. HABBERTON *Jericho Road* i. 7 If we get stuck way up the river, so's we have to lay up all summer, and you have to hoof it in deep water. **1888** 'BUFFALO BILL' *Story of Wild West* 531, I finally concluded that my prospects were good for 'hoofing' the whole distance. **1910** W. M. RAINE *B. O'Connor* iv. 58 He hoofed it back to the cabin. **1923** BELLOC *Sonnets & Verse* 111 A score of stout fellows who..Hoofed it amain, Rain or no rain. **1958** S. ELLIN *Eighth Circle* (1959) II. xvii. 177 They hoofed it all the way down to Barrow Street. **1972** C. WESTON *Poor, Poor Ophelia* (1973) xvii. 109 Man's not very sick if he's out hoofing around that early.

b. To dance. (Also with *it.*) *slang.*

1925 *Amer. Speech* I. 36/2 A 'hoofing act' is entirely made up of step dancing. **1926** C. VAN VECHTEN *Nigger Heaven* 13 Le's hoof, Ruby urged. Le's sit down, Anatole commanded. **1928** *Daily Express* 2 July 11/5 Mr. Tommy Nolan proposed to his partner, Miss Anna King. She accepted him, and they planned their wedding and honeymoon while 'hoofing'. **1958** 'A. GILBERT' *Death against Clock* iii. 27 A pretty nifty dancer himself in his young days and still able to hoof it quite neatly. **1972** I. HAMILTON *Thrill Machine* xv. 64 She sings, she hoofs a little, she does some straight narration.

2. a. *trans.* To strike with the hoof.

1864 BUSHNELL *Christ & His Salvat.* i. (1865) 15 All horning or hoofing each other, as hungry beasts in their stall.

b. To dismiss, expel, eject. Usu. with *out.*

1893 FARMER & HENLEY *Slang* III. 340/2 To hoof out. **1905** *Daily Chron.* 22 Apr. 9/2 Well, at least we know for certain..that he was hoofed out of the Guards. **1915** V. WOOLF *Voyage Out* xxiii. 376 They've hoofed out the prostitute. **1924** GALSWORTHY *White Monkey* III. viii, A packer we had, who got hoofed for snooping books. **1928** D. L. SAYERS *Unpleasantness at Bellona Club* i. 8 They'd hoof me out of the Club if I raised my voice beyond a whisper. **1959** *Punch* 6 May 600/2 They hoofed the London Museum out of Lancaster House. **1973** 'B. MATHER' *Snowline* v. 60 The Bengali doctor came in at that stage and hoofed Mukkerjee out of it.

3. *colloq. South. U.S.* 'To kill (game) by shooting it on the ground' (*Cent. Dict.*).

Hence ˈ**hoofer** *slang* (orig. *U.S.*), a dancer; ˈ**hoofing** *vbl. sb.*, going on foot; provision of hoofs.

1641 BROME *Joviall Crew* III. Wks. 1873 III. 395, I am sorely surbated with the hoofing already. **1654** WHITLOCK *Zootomia* 479 As much as Riding differs from Hoofing. **1872** SPURGEON *Treas. Dav.* Ps. lxix. 31 The horning and hoofing are nothing to him, though to Jewish ritualists these were great points. **1923** *N.Y. Times* 9 Sept. VII. 2/1 *Hoofer*, a dancer, also a heel-beater. **1928** [see FEMME 1]. **1928** *Sunday Express* 8 Apr. 5/7 To-morrow Roy Lloyd, who was the hoofer in 'Broadway', takes up the part. **1936** 'J. TEY' *Shilling for Candles* vi. 59 The little Broadway hoofer was blossoming into the song-and-dance star. **1959** *News Chron.* 19 June 8/2 Holly..gets herself involved with a no-good hoofer in a low night club. **1969** *Daily Tel.* 17 Jan. 21/5 An orthodox tale of stage success: unknown girl hoofer becoming overnight hit by breaking all the Ziegfeld rules. **1973** *Sunday Express* 8 July 6/4 She was impressed by one of the male dancers... The one-time hoofer ended up by working for her for 40 years.

ˈ**hoof-bound**, *a.* (*sb.*) *Farriery.* Affected with a painful dryness and contraction of the hoof; having the shoe put on too tight, causing the horse to go lame. Also *sb.* as a name of the affection.

1598 FLORIO, *Incastellare*,..a horse to haue his hoofe dride vp,..to be hoofe-bound. **1610** MARKHAM *Masterp.* II. c. 382 The hoofe-bound is nothing else but a shrinking in of the whole hoofe in the vpper part thereof, making the skinne to stare aboue the hoofe, and to grow ouer the same. **1727–41** CHAMBERS *Cycl.* s.v. *Hoof*, If the heel be narrow and tender, the horse will in time grow hoof-bound.

hoofed (hu:ft, ˈhu:fɪd), *a.* and *ppl. a.* Also hooved (hu:vd). [f. HOOF *sb.* and *v.* + -ED.]

1. Having hoofs; ungulate; often in *comb.*, as *broad-, flat-, solid-hoofed.*

1513 DOUGLAS *Æneis* VII. xiii. 179 From the tempil of Diane euermo Thir horny hovit horssis bene debarrit. **1586** FERNE *Blaz. Gentrie, Lacies Nobil.* 24 A deere and all hooued thinges of that nature. **1607** TOPSELL *Four-f. Beasts* (1658) 225 Greece therefore yeeldeth choice Horses, and well hoofed. **1663** BUTLER *Hud.* I. i. 435 Cæsar's Horse..Was not by half so tender-hooft. **1766** PENNANT *Zool.* (1768) I. 8 Most of the hoofed quadrupeds are domestic. **1838–9** HALLAM *Hist. Lit.* IV. viii. IV. §16. 346 Quadrupeds he was the first to divide into ungulate and unguiculate, hoofed and clawed. **1883** E. ARNOLD *Pearls Faith* 64 Hooved like a mule he was.

2. Beaten with hoofs.

1860 DOBELL in *Macm. Mag.* Aug. 327 Peace..From hoofed and trampled sod She leaps transfigured to a god.

3. *dial.* Callous or horny like a hoof.

1828 *Craven Dial.*, *Hooved*, callous, horny, as the hands of labouring people,..made hard or horny, like a hoof.

hoofish, hoofless: see under HOOF *sb.*

hooflet (ˈhu:flɪt). [f. HOOF *sb.* + -LET.] A small hoof; one of the divisions of a cloven hoof.

1834 MACGILLIVRAY *Zoologists* 211 A crackling noise..is produced by the hooflets striking against each other. **1880** HAUGHTON *Phys. Geog.* vi. 283 Pliohippus, which has lost the small hooflets, and is otherwise very equine.

hoofy (ˈhu:fɪ), *a.* [f. HOOF *sb.* + -Y.] Having or characterized by a hoof or hoofs.

a **1674** HERRICK *Hesper.*, *Farew. Poetry* 84 And softely on With numerous feete to Hoofy Helicon. **1880** G. MEREDITH *Trag. Com.* iii. (1881) 30 In the semblance of the hairy, hoofy, snouty evil one.

Hence ˈ**hoofiness**. [After *handiness.*]

1843 CARLYLE *Past & Pr.* III. v, Its handiness mere *hoofiness.* **1857** RUSKIN *Pol. Econ. Art* i. 27 The horse, with its inferior brains and its awkward hoofiness, instead of handiness.

hoo-ha (ˈhu:hɑ:). *colloq.* Also hoo-hah, hou-ha. [Orig. unknown.] A commotion, a rumpus, a row.

The use in quot. 1932 seems to be without parallel.

1931 *Punch* 14 Oct. 402/1 The devil of a hoo-ha in the papers about increasing the demand for English-grown corn. **1932** T. S. ELIOT *Sweeney Agonistes* 30 You've had a cream of a nightmare dream and you've got the hoo-ha's coming to you. **1937** N. MARSH *Vintage Murder* vi. 63 He came up under cover of all the hoo-hah on the stage some time after the event. **1944** 'N. SHUTE' *Pastoral* ix. 206 There's a bit of a hoo-hah on about your tea-party. **1954** *Times Lit. Suppl.* 24 Sept., After all the hou-ha in the *Observer* about the death of the novel, perhaps we ought to be wearing a mourning-band. **1955** E. C. R. LORAC *Ask Policeman* xvii. 187 He could cut off home after the hoo-ha died down and claim his inheritance. **1959** B. GOOLDEN *For Richer, for Poorer* xiii. 232, I don't think Mummy will make much of a hoo-hah if she knows it's not for long. **1963** *Sunday Express* 15 Sept. 8/7 What has all the houha about the prodigious jump in productivity meant to the housewife? **1968** *Listener* 27 June 837/1 And there was a terrific hoo-ha over this because they all thought I should go and be a termination case or something. **1971** *Country Life* 27 May 1328/2 Some of these lovely irises may..be grown ..successfully without much hoo-ha.

hook (hʊk), *sb.*[1] Forms: 1 hóc (hooc), 2–4 hoc, 3–5 hok, ? 3, 4–6 hoke, 4 *Sc.* houk, howk, 4–6 *Sc.* huke, 5–7 hooke, (6 hoocke, 7 *Sc.* hwick), 7– hook. [OE. *hóc* = MLG. *hôk*, MDu. *hoec*, Du. *hoek*, MLG. *hôk* corner, angle, nook, point of land. In ablaut relation with OE. *haca* 'pessulus', a (? hooked) bolt, and app. also with MDu. *hake* (? *hâke*), Du. *haak*, OHG. *hâko*, *hâkko* (also *hâggo*), mod.Ger. *haken*, ON. *haki*, Sw. *hake*, Da. *hage* hook: see HAKE *sb.*[2]]

I. 1. a. A length of metal, or piece of wood or other material, bent back, or fashioned with a sharp angle, often forming a part of something, as a pole, chain, etc., adapted for catching hold, dragging, sustaining suspended objects, or the like. (Frequently with a qualification indicating shape or use, as *boat-hook, chain-hook, chimney-hook, clip-hook, fire-hook, flesh-hook, gaff-hook, hat-hook, meat-hook, pot-hook, tenter-hook*, etc.)

c **900** tr. *Bæda's Hist.* I. ix. [xii.] (1890) 46 þa..worhton him hocas, and mid þam tuȝan hi earmlice adun of þam wealle. *c* **1000** ÆLFRIC *Gloss.* in Wr.-Wülcker 107/9 *Arpago, uel palum*, hooc. *c* **1150** *Semi-Sax. Voc.* ibid. 548/21 *Uncinus*, hoc. *c* **1290** *S. Eng. Leg.* I. 195/57 Hokes and witthene he let nime: and faste to hire breoste binde. *c* **1325** *Gloss. W. de Biblesw.* in Wright *Voc.* 170 *Cliket a cerure*, lacche and hok. *c* **1375** *Sc. Leg. Saints, Katerine* 852 Quhelis ..of þe quhilkis þe felyis all with scharpe houkis fichit be sall. *c* **1440** *Promp. Parv.* 242/1 Hooke [*v.r.* hoke], *hamus, uncus.* **1485** *Naval Acc. Hen. VII* (1896) 49 Hokes to fish the Ankre with..leche hokes..catte hokes. **1495** *Ibid.* 195 Hokes to hange the ketylles with a chayne of yron to the same. **1568** GRAFTON *Chron.* II. 243 They had great hookes and grappelers of Iron to cast out of one Ship into another. **1694** BURTHOGGE *Reason* 158 There needs no more of Hooks and Crooks to make the Latter..to stick and hold together. **1774** GOLDSM. *Nat. Hist.* (1776) VI. 20 The Avosetta is chiefly found in Italy,..the bill..turns up like a hook, in an opposite direction to that of the hawk or the parrot. **1823** SCORESBY *Whale Fishery* 69 *note*, The ice-anchor is a large iron hook, nearly of the shape of the letter S. **1874** BOUTELL *Arms & Arm.* iii. 53 Sometimes, this axe has an edge on one side only, when on the other side it has either a hook or a hammer.

fig. **1581** PETTIE tr. *Guazzo's Civ. Conv.* I. (1586) 9 When ..assailed..with the temptation of pleasures..breaking in sunder those hookes. **1818** JAS. MILL *Brit. India* II. v. vi. 564 The hooks and handles, which the ensnaring system of law, administered by them, afforded in such abundance.

b. *Zool.* and *Bot.* A recurved and pointed organ or appendage of an animal or plant.

1666 J. DAVIES *Hist. Caribby Isls.* 84 His mouth is arm'd with two hard hooks extreamly sharp. **1834** MCMURTRIE *Cuvier's Anim. Kingd.* 376 All the joints of the tarsi are entire, and the hooks of the last present one or two indentations beneath. **1841–71** T. R. JONES *Anim. Kingd.* (ed. 4) 329 Jaws armed with strong and penetrating hooks for seizing and securing active and struggling prey. **1866** *Treas. Bot.* 415/2 The hooks of the Teazels come in contact with the surface of the cloth, and thus raise the nap. **1888** ROLLESTON & JACKSON *Anim. Life* 657 Chitinoid hooks are present in some *Taeniadae.*

c. *pl. slang.* The fingers or hands. So *to get one's hooks on* or *into*: to get hold of.

1829 W. MAGINN tr. *Vidocq's Mem.* IV. 261 To his clies my hooks I throw in. **1877** *Five Years' Penal Serv.* iv. 259 In a week or two a man can bring his hooks and feelers into full working trim again. **1917** E. WALLACE *Just Men of Cordova* x. 169 Put your lamps over my shiners, run your hooks over me Astrakhan collar. **1926** *S.P.E. Tract* XXIV. 122 *Get one's hooks on*, get hold of. **1930** 'E. QUEEN' *French Powder Myst.* xxvii. 230 About these volumes... I noticed a queer hesitancy on your part when I first got my hooks into them. **1954** J. POTTS *Go, Lovely Rose* viii. 41 Maybe he's eloped with that fat Lang dame. She's been trying to get her hooks into him all winter.

d. A thief, a pickpocket. *slang.* (Cf. HOOK *v.* 6, HOOKER[1] 1.)

1863 *Once a Week* IX. 555/1 The party who picks the pocket while the 'stiff-dropper' is attracting the victim's attention is called 'the hook'. **1885** M. DAVITT *Leaves from Prison Diary* I. xi. 106 *Hooks*, these individuals, who are also known as 'gunns' and 'buzzers', in prison slang, constitute the pickpocket class in its various specialities. **1901** *Westm. Gaz.* 4 Sept. 4/1 The very same 'hook' was caught..a second time red-handed at another station. **1926** N. LUCAS *London & its Criminals* xviii. 246 The 'hook' is the 'whizzer' who actually picks the pocket. **1935** A. J. POLLOCK *Underworld Speaks* 57/2 *Hook*, the pickpocket who does the actual stealing. **1968** G. J. BARRETT *Guilty, be Damned* x. 116 We've nothing on him. But then we've nothing on half the hooks in Eastport.

2. a. A slender bent piece of wire, usually armed with a barb, which is attached to a fishing-line and carries the bait; a fish-hook; an angle.

c **950** *Lindisf. Gosp.* Matt. xvii. 27 Gae to sæ and sende ongul *vel* hoc. *c* **1000** in Cockayne *Narrat. Angl. Conscr.* 40 Ic eom..swa swa fisc on hoce. *c* **1175** *Lamb. Hom.* 123 Alswa deð mahȝe fisce þe..ne isihȝ na þene hoc þe sticað on þan ese. *c* **1300** *Havelok* 752 Mani god fish ther inne he tok, Bothe with neth, and with hok. *a* **1450** *Knt. de la Tour* (1868) 59 As the fysshe that takithe his bayte upon an hoke. **1573–80** Baret *Alv.* H 610 The fish runneth to the hooke hidden with the baite. **1617** Moryson *Itin.* III. 37 No man will fish with a golden hooke for a halfe penny fish. **1657** R. Ligon *Barbadoes* (1673) 5 The Engine we took this great Shark with, was a large Hook, baited with a piece of Beef. **1728–46** Thomson *Spring* 412 Then fix, with gentle twitch, the barbed hook. **1840** F. D. Bennett *Whaling Voy.* I. 10 Birds we captured by hook and line, baited with fat meat. **1867** F. Francis *Angling* xiii. (1880) 463 The angler might see fish rising but be unable to bring them to hook.

b. *fig.* That by which any one is attracted or ensnared and caught; a snare; a catch. ***on the hook***: in various *fig.* uses, e.g. ensnared, in the power (of someone); in one's grasp; attached to some occupation, habit, etc. Cf. *off the hook* (sense 15 f below).

1430–40 Lydg. *Bochas* VI. i. (1554) 146 b, Marius layd out hoke and lyne As I haue told, Metellus to confound. *a* **1541** Wyatt *Poems, Renouncing of loue*, Farewell, Loue..Thy bayted hokes shall tangle me no more. *a* **1635** Naunton *Fragm. Reg.* (Arb.) 36, I am to seek wherefore he suffered Parry to play so long on the hook, before he hoysed him up. **1730** Bolingbroke *Hist. Eng.* xxiii. (R.), This Solomon catched at the bait which was thrown out to him, and hung fast on the hook for seven years together. **1893** Farmer *Slang, Hook*,..3..A catch; an advantage; an imposture. **1895** *Daily News* 2 Jan. 5/1 We often..have a perfectly visible hook offered to us, in a young lady, a speculation..or what not. **1927** H. Crane *Let.* 12 Aug. (1965) 304, I do hope that I can count on your assistance to the extent of the monthly amount until I can get something on my hook. **1932** L. C. Douglas *Forgive our Trespasses* xii. 233 Presently Angela was again on the hook in twenty score of composing-rooms. **1958** 'J. Brogan' *Cummings Rep.* xii. 126 She had made me wretchedly conscious of my shortcomings; that is how she had me on the hook. **1963** 'D. Rutherford' *Creeping Flesh* i. 72 'He really is on the hook.' 'The hook?' 'This drug habit.' **1970** G. F. Newman *Sir, You Bastard* ii. 60 Poor bastard might as well have been fined today as kept on the hook.

3. A curved instrument with a cutting edge.

a. An agricultural implement with a crescent-shaped blade and sharp inner edge for lopping or cutting, as a ***weed-hook***; esp. a reaping-hook.

A hook used to be distinguished from a sickle by having the edge finely serrated.

a **700** *Epinal Gloss.* 887 *Sarculum*, uueadhoc. *a* **1310** in Wright *Lyric P.* 41 He sende hem thider [to the vineyard] fol son, to helpen hem with hoc. *c* **1375** *Sc. Leg. Saints, Ninian* 94 Gyf he in sic corne cuth set huke. **1398** Trevisa *Barth. De P.R.* IX. xv. (1495) 356 Iulius is paynted with an hoke repynge corne. *c* **1440** *Promp. Parv.* 242/1 Hooke to hewe wode,..*sirculus*. **1513** Douglas *Æneis* VII. iv. 67 The crukit huik vndir his weid held he. **1523** Fitzherb. *Husb.* §29 Pees and benes be..reped or mowen of diuers maners, some with sickles, some with hokes, and some with staffe hokes. **1643** *Sc. Acts Chas. I* (1814) VI. I. 251, 2000 hwickis and 100 sythes for sheiring and mawing. **1744–50** W. Ellis *Mod. Husbandm.* IV. III. 42 Here [Sandwich] they cut their drilled field-pease with what they call Hooks and Hincks. **1851** *Illustr. Catal. Gt. Exhib.* 610 The reaping and bagging hooks are made of cast-steel. **1889** *Daily News* 8 Aug. 5/1 The old saying applied to the bad harvestman, 'A bad shearer never had a good hook'.

†**b.** *Naut.* (*pl.*) = sheer-hooks. *Obs.*

c **1385** Chaucer *L.G.W.* 641 *Cleopatra*, Among the ropis rennyth the scherynge hokys. *Ibid.* 646 He rent the seyl with hokys lyk a sithe. **1627** Capt. Smith *Seaman's Gram.* xii. 58 Some haue vsed sheare hookes, which are hookes like sickels fixed in the ends of the yards armes, that if a ship vnder saile come to boord her, those sheares will cut her shrouds, and spoile her tackling.

†**c.** An 'inside' tool. *Obs.*

1703 Moxon *Mech. Exerc.* 186 The Hook is used when the Work stands on the right or left side the Workman... And the Hook is made so as to cut on the right or left side.

4. a. The crook or pin on which a door or gate is hung; forming the fixed part of the hinge.

c **1325** *Gloss. W. de Biblesw.* in Wright *Voc.* 170 *Gouns*, hokes. *Verteveles*, the bondes of hokes. **1377** Langl. *P. Pl.* B. v. 603 Of almes dedes ar þe hokes þat þe gates hangen on. **1535** Coverdale *1 Kings* vii. 50 The hokes of yᵉ dores on the insyde of the house..were of golde. **1581** J. Bell *Haddon's Answ. Osor.* 147 b, He doth not heave the doores of the hookes. **1624** in *Naworth Househ. Bks.* (Surtees) 215 A hooke and thimble for the parke gate. **1784** R. Bage *Barham Downs* I. 126 They contented themselves with throwing gates off the hooks.

b. A hook upon which (in early models) the telephone receiver rested. (The expression is still used when the reference is to the cradle upon which a telephone rests.)

1885 *List of Subscribers* (United Telephone Co.) p. iii, When your bell rings..take the Telephone *off the hook*... Unless the telephone is *on* the hook, the Subscriber *cannot call* or *be called* by the Exchange. **1921** *Conquest* Jan. 126/3 On removing the receiver from the hook, the subscriber's line is connected to a selector. **1955** W. Gaddis *Recognitions* II. v. 508 Otto hung the receiver back on its hook. **1970** G. F. Newman *Sir, You Bastard* 262 Another phone crossed Sneed's mind, the one in his own flat with its receiver off the hook.

5. A bent metal appliance for fastening together two parts of a dress, on one of which it is fixed so as to catch in a loop or an 'eye' on the other. See also hook and eye.

1525 *Jests Widow Edyth* xii. (1573) G iv b, This wydow borowed..A Cap: an Hat, and three kerchieues therto, A cople of syluer pinnes, a payr of Hokes and no mo. **1530** Palsgr. 231/2 Hoke for a womans gowne, *agraffe*. *a* **1659** Cleveland *Poems, Poor Cavalier* 36 Thy Hooks and Buttons sprung with Sherburns Mine. **1895** *Advt.*, The only hook made to keep the dress in its place. **1896** Edith Thompson in *Monthly Packet* Christm. No. 91 She..wrenched open the fastenings of her black dress, breaking two hooks and a loop.

†**6.** A shepherd's crook. *Obs.*

1523 Fitzherb. *Husb.* §40 Lette the shepeherde take that shepe with his hoke. **1635–56** Cowley *Davideis* III. Wks. (1684) 89 Some drive the crowding Sheep with rural hooks. **1636** Massinger *Bashf. Lover* III. i, My scrip, my tar-box, hook, and coat, will prove But a thin purchase. **1697** Dryden *Virg. Past.* III. 150 From Rivers drive the Kids, and sling your Hook.

†**7.** The barb of an arrow; the fluke of an anchor. *Obs.*

c **1470** Henry *Wallace* IV. 553 Ane angell hede to the hukis he drew, And at a schoyt the formast sone he sleu. *a* **1605** Montgomerie *Misc. Poems* xxviii. 57 Eviry shaft thairof must needs To haif als mony heeds, And euirie head als mony huikis. **1627** May *Lucan* II. 753 The anchors made No noise, when from thicke sands their hookes are weigh'd.

8. *Shipbuilding.* A bent piece of timber used to strengthen an angular framework. Cf. *breast-hooks, fore-hooks*, and futtocks.

1611 Cotgr., *Four*,..a great peece of timber in the prowe of a Ship, called the Hooke. **1627** Capt. Smith *Seaman's Gram.* ii. 3 Your rising timbers are the hookes, or ground timbers and foot-hookes placed on the keele. **1678** Phillips (ed. 4), *Hooks of a Ship*, those forked Timbers which are placed upright on the Keel, both in the rake and run of the Ship. **1820** Scoresby *Acc. Arctic Reg.* II. 191 The fore part of the ice-beams, which butt against the hook,..diverge. *c* **1850** *Rudim. Navig.* (Weale) 124 *Hook of the Decks.* See *Breast-hooks*.

9. A sharp bend or angle in the course or length of anything; esp. a bend in a river (now in proper names). [Perh. in some cases influenced by Du. *hoek* corner, nook.]

1563–87 Foxe *A. & M.* (1684) II. 338 The very straight way that hath neither hook ne crook. **1662** Stillingfl. *Orig. Sacr.* III. ii. §15 In order to the making of such hooks and angles, which are necessary for the contexture of bodyes. **1670** Narborough *Jrnl.* in *Acc. Sev. Late Voy.* I. (1694) 67 For the Bay lies up in a little hook North-west. **1749** W. Douglass *Summary* I. 402 Cape Cod harbour, safe, and deep water; but from the hook or flexure..vessels with difficulty get out to sea. **1863** *N.E. Hist. & Gen. Reg.* XVII. 321 He was often at Hallowell Hook; so called from a peculiar bend in the river. **1877** *N.W. Linc. Gloss., Hook*, a bend in a river. Thus in the Trent are—Morton Hook, Amcotts Hook, etc.

10. a. A hook-shaped symbol or character; a 'pot-hook' as an element of handwriting.

1668 Wilkins *Real Char.* 377 The first Rank doth contain the Characters for the six more simple Vowels..the former three being meer Rounds, the other Hooks. *Ibid.* 388 Abstracts may be expressed by a Hook at the left end of the Character... The Active and Passive voice may be expressed, one of them by a Hook, and the other by a Loop, at the left end of the Character. **1867** Pitman *Man. Phonogr.* (ed. 12) 30 Initial *l* or *r* hooks. *Ibid.* 33, *n* hook..*f* or *v* hook. *Ibid.* 34, *-tion* hook.

†**b.** *pl.* Brackets (in printing), parentheses: formerly also called *crotchets* and *crooks*; also, inverted commas. *Obs.*

1680 G. Hickes *Spirit of Popery* Pref. 5 He hath left out all betwixt the Hooks. **1707** Hearne *Collect.* 10 Feb. (O.H.S.) I. 325 Words..in hooks are his own. **1732** Bentley *Pref. Milton's P.L.*, Printing them in the Italic letter, and inclosing them between two hooks. **1788** Mad. D'Arblay *Diary* Feb., As if he had pronounced a sentence in a parenthesis, between hooks. **1806** R. Cumberland *Mem.* (1807) I. 64 What is within hooks is of my own composing.

c. *Mus.* One of the lines or marks at the end of the stem of a quaver (♪), semiquaver (♬), etc.

1782 Burney *Hist. Mus.* (ed. 2) II. iv. 303 [Called] crotchets: a name given by the French with more propriety, from the hook or curvature of the tail, to the..Quaver. **1880** W. S. Rockstro in Grove *Dict. Mus.* I. 476/2 The Semiquaver was..subdivided into Demisemiquavers, with three Hooks, and Half-Demisemiquavers, with four.

d. *Logic. colloq.* A name for the sign ⊃, used as the implication sign (cf. horseshoe 2 f.). Also, more commonly, a reading of the sign: thus '$p \supset q$' is read '*p*, hook, *q*'.

In colloquial use among logicians since 1955 or earlier.

1967 R. Neidorf *Deductive Forms* 65 'If...then'..will be symbolized by a hook, ⊃. **1971** G. Hunter *Metalogic* 54 We shall call the tilde and the hook the connectives of P.

11. A projecting corner, point, or spit of land.

[app. a. Du. *hoek*, as in *Hoek van Holland* Hook of Holland; cf. also Fris. *hôk*, point or tongue of land.]

1600 Hakluyt *Voy.* III. 743 A hooke or headland. **1832** E. C. Wines *Two Years in Navy* i, We were kept off the hook, waiting either for wind or tide. **1855** Motley *Dutch Rep.* (1861) I. 21 This narrow hook of land, destined, in future ages, to be the cradle of a considerable empire. **1860** Bartlett *Dict. Amer.* (ed. 3), *Hook*..This name is given, in New York, to several angular points in the North and East Rivers; as, Corlear's Hook, Powle's Hook, Sandy Hook. **1862** Dana *Man. Geol.* IV. 663 The course of the outflowing currents..determines the position of the channels and sand-bars, and causes the prolongation of hooks off prominent capes.

†**12.** Applied with certain qualifications to a person: ***unhappy hook***, unhappy wight. *Obs.*

1526 Skelton *Magnyf.* 1390 All hokes unhappy to me haue resorte. **1556** Heywood *Spider & F.* xvii, Why hast thou..thou vnhappy hooke No conscience to be a periurde wretche? **1562** *Jack Jugler* (1820) 26 Loo yender cumithe that vnhappye hooke.

13. a. *Cricket.* The act of hooking: see hook *v.* 8 c.

1896 *Badminton Mag.* Sept. 278 Leg-hitting..has found a goodly representative in the 'hook', as invented by E. M. Grace. **1897** Lang in *Longm. Mag.* Oct. 503 Playing on the leg in all its variety of 'glances'..varied by the 'pull' and 'hook' to the undefended area of the ground. **1904** F. C. Holland *Cricket* 26 Short-pitched balls are best disposed of by a hook. **1948** E. W. Swanton *Denis Compton* i. 14 The hook (that is the leg-side hit off the back foot) is another and more orthodox favourite. **1972** *Observer* 23 Apr. 24/8 Two regal hooks by Cowdrey were matched in the next over by two lordly cover-drives from Dexter.

b. *Boxing.* A short swinging blow with the elbow bent. Also *transf.*

1898 *Daily News* 9 Nov. 8/5 After Smith had put a left hook on the chin the issue was not in doubt. **1910** J. Driscoll *Ringcraft* 94 It only needs practice to convince anyone that the straight blow will always get there before the swing or the hook. **1929** *Evening News* 18 Nov. 16/4 With a couple of left hooks to the head. **1945** *Diamond Track* (Army Board, N.Z.) 7/1 The Division carried out the outflanking movements, the celebrated 'left hooks' which forced the enemy out of the two great strongholds. **1961** B. Fergusson *Watery Maze* x. 251 Some of the Mediterranean landing-craft had already been promised to India, to help the British mount amphibious hooks down the coast of Arakan. **1971** *Daily Express* 17 Feb. 14/7 Salah..was pinned and punished by Clark's jabs and hooks.

c. *Golf.* The act of hooking.

1890 W. Simpson in H. G. Hutchinson *Golf* vi. 204 Press ever so little when your club is turned in and yourself over-reached, and the hook is certain.

II. Phrases.

14. ***by hook or (and) by crook***, †***with h. or c.***: by all or any means, fair or foul; by one device or another. Usually implying difficulty in attaining the thing sought, which may necessitate the use of special or extraordinary means.

As to the origin of the phrase there is no evidence; although invention has been prolific of explanatory stories, most of them at variance with chronology. The Wycliffite quots. are of somewhat doubtful date, and may be later than that from Gower, which has hepe (q.v.) for 'hook'.

c **1380** ? Wyclif *Wks.* (1880) 250 þei schulle bie hem wiþ pore mennus goodis wiþ hook or wiþ crok. *c* **1383** —— *Sel. Wks.* III. 331 þei sillen sacramentis..and compellen men to bie alle þis wiþ hok or crok. [**1390** Gower *Conf.* II. 223 What with hepe and what with croke They [false Witness and Perjury] make her maister ofte winne.] *a* **1529** Skelton *Col. Cloute* 1240 Nor wyll suffre this boke By hoke ne by croke Prynted for to be. **1551** Robinson *More's Utop.* I. (Arb.) 41 By one meanes therefore or by other, either by hooke or crooke, they must needes departe awaye. **1561** *Schole-ho. Wom.* 847 in Hazl. *E.P.P.* IV. 138 So at length, by huch or by cruch, Lesse or more, euer they craue, Until thy hand be in thy pouch. **1621** Burton *Anat. Mel.* I. ii. III. xv. (1651) 137 Some..care not how they come by it per fas et nefas, hooke or crook, so they have it. **1651** N. Bacon *Disc. Govt. Eng.* II. xiii. (1739) 69 Title enough for a great Man that resolved to hold by hook, what he had got by crook. **1778** Foote *Trip Calais* II. Wks. 1799 II. 348 If you could put us in a way, by hook or by crook, to get her out of the convent. **1833** Marryat *P. Simple* lii, If you can't gain it by *hook*, you must by *crook*. **1842** Geo. Eliot in *Life* (1885) I. 112 Do come by hook or by crook.

15. ***off the hooks***. (Cf. *off the hinges*, hinge *sb.* 5.) †**a.** Out of proper condition; out of order; 'in a bad way'. †**b.** Out of ordinary bounds, to excess. †**c.** Out of humour or spirits, 'put out'; 'not quite right'. *Obs.* **d.** Straight off, at once, summarily. **e.** ***to drop*** (etc.) ***off the hooks***, to die (*slang*). **f.** ***off the hook***: out of a difficult situation. Cf. *on the hook* (sense 2 b above).

a. ? **16..** *Songs Lond. Prentices* (Percy Soc.) 64 In all this long season they were off o' th' hook. *a* **1659** Cleveland *Pet. Poem* 22 My Doublet looks Like him that wears it, quite off o' the Hooks. **1684** H. More *Answer* 240 But the application is, methinks, much off the Hooks.

b. **1612** *North's Plutarch* 1214 Agrippina began..to flye off the hookes: and coming to Nero himself, threatned to take his Empire from him. **1621** Molle *Camerar. Liv. Libr.* III. vi. 167 In time of prosperitie proudly flie off the hookes. **1676** D'Urfey *Mad. Fickle* I. i. (1677) 7 My Brothers a little off the Hooks; but..'tis only the over-flow of Wit.

c. **1662** Pepys *Diary* 28 Apr., One thing that hath put Sir William so long off the hooks. **1665** *Ibid.* 26 May, The Duke of Albemarle..mightily off the hooks, that the ships are not gone out of the River. **1779** *Sylph* II. 98 The Baronet is cursedly off the hooks, from the idea of its transpiring. **1824** Scott *St. Ronan's* xxx, Everybody..is a little off the hooks..in plain words, a little crazy, or so.

d. **1860** Trollope *Castle Richmond* (Tauchn.) II. 350 (Hoppe) Baronets with twelve thousand a year cannot be married off the hooks.

e. **1840** H. Cockton *Life Valentine Vox* xii. 95 No man was ever able to write his own life complete. He's certain to go off the hooks before he has finished it. **1842** Barham *Ingol. Leg., Blk. Mousquet.* 11, Our friend..has popp'd off the hooks! **1862** Trollope *Orley F.* (Tauchn.) II. 192 (Hoppe) If he fatigues himself so much as that often, he'll soon be off the hooks. **1886** Mrs. Lynn Linton *Paston Carew* iii, He..was not far from eighty when he slipped off the hooks without an ache or pain. **1894** Blackmore *Perlycross* 293 Is it true that old Fox is dropping off the hooks? **1921** Galsworthy *To Let* I. i. 9 Old Timothy; he might go off the hooks at any moment. I suppose he's made his Will.

f. **1864** Trollope *Small House at Allington* II. xxix. 296 'Poor Caudle!' he said to himself; 'he's hooked, and he'll never get himself off the hook again.' **1954** J. Potts *Go, Lovely Rose* xii. 77 'It's an idea,' said Dr. Craig... It would

get Hartley off the hook, sure enough. **1962** M. URQUHART *Frail on North Circular* xxv. 140 Let Broadbent think he's off the hook and then give it another twist. **1966** *New Yorker* 25 June 49 Then he smiled, and I knew I was off the hook. **1969** A. GLYN *Dragon Variation* vii. 199 You mean she lost the kid? Well! Well, that sure lets old Walter off the hook!

16. a. ***on one's own hook***: in dependence on oneself or one's own efforts; on one's own account; at one's own risk. *colloq.*

1812 *Boston Gaz.* 23 Nov. (Th.), They forget that Rodgers himself says that he went upon his own hook. **1836** D. CROCKETT *Exploits & Adv. Texas* (1837) 13 But now I start anew upon my own hook. **1845** *N.Y. Herald* Oct. (Bartlett), The time is fast approaching when we shall have our American Pope..and American Catholic every thing, on our own hook. **1849** THACKERAY *Pendennis* lxix, Do we come out as Liberal Conservative, or as Government men, or on our own hook? **1852** MRS. STOWE *Uncle Tom's C.* xiv, 'I'm a thinkin, that every man'll have to hang on his own hook, in them ar quarters.' **1861** HUGHES *Tom Brown at Oxf.* ii, I thought to-day I would go on my own hook, and see if I couldn't make a better hand of it. **1899** J. LONDON *Let.* 30 Mar. (1966) 26 When I was just sixteen I broke loose and went off on my own hook. **1927** E. W. SPRINGS *Nocturne Militaire* vi. 178 You know a man has to be crazy to go after a balloon on his own hook. **1940** M. LOWRY *Let.* Spring (1967) 21 They objected to my going east on my own hook ..because they would not trust me. **1952** F. YERBY *Woman called Fancy* xvi. 307 I'm not going out of this house with you on my own hook.

b. ***to sling*** or ***take one's hook***: to go away, be off, decamp. *slang* or *dial.*

1874, 1897 [see SLING *v.*[1] 3 d]. **1885** O. ALLAN *Sinbad the Sailor* 22, I 'took the office' and I took my hook. **1886** M. PEACOCK *Tales Lindsey Folk-Speech* 106 An' soa he teks his hook back agaain to steam-hoose yard. **1890** KIPLING *Barrack-Room Ballads* (1892) 34 Before you sling your 'ook, at the 'ousetops take a look. **1892** 'F. ANSTEY' *Mr. Punch's Model Music-Hall Songs* 130 Take your 'ook while you can. **1928** *Daily Express* 10 May 7 Magistrate: How is your husband cruel to you? Wife: He will not speak to me, and he tells me to sling my hook. **1955** L. P. HARTLEY *Perfect Woman* xxii. 193 Anyhow, she's gone, walked out, slung her hook. **1959** [see BREEZE *sb.*[2] 3 b].

17. ***hook, line, and sinker***: completely, without reservations.

1838 G. W. PATTERSON in T. W. Barnes *Mem. T. Weed* (1884) v. 60 We are gone, hook, line, and sinker. **1865** *Weekly New Mexican* 25 Aug. 1/3 Without him Chavez [*sc.* a candidate for Congress] is gone hook, line, and sinker. **1924** WODEHOUSE *Bill the Conqueror* ii. 59 The old man swallowed those references of yours, hook line and sinker. **1936** N. COWARD *To-night at 8.30* II. 58, I fell for it hook, line and sinker. **1945** E. WAUGH *Brideshead Revisited* I. ii. 38 You, my dear Charles,..have gone straight, hook, line and sinker, into the very worst set in the University.

III. Attributive uses and combinations.

18. a. *attrib.* (or *adj.*) Shaped like or resembling a hook, hook-like, hooked, as ***hook-head, -shoulder, -tool***; HOOK-BILL, -NOSE; furnished with a hook, as ***hook block, bolt, ladder, rope, tackle***; parasynthetic, ***hook-backed, -beaked, -handed***, †***-nebbed, -shouldered*** adjs.; also HOOK-NOSED.

1847–78 HALLIWELL, *Hook-backed, hump-backed, crooked. **1875** KNIGHT *Dict. Mech.*, **Hook-block*, a pulley-block strapped with a hook, in contradistinction to one with an eye or a tail. **1899** *Hook-bolt [in *N.E.D.*]. **1923** *Man. Seamanship* (H.M.S.O.) II. 300 It will be necessary [during salvage operations] to drill a few extra holes for hook bolts which will be used to secure the patch temporarily to the ship's side... The hook bolts are shipped in the holes ready for use. **1940** *Chambers's Techn. Dict.* 421/2 *Hook bolt*, a galvanised-iron bolt formed out of rod which is bent at one end into a hook serving as the head, and threaded at the other to take a nut; used for fixing corrugated sheeting. **1956** *Archit. Rev.* CXIX. 213/1 For fixing to metal purlins, a standard range of hook-bolts and U-bolts is available. *a* **1637** B. JONSON *Underwoods, Epigr. to Counsellor*, *Hook-handed harpies. **1756** ROLT *Dict. Trade, Hook-pins*, in architecture, are taper iron pins, only with a *hook-head, to pin the frame of a roof or floor together. **1519** *Churchw. Acc. St. Giles, Reading* 5 For sises pynnes and *hoke naylles. ?*a* **1400** *Morte Arth.* 1082 *Huke-nebbyde as a hawke. **1495–7** *Naval Acc. Hen. VII* (1896) 271 *Hoke ropes for fyssyng of ankers. **1801** NELSON 15 Aug. in Nicolas *Disp.* (1845) IV. 460 To be furnished with stout hook-ropes, to be the more ready to take them in tow. *a* **1678** MARVELL *Poems, On hill at Billborow*, Ye mountains Which do with your *hook-shoulder'd height The earth deform, and heaven fright.

b. objective and obj. gen., as ***hook-bearer, -bender***; **c.** similative, etc., as ***hook-crooked, -like, -shaped, -winged*** adjs.; **d.** instrumental and locative, as ***hook-armed*** adj., ***-fishing, -swinging***.

1627 MAY *Lucan* I. 456 The Belgæ *hooke-arm'd Chariots expert-guiders. **1883** *Fisheries Exhib. Catal.* 363 Various Tools for manufacturing Fishing Tackle and Gear, such as *Hook-benders [etc.]. *c* **1611** SYLVESTER *Du Bartas* II. iv. IV. *Decay* 883 With *hook-crookt hands upon the smoothest crawling. **1745** ELLIS *Mod. Husb.* VI. II. 67 Those poor People..may have the single Engines for *Hook-fishing fixed within their Houses. **1841** J. JOHNSON tr. *Van der Donck's New-Netherlands* in *N.Y. Hist. Soc. Coll.* 2nd Ser. I. 177 Those the people call weak crabs, and they make excellent bait for hook fishing. **1851** *Illustr. Catal. Gt. Exhib.* IV. 926/1 Hook-fishing is within 3 fathoms, either in the river or in open sea. **1616–61** HOLYDAY *Persius* 323 A *hook-like bearded dart. **1874** BOUTELL *Arms & Arm.* vi. 91 Projecting hook-like barbs. **1834** MEDWIN *Angler in Wales* I. 317 *Hook-shaped prickles. **1891** *Pall Mall G.* 18 Nov. 2/2 The horrible ceremony of '*hook-swinging',..the swinging aloft at the end of a long pole, for over an hour, of a man by means of two iron hooks embedded in the muscles of his back. **1894** *Daily News* 15 Nov. 5/3 The Government of Madras has passed orders giving Magistrates power to prevent..hook-swinging in the Southern Presidency. **1905** *Spectator* 7 Jan. 12/1 Every autumn the great coffee-coloured, *hook-winged skua-gulls come down from the North and patrol the midway air. **1939** L. MACNEICE *Autumn Jrnl.* vi. 27 A vulture hung in air..His hook-winged shadow wavered. **1968** T. KINSELLA *Nightwalker* 17 Hook-winged geese or hawks.

19. Special combs.: **hook and butt, hook-butt**, 'a mode of scarfing timber so that the parts resist tensile strain to part them' (Knight); **hook-and-ladder** *U.S.*, apparatus consisting of ladders and hooks used by firemen; often *attrib.*; **hook-book**, a book with flannel or parchment leaves in which anglers keep their hooks; **hook-climber**, a plant that climbs by means of its own hooklets, as members of the genera *Galium* and *Rubus*; **hook gauge**, an instrument for accurately determining the surface level of water and consisting of a hook and pointer attached to a fixed vernier, the hook being brought up until its tip just pierces the surface of the water; **hook-heal**, a name for Self-heal, *Prunella vulgaris*; **hook-hit** = 13 b above; **hook-ladder**, a ladder with hooks at one end by which it can be suspended; †**hook-land**, land ploughed and sown every year; †**hookman**, a manufacturer of fish-hooks; **hook-money**, a currency formerly in vogue in Ceylon, consisting of pieces of silver twisted into the form of fish-hooks; **hook-penny** (*Sc.*), a penny received by reapers every week in addition to the ordinary wages; **hook-pin**, a taper iron pin with a hooked head to pin the frame of a roof or floor together; a draw-pin; **hook-pot** (see quot. *a* 1865); **hook rug** = *hooked rug*; **hook-scarf, hook-scarf-joint** = *hook-butt*; **hook-seam** (see quot.); **hook shop** *slang*, a brothel; **hook-shot** *Basketball*, a twisting shot started when the player has his back to the basket and completed as he pivots round towards the basket; **hook-squid**, a decapodous cephalopod of the family *Onychoteuthididæ*, having long tentacles armed with hooks, the bases of which are furnished with suckers; **hook stroke** *Cricket*, a stroke made by hitting a short-pitched ball, after it has risen, round to leg with a horizontal swing of the bat; **hook-sucker**, a fish that takes a hook or bait with a sucking motion (*Cent. Dict.*); **hook-swivel**, the swivel of a gorge-hook; **hook tender** *N. Amer.* (see quot. 1905); **hook-tip**, a moth of the genus *Platypteryx*, having the tips of the wings hook-shaped; **hook-ward**, a ward of a lock having the shape of the letter L; †**hook-ware**, tools used in reaping; **hook-weed**, same as *hook-heal*; **hookwise** *adv.*, after the fashion, or in the manner of a hook; **hook-wrench**, a spanner with a bent end adapted to grasp and turn a nut or coupling piece.

1821 *Minutes Boston* (Mass.) *Selectmen* XXXIX. 187 Mr. George G. Channing..declines taking command of the Fire *Hook & Ladder company. **1865** *Chambers's Jrnl.* 29 July 469/2, 18 hook-and-ladder trucks. **1902** *Westm. Gaz.* 11 June 8/1 Other Americans pointed with pride to their hook-and-ladder system, which forms such an important aid to the New York fireman. **1909** *Strand Mag.* Apr. 363 There stood the engines and the 'hook-and-ladder'. **1949** *Los Angeles Times* 18 May 8/1 The Fire Department obligingly backed up a hook-and-ladder truck. **1859** SALA *Gas-light & D.* x. 118 The parchment *hook-books of the gentlemen fishermen. **1897** WILLIS *Flower. Pl.* I. 177 In the tropics many *hook-climbers grow to a great size and have stem- or leaf-structures modified into hooks. **1875** *Jrnl. Franklin Inst.* XCIX. 250 The depth on the weir was observed by means of a *hook-gauge. **1880** *Encycl. Brit.* XII. 477/2 The hook gauge used first by Mr. U. Boyden of Boston, in 1840. **1934** H. ADDISON *Text Bk. Appl. Hydraulics* xv. 304 Hook and point gauges. These are the simplest and most reliable gauges for measuring ranges of head not exceeding about 3 ft. (60 cms.) with a probable error of 1/1500 ft. (0·2 mm.). **1578** LYTE *Dodoens* I. xx. 133 The second kinde is also called ..in English Prunell..*Hooke heale. **1727** BRADLEY *Fam. Dict.* s.v. *Cut*, Take some Prunel or Hook-heal. **1890** R. G. A. ALLANSON-WINN *Boxing* (ed. 2) ix. 43 There is another half-arm hit, called the '*hook-hit', in which the elbow is not so much bent as it is with the real 'contracted-arm'. **1919** G. B. SHAW in *Manch. Guardian* 1 Nov. 7/6 He missed that chance of a hook hit at the white chokers. **1858** SIMMONDS *Dict. Trade*, *Hook-ladder. **1905** *Westm. Gaz.* 17 Oct. 7/1 The escape was rushed up, ladders extended, hook-ladders placed into position. **1972** *Times* 20 Sept. 3/3 Window cleaners..made their final assault on the upper storeys by jumping out of windows..by lowering a hook ladder from the summit. **1669** WORLIDGE *Syst. Agric.* (1681) 56 That Land which is so often tilled, which they call *Hook-land. **1706** PHILLIPS (ed. Kersey), *Hook-land, or Ope-land.* **1658** ROWLAND *Moufet's Theat. Ins.* 946 We have some bold bragging *hookmen..that ascribe it to their own invention. **1801** C. KEITH *Har'st Rig* cxxi. *note*, **Hook-penny*, which each shearer is in use to ask and receive weekly over and above their pay. **1637–8** in Willis & Clark *Cambridge* (1886) I. 94 Ashpoles for levers and *hookepinnes. **1703** MOXON *Mech. Exerc.* 123 The Hook-Pin is..to pin the Frame of a Floor, or Frame of a Roof together, whilst it is framing. *a* **1865** SMYTH *Sailor's Word-Bk.* (1867) 388 **Hook-pots*, tin cans fitted to hang on the bars of the galley range. **1886** R. BROWN *Spunyarn & Spindrift* v. 66 A hook-pot of tea a-piece. **1896** *Idler* Mar. 173/1 There you'd see them crowding about the doors at meal-times, flourishing their hook-pots. **1913** J. MASEFIELD *Daffodil Fields* 33 Tin dishes, sailors' hookpots. **1951** T. CAPOTE *Grass Harp* (1952) i. 12 There was a *hook rug on the floor. **1967** E. SHORT *Embroidery & Fabric Collage* iii. 83 The canvas [is] the one normally used for hook rugs, i.e. three holes to the inch. **1793** SMEATON *Edystone L.* §268 To be united to each other by *Hook-Scarf-Joints, so as to compose, in effect, one stone. **1828** *Craven Dial.*, **Hook-seams*, hooks or paniers to carry turf, lead, etc.; now nearly extinct, since the improvement of roads. **1889** BARRÈRE & LELAND *Dict. Slang* I. 473/1 **Hook shop*, a brothel. **1935** A. J. POLLOCK *Underworld Speaks* 57/2 *Hook shop*, a house of ill fame. **1954** J. STEINBECK *Sweet Thursday* vi. 49 This kid could be pure murder in a hook-shop. **1957** *Encycl. Brit.* III. 181B/1 Farther out..players use a one-hand shot from a stride, jump or standing position, and a *hook shot which is overhead. **1969** Z. HOLLANDER *Mod. Encycl. Basketball* 43 Washington, led by hook-shot artist Jack Nichols, defeated Oregon State. **1969** *New Yorker* 14 June 79/1 You go through Harlem and you'll see kids less than five feet tall with pretty good jump shots and hook shots. **1897** K. S. RANJITSINHJI *Jubilee Bk. Cricket* 175 Batsmen of the old school very much disliked the *hook-stroke on principle. **1908** *Daily Chron.* 15 May 8/2 He began exploiting the full drive and the hook stroke. **1911** C. B. FRY in P. F. Warner *Bk. Cricket* 226 Ranjitsinhji found almost as little difficulty in making his famous 'hook strokes'. **1945** N. CARDUS *Eng. Cricket* 38 Maclaren was the grand manner personified; with his hook-stroke he dismissed the fastest ball from his presence. **1893** *Atlantic Monthly* Feb. 196/1 Each man, being hired for a definite purpose, as chopper, *hook-tender, barker, [etc.]..keeps closely to his own job. **1901** *Daily Colonist* (Victoria, B.C.) 3 Nov. 5/2 Seventy-five cents was taken off hook-tenders and other men not necessarily expert. **1905** *Terms Forestry* (U.S. Dept. Agric.) 40 *Hook tender*, the foreman of a yarding crew; specifically, one who directs the attaching of the cable to a turn of logs. **1966** *Sun* (Vancouver) 12 Jan. 25/5 Moore said the industry needs more managers, logging operators, hook-tenders..'and even chokermen'. **1819** G. SAMOUELLE *Entomol. Compend.* 254 *Hooktip moths. **1869** E. NEWMAN *Brit. Moths* 205 The boundary line between the two colours is straight in the Hook-tips. *Ibid.* 206 The Scalloped Hook-tip. **1688** R. HOLME *Armoury* III. 301/2 **Hookward*, any cross Ward that cometh out from it [the Key]. **1541** *Aberdeen Reg.* V. 17 (Jam.) Tar, pik, hemp, irn, & *huik-wair. **1861** MISS PRATT *Flower. Pl.* IV. 205 Carpenter's-Herb, Sickle-wort, and *Hookweed. **1597** A. M. tr. *Guillemeau's Fr. Chirurg.* 16 b/2 A Spatula, may be vsede in place of a privet..and the same being *hookwise, is called Agrimeles.

hook, *sb.*[2] *local.* [Variant of HUCK *sb.*[1]] The projecting upper part of the thigh bones of cattle near the hip-joint. Also **hook-bone**. Cf. HUCK *sb.*[1] and HUCKLE-BONE.

1808 T. H. HORNE *Compl. Grazier* (ed. 3) 9 The roof [of a bull ought to be] wide, particularly over the chine and hips, or hooks. **1844** H. STEPHENS *Bk. Farm* II. 161 Between the shoulders and the hook. *Ibid.* III. 1253 The broad hook-bones, with the narrow chest, are not entirely occasioned in cows by calf-breeding. **1858** C. L. FLINT *Milch Cows* 17 The Ayrshire farmers prefer their dairy bulls..broad at the hook-bones and hips, and full in the flanks. **1900** *Westmorland Gaz.* 3 Feb., Advt. (E.D.D.), Strayed, two Herdwick ewes; marked red pop near shoulder and near hook. **1935** *Amer. Speech* X. 271/1 *Hooks*, hip bones of a cow. **1960** *Farmer & Stockbreeder* 8 Mar. 95/2 As is good breadth between the hookbones.

hook (huk), *v.* [f. HOOK *sb.*[1]]

1. *trans.* To make hook-like or hooked; to bend, crook, incurve. *rare.*

a **1250** *Owl & Night.* 377 ȝif hundes urneþ to him ward He ..hokeþ paþes swiþe narewe. **1483** *Cath. Angl.* 191/2 To Huke, *hamare.* **1570** LEVINS *Manip.* 159/32 To Hooke, *incuruare.* **1598** FLORIO, *Vncinare*, to hooke, to crooke.

2. *intr.* To bend or curve sharply; to have a hooked shape.

c **1420** *Pallad. on Husb.* IV. 202 It is so ferd of oiles, that therfro Hit hoketh, yf me sette it nygh thervnder. **1601** HOLLAND *Pliny* XIX. v, Melons cannot abide oile..let oile stand the like distance from them, shrink they wil from it, and hook upward. **1665** SIR T. HERBERT *Trav.* (1677) 383 Her bill hooks and bends downwards. **1704, 1774** [see HOOKING *ppl. a.* 2].

3. *intr.* To move with a sudden turn or twist. Now *slang* or *dial.* To make off. Also ***to hook it*** and (N.Z.) ***to hook off***.

c **1400** *Destr. Troy* 4621 All the company enclinet, cairyn to ship..Hokit out of hauyn, all the hepe somyn. **1824** W. IRVING *T. Trav.* II. 243 He..was always hooking about on mysterious voyages. **1851** MAYHEW *Lond. Labour* (1861) II. 137 (Farmer) He slipped from her and hooked it. **1862** H. KINGSLEY *Ravenshoe* III. xi. 184 When the experienced hunter sees him doing that, he, so to speak, 'hooks it'. **1886** BARING-GOULD *Crt. Royal* I. iii. 37 Hook up the steps, if you please. **1886** —— *Gold. Feath.* viii. 20 Anything does to burn ..human creatures as well, if they don't hook out of the windows. **1938** F. S. ANTHONY in D. M. Davin *N.Z. Short Stories* (1953) 219, I hooked off on my own and rambled aimlessly about. **1940** F. SARGESON *Man & Wife* (1944) 75 If Ted saw her coming up the road he'd hook off if he could before she got near. And if he couldn't I'd hook off while they had their barney.

4. a. *trans.* To lay hold of or grasp with a hook; to make fast, attach, or secure with a hook or hooks, or in the manner of a hook; to connect or fasten together with hooks, or hooks and eyes.

1611 COTGR., *Haver*,..to hooke, or grapple with a hooke. *c* **1626** *Dick of Devon* IV. i. in Bullen *O. Pl.* II. 63 Now the word is 'Come, hooke me'..the needle lance knights..put so many hookes and eyes to every hose and dubblet. **1634** HEYWOOD *Maydenh. Well Lost* I. Wks. 1874 IV. 112 At last we came to hooke our ladders, and By them to skale. **1682** N. O. *Boileau's Lutrin* IV. 222 A third..Had not due time to hook his dropping Breeches! **1710** J. CLARKE *Rohault's Nat. Phil.* (1729) I. xxii. 135 Their Particles are so hooked together, that they may be bent any way. **1820** SCORESBY

Acc. Arctic Reg. II. 287 When the harpoon..slipped out.. it luckily hooked the lines belonging to another boat. **1895** *The Season* Mar. 84 Stuff put plain or pleated over lining hooked down the middle in front. *Ibid.* 95 Cape hooked over at the side.

b. ***to hook on, in, up,*** to attach by means of a hook, e.g. a horse to a vehicle, etc.

1825 J. NICHOLSON *Operat. Mechanic* 428 There are many other ways by which the hooking up of the yarns may be effected. **1835** MARRYAT *Jac. Faithf.* xxxvii, Maintop, there, hook on your stays. **1844** MRS. HOUSTON *Yacht Voy. Texas* I. 5 After being hooked on to a steamer, we were tugged rapidly down the river. **1875** W. S. HAYWARD *Love agst. World* 16 They saw a horse hooked up to the post of the inn. **1883** *Chicago Advance* 23 Aug., The livery man hooked up for us as fine a team. **1897** *Cavalry Tactics* xvi. 112 The breast-harness horses in the cavalry ranks should be hooked in.

c. To make (rugs) with a hook: see HOOKED *a.* 4. *U.S.*

1882 *Harper's Mag.* Dec. 126/1 Cynthy Ann..hooked rugs from early in the morning until late into the night. **1945** B. MACDONALD *Egg & I* 66 A time to repair machinery, hook rugs, patch quilts, mend harness and perform other leisurely tasks.

d. *intr.* To use a crochet needle.

1854 C. M. YONGE *Castle Builders* vi. 81 Miss Townsend ..hooked away with her crochet needle.

e. ***to hook up***: to establish a link *with*, to make a connection *with*. Also const. *to*, and with direct object. Cf. HOOK-UP.

1925 H. CRANE *Let.* 27 Oct. (1965) 218 They want to hook the book up with an illustrious name. **1929** WODEHOUSE *Mr. Mulliner Speaking* v. 172 What I would propose is that we take a short cut through the fields to the station, hook up with the five-fifty express at Goresby, [etc.]. **1943** E. C. WICKS et al. *Shopwork* vi. 113 Whenever electricity is needed for any purpose, the particular job must be wired or 'hooked-up' to feed the electrical current to the necessary place. **1953** P. C. BERG *Dict. New Words* 94/1 *Hook-up*, v.t., to connect two or more broadcasting systems for the time needed to broadcast a common item on their otherwise different programmes. **1971** *Ink* 12 June 12/1 David Mercer's moving and intelligent portrait of a Marxist drama critic who can't hook up his ideology with his unresolved feelings towards his impossible working-class father. **1971** M. TAK *Truck Talk* 84 *Hook up*, to couple a tractor to a trailer. **1972** *Edmonton* (Alberta) *Jrnl.* 31 Aug. 3/4 RCMP and city police forces in Alberta have begun hooking up to a national computer system.

5. a. *intr.* (for *refl.*) To attach oneself or be attached with or as with a hook; to be coupled. ***hook on*** (fig.): to join on; to be consequent or continuous.

1597 SHAKS. *2 Hen. IV*, II. i. 175 Go with her, with her: hooke-on, hooke-on. **1774** C. J. PHIPPS *Voy. N. Pole* 181 Two small steel rods..hook into the ends of this board. **1777** SHERIDAN *Trip Scarb.* I. ii, If it had been tighter, 'twould neither have hooked nor buttoned. **1847** THACKERAY *Brighton in 1847* i, He hooked on to my arm as if he had been the Old Man of the Sea. **1885** T. A. GUTHRIE *Tinted Venus* viii. 93 Haven't you missed out a lot, sir?.. because it don't seem to me to hook on quite.

b. Usu. in pa. pple. ***hooked*** (*on*): addicted (to), captivated (by). *slang.*

1925 *Writer's Monthly* June 486/2 *Hooked*, to become a drug addict. **1931** D. RUNYON *Guys & Dolls* (1932) vi. 115 Waldo Winchester is hooked. **1953** W. BURROUGHS *Junkie* (1972) 11, I drifted along taking shots when I could score. I ended up hooked. *Ibid.* vi. 61 When you are hooked, the effects are not dramatic. **1964** *Daily Tel.* 25 Nov. 22/6 The chances are that he is hooked on opium, morphine or heroin. **1965** *New Statesman* 16 Apr. 620/3 Other cities have admirers, even lovers, but Liverpool has only addicts: either you are hooked the very first time you step out of Lime Street Station to be confronted by the bulk of St George's Hall, or you never get the message. **1966** E. MCGIRR *Funeral was in Spain* 137 She was half-way to being hooked: one of the punks she was with was a pusher. **1967** M. M. GLATT et al. *Drug Scene* ii. 21 Once you're registered, you're hooked. It's too depressing when you're hooked, besides a girl looks terrible on heroin. **1967** *New Scientist* 25 May 478 Hopes that the millions of men and women 'hooked' on tobacco may soon be able to satisfy their craving with a 'safe' cigarette are not supported by the facts. **1970** *Daily Tel.* 8 May 3/2 Hundreds of domestic pets die each year after becoming 'hooked' on slug bait.

6. *trans.* To snatch with a hook; to seize by stealth; to steal, pilfer. Cf. HOOKER¹ 1.

1615 TOMKIS *Albumazar* III. iii. in Hazl. *Dodsley* XI. 359 Picking of locks, or hooking clothes at windows. **1627–77** FELTHAM *Resolves* I. x. 14 Like Thieues, that hooking for clothes in the dark, draw the Owner which takes..them. **1631** WEEVER *Anc. Fun. Mon.* 47 To hooke or draw any thing from thence, is a sinne. **1785** BURNS *Jolly Beggars* Recitat. iv, Monie a pursie she had hooked. **1857** *N.Y. Tribune* (Bartlett), A maid hooked one of her mistress's dresses the other day. **1884** MARK TWAIN *Huckleb. Finn* xxx. 312 (Farmer) To hook the money and hide it.

7. a. To catch (a fish) with a hook: applied both to the external use of a large hook, and to that of the baited hook which is swallowed.

[**1700** WALLIS in *Collect.* (O.H.S.) I. 326 This bait..is to hook-in somewhat else.] **1771** MRS. GRIFFITH tr. *Viaud's Shipwreck* 178 A few small flounders, which are hooked up out of the water, with a sort of harpoon. **1772–84** COOK *Voy.* (1790) V. 1831 This day we hooked plenty of fine cod. **1885** W. C. SMITH *Kildrostan* I. i. 227 It is not every fish you hook that comes to the creel.

b. *fig.* To catch, secure, *e.g.* as a husband, etc.

a **1800** T. BELLAMY *Beggar Boy* (1801) II. 97 He was anticipating..the young spendthrifts whom he hoped to hook at the gaming-table. **1848** THACKERAY *Van. Fair* iv, The first woman who fishes for him, hooks him. **1893** F. J. FURNIVALL *Child-Marriages* Pref. 49 A man trying to hook a well-off widow.

c. To solicit as a prostitute. Cf. HOOKER¹ 4. *slang.*

1959 'E. MCBAIN' *Killer's Wedge* (1961) vi. 57 She's been in the city for almost a year, Pete. Hooking mostly. **1965** —— *Doll* (1966) v. 66 The girl was a prostitute... The girl had been hooking in the neighborhood for little more than a week. **1969** DISCH & SLADEK *Black Alice* v. 53 Bessie's girls didn't have to go out hooking in hotel lobbies or honkytonks, no indeedy. **1971** W. HANLEY *Blue Dreams* xix. 313 A high-class hooker couldn't be entirely without redeeming social value. Especially one who..taught English and hooked on the side.

8. *transf.* and *fig.* **a.** To catch hold of and draw as with a hook; to drag. **b.** To attach as with a hook.

1577 STANYHURST *Descr. Irel.* i. (R.), Neighbourhood bred acquaintance, acquaintance waffed in the Irish toong, the Irish hooked with it attire. **1611** SHAKS. *Wint. T.* II. iii. 7 The harlot-King Is quite beyond mine Arme..but shee, I can hooke to me. *a* **1661** FULLER *Worthies* (1840) I. 560 A Dictionary, or Vocabulary, hooking all words..within the compass thereof. *a* **1677** BARROW *Pope's Suprem.* (R.), There is nothing which each of these powers will not hook within the verge of its cognizance and jurisdiction. **1764** WESLEY *Wks.* (1872) III. 199 He hooked me, unawares, into a little dispute. **1842** TENNYSON *Day-dream, Moral* ii, If I Should hook it to some useful end.

c. In *Golf*, To drive (the ball) widely to the left hand. In *Cricket*, To play (the ball) round from the 'off' to the 'on' side without hitting it at the pitch. = DRAW *v.* 14; cf. *hook stroke* (HOOK *sb.*¹ 19). Also *absol.*

1857 *Chambers's Inform.* II. 695 (Golf) When standing too far, the ball is apt to be 'drawn' or 'hooked'—that is to say, struck with the point or 'toe' of the club, in which case the ball flies in to the left. **1896** *Badminton Mag.* Oct. 482 Gregory, in attempting to hook Peel, put the ball straight into Richardson's hands. **1897** A. LANG in *Longman's Mag.* Oct. 503, I remember Mr. Fry returning a simple ball as a yet simpler catch to bowler in his first over, all because he tried to hook it. **1898** C. B. FRY in *Windsor Mag.* June 26/1 His cutting and hooking are second only to Ranji's. **1898** K. S. RANJITSINHJI *With Stoddart's Team* (ed. 3) iii. 50 He [*sc.* C. Hill] seemed able to 'drive', or 'hook', or 'glance'..with equal skill and success. **1904** [see COVER *sb.*¹ 1 d]. **1955** [see BOUNDARY 2 b]. **1955** *Times* 9 May 15/2 Then, when he must have been looking ahead to a century, he was leg-before-wicket hooking at Heine. **1972** 'J. ROSS' *Here lies Nancy Frail* xii. 145 I'm bloody useless with a two wood... I hook like hell with it.

d. *Boxing.* To strike (one's opponent) a swinging blow with the elbow bent (cf. HOOK *sb.*¹ 13 b). Also *absol.*

1898 *Daily News* 24 Nov. 8/3 Corbett hooked with his right hard on Sharkey's jaw. **1910** J. DRISCOLL *Ringcraft* 86 Wild attempts to hook him on his well protected jaw. **1973** *Times* 14 Feb. 9/3 Bugner..clubs rather than hooks.

e. *Rugby Football.* To secure (the ball) with the foot, as hooker, when it is placed in the scrummage. Also *intr.*

1906 GALLAHER & STEAD *Compl. Rugby Footballer* vii. 110 In Britain it is the custom to hook the ball in the scrum with the outside feet crossing over those on the inside. **1913** *Daily Graphic* 24 Mar. 15/1 D. A. Greer..may be of use to Ireland henceforward, especially as 'hooking' is his forte. **1927** WAKEFIELD & MARSHALL *Rugger* 183 The front row tried trick hooking and foot-up tactics. **1955** *Times* 1 Aug. 2/3 Kroon's brilliant hooking has been a feature of the season's provincial matches.

9. ***hook in***: to draw in with or as with a hook; *fig.* to get hold of as best one may; to secure by hook or by crook; to bring or drag (a person) in unwillingly or against his judgement.

1551 ROBINSON tr. *More's Utop.* I. (Arb.) 56 An other.. aduiseth to hooke in the kynge of Castell. **1617** MORYSON *Itin.* I. 62 Mils..having an iron wheele, which doeth not onely drive the saw, but hooketh in, and turneth the boords to the saw. **1658** GURNALL *Chr. in Arm.* verse 14. III. xiii. (1669) 107/2 Servants standing at the door to hook in customers. **1683** KENNETT tr. *Erasm. on Folly* 114 Hooking in a larger revenue to their own Exchequer. **1772** BURKE *Corr.* (1844) I. 396 If they can hook in any job or patronage they will. **1836** J. HALLEY in Arnot *Life* (1842) 77, I have been hooked in for an essay.

10. To link by a hook or bent part.

1823 J. BADCOCK *Dom. Amusem.* 116 Holding the other extremity in your hand, or hooked over the arm. **1847** TENNYSON *Princ.* IV. 249 At last I hook'd my ankle in a vine. **1861** HUGHES *Tom Brown at Oxf.* xv, He hooked his arm into Tom's and led the way into the town.

11. To catch on the horns, attack with the horns, as a cow. Also *absol. U.S.*

1837–40 HALIBURTON *Clockm.* (1862) 225 As a hookin' cow does [carry] a board over her eyes to keep her from makin' right at you. **1865** WHITTIER *Snowbound* 86 The oxen lashed their tails and hooked.

12. To furnish with a hook (see HOOK *sb.*¹ 10 a).

1867 PITMAN *Man. Phonogr.* (ed. 12) 30 The downward *r* and *s* do not require to be hooked for *rr, sr.*

13. ***to hook Jack***: to play truant. *U.S. colloq.* (Cf. HOOKEY 1.)

1877 BARTLETT *Dict. Amer.* (ed. 4) 294 *Hook Jack*, to play truant. New England. **1890** *Dialect Notes* I. 22 *Hookey*, in 'to play hookey', meaning *to play truant*, used in Maine, but not usual in Boston, where the phrase was and is to 'hook Jack'. **1892** *Ibid.* 216 In all the period from 1840 to 1850 the current phrase among the boys was *to hook Jack.* **1905** J. C. LINCOLN *Partners of Tide* iv. 70 The boy 'hooked Jack' for a whole day. **1967** *Publ. Amer. Dial. Soc.* XLVII. 7 *Hook jack*, 'play hookey'.

‖**hookah** ('hʊkə). Also **hooker, houka, hooka, huk(k)ah, hooqqa.** [a. Arab. (Pers., Urdū) *ḥuqqah* casket, vase, cup, 'the bottle through which the fumes pass in smoking tobacco', extended in Urdū to the whole apparatus.] A pipe for smoking, of Eastern origin, having a long flexible tube, the smoke being drawn through water contained in a vase, to which the tube and the bowl are attached; the narghile of India.

1763 SCRAFTON *Indostan* iii. (1770) 86 A fellow entered.. and carried off the gold top of the hookah he was smoking. **1803** *Ann. Rev.* I. 209/2 It is a ceremony of friendship for the master of the house to offer the visitor his hookah. **1804** W. TENNANT *Ind. Recreat.* (ed. 2) I. 67 Smoking their hookers. **1820** T. S. HUGHES *Trav. Sicily* I. vi. 185 (Stanf.) He was seated..smoking his houka. **1893** EARL DUNMORE *Pamirs* I. 338 The hukkah is brought in.

b. *attrib.* and *Comb.*

1763 SCRAFTON *Indostan* (1770) 31 His Hookah, or pipe-bearer. **1872** E. BRADDON *Life India* i. 4 (Stanf.) A luxurious idler, whose life is spent in hookah-smoking.

hook and eye, hook-and-eye, *sb.* [HOOK *sb.*¹ 5.] A metallic fastening, esp. for a dress, consisting of a hook, usually of flattened wire, and an eye or wire loop on which the hook catches, one of the two being fixed to each of the parts to be held together.

c **1626** [see HOOK *v.* 4]. *a* **1697** AUBREY *Lives* (1898) I. 205 Then their breeches were fastened to the doubletts with points—then came in hookes and eies. **1812–16** J. SMITH *Panorama Sc. & Art* I. 330 The ends are united by a small steel hook and eye. **1838** DICKENS *Nich. Nick.* xvii, Now and then tying a string, or fastening a hook-and-eye. **1862** READE *Hard Cash* 9 My ladies did not..care a hook and eye about it.

fig. **1809–10** COLERIDGE *Friend* (1837) I. 20 All the hooks-and-eyes of the memory. **1860** EMERSON *Cond. Life, Worship* Wks. (Bohn) II. 394 The whole creation is made of hooks and eyes.

attrib. **1850** *Beck's Florist* Apr. 95 The lid attached by hook-and-eye hinges.

Hence **hook-and-eye** *v. trans.*, to fasten with or as with a hook and eye; *fig.* to connect, link.

1827 SOUTHEY *Lett.* (1856) IV. 82 That any combination of chances should hook-and-eye me with any near connection of absolute wisdom! *a* **1843** —— *Comm.-pl. Bk.* Ser. II. (1849) 230 A multitude of stories hooked and eyed together clumsily. **1855** J. LEECH *Pict. Life & Char.* 11 (Heading) Hooking and Eyeing.

hook-bill. [See BILL *sb.*¹ and ².]

1. A bill with a hook; a billhook.

1613 T. CAMPION *Entertainm. Ld. Knowles* Wks. (Bullen) 178 One of them in his hand bearing a hook-bill.

2. 'The curved beak of a bird' (Ogilvie). Cf. HOOK-NOSE.

3. 'A spent male salmon whose jaws have become hooked' (*Cent. Dict.*).

So '**hook-billed** *a.*, having a curved bill.

1695 *Lond. Gaz.* No. 3080/4 Hookbil'd Ducks. **1785** J. LATHAM *Gen. Synopsis Birds* III. 495 Hook-billed Duck, *Raii Syn.* p. 150.2. **1881** *Amer. Naturalist* XV. 182 The male [of hump-back salmon] is slab-sided, hook-billed and distorted. **1911** *Encycl. Brit.* XXII. 219 Among the breeds differing in structure may be mentioned..the hook-billed and tufted ducks.

Hooke (hʊk). The name of Robert *Hooke* (1635–1703), English inventor and natural philosopher, used, chiefly in the possessive, to designate his discoveries and inventions, as **Hooke('s) coupling**, a Hooke's joint; **Hooke's law**, the law, valid within the limits of elasticity, that the strain produced by a stress of any one kind is proportional to that stress; **Hooke's (universal) joint**, a kind of universal joint for transmitting rotary motion from one shaft to another.

1825 J. NICHOLSON *Oper. Mech.* 32 Hooke's universal joints are sometimes used to communicate motion obliquely. **1853** *Trans. R. Soc. Edin.* XX. 93 The fundamental assumption from which the following equations are deduced is an extension of Hooke's law. **1883** *Encycl. Brit.* XV. 762/2 Two Hooke's couplings. **1906** A. E. H. LOVE *Treat. Math. Theory Elasticity* (ed. 2) iv. 110 Many materials used in engineering structures, e.g. cast iron, building stone, cement, do not obey Hooke's Law for any strains that are large enough to be observed. **1930** *Engineering* 31 Jan. 134/1 A Hooke's joint is provided to allow for the vertical motion of the [gear] boxes. **1959** C. E. PEARSON *Theor. Elasticity* v. 83 The familiar Hooke's-law experiment in which a metal wire is stretched by a tensile load. **1968** R. H. BACON *Car* xx. 268 Most universal joints are based on the Hooke coupling.

Hence **Hookean, hookean** ('hʊkɪən) *a.* [-AN], obeying Hooke's law; linearly elastic.

1956 J. C. JAEGER *Elasticity, Fracture & Flow* ii. 99 (*heading*) The perfectly elastic or 'Hookean' substance. **1960** *McGraw-Hill Encycl. Sci. & Technol.* X. 476/2 On extension of polymeric materials, both rubberlike and Hookean elasticity may be present. **1968** C. G. KUPER *Introd. Theory Superconductivity* ix. 146 The elastic vibrations of a lattice of discrete point masses, coupled by Hookean springs. **1972** *Physics Bull.* Nov. 651/3 For most practical purposes alkali silicate glasses are hookean solids exhibiting a linear stress-strain curve to fracture.

hooke, obs. form of OAK.

hooked (hʊkt, 'hʊkɪd), *a.* [f. HOOK *sb.*¹ or *v.*]

1. Bent like a hook; hook-shaped; hamate.

c **1000** in Kemble *Cod. Dipl.* III. 434 Oð ðat hit cymþ to ðan hokedan garan. *a* **1250** *Owl & Night.* 1675 For þeo þe haveþ bile ihoked, And clivres scharpe and wel i-croked.

1413 *Pilgr. Sowle* (Caxton) II. xlv. (1859) 51 Somme hadden longe hoked clawes. **1552** HULOET, Hooked nose. **1665** SIR T. HERBERT *Trav.* (1677) 149 He holds a Sword not so hooked as the Damasco. **1766** PENNANT *Zool.* (1812) I. 218 The bill is strong, short, and very much hooked. **1834** MEDWIN *Angler in Wales* I. 291 *note*, The nose being larger and more hooked.

2. Having or furnished with a hook or hooks. **1362** LANGL. *P. Pl.* A. Prol. 50 Eremytes on an hep wiþ hokide staues. **1430–40** LYDG. *Bochas* I. xiv. (1554) 28 a, One sleeth the dere with an hoked arowe. *c* **1586** C'TESS PEMBROKE *Ps.* LXVIII. vi, Twice ten thousand.. Of hooked chariotts, clad in warrs array. **1687** A. LOVELL tr. *Thevenot's Trav.* II. 65 One of them with a hooked stick, took hold of my Horses bridle and stopt him. **1867** PITMAN *Man. Phonogr.* (ed. 12) 30 A series of curved hooked letters.

3. [f. HOOK *v.*] See the verb. **1611** COTGR., *Accroché*, hooked; clasped, grapled. *a* **1700** B. E. *Dict. Cant. Crew*, *Hookt*, over-reached. **1821** BYRON *Vis. Judgm.* xv, To bring to land a late-hook'd fish.

4. ***hooked mat, hooked rug***, a mat or rug made on a canvas ground with woollen yarn which is pulled through with a hook. orig. *U.S.* **1880** W. D. HOWELLS *Undiscovered Country* 415 Hooked rugs and embroidered tidies were as worthy a place in Mrs. Ford's simple house as most of the old-fashioned things. **1917** L. M. MONTGOMERY *Anne's House of Dreams* (1926) ii. 10 Nobody seems to want anything but hooked mats now. **1932** D. C. MINTER *Mod. Needlecraft* 223 (*heading*) Hooked rugs. **1960** G. LEWIS *Handbk. Crafts* 91 A hooked rug is a very satisfying thing to make. **1964** MRS. L. B. JOHNSON *White House Diary* 21 May (1970) 144 After the speech Mrs. Breathitt presented me with a beautiful hooked rug—an art still practiced by the old people in the area. **1969** H. A. HORWOOD *Newfoundland* 7 A hooked mat is a kind of tapestry made by Newfoundland women who got the art from their mothers who had it handed down to them from the first European settlers. **1970** *Globe & Mail* (Toronto) 26 Sept. 45/6 (Advt.), Superior antiques.. including.. hooked and braided rugs.

Hence **'hookedness** ('hʊkɪdnɪs). **1530** PALSGR. 231/2 Hokednesse, *crochuseté*. **1623** COCKERAM, *Aduncitie*, hookednesse.

hooker[1] ('hʊkə(r)). [f. HOOK *v.* + -ER[1].] One who or that which hooks.

1. A thief who snatched away articles with a hook; a pilferer, thief; (*mod. slang*) a watch-stealer. **1567** HARMAN *Caveat* (1869) 35 These hokers, or Angglers, be peryllous and most wicked knaues. **1592** GREENE *Art Conny-catch.* II. 24 The Courber, which the common people call the Hooker.. with a Curb.. or hook, doth pul out of a window any loose linnen cloth, apparell, or els any other houshold stuffe. **1672** WORTHINGTON in *Mede's Wks.* Life 42 The Hooker.. once began to draw away his Bed-cloaths whiles he lay awake. **1834** H. AINSWORTH *Rookwood* III. v, No strange Abram, Ruffler crack—Hooker of another pack. **1888** *Tit Bits* 17 Nov. 82/2 (Farmer) The hooker, having.. got a hold of the desired prize, detaches it from the chain by breaking the ring and passes it to number two.

2. One who fastens his clothes with hooks: see quot. **1880** *Libr. Univ. Knowl.* IX. 700 The Amish Mennonites .. are sometimes called Hookers, because they substitute hooks for buttons on their clothes.

3. ***hooker-on*** (*Coal-mining*): A 'hanger on' or hitcher. Also simply *hooker*; and in many other technical usages. **1881** *Instr. Census Clerks* (1885) 134/2 Hooker (to special trade when stated or determinable). Hooker (Undefined).. Factory Labourer. **1883** *Times* 9 Nov., These men found the fire-beater acting as hooker-on for the uninjured men, who were brought up with great rapidity. **1900** *Westm. Gaz.* 16 May 8/1 No one received injuries, the hookers having received warning by the clashing of the cage. **1919** *Camp Worker* (Vancouver) 26 Apr. 5/2 The best hooker that ever gave signals for the high-rigger, while his short-handed crew changed the haul-back without the assistance of a grass-line. **1921** *Dict. Occup. Terms* (1927) §043 *Onsetter*; .. *hooker, hooker-at-shaft*..; stands at bottom of shaft in coal or shale mine to push full tubs on to cage and remove empty ones. *Ibid.* §943 *Hooker, cloth hooker, piece hooker, hooker-and-lapper.* **1966** H. SHEPPARD *Dict. Railway Slang* (ed. 2) 6 *Hooker*, shunter. **1967** *Amer. Speech* XLII. 291 Hookers come and attach hooks on slings from the overhead cranes, or travelers, that move over the yard transferring loads between saws and stacks.

4. A prostitute. *slang* (chiefly *U.S.*). **1845** in N.E. Eliason *Tarheel Talk* (1956) 277 If he comes by way of Norfolk he will find any number of pretty Hookers in the Brick row not far from French's hotel. **1914** JACKSON & HELLYER *Vocab. Criminal Slang* 45 *Hooker*, a prostitute. **1929** T. WOLFE *Look Homeward, Angel* (1930) xxx. 435, I hope you have sense enough now to leave those old hookers alone? **1932** J. DOS PASSOS *1919* 43 Ain't you got the sense to tell a good girl from a hooker? **1952** J. STEINBECK *East of Eden* xlv. 504 Joe could find any hooker in any town in a few hours. **1964** *Esquire* Nov. 85/2 They were attractive but not very imaginative, they looked like hookers on horses. **1971** [see HOOK *v.* 7 c].

5. A cow or ox that 'hooks' (see HOOK *v.* 11). *U.S.* **1866** *Harper's Mag.* May 816/1 He.. asked 'Why that pipe [*sc.* a hookah] was like a cow?' having in mind the obvious answer that it was a *hooker*. **1885** 'C. E. CRADDOCK' *Prophet Gt. Smoky Mts.* ii. 48 The red cow jes' hooked down the bars, bein' a turrible hooker. **1902** G. H. LORIMER *Lett. Merchant* vii. 84 You want to.. distinguish between a cow that's a kicker, but whose intentions are good.. and a hooker, who is vicious on general principles.

6. a. *Rugby Football.* A player in the centre of the front row of the scrummage on either side who endeavours to obtain the ball by hooking it. Cf. HOOK *v.* 8 e. **1905** *Daily Chron.* 13 Sept. 7/4 The two front men—called 'hookers'—can get the ball just as well as three. **1906** [see BACK *a.* 1]. **1927** WAKEFIELD & MARSHALL *Rugger* 166 Some hookers prefer to have the weight on the loose-head side. **1963** *Times* 14 Jan. 3/1 Thorne had been on the fringe of this new honour as a hooker for several years, and Davis and Owen look a sound second row. **1971** *Times* 15 Feb. 9/2 For a hooker Pullin often showed up well in the loose.

b. *Cricket.* One who uses the hook stroke. **1900** W. J. FORD *Cricketer on Cricket* 102 Like Hill he is a splendid hooker. **1911** P. F. WARNER *Bk. Cricket* 208 He has a lovely shot over extra-cover's head,.. and on a slow wicket is a fine puller and hooker. **1972** *Cricket World* 1. 8/2 Keith [Stackpole] has long been regarded as only a puller, hooker and cutter but, last season, developed so much that he also drove strongly.

hooker[2] ('hʊkə(r)). Also howker, hawker. [App. orig. a. Du. *hoeker*, in Hexham '*hoecker-schip* a dogger-boat', in Kilian *hoeck-boot* 'a fishing-boat, so called from *hoeck* hook'.]

1. A two-masted Dutch coasting or fishing vessel. **1641** S. SMITH *Royal Fishings* 4 A Hooker or Wellboat. **1781** *Westm. Mag.* IX. 555 There were also two large Hookers, which I could not conveniently bring away. **1794** *Rigging & Seamanship* I. 237 *Howker*, a vessel of burthen with two masts (main and mizen) used by the Dutch and Northern nations. **1858** SIMMONDS *Dict. Trade*, *Howker*, a two-masted Dutch vessel.

2. A one-masted fishing smack on the Irish coast and south-west of England, similar to a hoy in build. Also *attrib.* **1801** *Naval Chron.* VI. 432 He was in a Cork hawker, which shipped a sea. **1807** SIR R. HOARE *Tour Irel.* 84 The whole morning was spent on board Mr. Newenham's hooker. **1813** *Q. Rev.* July 289 The cost of one of these hookers is from £130 to £150;.. the mode of fishing is by the hook and line. **1884** *West. Morn. News* 28 July 1/4 Hookers belonging to the Port of Plymouth. **1894** *Daily News* 15 June 5/6 The number of hooker boats in Achill is very limited.

3. Applied depreciatively or fondly to a ship. **1823** J. F. COOPER *Pioneer* xxiii, Where away did 'ee ever fall in with such a hooker? **1825** *Blackw. Mag.* XVIII. 50/2 You've the easiest birth in the hooker. **1865** *Daily Tel.* 6 Dec. 4/4 The voyage—fair or foul—has been made;.. people shake hands with one another, giving the ' old hooker' a hearty cheer before they leave her. **1867** SMYTH *Sailor's Word-bk.*, *Hooker*, or *Howker*... Also, Jack's name for his vessel, the favourite 'old hooker'. **1883** *Century Mag.* Oct. 945/1 The old hooker actually made two and a half knots, and answered her helm tolerably well.

Hence **'hookerman**. **1894** *Daily News* 15 June 5/6 The hookerman should have lowered her sail before jibing.

†**hooker**[3]. *Obs.* (See quots.) **1594** PLAT *Jewell-ho.* II. 30 Great stone pottes.. such as the Golde finers call their Hookers. **1602** —— *Delightes for Ladies* Receipt iii, An earthen potte hauing a narrow mouth, and being well leaded within (the Refiners of gold and siluer, call these pottes *hookers*).

hooker[4] ('hʊkə(r)). *dial.* and *N. Amer. colloq.* [Orig. unknown.] A glass of whisky, a dram; usu. with qualifying word (e.g. *stiff*), a drink (of brandy, etc.). **1833** J. KENNEDY *Geordie Chalmers* iv. 45 Ye'll be nane the waur o' a hooker after yer fricht. **1865** W. H. L. TESTER *Poems* 133 Sandy liket a hooker, an' brawlie I kent, The drap creatur' wad set him a speakin'. **1887** *Grip* (Toronto) 21 May 12/2 We went in and were served out with a pretty stiff hooker each. **1906** H. GREEN *At Actor's Boarding House* 62 A stiff hooker of whiskey, and then another had the expected effect. **1927** *Black Mask* Feb. 37/1 It took a stiff hooker of whiskey and a lot of words to thaw her into understanding. **1930** H. CRADDOCK *Savoy Cocktail Bk.* I. 97 The Juice of 1 Lemon. 4 Hookers Whiskey. **1939** C. MORLEY *Kitty Foyle* xxvii. 268 She gave me such a hooker of brandy I went right to sleep. **1955** 'T. P. KELLEY' *Black Donnellys* 63 Danny was quiet enough until he got about six hookers under his belt.

Hooker[5] ('hʊkə(r)). The name of William *Hooker* (1779–1832), botanical artist, used in the possessive in ***Hooker's green***, a bright green colour used in water-colour painting. **1853** *Dict. Archit.* (Archit. Publ. Soc.) II. 84/2 This method of imitating the mixture of ultramarine with yellow has grown into a system, but the colour is not durable: as in the cases of Hooker's green and Varley's green. **1886** *Jrnl. Bot.* XXIV. 52 His memory is associated by artists with the colour called after him, 'Hooker's Green'. **1948** F. A. STAPLES *Water-Color Painting* i. 2 For paints get the following water colors in tubes: Alizarin Crimson,.. Hooker's Green Dark. **1951** R. MAYER *Artist's Handbk.* ii. 51 *Hooker's green*, a mixture of Prussian blue and gamboge. Sold in two shades, yellowish and bluish.

hooker, var. of HOOKAH.

hookey ('hʊkɪ). Also hooky. [Cf. HOOK *sb.* 14, *v.* 6, *v.* 13, and HOOKY-CROOKY.]

1. *to play hookey*: to play truant. Also *transf. colloq.* (chiefly *N. Amer.*). **1848** in BARTLETT *Dict. Amer.* **1866** *Harper's Mag.* May 779/1 Kate used to.. entreat him not to get feruled, nor play 'hookey'. **1867** 'MARK TWAIN' *Amer. Drolleries* 20 He would not play hookey, even when his sober judgment told him it was the most profitable thing he could do. **1883** E. EGGLESTON *Hoosier School-Boy* ix. 47 They remembered that the geography lesson was a hard one, and so they played 'hookey'. **1904** W. N. HARBEN *Georgians* vii. 77 'I sorter feel like playin' hookey myself,' he admitted. **1908** C. E. MULFORD *Orphan* xii. 150 I'll play on them, too, when they gets home! Off playing hookey from work when we all of us aches from double shifts. **1923** WODEHOUSE *Inimitable Jeeves* xiv. 172 He's played hookey from the choir so often that the vicar told him.. he would fire him out. **1957** W. H. WHYTE *Organization Man* III. xi. 144 Such solitary contemplation during the office day.. is regarded.. as a form of hooky. **1960** I. WALLACH *Absence of Cello* (1961) 98 'I like to play hooky now and then.'.. 'You can't just call it hooky.' **1965** *Globe & Mail* (Toronto) 22 Apr. 23/8 Youngsters who play hooky are.. merely afraid of their classrooms.

2. **blind hookey**: see BLIND *a.* 16. Also *fig.* or *transf.* **1852** G. C. MUNDY *Our Antipodes* III. iii. 85 The process of emigration was formerly—as compared with its present gradual perfection—a very blind-hookey kind of game. **1909** J. R. WARE *Passing Eng.* 34/1 *Blind Hookey*, a leap in the dark; *e.g.*, 'Oh, it's Blind Hookey to attempt it.' **1925** *Blackw. Mag.* Aug. 286/2 It is.. the common practice of politicians to play blind hookey with the great interests entrusted to them.

Hookey Walker: see WALKER *int.*

'hooking, *vbl. sb.* [f. HOOK *v.* + -ING[1].] The action of the vb. HOOK; catching, fastening, or attachment by means of a hook or hooks. *c* **1430** *Pilgr. Lyf Manhode* IV. viii. (1869) 179 Sathan.. dooth al his entente to haue alle þilke þat ben in þe see by his fysshinge and bi his hookinge. **1658** R. WHITE tr. *Digby's Powd. Symp.* (1660) 72 The continuity of bodies results from some small hookings or claspings. *c* **1850** *Rudim. Navig.* (Weale) 124 *Hooking*, the act of working the edge of one plank, &c. into that of another, in such a manner that they cannot be drawn asunder endways.

'hooking, *ppl. a.* [f. as prec. + -ING[2].] That hooks.

1. That snatches, catches, or grasps as with a hook. **1598** SYLVESTER *Du Bartas* II. i. III. *Furies* 708 Avarise, all-armed in hooking Tenters And clad in Bird-lime. **1621** MOLLE *Camerar. Liv. Libr.* IV. iii. 229 To saue it from the hooking hands of the Spaniards. **1837–40** [see HOOK *v.* 11].

2. That bends or curves into a hook; hooked. **1704** *Lond. Gaz.* No. 4011/4 His Nose somewhat hooking. **1774** GOLDSM. *Nat. Hist.* (1776) V. 109 Beak straight in the beginning, but hooking at the point.

hookish ('hʊkɪʃ), *a.* [f. HOOK *sb.*[1] + -ISH.] Somewhat hook-like or hooked. **1597** A. M. tr. *Guillemeau's Fr. Chirurg.* 13 b/2 He is also hoockishe and recurvated. **1712** *Lond. Gaz.* No. 5053/3 Full Eyes, hookish Nose.

hookless ('hʊklɪs), *a.* [f. as prec. + -LESS.]

a. Without a hook. **1776** R. GRAVES *Euphrosyne* II. 173 Thus round the hookless bait the Pike will play. **1854** *Fraser's Mag.* L. 397 Your line springs into the air, hookless, and of course fishless.

b. Of a garment: having no hooks, with its hooks missing. **1906** *Westm. Gaz.* 25 Sept. 2/1 Blouses, in various stages of hookless decrepitude.

hooklet ('hʊklɪt). [f. as prec. + -LET.] A small or minute hook; esp. in *Nat. Hist.* **1836–9** TODD *Cycl. Anat.* II. 127/1 Hard transparent horny hooklets around the oral proboscis. **1872** NICHOLSON *Palæont.* 314 The spines, or hooklets, or denticles of Naked Molluscs and Annelides. **1897** ALLBUTT *Syst. Med.* II. 1007 The suckers and hooklets serve to attach the parasite to the mucous membrane of the alimentary canal of the host.

hook-nose. A nose of a hooked shape with a downward curve; an aquiline nose. **1687** *Lond. Gaz.* No. 2307/4 A tall black Man, with a Hook Nose. **1826** SCOTT *Jrnl.* 21 Oct., Figures, with black eyes and hook-noses.

hook-nosed, *a.* Having a hook-nose. **1519** HORMAN *Vulg.* 31 They that be hookenosed.. theyr spectacles shall nat lightly fal fro them. **1597** SHAKS. *2 Hen. IV*, IV. iii. 45, I may iustly say with the hooke-nos'd fellow of Rome, I came, saw, and ouer-came. **1682** *Lond. Gaz.* No. 1708/4 A.. raw-bon'd Man.. squint Eyed, hook Nos'd. [**1870** MORRIS *Earthly Par.* III. IV. 34 Thin-cheeked, hooked-nos'd, e'en as might be An ancient erne.] **1938** [see *fawn-eyed* s.v. FAWN *sb.*[1] 4]. **1958** L. DURRELL *Mountolive* ii. 55 Cherry-starred Japan, hook-nosed Lima.

hookster, obs. form of HUCKSTER.

hookum ('hu:kəm). *India.* Also hookm, hukm. [a. Hindi, a. Arab. *ḥukm*, f. *ḥakama* (cf. HAKIM).] A command, order, or instruction from a person in authority. Also *transf.* (see quot. 1925). **1838** E. EDEN *Let.* 17 Dec. in *Up Country* (1866) II. ii. 13 An officer came to ask his 'hookum', or orders. **1843** LADY SALE *Jrnl. Disasters Afghanistan* 39 The troops.. instead of receiving *hookm* to enter the city, the Shah almost rudely inquired why they had come! **1858** W. H. RUSSELL *Diary in India* 7 Oct. (1860) II. xii. 226 We had no hookum from the commissioner or deputy. **1886** [see DASTOOR, DASTUR(I)]. **1895** B. M. CROKER *Village Tales* (1896) 224 His coat was restored to him, with a 'hookum', to say that he was free. **1925** FRASER & GIBBONS *Soldier & Sailor Words* 120 *Hookum*, a regulation. The correct thing, *e.g.*, 'That's the hookum'. An old Army colloquial term.

hookum-snivey ('hʊkəm'snɪvɪ). *dial.* and *slang.* Also hook and snivey (snivvy), hook 'em snivey, hookem snivey, hookem-snivvy, hook um snivey. [app. orig. *hook and snivey*, prob. f. HOOK *sb.* or *v.*] An imposture or deceit; also, a contrivance

for undoing the bolt of a door from the outside. Also *attrib.* or *adj.*, deceitful, tricky.

1781 G. Parker *View Soc.* II. 81 He..would stand no Hook and Snivey, or Nix the Buffer. **1802** R. L. & M. Edgeworth *Irish Bulls* 129, I ranged them fair and even with my hook-em-snivey. **1823** 'J. Bee' *Dict. Turf* 98 Hook and Snivvy—practised by soldiers in quarters, when they obtain grub for *nix*, by connivance with the slavey, or her mistress. **1874** Hotten *Slang Dict.* 194 Sometimes used as an irrelevant answer, by street boys. As, 'who did that?'—'Hook um snivey'—actually no one. **1892** S. Hewett *Peasant Speech of Devon* 89, I tellee 'onesty is the best policy. Niver yü be up tü hookem-snivey ways. **1905** E. Phillpotts *Secret Woman* II. xi, An' some lying an' doing all manner of hookem-snivey deeds. **1928** —— *Ring Fence* xvi. 132 I'd a lot rather put my thoughts into work, so as you should have a wedding worthy of you and no hookem-snivey marrying in a corner. **1950** L. A. G. Strong *Which I Never* vi. 184 'Tisn't like him to do any sort of hookem-snivvy tactics.

hook-up ('hʊkʌp). orig. *U.S. colloq.* [f. phr. *to hook up*: HOOK *v.* 4b, 4e, 5.] A connection or combination, esp. of radio or television broadcasting facilities.

1903 A. H. Lewis *Boss* 116 It'll put us in line for a hook-up with th' reform bunch in th' fight for th' town next year. **1911** H. Quick *Yellowstone Nights* vii. 191 The Golden Fountain..had no lawyer against us. It was a funny hook-up. **1922** L. D. Brigham *How to make Vacuum Wireless Receiving Sets* 39 The remainder of the hook-up is just like the other amplifier hook-ups. **1927** *Observer* 11 Dec. 16/5 National appeals are possible by wireless when the various American 'Radio Corporations' agree to a 'national hook-up'. **1929** *Lit. Digest* 18 May 79/1 These lines are the skeleton of a gigantic aerial hook-up that now seems destined to cover South America. **1930** P. W. Slosson *Gt. Crusade* x. 278 A radio hook-up brought the whole nation to the [prize] ring side. **1932** E. Wallace *When Gangs came to London* xxi. 186 There had to be either a hook-up or one side had to go out of business. **1944** E. J. Teichert *Ferrous Metall.* (ed. 2) II. xi. 227 The electrical hook-up..is of such a nature that the two motors act as a unit. **1950** Wodehouse *Nothing Serious* 16 He could not have been better informed regarding it if the facts had been broadcast on a nation-wide hook-up. **1957** *Times* 31 Oct. 11/4 This American precedent of appearing in person on a nation wide hook-up. **1959** *Punch* 28 Oct. 360/3 Are you now in favour of a Lab-Lib hook-up? **1967** *Electronics* 6 Mar. 80/1 How do you create a galvanometer..that doesn't require hours of delicate dial twiddling, trapdoor adjustments or experimental hook-ups? **1970** *New Yorker* 12 Sept. 25 Discussing layouts, viewing charts, and getting computer information via a Picturephone/Computer hookup are just a few of the areas being pursued.

hook-worm. *Zool.* [Cf. G. *hakenwurm*, mod.L. *Uncinaria*, f. L. *uncīnus* hook (both coined by J. A. Fröhlich 1789, in *Naturforscher* XXIV. 136).] A parasitic nematode worm of the family Ancylostomatidæ, which infests man, other mammals, or birds, using hook-like organs to attach itself to the host's intestinal lining. Hence **hook-worm disease** = ANKYLOSTOMIASIS; also **hookworm-ridden** *a.*, infested with hookworms.

1902 *Rep. Bur. Anim. Industry 1901* (U.S. Dept. Agric.) 183 (*title*) The significance of the recent American cases of hookworm disease (Uncinariasis, or Anchylostomiasis) in Man. **1902** C. W. Stiles in *Amer. Med.* III. 777 (*title*) A new species of hookworm..parasitic in man. **1909** *Times* 29 Oct. 5/6 A commission of eminent medical men to investigate the hook-worm disease. **1925** R. W. G. Hingston in E. F. Norton *Fight for Everest: 1924* III. vi. 352 Porters should be vaccinated, and given suitable treatment for hook-worm. **1931** [see ANKYLOSTOMIASIS]. **1932** W. Faulkner *Light in August* I. 3 Department annals would not now even be remembered by the hookworm-ridden heirs-at-large. **1950** F. A. Brown *Selected Invertebr. Types* 237 It is believed that infected African Negroes brought into the United States established the hookworm in at least part of its present range. **1964** J. E. Larsh *Outl. Med. Parasitol.* xiii. 119 Long-continued anemia, characteristic in chronic hookworm disease, is most detrimental in children. **1968** N. D. Levine *Nematode Parasites* iii. 106 Prevention of hookworm infections in dogs and cats depends upon sanitation.

hooky ('hʊkɪ), *a.* [f. HOOK *sb.*[1] + -Y.] Having a hook or hooks; hook-shaped; hooked.

1552 Huloet, Hooky, or full of hookes, *hamosus.* **1611** Cotgr., *Racrocher*,..to make of a hookie forme. **1678** Cudworth *Intell. Syst.* I. v. 687 Strato derided Democritus his Rough and Smooth, Crooked and Hooky Atoms, as meer Dreams and Dotages. **1855–9** Singleton *Virgil* II. 171 Holding a hooky bill below his bust.

'hooky-'crooky, *a.* and *sb.* [Cf. HOOK *sb.*[1] 14.]

A. *adj.* Not straightforward, perverse, dishonest. **B.** *sb.* An underhand act or practice.

1830 Galt *Lawrie T.* V. iv. 205 He was coming round me with one of his hooky-crookies. **1833** *Fraser's Mag.* VIII. 201 [They] manage to keep themselves..by hookey-crookey gambling ways, as brother Jonathan would say.

hool, -e, obs. forms of HOLE, HULL, WHOLE.

hoold, obs. form of HOLD.

‖**Hoolee, Holī** ('huːliː, 'həʊliː). *E. Indies.* Also 7 **houly**, 7–9 **hooly**, 8–9 **huli**, 9 **hooley**, **hohlee**. [Hindi *holī*.] The great festival or carnival of the Hindus, held at the approach of the vernal equinox, in honour of Krishna and the Gopīs or milkmaids.

1687 A. Lovell tr. *Thevenot's Trav.* III. 67 That once in his life he might be present at the Feast of Houly. **1698** Fryer *Acc. E. India & P.* 180 In their Hooly, which is at their other Seed-time. **1789** Pearce in *Asiat. Res.* II. 333 During the *Húli*, when mirth and festivity reign among Hindus of every class. *Ibid.* 334 The late Shujául Daulah..was very fond of making *Húli*-fools. **1800** *Asiat. Ann. Reg.*, *Misc. Tr.* 280/1 The hooly, or saturnalia of India, when liberty of speech and action towards superiors are allowed to as great an extent as among the ancient Romans. **1809** T. D. Broughton *Lett.* (1813) 87 (Y.) We paid the Muha Raj the customary visit at the Hohlee. **1825** Heber *Narr. Journ.* (1828) II. 524 During all the time of Hoolee, drunkenness is common among the Hindoos. **1910** *Encycl. Brit.* XIII. 507/2 The *Holi*, the Indian Saturnalia in the month of Phālguna (February to March). **1921** E. M. Forster *Let.* 1 Apr. in *Hill of Devi* (1953) 58 My painted escort (they had been celebrating Holi) were all that is polite. **1958** *Listener* 13 Nov. 768/1 The great spring game of Holi that they play all over northern India. *Ibid.*, Holi used to be the loveliest of festivals. **1969** *Eve's Weekly* (Bombay) 20 Dec. 67/3 When I was a young girl every year brought Holi with its gay colours.

hooley ('huːlɪ), Chiefly *Irish.* Also **huly**, **wholee**. [Origin unknown.] A noisy party, a spree (see also quots.).

1877 Bartlett *Dict. Amer.* (ed. 4) 302 *Huly*, a noise, uproar. 'To raise *huly*.' New England. **1947** *Béaloideas* XVII. 273 *Hooley*, a dance or 'spree' in a private house, often to celebrate a wedding, etc. **1950** *Ibid.* XX. 191 *Wholee, Hooley*, a party or dance in a country house. *John gave a right wholee last night.* **1960** *News-Call Bulletin* (San Francisco) 4 Jan. 16/1 She can be seen at all the best hoolies in town. **1966** 'L. Lane' *ABZ of Scouse* 50 *'ooley*, a dispute, a fight or a riot. **1966** *Listener* 12 May 687/2 Sir Laurence tries to make it one of those peculiar Irish occasions, a hooley: swinging from wild hilarity to nostalgic sadness.

hooli, hoolly, obs. forms of WHOLLY.

hooligan ('huːlɪgən). [Origin unascertained.

The word first appears in print in daily newspaper police-court reports in the summer of 1898. Several accounts of the rise of the word, purporting to be based on first-hand evidence, attribute it to a misunderstanding or perversion of *Hooley* or *Hooley's gang*, but no positive confirmation of this has been discovered. The name *Hooligan* figured in a music-hall song of the eighteen-nineties, which described the doings of a rowdy Irish family, and a comic Irish character of the name appeared in a series of adventures in *Funny Folks*.]

A young street rough, a member of a street gang. Also *attrib.* and *transf.*; *spec.* **Hooligan Navy** *U.S. Naut. slang*, the U.S. Coast Guard Service.

1898 *Daily News* 26 July 5/1 It is no wonder..that Hooligan gangs are bred in these vile, miasmatic byways. *Ibid.* 8 Aug. 9/3 The constable said the prisoner belonged to a gang of young roughs, calling themselves 'Hooligans'. **1898** *Daily Tel.* 6 Aug. (Ware), William Lineker, decribed as a Hooligan, sets upon an inoffensive man. **1898** *Daily Graphic* 30 Aug. 4/4 Mr. White..stated that every Saturday and Sunday nights gangs like the 'Hooligan gang' came to his house, broke the windows, glass, &c., and made disturbances. **1898** *Westm. Gaz.* 15 Sept. 1/2 The Khalifa was, after all, only a sort of Soudanese Hooligan. **1901** *Pall Mall Mag.* Feb. 198 Nobody will claim honesty as a Hooligan virtue. **1922** L. Hisey *Sea Grist* 7 Haven't even been in the Hooligan Navy? Just land lubbers. **1932** H. Walpole *Fortress* III. 439 Crowds of roughs and hooligans, urged on by the more violent Chartists, drove their way towards the stands with shouts and threats. **1938** Auden & Isherwood *On Frontier* III. ii. 110, I always suspected that you and your gang of hooligans would rat. **1962** L. Farago *Tenth Fleet* 119 Thus was born the Coastal Picket Patrol or, as the Coast Guard called it, the Corsair Fleet. Its own personnel, mostly amateur yachtsmen, preferred to refer to it as the 'Hooligan Navy'. **1963** *Daily Tel.* 27 Dec. 1/6 Some driving he had seen amounted to 'downright hooligan behaviour'. **1971** *Guardian* 29 July 11/4 Rome's young black-shirted hooligans like to taunt the long-haired guitar-strummers by roaring around them on motor-cycles.

Hence **'hooligan** *v. intr.*, to act as a hooligan; also *trans.*, to treat (a person) roughly; **ˌhooliga'nesque** *a.*, like a hooligan; **hooli'ganic** *a.*, resembling that of hooligans; **'hooliganism**, the characteristic behaviour of hooligans, rough horseplay; **'hooliganize** *v. intr.*, to act as a hooligan.

These derivatives, with the exception of *hooliganism*, are only occasional, but they are inserted here because of their additional testimony to the currency of *hooligan*.

1898 *Pall Mall Gaz.* 19 Aug. 9/3 Any unauthorized person found trespassing on the aforesaid sphere would be Hooliganed without further notice. **1899** *Ibid.* 5 Jan. 2/3 The proprietor of Lord Tennyson (in wax) says that it was a certain young man, who, with others,..when called upon to desist, Hooliganed about and threw the late Laureate's head at him. *Ibid.* 1 Feb. 2/3 Larking about in the usual hooliganesque way. **1902** *Daily Chron.* 20 Sept. 5/6 Stay then your Hooliganic lark. **1898** *Daily Tel.* 12 Aug. 5/7 'Hooliganism', or youthful ruffianism. **1898** *Daily Graphic* 22 Aug. 14/2 The avalanche of brutality which, under the name of 'Hooliganism'..has cast such a dire slur on the social records of South London. **1900** *19th Cent.* July 90 To strike at the very roots of truancy, juvenile crime, and Hooliganism. **1911** *Catholic Times* 1 Sept., The recent outbreak of hooliganism [in Liverpool]. **1955** *Times* 14 June 6/6 In a talk with journalists he denied one by one the Government's charges of hooliganism against Catholics. **1973** *Oxford Mail* 23 Jan. 8/2 The ban had been imposed on safety grounds 'following incidents on Sunday night involving hooliganism by youngsters'. **1901** *Pall Mall Mag.* Feb. 198 The Hooligan..would Hooliganise less..if in his ruffianism he risked a cut of it [*sc.* the whip].

hoolivan ('huːlɪvæn). [Blend of HOOLIGAN and VAN *sb.*[3]] A popular name for a type of police van carrying photographic and video equipment for observing crowd behaviour and identifying trouble-makers at football matches and other events.

1985 *Daily Tel.* 9 May 3/6 The 'hoolivan' designed to detect trouble-makers in football crowds, was unveiled at the Chelsea-Luton match at Stamford Bridge last night. **1985** *Sunday Times* 11 Aug. 5/4 Development of the Hoolivan began in 1983 and a Mark 1 model was quietly undergoing trials at the end of last season. **1986** *Times* 15 Jan. 12/4 The Home Office has three public order surveillance vehicles nicknamed 'hoolivans'.

‖**hoolock** ('huːlɒk). Also **hulluk**, **hooluck**, **-ack**, **huluq**. [a. *hulluk*, the native name.] The Black Gibbon, *Hylobates Hoolock*, native of Assam.

c **1809** Buchanan *Rungpoor* in *E. Ind.* III. 563 (Y.) The Hulluks live in considerable herds. **1838** *Penny Cycl.* XII. 407/2 Three individuals of the species called the Hoolock. **1868** in T. Lewin *Fly on Wheel* (1885) 374 (Y.) A huluq monkey, a shy little beast.

hooly, huly ('huːlɪ, *Sc.* 'hʏlɪ), *adv.* and *a.* *Sc.* and *north.* Also 4 **holy**, 6 **hulie**, **hully**, 7 **hewly**. [ME. *hōly*, app. of Norse origin: cf. ON. *hófligr* moderate, *hófliga* with moderation, fitly, justly, f. *hóf* measure, moderation, HOVE *sb.*[2]; also, ON. *hógligr* adj. easy, gentle, *hógliga* adv. gently, calmly, meekly, fitly, f. *hóg-* in comb. easy, gentle, soft.]

A. *adv.* Gently, softly, cautiously; tardily. Often in phr. ***hooly and fairly***.

a **1340** Hampole *Psalter* xxxix. 24 My god cum not holy [Vulg. *ne tardaveris*]. *Ibid.*, God come ouer huly til oure bihofe. **1513** Douglas *Æneis* VI. v. 127 Huly and fair on to the cost I swam. **1598** Ferguson *Scott. Prov.* (1785) 13 (Jam.) Hooly and fairly men ride far journies. **1728** Ramsay *To R. Yarde* 114 Yet love is kittle and unruly, And shou'd move tentily and hooly. **1827** Scott *Jrnl.* 10 June, Cash difficulties, etc. all provided for..so that we go on hooly and fairly. **1830** Galt *Lawrie T.* VI. i. (1849) 253 'Hooly, hooly, Mr. Bradshaw', cried I.

B. *adj.* Gentle, cautious; slow, tardy.

1513 Douglas *Æneis* IX. xiii. 45 Turnus..Steppys abak wyth huly pays full styll. **1597** Montgomerie *Cherrie & Slae* 1283 Fulis hast cums huly speid. *a* **1810** Tannahill *Poet. Wks.* (1846) 55 In judging, let us be right hooly.

Hence **'hooliness**, **'huliness**, tardiness, delay.

a **1340** Hampole *Psalter* xxxix. 24 Þat hulynes þat he will not bifell. **1820** *Edin. Mag.* May 422/2 The trauchl't stag i' the wan waves lap, But huliness or hune.

hooly, obs. f. WHOLLY.

hoom(e, obs. ff. HOME.

hoom(m)ock(e, obs. ff. HUMMOCK.

hoon (huːn), *sb.*[1] *India.* Also **hun**. [Hindi (Skr. *hūna*).] A gold coin, the pagoda.

1807 F. Buchanan *Journ. Madras* II. 310 Huns, or Pagodas. **1876** J. Grant *Hist. India* I. xxvi. 140/1 The pagoda..was called a *hoon* by the Mohammedans, and a *varaha* by the Hindoos. **1877** J. Dowson *H. M. Elliot's Hist. India* VII. 84 Part of the two *lacs* of *huns* (pagodas), which was the stipulated amount of his annual tribute. **1962** R. A. G. Carson *Coins* 508 Gold was struck in two denominations, the heavier hun or pagoda and the smaller fanam.

hoon (huːn), *sb.*[2] *Austral. slang.* [Origin unknown.] A lout, a rough; a crazy person, a 'clot'; a ponce.

1938 X. Herbert *Capricornia* xxi. 309 'You flash hoon,' he went on. 'Kiddin' you're white, eh?' **1953** Baker *Australia Speaks* v. 124 Women whose activities are not organised by hoons..are called battlers. **1965** *Telegraph* (Brisbane) 5 July 8/4 *Hoon*, a crackpot. **1967** *Sunday Truth* (Brisbane) 9 July 32/4 Two louts..walked up behind him. The biggest hoon ruffled up his hair and tried to put his half-smoked cigarette in the young man's hair. **1969** *Courier-Mail* (Brisbane) 8 Jan. 2/4 Advertising these locations [*sc.* of radar speed traps], also advertises the locations where they are not being used, thus giving the hot-rod hoons an open go.

hoond(e, obs. ff. HAND.

hoondee, hoondi, hoondy, varr. HUNDI.

hoon(e), obs. ff. HONE.

hoong, obs. f. *hung*, pa. t. of HANG *v.*

Hoonoomaun, var. Hanuman.

hoop (huːp), *sb.*[1] Forms: 2 **hóp**, 2–5 **hop**, 4–6 **hope**, 5 *north.* **hupe**, 5–7 **hoope**, 6– **hoop**, (6 **howp(e**, **howpp**, **whop(e**, **whoope**, 6–7 **houpe**). [Late OE. *hóp* = OFris. *hôp*, MDu. *hoop*, *houp*, *hoep*, Du. *hoep*:—OTeut. type **hôpo-z*; but not known outside the Low German-Frisian group.]

1. a. A circular band or ring of metal, wood, or other stiff material; esp. a circle of wood or flattened metal for binding together the staves of casks, tubs, etc.

a **1175** *Hist. Holy Rood* (E.E.T.S.) 22 Ða het he wurcean ænne seolfrene hop of þrittigæ pundon..swa fela seolfrenæ hopæ. **1398** Trevisa *Barth. de P.R.* XVII. clxxiv. (1495) 716 Bendes and knyttynges made to bynde vp vynes and hopes for tonnes. **1417** *Durham MS. Almoner's Roll*, In j pari molarum cum hopys et rynd-spindellis. *c* **1440** *Promp. Parv.* 245/2 Hoope, vesselle byndynge (*K.* hope). **1485** *Ripon Ch. Acts* (Surtees) 373, ij hupes pro rota plaustri. **1522** *Churchw. Acc. St. Giles, Reading* 17 Paid for a whope of Iron to the

shafts of the churche gate iijd. **1555** EDEN *Decades* 28 The hoopes of his barrels cracked and brake. **1592** WARNER *Alb. Eng.* VIII. xlii. (1612) 202 A Stoole halfe backed with a houpe. **1617** MORYSON *Itin.* III. 174 This cap..is hollow..being borne up by little hoopes, and so cooles the head. **1750** JOHNSON *Rambler* No. 51 ¶12 A vessel of gooseberry wine had burst the hoops. **1851** *Illustr. Catal. Gt. Exhib.* 971 Model of a hoop for a mast, for the boom to work in, instead of a 'goose-neck'. **1875** *Ure's Dict. Arts* III. 244 The pieces of buhr-stones..are bound with iron hoops into large millstones. **1885** *Act 48 & 49 Vict.* c. 70 §9 Barrels made..with such hoops as may be approved by the Fishery Board.

fig. **1602** SHAKS. *Ham.* I. iii. 63 The friends thou hast, and their adoption tride, Grapple them to thy Soule, with hoopes of Steele. **1606** —— *Ant. & Cl.* II. ii. 117 What Hoope should hold vs staunch from edge to edge A th' world.

b. In tavern signs: see COCK-A-HOOP, *note*.

1403 *Add. Charter* 5313 Br. Mus., [A messuage called] the belle on the hoop. **1463** *Bury Wills* (Camden) 31 The hert of the hop [sign of inn at Bury]. **1631** *Deed* (in *J. Coleman's Bk. Catal.* 1889), Two Inns in Shoreditch, one called the Cock and Hoope, the other the Holy Lambe.

c. A circular ring, often with paper stretched over it, through which acrobats or performing animals leap. Also *fig.*, esp. in phr. ***to go*** (or ***jump***) ***through*** (***the***) ***hoop***(***s***: to undergo an ordeal or trial. Similarly ***to put through the hoop***(***s***.

1793 in T. Frost *Circus Life* (1875) 43 Through the Hoop on Fire, fourteen feet high, by Mr. Porter and Mr. Ducrow. **1869** B. CLARKE *Crocker* 88 When a rider..has been jumping through paper hoops held up at intervals round the ring. **1875** T. FROST *Circus Life* 185 All aspirants to saw-dust honours..are required to..hold hoops, balloons, banners, &c. **1914** W. W. GIBSON *Borderlands* 55 *Merry Andrew.* I missed a hoop This afternoon... I've not missed A hoop since I was six. I'm forty-two. **1917** WODEHOUSE *Man with Two Left Feet* 192 It was his business to make money, and, when called upon, to jump through hoops and sham dead at the bidding of his wife and daughter Mae. **1919** 'B. CABLE' *Old Contempt.* 209 Then Tommy Dodd got hold of his sergeant and 'put him through the hoop'. **1925** FRASER & GIBBONS *Soldier & Sailor Words* 120 *Hoop, through the*: up for punishment. **1926** GALSWORTHY *Silver Spoon* xi. 81 Let the papers jump through their hoops as much as they liked. **1930** M. KENNEDY *Fool of Family* xxvii. 275 Disagreeable thoughts were going to assail him... If he had ever let them get hold of him he would never have got through his hoop. *Ibid.* xxx. 314 'Let's hide..upstairs...' 'No use. They'll all come up to look at Henry VIII's bed.' 'Oh, well. Then it's through the hoops.' **1938** H. NICOLSON *Diary* 7 Apr. (1966) 333, I come back to find that the F.A. Committee have put Paul through the hoops also, asking whether he is 'pro-Chamberlain' or 'pro-Eden'. **1943** R. CHANDLER *Lady in Lake* (1944) xxxix. 205 She got the men that way, she could make them jump through hoops. **1958** *Economist* 1 Nov. 390/2 The most controversial new legislation may still be the bill which will oblige any British government to go through the parliamentary hoop when imposing certain economic controls. **1958** 'A. GILBERT' *Death against Clock* 139 He may have jumped through the hoop right away. **1969** *Times* 12 May 15/5 Their..irritations are put through nightly hoops.

2. a. Applied to rings, bands, or loops, having similar uses (see quots.); also to other contrivances for binding or confining, as 'the enclosing case of a run of stones' in a mill (Knight *Dict. Mech.*).

1867 SMYTH *Sailor's Word-bk.*, *Hoops*, the strong iron bindings of the anchor-stock to the shank, though square, are called hoops. **1875** KNIGHT *Dict. Mech.*, *Hoop*,..one of the rings to which the weather-leach of a fore-and-aft sail is bent, and by which it slides on the mast or stay as the sail is hoisted or lowered.

b. A circular wooden frame in which a cheese is moulded.

[**1790** W. H. MARSHALL *Rural Econ. Midl. Counties* I. 349 The cheese vats of this district are merely 'hoops' of ash, with a boarden bottom.] **1857** *Trans. Ill. Agric. Soc.* II. 181 These vats warm, scald, and work the curd ready for the hoop without being removed. **1877** *Rep. Vermont Board Agric.* IV. 54 Most of the cheese made about here was bought and shipped almost as soon as it was out of the hoops. **1951** *Oxf. Jun. Encycl.* VII. 156/1 The curd..is 'milled' or torn into small particles, mixed with salt, and packed into a hoop or mould.

3. A circle of wood or iron (orig. a barrel-hoop), which is trundled along as a plaything by children.

1792 MARY WOLLSTONECR. *Rights Wom.* iv. 150 When they ought to have been spinning a top, or twirling a hoop. **1801** STRUTT *Sports & Past.* IV. iv. §4 Trundling the hoop is a pastime of uncertain origin, but much in practice at present. **1848** DICKENS *Dombey* xviii, The rosy children..run past with hoops.

†**4.** One of the bands at equal intervals on a quart pot; hence, the quantity of liquor contained between two of these. *Obs.*

1592 NASHE *P. Penilesse* (ed. 2) 23 b, I beleeue hoopes in quart pots were inuented to that ende, that euery man should take his hoope, and no more. **1593** SHAKS. *2 Hen. VI*, IV. ii. 72 The three hoop'd pot shall haue ten hoopes, and I wil make it Fellony to drink small Beere. **1609** DEKKER *Gvll's Horne-bk.* 28 (N.) The Englishman's healths, his hoops, cans, half-cans [etc.].

5. a. A measure of corn, etc. of varying capacity. Now *local.*

1520 WHITINTON *Vulg.* (1527) 12 b, A mette or an hoope of oote mele. **1548** *Ludlow Churchw. Acc.* (Camden) 35 A busshelle and a whop of lyme. **1606** HOLLAND *Sueton.* Annot. 4 *Denosmodios*, in round reckoning may goe for ten peckes or hoopes with vs. **1654** *Manch. Crt. Leet Rec.* (1887) IV. 129 The Jury Amerce John Maulton for a halfe hoope and a Peck vndʳ measure. **1674** RAY *N.C. Words* 26 *A Hoop*, a Measure containing a Peck or Quarter of a Strike. Yorksh. **1810** W. DAVIES *Agric. N. Wales* xvii. §2. 466 In Montgomeryshire, a cylindrical vessel, containing 20 quarts, is called a hoop; two of such hoops make a strike or measure. **1845** PETRIE *Eccl. Archit. Irel.* 222 A hoop [i.e. a quarter of a peck] was sold for no less than five groates.

b. A short metal cylinder used as a shape for a cake.

1741 *Compl. Fam. Piece* I. ii. 193 Butter your Hoop, and let it stand 3 Hours in a moderate Oven.

6. A circle of flexible elastic material, as whalebone or steel, used to expand the skirt of a woman's dress; hence, the structure consisting of such hoops connected by some material, worn under a petticoat or skirt; a hoop-petticoat or -skirt.

Such a structure has appeared, with modifications, in the farthingale of the 16th–17th c., the extravagant hoop-skirt of the 18th, and the crinoline of the 19th.

1548 HALL *Chron., Hen. VIII* 67 b, Eight ladies in blacke velvet bordred about with gold, with hoopes from the wast downeward, and sleves ruffed. **1550** CROWLEY *Epigr.* 1318 Wyth whoopes at the skyrte. **1617** MORYSON *Itin.* III. 168 Women weare long fardingales..like hoopes, which our Women used of olde. **1717** PRIOR *Alma* II. 277 The swelling hoop sustains The rich brocade. **1738–9** MRS. DELANY in *Life & Corr.* (1861) II. 25 The fashionable hoops are made of the richest damask, trimmed with gold and silver, fourteen guineas a hoop. **1754** *Connoisseur* No. 36 ¶3 The hoop... At present it is nearly of an oval form, and scarce measures from end to end above twice the length of the wearer. **1800** MAR. EDGEWORTH *Belinda* (1832) I. v. 98 Everybody wears hoops, but..'tis a melancholy consideration—how very few can manage them. **1812** BYRON *Waltz* xiii, Hoops are no more, and petticoats not much. **1842** TENNYSON *Talking Oak* xvi, In teacup-times of hood and hoop, Or while the patch was worn. **1878** MRS. OLIPHANT *Dress* iv. 54 The hoop proper was not so abrupt as the farthingale, and the crinoline was greatly softened from the hoop.

7. A finger-ring.

1507 *Will of Oppy* (Somerset Ho.), My hoope of gold made like a crown of thorn. **1520** *Test. Ebor.* (Surtees) V. 117 My howpe of golde that I were on my finger. **1530** PALSGR. 233/1 Houpe a greate ryng, *signet.* **1596** SHAKS. *Merch. V.* v. i. 147 A hoope of Gold, a paltry Ring. **1668** DAVENANT *Man's the Master* II. i. Wks. 1874 V. 41, I know but one hoop in the world can bind us close together... A wedding-ring. **1857** C. KINGSLEY *Two Years Ago* II. vi. 226 She drew off a diamond hoop, and put it quietly into his hand. **1926** J. BLACK *You can't Win* xv. 199, I go in her joint and drop a hoop to one of her frowsy little brums for nine dollars. **1970** C. MAJOR *Dict. Afro-Amer. Slang* 67 *Hoop*, ring.

8. a. Any hoop-like or circular structure, conformation, or figure; a circle, ring, arc.

1530 PALSGR. 233/1 Houpe of a beestes fote, *corne.* **1570** B. GOOGE *Pop. Kingd.* II. 25 b, Scarce an ynche brode hoope of heare, about their pate appeares. **1684** T. BURNET *Th. Earth* I. 169 Saturn is remarkable for his hoop or ring, which seems to stand off from his body. **1719** D'URFEY *Pills* (1872) III. 315 His Knights around his Table in a Circle sate, d'ye see, And altogether made up one large Hoop of Chivalry. **1893** MCCARTHY *Red Diamonds* II. 41 Specimens of almost every herb under the hoop of heaven.

b. *Bot.* Applied to the overlapping edge of one of the valves of the frustule of the *Diatomaceæ*; called also the 'girdle'.

1884 *Challenger Reports, Botany* II. 3 These walls..are formed by two distinct plates or valves, each possessing its own hoop..This hoop, connecting zone or belt, may be single, double, or of complex structure.

c. *U.S. Basketball.* The (rim of the) basket. Also, a goal scored by throwing the ball through the basket.

1893 in Z. Hollander *Mod. Encycl. Basketball* (1969) 8 The baskets are strong iron hoops, with braided cord netting. **1937** F. C. ALLEN *Better Basketball* ii. 29 (*heading*) Standardized basketball nomenclature... Baskets—not Buckets,..hoops, nets, or strings. **1967** *Boston* (Mass.) *Herald* 1 Apr. 17/1 Jim Small scored the first hoop of the game. **1969** Z. HOLLANDER *Mod. Encycl. Basketball* xvii. 419 He drove for the hoop and tried to make contact while making the basket.

d. A band in contrasting colour on a jockey's blouse, sleeves, or cap. So **hooped** *a.*

1898 *Dorling's List Epsom Races* 27 May 1/3 Rose hoops, rose cap..black hooped sleeves. **1961** F. C. AVIS *Sportsman's Gloss.* 228/2 *Hoops*, narrow bands of white or coloured silks going round the jockey's blouse; also known as Rings. **1970** *Accent* June 35/1 Wives try to get colours as close to those of their husbands... The Duchess of Devonshire's silks are straw with a brown hoop on the cap. *Ibid.* 35/2 (*caption*) Maroon hooped sleeves.

e. *Austral.* A jockey.

1941 BAKER *Dict. Austral. Slang* 36 *Hoop*, a jockey. **1957** 'N. CULOTTA' *They're Weird Mob* (1958) v. 72 Best hoop in the country. **1963** *Sunday Mirror* (Sydney) 20 Jan. 43/1 Glamour hoop Athol Mulley in the saddle. **1967** E. MCGIRR *Hearse with Horses* ii. 33 Old Paddy was not a great deal more successful as a trainer than I was as a hoop.

9. A hoop- or ring-net.

1882 *Standard* 26 Sept. 2/2 They [whelks] are also caught in nets called 'hoops' or 'rings'.

10. One of the iron arches used in croquet.

1872 R. C. A. PRIOR *Croquet* 56 *Hoop* is now an established term, but is a wrong name for the arches set up on a croquet lawn. **1874** J. D. HEATH *Croquet Player* 17 The setting or arrangement of the hoops.

†**11.** The semicircular part of the spur which clasps the boot. *Obs.*

1620 SHELTON *Quix.* (1746) III. xiv. 93 Jagging his Spurs into his Horse to the very Hoops.

†**12.** *pl.* A canopy stretched upon hoops. *Obs.*

c **1520** *Mem. Ripon* (Surtees) III. 206 Item pro howpps pro sacrament ad summum altare, 1½d.

13. *attrib.* and *Comb.* **a.** General, as ***hoop-bender***, ***-dancer***, ***-girdle***, ***-maker***, ***-mill***, ***-roller***, ***-stuff***; ***hoop-crimping***, ***-dressing***, ***-fellied***, ***-horned***, ***-ribbed***, ***-riving***, ***-spined***, ***-splaying***, etc., adjs. Also HOOP-PETTICOAT, -STICK.

1858 GREENER *Gunnery* 99 In the *hoop-and-stave wrought iron gun. **1812** *Examiner* 7 Dec. 777/1 W. Rumsey, ..*hoop bender. **1875** KNIGHT *Dict. Mech.*, **Hoop-crimping Machine*, one for giving the bend to hoop-stuff to render the hoops tractable in fitting to barrels and casks. **1800** *Sporting Mag.* XV. 28 His most Christian Majesty was attended by several devils, *hoop-dancers and banner-bearers. **1799** *Ibid.* XIV. 28 *Hoop-fellied wheels. **1607** DEKKER *Knt.'s Conjur.* (1842) 74 A streame..clasps it round about like a *hoope girdle of christall. **1626** *Canterb. Marriage Licences* (MS.), Robert Claringbole of Barham, *hoopemaker. **1832** in Cobbett *Rur. Rides* (1885) II. 366 Beautiful cattle ..*hoop-ribbed, square hipped. **1825** J. NICHOLSON *Operat. Mechanic* 339 The *hoop-rollers are represented in fig. 351; the bar-rollers in fig. 352. **1884** *B'ham Daily Post* 28 July 3/4 Wanted, a thoroughly experienced..Hoop Roller. **1875** KNIGHT *Dict. Mech.*, **Hoop Splaying and Bending Machine*, a machine for spreading hoop-iron on one side so as to enable it to set snugly on the bilge.

b. Special combs.: **hoop-ash**, (*a*) a species of ash, *Fraxinus sambucifolia*, the flexible stems of which are used for making hoops; (*b*) the American Hackberry, *Celtis occidentalis* (Craig 1847); **hoop-back**, (a chair with) a hooped back; also *attrib.* in ***hoop-back chair***; **hoop-bee**, a burrowing bee of the genus *Eucera*; †**hoop-caul**, the chorion or outermost membrane enveloping the fœtus before birth; †**hoop-coat**, = HOOP-PETTICOAT; **hoop-cramp**, 'a ring-clutch for holding the ends of a hoop which are lapped over each other' (Knight *Dict. Mech.*); **hoop-driver**, a tool or machine by which the hoops of a cask are driven on; **hoop-iron**, (*a*) flat thin bar-iron of which hoops are made; (*b*) the iron rod with which a child's hoop is trundled; **hoop-lock**, a mode of connecting the ends of a wooden hoop by interlocking notches; also one of the notches themselves; †**hoop-man**, an acrobat who performs with hoops; **hoop-net**, a fishing-net, butterfly-net, etc. held open by a hoop or ring at its mouth; **hoop-pine**, the Moreton Bay Pine (*Araucaria Cunninghamii*) of eastern Australia (Morris); **hoop-pole**, a smooth straight sapling of green wood for making hoops; **hoop-ring**, a ring consisting of a plain band; also, a finger-ring encircled with stones in a cut-down setting; **hoop-shave**, a kind of spoke-shave for dressing hoop-stuff; **hoop-shaver**, (*a*) one who dresses wood for hoops; (*b*) a name given to a species of wood-boring bees; **hoop-shell**, a shell of the genus *Trochus*, a top-shell; **hoop-skirt** = HOOP-PETTICOAT; also *fig.*; †**hoop-sleeve**, a wide full sleeve, as though expanded by hoops; **hoop-snake**, a non-venomous American snake, *Farancia abacura*, popularly believed to roll like a hoop; = *horn-snake* (*b*) *s.v.* HORN *sb.* 30; **hoop stress**, the stress in a cylinder or in a spherical shell corresponding to the hoop tension; **hoop tension**, the circumferential tension in a transverse section of a cylinder or in a spherical shell subjected to radial pressure; **hoop-tree**, a semi-tropical low tree, *Melia sempervirens* (Miller 1884); †**hoop-wheel**, the detent-wheel of a clock; **hoop-withe**, **-withy**, a plant of the genus *Rivina* (Craig 1847); also *Colubrina asiatica* (Miller 1884); **hoop-wood**, a tree yielding wood suitable for making hoops; in Jamaica *Calliandra latifolia*; in U.S. the Hoop-ash; the black ash, *Fraxinus nigra*, or the winterberry, *Ilex lævigata*; in Jamaica, *Zygia latifolia*.

1763 *Hoop ash [see BUCK-EYE 1]. **1832** D. J. BROWNE *Silva Amer.* 133 On the Ohio it is called Hoop Ash and in Kentucky, Hack Berry. **1864** *Chambers's Encycl.* VI. 727 Another American species, *Celtis crassifolia*, often called Hackberry or Hagberry, and Hoop Ash. **1905** P. MACQUOID *Hist. Eng. Furnit.* II. viii. 198 Early *hoop-back chairs..were slow in obtaining favour. **1924** MACQUOID & EDWARDS *Dict. Eng. Furnit.* I. 244 The tall back is reminiscent of early eighteenth century walnut chairs... A deliberate attempt at Oriental effect may be seen in..the shaping of the hoop-back. **1934** *Burlington Mag.* Nov. 204/1 The chair..has a splat formed of framework..the uprights continue in the top-rail so as to form a fine 'hoop-back'. **1935** [see *comb-back* s.v. COMB *sb.*[1] 9]. **1952** J. GLOAG *Short Dict. Furnit.* 506 The two main types of design in Windsor chairs are: the comb back and the hoop back... In the latter, the back is shaped like a bow, into which the spindles are socketed. **1545** RAYNOLD *Byrth Mankynde* (1564) 34 b, Chorion or the *hoope cal. **1820** SCORESBY *Acc. Arctic Reg.* II. 511 A quantity of *hoop-iron and rivets. **1858** SIMMONDS *Dict. Trade*, *Hoop-iron*,..a child's toy for trundling a hoop. *a* **1668** DAVENANT *Play-House* I. Dram. Wks. 1873 IV. 24 Rich jugglers..*hoop-men, And so many tom-tumblers. **1481–90** *Howard Househ. Bks.* (Roxb.) 192 [The] netter..had sent home..ij. *hopenettes, prise viij. *d.* **1880** HUXLEY *Crayfish* i. 11 Hoop-nets baited with frogs are let down into the water. **1884** A. NILSON *Timber Trees N.S.W.* xv. 33 (*heading*) Araucaria. (Natural Order Coniferae.)..A. Cunninghamii.—Moreton Bay Pine; Colonial Pine; *Hoop

Pine.— A noble tree with a pyramidal or somewhat flattened head. **1920** B. Cronin *Timber Wolves* i. 21 Well, what wood are they using for their matches now? I'll tell you. Their substitute is Queensland hoop pine, and I ain't heard any complaints yet. **1956** M. West *Gallows on Sand* xv. 153, I showed her the great hoop-pines, whose seeds had been carried by birds from the mainland [of Australia]. **1969** T. H. Everett *Living Trees of World* 25/1 Another Australian species is the Richmond-river-pine or hoop-pine (*A. cunninghamii*), the latter name deriving from its bark, which has horizontal cracks in encircling bands. **1807** Vancouver *Agric. Devon* (1813) 247 Used for hop-poles, *hoop-poles, hurdles, faggots, and charcoal. **1545** Raynold *Byrth Mankynde* 39 It is compassed with this wrapper, as with a broode *hoope-ryng. **1629** Massinger *Picture* ii. ii, Good madam, what shall he do with a hoopring, And a spark of diamond in it? **1798** Jane Austen *Northang. Abb.* (1833) I. xv. 99 She saw herself with..a brilliant exhibition of hoop rings on her finger. **1885** *St. James's Gaz.* 2 Jan. 6/2 The long-bladed *hoop-shave, with the double handle. **1688** *Lond. Gaz.* No. 2318/4 A Man of about 30 years old..by Trade a *Hoopshaver, or Lathrender. **1771** G. White *Obs. Insects* in *Selborne* (1875) 348 It strips off the pubes, shaving it bare with the dexterity of a hoop-shaver. **1864–5** Wood *Homes without H.* viii. (1868) 180 One of the wood-boring bees..We will call it the Hoop-shaver. **1857** Underhill & Thompson *Elephant Club* 193 Lady with *hoop-skirt hails the driver. **1875** Knight *Dict. Mech.* 1118/2 The modern hoop-skirt is formed of braid-covered flat steel-wire hoops, united by tapes and shaped upon a former. **1892** A. E. Lee *Hist. Columbus* (Ohio) I. 735 The hoop-skirt gradually waned until the opposite extreme was reached. **1896** *Emporia* (Kan.) *Gaz.* 15 Aug., We have raked the old ash heap of failure..and found an old human hoop skirt who has failed as a business man. **1906** *Springfield Weekly Republ.* 19 July 1 Populism was a 'hoopskirt' article of statesmanship. **1916** E. Pound *Lustra* 54 You're a very depleted fashion, A hoop-skirt, a calash. *a* **1613** Overbury *Char., Lawyer* Wks. (1856) 85 Next tearme he walkes his *hoopsleeve gowne to the hall. **1784** J. F. D. Smyth *Tour in U.S.* I. 265 From the above circumstance, peculiar to themselves, they have also derived the appellation of *hoop snakes. **1840** *Southern Lit. Messenger* VI. 380/2, I never believed in the existence of hoop-snakes neither, until I went out into the western country. **1937** A. H. Verrill *Strange Reptiles* ii. 7 Thousands of otherwise intelligent and educated persons believe in the mythical 'hoop snake' which is supposed to take its tail in its mouth and roll like a hoop with incredible speed. **1956** C. H. Pope *Reptile World* 156 Tens of thousands of country people see hoop snakes rolling about like hoops, but these snakes quickly stop rolling and crawl when a herpetologist looms in sight. **1909** Webster, *Hoop stress. **1930** *Engineering* 23 May 679/2 S is the apparent hoop stress. **1966** C. C. Barnes *Power Cables* (ed. 2) xii. 179 The maximum pressure in the cable is therefore dictated by the hoop stress developed in the sheath. **1973** *Sci. Amer.* Dec. 18/1 The tensile strength must be sufficient to withstand the 'hoop stress' resulting from centrifugal forces, otherwise the [fly]wheel would fly apart. **1896** *Hoop tension [see stress *sb.* 5 c]. **1902** *Kynoch Jrnl.* Oct.–Nov. 17/1 Since the ratio of the inner to outer radius is now 1·595, the hoop tension at the inner surface = 62·8 tons. **1950** *Jrnl. R. Aeronaut. Soc.* LIV. 133 The earliest specimens of these [parachutes]..took account of 'hoop tensions', 'pressure across the fabric', etc. **1704** J. Harris *Lex. Techn., Detent-Wheel*, or **Hoop-Wheel* in a Clock, is that which has a Hoop almost round it, wherein there is a Vacancy at which the Clock locks. **1756** P. Browne *Jamaica* 279 Horse-wood, or *Hoop-wood, the wood is pretty tough, and sometimes cut for hoops. **1770** G. Washington *Writ.* (1889) II. 302, I marked two maples, an elm, and hoop-wood tree..I also marked..an ash and hoop-wood. **1821** J. Fowler *Jrnl.* (1898) 21 We get out at our ushal time; at ten miles pased a point of Rocks and a Hoop wood tree on them. **1908** N. L. Britton *N. Amer. Trees* 622 Winterberry—*Ilex lævigata*.. is also called the Smooth winterberry and Hoopwood. **1920** Fawcett & Rendle *Flora of Jamaica* IV. 150 (*heading*) Z[ygia] latifolia..Horse wood, hoop wood.

hoop, *sb.*^{2} Also 4 **houp**, 6 **howp**. [f. hoop *v.*^{2} Cf. hoop *int.*, whoop *sb.* and *int.*, F. *houp* int.]

1. A cry or call of 'hoop'; a whoop.

1340–70 *Alex. & Dind.* 167 Whan þei hurden [h]is houp, hastiliche aftur A lud to a litil boot lepus in haste. **1673** S. Parker *Reproof Rehears. Transp.* 26 (R.) You have run them all down with hoops and hola's. **1791** 'G. Gambado' *Ann. Horsem.* xvii. (1809) 135 His shouts..much resembled the war-hoops of the Indians. **1879** R. H. Elliot *Writ. on Foreheads* II. 6 The hoop-hoop-hoop of the large black-bodied, grey-bearded monkey.

2. The sonorous inspiration characteristic of hooping-cough. (Quot. 1538 is uncertain.)

[**1538** Bale *Thre Lawes* 195 For noyaunce of the howp, For easement of your toth.] **1811** Hooper *Med. Dict.* s.v. *Pertussis*, The cough..is attended with a peculiar sound, which has been called a hoop. **1871** Napheys *Prev. & Cure Dis.* ii. i. 370 The long, jerking cough, interspersed with a loud, sucking, drawing in of the air, known as the 'hoop', is known to every mother.

hoop, *sb.*^{3} Forms: 5 **huppe**, 6 **hupe**, **houupe**, 6–7 **houpe**, **hoope**, 7 **oope**, **whoope**, 7–8 **houp**, 7– **hoop**. [a. F. *huppe* (12th c. in Hatz.-Darm.), in Cotgr. *hupe*, *upe* 'a little woollen thread, or tuft in the top of a cap; also, the crest, or cop on the head of a bird; also, the Whoope or dunghill Cocke':—pop. L. *ūpupa*, for *upupa* hoopoe.]

†1. The hoopoe. (Formerly identified or confused with the lapwing on account of its crest.) *Obs.*

1481 Caxton *Myrr.* ii. xvi. 102 The huppe or lapwynche is a byrd crested, whiche is moche in mareys & fylthes. **1580** Hollyband *Treas. Fr. Tong*, *Hupe*, a bird called a Houpe. **1599** Minsheu *Sp. Dict.*, *Abubilla*, a bird called a Hoope. Some thinke it to be the Lapwing. **1601** Holland *Pliny* I. 287 The Houpe or Vpupa..is a nasty and filthy bird..but a goodly faire crest or comb it hath. **1607** J. *Barley-Breake* (1877) 32 Rookes, Pies, and Oopes. **1666** J. Davies *Hist. Caribby Isls* 92 That Bird which the Latines call *Upupa*, the English a *Whoope*. *a* **1682** Sir T. Browne *Tracts* (1684) 106 When Tereus was turned into an *Upupa*, or Hoopebird. **1708** Ockley *Saracens* (1848) 495 Solomon and the Queen of Sheba..had a bird called Hudhud (that is, the 'houp') who was the messenger of their amours.

2. A local name for the Bullfinch.

[It is not certain that this is the same word: cf. the names alp^2, olph, nope (= an *ope*).]

1798 F. Leighton *MS. Let. to J. Boucher* 11 May (Shropsh. Words), A Bullfinch—near Bath it is called a Hoop: in Norfolk an Olph. **1845** *P. Parley's Ann.* VI. 36 [The bullfinch] in some places..is called the Thickbill, the nope, and the hoop. It has a wild hooping note. **1848** *Zoologist* VI. 2290 The bullfinch is in G[loucestershire] a 'hoop'.

hoop, *v.*^{1} [f. hoop *sb.*^{1}]

1. *trans.* To bind or fasten round with a hoop or hoops; to confine with hoops.

c **1440** *Promp. Parv.* 245/2 Hoopyn, or settyn hoopys on a vesselle. **1531–2** *Act 23 Hen. VIII*, c. 4 §10 Euery bere brewer may kepe..coupers, to hoope and amende his barrelles. **1602** Marston *Ant. & Mel.* v. Wks. 1856 I. 65 And twere not hoopt with steele, my brest wold break. **1674** tr. *Martiniere's Voy. N. Countries* 18 A Tub of Wood, hoop'd about with Iron..in which we were let down into the Mine. **1693** R. Gould *Corrupt. Times by Money* 26 Tho your Tomb be hoop'd with Lead. **1809** W. Irving *Knickerb.* vi. iii. (1849) 327 The music of a cooper hooping a flour-barrel. **1887** Hall Caine *Deemster* xxx. 195 The smith was hooping a cart-wheel.

2. *transf.* and *fig.* To surround or confine as with a hoop; to encircle, embrace; to bind together or unite, as the staves of a tub.

a **1541** Wyatt *Of meane Estate* 77 in *Tottell's Misc.* (Arb.) 87 Although thy head were hoopt with golde. **1611** Shaks. *Wint. T.* iv. iv. 450 If euer henceforth, thou..hope his body more, with thy embraces. **1690** Leybourn *Curs. Math.* 457 An Island is a part of the Earth..hoopt as it were with a watery Girdle. **1821** T. Jefferson *Autobiog.* Writ. 1892 I. 107 During the war of Independence, while the pressure of an external enemy hooped us together.

hoop, *v.*^{2} Also 4 **howpe**, **hope**, 4–7 **houpe**, 6 **hoope**. [a. F. *houpe-r* (in 12th c. *huper*), f. *houp*, imitative of the cry: see hoop *sb.*^{2} ? Cf. OE. *hwōpan* to threaten, OHG., Goth. *hwôpan* to boast, from which some derive the Fr. vb. whoop (q.v.) is a later spelling, after *who*: cf. *whole*.]

1. *intr.* To utter a hoop; to whoop.

1362 Langl. *P. Pl.* A. vii. 159 Pers..hoped [B. vi. 174 houped; *v.r.* howpede] aftur hunger þo þat herde him atte furste. *c* **1386** Chaucer *Nun's Pr. T.* 580 Ther-with-al they shriked and they howped. *a* **1553** Udall *Royster D.* ii. i. (Arb.) 32 The howlet out of an yuie bushe should hoope. **1601** Holland *Pliny* I. 21 Ecchoes, answering one another ..when a man doth holla or houpe among them. **1664** Etheredge *Love in Tub* i. ii, You..hoop'd and hollow'd like madmen, and roar'd out in the streets. **1771** Mrs. Griffith tr. *Viaud's Shipwreck* 226, I intreated them to hoop and halloo..in hopes she might be able to hear. **1845** Mrs. S. C. Hall *Whiteboy* iv. 30 [He was] hooping and jumping like a half maniac.

†b. ***hoop and hide***: the game hide-and-seek.

1710–11 Swift *Tatler* 27 Jan. ⁋6 You played at Hoope and Hide with my Brother in the Garret.

†2. To shout with astonishment. *Obs.*

1599 Shaks. *Hen. V*, ii. ii. 108 Working so grossely..That admiration did not hoope at them. **1600** —— *A.Y.L.* iii. ii. 203 O wonderfull, and most wonderfull wonderfull, and yet againe wonderful, and after that out of all hooping.

3. To make the sonorous inspiration characteristic of hooping-cough.

1822–34 *Good's Study Med.* (ed. 4) I. 452 *note*, Dr. Gregory knew a lady who never hooped in the disease, but instead of doing so always fainted.

†4. *trans.* To greet with a 'hoop'. *Obs. rare.*

1781 W. Blane *Ess. Hunting* (1788) 122 Having met and hooped her, she [the hare] has redoubled back..and leaped off into some hedge.

b. ***hoop out***: to drive out with derisive cries.

1607 Shaks. *Cor.* iv. v. 84 By th' voyce of Slaues to be Hoop'd out of Rome.

hoop, *int.* [Cf. hoop *v.*^{2}] = whoop.

1709 Steele *Tatler* No. 2 ⁋2 Hey! Hoop! d'ye hear my damn'd obstrep'rous Spouse! **1792** Hohoop [see ho *int.*^{1} 5].

†'**hoopage**. *Obs.* [f. hoop *sb.*^{1}] (See quot.)

1611 Cotgr., *Droict de Liage*, hoopage; or a fee due vnto some Lords vpon euerie hooped vessell of wine which their vassalls haue, or sell.

hoop(e, obs. ff. hope; var. hoppe, boll of flax.

hooped (huːpt), *a.* [f. hoop *sb.*^{1} + -ed^2.]

1. a. Having a hoop or hoops; made with a hoop. (See also hoop *sb.*^{1} 8 d.)

1552 Huloet, Houped, *funetus*. **1630** in *Descr. Thames* (1758) 66 No Fisherman..shall..use or exercise any.. hooped Net. **1716** *Lond. Gaz.* No. 5464/4 One hoop'd Diamond Ring, with 19 Brilliants. **1794** W. Felton *Carriages* (1801) I. 111 There are three descriptions of wheels, viz. the straked, the hooped, and the patent rim. **1866** Rogers *Agric. & Prices* I. xxvi. 648 Hooped wooden goblets.

b. ***hooped petticoat*** = hoop-petticoat 1.

1712 *Spect.* No. 292 ⁋11, I wear the hooped Petticoat. **1881** Besant & Rice *Chapl. Fleet* I. 203 Skirts extended like a woman's hooped petticoat.

2. Wearing a hoop (sense 6).

1821–30 Ld. Cockburn *Mem.* i. 63 They had both shone as hooped beauties in the minuets. **1864** Sala in *Daily Tel.* 10 June, Are the stalls of the opera big enough to hold their hooped occupants?

3. Rounded like a hoop.

1852 *Trans. Mich. Agric. Soc.* III. 137 The breeder will do well to seek in his animal a proper form, viz...good, hooped ribs. **1934** M. F. McTaggart *Handbk. Horse Owners* ii. 40 The ribs should be well hooped and deep.

4. *Comb.* **hooped-back** *a.*, said of a chair with a hooped back. (Cf. *hoop-back*.)

1906 P. Macquoid *Hist. Eng. Furnit.* III. ii. 60 In the hooped-back chair..the splat begins to show signs of subdivision. **1941** *Burlington Mag.* June 187/1 Hooped-back chairs with compass seats were produced in the provinces until after Chippendale's *Director* made its appearance. **1960** H. Hayward *Antique Coll.* 145/1 Hooped-back chair.

hoop-ee, *int.* (Cf. hoop *int.* and whoopee.)

1846 J. J. Hooper *Adv. Simon Suggs* iii. 31 Hoop-ee! *won't* they roll over the floor.

hooper^1 ('huːpə(r)). [f. hoop *v.*^{1} + -er^1.] A craftsman who fits the hoops on casks, barrels, etc.; a cooper. Also, a maker of hoops.

1552 Huloet, Howper, *vietor*. **1554** T. Martin *Priests Marr.* Llij b, Euerye..tinker, tailour, hooper. **1765** J. Brown *Chr. Jrnl.* (1814) 55 Here stands the hooper: just now he set up the staves of his vessel. **1861** W. H. Russell in *Times* 12 July, A few of the Creole population..engaged as hoopers and stave-makers.

'**hooper**^{2}. [f. hoop *v.*^{2} + -er^1.]

1. One who hoops or cries 'hoop': only in ***hoopers hide***, an old name of hide-and-seek; cf. hoop *v.*^{2} 1 b.

1719 D'Urfey *Pills* I. 278 His Wife with Willy, Was playing at Hoopers-hide.

2. The Whooping, Whistling, or Wild Swan, *Cygnus musicus* (*ferus*): so called from its cry.

1556 Withals *Dict.* (1568) 5 b/1 A hooper or wilde swanne, *onocrotalus*. **1686** Plot *Staffordsh.* 228 Hoopers or wild-Swans whose feet are not black, but of a dusky yellow. **1750** R. Pococke *Trav.* (1888) 95 A sort of swan..call'd a hooper. **1851** J. Colquhoun *Moor & Loch* (1880) I. 77 Four hoopers were discovered close to the shore.

hooperyng, obs. f. *hoop-ring* (hoop *sb.*^{1} 13 b).

hooping ('huːpɪŋ), *vbl. sb.*^{1} [f. hoop *v.*^{1}]

1. The action of the verb hoop^1; the putting of hoops on casks, barrels, etc. Also *fig.*

1463 *Mann. & Househ. Exp.* (Roxb.) 193 Payd to Peter Garn for hopyng and hedyng and settyng in of hedys of pypys and barells. **1589** *Hay any Work* Bb, Your Cooper.. is..a deceitful workeman, and if you commit the hooping of your bishopricks vnto him, they wil leake. **1664** Butler *Hud.* ii. ii. 590 Kettle-drums, whose sullen dub Sounds like the hooping of a tub. **1803** *Naval Chron.* X. 477 The hooping of masts.

2. *concr.* Hoop-iron.

1823 Scoresby *Whale Fishery* 36 A coarse piece of iron-hooping, the substitute for a razor. **1831** J. Holland *Manuf. Metal* I. 145 Pieces of the old hooping properly straightened and cut into lengths.

†b. Something that girds like a hoop. *Obs. rare.*

1583 Stanyhurst *Æneis* ii. (Arb.) 50 His midil embracing with wig wag circuled hooping.

3. Trundling a hoop. *nonce-use.*

1844 *P. Parley's Ann.* V. 68 We had sober, steady, ashen hoops..and instead of hooping about in public thoroughfares..we used to take a range round greens, commons.

hooping, *vbl. sb.*^{2} [f. hoop *v.*^{2} + -ing^1.] The action of hoop *v.*^{2}; crying 'hoop'.

1557 F. Seager *Sch. Vertue* 257 in *Babees Bk.* 341 Hoopynge and halowynge as in huntynge the foxe. **1600** Holland *Livy* vii. x. 255 Without any houping, singing, and joyous vaunting of himselfe. **1811** Hooper *Med. Dict.* s.v. *Pertussis*, A convulsive strangulating cough, with hooping.

hooping, *ppl. a.*^{1} [f. hoop *v.*^{1} + -ing^2.] That secures with or as with a hoop.

1794 W. Felton *Carriages* (1801) II. Gloss., *Hooping Piece*, a strong timber, which unites the perch to the fore end of the carriage. *Hooping Wings*, two extending timbers, which unite the perch to the fore end.

hooping, *ppl. a.*^{2} [f. hoop *v.*^{2} + -ing^2.] That hoops or whoops. †**hooping-bird**, the Hoopoe. **hooping-crane**, *Grus americana*. **hooping turtle**, the Hawk's-bill Turtle.

1677 Plot *Oxfordsh.* 177 The Upupa, the Hoopoe, or Hooping-bird. **1712** W. Rogers *Voy.* 276 The very large hooping or logger-head Turtle. **1731** Mortimer in *Phil. Trans.* XXXVII. 177 *Grus Americana alba*, The Hooping Crane. **1837** M. Donovan *Dom. Econ.* II. 137 The brown crane and hooping crane are both edible species.

hooping-cough. Formerly the prevalent spelling of whooping-cough.

hoop-la ('huːplɑː). Also **houp-la**. [f. hoop *sb.*^{1} + la *int.*] A game in which persons throw rings on to a surface containing a number of articles, the object being to gain any of these as a prize by throwing a ring so as to encircle it completely. Also *attrib.*

[**1907** *Yesterday's Shopping* (1969) 1031/1 Hoopla!.. The players endeavour to throw balls..through circles poised on the Clown's head and hands.] **1909** *London Mag.* Sept. 26 A new game: Hoop-la! **1910** *Daily Chron.* 14 Jan. 3/5 A showman placed his 'hoopla' near the Promenade at Whitley, Northumberland, and invited the public to throw rings (at so many a penny) for prizes. **1912** A. S. M. Hutchinson *Happy Warrior* v. i. 279 All Maddox's

smaller-fry—coker-nut shies, hoop-la's, Living Mermaid. **1924** *Other Lands* Jan. 68/2 Houp-la stalls are a great attraction. **1927** *Blackw. Mag.* Sept. 358/2 We..finally sought refuge from the mob in a 'hoopla' stall, where we tried our luck. **1935** *Punch* 18 Sept. 319/1 One also tried one's hand at clock-golf, Houp-là! and throwing little balls into a bucket from which they instantly sprang out again. **1959** P. H. JOHNSON *Humbler Creation* xlviii. 329 His wife.. had the hoop-la [stall at a fête]. **1964** K. ROSEWALL in A. Trengove *Art of Tennis* 26 Most people do things like dealing cards, and playing table tennis and hoop-la backhanded. **1973** P. MOYES *Curious Affair of Third Dog* x. 135 You will not turn down my heartfelt appeal to you to preside over the Hoop-La stall.

hoop-la, var. HOUP-LA *int.*

hoopless ('huːplɪs), *a.* [f. HOOP *sb.*[1] + -LESS.] Having no hoop.

1885 A. MUNRO *Siren Casket* 65 Two hoopless pails.

hoopoe ('huːpuː). Also 7 hoopo, 7–8 hoopoop, 7– hoopoo. [app. an alteration of the earlier HOOP (*sb.*[3]), with partial assimilation to L. *upupa*, formed on the cry (*up up*) of the bird: cf. the form *hoopoop*.] A bird of the family *Upupidæ*, esp. the typical *Upupa epops*, a south European species, which occasionally visits England, conspicuous by its variegated plumage and its large erectile crest; formerly called HOOP (*sb.*[3]).

1668 CHARLETON *Onomasticon Zoicon* 92 *Upupa*,.. vernaculè an Hoopoop. **1675** RAY *Dict. Trilingue* 27 This bird [the lapwing] by a great mistake hath been generally taken to be the *upupa* of the Antients, which is now by all acknowledged to be the *Hoopo*. **1677** [see HOOPING *ppl. a.*[2]]. **1688** R. HOLME *Armoury* II. 254/2 A Upupa..is in our country speech called a Whoophoo, or Whopee, or Hoopoe, and Howpe. **1750** tr. *Leonardus' Mirr. Stones* 222 *Quirus*, is a juggling Stone, found in the Nest of the Hoopoop. **1789** G. WHITE *Selborne* ii. 31 The most unusual birds I ever observed in these parts were a pair of hoopoes. **1852** W. SMITH *Smaller Class. Dict.* (1874) 417 Procne, accordingly, became a nightingale.. Tereus a hoopoo. **1895** *Daily News* 5 Oct. 6/2, I saw to-day a pair of hoopoes on the road.. I could see the beautiful orange crest of the male, with its black tip going up and down as he walked, and after he flew into the tree he continued his cry of 'uup, uup'.

ˌhoop-'petticoat.

1. A petticoat or skirt stiffened and expanded by hoops of whalebone, cane, hoop-steel, or the like. (See HOOP *sb.*[1] 6.)

1711 ADDISON *Spect.* No. 127 ¶5 There are Men of Superstitious Tempers, who look upon the Hoop Petticoat as a kind of Prodigy. **1725** *Lond. Gaz.* No. 6391/6 John Lee, ..Hoop-Petticoat-Maker. **1770** GRAY in *Corr. with N. Nicholls* (1843) 112 With what grace..can she conduct her hoop petticoat through this auger-hole, and up the dark windings of the grand escalier? **1837** L. HUNT *Men, Women & B.* (1876) 310 We perceive a rustling of hoop-petticoats.

2. In full, ***hoop-petticoat narcissus*** or ***daffodil***. A plant of the species *Narcissus bulbocodium* or *N. cantabrica*, so called from the shape of the yellow or white flowers.

1731 P. MILLER *Gardener's Dict.* (*s.v.* Narcissus) 35 Rush-leaf'd Daffadil, with very narrow Petals, and a large tubulous Cup, commonly call'd The Hoop-Petticoat. **1790** *Curtis's Bot. Mag.* III. tab. 88 (*heading*) Narcissus Bulbocodium. Hoop Petticoat Narcissus. **1841** J. W. LOUDON *Ladies' Compan. Flower Garden* 190/1 The genus Narcissus is a very extensive one, embracing, as it does, the Jonquils, the Polyanthus Narcissus, the little Hoop Petticoat, the Poet's Narcissus, and the Daffodils, besides numerous others. **1866** *Treas. Bot.*, *Corbularia*, a genus of amaryllids, commonly called Hoop-petticoats... *C. Bulbocodium*, the common Hoop-petticoat. **1889** J. HABBERTON in *Harper's Mag.* Feb. 367/1 The daffodil, the 'pheasant-eye', and the 'hoop-petticoat' are all narcissuses. **1934** E. A. BOWLES *Handbk. Narcissus* xix. 211 It is hard to believe that the white Hoop Petticoat was ever found so far to the north as Cantabrica. **1952** C. E. L. PHILLIPS *Small Garden* xiii. 164 The 'hoop-petticoat daffodil' (*N. bulbocodium*), 6 ins., like a little bugle with virtually no perianth. **1961** P. M. SYNGE *Collins Guide to Bulbs* 232 Bulbocodium group. These are the hoop petticoats and they are nearly all subsp., varieties or forms of *N. bulbocodium*, a very large and variable sp., the exception being the early white-flowered forms known as *monophyllus* and *foliosus* which have now been separated under the name *N. cantabricus*. **1970** C. LLOYD *Well-Tempered Garden* 137, I dug up a congested clump of the hoop petticoat daffodil.

Hence **ˌhoop-'petticoated** *a.*, wearing a hoop-petticoat; having a flower of this shape (see sense 2 above).

1837 HAWTHORNE *Twice-Told T.* (1851) II. iv. 79 A hoop-petticoated phantom of Esther Dudley. **1893** *Daily News* 28 Mar. 2/2 Hoop-petticoated daffodils.

'hoop-stick.

1. A thin pliable stick or sapling such as is used for making cask-hoops.

1703 MOXON *Mech. Exerc.* 11 Your Punch fixed at the end of a Hoop-stick, or some such Wood. **1704** tr. *I. Lefevre's Mem.* 75 How many blows I have received with Cudgels and Hoopsticks.

2. One of the arched rails forming the framework of a carriage-head.

1794 W. FELTON *Carriages* (1801) I. 16 The compass rails, called hoopsticks, five or six in number, are shaped to the intended form of the roof. *Ibid.* 31 The flats and hoopsticks, or the timber-work for a square head to support the leather.

3. A stick for driving a toy hoop.

1852 W. JERDAN *Autobiog.* III. 174 A woman, bowling a hoop round the walks, with a hoop-stick in one hand and a book in the other.

hoor, obs. and dial. f. WHORE.

hoora, hooray, var. HURRAH.

hooray (hʊ'reɪ), *int. Austral.* and *N.Z.* [Var. of HURRAH.] Good-bye. Cf. HURROO *int.* (*sb.*)

1898 *Bulletin* (Sydney) 4 June (*red page*), In many places the salutation 'good-day' or 'good-night' is simply 'Hooray!' **1937** J. A. LEE *Civilian into Soldier* VI. 255 His companion ..thrust back his seat, stood erect, called 'Horray!' and was gone. **1945** BAKER *Austral. Lang.* xiv. 251 Some authentic local equivalents [of *so long!*].. are *hooray! aroo!* and *see you!* ..employed for many years, especially in rural areas, to denote 'good-bye'. **1948** D. BALLANTYNE *Cunninghams* (1963) I. vi. 35 'Bye-bye, Mr. Cunningham.' 'Hooray,' Gil said. **1960** N. HILLIARD *Maori Girl* 128 'Well, hooray.' 'Hooray.' **1963** A. LUBBOCK *Austral. Roundabout* 83 Be seein' yer soon in England. Hooray! Aroo! Good on yer, Pom. **1965** *N.Z. Listener* 15 Oct. 9/4 Best of luck on the lake. Hooray!

Hooray Henry (həˌreɪ 'hɛnrɪ, also 'huːreɪ ˌhɛnrɪ). *slang.* [f. HOORAY *int.* + *Henry*, man's personal name; cf. *hurrah boy* s.v. HURRAH 4.] A type of loud, rich, rather ineffectual or foolish young society man; now *spec.* a fashionable, extroverted, but conventional upper-class young man (see quot. 1976). Also *ellipt.* as **Hooray**. Cf. SLOANE RANGER. Also *attrib.* and as *adj.*

[**1936** D. RUNYON in *Collier's* 18 Apr. 8/2 He is without doubt strictly a Hoorah Henry, and he is generally figured as nothing but a lob as far as ever doing anything useful in this world is concerned.] **1959** C. MACINNES *Absolute Beginners* 76 That garden-party's for the ooblies and the Hooray Henries, anyway. **1974** L. DEIGHTON *Spy Story* vi. 59 No matter how slow you take the briefing, one of these hoorays is going to ask that very question. **1976** J. GODBOLT *All this & 10%* iv. 45 [We] watched with mounting amusement the dancing dervish antics of the Guardees and their debutante ladies... Their movements on the floor were, without exception, wild, totally unrhythmic and it was physically dangerous to be in proximity when they were in full thrash. A description hit me as we gazed... I had then recently read a selection of Damon Runyon stories. In one of them, 'Tight Shoes', there was a rich layabout called Calvin Colby. Runyon described him as 'Strictly a Hooray Henry'... Runyon's actual term was 'Hurrah Henry', which I misread as 'Hooray Henry', pronounced it as such and the phrase stuck. **1977** *News of World* 17 Apr. 4/8, I see that type of Hooray-Henry round London and I wince. They're a pain. **1979** *New Statesman* 30 Mar. 456/2 A gang of Hooray Henrys from Sotheby's travel round the country crying 'Bring out your junk'. **1982** BARR & YORK *Official Sloane Ranger Handbk.* 118/1 Hooray Henrys are the tip of the Sloane iceberg, visible and audible for miles. **1983** *Sunday Times* 12 June 35/7 It got a thorough Hooray-Henry going-over and they never came back. **1985** P. GEDDES *State of Corruption* iii. 26 She wrote off his companions as provincial Hooray Henrys, but he was quieter. **1986** *Expression!* July 31/2 A blanket or rug is also a good idea (tartans for hoorays; kilims for aesthetes).

hoord, -e, obs. ff. HOARD, HORDE.

hoore, obs. f. HOUR, WHORE; var. ORE *adv.*, before.

hoorle, obs. f. HURL.

hooroosh, var. HURRISH, HUR(R)OOSH *v.*

hoors, -e, hoos, -e, obs. ff. HOARSE.

hoose, hooze (huːz), *sb.* [app. related to **hwós-* root of OE. *hwésan* to wheeze, or to root of HOAST cough.] A parasitic bronchial disease of animals; = HUSK *sb.*[2] Cf. HOAST.

a **1722** [see HUSK *sb.*[2]]. **1797** DOWNING *Disord. Horned Cattle* 15 The symptoms are a great difficulty in breathing, attended with a cough or hoose. **1828** *Craven Dial.*, *Hoose*, a difficulty of breathing in cattle. **1890** *Yorksh. Weekly Post* 15 Nov. 4/1 Husk or Hoose in Calves, Lambs, Heifers, and Sheep. **1922** JOYCE *Ulysses* 309 A hoose drench for coughing calves. **1932** GAIGER & DAVIS *Vet. Path. & Bact.* xxxii. 440 Parasites are a frequent cause of bronchitis in animals, particularly in cattle, sheep and swine. The condition is popularly known as 'husk' or 'hoose'. **1960** W. R. WOOLDRIDGE *Farm Animals* (ed. 2) vii. 299 Husk: Hoose: Parasitic Bronchitis. This disease is caused by a heavy infestation of lambs, up to one year of age, with the round worm, *Dictyocaulus filaria*. Adult sheep are fairly resistant to infection.

hoose, hooze, *v.* [Belongs to prec. sb.] *intr.* To cough or wheeze. Hence **'hoosing** *vbl. sb.*

1846 *Jrnl. R. Agric. Soc.* VII. I. 204 In the early short-horns no hoosing or cough, no delicacy of constitution was known. **1868** ATKINSON *Cleveland Gloss.*, *Hooze*, to wheeze or breathe with difficulty and noise.

hoose, obs. f. HOSE; Sc. f. HOUSE.

hoosegow ('huːsgaʊ). *U.S. slang.* [ad. S. Amer. or Mex. Sp. *juzgao* = *juzgado* tribunal:—L. *jūdicātum*, pa. pple. of *jūdicāre* to JUDGE.] Prison.

1911 *Popular Mag.* 15 May 104/1 No thanks for th' little lady savin' th' bunch of you from th' 'hoose-gow'. **1920** *Public Opinion* 3 Dec. 560/3 Only the keeper and the kept in the hoosegow knew it. **1927** 'J. BARBICAN' *Confess. Rum-Runner* iv. 47, I have had one dose of the hoosegow, and I can tell you I don't want any more. **1937** J. WORBY *Other Half* x. 99 We soon got to the hoose-gow and I was once again frisked for weapons. **1940** WODEHOUSE *Quick Service* xix. 237 This guy Weatherby is a right guy, and he doesn't go to any hoosegow, not while I have my strength. **1955** *Beaver* Autumn 4 They would cheerfully accept ten years in the hoosegow before they would again face Ole the Terror. **1963** J. JOESTEN *They call it Intelligence* VI. xxxiii. 293 Since he had already spent..much time in the hoosegow..he was ..set free. **1973** D. RAMSAY *Deadly Discretion* 163 I'm not going to answer any questions... Okay. Off we go to the hoosegow.

hoosh (huːʃ), *sb. slang.* [Origin unknown.] A kind of thick soup.

1905 R. F. SCOTT *Voy. 'Discovery'* I. 445 The cook.. proceeded to prepare the ingredients of the *hoosh*, by which term the hot, thick soup that constituted the sledging meal was generally known. **1911** —— *Jrnl.* 29 Nov. in *Last Exped.* (1913) I. xvi. 479 They had some of Chinaman's undercut in their hoosh yesterday. **1919** E. H. SHACKLETON *South* xii. 239 The hoosh-pot with our precious limpets and seaweed was kicked over in the rush. **1922** *Chambers's Jrnl.* Jan. 73/2 The thick savoury 'hoosh' of pemmican and broken plasmon biscuit.

hoosh (huːʃ), *int.* An exclamation used in driving animals, etc.

1874 HARDY *Far from Madding Crowd* I. x. 131 Saying 'Hoosh!' to the cocks and hens when they go upon your seeds. **1900** *Contemp. Rev.* Oct. 512 A loud 'hoosh' from the Kaffir roused one of the Englishmen.

hoosh (huːʃ), *v. colloq.* [f. prec. word; cf. SHOO *int.* and *v.*] *trans.* To force or turn or drive (an animal, etc.) *off* (or *out*, etc.); also *intr.*, to move (rapidly). Cf. also quot. 1943.

1908 *Athenæum* 11 Apr. 450/1, I hooshed them, hooshed them all into the shed. **1928** A. A. MILNE *House at Pooh Corner* vi. 100 'Well done, Pooh... That was a good idea of ours... Hooshing you to the bank like that.' '*Hooshing* me?' said Eeyore in surprise. 'Hooshing *me*? You didn't think I was *hooshed*, did you? I dived. Pooh dropped a large stone on me, and so as not to be struck heavily on the chest, I dived and swam to the bank.' **1933** L. A. G. STRONG *Sea Wall* xvii. 283 We could hoosh the whole lot of them off of the line, and the train could go by. **1934** A. RUSSELL *Tramp-Royal in Wild Australia* iii. 27, I untied my camel, 'hooshed' it down and mounted it. **1936** A. THIRKELL *August Folly* ix. 283 Oh, she's dressing, and Aunt Palmer hooshed me out. **1939** JOYCE *Finnegans Wake* 112 Trust her to propagate the species and hoosh her fluffballs safe through din and danger! **1943** HUNT & PRINGLE *Service Slang* 39 *Hooshing*, purely an R.A.F. word, which means landing at great speed. **1956** 'A. BRIDGE' *Lighthearted Quest* ii. 37 Why do you go hooshing off to find him in this completely wild-cat way?

hooshtah ('huːʃtɑː), *int.* Also **hushdar**. [Echoic.] A shout of encouragement, etc., to a camel. Hence as *vb.* Also occas. as *sb.*, a camel.

1903 R. BEDFORD *True Eyes & Whirlwind* xxxvi. 201 Their string of five camels..were water-swollen, so that they looked like five great footballs set up on sticks. One by one Quinn and Lawler 'hooshta'ed' them to the ground. **1906** *Daily Chron.* 8 Jan. 6/7 So the camel was hooshtahed down and strapped. **1911** C. E. W. BEAN *'Dreadnought' of Darling* xxiv. 211 He made a noise, probably 'Hooshta', as he went—'Hooshta' seems to be the only noise an Afghan ever does make to a camel. **1936** F. CLUNE *Roaming round Darling* xxiv. 258, I remembered over in Cairo the cameliers used to shout 'Hooshta, hooshta' to their camels... Jack the Ripper..returned and wishtered and hooshtered to Galahad, who stopped, and gently genuflected himself while the sore torn-seated Poet dismounted. **1942** C. BARRETT *On Wallaby* iv. 62 Many a time we've been out in the Sinai desert guarding a grazing mob of 'hooshtas'. **1964** H. M. BARKER *Camels & Outback* 74 All the time the standard oriental 'hushdar' was hissed as if it were spelt with many 's's'.

Hoosier ('huːʒɪə(r)). *U.S.* Also **hoosher**. [Origin unknown.] **a.** A nickname for a native or inhabitant of the state of Indiana.

1826 in *Chicago Tribune* (1949) 2 June 20/3 The Indiana hoosiers that came out last fall is settled from 2 to 4 milds of us. **1834** *Knickerbocker* III. 441 They smiled at my inquiry, and said it was among the 'hoosiers' of Indiana. **1835** J. H. INGRAHAM *South-West* I. ix. 105 The primitive navies.. manned..by 'real Kentucks'—'Buck eyes'—'Hooshers' and 'Snorters'. **1860** EMERSON *Cond. Life* ii. 58 These Hoosiers and Suckers are really better than the snivelling opposition. **1885** *Outing* (U.S.) Nov. 152/2 Oh, say, papa. Did you notice that young Hoosier and his bride who sat opposite me at breakfast? **1947** *Harper's Mag.* Jan. 67/2 Other Hoosiers ridicule them as hillbillies. **1958** *Economist* 1 Nov. 417/2 Indiana, whose inhabitants go by the obscure name of Hoosiers, is a deeply conservative state.

b. An inexperienced, awkward, or unsophisticated person.

1846 J. GREGG *Diary & Lett.* 22 Aug. (1941) I. 212 Old King is one of the most perfect samples of a Hoosier Texan I have met with. Fat, chubby, ignorant, and loquacious as Sancho Panza..we could believe nothing he said. **1857** E. L. GODKIN in R. Ogden *Life E. L. Godkin* I. 157 The mere 'cracker' or 'hoosier', as the poor [southern] whites are termed. **1874** J. W. LONG *Amer. Wild-Fowl Shooting* viii. 144 'Greenhorns' and 'hoosiers', as the regular hunters call such fellows. **1926** *Amer. Mercury* Jan. 64/2 The word hoosier is applied to any one who is incompetent. **1955** *Publ. Amer. Dial. Soc.* XXIV. 174 Thus *hoosier grift* is the crowd at a country fair.

c. *attrib.* Of or belonging to Indiana. **Hoosier cake** (see quot. 1859).

1839 J. PLUMBE *Sk. Iowa* 46 (Th.), The Hoosier State has reason to rejoice in the amount and value of its waters. **1845** *Knickerbocker* XXV. 374 Three hundred miles of Hoosier mud. **1859** BARTLETT *Dict. Amer.*, *Hoosier cake*, a Western name for a sort of coarse ginger-bread, which, say the Kentuckians, is the best bait to catch a hoosier with, the biped being fond of it. **1871** E. EGGLESTON *Hoosier Schoolmaster* (1872) Pref., It has been in my mind since I was a Hoosier boy. **1878** J. H. BEADLE *Western Wilds* i. 18 No grammar of the 'Hoosier' language has ever been published. **1907** *Chicago Evening Post* 4 May 5 A rose

festival will be given by the Indiana Society of Chicago, comprising hoosier business men of the city. **1916** *Daily Colonist* (Victoria, B.C.) 23 July 1/2 He [*sc.* James Whitcomb Riley] made a study of the 'Hoosier' dialect. **1956** H. GOLD *Man who was not with It* (1965) xiv. 116 She left a print like feathers tipped with toes in the Hoosier loam. **1972** *Christian Science Monitor* 28 Sept. 16/3 Some folkway yarns about logrolling in the early Hoosier days.

Hence '**Hoosierism**, a peculiarity of Indiana, esp. in speech.

1843 'R. CARLTON' *New Purchase* 63 Thus the cabin lady kept on doing up her small stock of English into Hoosierisms and other figures. **1878** J. H. BEADLE *Western Wilds* i. 18 The native of Indiana finds..that he must drop some of his 'Hoosierisms'.

hoost, obs. form of HOAST, HOST.

hoosyl, obs. form of HOUSEL.

hoot (hu:t), *int. Sc.* and *north. dial.* Also **hout** (haʊt), **hut** (hʌt). [App. a natural utterance of objection or repulsion, there being parallel forms in many langs.: e.g. Sw. *hut* begone, used in taking one up sharply, Welsh *hwt* off! away!, Irish *ut* out! pshaw!, Gael. *ut! ut!* interj. of disapprobation or dislike. Possibly connected in origin with HOOT *v.*]

An ejaculation expressing dissatisfaction with, or impatient and somewhat contemptuous dismissal of, a statement or notion: nearly synonymous with *tut!*, with which also it appears to be combined in the more emphatic ***hoot toot*** (*hout tout, hut tut*).

1681 OTWAY *Souldiers Fort.* I. i, Hout ye Caterpillars, ye Locusts of the Nation. **1762** FOOTE *Orator* II. Wks. 1799 I. 216 Hut, hut, not spake, what should ail me? **1795** MACNEILL *Will & Jean* I, ('Wha can this new comer be?') 'Hoot!' quo' Tam, 'there's drouth in thinking—Let's in, Will, and syne we'll see'. **1815** SCOTT *Guy M.* xxiii, Hout tout, man! I would never be making a hum-dudgeon about a scart on the pow. **1825–80** JAMIESON, *Hoot, hout, howts,*.. equivalent to Eng. *fy. Hoot-toot*, of the same meaning, but stronger, and expressing greater dissatisfaction, contempt, or disbelief. **1879** MRS. WALFORD *Cousins* x. 133 'Hut, Emily! who said you were a tyrant?' **1883** MRS. OLIPHANT *Ladies Lindores* II. 130 'Hoot, mem, we'll just manage fine'. **1893** *Northumbld. Gloss.*, *Hoot! hoots! howt! hout! hut! huts!* an expression of impatience. Sometimes *hoot-toot*, or otherwise varied.

So **hoots** (*houts, huts*), *int.* [with advb. *-s*.]

1824 MACTAGGART *Gallovid. Encycl.*, *Howts*, huts..as 'howts—nonsense'; 'howts—ay'. **1826** J. WILSON *Noct. Ambr.* Wks. 1855 I. 240 Hoots! You're no serious in sayin you're gaun to smoke already. **1832** W. STEPHENSON *Gateshead Local Poems* 59 One with feelings cried, 'Hoots, hoots, Let's roll him up in wool'. **1871** C. GIBBON *Lack of Gold* v, Hoots, not so bad as that. **1893** [see above].

hoot (hu:t), *v.* Forms: 3 **huten**, (4 **huit**), 4–5 **houte(n**, **howte(n**, **hot(en**, 6–7 **howt**, **hout**, 7– **hoot**, (7–9 **whoot**). [ME. *hūten* is found *c* 1200: perh. echoic, representing an inarticulate sound like the hooting of owls or the 'toot' of a horn or pipe, of which the characteristic vowel is *u* (being that heard at the greatest distance, whence its use in distant calls, as *hoo! hoo!*, *cooee*, etc.). Cf. Swedish *huta ut* 'to take one up sharply', MHG. *hiuzen*, *hûzen* to call to the pursuit; also Da. *huie* to shout, cry, halloo, Fr. *huer* to hoot, and the exclamations mentioned under HOOT *int.* But the phonology presents difficulties: beside *hūten*, ME. had *hōten*, north. and Sc. *huit, hute*: perhaps a different word. ME. *hūten* regularly gave later *hout, howt*, down to 17th c., when its place appears to have been taken by *hoot*, which might either be the descendant of OE. *hōten*, or an alteration of *hout* under the influence of the natural sounds (cf. CUCKOO). The late spelling *whoot* was due to the influence of *who, whom, whose*.]

1. a. *intr.* To shout, call out, make an inarticulate vocal noise; to toot with a horn; now, esp., to utter loud sounds of disapproval or obloquy.

a **1225** [see HOOTING *vbl. sb.*]. *c* **1350** *Will. Palerne* 2387 þei ..went after þe werwolf..hotend out wiþ hornes. *c* **1380** *Sir Ferumb.* 3225 þanne by-gunne þay to grede & houte. *c* **1440** *Promp. Parv.* 251/2 Howtyn, or cryyn, *boo. Ibid.*, Howtyn, or cryen as shepmenn, ..*celeumo*. *c* **1450** *Cov. Myst.* (Shaks. Soc.) 182 Upon my spere, A gerle I bere, I dare welle swere Lett moderes howte. **1601** SHAKS. *Jul. C.* I. ii. 245 And still as hee refus'd it, the rabblement howted, and clapp'd their chopt hands. **1610** ROWLANDS *Martin Mark-all* 35 At this newes the whole fraternity of Vagabonds whooted for ioy. **1654** H. L'ESTRANGE *Chas. I.* (1655) 19 Recusants.. frequently passed through the Churches in time of Divine Service houting and ho-lo-ing. **1666** WOOD *Life* (O.H.S.) II. 76 They houted and hum'd all the way from the Scooles to Xt. Ch. **1711** ADDISON *Spect.* No. 131 ⁋7, I do not hoot and hollow and make a Noise. *Mod.* The crowd began to hoot.

b. To call out or shout opprobriously *at* (†*on*) or *after* any one. (With *indirect passive*.)

a **1300** *Cursor M.* 15833 þai huited on him viliker þan he had ben a hund. **1565** T. STAPLETON *Fortr. Faith* 118 What is more houted at, scoffed and scorned in Englande now. **1592** NASHE *P. Penilesse* (ed. 2) 28 b, Young children howted at her as a strumpet. **1611** SHAKS. *Winter's T.* v. iii. 116 [It] should be hooted at Like an old Tale. **1624** GEE *Foot out of Snare* v. 27 All who meet with their modern books, may hoot at them. **1741** RICHARDSON *Pamela* I. 67, I cannot wear those good things without being whooted at. **1820** W. IRVING *Sketch Bk.* I. 78 A troop of strange children ran at his heels, hooting after him.

c. To laugh. *colloq.*

1926 T. E. LAWRENCE *Seven Pillars* (1935) x. cxxii. 659 At this onslaught I cackled out like a chicken, with the wild laughter of strain... I hooted out again. **1928** S. VINES *Humours Unreconciled* xv. 201 The first time I came across it, 'Shakespeare has no bloody relation with Schiller', I just hooted. **1959** N. MAILER *Advts. for Myself* (1961) 168 The others hoot, they giggle, they are weak from the combination of their own remarks and the action of the plot. **1969** *New Yorker* 28 June 37/2 She'd mention him tragically, then hoot with laughter.

2. a. *trans.* To assail with shouts or sounds of disapproval, contempt, or derision.

c **1200** ORMIN 2034 ȝiff mann wollde tælenn þatt, & hutenn hire & þutenn. *Ibid.* 4875 Whærse icc amm bitwenenn menn Icc hutedd amm & þutedd. **1377** LANGL. *P. Pl.* B. II. 218 He was nawhere welcome..Ouer al yhowted and yhote trusse. **1508** DUNBAR *Tua mariit Wemen* 465 Fy on hir!.. Hutit be the halok. **1611** B. JONSON *Catiline* III. ii, The Owle of Rome, whom boys and girles will hoot! **1728** YOUNG *Love Fame* II. (1757) 90 Tho' hiss'd and whooted by the pointing crowd. **1740** C. PITT *Virg., Æneid* XII. (R.), How will the Latians hoot their hero's flight! **1875** JOWETT *Plato* (ed. 2) I. 132 They will not listen to him, but laugh at him, and hoot him.

b. To drive (a person) *out, away*, or in any direction, (a play) *off* or *from* (the stage), by shouts and sounds of disapproval.

1393 LANGL. *P. Pl.* C. III. 228 He was..Ouer-al houted out and yhote trusse. **1624** FLETCHER *Rule a Wife* I. i, I would give the Boys leave to whoot me out o' th' Parish. **1683** KENNETT tr. *Erasm. on Folly* 29 [He] could never recover himself but was houted and hissed home again. **1712** STEELE *Spect.* No. 443 ⁋7 There is neither Mirth nor Good-humour in hooting a young Fellow out of Countenance. **1843** MACAULAY *Ess., Mad. D'Arblay* (1887) 743 His play had not been hooted from the boards. **1895** *19th Cent.* Aug. 327 They can tell the public that work which they elect to hoot off the stage is first rate in quality.

3. a. *intr.* Applied to the cry of some birds, *spec.* of the owl.

a **1500** *Cuckow & Night.* 185 Thou shalt be as other that been forsake, And than thou shalt hoten as do I [the Cuckoo]. **1601** SHAKS. *Jul. C.* I. iii. 28 The Bird of Night did sit..vpon the Market place, Howting, and shreeking. **1618** WITHER *Motto, Nec Careo* Wks. (1633) 531 No more..Then doth the Moone [fear] when dogs and birds of night Doe barking stand or whooting at her light. **1750** G. HUGHES *Barbadoes* 153 Even doves..will not whoot, if deprived of these and bird-pepper. **1820** W. IRVING *Sketch Bk.* (1859) 131 The owl [shall] hoot from the shattered tower.

b. *trans.* To utter or express by hooting.

a **1687** COTTON *Fable* (R.), Perched on Parnassus all night long, He [an owl] hoots a sonnet or a song.

4. Applied to certain sounds mechanically produced, esp. that of a steam siren or 'hooter', used as a signal to workmen for beginning or ceasing work, a fog-signal, etc. Also, to emit the sound of a motor-horn (said of the horn, the motor vehicle, or the driver). Also *trans.* ***to hoot her way*** (of a ship): to make her way (as in a fog) with continuous hooting.

1883 STEVENSON *Silverado Sq.* (1886) 84 A cuckoo-clock ..hooted at intervals. **1890** *Daily News* 29 Sept. 6/6 It was not a dangerous fog, but our ship had to hoot her way for some distance down. **1896** R. KIPLING *Seven Seas* 3 Through the yelling Channel tempest when the siren hoots and roars. **1912** BEERBOHM in *Seven Men* (1919) 129 Our car neither slackened nor hooted. **1927** [see HONK *sb.* b]. **1957** A. CLARKE *Later Poems* (1961) 58 Badge and holy medal guide Your cars home, hooting through our dirtiest lanes. **1966** J. BETJEMAN *High & Low* 65 Who dares to come hooting at *me*? I only give way to a Jag.

hoot (hu:t), *sb.*[1] Forms: 6 **hute**, 6–7 **hout**, (7 **whout, whoote**), 7– **hoot**. [f. HOOT *v.*]

1. a. A loud inarticulate exclamation, a shout, outcry.

1600 HOLLAND *Livy* XXIII. xix. 487 Anniball made a hout at it [*exclamaret*], and cried alowd: What? shall we sit heere about Casilinum so long? *a* **1610** HEALEY *Epictetus' Man.* (1636) 70 But for the whootes, and cryes, and other turbulent motions avoide them utterly. **1859** T. G. BONNEY in Mrs. Cole *Lady's Tour Monte Rosa* App. 395 A marmot ..scampered rapidly away among the rocks at the hoot of our guides.

b. A sound produced mechanically by a motor-horn, factory whistle, or the like.

1904 A. B. F. YOUNG *Compl. Motorist* (ed. 2) xii. 258 You should have a connection from the exhaust pipe led into a small reservoir and thence into the horn, so that on turning a tap a prolonged hoot will be emitted. **1927** *Scots Observer* 14 May 17/1 An imperative horn hoot made him turn his head. **1963** H. GARNER in R. Weaver *Canad. Short Stories* (1968) 2nd Ser. 52 A long hoarse hoot of the factory whistle announced the lunch break.

c. A laugh; a cause of laughter, a joke, a very amusing situation. *colloq.*

1942 BERREY & VAN DEN BARK *Amer. Thes. Slang* §281/4 Something humorous,..*hoot*. *Ibid.* §408/1 Humorist; amusing person,..*hoot*. **1969** *Punch* 17 Dec. 990 All the chaps chuck their clubs in a heap, and the wives have to pick a club and go off with the owner; it's going to be an absolute hoot! **1970** 'D. HALLIDAY' *Dolly & Cookie Bird* iii. 23 Jansy can imitate anybody. So can I... We'd have the whole form in hoots. **1971** *Guardian* 27 Sept. 10/1 It's a little quaint ('a bit of a hoot,' Dews would say) to hear him mention Peter Brook first. **1973** 'D. HALLIDAY' *Dolly & Starry Bird* xiii. 188, I started talking shop, a hoot for Jacko, if he had heard me.

2. *spec.* A shout of disapprobation or obloquy.

1612 T. JAMES *Jesuits' Downf.* 53 Hee was hissed out the College with whouts and hobubs. **1660** FISHER *Rustick's Alarm* Wks. (1679) 103 For all the then Hout, and the still stout standing of thy Rout of rude ones to the contrary, I still say the same. **1893** LELAND *Mem.* I. 138, I heard certain mutterings and hoots among the students.

3. The cry or call of an owl. (Sometimes imitated as *to-hoot, too-hoot, to-hoo*.)

1795 WOLCOTT (P. Pindar) *Lousiad* III. Wks. 1812 I. 248 To-hoot of Owls amid the dusky vales. **1852** WOOD *Nat. Hist.* (1874) 281 The voice of the Brown Owl is a loud monotonous hoot. **1863** KINGSLEY *Water-Bab.* iv. (1886) 146 He..listened to the owl's hoot.

4. hoot owl, the Tawny Owl, *Syrnium aluco*.

1885 SWAINSON *Prov. Names Birds* 129 Tawny owl (*Syrnium aluco*), Hoot owl (Craven). **1893** *Northumbld. Gloss.* 384 The tawny owl (*Syrnium aluco*) is called brown owl, hoot owl and Jenny hoolet.

hoot (hu:t), *sb.*[2] *colloq.* (orig. *U.S.*). [Perhaps the same as HOOT *sb.*[1] or *int.* Cf. HOOTER[2].] The smallest amount or particle; a whit or atom. Chiefly with negative and in phrases ***to give (care, matter) two hoots (a hoot)***.

1878 J. H. BEADLE *Western Wilds* xxxviii. 615, I got onto my reaper and banged down every hoot of it before Monday night. **1923** R. D. PAINE *Comr. Rolling Ocean* xii. 214, I am glad of that even if he did tell me that as a supercargo I wasn't worth a hoot in hades. **1925** N. VENNER *Imperfect Imposter* iv, I can't see this place gives a hoot whether I'm here or not. **1925** FRASER & GIBBONS *Soldier & Sailor Words* 120 I don't care two hoots in hell. **1926** A. P. HERBERT *She-Shanties* 36 We did not care a hoot. **1926** T. E. LAWRENCE *Seven Pillars* (1935) VI. lxxx. 447 Not that my maimed will now cared a hoot about the Arab Revolt. **1927** *Observer* 9 Oct. 13 It doesn't matter two hoots how much Oxford is filmed. **1939** JOYCE *Finnegans Wake* 351, I did not care three tanker's hoots..for any feelings. **1943** K. TENNANT *Ride on Stranger* xix. 214, I don't see that it matters two hoots in hell if you don't function. **1947** O. SITWELL *Novels of G. Meredith* 4 The human being who is not worth a tinker's cuss,—or, in a more elegant simile, two hoots—does not exist. **1957** A. GRIMBLE *Return to Islands* iv. 78 Not that they gave a hoot for what I might say. **1963** V. NABOKOV *Gift* iv. 235 He most definitely did not give a hoot for the opinions of specialists. **1966** *Listener* 27 Oct. 613/1 Winston Churchill was idiosyncratic in that he did not care a hoot about being thought a gentleman.

hoot (hu:t), *sb.*[3] *N.Z. slang.* Also 9 **hootoo**, **hout**, **hutu**, etc. [ad. Maori *utu* UTU.] Money paid as recompense; (as a generic term) money.

1820 J. BUTLER in Barton *Earliest N.Z.* (1927) iii. 66 He and his people went and robbed Boyle for the (hutu) payment. **1828** W. HORTON *N.Z.* 1/3 He then seized one of our axes..saying that should be the *hutu* or payment for what he had done. **1830** G. L. CRAIK *New Zealanders* x. 242 What he now wanted, he said, was *hootoo*, or payment. **1834** E. MARKHAM *N.Z. or Recollections of it* (MS.) 5 The Cabin boy counted 8 Teeth marks and the Hout or Compensation money was 8 Figs of Tobacco. **1842** *N.Z. Jrnl.* LXI. 117/2 Ask them [*sc.* Maoris] what is the *hute* or price. **1879** J. BARR *Old Identities* xxxvii. 333 The land that's waste they'll parcel oot..And sell't to all that's got the hoot. **1917** *Chrons. N.Z.E.F.* 5 Sept. 28/1 Pig Island N.C.O.'s only go for the extra couple of bob a day..the hoot is all they're chasing. *c* **1926** 'MIXER' *Transport Workers' Song Bk.* 5 He gets his 'hoot', forgets his dues. **1938** X. HERBERT *Capricornia* xx. 274 On the construction you could make a pot of hoot in no time. **1953** *Landfall* VII. 250 Put on a quid for me, for a place—I've got the hoot. **1961** B. CRUMP *Hang on a Minute* 144 Reckon we ought to have something to aim at, like getting a bit of hoot together to buy a little farm or a place to live or something. **1967** K. GILES *Death & Mr Prettyman* ii. 57, I got the idea of starting a chain of those places..for blokes without much hoot and wanting a clean bed. **1970** *N.Z. Listener* 30 Jan. 12/2 'Hoot?' I said. I hadn't heard that word for money in years. I suppose in an isolated cut-off place..slang would ossify.

hoot, -e, obs. forms of HOT.

hootation, humorous for *hooting*: see -ATION.

hootch, var. HOOCH, HOOCHIE.

hootchy-kootchy ('hu:tʃɪ'ku:tʃɪ), *sb.* and *a.* Also **hoochie(-y)-coochie**, **hootchie-kootchie**, **hootchy-kootch**, etc. [Origin unascertained.] **A.** *sb.* A kind of erotic dance. **B.** *attrib.* and *Comb.*; also as *adj.*, indecent, 'suggestive'.

[**1890** B. HALL *Turnover Club* vii. 75, I have been told that one night 'Hoochy-Coochy' Rice, the minstrel man—they always call Billy 'Hoochy-Coochy' because he invariably says that whenever he comes on stage—entered [Charlie] Hoyt's room..and stole a new song.] **1898** F. P. DUNNE *Mr. Dooley in Peace & War* (1899) 18 He's seen th' hootchy-kootchy an' th' Pammer House barber shop. *Ibid.* 36 Hootchy-kootchy girls dancin' before him. **1901** *Everybody's Mag.* Oct. 437/2 The Doctor was too professional to relish the hootchie cootchie dance. **1904** [see BARK *v.*[1] 2 b]. **1925** *Manch. Guardian Weekly* Aug. 103/4 That hootchy-kootchy sort of intonation. **1931** 'D. STIFF' *Milk & Honey Route* xiv. 155 Enlivening them with the vitality of a hoochy-coochy dancer. **1934** F. SCOTT FITZGERALD *Tender is Night* xv. 273 There was the sound of a whining, tinkling hootchy-kootchy show. **1945** *Record Changer* (Fairfax, Virginia) Jan., The Chicago World Fair of 1893..gave the widest possible publicity to the new Negro dances..the cakewalk, the pasamala, the hoochie koochie, the bully dance and the bombershay. **1949** R. HARVEY *Curtain Time* v. 38 They expected a theatre man to be brassy and leering, like a sideshow barker at a hoochie-koochie tent. **1950** BLESH & JANIS *They all played Ragtime* viii. 149 A spate of exotic dances became the talk, from the hoochie-coochie to the bombashay. **1962** W. STEGNER *Wolf Willow* IV. iii. 256 A travelling group of hootchie-kootchie dancers pitched a

tent in the brush and sent their impressario through town advertising 'performances'. **1973** *Parade* 24 June 12/1 I'm trying to counteract the hootchy-kootchy aura that the dance has.

hoot(e)nanny, hootananny (ˈhuːt(ə)nænɪ). orig. *U.S. dial.* [Origin unknown.]

1. A 'thingumajig'. **2.** An informal session or concert of folk music and singing. Also *transf.*

1929 *Amer. Speech* V. 151 *Hootananny*, the same as gadget. **1940** *Washington* (Seattle) *New Dealer* 25 July 4 (Advt.), The New Dealer's Midsummer Hootenanny. You Might Even Be Surprised! **1959** [see CEILIDH]. **1962** W. SCHIRRA in *Into Orbit* 31 Don't worry about it. That's just the hootenanny valve on the watchamacallit fluttering a little. **1963** *Daily Mail* 11 Sept. 8/4 Hootenanny...is to the folk singer what a jam session is to the jazzman. **1964** *Radio Times* 5 Mar. 25/1 The Hoot'nanny Show. **1964** *Punch* 2 Sept. 348/1 A report of one of the side-shows in the psychiatrists' hootenanny held in London last week. **1964** MRS. L. B. JOHNSON *White House Diary* 13 Jan. (1970) 44, I love folk music, but the name 'Hootenanny' rather repels me. **1972** *Time* 5 June 4/2 Memorial Day: a three day national hootenanny.

hooter[1] (ˈhuːtə(r)). [f. HOOT *v.* + -ER[1].] One who or that which hoots.

a. A person or animal that hoots: esp. an owl.

1674–1828 [see GILL-HOOTER]. **1856** F. E. PAGET *Owlet of Owlst.* 12 Though he [an owl] was esteemed a good hooter in his youth, their hootings beat his hollow. **1884** *Chesh. Gloss.*, *Hooter*, an owl. *Mod.* A few hooters tried to disturb the meeting.

b. A steam whistle or siren; esp. one at large works, sounded as a signal for beginning or ceasing work.

1878 C. J. H. FLETCHER in *Oxford Chron.* 19 Oct., The conditions under which these 'hooters' or 'buzzers' are used in our northern manufacturing towns. **1881** *Daily News* 24 Feb. 5/3 Behind this apparent boiler stands the driver with brake, regulator and 'hooter' within easy reach. **1894** *Westm. Gaz.* 30 June 5/2 The accompaniment of indescribable din and noise from the sirens and hooters of all the steamers down below. **1897** BLACKMORE *Dariel* lv. 485 The Osset tongue..sounds like..a hooter at the junction.

c. The horn of a motor vehicle.

1908 *Lincoln Rutland & Stamford Merc.* 19 June 5 No hooter was sounded on the car when rounding this dangerous corner. **1972** M. IRVING *Mr Purpose* 10 Mike pulled up outside Joanna's house, beeped on the hooter and she appeared.

d. *slang.* The nose.

1958 F. NORMAN *Bang to Rights* 52 He held it [*sc.* a handkerchief] up to his face as though he was going to blow his hooter. **1972** *Times* 18 July 12/5 Derek Griffiths is a young coloured comedian with a face like crushed rubber.. and a hooter to rival Cyrano de Bergerac.

Hooter[2]. *U.S. colloq.* = HOOT *sb.*[2]

1839 *Havana* (N.Y.) *Republican* 21 Aug. (Th.), Now the Grampus [*sc.* a vessel] stopt, and didn't buge [= budge] one hooter. **1889** *Commercial* (Cincinnati) 17 Oct., It has not harmed the Republican cause in Ohio a hooter. **1896** *Harper's Mag.* XCII. 784/1 Now I can have all I want, I don't care a hooter! **1900** E. A. DIX *Deacon Bradbury* xii, 'Do you mean that you don't know anything about the matter at all?'..'Not a hooter.'

hooting (ˈhuːtɪŋ), *vbl. sb.* [f. HOOT *v.* + -ING[1].] The action of the verb HOOT in various senses.

a. Shouting, calling out, clamour; *spec.* calling out in execration or derision.

a **1225** *Juliana* 52 Ne make þu me nawt men to huting ant to hokere. *Ibid.*, Ant heo leac him efter hire endelong þe cheping chepmenne huting [*MS. B.* þe cheping chapmen to huting]. *a* **1330** *Syr Degarre* 577 Than was ther long houting and cri. **1480** CAXTON *Chron. Eng.* ccxliv. (1482) 298 The frensshmen made..moche reuel with houting and showtyng. **1583** STANYHURST *Æneis* II. (Arb.) 68, I stoutly.. raysed an howting. **1588** SHAKS. *L.L.L.* IV. ii. 61 (1623) The people fall a hooting. *a* **1611** BEAUM. & FL. *Philaster* II. iv, Your whootings and your clamours..Can no more vex my soul, than this base carriage. **1756** FOOTE *Eng. fr. Paris* I. Wks. 1799 I. 102 The hideous hootings of that *canaille*. **1844** THIRLWALL *Greece* VIII. lxvi. 447 They were obliged to retire amidst the jeers and hootings of the multitude.

b. The cry or call of an owl.

1837 W. IRVING *Capt. Bonneville* III. 143 The hooting of large owls, and the screeching of the small ones. **1856** [see HOOTER[1] a].

hooting (ˈhuːtɪŋ), *ppl. a.* [f. as prec. + -ING[2].] That hoots; spec. of certain species of owls.

1697 DRYDEN *Virg. Past.* VIII. 75 [Let] hooting Owls contend with Swans in Skill. **1702** ROWE *Tamerl.* III. ii, Like an idle Madman That wanders with a Train of hooting boys. **1819** CRABBE *T. of Hall* XIV. 398 The night-wolf answer'd to the whooting owl. **1821** CLARE *Vill. Minstr.* II. 71 Cracking whips, and shepherd's hooting cries.

hoouel, obs. f. HOVEL.

hoouer, obs. f. HOVER.

hoouge, obs. f. HUGE.

hoove: see HOOF, HOUVE, HOVE.

hoove (huːv). [f. OE. *hóf-*, ablaut-stem of HEAVE *v.*; perh. representing ME. *hove*, for *hoven* pa. pple.] A disease of cattle, characterized by an inflation of the stomach, usually due to eating too much green fodder.

1840 *Penny Cycl.* XVII. 81/2 At other times an unnatural fermentation commences, and the stomach is inflated with gas... This is termed hoove. **1846** J. BAXTER *Libr. Pract. Agric.* (ed. 4) II. 141 If there is hoove, this will combine with the extricated gas, and prevent the continued formation of it.

Hoover (ˈhuːvə(r)). Also **hoover**. **a.** (With capital initial.) The proprietary name of a make of vacuum cleaner (patented in 1927). **b.** *Loosely.* (With small initial.) Any vacuum cleaner. Hence as *v. trans.*, to clean with a Hoover (or, by extension, any vacuum cleaner). Also *intr.*

1926–7 *Army & Navy Stores Catal.* 115 (Advt.), A Hoovered room..is..free from dust. **1934** *Punch* 10 Jan. 36/1 Her bodywork's smart and strikes the eye Clean-swept as though with a Hoover. **1934** S. BECKETT *More Pricks than Kicks* 67 He waddled out of the bar..into the lowly public ..like a bit of dirt into a Hoover. **1939** N. STREATFEILD *Luke* 187, I was Hoovering my passage. **1940** H. G. WELLS *All Aboard for Ararat* iii. 91, I shall feel like a man trying to sell Hoover cleaners to an Arab encampment in a dust storm. **1944** M. SHARP *Cluny Brown* x. 68 Are you the one who hoovers the east corridor? **1946** M. DICKENS *Happy Prisoner* ix. 185 I've been swept out of the kitchen, and dusted out of the dining-room, and Hoovered out of the drawing-room. **1955** P. WENTWORTH *Vanishing Point* xi. 69 It was Miss Maxwell who hoovered the carpet and dusted all those innumerable ornaments. **1960** P. MORTIMER *Saturday Lunch with Brownings* 202 Louisa was vacuuming the sitting-room... 'Do you mind moving, because I want to Hoover over there?' **1960** C. WILSON *Ritual in Dark* I. v. 101 The carpeting was a plain fawn colour, and looked as if it had only just been hoovered. **1971** *Engineer* 11 Nov. 66/3 How many housewives Hoover the carpet with an Electrolux?

Hooverize (ˈhuːvəraɪz), *v. U.S.* [f. the name of Herbert C. *Hoover* (1874–1964), food commissioner 1917–19, and President of the U.S. 1929–33 + -IZE.] *intr.* To be sparing or economical, esp. in the use of food.

1917 H. B. GROSS in *N.Y. Tribune* 13 June 10/7 It is now assured that Mr. Hoover is about to become our food regulator..and since he has..exhorted the public to exercise the utmost economy in the use of foodstuffs..I suggest that 'to Hooverize' be universally adopted as expressing the assistance every one of us..can render in that direction. **1919** W. T. GRENFELL *Labrador Doctor* (1920) ii. 20 To make sure that there were no truants, all hands were forced to 'Hooverize'. **1932** *Blue Valley Farmer* (Okla. City) 7 Jan. 5/6 Once before he made us Hooverize When Wilson had his war.

Hence ˈ**Hooverizing** *vbl. sb.*

1918 *Lit. Digest* 12 Jan. 14/2 Hooverizing is commonly regarded as something new. **1918** *Harper's Bazaar* Mar. 62/2 The butter-colored straw with its horn of abundance, overflowing with many colored fruits.., is doubly significant to-day with our enforced Hooverizing.

Hooverville (ˈhuːvəvɪl). *U.S.* [f. the name of Herbert C. *Hoover* (see prec. word) + *-ville* terminal element in many place-names.] A temporary shanty town.

The reference is to the temporary accommodation provided for unemployed workers in the economic depression of the early 1930s.

1933 *New Republic* 24 May 40/1 Hoovervilles are in a separate nation, with separate codes. **1939** J. STEINBECK *Grapes of Wrath* xix. 319 There was a Hooverville on the edge of every town. **1946** V. LINCOLN in *55 Short Stories from New Yorker* (1952) 36, I found White Creek Row. It was the town's Hooverville..a tragic, shocking, sordid shanty town. **1949** *Sat. Rev.* 6 Aug. 116 They called them 'Hoovervilles'. Evicted families lived in tin-and-cardboard shacks. **1952** *Economist* 6 Sept. 554/2 A tragic island of unemployment, a new, 1952 Hooverville. **1973** J. JONES *Touch of Danger* xviii. 108 It was all like some weird.. Hooverville. They were cooking their suppers over the open fires.

hooze: see HOOSE.

hop (hɒp), *sb.*[1] Also 5–6 hoope, hopp, 5–7 hoppe, 6 hope. [In 15th c. *hoppe*, a. MDu. *hoppe*, Du. *hop* = late OHG. *hopfo* (MHG. *hopfe*, Ger. *hopfen*); med.L. *hupa* (for **huppa*); ulterior origin obscure.]

1. (Usually in *pl.*) **a.** The ripened cones of the female hop-plant (see 2), used for giving a bitter flavour to malt liquors, and as a tonic and soporific.

c **1440** *Promp. Parv.* 245/2 Hoppe, sede for beyre ..*hummulus, secundum extraneos.* **1500–1600** *Chester Pl.* (Shaks. Soc.) II. 82 When I was a brewer longe With hoopes I made my ale stronge. **1502**, **1542** [see BEER *sb.*[1] 1]. **1545** *Nottingham Rec.* III. 224 Duas libras hoppes pro vd. **1617** MORYSON *Itin.* III. 147 The English Beere is famous in Netherland..made of Barley and Hops; for England yeelds plenty of Hops. **1654** TRAPP *Comm. Job* xxxix. 13 They were wont to say here, that Peacocks, Hops, and Heresie, came first into England in one and the same ship. **1711** *Lond. Gaz.* No. 4848/1 An Act for laying a Duty upon Hops. **1881** WHITEHEAD *Hops* 61 The hops are picked into bins, long, light, wooden frames, with sacking bottoms.

b. Beer. Also (as *hop*) in *Comb.* Chiefly *Austral.* and *N.Z. slang.*

1929 W. R. BURNETT *Little Caesar* VI. iv. 218 That dame's full of hop. **1930** *Bulletin* (Sydney) 1 Jan. 11/4 The proprietor provided a beer party, and the riot that arose out of the hop-drinking led to the school's first raid. **1940** F. SARGESON *Man & Wife* 24 Before Bill came back half a dozen Maoris had shouted her, and each time she had less than half a glass of beer... She was keen enough on the hops he said, but she was like that.

2. a. A climbing perennial diœcious plant (*Humulus Lupulus*, N.O. *Urticaceæ*, suborder *Cannabineæ*), with rough lobed leaves shaped like those of the vine; the male plant bears pentamerous flowers which grow in drooping panicles; the female bears green cones or catkins consisting of broad scales each with two flowers at the base. The plant is a native of Europe, and is much cultivated for its cones, esp. in Bavaria, Belgium, England, and the United States: see 1.

The plant is believed to have been introduced into the south of England from Flanders between 1520 and 1524.

1538 TURNER *Libellus* B ij b, *Lupus salictarius*, hoppes. **1562** —— *Herbal* II. 42 b, I can fynd no mention of hoppes in any olde autor, sauing only in Pliny. **1572** MASCALL *Plant. & Graff.* (1592) 81 To choose your Hoppe. Ye shall choose your rootes best for your Hop, in the Sommer before ye shall plant them. **1647** SANDERSON *Serm.* II. 197 A hop, for want of a strong pole, will wind it self about a thistle or nettle or any sorry weed. **1754** HUME *Hist. Eng.*, *Jas. I*, App. (R.), The planting of hops increased much in England during this reign. **1872** OLIVER *Elem. Bot.* II. 232 The Hop..is remarkable amongst the Nettle Family for its twining stem.

b. Locally applied to *Medicago lupulina* and *Bryonia dioica*; in Australia to species of *Dodonæa* and *Daviesia*. ***bog hop***, a local name for Buckbean (*Menyanthes trifoliata*).

1866 *Treas. Bot.* 727/2 *M*[*edicago*] *lupulina*..generally known by farmers as the Hop Trefoil, or Hop. **1876** *Ibid.* Suppl., *Hop, Native*, the seed-vessels of *Dodonœa* which are used in the same manner as the common hop in the manufacture of beer. **1879** BRITTEN & HOLLAND *Plant-n.*, Hop, Bog..In allusion to its well-known bitter properties and place of growth.

3. Phr. ***as thick as hops*** (? referring to the plants when grown in rows, or to the crowded catkins of flowers); also ***as fast as hops***, ***as mad as hops*** (? with play on HOP *sb.*[2]).

1590 NASHE *Pasquil's Apol.* I. C, They must be throwne ouer the Pulpit as thicke as hoppes. **1630** J. TAYLOR (Water P.) *Wks.* (N.), At the bake-houses, as thicke as hops The tatling women..thy fourefold praises knead. **1677** NEEDHAM *2nd Packet Adv.* 54 'Tis to be answer'd too as fast as Hops now. **1700** T. BROWN tr. *Fresny's Amusem. Ser. & Com.* 110 Other Amusements presented themselves as thick as Hops. **1884** *Harper's Mag.* Oct. 695/2 Such a grin! It made me mad as hops.

4. A narcotic drug; *spec.* opium.

1887 *Lantern* (New Orleans) 14 May 4/2 As long as a smoker can obtain his 'hop'. **1903** ADE *In Babel* 110 Me settin' around on my shoulder-blades lookin' like one o' these bamboo boys full o' hop. **1911** C. B. CHRYSLER *White Slavery* xi. 89 When a 'fiend' is full of 'hop' he is cunning as the devil. **1916** [see COOK *v.*[1] 2 d]. **1924** G. BRONSON-HOWARD *Devil's Chaplain* vi. 97 It was he who controlled the available supply of 'hop'. **1933** C. DE LENOIR *Hundredth Man* iv. 63 'Sure,' I replied, 'but what are you going to do when you can't get a card of "hop" for love or money?' **1955** *U.S. Senate Hearings* (1956) VIII. 4161 Opium in the underworld is referred to [as]..'hop'.

5. *Comb.* **a.** General Combs., as ***hop-bud***, ***-cone***, ***-dealer***, ***-drier***, ***-duty***, ***-frame***, ***-growing***, ***-harrow***, ***-harvest***, ***-plantation***, ***-prop***, ***-setter***, ***-top***; (sense 4) ***hop-dream***, ***-pipe***.

1812 *Hop-dealer [see *hop-porter* in b]. **1896** H. M. BLOSSOM *Checkers* viii. 169 Half the time I think that I must be asleep, and trying to 'cash a *hop-dream'. **1931** E. LINKLATER *Juan in Amer.* v. 401, I listened like I was in a hop-dream. **1934** J. M. CAIN *Postman always rings Twice* xiv. 163 'That paper..was still in files, see?'..'You mean that hop dream she called a confession?' **1875** KNIGHT *Dict. Mech.*, **Hop-dryer*, a chamber in which hops are artificially dried..Also called *oast* or *hop-kiln*. **1891** *Daily News* 12 Sept. 3/6 Hop-dryers earn about 7*s.* per day. **1858** SIMMONDS *Dict. Trade*, **Hop-duty*, a tax of about two-pence per pound, levied on hops. **1887** *Lantern* (New Orleans) 21 May 4/1 The rising smoke that curls up from the bowl of the '*hop' pipe. **1926** H. CRANE *Let.* 19 Jan. (1965) 259 He might as well be in elfin land with a hop pipe in his mouth. **1807** VANCOUVER *Agric. Devon* (1813) 206 The valley in which are these *hop-plantations, is formed by sharp hills rising very abruptly from the plain below. **1664** EVELYN *Sylva* xvii. §6 The Timber [of the poplar] is incomparable ..for Vine, and *Hop-props, and divers viminious works.

b. Special Combs.: **hop-back** [BACK *sb.*[2]], a vessel with a perforated bottom for straining off the hops from the liquor in the manufacture of beer; **hop-bag**, a large bag of coarse cloth for packing hops; hence **hop-bagging**, the cloth of which this is made; **hop-bind, -bine**, the climbing stem of the hop-plant; **hop bitters**, a kind of unfermented liquor flavoured with hops; †**hop-boll**, the seed-vessel of the hop; **hop-bush**, an Australian shrub belonging to the genus *Dodonæa*; **hop-clover** = *hop-trefoil*; **hop-cushion** = *hop-pillow*; **hop-dresser**, one who cultivates hops, a hop-grower; **hop-factor**, a dealer in hops (Simmonds *Dict. Trade* 1858); **hop fiend** *slang* = HOPHEAD 1; **hop-flea**, a very small beetle (*Phyllotreta* or *Haltica concinna*), destructive to the hop-plant; **hop-fly**, a species of aphis (*Phorodon humuli*), destructive to the hop-plant; **hop frog-fly, hop froth-fly**, a species of froth-fly, (*Aphrophora interrupta* or *Amblycephalus interruptus*), destructive to the hop-plant; **hop-grower**, one who grows hops as a crop; **hop-hill** (see HILL *sb.* 3 b); **hop hornbeam** (see HORNBEAM); **hop-jack** = *hop-back*; **hop joint** *slang*, an opium den; **hop-kiln**, a kiln for drying hops; an oast; **hop marjoram, medick**, species of MARJORAM, MEDICK; **hop-mildew**, a parasitic fungus of genus

Sphærotheca, infesting the hop; **hop-nidget** (see NIDGET); **hop-oast,** a kiln for drying hops (Simmonds *Dict. Trade* 1858); **hop-oil,** an acrid oil obtained from hops; **hop-pad** *slang* = *hop joint*; **hop-pillow,** a pillow stuffed with hops to produce sleep; **hop-plant,** = sense 2; also applied to species of *Origanum*; **hop-planter** = *hop-grower*; **hop-pocket** (see POCKET); **hop-porter,** a man employed to carry sacks of hops; **hop-press,** a machine for expressing the liquid from hops after boiling; **hop-shim,** a horse-hoe used in hop cultivation; **hop-tier,** a person employed to tie the hop-bines to the poles; **hop toy** *slang*, a container used for smoking opium; **hop-tree,** a North American shrub or small tree (*Ptelea trifoliata*), N.O. *Rutaceæ*, with bitter fruit which has been used as a substitute for hops; **hop-trefoil,** a name for yellow clover (*Trifolium procumbens*), from the resemblance of its withered flower-heads to the cones of the hop; also applied to the hop medick, *Medicago lupulina*; **hop-vine,** the trailing stem or bine of the hop-plant, or the whole plant; **hop-yeast,** yeast prepared from an infusion of hops. Also HOP-DOG, GARDEN, etc.

1888 F. FAULKNER *Theory & Practice Mod. Brewing* (ed. 2) ix. 145 The well-boiled wort filtered from hops and coagulated precipitate—and what this amounts to is seen under the false-bottom plates of *hop-back—left on cooler floor..undergoes..evaporation. **1892** H. E. WRIGHT *Handy Bk. Brewers* i. 20 The boiling having lasted from one and a half to two hours..the copper is 'turned out' or 'struck', the boiling wort, hops and all, rushing out through an opened valve or tap into the *hop-back*, a vessel sometimes rectangular, sometimes circular in shape. **1937** 'N. BLAKE' *There's Trouble Brewing* ii. 51 'Shall I send a man to look in the hop-back?' he added. 'The hop-back?' asked Nigel mystified. 'That's right. Where the wort drains into.' **1604** T. M. *Black Bk.* Middleton's Wks. (Bullen) VIII. 22 Apparelled..in a wicked suit of coarse *hop-bags. **1733** P. MILLER *Gard. Dict.* (ed. 2) s.v. *Lupulus*, Two or three times in a Day the Binn must be emptied into a Hop-bag made of coarse Linen Cloth. **1705** *Wakes Colne* (Essex) *Overseers Acc.* (MS.), Paid for *hop baginge for Clarke and Woodward. **1845** *Encycl. Metrop.* VI. 58 Light wooden frames called *binges*..are clothed with hop-bagging, into which the hops are picked off the poles. **1733** *Act 6 Geo. II*, c. 37 §6 If any Person maliciously cut any *Hop-binds growing on Poles in any Plantation of Hops [etc.]. **1813** *Examiner* 3 May 279/2 The *hop bine said to come up very strong. **1846** SIR J. TYLDEN in J. Baxter *Libr. Pract. Agric.* (ed. 4) II. 33 Using the old hop-bines in the hop-garden, instead of burning or otherwise wasting them. **1894** *Lancet* 3 Nov. 1054 Other preparations affording excellent malt liquor substitutes are the *hop bitters and hop stout. **1649** BLITHE *Eng. Improv. Impr.* (1652) 179 It may do best if all of the *hop-bowl or husk be but cut and shattered as aforesayd. **1883** F. M. BAILEY *Queensland Flora* 82 (Morris) The capsules of many Dodonaeas are used for hops, and thus the shrubs are known as *hop-bushes. **1936** F. CLUNE *Roaming round Darling* xvii. 163 Lemon-bushes, minus the lemon, and a hop-bush, not hopping; but O'Malley said the old people used this bush for making bread. **1968** K. WEATHERLY *Roo Shooter* 108 A thick patch of hop bush. **1679** *Lond. Gaz.* No. 1383/4 A way to cleanse Trefoil or *Hopclover Seed from their husk. **1741** *Compl. Fam. Piece* III. 421 Hop-clover, Trefoil, or three-leav'd Grass, are both finer and sweeter than the great Clover-grass. **1685** in *Canterb. Marr. Licences* (ed. Cowper) Ser. IV. 397 Robert Rye of Barham, *hop dresser. May 21. **1898** L. J. BECK *N.Y. Chinatown* xviii. 165 A *hop fiend went on a weary stroll, In search of a friend who a pill could roll. **1911** C. B. CHRYSLER *White Slavery* xi. 89 Opium smokers, 'hop fiends' or 'hop heads' as they are called, are the fiercest of all the White Slavers. **1880** *Chambers' Encycl.*, **Hop-flea*..does much mischief in hop-plantations in spring. **1834** *Penny Cycl.* II. 156/2 We may refer to the *hop-fly. **1846** J. BAXTER *Libr. Pract. Agric.* (ed. 4) I. 404 On the 13th of May, 1845, the hop-fly made its appearance in my grounds. **1868** *Chambers' Encycl.* Suppl., **Hop Froth-fly*, or **Hop Frog-fly*..sometimes appears in great numbers in hop-grounds, and does considerable mischief. **1880** *Times* 10 Sept. 9/4 Our *hop-growers have continued to hold their own. *Ibid.*, It would be cause for general regret..were English *hop-growing to languish and die out. **1707–12** J. MORTIMER *Husb.* 145 Dissolved dung..to enrich your *Hop-hills. **1848** *Jrnl. R. Agric. Soc.* IX. 549 It will be wrong to attempt to grow any other crop between the rows of hop-hills. **1875** *Ure's Dict. Arts* I. 515 A shallow vessel or cooler, over which is placed the *hop-jack or sieve for straining out the spent-hops. **1887** *Lantern* (New Orleans) 4 June 5/2 The police..raided them '*hop joints'. **1905** J. LONDON *Jacket* xvi. 212 Chinatown dumps and hop-joints. **1923** E. WALLACE *Clue of New Pin* xix. 167 'Running a philanthropic hop joint?' asked the other sarcastically. **1931** D. RUNYON *Guys & Dolls* (1932) i. 25 They find they are nothing but speak-easies, although one is a hop joint. **1935** A. J. POLLOCK *Underworld Speaks* 58/2 *Hop joint*, a place where opium is bought and smoked by addicts. **1784** *Lett. to Honoria & Marianne* II. 75 By the way, he stopped to cheapen two hundred of hop-poles, and to inspect his new *hop-kiln. **1807** VANCOUVER *Agric. Devon* (1813) 205 The hop-kiln is occasionally otherwise employed than in drying hops. **1883** *Encycl. Brit.* XVI. 294/1 The **Hop-Mildew*..is a parasitic disease of the hop. **1818** TODD, **Hop-oast*, in Kent, a kiln for drying hops. *a* **1887** JEFFERIES *Field & Hedgerow* (1889) 106 The shapely cone of the hop-oast rises at the end. **1889** *Watts' Dict. Chem.* s.v., At the base of the membranous cones of the hop there is a bitter yellow powder called lupulin..When distilled with steam it yields *hop oil, which consists of a terpene $C_{10}H_{16}$, and various compounds containing oxygen. **1946** MEZZROW & WOLFE *Really Blues* (1957) xiv. 245 A little..coal bin..we cleaned out and converted into our *hop-pad. **1834** SOUTHEY *Doctor* I. 9 Lettuces, cow-slip-wine, poppy-syrup,..*hop-pillows, spiders-web pills. **1884** MARY WILKINS in *Harper's Mag.* Oct. 792/1 There was a hop pillow in a little linen case. **1817** J. BRADBURY *Trav. Amer.* 43 On the sides of the hills I noticed abundance of the *hop plant. **1866** *Treas. Bot.* 822/2 These last [*Origanum Dictamnus*, and *O. sipyleum*] are popularly called Hop plants, and are often seen in cottage windows. **1663–4** *Canterb. Marriage Licences* (MS.), Joh'es Dodd, civitatis Cant., *hopplanter. **1848** *Jrnl. R. Agric. Soc.* IX. 538, I would advise every young hop-planter never to stick a plough in his hop-ground. **1812** *Examiner* 5 Oct. 636/2 A *hop-porter..made oath, that..he hired himself..to Mr. G. S., a hop-dealer. **1805** R. W. DICKSON *Pract. Agric.* (1807) I. 44 **Hop-shim*, this implement is constructed with a frame, somewhat in the manner of the common wheel-barrow. **1848** *Jrnl. R. Agric. Soc.* IX. 555 It is not necessary for the *hop-tiers to wait until there are three bines for every pole long enough to tie. **1881** *N.Y. Medical Record* 5 Nov. 512/1, I procured a full outfit for smoking [opium]..: A pipe..and a buffalo-horn box (**hop toy*) for holding the opium. **1887** Hop toy [see COOK *v.*[1] 2d]. **1926** J. BLACK *You can't Win* xvii. 238 At last the little horn container, the 'hop toy', is empty. **1955** *U.S. Senate Hearings* (1956) VIII. 4162 Hop toy—container for smoking opium. **1877** BARTLETT *Dict. Amer.* (ed. 4), **Hop-tree*,..the fruit, a wafer-like seed, grows in clusters. **1890** *Chambers' Encycl.*, *Hop-tree*..also called Shrubby Trefoil, is planted as an ornamental plant. **1855** *Loudon's Encycl. Plants* 648 *Hop-trefoil..is cultivated along with the perennial clover. **1866** *Treas. Bot.* 1170/1 The Procumbent or Hop Trefoil of the botanist..must not be confounded with the Hop Trefoil of the farmer, which is the *Medicago lupulina*. **1707–12** J. MORTIMER *Husb.* (J.), Have the poles without forks, otherwise it will be troublesome to part the *hop vines and the poles. **1884** *Harper's Mag.* Aug. 440/1 The cultivation of the hop vine. **1884** MARY WILKINS *Ibid.* Oct. 790/1 She made *hop yeast.

hop (hɒp), *sb.*[2] [f. HOP *v.*[1]]

1. a. An act, or the action, of hopping; a short spring or leap, esp. on one foot.

1508 DUNBAR *Gold. Targe* 19 For mirth of May, wyth skippis and wyth hoppis. **1600** SURFLET *Countrie Farme* II. l. 323 [He] is lead by the hops and skips, turnings and windings of his braine. **1611** COTGR., *Cahot*, the iumpe, hop, or iog of a coach, etc., in a rugged, or uneven, way. **1834** BECKFORD *Italy* I. 125 All of a hop with toads and locusts. **1888** *Longm. Mag.* XI. 453, I thought I'd take the ball on the hop.

b. *humorously*, A leap or step in dancing: cf. 2.

1579 GOSSON *Sch. Abuse* (Arb.) 33 He gaue Dauncers great stipends for selling their hopps. **1812** W. TENNANT *Anster F.* IV. xiv, And scour with majesty of hop the ground.

c. *to catch* (or *take*) *on the hop*: to take unawares, to surprise, to catch in the act.

1868 *Broadside Ballad, The Chickaleary Cove* (Farmer), For to catch me on the hop..You must wake up very early in the morning. **1872** R. D. BLACKMORE *Maid of Sker* I. xxv. 301 He caught me on the hop; at a moment of rumours and serious warnings. **1887** *Brit. Med. Jrnl.* 21 May 1103/1 The attendants taking him, as it were, 'on the hop'. **1927** R. A. FREEMAN *Certain Dr. Thorndyke* I. xi, The police..caught him fairly on the hop with all the stolen property in his possession. **1947** 'N. SHUTE' *Chequer Board* iii. 68 But when you catch them on the hop, then you got to be plenty tough. **1959** *New Statesman* 14 Nov. 654/2 Some months ago our second child caught us on the hop and Jean had him here in this two roomed house. **1973** A. BEHREND *Samarai Affair* viii. 83 Ships are wayward things, and she may have taken a sudden turn which caught Gosling on the hop.

d. That distance which can be or is traversed in an aircraft or motor vehicle at one stretch; one stage of a long-distance journey.

1909 *Flight* 3 July 398/1 M. Breguet has a biplane there and has made one or two short 'hops'. **1927** *Daily News* 7 June 7/1 By flying from New York to Eisleben..in one hop. **1931** D. RUNYON *Guys & Dolls* (1932) x. 214 Finally after an extra long hop in an automobile we come to the outskirts of a..little burg. **1954** A. HUXLEY *Let.* 9 May (1969) 707 We leave for Cairo the day after tomorrow..then proceed to Beirut, Damascus and Istambul—short hops by air. **1958** *Observer* 10 Aug. 5/8 Companies..operate their jets on a number of economically valuable short hops. **1968** K. WEATHERLY *Roo Shooter* 69 They had about three hundred miles to go, and because of the road conditions they decided to do it in two hops.

e. *Radio.* A transmission path from one point on the earth to another that involves a single reflection from some region of the atmosphere.

1939 *Proc. Inst. Radio Engin.* XXVII. 640/2 The great-circle multiple-hop mode of propagation usually observed during all-daylight-path periods with 18-megacycle signals. **1966** *Electronics* 17 Oct. 137 This 178-mile tropo hop will connect Flyingsdales [*sic*] Moor, a ballistic missile early warning radar site..to Martlesham Heath.

f. *to go on the hop, to play the hop*: to play truant. *slang.* (Cf. HOP *v.*[1] 6 a.)

1959 I. & P. OPIE *Lore & Lang. Schoolch.* xvii. 372 A truant may also..be said to be..'hopping it' (in Rochdale 'going on the hop'). **1968** L. BERG *Risinghill* 15 Another boy said: I got the cane for playing the hop... Playing the hop, and fighting.

g. *long hop* (*Cricket*): see LONG *a.*[1] 18 d.

2. *slang* or *colloq.* **a.** A dance; a dancing-party, esp. of an informal or unceremonious kind.

1731 *Read's Weekly Jrnl.* 9 Jan., Near an hundred people of both sexes..dancing to the musick of two sorry fiddles..it was called a three-penny hop. **1744–5** MRS. DELANY in *Life & Corr.* (1861) II. 335 Our little hop..was appointed for Wednesday. **1771** SMOLLETT *Humph. Cl.* 5 June, The vulgar..now thrust themselves into all assemblies from a ridotto at St. James to a hop at Rotherhithe. **1797** *Sporting Mag.* X. 73 The most famous Dancing Assembly, or, as it is vulgarly called, the genteelest Hop, that ever was known in London. **1831** LADY GRANVILLE *Lett.* (1894) II. 98 On Friday, at my hop, it was known that there was a majority against us. **1880** *Scribner's Mag.* XX. 917/2 A party of youths and..maidens..dressed for a hop. **1892** KIPLING *Barrack-r. Ballads* 64 To dance with blowzy housemaids at the regimental hops. **1948** J. BETJEMAN *Sel. Poems* 115 You going to the Hanks's hop to-night? **1970** D. M. DAVIN *Not Here, Not Now* II. iii. 65 What about coming to the Arts Faculty bob hop on Saturday?

b. *on the hop*: on the go, with no chance to relax, busy, active; enjoying oneself.

1863 T. THOMPSON in E. Corvan et al. *Choice Collection Tyneside Songs* 129 Wiv some varry canny chiels, All on the hop and murry. **1892** E. J. MILLIKEN *'Arry Ballads* 22 A fierce-looking party, all elbows, was likeways A deal on the 'op. **1908** G. H. LORIMER *J. Spurlock* iv. 78 I'd been on the hop ever since morning, for being in love with Anita was a strenuous calling. **1923** J. MANCHON *Le Slang* 158 *To be on the hop*, être en bombe. **1952** A. HUXLEY *Let.* 29 Sept. (1969) 652 C is kept on the hop all the time, fetching, carrying, shopping etc.

3. hop, step, and jump (also ***hop, skip, and jump***; ***hop, step, and leap***, etc.). **a.** as *sb.* The action of making these three movements in succession; an athletic exercise in which the players try who can cover most ground with this sequence of movements. Also *spec.*, as an athletic event, and *transf.* and *fig.* Also ***hop, step, and long jump***. Hence ***hop, step, and jumper***.

a **1719** ADDISON (J.), When my wings are on, I can go above a hundred yards at a hop, step, and jump. **1760** STERNE *Tr. Shandy* (ed. 3) I. xii. 48 Yorick..would as often answer with a pshaw!—and if the subject was started in the fields—with a hop, skip, and a jump, at the end of it. **1785** BURNS *Holy Fair* iii, The third cam up, hap—step—an' lowp, As light as ony lambie. **1810** SCOTT *Let. to Southey* 20 May in *Lockhart*, I omitted no opportunity..of converting my dog-trot into a hop-step-and-jump. **1816** MAD. D'ARBLAY *Lett.* 2 Apr., Your kind father..instantly ran downstairs, with a hop, skip, and a jump. **1819** *Blackw. Mag.* V. 613/1 A match at hop-step-and-jump between Tickler and Dr. Scott. **1858** MAYHEW *Upper Rhine* v. §2 (1860) 265 It seems literally but a hop, skip, and a jump, from one..shelf of crags to the other. **1906** *Westm. Gaz.* 30 Apr. 7/1 The preliminaries of the hurdles, standing high jump, hop-step, and long jumps will also be decided. **1908** *Times* 7 July 16/5 July 25..10 a.m.—Athletics—hop, step, and jump. *Ibid.* 25 July 10/1 The hop, step, and jump fell to the United Kingdom, when an Irishman, T. J. Ahearne, created a British record of 48 ft. 11¼ in. **1909** *Daily Chron.* 24 Sept. 9/3 The hop-step-and-long-jump handicap. **1928** *Observer* 17 June 28/4 The only hop, step, and jumper of quality. **1935** *Encycl. Sports* 349/2 *Hop-Step-and-Jump*, Athletic event, of very ancient practice in the North of the British Isles. Now included in the Olympic Games, it has become the object of much specialization. Known also as the hop, skip and jump. **1961** CHAPMAN & ABRAHAMS *Track & Field Athletics* x. 71 It is not often that a Hop, Step and Jump athlete is able to use the more efficient Hitch-kick long jump action. **1966** *Publ. Amer. Dial. Soc.* XLVI. 21 The paper had to be a *hop, skip, and jump* through the various sorts of annotations that Schele De Vere had made.

b. *attrib.* or as *adj.* Of the nature of, or characterized by, such a saltatory motion. Also *fig.*

1783 WOLCOTT (P. Pindar) *Odes to R.A.'s* vi. Wks. 1812 I. 62 A hop and step and jump mode of inditing. **1808** SCOTT *Autobiog.* in *Lockhart* (1837) I. i. 44 Surprise that, after such a hop-step-and-jump perusal, I knew as much of the book. **1869** MRS. PALLISER *Brittany* 248 The dancers..sidle round in a kind of hop-skip-and-a-jump step. **1895–6** *Calend. Univ. Nebraska* 233 It is not designed to give a hop-skip-and-jump star lecture course.

c. as *vb. intr.* To make this movement; to proceed with irregular saltatory action. Also *fig.*

1815 SHERIDAN *Let. to Mrs. Sheridan* 27 Apr., Mind I don't hop, step, and jump through a book as some certain people do. **1891** MRS. WALFORD *Mischief Monica* III. 21 We pay the porter..and hop-skip-and-jump into the train.

d. Used as adv. phr.

1906 *Smart Set* June 102/1 To go hop, skip and jump over the earth's surface.

Hop (hɒp), *sb.*[3] *Austral. slang.* [Abbrev. of *John Hop*: see JOHN 1 c.] A policeman.

1923 D. H. LAWRENCE *Kangaroo* xvi. 356 It's our boys who've got things in hand. And handed them over to the Hops. **1933** *Bulletin* (Sydney) 8 Feb. 12 The Hops were taking the shattered body out of the water. **1959** BAKER *Drum* II. 118 *Hop*, a policeman.

hop (hɒp), *v.*[1] Pa. t. and pple. **hopped, hopt** (hɒpt). Also 2 **oppe,** 3–6 **hoppe,** 6– *Sc.* **hap.** [OE. *hoppian*, corresp. to ON., Sw. *hoppa*, Da. *hoppe*; also MHG., mod.G. *hopfen*, early mod.Fl. *hoppen* (Kilian):—OTeut. **hoppôjan*, co-radicate with **huppjan*, (see HIP *v.*[1]), also with High Ger. dial. *hoppen* (:—**hoppôn*:—**hubbôn*) and OE. *hoppetan* to jump about. The OTeut. stem *hupp-*, prob. represented a pre-Teut. *kupn-* from root *kup-*: cf. OSlav. *kŭpěti* to hop, leap.]

1. *intr.* **a.** To spring a short way upon the ground or any surface with an elastic or bounding movement, or a succession of such movements: said of persons, animals, and things. Formerly a general synonym of *leap*; now implying a short or undignified leap (perh. by association with b).

c **1000** ÆLFRIC *Hom.* I. 202 Da blissode min cild on minum innoðe, and hoppode ongean his Drihten. *c* **1230** *Hali Meid.* 17 And te deoueles hoppen. **1387** TREVISA *Higden* (Rolls) VII. 285 þanne Lanfrank hopped for joye. **1398** — *Barth. De P.R.* XVIII. iv. (1495) 751 The lambe hoppith and lepeth tofor the folke. *c* **1440** *York Myst.* xxxi. 164 O! my harte hoppis for joie. **1535** COVERDALE *1 Kings* xviii. 26 They [Baal's priests] hopped aboute the altare, as

their vse was to do. —— *Ps.* lxvii[i]. 16 Why hoppe ye so, ye greate hilles? **1590** SPENSER *F.Q.* II. i. 43 If any drop Of liuing bloud yet in her veynes did hop. **1597** MONTGOMERIE *Cherrie & Slae* 17, I saw the hurcheon and the hair..Wer happing to and fro. **1632** J. HAYWARD tr. *Biondi's Eromena* 181 The fawne..that plaid skipping and hopping round about him. **1758** GRAY *Let.* in *Poems* (1775) 261 Mr. Shenstone..goes hopping along his own gravel-walks, and never deviates from the beaten paths. **1758** in Doran '*Mann*' & *Manners* (1876) II. i. 18 Count Lorenzi hopped in, in the evening. **1824** SCOTT *Redgauntlet* Let. xi, Bullets happed aff his buff-coat like hailstanes from a hearth.

b. *spec.* Of animals: To move by leaps with both or all the feet at once, as opposed to walking or running: said esp. of small birds, frogs, grass-hoppers, sand-hoppers, fleas, and the like.

c **1440** *Promp. Parv.* 246/1 Hoppyn as fleys, or froschys, or other lyke, *salio.* **1590** SHAKS. *Mids. N.* v. i. 401 Hop as light as bird from brier. **1657** R. LIGON *Barbadoes* (1673) 60 They are a kind of Stares, for they walk, and do not hop as other birds. *a* **1813** A. WILSON *Discons. Wren* Wks. (1846) 98 But lanely, lanely aye I'll hap, 'Mang auld stane-dykes and braes. *a* **1845** HOOD *Mermaid Margate* ix, She hopt like a Kangaroo! *c* **1850** *Arab. Nts.* (Rtldg.) 405 The bird..flew upon the table..hopping from dish to dish. **1871** R. ELLIS *Catullus* iii. 9 The sparrow..Hopping round her, about her, hence or hither.

c. Of a person: To spring or leap on one foot, or move onwards by a succession of such leaps.

1700 T. BROWN tr. *Fresny's Amusem. Ser. & Com.* 57 They [women] Hop always upright with one Foot upon the Ground. **1711** STEELE *Spect.* No. 6 ¶2 A Man..hopping instead of walking. **1872** HUXLEY *Phys.* vii. 165 The thigh-bone of the leg..is bent up towards the body and not used, in the action of hopping.

2. To dance (for which it is now only a playful expression); also with cognate obj.

c **1386** CHAUCER *Reeve's Prol.* 22 We hoppen ay, whil that the world wol pype. *c* **1440** *Promp. Parv.* 246/1 Hoppyn, or skyppyn.., *salto.* **1500–20** DUNBAR *Poems* liii. 25 He hoppet lyk a pillie wantoun. **1546** J. HEYWOOD *Prov.* (1867) 71 Where all thy pleasure is, hop hoore, pipe theefe. **1791** WOLCOTT (P. Pindar) *Magpie & Robin* Wks. 1812 II. 475 And hops like modern Beaus in Country-dances. **1806** *Morn. Herald* in *Spirit Pub. Jrnls.* (1807) X. 266 She.. snapped the small bone of her right leg in hopping a reel with Lord Sligo. **1825** BROCKETT, *Hop*, to dance.

3. To limp.

1700 DRYDEN *Iliad* I. 769 The limping Smith..hopping here and there (himself a jest). **1724** DE FOE *Mem. Cavalier* (1840) 235 Away he hops with his crutch. **1814** D. H. O'BRIAN *Captiv. & Escape* 46, I insisted upon their leaving me in the rear, to hop on and struggle for myself..I.. limped on with the assistance of my club.

4. *trans.* **a.** To hop about (a place). **b.** To hop or jump over.

1791 WOLCOTT (P. Pindar) *Rights of Kings* Wks. 1812 II. 423 Poor Bird, whom fate oft cruelly assails..To hop a garden, and hunt snails. *Mod.* I could hop that easily.

c. To jump on to (a moving vehicle); to obtain (a ride, a lift) in this way; to catch (a train, etc.). *colloq.* (orig. *U.S.*).

1909 W. STEVENS *Let.* 21 Jan. (1967) 125, I used to 'hop' coal-trains and ride up the Lebanon Valley. **1918** in F. A. Pottle *Stretchers* (1930) 214 The other day, I hopped a truck and went 'to the front'. **1929** *Lit. Digest* 30 Nov. 30/2 Boys are predominantly the ones who 'hop' rides on trucks, trains and other vehicles. **1935** M. M. ATWATER *Murder in Midsummer* xiii. 117 Before midnight he intended to hop the twelve-twenty out. **1940** J. CARY *Charley is My Darling* xlii. 167, I hopped a lorry once with Su, half-way to Twyport. **1967** C. O. SKINNER *Madame Sarah* vi. 119 She and some friends hopped a train for Liverpool and drove to the Cross Zoo.

5. To cause to hop.

1860 LD. DUNDONALD *Autobiog. Seaman* I. xv. 260 These guns were got on board by means of hawsers carried from the frigate to the cliff, one end being made fast to the masthead. By the application of the capstan and tackles the guns were thus hopped on board.

6. Phrases. **a.** *hop the twig*: to depart, go off, or be dismissed suddenly; (also simply *hop, hop off*) to die. *to hop the wag*: to play truant. *slang.*

1797 MARY ROBINSON *Walsingham* II. 279 Must look in upon the rich old jade, before she hops off. *Ibid.* IV. 280 [He] kept his bed three days, and hopped the twig on the fourth. **1828** *Craven Dial.*, *Hop*, to die. *Ibid.*, *Hop*, 'to hop the twig', to run away in debt. **1861** MAYHEW *London Labour* III. 113, I used to hop the wag from school. **1870** MISS BRIDGMAN *R. Lynne* II. xiv. 289 If old Campbell hops the twig. **1903** J. LONDON *People of Abyss* xxiii. 280 The boy told a certain bishop, 'At ten we 'ops the wag...' Which is to say, at ten they play truant. **1959** *Guardian* 24 Oct. 4/5 Episodic truancy during the last year at school—known as 'hopping the wag'. **1964** M. TODD *Ever Such a Nice Lady* iii. 30 The two of them had 'hopped the wag' from school one afternoon.

b. *hop headless*: see HEADLESS 1 b. *hop step* (*skip*) *and jump*: see HOP *sb.*² 3 c.

c. *to hop it*: to be off, go away quickly.

1914 W. OWEN *Let.* 24 Aug. (1967) 279, I should hop it, immejit. **1915** *Scotsman* 13 Jan. 7/3 The Zeppelin kept a few miles in the rear of us, and finally hopped it. **1916** 'BOYD CABLE' *Action Front* 186 'Are we going to stick it here?' said one. 'Didn't the sergeant say something about 'opping it?' **1924** M. NEWMAN *Consummation* IV. xviii. 216 J. H. hopped it for all he was worth. A perfect tornado of bombs pursued him. **1934** T. S. ELIOT *Rock* i. 12 The commission bloke on the door looks at us and says: "op it!'

d. *to hop in* (*out*): to get into (out of) a car, etc.

1914 KIPLING *Diversity of Creatures* (1917) 388 Oh, hop in and drive... We want that beer! **1933** M. DE LA ROCHE *Master of Jalna* viii. 89 Why don't you hop in,..and go with them? **1955** M. GILBERT *Sky High* xiv. 196 Hop out, Rupert. **1963** B. S. JOHNSON *Travelling People* i. 23 I'm making for Aberfyllin,..but I think I can take you about thirty miles along this road... Hop in. **1972** D. DEVINE *Three Green Bottles* 8 A car had pulled up just down the road... 'Hop in. I'll take you.'

e. With *off.* To be off, depart; *spec.*, to start on a 'hop' (HOP *sb.*² 1 d) in an aircraft.

1922 C. E. MONTAGUE *Disenchantment* ii. 18 What the 'ell did you ever come to me for? 'Op off! Out of it! **1926** —— *Rough Justice* viii. 113 Molly and Auberon suddenly felt the breathless stillness of the place infringed by a low, earnest voice on the shore near them: 'It's 'im! 'Op orff!' It was the voice of an aged ferryman they knew. **1926** *Daily Colonist* (Victoria, B.C.) 7 July 5/5 The detailed story of Lieutenant Reece reveals the fact that on Friday morning..he had hopped off from Digby Island for Naden Harbor. The plane was heavily loaded, and it was not without some difficulty that he got away. **1930** *Morning Post* 5 Aug. 9/2 Given favourable weather, he will hop off for England to-morrow, his first stage to Bima..taking him across the Timor Sea. **1934** W. STEVENS *Let.* 12 Feb. (1967) 267 If all goes well, I shall hop off for Florida in a day or two.

f. Colloq. phr. *to hop into bed* (*with*): to have (casual) sexual intercourse (with). Cf. BED *sb.* 6 c.

1951 E. COXHEAD *One Green Bottle* viii. 229 Hopping quick into bed would be all you'd think of. **1968** 'J. WELCOME' *Hell is where you find It* iii. 44 His features were quite strikingly handsome... You'd think every woman he met would have only one thought and that was to hop into bed with him. **1971** C. WHITMAN *Death Suspended* i. 22 Duncan wouldn't waste too much time on her unless she was willing to hop into bed.

7. *Comb.* **hop-about**, (*a*) the action of hopping about, a dance; (*b*) name for an apple dumpling; **hop-ball**, some game with a ball; **hop-crease** = HOP-SCOTCH; **hop-frog** = LEAP-FROG *sb.*; †**hop-legged** *a.*, lame in the leg (cf. 3); †**hop-my-fool**, some gambling game; **hop-off** *Aeronaut.*, the take-off of an aircraft; **hop-over** *Army slang*, an assault; hence **hop over** *v.*, to attack, to go 'over the top'. Also HOP-O'-MY-THUMB.

1593 *Bacchus Bountie* in *Harl. Misc.* (Malh.) II. 275 The pots danced for joy the old *hop about commonly called Sellengar's Round. **1820** *Sporting Mag.* (N.S.) VI. 95 She made..four and twenty hop-a-bouts—apple dumplings—out of one pound of flour. **1811** *Ibid.* XXXVIII. 223 A particular game denominated *Hop-Ball. **1803** W. TAYLOR in *Ann. Rev.* I. 354 Flying kites, knuckling marbles, chuck-half-penny and *hop-crease. *a* **1825** FORBY *Voc. E. Anglia*, *Hop-crease*, the game among boys more commonly called *hop-scotch*..A *scotch* is a cut or *crease.* **1720** GORDON & TRENCHARD *Indep. Whig* No. 32 ¶13 He bows..and ducks his Head, as if he was playing at *Hop Frog. **1714** SAVAGE *Art Prudence* 257 *Hop-legg'd, Hump-back'd..never did any thing that was either Good or Honest. **1824** GALT *Rothelan* II. III. i. 8 The slouched and the slovenly.. wrangled at skittles and toss-my-luck, and bent eagerly over the *hop-my-fool tables. **1926** *Daily Colonist* (Victoria, B.C.) 13 Jan. 1/7 The expedition planes will be..flown..to Point Barrow, where the *hop-off for the Polar flight will be made. **1927** S. BENT *Ballyhoo* i. 36 To the mere hop-off by Lindbergh the *New York Times* gave three first page eight-column streamers. **1918** H. MATTHEWS in Murdoch & Drake-Brockman *Austral. Short Stories* (1951) 243 They didn't have the dash of the Australians in the *hop-over. **1929** *Papers Mich. Acad. Sci., Arts & Lett.* X. 299 *Hop over*, Australian for 'go over the top'. **1933** PARTRIDGE *Words, Words, Words!* III. 194 In the hop-over, many hoped for and some got a wound sufficiently serious to cause them to be sent 'home'.

hop (hɒp), *v.*² [f. HOP *sb.*¹]

1. *trans.* To impregnate or flavour with hops. (Chiefly used in *passive.*)

1572 J. JONES *Bathes Buckstone* 10 a, Ale, neyther to new, nor to stale, not ouerhopped. **1587** HARRISON *England* II. vi. (1877) I. 160 The drinke..being well hopped it lasteth longer. **1605** CAMDEN *Rem.* (1637) 287 A man of worship, whose beere was better hopped then maulted. **1738** SWIFT *Pol. Conversat.* 165, I never taste Malt Liquor; but they say, 'tis well hopt. **1830** M. DONOVAN *Dom. Econ.* I. 163 Malt liquors which have been highly hopped will at length lose all bitterness, and become powerfully acid.

2. *intr.* Of the hop-plant: To produce hops.

1848 *Jrnl. R. Agric. Soc.* IX. II. 554 They climb the poles fast..but do not..hop so well. *Ibid.* 557 The Goldings do not hop down generally so low as many other sorts.

3. To gather or pick hops: see HOPPING *vbl. sb.*²

hop, obs. form of HAP *v.*², HOPE.

Hop- in *Hop-Monday, -tide*, erron. form of HOCK-; cf. HOB-.

1528 *Churchw. Acc. St. Dunstan's, Canterb.*, Item the furst yere of Hopmunday of strayngers and the parysshyns vijs. iiijd. **1558** *Ibid.*, Money gathryd att Hopptyde last past.

'hop-dog. [f. HOP *sb.*¹ + DOG *sb.*¹.]

1. A tool for drawing hop-poles out of the ground. Also a cutting tool used in hop-gardens.

1796 J. BOYS *Agric. Kent* (1813) 56 A hop-dog, to wrench up the poles, costs 5*s.* **1880** C. M. MASON *40 Shires* 397 The cutter with his 'hop-dog' (which has a hook on one side and a knife on the other), cuts the vine near the roots. **1914** BLUNDEN *Waggoner* (1920) 50 Sharpened hopdog, at whose blow The stubborn cluster drops. *Ibid.* 70 *Hopdog*, long-handled curved knife for hop-gardens.

2. A green caterpillar which infests the hop-bine.

1872 C. M. YONGE *P's & Q's* iv. 30 The beautiful cocoon which the hopdog was spinning—a delicate apple-green fellow, with white tooth-brush tufts down his back, black velvet slashings..and a rose-coloured feather in his tail. **1887** in *Kent. Gloss.* **1961** R. SOUTH *Moths Brit. Is.* I. 117 As it is, or was previous to the modern 'washing', common in hop gardens at picking time, it was christened the 'hop dog'. **1968** P. JENNINGS *Living Village* 100 There are still people who use expressions such as..*hot cat* (hairy caterpillar), *hop dog* (green caterpillar).

hope (həʊp), *sb.*¹ Forms: 1 hopa, 2– hope; also 4 **hoppe, ope,** *Sc.* **hape,** 4–6 **hop,** 5 **hoype, howpe,** 5–6 **hoop(e,** 6 **hoape,** *Sc.* **hoip, houpe,** 6– *Sc.* **houp, howp** (haʊp). [Late OE. *hopa*, earlier *tó-hopa*, wk. masc., corresp. to OLG. *tôhopa*, MLG. and MDu. (m. and f.) *hope*, Du. *hoop*; not in OHG.; MHG., Ger. *hoffe*; Sw. *hopp*, Da. *haab* (from LG.). This word, with its cognate vb. (OE. *hopian*, MDu. etc. *hopen*), is recorded first in OE., and seems to have belonged originally to the Saxon and Low G. domain, and thence to have spread into HG. and Scandinavian.]

1. a. Expectation of something desired; desire combined with expectation.

c **1200** *Trin. Coll. Hom.* 193 Habbeð rihte bileue to brunie and hope to helme. *a* **1225** *Ancr. R.* 78 Ine silence & ine hope schal beon ower strencðe. **1382** WYCLIF *Rom.* iv. 18 The which Abraham aȝens hope bileuede in to hope. **1435** MISYN *Fire of Love* II. v. 78 Hoype my sawle chastisis. **1504** ATKYNSON tr. *De Imitatione* IV. vii. 269 Humble hoope. *c* **1560** A. SCOTT *Poems* (S.T.S.) xv. 3 Art thow noᵗ wantoun, haill, and in gud howp. **1579** TOMSON *Calvin's Serm. Tim.* 225/2 When the Churche was in bondage, and vtterly out of hope. **1597** MONTGOMERIE *Cherrie & Slae* 464 Luik quhair to licht before thou loup, And slip na certenty for Houp. **1690** LOCKE *Hum. Und.* II. xxi. §9 (R.) Hope is that pleasure in the mind, which every one finds in himself upon the thought of a profitable future enjoyment of a thing, which is apt to delight him. **1732** POPE *Ess. Man* I. 95 Hope springs eternal in the human breast. **1781** COWPER *Hope* 167 Hope, as an anchor firm and sure, holds fast The Christian vessel, and defies the blast. **1838** THIRLWALL *Greece* xliii. V. 293 While the public mind was thus suspended between hope and fear. **1850** TENNYSON *In Mem.* lv, I..call To what I feel is Lord of all, And faintly trust the larger hope. **1868** BAIN *Ment. & Mor. Sc.* III. xii. §5 This is the emotion of Hope, which is ideality coupled with belief.

b. Const. *of* (that which is hoped for), or with clause introduced by *that*, or (*arch.*) with *infin.*

c **1000** ÆLFRIC *Hom.* I. 568 Ne bepæce Ezechias eow mid leasum hopan, þæt God eow..ahredde. **1297** R. GLOUC. (1724) 456 Vor hope þat þer beþ mo. *a* **1300** *Cursor M.* 28355 In hope of forgiuenes. **1375** BARBOUR *Bruce* II. 89, I haiff gret hop he sall be king. *c* **1375** *Sc. Leg. Saints, Vincentius* 216 Men..sal hafe na hape til vndirstande. *c* **1386** CHAUCER *Prol.* 88 In hope to stonden in his lady grace. **1548** HALL *Chron., Hen. V* 68 b, Beyng in good hope that al his affaires should prosperously succede. **1603** SHAKS. *Meas. for M.* III. i. 4, I haue hope to liue, and am prepar'd to die. **1653** MILTON *Hirelings* (1659) 10 In hope..that preaching.. would prove gainful. **1781** GIBBON *Decl. & F.* II. 133 It was only in a field of battle that he could assert his innocence with any hope of success. **1842** TENNYSON *The Voyage* viii, And still we follow'd..In hope to gain upon her flight.

c. In plural; often in singular sense, esp. in phr. *in hopes.* Const. as in b.

1613 PURCHAS *Pilgrimage* (1614) 523 We will borrow of them to pay your hopes, by this long introduction suspended. **1659** B. HARRIS *Parival's Iron Age* 215 They continued still upon their guard in hopes of better times. **1660–1** MARVELL *Corr.* Wks. 1872–5 II. 44 God be praised, there is all good hopes of her recovery. **1702** J. LOGAN in *Pennsylv. Hist. Soc. Mem.* IX. 94 Hearing he was past hopes, I went to visit him the day before he departed. **1702** ADDISON *Dial. Medals* ii. Misc. Wks. 1727 III. 128, I was in hopes you would have shown us our own nation. **1849** MACAULAY *Hist. Eng.* v. I. 662 Great hopes were entertained at Whitehall that Cornish would appear to have been concerned: but these hopes were disappointed. **1864** TENNYSON *En. Ard.* 620 His hopes to see his own..Not yet had perish'd.

d. Personified; esp. as one of the three heavenly Graces. (1 Cor. xiii. 13.)

1382 WYCLIF *1 Cor.* xiii. 13 Now forsothe dwellen feith, hope, and charite, thes thre. **1782** HAN. MORE *David* v. 52 Fair Hope, with smiling face but ling'ring foot. **1799** CAMPBELL *Pleas. Hope* I, Oh! sacred Truth! thy triumph ceased a while, And Hope, thy sister, ceased with thee to smile. **18..** CHR. WORDSW. *Hymn 'Gracious Spirit'* v, Faith and hope and love we see Joining hand in hand agree.

2. Feeling of trust or confidence. *Obs.* exc. as biblical archaism, with mixture of sense 1.

c **1000** ÆLFRIC *Hom.* I. 350 Geleaffullum mannum mæȝ beon micel truwa and hopa to ðam menniscum Gode Criste. *c* **1200** *Vices & Virtues* 33 Ne haue ðu hope to golde ne to seluer. **1382** WYCLIF *Ps.* cxlv[i]. 5 His hope [is] in the Lord his God. *a* **1400–50** *Alexander* 1859 So sadly in soueraynete he set neuire his hope. **1500–20** DUNBAR *Poems* lxvi. 97 The formest hoip ȝit that I haue..Is in ȝour Grace. **1548** HALL *Chron., Hen. VII* 49 b, To the whiche saiynges..the freer perceaved hope to be geven. **1576** FLEMING *Panopl. Epist.* 99 Our private friendship,..upon hope and affiance whereof, I presume to be your petitioner. **1707** FREIND *Peterborow's Cond. Sp.* 174 My hopes then are all in you. **1867** G. MACDONALD *Disciple* xxv, Though the sky be dim, My hope is in the sky.

†**3.** Expectation (without implication of desire, or of a thing not desired); prospect. *Obs.*

13.. *E.E. Allit. P.* B. 713 Þenne arȝed Abraham..For hope of þe harde hate þat hyȝt hatz oure lorde. *c* **1375** *Sc. Leg. Saints, Clement* 193 Gret hope had he, þat his modir in þe se Was drownyt. *c* **1440** CAPGRAVE *Life St. Kath.* II. 419 To hem þat be in dwere And eke in hope for to be hange and drawe. **1535** STEWART *Cron. Scot.* I. 16 In hoip agane thai sould neuir meit.

4. *transf.* **a.** Ground of hope; promise. Freq. in negative in phr. *not a hope* (*in hell*). Also used ironically for: an expectation which has little or no chance of being fulfilled; esp. in ints., usu.

expressing resignation, ***some hope(s)!, what a hope!***

c **1375** *Sc. Leg. Saints, Nycholas* 579 Oyl rycht clere . . for seknes sere Gaf hop and but. **1535** Coverdale *Prov.* xxvi. 12 There is more hope in a foole then in him. **1613** Purchas *Pilgrimage* (1614) 850 He which at one blow can kill a Captive, is of the greatest hopes. **1633** Ford *Broken Ht.* v. ii, Never lived gentleman of greater merit, Hope or abiliment to steer a kingdom. **1676** tr. *Guillatiere's Voy. Athens* 349 A Child of great hopes. **1847** Tennyson *Princess* I. 167 Hills that look'd across a land of hope. **1899** R. Whiteing *No. 5 John St.* xxix. 297 What a hope for a night like this! **1915** F. Palmer *My Year of War* 231 'What hopes!' was the current phrase I heard among the men in these trenches. **1923** [see hell *sb.* 10 b]. **1929** J. B. Priestley *Good Companions* I. iv. 115 'Well, lads, wot's it yer want?' demanded their hostess. ''Cos if it's steaks and chips and feather beds, you've got a bloody hope.' *Ibid.* II. i. 249 If there was enough money behind to rent His Majesty's Theatre, it could go on better still. It amounted to *that.* 'What a hope!' she concluded bitterly. **1933** A. G. Macdonell *England, their England* xvi. 280 Not a hope! . . The dailies have gone to press ages ago. **1936** [see earthly *a.* 1 c]. **1940** 'G. Orwell' *Diary* 20 June in *Coll. Ess.* (1968) II. lvii. 352 There is a move on foot to get our police records . . at Scotland Yard destroyed. Some hope! The police are the very people who would go over to Hitler. **1948** C. Day Lewis *Otterbury Incident* v. 53 'Well, you'd better start giving back the money . .,' jeered Tuppy. 'What a hope!' **1959** S. Gibbons *Pink Front Door* xvii. 206 Not a hope . . not a single bloody ghost of a hope in hell. **1966** 'K. Nicholson' *Hook, Line & Sinker* v. 63 He . . wants to put on a good show for her. What a hope. **1966** F. Hoyle *Oct. First* vi. 60 I've given them the idea I might come up with some explanation. . . Some hopes. **1967** P. Moyes *Murder Fantastical* xv. 229 'His book is probably in the Lucky Dip.' . . Maud made a face. 'Some hope of finding it in that case,' she said. **1969** J. Ashford *Prisoner at Bar* iv. 33, I told Mrs. Green we hadn't a hope in hell, but she said it wasn't the money, it was the principle. **1971** C. Egleton *Last Post for Partisan* xvii. 176 'Make sure you get the right mix of weapons and explosives.' 'You've got a hope.'

b. A person or thing that gives hope or promise for the future, or in which hopes are centred.

a **1225** *Juliana* 65 þu art hope of heale; þu art rihtwises weole. *a* **1300** *Cursor M.* 23929 Leuedi . . þat es nu mi hope. **1382** Wyclif *1 Tim.* i. 1 Jhesu Crist oure hope. **1526** Tindale *Col.* i. 27 Christ in you, the hope of glory. **1702** Pope *Dryope* 9 Her tender mother's only hope and pride. **1876** E. Mellor *Priesth.* viii. 390 If the adult population are the despair of the priests, the children are their hope.

c. An object of hope; that which is hoped for.

1382 Wyclif *Prov.* xiii. 12 Hope that is deferrid tormenteth the soule. —— *Rom.* viii. 24 Hope that is seyn, is not hope. **1526** Tindale *Tit.* ii. 13 Lokinge for that blessed hope, and glorious apperenge of the mighty god. *c* **1600** Shaks. *Sonn.* cxliii, If thou catch thy hope, turn back to me. **1632** J. Hayward tr. *Biondi's Eromena* 122 The Prince thus frustrated of his first hope, came running. **1816** Shelley *Alastor* 32 Staking his very life on some dark hope.

¶ See also forlorn hope.

5. a. *Comb.* chiefly objective and instrumental.

1580 Sidney *Arcadia* III. (1724) II. 477 Hope-giving phrases. **1598** Sylvester *Du Bartas* II. ii. I. *Ark* 362 Then hope-cheer'd Noah . . Sends forth the Crow. **1817** Shelley *Pr. Athan.* I. 10 Baffled with blast of hope-consuming shame. **1822** Lamb *Elia* Ser. I. *Decay Beggars*, The cheerful and hope-stirring tread of the passenger. **1892** Jusserand *French Ambass.* 160 The hope-forbidding testimony of Pytheas.

b. Special comb. **hope chest** chiefly *U.S.*, a chest or box in which a young woman hopefully collects articles towards a home of her own in the event of her marriage; cf. *bottom drawer* bottom *sb.* 19.

1911 G. S. Porter *Harvester* xx. 504 It was a big, burl-maple box, designed after the hope chests that he saw advertised in magazines. **1922** M. B. Houston *Witch Man* vii. 80 The bedspread that three years before she had laid unfinished in Kaid's hope chest. **1959** 'J. R. Macdonald' *Galton Case* (1960) xi. 88 A metal box about the size of a hope chest. **1960** *New Left Rev.* Nov.–Dec. 12/2 The bride . . had a good six patents dealing with biochemistry in her hope chest. **1973** *Welcomat* (Philadelphia) 10 Oct. 12 Liza Minelli has just bought her third wedding dress and packed it away along with the others in her hope chest.

hope (həʊp), *sb.*[2] Forms: 1 hop, 4 hopp', 6 hoppe, *Sc.* hoip, 8 *Sc.* houp, 3– hope. [OE. *hop* app. recorded only in combination (e.g. *fenhop*, *mórhop*: see sense 1). It is doubtful whether all the senses belong orig. to one word. With sense 3 cf. ON. *hóp* 'a small land-locked bay or inlet, salt at flood tide and fresh at ebb' (Vigf.).]

1. A piece of enclosed land, e.g. in the midst of fens or marshes or of waste land generally.

a **1000** in Kemble *Cod. Dipl.* VI. 243 Mædwægan hop and wassan mæd oð ðone þreos dic. *c* **1200** *Merton Coll. Rec.* No. 1259 (Essex), Unam hopam marisci in villa de Westilleberie, quae hopa iacet in extrema hoparum mearum versus orientalem quae vocantur landhope, extendentem versus austrum a hopo Leuenoth. **1323–4** *Ibid.* No. 1260 (Essex), Unam hopam marisci continentem duas acras cum pertinentiis sicut fossatis undique includitur. **1468** *Will of Heyward* (Somerset Ho.), Mesuagium vocat. le Bakhous cum quadam domo vocat. le stable & vno hope & vna Wallia. **1500** *Will of N. Brown* (ibid.), Crofts lands marshes hopes & walles. **1607** Norden *Surv. Dial.* 205, I have planted an Ozier hope (for so they call it in Essex, and in some places an Ozier bed) in a surrounded ground, fit before for no vse, for the too much moisture and ouerflowing of it.

2. A small enclosed valley, esp. 'a smaller opening branching out from the main dale, and running up to the mountain ranges; the upland part of a mountain valley'; a blind valley. Chiefly in south of Scotl. and north-east of England, where it enters largely into local nomenclature, as in *Hopekirk, Hopetoun, Hopehead, Dryhope, Greenhope, Ramshope, Ridlees Hope*, etc.

1378 *Durh. Halm. Rolls* (Surtees) 143 Quod nullus eorum succidat bent infra le hopp' sine licencia. ? *a* **1400** *Morte Arth.* 2503 Thorowe hopes and hymlande hillys and oþer. *a* **1400–50** *Alexander* 5390 So þai come till a caue . . Be-twene twa hillis in a hope, and herberd all niȝt. **1542** *Newminster Cartul.* (Surt.) Introd. 18 Such as inhabyte in one of those hoopes, valyes, or graynes cannot heare the fraye, outecrye, or exclamac'on of suche as dwell in an other hoope or valley upon the other syde of the said mountayne. **1596** Dalrymple tr. *Leslie's Hist. Scot.* II. 163 Ouer hil and hoip, bank and bra. *a* **1697** Aubrey *Nat. Hist. Surrey* (1719) IV. 164 A long *Hope* (i.e. according to Virgil, *Deductus Vallis*) in the most pleasant and delightful Solitude. **1805** Forsyth *Beauties Scotl.* II. 151 The hills are every where intersected by small streams called *burns*. These flowing in a deep bed, form glens or hollows, provincially called *hopes*. **1893** *Northumbld. Gloss.*, *Hope*, . . the inch ordnance map of Northumberland gives seventy-three place names having this termination. In the county of Durham forty such occur. **1895** Crockett *Men of Moss-hags* ix. 67 Wide green holms and deep blind 'hopes' or hollows among the mountains.

3. An inlet, small bay, haven.

c **1425** Wyntoun *Chron.* VI. xx. 2499 And in Saynt Margretys Hope belyve Off propyre nede than till arryve. **1535** Stewart *Cron. Scot.* II. 673 Tha tuke land richt far vp into Forth, Into ane place . . Sanct Margaretis-hoip is callit at this da. **1587** Fleming *Contn. Holinshed* III. 1379/2 Being by contrarie winds driuen to staie against Erith, at Grauesend, in Tilberie hope. **1756** Rolt *Dict. Trade, Hope*, a station for ships in the mouth of the river Thames, below Gravesend. **1818** Scott *Br. Lamm.* xii, A little hamlet which straggled along the side of a creek formed by the discharge of a small brook into the sea . . It was called Wolf's Hope (*i.e.* Wolf's Haven). **1887** *Kent. Gloss.*, *Hope*, a place of anchorage for ships.

hope (həʊp), *v.* Forms: see hope *sb.*[1] [OE. *hopian*, ME. *hopien*, *hopen*, corresp. to MLG., MDu., Du. *hopen*:—OLG. **hopôn*. Not known in OHG.; in MHG. *hoffen* is rare, and chiefly MG., not the regular word for 'to hope'; like the corresp. sb. the vb. appears to have belonged orig. to the English and Saxon-Frankish domain, and thence to have spread in later times over Germany and Scandinavia.]

1. a. *intr.* To entertain expectation of something desired; to look (mentally) with expectation. Const. †*to*, †*after*, †*of* (obs.), *for*; also with indirect passive.

971 *Blickl. Hom.* 87 We to þinum hidercyme hopodan & hyhtan. *c* **1205** Lay. 17936 Ah ne hope þu to ræde of heom þat ligged dede. *c* **1290** *S. Eng. Leg.* I. 291/97 Ne hopie ich nouȝt þere-fore. *c* **1400** *Cato's Mor.* 203 in *Cursor M.* App. iv. 1672 Quen þou art atte disese, hope ofter better ese. **1553** Eden *Treat. Newe Ind.* (Arb.) 39 This nauigation . . was not brought to the ende hoped for. **1595** T. Bedingfeld tr. *Machiavelli's Florentine Hist.* 140 The Earle . . shut himselfe vp in Poppi, not hoping of any aide. *c* **1600** *My Ladyis Pulcritud* 26 in *Montgomerie's Poems* (1887) 279 Houping aganis all houp. **1659** B. Harris *Parival's Iron Age* 29, I can hope for no support in the equity of my cause. **1726** *Adv. Capt. R. Boyle* 16 Come, hope for the best, said I. **1850** Tennyson *In Mem.* cxii, Hope could never hope too much, In watching thee from hour to hour. *Mod.* I hoped for better things from him.

†**b.** With *to*, *for*: To look for, expect (without implication of desire): = 4. *Obs. rare.*

1303 R. Brunne *Handl. Synne* 6968 He yn þe feuer lay, And to þe deþe he hopede weyl. **1599** H. Buttes *Dyets drie Dinner* Ep. Ded. A vij, Neither can I hope for, at either of your hands, any ungentle or discourteous censure.

2. *intr.* To trust, have confidence. Const. †*to*, †*on* (obs.), *in* (obs. exc. as biblical archaism; now only a strong case of sense 1).

c **888** K. Ælfred *Boeth.* xlii, Hit nys no unnyt ðæt we hopien to Gode. *c* **1000** Ælfric *Hom.* I. 256 Ne hi ne hopian on heora unȝewissum welan. *c* **1200** *Moral Ode* 31 in *Trin. Coll. Hom.* 221 Ne hopie wif to hire were ne were to his wiue. *a* **1325** *Prose Psalter* li[i]. 7 He hoped in þe multitude of his riches. **1548** Hall *Chron., Hen. VI* 176 The lordes lyenge at Caleys, hoping in their frendes within the realme. *a* **1605** Montgomerie *Misc. Poems* li. 43 Bot I houp in the goddes Hemene. **1611** Bible *Ps.* cxix. 49 The word . . upon which thou hast caused me to hope. **1855** Cath. Winkworth *Hymn*, Leave God to order all thy ways, And hope in Him whate'er betide.

3. *trans.* To expect with desire, or to desire with expectation; to look forward to (something desired). **a.** with simple object (= *hope for*, sense 1). Now chiefly *poetic.*

c **1000** Ælfric *Hom.* I. 250 We beoð hæbbende ðæs ðe we ær hopedon. *a* **1240** *Ureisun* in *Cott. Hom.* 183 þu al þet ic hopie. *a* **1340** Hampole *Psalter* xxvi. 6 And hope þe victory thoro his help. *c* **1374** Chaucer *Boeth.* I. pr. iv. 10 By whiche lettres I am accused to han hooped the fredom of Roome. **1567** *Gude & Godlie B.* (S. T. S.) 124, I grant, I haif done wrang, Nocht hopeand help of the. **1603** B. Jonson *Sejanus* v. x. Wks. (Rtldg.) 172/2 Dost thou hope fortune to redeeme thy crimes? **1676** Dryden *Aurengz.* IV. i, Strange cozenage! none would live past years again; Yet all hope pleasure in what yet remain. **1792** S. Rogers *Pleas. Mem.* I. 350 With looks that asked yet dared not hope relief. **1837** Dickens *Pickw.* ii, The conviction that he had nothing to hope from his friend's fears. **1872** Ruskin *Fors Clav.* xxii. 28, I have not time to ask Mr. Sillar's permission, but hope his pardon for assuming it.

b. with obj. clause. (In mod. colloq. use often in weakened sense, expressing little more than a desire that the event may happen, or (with clause in pres. or past) that the fact may turn out to be as stated.)

c **1050** *Byrhtferth's Handboc* in *Anglia* VIII. 325 Ic hopiȝe þæt cherubin se mæra æt wesan wylle. *a* **1225** *Ancr. R.* 430 Ich hopie þet hit schal beon . . swuðe biheue. *c* **1350** *Will. Palerne* 1097, I hope to heuene king mi help schal nouȝt fayle. *c* **1449** Pecock *Repr.* II. xiii. 223 It is to hope that . . thei schulen no longer so erre. **1590** Shaks. *Com. Err.* III. i. 54 You'll let vs in I hope? **1660** Boyle *New Exp. Phys. Mech.* Pref. 4, I have in another treatise . . given a particular, and, I hope, a satisfactory account. **1738** Swift *Pol. Conversat.* 123 Thirty bad Bits, and Two good ones . . but I hope, you have got one of the two good ones. **1804** W. Gilpin *Serm.* III. xxxviii. (R.), He hoped you would consider the debt of little consequence. **1860** Tyndall *Glac.* I. xi. 70 We hoped that no repetition of the process would occur. **1865** W. G. Palgrave *Arabia* I. 114 He enters with a 'hope I don't intrude' air.

c. with infinitive.

1297 R. Glouc. (1724) 220 He . . hopede to wynne Rome, wanne he come eft aȝe. *c* **1305** *Judas Iscar.* 34 in *E.E.P.* (1862) 108 Glad heo was and hopede of him to habbe an heire. *c* **1400** *Destr. Troy* 8006 þai . . hopit in haste . . the mater to here. **1574** Churchyard *Wolsey* xlvi. in *Mirr. Mag.* (1815) II. 495, I hoapt to come before the king. **1659** B. Harris *Parival's Iron Age* 29 Cardinal Wolsey . . hoped to come to be Pope by the recommendation of the Emperour. **1738** Swift *Pol. Conversat.* 178 When may we hope to see you again in London? **1857** Buckle *Civiliz.* I. vii. 423 Violent measures, by which the King hoped to curb the colonies.

d. Phr. *to hope against hope* [after Rom. iv. 18]: to hope where there are no reasonable grounds for doing so; to hope very much. Hence **hope-against-hope** *sb.*

1813 J. Montgomery *World before Flood* 90 Hope against hope, and ask till ye receive. **1915** W. S. Maugham *Of Human Bondage* lxxviii. 403 He mentioned the place and time at which they were to meet, and hoping against hope kept the appointment. **1955** G. Greene *Quiet American* II. i. 93, I had hoped against hope that he would have gone before she returned. **1963** V. Nabokov *Gift* i. 69 Fyodor still hoped against hope that this was a metaphysical paradox and not a traitorous *lapsus*. **1968** W. Sansom *Grand Tour Today* ix. 181 Matisse's wonderful chapel of stained light . . has nothing to do with the usual hope-against-hope that modern concrete building will 'harmonise' with older surroundings.

†**4.** To expect or anticipate (without implication of desire); to suppose, think, suspect. *Obs.*

c **1330** R. Brunne *Chron. Wace* (Rolls) 4429, I hope Iulyus had drawen hit out. *Ibid.* 15842 Non hoped til hym no gyle. *a* **1340** Hampole *Psalter* ix. 1 *comm.*, I hope hat he beyne a rightwisman he had noght sayd swa. *c* **1386** Chaucer *Reeve's T.* 109 Our Manciple I hope he wil be deed. *a* **1400–50** *Alexander* 3548, I hope þou wenes at we be like to þire lethire Persyns. **15..** *Tanner Tamw.* in Puttenham *Eng. Poesie* (Arb.) 263, I hope I shall be hanged to morrow. **1571** *Satir. Poems Reform.* xxvi. 113 Quhat man did hoip of Grange now dois appeir . . He dois Rebell and will not serue the King. **1632** Rowley *Wom. never vexed* II. in Hazl. *Dodsley* XII. 132, I hope thou'lt vex me . . I shall rail and curse thee, I hope.

5. *trans.* To bring by hoping. *nonce-use.*

1720 *Lett. fr. Lond. Jrnl.* (1721) 60 Some hope themselves . . into a Halter, but few into their Wishes.

hope, obs. form of hoop.

hopeable ('həʊpəb(ə)l), *a. rare.* [f. hope *v.* + -able.] That may be hoped for.

1611 Cotgr., *Esperable*, hopeable, fit to be hoped for.

hoped (həʊpt), *ppl. a.* [f. hope *v.* + -ed[1].]

1. a. Expected with desire: see hope *v.* 3.

1573 Tusser *Husb.* cvi. (1878) 196 This was both God and man, of Jewes the hoped king. **1579** Spenser *Sheph. Cal.* Dec. 100 All my hoped gaine is turnd to scathe. **1625** *Modell Wit* 62 b, Shall . . all my hoped ioyes be defeated in a moment? **1685** H. More *Illustr.* 300 Which are the hoped Consequences thereof.

b. Now usually ***hoped-for***: see hope *v.* 1.

1593 Shaks. *3 Hen. VI*, IV. viii. 61 Cold biting Winter marres our hop'd-for Hay. **1694** Salmon *Bates' Disp.* Ded. (1713) A ij b, This Book, which, through your Benignity, cannot go without its hop'd-for Effects. **1860** Pusey *Min. Proph.* 485 Two-fifths only of the hoped-for produce was yielded. **1947** *Sci. News* IV. 37 The patience in collecting and sifting evidence that goes on steadily from the moment a body is found to the hoped-for sequel when a suspect is charged. **1967** *Listener* 30 Mar. 426/1 They gave the hoped-for succession of industries from 40,000 to 9,000 years ago.

†**2.** Viewed or contemplated with hope; about which hopes are entertained. *Obs.*

1581 Mulcaster *Positions* xli. (1887) 241 His most honored prince, and his best hoped pupill.

3. Possessed of or imbued with hope. *dial.*

1896 Barrie *Marg. Ogilvy* ii. (1897) 34 The Doctor says this morning that he is better hoped now, but at present we can say no more but only she is alive.

hopeful ('həʊpfʊl), *a.* (*sb.*) [f. hope *sb.*[1] + -ful.]

1. a. Full of hope; feeling or entertaining hope; expectant of that which is desired.

1594 Shaks. *Rich. III*, I. ii. 24 Childe . . Whose vgly and vnnaturall Aspect May fright the hopefull Mother at the view. **1665** Sir T. Herbert *Trav.* (1677) 124 Hopeful of some reward. **1822** Jeffrey *Let.* lxxxix. in Cockburn *Life* II, The . . happiest, hopefulest, creature that ever set fortune at defiance. **1886** Ruskin *Præterita* I. vii. 220 A time of active and hopeful contentment for both the young people.

b. Expressive of hope.

1607 Rowlands *Guy, Earl Warw.* 81 The comfort of a hopeful word bestowing. **1865** Dickens *Mut. Fr.* I. iii, It is

likely enough that ten thousand other young men..made the same hopeful remark in the course of the same evening.

2. a. Causing or inspiring hope; giving promise of success or future good, 'promising': said of a person or thing on which one's hope is set, or concerning which hope is entertained; sometimes ironically, of a young person who is likely to disappoint hopes.

1568 ELIZABETH *Let. to Cecil* in Strype *Ann. Ref.* (1709) I. li. 515 That she would allow honorary salaries to the acute and hopeful youth, for their maintenance in their studies there. **1592** SHAKS. *Rom. & Jul.* I. ii. 15 Earth hath swallowed all my hopes but she, Shee's the hopefull Lady of my earth. **1647** in *Wood's Life* (O.H.S.) I. 301 *note*, Money to maintain hopeful students at the University. **1732** SWIFT *Sacram. Test* Wks. 1761 III. 294 Which of the two is in the hopefullest Condition to ruin the Church. **1768** GOLDSM. *Good-n. Man* I. Wks. (Globe) 611/1 Here comes his hopeful nephew; strange, goodnatured, foolish, open-hearted. **1865–6** H. PHILLIPS *Amer. Paper Curr.* II. 92 Loans now seemed to afford a hopeful prospect of relief.

b. as *sb.* (*colloq.*) A 'hopeful' boy or girl: often ironical. (Sometimes as a *quasi*-proper name.)

1720 DUCHESS ORMOND *Let.* 18 Apr. in *Swift's Wks.* (1814) XVI. 363 Else young Hopeful might have been in danger. **1811** BYRON *Hints fr. Hor.* 256 O'er hoards diminish'd by young Hopeful's debts. **1842** C. WHITEHEAD *Richard Savage* (1845) III. vi. 381 Some of the young hopefuls make their parents pay pretty smartly for their love. **1860** G. H. LEWES *Let.* 26 Sept. in *Geo. Eliot's Lett.* (1954) III. 349 My hopeful and his parent will appear at the 'Bedford' on Monday morning. **1899** F. J. CROWEST *Beethoven* 41 He committed this hopeful, only now some nineteen years of age, to the care of an old lawyer friend. **1957** W. THIELENS in R. K. Merton *Student-Physician* 133 This difference is more than partially due to *anticipation* by medical school hopefuls of the more demanding entrance requirements. **1972** *Daily Tel.* (Colour Suppl.) 27 Oct. 9/2 A dozen new applications arrive each day and are filed away with all the other hopefuls anxious to establish themselves on the circuits.

hopefully ('həʊpfʊlɪ), *adv.* [f. prec. + -LY[2].]

1. In a hopeful manner; with a feeling of hope; with ground for hope, promisingly.

a **1639** WOTTON *Life Dk. Buckh.* in *Reliq.* (1672) 237 He left all his female kindred..either matched with peers of the realm actually, or hopefully with earls' sons and heirs. **1846** H. ROGERS *Ess.* (1860) I. 171 The limits within which the human understanding can hopefully speculate. *Mod.* He set to work hopefully.

2. It is hoped (that); let us hope. (Cf. G. *hoffentlich* it is to be hoped.) orig. *U.S.* (Avoided by many writers.)

1932 *N.Y. Times Book Rev.* 24 Jan. 11/4 He would create an expert commission..to consist of ex-Presidents and a selected list of ex-Governors, hopefully not including Pa and Ma Ferguson. **1965** T. L. BECKER *Political Behavioralism & Mod. Jurisprudence* p. v, Hopefully, this study, generated from the friction of highly polarized viewpoints, is the first of many steps directed towards satisfying a long-standing curiosity. **1965** *New Yorker* 27 Mar. 35/1 We asked her when she expected to move into her new apartment, and she answered, 'Hopefully on Tuesday.' **1966** in N. P. Vakar *Word Count Spoken Russian* p. viii, Professor Vakar's study will prove of enormous value... It should—and, hopefully, it will—be followed by a similar analysis of..syntactic patterns. **1967** *Lebende Sprachen* XII. 5/1 Machines will hopefully enable the scientist to find quickly the information he needs. **1969** *Language* XLV. 667 Hopefully, Tucker will publish supplements to this chapter. **1970** *Daily Tel.* 12 Feb. 21 The cost of developing a new 'Dash 50' series of engines, that hopefully will power Lockheed's 'extended range' jet, is put at around £75 million. **1970** *Sci. Jrnl.* May 27/2 By the time this issue..is on the bookstalls, *Apollo 13* should have completed its own trip to the Moon, hopefully with as little incident as its two predecessors. **1971** *Guardian* 13 Apr. 9/5 Prototype wooden rocking horses... Hopefully they will be available in the autumn at prices from £120.

hopefulness ('həʊpfʊlnɪs). [f. as prec. + -NESS.] The quality or state of being hopeful.

1. The state of feeling or expressing hope.

1628 WITHER *Brit. Rememb.* III. 170, I scarcely held it worth my hopefulnesse. **1858** J. H. NEWMAN *Hist. Sk.* II. II. ii, Perhaps he exaggerated his own hopefulness, in order to increase hers. **1886** HALL CAINE *Son of Hagar* III. ix, Greta's eyes were full of a radiant hopefulness.

2. The quality of inspiring hope; promisingness.

1651 *Fuller's Abel Rediv., Zanchius* 390 Zanchius in his youth shewing some testifications of his hopefulnesse. **1698** STRYPE *Life Sir T. Smith* ii. (R.), While he was thus a student here..notice was taken of his parts and hopefullness. *Mod.* The hopefulness of the political situation.

hopeite, hopite ('həʊpaɪt). *Min.* [Named 1823, after Dr. T. C. Hope of Edinburgh: see -ITE.] A phosphate of zinc found in greyish-white crystals, never accurately analyzed.

1824 *Trans. R. Soc. Edin.* X. 107 Description of Hopeite, a New Mineral. **1834** T. ALLAN *Min.* 24 Sir David Brewster ..distinguished it by the name of Hopeite.

hopeless ('həʊplɪs), *a.* [f. HOPE *sb.*[1] + -LESS.]

1. Destitute of hope; having or feeling no hope; despairing.

1590 SHAKS. *Com. Err.* I. i. 158 Hopelesse and helpelesse doth Egean wend. **1611** —— *Cymb.* IV. iv. 27 Hopelesse To haue the courtesie your Cradle promis'd. **1659** HAMMOND *On Ps.* cii. 6, I am as destitute and hopeless of it as the most solitary Pelican. **1823** SCORESBY *Whale Fishery* 460 On this [ice-floe] they spent a dismal and hopeless night. **1884** *Contemp. Rev.* May 629 Is it surprising that the great army of the hopeless should forget the way to church?

2. Of or concerning which there is no hope; despaired of, desperate. Also in weakened use: ineffectual, inadequate, unable to stand up for oneself; incompetent, stupid.

1566 DRANT *Horace*, Sat. II. ii. (R.), He..keepes it well, and warylye to helpe in hopelesse tyde. **1583** STANYHURST *Æneis* II. (Arb.) 50 Laocoon..al hoaples Hee striues. **1751** JOHNSON *Rambler* No. 87 ¶2 A sign of hopeless depravity, that though good advice was given, it wrought no reformation. **1849** MACAULAY *Hist. Eng.* vii. II. 185 He recovered from maladies which seemed hopeless. **1854** E. TWISLETON *Let.* 23 Oct. (1928) xiii. 245 Prussia is as *fainéant* as ever, and seems quite hopeless. **1867** FREEMAN *Norm. Conq.* I. v. 296 To reconcile the chronology is hopeless. **1922** W. S. MAUGHAM *Writer's Notebk.* (1949) 188 'You can't do a thing for people like that,' he said. 'They're hopeless.' **1932** R. LEHMANN *Invitation to Waltz* III. xiv. 240 But of course Mum's hopeless. She thinks virgins are sacred to all men. **1963** D. CORY *Hammerhead* ii. 26 'Who's this..?' 'That's Cary Grant, you are *hopeless*, Johnny.' **1967** O. NORTON *Now lying Dead* i. 3 'I'm *hopeless*,' she went on. 'I made a teapot once. It looked dinky. Only it wouldn't *pour*, don't you see.'

†**3.** Unhoped-for, unexpected. *Obs.*

1590 SPENSER *F.Q.* III. v. 34 His watry eies..He up gan lifte toward the azure skies, From whence descend all hopelesse remedies. **1624** CAPT. SMITH *Virginia* IV. 160 Giuing thanks to God for so hopelesse a deliuerance.

hopelessly ('həʊplɪslɪ), *adv.* [f. prec. + -LY[2].] In a hopeless manner; without or beyond hope; so that there is no hope; desperately.

1616 BEAUM. & FL. *Scornf. Lady* I. i, *El. Lo.* Brother, is your last hope past? *Y. Lo.* Hopelessly past. **1646** SIR T. BROWNE *Pseud. Ep.* I. iii. 8 Hopelesly continuing in mistakes, they live and dye in their absurdities. **1838** LYTTON *Alice* 162 You are hopelessly in love with Miss Cameron. **1873** BLACK *Pr. Thule* viii, Never was..sea-song sung so hopelessly without spirit.

hopelessness ('həʊplɪsnɪs). [f. as prec. + -NESS.] Hopeless condition; want of hope, despair; state of being despaired of, desperateness.

1809 HAN. MORE *Coelebs* II. 19 (Jod.) That discouraging superiority, which others might be deterred from imitating through hopelessness to reach. **1853** J. H. NEWMAN *Hist. Sk.* (1873) II. I. i. 13 A message which well illustrates the hopelessness of going to war with them. **1880** OUIDA *Moths* II. 287 The old heavy burden of hopelessness and apathy had fallen on her again.

† **hopelost** ('həʊplɒst, -lɔːst), *a.* and *sb. Obs.* [f. HOPE *sb.*[1] + LOST *ppl. a.*] **A.** *adj.* That has lost hope, despairing; lost to hope, desperate. **B.** *sb.* One who has lost hope.

1570 *Satir. Poems Reform.* xxii. 70 Fretting with feir in Inward conscience, As hoiplost wichtis without all pacience. **1587** FLEMING *Contn. Holinshed* III. 1548/2 His two gracelesse hopelost sonnes Shane and Alike Bourke. **1648** SYMMONS *Vind. Chas. I*, 148 Like a Company of poore Hope-losts..look up to that place of Honour, where erst they sat.

† **'hopely,** *a. Obs. rare.* [f. HOPE *sb.*[1] + -LY[1].] Of the nature of hope; fraught with hope.

1653 H. WHISTLER *Upshot Inf. Baptisme* 62 A noble instance of hopely probability by divine Providence.

hoper ('həʊpə(r)). [f. HOPE *v.* + -ER[1].] One who hopes.

1382 WYCLIF *2 Sam.* xxii. 31 God..a shelde is of alle the hopers [Vulg. *sperantium*] in hym. **1532** MORE *Confut. Tindale* Wks. 733/1 Such hopers and such louers..are yet no lesse begiled then are the beggers that dreme they finde great heapes of gold. *a* **1684** LEIGHTON *Comm. 1 Pet.* Wks. (1868) 196 Then shall these hopers be in eternal possession. **1788** MAD. D'ARBLAY *Diary* 23 Nov., She is no hoper; she sees nothing before us but despair and horror. **1889** W. WARD *W. G. Ward & Oxf. Movem.* 379 It would take a very enthusiastic hoper to look for success now.

hoper, obs. form of HOPPER.

'hop-ˌgarden. [f. HOP *sb.*[1]] A field or piece of land devoted to the cultivation of hops.

1573 R. SCOT (*title*) A Perfite Platforme of a Hoppe Garden, and necessarie Instructions for the making and mayntenance hereof. **1669** WORLIDGE *Syst. Agric.* (1681) 160 In the Winter, when little else can be done to the Hop-garden. **1766** GRAY *Let.* in *Poems* (1775) 322 Orchards, cherry-grounds, hop-gardens, intermixed with corn and frequent villages.

'hop-ground. [f. HOP *sb.*[1]] = prec.; also, ground suited to the cultivation of hops.

1679 *Essex's Excell.* 3 Coll. Mildmay came from his house to the place near the Hop-ground. **1715** *Lond. Gaz.* No. 5326/3 Four Acres of Hop Ground. **1855** MACAULAY *Hist. Eng.* xv. III. 611 The hopgrounds of Kent would be as the vineyards of the Neckar.

hop-harlot, var. HAP-HARLOT, *Obs.*

hophead ('hɒphɛd). **1.** [f. HOP *sb.*[1] 4 + HEAD *sb.*[1] 7 e.] An opium-smoker; a drug-addict. *slang* (orig. and chiefly *U.S.*).

1911 C. B. CHRYSLER *White Slavery* xi. 89 Opium smokers, 'hop fiends' or 'hop heads', as they are called, are the fiercest of all the White Slavers. **1915** G. BRONSON-HOWARD *God's Man* ii. 130, I told Beau to hunt up a skirt before, but you know these hop-heads—always putting things off. **1931** E. WALLACE *On the Spot* ii. 21 A hop-head will spill his friends' secrets to buy more hop. **1934** D. HAMMETT *Thin Man* xi. 72 'What's a junkie?' she asked. 'Hop-head.' **1947** E. E. CUMMINGS *Let.* 21 Sept. (1969) 180 Can someone imagine what any moujik coolie or hophead of any crevice of the Orient would sense, upon receiving such a gospel? **1959** J. CHRISTOPHER *Scent of White Poppies* ix. 144 Did you ever see a hophead when he's been kept short of what he wants? **1973** H. NIELSEN *Severed Key* vii. 75 I'll mail the letter to that hophead lawyer.

2. [HOP *sb.*[1] 1 b.] A drunkard, a tippler. *N.Z. slang.*

[**1942** *N.Z.E.F. Times* 17 Aug. 16/3 (*caption*) Private Harry Hophead seen leaving Shepheards after a brief visit (very).] **1948** D. BALLANTYNE *Cunninghams* (1963) II. ix. 166 It's Betty that can't hold the liquor... She's a real lily of a hophead. **1952** *Landfall* VI. 208 Among young people greetings like 'Hophead'..are accepted as flattery.

Hopi ('həʊpɪ). [Native name.] The name of a group of North American Indians living chiefly in north-eastern Arizona; also, a member of this people; their language. Also *attrib.*

1877 *Buffalo Soc. Nat. Sci. Bull.* 170 The title of '*Moquis*' has been applied to this confederacy by its enemies, and signifies the dying race. I understand that they usually speak of themselves as '*Ho-pees*' (our people). **1893** T. DONALDSON *Moqui Pueblo Indians* 13 The name which they call theselves by is Ho-pi, or Ho-pi-tuh-lei-nyu-muh, meaning 'peaceful people'. **1927** W. CATHER *Death comes for Archbishop* VII. i. 197 Last year, in May, he had been on his way to the Hopi Indians. **1927** D. H. LAWRENCE *Mornings in Mexico* 135 The Hopi country is in Arizona, next the Navajo country. *Ibid.*, The Hopis are Pueblo Indians, village Indians, so their reservation is not large. **1933** L. BLOOMFIELD *Language* iv. 72 The Shoshonean family.. including..Comanche, and Hopi. **1937** R. H. LOWIE *Hist. Ethnological Theory* vii. 82 Swanton has shown..that in North America..many higher tribes, like the Hopi, are strictly matrilineal. **1952** A. HUXLEY *Let.* 12 Oct. (1969) 657 The ways I look at the world, are determined—determined in profoundly different ways according to whether I speak Chinese, Maori, Hopi, or English. **1956** D. ABERCROMBIE *Probl. & Princ.* i. 12 Hopi is an example of a language which lacks expression..for concepts of time. **1957** C. F. & F. M. VOEGELIN in *Int. Jrnl. Amer. Linguistics Mem. No. 14* (*title*) Hopi domains, a lexical approach to the problem of selection. **1959** E. TUNIS *Indians* 25/2 Even today an elderly Hopi will jog trot twenty miles to his cornfield, work all day, and jog home again. **1969** *Observer* (Colour Suppl.) 18 May 34/1 She is a Hopi, one of the less-known tribes. **1973** HOLT & MARJORAM *Math. in a Changing World* ii. 65 The difference between a noun and a verb to a Hopi Indian, Whorf discovered, is that a noun is more permanent than a verb.

hoping ('həʊpɪŋ), *vbl. sb.* [f. HOPE *v.* + -ING[1].] The action of the verb HOPE; hope; †trust.

a **1300** *Cursor M.* 27016 Again þe toþer hoping þat es in werldes welth. *a* **1400–50** *Alexander* 4518 3e haue na hoping in þat hathill at on hi3e sittis. **1818** *Blackw. Mag.* III. 62 A few years of confident hopings and unreserved trustings.

'hoping, *ppl. a.* [-ING[2].] That hopes; hopeful. Hence **'hopingly** *adv.*, hopefully.

1602 WARNER *Alb. Eng.* x. lvi. (1612) 247 Contrarie to it that all did hopingly affect. **1842** MANNING *Serm.* (1848) I. 374 Out of a hoping timidity. **1883** VON BUNSEN in *Harper's Mag.* Aug. 367/2 Hopingly yet gravely did he ride into Versailles.

Hopkinsian (hɒp'kɪnzɪən), *a.* and *sb.* [f. the name of the New England theologian Samuel Hopkins (1721–1803): see -IAN.] **A.** *adj.* Belonging to or adhering to the theological system of Samuel Hopkins, a modification of Calvinism. **B.** *sb.* An adherent of this system. Hence **Hop'kinsianism**, the theological system of Samuel Hopkins.

1850 WHITTIER *Pr. Wks.* (1889) II. 132 Hopkinsianism.. held..that guilt could not be hereditary. **1860** J. GARDNER *Faiths World* II. 64/1 Some Christians..called from their leader Hopkinsians, though they prefer to be called Hopkinsian Calvinists. *Ibid.* 65/1 The Hopkinsian controversy is but little known in Britain. **1886** *Encycl. Amer.* III. 339 The founder of 'Hopkinsian divinity'.

hoplite ('hɒplaɪt). [ad. Gr. ὁπλίτης, f. ὅπλον weapon, piece of armour, heavy shield, pl. ὅπλα arms: see -ITE.] A heavy-armed foot-soldier of ancient Greece.

1727–41 CHAMBERS *Cycl.* s.v., A painting which represented two hoplites. **1846** GROTE *Greece* I. xx. (1849) II. 143 The hoplites, or heavy-armed infantry of historical Greece, maintained a close order and well-dressed line. **1857** BIRCH *Anc. Pottery* (1858) I. 408 Ares appears as a hoplite.

Hence **hoplitic** (hɒ'plɪtɪk) *a.*, belonging to or resembling a hoplite; **ho'plitics** (*nonce-wd.*), the drilling of hoplites.

1851 *Fraser's Mag.* XLIII. 251 The heavy-armed Hoplitic angler, as he may be called, returns generally from his expedition laden only with disappointment. **1886** SIDGWICK *Hist. Ethics* ii. 21 New pedantries of 'tactics' and 'hoplitics'.

hoplo- (hɒpləʊ), before a vowel **hopl-**, combining form of Gr. ὅπλον weapon, piece of armour, or of ὁπλή hoof, as in **'hoplarchy** (-ɑːkɪ), *nonce-wd.* [after *hierarchy*] (see quot.). †**'hoplochrism** [see CHRISM] (see quot. 1656); so †**hoplo'christical** *a.* **hoplognathous** (-'ɒgnəθəs) *a.* [Gr. γνάθος jaw], 'having the jaw armed' (*Syd. Soc. Lex.* 1886). **hoplology** (-'ɒlədʒɪ) [see -LOGY], the science of weapons or armour. **hoplomachic** (-'mækɪk) *a.* [ad. Gr. ὁπλομαχικός, f. ὁπλομάχος fighting in heavy arms (cf.

HOPLITE)], fighting in heavy armour (in quot. *fig.*); so **hoplomachist** (-ˈɒməkɪst), one who fights in heavy armour. **hoplonemertean** (-nɪˈmɜːtiːən), **hoplonemertine** (-nɪˈmɜːtaɪn) *Zool.*, *a.* belonging to those nemertean worms in which the proboscis is armed with a stylet; *sb.* one of these worms. **hoplophorous** (-ˈɒfərəs) *a.* [Gr. ὁπλοφόρος bearing arms], 'bearing armour; protected' (*Syd. Soc. Lex.*). **hoplopleurid** (-ˈpl(j)ʊərɪd) *Zool.* [Gr. πλευρά rib, side], a fish of the extinct family *Hoplopleuridæ*, having the body provided with four rows of sub-triangular scutes. **hoplopodous** (-ˈɒpədəs) *a. Zool.* [Gr. ὁπλή hoof, πούς, ποδ- foot], having the feet protected by hoofs.

a **1843** SOUTHEY *Doctor* (1847) VII. 498 The chiefs of the Hierarchy, the Iatrarchy, the Nomarchy, and the *Hoplarchy (under which title both sciences, naval and military, were comprised). **1650** CHARLETON *Paradoxes* Proleg. d iv b, Our disquisition of the δὶ ὅτι, or Casualties [? Causalities] of *Hoplochrisme. **1656** BLOUNT *Glossogr.*, *Hoplochrism*, an anointing of Armes or weapons; as they do in the use of the weapon-salve. **1650** CHARLETON *Paradoxes* Proleg. d iv e, Objection to the dignity of *Hoplochristicall Remedies. **1884** R. F. BURTON *Bk. of Sword* I The imperious interest of *Hoplology. **1832** *Fraser's Mag.* V. 696 That most pugnacious, or, to use the old term, *hoplomachic of universities. **1793** *Misc.* in *Ann. Reg.* 398 Dempster, the last of the formidable sect of *Hoplomachists, who fought every day.. either with sword or fist, in defence of his doctrines in *omni scibili*. **1854** MAYNE *Expos. Lex.*, *Hoplopodus*, applied by Goldfuss to an Order (*Hoplopoda*).. including those [mammals] which have their feet protected by hooves: *hoplopodous.

hop-merchant. [f. HOP *sb.*^{1}]

1. A merchant who deals in hops.

1639 *Canterb. Marriage Licences* 12 Nov., Henry Sum'ersole of the city of London, hopmarchant. **1849** MACAULAY *Hist. Eng.* iii. (1889) I. 156 He.. made bargains over a tankard with drovers and hop merchants.

2. *slang.* [with play on HOP *sb.*^{2}] A dancing-master; a dancer.

a **1700** B. E. *Dict. Cant. Crew, Hop-Merchant*, a Dancing-master. **1708** MOTTEUX *Rabelais* IV. xxxviii, Imitated by your Hop-Merchants.. in their.. Country Dances.

hopnyt, obs. pa. t. of OPEN *v.*

‖**hopo** (ˈhəʊpəʊ). [From an Afr. language.] A trap for game consisting of two converging hedges in the form of the letter V, with a pit at the angle, into which the game is driven.

1866 J. LEYLAND *Adv. Far Interior S. Afr.* iii. 124 Two hedges are formed (called the hopo) a mile long, and the same distance at the extremity, gradually narrowing till it comes to the sides of the pit. **1932** R. CAMPBELL *Taurine Provence* 50 That natural death-trap or hopo, where the plain treacherously converges into a triangular precipice.

hopoland, obs. f. HOUPLAND, a garment.

hop-o'-my-thumb (ˈhɒpəmɪˌθʌm). Also 6 hopthumb, 9 hop-me-thumb. [In 16th c., *hop on my thombe*, from HOP *v.*^{1} (in imperative mood), applied to a person so small that he may be hyperbolically told to hop on one's thumb: cf. *stick-in-the-mud, pick-me-up*.] A dwarf, a pygmy: the name of a pygmy hero of nursery lore. Cf. *Tom Thumb.*

1530 PALSGR. 232/1 Hoppe upon my thombe, *fretillon*. **1546** J. HEYWOOD *Prov.* (1867) 25 It is a small hop on my thombe. And Christ wot, It is wood at a woorde. **1583** STANYHURST *Æneis* IV. (Arb.) 106 A cockney dandiprat hopthumb. **1594** *Taming of Shrew* (N.), Plaine friend hop of my thum, know you who we are? **1681** OTWAY *Soldier's Fort.* IV. i, You little Hopo'-my-thumb, come hither. **1827** HONE *Every-day Bk.* II. 67 He was a hop-o'-my-thumb no higher than the window-locker. **1855** THACKERAY *Newcomes* II. 255 This hop-o-my-thumb of a creature has begun to give herself airs since her marriage and her carriage.

attrib. **1748** SMOLLETT *Rod. Rand.* (1812) I. 59 You pitiful hop o' my thumb coxcomb. **1819** *Sporting Mag.* IV. 272, I cannot.. help laughing at such hop-me-thumb fellows. **1889** *Pall Mall G.* 25 June 1/2 Austria is a mere Hop-o'-my-Thumb Power excepting so far as she is backed by Germany.

†**hoppe.** *Obs.* Also 5 hoop(p)e. [Cf. OE. *hoppe*, pl. *hoppan*, 'ornament, ? small bell' (Sweet). (Senses 1 and 2 are perhaps distinct words.)]

1. The seed-vessel of flax.

c **1325** *Gloss. W. de Biblesw.* in Wright *Voc.* 156 *Le boceaus* [*du lyn*] *Gloss.* hoppen [*Camb. MS.* flaxbolles]. **1398** TREVISA *Barth. De P.R.* XVII. xcvii. (1495) 663 Floures of flex ben.. blewe, and after comyth hoppys, and therin is the seed. And whan the hoppe begynnyth to wexe, thenne the flex is drawe vp. *c* **1440** *Promp. Parv.* 246/1 Hoope [*v.r.* hooppe], sede of flax. **1552** HULOET, Hoppes of flaxe or hemp, *lincidulum*.

2. The cornel tree, and its fruit.

1499 *Garlandia's Liber Equiv. Voc.* (W. de W.), *Corna, fructus corni*, hoppe: *cornus, quidam arbor*, hoppe tre, *ut quidam dicunt*.

hopped (hɒpt), *a.* [f. HOP *sb.*^{1} or *v.*^{2} + -ED.]

1. Furnished, mixed, or flavoured with hops.

1669 BOYLE *Contn. New Exp.* II. (1682) 174 A Receiver filled with hopped and fermented Beer. **1830** M. DONOVAN *Dom. Econ.* I. 203 Thirty-five barrels of hopped wort. **1897** *Daily News* 6 Sept. 7/3 The bines being lightly hopped without any 'tail', and the fruit all being within sight.

2. a. [f. HOP *sb.*^{1} 4 + -ED^2.] Chiefly with *up*. Stimulated by, or under the influence of, a narcotic drug. Also ***to hop up*** v. phr., to stimulate with a narcotic drug. *U.S. slang.*

1924 G. C. HENDERSON *Keys to Crookdom* 408 *Hopped up*, intoxicated on opium. **1927** C. F. COE *Me—Gangster* iii. 43 They do their shooting when they are all hopped up with dope. **1927** E. HEMINGWAY *Men without Women* (1928) 194 I'm not drunk. I'm hopped to the eyes. **1957** *Listener* 6 June 912/2 It is possible these men were physically hopped up, or perhaps 'mushroomed-up' would be the better word, by consuming a European fungus. **1958** J. D. MACDONALD *Executioners* (1959) vii. 108 A hopped-up kid can be bought for less, but the job would be bungled. **1968** 'J. WELCOME' *Hell is where you find It* vi. 80 Why didn't you go to his funeral? Too busy hopping yourself up in Paris? You do that for kicks, too, I suppose? **1973** *Guardian* 14 Apr. 10/3 Chuck Berry don't drink either but he gets hopped.

b. ***hopped-up.*** Excited, enthusiastic. *U.S. slang.*

1923 C. WITWER in *Collier's* 27 Jan. 28/4 He's especially hopped up about the piano down in the music room. **1935** WODEHOUSE *Let.* 4 Feb. in *Performing Flea* (1953) 79, I got all hopped up and felt that it wasn't possible to give 'em too much of this superb stuff. **1936** J. STEINBECK *In Dubious Battle* v. 69 You organize the stiffs and get 'em all hopped up with a bunch of bull. **1939** C. MORLEY *Kitty Foyle* xxii. 214 There were a lot of dames hopped up with culture and good grammar. **1973** 'I. DRUMMOND' *Jaws of Watchdog* viii. 107 A hopped-up son with anarchist-pacifist connections.

3. ***hopped-up.*** Of a motor vehicle: having its engine altered to give improved performance. Also *transf. U.S. slang.*

1945 *Amer. Speech* XX. 226/2 *Hopped up.* Applied to a plane built for speed. Taken from the 'hopped up' automobiles of the high-school set. **1946** *Sat. Even. Post* 14 Sept. 14/2 Today a hot rod is a hopped-up, stripped-down flivver. **1954** *Amer. Speech* XXIX. 98 *Hopped up*,.. 'souped up'; said of a car with any added speed equipment. **1958** *House & Garden* Mar. 62 The American housewife.. with her hopped-up central heating. **1971** *Islander* (Victoria, B.C.) 16 May 10/3 At the urge of the hopped-up motor in seconds they were tearing up Nanaimo Street.

hopper^1 (ˈhɒpə(r)). [f. HOP *v.*^{1} + -ER^1. OE. type **hoppere*, implied in the feminine *hoppestre*.

Sense 3 is naturally accounted for; but the origin of sense 5 is not clear, unless derived from resemblance to the mill-hopper, which is not favoured by the chronology of existing quotations.]

1. a. One who hops; a leaper, dancer.

c **1375** *Sc. Leg. Saints, Baptista* 442 þat fore a hoppare can hym sla. **1598** FLORIO, *Saltarino*,.. a iumper, a hopper. **1744-5** MRS. DELANY in *Life & Corr.* (1861) II. 335 The dancers are to be [etc.]. These are the rest of the hoppers. **1775-8** TYRWHITT *Notes on Chaucer's Knt.'s T.*, I conceive, a female hopper, or dancer, was called an hoppestere. **1829** *Chron.* in *Ann. Reg.* 21/1 A great hopper and runner. **1943** *N.Y. Times* 9 May II. 5/4 Listen, hoppers clot the action when the Duke or the Count start to beat it out.

b. *pl.* 'A kind of play in which the actor hops on one leg' (J.): see SCOTCH-HOPPERS, HOPSCOTCH.

c. *Baseball.* A ball which having been struck rebounds from the ground. *U.S. slang.*

Quot. 1914 appears to have a different sense.

1914 'B. L. STANDISH' in *Top-Notch Mag.* 30 Sept. 138/1 Courtney missed a hopper, though he almost fancied his bat lightly touched the whistling ball as it sped past. **1943** *Amer. Speech* XVIII. 104 *Baseball jargon*... Names for a grounder are *hopper*, [etc.]. **1968** [see BASEMAN].

2. An animal characterized by hopping, esp. an insect or insect-larva that hops.

Applied more or less spec. to a locust or grasshopper, a saltatorial beetle as the turnip flea, a saltatorial homopterous insect as a froth-hopper, a flea, the cheese-hopper or maggot of the cheese-fly; also dial. to a samlet; in Newfoundland to a seal of the second year. Also as a second element, in *cheese-hopper, grasshopper, sandhopper*, etc.

c **1250** *Gen. & Ex.* 3096 On wind cam fro westen, and ðo opperes nam, And warpes ouer in-to ðe se. **1797** POLWHELE *Hist. Devon* I. 120 The Samlet of Mr. Pennant, called here the hopper. **1822-34** *Good's Study Med.* (ed. 4) I. 278 *M*[*usca*] *putris*, the larvæ of which are known to the house-wife by the name of hoppers, as those of all of them by the name of maggots. *a* **1870** R. M. CHIPMAN *Notes on Bartlett* 202 *Hopper*, a grasshopper, especially the ravaging locust called grasshopper at the West. **1877** MRS. FLEMING *Life Arnot* (1879) 192 The armies of barbarous inhuman black hoppers are not greatly diminished. **1897** *Chamb. Jrnl.* XIV. 766/2 The locusts were attacked while still in the 'hopper' stage. **1933** *Bulletin* (Sydney) 5 July 21/2 One man says he counted 2000 hoppers [*sc.* kangaroos] in one paddock. **1946** *E. African Ann.* 1946-7 44/1 Youths have been out in the district beating and burning locusts... Besides these commendable efforts in destroying hoppers the Samburu have made a most useful war contribution. **1966** E. PALMER *Plains of Camdeboo* XV. 247 Our locust of the Karoo, the brown locust, *Locustana pardalina*, is well-known to us as a tiny dark hopper, later becoming black and orange.

3. In a corn or other grinding mill, a receiver like an inverted pyramid or cone, through which grain or anything to be ground passes into the mill; so called because it had originally a hopping or shaking motion (which is now usually transferred to the shaking-shoe, where that is present).

c **1386** CHAUCER *Reeve's T.* 119 Yet saugh I neuere.. How that the hopur wagges til and fra. *c* **1430** *Pilgr. Lyf Manhode* I. lxxiii. (1869) 43 In the hoper of the mille.. he was grounden broken and brused. *c* **1585** *Faire Em* I. ii. 175 in Simpson *Sch. Shaks.* II. 414 Now let me alone to pick the mill, to fill the hopper, to take the toll. **1786** BURNS *To Unco Guid* i, The heapet happer's ebbing still, And still the clap plays clatter. **1825** J. NICHOLSON *Operat. Mechanic* 158 The hopper.. is agitated by two iron pins on the axis.. that alternately raise the vessel containing the grain, which again sinks by its own weight. **1858** THOREAU *Maine W.* (1894) 204 A boy collecting the long edgings of boards as fast as cut off, and thrusting them down a hopper, where they were ground up beneath the mill. **1876** T. HARDY *Ethelberta* II. xl. 151 Modern developments have shaken up the classes like peas in a hopper.

4. Applied to similar contrivances for feeding any material to a machine, and, generally, to articles resembling a mill hopper in shape or use.

1763 W. LEWIS *Commerc. Phil.-techn.* 277 The space included between the pipes, at their lower end, under the bason, is a kind of hopper. *Ibid.* 278 The water issuing from the hopper is necessarily reduced into drops. **1832** BABBAGE *Econ. Manuf.* iii. (ed. 3) 28 To make the engine supply the fire with small quantities of fuel at regular intervals by means of a hopper. **1873** *Spon's Dict. Engin.* III. 2253 Receiving and weighing hoppers. *Ibid.* 2254 The sheet-iron funnel in which the grain is received before passing up into the weighing hopper. **1875** KNIGHT *Dict. Mech.*, *Hopper*, 1. a chute for feeding any material to a machine. 2. The basin of a water-closet. 3. (*Glass.*) A conical vessel suspended from the ceiling, containing sand and water for the use of the glass-cutter. **1878** F. S. WILLIAMS *Midl. Railw.* 626 The tickets are placed in a kind of tube or hopper, down which they descend, and.. are drawn one by one across a printing machine. **1883** *Daily News* 27 July 2/1 The new twelve-barrel Nordenfeldt gun.. Hoppers to fit on the feeders keep them constantly replenished, and so incessant is the fire that in half a minute 600 shots were discharged.

5. A basket; *esp.* a basket or other vessel in which the sower carries his seed. Now *dial.*

a **1300** *E.E. Psalter* lxxx. 7 [lxxxi. 6] His hend in hoper served pai. **1362** LANGL. *P. Pl.* A. VII. 57 He heng an Hoper on his Bac In stude of a Scrippe. *c* **1420** *Pallad. on Husb.* x. 43 Thyn hopur clothe hienys skyn; and throwe Thy seede therynne. **1523** FITZHERB. *Husb.* §10. **1649** BLITHE *Eng. Improv. Impr.* (1652) 179 Be sure ever and anon to stir up the bottom of your Hopper, or Seed-lop. **1821** CLARE *Vill. Minstr.* II. 106 What once were kernels from his hopper sown, Now browning wheat-ears.

6. A barge in attendance on a dredging machine, which carries the mud or gravel out to sea and discharges it through an opening in its bottom. Also ***hopper-barge***.

1759 in Brand *Hist. Newcastle* (1789) II. 588 A person invented a machine.. called a Hopper.. to take ballast out of ships.. convey the same to the sea, and there drop it. **1887** *Daily News* 14 Dec. 2/6 New steamer Giralda, when off Claxheugh, river Wear, came into collision with a laden hopper. **1894** *Ibid.* 8 Oct. 6/7 The men who were working the marine dredger and its attendant hoppers in the outer port of Port Said.

7. = *hopper-car*: see 10.

1862 *N.Y. Tribune* 10 June (Bartlett), Of the fifty-seven hoppers thrown over Opequan bridge, one half can be put into serviceable order again.

8. A funnel-shaped or hopper-like hollow.

1838 T. L. MITCHELL *3 Exp. E. Austral.* (1839) II. 319 We find among the features on these lofty river banks many remarkable hollows, not unaptly termed 'hoppers'.. from the water sinking into them, as grain subsides in the hopper of a mill. **1847** D. A. WELLS & S. H. DAVIS *Sk. Williams Coll.* 88 You find yourself on the edge of a gulf at least a thousand feet deep, the four sides of which apparently converge to a point at the bottom. This place, from its peculiar form, is called the Hopper.

9. *Pianoforte.* A piece attached at the back part of a key to raise the hammer and regulate the distance to which it falls back from the string after striking it. Also called *grasshopper*.

1840 *Penny Cycl.* XVIII. 140/1 The action of the square piano-forte, on its first introduction, consisted of a key, a lifter, a hammer, and a damper.. Longman and Broderip.. brought out a patented invention having two additional parts in the action, namely, the hopper, and the under-hammer. **1896** HIPKINS *Pianoforte* 37 The key, hopper, spring and set-off.

10. *attrib.* and *Comb.* **a.** appositive, as (sense 6) ***hopper-barge, -punt***. **b.** Of or belonging to a hopper, as (sense 3) ***hopper feed, form, head, mouth***; (sense 9) ***hopper button, lever, spring***. **c.** Shaped like or resembling the hopper of a mill, as ***hopper casement, closet, hip, pan, roof, ventilator, window***; **d.** parasynthetic, as (sense 5: cf. quot. 1787 s.v. HOPPET^1 1) ***hopper-arsed, -hipped, -rumped*** adjs. **e.** Special combs.: **hopper axis**, a contrivance for grinding apples, something like a coffee-mill; **hopper-boy**, 'a name given in mills to a rake which moves in a circle, drawing the meal over an opening through which it falls' (Craig 1847); **hopper-car**, a kind of car or truck for carrying coal, gravel, etc., shaped like a hopper, and emptying through an opening at the bottom; **hopper-cock**, a valve for water-closets, etc. (Knight *Dict. Mech.*); †**hopper-crow**, ? a crow that follows a seed-hopper during sowing; **hopper-dredge** or **-dredger**, a vessel combining the functions of a hopper and a dredger, being fitted with hoppers that receive the material dredged up and allow it to be discharged through the bottom at the place of deposit; **hopper-eared, -free** *adjs.* (see quots.); **hopper-hood**, a hooded seal in its second year.

a **1700** B. E. *Dict. Cant. Crew*, **Hopper-arst*, when the Breech sticks out. **1787** [see HOPPET^1 1]. **1807** VANCOUVER *Agric. Devon* (1813) 124 It performs all the operations of

thrashing, winnowing, grinding, and bolting, together with an iron *hopper axis for grinding apples. **1895** *Westm. Gaz.* 16 Oct. 4/2 The Admiralty *hopper barge..for use at the Gibraltar new Dry Dock and Extension Works, had an adventurous voyage. **1787** in *Rep. U.S. Comm. Patents* (1850) 574 The other [device], denominated an *hopper-boy, so constituted as to spread the meal over the floor of a mill to cool. **1813** *Niles' Reg.* V. Add. A. 6/2 Our Hopper-boy was an upright shaft revolving round with an arm. **1840** *Penny Cycl.* XVIII. 141/2 Hopper spring..Hopper lever ..*Hopper button..Sustaining spring..fixed in the front end of the hopper lever. **1862** *N.Y. Tribune* 10 June (Bartlett), There were one hundred and eighty-three iron *hopper-cars recovered in a condition to be restored. **1844** *Catholic Weekly Instr.* 103 *Hopper casements..should be inserted in almost all the windows, in order to secure due ventilation. *a* **1592** GREENE *Jas. IV*, v. ii, To gather feathers like to a *hopper-crow, And lose them in the height of all my pomp? **1896** *Engin. Index* II. 120 The *hopper dredge, 'Percy Sanderson', holding 1250 tons of debris and provided both with steel buckets and a suction pump. **1967** *Shipbuilding & Shipping Rec.* 6 July 21/1 (*heading*) 'McFarland'... A fully automated hopper dredge for the U.S. Army. **1876** SIMONS & BROWN *Brit. Pat. 4382*, This Invention, which relates to improvements in *hopper dredgers, has for its object..to effect the discharge of the load or contents of hopper dredgers on to the adjoining river or canal bank. **1969** R. HAMMOND *Mod. Dredging Pract.* iv. 101 Direct pumping ashore to disposal areas is another function performed by a hopper dredger. **1744-50** W. ELLIS *Mod. Husbandm.* III. I. 19 (E.D.S.) Such land would return an *hopper-eared crop at harvest, or, in plainer English, a little ear, with a few kernels. **1887** *Pall Mall G.* 12 Mar. 2/1 Mr. Maxim's next effort was also a 3-pounder, using a long cartridge, but having a very short action and a *hopper feed. **1829** J. HUNTER *Hallamsh. Gloss.* 51 When the tenants of the manor of Sheffield ground their corn at the lord's mill, some of them were called *hopper-frees, being privileged. **1898** *Edin. Rev.* Apr. 440 The 'hopper-free' tenants at Leeds.. had their corn grinded immediately upon the emptying of the hopper, though there were never so many attending. **1500-20** DUNBAR *Poems* lx. 55 With *hoppir hippis, and henches narrow. **1672** WYCHERLEY *Love in Wood* II. i, She is bow-legg'd, *hopper-hipp'd. **1793** SMEATON *Edystone L.* 198 The large square wooden pipe..terminates..in a *hopper-mouth proper for receiving in the burthen. **1884** *Health Exhib. Catal.* 59/2 Flushing Water Closet, with *Hopper Pan. **1867** SMYTH *Sailor's Word-bk.*, **Hopper-punt*, a flat-floored lighter for carrying soil or mud, with a hopper or receptacle in its centre, to contain the lading. **1626** MIDDLETON *Wom. Beware Wom.* II. ii, Her body straight, not *hopper-rump'd. **1840** *Hopper spring [see *hopper button*]. **1896** HIPKINS *Pianoforte* Gloss., *Hopper Spring*, the wire spring that regulates the angle of the sticker or hopper, and accelerates its return under the notch or roller. **1939** *Archit. Rev.* LXXXVI. 166 The windows have a side-hung casement and a long top-hung *hopper window for night ventilation.

Hence **hoppered** *a.*: cf. *hopper-hipped* (above).

1704 D'URFEY *Hell beyond Hell* 54 Holland, up to the ankles fine, But hopper'd still about the chine.

hopper² ('hɒpə(r)). [f. HOP *v.*² + -ER¹.]

1. One engaged in picking hops; a hop-picker.

1719 in Cowper *Canterb. Reg., St. George* (1891) 207 Edward Even and Alice his pretended wife, hoppers and way-going persons. **1751** SMOLLETT *Per. Pic.* lxxxvii, The venerable Society of weeders, podders, and hoppers. **1860** DICKENS *Uncomm. Trav.* xi, Many of these hoppers are Irish, but many come from London.

2. A brewer's vat in which the infusion of hops is prepared to be added to the wort (*Cent. Dict.*).

3. *attrib.*, as ***hopper-house***.

1883 J. Y. STRATTON *Hops & Hop-pickers* 45 The hopper-house is generally a long low-pitched building. **1884** *Daily News* 23 Sept. 3/2 Great efforts have been made..to provide suitable lodgings for the hoppers, and 'hopper-houses' catch the eye at every turn of the road.

hopper, erron. form of HOOPER², wild swan.

hopperdozer ('hɒpədəʊzə(r)). *U.S.* [f. HOPPER¹, perh. after *bull-dozer* (1876); see also quot. 1878.] A contrivance for catching and destroying insects, consisting essentially of an elongated pen or frame which is filled or smeared with some poisonous or glutinous substance and slowly drawn or pushed over the ground.

1877 *Pioneer Press* (St. Paul & Minneapolis) 19 May 5/4 (*heading of letter by A. B. Robbins*) A hopperdozer. *Ibid.* 22 May 1/5 The grasshoppers in this vicinity have hatched out very thickly... People are beginning to destroy them in various ways, principally with sheet iron hopperdozers covered with coal tar. **1878** *Ann. Rep. U.S. Entom. Commission 1877* xiii. 390 The simple pan..known as the Robbins' hopperdozer. [*Note*] A word that came into very general use last year among farmers..and which doubtless takes its origin from doze, in reference to the toxic effect of the coal-tar on the locusts. **1904** W. C. EDGAR *Story Grain Wheat* ii. 21 Large areas of wheat are saved by means of a machine termed in America the 'hopperdozer'. **1932** *Chieftain* (Tecumseh, Nebraska) 5 May, Mechanical 'hopperdozers' have some value in the control of grasshoppers of fairly level fields of alfalfa. **1962** METCALF & FLINT *Destructive & Useful Insects* (ed. 4) ix. 471 On the whole, hopperdozers are much more expensive to operate and less efficient than poisoning.

hoppergrass. orig. and chiefly *U.S. dial.* = GRASSHOPPER.

1829 *Virginia Lit. Museum* I. 458 *Hoppergrass.* This word is often used in the south for grasshopper. **1892** *Rep. Vermont Board Agric.* XII. 163 Alas! the 'hopper grasses' came and carried it away. **1934** R. CAMPBELL *Broken Record* viii. 200 Spectacles make men look like ridiculous hoppergrasses. **1955** E. POUND *Classic Anthol.* I. 7 'Chkk! chkk!' hopper-grass, Nothing but grasshoppers hopping past. **1970** C. MAJOR *Dict. Afro-Amer. Slang* 67 *Hopper grass*, grasshopper.

hopperings ('hɒpərɪŋz), *sb. pl.* [f. HOPPER¹ + -ING¹.] Gravel retained in the hopper in gold- or diamond-washing.

1893 *Westm. Gaz.* 29 Apr. 7/3 The yield of diamonds from the hopperings is 6¼ carats per 100 loads. **1898** *Daily News* 27 Jan. 9/5 Washed 197 loads from the mine, 3,725 loads lumps and hopperings producing 126 carats.

†**hoppestere.** *Obs.* [OE. *hoppystre*, f. *hoppian* to HOP: see -STER. The mod. form would be *hopster*; cf. Chaucer's *tappestere*, now *tapster*.] A female dancer, a danceress. In the quot. from Chaucer app. used attrib. = 'dancing'.

'Schippes hoppesteres' answers to *navi bellatrici* (= 'warlike ships') in Boccaccio's *Teseide*, which it is supposed that Chaucer misread as *ballatrici* (= dancers, dancing, pl. fem.). Speght (followed by Bullokar and Cockeram) erroneously explained 'hoppesteres' as 'pilots'. See Skeat, *Chaucer* V. 80.

c **1000** ÆLFRIC *Hom.* I. 484 He..ðæs mæran witeȝan deað þære lyðran hoppystran hire gliȝes to mede forȝeaf. *c* **1386** CHAUCER *Knt.'s T.* 1159 Yet saugh I brent the shippes hoppesteres [*Camb. MS.* hospesterys].

hoppet¹ ('hɒpɪt). Chiefly *north. dial.* Also 7- hobbet, 9 hoppett, -itt. [? f. HOPPER¹ with dim. suffix. Cf. also HOBBET.]

1. A basket, esp. a small hand-basket.

1671 SKINNER *Etym. Angl.*, *Hoppet*, vox agro Linc. usitatissima significat autem Corbem seu Calathum quo fructus circumferunt. **1674** RAY *N.C. Words* 26 A *Hoppet*, a little Handbasket. **1688** R. HOLME *Armoury* III. 392/1 An Hoppet, or Hobbet..is a Vessel of wood to carry corn in by him that soweth the same. **1787** GROSE *Prov. Gloss.*, *Hoppet*, a little basket, chiefly for holding seed-corn, worn by the husbandmen, in sowing, at their backs, whence a man with protuberant buttocks is compared to a man accoutered with a hoppet, and stiled hoppet-arsed, vulgarly hopper-arsed. **1828** *Craven Dial.*, *Hoppit*, a little basket. **1847-78** HALLIWELL, *Hoppet*,..the dish used by miners to measure their ore in. **1886** *S.W. Linc. Gloss.*, *Hoppet*, a small hand-basket with lids. 'She has ta'en a hoppet with her lunch.'

2. A large bucket, used for lowering and raising men and materials in the shaft of a mine or other excavation.

1865 *Ann. Reg.* 3 The engineer was astonished to find that the hoppet containing the men stopped in the shaft. **1888** *Times* 9 Apr. 6/5 The hoppet is a large iron bucket fastened by three hooks and chains to the rope. **1890** *Pall Mall G.* 8 Sept. 3/1 The workmen are raised by means of a 'hoppett', which a steam engine lifts or lowers as required. **1897** *Times* 10 Mar. 13/6 One hoppit came up with débris showing slight dampness.

3. A bee-hive; also ***bee-hoppet***. *dial.*

'**hoppet**². *local.* [? dim. of HOPE *sb.*²]

1. An enclosure; a yard, paddock, or the like.

1701 *Deed* [relating to properties called] 'a Barn and Hoppett'. **1864** *Gd. Words* 581/2 There is a hoppet big enough for the run of a pony. **1867** *Crim. Chronol. York Castle* 153 Crowther and Hoyle were interred in the hoppet at the back of the Castle.

2. A gaol or prison. [May perh. belong to prec. word: cf. *cage*, *coop* similarly used.]

1855 ROBINSON *Whitby Gloss.*, *Hoppet*, the jail. 'They were putten i' t' hoppet', imprisoned.

'**hoppet**³. *north. dial.* [dim. from HOP *v.*¹] An infant in arms.

1695 KENNETT *Par. Antiq.* II. Gloss. s.v. *Tremuta*, A young child danced in the arms is by metaphor called a little hoppet. **1828** *Craven Dial.*, *Hoppit*, an infant.

hop-picker. A labourer employed to pick the ripe hops from the bines; usually one of a large body who annually migrate to the hop-growing districts to do this work; also, a mechanical contrivance for picking, cleaning, and sorting hops. So **hop-picking**, the work of picking hops, which annually gives temporary employment in the country to large bodies of the poor.

1760 *Engraving of picture by G. Smith*, The Hop Pickers. **1777** BRAND *Pop. Antiq.* (1870) II. 20 To the festivities of Harvest Home must be referred the following popular custom among the hop-pickers in Kent. **1875** KNIGHT *Dict. Mech.*, *Hop-picker*,..a machine for picking hops. **1812** *Examiner* 5 Oct. 629/2 Hop-picking completed.

hoppill: see HOPPLE *v.*

hopping ('hɒpɪŋ), *vbl. sb.*¹ [f. HOP *v.*¹ + -ING¹.]

1. The action of the verb HOP, in various senses.

c **1290** *S. Eng. Leg.* I. 379/79 At þis bruydale was plei i-nouȝh: song and gret hoppingue. *a* **1340** HAMPOLE *Psalter* xxxix. 6 Hoppynge & daunceynge of tumblers & herlotis. **1576** NEWTON *Lemnie's Complex.* I. ii. 10b, Vndecent hopping and dauncing. **1879** H. SPENCER *Data Ethics* x. §66. 181 The perpetual hoppings of the canary from bar to bar of its cage.

2. A dance; a rural festival of which dancing forms a principal part.

c **1330** *Arth. & Merl.* 3545 Men made song and hopinges, Ogain the come of this kinges. *c* **1570** *Durham Depos.* (Surtees) 102 The day that one John Fletcher of Chester made a hopping. **1686** G. STUART *Joco-ser. Disc.* 32 To Horse-race, Fair, or Hoppin go. **1843** HARDY in *Proc. Berw. Nat. Club* II. No. 11. 55 These feasts, or as they are called elsewhere in Northumberland, hoppings, are held on the festival day of the patron Saint. **1889** *Archæol. Æliana* XIII. 322 At Newburn..the hopping is held about the feast of St. Margaret of Antioch.

hopping, *vbl. sb.*² [f. HOP *sb.*¹ or *v.*² + -ING¹.]

1. The gathering of hops; hop-picking.

1717 *Canterb. Parish Reg., St. George* (ed. Cowper) 206 One Robert Northborn, a stranger came hopping [= a-hopping]. **1751** SMOLLETT *Per. Pic.* lxxxvii, The profession of hopping. **1880** *Times* 10 Sept. 9/4 The return of the hopping season. *Ibid.* 9/5 A labourer, with his wife and children, may make from £6 to £8 by 'the hopping'.

2. The flavouring of malt liquor with hops.

1816 J. SMITH *Panorama Sc. & Art* II. 570 Of Boiling and Hopping. **1890** *Daily News* 14 Oct. 2/3 English hops suitable for fine ale brewing or dry hopping must prove to be in limited supply. **1894** *Times* 6 Mar. 4/1 When German hops were used for hopping down.

hopping, *ppl. a.*¹ [f. HOP *v.*¹ + -ING².]

1. That hops: see the verb.

1785 BURNS *Winter Night* iv, Ilk happing bird. **1790** BURKE *Fr. Rev.* 127 The little shrivelled, meagre, hopping, though loud and troublesome insects of the hour. **1799** COLERIDGE *Lett.* (1895) 280 A little hopping, over-civil sort of thing. **1916** H. G. WELLS *Mr. Britling* I. i. 24 The hopping inconsecutiveness of English conversation.

2. *Comb.* **hopping-dick**, local name for a species of thrush (*Merula leucogenys*) common in Jamaica, resembling the blackbird in appearance and song (*Maunder's Treas. Nat. Hist.*(1874) 325); **hopping-john** (*Southern U.S.* and *W.Ind.*), a stew of bacon with pease or pease and rice seasoned with red pepper; **hopping mad** *a.* (orig. *dial.* and *U.S.*), violently angry, so as to dance with rage.

1838 C. GILMAN *Recoll. Southern Matron* xviii. 124 Before me..was an immense field of **hopping John*. [*Note.* Bacon and rice.] **1856** OLMSTED *Slave States* 506 The greatest luxury with which they are acquainted is a stew of bacon and peas, with red pepper, which they call 'Hopping John'. **1969** *Daily Tel.* 13 May 24/6 The dinner consisted of such things as collard greens, fried chicken, water melon, cornbread and 'hopping John', a dish of black-eyed peas and rice that is supposed to bring luck. **1970** M. SLATER *Caribbean Cooking* 32 'Peas and Rice'..is cooked on every island, down from the Bahamas, where it is known as Hoppin' John, to the South American mainland. **1675** COTTON *Scoffer Scoft* 52, I us'd to make him *hopping mad. **1833** S. SMITH *Life & Writings Major J. Downing* 139, I had a long talk with the General t'other day—he was hopping mad. *a* **1860** *Widow Bedott Papers* 275 (Bartlett) Miss Fustick said Liddy Ann was too old to wear plumes..which made Liddy hoppin' mad, and led to an awful quarrel. **1915** WODEHOUSE *Psmith, Journalist* vii. 44 Dey was hoppin'-mad, de whole bunch of dem. **1922** [see CLAIM *v.* 2c]. **1954** [see EDITOR 3b]. **1960** *Guardian* 7 July 8/5 Would-be [telephone] subscribers get hopping mad. **1973** B. GRAEME *Two & Two make Five* vii. 67 Old Sourpuss must be hopping mad.

3. = *hopping mad*.

1894 'MARK TWAIN' in *Century Mag.* Jan. 338/1 Oh, my lan', ole Marse was jes a-hoppin'! **1942** I. GLEED *Arise to Conquer* vi. 57 David will be hopping. **1960** E. W. HILDICK *Boy at Window* xi. 80, I was mad, real hopping! **1973** R. HAYES *Hungarian Game* xxxi. 185 'I wonder what they're fishing for.' 'Whales... And they got everyone hopping about it.'

Hence '**hoppingly** *adv.*

1598 FLORIO, *Saltellone*, hoppingly, skippingly.

hopping, *ppl. a.*² [f. HOP *v.*² + -ING².] Engaged in hop-picking.

1860 DICKENS *Uncomm. Trav.* xi, The whole country side ..will swarm with hopping tramps.

'**hoppity**¹. [f. HOP *v.*¹] Another name for HALMA.

1894 L. B. SPERRY *Confid. Talks with Yng. Men* xvii. 164 Games of all sorts, base-ball, foot-ball,..checkers, hoppity. **1895** *Montgomery Ward Catal.* 235/1 The Game of 'Hopity' ..is a game of skill... The particular feature of the game is the popular jumping move, pieces being allowed to jump over friend and foe alike to reach the opposite side of the board. **1969** E. H. PINTO *Treen* 222 Halma or hoppity was introduced about 1890.

hoppity² ('hɒpɪtɪ). Also -ety. A fanciful extension of HOP *v.*¹, used adverbially or as *adj.*, often repeated or with the word *hop* to suggest a hopping or hobbling movement. Cf. HIPPETY.

1825, 1880, 1886 [see HIPPETY]. **1924** A. A. MILNE *When we were very Young* 60 Christopher Robin goes Hoppity, hoppity, Hoppity, hoppity, hop. **1936** W. DE LA MARE *Wind blows Over* 46 William had been even more lively and hoppity than usual. **1943** F. THOMPSON *Candleford Green* viii. 125 A tame thrush which he had found in the fields with a broken wing and brought home..would follow him round the garden, *hoppity-hop*. **1963** *Times* 10 May 5/3 Two no-balls from Greenhough, whose run up, like Christopher Robin, goes hoppity hoppity.

hopple ('hɒp(ə)l). *v.* [Origin obscure; it is exemplified earlier than HOBBLE *v.* in same sense, and can hardly be a later variant of that word; rather does the corresp. sense of *hobble* seem to be taken from *hopple*. But Kilian has early mod.Fl. *hoppelen* = MDu. *hobelen* to jump, dance; and see the German forms mentioned under HOBBLE *v.*]

trans. To fasten together the legs of (a horse or other beast) to prevent it from straying; also *transf.* to fetter (a human being); = HOBBLE *v.* 7.

1586 in *Scotter Manor Rec.* (*N.W. Linc. Gloss.*), That noe man hoppell noe cattell in the Forthe. **1630** *Ibid.*, That noe man shall leave his horsse or beaste loose in the fallowe feilde

but to hoppill tether or bringe him home att night. **1660** H. MORE *Myst. Godl.* IX. vii. §8 Superstitiously hoppled in the Toils and Nets of superfluous Opinions. *a* **1749** CHALKLEY *Wks.* (1766) 382, I think then he ought to be muzzled and hoppled too. **1807** P. GASS *Jrnl.* 223 We caught all our horses and hoppled them. **1876** MORRIS *Sigurd* I. 26 What of men so hoppled should be the tale to tell?

hopple ('hɒp(ə)l), *sb.* [f. HOPPLE *v.*]

1. An apparatus for hoppling horses, etc. (see prec.); also *transf.* a fetter; = HOBBLE *sb.* 3.

a **1825** FORBY *Voc. E. Anglia, Hopple.* **1886** *Guernsey News* 18 June 5/1 A pattern hopple for sheep..was submitted. **1888** W. MORRIS *Dream J. Ball* iv. 34, I..went up and down my prison what I could for my hopples. **1892** M. C. F. MORRIS *Yorksh. Folk-Talk* 113 When they are milking a cow they tie her hind legs with a hopple.

2. ? = HOBBLE-BUSH.

1856 BRYANT *Poems, Strange Lady* vii, A pebbly brook, where rustling winds among the hopples sweep.

‖**hoppo** ('hɒpəʊ). [See quot. 1882.] In China: The board of revenue or customs. Also (short for *hoppo-man*) an officer of the customs.

1711 C. LOCKYER *Trade in India* 101 (Y.) The Hoppos, who look on Europe Ships as a great branch of their Profits, will give you all the fair Words imaginable. **1726** SHELVOCKE *Voy. round World* 446 We should have met with great trouble from the Hoppo-men, or Custom-house Officers. *Ibid.* 448 The Bonita's boat..was..pursued by a Hoppo, or Custom-house boat. **1748** *Anson's Voy.* III. vii. 355 The Hoppo or Chinese Custom-house officer at Macao. **1882** *Fan Kwae at Canton* 36 (Y.) The 'Hoppo' (as he was incorrectly styled) filled an office especially created for the foreign trade at Canton... The Board of Revenue is in Chinese 'Hoo-poo', and the office was locally misapplied to the officer in question.

'hop-pole. [f. HOP *sb.*^{1}] A tall pole on which hop-plants are trained.

1573-4 in Willis & Clark *Cambridge* (1886) III. 583 For setting up the hop poles..vj^d. *a* **1687** COTTON *Poems, To J. Bradshaw* (R.), Like hop-poles in a hop-yard rear'd. **1784** [see *hop-kiln* s.v. HOP *sb.*^{1} 5 b]. **1892** *Spectator* 23 Jan. 118 Alder for charcoal, chestnut for hop-poles.

Hoppus ('hɒpəs). Also **hoppus**. The name of Edward *Hoppus*, 18th-century English surveyor, used *attrib.* and in the possessive to designate a method of measuring the cubic content of round timber used in the British Commonwealth, and tabulated in his *Practical Measuring now made Easy* (1736) (known in later editions as *Hoppus's Tables* and *Hoppus's Measurer*); it involves multiplying the length in feet by the square of the quarter-girth in inches and dividing the result by 144; **Hoppus foot**, a recent name for the 'cubic foot' as arrived at by the Hoppus method, approximately equal to 1·27 true cubic feet.

[**1820** R. MONTEATH *Forester's Guide* xxvi. 173 It will contain 2 solid inches and one-third of an inch, according to the measurement of Hoppus.] **1894** A. D. WEBSTER *Pract. Forestry* (ed. 2) xxv. 175 Timber-measuring is rather a vexed question, some following what is known as Hoppus's system, and others advocating that of Horton. **1924** A. C. DRUMMIE *Pract. Forestry* xxvii. 244 The standard usually adopted is the quarter girth Hoppus measure system, with the customary allowance for bark. **1941** S. E. WILSON *Decimal Hoppus Tables* 6 When the Hoppus system is employed to measure cylindrical bodies the solid foot amounts to 4/π or 1·273 cubic feet... To call the unit..a cubic foot is accordingly inaccurate and misleading... To avoid confusion we call the 'solid foot' of this system a 'Hoppus Foot', defining it as the unit of solid contents according to the Hoppus system of measuring round timber. **1947** H. L. EDLIN *Forestry & Woodland Life* xx. 144 The unit generally used in Britain for measuring round logs, trees, and plantations, is the customary cubic foot, or Hoppus foot. **1951** R. H. HORDERN *Woodworking Ind. Managem.* viii. 123 The 144 divisor used in the Hoppus System will show approximately 27 per cent less cubic content than the tree actually measures. **1970** *Timber Trades Jrnl.* 14 Mar. 53/3 Average volume of the trees was 25·4 Hoppus ft, and the price reached was 3s 5½d per Hoppus ft. **1971** *Daily Tel.* 7 Jan. 12/5 The hoppus foot, a traditional measure for timber,..will be replaced next month by the cubic metre and metric tonne.

hoppy ('hɒpɪ), *a.*^{1} [f. HOP *sb.*^{1} + -Y^1.] **1.** Tasting or smelling of hops; beery.

1893 *Harper's Mag.* Feb. 458 Jest so it don't tas'e hoppy, I ain't pertic'lar; but from hoppy bread *de*liver me! **1964** *Listener* 26 Mar. 534/3 Over cool dinner, the sour hoppy breath.

2. Of, pertaining to, or characterized by drugs or drug-taking. *U.S. slang.* (Cf. HOP *sb.*^{1} 4.)

1942 BERREY & VAN DEN BARK *Amer. Thes. Slang* §509/30 *Hoppy*, smelling of drugs. **1946** MEZZROW & WOLFE *Really Blues* (1957) vii. 98 Detroit is really a hoppy town—people must order their opium along with their groceries.

hoppy ('hɒpɪ), *a.*^{2} *colloq.* [f. HOP *sb.*^{2} + -Y^1.] Characterized by, or predisposed to, hopping; lively, full of movement; limping, lame.

1860 [implied in HOPPINESS]. **1902** in *Eng. Dial. Dict.* III. 232 'To go hoppy' is to walk rather lame. Among the working classes, lame persons are often nicknamed 'Oppy', as 'Oppy Smith', which denotes a certain Smith who is somewhat lame. **1914** JOYCE *Dubliners* 171 He had a game leg and for this his friends called him Hoppy Holohan. **1934** A. WOOLLCOTT *While Rome Burns* (1936) 42 Juventino Rosas..who once wrote a pleasant and rather hoppy waltz. **1942** BERREY & VAN DEN BARK *Amer. Thes. Slang* §53/15 *Rapid; quick*, hoppy. *Ibid.* §131/11 *Crippled; lame*, hoppy. **1968** K. WEATHERLY *Roo Shooter* 119 It's a damned good thing these hoppy bastards [*sc.* kangaroos] can't understand me.

Also **'hoppiness**, hopping manner or quality.

1860 J. WHITE *Hist. France* (ed. 2) 3 Animals [frogs]..the exact image of himself in hoppiness of motion.

hoppy ('hɒpɪ), *sb.*^{1} *colloq.* [f. HOP *sb.*^{2} + -Y^6.] A lame man.

1904 'No. 1500' *Life in Sing Sing* xiii. 249/2 *Hoppy*, a cripple. **1909** S. WATSON *Wops the Waif* iii. 5 Who-ay, Cully, here's Hoppy with the Rozin. **1962** J. FRANKLYN *Dict. Nicknames* 49 *Hoppy*, the nickname of anyone who walks with a limp.

hoppy ('hɒpɪ), *sb.*^{2} *U.S. slang.* [f. HOP *sb.*^{1} + -Y^6.] An opium addict. (Cf. HOP *sb.*^{3} 4.)

1922 E. F. MURPHY *Black Candle* II. i. 114 The Chinese here still furnish a large percentage of the 'hoppies'. **1924** G. C. HENDERSON *Keys to Crookdom* xxiv. 301 Even the 'hoppies' themselves look down on a user of cocaine. **1941** B. HECHT *1001 Afternoons in N.Y.* 129 A lush, a prosty, a hoppy, and a pain in the neck, say the police.

hoppyne, obs. form of OPEN.

hop-sack, hopsack ('hɒpsæk). [f. HOP *sb.*^{1}]

1. A sack in which hops are packed.

1481-90 *Howard Househ. Bks.* (Roxb.) 72 Item, making of the hopsakes iiij.*d.* **1612** ROWLANDS *More Knaves Yet* A iv, Great large abhominable breech Like Brewers Hop-sackes. **1753** *School of Man* 28 Vice may be said to get admittance to us habited in velvet, but comes from us in a Hopsack. **1869** *Punch* 10 July 10/2 He would come in a hop-sack, with a cabbage-leaf on his head.

2. = next, b. Also *attrib.*, and in form *hopsac*.

1892 *Daily News* 15 Oct. 7/1 Every variety of surface is supplied..from the sheeny 'faced cloth' to the rough 'hop-sack'. **1893** *Ibid.* 28 Mar. 2/3 'Horse-cloth', 'hopsack', and other similar kinds of material, which are only coarse in appearance, being really made of the finest wool. **1907** *Yesterday's Shopping* (1969) 831 Ascot Scarfs..made from ..Hopsack shot silk. **1923** *Daily Mail* 5 July 1 Hopsac suiting,..in pretty Heather Mixture grounds. **1930** *Daily Express* 8 Sept. 11/5 Hopsack Tweed. **1968** *Surfer Mag.* Jan. 27/1 Can you tell me the approximate weight of a piece of hopsack cloth secured with resin to the front third of my board?

hop-sacking. **a.** The material of which hop-sacks are made, a coarse fabric composed of hemp and jute. **b.** Applied to a woollen dress-fabric made with a roughened surface.

1884 *Girl's Own Paper* Feb. 211/1, I give the preference to unbleached linen and hop sacking. **1893** *Daily News* 17 July 6/3 A gown of hop-sacking, shot mauve and grey.

'hop-score. *local.* = HOPSCOTCH.

1829 J. HUNTER *Hallamsh. Gloss., Hop-score*, a child's game. **1890** *N. & Q.* 7th Ser. IX. 196 The game has always, I believe, been called in Yorkshire and the Northern countries 'hop-score'.

†**hop-scot.** *Obs. rare.* = HOPSCOTCH.

1789 *Archæol.* IX. 18 (D.) A very common game at every school called hop-scot.

hopscotch ('hɒpskɒtʃ). [f. HOP *v.*^{1} + SCOTCH *sb.* an incised line or scratch: a formation like *catchpenny, heal-all*, etc.] A children's game, consisting in hopping on one foot and driving forward with it a flat stone, fragment of a slate or tile, etc., from one compartment to another of an oblong figure traced out on the ground, so as always to hop over or clear each scotch or line. Also called *hop-score, hop-scot*, and (earlier) *scotch-hoppers*.

1801 STRUTT *Sports & Past.* IV. iv. 339 Among the school-boys in my memory there was a pastime called Hop-Scotch. **1840** R. H. DANA *Bef. Mast* xxiii. 72 Playing hopscotch and other games on the hard sand. **1886** *American* XII. 140 It would seem that the well-known boys' game of 'hop-scotch' dates back to the beginning of the Christian era.

attrib. **1897** *Pop. Sci. Monthly* Nov. 64 Streets and lanes cross and recross in delightfully hopskotch fashion.

'hopshackle, *sb. Obs.* exc. *dial.* [The second element is app. SHACKLE; the first is obscure: cf. HOPPLE, HAMSHACKLE.] 'A ligament for confining a horse or cow' (Jam.); a hopple or hobble.

a **1568** ASCHAM *Scholem.* II. (Arb.) 128 Soch runners..in the end..cum behind others and deserue but the hop-shakles, if the Masters of the game be right iudgers.

So **hopshackle** (in 6 *Sc.* **hap-**) *v. trans.*, to hopple or hobble. *Obs.* exc. *dial.*

1500-20 DUNBAR *Poems* liii. 12 He stackerit lyk ane strummall awer [*i.e.* aver, old horse] That hap shackellit war abone the kne. **1879** WAUGH *Chimney Corner* 17 Thou walks as if thou were hop-shackle't.

hopthumb: see HOP-O'-MY-THUMB.

hop-toad. *U.S.* [HOP *sb.*^{2} or *v.*^{1}] A toad.

1827 *Massachusetts Spy* 28 Nov. (Th.), An inhabitant of the Middle States talks of 'hop-toads',—as if all toads were not hoppers. **1830** F. TROLLOPE in *Dom. Manners* (1949) 428 Hop toads is little creatures what hop like a frog. **1844** MRS. STOWE *Mayflower* (1849) 157 I'd always find him stopping to chase hoptoads, or off after chip-squirrels. **1847** *Knickerbocker* XXIX. 183, I have so often..a tender leaning towards little pigs and hop toads. **1913** G. STRATTON-PORTER *Laddie* xiii. I like hop-toads, owls, and shitepokes. **1966** J. DOS PASSOS *Best Times* (1968) i. 12 We studied with passionate interest the egg-laying habits of the hoptoads that shrilled so loud.

Hopton wood ('hɒptən 'wʊd). Also **Hopton-Wood, Hoptonwood.** The name of a wood and neighbouring quarries close to Wirksworth, Derbyshire, used *attrib.* and *absol.* to designate a pale brownish- or greyish-white carboniferous limestone used for building and decorative purposes.

[**1811** J. FAREY *Gen. View of Agric. & Minerals Derbyshire* I. 419 *List of..Building-Stone Quarries, or Delphs*... Hopton-Wood, in Middleton by Wirksworth.] **1888** G. H. BLAGROVE *Marble Decoration* 86 *Hopton Wood*. This stone deserves to rank as a marble, for it will take an excellent polish. **1911** J. WATSON *Brit. & Foreign Building Stones* 117 Hopton Wood Stone has been employed for constructing many important buildings, including the Guildhall (1789), and the Imperial Institute (1881), in London. **1962** *Times* 3 Aug. 7/1 Any opaque stone—sandstone, bath, hoptonwood, basalt. **1967** G. SIMS *Last Best Friend* vii. 62 A fine example of lapidary art..cut on a panel of Hopton-Wood stone. **1973** *Times* 14 May 14/8 Later he began to experiment with native stones, such as Hopton Wood and Ancaster.

'hop-yard. [f. HOP *sb.*^{1}] = HOP-GARDEN.

1533-4 *L'Estrange Househ.-bk.* in *Archæol.* XXV. 538 For trymyng of the hopp yerd. **1552** HULOET, Hoppe yarde, *arbustum*. **1587** HARRISON *England* II. xiii. (1877) I. 259 There be now no houses at all, but hopyards. **1624** CAPT. SMITH *Virginia* II. 28 They hill it about like a hop-yard. *a* **1687** [see HOP-POLE]. **1881** WHITEHEAD *Hops* 22 The hop-yards in Worcestershire are..situated upon the better and richer clays and marls.

hopyn, hoqueton, obs. ff. OPEN, HAQUETON.

hor, var. HER *poss. pron. Obs.*, their; ME. var. of HAIR; obs. f. HOUR; var. HORE *Obs.*, filth.

‖**hora** ('hɔərə). Also **horah, horra.** [Rum. *horă*; Heb. *hōrāh*.] A Rumanian and Israeli round-dance; the music or song to which it is performed.

1878 J. W. OZANNE *Three Yrs. in Roumania* xii. 157 The *hora*, the Roumanian dance *par excellence*. **1911** *Encycl. Brit.* XXIII. 849 The popular songs of Rumania, the 'doine', the 'hora', [etc.]. **1923** *Chambers's Jrnl.* 20 Oct. 745/1 The favourite amusement of the Roumanian peasant is his dance, especially the traditional 'hora' danced in a circle. **1925** *Countries of World* V. 3431/2 Laughing girls..ready to dance the 'hora' with the men [in Rumania]. **1946** KOESTLER *Thieves in Night* viii. 61 [They] had formed the first ring of the horra, the stamping and swaying round-dance, a savage ring-polka. *Ibid.* 352 They were singing one of the popular horras, a folk-song with a passionate, almost hysterical tune. **1960** A. WESKER *I'm talking about Jerusalem* (1961) III. ii. 49 Let's do an Israeli dance..(*Starts doing a Zanny Hora on his own*). **1967** *Guardian* 15 July 6/2 Can you think of any other Army where officers and enlisted men would dance the hora together? **1967** *Observer* 8 Jan. 23/4 Catchy, minor-key *hora* strummings. **1969** *New Yorker* 6 Sept. 117/1 There is a scholarly argument over whether the Rumanian hora predates the Hebrew hora or vice versa. A diplomatic Rumanian-style answer is that both are of Mediterranean origin, the hora having been brought to Rumania by the Roman legions. **1971** *Observer* 17 Jan. 21/7 You were building, building, building. And on Friday nights I [*sc.* Mrs. Golda Meir] danced the Horah into the night.

†**hora'baptist.** *Obs. rare.* [irreg. f. Gr. ὥρα or L. *hōra* hour.] One who baptizes every hour.

a **1641** [see *holobaptist* s.v. HOLO-].

horæ ('hɔəriː). [L., pl. of *hōra* HOUR.] A book of hours (HOUR 5, 6).

1875 *Quaritch's Gen. Catal.* Suppl. 51 The earlier editions of Kerver's series of Horæ. **1927** *Observer* 27 Nov. 22/4 An exquisite Flemish Horæ of about 1500. **1967** D. DIRINGER *Illum. Book* (ed. 2) vii. 406 An interesting *Horae* of the Bodleian Library, at Oxford..was executed in France about 1430-40. A French Dominican *Horae* of the British Museum..was executed between 1425 and 1450.

horah, var. HORA.

horal ('hɔərəl), *a.* [f. L. *hōr-a* hour + -AL^1. Late L. had *hōrālis*.] Of or pertaining to an hour or hours; horary; hourly.

1717 PRIOR *Alma* III. 268 If the horal orbit ceases, The whole [watch] stands still. **1808** F. BALFOUR in *Asiat. Res.* VIII. 27 A column for the horal variations of sol-lunar power. **1896** *Daily News* 13 Nov. 7/7 The same rectification of the horal system that has already taken place in all Europe with the exception of France, Spain, and Portugal.

Hence **'horally** *adv.*, hourly, in relation to hours.

1623 COCKERAM, *Horally*, hourely.

horarious (hɒ'rɛərɪəs), *a. rare.* [f. late L. *hōrāri-us* HORARY + -OUS.] = next, 3.

1866 *Treas. Bot., Horarious*, enduring for an hour or two only; as the petals of *Cistus*.

horary ('hɔərərɪ), *a.* [ad. med.L. *hōrāri-us*, f. *hōra* HOUR: see -ARY and cf. F. *horaire*.]

1. Of, relating to, or indicating the hours. ***horary angle*** = HOUR-ANGLE. ***horary circle***: see CIRCLE *sb.* 2, 13 a; also, the circle of hours on a dial-plate.

1664 POWER *Exp. Philos.* III. 193 Understood no more of Nature, than a rude Countrey-fellow does of the Internal Fabrick of a Watch, that onely sees the Index and Horary Circle. **1688** BOYLE *Final Causes Nat. Things* I. 19 Furnished with a stile, with horary lines and numbers, and ..all the requisites of a sun dial. **1767** *Phil. Trans.* LVII. 390

The horary spaces, or angular distances of the hours on the dial. **1798** tr. *Pérouse's Voy. round World* III. 332 M. de Langle himself took the distances and horary angles. **1816** PLAYFAIR *Nat. Phil.* II. 13 The angle which the meridian of a star makes with the meridian of the place of observation, is called the star's Horary Angle. **1853** *Chr. Remembr.* Jan. 71 The general horary arrangement of time.

2. Occurring every hour, hourly.

1632 B. JONSON *Magn. Lady* I. vi, Horary shifts Of shirts and waste-coats. **1641** J. JACKSON *True Evang. T.* II. 152 A dayly, horary, momently breaking of that great Evangelicall precept. **1796** HUTTON *Math. Dict.* s.v., The Horary motion of the earth on her axis is 15°. **1881** *Nature* No. 620. 480 The horary average [of meteors] increased rapidly between the evening and morning hours.

†**3.** Lasting only for an hour, or for a short time; applied to fruits that will not keep. *Obs.*

1620 VENNER *Via Recta* vii. 114 These and such like horarie and quickly perishing fruites. **1698** FRYER *Acc. E. India & P.* 293 Melons, Cucumbers, and other Horary Fruits.

4. *Astrol.* ***horary question***, a question, the answer to which is obtained by erecting a figure of the heavens for the moment at which it is propounded. Hence, Relating to such questions, as ***horary astrology, prediction***.

1647 NEEDHAM *Levellers Lev.* 9 To perswade the Lady Arnabella to come to me, to be resolv'd 'bout some horary question. **1664** BUTLER *Hud.* II. iii. 985 Draw a Figure that shall tell you What you perhaps forget, befell you, By way of Horary inspection. **1790** SIBLY *Astrol.* (1792) I. 107 Calculating nativities or resolving horary questions. **1819** J. WILSON *Dict. Astrol.* s.v., The figure for a horary question is erected in the same manner as for a nativity. **1835** 'ZADKIEL' *Lilly's Introd. Astrol.* xxxv. 285 All these coincidences must be considered by the genuine searcher after truth as strong evidences of the truth of planetary influence, as evinced in *horary astrology*. **1911** 'SEPHARIAL' *Man. Occultism* vi. 98, I am quite convinced from experience that there is much that is both fictitious and erroneous in Horary Astrology. **1951** M. E. HONE *Mod. Text-bk. Astrol.* xv. 272 The practice of Horary Astrology was very popular in the Middle Ages, and its best known exponent was William Lilly (1602–81). *a* **1963** L. MACNEICE *Astrol.* (1964) i. 19 Casting horoscopes to answer questions is called 'horary' astrology.

horary, *sb. rare.* [ad. late L. *hōrāri-um* dial, book of hours, neut. sing. of *hōrāri-us* (see prec.).]

†**1.** *Eccl.* A book containing the offices for the canonical hours. *Obs.*

1631 HEYLIN *St. George* I. v. §11. 93 So was it in our Ladies *Horarie*, or *horarium*, according to the use of Sarum. **1789** BURNEY *Hist. Mus.* III. i. 9 This year [1549] all.. breviaries, offices, horaries.. were called in and destroyed.

2. a. An hourly account or narrative. (Cf. *diary*.)

1864 *Sat. Rev.* 31 Dec. 817/1 Todleben tells us that Canrobert deployed on the heights by two o'clock; Kinglake, that Bosquet.. crossed by the ford.. at 2·10; and so on through the horary of the battle.

b. A timed programme or plan. So **ho'rarium**.

1851 J. B. PAGANI *Life Rev. A. Gentili* III. ii. 151 He drew up a regular horary to promote recollection and compunction. **1921** *Ampleforth Jrnl.* Jan. 139 Adapting ourselves to the School horarium we began dinner at 5 p.m. **1922** *Westm. Gaz.* 7 Oct., His scheme of breaking the Germans in 24 hours on a meticulously timed 'horary'.

Horatian (hɒ'reɪʃ(ɪ)ən), *a.* (*sb.*) [ad. L. *Horātiān-us*, f. *Horāti-us* gentile name of the poet Horace.] **a.** Belonging to or characteristic of the Latin poet Horace (Quintus Horatius Flaccus, B.C. 65–8), or his poetry. So **Ho'ratianism**. **b.** as *sb.* The language of Horace.

1750 C. SMART (*title*) The Horatian canons of friendship. Being the third satire of the first book of Horace imitated. **1850** THACKERAY *Pendennis* II. iii. 25 According to the Horatian maxim, a work of art ought to lie ripening (a maxim, the truth of which may, by the way, be questioned altogether). **1851** TENNYSON in *Life* (1897) I. 341 A far-off echo of the Horatian Alcaic. **1891** S. MOSTYN *Curatica* 10 He capped my verse instantaneously, and for the next half-hour we conversed in Horatian. **1925** C. D. BROAD *Mind & its Place* xi. 492 It is wrong to live in accordance with the Horatian ethics. **1936** F. R. LEAVIS *Revaluation* iv. 137 [Matthew] Green, in his Horatianism, is a good positive Augustan. **1945** AUDEN *Coll. Poetry* 121 The bland Horatian life of friends and wine. **1964** *English Studies* XLV. (Suppl.) 217 It shows a deeply felt appreciation of ethical norms, a truly English horatianism that Cobbett, for all his lack of a classical education, inherited from the eighteenth century. **1965** B. SWEET-ESCOTT *Baker Street Irreg.* 14 Others may wonder whether such a book *ought* to have been published, even after an interval which now exceeds the Horatian decade.

horce, obs. form of HOARSE.

‖**horchata** (or'tʃata). Also **orchata**. [Sp.] A popular Spanish and Latin-American chufa-flavoured soft drink.

1859 in *Century Mag.* (1898) Dec. 312 *Orchata* is also a favorite drink; it is made from the juice of almonds, and is as white as milk. **1922** J. HERGESHEIMER *Bright Shawl* (1923) 63 She preferred rather than an ice, an orchata, and sipped it slowly. **1932** E. HEMINGWAY *Death in Afternoon* xx. 271 The taste of horchata, ice-cold horchata. **1968** J. M. WHITE *Nightclimber* ii. 9, I debate whether to order a *horchata* or a *zumo de limón*, and when the waiter arrives I ask for the latter. **1969** R. & D. DE SOLA *Dict. Cooking* 121/1 *Horchata*, almond-flavoured soft drink popular throughout Latin America and Spain.

†**horcop, horecop.** *Obs.* Also 6 *dial.* **hoorecup, -chup.** [ME. f. *hōr* whore + ? COP *sb.*²; but the analytical sense is not clear.] A bastard. Also as a term of abuse.

c **1430** *Syr Tryam.* 224 Hyt were not feyre, A horcop to be yowre heyre. *c* **1440** *Promp. Parv.* 246/1 Horcop, bastarde. *c* **1440** *Gesta Rom.* lxvii. 384 (Add. MS.), I gafe souke, and noryshed my ij. hore Coppis. **14..** *Nom.* in Wr.-Wülcker 694/9 *Hic pelinguis*, a horcoppe. **1578** WHETSTONE *Promos* II. iv, T'wyll teache the hoorecup wyt.

†**hord.** *Obs.* [ad. L. *horda* in same sense.] (See quot. 1623.)

1623 COCKERAM, *Hord*, a Cow great with Calfe. **1658** in PHILLIPS.

hord, obs. f. HOARD, HORDE; var. ORD *Obs.*

hor'darian. *rare.* [f. med.L. *hordāri-us*, ad. OE. *hordere* treasurer, HOARDER.] (See quot.)

1892 G. W. KITCHIN *Comp. Rolls* 32 The Hordarian, who had charge of the *home* or material resources of the Convent; providing bread and beer, meat and fish, for the Refectory. *Ibid.* 496 *Hordarius*, a Hordarian, officer in charge of the hoard or collection of property belonging to the Monastery [at Winchester].

So **'hordary** [ad. med.L. *hordāria*], the department of the monastery under the hordarian.

1892 G. W. KITCHIN *Comp. Rolls* Index 527 Hordary, Chaplain of the.

horde (hɔəd), *sb.* Forms: 6–8 **horda, hord,** 7 **hordia,** 7–8 **hoord,** 7– **horde.** [Ultimately ad. Turkī *ordā*, also *ordī, ordū, urdū* camp (see URDU), whence Russ. *ordá* horde, clan, crowd, troop, Pol. *horda*, Ger., Da. *horde*, Sw. *hord*, It. *orda*, Sp., Pr. *horda*, F. *horde* (1559 in Hatz.-Darm.). The initial *h* appears in Polish, and thence in the Western European languages. The various forms *horda, horde, hord* were due to the various channels through which the word came into Eng.]

1. a. A tribe or troop of Tartar or kindred Asiatic nomads, dwelling in tents or wagons, and migrating from place to place for pasturage, or for war or plunder. **b.** Also applied to other nomadic tribes.

Golden Horde, name for a tribe who possessed the khanate of Kiptchak, in Eastern Russia and western and central Asia, from the 13th century till 1480.

1555 EDEN *Decades* 280 Tartares are diuided by companies which they caule Hordas.. they consiste of innumerable Hordas. **1560** JENKINSON in Hakluyt *Voy.* (1886) III. 225 The Nagayans.. were diuided into diuers companies called Hords. **1594** BLUNDEVIL *Exerc.* v. (ed. 7) 560 The Tartarians are divided into certaine commonalties, and Colonies, called of them Hordes. **1600** FAIRFAX *Tasso* XVII. xxi, As the Scythian Hordas stray. **1613** PURCHAS *Pilgrimage* (1614) 421 Stayed with him in his hord (which consisted of about 1000 housholds of a kindred). **1740** THOMPSON & HOGG in Hanway *Trav.* (1762) I. IV. lii. 239 They are divided into three *hordas*, under the government of a *khan*. **1799** W. TOOKE *View Russian Emp.* II. 78 The Kirghises.. have always been divided into three hordes, the great, the middle and the little hordes. **1863** KINGLAKE *Crimea* (1877) I. i. 2 Nations trembled at the coming of the Golden Horde.

b. 1613 PURCHAS *Pilgrimage* (1614) 745 (Greenland) In which Tents they lived by hoords. **1695** TEMPLE *Hist. Eng.* Introd., Such were the Hords among the Goths, the Clans in Scotland, and Septs in Ireland. **1838–42** ARNOLD *Hist. Rome* (1846) II. xxxiii. 320 Of the Gauls, new hordes had lately arrived from beyond the Alps. **1847** DISRAELI *Tancred* VI. iv, I am sprung from a horde of Baltic pirates.

c. *Anthropol.* A loosely-knit social group consisting of about five families.

[**1894** H. CUNOW *Verwandtschafts-Organisationen der Australneger* iii. 28 In Dr. Hodgkinson's Werk 'Australia from Port Macquarie to Moreton Bay' (London 1845).. wird überall.. die Bezeichnung 'tribe' gebraucht, ich habe dafür den meines Erachtens besser passenden Ausdruck 'Horde' gewählt. Unter 'tribus' ist stets die aus mehreren verwandten Horden bestehende grössere Volksgemeinschaft, der Stamm, zu verstehen.] **1896** F. H. GIDDINGS *Princ. Sociol.* iii. 275 Practically the horde as a component of the tribe is nearly, but not quite, identical with the clan. **1918** A. A. BRILL tr. *Freud's Totem & Taboo* iv. 208 Man, too, lived originally in small hordes in which the jealousy of the oldest and strongest male prevented promiscuity. **1939** *Geogr. Jrnl.* XCIV. 89 Davidson points out that the horde, a unit of about five families, in all some thirty-five persons, was the largest political unit known to the Australians. **1948** W. MCDOUGALL *Introd. Soc. Psychol.* (ed. 29) Suppl. iv. 402 That.. primitive society took the form of a horde, the leader of which horde, the horde-father, actuated by his sexual jealousy, habitually treated his sons with extreme brutality.

2. *transf.* **a.** A great company, esp. of the savage, uncivilized, or uncultivated; a gang, troop, crew.

1613 PURCHAS *Pilgrimage* (1614) 426 Pillars of Stone, which sometimes were Hoords of Men and Beasts feeding, transformed. **1796** BURKE *Regic. Peace* I. Wks. VIII. 99, I hardly shall allow that with the horde of regicides we could .. obtain any thing at all deserving the name of peace. **1837** W. IRVING *Capt. Bonneville* II. 160 Eager to be out of the vicinity of such a piratical horde. **1883** *19th Cent.* May 901 In all our large cities there are hordes of little ragged urchins who live on the streets. **1888** H. E. SCUDDER in *Atlantic Monthly* Aug. 227/1 This great horde of young readers in America has created a large number of special writers for the young.

b. Of animals: A moving swarm or pack.

1834 LYTTON *Pompeii* IV. iv, The grass still moved to the stir of the insect horde. **1864** SWINBURNE *Atalanta* 823 Wolves in a wolfish horde.

Hence **horde** *v. intr.*, to form a horde; to congregate or live as in a horde.

1821 BYRON *Sardan.* v. i. 209 My fathers' house shall never be a cave For wolves to horde and howl in.

horde, obs. form of HOARD.

hordeaceous (hɔːdiː'eɪʃəs), *a.* [f. L. *hordeāce-us*, f. *hordeum* barley: see -ACEOUS.] Of the nature of barley; related to or resembling barley.

1854 in MAYNE *Expos. Lex.*

†**'hordeate.** *Obs.* [ad. med.L. *hordeāt-um*, f. *hordeum* barley. Cf. F. *orgeat.*] A drink made of barley; a decoction of barley.

1639 J. W. tr. *Guibert's Char. Physic.* I. 28 To make a Hordeat or mundified Barly. **1657** TOMLINSON *Renou's Disp.* 162* They may be used instead of apozems and Hordeates. **1676** WISEMAN *Chirurg. Treat.* VII. 60, I prescribed him that night a barly-cream.. We repeated the hordeat that night.

hordein ('hɔːdiːɪn). *Chem.* [f. L. *horde-um* barley + -IN.] A pulverulent substance obtained from barley-meal: see quots.

1826 HENRY *Elem. Chem.* II. 259 In this grain, Proust has discovered.. a peculiar substance.. to which he has given the name of hordein. **1830** M. DONOVAN *Dom. Econ.* I. 73 Dr. Thomson is of opinion that the hordein.. is merely starch in a particular state. **1865–72** WATTS *Dict. Chem.* III. 167 Barley-starch obtained by kneading barley-meal in water, and leaving the liquid to settle.. leaves a pulverulent substance, to which Proust gave the name *hordein*. It appears, however, to be, not a definite substance, but a mixture of starch, cellular tissue, and an azotised body.

horden, hordere, obs. ff. ORDAIN, ORDER.

hordeolum (hɔː'diːələm). *Path.* Pl. **hordeola.** [Altered form of late L. *hordeolus* a sty, dim. of L. *hordeum* barley.] A sty on the eyelid.

[**1622** R. BANISTER *Treat. Dis. Eyes* (ed. 2) IV. xiii. E 6 b (*heading*) Of the wart, or barly corne on the Eye-lidde, commonly called.. a Stian,.. in Latin, hordeum, or hordeolum.] **1806** J. BRIGGS tr. *Scarpa's Dis. Eye* ii. 75 The appearance of a white spot upon.. the hordeolum should not induce the surgeon to be hasty in opening it. **1833** W. LAWRENCE *Dis. Eye* xix. 341 Some hordeola form more quickly, with greater suppuration and no slough. **1908** *Practitioner* Feb. 288 Epiphora may be due to.. a hordeolum. **1966** S. LERMAN *Basic Ophthalm.* viii. 459 A hordeolum (stye) is caused by a purulent inflammation in the glands of Zeis at the base of the eyelashes.

†**hore, hor.** *Obs.* Also 4 **hoore.** [Com. Teut.: OE. *horh, horȝ* masc. and neut., clammy humour, phlegm; also *horu, horw-* m., dirt, filth, foulness = OFris. *hore*, OS. *horu*, OHG. *horo* (*horw-, horow-, horew-*), MHG. *hor* (*horw-es*) n., dirt, LG. *hor, hâr*, dirt, ON. *horr* m., mucus from the nose:—OTeut. **horwo-*:—pre-Teut. **korw-*, **korv-*; cf. OIr. *corbud* pollution.] Dirt, filth, defilement, foulness.

a **700** *Epinal Gloss.* 412 Flegmata, horh. *a* **1000** *Elene* 297 (Gr.) Ge mid horu speowdon on ðæs andwlitan. *c* **1000** *Sax. Leechd.* II. 174 Dracontjan wiþ fule horas on men. *c* **1000** ÆLFRIC *Hom.* II. 56 þæt aðweahð.. fram synna hore-wum. *c* **1200** *Trin. Coll. Hom.* 49 þe clenesse þe is bideled of þe hore þat is cleped hordom, þat is alre horene hore. *c* **1305** *Edmund Conf.* 8 in *E.E.P.* (1862) 71 So clene he cam fram his moder: wiþoute enie hore. *c* **1305** *Land Cokaygne* 34 (ibid. 157) þer nis schepe no swine no gote No non horwȝ. **1340** *Ayenb.* 137 Huet am ich bote esssse and spearken and hor and stench, wermes wynd ssed and smech. **1398** TREVISA *Barth. De P.R.* XIII. iii. (1495) 442 Fylthe and hore of cyttees ben cast in to ryuers. *Ibid.* XVI. vii. 557 The fome of syluer clensyth fylth and hoore of bodyes. *c* **1430** *Hymns Virg.* 83 On me was neiþer wem ne hore.

hore, ME. north. midl. form of HAIR; obs. f. HOAR, HOUR, OAR, WHORE; var. HER *pron. Obs.*, their, ORE *Obs.*, mercy.

horecop: see HORCOP.

horehound, hoarhound ('hɔəhaʊnd). Forms: 1 **háre húne, (háran húnan),** 3 **horehune,** 4 **-houne,** 5 **horho(w)ne, haarhounde,** 5–6 **horehounde,** 6– **horehound,** 8– **hoarhound.** [OE. *háre húne*, f. *hár* hoar, hoary + *húne* name of a plant, of uncertain origin; thence ME. *hôrhowne*, altered by popular etymology to *horehound*, which puts some appearance of meaning into the second element. The analogical spelling is *hoar-*, but this is much less usual in England than *hore-*.]

1. A labiate herb, *Marrubium vulgare*, having stem and leaves covered with white cottony pubescence; its aromatic bitter juice is much used as a remedy for coughs, etc. Hence extended to several allied herbs (see b), horehound proper being then distinguished as ***common*** or ***white horehound***.

c **1000** *Sax. Leechd.* II. 110 Genim þa haran hunan. *a* **1100** *Ags. Voc.* in Wr.-Wülcker 298/6 *Marubium*, hare hune. *c* **1265** *Voc. Names Pl.* Ibid. 554/4 *Marubium*, maruil, horehune. *c* **1400** *Lanfranc's Cirurg.* 80 Wiþ watir.. þat mirre wormode, horhone, sauge, pimpernelle hony symple or compounned ben soden yn. *c* **1425** in *Rel. Ant.* II. 9 An heved hor als horhowne. *c* **1440** *Promp. Parv.* 247/1

Horone, herbe..*marubium*. **1486** *Bk. St. Albans* C v b, Take the Juce of haarhounde. **1530** PALSGR. 232/1 Horehounde herbe, *langue de chien*. **1742** *Lond. & Country Brew.* I. (ed. 4) 38 That wholesome Herb Horehound, which, indeed, is a fine Bitter. **1794** MARTYN *Rousseau's Bot.* xxii. 308 Common White Horehound. **1897** WILLIS *Flower. Pl.* II. 242 *Marrubium vulgare*, white horehound.

b. With qualifying words: **base horehound**, White Dead-nettle, *Lamium album*; **black, fetid**, or **stinking h.**, *Ballota nigra*, a common weed with dull purple flowers; **water h.**, species of *Lycopus*, particularly *L. Europæus*.

1548 TURNER *Names of Herbes* (1881) 19 Ballote..is named in english stynkyng Horehounde or blacke Horehound. *Ibid.* 77 Stachys..maye be named in englishe litle Horehounde or strayte Horehound. **1578** LYTE *Dodoens* II. lxxxi. 255 There be foure kindes of Horehounde, in fasshion one like to another..The first kinde is our white Horehounde, the seconde is the blacke stinking Horehounde. The third is Stachys or field Horehounde. The fourth is water or Marrishe Horehounde. *Ibid.* 256 Stachys or wilde Horehounde. **1597** GERARDE *Herbal* II. ccxxi. 564. *a* **1625** FLETCHER *Faith. Sheph.* II. i, The Clote.. And this black Hore-hound, both are very good. **1741** *Compl. Fam.-Piece* II. iii. 380 Perennial shrubby Lamium or base Horehound. **1897** WILLIS *Flower. Pl.* II. 39 *Ballota Nigra*, the foetid horehound.

2. An extract or confection of the plant *Marrubium vulgare*, used as a remedy for coughs.

1562 TURNER *Herbal* II. 51 b, Horehounde..is good to be geuen with hony vnto them that syghg much. **1859** SALA *Tw. round Clock* (1861) 55 The relative merits of almond-rock and candied horehound. **1876** HARLEY *Mat. Med.* (ed. 6) 475 Horehound, an aromatic stimulant.

3. *attrib.* and *Comb.*, as ***horehound candy, drop, lozenge***, etc.; **horehound beer**, a fermented beverage containing horehound juice.

1855 MRS. GASKELL *North & S.* v, She..took the horehound drop that Margaret offered her. **1861** DELAMER *Kitch. Gard.* 127 Horehound lozenges are sold by most dispensing chemists, as expectorant medicine.

†**horel.** *Obs. rare*$^{-0}$. Also 6 horrel(l. [app. a var. of *holour*, assimilated to *hore*; cf. next.] A fornicator, adulterer.

c **1440** *Promp. Parv.* 246/2 Horel, or hullowre (*S.* hollowr, *P.* holour), *fornicator*..*fornicatrix*. **1552** HULOET, Horrell, or whoremonger, *concubitor, libidinarius*. **1570** LEVINS *Manip.* 56/11 An Horrel, *libidinosus*.

†**horeling, horling.** *Obs.* [f. ME. *hore*, WHORE + -LING.] A fornicator, whoremonger; an adulterer, a paramour.

c **1200** *Moral Ode* 103 in *Trin. Coll. Hom.* 223 Hwat sullen horlinges don? *c* **1325** *Poem Times Edw. II*, 25 in *Pol. Songs* (Camden) 324 If there be in countre an horeling, a shrewe, Lat him come to the court. **1340** *Ayenb.* 52 Þe drinkere and þe horling. **1387** TREVISA *Higden* (Rolls) III. 157 Horlynges and strompettes. *c* **1425** *Seven Sag.* (P.) 2189 Quod hire horlyng in the bede.

†**'horemint.** *Obs.* Some hoary species of mint; or perhaps horehound.

1533 ELYOT *Cast. Helthe* (1539) 60 Digestiues of fleume.. Horemint.

†**'horeness.** *Obs.* In 4 **hoornesse**. [f. HORE filth + -NESS.] Foulness, filth; mucus.

1398 TREVISA *Barth. De P.R.* IV. i. (1495), Heete.. dystroyeth superfluytees, and clensyth fylthe and hoornesse.

horestrong, var. of HARSTRANG.

†**'horewort.** *Obs. Herb.* [f. *hore* HOAR *a.* + WORT, in reference to its white downy covering.] An old name of Cudweed, *Filago Germanica*.

c **1400** *Alphab. Herb.* in MS. Arundel 42, lf. 94 b, *Filago* horswort [*error for* horwort]. *c* **1485** *MS. Bodl.* 536 lf. 27 Filago..a litell erb cald feld worte or hor worte And he groys in whete. **1597** GERARDE *Herbal* App., Horewort is *Filago*.

Hori ('hɒri:). *N.Z.* Also with lower-case initial. [Maori form of 'George'.] A contemptuous term for a Maori.

1933 F. E. BAUME *Half-Caste* 26 'Hori', he [*sc.* the driver] said to Paul (as a negro is 'Sambo' a Maori is 'Hori' to the poor white). 'You like a drink, eh?' **1942** *National Education* (N.Z.) Mar. 59/1, I looked at the eighty husky Horis in their gum-boots, denim trousers.., tattered shirts. **1944** J. H. FULLARTON *Troop Target* xi. 87 But all you Horis are related. **1960** N. HILLIARD *Maori Girl* III. vii. 219 All *horis* come off the farm, I think. **1963** *N.Z. News* 23 July 6/2 The Maori representative on the Dominion Council..asked the R.S.A. to lead a move to eliminate racial and other discords fostering Communism and instanced the use of *Hori*, as a general term for a Maori, as distasteful and creating friction.

hori, filth, filthy: see HORE *sb.*, HORY *a.*

horison, obs. form of ORISON, prayer.

horizon (hɒ'raɪz(ə)n), *sb.* Forms: *α.* 4 **orisont(e**, 4–5 **orizont(e**, 6 **orizunt**, 6–7 **horizont**. *β.* 4 **orisoun**, 5 **oryson**, 5–6 **orizon(e**, 6 **horyson**, 6– **horizon**. [a. OF. *orizonte* (13th c. in Hatz.-Darm.), *orizon* (14th c.), mod.F. *horizon* (= It. †*orizonte*, *orizzonte*, Sp., Pg. *horizonte*), ad. late L. *horīzont-em* (*horīzōn*), a. Gr. ὁρίζων (sc. κύκλος) the bounding circle, horizon, pres. pple. of ὁρίζειν to bound, f. ὅρος boundary, limit. In later OF. and Eng., conformed to the L. nom.; but at first stressed '*horizon* (Gascoigne, Shakspere, Sylvester); *ho'rizon* appears in Cowley, 1647.]

1. a. The boundary-line of that part of the earth's surface visible from a given point of view; the line at which the earth and sky appear to meet. In strict use, the circle bounding that part of the earth's surface which would be visible if no irregularities or obstructions were present (called the ***apparent, natural, sensible, physical***, or ***visible horizon***, as distinguished from 3), being the circle of contact with the earth's surface of a cone whose vertex is at the observer's eye. On the open sea or a great plain these coincide.

α. c **1374** CHAUCER *Troylus* v. 276 And whiten gan the Orisonte shene. *c* **1386** — *Frankl. T.* 289 Ffor Thorisonte hath reft the sonne his lyght. **1390** GOWER *Conf.* III. 108 By thorizont, as to us semeth. **1551** RECORDE *Cast. Knowl.* (1556) 21 The Horizonte is a cyrcle whiche parteth that parte of the worlde that wee see, from that whiche wee see not. *Ibid.* 179 The other horizont, whiche I thinke moste aptlye to bee called the Earthly horizont, bycause it.. reacheth not vnto the skie..his semidiameter excedeth not ..22 myles and a halfe. **1559** W. CUNNINGHAM *Cosmogr. Glasse* 149 Whan as the Mone shall shew her selfe above the Horizont.

β. **1398** TREVISA *Barth. De P.R.* VIII. vi. (Tollem. MS.), The circle to þe whiche þe sy3te strecchep and endeþ is calde Orizon, as it were þe ende of þe sy3te. **1413** *Pilgr. Sowle* (Caxton) v. xiv. (1859) 81 The sonne..hastyd hym vpward toward the eest oryson, to bringe ageyne the day. *c* **1550** *Sheph. Kal.* (1604) Contents xxxv, Of the rising and descending of the signes in the horyson. **1610** HOLLAND *Camden's Brit.* I. 631 Wilde Deere..feeding aloft..in the farthest Horizon or Kenning of their sight. **1667** MILTON *P.L.* IX. 52 Nights Hemisphere had veild the Horizon round. **1728–46** THOMSON *Spring* 961 Like far clouds That skirt the blue horizon. **1812** S. ROGERS *Columbus* I. 53 Stars rose and set, and new horizons glowed. **1887** BOWEN *Virg. Æneid* I. 181 Æneas explores meanwhile with his glance All the horizon of waters.

†**b.** *transf.* The part of the earth's surface bounded by this line; the region visible from any point. *Obs.*

1559 W. CUNNINGHAM *Cosmogr. Glasse* 137 The townes, and Villagies, about you adjacent in your Horizont. **1771** MRS. GRIFFITH tr. *Viaud's Shipwreck* 23 To open to us the horrid prospect of a boundless horizon and a devouring sea.

†**c.** The bounding limits, the compass. *Obs.*

1620 MELTON *Astrolog.* 9 If the Man..lies eyther within the Horizon of England, Fraunce, Spaine, Italy, or the Low-Countries, I will undertake to shew you him.

2. *fig.* †**a.** A boundary, the frontier or dividing line between two regions of being. *Obs.*

1387 TREVISA *Higden* (Rolls) II. 183 Mannis soule..is i-cleped orisoun, as it were þe next marche in kynde bytwene bodily and goostly þinges.

b. The boundary or limit of any 'circle' or 'sphere' of view, thought, action, etc. (often with direct reference to sense 1); that which bounds one's mental vision or perception; limit or range of one's knowledge, experience, or interest; formerly, sometimes = the region so bounded.

1607 TOPSELL *Four-f. Beasts* Ep. Ded., The Right Noble ..Earl of Surry, long ago departed out of this earthly Horizon. **1615** CROOKE *Body of Man* 261 Now at the second seauen yeares the heate begins to gather strength..and to rule in the Horizon of the body. **1639** T. BRUGIS tr. *Camus' Mor. Relat.* 179 Noe sooner did the new star appeare on the Horizon of Touraine, but her rayes strooke into the eyes of ..divers Sutors. **1659** B. HARRIS *Parival's Iron Age* 89 The Minister, who then began to climb the Horizon of favour. **1681** FLAVEL *Meth. Grace* vii. 148, I see no hope within the whole horizon of sense. **1826** T. JEFFERSON *Writ.* (1830) IV. 424 The present lowering aspect of our political horizon. **1849** RUSKIN *Sev. Lamps* 3 Their range necessarily includes the entire horizon of man's action. **1875** JOWETT *Plato* (ed. 2) II. 199 The danger..of substituting the definite and intelligible for the true but dim out-line which is the horizon of human knowledge.

3. a. *Astron.* A great circle of the celestial sphere, the plane of which passes through the centre of the earth and is parallel to that of the sensible horizon of a given place: distinguished as the ***astronomical, celestial, mathematical, rational, real***, or ***true h.***

right horizon, the celestial horizon of a place on the equator, the plane of which is perpendicular to that of the equinoctial; opp. to ***oblique horizon***, that of any place between the equator and either pole. ***geographical horizon***, the great circle on the earth's surface in the plane of the rational or astronomical horizon.

c **1391** CHAUCER *Astrol.* Prol., A suffisaunt astralabie as for owre orizonte, compowned after the latitude of Oxenford. *Ibid.* II. §26 This forseid rihte orisonte..diuideth the equinoxial in-to riht Angles. **1549** *Compl. Scot.* vi. 49 There is tua sortis of orizons, ane is callit the rycht orizon, the tothir is callit the oblique orizone. **1559** W. CUNNINGHAM *Cosmogr. Glasse* 39 The vj. great circles of the Sphere ar, as the Horizont, the Meridian, th' Equinoctiall, the Zodiake, the Equinoctiall and solsticiall Colures. **1634** SIR T. HERBERT *Trav.* 8 For the Æquator is Horizon to both Poles. **1704** J. HARRIS *Lex. Techn.* s.v., The Rational, Real or True Horizon, is a Circle which encompasses the Earth exactly in the Middle, and whose Poles are the Zenith and Nadir.

b. *transf.* The celestial hemisphere within the horizon of any place.

a **1577** GASCOIGNE *Hearbes, Praise of Countesse* v. 240 Dan Phœbus stands in dread, And shames to shine within our Horizon. **1593** SHAKS. *3 Hen. VI*, IV. vii. 81 When the Morning Sunne shall rayse his Carre Aboue the Border of this Horizon. **1600** F. WALKER *Sp. Mandeville* 122 a, Euery Prouince and Country hath an Orizon, which is that part of Heauen which they discouer in circling or compassing it about with theyr sight. **1642** MILTON *Apol. Smect.* viii, I leave you and your fellow stars, as you term them, of either horizon, meaning, I suppose, either hemisphere. **1650** TRAPP *Comm. Numb.* xxiii. 10 No more..then a man doth of the Sun, when it shines not in his own Horizon. **1825** SCOTT *Talism.* i, The burning sun of Syria had not yet attained its highest point in the horizon.

4. a. The broad ring (usually of wood) in which an artificial globe is fixed, the upper surface of which represents the plane of the rational horizon.

1592 DEE *Compend. Rehears.*, The theorick of the eighth spheare, the nynth and tenth, with an horizon and meridian of copper of Gerhardus Mercator his owne making. **1594–7** BLUNDEVIL *Exerc.* IV. Introd. (ed. 2) 437 To the Globe belongeth another Circle called the Horizon, which is a broad Circle of wood. **1674** MOXON *Tutor Astron.* I. i. §vi. (ed. 3) 6 The use of the upper Plain of the Horizon is to distinguish the Day from the Night; the rising and setting of the Sun, Moon, or Stars, etc. **1796** HUTTON *Dict. Math.*, *Horizon of the Globe*, a broad wooden circle.

b. ***artificial*** or ***false horizon***: a level reflecting surface, usually of mercury, used in taking altitudes.

1812 WOODHOUSE *Astron.* xl. 393 A *False Horizon*..in its simplest state, is a bason either of water, or of quicksilver. **1820** SCORESBY *Acc. Arctic Reg.* I. 442 Where the sea is.. smooth..an artificial horizon may be used with tolerable accuracy, even upon a ship's deck.

5. a. *Geol.* A plane or level of stratification assumed to have been once horizontal and continuous; a stratum or set of strata characterized by a particular fossil or group of fossils.

1856 WOODWARD *Mollusca* III. 411 Each [species] is most abundant in one horizon, and becomes gradually less frequent in the beds above and below. **1863** A. C. RAMSAY *Phys. Geog.* v. (1878) 65 The passage of species from lower to higher geological horizons. **1890** *Builder* LVIII. 89/2 A horizon that may give a bad stone in one quarry may improve.

b. *Soil Sci.* Any of several layers in the soil which lie roughly parallel to the surface and are distinguishable by differences in physical properties, as colour, texture, or structure, or in chemical reaction.

A typical soil shows the following horizons (from the surface downwards): the ***A-horizon***, generally the horizon of eluviation; the ***B-horizon***, generally the horizon of illuviation; and the ***C-horizon***, consisting of partly weathered parent material. Within the A-horizon and B-horizon further horizons may be distinguished (as B_1, B_2, B_3 horizons), though some writers refer to such horizons as zones or layers rather than as horizons.

1923 *Soil Sci.* XVI. 97 The soil assumes added importance as a factor when the chemical and physical differences of the separate horizons are studied in relation to root development. **1927** C. F. MARBUTT tr. *Glinka's Great Soil Groups* 9 Russian investigators use the word *Horizon* rather than stratum to designate the various layers in the soil profile. **1948** WHITE & RENNER *Human Geogr.* xxiv. 406 A marked zone of lime accumulation occurs at a moderate depth in the 'B' horizon. The 'C' horizon or sub-soil is brown. **1968** P. BURINGH *Introd. Study Soils Trop. & Subtrop. Regions* v. 74 A much lighter reddish A_2 horizon, much lower in clay and much higher in sand, is clearly visible. **1971** E. A. FITZPATRICK *Pedology* i. 4/1 In some cases the contrast between horizons is dramatic and self-evident, while in others it is very subtle.

c. *Archæol.* A level at which a particular group of remains is found, or which is taken as representing a particular culture or cultural period.

1926 D. A. E. GARROD *Upper Palaeolithic Age* i. 34 Thanks to his journal it is possible to attempt a reconstruction of the archeological horizons which existed at the time of excavation. **1935** *Nature* 6 Apr. 550/1 Mr. Harrod was able to indicate the horizon of discovery very closely. The spear-head was found at the base of the lowest draw of peat. **1959** J. D. CLARK *Prehist. S. Afr.* iv. 90 Nitrogen tests confirm that the remains are contemporary with the horizon in which they were found. **1962** R. MASON *Prehist. Transvaal* iv. 85 The Florisbad Peat 1 horizon has a radiocarbon age of more than 35,000 B.P. and may be associated with a Middle Stone Age industry...Four radiocarbon age estimations for Later Stone Age horizons in Matjes River Cave give ages varying from 11,250 ± 400 B.P. to 5,400 ± 250 B.P. **1973** *N.Y. Times* 15 July x. 1/1 Investigations have uncovered 15 distinct *horizons* (the archeological term for strata bearing traces of human habitation).

6. *Zool.* and *Anat.* A level or horizontal line or surface, as the horizon of the teeth, the horizon of the diaphragm. ***retinal horizon***, 'Helmholtz's term for the horizontal plane which passes through the transverse axis of the globe of the eye' (*Syd. Soc. Lex.*).

7. *Embryology.* One of a numbered sequence of stages in the development of the human embryo.

1942 G. L. STREETER in *Contrib. Embryol.* No. 197.213 (*heading*) Developmental horizons in human embryos. *Ibid.* 214 In searching for a suitable expression for the age groups under consideration..it was decided to follow the practice of other sciences and make use of the word 'horizons'. **1956** G. H. BOURNE *Biochem. & Physiol. Bone* xiii. 376 Each age group or 'horizon' is characterized by a certain degree of differentiation and organization of various tissues and organs. **1968** J. B. THOMAS *Introd. Human Embryol.* vi. 55 He [*sc.* Streeter] initially proposed 25 'horizons' for the

human embryonal period, but this was later revised to 23. *Ibid.* viii. 80 With the appearance of these branching villi proposed horizon VII is reached.

8. *Mining.* In horizon mining, a system of approximately horizontal tunnels lying in the same horizontal plane; the plane containing these tunnels.

1948 *Coal* Nov. 6/3 A further upper horizon was..fixed at a depth of 115 yards in the South Pit. **1960** J. SINCLAIR *Winning Coal* iii. 51 The coal lying between a pair of horizons is worked in such a manner that the coal flows downwards to the lower level and ventilation is ascensional. **1966** VOROBJEV & DESHMUKH *Advanced Coal Mining* II. xxxvi. 871 In steep and inclined coal seams (25°–9°) level division of the mining area with main workings on each horizon is preferable.

9. *attrib.* and *Comb.*, as ***horizon-bounded*** adj., ***horizon-line***; **horizon-blue** [Fr. *bleu horizon*], a light shade of blue, the colour of the uniform of the French Army during and after the war of 1914–18; such a uniform; also as *adj.*; **horizon-glass**, a small mirror of plate-glass fixed on the frame of a quadrant or sextant, having one half unsilvered so that the horizon-line or other object can be observed directly through it, and the reflected image of a heavenly body brought into optical coincidence with such object; **horizon mining**, a method of working inclined seams from approximately horizontal tunnels driven through the various strata to intersect the seams, there being several systems or 'horizons' of tunnels, one below another, connected by vertical shafts.

1919 J. BUCHAN *Mr. Standfast* xiv. 248 There was very little khaki or *horizon-blue about. **1926** 'C. BARRY' *Detective's Holiday* i. 9 'It is thus,' the man in horizon blue began... 'This morning..a fisherman..discovered..the body of a man who had been murdered.' **1942** E. PAUL *Narrow St.* xvii. 136 Monsieur Saint-Aulaire found himself over-stocked with horizon-blue material, the Chamber having agreed that French soldiers and officers should wear khaki in the future. **1954** W. FAULKNER *Fable* (1955) 14 The whole ring of..faces was stained with a faint,..reflected horizon-blue. **1972** J. WILLIAMS *Home Fronts* viii. 137 Little girls decked out in 'horizon-blue' policemen's caps and cloaks. **1812** BYRON *Ch. Har.* I. xxxi, Immense *horizon-bounded plains succeed. **1827** MOIR *Poems, To a Dead Eagle* iii, Outstretched, *horizon-girt, the maplike earth. **1774** M. MACKENZIE *Maritime Surv.* iv. 35 How to adjust the *Horizon-glass for Observation, by a horizontal Line. **1820** SCORESBY *Acc. Arctic Reg.* I. 388 Viewed through the horizon glass of a sextant. **1877** BLACK *Green Past.* v, At the far *horizon-line. **1947** *Coal* Nov. 16/3 *Horizon mining is planned to cut out heavy dip haulages, replacing them with locomotives. **1953** *Times* 15 Aug. 2/3 The site of the second modern horizon-mining development of the west Wales coalfield. **1963** J. SINCLAIR *Planning & Mechanized Drifting at Collieries* viii. 163 Probably the most important decision in planning a horizon-mining project is the position of the horizons and the vertical interval between them.

Hence **ho'rizonless** *a.*, having no definite horizon, visually boundless.

*a***1839** GALT *Demon Destiny* VI. (1840) 38, I that horizonless scene surveyed. **1892** *Chicago Advance* 7 July, The horizonless prairies of the West.

ho'rizon, *v.* [f. prec. sb.] *trans.* To furnish or bound with a horizon: chiefly in *pa. pple.* **ho'rizoned.**

1791 E. DARWIN *Bot. Gard.* I. 124 A thousand realms, horizon'd in his arms. **1859** CORNWALLIS *New World* I. 108 Far away to the west and north..the view was horizoned by a chain of rolling hills. **1863** MRS. WHITNEY *Faith Gartney* xxvi. 245 Her eyes away off over the lake, and..thoughts horizoned yet more distantly.

horizontal (hɒrɪ'zɒntəl), *a.* (*sb.*) [f. L. type **horīzontāl-is*, f. *horīzōn, horizont-* (see prec. sb.). Cf. F. *horizontal* (1545 in Hatz.-Darm.).]

A. *adj.* **1.** Of or belonging to the horizon; situated on or occurring at the horizon. Now chiefly in special collocations, as ***horizontal parallax***, the geocentric parallax of a heavenly body when on the horizon.

1555 EDEN *Decades* 9 The eleuation of the pole from the horizontal lyne. **1665** HOOKE *Microgr.* 236 The Astronomers..who have calculated the distance of the Planets from their Horizontal Parallax. **1667** MILTON *P.L.* I. 595 As when the Sun new ris'n Looks through the Horizontal misty Air. **1709** BERKELEY *Th. Vision* §77 He will ..declare the horizontal moon shall appear greater than the meridional. **1816** PLAYFAIR *Nat. Phil.* II. 74 The parallax at any given altitude..is to the horizontal parallax as the cosine of the altitude to the radius.

2. a. Parallel to the plane of the horizon; at right angles to the vertical line; level; flat; measured in a line or plane parallel to the horizon.

horizontal equivalent, the distance between two points or two adjacent contours measured in a horizontal plane (rather than along the ground). ***horizontal plane***, in *Perspective*, a plane at the level of the eye, intersecting the perspective plane at right angles, the line of intersection being the ***horizontal line***. ***horizontal plane of Camper*** in *Craniometry*, the plane passing through the centre of the external ear-holes and the inferior nasal spine; the intersection of this with the median plane of the head is the ***horizontal line (of Camper)***. ***horizontal rainbow***, a spectrum occasionally seen on or just above the surface of a lake, appearing as an oval or as an open curve with its arms pointing away from the observer.

1638 SIR T. HERBERT *Trav.* (ed. 2) 158 The Horyzontall plaine which is..discovered from thirty rising Turrets there, yeelds most pleasure [to look on]. **1665** HOOKE *Microgr.* 151 The bended part or Index of it lay horizontal. **1696** PHILLIPS (ed. 4), *Horizontal Projection*, a Projection of the Sphere in Arches of Circles, called *Stereographic*, wherein the Sphere is pressd into the plain of the Horizon and the Meridians and Parallels of the Sphere projected thereon. **1704** F. FULLER *Med. Gymn.* (1711) 27 Changing.. from an Horizontal to an Erect Position. **1706** PHILLIPS (ed. Kersey), *Horizontal Range* (in Gunnery), the Level-range of a piece of Ordnance, being the Line it describes parallel to the Horizon. **1834** MEDWIN *Angler in Wales* II. 210 The head is..circular in its horizontal section. **1886** R. C. LESLIE *Sea-painter's Log* 192 That strange family of fish which, commencing life on edge..change that position at an early age for a horizontal one. **1889** G. W. USILL *Pract. Surveying* x. 199 The known difference of height thereof are [*sic*] called the vertical intervals, and their distance apart upon the survey are termed the horizontal equivalents. **1906** *Nature* 26 Apr. 608/2 (*heading*) A horizontal rainbow. **1916** *Monthly Weather Rev.* (Wash.) XLIV. 66/1 In general these horizontal rainbows are confined to the early hours of the day. **1952** MONKHOUSE & WILKINSON *Maps & Diagrams* ii. 74 If two points on a hill-side are projected on to a horizontal plane, as they are on a map, the distance between them is known as the Horizontal Equivalent (H.E.). **1957** G. E. HUTCHINSON *Treat. Limnol.* I. vi. 419 The horizontal rainbow, or iris, is a relatively rare phenomenon, though it has been observed on a number of lakes in many parts of the world.

b. Applied to various mechanical contrivances, or artificial structures, of which the whole or the main part works or lies in a horizontal direction.

horizontal bar, a round bar fixed horizontally at some distance above the ground for gymnastic exercise. ***horizontal dial***, a dial with the face, or surface on which the hours are marked, horizontal. ***horizontal (steam) engine***, one in which the piston moves horizontally. ***horizontal escapement*** (in a watch), 'one in which the impulse is given by the teeth of a horizontal wheel acting on a hollow cylinder on the axis of the balance; invented by Graham about 1700' (Knight *Dict. Mech.*). † ***horizontal rudder*** Aeronaut., an elevator on an aircraft. ***horizontal watch***, one having a horizontal escapement. ***horizontal wheel***, a wheel the plane of which is horizontal, the axis being vertical; in a carriage, the wheel-plate or 'fifth wheel'.

1674 MOXON *Tutor Astron.* v. Prob. iii. (ed. 3) 150, I would make an Horizontal Dyal for Londons Latitude. **1688** R. HOLME *Armoury* III. 372/2 A Horizontal Dial..is a Dial for a Pillar or top of a Post. **1755** *Specif. Bosley's Patent* No. 698 The scapemt. of the ballance of these my horizontal watches. **1782** *Specif. T. Tyrer's Patent* No. 1311 [For a] Horizontal scapement for a Watch. **1794** W. FELTON *Carriages* (1801) I. 45 When the carriage is intended for a whole or horizontal wheel, the perch has no hooping-piece, but is bolted by the plates at each end to the inside of the transoms. *Ibid.* 46 Extending to the out circumference of the horizontal half-wheel. **1817** Horizontal rudder [see SAIL *sb.*[1] 1 d]. **1825** J. NICHOLSON *Operat. Mechanic* 139 Horizontal and vertical windmills. **1827** G. HAMILTON *Elem. Gymnastics* 55 The performer, taking hold of the horizontal bar, swings backward and forward. **1843** *Lancet* 27 May 302/1 [I] made her exercise twice a day on a horizontal bar erected for the purpose. **1875** T. FROST *Circus Life* ix. 161 The rising school of young gymnasts.. began to practise on..the horizontal bar, and the flying rings. **1875** *Aëronaut. Soc. Gt. Brit. 9th Ann. Rep. 1874* 56 This problem M. Renaud has solved by means of his automatic rudder... The idea occurred to him of placing a small horizontal rudder behind the sustaining planes. **1878** M. JEWRY *Warne's Model Cookery* Inside front cover (Advt.), Practical Instructions on the Horizontal Bar, Parallel Bars. **1884** *Punch* 8 Mar. 117/1 Let the Ladies learn gymnastics..They'll improve too pale complexions..After practice on the ladders and the horizontal bars. **1895** MACLAREN *Phys. Educ.* 254 It is important that every gymnasium should contain two forms of horizontal bar. **1903** A. BENNETT *Truth abt. Author* ii. 16 He..taught us to fence, and to do the lesser circle on the horizontal bar. **1909** C. C. TURNER *Aerial Navig.* viii. 121 The aviator must further correct this instability by control of the horizontal rudder. **1913** A. E. BERRIMAN *Aviation* vii. 71 Originally the elevator was often called the horizontal rudder. **1964** G. C. KUNZLE *Parallel Bars* i. 36 In this case it is very similar to position 2 (c)..on the Horizontal Bar.

c. *Bot.* Applied to parts or organs having a position at right angles to the stem or axis. **d.** *Zool.* and *Anat.* Applied to parts, organs, or markings parallel to a plane supposed to extend from end to end and from side to side of the body.

1753 CHAMBERS *Cycl. Supp.* s.v. *Leaf, Patent Leaf*..when it forms perfectly right angles, it is called *horizontal.* **1880** GRAY *Struct. Bot.* vi. §8. 277 Ovules are..horizontal, when borne on one or more sides of the cell and not directed either upward or downward. **1881** MIVART *Cat* 77 The rest is named the horizontal ramus.

3. a. Uniform; producing or based on uniformity. Chiefly *U.S.*

1842 *Congress. Globe* 17 Mar. 331 Was it expected that this committee would send in a horizontal tariff? **1872** *Ibid.* 28 Mar. 2016/2 The horizontal reduction of duties would do incalculable injury. **1890** *Ibid.* 9 May 4392/2 The Democratic bill made a horizontal cut of 20 per cent. **1907** *Daily Chron.* 23 Sept. 5/3 The 'Journal of Commerce' [N.Y.] says that the North German Lloyd Company announced yesterday a practically horizontal cut of 25 dols. on the eastward and westward passages. **1963** *Times* 22 May (Margarine Suppl.) p. viii, The Council of the European Community has already issued a directive in connexion with the use of colour additives. This follows what is known as the 'horizontal' system, meaning that it is of application to all food products.

b. In Industry: (see quots. 1959 and 1968). ***horizontal combination, integration, merger***, an industrial merger of firms engaged in the same stages or types of manufacture; so ***horizontal combine***, the organization resulting from such a merger.

1927 *Observer* 27 Mar. 5 Looking with a benevolent eye on horizontal combines. **1930** M. CLARK *Home Trade* 204 There have been the combinations of one business with one or more of the same type. To this type the term 'horizontal combine' is usually applied. **1930** *Economist* 29 Mar. 710/2 Horizontal integration took place in the alcohol and solvents industry. **1959** *Listener* 9 July 46/2 The cotton industry is what is called a horizontal industry... As a rule the processing is done in stages in which the goods pass from one producer to another. **1960** NANASSY & SELDEN *Business Dict.* 96 *Horizontal combination*, formation of a business by combining two or more concerns engaged in the same kind of business. **1962** H. O. BEECHENO *Introd. Business Stud.* v. 40 When business units of the same type combine..it is called horizontal integration. **1967** *Economist* 15 Apr. 253/3 He also held that all mergers must be judged by the same standards, whether they be vertical, horizontal or conglomerate. **1968** J. IRONSIDE *Fashion Alphabet* 232 The textile and fashion industry works in two ways—horizontal or vertical... The 'horizontal' system means that in each stage of its manufacture..the textile goes through different hands... In the 'vertical' system, everything from weaving ..to making up the garments..is done under one organisation.

c. Denoting a relationship, movement, etc., between a social group of a particular status, class, age-group, etc., and another of similar specifications, as opp. a 'vertical' relationship with a higher (or lower) authority, class, age-group, etc.

1931 H. G. WELLS *Work, Wealth & Happiness of Mankind* (1932) xi. 540 The only remaining physical differences between man and woman are becoming horizontal, i.e., differences between individuals in the same class, and not vertical differences, in which all women are put below all men, or vice versa. **1949** KOESTLER *Promise & Fulfilment* III. i. 289 The trend of social migrations is a 'horizontal' drift from village and agriculture to town and industry, and a 'vertical' drift from working-class to middle-class occupations. **1959** *Listener* 12 Feb. 280/2 When the children's interests turn outwards, when they develop loyalties of a horizontal sort. **1959** N. MAILER *Advts. for Myself* (1961) 374 The old exploitation was vertical—the poor supported the rich. To this vertical exploitation must now be added the horizontal exploitation of the mass by the State and by Monopoly. **1967** *Listener* 13 July 62/2 This horizontal integration of Saudi-Arabian Arab with Egyptian Arab ultimately gave way to the vertical integration of Egyptian peasant with Egyptian professional man.

d. ***horizontal union*** = ***craft union***.

1937 H. FELDMAN *Probl. Labor Relations* iv. 255 Shall the mass production industries..be organized on a 'horizontal' (craft union) basis, or in 'vertical' (industrial) unions? **1950** THEIMER & CAMPBELL *Encycl. World Politics* 425/1 Unions may be craft unions, also known as horizontal unions, or industrial unions, also known as vertical unions.

4. *Mus.* (See quots. 1955 and 1970.)

1886 G. B. SHAW *How to become Mus. Critic* (1960) 122 The fact that M. Gounod has put too much sugar in it for the palate of a British Protestant might be condoned if the music were not so very horizontal. There is nearly always a pedal flowing along, and the other parts are slipping chromatically down to merge in it. **1900** C. W. PEARCE *Composers' Counterpoint* iii. 28 Composers..have re-established the beautiful horizontal polyphony of the two-dimensional period, upon the perpendicular lines of the modern harmonic school. **1942** E. BLOM *Mus. in Eng.* ii. 21 Vertical hearing, i.e. listening to the chordal incidence of parts rather than to their separate horizontal flow. **1955** L. FEATHER *Encycl. Jazz* ii. 53 Similarly 'horizontal' or 'linear' refers to the relationship of the notes or chords as they are played one after the other, read horizontally across the manuscript. **1962** *Listener* 9 Aug. 225/3 In Webern's texture the distinction between the horizontal and vertical is in a process of complete liquidation. **1970** W. APEL *Harvard Dict. Mus.* (ed. 2) 842/1 Much like woven fabric, music consists of horizontal ('woof') and vertical ('warp') elements. The former are the successive sounds forming melodies, the latter the simultaneous sounds forming harmonies.

B. *sb.* (ellipt. use of the *adj.*)

†**1.** = HORIZON. *Obs.*

1555 EDEN *Decades* 10 They had euer the northe pole.. eleuate in sight aboue the Horizontal. *Ibid.* 185 It can not bee seene, bycause it is vnder the horisontal.

2. *ellipt.* A horizontal line, bar, member, etc.

Craniometry. 'The line drawn from the lower edge of the orbital cavity to the middle of the ear-cavity' (*Cent. Dict.*).

1674 MOXON *Tutor Astron.* v. Prob. iv. (ed. 3) 154 You may reduce all Verticals into Horizontals [in dialling]. **1755** YOUNG *Centaur* v. Wks. 1757 IV. 224 To confess, that, though we are not quite horizontals, yet neither are we quite upright. **1816** KEATINGE *Trav.* (1817) I. 162 The geology of Spain is an alternation of edges and horizontals. **1890** BOLDREWOOD *Col. Reformer* (1891) 225 The 'cap', or uppermost horizontal..of rounded..timber. **1955** *Oxf. Jun. Encycl.* VIII. 429/1 The theodolite is also used to measure vertical angles, that is, angles above or below the horizontal. **1962** *Listener* 15 Mar. 479/2 Bonnard derived his use of horizontals and verticals within the picture from Gauguin.

3. An evergreen Tasmanian tree or, in exposed positions, a shrub, *Anodopetalum biglandulosum*. Also *attrib.*, as ***horizontal scrub***, the mat of vegetation formed by interlocking branches of a group of trees.

1888 R. M. JOHNSTON *Geol. Tasmania* p. vi (Morris), The Horizontal is a tall shrub or tree. **1891** *Australasian* 4 Apr. (Ibid.), That stuff as they calls horizontal, a mess of branches and root. **1898** MORRIS *Austral Eng.* 202/2 Horizontal scrub. **1927** *Blackw. Mag.* Oct. 471/2 These tentacles of horizontal were generally clothed with a thick velvety covering of damp green moss. **1936** *Discovery* Jan. 15/1 If he meets with a patch of 'horizontal scrub', he will

clamber over the tree tops. **1949** D. Walker *We went to Australia* xxi. 200 Arid mountain country covered with 'horizontal scrub'. This extraordinary growth shoots upward for some twenty feet, the boughs then interlocking over very large areas; and so thickly matted is it that you can walk on the scrub some twenty feet from the ground. **1957** *Forest Trees Austral.* (Commonw. Forestry & Timber Bur.) 218/1 Associated species include myrtle beech.. and shrub species such as horizontal.

4. [Fr. (*grande*) *horizontale.*] A prostitute. Also ***grand horizontal***; also in French form. *slang.*

1888 E. Dowson *Let.* 13 Nov. (1967) 18, I shall let the liaison run its course—it will be very amusing & not as costly as an affair with a regular horizontale. **1909** J. R. Ware *Passing Eng.* 154/2 Horizontal. **1928** A. Philips *Boy at Bank* v. i, More than ten thousand professional 'horizontals' are light o' loves. **1963** *Times* 4 Apr. 16/2 The 'grand horizontals' were merely in the argot of the day the leading fashionable cocottes. **1967** *Observer* 8 Oct. 26/2 A *grisette* is cheaper than a regular *horizontale.* **1967** C. O. Skinner *Madame Sarah* iii. 44 La Païva, a contemporary 'grand horizontal', had attained respectability by marrying. **1970** *New Yorker* 28 Feb. 113/1 He is over-shadowed throughout by Aunt Augusta, the still unretired *grande horizontale* of seventy-three.

hori'zontalism. [f. prec. + -ism.] The quality of being, or of having some part, horizontal.

1848 B. Webb *Continent. Ecclesiol.* 19 At York the buttresses are too prominent; there is an over-great horizontalism apparent. **1853** Kane *Grinnell Exp.* xlviii. (1856) 449 Their slopes became less sudden, their horizontalism more diffused.

horizontality (ˌhɒrɪzɒn'tælɪtɪ). [f. as prec. + -ity.] The condition or quality of being horizontal (in sense 2); horizontal position.

1752 Short in *Phil. Trans.* XLVII. 352 The cause of this horizontality. **1797** *Ibid.* LXXXVII. 507 The whole instrument may be moved round without disturbing its horizontality. **1881** A. Geikie in *Macm. Mag.* Oct. 423 Mile after mile they can be followed.. always keeping their horizontality.

hori'zontalize, *v.* [f. as prec. + -ize.] **a.** *trans.* To place in a horizontal position. **b.** *to horizontalize it* (humorous): to lie down flat.

1837 T. Hook *Jack Brag* xxii, With his little legs horizontalised on his lodging-house sofa. **1843** *Fraser's Mag.* XXVIII. 39 My friend.. was still horizontalising it on the chairs.

Hence **hori,zontali'zation,** the action of making horizontal; *spec.* in *Craniometry,* the placing of the skull with the datum-plane truly horizontal.

horizontally (hɒrɪ'zɒntəlɪ), *adv.* [f. as prec. + -ly².] In a horizontal position or direction.

1646 Sir T. Browne *Pseud. Ep.* 259 An obelisk erected, & golden figures placed horizontally about it. **1715** Desaguliers *Fires Impr.* 80 The Wind.. blows horizontally. **1776** Withering *Brit. Plants* (1796) II. 143 Panicle spreading horizontally. **1871** Tyndall *Fragm. Sc.* (1879) I. iv. 96 A glass tube.. supported horizontally on two stands. **1934** *Hound & Horn* VII. 596 He [*sc.* Stravinsky] is tired of .. exploiting the folk tune, horizontally, vertically, atonally, seriously or comically. **1956** M. Stearns *Story of Jazz* (1957) xii. 126 Everybody had an interesting part, for the idea was to move horizontally rather than vertically. **1958** *Listener* 9 Oct. 547/2 Differences throughout the Arab sector run both vertically and horizontally: between religious sects, social strata, settlers and nomads. **1959** *Ibid.* 13 Aug. 245/1 A society so divided vertically as well as horizontally.

hori'zontalness. [f. as prec. + -ness.] The quality of being horizontal; horizontality.

1869 tr. *Hugo's By King's Command* II. i. 58 The horizontalness of the blasts.

†**hori'zontic,** *a. Obs. rare.* [f. L. *horīzōn, horīzont-* horizon + -ic.] Of or pertaining to the horizon; = horizontal 1. Hence †**horizontically** *adv.* = horizontally.

1651 Ogilby *Æsop* (1665) 169 The Four Winds muster'd .. From all their Horizontick Seats in Heaven. **1665** Boyle *Hist. Air* xvii. (1692) 100 Being placed on one of the Scales as Horizontically as we could.

horkey, var. of hockey¹.

horl(e, obs. ff. hurl.

horlege, obs. f. horologe.

Horlick ('hɔːlɪk). The name of the British-born American industrialist W. *Horlick* (1846–1936), used in the possessive to designate the trade-name of the malted milk-powder or the drink made from this, which was first manufactured by his firm in 1883.

1891 *Trade Marks Jrnl.* 19 Aug. 784 (*heading*) Horlick's. .. A desiccated and granulated preparation of malt extract and milk as a food for infants and invalids. James Horlick, .. London, E.C.; manufacturer. **1907** *Yesterday's Shopping* (1969) 510/3 Horlick's malted milk. **1932** L. Golding *Magnolia St.* II. iv. 324 The Horlick's mugs danced on the trestle tables. **1936** R. Lehmann *Weather in Streets* I. v. 152 'Hot milk?'.. 'No, thank you, Mum. Not even Horlick's.' **1958** J. Cannan *And be a Villain* vii. 150 A tray of 'night-caps', hot milk for Evadne, a whisky and soda for Laura, Horlick's for herself. **1966** J. Cleary *High Commissioner* iii. 53 A spoonful of Horlicks in a glass of Scotch and I'll be fine. **1973** J. Wilson *Truth or Dare* ii. 24 She.. rinsed out the Horlicks mugs.

horly-borly, obs. f. hurly-burly.

horme ('hɔːmiː). *Psychol.* Also **hormé.** [C. G. Jung's ad. Gr. ὁρμή impulse.] Vital or purposeful energy. Hence **'hormic** *a.*, of, pertaining to, or characterized by horme; **'hormism,** the theory of, or belief in, such purposeful energy; so **'hormist,** an adherent of hormism.

[*a* **1680** Cudworth *Treat. Freewill* (1838) 30 Now this love and desire of good,.. is not a mere passion or *horme,* but a settled resolved principle. *Ibid.* 57 Epicurus.. conceived that brutes were not merely passive to their own fancies and *hormae,* but that they could add something of their own to them.] **1915** Jung in *Jrnl. Abnormal Psychol.* IX. 396 The terminology—extraversion and introversion—depends upon my energic conception of mental phenomena. I assume a hypothetical energy which I designate as *hormé.* **1915** W. H. B. Stoddart *New Psychiatry* 4 This word 'horme' has a wide signification, applicable to all the instincts. **1920** T. P. Nunn *Education* ii. 21 To this element of drive or urge, whether it occurs in the conscious life of men and the higher animals, or in the unconscious activities of their bodies and the (presumably) unconscious behaviour of lower animals, we propose to give a single name—*horme.* **1926** W. McDougall *Outl. Abnormal Psychol.* 27 Jung says, 'I postulate a hypothetical fundamental striving which I designate *libido*'; and in a footnote.. 'This energy may also be designated as hormé. Hormé is a Greek word (ὁρμή)—force, attack, press, impetuosity, violence, urgency, zeal. It is related to Bergson's "élan vital". The concept hormé is an energetic expression for psychological values.' *Ibid.* 121 The vital or hormic energy of B's organism. **1927** *Contemp. Rev.* June 769 A kind of hormic determinism. **1931** R. S. Woodworth *Contemp. Schools Psychol.* 213 Purpose can properly be carried over into abnormal psychology, as has been done by the hormic psycho-pathologists, Freud especially. **1937** *Jrnl. Theol. Stud.* XXXVIII. 330 Miss Ikin is herself a thoroughly competent psychologist, with a Freudian training, but with a much wider interest in psychology of the hormic type than is usual in those whose concern has been with 'deep analysis' or psycho-analysis proper. **1944** L. Cohn in H. Treece *Herbert Read* 58 McDougall adheres to the same 'dionysian' or hormic conception of the soul which is to-day represented by Bergson, Freud, [etc.]. **1948** *Brit. Jrnl. Psychol.* June 187 The hormic-tension theory, (which explains pleasure as connected with the lowering of tension and unpleasure with its increase). **1948** W. McDougall *Introd. Soc. Psychol.* (ed. 29) Suppl. vii. 465 'Pleasure and pain are also motive forces depending upon individual experience.'.. To admit this is to combine hedonism with hormism. *Ibid.* 471 The hormist can find no clear instances that support Woodworth's thesis and can point to a multitude of instances which indicate an absence of.. power. **1953** Hinsie & Schatzky *Psychiatric Dict.* (ed. 2) 653/1 Hormism is.. opposed to hedonism. **1958** W. Stark *Sociology of Knowledge* 239 Though the sympherontic and hormic theories are commonly regarded as sociologies on knowledge.

†**hor'metic,** *a. Obs. rare.* [ad. Gr. ὁρμητικός, f. ὁρμά-ειν (vbl. adj. ὁρμητ-ός) to urge on, impel: see -ic.] Having the property of exciting or impelling. Hence †**hor'metically** *adv.*, by impulse.

1666 J. Smith *Old Age* (1676) 62 [The muscles] By their hormetick power and contraction into their own bodies.. can readily perform whatsoever motion the Organ is capable of. **1678** Cudworth *Intell. Syst.* I. iii. §18. 161 The plastick nature, acting neither by knowledge nor by animal fancy, neither electively nor hormetically.

hormogone ('hɔːməʊgəʊn), **-gon** (-gɒn). *Bot.* [ad. mod.L. *hormogonium,* f. Gr. ὅρμος chain, necklace, after *archegonium,* etc.] A special reproductive body in the Nostocs, consisting of a chain of roundish cells. Hence **hormogonous** (hɔː'mɒgənəs) *a.*, having or resembling a hormogone.

1886 *Syd. Soc. Lex., Hormogone,* in Nostocs, the portion of the filament included between two consecutive heterocysts.

hormogonium (hɔːməʊ'gəʊnɪəm). *Bot.* Pl. **hormogonia.** [mod.L.: see hormogone.] = hormogone.

1880 W. G. Farlow *Marine Algae* in *Rep. Commissioner Fish & Fisheries* 1879 (U.S. Senate Misc. Document 59, 46th Cong., 2nd Session) App. A. 12 The cells intermediate between the two heterocysts escape in the form of a small chain called a hormogonium. **1948** *New Biol.* V. 13 Most filamentous blue-green algae form hormogonia. **1965** F. E. Round *Biol. Algae* ii. 24 The short lengths of trichomes thus released are known as hormogonia.

hormonal (hɔː'məʊnəl, 'hɔːməʊnəl), *a. Physiol.* [f. hormon(e + -al.] Of, involving, or effected by a hormone or hormones; that is or acts as a hormone.

1926 *Chem. Abstr.* XX. 3029 (*heading*) The hormonal-nervous regulatory system of fat metabolism. **1949** M. Mead *Male & Female* xvi. 338 This domestic crisis.. is reinforced by the hormonal instability and emotional fears that surround the menopause. **1953** *Jrnl. R. Hort. Soc.* LXXVIII. 165 The use of hormonal regulators of plant growth. **1955** R. G. Harry *Mod. Cosmeticol.* (ed. 4) iv. 95 The remark is often made that the mother-to-be has never 'looked so young' or 'so beautiful'. Undoubtedly this effect is due to hormonal influences. **1968** *Times* 11 Nov. 10/8 Apes and most monkeys have menstrual cycles, and in some species the pattern of sexual activity is known to be under hormonal control.

Hence **hor'monally** *adv.*, by means of a hormone or hormones; as a hormone.

1939 B. Hanström *Hormones in Invert.* ix. 84 *Dixippus* shows a morphological and a physiological colour-change which are both hormonally regulated. **1955** R. I. Dorfman in Pincus & Thimann *Hormones* III. xii. 593 A group of hormonally active steroids, estrogens. **1970** *Sci. Jrnl.* June 68/1 They were both able to mate normal individulas to hormonally sex reversed animals which had exactly the same chromosomes.

hormone ('hɔːməʊn). *Physiol.* [ad. Gr. ὁρμῶν, pres. pple. of ὁρμᾶν to set in motion (f. ὁρμή onset, impulse), with assimilation to -one.]

1. a. Any of numerous organic compounds that are secreted into the body fluids of an animal, particularly the bloodstream, by a specific group of cells and regulate some specific physiological activity of other cells; also, any synthetic compound having such an effect.

1905 E. H. Starling in *Lancet* 5 Aug. 340/1 These chemical messengers, however, of 'hormones'.. as we might call them. **1906** —— *Recent Adv. Physiol. Digest.* 75 The first products of digestion act on the pyloric mucous membrane, and produce in this membrane a substance which is absorbed into the blood stream, and carried to all the glands of the stomach, where it acts as a specific excitant of their secretory activity. This substance may be called the gastric secretin or gastric hormone. **1924** [see *growth-hormone* s.v. growth¹ 5]. **1930** R. A. Fisher *Genet. Theory Nat. Selection* 131 The investigation of the influence of the sex hormones has shown how genetic modifications of the whole species can be made to manifest themselves in one sex only. **1931,** etc. [see gonadotrophic, -tropic *a.*]. **1951** A. Grollman *Pharmacol. & Therapeutics* xxvi. 581 The estrogenic hormones are responsible for certain secondary sex characteristics in the female, such as the plumage markings of some birds. **1955** *Sci. News Let.* 24 Sept. 198/3 Hormones are chemicals made by the adrenal, sex, pituitary and other body glands. **1959** A. .C. Guyton *Function Human Body* i. 11 Adrenocortical hormones secreted by the two adrenal cortices.. control the passage of proteins, salts, and perhaps other substances through the cell walls. **1967** *Martindale's Extra Pharmacopoeia* (ed. 25) 1277/2 Synthetic sex hormones have usually been developed from the basic steroid structure of the naturally occuring testosterone. **1968** Passmore & Robson *Compan. Med. Stud.* I. xxv. 40/1 Insulin is a powerful hormone whose actions affect the structure and function of every organ in the body. **1969** *Times* 16 June 3/8 Testosterone.. is the chief of the male sex hormones known as androgens. **1970** W. B. Yapp *Introd. Animal Physiol.* (ed. 3) ii. 59 The acid of the gastric juice is secreted under the action of gastrin, a hormone secreted and liberated into the blood by the stomach wall.. when it is mechanically stimulated.

b. Restricted to those compounds that have a stimulating (rather than an inhibiting) effect (cf. chalone). Now *rare.*

1914, etc. [see chalone]. **1955** J. T. & O. T. Lewis tr. *Houssay's Human Physiol.* (ed. 2) li. 561 The word 'hormone' is used also for substances that do not excite activity but rather inhibit it. According to Sharpey-Schafer, the term 'autocoid' would be appropriate for all chemical messengers; 'hormone' for chemical messengers that stimulate activity; and 'chalone' for those which inhibit it. This terminology has not been generally adopted.

2. Any of numerous organic compounds produced by plants which regulate growth and other physiological activities; also, any synthetic compound having such an effect.

1917 *Bot. Gaz.* LXIII. 50 In other plants the hypothetical geotropic substance might be associated with the shoot-forming hormone. **1927** *Biol. Abstr.* I. 244/2 Growth hormone of *Zea* coleoptile tips. **1951** *Jrnl. Chem. Education* XXVIII. 113 We now use plant hormones to propagate plants, prevent preharvest drop of apples,.. and defoliate plants without killing the stems. **1952** Meyer & Anderson *Plant Physiol.* (ed. 2) xxviii. 555 Other terms commonly used to designate plant hormones are phytohormones, growth hormones, growth substances, and growth regulators. **1960** *Biol. Abstr.* XXXV. 4920/1 The action of synthetic plant hormones on pathogenic fungi was studied. **1966** R. M. Devlin *Plant Physiol.* xxii. 532 Bud dormancy in woody species may be regulated by some balance or ratio between a dormancy-inducing hormone and gibberellins. **1968** Y. Vardar (*title*) Transport of plant hormones. **1970** [see cytokinin]. **1970** Wareing & Phillips *Control of Growth & Differentiation in Plants* iv. 62 Whereas the effects of most animal hormones are rather specific, a plant hormone can elicit a wide range of responses depending upon the type of organ or tissue in which it is acting.

3. *attrib.* and *Comb.*, as ***hormone activity, balance, therapy, treatment, weedkiller; hormone-like*** adj.; ***hormone-controlled*** ppl. adj.; **hormone cream,** a skin cream that contains one or more sex hormones.

1936 *Discovery* Nov. 362/1 Such complex subjects as inhibition, reflex action, hormone activity, etc. **1914** H. R. Harrower *Pract. Hormone Therapy* iii. 45 The intricacies of the hormone balance are fully as complicated as those of the nervous system. **1950** *Sci. News* XV. 134 Rheumatoid arthritis is related to the hormone balance of the body. **1963** A. Heron *Towards Quaker View of Sex* 54 In most mammals, the oestrous cycle of the female, hormone-controlled, is an important factor. **1938** *Encycl. Brit. Bk. of Yr. 1938* 588/1 The group of hormone and vitamin creams, etc., known collectively as 'biological' preparations. **1961** 'R. M. Dashwood' *Provincial Daughter* 85 A very good Hormone Cream which many clients find helpful after a certain age. **1962** *Punch* 12 Dec. 845/2 The Consumers' Association finds no reason for buying oestrogenic hormone creams. **1937** *Contrib. Boyce Thompson Inst.* VIII. 338 Characteristic responses of plants to hormone-like substances have been described. **1914** H. R. Harrower *Pract. Hormone Therapy* p. xii, At present the application of hormone therapy in general practice is the exception rather than the rule. **1921** *Endocrinology* V. 538 Convincing results of hormone therapy in gynecology. **1949** Koestler *Insight & Outlook* x. 138 Hormone therapy and neuro-surgery aim

at restoring equilibrium by action somewhere in the middle. **1955** A. HUXLEY *Let.* 5 Feb. (1969) 731 Hormone treatment is now being given. **1972** *Lancet* 3 June 1246/2 In 1 case hormone treatment was given for mastitis. **1950** *N.Z. Jrnl. Agric.* Apr. 328/3 There is no danger in using hormone weedkillers on pastures.

Hence **'hormonize** *v. trans.*, to treat with a hormone; **'hormonized** *ppl. a.*, treated with a hormone; containing a hormone.

1940 *Proc. Amer. Soc. Hort. Sci.* XXXVII. 1015 Hormonized Dust gave satisfactory results with many kinds of cuttings. *Ibid.* 1016 Forty-seven days after potting, plants rooted with Hormonized Dust were 7 days ahead of untreated plants in shoot production. **1947** *Biol. Abstr.* XXI. 2043/1 Field expts. with potatoes hormonized by heteroauxin. **1950** *Ibid.* XXIV. 1611/2 The germination of seeds of endive and Brussels sprouts is not improved by hormonizing the seeds or fruits with indole-acetic acid. **1959** *Times* 16 Feb. 15/5 Its carcass did not set well on cooling, and this had led to most of the butchers' complaints about hormonized beef. **1960** *Farmer & Stockbreeder* 16 Feb. 78/1 America's top authorities confirm there is absolutely no risk with hormonized meat.

hormonic (hɔːˈmɒnɪk, hɔːˈməʊnɪk), *a. Physiol.* [f. HORMON(E + -IC.] = HORMONAL *a.*

1914 [see CHALONE]. **1928** *Brit. Med. Jrnl.* 18 Feb. 255/1 The functional (hormonic) over-activity of the anterior lobe of the pituitary gland. **1933** T. C. MERRILL tr. *Voronoff & Alexandrescu's Testicular Grafting* 2 Animals which are too young and employed before the establishment of puberty and the production of free hormonic secretion, are unsuitable.

hormonology (hɔːməʊˈnɒlədʒɪ). *rare.* [f. HORMON(E + -OLOGY.] The study of hormones; endocrinology.

1918 *Endocrinology* II. 62 (*heading*) A bit of hormonology, with practical applications. **1944** KOESTLER in *Horizon* Mar. 170 The whole body of ideas had undergone a radical transformation: Relativity and Quantum mechanics, Hormonology and Psycho-analysis. **1970** *Sci. Jrnl.* June 44/1 It used to be a shibboleth of hormonology that such messenger molecules were not affected by the chemical process they influenced.

horn (hɔːn), *sb.* Forms: 1– horn; also 3 heorn, 5 horun, 4–7 horne. [Com. Teut.: OE. *horn* masc. = OFris., OS. *horn* masc., OHG., ON. *horn* neut., Goth. *haurn* neut.:—OTeut. **horno-*, cognate with L. *cornu*, Celtic *corn* 'horn': in ablaut relation with Gr. *κέρ-ας, κερ-ατ-*; cf. also Skr. *çṛṅ-ga* 'horn'.]

I. As an animal organ or appendage.

1. a. A non-deciduous excrescence, often curved and pointed, consisting of an epidermal sheath growing about a bony core, on the head of certain mammals, as cattle, sheep, goats, antelopes, etc., and serving as a weapon of offence or defence.

(True horns are common to male and female animals. They are usually produced in pairs, a right and a left; sometimes in two, or (in some extinct animals) even in three pairs. Horns also occur singly, or one in front of the other, as in species of rhinoceros.)

c **1000** ÆLFRIC *Gen.* xxii. 13 Anne ramm betwux þam bremelum be þam hornum ʒehæft. *a* **1225** *St. Marher.* 7 Leose.. mi meoke mildschipe af þe anhurnde hornes. *c* **1300** *Havelok* 700 Shep wit wolle, neth wit horn. **1382** WYCLIF *Rev.* xiii. 1 A beest.. hauynge seuen heedes and ten hornes. *c* **1440** *Promp. Parv.* 247/1 Horne, *cornu*. **1596** SPENSER *F.Q.* VI. vii. 47 A salvage Bull, whose cruell hornes doe threat Desperate daunger. **1626** BACON *Sylva* §753 No Beast that hath Hornes hath vpper Teeth. **1774** GOLDSM. *Nat. Hist.* (1776) IV. 287 The elephant is often found dead in the forests, pierced with the horn of a rhinoceros. **1854** OWEN *Skel. & Teeth* in *Circ. Sc., Organ. Nat.* I. 239 The term 'horn' is technically restricted to the weapon which is composed of a bony base, covered by a sheath of true horny matter. Such horns are never shed. *Ibid.* 240 The horn of the rhinoceros consists wholly of fibrous horny matter.

b. *fig.*

a **1659** OSBORN *Char.* etc. Wks. (1673) 632 Were You thrown upon it, by the Iron Horns of an unavoidable Compulsion. **1827** POLLOK *Course T.* v, The Church, Who with a double horn the people pushed.

c. That borne by the Ram (Aries) and Bull (Taurus) as figured among the constellations and zodiacal signs; the stars situated in those parts of the constellations; †also the constellation Ursa Minor [cf. It. *il Carro e'l Corno* the Wain and the Horn].

1390 GOWER *Conf.* III. 119 This bulle is eke with sterres set, Through which he hath his hornes knet. **1513** DOUGLAS *Æneis* VIII. Prol. 154 The son, the sevin sternis, and the Charll wane.. The horne and the hand staff, Prater John and Port Jaff. *a* **1605** MONTGOMERIE *Flyting w. Polwart* 419 Be the hornes, the handstaff, and the king's ell. **1726** tr. *Gregory's Astron.* I. 370 Copernicus and others.. reckon the distance of the Fix'd Stars in the Ecliptic towards the East, from the preceding of the two in the Horn of Aries.

d. Put for 'horned animal'. Cf. SHORTHORN.

1588 SHAKS. *L.L.L.* IV. i. 113 My Lady goes to kill hornes. **1846** J. BAXTER *Libr. Pract. Agric.* (ed. 4) II. 87 This property is almost peculiar to the improved short horn. **1890** L. C. D'OYLE *Notches* 85 They at last headed the drifting 'horns'.

2. Phrases and proverbs.

†**a.** ***horn and corn***: used symbolically for cattle and provisions in general. **b.** ***neither horn nor hoof***: not a trace or vestige. **c.** ***horn with horn***: see quots. **d.** ***all horn and hide***: nothing but skin and bone. **e.** ***in a horn*** (*slang*): 'a general qualification implying refusal or disbelief; over the left' (Farmer). [Cf. It. *un corno* as a negative.] **f.** ***to be squeezed through a horn, to come out at the little end of the horn***: to come off badly in an affair, esp. to fail conspicuously in a great or pretentious undertaking. **g.** Other phrases of obvious meaning. Also ***to take the bull by the horns***, etc.: see BULL *sb.*[1] 7 c; ***to carry hay in one's horn***: see HAY *sb.*[1] 3.

a. **1633** T. STAFFORD *Pac. Hib.* III. xv. 357 Their Troupes left neither Corne nor horne, nor house unburnt, betweene Kinsale and Rosse. **1819** *Sporting Mag.* IV. 274 Horn and corn were both up at a pretty vitty price.

b. **1664** H. MORE *Myst. Iniq.* 548 There is not any one horn or hoof of Anti-christianism left in our Church.

c. **1276** *Const. Rob. Dunelm.* in Spelman *Gloss.* (1626) s.v., Licet in vicinis parochijs, Horne with horne, secundum Anglicam linguam pascua quærant. **1490** in *Trans. Durh. Archæol. Soc.* IV. 294 He saith that all way the Priours bestes and the tenantes bestes went all, horne with horne. **1809** TOMLINS *Law Dict.* s.v., The commoning of cattle horn with horn, was properly when the inhabitants of several parishes let their common herds run upon the same open spacious common.

d. **1890** BOLDREWOOD *Col. Reformer* (1891) 219 The cattle were.. mostly old savage devils, all horn and hide.

e. **1847–78** HALLIWELL s.v., *In a horn when the devil is blind*, spoken ironically of a thing never likely to happen. *Devon.* **1858** *Washington Even. Star* 26 Aug. (Bartlett), I have mentioned before the innumerable comforts—in a horn—of the old White Sulphur Springs.

f. **1605** CHAPMAN, etc. *Eastw. Ho* I. i, You all know the deuise of the Horne, where the young fellow slippes in at the Butte end, and comes squesd out at the Buckall. **1624** FLETCHER *Wife for Month* III. iii, The prodigal fool.. That was squeezed through a horn. **1847** PORTER *Big Ben* etc. 37 (Farmer) How did you make it? You didn't come out at the little end of the horn, did you?

g. **1560** DAUS tr. *Sleidane's Comm.* 358 To geue God thankes yᵗ sent shrewed cowes short hornes. *a* **1640** DAY *Peregr. Schol.* (1881) 43 A Butcher.. sweares by the horne and the hoofe (a poore othe, yet proper enough to the trade). **1660** HOWELL *Prov.* 16 You will make a horn as soon of an Ape's tail. **1869** HAZLITT *Eng. Prov.* 208 Horns and grey hairs do not come by years.

3. a. Each of the two branched appendages on the head of a deer.

(These differ from a true horn in being osseous, deciduous, and (usually) borne only by the male.)

Beowulf (Z.) 1370 Heorot hornum trum. *c* **1000** *Sax. Leechd.* I. 334 Wiþ heafod sare, heortes hornes axan.. drinc. *c* **1290** *S. Eng. Leg.* I. 393/19 Ane heort.. Bi-twene is hornes he i-saiȝh ane croiz schine briȝhte. *c* **1386** CHAUCER *Frankl. T.* 463 Ther saugh he hertes with hir hornes hye. **1486** *Bk. St. Albans* E j b, The hornys that he then berith a bowte. **1607** TOPSELL *Four-f. Beasts* (1658) 98 Every year in the month of April, they [harts] loose their horns.. Their new horns come forth like bunches at the first. **1870** BLAINE *Encycl. Rur. Sports* (ed. 3) §1797 April is the most usual month for the shedding of the horns of the older deer.

b. Each of the erect and permanent bony processes, covered with hairy skin, growing on the head of a giraffe; also applied to a smaller protuberance in front of the other two.

[**1598** [implied by quot. s.v. GIRAFFE 1].] **1753** *Chamber's Cycl.* Suppl. s.v. *Zurnapa*, Its head is wholly of the make of the stag's, but differs in size, and has two little obtuse horns, which are not more than six fingers breadth long, and are hairy. **1840** tr. *Cuvier's Anim. Kingdom* 138 The Giraffe.. is characterized by conical horns in both sexes, that are always covered with a hairy skin, and never fall... In the middle of the forehead, there is an eminence or third horn, broader and much shorter, but equally articulated by suture. **1879** *Encycl. Brit.* X. 619/2 In captivity it [*sc.* the giraffe] is said to make use of its skin-covered horns as weapons of defence. **1965** D. MORRIS *Mammals* 393 The Giraffe is easily the tallest of all the mammals... Both sexes have short, hair-covered horns.

4. †The tusk of an elephant (*obs.*); the tusk of a narwhal.

1607 TOPSELL *Four-f. Beasts* (1658) 165 That there was nothing in an Elephant good for meat, except the trunck, the lips, and the marrow of his horns, or teeth. **1611** BIBLE *Ezek.* xxvii. 15 They brought thee for a present, hornes of Iuorie, and Ebenie. **1613** PURCHAS *Pilgrimage* (1614) 739 They found a great dead Fish.. twelve foote long, having a Horne of two yardes.. growing out of the Snout, wreathed and straight, like a Wax Taper. **1847** CARPENTER *Zool.* §212 The Monodon, or Narwhal, commonly known as the Sea Unicorn.. has been known to drive its horn, or rather tusk, deep into the thick oak timbers of a ship.

5. a. A projection or process on the head of other animals: e.g. the excrescence on the beak of the HORNBILL, the antennæ or feelers of insects and crustaceans, the tentacles of gastropods, esp. of the snail and slug; also, loosely, a crest of feathers, a plumicorn, as in the horned owl, etc. Also jocularly, the human nose (*slang*).

1340 *Ayenb.* 32 [He] þet ne dar naȝt guo ine þe peþe uor þane snegge þet sseaweþ him his hornes. **1398** TREVISA *Barth. De P.R.* XVIII. i. (Bodl. MS.), Snailes haue certayne hornes nasche and gleymyer, but þei beþ nouȝt proprelich hornes but þinges ȝeue to snailes for helpe and socoure. **1588** SHAKS. *L.L.L.* IV. iii. 338 The tender hornes of Cockled Snayles. **1657** R. LIGON *Barbadoes* (1673) 63 Flyes.. (from two inches long with the great horns, which we keep in boxes, and are shewed by John Tredescan amongst his rarities). **1665** HOOKE *Microgr.* 194 Resembling the long horns of Lobsters. **1774** GOLDSM. *Nat. Hist.* (1776) V. 236 It [the Hornbill] has a kind of horn standing out from the top, which looks somewhat like a second bill. **1834** MEDWIN *Angler in Wales* II. 47 The beetle being somewhat restless, they pinioned down his horns.. to the ground. **1893** FARMER & HENLEY *Slang* III. 351/1 *Horn*, the nose. **1935** ERSINE *Underworld & Prison Slang* 45 *Horn*, a man's nose, *bugle*. **1945** L. SHELLY *Jive Talk Dict.* 12/2 *Horn*, the nose.

b. ***to draw in*** (†***shrink, pluck, pull in***) ***one's horns***: to restrain one's ardour; to repress one's pride; to lower one's pretensions: in allusion to the snail's habit of drawing in its retractile tentacles (which bear the eyes), when disturbed. Also, to restrict one's expenditure, esp. of money.

13.. *Coer de L.* 3835 They.. gunne to drawen in her hornes, As a snayl among the thornes. **1430–40** LYDG. *Bochas* I. xx. (Bodl. MS.) lf. 83/1 Who is knowe ontrewe.. Shrynkith his hornis whan men speake of falsheede. *c* **1566** J. ALDAY tr. *Boaystuau's Theat. World* N iv b, As soone as man thinketh to spread out his horns, or rise against his god. **1589** *Hay any Work* 38 Mark how I haue made the bishops to pull in their hornes. **1678** WOOD *Life* (O.H.S.) II. 414 When the parliament was prorogued he plucked in his horne. **1741** RICHARDSON *Pamela* (1883) I. 115 So I began to pull in my horns, as they say. **1824** *Examiner* 434/1 We are to creep into our shells and draw in our horns. **1891** *Sat. Rev.* 19 Dec. 682/2 They are imploring the Council to draw in its horns. **1920** GALSWORTHY *In Chancery* I. i. 7 In the meantime, no more children! Even young Nicholas was drawing in his horns, and had made no addition to his six for quite three years. **1941** A. L. ROWSE *Tudor Cornwall* xiv. 363 His will was a very cautious affair: he had to draw in his horns. **1957** I. MURDOCH *Sandcastle* i. 16 If we don't get some extra money from somewhere we shall have to draw our horns in pretty sharply. No more Continental holidays, you know.

c. An erect penis; an erection. Also in phr. ***to have*** (***get***) ***the horn***, to be sexually excited. (Not in polite use.)

1785 GROSE *Dict. Vulgar T.*, *Horn Cholick*, a temporary priapism. **1879–80** *Pearl* (1970) 257 A man with light trousers, of decency shorn, Stop and talk to young ladies while having the horn. **1889** BARRÈRE & LELAND *Dict. Slang* I. 475/2 'To have the *horn*', to be in a state of sexual desire. **1922** JOYCE *Ulysses* 263 Got the horn or what? he said. **1968** J. R. ACKERLEY *My Father & Myself* xiii. 148 He remarked to me then with a chuckle that the thing that had worried him most was that he might not be able to 'get the horn' again. **1968** L. BERG *Risinghill* 121 'Why does a boy get the "horn"?' 'The "horn" or the erection of the penis is necessary to make sure that the sperm is placed well inside the body of the woman.' **1972** *Guardian* 3 Apr. 11/3 Dirty old goat... He only bows his head to get his horn up.

6. a. Horns (like those of quadrupeds) have been attributed to deities, demons, to Moses, etc., and are represented in images, pictures, etc. Cf. sense 16.

a **1400–50** *Alexander* 319 þis myȝty god.. How he is merkid & made is mervaile to neuyn With.. twa tufe hornes. *c* **1590** MARLOWE *Faust.* iv. 58 All he-devils has horns. **1603** SHAKS. *Meas. for M.* II. iv. 16 Let's write good Angell on the Deuills horne. *a* **1822** SHELLEY *Devil* II. 3 His horns were concealed by a *Bras Chapeau*. **1832** GEN. P. THOMPSON *Exerc.* (1842) II. 64 Horns and a tail would not be more decisive to a frightened child at midnight. **1895** ELWORTHY *Evil Eye* vi. 186 *note*, The belief that Moses had actual solid horns must have been firmly held in the Middle Ages. *Ibid.* 197 From Tahiti was exhibited an idol, with two large horns on its head carved in wood.

b. ***horns of consecration***: in Mycenæan art, a pictorial symbol or object, often found together with the double axe and pillar, connected with the Cretan worship of the ox.

1901 A. J. EVANS in *Jrnl. Hellenic Studies* XXI. 196 The columns of the Knossian shrine apparently approach the outer edge of the openings, leaving room, however, in front of them for the 'horns of consecration'. **1939** V. G. CHILDE *Dawn Europ. Civilization* (ed. 3) v. 73 The cult of the Mother Goddess, associated, as in Crete, with the symbols of the dove, the double-axe, the sacred pillar and horns of consecration. **1939** J. D. S. PENDLEBURY *Archæol. Crete* v. 274 The double axe itself is found as a votive offering and as a cult object between the horns of consecration. **1970** BRAY & TRUMP *Dict. Archaeol.* 149/2 Minoan religion is somewhat obscure, but includes a Mother Goddess who was worshipped in many shrines equipped with figurines.. the sacred double axe and horns of consecration.

7. a. Cuckolds were fancifully said to wear horns on the brow. ***to give horns to, to graft, plant horns on***: to cuckold.

[The origin of this, which appears in so many European langs., and, seemingly, even in late Gr. in phrase *κέρατα ποιεῖν τινί* (Artemidorus, *Oneirocritica* II. 12) is referred by Dunger (*Germania* XXIX. 59) to the practice formerly prevalent of planting or engrafting the spurs of a castrated cock on the root of the excised comb, where they grew and became horns, sometimes of several inches long. He shows that Ger. *hahnreh* or *hahnrei* 'cuckold', originally meant 'capon'.]

1430–40 LYDG. *Bochas* II. xxiii. (Bodl. MS.) lf. 128/1 A certeyn knyht Giges callid.. To speke pleyn inglissh made hym a cokold. Alas I was nat auysid weel beforne On-cunnyngli to speke such language; I sholde ha said how that he hadde an horn.. As in sum land Cornodo men them call. *c* **1530** *Hickscorner* in Hazl. *Dodsley* I. 180 My mother was a lady of the stews' blood born, And.. my father ware an horn. *c* **1537** *Thersites* Ibid. 412. **1594** GREENE & LODGE *Looking Glasse* (1598) H ij a, Nay, sir, he was a cuckoldly diuell, for hee had hornes on his head. **1599** SHAKS. *Much Ado* II. i. 28. **1600** —— *A.Y.L.* IV. ii. 18. **1606** —— *Ant. & Cl.* I. ii. 4 Oh that I knewe this Husband, which you say, must change his Hornes with Garlands. **1700** DRYDEN *Epil.* 25 Mar. 10 London a fruitful soil, yet never bore So plentiful a crop of horns before. **1728** YOUNG *Love Fame* I. 70 And the brib'd cuckold.. glories in his gilded horn. *a* **1796** BURNS *Cooper o' Cuddie* iii, On ilka brow she's planted a horn. **1822** SCOTT *Nigel* xxxvi, O what a generous creature is your true London husband! Horns hath he, but.. he goreth not. **1942** D. POWELL *Time to be Born* (1943) i. 24 Julian was almost pathologically jealous of her, fearing the final indignity of horns.

†**b.** ***to make horns at*** [F. *faire les cornes à*, It. *far le corna a*]: to hold the fist with two fingers extended like a pair of horns, as an insulting gesture.

[Cf. *c* **1530** *Crt. Love* 1390 This folissh dove will give us all an horn!] **1607** DEKKER & WEBSTER *Northw. Ho* I. D.'s Wks. 1873 III. 9 If a man be deuorst..whether may he haue an action or no, gainst those that make horns at him? **1627** DRAYTON *Agincourt* etc. 174 Some made mouthes at him, others as in scorne With their forkt fingers poynted him the horne. **1652** PEYTON *Catastr. Stuarts* (1731) 30 Denmark was so disquised, as he would have lain with the Countess of Nottingham, making Horns in Derision at her Husband the High Admiral of England.

8. In Biblical and derived uses: An emblem of power and might; a means of defence or resistance; hence ***horn of salvation*** (†***health***) is used of God or Christ. ***to lift up the horn***: to exalt oneself; to offer resistance, 'show fight'.

[Representing well-known uses of Heb. *qeren* horn, found also in Syriac, Arabic, and the Semitic langs. generally. Through the Septuagint and Vulgate also in late Gr. and Lat., and so in the mod. langs.: cf. F. *lever les cornes*. (Some would explain it from sense 16.)]

c **825** *Vesp. Psalter* lxxiv. [lxxv.] 5 Nyllað uphebban horn. *a* **1300** *E.E. Psalter* xvii. 3 Mi schelder, and of min hele horne. *Ibid.* lxxiv. 11 Alle hornes of sinful breke sal I þa, And up-hoven ben hornes of rightwys ma. **1382** WYCLIF *Luke* i. 69 He haþ rerid to vs an horn of helþe, in þe hous of dauiþ his child. **1570** *Tragedie* 277 in *Satir. Poems Reform.* x. 90 Than did sum Lords lyft vp yair hornis on hie. **1611** BIBLE *2 Sam.* xxii. 3 Hee is my shield, and the horne of my saluation. **1613** PURCHAS *Pilgrimage* (1614) 632 Fleeing then to his horne or defense in time of distresse. *a* **1703** BURKITT *On N.T., Luke* i. 79 The horn in Scripture signifies glory and dignity, strength and power. **1806** WOLCOTT (P. Pindar) *Tristia* Wks. 1812 V. 341 On Homer's birth-place, proud t'exalt their horn. **1844** E. ROBINSON tr. *Gesenius' Heb. Lex.* 954 s.v. *qeren*. Metaph. *horn* is put as the symbol of strength, might, power, the image being drawn from the bull and other animals which push with their horns. **1886** MRS. LYNN LINTON *Paston Carew* xliii, Pride, when it has lowered its horn as it skirted by ruin, now raises it again as it touches success.

II. As a substance, or an article made of it.

9. The substance of which the horns of animals consist, as a material for manufacturing purposes or the like. ***gate of horn***: see GATE *sb.*[1] 5.

1545 ASCHAM *Toxoph.* II. (Arb.) 135 Many countryes bothe of olde tyme and nowe, vse heades of horne. **1575** LANEHAM *Let.* (1871) 39 Horn..a substauns..nether so churlish in weight az iz mettall..nor roough to the lips, az wood iz. **1577** HARRISON *England* II. xii. (1877) I. 236 The Saxons..did make panels of horne in steed of glasse. **1599** SHAKS. *Much Ado* V. iv. 126 There is no staff more reuerend than one tipt with horn. **1647** H. MORE *Song of Soul* II. i. II. v, A lamp arm'd with pellucid horn. **1784** COWPER *Tiroc.* 120 Neatly secur'd from being soil'd or torn Beneath a pane of thin translucent horn..'Tis called a book, though but a single page. **1843** J. A. SMITH *Product. Farming* (ed. 2) 133 Horn is a still more powerful manure than bone,—that is to say, it contains a greater proportion of organized animal matter.

10. A structure of the nature of horn; the hardened and thickened epidermis or cuticle of which hoofs, nails, corns, the callosities on the camel's legs, etc. consist. (†Formerly also = hoof.)

c **1420** *Pallad. on Husb.* IV. 815 [A stallion] With holgh horn high yshood. **1483** CAXTON *Gold. Leg.* 164b/2 He knelyd so oft in prayers that his knees were as harde as the horne of a camel. **1599** SHAKS. *Hen. V*, III. vii. 17 The basest horne of his hoofe, is more Musicall than the Pipe of Hermes. **1607** TOPSELL *Four-f. Beasts* (1658) 287 Of the horns or hard knobs growing under the Sadle side. **1763** WESLEY *Nat. Philos.* (1784) I. I. iii. §5. 159 From three years old, [she] had Horns growing on various parts of her body.. they are fastened to the skin like warts..but toward the end are much harder. **1764** CROKER, etc. *Dict. Arts & Sc.* s.v. *Tanning*, When the skin has not been kept long enough in the lime, or in the tan-pit, upon cutting it in the middle there appears a whitish streak, called the horn or crudity of the skin. **1808–18** JAMIESON, *Horn*, an excrescence on the foot, a corn. **1867** *Jrnl. R. Agric. Soc.* III. II. 446 The straw in wet weather softens the horns of sheep's feet.

11. a. An article manufactured of horn; the side of a lantern; a thimble, esp. one used by cutpurses to catch the edge of the knife in cutting the purse-strings; a horn spoon or scoop, a SHOE-HORN.

1483 *Act 1 Rich. III*, c. 12 §2 That no merchaunt Straungier..brynge into this Realme lantern hornes. *c* **1560** PRESTON *Cambyses* in Hazl. *Dodsley* IV. 235 A horn on your thumb, A quick eye, a sharp knife, at hand a receiver. **1573–80** BARET *Alv.* H637 A shooing horne, *cornu calcearium*. **1607** TOPSELL *Four-f. Beasts* (1658) 86 To make hafts for knives, or else horns for Spectacles. **1683** WILDING in *Collect.* (O.H.S.) I. 258 For a horne in my Lanterne..00 00 02. **1810** CRABBE *Borough* xviii, How she, all patient, both at eve and morn Her needle pointed at the guarding horn. **1875** KNIGHT *Dict. Mech.*, *Horn*, a spoon or scoop of horn, in which washings are tested in prospecting.

b. In *Golf*, the substance of which part of the face of a wooden club is made.

1743 T. MATHISON *Goff* I. 5 Fenc'd with horn the head. **1801** J. STRUTT *Sports & Pastimes* II. iii. 81 Goff..is performed with a bat,..the curvature is affixed to the bottom, faced with horn and backed with lead. **1839** *Chambers's Jrnl.* 22 June 173/3 The curvature, made of thorn, is affixed to the bottom, faced with horn, and backed with lead. **1890** H. G. HUTCHINSON *Golf* iii. 65 There is, however, something to be said in favour of dispensing altogether with the 'horn' in the case of brass-soled clubs.

c. ***by the*** **(*great*)** ***horn spoon***: used as a fanciful oath or formula of asseveration. *U.S.*

1842 *Amer. Nat. Song Bk.* II. 222 He vow'd by the great horn spoon..He'd give them a licking, and that pretty soon. **1848** LOWELL *Biglow P.* 1st Ser. v. 16 'I should like to shoot The holl gang, by the gret horn spoon!' sez he. **1853** *Knickerbocker* XLI. 115 'By the horn spoons!' repeated the skipper suddenly. **1897** *Outing* (U.S.) XXX. 380/2 'By the Great Horn Spoon!' the voice shouted, 'here's a chunk of civilization.' **1948** *Time* 22 Nov. 25/1 Operators had sworn by the Great Horn Spoon that they would not negotiate with Harry ('The Nose') Bridges.

III. The hollow horn of an animal (without the core) used as a vessel or a musical instrument, with senses thence developed.

12. a. A vessel formed from the horn of a cow or other beast, or in later times shaped after this, for holding liquid (as drink, oil, or ink), powder, etc.; a drinking-horn; a powder-flask; also, a similarly shaped vessel for cupping. Hence a hornful; a draught of ale or other liquor.

c **1000** *Sax. Leechd.* II. 126 Sete horn on þa openan scearpan. **1073** *Charter* in *Dipl. Angl. Ævi Sax.* (Th.) 428, II ȝebonede hnæppas, and IIII. hornas. *a* **1300** *Cursor M.* 7345 Þou fill þi horn Wit oile, and weind þe forth. *a* **1300** *K. Horn* 1153 Heo fulde hire horn wiþ wyn, And dronk to þe pilegrym. **1382** WYCLIF *1 Sam.* xvi. 13. **1398** TREVISA *Barth. De P.R.* VII. xxi. (Bodl. MS.), Men shall..souke it oute oþer drawe it oute wiþ an horne oþer a copping cuppe. **1583** HOLLYBAND *Campo di Fior* 333 Give me a penne and ink-horne. **1587** MASCALL *Govt. Cattle* (1627) 11 Giue it the beast in the morning with a horne. **1634** T. JOHNSON *Parey's Chirurg.* XII. iv. (1678) 295 Ther shall you apply Cupping-glasses, or Horns. **1682** WOOD *Life* 31 May, He went to Queen's College..and had a horne of beere. **1719** DE FOE *Crusoe* I. iv, I took out..a horn of powder. **1804** WOLCOTT (P. Pindar) *Ep. to Ld. Mayor* Wks. 1812 V. 206 My horn's last drop of ink To raise her glory, lo, I'll shed it. **1851** D. JERROLD *St. Giles* xviii. 190 Take another horn of ale. **1868** G. STEPHENS *Runic Mon.* I. 323 The Runic Horn, so rich and rare, so barbarically magnificent, altogether unique, a splendid and mystic relic.

b. ***horn of plenty*** or ***abundance*** = CORNUCOPIA.

c **1586** C'TESS PEMBROKE *Ps.* LXXIII. iii, They see Their horne of plenty freshly flowing still. **1597** SHAKS. *2 Hen. IV*, I. ii. 52 He hath the horne of Abundance. **1707** *Curios. in Husb. & Gard.* 193 Holding in his Left Hand a Reed, and in his Right a Horn of Plenty. **1851** *Illustr. Catal. Gt. Exhib.* 826 Wood-carving, consisting of..flowers and two horns of plenty. **1886** BESANT *Childr. Gibeon* II. xxviii, Nature, very oddly, when the Horn of Plenty is quite empty, always fills it with babies.

c. ***horn of plenty grass***: see quot.

1866 *Treas. Bot.* 333/1 *Cornucopia cucullata*, the Horn of Plenty grass, a native of Greece and Asia Minor..frequently cultivated in gardens amongst curious annuals.

13. a. A wind instrument more or less resembling a horn in shape, and originally formed of the horn of some beast, now made of brass or other material. Also with qualifying words, as ***bugle horn, hunting-horn, post-horn, tin horn, valve horn***, etc.

c **825** *Vesp. Psalter* lxxx. 4 [lxxxi. 3] Singað in fruman monðes horne. *a* **1000** *Laws of Wihtræd* c. 28 (Schmid) He þonne nawðer ne hryme ne he horn ne blawe. *c* **1205** LAY. 25787 Hafe mine godne horn..and blawe hine mid maine. *a* **1300** *Cursor M.* 15011 Wit harp and pipe, and horn and trump. *c* **1400** *Sowdone Bab.* 2520 Thai..blewen hornes of bras. *c* **1420** *Anturs of Arth.* xxxiv. (Thornton MS.), We hunte at the herdis with hundes and with horne. **1596** SHAKS. *Merch. V.* V. i. 47 Ther's a Post come from my Master, with his horne full of good newes. **1617** MORYSON *Itin.* III. 267 The Vrij blow a horne of a wild Hart..but those of Lucerna use a horne of brasse. **1735** SOMERVILLE *Chase* II. 186 The clanging Horns swell their sweet-winding Notes. **1794** MRS. RADCLIFFE *Myst. Udolpho* iii, The hunter's horn hung from his belt.

b. ***to wind the horn***, to blow a blast on the horn, to sound the horn; also *fig.* of insects making a piping or humming sound. ***to blow*** (U.S. ***toot***) ***one's own horn***: 'to blow one's own trumpet' (see TRUMPET *sb.* 3).

1611 HEYWOOD *Gold. Age* II. Wks. 1874 III. 32 (*Stage directions*) Hornes winded..Winde hornes. **1617** MORYSON *Itin.* I. 7 Neither may the Citizens..winde a Horne in their night watches. **1637** MILTON *Lycidas* 28 What time the grey-fly winds her sultry horn. **1746** COLLINS *Odes, To Evening* iii, Or where the beetle winds His small but sullen horn. **1783–94** BLAKE *Songs Innoc., School-Boy* 3 The distant huntsman winds his horn. **1810** SCOTT *Lady of L.* I. xvii, But scarce again his horn he wound. **1859** 'MARK TWAIN' *Lett.* (1917) I. 43 Permit me to 'blow my horn'. **1860** G. D. PRENTICE *Prenticeana* 63 'Blowing your own *horn* I see,' said his comrade. **1903** A. W. PATTERSON *Schumann* 167 Surely these side-lights upon the straightforwardness and integrity of the man entirely free him from the calumny of ever being guilty of 'blowing his own horn'. **1940** A. E. HERTZLER *Doctor & his Patients* (1941) ii. 47 He that tooteth not his own horn, the same shall not be tooted. **1949** E. S. GARDNER *Case of Half-Wakened Wife* ii. 9 Gregory, on the other hand, had been reticent, inarticulate, sensitive, a man who modestly refrained from tooting his own horn and didn't like to hear others talk about themselves.

c. (More fully ***French horn***) An orchestral wind instrument of the trumpet class, developed from the hunting-horn, and consisting of a continuous tube some 17 feet in length, curved for convenience in holding, and having a wide bell and a conoidal mouthpiece.

1682 *Loyal Protestant & Domestick Intelligencer* 7 Mar. [2]/2 (Advt.), Any Gentleman may be furnished with Trumpets, French horns, Speaking Trumpets. **1742** POPE *Dunc.* IV. 278 The voice was drown'd By the French horn, or by the op'ning hound. **1753** *Scots Mag.* Sept. 427/1 A band of French horns. **1771** C. BURNEY *Pres. St. Mus.* 149 There were two organs, and two pair of French horns. **1856** MRS. C. CLARKE tr. *Berlioz' Instrument.* 129 All horns with the exception of the horn in C, are transposing instruments. **1879** W. H. STONE in Grove *Dict. Mus.* I. 748/1 The hunting horn finally adopted differs from the orchestral horn in consisting of an unbroken spiral of three turns, sufficiently large to be worn obliquely round the body, resting on one shoulder and passing under the opposite arm. *Ibid.* 748/2 The introduction of the Horn into the orchestra is attributed to Gossec. **1961** R. M. PEGGE in A. Baines *Mus. Instruments* xii. 297 In England [*sc.* in the 18th cent.]..the French horn was chiefly used for the purposes of entertainment in the pleasure gardens and on the river, two performers playing duets being the usual thing. Rich men of family and fashion sometimes included in their retinues French horn players, often Negroes, to add *panache* to their equipages.

d. ***English horn*** (Fr. *cor anglais*), a wind instrument of the oboe kind: see quots.

1838 *Penny Cycl.* XII. 292/2 The *English Horn*, or *Corno Inglese*, is a deeper-toned oboe, but of rather larger dimensions, somewhat bent, the lower end very open. **1879** W. H. STONE in Grove *Dict. Mus.* I. 488/2 *English horn*, the tenor oboe in F, intermediate between the ordinary oboe and the bassoon.

e. An 8-foot reed-stop on an organ.

1722–4 *Specif. Organ St. Dionis Backchurch* in Grove *Dict. Mus.* II. 596 Great Organ..10. Trumpet. 11. French Horn to tenor D. ['It appears to have been the earliest organ to contain a "French Horn" stop.'] **1834** *Specif. Organ York Minster* Ibid. 600 Swell Organ..42. Horn. 43. Trumpet.

f. An instrument attached to motor vehicles, etc., which is sounded as a warning signal. Also *attrib.*

1901 *Graphic* LXIV. 268/3 The hideous toot-toot of its horn. **1914** R. & E. SHACKLETON *Four on Tour in Eng.* 83 The horn was honked suddenly. **1939** H. HODGE *Cab, Sir?* 19 And plenty of hornwork. The more the toots the bigger the tip. **1965** *New Statesman* 22 Oct. 594/2 The car..is taking over this enchanting city [*sc.* Rome]... The official campaign to cut down horn-maniacs appears to be a total failure. **1969** *Highway Code* 49 You must not..sound your horn at night (11.30 p.m.–7 a.m.) in a built-up area. **1973** *Sat. Rev. Soc.* (U.S.) May 42 Horn alarms: many inexpensive devices that can be hooked into the automobile horn can now be bought for less than $10.

g. A horn-shaped pastry case; an ice-cream cornet.

1908, 1960 [see *cream horn*, CREAM *sb.*[1] 7]. **1927** 'R. CROMPTON' *William—in Trouble* viii. 202 In one hand it held a stick of rock; in the other an ice cream horn. It licked them alternately. **1933** —— *William—the Rebel* xi. 212, I c'n eat twenty ice-cream horns. **1951** *Good Housek. Home Encycl.* 426/1 For savoury horns use a mixture such as those suggested for bouchées. **1969** *Main Cookery Bk.* (ed. 14) 172 Pastry horns can only be made using a special cone-shaped pastry case.

h. *Jazz slang.* A trumpet.

1935 *Hot News* May 5/1 He just threw his horn away and went into a pawnshop and bought another. **1938** D. BAKER *Young Man with Horn* 9 And then he learned to play a horn—a trumpet, if there's anybody here who doesn't know what kind of a horn a horn is—and that was his proper medium. **1955** R. DAVIS in A. J. McCarthy *Jazzbook 1955* 40 Bunk was the subject of articles in the *New York Herald-Tribune* and the magazine *Time*, in which he was somewhat superlatively described as 'genius of the horn'. **1959** G. AVAKIAN in M. T. Williams *Art of Jazz* (1960) 68 Each of these trio cuttings ends with Bix picking up his horn to play the coda.

i. *Jazz slang.* Any kind of wind instrument.

1937 *Metronome* Jan. 25/1 Satchmo, I was only kiddin'. I'll give you your horn back. **1938** [see prec.]. **1966** *Melody Maker* 30 July 8/3 Every instrument became a horn. When a guy said 'Can I bring my horn for a sit in,' you never knew whether he'd show up with a goofus or a glockenspiel. **1966** *Crescendo* Aug. 21/2 If I'm happy with the horn I've got, the mouthpiece, the set-up, the reed and everything.

j. The player of a horn (sense 13c, h and i).

1945 L. SHELLY *Jive Talk Dict.* 35 *The Horn*, the famous trumpeter. **1947** R. DE TOLEDANO *Frontiers of Jazz* p. ix, Did you ever try to relax while some fine horns were blowing, like for instance, Maxey, Pee Wee, and Bird? **1955** KEEPNEWS & GRAUER *Pict. Hist. Jazz* i. 14 Freddie Keppard was among the very great New Orleans horns. **1955** S. WHITMORE *Solo* iv. 52 Take Buddy Bolden, if you will. A great horn. **1968** *Globe & Mail* (Toronto) 17 Feb. 26 'We've been lucky,' Harry Freedman, English horn, said. 'Ozawa has..done much to build up the orchestra.'

k. ***the horn***: the telephone. *U.S. colloq.*

1945 L. SHELLY *Jive Talk Dict.* 31/1 *On the horn*, telephoning. **1962** [see FLAT *adv.* 3b]. **1967** D. C. COOKE *c/o American Embassy* (1968) xi. 104 I've been on the horn half the night trying to get you. **1970** C. ARMSTRONG *Protégé* vii. 89 I'll have to get on the horn tomorrow and poke up my contacts.

14. a. The wind instrument as used in forms of legal process; e.g. in the Scotch ceremony of proclaiming an outlaw, when three blasts were blown on a horn by the king's messenger; hence ***to put*** (***denounce***) ***to the horn***, to proclaim an outlaw, to outlaw; † ***to be at the horn***, to be out of the protection of the law, proclaimed an outlaw.

1397 *Sc. Acts Rob. III* (1844) I. 574/1 [red] Qwhasa cumys nocht within þe said terme sal be at þe kyngis horne and þair landis and gudis eschete. **1432** *Sc. Acts Jas. I*, c. 11 (1814) II. 22/1 Ilk officiar of þe kingis as mare or kingis seriande.. sal nocht pass in þe cuntre na þe baroun seriande in þe barony but a horne and his wande. **1536** BELLENDEN *Cron. Scot.* XII. vi. (Jam.), Makbeth..syne confiscat Makduffis guddis, & put him to the horn. **1567** *Gude & Godlie B.* (S.T.S.) 76 For ȝe war all at Goddis horne. **1609** SKENE *Reg.*

Maj. IV. xxiii. §2 (Jam.) Gif ane man findes ane theif with the fang..in-continent he sould raise the blast of ane horne vpon him; and gif he hes not ane horne, he sould raise the shout with his mouth; and cry lowdly that his neighbours may heare. *c*1610 SIR J. MELVIL *Mem.* (1735) 397 Such as were denounced to the Horn. *a*1765 ERSKINE *Inst. Law Scot.* II. v. §56 (1773) 236 The messenger must..read the letters, also with an audible voice, and afterwards blow three blasts with an horn; by which the debtor is understood to be proclaimed rebel to the King... Hence the letters of diligence are called *letters of horning*, and the debtor is said to be denounced at the horn. 1895 CROCKETT *Men of Moss-Hags* 121 Both of us were put to the horn and declared outlaw.

†**b.** = HORNING *sb.* 4. *Obs. rare.*

1491 *Acta Dom. Conc.* 205 (Jam.) The lordis prolongis the execucioun of the horne in the meyntime. *a*1670 SPALDING *Troub. Chas. I* (1829) 31 He compears before the council, and upon his compearance he is released from the horn.

15. a. A trumpet- or cone-shaped accessory of early gramophones and phonographs that collects sound to be recorded and amplifies the sound reproduced; a similar structure in some kinds of loud-speaker that contains the diaphragm in its throat and is designed to transmit its vibrations to the air. Also *attrib.*

1897 *Sears, Roebuck Catal.* 485/2 The Graphophone or Talking Machine is a most wonderful invention... By using the horn they can be distinctly heard in every part of a large hall. 1904 S. R. BOTTONE *Talking Machines* 62 The horn or trumpet which collects the sounds should be of *papier mâché*, and not of metal. 1911 *Encycl. Brit.* XXI. 468/2 The person making the record sings or plays in front of a horn or funnel. 1927 *Wireless World* 16 Nov. 664 When broadcasting first started, the only type of loudspeaker on the market was one which had..a straight conical horn. 1931 B. BROWN *Talking Pictures* v. 121 Some of the first horns to be used in sound pictures were of the straight trumpet type. 1934 C. LAMBERT *Music Ho!* iv. 257 The old pre-electric horn recording, with its euphoniums instead of 'cellos, and its handful of Stroh violins. 1946 T. RATTIGAN *Winslow Boy* I. 12 He points to a gramophone—1912 model, with horn—lying on a table. 1956 C. FOWLER *High Fidelity* vi. 103 Most tweeters used in high-fidelity systems employ small diaphragms which work into a horn of some sort. 1957 L. DURRELL *Justine* II. 141 The same night, on the old horn gramophone..I heard some amateur's recording. 1969 *Listener* 23 Jan. 121/3 A pre-electric horn gramophone. 1970 R. D. FORD *Introd. Acoustics* v. 98 Horns are also very useful for improving the performance of loudspeakers at low frequencies.

b. *Radio.* Any hollow waveguide that increases in one or both transverse dimensions towards the open end and can consequently act as a transmitting or receiving aerial. Also *attrib.*, as ***horn aerial, antenna.***

1936 W. L. BARROW in *Proc. Inst. Radio Engin.* XXIV. 1328 [The pipe can be flared into a horn-shaped radiator]. *Ibid.*, The application of horn radiators is not confined to the hollow tube system, for they may be fed by a coaxial or other lines... Thus, electromagnetic horns may be used as radiators in the wave band below ten meters. 1939 *Ibid.* XXVII. 51 The operation of the electromagnetic horn 'antenna'. 1949 H. E. PENROSE *Princ. & Pract. Radar* xxii. 511 In general, the longer the opening of the horn, the more directive is the resulting field pattern. 1961 H. JASIK *Antenna Engin. Handbk.* x. 7 The pyramidal horn is frequently used as a standard horn of known gain in making measurements of other antennas. 1961 MICZAIKA & SINTON *Tools of Astronomer* viii. 261 Often a parabola is fed by a wave guide that terminates in a horn aimed at the disk. 1962 [see ANTENNA 5]. 1970 [see DESPIN *v.*]. 1972 *Daily Tel.* 28 June 11/8 Mounted inconspicuously in its front grille were two four-inch-square radar 'horns'—one for transmitting, the other for receiving.

IV. A horn-shaped or horn-like projection; one of two or more such; a corner, an angle.

16. A horn-like appendage or ornament worn on the head. (Cf. sense 6.)

Actual horns or antlers of beasts have been and are sometimes worn by savages; horns of metal have been from time immemorial worn by women in some eastern countries; the name was also given to part or the whole of head-dresses worn in England, and to forms in which the hair was done up in the 14th and 15th c.

1340 *Ayenb.* 176 Þo þet makeþ zuo greate hornes of hare here oþer of oþren þet hi semble þ wel fole wyfmen. *a*1450 *Knt. de la Tour* (1868) 62 Ladyes and gentilwomen, that were merveilously arraied..and hadde highe hornes. 1605 CAMDEN *Rem.* (1870) 214 Queen Anne, wife to King Richard the second..brought in high head attire piked with horns. 1613 PURCHAS *Pilgrimage* (1614) 536 About her forehead a haire-lace with two horns... The horned Beldame still muttereth certaine wordes. 1617 MORYSON *Itin.* III. 169 A hoyke or vaile which..hath a kinde of horne rising over the forehead. *Ibid.* 172 Women of Venice..raise up their hair on the forehead in two knotted hornes. 1859 THOMSON *Land & Bk.* I. vi. (1872) 74 The princesses of Lebanon and Hermon sported gold horns, decked with jewels. 1864 *Kitto's Cycl. Bibl. Lit.* s.v., The women among the Druses on Mount Lebanon wear on their heads silver horns of native make which are the distinguishing badge of wifehood.

17. A projection, like a horn, at each corner of the altar in the Jewish temple; one of the two outer corners of the altar in some churches.

*c*1000 *Ags. Ps.* (Spelm.) cxvii[i]. 27 Oð horn wibedes [*Thorpe* oð wiȝ-bedes..hornas]. *a*1300 *E.E. Psalter* ibid. Settes miri daie in thicknesse, Unto horn þat of weved esse. 1382 WYCLIF *1 Kings* i. 51 Adonyas dredynge kyng Salomon, holdith the horn of the auter. 1611 BIBLE *Exod.* xxvii. 2 Thou shalt make an Altar of Shittim wood..And thou shalt make the hornes of it vpon the foure corners thereof. 1816 KEATINGE *Trav.* (1817) I. 49 Delinquency, a garrison qualification, first clings to the horns of the altar. 1877 J. D. CHAMBERS *Div. Worship* 196 At the right horn of the Altar.

18. a. Each of the pointed extremities of the moon as she appears in her first and last quarters (or of Mercury or Venus in a similar phase); each end of a crescent; a cusp.

*a*1000 *Riddles* xxx. (Gr.), Ic wiht ȝeseah..hornum bitweonum huðe lædan. *c*1400 *Rom. Rose* 5340 The shadowe maketh her bemis merke, And hir hornes to shewe derke. 1617 MORYSON *Itin.* I. 5 The Idol Isis, bearing two hornes of the Moone. *Ibid.* 27 This City is of the forme of an half Moone..and..imbraceth betweene the two hornes the lesser City. 1667 MILTON *P.L.* x. 433 From the hornes Of Turkish Crescent. 1726–46 THOMSON *Winter* 125 The moon Wears a wan circle round her blunted horns. 1813 SCOTT *Trierm.* III. xi, Till..The moon renew'd her silver horn. 1816 PLAYFAIR *Nat. Phil.* II. 179 Certain periodical inequalities, observed in the Horns of the disk [of Mercury], seem to indicate a revolution on an axis. 1869 HUXLEY *Physiol.* xi. 286 This grey substance [of the spinal cord] is so disposed that..it looks something like a crescent... The two ends of the crescent are called its *horns* or *cornua.*

b. Each tip or end of a bow.

1611 COTGR. s.v. *Cornette, Les cornettes d'un arc*, the hornes, or hornie tips of a long Bow. 1697 DRYDEN *Virg. Georg.* I. 524 At either Horn the Rainbow drinks the Flood. —— *Æneid* IX. 854 He drew, And almost join'd the horns of the tough yew. 1772 COOK *1st Voy.* I. vii, The island was shaped exactly like a bow..The horns, or extremities of the bow, were two large tufts of cocoa-nut-trees. 1879 E. ARNOLD *Lt. Asia* 34 Drew the twisted string Till the horns kissed.

19. Each of the two wings of an army; = L. *cornu.*

1533 BELLENDEN *Livy* v. (1822) 457 The left horne of Romanis..fled to the brayis of Tiber. 1598 BARRET *Theor. Warres* III. ii. 70 Seruing for hornes or wings vnto the battell. 1636 E. DACRES tr. *Machiavel's Disc. Livy* II. 520 Quintius seeing one of the hornes of his Army beginning to fayle. 1834 MEDWIN *Angler in Wales* I. 106 [I] perceived the two horns, or wings, of the troop, making..to outflank, and then enclose us.

20. Each of two (or more) lateral projections, arms, or branches.

a. The two arms of a cross (late L. *cornua crucis*). **b.** The two projecting divisions of the uterus (*cornua uteri*). Also, any cornu. **c.** The branches of a river or estuary, the narrow arms of a bay (L. *cornua*).

a. *a* 13.. *Minor Poems fr. Vernon MS.* xxiii. 621 *In crucis cornibus a iudeis tentum*..þat on þe hornes of þe Croys Iewes helden wiþ-outen les. 1814 CARY *Dante, Paradise* XVIII. 30 On the horns..of the cross.

b. 1597 A. M. tr. *Guillemeau's Fr. Chirurg.* Q b/2 The Testicles or Hornes of the Wombe. 1802 C. BELL *Anat. Brain* 15 The Choroid Plexus..will be seen sinking backwards into the great inferior horn of the Ventricle. 1889 J. M. DUNCAN *Lect. Dis. Wom.* viii. (ed. 4) 43 The fœtus developed in a uterine horn. 1901 J. BERRY *Dis. Thyroid Gland* i. 6 Small portions of the larynx and pharynx are embraced by the upper horns [of the thyroid]. 1957 R. T. WOODBURNE *Essent. Human Anat.* iv. 300/1 The coccygeal horns..articulate with the horns of the sacrum and enclose the fifth sacral intervertebral foramen. 1972 *Nature* 22 Oct. 521/1 In the spinal cord..the motoneurones of the ventral horn..are subject to a variety of inhibitory influences.

c. 1697 DRYDEN *Virg. Georg.* IV. 409 With sev'n-fold Horns mysterious Nile Surrounds the Skirts of Egypt's fruitful Isle. 1840 E. FITZGERALD *Lett.* (1889) I. 61, I remember a ravine on the horn of the bay opposite the town where the sea rushes up. 1870 MORRIS *Earthly Par.* I. I. 50 Within the long horns of a sandy bay.

21. *pl.* **a.** The awns of barley. *dial.* **b.** *fig.* Rigid branches of leafless trees.

a. *a*1825 FORBY *Voc. E. Anglia, Horns*, the awns of barley. 1851 *Illustr. Catal. Gt. Exhib.* 386 A barley aveller..for..rubbing the horns or avels off barley. 1893 *Jrnl. R. Agric. Soc.* Dec. 696 The Himalayan barley which has three short horns to the flowering glume.

b. 1850 TENNYSON *In Mem.* cvii, The wood which grides and clangs Its leafless ribs and iron horns.

22. A pointed or tapering projection.

a. The beak of an ancient galley (*obs.*); of an anvil; the end of an ancient roll of bread: cf. Ger. *horn*, It. *cornuto* 'a kind of loafes or simnell bread cornered'.

*c*1205 LAY. 4538 Scip ærne to ȝen scip..horn a-ȝen horne. *c*1300 *Havelok* 779 For hom he brouthe fele siþe Wastels, simenels with þe horn. 1826 SCOTT *Diary* 10 Feb. in *Lockhart*, When I was a young man, I was able at times to lift a smith's anvil with one hand, by what is called the 'horn'.

b. Name of the projections or crutches on a side-saddle, which support or are grasped between the rider's knees; also the high pommel of a Spanish or half-Spanish saddle.

1849 F. PARKMAN *Calif. & Oregon Trail* iv. 41 My long heavy rifle encumbered me, and the low sound it made striking the horn of my saddle startled him. *a*1861 T. WINTHROP *Canoe & Saddle* (1862) 212, I threw Klale's bridle over his neck, and grasping the horn, swung myself into the saddle. 1947 *Harper's Mag.* July 42/1 He took off his battered gray hat and rested it on the horn of his saddle.

c. A piece of land projecting into the sea, etc.; a promontory.

1601 HOLLAND *Pliny* I. 135 Media..casting forth a crooked and winding horne as it were toward the West, seemeth to enclose within that compasse both the said realmes. 1612 DRAYTON *Poly-olb.* i. 505 The conquering Brute, on Corineus braue This horne of land [Cornwall] bestow'd. 1865 *Athenæum* No. 1947. 225/1 The extreme western horn of Brittany.

d. A mountain peak (sometimes *fig.*, sometimes = Swiss-Ger. *horn*).

1820 KEATS *Hyper.* II. 12 Rocks that..Forehead to forehead held their monstrous horns. 1846 MISS COSTELLO *Tour to & fr. Venice* 389 Strange-pointed rocks, piercing the skies, the *horns* of the dolomite mountains. 1861 SYMONDS in *Biog.* (1895) I. 156 The Bernese Alps..and their snow-capped horns. 1886 *Pall Mall G.* 4 Sept. 5/1 The highest point of the Cuchullins is Scuir Dearg, the 'Red Peak', a square-shaped mountain, topped with a strange-looking horn of rock.

e. A part of a plant shaped like a horn, beak, or spur.

1776 WITHERING *Brit. Plants* (1796) II. 434 Capsule when ripe lengthened out into a straight horn. 1804 in Charl. Smith *Convers.* I. 40 The woodbine's honied horn. 1819 *Pantologia, Horn* or Spur in Botany..The hinder hollow part of the nectary in some flowers, extended in a conical form: as in Orchis, Larkspur, etc.

f. The minute apex of a Hebrew letter, as at the top of ל or ר.

1879 FARRAR *St. Paul* ix. (1883) 103 They remembered what He had said about the permanence of every *yod* and horn of a letter in the Law.

g. *Electr.* Either of the pointed projections at the edge of a pole-piece of an electric motor or generator.

1886 S. P. THOMPSON *Dyn.-Electr. Machinery* (ed. 2) v. 88 The greatest amount of such eddy-currents will be generated..where the magnetic perturbations are greatest and most sudden... This should be at the leading corner or 'horn' of the pole-piece of the generating dynamo. 1923 A. S. LANGSDORF *Princ. Direct-Current Machines* (ed. 3) ii. 91 Increased area is secured by means of pole shoes bolted or dove-tailed to the core in the case of solid poles, or by means of projecting tips or horns punched integrally with the sheets composing a laminated pole.

h. *Aeronaut.* (i) A short lug or lever projecting from a control surface to which the wire for moving the surface is attached.

1920 H. WOODHOUSE *Textbk. Appl. Aeronaut. Engin.* 319/2 *Horn-control arm*, an arm at right angles to a control surface to which a control cable is attached, for example, aileron horn, rudder horn, elevator horn, etc. More commonly called a Mast. 1928 CHATFIELD & TAYLOR *Airplane* v. 75 The cables from the horns on the ailerons are led to the stick. 1952 A. Y. BRAMBLE *Air-Plane Flight* vii. 101 Notice the curved projecting pieces above and below on each aileron. These are called 'horns', and from these we see wires running forward into holes in the wing.

(ii) A part of an aileron or other control surface that extends across the axis of rotation over part of its length and serves to improve the balance of the surface; so ***horn balance, -balanced*** adj.

1921 *Aeronaut. Jrnl.* XXV. 539 The most common method of balancing ailerons is to have a 'horn' or projection on the aileron beyond the wing tip and forward of the aileron hinge. *Ibid.* 554 The horn method of balancing elevators. 1922 *Encycl. Brit.* XXX. 23/2 This so-called 'horn' balance proved unsatisfactory. 1939 *Jrnl. R. Aeronaut. Soc.* XLIII. 424 This effect was noticed during the war on horn-balanced rudders, and has now been used in the design of elevators. 1952 W. J. DUNCAN *Control & Stability Aircraft* vii. 195 A horn balance is a local protuberance of the control surface lying forward of the hinge axis... The horn may lie behind the main surface (shielded horn) or be exposed to the airstream. 1968 B. DICKINSON *Aircraft Stability & Control* x. 235 If the horn extends to the leading edge of the aerofoil it is referred to as an 'unshielded' horn.

23. *Arch.* †In OE. a pinnacle or gable (*obs.*); each of the Ionic volutes (likened to ram's horns); the projections of an abacus, etc.: see quots.

*c*1000 *Finnesburg* 4 (Gr.) Ne þisse healle hornas ne byrnað. 1847 CRAIG, *Horn*,..a name sometimes given to the Ionic volute. 1852–61 *Archit. Publ. Soc. Dict.* s.v., In general the word *Horn* (Fr. *corne*) is employed to express each of the four projecting portions of any abacus which has its faces curved on a plan... The terms *horn* or *side-arm* are also applied to the portions which project beyond the rest of a piece of framed work, as in the head of a solid door-frame.

24. *Naut.* See quots. (In quot. 1887 tr. L. *cornua* the ends of the sail-yards: cf. ANTENNA.)

1794 *Rigging & Seamanship* I. 167 *Horns*, the jaws, or semi-circular ends of booms and gaffs. 1867 SMYTH *Sailor's Word-bk.*, *Horn*, the arm of a cleat or kevel. *Horns*, the points of the jaws of the booms. Also the outer ends of the cross-trees. *Horns of the Rudder* = *Rudder-horns*. *Horns of the tiller*, the pins at the extremity. 1882 NARES *Seamanship* (ed. 6) 76 The foremost horn of the topmast trestle-tree. 1887 BOWEN *Virg. Æneid* III. 548 Windward pointing the horns of the sail-clothed yards of the fleet.

25. *Fortif.* = HORNWORK.

1709 LUTTRELL *Brief Rel.* (1857) VI. 497 One of our bombs fell into a magazine in the horn, blew it up, and ruin'd great part of the wall.

26. a. In various other technical applications.

1875 R. F. MARTIN tr. *Havrez Winding Mach.* 60 It is to be feared that the rope might slip down between its own coil and the horns of the rope rolls. 1875 KNIGHT *Dict. Mech.*, *Horn*..8. (*Milling*) One of the points of a driver, on the summit of a millstone spindle..which project into the coffins of the runner to convey the motion of the spindle thereto. 9. One of the prongs or crutches of an elevating screw or jack. 10. A curved projection on the forepart of a plane. 1884 *Ibid.* Suppl., *Horn* (*Railway U.S.*), One of the projecting parts of a pedestal, between which the journal-boxes work = *Horn-block.*

b. *Electr.* Each of a pair of rod conductors that diverge in a vertical plane from a narrow gap at the base, designed to extinguish any arc that forms in the gap and used to protect power lines from voltage surges; so ***horn arrester, gap***; also, a projecting rod conductor that protects an insulator by attracting away from it any arc that forms.

1911 *Trans. Amer. Inst. Electr. Engin.* XXIX. I. 582 The relief gaps were removed before the lightning season of 1908. The grounded horn was left in place to act as a

lightning rod. *Ibid.* 600 We placed the horn gaps on the towers, about 500 feet apart. **1930** *Engineering* 7 Mar. 314/2 Insulators on high-voltage lines are protected by arcing horns. **1968** P. J. FREEMAN *Electric Power* ix. 253 The shape of the horn gap forces the arc upwards by magnetic and thermal effects and the arc is self-extinguishing. **1969** L. CSUROS in *Power Syst. Protection* (Electr. Council) III. xii. 20 The arcing horns shown on the 132 kV bushings serve the main purpose of protecting the metal fittings on..the bushing by providing a suitable anchorage for the fault arc.

V. 27. Each of the alternatives of a dilemma (in Scholastic Lat. *argumentum cornutum*), on which one is figured as liable to be caught or impaled.

1548 UDALL *Erasm. Par. Luke* xx. 158 [verses 3–7] Thys forked questyon; which the sophisters call an horned question, because that to whether of both partyes a bodye shall make a direct aunswere, he shall renne on the sharpe poyncte of the horne. **1647** COWLEY *Mistr., Agst. Hope* i, And both the Horns of Fates Dilemma wound. **1668** H. MORE *Div. Dial.* I. xviii. (1713) 38 This seems a smart Dilemma at first..yet I think neither Horn is strong enough to push us off from our belief of the Existence of a God. **1755** YOUNG *Centaur* v. 183 That horn of the alternative wounds more than the former. **1853** W. JERDAN *Autobiog.* III. x. 137 [He] placed the King in a dilemma, from the horn of which he could not extricate himself. **1887** FOWLER *Deduct. Logic* v. 121 In disputation, the adversary who is refuted by a dilemma is said to be 'fixed on the horns of a dilemma'.

VI. *attrib.* and *Comb.*

28. a. Simple attrib. = of a horn or horns, as ***horn-call, colour, measurement, shavings.***

1632 B. JONSON *Magn. Lady* v. i, They burnt old shoes, goose-feathers, assafœtida, A few horn-shavings..And shee is well again. **1828** STARK *Elem. Nat. Hist.* II. 54 Shell.. yellowish horn colour. **1855** MORTON *Cycl. Agric.* II. 70 Horn shavings, from the large proportion of nitrogen in them, are a powerful manure. **1896** *Daily News* 13 Nov. 6/6 Records of horn measurements. **1912** G. MOORE *Hail & Farewell! Salve* vi. 102 If I knew Elgar, I'd write and ask him to send me a horn-call. **1954** J. R. R. TOLKIEN *Two Towers* i. 15 Suddenly the horn-calls ceased. **1959** D. COOKE *Lang. Mus.* ii. 57 Wagner..makes a musical demonstration of the natural 'rightness' of the harmonic series, for the horn-call is preceded by the low E flat on the basses. **1971** *Country Life* 18 Feb. 358/1 Siegfried promptly announces his arrival by horn-call and wastes no time in walking into the trap.

b. objective and obj. gen., as ***horn-bearer, -blower, -blowing, -player.*** **c.** similative, as ***horn-like, -shaped*** adjs. **d.** instrumental and locative, as ***horn-bind*** vb., ***horn-crested, -pushing, -yoked*** adjs.

1483 *Cath. Angl.* 188/2 An *Horne berer, *corniger.* **1679** *Prot. Conformist* 3 How they have *horn-bound for several years past the Bavarian Duke. *c* **725** *Corpus Gloss.* 454 *Cereacus*, *horn blauuere. **1483** *Cath. Angl.* 188/2 An Horne blawer, *cornicen.* **1830** GEN. P. THOMPSON *Exerc.* (1842) I. 314 The horn-blowers of arbitrary power in England. **1870** *Echo* 23 Nov., Vague—not to say unsatisfactory pieces of *hornblowing. **1848** C. C. CLIFFORD *Aristoph., Frogs* 9 *Horn-crested Pan. **1929** D. H. LAWRENCE *Pansies* 26 Honking *horn-like into the twilight. **1951** S. SPENDER *World within World* 162 The syllables which she unerringly chose to emphasize changed her speech into horn-like blasts. **1879** W. H. STONE in Grove *Dict. Mus.* I. 752/1 Rossini, the son of a *horn-player. **1776** WITHERING *Brit. Plants* (1796) II. 495 *Aquilegia*..nectaries 5, *horn-shaped. **1852–61** *Archit. Publ. Soc. Dict.* s.v., The horn-shaped leaf so often seen in English mediæval work.

29. *attrib.* passing into *adj.* Made of horn, as ***horn bow, cup, lantern, ring, spoon, ware***; formed naturally of horn, as ***horn foot, sheath.*** Hence parasynthetic combs., as ***horn-footed, -handled, -sheathed*** adjs.

c **1440** *York Myst.* xvi. 124 An horne spone. **1575** LANEHAM *Let.* (1871) 40 Wear it not in deede that hornz bee so plentie, hornware I beleeue woold bee more set by than it iz. **1611** SHAKS. *Wint. T.* IV. iv. 611 Not a Ribbon.. Shooe-tye, Bracelet, Horne-Ring. **1611** COTGR., *Corne-pied*, hoofed, horne-footed. **1665** DRYDEN *Ind. Emp.* II. i, The frighted satyrs..their horn-feet ply. **1698** FRYER *Acc. E. India & P.* 357 They draw their Bows with the Thumb armed with an Horn Ring. **1843** JAMES *Forest Days* ii, The horn cup, which the host set down beside the tankard. **1844** W. H. MAXWELL *Sports & Adv. Scotl.* ix. (1855) 93 The porrich..must be eaten with a horn spoon. **1847** TENNYSON *Princ.* II. 143 Horn-handed breakers of the glebe. **1854** OWEN *Skel. & Teeth* in *Circ. Sc., Organ. Nat.* I. 276 This edentulous and horn-sheathed condition of the jaws. **1877** J. D. CHAMBERS *Div. Worship* 251 Horn Chalices were forbidden. **1879** G. MACDONALD *P. Faber* (1883) 201 If it is a horn lantern you've got. **1885** tr. *Hehn's Wand. Pl. & Anim.* 408 Horn-bows were used as well as those of yew. **1885** TENNYSON *Tiresias* 10 Tramp of the hornfooted horse. **1922** JOYCE *Ulysses* 619 A blunt hornhandled ordinary knife with nothing particularly Roman or antique about it. **1925** W. DE LA MARE *Connoisseur* (1926) 51 His horn-handled and gold-mounted umbrella.

30. Special combs.: **horn aerial, antenna** (see HORN *sb.* 15 b); † **horn-back** = HORN-FISH; **horn balance** (see HORN *sb.* 22 h (ii)); **horn-band**, a band of musicians that play horns; **horn-bar**, the cross-bar of a carriage, or the gearing supporting the fore-spring stays; † **horn battle**, an army in battle array having horns or wings; † **horn-beast**, a horned beast, as an ox; † **horn-beaten** *a.*, cuckolded; **horn-beech** = HORNBEAM; **horn-bug**, a North American beetle, *Passalus cornutus*, having its head armed with a stout curved horn; **horn-card**, a transparent plate of horn bearing a graduated scale, or the like (Knight *Dict. Mech.* 1875); **horn-cattle** = horned cattle: see CATTLE 6; **horn cell** *Anat.*, any of the ganglion cells of the cornua of the spinal cord; **horn-centre**, a mathematical instrument: see quot.; † **horn-cod**, a carob; † **horn-coot** = HORN-OWL; **horn-core**, the central bony part of the horn of quadrupeds, a process of the frontal bone; **horn-distemper**, 'a disease of cattle, affecting the internal substance of the horn' (Craig 1847); **horn-drum** (*Hydraulics*), a water-raising wheel divided into sections by curved partitions (Knight *Dict. Mech.*); **horn-eyed** *a.*, having a horny film over the eye, dull-eyed; † **horn-face**, ? a stupid face, such as a cuckold might have; † **horn-fair**, 'a fair formerly held at Charlton in Kent' (Nares) for the sale of horn goods; used allusively by 17th and 18th c. writers with reference to cuckoldry; **horn-fisted** *a.*, having hands made horny by hard work; **horn-flint**, flint of a horn-like appearance and translucency; **horn-fly**, a dipterous insect, *Hæmatobia serrata*, so called from its habit of clustering on the horns of cattle; † **horn-foot, -feet** *a.*, having feet of horn, as horses; horn-footed; **horn-frog**, the horned frog: see HORNED; **horngarth** [GARTH[1]] (see quot. 1928); **horn gate** *Founding*, a horn-shaped gate (GATE *sb.*[4] 1 a) that curves downward from a runner and then upwards into a mould cavity, discharging through its narrow end; **horn grass**, a grass of the genus *Ceratochloa* (Craig 1847); **horn-hard** *a.*, as hard as horn; also advb.; † **horn-head**, a horn-headed being, a cuckold; **horn-hipped** *a.* (see quot.); **horn-lead**, a name given by the old chemists to chloride of lead, because it assumes a horny appearance on fusing: cf. CORNEOUS; **horn-machine**, a shoe-soling machine, so called because the shoe is placed on a horn-like projection; **horn-maker**, a maker of horns; †one who 'horns' or cuckolds; **horn-man**, a man with a horn; *spec.* in Jamaica among the Maroons, a man who blew the horn, giving signals; **horn-mercury**, chloride of mercury: cf. *horn-lead*; † **horn-mouth** *a.*, having a horn in the mouth; † **horn-nose**, a rhinoceros; **horn-nut**, the horned fruit of plants of the genus *Trapa*; **horn-ore**, 'a species of silver ore of a pearl-grey colour, bordering on white' (Craig); † **horn-penny** = HORNGELD; **horn-piece**, the skin (of an ox) with the horns attached; **horn-pike**, the horn-fish or garfish; **horn-pith**, the soft porous bone which fills the cavity of a horn; **horn-plant**, a seaweed, *Ecklonia buccinalis*; **horn-pock, -pox**, a mild form of smallpox or chicken-pox; **horn-poppy**, the Horned Poppy, *Glaucium flavum*; **horn porphyry** = HORNSLATE; **horn-pout** (*U.S.*), a name for some fishes of the genus *Amiurus*, esp. *A. catus*; **horn-press**, a form of stamping-machine for closing the side seams of tin cans and boxes (*Cent. Dict.*); † **horn-putter** (tr. Vulgate *cornupeta*), an animal that butts or gores with the horn; **horn-quicksilver**, same as *horn-mercury*; **horn-rimmed** *a.*, denoting spectacles having rims made of horn; **horn-rims**, horn-rimmed spectacles; **horn-ring** (see quot. 1928); **horn-schist** = HORNSLATE; **horn-shell** (see quot.); † **horn sickness**, humorous for 'jealousy due to being cuckolded'; **horn-snake**, (*a*) the Pine Snake or Bull Snake, *Coluber melanoleucus*; (*b*) the Red-bellied or Wampum Snake, *Farancia abacura* (local U.S.); **horn speaker**, a loud-speaker that incorporates a horn; **horn spectacles** = *horn-rims*; **horn-tail**, an insect of the family *Uroceridæ*, having a prominent horn on the abdomen of the male; † **horn-thumb**, a thumb protected by a thimble of horn such as was used by cutpurses; a pickpocket; **horn-tip**, the tip of a horn; a button or knob fixed on the point of a horn for a guard or ornament; **horn-weed**, (*a*) same as HORNWORT; (*b*) same as *horn-plant*; † **horn-wood** = HORNBEAM; **horn-worm** *U.S.*, the larva of moths of the genus *Protoparce*, which includes *P. sexta*, a pest of tobacco, and *P. quinquemaculata*, which attacks the tomato and certain other vegetables; also, the larva of other hawkmoths of the family Sphingidæ.

1598 FLORIO, *Acicula*, a horne fish or *hornebacke. **1849** J. G. DALYELL *Musical Memories Scotland* v. 170 The Russian *horn-band consists of a multitude of performers whose concert comprehends the most simple music... Each instrument emits only a single note. *Ibid.* 171, I heard the Russian horn-band in this country, in the year 1833. **1938** *Oxf. Compan. Mus.* 441/1 In Russia..in the middle of the eighteenth century, proprietors of large estates established *horn bands*, much on the principle of our present day handbell ringing, each player being provided with one instrument of the appropriate size for the easy production of one note... The horns were straight ones (not circular). **1879** *Cassell's Techn. Educ.* IV. 175/1 The *horn-bar which stands at the back of the top bed. **1635** BARRIFFE *Mil. Discip.* lxxv. (1643) 207 The *Horne Battell may be for the same occasion and use. **1600** SHAKS. *A. Y. L.* III. iii. 51 No Temple but the wood, no assembly but *horne-beasts. **1652** PEYTON *Catastr. Ho. Stuarts* (1731) 27 Silly Men, being *Horn-beaten. **1771** R. WARNER *Plant. Woodford.* 114 *Carpinus, Ostrya Ulmo similis*..the Horn, or Hard-beam Tree, called in some places, the Horse-beech or *Horn-beech, from some likeness of the leaves to the Beech. **1776** J. TRUMBULL *McFingal* (Th.), Thought *horn-bugs bullets, or, through fears, Muskitoes took for musqueteers. **1846** WORCESTER cites *Farm. Encycl.* for Hornbug. **1869** MRS. STOWE *Oldtown Folks* xxvii. 341 Youre saucy enough to physic a horn-bug. **1899** *Mem. Amer. Folklore Soc.* VII. 63 Horn-bugs, May-bees, May-flies, [etc.]. **1793** MISS SEWARD *Lett.* (1811) III. 257 Beauties of *horn-cattle. **1898** *Med. Chron.* IX. News 39 Collateral branches..are structures of enormous importance..representing the most direct path of nerve communication between the sensory surface..and the ventral *horn cells. **1969** J. H. GREEN *Basic Clin. Physiol.* xx. 114/2 When the anterior horn cell sends a nerve impulse along the motor nerve, every muscle fibre in the motor unit contracts. **1879** *Cassell's Techn. Educ.* I. 12/2 *Horn centres ..are small circular pieces of horn with three needle-points fixed in them. **1682** WHELER *Journ. Greece* VI. 446 The *Horncod-Tree or *Keratia.* **1650** EARL MONM. tr. *Senault's Man bec. Guilty* 306 To make lodgings for Owles, and to prepare habitations for *Horn-Coots. **1753** CHAMBERS *Cycl. Supp., Horn-coot*, a name given by fowlers to the great Horn owl. **1872** NICHOLSON *Palæont.* 424 In neither case are the horns supported by bony *horn-cores. **1843** *Knickerbocker* XXI. 254 Hence it is as important to keep the bee-moth out of hives as the *horn-distemper out of cattle. **1838** LYTTON *Alice* XI. ii, Self-conceit is *horn-eyed. **1843** CARLYLE *Past & Pr.* II. vii, All his flunkeyhood, and horn-eyed dimness. *a* **1668** DAVENANT *Man's the Mast.* Wks. (1673) 334 Dog! what will she say of thy *horn-face? **1669** *Newest Acad. Compliments* (N.), When..cuckolds forget to march to *Horn-fair. **1730** *Poor Robin* (N.), Now in small time comes on Horn-fair, Your horns and ladles now prepare. **1896** A. W. TUER *Hist. Horn-Bk.* I. vii. 91 Horn Fair was held at least as early as the time of Henry III, and was continued annually until abolished in 1872. **1929** F. C. BOWEN *Sea Slang* 69 **Horn-fisted*, a seaman with hands hardened with work. **1961** F. H. BURGESS *Dict. Sailing* 117 *Horn-fisted*, possessing tough hands, and a character to match, through hard work. **1802–3** tr. *Pallas's Trav.* (1812) II. 108 Its grain can with difficulty be perceived, and the whole is similar to *horn-flint. **1708** KERSEY, **Horn-fly*, an American Insect. **1897** BAILEY *Princ. Fruit-Growing* 25 A comparatively harmless insect in France becomes the dreaded horn-fly in America. *c* **1595** J. DICKENSON *Sheph. Compl.* (1878) 11 The *hornfeet halfe-gods, with all the progeny rurall. **1627** HAKEWILL *Apol.* (1630) 279 Horn-foote horses. **1807** PIKE *Sources Mississ.* (1810) II. 156 *note*, I have seen the Wishtonwish, the rattle snake, the *horn frog..and a land tortoise all take refuge in the same hole. **1779** L. CHARLTON *Hist. Whitby* II. 96 The *Hornegarth..seems to have been a certain stake and yether hedge, made up in the beginning of summer by all those in Whitby-Strand who held land of the Abbot. **1890** *Hornes' Guide to Whitby* 18 About the year 1315,..the *Horngarth* was made at the town of Whitby, with wood from the abbot's forest. **1894** J. C. ATKINSON *Memorials Old Whitby* 50 There is no reason whatever for questioning the conclusion that the Horngarth service.. must date back to pre-conquest times. **1928** *Daily Express* 24 May 3 What is the ceremony of 'planting the Horngarth'? .. Driving in a hedge of stakes near Whitby Harbour to the sound of a horn, a custom dating to feudal times, to prevent cattle from straying into the harbour. **1909** *Hawkins' Mech. Dict.* 287/1 *Horn gate. **1910** E. L. RHEAD *Princ. & Pract. Ironfounding* ix. 202 Horn gates are shown in Fig. 96... The tapering form and circular sweep allow of their removal without disturbance of the sand. **1934** LAING & ROLFE *Man. Foundry Pract.* vi. 126 The semi-circular in-gates are known as 'horn-gates'. **1768** ROSS *Helenore* 53 (Jam.) For now the lads are sleeping *horn hard. **1818** SCOTT *Br. Lamm.* xxv, The hearty shake of Mr. Girder's horn-hard palm. *a* **1625** FLETCHER *Love's Cure* II. i, And Vulcan a limping *horn-head, for Venus his wife was a Strumpet. **1727–41** CHAMBERS *Cycl.* s.v., A horse is said to be *Horn-hipped when the tops of the two haunch bones appear too high. **1782** KIRWAN in *Phil. Trans.* LXXIII. 22, 100 grs. of *horn lead, formed by precipitation, contain 72 of lead, 18 of marine acid, and 10 of water. **1812** SIR H. DAVY *Chem. Philos.* 397 Called horn lead by the old chemists. **1600** SHAKS. *A. Y. L.* IV. i. 63 Vertue is no *horne-maker: and my Rosalind is vertuous. **1803** R. C. DALLAS *Hist. Maroons* I. iii. 70 One of Quao's men, a *hornman,..consented to accompany Captain Adair. **1844** *Camp Refuge* I. 126 The horn-men blew might and main. **1957** J. KEROUAC *On Road* (1958) I. iv. 201 The hornman sat absolutely motionless. **1961** F. G. CASSIDY *Jamaica Talk* viii. 166 Among the Maroons an important person was the *horn-man*, who gave signals with a horn or conch. **1972** *Down Beat* 16 Mar. 26/2 Farmer and Heath are two of the best-matched hornmen at work in the idiom today. **1776** WOULFE in *Phil. Trans.* LXVI. 619 The *horn-mercury..was intermixed with minute globules of quicksilver. **1645** QUARLES *Sol. Recant.* xii. 58 The *horn-mouth Belman shal affright thy slumbers. **1598** FLORIO, *Rinoceronte*, a great beast or monster called a *horne nose. *c* **1320** in *Registr. Monast. de Winchelcumba* (1892) 291 Et acquietabimus omnia predicta de assisis.. wardepeni, hevedpeni, *hornpeni, et de omnibus servitiis secularibus. **1757** W. THOMPSON *R.N. Advoc.* 46 He will find the Legs, Shins..and *Horn Pieces of Oxen..pack'd into slight Casks. **1851** P. H. GOSSE *Nat. Sojourn Jamaica* 39 The Mexican *Horn-poppy (*Argemone*), the West Indian Vervain (*Stachytarpha*),..and others. **1909** *Chambers's Jrnl.* July 445/2 The wild wallflower and horn-poppy..bloom in mid-air. **1798** *Gaz. U.S.* (Philad.) 3 Aug. (Th.), The company concluded to go, for the sake of seeing a *horn pout —when at last I drew one up—and behold! what was it, but a cat fish! **1832** *Coll. New H. Hist. Soc.* III. 87 On each side of their body and close to the head is a formidable weapon called a *horn*, and hence the name *Horn-pout.* **1910** *Outlook* 9 July 529 On the other side of the pond we met Sam Noyes, who was catching horn-pouts. **1943** B. DAMON *Sense of Humus* 22 First he brought her a mess of horn pouts he had caught. **1822–34** *Good's Study Med.* (ed. 4) II. 360 Varicella, crystalline and *horn-pox. **1877** ROBERTS *Handbk. Med.* (ed.

3) I. 153 Horn-pock or Wart-pock is a mild and abortive form, in which the pocks..shrivel and dry up on the 5th or 6th day. **1796** KIRWAN *Elem. Min.* (ed. 2) I. 309 Leske in his voyage through Saxony often calls our stone [Hornslate] **hornporphyry.* **1860** O. W. HOLMES *Elsie V.* (1887) 26 Pond well stocked with *horn pouts. **1870** LOWELL *Among my Bks.* Ser. I. (1873) 247 Memories of going after pond-lilies, of angling for horn-pouts. **1382** WYCLIF *Exod.* xxi. 29 If an oxe be an *horn-putter. **1860** DANA *Man. Min.* 288 *Horn-quicksilver..Chloride of Mercury. **1894** *Idler* V. 452 Putting on a pair of *horn-rimmed eye-glasses, he read it through very carefully. **1901** KIPLING *Kim* i. 10 The lama mounted a pair of horn-rimmed spectacles of Chinese work. **1922** Horn-rimmed [see BEAVER[4]]. **1923** *Westm. Gaz.* 12 Apr., A long-necked youth who was talking to a horn-rimmed female. **1931** R. CAMPBELL *Georgiad* ii. 34 Women! .. Who mock at horn-rimmed spectacles. **1973** *Times* 16 June 1/4 The London strip club owner..heavily disguised with..a beard and thick, horn-rimmed spectacles..was approached by three detectives. **1927** *Punch* 20 Apr. 424/3 He removed his *horn-rims and began polishing them vigorously. **1959** *Encounter* July 59/1 In open-necked tennis shirt and heavy horn-rims. **1970** *New York* 16 Nov. 56/3 Junius glowers over his horn rims. **1928** *Daily Tel.* 16 Oct. 17 The *horn-ring, an attachment fitted on the steering wheel so that the motorist can sound his horn without lifting his hand from the circumference of the wheel. **1962** *Which?* Apr. (Suppl.) 74/1 Horn-ring assembly came adrift from steering wheel causing horn failure. **1973** J. M. WHITE *Garden Game* 189, I..put my hand on the horn-ring, pushed it down and held it there. The noise sounded shattering. **1799** W. TOOKE *View Russian Emp.* I. 151 Genuine *hornschist and jasper are here not to be found. **1883** *Cassell's Nat. Hist.* V. 209 *Cerithium*, or the '*Horn-shell', has a turreted, many-whorled shell. **1613** in *Crt. & Times Jas. I* (1849) I. 238 Langley..is lately dead of the *horn sickness. **1688** J. CLAYTON in *Phil. Trans.* XVIII. 134 The *Horn-Snake is, as they say, another sort of deadly Snake. **1705** R. BEVERLEY *Virginia* (1722) 260 They have likewise the Horn-Snake, so called from a sharp Horn it carries in its Tail. **1791** W. BARTRAM *Carolina* 276. **1928** L. S. PALMER *Wireless Princ. & Pract.* xi. 428 To reproduce such extremes without distortion is quite beyond the power of any existing *horn speaker. **1957** *Encycl. Brit.* XIV. 409/1 Horn speakers may be made quite efficient. **1893** M. BEERBOHM *Let.* 19 Aug. (1964) 53 An old sexton too with *horn-spectacles. **1915** J. BUCHAN *Salute to Adventurers* xi. 163 Then he produced some papers, and putting on big horn spectacles, proceeded to instruct me in them. **1923** V. WOOLF in *Dial* LXXV. 21 Mrs. Dalloway, remembering Kensington Gardens and the old lady in horn spectacles. **1884** J. S. KINGSLEY *Stand. Nat. Hist.* II. 507 The family Uroceridæ, or *horn-tails, includes insects which are closely allied to the saw-flies. **1594** GREENE & LODGE *Looking Glasse* Wks. (Rtldg.) 138/2, I cut this from a new-married wife by the help of a *horn-thumb and a knife. **1808** T. ASHE *Travels* III. xxxiii. 89 They sell them furs and *horn tips, and receive in exchange ball powder, whiskey, tobacco, beads, ornaments, and blankets. **1884** MILLER *Plant-n.*, Horn-wort or *Horn-weed, *Ceratophyllum demersum*. **1731** *Lunenburg* (Mass.) *Proprietors' Rec.* (1897) 137 There making an Angle and runing East..68 rod to a smale *horn wood tree. **1676** T. GLOVER in *Phil. Trans.* XI. 635 A Worm that devours the leaf, called a *Horn-worm. **1763** T. PRICE in B. M. Carew *Life* 110 The planters prune off the suckers, and clear them of the Horn-worm twice a week. **1784** J. SMYTH *Tour U.S.* II. 132 The other [species] is the horn-worm..of a vivid green colour, with a number of pointed excrescences or feelers, from his head like horns: these devour the [tobacco] leaf. **1850** *Rep. U.S. Comm. Patents, Agric. 1849* 459 The horn-worm is deposited on the smooth or upper surface of the leaf in an egg by the tobacco fly. **1962** METCALF & FLINT *Destructive & Useful Insects* (ed. 4) xiv. 656 The winter stage of the hornworms is very often spaded up or plowed out in the spring. *Ibid.* 657 In the tomato hornworm larvae the horn is black and there are eight stripes ..; while in the tobacco hornworm the horn is red and there are seven oblique stripes. **1972** *Sci. Amer.* June 73/2 The caterpillars of *Manduca sexta*..are the hornworms that feed on tobacco and tomato plants.

horn (hɔːn), *v.* [f. HORN *sb.*]

1. a. *trans.* To furnish with horns.

1694 R. L'ESTRANGE *Fables* lxxviii. (1714) 95 Jupiter instead of Horning the Camel, order'd him to be Cropt.

b. To tip, point, cover, etc. with horn.

1421–2 [see HORNING *sb.* 2]. **1605** *Eik to Seal of Cause of Skinners of Glasgow* 5 Feb. (Jam. Suppl.), That nane.. schaip or horne pointis, schaip or mak purssis.

2. To 'give horns to': to cuckold.

c **1550** *Pryde & Ab. Wom.* 76 in Hazl. *E.P.P.* IV. 237 Some wyll not stycke..To horne you on everye side. **1608** ROWLANDS *Humors Looking Glasse* 30 Being married to a iealous asse, He vowes she hornes him. **1702** STEELE *Funeral* I, This Wench I know has play'd me false, And horn'd me in my Galants. **1823** *New Monthly Mag.* VIII. 343 Milk and water husbands—horned, hen-pecked, and abused by virago wives. **1952** S. SELVON *Brighter Sun* viii. 157 Look at yuh, yuh nasty dog! Yuh suspect she horning yuh! Yuh ain't have no shame? Dat poor gul don't even look at any odder man but you. **1970** 'W. HAGGARD' *Hardliners* i. 5 She'd given him a daughter and called it a day, horning him quite shamelessly.

3. a. To butt or gore with the horns.

1599 MINSHEU *Sp. Dict.*, *Cornear*, to horne, to push with the horns. **1883** *Pall Mall G.* 12 Oct. 3/2 The cattle horn each other. **1891** *Melbourne Argus* 7 Nov. 13/5 A beast turned on me and horned my horse.

b. *fig.* To push, as an ox with its horns. *U.S.*

1851 J. J. HOOPER *Widow Rugby's Husb.* 69 You horned me off to get a chance to get gaming witnesses out of the way. **1881** *Times* (Philad.) 5 June (Th.), Mac Veagh is trying his best to horn Blaine out of the Cabinet herd, just as young buffalo bulls horn out the old ones.

c. *intr.* To push or butt *in* (*on* or *with*). *colloq.* (orig. *U.S.*).

1912 C. MATHEWSON *Pitching in a Pinch* 213 Many of them try hard to 'horn in' with the men who have made good as Big Leaguers. **1924** C. E. MULFORD *Rustlers' Valley* xviii. 201 Why did Chet horn in on Baldy's arrest? **1927** *Bulletin* 15 Apr. 12/3 'Well, your little playmate certainly queered things,' he said. Thorn shrugged. 'I'm sorry, chief; but I couldn't help it. You saw how he horned in.' **1932** D. L. SAYERS *Have his Carcase* xiv. 186 Glaisher might not like this horning in on his province. **1936** WODEHOUSE *Laughing Gas* xvi. 173, I suppose she felt she owed you something, after horning in on your big scene like that and trying to steal your publicity the way she did. **1939** *Airman's Gaz.* Dec., The lesson for today chicks is how to horn in on the radio racket. **1942** 'B. J. ELLAN' *Spitfire!* xii. 61 Hurricanes had probably been chasing this Dornier when I had come in and attacked. Perhaps after all I was horning in on them! **1970** G. F. NEWMAN *Sir, You Bastard* iv. 114 A proportion of detectives everywhere were at it; it was simply a question of finding them and horning in.

4. *Shipbuilding.* To adjust (the frame of a ship) so as to be at right angles to the line of the keel.

c **1850** *Rudim. Navig.* (Weale) 147 Standards..convenient to horn or square the frame. *Ibid.* 151 To *Square*, is to horn or form with right angles. **1869** SIR E. REED *Shipbuild.* xx. 442 Each frame being horned and plumbed in order to ensure the correctness of its position.

†**5.** *Sc. Law.* To put to the horn; to proclaim a rebel; to outlaw: cf. HORNING *sb.* 4. *Obs.*

1592 *Sc. Acts Jas. VI* (1814) 551 (Jam.) That ye nor nane of yow charge, horne, poynd, nor trouble the said Johnne Schaw. **1702** E. CHAMBERLAYNE *St. Gt. Brit.* II. xi. (1707) 142 Condemn'd, out-lawed, or Horned. **1705** HICKERINGILL *Priest-cr.* I. 3 They proclaim you to be Rebels to God, Horn you, as in Scotland.

6. *trans.* and *intr.* To sound a horn; to signal to (someone) with a horn; to proclaim (something) loudly (as if) by sounding a horn.

1874 HARDY *Far from Madding Crowd* II. xii. 147 Jan meanwhile merging his..thoughts..in a song:—'To-morrow-to-morrow!.. To-mor-row, to-mor—'. 'Do hold thy horning, Jan! said Oak. *Ibid.* II. xxvii. 335 'I am afeard your labour in keeping it close will be throwed away,' said Coggan... 'Labe Tall's old woman will horn it all over parish in half an hour.' **1892** G. MEREDITH *Poems* 77 He entreats..Compassion..For his fierce bugler horning onset. **1908** R. BROUGHTON *Mamma* v. 45 Silence save of the nightly traffic roaring and ringing and horning past outside. **1923** W. DE LA MARE *Riddle* 209 The screech of its engine, horning up into the windless air. **1946** A. M. WALTERS *Moondrop to Gascony* xv. 199 We horned the small convoy to a stop as we approached Tanet.

†**hornage.** *Obs. rare*[−0]. [f. HORN *sb.* + -AGE, after F. *cornage.*] Cornage, horngeld.

1611 COTGR., *Cornage*, hornage; an yearely duetie of corne exacted..vpon euerie Oxe that labours in the Winter-corne-ground.

hornbeak (ˈhɔːnbiːk). Now *dial.* The garfish or hornfish, *Belone vulgaris*, which has extremely long and slender tapering jaws.

1565–73 COOPER *Thesaurus*, *Acus*, a fish..of some called a hornebeake. **1598** *Epulario* G iij b, To seeth the Horne-beeke or Pipe fish. **1601** HOLLAND *Pliny* I. 266 The Horne-beaks or Needle-fishes, Belonæ..haue within them so great egs that their wombe cleaueth and openeth when they should lay them. **1706** PHILLIPS (ed. Kersey), *Horn-beak*, a kind of Fish. **1836** YARRELL *Brit. Fishes* I. 442.

hornbeam (ˈhɔːnbiːm). [f. HORN *sb.* + BEAM.]

1. a. A tree of the genus *Carpinus* (family Betulaceæ), native to Asia, Europe, and North America, esp. *C. betulus*, the common hornbeam, which is native to Great Britain, or *C. caroliniana*, the American hornbeam; so called from its hard, close-grained wood.

1577 B. GOOGE *Heresbach's Husb.* II. (1586) 101 b, Upon the plaines you shall have..the Hornebeame. **1664** EVELYN *Sylva* xii. § 1. 29 The Horn-beam, in Latine the *Carpinus*, is planted of Sets. **1671** in *Early Rec. Providence, R.I.* (1893) III. 107 Boundeth on..the norwesterne Corner with a horne beame or peckled tree marked on too sides. **1766** J. BARTRAM *Jrnl.* 6 Feb. in Stork *E. Florida* 62 A hammock of oak, hiccory, magnolia, and hornbeam. **1791** W. GILPIN *Remarks on Forest Scenery* I. iv. 48 Very nearly allied to the beech..is the hornbeam. It grows like it, when it is suffered to grow; but it is generally seen only in clipped hedges. **1897** WILLIS *Flower. Pl.* II. 71 The horn-beam is very like the beech in habit, but the leaves are not shiny. **1968** J. ARNOLD *Shell Bk. Country Crafts* xxxi. 330 When threshing was done with flails, the floors were made of hornbeam planks, and until lignum vitae came to this country hornbeam was used for bowls and still is for butchers' blocks.

b. hop hornbeam, the name of the genus *Ostrya*, closely allied to the common hornbeam, so called from the hop-like appearance of the ripe catkins; it has two species, *O. vulgaris* of Southern Europe, and *O. virginica* of America.

1794 MARTYN *Rousseau's Bot.* xxviii. 441 In the common Hornbeam the scales of the strobiles are flat; and in the Hop-Hornbeam they are inflated. **1866** *Treas. Bot.* 828/1 *Ostrya vulgaris*, the Common Hop Hornbeam, is a native of the south of Europe, but is quite hardy in the climate of England. **1884** MILLER *Plant-n.*, *Ostrya virginica*, Iron-wood (N. American), Hop-Hornbeam, Lever-wood.

c. *attrib.* †**hornbeam pollenger** (see quot.).

1597 GERARDE *Herbal* III. cix. 1295 Betulus, or the Horne-beame tree. **1706** PHILLIPS (ed. Kersey), *Horn-beam Pollengers*, trees of about Twenty Years Growth, that have been often lopp'd, and upon that Account not Tithable. *a* **1783** J. SCOTT *Ode to Leisure* (R.), Where Easna's horn-beam grove Its foliage o'er me interwove. **1838** *Murray's Hand-Bk. N. Germ.* 94 The avenues and high hornbeam hedges, with windows cut in them.

†**2.** A beam of light issuing like a horn from the head of a deity, etc. *Obs.*

1583 STANYHURST *Æneis* III. (Arb.) 91 Lyke..Phœbus his hornebeams.

3. = BEAM *sb.*[1] 12.

1861 WILDE *Catal. Antiq. R. Irish Acad.* 259 A horn-beam of an immense red deer.

hornbill (ˈhɔːnbɪl). [f. HORN *sb.* + BILL *sb.*[2]]

1. A bird of the family *Bucerotidæ*, so called from the horn-like excrescence surmounting the bill.

Formerly called *horned crow*, *horned pie*.

1773 PENNANT *Genera of Birds* p. xxix. and 8. **1781** LATHAM *Gen. Synops. Birds* I. 341. **1802** BINGLEY *Anim. Biog.* (1813) II. 89 Of the Hornbills in general..[Their bills] have frequently a protuberance, somewhat resembling another bill, on the upper mandible. **1854** OWEN *Skel. & Teeth* in *Circ. Sc., Organ. Nat.* I. 167 The enormous beak of the hornbill..forms one enormous air-cell. **1893** NEWTON *Dict. Birds* 435 The Hornbills, of which more than 60 species have been described, form a very natural and in some respects an isolated group.

2. *Comb.* **hornbill cuckoo**, the keel-billed cuckoo, *Crotophaga*, of N. America.

hornblende (ˈhɔːnblɛnd). *Min.* Also -blend. [a. Ger. *hornblende*, f. *horn* horn + BLENDE.]

1. A mineral closely allied to augite, and having as its chief constituents silica, magnesia, and lime. It is a constituent of many rocks, as granite, syenite, and diorite, and has numerous varieties, aluminous and non-aluminous, as actinolite, antholite, asbestos, dannemorite, nephrite, tremolite, etc., which are sometimes all included under the name AMPHIBOLE; it is usually of a dark brown, black, or greenish black colour.

1770 FORSTER tr. *Cronstedt's Min.* 95 The hornblende of the Swedes. **1796** KIRWAN *Elem. Min.* (ed. 2) I. 215 The great weight of the stone called *hornblende* made the miners at first imagine it contained some metal, but finding none except iron they called it *blind*. **1847** TENNYSON *Princ.* III. 344 Chattering stony names Of shale and hornblende, rag and trap and tuff, Amygdaloid and trachyte. **1876** PAGE *Adv. Text-bk. Geol.* v. 104 Hornblende is of a dark or dark-green colour, with a horny glistening lustre.

2. *attrib.* Of hornblende, as ***hornblende boulder***, etc.; containing or having hornblende as a chief constituent, hornblendic, as ***hornblende basalt, granite, porphyry, syenite***; **hornblende andesite** (see quot. 1885); **hornblende gabbro**, a variety of gabbro in which the diallage is more or less replaced by horneblende; **hornblende rock**, a green-stone consisting chiefly of hornblende; **hornblende schist, slate**, hornblende rock of a schistose nature.

1796 KIRWAN *Elem. Min.* (ed. 2) I. 354 Hornblende Porphyry. *Ibid.* 383 Hornblende Slate, penetrated with Talc or Mica. **1821** J. MᶜCULLOCH *Geol. Classif. Rocks* 298 Wherever hornblende rock occurs, it is only a portion of those beds of which the greater parts present the same characters as hornblende schist. **1862** B. TAYLOR *Poet's Jrnl., 2nd Eve* 23 Through hornblende bowlders, where the discus flung. **1880** BIRDWOOD *Ind. Art.* II. 4 The horn-blende slate or schist from which the magnetic iron used for ages in the manufacture of Damascus steel..is still obtained. **1885** GEIKIE *Text-bk. Geol.* (1893) 167 Hornblende-andesite consists of a triclinic felspar with hornblende, augite or mica... Hornblende-andesite is a volcanic rock of Tertiary and post-Tertiary date.

hornblendic (hɔːnˈblɛndɪk), *a. Min.* [f. prec. + -IC.] Of the nature of hornblende; containing hornblende; **hornblendic rock, schist, slate** = hornblende rock, etc.: see prec. 2.

1823 SCORESBY *Whale Fishery* 233, I obtained specimens of rocks..hornblendic mica-slate. **1858** GEIKIE *Hist. Boulder* xii. 239 Mineralogically they are..hornblendic, when the augite is replaced by hornblende. **1862** ANSTED *Channel Isl.* I. vi. (ed. 2) 126 Quarries of remarkably fine, tough hornblendic granite. **1865** LUBBOCK *Preh. Times* iv. (1878) 82 At the hornblendic extreme of the trap rocks we find the basalt, of which also celts were made.

hornblendite (ˈhɔːnblɛndaɪt). *Petrogr.* Also †-yte. [f. HORNBLEND(E + -ITE[1].] A granular rock largely or entirely composed of hornblende.

1874 J. D. DANA *Man. Geol.* (ed. 2) II. i. 70 Hornblendyte.—A very tough, granular, crystalline rock, consisting of hornblende, and hardly schistose in structure. **1901** *Jrnl. Chem. Soc.* LXXX. II. 170 Hornblendite from Brandberget, consisting essentially of hornblende. **1930** PEACH & HORNE *Geol. Scotl.* 26 The ultrabasic rocks (pyroxenites, hornblendites) generally form lenticles. **1967** P. J. WYLLIE *Ultramafic & Related Rocks* i. 2/2 Hornblendites vary widely in mineralogy, and various combinations of hornblende, pyroxene, olivine, and biotite are known.

horn-book (ˈhɔːnbʊk). A leaf of paper containing the alphabet (often with the addition of the ten digits, some elements of spelling, and the Lord's Prayer) protected by a thin plate of translucent horn, and mounted on a tablet of wood with a projecting piece for a handle. A simpler and later form of this, consisting of the tablet without the horn covering, or a piece of stiff cardboard varnished, was also called a BATTLEDORE (q.v. 3). For an exhaustive account see A. W. Tuer, *History of the Horn-Book* (1896).

1588 SHAKS. *L.L.L.* v. i. 49 Yes, yes, he teaches boyes the Horne-booke: What is Ab speld backward with the horn on

his head? **1589** *Pappe w. Hatchet* C iij, Such vnmannerlie knaues..must bee set againe to their A.B.C. and learne to spell *Our Father* in a Horne booke. **1639** *Bury Wills* (Camden) 176 For the buyeing and provideing of horne bookes and primers to be giuen to poore children. **1682** N. O. *Boileau's Lutrin* I. Argt., St. George oth' back-side of the Horn-book, The Dragon kills, to Humour Scorn-book. **1717** PRIOR *Alma* II. 463 To Master John the English maid A horn-book gives of gingerbread, And that the child may learn the better, As he can name, he eats the letter. **1763** *Brit. Mag.* IV. 131 Being ambitious to commence author, I was composing a new horn-book. *a* **1842** HONE in A. W. Tuer *Hist. Horn-Bk.* I. i. 7 A large wholesale dealer in.. school requisites recollects that the last order he received for Horn-books came from the country, about the year 1799. From that time the demand wholly ceased.. In the course of sixty years, he and his predecessors in business had executed orders for several millions of Horn-books. **1851** D. JERROLD *St. Giles* xiii. 135 A child at the horn-book might spell it. **1864** *Chambers' Book of Days* II. 233/1 The 'Horn-book' gradually gave way to the 'Battledore' and the 'Primer'.

b. *transf.* A treatise on the rudiments of a subject; a primer.

1609 DEKKER (*title*) The Gulls Horne-booke. **1757** *Connoisseur* No. 83 (Tuer) Under the title of the Rhymer's Play-thing, or Poetaster's Horn-Book. **1790** WOLCOTT (P. Pindar) *Adv. Fut. Laureat* iii. Wks. 1812 II. 339 Go find of Politics the lost Horn-book. **1847** H. PIDDINGTON (*title*) The Horn Book of Storms for Indian and China Seas. **1848** LYTTON *Harold* VI. vii, I come not here to learn the horn-book of war. **1874** MOTLEY *Barneveld* II. xi. 30 Ignorant of the very hornbook of diplomacy.

c. *attrib.*, as ***horn-book lore, school.***

1681 W. ROBERTSON *Phraseol. Gen.* (1693) 215 A Battle-dore boy or Horn-book-boy. **1766** ENTICK *London* IV. 403 The third school is the horn-book school, where 30 children are taught by the mistress. **1832** J. BREE *St. Herbert's Isle* etc. 154 The horn-book lore I early knew.

horned ('hɔːnɪd, hɔːnd), *a.*

I. [f. HORN *sb.* + -ED².(OE. had *hyrned*, from *hyrnan*:—**hurnjan*: cf. OHG. *gihurnet*.)]

1. a. Having horns or antlers; cornuted.

a **1400–50** *Alexander* 4267 Hald we no hors.. ne na horned stottis. **1413** *Pilgr. Sowle* (Caxton 1483) II. xlv. 51 Somme of them were horned, as boolys. **1590** SPENSER *F.Q.* III. x. 47 Emongst the horned heard. **1667** MILTON *P.L.* x. 525 Cerastes hornd, Hydrus, and Ellops drear. **1756–7** tr. *Keysler's Trav.* (1760) III. 175 The..horned cattle brought from Umbria. **1887** BOWEN *Virg. Eclogue* v. 33 Bull to the horned herd, and the corn to a fruitful plain.

b. *Logic.* ***horned syllogism*** (***argument***, etc.): the dilemma.

1548 Horned question [see HORN *sb.* 27]. **1551** T. WILSON *Logike* (1580) 34 b, Dilemna, otherwise..called a horned argument. **1620** T. GRANGER *Div. Logike* 285 *note*, Dilemma ..A forked or horned Syllogisme. **1837–8** SIR W. HAMILTON *Logic* xviii. (1866) I. 351 An hypothetico-disjunctive syllogism is called the dilemma or horned syllogism.

c. *fig.*

1889 W. B. YEATS *Wanderings of Oisin* 137 Between the hornèd hills. **1955** E. POUND *Classic Anthol.* III. 195 High spouts the water, from the hornèd spring.

2. a. Having, bearing, or wearing an appendage, ornament, etc., called a horn; having horn-like projections or excrescenses.

a **1300** *Cursor M.* 6655 Quen moyses had broght þe lagh ..þam thoght him hornd apon farr. **1382** WYCLIF *Exod.* xxxiv. 29 He wiste not that his face was horned of the cumpanye of the word of God. *a* **1450** *Knt. de la Tour* (1868) 63 He saide that the women that were so horned were lyche to be horned snailes and hertis and vnicornes. **1585** Horned beetle [see HORNET *sb.* 3]. **1650** SIR T. BROWNE *Pseud. Ep.* v. ix. (1686) 201 One side of a Silver Medal we find Moses horned. *c* **1695** J. MILLER *Descr. N. York* (1843) 6 In the middle of the line from thence northward is a horned work. **1850** H. W. TORRENS in *Jrnl. Asiat. Soc. Bengal* 33 A peculiar horned or crested helmet. **1856** BRYANT *Poems, Count of Greiers* i, The horned crags are shining. **1867** J. B. ROSE tr. *Virgil's Æneid* 13 Screened By the horned altar. **1882** MISS BRADDON *Mt. Royal* I. i. 14 That horned coast is said to have given its name to Cornwall.

b. horned adder, an African snake, *Bitis cornuta*, belonging to the viper family; **horned crow** or **pie**, old name of the hornbill; **horned dace** *U.S.*, a small freshwater fish, *Semotilus atromaculatus*, of the family Cyprinidæ; **horned frog**, (*a*) a lizard of the genus *Phrynosoma*, having the head and back covered with spikes (*U.S.*); also ***horned toad***; (*b*) a South American frog of the genus *Ceratophrys* which has horn-like projections on its eyelids; **horned helmet**, the gastropod mollusc, *Cassis cornuta*, or its shell, from which cameos are cut; **horned hog**, (*a*) the babiroussa: see HOG *sb.*¹ 3; †(*b*) a kind of fish with a horn on its head (*obs.*); **horned horse**, the Gnu; **horned lizard** = *horned frog* (*a*) (*s.v.* HORNED *a.* 2 b); **horned poppy**, the yellow sea-poppy, *Glaucium flavum*; **horned pout**, an American catfish, *Ictalurus* (formerly *Ameiurus*) *nebulosus*, introduced into western Europe about 1880, = *horn-pout* (HORN *sb.* 30); **horned rattlesnake**, a desert snake, *Crotalus cerastes*, found in the south-western U.S. and Mexico; = SIDE-WINDER²; **horned screamer**, a large black and white bird, *Anhima cornuta*, distinguished by a hornlike process on its forehead and found in marshy country in the northern half of South America; **horned snake**, (*a*) = *hoop-snake* (s.v. HOOP *sb.*¹ 13 b); (*b*) = *horned viper*; †**horned-snout**, the rhinoceros (*obs.*); **horned toad**, (*a*) = *horned frog* (*a*) (*s.v.* HORNED *a.* 2 b); (*b*) = *horned frog* (*b*); **horned viper**, a venomous African snake, *Cerastes cornutus*, distinguished by a horny scale above each eye. Also *horned* LARK, OWL, etc.

1878 A. AYLWARD *Transvaal of To-Day* xii. 244 The *horned adder—a rather rare variety—is one of the worst of these pests. **1929** W. ROSE *Veld & Vlei* 175 The Horned Adder..favours sandy localities, where, buried to the eyes, it watches for any lizards or mice that are unwary enough to approach within striking distance. **1947** J. STEVENSON-HAMILTON *Wild Life S. Afr.* xxxvi. 329 The Horned Adder. .. Also a dangerous viper, is usually found in sand regions. **1842** *Nat. Hist. N.Y., Zool.* IV. 199 The Horned Sucker is common in most of the fresh-water streams of this state... It is known under the various popular names of *Barbel, Dace*, and **Horned Dace*. **1896** JORDAN & EVERMANN *Fishes Amer.* I. 222 *Semotilus Atromaculatus*... Horned-dace; Creek-chub. **1963** P. A. PARSONS *Outdoor Life Compl. Bk. Fresh Water Fishing* iv. 45 They [*sc.* creek chubs] are often called horned dace, and are found in creeks and rivers from Montana and New Mexico to the Atlantic Coast and south to Florida. **1831** E. GRIFFITH et al. tr. *Cuvier's Animal Kingdom* IX. 395 It is of the *horned frogs, with concealed tympanum, that Gravenhorst has made his genus Stombus, but they have teeth like the others, and should not be approximated to the toads. **1841** CATLIN *N. Amer. Ind.* (1844) II. xliv. 78 The horned frog..specimens..with the horns of half and three-fourths of an inch in length and very sharp at the points. **1847** RUXTON *Adv. Mexico* 156 The cameleon is the 'horned frog' of the prairies of America. **1902** P. FOUNTAIN *Gt. Mountains & Forests S. Amer.* xi. 290 In all outward aspects they resemble toads... They are very revolting-looking creatures, and are mostly of the species known as South American horned frogs. The common horned frog of Brazil is among them. **1962** H. R. SMYTH *Amphibians & their Ways* xviii. 225 The Horned Frog possesses sharp teeth on his upper jaws and sharp bony processes on the lower jaw; what is more, he does not hesitate to use those teeth. **1863** *Horned Helmet-shell [see HELMET *sb.* 5]. **1876** *Encycl. Brit.* IV. 740/1 The black helmet (*Cassis tuberosa*) of the West Indian seas, the horned helmet (*C. cornuta*) of Madagascar..are also employed [for cameos]. **1966** A. G. MELVIN *Sea Shells of World* 92/2 *Cassis cornuta* L. Indo-Pac[ific]. Horned Helmet. Whitish... Interior is golden brown. **1702** *Collect. Voy.* (1729) III. 413 The *Horned-Hog. A small flat Fish, with a Horn on his Head, notcht on one Side only. **1806** W. CLARK in R. G. Thwaites *Lewis & Clark Exped.* (1905) IV. 325 The *Horned Lizzard is also common. **1844** J. GREGG *Commerce Prairies* II. 231 Horned frog..horned lizard, as those of earlier times more rationally called it. **1931** *Times Educ. Suppl.* 13 June p. iv/3 Among the new arrivals..some horned lizards known in America as 'horn toads' are of special interest. **1969** A. BELLAIRS *Life of Reptiles* II. xii. 498 The spiny little horned lizards (*Phrynosoma*) are able to squirt drops of blood from their eyes for several feet. **1548–1870** *Horned poppy [see POPPY *sb.* I. 3]. **1909** *Daily Mail* 5 Aug. 9/3 The horned poppy is particularly plentiful in Start Bay. **1938** R. GATHORNE-HARDY *Wild Flowers in Britain* vi. 41 The Yellow Horned Poppy..is named from the long curved fruit, which, like an orange tree, it bears at the same time as its blossom. **1963** W. BLUNT *Of Flowers & Village* 140 Of course you know the horned poppy—*Glaucium flavum*. **1837** *Horned pout [see POUT *sb.*¹]. **1839** STORER & PEABODY *Rep. Fishes Mass.* 102 The Horned Pout ..is highly esteemed as an article of food. **1890** K. D. WIGGIN *Timothy's Quest* 126 The baby horned-pouts rustled their whiskers drowsily. **1969** A. WHEELER *Fishes Brit. Isles & N.W. Europe* 222/1 Horned Pout... A common fish in still or slow-flowing waters, it is found in many ponds, canals and lowland rivers in western Europe. Not so far reported as feral in the British Isles. **1870** *Proc. Calif. Acad. Sci.* IV. 67 The following do not occur west of this region..*Horned Rattlesnake, [etc.]. **1888** *Buck's Handbk. Med. Sci.* VI. 166/1 Crotalus cerastes Hallowell, Horned Rattlesnake, 'Side-winder'. **1965** R. & D. MORRIS *Men & Snakes* viii. 193 This special form of locomotion.. occurs in..the horned rattlesnake or 'sidewinder' of North America. **1785, 1869–73** *Horned screamer [see SCREAMER 3 a]. **1970** R. MEYER DE SCHAUENSEE *Guide to Birds S. Amer.* 30/1 Horned screamer... General plumage glossy greenish black. **1775** J. ADAMS *Diary* 21 Sept. in *Wks.* (1850) II. 426 Every dip of his pen stung like a *horned snake. **1784** [see *bull-snake* (BULL *sb.*¹ 11)]. **1812** A. PLUMPTRE tr. *Lichtenstein's Trav. S. Afr.* I. i. vii. 95 The heat of the day brought out a great many snakes; we killed two of very venemous kinds, one the horned snake, as it is called (*coluber cerastes*). **1851** D. B. WOODS *Sixteen Months at Gold Diggings* 134 It answers the description of horned snake. It is said that, taking the end of its tail in its mouth, it will form a perfect hoop with its body, rolling rapidly over till it reaches the object at which it aims. **1864** T. BAINES *Explor. S.-W. Afr.* xiii. 374, I found and captured a cerastes, or horned snake, sixteen or eighteen inches long, lying in the path. **1661** LOVELL *Hist. Anim. & Min.* 79 *Hornd-snout. Rhinoceros. **1806** *Massachusetts Spy* 16 July (Th.), A venerable Philosopher [*sc.* Thomas Jefferson] sitting in the middle of an immense Map, marked with vast prairies, huge rivers, and mountains of salt: surrounded by piles of Mammoth's bones, stuffed squirrel skins, and *horned toads. **1883** *Harper's Mag.* Oct. 706/1, I put my horned toad in his cage out in the sun. **1914** E. G. BOULENGER *Reptiles & Batrachians* iv. 70 The genus *Phrynosoma*, the Horned Toads, as these small, much flattened lizards are often called, inhabit the Southern United States and Mexico. **1956** C. H. POPE *Reptile World* 282 The grotesqueness of horned toads makes their bluffing antics ludicrous in the extreme. **1901** H. GADOW in *Cambr. Nat. Hist.* VIII. vi. 218 These 'horned toads' make a squeaking noise when teazed. **1956** G. DURRELL *Drunken Forest* vii. 134 'Horned toads.. three beauties.'.. The largest..was about the circumference of a saucer, and three-quarters of his bulk seemed to consist of head. **1767** *Phil. Trans.* LVI. 287 The ..*horned viper of Egypt..is very rare, and scarce to be found in any of the cabinets of natural curiosities in Europe. **1863** [see CERASTES]. **1926** T. E. LAWRENCE *Seven Pillars* (1935) IV. xlvii. 269 This year the valley seemed creeping with horned vipers. **1957** SCHMIDT & INGER *Living Reptiles of World* 162/2 The sharp-tailed worm lizard..is thought erroneously by the natives to be the very poisonous young of the horned viper, *Cerastes cornutus*. **1973** 'A. HALL' *Tango Briefing* iii. 47 'Mine was a horned viper—see that?' He showed me the fang-marks.

3. a. Having crescent horns, crescent-shaped.

c **1400** LYDG. *Floure Curtesie* 2 In Fevrier, whan the frosty mone Was horned. *c* **1560** A. SCOTT *Poems* (S.T.S.) xiv. 3 Hornit Dyane, with hir paly glemis. **1624** MASSINGER *Renegado* II. v, These knights of Malta..with their crosses Struck pale your horned moons. **1810** VINCE *Elem. Astron.* viii. 89 Venus and Mercury appear, first horned.

b. horned cairn, a type of long barrow peculiar to Scotland.

1877 W. GREENWELL *Brit. Barrows* 481 They are in all particulars, except in shape, like the 'horned' long cairns. **1907** T. R. HOLMES *Anc. Brit.* I. iii. 106 Intimately related to certain chambered long barrows and the famous horned cairns, which exist only in Caithness. **1954** S. PIGGOTT *Neolithic Cultures* viii. 238 These 'horned cairns' as they have been known since the nineteenth-century definition of the type.

†**4.** Of a cuckold: see HORN *sb.* 7. *Obs.*

1626 MIDDLETON *Anything for Quiet Life* IV. ii, Thou art a beast, a hornèd beast, an ox! **1719** D'URFEY *Pills* I. 349 The horn'd Herd within yon City Wall. **1830** in *Roxb. Ball.* (1890) VII. 195 You horned fumbling Cuckolds, in city, court, or town.

†**5.** Applied to bishops with reference to the shape of the mitre. *Obs.*

c **1425** LYDG. *Pilgr. Lyf Manhode* 1663 Ye that han in subieccioun Peplys vnder your prelacye..Thogh ye be hornyd to syth [= sight] outward [etc.]. **1558** KNOX *Serm.* in *Sel. Writ.* (1845) 236 Our horned and mitred bishops. *a* **1651** CALDERWOOD *Hist. Kirk* (1843) II. 172 To the servants of the devill, to your dumbe dogges, and horned bishops.

6. Armed or furnished with horn or horny substance.

1590 SPENSER *F.Q.* III. x. 45 All day they [Satyrs] daunced ..And with their horned feet the greene gras wore.

7. Provided, fitted, or ornamented with horn.

1801 WOLCOTT (P. Pindar) *Tears & Smiles* Wks. 1812 V. 42 Of spectacles that rode his nose He wink'd through each horn'd glass. **1884** *Pall Mall G. Extra* 24 July 9/2 Specimens of horns mounted in silver and horned goods generally.

II. [f. HORN. *v.* + -ED¹.]

†**8.** *Sc. Law.* 'Put to the horn'; proclaimed a rebel. *Obs.*

1705 HICKERINGILL *Priest-cr.* I. (1721) 38 The horn'd Man has no Remedy but to fly out of the Kingdom of Scotland.

Hence **'hornedness**, horned condition.

1777 BRAND *Pop. Antiq.* (1849) III. 241 The hornedness of the moon. **1852** J. MARTINEAU *Ess., Rev.* etc. (1891) III. 417 The previous coexistence of hornedness and rumination in our conception.

†**hornen**, *a.* *Obs.* exc. *dial.* [f. HORN *sb.* + -EN⁴. OE. had *hyrnen*:—OTeut. **hurnîno-*.] Made of horn.

1382 WYCLIF *Ps.* xcvii[i]. 6 In vois of the hornene trumpe. *a* **1825** FORBY *Voc. E. Anglia* s.v., 'A hornen-spoon'.

horner ('hɔːnə(r)), *sb.*¹ [f. HORN *sb.* or *v.* + -ER¹.]

1. A worker in horn; a maker of horn spoons, combs, etc.

1421–2 [see HORNING *vbl. sb.* 2]. *c* **1440** *Promp. Parv.* 247/1 Hornare, or horne make[r], *cornutarius*. **1464** *Rolls Parl.* V. 567/1 The men of the Craft of Horners enfraunchised in the Cite of London. **1484** *Nottingham Rec.* II. 346 Georgius Hoton..horner. **1607** DEKKER *Knt.'s Conjur.* (1842) 18 The head-warden of the horners. **1766** ENTICK *London* IV. 309 The most reputable inhabitants are the horners, who prepare horn for petty manufacturers. **1896** A. W. TUER *Hist. Horn-Bk.* I. vii. 91 The Horners' Exhibition held in London in 1882.

†**b.** One who makes musical horns. *Obs.*

1530 PALSGR. 232/2 Horner a maker of hornes, *cornettier*. **1552** *Loseley MSS.* (Kempe 1835) 53 Horner for blowinge hornes, turner for daggers.

2. One who blows or winds a horn.

14.. *Voc.* in Wr.-Wülcker 575/31 *Cornicarius*, an hornere. **1611** COTGR., *Corneux*, a Horner; a winder of a Horne. **1677** N. COX *Gentlem. Recreat.* (ed. 2) A iv b, Mr. Michael Marsh, Horner..who teaches to blow the Horn. **1827** in Hone *Every-day Bk.* II. 121 The keeper..blew 'the death of the buck', and..the horners..answered him. **1894** F. R. STOCKTON *Pomona's Trav.* 25 The horner blew his horn until his eyes seemed bursting.

†**3.** One who cuckolds; a cuckold-maker. *Obs.*

1598 FLORIO, *Cornaro*,..a horner. **1690** D'URFEY *Collin's Walk* III. (D.), 'Till th' Jury..Their favour gave with sense adorn'd, Not to the horner, but the horn'd. **1717** BULLOCK *Woman a Riddle* I. i, A cornuted coxcomb, that cou'd not smell his Horner from his house-dog.

†**4.** A person who has been 'put to the horn' or declared a rebel. *Sc. Obs.*

1590 *Sc. Acts Jas. VI* (1814) III. 525/1 Thair names salbe deleit out of the catologe of hornaris and..they sall not be forder troublit for that horning in tyme cuming. **1598** *Ibid.* IV. 174/2 To the effect the haill horneris registrat thairin and remaneing vnrelaxt may be extractit and chargit.

Hence †**'horneress**, a female worker in horn or maker of horns.

1530 PALSGR. 232/2 Horneresse, a woman, *cornettiere*.

Horner ('hɔːnə(r)), *sb.*² The name of W. G. *Horner* (1786–1837), English mathematician, used *attrib.* and in the possessive (esp. in ***Horner's method***) to designate a method for finding the real roots of a polynomial equated to zero by means of successive approximations.

It involves finding by trial the largest integer a_1 less than the root (x); transforming the equation to one with a root x^1

$= x - a_1$ (or $10(x - a_1)$, to avoid fractions); finding the largest one-place decimal (or integer) a_2 less than the new root; and so on, each approximation a_1, a_2, etc., providing one digit of the solution.

1842 *Penny Cycl.* XXIV. 341/1 The use of Horner's method is very much more easy than that of Newton. **1875** L. HENSLEY *Scholar's Algebra* xiii. 197 Horner's process..is applicable to find the roots of equations of all degrees. **1879** *Encycl. Brit.* VIII. 500/2 Horner's method (1819) gives the root as a decimal, figure by figure. **1913** W. P. MILNE *Higher Algebra* viii. 352 The determination of the two consecutive integers between which the required root of $f_2(x) = 0$ lies is therefore an easy matter very early in the Horner approximating process. **1957** K. S. KUNZ *Numerical Analysis* ii. 23 The Horner method was devised to reduce such pencil work. **1966** W. E. GROVE *Brief Numerical Methods* i. 1 Horner's method is not used in computing, for it is designed for hand calculation.

‖**hornero** (or'nero). [Sp., baker.] A South American bird of the genus *Furnarius*, esp. *F. rufus*; also called baker-bird, OVEN-BIRD.

1880 E. GIBSON in *Ibis* IV. 16 Furnarius Rufus. (Red Oven-Bird) Native name 'Hornero'... This species is.. probably one of the best-known of our Buenos-Ayrean birds. **1911** J. A. THOMSON *Biol. Seasons* II. 163 A masterpiece along the line illustrated by swallow and martin is the nest of some of the South American oven-birds (Furnarius)—for instance, of that species (F. rufus) which is called the 'hornero' or baker. **1956** G. DURRELL *Drunken Forest* i. 21 The oven-bird appears to have more than his fair share of personality and charm... An elderly peon..solemnly told me that he would never harm an *hornero*. **1970** R. MEYER DE SCHAUENSEE *Guide to Birds S. Amer.* 201 The name 'ovenbirds' has often been applied to this family [*sc.* Furnariidæ] because of the oven-like mud nests built by horneros.

Horner's syndrome. *Med.* [Named after J. F. *Horner* (1831–86), Swiss ophthalmologist.] A condition marked by abnormalities on one side of the face (including a contracted pupil, drooping upper eyelid, sunken eye, and a local inability to sweat) and caused by damage to the sympathetic nerves on that side of the neck.

1929 *Arch. Surg.* XVIII. 2025 The symptom-complex known variously as Claude Bernard-Horner syndrome (in France),..but usually and more rightly as Horner's syndrome. **1968** PASSMORE & ROBSON *Compan. Med. Studies* I. xxiv. 89 Interruption of the cervical part of the sympathetic chain of ganglia produces a condition known as Horner's syndrome. **1971** *Brit. Med. Bull* XXVII. 33/2 The presence of a single underlying lesion can readily be inferred from the detection of several symptoms or signs (e.g. Horner's syndrome).

hornet[1] ('hɔːnɪt). Forms: α. 1 hyrnetu, hyrnet, 5 hernet. β. 4 harnette, 6 harnet. γ. 6– hornet, (6 -ette, 7 -ett). [OE. *hyrnetu*, *hyrnet*, earlier *hurnitu*, *hirnitu*, fem. corresp. to MDu. *hōrnete*, *hornte*, MLG. *hornte*, LG. *hörnt*, *hornke*, EFris. *hörnetje*, *hörntje*, OHG. *hornuz*, *-oz*, *-az*, masc., MHG. *hornuz*, *-iz*, etc., Ger. *hornisse* (with many variants: see Grimm).

These words have the appearance of being derivatives of *horn*, a presumption strengthened by the OS. *hornobero*, and early mod.Du. *horener* (Kilian), which mean both 'horner or horn-blower' and 'hornet', also by Kilian's *hornsel* as a var. of *horsel(e*, mod.Du. *horzel*. Many scholars however incline to the opinion that the latter contains the original root, and that *hornut-* represents an original *horz-nut-*, formed, like MD. *horsele*, from a radical **hors-* = pre-Teut. **kṛs-*, found in OSlav. *sršĭ*, Lith. *szirszŭ* wasp, and perh. in L. *crābrōn-* for **crāsrōn-*. If this were so, the association with *horn* would be later and due to popular etymology. See Kluge s.v. *Hornisse*, Franck s.v. *Horzel*.]

1. a. An insect of the wasp family, esp. the European *Vespa Crabro* and the American *V. maculata*, much larger and stronger than other wasps, and inflicting a more serious sting.

c **725** *Corpus Gloss.* 603 Crabro, waefs *vel* hurnitu. *a* **800** *Erfurt Gloss.* 275 Crabro, hirnitu. *a* **1000** *Ags. Voc.* in Wr.-Wülcker 215/3 *Crabro*, hyrnetu. *c* **1000** ÆLFRIC *Gloss.* Ibid. 121/11 *Crabro*, hyrnet. **1387** TREVISA *Higden* (Rolls) II. 211 Of calues i-rooted comeþ bees, and of hors i-roted comeþ harnettes. **14..** *Voc.* in Wr.-Wülcker 619/7 *Vespa*, a waspe (*et est vespa major illa*, an hernet). **1535** COVERDALE *Deut.* vii. 20 The Lorde thy God also shal sende hornettes amonge them. **1565–73** COOPER *Thesaurus*, *Crabro*, a great waspe called an hornet. **1602** *Narcissus* (1893) 647 Thou huge and humminge humblebee, thou hornett. **1709** SWIFT *Tritical Ess.* Wks. 1755 II. I. 143 Laws are like cobwebs, which may catch small flies, but let wasps and hornets break through. **1802** BINGLEY *Anim. Biog.* (1813) III. 261 It is chiefly in the hollow trunks of decayed trees that the Hornets form their nest. **1855** LONGF. *Hiaw.* xvii. 10 Words of anger and resentment, Hot and humming like a hornet.

b. In early glosses and vocabularies (continental as well as Eng.: see Verwijs and Verdam, *Middelndl. Wbk.*), there is some confusion between the hornet and hornet-fly or large gadfly, due app. to uncertain use of L. *œstrus*.

c **1000** ÆLFRIC *Gloss.* in Wr.-Wülcker 121/12 *Œstrum*, beaw *uel* hyrnette. **1530** PALSGR. 232/2 Hornet a flye. **1658** PHILLIPS, *A Hornet*, a kinde of Insect, called in Latin Crabro, which useth to infest horses and other creatures, and is ingendred of the carcases of dead horses.

2. *transf.* and *fig.* An enemy that attacks persistently and with virulence; esp. in phr. ***hornets' nest, nest of hornets. to bring a hornets' nest about one's ears, arouse a nest of hornets***: to stir up a host of enemies around one; also, trouble, opposition. Also, ***to stir up a hornets' nest.***

1590 NASHE *Pasquil's Apol.* I. C ij, They are no better then the Prophets, which dwelt as it were in a nest of Hornets. **1739–40** RICHARDSON *Pamela* (1740) I. xxvi. 78, I rais'd a Hornet's Nest about my Ears, that..may have stung to Death my Reputation. **1751–73** JORTIN *Eccl. Hist.* (R.), He dared not speak out, and provoke the hornets. **1857** TROLLOPE *Barchester T.* xiv, But Proudie, ass as he is, knows the world too well to get such a hornets' nest about his ears. **1921** GALSWORTHY *To Let* I. i. 21 An acid humour stirred in his Forsyte blood; a subtle pain divided by hair's-breadth from pleasure. If only June did not suddenly bring her hornets about his ears! **1921** H. CRANE *Let.* 26 Nov. (1965) 71 But I also find that I stirred up a hornet's nest in me this summer with his words about getting away from current formulae. **1928** G. B. SHAW *Intell. Woman's Guide Socialism* lxxiv. 360 It is unlikely that a Proletarian House of Commons will suffer the nation's children to go on being taught Capitalist and Imperialist morality in the disguise of religion; and yet, the moment the subject is touched, what a hornet's nest is stirred up! **1966** *Listener* 4 Aug. 177/3 Judges have stirred up a hornets' nest in the sacred territory of 'the right to strike'. **1969** I. KEMP *Brit. G.I. in Vietnam* xiii. 200 On the third landing zone we ran into a hornet's nest. **1973** W. TUTE *Resident* iv. 67 The Ambassador wants you removed. You've got a hornet's nest buzzing round your head in Whitehall.

†**3.** The horned beetle or stag-beetle. *Obs.*

1585 HIGINS tr. *Junius' Nomenclator* 72/2 *Cerf volant*, a horned beetle: a bullfie, or hornet. **1598** FLORIO, *Bucarone*, ..a beetle, a hornet.

4. An artificial fly for salmon-fishing.

1867 F. FRANCIS *Angling* xii. (1880) 434 The Hornets.. have fat bodies dressed after the fashion of the 'bumble' trout fly.

5. *attrib.* and *Comb.*, as **hornet host, sting**; ***hornet-haunted*** adj.; **hornet-clearwing, -hawk, -moth**, names for certain moths of the genus *Sesia* (see quots.); **hornet-fly**, a dipterous insect of the family *Asilidæ*, a hawk-fly or robber-fly; †**hornet worm**, ? the larva of the hornet.

1869 E. NEWMAN *Brit. Moths* 16 The *Hornet Clearwing of the Osier (*Sesia Bembeciformis*). The Hornet Clear-wing of the Poplar (*Sesia Apiformis*). **1752** SIR J. HILL *Hist. Anim.* 31 The *Hornet Fly. This is one of the largest of the fly kind; it equals the hornet in size. **1816** KIRBY & SP. *Entomol.* (1843) II. 290, I have often been amused in my walks with the motions of the hornet fly (*Asilus crabroniformis*). **1895** K. GRAHAME *Golden Age* 43, I scrambled through the hedge, avoiding the *hornet-haunted side. **1832** J. RENNIE *Conspectus Butterfl. & Moths* 27 The *Hornet Hawk (*Tr[ochilium] Crabroniformis*) appears in July. **1834** MARY HOWITT *Sk. Nat. Hist.*, *Hornet* (1851) 185 The *hornet-host is retreating to its den. *a* **1450** *Fysshynge w. angle* (1883) 25 In Juyll..the water docke leyf worme & the *hornet worme.

hornet[2]. *nonce-wd.* [f. HORN *sb.* + -ET[1].] A diminutive horn.

1825 LAMB *Vis. Horns* Misc. Wks. (1871) 381 It was the least little hornet of a horn that could be framed.

hornfels ('hɔːnfɛls), *sb. Petrogr.* [a. G. *hornfels*, f. *horn* horn + *fels* rock.] A fine-grained, non-schistose rock composed mainly of quartz, micas, and feldspars and formed by the contact metamorphism of an argillaceous rock. Hence **horn'felsic** *a.*, composed of, or having the character of, hornfels.

1854 DANA *Syst. Min.* (ed. 4) II. 246 The Hornfels of the Germans is a massive compound of quartz and feldspar breaking with a smooth flinty fracture. **1888** J. J. H. TEALL *Brit. Petrogr.* xii. 374 We use the term hornfels instead of its etymological equivalent, hornstone, because in many cases the rocks termed hornfels are distinctly crystalline and not at all like what is commonly termed hornstone in this country. **1951** TURNER & VERHOOGEN *Igneous & Metamorphic Petrol.* xv. 373 Structure is typically granoblastic (hornfelsic) or maculose. **1965** G. J. WILLIAMS *Econ. Geol. N.Z.* vii. 73/2 The conglomerates are quartzose in some places, and elsewhere contain granite, greywacke and hornfelsic components.

So **'hornfels** *v. trans.*, to metamorphose (a rock) to hornfels; **'hornfelsed** (-fɛlst, -fɛlzd) *ppl. a.*, **'hornfelsing** *vbl. sb.*

1901 *Rep. Brit. Assoc.* 634 The Old Red Sandstone is indurated and often hornfelsed to a varying distance from the margin. **1922** *Nature* 12 Jan. 62/1 Hornfelsed green rocks. **1930** PEACH & HORNE *Geol. Scotl.* ii. 70 The hornfelsing of the orthogneisses. **1947** *Q. Jrnl. Geol. Soc.* CII. 395 The hornfelsed graywacke is slightly silicated. **1970** G. NEWALL et al. *Mechanism of Igneous Intrusion* iv. 49 The granite is in contact with hornfelsed pillow lavas.

horn-fish.

1. The garfish, *Belone vulgaris*, so called from its long projecting beak.

a **1000** *Andreas* 370 (Gr.) Hornfisc pleȝode, glad ȝeond garsecg. **1599** MINSHEU *Sp. Dict.*, Hornefish, *enxarraco, xarraco.* **1611** FLORIO, *Cornuto*..Also the Horne-fish. **1752** SIR J. HILL *Hist. Anim.* 223 We call it the Gar-fish, and, in some places, the Horn-fish.

2. The sauger or sand-pike, *Stizostedium canadense.*

1885 J. S. KINGSLEY *Stand. Nat. Hist.* III. 229 Sauger, sand-pike, gray-pike, blue-pike, and horn-fish, are.. designations of a smaller pike-perch, the *Stizostedion canadense.*

3. A fish of the family *Syngnathidæ*; a pipe-fish: so called from the horny texture of the exoskeleton.

hornful ('hɔːnfʊl). [f. HORN *sb.* + -FUL.] As much as a (drinking) horn holds, or will hold.

1610 MARKHAM *Masterp.* I. xli. 86 Giue it the horse to drinke, one horne-ful at his mouth, and another at his nosthrels. **1868** BAKER *Cast up by Sea* iii. 48 He poured out a large hornful for the lad.

†**horngeld.** *Old Law. Obs.* [f. HORN *sb.* + GELD *sb.*[1]] A feudal 'service', being a form of rent fixed according to the number of horned cattle; cornage.

c **1170** *Newminster Cartul.* (Surtees) 197 Et geldis, et danageldis, et hornegeldis. *c* **1250** BRACTON *Note-Bk.* (Maitland, 1887) No. 1270 Quia dedit cornagium quod anglice dicitur horngelde. **1579** RASTELL *Expos.*, Hornegeld. **1598** KITCHIN *Courts Leet* (1675) 415 If he hold to give to the King Hornegeld..it is great Serjeantry. **1628** COKE *On Litt.* 107 a, Cornage..is called in old bookes horngeld.

'hornified, *ppl. a.* [f. HORNIFY *v.* + -ED[1].]

†**1.** Make horned, cuckolded. *Obs.*

a **1693** URQUHART *Rabelais* III. xlvi. 373 Hornified and cornuted. **1769** *Pub. Advertiser* 18 May 4/1 My hornified Situation.

2. Adorned with horns; of a horn-like texture.

1789 J. BYNG *Diary* 30 June in *Torrington Diaries* (1935) II. 113 We enter'd the old cloisters, now glazed up; and so hornified are their walls, as to give horrible presage; their being horns of all sorts of wild cattle. **1963** R. R. A. HIGHAM *Handbk. Papermaking* ii. 36 The hornified cellulose fibres are not capable of assuming their original shape because of the permanent set that has taken place in the structural walls of the fibres.

hornify ('hɔːnɪfaɪ), *v.* [f. HORNY *a.* + -FY.]

1. *trans.* To make horny or horn-like in texture.

1670–7 J. COVEL *Diary* (Hakluyt Soc.) 215 Of a dryed film, or skin hornifyed. **1859** *Specif. Siemens' Patent* No. 2053 in J. Dredge *Electr. Illumin.* (1882) I. App. 82/2 Of vulcanite, or hornified india-rubber.

†**2.** To make horned, 'give horns to'; to cuckold. Hence **'hornifying** *vbl. sb.*; also **'hornifier; hornifi'cation**, cuckoldry. *Obs.*

1607 *World of Wonders* 78 They hornifie their husbands. **1611** COTGR., *Apistoler*,..to hornifie, or giue the blow that smarts not. *a* **1693** URQUHART *Rabelais* III. xlvi. 373 Hornifyer. **1698** J. CRULL *Muscovy* 52 Opportunity of hornifying their Husbands. **1819** 'R. RABELAIS' *Abeillard & Heloisa* 69 Sad and vile hornification.

hornily ('hɔːnɪlɪ), *adv.* [f. HORNY *a.* + -LY[2].] In a horny fashion; in a manner like horn.

1873 MISS BROUGHTON *Nancy* I. 280, I am now becoming hornily hard.

horniness ('hɔːnɪnɪs). [f. as prec. + -NESS.]

1. Horny quality or character.

1885 *Athenæum* 7 Feb. 190/1 It [the painting] has none of the yellow horniness common in Dous. **1894** *Ibid.* 5 May 587/2 A certain horniness..injures the coloration.

2. A state of sexual excitement. Cf. HORNY *a.* 2 b.

1963 T. PYNCHON *V.* i. 37 He was visited on a lunar basis by these great unspecific waves of horniness, whereby all women within a certain age group and figure envelope became immediately and impossibly desirable. **1969** P. ROTH *Portnoy's Complaint* 102 Do I really experience this restlessness, this horniness? **1971** *Esquire* July 48/4 He establishes adolescent horniness as a condition too furtive and bewildered..to admit of real caring.

horning ('hɔːnɪŋ), *vbl. sb.* [f. HORN *sb.* or *v.*]

†**1.** Bleeding with a horn. *Obs.*

1398 TREVISA *Barth. De P.R.* VII. xxviii. (Bodl. MS.), Leting of blood vndur þe tunge..copping or hornyng in þe nekke and in þe schuldres.

†**2.** Covering or furnishing with horn. *Obs.*

1421–2 *York Minster Fabric Acc.* (Surtees) 46 Thomæ Hornar..pro hornyng et naillyng superscriptorum librorum.

†**3.** Cuckolding, cuckoldry. *Obs.*

1575 LANEHAM *Let.* (1871) 40 Too auoow that many an honest man..hath had his hoous by horning well vphollden. **1588** SHAKS. *Tit. A.* II. iii. 67 'Tis thought you haue a goodly gift in Horning. **1762** J. H. STEVENSON *Crazy Tales* 55 An hour convenient for horning.

4. *Sc. Law.* 'Putting to the horn' (see HORN *sb.* 14). ***letters of horning***: a process of execution issued under the signet directing a messenger to charge a debtor to pay or perform in terms of the letters, under pain of being 'put to the horn', i.e. declared rebel. (Now largely superseded by the simpler forms of diligence introduced by 1 & 2 Vict. c. 114; but not obsolete.)

1536 *Sc. Acts Jas. V*, c. 38 (1814) II. 350/1 Þaim þat sustenit sik process of hornyng ȝere and day as said Is. **1568** in Calderwood *Hist. Kirk* (1843) II. 426 Upon the said letters of horning, to direct letters to officers of armes..to uptake the escheats of the persouns denounced and putt to the horne. **1733** NEAL *Hist. Purit.* II. 315 Who were charged with letters of Horning for their disobedience. **1754** ERSKINE *Princ. Sc. Law* (1809) 57. **1873** BURTON *Hist. Scot.* V. lvii. 166 The Government..relaxed the hornings,—that is to say, restored the men for the time to the protection of the law.

†**5.** The fact of becoming a crescent. *Obs.*

a **1646** J. GREGORY *Posth.* (1650) 168 (T.) They account.. from the horning [of the moon].

6. *Shipbuilding.* See HORN *v.* 4.

1879 *Cassell's Techn. Educ.* IV. 190/1 A line or batten is stretched from some point in the middle-line of the keel to the corresponding heads or sirmarks on the opposite sides,

and the two measurements must..be equal when the timbers are in place; this operation is termed 'horning'.

7. *attrib.* **horning-tackle**: see quot. 1850.

c **1850** *Rudim. Navig.* (Weale) 147 Horning Tackles.. most convenient to horn or square the frame as wanted. **1895** CROCKETT *Men of Moss Hags* xvi. 113 This is not a 'horning' but a hanging job.

'horning, *ppl. a.* [f. HORN *v.* + -ING².] That horns or 'puts to the horn': see prec., 4.

1705 HICKERINGILL *Priest-cr.* II. iii. 36 In no Nation in the World, but the poor, rigid, horning Scots.

†**horning**, app. a corruption of HORNEN *a. Obs.*

1622 W. HORNBYE *Horn-bk.* (Tuer), My honest, humble, harmlesse horning-book, From whence young Schollers their first learning took. **1632** HEYWOOD *2nd Pt. Know not me* I. Wks. 1874 I. 258 The horning-busk and silken bridelaces are in good request with the parsons wife.

hornish ('hɔːnɪʃ), *a.* [f. HORN *sb.* + -ISH.] Of or pertaining to a horn; of the nature of horn.

1634 M. SANDYS *Prudence* 21 (T.) Temperance, as if it were of a hornish composure, is too hard for the flesh. *a* **1638** MEDE *Apost. Later Times* (1641) 71 This Hornish soveraignty is..the conclusion of the fourth beast. *Ibid.*, Daniels hornish tyrant.

'hornist. [f. HORN *sb.* + -IST.] One who plays a horn; a performer on the (French) horn.

1836 *Knickerbocker* VIII. 71 Some evil-disposed citizens having no taste for music went to his honor the Mayor, and lodged grievous complaints against the distinguished hornist. **1865** tr. *Spohr's Autobiog.* I. 39 The hornist Bornaus, and others. **1867** *Cornh. Mag.* Jan. 28 Hornists or trumpeters. **1906** *Westm. Gaz.* 1 Mar. 12/1 Vivier was solo hornist in the orchestra of the Imperial Opera.

‖**hornito** (or'nito). [Sp., dim. of *horno* (:—L. *furnu-s*) oven, furnace.] A low oven-shaped mound of volcanic origin, usually emitting smoke and vapour from its sides and summit: frequent in South American volcanoes.

1830 LYELL *Princ. Geol.* I. 378 The small conical mounds (called 'hornitos' or ovens) [at Jorullo]. **1853** HERSCHEL *Pop. Lect. Sc.* i. §43 (1873) 33 Out of which sprang thousands of little volcanic cones called *Hornitos* or ovens. **1877** LE CONTE *Elem. Geol.* (1879) 83 These subordinate cones about the base, and upon the slopes of the principal cone, are called *monticules* or *hornitos*.

†**hornkeck.** *Obs.* [f. HORN *sb.*: the second element is obscure; can it have originated in a scribal error for *bek*, *beke*, BEAK, copied by successive compilers?] The garfish or hornbeak.

c **1425** *Voc.* in Wr.-Wülcker 642/19 *Hec gamorus*, hornekek. *c* **1440** *Promp. Parv.* 247/1 Horn keke, fysche (*P.* horn-kek, or garfysshe). *c* **1475** *Pict. Voc.* in Wr.-Wülcker 765/12-13 *Hec rugella*, *Hoc rustiforum*, a hornkeke. **1530** PALSGR. 232/2 Hornkecke, a fysshe lyke a mackerell. **1611** COTGR. *Orphie*, the Hornebeake, Hornekecke.. Garre-fish.

hornless ('hɔːnlɪs), *a.* [f. HORN *sb.* + -LESS.]

1. Without horns; destitute of horns.

1398 TREVISA *Barth. De P.R.* XVIII. xviii. (Bodl. MS.), þe camel..þowȝe he be horneles. **1611** COTGR., *Vicugne*, a hornelesse wild beast in Peru. **1766** PENNANT *Zool.* (1776) I. 20 The cattle of the highlands of Scotland are exceeding small, and many of them..are hornless. **1812** W. TENNANT *Anster F.* I. xii, The hornless moon among her brilliant host.

2. Without a horn (HORN *sb.* 15 a).

1909 *Talking Machine News* Oct. 337 Portable hornless machine. **1913** B. CLEMENTS-HENRY *Gramophones & Phonographs* ix. 54 Some modern disc machines are hornless. **1934** N. W. MCLACHLAN *Loud Speakers* xv. 256 A hornless speaker with baffle 4 ft. square. **1957** *Encycl. Brit.* XIV. 409/1 In the direct-radiator or hornless speakers the diaphragm is made large enough to radiate directly into unconfined air.

Hence **'hornlessness**, hornless condition.

1887 *Amer. Naturalist* XXI. 897 Herodotus's opinion as to the cause of hornlessness has been accepted by many writers down to the present times.

hornlet ('hɔːnlɪt). [-LET.] A little horn.

a **1794** SIR W. JONES *Observ. Ind. Plants* Wks. 1799 II. 105 Wings oblate..embracing the keel and the hornlets of the awning. **1894** R. B. SHARPE *Birds Gt. Brit.* (1896) 80 The horned larks..recognised by the little tufts of black feathers, or hornlets, on each side of the hinder crown.

'horn-like, *a.* Resembling horn or a horn.

1579 J. JONES *Preserv. Bodie & Soule* I. xl. 87 Swordlike, tunlike, hornelike,..and such other. **1684** BOYLE *Porousn. Anim. & Solid Bod.* v. 93 This horn-like Silver did dissolve neither. **1835-6** TODD *Cycl. Anat.* I. 314/1 The Hornbills have..upon their enormous beaks horn-like prominences. **1885** *Pall Mall G.* 31 Mar. 4/1 Certain notes, full, hornlike ..which no horn or violoncello ever equalled in timbre.

horn-mad, *a. arch.* **a.** App. orig. of horned beasts: Enraged so as to be ready to horn any one. Hence of persons: Stark mad; mad with rage; furious. Cf. the earlier HORN-WOOD.

1579 TOMSON *Calvin's Serm. Tim.* 57/2 With it must we fight against these hornemad beastes. **1596** NASHE *Saffron Walden* 32 A Bulls..bellowing and running horne mad at euery one in his way. **1607** WALKINGTON *Opt. Glass* 47 We must not..drinke our selues horne madde. **1608** TOPSELL *Serpents* (1658) 660 The perillous and transpiercing stinging of these horn-mad Hornets. **1695** CONGREVE *Love for L.* v. viii, She's mad for a Husband, and he's horn mad, I think, or they'd ne'er make a Match together. *a* **1773** in Hone *Every-day Bk.* (1825) I. 157 They run horn mad to go to law. **1893** STEVENSON *Catriona* 265 Miss Grant..would be driven fair horn-mad if she could hear of it.

†**b.** Sometimes by word-play: Mad with rage at having been made a cuckold. *Obs.*

1590 SHAKS. *Com. Err.* II. i. 57 *E. Dro.* Why Mistresse, sure my Master is horne mad. *Adri.* Horne mad, thou villaine? *E. Dro.* I meane not Cuckold mad, But sure he is starke mad. **1658** J. JONES *Ovid's Ibis* 51 A loose wife makes her husband horn-mad and heart-sad. *a* **1700** B. E. *Dict. Cant. Crew*, *Horn-mad*, stark staring Mad because Cuckolded. **1822** SCOTT *Nigel* xxvi, The man is mad, horn mad, to boot.

c. Lecherous. Cf. HORN *sb.* 5 c. *slang.*

1893 FARMER & HENLEY *Dict. Slang* III. 356 *Horn-mad*,.. sexually excited; lecherous. **1937** in PARTRIDGE *Dict. Slang.* **1951** R. CAMPBELL *Light on Dark Horse* xvii. 251 The evil-minded and horn-mad levantine.

Hence †**,horn-'madded** *ppl. a.*, driven horn-mad; **horn-'madness**, horn-mad condition.

1661 NEEDHAM *Hist. Eng. Reb.* in *Harl. Misc.* (Park) II. 523 The Houses know not what to think; The Cits horn-madded be. **1868** BROWNING *Ring & Bk.* II. 832 Somebody courts your wife, Count? Where and when? How and why? Mere horn-madness: have a care!

horn-owl. A horned owl, or one having plumicorns on the head, as some species of *Asio* and *Otus*; formerly, a name for the Eagle-owl.

1601 HOLLAND *Pliny* II. 397 The fat of the Bistard or Horn-owle is verie good. **1674** RAY *Words, Eng. Birds* 83 The Horn-Owl, *Otus sive Noctua aurita.* **1678** RAY *Willoughby's Ornith.* 99 The great Horn-Owl or Eagle-Owl. **1774** GOLDSM. *Nat. Hist.* V. 140 The Brown Horn Owl is often seen to prowl along the hedges by day.

hornpipe ('hɔːnpaɪp).

1. An obsolete wind instrument. Said to have been so called from having the bell and mouthpiece made of horn. See *Penny Cycl.* XII. 297.

c **1400** *Rom. Rose* 4250 Controve he wolde, and foule fayle, With hornepypes of Cornewayle. **14..** *Voc.* in Wr.-Wülcker 575/37 *Cornubium*, an hornpipe. **1579** SPENSER *Sheph. Cal.* May 23 A..Tabrere That..a Horne pype playd. **1592** GREENE *Groat's W. Wit* (1637) 14 Desiring them to play on an horn pipe. **1697** DRYDEN *Æneid* XI. 1086 The shrill horn-pipe sounds to bacchanals. **1788** *Chambers' Cycl.*, *Hornpipe*, a common instrument of music in Wales, consisting of a wooden pipe, with holes at stated distances and a horn at each end. **1891** *Daily News* 5 Oct. 2/3 Among other instruments were..the original hornpipe, which has now given its name to the popular sailors' dance.

†**b.** One who played the instrument. *Obs.*

a **1693** URQUHART *Rabelais* III. xlvi. 373 You will be the Hornepipe of Busancay.

2. A dance of a lively and vigorous character, usually performed by a single person, orig. to the accompaniment of the wind instrument, and specially associated with the merrymaking of sailors.

c **1485** *Digby Myst.* (1882) v. *Stage direct, ad fin.*, Here mynstrallys, an hornpype. **1597** MORLEY *Introd. Mus.* 181 Many other kindes of daunces (as hornepypes Iygges and infinite more). **1709** STEELE *Tatler* No. 106 ¶6 Florinda.. having danced the Derbyshire Hornpipe in the Presence of several Friends. **1755** JOHNSON, *Hornpipe*, a country dance, danced commonly to a horn. **1833** HT. MARTINEAU *Manch. Strike* vii. 80 It appeared from the heavy tread and shuffling of feet that some were dancing hornpipes.

fig. **1798** WOLCOTT (P. Pindar) *Tales of Hoy* Wks. (1823) 169/1 The true heart dances no hornpipes on the tongue. **1849** LYTTON *Caxtons* 38 My father..could conjure wonderfully, make a bunch of keys dance a hornpipe.

3. A piece of music for such a dance.

1789 BURNEY *Hist. Mus.* III. vii. 397 Harry Carey's ballad ..is a slower kind of hornpipe. **1838** *Penny Cycl.* XII. 297/1 That the dance-tunes still called *Hornpipes* were originally composed for the instrument. **1879** GROVE *Dict. Mus.* I. 753/1 Hornpipes were much written in the last century.. The airs 'My love is but a lassie yet' and 'The British Grenadier', and the hymn tune 'Helmsley', are hornpipes.

4. *attrib.*, as *hornpipe dancer*, *fling*.

1797 *Monthly Mag.* III. 61 The hornpipe movement given to 'When on the ocean', is particularly pleasing. **1845** J. T. SMITH *Bk. for Rainy Day* 6 Nancy Dawson, the famous hornpipe dancer, died this year [1767].

Hence **'hornpiping**, playing or dancing a hornpipe.

1864 *Realm* 30 Mar. 8 When we have praised..Miss Lydia Thompson's lively hornpiping.

horn-plate. An iron frame attached to the lower part of a railway carriage or truck and having two guides in which the journal-box of the axle moves; an axle-guard, pedestal.

1856 S. C. BREES *Gloss. Terms* 29 Axle Guard or Horn-plate. **1861** *Ann. Reg.* 5 The cause of the disaster was the breaking of one of the 'horn-plates' of the engine. **1864** *Daily Tel.* 1 Dec., Adopting the old classic car system of rollers fixed on a shaft or axle, which revolves with them in hole pins, or what are now termed horn plates.

horn-silver. *Min.* [Cf. Ger. *hornsilber.*] Native chloride of silver, so called from its horny appearance; cerargyrite.

1770 FORSTER tr. *Cronstedt's Min.* 178 The author.. quotes the horn silver ore..as proof of his opinion. **1812** SIR H. DAVY *Chem. Philos.* 211 It appears that muriatic acid gas is formed when horn silver is blackened by light. **1875** tr. *Vogel's Chem. Light* i. 4 In the mines of Friburg is now and then found a vitreous dull-shining silver ore, which on account of its appearance, is called *horn silver*.

†**hornslate** ('hɔːnsleɪt). *Min. Obs.* [Cf. Ger. *hornschiefer.*] A schistous form of hornstone.

1791 BEDDOES in *Phil. Trans.* LXXXI. 60 The Scheibenberg, near Königsbruck, consists of a stone which Mr. Leske knows not whether to call hornslate, or corneous porphyry. **1796** KIRWAN *Elem. Min.* (ed. 2) I. 307 Hornslate..Schistose Porphyry of Werner. **1799** W. TOOKE *View Russian Emp.* I. 116 Pebbles of hornslate.

hornsman ('hɔːnzmən). [f. *horn's* poss. case: cf. *townsman*, etc.]

1. A man who plays a horn.

1897 *Q. Rev.* Apr. 521 The hornsman himself was cut down, and the famous horn captured.

2. The horned adder or plumed viper of Africa, *Clotho cornuta*.

1890 in *Cent. Dict.*

†**'horn-stock.** *Obs.*

1. The garfish or hornbeak.

a **1485** *Promp. Parv.* 247/1 (MS. S.) Horne stoke [*c* **1440** Horn keke; *Pynson*, or garfysshe].

2. A cuckold.

1611 CHAPMAN *May-Day* Plays 1873 II. 393 Alas, poore hornestocke, he thinks her to haue no fault.

hornstone ('hɔːnstəʊn). *Min.* [tr. Ger. *hornstein*: from its appearance.] A compact siliceous rock, resembling flint, but more brittle; chert.

1728 WOODWARD *Catal. For. Fossils* I 11 Rother Hornstein, i.e., Red Hornstone. **1796** KIRWAN *Elem. Min.* (ed. 2) I. 305 Hornstone differs from jaspers, often by its splintery fracture. **1816** KEATINGE *Trav.* (1817) II. 155 Here the sand-stone approaches to horn-stone; that is, assumes the rhomboidal conformation. **1833** LYELL *Princ. Geol.* III. 370. *a* **1862** THOREAU *Maine W.* iii. (1864) 180 This variety of hornstone I have seen..in..New England, in the form of Indian arrowheads, hatchets, chisels, &c.

b. *attrib.*, as *hornstone basis*, *porphyry*.

1796 KIRWAN *Elem. Min.* (ed. 2) I. 351 Hornstone Porphyry. *Ibid.* 368 [It] has for its ground a hornstone basis.

hornswoggle ('hɔːnswɒg(ə)l), *v. colloq.* (orig. *U.S.*). [Prob. fanciful.] *trans.* To get the better of; to cheat or swindle; to hoodwink, humbug, bamboozle.

1829 *Virginia Lit. Museum* I. 458 *Hornswoggle*, to embarrass irretrievably. **1834** W. A. CARRUTHERS *Kentuckian in N.Y.* I. 61, I wish I may be horn swoggled, if ever I thought [etc.]. **1860** *Oregon Argus* 12 May (Th.), P. F. is going to hornswoggle the Douglas Democrats. **1904** *Boston Herald* 27 June 6 One practical working theory in advertising circles is that the ad's chief function is to hornswoggle the consumer. **1911** H. QUICK *Yellowstone Nights* iii. 82 If you'll stand by..and see your old father hornswoggled out of his eye-teeth you'll never see a cent of my money. **1958** *Spectator* 11 Apr. 448/3, I am sure the manufacturers hornswoggle us and sell us a lot of useless trim and gadgets. **1968** *Guardian* 28 Feb. 18/8 In this wretched week we get a report from the Government Actuary which is quoted to hornswoggle us into increased insurance contributions. **1970** *Sunday Times* 28 June 11/3 The Americans look for value; you can't..hornswoggle them.

†**horn-'wood**, *a. Obs.* [f. HORN *sb.* + WOOD *a.* mad.] = HORN-MAD.

? *a* **1500** *Chester Pl.* (Shaks. Soc.) II. 68 Though Cayphas goe horne-wood therby. **1546** J. HEYWOOD *Prov.* (1867) 82 She was (as they say) horne wood. **1581** MARBECK *Bk. of Notes* 143 A Bull..of his hornewoode and madde fiercenesse, when he is well baited. **1600** HOLLAND *Livy* XXXI. xviii. 784 The King amazed and astonied to see them thus horne-wood, stayed the bloudie hand of his owne souldiours.

hornwork ('hɔːnwɜːk). [f. HORN *sb.* + WORK.]

1. *Fortif.* A single-fronted outwork, the head of which consists of two demi-bastions connected by a curtain and joined to the main body of the work by two parallel wings. It is thrown out to occupy advantageous ground which it would have been inconvenient to include in the original enceinte.

1641 EVELYN *Diary* 6 Aug., I watched on a horne worke neere our quarters. **1759** STERNE *Tr. Shandy* II. xii, The horn-work..is formed by two epaulments of demi-bastions. **1813** WELLINGTON in Gurw. *Desp.* XI. 61 *note*, A mine was exploded in the left angle of the counter-scarp of the horn-work, which did great damage.

2. Work done in horn; articles made of horn.

1642 MILTON *Apol. Smect.* xii, No helmet of salvation, but the meere mettle and horn-work of Papall jurisdiction. **1777** W. DALRYMPLE *Trav. Sp. & Port.* cxxxi, This town is famous for horn-work. **1887** DONALDSON *Suppl. to Jamieson* s.v. *Horner*, A few of the simpler branches of horn-work are still followed by tinkers and gipsies.

†**3.** Cuckoldry. *Obs.*

1738 *Common Sense* I. 344. **1759** STERNE *Tr. Shandy* II. xii. **1813** MOORE *Poems, Re-inforcem. for Duke.*

hornwort ('hɔːnwɜːt). [f. HORN *sb.*¹ + WORT, after Gr. κερατόφυλλον, i.e. horn-leaf: from the appearance of the branched stem.] A book-name of *Ceratophyllum demersum*, an aquatic plant with dense whorls of finely-divided leaves; also called *horned pondweed*.

1805 J. GALPINE *Brit. Bot.* (1806) 399. **1857** HENFREY *Bot.* 384 *Ceratophyllaceæ*, the Hornwort Order. **1885** GEIKIE *Text-bk. Geol.* (ed. 2) 880 Cones of Scotch fir and spruce,.. hornwort, blackthorn, bog-bean.

hornwrack ('hɔːnræk). [f. HORN *sb.* + WRACK, seaweed cast ashore.] A polyzoon of the genus

Flustra, resembling a seaweed in appearance, and of somewhat horny consistency.

1819 *Pantologia, Flustra*, horn-wrack. **1888** ROLLESTON & JACKSON *Anim. Life* 234 Broad-leafed Hornwrack (*Flustra foliacea*).

horny ('hɔːnɪ), *a.* (*sb.*) [f. HORN *sb.* + -Y.]

A. *adj.* 1. a. Consisting of horn; of a texture resembling that of horn; corneous.

1398 TREVISA *Barth. De P.R.* v. v. (Bodl. MS.), Foure [webbes] bene in the formest partye [of the eye]..the thredde de cornia, horny. **1530** PALSGR. 316/1 Horny, made or stored of hornes. **1615** tr. *De Monfart's Surv. E. Indies* 20 With a kind of hornie rinde. **1671** MILTON *P.R.* II. 267 Him thought, he..saw the Ravens with their horny beaks Food to Elijah bringing euen and morn. **1774** GOLDSM. *Nat. Hist.* (1776) VI. 253 These eggs [of the ray] are covered with a tough horny substance. **1864** H. SPENCER *Illustr. Univ. Progr.* 398 *Amœba*-like creatures, massed together in a frame-work of horny fibres, constitute Sponge.

†b. ***horny gate*** (*port*), the gate of horn: see GATE *sb.*[1] 5. *Obs.*

1592 SYLVESTER *Tri. Faith* I. i, Sad Morpheus, entring in Through's horny gate. *a* **1649** DRUMM. OF HAWTH. *Poems* Wks. (1711) 17/1 Dametas dream'd he saw his wife at sport, And found that sight was through the horny port.

†c. ***horny coronet***, humorously put for 'cuckold's horns'. *Obs.*

1688 CROWNE *Darius* Prol., He dubs this man a knave, a coxcomb that, Gives any brow a horny coronet.

2. *transf.* a. Callous or hardened so as to be horn-like in texture.

1693 TATE in *Dryden's Juvenal* (1697) 370 Who, wanting Weapons, clutch their horny Fists. **1697** DRYDEN *Virg. Georg.* IV. 172 Till his hard horny Fingers ake with Pain. **1875** HAMERTON *Intell. Life* v. ii. 177 It is observed that horny hands, in the colonies, get gold into them sooner than white ones. **1884** W. C. SMITH *Kildrostan* I. i. 84 Bronzed with weather, and horny of hand.

b. Sexually excited; lecherous. (Chiefly used of a man.) *slang*. Cf. HORN *sb.* 5 c.

1889 BARRÈRE & LELAND *Dict. Slang* I. 476/1 *Horny*, lecherous, in a state of sexual desire, in rut. **1918** *Dialect Notes* V. 25 *Horny*, amative. **1949** H. MILLER *Sexus* (1969) v. 104 Her thick, gurgling voice saying..: 'Get it in all the way...please, please do... *I'm horny*.' *Ibid.* x. 239 When I look at this thing I get horny again. **1965** J. L. HERLIHY *Midnight Cowboy* (1966) II. v. 120 You *are* a gorgeous-lookin' piece, Cass. Gets a guy all horny just *lookin'* at you. **1968** M. RICHLER *Cocksure* xi. 63 When..he used to make a habit of watching the hockey games..he always felt horny. **1970** T. LEWIS *Jack's Return Home* 43 The talk'd got filthier. It'd made me very horny. **1971** *Black World* Oct. 65/1 Ain't that the horny bitch that was grindin with the blind dude.

3. Semi-opaque like horn.

1652 BP. HALL *Invis. World* I. v, The [angels] do not, as we mortals are wont, look through the dim and horny spectacle of senses. **1830** M. DONOVAN *Dom. Econ.* I. 75 So affected as to be at least horny, if not in a slight degree transparent. **1859** GULLICK & TIMBS *Paint.* 202 The media afforded by expressed oils become horny or semi-opaque.

4. Bearing, having, or abounding in horns or horn-like projections.

1530 [see 1]. **1613** PURCHAS *Pilgrimage* (1614) 89 So it appeareth by her hornie head. *a* **1825** FORBY *Voc. E. Anglia*, *Horny*, abounding in horns. It is applied to a sample of barley, from which the awns have not been properly separated in the process of winnowing.

5. Consisting of beasts' horns.

a **1732** GAY *Birth of Squire* (T.), The horny spoils that grac'd the wall.

6. Of sounds: Like that of a horn.

1888 P. H. FITZGERALD *Fatal Zero* ix. 48 When they open their full lips out streams the twang, nasal and horny!

7. *Comb.*, parasynthetic, as ***horny-browed***, ***-eyed***, ***-fisted***, ***-handed***, ***-hoofed***, ***-knuckled***, ***-nibbed*** adjs.; **horny-head** (in full **hornyhead chub**) *U.S.*, a North American cyprinid fish, *Nocomis biguttatus*; occasionally also used for *Campostoma anomalum*, a smaller cyprinid.

1916 JOYCE *Portrait of Artist* iii. 158 Goatish creatures with human faces, *horny browed, lightly bearded and grey as indiarubber. **1912** W. OWEN *Let.* 2 July (1967) 148 A bushy-browed and *horny-fisted blacksmith's assistant. **1859** J. BROWN *Rab & F.* 8 That *horny-handed, snell, peremptory little man. **1892** *Spectator* 10 Dec. 847/2 He must have employed indirectly tens of thousands of the horny-handed. **1882** JORDAN & GILBERT *Synopsis Fishes N. Amer.* 212 C[eratichthys] *biguttatus*..*Horny Head; River Chub; Jerker. **1933** *Amer. Speech* VIII. 50/1 Horny-head... A chub-like fish with short, horny protuberances on the scales, those on top of the head being largest. **1963** P. A. PARSONS *Outdoor Life Compl. Bk. Freshwater Fishing* iv. 45 Hornyhead chubs, excellent bait for members of the pike family, are durable on the hook. **1965** A. J. McCLANE *Standard Fishing Encycl.* 891/2 Stoneroller. *Campostoma anomalum*. Also known as hornyhead and knottyhead, it is a brownish-olive minnow with a brassy luster. **1513** DOUGLAS *Æneis* VII. xiii. 179 From the tempil of Diane euermo Thir *horny hovit horssis bene debarrit. **1812** W. TENNANT *Anster F.* II. xxxvii, The *horny-knuckl'd kilted Highlandman. **1880** TENNYSON *Battle of Brunanburh* xiv, The *horny-nibb'd raven.

B. *sb.* 1. Usually ***Auld Hornie***: A name for the devil. *Sc.*

1785 BURNS *Addr. to Deil* i, O thou! whatever title suit thee, Auld Hornie, Satan, Nick, or Clootie. **1806** J. BLACK *Falls of Clyde* I. iv, I'm sure I wish them a' in hell Wi' Hornie their auld father there to dwell. **1840** GEN. P. THOMPSON *Exerc.* (1842) V. 44 As 'old Hornie', or somebody I took for him, once said to me.

2. A policeman. *slang*.

1753 J. POULTER *Discoveries* (ed. 2) 39 *A Horney*,..a Constable. **1789** G. PARKER *Life's Painter* xiv. 116 There's no horneys, traps, scouts, nor beak-runners amongst them. **1856** J. STRANG *Glasgow & its Clubs* 187 Town officers.. were then better known by the appellation of red-coat officers or *hornies*. **1922** JOYCE *Ulysses* 160 Can't blame them after all with the job they have especially the young hornies.

3. A cow; a bullock. *Sc.* and *Austral. slang*.

1808 A SCOTT *Poems* 81 Bedown the green the hornies rowt. **1879** G. MACDONALD *Sir Gibbie* I. xiv. 194 Hornie —so named, indeed, because of her readiness to use the weapons with which Nature had provided her..was in fact a malicious cow. **1933** *Bulletin* (Sydney) 18 Jan. 25 Polled cattle graded better than the hornies. **1938** X. HERBERT *Capricornia* (1939) xx. 273 Hornies, or beasts with ingrowing horns. **1943** BAKER *Dict. Austral. Slang* 40 *Horney-steerer*, a bullock driver.

†**horodix.** *Obs. rare*[−0]. [f. Gr. ὥρα hour + δεῖξις exhibition, f. δεικ- to show.] 'A kind of dial, or instrument to shew how the hours pass away' (Phillips 1658; thence in Bailey 1721, etc.).

horoeka (hɒrəʊ'iːka). [Maori.] A small, round-headed New Zealand tree, *Pseudopanax crassifolium*, which has a juvenile form with long, toothed leaves; = LANCEWOOD 2.

1831 G. BENNETT in *London Med. Gaz.* 5 Nov. 150/1 (*heading*) The Horoeka Tree of New Zealand. This tree.. has not yet been observed by botanists either in flower or fructification. **1838** J. S. POLACK *New Zealand* II. 399 *Horoeka*..is generally found on elevated lands, grows to the height of thirty feet. **1868** J. BUCHANAN in *Trans. N.Z. Inst.* I. Essays III. 33 Horoeka (*Panax crassifolium*). A singular-looking plant in all stages of its growth. Three varieties are found at Dunedin, only distinguishable, in the young state, by the method of inflorescence. **1899** T. KIRK *Students' Flora N.Z.* 222 P[*anax*] *crassifolium*... A round-headed tree ..20 ft.-60 ft. high... *Horoeka*. *a* **1939** 'R. HYDE' *Houses by Sea* (1952) 64 They cut the yellow twisted horoeka For sticks.

horograph ('hɒrəgrɑːf, -græf). *Math.* [f. Gr. ὅρο-ς boundary + -GRAPH.] (See quot.)

1879 THOMSON & TAIT *Nat. Phil.* I. I. §136 The *curvatura integra* of any given portion of a curved surface, is the area enclosed on a spherical surface of unit radius by a straight line drawn from its centre, parallel to a normal to the surface, the normal being carried round the boundary of the given portion. The curve thus traced on the sphere is called the *Horograph* of the given portion of curved surface.

horography (hɒ'rɒgrəfɪ). [a. F. *horographie* (1644 in Hatz.-Darm.), f. ὥρα time, season + -γραφία writing.] (See quots.)

1727-41 CHAMBERS *Cycl.*, *Horography*, the art of making or constructing dials; called also horologiography. **1755** JOHNSON, *Horography*, an account of the hours. **1798** J. GILCHRIST in *Asiat. Res.* V. 81 [They] reckon and divide time in the following manner, which exhibits a horography so imperfect..that [etc.].

So **ho'rographer**, a horologer, horologist.

In recent Dicts.

horologe ('hɒrəlɒdʒ). Forms: α. 4 orlogge, 4-5 orloge, 4-6 orlege, 4-7 -lage, 5 -legge, -lyge, horlege, (6 orlache, horleige). β. 4 orologe, 4-5 oriloge, 5 oro-, oryloge, orrelegge, (horolage, 6 hora-, horyloge, horrelage), 5- horologe. [a. OF. *orloge*, *oriloge*, mod.F. *horloge* (= It. *orologio*, Sp. *reloj*, Pg. *relogio*, Pr. *reloge*):—L. *hōrologium*, a. Gr. ὡρολόγιον instrument for telling the hour or time, dim. of ὡρολόγος hour-teller, f. ὥρα time + -λογος telling. The initial *h* in Fr. and Eng., and the medial *o* in Eng. are owing to later conformation to L.]

1. An instrument for telling the hour; a timepiece; a dial, hour-glass, or clock.

1382 WYCLIF *Isa.* xxxviii. 8 The shadewe of lynes bi the whiche it hadde go doun in the oriloge [**1388** orologie] of Acath. *c* **1386** CHAUCER *Nun's Pr. T.* 34 (Ellesm. MS.) Wel sikerer was his crowyng in his logge Than is a Clokke or an abbey Orlogge. **1413** *Pilgr. Sowle* (Caxton 1483) v. xiv. 81 And by this tyme the Horologe had fully performed half his nyghtes cours. *c* **1449** PECOCK *Repr.* I. xx. 118 Orologis, schewing the houris of the daie bi schadew maad bi the sunne in a cercle. **1481** CAXTON *Myrr.* III. x. 152 By hym were founden first the oryloges of the chirches whiche begynne the houres of the dayes & of the nyghtes. *a* **1535** MORE *7th Pageant*, *Tyme* (R.), I, whom thou seest with horyloge in hande, Am named Tyme. **15..** *Aberdeen Reg.* V. 16 (Jam.) The tolbuith horrelage. **1627** in J. Irving *Hist. Dumbarton* (1860) 478 The paynting and cullaring of the orlage. *a* **1652** J. SMITH *Sel. Disc.* v. 142 This world indeed is a great horologe to itself, and is continually numbering out its own age. **1853** G. JOHNSTON *Nat. Hist. E. Bord.* I. 101 The flower affords a horologe of a primitive sort. **1884** TENNYSON *Becket* II. ii, Always in suspense, like the tail of the horologe—to and fro—tick-tack.

b. *transf.* and *fig.* Applied to the cock, chanticleer; and in other applications. ***horologe of Flora***, ***Flora's horologe*** (*Horologium Floræ*, Linnæus *Philos. Bot.* (1750) §335): see quot. 1789.

c **1381** CHAUCER *Parl. Foules* 350 The kok, that orloge ys of thorpis lyte. **1513** DOUGLAS *Æneis* I. Prol. 346 Thocht venerable Chaucer, principall poet but peir, Hevinlie trumpat, horleige [**1553** orlege] and reguleir. **1604** DRAYTON *Moses* II. (L.), The cock, the country horologe, that rings The chearful warning to the sun's awake. **1659** T. PECKE *Parnassi Puerp.* 88 The Countrey Horologe, first claps his wings; Before he News of grateful Day-light brings. **1691** E. TAYLOR *Behmen's Philos.* 396 This Soul, the Horologe of Nature. **1789** E. DARWIN *Bot. Garden* 62 *note*, Many other flowers close and open their petals at certain hours of the day; and thus constitute, what Linneus calls the Horologe, or Watch of Flora. **1798** CHARL. SMITH *Young Philos.* IV. 59 *note*, Notes on..the horologe of Flora, in the Oeconomy of Vegetation. **1817** SOUTHEY *Ess.* (1832) II. 23 The hand of the political horologe cannot go back. **1837** SIR F. PALGRAVE *Merch. & Friar* iv. (1844) 157 Make your government horologe go right. **1845** LONGF. *Old Clock on Stairs* ix, The horologe of Eternity Sayeth this.

†2. Phrase. ***the devil in the horologe***: the devil in the clock playing pranks with its works and making chaos of its time-keeping; a type of the confusion and disorder caused by a mischievous agent in any orderly system. *Obs.*

1519 HORMAN *Vulg.* 232 b, Some for a tryfull pley the deuyll in the orlege. *a* **1553** UDALL *Royster D.* III. ii. (Arb.) 43 *Cust.* What will he? *Me.* Play the deuill in the horologe. **1562** J. HEYWOOD *Prov. & Epigr.* (1867) 149 The diuell is in thorologe, the houres to trye, Searche houres by the sunne, the deuyls dyall wyll lye. **1589** R. HARVEY *Pl. Perc.* (1590) 18 Martins clocke goes true, though the Diuell were in the Horologe.

3. *attrib.*

1483 *Cath. Angl.* 188/2 An Horlege loker, *horuspex*.

horologer (hɒ'rɒlədʒə(r)). Forms: 5-6 orloger(e, 6 orla-, orliger(e, 6-7 orleger(e, 7 horaloger, 9 horologer. [ME. and AFr. *orloger* = OF. *orlogier*, f. *orloge*: see prec. and -ER[2]. The mod. word is a new formation from *horologe*.]

1. A clock-maker, horologist.

[**1368** *Pat. Roll 42 Edw. III*, I. 5 in Rymer *Fœdera* (1830) III. II. 845 Johannem Vueman, Willielmum Vueman, et Johannem Lietuyt de Delft, orologiers, veniendo in regnum nostrum.] **1496** *Dives & Paup.* (W. de W.) I. xviii. 52/2 Thou mayst not knowe by the orloge what tyme the orloger wyll sett it. **1822** SCOTT *Nigel* vi, The young lord naturally addressed himself next to the old horologer's very pretty daughter. **1865** *Pall Mall G.* 10 Nov. 9 We advise that facetious horologer to offer to take down his clock.

2. A proclaimer of the hours.

c **1420** LYDG. *Story of Thebes* Prol., I will myself, be your Orlogere. **1513** DOUGLAS *Æneis* VII. Prol. 113 Phebus crownit byrd, the nychtis orloger [**1553** orlagere]. **1616** J. LANE *Cont. Sqr.'s T.* VI. 1 Chaunticleer, the sadd nightes horaloger, vp thrilld the poize that his clockes watch gann sterr.

†**horo'logial**, *a. Obs.* = HOROLOGICAL.

1662 J. CHANDLER *Van Helmont's Oriat.* 127 Seven points after the ninth houre Solar or according to the Sun, and not horologiall or according to the Diall or Clock.

horologic (hɒrəʊ'lɒdʒɪk), *a.* [ad. L. *hōrologic-us*, a. Gr. ὡρολογικός, f. ὥρα HOUR + -λογος telling: see -IC.] Of or pertaining to horology.

1665 SIR T. HERBERT *Trav.* (1677) 377 Horologic knowledge they want, as may be supposed by that..King who upon first view of a Watch..believed it a living creature. **1850** LEITCH tr. *C.O. Müller's Anc. Art* §153 (ed. 2) 128 The octagonal horologic building of Andronicus Cyrrhestes. **1859** WRAXALL tr. *R. Houdin* iii. 21 Blois, a town which has long excelled in the horologic art.

b. *Bot.* Of a flower: Opening and closing at certain hours.

1882 in OGILVIE, and later Dicts.

horological (hɒrəʊ'lɒdʒɪkəl), *a.* [f. as prec. + -AL[1].] Of or pertaining to a horologe or to horology; measuring or recording time.

1593 FALE *Dialling* A iij b, The making of the Horologicall Cylindre..we have presently omitted. **1653** W. OUGHTRED (*title*) Description and Use of the General Horological Ring, and the Double Horizontal Dial. **1838** *Penny Cycl.* XII. 297/2 The middle of the fourteenth century seems to be the time which affords the first certain evidence of the existence of what would be now called a clock, or regulated horological machine. **1867** A. BARRY *Sir C. Barry* vi. 177 Mechanical ingenuity, and horological knowledge.

Hence **horo'logically** *adv.*, in a horological manner.

1727 in BAILEY vol. II. **1851** *Tait's Mag.* XVIII. 469 Chronologically, or rather horologically, the most convenient course.

†**horologiography** (ˌhɒrəʊlɒdʒɪ'ɒgrəfɪ). *Obs.* [f. Gr. ὡρολόγιο-ν HOROLOGE + -GRAPHY.] a. A description of horologes or timepieces. b. The art of constructing horologes; dialling.

[**1570** DEE *Math. Pref.* d ij, Horometrie..called..of late *Horologiographia*.] **1639** WYBARD (*title*) Lunar Horologiographie. **1653** W. OUGHTRED (*title*) Mathematicall Recreations, a collection of problems, as secrets and experiments in Arithmetick, Cosmographie, Horologiography [etc.]. **1696** PHILLIPS (ed. 5), *Horologiography*, the Art of making or treating of the Properties of Dials, Clocks [etc.].

Hence †**horologio'graphian**, †**horologi'ographer**, a maker of timepieces; a horologist. †**horologio'graphic** *a.*, pertaining to dialling.

1688 R. HOLME *Armoury* III. 372/1 An Horologiographian [is] a Sun Dial maker. **1727** BAILEY vol. II, *Horologiographer*, a maker of Dials [etc.]. **17..** CHAMBERS (T.), The gnomonick projection is also called the horologiographick projection, because it is the foundation of dialling.

horologist (hɒ'rɒlədʒɪst). [mod. f. HOROLOGE or HOROLOGY + -IST.] One who is skilled in horology; a maker of timepieces; a clock- or watch-maker.

1798 J. GILCHRIST in *Asiat. Res.* V. 86 The grand horologist himself is about to inform them, that now is the time. *a* **1857** LD. ELLESMERE *Addr.* etc. 54 (L.) The name of Mr. B. L. Vulliamy is one well known as connected with the highest eminence in his profession as an horologist. **1884**

Spectator 12 July 923/2 The..advocate..was a journeyman horologist.

‖**horologium** (hɒrəʊ'lɒdʒɪəm, -'ləʊdʒɪəm). Also (in sense 3) -on. [L. *hōrologium*, Gr. ὡρολόγιον: see HOROLOGE.]

1. = HOROLOGE 1; a dial, clock, or chronometer.

horologium Floræ: see HOROLOGE 1 b.

a **1661** FULLER *Worthies* II. (1662) 72 He presented King Henry the 8. with a Horologium..observing the shadow of the sun. **1846** ELLIS *Elgin Marb.* I. 29 The horologium, or water clock. **1866** *Treas. Bot.*, *Horologium Floræ*, a time-paper of flowers; a table explaining the time at which the same flowers expand in different latitudes.

2. *Astrol.* One of the southern constellations.

1819 *Pantologia*, *Horologium*,..a new southern constellation. **1838** *Penny Cycl.* XII. 297/1 *Horologium*, the Clock, a southern constellation of Lacaille. It is cut by a line passing through Canopus to the southern part of Eridanus.

3. *Gr. Ch.* A book containing the offices for the canonical hours; corresponding to a certain extent with the Western breviary.

1724 WATERLAND *Athan. Creed* vi. 56 This Horologion belong'd to a monk of Constantinople. **1727–41** CHAMBERS *Cycl.*, *Horologium, Horologion*, is also a name the Greeks give to their liturgy, or breviary. **1875** *Smith's Dict. Chr. Antiq.* I. 784 The contents of the *Great Horologium*, which is the fullest form. *Ibid.*, The *Horologion* is often prefaced by the calendar of the Menology, which begins with September.

horology[1] (hɒ'rɒlədʒɪ). Also 4 orologie, 6 horologie. [ad. L. *hōrologi-um*, ad. Gr. ὡρολόγιον.]

†**1.** = HOROLOGE 1; a dial, clock, or timepiece.

1388 [see HOROLOGE 1]. **1509** HAWES *Past. Pleas.* XLIV. ii, In his left hande he had an horology. **1594** BLUNDEVIL *Exerc.* III. I. xlviii. (ed. 7) 363 The most part of Horologies or clocks in the East country. **1639** DRUMM. OF HAWTH. *Consid. to Parlt.* Wks. (1711) 186 That great horologies of towns be reformed according to the small sun-dials. **1798** J. GILCHRIST in *Asiat. Res.* V. 87 The simple rude horology described above suffices..the Asiatics in general. **1836** I. TAYLOR *Phys. Th. Another Life* 29 This stupendous machinery [nature] is a vast horology—a register of duration to all rational tribes.

2. A rendering of HOROLOGIUM 3.

1890 in *Cent. Dict.*

ho'rology[2]. [f. Gr. ὥρα time, HOUR + -(O)-LOGY, after Gr. type *ὡρολογία.] The art or science of measuring time; the construction of horologes.

1819 *Pantologia* s.v., The term horology is at present more particularly confined to the principles upon which the art of making clocks and watches is established. **1848** CARPENTER (*title*) Mechanical Philosophy, Horology, and Astronomy. **1872** YEATS *Techn. Hist. Comm.* 381 About this time.. horology was first applied to astronomical purposes.

horomai, var. HAEREMAI.

horometer (hɒ'rɒmɪtə(r)). [f. Gr. ὥρα time + -METER.] An instrument for measuring the time.

1775 in ASH. Hence in MAUNDER, WORCESTER, etc.

horometrical (hɒrəʊ'mɛtrɪkəl), *a.* [f. as prec. + -IC + -AL[1].] Of or pertaining to horometry; relating to the measurement of time.

1691 T. H[ALE] *Acc. New Invent.* 119 Magnetical, Horometrical, and Optical Instruments. **1694** W. LEYBOURN (*title*) Pleasure and Profit, consisting of Recreations of divers kinds, viz: Numerical, Geometrical,.. Astronomical, Horometrical, Cryptographical [etc.]. **1798** J. GILCHRIST in *Asiat. Res.* V. 84 The Indian horometrical system.

horometry (hɒ'rɒmɪtrɪ). [f. Gr. ὥρα time, HOUR + -METRY, Gr. -μετρία measurement.] The measurement of time; also, 'the determination of the exact error of a timepiece by observation'.

1570 DEE *Math. Pref.* d ij, Horometrie, is an Arte Mathematicall, which demonstrateth, how..the precise vsuall denomination of time, may be knowen..Some parte of this Arte..may be termed Dialling. **1646** SIR T. BROWNE *Pseud. Ep.* v. xviii. 260 It is I confesse no easie wonder how the horometry of Antiquity discovered not this Artifice. **1798** J. GILCHRIST in *Asiat. Res.* V. 81 Account of the Hindustanee Horometry. **1819** H. BUSK *Vestriad* IV. 851 Pleas'd her horometries and signs foretell Fortunes to those.

horone, obs. form of HOREHOUND.

horopito (hɔə-, hɒrəʊ'piːtəʊ). [Maori.] A small, aromatic, evergreen New Zealand tree, *Pseudowintera axillaris*; = PEPPER-TREE b.

1847 G. F. ANGAS *Savage Life* II. 17 A straggling shrub, with bright green shining leaves, resembling those of the nutmeg-tree; and a profusion of rich and delicate blossoms, looking like waxwork... The natives call this plant horopito. **1889** T. KIRK *Forest Flora N.Z.* pl. 2 (*caption*) The horopito, or pepper-tree of the settlers. **1963** POOLE & ADAMS *Trees & Shrubs N.Z.* 40 *Pseudowintera axillaris* (J. R. & G. Forst.) Dandy. (Flowers borne in the axils of the leaves.) Horopito. Small tree reaching 8 m. **1966** *Encycl. N.Z.* II. 117/1 Horopito..is unpalatable to deer.

horopter (hɒ'rɒptə(r)). *Optics.* [mod. f. Gr. ὅρο-ς boundary, limit + ὀπτήρ one who looks. Cf. F. *horoptère* (1694 in Hatz.-Darm.).] A line or surface containing all those points in space, of which images fall on corresponding points of the two retinæ; the aggregate of points which are seen single in any given position of the eyes.

1704 J. HARRIS *Lex. Techn.*, *Horopter*, in Opticks, is a Right Line drawn thro' the Point of Concourse, parallel to that which joyns the Center of the Eye[s]. **1876** BERNSTEIN *Five Senses* vii. 135 The imaginary figure in space, in which all points are seen single, is called the *Horopter*. **1876** FOSTER *Phys.* III. ii. (1879) 507 For any given position of the eyes there exists in the field of vision a certain line or surface of such a kind that the images of the points in it all fall on corresponding points of the retina. A line or surface having this property is called a Horopter.

Hence **horopteric** (hɒrɒp'tɛrɪk), **ho'roptery** *adjs.*, pertaining to or forming a horopter; ***horopteric circle***, the horopter.

1876 BERNSTEIN *Five Senses* vii. 136 For other positions of the eye complicated Horoptery figures have been constructed. **1881** LE CONTE *Sight* 99 This circle has been called the horopteric circle of Muller. *Ibid.* 210 The increasing inclination of the horopteric line with increasing nearness of the point of sight.

horoscopal (hɒ'rɒskəpəl), *a.* [f. L. *horoscop-us* HOROSCOPE + -AL[1].] Of or pertaining to a horoscope.

a **1649** DRUMM. OF HAWTH. *Poems* Wks. (1711) 39/2 The Speeches at the horoscopal Pageant by the Planets. **1658** SIR T. BROWNE *Hydriot.* v. 75 Disparaging his Horoscopal Inclination and Judgement of himself. *a* **1693** URQUHART *Rabelais* III. xxxviii. 320 Genethliack and Horoscopal fool. **1873** MASSON *Drumm. of Hawth.* x. 199.

†**ho'roscopate**, *v. Obs.* [f. L. *hōroscopāre* to draw a horoscope, to cast the nativity of.] *intr.* = HOROSCOPE *v.*; to be in the ascendant.

1647 LILLY *Chr. Astrol.* clxxvi. 747 Forme and Stature. Designed principally from the Signe horoscopating, viz. ♑.

horoscope ('hɒrəskəʊp), *sb.* [In current form, a. F. *horoscope* (= Sp. *horoscopo*, It. *oroscopo*), ad. L. *hōroscopus*, a. Gr. ὡροσκόπος nativity, horoscope (also observer of the hour of nativity, caster of nativities), f. ὥρα time, hour + σκοπός observer, watcher. In early use the L. form also occurs.]

1. *Astrol.* An observation of the sky and the configuration of the planets at a certain moment, as at the instant of a person's birth; hence, a plan or scheme of the twelve houses or twelve signs of the zodiac, showing the disposition of the heavens at a particular moment. In early use, *spec.* = ASCENDANT, or *house of the ascendant*.

to cast a horoscope (see CAST *v.* 39), to calculate the degree of the ecliptic which is on the eastern horizon at a given moment, e.g. at the birth of a child, and thence to erect an astrological figure of the heavens, so as to discover the influence of the planets upon his life and fortunes.

c **1050** *Byrhtferth's Handboc* in *Anglia* VIII. 298 An circul ys þe uðwitan hatað zodiacus oððe horoscopus. *c* **1391** CHAUCER *Astrol.* II. §3 To knowe by nyht or by day the degree of any signe þat assendith on the est Orisonte, which þat is cleped communly the assendent or elles oruscupum. *Ibid.* §4 Yif þat any planet assende at þat same tyme in thilke for-seide [degre of] his longitude, Men seyn þat thilke planete is in *horoscopo*. **1568** GRAFTON *Chron.* I. 45 The Horoscope of the beginning of the said woorke first considered. **1594** BLUNDEVIL *Exerc.* IV. xxxvi. (ed. 7) 493 This word Horoscope doth not only signifie the degree of the Ecliptique, otherwise called the ascendent,..but also somtimes the whole figure of heaven containing the 12 houses, and doth shew the very secrets of nature. **1602** FULBECKE *2nd Pt. Parall.* 60 The Horoscope in Astronomy, if it be formally taken is nothing els but *horæ inspectio*, if it bee materially taken, it is that part of the Zodiacke which ascendeth vpon our hemisphere. **1692** BENTLEY *Boyle Lect.* iii. 101 Drawing Schemes of their own Horoscopes. **1828** SCOTT *F.M. Perth.* xvi, I have a strong horoscope, and shall live for fifty years to come. **1837** WHEWELL *Hist. Induct. Sc.* (1857) I. 229 The most important part of the Sky in the astrologer's consideration, was that sign of the Zodiac which rose at the moment of the child's birth, this was, properly speaking, the *horoscope*, the ascendant or the first house. **1886** *Pall Mall G.* 7 July 4/2 This able and gifted lady..also makes horoscopes, but only 'to order'; price, 100 francs.

fig. **1641** MILTON *Ch. Govt.* I. vi, A Lordly ascendent in the horoscope of the Church from Primate to Patriarch, and so to Pope. **1856** FROUDE *Hist. Eng.* (1858) I. iv. 309 Catholics and protestants had alike their horoscope of the impending changes. **1867** LONGF. *Wind over Chimney* vi, These are prophets, bards, and seers; In the horoscope of nations..They control the coming years. **1886** *Pall Mall G.* 26 July 1/1 If we were to cast the horoscope of the new Government solely from the signs afforded us in some quarters.

†**2.** A figure or table on which the hours are marked. **a.** A dial. **b.** A table showing the length of the days and nights at different places and seasons. **c.** A kind of planisphere, invented by John of Padua. *Obs.*

1623 COCKERAM, *Horoscope*, wherin houres bee marked, as in a dyall. *a* **1656** USSHER *Ann.* VI. (1658) 98 He also invented ..the Horoscope, or instrument whereby to observe the Equinoctials, and the Tropicks, or the summer and winter solstice. **1696** PHILLIPS (ed. 5), *Horoscope*..is also a Mathematical Instrument, made in the form of a planisphere, invented by John Paduanus.

'**horoscope**, *v.* [f. prec. sb.] **a.** *intr.* To form a horoscope; to inquire into futurity. **b.** *trans.* To cast the nativity of.

1673 MARVELL *Reh. Transp.* II. 77 He spent a considerable time in creeping into all Corners and Companies, Horoscoping up and down concerning the duration of the Government. **1888** *Daily News* 16 Feb. 4/8 It would be a good deal more convincing if, instead of horoscoping people dead and gone, he would prophesy about the living.

Hence **horoscoper** ('hɒrəskəʊpə(r)), one who casts horoscopes; an astrologer.

1561 EDEN *Arte Nauig.* Pref., The superstitious Horoscopers (astrologiers I meane and not Astronomers). **1710** SHAFTESB. *Charac.*, *Adv. Author* III. i. (1737) I. 289 Astrologers, horoscopers, and other such, are pleas'd to honour themselves with the title of mathematicians.

horoscopic (hɒrəʊ'skɒpɪk), *a.* [ad. L. *hōroscopic-us*, f. *hōroscop-us*: see -IC.] Of or pertaining to a horoscope. So **horo'scopical** *a.*

1790 SIBLY *Occult Sc.* (1792) I. 97 Those persons in whose nativity ♈ ♉ ♌ ♑ are horoscopical, have a constant hoarseness. **1850** KITTO *Daily Bibl. Illustr.* XXXIII. vi. (1881) 241 Under certain horoscopic and astrological aspects.

horoscopist (hɒ'rɒskəpɪst). [f. L. *hōroscop-us* + -IST.] = HOROSCOPER.

1652 GAULE *Magastrom.* 3 He would not give the least occasion to planetary horoscopists and monethly prognosticators. **1883** *Contemp. Rev.* June 849 The astronomical writings and tables of the ancient horoscopists are lost.

horoscopy (həʊ'rɒskəpɪ). [f. HOROSCOPE (or its source) + -Y: cf. L. *horoscopium*, *-opium*, Gr. ὡροσκοπεῖον, -όπιον, a horoscopic instrument, a horoscope.] **a.** The casting of horoscopes. **b.** The aspect of the heavens at a given moment, esp. at that of nativity.

1651 HOBBES *Leviath.* I. xii. 56 Sometimes in the aspect of the Starres at their Nativity; which was called Horoscopy. **1664** BUTLER *Hud.* II. iii. 207 He had been long t'wards Mathematicks..Magick, Horoscopie, Astrologie, And was old dog at Physiologie. **1823** LAMB *Elia* Ser. II. *New year's coming of age*, Good Days, bad Days, were so shuffled together, to the confounding of all sober horoscopy.

horow, var. HARROW *int.*, or HARRO *v. Obs.*

c **1460** *Towneley Myst.* xvi. 391 Veniance for thi blod thus spent, out! I cry, and horow!

horowe, var. HORY *Obs.*, filthy.

horpyd, var. ORPED *a. Obs.*, bold.

horra, var. HORA.

†**horre**, *v. Obs.* [ad. L. *horrēre* to stand on end (as hair), to bristle, to be rough; to shake, tremble, shiver, shudder, quake; to shudder at, dread, loathe: cf. ABHOR *v.*] *trans.* To abhor.

c **1430** *Life St. Kath.* (1884) 31 þay horre not þe foule ymage of eny myschape þyng. *Ibid.* 47 Had not oure lawe horred þe sect of cristen puple. **1450–1530** *Myrr. our Ladye* 120 When thou shuldest take vpon the mankynde for the delyueraunce of man; thow horydest not the vyrgyns wombe.

†**ho'rrend**, *a. Obs. rare.* [ad. L. *horrēnd-us* dreadful, horrible, gerundive of *horrēre*: see prec. Cf. OF. *horrende* in same sense.] = next.

c **1420** *Pallad. on Husb.* I. 1035 Fer awey propelle Horrende odour of kitchen, bath, gutteris.

horrendous (hɒ'rɛndəs), *a.* [f. as prec. + -OUS: cf. *tremendous*, *stupendous*.] Fitted to excite horror; terrible, dreadful, horrible.

1659 HOWELL *Twelve Treat.* (1661) 399 Your horrendous Sacriledges the like whereof was never committed. **1683** E. HOOKER *Pref. Ep. Pordage's Mystic Div.* 15 Damnings most dreadfull..Execrations horrendous, Blasphemies stupendous. **1702** C. MATHER *Magn. Chr.* I. App. (1852) 100 The preservation of the town from horrendous earthquakes. **1897** *Blackw. Mag.* May 675 A man alone..could compass an effect so horrendous. **1952** S. KAUFFMANN *Philanderer* (1953) vi. 97 The effect on the family of this drastic change in their financial status was horrendous. **1963** *Daily Tel.* 31 July 10/2 Blackmail and horrendous tales of Western avengers on their heels are probably as effective instruments as any. **1972** *Nature* 28 Apr. 434/2 Elsewhere there are horrendous accounts of how organochlorine pesticides contaminating food have killed large numbers of people.

horrent ('hɒrənt), *a.* Chiefly *poet.* [ad. L. *horrĕnt-em*, pres. pple. of *horrēre*: see HORRE *v.*]

1. Bristling; standing up as bristles; rough with bristling points or projections.

1667 MILTON *P.L.* II. 513 Inclos'd With bright imblazonrie, and horrent Arms. **1744** AKENSIDE *Pleas. Imag.* II. 699 Terror's icy hand Smites their distorted limbs and horrent hair. **1829** CARLYLE *Voltaire* Misc. 1857 II. 30 A life ..horrent with asperities and chasms. **1847** SIR A. DE VERE *1st Pt. Mary Tudor* V. v, The snakes of the Eumenides Brandish their horrent tresses round my head! **1847** W. E. STEELE *Field Bot.* 55 Excessively hirsute; calyx horrent; leaves jagged. **1878** H. S. WILSON *Alp. Ascents* i. 15 The horrent peak of the fatal Matterhorn.

2. Shuddering; feeling or expressing horror.

1721 BAILEY, *Horrent*,..abhorring. **1799** CAMPBELL *Pleas. Hope* II. 173 There shall he pause with horrent brow, to rate What millions died—that Cæsar might be great. **1825** SOUTHEY *Tale Paraguay* II. xxvi, Horrent they heard; and with her hands the Maid Prest her eyes close as if she strove to blot The hateful image which her mind portray'd. **1876** J. ELLIS *Cæsar in Egypt* 145 Then went a shout of flame, a horrent cry.

horrescent (hɒ'rɛsənt), *a. rare.* [ad. L. *horrēscĕnt-em*, pres. pple. of *horrēscĕre*,

inchoative of *horrēre* (see prec.).] Shuddering; expressive of horror.

1865 De Morgan in *Athenæum* 14 Oct. 504/2, I agree in the main with A.B.; but can..make none but horrescent reference to his treatment of the smaller philosopher.

‖**horribile dictu** (hɒ'ri:bɪleɪ 'dɪktu:). [mod.L., by analogy with mirabile dictu.] Horrible to relate.

1854 Geo. Eliot in *Westm. Rev.* Oct. 467 In some circles the effort is, who shall make the best puns, (*horribile dictu!*) or the best charades. **1883** G. Meredith *Let.* 16 Mar. (1970) II. 691 Louis Stevenson wrote to me from Marseilles in the winter... I, *horrible* [sic] *dictu*, have not yet replied to him. **1935** Huxley & Haddon *We Europeans* ii. 64 Puffed up with pride and, *horribile dictu!*, even with wealth.

horribility (hɒrɪ'bɪlɪtɪ). Now *rare*. [ME. (*h*)*orriblete*, etc., a. OF. *horribleté, horribilité*, f. *horrible* (see next); in mod. use f. horrible, after such words as *possibility*, etc.]

1. The quality of being horrible, horribleness; †something horrible or to be abhorred (*obs.*).

13.. *St. Bernard* (Horstmann) 528 Seint Bernard wolde hire not se, As a þing of horriblete. *c* **1400** *Rom. Rose* 7187 Full many another orribilite May men in that book se. **1413** *Pilgr. Sowle* (Caxton) ii. lviii. (1859) 56 Of al my fowle horribilite thy self art the cause. **1481** Tiptoft *Tulle on Friendsh.* (Caxton) E vij b, The horrybylyte of his sharp lyf. **1826** Disraeli *Viv. Grey* ii. i, The horribility of 'committing' puns.

†**2.** Abhorrence = horribleness 2. *Obs. rare.*

1496 *Dives & Paup.* (W. de W.) vi. x. 247/1 Comonly wymen haue more horrybylyte of synne than men doo.

horrible ('hɒrɪb(ə)l), *a.* (*sb.*, *adv.*) Forms: 4–6 or(r)i-, hor(r)i-, h)or(r)y-, -bel(l, -bil(l, -ble, -bull(e, -byl(le, (4 orebil, orble, 5 arrable, horreble, horebyl, 5–6 horrable, -bul, 6 orabill), 4– horrible. [a. OF. (*h*)*orrible* (12th c. in Hatz.-Darm.) ad. L. *horribilis*, f. L. *horrēre*: see horre and -ble.] **A.** *adj.* **a.** Exciting or fitted to excite horror; tending to make one shudder; extremely repulsive to the senses or feelings; dreadful, hideous, shocking, frightful, awful.

1303 R. Brunne *Handl. Synne* 4472 So grete hyt was and so orryble. **1340** *Ayenb.* 43 Ane greate zenne, dyadlich, and orrible. *c* **1375** *XI Pains Hell* 201 in *O.E. Misc.* 217 Orebil wormys devouryd hem þere. *c* **1386** Chaucer *Frankl. T.* 282 Thanne moot I dye of sodeyn deth horrible [*v.r.* orrible]. **14..** *MS. Cantab.* Ff. v. 48 lf. 45 (Halliw.) Fendis led hir with arrable song. **1483** Caxton *Gold. Leg.* 397 a/1 He made the horryblest crye that myght be herde. **1535** Coverdale *Job* xxxvii. 5 It geueth an horrible sownde, when God sendeth out his voyce. **1535** Stewart *Cron. Scot.* II. 152 That orabill wes to euerie Cristin man. **1568** Turner *Herbal* iii. 35 Bitter and horrible thinges destroye the appetite. **1604** Jas. I *Counterbl.* (Arb.) 112 The horrible Stigian smoke of the pit that is bottomelesse. **1667** Milton *P.L.* i. 61 A Dungeon horrible, on all sides round As one great Furnace flam'd. **1727** De Foe *Hist. Appar.* iv. (1840) 31 An apparition and a horrible monster in the night. **1856** Kane *Arct. Expl.* I. xxvi. 343 It is horrible—yes, that is the word —to look forward to another year of disease and darkness. **1870** Swinburne *Ess. & Stud.* (1875) 311 Superb instances of terrible beauty undeformed by horrible detail.

b. as a strong intensive (now *colloq.*): Excessive, immoderate. (Primarily of things objectionable, but often without such qualification. Cf. *awful, dreadful, frightful, tremendous.*)

1460 Capgrave *Chron.* 155 The Kyng of Frauns [was] toke prisonere be the Soudan, and raunsond to a horibil summe. *c* **1489** Caxton *Blanchardyn* vii. 28 Suche an horryble and dysmesurable a strok. **1529** More *Comf. agst. Trib.* (1573) 36 [Solomon] multipliyng wiues to an horrible number. **1632** J. Hayward tr. *Biondi's Eromena* 178 [He] ranne his head at the wall with such a horrible force as he therewith dash'd out his braines. **1676** Lady Chaworth in *12th Rep. Hist. MSS. Comm.* App. v. 33, I cannot get rid of my horrible cold heere. **1676** Temple *Let. to Chas. II* Wks. 1731 II. 423 They had a horrible mind to the Peace. **1718** Lady M. W. Montagu *Let. to C'tess Bristol* 10 Apr., This letter is of a horrible length.

c. In combination (*parasynthetic*).

1552 Huloet, Horrible sowned, or voyced, *horrisonus, horriuocus*. **1719** De Foe *Crusoe* ii. xv, Horrible-shaped animals.

B. as *sb.* A horrible person or thing; †a being inspiring awe or dread (quot. 1400); a horrible attribute or characteristic; a story of horrible crime or the like (cf. dreadful C.).

c **1400** *Destr. Troy* 13260 An old temple..I founde, Of a god, þat with gomes was gretly honouret. At þat orribill I asket angardly myche, Of dethe, & of deire, as destyny willes. **1726** De Foe *Hist. Devil* ii. vi. (1840) 242 Among all the horribles that we dress up Satan in. **1851** H. Melville *Moby Dick* I. xxxviii. 273 Such a waggish leering as lurks in all you horribles! **1890** *Pall Mall G.* 2 Sept. 7/2 Those children of this world, the writers of 'penny-dreadfuls' and 'halfpenny horribles'. **1899** [see *penny horrible* s.v. penny 11]. **1909** *Daily Chron.* 3 Sept. 1/6 Both boys said yesterday that they had been reading 'penny horribles' about burglaries. **1917** A. Conan Doyle *His Last Bow* i. 51 There is but one step from the grotesque to the horrible.

C. as *adv.* Horribly, terribly; usually as a mere intensive = Exceedingly (cf. horribly).

c **1400** *Apol. Loll.* 24 Þei curse more souare & horribelare hem þat þei hatun. *c* **1489** Caxton *Sonnes of Aymon* xxiii. 496 By cause of the grete stone that was at his necke whiche was horryble hevy. **1513** Q. Kath. *Let.* 13 Aug. in Ellis *Orig. Lett.* Ser. i. I. 83, I am horrible besy with making standerds, banners, and bagies. **1605** Shaks. *Lear* iv. vi. 3 *Glou.* Me thinkes the ground is eeuen. *Edg.* Horrible steepe. **1611** Middleton & Dekker *Roaring Girle* D.'s Wks. 1873 III. 182 Shee has a horrible high colour indeed. **1623** Webster *Devil's Law-Case* ii. iii, I am horrible angry. **1708** Ozell tr. *Boileau's Lutrin* v. 84 Her Den groan'd horrible. **1843** Carlyle *Past. & Pr.* ii. vi, A far horribler composed Cant.

horribleness ('hɒrɪb(ə)lnɪs). [f. prec. + -ness.]

1. The quality of being horrible; shocking repulsiveness; dreadfulness, hideousness.

1398 Trevisa *Barth. De P.R.* iii. xx. (1495), As it faryth in the taast of an aloe and other that ben passynge bytter, for by her horryblenes therof the taast is sore greuyd. *a* **1450** *Knt. de la Tour* (1868) 69 None might endure to loke theron for orriblenesse. **1587** Golding *De Mornay* xxx. (1617) 525 To make him know the horriblenesse of his sin. **1683** Cave *Ecclesiastici* 409 You do not rightly apprehend the horribleness of the Massacre. **1827** D. Johnson *Ind. Field Sports* 198 A bite from a mad dog is more dreaded..from the horribleness of the disease.

†**2.** *subjectively.* A feeling of horror or repulsion. *Obs.* (Cf. hideousness 2.)

1398 Trevisa *Barth. De P.R.* viii. xxxi. (Bodl. MS.), [An eclipse] smyteþ in men and beestes many maner feere and horriblenesse [*timoris et horroris*]. *Ibid.* ix. xxv, Nyȝt of it silfe greueþe in horriblenes and feere. **1548** Udall, etc. *Erasm. Par. John* xi. 78 b, By horriblenesse of spirite, and by trouble of minde. **1577** Frampton *Joyful News* iii. (1596) 108 Although it bee taken, it maketh not any horribleness, as the other Balsamo doeth.

horribly ('hɒrɪblɪ), *adv.* [f. as prec. + -ly².] In a horrible manner, or to a horrible degree; so as to make one shudder or tremble; dreadfully, awfully, frightfully: sometimes as a strong intensive = Exceedingly (properly before an adj. having an objectionable sense).

1340 Hampole *Pr. Consc.* 2340 Foule devels of helle.. horribely defygurd thurgh syn. **1382** Wyclif *Wisd.* vi. 6 Orribleli [**1388** Hidousli] and soone he shal apere to ȝou. *c* **1386** Chaucer *Monk's T.* 627 He stank horriblely That noon of al his meynee þat hym kepte..Ne myghte noght for stynk of hym endure. *c* **1450** *St. Cuthbert* (Surtees) 4864 He cryed orrybelly and confest clene. **1480** Caxton *Chron. Eng.* clxxxi. 161 Horrybelyche they tormented the body. **1535** Coverdale *Esther* (Apocr.) xvi. 24 All cities and londes that do not this, shal horribly perish. **1599** Shaks. *Much Ado* ii. iii. 243, I wil be horribly in loue with her. **1671** Milton *Samson* 1510 What hideous noise was that? Horribly loud, unlike the former shout. **1711** Swift *Lett.* (1767) III. 261, I am horribly down at present. **1818** Byron *Ch. Har.* iv. lxxii, A matchless cataract, Horribly beautiful. **1884** F. M. Crawford *Rom. Singer* I. 8 Suddenly his voice cracked horribly.

horrid ('hɒrɪd), *a.* (*adv.*) Also 7 horred, horride. [ad. L. *horrid-us* bristling, rough, shaggy; rude, savage, unpolished; terrible, frightful, f. *horrēre*: see horre *v.* Cf. It. *orrido.*]

A. *adj.* **1.** Bristling, shaggy, rough. (Chiefly *poetic.*)

1590 Spenser *F.Q.* i. vii. 31 His haughtie Helmet, horrid all with gold. **1621** Burton *Anat. Mel.* i. ii. iii. xiv. (1651) 125 A rugged attire, hirsute head, horrid beard. **1654** Evelyn *Diary* 27 June, There is also on the side of this horrid Alp a very romantic seate. *a* **1700** Dryden (J.), Horrid with fern, and intricate with thorn. **1717** Pope *Eloisa* 20 Ye grots and caverns shagg'd with horrid thorn! **1740** Gray *Let.* in *Poems* (1775) 72 They [Apennines] are not so horrid as the Alps, though pretty near as high. **1772–84** Cook *Voy.* (1790) IV. 1255 Nothing in nature can make a more horrid appearance than the rugged mountains that form Table Bay. **1817** G. S. Faber *Eight Dissert. Mighty Deliv.* (1845) II. 179 The Roman Capital was horrid with sylvan thickets.

fig. **1731** Blackwall *Sacr. Class.* II. 132 (T.) This makes the style look rough and horrid.

2. Causing horror or aversion; revolting to sight, hearing, or contemplation; terrible, dreadful, frightful; abominable, detestable.

In earlier use nearly synonymous with *horrible*; in modern use somewhat less strong, and tending to pass into the weakened colloquial sense (3).

1601 Shaks. *Twel. N.* iii. iv. 220, I wil meditate the while vpon some horrid message for a Challenge. **1602** Marston *Ant. & Mel.* i. Wks. 1856 I. 16 We might descry a horred spectacle. **1616** Bullokar, *Horride*, terrible: fearefull to looke on. *c* **1645** Howell *Lett.* (1650) III. 2 Within these twelve yeers ther have the strangest revolutions, and horridst things happen'd. **1662** Dryden *Astræa Redux* 7 An horrid stillness first invades the ear, And in that silence we the tempest fear. **1678** Lady Chaworth in *12th Rep. Hist. MSS. Comm.* App. v. 53 The horrid murther of Sir Edmondbury Godfrey is not yet discovered. **1720** De Foe *Capt. Singleton* iv. (1840) 66 They set up the horridest yell. **1751** *Act 25 Geo. II*, c. 37 *title*, An Act for better preventing the horrid Crime of Murder. **1827** D. Johnson *Ind. Field Sports* 77 The fierce horrid look of the tiger. **1827–39** De Quincey *Murder* Wks. 1862 IV. 105 Stupefied with the horrid narcotic which he had drunk.

3. *colloq.* in weakened sense. Offensive, disagreeable, detested; very bad or objectionable.

Noted in *N.E.D.* as especially frequent as a feminine term of strong aversion.

1666 J. Davies *Hist. Caribby Isls* 281 Making horrid complaints that..treated them ill. **1668** Pepys *Diary* 23 Oct., My Lord Chief Justice Keeling hath laid the constable by the heels..which is a horrid shame. **1676** Wycherley *Pl. Dealer* ii. Wks. (Rtldg.) 110/2 O horrid! marriage!.. I nauseate it of all things. **1697** Dampier *Voy.* I. 362 We began to work on our Ships bottom, which we found very much eaten with the Worm: for this is a horrid place for Worms. **1749** Fielding *Tom Jones* xi. i, Neither can any one give the names of sad stuff, horrid nonsense, &c. to a book, without calling the author a blockhead. **1782** Miss Burney *Cecilia* iv. ii, He said he supposed we were only talking some scandal, and so we had better go home, and employ ourselves in working for the poor! Only think how horrid! **1858** Lytton *What will he do* i. vi, I should not wear those horrid dresses. **1864** P'cess Alice in *Mem.* (1884) 78 The horrid weather has kept me in these three days. **1883** *Harper's Mag.* 866/1 She's so horrid, you know.

B. as *adv.* 'Horridly', 'abominably', very objectionably. *colloq.* or *vulgar.*

1615 Crooke *Body of Man* 410 All things become horred wanne and pale. **1697** tr. *C'tess D'Aunoy's Trav.* (1706) 214 His Father in Law..lives at a horrid profuse rate. **1753** *Scots Mag.* XV. 37/2 Went to bed horrid soon. *a* **1899** (*Cockney*) It's 'orrid 'ot. **1867** S. Hale *Lett.* (1919) 25 I'm horrid sorry there was such a gap in my letters then. **1899** Kipling *Stalky & Co.* 135 Fags bully each other horrid. **1932** —— *Limits & Renewals* 80 The New Armies are horrid quick on the trigger.

horridity (hɒ'rɪdɪtɪ). [ad. med.L. *horriditās*, f. *horridus* horrid. Cf. obs. F. *horridité.*] †**a.** (See quot. 1623.) *Obs.* **b.** The quality of being horrid, horridness; *concr.* something horrid.

1623 Cockeram, *Horriditie*, a fearefull trembling. *a* **1641** Bp. Mountagu *Acts & Mon.* (1642) 285 Most of them dyed in the Tormentors hands upon the rack, with horridity of paine. **1892** *Illustr. Sporting & Dram. News* 20 Aug. 842/1 A taste for beetles, butterflies..in fact, horridities of all kinds.

horridly ('hɒrɪdlɪ), *adv.* [f. horrid + -ly².] In a horrid manner, or to a horrid degree; dreadfully, frightfully, abominably: often *colloq.* as a strong intensive before adjectives denoting qualities that are disliked.

1602 Shaks. *Ham.* i. iv. 55 That thou dead Coarse.. Reuisits thus the glimpses of the Moone..So horridly to shake our disposition. **1660** F. Brooke tr. *Le Blanc's Trav.* 88 Idols strangely and horridly shap'd. **1742** H. Walpole *Lett. H. Mann* (1834) I. li. 200 Lord, I am horridly tired of that romantic love and correspondence. **1798** Lady Chatham in G. Rose *Diaries* (1860) I. 208 The weather is.. horridly bad. **1857** Mrs. Carlyle *Lett.* II. 309, I was horridly sick and uncomfortable.

horridness ('hɒrɪdnɪs). [f. as prec. + -ness.] The quality or condition of being horrid: see adj.

a **1612** Donne *Βιαθανατος* (1644) 24 Disorderly long haire which was pride and wantonnesse in Absolon, and squallor and horridnes in Nebuchodonozor. **1638** F. Junius *Paint. of Anc.* 350 In old pictures, we are most of all affected with their decaying horridnesse. **1649** Bp. Hall *Cases Consc.* 177 Conscience of the horridnesse of a crime done. **1659** D. Pell *Impr. Sea* 270 [The Alpes] the difficulty of their ascent is admirable, the horridness of their crags is wonderful. *a* **1791** Wesley *Serm.* lxv. iii. 4 Wks. 1811 IX. 199 The horridness of their appearance..the deformity of their aspect will vanish. **1896** Mrs. Caffyn *Quaker Grand-mother* 160 His not having come for so untold a time..formed part of the general horridness.

†**ho'rriferous**, *a.* *Obs. rare.* [f. L. *horrifer*, f. stem of *horrēre* (see horre) + *-fer* bearing: see -ferous.] Bringing or inducing horror. Hence **ho'rriferously** *adv.*, in a way that induces horror, horribly.

c **1626** *Dick of Devon* iv. i. in Bullen *O. Pl.* II. 61, I heard one of you talke most stigmatically in his sleepe—most horriferously. **1727** Bailey, *Horriferous*, bringing horror.

horrific (hɒ'rɪfɪk), *a.* [a. F. *horrifique* (1532 Rabelais) or ad. L. *horrific-us*, causing tremor or terror, frightful, f. stem of *horrēre*: see horre *v.* and -fic.] Causing horror, horrifying.

1653 Urquhart *Rabelais* ii. xxxiv. 219 Now (my Masters) you have heard a beginning of the horrifick history. **1730–46** Thomson *Autumn* 782 The huge encumbrance of horrific woods. **1799** Jane West *Tale of Times* I. 5 The lover of the wonderful and the admirer of the horrific. **1817** Coleridge *Biog. Lit.* II. xxiii. 259 To add the horrific incidents. **1856** Masson *Ess., Three Devils* 83 The horrific plays a much less important part in human experience than it once did. **1879** G. Macdonald *Sir Gibbie* I. xviii. 243 A thrill of horrific wonder and delight.

Hence **ho'rrifically** *adv.*, in a horrific manner.

a **1693** Urquhart *Rabelais* iii. xxiii. 193 Mars..did raise his Voice..horrifically loud. **1830** *Westm. Rev.* XIII. 364 Something horrifically picturesque. **1972** *Daily Tel.* 24 Feb. 2/6 The Aldershot explosion which caused the deaths of seven people went 'horrifically wrong' as an act of IRA retaliation, said Miss Bernadette Devlin. **1972** *Oxford Times* 27 Oct. 19/1 A young doctor is promised a job..if he can discover which of four horrifically insane patients is really the head of the asylum.

horrification (hɒrɪfɪ'keɪʃən). [n. of action f. L. *horrificāre* to horrify: see -ation.] The action of horrifying or condition of being horrified; *concr.* something horrifying.

1800 Mar. Edgeworth *Belinda* (1831) I. iii. 60, I could almost have thought of 'Sir Bertrand', or of some German horrifications. **1827** J. F. Cooper *Prairie* II. vii. 105 Among the horrifications and circumventions of Indian warfare! **1891** G. Meredith *One of our Conq.* I. viii. 139 To the horrification of the prim.

horrifiedly ('hɒrɪfaɪdlɪ), *adv.* [f. horrified *ppl. a.* + -ly².] In a horrified manner.

1908 R. Broughton *Mamma* v. 49 A thought which they have been horrifiedly chasing like a rat or a scorpion out of his or her own mind. **1923** J. S. Huxley *Ess. Biologist* i. 56 It is easy enough to see items on the debit side, and indeed to be so horrifiedly fascinated by it as not to have eyes for anything else. **1951** *Theatre Arts* Dec. 78 He is fondling her white throat with his fingers and she horrifiedly realizes it is

these same clutching digits that have strangled his earlier victims.

horrify ('hɒrɪfaɪ), *v.* [ad. L. *horrificāre* to cause horror, f. *horrific-us* HORRIFIC: see -FY.

Not in Johnson, Ash, Todd, Richardson, nor in Webster 1828.]

trans. To cause or excite horror in; to move to horror. Hence **'horrified, 'horrifying** *ppl. adjs.*

1791 W. BARTRAM *Carolina* 190 The thundering alligator has ended his horrifying roar. **1836** T. HOOK *G. Gurney* (L.), I was horrified at the notion. **1866** J. MARTINEAU *Ess.* I. 7 In a way horrifying to Quakers. **1875** JOWETT *Plato* (ed. 2) III. 160 We start back horrified from this Platonic ideal. *Mod.* He horrified me by playing cards on Sunday. I looked at him with a horrified air.

†**'horring,** *vbl. sb. Obs. rare.* [f. HORRE *v.* + -ING[1].] Abhorrence, horror: = ABHORRING.

*c*1568 in H. Campbell *Love Lett. Mary Q. Scots* App. (1824) 25, I haif horring thairat.

†**horrious,** *a. Obs. rare.* [irreg. f. *horri-* in L. *horrificus* + -OUS.] Causing horror, horrible.

*c*1520 BARCLAY *Jugurth* 48 a, The sounde of the armoure and horrious strokes mounted to the ayre.

horripilation (hɒrɪpɪ'leɪʃən). [ad. late L. *horripilātio* (Vulgate), n. of action f. *horripilāre*, f. stem of *horrēre* to bristle (see HORRE *v.*) + *pilus* hair.] Erection of the hairs on the skin by contraction of the cutaneous muscles (caused by cold, fear or other emotion, or nervous affection), producing the condition known as 'goose-flesh'; 'creeping of the flesh'.

1656 BLOUNT *Glossogr.*, *Horripilation*, the standing up of the hair for fear..a sudden quaking, shuddering or shivering. **1659** R. GELL *Ess. Amendm. Transl. Bible* 591 That formidable doctrine which causeth horripilation, and makes the hair stand on end through fear. **1776** CULLEN *1st Lines Pract. Phys.* I. i. Wks. 1827 I. 480 The horripilatio is confined to diseases from internal causes. **1822–34** *Good's Study Med.* (ed. 4) I. 617 When the shivering or horripilation produced by the cold-water has not been followed by a stimulant effect. **1896** *Times* 18 Dec. 6/3, I.. never in my life felt more keenly that uncomfortable sense.. known as 'horripilation'. **1898** J. HUTCHINSON in *Archives Surg.* IX. No. 34. 133 Spasmodic contraction of the muscular coats of the blood vessels is probably the essential cause of true shivering, whilst spasm of the *arrectores pili* is that of horripilation.

So **ho'rripilant** *a.*, causing horripilation; **ho'rripilate** *v. intr.*, to undergo horripilation; *trans.* to cause horripilation in, make (the flesh) to creep.

1623 COCKERAM, *Horripilate*, to grow rough with hair. **1835–40** J. M. WILSON *Tales Borders* (1851) XX. 238 Rendered the sight appalling and horripilant. **1887** L. HEARN *Some Chinese Ghosts* vi. 149 Flesh made to creep by the utterance of such words as poets utter—flesh moved by an Idea, flesh horripilated by a Thought!

horrisonant (hɒ'rɪsənənt), *a.* [f. stem of L. *horrēre* (see prec.) + *sonānt-em* sounding, f. *sonāre* to sound.] Sounding horribly; of terrible sound.

1656 BLOUNT *Glossogr.*, *Horrisonant*, roaring, having a terrible sound. **1709** *Brit. Apollo* II. No. 64. 2/2 A Multiplicity of Horisonant Phrases. **1772** NUGENT tr. *Hist. Fr. Gerund* II. 97 The horrisonant bam, bim, bom, of the bombs resounded throughout all the fields. **1835** SOUTHEY *Doctor* lxxxvi. III. 105 To exact implicit and profound belief by mysterious and horrisonant terms.

ho'rrisonous, *a.* [f. L. *horrison-us* (f. stem of *horrēre* + *-sonus* sounding) + -OUS.] = prec.

1631 *Celestina* VII. 84 Words of most horrisonous roaring. **1901** *Daily Chron.* 31 Dec. 5/1 Sophie oft wakes on my snorting horrisonous. **1962** L. DEIGHTON *Ipcress File* XV. 91, I listened to the ululating wail and horrisonous mewl.

horror ('hɒrə(r)), *sb.* Forms: 4–5 **orrour**, 5 **orrowre, horreur**, 6 **horrure**, 4–9 **horrour**, 6– **horror**. [a. OF. *orror*, (*h*)*orrour* (mod.F. *horreur*) = Pr. and Sp. *horror*, It. *orrore*:—L. *horrōr-em*, f. *horrēre* to bristle, shudder, etc. (see HORRE *v.*). For the spelling cf. ERROR.]

1. a. Roughness, ruggedness. (In 1382 a literalism of translation; now *poet.* or *rhet.* Cf. HORRID 1.)

1382 WYCLIF *Deut.* xxxii. 10 The Lord..foond hym in a deseert loond, in place of orrour [**1388** ethir hidousnesse], and of waast wildernes. **1697** DRYDEN *Æneid* VII. 41 Which thick with Shades, and a brown Horror, stood. **1774** PENNANT *Tour Scotl. in 1772*. 39 The horror of precipice, broken crag or overhanging rock.

†**b.** *transf.* Roughness or nauseousness of taste, such as to cause a shudder or thrill. *Obs.*

1477 NORTON *Ord. Alch.* v. in Ashm. (1652) 73 Over-sharpe, too bitter, or of greate horrour.

2. a. A shuddering or shivering; now *esp.* (*Med.*) as a symptom of disease.

1533 ELYOT *Cast. Helthe* (1541) 52 b, Horrour or shrovelynge of the body myxt with heate. **1626** BACON *Sylva* §700 Squeaking or Skriching Noise, make a Shiuering or Horrour in the Body, and set the Teeth on edge. *a* **1693** AUBREY *Lives, Harvey* (1898) I. 301 His way was to rise out of his bed and walke about his chamber in his shirt till he was pretty cool, i.e., till he began to have a horror. **1706** PHILLIPS (ed. Kersey), *Horrour*..Among Physicians 'tis taken for a shivering and trembling of the Skin over the whole Body, with a Chilness after it. **1743** tr. *Heister's Surg.* 192 It generally seizes the Patient with a Horror or Shivering. **1822–34** *Good's Study Med.* (ed. 4) I. 615 The first attack generally commences with a horror.

†**b.** Ruffling of surface; rippling. *Obs.* (Cf. 1.)

a **1634** CHAPMAN (Webster 1864), Such fresh horror as you see driven through the wrinkled waves. **1765** *Antiq.* in *Ann. Reg.* 181/1 A gentle horror glides over its [the sea's] smooth surface.

3. a. A painful emotion compounded of loathing and fear; a shuddering with terror and repugnance; strong aversion mingled with dread; the feeling excited by something shocking or frightful. Also in weaker sense, intense dislike or repugnance. (The prevalent use at all times.)

c **1375** *Sc. Leg. Saints, Mathias* 47 Gret horroure had þai alsa, For sic dremynge. **1382** WYCLIF *Ezek.* xxxii. 10 The kyngis..with ful myche orrour shulen be agast vpon thee. *c* **1386** CHAUCER *Pars. T.* ¶ 149 Ther shal horrour and grisly drede dwellen with-outen ende. *c* **1440** *Promp. Parv.* 371/1 Orrowre, *horror*. **1526** *Pilgr. Perf.* (W. de W. 1531) 90 b, Affeccyon & loue to this present worlde, horrour & despeccyon of the worlde to come. **1602** MARSTON *Ant. & Mel.* IV. Wks. 1856 I. 54 A sodden horror doth invade my blood. **1632** J. HAYWARD tr. *Biondi's Eromena* 30 Foure bodies..whereof (to their great horror) they knew at the first sight their Mistresse and the Prince. **1697** DRYDEN *Virg. Georg.* I. 451 Deep Horrour seizes ev'ry Humane Breast. **1725** DE FOE *Voy. round World* (1840) 192 The mountains of Andes..so frightful for their height, that it is not to be thought of without some horror. **1756** BURKE *Vind. Nat. Soc.* Wks. 1842 I. 11 On the return of reason he began to conceive a horrour suitable to the guilt of such a murder. **1833** N. ARNOTT *Physics* (ed. 5) I. 349 What was called nature's horror of a vacuum. **1866** G. MACDONALD *Ann. Q. Neighb.* iii. (1878) 24, I had a horror of becoming a moral policeman as much as of 'doing church'. **1872** DARWIN *Emotions* xii. 304 He who dreads, as well as hates a man, will feel, as Milton uses the word, a horror of him.

b. pl. ***the horrors*** (*colloq.*): a fit of horror or extreme depression; *spec.* such as occurs in delirium tremens.

1768 GOLDSM. *Good-n. Man* IV. Wks. (Globe) 631/2 He is coming this way all in the horrors. **1780** J. ADAMS in *Fam. Lett.* (1876) 382 London is in the horrors. Governor Hutchinson fell down dead at the first appearance of mobs. **1818** MISS FERRIER *Marriage* iii. (D.), As you promise our stay shall be short, if I don't die of the horrors, I shall certainly try to make the agreeable. **1889** BOLDREWOOD *Robbery under Arms* (1890) 3 He does drink, of course..the worst of it is that too much of it brings on the horrors. **1893** C. G. LELAND *Mem.* II. 20 To be regarded as a real Bohemian vagabond..would..have given me the horrors.

c. As *int.* (usu. *pl.*). An exclamation indicating shock, surprise, fear, etc.

1879 L. TROUBRIDGE *Life amongst Troubridges* (1966) xi. 152 Went to Shepherd's Bush. Oh, horror—stinking underground. *Ibid.* 153 The train went off without us! Oh, horror, no other train to Penzance. **1893** *Ladies' Home Jrnl.* Feb. 6/4 Horrors!.. You don't mean that you're going to carry it any further? **1914** E. R. BURROUGHS *Tarzan of Apes* (1917) xvi. 137 Horrors! The lion was bounding along in easy leaps scarce five paces behind. **1928** 'BRENT OF BIN BIN' *Up Country* xvi. 284 After that was Miss Oswald—horrors, supposing she proposed too! **1973** *Times Lit. Suppl.* 31 Aug. 1007/3 Lord Crouch pulls strings to get..the Yard for the murder near his stately home, but horrors!—for him, anyway—when what he gets is [Inspector] Dover.

†**4.** A feeling of awe or reverent fear (without any suggestion of repugnance); a thrill of awe, or of imaginative fear. *Obs.*

1579 FULKE *Heskins' Parl.* 129 That sacrifice most full of horror and reuerence, where the uniuersall Lorde of all thinges is daily felt with handes. *a* **1670** HACKET *Abp. Williams* (1692) II. 56 (D.) That super-cœlestial food in the Lord's Supper which a Christian ought not once to think of without a sacred kind of horror and reverence. **1715–20** POPE *Iliad* VIII. 36 A reverend horror silenced all the sky. [**1820** HAZLITT *Lect. Dram. Lit.* 321 The interest will be instantly heightened to a sort of pleasing horror.]

5. *transf.* **a.** The quality of exciting repugnance and dread; horribleness; a quality or condition, and *concr.* a thing, or person, which excites these feelings; something horrifying.

Chamber of Horrors, the name given to a room in Madame Tussaud's waxwork exhibition, containing effigies of noted criminals and the like; hence *transf.* a place full of horrors.

c **1375** *Sc. Leg. Saints, Jacobus Minor* 695 To þe thefys horroure alvay. **1413** *Pilgr. Sowle* (Caxton 1483) III. x. 56 The grete horrour therof may not be lykened ne declared. **1489** CAXTON *Faytes of A.* III. xvii. 208 To putte a man in an euyl pryson and constrayne by tormentynges..is an homynable horreur. **1594** DANIEL *Cleopatra* III. ii, This solitary Horror where I bide. **1605** SHAKS. *Macb.* II. iii. 85 As from your Graues rise vp, and walke like Sprights, To countenance this horror. *Ibid.* V. v. 13, I haue supt full with horrors. **1748** *Anson's Voy.* III. vii. 357 The *Centurion*, fitted for war..was the horror of these dastards. **1805** E. FREMANTLE in A. Fremantle *Wynne Diaries* (1940) 4 Mar. III. 160 He [Count Barlowsky] is a little horror. **1831** PRAED *Poems, Where is Miss Myrtle* ii, I brought her, one morning, a rose for her brow..She told me such horrors were never worn now. **1846** E. HALL *Diary* 11 June in O. A. Sherrard *Two Victorian Girls* (1966) xvii. 162 Took the horrors for a drive, and even in the carriage Sydney and Cornelia could not behave themselves. **1849** THACKERAY *Pendennis* I. xxxvii. 362 That collection of old fogies..ought to be cast in wax, and set up at Madame Tussaud's—..In the chamber of horrors! **1856** *Amy Carlton* 126, I want to see the Chamber of Horrors. It is full of wax models of the most wicked people that ever lived. **1859** *Macm. Mag.* Dec. 132/2 A series of magic lantern slides from some 'chambers of horrors', which he presumes to call the *Legend of the Ages*. **1861** DU CHAILLU *Equat. Afr.* xi. (ed. 2) 144, I dreamed.. of serpents that night, for they are my horror. **1889** BARRÈRE & LELAND *Dict. Slang* I. 235 *Chamber of Horrors*, the Peeresses' gallery at the House of Lords, from its being railed round as if it contained objectionable or repulsive inmates. **1891** FARMER *Slang* II. 69 *Chamber of Horrors*, sausages. **1895** R. L. DOUGLAS in *Bookman* Oct. 22/2 Louis was in a large measure responsible for the horrors of the Revolution. **1899** *Daily Chron.* 2 Mar. 9/1 This..room..is one of terrible interest, for the 'flimsies' record the lost and overdue vessels, and the place bears the gruesome and apt title of 'Chamber of Horrors'. **1909** J. R. WARE *Passing Eng.* 69/2 *Chamber of Horrors*, the name of the corridor or repository in which Messrs Christie..locate the valueless pictures that are sent to them. **1922** JOYCE *Ulysses* 613 He stowed the weapon in question away as before in his chamber of horrors, otherwise pocket. **1958** *Spectator* 6 June 746/2 Children adore reading about little horrors being taken down a peg. **1959** A. HUXLEY *Let.* 13 Feb. (1969) 866 Passages on infant damnation from St. Augustine... Passages on Jesus as a salesman from Bruce Barton. And so forth. A few pages of these wd constitute a stimulating Chamber of Horrors. **1959** *Times Lit. Suppl.* 10 July 409/2 A diary kept by an elderly horror whose name we never learn.

b. = *horror film*.

1958 *Vogue* July 47 The American horrors pour out at an average of three a month: The Man without a Body, Back from the Dead, etc. **1958** *Economist* 6 Dec. 868/2 'Horror' is a generic term covering a wide range of films whose only common link is that they all contain a monster.

6. *Comb.*, as ***horror joke, magazine, -monger, -mongering, -photograph, story***; ***horror-crowned, -fraught, -inspiring, -loving, -stricken, -struck*** adjs.; ***horror-strike*** vb. (*rare*); **horror comic**, a children's comic (sense B. 2) in which the principal ingredients of the pictures and stories are violence and sensationalism; **horror film, movie, picture**, a film designed to horrify, usu. by the depiction of violence and the supernatural.

1954 *Time* 8 Nov. 60/3 Public criticism of *horror comics. **1959** J. CARY *Captive & Free* lvi. 244 She had been all for the Bill putting down the horror comics, though her husband had been against it. **1964** M. ARGYLE *Psychol. & Social Probl.* iv. 51 There has been considerable public anxiety about the possible effect of television shows, films and horror comics on children. **1973** *Guardian* 28 Mar. 10/6 It was jokey in a horror-comic way, but I don't think horror is a reasonable reaction to a horror-comic. **1851** C. L. SMITH tr. *Tasso* v. xliv, Engirt with steel, and *horror-crowned. **1936** *Variety* 1 July 1/5 Recently showed..*horror films and Sino-Japanese War cruelty shots. **1952** M. MCCARTHY *Groves of Academe* (1953) iii. 31 Miss Rejner and her boy-tutee..sat transfixed, as in a horror-film, watching the knob turn. **1965** *Listener* 18 Nov. 805/1 The connoisseur of the horror film knows instinctively that *Son of Dracula* will lack the blood chilling quality of *Dracula*. **1971** B. W. ALDISS *Soldier Erect* 10 My eyelids flickered like an ancient horror film, revealing acres of white-of-eye. **1812** G. COLMAN *Br. Grins, Lady of Wreck* I. xviii, A moment *horror-fraught. **1963** AUDEN *Dyer's Hand* 372 A few years ago, there was a rage in New York for telling '*Horror Jokes'. **1909** *Westm. Gaz.* 1 May 13/2 The same *horror-loving multitude flocks to its haunts of pleasure. **1939** R. CHANDLER *Big Sleep* x. 75 A fresh-faced kid was reading a *horror magazine. **1797** MRS. BENNETT *Beggar Girl* (1813) IV. 225 Her reality might have set the best *horror-monger of the age at a distance. **1887** SAINTSBURY *Hist. Elizab. Lit.* xi. (1890) 425 A specimen of *horror-mongering. **1965** MRS. L. B. JOHNSON *White House Diary* 3 June (1970) 280 Tall plants called gorgonian..for all the world like those plants you see in *horror movies. **1972** 'R. CRAWFORD' *Whip Hand* I. iii. 11 A horror movie, vehicle for a Hollywood godling who had been in his grave for a decade. **1954** KOESTLER *Invis. Writing* xxxi. 333 He insisted on adding to the book a supplement of *horror-photographs on glossy paper. **1937** *New Yorker* 9 Jan. 13/2 Mr. Arthur L. Mayer took over the..theatre, put in *horror pictures (zombies and draculas), and he has made it pay every week. **1960** *Times* 14 Jan. 6/3 The world-wide success of the so-called 'horror' pictures made by Hammer Films. **1937** E. SNOW *Red Star over China* I. i. 22 A torrent of *horror-stories about Red atrocities. **1963** *Listener* 7 Mar. 428/1 The horror story afforded scope for the more primitive fears and desires that had gradually been squeezed out of the English novel. **1970** *Nature* 5 Dec. 900/2 Both argued that the 'horror stories' of genetic engineering are completely out of the question, at least in the foreseeable future. **1805** E. DE ACTON *Nuns of Desert* I. 41 The *horror-stricken witnesses. **1818** COBBETT *Pol. Reg.* XXXIII. 41 She seemed horror-stricken when some of her own agents..took the liberty to trade in human blood. **1876** BLACK *Madcap V.* v, He looked so horror-stricken that she nearly laughed. **1811** COLERIDGE *Own Times* (1850) 906 Though [they should] attempt to *horror-strike us with the signature of Cambro-Hibern-Anglo-Scotus! **1814** JANE AUSTEN *Mansf. Park* III. vi. 134 William and Fanny were *horror-struck at the idea. **1821** J. W. CROKER in *Diary* 14 Aug. (1884), He looked horrorstruck and stopped short. **1857** RUSKIN *Pol. Econ. Art* 20 We should be utterly horror-struck at the idea. **1953** R. LEHMANN *Echoing Grove* 23 Horror-struck, they continued to stand watching.

Hence †**'horror, 'horrorize** *vbs. trans.*, to affect with horror, horrify; **'horrorful, 'horrorish, 'horrorous, 'horrorsome** *adjs.*, full of, characterized by, or producing horror; †**horrorie**, horror.

1642 SIR E. DERING *Sp. on Relig.* 85 Truly (Sir) it *horrors me to thinke of this. **1600** TOURNEUR *Transf. Metamorph.* Prol. 10 The ecchoized sounds of *horrorie. **1847** J. MACKINTOSH *Diary* 10 June in Macleod *Mem.* (1854) 124 Pensive but not *horrorish. **1820** SOUTHEY in *Life* (1850) V. 19 In my next letter I shall probably *horrorize you about these said verses. **1856** T. GWYNNE *Young Singleton* xv. 250 The corpse lay..with the same horrorized yet defying expression of face. **1756** *Gentl. Mag.* XXVI. 254 That they should gall a reeking wound, and produce *horrorous effects. **1593** NASHE *Christ's T.* (1613) 77 Some part of thy ..description would I borrow, to make it more *horrorsome.

‖**horror vacui** (hɒrə 'vækjuːaɪ). *Art.* [mod.L., lit. 'the horror of a vacuum'.] The dislike of

leaving empty spaces, e.g. in an artistic composition.
1845 W. PLATE *Ptolemy's Knowl. Arabia* 5 Ptolemy had a tendency towards putting the inland towns too far east; but whether it was a mere *horror vacui*, or some misunderstanding, that induced him to do so, cannot be decided. **1937** *Burlington Mag.* Apr. 183/1 Pictures.. showing looser compositions, less *horror vacui*, and a less trenchant treatment of light and drapery. **1954** M. RICKERT *Painting in Britain* v. 108 True to the thirteenth century artist's *horror vacui*, he fills the lower corner of his miniature with more architecture..to balance that on the other side. **1960** R. LISTER *Decorative Cast Ironwork* iv. 123 Castings were used in place of hand-carved or forged iron fittings,.. loading them with detail with which to placate the current *horror vacui*. **1968** *Listener* 5 Dec. 774/2 A further tension builds up between the desire to create space and the desire to fill it. Sometimes the space-filling seems compulsive... *Horror vacui* struggles with claustrophobia. **1972** E. LUCIE-SMITH *Eroticism in Western Art* ix. 180 Nudes..fill the whole picture-space as if the artist suffered from *horror vacui*.

†'**horsage.** *Obs. rare.* [f. HORSE *sb.* + AGE.] Provision or supply of horses.
1586 EARL LEICESTER *Corr.* (Camden) 323, I shall neither haue the allowance for horsage, nor for myself.

‖**hors concours** (ɔr kɔ̃kur), *adv.* [Fr.] Not competing; hence, without a rival; unequalled.
1884 *Tablet* LXIII. 804/2 A work such as..would, were it shown in the *Salon*, range him Hors Concours. **1931** *Times Lit. Suppl.* 7 May 353/3 Dickens and Wilkie Collins were regarded as *hors-concours*; Trollope, however, he despised. **1941** V. NABOKOV *Real Life S. Knight* (1945) xvi. 138 Most husbands are fools, but that one was *hors concours*.

‖**hors de combat** (ɔr də kɔ̃ba, (h)ɔː də'kɒmbɑː) *adv.* [Fr., lit. 'out of fight'.] Out of fight, disabled from fighting; also *fig.* and *transf.*
1757 CHESTERF. *Lett.* II. cxii. Misc. Wks. 1777 II. 439 The King of Prussia..is now, I fear, *hors de combat*. **1767** *Ibid.* (1774) II. cxciii. 525 Lord C—— is *hors de combat*, as a Minister. **1776** FRANKLIN *Lett.* Wks. 1889 VI. 2 An arrow sticking in any part of a man puts him *hors du combat* till it is extracted. **1834** *Blackw. Mag.* XXXVI. 18/1 Colonsay, turning tail, flings out savagely, and puts him *hors de combat*. **1894** G. ARMATAGE *Horse* iv. 48 It will be generally found that out of a stud of four [hunters], one will be *hors de combat*.

‖**hors d'œuvre** (ɔr dœvr, (h)ɔː'dɜːvr), *adv.* and *sb.* [Fr., lit. 'outside (the) work'.]
A. *adv.* Out of the ordinary course of things.
1714 ADDISON *Spect.* No. 576 ⁋5 The Frenzy of one who is given up for a Lunatick, is a Frenzy *hors d'œuvre*.. something which is singular in its Kind.
B. *sb.* [The pl., which remains unchanged in Fr., usually has *-s* in Eng.]
1. Something out of the ordinary course.
1783 H. WALPOLE *Lett. to Mann* 11 June (1858) VIII. 379 This is a *hors d'œuvre*, nor do I know a word of news.
2. An extra dish served as a relish to whet the appetite between the courses of a meal or (more generally) at its commencement.
1742 POPE *Dunc.* IV. 317 He..Try'd all *hors-d'œuvres*, all *liqueurs* defin'd, Judicious drank, and greatly-daring din'd. **1771** SMOLLETT *Humph. Cl.* 8 Aug., I have seen turnips make their appearance, not as a dessert, but by way of *hors d'œuvres*, or whets. **1898** *Pall Mall Mag.* Jan. 85 The more unpalatable is an *hors d'œuvre* [to him], the more fashionable is the dinner which it precedes.
fig. **1877** L. M. W. LOCKHART *Mine is Thine* xiii, Art and literature were for him the *hors d'œuvres* of life.

horse (hɔːs), *sb.* Forms: *sing.* 1–6 hors, (3 *Orm.* horrs, 4 horce, ors, 5 orse, 6 horsse), 4– horse; *pl.* 1–6 hors, 4– horse, 3– horses. [Com. Teut.: OE. *hors* = OFris. *hors, hars, hers* (Fris. *hoars*), OS. *hros* (MLG. *ros, ors*, MDu. *ors*, LG. and Du. *ros*), OHG. *hros, ros*, MHG. *ros, ors*, G. *rosz*, all neuter, ON. *hross* masc.; not recorded in Goth. The affinities of the word outside Teutonic are uncertain: the conjecture that OTeut. **horso-*, pre-Teut. **kurso-* was from the root **kurs-* of L. *currere* 'to run' is favoured by many; but other derivations have also been suggested. Like several other names of animals (*sheep, swine, neat, deer*), this was originally neuter, applicable to the male and female alike; and like these words and other neuters in a long syllable, the nom. plural was the same as the singular. The plural *horses*, and the tendency to restrict the name to the male came in later: see 1 b, c.]
I. The animal, and senses immediately related.
1. a. A solid-hoofed perissodactyl quadruped (*Equus caballus*), having a flowing mane and tail, whose voice is a neigh. It is well known in the domestic state as a beast of burden and draught, and esp. as used for riding upon.
c **825** *Vesp. Psalter* xxxi[i]. 9 Nyllað bion swe swe hors & mul in ðæm nis ondȝet. *c* **1205** LAY. 21354 Þe king..his hors he gon spurie. *c* **1290** *Beket* 1151 in *S. Eng. Leg.* I. 139 Hors ne hadde he non. *c* **1300** *Havelok* 126 Mi douhter..Yif scho couþe on horse ride. *c* **1380** WYCLIF *Sel. Wks.* III. 231 A horce..þat haves a sore back, wynses when he is oght touched. *c* **1400** MAUNDEV. (1839) xxii. 237 [Thei] presenten the white Hors to the Emperour. **1567** *Gude & Godlie B.* (S.T.S.) 9 Nor wis His hors, his oxe, his maide nor page. **1584** POWEL *Lloyd's Cambria* 288 Falling off his horsse. **1594** SHAKS. *Rich. III*, v. iv. 7 A Horse, a Horse, my Kingdome for a Horse! **1654** WHITLOCK *Zootomia* 143, I believe Banks his Horse was taught in better language, then some would have Christians taught. **1782** COWPER *Gilpin* 45 John Gilpin at his horse's side Seized fast the flowing mane. **1848** W. H. BARTLETT *Egypt to Pal.* v. (1879) 116 Not a horse appears on the monuments prior to Thothmes III, who clearly in his conquests brought them from Asia.
b. *Plural.*
The plural was in OE. the same as the sing.; *horse* plural was in general use down to 17th c., and is still frequent dialectally; but *horses* appears as early as Layamon (*c* 1205), and its use increased till in 17th c. it became the usual plural in the literary language; sometimes *horse* appears as the collective and *horses* as the individual plural, which explains the retention of *horse* in military language as in 'a troop of horse'. The OE. dat. pl. *horsum* appears in early ME. as *horsen, horse*.
α. *a* **900** in *O.E. Texts* 177 Fiow(er) wildo hors. *Ibid.* 178 Ða cwom Godes engel..and ȝestillde ðæm horssum. *c* **1200** *Trin. Coll. Hom.* 179 Hundes and hauekes, and hors and wepnes. *c* **1205** LAY. 1025 He sculde beon..mid horsen [*c* **1275** horse] to-drawen. **1375** BARBOUR *Bruce* VIII. 446 Syne thame lay Apon their horss. **1387** TREVISA *Higden* (Rolls) VII. 121 Two gentil hors. **1422** tr. *Secreta Secret., Priv. Priv.* (E.E.T.S.) 219 We seen that knyghtis knowyth the goodnys of horsyn. **1480** CAXTON *Chron. Eng.* clxxxix. 167 Oftymes the poure peple..ete also the houndes..and eke hors and cattes. *a* **1533** LD. BERNERS *Huon* lxii. 215 Gerames..bought horse and mules to ryde on. **1588** SHAKS. *Tit. A.* II. ii. 18 Come on then, horse and Chariots let vs haue. **1702** *Lond. Gaz.* No. 3783/3 We brought away.. above 500 Horse belonging to their Cavalry and Artillery. **1818** BYRON *Mazeppa* xvii, A thousand horse—and none to ride! **1832** LANDER *Adv. Niger* I. iv. 177 A few rough, ragged-looking ponies are the only 'horse' of which he has the superintendence.
β. *c* **1205** LAY. 3561 Hundes & hauekes & durewurðe horses [*c* **1275** hors]. **1297** R. GLOUC. (1724) 50 Here folc heo loren..& heore horses [*MS. A* hors] ney echon. **1382** WYCLIF *Rev.* xix. 14 The hoostes..sueden him in whijte horsis [*v.r.* hors]. **1434** *Priv. Purse Exp. Eliz. of York* (1830) 262/2 Three of her best horses. *c* **1511** *1st Eng. Bk. Amer.* (Arb.) Introd. 33/2 They haue horseys as great as a great dogge. **1584** POWEL *Lloyd's Cambria* 41 They were driuen to eat their own horsses. **1697** DRYDEN *Virg. Georg.* III. 178 Bold Ericthonius was the first, who join'd Four Horses for the rapid Race design'd. **1735** SOMERVILLE *Chase* III. 322 Intrepid Bands, Safe in their Horses Speed. **1859** F. A. GRIFFITHS *Artil. Man.* (1862) 156 The ride and spare horses will be on the left when picketed, the gun horses on the right.
c. *spec.* The adult male of the horse kind, as distinguished from a mare or colt: a stallion or gelding. ***to take the horse***: (of the mare) to conceive.
c **1485** *Digby Myst.* (1882) II. 119 He was nother horse ne mare, nor yet yokyd sow. **1549** *Compl. Scot.* vi. 39 Baytht horse & meyris did fast nee, & the folis nechyr. **1577** B. GOOGE *Heresbach's Husb.* III. (1586) 117 What age doe you thinke best for the Mare to go to the horse? *Ibid.* 117 b, To put the Mare to the Horse. **1606** SHAKS. *Ant. & Cl.* III. vii. 7. **1617** MORYSON *Itin.* III. 56 They have goodly Mares to draw these Waggons, using Horses for the troops in their Army. **1697** DRYDEN *Virg. Georg.* III. 223. **1854** OWEN *Skel. & Teeth* in *Circ. Sc., Organ. Nat.* I. 285 Upon the rising of the third permanent incisor, or 'corner nipper'..the 'colt' becomes a 'horse', and the 'filly', a 'mare'. **1870** BLAINE *Encycl. Rur. Sports* §1013 Having taken the horse, i.e. being fecundated, is therefore a matter of uncertainty usually for three or four months, particularly in pastured mares.
d. In *Zool.* sometimes extended to all species of the genus *Equus*, or even of the family *Equidæ*.
e. With qualifications denoting origin, variety, or use, as *Arabian, Barbary, Flemish, wild horse*. Cf. also CART-, DRAY-, SADDLE-, WAR-HORSE, etc.
c **1000** ÆLFRIC *Gloss.* in Wr.-Wülcker 119/33 *Equifer*, wilde cynnes hors. *a* **1400–50** *Alexander* 1250 Þe multitude was sa mekill..Of wees & of wild horsis [*v.r.* horse]. **1577** B. GOOGE *Heresbach's Husb.* I. (1586) 13, I have an other stable ..for my Horses of service, and Hackneyes. **1607** TOPSELL *Four-f. Beasts* (1658) 252 Single horses, which therefore they called Coursers, and now a days a Horse for Saddle. **1889** *Spectator* 21 Sept., As good, if not better, than the shire or cart-horse. **1890** BESANT *Demoniac* xv. 179 To have his flesh wrenched off with red-hot pincers and to be torn to pieces by wild horses.
f. Colloq. abbreviation of HORSE-POWER.
1904 [see TONNEAU]. **1931** *Star* 8 May 13/1 Each of them with a few 'horses' in reserve. **1932** KIPLING *Limits & Renewals* 341 Sign—refill, and let me away with my horses (Seventy Thundering Horses!). **1973** R. C. DENNIS *Sweat of Fear* vi. 41 The Mercedes..pointed north at high speed, but there was never any chance of its outdistancing me. I had too many horses under my foot.
2. a. A representation, figure, or model of a horse. Cf. also HOBBY-HORSE *sb.*, ROCKING-HORSE.
c **1400** *Destr. Troy* 11848 The grekes..Prayd to Priam.. ffor to hale in a horse hastely of bras, Palades to ples with. *a* **1547** SURREY *Æneid* II. 44 Astonnied some the scathefull gift beheld..All wondring at the hugenesse of the horse. *c* **1600** *Timon* I. iv, Dost thou knowe where Are any wodden horses to be sould, That neede noe spurre nor haye? **1639** DU VERGER tr. *Camus' Admir. Events* To Rdr. A iv b, The horse of Troy, out of which came armed soldiers. **1738** F. WISE *Lett. Antiq. Books* 26 No one can be ignorant, that the Horse was the Standard which the Saxons used, both before and after their coming hitherto. **1760** TOLLETT in *Shaks. Plays* (1813) XI. 439 Our Hobby is a spirited horse of pasteboard. *Mod. Advt.*, Pole Horses, well made, 2*s.* 6*d.*
b. = The constellation of Pegasus: cf. *flying-horse* (sense 20). Also the equine part of Sagittarius (represented as a centaur).
[**1565–73** : see 7 c.] **1697** CREECH *Manilius* v. 69 When this Centaur hath advanc'd his Fire Thrice Ten Degrees, and shews his Horse entire; The Swan displays his Wings. *Ibid.* 80 With Pisces twenty first Degree to fly The Horse begins, and beats the yielding Sky.
3. *Mil.* A horse and his rider; hence a cavalry soldier. †**a.** In sing., with pl. *horses*. *Obs. rare.*
1548 HALL *Chron., Edw. IV* 231 The Duke..came in no small hast..onely accompaignied with sixtene horses. *Ibid., Hen. VIII* 32 The kyng contynually sent foorth his light horses to seke the country.
b. Collective pl. *horse*: Horse soldiers, cavalry. ***light horse***: see quot. 1853, and LIGHT-HORSE.
1548 HALL *Chron., Hen. IV* 13 King Henry..with a fewe horse in the night, came to the Tower of London. **1549** *Compl. Scot.* xi. 89 He furnest..tua hundretht lycht horse. **1597** SHAKS. *2 Hen. IV*, II. i. 186 Fifteene hundred Foot, fiue hundred Horse Are march'd vp. **1698** *Lond. Gaz.* No. 3445/1 First marched an Alai Beg with about 50 Horse. **1777** ROBERTSON *Hist. Amer.* (1783) I. 157 The body..consisted only of two hundred foot, twenty horse, and twenty.. Indians. **1853** STOCQUELER *Milit. Encycl.*, *Light horse*, all mounted soldiers that are lightly armed and accoutred, for active and desultory service. Thus light dragoons, fencible cavalry, mounted yeomanry, etc. are, strictly speaking, light horse.
c. ***horse and foot***: both divisions of an army; hence, whole forces; †*advb.* with all one's might.
c **1600** I. T. *Grim* IV. in Hazl. *Dodsley* VIII. 448, I made a dangerous thrust at him, and violently overthrew him horse and foot. **1607** MIDDLETON *Phœnix* IV. i. 66, I hope I shall overthrow him horse and foot. **1740** H. WALPOLE *Lett.* (1820) I. 87 (D.) She played at pharaoh two or three times at Princess Craon's, where she cheats horse and foot. **1930** W. FAULKNER *Rose for Emily* in *Coll. Stories* (1951) II. 121 So she vanquished them [*sc.* the city authorities] horse and foot, just as she had vanquished their fathers thirty years before.
4. *fig.* Applied contemptuously or playfully to a man, with reference to various qualities of the quadruped.
1500–20 DUNBAR *Poems* lxi. 68 Tak in this gray horss, Auld Dunbar. **1596** SHAKS. *1 Hen. IV*, II. iv. 215 If I tell thee a Lye, spit in my face, call me Horse. **1606** —— *Tr. & Cr.* III. iii. 126 The vnknowne Aiax; Heauens what a man is there? a very Horse, That has he knowes not what. **1648** *Brit. Bellman* 20 Your Maior (a very Horse, and a Traitour to our City). **1806** SIR R. WILSON *Jrnl.* 17 Jan. in *Life* (1862) I. v. 302 His wife somewhat pretty and amiable..his eldest daughter good-looking, but his youngest a *third horse*. **1840** R. H. DANA *Bef. Mast* (1854) xxii. 125 Though 'a bit of a horse'..yet he was generally liked by the crew. **1844** *Southern Lit. Messenger* X. 489/2 'Huzzah!..went round the crowd, while Jeptha's..friends swore he was 'a horse'. **1847** ROBB *Squatter Life* 70 (Bartlett) None of your stuck-up imported chaps from the dandy states, but a real genuine westerner—in short, a hoss! **1867** SMYTH *Sailor's Word-bk.*, *Horse*..is a term of derision where an officer assumes the grandioso, demanding honour where honour is not his due. Also, a strict disciplinarian, in nautical parlance. **1925** J. METCALFE *Smoking Leg* 26 There you are, old horse; don't say I never did you a good turn. **1930** D. L. SAYERS *Strong Poison* iv. 48 It's your triumph at having secured a disagreement that gives you away, old horse. **1973** 'A. HALL' *Tango Briefing* i. 10 'It *is* a joke, isn't it?' 'As far as I know, old horse.'
5. Applied to other animals. **a.** = BLUE-FISH. **b.** See SEA-HORSE. **c.** ***horned horse***, an appellation of the GNU, a species of antelope.
1672 JOSSELYN *New Eng. Rarities* 96 Blew Fish, or Horse, I did never see any of them in England; they are as big usually as the Salmon, and better Meat by far.
II. Things resembling the quadruped in shape, use, or some characteristic real or fancied.
6. A contrivance on which a man rides, sits astride, or is carried, as on horseback.
a. *gen.* and *fig.* esp. with qualification, as ***iron*** or ***steam horse***, the locomotive engine; †a bier. *spec.* **b.** An ancient instrument of torture; a wooden frame on which soldiers were made to ride as a punishment; also called *timber mare*. **c.** A vaulting block in a gymnasium. **d.** A wooden block on which, sitting astride, a man is lowered down a shaft. **e.** A low wooden stool or board on which a workman sits in various occupations.
a. 1597 J. PAYNE *Royal Exch.* 10 To think often on the wooden horse or foure foted bere, so sodaynly comminge from other mens doores to theires..to carie them a waye for ever. **1606** *Choice, Chance* etc. (1881) 9, I saw how woodden horses went with the wind, which carried men and Merchandize, ouer the water. **1659** D. PELL *Impr. Sea* 20 He got his foot into the stirrup of a Wooden Horse, and rid as proudly over the waves..as any Commander. **1754** RICHARDSON *Grandison* (1812) IV. 299 (D.) A kind of horse, as it is called with you, with two poles like those of chairmen, was the vehicle; on which is secured a sort of elbow-chair in which the traveller sits. **1874** LONGF. *Monte Cassino* xxi, I saw the iron horses of the steam Toss to the morning air their plumes of smoke. **1898** *Daily Chron.* 26 May 7/7 It [a locomotive] was a powerful and quick-moving horse, only the run to London was not done under any sort of pressure. **1937** *Times* 13 Apr. (Brit. Motor Suppl.) p. vi/3 Good progress..is most noticeable with the mechanical horse .. and the trolley omnibus. **1963** *Amer. Speech* XXXVIII. 44 *Horse*.., a tractor or power unit.
b. 1648 JENKYN *Blind Guide* iii. 33 A wooden horse for unruly Souldiers is no living creature. **1705** FARQUHAR *Recruiting Officer* v. iv. **1788** GROSE *Milit. Antiq.* II. 200 The remains of a wooden horse was standing on the parade at Portsmouth, about the year 1760. **1895** J. J. RAVEN *Hist. Suffolk* 37 If they were suspected of falsifying their accounts, they might be tortured by a kind of rack called the horse.
c. *c* **1785** J. WESLEY *Let.* 17 July (1931) VIII. 281 Constant exercise. If you can have no other, you should daily ride a wooden horse, which is only a double plank nine or ten feet long, properly placed upon two tressels. **1875–98** [see VAULTING *vbl. sb.*[2] 2 b]. **1949** E. WILLIAMS *Wooden Horse* ii. 37 A vaulting horse, a box horse like we had at school. You know, one of those square things with a padded top and sides that go right down to the ground. **1962** *T.V. Times* 9 Mar. 22/3 Trampoline, pommelled horse and vaulting box. **1973**

J. Burrows *Like an Evening Gone* iii. 40 Sporting equipment of a modest kind.. a vaulting horse and a set of P.E. mats.

d. **1747** Hooson *Miner's Dict.* K ij b, *Horse*, a strong thick piece of Wood, with a Hole bored in the middle of it, and.. the Rope being put through the Hole.. the Miner places between his Legs and sits on it and so rides down and up the Shafts. **1894** *Times* 10 Jan. 11/3 He was seated on the 'horse'.. and the engineman heard him give the signal to 'lower'.

e. **1865** J. T. F. Turner *Slate Quarries* 14 These sheets of slate are then passed to the 'dressers', or cutters.. seated on a wooden 'horse'.. The 'horse' is a low wooden stool, on one end of which the cutter sits astride. **1921** [see broom *sb.* 6].

7. A frame or structure on which something is mounted or supported. (Often having legs.)

a. A horizontal board or beam resting upon two or four vertical legs, and used as a support. **b.** A sawyer's frame or trestle, a saw-horse. **c.** A clothes-horse, on which washed linen, etc. is dried; a frame on which towels are hung. **d.** A frame, board, block, or plank, used in various trades, to support the material or article which is being operated on. (See quots.)

a. **1703** T. N. *City & C. Purchaser* 3, Horses, or Trussels.. to lay the Poles.. on whilst they are boring. **1727–41** Chambers *Cycl.*, *Horse*.. is also used in carpentry for a piece of wood jointed across two other perpendicular ones, to sustain the boards, planks, etc. which make bridges over small rivers. **1874** J. H. Collins *Metal Mining* 82 The horses are placed one on each side of the shaft, about 5 or 6 feet apart, the centre of the space between being in line with the span-beam of the whim. **1875** Knight *Dict. Mech.*, *Horse*,.. 6. That on which the mooring of a flying-bridge rides and traverses, and which consists of two masts with horizontal beams at their heads.

b. **1718** *Law French Dict.* (ed. 2) s.v., A horse to saw wood on, *cantherius*. **1769** Falconer *Dict. Marine* (1789), *Baudet*, a sawyer's frame, horse, or trestle. **1846** D. Corcoran *Pickings* 83 One carried his saw slung on his arm, and the other had his 'horse' mounted on his shoulder. **1850** N. Kingsley *Diary* (1914) 103 Worked at hewing some sticks for horses to use the Pit Saw.

c. [**1565–73** Cooper *Thesaurus*, *Pegasus*, A winged horse. A signe of starres so named. An instrument in an house whereon garments and other things be hanged.] **1706** Phillips (ed. Kersey), *Horse*,.. also a wooden Frame to dry wash'd Linnen upon. **1826** H. N. Coleridge *West Indies* 171 Converted into drying horses for their clothes. **1852** Mrs. Smythies *Bride Elect* xxiii, She.. wrung out the wretched rags, and hung them on an old horse to dry.

d. **1727–41** Chambers *Cycl.* s.v., The horse used by tanners and skinners.. upon which they pare their skins. **1750** Blanckley *Naval Expos.*, *Horse*.. is also a Frame of Wood the Riggers make use of to woold Ships Masts, which hath a Rowl fixed in it, whereon several Turns are taken for the heaving the Robe taught round the Mast. **1791** Hamilton *Berthollet's Dyeing* II. ii. ii. v. 107 Passing the piece successively from the winch to the horse or board. **1823** Crabb *Technol. Dict.*, *Horse*, the form, or bench, on which the pressmen set the heaps of paper; also the pressmen themselves were jocosely so called because they worked the horse. **1839** T. Beale *Sperm Whale* 187 Strips of fat or blubber.. being cut up into thin pieces upon blocks called 'horses'. **1850** W. B. Clarke *Wreck Favorite* 31 The 'horse', used for supporting the blubber whilst it is being cut into the tubs, consists of a piece of board, about one foot wide by one foot and a half long, having a ledge.. on each side. **1853** C. Morfit *Tanning* etc. 156 The working and softening of the hides upon the horse, or beam. *Ibid.* 447 (in parchment manufacture) A horse, or stout wooden frame.. formed of two uprights and two crossbars, solidly joined together by tenons and mortises. **1875** Knight *Dict. Mech.* s.v., A *shaving-horse* is a beam supported by legs, and having a jaw.. to hold a shingle, axe-handle, spoke, or other article while being shaved by a drawing knife. *Ibid.*, *Horse*,.. 4. A slanting board at the end of the bank or table, to hold a supply of paper for a press. **1884** F. J. Britten *Watch & Clockm.* 122 [A] Horse [is] a wooden standard for supporting a small clock movement while it is being brought to time.

8. An instrument, appliance, or device, for some service suggesting or taken to suggest that of a horse.

†**a.** A wedge passed through the pin which holds pieces together to tighten their contact. *Obs.* **b.** A clamp for holding screws for filing. **c.** A hook-shaped tool used in making embossed or hammered work. **d.** A cooper's tool used in driving the staves of a cask closely together. †**e.** A kind of battering-ram. *Obs.* **f.** In a malt-kiln: see quot. 1848. **g.** A wooden faucet (Jam.). **h.** A groyne. *local.*

c **1391** Chaucer *Astrol.* i. §14 Thorw wich pyn ther goth a litel wegge which þat is cleped the hors, þat streyneth alle this parties to hepe. **1601** Holland *Pliny* I. 189 The engine to batter wals (called sometime the horse, and now is named the ram). **1610** W. Folkingham *Art of Survey* i. xiii. 45 Engines are.. Militarie; as Battering-Rams, Sowes, Horses, Tortuses. **1611** Cotgr., *Sergeant de tonnelier*, the Coopers horse; an yron toole which he vseth in the hooping of Caske. **1669** Worlidge *Syst. Agric.* (1681) 153 In the midst of this Room on the Floor, must the Fire-place be made.. it is usually called a Horse, and is commonly made in Mault-Kilns. **1848** *Jrnl. R. Agric. Soc.* IX. ii. 570 It is a very good precaution.. to have horses or hogs (as these plates, resting upon open brickwork, are called) over the fires, when there are three to the same space. **1852** J. Wiggins *Embanking* x. 232 Expensive works.. such as those called '*horses*' in Essex, and '*groins*' in Sussex and Hants.

i. In other uses (see quots.).

1904 Goodchild & Tweney *Technol. & Sci. Dict.* 290/2 *Horse*, (*Plast.*) the wood backing of a zinc mould, used by plasterers for running mouldings. (*Plumb.*) A wooden finial, etc., forming a core which is to be covered with lead. **1946** N. Wymer *Eng. Country Crafts* vi. 62 When the sticks are well 'cooked' the craftsman takes them, one by one, from the sand and pulls them through a 'horse'.. a wooden plank with niches cut out of the side—to straighten them. **1957** R. Lister *Decorative Wrought Ironwork* 229 *Horse*, a kind of stake.. with perforations for holding other tools. **1964** W. L. Goodman *Hist. Wood-working Tools* 153 Holding his work in a vertical pedal-operated vice or 'horse'.

9. *Nautical.*

a. A rope stretched under a yard, on which sailors stand in handing sails; a foot-rope. **b.** A rope for a sail to travel on, also called ***traverse-horse***. **c.** A jack-stay on which a sail is hauled out. **d.** Applied to various other ropes used to support or to guide. **e.** A horizontal bar of iron or wood used as a traveller for the sheet-block of a fore-and-aft sail. **f.** Applied to various other bars used as protections, etc. (See quots. and Smyth *Sailor's Word-bk.* 1867).

1626 Capt. Smith *Accid. Yng. Seamen* 14 The fore top sayle hallyard.. the horse, the maine sheats. **1627** —— *Seaman's Gram.* v. 21 A Horse is a rope made fast to the fore mast shrouds, and the Spretsaile sheats, to keepe those sheats cleare of the anchor flookes. **1692** *Ibid.* i. xiv. 64 The Horse for the main Topsail yard. *Ibid.* The Main Horse and Tackle. *Ibid.* 65 The Horse on the Bowsprit. **1706** Phillips, *Horse*,.. also a Rope made fast to the Shrowds, to preserve him that heaves out the Lead there from falling into the Sea. *Ibid.* s.v. *Wapp*, Those little short Wapps which are seized to the Top-mast and Top-gallant-mast Stay, wherein the Bowlings of the Top-sail and Top-gallant-sail are let thro', are also call'd Horses. **1711** W. Sutherland *Shipbuild. Assist.* 114 Horses for the Yards; a Conveniency for the Men to tread on, in going out to furl the Sails. **1727–41** Chambers *Cycl.*, *Horse*.. is also a rope in a ship, made fast to one of the foremast shrouds; having a dead man's eye at its end, through which the pennant of the sprit-sail sheets is reeved. **1794** *Rigging & Seamanship* I. 6 *Horse*, a thick iron rod, fastened at the ends to the inside of the stern of vessels that carry a fore and aft mainsail, for the main sheet to travel on. *Ibid.* 167 *Bowsprit-horses*.. serve as rails for the men to hold by, when.. out upon the bowsprit. *Flemish-horses* are small horses under the yards without the cleats. *Jib-horses* hang under the jib-boom. *Traverse-horses* are of rope, or iron, for sails to travel on, &c. **1815** W. Burney *Dict. Marine* s.v., *Flemish Horse*.. placed at the top-sail-yard-arms, on which the man who passes the earing usually stands. *Ibid.*, *Iron Horse*, in ship building, the name given to a large round bar of iron, fixed in the heads of ships, with stanchions and netting. *c* **1850** *Rudim. Navig.* (Weale) 125 *Horse*, the round bar of iron which is fixed to the main rail and back of the figure in the head, with stanchions, and to which is attached a netting for the safety of the men who have occasion to be in the head. **1854** H. Miller *Sch. & Schm.* i. (1858) 15, I was stationed a-head on the out-look beside the foresail horse. *c* **1860** H. Stuart *Seaman's Catech.* 17 What is the name of the standing rigging for jib and flying jibbooms? Foot ropes or horses, inner and outer jib guys,.. flying jib foot ropes or horses. **1867** Smyth *Sailor's Word-bk.* s.v., Horses are also called jackstays, on which sails are hauled out, as gaff-sails.

†**10.** **a.** A lottery ticket hired out by the day. **b.** A day-rule. *legal slang.*

1726 *Brice's Weekly Jrnl.* 14 Oct. 2 Tis computed that 6000 Tickets, called Horses, are hired every Day in Exchange-Alley. **1727–41** Chambers *Cycl.* s.v. *Horse*.. To determine the value of a horse.—Multiply the amount of the prizes in the lottery by the time the horse is hired for [etc.]. **1731** Fielding *Lottery* i, Does not your worship let horses, Sir! I have a little money.. and I intend to ride it out in the lottery. **1825** C. M. Westmacott *Eng. Spy* I. 317 King's Bench rulers with needy habiliments, and lingering looks sighing for term time and a horse. [*Note*] A day-rule, so called.

11. **a.** A mass of rock or earthy matter enclosed within a lode or vein (usually part of the rock through which the lode runs); a fault or obstruction in the course of a vein; hence ***to take horse***.

1778 W. Pryce *Mineralogia Cornubiensis* 323 *Horse*, a portion of dead ground in a Lode, which widens like a horse's back from the spine. **1789** Mills in *Phil. Trans.* LXXX. 74 Examining the cliffs at Ballycastle, I found the horses (or faults) of which there are several between the coals, where veins of lava.. standing vertically. **1828** *Craven Dial.*, *Horse*, an obstruction of a vein or stratum, called also a rider. **1855** *Cornwall* 88 When a lode divides into branches, the miners say it has *taken horse*. **1872** Raymond *Statist. Mines & Mining* 302 One vein, which is divided into two parts by an intervening 'horse' of ground. **1874** J. H. Collins *Metal Mining* 27.

b. A mud or sand bank. *dial.*

1926 H. A. Tripp *Suffolk Sea Borders* vi. 109 Below Waldringfield is a 'horse' in mid-channel—'horse' being the name given to banks that crop up with rounded backs like the back of a horse. **1929** E. A. Robertson *Three came Unarmed* ix. 149 Now the shoal-water of this coast is.. full of under-water mud-banks or 'horses' which come dry or are barely covered at low tide.

12. (See quot.)

1871 *Trans. Amer. Inst. Mining Engineers* I. 112 Metallic iron, not finding heat enough in a lead-furnace to keep it sufficiently fluid to run out with the slag, congeals in the hearth, and forms what smelters term 'sows', 'bears', 'horses' or 'salamanders'.

13. A translation or other illegitimate aid for students in preparing their work; a 'crib'. *U.S.*

14. *slang.* Among workmen, work charged for before it is executed. See *dead horse* (sense 19). Also ***live horse***: work done and not charged for.

1770 P. Luckombe *Conc. Hist. Printing* 499 If any journeyman set down in his bill on Saturday night more work than he has done, that surplus is called Horse. **1823** Crabb *Technol. Dict.*, *Horse*, is the surplusage of work which a journeyman printer sets down in his bill on Saturday night above what he has done, which he abates in his next bill. This was formerly called *Horse-flesh*. **1859** Bartlett *Dict. Amer.* 247 *Live horse*, in printers' parlance, work done over and above that included in the week's bill.

15. Heroin. *slang* (orig. *U.S.*).

1950 *Time* 28 Aug. 2/2 There are the usual thrill-seekers who take goof balls.. quite often ending up as confirmed addicts of.. heroin (H, horse, white stuff). **1951** *N.Y. Times* 13 June 24/3 Then one day we met another fellow and he offered us some heroin. I sniffed this too. We called it 'horse' and 'H'. **1961** *John o' London's* 16 Nov. 548 'Pot' is marijuana, and 'horse' heroin. **1962** J. Baldwin *Another Country* (1963) i. i. 14 His first taste of marijuana, his first snort of horse. **1963** L. Deighton *Horse under Water* xl. 158 Diacetyl-morphine. Which is what you would call 'heroin', or 'H', or 'horse'. **1969** *Daily Tel.* 31 Jan. 24/6 He had seen the effects of an overdose of 'horse' before. The skin becomes greenish and there was frothing at the mouth.

III. Phrases. * *With governing prep.*

16. **on horse.** On horseback.

on horse of ten toes (humorous), on foot; so ***on foot's horse*** (foot *sb.* 29, quot. 1883).

c **1250** *Gen. & Ex.* 3217 On horse fifiti ðhusent men. *a* **1300** *Cursor M.* 6267 He folud wit ost on hors and fote. *a* **1661** Fuller *Worthies, Somerset* (1662) 31 Mounted on an horse with ten toes.

17. **to horse.** **a.** To horseback, to mounting a horse; used absolutely as an order to mount.

c **1350** *Will. Palerne* 1947 Whan þe gomes of grece were alle to horse, araied wel redi. *a* **1400–50** *Alexander* 777 Ilk a hathill to hors [*Dubl.* to hys hors] hiȝis him be-lyue. **1593** Shaks. *Rich. II*, ii. i. 299 To horse, to horse, vrge doubts to them yᵗ fear. **1617** Moryson *Itin.* i. 106 As soone as the mules are grast, they must to horse againe, every man. **1847** Tennyson *Princ.* iv. 148 'To horse!' Said Ida; 'home! to horse!' **1849** Macaulay *Hist. Eng.* viii. II. 288 His trumpets had been heard sounding to horse through those quiet cloisters.

b. Of a mare: To the stallion. See 1 c, quot. 1577.

** *With governing verb.*

18. ***to change horses***, to substitute a fresh horse for that which has been ridden or driven up to this point; ***to change (swap) horses in midstream (while crossing a stream)***: to change one's ideas, plans, etc., in the middle of a project, progress, etc.; ***to hitch, set,*** or ***stable horses together***, to agree, combine, get on with each other; ***to play horse with*** (U.S.): to treat roughly or unceremoniously; ***to take horse***, to mount, start, or proceed, on horseback: see also 1 c and 11; ***to talk horse***, to talk the language of 'the turf'; to talk big or boastfully; ***to hold one's horses***: see hold *v.* 11 c.

1617 Moryson *Itin.* iii. 12 Being ready to take Horse. **1632** J. Hayward tr. *Biondi's Eromena* 29 They rode all night, having twise changed horse. **1651** *Ep. Ded. to Donne's Lett.*, The Cavaliers and They (that were at such enmity here) set their horses together there. *a* **1704** T. Brown *Wks.* (1760) III. 198 (D.) Faith and reason, which.. can never be brought to set their horses together. *c* **1800** R. Cumberland *John de Lancaster* (1809) I. 258 They'll never set their horses up together. **1821** Scott *Kenilw.* vii, The earl and his retinue took horse soon after. **1837–1862** [see hitch *v.* 5 d]. **1855** T. C. Haliburton *Nat. & Hum. Nat.* II. 337 Doctor, I am a borin of you, but the fact is, when I get a goin 'talkin hoss', I never know where to stop. **1864** A. Lincoln in *Compl. Wks.* (1894) II. 531, I do not allow myself to suppose that either the Convention or the League have concluded to decide that I am either the greatest or best man in America, but rather they have concluded that it is not best to swap horses while crossing the river, and have further concluded that I am not so poor a horse that they might not make a botch of it in trying to swap. **1891** *Melbourne Argus* 7 Nov. 13/2 In the stand [at a race].. I was privileged to hear the ladies talk horse. **1891** R. Kipling *Life's Handicap* 209 Half-a-dozen planters.. were talking 'horse' to the biggest liar in Asia, who was trying to cap all their stories. **1896** Ade *Artie* xvii. 163 Do you think I'm goin' out ridin' with her and have a lot o' cheap skates stoppin' to play horse with her everywhere we go? **1904** W. H. Smith *Promoters* x. 169 You've got to have some well-matured plan.. if they try to play horse with you again. **1911** L. J. Vance *Cynthia* x. 157 Why does Madame Savaran insist on coming along to see that he doesn't play horse with her stake in the venture? **1923** —— *Baroque* viii. 49 Remember the Wop detective that used to play horse with the Black Handers. **1940** 'H. Pentecost' *24th Horse* v. 42 Don't come if you don't want to... Change horses in midstream if you want to. **1948** A. J. Toynbee *Civilization on Trial* 195 'Herodianism'.. does not really offer a solution. For one thing, it is a dangerous game... It is a form of swapping horses while crossing a stream, and the rider who fails to find his seat in the new saddle is swept.. to a death. **1951** H. S. Davies *Gram. without Tears* vi. 56 From the point of view of strict old-fashioned grammar, this is obviously bad; it involves a change from the singular to the plural horse in mid-stream of the sentence. **1969** *Listener* 13 Mar. 360/1 Another play which changed horses in midstream was William Ingram's *Double Take*. The long dialogue between the nervous kidnapper and his oddly calm victim was inconsequential and tense and had one thinking hopefully of Pinter.

*** *With qualifying adjective or attribute.*

(dark, salt, willing *horse*, etc.: see the adjs.)

19. **dead horse.** Taken as the type of that which has ceased to be of use, and which it is vain to attempt to revive.

to work, etc. ***for a dead horse***, or ***to work the dead horse***: to do work which has been paid for in advance, and so brings no further profit: cf. sense 14 and horseflesh 3 b. ***to flog*** (also ***to mount on***) ***a dead horse***: to attempt to revive a feeling or interest which has died out; to engage in fruitless effort.

1638 Brome *Antipodes* i. Wks. 1873 III. 234 His land.. 'twas sold to pay his debts; All went That way, for a dead horse, as one would say. **1668** *Nicker Nicked* in *Harl. Misc.* (Park) II. 110 Sir Humphry Foster had lost the greatest part of his estate, and then (playing, as it is said, for a dead horse) did, by happy fortune, recover it again. **1830** Gen. P. Thompson *Exerc.* (1842) I. 271 What can have led any sensible man to mount on a dead horse like this? **1832** E. C. Wines *Two Years in Navy* I. 73 Most of us had not 'worked out our dead horses'. *Ibid.*, Dead horses are debts due to the purser on account of advances of pay. **1857** *N. & Q.* 2nd Ser. IV. 102/1 When he charges for more.. work than he has really done.. he has so much unprofitable work to get through in the ensuing week, which is called 'dead horse'. **1863** S. Butler *First Yr. Canterbury Settlement* x. 146 Some good hands are very improvident... They will come back

possibly with *a dead horse to work off*—i.e. a debt at the accommodation house. **1872** *Globe* 1 Aug. 3/1 For..twenty minutes..the Premier..might be said to have rehearsed that..lively operation known as flogging a dead horse. **1886** F. T. ELWORTHY *W. Somerset Word-Bk.* 186 Work done in redemption of debt is called working out the dead-horse. **1887** MORLEY in *Dict. Nat. Biog.* XI. 151/2 In parliament he again pressed the necessity of reducing expenditure. Friends warned him [R. Cobden] that he was flogging a dead horse. **1907** *Westm. Gaz.* 7 Mar. 5/2 Mr. Philip S. Head, auctioneer and house agent, stated that 'Hillside' had been on his books for three years. Some people when asking for a house had stated that they did not want 'the haunted house'... His Lordship: Do you think 'Hillside' will always be 'a dead horse'? **1927** J. SAMPSON *Seven Seas Shanty Bk.* 45 For the first month at sea he was working for nothing —in other words he was working out the 'dead horse'. **1935** *Yachting* Dec. 82/3 *Dead horse.* The common sailor was advanced one month's pay at time of signing the articles. This usually went to his boarding-house keeper for alleged debts. During the first month out, he was said to be 'working off the dead horse'; and at the end of this period it was the custom..to make an effigy of a horse and throw it overboard with suitable ceremonies. **1970** *New Yorker* 10 Oct. 109/1 All this critical analysis would be a flogging of a dead horse. **1971** *Cabinet Maker & Retail Furnisher* 1 Oct. 14/2 If this is the case, we are flogging a dead horse in still trying to promote the scheme.

20. flying horse. The mythical winged horse of the Muses, Pegasus; hence, *Astron.* the constellation Pegasus; see also FLYING *ppl. a.* 1 d.

1551 RECORDE *Cast. Knowl.* (1556) 265 Harde by him is the Flying horse, named Pegasus: and doth consiste of 20 starres. **1559** W. CUNNINGHAM *Cosmogr. Glasse* 54 To have shewid me..the flieng Horse, mightie Orion [etc.].

21. gift horse. (Earlier ***given horse.***) A horse bestowed as a gift. ***to look a gift*** **(†*given*)** ***horse in the mouth***, to criticize and find fault with a gift.

1546 J. HEYWOOD *Prov.* (1867) 11 No man ought to looke a geuen hors in the mouth. **1616** B. R. *Withals' Dict.* 578. **1663** BUTLER *Hud.* I. i. 490 He ne'er consider'd it, as loth To look a Gift-Horse in the mouth. **1707** J. STEVENS tr. *Quevedo's Com. Wks.* (1709) 334 It is a madness..to look a gift Horse in the Mouth. **1888** J. PAYN *Myst. Mirbridge* xxxii, He would be a fool..to look such a gift horse in the mouth.

22. great horse. The horse used in battle and tournament; the war-horse or charger [= F. *grand cheval*]. *fig.* (quot. 1800) = *high horse*, 23 b.

1466 CLEMENT PASTON in *P. Lett.* No. 540 II. 259 The Kyng..is nowther horsyd nor harneysyd, for his grett hors is lykly to dye. **1553** T. WILSON *Rhet.* (1580) 13, I maie commende hym for plaiyng at weapons, for runnyng uppon a greate horse. **1615** in *Crt. & Times Jas. I* (1849) I. 383 The king hath sent for some of his great horses to Newmarket, and for St. Anthony, the rider. **1623** MASSINGER *Bondman* I. iii, His singing, dancing, riding of great horses. **1700** WALLIS in *Collect.* (O.H.S.) I. 319 Here was, Not many years since, one..Mr....in Oxford,..to teach riding the great horse. **1771** R. BERENGER *Horsemanship* I. 170 Those persons who professed the science of arms were obliged to learn the art of managing their horses, in conformity to certain rules and principles; and hence came the expression of learning to 'ride the great Horse'. **1800** I. MILNER in *Life* xii. (1842) 204, I hope our people will not ride the great horse. *a* **1817** R. L. EDGEWORTH *Mem.* (1844) 166 To compel his antigallican limbs..to dance, and fence, and manage the *great horse.* **1858** *Sat. Rev.* V. 421/2 They learned fencing, or rode the great horse, with a skill unknown to the vulgar.

23. high horse. a. *lit.* = *great horse.*

c **1380** WYCLIF *Wks.* (1880) 475 þe emperour..made hym & his cardenals ride in reed on hye ors. *a* **1400–50** *Alexander* 883 Heraudis on heȝe hors hendly a-rayed.

b. ***to mount*** or ***ride the high horse*** (colloq.): said of a person affecting airs of superiority, or behaving pretentiously or arrogantly. So ***on the high horse.*** Cf. *high-horsed* in HIGH *a.* 22 b. ***to come***, etc., ***off one's high horse***, to climb down, to become less arrogant.

1782 T. PASLEY *Private Sea Jrnls.* (1931) 252 Whether Sir George will mount his high Horse or be over-civil to Admiral Pigot seems even to be a doubt with himself. **1805** F. AMES *Wks.* I. 339, I expect reverses and disasters, and that Great Britain, now on the high horse, will dismount again. **1809** MALKIN *Gil Blas* II. vii. ¶5 Riding the high horse with all the arrogance of greatness. *Ibid.* IX. i. ¶2 Do not ride a higher horse than a thousand jockeys of quality whom I could name. **1831** LD. GRANVILLE *Let. to Palmerston* 4 Feb. in Bulwer *Palmerston* (1870) II. VIII. 38 *note*, At one o'clock he [Sebastiani] was warm, warlike, and mounted on his highest horse. **1833** LONGF. *Outre-Mer* Prose Wks. 1886 I. 118 My radical had got upon his high horse again. **1843** THACKERAY in *Fraser's Mag.* Apr. 469/2 It would be *his* turn to sneer and bully, and ride the high horse. **1848** C. BRONTE *J. Eyre* xvii, She appeared to be on her high horse to-night. **1869** LOWELL *Wks.* (1890) III. 213 To be sure Châteaubriand was apt to mount the high horse. **1887** G. R. SIMS *Mary Jane's Mem.* 116 They were awfully civil, and let Mrs. Master John ride the high horse over them. **1920** A. CHRISTIE *Mysterious Affair at Styles* x. 224, I decided that I would descend from my high horse, and once more seek out Poirot at Leastways Cottage. **1928** W. S. MAUGHAM *Ashenden* ix. 153 Come, come, my dear fellow, do not try to ride the high horse. You do not wish to show me your passport and I will not insist. **1928** *Sunday Express* 15 Jan. 6/4 The cable companies have come off the high horse at last in entering into negotiations with the wireless group. **1936** A. CHRISTIE *Murder in Mesopotamia* xix. 162 I'd like to see Sheila honest enough to come off her high horse and admit that she hated Mrs. Leidner for good old thorough-going personal reasons. **1950** W. SAROYAN *Assyrian & Other Stories* 219 Only his mother felt that Mayo was not a rude boy, but his father frequently asked Mayo to get down off his high horse and act like everbody else. **1959** *Economist* 20 June 1079/1 Politicians..riding on high horses.

24. a. White Horse. The figure of a white horse, reputed (by later writers) as the ensign of the Saxons when they invaded Britain, and the heraldic ensign of Brunswick, Hanover, and Kent; also, the figure of a horse cut on the face of chalk downs in England, and popularly supposed to represent the 'white horse' of the Saxons; notably that near Uffington in Berkshire.

[*c* **1171** *Cartul. Abbey Abingdon* in Hughes *Scouring White Horse* (1859) App. i. 215 Juxta locum qui vulgo mons Albi Equi nuncupatur]. **1368–9** *Close Roll 42 Edw. III* (ibid.) En la vale de White Horse. **1607** CAMDEN *Brit.* 202 In vallem.. quam a nescio qua albi equi forma, in candicanti colle imaginata, The Vale of Whitehorse vocant. **1720** *Magna Britania et Hibernia* I. 171/1 Some fancy it to be the Monument of Uter Pen Dragon, with as much Reason..as others imagine Hengist to have made the White Horse on the Edge of the Hill. **1738** F. WISE (*title*) A Letter to Dr. Mead..shewing that the White Horse is a monument of the West Saxons. **1780** *Reading Mercury* 22 May in Hughes *Scouring White Horse* (1859) v. 93 The ceremony of scowering and cleansing..the White Horse, was celebrated on Whit-Monday. **1814** SCOTT *Wav.* xi, May the white horse [of Hanover] break his neck over a mound of his making! **1856** KNIGHT *Pop. Hist. Eng.* I. vii. 98 [On] the chalk-hills about Wantage..the White Horse of the Saxon race has been held to be a monument of the Saxon victory. *Ibid.* 100 The banner of the White Horse floated triumphantly over the Danish raven. **1859** TENNYSON *Enid* 1784 As now Men weed the white horse on the Berkshire hills To keep him bright and clean. —— *Guinevere* 16 He [Modred]..tamper'd with the Lords of the White Horse. **1869** FREEMAN *Old Eng. Hist. for Childr.* v. 33; viii. 124.

b. A high white-crested racing wave.

1833 MRS. OPIE in *Mem.* (1854) xix. 298 The sea a succession of foaming billows, and the white horses galloping towards us. **1834** MEDWIN *Angler in Wales* I. 174, I like to see the pool..full of what the Genevese call 'moutons' and the Irish 'white horses'. **1848** C. A. JOHNS *Week at Lizard* 102 As mariners say, the sea is covered with 'white horses'. **1849** ARNOLD *Forsaken Merman* 6 The wild white horses play, Champ and chafe and toss in the spray.

†25. wooden horse. The scaffold, the gallows (cf. *a horse foaled of an acorn*: 26 b); an instrument of torture. See also 6 b. *Obs.*

1642 FULLER *Holy & Prof. St.* IV. ii. 247 He becomes Mordecai's Herauld and Page..(who he hoped by this time should have mounted the wooden horse). *Ibid.* v. xv. 419 The wooden horse hath told strange secrets.

****** 26.** *Proverbial phrases and locutions.* **a.** In comparisons: ***as holy, as sick, as strong as a horse; to eat, or work like a horse. a horse of another*** (***the same***, etc.) ***colour***, a thing or matter of a different (etc.) complexion.

1530 PALSGR. 620/1 He maketh as thoughe he were as holy as a horse, *il pretent la saincteté dung cheual.* **1601** SHAKS. *Twel. N.* II. iii. 181 My purpose is indeed a horse of that colour. **1707** LD. RABY in Hearne *Collect.* 14 Sept. (O.H.S.) II. 43 He eats like a Horse. **1798** *Aurora* (Philad.) 27 Aug. (Th.), Whether any of them may be induced..to enter into the pay of King John I. [i.e. President Adams] is 'a horse of another colour'. **1829** G. GRIFFIN *Collegians* II. xxii. 160 'I never tought o' dat,' said Danny... 'Dat's a horse of anoder colour.' **1853** [see COLONIALISM 1 b]. **1856** C. READE *Never too Late* I. ii. 47 A gentleman is a horse of another colour than this Robinson. **1860** O. W. HOLMES *Prof. Breakf.-t.* vii. (Paterson) 143 It is a common saying of a jockey that he is 'all horse'. **1867** TROLLOPE *Chron. Barset* I. xxiv. 216 What did you think of his wife? That's a horse of another colour altogether. **1877** [see HOSS 1]. **1937** W. S. MAUGHAM *Theatre* ii. 23 I'll give you a three years' contract, I'll give you eight pounds a week and you'll have to work like a horse. **1937** K. A. PORTER *Noon Wine* 38 He never got married, for one thing, and he works like a horse. **1948** J. CARTER *Taste & Technique in Book-Collecting* (1949) ii. 24 Buxton Forman's *A Shelley Library*, however, was a horse of a different colour: no mere handlist but a fully annotated and richly informative study of Shelley's original editions. **1952** 'N. SHUTE' *Far Country* 80 Going into the saloon for every meal, and eating like a horse. **1966** *Listener* 5 May 661/1 A horse of a somewhat different colour is that tycoon of the brush, pop-man Salvador Dali. **1971** J. PHILIPS *Escape a Killer* (1972) I. ii. 18 She could now 'eat like a horse'.

b. ***a horse that was foaled of an acorn***, the scaffold, the gibbet. †***to come for horse and harness***, i.e. for one's own ends. †***to run before one's horse to market***, to count one's gains prematurely. ***horse and foot***: see 3 c.

1483 CAXTON *G. de la Tour* E viij, [She] dyde come thyder only for hors and harnois, that is to wete to accomplisshe her fowle delyte. **1594** SHAKS. *Rich. III*, I. i. 160 But yet I run before my horse to Market: Clarence still breathes, Edward still liues and raignes, When they are gone, then must I count my gaines. **1678** RAY *Prov.* 253 You'll ride on a horse that was foal'd of an acorn. That is the gallows. **1708** MOTTEUX *Rabelais* v. xxviii. (1737) 128 May I ride on a Horse that was foal'd of an Acorn. **1828** LYTTON *Pelham* III. xviii. 296 As pretty a Tyburn blossom as ever was brought up to ride a horse foaled by an acorn.

c. Other phrases and proverbs. ***horses for courses***: a theory that each racehorse is suited to a particular race-course, and will do better on that course than on any other; also *fig.*; ***horse and horse*** (U.S.): equally matched, neck and neck; ***the horse's mouth***: the original, authentic source of information, esp. in phr. ***straight from the horse's mouth***; ***horse-and-buggy*** (U.S.): bygone, old-fashioned (app. used as quasi-*sb.* in quote. 1926).

c **1175** *Lamb. Hom.* 9 Hwa is þet mei þet hors wettrien þe him self nule drinken? *c* **1300** *Prov. Hending* xxvii, He is fre of hors þat ner nade non, quoþ Hendyng. **1390** GOWER *Conf.* II. 392 What man hath hors men yiven him hors. **1541** *Schole-ho. Wom.* 1013 in Hazl. *E.P.P.* IV. 145 Rub a scald horse vpon the gall, and he wil bite. **1546** J. HEYWOOD *Prov.* (1867) 27 A man maie well bring a horse to the water, But he can not make him drinke without he will. *Ibid.* 75 That some man maie steale a hors better Than some other maie stande and looke vpone. *Ibid.* 81 For it is..A prowde horse that will not beare his own prouander. **1573** J. SANFORD *Hours Recreat.* (1576) 208 He that can not beate the Horsse, beateth the saddle. **1577** B. GOOGE *Heresbach's Husb.* I. (1586) 16 b, The weather being faire, you bring a Horse to the Feelde (as they say) when you speake to me of going abrode. **1611** COTGR. s.v. *Cheval*, The best-shod horse doth slip sometimes. **1640** HERBERT *Outland. Prov.* Wks. (Warne) 383 Choose a horse made and a wife to make. **1659–60** PEPYS *Diary* 2 Feb., After this we went to a sport called, *selling of a horse for a dish of eggs and herrings*, and sat talking there till almost twelve at night. **1672** W. WALKER *Paræmiol.* 37 It is a good horse that never stumbles. *a* **1859** in BARTLETT *Dict. Amer.* (1859) 204, I sot down to old sledge along with Jake Stebbins. It was horse and horse, and his deal. **1869** HAZLITT *Eng. Prov.* 215 I'll not hang my bells on one horse: That is, give all to one son. **1897** MARQ. SALISBURY in *Ho. Lords* 19 Jan., Many members of this House will keenly feel the nature of the mistake that was made when I say that we put all our money upon the wrong horse. **1898** A. E. T. WATSON *Turf* vii. 160 A familiar phrase on the turf is 'horses for courses'. **1908** G. H. LORIMER *J. Spurlock* i. 3 It was horse and horse between the professors. **1926** MAINES & GRANT *Wise-Crack Dict.* 9/2 *Horse and buggy*, young lady out of date—with long hair. **1927** K. EUBANK (*title*) Horse and buggy days. **1928** WODEHOUSE in *Strand Mag.* Aug. 114/1 The prospect of getting the true facts—straight, as it were, from the horse's mouth—held him..fascinated. **1929** *Daily Express* 7 Nov. 18/4 Followers of the 'horses for courses' theory. **1929** A. HUXLEY *Let.* 1 Dec. (1969) 320 One or other of us may very likely be over..when there will be a chance of getting your news 'straight from the horse's mouth'. **1930** F. YEATS-BROWN *Bengal Lancer* xii. 172 We discuss..what Sir Mark Sykes said, straight from the horse's mouth. **1934** C. DAY LEWIS *Hope for Poetry* vi. 29 A pandemonium of slogans,..tips from the horse's mouth, straight talks,..etc. **1944** J. CARY (*title*) The horse's mouth. **1949** *This Week Mag.* 9 Jan. 5/1 Wherever this horse-and-buggy court is held, your chances of going scot-free are slim. **1957** *Times Lit. Suppl.* 11 Oct. 609/1 She thinks that our docility, our patience, our contentedness or even complacency with charming, outmoded, horse-and-buggy ways of doing things are, as reflected in the public will, endangering our country's future. **1958** *Listener* 7 Aug. 207/1 Keats' letters remain the horse's mouth. **1958** *Ibid.* 2 Oct. 536/1 Mr. Butler [*sc.* a sculptor] spoke his own commentary: it was an odd mixture of naïveté and insight, a 'horse's mouth' statement vastly preferable to some smooth literary piece by an art critic. **1962** *Daily Tel.* 23 Oct. 15/3 (*headline*) End of 'horse and buggy' medicine. **1963** *Punch* 18 Sept. 430/1 People enjoy what they are capable of enjoying—horses for courses. **1972** *Daily Tel.* 12 July 10/5 Horses for courses is a sound adage in motoring as well as the turf, and few British motorists would look to Czechoslovakia for their car. **1972** J. L. DILLARD *Black English* vi. 242 Such horse-and-buggy terms as *whiffletree* and *singletree.*

IV. *attrib.* and *Comb.*

27. a. appositive, as ***horse-beast, -foal***, etc.

1573 in W. H. Turner *Select. Rec. Oxford* 347 Every beast as well *horsebeast as other. **1587** FLEMING *Contn. Holinshed* III. 1543/1 They wrought altogether with hors-beasts. **1535** COVERDALE *Ecclus.* xxiii. 30 A yonge *horse foale. **1822** LAMB *Elia* Ser. I. *Decay Beggars*, He was as the man-part of a centaur, from which the *horse-half had been cloven in some dire Lapithan controversy.

b. Of, pertaining or relating to, or connected with a horse or horses, as ***horse-beef, -body, -craft***, †***-crag*** (= neck), ***-dentist, -dropping, -factor, -hide, -kick, -length, -line, -mane, -market, -marrow, -merchant, -muck, -piss, -sausage, -serum, -show, -side, -supply, -team, -tread, -trick***, etc.,

1716 B. CHURCH *Hist. Philip's War* (1865) I. 161 They fell to roasting their *Horse-beaf. **1817** *Edin. Rev* XXVII. 306 Half a dozen prime joints of horse-beef. **1767** YOUNG *Farmer's Lett. to People* 106 It has been objected, that oxen are not proper for all work—and in the *horse counties there is quite an abhorrence against their use. **1832** J. P. KENNEDY *Swallow B.* ii. (1860) 36 The mystery of *horse-craft. *c* **1470** HENRY *Wallace* x. 368 Sper and *horscrag in till sondyr he drave. **1796** *Instr. & Reg. Cavalry* (1813) 124 The serrefiles ..place themselves in rank behind their squadrons, at half a *horse distance. **1871** SMILES *Charact.* iv. (1876) 111 De Foe was by turns *horse-factor, brick and tile maker, shopkeeper. **1887** *Daily News* 27 July 6/3 He had complained to the *horse-foreman that the animal he drove was vicious. *a* **1300** *Cursor M.* 2250 Bath wit *hors and camel hide. **1843** *Ainsworth's Mag.* IV. 116 There were.. coracles or boats of horse-hides..to be seen. **1900** *Westm. Gaz.* 16 May 7/3 Horse-hide brawn is now being extensively made. **1959** *Sears, Roebuck Catal.* Spring & Summer 528/3 Work Gloves... Top grain horsehide or cowhide drivers. **1811** *Sporting Mag.* XXXVIII. 292 With the force of a *horse-kick. **1673** *Providence (R.I.) Rec.* (1893) III. 248 Vntill the Comon be divided to say Cow-kind or *horse kind and sum swine. **1880** BROWNING *Muleykeh* 89 A *horse-length off. **1902** J. H. M. ABBOTT *Tommy Cornstalk* 27 If you have the last couple of hours' 'watch' on the *horse-lines, you see it all. **1932** *Times Lit. Suppl.* 3 Mar. 146/3 In the night a boy on the horse-lines was killed and the flag was taken. **1934** BLUNDEN *Mind's Eye* 79 We were transferred to some old horse-lines. *c* **1425** *Voc.* in Wr.-Wülcker 638/28 *Hic juba*, *horsemane. **1817** V. BROWN *Jrnl.* 11 Jan. in *Maryland Hist. Mag.* (1916) XI. 372 This day spent in the *Horse Market trying to sell the two Horses. **1894** *Westm. Gaz.* 13 Sept. 1/3 Of palpable material advantage to this country, the horse-market of the nations. **1909** *Daily Chron.* 15 Apr. 4/6 The plum pudding and *horse-marrow sauce. **1711** *Lond. Gaz.* No. 4849/4 Thomas Skitt of Newport, ..*Horse-Merchant. **1607** MARKHAM *Caval.* I. (1617) 24 Some..out of curiositie..would become *Horse-midwiues.

1727 S. Switzer *Pract. Gard.* II. vii. 55 The water that procceds from a *horse-mixen is reckoned some of the best ..for a melonry. **1601** Holland *Pliny* I. 507 They prefer it before *hors-muck, and such like. **1610** Shaks. *Temp.* IV. i. 199 Monster, I do smell all *horse-pisse. **1922** Joyce *Ulysses* 75 The sweet oaten reek of horsepiss. **1935** L. Durrell *Spirit of Place* (1969) 33 It cost 6 dracks—3d per bottle... In England I couldn't buy a bottle of horse-piss for 3d. **1973** H. Miller *Open City* xv. 170 Dominic looked straight at Michael. 'Horse piss... You're talking baloney.' **1900** *Westm. Gaz.* 16 May 7/3 Breakfast consisted of *horse sausages. **1908** *Daily Chron.* 17 Jan. 5/3 The horse-sausage boat. **1909** *Practitioner* Dec. 867 The introduction of such large quantities (200 c.c.) of *horse-serum. **1926** *Encycl. Brit.* II. 772/1 Particular reference may..be made to the recent therapeutic use of horse serum in the treatment of.. blackwater fever. **1964** M. Hynes *Med. Bacteriol.* (ed. 8) vii. 74 The illustration is that of a rabbit immunized with horse-serum. **1856** *Porter's Spirit of Times* 181/2 The performances at the *horse show..were very interesting. **1865** *Once a Week* XIII. 133/1 Within the last few years there has been a mania for shows; we have had dog shows, donkey shows, baby shows, and last, not least, horse shows. **1931** Horse-show [see astride c *adj.*]. **1973** *Country Life* 8 Mar. 652/1 Royal Windsor horse show, Home Park, Windsor. **1596** Spenser *F.Q.* VI. ii. 10 His Ladie..by his *horse side did pas. **1817** S. R. Brown *Western Gaz.* 107 [The walls] are..wide enough on the top to admit a *horse team and waggon. **1866** *Rep. Indian Affairs* 294 At Leech lake and Winnepeg, eight government oxen and two horse teams were employed ploughing during the season. **1908** *Westm. Gaz.* 27 June 6/3 Hannah's husband was drowned whilst swimming his horse-team across the flooded river. **1570** *Tragedie* 340 in *Satir. Poems Reform.* x, Sum saw him weill, and followit his *hors tred. **1851** Mayne Reid *Scalp Hunt.* xli, It [the sound] was the horse-tread of the approaching Navajoes! **1599** Massinger, etc. *Old Law* III. ii, Look you, here's your worship's *horsetrick, sir. (Gives a spring.) **1608** *Merry Devil Edmonton* in Hazl. *Dodsley* X. 221 Make her leap, caper, jerk, and laugh, and sing, And play me horse tricks.

c. For a horse; for the use, pasturage, accoutrement, housing, transport, etc. of horses, as ***horse-ball***, ***-barn***, ***-bell***, ***-bin***, ***-blanket***, ***-blister***, ***-close***, ***-corn***, ***-feed***, ***-ferry***, ***-fleam***, †***-garth***, ***-girth***, ***-grass***, ***-hames***, ***-harness***, ***-heck***, ***-lighter***, ***-manger***, ***-measure***, ***-medicine***, ***-net***, ***-paddock***, ***-path***, ***-pen***, ***-rack***, ***-road***, ***-rod***, ***-rug***, ***-shed***, ***-ship***, ***-stable***, ***-track***, ***-transport***, ***-trappings***, ***-trough***, ***-yard***, etc.

1826 Miss Mitford *Village* Ser. II. (1863) 421 Think of giving a *horse-ball to my May! **1854** M. J. Holmes *Tempest & Sunshine* xix. 266 I'd as soon be married in the *horsebarn as there. **1885** *Rep. Indian Affairs* 130 The horse-barn, carpenter-shop, warehouse, and some small buildings. **1685** *Lond. Gaz.* No. 1998/4 It had a Coller and *Horse Bell about his Neck. **1818** in *Knickerbocker* XXIX. 470 But wiser Bill Van Snort the jockey,..Spread his *horse-blanket in the manger. **1851** *Illustr. Catal. Gt. Exhib.* 497 Horse blankets of various qualities. **1884** 'Mark Twain' *Huck. Finn* vi. 40 There was an old horse-blanket nailed against the logs at the far end of the cabin. **1967** S. Beckett *No's Knife* 23 He spread a horse blanket on the ground in a corner on the straw. **1701** C. Wolley *Jrnl. N. York* (1860) 59 A Curry Comb and *Horse-brush. *c* **1440** *Durham MS. Hostillar's Roll*, In clausura circa le *horscloce. **1577** Harrison *England* II. vi. (1877) I. 153 The poore laboring man..is driuen to content himselfe with *horssecorne, I meane, beanes, otes [etc.]. **1785** J. Phillips *Treat. Inland Navig.* 11 Land, now occupied to grow horse-corn only. **1632** J. Hayward tr. *Biondi's Eromena* 29 They must have taken them up behind them on their *horse-croppers. **1610** Holland *Camden's Brit.* I. 444 Tenements were demised with a spurre, or *horse-cury-combe. **1818** J. Owen *Jrnl.* 13 Dec. in *Southern Hist. Assoc. Publ.* (1897) I. 96 No provisions to be had for *horse feed. **1823** Horse-feed [see feed *sb.* 3b]. **1894** *Country Gentlemen's Catal.* 23/2 The Metropolitan Tram and 'Bus Companies..have not gone scientifically into the question of horse feed. **1968** R. M. Patterson *Finlay's River* 91 They had no time to linger on that good horse-feed: summer was already on its way. **1682** *Lond. Gaz.* No. 1782/4 At the White-Hart-Inn, by the *Horse-Ferry, in Westminster. **1776** Withering *Brit. Plants* (1796) II. 512 On the Thames shore, over against Lambeth palace; and..above the horse ferry. **1771** Smollett *Humph. Cl.* 4 Oct. Let. iv, Pulling out a *horse-fleam, [he] let him blood in the farrier style. **14..** *Nom.* in Wr.-Wülcker 727/37 *Hec singula*, a *horsgarthe. *a* **1000** in Kemble *Cod. Dipl.* III. 414 Onbutan ðone *horsgærstun. **1493** *Mem. Ripon* (Surtees) III. 164 Pro j *hors gresse in parya prata apud Topclyf. **1887** Rogers *Agric. & Prices* V. 304 The charges for a horse-grass..are common in the accounts. *c* **1325** *Gloss. W. de Biblesw.* in Wright *Voc.* 171 *Hors-hames, *hesteles de chival*. **1483** *Act 1 Rich. III*, c. 2 Sadeles, sadel trees, *hors harnes. **1577** B. Googe *Heresbach's Husb.* III. (1586) 119 Bridles and other horse harneies. **1400–1** *Durham MS. Almoner's Roll*, Pro uno *Horshek et senevectorio. *a* **1656** Ussher *Ann.* VI. (1658) 258 How far every barge, how far every *horse-lighter, how far every ship of war should steer off from each other. **1457–8** *Durham MS. Bursar's Roll*, Pro emendacione le *horsmaunger in stabulo. **1706** Phillips (ed. Kersey), **Horse-measures*, a Rod of Box..divided into Hands and Inches, to measure the Height of Horses. **1873** Trollope *Harry Heathcote* (1874) ii. 33 While they were still in the *horse-paddock, Harry turned from the track. **1966** G. W. Turner *Eng. Lang. Austral. & N.Z.* vii. 144 Before the school bus was common country schools used to provide a horse-paddock for children who rode to school. **1784** Cowper *Lett.* 19 July, Some geese were in the *horse-path, and in danger of being run over. **1847** James *Convict* xvii, A narrow horse-path across the downs. **1738** in L. Chalkley *Chron. Scotch-Irish Settlement Virginia* (1912–13) II. 376 One of ye corners of Col. Carter's *Horsepen. **1839** J. K. Townsend *Narr. Rocky Mts.* v. 210 Most of the men were immediately put to work making horse-pens. **1846** J. W. Webb *Altowan* I. iv. 116 Pointing out a spot for a horse-pen ..he was not long in disappearing. **1633** in *Country Life* (1972) 24 Feb. 470/1 In the stable a *horsracke. **1887** *Harper's Mag.* Jan. 231/2 They alighted at the horse-rack nearest the law-office. **1739–40** Richardson *Pamela* (1740) I. 185 This Pasture..is about half a Mile, and then comes to a Common, and near that a private *Horse-road. **1803** D. Wordsworth *Jrnl.* 1 Sept. in *Tour Scotland* (1874) 146 There was no horse-road..but a person on foot..might make his way. **1824** Scott *St. Ronan's* ix, The horse-road which winded down the valley. **1876** Bancroft *Hist. U.S.* II. xlii. 570 Trees had been blazed all the way for a 'horse road'. **1843** W. Carleton *Traits* I. p. xiii, Beaten on the.. head, with a kind of stick between a *horse-rod & a cudgel. **1968** D. Braithwaite *Fairground Archit.* iii. 49 The horse rods extended below the platform, passing through radial slots. **1869** C. Gibbon *R. Gray* xxxi, With a coarse *horse-rug rolled in a bundle on his shoulder. **1768** *Penn. Gaz.* 28 Jan. in *N.J. Archives* (1904) 1st Ser. XXVI. 24 There are belonging to the premises..a new large *horse-shed, [etc.]. **1836** W. Dunlap *Mem. Water Drinker* (1837) I. 120 He.. seated himself upon a bench under..the horse-shed in front of the house. **1849** Thoreau *Week on Concord & Merrimack Rivers* 80 Driving a poor beast to some meeting-house horse-sheds among the hills. **1959** W. R. Bird *These are Maritimes* ii. 53 We remembered seeing many little country churches with ancient horse sheds still at the rear. **1625** in *Crt. & Times Chas. I* (1848) I. 63 You must add five victuallers, and as many *horse-ships. **1803** in W. P. & J. P. Cutler *Life & Corr.* (1888) II. 125 Keep your *horse-stable free from dung. **1854** R. Glisan *Jrnl. Army Life* (1874) xii. 160 All the hotels and public buildings have carriage houses and horse stables. **1904** T. Watson *Bethany* i. 8 Among corn-cribs, cow-pens, horse-stables, pig-styes..and worm-fenced cotton fields. **1836** *Penny Cycl.* V. 225/1 There is a *horse-track across the well-known pass of Sty Head to Wasdale. **1836–48** B. D. Walsh *Aristoph.* 191 *note*, 200 cavalry in *horse-transports. **1480** Caxton *Chron. Eng.* (1510) 23a/2 Theyr cotes, theyr armure, sheldes, *hors trappure..all was whyte hertes. *c* **1826** D. W. Jerrold in M. R. Booth *Eng. Plays of 19th Cent.* (1973) IV. 106 Oh dear, and I shall go off at last without knowing the secret. I'll stay in the *horse-trough. **1837** Dickens *Pickw.* lii, Immersing Mr. Stiggins's head in a horse-trough full of water. **1867** 'T. Lackland' *Homespun* I. 140 There were times..when the horse trough was tight frozen. **1973** P. Moyes *Curious Affair of Third Dog* i. 13 The village green, with its Victorian stone horse-trough and ugly but touching war memorial.

d. Carried, drawn, or worked by a horse or by horse-power, as ***horse-barge***, ***-broom***, ***-burden***, ***-bus***, ***-cab***, ***-capstan***, ***-cart***, ***-drill***, ***-gin***, ***-harrow***, ***-pack***, ***-railroad***, ***-railway*** (U.S.), ***-rake*** (hence ***horse-rake*** vb., ***horse-raking***), ***-roller***, ***-shaft***, ***-sled***, ***-tram***, ***-wain***, ***-whim***, etc.

1858 Simmonds *Dict. Trade*, **Horse-barge*, one towed by horses on a canal or narrow river. **1892** J. Lucas tr. *Kalm's England* 412 The *horsebreak is much used here to plough and clean away the weeds. **1840** *Picayune* (New Orleans) 22 Aug. 2/5 A new thing has appeared in the streets of New York in the shape of a *horse broom for street sweeping. **1908** *Daily Chron.* 11 Nov. 5/2 Last night the Bermondsey Borough Council decided to dispense with ten horse-brooms for street-sweeping and to employ fifty men to take their place. *a* **1400** in *Eng. Gilds* (1870) 353 Euerych *horse-burdene of fresh fysh. **1905** *Westm. Gaz.* 14 Dec. 6/3 This applies equally to motor-'buses as to *horse-'buses. **1963** *Times* 24 May p. vi/3 One critic described the dozen passengers sitting six a side, opposite each other, in the poorly designed, inadequately ventilated, boxlike structures of the early London horsebus as 'trussed fowls in a poulterer's window'. **1973** G. Butler *Coffin for Pandora* vi. 135, I had not walked all the way back. There was a horse bus to Folly Bridge. **1906** *Westm. Gaz.* 31 May 12/1 Ordinary *horse-cab fares. **1907** *Daily Chron.* 3 July 5/2 The immediate doom of the horse cab. **1964** in S. Nowell-Smith *Edwardian England* iii. 122 Six years later, the number of motor-taxis had grown to over 6,300 and there were now fewer than 5,000 horse-cabs. **1658** *Rec. Early Hist. Boston* (1877) II. 147 Henceforth all *horse-carts shall bee led by the carters with a rayne. **1774** Abigail Adams in *J. Adams' Fam. Lett.* (1876) 34 About two hundred men, preceded by a horsecart. **1821** Horse-cart [see ass *sb.* 5b]. **1863** D. G. Mitchell *My Farm* 135 An active man with a sharp scythe, a light horse-cart and a Canadian pony. **1756** in *N. Eng. Hist. & Gen. Register* (1869) XXIII. 159 My Saddle horse which I usually Ride, and my part of the *Horse Chair, and Tackling. **1770** J. R. Forster tr. *Kalm's Trav. N. Amer.* (1772) II. 327 The governor-general and a few of the chief people in town have coaches, the rest make use of horse-chairs. **1886** T. Hardy *Mayor Casterbr.* xxiv, The new-fashioned agricultural implement called a *horse-drill. **1881** Raymond *Mining Gloss.*, **Horse-gin*, gearing for hoisting by horse-power. **1523** Fitzherb. *Husb.* §15 The harrowe is good to breake the greatte clottes..and then the *horse-harowes to come after, to make the clottes small. **1791** *Gentl. Mag.* LXI. II. 719 Capt. Lloyd, of Killgwyn.. invented, about eight years ago, a horse-harrow. **1696** *Lond. Gaz.* No. 3228/4 A *Horse-Pack of Goods lost or mislaid. **1858** O. W. Holmes *Aut. Breakf.-t.* vii. (1891) 165 Busy Cambridge Street with its iron river of the *horse-railroad. **1892** *Aberdeen* (S. Dakota) *Sun* 24 Nov. 6/5 The longest horse-railroad in the world runs from Buenos Ayres to San Martin..the distance being about fifty miles. **1863** W. Whitman *Specimen Days* (1882–3) 31 At the end of the then *horse railway route on Seventh street. **1878** *Harper's Mag.* Jan. 192 He..thought some hunting grounds might be found near the terminus of the horse-railway. **1817** in *Trans. Ill. State Hist. Soc. 1910* 147 The ground has to be cleared of the Cornstock by..cutting them down and drawing them together with a *horse Rake. **1822** J. Flint *Lett. Amer.* 17 A horse rake has been recently invented. **1913** D. H. Lawrence *Sons & Lovers* ix. 249 He had been on the horse-rake, and, having finished, came to help her to put the hay in cocks. **1945** 'G. Orwell' *Animal Farm* iii. 24 Boxer and Clover would harness themselves to the cutter or the horse-rake (no bits or reins were needed in these days, of course). **1887** I. R. *Lady's Ranche Life Montana* 95 If people tried *horse-raking when they are ordered carriage exercise, they would get a little of the latter. **1848** Thoreau *Maine W.* (1894) 37 A *horse-sled made of saplings. **1895** *Daily News* 29 Oct. 2/7 The lessees of the present *horse trams. *c* **1000** Ælfric *Gloss.* in Wr.-Wülcker 140/4 *Carpentum, currus*, *horswæn. **1838** Soames *Anglo Sax. Ch.* (ed. 2) 283 To travel about in a horse-wain.

e. Mounted upon a horse or horses; used by or for the service of mounted soldiers; as ***horse-armoury***, ***-arms***, ***-artillery***, ***-barrack***, ***-bowman***, ***-camp***, ***-dragoon***, ***-forces***, ***-grenadier***, ***-lancer***, ***-officer***, †***-petrel***, ***-quarters***, ***-soldier***, ***-troop***, ***-trooper***, etc.; performed on horseback, as ***horse-exercise***.

1766 Entick *London* IV. 343 The *horse-armoury is a little eastward of the White Tower. **1688** Luttrell *Brief Rel.* (1857) I. 457 The Dutch..are getting ready..saddles and *horse armes. **1842** *Penny Cycl.* XXIII. 510/1 Should the enemy's line become disordered, the *horse-artillery gallops up to within range of grape-shot, and completes the victory. **1778** J. Wesley *Jrnl.* 22 June (1938) 201 A new-built *horse-barrack. **1783** W. Dyott *Diary* 28 Feb. (1907) I. 10 There is a horse barracks with one troop of the 2nd horse. **1822** in Cobbett *Rur. Rides* (1885) I. 92. The first thing you see..is a splendid horse-barrack on one side of the road. **1840** Thirlwall *Greece* liii. VII. 20 Alexander..sent the *horse-bowmen forward to reconnoitre. **1712** *Lond. Gaz.* No. 5000/2 Threescore *Horse Dragoons. **1807** Coleridge *Lett. to Davy* 11 Sept. (1895) 515, I have.. received such manifest benefit from *horse-exercise. **1632** J. Lee *Short Surv.* 38 Their *horse-forces are raised both from among the Gentrie and the common people. **1702** *Lond. Gaz.* No. 3807/1 First a Troop of *Horse-Granadiers, Knight Marshal's Men, Kettle-Drum. **1772** *Ann. Reg.* 67 The trial of the horse-grenadier for imprisoning Mr. Rainsford. **1811** *Hist. Eur.* in *Ann. Reg.* 106/1 A body of Polish *Horse-lancers. **1716** *Lond. Gaz.* No. 5472/3 The Westminster Troop of *Horse-Militia. **1709** Steele *Tatler* No. 17 ¶2 The same Man pretended to see in the Style, that it was an *Horse-Officer. **1823** *Spirit Pub. Jrnls.* (1824) 210 Every horseman on the road, with the *horse-patrol.. scampered after him. **1844** Ld. Brougham *Brit. Const.* xix. §3 (1862) 325 The horse patrol put an end to highway robbery near London. **1580** Hollyband *Treas. Fr. Tong.*, *Poictrail de Cheval*, a *Horse petrell. **1641** Evelyn *Diary* 8 Aug., I din'd in the *Horse quarters with Sir Rob. Stone and his Lady. *a* **1674** Clarendon *Hist. Reb.* xv. §141 It [Hochstrade] is always a Horse-quarter in the Winter Season, who use great licence. **1849** Macaulay *Hist. Eng.* iii. I. 294 The dragoon..has since become a mere *horse soldier. **1600** Dymmok *Ireland* (1843) 32 The rest of the *horse troopes fell in before the reare-warde. **1661** *Barriffe's Mil. Discip.* (*title-p.*), Instructions for the exercising of the Cavalry of *Horse Troopers.

f. objective and objective genitive, as ***horse-breeder***, ***-cabby***, ***-catcher***, ***-dealer***, ***-duffer*** (Austral.), ***-feeder***, ***-gelder***, ***-jobber***, ***-painter***, ***-seller***, ***-stealer***, ***-tamer***, ***-tender***, ***-thief***, ***-trader***, ***-trainer***, ***-waterer***, etc.; ***horse-boiling***, ***-breeding***, ***-broking***, ***-clipping***, ***-docking***, ***-duffing***, ***-eating***, ***-hitching***, ***-hunting***, ***-maiming***, ***-owning***, ***-slaughtering***, ***-stealing***, ***-taming***, ***-thieving***, etc., sbs. and adjs.

1898 *Westm. Gaz.* 22 Jan. 7/2 Horse-slaughtering and *horse-boiling establishments. **1607** Markham *Caval.* I. (1617) 54 Advising all *Horsebreeders and Horsemen whatsoever. **1890** Boldrewood *Col. Reformer* (1891) 260, I should begin to think there was something in *horse-breeding after all. **1889** *The County* xxii, Mrs. Stuart..does a good bit of *horse-broking in a quiet way. **1939** H. Hodge *Cab, Sir?* 270 The old *horse-cabby. **1740** *Hist. Jamaica* vii. 170 No common *Horse-catcher shall ride or drive in any Savannah, without giving 100*l*. Bond. **1761** J. Thompson (*title*) The Compleat *Horse-dealer; or, Farriery made plain and easy. **1865** W. G. Palgrave *Arabia* I. 36 Their trade is ..a little in the *horse-dealing line. **1895** *Daily News* 22 Oct. 6/4 Fined for *Horse Docking. **1963** A. Lubbock *Austral. Roundabout* 161 *Horse- and cattle-duffers. **1888** Boldrewood *Robbery under Arms* I. i. 9 Poaching must be something like cattle and *horse duffing. **1936** M. Franklin *All that Swagger* x. 92 Cattle- and horse-duffing became staple industries in the wilds of Monaro. **1910** *Daily Chron.* 14 Jan. 1/5 Saxony is not the only *horse-eating part of Germany. **1960** A. Clarke *Later Poems* (1961) 87 Horse-eating helps this ill-fare state To Sunday plate. **1552** Huloet, *Horse-feader, *hippobotos*. **1750** *Phil. Trans.* XLVII. xii. 89 This phænomenon surprized..the *horse-flayer who attended me. **1593** *Nottingham Rec.* IV. 239 William Yates, *horsegelder. **1848** H. W. Haygarth *Recoll. Bush Life Austral.* vi. 61 Cattle-hunting in Australia is excellent sport..with less speed than in *horse-hunting. **1908** *Daily Chron.* 24 Oct. 1/2 Apart from the horse-hunting we had harness to repair. **1795** *Sporting Mag.* V. 49 A number of *horse jobbers were there. **1890** Boldrewood *Col. Reformer* (1891) 279 Drawing forth..encomiums from the *horse-loving..Colonel. **1907** *Westm. Gaz.* 6 Sept. 5/1 Another case of *horse-maiming. **1908** *Daily Chron.* 14 Aug. 8/6 Three horse-maiming outrages. **1820** *Sporting Mag.* VI. 157 Stubbs, the prince of *horse-painters. **1552** Huloet, *Horse seller, *hippoplanus*. *Ibid.* *Horse stealer, *hippolegus*. **1600** Shaks. *A.Y.L.* III. iv. 25 Yes, I thinke he is not a picke purse, nor a horse-stealer. **1730** in *Man. Corpor. N.Y.* (1864) 677 That one Solomon Jennings hath been a notorious Horse-Stealer for many years past. **1837** W. Irving *Capt. Bonneville* (1895) I. 41 One of the most.. predatory tribes of the mountains; horse-stealers of the first order. **1737** *London Mag.* Aug. 456/1 At Norwich, 2 Men receiv'd Sentence of Death for *Horse-stealing. **1837** W. Irving *Capt. Bonneville* (1895) I. 43 This wild, horse-stealing tribe. **1858** T. Vielé *Following Drum* 123 Horse-stealing from the Mexicans is a..branch of their business. **1871** E. Eggleston *Hoosier Schoolmaster* (1872) vi. 70 The whole region..had the reputation of being infested with thieves, who practiced horse-stealing. **1937** *Discovery* Aug. 245/2 The horse-stealing scenes in *The Merry Wives*. **1530** Palsgr. 232/2 *Horse tamer, *domptevr de cheuavlx*. **1859** *Art Taming Horses* i. 3 Mr. Rarey..as an invincible Horse-Tamer. **1836–48** B. D. Walsh *Aristoph.* 365 *note*, Pallas, the *horse-taming goddess of frowns. **1898** W. J. Locke *Idols* xxiii. 323 Two sturdy and swarthy peasants..pausing by the *horse-tender, received a voluble account of the situation. **1907** *Daily Chron.* 12 Nov. 8/1 He pushed close to the horse-tender, a Somali. **1768** *Boston Chron.* 10 Oct. 388/3 People ..who have assembled..with the view of driving all *horse thieves..from amongst them. **1891** M. E. Ryan *Told in*

Hills II. v. 61 She intimated yesterday that he might be a horse-thief. **1893** KIPLING *Land & Sea T.* (1923) 230 Murderers, horse-thieves, and cattle-lifters. **1835** R. M. BIRD *Hawks of Hawk-Hollow* II. xiii. 137 Down you rogue, or I'll indict you for *horse-thieving. **1874** R. GLISAN *Jrnl. Army Life* xxxii. 463 A band of.. horse-thieving, prairie Indians. **1945** DYLAN THOMAS *Let.* 28 Aug. (1966) 283 Mean, green, horse-thieving Wales. **1889** *Cent. Dict.*, *Horse-trainer. **1906** *Daily Chron.* 4 Jan. 7/1 Only one British subject is reported to have been killed during the rising—a horse-trainer, who was accidentally shot. **1921** *Daily Colonist* (Victoria, B.C.) 9 Oct. 36/2 Mr. Carley, of Epsom, England, licensed horse-trainer under the English Jockey Club. **1872** *Daily News* 2 Aug., Goodwood, as a *horsewaterer phrased it, is a 'quality' meeting.

g. instrumental, as ***horse-bitten, -drawn, -driven, -nibbled, -raised*** adjs.; ***horse-tower, -towing.***

1677 *Lond. Gaz.* No. 1238/4 The further shoulder full of spots, having been *Horse-bitten. **1890** O. WILDE in *19th Cent.* July 140 On foot, or in *horse-drawn chariot, the warriors go forth to battle. **1969** *Times* 25 Apr. 11/3 The modern equivalent of the correspondents who no doubt wrote to you when the first steam train appeared and said that we should.. travel as God intended, by horse-drawn carriage. **1900** *Daily News* 2 Oct. 7/1 To his efforts.. the cities of Philadelphia and Chicago owe their emancipation from the.. delay of *horse-driven public conveyances. **1936** *Discovery* Mar. 75/1 An ancient horse-driven windlass. **1968** C. A. DOXIADIS *Between Dystopia & Utopia* 8 We still cross our big cities at nine miles per hour, which was the speed of a horse-driven cart at the beginning of the century. **1973** *Guardian* 18 May 10 A petition.. was taken in a horse-driven carriage to Kensington Town Hall yesterday. **1638-48** G. DANIEL *Eclog* v. 106 *Horse-rais'd Hyppocrene. **1783** *Rules for Bargemasters* etc. 9 No such *horse-tower shall take, for the towing of any barge, more than the usual price. **1795** *Act 35 Geo. III*, c. 106 *Preamble*, In making *Horse Towing-Paths.

h. *attrib.* Like a horse, or like that of a horse, horse-like; hence coarse, unrefined: in construction sometimes approaching an adj.; as ***horse face*** (hence ***horse-faced*** adj.), ***joke, language, mouth, smile, vein***; ***horse-headed*** adj. See also HORSE-LAUGH, HORSE-PLAY.

1630 DAVENANT *Just Ital.* II. Dram. Wks. 1872 I. 227 See his horse veins, th' are large as conduit pipes. **1672** JOSSELYN *New Eng. Rarities* 99 The Men are somewhat Horse Fac'd. **1681** OTWAY *Soldier's Fort.* v. i, With a Horse-face, a great ugly head. **1748** RICHARDSON *Clarissa* (1811) III. lxii. 356 She prims up her horse-mouth. **1845** DISRAELI *Sybil* (1863) 213 Here he [Tadpole] broke into a horse smile. **1865** *Pall Mall G.* No. 208. 3/1 A vulgar, insolent horse-joke. **1910** W. J. LOCKE *Simon* xii. 146 The horse-headed Englishman cried '*banco*'. **1916** E. POUND *Lustra* 53 The horse-faced lady of just the unmentionable age. **1937** C. S. FORESTER *Happy Return* 113 One of the horsefaced mannish women whom he particularly disliked.

28. Special combs.: **a. horse aloes** (see quot.); **horse arm** (*Mining*), that part of a horse-whim to which horses are attached (Cassell); **horse-billiards**, a game played on board ship with wooden disks, on a diagram chalked on the deck; **horse-bite**, (*a*) a bite given by a horse; (*b*) *colloq.*, a rough pinch on the thigh with the hand; **horse-book**, (*a*) a book about horses; (*b*) a betting-book; **horse-boot**, a leather covering for the hoof and pastern of a horse designed to protect them against over-reaching or interfering; **horse brass** (see quot. 1963); **horse-bridge**, a bridge for horses to pass over; **horse-bucket** (see quot.); **horse butcher**, a man who kills horses, esp. for food; also, a man who sells horse-meat (HORSE-MEAT 2); so **horse-butchery; horse-cadger** a horse-coper; **horse-chanter** = CHANTER *sb.*[1] 7; so **horse-chanting; horse-clipper**, a man who clips horses; a pair of shears used in clipping horses; † **horse-coal** (see quot.); **horse-doctor**, one who treats the diseases of horses; so **horse-doctoring; horse-drench**, a draught of medicine administered to a horse; also, a horn or other vessel by which it is administered; **horse feathers** *U.S. slang*, nonsense, rubbish, balderdash; **horse-fettler**, a man who 'fettles' or attends to horses in a coal-mine (Heslop *Northumb. Gloss.* 1893); **horse-fiddle** *U.S.* (see quot. 1872); **horse-fight**, (*a*) a fight on horseback; (*b*) a fight between horses; **horse-furniture**, the trappings of horses; **horse-gang** = *horse-walk* (Heslop *Northumb. Gloss.* 1893); **horse-gentler** (*local*), a horse-tamer or breaker; **horse-high** *a. U.S.*, (*a*) as high as a horse; (*b*) too high for a horse to jump over; also *fig.*; **horse-holder**, (*a*) a slinging frame for holding unruly horses while being shod, or for supporting sick or disabled horses (Knight *Dict. Mech.* 1875); (*b*) *Mil.*, each of the mounted horse artillery gunners who take charge of the dismounted horses while the gun is in action; † **horse-holy** *a.* (cf. 'as holy as a horse' 26 a); **horse-hook**, an iron hook on a railway carriage or truck by which a horse may be attached to draw it; **horse-iron** (see HORSE *v.* 11); **horse-knacker**, one who buys up old or wornout horses, and slaughters them for their commercial products; † **horse-knave** = HORSE-BOY; **horse-lease** = HORSE-GATE[2]; † **horse-lede**, horsemen; **horse lot** *U.S.*, a piece of ground on which horses are pastured; **horse manure**, (*a*) = HORSE-DUNG; (*b*) = *horse shit*; † **horse marshal**, one who has the charge or care of horses; a horse-doctor; † **horse-match**, a race between two horses; † **horse-meal**, a dry meal without drink, such as a horse's is; **horse-milliner** (quasi-*arch.*), one who supplies ornamental trappings for horses; † **horse-mithridate**, an antidotal medicine for horses; **horse-monger**, a dealer in horses; † **horse-nest** = MARE'S NEST; **horse-nightcap**, grimly humorous for a hangman's halter; **horse opera** *colloq.* (orig. *U.S.*), a 'Western' film or television series; **horse-pew**, a large pew with high sides, = HORSE-BOX 2; **horse-pick, -picker**, a hooked instrument, sometimes forming part of a pocket knife, used for removing a stone from a horse's foot; **horse-piece**, a large piece of whale's blubber; esp. a tough piece put under the pieces to be cut in order to protect the edge of the knife; **horse pistol**, a large pistol carried at the pommel of the saddle when on horseback; † **horse-plea**, a sort of special plea for delaying the cause and carrying it over the term; **horse-post**, a letter-carrier who travels on horseback; postal delivery by means of such carriers; **horse-protector**, a spiral spring for reducing the strain upon a horse in starting a vehicle; **horse-ride**, (*a*) a road for horse-traffic; (*b*) a ride taken mounted on a horse; **horse-rough**, a calk fitted to a horse's shoe to prevent slipping on frozen ground; **horse-run** (see quot.); † **horse-running** = HORSE-RACING; **horse shit** *U.S. slang*, nonsense; **horse-sickness**, an acute virus disease of horses and related animals, marked by fever, difficulty in breathing, or swelling of the head, and endemic in Africa; † **horse-smith**, a farrier; **horse's neck** *slang* (orig. *U.S.*), a beverage of ginger ale flavoured with lemon-peel, with or without the addition of whisky, brandy, or gin; **horse's tail** (see HORSE-TAIL 1 c); **horse-steps** = HORSE-BLOCK 1; **horse-tailer** [TAIL *v.*[1] 5] *Austral.*, one who 'tails' or follows horses; **horse-towel**, a coarse towel, hung on a roller, for general use; a jack-towel; **horse-trade** *U.S.*, a deal in horses; also *fig.* or *transf.*; hence **horse-trader** (in quots. 1963 and 1972 = heroin-trader; cf. sense 15 above); **horse-trading** *vbl. sb.*, (*a*) *U.S.* dealing in horses; (*b*) *transf.*, hard or unfair bargaining; **horse-tree** (see quots. 1787 and 1828); **horse-trot** (*U.S.*), a trotting match; † **horse-twitcher** (see quot.); **horse-walk**, the path which a horse follows in working a machine, as a gin, whim, etc.; **horse-watcher** (*Horse-racing*), one who watches the performances of racing horses and calculates their chances for particular races; **horse-wrangler**, in the Western U.S.: a herder having charge of a string of ponies.

1881 *Syd. Soc. Lex.*, *Aloë caballina*, caballine, *horse, or fetid aloes. An inferior variety.. at one time used in veterinary medicine... It is black, opaque, dull in fracture, and very nauseous. **1872** 'MARK TWAIN' *Innoc. Abr.* iv, *Horse-billiards is a fine game. **1897** —— *More Tramps Abr.* iv. **1885** 'MARK TWAIN' in *Century Mag.* Dec. 197/1 Bowers, already irritated by the pain of the *horse-bite. **1949** F. SARGESON *I saw in my Dream* II. xiii. 117 He brought his hand down smartly on Len's leg, giving him a horse-bite that made him jump. **1643** in *Essex Co. Prob. Rec.* (1916) I. 30, I give to him my *horse booke alsoe a pitchforke. **1909** *Times Lit. Suppl.* 21 Jan. 23/1 Colonel.. Dodge.. is the author of two admirable horse-books. **1962** K. ORVIS *Damned & Destroyed* xiv. 91 A guy I know runs a horse-book on University. **1911** E. LOVETT *Folk Lore Horse* 3 (*heading*) *Horse brasses. It is almost impossible to walk through any of our towns without meeting with horses.. bedecked with certain brass ornaments. *Ibid.* 7 We now turn to the other typical horse brass, viz., the crescent. **1945** 'G. ORWELL' *Animal Farm* iv. 34 It consisted of a brass medal (they were really some old horse-brasses which had been found in the harness-room). **1960** 'R. EAST' *Kingston Black* xiv. 135 A great glittering display of silver darts trophies and horse brasses. **1963** BLOODGOOD & SANTINI *Horseman's Dict.* 107 *Horse brasses*, decorative metal ornaments in a great variety of designs hung on draft-horse harness. Probably originating in the amulets used on camels in the East and horses in Mediterranean countries to ward off the 'evil eye'. **1637** in *N. Riding Rec.* IV. 69 Not repairing the *horse-bridge near by Button Oak. **1647** *Mass. Colony Rec.* (1854) III. 113 There shalbe a sufficyent horsbridge made on the riuer neere Watertowne Mill. **1791** R. MYLNE *Rep. Thames & Isis* 50 Towing path on South side requires two horse-bridges. **1827** J. F. COOPER *Red Rover* II. viii. 134 There was a *horse-bucket kicking about her decks. **1867** SMYTH *Sailor's Word-bk.*, *Horse-buckets*, covered buckets for carrying spirits or water in. **1815** *Sporting Mag.* XLVI. 19 A *horse-butcher's cart draws up. **1896** *Westm. Gaz.* 28 July 10/1 There are.. at least 200 horse-butcher shops in Paris. **1905** *Daily Chron.* 26 May 5/6 Whole families have been affected by the meat, and even the horse-butcher himself who sold the meat is among the victims. **1942** E. PAUL *Narrow St.* vi. 48 A golden horse above the green and white awning.. was the emblem of the horse butcher, M. Monge. **1892** *Daily News* 2 Mar. 5/4 In the year 1866 the then Prefect of the Seine.. authorized the first *horse butchery in Paris. **1886** *Westm. Rev.* April 380 A combination of a Yorkshire *horse-cadger and a Whitechapel bully. **1835** SIR G. STEPHEN *Adv. Search Horse* v. 71 Even the knavery of a professed *horse-chaunter is at fault to hide it. **1841** J. T. HEWLETT *Parish Clerk* II. 7 The mysteries of horse-couping, *horse-chanting. **1552** *Will of R. Turke* (Somerset Ho.), Cooles which are brought to London on horsback called *Horse cooles. **1672** J. LACY *Dumb Lady* I. Dram. Wks. (1875) 25, I understand myself to be a great *horse-doctor, sir. **1723** *Lond. Gaz.* No. 6139/3 Rope Dancers, Horse-Doctors, Poppet-Shewers. **1810** M. L. WEEMS *Lett.* (1929) III. 11 A collection in which there is not a single Bible.. nor Dream-book, nor Horse Doctors. **1894** *Congress Rec.* 1 Mar. 2500/1 We found.. that he was a veterinary surgeon, called in New England a 'horse doctor'. **1930** T. S. ELIOT tr. *St. J. Perse's Anabasis* 65 The vast court of the horse-doctor. **1807** W. IRVING et al. *Salmagundi* (1814) xv. 345 He is.. resorted to as an oracle to resolve any question about.. *horse-doctoring. **1607** SHAKS. *Cor.* II. i. 129 The most soueraigne Prescription.. of no better report then a *Horse-drench. **1928** *Amer. Speech* IV. 98 Mr. William De Beck, the comic-strip comedian.. assumes credit for the first actual use of the word *horsefeathers. **1934** J. O'HARA *Appointment in Samarra* (1935) vi. 163 'And my orders is to see that you keep your knees together, baby.' 'Horse feathers,' she said. **1936** [see BUTTON *v.* 3]. **1936** WODEHOUSE *Laughing Gas* xvi. 173 'Oh, horse-feathers!'.. The expression which she used was new to me, but one could gather its trend. Her ribald and offensive tone jarred upon me. **1966** A. A. FAIR *Widows wear Weeds* xiv. 160 'We lose our licence; Sellers gets fined and maybe you get prosecuted for perjury.' 'Horsefeathers!' Bertha snorted. **1967** J. GARDNER *Madrigal* ii. 21 Mostyn pointed out that.. they could court-martial him *in camera*... On reflection, Boysie realised that this was all a load of horse feathers. **1807** J. JENNINGS *Let.* 19 Sept. in *Ind. Hist. Coll. Soc. Publ.* (1932) X. 164 The French.. convened around the house of the new couple.. playing on *horse fiddles. **1843** *Knickerbocker* XXI. 46 The clangor of trumpets, the clattering of pans, the grinding of horse-fiddles. **1872** E. EGGLESTON *End of World* xlvi. 294 Bill Day had a gigantic watchman's rattle, a hickory spring on a cog-wheel. It is called in the West a horse-fiddle, because it is so unlike either a horse or a fiddle. **1911** H. QUICK *Yellowstone Nights* viii. 212 In addition to the horse-fiddles and bells and horns Absalom had arranged some private theatricals. **1601** R. JOHNSON *Kingd. & Commw.* (1603) 58 The Persians have sometime prevailed in *horse-fights. **1897** *Edin. Rev.* Oct. 394 Savage horse-fights, and sombre legends of Lapland witch-women. **1613** PURCHAS *Pilgrimage* (1614) 654 All his *horse-furniture.. were of Gold. **1851** MAYNE REID *Scalp Hunt.* xxvi, They strip the animals, and bring away their horse-furniture. **1889** HISSEY *Tour in Phaeton* 140 Over a house.. we read the inscription '*horse-gentler'. **1859, 1879** *Horse-high [see *hog-tight* adj. s.v. HOG *sb.*[1] 13 a]. **1896** W. A. WHITE *Real Issue* 147 In the summer the field stood horse-high with corn. *a* **1930** D. H. LAWRENCE *Sex, Lit. & Censorship* (1955) 12 The Clean Books League, whose object was to make the law.. 'horse-high, pig-tight, and bull-strong'. **1972** *Christian Science Monitor* 28 Sept. 16/4 The pioneers.. tipped the stumps up with their roots in the air, and lined them along so they were, as the saying went, 'horse-high, hog-tight, and bull-strong'. **1837** A. F. OAKES *Madras Horse Artillery* 18 The rear rank are *horse-holders. **1875** *Man. Field Artillery Exerc.* VIII. 285 The horse-holders do not dismount. **1902** J. H. M. ABBOTT *Tommy Cornstalk* 35 When calvary are dismounted for skirmishing, one man of every four—the horse-holder, or number three—is out of action. **1936** C. S. FORESTER *General* 7 In a long straggling line.. lay the troopers of the squadron.. firing away. In a gully to the rear.. were the horses and horseholders. **1589** NASHE *Almond for Parrat* 18 a, This *hors-holy father preaching. **1750** BLANCKLEY *Naval Expos.*, **Horse Irons*, used by the Caulkers, when they cannot come at a Seam with their common Irons. *c* **1850** [see HORSE *v.* 11]. **1937** *John o' London's* 5 Feb. 762/2 [A girl] promised to wait for me. She didn't, though. Too impatient. Married a *horse-knacker. *c* **1300** *Havelok* 1019 It ne was non *horse-knaue. **1390** GOWER *Conf.* II. 48, I must nedes sue her route.. And am but as her horse knave. **1887** E. GILLIAT *Forest Outlaws* 235 More I heard, mostly from Alan her horse-knave. **1721** *Lond. Gaz.* No. 5930/3 A Fishpond and *Horse-Lease in the Common. *c* **1205** LAY. 23012 His wepnen and his weden & his *hors-leden. **1847** W. T. THOMPSON in *Spirit of Times* 24 July 250/2 Way he went.., down around the house, through the *horse lot, and into the old field. **1850** *Rep. Comm. Patents 1849: Agric.* 144 The man.. has.. no time to make manure, or to haul out and spread the little that is dropped in his horse-lot. **1889** *Harper's Mag.* June 123/2 In the horse lot she found her father putting on his coat. **1966** *Publ. Amer. Dial Soc.* XLII. 19 *Horselot*, the enclosure around a stockbarn. **1843** S. L. DANA *Muck Man. Farmers* (ed. 2) vi. 135 The dung of pigeons is 2-7ths stronger than *horse manure. **1954** A. G. L. HELLYER *Encycl. Garden Work* 127/2 Horse manure can be used safely for all plants and crops for which animal manure is desirable. **1956** *Dict. Gardening* (R. Hort. Soc.) (ed. 2) II. 1011/1 Horse manure is especially valuable in mushroom growing. **1957** J. OSBORNE *Entertainer* viii. 67 She's not interested in all that horse manure about Canada. **1964** *New Statesman* 1 May 674/1 Imagine his furious indignation if a similar *contre-temps* had arisen (as well it might) at a Washington club because one had been reported as saying on television that federal policy on racial discrimination in the South is a load of horse-manure. **1508** KENNEDIE *Flyting w. Dunbar* 475 A *horse marschall thou call the at the mute. **1670** RAY *Prov., Scott. Prov.* 296 Unskild mediciners and horsemarshels. **1632** SANDERSON *Serm.* I. 299 Who can reasonably say, that *horse-matches.. are in themselves wholly unlawful? **1707** *Lond. Gaz.* No. 4371/4 Two Horse Matches will be run for on Wakefield out-wood.. for Two Plates. **1760** C. JOHNSTON *Chrysal* II. I. ii. 12 *Horse-meals.. are enough to choak human creatures! *a* **1770** CHATTERTON *Balade Charitie* 56 in *Rowley Poems* (1778) 207 The *horse-millanare his head with roses dighte. **1829** W. IRVING *Conq. Granada* lxxvii. (1850) 417 Saddlers and harness-makers and horse-milliners, also, were there. **1614** MARKHAM *Cheap Husb.* I. i. (1668) 7 Give him.. 2 spoonfuls of Diapente, or such like, which is called *Horse-Mithridate. *a* **1400** *Octouian* 836 What thenkest dow be an *horsmonger? *c* **1425** *Voc.* in Wr.-Wülcker 650/18 *Hic mango*, a horsemowngner. **1583** STANYHURST

Æneis To Rdr. (Arb.) 14 Soom grammatical pullet..would stand clocking agaynst mee, as thogh hee had found an *horse nest. *a* **1639** BRETON *Sch. Fancie* (1879) 6 (D.) To laugh at a horse nest, And whine too like a boy. **1593** *Bacchus Bountie* in *Harl. Misc.* (Park) II. 304 His very head so heavie, as if it had beene harnessed in an *horse-nightcap. **1681** *Dial. Oxford Parl.* II. 28 He better deserves to go up Holborn in a Wooden Chariot, and have a Horse Night-Cap put on at the farther end. **1927** *Motion Picture Classic* 2 July 26/1 *Horse Opera..is an opus of the West where men are cowboys. **1948** 'J. TEY' *Franchise Affair* xix. 227 That happens only in detective-stories and the last few minutes of horse-operas. **1957** E. HYAMS *Into Dream* 244 An officer who looked like a bad-man Mexican in an early horse-opera. **1958** *Times* 17 Nov. 8/6, 21 per cent. of the available time is devoted to westerns (28 of these 'horse-opera' series are being broadcast). **1778** *Learning at a Loss* II. 24 He..began digging his Jaw-bone with his *Horse-picker..as if it had been the Hoof of the Animal. **1840** F. D. BENNETT *Whaling Voy.* II. 211 The blubber is..cut with spades into slips, or '*horse-pieces', which, (after they have been 'minced'.. upon an elevated block of wood, termed the 'horse') [etc.]. **1874** C. M. SCAMMON *Marine Mammals* 119 The fat [of the sea elephant].. is cut into 'horse-pieces', about eight inches wide, and twelve to fifteen long. **1704** *Lond. Gaz.* No. 4055/4 One Pair of *Horse Pistols. **1814** SCOTT *Wav.* xxxix, Discharging one of his horse-pistols at the battlements. **1796** J. ANSTEY *Pleader's Guide* (1803) 116 Of *Horsepleas, traverses, demurrers, Jeofails, imparlances and Errors. **1668** *Lond. Gaz.* No. 304/4 A new *Horse-Post is setled, to carry Letters twice every week between Exeter and Lawnston. **1711** *Ibid.* No. 4866/1 Any Offender..that shall presume to ..employ any Foot-Post, Horse-Post, or Packet-Boat. **1887** *Pall Mall G.* 3 Sept. 5/1 The '*Horse Protector', only just introduced into this country..consists of a series of spring coils of great strength connecting the vehicle with the traces of the horses. **1903** *Daily Chron.* 6 Nov. 3/3 On one side of it there will be a *horse-ride, and on the other..a gravelled walk for foot passengers. **1906** W. OWEN *Let.* 15 Aug. (1967) 31 Mr. Smallpage has just been for a horse-ride. **1842–67** GWILT *Archit.* Gloss., **Horse-run*, a contrivance for drawing up loaded wheelbarrows of soil from the deep cuttings..by the help of a horse, which goes backwards and forwards instead of round, as in a horse-gin. **1601** HOLLAND *Pliny* II. 490 Those *horse-runners they called Celeres. **1504** *Ld. Treas. Acc. Scotl.* in Pitcairn *Crim. Trials* I. *121 He wan fra þe King on *hors-rynnyng, xxviiij.*s.* **1601** HOLLAND *Pliny* I. 222 The horses..who had woon the price in the horse-running at Veij. **1955** M. MCCARTHY *Charmed Life* (1956) iii. 66 Pardon me if I say that's *horse shit. **1959** W. BURROUGHS *Naked Lunch* 98 Gentlemen of the jury,.. are we to gulp down this tissue of horse shit? **1970** *It* 12–25 Feb. 2 'This is definitely the weekend of the big bust!' 'Horseshit! You've said the same thing for the past six weekends!' **1822** J. CAMPBELL *Trav. S. Afr. 2nd Journey* I. ii. 32 The *horse sickness..was prevailing much at that time. **1885** *Manch. Exam.* 13 June 5/3 Horse-sickness is one of the drawbacks of these fat plains. **1897** MARY KINGSLEY *W. Africa* 637 The horse-sickness and tsetse fly..occur as soon as you get into the forest behind the littoral region. **1899** W. J. K. LITTLE *Sk. & Stud. S. Afr.* (ed. 2) iv. 93 Let us hope..rinderpest, horse-sickness, and the locusts will yet be conquered. **1947** J. STEVENSON-HAMILTON *Wild Life S. Afr.* vi. 50 The zebra..has..the immense advantage of being entirely immune from Horse Sickness and Nagana disease. **1963** JUBB & KENNEDY *Path. Domestic Anim.* II. 585/1 Even in districts where horsesickness recurs annually, the distribution tends to be limited to low-lying areas such as valleys, swamps, and areas with summer rain. **1580** HOLLYBAND *Treas. Fr. Tong, Vn Mareschal*, a Ferrier, a *horse smith. **1903** 'C. E. MERRIMAN' *Lett. from Son* 177 Every man then visited the tool-house, where a tin wash-boiler filled with what they call here '*horse's neck', a savage compound of whiskey and hard cider, occupied the place of honor. **1925** J. METCALFE *Smoking Leg* 138 A tall young man in a grey suit whose drink was horse's neck in summer and Burton in the winter. **1936** E. AMBLER *Dark Frontier* xiii. 219, I ordered a Horse's Neck, remembered how bad the gin was..and had a small beer instead. **1938** L. MACNEICE *I crossed Minch* II. xv. 211 If I could sit in a garden shady With a Horse's Neck or a White Lady. **1968** *Daily Tel.* (Colour Suppl.) 13 Dec. 43/3 Brandy and soda, or brandy and some soft drink like ginger ale—the Horse's Neck—have become women's drinks. **1828** *Craven Dial.*, **Horse-steps*, steps for the convenience of mounting a horse, a horse-block. **1933** *Bulletin* (Sydney) 16 Aug. 20/2 Then the *horse-tailer pulled out, and an abo. was given the job. **1954** B. MILES *Stars my Blanket* xxiii. 202 The 'horse tailers', whose job it was to look after the mob of spare horses. **1968** K. WEATHERLEY *Roo Shooter* 100, I was only twenty at the time and working as horse-tailer for a cattle-drover. **1861** J. G. SHEPPARD *Fall Rome* xiii. 744 The rough *horse-towel which hung on a roller before the door. **1846** *Knickerbocker* XXVIII. 361 He was employed in..an action brought by a man against another for cheating him in a '*horse-trade'. **1902** A. D. MCFAUL *Ike Glidden* iii. 22 His self-confidence could not admit of a thought that he could be fooled in a horse trade. **1923** *Daily Mail* 15 June 9 [New York World] We hope that foreign Powers will not be weak enough to consent to such unprincipled horse trade. **1850** L. H. GARRARD *Wah-to-Yah* vii. 109 The unfair *horsetrader might have taken my scalp. **1912** I. S. COBB *Back Home* 3 The swapping ring below the wagonyard was..clamorous with the chaffer of the horse-traders. **1932** W. FAULKNER *Light in August* xiii. 283 A room where it will be quiet when her time comes, and not every durn horsetrader or courtjury that passes through the hallway. **1963** T. TULLETT *Inside Interpol* iv. 44 There is another process..that of turning the morphine into heroin, and the price then soars to £600 a pound. Even this gigantic profit is not enough for the 'horse-traders', as these criminals are known. **1972** H. C. RAE *Shooting Gallery* II. 67 And how many hose-traders are there in this part of the world? **1826** T. FLINT *Recoll.* 64 *Horse-trading..seems to be a favorite and universal amusement. **1853** J. G. BALDWIN *Flush Times Alabama* 273 An enterprising young gentleman..engaged..in the horse-trading line. **1891** C. ROBERTS *Adrift Amer.* 190 We stayed in camp here for two days, during which time we did some horse-trading. **1902** A. D. MCFAUL *Ike Glidden* iv. 28 A horse-trading expedition. **1939** I. BAIRD *Waste Heritage* xix. 262 There is too damn much horse-trading going on around here. **1947** *Forum* 24 May 4/3 It was certain that some hard bargaining had taken place in that upstairs conference room, political horse-trading at which South Africa's politicians are adept. **1969** *Times* 25 Apr. 28/3 Employers in the Lancashire textile industry were accused..of 'horse trading'. **1971** *New Scientist* 20 May 460/1 A powerful ingredient in all this horsetrading is the continually deteriorating employment situation in the aerospace industry. **1787** W. MARSHALL *Norfolk* Gloss. (E.D.S.), **Horse-tree*, whippin; or swingletree. **1828** *Craven Dial.*, *Horse-tree*, the beam on which timber is placed previous to sawing. **1882** BURDETTE *Life of W. Penn* viii. 134 The agricultural *horse-trot of the county fair. **1858** O. W. HOLMES *Aut. Breakf.-t.* (1865) 13 Horse-racing is not a republican institution; *horse-trotting is. **1706** PHILLIPS (ed. Kersey) s.v. *Barnacle*, Among Farriers, *Barnacles*, **Horse-twitchers*, or *Brakes*, are Tools put on the Nostrils of Horses, when they will not stand quietly to be Shoo'd, Blooded, or Dress'd of any sore. **1807** VANCOUVER *Agric. Devon* (1813) 124 Lord Clifford has erected a thrashing machine the *horse-walk of which is 28 feet in diameter. **1894** ASTLEY *50 Years Life* II. 303 Meeting any of the numerous touts and *horse-watchers. **1894** *Daily News* 10 Sept. 3/1 The horse-watchers were, however, wrong, and the real spin was decided on Friday. **1888** *Century Mag.* Apr. 851/2 There are two herders, always known as '*horse-wranglers'—one for the day and one for the night. **1902** O. WISTER *Virginian* x. 109 The foreman of the 76 outfit, and the horse-wrangler from the Bar Circle-L. **1968** R. M. PATTERSON *Finlay's River* 102 Various packers and horse wranglers, with their pack-trains, moved with the party or made rendezvous with them as the work demanded.

b. In names of animals (sometimes denoting a large or coarse kind, sometimes with the sense of 'infesting horses'): **horse ant**, a large species of ant; **horse bot**, the fly *Gasterophilus intestinalis*, esp. its larva which is a parasite of horses; also **horse bot-fly**; **horse-conch**, a large shell-fish (*Strombus gigas*); **horse-crab** = HORSESHOE-*crab*; †**horse-eel** = HORSE-LEECH; **horse-emmet** = *horse-ant*; **horse-finch**, a local name of the chaffinch (Swainson *Prov. Names Birds*); **horse-lark**, name in Cornwall for the corn bunting (Swainson); †**horse-marten**, 'a kind of large bee' (Johnson, citing Ainsworth); **horse-masher, -musher** = next (*a*); **horse-match, -matcher**, local names for two different birds: (*a*) the Stonechat or Wheatear (*Saxicola œnanthe*); (*b*) the Redbacked Shrike (*Lanius collurio*); **horse-mussel**, a large and coarse kind of mussel of the genus *Modiola*; also a freshwater mussel, *Unio* or *Anodonta*; **horse-smatch** = *horse-match* (*a*); **horse-sponge**, the commercial bath-sponge (*Spongia equina*), found in the Mediterranean; **horse-stinger**, a popular name for the Dragon-fly; **horse-thrush**, local name for the missel thrush (Swainson); **horse-tick** = HORSE-FLY; †**horse-whale**, the walrus; **horse-winkle**, the common periwinkle (*Littorina littorea*); **horse-worm**, a 'worm' or maggot infesting horses, as the larva of the common bot-fly.

1721 BRADLEY *Philos. Acc. Wks. Nat.* 132 There are several sorts of Ants, some of which are larger than our common House Flies; these are call'd *Horse-Ants. **1747** GOULD *Eng. Ants 2 note*, They [Hill Ants] are also called Horse Ants, or Hippomyrmaces..probably on Account of their being superior in Size to the other species. **1815** KIRBY & SP. *Entomol.* I. viii. 230 Ants will sometimes plant their colonies in our kitchens (I have known the horse-ant, *Formica rufa*, do this). **1908** *Westm. Gaz.* 16 Apr. 10/3 The 'horse-ant',..(*Formica rufa*), the big fellow which builds the great heaps, usually of pine-needles. **1945** C. P. HASKINS *Of Ants & Men* ix. 167 Typical of this group [*sc.* raiding ants] is *Formica rufa*, the 'horse ant' or 'fallow ant' of England and Europe, whose great thatched mounds form a conspicuous feature of the German forests. **1744–50** W. ELLIS *Mod. Husbandm.* IV. I. 132 (E.D.S.) If the fly, dar, or *horse-bee should happen to blow your sheep. **1840** J. & M. LOUDON tr. *Köllar's Treat. Insects* I. 53 The *Horse-bot, a larva proceeding from a fly resembling a humble-bee with two wings. **1925** A. D. IMMS *Gen. Textbk. Ent.* III. 652 The horse bot-flies..lay their eggs on the hair. **1928** METCALF & FLINT *Destructive & Useful Insects* xxii. 779 The common horse bot may easily be told by the faint smoky spots on the wings. **1968** *Oxf. Bk. Insects* 138/2 *Horse-bot fly* (Gasterophilus intestinalis). This belongs to a separate sub-family in Muscidae—the Gasterophilinae. **1885** C. F. HOLDER *Marvels Anim. Life* 85 The hermit-crab..that hauled about a shell of the *horse conch. *c* **1400** MAUNDEV. (Roxb.) xxi. 98 Þare er in þe lowgh *hors iles of wonderfull greteness. **1483** *Cath. Angl.* 189/2 An Horse ele [*v.r.* eylle] *sanguis-suga*. **1755** JOHNSON, **Horseemmet*, ant of a large kind. **1885** SWAINSON *Prov. Names Birds* 9 Wheatear (*Saxicola œnanthe*)..Horse smatch, or Horse musher. *Ibid.* Index, *Horse masher. **1736–52** AINSWORTH *Lat. Dict.*, The *horse match (bird), *œnanthe*. **1848** *Zoologist* VI. 2290 The red-backed shrike is in G[loucestershire] a 'French magpie' or a 'horse match'. **1879** JEFFERIES *Wild Life in S. Co.* x. 159 *Horse-matchers or stonechats also in summer often visit the rickyard. **1882** —— *Bevis* III. vi. 85 The horse-matcher is the bold hedge-hawk or butcher bird. **1626** BACON *Sylva* §875 The great *horse-Mussle, with the fine shell, that breedeth in Ponds, do..gape and shut as the oysters do. **1661** J. CHILDREY *Brit. Bacon.* 178 In the Rivers Dee and Done is..a shel-fish called the Horse-Muskle, in which there grow Pearls, as Orient as the best. **1791** *Statist. Acc. Scotl., Lanark.* II. 179 (Jam.) A large bivalvular shell-fish known here by the name of the horse-muscle..in some of them are found small pearls. **1772** *Ann. Reg.* 207 Large insects, about the size of a *horse-stinger. **1910** *Encycl. Brit.* VIII. 468/1 Dragon-fly... In many parts of England are termed 'horse-stingers'. It is almost needless to say that (excepting to other insects..) they are perfectly innocuous. **1966** 'J. HACKSTON' *Father clears Out* 134 Flies, mosquitos, beetles, March flies, blowflies, and horsestingers. *c* **893** K. ÆLFRED *Oros.* I. i. §15 For þæm *horsc-hwælum, for ðæm hie habbað swiþe æþele ban on hiora toþum. **1598** HAKLUYT *Voy.* I. 5 For the more commoditie of fishing of horsewhales. **1863** KINGSLEY *Water-Bab.* vii. 275 Right whales and horse-whales.

c. In names of plants, fruits, etc. (often denoting a large, strong, or coarse kind: cf. similar use of *Rosz-* in German, in *Roszveilchen*, etc.): **horse-balm**, a strong-scented labiate plant of the North American genus *Collinsonia*, with yellowish flowers (Webster 1864); **horse-bane**, name for species of *Œnanthe*, esp. *Œ. Phellandrium*, supposed to cause palsy in horses; **horse-bean**, a leguminous plant grown as food for cattle, as *Vicia faba*, *Canavalia ensiformis*, *Parkinsonia aculeata*, or their seeds; **horse-beech**, the Hornbeam (see BEECH 2); **horse-blob**, local name of the Marsh Marigold (*Caltha palustris*); **horse-bramble**, local name of the wild rose (W. Marshall *Norfolk* II. Gloss. 1787); **horse-brier**, 'the common greenbrier or cat-brier of N. America, *Smilax rotundifolia*' (*Cent. Dict.*); **horse-cane**, the Great Ragweed of N. America, *Ambrosia trifida* (*Syd. Soc. Lex.* 1886); **horse-cassia**, a leguminous tree (*Cassia marginata* or *Cathartocarpus marginatus*), bearing long pods containing a purgative pulp used in the East Indies as a medicine for horses (Webster 1864); †**horse-chire**, an old name for Germander (*Teucrium Chamædrys*); **horse-cress**, local name for Brooklime (*Veronica Beccabunga*); **horse-cucumber** (see quot.); **horse-daisy**, the Ox-eye Daisy (see DAISY *sb.* 2); †**horse-elder**, corrupt form of HORSEHEAL, elecampane; **horse-eye, horse-eye bean**, the seed of the Cowage (*Mucuna pruriens*), a West Indian leguminous plant; also that of *Dolichos Lablab*; **horse-fennel** (see FENNEL); †**horse-flower**, a species of Cow-wheat (*Melampyrum arvense*); †**horse-gall**, an old name for *Erythræa Centaureum*; **horse-gentian, -ginseng**, a North American caprifoliaceous plant of the genus *Triosteum*, having a bitter root; **horse-gog**, local name for different varieties of plum, having a harsh taste; **horse-gowan**, name given in Scotland to the Ox-eye Daisy and other large composites with similar flowers; **horse-gram**, a leguminous plant (*Dolichos biflorus*) grown in India as food for horses; **horse-jag, -jug** (*dial.*) = HORSE-PLUM 1; **horse-knob, -knop, -knot** (*dial.*), the head of the Knapweed, also the plant itself; **horse mushroom**, a species of edible mushroom, *Agaricus arvensis*, larger and coarser than the common mushroom; **horse-nettle**, a North American weed of the nightshade family (*Solanum carolinense*); **horse-nicker**, a large West Indian shrub, *Cæsalpinia bonduc*, or its seeds; **horse-parsley**, a large-leaved umbelliferous plant, *Smyrnium Olusatrum* (Prior *Plant-n.* 1879); †**horse-pear**, ? a large or coarse variety of pear; **horse-pipe**, local name for several species of *Equisetum* or Horsetail; **horse poison**, a West Indian plant, *Isotoma longiflora*; **horse-poppy** = *horse-fennel*; **horse-purslane**, a West Indian plant, *Trianthema monogyna* (Webster 1828); **horse-sorrel**, the Water-dock, *Rumex Hydrolapathum*; **horse-sugar**, a shrub (*Symplocos tinctoria*) found in the southern United States, also called *sweetleaf*, the leaves of which are used as fodder (Webster 1864); **horse-thistle**, †(*a*) an old name for 'Wild Endive' or Succory (*Cichorium Intybus*), and for Wild Lettuce (*Lactuca virosa*); (*b*) a thistle of the genus *Cirsium* (sometimes reckoned a subgenus of *Cnicus*) (Miller *Plant-n.* 1884); †**horse-thyme**, Turner's name for Wild Basil (*Calamintha Clinopodium*); **horse-tongue**, (*a*) the shrub *Ruscus Hypoglossum* (= DOUBLE-TONGUE 2); (*b*) the Hart's-tongue Fern (Miller *Plant-n.*); **horse-vetch** = HORSESHOE-*vetch* (Webster 1828); **horse-violet**, local name for the Dog-violet, in Essex, etc.; **horse-weed**, name for two North American plants, *Erigeron canadensis* (N.O. *Compositæ*), also called *butter-weed* (now frequent in England), and *Collinsonia canadensis* (N.O. *Labiatæ*), also called ***horse-mint*** (Miller *Plant-n.*); **horse-wellgrass** (*Sc.*) = *horse-cress* (cf. *well-grass*, watercress) (Jam.); †**horse-willow** = HORSETAIL 2; **horse-wood**, name for various West Indian shrubs or trees of the genus *Calliandra*.

1894 *Harper's Mag.* Mar. 562, I passed a luxuriant clump of..*horse-balm. **1818** *Withering's Brit. Pl.* (ed. 6), *Phellandrium aquaticum*..Water Hemlock, or *Horsebane. **1684** I. MATHER *Remark. Prov.* (1890) 216 The stone weighed about seven grains, being much in the shape of our ordinary *horse-beans. **1707–12** MORTIMER *Husb.* (J.), Only

the small horsebean is propagated by the plough. **1787** WINTER *Syst. Husb.* 253 A bushel of horse beans weighed sixty four pounds. **1811** *Sporting Mag.* XXXVIII. 137 A fricasee of horse-beans. **1942** CASTETTER & BELL *Pima & Papago Agric.* 60 Of somewhat less importance were the seeds of..Jerusalem thorn or horsebean (*Parkinsonia aculeata*). **1964** J. M. KINGSBURY *Poisonous Plants of U.S.* 43 *Parkinsonia aculeata*, horsebean. *Ibid.* 362 *Vicia faba* L. Fava bean, broad bean, horse bean. **1965** E. G. B. GOODING et al. *Flora of Barbados* 198 *Canavalia ensiformis* (L.) DC. (Horse bean, Overlook bean, Sword bean, etc.) is sometimes grown as a vegetable. The young pod is sliced, and eaten like French beans. **1731** GRAY in *Phil. Trans.* XXXVII. 36 It was that Sort of Wood they call *Horse-Beech. **1821** CLARE *Vill. Minstr.* II. 120 The *horse-blob swells its golden ball. **1597** GERARDE *Herbal* App., *Horsechire is Germander. **1879** BRITTEN & HOLLAND *Plant-n.*, *Horse Cress, *Veronica Beccabunga*.—E. Yks. One of its French names is *Cresson du cheval.* **1707–12** MORTIMER *Husb.* (J.), The *horse-cucumber is the large green cucumber, and the best for the table, green out of the garden. **1597** GERARDE *Herbal* App., *Horselder is *Enula campana.* **1700** W. KING *Transactioneer* 23 The Second sort of Bean is called the *Horse Eye-Bean, for its resemblance to the Eye of that Beast by reason of a Hilus almost surrounding it. **1707** SLOANE *Jamaica* I. 179 Horse-eye Bean..of a light-brown colour, with a black ledge or hilus almost round them, looking something like a horses eye, whence the name. **1750** G. HUGHES *Barbadoes* 215 A large downy pod inclosing from one to three beans, called Horse-Eyes. **1578** LYTE *Dodoens* II. xiv. 163 Of *Horse floure or Cowe wheate..They call this herbe..in Brabant Peertsbloemen: that is to say, Horse floure. *a* **1500** *Gl. Sloane* 5 in *Sax. Leechd.* III. 333/1 *Horsegalle, *centaurea minor.* **1864** WEBSTER, **Horse-gentian*..called also fever-wort. **1842** HARDY in *Proc. Berw. Nat. Club* II. No. 10. 16 The corn-feverfew..the great ox-eye..and the corn-chamomile..have been, in Berwickshire, denominated *horse-gowans, and in Northumberland white-gowlons. **1886** A. H. CHURCH *Food Grains India* 162 *Horse-Gram, this species of Dolichos is either suberect or twining in habit. **1886** *Cheshire Gloss.*, **Horse-jug*, or *horse plum*, a small red plum. **1730–6** BAILEY (folio), **Horse-Knobs*, Heads of Knap-weed. **1876** *Whitby Gloss.*, *Horse-knobs*,.. knob weed, or black knapweed, *Centaurea nigra.* **1674–91** RAY *N.C. Words* 30 **Horseknops*, Heads of Knapweed so called. **1868** ATKINSON *Cleveland Gloss.*, *Horse-knops*, the plant black knapweed..Also called Hard-heads. **1866** LINDLEY & MOORE *Treas. Bot.* II. 598/1 The *horse-mushroom need not be excluded on account of its supposed unwholesomeness. **1890** R. D. BLACKMORE *Kit & Kitty* III. iii. 39 Mingling with the true Agaric some very fine 'Horse-mushrooms'. **1966** *Times* 28 Apr. 16 Horse mushrooms are bigger and stronger flavoured than proper field mushrooms. **1860** BARTLETT *Dict. Amer.* (ed. 3), **Horse-Nettle*,..a plant well known for its orange yellow berries. **1750** *Horse-nicker [see NICKER *sb.*[4]]. **1871** C. KINGSLEY *At Last* I. i. 36 The grey horse-nicker-beads of our childhood. **1965** E. G. B. GOODING et al. *Flora of Barbados* 176 *Caesalpinia bonduc.* .. Grey nicker, Horse-nicker... Shrub, often scrambling by means of prickles. **1657** BEALE in *Phil. Trans.* XLIII. 517 The croft Crab and white or red *Horse-pear do excel them and all others [for cider]. **1671** *Ibid.* VI. 2147 The Horse-pears..the white and the red of several kinds, yield abundance of pleasant liquor. **178.** *Ann. Agric.* IV. 431, *Staff.*, *Horse-pipe, *Equisetum arvense.* **1851** P. H. GOSSE *Nat. Sojourn Jamaica* 80 One of the most venomous of plants (*Isotoma longiflora*) commonly called *Horse-poison. **1955** *W. Indian Med. Jrnl.* IV. 73 *Isotoma longiflora*.. Madam Fate; Star Flower; Horse Poison. **1578** LYTE *Dodoens* V. ix. 559 Called..in Englishe, Great Sorrel, Water Sorrel, and *Horse Sorrel. *c* **1450** *Herbal* in *MS. Douce* 290 lf. 142 Endive is an herbe þat som men callet *hors þistel. **1597** GERARDE *Herbal* App., Horse Thistle is wild Lettuce. **1548** TURNER *Names of Herbes, Clinopodium*..may be called in englishe *horse Tyme, because it is like greate Tyme. **1562** —— *Herbal* II. 15 a, A Garland made of the leaues of *hors tong. **1736–52** AINSWORTH *Lat. Dict.* (1783) II, *Hippoglossum*,..the herb horse-tongue, or tongue-wort. **1790** L. CASTIGLIONI *Viaggio negli Stati Uniti* II. 333 *Collinsonia canadensis*, Lin. *Horse-weed. **1874** J. W. LONG *Amer. Wild-Fowl Shooting* xxiii. 239 The hunter usually selects a position..amongst the high 'horse-weeds' bordering the field. **1892** B. TORREY *Foot-path Way* 72 Acres and acres of horseweed. **1963** H. A. GLEASON *Illustr. Flora North-eastern U.S.* III. 475/1 *Conyza canadensis* (L.) Cron. Horseweed. Coarse annual... A weed in waste places. **1611** COTGR., *Queuë de cheval*, Shaue-grasse, *Horse-willow, horse-taile. **1756** P. BROWNE *Jamaica* 279 *Horse-wood or Hoop-wood. This shrub is very common in St. Mary's.

horse, *v.* [f. prec. sb.]

1. a. *trans.* To provide with a horse or horses; to set on horseback.

a **1100** *O.E. Chron.* an. 881 þær þa warð se here horsad æfter þam ȝefeohte. *Ibid.* an. 1015 West Seaxe buȝon..& horsodon þone here. *c* **1330** R. BRUNNE *Chron. Wace* (Rolls) 12715 Of þem alle last horsed he was. **1470–85** MALORY *Arthur* I. xiv, Syre kay..lad his hors vnto syr gryflet & horsed hym ageyne. **1582–8** *Hist. James VI* (1804) 250 He suddainlye horsit himselff for saifftie of his lyffe, and came furth of the village. **1611** CORYAT *Crudities* 80 Maron of Turin, who horsed oure Company from Lyons to Turin. **1688** in Gutch *Coll. Cur.* I. 429 He horst a servant, and sent him with a Letter to the Bishop. **1799** SHERIDAN *Pizarro* Prol., Horsed in Cheapside. **1867** FREEMAN *Norm. Conq.* I. v. 324 The Danes horsed themselves and ravaged the whole western part of the shire.

b. To furnish (a vehicle) with horses; esp. to provide horses for carriages and coaches on a given length of road. Also *transf.*, to provide the engine for a railway train.

1755 WASHINGTON *Lett.* Writ. 1889 I. 167 We set out with less than thirty carriages..all of them strongly horsed. **1809** TAUNTON *Cases in Com. Pl.* 50 On the road..the separate Defendants horsed the separate stages. **1812** COL. HAWKER *Diary* (1893) I. 47 One Kitty Lockey, who horses the mail. **1842** *P. Parleys Ann.* III. 85 He immediately gave orders that his carriage should be horsed. **1888** *Pall Mall G.* 23 July 6/2 Twelve 16-pounder guns, horsed for service. **1897** *Westm. Gaz.* 30 Dec. 3/2 The North-Eastern again took up the 'horsing'—as the original agreement terms it—of the northern portion of the East Coast triumvirate.

2. *intr.* To mount or go on horseback.

c **1400** *Destr. Troy* 11044 Polidamas..Horsit in hast. **1535** STEWART *Cron. Scot.* II. 234 King Loth thair lord..syne horsit hes agane. **1661** PEPYS *Diary* 19 Sept., Then we all horsed away to Cambridge. **1670–98** LASSELS *Voy. Italy* I. 52 We dined, horsed, and went that night to Susa. **1853** G. JOHNSTON *Nat. Hist. E. Bord.* I. 90 He had to horse it with guides, and carry all necessaries.

†**3. a.** *trans.* To raise or hoist up. *Obs.*

c **1460** *Towneley Myst.* xxiii. 108 Stand nere, felows, and let se how we can hors oure kyng so fre. **1542** *Ludlow Churchw. Acc.* (Camden) 11 Item, for vj. peces of tymbere to horse the belles..iijd. **1613** PURCHAS *Pilgrimage* (1614) 849 Three of them stole a horse..but were therefore horsed on a Gibbet. **1637** T. MORTON *New Eng. Canaan* (1883) 202 If hee tread on the trapp hee is horsed up by the legg, by meanes of a pole that starts up and catcheth him.

b. *Salt-making.* (See quot.)

1886 *Cheshire Gloss.*, *Horse*,..to set the lumps of salt upon the top of each other in the hothouse.

4. a. To carry on a man's back or shoulders.

c **1560** A. SCOTT *Poems* (S.T.S.) v. 58 Madynis..hes their mynȝonis on the streit To horss thaim quhair the gait is ruch. *a* **1680** BUTLER *Rem.* (1759) II. 93 Horsing the deer on his own Back, and making off. **1780** A. YOUNG *Tour Irel.* II. 250 They send to the fair one's cabin to inform her that on the Sunday following 'she is to be horsed', that is carried on men's backs. *a* **1843** SOUTHEY *Comm.-pl. Bk.* IV. 563 [The] Irish custom of horsing a girl, and then hurling for her, that the winner may marry her.

b. To elevate on a man's back, in order to be flogged; hence, to flog.

1563–87 FOXE *A. & M.* (1596) 81 (R.) The capteine commanded the child to be horsed up and scourged. **1647** NEEDHAM *Levellers Lev.* 13 Ile make the House of Lords horse one another, while I doe lash their Buttocks. **1767** H. BROOKE *Fool of Qual.* (1859) I. 232 (D.) Andrew was ordered to horse, and Frank to flog the criminal. **1822** *New Monthly Mag.* V. 462 A judicious teacher, when he is compelled to punish a wicked boy, horses him (as the phrase is) on the back of a dunce. *a* **1863** THACKERAY *Fatal Boots* ii, The biggest boy..horsed me—and I was flogged.

†**5.** *Naut.* Of a current, tide, etc.: To carry with force (a ship or its crew). *Obs.*

1698 FRYER *Acc. E. India & P.* 184 The Tides horsed us to the Northward. **1726** G. ROBERTS *4 Years Voy.* 143 A strong Lee Current, which we perceiv'd to horse us down to Leeward apace. **1726** SHELVOCKE *Voy. round World* 298 We were in eminent danger of being horsed by the current upon two rocks.

6. Of a stallion: To cover (a mare).

c **1420** [see HORSED 3]. **1530** PALSGR. 588/1 Your genet hath horsed my mare. **1605** A. WILLET *Genesis* 319 The fashion is in Spaine to set before the mares, when they are horsed, the most goodly beasts. **1650** BULWER *Anthropomet.* 209 Mares, which they would not have horsed.

7. To set astride, bestride. *rare.*

1607 SHAKS. *Cor.* II. i. 227 Windowes are smother'd vp, Leades fill'd, and Ridges hors'd With variable Complexions.

8. *Naut.* To drive or urge at work unfairly or tyrannically; also (*workmen's slang*), 'to work to death', to out-work.

1867 *All Year Round* 13 July 59 (Farmer) To horse a man, is for one of two men who are engaged on precisely similar pieces of work to make extraordinary exertions in order to work down the other man.

9. *Hop-growing.* (See quot.)

1887 *Kent. Gloss.*, *Horse*, to tie the upper branches of the hop-plant to the pole.

†**10.** ***horse away***: to spend in a lottery. *Obs.* See HORSE *sb.* 10 a.

1731 FIELDING *Lottery* Prol., Should we behold poor wretches horse away The labour of a twelvemonth in a day.

11. ***horse up***: to drive (oakum) between the planks of a ship.

c **1850** *Rudim. Navig.* (Weale) 125 *Horse iron*, an iron fixed in a handle, and used with a beetle by caulkers, to *horse-up* or harden in the oakum.

12. ***horse it***: to charge for work before it is done: cf. HORSE *sb.* 14 and 19.

1857 *N. & Q.* 2nd Ser. IV. 192/1 A workman 'horses it' when he charges for more work than he has really done.

13. a. To make fun of, to 'rag', to ridicule; to indulge in horseplay; to fool *about* or *around*. orig. *U.S.*

1901 *Munsey's Mag.* XXV. 407/1 Because we chose to chew his statements and remove the bones before we swallowed them, he developed the idea that we had no interest in the work and were trying to 'horse' him. **1901** F. H. SPEARMAN *Held for Orders* 173 'Are you horsing me?' he exclaimed, raising his voice angrily. **1928** P. BURANELLI et al. *Cryptogram Bk.* p. i, Always playing jokes on each other, they began to 'horse' each other cryptographically. **1928** *Amer. Speech* III. 219 *Horse around*, to indulge in ill-timed trifling or horse-play. **1939** R. CHANDLER *Trouble is my Business* (1950) 8 Quit horsing around. **1942** *R.A.F. Jrnl.* 2 May 15 Why must you continually horse around, Ginger? **1952** W. G. HARDY *Unfulfilled* 48 Peter horsed around and ducked Elise and she ducked him. **1954** 'W. HENRY' *Death of Legend* 32 Dingus was really mad about it; he wasn't just horsing now. **1959** E. ALLEN *Man who chose Death* v. 49 You saw scores like him..laughing and horseing with the pretty ..young Italian girls. **1959** *Punch* 10 June 776/2 The professor thought I was horsing about and came down to me. **1961** WODEHOUSE *Ice in Bedroom* vi. 47 When you've cleaned up pretty good, you don't want to be horsing around down in the suburbs. **1961** J. HELLER *Catch-22* (1962) xxxii. 340 They were having a whale of a good time as they helped each other set up their cots. They were horsing around. **1971** *It* 2–16 June 7/1 Two black kids..were horsing around just outside the club.

b. To philander; to 'sleep *around*'.

1952 S. KAUFFMANN *Philanderer* (1953) ii. 32 It isn't as if I didn't love her. I'd die for her. Literally. Then why do I have to go horsing around with dames? **1956** S. LONGSTREET *Real Jazz* 67 'This is a respectable band,' he said, 'and there ain't goin' to be any immoral horsin' goin' on. Whoever you start sleepin' with this trip, that's how you end the tour!' **1956** C. SMITH *Deadly Reaper* xxv. 201 She'd be horsing around with Nicky, giving me grounds for divorce.

horse, obs. f. HOARSE; erron. f. HAUSE.

horse-back, horseback, *sb.* (*adv.*)

A. *sb.* † **1.** ('hɔːs'bæk). The back of a horse. *Obs.*

1484 CAXTON *Fables of Poge* iv, He sawe a fayr yong man on a horsbak. **1589** *Marprel. Epit.* F iij b, They are no sooner on their horse backes, then..the horse [etc.]. **1595** SHAKS. *John* II. i. 289 Saint George that swindg'd the Dragon, And ere since sit's on's horsebacke at mine Hostesse dore. **1688** R. HOLME *Armoury* III. vii. 320/2 Water Bags, with the Leather under it which covers the Horse-Back. **1704** N. N. tr. *Boccalini's Advts. fr. Parnass.* II. 219 So soon as he had alighted of his Horse-back.

2. ('hɔːsbæk). *esp.* in Phrases. ***on horseback*** († ***a horseback***). **a.** Sitting or riding on a horse; **b.** of motion: (Mounting) upon a horse. So ***from, off horseback.***

a. **1390** GOWER *Conf.* I. 260 This knight, whiche hoved and abode Embuisshed upon horsebake. *c* **1400** MAUNDEV. (1839) v. 58 Be this Desert, no Man may go on Hors back. **1523** LD. BERNERS *Froiss.* I. xvii. 18 They are all a horsbacke. **1535** COVERDALE *Esther* vi. 11 Aman..broughte him on horszbacke thorow the strete of the cite. **1611** COTGR. s.v. *Maladie*, Diseases come a horsebacke, and returne on foot. **1627** *Lisander & Cal.* I. 21 Many of the chiefe courtiers were a horse-backe. **1667** FLAVEL *Saint Indeed* (1754) 75 That such a beggar should ride on horse-back, and such a prince run after it on foot! **1771** SMOLLETT *Humph. Cl.* 26 June, A couple of robbers a-horseback suddenly appeared. **1849** MACAULAY *Hist. Eng.* iii. I. 351 In an age when even princesses performed their journeys on horseback.

b. *c* **1489** CAXTON *Blanchardyn* vii. 28 The knyght mounted hastely on horsbake. **1513** MORE in Grafton *Chron.* (1568) II. 764 They found the king with his companie readie to leape on horsebacke. **1613** PURCHAS *Pilgrimage* (1614) 420 Counterfeit shapes of men set on horseback. **1704** N. N. tr. *Boccalini's Advts. fr. Parnass.* III. 175 A certain Great King..fell off Horse-back. **1724** DE FOE *Mem. Cavalier* (1840) 269 The dragoons..get a horseback. **1740** tr. *De Mouhy's Fort. Country Maid* (1741) II. 297 A Man just alighted from Horseback. **1809** COBBETT *Pol. Reg.* XV. xii. 429 Set a beggar on horse-back, and he'll ride to the devil. *Mod.* He had some difficulty in climbing on horseback.

† **c.** ***to horseback***, (to mount) upon horseback; to horse. *Obs.*

c **1435** *Torr. Portugal* 2466 To hors-back went thay in fere. *c* **1500** *Melusine* liv. 331 He made to go to horsback hys brother and his x knightes. **1562** J. HEYWOOD *Prov. & Epigr.* (1867) 202 Then must she to horsbacke. **1594** R. ASHLEY tr. *Loys le Roys Interchang. Var. Things* 108 a, A stool to help him to horsback. **1607** TOPSELL *Four-f. Beasts* (1658) 240 Before you go to Horseback first stroke your Horse.

d. Short for: Riding on horseback.

1878 GEO. ELIOT in *Life* (1885) III. 332 Mr. Lewes did once try horseback, some years ago.

3. *Geol.* ('hɔːsbæk). A low and somewhat sharp ridge of gravel or sand; a hog-back. *U.S.*

1851 J. S. SPRINGER *Forest Life* 41 The pumpkin Pine is ..found..also on abrupt ridges, called horse-backs. **1857** THOREAU *Maine W.* (1894) 390 There were singular long ridges hereabouts, called 'horsebacks', covered with ferns. **1884** G. NASH in *Hist. Norfolk County* (Mass.) 561/2 The sharp, linear hills, called horse-backs or kams.

4. *Coal Mining* (*Newc.*). 'A portion of the roof or floor which bulges or intrudes into the coal.'

1881 in RAYMOND *Mining Gloss.* *a* **1886** C. M. INGLEBY *Ess.* (1888) 45 What miners call a 'horse's back', which is an upheaving of the strata which underlie the coal.

5. *attrib.* and *Comb.*, as ***horseback-breaker, -ride, -riding***; ***horseback-fashion*** adv.; **horseback opinion** *U.S.*, an opinion given (as) from horseback, without opportunity for full consideration of the question.

horseback ride, riding, are expressions used chiefly in U.S.; in England, *ride, riding* are understood to be on horseback, unless otherwise expressed or implied, as 'a ride in a wagon', 'a bicycle ride'. See RIDE, DRIVE. (*N.E.D.*)

1596 SHAKS. *1 Hen. IV*, II. iv. 268 This Hors-back-breaker, this huge Hill of Flesh. **1821** COL. TRIMBLE in *Open Court* XI. 245 A horseback ride over the country. **1843** MARRYAT *M. Violet* xxxii, Seated, horseback-fashion, upon parallel low benches. **1878** G. DURANT (*title*) Horseback Riding from a Medical Point of View. **1879** *Congress. Rec.* 23 Apr. 728/1, I am not here as a judicial authority or oracle. I can only give a horseback opinion. **1884** *Cassell's Encycl. Dict.* s.v., The American use is to speak of the latter [*i.e.* driving in a carriage or riding in an omnibus] as riding, distinguishing the former as horseback-riding. **1903** A. ADAMS *Log of Cowboy* vi. 72 My sister gives it as a horseback opinion that she'd been engaged to this fellow nearly eight months.

B. *adv.* Short for *on horseback*.

1727 S. WESLEY in Eliza Clarke *Susanna Wesley* (1886) 152 We can neither go afoot or horseback. **1756** FRANCES BROOKE *Old Maid* No. 26 ¶ 11 Upon the Champion's entry horse-back, he burst into..an immoderate fit of laughter. **1890** BOLDREWOOD *Col. Reformer* (1891) 129, I rode horse-back to the next stage.

†**horse-belly.** *Obs.* An old name for a retort or alembic of some kind.

1660 tr. *Paracelsus' Archidoxis* I. IV. 53 Let this be put in a Horse-belly to distil off all the moisture.

†**horse-bier.** *Obs.* [OE. *horsbǣr, -bér*, f. *hors* HORSE + *bǣr, bér*, BIER.] A horse-litter.

c **900** tr. *Bædas Hist.* IV. vii. [vi.] (1890) 282 His horsbær, þe hine mon untrumne on bær. *c* **1205** LAY. 19598 Ich wæs here ilad inne horse-bere. **1297** R. GLOUC. (Rolls) 3400 þuder he sede he wolde..3if eny horsbere him wolde bere. **1387** TREVISA *Higden* (Rolls) VII. 413 þe Kyng was i-leide on an horsbere. *c* **1440** *Promp. Parv.* 247/2 Horse-bere, *lectica, bajulum.* **1470–85** MALORY *Arthur* IV. xii, Whan Accolon was dede, he lete sende hym on a horsbere..vnto Camelot. **1480** CAXTON *Chron. Eng.* ccxliii. (1482) 289 Thens he [the deceased knight] was brou3t to london vpon a hors bere with moche torche lyght.

'horse-block.

1. A small platform, usually of stone, ascended by 3 or 4 steps, for convenience in mounting a horse; also a portable structure of wood, or the like, for the same purpose.

1753 CHAMBERS *Cycl. Supp., Horse-block*, in the manege. **1798** *Sporting Mag.* XI. 79 Near the gate a horse block, for the conveniency of mounting. **1854** EMERSON *Lett. & Soc. Aims, Poet. & Imag.* Wks. (Bohn) III. 143 The old horse-block in the yard. **1889** CONSTANCE F. WOOLSON *Jupiter Lights* i. 9 A horse-block with a flight of steps attached was brought, and placed in position for the visitor's descent.

2. 'A square frame of strong boards, used by excavators to elevate the ends of their wheeling-planks' (Gwilt *Archit.* 1842–76).

1825 J. NEAL *Bro. Jonathan* II. 12 Lolling about over the horse-blocks, timber, and shingles.

3. *Ship-building.* 'A grating or platform elevated above the deck at the height of the rail, for the use of the officers of the deck' (*Cent. Dict.*).

'horse-boat.

1. a. A ferry-boat for conveying horses or carriages.

1591 PERCIVALL *Sp. Dict., Tafurea*, a horse boate, *Hippagium.* **1665** PEPYS *Diary* 31 July, The horse-boat could not get off on the other side the river to bring away the coach. **1755** JOHNSON, *Horseboat*, a boat used in ferrying horses. **1849** E. B. EASTWICK *Dry Leaves* 22 In another.. boat, I embarked my horses. My horse-boat [etc.].

b. A type of landing-craft.

1907 *Daily Chron.* 25 Feb. 6/3 Exercises with the new form of steel horse-boat were carried out..on Saturday by an A.S.C. contingent... At the stern is a large flap which falls down to facilitate landing. **1923** *Man. Seamanship* (H.M.S.O.) II. 215 Horseboats would be excellent for landing troops except for the fact that they are unhandy.

2. *N. Amer.* A boat whose paddle-wheels are driven by horses working a tread-mill. †*Obs.* exc. *Hist.*

1823 I. HOLMES *Account U.S.A.* 315 One of the horse-boats which cross the North River..is of a very peculiar construction. **1828** WEBSTER, *Horseboat*..a boat moved by horses; a new species of ferry-boat. **1829** *Brockville* (Upper Canada) *Gaz.* 28 Aug. 2/5 In crossing the lake..the Steamboat Montreal and the horse-boat came in contact with each other. **1897** R. E. ROBINSON *Uncle Lisha's Outing* 257 They wended their way to the ferry just in time to see the horse boat come splashing into port, the four horses plodding their unprogressive journey on the revolving wheel. **1928** *Old-Time New Eng.* Apr. 161 Before the wreck of the *Belknap* a new type of freighter, the horse-boat, appeared on the lake. The first one of its kind was built on Long Island in 1838. It was an open scow propelled by paddle-wheels, the motive power being supplied by a pair of horses tramping a treadmill.

'horse-box.

1. A closed carriage or vehicle for transporting horses by railway; an enclosure for a horse to be slung into or conveyed in a vessel.

1846 [see BOX *sb.*[1] 12]. **1849** SIR F. HEAD *Stokers & Pokers* iii. (1851) 41 Embarking in carriages, horse-boxes, and trucks. *Mod. Railw. Time Table*, Horse Boxes and Carriage Trucks are not conveyed by these Trains.

2. Humorously applied to large pews with high sides, formerly common, esp. in country churches.

1884 *Sat. Rev.* 16 Aug., The interior is encumbered with huge horse-boxes, lined with mangy baize. **1891** P. G. STONE *Archit. Antiq. Isle Wight* 6 In 1744 the pewing was re-arranged..on the 'horse-box' principle.

'horse-boy. A boy employed to attend to horses; a stable-boy. (Often contemptuous.)

1563 WINȜET *Four scoir thre Quest.* lxxiii. Wks. 1888 I. 122 Except ȝe will euiry lady in the land to be subdeuit to hir awin cuik or horsboy. **1617** MORYSON *Itin.* II. 127 Though thereby their state bee no better then horseboyes. **1808** SCOTT *Marm.* II. xxvii, For three long years I bowed my pride, A horse-boy in his train to ride. **1847** EMERSON *Repr. Men, Napoleon* Wks. (Bohn) I. 375 Every horse-boy and powder-monkey in the army.

'horse-bread. Bread made of beans, bran, etc. for the food of horses.

Horse-bread is still in use in many parts of Europe.

1467 in *Eng. Gilds* (1870) 406 That non Baker that shalle bake eny horsbrede, kepe eny hostre. **1540** *Act 32 Hen. VIII*, c. 41 No hosteler or inholder shuld make any horse breadde. **1590** WEBBE *Trav.* (Arb.) 20 The foode which I and others did eat, was very blacke, far worse then Horse-breade. **1622** *Naworth Househ. Bks.* (Surtees) 196 Horsbread for Mr. Howard brought from Newcastell. **1704** *Dict. Rust.* s.v. *Bread*, make your Loaves like to Horse-bread, but not too thick. **1753** CHAMBERS *Cycl. Supp., Horse-bread*, is often given Horses to hearten and strengthen them.

Comb. **1599** B. JONSON *Ev. Man out of Hum.* III. ii, You thread-bare, horse-bread-eating rascals.

'horse-breaker. 1. One who breaks in horses or trains them to the bridle or collar.

1550 COVERDALE *Spir. Perle* vi. (1588) 66 Whan the horsse breaker geueth vnto a lusty freshe yong horsse, too much of the bridle, he is wilde and wanton. **1601** HOLLAND *Pliny* I. 222 Hereupon horse-breakers..haue an art by cords to bring a horse to the like amble. **1660** R. COKE *Justice Vind.* 9 The most furious and robust man is not the best horse-breaker and pacer. **1864** J. PAYN *Sir Massingberd* 58 If he had been a horsebreaker by profession, he could not have taken greater pains with the animal.

†**2.** A courtesan; a demi-mondaine; a prostitute. Freq. ***pretty horsebreaker.*** *Obs.*

1861 *Times* 28 June 12/4 They are, in the end, only fit for the company of 'horsebreakers'. *Ibid.* 12/5 If she thinks men prefer the society of 'pretty horsebreakers'..she never was more mistaken. **1861** *Punch* 13 July 13 *(caption)* *Stout Equestrian.* 'Dou [*sic*] you know, love, I'm rather sorry I got this hat, for suppose I should be taken for a "pretty horsebreaker"!' **1865** *Public Opinion* 30 Sept. 352/2 These *demi-monde* people,..horsebreakers, hetairæ..are by degrees pushing their way into 'society'. **1865** C. KNIGHT *Shadows of Old Booksellers* v. 112 He..was intimate with all the high —— (read 'pretty horse-breakers') in town... Some of these girls he often asked to dine with him. **1966** D. CROW *Theresa* xvi. 189 While Brewster's aim was to show her up as a pretty horse-breaker, hers was to proclaim her purity. **1970** G. GREER *Female Eunuch* 265 The vestiges of sensual innocence hung around long enough to endow us with obsolete terms like..*pretty horsebreaker.*

'horse-car. *U.S.*

1. A tramcar (or railway-car) drawn by a horse or horses. Also *attrib.*

1864 WEBSTER, *Horse-car*, a railroad car drawn by horses. **1883** *Century Mag.* June 240/1 Everything she had in her portemonnaie except some horse-car tickets. **1888** BRYCE *Amer. Commw.* II. III. lxx. 556 The horse-cars can scarcely penetrate the throng. *Ibid.* lxxv. 621 *note*, The right of laying a horse-car line in Broadway.

2. A railway-car for the transport of horses. (*Cent. Dict.*)

†**horse-charge.** *Obs.* [See CHARGE *sb.*]

1. A horse-load; the load of a pack-horse.

c **1350** *Usages Winchester* in *Eng. Gilds* (1870) 358 An halpeny of custome as many tyme as he comeþ, and þe horsecharche a ferthynge. *Ibid.*, An horse-charche, a peny.

2. A cavalry charge.

1650 R. ELTON *Compl. Body Art Milit.* I. iii. (1668) 2, I conceive it to be of little use to receive a desperate charge of the Horse..The best way of opposing the Horse-charge.

'horse-'chestnut. [tr. obs. Bot. L. *Castanea equina*; cf. Ger. *Roszkastanie.*

The statement in Gerarde as to the origin of the name (quot. 1597) goes back to Matthiolus *Comment.* I. cxxii. (Venice 1548). See also N. & Q. 3rd Ser. X. 452, 523, *Gard. Chron.* 1878 II. 53.]

1. The hard smooth shining brown seed or 'nut' of the tree described in 2.

1611 COTGR., *Chastaigne chevaline*, the horse Chestnut. **1698** *Lond. Gaz.* No. 3366/4 A parcel of Horse Chesnuts lately brought from beyond Sea..to be sold by Mr. Edw. Fuller. **1789** WOLCOTT (P. Pindar) *Expost. Odes* xvi. 24 Wks. (1823) 230/2 On hard horse chesnuts make them dine and sup. **18..** *Chapter on Logic* 40 (Bell's *Stand. Elocut.*, 1883, 471) Down fell A fine horse-chestnut in its prickly shell.

2. A large ornamental tree, *Æsculus Hippocastanum* (N.O. *Sapindaceæ*), probably a native of Asia, said to have been introduced into England *c* 1550; it bears large digitate leaves, and upright conical clusters of showy flowers; the fruit resembles the edible chestnut, consisting of a soft thick prickly husk inclosing two or three large seeds of a coarse bitter taste. The name is also extended to some American species of *Æsculus* and the allied genus *Pavia*, usually called *buck-eye.*

1597 GERARDE *Herbal* III. lxxxv. 1254 Called..in English Horse Chestnut; for that the people of the East countries do with the fruit thereof cure their horses of the cough..and such like diseases. **1664** EVELYN *Sylva* vii. §4 The Horse-Chessnut..bears a most glorious flower. **1794** MARTYN *Rousseau's Bot.* xix. 255 The form of the Horse-Chesnut is grand, the pyramids of flowers beautiful. **1866** *Treas. Bot.* 853/2 *P[avia] rubra*, often called Red-flowered Horse-chestnut, is a slender-growing tree..from the mountains of Virginia and Carolina. **1884** MILLER *Plant-n.*, *Pavia* (*Æsculus*), Buck-eye, Smooth-fruited Horse-Chestnut.

'horse-cloth. A rug or cloth used to cover a horse or as part of its trappings.

1530 PALSGR. 232/2 Horse clothe, *couuerture a cheual, couuertoir.* **1600** J. PORY tr. *Leo's Africa* II. 46 Base and harsh stuffe..much like unto the stuffe which is brought hither.. to serve for horse-cloathes. **1704** STEELE *Lying Lover* II. i. 24 The Furniture, and the Horse-Cloaths will be all your own Device for the Wedding, and the Horses. **1865** W. G. PALGRAVE *Arabia* II. 93 [Horses] tied up at their stalls; some, but not many, had horse-cloths over them. **1866** ROGERS *Agric. & Prices* I. xxi. 533 Surcingles are mentioned in the year 1305, as also horse-cloths.

b. A strong rough material for dresses akin in quality to shepherd's plaid: chiefly *attrib.* or as *adj.*

1892 *Pall Mall G.* 30 June 1/2 Shepherd's plaids, and 'horsecloth' materials will be the fashion for dresses this autumn. **1893** [see HOP-SACK 2].

'horse-collar. The COLLAR of a horse.

to grin through a horse-collar: see quot. 1801. Hence allusively, as in quot. 1878.

c **1440** *Promp. Parv.* 247/2 Horsys colere, *eph(ipp)ium, columbar.* **1497** *Naval Acc. Hen. VII* (1896) 101 Hors-colers, l. vij. **1591** PERCIVALL *Sp. Dict., Meléna*, a horse collar. **1801** STRUTT *Sports & Past.* IV. iii. §31 The Grinning Match is performed by two or more persons..each of them having his head thrust through a horse's collar. **1878** BLACK *Goldsmith* xiii. 111 The jokes..are of the poorest sort. The horse-collar is never far off. **1881** BESANT & RICE *Chapl. of Fleet* I. x, Bawling a comic song while he grins through a horse-collar.

b. *Comb.*, as ***horsecollar-maker.***

1580 *Faversham Reg.* (MS.), Richard Cookes, a horse-kollermaker. **1897** *Daily News* 30 Apr. 3/5 A horse-collar maker, an Army Reserve man.

'horse-colt. A young (male) horse.

1382 WYCLIF *Ecclus.* xxiii. 30 As an horsecolt he shal be dryue. *c* **1440** *Jacob's Well* (E.E.T.S.) 39 þe tythes owyth to be payed of folys of hors, þat is, of hors-coltys. **1544** *Will of J. Welles* in *B.M. Addit. MS.* 24,925 lf. 22, iij coltes, one horse colt and ij mare coltes. **1760** WASHINGTON *Writ.* (1889) II. 168 My Great Chestnut foalded a horse colt on the 6 Instant. **1809** *Portfolio* Ser. II. II. 309 Horse-colts and mare-colts.

horse-comb ('hɔːskəʊm). An instrument for combing the hair of horses; a curry-comb.

a **1100** *Ags. Voc.* in Wr.-Wülcker 331/9 *Strigil, uel strigilis*, horscamb. **1387** TREVISA *Higden* (Rolls) IV. 25 3onge-lynges ..frotede þe oliphauntes in þe forhedes wiþ hors-combes. **1398** —— *Barth. De P.R.* XVIII. xl. (Bodl. MS.), þe colte is nou3t..icoreyed wiþ hors combe. **1465** *Durham MS. Almoner's Roll*, Item j horskam. **1584** R. SCOT *Discov. Witchcr.* XII. xiv. (1886) 197 Horssecombs and sickles that have so many teeth. **1679** BLOUNT *Anc. Tenures* 46 A certain Horse-comb or Curry-comb. **1866** ROGERS *Agric. & Prices* I. xxi. 532 Among other stable implements..*strigils*, which I conceive to be horsecombs.

'horse-coper (-ˌkəʊpə(r)), **-couper** (-ˌkaʊpə(r)). Also 7 **-cooper**, 8 **-koper**, 9 *dial.* **-cowper.** [f. HORSE + COPER[1], COUPER. Practically, *horse-couper* is treated as a northern variant of *horse-coper.*] A horse-dealer.

α. **1681** COLVIL *Whigs Supplic.* (1695) 25 Some turnd Horse-Coopers, some pedlers. *a* **1734** NORTH *Lives* I. 287 There were horsecopers amongst them. **1748** *De Foes Tours Gt. Brit.* (ed. 4) II. 397 (D.) There were not less than an hundred jockeys or horse-kopers, as they call them there [Penkridge, Staffs.] from London, to buy horses for sale. **1882** *Pall Mall G.* 2 June 4/2 Horse-copers..are singularly at one with respect to stolen nags.

β. **1755** JOHNSON s.v. *Horsecourser*, The word now used in Scotland is *horsecouper*, to denote a jockey, seller, or rather changer of horses. **1814** SCOTT *Wav.* xxxix, I was bred a horse-couper, sir. **1847** J. WILSON *Chr. North* (1857) II. 25 Newcastle horse-cowpers, who laid their money thick. **1859** THACKERAY *Virgin.* xiii, Moping at the taverns..with horse-coupers and idle company.

So **'horse-coping, -couping** *sb.* and *a.*, horse-dealing.

1841 J. T. HEWLETT *Parish Clerk* II. 7 The mysteries of horse-couping, horse-chanting. **1861** WHYTE MELVILLE *Mkt. Harb.* ii, The stables of a certain horse-coping worthy. **1882** *Pall Mall G.* 2 June 4/2 Three horses..carried south by a horse-coping gang.

†**'horse-corser, -courser.** *Obs.* Also 6 **-coarser, -scorser**, 7 **-scourser**, 9 **-coser.** [See CORSER, SCORSER; also Skeat in *Trans. Phil. Soc.* (1888–9), where AF. *cossour* (1310), *corsour* (1372) broker:—L. *cociatōr-em*, is cited.]

A jobbing dealer in horses.

1552 HULOET, Horsecorser, whiche let horse to hyre, *veterinarius.* **1567** THOMAS *Ital. Gram.*, *Cozzone*, an horscoarser, or the rider that tameth wilde horses. **1576** GASCOIGNE *Steele Gl.* (Arb.) 79 When horsecorsers beguile no friends with Iades. **1585** HIGINS tr. *Junius Nomencl.* 514/1 *Mango equorum*, a horse scorser: he that buyeth horses, and putteth them away againe by chopping and changing. **1605** *Nottingham Rec.* IV. 277 Horssecorsers and diuers other that do buy and sell horsses. *a* **1613** OVERBURY *A Wife* (1638) 136 Which..were as strange a thing to doubt, as whether there be knavery in Horse-coursers. **1617** MINSHEU *Ductor*, a horse Courser, or horse scourser ..*mango equorum.* **1704** *Dict. Rust.* s.v. *Horse*, This manner of making a Horse to look Young, is called by Horse-coursers, Bishoping. **1801** *Sporting Mag.* XVIII. 101 *Horse Coser*, a dealer in horses, vulgarly and corruptly called horse-courser. **1808** SCOTT *Marm.* VI. xvi, Thou sworn horse-courser, hold thy peace. **1818** W. H. SCOTT *Brit. Field Sports*, No credit to the discernment of those practical Horse Coursers.

†**'horse-corsing, -coursing.** *Obs.* [See CORSE *v.* and prec.] Horse-jobbing. Applied also to dishonest modes of 'raising the wind' by means of a horse: see context of quot. 1602.

1602 ROWLANDS *Greenes Ghost* 14 There is a certain kind of cosonage called horse coursing. **1607** MARKHAM *Caval.* VIII. i. 2 This deceit or impostume vpon the face of Horse manshippe which wee call Horse-corsing. **1611** COTGR., *Maquignonnage*, deceitfull brokage..also the trade of hors-scoursing. **1644** BULWER *Chirol.* 105 Wil not set forth the art of Hors-coursing. **1673** R. HEAD *Canting Acad.* 192 If they catch him horse-coursing he's noozed.

'horse-course. 1. A horse-race.

1715 LEONI *Palladios Archit.* (1742) II. 83 The Hippodromus for Horse-courses. **1727** SWIFT *Art Polit. Lying* Wks. 1755 III. I. 121 Fox-chases, horse-courses, feats of activity in driving of coaches. **1759** GOLDSM. *Wks.* (1854) II. 68 The ambition of being foremost at a horse course.

2. A place for horse-races; a race-course.

1766 PENNANT *Zool.* (1768) I. 5 Croydon in the south, and Garterly in Yorkshire, were then famous horse-courses. **1778** *Eng. Gazetteer* (ed. 2) s.v. *Nottingham*, Here is a fine plain on the north side of the town for a horse-course. **1841**

LANE *Arab. Nts.* I. 86 [He] directed him to repair to the horse-course.

horse-courser¹, -coursing¹: see HORSE-CORSER, -CORSING.

horse-courser². [See COURSER¹.

(It appears first in Johnson, identified with HORSE-CORSER, of which it is put down as the primary sense, without quot.; but the sense is perh. only conjectural.)]

1755 JOHNSON, *Horsecourser*, one that runs horses, or keeps horses for the race. Hence in later Dicts.

†**ˈhorse-coursing².** *Obs.* [See COURSING *vbl. sb.*¹] Horse-racing.

1764 J. KIRBY *Suffolk Trav.* (ed. 2) 190 There [Newmarket] are many good modern Houses built by Noblemen and Gentlemen who delight in Horse-coursing.

horsed (hɔːst), *ppl. a.* [f. HORSE *v.* + -ED¹.]

1. Mounted on horseback.

c **1400** *Destr. Troy* 6470 All horset but he. *c* **1470** HENRY *Wallace* v. 795 Horssyt archaris schot fast. *a* **1533** LD. BERNERS *Huon* lviii. 197 Then Gerames yssued out clene armed, well horsed. **1612** ROWLANDS *More Knaves Yet* 42 The seauen deadly Sins all Horst and riding to Hell. **1807** WORDSW. *White Doe* II. 82 All horsed and harnessed with him to ride. **1865** KINGSLEY *Herew.* vii, Footpad-churls.. who fancy they can face horsed knights.

b. Furnished with or drawn by a horse.

1884 *Times* (weekly ed.) 19 Sept. 5/2 A number of well-horsed cars. **1898** *Daily News* 27 July 2/5 A horsed ambulance was speedily brought to the court.

2. Propped, supported.

1745 tr. *Columellas Husb.* v. iv, Those which leaning upon props are placed upon single frames. These the peasants call *under-propped* or *horsed* vines.

3. Of a mare: Covered by a horse.

c **1420** *Pallad. on Husb.* I. 984 An horsid asse or mare.

†**horse de frise**, partial trans. of CHEVAL DE FRISE.

1688 J. S. *Fortif.* 120, *Horse de Freeze*, or Turnpikes. **1702** *Milit. Dict.* (Stanf.) *Chevaux de Frise*, or *Horse de Frise*, the same as Turnpikes.

ˈhorse-dung. The excrement of horses.

1460-70 *Bk. Quintessence* I. 6 Distillid in hors dounge contynuely digest. **1606** PEACHAM *Gentl. Exerc.* I. xxii. (1612) 73 Let it rot in hot horse dung. **1796** H. HUNTER tr. *St.-Pierres Stud. Nat.* (1799) II. 41 This last insect takes delight in a hillock of horse-dung. **1823** J. BADCOCK *Dom. Amusem.* 21 A luting of clay and horse-dung.

ˈhorse-fair. A fair or annual market for the sale of horses. **b.** Hence the name of the square, place, or street where such a fair is or was held. (Cf. *Mayfair*, *Haymarket*, *Cornmarket*, etc., as place-names.)

1369 *Mem. Ripon* (Surtees) II. 127 In le Horsefaire. **1504** *Ripon Ch. Acts* (Surtees) 321 In le horsffayr, aliter dicto horstreyt gaytt.. al. dicto horsgaitstreyt. **1688** *Lond. Gaz.* No. 2323/4 The Horse-Fairs at Ripon in Yorkshire, will be holden. **1689-90** TEMPLE *Ess. Trade Irel.* (Jod.), There may be set up both a horsefair and races. **1828** CARLYLE *Misc.*, *Voltaire* (1840) II. 101 Figure Mahomet, in his youthful years, 'travelling to the horse-fairs of Syria!' *Mod.* Barnet is celebrated for its annual horse-fair.

c. *attrib.* Such as is used in a horse-fair: dishonest, equivocating.

1606 *Sir G. Goosecappe* IV. i. in Bullen *O. Pl.* III. 58 Away with these same horse-faire allegations; will you answer the letter?

ˈhorse-fish. A name given to various fishes with heads more or less like that of a horse. **a.** The carangoid fish *Vomer setipinnis* (also called *dollar-fish* or *moonfish*), and the allied *Selene vomer*. **b.** 'The sauger, *Stizostedion canadense*. (Western U.S.)' (*Cent. Dict.*). **c.** The *Hippocampus* or sea-horse.

1723 S. MORLAND *Spec. Lat. Dict.* 7 Here I shall beg leave to show the difference between the Sea-horse and Horse-fish, i.e. the Hippocampus. **1883** *Fisheries Exhib. Catal.* (ed. 4) 98 The tufted gilled fishes, represented by the pipe- and horse-fishes.

horseflea-weed, var. of HORSE-FLY *weed*.

ˈhorse-flesh, horseflesh.

1. The flesh of a horse, esp. as an article of food.

c **1532** DEWES *Introd. Fr.* in *Palsgr.* 921 Horse flesshe, *cher de cheual.* **1613** PURCHAS *Pilgrimage* (1614) 421 They preferre horse-flesh before other meats, esteeming it stronger nourishment. **1699** DAMPIER *Voy.* II. I. ii. 31 The Horseflesh comes to Market at Cachao very frequently, and is as much esteemed as Beef. **1709** STEELE *Tatler* No. 59 ¶6 They were reduced to eat Horse-Flesh. **1855** MACAULAY *Hist. Eng.* xii. III. 228 So early as the eighth of June horseflesh was almost the only meat which could be purchased.

2. Living horses collectively, usually with reference to riding, driving, or racing.

a **1400-50** *Alexander* 2161 What aylez you nowe?.. Wheþer euer your hertes for horse-fleshez abaytez? **1492** W. PASTON in *P. Lett.* No. 929 III. 376 Hors flesche is of suche a price here that my purce is schante able to bye one hors. **1548** HALL *Chron., Edw. IV* 202b, Herauldes spared no horseflesh in riding betwene the kyng and the erle. **1601** HOLLAND *Pliny* II. 614 As for horse-flesh, I haue alwaies heard.. That the breed of Italy passeth al others. **1711** STEELE *Spect.* No. 157 ¶7 A Person.. profoundly learned in Horse-flesh. **1791** 'G. GAMBADO' *Ann. Horsem.* iv. (1809) 85 As honest a man as any that deals in horse flesh. **1861** HUGHES *Tom Brown at Oxf.* xl, Anything that horse-flesh is capable of, a real good Oxford hack.. will do.

†**3.** In technical uses: **a.** *Surgery* (see quot.).

1658 A. FOX *Wurtz Surg.* II. xxvi. 175 The flesh holds the two ends of the [fractured] bone together, for that reason is it called Horse-flesh, because it is harder then other flesh.

b. = *dead horse*: see HORSE *sb.* 14.

1688 R. HOLME *Armoury* III. iii. 122/1 (Printing) If any Journeyman set down in his Bill.. more Work then he hath done that Week, that surplusage is called Horse Flesh.

c. (In full ***horse-flesh wood, mahogany.***) The sabicu tree, *Lysiloma Sabicu*, a native of Bahama. (So called from its colour.)

1851 *Illustr. Catal. Gt. Exhib.* 195 Horseflesh-wood, Rio Janeiro. *Ibid.* 813 Horse-flesh, or Bahama mahogany. Nassau. **1883** *Fisheries Exhib. Catal.* (ed. 4) 160 The timbers being of native hard wood (horse-flesh).

4. *attrib.*, usually in reference to the colour, a peculiar reddish bronze. **horse-flesh ore**, an ore of copper, bornite.

1530 PALSGR. 232/2 Horse flesshe colour. **1552** *Inv. Ch. Goods Surrey* in *Surrey Archæol. Collect.* (1869) IV. 97 Item iij dekyns of sylke one of blew another of grene and the other of horse flesh color. **1597** GERARDE *Herbal* II. clxxii. 472 Some are called Carnations, others Cloue Gilloflowers,.. some Pagiants or Pagion colour, Horseflesh, blunket, purple, white.. Gilloflowers. **1787** BEST *Angling* (ed. 2) 101 April.. The Horseflesh Fly. This fly is taken all the month two hours before sun set till twilight. **1868** DANA *Min.* (ed. 5) 45 Crystalline varieties [of bornite] are found in Cornwall.. called by the miners 'horse-flesh ore'.

ˈhorse-fly¹. [f. FLY *sb.*¹ 2.] One of various dipterous insects troublesome to horses, as the horse-tick (family *Hippoboscidæ*), the breeze or gadfly (*Tabanidæ*), the bot-fly (*Œstridæ*).

1382 WYCLIF *Josh.* xxiv. 12, I sente before ȝou hors fleeȝis [Vulg. *crabrones*]. **1556** WITHALS *Dict.* (1568) 7 a/1 A horse flye, *cantholarethrus.* **1578** LYTE *Dodoens* II. lvi. 221 The third [*Serapias Orchis*] hath small floures like to a kinde of Horseflies. **1645** MILTON *Colast.* (1851) 377 Infested, somtimes at his face, with dorrs and horsflies. **1822** LOUDON *Encycl. Gard.* II. iv. (L), The horse-flies cause much distress to horses in the vicinity of the New Forest. **1861** HULME tr. *Moquin-Tandon* II. IV. i. 227 The Horse Fly (*Hippobosca Equina*).. of a brown colour mottled with yellow and white.

b. *attrib.* **horse-fly-weed**, a North American leguminous plant, *Baptisia tinctoria*, called also *wild indigo*.

1884 in MILLER *Plant-n.*

†**ˈhorse-ˈfly².** *Obs.* [f. FLY *sb.*² 3 b.] A covered carriage drawn by a horse. (Subsequently simply *fly*.)

1826 MISS MITFORD *Village* Ser. II. (1863) 355 A much more dignified conveyance.. than any of the race of flies, whether horse-fly or man-fly. **1830** T. HOOK *Maxwell* II. ii. 53 [To] go and get a fly.. not to bring a horse-fly.

horse-foot.

†**1.** A horses foot. *Obs.*

1375 BARBOUR *Bruce* II. 359 Knychtis.. Wndyr horss feyt defoulyt thar. *c* **1400** *Destr. Troy* 5834 The Troiens.. Harlet hym fro horsfet, had hym away. **1597** GERARDE *Herbal* II. cclxxvii. 666 *Tussilago* or Folefoote hath.. many great broad leaues.. fashioned like an horse foote.

b. *attrib.* (See HIPPOCRENE.)

1591 SPENSER *Tears Muses* 271 The sacred springs of horsefoot Helicon.

†**2.** The plant Coltsfoot (*Tussilago Farfara*); also applied to *T. alpina* (Mountain Horse-foot).

1597 GERARDE *Herbal* II. cclxxvii. 666 Of Coltes foote, or Horse foote. **1633** JOHNSON *Gerardes Herbal* II. ccxcii. 815 This plant.. I have thought good to name in English Horse-foot, for that the leaves exceed Colts-foot in bignesse, yet are like them in shape.

3. a. A crustacean of the genus *Limulus*, also called *horseshoe-crab* or *king-crab*. **b.** A fossil molluscan shell (*Hippopodium ponderosum*) found in the Lias, so called from its shape.

1672 JOSSELYN *New Eng. Rarities* 13 They feed.. upon a shell-fish called a Horse-foot. **1860** BARTLETT *Dict. Amer.* (ed. 3), *Horse-Foot*,.. a crustacean found in our waters from Massachusetts to Virginia, and in some places so abundant as to be used for manure. **1883** *Pall Mall G.* 21 Sept. 12/1 [The eels] are fed regularly every day on 'horse-feet', a peculiar shell-fish.

ˈhorsefully, *adv. nonce-wd.* [After *manfully*; cf. *dogfully*.] As becomes a horse.

1837 *New Monthly Mag.* L. 535 Brown George.. had stepped out manfully, or rather horsefully. **1864** G. DYCE *Bella Donna* I. 163 Both horses were fresh, and went over hedges and ditches, and smooth field, horsefully.

ˈhorsegate¹. [f. GATE *sb.*¹] A gate for the passage of horses.

1535 COVERDALE *Jer.* xxxi. 40 From thence vnto the corner of the horsgate. **1894** *Daily News* 5 Feb. 6/6 The crew then proceeded on to Sandford, and paddled to the horsegate.

ˈhorsegate². [f. GATE *sb.*², going, walk.] A right of pasturage for a horse, e.g. in a common field. Cf. COW-GATE.

1619 *N. Riding Rec.* (1894) I. 17 Whether anie tenante.. hath sold anie Oxegates, Cowgates, horsegates or the like. **1776** *Foston Inclos. Act* 2 The Reverend Joseph Sommers is entitled.. to a horsegate in the car.

ˈhorse-gear.

1. Harness or trappings for horses.

1653 H. MORE *Antid. Ath.* II. vii. (1662) 60 Roaps for the horse-gears to pull by. **1894** H. SPEIGHT *Nidderdale* 384 Bits.. and other metal work required for horse-gear. **1941** *Proc. Prehist. Soc.* VII. 130 The bulk of the hoard is Celtic horse-gear. **1960** G. E. EVANS *Horse in Furrow* xvii. 220 An unorthodox use of a piece of horse-gear.. should be recorded.

2. A mechanism by which horse-power is applied to drive machinery.

a **1899** *Mod. Manufacturer's Catal.*, Very Powerful two-horse Gear, with covered Driving Wheel and poles and fittings for two horses. Light One Horse Gear, 33 in. Driving Wheel, speed 6½ to one. **1904** GOODCHILD & TWENEY *Technol. & Sci. Dict.* 291/1 *Horse gear*, the device used for yoking horses to machinery. **1940** *Chambers's Techn. Dict.* 119/2 *Horse gear*, a device for producing mechanical power by means of a lever attached to gears, which is operated by.. [a] horse walking in a circle.

ˌhorse-ˈgodmother. *dial.* and *vulgar.* A large coarse-looking woman.

1569-70 *Durham Depos.* (Surtees) 91 In causa diff. viz. that she was a horse goodmother water wych. **1785** GROSE *Dict. Vulg. T.*, *Horse Godmother*, a large masculine woman. **1809** MALKIN *Gil Blas* I. v, A kitchen girl.. a great bloated horse-god-mother. **1848** THACKERAY *Van. Fair* xxxix, You aint like that old horse-godmother your mother.

horse guard (ˈhɔːs ˌgɑːd).

1. a. One of a body of picked cavalry for special service as a guard; formerly also *collective*.

1647 SPRIGGE *Anglia Rediv.* (1854) 104 Sallied out.. in a full career, and came upon our horseguards. **1670** COTTON *Espernon* I. IV. 157 They furiously set upon the Duke's Horse-Guard; who were all presently cut to pieces. *a* **1674** CLARENDON *Hist. Reb.* IX. §37 In the Reserve were the King's life-Guard.. with the King's horse-Guards. **1815** R. TWEDDELL in *J. Tweddell's Rem.* 207 *note*, Potemkin.. was an ensign in the horseguards. **1824** HEBER *Jrnl.* (1828) II. 62 His [King of Oudes] horse-guards are fine tall men, and well-mounted.

b. *pl.* The cavalry brigade of the English Household troops; *spec.* the third regiment of this body, the ***Royal Horse Guards*** (formerly the *Oxford Blues*).

1661 in Sir S. D. Scott *Brit. Army* (1880) 82 His Majestys Regiment of Horse Guards under the command of.. Aubrey Earl of Oxford, was mustered this day [16 Febr.] in Tuthill Fields. **1666** PEPYS *Diary* 9 Nov., Drums beat and trumpets, and the Horse Guards everywhere spread running up and down the street. **1707** J. CHAMBERLAYNE *St. Gt. Brit.* II. xiv. 183 Of the Troops of the Houshold: And first of the Horse-Guards. —— *List Govt. Officers* ibid. 559 First troop of Horse-guards.. Second Troop of the Guards.. Third Troop of the Guards. *Ibid.* 560 Regiment of Royal Horse Guards. **1727-41** CHAMBERS *Cycl.* s.v. *Guard*, The English horse guards are distinguished by troops: first, second, third, and fourth troop of horse guards. **1840** DICKENS *Barn. Rudge* xlix, The Horse-guards came riding in among the crowd.

2. *pl.* The barracks, head-quarters or guard-house of such cavalry; *spec.* a building in London, opposite Whitehall, bearing this name.

The building in London orig. served as the guard-house of the palace of Whitehall and, on the establishment of the Horse Guards, as their guard-house and barracks; later, while remaining a guard-house, it became the head-quarters of the whole army organization, and subsequently that of the Commander-in-Chief and the military authorities, as distinct from the Secretary of State for War and the civil authorities (whence the uses in 3). The buildings serve now (1899) as offices for some of the departments of the War Office, the head-quarters of several regiments of the Guards, etc. The fact that soldiers of the Household cavalry still perform the duties of the guard helps to keep the name in popular use.

1645 EVELYN *Diary* 12 Dec., Next to this is the Inquisition house.. To this joins his Holinesse's Horse-guards. [**1659** LUDLOW *Mem.* (1698) II. 776 Next morning I went with Sir Henry Vane and Major Saloway to the Chamber of the Horse Guards, at Whitehall, where the principal officers use to meet.] **1666** PEPYS *Diary* 9 Nov., News that White Hall was on fire; and presently more particulars, that the Horse-guard was on fire. **1666** *Lond. Gaz.* No. 103 Nov. 9.—Between 7 and 8 at night there happened a fire in the Horse Guard House in the Tilt Yard, over against Whitehall. **1679** *Ibid.* No. 1455/4 Whoever gives notice of him to Mr. John Bird Sutler at the Horse Guard, shall be well rewarded. **1691** LUTTRELL *Brief Rel.* (1857) II. 212 An order is fixt on the horse guards door by Whitehal. **1713** *Lond. Gaz.* No. 5105/2 The Lords and other Commissioners of Her Majesty's Royal Hospital near Chelsea.. will meet at the Horse-Guards on [etc.]. **1763** *Brit. Mag.* Apr. 542/1, I heard a bunter at the Horse-guards.. swear she would not venture into the Park. **1842** GEN. P. THOMPSON *Exerc.* Pref. 3 Like the mounted sentries at the Horse Guards.

3. *pl.* The personnel of the office of the Commander-in-Chief and the military authorities at the head of the army, esp. as distinct from the Secretary of State for War and the civil authorities.

1826 WELLINGTON in *Croker Papers* (1884) I. xi. 342, I cant say that I owe my successes to any favour or confidence from the Horse Guards. **1867** GOLDW. SMITH *Three Eng. Statesmen* (1882) 37 [The question who shall control the army] does partly present itself whenever an attempt is made to bring the Horse-Guards under constitutional control. **1880** *Chambers Encycl.* s.v., The word Horse-guards is used conventionally to signify the military authorities at the head of army affairs, in contradistinction to the civil chief, the Secretary of State for War.

4. A sentinel in charge of a horse or horses. *N.Amer.*

1828 A. WETMORE *Diary* 30 May in *Mo. Hist. Rev.* (1914) VIII. 185 Formed our Wagons into an oblong square, and set a horse guard. **1851** MAYNE REID *Scalp Hunt.* xlii, The horse-guard stood leaning upon his rifle silent and watchful.

1907 J. R. Cook *Border & Buffalo* (1938) 279 The horse-guard brought in the horses. **1971** J. McDougall *Parsons on Plains* v. 40 When you reach the horse guard.. tell him to catch my horse Badger for you.

Hence **horse-'guardsman**, a man of the Royal Horse Guards.

1817 J. Scott *Paris Revis.* (ed. 4) 147 A Horse-guardsman ..was left upon the ground..wounded in a charge.

horsehair ('hɔːshɛə(r)). **a.** A hair from the mane or tail of a horse.

animated horsehair = *horsehair worm*: see c.

1387 Trevisa *Higden* (Rolls) III. 323 A briȝt swerd and a scharp euene aboue his heued by an hors here. **1422** tr. *Secreta Secret., Priv. Priv.* (E.E.T.S.) 155 Nothynge the Swerde held, Saue oone hors-here. **1611** Shaks. *Cymb.* II. iii. 33 A voyce in her eares which Horse-haires, and Calues-guts..can neuer amend. **1672** *Phil. Trans.* VII. 4064 *(heading)* Extract of a letter..concerning animated horse-hairs, rectifying a Vulgar Error. **1753** Chambers *Cycl. Supp.* s.v., *Animated Horse-Hairs*,..a sort of long and slender water-worm..generally, by the vulgar, supposed to be the hair fallen from a Horse's mane into the water. **1796** Withering *Brit. Plants* (ed. 3) III. 655 Fruit-stalks hardly thicker than horse hair. **1816** J. Smith *Panorama Sc. & Art* II. 82 Suspended by means of a horse hair.

b. A mass or collection of such hair.

In quot. 1850 = legal verbiage, horsehair being use to make barrister's wigs. ***vegetable horsehair***: see quote. 1897.

c **1305** *Edmund Conf.* 158 in *E.E.P.* (1862) 75 Seint Edmund werede strong here..Of hard hors-her ymaked. **1494** *Act 11 Hen. VII*, c. 19 Preamb., Cussions stuffed with horse here. **1638** Sir T. Herbert *Trav.* (ed. 2) 233 The Chynaes..they write with pencils made of horse hayre. **1812** J. Smyth *Pract. of Customs* (1821) 203 The Hair cut from the manes and tails of Horses is considered and passed in London as Horse Hair, and no other. **1850** Carlyle *Latter-d. Pamph.* ii. (1827) 67 In spite of all this..blotting-out of Heaven's sunlight by mountains of horsehair and officiality. **1897** Willis *Flower. Pl.* II. 372 *Tillandsia usneoides*, L. (long moss, old man's beard, vegetable horsehair).

c. *attrib.* and *Comb.*, as ***horsehair crest***, ***-crested*** *adj.*, ***-dresser***, ***glove***, ***plume***, etc.; in sense 'covered with a fabric woven of horsehair', as ***horsehair chair***, ***cushion***, ***sofa***, etc.; **horsehair-lichen** = *horsetail-lichen*; **horsehair snake** *U.S.* = *horsehair-worm*; **horsehair-worm**, a hairworm or Gordius.

1753 Chambers *Cycl. Supp., Horse Hair Worms.* **1822–34** *Good's Study Med.* (ed. 4) I. 276 The Gordius is the *seta equina* or horse-hair-worm of the old writers. **1838** Dickens *O. Twist* xxvii, The very horse-hair seats of the chairs. **1852** Miss Sewell *Exper. of Life* xiv. (1858) 95 A set of black horsehair chairs and a horsehair sofa. **1853** Hickie tr. *Aristoph.* (1872) II. 572 Strife of horse-hair-crested words. **1864** Earl Derby tr. *Iliad* VI. 546 Scar'd by the brazen helm and horse-hair plume. **1875** B. Meadows *Clin. Observ.* 61 Friction with horse hair gloves. **1897** *Daily News* 30 Apr. 3/3 The daughter of a horsehair dresser. **1897** *Outing* (U.S.) XXX. 434/2 The creature referred to as a mystery is what is termed the 'horsehair snake', in reality, a hairworm. **1949** *Sci. Monthly* Jan. 56/2 Another mythical serpent, confined to the rural scene, is the horsehair snake..the worm *Paragordius varius*. **1966** *Publ. Amer. Dial. Soc.* XLII. 19 Horsehair snake. Actually a long slender worm (*Gordius*, sp.), which spends one portion of its life in the body of a large insect and the other in shallow water, as in a watering trough. Thus arose the folk belief that these worms were originally horsehairs.

So **'horse-haired** *a.*, covered or furnished with horsehair; in quot. = bewigged.

1887 *Pall Mall G.* 4 Mar. 1/1 Glozing phrases..which horse-haired pedants of Attorney-Generals in every age have employed.

'horse-head.

1. a. The head of a horse. **b.** A head like that of a horse. **c.** The representation of a horse's head.

?*a* **1400** *Arthur* 394 Hyt was so oryble & so greet, More þan any Horse heed. **1551** T. Wilson *Logike* (1580) 21 b, What idiote knoweth not, except he had a Horse hedde, that here the sence is altered? **1601** Holland *Pliny* II. 337 The haire which is curried from the horsehead or buttock. **1610** Guillim *Heraldry* III. xiii. (1611) 126 He beareth gules a Horsehead couped argent. **1827** 'Mark Twain' *More Tramps Abr.* lxvii, The long horse-heads and very sharp chins of the negroes of the picture-books.

2. *Racing.* The length of a horse's head. Cf. HEAD *sb.*[1] 1 c.

1623 Massinger *Dk. Milan* II. Wks. (Rtld.) 55/2 A devil of this size, Should they run for a wager to be spiteful, Gets not a horse-head of her.

3. The stony inner cast of the fossil Trigonia.

1708 *Phil. Trans.* XXVI. 78 The Horse-head. This is only the Kernel or Stone included in the Wry-neb. **1851–6** Woodward *Mollusca 272* Casts of the interior are called 'horse-heads' by the Portland quarry-men.

4. *Zool.* A name of various fishes whose heads more or less resemble that of a horse, as the moon-fish, *Selene vomer*, and the *Hippocampidæ*.

1884 *Bull. U.S. Nat. Museum* No. 27. 438 *Selene argentea* ..Horsehead. **1905** D. S. Jordan *Guide to Study of Fishes* II. xvii. 276 *Selene vomer*, the horse-head-fish, or look-down, is similarly but even more distorted. **1966** Leim & Scott *Fishes of Atlantic Coast of Canada* 251 Atlantic lookdown... *Selene vomer* (Linnaeus) 1758. Other common names: horsehead, moonfish.

†**5.** *Mining.* A kind of ventilator: see quots.

1747 Hooson *Miner's Dict.* K iij, *Horsehead*, a large kind of Trunk standing on the Top of the Rest..it is made broad and wide in the Top, and open on one side, and conveniently made to catch the Wind. **1789** *Trans. Soc. Arts* VII. 193 Thus the horse-head..drives the wheel..to the right or left. **1802** J. Mawe *Min. Derbysh.* Gloss. (E.D.S.), *Horsehead*, a large opening made of wood, to turn and put on to a fang or trunk, to convey wind from day-light.

†**horseheal, -heel** ('hɔːshiːl). *Obs.* or *dial.* Forms: 1 **horselene, horshelene,** 3–5 **horselne,** 5 **horshelne, horshelyn, horselle, horshalle,** (5–7 **horshelm(e),** 6 **horshele, horseheele,** 6–7 **horseheale,** 7– **horseheal,** 9 **horseheel.** [OE. *horselene, horshelene*, f. *hors* HORSE + *elene, helene*, the latter of which appears by itself as a name of the same plant, also in form *eolone*, representing med.L. *elena, helena*, given, along with *ynula, enula, enela, elna, elenia, ellenium*, as names of this plant in *Alphita* and other med.L. lists. Some of these go back immediately to ancient L. *inula*, whence others are formed by metathesis, and by influence of another L. name *helenium* = Gr. ἐλένιον. The prefix *hors-* prob. meant 'wild' or 'coarse', as in other plant-names in *horse-*. The later phonetic history of the word is somewhat parallel to that of ELL; but there was prob. association with *hele*, HEAL *sb.*]

A tall strong composite plant, with very large yellow flowers; Elecampane (*Inula Helenium*).

c **1000** Ælfric *Gloss.* in Wr.-Wülcker 136/23 *Helena*, horshelene. *a* **1100** *Ags. Voc.* ibid. 323/8 *Helena*, horselene. *c* **1265** *Voc. Names Pl.* ibid. 557/5 *Enula*, [Fr.] alne, [Eng.] horselne. *c* **1450** *Alphita* (Anecd. Oxon.) 53/1 *Elena campana* uel *enula* [v.r. *enela*],..horshelne [*v.r.* horselle]. *Ibid.* 163/2 Horselne. **14..** *Voc.* in Wr.-Wülcker 580/12 *Enula campana*, horshelyn. **14..** *Nom.* ibid. 712/19 *Hec elena campana*, horshalle. **1483** *Cath. Angl.* 189/2 Horselle, *herba, enula campana.* *c* **1516** *Grete Herball* cl. I v b/2 *De Enula campana*,..Scabwoort or horshele. **1578** Lyte *Dodoens* III. xiv 336 This herbe is called..in Englishe Elecampane..and Horseheele. **1640** Parkinson *Theat. Bot.* v. lxxxiii. 655 This herb we [call] Elecampane generally, yet in some countries of this kingdome Scabwort and Horseheale.

'horse-herd. [f. HERD *sb.*[2]] One who herds or tends horses. (In quot. 1175, tr. L. *stabularius* hostler, innkeeper: cf. HORSE-HOUSE.)

c **1000** Ælfric *Gram.* ix. (Z.) 35 *Agaso*, horshyrde. *c* **1175** *Lamb. Hom.* 79 [He] bitahte hine þe hors horde to witene. *c* **1475** *Pict. Voc.* in Wr.-Wülcker 814/12 *Hic equiarius*, a horsheyrd. **1552** Huloet, Horse herd, *hipponomus.* **1884** Gilmour *Mongols* 120 A horse-herd appeared inside the door.

'horse-hire. The hire of a horse; payment for the use of a horse.

1464 *Nottingham Rec.* II. 375 For his horshire the said ij tymes viijd. **1589** Puttenham *Eng. Poesie* III. xv. (Arb.) 183 The Sergeant, for sparing of hors-hire, said he would goe with the Carrier on foote. **1646** J. Harrington in *Monthly Mag.* (1800) X. 240 For victuals, drink, and horse-hire. **1887** Jessopp *Arcady* vii. 216 He turns an honest penny by horse hire.

'horse-hoe, *sb.* [f. HORSE *sb.* + HOE *sb.*] A frame mounted on wheels and furnished with ranges of shares at such intervals as to work in the spaces between drills or rows of plants, in which each acts like a hoe in stirring up the soil, rooting up weeds, etc.

1731 Tull *Horse-hoeing Husb.* xviii (1733) 121 Proper for the regular operation of the Horse-Hoe. **1789** *Ann. Reg.* 64 Of the utility of the horse-hoe I am inclined to entertain a very high opinion. **1826** Loudon *Encycl. Agric.* (1831) 405 Of horse hoes there is a great variety, almost every implement-maker having his favourite form.

'horse-hoe, *v.* [f. HORSE *sb.* + HOE *v.*[1]]

trans. or *absol.* To hoe (or stir up the earth as in hoeing) with an implement drawn by a horse; to work with a horse-hoe. Hence **horse-hoed** *ppl. a.*, **horse-hoeing** *vbl. sb.*; also **horse-hoer**.

1731 J. Tull (*title*) Specimen of a Work on Horse-Houghing Husbandry. **1732** W. Ellis *Pract. Farmer* Gloss. (E.D.S.), *Horse-houghing* is so called by reason it saves man's houghing, not that a hough is used by horses, but their drawing a plough in a particular manner supplies the use of a hough. **1744** W. Ellis *Mod. Husb.* I. 145 It will be a difficult Point for the Horse-hougher to keep his Horse and Instrument..exact. **1780** A. Young *Tour Irel.* I. 14 Horse hoed, hand hoed and weeded. **1808** J. Walker *Hist. Hebrides* I. 245 All horse-hoed grain should be avoided for seed-corn. **1846** J. Baxter *Libr. Pract. Agric.* (ed. 4) II. 24 As soon as the plants get about three inches high, the intervals should be horse-hoed. **1935** J. Joyce *Let.* 19 Feb. (1966) III. 345 If they put on *Floradora* with George Robey in the name part the horsehoers would not notice.

'horsehood. The quality proper to a horse.

1654 Gayton *Pleas. Notes* III. i. 65.

'horse-hoof. Also (in sense 2) 5 **-howve,** 6 **-hove.** [f. HORSE *sb.* + HOOF.]

1. The hoof of a horse.

1539 Bible (Great) *Judg.* v. 22 Then were the horse hoffes smytten asunder. **1638–48** G. Daniel *Eclog* iii. 273 The true fountaine which The Muses Love..The Horse-hoofe never rais'd [cf. HIPPOCRENE]. **1843** Macaulay *Lays Anc. Rome, Lake Regillus* xxxvii, To listen for the rushing Of horse-hoofs from the east. **1896** *Black Horse Gaz.* Jan. 8/2 Loud thunder of horse hooves, low curtain of dust.

2. The plant Coltsfoot (*Tussilago Farfara*).

1398 Trevisa *Barth. De P.R.* XVII. xciii. (Bodl. MS.), Many men cleþeþ it Caballina an hors huoue. **1562** Turner *Herbal* II. 158 b, Tussilago is named..in Englishe Horse houe, or Bullfoote. **1578** Lyte *Dodoens* I. xii. 20 It is called ..Fole foote, Horse houe, Coltes foote. **1893** *Northumbld. Gloss.*, *Horse-hoof*, the colt's-foot, *Tussilago farfara*.

3. = HORSE-FOOT 3 a.

1699 Dampier *Voy.* II. II. ii. 40 Horse-hoof-fish. *Ibid.* 44 By the shore, you find abundance of Shell-fish, called by the English, Horse-hoofs..the shell is thin and brittle, like a Lobsters; with many small Claws.

†**'horse-house**[1]. [f. HOUSE[1].] A stable: in quot. tr. L. *stabulum* stable, hostelry, inn.

c **1175** *Lamb. Hom.* 79 [He] brohte him to an hors huse. *Ibid.* 85 Hwet is þis hors-us? þet is hali chirche..In hors-huse boð fule and clene.

†**'horse-house**[2]. *Obs.* [f. HOUSE *sb.*[2]] Housings or trappings for a horse.

1316 *Durham MS. Cell. Roll*, In ij Horsehous', ij capistris ..empt. **1480** *Wardr. Acc. Edw. IV* (1830) 125 For the making and garnysshing of x hors houses. **1483** in Grose *Antiq. Repert.* (1807) I. 50 To the queen for her use, xvj horshouses, made of..rede clothe engreyled.

'horse-jockey. a. One hired to ride a horse in a race. (Now usually simply *jockey*.)

1782 Wolcott (P. Pindar) *Odes R. Acad.* I. i. Wks. 1812 I. 15 My Cousin Pindar, in his Odes Applauded Horse-jockeys and Gods. **1812** *Sporting Mag.* XXXIX. 66 The parties were both horse-jockeys. **1858** in Hughes *Tom Brown* Pref. to ed. 6, Horse-jockeys have learnt to be wiser.

attrib. **1848** Thackeray *Van. Fair* lxiv, His horse-jockey jokes and prize-ring slang.

b. *U.S.* One who traffics in horses. Hence **'horse-jockeying** *vbl. sb.*

1744 A. Hamilton *Itinerarium* (1907) 31 May 3, I met one Matthew Baker, a horse-jockey. **1783** in S. E. Baldwin *Simeon Baldwin* (1919) 120 The conversation was upon News—horsejockeying—& other indifferent subjects. **1784** in *Connecticut Hist. Soc. Coll.* (1930) XXIII. 204 Ship Building is carried on with Vigor in this State, & the Horse Jockey business flourishes. **1792** J. Belknap *Hist. New-Hampshire* III. ix. 144 Few [horses] live and die on the plantations where they are bred; some are exported..; but the most are continually shifted from one owner to another, by means of a set of contemptible wretches called horse-jockies. **1866** 'Mark Twain' *Lett. fr. Hawaii* (1967) 50 The Kanaka horse jockey is fertile in imagination and elastic in conscience. *Ibid.* 288 Brown bought a horse from a native at Waiohinu for twelve dollars, but happening to think of the horse-jockeying propensities of the race, he removed the saddle and found that..recent hard riding had polished most of the hide off his back.

'horse-keeper. One who has the care of horses: in various shades of meaning.

c **1440** *Promp. Parv.* 247/2 Horskepare,..*equarius.* *c* **1515** *Cocke Lorell's B.* (Percy Soc.) 14 Carryers, carters, and hors-kepers. **1581** Savile *Tacitus' Hist.* II. lxxxvii. (1591) 104 Of lackeyes and horsekeepers a greater number. **1673** R. Head *Canting Acad.* K iij, The Oates which his Horse-keepers had given his Horses. **1789** Madan *Persius* (1795) 132 *note*, A horse-keeper, a groom that looks after his master's horses. **1891** S. C. Scrivener *Our Fields & Cities* 160 Ploughmen who want to 'get on' by being thought able horse-keepers. **1893** *Northumbld. Gloss.*, *Horse-keeper*, the person in a [coal] pit who attends to the feeding and grooming of the horses and ponies.

So **'horse-keeping.**

1777 Abigail Adams in *J. Adams' Fam. Lett.* (1876) 262 By your accounts of board, horsekeeping, etc., I fancy you are not better off than we are here.

horse latitudes, *sb. pl.* [Origin of the name uncertain: see the quots. for statements and conjectures.] The belt of calms and light airs which borders the northern edge of the N.E. trade-winds.

1777 G. Forster *Voy. round World* II. 581 The latitudes where these calms chiefly reign, are named the horse-latitudes by mariners..because they are fatal to horses and other cattle which are transported to the last mentioned continent [America]. **1826** H. N. Coleridge *West Ind.* 330 A dead calm for five days in the horse latitudes. **1850** Maury *Notice to Mariners* (ed. 2) 10. **1851** —— *Winds & Currents* 38. **1860** —— *Phys. Geog. Sea* (Low) §514. **1883** R. H. Scott *Elem. Meteorol.* xiv. 268 The Horse Latitudes, a title which Mr. Laughton derives from the Spanish *El Golfo de las Yeguas*, the Mares' Sea, from its unruly and boisterous nature..in contradistinction to the Trade-wind zone, *El Golfo de las Damas*, so called from the pleasant weather to be met with there.

horse-laugh ('hɔːslɑːf, -æ-). [See HORSE *sb.* 27 h.] A loud coarse laugh.

1713 Steele *Guardian* No. 29 ⁋24 The Horse-Laugh is a distinguishing characteristick of the rural hoyden. **1751** Lavington *Enthus. Method & Papists* (1754) II. 46 Treating the holy Men with Derision, Scoffs, Taunts, Horse-Laughs. **1847** Alb. Smith *Chr. Tadpole* xlv. (1879) 394 They..burst into a loud horse-laugh in his face. **1874** L. Stephen *Hours in Library* (1892) I. x. 353 Jovial squires laughed horse-laughs at this mincing dandy.

So (*nonce-wds.*) **horse-laugh** *v. intr.*, to give vent to a horse-laugh or a series of horse-laughs; hence **horse-laugher**. Also **horse-laughter**.

1713 Steele *Guardian* No. 29 ⁋5 Several kinds of laughers..The Dimplers. The Smilers..The Horse-laughers. **1763** *Brit. Mag.* IV. 660 For ministers had done the like before, And like him horse-laugh'd at the nation. **1821** *Blackw. Mag.* X. 572/2 Whisperings, and titterings, and horse laughter, and loud guffaws.

horse-leech ('hɔːsliːtʃ), *sb.* [f. HORSE + LEECH:—OE. *lǽce, léce*, physician.]

†**1.** A horse-doctor, farrier, veterinary surgeon.

1493 *Mem. Ripon* (Surtees) III. 165 Item Johanni Hors-leych pro medicacione j equo magistri Langton, 7*d.* *c* **1515**

Cocke Lorell's B. (Percy Soc.) 9 Bokell smythes, horse leches, and gold beters. **1529** MORE *Dyaloge* II. x. 52 b/2 Saynt Loy we make an horsleche, and must let our horse rather renne vnshodde and marre hys hoofe than to shoo hym on hys daye. **1653** BOGAN *Mirth Chr. Life* 234 The horse.. will not endure the hand of the horseleech.

2. An aquatic sucking worm (*Hæmopsis sanguisorba*) differing from the common leech in its larger size, and in the formation of the jaws.

(In some early quots. it seems to mean the common medicinal leech.)

14.. *Nom.* in Wr.-Wülcker 706/26 *Hec sanguissuga*, a horsleche. **1530** PALSGR. 232/2 Horse leche, a worme, *sansue.* **1535** COVERDALE *Prov.* xxx. 15 This generacion (which is like an horsleche) hath two doughters [**1388** WYCLIF The watir leche hath twei douȝtris]: yᵉ one is called, fetch hither: the other, brynge hither. **1573-80** BARET *Alv.* H. 663 An Horse leach, or bloudsucker worme, *hirudo.* **1581** MARBECK *Bk. of Notes* 503 The Horse-leach hath two daughters.. that is, two forks in her tongue, which he heere calleth her daughters, wherby she sucketh the bloud, and is neuer saciate. **1625** HART *Anat. Ur.* I. ii. 15 Horse-leaches were wont to taste of the horses dung. **1802** BINGLEY *Anim. Biog.* (1813) III. 412 Horse-leeches are.. so extremely greedy of blood, that a vulgar notion is prevalent, that nine of them are able to destroy a horse. **1880** *Chambers' Encycl.* VI. 74/2 The Horse-leech.. is much larger than the medicinal species.. but its teeth are comparatively blunt, and it is little of a blood-sucker—notwithstanding the popular notion.. It feeds greedily on earth-worms.

3. *fig.* A rapacious, insatiable person.

1546 *Suppl. Poor Commons* (1871) 63 Besides the infinit number of purgatory horseleches. **1608** SYLVESTER *Du Bartas* II. iv. IV. *Decay* 192 Thou life of strife, thou Horse-leach sent from hell. **1705** HICKERINGILL *Priest-cr.* I. (1721) 18 Of all Priests, the Popes have been in several Ages the great Horse-leaches and Blood-suckers. **1836-48** B. D. WALSH *Aristoph., Clouds* I. i, He has disregarded my advice, and stuck horse-leeches on to my estate.

Hence †**horse-leech,** *v. trans.* to suck insatiably (as reputed of the horse-leech): †'**horse-,leechery, -leechcraft**, veterinary medicine.

1679 *Prot. Conformist* 3 They have thereby Horse-leach'd a great deal of the best blood in Europe. **1688** R. HOLME *Armoury* II. 149/2 Horse Leachery, or Leach-craft, is the Art of curing Horses of Diseases.

horseless ('hɔːslɪs), *a.* Without a horse. Applied *c* 1895–1910 to motor vehicles.

1671 H. M. tr. *Erasm. Colloq.* 429 The horseless Horse-man. **1790** COWPER *Let. to Bull* 8 Sept., We rejoice that though unhorsed, or rather horseless, you are come safe home again. **1878** *Lond. Rev.* Jan. 338 It is from the apparently horseless Continent of America that the finest geological evidence of the pedigree of the horse is to be traced. **1895** *Chamb. Jrnl.* XII. 673/1 Horseless carriages threaten to give a new aspect to road traffic. **1900** *T. Eaton & Co. Catal.* Christmas 5/1 Horseless carriage, large size, wind with key, best spring, 50 c. **1901** *Chambers's Jrnl.* Jan. 14/2 The three great trusts that control the making and using of these horseless machines. **1905** *Ibid.* Jan. 111/1 Farmers, who now look askance at horseless vehicles. **1973** J. WAINWRIGHT *Devil you Don't* 144 An Olde Worlde coaching town which hadn't yet got round to noticing the arrival of the horseless carriage.

'**horse-like,** *a.* Like or resembling a horse.

1530 PALSGR. 316/1 Horselyke, belongynge to an horse, *cheualin.* **1598** SYLVESTER *Du Bartas* II. ii. III. *Colonies* 453 Bunch-backed Calves, with Horse-like manes.

'**horse-,litter.** Forms: see LITTER.

1. A litter hung on poles, carried between two horses, one in front and the other behind.

1388 WYCLIF *2 Macc.* iii. 27 Putte in a pakke sadil [*gloss*] ether hors litir. *c* **1465** *Eng. Chron.* (Camden 1856) 46 He was brought in a horsliter to Westmynstre. **1600** HOLLAND *Livy* XXVI. xxix. 650 Scarce able to endure the shogging and shaking of the horselitter, for pain and greefe of his wounds. **1775** R. TWISS *Trav. Port & Sp.* 49 Chairs and horse-litters are used here in bad weather. **1851** DICKENS *Child's Hist. Eng.* xvi, The King, now weak and sick, followed in a horse-litter.

b. Sometimes on wheels, esp. as a funeral car.

1591 PERCIVALL *Sp. Dict.*, *Carro con andas*, a horslitter, *rheda.* **1663** WOOD *Life* July (O.H.S.) I. 479 Then the wain or hors-litter on four wheeles.

2. A bed of straw or hay for horses to rest upon. **b.** The manure consisting of such straw mixed with the excrements of horses.

1624 BURTON *Anat. Mel.* I. ii. IV. vii. 146 Olde monuments and books, made horse-litter, or burned like straw. **1721** BRADLEY *Coffee* 33 A bed prepared with horse-litter. —— *Philos. Acc. Wks. Nat.* 20 It must be cover'd, the Top and Sides with Horse-litter to lie upon it undisturb'd.

'**horse-load.** A load for a horse; sometimes, a determinate weight: cf. LOAD.

c **1350** in *Eng. Gilds* (1870) 358 Tonnes and barelles þᵗ comeþ in carte, sholde custome a peny; an horselode an halpeny. *c* **1400** MAUNDEV. (Roxb.) xxxiv. 153, cccᵐ hors lade of corne and als many of ryess. **1483** *Cath. Angl.* 189/2 An Horse lade, *clitella.* **1580** HOLLYBAND *Treas. Fr. Tong, Somme ou charge de charbon*, a horse lode of coles. **1641** VICARS *Jehovah-Jireh* 160 His Souldiers took horse-loads of Provision, Bisket, Meal and other necessaries. **1667** PRIMATT *City & C. Build.* (1680) 6 Some [lead] Oare.. yeilding Thirty-six shillings.. a Horse-load (which is nine dishes, as they compute, weighing about Four hundred and Fifty pound). **1700** TYRRELL *Hist. Eng.* II. 997 A Horse-load of Corn was sold for Ten Shillings. **1776** PENNANT *Zool.* III. 63 If a Porpesse should be too big for a horse-load, allowance should be made to the purveyor.

b. *loosely* or *fig.* A large load or quantity.

c **1500** *How Plowman learned Pater-Noster* 116 in Hazl. *E.P.P.* II. 213 They thought to longe that they abode, Yet eche of them had an hors-lode. **1641** MILTON *Ch. Govt.* II. Pref., They have.. laid ye down their horseload of citations and fathers at your door. **1681** OTWAY *Soldier's Fort.* I. i., A Horse-load of Diseases. **1837** HAWTHORNE *Twice-Told T.* (1851) I. v. 75 Toiling through the difficult woods, each with a horseload of iron armor to burden his footsteps.

†'**horse-loaf.** *Obs.* A loaf of HORSE-BREAD.

c **1468** in *Stow's Surv.* (ed. Strype 1720) v. 341 The horse lof shal wey two halfpeny white lofis. **1483** in *Eng. Gilds* (1870) 337 Thath all Bakers.. make butt ij. horselofys to a peny, and of clene beanys. **1591** HARINGTON *Orl. Fur.* VII. lxii. (N.), Her stature scant three horse-loaves did exceed. **1611** COTGR., *Nain*, a dwarfe,.. one thats no higher then three horse-loaues. **1681** *Manch. Crt. Leet Rec.* (1888) VI. 126 James Smith, 1 horse loafe 4 ounce too light.

†'**horse-lock.** *Obs.* A shackle for a horse's feet = FETLOCK *sb.* 2; hence, app. any hanging lock, a padlock.

1486 *Nottingham Rec.* III. 255 For a horse lok.. vjd. **1530** YATTON CHURCHW. ACC. (Som. Rec. Soc.) 145 Payd for a horse locke to yᵉ cherche yatte, viijᵈ. **1573** TUSSER *Husb.* xvii. (1878) 38 Soles, fetters, and shackles, with horselock and pad. **1623** FLETCHER & ROWLEY *Maid of Mill* III. i, Horse-locks nor chains shall hold her from me. **1680** *Lond. Gaz.* No. 1569/4 A little.. Nag.. a Horse-lock on his near foot before. **1736** *N. Jersey Archives* (1894) XI. 483 He [one escaped from prison] had a Horse-Lock on one of his Legs.

†'**horsely,** *a. Obs.* Also horsly(e. [f. HORSE + -LY¹; cf. *manly.*] Of or pertaining to a horse; of the nature of a good horse.

c **1386** CHAUCER *Sqr.'s T.* 186 This hors.. so horsly [*v.r.* horsely] and so quyk of eye. **1552** HULOET, Horsly, or parteynynge to a horse, *equarius.*

'**horse-'mackerel.** A name for several fishes allied to the mackerel; *esp.* the Cavally or Scad (*Caranx vulgaris*).

Also in various parts of U.S. the common Tunny, the Jurel (*Caranx pisquetus*), the Bluefish (*Pomatomus saltatrix*), the Black Candle-fish (*Anoplopoma fimbria*), the Californian Hake (*Merlucius productus*), and the Ten-pounder (*Elops saurus*). (*Cent. Dict.*)

a **1705** RAY *Synops. Pisc.* (1713) 92 *Tracherus*.. A Scad.. a Horse Mackrell. **1777** G. FORSTER *Voy. round World* I. 126 Scorpens, mullets, horse-mackrel, and many other sorts. **1838** JOHNSTON in *Proc. Berw. Nat. Club* I. No. 6. 171 The Scad or Horse-Mackerel. **1860** BARTLETT *Dict. Amer.* (ed. 3), *Blue-Fish*,.. on the Jersey coast.. called Horse-Mackerel. **1862** ANSTED *Channel Isl.* II. ix. (ed. 2) 212 The horse-mackarel also is considered poor and dry.

horseman ('hɔːsmən). Pl. -men.

1. One who rides on horseback, a rider; one skilled in riding and managing a horse.

c **1400** *Ywaine & Gaw.* 401 Another noyse than herd i sone, Als it war of horsmen. **1583** HOLLYBAND *Campo di Fior* 277 O there is a good horseman: O brave rider. **1673** S. C. *Art of Complaisance* 131 To pass simply for a good horseman, or a fine dancer. **1780** HARRIS *Philol. Enq.* Wks. (1841) 542 These Spanish Arabians.. were great horsemen, and particularly fond of horses. **1849** MACAULAY *Hist. Eng.* viii. II. 349 These letters.. were sent by horsemen to the nearest country post towns on the different roads.

†**b.** *spec.* A mounted soldier. *Obs.*

c **1205** LAY. 26641 Heo letten alle þa horsmen i þan wude alihten. *c* **1302** in *Pol. Songs* (Camden) 189 Sixtene hundred of horsmen asemblede o the gras. **1382** WYCLIF *Rev.* ix. 16 The noumbre of the hoost of horsemen twenty thousynd. **1548** HALL *Chron., Hen. VIII* 28 Among the Frenchmen were certain light horsmen called Stradiotes. **1655** STANLEY *Hist. Philos.* III. (1701) 116/1 Notwithstanding he had also a Horse-man's Cuirass. **1855** MACAULAY *Hist. Eng.* xxi. (1880) II. 529 A horseman in the uniform of the Guards spurred through the City, announcing that the King had been killed.

c. A knight. (*transl.* L. *eques*, Gr. ἱππεύς.)

1596 DALRYMPLE tr. *Leslie's Hist. Scot.* I. 13 In Galloway ar horsmen, Barounes, and vthiris noble men mony. **1807** ROBINSON *Archæol. Græca* IV. ii. 337 Both at Athens and Sparta ἱππεῖς, horsemen, composed the second order in the commonwealth. **1849** GROTE *Greece* II. lxxii. (1862) VI. 347 The Knights or Horsemen, the body of richest proprietors at Athens, were the mainstay of the Thirty.

d. ***horseman's bed*** (in Ireland), a tenement of a certain size. ***horseman's hammer***, a hammer-shaped mace, a mediæval weapon. ***horseman's weight***, the weight by which a jockey is weighed, applied to the legal stone of fourteen pounds.

1672 PETTY *Pol. Anat.* (1691) 107 As to these town-lands, plough-lands, colps, greeves.. horseman's beds, etc., they are at this day manifestly unequal. **1828** J. M. SPEARMAN *Brit. Gunner* 413 Also, 14 pounds make 1 stone, horseman's weight, and 8 pounds 1 stone, in the London markets.

2. A man who attends to horses.

1882 HOWELLS in *Longm. Mag.* I. 55, I heard myself indicated in a whisper as 'one of the horse-men'. **1889** *N.W. Linc. Gloss.* (ed. 2), *Horseman*, the man who attends upon and travels with a stallion. **1898** R. HAGGARD in *Daily News* 28 Sept. 6/5 The agricultural labourer.. works from six to six.. horsemen and cattlemen work longer.

3. A variety of fancy pigeons: see quot. 1867.

1735 J. MOORE *Columb.* 31 The oftener it is thus bred [from a Carrier] the stouter the Horseman becomes. **1741** *Compl. Fam.-Piece* III. 512. **1867** TEGETMEIER *Pigeons* vii. 79 In many of the older treatises an inferior variety of the Carrier was described under the name of the *Horseman.*

4. *Ichthyol.* A sciænoid fish of the genus *Eques* found on the coasts of Central America.

5. See also LIGHT-HORSEMAN.

Light and *Heavy Horsemen*, slang names for certain Thames thieves.

1849 MARRYAT *Valerie* xviii, 'There's a lighter adrift', said I. 'The Light Horsemen have cut her adrift.' *Ibid.*, Light Horsemen—that's a name for one set of people who live by plunder... Then we have the Heavy Horsemen—they do their work in the daytime, when they go on board as lumpers to clear the ships.

horsemanship ('hɔːsmənʃɪp). [f. prec. + -SHIP.] The art of riding on horseback; skill or expertness in riding, equestrian performance. Formerly including the breeding, rearing, and management of horses; the duties of the *manège*.

1565 BLUNDEVIL (*title*) The Fower Chiefest Offices belonging to Horsemanshippe, that is to say, The Office of the Breeder, of the Rider, of the Keeper, and of the Ferrer. **1577** B. GOOGE *Heresbach's Husb.* III. (1586) 19 When we entreat of horsemanship, and breaking of horses. **1601** R. JOHNSON *Kingd. & Commw.* (1603) 205 The nature of the countrey is not fitte for horsemanshippe. **1727-41** CHAMBERS *Cycl.*, *Horsemanship*, in its latitude, includes what relates to the make, colour, age, temper, and qualities of horses. **1796** MORSE *Amer. Geog.* II. 479 The Tartars are inured to horsemanship from their infancy: they seldom appear on foot. **1816** KEATINGE *Trav.* (1817) II. 102 The show exhibited very capital horsemanship. **1875** JOWETT *Plato* (ed. 2) V. 375 Gymnastic and horsemanship are as suitable to women as to men.

attrib. **1825** SCOTT *Fam. Lett.* 5 Nov. (1894) II. 369, I hope in God you will not break Jane's neck with your horsemanship experiments.

†**horse-marine**¹. *Her. Obs.* [f. HORSE *sb.* + MARINE *a.*] A sea-horse.

1705 *Lond. Gaz.* No. 4162/4 On a Torse a Demy Horse-Marine.

horse-marine² ('hɔːsmə'riːn). [f. HORSE *sb.* + MARINE *sb.*]

1. A marine mounted on horseback, or a cavalryman doing a marine's work.

1878 *N. Amer. Rev.* CXXVII. 225 This old sea-dog.. organized a body of horse-marines to patrol the shore. **1886** *Tinsley's Mag.* Apr. 321 The 17th Lancers were once christened the 'Horse marines'. Two troops of this showy corps were employed as marines on board the Hermione frigate during some severe fighting in the West Indies.

2. *humorously.* (*pl.*) An imaginary corps of mounted marine soldiers, considered as a type of men out of their element; hence, *sing.* a man doing work for which he is not fitted; a 'landlubber' on shipboard. Phr. ***tell that to the horse marines***: a colloquial expression of incredulity. Cf. MARINE *sb.* 4 c.

1824 SCOTT *St. Ronan's* xxi, 'What the devil has a ship to do with horse's furniture?—Do you think we belong to the horse-marines?' **1860** O. W. HOLMES *Sea Dial.* 45 Belay y'r jaw, y' swab! y' hoss-marine! **1892** *Wops the Waif* i. 1 (Farmer) You'd better tell that to the hoss marines; I've lived a sight too long in Shoreditch to take that in. **1921** W. S. MAUGHAM *Circle* II. 65 *Elizabeth*: He's never even kissed me. *Arnold*: I'd try telling that to the horse marines if I were you.

3. 'A man or youth who is engaged in leading and attending to the horse drawing a canal-boat' (*Lab. Comm. Gloss.* 1894).

c **1850** [Correspt. writes 'In general use on Regent's Canal'.] *c* **1860** [Used by a witness at the Lindsey Sessions, Lincolns.]. **1881** *Census-returns* in *Brit. Alm. Comp.* (1885) 94.

'**horse-master.** One who owns or manages horses; also, a horse-breaker.

1523 FITZHERB. *Husb.* §120 A Horse-mayster is he, that bieth wylde horses, or coltes, and bredeth theym, and selleth theym agayne wylde, or breaketh parte of them, and maketh theym tame, and then selleth them. **1567** *Triall Treas.* (1850) 22 Suche horse maisters will make a colte quickely tame. **1607** TOPSELL *Four-f. Beasts* (1658) 249 Of the greatest Horse-masters and nourishers of Horses. **1766** W. SMITH tr. *Bouquet's Exp.* (1868) 43 Four divisions.. of pack-horses, each conducted by a horse master. **1897** *Cavalry Tactics* ii. 8 The good horse master in stables is much more likely to be a good horse master under any circumstances.

'**horse-,mastership.** [See -SHIP.] Skill in managing horses.

1904 *Westm. Gaz.* 21 Sept. 10/1 Thereupon a trumpeter, who knew something about horse-mastership, instantly sounded the forage-call. Two minutes later every animal was standing quietly in its appointed place. **1925** E. O. SHEBBEARE in E. F. Norton *Fight for Everest, 1924* 365 Unless any other member of the Expedition better fitted by his knowledge of horsemastership undertakes the care of the mess mules. **1927** *Daily Tel.* 26 Apr. 16/7 The Army in India Polo team.. has undertaken a very difficult and interesting feat of horse-mastership. The problem to be solved is that of transporting a large stable of ponies from India to America. **1937** H. BELLOC *Crusade* iii. 67 The rest of the work was foot-slogging and horsemastership. **1971** *Country Life* 30 Dec. 1829/3 The present upsurge of interest in all aspects of horsemanship and horsemastership.

'**horse-meat.** [See MEAT.] **1.** Food or provender for horses.

1404 *Durham MS. Sacr. Roll*, j sythe pro horsmet falcand. **1475** *Bk. Noblesse* 30 Finding bothe horsmete and mannys-mete to youre soudeours riding be the contre. **1528** SIR B. TUKE in Ellis *Orig. Lett.* Ser. I. I. 286, I sent a phisician.. promysing hym a mark by day, horsmete, and mans mete. **1677** PLOT *Oxfordsh.* 256 Oats, and all mixed Corns called Horse-meat, are Harvested somtimes with two reaping hooks. **1742** FIELDING *J. Andrews* II. ii, The sum due for horsemeat was twelve shillings.

2. = HORSE-FLESH 1.

1853 S. N. CARVALHO *Jrnl.* 1 Feb. in J. Bigelow *Mem. J. C. Fremont* (1856) xvii. 441 He sent a Mexican.. with cooked horsemeat. **1868** *All Year Round* 22 Feb. 252/2 Horse-meat is a common.. article of food. **1870** *Food Jrnl.* 1 Dec. 620 The almost impossibility of obtaining beef and mutton naturally forced the use of horsemeat upon the

people. **1904** *Westm. Gaz.* 23 Dec. 10/1 Every day the purveyors and the consumers of horsemeat increase in numbers. **1910** *Daily Chron.* 14 Jan. 1/5 The price of horse meat was 3½d. a lb. **1972** T. P. McMahon *Issue of Bishop's Blood* (1937) xi. 171 A very suave-type fellow then came to Hymie with a tale about.. buying frozen horse meat to meet the chain's need for huge quantities of frozen beef.

'horse-mill. **a.** A mill driven by a horse; usually, by one walking in a circle or in a wheel.

1530 Palsgr. 232/2 Horse myll, *movlin a cheual.* **1559** in Boys *Sandwich* (1792) 738 The water must be conveyed awaye with horse mylnes. **1769** Falconer *Dict. Marine* (1789) L ij, Like the machinery of a horse-mill. **1828** P. Cunningham *N. S. Wales* (ed. 3) II. 65 Ten water-mills, eighteen windmills, and two horse-mills. **1848** E. Bryant *California* xxi. 269 The flour consumed by Captain Sutter is ground by a very ordinary horse-mill. **1889** *Century Mag.* Feb. 520/2 A horse-mill—a long pole on which a man sits, and to which a horse or mule is hitched. **1971** *Country Life* 30 Sept. 848/1 Some of these groups of stone-built barns, byres and arcaded cartsheds, relieved on occasion by a circular horse-mill, [etc.].

b. *fig.* A monotonous round.

1621 Burton *Anat. Mel.* I. ii. III. xi. (1651) 112 Desire hath no rest, and is infinite in it selfe, endlesse, and as one cals it, a perpetuall racke, or horse mill.. still going round as in a ring.

'horse-mint. [See horse 28 c.]

1. 'A name applied generally to the wild mints' (Britten and Holland), esp. *Mentha sylvestris* and *M. aquatica.*

c **1265** *Voc. Names Pl.* in Wr.-Wülcker 555/5 *Mentastrum*, ..horsminte. *a* **1387** *Sinon. Barthol.* (Anecd. Oxon.) 30 *Menta aquatica*, an horsment. *c* **1440** *Promp. Parv.* 248/1 Horsmynte, herbe, *balsamita, mentastrum.* *c* **1516** *Grete Herball* cclxxv. P v b, Agaynst colde cough bethe dry fygges with horsmynt in wyne, and vse it. **1646** Sir T. Browne *Pseud. Ep.* 102 So are they deceived in the name of Horse-raddish, Horse-mint, Bull-rush, and many more.. that expression is but a Grecisme.. intending no more then great. **1787** Winter *Syst. Husb.* 97 Coarse grass, rushes, horse-mints.. general productions of lands overcharged with moisture. **1861** Miss Pratt *Flower. Pl.* IV. 152.

2. Applied in North America to other aromatic labiates, as various species of *Monarda, Collinsonia canadensis*, and *Cunila Mariana* (Sweet Horse-mint, also called *dittany*). (See Miller *Plant-n.*, and *Cent. Dict.*)

†**'horsen,** *a.* *Obs. rare.* [See -en⁴.] Of or belonging to horses.

1558 Warde tr. *Alexis' Secr.* I. vi. (1580) 108 a, Let hym put the Yearth onely, the Floxe, and the Horsen doung.

'horse-nail.

1. A horseshoe-nail.

1598 Barret *Theor. Warres* 135 Horse nayles and horse shoes of all sizes. **1695** Congreve *Love for L.* III. ix, Poring upon the Ground for a crooked Pin, or an old Horse-Nail. **1858** Greener *Gunnery* 148 The inferior iron of which we make horse-nails.

2. A tadpole. *local.*

1608 Topsell *Serpents* (1658) 719 The heads of these young Gyrini, which we call in English Horse-nails; because they resemble a Horse-nail in their similitude, whose head is great, and the other part small. **1887** in *Kent. Gloss.*

'horseness. *nonce-wd.* The abstract quality of a horse (tr. Gr. ἱππότης).

1864 *Q. Rev.* July 72, 'I see a horse', said Antisthenes to Plato, 'but I do not see horseness'.

'horse-play.

†**1.** Play in which a horse is used or takes part; theatrical horsemanship. Also *transf. Obs.*

1599 Massinger, etc. *Old Law* III. ii, Horse-play at four-score is not so ready. *a* **1627** Middleton *Mayor of Queenborough* v. i, *Second Play.* We have a play wherein we use a horse. *Sim.* Fellows, you use no horse-play in my house. **1668** Dryden *Evening's Love* I. ii, *Bel.* They get upon their jennets, and prance before their ladies' windows... *Wild.* And this horseplay they call making love.

2. Rough, coarse, or boisterous play, passing the bounds of propriety.

1589 R. Harvey *Pl. Perc.* (1590) 9, I am a stranger, and cannot tel what your horse play meanes. **1700** Dryden *Fables* Pref. Wks. (Globe) 506 He [Collier] is too much given to horse-play in his raillery. **1749** Chesterf. *Lett.* (1792) II. clxxix. 166 No aukward overturns of glasses, plates, and salt-cellars; no horse-play. **1856** Masson *Ess.* iv. 121 Dryden's best comic attempts were but heavy horse-play. **1871** L. Stephen *Playgr. Europe* vi. (1894) 149 Explosions of animal spirits, bordering at times upon horse-play.

Hence **horse-playish** *a.*, given to horse-play.

1882 *Daily News* 22 Sept. 2/1 The younger men were somewhat horse-playish in their behaviour.

'horse-plum.

1. A small red variety of plum.

1530 Palsgr. 232/2 Horse plome, frute, *jorroise.* **1546** J. Heywood *Prov.* (1867) 20 Her cheekes are purple ruddie lyke a horse plumme. **1648** Gage *West Ind.* 28 A great black kernell as big as our horse Plums. **1886** Britten & Holland *Plant-n.*, *Horse Plum*, a small red plum.

2. *N. Amer.* Either of the two common wild plums, *Prunus americana* or *P. nigra.*

1790 S. Deane *New-Eng. Farmer* 222/2 The horse-plum, a very pleasant tasted juicy fruit, of a large size. **1827** *Western Monthly Rev.* I. 322 The fruit is of the size of a common horse plum. **1908** N. L. Britton *N. Amer. Trees* 494 Canada Plum.. *Prunus nigra* Aiton. Also called Horse plum, this is a small, bushy tree, occurring in woods and neglected lands from Newfoundland to Alberta, and southward to Georgia.

'horse-pond, *sb.* A pond for watering and washing horses; proverbial as a ducking-place for obnoxious persons.

1701 Cibber *Love Makes Man* I. i, I han't much Land to spare; but I have an admirable Horse-Pond—I'll settle that upon him, if you will. **1713** Addison *Guardian* No. 136 ¶4 Led into a horsepond by a Will of the Whisp. **1746** *Brit. Mag.* 101 If old Bettenson had ordered him to have been dragg'd through a Horse-pond. **1843** Bethune *Sc. Fireside Stor.* 62 He intended.. to take a third individual to a horse-pond.. and duck him head and ears three times.

'horse-pond, *v.* [f. prec. sb.] *trans.* To duck in or drag through a horse-pond.

1757 Garrick *Male Coquette* I. 13 If I go again, Sir, may I be caned, kicked, and horseponded for my pains. **1782** Miss Burney *Cecilia* VI. x, Not only horsewhipt, but horse-ponded. **1884** *Church Reformer* III. 79 [They] will not readily forget his suggestion of horse-ponding their leaders as a substitute for redressing their grievances.

'horsepower. Also horse-power.

1. **a.** The power or rate of work of a horse in drawing; hence, in *Mech.*, a conventional unit for measuring the rate of work of a prime motor, commonly taken (after Watt) as = 550 foot-pounds per second (which is about 1⅓ times the actual power of a horse). Abbreviated H.P.

1806 O. Gregory *Mech.* (1807) II. 357 The usual method of estimating the effects of engines by what are called 'horse powers' must inevitably be very fallacious. **1891** *Electrician* Sept. 551 A new and shockingly unscientific unit, the electrical horse power, is insensibly coming into use. **1897** Preece in *Glasgow Herald* 6 Feb. 3/5 The term 'horse-power' has probably seen its best days.. As a scientific term it has been much abused, and as a commercial term it conveys no meaning.

b. With prefixed numeral, expressing the power or rate of work of an engine, etc.; as 'an engine of 40-horse power', or 'a 40-horse-power engine'.

Properly the numeral + 'horse' form an attrib. phrase qualifying 'power' (as in 'four-horse coach'; cf. *two-foot rule, half-mile race*); but the whole phrase (esp. when used *attrib.*) is often analyzed as numeral + 'horse-power'.

1823 Byron *Juan* X. xxxiv. *note*, A metaphor taken from the 'forty-horse power' of a steam-engine. **1835** Marryat *Olla Podr.* iv, She.. preferred the three-horse power of the schuyt to the hundred-horse power of the steam-packet. **1851** *Illustr. Catal. Gt. Exhib.* 214 Oscillating steam-engine, of 10-horse power. **1872** R. B. Smyth *Mining Statist.* 50 One 25 horse-power engine, 16-inch cylinder.

c. With qualifying words, esp. **brake horsepower**, the power available at the shaft of an engine, measurable by means of a brake; **indicated horsepower**, the power produced within the cylinders, as shown by an indicator.

1859 W. J. M. Rankine *Man. Steam Engine* v. 479 Nominal Horse-power is a conventional mode of describing the dimensions of a steam engine, for the convenience of makers and purchasers of engines, and bears no fixed relation to indicated or to effective horse-power. **1881** *Encycl. Brit.* XII. 207/1 Nominal horse-power is a purely conventional term adopted by makers of steam-engines, and has no fixed relation to indicated horse-power. **1887** *Encycl. Brit.* XXII. 493/2 The efficiency of the mechanism is the ratio of the 'effective' or 'brake' horse power to the indicated horse power. **1904** *Westm. Gaz.* 30 Mar. 10/2 The *Good Hope* and the *Drake*.. are of 14,100 tons displacement and 30,000 indicated horse-power. **1943** A. P. Fraas *Aircraft Power Plants* vi. 110 The power required to turn the engine over, or friction horsepower,.. increases rapidly with rpm. **1968** R. H. Bacon *Car* ii. 17 The power developed in the cylinder.. is called the indicated horsepower or i.h.p. Some of this power is absorbed by the friction of various parts of the engine. The power remaining, that is the power that can be used for work, is called the brake horsepower or b.h.p. **1972** *Daily Tel.* 15 Mar. 11/5 The latest car is almost a hundredweight heavier while the net brake horsepower is only up by six.

2. *transf.* Power or rate of work as estimated by this unit; number of horse-powers. Also *fig.*

1860 Maury *Phys. Geog. Sea* iv. §268 What is the horse-power of the Niagara? **1867** Emerson *Lett. & Soc. Aims, Progr. Culture* Wks. (Bohn) III. 235 Enthusiasm is the leaping lightning, not to be measured by the horse-power of the understanding. **1871** Tyndall *Fragm. Sc.* I. xx, [He] calculates the equivalent of that heat in horse-power.

3. The power or agency of a horse or horses as employed in driving machinery; hence, a machine by which the pull or weight of a horse is converted into power for driving other machinery.

1853 *Catal. R. Agric. Soc. Show Gloucester* 50 A One Horse Power Portable Horse Gear. *Ibid.* 51 A useful and economical thrashing machine to be either worked by hand or horse power. **1864** Webster, *Horse-power*.. 3. A machine operated by one or more horses; a horse-engine. **1875** Knight *Dict. Mech.* s.v., An ordinary horse-power, such as is used for thrashing-machines, drag-saws, clover-hullers.

4. *Comb.* **horsepower-hour**, a unit representing the work performed or energy consumed in working at the rate of one horsepower for one hour.

1899 J. Perry *Steam Engine* xvi. 250 Units of Energy used Commercially. 1 horse-power hour = ..1,980,000 foot-pounds. **1906** *Westm. Gaz.* 28 June 2/1 An output of 36 cubic feet of oxygen per horse-power hour. **1949** G. P. Sutton *Rocket Propulsion Elem.* i. 18 The specific fuel consumption is based on the horsepower output, and its units are pounds of fuel per horsepower-hour. **1963** F. D. Jones & Schubert *Engin. Encycl.* (ed. 3) 662, 1 horsepower-hour = 0·746 kilowatt-hour.

'horse-pox. [See pox.]

†**1.** A severe or virulent pox. (Used in coarse execrations.) *Obs.*

1656 S. Holland *Zara* (1719) 115 With a Horse-pox and a Murrain. **1667** Dk. Newcastle & Dryden *Sir Martin Mar-all* IV. i, Leave off your winking and your pinking, with a horse-pox t'ye. **1694** Echard *Plautus* Pref. A iij, I'll fetch ye out with a Horse-pox for a damnable, prying, nine-eyed Witch.

2. A pustular disease of horses, said, when communicated to cows, to produce cow-pox.

1884 *N.Y. Med. Jrnl.* 15 Nov. 548 An outbreak of casual 'horse-pox' among the she-asses. **1897** Allbutt *Syst. Med.* II. 636 He explained the failure on the part of many experimenters to transmit horse-pox to the cow.

'horser. [f. horse *v.* + -er¹.] One who provides horses for a coach; a postmaster.

1851 'Nimrod' *Road* 35 The horser's profits depend upon the luck he has with his stock.

'horse-race. A race by horses (with riders).

1581 Sidney *Apol. Poetrie* (Arb.) 46 Phillip of Macedon reckoned a horse-race wonne at Olimpus among hys three fearefull felicities. **1617** Moryson *Itin.* I. 198 No meane Lordes.. and Gentlemen in our Court had in like sort put out money upon a horserace, or speedie course of a horse, under themselves. *a* **1626** Bacon (J.), In horseraces men are curious that there be not the least weight upon one horse more than upon another. **1712** Steele *Spect.* No. 462 ¶4 To glory in being the first Man at Cock-matches, Horse-races. **1821** Byron *Juan* III. lxxxv, Pindar sang horse-races.

attrib. **1629** J. Maxwell tr. *Herodian* (1635) 426 Cirque (*margin*, Or Horse-race-yard, able to hold above 20000).

'horse-ˌracer. [f. horse-race + -er¹, after *race, racer.*] One who keeps horses for racing; one who rides horses in races, a jockey.

c **1618** J. Bruen in Hinde *Life* xi. (1641) 38 A good rule for our horse-racers, rank riders, and hot-spurre hunters. **1733** *Weekly Reg.* 8 Dec., Song-singers, horse-racers, valets-de-chambre. **1888** *Athenæum* 22 Sept. 381/1 The first Lord Godolphin was a horse-racer as well as gambler undoubtedly.

'horse-ˌracing, *sb.* [f. horse + racing *vbl. sb.*, after *horse-race.*] The practice or sport of running horses in competitions of speed.

c **1654** G. Fox *Jrnl.* (1827) I. 250 Each taking his horse.. and so go to horse-racing. **1780** T. Davies *Garrick* (1781) I. xxvi. 297 The wretched attachment of our young nobility and gentry to horse-racing. **1837** W. Irving *Capt. Bonneville* III. 201 All ardently addicted to gambling and horse-racing. **1894** *Westm. Gaz.* 13 Sept. 1/3 Horse-racing.. is a sport which gives more employment to more thousands of deserving persons than can be claimed for any other.

b. *Comb.* **horseracing-board**, a board used for a gambling game played with figures of horses.

1883 *Pall Mall G.* 13 Mar. 7/2 Charged with gambling with a horseracing-board in the New-cut, and carrying on a system of swindling.

So **'horse-ˌracing** *a.*, addicted to horse-racing.

1814 *Last Act* II. ii, A bold, dashing, horse-racing, fox-hunting heroine.

'horse-ˌradish. [See horse *sb.* 28 c.]

1. A cruciferous plant (*Cochlearia Armoracia*), with white flowers and broad rough leaves, a native of middle Europe and western Asia, commonly cultivated for its root (see 2).

1597 Gerarde *Herbal* II. vii. 186 Horse Radish bringeth foorth great leaues. **1732** Arbuthnot *Rules of Diet* 263 Vegetables which abound with a pungent volatile Salt and Oil as.. Horse-Radish, Cresses. **1876** Harley *Mat. Med.* (ed. 6) 732 Horse-Radish is a Native of most hilly situations in Europe,.. flowering in May.

2. The thick rootstock of this plant, which has a very pungent flavour, and is scraped or grated down as a condiment.

1625 Hart *Anat. Ur.* Pref. B b, The Germanes in diuerse places.. boyle wilde or horse radishes with their beefe. **1769** Mrs. Raffald *Eng. Housekpr.* (1778) 351 Pour it on your parsley, with two or three slices of horse-radish. **1881** Besant & Rice *Chapl. of Fleet* I. vi. 150 His prejudices as a gentleman and a scholar were offended by the absence of horse-radish.

fig. **1830** Galt *Lawrie T.* VI. iii, With a plentiful garnishing of the horse radish of their petulance.

3. *attrib.* and *Comb.*, as ***horse-radish root***; †**horse-radish ale**, ? ale flavoured with horse-radish; **horse-radish tree**, (*a*) a tree (*Moringa pterygosperma*), a native of India, cultivated in tropical countries for its pod-like capsules, which are eaten fresh or pickled, and for its winged seeds (*ben-nuts*), from which oil of ben is obtained; the root resembles horse-radish in flavour; (*b*) in Australia, a name for *Codonocarpus cotinifolius* (N.O. *Phytolaceæ*): see quot. 1889.

1664 Pepys *Diary* 16 Sept., He would needs have me drink a cup of horse-radish ale. **1694** Salmon *Bates' Disp.* (1713) 437/2 On the edulcorated Pouder, affuse Oil of Turpentine drawn off from Horse-radish-roots. **1859** *All Year Round* No. 32. 127/1 Horse-radish trees, giving perfumers and watchmakers that famous oil of Ben, which can hardly ever be obtained pure. **1889** J. H. Maiden *Usef. Nat. Plants Australia* 164 Called also 'Horse-radish Tree', owing to the taste of the leaves.

ˈhorse-ˌrider. One who rides a horse; a professional performer on horseback; a circus-rider. So **ˈhorse-ˌriding** *vbl. sb.* and *ppl. a.*

1580 LYLY *Euphues* To Gentlem. Rdrs. (Arb.) 223 The cholaricke Horse-rider, who..not daring to kill the Horse went into the stable to cutte the saddle. *c* **1610** SIR J. MELVIL *Mem.* (1735) 317 His Pastimes of Hunting, Hawking and Horse-riding. **1854** DICKENS *Hard T.* I. iii, The clashing and banging band attached to the horse-riding establishment..A flag..proclaimed..that it was 'Sleary's horse-riding'. *Ibid.* III. v, The horse-riders never mind what they say, sir; they're famous for it. **1885** tr. *Hehn's Wand. Pl. & Anim.* 48 Those north-eastern branches..as far as the light of history reaches, are..found a horse-riding race.

horse-scorser, -scourser: see HORSE-CORSER.

ˈhorse-ˈsense. *colloq.* (orig. *U.S.*) Strong common sense; 'a coarse, robust, and conspicuous form of shrewdness often found in ignorant and rude persons; plain, practical good sense' (*Cent. Dict.*).

1832 J. K. PAULDING *Westward Ho!* II. 60 He's a man of good strong horse sense. **1870** *Nation* (N.Y.) 18 Aug. 105 The new phrase—born in the West, we believe—of 'horse-sense', which is applied to the intellectual ability of men who exceed others in practical wisdom. **1872** C. D. WARNER *Backlog Studies* 124 He was a plain man..he had what is roughly known as 'horse-sense', and he was homely. **1884** *New Eng. Jrnl. Educ.* XIX. 377 The latent 'horse-sense' of the American people may be relied on, in the end, to abate this nuisance. **1911** H. S. HARRISON *Queed* xviii. 223 A rich vein of horse-sense underlay Byrd's philanthropic enthusiasms. **1920** R. MACAULAY *Potterism* II. iii. 88, I am sure both parties credited them with too much idealism and too little plain horse-sense. **1930** CHESTERTON *Four Felons* 252 What I say is horse-sense, for all that. **1942** *Short Guide Gr. Brit.* (U.S. War Dept.) 2 We can defeat Hitler's propaganda with..plain, common horse sense; understanding of evident truths. **1960** I. WALLACH *Absence of Cello* 72 Summoning up his best horse sense (and trying to forget that the horse is an uncommonly stupid animal), Andrew said, 'I agree with Mr. Clifton.' **1973** E. LEMARCHAND *Let or Hindrance* v. 41 All horse sense on your part, old man, but I've got a tiresome hunch that it's not going to be as straightforward as all that.

horseshoe, horse-shoe (ˈhɔːsʃuː), *sb.*

1. a. A shoe for a horse, now usually formed of a narrow iron plate bent to the outline of the horse's hoof and nailed to the animal's foot.

Widely employed by the superstitious as an amulet, a protection from witchcraft, omen of good luck, etc.

1387 TREVISA *Higden* (Rolls) VI. 255 Foure hors schoon. **1485** *Nottingham Rec.* III. 245 Item for a hors shoo..jd. ob. **1596** DALRYMPLE tr. *Leslie's Hist. Scot.* VII. 39 Makdonald..with horschone he schod his wife, and set thame on her solis with nailis. **1598** SHAKS. *Merry W.* III. v. 123 To be throwne into the Thames, and coold, glowing-hot..like a Horse-shoo. **1665** BOYLE *Occas. Refl.* (1845) 348 The common People of this Country have a Tradition, that 'tis a lucky thing to find a Horse-shoe. **1751** *Univ. Mag.* in Hone *Every-day Bk.* II. 1457 No horseshoe nor magpye shall baffle our skill. **1824** SCOTT *Redgauntlet* ch. xi, Your wife's a witch, man; you should nail a horse-shoe on your chamber door. **1851** D. WILSON *Preh. Ann.* (1863) II. III. iv. 124. One of the ancient horse-shoes is described as consisting of a solid piece of iron. **1895** ELWORTHY *Evil Eye* vi. 217 Here in Somerset, horseshoes are nailed on stable doors, hung up to the ceilings above the horses, or fastened to the walls of the cow-house, 'to keep off the pixies'.

b. *horseshoes*, the game of quoits. *dial.*

1825 in BROCKETT. **1846** *Ibid.* (ed. 3) I. 228 The game of quoits is called 'horse-shoes' in the North because sometimes played with horse-shoes.

2. Applied to things shaped like a horseshoe, or a circular arc larger than a semi-circle.

a. generally.

1489 CAXTON *Faytes of A.* I. xxiv. 73 The batayIle ought to be then ordred and made in manere of a hors-shoo. **1725** DE FOE *Voy. round World* (1840) 130 The river making a kind of a double horse-shoe. **1770** WASHINGTON *Writ.* (1889) II. 298 The Ohio running round it in the nature of a horse-shoe. **1799** KIRWAN *Geol. Ess.* 337 When the dip forms what is called a horse-shoe, descending from one mountain or hill, and ascending on the opposite. **1866** ROGERS *Agric. & Prices* I. xx. 507 The horseshoe which lies between the wooded hills of Maidenhead, Wycombe and Marlow.

b. *Fortification.* (See quot. 1704.)

1698 FROGER *Voy.* 108 Three pieces of Fortification call'd Horse-Shooes. **1704** J. HARRIS *Lex. Techn.*, *Horse-Shooe*, in Fortification, is a Work sometimes of a round, and sometimes of an Oval Figure, raised in the Ditch of a Marshy Place, or in low Grounds, and border'd with a Parapet. **1717** tr. *Frezier's Voy.* 312 That Fortress has no other Out-works, besides a Horse-shooe next the Port, and a little Cover'd-way.

c. *Ship-building.* = *horseshoe clamp* in 5 d.

c **1850** *Rudim. Navig.* (Weale) 125 *Horse-shoes*, large straps of iron or copper shaped like a horse-shoe and let into the stem and gripe on opposite sides, through which they are bolted together to secure the gripe to the stem.

d. *Turning-lathe.* (See quot.)

1875 KNIGHT *Dict. Mech.*, *Horseshoe*..2. A movable support for varying the gearing and the velocity of the screw which moves the slide.

e. A horseshoe bend. *U.S.*

1795 in *Amer. Speech* (1963) XXXVIII. 183 In the bend, or horse shoe..is a neck of land about 4 or 500 yards wide. *a* **1910** [see FETCH *v.* 9].

f. *Logic.* (See quots. 1926, 1954.) Cf. HOOK *sb.*[1] 10 d.

1926 H. M. SHEFFER in *Isis* VIII. 231 The authors (1)..inform us, 'unofficially', that they are privately convinced that 'either *p* is false or *q* is true' (2) *means* '*p* implies *q*'; and they henceforth regard '*p* horseshoe *q*' as *meaning* '*p* implies *q*'. **1952** F. B. FITCH *Symbolic Logic* 15 The horseshoe symbol can be read as 'implies', but a more accurate reading is the *if-then* reading. **1954** I. M. COPI *Symbolic Logic* ii. 17 We introduce the new symbol '⊃', called a horseshoe, to represent the partial meaning common to all conditional statements. **1959** *Listener* 30 Apr. 757/2 He spent another [term] worrying about the ordinary use of the words 'if-then' whereas logicians had assured us that nothing but the 'horse-shoe' was worth talking about.

3. *Bot.* The same as *horse-vetch*: see 5 d.

1578 LYTE *Dodoens* IV. xxxi. 490 The thirde kinde is called ..in English Horse shoe. **1597** GERARDE *Herbal* II. d. 1057 Horse shooe commeth vp in certaine vntilled and sunny places of Italy and Languedock. **1711** J. PETIVER in *Phil. Trans.* XXVII. 387 *Horse-shoes*..The Pods of this elegant Plant resemble a Half moon, or Horse-shoe.

4. *Zool.* **a.** A horseshoe-crab: see 5 d. **b.** An American name of a bivalve mollusc, *Lutraria elliptica*, the oval otter-shell.

1775 ROMANS *Florida* 302 A crab..called in the southern province a king crab, and to the northward a horse-shoe. **1850** HAWTHORNE *Scarlet L.* xv. (1883) 213 She seized a live horseshoe by the tail.

5. *attrib.* and *Comb.* **a.** Simple attrib. 'of a horseshoe', as in ***horseshoe-fashion, form, shape.***

1712 J. JAMES tr. *Le Blond's Gardening* 26 Great Stairs made Horse-shoo-Fashion. **1837** *Penny Cycl.* VII. 23/2 Nose..bordered by a wide crest of a horseshoe shape. **1874** PARKER *Goth. Archit.* I. iii. 66 Norman arches are not unfrequently of the horse-shoe form.

b. *attrib.* passing into *adj.* 'Of the form of a horseshoe, or arc larger than a semicircle', as ***horseshoe arch, bend, brooch, curve, door, moustache, table.***

1770 DUCHESS OF NORTHUMBERLAND *Diary* 10 June (1926) 139 In the midst of the Room were two Horse Shoe Tables the ends of which pretty near touching form'd a Kind of Oval. **1796** COMBE *Boydell's Thames* II. 71. The horse-shoe bend that begins at Mortlake. **1812–16** J. SMITH *Panorama Sc. & Art.* I. 131 A horse-shoe arch has its centre above the spring. **1857** C. M. YONGE *Let.* 1 Oct. (1903) viii. 212 A great horse-shoe table, holding 116 people. **1873** HAYNE in Tristram *Moab* 375 Arches distinctly horse-shoe. **1875** 'MARK TWAIN' in *Atlantic Monthly* Aug. 192/2 The water cuts the alluvial banks of the 'lower' river into deep horseshoe curves. **1884** *Graphic* 22 Nov. 538/1 The delegates took their places to the right and left of him at a horseshoe table. **1893** T. B. FOREMAN *Trip to Spain* etc. 64 Through the usual horse-shoe door, we enter an open court. **1926** F. M. FORD *Man could stand Up* I. i. 17 The gentlemen with sergeant-majors' horse-shoe moustaches. **1950** G. BRENAN *Face of Spain* ii. 42 The double horseshoe arches, striped buff-white and brick-rose, arrest one by their strangeness and novelty.

c. similative, parasynthetic, etc., as ***horseshoe-shaped, horseshoe-like*** adjs.

1776 PENNANT *Zool.* IV. 48 A horse-shoe-shaped mark of deep purple. **1892** E. REEVES *Homeward Bound* 276 A small room entered by a horse-shoe-like arch. **1895** *Westm. Gaz.* 4 Sept. 3/3 The tunnel..is 21 ft. high and 19 ft. broad, and is horseshoe-shaped.

d. Special combs.: **horseshoe anvil** (see quot.); **horseshoe-bat**, any species of bat having a nose-leaf more or less horseshoe-shaped, esp. *Rhinolophus ferrum-equinum*, *R. hipposideros*, and *Phyllorhina armigera*; **horseshoe clamp** (see quot.); **horseshoe-crab**, a crab-like animal of the genus *Limulus*, so called from the shape of its shell; a king crab; **horseshoe-fern**, (in New Zealand) *Marattia fraxinea*, called in Australia *potato-fern* (Morris *Austral Eng.* 1898); **horseshoe goose, head, kidney, magnet**, (see quots.); **horseshoe-nail**, a nail of soft iron for fastening on horseshoes; hence ***horseshoe-nail machine, rod***; **horseshoe-vetch**, a leguminous plant (*Hippocrepis comosa*) bearing umbels of yellow flowers, and jointed pods each division of which resembles a horseshoe.

1875 KNIGHT *Dict. Mech.*, **Horseshoe-anvil*, one which corresponds in shape and size to the hoof of a horse, and has shanks which permit its adjustment in the socket-hole of the anvil, in either a natural or a reversed position. **1774** GOLDSM. *Nat. Hist.* IV. 140 The *Horse shoe Bat, with an odd protuberance round its upper lip, somewhat in the form of an horse-shoe. **1847** CARPENTER *Zool.* §169 Two species are known in England under the name of the Greater and Lesser Horse-shoe Bats. **1875** KNIGHT *Dict. Mech.*, **Horseshoe-clamp* (*Ship-building*), an iron strap by which the gripe and fore-foot are attached. **1865** PARKMAN *Champlain* iii. (1875) 231 The *horseshoe-crab awakened his especial curiosity. **1849** *Zoologist* VII. 2393 The Egyptian goose is the '*horse-shoe goose'. **1727–41** CHAMBERS *Cycl.*, **Horse-shoe Head*, a disease in infants, wherein the sutures of the skull are too open, or too great a vacuity is left between them. **1887** *Syd. Soc. Lex.*, **Horse-shoe kidney*..a variety of the kidneys in man in which they are connected by their lower ends, so as to make one horseshoe-shaped organ. **1785** G. ADAMS *Ess. Magnetism* (ed. 2) 419 To touch horseshoe magnets. **1822** IMISON *Sc. & Art* I. 409 A magnet, bent so that the two ends almost meet, is called a horse-shoe magnet. **1871** TYNDALL *Fragm. Sc.* (1879) II. xvi. 441 He bent it into a continous ring, which..he caused to rotate rapidly close to the poles of a horse-shoe magnet. **1415–16** *Durham MS. Sacr. Roll*, Et in furfure et *horsescho-nayle, xixs. xjd. **1800** tr. *Lagrange's Chem.* II. 97 Six parts of iron in small fragments, as points of horse-shoe nails. **1888** *Law Rep.* 13 App. Cas. 401 A patent for the manufacture of horse-shoe nails. **1875** KNIGHT *Dict. Mech.*, **Horse-shoe Nail-machine*, one in which rods of iron are shaped into nails for the purpose stated. **1894** *Daily News* 22 Jan. 7/4 Rolled horseshoe nail rods (charcoal) are priced at £16 10s. **1706** J. LEE *Introd. Bot.* (1788) 282 *Hippocrepis*, *Horseshoe Vetch.

ˈhorseshoe, *v.* [f. prec. sb.: cf. SHOE *v.*]

1. *trans.* To provide with horseshoes.

2. *Arch.* To make (an arch) horseshoe-shaped.

1874 J. FERGUSSON *Hist. Archit.* (ed. 2) I. IV. vi. I. 391 A Sassanian arch..horse-shoed to the extent of one-tenth of its diameter.

So **horse-shoer** (-ʃuːə(r)), one who makes horseshoes, or shoes horses; **ˈhorse-shoeing,** the art or craft of shoeing horses.

1591 SPARRY tr. *Catton's Geomancie* 76 Craftsmen working by yron, as horse-shooers, locke-smiths, and such like. **1869** G. FLEMING (*title*) Horse-Shoes and Horse-Shoeing. **1888** *Pall Mall G.* 24 Sept. 11/2 The horse-shoers wore new russet leather aprons, with blood-red horseshoe stamped in the centre.

ˈhorse-skin. The skin of a horse; leather made of a horse's skin. Also *attrib.*

c **1340** *Cursor M.* 2250 (Fairf.) þai dight ham..wiþ hors skynnys and camel hide. **1654** tr. *Martini's Conq. China* 35 Their Boots..of Horse-skin very neatly drest. **1851** MAYNE REID *Scalp Hunt.* v, The soft clinging sand already overtopped my horse-skin boots.

horse-tail, ˈhorsetail.

1. a. A horse's tail.

c **1400** *Destr. Troy* 10311 He..Festnyt hym..by his fete euyn, Hard by the here of his horse tayle. *a* **1533** LD. BERNERS *Huon* lxxxi. 251, I say and iuge that Gerarde be drawen at horse taylles, and then hangyd. **1596** SHAKS. *Tam. Shr.* IV. i. 96 Let them..not presume to touch a haire of my Masters horse-taile, till they kisse their hands. **1737** POPE *Hor. Epist.* II. i. 63 Then by the rule that made the Horse-tail bare, I pluck out year by year, as hair by hair. **1846** H. TORRENS *Rem. Milit. Hist.* I. 162 The Turk..made his standard of a horse-tail.

b. Used in Turkey as an ornament, as a military standard, the symbol of war, and as an ensign denoting the rank of a pasha: see TAIL; hence, †the office of a pasha (*obs.*). Anciently used also by the Bulgarians.

1613 PURCHAS *Pilgrimage* (1614) 695 Horse-tailes are great jewels, and two slaves will be given for one taile. **1683** *Lond. Gaz.* No. 1860/6 The King of Poland has taken two Horse Tails (which are the Turks Signals of War). **1703** MAUNDRELL *Journ. Jerus.* (1721) 127 Next were brought the Bassa's two Horse Tails. **1711** LUTTRELL *Brief Rel.* (1857) VI. 709 The sultan has resolved..to renew the war against Muscovy, having for that end caused the horse tail (their signal of war) to be placed again before the seraglio. **1771** SMOLLETT *Humph. Cl.* 5 June, The dey will make you a horse-tail. **1840** *Blackw. Mag.* XLVII. 219 While all Christendom trembled at the sight of the horse-tails, Soliman died. **1847** DISRAELI *Tancred* VI. x. **1855** MILMAN *Lat. Chr.* v. viii. II. 423 They [the Bulgarians] were to go to battle no longer under their old national ensign, the horse-tail, but under the banner of the Cross.

c. Usu. **horse's tail.** A woman's hair-style in which the hair is arranged to resemble the shape of the tail of a horse; a 'pony-tail'.

1872 TROLLOPE *Eustace Diamonds* (1873) II. xxxiv. 100 How a man can like to kiss a face with a dirty horse's tail all whizzling about it, is what I can't at all understand. **1953** R. FULLER *Second Curtain* v. 79 Her hair done in a fringe and horse's tail. **1955** G. FREEMAN *Liberty Man* I. iii. 48 She had blondish hair tied into a horse's tail with a piece of black ribbon. **1960** 'J. & E. BONETT' *No Grave for Lady* ii. 27 She wore jeans and a cotton sweater, her hair was in a horse-tail.

d. (See quots.)

1880 L. HIGGIN *Handbk. Embroidery* i. 8 'Japanese gold thread'..must..be laid on, and stitched down with a fine yellow silk, known as 'Maltese', or 'Horse-tail'. **1960** B. SNOOK *Eng. Hist. Embroidery* 104 A woman's court dress (1780)... Variation is obtained by the use of floss silk and horsetail, a tightly twisted silk.

2. a. The common name of the genus *Equisetum*, consisting of cryptogamous plants with hollow jointed stems, and whorls of slender branches at the joints; the whole having some resemblance to a horse's tail.

1538 TURNER *Libellus*, *Hippuris*, latinis dicitur equisetum, aut cauda equina..aliquibus dicitur Hors tayle, non-nullis Hally Water stryncle, Dysshewasshynges. **1577** B. GOOGE *Heresbach's Husb.* I. (1586) 45 For Pasture or Meddowe..the woorst as Plinie saith, is Russhes, Fearne, and Horsetayle. **1664** POWER *Exp. Philos.* I. 31 The Water spider, hath two hairy geniculated horns, knotted or joynted at several divisions like..Hors-tayl. **1794** MARTYN *Rousseau's Bot.* xxxii. 488 Wood Horsetail has the leaves compound or divided, and the spikes at the end of the same stems. **1873** MRS. KING *Disciples, Ugo Bassi* iv. (1877) 146 Brushing past the rigid arms Of hideous giant horsetails.

b. †**female horse-tail**, an old name for *Hippuris* or MARE'S-TAIL, a phanerogamous plant somewhat resembling *Equisetum* in habit. **shrubby horse-tail**, name for shrubs of the genus *Ephedra* (N.O. *Gnetaceæ*), having small scale-like leaves resembling the branches of *Equisetum*. **tree horse-tail** = *horsetail-tree*: see 5.

1597 GERARDE *Herbal* II. ccccxlii. 957 *Cauda equina fœmina*, the female Horse taile. **1794** MARTYN *Rousseau's Bot.* xi. 116 In the books it [Hippuris] is called Female Horsetail or Mare's-tail. **1884** MILLER *Plant-n.*, Horse-tail, Great Shrubby, *Ephedra distachya*. *Ibid.*, *Casuarina equisetifolia*...Swamp Oak of Australia, Tree-Horse-tail.

3. 'A hippurite.' (*Cent. Dict.*)

4. *Anat.* The leash of nerves in which the spinal cord ends: called in mod.L. *cauda equina*.

5. *attrib.* and *Comb.*, as ***horsetail-like*** adj., ***horse-tail standard*** (see 1 b); resembling a horse's tail, as ***horse-tail cloud, lock***; also

horsetail-lichen, name for various species of *Alectoria*, esp. *A. jubata*, having a slender pendulous thallus; **horsetail-tree**, a tree of the genus *Casuarina*, esp. the Australian *C. equisetifolia*, so called from the resemblance of the leafless jointed branches to those of *Equisetum*.

1600 ROWLANDS *Lett. Humours Blood* C, Aske Humors, why a Feather he doth weare?.. Or what he doth with such a Horse-taile locke? **1612** *Pasquil's Night-Cap* (1877) 7 His sweet worship with his horse-taile locke. **1831** HOWITT *Seasons* (1837) 228 The vault of heaven was strewn with what are called horse-tail clouds. **1891** *Pall Mall G.* 23 Oct. 3/2 [A yucca with] enormous horsetail-like panicles of white flowers.

'horseward, orig. *to horse-ward*: see -WARD.

1611 SPEED *Hist. Gt. Brit.* IX. xviii. (1632) 901 Giuing command to make themselues shortly ready, for their Lords were to horse-ward.

'horse-way. A road by which a horse may pass; a bridle-road; sometimes = cart-road.

985 *Charter of Æthelred* in Kemble *Cod. Dipl.* III. 219 To horswegеs heale. **1517** TORKINGTON *Pilgr.* (1884) 66 With owt the Citys ys an horse wey vnder neth a mownteyn. **1532-3** *Act 24 Hen. VIII*, c. 5 Any common high-way cartway horseway or fotewayes. **1605** SHAKS. *Lear* IV. i. 58 *Glou.* Know'st thou the way to Douer? *Edg.* Both style and gate; Horseway and foot-path. **1766** GOLDSM. *Vic. W.* x, I therefore walked back by the horse-way, which was five miles round, though the footway was but two. **1875** POSTE *Gaius* IV. §3 A right of horse-way or carriage-way through his land.

horsewhip ('hɔːshwɪp), *sb.* A whip for driving or controlling a horse.

1694 G. FOX *Jrnl.* (1827) I. 108 Then they.. put me into the stocks,.. and they brought dog-whips and horse-whips, threatening to whip me. **1766** SMOLLETT *Trav.* I. xv. 254 (Jod.) Riding out.. with his horsewhip in his hand. **1809** MALKIN *Gil Blas* x. xi. (Rtldg.) 377 Those impracticable beings, on whom good example, good advice, and a good horsewhip, are equally thrown away. **1843** *Knickerbocker* XXII. 56 I'd like to have some on 'em tied to a tree, and have fair play at 'em with this horse-whip. **1856** P. CARTWRIGHT *Autobiogr.* (1858) viii. 74 They came drunk, and armed with .. horse-whips. **1965** S. HULT tr. *G. de Coulteray's Sadism in Movies* 111 It is horsewhips with which Christine Nordeu and Bery Baxter are armed in *Idol of Paris*.

'horsewhip, *v.* [f. prec.: cf. WHIP *v.*] *trans.* To chastise with a horsewhip.

1768 BICKERSTAFF *Lionel & Clarisse* III. ii, If you are a gentleman, you shall fight me; if you are a scrub, I'll horsewhip you. **1829** LYTTON *Devereux* V. v, I will fulfil your errand, and horsewhip him soundly. **1877** BLACK *Green Past.* viii, If I were a man I would horsewhip him.

fig. **1790** J. B. MORETON *Mann. W. Ind.* 183 That he horsewhips and shoots you dead with a murdering infamous tongue.

Hence **'horsewhipped** *ppl. a.*, **'horsewhipping** *vbl. sb.* Also **'horsewhipper**, **'horsewhipship**.

c **1774** T. ERSKINE in *Spirit Pub. Jrnls.* (1799) III. 320 To save thy horse-whipp'd back from daily fears. **1808** —— *Ep. to Mrs. Clarke* ibid. V. 405 A horse-whipper of carpets. **1829** LYTTON *Devereux* V. v, If ever you meet him, give him a good horse-whipping on my account. **1842** *Tait's Mag.* IX. 457 Ballinasloe, where this person performed his feat of horsewhipship. **1875** W. S. HAYWARD *Love agst. World* 20 If he tamely submits to a horsewhipping, he must be more or less than man.

horsewoman ('hɔːsˌwʊmən). A woman who rides on horseback; a female equestrian. Usually with qualifying adj.

1564-78 BULLEYN *Dial. agst. Pest.* (1888) 58 Your mother was a good horsewoman, and loued ridyng well as any gentlewoman that euer I knewe in my life. **1626** MIDDLETON *Wom. Beware Wom.* II. i, Sh'ad need be a good horsewoman, and sit fast. **1814** JANE AUSTEN *Mansf. Park* vii, His comments on Miss Crawford's great cleverness as a horsewoman. **1887** FRITH *Autobiog.* I. xxi. 279 Miss Gilbert was a most accomplished horsewoman.

Hence **'horsewomanship**.

1857 *Tait's Mag.* XXIV. 332 Her excellent and bold horsewomanship attracted.. admiration. **1882** 'ANNIE THOMAS' *Allerton Towers* II. vi. 105 A severe critic upon horsewomanship.

horsfordite ('hɔːsfədaɪt). *Min.* [f. the name of E. N. *Horsford* (1818–1893), American chemist: see -ITE[1].] A brittle, silvery white antimonide of copper, perhaps Cu_5Sb.

1888 LAIST & NORTON in *Amer. Chem. Jrnl.* X. 62 This new mineral is named horsfordite, in honor of Professor Horsford, formerly Rumford Professor of Chemistry at Harvard University. **1923** J. W. MELLOR *Inorg. & Theoret. Chem.* III. xxi. 7 The antimonide: horsfordite, Cu_6Sb. **1970** *Min. Abstr.* XXI. 340/2 The properties of cuprostibite are compared with and differ considerably from those of horsfordite, chalcostibite, tetrahedrite, and famatinite.

horsiness ('hɔːsɪnɪs). [f. HORSY *a.* + -NESS.] The quality of being horsy, esp. in sense 2.

1864 *Daily Tel.* 19 July, There is no keeping clear of 'horsiness' and the horsey. **1875** TENNYSON *Q. Mary* III. v, It shall be all my study for one hour To rose and lavender my horsiness, Before I dare to glance upon your Grace. **1882** MISS BRADDON *Mt. Royal* III. vi. 117 The St. Aubyn girls .. finding him a kindred spirit in horseyness and doggyness, took him at once into their confidence.

'horsing, *vbl. sb.* [f. HORSE *v.* + -ING[1].]

1. Provision of horses or cavalry.

1382 WYCLIF *Deut.* xvii. 16 Bi noumbre of horsynge arered [Vulg. *equitatus numero sublevatus*]. *c* **1400** *Rowland & O.* 389, I hafe horssynge at my will. *c* **1650** *Don Bellianis* 72 Send half of your men.. taking with them double horsing that when we arrive.. we may find fresh horses. *c* **1896** *N.B. Daily Mail* 17 June 4 The ordinary expenses for horsing, traffic, and general management [of a tramway].

2. The 'covering' of a mare.

1552 HULOET, Horsynge of a mare. **1565-73** COOPER *Thesaurus*, *Catulio*, to desire the male:.. to go to rutter: to horsing: to blissoning. **1577** B. GOOGE *Heresbach's Husb.* III. (1586) 125 b, She.. is taken to be barren.. yᵗ takes not at yᵉ first horsing. **1727** POPE, etc. *Mart. Scribl.* I. vi.

3. A mounting as on a horse; a flogging inflicted while on another's back: see HORSE *v.* 4 b.

1688 R. HOLME *Armoury* III. 105/1 *Horsing*, of Beer, is the setting of one Barrel upon two. **1824** W. IRVING *T. Trav.* I. 261, I felt so indignant at the ignominious horsing I had incurred.

4. *Cutlery trade.* (See quot.)

1831 J. HOLLAND *Manuf. Metal* I. 292 What is technically called the *horsing*, being in fact, the seat or saddle upon which the grinder sits astride while at work. **1870** READE [see sense 5].

5. *attrib.* and *Comb.*: **horsing-block, stone** = HORSE-BLOCK 1 and 2; **horsing-chain**, the chain that fastens a grinder's seat to the framework of the grindstone.

1661 *Manch. Court Leet Rec.* (1887) IV. 300 For a Horseing stone att Hyde Crosse. **1662** GURNALL *Chr. in Arm.* verse 18. viii. §3 (1669) 452/2 [He] makes his seeming piety to God but as a horsing-block to get into the Creatures Saddle. **1708** THORESBY *Diary* (Hunter) II. 13 We met with a great number of horsing-stones, each of three steps, but cut out of one entire stone. **1856** S. C. BREES *Gloss. Terms*, *Horsing block*, a square timber framing, used in forming excavations for raising the ends of the wheeling planks. **1807** E. PEACOCK *Ralf Skirl.* II. 23 A stone horsing-block stood near the doorway. **1870** READE *Put yourself in his place* I. 201 The stone went like a pistol-shot, and snapped the horsing-chains like thread.. the grinder.. had fallen forward on his broken horsing.

'horsing, *ppl. a.* [f. as prec. + -ING[2]; but in sense 1, app. for phrase *a-horsing*.]

1. Of a mare: Desiring the horse; in heat.

1577 B. GOOGE *Heresbach's Husb.* III. (1586) 126 b, When you perceive yᵗ she is Horsing.. put to your stallion. **1870** BLAINE *Encycl. Rur. Sports* (ed. 3) §1011 Mares come into season about February, and continue to be horsing, as it is called, until the end of June or middle of July.

†**2.** Riding on or having to do with horses; horsy.

c **1613** MIDDLETON *No Wit like a Woman's* II. iii, A young horsing gentleman.

horsly, obs. f. HOARSELY, HORSELY.

horson, obs. f. WHORESON.

horst (hɔːst). *Geol.* [a. G. *horst* heap, mass, cluster, sandbank, etc.; introduced in its geol. sense by E. Suess (*Antlitz d. Erde* (1883) I. I. iii. 167).] A block of the earth's surface which has been raised relative to the surrounding land and is bounded by faults on some or all sides.

1893 *Q. Jrnl. Geol. Soc.* XLIX. 77 We have, therefore, sunken *massifs* both west and east of the Dürrenstein; that mountain itself remains at a higher level between the two, and may be called a 'Horst' in the sense originally applied by Suess. **1904** H. SOLLAS tr. *Suess's Face of Earth* I. I. iii. 126 If the outer borders of two fields of subsidence approach each other so that a ridge is left between them, on both sides of which the two areas of depression descend more or less in the form of steps, then we have what we shall distinguish, making use again of a common mining word, as a *horst*. **1910** [see GRABEN]. **1914** G. A. J. COLE *Growth of Europe* ii. 22 Far older masses have asserted themselves.. as horsts, that is, as upstanding blocks from which material has been faulted down on all sides. **1942** M. P. BILLINGS *Struct. Geol.* xi. 205 Horsts range in size from those that are only a few inches wide to those that are many miles wide. **1944** A. HOLMES *Princ. Physical Geol.* xix. 416 Between the horsts of the Vosges and the Black Forest the Rhine flows through a rift valley. **1970** *Sci. Amer.* Feb. 37/3 The evidences of crustal movement are in plain view as wide-open fissures, horsts and grabens that form a classic graben structure of steps down the sides of a major depression.

horst, dial. f. HURST.

Horst Wessel (hɔːst 'vɛsəl). The name of the author (1907–1930) of the words of the official anthem of the German Nazi party, used *attrib.* in ***Horst Wessel lied, song***. Also *ellipt.*

1937 V. BARTLETT *This is my Life* x. 165 Hundreds of arms went out in the Hitler salute, hundreds of voices yelled the *Horst Wessel Lied*. **1968** R. COLLIN *Locust on Wind* xv. 137 This time it will be lounge suits instead of brownshirts, and no Horst Wessel while we're on television. **1968** J. BLACKBURN *Young Man from Lima* xvii. 173 The Horst Wessel song was one of the greatest hymns of hate that had ever been composed. **1969** *Guardian* 6 Oct. 10/6 In spite of the fears of churchmen, 'Lay, lady, lay' is likely to cause less damage than the 'Horst Wessel Lied'. **1970** *New York* 16 Nov. 35/2 Someone wondered when the cornball band.. was going to.. get down to the serious strains of the Horst Wessel Song.

horsy ('hɔːsɪ), *a.* Also **-ey**. [f. HORSE *sb.* + -Y.]

1. Of, pertaining to, or of the nature of a horse or horses.

1591 SPENSER *Virg. Gnat* 41 Th' halfe-horsy people, Centaures hight. **1864** *Daily Tel.* 19 Oct., Elk-flesh is a decidedly horsey species of game.

2. Having to do with horses; addicted or devoted to horses, horse-racing, and matters of the stable; affecting the dress and language of a groom or jockey.

1852 R. S. SURTEES *Sponge's Sp. Tour* i. 3 [His] groomy gait and horsey propensities. **1858** *Almae Matres* 6 The horsy individual then related an anecdote. **1881** *Athenæum* 19 Mar. 392/1 'In Luck's Way' is a horsy, if not a racy story. **1882** MISS BRADDON *Mt. Royal* II. v. 111 They.. were both horsey and doggy, and plain-spoken to brusqueness.

3. Of the mare: Desiring the horse.

1870 BLAINE *Encycl. Rur. Sports* §1012 Separated from other mares, which, becoming horsy, will kick them.

4. *Comb.*, as ***horsy-looking***, ***-minded***.

1852 R. S. SURTEES *Sponge's Sp. Tour* lxiv. 361 He's a horsey lookin' sort o' man. **1886** *Cycl. Tour. Club Gaz.* May 183/2 Horsey-minded road trustees and sheriffs.

Hence **'horsyism**, horsy quality and practice; **'horsily** *adv.*, in a horsy manner.

1882 *Daily News* 31 Jan. 5/7 Horseyism is a word that has been coined to express that inexplicable affinity which equine pursuits seem to have in some countries with rough manners and loud oaths. **1889** *Sat. Rev.* 30 Nov. 614/2 If he be horsily inclined.

hort, obs. form of HURT.

†**'hortal**, *a. rare.* [f. L. *hort-us* garden + -AL[1]: cf. med.L. *hortāle*, *-ālis* (Du Cange).] Growing in a garden; cultivated.

c **1700** A. DE LA PRYME *Diary* (Surtees) 316 Flowers, as well hortal as wild. **1926** G. C. DRUCE in J. J. Walker *Nat. Hist. Oxford Distr.* 119 Other hortal plants which have become established are several species of North-American Asters.

hortation (hɔː'teɪʃən). [ad. L. *hortātiōn-em*, n. of action f. *hortārī* to encourage, exhort.] The action of exhorting or inciting; exhortation.

1536 BELLENDEN *Cron. Scot.* (1821) I. 98 The Albianis, inflammit.. be this hortation, come forthwart weill arrayait on thair ennimes. **1620** GRANGER *Div. Log.* 4 Propounded in forme of a commandement, counsell, hortation. **1721** STRYPE *Eccl. Mem.* an. 1548 (R.) That he should by his hortation set the commons against the nobility and gentlemen.

hortative ('hɔːtətɪv), *a.* and *sb.* [ad. L. *hortātīv-us*, f. *hortārī* to exhort: see -IVE.]

A. *adj.* Characterized by exhortation, serving or tending to exhort.

1623 COCKERAM, *Hortatiue*, belonging to exhortation. **1651** HOWELL *Venice* 63 Hereupon Pope Vrban came.. and made this hortative Oration. **1854** *Tait's Mag.* XXI. 364 The narrative.. is vastly more interesting than the didactic or hortative. **1882** FARRAR *Early Chr.* I. 445 Many hortative and illustrative digressions.

B. *sb.* A hortatory speech; an address intended to exhort or encourage.

1607-12 BACON *Ess.*, *Marriage & Single Life* (Arb.) 268 Generalls commonlye in theire hortatives putt Men in minde of theire wives and Children. *c* **1645** HOWELL *Lett.* (1650) I. 72 Others incited him to it, and among other hortatives they told him [etc.]. **1884** *Jaunt in Junk* 253 So encouraging [were] the hortatives of Kinioch.

Hence **'hortatively** *adv.*, in a hortative manner; by way of exhortation.

1882 FARRAR *Early Chr.* II. 44 Are we to understand this phrase hortatively?

hortator (hɔː'teɪtə(r)). [a. L. *hortātor*, agent-n. f. *hortārī* to exhort.] One who exhorts or encourages; an exhorter.

1880 L. WALLACE *Ben-Hur* 140 With an angry crash, down fell the gravel of the hortator.

hortatory ('hɔːtətərɪ), *a.* [ad. late L. *hortātōri-us*, f. *hortārī* to exhort: see -ORY.] Of, pertaining to, or characterized by, exhortation or encouragement; hortative, exhortatory.

1586 A. DAY *Eng. Secretary* I. (1625) 20 Hortatorie and Dehortatorie. **1612** T. TAYLOR *Comm. Titus* i. 9 After the doctrinall part followeth the hortatorie. *a* **1784** JOHNSON in *Boswell* (1831) I. 381 'Law's Serious Call' [he said] was the finest piece of hortatory theology in any language. **1878** W. C. SMITH *Hilda* (1879) 173 That night he went on, ceaseless, in his hortatory tone.

hortensia (hɔː'tɛnsɪə). [mod.L. (P. Commerson in A. L. de Jussieu *Genera Plantarum* (1789) 214), f. *Hortense*, adopted Christian name of the wife of J.-A. Lepaute (1720–*c* 1787), French clockmaker.] A variety of the common hydrangea, *Hydrangea macrophylla*, var. *hortensia*.

1799 *Curtis's Bot. Mag.* XIII. 438 Authors have entertained very different opinions as to what this plant really is; Jussieu following Commerson makes it an Hortensia,.. Dr. Smith an Hydrangea. **1866** LINDLEY & MOORE *Treas. Bot.* II. 598/2 Hortensia. (Fr.) *Hydrangea Hortensia*. **1906** *Daily Chron.* 9 Feb. 5/1 The bouquet was of artificial hortensias. **1961** *Amateur Gardening* 7 Oct. 25/1 A medium sized pure white 'hortensia'. **1969** *Dict. Gardening* (R. Hort. Soc.) Suppl. 42/1 Hydrangea. Cultivars of *H.* × *macrophylla*... (*a*) Hortensias. Globose corymbs of mostly sterile flowers.

hor'tensial, *a.* ? *Obs.* [f. L. *hortensis*, *-ius*, of or belonging to a garden (f. *hortus* garden) + -AL[1].] Of or belonging to a garden; growing or cultivated in gardens.

1655 W. HOW *Let.* 20 Sept. in *Sir W. Browne's Wks.* (1848) III. 517 Wee shall adde our experiments; to this,

hortensiall..to that, *medicinall*. **1664** EVELYN *Sylva* Introd. §3 Such [trees] as are sative and hortensial.

hor'tensian, *a.* ? *Obs.* [f. as prec. + -AN.] = prec.

1657 TOMLINSON *Renou's Disp.* 229 Mallows..is either Hortensian..or Sylvestrian. **1807** ROBINSON *Archæol. Græca* III. i. 188 Venus was named οὐρανία, the celestial;..ἡ ἐν κήποις, the hortensian.

horter, obs. form of HURTER *sb.*

horteyard: see HORTYARD.

horticolous (hɔː'tɪkələs), *a. rare.* [f. L. *hortus* garden + *col-ĕre* to inhabit + -OUS. Cf. mod.F. *horticole*.] 'Inhabiting or growing in the garden' (Mayne *Expos. Lex.* 1854).

†**hor'ticulist.** *Obs. rare.* [f. med.L. *horticula, -ulus* (Du Cange), 'gardener' (? for L. **horticola*, like *agricola*), f. *hortus* garden + *col-ĕre* to cultivate + -IST. (Cf. *agricolist* in same poem.)] A horticulturist.

1754 DODSLEY *Pub. Virtue, Agric.* II. 135 On Culture's hand Alone, do these Horticulists rely?

†**'horticultor.** *Obs. rare.* [ad. L. type **horticultor*, f. *hortus* garden + *cultor* cultivator. Cf. mod.F. *horticulteur*.] = HORTICULTURIST.

1760 BP. HILDERSLEY in W. Hanbury *Charities Church Langton* (1767) 114 To have paid my respects to the renowned horticultor at Church-Langton.

horticultural (hɔːtɪ'kʌltjʊərəl, -tʃər-), *a.* [f. as HORTICULTURE + -AL[1].] **1.** Of or pertaining to horticulture; connected with the cultivation of a garden.

1778–9 V. KNOX *Ess.* cxv. (R.), I should not hesitate to allot the first place, in an estimate of horticultural graces, to the weeping willow. **1805** T. A. KNIGHT (*title*) Report of a Committee of the Horticultural Society of London. **1820** SHELLEY *Witch Atl.* xxxii, Like an horticultural adept, Stole a strange seed, and wrapt it up in mould. **1872** YEATS *Growth Comm.* 141 [Haarlem] early celebrated for its horticultural produce.

2. Comb. ***horticultural exhibition, fête, show.***

1847 F. A. KEMBLE *Let.* 23 June in *Rec. Later Life* (1882) III. 204 Some *unique* foreign flower, sent..to blossom at the Chiswick *horticultural exhibition. **1840** J. ROMILLY *Diary* 16 July (1967) 197 We then went to the *Horticultural Fete in the dining room..at Downing. **1843** *Ainsworth's Mag.* IV. 100 A dazzling conservatory that looked like a *horticultural show. **1853** C. M. YONGE *Heir of Redclyffe* i. 3 This [camellia] is to go to the horticultural show. **1858** QUEEN VICTORIA *Let.* 21 Apr. in R. Fulford *Dearest Child* (1964) 93 We have just returned from a horticultural show in St. James's Hall. **1952** *Oxf. Jun. Encycl.* VI. 14 The most important horticultural show is the Chelsea Flower Show. **1973** P. MOYES *Curious Affair Third Dog* viii. 104 A sort of scroll proclaiming that Henry Heathfield had taken second prize for tomatoes at the County Horticultural Show.

horticulturally (hɔːtɪ'kʌltjʊərəlɪ, -tʃər-), *adv.* [See -LY[2].] In the way of horticulture.

1899 O. WILDE *Importance of being Earnest* II. 69, I spoke horticulturally. My metaphor was drawn from fruits. **1927** *Observer* 27 Nov. 13/3 It is not only horticulturally that the Riviera is making ready.

horticulture ('hɔːtɪˌkʌltjʊə(r), -tʃə(r)). [ad. L. type **horticultūra* cultivation of a garden, f. *hortus* garden + *cultūra* CULTURE: after *agriculture*. Cf. mod.F. *horticulture*, admitted by Acad. 1835.]

The cultivation of a garden; the art or science of cultivating or managing gardens, including the growing of flowers, fruits, and vegetables.

1678 PHILLIPS (ed. 4) App., *Horticulture*, the tillage, dressing, or improvement of Gardens, as Agriculture of other Grounds. **1699** EVELYN *Acetaria* Ep. Ded. a j b, The Product of Horticulture, and the Field. **1713** A. EVANS *Vertumnus* xix, Hail, Horticulture's Sapient King! Receive the Homage which we bring. **1849** MACAULAY *Hist. Eng.* iii. I. 410 Temple, in his intervals of leisure, had tried many experiments in horticulture.

horticulturist (hɔːtɪ'kʌltjʊərɪst). [f. prec. + -IST.] One who practises the art of horticulture; a gardener; esp. one who practises gardening scientifically as a profession.

1818 TODD, *Horticulturist*, one who is fond of, or skilled in, the art of cultivating gardens. **1820** SCOTT *Abbot* xxviii. **1836** PRICHARD *Phys. Hist. Man* I. i. §5. 139 Hybrid plants are continually produced in gardens..by a process well known to horticulturists.

hortle, obs. form of HURTLE.

hortolan, hortulan(e, obs. ff. ORTOLAN.

hortonolite (hɔː'tɒnəlaɪt, 'hɔːtənəlaɪt). *Min.* [f. the name of Silas Ryneck *Horton* (b. 1820), American amateur mineralogist + -O + -LITE.] A silicate mineral, $(Fe, Mg)_2SiO_4$, yellow or greenish-yellow on fresh fracture, having a preponderance of iron over magnesium and often some substitution by manganese (see also quot. 1955).

1869 G. J. BRUSH in *Amer. Jrnl. Sci.* XCVIII. 19 It is proper to designate this new variety with a special name, and I propose for it the name *Hortonolite*, after Mr. Horton, who first discovered the mineral. **1939** *Amer. Mineral.* XXIV. 24 At present the names commonly accepted, in order of increasing richness [of Fe_2SiO_4] in the fayalite molecule are forsterite, chrysolite, hyalosiderite, hortonolite and fayalite. **1955** M. H. HEY *Index Min. Species* (ed. 2) 124 *Hortonolite*. $4[(Fe, Mg)_2SiO_4]$, with Fe··> Mg (in Hortonolite proper, Fe_2SiO_4 50 to 70 mols. %)... The original Hortonolite contained 4% MnO. Olivine family. **1968** EMBREY & PHEMISTER tr. *Kostov's Mineralogy* 291 Titanolivine is rich in Ti; hortonolite is rich in iron.

hortour, obs. form of HURTER *sb.*[1]

hortulan ('hɔːtjʊlən), *a.* (*sb.*) Also 7–9 hortulane, 8 hortuline. [ad. L. *hortulān-us* of or belonging to a garden, sb. a gardener, f. *hortulus* dim. of *hort-us* garden. In earlier form ORTOLAN, from It. *ortolano*.] Of or belonging to a garden or gardening; garden-.

1664 EVELYN *Kal. Hort.* Ep. Ded., This Hortulan Kalendar is yours. **1669** J. ROSE *Eng. Vineyard* Pref., All things which concern his hortulan profession. **1783** W. F. MARTYN *Geog. Mag.* II. 236 Fruits and other hortulane productions are drawn by dogs round the streets. *a* **1817** T. DWIGHT *Trav. New Eng.* (1821) II. 311 The hortulan vegetables, common to other parts of New-England. **1822** *New Monthly Mag.* IV. 83 A rarer display of architectural and hortulan splendour.

†**B.** *sb.* A gardener. *Obs. rare.*

1526 [see ORTOLAN].

†**hortu'lanary**, *a. Obs. rare.* = HORTULAN *a.*

1715 PITTIS *Life Dr. Radcliffe* 24 The Doctor's servants made such a Havock amongst his Hortulanary Curiosities.

‖**hortus conclusus** ('hɒtəs kən'kluːsəs). [Lat., = enclosed garden, in reference to *Song Sol.* iv. 12.] **a.** An enclosed, inviolate garden; in spiritual and exegetical tradition, the symbol of the soul, the Church, or the virginity of Mary. **b.** In Art, a painting of the Madonna and Child in an enclosed garden. Freq. *transf.*

1624 DONNE *LXXX Sermons* (1640) xvii. 165 The University is a Paradise, Rivers of knowledge are there, Arts and Sciences flow from thence. Counsell Tables are *Horti conclusi* (as it is said in the Canticles). **1852** A. B. JAMESON *Legends Madonna* p. xlviii, The Enclosed Garden (*Hortus conclusus*)... I have seen this enclosed garden very significantly placed in the background of the Annunciation, and in pictures of the Immaculate Conception. Sometimes the enclosure is formed of a treillage or hedge of roses, as in a beautiful Virgin by Francia. **1940** 'M. INNES' *There came both Mist & Snow* i. 7, I shall get more surely on the rails if I drop ancestry and the *hortus conclusus* of history and begin again with some account of the Priory itself. **1947** 'N. BLAKE' *Minute for Murder* ix. 208 People that would trample over her little *hortus conclusus*. **1956** M. SWAN *Paradise Garden* xvii. 161 The protective hedges of his *hortus conclusus* were rotten and useless with disease. **1957** N. FRYE *Anat. Criticism* 152 The symbol of the body of the Virgin as a *hortus conclusus*. **1963** *Listener* 21 Mar. 520/2 Nepal has long been the *hortus conclusus* of the fabulous Ranas.

‖**hortus siccus** ('hɔːtəs 'sɪkəs). [Lat., = dry garden.] An arranged collection of dried plants; a herbarium.

1687 A. LOVELL tr. *Thevenot's Trav.* Pref. Bij, It is a Collection of all the Plants of those Countries, which in Botanick terms is called a *Hortus Siccus*. **1759** JOHNSON *Idler* No. 64 ⁋5, I..bought a *Hortus Siccus* of inestimable value. **1824** MISS MITFORD *Village* Ser. I. (1863) 38 Flowers in the court looking fit for a *hortus siccus*. **1853** KANE *Grinnell Exp.* vi. 48 (Stanf.) The furs were packed, my sketches and wet *hortus siccus* [mosses, etc.] properly combined, and we started again.

fig. **1763** GRAY *Let. to Wharton* 5 Aug., [At Cambridge] where no events grow, though we preserve those of former days, by way of *Hortus Siccus* in our libraries. **1790** BURKE *Fr. Rev.* (ed. 3) 15 The ample collection of known classes, genera, and species, which at present beautify the *hortus siccus* of dissent.

†**'hortyard.** *Obs.* Also 6–7 horteyard, hort-yard. [An affected alteration of *orchard*, frequent in 16–17th c., influenced by L. *hortus* garden. The earliest OE. form was *ortȝeard*, whence later *orceard*, ME. *orchard* (from *c* 1200); in 16th c. this was written by some *ortyard*, after med.L. *ortus* or It. *orto* garden, and still later *hortyard*.] A garden of fruit trees, an ORCHARD; sometimes a garden in general.

1555 W. WATREMAN *Fardle Facions* App. 323 He that planteth an horteyarde. **1562** TURNER *Herbal* II. 60 a, The hortyard of Pembrok hall in Cambridge. **1579–80** NORTH *Plutarch* (1895) I. 226 Pety larceny, as robbing mens horteyards and gardens of fruite. **1677** PLOT *Oxfordsh.* 15 Any one that suspects the Echo to be really in the Hortyard, and not in the Garden, go but into it. **1699** EVELYN *Acetaria* Plan, Of the Hort-Yard and Potagere; and what Fruit-Trees ..may be admitted into a Garden.

Horus ('hɔərəs). [late L., ad. Gr. Ὧρος, ad. Egyptian *Hor*.] The name of an Egyptian deity, represented in art as having the head of a hawk, used *attrib.* to designate an image of this deity.

1851 [see HATHOR]. **1875** *Encycl. Brit.* VII. 715/2 Hathor is associated with Horus, but her genealogical place is not clear. **1923** *Glasgow Herald* 13 Feb. 8 The horus birds. **1923** D. H. LAWRENCE *Birds, Beasts & Flowers* 199 The golden Great and glistening-feathered legs of the hawk of Horus. **1972** *Times* 18 May (Egypt Suppl.) p. iv/3 The falcon was sacred to Horus, the sky god who bore the sun on his head.

horwed: see HORY *v.*

horwȝ, horȝ(e, filth: see HORE *sb.*

hory, horry, *a. Obs.* exc. *dial.* Forms: α. 1 horiȝ, 3–4 hori, hore, 4 horie, 4–5 hory, hoory, 8 horry, 9 *dial.* howry; β. 4–5 horow(e, (7 horrow). [OE. *horiȝ*, f. *horh, horw-, hor-*, HORE *sb.* + -Y. The ordinary OE. *horiȝ* naturally gave ME. *hori, hory*. Chaucer's *horowe* (cited by Bullokar and Cockeram as *horrow*) attaches itself app. to the inflexional *horȝ-* in *horȝ-um*, etc.: cf. HOLY, HALLOW.]

Foul, dirty, filthy; slanderous.

α. *c* **1000** *Canons of Ælfric* §22 in Thorpe *Laws* II. 350 Ðæt his reaf ne beo horiȝ. *c* **1000** ÆLFRIC *Hom.* I. 528 Mid horium reafe. *c* **1200** *Trin. Coll. Hom.* 141 Clensunge þat is þat brinð hori to clene. *a* **1300** *Sev. Sins, Pride* 13 in *E.E.P.* (1862) 19 Hit nis bote hori felle. **1382** WYCLIF *Lev.* xxii. 5 He that..shal touche..eny vnclene, whos touchynge is hoory [**1388** foul], shal be vnclene vnto the euen. *c* **1400** *Lanfranc's Cirurg.* 82 An hory wounde shal be heelid, in remeuynge awey þe crust eiþere filþe þat is in him. *c* **1420** *Chron. Vilod.* 1870 þis synfulle worlde þat so horry ys. **1746** *Exmoor Scold.* (E.D.S.) 155 Thy Waistcoat oll horry. **1880** TENNYSON *Village Wife* vii, A howry owd book. **1881** *N. Linc. Gloss., Howery*, dirty, filthy.

β. [*c* **1000** *Appollonius* (1834) 13 Mid horhgum scicelse.] *c* **1374** CHAUCER *Compl. Mars* 206 Somtyme envyous folke with tunges horowe departen hem alas. ? *c* **1400** *Plowman's T.* 1097 They were noughty, foule, and horowe. **1616** BULLOKAR, *Horrow*, beastlie; base, slaunderous.

Hence †**'horyness.** *Obs.*

c **1425** *Eng. Conq. Irel.* xxviii. 66 Mych horynesse [*Rawl. MS.* felth] or oryble synnes, that me ne aght nat to speke of.

†**hory**, *v. Obs.* Forms: 2–3 horeȝ-en, horyen, 4 horew-en, horw-en. [OE. type **horȝian*, f. *horiȝ* (see prec.): cf. *herȝian*, HARRY.] *trans.* To make hory, foul, or filthy; to defile, pollute.

c **1200** *Trin. Coll. Hom.* 201 We habbeþ don of us þe ealde man þe us horeȝede alle. *c* **1275** in *O.E. Misc.* 92 Lest he schulde his saule horyen and schede. **13..** *E.E. Allit. P.* B. 335 Of vche clene comly kynde enclose seuen makez Of vche horwed, in ark halde bot a payre.

horydest, 2nd sing. pa. t. of HORRE *v. Obs.*

hos, obs. form of HOARSE.

hosanna (həʊ'zænə), *int.*, *sb.* and *v.* Forms: 1 osanna, 4 ossanna, 4–7 osanna, 6 hosianna, osan, 7 hosannah, 6– hosanna. [ad. late L. *osanna, hosanna* (Vulg.), ad. Gr. ὡσαννά, ὡσαννά, repr. the Heb. *hōshaᵉ-nā*, abbreviated form of *hōshīᵉāh-nnā* save, pray! Cf. Ps. cxviii. 25, lxxxvi. 2. In Rabbinical literature the phrase occurs as a word in *yōm-hōshaᵉnā*, 'hosanna-day', the seventh day of the Feast of Booths, also as a name for the palm (or willow) branches carried in procession.]

A. *int.* An exclamation, meaning 'Save now!' or 'Save, pray!', occurring in Ps. cxviii. 25, which forms part of the Hallel at the Passover, and was in frequent liturgical use with the Jews, as an appeal for deliverance, and an acclamation or ascription of praise to God. At the entry of Jesus in Jerusalem it was shouted by the Galilean pilgrims in recognition of His Messiahship (Matt. xxi. 9, 15; Mark xi. 9, 10; John xii. 13), and it has been used from early times in the Christian Church as an ascription of praise to God and Christ.

c **1000** *Ags. Gosp.* Mark xi. 9, 10 Osanna [*Lindisf.* la hæl wusiȝ] sy ȝebletsod se þe com on drihtnes naman..Osanna on heahnessum. *a* **1300** *Cursor M.* 15031 Osanna, lauerd! welcum þou be, Quar has þou ben sa lang? *Ibid.* 15106 Nu sais alle ossanna! **1377** LANGL. *P. Pl.* B. XVIII. 9 How osanna by orgonye [*C.* orgone] olde folke songen. **1382** WYCLIF *Matt.* xxi. 9 The cumpanyes that wenten before, and that sueden, crieden, seyinge, Osanna [*gloss* that is, I preie, saue], to the sone of Dauith..Osanna in the heeȝist thingis. [**1526** TINDALE, **1535** COVERD. hosianna, **1534** TINDALE hosanna]. **1567** *Gude & Godlie B.* (1897) 198 For our gude man in heuin dois regne..Quhar Angellis singis euer Osan. **1625** SANDERSON *Serm.* I. 117 The abridgment..which some have made of the whole Book of Psalms, but into words, Hosannah, and Hallelujah. **1718** WATTS *Ps.* cxviii. IV. v, Hosanna in the highest strains The church on earth can raise. **1811** HEBER *Hymn*, Hosanna to the living Lord..To Christ, Creator, Saviour, King, Let earth, let heaven, Hosanna sing.

B. *sb.* **1.** A cry or shout of 'hosanna': a shout of praise or adoration.

1641 MILTON *Ch. Govt.* II. iii, All men with loud hosannas will confess her greatness. **1673** *Lady's Call.* I. iv. §13. 29 The acclamations and hosannahs of the multitude. **1717** POPE *Eloisa* 353 When loud Hosannas rise. **1866** BRYANT *Poems, Death Slavery* ii, Our rivers roll exulting, and their banks Send up to hosannas to the firmament!

2. *attrib.* **Hosanna Sunday**, Palm Sunday.

1868 M. E. C. WALCOTT *Sacred Archæol.* 422 Hosanna (save us, we pray) Sunday, in the East and Southern Europe. **1899** J. HASTINGS *Dict. Bible* II. 418/2 In Christian usage, Palm Sunday, to which our Lord's entry has given name, has in certain periods and regions been called 'Hosanna Sunday' or 'Day of Hosannas', or simply 'Osanna'.

C. *vb. trans.* To address, applaud, or escort with shouts of 'hosanna'.

1697 C. LESLIE *Snake in Grass* (ed. 2) 46 This James Naylor suffer'd himself to be Hosanna'd into Bristol, as

Christ was into Jerusalem. **1775** P. Oliver in *T. Hutchinson's Diary* 31 Oct. (1886) II. 110 They Hosanna'd a man who was known to be infamous in all vices. **1851** H. Angus *Serm.* (1861) 143 The act of him who has been much hosannaed as if he were a Saviour.

hosband, -bond, obs. ff. HUSBAND.

hosch, obs. form of HUSH.

hose (həʊz), *sb.* Forms: *Sing. and collect. pl.* 1 **hosa,** 3- **hose;** 3-6 **hosse,** 4-7 **hoose,** 5 **hoyse,** 5-6 *Sc.* **hois,** 6 **hoys,** *Sc.* **hoss, hoiss, hoyss, hoess, howis,** 6-8 **hoase,** 7 *Sc.* **hoise,** 8-9 erron. *Sc. sing.* **ho.** *Pl.* α. 3- **hosen,** (5 **hoosen, hausyn, hosin,** 5-6 **-yn,** 6 **-one, hozen);** β. 4-7 **hoses,** (4 **hoosis,** 4-6 **hosis,** 5 **hossys,** 6 **hosys).** [OE. *hosa* (? *hose, hosu*) = OHG. *hosa* (MDu., MLG., MHG., Ger. *hose* hose, trousers, Du. *hoos* stocking, water-hose), ON. *hosa,* Da. *hose* stocking; app.:—OTeut. **hosôn-*. Of German origin are the Romanic forms, med.L. *hosa, osa,* OF. *hose, heuse,* It. *uosa,* OSp. *huesa,* OPg. *osa,* Pr. *oza* legging; Welsh and Corn. *hos* are from Eng.]

I. 1. a. An article of clothing for the leg; sometimes reaching down only to the ankle as a legging or gaiter, sometimes also covering the foot like a long stocking. †α. *sing. Obs.*

a **1100** *Ags. Voc.* in Wr.-Wülcker 327/29 *Caliga, uel ocrea,* hosa. *c* **1205** Lay. 15216 þat ælc nome a long sax & læiden bi his sconke wið inne his hose. *c* **1477** Caxton *Jason* 49 The firste man that he mette with an hose on that one foot and none on that other. **1483** *Cath. Angl.* 189/2 An Hose (*A.* Hoyse), *caliga, caligula.* **1490** Caxton *Eneydos* xxiv. 89 Dydo beynge ther present .. with one fote bare and the other hosse on. **1573-80** Baret *Alv.* H 664 An Hose, or nether stock, *crurale.* **1682** N. O. *Boileau's Lutrin* iv. 218 One Chanon ran With one hose off, the other scarcely on.

β. *pl.* **hosen,** *arch.* or *dial.*; **hoses,** *obs.* Sense as in γ.

a **1225** *Ancr. R.* 420 Ine sumer ȝe habbeð leaue uorto gon and sitten baruot; and hosen wiðuten uaumpez, and ligge ine ham hwoso likeð. **1297** R. Glouc. (Rolls) 8013 Is chanberlein him broȝte .. Amorewe uor to werie a peire hosen [*v. rr.* hoses, hose] of say. *c* **1300** *Havelok* 860 Hauelok .. Hauede neyþer hosen ne shon, Ne none kines oþe[r] wede. **1382** Wyclif *Acts* xii. 9 Be thou gurd bifore, and do on thi hosis [Vulg. *caligas*]. *c* **1386** Chaucer *Prol.* 456 Hir hosen weren of fyn scarlet reed. *c* **1400** Maundev. 1839 v. 59 Oure lord seyde to Moyses, 'Do of þin hosen and thi schon: for the place þat þou stondest on is lond holy and blessed'. *c* **1460** Fortescue *Abs. & Lim. Mon.* iii. (1885) 114 Thair hausyn beth of lyke caunuas, and passyn not thair kne, wher fore thai beth gartered and ther theis bare. **1530** Palsgr. 232/2 Hosyn and shossys, *chaussure.* **1557** North tr. *Gueuara's Diall Pr.* 190 b/1 Wearing their hosen very close. *a* **1732** Gay *Past.* (J.), Will she thy linen wash, or hosen darn? **1882** *Gd. Words* 602 With their spruce knee-breeches, hosen and buckles.

γ. *collect. pl.* **hose.** In mod. use = Stockings reaching to the knee. ***half-hose,*** short stockings or socks.

From *hose* (as if = *hoes*), a false sing. *ho,* stocking, is found in Sc.

1297 [see β]. *c* **1400** Maundev. (Roxb.) viii. 31 þai putte off þaire hose and þaire schone. **1538** *Aberdeen Reg.* V. 16 (Jam.) To pay him x sh. & the wtter part of a pair of hoyss. **1553** T. Wilson *Rhet.* (1567) 82 b, Some .. go with their hose out at heles. **1579** *Inv. R. Wardr.* (1815) 282 Ten howis sewit with reid silk, grene silk and blak silk. **1591** Shaks. *Two Gent.* II. i. 83 Hee beeing in loue, could not see to garter his hose. **1660** *Acts Council Rutherglen* in D. Ure *Hist. Rutherglen* (1793) 65 A paire of shooes and hoise. **1715** Ramsay *Christ's Kirk Gr.* II. xxi, Her left leg ho was flung. **1776-81** Gibbon *Decl. & F.* lxv. (R.), The legs and feet were clothed in long hose and open sandals. **1807** Hogg *Mount. Bard* 193 His shoon was four pound weight a-piece; On ilka leg a ho had he. **1851** *Illustr. Catal. Gt. Exhib.* 588 Merino hose, half-hose, and socks. **1892** *Labour Commission* Gloss. s.v., *Wrought-hose,* a very elastic class of hosiery made wholly upon a hand-machine.

fig. **1670** Eachard *Cont. Clergy* 59 We must put on the hose of faith.

b. *pl.* Coverings for the legs forming part of a suit of armour; greaves.

c **1205** Lay. 21136 His sconken he helede mid hosen of stele. **13..** *Guy Warw.* (A.) 3851 Hosen of iren he haþ on drawe. *c* **1380** *Sir Ferumb.* 235 Wiþ is hosen of mayle he by-gon. *c* **1440** *Partonope* 1907 Armed wele Wyth hosyn of mayle made of stele.

c. ***one's heart in one's hose***: see HEART 54 a.

†**2.** Sometimes an article of clothing for the legs and loins, = breeches, drawers; esp. in phrase DOUBLET *and hose,* as the typical male apparel. **a.** Usually in *pl.*, **hosen, hoses, hose,** also (with reference to its original divided state) ***a pair of hose.***

c **1460** J. Russell *Bk. Nurture* 895-7 Then drawe on his sokkis & hosyn .. Strike his hosyn vppewarde .. þen trusse ye them vp strayte to his plesure. *Ibid.* 961 His shon, sokkis, & hosyn to draw of be ye bolde. *c* **1485** *Digby Myst.* (1882) III. 502 My dobelet and my hossys euer to-gether a-byde. **1535** Coverdale *Dan.* iii. 21 So these men were bounde in their cotes, hosen, shues [**1611** in their coates, their hosen, and their hats]. **1542** *Inv. R. Wardr.* (1815) 93 Ane pair of hois of cramasy velvott, all the theis laid out with small frenyeis of gold. **1563-4** *Rolls Parlt.* V. 505/2 Nor that eny of the same Servauntez nor Laborers .. use or were eny close Hoses, nor eny Hoses wherof the peyre shall excede in price xiiii *d.* **1586** B. Young tr. *Guazzo's Civ. Conv.* IV. 227 Not knowing how to put on a paire of hose, made his wife holde them with both her hands abroade, and then rising .. in the bed, leapt downe into his breeches. **1596** Shaks. *1 Hen. IV,* II. iv. 239 *Falst.* Their Points being broken. *Poin.* Downe fell his Hose. **1647** Ward *Simp. Cobler* 36 They have carried away with them all that was in the pockets of their Holliday hose. **1650** Fuller *Pisgah* IV. vi. II. 109 By *hosen* we understand not stockins, but breeches. [**1849** James *Woodman* xxiii, You have got a new coat and hosen, I see.]

†**b.** app. sometimes in *sing.* with same sense.

1465 J. Paston in *P. Lett.* No. 526 II. 233, I have not an hole hose for to doon. **1560** J. Heywood *Prov. & Epigr.* (1867) 134 A hart in a heelde hose, can neuer do weele.

†**c.** ***shipman's hose,*** wide trousers worn by sailors.

(Contrasted with the tight-fitting hose then worn.)

1553 T. Wilson *Rhet.* (1567) 51 b, Not made as a shippe mannes hose, to serue for euery legge. **1565** Jewel *Def. Apol.* (1611) 416 Hereunto they adde a similitude not very agreeable, how the Scriptures be like to a Nose of Wax, or a Shipmans Hose: how they may .. serue all mens turns. *a* **1625** Boys *Wks.* (1629-30) 414 Making the Scriptures a shipmans hose to cover their own malitious humours.

II. 3. A flexible tube or pipe for the conveyance of water or other liquid to a place where it is wanted.

1495-7 *Naval Acc. Hen. VII* (1896) 229 Halff an Oxe hyde .. spent abought makyng of hoses for the pompes of the seid ship. **1727** Bradley *Fam. Dict.* s.v. *Building,* A Parish-Engine compleat, with Socket, Hose, and Leather-Pipe. **1748** *Anson's Voy.* II. iii. 141 The casks may be filled in the long-boat with an hose. **1788** *Chambers' Cycl.*, *Hoase* in Sea-Language, is a long flexible tube, formed of leather or tarred canvas .. to conduct the fresh water .. into the casks. **1825** J. Nicholson *Operat. Mechanic* 272 That if any of the hoses burst, the water may not escape from the receiver at the nozle. **1854** *Hull Improvem. Act* 36 Fire-plugs, hose and all necessary works .. in case of fire. **1868** *Daily Tel.* 28 July, If it were watered every evening by a hose.

4. A sheath or sheathing part; *spec.* the sheath inclosing the ear or straw of corn; the sheath or spathe of an Arum.

(In Halliwell, *sheath* is erron. printed *sheaf,* which is copied by other Dicts.)

a **1450** *Fysshynge with an Angle* (1883) 15 Thenne put your threde in at the hose twys or thries & lete it goo at eche tyme rounde abowte the yerde of your hoke. Thenne wete the hose & drawe it tyll that it be faste. **1495** *Trevisa's Barth. De P.R.* XVII. clvii. (W. de W.) Stobble is properly that strawe wyth leues and hosen that is lefte in the felde after that repers haue repen the corn. **1578** Lyte *Dodoens* III. vii. 323 It [Arum] carieth a certayne long codde, huske, or hose. **1620** *Thomas' Lat. Dict.*, *Folliculus,* .. the greene huskes or hose of wheate or any other graine being young, and beginning to spire. **1656** [see HOSED *ppl. a.* 3]. **1657** W. Coles *Adam in Eden* xxxii. 65 (*Arum*) At the top .. standeth a long hollow Hose or Husk, close at the bottom, but open from the middle upwards, ending in a point. **1744-50** W. Ellis *Mod. Husbandm.* II. I. 2 The Honey-dews .. will then .. so close and glew up the tender Hose of the Ear, that the unripe Wheat-kernels cannot expand themselves. **1813** Headrick *Agric. Surv. Forfarsh.* 299 The disease of smut .. is found in the ears before they have burst from the hose or seed-leaves. *a* **1825** Forby *Voc. E. Anglia, Hose,* the sheath or spathe of an ear of corn.

5. A socket. *spec.* **a.** The socket of any metal tool (as a spade or rake) which receives the handle or shaft. **b.** In a printing press of the old type: A square wooden frame inclosing part of the spindle and serving as a support for keeping the platen level.

1611 Cotgr., *Planche,* .. the Till of a Printers Presse, or the shelfe that compasseth the Hose. **1743** Maxwell *Sel. Trans.* 96 (Jam.) With a hose or socket .. made for holding of a pole or shaft; which being fixed into the hose, it may be thrust down into the earth. **1765** Croker, etc. *Dict. Arts* II. s.v. *Printing,* At each corner of the hose, there is an iron-hook fastened with pack-thread to those at each corner of the platten.

c. *Golf.* The socket into which the shaft of an iron club is fitted.

1893 H. Hutchinson *Golfing* 21 A method of obviating the trouble of occasionally hitting the ball on the hose of these short-faced clubs. **1953** R. Harris *Sixty Yrs. Golf* iii. 37 The sand-track iron is a most formidable looking bludgeon... The hose or socket is $6\frac{1}{4}$ inches.

†**6.** The bag at the lower end of a trawl-net or other fishing net: = COD *sb.*[1] 5. *Obs.*

1630 *Order* in *Descr. Thames* (1758) 72 The Hose not to exceed eleven feet in length, and in compass sixty Meishes. *Ibid.* 73 To have the Hose or Cod of his Net full Inch and half.

III. 7. *attrib.* and *Comb.*, as (senses 1 and 2) ***hose-cloth, -factor, -garter, -heeler, -maker, -yarn;*** (sense 3) ***hose-carriage, -carrier, -cart, -coupling, -maker, -making, -man, -reel, -tender, -trough, -van;*** **hose-bridge, -jumper, -protector, -shield,** devices for the protection of firemen's hose lying across a street or road; **hose company** *U.S.*, a company in charge of a fire-hose; **hose-grass,** a local name for *Holcus lanatus;* **hose-hook,** (*a*) a hook for raising the hose of a fire-engine; †(*b*) a hook by which the platen was attached to the hose (see sense 5 b); **hose-husk,** a husk resembling a hose or stocking; **hose-pipe** = HOSE *sb.* 3; hence as *v.*, to spray (as) with a hose; **hose-ring** (*humorous*) a fetter.

1829 *Massachusetts Laws* XI. 237 If any person shall .. damage .. any Engine, *Hose Carriage ... he shall be convicted. **1893** *Daily News* 12 Jan. 5/5 The bodies were conveyed on two hose carriages, on each of which were twelve fire-men in their helmets and uniforms. **1894** *Westm. Gaz.* 9 Oct. 5/2 As the *hose-carrier was crossing the market-place the wheels skidded and the carrier turned over. **1865** *Trans. Ill. Agric. Soc.* VI. 320 A large amount of three-inch hose always ready on *hose carts. **1887** *Times* 19 Sept. 7 The firemen had run out the telescopic escape and the hose-cart, and were on the scene. **1906** *Westm. Gaz.* 27 July 6/2 Two new .. fire-stations, .. with a horsed-escape, a manual fire-escape, and a hose-cart. **1478** W. Paston in *P. Lett.* No. 824 III. 237 Also I beseche yow to sende me a *hose clothe. **1543-4** *Old City Acc.-Bk.* in *Archæol. Jrnl.* XLIII, Itm for iiij yards of hoose cloth. **1806** *Massachusetts Spy* 21 May (Th.), The efforts of several *hose and fire companies at length prevailed. **1860** O. W. Holmes *Prof. Breakf.-t.* iv. 106 More widely known through the Movamensing Hose-Company, and the Wistar parties. **1948** *Times-Picayune Mag.* (New Orleans) 5 Dec. 21/2 The next and last contestant is Sound Point Protection Hose Company Number One! **1703** *Lond. Gaz.* No. 3879/4 He .. for many years was a *Hose-Factor in Freeman's-Yard. **1894** *Westm. Gaz.* 10 Sept. 8/2 He [Defoe] did not consider himself a 'hosier', that is, one who stood behind the counter selling hosiery, but 'a hose factor'—a warehouseman in a small way. **1563** W. Fulke *Meteors* (1640) 30 b, Her *hose garters untyed. **1811** W. Aiton *Agric. Surv. Ayrsh.* 287 (Jam.) *Hose-grass or York-shire fog (*Holcus lanatus*), is next to rye-grass the most valuable grass. *a* **1625** Fletcher *Martial Maid* II. i, Thou woollen-witted *hose-heeler. **1727-41** Chambers *Cycl.*, **Hose-Husk,* in botany, a long round husk; as in pinks, julyflowers, &c. **1483** Caxton *Cato* C ij, We reden of two *hosemakers. **1863** P. Barry *Dockyard Econ.* 113 Twenty-third in order stand the hosemakers' shops. **18..** *Elect. Rev.* (U.S.) XI. 2 (Cent.) The *hosemen managing the apparatus. **1835** J. Martin *Gaz. Virginia* 139 The height of the reservoir, above these streets, .. gives a jet of water by means of *hose pipes, of some 60 to 80 feet elevation. **1872** Raymond *Statist. Mines & Mining* 64 The water of seven or eight ordinary hose-pipes. **1884** *Pall Mall G.* 15 Aug. 4/2 A friendly hand turned the hose-pipe upon them. **1928** *Daily Express* 27 Sept. 8 A stream of the chief's choicest acid would be hosepiped his way. **1930** R. Campbell *Poems* 17 With your fountainpen to spray the flowers, The hosepipe of your literary hours. **1940** *Flight* 5 Dec. 468*a*/1 A stripped Lewis gun as used on trawlers and such-like ships for 'hose-piping' dive-bombers and low-fliers. **1948** Partridge *Dict. Forces' Slang* 96 *Hosepipe,* to spray liquid fire from a flame-thrower. **1973** J. Fleming *You won't let me Finish* xvii. 133 Around the cage were elephantine hose pipes to be used in case of emergency to protect the people at ground level. **1837** W. Baddeley in *Mech. Mag.* XXVII. 34 A little invention which I have termed a *hose-reel. *c* **1530** *Hickscorner* in Hazl. *Dodsley* I. 172, I will go give him these *hose rings. **1851** J. S. Macaulay *Field Fortif.* 197 The *hose-troughs are small wooden tunnels, in which the powder-hose intended to communicate the fire to the charge is placed. **1581** *Act 23 Eliz.* c. 9 § 1 Wools, .. Cottons, *Hose-Yarn.

hose (həʊz), *v.* Also 3 **ose,** 6 **hoose, hoase.** [f. HOSE *sb.*]

1. *trans.* To furnish or provide with hose.

c **1300** *Havelok* 971 Hwan he was cloþed, osed, and shod. **1387** Trevisa *Higden* (Rolls) I. 29 Boþe i-hosed and i-schod. *c* **1430** *Pilgr. Lyf Manhode* II. xxxii. (1869) 87 Thou wolt hose him, and take him noble robes. **1530** Palsgr. 588/1 It costeth me monaye in the yere to hose and shoe my servauntes. **1599** Thynne *Animadv.* (1875) 13 The name of Chaucer .. (being frenche, in Englishe signyfyinge one who shueth or hooseth a manne). **1610** W. Folkingham *Art of Survey* To Rdr., 3 shillings, which now will scarce hose a frugall Peasant. **1834** *Fraser's Mag.* X. 416 The men degenerate shirted, cloaked, and hosed.

2. To water or drench with a hose. (HOSE *sb.* 3.) Also with *down.* Also *fig.* and *transf.* and as *sb.*

1889 Lady Brassey *Last Voy.* iv. 92 In the morning we go on deck at a very early hour... Then we are most of us hosed. **1898** *Westm. Gaz.* 15 Feb. 11/3 All the .. animals able to stand the application of water were repeatedly hosed. **1931** E. E. Cummings *Let.* 7 Jan. (1969) 119 Precisely as a cannon exploded, searchlights hozed the environs. **1936** [see BALDY]. **1939** H. Hodge *Cab, Sir?* ii. 15 A shirt-sleeved washer .. is hosing down a late-night cab. **1947** *Book Nine* (Caxton Press, N.Z.) 23 Treat him [*sc.* the patient] sweet, Floss. Hose him out and get him clean for us. **1961** W. Vaughan-Thomas *Anzio* v. 86 SP guns, out on the right, hosed them with fire, but they pushed on resolutely. **1964** C. Willock *Enormous Zoo* ix. 170 Roger Wheater hoses him with a blistering swathe of Swahili. **1969** *Gloss. Landscape Work* (*B.S.I.*) v. 25 *Hosing down,* the application of water by means of a hose to clean down buildings or other surfaces; or as a daily routine to control pests, dirt and humidity. **1971** *Guardian* 26 Aug. 22 Visitors to Piccadilly Circus, London, keeping out of the way of the regular hose-down.

hose: see HOARSE, HALSE, HAUSE.

hoseband, -bond, obs. forms of HUSBAND.

hosed (həʊzd), *a.* [f. HOSE *v.* or *sb.* + -ED.]

1. Provided with hose; wearing hose.

a **1310** in Wright *Lyric P.* xxxix. 111 Hupe forth, Hubert, hosede pye. **1480** Caxton *Chron. Eng.* (1510) s j b/2 With a swerde gyrde aboute hym, & hosyd and sporyd. **1565-73** Cooper *Thesaurus, Caligatus,* hoased. **1825** Scott *Betrothed* x, The scarlet-hosed Gillian.

2. Of a horse: Having the lower parts of the legs covered with white hair so as to present the appearance of wearing white stockings.

1720 W. Gibson *Dict. Horses* i. (ed. 3) 5 When the White .. happens to be on all the four feet, or only before, or behind, rising pretty high, the Horse is then said to be *hosed.* **1737** Bracken *Farriery Impr.* (1757) II. 5 When a Horse is what we call hosed, it is a Sign he is of a washy Constitution.

3. Inclosed in a sheath or glume.

1656 W. D. tr. *Comenius' Gate Lat. Unl.* § 91. 31 Corn bringeth grains; that which is eared, in ears; the hosed in hosen; the codded in codds.

hose-in-hose, *a.* and *sb.* [See HOSE *sb.* 4.] Said of flowers which appear to have one corolla within another, esp. a well-known variety of *Primula* or Polyanthus.

1688 R. Holme *Armoury* II. iv. 67/2 Another kind [of Thorn Apple] having the Flower Ingeminated, or Hose in Hose, that is one coming out of another. **1727-41** Chambers *Cycl., Hose in Hose*.. signifies one long husk within another; as in the polyanthos. **1879** Britten & Holland *Plant-n., Hose-in-hose*, a peculiar variety of garden Polyanthus, where the calyx becomes petaloid, giving the appearance of one corolla within another. **1882** *Garden* 20 May 343/1 Hose-in-Hose Polyanthuses.

hosel(e, hosil, obs. forms of HOUSEL.

hoseless ('həʊzlıs), *a.* [f. HOSE *sb.* + -LESS.] Without hose; wearing no hose.

1594 Carew *Huarte's Exam. Wits* xi. (1596) 156 A.. hosier.. if none agree with the buiers measure.. must send him away hoselesse. **1658** Cleveland *Rustic Ramp.* Wks. (1687) 416 Among such hoseless Ribaulds. **1823** *New Monthly Mag.* VIII. 397 The shoeless, hoseless, shirtless, and houseless peasantry.

'hose-net. Chiefly *Sc.* A small net resembling a stocking, affixed to a pole (Jam.); *fig.* a position from which it is difficult to escape.

1552 Lyndesay *Monarche* 4762 They.. with their hois net dayly drawis to Rome, The maist fine gold, that is in Christindome. **1589** R. Bruce *Serm. Sacrament* M iv b, Sa .. yee haue drawne your selfes in a hose-net, and crucified your messe. **1743** Pitt in *Anecd. Earl Chatham* (1797) I. v. 149 If the French had not.. caught our army in a hose net, from which it could not have escaped. **1824** Scott *Redgauntlet* Let. xiii, I had him in a hose-net.

hosere, obs. f. WHOSOEVER.

hosewif, obs. f. HOUSEWIFE.

hoshen, var. HUSHION.

hosier ('həʊʒ(ı)ə(r), 'həʊzıə(r)). Forms: 5 hoseer, hoseare, hoseȝere, hosiare, hoser, (hosyrer), 5-6 hosyer, 8 hozier, 6- hosier. [f. HOSE *sb.* + -IER.] One who makes or deals in hose (stockings and socks) and frame-knitted or woven underclothing generally. Also used more generally for a men's outfitter or haberdasher.

[**1403** in *York Myst.* Introd. 20 *note*, Touz hosyers que vendront chauuces ou facent chauuces a vendre.] *c* **1440** *Promp. Parv.* 248/2 Hoseare, or he þat makythe hosyne (*K.* hoseȝere, *S.* hosiare, *P.* hoser). **1465** J. Paston in *P. Lett.* No. 526 II. 233, ij peyir hose.. redy made for me at the hosers. **1574** J. Dee in *Lett. Lit. Men* (Camden) 38 Vulgar, obscure persons, as hosiers and tanners. **1731** Swift *Lett.* 10 Sept., You are as arrant a cockney as any hosier in Cheapside. **1837** N. Whittock et al. *Compl. Bk. Trades* 289 *Haberdasher and hosier*. Each of those trades merge in the other, occasionally;.. our Hosiers seldom confine their dealings to the wares which clothe our legs. **1855** Macaulay *Hist. Eng.* xx. IV. 503 It had been necessary for the Chancellor of the Exchequer to go, hat in hand,.. borrowing a hundred pounds from this hosier, and two hundred pounds from that ironmonger. **1892** P. L. Simmonds *Comm. Dict. Trade Products* 197/2 *Hosier*, one who deals in stockings, shawls, gloves, braces, laces, and under garments, etc. **1921** *Dict. Occup. Terms* (1927) 344/3 *Hosier*,.. is usually also an outfitter. **1935** Wodehouse *Luck of Bodkins* xvi. 192 Monty passed a finger round his collar. A perfect fit, made to measure by the finest hosier in London, it seemed to be too tight. **1936** —— *Laughing Gas* xii. 119 In the matter of pyjamas I've always been a trifle on the choosy side. I'm not one of those fellows who just charge into a hosier's and grab anything.

hosiery ('həʊʒ(ı)ərı, 'həʊzıərı). [f. prec.: see -ERY.]

1. Hose collectively; extended to other frame-knitted articles of apparel, and hence to the whole class of goods in which a hosier deals.

1790-1826 Fleecy Hosiery [see FLEECY 1 b]. **1796** Morse *Amer. Geog.* I. 259 Hosiery of wool, cotton and thread. **1839** E. E. Perkins *Haberdashery & Hosiery* (ed. 6) 98 Socks and stockings legitimately constitute Hosiery, but.. caps, waistcoats, drawers, and petticoats,—being made of the same materials.. are now included under the term 'Hosiery'. **1875** *Ure's Dict. Arts* (ed. 7) II. 813 There are many different fabrics of stocking-stitch for various kinds of ornamental hosiery. *Ibid.*, The first kind of frame.. is that for knitting plain hosiery, or the common stocking-frame.

2. The business or trade of a hosier.

1789 J. Pilkington *View Derbysh.* II. 51 The business of hosiery is carried on extensively in that part of the county.

3. A factory where hose are woven.

4. *attrib.* and *Comb.*

1803 *Med. Jrnl.* IX. 550, I adopted the use of fleecy hosiery stockings. *Ibid.* X. 283 The patent fleecy hosiery jackets sold in the shops. **1897** *Daily News* 23 Apr. 3/4 Manager in the hosiery department. *Ibid.*, The question had never been previously raised as to hosiery goods.

hosing ('həʊzıŋ), *vbl. sb.* [f. HOSE *v.* + -ING[1].] The providing with hose; *concr.* material for hose, hose collectively.

1340 *Ayenb.* 154 Ine mete and ine drinke and ine cloþinge and ine hosiynge and ine ssoinge. **1513** Douglas *Æneis* XI. xv. 23 Hys hosing schane of wark of Barbary. **1580** Hollyband *Treas. Fr. Tong, Chaussure*, hosing.

hospetes, obs. f. *hostess*: see HOSPTE.

hospice ('hɒspıs). [a. F. *hospice*, ad. L. *hospitium* hospitality, entertainment, a lodging, inn, f. *hospit-em*: see HOST *sb.*[2]]

1. A house of rest and entertainment for pilgrims, travellers, or strangers, esp. one belonging to a religious order, as those of the monks of St. Bernard and St. Gotthard on the Alps; also, generally, a 'home' for the destitute or the sick.

1818 *Blackw. Mag.* IV. 88 The *Hospice* of St Bernard. G. Downes *Lett. Cont. Countries* I. 275 Beyond this spot are the *Hôpital*, an ancient hospice, and a new but unfinished one, commenced by Napoleon. **1862** Merivale *Rom. Emp.* (1865) VI. xlviii. 62 The establishment of a hospice in the wilderness of snows. **1894** *Times* 18 Dec. 13/1 The hospice provides 20 beds, soup, bread, and coals to families, and penny dinners to sandwich-men.

2. A hostel for students; = HOSPITIUM 2.

1895 Rashdall *Univ. Europe* I. v. §5. 497 There was more chance of the rule.. being enforced [in a college] than in the private Hospice.

3. A nursing-home for the care of the dying or the incurably ill.

1893 R. Mulholland in Baroness Burdett-Coutts *Woman's Mission* (R. Brit. Commission, Chicago Exhib.) 246 The Sisters of Charity at Harold's Cross, Dublin.. is simply a 'hospice', where those are received who have very soon to die, and who know not where to lay their weary heads. **1905** *Catholic Herald* 3 Feb. 12/3 The Hospice for the Dying in Cambridge Road, which is.. under the management of the Irish Sisters of Mercy, has already a few inmates. **1922** Joyce *Ulysses* 96 Ward for incurables there. Very encouraging. Our Lady's Hospice for the dying. Dead-house handy underneath. **1967** *Nursing Times* 28 July 981/1 This week has seen the opening of a hospice where the whole atmosphere is one of leisurely time; time to die. *Ibid.*, St. Christopher's Hospice has been planned.. to enable patients who are in the last stages of their illness to have.. a tranquil end. **1979** M. Campion *Making of Hospice* iii. 10 A hospice it was.., the choice of name reflecting the Christian belief that death is but the close of one stage of life and the beginning of another and deeper life in Christ. **1985** *Washington Post* 30 Aug. B1/1 Mother Frances is best known as the founder.., fundraiser and administrator of Helen House, in Oxford, England, probably the world's first hospice for dying or acutely afflicted children.

4. Special Comb. **hospice movement**, a movement for the establishment of hospices (sense 3).

1979 M. Campion *Making of Hospice* vii. 31 The *hospice movement both national and international, is not in competition with hospitals. **1981** *Times* 13 May 4/7 What has become known as the 'hospice movement' for the specialized treatment of the incurably ill or dying. **1986** *Church Times* 8 Aug. 7/3 He pays full tribute to his inspirer, Dame Cicely Saunders, who pioneered the hospice movement.

hospitable ('hɒspıtəb(ə)l), *a.* [a. obs. F. *hospitable* (Cotgr. 1611), or ad. L. type **hospitābilis*, f. *hospitā-re*: see HOSPITATE and -BLE.]

1. Offering or affording welcome and entertainment to strangers; extending a generous hospitality to guests and visitors.

a. Of persons.

1570 Levins *Manip.* 3/28 Hospitable, *hospitabilis.* **1638** Sir T. Herbert *Trav.* (ed. 2) 340 They are very hospitable one to another. **1816** Keatinge *Trav.* I. 330 *note*, The savages in America are extremely hospitable. **1859** C. Barker *Assoc. Princ.* i. 9 They were.. hospitable to travellers.

b. Of things, feelings, qualities, etc.

1595 Shaks. *John* II. i. 244 Then the constraint of hospitable zeale, In the releefe of this oppressed childe. **1612** Drayton *Poly-olb.* ii. (R.), His hospitable gate The richer and the poor stood open to receive. **1727** Swift *Gulliver* III. iv, Entertained in a most hospitable manner. **1838** Thirlwall *Greece* xxxviii. V. 55 He is said to have inherited his father's hospitable relation to Sparta.

2. *transf.* Disposed to receive or welcome kindly; open and generous in mind or disposition.

1655 Evelyn *Lett.* 8 June, Ostende may prove as hospitable to our shippinge as Brest hath bene. **1661** Boyle *Style of Script.* (1675) 134 We must.. make our faculties as hospitable to it [God's Word] as we can. **1887** *Amer. Jrnl. Philol.* VIII. 86 The religion of the Greeks.. was hospitable to novelties and was composite in character.

Hence **'hospitableness**, hospitable quality or character.

1612-15 Bp. Hall *Contempl., N.T.* IV. xvii, Charity and hospitableness. **1665** Boyle *Occas. Refl.* (1845) 73 Such a constant kindness and hospitableness to such thoughts.. they will, as it were, come to the mind without calling. *a* **1677** Barrow *Serm.* Wks. 1687 I. xxxi. 428 His benignity to strangers, and hospitableness, is remarkable.

hospitably ('hɒspıtəblı), *adv.* [f. prec. + -LY[2].] In a hospitable manner; with hospitality.

a **1721** Prior *Ladle* 119 Ye thus hospitably live, And strangers with good cheer receive. **1774** Goldsm. *Nat. Hist.* (1776) IV. 327 He makes a virtue of necessity, and hospitably rows him to shore. **1849** Macaulay *Hist. Eng.* v. I. 530 They received him most hospitably.

hospitage ('hɒspıtıdʒ). *Obs.* or *arch.* [ad. med.L. *hospitāgium*, f. *hospit-em*: see HOST *sb.*[2] and -AGE.]

†**1.** The position of a guest; guestship. *Obs.*

1590 Spenser *F.Q.* III. x. 6 That his ungentle hoste n'ote him appeach Of vile ungentlenesse, or hospitages breach.

†**2.** Lodging, entertainment as a guest. *Obs.*

1611 Speed *Hist. Gt. Brit.* IX. ix. §77 No where contenting himself with his dyet and hospitage.

3. A place of hospitality.

1855 Singleton *Virgil* I. 312 That a hospitage Defiled should be abandoned.

hospital ('hɒspıtəl), *sb.* Also 4 -ayle, 4-6 hospyt-, 4-7 -ale, 5-7 -alle, 5-8 -all. [a. OF. *hospital*, mod.F. *hôpital*, ad. med.L. *hospitāle* place of reception for guests, neut. sing. of *hospitālis* (see next). Of this word, HOSTEL and HOTEL are doublets, and SPITAL an aphetized form.]

1. A house or hostel for the reception and entertainment of pilgrims, travellers, and strangers; a hospice. Hence, one of the establishments of the Knights Hospitallers.

c **1300** *Beket* 84 Ther is nouth an hospital arerd of Seint Thomas. *c* **1330** R. Brunne *Chron.* (1810) 135 To temples in Acres he quath fiue þousand marke, & fiue thousand to þe hospitale. *c* **1400** Maundev. (Roxb.) x. 40 Before þe kirke.. es a grete hospitale.. of whilk þe hospitalleres hase þaire first fundacion. **1500** *Melusine* xxi. 122 How they chaced two galleyes of the hospytal of Rodes. **1540** *Act 32 Hen. VIII*, c. 24 §2 The said William Weston or any of his bretherne or confreers of the said Hospitall or house of Sainct John of Hierusalem in England. **1598** Hakluyt *Voy.* I. 102 (R.) The countrey of Prussia, which the Dutch knights of the order of Saint Maries hospitale of Jerusalem haue of late wholly conquered and subdued. **1765** H. Walpole *Otranto* iii. (1798) 52 An adjacent hospital founded by the princess Hippolita for the reception of pilgrims.

2. a. A charitable institution for the housing and maintenance of the needy; an asylum for the destitute, infirm, or aged. *Obs.* exc. in Eng. legal use and in proper names like ***Greenwich Hospital***, orig. a home for superannuated seamen.

1418 *E.E. Wills* 31, I bequethe to þe pore hospitales.. to eueryche hospitall, to parte a-monge pore folk, there xx *s.* **1548** Hall *Chron., Edw. IV* 200 An olde and riche Hospitall, dedicated to Saincte Leonarde, in the whiche Almose-house the poore and indigente people were harbored. **1581** W. Stafford *Exam. Compl.* I. (1876) 18 Yee knowe the hospitall at the townes ende, wherein the freemen decaied are releaued. **1657** R. Ligon *Barbadoes* (1673) 44 Send into England for rug Gowns, such as poor people wear in Hospitals. *c* **1710** Celia Fiennes *Diary* (1888) 38 We go by St. Cross [Winchester] a large hospitall for old men and I thinke most is for ye decayed schollars. **1838** *Penny Cycl.* XII. 316/2 Hospitals intended merely for the relief of poor and indigent persons in England are peculiarly called Alms-houses.

†**b.** A house for the corporate lodging of students in a university; a hostel or hall. *Obs.*

1536 *Act 27 Hen. VIII*, c. 42 §1 Halles Hostelles Hospitalles. **1589** Nashe *Pref. to Greene's Menaphon* (Arb.) 11 Saint Johns in Cambridge, that at that time was.. shining so farre aboue all other Houses, Halls, and Hospitalls. **1706** Estcourt *Fair Examp.* III. i, England, instead of being.. the Hospital of Fools wou'd be an entire College of Learned Men.

c. A charitable institution for the education and maintenance of the young. Now only in Sc. legal use and in names of ancient institutions such as Christ's Hospital, London, and Heriot's Hospital, Edinburgh.

1552 Huloet, Hospitall for children to be brought up, *brephotrophia.* **1598** B. Jonson *Ev. Man in Hum.* II. i, I tooke him of a child, up, at my doore.. gave him mine owne name Thomas, Since bred him at the hospitall. **1691** Wood *Ath. Oxon.* I. 164 Among the blew coats in Ch. Ch. Hospital. **1837** *Penny Cycl.* VII. 347/2 An hospital.. is sometimes a place of learning, as Christ's Hospital, London. *Ibid.* IX. 275/1 Edinburgh has some noble hospitals and charitable institutions. Among these are.. Heriot's Hospital.. Watson's Hospitals, Merchant-Maiden and Trades'-Maiden Hospitals, Orphan Hospital, and Gillespie's Hospital. **1870** Ramsay *Remin.* v. (ed. 18) 118 She was brought up in one of the hospitals here. **1880** *Chambers' Encycl., Hospital*, in Law.. in Scotland more frequently signifies a mortification or endowment for the education as well as support of children.

3. *spec.* **a.** An institution or establishment for the care of the sick or wounded, or of those who require medical treatment. (The current sense.)

Such institutions are either public or private, free or paying,—or both combined,—general or special with respect to the diseases treated.

[*c* **1425** *Found. St. Bartholomew's* (E.E.T.S.) xliii, Oure hoely places, callyd the Priory of seynt Bartholomew yn Smythfyld, and.. the hospital by olde tyme longyng to the same.] **1549** *Order resp. St. Barthol.* in *Vicary's Anat.* (1888) App. iii. 137 For the better sustentation and comforte of the diseased and impotent persons within the said hospitall. **1552** *Ordre Hosp. St. Barthol.* Pref. A v, This Hospital.. where.. there haue bene healed of the pocques, fystules, filthie blaynes and sores, to nombre of .viij. hundred. **1573-80** Baret *Alv.* H 665 An Hospitall, or spittle for poore folkes diseased. **1613** Purchas *Pilgrimage* (1614) 299 The money.. is sent to the Hospitals of the diseased. **1789** W. Buchan *Dom. Med.* (1790) 81 Physicians, surgeons, and others who attend hospitals, ought, for their own safety, to take care that they be properly ventilated. **1869** Lecky *Europ. Mor.* II. i. 85 A Roman Lady.. founded at Rome as an act of penance the first public hospital.

transf. and *fig.* **1643** Sir T. Browne *Relig. Med.* II. §11 For the world, I count it not an Inne, but an Hospitall, and a place, not to live, but to die in. **1681** Flavel *Meth. Grace* x. 217 The world is a great hospital full of sick and dying souls, all wounded by one and the same mortal weapon, sin.

b. A similar establishment for the treatment of sick or injured animals.

1613 Purchas *Pilgrimage* (1614) 482 The publike Hospitall, which the Citizens.. had founded for all kindes of Birds, to cure them in their sicknesse. **1884** *Daily News* 23 July 7/1 The Great Northern Railway has just set up a hospital for their sick or injured horses.

c. Short for *hospital-ship*.

1709 *Lond. Gaz.* No. 4562/3 Her Majesty's Ships the Dover..Pembroke-Hospital, and Carcass-Bomb. **1723** *Ibid.* No. 6141/3 Serpent Bomb, Smirna Factor Hospital.

d. ***in*** **(*into*)** ***hospital***: under medical treatment in a hospital. In quot. 1885, *transf.* of vessels.

1844 H. H. WILSON *Brit. India* III. 113 More than half the survivors were in hospital. **1885** U. S. GRANT *Pers. Mem.* xxii. I. 305, I saw the absolute necessity of his gun-boats going into hospital.

†**4.** A house of entertainment; 'open house'.

c **1400** *Apol. Loll.* 33 Ne coueytous of foul wynning, but to holde hospital. **1592** GREENE *Groat's W. Wit* (1617) 9 The house where Lamilia (for so we call the Curtezan) kept her Hospitall.

†**5.** A place of lodging. In first quot. *fig.* *Obs.*

1500–20 DUNBAR *Poems* lxxxv. 77 (To the Virgin Mary) Hospitall riall, the lord of all Thy closet did include. **1548** UDALL, etc. *Erasm. Par. Matt.* xii. 74 An unclene spirite.. banished from his olde hospital. **1590** SPENSER *F.Q.* II. ix. 10 They spide a goodly castle..Which choosing for that evening's hospitale, They thither marcht.

6. *attrib.* and *Comb.*, as ***hospital-assistant, management, nurse, practice, surgeon, tent***, etc.; ***hospital-treated*** adj.; **hospital bed**, (*a*) a (metal) bed as used in hospitals, higher than an ordinary bed to facilitate nursing, and freq. adjustable in several ways; also ***hospital bedstead***; (*b*) an available place in hospital for a bed patient; **hospital blue(s)**, the blue uniform worn by wounded soldiers in the wars of 1914–18 and 1939–45; **hospital-boy**, a boy brought up at a hospital, a charity-boy; **hospital corps**, the medical corps in the U.S. Navy; so **hospital corpsman**; cf. CORPSMAN; **hospital fever**, a kind of typhus fever arising in crowded hospitals from the poisonous condition of the atmosphere due to exhalations from diseased bodies; **hospital gangrene**, a spreading, sloughing, gangrenous inflammation starting from a wound and arising in crowded hospitals; also called *sloughing phagedæna*; **hospital letter**, a letter referring a patient for free treatment in a hospital; **hospital-man, mate**, an assistant in a hospital on board ship; **hospital paper** = *hospital letter*; **hospital pass** *Football*, etc., a pass to a player likely to be tackled heavily as soon as he receives it; **hospital porter** (see PORTER *sb.*[2]); **Hospital Saturday**, a particular Saturday in the year on which collections of money for the local hospitals are organized in workshops, in the streets, and elsewhere; **hospital ship**, (*a*) a vessel fitted up for the reception and treatment of sick and wounded seamen; so ***hospital berth, cabin, hulk, vessel***; (*b*) a ship for conveying sick and wounded soldiers to their own country or to an area remote from the battlefield; **hospital steward**, (*a*) a non-commissioned staff-officer in the U.S. army who makes up prescriptions, administers medicine, and has general charge, under the direction of an army surgeon, of the sick and of hospital property; (*b*) in the navy, the designation formerly given to the apothecary (*Cent. Dict.*); **Hospital Sunday**, a particular Sunday in the year on which collections of money are made in the places of worship of a town or district for the local hospitals; **hospital train**, a train for conveying wounded soldiers from the front to the base hospitals; **hospital ulcer** = *hospital gangrene*.

1816 A. C. HUTCHISON *Pract. Obs. Surg.* (1826) 168 Examined during the night by the nurse of the ward, or by an *hospital-assistant. **1823** C. MATHEWS *Let.* 7 Feb. in A. Mathews *Mem. Charles Mathews* (1838) III. 365, I slept in a bed on the road without even posts for curtains—a regular *hospital-bed. **1952** *Oxf. Jun. Encycl.* X. 190/2 Small sums paid weekly during health might entitle contributors to a hospital bed in time of need. **1970** *New Yorker* 29 Aug. 55/1 He lends people hospital beds, which he happened to get at a good price. **1973** C. MULLARD *Black Brit.* iv. 46 Overnight, blacks were suddenly held responsible for the unemployment figures.., lack of adequate social services, schools and hospital beds. **1860** F. NIGHTINGALE *Notes on Nursing* viii. 47 *Hospital bed-steads are..very much less objectionable than private ones. **1758** J. BLAKE *Plan Mar. Syst.* 53 That the *hospital-birth be appointed..between decks. **1919** 'I. HAY' *Last Million* vi. 67 Convalescent soldiers in *hospital blue. **1920** J. M. BARRIE *Kiss for Cinderella* (1928) III. 445 Danny, who is slightly lame and is in hospital blue. **1920** [see AIRER]. **1957** R. CAMPBELL *Portugal* ii. 29, I was clothed in army hospital-blues. **1973** B. TURNER *Hot-Foot* iv. 20 Some day I would be spotted as a wanted man by someone who knew me either in khaki or in hospital blues. **1677** HORNECK *Gt. Law Consid.* iv. (1704) 210 A thing only fit for alms-men and *hospital-boys. **1899** *Statutes at Large U.S.A.* XXX. 474 June 17, 1898..Be it enacted..That a *hospital corps of the United States Navy is hereby established. **1945** *Amer. Handbk.* (Office War Information) xxvi. 386 Men of the Hospital Corps include pharmacists... They may be found in the amphibious units of the Marine Corps, in the dressing stations of warships, and in submarines. **1901** E. ROOT in Bacon & Scott *Mil. & Colonial Policy U.S.* (1916) 374 An order was made fixing the enlisted strength..exclusive of *hospital corps men, at 77,287. **1943** *Sci. News Let.* 29 May 343 Soon a Hospital Corpsman with a larger kit of supplies comes along and quickly ministers to the wounded man. **1750** PRINGLE (*title*) Observations on the Nature and Cure of *Hospital and Jail Fevers. **1822–34** *Good's Study Med.* (ed. 4) I. 690 It [putrid fever] possesses the additional names of Jail, Camp, and Hospital Fever. **1813** J. THOMSON *Lect. Inflam.* 456 The particular ulcer, to which surgeons now give the name of malignant ulcer, or *hospital gangrene. **1890** W. BOOTH *In Darkest Eng.* I. iii. 26 He had hoped to have obtained a *hospital letter at the Mansion House so as to obtain a truss for a bad rupture. **1828** P. CUNNINGHAM *N.S. Wales* (ed. 3) II. 217, I also allow each captain of the deck and *hospital-man two pounds of tobacco for use on the voyage. **1809** WELLINGTON *Let. to Ld. Liverpool* 7 Dec. in Gurw. *Desp.* (1838) V. 341, I also hope your Lordship will..send us out *Hospital Mates. **1848** THACKERAY *Van. Fair* lvii. 514 Women..who are *hospital-nurses without wages. **1893** O. WILDE *Lady Windermere's Fan* IV. 120 You would like me to retire into a convent or become a hospital nurse, or something of that kind. **1936** A. THIRKELL *August Folly* ix. 265 Jessica got up and the hospital nurse left. **1962** A. CHRISTIE *Mirror Crack'd* ii. 13 In real illness you could have a proper hospital nurse, at vast expense and procured with difficulty, or you could go to hospital. **1838** C. M. YONGE *Let.* 25 Sept. in C. Coleridge *C. M. Yonge* (1903) iv. 139 Mr. Rudd, the tall man we took the *hospital paper to, is dead. **1890** —— *More Bywords* 260 Jane Cox is come for a hospital paper, ma'am. **1978** *Times* 27 Nov. 9/3 The centres were always cramped for room, but the distribution was not always quick or accurate enough and *hospital passes were not unknown. **1986** *Guardian* 17 Mar. 29/7 It was not exactly a hospital pass but... He made three yards before he was smothered. **1683** *Lond. Gaz.* No. 1877/4 The Swallow is arrived in the Downs..as likewise an *Hospital Ship, with old and sick Soldiers. **1758** J. BLAKE *Plan Mar. Syst.* 51 It is proposed, that..an hospital-ship be appointed. **1888** E. J. MATHER *Nor'ard of Dogger* 282 Numbers of poor fellows.. eager to seize the first opportunity of boarding the hospital-ship. **1899** *Westm. Gaz.* 20 Nov. 6/2 The American hospital-ship *Maine*. **1916** 'BOYD CABLE' *Action Front* 172 Swinging at top speed down the line to the base and the hospital ship and home. **1944** F. CLUNE *Red Heart* 12 I've seen my mates consigned to the deep on a hospital ship..in war-time. **1856** R. GLISAN *Jrnl. Army Life* (1874) 350 Besides the sick, *hospital steward, hospital attendants, and some three others, there will be no troops. **1895** *Outing* (U.S.) Dec. 255/2 The non-commissioned staff comprises a sergeant-major, a quarter master-sergeant, a commissary-sergeant, and a hospital steward. **1873** *Punch* 1 Feb. 43/2 Munificence to medical charities upon '*Hospital Sunday'. **1876** J. IRVING *Ann. Time* Suppl. (ed. 2), [June] 15 [1873]. —The first 'Hospital Sunday' held in London; above 27,400*l.* collected in connection with the different services. **1822–34** *Good's Study Med.* (ed. 4) I. 687 One reason why nurses, and perhaps *hospital-surgeons, escape so often without injury. **1812** *Niles' Reg.* II. 131/1, 300 *hospital, horsemen's and common tents. **1862** G. B. MCCLELLAN *Let.* 31 July in *Own Story* (1887) 458 They are nearly all in hospital-tents and are well provided for. **1936** C. DAY LEWIS *Friendly Tree* i. 14 Holding the wound shut..until he reaches the hospital tent. **1874** B. F. TAYLOR *World on Wheels* I. xxiv. 162 The saddest train upon which the writer ever took passage was the *Hospital Train, with its maimed and mangled burden. **1916** 'BOYD CABLE' *Action Front* 172 That he might be lying warm and comfortable in the soothing ease of a bed in the hospital train. **1937** V. BARTLETT *This is my Life* iv. 51, I spent my twenty first birthday in a hospital train... The Medical Officer in charge ..was an old school friend. **1799** *Med. Jrnl.* I. 430 Ulcers.. which are known by the term of *hospital ulcers. **1897** MARY KINGSLEY *W. Africa* 620 The true sanatorium for the Coast would be a *hospital vessel attached to each district.

Hence '**hospital** *v. trans.*, to place in a hospital.

1840 *Fraser's Mag.* XXII. 182 Like a deserving pensioner, hospitalled in the comfort..of fond protection.

†'**hospital**, *a.* *Obs.* [ad. L. *hospitālis* hospitable, f. *hospes, hospit-em* host, guest: see HOST *sb.*[2] and -AL[1].]

1. = HOSPITABLE. **a.** Of persons.

1570 LEVINS *Manip.* 14/28 Hospitall, *hospitalis*. **1600** ABP. ABBOTT *Exp. Jonah* 307 And it is said that a Bishop..should be hospitall, that is an entertainer of strangers. **1616** PURCHAS *Pilgrimage* (1614) 482 For Men they had not an Hospitall, that were thus Hospitall to Fowles. **1680** MORDEN *Geog. Rect., Wales* (1685) 27 Their Gentry brave and Hospital.

b. Of things, qualities, feelings, etc.

1600 HOLLAND *Livy* XLII. xl. 1138 Hospitall and friendly courtesies. **1638** HEYWOOD *Lucrece* Wks. 1874 V. 222 Her kinde hospitall grace. **1697** POTTER *Antiq. Greece* IV. xxi. (1715) 416 He had contemn'd the Salt, and overturn'd the Hospital Table.

2. In phr. ***hospital Jove, Jupiter***, or ***God***, a translation of L. *hospitālis* or Gr. *ξένιος* 'protector of the rights of hospitality'; also of Gr. *ξενικός*.

1382 WYCLIF *2 Macc.* vi. 2 Thei weren, that enhabitiden the place, of Iouis hospitale [Vulg. *Iovis hospitalis*]. **1609** HOLLAND *Amm. Marcell.* XXX. ii. 380 In the very sight of the Hospitall God. **1658** ROWLAND tr. *Moufet's Theat. Ins.* 1052 They are sacred to hospital Jupiter. **1697** POTTER *Antiq. Greece* IV. xxi. (1715) 416 Out of a pious regard to the Hospital Alliance. **1807** ROBINSON *Archæol. Græca* I. xx. 93 *Στέφανοι ξενικοί*, hospital crowns.

hospita'larian. *rare*. [f. med.L. *hospitālārius* + -AN.] = HOSPITALLER 1.

1745 A. BUTLER *Lives Saints* (1836) I. 40 Dedicated under the name of St. Julian the hospitalarian and martyr.

†'**hospitalary**. *Obs. rare*. [ad. med.L. *hospitālāri-us* HOSPITALLER.] = HOSPITALLER 3.

1598 HAKLUYT *Voy.* I. 144 The Order of the Dutch knights, commonly called the Hospitalaries of Ierusalem. *Ibid.* 150 Sifridus Walpode de Bassenheim, chiefe hospitalary commander in Elburg.

†**hospi'talious**, *a.* *Obs. rare*. [irreg. f. L. *hospitāli-s* hospitable + -OUS.] Hospitable.

1602 WARNER *Alb. Eng.* IX. liii. (1612) 238 Be hospitalious, Churchmen. *Ibid.* XII. lxxvii. 313 Lesse hospitalious too.

hospitalism ('hɒspɪtəlɪz(ə)m). [f. HOSPITAL *sb.* + -ISM.] The hospital system: used esp. with reference to the hygienic evils incident to old, crowded, and carelessly conducted hospitals.

1869 SIR J. Y. SIMPSON (*title*) Hospitalism: its effects on the results of surgical operations. —— *Our existing System of Hospitalism* 4 We cannot..hope for adequate..progress in the..healing art, till our system of hospitalism is more or less changed and revolutionized. **1897** ALLBUTT *Syst. Med.* II. 146 That unknown conjunction of ward influences known as Hospitalism.

hospitality (hɒspɪ'tælɪtɪ). [a. OF. *hospitalité* (12–13th c. in Hatz.-Darm.), ad. L. *hospitālitās*, f. *hospitālis* (see HOSPITAL *a.*).]

1. a. The act or practice of being hospitable; the reception and entertainment of guests, visitors, or strangers, with liberality and goodwill.

c **1375** *Sc. Leg. Saints, Thomas* 424 [þe] aucht wel ma be, for to luf hospitalyte. **1382** WYCLIF *Rom.* xii. 13 Hospitalite, that is, herboringe of pore men. *c* **1460** FORTESCUE *Abs. & Lim. Mon.* xviii. (1885) 153 Euery abbey priory, and oþer howses founded vpon hospitalite. **1550** CROWLEY *Last Trump* 705, I can kepe hospitalitye, And geue as much vnto the pore. **1617** MORYSON *Itin.* III. 151 That the old English Hospitality was..a meere vice, I have formerly shewed. *a* **1661** FULLER *Worthies* (1840) II. 421 Keeping good hospitality in the Christmas at Bromley. **1771** SMOLLETT *Humph. Cl.* 26 June, Living in the country and maintaining 'old English hospitality'..This is a phrase very much used by the English themselves, both in words and writing; but I never heard of it out of the island, except by way of irony and sarcasm. **1810** SCOTT *Lady of L.* I. xxix, Every courteous rite was paid, That hospitality could claim. **1865** LIVINGSTONE *Zambesi* xxviii. 580 We accepted his hospitality after the weather had moderated.

b. with *pl.* An instance of this.

1856 EMERSON *Eng. Traits, Aristocr.* Wks. (Bohn) II. 82 In matters of state, and of expense..in convivial and domestic hospitalities. **1890** *Spectator* 14 June, The mind has various hospitalities to offer, and may treat its guests.. with a caprice we cannot wholly over-reach.

c. Applied in conventional phr. to the admission of correspondence, etc., to a newspaper.

1913 *Punch* 16 Apr. 298, I thank you for the hospitality of your columns.

d. ***to partake of*** (or ***enjoy***) ***His*** (or ***Her***) ***Majesty's hospitality***: to be in prison. *jocular*.

1894 *Strand Mag.* Sept. 296/2 Partaking of Her Majesty's hospitality, in a building specially erected for gentlemen who need a compulsory holiday. **1938** F. D. SHARPE *Sharpe of Flying Squad* xiv. 157 One awful thug I know, who is now enjoying His Majesty's hospitality, beat his woman up regularly.

†**2.** Hospitableness. *Obs.*

1706 PHILLIPS (ed. Kersey), *Hospitality*, a being well disposed to entertain. **1711** SHAFTESB. *Charac.* II. II. §3 (1737) II. 166 The noble Affection, which, in antient Language, was term'd Hospitality, viz. extensive Love of Mankind, and Relief of Strangers.

†**3.** A hospitable institution or foundation; a hospital (sense 2). In quot. 1571, ? Hospitable institutions generally. *Obs. rare*.

1571 *Act 13 Eliz.* c. 10 §2 The Dilapidations and the Decaye of all Spyrituall Lyvynges and Hospitallytie. **1761** HUME *Hist. Eng.* II. xxii. 45 The hospitality of St. Leonard's near York.

4. *attrib.* and *Comb.* Now commonly used of a room, suite of rooms, etc., in a hotel, TV studio, etc., set aside for the entertainment of guests with drinks.

1552 HULOET, Hospitalitie keper, or he who kepeth a good howse of meat and drinke, *philoxenus*. *Ibid.*, Hospitalitie kepynge, *larem fouens*. **1897** *Daily News* 5 Oct. 5/3 The women..have formed a strong 'hospitality' committee. **1959** *Encounter* Aug. 8/1 The eminent person is ushered into ..the 'hospitality' room [at the BBC]. **1960** *News Chron.* 2 Mar. 4/4 The drinks, consumed rather dismally in the hospitality room,..conspire to make a TV appearance an ordeal. **1963** J. N. HARRIS *Weird World Wes Beattie* (1964) ii. 20 At these conventions a lot of big companies put in hospitality suites—snake rooms, they call them. **1966** M. HASTINGS *Cork on Telly* i. 10 There was no time to talk to him in the hospitality room before the programme. **1969** *Observer* 8 June 38/1 The Americans led off by introducing Shatalov and Yeliseyev to the taste of bourbon from the hospitality cupboards of the private room at the American exhibition stand. **1970** *Globe & Mail* (Toronto) 25 Sept. 40/1 Opportunities..in the ever-growing hospitality field [in motels]. **1970** *Globe Mag.* (Toronto) 26 Sept. 6/3 There aren't many bands or hospitality suites or funny hats. **1971** *Bahamas* XXIII. III. 34/1 She moved into the hospitality industry where her personality assets were plus factors. **1972** *Guardian* 20 Mar. 11/1 She said it in the Hospitality Room..right after the show.

hospitalize ('hɒspɪtəlaɪz), *v.* [f. HOSPITAL *sb.* + -IZE.] *trans.* To place or accommodate in a hospital.

Freq. commented on as an unhappy formation.

1901 *Daily Chron.* 10 Sept. 6/2 The disease was spreading rapidly owing to the people refusing to hospitalise first cases. **1904** *Ibid.* 28 Oct. 8/3 The pauper who is hospitalised in an English casual ward. **1946** *Nature* 3 Aug. 170/1 Cases hospitalized in the Carmichael Hospital for Tropical Diseases, Calcutta. **1955** *Sci. News Let.* 15 Jan. 39/3 Surgery ..was performed on 70% of the hospitalized children. **1961** *Observer* 19 Nov. 29/6 On the second day after the mutiny the ship's doctor insisted that the lives of a passenger and a wounded member of the crew depended on their being hospitalised. **1970** G. GREER *Female Eunuch* 239 The more the state undertakes to protect a man from illness..the more it has the right to sacrifice him..to hospitalize his children.

Hence ˌ**hospitaliˈzation**, confinement to, or accommodation in, a hospital.

1909 in WEBSTER. **1918** A. WOOLLCOTT *Let.* 12 Jan. (1946) 40 My present brief hospitalization is traceable to eye-strain. **1932** *Nation* 25 May 604 The activities of the Legion ..began with a demand for pensions and hospitalization for those disabled in war service. **1937** R. S. MORTON *Woman Surgeon* vi. 70 The systematic hospitalization of the sick poor furnished a wealth of clinical material. **1967** *Spectator* 28 July 114/1 Private hospitalisation and medicine has been increased in price by this Government so that, while the rich people can cope, the moderately well off can no longer do so. **1971** COWDRY & STEINBERG *Care of Geriatric Patient* (ed. 4) xxvii. 352/1 Application of new scientific knowledge to clinical medicine has profoundly affected the hospitalization requirements of elderly patients.

hospitaller, -aler (ˈhɒspɪtələ(r)). Forms: 4–6 hospiteler, -yteler, 5 -ytler, hosspituller, hospituler, ospitallere, 6 hospytelar, 7–8 -itler, 4– hospitaler, 5 -aller. [a. OF. *hospitalier* (12–13th c. in Hatz.-Darm.), ad. med.L. *hospitālārius* hospitaller (senses 1 and 2), f. *hospitāle* (see HOSPITAL *sb.*). HOSTELER, OSTLER are doublets.]

1. In a religious house or hospice, the person whose office it is to receive and attend upon visitors, pilgrims, and strangers; = HOSTELER[1] 1.

1483 *Cath. Angl.* 190/1 An Hosspituller, *cenodochiaria, cenodochiarius.* **1745** A. BUTLER *Lives Saints* (1836) I. 67 St. Isidore, Priest and Hospitaller..of Alexandria. **1864** GREENSHIELDS *Ann. Lesmahagow* 13 The hospitaler received strangers and the wayfaring poor.

2. *spec.* A member of a religious order, brotherhood, or sisterhood, formed for charitable purposes, esp. for the care of the sick and infirm in hospitals. Many such have existed from the 13th c. or earlier. Such were originally the *Knights Hospitallers* (see 3).

c **1386** CHAUCER *Pars. T.* ¶817 Folk that been entred in-to ordre as subdekne or preest or hospitaliers. *c* **1430** LYDG. *Venus-Mass* Ep. in *Lay Folks Mass Bk.* 394 To all the holy ffraternite and Confrary of the same bretherhede. And to alle hospytlerys and Relygious nat spottyd nor mad foul wyth no cryme. **1686** J. SERGEANT *Hist. Monast. Convent.* 52 The Hospitalers of the Holy Ghost took their beginning at Rome, about..1201. **1727–41** CHAMBERS *Cycl.* s.v., The appellation is chiefly given to certain communities of religious; as, the hospitalers of Elsefort in Essex, instituted to take care of lepers; hospitalers of S. John Baptist of Coventry; hospitalers of S. Julian; hospitalers of S. Leonard at York, etc. **1746** in *Acc. French Settlem. N. Amer.* 24 This house is serv'd by the nuns hospitalers of St. Augustine of the congregation of the mercy of Jesus. **1880** *Chambers' Encycl.* s.v., The hospitallers of Our Lady of Christian Charity were founded near Chalons in the end of the 13th c., by Guy de Joinville;..and the hospitallers of Our Lady Della Scala about the same time at Siena.

3. More fully, ***Knights Hospitallers***, an order of military monks, following chiefly the rule of St. Augustine, which took its origin from a hospital founded at Jerusalem, *c* 1048, by merchants of Amalfi, for the succour and protection of poor pilgrims visiting the Holy Land, but subsequently grew to be a wealthy fraternity, received a military organization, and became one of the chief bulwarks of Christendom in the East, besides having dependent 'hospitals' and possessions throughout the Christian lands. (See COMMANDERY.) ***Grand Hospitaller***, the third in dignity of the order, after the Grand Commander and Grand Marshal; also an officer in some other orders.

After the taking of Jerusalem by Saladin in 1187, the chief seat of the order was successively at Markab in Phoenicia, Acre 1193, Cyprus 1291, Rhodes 1310, Malta 1530 to 1798. Their possessions were confiscated in England in 1540, and the order was suppressed in most European countries in or after 1799. They were known at various times, and in their various capacities, as *Brothers of the Hospital of St. John the Baptist, Knights of the Hospital of St. John of Jerusalem, Knights of Rhodes, Knights of Malta*, etc. (This is the earliest sense of the word in English.)

c **1330** R. BRUNNE *Chron.* (1810) 178 He toke it wikkedly out of þe Hospitelers hond. *c* **1400** MAUNDEV. (Roxb.) iv. 13 Þe ile of Rodes, þe whilk þe Hospitelers haldez and gouernes. *Ibid.* x. 40 [see HOSPITAL *sb.* 1]. **1531** *Dial. on Laws Eng.* II. xlii. (1638) 136 The Hospitelers and Templers be prohibit they shall hold no plee that belongs to the Kings Courts. **1603** KNOLLES *Hist. Turks* (1638) 13 He entred into a deepe discourse thereof with..the master of the Hospitalers. **1703** MAUNDRELL *Journ. Jerus.* (1721) 55 The Convent of the Knights Hospitallers. **1756–7** tr. *Keysler's Trav.* (1760) I. 274 As to the order of St. Maurice, it has the king for grand master... The marquis de Morus, chancellor of the order. The count de Provana, great hospitaler. **1776–81** GIBBON *Decl. & F.* lviii. **1858** W. PORTER *Knights Malta* I. i. 13 Such was the original establishment of the Hospitallers of Jerusalem, which may justly be considered as the cradle of the Order of St. John.

4. In some of the London hospitals, which were orig. religious foundations (and thus a direct development of sense 1): The title of the chief resident official whose office included that of religious superintendent; hence it is retained in some cases, e.g. St. Bartholomew's Hospital and St. Thomas's Hospital, as the title of the chaplain.

1552 *Ordre Hosp. St. Barthol.* D iiij, The office of the Hospiteler. **1557** *Order of Hospitalls* E j b, Your warrant in sending any [sick folk] to the Hospitalls, shalbe sufficient to the Hospitaller for the receaving of the same. **1624** in *Vicary's Anat.* (1888) App. iii. 146 To haue a revercion of the Hospitlers place of Saint Bartholomewes. **1726** LEONI *Alberti's Archit.* I. 86/1 Sick Strangers..distributed regularly to inferior Hospitlers, to be looked after. **1737** J. CHAMBERLAYNE *St. Gt. Brit.* 248 (St. Thomas's Hospital, Southwark) In the same court are the houses of the Treasurer, Hospitaler, Steward, Butler and Cook. **1766** ENTICK *London* IV. 382 An hospitaller or chaplain, 4 physicians. **1898** *St. Barthol. Hosp., Charge of the Vicar and Hospitaller.* **1898** *St. Thomas's Hosp., Duties of Hospitaller*, You shall enjoin the Sisters to send for you, or the Assistant Hospitaller, whenever any Patients shall desire such [religious] Ministrations.

5. An inmate of a hospital. *rare.*

1854 HAWTHORNE *Eng. Note-Bks.* (1879) II. 325 There is an old man's hospital..Life-like tales might be written on the..experiences of these Hospitallers.

6. *attrib.* † ***Hospitaller Knight*** = 3. *Obs. rare.*

1613 PURCHAS *Pilgrimage* (1614) 521 It was the Seat of the Hospitular-knights, which now reside in Malta.

† **ˈhospitary**, *a. Obs. rare.* [ad. med.L. *hospitāri-us*, f. *hospes, hospit-*: see HOST *sb.*[2] + -ARY.] Connected or having to do with entertainment or housing.

1658 ROWLAND *Moufet's Theat. Ins.* 900 Untill the publick overseers and hospitary Bees have found a fit place for the Swarm to settle in.

hospitate (ˈhɒspɪtət), *a. rare.* [ad. med.L. *hospitāt-us*: see Du Cange.] Devoted to the purposes of a hospice.

1869 R. WILLIS *Hist. Monast. Christ Ch. Canterb.* v. (*heading*), Hospitate and private buildings of the prior. *Ibid.* Index, Hospitate buildings of the Monastery.

hospitate (ˈhɒspɪteɪt), *v. rare.* [f. L. *hospitāt-*, ppl. stem of *hospitārī* to be a guest, med.L. *hospitāre* to receive as a guest, f. *hospit-em* guest, HOST *sb.*[2]]

† **1.** *trans.* To lodge or entertain. *Obs. rare*$^{-0}$.

1623 COCKERAM, *Hospitate*, to lodge one.

† **2.** *intr.* To lodge, take up one's abode. *Obs.*

1681 GREW *Museum* (J.), This hospitates with the living animal in the same shell.

3. Repr. Ger. *hospitieren*, To attend university lectures as an occasional student.

a **1886** W. B. ROBERTSON *Martin Luther* etc. II. (1892) 113 You may *hospitate*, as it is called, though you are not a Bursch.

So **hospiˈtation**, reception as a guest, hospitable entertainment. **ˈhospitator** (L. *hospitātor*), one who receives or entertains hospitably.

1851 *Illustr. Calend. Angl. Ch.* 251 From his great liberality to travellers and wayfarers, he [Saint Julian] is called Hospitator, and is considered the patron saint of travellers, ferrymen, and wandring minstrels. **1863** J. R. WALBRAN *Mem. Fountains Abbey* (Surtees) 188 He..was admitted by the grace and favour of Queen Margeret to her household and hospitation. **1894** J. A. WHITLOCK *Hosp. God's House, Southampt.* 28 The traditionary life of St. Julian, Hospitator.

hoˈspiticide. *rare*$^{-0}$. [ad. rare L. *hospiticīda*, f. *hospes, hospit-* guest + *-cīda*, -CIDE 1.] One who kills his guest or host. (Blount *Glossogr.* 1656.)

† **hospitious** (hɒˈspɪʃəs), *a. Obs.* [f. L. *hospitium* (see HOSPICE) + -OUS: cf. *auspicious, officious.*] Hospitable. (Sometimes repr. L. *hospitālis*: see HOSPITAL *a.* 2.)

1588 GREENE *Dorastus & F.* 22 Where I shall hope hospitious friends to find. *c* **1611** CHAPMAN *Iliad* VI. 240 We glory in th' hospitious rites our grand-sires did commend. **1622** DRAYTON *Poly-olb.* xxii. (1748) 341 The shire's hospitious town. **1784** in Sir B. Burke *Viciss. Fam.* Ser. II. (1860) 316 He got the name of Na Feile, or the Hospitious.

‖ **hospitium** (hɒˈspɪʃɪəm). [L.: see HOSPICE.]

1. = HOSPICE 1.

1650 TRAPP *Comm. Gen.* i. 9–10 God..will not faile to provide us an *hospitium*, a place to reside in, when cast out of all. **1700** tr. *Angelo & Carli's Congo* in Pinkerton *Voy.* (1814) XVI. 156 (Stanf.) Attended by this croud, we proceeded to our *hospitium* or house for our reception. **1830** SCOTT *Monast.* xvi, Inform us why you will not approach our more pleasant and better furnished *hospitium.* **1878** MACLEAR *Celts* xi. 181 The Church at Iona, as well as the hospitium, the refectory, etc. were thus made of wattles.

2. A place of residence for students in a university; a hall or hostel.

1895 RASHDALL *Univ. Europe* I. v. §5. 481 The original Hospicium or Hall (as it was usually called at Oxford) was a democratic, self-governing Society. *Ibid.* 482 The College was, in its origin, nothing but an endowed Hospicium or Hall. *Ibid.* II. II. xii. §9. 558 At Cambridge..the more usual name was Hospicium or Hostel—not the only instance in which a Parisian usage has been preserved more faithfully at Cambridge than at Oxford.

hospitize (ˈhɒspɪtaɪz), *v. rare.* [f. L. *hospit-em* guest + -IZE.]

1. *trans.* To lodge or entertain with hospitality.

1895 *Ch. Chron.* (N. Zealand) May 597 His Lordship.. was driven to the residence of Mr. Aldrich, where they were hospitised till the following evening.

2. *intr.* = HOSPITATE 3.

1895 A. STODDART *J. S. Blackie* iii. 54 By the rule of 'hospitising' practised in the University, he found himself free to visit the classes under Hausmann [etc.].

‖ **hospodar** (ˈhɒspəʊdɑː(r)). [a. Romanian *hospodár*, of Slavonic origin: possibly from Little Russ. *hospodárĭ* = Russ. *gospodárĭ* (in South Russia 'master of a house'), deriv. of *gospódĭ* lord. Another Russian form of the word is *gosudárĭ* sovereign, king, lord, sir.]

A word meaning 'lord', formerly borne as a title of dignity by the governors appointed by the Ottoman Porte for the provinces of Wallachia and Moldavia.

[**1630** *R. Johnson's Kingd. & Commw.* 476 (Russia) And all this for the honour of Hospodare, viz. the Prince.]

1684 *Scanderbeg Rediv.* iv. 86 The Hospodars of Wallachia and Moldavia..revolted from the Turks. **1796** MORSE *Amer. Geog.* II. 461 (Stanf.) The Hospodars, or princes of Wallachia and Moldavia, pay very large sums to the Grand Sultan for their dignities. **1838** *Penny Cycl.* XII. 317/1 These Hospodars or governors assumed the title of princes, and were addressed as 'Most Serene Highness'. **1886** DOWDEN *Shelley* II. ix. 362 His father, for a time hospodar of Wallachia, had retired into private life.

Hence **hospoˈdariat, -iate** (erron. **-iot, hospodorate**), the office of a hospodar, the territory governed by a hospodar.

1833 *Fraser's Mag.* VII. 196 The hospodariats were sure to become dependencies of Muscovy. **1866** *Ch. Times* 3 Mar., The deposition of Prince Couza from the Hospodariate of Wallachia and Moldavia has been accomplished. **1878** SEELEY *Stein* III. 529 Hampering negotiations, with the ideas of an Hospodorate, an annexation of Candia.

hospray, obs. form of OSPREY.

† **hospte**, a variant of HOST, assimilated to L. *hospit-em.* So † **hospetes** for HOSTESS *sb.*

1549 COVERDALE, etc. *Erasm. Par. 2 Tim.* 25 Salute Prisilla and Aquila myne hospte and myne hospetes.

hospyt-, obs. form of HOSPIT-.

hoss (hɒs), *sb.* Dial. and U.S. var. of HORSE *sb.*

1. = HORSE *sb.* 1 and 26 a.

1815 D. HUMPHREYS *Yankey in Eng.* v. 77 The boys..see a ghost in the form of a white hoss; and an Indian in every black stump. **1849** N. KINGSLEY *Diary* (1914) 88 My supper consisted of beans, old hoss, and hard bread. **1877** J. M. BAILEY *Folks in Danbury* 37 But this is a hoss of another colour. **1877** F. ROSS et al. *Gloss. Holderness* 78 *Hoss*, a horse. **1887** T. DARLINGTON *Folk-Speech S. Cheshire* 225 *Hoss-wesh*, a horse-pond. **1888** F. R. STOCKTON *Dusantes* 15 'These hosses won't do much at holdin back,' he said. **1889** M. PEACOCK *Taales fra Linkisheere* 130 In cums a greät black hoss, all drippin' wi' wet. **1958** S. E. HYMAN in A. Dundes *Mother Wit* (1973) 55/1 He had him a big black hoss.

2. *U.S.* = HORSE *sb.* 4.

1843 in *Amer. Speech* (1965) XL. 130 Sez he old hoss, I'll eat you up jis like I would a cabbage. **1844** *Yale Lit. Mag.* X. 168 Well, hoss, I reckon I will. **1847** *Knickerbocker* XXIX. 204 We've sworn to give the first strange old hoss that comes along this road an up-and-down beating. **1847** W. T. PORTER *Quarter Race Kentucky* 39 Good mornin', old hoss. **1857** T. H. GLADSTONE *Englishm. in Kansas* iv. 41 Step up this way, old hoss, and liquor. **1904** W. N. HARBEN *Georgians* xv. 148 'Went back on us, ole hoss,' Jim said, cordially. **1940** *Amer. Speech* XV. 216/1 Varmint might be applied to a contemptible person..but in Florida hound or hoss would as likely be used.

3. = HORSE *sb.* 15. *U.S. slang.*

1968 *Sun Mag.* (Baltimore) 13 Oct. 19/3, I was square to them, one step lower because I wasn't on hoss.

4. *attrib.* and *Comb.* = HORSE *sb.* 27 and 28.

1837 R. M. BIRD *Nick of Woods* II. iv. 63, I do [know].. all the parts injacent and outjacent, circumsurrounding the hoss-stump. **1877** J. HABBERTON *Jericho Road* xv. 142 Losin' your health when you started with Sam Reeves' hoss-gang. **1909** 'O. HENRY' *Roads of Destiny* xvi. 263 Amos Colvin and me were thicker than two hoss thieves more than ten years. **1942** BERREY & VAN DEN BARK *Amer. Thes. Slang* §608/9 *Western picture*, hoss opera, opery.

† **hoss**, *v. Obs. rare*$^{-0}$. [An onomatopœic form akin to HUZZ.] *intr.* To buzz.

1530 PALSGR. 588/1, I hosse, as a bee or flye dothe..It is a perylous noyse..to here a bee hosse in a boxe.

hoss, -e, hossell, obs. ff. HOSE *sb.*, HOUSEL.

host (həʊst), *sb.*[1] Forms: α. 3–6 ost(e, 4–5 oost, 4–6 ooste, 6 oast, 6–7 *Sc.* oyst. β. 4–6 hoost, 4–7 hoste, 5–6 hooste, 6–7 hoast, *Sc.* hoist, 4– host. [a. OF. *ost, host, oost, hoost* army (10th c. in Godef.) = It. *oste*, Sp. *hueste*, Pg. *hoste*:—L. *hostem* (*hostis*) stranger, enemy, in med.L. army, warlike expedition. The Latin *h*, lost in Romanic, was gradually readopted in OF. and ME. spelling, and hence in mod.Eng. pronunciation.]

1. An armed company or multitude of men; an army. Now *arch.* and *poet.*

c **1290** *S. Eng. Leg.* I. 13/431 His sone a-ȝein þe Aumperour with is ost he wende. *a* **1300** *Cursor M.* 6160 Of egypte godds ost [*Trin.* hoost] vte vend. *c* **1330** R. BRUNNE *Chron. Wace* (Rolls) 14336 Þey..gadered folk, & hostes ledde. **1362** LANGL. *P. Pl.* A. III. 252 Weend þider with þin host [*v. rr.* ost, oost]. **1398** TREVISA *Barth. De P.R.* XV. cxxvii[i]. (Bodl. MS.), Þer was no corner of þe worlde wide but he feelde þe swerd of þe oste of Rome. **1526** TINDALE *Acts* xxviii. 16 The chefe captayne of the host. *a* **1555** LYNDESAY *Tragedie* 163, I rasit ane oyste of mony bald Baroun. *a* **1592** H. SMITH *Serm.* (1637) 148 As Samuel would not come to Saul, so wisdome will not come to that oast. **1605** SHAKS. *Macb.* v. iv. 6 Thereby shall we shadow The numbers of our Hoast. **1609** SKENE *Reg. Maj.*, *Stat.*

Will. 7 Of them qvha comes to the hoist. **1700** Dryden *Ajax & Ulysses* 214 Who better can succeed Achilles lost Than he who gave Achilles to your hoast? **1715–20** Pope *Iliad* II. 201 Haste, goddess, haste! the flying host detain. **1840** Thirlwall *Greece* lvii. VII. 211 She was..not daunted by the sight of the armed host which surrounded her. **1871** Freeman *Norm. Conq.* IV. xvii. 30 The leaders of the host were exhorted to gentleness and moderation.

b. *fig.* and *transf.*

[*c* **1315** Shoreham 15 A prince of Godes ost Schel do thė confermynge None loȝer, Therfore hit mot a bisschope be.] **1340** Hampole *Pr. Consc.* 4475 Gog and Magog es noght elles Bot þe host of anticrist. *c* **1400** *Rom. Rose* 5859 Fonde Shame adowne to brynge, With alle her oost erly and late. **1573** J. Sanford *Hours Recreat.* (1576) 56 That an host of Hartes is more to be feared that is ruled by a Lyon, than an hoste of Lyons ruled by an Hart. **1629** Milton *Hymn Nativ.* 21 All the spangled host keep watch in squadrons bright. **1773** Burke *Corr.* (1844) I. 417 He was a host of debaters in himself. **1862** Stanley *Jew. Ch.* (1877) I. xix. 374 It is a word which..is a host of imagery and doctrine in itself. **1866** G. Macdonald *Ann. Q. Neighb.* xxvii. (1878) 470 Arcturus and his host.

†**c.** A warlike gathering; cf. hosting. *Sc. Obs.*

1807 Grierson *St. Andrews* 74 A clause binding the latter to attend and protect the former in all reids and hosts.

2. *transf.* A great company; a multitude; a large number.

[*c* **1440** *Gesta Rom.* xii. 38 (Harl. MS.) The king maade him redy to come to þe Emperour, with a gret oost, for to wedde his dowter.] **1613** Purchas *Pilgrimage* (1614) 269 The three Hostes [caravans] cast themselves into a triangle. **1797** Mrs. Radcliffe *Italian* xii, Defend this lady against your host of Monks. **1840** Mrs. F. Trollope *Widow Married* viii, The examination of a host of trunks just arrived from France. **1845** M. Pattison *Ess.* (1889) I. 11 What a host of thoughts and images that one name carries! **1875** Jowett *Plato* (ed. 2) III. 234 They produce a host of books written by Musaeus and Orpheus.

†**b.** A name for a 'company' of sparrows. *Obs.*

1486 *Bk. St. Albans* F vj b, An Ost of sparowis.

3. In Biblical and derived uses: **a.** ***host*** or ***hosts of heaven*** (Heb. *ts'bā hashshāmayim*) is applied to (*a*) the multitude of angels that attend upon God, and (*b*) the sun, moon, and stars.

1382 Wyclif *1 Kings* xxii. 19, I saw the Lord vpon his see sittynge, and al the oost of heuene stondynge neeȝ to hym. **1535** Coverdale *Gen.* ii. 1 Thus was heauen and earth fynished with all their hoost. —— *Deut.* xvii. 3 Sonne or Mone, or eny of the hooste of heauen. **1611** Bible *Josh.* v. 14 As captaine of the hoste of the Lord am I now come. **1667** Milton *P.L.* iv. 606 Hesperus that led The starrie Host. *Ibid.* v. 710 His count'nance..Drew after him the third part of Heav'ns Host. **1839** Yeowell *Anc. Brit. Ch.* i. (1847) 5 The worship of the host of heaven.

b. ***Lord*** (***God***) ***of Hosts*** (***Jehovah Ts'bāōth***): a frequent title of Jehovah in certain books of the Old Testament; app. referring sometimes to the heavenly hosts (see a), sometimes to the armies of Israel, and hence in modern use with the sense 'God of armies' or 'of battles'.

1382 Wyclif *1 Sam.* xvii. 45 Y come to thee in the name of the Lord God of oostis, God of the cumpanyes of Israel. —— *Zech.* i. 3 Be ȝe conuerted to me, saith the Lord of oostis. **1535** Coverdale *Zech.* xiv. 21 All the kettels in Ierusalem and Iuda, shalbe holy vnto the Lorde of hoostes. **1569** in *Q. Eliz. Prayer Bk.* App. v. (1890) 225 O most myghtie God, the Lorde of hoastes..the only geuer of all victories. **1860** Pusey *Min. Proph.* 78 The Lord of Hosts, i.e. of all things visible and invisible..of all things animate and inanimate, which, in the history of Creation, are called, the host of heaven and earth, the one host of God. **1891** A. F. Kirkpatrick in *Camb. Bible for Schools, Psalms* xxiv. 10 *note.* **1897** R. Kipling *Recessional*, Lord God of Hosts, be with us yet, Lest we forget—lest we forget.

host (həʊst), *sb.*[2] Forms: α. 3–7 **oste**, 4–5 **ost**, 5–6 **ooste**, 6–8 **oast**. β. 4– **host**; also 4–6 **hoost(e**, 4–7 **hoste**, 6 *Sc.* **hoist**, 6–7 **hoast**. [a. OF. *oste*, *hoste* (12th c. in Littré), mod.F. *hôte* host, guest = It. *oste*:—L. *hospit-em* (*hospes*) host, guest, stranger, foreigner. For resumption of *h*, cf. prec.]

1. A man who lodges and entertains another in his house: the correlative of *guest*.

1303 R. Brunne *Handl. Synne* 4601 And ȝyt shall he make sum robbery, Or begyle hys hoste þer he shal lye. **1388** Wyclif *Rom.* xvi. 23 Gayus myn oost [**1382** my herborgere; **1526** Tindale myne hoste; **1611** mine hoste] greeteth ȝou wel. **1531** Tindale *Exp. I John* (1537) 98 Gaius..whome Paule..calleth hys ooste and the ooste of all the congregacion. **1580** Sidney *Arcadia* II. (1622) 173 A tedious guest to a loathsome oast. **1605** Shaks. *Macb.* I. vi. 29 Conduct me to mine Host, we loue him highly. **1700** Dryden *Baucis & Phil.* 118 But the kind hosts their entertainment grace, With hearty welcome, and an open face. **1708** E. Cook *Sot-weed Factor* (1865) 10 Pleas'd with the Treatment I did find, I took my leave of Oast so kind. **1870** Dickens *E. Drood* viii, You are almost in the position of host to-night.

2. *spec.* A man who lodges and entertains for payment; a man who keeps a public place of lodging or entertainment; the landlord of an inn. Often in archaic phr. ***mine*** (***my***) ***host*** = the landlord of such and such an inn.

c **1290** *Beket* 1176 in *S. Eng. Leg.* I. 140 At one gode mannes house his In a-niȝt he nam..his oste nam wel god ȝeme hov heo heom alle bere. *c* **1386** Chaucer *Prol.* 747 Greet chiere made oure hoost [*v. rr.* ost, oste, hooste] vs euerichon. *c* **1400** *Ywaine & Gaw.* 222 Efter soper, sayd myne oste, That he cowth noght tel the day That ani knight are with him lay. **1573** J. Sanford *Hours Recreat.* (1576) 145 Lodged in an Inne..Whereuppon the Hoste asked him payment. **1598** Shaks. *Merry W.* II. i. 100 Mine Host of the Garter. **1653** Walton *Angler* ii. 45 Tell me freely how you like my Hoste, and the company? is not mine Hoste a witty man? **1805** Wordsw. *Waggoner* I. 90 Who does not know the famous Swan? Object uncouth! and yet our boast, For it was painted by the Host. **1858** *Murray's Hand-bk. N. Germ.* 58 The two daughters of mine host are both fair and graceful in their national costume. **1860** Tyndall *Glac.* I. xvii. 121, I was informed by my host that [etc.]. **1909** Wodehouse *Mike* xii. 66 That was the supreme moment in mine host's life. **1934** —— *Right Ho, Jeeves* x. 123, I entered the saloon bar and requested mine host to start pouring. **1973** J. Porter *It's Murder with Dover* vii. 67 Dover set about cross-questioning the landlord... Mine host stuck to his guns.

b. Prov. ***to reckon*** (†***count***) ***without*** (†***before***) ***one's host***: to calculate one's bill or score without consulting one's host or landlord; to come to conclusions without taking into consideration some important circumstance of the case.

c **1489** Caxton *Blanchardyn* lii. 202 It ys sayd in comyn that 'who soeuer rekeneth wythoute his hoste, he rekeneth twys for ones'. **1533** More *Debell. Salem* Wks. 991/2 He fareth lo lyke a geste, that maketh hys rekening himselfe without hys hoste. **1548** Hall *Chron., Hen. VI* 131 b, Thei reckened before their host, and so paied more then their shotte came to. **1597** Montgomerie *Cherrie & Slae* 649 He that countis without his oist, Oft tymes he countis twyse. **1698** Vanbrugh *2nd Pt. Æsop* iii, But here, alas! he found to's cost, He had reckon'd long without his host. **1824** Scott *St. Ronan's* xv, But hostess as she was herself,..she reckoned without her host in the present instance. **1877** [see count *v.* 7]. **1886** Symonds *Catholic React.* II. 174 He [Bruno] reckoned strangely in this matter, without the murderous host into whose clutches he had fallen.

3. a. *Biol.* An animal or plant having a parasite or commensal habitually living in or upon it.

1857 Lankester tr. *Küchenmeister's Anim. Paras.* I. Introd. 4 They usually emigrate once into the external world, generally with the excrements of the hosts of their parents. *Note*, Host is a literal translation of the German 'Wirth', and although not perhaps previously used in the above sense in the English language, I have adopted it to prevent a somewhat tedious circumlocution. **1862** *Intell. Observ.* I. 115 The mode in which the liver flukes gain access to their hosts, or in other words to the bodies of the herbivorous animals they frequent. **1875** Bennett & Dyer *Sachs' Bot.* 733 Cuscuta is nourished exclusively by the haustoria which penetrate into the tissue of the host. **1892** Brady *Addr. Tyneside Field Club* 9 To complete the life-cycle of any one of these creatures [tape-worms], successive residence is necessary in the bodies of two distinct species of animal,..thus called the 'intermediate host' and the 'final host'.

b. *Biol.* and *Med.* An animal or person that is the recipient of tissue, an organ, etc., that has been transplanted into it from another.

1906 *Brit. Med. Jrnl.* 22 Dec. 1796/1 Entire organs may be transplanted by anastomosis of their blood vessels to suitable points on the circulatory apparatus of the host. **1923** H. Neuhof *Transplantation of Tissues* i. 9 Experiments.. continued from six to nine months showed the transplant completely replaced by a connective tissue derived from the host. **1958** *New Biol.* XXVII. 42 The host reacts to the antigens of the graft by producing antibodies. **1961** *New Scientist* 5 Jan. 45/3 Cells of both the donor of the graft tissue, and the recipient host, played a part in the immune reaction.

†**4.** A guest. Cf. hoastman. *Obs.*

1390 Gower *Conf.* III. 205 How he [Lichaon]..His hostes slough and into mete He made her bodies to ben ete. **1490** Caxton *Eneydos* xviii. 68 An hoste that lightly forgeteth his lodgynge..and departeth Ioyously wythout to haue eny rewthe. **1518** *Merch. Adv. Newcastle* (Surtees) 51 The ostmen that byes any merchaundyse of ther hosts. **1559** *Mirr. Mag., Jas. I*, vii, They took me prisoner, not as oste.

5. a. *Geol.* A mineral mass containing a different mineral; a rock containing an ore deposit or foreign rock. Freq. *attrib.*

1889 *Cent. Dict.* III, *Host*, a mineral which incloses another. **1950** E. E. Wahlstrom *Introd. Theor. Igneous Petrol.* iv. 80 Perthites are intergrowths of two feldspars. Commonly the host mineral (that is, the more abundant mineral) is potash feldspar. **1965** G. J. Williams *Econ. Geol. N.Z.* i. 1/1 These are the host-rocks of the gold mineralization west of the Alps.

b. *Physics* and *Chem.* A crystal lattice or molecular structure containing a foreign ion, atom, or molecule; *spec.* (i) a crystal or a crystalline material to which a small amount of some impurity has been added to make it luminescent; (ii) that component of a clathrate compound that encloses or surrounds the other component. Usu. *attrib.*

1939 *Trans. Faraday Soc.* XXXV. 126 It may be imagined that the function of the activating impurity is to enter the host lattice and produce therein centres of distortion. **1950** H. W. Leverenz *Introd. Luminescence of Solids* vi. 369 A host crystal should not be strongly absorbing in the spectral region where efficient luminescence emission is to be produced. **1956** *Nature* 22 Dec. 1410/1 Various instances are known of continuous crystalline 'host' lattices within which 'guest' molecules may be trapped... Among inorganic lattices the best known are the crystalline zeolites. **1961** L. F. & M. Fieser *Adv. Org. Chem.* xxii. 771 They are similar to the urea inclusion complexes..except that the host is a covalently bonded molecule with a hole in it. **1967** Vanders & Kerr *Mineral Recognition* v. 85/2 At high temperatures, foreign ions are dissolved in the solid host crystal. **1968** *Proc. Internat. Conf. Luminescence Budapest* (1966) I. 1289 Luminescence of crystalline phosphors is strongly connected with the structure of the host crystal.

6. *attrib.* and *Comb.*, as (sense 1) ***host country***, ***government***, ***population***, ***society***; (sense 3) ***host animal***, ***cell***, ***-parasite*** (used appos.), ***plant***; ***host-specific*** adj. (so ***host-specificity***); ***host-controlled***, ***-induced*** adjs. See also sense 5.

1956 *Nature* 10 Mar. 453/1 It is reasonable to attribute these changes to the high dose of radiation delivered to the *host-animal and so to identify the cells containing them as host cells. **1954** *Science* 16 July 110/1 (*heading*) Action of T_2r^+ bacteriophage on *host-cell membranes. **1958** *Spectator* 22 Aug. 252/1 The life of the virus is so closely linked with that of the host cell that one cannot be attacked without injury to the other. **1965** *Ann. Rev. Microbiol.* XIX. 365 *Host-controlled modification of viruses is a general term applied to those cases in which passage through certain host strains imparts one or more new, nonheritable properties to the virus without altering its genetic information content. **1959** *Manch. Guardian* 21 July 1/7 The technical staff of control posts..should consist of one-third *host-country nationals. **1962** *Times* 18 Dec. 11/7 The 'host countries'..are [not] able economically to absorb the refugees permanently. **1969** H. MacInnes *Salzburg Connection* ix. 131 Switzerland is the host country. **1960** *Economist* 15 Oct. 263/1 Certain of the important '*host governments' of countries where the oil is actually produced chose not to come. **1953** *Cold Spring Harbor Symp. Quant. Biol.* XVIII. 237 (*heading*) *Host-induced modifications of viruses. **1946** *Nature* 6 July 30/2 *Host-parasite relations. **1964** V. J. Chapman *Coastal Veget.* iii. 77 Plants of course may exhibit host-parasite relations. **1888** *Athenæum* 28 Jan. 119/1 Preparations showing the entrance of the potato fungus into the *host-plant. **1889** *Scot. Leader* 19 June 7 The part played by the barberry as a 'host plant' in producing mildew. **1959** Southwood & Leston *Land & Water Bugs* viii. 239 This species may be found in great abundance on its host-plant. **1971** *Guardian* 24 July 7/2 The feelings of any *host population towards immigrants included suspicion, fear, and irritation. **1961** S. R. Herman in J. A. Fishman *Reading Sociol. Lang.* (1968) 509 Our analysis implies a cautionary note for the attitude of a *host society to newcomers. The host society may legitimately wish to encourage the use of its language by the newcomers, but it may aggravate the problem of adjustment if it insists too strictly on the adherence to its language norms. **1969** *Listener* 13 Nov. 664/1 Just one sign of the equivocal welcome meted out by the host society. **1972** *Jrnl. Social Psychol.* LXXXVI. 159 The changers displayed more of behavioral and psychological affinities toward the host society than the nonchangers. **1969** *New Scientist* 13 Mar. 23/1 WHO workers introduced a *host-specific pathogenic fungus which kills mosquito larvae. **1951** Whitby & Hynes *Med. Bacteriol.* (ed. 5) xxiv. 376 The viruses have the same wide range of *host-specificity as the bacteria.

†**host**, *sb.*[3] *Obs.* Forms: 4 **ooste, hoost(e**, 5 **ost(e, host(e**. [? ad. OF. *hosté*, *osté*, var. of *hostel*, *ostel* hostel. The pl. of the latter was often *ostez*, *ostes*, whence by reaction the sing. *osté*; mod.F. dialects have *hôté*, *ôté*. For the loss of final *-e* in Eng. cf. *assign* sb., *avowe* sb.] A place of lodging or entertainment; a hostel, inn.

1382 Wyclif *Acts* xxviii. 23 Mo camen to him in to the hoost, or herbore [1388 the in]. —— *Philem.* 22 Make redy to me an ooste [*gloss* or hous for to dwelle inne]. *c* **1440** *Gesta Rom.* xxiv. 89 (Harl. MS.) Thes two yong knyghtes yede to her oste in þe cite. *Ibid.* lxi. 257 His squier soȝte an host, for swiche a worthi knyȝt to be eside ynne. *c* **1450** Lonelich *Grail* xxxv. 26 An old vauasour that kepte An Ost, & was A Man of honour.

b. Phr. ***to be*** (or ***lie***) ***at host***: to be lodged or entertained; to be put up at an inn; *fig.* to be on familiar terms or at home *with*.

c **1450** *Merlin* 171 This mayden..was at hoste with a riche burgeys. **1554** H. Weston in *Latimer's Serm. & Rem.* (Parker Soc.) 264, I will be at host with you anon. **1565–73** Cooper *Thesaurus*, *Diuerti ad aliquem in hospitium*,..to be at host with one. **1589** Nashe *Anat. Absurd.* 35 Crowes and Rauens..are at hoste with euery kind of fruite in the Orchard. **1590** Shaks. *Com. Err.* v. i. 410 Your goods that lay at host..in the Centaur.

host (həʊst), *sb.*[4] Forms: α. 4 **oyst**, 4–5 **oost**, 4–7 **ost(e**, 6 **oast**. β. 4–6 **hoost(e, hoste**, 6–7 **hoast(e**, 5– **host**. [a. OF. *oiste*, *hoiste*:—L. *hostia* victim, sacrifice. At an early stage the Eng. word became assimilated in form to the prec. sbs., of which *ost*, *oost*, *hoost*, etc. were the normal etymological forms. See also hostie.]

†**1.** A victim for sacrifice; a sacrifice (*lit.* and *fig.*): often said of Christ. *Obs.*

a **1340** Hampole *Psalter* xxvi. 11, I offird in his tabernakile þe hoste of heghynge of voice. **1382** Wyclif *Phil.* iv. 18 A couenable oost [*gloss* or sacrifice], plesynge to God. —— *1 Pet.* ii. 5 To offre spiritual hoostes [*gloss* or offringes] acceptable to God bi Jhesu Crist. *c* **1430** *Life St. Kath.* (1884) 44 þat I myght offre my self an acceptable oost to hym. **1563** *Homilies* II. *Sacram.* II. (1859) 448 Let us..offer always to God the host or sacrifice of praise by Christ. **1605** Sylvester *Du Bartas* II. iii. II. *Fathers* 287 Anon said Isaac ..But where's your Hoste? **1609** Holland *Amm. Marcell.* XXIII. vi. 232 To goe unto the altars, or to handle an ost or sacrifice. **1653** Ld. Vaux *Godeau's St. Paul* 310 Jesus Christ having once offered the Host of His body, is seated at the right hand of God.

2. *Eccl.* The bread consecrated in the Eucharist, regarded as the body of Christ sacrificially offered; a consecrated wafer. Also applied to the wafer before consecration (quots. 1687, 1881).

1303 R. Brunne *Handl. Synne* 8849 He stode and heylde þe oste. **1387** Trevisa *Higden* (Rolls) V. 9 He ordeyned þat þe oyst schulde be of þerf brede. *c* **1400** *Apol. Loll.* Introd. 7 The sacred oost is no maner breed, but either nowȝt, or accident withouten ony subiect. **1526** *Pilgr. Perf.* (W. de W. 1531) 259 The host betokeneth the body of Chryst. *a* **1583** Grindal *Fruitf. Dial.* Rem. (1843) 46 If a little mouse get an host, he will crave no more meat to his dinner. **1687** A. Lovell tr. *Thevenot's Trav.* II. 164 They make their Hosts of Flower kned with Wine and Oil. **1756–7** tr. *Keysler's Trav.* (1760) IV. 28 Such as scruple to kneel at the host. **1845** S. Austin *Ranke's Hist. Ref.* II. 19 Omitting the words

which convey the idea of a sacrifice, and the ceremony of the elevation of the host. **1881** SHORTHOUSE *J. Inglesant* I. x. 191 An apothecary, who also was useful to the Catholics, making 'Hosts' for them.

3. *attrib.*, as (sense 2) ***host-bearer***, **-*cup***.

1688 R. HOLME *Armoury* III. 465/1 Host Cup. **1890** O. CRAWFURD *Round Calend. Port.* 4 The solemn chant of the Host-Bearers.

†**host**, *v.*[1] *Obs.* [f. HOST *sb.*[1]]

1. *trans.* To gather into a host; to assemble in battle array, to encamp. (Cf. HOSTING *vbl. sb.*)

1297 R. GLOUC. (Rolls) 1190 Betere hom adde ibe at rome, þan iiousted [*MS.B.* y osted] þere. *c* **1425** *Eng. Conq. Irel.* 16 The whill the host was thus in Ossory .. these tweyn, as har wone was, weren both I-hosted to-gedderes.

2. *intr.* To be assembled or gather in a host.

1430–40 LYDG. *Bochas* II. i. (1554) 42a, As they lay hostyng Not farre asonder, and Saul lay an slepe. **1787** J. BARLOW *Vis. Columbus* VI. 173 With scanty force, where should he lift the steel, While hosting foes immeasurably wheel?

host, *v.*[2] [f. HOST *sb.*[2]]

1. a. *trans.* To receive (any one) into one's house and entertain as a guest. Also, to receive into one's town, country, etc.; to be the host at (a party, dinner, etc.); to compère (a television show, etc.).

1485 *Act 1 Hen. VII*, c. 10 §3 That no Straunger .. shuld oste or take to sojourne with hym within this Realme of England any Merchaunt Straunger. **1531** ELYOT *Gov.* II. xii, Fuluius .. caused him to be hosted with a worshipfull man. **1596** SPENSER *F.Q.* IV. viii. 27 Such was that Hag, unmeet to host such guests. **1613** T. MILLES tr. *Mexia's Treas. Anc. & Mod. Times* I. 20/2 Nowhere should he account himselfe eyther a Stranger, or to be Hosted. [**1894** R. LEIGHTON *Wreck Golden Fleece* 61 They [fishing smacks] were 'hosted' by Lowestoft merchants, to whom they sold their fish.] **1939** *John o' London's* 7 Apr. 42/3, I am not surprised that Messrs. Auden and Isherwood came away with a sense of deep and humble respect for the people and the country who had hosted them. **1957** J. KEROUAC *On Road* (1958) 87 He went right out and bought a pint of whisky to host me proper. **1958** I. ASIMOV *Whiff of Death* (1968) vi. 55 Those comments applying to him were read at the celebration dinner hosted (invariably) by Anson himself. **1967** *Boston Sunday Herald* 26 Mar. I. 12/2 Dorchester man has been hosting a series of unusual farewell parties. **1967** *Boston Globe* 30 Mar. 15/2 The delegation of 25 men and women .. will be hosted by the Greater Boston Chamber of Commerce and Burlington town officials. **1967** *New Yorker* 1 Apr. 129 (Advt.), Bob Hope hosts the annual Academy of Motion Picture Arts and Sciences presentation. **1969** N. COHN *AWopBopaLooBop* (1970) ix. 88 He .. sold Murray the K T-shirts and hosted albums of Murray the K's Golden Gassers. **1969** *New Yorker* 29 Mar. 24/1 Let us host you at the Kahala Hilton, on one of Oahu's most beautiful beaches. **1969** *Guardian* 19 July 9/1 There will be David Frost, hosting ITV's night-long bonanza of touchdown and pop stars. **1973** *Times* 9 Feb. 8/8 The session was hosted by Mr. William Fulbright.

b. *intr.* To play the host.

1868 BP. WILBERFORCE in *Collect. & Recoll.* xv. (1898) 202 The great power of charming and pleasant host-ing possessed by Salisbury. **1957** *Time* 2 Sept. 34/2 Critic John Crosby, currently on leave from his TV syndicated column to polish up on his broadcast manners, will host. **1962** H. KANE *Killer's Kiss* xxviii. 216, I must do a bit more hosting —I'm expecting some special people.

†**2.** *intr.* To be a guest; to lodge, put up. *Obs.*

c **1450** *St. Cuthbert* (Surtees) 3978 He ostyd at haly eland. **1546** J. HEYWOOD *Prov.* (1867) 30 Great bost and small roste, Maketh vnsauery mouthes, where ever men oste. **1590** SHAKS. *Com. Err.* I. ii. 9 Goe beare it to the Centaure, where we host. *a* **1656** USSHER *Ann.* VI. (1658) 386 Antiochus, falling in love with .. the daughter of Cleoptolemus, where he hosted.

host, var. HOAST *sb.* and *v.*, cough.

hosta ('hɒstə). [mod.L. (L. Trattinick 1812, in *Archiv der Gewächskunde* I. 55; formerly used by N. J. Jacquin *Icones Plantarum Horti Schönbrunnensis* (1797) I. 60 for a plant now included in the genus *Cornutia*), f. the name of N.T. *Host* (1761–1834), Austrian physician.]

A plant of the genus so named (formerly called FUNKIA), native to Japan and eastern Asia and belonging to the family Liliaceæ; a plantain-lily.

[**1828** *Bot. Reg.* XIV. 1204 Willdenow proposes to unite Hosta with Cornutia. **1930** L. H. BAILEY in *Gentes Herbarum* II. 119 Mostly they [*sc.* plantain lilies] are known as species of Funkia, but Hosta is now the accepted name to those who follow the International Rules of nomenclature.] **1931** W. T. STEARN in *Gardeners' Chron.* 11 July 27/1 The Hostas, or Funkias, as they are commonly called, are hardy Liliaceous perennials, well-known in gardens on account of their decorative foliage. **1961** *Amateur Gardening* 4 Nov. 23/1 For the moist but well-drained part plants that you could grow are .. hydrangeas, .. hemerocallis, hostas. **1971** *Country Life* 25 Feb. 438/1 All hostas have good leaves, but there are some which we more particularly grow for foliage, than for flowers.

hostage ('hɒstɪdʒ), *sb.*[1] Also 4–7 **ostage**. [a. OF. *ostage* (11th c.), *hostage* (12–16th c. in Littré; Cotgrave 1611, *hostage* and *ostage*), mod.F. *otage*, = Pr. *ostatge*, OCat. *hostatge*, OSp. *hostage*, It. *ostaggio*, going back through **ostāticum*, to a late pop.L. type **obsidāticum*, f. L. *obsidātus* condition of a hostage, hostageship, f. *obses*, *obsidem* hostage. The initial *h* appears to have been added in OF., etc., through association with the family of L. *hospit-em*: see HOST *sb.*[2] Cf. med.L. *ostāticum*, *hostāticum* in sense 1, *hostāticus*, *ostagius*, *hostagius*, in sense 2 (Du Cange).]

†**1.** Pledge or security given to enemies or allies for the fulfilment of any undertaking by the handing over of one or more persons into their power; the standing, state, or condition of the persons thus handed over; chiefly in phrases ***in, into, to hostage***. (No plural.) *Obs.*

c **1275** LAY. 5317 Hii wolleþ habbe hure children to hostage [*c* 1205 ȝisle]. *c* **1290** *S. Eng. Leg.* I. 399/231 Heo and manie oþer in ostage weren itake. *a* **1300** *Cursor M.* 4987 Þijs oþer ten .. Duel in ostage her wit me. *a* **1420** HOCCLEVE *De Reg. Princ.* 3680 There was a maide sent hym into hostage. **1483** CAXTON *Gold. Leg.* 432 b/1 He was ledde .. with hys two brethren in ostage or pledge for the delyueraunce of the sayd kyng theyr fader. *a* **1533** LD. BERNERS *Huon* lxv. 223 Your brother layd hostage, promysynge that he wolde neuer retourne without he brought with hym ye admyrall Gaudys berde. **1555** EDEN *Decades* 80 Violatinge the lawe of hostage. **1588** SHAKS. *Tit. A.* IV. iv. 105 If he stand in Hostage for his safety. **1634** SIR T. HERBERT *Trav.* 6 [They] desired one or two of our men to goe ashoare, leaving hostage in our ship for their safe returne. **1726–31** TINDAL *Rapin's Hist. Eng.* (1743) II. XVII. 97 To give the young King .. in Hostage to the Queen.

2. (with *pl.*) A person thus given and held in pledge. Cf. HOSTAGER.

c **1275** LAY. 20909 Four and twenti hostages [*c* 1205 ȝisles] Childrich þar bitahte. *c* **1330** R. BRUNNE *Chron.* (1810) 78 William .. gaf ageyn þo fees, of whilk he toke ostages. **1520** *Caxton's Chron. Eng.* v. 46 b/1 Upon assuraunce of this same thynge they gave him good hostages. **1579** FENTON *Guicciard.* III. (1599) 101 He laboured secretly that the Genoways should not deliuer in their ostages to the King. **1665** MANLEY *Grotius' Low C. Warres* 85 He .. kept the Prince of Aurange's Son .. as an Hostage for his Fathers Actions. **1781** GIBBON *Decl. & F.* III. 225 Ambassadors .. to solicit the exchange of hostages. **1871** FREEMAN *Norm. Conq.* IV. xviii. 155 [At the siege of Exeter in 1068] one of the hostages was brought close to the East Gate, and his eyes were put out in the sight of both armies. **1879** FROUDE *Cæsar* xvi. 254 They had given hostages for their good behaviour.

3. *generally*. A pledge or security. spec. in phr. ***to give***, etc., ***a hostage to fortune***: to deliver one's future happiness, success, etc., into the hands of fate.

c **1400** *Rom. Rose* 7312 Though ye borowes take of me, The sikerer shal ye never be For ostages, ne sikirnesse, Or chartres. **1597** DANIEL *Civ. Wars* II. xxiii, The ost of Christ, an ostage for his troth. **1606** SHAKS. *Tr. & Cr.* III. ii. 115 You know now your hostages: your Vnckles word and my firme faith. **1607–12** BACON *Ess., Marriage* (Arb.) 264 He that hath wife and children, hath given hostages to fortune; for they are impedimentes to great enterprizes, either of vertue, or of mischief. **1732** T. FULLER *Gnomologia* 253 Wife and Children are Hostages given to Fortune. **1865** WHITTIER *Snow-bound* 483 One who wisely schemed, And hostage from the future took In trained thought and lore of book. **1875** M. E. BRADDON (*title*) Hostages to fortune. **1934** J. E. NEALE *Queen Elizabeth* xiv. 235 But to enter on war was to give hostages to fortune. Her instinct was to gamble on avoiding it. **1950** W. S. CHURCHILL *Second World War* IV. I. xi. 194 Once several good outfits are prepared, any one of which can attack a Japanese-held base or island and beat the life out of the garrison, all their islands will become hostages to fortune. **1965** *Listener* 4 Nov. 728/2 Every manufacturer who indulges in advertising is giving a hostage to fortune in that he is inviting public confidence in his goods and service, and he will rapidly go out of business if he cannot live up to his claims. **1968** *Ibid.* 28 Nov. 710/2 Denmark was almost a hostage to fortune by being in Nato at all.

†**4.** A treaty to which parties are pledged. *rare.*

1470–85 MALORY *Arthur* x. xxx, And there with alle was made hostage on bothe partyes, and made hit as sure as hit myghte be.

5. *attrib.*

1905 *Westm. Gaz.* 26 Sept. 8/2 The hostage camps [in the Gaboon]. **1909** *Daily Chron.* 18 Nov. 1/7 The dragging of a man to the hostage house [in the Congo]. **1931** H. G. WELLS *Work, Wealth, & Happiness of Mankind* (1932) vii. 275 Here all over again were the murders, the mutilations .. the hostage houses, and the atrocities.

Hence **'hostage** *v. trans.*, to give as a hostage.

1624 CAPT. SMITH *Virginia* IV. 158 Nor is it likely now they would have so hostaged their men .. had they intended any villany.

†**'hostage**, *sb.*[2] *Obs.* [a. OF. (*h*)*ostage*:—late L. type **hospitāticum*, f. *hospes*, *hospit-em* HOST *sb.*[2]: see -AGE. (Med.L. had *hospitāgium* and *hostāgium*, from Fr.)] A hostel, hostelry, inn. Also *attrib.*

c **1440** *Ipom.* 1292 His owne mayde, that was so bryght, To his ostage she went right. *c* **1450** *Cov. Myst.* (Shaks. Soc.) 147 Ostage in this towne know I non, Thin wyff and thou in for to slepe. **1547** BOORDE *Introd. Knowl.* xxxii. (1870) 205, I, hauynge pitie .. poynted them to my hostage. *a* **1828** *Willie Wallace* x. in Child *Ballads* (1882–98) III. 271 He's on to the hostage gone Asking there for charitie. *Ibid.* iv, Fifteen lords in the hostage-house Waiting Wallace for to see. **1852** *Act 15 & 16 Vict.* cxxxvi. Preamb. (Hull Shipping Dues), Certain Dues called .. Hostage Dues.

†**hostager.** *Obs.* Also 4 **ost-**. [a. OF. (*h*)*ostagier*, *-ger* hostage, pledge, security, f. *hostage* + *-ier*:—L. *-ārius*.] = HOSTAGE *sb.*[1] 2.

c **1330** R. BRUNNE *Chron.* (1810) 139 Þe castels and ostagers he ȝald þorgh curteysie. —— *Chron. Wace* (Rolls) 4983 Sende he scholde hym hostagers, Men of gode, barons, pers. **1523** LD. BERNERS *Froiss.* I. ccxlvi. (R.), Ther wer styll in England hostagers, the erle Dolphyn of Auuergne, therle of Porseen .. and dyuers other. **1530** PALSGR. 232/2 Hostager, one that is pledge for another, *hostagier*.

hostageship ('hɒstɪdʒʃɪp). [f. HOSTAGE *sb.*[1] (sense 2) + -SHIP.] The condition of a hostage; = HOSTAGE *sb.*[1] 1.

1848 LYTTON *Harold* IV. iii, The time of the hostageship rests with the King and the Duke. **1865** J. M. LUDLOW *Epics Mid. Ages* II. 249 By this act .. the terms of his hostageship are forfeited. **1867** *Contemp. Rev.* VI. 256 For a companion of his exile and hostageship.

hostay(e, var. of HOSTEY *v. Obs.*

hosted ('həʊstɪd), *a.* [f. HOST *sb.*[1] + -ED. Cf. HOST *v.*[1]] Assembled in a host; in hosts.

1808 J. BARLOW *Columb.* I. 576 Indignant Frost .. plies His hosted friends that vex the polar skies. **1830** W. PHILLIPS *Mt. Sinai* II. 91 The hosted Hebrews to their several tents .. betake them. **1892** STOPF. BROOKE *E.E. Lit.* x. 243 The hosted waves of ocean.

hostel ('hɒstəl), *sb.*[1] Forms: α. 3–4 **ostel**, 4 **osteyl**, 5 **osteill**, **-tell**, 6–7 **ostle**. β. 3– **hostel**; also 4 **hostil**, 4– 7 **hostell**, 6 **hostle**, **hostelle**. [a. OF. *ostel*, *-eil*, *hostel*, mod.F. *hôtel* = Pr. (*h*)*ostal*, Sp. *hostal*:—med.L. *hospitāle* (see HOSPITAL).]

†**1. a.** A place of sojourn; a house where one lodges; a lodging. *Obs.*

c **1250** *Gen. & Ex.* 1056 He .. bead hem hom to is ostel To herberȝen wið him. **13..** *Gaw. & Gr. Knt.* 251 Þe hede of þis hostel Arthour I hat. *c* **1450** *Merlin* 130 The kynge wolde not haue hem at noon other osteill but in his house.

b. *transf.* and *fig.*

a **1300** *Cursor M.* 22623 Lauerd .. yeild us gain vr ostel nu, þat us es reft. **1450–1530** *Myrr. our Ladye* 326 Whiche gaue to the lorde of heuen the hostell of her moste holy body. **1610** HOLLAND *Camden's Brit.* I. 495 That this Island is an Hostell of Charity, an harbour of honesty.

2. *spec.* **a.** A public house of lodging and entertainment for strangers and travellers; an inn, a hotel.

Obs. after 16th c. till revived in 19th by Scott.

c **1384** CHAUCER *H. Fame* II. 514 Seynt Iulyane loo bon hostele Se her the house of Fame lo. **1393** LANGL. *P. Pl.* C. XIV. 64 As safliche passe as the messager and as sone at hus hostil. **1550** LEVER *Serm.* 14 Dec. (Arb.) 121 One hundred also of an other sorte .. dyd lyue of theym selues in Ostles and Innes. **1808** SCOTT *Marm.* III. (*heading*), The hostel, or inn. **1847** LYTTON *Lucretia* (1853) 264 As is the usage of hostels, a pair of boots stood ouside the door, to be cleaned betimes in the morning. **1880** WATSON *Prince's Quest* (1892) 25 But, being wearied sore in every limb Sought out a goodly hostel, where he might Rest him and eat and tarry for the night.

b. = *youth hostel*. Hence **'hosteller**; **'hostelling** *vbl. sb.*

1931 *Times* 21 Jan. 11/6 The Youth Hostels Association. .. It is hoped that this summer there will be 50 hostels where .. a night's lodging may be obtained. **1932** *Y.H.A. Handbk. Hostels* 19 Much of the Y.H.A. Insurance of property in Hostels is now undertaken by the National Office. *Ibid.*, Write to the Warden at the Hostel and quote your membership number. **1951** E. COXHEAD *One Green Bottle* i. 26 House used to be a climbing centre, but now it's been taken for one of those youth hostels. Pity. Some of the hostellers climb, I believe. *Ibid.* x. 256, I treated myself to a few days' hostelling. **1961** *Countryman* LVIII. 434 There were always plenty of hostellers to fill the boat. **1967** *Rambling & Youth Hostelling* ('Know the Game' Series) 31 The YHA Map is useful for tour planning. It will enable you to see the network of hostels in the area you are visiting. **1970** P. CARLON *Souvenir* xii. 106 Her daughter's friends were allowed to go hostelling and hiking. **1973** *Guardian* 1 Jan. 6/3 In the most expensive .. hostels, the overnight charge will go up from 35p to 40p for young hostellers.

3. A house of residence for students at a university or elsewhere; esp. (in recent times) for students connected with a non-resident college; = HALL[1] 4a.

The term was never in official use at Oxford, though 'Halls' have been spoken of as 'hostels'; at Cambridge it has a recognized standing.

1536 *Act 27 Hen. VIII*, c. 42 §1 Provostshippz Maistershippz Halles Hostelles. **1547** *Act 1 Edw. VI*, c. 14 §15 Any of the Colleges Hostelles or Halles being in the same Universities. **1577** HARRISON *England* II. iii. (1877) I. 87 There is mention and record of diuerse other hals or hostels, that haue beene there [at Oxford] in times past, as Beefe hall, Mutton hall [etc.]. **1629** in Willis & Clark *Cambridge* (1886) I. 41 The clearing of the ground .. was begun in May 1628, by taking down the 'litle Ostle'. *a* **1661** FULLER *Worthies* (1840) III. 436 Bred in some of the hostels after-wards united thereunto [Trinity College, Cambridge]. **1894** *Times* (weekly ed.) 2 Feb. 98/3 (St. Deiniol's Library, Hawarden) These [readers] are expected to reside in the hostel belonging to the library. **1895** RASHDALL *Univ. Europe* I. v. §1. 296 The Provost of Paris at the head of an armed band of citizens in return attacked a Hall or Hostel (*hospitium*) of students. **1898** *Cambridge Calendar* 876 Selwyn College .. was recognised as a Public Hostel of the University by Grace of the Senate, Feb. 8, 1883.

†**4.** A town-mansion; = HOTEL 1. *Obs.*

1587 FLEMING *Contn. Holinshed* III. 1381/1 The said duke de Montpensier .. met the earle of Derbie and the English traine .. and did accompanie him vnto hostell de Longueuille, sometime called the hostle of Aniou. *a* **1648** LD. HERBERT *Life* (1886) 105, I went sometimes also to the court of Queen Margaret at the Hostel, called by her name. **1661** MORGAN *Sph. Gentry* III. vi. 60 Doth belong to Serjeants Inne in Fleet street and as they were anciently called *Hostels* by being Houses of Nobles. **1670** COTTON *Espernon* I. II. 61 His Hostel at Paris .. was then the best House next to the Queen Mothers, now call'd the *l'Hostel de Soissons*.

†**5.** Lodging, entertainment; esp. in *to take hostel*, to lodge, put up. *Obs.*

c **1250** *Gen. & Ex.* 1397 Laban..fond good grið and good hostel, Him, and hise men, and hise kamel. **1303** R. Brunne *Handl. Synne* 12472 Whan synne ys shryue ande clene eche deyl þere wyl Gode holde hys hostele. *c* **1400** *Ywaine & Gaw.* 3404 Syr Ywayn and his damysell In the town toke thaire hostell. *c* **1450** *Merlin* 606 For his love shull ye haue hostell at youre volunte.

6. *attrib.*

c **1610** in Gutch *Coll. Cur.* II. 13 A barrel of Hostel Ale. **1808** Scott *Marm.* III. xxvi, Slumbering on the hostel floor.

†**hostel**, *sb.*[2] *Obs. rare*$^{-1}$. A dyslogistic diminutive of HOST *sb.*[4]

1624 Darcie *Birth of Heresies* xv. 62 Your round hostel, which you cause to be ador'd.

hostel, *v.* *Obs.* exc. *dial.* Also 5 **hostyl**, 9 **hostle.** [f. HOSTEL *sb.*[1]]

†**1.** *trans.* To lodge, put up. *Obs.*

c **1330** R. Brunne *Chron. Wace* (Rolls) 5557 In Wynchestre were þey hosteld boþe. **1377** Langl. *P. Pl.* B. xvii. 118 Hope shal lede hem forth..And hostel hem and hele. *a* **1400** *Stac. Rome* 548 Boþe þei weoren hostelled þere.

2. *intr.* To lodge. Now *dial.*

c **1460** *Towneley Myst.* xxviii. 263 Ther hostyld thai all thre. **1855** Robinson *Whitby Gloss.* s.v., 'Where do you hostle at?' lodge at.

hostelar. Also **-ilar**, **-illar.** Sc. form of *hostellary*, HOSTELRY.

(The 15th c. instances may be plurals of *hostelarie.*)

1424 *Sc. Acts Jas. I* §25 (1814) II. 6/2 þ^{t} in all burrowis townys..þar be ordanyt hostilaris and resettis haifande stabillis and chawmeris to ridaris and gangaris. **1425** *Ibid.* §11 (1814) II. 10/1 þe king..forbids þat ony liege man..herbery or luge þaim in ony vthir place bot in þe hostelaris forsaide. **1819** W. Tennant *Papistry Storm'd* (1827) 125 Spers'd about in search o' beds Throu' houses, hostillars, and sheds.

hosteler ('hɒstələ(r)). Now *arch.* or *Hist.*, exc. in sense 4 b. Forms: α. 3–5 (9) **hostiler**, 4– **hosteler**, (4 **hostyller**, 4–5 **hostilere**, **-ellere**, 5–6 **-iller**, **-elere**, 5–6 (9) **-illar**, 6 (9) **-elar**, 7 (9) **-eller**; also 5–8 **hostler.** β. 4–5 **ostiler**, 4–6 **osteler**, 5–6 **-ere**, 5–7 **ostler**, 6 **ostleir**, 7 *Sc.* **oistlar.** [a. OF. *ostelier* (12th c. in Hatz.-Darm.), *hostelier*, mod.F. *hôtelier*, f. *hostel*: see -ER. Cf. med.L. *hospitā lārius*, *hostalārius*, *hostel(l)ārius*. See also HOSTLER, OSTLER, variants of this word.]

†**1.** One who receives, lodges, or entertains guests and strangers; *spec.*, in a monastery or religious house, one whose office was to attend to guests and strangers. *Obs.* exc. *Hist.*

c **1290** *S. Eng. Leg.* I. 361/61 þe Abbot sende him out to one of heore celles; hostiler he was þare i-mad gistes to onder-fongue. *c* **1430** *Pilgr. Lyf Manhode* I. lxi. (1869) 37, I am norishe of orphanynes, osteleer of pilgrimes. **1483** Caxton *Gold. Leg.* 149 b/2 Thabbot..sente hym..to be hosteler for to receyue there ghestes. **1877** J. Raine in Smith & Wace *Dict. Chr. Biog.* I. 725 In this establishment Cuthbert was the hostillar. **1897** J. W. Clark *Priory Barnwell* p. lii, It was the duty of the Hosteller..to entertain the guests who sought the hospitality of the monastery.

2. A keeper of a hostelry or inn; an innkeeper. *arch.*

1365 *Munim. Gildh. Lond.* (Rolls) III. 422 Ricardus le Yonge, hostyller. **1388** Wyclif *Luke* x. 35 He brouȝte forth twey pans, and ȝaf to the ostiler. *c* **1440** *York Myst.* xlvii. *heading*, The Osteleres. Alias Inholders. **1531** *Dial. on Laws Eng.* II. xlii. (1638) 138 If a man desire to lodge with one that is no common Hosteler. **1592** Nashe *P. Penilesse* (ed. 2) 5 a, An Hostler that had built a goodly Inne. *a* **1635** Corbet *Iter Bor.* 174 The inne-keeper was old, fourescore allmost..God and Time decree To honour thrifty ostlers, such as hee. *a* **1670** Spalding *Troub. Chas. I* (1829) 12 [They] crossed the water, and breakfasted in William Stewart's, ostler. **1862** J. Grant *Capt. of Guard* xxv, Gray had been repeatedly warned by the friendly hosteller..to beware of travelling in the dusk.

3. A stableman: see HOSTLER, OSTLER.

4. †**a.** A student who lives in a hostel (sense 3). *Obs.*

1577 Harrison *England* II. iii. (1877) I. 87 The students also that remaine in them, are called hostelers or halliers. Hereof it came of late to passe, that..Thomas late archbishop of Canturburie, being brought vp at such an house at Cambridge, was of the ignorant sort of Londoners called an 'hosteler', supposing that he had serued..in the stable. **1655** Fuller *Hist. Camb.* 29 We infer them to be no Collegiates, but Hostelers, not in that sense which the spitefull Papists charged Dr. Cranmer to be one (an attendant on a stable), but such as lived in a learned Inn or Hostle not endowed with revenues.

b. A youth hosteller: see HOSTEL *sb.*[1] 2 b.

5. *attrib.*, as ***hosteler-house*** [= OF. *maison hosteliere*; cf. med.L. *hospitālāria* (sc. *domus*) hostelry]; **hosteler-wife**, the mistress of an inn.

c **1470** Henry *Wallace* III. 71 A trew Scot, quhilk hosteler house thair held. **1820** Scott *Abbot* xviii, The hostler-wives,..are like to be the only losers by their miscarriage.

Hence '**hosteleress**, a female student in a hostel.

1850 *Fraser's Mag.* XLII. 251 The female college, with its professoresses and hostleresses, and other Utopian monsters.

†**ho'stelity.** *Obs. rare.* Also -illity. [? f. *hostel* = hospital + -ITY.] Hospitality.

1593 *Jack Straw* III. in Hazl. *Dodsley* V. 398 Defacing houses of hostelity [Old copy, *hostilltie*].

hostelry ('hɒstəlrı). Now *arch.* Also 4–5 **ostelrie**, **(h)ostellerie**, **-elerie**, **-ye**, 4–6 **ostlerye**, **-ie**, 5 **hostillary**, 7 **hostilerie**, 4–7, 9 (*arch.*) **hostelrie.** [a. OF. *(h)ostelerie* (12th c. in Hatz.-Darm.), mod.F. *hôtellerie*, f. *(h)ostelier* HOSTELER[1]: see -ERY 3, -RY. The word is sparsely exemplified before the 19th c., when it was taken up by Scott, and thence became common as a literary form.]

1. A house where lodging and entertainment are provided; an inn, a hostel. Also, the place in a convent for the reception of strangers.

c **1386** Chaucer *Prol.* 718 In Southwerk at this gentil hostelrye [*v.r.* ostelry, *Petw.* hostrye, *Lansd.* hosterie] That highte the Tabard. —— *Knt.'s T.* 1635 In the hostelryes [*v. rr.* ostelleryis, hostelleries, *Lansd.* hostries] al aboute. *c* **1430** *Pilgr. Lyf Manhode* IV. xxxii. (1869) 193 To þe ostelrye j wente at þe firste, thinking to herberwe me þere. **1597–8** Bp. Hall *Sat.* III. i. 73 The under-groome of the ostlerie. **1630** B. Jonson *New Inn* II. i, A bashful child, homely brought up, In a rude hostelrie. **1808** Scott *Marmion* III. ii. *note*, The accommodations of a Scottish hostelrie, or inn, in the sixteenth century, may be collected from..the 'Friars of Berwick'. **1823** —— *Peveril* xxi, Peveril entered the kitchen, which indeed was also the parlour and hall of the little hostelry. **1840** Dickens *Old C. Shop* xviii, Codlin diminished the distance between himself and the hostelry. **1886** Ruskin *Præterita* I. vi. 188 Dining at any nice village hostelry.

2. Hostel business. *nonce-use.*

1855 Thackeray *Newcomes* I. x. 101 A gay sight was the road..in those days, before steam-engines arose and flung its hostelry and chivalry over.

Hence '**hostelric** *a. nonce-wd.*, pertaining to a hostelry or inn.

1860 *All Year Round* IV. 78 He looks at things in an eminently hostelric view.

†**hoster**[1]. *Obs. rare.* [f. HOST *v.*[2]] A hosteler or innkeeper.

c **1500** in *Arnolde's Chron.* Index (1811) 5 That commen hosters be partyners of all charges so as free hosters. **1598** Florio, *Hosteriero*, an hoste, an hoster, an inholder.

hoster[2] ('həʊstə(r)). *rare.* [f. HOST *sb.*[1]] One who serves in a host or army.

1892 Stopf. Brooke *E.E. Lit.* viii. 183 The hosters grim Sent the showers of arrows.

hosteria, obs. f. OSTERIA, (Italian) hostelry.

hostery, var. HOSTRY.

hostess ('həʊstıs), *sb.* Forms: α. 3–7 **ostesse**, (5 **ostes**, 7 **oastess**). β. 4 **hoostesse**, 4–6 **hostes**, 4–7 **hostesse**, 6–7 **hostis**, 7– **hostess.** [a. OF. *ostesse* (12th c. in Littré), mod.F. *hôtesse*, f. *(h)oste* HOST *sb.*[2]: see -ESS.]

1. A woman that lodges and entertains guests.

c **1385** Chaucer *L.G.W.* 2496 *Phyllis*, Ostesse [*v.rr.* hostesse, ostes] thyn quod she O demophon Thyn Philis whiche that is so wo begon. **1589** *Hay any Work* 48 He has also a charge to prouide for, his hostesse and cosin. **1592** Warner *Alb. Eng.* VIII. xlii. 19 Thanks, and welcome too, he sayd Unto his Oste and Ostesse. **1598** Barnfield *Pecunia* xxi, Your Hostis presently will step in Place. **1605** Shaks. *Macb.* I. vi. 10 See, see, our honor'd Hostesse. **1632** T. Deloney *Thomas of Reading* xi. (ed. 6) Hj b, Beholding his Oast and Oastesse earnestly. **1808** Pike *Sources Mississ.* III. 235 At one o'clock we bid adieu to our friendly hostess. **1880** Mrs. Forrester *Roy & V.* I. 28 'Come and look at the conservatory', smiled his hostess.

fig. **1402** Hoccleve *Letter of Cupid* 461 O womman that of wertu art hostesse.

2. *spec.* **a.** A woman who keeps a public place of lodging and entertainment; the mistress of an inn. Also in archaic phr. ***mine hostess.***

c **1290** *S. Eng. Leg.* I. 325/96 þare-with heo fedde hire swiþe wel and hire ostesse al-so. *c* **1305** *Edmund Conf.* 98 in *E.E.P.* (1862) 73 His ostesce had a dowȝter þer he was at inne. **1375** Barbour *Bruce* IV. 635 His hostes com rycht till hym thar. **1474** Caxton *Chesse* 115 Al tho thynges that ben delyuerd to kepe to the hoste or hostessis they ought to be sauf. **1596** Shaks. *1 Hen. IV*, II. iv. 305 Hostesse, clap to the doores: watch to night. **1653** Walton *Angler* iii. 82 Come Hostis, give us more Ale. **1716** Swift *Phillis* 98 John is landlord, Phillis hostess: They keep at Staines the Old Blue Boar. **1832** W. Irving *Alhambra* I. 30 [He] had a good understanding with the brother of mine hostess. **1962** *Listener* 19 July 113/3 *Mine Hostess*, as *La Locandiera* is called in Clifford Bax's otherwise excellent English translation, is one of the dozen or so greatest comedies.

b. A woman employed to entertain customers at a night-club, etc.; also in derogatory sense: a prostitute.

1931 Durante & Kofoed *Night Clubs* xxi. 190 Joan Sawyer—and what a girl she was!—the foremost dancer and hostess of the day, ran the shows. **1933** *New Statesman* 18 Mar. 331/2 If a young man dances with a 'hostess' he scurries back at the finish. **1937** C. R. Cooper *Here's to Crime* ix. 189 Women, reaching the dregs, become the 'hostesses' in what are known as 'jukin' joints'. **1959** *Economist* 11 Apr. 105/2 This question of hostesses is one of the most hotly debated in the night club business. It is also revealing since, broadly speaking, it is a management's policy towards hostesses that determines the standing of a night club. **1963** *Listener* 7 Feb. 260/3 American Bunny Clubs, with their Freudian fantasy-tease hostesses. **1968** *Sunday Times* 30 June 5/5 He..got Miss C. to admit..'that the word hostess is a polite euphemism for prostitute'. **1970** G. Greer *Female Eunuch* 131 Many a prostitute, whether she calls herself a..hostess, or a common whore, imagines that she is exploiting the male sex. **1970** *Guardian* 22 Aug. 8/6 The French authorities have been able to organise a traditional Legion recreation centre, whose Somali hostesses are under regular medical supervision. **1972** P. A. Whitney *Snowfire* (1973) i. 2 Juniper Lodge in the Poconos was looking for an après-ski hostess to help with guests during the evening hours. **1973** *Times* 30 May 4/3 We were able to call it Europe's biggest hostess service and had an interesting offer of more than 200 girls.

c. = *air hostess*; also, a woman similarly employed on a train.

1936 *Jrnl. R. Aeronaut. Soc.* XL. 525 On American aeroplanes for many years now we have had, as part of the staff, 'hostesses', young women of 20 to 30 years of age, generally trained nurses, whose duties are to make passengers 'feel at home' aloft. **1940** *Amer. Speech* XV. 213/2 *Hostess*..now suggests a professional person paid for her services, as the hostess at a hotel, on an airplane, or on pullman cars. **1953** R. Lehmann *Echoing Grove* 252 She'll be a hostess on a transglobal airline. **1958** *Times Lit. Suppl.* 17 Oct. 598/4 Illuminating testimonies by hostesses of various air lines. **1970** *Times* 17 Nov. 19/7 Five years ago..she was one of the first Gatwick hostesses. They're British Rail's answer to an air hostess.

†**3.** A female guest: cf. HOST *sb.*[2] 4. *Obs. rare.*

1388 Wyclif *Exod.* iii. 22 A womman schal axe of hir neiȝboresse and of her hoosteesse [1382 gest] siluerne vesselis.

4. *Comb.* ***hostess apron, dress, gown, pyjamas, robe, skirt, trolley.***

1968 *Wanganui* (N.Z.) *Chron.* 15 Nov. 8/3 (*winner of competition*) *Hostess apron: Mrs. S. 1, Mrs. A. J. M. 2. **1970** N. Armstrong et al. *First on Moon* xiv. 352 Kate Collins, wearing her mother's pink hostess apron, was passing coffee. **1951** *Country Life* 16 Nov., The picture or *hostess dress has been re-instated for informal evenings. **1963** *Times* 27 Feb. 12/5 Sleeveless hostess dresses. **1968** *Guardian* 30 Apr. 7/1 Full-length hostess dresses, long-sleeved or sleeveless. **1938** 'E. Queen' *Four of Hearts* (1939) x. 143 She looked ravishing in a silver lamé *hostess-gown. **1945** E. Bowen *Demon Lover* 178 Her cretonne house-coat, the nearest thing to a hostess gown that she had. **1963** M. McCarthy *Group* v. 92 Instead of a dress, Kay was wearing a cherry-red velvet sleeveless hostess gown. *a* **1774** Goldsm. tr. *Scarron's Comic Rom.* (1775) II. 199 She spoke with so grave and *hostess-like a tone. **1945** F. & R. Lockridge *Payoff for Banker* (1948) vi. 58 Dorian did not have *hostess pyjamas of quite this cut—quite this daring—and would hardly have worn them if she had. **1970** *Daily Progress* (Charlottesville, Va.) 21 Mar. C 2/3 It's time to turn to wearing the long 'hostess pyjamas' for seasonal glamour in entertaining. **1964** *N.Y. Times* 15 Nov. Sect. XI. 9 (Advt.), Button-front *hostess robe of soft fleece. **1966** Mrs. L. B. Johnson *White House Diary* 6 Aug. (1970) 406, I put on my white hostess robe that Lyndon had bought me in Paris ten years ago and went in to see Luci. She was eating breakfast. **1966** *Daily Tel.* 19 Dec. 9/4 The kilt that grew—and grew—and grew—becomes the Christmas *hostess skirt that's on view at all the cosiest fireside parties. **1963** *Guardian* 25 Nov. 6/3 The latest model of the L. G. Hawkins *hostess trolley..in which you can carry four dishes and a joint from the kitchen.

Hence '**hostessship**, the office of hostess.

1611 Shaks. *Wint. T.* IV. iv. 72 It is my Fathers will, I should take on mee The Hostesseship o' th' day: you're welcome sir.

hostess ('həʊstıs), *v.* [f. the sb.] *trans.* and *intr.* To be the hostess at (a party, etc.); to act as hostess. So '**hostessing** *vbl. sb.*

1928 *Sunday Express* 6 May 16 She observed herself think that possibly Athene felt political 'hostessing' to be her vocation. **1946** *Lincoln State Jrnl.* 24 Jan., Wednesday was the day of the party which Mrs. Herbert Folsom..hostessed..in honor of Mr. Thomas Mauck. **1951** 'J. Wyndham' *Day of Triffids* xii. 215 She had led one of those fringe careers—modelling dresses,..hostessing for obscure clubs. **1957** J. Frame *Owls do Cry* xxviii. 123 It will be my first *real* experience of hostessing to people who really matter. **1961** *Spectator* 27 Oct. 605 The hell of hostessing is..that one can know..what things make a good hostess and still be quite unable to achieve them. **1962** *Aeroplane* CII. 229/2 The book..details the growth of the aviation industry. This is vital for anyone interested in 'Hostessing', because a proper appreciation of the industry's background is invaluable in assessing the job as a whole and its importance in helping to 'sell' the airlines. **1968** C. Nicole *Self Lovers* ii. 22 Vanessa thought hostessing large political gatherings would grow easier with experience.

hostessy ('həʊstısı), *a.* [f. HOSTESS + -Y[1].]

Pertaining to, or typical of, a hostess; hospitable.

1930 J. B. Priestley *Angel Pavement* iii. 108 And then, too, all the time you were so worried and anxious about the food and the serving, you were expected to be keeping the conversation going, terribly bright and hostessy. **1939** 'N. Blake' *Smiler with Knife* 21 She would assume a gushing, hostessy manner. **1945** *Penguin New Writing* XXVI. 62 Betty Mordon began by being affably hostessy towards him. **1967** D. Francis *Blood Sport* i. 13 Idle hostessy chat. **1973** J. Burrows *Like an Evening Gone* i. 18 Greta has been making hostessy interested noises.

†'**hostey**, *v.* *Obs.* Also **h)osteye**, **hostaye**, **(hostie).** [a. OF. *(h)osteie-r*, *-aier*, *-oier*:—L. type **hosticāre*, f. *hostis* (med.L.) army, warlike expedition: see HOST *sb.*[1]] *intr.* To wage war, make a warlike expedition.

? *a* **1400** *Morte Arth.* 555, I ettylle my selfene, To hostaye in Almayne with armede knyghtez. *Ibid.* 3503 Ffor he es in this empire..Ostayande in this oryente with awfulle knyghtes. **1430–40** Lydg. *Bochas* III. ix. (1554) 80 b, Neuer prince..Hosteyed at once with such a multitude. *c* **1450** *Merlin* 70 Arayed for to osteye. **1475** *Bk. Noblesse* 13 Full noble erle of Darby havyng rule..in the duchie of Guyen, hostied the said tyme and yere.

host-house. Now *dial.* [Cf. Ger. *gasthaus.*] A house for the reception of guests or strangers; a hostelry; an inn.

1563-87 FOXE *A. & M.* (1684) III. 591 To go with him to the free Ostehouses amongst the English Merchants. **1634** W. TIRWHYT tr. *Balzac's Lett.* (vol. I.) 352 One night in a bad Host-house. **1855** ROBINSON *Whitby Gloss., Host-house,* ..a farmer's inn at market. **1893** *Northumbid. Gloss.* s.v. *Hoast-hoos,* The inns where farmers put up..have *oast-hooses* attached. They are the waiting rooms used by wife and daughters, and the reception place for parcels or goods.

hostiary, obs. form of OSTIARY.

†**'hosticide.** *Obs. rare*—⁰. [ad. L. **hosticīda,* f. *hostis* enemy: see -CIDE 1.] One that kills his enemy (Blount *Glossogr.* 1656).

1848 in WHARTON *Law Lex.*

hostie ('hɒstɪ). *Obs.* or *arch.* Also 4-5 **hostye,** 5 **hoostye.** [a. F. *hostie* (14th c. in Littré), ad. L. *hostia* victim, HOST *sb.*⁴]

1. = HOST *sb.*⁴ 1.

1483 CAXTON *Gold. Leg.* 57 b/1 Moyses saide we shal take with us suche hostyes & sacrefyses as we shal offre. **1495** *Trevisa's Barth. De P.R.* IX. xxvii. (W. de W.) 363 The feest ..was worshypped wyth spyrytuell hostyes [*Bodl. MS.* hoistes] and offrynges. **1681** R. FLEMING *Fulfill. Script.* (1801) II. 287 There is no necessity to offer daily Hosties for the sins of the people.

2. = HOST *sb.*⁴ 2.

1641 R. BAILLIE *Parall. Liturgy with Mass-bk.* 51 The Papists injoyne all the relickes of the Hostie and wine..to be gathered together. *a* **1715** BURNET *Own Time* (1766) I. 11 Some of his seamen went ashore and met the Hostie carried about. **1837** CARLYLE *Fr. Rev.* III. VI. i, Saint-Just..'carries his head as if it were a *Saint-Sacrement*', adorable Hostie, or divine Real-Presence!

hostie, rare var. HOSTEY *v. Obs.*

hostile ('hɒstaɪl, -tɪl), *a.* (*sb.*) Also 7 **hostill.** [ad. L. *hostīlis,* f. *hostis* enemy (see -ILE): perh. through F. *hostile* (15-16th c. in Hatz.-Darm.).]

A. *adj.* **1. a.** Of, pertaining to, or characteristic of an enemy; pertaining to or engaged in actual hostilities.

1594 SHAKS. *Rich. III,* IV. iv. 236 (Qos.) My dangerous attempt of hostile armes. **1596** —— *1 Hen. IV,* I. i. 9 Nor bruise her Flowrets with the Armed hoofes Of hostile paces. **1659** B. HARRIS *Parival's Iron Age* 246 The King of Denmark, who entred Germany in an hostile manner. **1698** FRYER *Acc. E. India & P.* 337 By these Bars..the Hostile Arms of the Turks have been put to a stop. **1725** POPE *Odyss.* XI. 656 Thus, great in glory, from the din of war, Safe he return'd without one hostile scar. **1810** WELLINGTON in Gurw. *Desp.* (1838) VI. 114 The operations of hostile armies. **1847** EMERSON *Repr. Men, Napoleon* Wks. (Bohn) I. 371 On a hostile position [he] rained a torrent or iron.

b. Of the nature or disposition of an enemy; unfriendly.

1782 PRIESTLEY *Corrupt. Chr.* I. Pref. 4 They all came in from a foreign and hostile quarter. **1821** JOANNA BAILLIE *Metr. Leg., Lady J. B.* li, The dame held fast the hostile door. **1840** F. D. BENNETT *Whaling Voy.* II. 88 A second hostile rajah..was for some time kept as a state-prisoner. **1876** FREEMAN *Norm. Conq.* V. xxiv. 392 Men of different and hostile races.

2. *transf.* and *fig.* **a.** Unfriendly in feeling, action, nature, or character; contrary, adverse, antagonistic.

1791 BOSWELL *Johnson* an. 1748 The natives of North Britain, to whom he is supposed to have been so hostile. **1800** *Med. Jrnl.* IV. 114 The principal of putrefaction, or azote, the element hostile to life. **1849** MACAULAY *Hist. Eng.* ii. I. 231 A long succession of princes, hostile to the established faith, might sit on the English throne. *a* **1862** BUCKLE *Civiliz.* (1873) III. v. 413 It is possible for two hostile principles to flourish side by side, without ever coming into collision.

b. *to go hostile*: to become angry. *Austral.* and *N.Z. colloq.*

1941 W. D. HAYDON *N.Z. Soldiers* 17 Wouldn't he go hostile if he knew who pinched his bacon. **1945** BAKER *Austral. Lang.* II. xv. 23 *To go hostile* means to become angry.

3. *Comb.* **hostile ice** (see quot. 1966); **hostile ord** *Naval slang,* an ordinary seaman who joins the Navy in wartime for the period of hostilities only.

1964 *Polar Record* XII. 197 *Hostile ice. **1966** T. ARMSTRONG et al. *Gloss. Snow & Ice* 19 *Hostile ice,* from the point of view of the submariner, an ice canopy containing no large ice skylights or other features which permit a submarine to surface. **1919** W. LANG *Sea-Lawyer's Log* iii. 37 To the active service man the '*hostile ord', as the temporary seaman is called, is a mere interloper, one who has joined the Navy to 'dodge Kitchener', as they put it, and they do not hesitate to tell him so.

B. *sb.* A hostile person; *spec.* (*U.S.*) a North American Indian unfriendly to the Whites.

1838 *N. Y. Mirror* 27 Jan. 245/3 Yesterday five Delaware chiefs, who had gone from the main army to the stronghold of the hostiles, reappeared with four Indians. **1860** BARTLETT *Dict. Amer., Hostiles,* enemies. *Western.* **1880** *Libr. Univ. Knowl.* X. 431 They were formerly hostiles, but ..at present peaceable and industrious. **1885** *Milnor* (Dakota) *Teller* 24 Apr. 5/3 Saturday a scouting-party.. captured three hostiles. **1890** *Pall Mall G.* 18 Dec. 5/2 A courier has just arrived, and reports..that the hostiles are fighting with the friendly Indians on the Grand River. **1963** *Guardian* 8 Sept. 6/6 There were rumours that Naga hostiles were getting help from China. **1966** A. FIRTH *Tall, Balding, Thirty-Five* iv. 48 It is most unlikely that a hostile could select such a person as yourself to assist them. **1969** *Hindu* 3 Aug. 1/5 A strong contingent of security forces has been rushed to..Ukhrul..to intercept over 400 China-trained Naga hostiles.

Hence †**hostile** *v. Obs.,* in *to hostile it,* to be hostile, engage in warlike hostilities.

1656 S. H. *Gold. Law* 8 Why may not Clients clearly injured by their Lawyer, or their Adversary, hostile it, and gather an Army? *Ibid.* 96 Had you just cause to invade and hostile it against us.

hostilely ('hɒstaɪllɪ), *adv.* Also 7 **hostilly, hostily.** [f. HOSTILE *a.* + -LY².] In a hostile manner; as or in the manner of an enemy. **b.** With opposition or antagonism.

1609 BP. W. BARLOW *Answ. Nameless Cath.* 238 Hostily to inuade another Kings Land. **1611** SPEED *Hist. Gt. Brit.* IX. xvi. (1632) 856 The Scots hostilly entred into Northumberland. **1649** *Bounds Publ. Obed.* (1650) 52 D. Hamilton entred England hostilely. **1762** *St. Papers* in *Ann. Reg.* 198/1 To act hostilely against Great Britain. **1876** GEO. ELIOT *Dan. Der.* IV. xxx, He could not shake her nor touch her hostilely.

hostil(e)ment, var. HUSTLEMENT.

hostility (hɒ'stɪlɪtɪ). [ad. late L. *hostīlitās,* f. *hostīlis* HOSTILE; perh. through F. *hostilité* (15-16th c. in Hatz.-Darm.).]

1. a. The state or fact of being hostile; hostile action exercised by one community, state, or power against another; *esp.* such as involves war.

1531 ELYOT *Gov.* I. xxiv, With outwarde hostilitie or martiall businesse. **1548** HALL *Chron., Hen. VI* 172 Ye feare of outward hostilitie, and foren invasion. **1665** MANLEY *Grotius' Low C. Warres* 101 Now these private Quarrels were broke out into open Hostility. **1706** E. GIBSON *Assize Serm. Croydon* 15 Open acts of sedition and hostility. **1876** MATHEWS *Coinage* ii. 16 Prusias dared the hostility of the Romans by giving a shelter at his Court to Hannibal.

b. *pl.* Hostile acts; acts of warfare, war.

1613 PURCHAS *Pilgrimage* (1614) 837 Howsoever they exercise hostilities, and mutuall disagreements. **1699** BENTLEY *Phal.* 488 Declar'd no War..nor committed the least Hostilities. **1781** LD. CORNWALLIS *Let. Washington* 17 Oct., I propose a cessation of hostilities for twenty-four hours. **1855** PRESCOTT *Philip II,* viii. (1857) 141 A suspension of hostilities was agreed on.

c. *hostilities, -y only*: used in the Navy to describe a seaman enlisted only for the duration of a war, or such an enlistment.

[**1917** 'TAFFRAIL' *Off Shore* 81 Even in our small ships we carry some of the 'hostility men'.] **1942, 1961** [see *H.O.* s.v. H III]. **1946** J. IRVING *Royal Navalese* 7 Once again the 'Hostility Only' man took his silent stand beside the slender handful of us professional seamen. **1948** *Hansard Commons* 17 Mar. 2083 Recruiting on a hostilities only engagement was not open in the branch of their choice in the Royal Navy and Royal Marines. **1973** *Times* 31 Jan. 16/7 He enrolled in the Royal Navy as a 'hostilities only' rating.

2. *transf.* and *fig.* Opposition or antagonism in action, thought, or principle.

1632 J. HAYWARD tr. *Biondi's Eromena* 63 There being not betweene us any cause of hostility. **1704** J. HARRIS *Lex. Techn.* s.v. *Duellist,* Explicate all the Phænomena of Nature from the Doctrine of Alkali and Acid, and the supposed Hostility that there is between them. **1849** MACAULAY *Hist. Eng.* iii. I. 400 The hostility excited by a grotesque caricature of virtue did not spare virtue herself.

'hostilize, *v. rare*⁻¹. [f. HOSTILE *a.* + -IZE; cf. Sp., Pg. *hostilizar.*] *trans.* To render hostile; to cause to be an enemy.

1794 ANNA SEWARD *Lett.* (1811) III. 376 The powers already hostilized against an impious nation.

hosting ('həʊstɪŋ), *vbl. sb. Obs.* exc. *Hist.* [f. HOST *v.*¹] The raising of a host or armed multitude; hostile encounter or array; formerly, esp. in Ireland, a military expedition.

1422 tr. *Secreta Secret., Priv. Priv.* (E.E.T.S.) 204 This Erle a litill afore the forsayd hostynge rode Thomon xl. dayes, the wyche is the moste Inly Streynth of Iryssh of al the land. **1537** *Act 28 Hen. VIII* in *Stat. Irel.* (1621) 130 Going, riding or abiding in any hostings, jorney, or rode. **1596** SPENSER *State Irel.* Wks. (Globe) 673/2, I have often hearde, that when the Lord Deputye hath raysed any generall hostinges, the noblemen have claymed the leading of them. **1617** MORYSON *Itin.* II. 102 The foresaid generall hoasting is a rising out of certaine foote and horse, found by the subject..to assist the Queenes forces. **1667** MILTON *P.L.* VI. 93 Strange to us it seemd At first, that Angel should with Angel warr, And in fierce hosting meet. **1708** J. PHILIPS *Cyder* (1807) 98 From him, Two branches, that, in hosting, long contend For sov'reign sway. **1715** *Act 1 Geo. I* Stat. II. c. 54 § 10 The annual Value of the Services, commonly called personal Attendance, hosting, hunting, watching and warding, due by virtue of any Charter..shall be paid in Money annually instead of them. **1884** LOW & PULLING *Dict. Eng. Hist.* s.v. *Pale,* The small English freeholders were forced to follow the Lord-Deputy in his 'hostings'. Their abandoned farmsteads were robbed and burnt by English and Irish alike.

b. *attrib.*

1575 MAITLAND *Scot. Poems* 318 My hors, my harnes, and my speir; And all uther, my hoisting geir, Now may be sald. **1577** HOLINSHED *Chron.* II. 973/1 The Prince..aduanced forwarde..towarde his enimies, an hosting pace. **1620** *Thomas' Lat. Dict., Simplares armaturæ,* hosting harnesse.

hostis, obs. form of HOSTESS *sb.*

'hostler. Forms: 4-5 **hosteler (-eller, -iler, -iller),** 5- **hostler.** See also OSTLER. [A syncopated form of *hosteler,* found also in the sense 'keeper of a hostelry, innkeeper' (HOSTELER 2), but from 16th c. usually appropriated as below; in this popular sense it has always varied with the form OSTLER ('ɒslə(r)), now more prevalent. The Shakspere Folio of 1621 has *hostler* once, *ostler* six times.

As a variant spelling of *ostler,* ordinarily pronounced like the latter, with *h* and *t* mute; but, if used in the sense of *hosteler,* both letters would now usually be sounded.]

A man who attends to horses at an inn; a stableman, a groom.

c **1386** CHAUCER *Pars. T.* ¶366 Thilke that holden hostelries, sustenynge the thefte of hire hostilers [*v.rr.* hostelers, hostelleris, ostelers, ostilers]. *c* **1400** *Three Kings Cologne* 23 Þis was a comune custome to diuers hostlers..to bring her hors to þat plaas. *c* **1485** *Digby Myst.* (1882) II. 85 How, hosteler, how, a peck of otys and a botell of haye. **1570** LEVINS *Manip.* 73/46 Hostler, *caupo, stabularius.* **1651** C. WALKER *Hist. Independ.* III. 10 To make Religion but a stalking horse..and the Ministers thereof but hostlers, to rub down, curry and dresse it for their riding. *a* **1713** ELLWOOD *Autobiog.* (1756) 20 Having ordered the Horstler to take Care of my Dog. **1837** HAWTHORNE *Twice-Told T.* (1851) II. x. 139 The landlord himself, or his loutish hostler. **1848** DICKENS *Dombey* vii, Where hostlers were continually accompanying themselves with effervescent noises.

b. *U.S.* (See quot.)

1890 COOLEY, etc. *Railw. Amer.* 232 The compartments in the round-houses for sheltering locomotives are termed the stalls, and the keeper of the round-house is called the hostler.

Hence **'hostlership,** the function of a hostler, or the discharge of such function.

1626 W. SCLATER *Exp. 2 Thess.* (1629) 123 To hold his stirrop, and beare the checke for ill hostlership.

hostler, hostleress: see HOSTELER.

hostless ('həʊstlɪs), *a. rare.* [f. HOST *sb.*² + -LESS.] Destitute of a host; †inhospitable.

1590 SPENSER *F.Q.* III. xi. 3 Forth ryding from Malbeccoes hostlesse hous. **1891** *St. James's Gaz.* 19 Mar. 6/1 A 'Frisco millionaire, who apparently prefers his friends to dine host-less.

hostly ('həʊstlɪ), *a.* [f. HOST *sb.*² + -LY¹.]

Belonging or proper to a host; host-like.

1893 *Star* 6 June 1/7 To resume their hostly functions. **1894** *Bedford Times* 2 June 2/2 A hostly host and trusty citizen.

†**hostry** ('həʊstrɪ). *Obs.* or *arch.* Forms: α. 4-6 **ostrye,** 5 **oostre,** 5-7 **ostry, -ie,** 5-8 **ostery,** 6 **ostrey.** β. 4-6 **hostrye,** 5-6 **hostre,** 5-7 **hostrie,** 5-8 **hostery, hostry,** 6 **-trey,** 6-8 **-terie,** 8 *arch.* **hoastrie.** [a. OF. *hosterie, hostrie* (= It. *osteria,* Sp. *hosteria*), f. *hoste* (mod.F. *hôte*) HOST *sb.*²: see -ERY, -RY.] = HOSTELRY.

1377 LANGL. *P. Pl.* B. XVII. 73 He..Herberwed hym at an hostrye. *c* **1400** MAUNDEV. (Roxb.) xxv. 119 Þus þ ai do fra ostrie to ostrie till þai comme at þe emperour. *c* **1460** *Towneley Myst.* iii. 329, I was neuer bard ere..In sich an oostre as this. **1483** CAXTON *Gold. Leg.* 210 b/2 This wenche went to another that laye in the same hostery. **1526** TINDALE *Luke* ii. 7 There was no roume for them with in, in the hostrey. **1598** STOW *Surv.* xxxvi. (1603) 350 Now a common ostrey for receipt of travellers. **1630** *R. Johnson's Kingd. & Commw.* 88 The Princes sit at meat like Carriers in an Hostry. **1652** PEYTON *Catastr. Ho. Stuarts* (1731) 31 She.. accompanied him to some Hostery. **1756** CIBBER *Apol.* II. *Dial. Old Pl.* 165 Five inns or common osteries. **1790** PENNANT *London* 458 (R.) In Stow's time it was altered to a common hosterie or inn, having a black bell for a sign.

b. *attrib.,* as **hostry bottle, court, house, press, roof;** **(h)ostry faggot,** a faggot used to light hostelry fires; so **hostry-wood**: see quot. 1769.

1507-8 *Durham MS. Terr. Roll,* Le hostre house ibidem. **1594** GREENE & LODGE *Looking Glasse* G.'s Wks. (Rtldg.) 133/1 Think, mistress, what a thing love is: why, it is like to an ostry-faggot, that, once set on fire, is as hardly quenched as the bird crocodile driven out of her nest. **1644** QUARLES *Sheph. Orac.* ii, It must be served in locks And ostry bottles. **1671-2** *Overseers' Acc. Holy Cross, Canterb.,* For six ostery fagotes..£o. os. 6d. **1769** *De Foe's Tour Gt. Brit.* (ed. 7) I. 139 Here they make those Faggots, which the Woodmongers call Ostreywood, and in particular those small light Bavins which are used in Taverns in London to light their Faggots. *a* **1770** CHATTERTON *Eclogue* i. 26 in *Rowley P.* (1778) 3 The joyous daunceynge ynn the hoastrie courte. **1881** T. WATTS in *Athenæum* 10 Sept. 337/1 To have the grass for his bed and the sky for his hostry-roof.

hostryche, -yge, obs. forms of OSTRICH.

†**'hostryinge.** *Obs.* [f. HOSTRY.] Lodging, entertainment.

c **1470** HARDING *Chron.* ccxl. *note* (Harl. MS.), All this cuntrey is goode hostryinge and full of uitaile.

hostship ('həʊst-ʃɪp). [f. HOST *sb.*² + -SHIP.] The function of a host, entertainment of guests.

1874 HELPS *Soc. Press.* x. (1875) 142 The prime minister whose excellence..in hostship was to be attributed to his wife.

hosyl, obs. form of HOUSEL.

hot, hott (hɒt), *sb.*¹ *Obs.* exc. *dial.* [a. OF. *hotte* a pannier or creel, supposed to be of Ger. origin: cf. Ger. *hotte,* Swiss *hutte* a vintager's dorser, a tub or basket carried on the back. (See also HOD *sb.*¹) Sense 3 is possibly a different word.]

1. A kind of basket or pannier for carrying earth, sand, lime, manure, etc. *north. dial.*

a 1300 *Cursor M.* 5524 Apon þer neckes sal þai bere Hott wit stan and wit morter. *c* 1384 CHAUCER *H. Fame* III. 850 Twigges.. Swiche as men.. maken of these paniers, Or elles hottes or dossers. 1434–5 *Durham MS. Almoner's Roll*, j par de hottys pro sabulo et luto cariand. 1483 CAXTON *Gold. Leg.* 109 a/2 And bare on hys sholders vii hottis or baskettis fulle of erthe. 1661 *Wit & Drollery* 74 Ise lay down my hot. 1781 J. HUTTON *Tour to Caves* Gloss. (E.D.S.), *Hots*, a sort of panniers to carry turf or slate in. 1825 BROCKETT, *Hot*, a sort of square basket formerly used for taking manure into fields of steep ascent. 1878 *Cumberld. Gloss.*, *Muck hots*.. panniers for conveying manure on horseback.

2. A small heap (e.g. of dung, dust, sand, etc.). *Sc.* and *north. dial.*

a 1800 *Song* in *Edinb. Month. Mag.* (1817) June 238 There was.. An hunder hotts o' muck to spread. 1822 HOGG *Perils of Man* II. vii. 255 Will then laid his arm over the boy and the hott o' claes, and fell sound asleep. 1841 *Jrnl. R. Agric. Soc.* II. I. 126 The field.. was left by the cattle in tufts or hots not eaten regularly off. 1878 *Cumberld. Gloss.*, *Muck hots*.. (N.E.) heaps of muck or lime in the field.

†**3.** (Also **hut(t)**.) A padded sheath for the spur of a fighting cock. *Obs.*

1615 MARKHAM *Pleas. Princes* (1635) 48 Hots are soft bumbasted roules of Leather, covering their Spurs, so that they cannot hurt or bruise one another. 1649 G. DANIEL *Trinarch.* To Rdr. 92 Hee without Cloake Is a Witt in Hutts, a pretty spurringe Cocke. 1688 R. HOLME *Armoury* II. xi. 252/2 *Hotts* or *Hutts*, are the Pounces or round Balls of Leather stuffed and clapped or tied on the sharp end of the Spurs, to keep Cocks that they shall not hurt one another in sparing, or breathing themselves. 1806 *Sporting Mag.* XXVII. 140 Cover your Cock's heels with hots made of leather.

hot (hɒt), *a.* (*sb.*²) Forms: α. 1 **hát**, 2–4 **hat**, (4–5 *north.* **hatt(e, hate)**; 5 **hayt**, 5–6 **hait**, 6 **haet**, **heit**. β. 2– **hot**; 4–6 **hoot**, **-e**, 4–7 **hote**, 6 **hoat(e**, 6–7 **hott(e**. γ. 5–6 **whote**, **whoot(e**, 6 **whot**, **whott(e**, **whoat(e**, **woght**. *Comp.* 1 **hattra**, 2–3 **hattre**, **hattere**, **hatere**, 3 **hatture**, 3–4 **hattore**, 4– **hotter**. *Sup.* 1 **hattost**, 3–7 **hotest**, 4– **hottest**. [Com. Teut.: OE. *hát*, corresp. to OFris., OS. *hêt* (MDu., Du. *heet*, LG. *hêt*), OHG. (MHG.) *heiz* (Ger. *heisz*), ON. *heitr*:—OTeut. **haito-z*, f. ablaut-stem *hit-*, *hît-*, *hait-*, whence also Goth. *heitô* fever, and OE. *hǽtu* HEAT. The normal phonetic representatives of OE. *hát* were ME. northern *hāt* (*hate*, *hait*), southern *hôt* (*hote*, *hoot*, *hoat*); the former came down to 16th, the latter to 17th c.; but as early as 1550 we find the shortened *hot*, *hott*. This was app. taken from the inflected comparative, OE. *hátra*, later *hattre*, found as late as 1400 as *hatter*, beside which *hotter* shortened from *hôter* is found in 14th c. (cf. *out*, *utter*, *late*, *latter*). The forms in *wh* are parallel to those of WHOLE.

The phonology of *hot* in the dialects presents many points of difficulty. Cf. HET.]

1. The proper adjective expressing a well-known quality or condition of material bodies, due to a high degree of the molecular energy known as *heat* (HEAT *sb.* 1, 2), and producing one of the primary sensations (HEAT *sb.* 1 b); having or communicating much heat; of or at a high temperature; the opposite of *cold*. (Distinguished from *warm* by the high degree of this quality.) **a.** Of the sun, the air, and atmospheric conditions.

c 1000 *Sax. Leechd.* I. 228 Ðeos wyrt.. byþ cenned neah sæ and on hatum stowum. *Ibid.* III. 280 Swa hattra sumor, swa mara ðunor and liȝet. *c* 1250 *Old Kent. Serm.* in *O.E. Misc.* 35 At middai wanne þo dai is al þer hotesd. 1297 R. GLOUC. (Rolls) 10960 þut somer so druye & so hot, þat.. none hattore me not. *a* 1300 *Cursor M.* 2703 Quen it was hate [*later MSS.* hat, hoot] a-pon a tide Abram satt his hus be side. *c* 1375 *Sc. Leg. Saints, Ninian* 564 It wes hate [*rime* gate]. *c* 1440 *Partonope* 2141 The day was whote and longe. 1548 HALL *Chron.*, *Hen. VIII* 34 b, The wether was hoat. 1633 BP. HALL *Hard Texts* 331 In an hote scorching season. 1653 WALTON *Angler* iv. 118 In a hot day, but especially in the evening of a hot day. 1727 SWIFT *Gulliver* III. i, The sun so hot, that I was forced to turn my face from it. 1833 STURT *S. Austral.* II. iii. 66 The hot winds in the interior.

b. Of fire, or anything burning or glowing.

c 1000 *Sax. Leechd.* II. 124 Stæppe on hat col, cele mid wætre; stæppe on swa hat swa hatost mæȝe. *c* 1200 *Vices & Virtues* 63 On ðe wallende brene of ðe hote fiere. *c* 1386 CHAUCER *Can. Yeom. Prol. & T.* 402 The fir was ouer hoot [*v.rr.* hot, hote]. *c* 1489 CAXTON *Sonnes of Aymon* vi. 136 Whan the yron is well hoote, hit werketh the better. 1598 *Epulario* B iv b, Almonds scorched on whote embers. 1772 H. BROOKE *Redempt.* (R.), The Sun himself [shall] consume with hotter fire. 1819 SHELLEY *Prometh. Unb.* I. 532 From the furnace, white and hot.

c. Of material objects in general (as affected by the sun, fire, chemical action, the vital heat of animals, subterranean heat, etc.).

a 1000 *Guthlac* 1055 in *Exeter Bk.*, He hate let torn þoliende tearas geotan. *c* 1200 *Trin. Coll. Hom.* 83 Ne wepeð none hote teres. *c* 1290 *S. Eng. Leg.* I. 360/53 Seoth it to-gadere.. and leie it al hot þar-to. *c* 1330 R. BRUNNE *Chron. Wace* (Rolls) 2243 Hote bathe he dide make. 1398 TREVISA *Barth. De P.R.* IV. vii. (1495) 91 Blode is hotter in the ryght syde.. strengthe of hote blode is in the ryght syde. *c* 1440 *Promp. Parv.* 249/1 Hoott bathe, *murtetum*. 1546 J. HEYWOOD *Prov.* (1867) 25 Little potte soone whot. *a* 1674 CLARENDON *Hist. Reb.* XIV. §105 This place is famous for its hot baths. 1744 BERKELEY *Siris* §221 A body heated so hot as to emit light. 1860 TYNDALL *Glac.* II. xxiii. 351 When the water.. is as hot as the hand can bear.

d. Of food or drink prepared with the aid of fire, and served before it becomes cool. Cf. *hot and hot* 11 b.

a 1300 *Land Cokayne* 104 in *E.E.P.* (1862) 159 'Gees al hote, al hot.' 1362 LANGL. *P. Pl.* A. Prol. 104 Cookes and heore knaues cryen 'hote pies, hote!' *c* 1430 *Two Cookery-bks.* 12 Serue forth alle hote as tostes. 1548 HALL *Chron.*, *Hen. VII* 4 To take no more drynke neither hote nor colde. 1687 WOOD *Life* 5 Sept. (O.H.S.) III. 235 Three hot dishes, which he fed upon. 1853 SOYER *Pantroph.* 290 A kind of cake.. designated hot-cross-bun. 1896 *Daily News* 2 Jan. 5/7 Nothing is eaten as hot as it is boiled.

e. At a high voltage, 'live'. Esp. in U.S. slang phrs. ***hot chair***, ***seat***, ***squat***, the electric chair.

1925 *Sat. Even. Post* 29 Aug. 18/3 A judge sentenced a boy fifteen years old to the electric chair... A newspaper reporter said he heard the lad announce that he was not afraid to die 'in the hot seat'. 1927 *Flynn's Weekly* 1 Jan. 819/1, I never shot nobody... Lotsa times I don't carry a gun. That's one thing I try to dodge—the hot chair. 1928 J. P. MCEVOY *Showgirl* xii. 180, I ought to get something for that don't you think? The chair maybe—better known as the hot squat. 1930 *Sel. Gloss. Motion Pict. Techn.* (Acad. Motion Pict., Hollywood), *Hot*, electrically charged, particularly when dangerous. 1937 *Printers' Ink Monthly* Apr. 54/2 *Hot mike*, a microphone in which the current is flowing. A live microphone. 1940 *Chambers's Techn. Dict.* 424/1 *Hot*, said of a conductor which is charged to a dangerously high potential. Colloquial. 1944 'P. QUENTIN' *Puzzle for Puppets* ix. 74 When they get me on to the hot seat, I won't even burn. 1952 R. CHANDLER *Let.* 11 Jan. in *R. Chandler Speaking* (1966) 128 That scene at the end where the girl visits him in the condemned cell a few hours before he gets the hot squat!

2. a. Of a person or animal: Having the sensation of heat (in a high degree). Usually in predicate.

c 1400 *Rom. Rose* 2396 Thou shalt no while be in oo state, But whilom colde & whilom hate. 1577 B. GOOGE *Heresbach's Husb.* I. (1586) 15 There must be heede taken, that they drinke not when they be hotte. 1595 SHAKS. *John* IV. iii. 74 Lords, I am hot with haste, in seeking you. 1698 FROGER *Voy.* 10 'Tis very pleasant to drink when one is hot. 1880 A. RALEIGH *Way to City* 105 He is weary like other men and hungry and hot.

b. Of bodily conditions or affections producing or accompanied by this sensation, as fevers, etc.

a 1533 LD. BERNERS *Gold. Bk. M. Aurel.* (1546) M vij, He was vexed with hote feuers. 1600 J. PORY tr. *Leo's Africa* I. 52 Taken with an hot and a cold fit of an ague. 1702 J. PURCELL *Cholick* (1714) 101 Violent Hot Pains in the Lower-Belly. 1882 *Century Mag.* XXV. 103/2 The girl acknowledged his salute by a hot blush.

3. *transf.* Having to do with things that are hot; associated with heat. *rare.*

1658 J. JONES *Ovid's Ibis* 34 Brewers, Bakers, Smiths, and such hot artificers. 1876 L. MORRIS *Epic Hades* I. 3 The hot noise of bees.

4. In the physiology of the Middle Ages, expressing one of the fundamental qualities of humours, elements, planets, and bodies in general: see COLD *a.* 6. (Often passing into 5.) Now in astrological usage.

c 1000 *Sax. Leechd.* I. 284 Ðeos wyrt.. hys ȝecynde is swiþe hat. 1387 TREVISA *Higden* (Rolls) I. 53 Norþeren men, in þe whiche colde.. makeþ hem fatter, gretter, and whitter and hatter with inne. 1398 —— *Barth. De P.R.* XIX. xxvi. [xxxviii.] (Bodl. MS.), Alle þinges wiþ odoure is accounted hote amonge Auctours as.. vinegre, caumfer and rose. 1460–70 *Bk. Quintessence* 2 Oure quinta essencia.. is not hoot and drie wiþ fier, ne coold and moist wiþ watir, ne hoot and moist with eyr, ne coold and drie wiþ erþe. 1551 TURNER *Herbal* I. A v a, Pontike Wormwoode is hote in the first degree and drye in the thirde. 1578 LYTE *Dodoens* VI. lxxxiii. 705 The liquor Cedria.. is almost whoate in the fourth degree. 1599 H. BUTTES *Dyets drie Dinner* N vij b, Pepper.. Hurtful to hot constitutions. 1670 W. CLARKE *Nitre* 52 It is ..controverted whether Nitre be cold or hot. 1819 J. WILSON *Dict. Astrol.* 268 Aries.. is a vernal, hot, dry, fiery, cardinal,.. fortunate, hoarse, bitter sign. 1889 R. BAUGHAN *Influence of Stars* 12 Aries.. is a hot and fiery sign, and produces a lean body. 1909 KIPLING *Rewards & Fairies* (1910) 257 Between Mars and Luna, the one red, t' other white, the one hot, t' other cold.., stands.. a natural antipathy.

5. a. Producing an effect as of heat or burning, esp. on the nerves of taste or the mucous membrane; pungent, acrid, biting; corrosive; heating, ardent.

1548 HALL *Chron.*, *Hen. VIII* 18 The Englishemen.. dranke hote wynes in the hote wether, and did eate all the hote frutes.. that there fell sicke [etc.]. 1596 SHAKS. *Tam. Shr.* IV. iii. 25 The Mustard is too hot a little. 1600 —— *A.Y.L.* II. iii. 49, I neuer did apply Hot and rebellious liquors in my bloud. 1702 J. PURCELL *Cholick* (1714) 171 We may.. give Hotter Remedies in this, than in any other Cholicks. 1806 A. HUNTER *Culina* (ed. 3) 166 The dish is.. too hot of pepper. 1838 T. THOMSON *Chem. Org. Bodies* 488 Camphor [has] a strong hot acrid taste.

b. Affected with this sensation. *rare.*

1870 H. SPENCER *Princ. Psychol.* (ed. 2) §45 While the palate is still hot with a curry, an unflavoured dish seems insipid.

6. *transf.* Excited (this being naturally accompanied by a sensible increase of temperature). **a.** Having or showing intensity of feeling; fervent, ardent, passionate, enthusiastic, eager, keen, zealous. (Of persons, their affections, actions, etc.) Freq. const. *for* or *on* (= keen on, eager for), or with *inf.* With negative construction: unsuccessful, not good or skilful.

971 *Blickl. Hom.* 225 Wæs him.. seo Godes lufu toðæs hat and toðæs beorht on his heortan. *c* 1200 ORMIN 15580 Hat lufe towarrd Godess hus. *c* 1200 *Trin. Coll. Hom.* 119 He.. makede hem hattere on soðe luue to gode and to men. *a* 1225 *Ancr. R.* 400 Forði þet tu ert.. nouðer cold ne hot.. ich chulle speouwen þe ut, bute ȝif þu i-wurðe hattre. *c* 1374 CHAUCER *Troylus* I. 956 (1012) Hotter wex his loue. *c* 1470 HENRY *Wallace* v. 834 Hardy and hat contenyt the fell melle. *a* 1553 UDALL *Royster D.* I. i. (Arb.) 12 In all the hotte haste must she be hys wife. 1573 G. HARVEY *Letter-bk.* (Camden) 14, I.. was then whottist at mi book when the rest were hardist at their cards. *c* 1620 A. HUME *Brit. Tongue* (1865) 18 Ther rease.. a hoat disputation betuene him and me. 1667 PEPYS *Diary* 12 July, The Duke of York.. is hot for it. 1779–81 JOHNSON *L.P.*, *Pope* Wks. IV. 15 Her desires were too hot for delay. 1844 DISRAELI *Coningsby* VI. ii, In the days of his hot youth. 1862 [see DUSTY *a.* 4 d]. 1865 G. MEREDITH *Let.* ?8 Dec. (1970) I. 320, I am very hot upon *Vittoria*. Lewes says it must be a success. 1870 BRYANT *Iliad* II. xv. 107 The foe poured after them In hot pursuit. *a* 1877 SWINBURNE *Lesbia Brandon* (1952) iii. 75 He was always rather hot upon that song. 1897 *Bookman* Jan. 119/1 He was .. a hot patriot in '70. 1924 P. MARKS *Plastic Age* xi. 112, I didn't flunk out but my record isn't so hot. 1925 T. E. LAWRENCE *Let.* 7 Sept. (1938) 485 The Squadron Leader is hot on punishment. 1932 *Blue Valley Farmer* (Okla. City) 28 Jan. 2/3 For president he's not so hot. Business won't support him. 1934 J. M. CAIN *Postman always rings Twice* vi. 57 He was all hot to show me something. 1934 N. COWARD *Play Parade* I. p. x, It.. established me both as a playwright and as an actor... Until then I had not proved myself to be so hot in either capacity. 1937 'J. BELL' *Murder in Hospital* vii. 133 They're quite hot on First-Aid at these race tracks and he had a tourniquet on. 1937 *Tablet* 23 Oct. 553/2 Reviewed long ago with hot delight. 1946 MEZZROW & WOLFE *Really Blues* 375 *Hot for*, enthusiastic about, in favor of. 1952 *Manch. Guardian Weekly* 8 May 5/4 American radio listener, hot for news and excitement, leans forward. 1960 S. KAUFFMANN *If it be Love* II. i. 121 He's very hot on the Babbage Square move. He thinks it's a good idea. 1967 R. RENDELL *New Lease of Death* ii. 22 The Victorians.. were not too hot on design. 1969 D. GRAY *Murder on Honeymoon* xix. 118 Bryce was very hot on never having a drink in the bar.

b. Excited with anger; angry, wrathful, 'in a passion'; *rarely*, of a wrathful disposition, violent-tempered, passionate.

a 1225 *Leg. Kath.* 2147 He.. het, on hat heorte, unhende-liche neomen hire. 1390 GOWER *Conf.* III. 148 Whan he was hottest in his ire. *a* 1450 *Knt. de la Tour* (1868) 19 The eldest chidde with the knight that plaied with her, and gaue hym angri, hasti, and hote langage. 1535 COVERDALE *Gen.* xxxi. 36 What haue I trespassed or offended yᵗ thou art so whote upon me? 1590 SHAKS. *Com. Err.* I. ii. 47 She is so hot because the meate is colde. 1684 BUNYAN *Pilgr.* II. 112 Come man be not so hot, here is none but Friends. 1784 COWPER *Task* II. 179 God proclaims His hot displeasure. 1849 MACAULAY *Hist. Eng.* vi. II. 113 Men of hot temper and strong prejudices. *a* 1863 THACKERAY *D. Duval* i, He had parted, after some hot words.. from his mother. 1877 MRS. OLIPHANT *Makers Flor.* i. 23 Donati was a hot and arrogant noble.

c. Excited with sexual desire; lustful; of animals, 'in heat' (see HEAT *sb.* 13). Also of a play, book, etc.: licentious. Phr. (U.S. slang) ***to have*** (or ***get***) ***hot pants***, to be (or become) aroused with sexual desire. Also, ***hot pants***, a highly sexed (young) woman. Cf. senses 10 b and 12 c.

1500–20 DUNBAR *Poems* xiii. 52 Thair cumis ȝung monkis ..And in the courte thair hait flesche dantis. *c* 1511 *1st Eng. Bk. Amer.* (Arb.) Introd. 27 Very hoote and dyposed to lecherdnes. 1604 SHAKS. *Oth.* III. iii. 403 Were they as prime as Goates, as hot as Monkeyes. 1797 *Phil. Trans.* LXXXVII. 199, I took a female rabbit, hot, (as the feeders term it) that is, ready to be impregnated. 1892 E. J. MILLIKEN *'Arry Ballads* 37 As most of our plays are now cribbed from the French, wy they're all pooty 'ot. 1898 J. D. BRAYSHAW *Slum Silhouettes* 31 She was a 'an'some gal, was Daisy.. but.. she wos a fair scorcher, jist abart as 'ot as they make 'em. 1908 *Daily Chron.* 22 June 6/5 Publishing firms ..discovered that money was to be made out of what they called 'the hot novel'. 1927 K. NICHOLSON *Barker* II. ii. 112 When you had him all hot pants you married him. 1933 D. L. SAYERS *Murder must Advertise* viii. 148 He said to Mr. Tallboy he thought the headline was a bit hot. And Mr. Tallboy said he had a nasty mind. 1935 J. T. FARRELL *Judgement Day* xvi. 383 A burlesque show. The hottest ones were south of Van Buren. 1936 J. STEINBECK *In Dubious Battle* 64 Every time the sun shines on my back all afternoon I get hot pants. 1961 S. PRICE *Just for Record* v. 36 You've got the hot-pants for some good-looking piece. 1963 M. MCCARTHY *Group* iii. 48 I've still got hot pants for her, if you want to call that love. 1963 L. MEYNELL *Virgin Luck* ii. 30, I was just a hot little bit throwing myself at the head of the nearest presentable male. 1966 C. ROBERTSON *Judas Spies* iii. 31 His second wife, this blonde hot pants. 1968 K. AMIS *I want it Now* i. 39 It would help to hold off little hot-pants, and might distract him from the thought of what he was so very soon going to be doing to her. 1968 O. WYND *Sumatra Seven Zero* x. 159 'You ought to marry.' 'That can wait. I haven't got as hot pants as I look.' 1971 W. HANLEY *Blue Dreams* xiii. 221 'I'm hot as a firecracker is what I am,' she said demurely.

d. Of an action: exceptionally good or fine. Of a person: exceptionally smart or skilled or successful (in some action or kind of work). Of dice, cards, etc.: unusually lucky or successful.

1895 S. CRANE *Red Badge of Courage* xvii. 169 'Hot work!' cried the lieutenant deliriously. 1914 *Daily Express* 30 Nov. 5/7 The Deutsches have some pretty hot snipers. 1919 A. A. MILNE *First Plays* 44 He did the ninth [hole in golf] in three. .. How's that for hot? 1934 J. T. FARRELL *Young Manhood* iv. 61 I'm shakin' fair, brother. They're just hot for me this time. The dice get hot for a guy like this maybe once in his whole life. 1944 D. RUNYON *Runyon à la Carte* (1946) 101 Here is Big Nig hotter than a stove, and here I am without a bob to follow him with... Nig can make sixes all night

when he is hot. **1968** *Surfer* IX. 63 Cabell is really ripping it up in Hawaii now, too, but Young and McTavish are so hot it's unbelievable. **1970** *Surf '70* (N.Z.) 17/3 Walsh is not the only hot surfer in New Plymouth.

7. a. Attended with feverish or violent exertion, suffering, discomfort, or danger; intense, violent; raging, severe, sharp, keen. (Chiefly of conflict or the like; formerly also of pestilence or epidemics.)

a **1000** *Guthlac* 979 in *Exeter Bk.* 57 Wæs seo adl þearl, hat, and heoro-grim. *a* **1000** *Phœnix* 613 ibid. 64 b, Hungor se hata. *c* **1000** *Andreas* 1544 (Grein) Hatan heaðo-wælme. *c* **1374** CHAUCER *Troylus* III. 1601 (1650), I hadde it neuere half so hote as now. *c* **1400** *Destr. Troy* 9377 Hongur full hote harmyt hom þen. **1548** UDALL, etc. *Erasm. Par. John* 21 b, The feast was at the hottest. **1581** PETTIE *Guazzo's Civ. Conv.* I. (1586) 7 Vices, which began to growe hot in the Cities. **1590** SIR J. SMYTH *Disc. Weapons* 19 Great skirmishes and encounters that have been verie hot. **1613** PURCHAS *Pilgrimage* (1614) 587 The Plague is sometime so hotte at Cairo, that there die twelve thousand Persons dayly. **1683** WOOD *Life* (O.H.S.) III. 67 Small pox hot and frequent in Oxon. **1709** STEELE *Tatler* No. 80 ¶9 The Fire of Bombs and Grenades..was so hot, that the Enemy quitted their Post. **1722** DE FOE *Plague* (1884) 161 The Plague grows hot in the City. **1845** S. AUSTIN *Ranke's Hist. Ref.* I. 381 In the hottest of the fight.

b. *transf.* Said of a place, position, etc. in which intense action of some kind is going on, or in which one suffers severe discomfort.

1855 *Cornwall* 250 As to the 'hot-lode' at the United Mines..the discovery of which sent up shares from £40 to £450 each—both the heat of the lode and the ardour of the shareholders have considerably declined, and so have the shares. **1872** W. F. BUTLER *Gt. Lone Land* xx. (1878) 318, I have been compelled to seek my sport in hot climates instead of in hot corners. **1892** *Daily News* 15 Feb. 6/2, I have seen many roaring camps; they are hot places, when men lose their money at the gambling-tables and when the bullets begin to fly about. **1896** *Tablet* 22 Feb. 291 We got into as hot a corner as a lot of men ever got into.

c. Of a ball: hit or thrown hard, and difficult for the other side to deal with.

1867 *Ball Players' Chron.* 6 June 3/4 The hot one he sent to pitcher. **1868** H. CHADWICK *Game of Base Ball* 41 *Hot Balls.* This term is applied to balls sent very swiftly to the hands from the bat, or thrown in swiftly. **1882** *Australians in Eng.* 37 Lockwood gave Murdoch a hot chance at point. **1886** F. H. BURNETT *Little Lord Fauntleroy* (1887) vi. 122 He ..gave a dramatic description of a wonderful 'hot ball' he had seen caught. **1917** C. MATHEWSON *Second Base Sloan* 125 The players..had not handled a ball since the summer before and the 'hot ones' made them wince and yell.

d. Associated with or affected by a trade-union dispute. orig. *U.S.*

1901 *Denver Republican* 19 Aug. 1/1 (*headline*) Non-union men invading 'hot' section. **1940** F. RIESENBERG *Golden Gate* 312 Docks had become dangerously congested, for the teamsters joined with the I.L.A., refusing to haul 'hot cargo'. **1947** *Seafarers Log* 25 Apr. 13/2 Officers would no longer go through a picket line to move a hot ship. **1959** *Economist* 2 May 423/2 'Hot cargo' clauses in transportation contracts, under which a lorry-owner agrees not to handle freight coming from another employer with whom the union has a dispute.

e. Of stolen property: easily identifiable and so difficult to dispose of. In extended use: stolen. Also applied to a person wanted by the police.

1925 *Collier's* 8 Aug. 30/2 Stolen bonds are 'hot paper'; stolen diamonds 'hot ice'. **1926** [see *hock-shop* s.v. HOCK *sb.*[7] b]. **1931** *Amer. Speech* VII. 109 *Hot car hustler*, car thief. **1931** 'D. STIFF' *Milk & Honey Route* 207 A person is hot when he is wanted by the law. No hobo will travel with a man who is hot. **1942** M. SCHLAUCH *Gift of Tongues* (1943) 269 Jewels become 'ice', and stolen jewels..'hot ice'. **1943** P. CHEYNEY *You can always Duck* ix. 151 Look, I'm hot, see? The cops here are after me. **1943** R. CHANDLER *Lady in Lake* (1944) xi. 64 The best stunt would be to unload it on a hot car dealer. **1953** W. BURROUGHS *Junkie* (1972) iii. 36 Herman pulled out a silk dress he had under his coat—as I recall somebody unloaded a batch of hot dresses on us for three grains of morphine. **1958** 'A. GILBERT' *Death against Clock* 70 It [*sc.* a stolen brooch] was too hot to touch at present. **1960** H. L. LAWRENCE *Children of Light* ii. 34 You come here, in a hot car... And the police know. **1969** *Times* 4 July 3/8 Many stolen works of art have been recovered recently..which suggests that thieves are finding them too hot to handle. **1973** P. MOYES *Curious Affair of Third Dog* xv. 207 Griselda was 'hot'. Griselda had to disappear.

f. Of a motor vehicle or aircraft: fast or powerful (esp. in relation to size). *colloq.* Cf. HOT ROD.

[**1924** T. E. LAWRENCE *Let.* 20 Feb. (1938) 456 Hot speed on a motor-bike.] **1944** *Sat. Even. Post* 24 June 80/2 PV's can outrun all but the fastest of Jap fighters, but they pay for their speed by landing hot. **1951** *N.Y. Times Mag.* 21 Oct. 59/2 Certainly, the pure jet does land a little 'hotter' than the propeller plane. **1966** T. WISDOM *High-Performance Driving* ii. 31 Small 'hot' machines like a Mini Cooper and a Renault Gordini. **1968** *Hot Car* Nov. 7 It was a 'hot little car'.

8. Technical uses. **a.** *Hunting.* Of the scent: Strong, intense; opp. to COLD *a.* 12. ***to get*** (or ***be***) ***hot***: in a game or pursuit, to come (or be) near the discovery of something concealed. Also *transf.*

Hence, in nursery and parlour games which involve searching or guessing on the part of some of the players, *hot* means close on the track of the object hidden or the solution to be guessed.

1648 MILTON *Tenure Kings* (1650) 60 Hungrie Church-wolves following the hot sent of double Livings. **1781** W. BLANE *Ess. Hunt.* (1788) 111 The scent lying hotter, and encreasing. **1875** W. S. HAYWARD *Love agst. World* 5 He could halloo them off the hottest scent that ever lay on Warwickshire grass. **1876** [see COLD *a.* 12 b]. **1879** TOURGEE *Fool's Err.* xliv. 326 A pack of hounds running on a hot trail. **1882** *Cassell's Bk. In-Door Amusem.* (ed. 2) 29 The progress of the player is usually announced by assuring him that he is 'very cold', 'cold', 'warmer', 'warm', 'hot', 'very hot', or 'burning', according as he is far from or near to the article to be discovered. **1899** E. W. HORNUNG *Amat. Cracksman* 252 'Not there, not there,' said Raffles; 'but you're getting hot. Try the cartridges.' **1931** *Times Lit. Suppl.* 29 Oct. 832/4 He needs it [*sc.* personality] to act quickly and effectively when an appliance fails, or when an investigator gets 'hot'.

b. Of a colour: intense, vivid, glowing.

1896 SIR E. M. THOMPSON in *Proc. Soc. Antiq.* 221 The colours employed are vivid, sometimes even rather hot. **1933** *Burlington Mag.* Apr. 176/2 De Vos had long admired Rubens and emulated his hot tones. **1958** *Vogue* Mid-Sept. (Extra Issue) 87 Hot pink velour hat. **1962** *Harper's Bazaar* Oct. 124/3 A new hot orange lipstick. **1967** D. FRANCIS *Blood Sport* xii. 144 A..hot pink-orange tunic.

c. Dry and absorbent of moisture.

1883 in Spon *Workshop Receipts* Ser. II. 252/2 If the ceiling is 'hot'—*i.e.* porous, and soaks in the moisture very quickly.

d. In constant use or action; figured as heated by friction, etc.

1888 *Harper's Mag.* Oct. 679/2 The New York and Washington wire is kept 'hot' for eight hours every night.

e. *Racing slang.* Said of a 'favourite' on which the betting is specially keen.

1894 *Daily News* 4 June 4/1 The possessor of one of the hottest favourites on record.

f. *Metallurgy* and *Founding.* Of metal, esp. iron: completely fluid; sufficiently above the melting point to flow readily (see also quots. 1904, 1908[1]). So ***hot-metal***, in the sense 'molten iron', is used *attrib.*, as in ***hot-metal process***, a steel-making process in which the charge consists wholly or chiefly of molten iron. (See also *hot metal* in sense 12 c below.)

1888 *Lockwood's Dict. Mech. Engin.* 182 *Hot metal.* Molten iron and brass are said to be hot when their temperature is higher than that required for the class of work for which they are intended. **1902** G. R. BALE *Mod. Iron Foundry Pract.* I. x. 177 In pouring..the metal should be run 'hot'.., for when the metal is poured 'dull'..it is too sluggish to expel its gases. **1904** GOODCHILD & TWENEY *Technol. & Sci. Dict.* 291/1 Metal of any kind is said to be 'hot' when it is at a temperature sufficiently high for some definite operation to be carried out. Thus a smith may say iron is hot when it is just at a welding or a forging heat. **1908** B. STOUGHTON *Metall. Iron & Steel* ii. 37 The term 'hot iron' has come to be synonymous in the minds of blast-furnace foremen with iron high in silicon and low in sulphur. *Ibid.* xiii. 361 When I say 'hot iron' here, I mean 'fluid iron', i.e., the degree of heat above the melting-point. **1929** C. R. HAYWARD *Outl. Metall. Pract.* xxii. 463 (*caption*) Hot-metal mixer at South Chicago... A ladle supported by a crane is delivering metal. **1946** *Firth Brown Gloss. Metall. Terms* 11 In the hot-metal process, iron from the blast furnace goes through the mixer to the open hearth furnace, and constitutes 75% or more of the charge. **1951** G. R. BASHFORTH *Manuf. Iron & Steel* II. xii. 356 The cupola metal replaces the molten pig iron employed in the hot-metal open-hearth process. **1966** J. D. SHARP *Elem. Steelmaking Pract.* viii. 160 Ore, if used, is normally placed directly on top of the lime, or fed to the furnace immediately after the hot metal.

g. orig. *U.S.* Applied to jazz or highly elaborated and florid dance music with a marked beat and strong emotional appeal, freq. improvised; also to the performer or to the place where played and in other uses; opp. COOL *a.* 4 d; *hot lick* (see LICK *sb.* 7).

1924 *Variety* 9 July 9/3 The style in vaudeville jazz bands this coming season will tend toward the 'sweet' and 'hot' dance orchestras. *Ibid.* 24 Sept. 26-c/1 Leon Beiderbecke is a 'hot' trumpet. *Ibid.* 26-c/2 The boys step on it and get 'hot' at various intervals. **1926** [see CHORUS *sb.* 6 c]. **1927** *Dancing Times* Apr. 117 We are in the days of the '*hot*' chorus. *Ibid.* May 149 'Hot Music' is still so much in its infancy over here that I do not propose to deal fully with it for the moment. **1927** *Melody Maker* June 531/3 A rendering from an orchestration or an extemporisation made in this way is usually termed..'hot', the word 'hot' being intended to convey lilting, dance-inspiring rhythm with the accents irregularly placed but strongly portrayed, modern, or as some call them, extreme harmonies, and phrases based on these harmonies worked round the melody. **1928** *Gramophone* VI. 300/2 It is not a question of 'hot' dance music or 'straight' dance music. **1933** *Fortune* Aug. 47/1 Continuing in the language of jazz, it may be explained that Lawrence Brown is a *hot* trombonist with Duke Ellington's famous Negro jazz orchestra. That is to say, he excels in spontaneous, highly syncopated solos. **1933** *Punch* 18 Oct. 441/3 Miss Elizabeth Welch, a coloured lady,..sings what is known as a hot jazz song about Solomon in a startling but rather fascinating way. **1934** [see CHORUS *sb.* 6 c]. **1935** *Vanity Fair* (N.Y.) Nov. 38/3 Hot artists often escape from the routine of their commercial work to the night clubs of Harlem. *Ibid.*, These are the only truly hot bands. **1938** *Oxf. Compan. Mus.* 777/2 Louis Armstrong (claimed by one of his admirers as 'certainly the greatest of all hot musicians ..'). **1946** MEZZROW & WOLFE *Really Blues* xi. 195 Hugues [Panassié]..sure kept himself busy.., launching the Hot Clubs of France. **1947** [see BEAT *v.*[1] 30 d]. **1947** AUDEN *Age of Anxiety* (1948) ii. 40 Emble did likewise but his choice was a hot number. **1949** F. MACLEAN *Eastern Approaches* I. vi. 78 In the station buffet an extremely 'hot' band with a good sense of rhythm played fairly recent jazz from New York. **1953** J. G. MOORE *Relig. Jamaican Negroes* 126 *Hot*, said of drums at Cumina ceremony when the fast rim beat indicates the presence of zombies in the drum. **1956** H. LYTTELTON in S. Traill *Play that Music* 79 Shall it be a trumpet or a cornet? I have no strong views either way—a good 'hot' style can be achieved on either instrument. *Ibid.* 84 'Hot' tone cannot be defined on paper... It can be heard in essence in the playing of Bunk Johnson, Tommy Ladnier..and Louis Armstrong. *Ibid.* 85 Vibrato plays an important part in hot jazz, being used as a means of expression. **1970** P. OLIVER *Savannah Syncopators* 31 The idea of 'hot rhythm' is one which Richard A. Waterman borrowed from jazz and applied to African drumming.

h. Of a Treasury bill: newly issued.

1928 *Evening News* 18 Aug. 11/6 The hot Treasuries were offered at 4 3-16 per cent., without finding buyers. **1929** *Times* 16 Nov. 18/1 The 'hot' Treasury Bills were dealt in at 5 13-32 per cent. **1929** *Observer* 17 Nov. 3/3 'Hot' bills yesterday morning changed hands in very small amounts at 5 5-16 per cent. **1959** *Times* 15 Sept. 17/5 'Hot' bills were again sold to the clearing banks.

i. Radioactive; *esp.* so radioactive as to be dangerous; so ***hot laboratory***, a laboratory designed for the safe handling of highly radioactive material; also ***hot atom***, an atom that has high kinetic or internal energy as a result of a nuclear process.

1942 POLLARD & DAVIDSON *Appl. Nucl. Physics* vii. 139 Almost all the 'hot' sodium was in the form of NaOH. **1945** H. D. SMYTH *Gen. Acct. Devel. Atomic Energy Mil. Purposes* viii. 84 Later a 'hot laboratory', i.e., a laboratory for remotely-controlled work on highly radioactive material, was provided. **1946** *Sci. News Let.* 10 Aug. 84/1 A large part of Bikini lagoon remained..'hot' with radioactivity. **1947** *Time* 10 Nov. 82/2 'Hot' (radioactive) atoms have already caused plenty of trouble in laboratories. **1950** *Sci. Amer.* Mar. 44/3 The bizarre chemical effects sometimes produced by radioactive atoms have given rise to a fascinating new branch of investigation known as hot atom chemistry. *Ibid.* 47/1 The immense recoil energy of the hot carbon atoms will effect chemical reactions that would not ordinarily occur. **1955** *Times* 12 Aug. 6/4 The elaborate precautions needed in so-called 'hot' laboratories—those in which large quantities of radioactive materials are manipulated. **1955** *Sci. News Let.* 27 Aug. 134/3 At Hanford atomically 'hot' strontium is kept in large tanks until it cools down. **1958** H. ETHERINGTON *Nuclear Engin. Handbk.* VII. 48 The building arrangement should be such that one cannot pass from a hot to a 'cold' area without going through a clothing-change facility. **1964** M. GOWING *Britain & Atomic Energy* x. 286 The new laboratories at Chalk River..included a 'hot' laboratory for remote handling. **1972** *Nature* 25 Feb. 443/1 The Mössbauer effect has been used to elucidate..hot atom effects, nuclear lifetimes, [etc.].

9. a. That has not had time to cool down or grow stale or unexciting; fresh, recent: said *esp.* of acts; also of a person fresh from such an act.

c **1330** R. BRUNNE *Chron. Wace* (Rolls) 8627 Wyþ þe dom al hot, Hengistes heued of he smot. **1513** DOUGLAS *Æneis* XIII. iv. 45 Turnus be his hait and recent deid [= death] Had wyth his blude littit the grond al reid. **1659** B. HARRIS *Parival's Iron Age* 246 Which murther being discovered, whilest it was hot, made the Citizens take Arms. **1887** HALL CAINE *Deemster* xxii. 142 The horrible thought that he..was going, hot and unprepared, to an everlasting hell.

b. Of news: sensational, striking, exciting. Phr. ***hot from*** (or ***off***) ***the press***: just printed.

In quot. 1945[2] a fanciful use.

1908 [see HEADLINE 2 d]. **1914** *Daily Express* 30 Sept. 4/5 'Hot news'..must be provided for the people, and thus we learn from the Vienna 'Abendblatt' that General French is a prisoner. **1945** KOESTLER *Twilight Bar* I. 34 News? You bet it is news... Hot? You bet it is hot. **1945** *Tee Emm* (Air Ministry) V. 52 The gen it contains is hot from the griddle. **1955** *Times* 19 Aug. 2/5 But it is for novelties, hot from the press or the copyist's desk, that discontent is calling. **1958** *New Statesman* 3 May 557/2 Television: Curran comments that to this the response of the American press (as it is to some extent that of the British press) is to leave aside all but the hottest news because radio and television can cover it with more actuality and immediacy and to concentrate instead on..personalities. **1969** *Times* 5 July 8/6 There has just arrived hot off the..presses a new publication called The Open Secret.

†**10. a.** *absol.* as *sb.* Hot condition, heat. *Obs.*

c **1200** ORMIN 3734 Wiþþ hat & kald, wiþþ nesshe & harrd. **1340** *Ayenb.* 139 He soffreþ and honger an þorst, and chald and hot. **1398** TREVISA *Barth. De P.R.* v. iii. (Bodl. MS.), Hoote and colde greueþ suche one. **1667** MILTON *P.L.* II. 898 Hot, cold, moist, and dry, four Champions fierce Strive here [in Chaos] for Maistrie.

b. *absol.* as *sb. pl.* Strong sexual desire. *slang.*

1947 in Wentworth & Flexner *Dict. Amer. Slang* (1960) 274/1 I'd never get the deep undying hots for that rah rah collitch [boy]. **1951** AUDEN *Nones* (1952) 18 Jack likes Jill who worships George Who has the hots for Jack. **1961** S. PRICE *Just for Record* vi. 49 One day Lamb was going to get the hots for some painted woman. **1968** M. RICHLER *Cocksure* vi. 44 Well, me, I've got the hots for Polly Morgan. **1973** *Times Lit. Suppl.* 10 Aug. 921/5 It is Blodgett who has the hots for Smackenfelt's mother-in-law.

11. Phrases. **a.** † ***hot and cold*** (also ***in hot and cold***): in all conditions and circumstances (*obs.*). ***to blow hot and cold***: see BLOW *v.*[1] 2 b. ***hot and cold***: short for 'hot and cold water' (in a hotel, etc.). ***to go hot and cold*** (***all over***), ***to go all hot and cold***: to experience alternate sensations of heat and cold as from shock or embarrassment. Also used trivially.

13.. *Gaw. & Gr. Knt.* 1844 Euer in hot and colde To be your trwe seruaunt. *c* **1430** *Deuelis Perlt.* 161 in *Hymns Virg.* 46 Neiþer in hoot ne coolde I may not make him stumble. **1650** B. *Discolliminium* 30 He that pleadeth for a generall.. Toleration, hot and cold, I meane constantly and deliberately.. shall finde himselfe a very Atheist. **1908** *Sears, Roebuck Catal.* 610/4 Brass nickel plated compression bath cocks. Combination hot and cold. **1910** *Bradshaw's Railway Guide* Apr. 1012/1 High-class boarding establishment... Bath (hot and cold). **1914** BARRIE *Admirable Crichton* III. 130 He's working out that plan for laying on hot and cold. **1928** *Daily Mail* 3 Aug. 10/6 The figures given..as to my earnings..made me go all hot and cold—I wonder what I can have done with all that money! **1931** *Times* 16 Mar. 1/5 (Advt.), First-class guest house,.. fitted hot and cold and gas fires. **1944** A. THIRKELL *Headmistress* i. 23 'There is a basin with hot and cold,' she

said. **1973** A. PRICE *October Men* v. 64 His wife had said.. that she had gone 'all hot and cold' after nearly being run over.

b. ***hot and hot***: said of dishes of meat, etc. served in succession as soon as cooked; also *absol.* as *sb.* food thus served. Also *fig.*

1771 SMOLLETT *Humph. Cl.* 4 Oct. Let. iv, I will give you them like a beef-steak at Dolly's, *hot* and *hot.* **1842** TENNYSON *Will Waterproof* xxix, Thy care is, under polish'd tins, To serve the hot-and-hot. **1848** DICKENS *Dombey* viii, Mutton-chops, which were brought in hot and hot, between two plates.

†**c.** ***hot of the spur***: very eager about something. (Cf. HOTSPUR.) *Obs.* (*hot at hand*: see HAND *sb.* 25c.)

1652 SHIRLEY *Doubtf. Heir* v. 62 (N.) Speed, an you be so hot o' the spur.

d. ***to give it*** (a person) ***hot***: to administer a severe chastisement. So ***to get*** or ***catch it hot.*** Also, ***to give it*** (to a person) ***hot and strong*** (and similar phrases). (Cf. 7.) *colloq.*

1679 *Hist. Jetzer* 24 St. Catherine.. gave him as hot as he brought. **1826** SCOTT *Jrnl.* 26 Feb., I would give it them hot. **1877** *5 Yrs.' Penal Servit.* iv. 287 He 'got it hot' for such a crime. **1880** E. W. HAMILTON *Diary* 25 July (1972) I. 27 Wilfrid Blunt goes in 'hot and strong' for making the Province a sort of independence. **1881** [see BITE *v.* 1 b]. **1931** T. R. G. LYELL *Slang* 412 *To give it a person hot and strong*, to punish a person severely, either physically or verbally; to give a good scolding to. **1938** A. G. MACDONELL *Autobiogr. of Cad* ii. 14 Jedediah never spent a penny on the estate unless he was legally compelled to—and then the man who legally compelled him got it hot and strong in double quick time.

e. ***to make it hot for***: to make the position decidedly uncomfortable for. ***too hot for*** or ***too hot to hold*** (a person): said of a place, etc. which is made, through persecution or the like, too disagreeable for him to continue in.

1618 BOLTON *Florus* IV. xii. (1636) 322 Cæsar Augustus thought good to make that practice too hot for them. **1648** NEEDHAM *Plea for King* Ep. A ij, They will make your House too hot to hold you. **1660** HICKERINGILL *Jamaica* (1661) 43 'Ere they make the Island too hot for the English. **1771** FOOTE *Maid of B.* I. i, The share he had in your honour's intrigue.. soon made this city too hot for poor Ned. **1877** MISS YONGE *Cameos* Ser. III. xiii. 110 She.. made St. Albans too hot to hold her. **1890** 'BOLDREWOOD' *Col. Reformer* (1891) 298 A pocket Derringer, which.. had a trick of going off unexpectedly, and had once 'made it hot' for a friend.

f. With qualifying word prefixed, denoting the degree of heat, as BOILING *hot*, BROILING *hot*, PIPING *hot*, RED-HOT, WHITE-HOT, etc.: see these words.

g. ***hot under*** (or occas. ***in, around***) ***the collar***: feeling anger or resentment, agitated (cf. sense 6b); ***hot and bothered***: in a state of exasperated agitation; also used (with hyphens) as attrib. phr.

1895 *Horse Rev.* 31 Dec. 1840/3 He would storm erround' dat room an' git hot under de collar. **1906** J. LONDON *Let.* 1 Nov. (1966) 217, I must confess that he got me rather hot in the collar. **1918** E. POUND *Let.* 4 June (1971) 138 After years of this sort of puling imbecility one gets hot under the collar and is perhaps carried to an extreme. **1919** *Red Cross Mag.* Dec. 3/1 He fumbles around, gets hot under the collar and falsely accuses them of being a nuisance. **1921** M. ARLEN *Romantic Lady* IV. v. 161, I was getting very hot and bothered about the whole thing. **1923** KIPLING *Independence* 16 It [*sc.* each generation] goes to its grave hot and bothered, because no new birth has been vouchsafed for its salvation. **1930** A. P. HERBERT *Water Gipsies* 279 She was delighted, though she had been caught in that rag, and still felt hot and bothered. **1932** *N.Y. Times Bk. Rev.* 7 Feb. 18/4 We thought it must belong to the 'Hot-and-Bothered Virgin on a Gunboat', 'Hot-and-Bothered Virgin at the South Pole' series. **1941** *Q. Jrnl. Speech* Oct. 361 [speech of the Frontier] Hamilton.. spoke sharply to some of the men and Ike, with the licence allowed to an old retainer, suggested that there was no need to 'get hot under the collar'. **1941** F. REINFELD *Keres' Best Games of Chess* 43/2, I suddenly began to go hot under the collar as I noticed the powerful move. **1958** *Listener* 23 Oct. 649/2 Then she emerged, hot and bothered, glasses half down her nose. **1961** J. BARLOW *Term of Trial* I. ii. 22 Most of the teachers.. urged silence in hot-and-bothered threats. **1969** *Bucks Examiner* 25 July 7/1 Very few subjects can get parents as hot under the collar as education. **1970** J. PORTER *Dover strikes Again* i. 7 Twenty-five years in the police had not tarnished Superintendent Underbarrow's basic serenity... He made it a point of honour never to get hot around the collar about anything.

h. ***hot dog***: see as main entry.

i. ***a bit hot***: somewhat unreasonable.

1931 T. R. G. LYELL *Slang* 410 To dismiss the lad just because he forgot to post a letter is a bit hot. **1946** K. TENNANT *Lost Haven* (1947) xiii. 204 She has to be humoured although I do think it's a bit hot her boy friend calling just as if she owned the place.

j. ***hot as*** (in hyperbolic comparisons), esp. (***as***) ***hot as hell.***

1849 N. KINGSLEY *Diary* (1914) 19 Hot as blazes—glad to get under awnings. **1850** W. M'COLLUM *California* 20 It was a delightful, salubrious spot—'hot as blazes' to be sure, but fanned by gentle breezes. **1889** FARMER *Americanisms* 293/2 Hot as the Devil's kitchen. **1896** *N.Y. Dramatic News* 4 July 7/1 This afternoon was as hot as blazes. **1912** *Dialect Notes* III. 579 Hot as hammered hell. **1922** E. O'NEILL *Hairy Ape* (1923) vi. 62 I'll be fire—under de heap—fire dat never goes out—hot as hell. **1935** A. J. POLLOCK *Underworld Speaks* 58/2 *Hot as a 45*, wanted by the police. **1935** DYLAN THOMAS *Let.* July (1966) 159 He's got a.. hot-as-hell conservatory with a fountain. **1953** R. GRAVES *Poems* 29 From every-which-a-way, hot as a two-buck pistol. **1967** *Word Study* Dec. 4/1 One of the most common comparisons in English —is probably 'as hot as hell'.

12. *Comb.* **a.** Parasynthetic, as ***hot-breathed, -eyed, -hearted, -looking, -mettled, -spirited, -stomached, -tailed, -tempered, -toned*** adjs. **b.** With another adj., expressing a union of qualities (*poet.*), as ***hot-bright, -cold, -dry, -humid, -moist*** adjs. **c.** Special combinations and collocations: **hot-ache** (*dial.*), a pain felt in the hands when warmed after being very cold; hence **hot-aching** *a.*; †**hot-backed** *a.*, lustful; **hot beef**, rhyming slang for 'Stop thief!' e.g. in phr. ***to give*** (a person) ***hot beef***; **hot bottle**, a hot-water bottle; **hot box** *U.S.*, an overheated journal-box, esp. of a railway carriage; also *fig.* or *transf.*; **hot bricks**, chiefly in phr. ***like a cat on hot bricks***, denoting a situation of extreme discomfort and restiveness, or expressing swiftness or nimbleness of movement; **hot bulb**, in a semi-Diesel engine, an uncooled chamber connected to the cylinder head which is maintained at a sufficiently high temperature to vaporize fuel oil injected into it prior to compression in the cylinder; any mass of metal that performs the same function in such an engine, usu. *attrib.*; **hot cakes** orig. *U.S.*, (*a*) griddle-cakes, flannel-cakes; (*b*) in phr. ***to sell*** or ***go*** (***off***) ***like hot cakes***, to be sold or disposed of very rapidly; to be in great demand; **hot cathode**, a cathode intended to be heated, so that electrons are emitted thermionically; also *attrib.*; **hot chisel**, a short thick chisel used for cutting or nicking hot metal and having a sharper edge than a cold chisel; **hot-closet** (see quot.); **hot coppers** (see COPPER *sb.*[1] 8); **hot cross bun** (see BUN *sb.*[2] 1, CROSS-BUN); **hot cupboard**, (*a*) an airing cupboard; also *fig.*; (*b*) a cupboard in which plates, dishes, etc., may be made warm; **hot diggety (dog)** *U.S. slang*, an exclamation of joy or surprise; cf. HOT DOG 3; **hot-dip** *a.*, involving, used for, or applied by hot dipping; **hot dipping**, the application of a coating to an article either by dipping it in a bath of hot liquid (e.g. molten metal), or by dipping it hot in a bath of liquid; so **hot-dipped** *a.*, said of the coating; **hot flashes, flushes** *pl.*, a menopausal symptom which manifests itself by a momentary sensation of heat, freq. accompanied by a heightening of facial colour and perspiration; **hot-flue**, a heated chamber for drying cloth or other articles; **hot-hoof** *adv.*, with haste or rapid progress (of horses or cattle: cf. HOT-FOOT); **hot iron** (see sense 8f above); **hot-iron test** *Cheesemaking*, a test to determine the acidity of the curd; **hot line**, a direct, exclusive communication channel between two points; *spec.* the direct telephone link between Washington and Moscow (and similar lines); also *attrib.* and *fig.*; †**hot-livered** *a.*, hot-tempered, excitable, irascible; **hot-making** *a. colloq.*, embarrassing; **hot-melt** *a.*, solid at normal temperatures but capable of being melted for application (e.g. as a coating); **hot metal**, (*a*) molten iron: see sense 8f above; (*b*) used *attrib.* to designate printing machines and methods in which type made by the machine from molten metal is used; **hot money**, capital which is transferred from one country to another in order to avoid the effects of currency devaluation or to profit from high interest rates or possible revaluation; also *attrib.*; †**hot-mouthed** *a.*, restive or ungovernable, as a horse whose mouth is irritated by the bit; **hot pants**, brief shorts worn by girls and young women as a fashion in the early 1970s; cf. ***to have*** (or ***get***) ***hot pants*** s.v. sense 6c above; hence **hot-panted, hot-pantsed** *adjs.*; **hot pint**, a drink consisting of ale sweetened, spiced, and heated: so-called in Scotland; †**hot piss** = CHAUDPISSE; **hot-plate**, (*a*) a heated flat surface on a stove, etc., for cooking or similar purposes; also, a heating element on an electric cooker; (*b*) a plate with a cover for keeping food hot; (*c*) a low, portable heating appliance with a flat top for keeping food hot or heating vessels, food, etc., placed on it; **hot potato**, in fig. phr. (to drop something) ***like a hot potato***; also, a ticklish subject, an embarrassing problem; *rhyming slang*, a waiter; †**hot-reined** *a.*, 'fiery, high-spirited' (Jodrell); **hot-saw**, a buzz-saw for cutting up hot bar-iron into pieces to be re-heated, and re-rolled (Knight); **hot seat**, (*a*) (see sense 1e above); (*b*) used as in sense 7b; (*c*) (see quots. 1933 and 1938); (*d*) an ejection seat in an aircraft; **hot set**, a hot chisel, esp. one with a wooden handle; **hot shift** orig. *U.S.*, a mechanism enabling a change of gear to be made while a vehicle is moving without interrupting the drive to the wheels; **hot shoe**, a socket on a camera incorporating electrical contacts for a flash, etc.; **hot-skull** = HOT-HEAD; **hot spring**, any spring whose waters issue forth at a temperature appreciably higher than that of the ground; **hot squat** (see sense 1e above); **hot-stopping** (*slang*), hot spirits and water; **hot-stove** *N. Amer.*, used *attrib.* of a discussion about a particular sport (e.g. baseball or ice hockey) between periods of play or in an off-season; also applied to anyone discussing a sport in this way; **hot tear** *Metallurgy*, a rupture produced in a casting or ingot as the metal cools and contracts; so **hot tearing** *vbl. sb.*; **hot top** *Metallurgy*, a refractory container for holding a reservoir of molten metal at the top of a mould during the solidification of an ingot; **hot-trode**, fresh or recent trail; **hot tube**, in some early internal combustion engines, a metal or porcelain tube, closed at the end, which projected from one end of the cylinder and was heated externally by a flame, so that it ignited the mixture forced into it during the compression stroke; usu. *attrib.* in ***hot-tube ignition***; **hot-wall**, 'a wall with included flues to assist in ripening the fruit of trees trained against it' (Knight); **hot war**, an open war, involving active hostilities (opp. *cold war*); hence ***hot-warrior***; **hot wave**, a spell of exceptionally hot weather, a heat wave; **hot wind**, a dry, very hot wind that blows over land for large distances from the interior in Australia, the United States, and elsewhere; **hot-wire** *attrib.*, denoting electrical instruments the indications or operation of which are based on the change in the length or resistance of a wire with changing temperature; as *v. trans.* (*N. Amer. slang*), to by-pass the ignition systm of a motor vehicle (as a preliminary to stealing the vehicle); hence **hot-wired** *ppl. a.*; **hot with** (*colloq.*), hot spirits and water with sugar (cf. *cold without*); in quot. 1862 *fig.*

1697 LISTER in *Phil. Trans.* XIX. 379 The tops of my Fingers.. did boaken and ake, as when after extream cold, one has the *hot-ach in them. **1791** E. DARWIN *Bot. Gard.* I. 131 *note*, The pain called the hot-ach after the hands have been immersed in snow. **1917** D. H. LAWRENCE *Look! We have come Through!* 155 Their scent is lacerating and repellent, it smells of burning snow, of hot-ache. *Ibid.* 156 What kind of ice-rotten, hot-aching heart must they need to root in! **1607** TOURNEUR *Rev. Trag.* I. ii. Wks. 1878 II. 21 A *hot-back'd Diuill. **1879** *Macm. Mag.* XL. 506/2 He followed, giving me *hot beef (calling 'Stop thief'). **1896** A. MORRISON *Child of Jago* x. 95 It was now that he first experienced 'hot beef'—which is the Jago idiom denoting the plight of one harried by the cry 'Stop thief'. **1973** G. BUTLER *Coffin for Pandora* vii. 157 'Hot beef, hot beef,' cried the schoolboys. 'Catch him...' **1845** MRS. GASKELL *Lett.* (1966) 824 Please let Meta's feet be warm in bed (a *hot bottle she has here by Dr. H' direction). **1860** F. NIGHTINGALE *Notes on Nursing* i. 11 Hot bottles, hot bricks, or warm flannels.. should be made use of until the temperature is restored. **1967** S. KNIGHT *Window on Shanghai* xxxi. 139 The Chinese don't use hot-bottles unless they're ill. **1848** *Merchant's Mag.* XIX. 656 Such a thing as a '*hot box' to a car has not been known,.. since the sprinkler has been in use. **1873** 'MARK TWAIN' & WARNER *Gilded Age* xlvi. 419 A hot box had to be cooled at Wilmington. **1899** S. HALE *Lett.* (1919) 343 He was excellent with the horses and very careful about hot-boxes and watering. **1910** J. HART *Vigilante Girl* x. 140 If that near hind box was to begin to talk different, I'd pull up and examine it right away. Mebbe I'd save a hot box by doin' it. **1971** D. J. SMITH *Discovering Railwayana* x. 56 *Hot box*, axle box overheated through lack of lubricants or overwork. **1971** *Flying* (N.Y.) Apr. 48/3 Lovely airplane but its another hotbox. **1591** SYLVESTER *Du Bartas* I. iv. 301 Orion, Eridanus.. and *hot-breath'd Sirius. [**1678** J. RAY *Coll. Eng. Proverbs* (ed. 2) 285 To go like a cat upon a hot bake-stone.] **1862** WHYTE-MELVILLE *Inside Bar* ii. 248 A well-bred, raking-looking sort of mare... Beautiful action she had, stepped away like a cat on *hot bricks. **1886** 'J. S. WINTER' *Army Society* xvi, Lady Mainwaring looked.. like a cat on hot bricks. **1958** 'A. GILBERT' *Death against Clock* 165 Crook also was like a cat on hot bricks. **1961** WODEHOUSE *Service with Smile* iii. 42 Having become accustomed to this kind of thing myself.. I have lost that cat-on-hot-bricks feeling which I must have had at one time. *a* **1649** DRUMM. OF HAWTH. *Poems* Wks. (1711) 33 Night neither here is fair, nor day *hot-bright. **1911** *Motor Boat* 26 Jan. 66/3 If you are nervous of electric ignition you should choose a *hot-bulb ignition engine. **1919** W. POLLOCK *Hot Bulb Oil Engines* i. 2 All engines of the low compression type using heavy oils, and hot surface ignition of the injected spray are included under the title of hot bulb oil engines, although some makers use plates or discs, instead of bulbs. **1922** *Encycl. Brit.* XXXI. 519/1 Prior to starting the hot-bulb is blow-lamp-heated for 10 to 15 minutes. **1958** *Van Nostrand's Sci. Encycl.* (ed. 3) 823/1 It [*sc.* the semi-Diesel engine] has a hot bulb, which is a certain mass of metal incorporated in the cylinder head in such a way that a portion of it projects slightly in the combustion space. **1683** W. PENN *Sel. Works* (1782) IV. 309 Their entertainment was.. twenty bucks, with *hot cakes of new corn. **1839** C. F. BRIGGS *Adventures H. Franco* I. xi. 74 'You had better buy 'em, Colonel,' said Mr. Lummucks, 'they will sell like hot cakes.' **1879** *Congress. Rec.* 15 May 1368/1 Four per cent bonds.. go off like hot cakes. **1891** FARMER *Slang* II. 18/2 s.v. *Cake*, Buckwheat and other hot cakes form a staple dish at many

American tables. **1893** P. H. Emerson *Signor Lippo* xii. 37 It went off like hot cakes. **1908** *Daily Chron.* 4 Aug. 3/4 Ice creams at 3d. a time went 'like hot cakes'. **1925** J. Gregory *Bab of Backwoods* xi. 141 So they got the blaze going, bacon sizzling, the frying-pan balanced on the fire, hot-cakes mixed and coffee set to boil. **1930** E. Waugh *Vile Bodies* x. 183 Those who were fortunate enough to own cottages or public houses at the more dangerous corners..were selling tickets like very expensive hot cakes. **1949** H. Kurath *Word Geogr. Eastern U.S.* 34 Flannel cake is..rather uncommon in..Philadelphia, where hot-cake is in common use. *Ibid.* 35 Hot-cakes for griddle cakes made of flour. **1966** *Publ. Amer. Dial. Soc.* 1964 xlii. 16 *Flapjacks*, the commonest name for pancakes. *Batter* (or *batty*) *cakes*, *flitters* (or *flitter cakes*), *fritters*, *griddle cakes*, *hot cakes* are all known. **1971** *Petticoat* 17 July 3/1 You'll find amazing hessian bags..selling like hot cakes for only £1.50. **1913** *Physical Rev.* II. 412 The idea of using a *hot cathode in a Röntgen tube was not new. **1930** *Engineering* 31 Oct. 560/2 The hot-cathode discharge tube was free from these restrictions. **1943** *Electronic Engin.* XVI. 260/3 The instrument incorporates a hot-cathode, low-voltage, cathode-ray tube. **1959** *Listener* 12 Mar. 454/1 The hot cathode, as it was called in 1930, consisted of a small rod of alkaline earth oxide held in a tungsten coil. **1889** *N. & Q.* 23 Feb. 151/1 Cold and *hot chisels are used for cutting cold and hot iron (or metal) respectively. **1964** S. Crawford *Basic Engin. Processes* xiii. 274 The process used to remove surplus metal from the forging with the aid of hot chisels or hot sets. *a* **1817** Jane Austen *Northanger Abbey* (1818) II. viii. 148 The ancient kitchen..rich in the massy walls and smoke of former days, and in the stoves and *hot closets of the present. **1875** Knight *Dict. Mech.*, *Hot-closet.* 1. One attached to a stove to keep victuals or plates warm.. 2. (*Candle-making.*) A chamber in which candle-molds are kept at a heat of 150° Fah., previous to pouring, to prevent the chilling of the stearic acid. **1597** Middleton *Wisd. Solomon* ix. v, Behold his poore estate, his *hot-cold fire. **1614** Sylvester *Little Bartas* 456 The Fits of th' hot-cold cruell Fever. **1733** *Hot cross bun [see cross-bun]. **1825** [see bun *sb.*² 1]. **1880** A. Beardsley *Let.* 1 Apr. (1971) 12 On Good Friday we had hot cross buns for breakfast. **1908** A. Huxley *Let.* 17 Apr. (1969) 26, I am almost prostrated just now by an *Enourmous* [sic] Hot cross Bun. **1941** C. Hole *Eng. Custom & Usage* iv. 43 Hot-cross buns are eaten throughout England on Good Friday... These little cakes ..seemed to be descended from the wheaten cakes eaten at the Spring Festival alike by Greeks, Romans and Saxons. **1970** Simon & Howe *Dict. Gastron.* 90/2 Hot Cross buns are heavily spiced and eaten on Good Friday. **1930** S. Beckett *Whoroscope* 2 Them were the days I sat in the *hot-cupboard throwing Jesuits out of the skylight. **1931** —— *Proust* 51 The Cartesian hotcupboard of the Guermantes library. **1950** *Chambers's Encycl.* VII. 256/2 One [electric cooker] for an ordinary family..would include..a hot cupboard enclosed by a drop door between the hob and the oven, and an oven. **1953** M. Dickens *No More Meadows* i. 20 The bathroom, which housed a boiler and a monstrous hot cupboard. **1959** *Observer* 12 Apr. 14/5 The bathroom.. is assumed to be on first-floor level, adjoining a bedroom with access to water-heater hot-cupboard from the passage. **1967** N. Freeling *Strike Out* i. 11 Saskia took a plate from the hot cupboard. **1924** *Dialect Notes* V. 270 *Hot diggity. **1927** *Sun* (Baltimore) 3 Apr. ii. 1. 12/2 When it comes to 'hot dog', there's no more to be said, unless it is, perhaps, to add a frill and make it 'hot diggety dog'. **1939** Ryerson & Clements *June Mad* iii. 178 I'll..get cleaned up and into my..tux!..Hot diggity! **1947** M. Lowry *Let.* May (1967) 142 All I wanted was..a single word or phrase like: O.K., Hot Diggety, or even We are not amused. **1952** M. R. Rinehart *Swimming Pool* xi. 104 Hot diggety dog! Ain't that something? **1923** *Foundry* (Cleveland) 1 June 454/3 It has been shown that the deterioration of malleable in the *hot-dip galvanizing process is intimately connected with the phosphorus and silicon content of the iron. **1960** *Farmer & Stockbreeder* 22 Mar. 138/2 (Advt.), Rust-proofing by the Hot-dip Galvanizing process ensures complete protection against weather. **1961** *New Scientist* 13 Apr. 38/2 The industrial process for the hot dip tinning of steel has been practised successfully for many years. **1971** *Engineering* Apr. 61/2 Croda Chemicals Ltd..supply both hot-dip strippable wax coatings as well as plastics. *Ibid.* 63/1 These are hot-dip compounds and provide coats impervious to moisture. **1936** *Jrnl. Amer. Zinc Inst.* XVII. 70 We began to collect samples of *hot dipped spelter coated or galvanized sheets that had been subjected to varying periods of service. **1952** Kirk & Othmer *Encycl. Chem. Technol.* VIII. 901 The normal hot-dipped coating consists of an alloy layer covered with a layer of pure coating metal. **1931** *Amer. Machinist* 8 Jan. 59/2 In *hot dipping, crevices are sealed shut and filled with metal. **1954** *Plastics Engin. Handbk.* (Soc. Plastics Industry, Inc.) x. 300 Successive hot-dipping of objects in a tank of plastisol over the course of several hours will raise the temperature of the plastisol. **1605** —— *Du Bartas* ii. iii. iii. *Law* 1167 Some *hot-dry Exhaling, Or Blazing-Star. **1924** A. J. Small *Frozen Gold* 222 *Hot-eyed, livid-faced men. **1936** *Times Lit. Suppl.* 3 Oct. 788/4 The Herr Doktor, who was hot-eyed, not weary-eyed. **1969** *Listener* 5 July 21/3 For some tastes, to embark on a Doris Lessing book has always meant a tough regime of entrail-inspection and hot-eyed political pamphleteering. **1910** H. S. Crossen *Diagn. & Treatm. Dis. Women* (ed. 2) xiv. 851 '*Hot flashes'..can hardly be classed as pathological. **1933** R. G. Hoskins *Tides of Life* xii. 282 This..phenomenon is accompanied by..the well-known 'hot flashes'. **1959** M. F. Willis *Let.* in 'I. Devi' *Yoga for You* (1960) 200 These benefits have continued with the extra good fortune of getting rid of seventy-five per cent of the hot flashes. **1875** *Ure's Dict. Arts* II. 820 *Hot-flue is.. an apartment heated by stoves or steam-pipes, in which.. calicoes are dried hard. **1910** W. B. Bell *Princ. Gynaecol.* iii. 89 The '*hot flushes'..are produced by rapid changes in the condition of the vaso-motor system. **1946** P. M. F. Bishop *Gynaecol. Endocrinol.* iii. 33 A premature menopause complete with hot flushes becomes established. **1948** L. Martin *Clinical Endocrinol.* viii. 185 The general symptoms of the menopause are well marked in over 50 per cent of women, but some entirely escape and others suffer only minor discomfort from 'hot flushes'. **1971** M. Lee *Dying for Fun* xxxvi. 174, I keep getting hot flushes. It's my age. **1897** *Blackw. Mag.* Dec. 722 To take..a hundred head of beestial *hot-hoof over hill and moor. *a* **1618** Sylvester *Panaretus* 1284 The Angell..found her out in a *hot-humid Cell. **1889** *Jrnl. Brit. Dairy Farmers' Assoc.* V. ii. 70, I depend entirely on the *hot iron test at this stage [of cheese-making]. *Ibid.*, To determine when the curd is ready for salting the hot iron test is again resorted to. **1955** J. G. Davis *Dict. Dairying* (ed. 2) 209 *Hot iron test.* This test is held in great esteem by some cheesemakers, but is very crudely carried out. **1955** *N.Y. Times Mag.* 7 Aug. 10/1 To hold this breakthrough to a minimum is 'ConAd's' job. It has twelve air divisions, tied in by '*hot line' communications with one another and with the Army, Navy and Civil Defense Administration. **1962** *Flight Internat.* LXXXI. 401/1 'Hot line' communications are by radio. **1963** *Guardian* 6 Apr. 1/3 Mr. Tsarapkin's acceptance of a 'hot' White House-Kremlin telephone or teleprinter line. **1963** *Daily Tel.* 21 June 16 *Hot line.* At Geneva yesterday the United States and Russia signed an agreement to set up a direct link between the Kremlin, the Pentagon and, presumably, the White House. **1963** *Ibid.* 6 Sept. 23/4 The British Overseas Airways Corporation yesterday opened its own 'hot line'. It is an instantaneous electronic reservations system between London and New York. **1965** *New Statesman* 17 Sept. 390/2 The hand [of the Pope] hesitates to reach for the hot-line to the Holy Ghost. **1966** *Maclean's Mag.* 17 Sept. 3 About 20 orators arose, one after another, to espouse everything from (predictably enough) free university tuition to local night shopping and radio hot lines. **1966** *Melody Maker* 15 Oct. 6 Is he a mystic with a direct hot-line to heaven? **1969** *Times* 9 Aug. 4/2 President Nixon and..the West German Chancellor, announced today that they had agreed to set up a 'hot line' for communication between Washington and Bonn. **1970** *Daily Tel.* 17 Mar. 13/2 'Hot lines' are becoming *de rigueur* these days—Washington-London-Moscow, to say nothing of London-Canberra. **1971** *Ibid.* 26 July 3/3 On five days during the Moon mission, ITN will have a 'hot line' over which viewers can put questions to a panel of experts. **1599** *Broughton's Let.* ix. 29 Ignorant *hotliuered fellowes, of an vnseasoned zeale. **1641** Milton *Animadv.* (1851) 188 A capricious Pædantie of hot-liver'd Grammarians. **1936** J. Curtis *Gilt Kid* v. 50 She wasn't quite so *hot-looking as Maisie... That judy certainly had passion. **1959** *Tamarack Rev.* xii. 23 How could a hot-looking girl turn out so cold? **1931** *Sunday Times* 22 Feb. 4/1 This, to use the current phrase, *hot-making play. **1958** B. Nichols *Sweet & Twenties* i. 34 How was it that Queen Marie delivered such hot-making effusions? **1939** *Manuf. Pulp & Paper* (ed. 3) V. §4. 84 *Hot-melt coatings will probably become familiar as paper coatings in the near future. **1946** *Nature* 30 Nov. 801/1 The production of hot-melt inks for carbon paper. **1954** *Plastics Engin. Handbk.* (Soc. Plastics Industry, Inc.) viii. 234 Hot-melt compounds of ethyl cellulose have become available..as another tooling material... Worn or damaged tools..can be reclaimed by remelting and recasting. **1969** *New Scientist* 19 June 641/3 The process is based on the use of papers precoated during production with a very thin film of 'hot-melt' plastic resin. **1960** *McGraw-Hill Encycl. Sci. & Technol.* X. 601/2 If type produced on '*hot metal' machines is to be used, the type is set, proved, read, and corrected. **1964** Turnbull & Baird *Graphics of Communication* v. 83 Hot-metal composition is done on various type-casting machines. **1971** *Brit. Printer* Aug. 61/1 Harris-Intertype has introduced a low-cost photo text setter, the price of which is said to be comparable to that of a modern, manual hot-metal machine. **1698** Fryer *Acc. E. India & P.* 34 Their Horses..are small and *hot-mettled. **1591** Sylvester *Du Bartas* i. ii. 261 The cold-dry Earth to *hot-moist Aire returnes not. **1936** P. J. O'Brien *Forward with Roosevelt* xi. 191 The movements of 'refugee capital', or as President Roosevelt and other financiers..described it, '*hot money', was an important consideration in the question of currency stabilization. **1951** J. R. Winton *Dict. Econ. Terms* (ed. 3) 45 *Hot money*, a term used to describe the movement between different countries of balances and capital assets, withdrawn from one country through a loss of confidence as a result of war scares, possibilities of currency depreciation, [etc.]. **1958** *Spectator* 24 Jan. 117/2 Anybody who can afford to pay the 'hot' money price. **1971** *Daily Tel.* 3 Feb. 15 The huge volume of 'hot money' coming from abroad to chase high interest rates in Britain. **1645** Quarles *Sol. Recant.* vii. 9 Let not thy *hot-mouth'd spirit entertain Too sudden passion with too slack a rain. **1681** Dryden *Sp. Friar* iii. iii, That hot-mouthed beast, that bears against the curb. **1971** *New Scientist* 25 Feb. 428/2 Where we once had ladies in gowns and earrings to elocute the score at us, we now have *hot-panted dolly-birds who can't add up. **1972** *Guardian* 29 May 8/1 The miniskirted or hotpanted lass. **1970** *Women's Wear Daily* 23 Nov. 31/2 As for *hotpants, we haven't seen anything in the market... They're going to have to be styled very imaginatively. Otherwise, they're going to look like old-fashioned short shorts. **1971** *Daily Tel.* 26 Jan. 4/8 'Hot pants', the fashion craze for abbreviated shorts for day or evening wear, is becoming the dominant fashion in the children's wear field, according to designers and manufacturers in New York. *Ibid.* 8 Nov. 12/8 Hotpants have rather quickly died a fashion death. **1971** *Daily Colonist* (Victoria, B.C.) 26 May 2A/1 Bibbed hot pants in easy care cotton. Styled with back zip. **1971** W. Hanley *Blue Dreams* xi. 178 But, she couldn't wait! *Hot-pantsed little... It was all perfectly clear now! **1863** *Chambers' Bk. of Days* I. 28 On the approach of twelve o'clock, a *hot pint was prepared—that is, a kettle or flagon full of warm, spiced, and sweetened ale, with an infusion of spirits. **1578** Lyte *Dodoens* iii. lxvii. 408 Good against the strangurie, the *hoote pisse, the stone in the bladder. **1845** E. Acton *Mod. Cook.* vii. 159 The *hot plates, or *hearths* with which the kitchens of good homes are always furnished. **1846** S. Etievant *Brit. Pat. 11,096*, In the Drawing,..the spit on to which the material to be roasted is placed is affixed to the hot plate J, which carries the pots for charcoal K. **1861** C. E. Francatelli *Cook's Guide* 3 (Advt.), Smoke Jacks, Hot Plates,.., Steam Tables, and..other description of.. Cooking Apparatus. **1925** G. L. Hill *Ariel Custer* vii. 99 A gas hot plate with two burners. **1925** L. Stallings *Plumes* vii. 175 The hot plate..was set upon a bracket next the water closet. **1936** *Catal. Chem. Apparatus* (F. E. Becker & Co.) (ed. 25) 436 Gas Heated Hot Plate, polished smooth steel top on wrought-iron stand. **1938** *Trans. Amer. Soc. Mech. Engin.* LX. 70/1 Cores, crossbands and veneers.. were glued on a hydraulic hot-plate press with hide or bone glue. **1966** *Which?* Feb. 45/2 All the other cookers had spiral hotplates with continuously variable controls. **1969** Hotplate [see cordless *a.*]. **1971** *Sci. Amer.* Aug. 108/3, I use butyl phthalate..and heat it with small laboratory hot plates operated at a temperature of 350 degrees Fahrenheit. [**1840** *Picayune* (New Orleans) 11 Sept. 2/2 Let's drop Nancy Daly like a hot praytee and proceed.] **1846** *Spirit of Times* 6 June 170/1, I dropped the divine's arm 'like a *hot potatoe'. **1861** H. Rhys *Theatr. Trip Canada & U.S.* xi. 96 A deep growl..made the article like a hot potato. **1886** B. P. Poore *Perley's Reminisc.* I. 448 They dropped him like a hot potato when they learned that he had accepted a place on the Republican Committee of his State. **1909** J. R. Ware *Passing Eng.* 155/1 *Hot potato* (False Rhyming—Music Hall, 1880). Waiter. **1930** W. S. Maugham *Cakes & Ale* xiv. 169 She dropped him, but not like a hot brick or a hot potato. **1952** M. McCarthy *Groves of Academe* (1953) xiii. 257 It was a very hot potato... I chose to ignore the question. **1958** *Economist* 20 Dec. 1062/2 It has..dropped the hot-potato question of future UN forces. **1961** C. McCullers *Clock without Hands* x. 199 The Judge had been distressed when Johnny agreed to take the case, was amazed at first at the way he handled it—hot potato that it was. **1963** *Listener* 14 Feb. 308/1 Tories continue to treat *laissez-faire* enterprise as a political hot potato. **1969** *New Scientist* 16 Oct. 116/1 The current hot potato in the sociological field is the question of poverty in Britain today. **1639** Massinger *Unnat. Combat* iv. ii, Like a *hot-rein'd horse. **1933** C. E. Leach *On Top of Underworld* xii. 185 No catalogue of the methods of con-men would be complete without an exposure of this time-honoured 'ramp' [the 'Rosary' confidence trick], and of its companion, the '*Hot Seat'. **1938** F. D. Sharpe *Sharpe of Flying Squad* xxviii. 286 You've got to hand it to the Hot Seat Boys. They're clever little devils. For the benefit of the great overworld public —Hot Seat Mob is the title bestowed by the Underworld on the gentlemen we so often read about under the heading of Confidence Tricksters. **1942** *Time* 6 Apr. 49/1 We are an entire nation of people who are trying to wage a war and everyone is trying, himself, to keep out of the hot seat. **1950** *Nat. Geogr. Mag.* Sept. 311/1 (*heading*) Jets' 'Hot Seat' saves lives. **1959** *Observer* 11 Oct. 21/4 The cosy climate of gracious-uxorious living shattered by hot-seat-phobia. **1961** *Economist* 2 Dec. 913/1 The 'hot seat' issue of Chinese representation. **1966** *Listener* 28 July 143/1 After fifteen months in this critical hot seat..between listeners and the BBC I am saying my farewell. **1969** *Times* 24 June 25/1 (*headline*) Return to the hot seat. **1888** *Lockwood's Dict. Mech. Engin.* 183 *Hot set*, a smith's set,..used for the nicking and cutting of hot metal. **1894** G. Hughes *Construction Mod. Locomotive* iii. ii. 155 Upon each side of the vertical an angle of 45° is marked, that is, nicked cold and afterwards heated and removed by a hot set. **1964** S. Crawford *Basic Engin. Processes* xiii. 270 The hot set is used for cutting or marking hot material, often used in conjunction with a hardie. **1971** *Power Farming* Mar. 15/4 The tractor of the late seventies would be similar in layout to present-day models... The main differences would be in driver comfort,..greater use of *hot-shift transmission and quick-attach systems for implements. **1972** *Good Motoring* Dec. 12/1 Driver-controlled epicyclic gearboxes in which various ratios were engaged or disengaged under load ('hot shift' is the American phrase) by means of friction clutches. **1971** *Amat. Photographer* 13 Jan. 57/1 (Advt.), Center flash contact (*hot shoe). **1972** *Ibid.* 12 Jan. 71/2 (Advt.), Dual flash synchronisation system accepts virtually every type of flash unit with 'hot shoe' or plug-in coupling. **1972** L. Gaunt *Praktica Way* 118 Their single flash contact is in the accessory shoe and is designed for use with flashguns with a contact in the foot (the so-called 'hot-shoe' contact). **1608** Day *Hum. out of Br.* iv. i. Wks (1881) 53 *Hot-sprighted youthes. **1669** W. Simpson *Hydrologia Chymica* 154 Some other causes there are of *hot springs, *viz.* subterraneal fires. **1780** [see geyser 1]. **1850** [see spring *sb.*¹ 2 b]. **1961** *Times* 18 Mar. 11/1 Hot springs are found throughout the island [*sc.* Iceland]. **1549** Coverdale, etc. *Erasm. Par. Phil.* 5 Peace and concorde can not..continue among them, that are *hote stomaked and hyghe mynded. **1861** Whyte Melville *Mkt. Harb.* ii. (ed. 12) 13 No man can..drink *hot-stopping the last thing at night, and get up in the morning without remembering that he has done so. **1952** *Time* 18 Feb. 55 **Hot stove leaguer*, in the U.S., anyone who likes to talk at length..about recent developments in his favorite sport—which is usually baseball. **1959** *Ottawa Citizen* 25 June Suppl. 7/1 The auto industry has its own hot-stove league —the off-season gatherings of stylists, planners and engineers who talk of what might have been or what might yet be. **1962** *Hockey Canada* Nov. 12/2 Things we have missed may be mulled over in Hot Stove sessions which are as old and as popular as the sport of hockey itself. **1965** *Globe & Mail* (Toronto) 13 Jan. 26/4 King Clancy..joined Bower ..on the Hot Stove panel yesterday. **1680** ? Buckhurst in Rochester *Poems* 78 Until her *Hot-Tail'd Majesty..Had worne her Gems on Holy Days. **1933** *Jrnl. Iron & Steel Inst.* CXXVII. 566 The application of certain principles of casting design is important in eliminating the danger of *hot-tears. **1955** Heine & Rosenthal *Princ. Metal Casting* xvi. 350 A rigid mold is also a potential cause of hot tears. **1945** *Jrnl. Iron & Steel Inst.* CLI. 380P The degree of *hot tearing..can be minimised or often eliminated by using steel with a lower sulphur content. **1967** A. H. Cottrell *Introd. Metall.* xiii. 180 Another practical problem of shrinkage is hot tearing. **1873** Symonds *Grk. Poets* vii. 196 Oedipus, the *hot-tempered king. **1961** *New Left Rev.* July–Aug. 43/1 A swinging musician with a great sense of the Blues, and '*hot-toned'. **1928** *Jrnl. Iron & Steel Inst.* CXVII. 831 Corrugated ingots of acid steel cast with *hot tops to eliminate segregation and piping are used for the larger forgings. **1954** A. R. Bailey *Text-bk. Metall.* ix. 388 A 'hot top'..acts as a reservoir for feeding the ingot, the pipe eventually occurring in this portion, which is discarded. **1774** Pennant *Tour Scotl.* in 1772, 68 Persons who were aggrieved..were allowed to pursue the *hot-trode with hound and horn. **1805** Scott *Last Minstr.* v. xxix. *note*, The pursuit of Border marauders was followed..with bloodhounds and bugle-horn, and was called the *hot-trod*. **1890** W. Robinson *Gas & Petroleum Engines* iii. 35 The *hot tube gives a good regular ignition. *Ibid.*, With hot-tube ignition..there is the possibility of premature and irregular explosions. **1912** Askling & Roesler *Internal Combustion Engines* ii. ii. 122 Ignition by hot tube is only employed for small engines. **1963** Bird & Hutton-Stott *Veteran Motor Car* 67, 1899 Clément-Panhard... Engine: Transverse, inclined, rear, 1-cyl., 90 × 120 mm., A.I.V. (i.o.e.), hot-tube ignition. **1777** W. Wilson (*title*) The Forcing of Early Fruits, and the Management of *Hot Walls. [**1768** J. Lees *Jrnl.* (1911) 39 The Chipawas..were at this time in a hot war with the *Sous*.] **1947** *Newsweek* 17 Nov. 25/2 The ideological war of the Communists is as ruthless and as determined..as a *hot war. **1955** *Times* 5 July 11/6 It is a reasonable

assumption that a hot war would be measured in months if not weeks. **1973** R. Hayes *Hungarian Game* 340 U.K. Counterintelligence..blew the cover of every *Abwehrabteilung*..agent in Britain during the hot war. **1966** *New Statesman* 22 July 116/2 It is more likely that the *hot warriors..want to use rash behaviour in Hanoi to authenticate the next escalation. **1888** *Encycl. Brit.* XXIII. 805/1 The occasional occurrence of '*hot waves' which sweep over large areas of country, raising the temperature much above its normal height, is one of the most striking and most disagreeable features of the climate of the country [*sc.* the U.S.A.]. **1901** *Daily Colonist* (Victoria, B.C.) 23 Oct. 5/2 The 'hot wave', as the weather man calls it, was general along the coast and extended some way east. **1936** *Discovery* Mar. 78/2 The only periods when Buchan's spells appear to be at all true in London and the south are his cold wave of February 7th to 14th, and the hot wave from July 12th to 15th. **1968** G. R. Rumney *Climatol.* xi. 198 The familiar but unwelcome heat wave, or hot wave, of eastern North America. **1797** *Encycl. Brit.* VI. 402/1 A sign of the approaching *Simoom* or *hot wind. **1804** Wellington *Disp.* (1837) III. 180 A desire to give his troops some repose, and not to expose the Europeans to the hot winds in Hindustan. **1850** R. G. Cumming *Five Yrs. Hunter's Life S. Afr.* I. 60 At certain seasons..northerly breezes prevail: these are termed by the colonists 'hot winds'. **1900** W. Stebbing *C. H. Pearson* 289 He revelled in the Victoria hot-wind days which shrivelled up everybody else. **1910** W. L. Moore *Descr. Meteorol.* x. 187 The 'hot winds' of our western plains [in the U.S.A.]. **1971** J. Gentilli *Climates of Austral. & N.Z.* v. 68 In the southern interior, especially in Victoria, these hot winds laden with dust are known as brick-fielders. **1871** 'Dingo' *Austral. Rhymes* 18 The dust and the *hot-windy weather. **1889** *Telephone* 15 Mar. 136/1 The actual stress in the platinum silver wire in our *hot-wire voltmeter was not sufficient. **1904** *Electrician* Nov. 150/1 An oscillating circuit containing..a delicate hot-wire ammeter. **1914** *Phil. Trans. R. Soc.* A. CCXIV. 404 (*heading*) On the design of portable hot-wire anemometers. *Ibid.* 405 Standard thermometer wire is the most suitable for the purpose of hot-wire anemometry. **1922** *Encycl. Brit.* XXXI. 186/2 A case of great importance from its industrial application in hot wire valves is one where all the ions are negative and are emitted from the cathode. **1923** E. W. Marchant *Radio Telegr.* iv. 44 Other forms of detector for wireless circuits are the electrolytic, the hot wire 'barretter' and the crystal. **1933** *Phil. Mag.* XVI. 50 The sound recording instrument was a tuned hot-wire microphone. **1957** Haltiner & Martin *Dynamical & Physical Meteorol.* xiv. 218 Hot-wire anemometers are..highly sensitive instruments capable of measuring mean wind velocities over very short periods (down to 0·1 sec.). **1957** E. G. Richardson *Techn. Aspects Sound* II. ix. 361 The turbulence data..were measured inside the jet stream by the use of hot wire equipment. **1966** R. Thomas *Spy in Vodka* (1967) i. 7, I was pleasantly surprised to find my car intact. The German juvenile delinquents..can hot-wire a car in a time that makes their American counterparts look sick. **1968** *Daily Colonist* (Victoria, B.C.) 5 Sept. 19/2 Newton told court he yelled his intention to 'hot-wire' the Thomas car (bypass the need for an ignition key). **1962** *Amer. Speech* XXXVII. 269 **Hot-wired*, designating a motor vehicle which has had the ignition switch short-circuited by a thief. **1843** *Ainsworth's Mag.* IV. 437 The '*hot with' set our tongues in motion. **1856** C. Reade *Never too Late* III. xxx. 289 'Hot with,' demanded the waiter in a sharp mechanical tone... The landlady..poured first the brandy then the hot water into a tumbler. **1862** Thackeray *Wks.* (1872) X. 211 How do you like your novels? I like mine strong, 'hot with'.

d. Used before numerous vbl. sbs. and pa. pples. (ppl. adjs.) that denote an industrial or manufacturing process or its result, from which arise transitive vbs. as back-formations; so **hot drawing**, the drawing of wire, tubing, or the like with the application of heat or while hot; ***hot-drawn*** adj.; ***hot-draw*** vb.; **hot-gilding**, 'a name applied to amalgam gilding, in which the mercury is driven off by heat' (Knight *Dict. Mech.* 1875); **hot moulding**, moulding in which heat is applied either to the material to be moulded (as in injection moulding) or to the mould (as in compression moulding); ***hot-moulded*** adj.; ***hot-mould*** vb.; **hot rolling**, the rolling of metal while it is at an elevated temperature; ***hot-rolled*** adj.; ***hot-roll*** vb. Also HOT-PRESS *v.*, HOT-WORK *v.*

1899 Hot-drawn [in N.E.D.]. **1910** H. P. Tiemann *Iron & Steel* 336 With hot drawing the thickness of the walls is not generally carried below ¼ in. **1952** J. Delmonte *Plastics Molding* xiii. 409 It is much more feasible to stock a few sizes and then, when a special tubing is required, hot-draw the tubing down to the required dimension. **1963** H. R. Clauser *Encycl. Engin. Materials* 685/1 Typical applications for these steels are..hot-drawing dies..and die casting dies. **1938** H. I. Lewenz tr. *Brandenburger's Processes & Machinery Plastics Industry* i. 1 *Hot moulding, where the hardening process..takes place to some extent simultaneously with the moulding of the paste by tools, which..are heated. *Ibid.* 7 Hot-moulded articles. **1962** *Times* 13 Feb. 4/6 They have offered to build a racing eight by the hot-moulded method. **1964** N. G. Clark *Mod. Org. Chem.* xvii. 359 The product is a colourless, transparent solid which may be machined, or hot-moulded. **1878** *Hot-rolled [see *cold-rolled* (COLD *a.* 18)]. **1888** *Proc. Inst. Civil Engineers*, XCIV. 236 (*caption*) Billet [of mild steel]. Reduced by hot rolling to wire rod. **1925** Hot-roll [see *base box* (BASE *sb.*[1] 20)]. **1928** *Jrnl. Iron & Steel Inst.* CXVII. 840 A description of the hot-rolling, cold-rolling and drawing operations in the manufacture of nickel steel. **1955** *Times* 12 July 8/3 The new Duisburg mill will be able..to produce 180,000 tons of hot-rolled steel products a month. **1967** A. H. Cottrell *Introd. Metall.* xxii. 439 In steel-making..the ingots are taken from their moulds while still hot and then stored in a soaking pit or furnace ready for hot-rolling at 1000–1200° C.

hot, *adv.* [OE. *háte* = OS. *hêto*, OHG. *heizo*; afterwards levelled with the adj.] In a hot manner, hotly. (Usually hyphened to a following adj. or pple. used attrib.)

1. With great heat, at a high temperature; pungently.

c **1000** Ælfric *Hom.* I. 424 Isenan clutas hate glowende. **13..** *K. Alis.* 572 (Bodl. MS.) Þe briȝth sonne so hoote shoon. **1340** Hampole *Pr. Consc.* 6572 With melles of yren hate glowand. **1513** Douglas *Æneis* I. vi. 185 Ane hundreth altaris..Hait birning full of Saba sence. **1593** Shaks. *3 Hen. VI*, IV. viii. 60 The Sunne shines hot. **1730–46** Thomson *Autumn* 438 Adhesive to the track Hot-steaming. **1856** Kane *Arct. Expl.* II. xxix. 292 With hot-tingling fingers.

2. *fig.* Ardently, eagerly, violently, severely, angrily, etc.: see the adj.

1375 Barbour *Bruce* x. 693 Þe Erll was handlyt þair sa hat. *c* **1385** Chaucer *L.G.W.* Prol. 59 Ther loved no wight hotter in his lyve. *c* **1460** *Towneley Myst.* xiii. 228 A sekenes I feyll that haldys me fulle haytt. **1551** T. Wilson *Logike* (1580) 83 b, He tooke the matter very hotte. **1593** Shaks. *Lucr.* 247 'Tween frozen conscience and hot-burning will. **1795** Nelson 27 Aug. in Nicolas *Disp.* (1845) II. 75 The French cavalry fired so hot on our Boats. **1816** Byron *Siege Cor.* vi, Fast and hot Against them pour'd the ceaseless shot. **1884** 'Mark Twain' *Huck. Finn* xv. 126 As soon as I got started I took out after the raft, hot and heavy, right down the tow-head. **1922** Joyce *Ulysses* 160 If a fellow gave them trouble being lagged they let him have it hot and heavy in the bridewell. **1924** T. E. Lawrence *Let.* 19 Mar. (1938) 459 *A*[*rabia*] *D*[*eserta*] is selling hot in U.S.A. **1927** *Melody Maker* Aug. 782/2 The verse is then taken 'hot' by the trumpet. **1928** *Ibid.* Feb. 184/2 They are..played 'hot'. **1934** T. S. Eliot *Rock* i. 12 The shareholders ain't there, and their divvies ain't 'ardly there either, 'cos they paid too 'ot for their shares.

hot (hɒt), *v.* [OE. *hátian*, f. *hát* HOT *a.*: cf. OHG. *heizên* to be hot. In later use formed afresh from the adj.]

†**1. a.** *intr.* To be or become hot. (Only in OE.)

c **825** *Vesp. Psalter* xxxviii. 4 [xxxix. 3] Hatade heorte min binnan me.

b. With *up*. To become hot. Also *fig.*

In quot. 1909 the passive use is somewhat unusual.

1909 W. Owen *Let.* 23 Aug. (1967) 55, I *did* take a holiday, on account of the day being so 'hotted up'. **1936** Wodehouse *Laughing Gas* xiii. 146 It did not need a razorlike intelligence to show me that things were hotting up, and that flight was the only course. **1958** *Daily Mail* 3 Sept. 1/2 The cold war being fought out between Britain and Iceland in the rich fishing grounds of the northern seas hotted up yesterday. **1967** M. Chandler *Ceramics in Mod. World* iv. 132 The higher the frequency the more the insulator will hot up. **1969** *Times* 28 July 18/6 (*heading*) Pacific air route battle hots up.

2. *trans.* To heat. (Now *colloq.* or *vulgar.*)

1561 Hollybush *Hom. Apoth.* 7 a, Take two tyles that be hoted. **1610** Healey *St. Aug. Citie of God* 680 Pele-thronian Lapitho gave the bit And hotted rings. **1847–78** Halliwell, *Hot*, to heat, or make hot. *Notts.* **1878** Miss Braddon *Open Verd.* xix. 139 I'll go and get things hotted up for you. **1881** *Society* 2 Feb., Water hotted and a steaming bowl of punch prepared. **1903** M. Crommelin *Crimson Lilies* (1913) xxiv. 176 You put something on your outside, while I hot up some tea..to put in your inside. **1928** Galsworthy *Swan Song* II. iv. 138 Let me hot up your stew. **1952** S. Selvon *Brighter Sun* ix. 188 Urmilla went to hot the food.

3. *fig.* or *transf.* with *up*. *spec.* (*a*) To become 'warm' or unpleasantly excited, near the point of anger. Cf. also sense 1 b. (*b*) *pass.* Of an internal-combustion engine, a car, etc.: to be 'tuned up'; to have the power increased so as to be capable of higher speeds. Also *trans.* and in *ppl. a.*, and in extended uses.

1923 Wodehouse *Inimitable Jeeves* x. 108 The atmosphere was consequently more or less hotted up when Cyril..breezed down centre. **1928** *Morning Post* 20 Oct. 10/7 This car..is not in any sense a 'hotted up' Morris six-cylinder. **1939** R. Lehmann *No More Music* 56 *Jan*: Excitable girl. *Miriam*: You seem to have hotted her up nicely. **1945** *Jrnl. R. Aeronaut. Soc.* XLIX. 205/1 The Americans have had considerable success in 'hotting up' engines once intended for airline use. **1946** A. Lee *German Air Force* 13 The special hotted-up engines flown by ace pilots. **1950** *Hansard Commons* CCCCLXXII. 2036 Our present submarines are being 'hotted-up' with fast battery drive. **1958** J. Carew *Wild Coast* xii. 161 The drummerboys hotted up the rhythm. **1958** *Spectator* 6 June 740/2 The *Observer* complains that Mr. Allsop's style has 'the hotted-up, black-and-white, metaphor- and smart-allusion-besotted quality typical of one kind of popular journalism'. **1958** *Times* 12 Aug. 7/2 The General Assembly is the place to hot things up. **1959** *Listener* 9 Apr. 628/1 Hotting up hymn tunes was the absolute end. **1960** *Guardian* 5 Jan. 4/4 A rather hotted-up radio receiver. **1962** *Listener* 5 Apr. 595/2 The hotted-up economic and ideological conflicts of the latter part of the nineteenth century. **1968** *Hot Car* Oct. 61 If you hot up your car, don't forget to step up your braking power. **1973** 'M. Innes' *Appleby's Answer* xvii. 150 Far from cooling up, he might hot up, and simply jump the gun. **1973** *Guardian* 28 May 2 Sir Alec Douglas-Home..was launching into..the need to avoid actions which would 'hot up this cod war'.

hot, obs. pa. t. and pple. of HIT; see also HIGHT.

hot air. 1. *attrib.* or as *adj.* Of hot air, or in which hot air is used.

1813 M. Edgeworth *Let.* 26 Apr. (1971) 27 When first the hot air flues were opened..the hot air all escaped. **1841** C. Cist *Cincinnati* (Advt.), Manufacturers of Hot Air Furnaces, Stoves, &c. **1853** *Hunt's Merchant's Mag.* XXVIII. 282 Hot-air vessels are to take the place of steamships. **1854** Ronalds & Richardson *Chem. Technol.* (ed. 2) I. 233 No fear of smoke being mingled with the hot-air current... A hot-air stove. **1861** Mrs. Beeton *Bk. Housek. Managem.* 1009 A better arrangement is to have a hot-air closet,..heated by hot-air pipes,..and clothes-horses on castors..for drying purposes. **1892** Stevenson & Osbourne *Wrecker* i. 24, I designed.. a hot-air grating for the offices. **1905** G. Bacon *Balloons* i. 23 To this day large hot-air balloons inflated by the same methods employed a hundred years ago occasionally take passengers aloft. **1908** *Sears, Roebuck Catal.* 606/3 Standard American Plumbing. Hot Air and Hot Water Heating. **1940** *Chambers's Techn. Dict.* 424/1 *Hot-air heater*, one which supplies warm air through gratings in the floor or openings in the walls. *Ibid.*, Hot-air turbine. **1964** M. Hynes *Med. Bacteriol.* (ed. 8) iii. 27 The syringe, clean, assembled and lubricated, is packed in a glass or metal tube and subjected to a temperature of 160° C for 1 hour in the hot-air oven. **1970** *New Yorker* 3 Oct. 28/2 We can..move hot-air registers around simply by making holes in the floor. **1973** *Times* 8 Jan. 2/5 (*caption*) A hot-air airship, claimed to be the world's first, making its maiden flight yesterday from Newbury, Berkshire.

2. *colloq.* (orig. *U.S.*). Vaporous or boastful talk, pretentious or unsubstantial statements or claims; also *attrib.*, as in ***hot-air artist*** or ***merchant***, one who indulges in talk of this kind.

1873 'Mark Twain' & Warner *Gilded Age* xliv. 399 The most airy scheme inflated in the hot air of the Capital only reached in magnitude some of his lesser fancies, the by-play of his constructive imagination. **1900** Ade *Fables in Slang* 126 They strolled under the Maples, and he talked what is technically known as Hot Air. **1906** [see BLUE SKY 2]. **1910** *Sat. Even. Post* 2 July 13/3 'Hot-air artists' was a phrase uncoined; the farmer called them 'jawsmiths'. **1911** H. B. Wright *Winning of Barbara Worth* 327 The presence av sich..a hot air merchant..is a disgrace to any..company. **1914** [see BULL *sb.*[4] 3]. **1920** 'Sapper' *Bull-Dog Drummond* xii. 308 Author—so-called. Hot-air factory, but useful up to a point. **1922** *Daily Mail* 20 Nov. 8 Much 'hot air' from the politicians. **1932** [see BULL *sb.*[4] 3]. **1956** A. Wilson *Anglo-Saxon Att.* II. iii. 365 Gerald in his new mood thought only he shouldn't have poll-parroted his life away in humbug and hot air. **1963** *Times* 17 May 13/7 Anti-European slogans shouted by politicians were mere hot air.. **1970** T. Coe *Wax Apple* (1973) xxiv. 170, I think you're just full of hot air... I don't believe you know anything.

'hotbed, 'hot-bed.

1. A bed of earth heated by fermenting manure, and usually covered with glass, for raising or forcing plants.

1626 Bacon *Sylva* §401 The Bed we call a Hot-Bed. **1664** Evelyn *Kal. Hort.* 64 Fine and tender Seeds that require the Hot-bed. **1719** London & Wise *Compl. Gard.* 217 The bright curled Lettuces..do well upon Hot-Beds, and especially under Bell-Glasses, or Glass Frames. **1879** D. J. Hill *Bryant* 117 Numerous hotbeds assist the tender plants in spring.

2. *fig.* A place that favours the rapid growth or development of any condition, esp. of something evil.

1768 Bickerstaff *Hypocrite* I. i, The seeds of wickedness ..sprout up every where too fast; but a play-house is the devil's hot-bed. **1771** Smollett *Humph. Cl.* 8 Aug. Let. ii, Edinburgh is a hot-bed of genius. **1827–48** Hare *Guesses* II. (1873) 559 Those hotbeds of spurious, morbid feelings, sentimental novels. **1851** Kingsley *Yeast* iii, These picturesque villages are generally the perennial hotbeds of fever and ague. **1883** S. C. Hall *Retrospect* II. 397 Both Houses of Parliament were hot-beds of corruption.

3. 'A platform in a rolling-mill on which rolled bars lie to cool' (Raymond *Mining Gloss.* 1881).

4. *U.S. slang.* A bed, usu. in a flop-house, used continuously, day and night, by different people for limited periods. Also, the flop-house in which such beds are found.

1945 L. Shelly *Jive Talk Dict.* 26/1 *Hot bed*, cheap flop house. **1953** Pohl & Kornbluth *Space Merchants* (1955) vii. 77 The dorm was jammed with about sixty bunks... Since production went on only during daylight hours, the hot-bed system wasn't in use. My bunk was all mine. **1968** P. Oliver *Screening Blues* vi. 253 In city streets where hot-bed apartments and kitchenettes were the only dwelling units available to Negroes,..the automobile parked in the street became the front parlour. **1970** C. Major *Dict. Afro-Amer. Slang* 67 *Hotbed*,..in a flophouse a public bed for the price of 25 cents per eight hours.

5. *attrib.* (in senses 1 and 2).

1810 Crabbe *Borough, Relig. Sects* (L.), First comes the hotbed heat, and while it glows, The plants spring up. **1848** Kingsley *Saint's Trag.* Notes 250 Hot-bed imaginations.

Hence **hotbed** *v.* (*nonce-wd.*) *trans.*, to force as in a hotbed.

1892 *Sat. Rev.* 9 Apr. 411/2 Men forced and hot-bedded into honours without any genius for study.

hot blast. A blast of heated air forced into a furnace. Also *attrib.*, and short for *hot-blast process*, etc.

1836 J. B. Neilson in *Trans. Inst. Civ. Engin.* I. 83 Were the Hot Blast generally adopted, the saving..in..coal would be immense. **1860** W. Fordyce *Coal* etc. 112 Neilson ..distinguished for his invention of the hot-blast..'hot-blast Iron' is familiar all over the country.

hot-blooded ('hɒtˌblʌdɪd), *a.* Having hot blood; ardent or excitable; passionate.

1598 Shaks. *Merry W.* v. v. 2 Now the hot-bloodied-Gods assist me. **1837** Macaulay *Ess.*, *Bacon* (1887) 379 The proud and hot-blooded Tudors. **1879** Froude *Cæsar* xvi. 259 The Germans, being undisciplined and hot-blooded, were less easy to be restrained.

'hot-brain. A person of a hot or excitable brain; = HOT-HEAD.

1605 *Play Stucley* 2024 in Simpson *Sch. Shaks.* (1878) I. 238 This English hot-brain. **1625** Jackson *Creed* v. v. §6 A practicall head skillfull in humoring such an hot braine.

1827 G. DARLEY *Sylvia* 29 He is all unversed In these wild paths, and is a hot-brain, too.

hot-brained ('hɒtbreɪnd), *a.* Having a 'hot' or excitable brain; = HOT-HEADED 2.

1553 GRIMALDE *Cicero's Offices* I. (1558) 36 Daungerous and hotebrained deuises. 1687 SHADWELL *Juvenal* x. 251 Run o're the rugged Alps, thou hot-braind Fool! 1702 ROWE *Tamerl.* I. i. 23 Furious zeal inspir'd by hot-brain'd Priests. 1837 CARLYLE *Fr. Rev.* I. I. ii, Hot-brained Sciolists.

hotch (hɒtʃ), *v. Sc.* and *north. dial.* [Corresponds to Du. *hotsen, hossen*, to jog, jolt, MHG. and Ger. dial. *hotzen* to move up and down; also in form to F. *hocher* (12th c. *hocier* in Littré) to shake; but the original relations between these words are obscure.]

1. *intr.* To move up with a short jerk and sink back by one's own weight; to make a succession of such movements, to jog; to move or leap forward in a sitting position; to fidget, to move uneasily or with impatience.

? *a* 1400 *Morte Arth.* 3688 Archers of Inglande fulle egerly schottes.. Sonne hotchene in holle the heþenne knyghtes. 1585 JAS. I *Ess. Poesie* (Arb.) 68 Quhen our gude nichtbors rydis.. Some hotcheand on a hemp stalk, hovand on a heicht. *a* 1605 MONTGOMERIE *Sonn.* lxvi, With old bogogers, hotching on a sped. *c* 1746 J. COLLIER (Tim Bobbin) *View Lanc. Dial.* Gloss. Wks. (1862) 88 *Hotching*, to limp, to go by jumps, as toads. 1790 BURNS *Tam o' Shanter* 186 Even Satan glowr'd, and fidg'd fu' fain And hotch'd and blew wi' might and main. 1825–80 JAMIESON, *Hotch*,.. 2. To move by short heavy leaps as a frog or toad does. 1847–78 HALLIWELL s.v., The old woman said, 'I bustled through the crowd, and she hotched after me'. 1893 STEVENSON *Catriona* 144 Here am I, fair hotching to be off.

2. *trans.* To cause to move in this way; to shake up with a jerky motion; to jog, hitch.

1824 SCOTT *St. Ronan's* xv, Are ye sure ye hae room eneugh, sir? I wad fain hotch mysell farther yont. 1847–78 HALLIWELL s.v., When they shake potatoes in a bag, so that they may lie the closer, they are said to hotch them. 1866 *Durham Lead-m. Lang.*, *Hotch*, to shake with a sharp jerk a trough with a grated bottom, suspended in water, at the end of a long lever, and containing crushed lead ore.

3. *intr.* To swarm.

a 1779 in *E.D.D.* 1797 *Edin. Mag.* Dec. 458 The floor i' now is just a hotchin' thrang. 1825 *Blackw. Mag.* Mar. 369 When there's sae strong a spirit of life hotchin' ower yearth and sea in this very century. 1893–4 R. O. HESLOP *Northumb. Words* II. 387 The place is fair hotchin wi' rabbits. 1909 *Daily Chron.* 17 May 4/4 'The county,' he said, in his broad Ayrshire accent, 'is fair "hotching".. with them.' 1961 B. FERGUSSON *Watery Maze* v. 111 They found themselves delayed in Lisbon, a city then hotching with spies. 1965 J. CAIRD *Murder Reflected* ix. 108 Tripped over a stool. The place hotches with them. 1967 'H. CALVIN' *DNA Business* xiii. 148, I expect the office will be simply hotching with typists.

hotch, *sb. Sc.* [f. HOTCH *v.*] A jerk or jolt.

1721, 1824 in *E.D.D.* 1773 R. FERGUSSON *Poems* (1956) II. 124 Uncanny hotches Frae clumsy carts or hackney-coaches. 1914 N. MUNRO *New Road* ii. 24 *She* never mentioned it, but every time I did, I saw her give a hotch upon her chair.

hotcha ('hɒtʃə), *phr., int.*, and *a. slang* (chiefly *U.S.*). Also **hotcha cha, hot-cha(-cha)**, etc. [Fanciful extension of HOT *a.*] **1.** Used in combination with the traditional interjection *hey nonny nonny* (cf. HEY 2).

1932 KAUFMAN & RYSKIND *Of thee I Sing* in *Famous Plays* (1933) 694 With a hey, nonny nonny, and a ha cha cha! 1937 WODEHOUSE *Lord Emsworth & Others* ii. 99 Good morning, Phipps. What ho, what ho, with a hey nonny nonny and a hot cha-cha. 1954 *Word Study* Oct. 6/1 Many of us.. find Shakespeare's *Hey nonny nonny* a bit naked without the *hotcha cha.*

2. *int.* Expressing enthusiastic approval. Also as *adj.*, attractive, desirable.

1934 J. O'HARA *Appointment in Samarra* (1935) i. 21 Did you ever see her in a bathing suit? Hot-cha! 1939 R. CHANDLER *Big Sleep* ix. 71 He run Sternwood's hotcha daughter,.. off to Yuma.

3. *adj.* Of jazz: hot.

1937 S. KING-HALL *King-Hall Survey 1936* ix. 93, I seemed to notice a tendency, towards the end of 1936, for what one of my daughters calls 'Hotcha' music to be replaced by 'Swing' music. 1947 R. DE TOLEDANO *Frontiers of Jazz* ii. 13 In 1934.. the number of people who had anything more than a hotcha idea of jazz could be numbered on the fingers of a hand. 1957 W. C. HANDY *Father of Blues* vii. 98 Hot-cha music was the stuff we needed, and it had to be mellow. 1960 C. RAY *Merry Eng.* 60 There are hotcha gramophone records.

hotche, obs. form of HUTCH *sb.*

hotchi witchu ('hɒtʃɪ 'wɪtʃuː). Also **hotchi witchi.** [Romany.] The gypsy name for a hedgehog.

1843 BORROW *Zincali* (ed. 2) I. I. v. 98 They [*sc.* gypsies] have been seen.. to roast hotchiwitchu or hedgehog. 1928 *Sunday Dispatch* 2 Sept. 3/3 The gypsies call the animal 'Hotchi witchu', we speak of him as the hedgehog. 1935 'X. PETULENGRO' *Romany Life* xix. 79 As we sat.. eating our *hotchi-witchi*, some gentlemen.. passed near us and were curious to see what smelt so good. 1963 C. DUFF tr. *Clébert's Gipsies* v. 185 One of the dishes peculiar to Gypsies is the hedgehog.. (in English Gypsy *hotchi-witchi*).

Hotchkiss ('hɒtʃkɪs). The name of B. B. *Hotchkiss* (1826–85), American inventor, used *attrib.* to designate certain cannon and rifles invented by him, and a machine-gun developed by his successors.

1878 W. MORGAN-BROWN *Brit. Pat. 3017* 30 July, This Invention consists in several important improvements on the Hotchkiss revolving cannon and other machine guns. *Ibid.*, The gunner may have entire control over the laying, sighting, and firing of a Hotchkiss revolving cannon. 1880 *Encycl. Brit.* XI. 285/1 Hotchkiss Magazine Gun. 1886 *Harper's Mag.* Oct. 793/2 The types adopted by the United States navy are the Hotchkiss revolving cannon and rapid-firing single-shot guns. 1890 *Handbk. Six-Pounder Hotchkiss Quick-Firing Gun* 12 The shell is fitted with.. a brass Hotchkiss band. *Ibid.*, The fuze may be either the Nordenfelt or the Hotchkiss, Mark II, pattern. 1890 G. S. CLARKE *Fortification* xiii. 191 Twelve Hotchkiss machine guns. 1899–1900 *Kynoch Jrnl.* Dec.–Jan. 31/2 The Hotchkiss Automatic Gun. 1900 [see POM-POM]. 1902 *Encycl. Brit.* XXIX. 166/1 In the Hotchkiss and also in the Skoda systems the mechanism is of the vertical breech block type. 1908 *Trade Marks Jrnl.* 3 June 906 Hotchkiss... Guns, gun mountings, gun carriages, and other appurtenances and accessories for guns... The Hotchkiss Ordnance Company, Limited,.. London,.. manufacturers. *Ibid.*, Hotchkiss... Ammunition (explosive). The Hotchkiss Ordnance Company, Limited,.. London,.. manufacturers. 1926 T. E. LAWRENCE *Seven Pillars* (1935) III. xxviii. 168 The Frenchman began by presenting six Hotchkiss automatics complete with instructors. 1959 *Chambers's Encycl.* V. 676/2 The Hotchkiss light machine-gun.. was adopted for cavalry use.

hotchpot, hotch-pot ('hɒtʃpɒt). Forms: 3–6 **hochepot,** 5 **-pote, hoche potte,** 6 **hoch-, hotch(e)potte,** 6–7 **hochpot, hotch pot,** (8 **hotch-poe**), 6– **hotchpot, hotch-pot.** [a. F. *hochepot*, f. *hocher* to shake, shake together + *pot* POT. Used in 1292 as an AF. law term; as a term of Cookery it is known in 15th c., but may be earlier; *Ouchepot* as a personal sobriquet occurs in 1265 (Hatz.-Darm.). Its precise original application is thus uncertain, since it may have had reference to the shaking together of things in a pot for other than a culinary purpose. Cf. also Du. *hutspot* hodge-podge. Corruptions of this are HOTCHPOTCH, HODGEPOT, HODGE-PODGE.]

1. = HOTCHPOTCH 1.

c 1440 *Anc. Cookery* in *Househ. Ord.* (1790) 432 Goos in Hochepot. *a* 1481 LITTLETON *Inst.* III. ii. §267 Cest parol (*Hotchpot*) est en English A Pudding.. un chose avec autres choses ensembles. 1530 PALSGR. 233/1 Hotchepotte of many meates, *haricot.* 1591 PERCIVALL *Sp. Dict.*, *Almodrote*, a hotchpot of garlicke and cheese. *a* 1648 DIGBY *Closet Open.* (1669) 179 The Queen Mothers Hotchpot of Mutton, is thus made. 1853 KANE *Grinnell Exp.* xxxiv. (1856) 303 Cold merriment, but it concluded with hotchpot and songs.

2. *Eng. Law.* The blending or gathering together of properties for the purpose of securing equality of division, *esp.* as practised in certain cases in the distribution of the property of an intestate parent; answering in some respects to the *collatio bonorum* of the civil law: cf. COLLATION *sb.* 1 b.

[1292 BRITTON III. viii. §1 Touz heritages ne cheent mie uniement en divisioun ne en hochepot, a partir entre parceners. 1303 *Year-Bk. 30–1 Edw. I*, 373 Touz les tenemenz qe sont donez.. cherront en hochepot ovesqe les altres tenemenz.] 1552 HULOET, Hotchpot is also a maner of particion at the common lawe of landes geuen in franck mariage. 1574 tr. *Littleton's Tenures* 56 b, No lands shalbee put in hotchpot, with other, but lands that bee geeven in frank mariage alonelye. 1741 T. ROBINSON *Gavelkind* ii. 15 Having put all their Possessions in Hotchpot, made a new Partition. 1767 BLACKSTONE *Comm.* II. xxxii. (1809) 516 With regard to lands descending in co-parcenary, that it hath always been, and still is, the common law of England, under the name of *hotchpot.* 1848 J. WILLIAMS *Pers. Prop.* IV. iv. (1878) 403 Bring the amount of their advancement into hotchpot. 1875 POSTE *Gaius* III. Comm. (ed. 2) 321 On condition that the latter brought their goods into hotchpot (*collatio bonorum*).

fig. 1802–12 BENTHAM *Ration. Judic. Evid.* (1827) V. 510 Putting all causes together in hotch-pot, the average upon the sum total may thus come to be doubled or trebled. 1883 F. GALTON *Human Faculty* 190 Throwing these results into a common statistical hotchpot.

3. *transf.* = HOTCHPOTCH 2.

(In early use prob. from the legal sense, but in later chiefly from the dish.)

c 1386 CHAUCER *Melib.* ¶291 Ye han cast alle hire wordes in an hochepot [*Harl. & Lansd. MSS.* hoche poche]. 1588 J. UDALL *Demonstr. Discip.* (Arb.) 4 Schismes, that make a hotchpot of true religion and poperye. 1652–62 HEYLIN *Cosmogr.* IV. (1682) 5 An Hochpot or Medly of many Nations. 1871 TYLOR *Prim. Cult.* II. 230 The wonderful hotchpot of Hindu and Arabic language and religion.

4. *attrib.* or as *adj.*

1588 FRAUNCE *Lawiers Log.* Ded. ¶iij, That Hotchpot French, stufft up with such variety of borowed words, wherein our law is written. 1795 J. S. HOBART in *J. Jay's Corr. & Pub. Papers* (1893) IV. 95 Henry the 8th.. made a kind of hotch-pot business of it, by uniting the ecclesiastical and civil power in his own hands.

hotchpotch, hotch-potch ('hɒtʃpɒtʃ), *sb.* Forms: 5–6 **hoche poche,** 6 **hoche-poche,** 6–7 **hoch-poch,** 6–8 **hotch potch,** 6– **hotchpotch, hotch-potch.** [A corruption of prec., with riming assimilation of the second part of the compound to the first, as in reduplicated words.]

1. *Cookery.* A dish containing a mixture of many ingredients; *spec.* a mutton broth thickened with young vegetables of all sorts stewed together.

1583 GOLDING *Calvin on Deut.* lxxii. 443 We make a hotchpotch of halfe figges and half reysons as they say. 1692 DRYDEN *Ess. Sat.* Ess. (1882) 44 A kind of olla, or hotchpotch, made of several sorts of meats. 1797 *Sporting Mag.* IX. 327 [She] had got ready what is there [Scotland] called hotchpotch, for dinner. 1891 MRS. OLIPHANT *Railway Man* I. xi. 178 The hotch-potch.. was excellent. It is a soup made with lamb and all the fresh young vegetables.

attrib. 1851 *Illustr. Catal. Gt. Exhib.* 1060 Large tureen, or hotch-potch dish, with lid.

2. *fig.* A mixture of heterogeneous things, a confused assemblage, a medley, jumble, farrago.

14.. [see quot. 1386 in prec. 3.] 1549 LATIMER *3rd Serm. bef. Edw. VI* (Arb.) 98 They.. made a myngle mangle and a hotchpotch of it.. partely poperye, partelye true religion mingeled together. 1605 *Tryall Chev.* III. i. in Bullen *O. Pl.* III. 306 Hang the hotch-potch up in a fathom or two of match. 1652–62 HEYLIN *Cosmogr.* II. (1682) 32 A Hotch-potch of all sorts of men. 1728 *Wodrow Corr.* (1843) III. 371 A hotch-potch of errors. 1783 LEMON *Eng. Etymol.* Pref. 4 The English language, which, say they, is only a hotch-potch, composed of all others. 1890 HUXLEY in *19th Cent.* Nov. 761 That wonderful ethnological hotch-potch miscalled the Latin race.

3. *Eng. Law.* = HOTCHPOT 2.

1602 *2nd Pt. Return fr. Parnass.* IV. ii. 1586 If that fee-simple, and the fee taile be put together it is called hotch potch. 1646 SIR J. TEMPLE *Irish Rebell.* 9 *note* He assembled the whole Septs, and having put all their possessions together in hotch-potch, made a new partition among them. *a* 1656 USSHER *Ann.* VI. (1658) 189.

fig. 1838 SOUTHEY *Lett.* (1856) IV. 560 Throwing all the collections into hotch-potch, and then re-arranging the materials according to the subjects.

4. as *adj.* Like a hotchpotch or medley, confused.

1599 MARSTON *Sco. Villanie* III. ix. 219 What hotch-potch giberidge doth the Poet bring? 1613 PURCHAS *Pilgrimage* (1614) 87 Of those Drusian Robbers.. and of this hotch-potch Religion. 1769 E. BANCROFT *Guiana* 287 The hotch-potch officinal compositions of pharmacy.

Hence **'hotch-potch** *v. trans.*, to make a hotchpotch of, to jumble *up*; **'hotchpotchly** *a.*, of the nature of a hotchpotch, confusedly mingled.

1593 NASHE *Christs T.* (1613) 132 Scripture we hotch-potch together. 1596 —— *Saffron Walden* 77 He can hotch-potch whole Decades vp of nothing. 1674 R. GODFREY *Inj. & Ab. Physic* 181 Unmasked and singled from their hotch-potchly adjuncts.

hot cockles. *Obs.* exc. *Hist.* [f. HOT *a.* + COCKLE ? *sb.*[2]; origin of the name unknown.

(The F. *hautes coquilles*, alleged by Skinner, is a figment.)]

A rustic game in which one player lay face downwards, or knelt down with his eyes covered, and being struck on the back by the others in turn, guessed who struck him. Also *attrib.*

1580 SIDNEY *Arcadia* II. (1629) 224 How shepheards spend their dayes, At blow point, hot cockles, or else at keeles. 1676 MARVELL *Mr. Smirke* 13 They.. leave men, as if it were at Hot-Cockles, to guesse blind-fold who it is that hit them. *a* 1708 HICKERINGILL *Wks.* (1716) I. 368 Upon pretence of Hot-cockles sport, or a Christmas-game. 1714 GAY *Sheph. Week* Monday 99 As at Hot-cockles once I laid me down, And felt the weighty hand of many a clown. 1823 H. RAVELIN *Lucubr.* 303 Farmer Flamborough over his tankard.. and his daughters.. at hot-cockles upon the floor.

†**b.** *to sit upon hot cockles*: to be very impatient, to 'sit on pins and needles'. *Obs. rare*

1607 WALKINGTON *Opt. Glass* 90 He.. sits vpon hote cockles till it be blaz'd abroade.

Hence (app.) †**hot-cockled** *a.*, ? resembling a game of hot-cockles, as involving the infliction of strokes or buffets.

1549 COVERDALE, etc. *Erasm. Par. Phil.* 3 In case throughe theyr earnest hoote cockled ghospellyng, they coulde haue broughte vs in to more haynous displeasure.

hot damn, *int. phr. U.S.* An intensified form of 'damn!'.

1936 J. STEINBECK *In Dubious Battle* 90 Hot-damn, listen. 1957 J. KEROUAC *On Road* (1958) IV. ii. 257 Hot damn, I could go with you? 1971 *Black World* Apr. 73 Pop pulled garbage in an old-law tenement building. Hot-damn.. every night.

hot dog. [DOG *sb.*[1]] **1. a.** *N. Amer. slang.* One who is skilled or proficient in some pursuit (see also quot. 1900). Also *attrib.* or as *adj. phr.*, good, superior.

Freq. with connotations of 'showing off'. In some sports, e.g. Skiing, applied to 'trick' or 'stunt' or spectacular variations of normal movements.

1896 W. C. GORE in *Inlander* Jan. 148 *Hot-dog*, good, superior. 'He has made some hot-dog drawings for ——.' 1900 *Dialect Notes* II. I. 42 *Hot-dog.* 1. One very proficient in certain things. 2. A hot sausage. 3. A hard student. 4. A conceited person. 1966 *Atlantic Monthly* Mar. 131 We had this one [basketball] player, Alston Mackintosh,.. who could hit nine out of ten from the foul line with his back to the basket. He was a real hot dog. 1968–70 *Current Slang* (Univ. S. Dakota) III–IV. 71 *Hot dog*, one who shows off by squealing his tires and gunning his motor as he drives around among his friends. A crowd pleaser who is actually obnoxious. A showoff. To show off. 1973 *Internat. Herald Tribune* 9 Feb. 13/1 'Hot dog', or acrobatic, skiing has become a fast-growing sport in the United States. 1973 *Times* 23 Feb. (Canada Suppl.) p. vii/8 The local 'hot dogs', mostly teenagers who probably learnt to ski almost as soon as they could stand up, skate over mounds of hard-packed snow 4 ft high like sprinters over hurdles. 1973 *Time* (Canad. ed.) 16 July 51/1 Cedeno pulls off so many flashy plays in the field that some National League players accuse him of being a 'hot dog'—baseballese for show-off. 1973

Globe & Mail (Toronto) 1 Sept. 35/1 This year..it was generally agreed that McQuay must change his hotdog antics or go. **1974** *Ibid.* 20 Feb. 34/5 Dan Genge..admits that it was those same little hills that made him what he is—one of Ontario's coolest hot-dog skiers. *Ibid.* 34/8 There has to be something of the mountain climber in the hot-dog skier. They must do something harder, tougher, higher each year. **1974** *Hockey News* (Montreal) 22 Feb. 35/1 Critics label him a 'hot dog' and a 'show-off' and several unprintable things.

b. *Surfing slang.* A particular kind of surf-board, somewhat smaller than a 'gun' (GUN *sb.* 15). Also *attrib.* or as *adj. phr.*

1963 *Observer* 13 Oct. 15/6 He always owns two boards at any one time, one 'hot dog' board and a 'big gun' (which is a foot or so longer) for riding really big waves. **1965** [see GUN *sb.* 15]. **1966** *New Yorker* 31 Dec. 28 He's a hot-dog surfer and he used to be real wigged on Zen. **1967** *Surfabout* III. VII. 38/1 Joey Hamasaki is an excellent surfer and she could possibly beat Joyce in small hot-dog surf. **1970** [see GUN *sb.* 15].

So **hot dogger**, a surfer who rides a 'hot dog'; **hot dogging**, the action of riding such a board (see also quot. 1963²). Hence (as a back-formation) **hot-dog** *v.*

1961 *Life* 1 Sept. 48 Almost every wave carries a 'hot dogger' doing tricks or sometimes even dressed in outlandish garb. **1962** T. MASTERS *Surfing made Easy* 64 *Hot dogging*, performance surfing, fast turns, quick movements, etc. **1963** *Pix* (Austral.) 28 Sept. 63 Looking good on a little wave is hard. If you can hot dog on two foot waves you are 'king'. **1963** *Observer* 13 Oct. 15/4 From all these movements..has developed the modern style of surfing known as 'hot dogging': a spectacular, virtuoso style which concentrates on fast slides across the face of the waves, rapid turns, cut-backs, flick-offs and a repertoire of classic riding stances which have evolved in much the same way as the classic passes of the Spanish bullfight. **1966** Hot dogging [see BOMBORA]. **1966** *Surfer* VII. IV. 39 There were plenty of hot-doggers—or trick riders as we called them then—in Hawaii when I was surfing there during the 1920's.

2. A hot sausage enclosed as a sandwich in a bread roll. orig. *U.S.*

1900 [see sense 1 a above]. **1908** 'O. HENRY' *Gentle Grafter* vii. 97 Sitting on a cake of ice we ate seven hot dogs. **1920** S. LEWIS *Main St.* 304 Lining one block of Main Street were the 'attractions'—two hot-dog stands, [etc.]. **1926** *Spectator* 11 Sept. 373/1 The President of the Brooklyn team asked them to his box and gave them hot dogs. **1928** S. VINES *Humours Unreconciled* ii. 35 If one trained on hot dog, pumpkin pie, graham flour, ice-cream sundaes. **1932** E. WILSON *Devil take Hindmost* i. 1 The hot-dog stands on the motor roads sell gin. **1955** *Times* 3 Aug. 10/5 Tell the miners what Yarmouth has to offer—Tommy Trinder, Charlie Chester, Ronnie Ronalde, 'hot-dogs', bathing beauties, and all. **1957** *London Mag.* Dec. 19 There is a pier with all the usual sideshows, hot dogs, hamburger and ice cream stands. **1970** *New Yorker* 12 Sept. 50/3 She came back with a hot dog... The smell..was..persuasive.

3. *int.* Expressing delight or strong approval. Cf. *hot diggety* (*dog*) s.v. HOT *a.* 12 c. *U.S. slang.*

1906 *Dialect Notes* III. II. 141 *Hot dog*,..bravo! **1924** [see ATTABOY *int.*]. **1934** WODEHOUSE *Right Ho, Jeeves* x. 113 Hot dog! Tell me more. **1935** M. M. ATWATER *Murder in Midsummer* xv. 138 'Hot dog!' cried Wally, his eyes shining. 'That's the old fight!' **1944** T. RATTIGAN *While Sun Shines* I. 202 Hot dog! There's some Scotch. **1965** *Amer. Speech* XL. 85 The ubiquitous *hot dog*!

†**hote.** *Obs.* Forms: 1 **hát**, 2–3 (4 *north.*) **hat**, 3–4 **hot**, 4–5 **hote**. [OE. *hát*, also *ȝehát* = OHG. *gaheiz*, MHG. *heiz*, ON. *heit*, f. stem *hait-* of *haitan*, OE. *hátan*: see HIGHT *v.*¹] A promise; a vow: = HIGHT *sb.*¹ 2.

c **950** *Lindisf. Gosp.* Luke xxiv. 49 Ic sendo hat fadores mines in iuih. *c* **1200** ORMIN 13822 þiss hat tatt wass Natanæl Bihatenn and Filippe. *c* **1250** *Gen. & Ex.* 936 Abram leuede ðis hot in sped. *a* **1300** *E.E. Psalter* xlix. 14 (Mätz.) Yelde til Hegheste þi hates. *c* **1340** *Cursor M.* 2349 (Fairf.) For þis hote [*Cott.* hight, *Gött.* hith, *Trin.* biheest] miȝt be na fabil. *c* **1460** *Towneley Myst.* vi. 46 Lord of heuen, that all wote, here to the I make a hote.

hote, obs. f. HOT, OAT: see also HIGHT *v.*¹

hotel (həʊ'tɛl, old-fashioned əʊ'tɛl), *sb.* [a. F. *hôtel*, later form of *hostel* (see HOSTEL *sb.*¹).]

1. (In French use.) **a.** A large private residence, a town mansion. ‖**b.** A public official residence, ***hôtel de ville***, the mansion house of a *maire*, a town hall. ‖**c.** ***hôtel-Dieu***, a hospital.

1644 EVELYN *Diary* 4 Feb., Above all is the Hôtel Dieu for men and women, near Notre Dame. **1684** tr. *Tavernier's Grd. Seignor's Serag.* 36 (Stanf.) Ceremonies of their march from the Hôtel, or great House of Perra. **1744** M. W. MONTAGU *Let.* 12 June (1966) II. 331 Here [*sc.* in Avignon] are 2 Consuls chose every year..and there is as much struggling for that Dignity in the Hotel de ville as in the Senate. **1746** in *Acc. Fr. Settlem. N. Amer.* 24 The Hotel Dieu, or hospital, of Quebec has two great halls. **1749** CHESTERF. *Lett.* (1792) II. cxcix. 249, I hope I have domesticated you at his *hotel* there. **1768** STERNE *Sent. Journ.* (1778) II. 48 (*Versailles*), I bid Le Fleur..enquire for the Count's hotel. **1789** A. YOUNG *Jrnl.* 30 July in *Trav. France* (1792) I. 149 Two bourgeois musketeers conducted me to the hotel de ville. **1797** *Encycl. Brit.* VIII. 683/1 The *hotel de ville* is what we call a *town-house* or town-hall. **1827** SCOTT *Chron. of Canong.* Introd. vi, She inhabited, when in Edinburgh..one of those old hotels. **1841** C'TESS BLESSINGTON *Idler in France* I. 4 It was then given to a certain Pierre Boys, in exchange for a piece of ground to erect a new hôtel-de-ville. **1846** DICKENS *Pictures from Italy* 9 Sometimes an hotel de ville, sometimes a guard-house. **1849** MACAULAY *Hist. Eng.* iii. I. 356 A few great men still retained their hereditary hotels between the Strand and the river. **1858** HAWTHORNE *Fr. & It. Jrnls.* (1883) 35 We stood a few moments on the steps of the Hôtel Dieu. **1957** J. S. BROMLEY in Wallace-Hadrill & McManners *France: Govt. & Society* 147 Louis XIV made his first formal visit to the Hôtel de Ville, in 1687, to 'forgive' the City [of Paris] for its share in the Fronde. **1973** *Times* 22 Feb. 5/1 M Louis Pradel ..dominates the hôtel de ville.

d. hôtel garni, a furnished apartment; an hotel or boarding-house supplying breakfast.

1774 H. WALPOLE *Let.* 7 Sept. (1857) VI. 114, I now live in dread of my biennial gout, and should die of it in an *hôtel garni*. *Ibid.* 28 Sept. 126 Take care of your papers at Paris, ..In the *hôtels garnis* they have double keys to every lock. **1858** GEO. ELIOT *Let.* 17 Apr. (1954) II. 450 He took us to two Hôtels Garnis—places where you get lodgings and attendance and coffee and nothing else. **1896** E. DOWSON *Let.* c. 12 Jan. (1967) 339, I have just risen from a bed of sickness, incomparably uncomfortable, as in my *hotel garni*, one is reduced under such circumstances to living entirely on milk the only nourishment that one can procure. **1968** *Guardian* 28 Dec. 5/5 The cheapest alternative to *le camping* ..is the *hotel garni*, providing only bed and breakfast.

e. hôtel particulier, a large privately owned town house or block of flats.

1934 JOYCE *Let.* 13 July (1966) III. 309 Right opposite is a hotel particulier of 2 storeys. **1964** *Time Off in Paris* (Observer) 16 The big Haussman-period blocks of flats (*hotels particuliers*), that are still the main form of housing in central Paris, were built each to contain different social strata, and so they still do today. **1969** N. FREELING *Tsing-Boum* xx. 144 There were still some hôtels particuliers, last bastions of privilege. **1970** *Times* 28 Nov. 12/5 Their *hotel particulier* in Paris contains countless treasures.

†**2.** A HOSTEL in a university. *Obs.*

1748 SALMON *Comp. through Univ.* 18 Hugh de Balsham ..purchased two Halls or Hotels near St. Peter's Church.

3. A house for the entertainment of strangers and travellers, an inn; *esp.* one that is, or claims to be, of a superior kind.

1765 SMOLLETT *Trav.* xxxix. (1766) II. 235 The expence of living at an hotel is enormous. **1775** ASH, *Hostel*, an inn, an hotel. **1776** R. KING in *Life & Corr.* (1894) I. 20 By a Gentlemen who lately came out of Boston I was informed that they have two bake houses constantly employed in baking for their hotels. **1783** *Let.* in H. Arnot *Hist. Edinburgh* App. 512 In 1763 there was no such place as an Hotel: the word indeed was not known, or only intelligible to French scholars. **1806–7** J. BERESFORD *Miseries Hum. Life* (1826) XIV. i, Groping your way to the inn—(I beg pardon—hotel). **1817** WALKER, *Hostel, Hotel*, a genteel inn: this word is now universally pronounced and written without the *s*. **1834** MEDWIN *Angler in Wales* II. 118, I..returned slowly..to my hotel.

4. *attrib.* and *Comb.* ***hotel-bill, bus, clerk, garage, -keeper, -keeping, lobby, manager, omnibus, porter, prowler, register, room, tout.***

1872 GEO. ELIOT *Middlem.* IV. VII. lxx. 123 Raffles's pockets..were sure to carry..*hotel-bills of the places he had stopped in. **1903** JOYCE *Let.* 26 Feb. (1966) II. 31, I was favoured with my hotel-bill on Tuesday. **1973** P. AUDEMARS *Delicate Dust of Death* xii. 175 The 10 per cent surcharge would have been added to the hotel bill. **1878** *Harper's Mag.* Jan. 194 The traveller reaches his stopping-place by *hotel 'bus, carriage, or by the democratic street cars. **1923** E. F. WYATT *Invis. Gods* IV. iii. 221 He was marshalling them all toward a hotel bus. **1875** KNIGHT *Dict. Mech.* (U.S.), **Hotel-car*, one arranged for affording meals to passengers on board while on a journey. **1856** F. L. OLMSTED *Journey Slave States* (1861) V. 333 An easy and gentleman-like employment as that of *hotel-clerk and bar-keeper. **1945** L. R. TRYON *Poor Man's Doctor* 185, I suppose the actor is better trained than most of us at inventing stratagems for getting past the hard and watchful eyes of hotel clerks. **1910** *Bradshaw's Railway Guide* Apr. 1101 Best *Hotel Garage in London. **1829** *Virginia Lit. Museum* 336/1 The Proctor is required to make a monthly report..of any matters relating to the students or *hotel-keepers which may be worthy of being noticed. **1869** W. H. H. MURRAY *Adventures in Wilderness* 35 The 'hotel guides' are paid so much per month by the hotel-keepers. **1879** *Scribner's Monthly* June 242/1 Her husband had left town suddenly on a horse belonging to the hotel-keeper. **1916** JOYCE *Portrait of Artist* (1969) i. 29 He..began to speak with the voice of the hotelkeeper. **1870** 'F. FERN' *Ginger-Snaps* 247 Having then left what, in my opinion, is the perfection of *hotel-keeping. **1959** *News Chron.* 19 Aug. 6/2 French small hotel-keeping at its most terrible. **1912** M. NICHOLSON *Hoosier Chron.* 182 A number of idlers in the *hotel lobby regarded him with a new interest. **1964** M. MCLUHAN *Understanding Media* (1967) II. xxxi. 341 Shoddy match-wood bars and hotel lobbies. **1910** W. J. LOCKE *Simon* XV. 199 The correctly attired *hotel manager in the attitude in which he habitually surveyed the lay-out of the *table d'hôte*. **1972** I. HAMILTON *Thrill Machine* viii. 34 The hotel manager led her and her group towards the lift. **1878** R. L. STEVENSON *Inland Voyage* 37 The driver of the *hotel omnibus. **1910** *Bradshaw's Railway Guide* Apr. 1049 The Hotel omnibus meets the principal London trains. **1847** F. A. KEMBLE *Let.* 31 May in *Rec. Later Life* (1882) III. 190, I..despatched one of the *hotel porters thither to hunt for her. **1881** LADY C. SCHREIBER *Jrnl.* (1911) II. 343 The officious Hotel porter had told a lot of other people. **1968** *Guardian* 11 Apr. 5/2 Now we are going to set off along the A 10—the hotel porter will direct you to it. **1928** M. C. SHARPE *Chicago May* 286 *Hotel Prowlers, sneak thieves. **1962** K. ORVIS *Damned & Destroyed* v. 40 Hotel-prowlers and house-prowlers. **1860** in *Abraham Lincoln Q.* (1949) Mar. 262, I found the name of Mr Bates on the *hotel register. **1899** E. WHARTON *Greater Inclination* iv. 99 She must take her place in the hotel register as Mrs. Garnett. **1971** P. M. HUBBARD *High Tide* i. 10 The hotel register still lay open on the desk where I had signed it. **1946** E. O'NEILL *Iceman Cometh* (1947) IV. 202 You know how it is, traveling around. The damned *hotel rooms. **1972** R. LOCKRIDGE *Something up Sleeve* i. 13 The jurors had been escorted back to their hotel rooms. **1858** HAWTHORNE *Fr. & It. Jrnls.* (1872) I. 47 A crowd of cab-drivers, *hotel-runners, and commissionaires. **1837** HT. MARTINEAU *Soc. Amer.* III. 89 The celerity at *hotel-tables is remarkable. **1881** *Hotel tout [see TOUT *sb.*¹ 2]. **1922** S. LESLIE *Oppidan* i. 7 He had picked them up at the station like a hotel-tout.

Hence **ho'tel** *v.*, to put up or lodge at an hotel (*intr.* and *trans.*; also *to hotel it*). **ho'telhood**, the state of an hotel. **ho'telify, ho'telize** *vbs.*, *trans.* to make into, or like, an hotel; also *intr.* for *pass.* **ho'telless** *a.*, without an hotel. **ho'tellish** *a.*, like an hotel. **ho'telward** *adv.*, towards the hotel. (All more or less *nonce-wds.*)

1883 BURTON & CAMERON *Gold Coast* I. ii. 49, I was *hotelled at the 'Royal Edinburgh'. **1894** HOWELLS in *Cosmopolitan* XVII. 52 We tried hotelling it. **1834** *Blackw. Mag.* XXXV. 178 It was, for lack of a better word, to coin one, *hotelified. **1886** H. MERIVALE in *Temple Bar Mag.* LXXVI. 551 A fine old palace of the kind which *hotelize so well. **1891** *Sat. Rev.* 29 Aug. 244/2 Most of the smaller towns were *hotelless. **1851** NEWLAND *The Erne* 252 Rooms ..of a towny and *hotellish character.

hoteldom (həʊ'tɛldəm). [f. HOTEL *sb.* + -DOM.] The realm of hotels, hotels collectively.

1904 *Westm. Gaz.* 1 June 9/2 Then our representative turned his attention to hoteldom. **1927** *Glasgow Herald* 28 Mar. 11/1 There is to be an addition to London hoteldom. **1964** *Sat. Rev.* (U.S.) 21 Mar. 28 The biggest thing in hoteldom lately is non-eating.

hotelier (‖otɛlje, (h)əʊ'tɛlɪeɪ, həʊ'tɛlɪə(r)). Also **hôtelier**. [Fr.] The keeper or proprietor of an hotel.

1905 *Westm. Gaz.* 10 Mar. 12/1 Some enterprising hotelier. **1907** *Ibid.* 7 Sept. 11/2 He grudges the lucky Swiss hôtelier his millions. **1930** *Observer* 20 Apr. 7 That prince of hoteliers, the late M. Ritz. **1956** R. BRADDON *Nancy Wake* i. 6 He was an immaculately dressed *hôtelier*, a director-manager of the Palm Beach Hotel. **1959** F. STARK *Riding to Tigris* 12 In all which countries hotelier schools exist. **1966** *Illustr. London News* 3 Sept. 11 He is on the board of 36 companies, and..can fairly claim to be the biggest hotelier in Europe. **1972** L. P. BACHMANN *Ultimate Act* iv. 33 One has to learn many languages to be a proper hôtelier... I attended hôtelier school in Switzerland.

†**'hoten,** *ppl. a. Obs.* [pa. pple. of HIGHT *v.*¹, q.v.] Promised.

c **1250** *Gen. & Ex.* 2508 He sal ȝu leden..Heðen to ðat hotene lond.

'hot-foot, *adv.* and *sb.* Also 6 Sc. hait-fute. [f. HOT *a.* + FOOT *sb.* See also FOOT-HOT.]

A. *adv.* **1.** With eager or rapid pace; in hot haste; hastily.

a **1300** *Body & Soul* in *Map's Poems* (Camden) 339 Ʒwan tho fendes hot fot come to fette me away. **1536** BELLENDEN *Cron. Scot.* (1821) II. 139 King Athelstane..followit, hait-fute, on the Pichtis. **1647** TRAPP *Comm. Matt.* vi. 12 An evil conscience..follows him up..like a blood-hound, hot foot. **1827** SIR J. BARRINGTON *Pers. Sketches* I. 154 If your honour's in a hurry, I can run on hot-foot and tell the squire your honour's galloping after me. **1893** STEVENSON *Catriona* 4 To go to him hot-foot from Appin's agent.

2. *attrib.* or as *adj.* Acting with haste or promptitude.

1901 *Spectator* 2 Nov. 631/1 He had to make the most arduous hot-foot journeys across the country. **1904** 'O. HENRY' *Cabbages & Kings* v. 90 He was private secretary of the late hot-foot president of this grocery and fruit stand that they call a country. **1940** C. DAY LEWIS tr. *Georgics of Virgil* I. 28 If you observe the hotfoot sun and the moon's phases, To-morrow will never cheat you.

B. *sb.* **1.** Prompt or rapid action or movement; a quick escape, as in the phrases ***to do a hot foot*** (or *foots*), ***to give*** (someone) ***the hot foot, to come*** (or *go*) ***on the hot foot.*** *U.S. slang.*

1869 *Congress. Globe* 15 Jan. 389/3 The honorable Senator ..admonishes us of the importance of hot-foot in this business, if I may say so, of allowing the testimony to be taken at once. **1897** *Pop. Sci. Monthly* Apr. 833 To run from a police officer is *to do a hot foot*. **1903** 'H. MCHUGH' *Back to Woods* iv. 66 Did somebody give you the hot-foot and make a quick exit? **1905** —— *You can search Me* iii. 55 If somebody ever steals his hammer he'll be doing hotfoots for the handout. **1915** H. L. WILSON *Ruggles of Red Gap* (1917) ii. 27 We'd better report to her before she does a hot-foot over here. **1926** *Flynn's* 16 Jan. 639/1, I know that th'fly was jerry because he gave me th'once over as I was comin' out and I went on th' hoot-foot... I beat it. **1929** C. F. COE *Hooch!* x. 241 You dress an' grab a cab, see? Come down here to Zuroto's on the hot foot.

2. A beating on the soles of the feet; more usually, a practical joke in which a match is put against the victim's foot and then lit. Also *fig.*

1906 A. H. LEWIS *Confessions of Detective* I. iii. 32 I'd become learned in certain mysteries, among others, the 'hot foot'... Given a man, unconscious by..rum,..you can restore him..by smartly beating the soles of his feet. **1934** D. RUNYON in *Hearst's International* Sept. 84/1 The way you give a hot foot is to sneak up behind some guy..and stick a paper match in his shoe between the sole and the upper along about where his little toe ought to be, and then light the match. **1943** J. MITCHELL *McSorley's Wonderful Saloon* (1946) 18 Drunks reel over from the Bowery and.. the kids give them hotfoots with kitchen matches. **1948** MENCKEN *Amer. Lang.* Suppl. I. v. 392 The Army also discourages the old soldiers' game of *hot-foot*, which consists in inserting matches between the soles and uppers of a sleeping comrade's shoes, and then lighting them. **1959** *Encounter* Dec. 30/2 His prose should never be quiet. It must always shock with the hot-foot.

hot-foot, *v. colloq.* (chiefly *U.S.*). [f. prec.] *intr.* To go hot-foot; to make haste. Also with *it*. Hence **hot-'footed** *ppl. a.*

1896 ADE *Artie* iii. 22, I hot-foots up to the dance. **1896** [see DINKY *a.*¹]. **1903** W. B. YEATS *In Seven Woods* 37 The hot-footed sun, And the cold sliding slippery-footed moon. **1904** *Sun* (N.Y.) 27 Aug. 10 Thousands hot footed to the

corner of Broadway. **1906** *Dialect Notes* III. II. 141 *Hotfoot it*, to hasten. **1911** R. D. SAUNDERS *Col. Todhunter* ii. 34 Great Scott and Maria, you must have hot-footed it away from your vittles, young man! **1926** C. HARRIS *Flapper Anne* ii. 92 At the present nothing was further from her thoughts than marrying Sealy, but she craved the triumph of bringing him hotfooted to Milledge. **1928** *Observer* 29 Jan. 22/3 Words of such enthusiasm send one at once hot-footed to the [Crystal] palace to see for oneself. **1934** J. O'HARA *Appointment in Samarra* (1935) vii. 214 When O'Dowd did hear.. he would hot-foot out to Quilty and make the sale. **1951** *Manch. Guardian Weekly* 18 Jan. 15 He short-circuits Mr. Kingley's pedestrian approach and makes a bee-line for Koestler's original like the prodigal hot-footing it home. **1970** G. GREER *Female Eunuch* 195 She hotfoots to Mexico.

hot gospeller. [HOT *a.* 6.] An abusive nickname for a zealous Protestant or Puritan, esp. a revivalist preacher. Also *transf.* Hence **hot gospelling** *vbl. sb.* and *ppl. a.*; **hot-gospel** *v. trans.* and *intr.*

1562 E. UNDERHILL in *Narr. Days Reform.* (Camd. Soc.) 159, I was also callede 'the hoote gospellar', jestynge and mokynge me, saynge 'he is alle off the sprete'. **1874** MOTLEY *Barneveld* I. vii. 330 Those hot gospellers. **1875** TENNYSON *Q. Mary* 271 There are Hot Gospellers even among our guards. **1899** R. WHITEING *No. 5 John St.* viii. 71 That terrible old Hot Gospeller who.. screams undying hate of all institutions. **1923** W. S. CHURCHILL *World Crisis 1911–14* ii. 29 Like Henry VIII, he [*sc.* A. J. Balfour] decapitated Papists and burned hot Gospellers on the same day for their respective divergencies.. from his.. compromise. **1923** J. M. MURRY *Pencillings* 107, I do not think.. I can fairly be accused of advocating hot-gospelling or holy-roaring as the short road to good writing. *Ibid.* 275 He has made me bold, not to say thrasonical. I am become a hot-gospeller, a crusader. Dr. Henry Bradley himself is timid and lukewarm compared to me. **1931** R. LEHMANN *Let. to Sister* 9 Do you remember that frothing hot-gospelling temperance-man?.. He told them how he himself had found salvation when going upstairs late one night—drunk, he manfully admitted. **1933** *Times Lit. Suppl.* 19 Oct. 713/1 The hot-gospeller Spooner marries the thin-lipped Harriet. **1952** R. CAMPBELL *Lorca* i. 7 Every sub-poetaster is hot-gospelling world-messages. **1955** A. L. ROWSE *Expansion Eliz. Eng.* ix. 331 The hot-gospelling of Knox and the spread of Calvinism. **1958** *Spectator* 31 Jan. 124/3 Mr. Dulles's hot-gospelling speech. **1965** G. MCINNES *Road to Gundagai* vi. 110 In the true.. hot-gospelling tradition, he ladled out the brimstone. **1968** *Times* 6 Nov. 3/4 The hot-gospeller H. H. Nininger, who preached the value and importance of meteorites. **1970** *Daily Tel.* (Colour Suppl.) 13 Mar. 47/1 He was not hot-gospelling for pop or for the American way of life. **1972** *Daily Tel.* 4 Dec. 11/3 The film.. is 'Marjoe', a .. deeply cynical documentary on the American weakness for hot-gospelling revivalists.

hot-head, hothead ('hɒthɛd). A hot-headed person: see next, 2.

1660 *Lauderdale Papers* (Camden) I. 57 Which will daunt the rest of the hottheads. **1895** BESANT *Westminster* vii. 177 Certain English sailors—young hotheads.

hot-headed ('hɒtˌhɛdɪd), *a.*

1. Having a hot head (in *lit.* sense); in quot. 1712, having the head heated, as with liquor. *rare.*

a **1693** AUBREY *Lives, Harvey* (1898) I. 301 He was hott-headed, and his thoughts working would many times keepe him from sleepinge. **1712** E. COOKE *Voy. S. Sea* 77 The women do not dance till they are a little hot-headed.

2. *fig.* Of an unduly excitable nature or temperament; impetuous, headstrong, fiery, rash.

1641 MILTON *Reform.* I. (1851) 20 The blasphemous Jesuits presum'd.. to give their judgement of S. Paul, as of a hot headed person. **1688** LD. DELAMER *Wks.* (1694) 17 A hot-headed or rash action. **1771** SMOLLETT *Humph. Cl.* 12 June, The hot-headed boy is more than ever incensed against Wilson. **1887** *Spectator* 26 Mar. 413/2 Too hot-headed and violent for a diplomatist.

Hence **hot-'headedly** *adv.*, **hot-'headedness.**

1872 BLACK *Adv. Phaeton* xxvi, The hotheadedness.. of boys in love. **1895** *Forum* (N.Y.) Jan. 524 Some isolated.. workmen.. did throw themselves hot-headedly into the fray.

hot-house, hothouse ('hɒthaʊs), *sb.*

†**1.** A bathing-house with hot baths, vapour-baths, etc.; = BAGNIO 1. *Obs.*

1511 *Churche of yvell Men* A iv, Bordelles, tauernes, sellers, and hote houses dissolute, there as is commytted so many horryble synnes. **1544** PHAER *Regim. Lyfe* (1560) C vj, The pacient must.. sweate in baths, or whote houses. **1552** HULOET s.v. *Annoyntyng*, A place nighe unto a hotte house, or stewsse wherin men be annoynted. **1625** HART *Anat. Ur.* I. ii. 15 The.. sweate that was rubbed off the bodie in the hotehouses. **1664–5** PEPYS *Diary* 21 Feb., My Wife busy in going.. to a hot-house to bathe herself. **1759** JOHNSON *Idler* No. 61 ⁋6 He could shiver in a hothouse.

†**2.** A brothel. (Cf. BAGNIO 3, STEW.) *Obs.*

1511 [see 1]. **1602** *2nd Pt. Return fr. Parnass.* I. ii. 257 Hee cannot swagger it well in a Tauerne, nor dominere in a hot house. **1603** SHAKS. *Meas. for M.* II. i. 66 Now shee professes a hot-house; which, I thinke is a very ill house too. **1699** GARTH *Dispens.* II. 22 A Hot-house he prefers to Julia's Charms.

3. a. A structure, usually with glass roof and sides, kept artificially heated for the growth of plants belonging naturally to warmer climates, or of native flowers and fruits out of season.

1749 LADY LUXBOROUGH *Lett. to Shenstone* 29 Aug., A Ménagerie; and as well as I love pine-apples, would prefer it to a hot-house. **1838** LYTTON *Alice* II. v, The hothouses yielded their early strawberries.

attrib. **1771** W. MALCOLM (*title*) A Catalogue of Hot-house and Greenhouse Plants. **1836** *Lett. fr. Madras* (1843) 26 English hot-house flowers, growing wild. **1882** *Printing Times* 15 Feb. 27/1 Hothouse forcing by the aid of outside subsidies. **1889** J. K. JEROME *Three Men in Boat* 84 Hot-house grapes.

b. *fig.* (Cf. HOTBED 2.) Also *attrib.*

1802–12 BENTHAM *Ration. Judic. Evid.* (1827) V. 121 The technical system is a hot-house of mendacity. **1811** BYRON *Farew. Malta* 46 Thou little military hothouse! **1838** DICKENS *Nickleby* (1839) xxi. 201 Mrs. Wititterly is of a very excitable nature, very delicate, very fragile; a hothouse plant. **1840** MILL *Let.* 3 Dec. (1910) I. 119 *You* will be interested in the modern German art;.. it appears to me a feeble, hot-house product. **1851** ROBERTSON *Serm.* Ser. II. x. (1864) 135 Men nurtured in the hothouse of religious advantages. **1853** C. READE *Peg Woff.* ii. 46 She is so fresh and natural. They are all hot-house plants. **1911** G. B. SHAW *Getting Married* Pref. 156 A hothouse atmosphere of unnatural affection. **1964** *English Studies* XLV. 50 Those delicate, hot-house feelings. **1966** *Listener* 28 July 143/2 Opera will never cease to be a hothouse plant in this country until a wider public appreciates it. **1973** 'E. PETERS' *City of Gold & Shadows* ii. 31 This hot-house community of time-expired settlers and pay-happy leave-men.

4. A heated chamber or building for drying something.

1555 EDEN *Decades* 259 Theyr corne and other grayne.. doo seldome waxe rype on the ground by reason wherof they are sumtimes inforced to rype and dry them in theyr stooues and hottes houses. **1585** T. WASHINGTON tr. *Nicholay's Voy.* II. xxi. 58 A furnace like unto the hotte houses of Germanye serving too drye the shyrtes and other linnen. **1674–91** RAY *N.C. Words, Making Salt* 207 The Hot-House where they set their Salt to dry. **1875** KNIGHT *Dict. Mech.*, *Hot-house*. 1. (*Pottery*.) A room where strong heat completes the drying of green ware, previously to.. firing in a kiln.

†**5.** Among the North American Indians, a separate hut kept heated for winter residence. *Obs.*

1765 H. TIMBERLAKE *Mem.* 35, I retird to Kanagatucko's hot-house. *Note.* This Hot-house is a little hut joined to the house, in which a fire is continually kept. **1791** W. BARTRAM *Carolina* 367 Each.. habitation has besides a little conical house, covered with dirt, which is called the winter or hot-house.

6. In the West Indies, A hospital.

1707 H. SLOANE *Voy. to Jamaica* I. p. ciii, One Prince, a lusty Negro, had been ill of the Yaws.. and flux'd for it in one of the Chirurgeons Hot-Houses. **1788** H. MACNEILL *Observ. Treatm. Negroes Jamaica* 8 He [*sc.* a sick slave] is put into a house particularly appropriated to the purpose, (a lazaretto or *hot-house*, as it is generally called). **1790** W. BECKFORD *Descr. Acct. Jamaica* II. 17 This building has a narrow piazza in front, at the end of which is a small apartment for the nurse or hot-house woman. **1827** *Hamel, the Obeah Man* I. xxii. 244 The hothouse-keeper indulged him with a plentiful dose of grog. **1828** *Life Planter Jamaica* 49 He went to the hot-house or hospital. *Ibid.* 153 Several of the negroes complained of sickness, and in consequence were sent to the hot-house. **1834** R. R. MADDEN *Let.* 4 Apr. in *Twelvemonth's Residence W. Indies* (1835) I. 154 The hot-house doctor is generally a negro disqualified by age or infirmity for labour in the field. He has charge of the medicines.

Hence **'hothouse** *v. trans.*, to place or cultivate in a hothouse. Also *fig.*

1833 FONBLANQUE *Eng. under 7 Administ.* (1837) II. 355 Hot-housing and the manure of Mammon. **1892** *Standard* 23 Dec. 2/2 Every trivial incident.. had been hot-housed, gloated over.. and treated as a dainty dish. **1898** *Atlantic Monthly* Apr. 464 No fretful orchid hot-housed from the dew, But hale and hardy as the highland heather.

‖**hoti** ('hɒtɪ). *Obs.* Pl. **hoties** ('hɒtɪz). [Gr. ὅτι conj., that, because.] **a.** A statement introduced by 'because', or the fact denoted by such a statement; a cause, reason (= DIOTI); a piece of reasoning or inference. **b.** A statement introduced by 'that'; an assertion, or fact asserted (opp. to DIOTI).

1638–48 G. DANIEL *Eclog* v. 44 T' insert our Interests, or wand'ring be In Selfe-borne Hoti'es, from the Historie. *c* **1645** HOWELL *Lett.* III. iii. (1655) 5 Poor sciolists who scarce know the Hoties of things. **1646** SIR T. BROWNE *Pseud. Ep.* I. viii. 34 Unto him that desireth Hoties, or to replenish his head with varieties. **1656** BLOUNT *Glossogr.*, *Hoti* and *Dioti* (Gr.) two terms used in Logick.. the one the thing it self, and the other the cause or reason of it. **1734** WATTS *Reliq. Juv.* (1789) 79 He.. shewed the *Hoti* and the *Dioti* (i.e. that it was so, and why it was so).

hoting, var. *highting*: see HIGHT *v.*[1]

hot line: see HOT *a.* 12 c.

hotly ('hɒtlɪ), *adv.* Forms: see HOT *a.* [f. HOT *a.* + -LY[2].] In a hot manner or degree.

1. With great heat, at a high temperature; so as to be 'hot' or pungent.

1592 SHAKS. *Ven. & Ad.* 178 The shadow had forsook them, And Titan.. With burning eye did hotly overlook them. *Ibid.* 332 An oven that is stopp'd.. Burneth more hotly. **1809** PINKNEY *Trav. France* 8 Gingerbread nuts.. hotly spiced. **1871** R. ELLIS *Catullus* lxiv. 93 Flame blazed hotly within her, in all her marrow abiding.

2. *fig.* With 'heat' or fervour; ardently, fervently, eagerly, passionately, keenly; angrily, excitedly.

1525 LD. BERNERS *Froiss.* II. xxxiv. 101 They wolde haue you hotely to sette on your enemyes. **1546** J. HEYWOOD *Prov.* (1867) 74 Louyng hir.. As whotly as euer. **1607** ROWLANDS *Diog. Lanth.* 32 They hotly fell to wordes, And out in choller brake. **1727** DE FOE *Syst. Magic* I. iii. (1840) 85 If he.. was.. so hotly pursued, he should certainly be discovered. **1874** GREEN *Short Hist.* iii. §7. 148 The King hotly retorted that he was bound by no promise to a false traitor. **1876** SWINBURNE *Erechth.* 1276 Whom his own crime tracks hotlier than a hound.

hotness ('hɒtnɪs). [f. as prec. + -NESS.] The quality or state of being hot; heat.

1530 PALSGR. 232/1 Hotenesse, *chalevr*. **1586** BRIGHT *Melanch.* i. 2 The bloud.. which by.. immoderate hotenesse .. surchargeth the bodie. **1650** BULWER *Anthropomet.* 235 The hotnesse of the Country. **1852** M. ARNOLD *Empedocles* II, The day in his hotness. *Mod.* The hotness of the pepper. The hotness of his temper contrasts remarkably with the coolness of his judgement.

Hotnot ('hɒtnɒt). *S. Afr.* An abbreviated pejorative form of Hottentot.

1913 C. PETTMAN *Africanderisms* 217 *Hotnot*, a common Dutch pronunciation of Hottentot. **1939** J. S. MARAIS *Cape Coloured People* i. 31 The 'colloquial Afrikaans' for Coloured People is not, as Professor Macmillan thinks, ..'Hotnots'— at any rate in the western Cape—but 'bruin mense'. 'Hotnot' is a term of contempt. **1949** *Cape Times* 8 July 8 His uncouth remarks about 'Hotnots, Coolies and Kafirs'. **1956** A. SAMPSON *Drum* xv. 201 They joked and laughed about apartheid, and about being mistaken for white men, and being called bushmen, hotnots, coolies, with compulsory wounding laughter. **1966** A. SACHS *Jail Diary* xvi. 133 That was my Grandfather's place.. before the British took it away, and he even allowed a few Hotnots to sleep in the house.

'hot-pot, hot pot.

1. A hot drink composed of ale and spirits, or ale sweetened and spiced. *local.*

a **1700** B. E. *Dict. Cant. Crew*, *Hot Pot*, Ale and Brandy boyled together. *c* **1730** *Royal Remarks* 49 All of them in a loving Way, over a Hot Pot. **1825** BROCKETT, *Hot-Pot*, warmed ale with spirit in it. **1855** ROBINSON *Whitby Gloss.*, *Heeat pots*, pots of hot ale sweetened and spiced, with which the friends of a bridal party meet them on the road from church after the marriage ceremony.

2. A dish composed of mutton or beef with potatoes, or potatoes and onions, cooked in an oven in an earthenware pot with a tight-fitting cover. Also *attrib.*

1851 *London at Table* I. 21 At the bottom of the table,.. let there be a hot-pot. **1854** MRS. GASKELL *North & S.* xlii, Master, there's hot-pot for dinner to-day. **1855** THACKERAY *Newcomes* I. xvi. 160 The Colonel.. was great at making hash mutton, hot-pot, curry and pillau. **1889** *Daily News* 26 Dec. 2/7 Yesterday over 30,000 poor people in Liverpool, were provided with 'hot pot' dinners.. Each 'hot pot' weighed ten pounds. There were used 13,000 lbs. of beef, 15 tons of potatoes, and a ton and a half of onions.

3. *Racing slang.* (See quots. and cf. HOT *a.* 8 e.)

1922 *N. & Q.* 23 Sept. 206/2 *Hot pot*, a horse which has been heavily backed. **1945** BAKER *Austral. Lang.* xvii. 299 'Truth' has always devoted special attention to sporting news and, as a consequence, has developed racing jargon considerably... A favourite is a hot-pot.

hot-press, *sb.* A contrivance for pressing paper or cloth between glazed boards and hot metal plates, to make the surface smooth and glossy. Also, a similar apparatus used in making plywood (see next). Also *attrib.* = *hot-pressed.*

1631 T. POWELL *Tom All Trades* 163 Hot Presses for Cloth. **1712** H. NEVILL in *Phil. Trans.* XXVIII. 253 He wanting a flat Stone to make him a Hot-press (for so they do, who want an Iron Plate to Press their Cloth on). **1798** T. JEFFERSON in *Harper's Mag.* (1885) Mar. 542/2 A hot-press bible. **1821** BYRON *Juan* IV. cix, A ball-room bard, a foolscap, hot-press darling. **1875** KNIGHT *Dict. Mech.*, *Hot-press*, a means of calendering and smoothing paper by subjecting it to pressure between glazed boards; a hot iron plate is placed at every 20 sheets or so, to heat the pile. **1938** *Trans. Amer. Soc. Mech. Engin.* LX. 60/1 The great scarcity of hot presses in plywood plants. *Ibid.* 60/2 In the hot-press operation with resin film, the resin film is cut to dimension and laid between the sheets of veneer. **1943** SIMONDS & ELLIS *Handbk. Plastics* xi. 433 The panels are formed in these hot presses under pressures ranging from 100 to 300 lb. per sq. in. *Ibid.*, At 220° F., hot-press panels are completely bonded in from 3 to 10 minutes' cure in a hot press. **1968** KIRK & OTHMER *Encycl. Chem. Technol.* (ed. 2) XV. 903 By far the largest production [of plywood] is in a hot press in which thermo-setting resins are the adhesive basis.

hot-press, *v. trans.* Usu. in pa. pple. (ppl. adj.) **hot-pressed**, or vbl. sb. **hot-pressing. a.** To subject to pressure in a hot-press; to make (paper or cloth) smooth and glossy by pressure between hot plates. Also, to press (veneers, etc.) between heated platens for a period in order to bond them together to make plywood.

1745 *De Foe's Eng. Tradesman* xx. (1841) I. 193 Every false gloss put upon our woollen manufactures by hotpressing, folding, dressing [etc.]. **1794** MATHIAS *Purs. Lit.* (1798) 223 In one glaz'd glare tracts, sermons, pamphlets vie, And hot-press'd nonsense claims a dignity. **1859** F. A. GRIFFITHS *Artil. Man.* (1862) 191 The serge is to be.. hot-pressed. **1874** R. TYRWHITT *Sketch. Club* 17, I wish you would all use hot-pressed paper. **1932** *Trans. Amer. Soc. Mech. Engin.* LIV (sect. WDI). 1/2 The necessity for hot-pressing is the chief disadvantage [of blood-albumin glues]. **1943** SIMONDS & ELLIS *Handbk. Plastics* xi. 433 Wherever the type of plywood permits it, hot pressing offers quite a few advantages to the manufacturer over cold pressing. **1957** *Times* 23 Dec. 11/2 A decision was taken to introduce hot-pressing in the veneer mills. **1968** J. ARNOLD *Shell Bk. Country Crafts* 214 After the drying, the cloth is 'hot-pressed'.

b. To shape under pressure in a heated die or mould.

1913 J. V. WOODWORTH *Drop Forging* viii. 254 The Burdict hot-pressed nut-machine. **1938** H. I. LEWENZ tr.

Brandenburger's Processes & Machinery Plastics Industry i. 5 Constant improvements..have taken place in the production of paste for hot pressing. **1947** KIRK & OTHMER *Encycl. Chem. Technol.* I. 561 Alloys that can be made in no other way can be produced by compressing and sintering metal powders or by hot pressing loosely compacted slugs. **1967** M. CHANDLER *Ceramics in Mod. World* vi. 173 An alternative technique for forming silicon nitride is to hot-press it.

hot-presser. One whose occupation is the hot-pressing of paper or cloth. Also *fig.*

1646 JENKYN *Remora* 24 A few strict, precise legalists.. hot-pressers of uniformity. **1706** *Lond. Gaz.* No. 4292/4 Thomas Freeman, of London, Hot-presser. **1886** *Pall Mall G.* 3 June 12/1 To take the work direct from the manufacturer..deducting only from his price the cost of foreman, hot-presser, and hire of the distributing room.

hot rod. orig. *U.S.* A motor vehicle specially modified to give high power and speed; the driver (also **hot rodder**) of a hot rod. Hence **hot-rod** *v. intr.*, **hot-rodding** *vbl. sb.* Also *attrib.* and *fig.*

1945 *Life* 5 Nov. 87 A 'hot rod'..is an automobile stripped for speed and pepped up for power until it can travel 90 to 125 mph. Most hot rods are roadsters. **1949** *Life* 7 Nov. 123 *(caption)* Policeman holds fistful of licenses confiscated from hot-rodders. *Ibid.*, In Los Angeles and Dallas, where 'hot-rodding' is at its peak, hundreds of youngsters spend their spare time in suicidal games on wheels. **1953** J. N. LEONARD *Flight into Space* 87 All over the United States and in many other parts of the world are groups of enthusiasts who dream of hot-rodding off the tedious earth. **1953** *Time* 21 Sept. 85/1 Every day during the show he thrilled the crowds with the airborne hot-rodding that Britain encourages at Farnborough. **1955** *Sci. News Let.* 1 Oct. 213/1 Teenagers are as accident prone with shotguns as they are with hot rods. **1957** J. KEROUAC *On Road* (1958) 15 A hotrod kid came by with his scarf flying. **1958** J. D. MACDONALD *Executioners* (1959) iv. 52, I don't want her hot-rodding around in the night, going to those drive-ins. **1958** *Woman* 9 Aug. 14/1 Hot-rod road scorchers. **1958** *Observer* 30 Nov. 10/5 Bernstein and his direct knowledge of hot-rodders and what they are after. **1959** *Observer* 25 Jan. 7/4 Mike Hawthorn, champion racing driver and the idol of hot-rods all over the world. **1959** *Sunday Times* 22 Mar. 24/8 My old two-litre hot-rod after its last disastrous tune-up. **1959** *Encounter* Dec. 30/2 Almost every popular magazine nowadays is likely to be written in a hot-rod style which bursts with energy in every sentence. **1962** *Punch* 17 Oct. 559/3 The youth of these islands.. looked on the motor-cycle as their hot rod. **1967** *Listener* 23 Nov. 682/1 The Beach Boys made their reputation.. ostensibly by taking surfing and hotrodding as their subject. **1971** *Daily Tel.* (Colour Suppl.) 3 Sept. 41/1 The first hair freaks I ever saw in California were not hippies, but surfers and hotrodders.

'hot-short, *a.* [f. HOT *a.* + *short*, after the earlier RED-SHORT: cf. also COLD-SHORT.] Of iron: Brittle in its hot state; opp. to *cold-short.* Hence **hot-'shortness,** the quality or state of being hot-short.

1798 D. MUSHET in *Phil. Mag.* II. 160 Hot short iron is possessed of an extreme degree of fusibility. **1875** *Ure's Dict. Arts* II. 956 The tendency of the [sulphur] is to make the metal what is called 'hot short', so that it cannot be worked while hot under the hammer. **1877** M. REYNOLDS *Locom. Engine Driving* IV. (ed. 5) 230 Cracks on the edges of bars, sign of hot-short iron. **1890** H. M. HOWE *Metall. of Steel* I. iv. 42/1 Manganese..by bodily removing sulphur from cast-iron and probably from steel,..prevents hot-shortness, both red and yellow. **1961** S. A. HISCOCK *Lead & Lead Alloys for Cable Sheathing* vii. 221 By subtracting 20° C. from the 'cracking-temperature'..some indication will be obtained of the extrusion temperature which must not be exceeded if 'hot-shortness'..is to be avoided.

'hot-shot. Also hot shot, hotshot. [See SHOT *sb.*]

1. † **a.** One who shoots (with a fire-arm) 'hotly' or eagerly; a reckless or hot-headed fellow. *Obs.*

1604 MIDDLETON *Father Hubburd's T.* Wks. (Bullen) VIII. 90 To the wars I betook me, ranked myself amongst desperate hot shots. **1609** *Ev. Woman in Hum.* v. i. in Bullen *O. Pl.* IV, He railes against women like a whot-shot. *c* **1626** *Dick of Devon.* I. iii. Ibid. II, A company of hott shotts are abroad. **1665** COTTON *Poet. Wks.* (1765) 110 Straight to the Wharf repairs the Hot-shot.

b. An important or exceptionally capable person. Also *attrib. colloq.* (orig. *U.S.*).

1933 *Amer. Speech* Oct. 35/2 *Hot shot*, a champion, a leading contender, an excellent fighter. **1943** 'B. HALLIDAY' *Murder wears a Mummer's Mask* xviii. 205 All the important critics were there—the hot shots from the East whose wire stories to their papers could make or break an actress. **1951** J. D. SALINGER *Catcher in Rye* iii. 23 He was telling us all about what a swell guy he was, what a hot-shot and all. **1952** S. KAUFFMANN *Philanderer* (1953) xiv. 234 The only relaxation I would have would be going out with the local hot-shots. **1961** J. HELLER *Catch-22* (1962) xxii. 230 How about getting us a hotel-room if you're such a hotshot? **1973** J. WAINWRIGHT *Pride of Pigs* 103 These hot-shot scientists. They love the limelight.

† **2.** (Also *hot-shoot.*) See quots. *Obs.*

1673 RAY *Journ. Low C.* 58 They use also for Fewel a sort of round Balls made of Clay mixed with a certain proportion of coal..which they call Hotshots. **1727–41** CHAMBERS *Cycl.*, *Hot-Shoots*, or *Hovilses*, a sort of factitious or compound fuel, made of a third part of any coal..mixed with two thirds of loam.

3. *U.S. slang.* (See quots.)

1925 *Writer's Monthly* May 486/2 *Hot shot*, a fast freight. **1931** 'D. STIFF' *Milk & Honey Route* 207 *Hot shot*, a fast freight or passenger train.

4. *U.S. slang.* (See quots.)

1953 W. BURROUGHS *Junkie* (1972) 157 *Hot Shot*... Poison, usually strychnine, passed to an addict as junk. The peddler sometimes slips a hot shot to an addict because the addict is giving information to the law. **1971** E. E. LANDY *Underground Dict.* 106 *Hot shot*,.. 1. Injection of poison that user believes to be good drugs, a method of getting rid of police informers. 2. Injection of a drug that is of higher potency than the addict is accustomed to.

5. Used *attrib.* to designate a wind tunnel in which an arc discharge in a pressurized chamber is used to produce a hypersonic pulse of gas in an evacuated test chamber, the two chambers being separated initially by a diaphragm that is ruptured by the discharge.

1959 *Engineering* 13 Feb. 219/2 A wind tunnel, which will test models at the speed of satellite rockets, is expected to be in use in the United States toward the end of this year... Known as a 'hotshot' tunnel, it makes use of a powerful electric arc to pressurise the air. **1971** *Sci. Amer.* Sept. 14/2 The heated gas in the arc chamber is the working gas of a hotshot tunnel with a working section of 2·5 meters and a Mach number of about 20.

hot spot. Also hot-spot. **I. 1.** *Physiol.* One of numerous small areas on the skin that are specially sensitive to heat.

1888 W. STIRLING tr. *Landois's Text-bk. Human Physiol.* (ed. 3) xiv. 836 The chain of the 'cold-spots' usually does not coincide with those of the 'hot-spots'. **1911** *Encycl. Brit.* XXVII. 97/1 There are points [on the skin], stimulated by addition of heat, hot spots, while others are stimulated by withdrawal of heat, cold spots. **1926** S. WRIGHT *Applied Physiol.* I. 21 If all the 'hot' and 'cold' spots are marked out, the areas of skin between them are found to be insensitive to punctate thermal stimuli.

II. A spot that is hot (*lit.* and *fig.*). **2.** [SPOT *sb.*^{1}10.] A small area in a surface or body that is at a higher temperature than its surroundings.

1919 G. KAPP *Princ. Electr. Engin.* II. vi. 143 The average internal temperature of a winding can be more accurately deduced from a resistance test, whilst for the discovery of so called 'hot spots' thermo-couples must be used. **1936** D. M. ROBINSON *Dielectric Phenomena in High Voltage Cables* ii. 16 A cable subjected to excess voltage may develop local hot spots, and..frequently fails at or near the hottest of these points. **1947** *Sci. News* IV. 150 With a metal sliding on glass with a load of a few pounds, visible hot spots (temp. 520–570° C.) can be seen when the sliding speed is as low as one or two feet per second. **1958** H. ETHERINGTON *Nuclear Engin. Handbk.* XII. 17 Hot-spot effects usually require a correction in the calculation of maximum temperature. **1959** H. F. TAYLOR et al. *Foundry Engin.* x. 277 Under normal conditions of cooling, metal at the center of the *d* region is a hot spot, the last to solidify. **1970** *Times* 30 Oct. 23/2 A small ..infra-red television camera..for detecting the 'hot spots' in overhead power lines and substations which can lead to serious breakdowns. **1972** *Physics Bull.* May 284/2 This effect has been used to detect hot spots and hence structural flaws in systems as diverse as integrated circuits and the human body.

3. [HOT *a.* 7 b, SPOT *sb.*^{1} 8.] **a.** A night-club or other place of lively public entertainment.

1931 D. RUNYON *Guys & Dolls* (1932) iii. 53 There are very seldom any customers in Good Time Charley's until along about five o'clock in the morning..and then it is sometimes a very hot spot indeed. **1937** J. WEIDMAN *I can get it for you Wholesale* xxv. 227 The line in Winchell's column: Martha Mills..is doing the hot spots with what prominent young manufacturer of feminine haberdashery? **1940** *Time* 15 Apr. 98/2 Eschewing Hollywood hotspots, they prefer at-homes with the quieter younger set. **1954** G. SMITH *Flaw in Crystal* iv. 39 The Wind in the Willows [a roadhouse] had been a noted hot-spot when I was a schoolboy. **1954** *Manch. Guardian Weekly* 26 Aug. 7/1 Intellectuals..went on a kind of jazz-slumming in the Harlem hot spots.

b. A place of danger; *spec.* a place where war is being actively engaged in or experienced.

1941 *Illustr. Lond. News* CXCIX. 200 *(caption)* Miss Cowles, an American journalist, whose pre-war assignments took her to most of the 'hot-spots' of Europe [*sc.* Prague, Berlin, Warsaw, etc.]. **1966** *Economist* 19 Feb. 711/2 The Administration wanted to distinguish financially between men who had been in 'hot spots' and those who had only served in non-combat zones. **1973** G. BEARE *Snake on Grave* xii. 62 You're putting yourself on the hot-spot, Sammy.

4. Specific technical applications in the literal sense.

a. In an internal combustion engine, a portion of the manifold or combustion chamber that is heated in order to facilitate vaporization of the liquid fuel; also, a region of overheating that tends to cause pre-ignition. **b.** *Astr.* A region in the sun's corona (generally associated with a solar flare) that is temporarily at a higher temperature than normal and is emitting a characteristic spectrum of radiation. **c.** *Electronics.* In a mercury-arc rectifier with a pool cathode, that part of the pool of mercury with which the arc is in contact and from which electrons are emitted.

a. 1924 *Motor Manual* (ed. 25) ii. 32 As an additional means towards obtaining efficient carburation a 'hot spot' arrangement is provided on a number of cars. **1929** *Times* 2 Nov. 4/7 The inlet manifold is jointed to the exhaust centrally, and thus a hot-spot is provided. **1934** *Jrnl. R. Aeronaut. Soc.* XXXVIII. 960 Thus making absolutely sure of high compression without hot spots acting as sparks in the combustion chamber. **1959** *Chambers's Encycl.* VII. 639/1 [In the petrol engine] pre-ignition is usually caused by an unsuitable plug or some local hot-spot, e.g. the exhaust valve head. **1968** *Practical Motorist* Dec. 459/1 Some hot spots are fitted with a thermostatically controlled flap which diverts the mixture away from the hot spot once the engine is running at normal temperature.

b. 1936 *Harvard Coll. Observatory Circ.* No. 410. 22 This region [of the chromosphere] appears to be one of abnormal excitation, possibly caused by a 'hot spot' near the limb of the sun at the time of the eclipse. **1958** *Sci. Amer.* Aug. 41/2 When the sun is observed with a radio telescope tuned to 10 centimeters, the hot spots in its atmosphere stand out brilliantly. **1966** *McGraw-Hill Encycl. Sci. & Technol.* XIII. 282/2 Coronal hot spots, indicated by emission of the yellow line of Ca XV at 5694 A above the photosphere by some 30,000 km, have been found in all spectrographic observations of the corona over a limb flare.

c. 1937 W. G. DOW *Fund. Engin. Electronics* xix. 426 The cathode 'hot spots' of mercury-pool-type mercury vapor rectifiers dodge about erratically on the mercury surface. **1971** B. SCHARF *Engin. & its Lang.* xx. 277 Where the arc terminates on the surface of the mercury a 'hot spot' occurs which forms the source of electronic emission.

5. Technical senses representing transferred senses either of *hot* or of the phr. as a whole.

a. In an ingot or casting (see quot. 1908). **b.** A particularly active part of a forest fire; so **hot-spotting** *vbl. sb.* (see quot. 1953). **c.** *Theatr.*, *Photogr.*, etc. An area that is markedly brighter than its surroundings. **d.** *Nuclear Sci.* An area where the radiation level is much higher than in the surroundings; a local concentration of radioactivity. **e.** *Genetics.* A part of a gene especially liable to undergo mutation.

a. 1908 B. STOUGHTON *Metall. Iron & Steel* xii. 349 These localities, where the segregation is high, and which are known, when very bad, as 'hot spots', are sometimes porous or surrounded by porous parts of the casting. **1938** ROSENHOLTZ & OESTERLE *Elem. Ferrous Metal.* ii, Hot spots are irregularities occasioned by the uneven distribution of the coarse and fine parts of the charge in such a way that the coarse parts are concentrated near the furnace walls.

b. 1938 *Fire Control Notes* Oct. 26 This work includes such jobs as..burning out material between the line and the fire edge, and reduction of hot spots. **1940** *Ibid.* July 141 It is well for the scout to carry a pulaski or light ax for blazing or hot-spotting. **1953** *Brit. Commonw. Forest Terminol.* I. 77 *Hot-spotting*, checking the spread of fire on hot spots alone or at salient points, as an emergency measure employed in advance of control-line construction.

c. 1952 GRANVILLE *Dict. Theatr. Terms* 99 *Hot spot*, a bright spot in an area of uneven lighting. **1958** *New Scientist* 25 Dec. 1569/3 Some areas on the document will be reproduced as dark grey.., while on others, known colloquially as 'hot spots', there will be such a powerful reflection of light that any markings on such areas may be completely blotted out. **1971** L. B. HAPPÉ *Basic Motion Pict. Technol.* vii. 218 A brighter central area, or hot spot, is particularly obvious when a short focal length lens is used on a camera and a long focal length on the projector.

d. 1955 *Bull. Atomic Sci.* Feb. 46/2 One would expect 'hot spots' even far downwind but since the history of the bomb cloud would already be several hours 'old' by then, there would be a corresponding drop in intensity. **1955** *Sci. Amer.* Aug. 37/1 A particularly malignant feature of some of the radioisotopes is their tendency to concentrate in 'hot spots' instead of distributing themselves evenly through the bone or other tissue they invade. **1962** *Listener* 19 July 104/2 The concentration of radio-active substances into 'hot spots' may well be exaggerated in the rapidly dividing cells of the foetus.

e. 1958 BENZER & FREESE in *Proc. Nat. Acad. Sci.* XLIV. 115 A striking feature of the map is the existence of certain 'hot spots', where mutations recur with high probability. **1964** W. HAYES *Genetics of Bacteria & their Viruses* viii. 171 Out of 1,612 spontaneous mutations..more than 500 occur at a single site or 'hot spot' in the B cistron. **1967** E. STEINER tr. *Esser & Kuenen's Genetics of Fungi* v. 300 A hot spot probably consists of a single base pair, at least one member of which is particularly sensitive to a specific mutagen.

hots-potch, obs. form of HOTCHPOTCH.

hotspur ('hɒtspɜː(r)).

1. One whose spur is hot with impetuous or constant riding; hence, one who spurs or pushes on recklessly; a heady or rash person. (First occurring, and best known, as surname of Sir Henry Percy, son of the Earl of Northumberland, who fell in the rebellion against Henry IV, in 1403.)

1460 CAPGRAVE *Chron.* (Rolls) 243 Herry Percy the yonger, whom the Scottis clepid Herry Hatspore. **1586** J. HOOKER *Girald. Irel.* in *Holinshed* II. 97/2 He was..in matters of importance an headlong hotspur. **1596** SHAKS. *1 Hen. IV*, v. ii. 19 A haire-brain'd Hotspurre, gouern'd by a Spleene. **1600** HOLLAND *Livy* XXXVI. vi. 922 Some hot-spurres..gave councell to goe against them with all their forces. **1726** DE FOE *Hist. Devil* (1822) 287 As we say of some hot-spurs who ride post, they whip the post boy. **1895** *Daily News* 19 Apr. 5/5 The 'Vossische Zeitung'..says: 'Perhaps this sudden coolness on the part of England gives certain Hot-spurs in our own Fatherland something to think about'.

† **2.** Name for a very early kind of pea: also ***hotspur-pease.*** (Cf. HASTING B. 1.) *Obs.*

a **1700** B. E. *Dict. Cant. Crew*, *Hot Spur*,..also early or forward Peas. **1707** *Lond. Gaz.* No. 4357/4 To be sold.. Rogue-Pease, and Hotspur-Pease. **1707–12** MORTIMER *Husb.* (J.), The hotspur is the speediest of any in growth.

3. *attrib.* or *adj.* Fiery-spirited, hasty, rash.

1596 SPENSER *F.Q.* IV. i. 35 The hot-spurre youth so scorning to be crost. *c* **1618** [see HORSE-RACER]. **1660** HICKERINGILL *Jamaica* (1661) 71 A wary plodding Fabius signifying more than a hot Spur Marcellus. **1883** *Harper's Mag.* Feb. 425/1 After the union of the States..the political conduct of South Carolina was so imperious..that she was not uncommonly known as the 'Hotspur State'.

So **hot-spurred** ('hɒtspɜːd) *a.* = 3.

1594 NASHE *Unfort. Trav.* 60 Such a hotspurd plague as hath not bin heard of. **1683** CHALKHILL *Thealma & Cl.* 41 (N.) A hot-spurr'd youth height Hylas.

hot stuff. a. A person or thing out of the ordinary run, something of surpassing excellence or merit; sometimes with implication of moral censure; also, specif., a woman reputed to be highly sexed. Also *attrib.*, esp. (i) sexually explicit, (ii) extremely capable or efficient. *colloq.* (orig. *U.S.*).

1889 *Kansas City* (Missouri) *Times & Star* 14 Nov., 'Miss Middleton's Lover.' Were there room for two words in that

last line, 'Hot Stuff' might be appropriate. **1900** *Dialect Notes* II. 42 Hot stuff. 1. A person of good quality; often ironical. 2. A person having merit. **1905** WODEHOUSE *Head of Kay's* 252 Kay's are hot stuff, Jimmy. **1908** *Varsity Vices* May 5/1 Gad, though, but she's tremendously hot stuff, the little devil. Stood her a bust at the Zoo. **1909** WODEHOUSE *Mike* xvii. 101 The book was obviously the last word in hot stuff. **1911** F. SWINNERTON *Casement* i. 41, I say, Trevell.. you had any dealings with Jimpton? Eh? He's hot stuff.. what! **1912** C. MACKENZIE *Carnival* x. 111 I'm not going to have fellows say my sister's hot stuff. **1912** *Strand Mag.* Jan. 22/2 Clarence in goal was the nearest approach to an indiarubber acrobat.. to be seen off the music-hall stage. He was, in brief, hot stuff. **1915** H. WILSON *Diary* 9 Sept. (1927) I. 249 Here is Sarrail.. to urge a plan about which he knows nothing. And all because he is a Radical-Socialist. Hot stuff. **1917** A. WAUGH *Loom of Youth* II. i. 111 This side [*sc.* a Rugby football team] was certainly 'pretty hot stuff'. **1923** H. G. WELLS *Men like Gods* I. vi. 102 'Raced us from Hounslow,' said Mr. Burleigh's driver. 'Real hot stuff.' **1928** *Punch* 21 Mar. 328/1 His father had influence.., being a frightfully hot-stuff surgeon. **1931** *Amer. Speech* Feb. 204 *Hot stuff*, new, up-to-date material or new incidents; approved as being startling, or the 'latest'. **1931** W. DEEPING *Road* viii. 86 I'm getting my new M.-B. next week. Hot stuff. She'll do eighty. **1936** E. M. FORSTER *Abinger Harvest* 43 During the interval we discussed, not whether the Scallies were good, but whether they were better or worse than the Wags. They were less hot stuff, that was admitted on all sides. **1940** GRAVES & HODGE *Long Week-End* iv. 52 Elinor Glyn was the reigning queen of popular love literature and considered 'very hot stuff'. **1944** M. PANETH *Branch Street* 64 The men say of her, 'Joan is hot stuff.' **1965** D. LODGE *Brit. Mus. is falling Down* vii. 125 A sort of novel, ..the story of his affair with Mother, with just the names changed. It's hot stuff, as we used to say at school. **1965** H. PORTER *Cats of Venice* 91 Singapore boy hot stuff, hot stuff!

b. *slang*. Stolen goods. Cf. STUFF *sb.*[1] 10 b.

1924 G. C. HENDERSON *Keys to Crookdom* ix. 117 Pawnshops and second-hand stores establish a reputation for handling 'hot stuff' and there are very few such establishments that will refuse to buy from a known thief. **1962** K. ORVIS *Damned & Destroyed* vii. 51 So you're handling a bit of hot stuff as well as joy-popping?

So **hot-stuff** *v. trans.* (Army slang), to scrounge, steal; **hot-stuffed** *ppl. a.*; **hot-stuffer**, a scrounger.

1914 H. ROSHER *In R.N.A.S.* (1916) 36, I at once hot-stuffed one of his inlet valves and set the men to work changing it. **1929** *Papers Mich. Acad. Sci., Arts & Lett.* X. 300/1 *Hot-stuffed*, stolen. *Ibid.*, *Hot-stuffer*, a thief. **1950** E. PARTRIDGE *Here, There & Everywhere* 81 *Hotstuff*, to appropriate illicitly, to steal.

hotsy-totsy ('hɒtsɪ'tɒtsɪ), *a. slang* (orig. *U.S.*). ['Coined *c* 1926 by Billie De Beck, Amer. cartoonist' (Webster).] Comfortable, satisfactory, just right. Hence ˌ**hotsy-'totsiness**.

1926 B. REYNOLDS *Cocktail Continentale* ii. 29 And they sure can fix up a rip-snotin', raring, tearing, hotsy-totsy time, honey boy. **1927** DUNNING & ABBOTT *Broadway* xx. 205 They complimented Steve in the lingo of the night clubs. 'Everything is hotsy-totsy!' whooped the loud Ruby. **1927** WODEHOUSE *Small Bachelor* vi. 95 It seemed to me that I was absolutely hotsy-totsy. **1935** —— *Luck of Bodkins* xxii. 282 And a fat chance..there is of any hotsy-totsiness resulting from anything Ambrose can do. **1940** N. MARSH *Surfeit of Lampreys* (1941) xviii. 281 Daddy's all hotsy-totsy now as regards money. **1944** H. CROOME *You've gone Astray* xxi. 214 Now she thinks another man would be all hotsy totsy. **1952** [see BABE 3 b]. **1958** L. A. G. STRONG *Treason in Egg* ix. 165 All is hotsy-totsy. **1964** W. MARKFIELD *To Early Grave* (1965) iv. 77 He became a big-time hotsy-totsy critic. **1973** J. MANN *Only Security* xii. 162 What the law allows me, is mine... So that's all hotsy totsy.

hott(e, obs. forms of HOT.

hotte. *Obs.* (14th c.) Of uncertain meaning.

(Although the sense is obscure, it is prob. the same word as HOT *sb.*[1] 'panier, creel'. The suggestion that it is a variant of HUT is, from the history of that word, inadmissible.)

c **1300** *Langtoft's Chron.* (Rolls) II. 236 Skaterd be the Scottes, Hoderd in thar hottes, Never thay ne the [in R. BRUNNE (1810) 273 For scatred er þi Scottes, & hodred in þer hottes, neuer þei ne the]. *c* **1330** R. BRUNNE *Chron.* (1810) 282 Þou scabbed Scotte, þi nek, þi hotte, þe deuelle it breke, It salle be hard to here Edward, ageyn þe speke.

Hottentot ('hɒt(ə)ntɒt). Also 7 **hatten-tote, hottantot**: see also HODMANDOD 2. [a. Du. *Hottentot* (also *Ottentot*, *Hottentoo*, Riebeck's Journal, Jan. 1652); according to Dapper, *Beschryvingh der Afrikansche Gewesten*, 1670, a word meaning 'stutterer' or 'stammerer', applied to the people in question on account of their clucking speech: see *Trans. Philol. Soc.* 1866, 6–25.]

1. a. One of the two sub-races of the Khoisanid race (the other being the Sanids or Bushmen), characterized by short stature, yellow-brown skin colour, and tightly curled hair. They are of mixed Bushman-Hamite descent with some Bantu admixture, and are now found principally in South-West Africa. Also, a member of this race.

1677 SIR T. HERBERT *Trav.* 17 While these Hatten-totes were in our company. **1697** DAMPIER *Voy.* (1729) I. 536 The word *Hottantot*..is the Name by which they call to one another..as if every one of them had this for his Name. **1715** BURNET *Hist. Ref.* III. Introd. 18 Would these Men reduce us to be a Sort of Hottentots? **1766** WESLEY *Wks.* (1872) III. 253, I found her as ignorant of the nature of religion as an Hottentot. **1886** MARQ. SALISBURY *Sp.* 15 May, You would not confide free representative institutions to the Hottentots, for instance. **1897** BRYCE *S. Africa* 76 The second native race was that which the Dutch called Hottentot. *Ibid.* 78 In the settled parts of the Colony, the Hottentot..has vanished more completely than has the Red Indian from the Atlantic States of North America. **1924** A. C. HADDON *Races of Man* (ed. 2) 41 An early migration of Hamites mixed with this population [*sc.* Bushmen] and gave cattle and elements of their language to the mixed people who in South Africa are known as Hottentots. **1930** I. SCHAPERA *Khoisan Peoples of S. Africa* III. x. 239 There is little information as to the existence of food taboos among the Hottentots in more recent times. **1965** H. B. ISHERWOOD *Racial Contours* viii. 308 Opinion seems to be gaining ground that the Bushman and the Hottentot bear so many features indicating a divergent evolutionary history that they should be classed as a separate race altogether and not grouped under the heading of Negroid. The title provisionally proposed is Khoisanoid, based on the name by which these people know themselves. **1970** P. OLIVER *Savannah Syncopators* 31 Alan P. Merriam has identified as distinct musical regions those of the Hottentot-Bushman. **1974** J. R. BAKER *Race* xvii. 318 The Hottentots, Korana, and Bushmen are not to be regarded as people adapted by natural selection to a desert life.

b. *transf.* A person of inferior intellect or culture; one degraded in the scale of civilization, or ignorant of the usages of civilized society. (This derogatory sense, which was based on a failure to understand an alien culture, appears now to be very rare.)

1726 AMHERST *Terræ Fil.* xxxv. 190 Surprized..to find a place, which he had heard so much renown'd for learning, fill'd with such grey-headed novices and reverend hottentots. **1751** CHESTERF. *Lett. to Son* 28 Feb., The utmost I can do for him, is to consider him a respectable Hottentot. **1763** *Brit. Mag.* July 338/2 England..yet abounded greatly with such kinds of Hottentots.

c. (In full ***Hottentot fish***.) A South African marine food fish of the genus *Pachymetopon*, esp. *P. blochii*.

1798 S. H. WILCOCKE tr. *Stavorinus' Voy. E. Indies* I. 560 The Hottentot-fish, which is like a sea-bream. **1838** J. E. ALEXANDER *Exped. Disc. Int. Afr.* I. 88 The delicious Roman fish, Hottentot. **1921** *Ann. S. Afr. Mus.* XXI. 721 The Hottentot is one of the commonest Cape fishes. **1949** J. L. B. SMITH *Sea Fishes S. Afr.* 276 The Hottentot slipped away with the next wave.

d. The Khoisan language spoken by the Hottentots.

1884 [see CLICK *sb.*[1] 5]. **1910** *Encycl. Brit.* IV. 871/2 Their language..has in common with Hottentot..the peculiar sounds known as 'clicks'. **1921** E. SAPIR *Lang.* iii. 55 Certain languages, like the South African Hottentot and Bushman, have also a number of inspiratory sounds. **1953** J. B. CARROLL *Study of Language* ii. 57 He..doubts very much the validity of certain early theories that such languages..as Bantu and Hottentot are in any way related to the Semitic-Hamitic group. **1972** *Stand. Encycl. S. Afr.* V. 605/1 Afrikaans and South African English have taken over words from Hottentot, such as *buchu*, *dagga*, *kanna*.

2. *attrib.* or as *adj.* Of or belonging to this race.

1718 *Entertainer* No. 28. 187 The Spiritual is reduc'd to a Hottentot Way of Government. **1731** MEDLEY *Kolben's Cape G. Hope* I. 81 The Hottentot stammering or clashing of the tongue in speaking. **1797** *Encycl. Brit.* VIII. 684/2 The Hottentot language is..said to be a composition of the most strange and disagreeable sounds. *Ibid.* 685/1 A general opinion has prevailed that the Hottentot women have a kind of natural vail which covers the female parts. *Ibid.* 687/2 In a craal, or Hottentot village, the huts are most commonly disposed in a circle. **1811** in W. J. BURCHELL *Trav. S. Afr.* (1822) I. xv. 371 The most dangerous malady is a kind of cancerous sore or ulcer, called in the colony the *Hottentots Zeer* (Hottentot Sore). **1828** J. PHILIP *Res. S. Afr.* I. p. xviii, The missionaries..were called 'Hottentot predicants' (ministers), by way of contempt. **1836** *Penny Cycl.* VI. 257/1 The latter [the Koranna Hottentots] are one of the few Hottentot tribes that have retained their independence. **1846** MRS. GORE *Eng. Char.* (1852) 104 In what Hottentot ignorance these poor creatures are at present reared. **1865** WATERMEYER in *Trans. Philol. Soc.* (1866) 17 The Hottentot national name is 'Khoikhoip', plural 'Khoikhoin', and is still in use among the Namaquas. **1897** BRYCE *S. Africa* 77 From unions between Hottentot women and the Dutch sprang the mixed race whom the Dutch call Bastards and the English Griquas. **1924** *Internat. Jrnl. Psycho-Anal.* V. 41 It might perhaps be not without significance that three of the five patients informed me of their own accord that they possessed 'Hottentot nymphae'. **1933** I. SCHAPERA *Early Cape Hottentots* p. xii, In Hottentot mythology ||Gaunab figured as a malevolent chief. **1965** H. B. ISHERWOOD *Racial Contours* viii. 308 Associated with the Naman and talking their language are the primitive Bergdama or Hankhoin people, who are virtually under Hottentot tribal rule. **1974** J. R. BAKER *Race* vi. 97 When Van Riebeck and his little company of emigrants from the Netherlands landed at Table Bay in 1652, they were met by Hottentot herdsmen.

3. Special comb.: chiefly names of South African plants: **Hottentot apron** (see APRON *sb.* 5 c); **Hottentot('s) bean (tree)** *S. Afr.*, a shrub or tree of the genus *Schotia*, esp. *S. latifolia*, or its fruit; **Hottentot('s) bread**, *Testudinaria elephantipes*; formerly, also, the root of *Richardia* (*Calla*) *æthiopica*; **Hottentot cherry**, *Cassine maurocenia*; **Hottentot('s) fig**, *Mesembryanthemum edule*; **Hottentot fish** (see sense 1 c above); **Hottentot('s) god** *S. Afr.*, a praying mantis, formerly worshipped by the Hottentots; **Hottentot's head**, *Stangeria paradoxa*, a cycad with a thick trunk like a turnip; †**Hottentot pie**, a kind of meat pie (see Mrs. Raffald *Eng. Housekpr.* (1778) 154); **Hottentot rice**: see quot.; **Hottentot('s) tea**, *Helichrysum serpyllifolium*.

1801 J. BARROW *Acct. Trav. S. Afr.* I. 189 Not so with the *Hottentot bean... This plant is the African *Lignum vitae*. **1833** S. KAY *Trav. Caffraria* 106 The Hottentot's bean tree. **1921** T. R. SIM *Native Timbers S. Afr.* 192 Hottentots Bean Tree. *Schotia*, sps. **1965** F. VON BREITENBACH *Indigenous Trees S. Afr.* II. 327 *Schotia afra*... Hottentot's Bean... The roasted beans are eaten by some tribes. **1731** MEDLEY *Kolben's Cape G. Hope* II. 223 The root of the Arum..is ordinarily call'd *Hottentot-Bread. They boil out its acrimony in two or three fresh waters, and then dry it in the sun. **1858** HOGG *Veg. Kingd.* 718 The root-stock of *Testudinaria elephantipes*, called Elephant's Foot or Hottentot's Bread, forms a large, fleshy mass covered with a rough and cracked bark. **1818** TODD cites *Chambers* for *Hottentot Cherry. **1880** *S. Africa* (ed. 3), Hottentot Cherry is the fruit of *Maurocenia Capensis*..a shrub growing in the ravines of Table Mountain. **1731** MEDLEY *Kolben's Cape G. Hope* I. 141 Some women go into the field to gather the stalks of what they call *Hottentot-figs. **1882** *Garden* 4 Feb. 75/3 The Hottentot Fig..sometimes used as a substitute for Spinach. **1785** G. FORSTER tr. *Sparrman's Voy. Cape G. Hope* I. 211 A genus of insects (the *mantis*) called by the colonists the **Hottentot's god*. **1957** W. TAPSON *Old Timer* i. 10 Flyingants and glowworms and dragonflies and hottentot-gods. **1961** L. VAN DER POST *Heart of Hunter* xii. 161 When they noticed the reverence in which the Mantis was held by some of the aborigines of the Cape, they inaccurately called him the Hottentot's God. **1962** *Cape Times Week-end Mag.* 10/1, I like Hottentot Gods, bloodthirsty little savages as they may be. **1884** MILLER *Plant-n.*, *Hottentot's-head, *Stangeria paradoxa*. **1775** MASSON in *Phil. Trans.* LXVI. 315 They also eat the eggs of a large species of ant. They are commonly called *Hottentot's rice. **1850** L. PAPPE *Florae Capensis Medicae Prodromus* 17 *Helichrysum serpyllifolium*..goes by the name of **Hottentot's tea*,..and is much liked by the coloured people, who infuse it as tea. **1972** *Stand. Encycl. S. Afr.* V. 611/1 Hottentot tea... *Helichrysum orbiculare* = *H. serpyllifolium*... Another species, which is also called Hottentot-tea, is *H. nudifolium*.

Hence '**Hottentot** *v. intr.*, to become, or live as, a Hottentot; **Hottento'tese**, the speech of the Hottentots; **Hotten'totic**, '**Hottentotish** *adjs.*, of, pertaining, or relating to Hottentots, or to races in a similar condition; after the manner of a Hottentot. '**Hottentotism**, a practice characteristic of Hottentots, a species of stammering.

1787 MAR. EDGEWORTH *Leonora* (1833) 172 It is lost labour to civilize him, for sooner or later he will *hottentot again. **1873** F. HALL *Mod. Eng.* 39 They might as well address Roger in *Hottentotese or Kamschadalian. **1884** I. TAYLOR in *Academy* 26 Jan. 63/1 [A method of explaining myths, which] may be provisionally designated as the *Hottentotic heresy. *Ibid.* 16 Feb. 115/3 Interpreted by the Hottentotic process. **1795** in Polwhele *Trad. & Recoll.* (1826) II. 427 The survey of a *Hottentottish pilchard cellar. **1817** COLERIDGE *Own Times* (1850) III. 957 Some Hottentots were converted from *Hottentotism through the pious labours of the Missionary Society. **1871** TYLOR *Prim. Culture* I. v. 156 The term Hottentotism has been thence adopted as a medical description of one of the varieties of stammering.

hotter ('hɒtə(r)), *v. Sc.* and *north. dial.* Also **hatter, hutter.** [Has an iterative ending as in *batter*, *totter*, *stagger*; perh. related to MDu. *hotten*, in Flemish also *hotteren* to shake up; also *hotten* to cluster or run together, to coagulate, as milk.]

1. *intr.* To move up and down with vibration; to clatter; to shake, tremble, as water in boiling, or a person in rage, fear, etc.

1813 W. BEATTIE *Tales* 5 (Jam.) Twa pots..Forby ane hott'rin' in the crook. **1854** DICKENS *Hard T.* I. xi, Haply, but for her, I should ha' gone hottering mad. **1857** J. SCHOLES *Jaunt to see Queen* 28 (Lanc. Gloss.) Hoo wur fayr hotterin' wi' vexashun.

2. To move along with vertical vibration as over a rough surface; to run totteringly.

1796 W. MARSHALL *Yorksh.* (ed. 2) Gloss. (E.D.S.), *Hotter*, to shake; as a carriage on a rough stoney road. **1804** TARRAS *Poems* 73 (Jam.) Tho' age now gars me hotter. **1805** J. NICOL *Poems* II. 102 (Jam.) 'Twas a muir-hen, an' monie a pout Was rinnin, hotterin round about. **1880** GORDON *Bk. Chron. Keith* 148 The primitive mill hottered away at the rate of six bolls of meal ground in a week.

3. a. To make a clattering noise; to rattle. **b.** To speak unsteadily or stammeringly.

a **1823** *Baronne o' Gairtly* vii. in A. Laing *Thistle Scotl.* 13 Athwart the lyft the thun'er rair'd, Wi' awfu' hottrin din. **1828** *Craven Dial.*, *Hutter*, to speak confusedly.

4. To cluster in a confused mass, to swarm.

1808–18 JAMIESON, To *hotter*, to crowd together, expressive of individual motion. **1891** MRS. WALFORD *Mischief of Monica* xxxii, If we had been..huttering over the fire in that wretched little Albion Street on this Christmas Eve!

hotter, *sb. Sc.* and *north. dial.* Also **hatter.** [f. prec. vb.] **a.** Vibratory or shaky motion as over a rough road; vertical shaking. **b.** The confused motion of a crowd or swarm of small things. **c.** A large number of things crowded irregularly together; a clustered mass or heap.

1825–80 in JAMIESON. **1836** J. STRUTHERS *Dychmont* II. 448 Ah me! a perfect hotter. **1871** W. ALEXANDER *Johnny Gibb* xliii. (1873) 241 I've stan't mony a roch hotter afore noo i' the wye o' duty, as ye ken brawly, Meg.

Hence '**hottery** *a.*, uneven so as to cause vibration.

1796 W. MARSHALL *Yorksh.* (ed. 2) Gloss. (E.D.S.), *Hottery*, rough, as a road. **1876** *Whitby Gloss.* s.v., 'A hottery journey', said of a course over uneven tracks.

hottie, hotty ('hɒtɪ), *sb. colloq.* [f. HOT *a.* + -Y[6].] A hot-water bottle.

1947 H. WALSH *Fourth Point of Star* xx. 102, I am going to..rub my feet with meth., then get into bed with a hotty. **1956** D. M. DAVIN *Sullen Bell* vi. 40 Get a hotty for yourself. **1960** V. ANDERSON *Daughters of Divinity* vi. 51 And show her where to fill her hotty? **1967** R. HARRIS *All my Enemies* xiii. 117 You look rotten, Jenny. At least have a hottie to clutch.

†**hottie-tottie.** *Obs.* Variant of HODDY-DODDY.

c **1580** J. JEFFERE *Bugbears* III. ii. in *Archiv Stud. Neu. Spr.* (1897), Though the hottie-tottie be old, yet he wooeth a yoong wyfe.

hottish ('hɒtɪʃ), *a.* [f. HOT *a.* + -ISH.] Somewhat hot, rather hot.

1593 Q. ELIZ. tr. *Boeth.* III. met. x. 65 Or Indian dwelling nire to hottische Circle. **1870** H. SMART *Race for Wife* iii, It will be a hottish Monday for some of them.

hot water.

1. a. Water at a high temperature, either naturally as in a hot spring, or artificially heated for cookery, washing or other purposes.

c **1400** *Lanfranc's Cirurg.* 42 Hoot watir, þouȝ it aswage akþe, to þe prickynge of a senewe is most greuaunce. *c* **1430** *Two Cookery-bks.* 24 Sethe hem in hot water. **1613** PURCHAS *Pilgrimage* (1614) 524 A certaine herb called Chia, of which they..drinke with hot water. **1858** LARDNER *Hand-bk. Nat. Phil., Hydrost.* etc. 277 If cold water be poured into a vessel ..and hot water be carefully poured over it,.the hot water will float on the cold.

attrib. **1825** J. NICHOLSON *Operat. Mechanic* 171 The hot-water cistern. **1855** MRS. GASKELL *Lizzie Leigh* 163 Pack up for each his portion of the dainty dish, and send it separately, in hot-water trays. **1872** *Young Englishwoman* Nov. 610/2 Cover for a hot-water tin. **1877** E. S. DALLAS *Kettner's Bk. of Table* 332 Hot-water paste for raised pies. **1895** KIPLING *Day's Work* (1898) 373 He turned to explore the hot-water dishes on the sideboard. **1904** GOODCHILD & TWENEY *Technol. & Sci. Dict.* 291/1 *Hot water system*, a method of warming effected by means of hot water or steam circulating in a system of closed pipes. **1921** *Daily Colonist* (Victoria, B.C.) 24 Mar. 3/1 Attractive modern home, hot water heating, lot 90 × 180, three bedrooms, [etc.] **1926** W. DE LA MARE *Connoisseur* 48 In spite of the hot-water-fountain on the counter it was..cooler in here. **1926** S. T. WARNER *Lolly Willowes* I. 46 The maid..laid the folded towel across the hot-water can. **1932** *Edinburgh Bk. Plain Cookery Recipes* 149 Hot-Water Crust. Used for Savoury Dishes. **1950** *N.Z. Jrnl. Agric.* Dec. 575/1 In almost all houses the hot-water cupboard was used for airing clothes. **1956** G. TAYLOR *Silver* ix. 191 Hot-water jugs were set on classical tripod legs with a spirit lamp between. **1970** SIMON & HOWE *Dict. Gastron.* 290/2 Hot-water crust is a stiff dough moulded to make a filling of meat or game.

b. Special comb.: **hot-water bottle**, a receptacle made of rubber, metal, or other material that may be filled with hot water and used for warming a bed, or for applying local heat to the body; **hot-water pipe** usu. *pl.*, the pipe(s) in a water-heating system.

1895 *Montgomery Ward Catal.* 107/1 Challenge *Hot Water Bottles, pure rubber. **1897** ALLBUTT *Syst. Med.* III. 331 A hot-water bottle..placed at his feet. **1900** J. VAIZEY *About Peggy Saville* xxv. 229 I'd have a fire and an india-rubber hot-water bottle, and I'd lie and sleep. **1926–7** *Army & Navy Stores Catal.* 151/1 Aluminium hot water bottles. Round 9 in. **1932** D. C. MINTER *Mod. Needlecraft* 248/1 Hot-water bottle cover..cut to fit. **1946** G. MIKES *How to be an Alien* 25 Continental people have sex life; the English have hot-water bottles. **1972** S. HYNES *Edwardian Occasions* 169 The narrative is slacker and more trivial, begins to take note of the hot-water bottle and the nine o'clock news. **1842** *Trans. Hort. Soc.* II. 435 All the experience obtained at the Garden goes to demonstrate the great inferiority of flues to *hot water pipes as a mode of heating. **1852** DICKENS *Bleak Ho.* (1853) xxviii. 274 The hot-water pipes that trail themselves all over the house..fail to supply the fires' deficiencies. **1912** BEERBOHM *Christmas Garland* 26 The faint yet heavy fragrance exhaled from the hot-water pipes. **1973** G. BUTLER *Coffin for Pandora* v. 106 The luxurious ways of Sarsen House kept all the rooms warm with hot-water pipes.

†**2.** ***hot waters***: ardent spirits, spirituous liquors.

1643 *Let.* 28 Oct. in Clarendon *Hist. Reb.* VII. §351 Selling hot Waters. **1660–86** *Ord. Chas. II*, in *Househ. Ord.* (1790) 352 Tents, boothes..employed for tipling-houses; selling or takeing tobacco, hott waters [etc.].

3. *fig.* (from 1.) A state of ferment, trouble, or great discomfort; a 'scrape'. *colloq.*

1537 *Lisle Papers* XI. 100 (P.R.O.) If they be to be had, I will have of them, or it shall cost me hot water. **1765** in *Priv. Lett. Ld. Malmesbury* (1870) I. 125 We are kept, to use the modern phrase, in hot water. **1840** R. H. DANA *Bef. Mast* xiii. 32 This poor fellow was always getting into hot water. **1857** KINGSLEY *Two Y. Ago* i, In everlasting hot water, as the most incorrigible scapegrace for ten miles round.

hot well, hot-well.

1. A spring of naturally hot water, a hot spring.

c **1400** MAUNDEV. (Roxb.) xiv. 64 þe cite of Phenice, whare er hate welles and hate bathez. **1752** CANTON in *Phil. Trans.* LVII. 203 The hot-well near Bristol, the water of which raised the thermometer to 76°. **1793** J. NOTT (*title*) A treatise on the Hot-Well Waters, near Bristol.

2. A reservoir in a condensing steam-engine, into which the heated water passes from the condenser, and from which it is drawn to supply the boiler.

1766 *Specif. Barber's Patent* No. 865. 3 The water hastens through the sinking clack into the trunk or hot well. **1827** FAREY *Steam Eng.* 354 The hot well..is part of the condensing cistern..for the reception of the hot water which is discharged by the air-pump.

hot-work, *v.* [f. HOT *a.* 12 d + WORK *v.* 12 e.] *trans.* To work (metal), e.g. by rolling, forging, etc., while it is hot and above the temperature at which recrystallization takes place. Usually in vbl. sb. **hot working.**

1896 H. H. CAMPBELL *Manuf. Structural Steel* xiv. 192 (*heading*) Influence of hot working on steel. **1916** D. K. BULLENS *Steel & its Heat Treatment* ii. 38 Steel which has been hot-worked down to the Ar1 point will show a finer grain. **1932** E. GREGORY *Metall.* ii. 59 The modification of structure which is brought about by hot-working is of greater importance. **1967** A. H. COTTRELL *Introd. Metall.* xviii. 313 This is one of the reasons for hot working such metals. *Ibid.* xxi. 405 This is the basis of industrial hot working processes in which metal ingots or billets are given massive deformations by comparatively small applied stresses.

Also **hot work** *sb.*, hot working.

1905 J. W. MELLOR *Crystall. Iron & Steel* 77 Hot work has no direct action upon the structure of the steel. **1928** H. M. BOYLSTON *Introd. Metall. Iron & Steel* xiii. 369 All mechanical treatment may be divided into two classes, namely, hot work and cold work. **1961** J. N. ANDERSON *Appl. Dental Materials* (ed. 2) v. 44 Hot work, on the other hand, involves simultaneous deformation and recrystallization.

hotys, obs. form of OATS.

hou: see HOUVE, HOW, HOWE.

houbara (hʊ'bɑːrə). Also **hobara, hubara, oubara, ubara.** [mod.L. (C. L. J. L. Bonaparte *Saggio d'una Distribuzione Metodica degli Animali Vertebrati* (1832) 84), f. Arab. *hubārī* bustard.] A bustard, *Chlamydotis undulata*, found in North Africa and Asia as far east as India and Persia, and formerly included in a genus *Houbara*.

1827 J. MALCOLM *Sk. Persia* I. 56 The beautiful speckled Hubara, with his head erect and wings out-spread. **1836** *Penny Cycl.* VI. 59/2 Arabs are accustomed to compare the eyes of their most beautiful women to those of the *Oubara*. **1876** *Encycl. Brit.* IV. 579/1 Two species, known indifferently by the name of Houbara (derived from the Arabic), frequent the more southern portions of the [Palæarctic] Region. **1883** *List Animals* (Zool. Soc.) (ed. 8) 517 *Houbara Bustard.* **1905** J. I. S. WHITAKER *Birds Tunisia* II. 285 North of the Mediterranean the Houbara is of merely accidental occurrence, but it inhabits North-east Africa. **1925** *Blackw. Mag.* Mar. 339/1 The hobara, or lesser bustard. **1963** *Times* 24 May 13/7 The great Houbara bustard yielded, as evidence of its continued presence..only a single stray feather in one area and a couple of sucked eggs.

houce, obs. f. HOUSE *sb.*[2]

houch, Sc. f. HOUGH.

houche, obs. f. HUTCH.

houchin ('haʊtʃɪn). *local.* An owl: cf. HOBHOUCHIN.

1744–50 W. ELLIS *Mod. Husbandm.* V. II. 101 In our Church steeple..a Nest of Houchin's Eggs, to the Number of two large whitish ones, has been found.

houck, var. *houk, howk,* HOLK *v.*, to dig.

1681 in *Archæol. Æliana* XIX. 211 He was houcking for coales.

houd, rare obs. f. HOOD.

houdah: see HOWDAH.

Houdan ('huːdən). Name of a town in the department of Seine-et-Oise, France, used to designate a breed of domestic fowl characterized by black and white plumage, a heavy crest, five toes on each foot, and by its prolific laying.

1871 W. M. LEWIS *People's Pract. Poultry Bk.* 23 The Brahma, Cochin, Leghorn, Poland, and Houdan stand relatively in the position here named [as egg-layers]. **1873** C. M. YONGE *Pillars of House* I. ii. 28, I am hardly prepared to say whether it is a Hamburg or a Houdan, or a more unambitious Dorking. **1883** [see CRÈVECŒUR]. **1902** *Encycl. Brit.* XXXI. 876/2 A race originated in France by crossing Houdans with Dorkings and Light Brahmas, and known as the Faverolles. **1925** *Glasgow Herald* 16 Jan. 6 During the war I had a houdan who ruled my hen run. **1960** *British Poultry Standards* (ed. 2) 72 Introduced into England in 1850, the Houdan is one of the oldest French breeds.

houdge, obs. f. HUGE.

Houdini (huː'diːnɪ). The professional name (Harry *Houdini*) of an American escapologist, Erich Weiss (1874–1926), used to denote an ingenious escape, or a person who embodies the characteristics of Houdini. Also *attrib.* Hence (occas.) as *v. intr.*, to escape.

1923 *N.Y. Times* 9 Sept. VII. 2/1 *Houdini*, to get out of something, to escape. **1923** J. E. BAXTER *Locker Room Ballads* 20 With a dozen balls in play at once And each of them doing Houdini stunts. **1930** J. FAIT *Big House* 120 Don't do no Houdini, or we'll lay you out. **1946** MEZZROW & WOLFE *Really Blues* 373/1 *Do a Houdini*, disappear. **1958** [see ESCAPOLOGIST]. **1962** L. DEIGHTON *Ipcress File* xxv. 164 There was no chance of a 'Houdini' through the boltwork. **1967** L. J. BROWN *Cat who ate Danish Modern* xiii. 117, I have to buckle the harness good and tight or he'll wiggle free... That cat's a Houdini. **1971** *Guardian* 24 Aug. 7/4 Houdini act saved injured climber in air crash.

houdle: see HUDDLE.

houe, obs. f. HOE, HOVE, var. HOW *sb.*[2]

houene, obs. f. HEAVEN, OVEN.

houff: see HOVE, HOWFF.

hougat(e: see HOWGATE.

houge, -ly, obs. ff. HUGE, HUGELY.

hough (hɒk), *sb.* Forms: 4–5 **hoȝ, houȝ,** 5 **howh, howgh, how,** 5–7 **hogh,** 6–7 **houghe,** 5– **hough;** see also HOCK *sb.*[2]; *Sc.* 5–6 **hoch, houch,** 6– **howch;** *pl.* 6 **howis,** 6– **howes:** see also HOUX. [Known from 14th c. as *hoȝ, houȝ*. In Scotland still pronounced (hɔx); pl. also (hɔʊz); in some parts of England the local pronunciation appears to be (hɒf, hʌf, haʊ, or hɔʊ). The now usual (hɒk) appears to be an anglicizing of *hoch* (hox): cf. *loch, lough, shough.* Its general prevalence appears to have given origin to the parallel spelling *hock*: see HOCK *sb.*[2] Evidently identical with OE. *hóh*, HO *sb.*[1], 'heel'; as to difficulties of sense and phonology, see Note below.]

1. The joint in the hind leg of a quadruped between the tibia and the metatarsus or cannon-bone, the angle of which points backward; the hock.

(This joint, though elevated high in the leg of ruminants and perissodactyls, is homogenetic with the human heel and ankle, the cannon-bone being the homogen of the bones of the instep in man.)

13.. *Gaw. & Gr. Knt.* 1357 Þay..henged þenne a[y]þer bi hoȝ es of þe fourchez. **1450–70** *Golagros & Gaw.* 674 Thair hors vith thair hochis sic harmis couth hint. **1486** *Bk. St. Albans* E viij a, She [the hare] hurcles vppon hir houghis ay. **1587** MASCALL *Govt. Cattle* (1600) 228 Put a small cord about the houghs of both the lambs feete. **1596** DALRYMPLE tr. *Leslie's Hist. Scot.* I. 99 The horses in lyke maner thay vse to bow thair hochis and to pase throuch mony partes. *a* **1605** POLWART *Flyting w. Montgomerie* 704 Thou puts the spauen in the forder spauld, That vses in the hinder hogh to bee. **1607** TOPSELL *Four-f. Beasts* (1658) 309 Griefs in the shoulders, legs, hips, houghes, joynts and hoofs, causing the Horse most commonly to halt. **1611** BIBLE *2 Esdras* xv. 36 Doung of men vnto the camels hough. **1646** SIR T. BROWNE *Pseud. Ep.* III. i. 106 The hough or suffraginous flexure behinde. **1796** W. MARSHALL *Yorksh.* (ed. 2) Gloss. (E.D.S.), *Hoff*, the hough, hock, gambrel, or hind-knee. **1816** SCOTT *Old Mort.* xvii, Wae betide ye!..and cut the houghs of the creature whase fleetness ye trust in! **1822** W. J. NAPIER *Pract. Store-farm.* 139 The quarters long and full with the mutton quite down to the hough.

2. The hollow part behind the knee-joint in man; the adjacent back part of the thigh. Chiefly *Sc.*

1508 DUNBAR *Flyting w. Kennedie* 190 His cair is all to clenge thy cabroch howis. **1513** DOUGLAS *Æneis* IX. xii. 82 Of quham the howchys bath he smate in twa. *a* **1550** *Christis Kirke Gr.* xix, Syn traytourlie behind his back They hewit him on the howiss Behind [*rimes* mowis, powis, bowis]. **1550** LYNDESAY *Sqr. Meldrum* 1347 And hackit on his hochis and theis. **1609** HOLLAND *Amm. Marcell.* XXVI. xi. 298 The hindmost resting upon their houghes or hammes, made a shew of an arched building. **1681** COLVIL *Whigs Supplic.* (1751) 52 After a pause and a cough, And sundry clawings of his hough. **1818** SCOTT *Hrt. Midl.* x, That ony ane.. should ever daur to crook a hough. **1822** —— *Nigel* v, Clap your mule between your houghs and god-den with you.

3. A joint of beef, venison, etc., consisting of the part extending from the hough (sense 1) some distance up the leg: also technically called 'leg' of beef; it corresponds to the knuckle of veal, the knuckle-end or hock-end of a gammon of bacon, and the shank-end of a leg of mutton; cf. HOCK *sb.*[2] 2.

c **1430** *Two Cookery-bks.* 25 Howhys of Vele. *Ibid.* 37 An howe of vele. *Ibid.* 51 Hoghes of Venyson. **1611** COTGR., *Trumeau de boeuf*, a knuckle, hough, or leg, of Beefe. **1826** SCOTT *Woodst.* xviii, When hough's in the pot, they will have share on't.

†**4.** ***hough and ham***: ? with thin and thick ends laid side by side alternately. *Obs.*

1776 G. SEMPLE *Building in Water* 55 The thorough Foundation..is laid over with large Stones, Hough and Ham, and some pitched upon their Ends.

5. *Comb.*, as ***hough-bone, -string***; †**hough-bony** (see BUNNY[1]). Also HOUGH-BAND, -SINEW.

1470–85 MALORY *Arthur* XII. iii, The bore rafe hym [Sir Lancelot] on the brawne of the thyȝ vp to the *houghbone [*ed.* 1529 huckle bone]. **1607** TOPSELL *Four-f. Beasts* (1658) 317 Therefore I thought good to call it the *hough-bony. This sorance cometh of some stripe or bruise. **1688** R. HOLME *Armoury* II. 152/2 The Hough boony is a swelling upon the tip or elbow of the Hough. **1609** HOLLAND *Amm. Marcell.* 129 (R.) Many men for old age feeble..had the calves of their legges or *hough-strings cut, and so were left behind.

Note. OE. *hóh* (HO *sb.*[1]) has been noted only in the sense '(human) heel', which does not at all correspond to 2 above. But the OE. compound *hóhsinu*, HOUGH-SINEW, used of horses, implies that *hóh* was also the hough or hock of a horse, as in sense 1 above. From the latter, 2 may have been transferred after the OE. sense 'heel' was obsolete and forgotten; the hough of a horse being in position analogous to the knee of man, and often popularly called the 'hind-knee'. As to the phonology, OE. *hóh* would regularly give Sc. *heuch*, HEUGH (hyx), as in *eneuch, teuch, pleuch*, etc., while Sc. *hoch, howch* (hɔx) goes back to a form with short *o*, as in *cough, trough, thocht*, etc. The words can then be identical only if the *ó* in OE. *hóh* was shortened early enough to give

howch, and not *heuch*, in Sc. The only apparent solution of this is that, as the compound *hóhsinu* (HOUGH-SINEW) was evidently shortened to *hohsin, hoxen, hockshin, huckson, huxen* (*ó* before the consonant-group becoming *o*), this reacted in some way upon the simple word, so as to give early ME. *hoh, hoȝ, hogh*, with short *o*, whence in later times Sc. *hoch*, Eng. *hock*. Perhaps the compound, with its derived verb, was in more general use than the simple word.

hough (hɒk), *v.*[1] Forms: see prec. [f. prec. sb.: cf. also HOCK *v.*[1], HOX *v.*] *trans.* To disable by cutting the sinew or tendons of the hough (see HOUGH-SINEW); to hamstring.

c **1440** *Promp. Parv.* 251/2 Howhyn (*K.* howghyn, *H.* howwhyn), *subnervo.* **1548** W. PATTEN *Exped. Scotl.* in Arb. *Garner* III. 123 Some [corpses] with their legs off; some but hought and left lying half dead. **1551** BIBLE *Josh.* xi. 6 (R.) Thou shalt hough theyr horses, and burne their charettes with fyre. **1580** *Acts Privy Council* in *Life of Melville* I. 437 (Jam.) He sould hoch and slay him. **1592** NASHE *P. Penilesse* (1842) 25 They account of no man that hath not a battle axe at his girdle to hough dogs with. **1607** HEYWOOD *Wom. Kilde with Kindn.* Wks. 1874 II. 113 Hath he not hamstrings That thou must hogh? **1681** COLVIL *Whigs Supplic.* (1751) 18 Some sythes had, men and horse to hough. **1851** HT. MARTINEAU *Hist. Peace* IV. ix. (1877) III. 28 His cattle were houghed in the night.

Hence **houghing** *vbl. sb.*

1581 *Sc. Acts Jas. VI* (1597) §110 *heading*, Against the schamefull oppression of slaying and houching of Oxon. **1611** COTGR., *Iarretade*, a houghing, a slash ouer the hammes. **1878** LECKY *Eng. in 18th C.* II. 393 We have seen how the houghing in 1711 and 1712 was attributed by many to a Jacobite source.

†**hough**, *v.*[2] *Obs.* [Echoic.] *intr.* To clear the throat.

1600 W. VAUGHAN *Direct. Health* (1633) 81 (misp. 79) After long houghing, halking, and hacking, hauing their throats well washed with dreggish drugs. **1670–1710** GREW (J), Neither could we hough or spit from us; much less could we sneeze or cough. **1755** JOHNSON, *To hough*, to hawk. (This orthography is uncommon.)

†**hough**, *int.* obs. spelling of HO *int.*[1]

a **1553** UDALL *Royster D.* I. ii. (Arb.) 13 Hough, Mathew Merygreeke, my friend, a worde with thee. **1598** B. JONSON *Ev. Man in Hum.* I. iv, I think this bee the house: what, hough!

hough: see HOE *sb.*[2] and *v.*[1], HOW, HOWE.

hough-band, *sb.* In Sc. also **hoch-ban'**. 'A band which confines one of the legs of a restless animal; it passes round the neck and one of the legs' (*Gallovid. Encycl.* 1824).

1568 *Satir. Poems Reform.* xlvi. 12 Gar heiss hir quhill hir howbandis skaill. **1686** G. STUART *Joco-ser. Disc.* 14 Nae hough-bands now for Godly helping.

Hence **hough-band** *v.*, *trans.* 'to tie a band round the hough of a cow, or horse, to prevent it from straying' (Jam.); *fig.* to confine, put restraint upon, coerce.

1687–8 D. GRANVILLE *Let. to Mr. Lumley* 19 Mar. in *Misc.* (Surtees 1858) 228 Nor will I hough-band, or so much as hamper or fetter my Soveraign, God's deputy.

houghel. *north. dial.* Also **hoffle.** (See quots.)

c **1570** *Durham Depos.* (Surtees) 264 He cut 4 kidgells or houghells to hange salmon netts upon. **1893** *Northumbld. Gloss.*, *Hoffle*, a stake on which salmon nets are dried. In a row of hoffle stakes one is higher than the others, and is called the bosom-hoffle.

hougher ('hɒkə(r)). [f. HOUGH *v.*[1] + -ER[1].]

1. One who houghs or hamstrings; in Ireland, a member of an association of law-breakers who arose in 1711, and practised the houghing of cattle; afterwards identified with the Whiteboys.

1581 *Sc. Acts Jas. VI* (1597) §110 *heading*, Sik slayeris and houcheris of Horses and Oxen. **1712** SWIFT *Jrnl. to Stella* 26 Mar., Your houghers of cattle. **1842** S. C. HALL *Ireland* II. 119 In the course of twenty years the Rapparees were succeeded by the Houghers. **1878** LECKY *Eng. in 18th C.* II. 354 Large rewards were offered for the apprehension of houghers.

2. In Newcastle-upon-Tyne, the name of an inferior officer appointed by the Corporation, called also ***Whipper and Hougher***.

1789 BRAND *Hist. Newcastle* II. 365 He is called hougher from the power that he is said to have had formerly of cutting the sinews of the houghs of swine that were found infesting the streets. **1827** BROCKETT s.v., The hougher is the public whipper of criminals, the executioner of felons, in Newcastle—still a regular officer of the town, with a yearly salary of £4 6*s.* 8*d.*

hough goe, obs. form of HOGO.

houghite ('hʌfaɪt). *Min.* [Named in 1851 after F. B. HOUGH.] A variety of hydrotalcite, derived from an alteration of spinel.

1851 *Amer. Jrnl. Sc.* Ser. II. XII. 210 Some of his specimens are spinel crystals..in one part, and true Houghite in another. **1868** DANA *Min.* (ed. 5) 179 Houghite ..occurs in flattened nodules.

houghmagandy (hɒxmə'gændɪ). Chiefly *Sc.* (now *rare*). Also **hochmagandy, houghmagandie.** [Fanciful formation, perh. f. HOUGH *sb.* + CANTY *a.*] Fornication.

a **1700** J. MAIDMENT *New Bk. Old Ballads* (1885) 11 And well I wot he kens the gate To play at hough-magandy. **1785** BURNS *Holy Fair* in *Poems & Songs* (1968) I. 137 An' monie jobs that day begin, May end in *Houghmagandie*. **1805** R. TANNAHILL *Poems* (1876) 44 The priest convenes his scandal court, Tae ken what houghmagandie sport Has been gaun on within the parish. **1962** V. NABOKOV *Pale Fire* 212 She would have preferred him to have gone through a bit of wholesome houghmagandy with the wench.

†**hough-sinew**, *sb. Obs.* [OE. *hóhsinu*, f. *hóh* (see HOUGH *sb.*) + *sinu* SINEW.

OE. *hóhsinu* corresponds in formation to OFris. *hôxene, hoxne*, ON. *hásin*, OHG. **hâhsina, hâhsna*, MDu. *haessene*, Du. *haassen*, later *haasse, haas*, in same sense (OTeut. type **haŋha-sinu*). The analytical meaning in OE. is 'heel sinew', but the quots. show it applied to the hamstrings of horses. The original long *ō* was shortened before the consonant group, so that it gave the later *hoxen* (HOX), HOCKSHIN, *huckson*, HUXEN. The uncontracted form in late ME. and Sc. may be a new formation from the elements.]

The sinew of the hough or hock; applied, in man, to the popliteal tendons, or hamstrings, at the back of the knee; in a quadruped, to the tendon of Achilles.

c **1000** ÆLFRIC *Josh.* xi. 6 Þu soþlice forcirfst heora horsa hohsina. *Ibid.* 9 He forcearf þa hohsina ealra þæra horsa. *c* **1000** *Sax. Leechd.* II. 146 Gif hoh sino forad sie. *a* **1430** *Wyclif's Bible* 1 Chron. xviii. 4 (MS. Corpus Coll., Camb.) He oxide, *that is*, he kitte asonder the houȝ senues of alle the horsis. *c* **1470** HENRY *Wallace* I. 322 His houch [*ed.* **1570** hoch] senons thai cuttyt in that press: On kneis he faucht. **1513** DOUGLAS *Æneis* x. xii. 29 Palmus hough sennonis [he] smayt in tuay.

†**hough-sinew**, *v. Obs.* [f. prec.: cf. OHG. *hâhsinôn* to hamstring, f. **hâhsina, hâhsna* (see prec.), also HOXEN *v.*] *trans.* To hough, to hamstring.

1577–87 HOLINSHED *Chron.* III. 1033/2 The rebelles.. when they were thrust through the bodies or thighs, and some of them hough-sinewed, would yet seeke revenge in striking at their adversaries. **1590** COKAINE *Treat. Hunting* D j b, Your Huntsmen must be carefull to..houghsnew him with their swords. **1609** BIBLE (Douay) *Josh.* xi. 6 Their horses thou shalt hoghsinew.

hougie, -y, var. of HUGY *Obs.*, huge.

hougly, obs. f. UGLY.

houhere ('haʊhɪəriː). *N.Z.* [Maori, f. *hou* to bind together + *here* tie.] A small tree of the native genus *Hoheria*, esp. *H. populnea*; also called lacebark or ribbonwood.

1879 J. HECTOR *Handbk. N.Z.* 93 Houhere, ribbon-wood of Dunedin. **1906** T. F. CHEESEMAN *Man. N.Z. Flora* 79 The Maoris apply the names *hoihere* or *houhere* to varieties *a* and *b* indifferently; the European settlers usually call all the forms 'ribbon-wood' or 'lacebark', names which are, unfortunately, also used for *Plagianthus betulinus*. **1946** *Jrnl. Polynesian Soc.* LV. 149 *Houhere*, a tree (*Hoheria populnea*), ribbonwood, lace-bark, thousand-jacket. One of the three or four deciduous Maori trees. **1968** *Landfall* XXII. 255 White edge of the sea White as the flower Of lace-bark, Te houhere, White edge of the sea Eating the land.

houhful, var. HOWFUL *Obs.*, careful, anxious.

houir, obs. Sc. form of HOVER.

houk, obs. f. HOOK, dial. f. HOLK *v.*

houka, var. of HOOKAH.

houkel, obs. f. HUCKLE.

houkester, obs. f. HUCKSTER.

hould, obs. f. HOLD.

houldbeard, obs. f. HALBERD.

houle, obs. f. HOLE *sb.*, HOWL, OWL.

houlet, obs. f. HOWLET.

houlour, var. of HOLOUR *Obs.*

houlse, rare obs. f. HAWSE *sb.*

hoult, var. HOLT.

hounce (haʊns). *East dial.* [Origin obscure.

(It has been conjectured to be a nasalized form of Fr. *housse* (see HOUSE *sb.*[2], but this does not give the sense.)]

An ornament on the collar of a horse.

1565 GOLDING *Ovid's Met.* II. 16 b, The chrysolites and gemmes That stood upon the collars, trace, and hounces in their hemmes. **1674–91** RAY *S. & E.C. Words* (E.D.S.), *Hounces*, that part of the furniture of a cart-horse, which lies spread upon his collar. *Ess. a* **1825** FORBY *Voc. E. Anglia*, *Hounce*, the ornament of red and yellow worsted spread over the collars of horses in a team. **1840** SPURDENS *Suppl. Forby* (E.D.S.), *Houncings*, housings; *phaleræ*.

hound (haʊnd), *sb.*[1] Forms: 1–6 **hund**, (3–5 **hond**, 4–6 **hunde, hounde**, 5–7 **hownd, -e**; 5 **howne**, 6 **hown**, 7 **huin**), 3– **hound.** [Com. Teut.: OE. *hund* = OFris. *hund, hond*, OS. *hund* (LG. *hund*, MDu. *hont* (*d-*), Du. *hond*), OHG. *hunt* (*d-*), (MHG. *hunt*, G. *hund*), ON. *hundr* (Sw., Da. *hund*), Goth. *hunds*:—OTeut. **hundo-z*, generally held to be a derivative of base **hun-*, pre-Teut. **kun-*, in Gr. *κύων, κυν-*, Skr. *çwan-, çun-*, Lith. *szū, szun-*, OIr. *cu* dog; cf. also L. *can-is*.

For the *d* (*dh*) of Teut. *hund*, the suggestion has been made of association with the vb. *hinþan* to seize, as if the word were understood to mean 'the seizer'.]

1. A dog, generally. (Now only *arch.* or *poetic.*) ***to wake a sleeping hound***: cf. DOG *sb.*[1] 17 k.

c **897** K. ÆLFRED *Gregory's Past.* xv. 89 Dumbe hundas ne maȝon beorcan. *a* **1225** *Ancr. R.* 60 Hund wule in.. hwar se he ivint hit open. *Ibid.* 324 Monie hundes..habbeð biset me. *c* **1290** *S. Eng. Leg.* I. 99/248 Houndes it scholden ete. *c* **1374** CHAUCER *Troylus* III. 715 (764) It is nought good a slepyng hound to wake, Ne yeue a wyght a cause to deuyne. **1382** WYCLIF *Luke* xvi. 21 Houndis camen, and lickiden his bylis. *c* **1400** MAUNDEV. (Roxb.) xiv. 64 Þai ete cattes and hundes, ratouns and myesse. **1508** DUNBAR *Tua Mariit Wemen* 273, I hatit him like a hund. **1841** LONGF. *Excelsior* viii, A traveller, by the faithful hound, Half-buried in the snow was found.

2. *spec.* A dog kept or used for the chase, usually one hunting by scent. Now esp. applied to a foxhound; also to a harrier; (*the*) ***hounds***, a pack of foxhounds.

to ride to hounds, to follow the hounds, to follow on horseback the hounds in the chase. ***to hold with the hare and run with the hounds***, etc.: see HARE.

c **1200** *Vices & Virtues* 69 Hundes and hauekes, and alle ðo þing ðe ȝeu hier gladien mai. *a* **1300** *Cursor M.* 687 Þe hund ne harmed noght þe hare. *a* **1440** *Sir Degrev.* 233 He uncouplede his houndus. **1526** *Pilgr. Perf.* (W. de W. 1531) 49 A kenel of houndes folowynge theyr game. **1576** FLEMING tr. *Caius' Dogs* in Arb. *Garner* III. 264 Hound signifieth such a dog only as serveth to hunt. **1596** SHAKS. *Tam. Shr.* Induct. i. 61 Another tell him of his Hounds and Horse. *c* **1710** LADY M. W. MONTAGU *Lett. to Mrs. Hewet* (1887) I. 30 Their mornings are spent among hounds. **1724** DE FOE *Mem. Cavalier* (1840) 244, I was as ravenous as a hound. **1758** JOHNSON *Idler* No. 30 ¶5 Another..follows his hounds over hedges and through rivers. **1848** THACKERAY *Bk. Snobs* xvii, They all..ride to hounds. **1877** *Encycl. Brit.* VII. 330/1 The Dalmatian Dog is a remarkably handsome breed, apparently intermediate between hound and pointer. **1881** BLACK *Sunrise* xxi, He would like to have a good looking wife..to go riding to hounds with him.

b. Preceded by defining word. See BLOOD-, BUCK-, DEER-, FOX-, GREY-, STAG-HOUND, etc.

3. *fig.* and *transf.* Often in phrases, as ***the hound of hell***, Cerberus; ***Orion's hound***, the constellation of the Greater Dog, the dog-star; ***winged hound***, an eagle; ***Gabriel's hounds***, see GABRIEL.

c **888** K. ÆLFRED *Boeth.* xxxv. §6 Þa sceolde cuman þære helle hund, þæs nama..wæs Ceruerus. **1579** SPENSER *Sheph. Cal.* Oct. 30 His musicks might the hellish hound did tame. **1587** *Mirr. Mag.*, *Forrex* v, Iarring like two hounds of hell. **1590** SPENSER *F.Q.* I. iii. 31 Scorching flames of fierce Orions hound. **1792** COWPER *Let. to Hayley* 29 July, I am hunted by spiritual hounds in the night-season. **1808** J. BARLOW *Columb.* x. 378 War's hosted hounds shall havoc earth no more. **1821** SHELLEY *Prometh. Unb.* I. i. 34 Heaven's winged hound..tears up My heart. **1866** B. TAYLOR *Poems, The Bath* 49 Press on, ye hounds of life. **1871** H. KING tr. *Ovid's Met.* IV. 534 The Hound of Hell.. reared his triple head, and thrice at once Howled greeting.

4. Transferred, in various senses, to persons.

a. Applied opprobriously or contemptuously to a man: cf. DOG *sb.*[1] 3 a; a detested, mean, or despicable man; a low, greedy, or drunken fellow.

c **1000** *Judith* x. (Thwaites) 23 Ðone hæþenan hund. *c* **1290** *S. Eng. Leg.* I. 11/365 'þou luþere hound', þis oþur seide. *c* **1340** *Cursor M.* 16636 (Trin.) Þei spitten on his louely face þo houndes alle of helle. *c* **1380** *Sir Ferumb.* 2155 Þys ȝonder day at morymond, conquered for soþ was hee, With a þef, a cristene hond, þar many men dide hit see. *c* **1400** *Sowdone Bab.* 164 From this cursed hethen houne. **1607** SHAKS. *Cor.* v. vi. 113 Boy, false Hound: If you haue writ your Annales true, 'tis there, That [etc.]. **1845** BROWNING *Soul's Trag.* I. 297 Miserable hound! This comes of temporising, as I said!

b. *Cambridge slang*: see quot. 1879. **c.** *U.S.* One of an organized gang of ruffians in San Francisco, in 1849; also called 'Regulators'.

1859 J. W. PALMER *New & Old* I. iii. 70 (Funk) Sam Roberts..mustered his 'hounds', parading them in.. Mexican and Chinese costume. **1879** E. WALFORD in *N. & Q.* 5th Ser. XII. 88 In the Anecdotes of Bowyer..we are told that a Hound of King's College..is an undergraduate not on the foundation, nearly the same as a 'sizar'.

d. *transf.* A player who follows the 'scent' laid down by the 'hare' in the sport *hare and hounds* or paper-chase. Cf. HARE 3 b.

1857 HUGHES *Tom Brown* I. vii, The hounds clustered round Thorne, who explained shortly, 'They're to have six minutes' law'. **1883** W. H. RIDEING in *Harper's Mag.* July 178/2 A flushed little 'hare' bounds past us, distributing the paper 'scent' in his course, and followed a quarter of an hour afterward by the panting and baffled 'hounds'.

e. Used with a preceding substantive to designate a person who has a particular enthusiasm for, or interest in, the object or activity specified; esp. in *news-hound* (see NEWS *sb. pl.* 6 c). *colloq.* (orig. *U.S.*).

1926 *Amer. Speech* II. 45 *Comma hound*, applied to teachers of English composition. **1928** L. NORTH *Parasites* 270 Much was made by the Zimski publicity hounds of this one hundred-per-cent Americanism of the little [film] star. **1968** *Word Study* Dec. 2/2 The enthusiast is a *bug* or a *hound*, as in *radio bug* or *hi-fi hound*. Closely related to this use of *hound* is its use as 'one who frequents', as in *tavern hound*. **1973** *Sat. Rev. Soc.* (U.S.) May 65/3 A real fun guy,..a super-duper party hound.

5. Short for HOUNDFISH. Also called SEA-HOUND.

rough and ***smooth hound***, Large and Small Spotted Dogfish; ***nurse hound***, *Scyllium stellaris*; ***white hound***, the Penny or Miller's Dog, *Galeus canis*.

1603 OWEN *Pembrokesh.* (1891) 123 [In list of Fish] Roughe hounds, smothe houndes. **1674** RAY *Collect. Words, Sea Fishes* 98 Rough Hounds; *Mustelus, an lævis primus Salviani?* **1758** *Descr. Thames* 235 There is another Dog-Fish, called the smooth, or unprickly Hound. **1836** YARRELL *Brit. Fishes* (1841) II. 487, 493 and 512. **1861** COUCH *Brit. Fishes* I. 11, 14, 45 and 47.

6. In north-eastern Canada: the old squaw or long-tailed duck, *Clangula hyemalis*.

1623 N. H. in Whitbourne *Newfoundland* 114 The Fowles and Birds..of the Sea are..Teale, Snipes, Penguyns, Murres, Hounds..and others. **1779** G. CARTWRIGHT *Jrnl.* 19 May (1792) II. 440 There were several hounds and gulls, with some pigeons and black-divers among them. **1861** L. DE BOILIEU *Recoll. Labrador Life* 160 The bird called the Hound—a graceful fowl, rather larger than a teal—is very abundant. **1959** W. L. MCATEE *Folk-Names Canad. Birds* (ed. 2) 14 Old Squaw [is also called] hound (the Chorus of sound from a number of these birds suggests the baying of a pack of hounds).

7. *attrib.* and *Comb.* **a.** simple attrib. (mostly in sense 2), as ***hound collar, -dog, hunger, list, music, -pup, show***; objective, ***hound-keeping, -poisoning***; similative, etc., ***hound-hungry, -like, -shaped*** adjs.

1483 *Cath. Angl.* 192/1 An *Hunde colar, *copularius, collarium, millus.* **1649** *Early Rec. Dedham, Mass.* (1892) III. 162 That care can be taken that the young *hound doges be in time taught to hunt. **1911** R. D. SAUNDERS *Col. Todhunter* ii. 24 I'm as hungry as a young hound-dog this very minute. **1949** *Chicago Daily News* 6 July 14/3 He's got about nine houn' dawgs. **1825–80** JAMIESON, **Hund-hunger*, the ravenous appetite of a dog or hound. *Ibid.*, **Hund-hungry*, ravenous as a dog. **1791** WOLCOTT (P. Pindar) *Loyal Odes* VIII. vi, Thus, *hound-like..A common-councilman ..On every seasoned dish so hungry stuffs. **1892** W. BLEW *Pref. to Vyner's Notit. Venat.*, The *hound lists of the more famous packs. **1889** *Daily News* 19 Dec. 3/3 A ringing chorus of *hound music shook the air. **1857** F. L. OLMSTED *Journey Texas* (1861) 52 The child..five miles from a neighbor;..[with] *hound-pups and negroes for playmates. **1878** J. H. BEADLE *Western Wilds* xxviii. 439 What he wouldn't steal, a hound pup wouldn't pull out of a tan-yard. **1932** KIPLING *Limits & Renewals* 293 Though well-meaning as a hound-pup..her face and figure were against her. **1889** *Dogs* iii. 15 The body *hound-shaped, but..much heavier than the foxhound. **1898** *Westm. Gaz.* 8 July 4/1 Twenty-one packs were represented in the annual *hound show at Peterborough.

b. Special comb.: **hound-bitch**, †**-brach**, a bitch-hound; †**hound-fennel, finkle**, a plant, ? = DOG-FENNEL; **hound-grass** (see quot.); **hound-meal**, meal prepared as dog's food; **hound-shark**, *U.S.*, a small species of shark, *Galeus canis*, common on the Atlantic coast of North America; †**hound's head**, applied opprobriously to a person; †**hound's-swain**, a man in charge of hounds; †**hound's thorn**, ? the dog-rose, or some species of bramble; †**hound-stone** (see quot.); **hound-work**, the work done by the hounds in hunting. Also HOUND-FISH, etc.

1677 N. COX *Gentl. Recreat.* I. (ed. 2) 28 A Brach is a mannerly name for all *Hound-bitches. **1688** R. HOLME *Armoury* II. ix. 184/2 The Brache is the Bitch to all hunting dogs..they are so called, not Bitches, but a *Hound Brache. *a* **1387** *Sinon. Barthol.* (Anecd. Oxon.) 19 *Emeroc*..*hounde fenel. **1483** *Cath. Angl.* 192/1 *Hunde fenkylle, *ferula*. **1565–73** COOPER *Thesaurus*, *Canaria*,..*houndgrasse wherwith dogs prouoke vomite. **1892** *Pall Mall G.* 29 Nov. 6/3 The animals get exercise..and good food, dog biscuits and *hound meal alternated. **1633** FORD *Broken H.* II. i, I'll tear thy throat out, Son of a cat, ill-looking *hounds-head. *c* **1420** *Avow. Arth.* v, The hunter and the *howundus-squayn, Hase ȝarket hom ȝare. *c* **1420** *Pallad. Husb.* I. 793 Brembil seed and seed of *houndis thorn. **1585** LUPTON *Thous. Notable Th.* (1675) 28 An Herb called *Hound-stone ..being so tyed to the neck of a Dog, that he cannot get it away; you shall see him turn about so long, that he will fall down. **1928** *Isis* (Oxf.) 14 Nov., Some very pretty *houndwork now ensued. **1932** *Morning Post* 19 Nov. 14/4 (*heading*) Pytchley Houndwork. **1971** *Country Life* 7 Oct. 897/2 The fascination of good hound-work.

hound (haʊnd), *sb.*² [app. a corruption of an earlier **houn*, early ME. *hūn*, a. ON. *húnn* 'knob', esp. 'the knob at the top of the mast-head'. Cf. the synon. *huin*, HUNE from French. (The final *-d* is excrescent, as in *horehound*, *sound*, etc., assisted by assimilation to HOUND *sb.*¹, which conversely was sometimes made *hown, houne*.)

Hound is less likely to be from the French *hune*, since *ou* represents a ME. *ū*, not *ŭ*.]

1. *Naut.* A projection or cheek, of which one or more are fayed to the sides of the masthead to serve as supports for the trestle-trees; see also quot. 1627.

[*c* **1205** LAYAMON 28978 Seil heo droȝen to hune.] **1495** *Naval Acc. Hen. VII* (1896) 190 Shevers of Brasse in the hownde of the foremaste. **1532** *Invent. Gt. Barke* 6 Oct. (MS. Cott. App. xxviii. lf. 1) Item, a nyew mayne mast of spruce with a nyew staye hounsyd and skarvyd with the same wood, whyche mast ys of length from the Hounse to the step 25 yards. **1627** CAPT. SMITH *Seaman's Gram.* iii. 16 At the top of the fore Mast and maine Mast are spliced cheeks, or thicke clamps of wood, thorow which are in each two holes called the Hounds, wherein the Tyes doe runne to hoise the yards, but the top Mast hath but one hole or hound, and one tye. **1749** CHALMERS in *Phil. Trans.* XLVI. 367 The Head of the Mast above the Hounds was not splintered. **1840** R. H. DANA *Bef. Mast* xxxiii. 127 The ice ..in the tops and round the hounds of the lower masts.

2. a. One of the wooden bars, of which there are two or more, connecting the fore-carriage of a springless wagon, the limber of a field-gun, etc., with the splinter-bar or shaft; also occasionally applied to supports of the connexion of the perch with the hind-carriage. *U.S.* and *local Eng.*

1847 *Rep. U.S. Comm. Patents 1846* 264 The placing on the rear ends of the extended hounds..the adjustable sway bar. **1854** BARTLETT *Pers. Narr. Explor. Texas* II. xl. 456 Mr. Flotte's large carriage got mired; and in the struggle to extricate, the tongue and hounds were broken. **1860** BARTLETT *Dict. Amer.*, *Hounds*, the portions of a wagon, which projecting from the forward axle, form a support for the tongue or pole. The term is borrowed from nautical language. **1875** KNIGHT *Dict. Mech.* s.v., In wagons, the hounds of the fore-axle pass forward and on each side of the tongue, to which they are secured by the tongue-bolt. The hounds of the hind-axle unite and are fastened to the coupling-pole by the coupling-pin. **1875** *Sussex Gloss.*, *Hounds*, the part of a wagon to which the fore-wheels and shafts are attached. **1886** ELWORTHY *W. Somerset Word-bk.* s.v. *Wagon*, In front the hounds support and connect the sharp-bar to which the shafts are hinged..the hounds.. bear all the pull or draught.

b. *Comb.* **hound-plate**, a bracing plate for the hounds of a carriage.

hound (haʊnd), *v.* [f. HOUND *sb.*¹]

1. *trans.* To hunt, chase, or pursue with hounds, or as a dog does. Also *absol.*

1528 LYNDESAY *Dreme* 902 Geue the wolffis cumis.. Thame [the flokis] to deuore, than ar thay put to flycht, Houndit, and slane be thare weill dantit doggis. **1617** ASSHETON *Jrnl.* (Chetham Soc.) 17, I hounded and killed a bitch-fox. *a* **1676** GUTHRY *Mem. Affairs Scotl.* (1748) 26 To direct them to hound fair, and encourage them to go on. **1706** PHILLIPS (ed. Kersey), *To Hound a Stag* (among Hunters), to cast the Dogs at him. **1842** CAMPBELL *Pilgrim Glencoe* 65 'Twas Luath [a sheep-dog], hounding to their fold the flock. **1873** *Forest & Stream* 25 Sept. 101/2 Parties ..hounded or killed by jack-light 15 or 18 deer.

2. *fig.* and *transf.* To pursue, chase, or track like a hound, or as if with a hound; esp. to pursue harassingly, to drive as in the chase. Also with *out*, to drive away.

1605 BACON *Adv. Learn.* II. i. §4 It is..by following, and as it were, hounding nature in her wandrings, to bee able to leade her afterwardes to the same place againe. **1672** J. WORTHINGTON *Pref. to Mede's Wks.* 41 As God began to punish it [Sacrilege] very early, even in Paradise itself..so hath he continually pursued and hounded this Sin. *c* **1730** BURT *Lett. N. Scotl.* (1760) II. xxiii. 233 They are hounded (as they phrase it) into the Bounds of an other chief. **1897** FARRAR *St. Paul* I. 516 The watchword would have been given to hound the fugitives from place to place. **1922** JOYCE *Ulysses* 628 Spain decayed when the Inquisition hounded the jews out. **1930** G. B. SHAW *Apple Cart* I. 41 If I attempt to fight them I shall be hounded out of public life. **1945** E. WAUGH *Brideshead Revisited* ii. 50 He daren't show his great purple face anywhere. He is the last, historic, authentic case of someone being hounded out of society.

3. To set (a hound, etc.) *at* a quarry; to incite or urge *on* to attack or chase anything.

1652 EARL MONM. tr. *Bentivoglio's Hist. Relat.* 53 Sometimes she..will Hound her Hawk, and Govern the Chase. **1656** BRAMHALL in Hobbes *Lib., Necess. & Chance* 94 He who only lets loose a Greyhound out of the slip, is said to hound him at the Hare. **1826** J. WILSON *Noct. Ambr.* Wks. 1855 I. 266 Why should he suffer ony o' his yelpin curs to bite the heels o' the Shepherd—perhaps hound him on wi' his ain gleg voice and ee?

4. *transf.* To incite or set (a person) *at* or *on* another; to incite or urge *on*.

1570 BUCHANAN *Admonit.* Wks. (1892) 25 Nor ȝit haif hundit furth proud..ȝoung men to herry, slay [etc.]. *a* **1616** BEAUM. & FL. *Bonduca* III. iii, Hold good sword, but this day, And bite hard where I hound thee. **1679** *Lond. Gaz.* No. 1406/2 Who shall discover his Complices, and such as hounded them out. **1833** MRS. BROWNING *Prometh. Bound* Poems 1850 I. 143 Will hound thee at this quarry! **1860** MOTLEY *Netherl.* (1868) II. xv. 223 It was idle..to hound the rabble upon them as tyrants and mischief-makers. **1874** GREEN *Short Hist.* viii. §2. 472 The Ecclesiastical Commission was hounded on to a fresh persecution.

Hence **'hounded, 'hounding** *ppl. adjs.* Also **'hounder**, one who hounds, incites, or urges.

1573 *Satir. Poems Reform.* xxxix. 216 Doun fra that Crage Kirkcaldy sall reteir, With schame and sclander lyke ane hundit fox. **1597** R. BRUCE in Wodrow *Life* (1843) 178 If we were the hounders, then, I ask, who stayed it? **1848** LYTTON *Harold* x. ii, The Orestes escapes from the hounding Furies. **1866** *Ch. Times* 10 Feb., A hounder-on of popular clamour against the self-same law in England.

'hound-fish, 'houndfish.

†**1.** A name given to various small sharks; = DOGFISH. *Obs.*

c **1386** CHAUCER *Merch. T.* 581 With thilke brustles of his berd vnsofte Lyk to the skyn of houndfyssh sharpe as brere. ? *a* **1400** *Morte Arth.* 1084 Harske as a hunde-fisch..So was þe hyde of þat hulke hally al over! *c* **1440** *Promp. Parv.* 250/2 Howndе fyshe, *canis marinus*. **1513** *Bk. Keruynge* in *Babees Bk.* (1868) 282 Mortrus of houndes fysshe. **1668** WILKINS *Real Char.* II. v. §3. 132 The Greater and the Lesser Hound Fish. **1753** CHAMBERS *Cycl. Supp.*, *Hound-Fish*,..two different fish of the squalus kind, the one called the smooth, and the other the prickly Hound. **18..** H. MILLER *Lett. on Herring Fish.*, The..hun-fish..a voracious animal of the shark species.

b. *attrib.*, as ***houndfish-skin***.

1449–50 in Willis & Clark *Cambridge* (1886) I. 402, j hownd-fissch skyn..ad officium carpentariorum. **1545** ASCHAM *Toxoph.* II. (Arb.) 161 A Hunfysh-skin and a cloth.

2. Applied to other species of fish: **a.** Species of garfish of genus *Tylosurus*, such as the *T. jonesi* (Bermuda) and *T. acus*; **b.** ***blue hound-fish***, a former name in Massachusetts of *Pomatomus saltatrix*, now called the Bluefish; **c.** ***speckled hound-fish***, a former name of the Spanish mackerel.

1672 JOSSELYN *New Eng. Rarities* 24 Blew Fish or Hound Fish, two kinds, speckled Hound Fish, and blew Hound Fish called Horse Fish.

†**hound-fly.** *Obs.* Also **hound's fly.** A fly troublesome to dogs: cf. DOG-FLY.

c **1000** *Ags. Ps.* (Th.) lxxvii[i]. 45 Sette him heard wite, hundes fleoȝan. *a* **1300** *Cursor M.* 5956 Bath þai clang on man and best, To hund-flee [*Fairf.* fleys of hounde] war þai lickest. **1483** *Cath. Angl.* 192/1 An Hundeflee, *cinomia*. **1495** *Trevisa's Barth. De P.R.* XII. xiii. (W. de W.), Cynomia, a houndes flye, is the werste kynde of flyes wyth gretter body and broder wombes than other flyes and lesse flyghte.

houndgild, -gilt: see HUNGIL.

†**hounding,** *sb.*¹ *Obs.* [f. HOUND *sb.*¹ + -ING.] A fabulous animal, partly dog and partly man; a cynocephalus.

13.. *K. Alis.* 4948 [4963] (Bodl. MS.) Anoþer folk there is biside; Houndynges men clepeþ hem wide, From þe brest to þe grounde Men hij ben, abouen houndes.

'hounding, *sb.*² *Naut.* [f. HOUND *sb.*²] The lower part of the mast, below the hounds.

c **1860** H. STUART *Seaman's Catech.* 74 From deck to the hounds it is called hounding. **1882** NARES *Seamanship* (ed. 6) 8 *Hounding*, from the upper deck, to where the rigging is placed.

hounding ('haʊndɪŋ), *vbl. sb.* [f. HOUND *v.*]

1. The action or practice of pursuing, driving, or tracking game with hounds; *spec.* the tracking and driving of a deer, etc., by a hound or hounds, until it is brought under the hunter's gun.

1854 THOREAU *Walden* xv. (1863) 299 The old hound burst into view with muzzle to the ground..but spying the dead fox she suddenly ceased her hounding. **1889** *Athenæum* 22 June 786/3 Mr. Phillipps-Wolley says that 'hounding' is the universal form of sport in the Adirondacks. **1894** *Century Mag.* Jan. 349/1 When they [hunters] introduced hounding, the moose simply left the country.

2. *fig.* Worrying, persecution.

1887 in *Pall Mall G.* 13 Jan. 12/1 When we reflect on the harrying and hounding to which this distinguished son of our country has been exposed.

'houndish, *a.* [f. HOUND *sb.*¹ + -ISH.] Of the nature of, pertaining to, or characteristic of a hound; doggish, canine.

1398 TREVISA *Barth. De P.R.* v. xx. (1495), Two of the teeth hyghte Canini, houndysshe, to the lyknesse of houndes teeth. **1633** T. ADAMS *Exp. 2. Peter* ii. 22 The houndish servility of base minds. **1830** *Examiner* 563/1 They have a houndish regard to the troughs of the kennel. **1849** ROCK *Ch. of Fathers* I. 279 [They] employed snaky, houndish, and dragon-like animals for ornaments upon their crosses.

houndreth, obs. form of HUNDRED.

†**'hound's-berry.** *Obs.* Also **hound-berry.**

1. The Black Bryony, *Tamus communis*.

c **1265** *Voc. Names Pl.* in Wr.-Wülcker 558/16 *Labrusca*, hundesberien.

2. The Black Nightshade, *Solanum nigrum*.

c **1485** *MS. Bodl.* 536 *Morella* i. morell or hondesbery. *a* **1500** *Gloss. Sloane* 5 lf. 38c. in *Sax. Leechd.* III. 333/1 *Morella medica*, Nyghtshade oþer pety morell oþer hound berry. **1597** GERARDE *Herbal* App., Houndberrie is *Solanum*.

3. The Wild Cornel or Dogwood.

1578 LYTE *Dodoens* VI. li. 726 *Cornus fœmina*, in Englishe, the female Cornel tree; Houndes tree, and Hounde berie, or Dogge berie tree. [**1858** HOGG *Veg. Kingd.* 336.]

†**'houndsfoot.** *Obs.* Also **hounsfoot.** [ad. Du. *hondsvot*, Ger. *hundsfott*, scoundrel, rascal, lit. *cunnus canis*: see Grimm, Kluge and Franck.] A scoundrel, a rascal, a worthless fellow.

1710 *Acc. Last Distemp. T. Whigg* I. 16 O pox! It's that Hounsfoot Tom Whigg. **1712** ARBUTHNOT *John Bull* III. ix, What houndsfoot is it that puts these whims in thy head?

attrib. **1814** SCOTT *Wav.* xlviii, If you play any of your hounds-foot tricks.

hound's-tongue. [trans. Gr. *κυνόγλωσσον*, L. *cynoglossum*.] The genus *Cynoglossum* of boraginaceous plants, esp. the species *C. officinale*; also called Dog's-tongue.

c **1000** *Sax. Leechd.* I. 144 Deos wyrt þe..engle glofwyrt, & oðrum naman hundes tunge hatað. *c* **1265** *Voc.* in Wr.-Wülcker 557/37 *Lingua canis*,..hundestunge. **1544** PHAER *Regim. Lyfe* (1553) B vij b, It is verye good to laye vpon them [wounds] the herbe called houndstong stamped with a litle hony. **1678** PHILLIPS (ed. 4), *Hounds tongue*..an Herb whose Leaves are like the Tongue, and smell like the Piss of an Hound. **1858** HOGG *Veg. Kingd.* 542 *Cynoglossum officinale*, or Hound's-tongue, grows in some parts of Britain. The whole plant has a disagreeable odour.

'houndstooth. Also **hound's tooth, hound's-tooth, hounds' tooth, houndtooth.** [f. HOUND *sb.*¹ + TOOTH *sb.*] A small irregular design of broken

check. Also, a fabric of this design; a suit, coat, etc., of such fabric.

1936 *New Yorker* 7 Mar. 44/2 (Advt.), We carry sports jackets in checks, plaids, and hound's tooth patterns. **1951** J. D. SALINGER *Catcher in Rye* ii. 32 If you're not going out any place special, how 'bout lending me your hound's tooth jacket? *Ibid.*, No kidding, you gonna use your hound's tooth to-night, or not? **1957** *Observer* 1 Dec. 11/5 Giant houndstooth designs made day dresses with jackets: so did imitation tweeds. **1959** *Woman's Own* 6 June 11/3 Clare.. put on her 'good' hounds-tooth check. **1959** *Sunday Express* 14 June 14/3 Patterns are clean and singularly chic—a bold hounds' tooth check or a variety of confetti spots. **1959** *Times* 23 Sept. 5/2 The choice of cloths is famous for its variety—ranging from subdued houndstooths to full-blooded overchecks. **1959** *Guardian* 4 Dec. 6/5 In the woollens, small houndtooth designs and overchecks are liked. **1959** G. FREEMAN *Jack would be Gent.* i. 18 Moyra glanced at James, covertly admiring his hound's-tooth check suit. **1971** *Homes & Gardens* Aug. 57/1 The dining chairs are covered in a toffee and black houndstooth check. **1972** P. CLEIFE *Slick & Dead* xix. 143 Wearing my natty houndstooth instead of uniform.

†**hound's-tree.** *Herb. Obs.* A name in the herbalists for the Common Dogwood.

1578 [see HOUND'S-BERRY 3]. **1598** FLORIO, *Cornio*.. Houndes tree. **1776** WITHERING *Brit. Pl.* (1801) II. 198 *Cornus sanguinea*, Dogberry tree, Hounds tree, Houndsberry. [**1861** MISS PRATT *Flower. Pl.* III. 109.]

houndy ('haʊndɪ), *a.* [f. HOUND *sb.*¹ + -Y.] Of the nature or character of a hound.

1890 *Field* 8 Mar. 355/1 Transit [a pointer].. is.. inclined to be houndy in character. **1893** *Kennel Gaz.* Aug. 222/2 Too short in head and flaggy in ear.. a good houndy coat.

houngan ('huːŋgən). Also **hougan, hungan.** [Native name in Haiti.] A priest of the Voodoo cult.

1929 W. B. SEABROOK *Magic Island* 304 There are many things my father (who was one of the great *hougans* of the past generation) could do which I cannot do. He could make thunder. **1932** J. J. WILLIAMS *Voodoos & Obeahs* iii. 91 Is there a Voodoo initiation whereby a neophyte, it matters not who he is, thanks to the good will of the hougan, may be admitted to the congregation? **1937** M. J. HERSKOVITS *Life Haitian Valley* xii. 223 Persistent failure to achieve cures will lose a *hungan* his reputation and his practice. **1941** J. G. LEYBURN *Haitian People* viii. 168 While the Vodun houngan sits quietly by, a special officiant.. reads or pretends to read from the Catholic prayer book. **1966** G. GREENE *Comedians* I. iii. 83 A zombie who has left his grave at the command of an *houngan*.

hounge, obs. f. *hung*, pa. t. of HANG *v.*

hounger, houngrie, obs. ff. HUNGER, -GRY.

†**hounsyd,** *a. Obs. rare.* ? Furnished with hounds.

1532 [see HOUND *sb.*² 1].

hount, obs. f. HUNT.

hountage, hountee: see HONT-.

houp, Sc. f. HOPE, obs. f. HOOP.

houp-la ('huːplɑː), *int.* Also **hoop-la.** [Cf. F. *houp-là!*] An exclamation accompanying a quick or sudden movement. Also as *sb.*, commotion, ballyhoo.

1870 O. LOGAN *Before Footlights* xxiii. 280 But the tearful clown cries 'houp-la!' while his baby is lying dead at home. **1877** *N.Y. Tribune* 2 Mar. 7/1 The Stock Exchange to-day commenced its business of speculation with a grand 'hoop la'. **1917** H. GARLAND *Son of Middle Border* xxiii. 286 Hoopla! We had taken wing! **1917** *Punch* 23 May 340/2 A beam of pleasure, succeeded by a falling of the countenance, then a look of decision, ended in a 'Houp-là' as the Japanese doll descended into the basket. **1925** F. M. FORD *No More Parades* I. ii, But.. Hoopla!.. He executed with his gloved right thumb in the moonlight a rapid pirouette. **1929** C. A. N. GARSTIN *Houp La!* xxiv. 308 'Houp la!' Bill sighed, letting his head fall back. **1948** *Carpenter* Mar. 16 Organized some three years ago amid a great hoopla of Communist propaganda and promotion, it has creaked along in a very erratic and unpredictable manner. **1973** *Guardian* 16 Mar. 10/3 There is sometimes so much surrounding hoop-la that you lose sight of the various tactics.

houp-la, var. HOOP-LA.

†'**houpland.** *Obs.* exc. *Hist.* in Fr. form. Also 4 houpelond, 5 hopoland. [a. F. *houppelande* (1281, *hoppelande*, in Hatz.-Darm.) of unknown origin: see Littré. Cf. Sp. *hopalanda* tunic with a train attached.] A tunic with a long skirt.

1392–3 *Earl Derby's Exp.* (Camden) 285 Pro factura j houpelond longe et j jupe pro domino. **1415** in Nicolas *Test. Vetust.* (1826) I. 187, I will that all my hopolandes huykes not furred, be divided among the servants. **1614** CAMDEN *Rem.* 231. [**1834** PLANCHÉ *Brit. Costume* 172 The lords wore a long tunic called a *houppelande*, of scarlet.]

hour (aʊə(r)). Forms: 3–4 ure, (hure), 3–5 oure, 4 ore, vure, hor, 4–5 owre, 4–6 our, hore, 4–7 howr(e, houre, 5 oware, heure, 6 ower(e, howere, 6–7 hower, 7 hoore, 4– hour. [a. OF. *ure, ore,* later *hure, hore, h)eure,* AF. *houre,* mod.F. *heure,* = Pr. *h)ora,* It. *ora,* Sp., Pg. *hora*:—L. *hōra* hour, a. Gr. ὥρα season, time of day, hour. The *h* became mute in Romanic, and though since written in F., Sp., and Eng. has never been pronounced. (The OE. was *tíd*; in some uses *stund*.)]

1. a. A space of time containing sixty minutes; the twenty-fourth part of a civil day.

Formerly the hours were commonly reckoned as each equal to one-twelfth of the natural day or night, whatever its length (called *planetary, temporary,* or *unequal* hours); the *equal* hours were sometimes distinguished as *equinoctial*, being each equal to a *temporary* hour at the equinoxes. ***sidereal, solar hour***, 24th part of a sidereal, or solar, day.

As with other nouns of time, the genitive is freely used: e.g. *an hour's space, time, work, wages, sermon, notice,* etc.

c **1250** *Old Kent. Serm.* in *O.E. Misc.* 34 Þos laste on ure habbeþ i-travailed. *c* **1330** R. BRUNNE *Chron.* (1810) 23 Þe foure & tuenty houres he spended in holy life. **1382** WYCLIF *John* xi. 9 Wher ther ben not twelue ouris of the day? [*Ags. Gosp.* Hu ne synt twelf tida þæs dæges?]. *c* **1430** *Two Cookery-bks.* 37 Late hym ben stepid .ij. or .iij. owrys in clene Water. **1548** HALL *Chron., Hen. V* 50 Thus this battaile continued .III. long houres. *Ibid., Hen. VIII* 37 b, What number.. they were able to make within an houres warnynge. **1561** EDEN *Arte Nauig.* II. xiv. 40 The houre naturall or equall, is a .24. parte of the day naturall... The artificial or temperall houre, is a twelfth parte of the daye arcke or the nyght arcke. **1601** SHAKS. *Jul. C.* II. ii. 121, I haue an houres talke in store for you. **1607–12** BACON *Ess., Youth & Age* (Arb.) 256 A man that is yong in yeares maie be old in howers, if he have lost noe tyme. **1674** MOXON *Tutor Astron.* IV. (ed. 3) 129 Astrologers divide the Artificial day (be it long or short) into 12 equal parts, and the Night into 12 equal parts: these parts they call Planetary Hours. **1777** SHERIDAN *Sch. Scand.* II. ii, She's six-and-fifty if she's an hour! **1793** SMEATON *Edystone L.* §339 It might be applied.. on an hour's notice. **1887** RIDER HAGGARD *Jess* xv, On he went, hour after hour.

b. In *pl.* (rarely *sing.*) with numeral, expressing the number of hours since midnight or noon, and thus denoting a particular time of the day (sense 3): as *ten hours* = ten o'clock (*obs.*, chiefly *Sc.*). In *pl.* with numerals rendered in figures (followed by those of minutes), expressing the number of hours since midnight (chiefly in the armed services and in passenger timetables). Cf. HUNDRED *sb.* and *a.* 1 d.

1427 *Sc. Acts Jas. I*, c. 118 Fra ten houres to twa efter nune. *c* **1470** HENRY *Wallace* IV. 121 Schyr Ranald come by x houris of the day. **1567** *Satir. Poems Reform.* iii. 1 To Edinburgh about vj. houris at morne, As I was passand. *c* **1620** A. HUME *Brit. Tongue* (1865) 31 At four hoores I was wryting. **1634–5** BRERETON *Trav.* (Chetham Soc.) 138 There is a sermon euery sabbath at 10 hour. **1657** *Edin. Kirk Sess. Reg.* in *Scott. Antiq.* (1898) June 35 The first Bell shall ring at half-hour to seven hours on the week dayes, the second Bell at seven hours. **1681** COLVIL *Whig's Supplic.* I. (1710) 34 He sees what hours it is in France. **1939** *Punch* 2 Aug. 124/1 It is 21.00 hours on the last day of our month's training. **1941** *Punch* 21 May 486 A lorry is leaving R.M.P. at 0915 hours. **1967** [see HOVERING *vbl. sb.* a (ii)]. **1968** A. HAMMERSLEY *Weather & Life* iv. 49, 6 hours G.M.T., i.e. 6 a.m. **1971** R. BUCKNALL *Trains* 46 With this time scale, 6 minutes would represent six hours, or 06.00.

c. Used to denote the distance of the sun above the horizon in the morning or afternoon. *U.S.*

1637 in *Essex Inst. Hist. Coll.* (1869) IX. 66 The keeper ..[is] to take the Cattle at the pen at Sun halfe an hour highe. **1683** in *New Hampsh. Hist. Soc. Coll.* (1866) VIII. 133 At night, about sun half an hour high. **1762** in *Narragansett Hist. Reg.* (1883–4) II. 219 We.. got to the Ferry the sun about two hours high at night. **1824** *New Hampsh. Hist. Soc. Coll.* I. 244 Though the sun was an hour above the horizon, it was now as dark as midnight. **1836** *Knickerbocker* VIII. 352 The sun is two hours up yet. **1907** M. H. NORRIS *Veil* i. 3 The sun was an hour high when he entered a narrow road overgrown with grass.

d. (orig. *hour-mile*.) The distance which can be traversed in an hour.

[*a* **1646** J. GREGORY *Posthuma* (1650) 318 One Hour-Mile of a Journie upon Hors, answereth to four English Miles.] **1785** G. FORSTER tr. *Sparrman's Voy. Cape G. Hope* II. 81 This place is situated at the distance of two hours (uurs) from that which we had just quitted. **1792** E. RIOU tr. *J. van Reenen's Jrnl. Journey from Cape G. Hope* p. xii, Throughout the journal the word hour is to be considered as distance, and not time. Travellers at the Cape of Good Hope reckon distance by hours: one hour being supposed equal to about a league. **1798** S. H. WILCOCKE tr. *Stavorinus' Voy. E. Indies* I. 58 A Dutch mile, which they in general call an hour, is about three miles and a half English. **1877** J. C. GEIKIE *Life & Words Christ* I. 388 Three hours from Jerusalem. **1907** in A. H. Anderson *Reading* Advts. p. xlviii a, Dulverton... 4 Hours from London, 1 Hour from Taunton and Exeter. **1970** *Country Life* 2 July 62/1 (Advt.), Radnorshire... Kington 6½ miles. Birmingham 1½ hours. An attractive period house.

e. Used as the second element, representing 'for one hour', in the names of some units of measurement, as ***ampere-hour, horsepower-hour, kilowatt-hour, man-hour*** (see under the first element).

f. A unit of measure of work done.

1900 *Daily News* 10 Jan. 8/3 It should be understood that the tailors' 'hour' is not one of time, but merely the word employed for an unit of calculation.

2. a. Used somewhat indefinitely for a short or limited space of time, more or less than an hour.

a **1310** in Wright *Lyric P.* xxv. 71 This hure of love to drynke so, That fleysshliche lust be al for-do. **1576** FLEMING *Panopl. Epist.* 310 If wee looke to live, till our last day and houre, without troublesome thoughtes. **1592** SHAKS. *Rom. & Jul.* I. i. 167 Sad houres seeme long. **1673** *Humours of Town* 52 They have made Love to be the hot passion of an hour. **1789** E. DARWIN *Bot. Gard.* 47 In dreams, we cannot compare them with our previous knowledge of things, as we do in our waking hours. **1838** THIRLWALL *Greece* V. 345 In a convivial hour, when they were all conversing on the subject. **1842** TENNYSON *Love & Duty* 56–7 The slow sweet hours that bring us all things good, The slow sad hours that bring us all things ill. **1864** BROWNING *Abt Vogler* x, When eternity affirms the conception of an hour.

b. *pl.* Stated time of occupation or duty.

1852 *12th Rep. Col. Land & Emigr. Comm.* in *Parl. Papers* XVIII. 151 They are not required to work 'long hours', five hours a day is what is required of them. **1857** HUGHES *Tom Brown* I. iii, But the school hours were long and Tom's patience short. **1865** MILL *Pol. Econ.* (ed. 6) v. xi. §12 A reduction of hours without any diminution of wages. **1878** JEVONS *Prim. Pol. Econ.* 63 The employer would generally prefer long hours. **1890** 'L. FALCONER' *Mlle. Ixe* ii. (1891) 35 Extra lessons had to be learnt, play-hours were curtailed. *Mod.* After office hours he goes for a ride.

c. (See quot. 1955.) Cf. *children's hour* (CHILD *sb.* 22).

1930 *Economist* 3 May 985/1 It is argued that an advertiser who broadcasts tedious over-vulgar, or over-highbrow material in his 'hour' will eventually discover that he is losing money. **1955** M. REIFER *Dict. New Words* 102/1 *Hour*, a scheduled radio or television feature, originally one hour long; the term now refers to any length program. **1972** *Daily Tel.* 20 Apr. 12/5 The star of *The Bob Monkhouse Comedy Hour* (ITV).. is almost guaranteed to turn me off.

3. a. Each of those points of time at which the twelve successive divisions after noon or midnight, as shown by a dial or time-piece, are completed; by extension, any definite point or 'time of day'. ***the eleventh hour***: see ELEVENTH.

a **1300** *Cursor M.* 8933 Ilk dai a certain hore, þar lighted dun of heuen ture Angels. *c* **1315** SHOREHAM 87 At evesanges oure. **1382** WYCLIF *Matt.* xx. 6 Aboute the elleuenthe houre [**1388** oure] he wente out, and foond other stondynge. *c* **1391** CHAUCER *Astrol.* Prol., A table of the verray Moeuyng of the Mone from howre to howre. *c* **1465** *Chevy Chase* xxix. in *Percy Reliq.*, It drewe to the oware off none. **1526** TINDALE *John* iv. 6 Hit was about the sixte houre. **1559** W. CUNNINGHAM *Cosmogr. Glasse* 158 By this Compasse (the Sonne shynynge) men shall perfitly knowe the houre of the day. **1663** BUTLER *Hud.* I. i. 125 What hour o' th' day The clock does strike. **1791** MRS. RADCLIFFE *Rom. Forest* ii, She awoke at an early hour. **1871** G. MACDONALD *Parables, Love's Ordeal* viii, The little clock rung out the hour of ten. **1882** SERJT. BALLANTINE *Exper.* I. ii. 24 Watchmen.. called the hours of the night.

b. ***small hours***: the early hours after midnight denoted by the small numbers, one, two, etc.

1836–7 DICKENS *Sk. Boz* vii. (1883) 30 He invited friends home, who used to come at ten o'clock, and begin to get happy about the small hours. **1859** FARRAR *J. Home* viii, Often beguiled by his studies into the 'wee small' hours of night. **1865** W. G. PALGRAVE *Arabia* II. 335 Conversation is prolonged to midnight or even to the small hours.

c. *pl.* Habitual time of getting up and going to bed, esp. the latter; usually with such adjs. as *good, regular, early, bad, late,* etc.

1601 SHAKS. *Twel. N.* I. iii. 6 You must come in earlyer a nights: your Cosin, my Lady, takes great exceptions to your ill houres. *a* **1744** POPE (J. s.v. *Keep*), I rule the family very ill, and keep bad hours. **1749** FIELDING *Tom Jones* XI. iii, The Sun.. keeps very good hours at this time of year. **1775** SHERIDAN *Rivals* I. i, Their regular hours stupify me—not a fiddle nor a card after eleven! **1816** JANE AUSTEN *Emma* II. vii. 123, I am not fond of dinner-visiting... Late hours do not agree with us. **1821** BYRON *Don Juan* III. lxvi. 36 Late hours, wine, and love are able To do not much less damage than the table. **1832** L. HUNT *Sir R. Esher* (1850) 81, I was nearly killed with his Grace's hours. **1834** *W. India Sketch Bk.* I. 18 The fatigues and late hours of the preceding night. **1891** MRS. S. EDWARDS *Secret of P'cess* II. xvi. 195, I keep early hours. **1970** *Brewer's Dict. Phr. & Fable* (rev. ed.) 550/2 *To keep good hours*, to go home early every night; to go to bed betimes; to be punctual at one's work.

d. *to* (or *till*) *all hours*: late at night; after midnight.

1931 BELLOC *Hist. Eng.* IV. I. 161 She.. had had him, and one, Culpepper, in her room up to all hours. **1932** A. J. WORRALL *Eng. Idioms* viii. 58, I sat up to all hours trying to finish my work. **1934** B. DE HOLTHOIR tr. *Duhamel's News from Havre* xiii. 196 She made up for lost time by sitting up till all hours of the night. **1945** E. WAUGH *Brideshead Revisited* iv. 264 She sits up to all hours with her wireless. **1961** R. CHAPMAN *Father Faber* viii. 161 He read till all hours and undertook heavy penances.

4. a. A definite time in general; an appointed time; an occasion. *spec.* ***of the hour***: of the present hour, of the very time that is now with us; as in 'the question of the hour'.

a **1300** *Cursor M.* 4665 His nam þai chaunged fra þat our. *c* **1380** WYCLIF *Serm.* Sel. Wks. II. 222 Seiþ Poul here þat our is now to rise fro sleep. **1490** CAXTON *Eneydos* lii. 147 The ladyes.. cursed turnus and the owre in whiche he bigan first the bataylle. **1526** TINDALE *John* ii. 4 Myne houre is not yett come. **1548–9** (Mar.) *Bk. Com. Prayer, Litany*, In the houre of death, in the daye of iudgement: Good lorde deliuer us. **1553** T. WILSON *Rhet.* (1580) 150 Sir Thomas More.. whose witte even at this hower, is a wonder to all the worlde. **1603** SHAKS. *Meas. for M.* II. ii. 16 Shee's very neere her houre. **1698** FRYER *Acc. E. India & P.* 373 Twelve Ships were sent to the bottom, in a well-chosen hour. **1750** GRAY *Elegy* ix, The boast of heraldry, the pomp of power.. Await alike th' inevitable hour. **1849** MACAULAY *Hist. Eng.* ii. I. 173 To hasten the hour of his own return. **1887** JESSOPP *Arcady* v. 136 The subject of the hour.. [is] the housing of the working classes.

b. Phr. ***in a good*** (***happy***, etc.) ***hour*** [partly = F. *à la bonne heure*]: at a fortunate time; happily, fortunately: so ***in an evil*** (***ill***, etc.) ***hour***. †***in good hour*** [F. *de bonne heure*]: in good time, early; so †***in due hour*** (obs.).

c **1450** *Merlin* 340 Arthur.. thought that in goode houre were he born that it myght conquere. *c* **1489** CAXTON *Sonnes of Aymon* i. 38 In an euyll oure was he put to deth. **1603** HOLLAND *Plutarch's Mor.* 1294 As if a man should say, In good houre and happily may this or that come. **1620**

SHELTON *Quix.* IV. xvi. II. 198 He resumes his Musick.. In a good Hour, quoth Donna Clara, and then because she herself would not hear him, she stoppd her Ears with her Fingers. **1634** SIR T. HERBERT *Trav.* 126 In a happy houre, the king.. tooke notice of him. **1685** EVELYN *Diary* 17 Sept., The next morning [we] set out for Guildford, where we ariv'd in good hour. **1689** —— *Let. to Pepys* 12 Aug., Retiring in due hour. **1719** DE FOE *Crusoe* I. i, In an ill hour.. I went on board. **1806–7** J. BERESFORD *Miseries Hum. Life* (1826) IV. Introd., In an evil hour I.. changed my lodgings.

5. *Eccl.* (*pl.*) The prayers or offices appointed to be said at the seven stated times of the day allotted to prayer (***canonical hours***: see CANONICAL 1 b); also (short for *book of hours*), a book containing these. Rare in *sing.* (The earliest recorded use, = L. *horæ*, OF. *ures*; in OE. (*seofon*) *tída.*)

a **1225** *Ancr. R.* 6 Sum is clergesse, & sum nis nout & mot te more wurchen, & an oðer wise siggen hire ures. **1377** LANGL. *P. Pl.* B. Prol. 97 Here messe and here matynes and many of here oures Arn don vndeuoutlych. *c* **1400** *St. Alexius* (Laud 622) 30 Forto seruen god almiȝth By tides and by houres. *c* **1450** *St. Cuthbert* (Surtees) 1427 When þe oure of terce was done. **1450–1530** *Myrr. our Ladye* 164 Complyn ys the Seuenthe and the laste houre of dyuyne seruyce.. in the ende therof the seuen howres of dyuyne seruyce ar fulfylled. **1669** WOODHEAD *St. Teresa* II. xviii. 121 They recited their Canonical Hours. **1873** DIXON *Two Queens* I. III. i. 119 Illuminated hours, and golden missals. **1894** BARING-GOULD *Deserts S. France* II. 130 A nun saying her hours.

6. *Mythol.* (*pl.*, with capital H, = L. *Horæ*, Gr. Ὧραι.) Female divinites supposed to preside over the changes of the seasons.

1634 MILTON *Comus* 986 The Graces and the rosy-bosomed Hours. **1751** GRAY *Odes, Spring* i, Lo! where the rosy-bosom'd Hours, Fair Venus' train, appear. **1835** THIRLWALL *Greece* vi. I. 221 The goddesses who preside over them [the seasons]—the Hours—were originally three in number. **1851** *Illustr. Catal. Gt. Exhib.* 1286 The Hours bringing the horses to the chariot of the Sun; from the basso-relievo.. by John Gibson, R.A.

7. *Astr.* and *Geog.* An angular measure of right ascension or longitude, being the 24th part of a great circle of the sphere, or 15 degrees.

[**1727–41** CHAMBERS *Cycl.* s.v., Fifteen degrees of the equator answer to an hour.] **1777** ROBERTSON *Hist. Amer.* (1783) I. 316 The longitude.. is seven hours, or one hundred and fifteen degrees from the meridian of the Canary Islands. **1877** G. F. CHAMBERS *Astron.* v. iii. (ed. 3) 460 Right Ascension.. is.. reckoned.. either in angular measure.. or in time, of hours, minutes, and seconds.

8. *Comb.*: **hour-angle**, *Astr.* the angular distance between the meridian and the declination-circle passing through a heavenly body, which is the measure of the sidereal time elapsed since its culmination; **hour-bell**, a bell rung every hour, or that sounds the hours; **hour-book**, *Eccl.* a book of hours (sense 5); **hour-cup**, a cup in a clepsydra that empties itself hourly; **hour-figure**, a figure denoting the hour, esp. on a dial-plate; **hour-hand**, the short hand of a clock or watch which indicates the hours; **hour-index**, an index or pointer which can be turned to any hour marked on the hour-circle of an artificial globe; **hour-line**, a line on a dial indicating the hour by the passage of the shadow across it; **hour-long** *a.*, lasting for an hour; **hour-plate**, the dial-plate of a clock or watch, inscribed with figures denoting the hours; **hour-stroke**, one of the strokes or marks on a dial-plate indicating the hours; **hour-watch**, a watch indicating only the hours; **hour-wheel**, (*a*) = HOUR-CIRCLE 2; (*b*) that wheel in a clock which carries the hour-hand.

1837 *Penny Cycl.* IX. 488 (s.v. *Equatorial*) The difference between the observed *hour angle and true hour angle. **1784** COWPER *Task* v. 404 To count the *hour-bell and expect no change. **1891** *Pall Mall G.* 15 Jan. 2/3 The hour bell in the clock-tower. **1896** *Daily News* 28 Nov. 3/6 An *Hour book ..illustrated with richly painted miniatures. **1799** J. GILCHRIST in *Asiat. Res.* V. 87 The water gradually fills the cup, and sinks it, in the space [of time] to which this *hour-cup or *kutoree* has previously been adjusted. **1690** LEYBOURN *Curs. Math.* 703 b, Before you can calculate the *Hour distances for these Plains, there are three Requisites to be first enquired. **1675** *Lond. Gaz.* No. 1052/4 The hour of the day, pointed at by an Archer engraved on the Plate within the *hour-figures. **1669** *Phil. Trans.* IV. 944 In case the *Hour-hand hath.. pass'd that hour. **1895** *Q. Rev.* July 222 The two failures.. put back the hour-hand of time for centuries. **1674** MOXON *Tutor Astron.* III. (ed. 3) 112 Turn the Globe Westwards till the *Hour-Index points at the Hour of the Night. **1593** FALE *Dialling* 6 From the centre C. by these markes the *houre-line must be drawne. **1767** FERGUSON in *Phil. Trans.* LVII. 390 The true hour-lines for a horizontal dial. **1803** BEDDOES *Hygëia* xi. 91 Requiring no *hour-long harangues. *a* **1704** LOCKE (J.), The characters of the *hourplate. **1674** N. FAIRFAX *Bulk & Selv.* 121 The hand or Index on the Dial-plate.. creeping from *hour-stroke to hour-stroke. **1697** *Lond. Gaz.* No. 3352/4 A plain *hour Watch. **1594** BLUNDEVIL *Exerc.* IV. Introd. (ed. 7) 437 Upon this brazen Meridian is placed at the North Pole another little brazen Circle.. called the *houre-wheele. **1704** J. HARRIS *Lex. Techn.* s.v. *Pinion*, The Hour Wheel [of a clock].

hourage ('aʊərɪdʒ). *rare.* [f. HOUR + -AGE.] The aggregate number of hours spent in working or travelling; extent or distance in hours. Also, rate of travel in hours.

1924 *Glasgow Herald* 29 Dec. 7, 52,000 individuals.. were taken for short flights, the total 'hourage' being 2400. **1968** *Times* 19 Feb. 5/2 When you've finished your optimum hourage you must stop clean and briskly.

'hour-circle.

1. Any great circle of the celestial sphere passing through the poles; a meridian or declination-circle. Twenty-four of these are commonly marked on the globe, each distant from the next by one hour of right ascension.

1690 LEYBOURN *Curs. Math.* 359 Through either of the Poles.. there are drawn 12 Meridians or hour-Circles. **1812–16** J. SMITH *Panorama Sc. & Art* I. 518 Twenty-four of these circles of declination are called hour-circles.

2. A small brass circle at the north pole of an artificial globe, graduated into hours and divisions of an hour.

1674 MOXON *Tutor Astron.* I. (ed. 3) 6 The Hour Circle is a small Brasen Circle, fitted on the Meridian whose Center is the Pole of the world. *Ibid.* III. 119 Turn about the Globe till the Index of the Hour Circle points to the Hour of the Day or Night.

3. A graduated circle upon an equatorial telescope, parallel to the plane of the equator, by means of which the hour-angle of a star is observed.

1837 *Penny Cycl.* IX. 486 (s.v. *Equatorial*) The hour-circle is made to read 0^h, when the telescope is in the meridian of the place. **1877** G. F. CHAMBERS *Astron.* VII. iii. (ed. 3) 650 The hour-circle has a female screw cut on its outer edge, in which an endless screw.. is arranged to work so as to give a slow motion in Right Ascension.

hourd(e, obs. form of HOARD.

houre, obs. form of OUR, WHORE.

houred (aʊəd), *a.* [f. HOUR + -ED².]

†**1.** Defined by a particular hour; definite. *Obs.*

c **1475** *Partenay* 528 A wilde swine chasing at that houred tyde. *Ibid.* 2695 This goth well at thys houred braid.

2. (in *comb.*) Of a specified number of hours.

1665 SIR T. HERBERT *Trav.* (1677) 330 Turning the four-hour'd glass. **1890** *Pall Mall G.* 2 Apr. 3/2 In a good 'short-houred' firm an assistant's lot compares very favourably with that of many a toiler.

'hour-glass. 1. a. A contrivance for measuring time, consisting of a glass vessel with obconical ends connected by a constricted neck, through which a quantity of sand (or sometimes mercury) runs in exactly an hour; a sand-glass that runs for an hour.

c **1515** *Cocke Lorell's B.* (Percy Soc.) 12 One kepte yᵉ compas, and watched yᵉ our glasse. **1591** *Churchw. Acc. St. Helen's, Abingdon* (Nichols 1797) 143 Paid for an houre glass for the pulpitt, 4d. **1596** SHAKS. *Merch. V.* I. i. 25. **1642** FULLER *Holy & Prof. St.* II. xxi. 139 America is not unfitly resembled to an Hour-glasse, which hath a narrow neck of land.. betwixt the parts thereof. **1711** ADDISON *Spect.* No. 63 ¶4 The figure of Time with an Hour-glass in one hand, and a Scythe in the other. **1852** HOOK *Ch. Dict.* (1871) 375 For the measurement of the time of sermon, hour-glasses were frequently attached to pulpits.

b. Often *fig.* or *allusively*, in reference to the passage of time; sometimes = an hour's space; a strictly finite space of time.

1588 FRAUNCE *Lawiers Log.* I. iv. 28 b, If a preacher.. should talk out his houre-glasse in discoursing of Bell the dragon. **1605** BACON *Adv. Learn.* II. Ded. §15 Those things ..may be done in succession of ages, though not within the houre-glasse of one mans life. **1644** QUARLES *Barnabas & B.* 26 What mean these strict reformers thus to spend their hour-glasses? **1714** GAY *Sheph. Week* Friday 142 He.. spoke the hour-glass in her praise—quite out. **1846** TRENCH *Mirac.* vi. (1862) 185 When death was shaking the last few sands in the hour-glass of his daughter's life.

c. *attrib.*, referring to the shape of an hour-glass.

1822–34 *Good's Study Med.* (ed. 4) IV. 173 If the uterus ..should contract.. transversely so as to form what has been called an Hour-glass contraction. **1860** G. H. K. *Vac. Tour.* 119, I used to think that the Pechts.. built them hour-glass fashion to prevent the said enemy scrambling into them.

d. A marking (as on a spider) in the shape of an hour-glass.

1937 *Discovery* Dec. 368/1 Two female Black Widows, showing the 'hour-glass' markings. **1962** METCALF & FLINT *Destructive & Useful Insects* (ed. 4) xxi. 1009 (*caption*) The black widow spider, *Latrodectus mactans*. At left, the female from the underside, showing the characteristic hourglass-shaped spot.

2. Special Comb.: **hour-glass structure** *Petrol.*, a structure present in certain rocks in which the mineral crystals have the shape of an hour-glass.

1888 J. J. H. TEALL *Brit. Petrogr.* vii. 159 The hour-glass structure already mentioned as occurring in the picrites is occasionally found in the normal plagioclaseaugite rocks. **1932** F. F. GROUT *Petrogr. & Petrol.* 100 'Hourglass' structure is occasionally noted in augite. **1959** W. W. MOORHOUSE *Study of Rocks in Thin Section* vi. 166 The larger grains and phenocrysts may be zoned, or they may show hourglass structure.

‖**houri** ('hʊərɪ, 'haʊərɪ). [a. F. *houri* (1654 in Hatz.-Darm.), a. Pers. *ḥūrī*, f. Arabic *ḥūr* pl. of *ḥaurāʼ* fem., in *ḥūr-al-ʻayūn* (females) gazelle-like in the eyes, f. *ḥawira* to be black-eyed like a gazelle.] A nymph of the Muslim Paradise. Hence applied allusively to a voluptuously beautiful woman.

1737 JOHNSON *Irene* IV. v, Suspend thy passage to the seats of bliss, Nor wish for houries in Irene's arms. **1745** H. WALPOLE *Lett.* (1857) I. 343 (Stanf.) Handsomer than one of the houris. **1816** BYRON *Siege Cor.* xii, Secure in paradise to be By Houris loved immortally. **1820** SCOTT *Ivanhoe* vii, What is she, Isaac? Thy wife or thy daughter, that Eastern houri that thou lockest under thy arm? **1827** LYTTON *Pelham* I. (Stanf.), This speech somewhat softened the incensed Houri of Mr. Gordon's Paradise.

hourless ('aʊəlɪs), *a.* Without hours; having no reckoning of time.

1855 BAILEY *Mystic* 11 The hourless mansions of the dead.

hourly ('aʊəlɪ), *a.* [f. HOUR + -LY¹.]

1. Of or belonging to an hour; of an hour's age or duration; very recent or brief. *rare.*

1513 MORE *Rich. III* (1883) 14 That an houerly kindnes, sodainely contract in one houre.. shold be deper setled.. then a long accustomed malice many yeres rooted. **1821** BYRON *Two Foscari* I. i. 376 For the present, Foscari Has a short hourly respite.

2. Occurring or performed every hour; done, reckoned, etc. hour by hour; frequent, continual.

?*c* **1530** *Crt. of Love* 353 With hourly labour and gret attendaunce. **1599** SHAKS. *Much Ado* II. i. 188 This is an accident of hourely proofe. **1659** B. HARRIS *Parival's Iron Age* 189 In hourly expectation of the Hangman. **1797** GODWIN *Enquirer* I. xi. 97 The hourly events of his life. **1808** MURDOCH in *Phil. Trans.* XCVIII. 126 An hourly supply of 1250 cubic feet of the gas. **1883** *Wom. Suffrage Jrnl.* Nov. 198/1 Whether he was paid an hourly, daily, or weekly wage.

b. as *sb.* (*U.S.*) A public conveyance that runs every hour.

1877 BARTLETT *Dict. Amer.* 299 *Hourly*, formerly used in and about Boston for an omnibus. **1881** *Harper's Mag.* Feb. 388 The terrors of the 'hourly' or omnibus.

hourly ('aʊəlɪ), *adv.* [f. HOUR + -LY².]

1. Every hour; hour by hour; from hour to hour; continually, very frequently.

1470 in Ellis *Orig. Lett.* Ser. II. I. 136 As dayly and howrlye is now.. proved. **1509** FISHER *Fun. Serm. C'tess Richmond* Wks. (1876) 306 The perylles.. innumerable, whiche dayly & hourly myght haue happed. **1611** SHAKS. *Cymb.* II. i. 64 A Mother hourely coyning plots. **1776** GIBBON *Decl. & F.* I. 303 The barbarians were hourly expected at the gates of Rome. **1811** BYRON *Farew. Malta*, Two spoonfuls hourly.

†**2.** For the space of an hour; for a short time; quickly, cursorily. *Obs.*

1529 MORE *Dyaloge* I. Wks. 105/2 Partes.. suche.. as rather nede to be attentely redde and aduised, than houerly harde and passid ouer. **1532** —— *Confut. Tindale* Ibid. 694/1. **1549** COVERDALE, etc. *Erasm. Par. Cor.* 43 With you peraduenture will I abyde for a whyle.. but I would not see you now houerly, & in my passage.

†**hoursch**, *v. Obs. rare.* [?:—OE. *hryscan*, 'stridere'.] *intr.* ? To rattle, make a din.

?*a* **1400** *Morte Arth.* 2110 Þe hathelieste on hy, haythene and oþer; All hoursches over hede harmes to wyrke.

hourte, obs. form of HURT.

housage ('haʊzɪdʒ). [f. HOUSE *v.*¹ + -AGE.]

1. A fee paid for housing goods.

1617 MINSHEU *Ductor*, *Housage* is a fee that one payes for setting vp any stuffe in a house, either for a Carrier, or at a wharfe, or such like. [Hence in later Dicts.]

2. The action of housing or condition of being housed.

1803 COLERIDGE *Lett.* (1895) 430 The former cargo is in safe housage.

†**housal**, *a. Obs.* In 7 housall, -ell, houseall. [app. irreg. f. HOUSE *sb.*¹ + -AL¹; but possibly worn down from *household*.] Belonging to the house; domestic; domesticated; household-.

1611 COTGR., *Addomestiqué*,.. inward, familiar, housall. *Ibid.*, *Ichneumon*,.. the Ægyptian Rat.. vsually tamed, and made housall, by the people of Ægypt. **1627** in E. D. Neill *Virginia Carolorum* (1886) 404 *note*, Goods moveable or housell stuffe or chattels. **1668** *N. Riding Rec.* VI. 126 Her goods and houseall stuff.

housband, etc., obs. form of HUSBAND, etc.

house (haʊs), *sb.*¹ Pl. houses ('haʊzɪz). Forms: 1 hús, 2–4 (6 *Sc.*) hus, 3–5 hows, 3–6 hous, 4– house, (4 huus, houus, huse, huis, *Sc.* howise, 4–6 *Sc.* houss, 4–7 howse, 6 owse, *Sc.* hws(z, housse). For the plural forms see 1 β. [Com. Teut.: OE. *hús* = OFris., OS. *hûs* (Du. *huis*, LG. *huus*), OHG., MHG. *hûs* (Ger. *haus*), ON. *hûs* (Sw., Da. *hus* (*huus*)), Goth. *-hûs* (known only in *gudhûs* temple, the usual word being *razn*). The ulterior etymology is uncertain: it has been with some probability referred to the verbal root *hud-*, *hûd-* of *hýdan* to HIDE, Aryan *keudh-*, OTeut. *hûso-*, from *hûsso-*, going back to *hûþto-*; but other suggestions have also been offered.]

I. The simple word.

1. A building for human habitation; *esp.* a building that is the ordinary dwelling-place of a family.

Beowulf (Z.) 286 On heah-stede husa selest. *c* **1000** *Ags. Gosp.* Matt. vii. 27 þæt hus feoll and hys hryre wæs mycel. *c* **1250** *Gen. & Ex.* 2010 Putifar luuede ioseph wel, bi-taȝte him his hus euerilc del. *c* **1290** *S. Eng. Leg.* I. 17/548 A rode he hadde in is hous. **1362** LANGL. *P. Pl.* A. II. 40 Þer nas halle ne hous þat miht herborwe þe peple. **1483** *Cath. Angl.* 190/2 To make an Howse, *domificare*. **1539** TAVERNER *Erasm. Prov.* (1552) 66 A lytle house wel fylled A lytle grounde well tylled And a litle wife wel willed is best. **1548-9** (Mar.) *Bk. Com. Prayer, Communion* (Rubric), When the holy Communion is celebrate.. in priuate howses. **1581** MULCASTER *Positions* xl. (1887) 222 His house is his castle. **1676** LADY CHAWORTH in *12th Rep. Hist. MSS. Comm.* App. v. 33 To be quit of itt I confine myself to the house. **1710** M. HENRY *Comm., Luke* xxii. 10 Whether it was a friend's house or a public house does not appear. **1855** TENNYSON *Maud* I. vi. 8 Living alone in an empty house.

β. The plural was in OE. *hús*, in 12th c. *husas*, *huses*, from 14th c. *houses*; also in various writers from *c* 1550, and still dialectally, *housen*, which is sometimes collective.

c **1000** *Ags. Gosp.* Mark x. 30 Þe hund-feald ne onfo.. hus & broðru & swustru [*Lindisf.* huso, *Rushw.* huse, WYCLIF housis, TINDALE houses]. *a* **1123** *O.E. Chron.* an. 1116 Bærnde.. eallæ þa husas. *c* **1175** *Lamb. Hom.* 49 Riche men ..þe habbeð feire huses. *c* **1205** LAY. 1937 Þa makeden heo hus. *a* **1300** *Cursor M.* 6117 An soght þair huses [*Gött.* housis, *Fairf.* houses] all bi-dene. **1529** WOLSEY in *Four C. Eng. Lett.* 10 My howsys ther be in decay. **1557** NORTH tr. *Gueuara's Diall Pr.* 194 a/2 The housen wherin they dwel. **1600** HOLLAND *Livy* 218 Sacking, rifling and flinging the goods out of their enemies housen. **1605** *Lond. Prodigal* II. iv, Two housen furnished well in Coleman Street. **1645** in *N. Eng. Hist. & Gen. Reg.* (1849) III. 82 After the death of my wife I giue unto the children of my brother John all my housen and lands. **1855** ROBINSON *Whitby Gloss., Housen*, houses, property in bricks and mortar.

b. The portion of a building, consisting of one or more rooms, occupied by one tenant or family. *Sc.* and *dial.*

c **1020** *Rule St. Benet* (Logeman) 54 Candel æfre on ðam ylcan huse byrne oð merien. **1529** *Will* in Harding *Hist. Tiverton* (1847) II. 31 Every one of them shall have in the [alms] house a siverall house and chamber by himself. **1600** in Bisset *Ess. Hist. Truth* v. (1871) 217 At the last, his Majesty passing through three or four sundry houses, and all the doors locked behind him, his Majesty entered into a little study. **1885** *2nd Rep. R. Comm. Housing Wrkg. Classes* 4 The single-room system appears to be an institution co-existent with urban life among the working classes in Scotland.. even in modern legislation the word 'house' is used for any separately occupied portion of a building, while the word 'tenement' represents the whole edifice, the English use of the terms being reversed.

c. The living-room in a farmhouse, etc.; that which the family usually occupy, as distinguished from the parlour, bedrooms, etc. *dial.*

1674 RAY *N.C. Words* 26 *The House*, the Room called the Hall. *a* **1825** FORBY *Voc. E. Anglia, House*, the family sitting room, as distinguished from the other apartments. **1828** *Craven Dial., Howse*, the principal room in a farm-house. **1893** S. O. ADDY *Hall Waltheof* 182 In this neighbourhood [Sheffield] the kitchen of a cottage is known as 'the house'.

2. A building for human occupation, for some purpose other than that of an ordinary dwelling. (Usually with defining prefix: see ALMSHOUSE, BAKEHOUSE, BREWHOUSE, LIGHTHOUSE, SUMMER-HOUSE, WORKHOUSE, etc., etc.) ***the House***, a popular euphemism for the workhouse.

1552 in *Vicary's Anat.* (1888) App. iii. 151 The house.. for the relief and socour of the poore, called the house of woorke. **1598** in *Antiquary* (1888) May 212 To Constables of the hundred for the housen of the hospitalls iij[s] iiij[d]. **1722** DE FOE *Col. Jack* (1840) 42, I.. went to a boiling house.. and got a mess of broth. **1781** R. KING *Mod. Lond. Spy* 63 Here once were many more of these houses of Resort. **1801** T. A. MURRAY *Rem. Situat. Poor* title-p., A Plan for the Institution of Houses of Recovery for Persons affected with Fever. **1835** DICKENS *Sk. Boz* (1836) 1st Ser. I. 3, I suppose you must have an order into the house. **1839-40** MRS. F. TROLLOPE *M. Armstrong* I. iv. 100 Not the quarter of a farthing, unless you'll come into the house. **1865** DICKENS *Mut. Fr.* I. xvi, 'He was brought up in the'—with a shiver of repugnance—'the House'. **1888** MRS. H. WARD *R. Elsmere* II. III. xix. 140 If they turn us out.. there'll be nothing left but the House for us old 'uns.

b. A place of worship (considered as the abode of the deity); a temple; a church. (Usually ***house of God***, ***the Lord's house***, ***house of prayer***, etc.) ***to bow down*** (or ***worship***) ***in the house of Rimmon*** (after 2 Kings v. 18): to pay lip-service to some principle which one does not accept; to sacrifice one's principles for the sake of conformity.

c **1000** *Ags. Gosp.* Matt. xxi. 13 Hyt ys awriten min hus ys ȝebed-hus. —— Luke vi. 4 He eode into godes huse. *c* **1000** *Ags. Ps* (Th.) lxxxiii[i]. 11 Ic.. wel ceose þæt ic hean gange on hus Godes. *c* **1200** *Vices & Virtues* 33 Alle hem ðe on godes huse wunien. *a* **1340** HAMPOLE *Psalter* xxii. 9 Þat i won in þe hows of lord in lenght of dayes. **1535** COVERDALE *2 Kings* v. 18 Yf I worshippe in the house of Rimmon, whan my lorde goeth there in to ye house to worshippe. **1585** T. WASHINGTON tr. *Nicholay's Voy.* III. xxi. 110 b, The first house of prayer whiche Abraham buylded. *a* **1708** BEVERIDGE *Thes. Theol.* (1710) II. 291 Where God is pleased to reveal Himself most, is called His house. **1718** DEFOE in W. Lee *Life & recently discovered Writings Defoe* (1869) I. p. xiii, Thus I bow in the House of Rimmon, and must humbly recommend myself to his Lordship's Protection. **1811** HEBER *Hymn, 'Hosanna to the living Lord'* iii, O Saviour! with protecting care Return to this thy house of prayer. **1842** TENNYSON *Two Voices* 409 On to God's house the people prest. **1903** KIPLING *Five Nations* 104 Duly with knees that feign to quake—Bent head and shaded brow,—Yet once again, for my father's sake, In Rimmon's House I bow. **1956** N. ANNAN in J. Morris *From Third Programme* 150 If you bow down in the house of Rimmon you admit that its values are more important than yours.

c. A building for the entertainment of travellers or of the public generally; an inn, tavern. (See also ALE-HOUSE, COFFEE-HOUSE, EATING-HOUSE, PUBLIC HOUSE, etc.) Also, used *attrib.* of wines selected and bought in bulk by the management in a restaurant, hotel, etc., to be offered at a special price, and often served from a carafe or by the glass. † ***house!*** an exclamation to summon the landlord or waiter (*obs.*). ***on the house***: at the expense of the tavern, saloon, etc.; also *transf.* and *fig.* (orig. *U.S.*).

1550 CROWLEY *Epigr.* 285 In taverns and tiplyng houses. **1638** SIR T. HERBERT *Trav.* (ed. 2) 220 The Coho house is a house of good fellowship.. in the Coho house they also inebriate their braines with Arace and Tobacco. **1668** ETHEREDGE *She Would if She Could* I. ii, He has engaged to dine with Mr. Courtal at the French house. **1696** DOGGET *Country Wake* v. i, House! house! (beating on the Table). What, are you all dead here? house! **1773** GOLDSM. *Stoops To Conq.* IV. Wks. (Globe) 665/2 Were you not told to drink freely, and call for what you thought fit, for the good of the house? **1834** MEDWIN *Angler in Wales* I. 143 It was a great thing for the house. **1889** *Kansas City* (Missouri) *Times & Star* 30 Nov., The first drink Thursday was 'on the house' in the leading saloons. **1891** *Times* 12 Sept. 10/3 A tied house .. is one.. owned by a brewer for the sale of his goods. **1934** J. A. LEE *Children of Poor* (1949) 26 'I must have a drink.' Here, have one on the house. **1944** AUDEN *For Time Being* (1945) 77 A voice I'd heard before, I think, Cried: 'This is on the House.' **1958** M. DICKENS *Man Overboard* xiii. 214 Laundry and cleaning were on the house. **1959** N. MAILER *Advts. for Myself* (1961) 95 One night just for the hell of it he has one on the house with the society gal, and she gets pregnant. **1967** W. SOYINKA *Kongi's Harvest* 18 *Daodu*:... Naturally it's on the house. *Secretary*: No, thank you. I prefer to pay for my drinks. **1967** O. LANCASTER *With Eye to Future* v. 120 The food was good and cheap, the house burgundy at five bob a bottle excellent. **1973** *Good Food Guide* 313 Small family guest house... House wine only (Hirondelle), £1 a carafe, 15p the glass. **1973** K. GILES *File on Death* ii. 28 The Chief Inspector.. signed the bill in defiance of Honeybody's pleas for welsh rarebit and a trial run of the house port. **1976-7** *Art N.Z.* Dec./Jan. 46/3 (Advt.), *Havelock red*: unlike other house reds has avoided becoming too functional and is not at all cliché. **1979** *Tucson Mag.* Apr. 77/3 Best deal is probably the dinner package for $5.45, including.. house wine with the meal. **1986** *Times* 31 May 15/2 My companion's smoked salmon salad.. was nicely complemented by the sprightly Californian house wine (£6.75).

3. A building for the keeping of cattle, birds, plants, goods, etc. (See also COW-HOUSE, DOVEHOUSE, GREENHOUSE, HEN-HOUSE, HOTHOUSE, OUTHOUSE, STOREHOUSE, WAREHOUSE, etc.)

1503-4 *Act 19 Hen. VII*, c. 37 §5 Too Cotages or Meses wyth Howses & Wharfes.. in Stepeney. **1523** FITZHERB. *Surv.* xx. (1539) 41 An oxe hous, a hey howse. **1577** B. GOOGE *Heresbach's Husb.* I. (1586) 13 These.. be Barnes to laye Corne in. In some places they use.. stackes set upon proppes.. but the houses are a great deal better. *Ibid.*, Next are houses for my sheepe, and next them for Kine, Calves, and Heyfers. **1591** SHAKS. *1 Hen. VI*, I. v. 24 So.. Doues with noysome stench Are from their.. Houses driven away. **1669** W. SIMPSON *Hydrol. Chym.* 216 Garden houses built at convenient distances. **1726** *Adv. Capt. R. Boyle* 28 A little House, meant for a Green-house. *Mod.* The gardener who has charge of the houses.

4. a. The place of abode of a religious fraternity, a religious house (cf. *house of religion*, sense 15), a convent; *transf.* the religious fraternity itself.

c **1375** *Sc. Leg. Saints, Eugenia* 265 Quhen þe abbot wes dede, Ewyne chosine wes in his stede; And sa wele gouernyt þe houss. *c* **1400** *Rom. Rose* 6692 Houses that han proprete, As templers and hospitelers, And as these chanouns regulers. **1492** *Bury Wills* (Camden) 73 Item I bequethe to euery hows of ffryeres in Cambredge, Lynne, Norwiche, Thetford, Clare, Sudbury, to eche of thes howses vjs. viijd. **1556** *Chron. Gr. Friars* (Camden) 32 One of that owse John Forrest was comandyd to preche at Powlles crosse the sonday after. **1631** WEEVER *Anc. Fun. Mon.* 813 A famous religious house of Carmelite Friers. **1855** PRESCOTT *Philip II*, II. vi. (1857) 259 The abbots.. were indebted for their election to the religious houses over which they presided.

b. A college in a university (i.e. either the building, or the fellows and students collectively). Chiefly in traditional phrases and uses, esp. in ***the House***, familiar name for Christ Church, Oxford, and ***Peterhouse***, for St. Peter's College, Cambridge.

1536 *Act 27 Hen. VIII*, c. 42 §1 Colleges, Houses, Howses Collegiate. **1553** T. WILSON *Rhet.* (1580) 166 When I was in Cambrige, and a student in the kynges College.. the Provost of that house [etc.]. **1576** *Act 18 Eliz.* c. 6 Chief Ruler of any Colledge Cathedrall Churche Halle or Howse of Learninge. **1583**, **1780** [s.v. HEAD *sb.*[1] 25 b] Heads of houses. **1642-6** in Quincy *Hist. Harvard* (1840) I. 517 If any scholar shall transgress any of the laws of God, or the House.. after twice admonition, he shall be liable.. to correction. **1748** J. BELCHER in J. Maclean *Hist. Coll. N. Jersey* (1877) I. 147 If, finally, money cannot be raised for the House.. the thing must be given up. **1856** *Oxf. Univ. Cal.* 16 (*List of Officers*) The Hebdomadal Council. Official.. Heads of Houses.. Professors.. Members of Convocation. **1868** [see HOUSEMAN 3]. **1894** in *Westm. Gaz.* 5 July 2/2 The indignation.. felt by the present undergraduates of Christ Church against the individuals who deliberately introduced outsiders for the express purpose of wrecking the house.

c. A boarding-house attached to and forming a portion of a public school; the company of boys lodged in such a house. Also, in day schools, a division of the school for purposes of organization and games or other competition. Also *attrib.*

1855 J. A. SYMONDS *Let.* Oct. (1967) I. 64 Tom Parr who has just joined his regiment came down here today with an old house fellow. **1856** —— *Let.* June I. 73, I had them sent to the Head of the House who flogged two. **1857** HUGHES *Tom Brown* I. vi, I'm as proud of the house as any one. I believe it's the best house in the school, out-and-out. **1857** —— *Let.* 15 Nov. I. 126 Yesterday I played in a house match. **1891** *Pall Mall G.* 6 Oct. 2/3 The real unit in most of the large public schools is the 'house', and it is the house-master who has the most powerful influence over his pupils. *Mod.* A football match between two houses. **1899** KIPLING *Stalky & Co.* 124, I thought the house-prefects might know more about it than I did. They ought to. They're giddy palladiums of public schools. **1908** A. HUXLEY *Let.* Nov. (1969) 29 M'tutor, who is also my house tutor and my division beak, is a dear man. **1922** C. E. MONTAGUE *Disenchantment* vii. 93 A boy of this kidney, while looking on at a vital house match, will give his mind ease by telling a friend what 'a lot of stinkers' the other house are. **1925** *City of Oxford Sch. Mag.* Mar. 8 Kerry House hold the new cup for the winning House for the first year. *Ibid.* July 33 In the points counting for the House Shield. **1949** W. B. GALLIE *Eng. School* ii. 31 He managed to infuse his ideas into the masters who coached the school's junior fifteens, house fifteens, and so on. **1965** A. NICOL *Truly Married Woman* 76 An important football house-match was scheduled for that afternoon. **1966** P. WILLMOTT *Adolescent Boys E. London* v. 93 After registration I took house prayers as House Captain.

d. The building in which a legislative or deliberative assembly meets; *transf.* the assembly itself; a quorum of such an assembly, esp. in the phrases ***to make a house***, ***keep a house***. (See also *House of* COMMONS, *of* DELEGATES, *of* LORDS, *of* REPRESENTATIVES, *Houses of* PARLIAMENT, etc., under these words.)

1545 BRINKLOW *Compl.* 3 b, All the degreys of men in the Parlament howse. **1548** HALL *Chron., Hen. VI* 158 The commons of the lower house, not forgettyng their olde grudge. **1559** in Strype *Ann. Ref.* (1824) I. App. vi. 399 What fourther authoritie can this howse give unto her highness, then she hath already? *a* **1577** SIR T. SMITH in Strype *Eccl. Mem.* (1721) III. v. 55 Do you remember then the motion of the Speaker and the request of the Commons' house? **1624** in *Crt. & Times Jas. I* (1849) II. 450 Sir Edward Coke is of the house. *a* **1635** NAUNTON *Fragm. Reg.* (Arb.) 39 Sir Henry Norris, whom she called up at a Parliament, to sit with the Peers in the higher House, as Lord Norris of Ricot. **1648** DK. HAMILTON in *H. Papers* (Camden) 160 By his submission to the 2 Houses. **1648** HERRICK *Hesp.* (1869) 326 As when the disagreeing Commons throw About their House, their clamorous I, or No. **1716** B. CHURCH *Hist. Philip's War* (1867) II. 93 Maj. Church being at Boston, and belonging to the House of Representatives. **1741** MIDDLETON *Cicero* I. vi. 485 Cicero .. made the petition so ridiculous that the house rejected it. **1775** J. ADAMS *Fam. Lett.* (1876) 99 There had not been members enough to make a House, several colonies being absent. **1789** *Constit. U.S.* i. §1 A Congress of the United States, which shall consist of a Senate and a House of Representatives. **1827** HALLAM *Const. Hist.* (1876) II. x. 226 The greatest part of the people of England were not yet satisfied whether the King levied war first against the houses, or the houses against him. **1845** DISRAELI *Sybil* (1863) 164 'Are you going down to the house, Egerton?' inquired Mr. Berners at Brooks', of a brother M.P. **1885** *Manch. Exam.* 21 May 6/1 A House had hardly been made, and Mr. Speaker was scarcely in his chair. **1890** *Blackw. Mag.* CXLVIII. 703/2 Not only must the Government Whips keep a house, but they must keep a majority. **1892** *Chamb. Jrnl.* 20 Feb. 114/2 Those who remain.. for the sake of 'keeping a house'.

e. Applied also to the deliberative assemblies of the Convocation of an ecclesiastical province, of the Convocation and Congregation of a University, etc.; formerly also to a municipal corporation.

1562 in W. H. Turner *Select. Rec. Oxford* 293 At the same Counseyll yt is ordered that Thomas Furres.. be dismyssed this howse [City Corporation]. **1576** *Ibid.* 380 Every suche person, being of thys worshippful howse, shalbe dyscharged of the same howse. **1666** WOOD *Life* 20 Oct. (O.H.S.) II. 90 The maior, bailive[s], and some of the house after him. **1705** HEARNE *Collect.* 31 Oct. (O.H.S.) I. 61 There was a full House [of Convocation]. **1831** SIR W. HAMILTON *Discuss.* (1853) 407 In Oxford it behoved that the regents constituted the House of Congregation.. through which, every measure should pass, before it could be submitted to the House of Convocation. **1871** G. R. CUTTING *Student Life Amherst Coll.* 93 In the summer term of 1828, a legislative body was formed in college, known as the 'House of Students'. Its object was to enact such laws.. as the good of a college community would seem to require.

f. A place of business; *transf.* a business establishment, a mercantile firm. ***the House*** (colloq.): the Stock Exchange. (See also CLEARING-HOUSE, COUNTING-HOUSE, CUSTOM-HOUSE, INDIA-HOUSE, etc.)

1582 N. LICHEFIELD tr. *Castanheda's Conq. E. Ind.* xvi. 41 Treasurer of the house of the Indias. **1756** ROLT *Dict. Trade, House*,.. particularly applied, in partnerships of trade, to that house where the business is carried on. **1814** *Stock Exchange Laid Open* 31 Now for the House itself; that is, the Stock Exchange. **1824** J. JOHNSON *Typogr.* II. iii. 27 Hurrying works through the press.. by dividing them among a variety of houses. **1861** M. PATTISON *Ess.* (1889) I. 41 Some of the large German houses in London.. advanced large sums. **1891** *Daily News* 5 Feb. 3/3 Business in the 'House' does not improve much.

Also, *spec.* (i) = *house of ill fame* (see 11 below).

c **1810** W. HICKEY *Memoirs* (1960) iv. 63, I was informed with vast glee by these wild young men that.. they had discovered two new houses of infinite merit. *a* **1922** T. S. ELIOT *Waste Land Drafts* (1971) 5 I've kept a decent house for twenty years. **1931** R. CAMPBELL *Georgiad* ii. 45 The old 'Matronas' of the Southern Race Can run their 'houses' with a smiling face, Business and pleasure to one end unite. **1954** P. ADLER (*title*) A house is not a home. **1962** *John o' London's* 1 Feb. 115/1 The girls who had worked in 'houses' were unfitted, by temperament and training, for any other sort of life. **1968** L. DURRELL *Tunc* ii. 47 'You see,' said Mrs. Henniker piteously 'what we are up against all the time? How to run a respectable house what I mean?'

(ii) A couture establishment.

1864 *2nd Rep. Children's Employment Comm.* 39 in *Parl. Papers* XXII. 1 At some houses all in the show-room are expected to wear black glacé silk. **1880** in L. de Vries *Victorian Advts.* (1968) *Messrs. Jay* import from the first houses in Paris Models of every style. **1931** S. JAMESON *Richer Dust* v. 145, I have good taste. I could think of dresses. I should have to go round the various houses. **1938** D. SMITH *Dear Octopus* III. i. 108, I can go to Raquelle's London house if I like. **1967** *Guardian* 24 July 4/6 Instead of showing their collections four weeks after the other houses, Givenchy and Balenciaga.. show on August 3.

(iii) A printing or publishing house.

1683–4 J. MOXON *Mech. Exerc., Printing* (1962) 16 A Printing-House may admit of a twofold meaning; one.. relative to the House or Place wherein Printing is used; the other.. only the Printing Tools... Thus they say.. such a one has remov'd his Printing-House, when thereby they only mean he has remov'd the Tools us'd in his former House. **1871** G. MEREDITH *Let.* 3 July (1970) I. 448 The debt has been left unsettled owing to my having kept back my work to perfect it more. It was honourably incurred by me out of consideration for your house. **1935** *Times Lit. Suppl.* 4 Apr. 217/4 Already there obtained something approaching what is now called 'the style of the house'. **1959** N. MAILER *Advts. for Myself* (1961) 399 There was no one in the house who had guts enough to say that *Some Came Running* was a washer-woman at 1,200 pages, and could be fair at 400.

(iv) Used *attrib.*, in ***house journal, magazine,*** etc., a publication written for and circulated within a business firm, group, etc.

1907 *Electr. World* XLIX. 674/1 The subject of 'house organs' for manufacturing concerns was discussed. **1915** *Writer's Bulletin* Jan. 75/1 *The Hoggson Magazine*.. is an example of the artistic heights to which the 'house organ' may attain. **1925** *Writer's Monthly* June 466/1 These little magazines, or internal house organs, as they are called by the advertising fraternity, are usually of an inspirational character. **1959** *Times Rev. Industry* Mar. 5/2 Publications such as.. house magazines. **1962** *Punch* 7 Mar. 375/2 Forty per cent of Sixth Form boys.. read *Punch*, or so.. their house-journal, *Sixth Form Opinion*, tells us. **1969** 'E. LATHEN' *Murder to Go* xvii. 171 *Chicken Feed*, house organ of the Chicken Tonight organization, was not due for three weeks. **1970** T. HILTON *Pre-Raphaelites* ii. 49 *The Germ*.. was the first house journal of a self-consciously avant-garde artistic group. **1970** *Vogue* May 48/2 They want.. to make the cinema altogether a pleasant experience, with programmes, discussions, attractive usherettes.. and a house magazine. **1971** *Nature* 5 Mar. 3/1 *Physical Review*, the house journal of the American Physical Society.

g. A theatre, PLAYHOUSE; *transf.* the audience or attendance at a theatre, or other place of entertainment. Also, of stage or cinema performances closely following each other, ***first, second house***. ***house full***: the announcement posted outside a place of entertainment to indicate to the public that there is no room available; also *transf.*

1662–3 PEPYS *Diary* 8 Jan., The famous new play acted ..'The Adventures of Five Hours' at the Duke's house... We.. were forced to sit.. at the end of the lower formes, so full was the house.. The house, by its frequent plaudits, did show their sufficient approbation. **1739** CIBBER *Apol.* (1756) II. 11 Acted every day for a month to constantly crowded houses. **1756** *Connoisseur* No. 133 ¶4 He.. seldom or never misses appearing at one house or the other, in the green boxes. **1815** W. IRVING in *Life & Lett.* (1864) I. 344 In consequence of acting so often before indifferent houses. **1835** DICKENS *Sk. Boz* (1836) 1st Ser. II. 202 There'll be a full house to-night—six parties in the boxes already. **1891** *Daily News* 3 Oct. 5/6 The familiar London theatre legend, 'House full', might have been hung outside the doors. **1898** J. HOLLINGSHEAD *Gaiety Chron.* ii. 115 No 'house full' boards were exhibited outside the theatre. **1906** J. M. SYNGE *Lett. to Molly* (1971) 49, I dreamed also that Tolstoi.. came to our plays.. and that there was a very bad house. **1906** *Daily Chron.* 23 Dec. 3/2 It would be natural to suppose that the book trade this Christmas has been a 'house full' affair. **1914** *Aeroplane* 2 Sept. 211/1 Both Services have practically put up the 'House Full' sign, and have a waiting list yards in length. **1921** G. B. SHAW *Let.* 27 Dec. in *To a Young Actress* (1960) 12 Until you can hit the boy at the back of the gallery in a three hundred pound house. **1924** in L. Warwick *Death of Theatre* (1960) vi. 62 The management have long felt that many first-class productions have been spoilt by the rush of two houses. **1930** J. B. PRIESTLEY *Angel Pavement* vii. 358 If I can get two seats for the first house tomorrow night, will you come with me? **1939** JOYCE *Finnegans Wake* 62 It was after the show at Wednesbury that one tall man.. returning late.. from the second house.. had a barkiss revolver placed to his face. **1940** H. G. WELLS *Babes in Darkling Wood* II. i. 137 He might go into some cinema... Or he might get in for the second house at the Holborn or Pavilion? **1968** *Blues Unlimited* Dec. 4 He played little guitar the first house but sang 'Two ways to skin a cat'.

h. Used *attrib.* of a permanent or resident band, jazz group, etc.

1934 S. R. NELSON *All about Jazz* iv. 76 There are many combinations which only record and play over the radio... These orchestras are often composed of prominent members of famous bands, in which case they are known as 'house' combinations. **1958** J. C. HOLMES *Horn* (1959) 34 The drummer for the house band good-naturedly chased Wing's warm-up runs with precise rim-shots. **1966** *Crescendo* Nov. 23/1 He was part of the house rhythm section for Prestige Records. **1968** *Blues Unlimited* Nov. 26 The earlier Tampas are better—though hardly classifiable as 'house band'.

5. The persons living in one dwelliing; the inmates of a house collectively: a household, family. Also ***son, daughter of the house.***

c **950** *Lindisf. Gosp.* John iv. 53 Gelefde ðæ ilca & hus his all [*Ags. Gosp.* eall his hiw-ræden]. *c* **1230** *Hali Meid.* 3 Forȝet ti folc & tine fader hus. **1382** WYCLIF *Acts* xvi. 33 And he is baptysid, and al his hous anoon. *c* **1386** CHAUCER *Sqr.'s T.* 16 In Armes desirous As any Bacheler of al his hous. **1535** COVERDALE *1 Kings* xvii. 15 He ate, & she also, and hir house a certayne season. **1592** SHAKS. *Rom. & Jul.* III. iii. 156 Commend me to thy Lady, And bid her hasten all the house to bed. **1768** JOHNSON *Lett. to Mrs. Thrale* 23 May, I count the friendship of your house among the felicities of life. **1802** C. WILMOT *Let.* 3 Jan. in *Irish Peer* (1920) 32 Lady Mount Cashal was handed out of the Room by Monsieur l'Abbé Sièyes, and I by Monsieur, the Son of the House. **1894** GLADSTONE *Horace, Odes* III. xvii. 16 Tomorrow a young porker slay, And let thine house make holiday. *Mod.* The whole house was down with influenza. **1926** WODEHOUSE *Heart of Goof* ii. 54 The modern butler.. looks like the son of the house. **1949** 'M. INNES' *Journeying Boy* xiii. 167 Mr. Thewless.. felt that the son of the house might turn out to be someone to rely upon. **1968** 'D. TORR' *Treason Line* 30 The daughter of the house, a slim, petite girl.

6. A family including ancestors and descendants; a lineage, a race: esp. one having continuity of residence, of exalted rank, or high renown.

c **1000** *Ags. Ps.* (Th.) cxiii. 21 [cxv. 12] Þu ȝebletsadest bearn Israhela, Aarones hus. *c* **1340** *Cursor M.* 10863 (Trin.) In iacobes hous regne shal he. **1382** WYCLIF *Luke* ii. 4 He was of the hous and meyne of Dauith. *c* **1477** CAXTON *Jason* 53 Honour and worship to me and of oure house. **1548** HALL *Chron., Edw. IV* 213 The Duke of Burgoin loved better the house of Lancastre, then the house of Yorke. **1592** SHAKS. *Rom. & Jul.* III. i. 111 A plague a both your houses! **1617** MORYSON *Itin.* III. 263 Subject to the house of Austria. **1789** BELSHAM *Ess.* I. iii. 51 The right of blood clearly rested in the house of Stuart. **1849** MACAULAY *Hist. Eng.* v. I. 629 Not far off sleep two chiefs of the great house of Howard. **1872** RUSKIN *Eagle's N.* §171 To read the shields, and remember the stories, of the great houses of England.

7. *transf.* and *fig.* (from 1). **a.** *fig.* Dwelling-place; place of abode, rest, deposit, etc.

a **1000** *Elene* 1237 (Gr.) Þus ic frod and fus þurh þæt fæcne hus, wordcræft wæf and wundrum læs. *c* **1200** *Grave* in *Erlanger Beitr.* (1890) 11 Dureleas is ðæt hus. *c* **1205** LAY. 32155 Þe pape hatte Sergius, he weteð Peteres hus. *a* **1310** in Wright *Lyric P.* 73 For sunful folk, suete Jesus, Thou lihtest from the heȝe hous. **1382** WYCLIF *Job* xxx. 23 For thou shalt take me to deth, wher is sett an hous to alle liuende. **1500–20** DUNBAR *Poems* xxi. 67 Quhen na houss is bot hell and hevin. **1580** SIDNEY *Arcadia* III. Wks. 1724 II. 420 The house of death had so many doors, as she would easily fly into it. **1598** B. JONSON *Ev. Man in Hum.* II. i, Like a pestilence, it doth infect The houses of the brain. *c* **1610** *Women Saints* 135 Breathing out as much as my poor little breath could afforde from my house of haye [cf. 'All flesh is grass']. **1784** COWPER *Task* II. 458 A heavenly mind May be indifferent to her house of clay. **1814** SCOTT *Ld. of Isles* IV. iv, The peaceful house of death. **1850** TENNYSON *In Mem.* xxxv, Yet if some voice that man could trust Should murmur from the narrow house.

b. *transf.* The habitation of any animal; a den, burrow, nest; the shell of a snail, tortoise, etc., in which the animal lives or into which it retires.

a **1000** *Phœnix 202* in *Exeter Bk.*, Þær se wilda fuȝel.. ofer heanne beam hus ȝetimbreð. *a* **1250** *Owl & Night.* 623 Hwane min hus stont briht and grene Of þine nis nowiht isene. **1398** TREVISA *Barth De P.R.* XVIII. cvii. (Bodl. MS.), The snaile hatte testudo and haþ þat name, for he is heled in his hous in a chambre. *c* **1566** J. ALDAY tr. *Boaystuau's Theat. World* B vij, Snayles.. beare with them their houses easely on their backes. **1638** SIR T. HERBERT *Trav.* (ed. 2) 25 The Sea Tortoise is not much differing from those at land, her house or shell is only flatter. **1728–46** THOMSON *Spring* 654 The swallow.. to build his hanging house Intent. **1748** H. ELLIS *Hudson's Bay* 160 The Constructions of these Creatures [Beavers] Dens, Burroughs, or, as they are commonly called, Houses are.. built of Wood, Stone, and Clay.

c. A receptacle of any kind.

1610 T. GODWIN *Moses & Aaron* I. x. 43 They did put them into one skin in which there was the proportion of four housen or receptacles, and not into four skins. **1881** RAYMOND *Mining Gloss.*, *House of water*, a cavity or space filled with water. *Cornwall.*

8. *Astrol.* **a.** A twelfth part of the heavens as divided by great circles through the north and south points of the horizon; the whole sky, excluding those parts that never rise and that never set, being thus divided into twelve houses, numbered eastwards, beginning with the ***house of the ascendant*** (see ASCENDANT B. 1), and each having some special signification attached to it. **b.** A sign of the zodiac considered as the seat of the greatest influence of a particular planet; each of the seven planets, except the sun and moon, having two such houses, a ***day house*** and a ***night house***.

c **1391** CHAUCER *Astrol.* II. §4 The hows of the assendent, þat is to seyn, the firste hous or the est Angle, is a thing more brod & large. **1398** TREVISA *Barth. De P.R.* VIII. ix. (1495), Amonge triplycytees of howses those that ben in the Eest ben stronger in theyr werkynge. **1477** EARL RIVERS (Caxton) *Dictes* 5 b, Whan the planetes entre in to their houses. **1583** STUBBES *Anat. Abus.* II. (1882) 58 The houses, aspects, and locall places of the signes and planets. **1594** BLUNDEVIL *Exerc.* IV. xxxvi. (1636) 494 A general figure of the 12. houses of Heauen, according to the Iudicial of Astrology. **1632** MASSINGER *City Madam* II. ii, Venus, in the west angle, the house of marriage the seventh house, in trine of Mars, in conjunction of Luna. **1695** CONGREVE *Love for L.* II. iii, This is the effect of the malicious conjunctions and oppositions in the third house of my nativity. **1819** WILSON *Compl. Dict. Astrol.* s.v., There are two kinds of houses.. mundane and planetary. **1897** *Zadkiel's Almanac* 57 When Saturn and Uranus are in the first house.

†**9. a.** Each square of a chess-board. *Obs.*

1656 BEALE *Chess*, His [the king's] draught is but one house at a time. **1688** R. HOLME *Armoury* III. 263/2 (Chess) House is every one of the squares, whether they be white or black. **1829** A. JAMIESON *Dict. Mech. Science* s.v. *Chess*, A board divided into 64 squares or houses.

b. *Curling.* The space within the outermost circle drawn round the tee.

1883 J. MACNAIR *Channel-Stane* 1st Ser. 50 The stone draws past everything save the winner, which is knocked clear of the house. **1914** J. G. GRANT *Complete Curler* II. vii. 91 The space within the 7-foot ring is colloquially known as the 'house' (*Scotice*, 'hoose'), or sometimes 'parish'. **1969** R. WELSH *Beginner's Guide Curling* xii. 89 A player will strike out the shot and his own stone will also roll out, leaving an empty house.

c. Lotto played (orig. in the Army) as a gambling game with special cards and checks. Also, the ***house-caller*** or ***house-man*** who organizes the game, the winning of the game or the call announcing this, or the prize given. See also HOUSEY-HOUSEY.

1900 *Strand Mag.* Apr. 419/2 When they were not drilling they were playing 'House'. **1917** A. G. EMPEY *From Fire Step* 125 The two most popular games are 'Crown and Anchor' and 'House'. *Ibid.* 126 As soon as the *estaminet* is sufficiently crowded the proprietors of the 'House Game' get busy. **1918** R. D. HOLMES *Yankee in Trenches* v. 60 If you get all your numbers covered, you call out 'house', winnng the pot. **1919** [see *clickety-click* (CLICK *sb.*[1] 8)]. **1920** G. K. ROSE *2/4th Oxf. & Bucks Lt. Infty.* 200 On the air floated the monotonous enumeration of 'House'. **1923** *Daily Mail* 9 June 7 The game of 'house', or 'box and numbers'. **1933** [see *clickety-click* (CLICK *sb.*[1] 8)]. **1936** F. RICHARDS *Old-Soldier Sahib* iii. 69 It takes two men to work a game of House: one calls out the numbers, the other collects the money and issues the cards. **1945** *Gen* 30 June 27/1 The house-caller announced that the amount of the house was two and a half piastres short of ten pounds. **1951** *Amer. Speech* XXVI. 99/1 *House*, the man who runs the game is spoken of as the 'house' or the 'house man'. **1973** *Guardian* 12 June 20 They were in a crooked [Bingo] game... Certain cards were stacked for a quick House against others which were.. distinct long-shots.

II. Phrases. * With nouns. (See also *house of* CORRECTION, *house of* DETENTION, *house of* EASE, etc., under these words.)

10. ***house of call***: **a.** a house where journeymen of a particular trade assemble, where carriers call for commissions, or where various persons in request may be heard of; **b.** *gen.* a house at which one is wont to call or pay a visit.

a **1700** B. E. *Dict. Cant. Crew*, *House of Call*, the usual lodging Place of Journey-men Tailers. **1756** ROLT *Dict. Trade*, *House of Call*, a house where journeymen taylors, shoemakers, and all other artificers meet, and may be heard of. **1844** DICKENS *Mart. Chuz.* xiii, This poor waggoner's house-of-call. **1845** DARWIN in *Life & Lett.* (1887) I. 345, I shall feel a lost man in London without my morning 'house of call' at Hart Street.

11. ***house of ill*** (***evil***) ***fame*** (***repute***): a disreputable house; *esp.* a brothel. Also ***house of accommodation*** (cf. ACCOMMODATION 7 b), ***house of assignation*** (cf. ASSIGNATION 10).

a **1726** VANBRUGH *Journ. London* 1, He was kidnapped into a house of ill repute. **1749** J. CLELAND *Mem. Woman Pleasure* II. 12 This was the safest, politest, and, at the same time, the most thorough house of accommodation in town. **1756–7** tr. *Keysler's Trav.* (1760) II. 76 A particular part of the city, noted for houses of ill-fame. **1790** J. B. MORETON *Mann. W. Ind.* 187 Should business call you into a Grog-shop, or other house of ill fame. **1821** COMBE *Dr. Syntax, Wife* (1869) 317/2 This is a house of evil-fame. **1834** *Sun* (N.Y.) 10 Apr. 2/2 Such men as Samuel Q. Wright, (a bank man) the keeper of a notorious house of assignation, and prostitution. **1861** B. HEMYNG in H. Mayhew *London Labour* Extra vol. (1862) 255/1 Keepers of houses of assignation, where the last-mentioned class [sc. ladies of intrigue] may carry on their amours with secrecy. **1886** N. H. DOLE tr. *Tolstoi's Anna Karénina* xxv, She wanted to escape from the house of ill-fame where she was. **1928** 'BRENT OF BIN BIN' *Up Country* x. 146 They started a house of accommodation in the most unlikely place for patrons. **1973** G. BUTLER *Coffin for Pandora* i. 26 Just as some of them could rise to an elegant house in Brompton, others could sink to a house of accommodation off the Haymarket or even worse.

12. ***house and home***: and alliterative strengthening of 'home'; usually in phr. ***to cast, drive, hunt,*** etc. ***out of house and home***; see also EAT *v.* 4 a. So ***house and harbour***.

c **1200** *Vices & Virtues* 35 Wif and children, hus and ham. **1297** R. GLOUC. (Rolls) 7702 He caste out of house & hom of men a gret route. **1387** TREVISA *Higden* (Rolls) V. 229 Men of þe lond were i-dryve out of hir hous and hir home. **1527** TINDALE *Doct. Treat.* (1848) 122 The prayers of them that.. eat the poor out of house and harbour. **1576** FLEMING *Panopl. Epist.* 204 Hunted out of house and home. **1597–1832** [see EAT *v.* 4 a]. **1885** *Scribner's Mag.* XXX. 394/1 To keep the friends of the deceased from eating and drinking his widow and orphans out of house and home.

13. ***house-to-house*** attrib. phr. (usually with a noun of action, as *visitation*, etc.): Performed or

carried on from house to house in succession. Also *ellipt.* or as *sb.*, = a house-to-house collection, search, etc.

1859 KINGSLEY in *Life* (1879) II. 96 (D.) Unless you had a complete house-to-house visitation of a government officer. **1879** FARRAR *St. Paul* II. 27 An earnest, incessant, laborious, house-to-house ministry. **1893** *Times* 27 Apr. 7/2 A house to house canvass by the registrar would be far cheaper. **1936** 'F. O'CONNOR' *Bones of Contention* 37 We'll make a house-to-house. **1969** B. WEIL *Dossier IX* vi. 44 The house-to-house paid off. We got someone in the mews to talk. **1970** R. RENDELL *Guilty Thing Surprised* xii. 142 Three of us have done a house-to-house in Myfleet. **1973** W. J. BURLEY *Death in Salubrious Place* v. 93 The house-to-house and the questionnaire both appear to have covered the ground pretty well.

14. ***house of office***: † **a.** a building or apartment for some domestic purpose, e.g., a pantry (*obs.*); **b.** a privy.

c **1460** *Towneley Myst.* iii. 134 Make in thi ship also, parloures oone or two, And houses of offyce mo. **1568** GRAFTON *Chron.* II. 161 All houses of office belonging to the same Abbey, were cleane brent. **1613** PURCHAS *Pilgrimage* (1614) 292 They..goe first to the house of office, and there purge their bodie. **1652** *Boston Rec.* (1877) II. 109 It is ordered that noe house of Office..shall stand within twentie foot of any high way. **1823** BYRON *Juan* XI. xl, The very clerks—those somewhat dirty springs Of office, or the house of office.

†**15.** ***house of religion*** (also ***house of piety***): a religious house, a convent. *Obs.*

1419 EARL OF SHREWSBURY in *Excerpta Historica* (1831) 42 No Hous of religion, ne non other place having saufgarde. **1517** TORKINGTON *Pilgr.* (1884) 5 A howse of Religion, of Chanons reguler, and ffryers Austyns. **1599** SANDYS *Europæ Spec.* (1632) 22 Another thing very memorable and imitable in Italy, is the exceeding good provision of Hospitalls and houses of Pietie.

** With verbs. (***break up house***: see BREAK *v.* 57 d. ***bring down the house***: see BRING 15 f. ***set up house***: see SET.)

†**16.** ***hold house***: = keep house, 18 a. *Obs.*

c **1325** *Metr. Hom.* 107 Thar als hoswif held scho house. *c* **1394** *P. Pl. Crede* 51 And þerwiþ holden her hous in harlotes werkes. **1563–7** BUCHANAN *Reform. St. Andros* (Wks.) 1892. 6 And he be maryit, or hald hous out of the college.

17. ***to play*** (***at***) ***house***(***s***): to play at being a family and running a house (see also quot. 1968).

1871 J. H. EWING *Flat Iron for Farthing* (1873) vii. 67 Polly and I had nothing to do.., which led us into the very reprehensible habit of 'playing at houses' in Uncle Ascott's gorgeously furnished pew. *Ibid.* 71 You know we *couldn't* play houses in the church where papa goes. **1918** K. MANSFIELD *Lett. to J. M. Murry* (1951) 220 They always seem to think we were so very very young at the Villa Pauline—playing houses—going to bed under the table for a minute with the cloth pulled down for a blind. **1957** J. KIRKUP *Only Child* ix. 120 If we were lucky, and the weather was fine, we would be allowed to have tea in our tent, and to play houses with the fireside things—the tongs, the little brush, the shovel and the ash-rake. **1959** H. GARDNER *So what else is New?* xiv. 140 'Let's play house, Sally,' the boy said. **1968** *Sun* (Baltimore) 18 Sept. B7/8 He's tried several times to get me to go to his apartment. I've always refused... I'm not ready to play house yet. **1969** GISH & PINCHOT *Lillian Gish* ii. 17 Whenever Dorothy and I were in the same company with Mother, our favorite game was to go to the theater early, dress in Mother's clothes, and play house on stage.

18. ***keep house.*** **a.** To maintain and preside over a household; also (usually ***to keep one's house***), to have one's abode, reside (*in* a place); also *fig.*

1535 COVERDALE *Ps.* cxii[i]. 9 Which maketh the baren woman to kepe house. **1548** HALL *Chron., Rich. III* 52 Kynge Rycharde at this season kepynge his howse in the Castell of Notyngham. **1608** DAY *Hum. out of Br.* I. i. (1881) 8 When the fiery spirit of hot youth Kept house within me. **1702** LUTTRELL *Brief Rel.* (1857) V. 172 Her majestie will not begin to keep house as queen till the 1st of July. **1864** TENNYSON *En. Ard.* 24 In this the children play'd at keeping house. **1890** *Temple Bar Mag.* Sept. 43 The pair began to keep house upon love and hope.

b. With qualifying words: To provide (well, liberally, etc.) for the household, or (esp.) for visitors or guests; esp. ***to keep open house***, to provide hospitality for visitors generally.

1530 PALSGR. 597/1 The kyng is determyned to kepe house or open house this Christemas. **1548** HALL *Chron., Hen. V* 65 b, He kept a liberall hous to all commers. **1608** SHAKS. *Timon* III. i. 24 Alas, good Lord, a Noble Gentleman 'tis, if he would not keep so good a house. **1662** GURNALL *Chr. in Arm.* verse 18 xiv. §2 (1669) 461/2 If the Trade fails in the Shop, there is but a poor house kept within. **1712** ADDISON *Spect.* No. 269 ¶8 Sir Roger..always keeps open House at Christmas. **1849** MACAULAY *Hist. Eng.* iii. I. 366 The King kept open house every day, and all day long, for the good society of London.

c. To manage the affairs of a household; to take charge of the house, and perform or direct domestic duties or work. (See also HOUSEKEEPER, -KEEPING.)

c **1386** CHAUCER *Merch. T.* 138 Ther nys no wyf the hous to kepe. **1598** SHAKS. *Merry W.* I. iv. 101, I may call him my Master..for I keepe his house; and I wash, ring..make the beds, and doe all my selfe. **1796** JANE AUSTEN *Pride & Prej.* iv. (1813) 11 Miss Bingley is to live with her brother, and keep his house. **1891** *Cornh. Mag.* July 57 She meant to keep house for her father.

d. (Usually ***to keep one's house*** or ***the house***): To stay indoors; to be confined to the house, as by illness; also *fig.*; to stay in the house for the purpose of guarding it.

1542–3 *Act 34 & 35 Hen. VIII*, c. 4 Sundrie persons.. kepe their houses, not mindinge to paie..their debts. **1553** T. WILSON *Rhet.* (1580) 146 Beyng sicke, and therefore kepyng his house. **1608** BP. HALL *Char. Virtues & V.* I. 6 Both his eyes are never at once from home, but one keeps house while the other roves abroad for intelligence. **1794** MRS. A. M. BENNETT *Ellen* II. 62 Sure, there is no necessity for us to keep house till she arrives. **1822** SIR C. ABBOTT in Barnewall & Cr. *Rep.* I. 61 Did not the bankrupt begin to keep house as a mode of absenting himself with an intent to delay his creditors? **1864** TENNYSON *En. Ard.* 822 Weakening the man, till he could do no more, But kept the house, his chair and last his bed.

e. ***to keep a house***: see 4 d.

19. Proverbial Phrases. (All *colloq.*) † ***to pull*** (***bring***) ***an old house on one's head***: to get oneself into trouble (*obs.*). Also, ***to pull a house over one's head.*** † ***atop of the house***: in a state of excitement or passion (*obs.*); cf. *up in the house-roof* (sense 19). ***to throw*** (***fling***) ***the house out of the windows*** (= Fr. *jeter la maison par les fenêtres*): to put everything into confusion. ***like a house on fire*** (***afire***): as fast as a house would burn; very fast or vigorously. ***as safe as houses***: perfectly safe. ***to go*** (***all***) ***round the houses***: *fig.* to beat about the bush, to reach the point in a lengthy or roundabout way. ***to put*** (or ***set***) ***one's*** (***own***) ***house in order***: to arrange one's affairs properly.

1608 TOPSELL *Serpents* (1658) 658 You shall pull an old house over your own head by a further provocation. **1611** BEAUM. & FL. *Knt. Burn. Pestle* III. v, We are at home now; where, I warrant you, you shall find the house flung out of the windows. **1611** BIBLE *2 Kings* 20:1 And the Prophet Isaiah the sonne of Amos came to him, and saide vnto him, Thus saith the Lord, Set thine house in order: for thou shalt die, and not liue. **1673** S. C. *Art of Complaisance* 130 If any trick or foul play be offered, we are not to be presently a top on the house. **1739** J. HILDROP *Regul. Freethinking* 7 He.. will have good Luck if he does not pull an old House upon his Head. **1809** W. IRVING *Knickerb.* (1824) 291 At it they went like five hundred houses on fire. **1837** DICKENS in Forster *Life* I. vi. 107, I am getting on..like 'a house o'fire', and think the next Pickwick will bang all the others. **1844** W. H. MAXWELL *Sport & Adv. Scotl.* vi. (1855) 77 Would not ..Stubbs throw the house out of the windows? **1859** CORNWALLIS *New World* I. 79 The owner of the weapon assured him that he was as safe as houses. **1861** GEO. ELIOT *Silas Marner* iii. 53 You'll have less pleasure in pulling the house over my head, when your own skull's to be broken too. **1871** HARDY *Desp. Rem.* III. iv. 92, I shall be high-treasoned—as safe as houses. **1880** E. W. HAMILTON *Diary* 25 Apr. (1972) I. 3 Layard has telegraphed from Constantinople that the Turk is becoming really alive to the necessity of 'putting his house in order'—(if that broken-down establishment will admit of repair). **1913** E. PHILLPOTTS *Widecombe Fair* v. 36 They say things, and do things, and even think things, that you'd fear must throw the house out of windows, and wreck the home for evermore. **1923** J. S. HUXLEY *Ess. Biologist* vii. 292 The theologians..fail in the majority of cases to set their own house in order, to organize the inner reality to react with the outer. **1932** 'A. BRIDGE' *Peking Picnic* xix. 238 Kidnapping Frenchmen is simply too unremunerative for words, whereas we're a perfect gold mine, safe as houses. **1949** A. WILSON *Wrong Set* 49 You had better put your own house in order before you go listening to wicked lies. **1955** *Times* 31 Aug. 7/5 If the conservative parties did not put their houses in order, Japan would soon see a Socialist Government in power. **1958** F. NORMAN *Bang to Rights* 129 Alright but I wish you wouldn't go all round the houses. **1965** V. CANNING *Whip Hand* iv. 43 You mean your little story..wasn't true?.. You went a hell of a way round the houses about this. **1965** *New Statesman* 14 May 749/3 Such a policy of firmness would make it clear to all that we are determined to put our economic house in order.

III. Attributive uses and Combinations.

20. *attrib.* Of or belonging to a house. **a.** Forming part of, or an adjunct to, a house; as ***house-back, -bell,*** †***-cop*** (= HOUSE-TOP), ***-drain, -eaves*** (***-eavesing***), ***-end, -front, -gate, -gutter, -number, -paddock*** (Austral.), ***-pile, -plat, -plot, -roof, -side, -site, -wall, -window, -wiring,*** †***-wough*** (= wall); HOUSE-DOOR. **b.** Used or kept in a house, as ***house-broom, -clock, -cloth, -flannel, -linen, -plant, -sand, -telephone*** (also ***-phone***); worn in the house, as ***house-boot, -dress, -frock, -gown, -jacket, -shoe, -slipper.*** **c.** Belonging to or connected with a house or household; performed or carried on in the house; domestic; as ***house affairs, business, education, expense, fire, game,*** † ***hire, life, rent, service, sport, talk, work.*** **d.** Of persons: Belonging to the household; dwelling in, or employed in or about, a house; as ***house-chaplain, -child, -folk, -priest, -servant, -slave, -steward***; also HOUSE-FATHER, etc.

1604 SHAKS. *Oth.* I. iii. 147 Still the *house Affaires would draw her hence. **1862** D. G. ROSSETTI *Let.* 22 Feb. (1965) II. 443 House-affairs get still further complicated. **1913** C. MACKENZIE *Sinister St.* I. ii. 29 He..wished that he could disappear in such company round corner after corner of the world beyond the grey *house-backs. **1948** C. DAY LEWIS *Otterbury Incident* 69 Between this path and the house-backs there are some small yards. *a* **1817** JANE AUSTEN *Northanger Abbey* (1818) II. xiii. 249 The loud noise of the *house-bell. **1834** *Chambers's Edin. Jrnl.* III. 414/1 He rung the teacher's house-bell. **1921** W. DE LA MARE *Crossings* 88 The far-away house-bell clangs into the room. **1652** R. VERNEY *Let.* in M. M. Verney *Mem.* (1894) III. ii. 46 Sir Ralph is much taken with some 'old men's *house boots', called Scarfaroni. **1914** JOYCE *Dubliners* 123 Then she took off her working skirt and her house-boots. **1823** J. BADCOCK *Dom. Amusem.* 168 Lime-wash..applied..with a brush or *house-broom. **1669** WOODHEAD *St. Teresa* II. xxx. 189 Humble and desirous of doing all the *House-business. **1690** *Lond. Gaz.* No. 2578/4 A Large *House-Clock..is now in the hands of Jonathan Puller. **1597** T. DELONEY *Jacke Newb.* (1630) sig. G3, [They] put an *house-cloath about his necke in stead of a fine towell. **1934** H. G. WELLS *Exper. Autobiogr.* I. iv. 149 Rolls of crash, house cloth, ticking and the like. **1388** WYCLIF *Ps.* cxxviii[i]. 6 Be thei maad as the hey of *hous coppis. **1897–8** *Kalendar R. Inst. Brit. Archit.* 278 Ventilation of *house-drains. **1897** *McClure's Mag.* X. 66 She looked charming in her long, soft *house-dress. **1921** *Daily Colonist* (Victoria, B.C.) 2 Apr. 9/5 House Dresses in V-neck style with kimona sleeves, pockets and belt, open down the front and come in stripes, checks and plain colors. **1966** 'S. RANSOME' *Hidden Hour* iv. 50 A woman wearing a house dress, evidently one of the tenants. **1382** WYCLIF *Ps.* ci[i]. 7 As a nyȝt rauen in the *hous euese. **1603** SHAKS. *Meas. for M.* III. ii. 186 Sparrowes must not build in his house-eeues. **1500–20** DUNBAR *Poems* xxx. 49 With him me thocht all the *houshend [*v.r.* hous end] he towk. **1682** BUNYAN *Holy War* (Cassell) xi. 248 Nor had he stood long under the house-end. **1595** SPENSER *Epithal.* 340 Ne let *housefyres..Fray vs. *c* **1250** *Gen. & Ex.* 3139 Euerilc *hus-folc ðe mai it ðauen. **1925** *Sears, Roebuck Catal.* 28 A neat, trim gingham *house or porch frock is an asset to every woman's wardrobe. **1952** C. W. CUNNINGTON *Eng. Women's Clothing* iv. 135 House-frocks are now all-important as a result of the war economies. **1838** DICKENS *O. Twist* l, *House-fronts projecting over the pavement. **1905** *Westm. Gaz.* 12 Dec. 9/1 The house-fronts of miles and miles of London streets are entirely carried on iron girders. **1963** *Times* 4 June 11/7 The drabness of house-fronts, that so deceive the casual visitor. **1832** *Chambers's Edin. Jrnl.* I. 121/3 Sometimes the fit takes the direction of a new gown for going out with on bad days,..at another time 'a *house gown'. **1896** *Westm. Gaz.* 23 Apr. 3/3 Alpaca makes a practical and pretty house-gown. *c* **1475** *Pict. Voc.* in Wr.-Wülcker 800/20 *Hoc stellocidum*, a *howsegoter. *c* **1325** *Poem Times Edw. II* 159 in *Pol. Songs* (Camden) 330 For *hous-hire ne for clothes he ne carez noht. **1922** JOYCE *Ulysses* 452 In *housejacket of ripplecloth. **1926** *Daily Colonist* (Victoria, B.C.) 1 Jan. 11/1 (Advt.), Christmas Goods Now on Sale. Dressing Gowns, House Jackets, Ties, [etc.]. **1857** MRS. GASKELL *Let.* 7 Dec. (1966) 492 Then we came home; and have been desperately busy ever since, looking over stores, and clothes, and *house-linen, and preserves. **1905** *Westm. Gaz.* 8 Nov. 5/2 No arrangements had been made for her reception. There was no silver, no house-linen. **1850** MRS. CARLYLE *Lett.* II. 135 My *house-money is utterly done. **1895** *Montgomery Ward Catal.* 396/2 *House numbers, 3 inch, made of brass and nicely nickel plated. **1972** C. WESTON *Poor, Poor Ophelia* (1973) vi. 29 Casey began looking for house numbers. **1908** MRS. A. GUNN *We of Never-Never* vi. 64 To the north-west are the stock-yards and *house paddock—a paddock of five square miles. **1951** J. K. EWERS in Murdoch & Drake-Brockman *Austral. Short Stories* 335 The scrawny gums by the house-paddock. **1908** S. FORD *Side-Stepping with Shorty* ix. 137 There was no answer to the call on the *house 'phone. **1935** *Archit. Rev.* LXXVIII. 73 Raymond McGrath designed standard signal lights, clocks, buzzer and house-phone mountings. **1970** 'W. HAGGARD' *Hardliners* i. 11 There was a house-phone on the impressive desk. **1930** M. MEAD *Growing up in New Guinea* ii. 13 Around the stout *house-piles the tides run. **1970** R. LOWELL *Notebk.* 47 Where the Brook Trout dolphins by the housepiles, Grows common..as hamburger. **1873** *Young Englishwoman* Nov. 562/2 Those who have cultivated *house plants for years. **1889** *Boston* (Mass.) *Jrnl.* 19 Jan. 2/4 On the cultivation of house-plants. **1970** D. BARTRUM *Exotic Plants for Home* ii. 29 All the house plants we buy from the florists are amenable to pot culture. **1636** *Boston Rec.* (1877) II. 12 William Hudson hath sould an *housplott and garden. **1531** *MS. Acc. St. John's Hosp., Canterb.*, Rec. for *house rent. **1776** ADAM SMITH *W.N.* I. x. I. (1869) I. 123 There is no city in Europe, I believe, in which house-rent is dearer than in London. *c* **1220** *Bestiary* 463 Ðe spinnere..festeð atte *hus rof. **1546** J. HEYWOOD *Prov.* (1867) 54 He is at three woordis vp in the house roufe. **1860** TYNDALL *Glac.* I. xviii. 126 An edge like the ridge of a house-roof. **1743** W. ELLIS *Mod. Husbandman* Oct. xxii. 238 There are two Sorts of Men Taskers, the Day Labourer, and the constant *House Servant. **1791** BOSWELL *Johnson* 11 Apr. an. 1773 Our female house-servants work much harder than the male. **1882** W. D. HAY *Brighter Britain* I. 37 That's a new dairy-maid and house-servant my friend's just engaged. **1916** *Gilbert & Ellice Islands Protect. Rep. for 1914–15* 15 The Ellice boy, who is much inferior to the Gilbertese in all things that really matter, makes a better house servant. **1966** B. KIMENYE *Kalasanda Revisited* 23 His house servant was away on leave, and the drawbacks of bachelorhood were making themselves acutely felt. **1881** BESANT & RICE *Chapl. of Fleet* I. ii. (1883) 10 *House-service is no disgrace to a gentlewoman. **1892** *Pall Mall G.* 22 Aug. 1/3 Ladies in their *house-shoes and light dresses. **1600** J. PORY tr. *Leo's Africa* I. 52 Vines..planted by an *house-side. **1719** DE FOE *Crusoe* I. iv, Steep as a house-side. **1913** J. LONDON *Let.* 1 Mar. (1966) 373 The hedges around the *house-site. **1949** M. MEAD *Male & Female* ii. 40 Considerations..that one would normally consider in choosing a house-site. **1738** F. MOORE *Trav. Inland Afr.* 110 Some people have a good many *House-Slaves..and they live so well and easy, that it is sometimes a very hard Matter to know the Slaves from their Masters. **1962** S. WYNTER *Hills of Hebron* vi. 81 His master was fond of him and made his mother a house-slave so that Cato could grow up in the big house. **1972** *Village Voice* (N.Y.) 1 June 24/1 Whitey has always pitted one black against the other. The field slaves and the house slaves. **1895** *Montgomery Ward Catal.* 512/1 Ladies' toilet and *house slippers. **1965** B. SWEET-ESCOTT *Baker St. Irreg.* vi. 161 His feet encased in a pair of black velvet house-slippers embroidered in white with the letters 'A.E.' **1607** MARKHAM *Caval.* III. (1617) 1 What *House-sport is it which hath not from it [Hunting] some imitation? **1758** JOHNSON *Idler* No. 29 ¶8 The *house-steward used to employ me. **1922** JOYCE *Ulysses* 304 The house-steward of the amalgamated cats' and dogs' home was in attendance. **1854** EMERSON *Soc. Aims* Wks. (Bohn) III. 174 In their games and in their *house-talk. **1889** *Telephone* I. xxiii. 534/1 The installation of a *house telephone recommends

itself in large hotels. **1921** [see CAMOUFLAGE *v.*]. **1950** T. S. ELIOT *Cocktail Party* II. 94 The house-telephone rings. **1968** J. FLEMING *Hell's Belle* i. 34 The humblest hotel in Paris has a house-telephone. **1856** W. L. LINDSAY *Brit. Lichens* 35 In a scale-like or *house-tile-like manner. **1836–48** B. D. WALSH *Aristoph., Acharn.* I. iv, Scribbling on the *house-walls. **1580** SIDNEY *Arcadia* I. Wks. 1725 I. 41 With..shot from corners of streets, and *house-windows. **1901** *Chambers's Jrnl.* Sept. 616/1 We now propose to consider installations which require, in addition to the ordinary *house-wiring, the machinery necessary for the production of the electric current. **1963** *Times* 6 May p. vii/2 The traditional type of housewiring involved separate circuits for the different kinds of load. *a* **1899** *Mod. Advt.*, A young girl to do general *housework. *c* **1325** *Femina* (MS. Trin. Coll. Cambr. B 14. 39 lf. 122 b), *Houswoghes makyn hous sur.

21. Applied to animals kept in or about a house (= domestic, tame), as ***house-bee***, ***-cat***, ***-cock***, ***-hen***, ***-pigeon***, ***-weasel***; or frequenting or infesting houses, as ***house-ant***, ***-finch***, ***-lizard***, ***-wren***: see also 24; (cf. FIELD *sb.* 19). Also HOUSE-DOG, -DOVE, -LAMB.

1601 HOLLAND *Pliny* I. 320 Of domestical and tame *house-Bees, there are two sorts. **1607** TOPSELL *Four-f. Beasts* 107 Her tayle longer then an ordinary *house cats. **1726** SHELVOCKE *Voy. round World* (1757) 259 They are in size and colour exactly the same with our house-cats. **1963** B. VESEY-FITZGERALD *Cat Owner's Encycl.* 54 But we do not know which species it was that first became the house-cat. **1973** R. LUDLUM *Matlock Paper* vii. 61 His clumsy, long-haired house cat had knocked over a stray glass. **1577** B. GOOGE *Heresbach's Husb.* IV. (1586) 166 b, Of the *house Cocke and the Hen. **1399** LANGL. *Rich. Redeles* II. 143 Rith as þe *hous-hennes..hacchen, And cherichen her chekonys. **1599** H. BUTTES *Dyets drie Dinner* K vij, The *house or tame Pigeon. *c* **1613** MIDDLETON *No Wit like a Woman's* v. i, Not toy, nor bill, and imitate house-pigeons.

22. Objective and obj. genitive, as ***house-bearing*** adj., ***-burner***, ***-burning***, ***decoration***, ***-decorator***, ***-furnisher***, ***-furnishing***, ***house-hunt*** vb. (HUNT *v.* 3), ***house-hunter***, ***-hunting***, ***-letting***, ***-move*** sb., ***-moving***, ***-owner***, ***-robbing***, ***-sweeper***, etc.

1708 J. PHILIPS *Cyder* I. 26 Large Shoals of slow *House-bearing Snails. *c* **1250** *Old Kent. Serm.* in *O.E. Misc.* 30 Manslechtes, *Husberners, Bakbiteres, and alle oþre euele deden. **1876** BANCROFT *Hist. U.S.* VI. xlviii. 293 Among the captives there were house-burners and assassins. *a* **1300** *Cursor M.* 26235 Mans slaghter and *hus brening. **1651** G. W. tr. *Cowel's Inst.* 267 House-burning doth not onely extend to Houses and Barnes wherein Corn is laid up; but also to those heaps which we call Mowes, Stacks, or Reeks, if they be near unto Houses. **1880** H. C. ST. JOHN *Wild Coasts Nipon* 224 Their younger sisters..go about their duties of *house-caring and nursing. **1881** C. C. HARRISON *Woman's Handiwork* I. 4 Industrial arts applied to *house-decoration. **1914** W. OWEN *Let.* 11 Aug. (1967) 276 She has an important business..selling House Decorations, Embroideries, and so on. **1911** G. S. PORTER *Harvester* xv. 321 As a *house decorator you surpass yourself. **1929** F. M. FORD *Let.* 14 Sept. (1965) 189 House-decorators find that books work into rooms with admirable effect. **1935** *Burlington Mag.* July 44/2 The colouring of cupboards and friezes and similar house-decorators' tasks. **1812** BYRON *Ch. Har.* II. xiv. (Orig. Draft), *House-furnisher withal, one Thomas hight. **1896** *Daily News* 21 May 8/1 The Lares, the *house-haunting spirits of ancestors. **1888** *Athenæum* 15 Dec. 806/1 Mrs. Austin at this time..*house-hunted for the Carlyles. **1821** SHELLEY *Let. To Mrs. S.* 1 Aug., That which is necessary for *house-hunting. **1831** A. A. WATTS *Scenes Life & Shades Char.*, *House-hunting*, A tolerable..insight into the mysteries of House-hunting. **1930** *Times Lit. Suppl.* 31 July 625/2 To engage playfully in house-hunting. **1960** *Guardian* 15 Feb. 4/2 Her recent house-hunting in London. **1839** DICKENS *Let.* 19 Nov. (1965) I. 603, I am in the agonies of *house-letting, house-taking, title-proving, [etc.]. **1909** *Westm. Gaz.* 1 Oct. 2/2 The Scotch House-Letting and Rating Bill. **1923** E. BOWEN *Encounters* 92, I shouldn't have thought that a *house-move was exactly the most leisurely time. **1961** *Times* 17 Aug. 11/2 Rearranging my books..after a house-move. **1926** R. MACAULAY *Crewe Train* II. x. 184 I'm extraordinarily sleepy, with all this *house-moving. **1898** *Edin. Rev.* Apr. 417 He wrote..for cultivated *house-owners. **1670** BLOUNT *Law Dict.*, *House-robbing or House-breaking. **1580** HOLLYBAND *Treas. Fr. Tong*, *Ballieur de maison*, a *house sweeper. **1897** *Daily News* 16 Mar. 6/5 If there are many odd trades there are also some very disagreeable ones. None more so, I should fancy, than that of the *housewrecker.

23. Locative, instrumental, etc., as ***house-burial***, ***-wear***; ***house-bred***, ***-fed***, ***-feeding***, ***-going*** adjs.; ***house-encompassed***, ***-proud*** adjs.; ***house-feed*** vb.

1848 KINGSLEY *Saint's Trag.* II. ii. 67 Our *house-bred foe, the adder in our bosoms. **1891** *Tablet* 12 Sept. 437 The tradition of *house-burial seems maintained in other ways. **1895** *Daily News* 20 Dec. 2/6 *House-fed lambs and Berkshire pigs are here in abundance. **1846** WARNES in J. Baxter *Libr. Pract. Agric.* (ed. 4) II. 115 One acre will *house-feed three bullocks, whereas it will require three acres to graze them in the field. **1804** W. TENNANT *Ind. Recreat.* (ed. 2) II. 81 Turnips, cabbages, clover, and all the articles of *house-feeding. **1885** *Times* (weekly ed.) 16 Oct. 15/2 A *house-going clergy would make a church-going people. **1898** *Daily News* 10 Jan. 6/5 For *housewear it is admirable.

24. Special Combinations: **house-agent**, an agent employed (by the landlord or owner) in the sale and letting of houses, the collection of rents, etc.; **house appointment**, a position as a house-physician or house-surgeon in a hospital; **house arrest**, detention in one's house; also (with hyphen) as *vb.*; **house-author**, an author employed by a theatre; **house-ball**, a boys' game in which one player throws a ball against the wall of a house, and the other strikes it with a bat when it rebounds; **house-barge** = HOUSE-BOAT; **house bill**, (*a*) a poster or programme describing a theatrical performance; (*b*) a bill of exchange drawn by a business house on itself; †**house-bird** = HOUSE-DOVE 2; **house-book**, a book for household accounts; **house-bound** *a.*, confined to the house; **house-boy**, a boy employed as servant in a house; **house-burnt** *a. U.S.*, designating tobacco which in the course of being cured in a tobacco-house has been injured or spoilt by disease; so **house-burn** *v. intr.* and (rare) *trans.*, to become or render house-burnt; also **house-burning** *vbl. sb.*; **house call**, a visit made to a patient in his own home by a doctor, chiropodist, etc.; **house cap**, a school cap made of the colours adopted by a particular house, esp. one awarded for proficiency in games; **house-car** (*U.S.*), 'a box-car; a closed railroad-car for carrying freight'; **house-carpenter**, a tradesman who does the wood-work of a house; **house-caucus** (see quot.); **house-chambermaid**, a servant combining the functions of housemaid and chambermaid; **house church** (see quot. 1967); **house-cleaning** *sb.*, the cleaning of the inside of a house; hence (as a back-formation) **house-clean** *v.*; also *transf.*; **house-cleaner**, one who cleans the inside of a house; **house-club**, a club (athletic or other) in a house of business; **house-coal**, coal suitable for house fires; **house-coat**, a woman's informal coat-dress for wearing at home; **house colours** [COLOUR *sb.*[1] 6 c], colours representing a house (sense 4 c above) at a school; **house-cricket**, the common species of cricket (*Acheta domestica*) frequenting houses (as distinguished from the *field-cricket*); **house detective**, a private detective employed by a business firm, hotel, etc.; **house detention** = *house arrest*; **house dinner**, a dinner given to the staff or the occupants of a house at a school, etc.; **house-duty**, a tax imposed on inhabited houses in England; **house-dweller**, one who lives in a house (opp. a nomad, etc.); so **house-dwelling**; **house-engine** (*Mech.*), a steam-engine structurally dependent on the building in which it is contained; **house-factor** = *house-agent*; **house-farmer** (see quot.); so *house-farming*; **house-fast** *a.* (*dial.*) = *house-bound*; **house finch**, a red-headed N. American finch of the genus *Carpodacus*, esp. *C. mexicanus*; **house-flag**, the distinguishing flag of a shipping or other business house; **house-fly**, the common fly (*Muscadomestica*); **house-furnishing**, the furnishing of a house; also *pl.* in concrete sense; **house-girl**, a female domestic servant or, formerly, a slave; **house-god**, a household god; pl. = *penates*; **house governor**, the head of administration in a hospital; **house-green**, a name for the houseleek; **house guest**, a guest staying in a private house; †**house-head** = HOUSE-TOP; **house-help** (*U.S.*), a domestic servant or 'help' (see HELP *sb.* 3 c); **house-husband** orig. *U.S.*, a husband who carries out the household duties traditionally associated with the role of housewife; **house-jobber**, **-knacker** = *house-farmer*; **house journal**: see sense 4 f (iv) above; †**house-lady**, lady or mistress of the house; †**house-lewe** (OE. *hús-hleow*, ME. *hus lewe*), **-lewth**, shelter of a house; **house-lighter** (see quot., and cf. HOUSE-BOAT); **house lights**, lights on the audience side of the stage curtain in a theatre; **house-line** *Naut.*, a small line of three strands, used for seizings, etc. (also called *housing*); **house longhorn**, **longicorn (beetle)**, *Hylotrupes bajulus*, a wood-boring beetle of the family Cerambycidæ; †**house-loom** = HEIRLOOM; †**house-lord** (OE. *hús-hlaford*), lord or master of the house; **house magazine**: see sense 4 f (iv) above; **house-manager**, the manager of a theatre, club, concert-hall, etc.; **house-martin**, the common martin (*Chelidon urbica*); **house-monger**, a dealer in houses (*opprobrious*); **house moth**, either of two moths, *Hofmannophila pseudospretella* or *Endrosis sarcitrella*; **house mouse**, *Mus musculus*, which lives in buildings as well as in open fields; **house-mover** *N. Amer.*, (*a*) a person whose business is to move furniture; (*b*) a machine or apparatus for the physical removal of houses; **house Negro, house nigger** *U.S.* (*rare* exc. *Hist.*), a Negro household servant; **house officer**, a junior full-time member of the medical staff of a hospital, usually (but not always) resident; *esp.* one whose post is tenable by qualified doctors who are not yet fully registered; **house organ**: see sense 4 f (iv) above; **house-painter**, an artificer who paints and decorates houses; so ***house-painting***; **house-parent**, a house-mother or house-father acting singly or jointly as head of a community of (young) persons living together as a family; **house-parlourmaid** (cf. *house-chambermaid*); **house-parlourman**, a male servant who does work corresponding to that of a house-parlourmaid; **house-party**, the guests staying in a house, as distinguished from those invited for the day or less; also = *house-rent party* (below); †**house-pentice**, a 'pentice' or penthouse; **house physician**, a resident physician in a hospital or other public institution, now usually (in Great Britain) a house officer working in the field of general medicine; **house-pride**, pride in one's house, desire to keep one's house clean and tidy; so **house-proud** *a.*, proud of one's house, desirous to see it always at its best (sometimes implying excessive preoccupation with it); **house-raiser**, one who raises or builds a house; **house-raising** (*U.S.*), 'a gathering of the inhabitants in a thinly settled district to assist a neighbor in raising the frame of his house' (*Cent. Dict.*); **house-rent party** *U.S.*, orig. a party aimed at raising money to pay the rent of a house; later, any 'jam' session in a house or apartment; also ***house-rent stomp***, ***strut***; **house-ridden** *a.*, confined to the house (after *bedridden*); **house seat**, a seat in a theatre, etc., reserved by the management for special guests; †**house-shouldered** *a.*, having shoulders sloping on each side like the roof of a house; **house-shrew**, the common shrew-mouse (*Crocidura* (*Sorex*) *aranea*); †**house-sin**, a private or secret sin; †**house-snail**, a shell-snail (cf. 7 b); **house-sparrow**, the common sparrow (*Passer domesticus*), which builds in the eaves and roofs of houses; **house-spider**, any species of spider infesting houses, as *Tegenaria domestica* or *Theridium vulgare*; **house style**, the distinctive printing methods and regulations, including the preferred spellings and conventions of punctuation, of a publishing or printing business; also *transf.*; **house surgeon**, a resident surgeon in a hospital, now usually (in Great Britain) a house officer working in the field of surgery; **house-swallow**, the common swallow (*Hirundo rustica*); **house-tablemaid** (cf. *house-chambermaid*); **house-tax**, a tax levied on houses (= *house-duty*); **house-trap**, a portable bird-trap made of wire netting in which bait has been laid; **house-type**, a type of house; **house-urn**, a cinerary urn of the form of a round cabin with a conical roof, also called *hut-urn*; **house-wagon**, a wagon serving as a house for a company of travellers, a caravan; **house-waitingmaid** (cf. *house-chambermaid*); **housewares** *sb. pl.* (chiefly *N. Amer.*), kitchen utensils and other utilitarian household articles; †**house-wood**, wood for housebote; **house-work**, the work required to keep a house clean and in order; **house-wrecker** = HOUSEBREAKER 2; **house wren**, the common N. American brown wren, *Troglodytes aedon*.

1843 *Ainsworth's Mag.* IV. 64 *House-agents and auctioneers are their attendant sprites. **1873** MISS THACKERAY *Wks.* (1891) I. 362 He had begun life as a house-agent. **1922** T. S. ELIOT *Waste Land* (1923) III. 16 A small house agents' clerk. **1961** *Lancet* 26 Aug. 497/1 After *house-appointments he graduated M.D. in 1900. **1963** *Ibid.* 19 Jan. 176/1 After holding house-appointments, he became an assistant bacteriologist in the Glasgow public-health laboratories. **1936** F. L. SCHUMAN *Hitler & Nazi Dictatorship* Epilogue ii. 441 He was subjected to '*house arrest' for his protection. **1945** M. ALLINGHAM *Coroner's Pidgin* xv. 126 In the normal way when I put a person under house arrest and she breaks it, I pull her in. **1948** A. KOESTLER in *Partisan Rev.* XV. I. 33 All of them are..in fact, under a kind of curfew or house arrest. **1958** *Listener* 13 Nov. 762/2 Galileo lived the remaining years of his life under house arrest. **1963** *Economist* 31 Aug. 732/2 The Hodgsons, banned, house-arrested and persecuted in South Africa. **1970** *New Yorker* 17 Oct. 179/1 The Chinese continue to support Prince Sihanouk, who is said to be living under house arrest in Peking. **1971** *Rand Daily Mail* 4 Sept. 12/4 Father Desmond was banned and house arrested after the book was published, probably for daring to write it. **1864** P. PATERSON *Glimpses Real Life* xxvii. 262 August, or even earlier, when the '*house-author' and the manager determine what it [*sc.* the pantomine] is to be. **1903** *Daily Chron.* 6 July 7/4 He was house-author to a theatre at Sydney. **1884** *Times* (weekly ed.) 19 Sept. 124 A crannoge must have united..the charms of solitude and social facilities. A *house barge could scarcely be better. **1829** H. FOOTE *Compan. to Theatres* 138 The usual bills of the theatres are termed *house bills. **1909** *Daily Chron.* 2 Mar. 3/2 That particular bill of exchange, the 'house bill'—a bill drawn by a firm or company on itself. **1623** tr. *Favine's Theat. Hon.* I. vi. 50 They were reputed no other than

*hous-birds or homelings. **1768** WILKES *Corr.* (1805) III. 286, I beg my dear girl to buy a *house-book, and to set down all expences. **1878** *Harper's Mag.* Jan. 277/1 The rains set in furiously, and I was completely *house-bound. **1960** *Sunday Express* 10 July 11/4 His ailing, house-bound wife is attended to by a home help. **1966** *New Statesman* 21 Jan. 80/3 Housebound married graduates. **1899** *Daily News* 8 June 5/7 Odd jobs as boot and knife cleaning, or where the boys are described as '*house-boys'. **1910** *Cape Times* 8 Oct. 2 House-boy; good references;..apply 6, St. Barnabas Street. **1926** S. G. MILLIN *S. Africans* III. i. 74 There might be black houseboys instead of white housemaids. **1944** *Living off Land* viii. 159 He [*sc* . a Papuan] may be an experienced 'house-boy' in which case he will make his own arrangements for employment. **1955** B. MANVERS *Shadow of Happiness* i. 19 That's my houseboy; he has an unpronounceable name, so I call him John. **1971** *E. Afr. Jrnl.* Mar. 5/1 She is procured by the African houseboys for their employer—a white expatriate. **1640** *Archives of Maryland* (1883) I. 98 Bad Tobacco shall be judged ground leafes, Second Crops leafs, notably brused or worm eaten, or leaves *house burnt, sun burnt, [etc.] . **1772** *Maryland Hist. Mag.* (1919) XIV. 363 For 3 weeks past the Weather has been very unfavourable for the tob[acc]o Cured by fier very much & I suppose has House burnt all tob[acc]o not fierd. **1850** *Rep. Comm. Patents Agric. 1849* (U.S. Dept. Agric.) 321 Splitting tobacco is admired by many who contend that it cures brighter..and [is] less likely to house-burn. *Ibid.* 324 In this crop every leaf was saved, none lost by worms nor by 'house-burning' (that is suffering, or even rotting from being hung too thick). **1897** *Bradstreet's* 25 Oct. 1/4 Some of the leading growers report several crops as 'house burnt' and inclined to rot. **1966** *Publ. Amer. Dial. Soc.* XLV. 16 Tobacco will house burn in wet weather if you don't fire it. **1960** R. H. BLUM *Managem. Doctor–Patient Relationship* ix. 203 The readiness of the physician to make *house calls is important to patients. **1973** R. C. DENNIS *Sweat of Fear* xii. 85, I opened the door, and there she was... I said, 'Doctor, I didn't know you made house calls.' **1899** KIPLING in *Windsor Mag.* Dec. 33/1 'S'pose we're collared?' said Beetle, cramming his red and black *house-cap into his pocket. **1907** *Daily Chron.* 15 June 4/7 The pride of a little boy who wins his house cap at school. **1856** W. FERGUSON *Amer. by River & Rail* 338, I was glad to withdraw myself and my stool within the doorway of a *house-car, as the covered freight-trucks are called. **1858** *Pennsylvania Rail Road Ann. Rep.* 14 The Rolling Stock..consisted..of..Eight-wheeled House Cars. **1688** *Lond. Gaz.* No. 2380/4 William Bowell of Brighthelmston..*House-Carpenter. **1741** W. STEPHENS *Jrnl.* 1 Apr. in *Colonial Rec. Georgia* (1908) IV. Suppl. 118 The other was looked on as a Master House-Carpenter of Repute. **1758** in S. M. Hamilton *Lett. to Washington* (1899) II. 365 And all this without one farthing expence (except about nine pence per day to the best house Carpenters). **1855** *Knickerbocker* XLVI. 222 Beech timber is held in great esteem by ship-builders and house-carpenters. **1888** BRYCE *Amer. Commw.* II. III. lxxiii. 596 What the Americans call '*House caucuses', i.e. meetings of a party in the larger House of the legislature, are not uncommon in England. *Mod. Advt.*, As *House-chambermaid in Hotel. Commercial preferred. **1964** *New Society* 26 Mar. 5/2 Four *house-churches meet regularly on week nights in people's homes in Notting Hill. They are a mixture of discussion, worship, sharing of problems and a social occasion. **1967** D. T. KAUFFMAN *Dict. Relig. Terms* 239/1 *House Church*, church program carried out and centered in homes rather than ecclesiastical structures. **1970** *Daily Tel.* 7 Aug. 10 At the 'house church' each member is given a duplicated sheet with questions and information on the subject for discussion. **1865** MRS. STOWE *House & Home Papers* 45 He could not come in the spring for then they were *house-cleaning. **1942** PARTRIDGE *Usage & Abusage* 154/2 *House-clean* or *houseclean* 'to clean (the) house', seems to me to be a permissible—and very convenient—word. **1954** *Manch. Guardian Weekly* 1 July 2 The sub-committee should houseclean its staff. **1959** 'J. R. MACDONALD' *Galton Case* (1960) xii. 93 With all the outside work I do, I don't get time to houseclean. **1959** *Time* 12 Jan. 26/3 Seldom had a government been so thoroughly housecleaned between midnight and dawn. **1905** *Daily Chron.* 16 May 5/5 A *house-cleaner..who was maddened with liquor, to-day shot..his landlady. **1863** B. TAYLOR *Hannah Thurston* ii. 26 The first thing..was immediately to summon old Melinda ..whose speciality was *house-cleaning. **1928** FOY & HARLOW *Clowning through Life* 294 The Chicago horror was a blessing in one respect—namely, in that it brought about a country-wide house-cleaning. **1936** *Discovery* Jan. 16/2 For one beautiful little specimen [of worked flint] the writer was indebted to the house-cleaning of a busy rabbit. **1951** H. REICHENBACH *Rise Sci. Philos.* xviii. 310 A good deal of house-cleaning is necessary before a philosophy of the social sciences can be constructed. **1959** *Times* 8 June (Latin Amer. Suppl.) 1/3 The new Cuban leaders are bitter that world opinion is now outraged by their house-cleaning methods. **1965** F. SARGESON *Mem. Peon* iv. 91 A char whom she employed for house-cleaning duties. **1969** *New Yorker* 31 May 72/3 A real political house-cleaning. **1867** W. W. SMYTH *Coal & Coalmining* 69 The uppermost notable seam is the well-known *house coal. **1916** in *Vogue* (1966) 15 Oct. 3/1 (Advt.), Artificial Silk Sports or House Coat in pretty, quiet striped colourings. **1937** *New Yorker* 16 Jan. 48/2 The Bendel negligee department is famous for its housecoats. **1946** 'S. RUSSELL' *To Bed with Grand Music* viii. 105 He came back..to find Deborah in a house-coat, cooking supper. **1958** 'A. GILBERT' *Death against Clock* 45 She was in a house-coat—that's what they call dressing-gowns these days. **1973** J. WAINWRIGHT *Pride of Pigs* 50 She..slipped a housecoat over her nightdress and made her way downstairs. **1914** 'I. HAY' *Lighter Side School Life* viii. 224 Have you got your *House colours? **1939** 'G. ORWELL' in *Crit. Ess.* (1946) 63 That mystic world of quadrangles and house-colours. **1961** D. BATES *Fly-Switch from Sultan* xix. 106 So I started a brothel... It was run on the best public-school lines, and there were prefects and houses and in a manner of speaking there were house colours as well. **1774** GOLDSM. *Nat. Hist.* (1776) VII. 349 The *House-cricket, whose voice is so well known behind a country fire in a winter's evening. **1898** *McClure's Mag.* X. 525/2 A *house detective [had] observed the whole transaction. **1922** F. SCOTT FITZGERALD *Beautiful & Damned* II. i. 135 The group was joined by the hastily summoned house-detective. **1939** M. ALLINGHAM *Mr Campion & Others* 178 [He] was quite an ornament in the City police... When he retired he received the job of house detective here. **1969** J. WAINWRIGHT *Take-Over Man* v. 75 It's your reputation. Don't blame me if the house detective finds us and boots us out of the servants' entrance. **1958** *New Statesman* 3 May 555/2, I found an old journalist friend in his second year of *house detention because he had been courageous enough to buck the army. **1870** E. L. BLANCHARD *Diary* 7 Apr. in C. W. Scott *Life E. L. Blanchard* (1891) II. 382 Dine at 7 at Arundel [Club], being the first '*house' dinner proposed. **1851** HT. MARTINEAU *Hist. Peace* (1877) III. IV. xi. 85 The *houseduty—that is nearly the best tax we have. **1909** *Westm. Gaz.* 1 Oct. 3/3 Many of them who dwell in tents during summer and autumn become *house-dwellers in Wandsworth..during winter. **1954** J. R. R. TOLKIEN *Fellowship of Ring* I. iv. 101 Most of the inhabitants..were house-dwellers. **1941** 'R. WEST' *Black Lamb* II. 103 The gypsies..would not dream of going into the church while the *house-dwelling Christians were still about. **1885** *1st Rep. R. Comm. Housing Wrkg. Classes* 21 The system of middlemen, of house jobbers, *house farmers, or house knackers, for by all these titles are designated those persons who stand between the freeholder and the occupier. **1887** *Daily News* 16 Mar. 2/5 It is generally within the last ten years of a building lease that houses in London come into the hands of the house farmer, who lets them out in tenements and asks the maximum of rent while doing the minimum of repairs. **1887** *Daily News* 16 Mar. 2/5 *House farming is admittedly a trade. **1855** ROBINSON *Whitby Gloss.*, **Housefast*, confined by illness or otherwise, to the house. **1891** ATKINSON *Moorland Par.* 51 She..was still house-fast, or unable to leave the house. **1869** *Amer. Naturalist* III. 183 About the gardens [in California] is the *House Finch. **1917** T. G. PEARSON *Birds Amer.* III. 7 House Finch... Other names [include] Crimson-fronted Finch; Red-headed Linnet [etc.]. **1961** O. L. AUSTIN *Birds of World* (1962) 302/2 Very similar to the Purple Finch is the slightly smaller and brighter Mexican House Finch, a common garden bird from California southward through Mexico. **1884** W. C. RUSSELL *Jack's Courtship* II. iv. 62 [I] turned my eyes aloft where the *house flag..was rattling..at the main royal masthead. *a* **1450** *Fysshynge w. angle* (1883) 29 Ye maye angle for hym wyth an *house flye. **1831** BREWSTER *Nat. Magic* x. (1833) 259 The house-fly is well known to have the power of walking in an inverted position upon the ceilings of rooms. **1791** COWPER *Let.* 30 Aug. in *Corr.* (1904) IV. 117 Such [chairs] as will suit may be found probably at Maurice Smith's, of *house-furnishing memory. **1858** *Leslie's Illustr. Weekly* 23 Jan. 127 Goods for Winter Use in the Housefurnishing Line. **1865** MRS. STOWE *House & Home Papers* 61 That such is not always the case in the real home comes often from the mistakes in the house-furnishing. **1904** *Sun* (N.Y.) 9 Aug. 8 The feminine preference for garments and house furnishings over locomotives and drop forgings. **1835** M. MORRISON *Let.* 5 Nov. in N. E. Eliason *Tarheel Talk* (1956) 277 We have been intending for some time to buy a *house girl. **1884** J. C. HARRIS *Mingo* 91 Jenny, the house-girl, refused to sleep at the quarters. **1906** *Dialect Notes* III. 141 *House-girl*, maid of all work. **1945** B. A. BOTKIN *Lay my Burden Down* 55 Part white children sold for more than black children. They used them for house girls. **1951** R. CAMPBELL *Light on Dark Horse* xxiii. 335 We had, at that time, two fine house-girls, the sisters Eugenia and Florentina Diaz y Medina. **1971** *E. Afr. Jrnl.* Mar. 6/1 Lawino condemns the missionaries who only wanted to make her a house-girl. **1600** HOLLAND *Livy* II. xl. 70 There are my *house gods, my mother, my wife, my children. **1634** SIR T. HERBERT *Trav.* 54 These Nomades..wander with their House-gods, day and night. **1905** M. F. REANEY *Med. Profession* iii. 39 The actual daily command is vested in the secretary or *house-governor. **1934** E. MACMANUS *Hosp. Admin. Women* I. i. 13 The Secretary or Superintendent, who may be known either as House Governor, or by some other title, may be..a member of the Medical Staff of the Hospital—with wide experience and a gift for administration. **1961** *Times* 18 July 3/2 (Advt.), Hospital.. House Governor and Secretary. **1964** G. L. COHEN *What's Wrong with Hospitals?* iii. 47 Matron will hand complaints to the Catering Officer, who refers to the House Governor, who sends a memo to the management committee. **1688** R. HOLME *Armoury* II. 88/2 House-leeke..is called generally with us by the name of *House-green. **1921** *Daily Colonist* (Victoria, B.C.) 1 Apr. 8/3 Miss Helen MacDonald.. invited a number of her girl friends to meet her *house guest, Miss Helen Whiteside. **1961** *Times* 27 Sept. 16/5 His house-guests hunt in the day. **1970** N. ARMSTRONG et al. *First on Moon* iii. 61 She was conscious about getting ready for houseguests—her father and stepmother. **1513** DOUGLAS *Æneis* II. vii. [vi.] 9 Syne to the *hous heid ascendis anone. **1835** T. C. HALIBURTON *Clockmaker* (1837) 1st Ser. viii. 62 Well, he roared like a bull, till black Lucretia, one of the *house helps, let him go. **1958** *Listener* 14 Aug. 249/1 Foreign house-helps in London, S.W. **1970** *Canadian Antiques Collector* Feb. 24/1 Presently in came two well-dressed house-helps, one with a splendid gilt lamp..and another with a tea-tray. **1955** *Sci. Amer.* Apr. 4/2 To a chemist 'kitchen-sink fluoridation' is only a minor nuisance, well worth the little trouble and infinitesimal cost, but the average housewife and *househusband may find it less easy. **1961** *Spectator* 9 June 857/3 Housewives, and I suppose househusbands, like to find that every well-known branded article (as advertised on television) costs precisely the same from Land's End to John o' Groats. **1986** *Sunday Express Mag.* 12 Oct. 31/1 John Lennon tried being the house husband for some years, but I'd prefer not to give up my work. **1885** LD. W. COMPTON in *Pall Mall G.* 14 Apr. 1/2 To show the evil results of the middleman or '*house-knacker' system. *a* **1225** *Ancr. R.* 414 Marthe mester is uorto ueden & schruden poure men, ase *huselefdi. *c* **1000** *Leges Penit.* c. 15 in Thorpe *Laws* II. 282 Gife his *hus-hleow and mete and munde þam þe þæs beþurfe. *a* **1240** *Wohunge* in *Cott. Hom.* 277 Iþi burð tid in al þe burh of belleem ne fant tu hus lewe. *c* **1380** WYCLIF *Wks.* (1880) 211 Lie wiþ-outen or geten *houslewth at pore men. **1920** WODEHOUSE *Jill the Reckless* (1922) xviii. 260 The *house-lights went up. **1957** *Oxf. Compan. Theatre* (ed. 2) 465/2 After 1765 the house lights and concealed footlights on traps cover the area in front of the proscenium. **1891** A. J. FOSTER *Ouse* 170 The *house-lighter, so called because a part of it makes a cabin for the men. **1769** FALCONER *Dict. Marine* (1789), *Marline*, a small line, somewhat less than *house-line. **1815** *Sporting Mag.* XLV. 153 My houseline and marline..are equal to any. **1867** [see HOUSING *sb.*[1] 4]. **1938** *Leaflet Forest Prod. Res.* XIV. 1 The *House Longhorn beetle (*Hylotrupes bajulus* L.) ..confines its attack to seasoned softwood timbers. *Ibid.* 2 This leaflet has been prepared to bring the House Longhorn beetle to the notice of architects, builders and property owners. **1962** *New Scientist* 15 Mar. 614/3 Massive timber struts..were already known to harbour death-watch beetles and the house longicorn. **1964** N. E. HICKIN *Househ. Insect Pests* viii. 83 The House Longhorn Beetle is a pest of softwood. **1697** EVELYN *Numism.* iii. 68 They..fixt them as *House-looms to the Inheritance. *c* **1000** *Ags. Gosp.* Luke xxii. 11 And secgeað þam *hus-hlaforde. *a* **1240** *Sawles Warde* in *Cott. Hom.* 245, I þis hus is þe huse lauerd. **1906** *Westm. Gaz.* 7 Nov. 10/2 Lord Selborne..was once the *house-manager of the club. **1924** WODEHOUSE *Bill the Conqueror* xviii. 269 Give it to the house-manager at the Bijou and he'll fix you up with a couple of seats any night you want. **1968** M. CULPAN *Vasiliko Affair* ii. 14 The house-manager, a courteous but wary young man in a dinner jacket. **1767** G. WHITE *Selborne* x. (1875) 34 The swallow and *house-martin. **1767** *Ibid.* xvi. 185 House-martins are distinguished..by having their legs covered with soft downy feathers down to their toes. **1604** ROWLANDS *Looke to it.* 32 *House-mongers, that on earth would ever dwell: Grinding the poore, as their distresses shoe. **1884** *Pall Mall G.* 20 Mar. 1 The purchase of fag ends of leases by speculating housemongers. [**1897** *Proc. Dorset Nat. Hist. & Antiq. Field Club* XVIII. 147, I think that this moth is one of the most universally distributed, being found, I expect, in pretty nearly every house in the kingdom.] **1932** *Entomologist's Monthly Mag.* LXVIII. 77 (*title*) *Borkhausenia pseudospretella* and other *house moths. **1966** J. R. BUSVINE *Insects & Hygiene* (ed. 2) xiii. 354 The house moths are probably species which originated as feeders on dry vegetable matter and have become adapted to dry animal remains. **1835** L. JENYNS *Man. Brit. Vertebr. Animals* 31 M[*us*] *Musculus*, Linn. (*House Mouse.)—Fur dusky gray above with a tinge of yellow; beneath cinereous. **1909** *Westm. Gaz.* 17 Sept. 3/1 We do not suppose that the creation of the first house mouse awaited the building of the first house. **1916** G. E. H. BARRETT-HAMILTON *Hist. Brit. Mammals* II. 635 In all probability the House Mouse is of Asiatic origin. **1964** H. N. SOUTHERN *Handbk. Brit. Mammals* v. 86 Break-back traps used on a large scale for catching House Mice can produce useful figures [for population studies]. **1838** D. STEVENSON *Sk. Civ. Engin. N. Amer.* 316 He and his father..had followed the business of '*house-movers' for fourteen years. **1867** *Atlantic Monthly* Jan. 106/2 Jedwort had over a house-mover from the North Village. **1959** *Times* 18 June (Suppl. Queen in Canada) p. vi/3 In all, 525 homes were lifted from their old foundations and, cradled in the steel framework of the housemovers, moved to their new locations. **1711** *Boston News-Let.* 21 May 2/2 (Advt.), A Young *House-Negro Wench of 19 Years of Age that speaks English to be Sold. **1771** in *Maryland Hist. Mag.* (1919) XIV. 135 You will have it that my People are not well fed, it is true they do not live so well as our House negroes, But full as well as any Plantation negroes. **1884** J. C. HARRIS *Mingo* 191 The house negroes stood in mortal dread of Blue Dave. **1936** M. MITCHELL *Gone with Wind* iii. 49 The house-negroes..considered themselves superior to white trash. **1880** J. C. HARRIS *Uncle Remus* (1884) 116 Dey er mighty biggity, dem *house niggers is, but I notices dat dey don't let nuthin' pass. **1970** G. JACKSON *Let.* 4 Apr. in *Soledad Brother* (1971) 207 This running dog..was transmitting the credo of the slave to our youth, the mod version of the old house nigger. **1971** K. WHEELER *Epitaph for Mr. Wynn* (1972) xii. 149 Barton called him a house nigger... By Barton's lights, I suppose he was. **1973** *Black World* June 13/1 The murder of Mrs. Mann by the Black maid in the Bullins play affirms the maid's Blackness and consummates her transition from a foot-shuffling house nigger to a proud Black woman. **1934** E. MACMANUS *Hospital Admin. Women* II. iii. 65 When doing 'a morning round' with a House Physician or Surgeon, the Ward Sister will put him in possession of any new facts relating to each patient before they reach that patient's bed. The Sister should stand on one side of the bed, the *House Officer on the other. **1966** *Lancet* 24 Dec. 1399/1 A man holds a senior house-officer post for up to eighteen months. **1969** S. G. HILL in Milne & Chaplin *Mod. Hosp. Managem.* iii. 46 In most hospitals and in most specialties, the medical team comprises the consultant who is the senior doctor, the registrar (a doctor of some four or five years' experience), and either a junior house officer (a newly qualified doctor holding a pre-registration post) or senior house officer (a doctor with rather more experience, often from overseas). **1973** *Lancet* 17 Feb. 17 (Advt.), Burton Road Hospital, Dudley... Applications are invited for the post of Senior House Officer in Geriatrics... Resident staff comprises of 1 Registrar and 2 Senior House Officers. *Ibid.* (Advt.), Chester City Hospital... Applications are invited for the post of House Officer (Geriatrics), pre- or post-registration... Accommodation will be available. **1689** *Lond. Gaz.* No. 2416/4 William Bishop of Reading, a *House Painter. **1756** ROLT *Dict. Trade* s.v. *Painter*, *House-painter*, one who paints things with plain colours, as wainscotting, doors, windows, frames. **1875** E. SPON *Workshop Receipts* 105/1 *House-Painting.—To produce the different tints, various colours are added to the white-lead base. *a* **1877** KNIGHT *Dict. Mech.* II. 1597/2 In house-painting, the pigment most extensively used is white-lead. **1929** D. H. LAWRENCE *Phoenix II* (1968) 602 There were several brushes for house-painting. **1951** M. BUCHANAN *Children's Village* 18 There are almost 200 children in the Village now. Each house has in it 15 or 16 boys and girls, their *house-parents,..and a teacher-help. **1964** *New Statesman* 10 Apr. 582/1 (Advt.), House-parents for African-Asian married students' hostel. *Mod. Advt.*, *House-parlourmaid wanted. Must wait well at table. **1923** *Daily Mail* 25 Jan. 5 A number of men are becoming *house-parlourmen. **1931** *Morning Post* 10 Aug. 16/6 House-parlourman Required for maisonette. **1961** *Times* 17 Oct. 1/3 House-Parlourman wanted. **1876** TROLLOPE *Amer. Senator* (1877) I. xxiv. 248 Partners were selected within the *house party. **1880** OUIDA *Moths* I. 168 Anybody who is in the same house-party with yourself. **1895** M. CORELLI *Sorrows Satan* xxi, Invitations to our dinners and house-parties. **1956** M. STEARNS *Story of Jazz* (1957) xiii. 145 Its ancestry was long obscured by labels such as 'house-party', 'rent-party', 'parlor social', or simply 'Harlem' piano style. **1968** *Blues Unlimited* Nov. 11 He was around here in town then playing houseparties. **1613** T. GODWIN *Rom. Antiq.* (1658) 16 Sheltred from the rain by the help of boards upheld with forks in manner of *house-pentices. **1753** N.

TORRIANO *Gangr. Sore Throat* 6 The Fever increasing every Moment, they..sent in the Evening for the *House-Physician. **1905** M. F. REANEY *Med. Profession* iii. 39 Finally, there is a junior staff of house physicians and surgeons and the like, working directly under the visiting staff, and responsible for the treatment of the patients in their absence. **1934** House physician [see *house officer* above]. **1962** D. MARGERSON *Med. as Career* vi. 42 Two pre-registration posts, those of house physician and house surgeon, must be held before full registration is granted. **1970** *New Yorker* 23 May 73/3 Alek Primrose plays..a house physician so nearsighted that he sometimes consults closets. **1908** *Daily Chron.* 3 Nov. 4/7 'A Quoi Tient la Superiorité des Anglo-Saxons?' It is in '*house pride'. **1909** *Ibid.* 7 Dec. 1/2 The 'instinct of house-pride' seems almost never entirely wanting in the home studied. **1936** *Punch* 19 Oct. 600/1 The joke of Felix's housepride continues a trifle too long. **1849** C. BRONTË *Shirley* II. vii. 169 You are what you call *house-proud; you like to have everything handsome about you. **1899** *Daily News* 17 Oct. 4/7 It is a bad thing for the mother of a family if she cannot be a little 'house-proud'. **1932** *Times Lit. Suppl.* 1 Sept. 603/2 His wife, house-proud as most North Country women are. **1960** *Times* 4 Mar. 13/7 Even under discouraging conditions.. you will see ample proof of house-proud families. *a* **1639** WOTTON *Parall.* (J. s.v. *House-keeper*), We know the people are apter to applaud housekeepers than *houseraisers. **1704** in *Essex Inst. Hist. Coll.* (1866) VIII. 223, I was at my L[and-]Lords *house raising. **1829** *Vindicator* (Montreal) 22 Dec. 3/2 A man..who, with some others, attended at a house-raising six miles from this town. **1843** *Amer. Pioneer* II. 451 The frequent necessity for united efforts at house-raisings, log-rollings, corn-huskings, &c. **1857** J. SMITH *Hist. Jefferson Coll.* 17 Conferences..held at log-rollings, house-raisings, or corn-huskings. **1927** J. D. FREEMAN *When West was Young* 415 They would..reach the West in time for a big house-raising which would be given them by the entire neighborhood. **1949** *Time* 2 May 22/2 It was just like an old-fashioned house-raising bee. **1925** *Inter-State Tattler* 27 Feb. 8/2, I am a tamer of wild women and bitterly against *house-rent parties. **1926** WHITEMAN & MCBRIDE *Jazz* viii. 177 Big sessions of blues were held in the South among the colored people, the biggest of all at 'house rent stomps' when a negro found himself unable to pay his rent. **1938** [see DOWN *prep.* 2 e]. **1955** SHAPIRO & HENTOFF *Hear me talkin to Ya* xii. 210 Joe..would bash at numerous functions and house-rent stomps along Carlisle and John Streets. **1956** M. STEARNS *Story of Jazz* (1957) xv. 168 A house-rent party, an unstable social phenomenon that was stimulated by Prohibition and made necessary by the Depression. **1964** W. R. DIXON in J. H. Clarke *Harlem* 138 The legends of the house rent parties are legion. **1968** *Blues Unlimited* Nov. 22 There are the more 'functional' Texas and Chicago house-rent pianists. **1895** *N. & Q.* 8th Ser. VIII. 468/2 A poor *house-ridden octogenarian. **1952** W. GRANVILLE *Dict. Theatr. Terms* 100 **House seats*, free seats given by courtesy of the house. **1552** HULOET, *House shouldred, *dimissis humeris*. **1645** RUTHERFORD *Tryal & Tri. Faith* xv. (1845) 162 Kept from the incursion of a *house-sin, and a home-bred corruption. **1610** GUILLIM *Heraldry* III. xvii. (1611) 154 These are called *House-snailes, either because they so carrie their houses upon their backe..or because vsually they breed about old houses. **1660** BOYLE *New Exp. Phys. Mech.* Digress. 372 A great, gray, House-Snail (as they call it). **1674** RAY *Collect. Words, Eng. Birds* 88 The *House-sparrow. **1897** *Times* 5 Jan. 10/4 House sparrows feed on grain during the winter. **1721** BRADLEY *Philos. Acc. Wks. Nat.* 135 The black *House Spider, whose Antennæ are seemingly pointed with Diamonds. **1883** J. G. WOOD in *Gd. Words* Dec. 762/1 The common House-spider ..sometimes grows to an enormous size. **1810** *Irish Mag.* Feb. 67/2 The true riding *housestile is distinguished in every page. **1940** GRAVES & HODGE *Long Week-end* xxv. 434 The publisher..has discovered..the 'house-style'. **1960** *Design* July 40/1 The present house style is by no means the first evidence of Watneys' interest in design. **1967** L. B. ARCHER in Wills & Yearsley *Handbk. Managem. Technol.* 128 The range of design activities which can be loosely termed 'house style' design. *Ibid.* 139 *House style*, the characteristic shapes and colours by which the products, paperwork, and property of a firm may be recognized. **1967** *Listener* 17 Aug. 220/2 It is the galleries which tend to have a 'house style'..which mount the most coherent exhibitions. **1825** J. MORISON in *Morisoniana* (1831) 240 The *house-surgeon having neglected to retain the elastic. **1836–9** DICKENS *Sk. Boz.* (1850) 146/2 A certificate was read from the house-surgeon of a neighbouring hospital. **1905**, **1962** House surgeon [see *house physician* above]. **1934** House surgeon [see *house officer* above]. **1674** RAY *Collect. Words, Eng. Birds* 86 The common *House-swallow; *Hirundo domestica*. **1766** PENNANT *Zool.* (1776) I. 399 The house-swallow is distinguished..by the superior forkiness of its tail, and by the red spot on the forehead, and under the chin. *Mod. Advt.*, *House-tablemaid..wanted at once. **1787** in O. Browning *Despatches fr. Paris* (1909) I. 207 It is said that the Timbre, the *House-Tax, and *le commerce des Grains* will be strongly oppos'd. **1825** MALTHUS *Diary* 17 June (1966) 232 Complaints of the weight of taxes—Capitation tax. House tax. **1833** J. S. MILL in *Monthly Repos.* VII. 580 A tradesman in Regent Street pays precisely as much house-tax (56l. 13s. 4d.) as the Duke of Devonshire pays for Chatsworth. **1844** H. H. WILSON *Brit. India* I. 469 The house-tax excited the discontent of its inhabitants. **1868** ROGERS *Pol. Econ.* xxii. (1876) 20 In the case of the poor, a house-tax has special disadvantages. **1939** *Brit. Birds* XXXIII. 32 Descriptions of some well-known methods such as the..*house-trap, and bat-fowling have already been received. **1960** E. ENNION *House on Shore* iv. 37 House traps of one kind or another, aviaries to all appearances, are to be found in many enthusiastic ringers' gardens. **1936** *Discovery* Apr. 99/2 A distinctive Irish *house-type. **1953** L. KUPER *Living in Towns* i. 7 A single house-type has been used in such a way as to create variety and interest, by the grouping of the units in different numbers and relationships. **1955** D. CHAPMAN *Home & Social Status* vi. 84 The families living in different house-types have different social and economic characteristics. **1891** *Tablet* 12 Sept. 437 To bring the Italian and German *house-urns into direct connection. **1886** *Pall Mall G.* 12 Oct. 4/1 The highways are blocked for miles with '*house-waggons'. *Mod. Advt.*, Wanted, a *House-waitingmaid, with good references. **1921** *Daily Colonist* (Victoria, B.C.) 1 Apr. 7/1 (Advt.), Extra values in reliable *house wares today and Saturday. **1969** *Sears, Roebuck & Co. Spring Catal.* 565/3 Housewares. **1970** *Toronto Daily Star* 24 Sept. 29/2 (Advt.), 'Perma-Glo' 9-pc. Teflon Cookware Set..Housewares. **1971** *Sunday Express* (Johannesburg) 28 Mar. (Home Jrnl.) 9/3 (Advt.), Housewares..Grapefruit knife..Bathroom Scales. **1602** FULBECKE *2nd Pt. Parall.* 52 The termor hath *house-wood..fire-woode belonging to his tearme of common right. **1841** A. BACHE *Fire-Screen* 119 Mrs. Gibbs, a woman who sometimes came to assist in doing *house-work, had followed Mrs. Brown into the parlour. **1871** *Rep. Indian Affairs* (U.S.) (1872) 378 While the boys are engaged in out-door work, the girls could be employed in sewing or house-work. **1928** D. H. LAWRENCE *Phoenix II* (1968) 531 No woman does her housework with real joy unless she is in love. **1896** A. MORRISON *Child of Jago* xvii. 177 The old buildings were sold..to the *house-wreckers. **1903** *Westm. Gaz.* 7 Sept. 8/2 The hand of the housewrecker. **1936** House-wrecker [see DEMOLITION 3]. **1808** A. WILSON *Amer. Ornith.* I. 133 The *House Wren inhabits the whole of the United States, in all of which it is migratory. **1848** [see WREN 1 b]. **1872** *Amer. Naturalist* VI. 275 Here the common 'house' wren is bleached and faded. **1904** E. GLASGOW *Deliverance* v. i. 442 A half-finished nest which a house-wren had begun to build. **1961** O. L. AUSTIN *Birds of World* (1962) 248/2 Most familiar of these [cavity-nesting species] is the common House Wren, a widespread species of 30-odd races which ranges from southern Canada south to Cape Horn and the Falkland Islands.

house (haʊs), *sb.*[2] Forms: (3 huce), 4 hous, houce, 4–7 houze, 5 howse, 6 howss, 6–7 houss, 7 housse, houche, 5– house. [a. OF. *huche* (12th c. in Littré), *houce* (13th c. in Hatz.-Darm.), mod.F. *housse* (med.L. *hucia, houcia, hussia, housia*).

According to Darmesteter-Thomas, perh. adopted during the Crusades from Arabic *ɣûshiah*, 'tegumentum, velum'. See other suggestions in Diez, Littré, etc.]

A covering of textile material; esp. and usually, a covering attached to a saddle, so as to cover the back and flanks of the horse; a housing.

c **1283** GRAYSTANES in *Script. Tres* (Surtees) 64 Ex eo [panno] palefridis tuis coopertoria quæ huces nuncupantur fecit. **1312–3** *Durham MS. Cell. Roll*, j Houce empt. pro j equo. **1333–4** *Durham MS. Burs. Roll*, In panno..empt. pro houzes equorum, pro j houze ad palefr. missam domino Regi. **1391** *Earl Derby's Exp.* 7 Pro j hous pro le baner. *Ibid.* 247 Pro j house pro sella domini de coreo. **1483** *Cath. Angl.* 190/1 A Howse of a horse, *sandalum, sudaria*. **1500–20** DUNBAR *Poems* lxi. 21 With ane new houss I wald be happit. **1601** F. TATE *Househ. Ord. Edw. II* §56 (1876) 40 He shal.. carri the houche of those horses the kinge shalbe mounted on. **1687** A. LOVELL tr. *Thevenot's Trav.* I. 86 A stately Horse, covered with a Housse all Embroidered with Gold. *a* **1700** DRYDEN tr. *Ovid's Met.* XII. (R.), The houss and trappings of a beast. **1756** ROLT *Dict. Trade, Housing or House*, a Cover laid over the Saddle of a horse, in order to save it from the weather and dirt.

house (haʊz), *v.*[1] [OE. *húsian* (in sense 1) = OHG. *hûsôn* (MHG., MLG., MDu. *husen*, Ger. *hausen*, Du. *huizen*), ON. *husa*; f. *hús* HOUSE *sb.*[1]]

I. Transitive senses.

1. a. To receive or put into a house; to provide with a house to dwell in; to keep or store in a house or building.

c **1000** *Leges Penit.* c. 14 in Thorpe *Laws* II. 282 Fede þ earfan and scryde and husiȝe. **1390** GOWER *Conf.* III. 18 Whan that they were alle housed And set and served ate mete. **1432** *Sc. Acts Jas. I* in *Stat. Scotl.* (1814) II. 21/1 The sheref..sal..forbide at ony man houss, herbery or resett hym. *c* **1440** *Promp. Parv.* 251/1 Howsyn, or puttyn yn a howse, *domifero*. **1577** B. GOOGE *Heresbach's Husb.* III. (1586) 118 b, That if the Mare be housed, there be roome enough for her and her foale. *c* **1586** C'TESS PEMBROKE *Ps.* LXXVIII. xxi, A shepheard wise to howse his flock doth haste. **1626** BACON *Sylva* §412 As wee House Hot-Countrey Plants ..to saue them; So wee may House our owne Countrey Plants to forward them. **1768** G. WHITE *Selborne* xiii. (1875) 50 A neighbour housed an oat-rick lately. **1773** GOLDSM. *Stoops to Conq.* v. ii. Wks. (Globe) 672/1 Where did you leave your fellow-travellers? Are they in safety? Are they housed? **1832** HT. MARTINEAU *Weal & W.* i. 3 There were nine children to be housed. **1885** *Manch. Exam.* 21 May 5/1 The arrangements for housing the art collection of the Museum Committee at Queen's Park.

b. *refl.* To enter a house; to take refuge or shelter in a house.

? *a* **1400** *Sir Beues* 142 (MS. C.) Thereaboute ye shalle yow howse And sone after that shalt be hur spowse. **1589** R. HARVEY *Pl. Perc.* (1590) A iij b, House your selues in the next Tauerne. **1685** TRAVESTIN *Siege Newheusel* 49 The rest of the Turks housing themselves. **1848** J. GRANT *Aide-de-camp* xxxiv, Each person housed himself where he could.

†**c.** To drive or pursue into a house. *Obs.*

1590 SHAKS. *Com. Err.* v. i. 188 Euen now we hous'd him in the Abbey heere. **1694** PENN *Trav. Holland* etc. 249 the Priest run away, they followed him till they housed him. **1701** STRYPE *Aylmer* (R.), Yet the said Bishop, as he understood, his single man housed them all.

2. To receive, as a house does; to give shelter to.

1610 G. FLETCHER *Christ's Vict.* II. xiv, Him the silent wildernesse did house. *a* **1652** J. SMITH *Sel. Disc.* i. 10 When we have broken through the outward shell of words and phrases that house it [truth] up. **1773–83** HOOLE *Orl. Fur.* XXIII. (R.), When the place No knight has hous'd. **1832** TENNYSON *Œnone* 36 O Caves That house the cold-crowned snake! **1877** T. A. TROLLOPE *Peep behind Sc. at Rome* xi. 140 The building was capable of comfortably housing a very much larger number.

3. *transf.* and *fig.* To place or enclose as in a house; to cover as with a roof; to harbour, lodge.

1577 B. GOOGE *Heresbach's Husb.* II. (1586) 65 b, Some use to house it with Strawe and Horse doung, and so leave it in the Garden. **1599** B. JONSON *Ev. Man out of Hum.* III. i. Wks. (Rtldg.) 49/1 Nay, good sir, house your head. **1643** MILTON *Divorce* To Parlt. Eng., The piety, the learning and the prudence which is hous'd in this place. **1791–1823** D'ISRAELI *Cur. Lit.*, *Puck the Comm.*, Some collector.. houses the forlorn fiction—and it enters into literary history. **1841** EMERSON *Meth. Nat.* Wks. (Bohn) II. 226 The universal does not attract us until housed in an individual.

4. a. *Naut.* To place in a secure or unexposed position: *e.g.* a gun, by running it in on deck and fastening it by tackle, muzzle-lashing, and breeching; a topmast or topgallant-mast, by partly lowering it and fastening its heel to the mast below it.

1769 FALCONER *Dict. Marine* (1789), *Canon à la serre*, a gun housed athwart, with the top of its muzzle bearing against the upper edge of the port. **1835** MARRYAT *Pirate* vii, In bad weather it [the gun] can be lowered down and housed. **1840** R. H. DANA *Bef. Mast* xv. 41 A large ship, with her top-gallant-masts housed. **1874** THEARLE *Naval Archit.* 77 Provision is made for housing the screw shaft by giving a swell to the post, as in a wood ship.

b. *Naut.* To cover or protect with a roof.

1821 A. FISHER *Voy. Arctic Reg.* 151 As the ships are now housed and secured, and the days getting so short. **1867** SMYTH *Sailor's Word-bk.* s.v. *Housed*, Ships in ordinary, not in commission, are housed over by a substantial roofing.

c. *Hop-growing.* (See quot.) Cf. HOUSLING.

1875 *Sussex Gloss.*, When hops have a great deal of bine, and the poles are thickly covered over the top, so as almost to shut out the light and sun, they are said to be 'housed'.

d. *Carpentry.* To fix in a socket, mortice, or the like: cf. HOUSING *sb.*[1] 5.

1856 S. C. BREES *Gloss. Terms* s.v. *Housing*, The steps of a staircase are housed into the stringboard, and the ends of a pair of rafters are sometimes housed into the head of a king-post. **1884** F. T. HODGSON *Stair-building* 12 Wall strings are the supporters of the ends of the treads and risers that are against the wall. They may be 'housed' or left solid.

†**5.** To build. (transl. L. *ædificare*.) *Obs. rare.*

a **1400** *Prymer* (1891) 35 [Ps. cxxii. 3] Iherusalem that is housed as a cite, whas delynge is in him self.

II. Intransitive senses.

†**6.** To erect a house or houses; to build. *Obs.*

1297 R. GLOUC. (Rolls) 492 Hii housede & bulde vaste & herede & sewe. *c* **1430** *Pilgr. Lyf Manhode* I. xlix. (1869) 30 The carpentere with his ax to howse and to hewe. **1496** *Dives & Paup.* x. viii. (W. de W.) 383/1 Thou shalt house & other shall dwelle therin.

7. To dwell or take shelter in (or as in) a house; to harbour. Also with *up*.

1591 SPENSER *M. Hubberd* 828 He would it drive away, Ne suffer it to house there. **1592** SHAKS. *Rom. & Jul.* III. v. 190 Graze where you will, you shall not house with me. **1697** DRYDEN *Virg. Georg.* I. 460 Observe the starry Signs, Where Saturn houses, and where Hermes joins. **1803** S. & HT. LEE *Canterb. T.* II. 342, I again housed with my peasants. **1828** *Blackw. Mag.* XXIV. 442 Surely the Devil houses here! **1873** J. H. BEADLE *Undevel. West* i. 40 We can house up, you know, and keep warm on the prairie in winter, but we can't house up and keep cool in the timber in the summer. **1880** WATSON *Prince's Quest* (1892) 32 If..unbelief House in thy heart.

†**8.** ***house in*** (also in *pass.*): said of a ship of which the upper works are built narrower than the lower. (Cf. HOMING *vbl. sb.* 1.) *Obs.*

1627 CAPT. SMITH *Seaman's Gram.* xi. 52 Flaring..is when she is a little howsing in, neere the water. **1704** J. HARRIS *Lex. Techn.* s.v. *Housed*, She is Housed-in, or Pinched-in too much. **1711** W. SUTHERLAND *Shipbuild. Assist.* 165 Tumbling home; when the Ship-side declines from a Perpendicular upwards, or, as some call it, houses in.

house (haʊz), *v.*[2] [f. HOUSE *sb.*[2]: cf. F. *housser* (OF. *houchier* 13th c. in Hatz.-Darm.).] *trans.* To cover (a horse) with a house or housing.

1500–20 DUNBAR *Poems* lxi. 71 Tak in this gray horss, Auld Dunbar,..Gar howss him now aganis this ȝuill. **1580** BLUNDEVIL *Horsemanship, Diet. Horses* (1609) 11 Horses.. would be housed in Summer season with canuas to defend the flies, and in Winter with a thicke woollen housing cloth, to keepe them warme. **1658** EVELYN *Diary* 22 Oct., A velvet bed of state drawn by six horses, houss'd wth y[e] same. **1844** MRS. BROWNING *Swan's Nest* vi, And the steed it shall be shod All in silver, housed in azure.

house *v.*[3], var. of HOISE *v.*: cf. HOWES.

c **1515** *Cocke Lorell's B.* (Percy Soc.) 14 Cocke wayed anker, and housed his sayle.

houseale, -all: see HOUSAL, HOUSEL.

houseband, obs. form of HUSBAND.

ˈ**house-boat**. A boat roofed over and fitted up as a house, for living in permanently or temporarily.

1790 G. WHITE *Let.* in *Selborne* (1877) II. 175 To enquire what small craft they had on the Rhine, and whether any house-boat. **1887** MISS BRADDON *Like & Unlike* i, The summer days we spent together on his lordship's house-boat at Henley. **1887** *Spectator* 9 July 920/2 Summer life in a house-boat on the Thames.

ˈ**housebote**. *Law.* Forms: 2–3 husbote, 6– housebote, (6–8 -boot, 7 -boote). [OE. **húsbót*, f. *hús* HOUSE *sb.*[1] + *bót* BOOT *sb.*[1] 5.] The repair of a house; wood for this purpose; the right of a tenant to take this from the landlord's estate.

? **1170** *Charter* in *Mon. Angl.* (1830) VI. i. 263–4 [H]usbotam et heybotam ad sufficientiam in bosco meo. **1235–52** *Rentalia Glaston.* (Som. Rec. Soc.) 83 Debet habere husbote ad aulam suam de bosco domini. **1292** *Year-bk.* *20–21 Edw. I* (Rolls) 121 Willem Chandez granta a ly ousbote e heybote en son boys. **1565**, **1594** [see HEDGEBOTE,

HAYBOTE]. **1641** *Termes de la Ley, Houseboote.* **1726** AYLIFFE *Parergon* 506 If a man cuts Trees for Houseboot, Hedgeboot, Cartboot, Ploughboot, and Fireboot, Tithes shall not be paid of them. **1818** CRUISE *Digest* (ed. 2) I. 323 It was resolved in 8 Ja. I. that every copyholder may of common right..take housebote, hedgebote, and ploughbote.

†**'housebreach.** *Obs. rare.* In 2 husbreche. [OE. *húsbrice*, f. *hús* HOUSE *sb.*¹ + *brice* BREACH = OFris. *hûsbreke.*] Housebreaking.

c **1025** *Cnut's Secular Laws* c. 64 [65] (Schmid) Hus-bryce [*v.r.* brec] and bærnet..æfter woruld-laȝe is botleas. *c* **1150** *Laws Hen. I*, c. 12 §1 (Schmid) Ex hiis placitis..quaedam non possunt emendari..husbreche et bernet. **1678** PHILLIPS (ed. 4) App., Housebreach, or House-breaking.

house-break ('haʊsbreɪk), *v.* [Back-formation from next or *house-breaking*; cf. *housekeep.*]

1. *intr.* To break into a house with felonious intent.

1820 SHELLEY *Hymn Mercury* xlix, The lord of those Who swindle, house-break, sheep-steal, and shop-lift. **1896** *Westm. Gaz.* 22 Oct. 3/1 To housebreak in his own humorous fashion.

2. *trans.* To train (a domestic animal) to be clean in the house. Also *transf.*, to train (a person) to adopt a specified mode of behaviour within a house. Freq. in pa. pple. or ppl. a. ***house-broken.*** Chiefly *U.S.*

1900 *Daily Chron.* 27 Aug. 7/4 Malcourt, house-broken, runs to heel with the rest. **1905** T. ROOSEVELT *Let.* 14 May in *Works* (1926) XIX. 487 Skip is housebroken, but he is like a real little Indian. **1922** *Hotel World* 20 May 6/2, I am 'bawled out' by the dog owner saying that the management of such and such a hotel never objects to a house-broke dog being taken care of in a room. **1932** WODEHOUSE *Hot Water* xii. 207 House-broken husband though he was, he still had an eye for beauty. **1945** J. STEINBECK *Cannery Row* xx. 82 He didn't even house-break her [*sc.* a puppy]. **1948** G. VIDAL *City & Pillar* II. x. 256 We weren't like all these other people here; we weren't housebroken. **1955** W. W. DENLINGER *Compl. Boston* 148 Some prospective dog owners fear the ordeal of housebreaking a dog. **1961** WODEHOUSE *Service with Smile* (1962) ii. 36 You won't mind if I bring a friend with me?.. He is house-broken and eats whatever you're having yourself.

housebreaker ('haʊsbreɪkə(r)).

1. One who breaks open and enters a house with intent to commit robbery or other felony.

c **1340** *Cursor M.* 6747 (Fairf.) Thefe housbreker in any stounde. **1483** *Cath. Angl.* 190/2 An Howse breker, *apercularius.* **1662** J. DAVIES tr. *Olearius' Voy. Ambass.* 280 A House-breaker coming one night into his House. **1727** SWIFT *What passed in London*, Highway-men, house-breakers, and common pick-pockets. **1855** MACAULAY *Hist. Eng.* xix. IV. 295 During the autumn of 1692 and the following winter, the capital was kept in constant terror by housebreakers.

2. One whose business it is to demolish houses.

1875 [Remembered in use by a correspt.]. **1892** *Times* 6 Dec. 11/4 The whole of the block of houses..is in process of demolition..the 'house-breakers' being already at work. **1898** *Daily News* 22 July 6/1 The house-breaker—the man of the pick, not the jemmy—is hard at work.

'housebreaking. [Cf. HOUSEBREACH.] The crime of breaking open and entering a house with intent to commit robbery or other felony. (See quots.) Also *attrib.* Formerly usu. denoting such a crime committed by day, for which *burglary* was the equivalent at night; now applied to such an act committed by day or night.

1617 MINSHEU *Ductor, Burglary*,..the Common Law restraines it to robbing of a house by night...The like offence committed by daie they call house breaking or robbing. **1670** BLOUNT *Law Dict.* s.v. **1769** BLACKSTONE *Comm.* IV. xvi. (1809) 223 Burglary, or nocturnal housebreaking..has always been looked upon as a very heinous offence. **1838** DICKENS *O. Twist* xix, Producing his box of housebreaking tools. **1897** *Daily News* 9 Dec. 10/7 Housebreaking, which means entry before nine o'clock at night, is commoner with these retail criminals than burglary. **1966** *8th Rep. Crim. Law Rev. Comm.* 85 in *Parl. Papers 1966–7* (Cmnd. 2977) XXXIX. 1 The present offence of housebreaking, by day at least, is not regarded as within that class, for many cases are dealt with by fine. **1966** *New Statesman* 7 Oct. 504/2 All this will be the result of abolishing a host of anomalies in the ancient law of burglary and housebreaking (a distinction which..will itself disappear). The Bill makes a bonfire of them. **1973** 'J. PATRICK' *Glasgow Gang Observed* iii. 27 Under the law of Scotland 'housebreaking' covers the forced entry of 'any roofed building', i.e. shops, factories, garages, as well as private houses.

'house-builder. One who builds a house; one whose business is the building of houses; a builder.

1769 *Junius Lett.* xxxiv. 152 [He]..descends to apply to his house-builder for assistance. **1895** *Educat. Rev.* (N.Y.) Sept. 158 A house-builder is not likely to excel as an architect.

b. *attrib.* **house-builder moth**: see quots.

1864–5 WOOD *Homes without H.* xiv. (1868) 283 This is the House-Builder Moth (*Oiketicus Sandersii*) an insect which is common in many parts of the West Indies.

So **house-building**, the building of houses.

1796 MORSE *Amer. Geog.* II. 258 Timber..is employed in house-building instead of bricks, stones and tiles. **1865** MRS. STOWE *House & Home Papers* 270 Why don't you write a paper on house-building? **1946** *Nature* 5 Oct. 462/1 The various forms of co-operative activity undertaken by the village.., such as road-making, bridge-building or house-building. **1969** *Times* 16 July 22/5 There are doubts about the growth pattern of house-building in this country.

housecarl ('haʊskɑːl). *Hist.* Forms: 1 húscarl, -karl(l, 7–9 hus-, housecarle, 9 hus-, housecarl. [Late OE. *húscarl*, a. ON. *húskarl* manservant, pl. king's men, body-guard, f. ON. *hús* house + *karl* man: see CARL.]

A member of the body-guard or household troops of a (Danish or late Old English) king or noble.

10.. *O.E. Chron.* (Laud MS.) an. 1036 þæt Ælfȝifu, Hardacnutes modor, sæte on Winceastre, mid þæs cynges huscarlum hyra suna. *a* **1066** *Charter of Eadweard* in Kemble *Cod. Dipl.* IV. 202 Swa ðurstan min huskarll hit furmest of me heold. *a* **1125** *O.E. Chron.* (Laud MS.) an. 1070 þa comen into Eliȝ Xp̄istien þa Densce biscop..and þa Densca hus carles mid heom. **1610** HOLLAND *Camden's Brit.* I. 576 They had slaine his Huscarles. **1670** MILTON *Hist. Eng.* VI. Wks. (1851) 272 Hardecnute sending his Housecarles, so they call'd his Officers, to gather the Tribute impos'd. **1761** HUME *Hist. Eng.* I. App. i. 97 He summoned from all parts his huscarles or householders and retainers. **1870** FREEMAN *Norm. Conq.* (ed. 2) I. vi. 440 Cnut now organized a regular paid force..These were the famous Thingmen, the Housecarls. *Ibid.* 441 The Housecarls were in fact a standing army. **1873** EDITH THOMPSON *Hist. Eng.* vii. 26 The thanes and house-carls were slaughtered almost to a man around their fallen standard.

housecraft ('haʊskrɑːft, -æ-). [f. HOUSE *sb.*¹ + CRAFT *sb.* 12.] The art of managing a house; skill in domestic duties. Also *attrib.*

1906 L. H. YATES (*title*) Modern housecraft. **1910** *Daily Chron.* 1 Mar. 9/1 Ignorance of housecraft is the favourite reproach brought against the modern woman. *Ibid.*, St. Martha's College of Housecraft. **1914** J. COLLINGS *Colon. Rural Brit.* I. vi. 116 Among the 'optional' subjects contained in the 'Regulations for the Training of Teachers for Elementary Schools' is that of 'Rural Science' (and 'Housecraft' for girls). **1930** *Birmingham Post* 10 Dec. 4/3 Housecraft classes at the Victoria Institute. **1951** *Archit. Rev.* CIX. 285/1 As housecraft activities take up more space than science, the housecraft centre is on the first floor. **1956** W. H. G. ARMYTAGE in D. L. Linton *Sheffield* 206 This was the ancestor of the present handsome College of Housecraft opened at Totley after the Second World War.

housed (haʊzd), *ppl. a.*¹ [f. HOUSE *v.*¹ or *sb.*¹]

1. Lodged, enclosed, or shut up in or as in a house; provided with a house or houses.

1549 CHEKE *Hurt Sedit.* (1641) 14 Which haue fled from housed conspiracies to encamped robberies. **1577** B. GOOGE *Heresbach's Husb.* III. (1586) 141 b, Thus much of housed sheepe. **1664** EVELYN *Kal. Hort.* (1729) 194 Air your hous'd Carnations. **1829** *Blackw. Mag.* XXVI. 204 The richly housed and planted acclivity. *a* **1862** BUCKLE *Civiliz.* (1869) III. v. 471 A badly fed, badly housed, and not over-cleanly people.

2. *Naut.* (See HOUSE *v.*¹ 4 a.)

1893 *Westm. Gaz.* 14 Oct. 5/3 It would have been better if both boats had sailed under housed topmasts.

housed (haʊzd), *ppl. a.*² [f. HOUSE *v.*² or *sb.*²] Covered with a house or housing.

1560 BECON *New Catech.* Wks. (1560–3) I. 323 To se a sorte of Popettes standing in euerye corner of the Church some holdinge in theyr handes a Swoorde, some a Scepter.. som housed, some vnhoused.

house-dog. A dog kept to guard the house; a watch-dog; a domestic dog.

1711 ADDISON *Spect.* No. 7 ¶4 She..was..almost frighted out of her Wits by the great House-dog. **1792** MARY WOLLSTONECR. *Rights Wom.* xii. (1891) 250 To love with reasonable subordination their whole family, from their husband to the house dog. **1882** OUIDA *In Maremma* I. 24 Of a fox never can you make a house-dog.

fig. **1848** THACKERAY *Van. Fair* xl, Briggs was the house-dog whom Rebecca had provided as guardian of her innocence and reputation.

house-door. The door of a house; the main or front door.

1666 PEPYS *Diary* 25 Sept., To the Parliament House.. and then delivered it [a letter] at the House-door. **1848** DICKENS *Dombey* iii, The butlers..began to stand at the house-doors in the twilight.

attrib. **1879** BROWNING *Halbert & Hob* 40 A yard from the house-door-sill.

house-dove.

1. A dove kept in a dove-house; a tame dove or pigeon.

1530 PALSGR. 233/1 Housedove, *coulomb.* **1625** BACON *Ess., Plantat.* (Arb.) 531 Cockes, Hennes,..House doues.

2. *fig.* Formerly commonly applied to a person (esp. a woman) that stays in the house; a stay-at-home.

1579–80 NORTH *Plutarch* (1595) 242 Then the home-tarriers and house-doues that kept Rome still, began to repent them that it was not their hap to go with him. **1589** GREENE *Menaphon* (Arb.) 85 You are proude such a house doue of late, or rather so good a Huswife, that no man may see you vnder a couple of Capons. **1639** DU VERGER tr. *Camus' Admir. Events* 20 Take me not as a house Dove, to imploy my selfe in spinning, sowing, and keeping the chimney corner.

housee: see HOUSEY-HOUSEY.

'house-father. [transl. of L. *paterfamilias*, or of Ger. *hausvater.*] The father of a household or family; the male head of a community or collection of persons living together as a family.

1552 LATIMER *Serm. Lincoln* i. 65 What a costly dyshe the housefather hath ordayned at the wedding of his son. **1859** THACKERAY *Virgin.* xxxii, He was dozing after the fashion of honest housefathers. **1879** W. E. HEARN *Aryan Househ.* ii. §1. 39 The simple minds of uncultured men unhesitatingly believed that the spirit of the departed House Father hovered round the place he loved in life. **1884** *Lutheran* 28 Feb. 3 Arranging the present building for the residence in it of a housefather which is a necessity for the institution [a theological seminary]. **1887** *Pall Mall G.* 7 Dec. 9/1 There were in these places no 'house-fathers' for the girls, though there were 'house-mothers' for both girls and boys.

houseful ('haʊsfʊl). [See -FUL.] As much or as many as a house will hold.

1610 BP. HALL *Apol. Brownists* §13 The tumultuarie Discipline of the refined house-full at Amsterdam. **1665** PEPYS *Diary* 19 Sept., The whole house-full there at cards. **1842** E. FITZGERALD *Lett.* (1889) I. 96 A housefull of the most delightful children. **1867** DICKENS *Lett.* (1880) II. 270 Having my annual houseful, I have, as yet, seen nothing.

'house-heating.

1. *lit.* The heating of a house. Also *attrib.*

1887 *Westm. Rev.* June 323 Our house-heating furnaces.. are not to be commended. **1895** *Daily News* 25 Apr. 7/2 It is applicable..to house-heating, to kitchen and baking-ovens, to steamers, locomotives, and other steam engines.

2. *fig.* = HOUSE-WARMING 2.

1819 *Blackw. Mag.* V. 631/2 His celebrated master-piece, 'Hogg's Househeating'. **1864** CARLYLE *Fredk. Gt.* XVI. i. IV. 245 A grand House-heating, or First Dinner.

household ('haʊshəʊld). Forms: 4–7 housholde, houshould, 4–8 houshold, 5 houshoold, housold, 5–6 howsold(e, householde, *north.* hous-, howshald(e, 5–7 howshold(e, 6 houssold, howseholde, howshould, 5– household. [f. HOUSE *sb.*¹ + HOLD *sb.*¹ Cf. MDu. *huushoud, huysholt*, Ger. *haushalt* housekeeping, Sw. *hushåll* household, family; also Ger. *haushaltung* in senses 1, 2, 3.]

I. †**1.** The 'holding' or maintaining of a house or family; housekeeping; domestic economy. (In quot. 1585, Dwelling, residence: see also 5.) *Obs.*

1489 CAXTON *Faytes of A.* I. i. 2 To spynne on the distaf & ocupie theim in thynges of houshold. **1529** WOLSEY in *Four C. Eng. Lett.* 10 Evry thyng mete for houssold vnprovydyd and furnyshyd. **1542** BOORDE *Dyetary* i. (1870) 242 That he begyn howseholde. **1576** NEWTON *Lemnie's Complex.* (1633) 76 The pleasant and delightfull furniture in every point for household, wonderfully rejoyced me. **1585** T. WASHINGTON tr. *Nicholay's Voy.* IV. xv. 129 Tharse.. being the place of birth and houshold of S. Paul.

†**2.** The contents or appurtenances of a house collectively; household goods, chattels, or furniture; household-stuff. *Obs.*

1382 WYCLIF *Ezek.* xxxviii. 13 And take pertenaunce of houshold and substaunce. **1420** *E.E. Wills* (1882) 52 Also I will þat my wyffe haue all my housholde holy. **1484** CAXTON *Fables of Poge* (1889) 1 Dysshes, pottes, pannes, and suche other houshold. **1621** *Bury Wills* (Camden) 167 Desiringe him..he would bestowe some of my howsholde of my brother Nicke. **1709** E. W. *Donna Rosina* 110 Devout Souls ..have sent their Beds hither and some other Household.

3. a. The inmates of a house collectively; an organized family, including servants or attendants, dwelling in a house; a domestic establishment.

1387–8 T. USK *Test. Love* II. iii. (Skeat) l. 126 In to myne housholde hastelye I woll that thou entre. *c* **1400** MAUNDEV. (1839) xix. 209 In on House men maken 10 Housholdes. *c* **1440** *Promp. Parv.* 250/2 Howsholde, *familia.* **1529** MORE in *Four C. Eng. Lett.* 12 Be of good cheere, and take all the howsold with you to Church. **1584** POWEL *Lloyd's Cambria* 105 With all his children and houshold to be murthered. **1624** SANDERSON *12 Serm.* (1637) 113 To give to every one of the houshold his appointed portion at the appointed seasons. **1719** YOUNG *Busiris* III. i, The gates are barr'd, And all the houshold is compos'd to rest? **1841** W. SPALDING *Italy & It. Isl.* III. 87 The pomp of the vice-regal household was no small addition to the other national burdens. **1875** JOWETT *Plato* (ed. 2) V. 103 The master of the household should be up early and before all his servants.

fig. **1526** *Pilgr. Perf.* (W. de W. 1531) 90 b, Certaynly they be yᵉ housholde of Sathan and progeny of pryde. **1526** TINDALE *Gal.* vi. 10 Vnto them which are off the housholde of fayth. **1548–9** (Mar.) *Bk. Com. Prayer* Collect 22nd Sund. after Trin., To kepe thy housholde the churche in continuall godlines.

b. spec. ***the Household*** = the royal or imperial household.

c **1400** MAUNDEV. (Roxb.) xxiii. 108 To kepe þat nane entre in at þe dure bot þai þat þe emperour will, oless þan he be of þe houshald. **1647** CLARENDON *Hist. Reb.* III. §213 The earl of Pembroke..Lord Chamberlain of the household. **1707** *Chamberlayne's St. Gt. Brit.* II. xiv. 183 (*heading*) Of the Troops of the Houshold. **1855** MACAULAY *Hist. Eng.* xviii. IV. 121 He had two good places, one in the Treasury, the other in the household. *Ibid.* xxii. IV. 776 Retaining his place of Comptroller of the Household. **1880** DISRAELI *Endym.* lxx, Gentlemen expecting high places in the Household, and under-secretaryships of state.

4. *techn.* Elliptically for *household bread, coal*, etc.: see 8.

1638 PENKETHMAN *Artach.* C ij b, The 1*d.* houshold (being Bread made of common wheat,) ought to weigh two penny white of the same course Cocket. **1854** RONALDS & RICHARDSON *Chem. Technol.* I. Pref. 6 [Coal] Household 19,000,000, Iron Works 13,000,000. **1863** S. L. J. *Life in South* I. xv. 301 Such a display of 'households' and 'calicos',

as coloured prints are called. **1875** *Ure's Dict. Arts* I. 477 Batch bread is made of best flour and of households, or flour of second quality. **1886** FALLOWS *Suppl. Dict., Households*, a technical name among millers for the best flour made from red wheat, with a small portion of white wheat mixed.

†5. Phrases. ***to hold*** or ***keep*** (*a, one's*) ***household***: to 'keep house'; ***to keep open household*** = to keep open house (see HOUSE *sb.*[1] 18 a, b). ***in*** or ***of household with***: in or of the same household with; familiar with. *Obs.*

c **1430** *Hymns Virg.* 61 þanne comeþ þe .vij. deedli synnes With þe wickid aungil housholde to holde. **1463** *Paston Lett.* No. 469 II. 129 Ther to dwelle and abide, and kepe howsold. **1467** *Ord. Worcester* c. 33 in *Eng. Gilds* (1870) 389 Eny craftiesman, artificer, or other, dwellynge or holdynge houshold, in Cites, Boroughez. **1548** UDALL, etc. *Erasm. Par. Matt.* iv. 33 Desire to haue in houshold with them, men, &c. **1568** GRAFTON *Chron.* II. 215 At Christmasse, at which tyme she promissed to keepe open houshold. **1581** PETTIE *Guazzo's Civ. Conv.* II. (1586) 52 Those that be of householde with us.

II. *attrib.* and *Comb.*

6. *attrib.* passing into *adj.* **a.** Of or belonging to a household, domestic.

1382 WYCLIF *Matt.* x. 25 ȝif thei han clepid the husbonde man Belzebub, hou myche more his housholde meynee? **1535** COVERDALE *Ecclus.* vi. 11 Deale faithfully with thy housholde folke. **1578** TIMME *Caluine on Gen.* 301 Abram.. with his housholdarmie, fell upon their enemies. **1613** PURCHAS *Pilgrimage* (1614) 524 All their most precious houshold furniture. **1643** MILTON *Divorce* To Parlt. Eng., This houshold unhappines. **1726** AYLIFFE *Parergon* 338 A Legacy of Housholdgoods or Furniture. **1738** WESLEY *Ps.* LXXX. vii, Our bitter Household Foes abound. **1841** W. SPALDING *Italy & It. Isl.* I. 299 Statues, mosaics, household utensils, and other antique treasures. **1847** EMERSON *Poems, Saadi* 176 That blessed gods in servile masks Plied for thee thy household tasks.

b. Of or belonging to the royal household, as ***household appointment, office***, etc.; **household troops**, troops specially employed to guard the person of the sovereign: in Great Britain the Life Guards, the Royal Horse Guards, and the Grenadier, Coldstream, Scots, Irish, and Welsh Guards; so ***household brigade, cavalry, infantry***, etc.

1711 *Lond. Gaz.* No. 4843/2 The Houshold Troops are under the Gates of Cambray. **1841** ELPHINSTONE *Hist. Ind.* II. 183 In most Asiatic despotisms, the king first trusts to the army against the people, and then to a body of foreign household troops, or Mamlúks, against the rest of the army. **1849** MACAULAY *Hist. Eng.* iii. I. 295 The household infantry consisted of two regiments.

c. *fig.* Familiar, intimate, homely. *arch.*

c **1450** tr. *De Imitatione* III. xxiv. 95 þine familiars & householde men. **1592** R. D. *Hypnerotomachia* 39 b, Growing into some houshold familiaritie. **1761** STERNE *Tr. Shandy* III. 94 Good plain houshold judgment. **1840** DE QUINCEY *Style* IV. (1860) 291 More household, more natural, less elaborate. **1852** HAWTHORNE *Tanglew. T., Circe's P.* (1879) 182 What a domestic, household, homelike sound it is!

7. Objective Combs., as ***household-keeper, -keeping*** (see 5), ***-orderer, -ordering***.

1479 *Bury Wills* (Camden) 51 Euery housold keper in the town that I dwelle jnne. **1552** HULOET, Housholde kepynge, *familiam fouens. Ibid.*, Housholde orderer, or gouernor, *oeconomicus. Ibid.*, Houshold orderyng, . . *oeconomia.*

8. Special Combs.: **household appliance**, a piece of equipment (e.g. a vacuum cleaner) used in the house; **household beer**, beer of ordinary quality for household use; **household book**, a book in which household accounts are noted; **household bread**, bread for ordinary household use: the application has changed several times between the 16th c., when it was brown bread, and the end of the 19th, when it is white bread made of a second or third quality of flour; **household effects**, the movable contents of a house; **household franchise, suffrage**, the right of voting in parliamentary or other elections, consequent upon being a householder within an electoral division: see HOUSEHOLDER; **household gods** (*Rom. Antiq.*), the *Lares* and *Penates*, divinities supposed to preside over the household, whose images were kept in the *atrium* or central room of the house; *fig.* the essentials of home life; **household linen**, linen for the bedroom, table, etc.; **household loaf**, a loaf of *household bread*; †**household-man**, a domestic male servant or attendant; **household management**, the art of running a house; **household name**, a name familiar to everyone; **household science** orig. *N. Amer.* = *domestic science*; **household servant**, a servant belonging to the household, a domestic servant; **household snake** = HOUSE SNAKE 2; **household word**, a word or saying in familiar use; a name familiar to everybody.

1926 *Encycl. Brit.* II. 375/2 The outstanding feature in the development of *household appliances..has been the greatly extended use of those operated electrically. **1935** *Discovery* Sept. 247/2 The fame of Norwich is also spread by its mustard and starch, electrical machinery and household appliances, aircraft, ironwork and other progressive industries. **1957** *Encycl. Brit.* XI. 813/2 Modern household appliances can be divided into two main headings, electrical and nonelectrical. **1599** M. HOBY *Diary* 18 Feb. (1930) 104 Then to supper: after, I looked of the *Houshould book, and then went to priuat praers. **1780** S. PEGGE in *Forme of Cury* p. xxxv, The present dean of Carlisle, to whom I stand indebted for his useful notes on the Northumberland-Household Book. **1866** TROLLOPE *Belton Est.* (ed. 3) II. vi. 145 Though she could not succeed in making retrenchments, she could and did succeed in keeping the household books. **1931** S. JAMESON *Richer Dust* xviii. 503 Mrs. James, pen stirring the clotted ink at the bottom of the bottle, bent close over the pages of her Household Book. **1577** B. GOOGE *Heresbach's Husb.* I. (1586) 10 b, Two Ovens, one serving for *householde bread, the other for manchet for myne owne table. **1620** VENNER *Via Recta* i. 18 A browne houshold bread agreeable enough for labourers. **1737** OZELL *Rabelais* I. 256 A Loaf of Houshold (or Brown) Bread. **1818** TODD, *Household-bread*, bread not of the finest quality: see *Cheat-bread*. **1859–60** *Ure's Dict. Arts* s.v. *Bread* (L.), Our household bread [is made], of the whole substance of the grain without the separation either of the fine flour or coarse bran. **1891** [see EFFECT *sb.* 4 b]. **1933** *Burlington Mag.* May p. xv/2 The English furniture generally is of better quality than that associated with '*household effects'. **1866** BRIGHT *Sp. Ho. Com.* 13 Mar., If..he approved a 10*l.* *household franchise in boroughs he must do so also in the counties. **1884** GLADSTONE *Sp. Ho. Com.* 28 Feb., The household franchise..now..the principal franchise of the cities and towns of this country. **1614** T. ADAMS *Devil's Banquet* 32 Those [*Lares et Lemures*] *household-Gods, or rather household-Goblins and Deuils. **1697** DRYDEN *Virg. Georg.* III. 535 And with him all his Patrimony bears: His House and Houshold Gods! **1818** BYRON *Lett.* 10 Sept., The deliberate desolation piled upon me, when I stood alone upon my hearth, with my household gods shivered around me. **1642** LADY SUSSEX *Let.* in F. P. Verney *Memoirs* (1892) I. xi. 253 She gives all her linen to to of hur grand-children not naminge hur *householde linen, but in generly hur linen. **1811** JANE AUSTEN *Sense & Sens.* I. v. 56 Household linen, plate, china, and books. **1967** E. SHORT *Embroidery & Fabric Collage* iii. 72 (*caption*) A basically simple design which could be adapted to almost any article of household linen. **1594** CROMPTON *Jurisdiction* 226 b, A penie wheaten loafe, A halfe-penie *houshold loafe. **1710** *Abstr. Act 8 Anne* c. 19 in *Lond. Gaz.* No. 4681/1 The White Loaves are One Half, and the Wheaten Three Quarters of the Weight of Houshold Loaves. **1477** NORTON *Ord. Alch.* iv. in Ashm. (1652) 49 Take never thereto no *Houshold-man, Thei be soone weary as I tell cann. **1591** LAMBARDE *Archeion* (1635) 195 The like [penaltie] upon the taker of any Liverie, except he were his Household-man. **1742** RICHARDSON *Pamela* (ed. 3) III. ix. 50 Let your Servants, under your Direction, do all that relates to *Houshold Management. **1801** JANE AUSTEN *Let.* 14 Jan. (1932) I. 111 It will be an amusement to Mary to superintend their Household management, and abuse them for expense. **1861** MRS. BEETON (*title*) The book of household management. **1862** TENNYSON *Idylls of King, Dedication* l. 40 A Prince indeed, Beyond all titles, and a *household name, Here-after, thro' all times, Albert the Good. **1907** W. RUSSELL *Arterial Hypertonus* v. 34 The names of Claude Bernard, Brown-Séquard, Waller, and Schiff are 'household names' in this connection. **1958** *Times* 27 Feb. 11/2 Our first encounter with so many household names in his list which were then unknown. **1969** *New Yorker* 29 Nov. 166/2 Spiro Agnew was then a household name only in his own household. **1970** *Times* 11 Mar. 21/1 (Advt.), We produce packs for a lot of household names. **1938** *Univ. Toronto Cal. 1938–39* (verso of title-p.), In the Faculty of *Household Science, the University offers courses leading to the degree of Bachelor of Household Science. **1953** *Univ. London Cal. 1953–54* 464 Queen Elizabeth College... Admitted in 1928 as a School of the University for the B.Sc. Degree in Household and Social Science and for the Degree of B.Sc. (Nutrition) and B.Sc. (Household Science) in 1953. **1963** F. F. LAIDLER *Gloss. Home Econ. Educ.* 46 *Household science*, a comprehensive study of the scientific, technological and sociological aspects of the household. **1495** *Trevisa's Barth. De P.R.* VI. xxii. (W. de W.), *Housholde seruauntes besyly helpe and folowe eche other. **1840** THIRLWALL *Greece* VII. 335 He sent back his brother Menelaus..together with his private baggage, and household servants. **1894** W. CROOKE *Pop. Relig. & Folk-Lore N. India* vii. 276 (*heading*) The *household snake. **1921** A. EVANS *Palace of Minos* I. 509 Such a household snake is known, indeed, as *domachitsa* or 'house-mother'. *Ibid.*, In its homely origin, from the religious tending of the household snake, the cult itself may be supposed to be of old indigenous tradition. **1962** R. W. HUTCHINSON *Prehist. Crete* viii. 208 The cult of the household snake has not entirely died out even now. **1866** BRIGHT *Sp. at Manchester* 20 Nov., *Household or rating suffrage has existed for centuries in our parishes. **1599** SHAKS. *Hen. V*, IV. iii. 52 Our Names, Familiar in his mouth as *household words. **1833** L. RITCHIE *Wand. by Loire* 157 The children of genius, whose names are as house-hold words in the mouths of their fellow-men. **1888** BURGON *Lives 12 Gd. Men* I. iv. 375 A household word wherever the English language is spoken.

Hence (*nonce-wds.*) †**'householdment**, a piece of household furniture. **'householdness** (see 6 c), domestic quality. †**'householdy** *a.* [cf. early mod.Du. *huyshoudigh* (Kilian)], belonging to or befitting a household.

1557 TUSSER *100 Points Husb.* v, At no tyme to much, but haue alway ynough: is housholdy fare, and the guyse of the plough. **1717** *N. Riding Rec.* VIII. 171 One oak chest, one arm chair with some other odd householdments within the Township. **1833** LYTTON *England* IV. ii, Wordsworth is German from his singular householdness of feeling.

householder ('haʊshəʊldə(r)). Forms: see HOUSEHOLD. [ME., f. HOUSE *sb.*[1] + HOLDER 2: cf. Du. *huishouder* (Kilian *huyshouder*), LG. *hushölder*, MHG., Ger. *haushälter*, Da. *huusholder*, Sw. *hushållare*; also Gr. οἰκονόμος.]

The person who holds or occupies a house as his own dwelling and that of his household; esp. *Hist.* in the law on parliamentary elections in the United Kingdom, one qualified to exercise the franchise by the occupancy, as legally defined, of a house or tenement.

c **1386** CHAUCER *Prol.* 339 An housholdere and that a greet was he, Seint Iulian was he in his contree. **1434** *E.E. Wills* (1882) 101 Sellè hite..& yeue to pore housholders in coles. **1547** in *Vicary's Anat.* (1888) App. iii. 161 Thaldermen.. shall cause euerye howseholder of their seuerall wardes..to [etc.]. **1679** *Establ. Test* 23 His Majesty.. has commanded all Papists who are not Householders, Travellers, &c. to depart from this..City. **1831** MACAULAY in *Life & Lett.* (1880) I. 253 With your head full of ten-pound householders. **1846** J. BAXTER *Libr. Pract. Agric.* (ed. 4) II. 309 Every householder in the country might practise this part of domestic economy. **1884** LOW & PULLING *Dict. Eng. Hist.* 424/1 By the Reform Bill of 1867..the franchise..was extended to all resident householders or rated occupants of dwelling houses, after payment of one year's rates.

b. Hence, the head of a household or family.

c **1440** *Promp. Parv.* 251/1 Howsholdare (*K.* howsalder), *pater familias, yconomus.* **1553** T. WILSON *Rhet.* (1580) 194 If an housholder will deale justly with his servauntes. **1588** J. UDALL *Demonstr. Discip.* xiv. (Arb.) 65 Euery kingdome or houshold, must be gouerned onely by the laws of the king, or orders of the housholder. **1645** PAGITT *Heresiogr.* (1661) 50 It was the Apostles practice..to baptize both the householders themselves that believed, and their housholds also. **1870** SCHAFF *Comm. Prov.* xxi. 25–6 Wishers and woulders are neither good householders nor long livers.

c. *fig.* Of God in reference to His providence.

1571 GOLDING *Calvin on Ps.* lxviii. 10 A most loving and carefull householder, bicause he alwayes sent them rayne to prepare them foode. **1872** SPURGEON *Treas. Dav.* Ps. lxv. 9 Blessed be the great Householder; he does not suffer the harvest to fail.

Hence **'house,holdership**, the position or status of a householder.

1817 BENTHAM *Plan Parl. Reform* Introd. 106 *note*, Evidence of Householdership. **1872** *Daily News* 30 Sept., His householdership..is rather in a peculiar position; for the house..which he inhabits he pays no rent, but he is allowed the use of it..in addition to his money wage.

householding ('haʊshəʊldɪŋ), *sb.* [f. HOUSE *sb.*[1] + HOLDING *vbl. sb.* Cf. Ger. *haushaltung*, Du. *huishouding* (Kilian *huyshoudinghe*). The other Teut. langs. have the vb., Ger. *haushalten*, Du. *huishouden*, Sw. *hushålla* to keep house.]

†**a.** Management of a household; housekeeping. *Obs.* **b.** Occupation of a house. Also *attrib.*

?*a* **1366** CHAUCER *Rom. Rose* 1132 A yong man fulle of semelyhede..His lust was mich in housholding. **1565–73** COOPER *Thesaurus* s.v. *Consuetudo*, Cicero translated Xenophons booke of housholding into the latine tongue. **1569** J. SANFORD tr. *Agrippa's Van. Artes* 107 Economie, or housholdinge cannot truely be termed neether Art nor Science. **1865** *Daily Tel.* 25 Oct. 6/5 Champions of 'fancy franchises' and those who insisted upon the householding test. **1884** GLADSTONE *Sp. Ho. Com.* 28 Feb., There will be a fourfold occupation franchise, or householding franchise.

'householding, *a.* [f. as prec. + HOLDING *ppl. a.*] That occupies, or manages, a house.

1866 DICKENS *Repr. Pieces* 129 The householding population of our watering-place. **1871** G. MACDONALD *Story Sea-Shore* in *Wks. Fancy & Imag.* II. 4 Householding Nature from her treasures brought Things old and new.

householdry ('haʊshəʊldrɪ). [f. HOUSEHOLD: see -ERY, -RY.]

1. The management of a household; housekeeping; domestic economy or occupations.

1581 MULCASTER *Positions* v. (1887) 35 Writing and reading do minister much helpe to trafficque, to householdrie, to learning, and all publicke dealinges. **1832** *Blackw. Mag.* XXXII. 645, I told her to mind her householdry. **1865** E. BURRITT *Walk Land's End* 426 Pre-historic prototypes or models of human householdry.

†**2.** *concr.* Household-stuff. *Obs.*

1573 TUSSER *Husb.* viii. (1878) 16 So houshold and housholdrie I doe define, for folke and the goodes that in house be of thine. *Ibid.* ix. 17 To furnish house with housholdry.

household-stuff. *arch.* The goods, utensils, vessels, etc. belonging to a household; the furniture of a house.

c **1511** *1st Eng. Bk. Amer.* (Arb.) Introd. 28/2 The women bere there chyldren & theyr householde stuffe. **1553** EDEN *Treat. Newe Ind.* (Arb.) 24 Theyr housholde stuffe is of golde and syluer. **1676** TEMPLE *Lett. to Sir J. Williamson* Wks. 1731 II. 419, I have given Order for shipping away the best Part of my Houshold-stuff To-morrow. **1719** DE FOE *Crusoe* II. i, Household-stuff, particularly kitchen utensils. **1869** FREEMAN *Norm. Conq.* III. xii. 211 Horses, arms, household stuff of every kind, were found in plenty.

housekeep ('haʊskiːp), *v.* [Back-formation from next or HOUSEKEEPING: cf. *housebreak.*] *intr.* To act as housekeeper, keep house.

1842 MRS. PEABODY in *N. Hawthorne & Wife* (1885) I. 251, I housekeep, paint, sew, study German, read. **1892** *Blackw. Mag.* CLI. 84/2 Kate shall come and housekeep. **1900** KIPLING in *Daily Express* 26 June 4/5 One or other of them would housekeep for him the year round. **1947** N. MARSH *Final Curtain* ii. 26 Millamant who, since the death of her husband, has house-kept for her father-in-law. **1954** *Encounter* May 20/1 The widow whom she housekeeps for.

housekeeper ('haʊskiːpə(r)). [f. HOUSE *sb.*[1] + KEEPER *sb.*, i.e. keeper of a house.]

1. = HOUSEHOLDER. Now *rare* or *Obs.*

c **1440** *Promp. Parv.* 251/1 Howskepare, *edituus, editua.* **1536** STAPLETON in *Lett. & Pap. Hen. VIII* (1890) XII. 189 At the request of honest men, he, being a house-keeper, was suffered to go unpunished. **1605** *Lond. Prodigal* I. ii, She hath refused seven of the worshipfull'st And worthiest

housekeepers this day in Kent. **1685** in Picton *L'pool Munic. Rec.* (1883) I. 329 None but housekeepers shall sitt in the seate on ye north side..and..none but the wives and widdows of housekeepers..'twixt the baylives wives and ye font. **1766** Entick *London* IV. 128 A handsome street, inhabited..by private housekeepers. **1833** Ht. Martineau *Brooke Farm* ii. 21 A piece of ground will be given to every housekeeper in return for his right of common.

fig. **1645** Bp. Hall *Remedy Discontents* 38 The great Housekeeper of the world knows how to fit every palate with that which either is, or should be agreeable.

†**2.** (With qualifying adj.) One who 'keeps a (good, bountiful, etc.) house' (see HOUSE *sb.*^{1} 18 b); a hospitable person. *Obs.*

1538 Latimer *Serm. & Rem.* (1845) 411 The man is ..a good housekeeper, feedeth many, and that daily. **1586** J. Hooker *Girald. Irel.* in *Holinshed* II. 137/2 Bountifull and liberall..a great housekeeper, and of great hospitalitie. *a* **1661** Fuller *Worthies* (1840) I. 281 John Barnston..a bountiful house-keeper. *a* **1707** Bp. Patrick *Autobiogr.* (1839) 71 Her grandmother, being a person of quality, a great housekeeper and very religious.

3. a. A person in charge of a house, office, place of business, etc.

1632 J. Hayward tr. *Biondi's Eromena* 6 The day following came to court the housekeeper of Poggio. **1709** Strype *Ann. Ref.* I. xv. 191 Nonsuch, another of her houses, of which the noble earl of Arundel seems to be now housekeeper. **1714** *Lond. Gaz.* No. 5274/8 Matthew Aylmer, Esq. ..to be..Housekeeper of His Majesty's Royal Palace of Greenwich Park. **1768** Ellis in *Phil. Trans.* LVIII. 78 Mr. Robertson, housekeeper to the Royal Society. *Mod.* The Bank occupies the three floors; the housekeeper and his family live in the attics.

†**b.** A dog kept to guard the house; a watch-dog. *Obs.*

1605 Shaks. *Macb.* III. i. 97 The valued file Distinguishes the swift, the slow, the subtle, The House-keeper, the Hunter. **1688** R. Holme *Armoury* II. ix. 186/1 The Village-Dog, or House-keeper..bigly barking, so as to terrifie Rogues and Theives.

4. A woman engaged in housekeeping or domestic occupations (see HOUSE *sb.*^{1} 18 c); a woman who manages or superintends the affairs of a household; *esp.* the woman in control of the female servants of a household.

1607 Shaks. *Cor.* I. iii. 55 How do you both? You are manifest house-keepers. What are you sowing [sewing] heere? **1724** Swift *Stella's Birthday* 9 Merry folks..Call the old house-keeper, and get her To fill a place. **1766** Fordyce *Serm. Yng. Wom.* (1767) I. vi. 226 Mistresses that leave all to housekeepers and other servants. **1834** Ht. Martineau *Demerara* xii. 140 The little pining thing that was kept in the housekeeper's room. **1859** Dickens *Lett.* (1880) II. 87 My eldest daughter is a capital housekeeper.

5. One who 'keeps the house', or stays at home (see HOUSE *sb.*^{1} 18 d).

c **1710** Celia Fiennes *Diary* (1888) 75 They..scarce ever go 2 or 10 mile from thence especially the women, so may be termed good housekeepers. **1826** Scott *Jrnl.* 12 June, Grief makes me a housekeeper, and to labour is my only resource.

Hence (in sense 4) **'housekeeper-like, 'house,keeperly** *adjs.*, like or characteristic of a housekeeper. **'house,keepership**, the position or office of a housekeeper.

1839 *Lett. fr. Madras* xxvii. (1843) 294 A sort of good-natured, housekeeper-like bodies, who talk only of ayahs and amahs. **1883** Howells *Woman's Reason* iii. I. 60 Marian ..turned to her mother with an air of house-keeperly pre-occupation to ask something about the lunch. **1896** *Daily News* 2 May 7/2 Her grandson..wrote to contradict the story of the housekeepership.

housekeeping ('haʊskiːpɪŋ), *sb.* [f. HOUSE *sb.*^{1} + KEEPING *vbl. sb.*]

1. The maintenance of a household; the management of household affairs: cf. HOUSE *sb.*^{1} 18 a, d. Also *transf.*

1550 Crowley *Last Trump.* 1316 In thine housekeping and thy chere. **1576** Fleming *Panopl. Epist.* 274 Democritus..being wearie of house keeping. **1640** in *Lismore Papers* Ser. II. (1888) IV. 122 It was Reported..that your honnor had giuen ouer houskiping. **1791** Mrs. Radcliffe *Rom. Forest* iii, At my mother's death my father gave up house-keeping. **1856** Kane *Arct. Expl.* II. xxii. 217 They had learned house-keeping. *a* **1899** *Mod.* He has married a scholar like himself, and the censorious ask 'Who is to do the housekeeping?' **1966** *Listener* 29 Sept. 448/1, I do not wish to consider..this..in terms of national housekeeping. **1969** *Times* 2 June (Fire Protection Suppl.) p. i, One of the most important things in industrial fire protection..is what we call good housekeeping—cleanliness, tidiness, the careful removal of rubbish.

†**2. a.** The keeping of a good (or other) table; hospitality. (Usually with qualifying adj.) Cf. HOUSE *sb.*^{1} 18 b. *Obs.*

1538 Latimer *Serm. & Rem.* (Parker Soc.) 411 To maintain..good housekeeping; for to the virtue of hospitality he hath been greatly inclined from his beginning. **1548** Hall *Chron., Hen. VI* 167 b, He obteined greate love ..by his abundant liberalitie, and plentifull house kepynge. **1593** Shaks. *2 Hen. VI*, I. i. 191 Thy deeds, thy plainnesse, and thy house-keeping, Hath wonne the greatest fauour of the Commons. **1687** A. Lovell tr. *Thevenot's Trav.* I. 32 It is never heard in Turkie, that a man hath undone himself by Housekeeping. **1849** Macaulay *Hist. Eng.* viii. II. 295 A banquet worthy of the fame which his splendid housekeeping has won for him.

†**b.** *concr.* Provisions for household use. *Obs.* (or *pseudo-arch.*).

1826 Scott *Woodst.* iii, 'Tell me softly and hastily, what is in the pantry?' 'Small housekeeping enough', said Phoebe.

3. Used *attrib.* of a rented holiday cabin or cottage equipped for light housekeeping; similarly, ***housekeeping rooms, suite***, etc., furnished accommodation with cooking facilities. *N. Amer.*

1935 M. M. Atwater *Murder in Midsummer* xx. 190 The house in which she had her tiny suite of 'housekeeping rooms'. **1968** *Globe & Mail* (Toronto) 15 Jan. 24/3 (Advt.). In sunny warm Grand Cayman. Furnished for 4, housekeeping ocean front cottages. **1968** W. Muir *Belonging* xx. 285 We had booked 'a house-keeping suite' without knowing what that was and found a sitting-room and bedroom..with a small kitchenette and a shower. **1970** *Globe & Mail* (Toronto) 26 Sept. 47/3 (Advt.), Housekeeping cabins fully equipped. **1972** *Amer. Automobile Assoc. Tour Book 1972–73* (Southwestern states) 214 (Advt.), Kinnikinnik Motor Lodge..Featuring 1 & 2 Rm. Units... Large Housekeeping Cottage. **1972** *Prince Edward Island Tourist Accommodations* 49 (Advt.), Brudenell Resort... Housekeeping chalets: single £16 to £20, double £20 to £28, extra person £4. **1973** *Kingston* (Ont.) *Whig-Standard* 5 Mar. 28 (Advt.), Single furnished light housekeeping room, refrigerator, stove and sink. *Ibid.* 8 Mar. 37/9 (Advt.), Near Kingston General Hospital, Queen's on Union Street. All housekeeping facilities.

4. Short for *housekeeping allowance, money.*

1946 G. Kersh *Clean, Bright & Slightly Oiled* ii. 16 He never give her no housekeeping. **1966** 'O. Mills' *Enemies of Bride* ii. 20 'Do you want some money?' 'No, it doesn't matter. I haven't got the housekeeping off the Gaffer yet, that's all.' **1970** J. Porter *Rather Common Sort of Crime* ii. 25 You'll go throwing your money around but if I ask you for a bit more housekeeping, that's a different story.

5. Those operations of a computer, organization, etc., which make its work possible but do not directly constitute its performance. Freq. *attrib.*

1956 *Jrnl. Assoc. Computing Machinery* III. 269 Most of the errors..turned up in the logical or housekeeping operations, building loops, tallying, etc. **1958** Gotlieb & Hume *High-Speed Data Processing* v. 80 In programming a problem for a data-processing machine many of the instructions are not of an arithmetic nature but fall into a class called organizational or housekeeping instructions. **1962** *IBM Systems Jrnl.* I. 72 The necessary routines such as housekeeping, timekeeping, utility routines, association of equipment, etc. **1966** *Sunday Mail Mag.* (Brisbane) 2 Jan. 12/6 The airline industry calls this process 'housekeeping'. It [*sc.* inspection of aircraft fuel tanks for traces of fungus, etc.] has to be done with painstaking thoroughness. **1967** *Oxford Computer Explained* 15 Housekeeping Suites are run on demand, usually twice a week. **1970** A. Chandor et al. *Dict. Computers* 182 Housekeeping functions include the setting of entry conditions, clearing areas of store if the program expects these to be set to some initial condition,..performing standard input/output routines. **1971** *Sci. Amer.* June 66/1 The computer provides status information on the equipment and performs many routine 'housekeeping' chores, such as adjusting currents in the spectrometer magnets and logging beam currents and other quantities of interest. **1971** *Nature* 27 Aug. 662/3 Mechanized methods of library housekeeping are also considered.

6. *attrib.* and *Comb.*, as ***housekeeping book, goods, keys***; **housekeeping allowance, money**, a sum of money regularly set aside for housekeeping expenses.

1914 A. Bennett *Price of Love* xvi. 309 She had received no *housekeeping allowance for more than a week. **1965** in P. Jennings *Living Village* (1968) 123 Housekeeping allowance £7. **1849** Dickens *Dav. Copp.* (1850) i. 7, I kept my *housekeeping-book regularly, and balanced it with Mr. Copperfield every night. **1930** A. Bennett *Imperial Palace* xxx. 200 The figures of the housekeeping-books had.. startled her. **1899** *Daily News* 26 June 10/6 There is a satisfactory trade doing in damasks, and *housekeeping goods. **1900** *Ibid.* 17 Sept. 2/7 Housekeeping goods and damasks. **1852** Dickens *Bleak Ho.* (1853) vi. 48 The *housekeeping keys, Miss. **1885** C. M. Yonge *Two Sides of Shield* I. i. 12 She gave him money—not father's *housekeeping money, but what she got for herself by writing. **1962** E. O'Brien *Lonely Girl* ix. 107 My father forgot about housekeeping money when he drank. **1966** L. Southworth *Felon in Disguise* vi. 86 Her husband had provided her with sufficient housekeeping money for her immediate needs.

'housekeeping, *a.* [f. HOUSE *sb.*^{1} + *keeping*, pr. pple. of KEEP *v.*] That 'keeps house'.

1552 Huloet, House kepynge, *larem fovens.* **1802–12** Bentham *Ration. Judic. Evid.* (1827) V. 16 A parcel of.. housekeeping tradesmen. **1892** *Daily News* 26 Feb. 5/7 [The price] that housekeeping consumers pay for their coal.

housel ('haʊz(ə)l), *sb. Obs.* exc. *Hist.* Forms: 1 **húsel, húsul, húsl,** 2 **husul,** 3 (*Orm.*) **husell,** 3–6 **husel, hosel,** 4– **housel,** (4–5 **hou-, how-, hosele,** 4–6 **hou-, how-, ho-, hoo-, -sil(l, -syl(l,** 5 **hossell, howsul, houzell,** 5–7 **howsel(l,** 6 **houseale, houssel, hussyll, -el, hushel,** 6–7 **housell,** 7 **houzle**). [OE. *húsl, -ul, -el* = ON. *húsl*, Goth. *hunsl* sacrifice, offering; prob. from a Teut. stem **hunþ-*, pre-Teut. **kwn̥t-*, whence Lith. *szweñtas* holy, devoted to God, Lett. *swéts*, OPruss. *swints*, OSlav. *svẽtŭ* holy, Zend *çpəñta* holy; Skr. *çwāntá* tranquil.]

†**1.** A sacrifice. *rare*$^{-1}$. *Obs.*

c **950** *Lindisf. Gosp.* Matt. xii. 7 Miltheortnisse ic willo and nis husul.

2. The consecrated elements at the Communion; the Mass or Eucharist; the administration or receiving of the Eucharist.

c **900** tr. *Bæda's Hist.* IV. xxv. [xxiv.] (1891) 348 He frægn, hwæðer heo æniȝ husl inne hæfdon. *c* **1000** *Canons of Ælfric* c. 36 in Thorpe *Laws* II. 360 Ðæt husl is Cristes lichama na lichamlice ac gastlice, na se lichama ðe he on þrowode ac se lichama ðe he embe spræc ða ða he bletsode hlaf and win to husle. *c* **1175** *Lamb. Hom.* 25 Er he me ȝefe husul. *c* **1200** *Trin. Coll. Hom.* 61 þer after ben alesd of pine þurh þat holie husel. **1297** R. Glouc. (Rolls) 8661 He..deide wiþoute speche Wiþoute ssrift & hosel. *c* **1375** *Lay Folks Mass Bk.* (B) 235, I trow þat housel es bothe flesshe & blode. *c* **1430** Lydg. *Min. Poems* (Percy Soc.) 198 Contricioun, shrifft, hoosyl at thy partyng. *c* **1449** Pecock *Repr.* 461 An ordynaunce..that thei schulde not take her hosil (that is to seie the holi Eukarist) at nyȝt tyme aftir her soper. **1534** More *Treat. on Passion* Wks. 1331/1 Holy men..haue in their writinges called this blessed holy housell, by the name of a sacrament, a signe, a memoriall and a figure. *c* **1550** Crowley *Inform.* (1872) 155 To begge money to paye for theyr housel, as they call it. **1564** Becon *Comp. Lord's Supper & Mass* Wks. (1560–3) III. 113 To celebrate the Lordes Supper, or as the Papistes terme it, to take their Hushel, or to receaue their maker. **1625** Ussher *Answ. Jesuit* 79 Christ hallowed bread and wine to housel before his suffering. **1844** Lingard *Anglo-Sax. Ch.* (1858) I. vii. 298 From the arrival of Augustine till the Reformation, the English name for the eucharist was the *housel.* **1859** Tennyson *Guinevere* 146 So the stately Queen abode..nor sought, Wrapt in her grief, for housel or for shrift.

3. *Comb.* †**housel-box**, a box containing the consecrated host; †**housel-bread**, the host.

c **1375** *Lay Folks Mass Bk.* (MS. B) 597 We praye þis messe vs stande in stede of shrift, & als of housel-brede. **1598** Hakluyt *Voy.* I. 115 Like vnto a deacon carying the houssel-boxe in time of lent.

housel ('haʊz(ə)l), *v. Obs.* exc. *Hist.* Forms: 1 **húslian,** 3–6 **husel, hosel,** etc.: see prec. [OE. *húslian* (= ON. *húsla*), f. *húsl* HOUSEL *sb.*]

1. *trans.* To administer the Communion or Eucharist to; = COMMUNICATE *v.* 7.

c **1000** *Canons of Edgar* c. 65 in Thorpe *Laws* II. 258 We lærað þæt ælc preosta..seoce men husliȝe þonne heom þearf si. *c* **1200** Ormin 6129 He shall shrifenn þe & huslenn ec. *c* **1290** *Michael* 96 in *S. Eng. Leg.* I. 302 þat folk he dude hoseli al. *c* **1400** *Rom. Rose* 6338 He shal housel me anoon. *c* **1450** *St. Cuthbert* (Surtees) 1964 To howsil her or she sulde dy. **1548** tr. *Luther's Art. Faith* Bj, One would pretend to husel or Communicate himself. **1590** Greenwood *Collect. Sclaund. Art.* G, Your popish and Idolatrous housling the sick with this Sacrament. **1616** Bullokar, *Howsell*, to minister Sacraments to a sicke man in danger of death. *a* **1650** *Sir Aldingar* xlvi. in Child *Ballads* (1885) lix. II. 46/2 'A preist, a preist', sayes Aldingar, 'Me for to houzle and shriue!' **1877** J. D. Chambers *Div. Worship* 395 In England, the Deacon might baptize and housel the people.

fig. *a* **1619** Beaum. & Fl. *Wit without M.* III. i, May zealous smiths So housel all our Hackneys, that they may feel Compunction in their feet.

b. *pass.* (and *refl.*) To receive the Communion; = COMMUNICATE *v.* 6.

c **1200** *Trin. Coll. Hom.* 101 Ðanne we hauen ure sinnes forleten and bireused and bet and ben huseled. *a* **1300** *Cursor M.* 28455 Efter þat i huseld was. *c* **1386** Chaucer *Pars. T.* ¶953 Oones a yeere atte leeste wey it is laweful for to been housled. *c* **1400** Maundev. (1839) xxv. 261 þei schryuen hem & howselen hem euermore ones or twyes in the woke. And þere ben manye of hem þat howselen hem euery day. *c* **1440** *Jacob's Well* (E.E.T.S.) 176 He was howselyd & anelyd, & dyed, & apperyd to oon of his frendys in lyknes of a deuyl, & seyde, he was dampnyd. **1541** Barnes *Wks.* (1573) 302/2 In the begynning of the church, all Christen men were houseled vnder both kyndes. **1870** Morris *Earthly Par.* I. I. 336 And then being houselled, did he eat and drink.

c. *intr.* or *absol.* To administer the Communion.

1504 in *Ripon Ch. Acts* (Surtees) 295, I witte unto the alter ..to serve at Pasch to howsell with, oon twill towel. **1516** in E. A. Tillett *St. George Tombland, Norwich* (1891) 40 A towel of plein cloth for to howsel with of iiij or v ellys.

†**2.** *transf.* To purify by ceremonial expiation or lustration. *Obs.*

1607 Topsell *Four-f. Beasts* (1658) 523 The Athenians, when they housled their army..did it with Hogs, Sheep or Buls..and at last slew and offered them to Mars.

house-lamb.

1. A lamb kept in or near the house; a pet lamb; a lamb kept and fattened for the table.

1574 Hellowes *Gueuara's Fam. Ep.* (1584) 141 So quiet and so gentle, as if it had beene a house lambe brought up by hand. **1826** in Cobbett *Rur. Rides* (1885) II. 193 The house-lambs and the early Easter-lambs. **1848** Dickens *Dombey* xxv, Mild and placid as a house-lamb.

2. The flesh of such a lamb used as food.

1727 *Philip Quarll* (1816) 30 It eat as delicious as house lamb. **1827** Mrs. Rundell *Dom. Cookery* II. 32 House-lamb may be had in great towns almost all the year.

houseleek ('haʊsliːk). Forms: see HOUSE and LEEK: also 6–7 **houselike,** 7 **houslicke.** [OE. type **húsléac*, f. *hús* HOUSE *sb.*^{1} + *léac* LEEK = MDu. *huuslooc*, MLG. *hûslôk*, Du. *huislook*; MHG. *huslouch*, Ger. *hauslauch*; Da. *huuslög*, Sw. *huslök*.] The plant *Sempervivum tectorum*, a succulent herb with pink flowers and thick stem and leaves, the latter forming a dense rosette close to the root, which grows commonly on walls and the roofs of houses. Hence extended to all species of the genus *Sempervivum*, N.O. *Crassulaceæ*.

c **1440** *Promp. Parv.* 251/1 Howsleke, herbe, or sengrene, *barba Jovis, semper viva, jubarbium.* **1538** Turner *Libellus*, *Sedvm*, housleke. **1562** —— *Herbal* II. 133 a, *Hous-leke* ..groweth in mountaynes and hylly places, som vse to set it vpon theyr houses. **1617** Markham *Caval.* VII. 39 Two

spoonefull of the iuyce of houslicke. **1656** Ridgley *Pract. Physick* 151 Housleek on houses is full of juyce in the greatest heat. **1832** Lytton *Eugene A.* i. ii, Roofs green with mosses and house-leek.

attrib. c **1540** in *Vicary's Anat.* (1888) App. ix. 227 Take.. of nightshade leaves.. howseleke leaves, plantaigne leaves. **1694** Salmon *Bates' Disp.* (1713) 645/1 Drink after it a Draught of Housleek Whey.

b. tree houseleek, or **houseleek-tree**: a shrubby plant with yellow flowers (*Sempervivum* or *Æonium arboreum*), allied to the Common Houseleek. **sea housleek**: see quot. 1611.

1611 Cotgr., *Ioubarbe arborée*, Tree Housleeke.. *Ioubarbe marine*, Sea Housleek, Sea Aygreen, hearb Aloes. **1866** *Treas. Bot.* 23/2 *Æonium arboreum* is well known to gardeners as the tree houseleek; its loose panicles, with a profusion of clammy yellow blossoms, are very elegant. **1884** Miller *Plant-n.*, House-leek Tree.

houseless ('haʊslɪs), *a.* [f. house *sb.*^{1} + -less.]

1. Not having or dwelling in a house; having no shelter or place of refuge; homeless.

c **1430** *15 Tokens* in *Adam Davy* etc. (1878) 93 Herberewe þe housles. **1605** Shaks. *Lear* iii. iv. 30 Your House-lesse heads, and vnfed sides. **1764** Goldsm. *Trav.* 4 Where the rude Carinthian boor Against the houseless stranger shuts the door. **1838** H. Blunt 7 *Ch. Asia* 77 We all feel for the houseless and destitute. **1886** *American* XIII. 21 The homeless and houseless poor.

2. Destitute of houses and the shelter they yield.

c **1586** C'tess Pembroke *Ps.* cxx. v, In a tent, in a howselesse harbour. **1798** Wordsw. *Tintern Ab.* 20 Vagrant dwellers in the houseless woods. **1829** Lytton *Disowned* ii. 8 Our home is the houseless sward.

†**b.** Inhospitable. *Obs. rare*$^{-1}$.

1387 Trevisa *Higden* (Rolls) I. 351 Men of þis lond beeþ.. housles, and grete fiȝteres [= *gens inhospita, bellicosa*].

Hence '**houselessness**, houseless condition.

1819 *Blackw. Mag.* V. 229 The night—the storms—the houselessness. **1860** Dickens *Uncomm. Trav.* xiii, A cry of loneliness and houselessness.

houselet ('haʊslɪt). *nonce-wd.* [f. house *sb.*^{1} + -let.] A very small house.

1802 W. Taylor in Robberds *Mem.* I. 410 The squeezed cabin-parloured houselets of Dover.

†**houseling** ('haʊslɪŋ), *sb. Obs.* or *dial.* [f. house *sb.*^{1} + -ling.] One that stays in the house; a stay-at-home. **b.** (See quot. 1847-78.)

1598 Florio, *Mansionaro*, a homekeeper, a houslin [**1611** houseling], one that seldome goes abroad. **1847-78** Halliwell, *Houselings*, tame animals, or rather animals bred up by hand. *North.*

houseling, -lling ('haʊz(ə)lɪŋ), *vbl. sb. Obs.* exc. *Hist.* [f. housel *v.* + -ing^1.]

1. The action of the verb housel; administration of the Eucharist; communion.

c **1000** Ælfric *Hom.* II. 548 Æfter þære huslunge. c **1315** Shoreham 25 Alle taketh that ryȝt body Thyse men at hare houslynge. c **1450** Myrc 253 After that holy hoselynge. **1548** *Confess. Faith Ch. Switzerland* in *Wodrow Soc. Misc.* (1844) I. 18 There is twayne whiche are named in the Churche of God Sacramentes, Baptyme, and Howslynge. **1642** Jer. Taylor *Episc.* (1647) 255 Houseling of people is the office meant, communicating them at home. **1886** M. K. Macmillan *Dagonet the Jester* i. 51 When all the houselling was done, the chaplain led me again to the bed.

2. *attrib.* **a.** Used at the celebration of the Eucharist; sacramental (in quot. 1590 *transf.*).

1474 *Will of Selby* (Somerset Ho.), Howseling towell. **1532** *Yatton Churchw. Acc.* (Som. Rec. Soc.) 147 Payd for xxviij yards of Irys cloth for a hussyllyng cloth. **1566** in Peacock *Eng. Ch. Furniture* 86 One howslinge bell. **1590** Spenser *F.Q.* i. xii. 37 His owne two hands.. The housling fire did kindle and provide, And holy water thereon sprinckled wide. **1872** *N. & Q.* 4th Ser. IX. 318 It is not generally known that houseling cloths are still used [in the Church of England], but only in one place that I know of in England—viz., in Wimborne Minster.

b. houseling people: communicants, or people of age to receive the Communion. (Cf. OE. *húslbearn, -wer.*)

1519 in *Pleadings Duchy Lancast.* (1896) 83 A gret paroch and hath seven thousand howseling peple and moo. **1568** *Reg. Parish Ulcombe, Kent* (MS.), Ther are housholders in the said paroch xl^{ti}. Ther are houslinge people 165. **1895** W. Page *Yorksh. Chantry Surv.* (Surtees) II. Pref. 16 Every one over 14 would be accounted a houseling person, or one who received the sacrament.

housell, var. housal, housel, *Obs.*

house-lot. *U.S.* A lot or portion of land sufficient for building a house on; a building plot; cf. home-lot and homestead 3.

1661 in C. Butler *Hist. Groton, Mass.* (1848) 16 That these lands and meadows be so divided.. that none have less than ten acres for their houselots and five acres of meadow. **1693**, **1706** [see homestead 3]. **1841** Emerson *Lect., Conservative* Wks. (Bohn) II. 269 'Touch any wood, or field, or house-lot, on your peril', cry all the gentlemen of this world. **1844** — *Yng. Amer.* ibid. 295 The selection of a fit houselot.

housemaid ('haʊsmeɪd). **a.** A female domestic servant, having charge especially of the reception-rooms and bed-rooms.

1694 *Dunton's Ladies Dict.* 183/2 *House-Maids*, Your principal Office is to make clean the greatest part of the House;.. so that you suffer no room to lie foul. c **1731** Swift *Direct. Servants* Wks. 1814 XII. 399 The house-maid may put out her candle by running it against the looking-glass. **1837** Carlyle *Fr. Rev.* I. vii. iv, The House-maid, with early broom.

b. *attrib.*

1833 Lady Granville *Lett.* (1894) II. 144 There is a vulgar, housemaid, common look in her features. **1884** *Girl's Own Paper* Nov. 58/1 The 'housemaid skirt', with its straight folds, lack of gores, and three or four tucks at the edge, seems to be.. worn.. by all the young girls.

c. ***housemaid's knee***: an inflammation of the bursa over the knee-cap, induced by kneeling on hard floors. (*Syd. Soc. Lex.* 1886.)

1831 *Lond. Med. & Physical Jrnl.* LXVII. 42 The third of the cases.. was of the common description: the bursa very slightly thickened, but distended with fluid, uneasy, and painful, the most ordinary state of the housemaid's knee. **1889** J. K. Jerome *Three Men in Boat* i. 3 The only malady I could conclude I had not got was housemaid's knee. **1912** Adami & McCrae *Text-bk. Path.* xii. 678 'Housemaid's knee', 'miner's elbow', and 'weaver's bottom' are all well-known forms of bursitis. **1971** *Daily Tel.* 19 Apr. 2 Occupational rheumatism known by a variety of names like weaver's bottom, housemaid's knee, and golfer's shoulder, is costing the country.. millions of pounds a year.

d. Other collocations containing the possessive form, as ***housemaid's box***, a box with a container for ashes and a tray above for brushes, dusters, etc.; ***housemaid's closet, cupboard***, a cupboard or small room where brooms, cleaning materials, etc., are kept, slops emptied, etc., ***housemaid's gloves***, gloves worn for protection when cleaning grates, etc.

1861 Mrs. Beeton *Bk. Househ. Managem.* 988 Her *housemaid's box, containing black-lead brushes.. and all utensils necessary for cleaning a grate. **1909** H. G. Wells *Tono-Bungay* iii. i. 266 Housemaid's boxes it'll be a pleasure to fall over. **1950** J. Cannan *Murder Included* viii. 146 Sylvia, carrying a housemaid's box, fled at their approach. **1857** C. M. Yonge *Dynevor Terr.* I. xiv. 229 Mrs. Martha might some day let her stand in the *housemaid's closet, to behold her idol issue forth in the full glory of an evening dress. **1873** — *Pillars of House* II. xix. 162 From a housemaid's closet half-way up, Alda was bringing to light a basin. **1906** M. H. Baillie-Scott *Houses & Gardens* x. 31 The housemaid's closet with its slop sink and spaces for pails and brooms. **1911** L. Weaver *House & its Equipment* 103 In small houses where there is not a housemaid's closet. **1950** J. Cannan *Murder Included* iii. 55 There's a sort of housemaids' closet just at the head of the main staircase, and.. they had an electric heater put in there so that the housemaid could make the early morning tea for everybody. **1873** L. Troubridge *Life amongst Troubridges* (1966) vi. 52 He.. spent nearly all the evening sulking and sobbing in the sink (in the *housemaid's cupboard). **1952** G. Raverat *Period Piece* iv. 68 They.. used to cry.. in the housemaids' cupboard. **1863** Dickens *Uncomm. Trav.* (1866) xxvii. 194/2 A tall straight sallow lady.. who does her household work in *housemaid's gloves. **1962** G. Avery *Greatest Gresham* vii. 132 Mabel.. wearing housemaid's gloves, was cleaning the brass.

Hence (chiefly *nonce-wds.*) '**house,maidenhood** (after *maidenhood*), the personality or honour of a housemaid. '**house,maidenly** *a.* (after *maidenly*), of or belonging to a housemaid. '**housemaiding**, housemaid's work.

1859 Mrs. Carlyle *Lett.* III. 17, I had a deal of housemaiding to execute during the week. **1876** Mrs. Oliphant *Curate in Charge* (ed. 5) I. iii. 62 That's why the girls have so much housemaiding to do. **1878** Besant & Rice *Celia's Arb.* II. xiii. 210 The domestic mop used to be.. a weapon for the defence of housemaidenhood. **1893** 'B. Abbotsford' *But* 49 A housemaid without the housemaidenly cap.

house-man, houseman ('haʊsmən).

1. (See quot.)

1798 Malthus *Popul.* ii. i. (1806) I. 310 The Norway farms have in general a certain number of married labourers employed upon them.. who are called housemen. *Ibid.* 311 A houseman's place becomes vacant.

2. A man who lives habitually in a house.

1843 E. Jones *Poems, Sens. & Event* 86 When the rich hedges Sleep.. so still and sunnily That housemen long to go and lie beside them.

3. ('*House,man*) A member of the college of Christ Church, Oxford: see house *sb.*^{1} 4 b.

1868 *Oxford Spect.* (1869) 102 While their dwelling is called Christ Church by strangers, by others it is called the House, and they themselves Housemen. **1895** *Daily News* 20 Sept. 4/7 Lord Rosebery (himself a Houseman).

4. *U.S. slang.* A burglar.

1904 'No. 1500' *Life in Sing Sing* 255/2 *Houseman*, a burglar. **1911** G. Bronson Howard *Enemy to Society* v. 147 Say a 'house man' or a 'sneak' or a 'second-story' man or a 'peteman'—anything but a 'cracksman'. **1924** G. C. Henderson *Keys to Crookdom* App. B. 408 *Houseman* burglar, prowler.

5. A person responsible for general duties in a private house, hotel, etc.

1934 in Webster. **1960** 'N. Shute' *Trustee from Toolroom* 277 She went through to tell the house-man to clear away the tea. **1961** *Times* 20 July 3/1 Houseman-Handyman.. Valet/Houseman. **1968** *Daily Tel.* (Colour Suppl.) 13 Dec. 24/4 His marvellous home.. with a Spanish houseman and an Italian cook.

6. A house physician or house surgeon; now usually (in Great Britain) a junior doctor who, having passed all the qualifying examinations, is working for a time in a hospital under a certain amount of supervision prior to being fully registered as an independent medical practitioner.

1938 *Amer. Speech* XIII. 228/2 House men (residents and interns) and 'O.R.' (operating room) nurses take their turn being on call for emergency operations. **1942** M. Dickens *One Pair of Feet* vi. 83, I hate these Housemen—stuck-up little boys, they think they know everything. **1962** *Becoming a Doctor* (B.M.A.) 27 The law requires that newly qualified doctors shall be 'provisionally registered' for a year immediately after they have taken their Finals. They are qualified doctors, but full registration must wait upon the results of two obligatory six-month appointments in hospitals specially approved for the purpose. These hospital appointments are in medicine, surgery, or obstetrics—that is to say, in any two of these three. During this time the young doctor is what is called a 'houseman' or, more correctly, a junior house officer. **1962** D. Margerson *Med. as Career* ix. 57 What are the houseman's duties? The *complete* care of the patients. When they come into hospital he takes down the full story of their illnesses; examines them; arranges for the special tests which aid diagnosis; and prescribes the initial treatment. At least once a day.. the houseman visits all his patients. *Ibid.*, The houseman is the patient's *personal* doctor while he is in hospital. Other doctors—the consultants and his registrar assistants—will be involved in diagnosis and treatment, but none will be as close to the patient.. as the houseman. **1965** N. Wymer *Behind Scenes Hospital* iii. 31 The registrars, in turn, are assisted by the house physicians and house surgeons, who, unlike their seniors, live in the hospital and therefore are known as 'housemen'. **1970** *Times* 25 Nov. 11/4 Either consultant or houseman may be called from the clinic for consultation.

Hence '**housemanship**, the state or position of being a houseman (sense 6).

1969 *Guardian* 10 Mar. 5/4 After six years of concentrated study.. the girl is hurled into her first housemanship. The pressure of her first hospital can terrify her. **1972** *Times* 31 Oct. 6/8 Many [doctors] will be completing their housemanship this year.

housemaster ('haʊs,mɑːstə(r), -æ-).

1. The master of a house or household. *rare.*

1878 W. E. Hearn *Aryan Househ.* xii. §5. 289 The Aryan House-master was the member of an organized clan under the presidency of a chief. **1882** *Queen's Printers' Bible-Aids* Gloss. s.v. *Goodman*, The 'goodman' of Prov. vii. 19 was the house-master or husband.

2. ('*house-'master.*) The master of one of the boarding-houses at a public school (house *sb.*^{1} 4 c). Also in some day schools, and *transf.*

1884 *Pall Mall G.* 4 Sept. 4/2 It is to be wondered whether parents.. ever realize the multifarious duties of a house-master. **1891** *Ibid.* 6 Oct. 2/3 The real unit in most of the large public schools is the 'house', and it is the house-master who has the most powerful influence over his pupils. **1963** R. Pedley *Comprehensive School* iii. 124 The house in a day school simply has not got this basis... Take, for example, a housemaster who does quite a lot of administration. **1965** H. Davies *Culture & Grammar School* v. 85 Where senior house masters exist.. they should be able to exercise an effective supervision over the boys in their care. **1966** *Listener* 10 Mar. 342/2 We continue to put some offenders.. under the care of individual probation officers and Borstal housemasters.

Hence (in sense 2) ,**house'mastering**, the work or functions of a housemaster; '**housemasterly** *adj.*, like or characteristic of a housemaster; ,**house'mastership**, the position or office of a housemaster.

1884 *Pall Mall G.* 4 Sept. 4/2 With other duties to perform besides housemastering. **1886** *Athenæum* 17 July 80/1 The unfelt gradual pressure of this system, that is so apt to make of a housemastership what fellowships have been said to be—'the grave of learning', and of other things besides learning which can ill be spared. **1961** A. Wilson *Old Men at Zoo* ii. 112, I should have to hear myself speak in these housemasterly tones many times before I had done with the business. **1963** *Times Lit. Suppl.* 8 Feb. 87/2 The effect is at once toughly moral and academic, a house-masterly harangue.

housemate ('haʊsmeɪt). One who lives in the same house with another; a household companion. Also *fig.*

1809-10 Coleridge *Friend* (1837) III. 325 Knowledge to be gained from books, children, housemates and neighbours. **1847** Emerson *Repr. Men, Uses Gt. Men* Wks. (Bohn) I. 284 It is observed in old couples, or in persons who have been housemates for a course of years, that they grow alike. **1861** Lowell *E Pluribus Unum* Pr. Wks. 1890 V. 74 Peace.. is a blessing that will not long be the housemate of cowardice.

Hence '**housemating**, living together in a house.

1882 Hall Caine *D. G. Rossetti* 273 Remaining.. in the same mind relative to our mutual housemating.

'**house-,mistress**. **1.** The mistress of a house.

1875 Ruskin *Fors Clav.* V. lviii. 293 Permitted to the house-mistresses on great occasions. **1887** *Pall Mall G.* 13 May 14/1 This is the sign that she [the bride] may henceforward regard herself as the true housemistress. She crosses the threshold, and the whole party follows.

2. At a girls' school, a person responsible for certain aspects of the supervision of the pupils; in a boarding school, the mistress in charge of one of the boarding houses.

1912 A. Brazil *New Girl at St. Chad's* iii. 42 Her house-mistress would not have been ready to overlook any deficiency in punctuality. **1961** *Evening Standard* 26 July 25/6 (Advt.), Education Committee.. House-mistress (non-teaching) required.. Technical School for Girls. **1972** *Daily Tel.* 24 Nov. 6/6, I shall continue as housemistress and shall teach mathematics and religious education. **1973** *Radio Times* 8 Nov. 81/1 Miss Gee, housemistress of Guldeford House at Benenden School, recalls Princess Anne's time there.

'**house-mother**. [Cf. Ger. *hausmutter.*] The mother of a household or family; the female

head of a community living together as a family. Also in extended uses.

1834 CARLYLE *Sart. Res.* II. i, in *Fraser's Mag.* Feb. 177/2 The good Gretchen..hovered round him, as only a true housemother can: assiduously she cooked and sewed and scoured for him. **1837** CARLYLE *Fr. Rev.* I. VII. iii, Men know not what the pantry is, when it grows empty; only house-mothers know. **1860** THACKERAY *Round. Papers* xviii. (D.), The house-mother comes down to her family with a sad face. **1882** *Standard* 16 Nov. 1/6 The Managers require a..woman to take charge of and act as House-Mother of a House containing from 20 to 25 Girls and Infants, at their Separate Home School. **1936** *Variety* 8 July 46/1 The cynical college man who dominates his fair-haired pal, the prim house mother—they're all here and more. **1959** *Tablet* 7 Mar. 240/1 Resident Roman Catholic Housemother required to act as Deputy to Housemother-in-charge. **1970** *Observer* 25 Jan. 6/5 The house mother—a woman who calls daily to look after a family in their own home. **1971** 'M. INNES' *Awkward Lie* iv. 71 Calling young women housemothers must be one of Overbury [School]'s notably few concessions to the march of time.

Hence **'house-,motherly** *a.*, belonging to or characteristic of a house-mother.

1880 MISS BROUGHTON *Sec. Th.* I. i, Gillian, wrapping.. with house-motherly care, a woolly shawl round..Emilia.

'house-place, houseplace. The name in many parts of England of the common living-room in a farm-house or cottage; = HOUSE *sb.*[1] 1 b.

1812 *Examiner* 7 Sept. 564/1 His mistress met him in the house-place. **1859** GEO. ELIOT *A. Bede* I. iv, Gyp..followed Lisbeth into the house-place. **1865** MISS METEYARD *Josiah Wedgwood* I. 200–1 From this garden you entered at once, as was then universally the custom, into the roomy house-place or kitchen. **1894** *Athenæum* 6 Oct. 459/1, I can take him into a farmhouse close to my residence, where he will find a very picturesque old 'houseplace' (always spoken of as such), that is, half best kitchen and half sitting-room, where the family ..live and sit at nights.

houser[1] ('haʊzə(r)). *rare.* [f. HOUSE *v.*[1] + -ER[1].]

†**1.** One who erects a house; a builder. *Obs.*

a **1400** *Prymer* (1891) 32 [Ps. cxviii. 22] The stoon þ^t the houseres reproueden her hit is maad in to the heued of the corner.

2. One who 'houses' or makes his habitation somewhere; a dweller, an inhabitant.

1871 R. ELLIS *Catullus* lxiii. 54 To be with the snows, the wild beasts, in a wintery domicile, To be near each savage houser that a surly fury provokes.

†**houser**[2] ('haʊzə(r)). *Obs.* Also 6 **howsour, houssour.** [a. OF. *houssure, -eure*, f. *housser* to cover, HOUSE *v.*[2]] A covering, housing.

1513 DOUGLAS *Æneis* VII. v. 192 The king With purpoure howsouris bad ane coursour bring. **1785** R. CUMBERLAND *Observer* No. 89 ¶2 He loaded and primed his pistols, and carefully lodged them in the housers of his saddle.

'house-room. Room or accommodation in a house for a person or thing; lodging.

1596 SPENSER *F.Q.* VI. iii. 41 Here is at his gate an errant Knight, That house-rome craves. **1601** *Death Earl Huntington* IV. ii. in Hazl. *Dodsley* VIII. 296 And thou find'st house-room in this nunnery. **1698** FRYER *Acc. E. India & P.* 370 They dare hardly give it House-room, or afford it a place in their Libraries. **1862** MRS. WOOD *Mrs. Hallib.* II. ix. 193, I must trouble you to give this man house-room for a few days. *Mod.* The amount of rubbish for which he finds house-room is incredible.

fig. **1586** *Praise of Mus.* 29 A precious stone may be set in ledde, and [etc.], in which cases wee..pittie their vnfortunate houserome. *a* **1618** RALEIGH *Advice of Son* Rem. (1661) 116 Being..turned both out of service and house-room of this wicked world. **1892** A. B. BRUCE *Apologetics* Introd. i. 25 His [Lessing's] large genial nature gave house-room to ideas and tendencies not easily reconciled.

†**'house-roomth.** *Obs. rare.* = prec.

1579 TWYNE *Phisicke agst. Fort.* II. xlvii. 222 b, The first gaue thee house-romth the space of a few monethes.

†**house-row** ('haʊsrəʊ). *Obs.* A row or series of houses. *by (in) house-row*: according to the order or succession of houses, house by house.

c **1586** in *Rel. Ant.* I. 255 The parishe by howserowe to fynde every sundaye in the yeare j. penye white lofe for holye bread. **1676** *N. Riding Rec.* VI. 264 That due watch and ward be kept by persons fit and of able body by house-row. *a* **1791** WESLEY *Wks.* (1872) VIII. 320 Take a regular catalogue of your societies, as they live in house-row. [**1896** T. BLASHILL *Sutton-in-Holderness* 186 For more important objects, collections were sometimes made by 'house-row'.]

†**'houseship.** *Obs.* In 3 husshipe. [f. HOUSE *sb.*[1] + -SHIP. Cf. OE. *húsȝescipe.*] Household, family.

c **1200** *Trin. Coll. Hom.* 197 His seuen sunes and þrie dochtres and al þat muchele husshipe þe him sholde heren.

house snake. 1. One of several North American snakes belonging to the genera *Elaphe* and *Lampropeltis.*

1807 in *Mass. Hist. Soc. Coll.* (1815) 2nd Ser. III. 54 The milk or house snake, speckled like a rattlesnake. **1884** 'MARK TWAIN' *Huck. Finn* xxxix. 396 We went for the snakes, and grabbed a couple of dozen garters and house-snakes. **1958** R. CONANT *Field Guide Reptiles U.S.* 171 Sometimes called 'house snake', but 'barn snake' would be more descriptive, for it would reflect the frequency with which farm buildings are entered in search of rodents.

2. A snake kept as a household god.

[**1742** C. OWEN *Ess. towards Nat. Hist. Serpents* 218 Ælian speaks of domestick Serpents, that were in the Houses of the Egyptians, and look'd upon as household Gods. *Ibid.*, The Arabians reputed Serpents sacred Beings... They take them into their Houses, feed and worship them as Genii, or Guardians of the Place. **1868** J. FERGUSSON *Tree & Serpent Worship* 25 There are house serpents which are accounted in the northern parts of Sweden as household gods.] **1894** W. CROOKE *Pop. Relig. & Folk-Lore N. India* vii. 276 Should rain drive the house snake out of his hole, he is worshipped. **1935** A. EVANS *Palace of Minos* IV. I. 153/2 When the house snakes died the master and mistress of the house died too. **1962** R. W. HUTCHINSON *Prehist. Crete* viii. 124 It was the house snake that was fed and revered as the genius, the guardian angel of the house. **1965** R. & D. MORRIS *Men & Snakes* ii. 47 A gallant housesnake..refused to desert the Macedonian village of Kalenova when the human inhabitants fled.

3. A southern African snake of the genus *Boædon.*

1907 R. L. DITMARS *Reptile Bk.* xxxii. 300 (*heading*) The Red Coluber; Corn Snake; Red Chicken Snake; Mouse Snake; Scarlet Racer; House Snake *Coluber guttatus*, (Linn.). **1911** *East London* (Cape Province) *Dispatch* 1 Sept. 7 These house snakes are more serviceable to man than cats, for they can follow rats and mice into their hiding places. **1932** *Discovery* XIII. 364/2 The brown house snake, *Boodon* [sic] *lineatus*, is far more efficient than a cat in keeping down rats and mice, as it penetrates into their holes and destroys the young. **1962** V. F. M. FITZ-SIMONS *Snakes S. Afr.* 123/1 In search of its prey it is often attracted to, and found in and about, human settlements, and has thus got the name of House Snake.

housestead ('haʊsstɪd). Also 7 **housted.** [OE. *hús-stede*, f. *hús* HOUSE *sb.*[1] + *stede* STEAD. Cf. OS. *hûs-stedi*, OFris. *hûs-stede*, OHG. *hûs-stat.*] A place or piece of ground on which a house stands; the site of a house; cf. HOMESTEAD 3.

c **1000** *Sax. Leechd.* I. 154 Ðeos wyrt..byþ cenned on ealdum hus stedum. *a* **1687** PETTY *Pol. Arith.* 18 The 82 thousand Families of Paris stand upon the equivalent of 65 thousand London Housteds.

,house-'top. a. The top or roof of a house.

1526 TINDALE *Matt.* xxiv. 17 Lett hym whych is on the housse toppe not come doune to take enythinge out of his housse. **1530** PALSGR. 233/1 Housetoppe or treetoppe, *coypeau de la maison.* **1582** N. T. (Rhem.) *Luke* xii. 3 That which you haue spoken into the eare in the chambers shal be preached in the house-toppes. **1828** CARLYLE *Misc.* (1857) I. 238 Mounting to the house-top to reach the stars. **1855** MACAULAY *Hist. Eng.* xi. III. 1 The streets, the balconies, and the very housetops were crowded with gazers.

b. *fig.* A public place; esp. (with allusion to Luke xii. 3) in phrase ***to proclaim, declare;*** or ***cry on*** or ***from the house-top***(*s*), to make public, to proclaim so that everyone knows. Also *attrib.*

1870 *Brewer's Dict. Phr. & Fable* 712/1 *Proclaim on the housetop*, to proclaim or make known to every one; to blab in public. **1895** *Ibid.* (rev. ed.) 632/1 To cry from the house-top. To proclaim (it) from the house-top. **1899** *Westm. Gaz.* 15 Nov. 3/2 The policy of house-top virtue. **1906** J. JACKSON tr. *Thoughts of Marcus Aurelius* 35 A man who has done a good deed should be like a horse that has run its race ..: in other words, he ought not to proclaim it from the house-tops. **1911** C. G. ROBERTSON *Eng. under Hanoverians* II. iv. 345 To cry on the house-tops that it was merry in England before the new industry came up. **1931** L. BIRCH *Pyramid* xviii. 233 Someone should come forward and cry from the housetops that all friendships that are romantic are not, for that reason, immoral. **1934** 'G. ORWELL' *Burmese Days* iii. 52 My friend, you do not think that. If truly you disapprove of the British Empire, you would not be talking of it privately here. You would be proclaiming from the housetops. **1955** L. P. HARTLEY *Perfect Woman* xxiii. 200 Don't worry; I didn't expect you to proclaim it on the house-tops, and I shan't either.

'house-train, *v.* [TRAIN *v.*[1]] *trans.* To train (a domestic animal or infant) to be clean in the house. Also *transf.*, esp. = HOUSE-BREAK *v.* 2 *transf.*; and *fig.*

1924 W. J. LOCKE *Coming of Amos* vii. 89 If you hadn't been house-trained by your excellent mother I should say that you've been making a beast of a night of it. **1928** *Punch* 25 Apr. 455/1 It [*sc.* a cheque] is house-trained and was clean about the bank. **1930** KIPLING *Thy Servant a Dog* 70 It are that dash-Toby-Dog! C'm with, and house-train him! **1937** A. HUXLEY *Ends & Means* xii. 180 The work of the late Dr. Suttie, whose book, *The Origins of Love and Hatred*, contains an interesting chapter on the effects of early house-training upon the emotional life of human beings. **1939** S. SPENDER tr. *Toller's Pastor Hall* I. 41 Goethe wasn't quite house-trained either, you know. First place he was a Freemason, and second too much of a cosmopolitan. **1944** N. STREATFEILD *Myra Carrol* 100 Birds aren't ever house trained. **1950** B. RUSSELL *Unpop. Ess.* vii. 127 Some boys never learn to be what, in animals, is called 'house-trained'. **1955** M. HASTINGS *Cork & Serpent* xvii. 243 After thirty years of marriage, I haven't been able to house-train him yet. **1956** A. HUXLEY *Adonis & Alphabet* 155 It is easy to house-train a cat or a dog. **1958** [see BILLETEE]. **1959** *Elizabethan* Apr. 22/2 Mr. Rochester has a lot of the Wild Man in him... But he is also a good deal more house-trained than Heathcliff. **1961** *Listener* 26 Oct. 645/2 We house-train puppies on a similar basis. **1969** AUDEN *City without Walls* 63 Rumours ran through the city That the Tsar's bodyguard Was not house-trained. **1969** *Times* 11 July 20/5 (Advt.), Capable girl, willing help run..Highland fishing cottage and two house trained small boys. **1973** J. WAINWRIGHT *Devil You Don't* 37 You house-trained him, when he was a kid. Trained him to use the totty. Trained him in table-manners.

houseward ('haʊswəd), *adv.* [See -WARD.] Towards the house. Formerly *to (the) houseward.*

1535 COVERDALE *2 Chron.* iii. 13 Their face was turned to the house warde. **1876** LANIER *Poems, Psalm of West* 134 Stride again To houseward all aghast. **1889** STEVENSON *Master of B.* 157 As we went houseward.

house-warm, *v.* [Back-formation from HOUSE-WARMING.] *intr.* To give, or take part in, a house-warming (sense 2); *trans.* to entertain at a house-warming. (*rare* in finite vb.)

1666 PEPYS *Diary* 1 Nov., A very noble cake, which I presently resolved to have my wife go with to-day, and some wine, and house-warm my Betty Michell. *c* **1810** L. HUNT *Blue-Stocking Rev.* I. 64 Tasteful shade of magnificent house-warming Guelph.

'house-warming.

1. *lit.* The warming or heating of a house; in quot. (?) fuel for warming a house.

c **1150** in *Registr. Monast. de Winchelcumba* (1892) 81 Concessit, etiam nobis..husbote et heibote et huswerminge.

2. The action of celebrating the entrance into the occupation of a new house or home with a feast or entertainment. **b.** The entertainment given on such an occasion.

1577 FLEETWOOD in Ellis *Orig. Lett.* Ser. II. III. 56 The Shomakers of London, having builded..a newe Hall, made a royall feast for theire frends, which they call their howse warming. **1661** EVELYN *Diary* 28 Nov., I dined at Chiffinch's house-warming, in St. James's Park. **1678** DRYDEN *Limberham* v. i. **1712** STEELE *Spect.* No. 518 ¶1, I must make the present entertainment like a treat at an house-warming, out of such presents as have been sent me by my guests. **1880** MRS. RIDDELL *Palace Gard.* ii. (1881) 21 We shall have to give a house-warming, I suppose.

attrib. **1844** J. T. HEWLETT *Parsons & W.* xxxiv, He had given the usual house-warming dinner.

housewife ('haʊswaɪf, formerly also 'hʌzwɪf, 'hʌzɪf), *sb.* Pl. **housewives** ('haʊswaɪvz, 'hʌz(w)ɪvz). Forms: α. 3–4 **husewif,** 4 **husewijf, hūswif, -wijf; house-, houswif, -wyf; hosewif, -wyf,** (*pl.* **-wyves**); 4–5 **houswif, -wijf, -wyff,** 6 **howswyff, housewyfe, (-wyfes -wyves),** 6–8 **houswife,** 6– **housewife, (-wives).** β. 5–6 **hŭswif, -wijf, -wyf(f,** 5–6 **huswyfe,** 6–8 (–9 in sense 3) **huswife,** 7 **-wiffe;** also (in sense 3) 8 **hussive,** 9 **huzzif, hussif,** *pl.* **hussives.** See also HUSSY. [ME. *hus(e)wif*, f. *hús* HOUSE *sb.*[1] + *wif* woman, WIFE: cf. Ger. *hausweib*, early mod.Du. *huyswijf* 'materfamilias' (Kilian); but the sense in Ger. and Du. is usually expressed by *hausfrau, huisvrouw.* In early ME., usually with a connective *e*, as in *husebond*, HUSBAND, which is not found in OE. compounds of *hús-*, and has not been clearly explained. When this was absent, in the form *hūswīf*, the *ū* tended to be shortened by position, as in *husband*, giving the form *hŭswife*, in literary use till the 18th c., and still common in transf. senses and dialectally. Elision of *w* (cf. *Chiswick, Keswick*), and (dialectally) of final *f, v*, gave the forms *huzzif, hussive, huzzy*, HUSSY q.v. But the analytical form with long vowel, *hūsewīf, hūswīf, houswif, housewife*, continued in use, and became frequent in sense 1 in the 16th c., esp. when the shortened *hŭswife* began to lose caste, through its depreciatory use in sense 2 (see HUSSY). But many still pronounce *huzwif, huzzif* in sense 1, even when they write *housewife.*]

1. A woman (usually, a married woman) who manages or directs the affairs of her household; the mistress of a family; the wife of a householder. Often (with qualifying words), a woman who manages her household with skill and thrift, a domestic economist.

α. *a* **1225** *Ancr. R.* 416 Heo nis nout husewif; auh is a chirche ancre. *a* **1240** *Sawles Warde* in *Cott. Hom.* 247 To cwemen wel þe husewif. *a* **1300** *Cursor M.* 14088 Martha was huswijf [*v.rr.* houswif, husewijf, hosewif] o þat hus. *c* **1325** *Gloss. W. de Biblesw.* in Wright *Voc.* 156 *Mesounere*, house wyf. **1382** WYCLIF *1 Tim.* v. 14, I wole, ȝongere for to be weddid..for to be hosewyues. **1393** LANGL. *P. Pl. C.* XIV. 9 By nom hym ys housewif, and heeld here hym self. **1465** MARG. PASTON in *P. Lett.* No. 506 II. 198 By your faynt houswyff at thys tyme. **1535** COVERDALE *Prov.* xxx. 21 The earth is disquieted..thorow an ydle houswife. **1600** SHAKS. *A.Y.L.* I. ii. 33 Let vs sit and mocke the good housewife Fortune from her wheele. **1710** *Brit. Apollo* III. No. 91. 3/2 There is..but An Hour in one whole Day between A Housewife and a Slut. **1832** W. IRVING *Alhambra* II. 85 Loitering housewives and idle maid-servants. **1857** RUSKIN *Pol. Econ. Art* i. (1868) 13 You will see the good housewife taking pride in her pretty table-cloth, and her glittering shelves.

β. *c* **1440** *Promp. Parv.* 255/1 Huswyfe, *materfamilias.* **1529** MORE *Comf. agst. Trib.* II. Wks. 1184/1, I bryng home a gose & not out of the pulters shoppe..but out of the huswiues house, at the fyrst hand. **1573** TUSSER *Husb.* lxx. (1878) 162 Take huswife from husband, and what is he than? **1579** LYLY *Euphues* (Arb.) 37 As good a huswife as she was a happy wife. *a* **1592** H. SMITH *Wks.* (1866–7) I. 29 We call the wife huswife, that is, house-wife. **1607** SHAKS. *Timon* IV. iii. 423 The bounteous Huswife Nature. **1635** BROME *Sparagus Gard.* III. vi. Wks. 1873 III. 166 We would be Much better huswifes. **1712–14** POPE *Rape Lock* v. 21 Who would not scorn what huswife's cares produce. **1762** [see 5].

†**b.** *housewife's cloth*: see quot. 1727. *Obs.*

1571 in Beck *Draper's Dict.* s.v., iij yeardes and half of howswyff clothe iijs. vjd. **1625** HART *Anat. Ur.* I. iv. 44, I discerne..neither carded wooll, flaxe, nor huswiues cloth.

1727–41 CHAMBERS *Cycl.*, House-wife's Cloth is a middle sort of linnen cloth between fine and coarse, for family uses.

†**2.** A light, worthless, or pert woman or girl. *Obs.* Usually *huswife*; now HUSSY, q.v.

1546 J. HEYWOOD *Prov.* (1867) 20 Ye huswife, what wynde blowth ye hyther thus right? **1599** *Broughton's Lett.* vii. 21 Sampsons heyfer was his wife, a skittish huswife. **1613** R. C. *Table Alph.* (ed. 3), *Concubine*, harlot or light huswife. **1655** FULLER *Ch. Hist.* II. i. §4 Some gigling Huswives, (Light Leaves will be wagg'd with Little Wind) causelesly fell a flouting at them. **1691** WOOD *Ath. Oxon.* II. 163 Afterwards he married a light Huswife. **1705** VANBRUGH *Confed.* v. ii, Impudent housewife!

3. Usually ('hʌzɪf). A pocket-case for needles, pins, thread, scissors, etc. (In this sense still often spelt *huswife, hussive.*)

1749 P. SKELTON *Deism Revealed* viii. (T.), Women.. spending their time in knotting, or making an housewife. **1762** STERNE *Tr. Shandy* V. xvi, To bring whatever he had to say, into so small a compass, that..it might be rolled up in my mother's housewife. **1768** —— *Sent. Journ.* (1775) I. 112 (*Temptation*) [She] without saying a word, took out her little hussive, threaded a small needle, and sewed it up. **1851** D. JERROLD *St. Giles* xv. 158 He placed a little silken huswife in her trembling hand. **1868** HOLME LEE *B. Godfrey* x. 54 She drew a thread of silk from the housewife. **1871** CARLYLE in *Mrs. C.'s Lett.* I. 161 She tried anxiously all her 'hussives', boxes, drawers.

†**4.** A local name of some kind of fish. *Obs.*

c **1640** J. SMYTH *Hundred of Berkeley* (1885) 319 The Dory, the huswife, the herring, the sprat.

5. *attrib.* and *Comb.* **a.** appositive; **b.** of or belonging to a housewife; **c. housewife-case** = sense 3; **housewife-cloth** (see 1 b).

1762 CHURCHILL *Ghost* III. 1 It was the Hour, when Huswife Morn, With Pearl and Linen hangs each thorn. **1856** BRYANT *June* iii, The housewife bee and humming-bird. **1856** KANE *Arct. Expl.* II. xxii. 217 They bestirred themselves real housewife-fashion to..make us comfortable. **1859** SALA *Gas-light & D.* xviii. 204 Walking-sticks, housewife-cases, knives.

'housewife (see prec.), *v.* Now *rare.* Also 7 -wive. [f. prec. sb.]

1. *intr.* (also *to* ***housewife it***): To act the housewife; to manage a household with skill and thrift; to practise economy.

1566 DRANT *Horace, Sat.* I. A ij b, She [the ant] huswyfes it right well. **1603** BRETON *Dial. Dignity or Indig. Man* 15 Shee Huswifeth at home for their owne profit and theyr Childrens comfort. **1766** MRS. GRIFFITH *Lett. Henry & Frances* III. 254 She neither reads, converses, works, visits, housewifes, coquets, intrigues, nor prays. **1894** *Westm. Gaz.* 28 June 1/3 All her daily dusting and careful housewifing.

2. *trans.* To manage as a good housewife, or with skill and thrift; to economize, be sparing of, make the most of. (Cf. *to husband.*)

1632 BROME *North. Lasse* III. ii. Wks. 1873 III. 57 If you ..huswife the entertainment to make it brave for my credit. **1649** G. DANIEL *Trinarch., Rich. II*, ccxxxix, The vndrest Hearth, and the ill house-wif'd roome Lay all on heaps. **1721** DE FOE *Moll Flanders* (1840) 116, I must housewife the money. **1798** F. LATHOM *Midnt. Bell* III. 55 In order to housewife the money we possessed..we resolved to buy a loaf.

housewifely ('haʊswaɪflɪ, 'hʌz(w)ɪflɪ), *a.* Also 6–7 hus-. [f. as prec. + -LY¹.]

1. Of the character of a housewife; skilful and thrifty in the management of household affairs.

1526 TINDALE *Titus* ii. 5 To be of honest behaveoure, chast, huswyfly. *a* **1639** W. WHATELEY *Prototypes* I. xi. (1640) 140 Sarah was huswifely in her house. **1677** *Compl. Servant-Maid* 2 Be neat, cleanly, and huswifely, in your clothes. **1741–70** ELIZ. CARTER *Lett.* (1808) 110 Whether Telemachus (like a notable housewifely young man as he was) hung his cloaths upon a peg. **1864** MISS YONGE *Trial* I. iv. 77 The homely housewifely mother.

2. Belonging to or befitting a housewife; relating to or showing skill in domestic economy.

1560 *Nice Wanton* in Hazl. *Dodsley* II. 165 Learn..to spin and sew, And other honest housewifely points to know. **1624** CHAPMAN *Homer's Hymn to Vesta*, Grace this house with thy housewifely repair. **1755** *Connoisseur* No. 60 ⁋1 Housewifely accomplishments are now quite out of date among the polite world. **1848** C. BRONTË *J. Eyre* xi, She produced from her pocket a most housewifely bunch of keys. **1869** MRS. LYNN LINTON *Girl of Period* Ess. 1883 I. 43 The snobbish half of the middle classes holds housewifely work as degrading.

Hence **'housewifeliness**, housewifely character.

1561 BECON *Sick Man's Salve* Wks. II. 245 Her quietnes, honestie, howsewiuelines, and such other fruites of Godes spirit. **1869** *Daily News* 8 Oct., One signal merit of domestic statesmanship in Prussia is..its housewifeliness. **1878** *Scribner's Mag.* XVI. 731/2 There was a quiet air of housewifeliness about her.

'housewifely, *adv.* ? *Obs.* [f. as prec. + -LY².] In a manner befitting a housewife.

c **1430** *How Good Wijf* 153 in *Babees Bk.* (1868) 43 Houswijfli þou schalt goon on þe worke day. **1551** T. WILSON *Logike* (1580) 58 She handleth all thinges housewifely. **1573** TUSSER *Husb.* lxxiii. (1878) 164 That all thing in season be huswifelie fed. **1693** SOUTHERNE *Maid's Last Prayer* v. i, You were more housewifely employ'd.

housewifery ('haʊswaɪfrɪ, 'hʌz(w)ɪfrɪ). Forms: see HOUSEWIFE; also 6–7 **-wivery**, etc., 6–8 **-wifry**, etc., 7 **husfrey**. [f. as prec. + -RY.]

1. The function or province of a housewife; management of household affairs; domestic economy; housekeeping.

c **1440** *Promp. Parv.* 255/1 Huswyfery, *yconomia.* **1481–4** E. PASTON in *P. Lett.* No. 859 III. 279, I deme her mynde hathe ben other weys ocapyed than as to huswyfery. **1550** CROWLEY *Way to Wealth* (1872) 139 Womanlike behauiour and motherlike housewifry. **1570** TUSSER (*title*) A hundreth good pointes of husbandry, lately maried unto a hundreth good poynts of huswifery. *c* **1611** CHAPMAN *Iliad* XXIII. 242 Skilled in housewiferies Of all kinds fitting. **1694** R. L'ESTRANGE *Fables* lxxxvii. 104 The very Point of Manage and Huswiv'ry. **1707** *Reflex. upon Ridicule* 225 Women of great Figure look upon Huswifery as a City Vertue. **1886** RUSKIN *Præterita* I. vii. 208 My mother..learned severely right principles of truth, charity, and housewifery.

†**b.** *fig.* Thrift, economy; making the most of something. *Obs.*

1638 BROME *Antipodes* III. vi. Wks. 1873 III. 288 To cease your huswifry in spinning out The Play at length thus. **1775** MAD. D'ARBLAY *Early Diary* (1889) II. 11 Trying on a coat she was altering in a fit of housewifery.

2. *concr.* Things pertaining to housekeeping; articles of household use; in quot. 1673–4, economic product. ? *Obs.*

1552 HULOET, Huswiferye, *lana et tela.* *c* **1590** GREENE *Fr. Bacon* i. 79 Amongst the cream-boles did she shine, As Pallas, mongst her Princely huswiferie. **1616** SURFL. & MARKH. *Country Farme* 156 Your Hedge..which shall part your Garden of Huswiferie and Pulse. **1673–4** GREW *Veget. Trunks* vii. §12 Scotch-Cloath, is only the House-wifery of the same parts of the Barque of Nettle. **1822** L. HUNT *Indicator, Old Lady*, She..is a great..connoisseur in butcher's meat and all sorts of house-wifery.

3. *attrib.*

1580 TUSSER *Husb.* Introd. (1878) 2 More lessons..Than Huswifery book doth utter or tell. **1891** *Review of Rev.* IV. 584/1 Housewifery schools were established.

'housewifeship. Forms: see HOUSEWIFE; also *Sc.* **hussyfskap, hussyskep, hissieskip, housewifeskep.** [f. as prec. + -SHIP: in north. dial. after ON. *-skapr.*] = prec.

a **1225** *Ancr. R.* 414 Husewifschipe is Marthe dole; and Marie dole is stilnesse. *c* **1449** PECOCK *Repr.* II. xiv. 230 Sche schulde make badde husewijfschip. *a* **1568** *Wife Auchtermuchty* iv, Sin' that ye will hussyskep ken, First ye sall sift and syne sall knead. **17..** *Barring o' the Door* iii. in Ritson *Sc. Songs* (1794) I. 227 My hand is in my hussyfskap, Goodman, as ye may see. **1825–80** JAMIESON s.v. *Hissieskip*, Mair by chance than guid hissieskip. **1854** MRS. OLIPHANT *Magd. Hepburn* III. 78 'Naething less than my mantle and my housewifeskep..a' to change with your jack and bonnet.'

housewifish ('haʊswaɪfɪʃ), *a.* [f. as prec. + -ISH.] Appertaining to, like, or partaking of the character of, a housewife.

1835 MOTLEY *Let.* 27 July (Corr. 1889 I. 60), I thought the whole scene at first too tidy..too housewifish. **1855** BAGEHOT *Lit. Stud.* (1879) I. 287 By tact and instinct motherly and housewifish. **1877** MRS. OLIPHANT *Makers Flor.* vi. 167 Foolish housewifish cares.

housewright ('haʊsraɪt). Now *rare.* [f. HOUSE *sb.*¹ + WRIGHT.] A builder of houses (esp. of timber); a house-carpenter.

1549 CHALONER *Erasm. on Folly* F iv b, What housewright by Geometrie found ever out such maner buildyng, as theyr [bees'] commes are of? *c* **1575** *Durham Depos.* (Surtees) 289 William Gelson, of Lanchester, houswright. *a* **1619** FOTHERBY *Atheom.* II. i. §8 (1622) 193 Some, Housewrights; ..some, Cartwrights. **1890** A. W. MOORE *Surnames Isle Man* 88 A housewright and church-builder by trade.

housey: see HOUSY.

housey-housey ('haʊsɪ'haʊsɪ). Also **housie-housie, housy-housy** and abbrev. **housey, housie,** (*rare*) **housee.** [f. HOUSE *sb.*¹ 9 c + -Y⁶.] A later name for the game of 'house' (see also quot. 1964).

1936 F. RICHARDS *Old-Soldier Sahib* iii. 69 To draw a crowd they would shout: 'Housee, housee, housee!' **1937** PARTRIDGE *Dict. Slang* 410/2 Housey-housey! **1938** in Mencken *Amer. Lang.* Suppl. (1945) I. 461/1 The game so popular in army circles in Hong Kong under the name of *tombola* is now sweeping South London as a craze called *housey-housey.* It is played for the most part by housewives who are attracted to open-door booths by a glittering display of cutlery and chromium-plated clocks. **1945** *Penguin New Writing* XXVI. 30 He was shouting numbers hoarsely from the Housey-Housey stall. **1949** S. P. LLEWELLYN *Troopships* 3 Men playing housie-housie (tombola). **1949** E. DE MAUNY *Huntsman in Career* 163 Someone started up a 'housey' school. **1957** J. FRAME *Owls do Cry* 42 Like the woman down the road..having parties every Saturday night with housey-housey and drink. **1960** *Times* (Canada Suppl.) 16 Mar. p. xv/5 Gala dances and housie-housie at night, bring people into contact. **1964** A. WYKES *Gambling* x. 249 The call used to assemble a group for a game of house was 'housey-housey'. **1967** *Stage* 2 Mar. 4/1 'Housey'-addicts never had it so good! **1971** B. W. ALDISS *Soldier Erect* 30 Desperate till now to get off the hated boat with its hated routines of exercise and housey-housey, I was suddenly reluctant to leave the shelter of a familiar place.

housing ('haʊzɪŋ), *sb.*¹ [f. HOUSE *v.*¹ or *sb.*¹ + -ING¹.]

1. The action of the verb HOUSE, in various senses: †building of houses (*obs.*); putting or enclosing in a house; furnishing or provision of houses; dwelling or lodging in a house.

1377 LANGL. *P. Pl.* B. xv. 76 Freres..folilich spenen In housyng, in haterynge, and in-to hiegh clergye shewynge. **1626** BACON *Sylva* §412 The Housing of Plants..will.. Accelerate Germination. **1681** N. RESBURY *Serm. Fun. Sir A. Broderick* 6 Noah's housing in the Ark. **1698** FRYER in *Phil. Trans.* XX. 346 Their Constitutions, and Customs, Housing, Cloathing. **1848** *Rep. U.S. Comm. Patents 1847* 168 The tobacco was hardly worth the housing. **1850** *Rep. Comm. Patents: Agric. 1849* (U.S. Dept. Agric.) 321 This mode is pursued easily by simply splitting..the plant.. before it is cut down for housing. **1930** A. P. HERBERT *Water Gipsies* viii. 96 Honest John Raven worked hard and late at the office, and sometimes brought home papers with him, or if not he talked 'housing' or threw off little anecdotes about 'National Insurance'. **1973** *Oxford Times* 9 Nov. 9/4 One problem we both have is of course that of housing.

2. a. Shelter of a house, or such as that of a house; house accommodation; lodging.

a **1300** *Cursor M.* 8591 Þai had husing nan to wale. *c* **1330** R. BRUNNE *Chron. Wace* (Rolls) 11073 Of wode and water, hey and gres, Of housyng. *c* **1489** CAXTON *Blanchardyn* liii. 204 Noo housyng nor no retrayt was nyghe..where they myght be lodged. **1589** PUTTENHAM *Eng. Poesie* I. ix. (Arb.) 39 The shepheardes tente or pauillion, the best housing. **1690** LOCKE *Govt.* II. xiii. (Rtldg.) 157 Scarce so much housing as a sheepcote. **1702** C. MATHER *Magn. Chr.* III. III. (1852) 558 Their housing is nothing but a few mats tyed about poles fastened in the earth. **1849** RUSKIN *Sev. Lamps* iv. §5. 98 The soft housing of the bird's nest.

b. Houses or buildings collectively; house-property; *spec.* a collection of outhouses or adjoining buildings attached to a house (dial. sometimes confused with *housen*, pl. of HOUSE).

? *a* **1400** *Morte Arth.* 1284 Thise hende..Be-helde þe howsyng fulle hye of Hathene kynges. **1446** in Willis & Clark *Cambridge* (1886) I. 339 Housyng sufficeant as wel for stables and hayhouses as for other of his beestis to be eased in. *c* **1550** LEVER in Strype *Mem. Eccl.* (1721) II. II. xxiv. 449 It is the common Custom with covetous Landlords, to let their Housing so decay, that the Farmer shall be fain..to give up his Lease. **1682** WOOD *Life* 6 Nov. (O.H.S.) III. 28 These housing belongs to Arthur Tyllyard by vertue of a lease from Oriel. **1716** B. CHURCH *Hist. Philip's War* (1867) II. 107 He..coming there found several Housing and small Fields of Corn. **1818** HALLAM *Mid. Ages* iii. II. (1872) I. 465 Our housing is valued at 7,000,000 ducats; its annual rental at 500,000.

c. A house or building.

1399 LANGL. *Rich. Redeles* III. 217 He wondrid..þat þe hie housinge herborowe ne myghte Halfdell þe houshould. **1483** CAXTON *Gold. Leg.* 424 a/1 He must make his habytacyon or howsyng more spacious & gretter than hit was. **1588–9** *Act 31 Eliz.* c. 7 §1 Nor convert..anye Buyldinge or Howsinge..as a Cottage for habitacion. **1831** LANDOR *Misc.* Wks. 1846 II. 637 Above the housings of the village dames.

†**3.** *Arch.* A canopied niche for a statue, a 'tabernacle'; also *collect.* tabernacle-work. *Obs.*

1463 *Bury Wills* (Camden) 37 An ymage of our lady, sitting or stondyng, in an howsyng of free stoon. **1516** in Willis & Clark *Cambridge* (1886) II. 243 A Rodeloft..wyth Imagery and howsynge. **1521** in C. Welch *Tower Bridge* 66 [New statues] set in howsinges of frestone. [**1879** S. WATERTON *Pietas Mariana* 262 Tabernacles were canopied niches. In ancient contracts they were also called *maisons*, habitacles, hovels, and howsings.]

4. *Naut.* **a.** A covering or roofing for a ship when laid up, or under stress of weather. **b.** The part of a lower mast between the heel and the upper deck, or of the bowsprit between the stem and the knight-heads. **c.** = *house-line*: see HOUSE *sb.*¹ 24. †**d.** ***housing-in***: see HOUSE *v.*¹ 8 (*obs.*).

1627 CAPT. SMITH *Seaman's Gram.* xi. 52 The howsing in of a Ship is when shee is past the bredth of her bearing shee is brought in narrow to her vpper workes. **1821** A. FISHER *Voy. Arctic Reg.* 142 We have now got the housing over the ships. **1853** KANE *Grinnell Exp.* xxviii. (1856) 232 A housing of thick felt was drawn completely over the deck. *c* **1860** H. STUART *Seaman's Catech.* 74 From the heel to the upper deck is called housing. From the step to the stem [of bowsprit] is called housing. **1867** SMYTH *Sailor's Word-bk.*, *Housing*, or *House-line*, a small line formed of three fine strands smaller than rope-yarn.

5. *Carpentry.* (See quot.)

1823 P. NICHOLSON *Pract. Build.* Gloss. 586 *Housing*, the space excavated out of one body for the insertion of some part of the extremity of another, in order to unite or fasten the same together. **1858** *Skyring's Builders' Prices* (ed. 48) 57 Housings under four inches girt.

6. *Mech.* **a.** 'One of the plates or guards on the railway-carriage or truck, which form a lateral support for the axle-boxes.' **b.** 'The framing holding a journal-box.' *spec.* A massive metal frame or pillar that supports one end of a set of rolls in a rolling mill. **c.** 'The uprights supporting the cross-slide of a planer' (Knight *Dict. Mech.* 1875).

1869 H. S. OSBORN *Metallurgy of Iron & Steel* III. iv. 771 (*heading*) View of a housing, and section of rollers and foundation. **1882** *Engineer* 24 Feb. 133/1 The screw in each housing is turned to reduce the space between the rolls. **1938** *Extension Course Ferrous Metall.* (Penn. State Coll.) (ed. 2) II. xii. 203 The housings are very heavy cast iron or steel frames, designed to support the rolls and adjusting mechanism securely in place. **1965** M. H. T. ALFORD tr. *Tselikov & Smirnov's Rolling Mills* v. 135 The weight of housings is taken by their feet which bear on the foundations through girders.

d. A structure that supports and encloses the bearings at the end of an axle or shaft; a journal-box. Hence more widely, a rigid case or cover

that encloses and protects an axle or any other mechanism or piece of apparatus.

1889 *Cent. Dict.*, *Housing*, a housing-box; a journal-box. **1915** V. W. PAGÉ *Model T Ford Car* iii. 111 The bevel pinion meshes with a large bevel gear..which is attached to the differential housing. **1916** J. E. HOMANS *Automobile Handbk.* xvi. 177 The housings of the oil pump, water pump, [etc.]. **1922** L. BELL *Telescope* x. 242 The housing, just big enough to take in the equatorial with the tube turned low, opens on the south side and then can be rolled northward on its track..well clear of the instrument. **1935** *Times* 2 Oct. 6/5 Helical springs working in a closed oil-filled housing. **1949** FRAZEE & BEDELL *Automotive Fundamentals* viii. 458 In conventional automobiles and trucks, the rear-axle housing supports the rear-end load on the road wheels. In addition, the housing contains the driving mechanism and carries the rear-wheel bearings. **1958** *Times* 9 May 13/7 The safety housings on the toggle switches. **1962** *Which? Car Suppl.* Oct. 139/2 The water pump to heater hose was chafing on thermostat housing. **1968** P. H. SMITH *Triumph Autobk. Two* (ed. 2) vii. 101/1 The outer ends of the axle-shafts are carried in trunnion mounted bearing housings which are attached to vertical pressed steel links. **1972** *Sci. Amer.* Jan. 68 (Advt.), A large diascopic illuminator and a set of episcopic illuminators; a 4 × 5″ bellows..; a mirror reflex housing; and a sensitive spot meter.

7. *attrib.* and *Comb.* as ***housing association, problem, project, question, reform, scheme, site, unit***; **housing-bearer, -frame**, the frame in which the rollers of an iron-rolling mill are set; **housing-bolt**, a bolt used in housing a gun on deck; **housing-box** = JOURNAL-BOX; **housing development** [DEVELOPMENT 3 d], the act or process of planning and building a group of houses (a **housing estate**) and associated services on a site; **housing list**, a waiting-list for council houses; **housing-ring** (see quot. 1867); **housing-sail**, a sail used for housing a ship; **housing screw**, a screw by means of which the rollers in a rolling mill can be adjusted and the thickness of the metal controlled.

1957 *Act* 5 & 6 *Eliz. II* c. lvi. §189 '*Housing association' means a society, body of trustees or company established for the purpose of..facilitating or encouraging the construction or improvement of houses. **1970** *Internat. & Compar. Law Q.* XIX. II. 205 Discussion inevitably ranged into such related topics as..housing associations and co-operatives. **1971** P. GRESSWELL *Environment* 131 The main object of Housing Associations is to provide houses to let for local people. **1859** F. A. GRIFFITHS *Artil. Man.* (1862) 236 No. 1 ..sees the gun laid square between the *housing-bolts. **1951** *Amer. City* Sept. 104/1 The builders of Lakewood Park.. envisioned the building of a community, including parks, play grounds, schools, churches, and a major shopping center. More than 30,000 people are already living in the 7,200 homes..that have been completed. There is a fact more than bigness, however, that puts this *housing development among the pioneers. **1959** N. MAILER *Advts. for Myself* (1961) 153 He looks down six stories into the giant quadrangle of the Queens housing development. **1920** *Times* 18 Nov. 9/4 It will afford.. much-needed means of access to the L.C.C. *Housing Estate at Dagenham. **1931** *Economist* 12 Dec. 1136/2 Weaker [building] societies may become mere appanages of speculative builders, agents, and other interests concerned with 'housing-estate' exploitation. **1936** W. HOLTBY *South Riding* I. vi. 68 More land for housing estates. **1956** J. M. MOGEY *Family & Neighbourhood* 73 The housing-estate family developed a much more critical attitude. **1964** M. ARGYLE *Psychol. & Social Probl.* xv. 183 The Census of 1961 showed that more people than before live in suburbs and housing estates. **1952** M. LASKI *Village* xiii. 181 Roy had put his name down on the *housing-list at the Town Hall. **1968** L. BERG *Risinghill* 46 The bannisters broke and she fell down the stairs and broke her leg. She's been on the housing list twenty-five years. **1899** S. A. BARNETT in H. Barnett *Canon Barnett* (1918) II. xlix. 311 The *housing problem..is bound up with the industrial problem, with the education problem, with the social problem, and with the religious problem. **1911** G. B. SHAW *Getting Married* Pref. 117 They were content to have the whole national housing problem treated on a basis of one room for two people. **1947** *Tribune* 24 Jan. 12/1 They began talking about the housing problem. **1973** *Guardian* 18 May 16/1 One of the reasons for Britain's housing problem is that many houses are in the wrong place. **1938** *Jrnl. Social Forces* May 528 (*title*) Some eighteenth century *housing projects in France. **1967** S. SONTAG *Death Kit* (1968) 10 All the housing projects are unadorned boxes built of brick. **1970** *Globe & Mail* (Toronto) 25 Sept. B7/5 A $1,644,512 loan for a 139-unit apartment house in a Hamilton low rental housing project. **1899** *Daily News* 19 July 5/5 Milner had charge of the *Housing Question after the boom was launched. **1867** SMYTH *Sailor's Word-bk.*, *Housing-rings, ring-bolts over the lower deck-ports, through the beam-clamps, to which the muzzle-lashings of the guns are passed when housed. **1856** KANE *Arct. Expl.* II. iii. 42 The *housing-sails have been blown off by the storm. **1903** W. THOMPSON *Housing Handbk.* p. v, The past twelve years, spent in..the promotion of a number of *housing schemes. **1918** LLOYD GEORGE *Slings & Arrows* (1929) 199 Your housing schemes must, in the majority of cases, be schemes outside the house. **1966** J. BETJEMAN *High & Low* 22 We pounded through a housing scheme. **1874** *Jrnl. Iron & Steel Inst.* I. 352 The top and bottom rolls are simultaneously raised or lowered by four *housing screws. **1951** *Engineering* 5 Jan. 2/1 The housing screws are of 0·5 per cent. forged carbon steel. **1926** *Daily Chron.* 13 May 2/7 Work on a Bristol *housing site has stopped owing to transport difficulties. **1972** *Country Life* 30 Nov. 1487/1 Every housing site has its own unique character. **1951** M. MCLUHAN *Mech. Bride* 38/2 It means an extension of *housing units. **1970** G. GREER *Female Eunuch* 227 No clever orientation of clean and efficient housing units..can break down the suspicion that the Oedipal unit feels.

housing ('haʊzɪŋ), *sb.*^{2} Forms: 5 **howssynge, husynge**, 7 **howzen**, 7–9 **howsing**, 7– **housing**. [f. HOUSE *sb.*^{2} and *v.*^{2} + -ING^1.]

1. A covering, esp. of cloth or the like. (Often in *pl.*) Rare in gen. sense.

c **1400** *Rowland & O.* 749 Ryalle howssynges þay by-gan Of pauylyouns proudly pighte. **1483** *Cath. Angl.* 193/2 An Husynge of a nutte, *folliculus..theca*. **1585** LUPTON *Thous. Notable Th.* (N.), Be sure you cover them with warm housings of straw. **1748** SMOLLETT *Rod. Rand.* (1812) I. 293 A pair of silver mounted pistols with rich housings. **1858** HOLLAND *Titcomb's Lett.* i. 92 [They] will see you, and not your housings and trappings. **1871** R. ELLIS *Catullus* lxiv. 234 See that on each straight yard down droop their funeral housings. **1890** W. H. ST. JOHN HOPE in *Archæol.* LII. 692 Interesting from preserving entire its original case or howsing.

2. *spec.* A cloth covering put on a horse or other beast for defence or ornament; caparison, trappings.

1645 EVELYN *Diary* May, The cattle used for draught.. are cover'd with housings of linnen fring'd at the bottome, that dangle about them, preserving them from flyes. **1782** J. ADAMS *Diary* 14 Sept. Wks. 1851 III. 274 He was mounted upon a noble English horse, with an embroidered housing, and a white silk net. **1808** SCOTT *Marm.* IV. vii, From his steed's shoulder, loin, and breast, Silk housings swept the ground. **1892** STEVENSON *Across the Plains* 92 A horse or two ..making a fine figure with their Mexican housings.

b. 'A small square pad, which lies on the horse's back, to which most of the harness is fixed' (Felton *Carriages*, Gloss.).

1794 W. FELTON *Carriages* (1801) II. 132 The housing or pad, a small saddle cut in different shapes, but mostly of a long square.

c. 'The leather fastened at a horse's collar to turn over the back when it rains' (Halliwell).

3. *attrib.* and *Comb.*, as **housing-cloth**, a cloth used for a housing.

1607 TOPSELL *Four-f. Beasts* (1658) 287 Lay a housing cloth upon the same to keep his back as warm as may be. **1617** ASSHETON *Jrnl.* (Chetham Soc.) 94 My housing-cloth stolen out of the stable. **1794** W. FELTON *Carriages* (1801) II. 135 The Newmarket strap; a strap with a buckle and loop, by which the collar is hung to the housing, at a proper distance; it is placed round the collar-buckle and housing-bridge. *Ibid.* Gloss., *Housing Cushion*, the soft stuffed under part of the housing.

housing ('haʊzɪŋ), *ppl. a.* [f. HOUSE *v.*^{1} + -ING^2.] That houses: see quots. and HOUSE *v.*^{1}

1627 [see HOUSE *v.*^{1} 8]. **1703** T. N. *City & C. Purchaser* 182 When a Tile, or Brick is warped, or cast crooked or hollow in burning, they then say such a Brick, or Tile is Housing; they are apt to be housing..on the struck side. **1810** SCOTT *Lady of L.* VI. xxix, Hum of housing bee.

†**housling**, *vbl. sb.* [? error for *housing*, from HOUSE *v.*^{1} 4 c; cf. HOUSY.] The growing of the hop-bine into a dense mass at the top of the poles.

1669 WORLIDGE *Syst. Agric.* viii. §1. 128 Let the Poles lean outward the one from the other..to prevent housling as they term it..that is, they will grow one amongst another, and cause so great a shade that you will have more Hawm than Hops. Hence **1707** MORTIMER *Husb.* 137; **1727–41** CHAMBERS *Cycl.* s.v. *Hop*; etc.

housling: see HOUSELING.

houss, var. HOUSE *sb.*^{2}

houssour, obs. f. HOUSER^2.

housted, obs. f. HOUSESTEAD.

‖**Houstonia** (huː'stəʊnɪə). *Bot.* [mod.L., named after Dr. William Houston, an 18th c. botanist (died 1733).] A North American genus of plants (N.O. *Rubiaceæ*), with delicate four-parted flowers of various colours; by some botanists included in the genus *Hedyotis* or *Oldenlandia*.

About 20 species are known; the best-known being *H. cærulea*, the Bluet.

1838 MRS. HAWTHORNE in *N. Hawthorne & Wife* (1885) I. 187 Mother brought me some Houstonias in their own bit of earth. **1841–4** EMERSON *Ess.*, *Nature* Wks. (Bohn) I. 225 The mimic waving of acres of houstonia, whose innumerable florets whiten and ripple before the eye.

†**housty**. pseudo-*arch.* or *dial.* [Cf. HOAST.]

1855 KINGSLEY *Westw. Ho* xv. (1861) 255 Lady Grenvile ..always sent for her if one of the children had a 'housty', i.e. sore-throat.

housy ('haʊzɪ), *a. local.* Also **housey**. [f. HOUSE *sb.*^{1} or *v.*^{1} + -Y.] Said of hop-bines when growing thickly at the top so as to form a kind of roof or covering. (Cf. HOUSE *v.*^{1} 4 c.)

1848 *Jrnl. R. Agric. Soc.* IX. II. 544 The hop growing and flourishing more under what is called housy bine than any other variety. *Ibid.* 553 Prevent the bine from being too rough and housy at the top. **1894** *Times* 30 July 12/1 The bine is very thick and 'housey'.

hout, var. of HOOT *sb.*, *v.*, *int.*

houting ('haʊtɪŋ). A species of whitefish, *Coregonus oxyrhynchus*, found in some fresh-water lakes.

1880–84 DAY *Fishes Gt. Brit.* II. 126.

†**houve, hoove**. *Obs.* or *Sc.* Forms: 1 **húfe**, 3–4 **houue**, 4 **houwe, howue, houe**, 4–8 *Sc.* **hou, how**, 5 **houffe, howfe, huve**, 6 **hove, hooue**, 8–9 *Sc.* **hoo**. [OE. *húfe* = MLG., MDu. *hûve*, Du. *huif*, OHG. *hûba* (MHG. *hûbe*, Ger. *haube*), ON. *húfa* (Sw. *hufva*, Da. *hue*):—OTeut. **hūbōn* wk. fem.] A covering for the head; a turban, a coif; a cap, a skull-cap; the quilted skull-cap worn under a helmet; in Sc. (*how, hoo*) a night-cap (Jam.).

to glaze one's houve, give him a houve of glass or ***glasen houve***: to mock, delude, cajole. See Skeat *Chaucer*, *Notes to C.T.* p. 237.

c **1000** ÆLFRIC *Gloss.* in Wr.-Wülcker 152/24 *Cidaris, uel mitra*, hufe. *c* **1050** *Suppl. Ælfric's Gloss.* ibid. 188/20 *Flammeolum, uel flammeum*, biscopes huf. *a* **1300** *Body & Soul* 246 in *Map's Poems* (Camden) 337 Tou..madest me an houue of glas. **1362** LANGL. *P. Pl.* A. Prol. 84 Þer houeþ an Hundret In Houues of selk, Seriauns hit semeþ to seruen atte Barre. *c* **1374** CHAUCER *Troylus* III. 726 (775) To holde in love a man in honde, And him hir 'leef' and 'dere herte' calle, And maken him an howve above a calle. *Ibid.* v. 469 Fortune his howue entendeth bet to glaze. *c* **1375** *Sc. Leg. Saints, Adrian* 228 þu did nocht ellis, I se now, Bot to god mad a clasine [= glasine] how. *Ibid.*, *Ninian* 1046 He ves hynt be how and hayre. **1377** LANGL. *P. Pl.* B. xx. 171 A glasen houve. *c* **1386** CHAUCER *Reeve's Prol.* 57, I pray yow alle that ye nat yow greue Thogh I answere and somdeel sette his howue [*v. rr.* howe, houve, houwe]. *c* **1430** LYDG. *Min. Poems* (Percy Soc.) 56 To be my frend, and gyve me false counsaile, To breke myn hede, and yeve me a houffe. *c* **1440** *Promp. Parv.* 249/2 Howe..heed hyllynge. **1483** *Cath. Angl.* 190/2 An Howfe, *tena*. **1513** DOUGLAS *Æneis* v. x. 22 Thair haris all..That..with how and helm wes thristit down. **1535** COVERDALE *Isa.* iii. 18 Bracelettes and hooues. —— *Judith* xvi. 8 She anoynted hir face, and bounde vp hir hayre in an hooue. **1721** KELLY *Scott. Prov.* 61 Break my head, and put on my hoo.

b. A child's caul.

1530 PALSGR. 233/1 Hove that a chylde is borne in, *taye*. **1616** ROBERTS *Treat. Witchcr.* 66 (Jam.) That natural couer wherewith some children are borne, and is called by our women the sillie how. **1646** SIR. T. BROWNE *Pseud. Ep.* v. xxi. 269. **1710** RUDDIMAN *Gloss. Douglas' Æneis* s.v. *How*, In Scotland the women call a haly or sely How (i.e. holy or fortunate cap or hood), a film or membrane stretched over the heads of Children new born.

houve: see HOVE.

†**houx**, *sb. pl.*, obs. var. pl. of HOUGH or HOCK.

1555 EDEN *Decades* 260 Alces..with longe legges withowt any bowinge of theyr houx or posternes. **1609** HOLLAND *Amm. Marcell.* xxv. ii. 264 Our light armed companies.. charging them behind, layd at the houx and backe parts as well of the beasts as the Persians themselves, and all to cut and hacked them.

houyhnhnm ('hwɪhn(ə)m, 'hwɪn(ə)m). [A combination of letters app. intended to suggest the neigh of a horse.] The name given by Swift in *Gulliver's Travels* to one of a race of beings described as horses endowed with reason and bearing rule over a degraded brutish race of men, called the Yahoos. Hence *transf.* A horse having, or considered as having, human characteristics.

1727 SWIFT *Gulliver* IV. i, Then the bay tried me with a second word, much harder to be pronounced; but reducing it to the English orthography, may be spelt thus, Houyhnhnms. *Ibid.* iii, The word Houyhnhnm, in their tongue, signifies a horse, and, in its etymology, the perfection of nature. *Ibid.* xii, The two Yahoos, said to have been seen many years ago upon a mountain in Houyhnhnmland. **1727** POPE (*title*) To Mr. Lemuel Gulliver, the grateful address of the unhappy Houyhnhnms, now in slavery and bondage in England. *Ibid.* i, Accept our humble lays, And let each grateful Houyhnhnm neigh thy praise. —— *Mary Gulliver to Capt. Lemuel Gulliver* 107 I'd call thee Houyhnhnm, that high-sounding name. **1773** MRS. GRANT *Lett. fr. Mount.* (1807) I. iii. 30, I should be very sorry to have my poor houyhnhnms where I could neither hear them neigh, nor see them shake their necks. **1833** L. RITCHIE *Wand. by Loire* 30 'Get on, you Houyhnhnm!' exclaimed we. The animal coughed banteringly.

houzle, houzell, obs. forms of HOUSEL.

hov, obs. form of HOW *adv.*

Hova ('həʊvə, 'hʌvə), Also **Ovah**. [Malagasy.]

a. A member of the dominant race of Madagascar; also, in restricted use, one of the middle class, as distinct from the nobles and the slaves. Also *collect.* **b.** The language of this race. Also *attrib.*

1839 *Penny Cycl.* XIV. 259/2 The Ovahs, who inhabit the elevated plains in the interior, are in height rather above the European standard. **1858** W. ELLIS *Three Visits to Madagascar* 468 In Madagascar itself different dialects exist. The spoken language of the Hovas..differs from that on the coasts. **1883** *Encycl. Brit.* XV. 171/1 The Hòva, who occupy the central province of Imérina. *Ibid.* 172/2 The majority of Hòva houses are built of layers of the hard red clay of the country. **1887** *Fortn. Rev.* Mar. 435 Only a few months ago French politicians..called the Hovas barbarians. **1911** J. G. FRAZER *Golden Bough: Magic Art* (ed. 3) I. vii. 397 The Hovas and other tribes of Madagascar. **1915** J. SIBREE *Naturalist in Madagascar* xxii. 299 Their [*sc.* Sàkalàva] language presents a good deal of difference from the Hova form of Malagasy, both in vocabulary and in pronounciation, yet the groundwork and the grammar is essentially the same. **1972** A. SILLERY *Africa* (ed. 2) ii. 114 The most important native people, as well as the most numerous and advanced, are the Merina or Ambaniandro, commonly called Hova, whose homeland is Imerina on the plateau near Antananarivo.

†**hovable**, shortened form of BEHOVABLE *a.*, advantageous, suitable.

1508 FISHER *7 Penit. Ps.* Wks. (1876) 46 Whan tyme was houable and conuenyent. *Ibid.* 51 A conuenyent and houable remedy.

†**hove**, *sb.*[1] *Obs.* [OE. *hófe*, also in the comb. *túnhófe* ? 'garden hove', and in ME. *heihove* HAYHOVE, and *ale-hove* ALEHOOF, names of ground-ivy.] The name of some plant, considered by an early glossator to be a 'viola' or violet; in the Promptorium identified with *hayhove*, Ground Ivy.

c **1000** *Sax. Leechd.* II. 20 Wiþ heafod ece ȝenim hofan and win and eced. *Ibid.* 34 Wiþ eaȝna ece, ȝenim þa readan hofan. *c* **1000** ÆLFRIC *Gloss.* in Wr.-Wülcker 134/39 *Viola*, hofe. *c* **1440** *Promp. Parv.* 250/1 Hove, or grownd yvy.

†**hove, hof**, *sb.*[2] *Obs.* [a. ON. *hóf* moderation, measure, f. *hefja*, *hóf*, to take up, lift, raise, exalt, etc.] Measure, moderation, temperateness.

c **1200** ORMIN 4742 A33 att rihht time, and a33 att hof, Forr þatt iss Drihhtin cweme. *a* **1300** *Cursor M.* 11973 Iesus þat was fulfild o houe, His moder mode wald he noght droue. *Ibid.* 23291 þai sal be beft wit-vten houe. *Ibid.* 26990 Hop es god at hald wit houe, Bot til vnskil not worth a gloue.

†**hove**, *sb.*[3] *Sc. Obs.* Forms: 4–6 hove, 6 huyfe, hufe, hoif, 6–7 hoff(e. [perh. f. HOVE *v.*[1]; or ? from OE. *hof*, hall, dwelling, ON. *hof* temple, Ger., Du. *hof* court.] In ***Arthur's hove, Julius' hove***: names applied by various authors to a remarkable round edifice which formerly stood near Carron in Stirlingshire: see Jamieson, s.v. *Hoif*.

The local name appears to have been *Arthur's Oon* (oven); it is called *Furnus Arthuri* in the Newbottle Chart. 1293.

c **1377** FORDUN *Scotichron.* II. xvi. (1759) I. 51 Quam cum Arthurus rex..recreandi gratiâ invisere soleret, a plebeis propterea Arthuris Hove dicebatur. **1526** BOETHIUS *Scot. Hist.* III. iv. (Jam.), Hancque Iulis Hoff, id est, Iulis aulam seu curiam, quod nomen ad nos devenit ab incolis exinde appellatum. **1535** STEWART *Cron. Scot.* III. 193 The laif.. He gart lat stand and wrait vpoun the wall 'Arthuris hufe', quhilk is to say, his hall. **1536** BELLENDEN *Cron. Scot.* XIV. vii. (Jam.), Thai put away the armes of Julius Cesar, and ingrauit the armis of King Arthour, commanding it to be callit Arthouris hoif. *a* **1639** SPOTTISWOODE *Hist. Dict.* (MS.) s.v. *Arthur's Oon* (Jam.), As to K. Edward giving it the name of Arthur's Hoff or house, it had the name of Arthur's Oon or Kiln long before. **1639** USSHER *De Brit. Eccl. Primord.* xv. 586 Arthurs Oven et Julius hoff appellant hodie.

b. See ARTHUR'S HUFE.

†**hove**, *sb.*[4] Also hofe. [f. HOVE *v.*[1]] The action of tarrying or lingering; in phr. ***on hove***, in waiting, in suspense.

c **1400** *Destr. Troy* 12699 Held hom on hofe in the hegh sea.

†**hove**, *sb.*[5] *Obs. rare*$^{-1}$. [A doubtful form; perh. a scribal error for *heve* = MDu. *heve*, Ger. *hefe*, yeast, barm, lees, dregs. Cf. also OE. *hæfe* (= *hefe*) yeast, leaven; f. root of *heven*, HEAVE *v.*] Lees, dregs, sediment (of oil, ale, etc.).

c **1440** *Promp. Parv.* 250/1 Hove of oyle, as barme, and ale ..*amurca*.

†**hove**, *v.*[1] *Obs.* Forms: 3–6 houe, (5 hofe), 4– hove, (6 hoove); *Sc.* (and *north.*) 4 houffe, 4–5 huf(e, 4–6 huve, 5 huwe, hue, 5–6 huif, 6 huff. [Of great frequency in ME. from 13th c.; in 16th c. largely superseded by HOVER. Derivation unknown.

The usual rimes with *move*, *prove*, *love*, the 16th c. spelling *hoove*, and above all the Sc. forms *huve*, *huive*, show that the early ME. was *hōven*, = OE. **hófian* with long *ó*. This severs it from the family of OE. *hof*, hall, dwelling, to which it has sometimes been referred.]

1. *intr.* To remain in a suspended or floating condition, as a bird in the air or a boat on water; to be poised, to HOVER.

c **1220** *Bestiary* 69 So riȝt so he cunne he [eagle] houeð in ðe sunne. *c* **1290** *S. Eng. Leg.* I. 269/298 Euere houede þis clere liȝt ouer hire faire and heiȝe. *a* **1352** MINOT *Poems* (Hall) iii. 83, viij. and xl. galays..houed on þe flode. *c* **1420** LYDG. *Assembly Gods* 1608 Ouer her heede houyd a culuer fayre & whyte. *c* **1440** *Promp. Parv.* 251/2 Hovyn yn watur, or oþer lycoure, *supernato*. **1550** HUTCHINSON *Image of God* vii. (1560) 26 Elias..making the Iron which is heuy to houe aboue the waters. **1590** SPENSER *F.Q.* III. vii. 27 A little bote lay hoving her before.

b. To lie at anchor.

c **1540** tr. *Pol. Verg. Eng. Hist.* (Camden) I. 52 Abowte the iiijth hower of the nexte daye hee [Cæsar] hooved beefore Brittaine.

2. To wait, tarry, linger, stay, remain; often *spec.* to remain on horseback.

c **1220** *Bestiary* 525 [He] stireð up and houeð stille. **1297** R. GLOUC. (Rolls) 4468 Moroud erl of gloucestre mid is ost bi syde In an valeye houede þe endinge uor to abyde. **1375** BARBOUR *Bruce* XVIII. 299 He hufit in-till ane enbuschement. *c* **1430** *Syr Generides* (Roxb.) 9101 She houed on hir palfray To wit what he wold say. *c* **1440** *Promp. Parv.* 252/1 Hovyn on hors, and a-bydyn, *sirocino*. **1508** DUNBAR *Poems* iii. 4 Quhairof I hovit..in dowt. **1513** DOUGLAS *Æneis* V. x. 59 All redy hufand thar coursis for to tak. **1535** STEWART *Cron. Scot.* II. 245 On to this erle quhair he wes huifand by. **1568** GRAFTON *Chron.* II. 288 Syr Geoffrey hoved still in the fields prively with his Banner before him. **1577–87** HOLINSHED *Chron.* II. 22/1 Being intercepted by them that laie hoouing in ambush. **1585** JAS. I *Ess. Poesie* (Arb.) 57 That ȝe make not *proue* and *reproue* ryme together, nor *houe* for houeing on hors bak, and *behoue*. **1590** SPENSER *F.Q.* III. x. 20 A couple..Which hoved closed under a forest side, As if they lay in wait, or els them selves did hide. **1595** —— *Col. Clout* 666 The which in court continually hooved [*rime* prooved].

b. *fig.* To linger or dwell *on*.

c **1440** CAPGRAVE *Life St. Kath.* II. 915 Ffy on þo hertes þat euer on swech þing houe!

3. To come or go floating or soaring; to be borne (as on horseback), move, or pass away; to pass *on*, pass *by*.

1390 GOWER *Conf.* I. 323 Hove out of my sonne And lete it shine into my tonne. *c* **1400** *Melayne* 1490 He sawe come houande ouer a felle Many a brade Banere. **1509** HAWES *Past. Pleas.* III. v, Ymages of golde..whiche with the wynde aye moved..About the towers in sundry wyse they hoved. **1535** STEWART *Cron. Scot.* II. 234 Tua pert Pechtis on hors wer huvand by. *a* **1650** *Flodden F.* 281 in Furniv. *Percy Folio* I. 330 The hind Hassall hoved on fast.

4. *trans.* To brood over, as a bird: = HOVER *v.*[1] 5.

1399 LANGL. *Rich. Redeles* II. 146 Þe..Egle..Hasteth him in heruest to houyn his bryddis. *Ibid.* III. 50 Anoþer proud partriche..houeth þe eyren þat þe hue laide And with hir corps keuereth hem.

†**hove**, *v.*[2] *Obs.* or *dial.* Also 7 houve, hoove, hoave. [app. a derivative of HEAVE *v.* (pa. t. *hove*, pa. pple. *hoven*).]

1. *trans.* To raise, lift.

(The first quot. is from its date doubtful; the word may be *hewand* for *hevand* from HEAVE *v.*)

c **1375** *Sc. Leg. Saints, Jacobus minor* 675 Howand his handis to þe hewyn. *c* **1570** *Marr. Wit & Science* V. v. in Hazl. *Dodsley* II. 392 Hove up his head upon your spear, lo, here a joyful sign!

2. *trans.* To swell, inflate, puff up or out. Chiefly in pa. pple. **hoved** = HOVEN.

1601 HOLLAND *Pliny* I. 255 Like unto bladders puft up and hooved with wind. *Ibid.* II. 560 Their bread is lighter and more houved vp than any other. **1639** HORN & ROB. *Gate Lang.* xxxiv. §407 The crum light and hoaved (puff'd) within. **1785** BURNS *Death & Dr. Hornbook* xxviii, Some ill-brewn drink had hov'd her wame. **1795** *Gentl. Mag.* LXV. II. 894 Cattle that are hoved or swelled. **1828** *Craven Dial.*, *Hoven*, to swell, to puff up.

3. *intr.* (for *refl.*) To rise; to swell up.

1590 SPENSER *F.Q.* I. ii. 31 Astond he stood, and up his heare did hove. **1601** HOLLAND *Pliny* I. 500 The earth.. swelleth and houeth as it were with a leauen. **1811** [see HOVING *vbl. sb.*]

hove, *v.*[3] Abbreviated for BEHOVE.

c **1450** LYDG. *Secrees* 1184 *heading*, How a kyng hovith to haue a leche to kepe his body. **1483** CAXTON *Gold. Leg.* 252 b/2 That we myght make thyn exequyes couenable as it houeth and is dygne and worthy. **1594** CAREW *Tasso* (1881) 9 A zeale How great, of host thy charge hooues thee to heat.

hove, pa. t. and pple. of HEAVE (see also HOVEN); var. HOUVE.

†**hove-dance.** *Obs.* [cf. MDu. *hof-dans*, lit. court dance, 'a dance usual at the court, the dance that is in fashion' (Verwijs and Verdam), 'saltatio numerosa, chorea aulica, circularis' (Kilian) = MHG. *hovetanz*.] A 'court dance'; app. a particular dance of a lively character.

1390 GOWER *Conf.* III. 6 Where as I muste daunce and singe The hove daunce and carolinge. **1481** CAXTON *Reynard* (Arb.) 54 Ther was daunsed..the houedaunce with shalmouse trompettis and alle maner of menestralsye. **1483** *Chaucer's H. Fame* (Caxton) III. 145 To lerne houe dauncis [*Fairf. MS.* loue Daunces] sprynges Reyes. [**1894** F. S. ELLIS *Reynard* 168 In the merry hovedance See the Elephant prance As lissom and light as a fawn.]

hovel ('hɒv(ə)l, 'hʌv(ə)l), *sb.*[1] Also 5 -yl, 5–7 -ell, 6 -elle. [Known from 15th c.: origin uncertain.

A conjectured derivation from OE. *hof* court, dwelling, with Romanic suffix *-el*, is etymologically and chronologically inadmissible. Heyne, in Grimm, favours a connexion with MHG. *hobel* 'cover, covering, lid': if this word occurred in LG., its form would be **hovel*, but it does not seem to be known, so that the connexion is not made out. Another conjecture is an AF. **huvel*, whence OF. *huvelet* 'petit toit en saillie' (Godef.).]

1. An open shed; an outhouse used as a shelter for cattle, a receptacle for grain or tools.

1435 *Nottingham Rec.* II. 357 Also a garthyn with a hovell' on it. *c* **1440** *Promp. Parv.* 250/1 Hovyl for swyne, or oþer beestys, *cartabulum*. **1555** W. WATREMAN *Fardle Facions* Pref. 7 Eche man..passed his daies..vnder the open heauen, the couerte of some shadowie Trees or slendre houelle. **1573** TUSSER *Husb.* lii. (1878) 116 Make drie ouer hed, both houell and shed. **1620–55** I. JONES *Stone-Heng* (1725) 8 They raise Cabbins and Cottages for themselves, and Hovels for their Cattel. **1796** *Trans. Soc. Arts* XIV. 301 It may be used as a stable, ox-stall, hovel, or cart-house. **1873** *Act 36 & 37 Vict.* c. 72 §1 Barns, hovels, or other like structures of wood.

2. A shed used as a human habitation; a rude or miserable dwelling-place; a wretched cabin.

a **1625** FLETCHER *Love's Cure* V. iii, No town in Spain, from our metropolis Unto the rudest hovel. **1698** FRYER *Acc. E. India & P.* 52 Their Houses are little Hovels or Hogsties, the best of them scarce worthy the name of a Booth. **1711** ADDISON *Spect.* No. 117 ⁋5 Her Hovel, which stood in a solitary Corner under the side of the Wood. **1806** *Gazetteer Scotl.* s.v. *Tammtoul*, It is entirely composed of turf-covered hovels. **1865** W. G. PALGRAVE *Arabia* II. 151 In it every description of dwelling is to be seen..for high and low, palace or hovel.

3. In various technical uses.

†**a.** *Arch.* A canopied niche for an image. Also ***hovel-house, -housing***. *Obs.*

1463 *Bury Wills* (Camden) 19, I wil that the ymage of oure lady..be set vp ageyn the peleer..and a hovel with pleyn sydes comyng down to the baas. **1875** PARKER *Gloss. Archit.*, *Hovel*, sometimes used in the sense of tabernacles for images. **1879** E. WATERTON *Pietas Mariana* 262 Tabernacles were canopied niches. In ancient contracts they were also called maisons, habitacles, hovels, and howsings. **1888** *Archit. Jrnl.* 241 Thirty-six 'weepers' standing in niches under simple canopies, or, as they were called, 'hovels'.

†**b.** A structure of reeds, broom, etc. on which brine is concentrated by natural evaporation. *Obs.*

1686 PLOT *Staffordsh.* ii. 95 Were the brine..laved on hovels cover'd with Mats, made of reeds, straw or flaggs.

c. The hood of a smith's forge.

1688 R. HOLME *Armoury* III. vii. 323/2 The Hovel or Covel of the Hearth [of a Smith's Forge] which ends in a Chimney to carry the Smoak away. **1703** MOXON *Mech. Exerc.* 2.

d. The conical building enclosing a porcelain oven or kiln.

1825 J. NICHOLSON *Operat. Mechanic* 468 Most ovens are surrounded by a high conical building, called a hovel, large enough to allow the man to wheel coals to the requisite places, and to pass along to supply each mouth with fuel. **1851** *Illustr. Catal. Gt. Exhib.* 724 The hovels in which the ovens are built form a very..striking feature of the pottery towns..resembling..a succession of gigantic bee-hives.

4. A stack of corn, etc. Hence ***hovel-frame***.

1591 PERCIVALL *Sp. Dict.*, *Gavilla*, a stacke of corne, a hoile of corne, a bauen, *fasciculus*. **1599** MINSHEU *Sp. Dict.*, *Gavilla*, or *Gavila*, a stacke or houell of corne, a bauen or fagot. **1722** *Act 9 Geo. I*, c. 22 §1 If any Person..set Fire to ..any Hovel, Cock, Mow, or Stack of Corn, Straw, Hay or Wood. **1782** BARKER in *Phil. Trans.* LXXII. 282 Some of the pease, which were either not got in, or the hovels not thatched, when the great rain came September 2. **1881** *Leicestersh. Gloss.*, *Hovel-frame*, a 'stack-frame', the wooden frame or platform on which stacks or ricks are built up.

'**hovel**, *sb.*[2] [ad. Du. *heuvel*, MDu. *hövel*, in Kilian *hovel* 'hill', also 'hump, boss, knob'.] The bump on the top of a whale's head.

1694 *Acc. Sev. Late Voy.* II. 126 He hath also an Hoffel [*printed* Hossel] on his Head like a Whale. *Ibid.* 134 Upon his Head is the Hovel or Bump before the Eyes and Finns. **1821** R. TURNER *Arts & Sc.* (ed. 18) 203 Its head is about one third part of its whole length, on the top..is what they call the hovel or bump; in this are two spout-holes.

hovel, *v.*[1] [f. HOVEL *sb.*[1]]

a. *trans.* To shelter as in a hovel or shed.

1583 STANYHURST *Æneis* IV. (Arb.) 98 They shal be in darcknes al hooueld. **1605** SHAKS. *Lear* IV. vii. 39 To houell thee with Swine and Rogues forlorne.

b. To provide with a roof or covering.

1688 R. HOLME *Armoury* III. ix. 400/2 Round Towers, Hoveled or Roofed.

c. (*Archit.*) To form like an open hovel or shed; as, 'to hovel a chimney'.

1823 P. NICHOLSON *Pract. Build.* Gloss. 586/2 *Hoveling*, carrying up the sides of a chimney, so that when the wind rushes over the mouth, the smoke may escape below the current or against any one side of it. **1858** *Skyring's Builders' Prices* (ed. 48) 71 Chimney pots..Hovilled second size..7*s.*

d. *intr.* To stack corn in a 'hovel'. *dial.*

1744–50 W. ELLIS *Mod. Husbandm.* V. I. 5 (E.D.S.) Be sure never to want a hand that can hovel; that is, a man who is capable of placing wheat-sheaves or other corn on a hovel, so as to lie in that advantageous position as is necessary to prevent the damage of weather.

hovel, *v.*[2] [Etymology uncertain: perh. a back-formation from HOVELLER, q.v.] **a.** *intr.* To pursue the occupation of a hoveller. **b.** *trans.* To bring (a vessel) into harbour, moor and unload it, etc. Hence **hovelling** *vbl. sb.*, the business of a hoveller, piloting.

1880 *Chambers' Encycl.* III. 445/2 s.v. *Deal*, The chief branches of industry are..boat-building, sail-making, piloting or hovelling [etc.]. **1891** J. SIMSON *Historic Thanet* 110 Hovelling and Foying are to a great extent synonymous terms. The latter has been described as 'going off to ships with provisions, and assisting them when in distress'; the same definition may with some amplification be applied to hovelling. **1891** ELWORTHY *Let. to Editor* 8 May, To *hovel* or *hobble* a vessel is to do the rough work of helping to bring her into harbour—mooring and unloading, &c. It is very unskilled labour.

hoveller ('hɒv(ə)lə(r), 'hʌv(ə)lə(r)). Also -eler. [Of obscure origin; it has been suggested that they were so called 'from their use of hovels on shore for shelter'; but cf. HOBBLER[2], HUFFLER.]

1. An unlicensed pilot or boatman, especially on the Kentish coast; frequently applied to a boatman who goes out to wrecks, sometimes with a view of plunder. Cf. HOBBLER[2] 3 a.

1769 FALCONER *Dict. Marine* (1789), *Vagans*, vagrants or hovellers, who infest the sea-coast in a tempest, in expectation of plunder from some ship-wrecked vessel. **1809** *Naval Chron.* XXIV. 105 Pilots, boatmen, hovellers. **1864** R. M. BALLANTYNE *Lifeboat* (ed. 2) 87 In olden time the owners of these nautical huts dwelt in them, hence the name 'hoveller' which is used at the present day. **1866** *Daily Tel.* 3 Nov., The vessel must go to pieces; and the hoveller's instinct is to clutch as much as he can from it. **1884** *Daily News* 23 Sept. 3/1 The Deal boatman..is often called a 'hoveller', and his most profitable work seems to be in knocking about at sea ready to afford aid to ships needing it. **1886** *N. & Q.* 7th Ser. II. 476/1.

2. The craft used by these boatmen.
1880 CLARK RUSSELL *Sailor's Sweetheart* I. iii. 97 There'll be a whole fleet of hovelers around 'em before another hour's gone. 1881 *Daily Tel.* 24 Feb., I made the journey in a hoveller, and reached the lightship half an hour before sunset.

hoven ('həʊv(ə)n), *ppl. a.* (and *sb.*) Now *dial.* Also hove. [pa. pple. of HEAVE *v.*, q.v.] Swollen, bloated, puffed out; esp. applied to cattle when swollen with over-feeding: cf. HOOVE. Also *fig.* and as *sb.*
1555 *Will of J. Pyshe* (Somerset Ho.), A brown hove cow. 1573 TUSSER *Husb.* xlix. (1878) 108 Tom Piper hath houen and puffed vp cheekes; If cheese be so houen, make Cisse to seeke creekes. 1599 *Broughton's Let.* iii. 13 Your houen imaginations. 1674–91 RAY *N.C. Words* 143 Hoven-bread, *zymites.* 1688 R. HOLME *Armoury* III. v. 244/1 Bad Cheese ..is..full of Eyes, not well prest but hoven and swelling. 1845 S. JUDD *Margaret* II. v. 284 Glad you got through with the pock so well...its worse than horn-ail, hoven or core. 1851 *Illustr. Catal. Gt. Exhib.* 419 Veterinary..stomach pump..for hove cattle. 1865 H. H. DIXON *Field & Fern* V. ii. 38 Sometimes a whole lot will get hoven with clover. 1877 *Rep. Vermont Dairym. Assoc.* VIII. 107 Hoven in cattle is caused by over-feeding upon succulent food like green clover. 1878 [see BLOAT *sb.* 1 b]. 1891 [see BLOWING *vbl. sb.*[1] 2 d]. 1902 *Phil. Trans. R. Soc.* CXCIX. A. 400 The symptoms of 'hoven' are not unlike those of prussic acid poisoning. 1962 [see BLOAT *sb.* 1 b].

hover ('hɒvə(r), 'hʌvə(r)), *sb.* [f. HOVER *v.*[1]]
1. a. An act of hovering, as of a bird or other winged creature. Also, a state of hovering.
1893 G. D. LESLIE *Lett. to Marco* xvi. 105 A circular sort of hover. *a* 1899 *Mod. Newspaper*, The hover of a hawk's wing is dimly sighted far away upon the horizon. 1961 *Hovering Craft & Hydrofoil* Oct. 32/2 Floatation and sea-keeping capability while floating and during transition from hover to high forward speed. 1962 *Air-Cushion Vehicles* July 16 The skirts have withstood the early trials well, most of the wear having occurred during tethered hovers on hard standing. 1967 B. W. MCCORMICK *Aerodynamics of V/Stol Flight* v. 106 The helicopter rotor in hover or in vertical climb is relatively easy to analyze. 1969 I. KEMP *Brit. G.I. in Vietnam* iii. 61 Major Bracken eased back on the cyclic.. and our speed dropped until we were almost in a hover. 1971 *Physics Bull.* Nov. 655/3 With careful design the tilting rotor propeller can be efficient in both hover and cruise.
b. A hovering host (of birds).
1826 J. WILSON *Chr. North* (1857) II. 328 A mile-square hover of crows darkens air and earth.
2. The action or condition of remaining in suspense.
1513 DOUGLAS *Æneis* XII. xiv. 129 Abydand lang in hovir quhat he suld do. *c* 1565 LINDESAY (Pitscottie) *Chron. Scot.* (1728) 537 (Jam.) They stood in hover, and tuik consultatioun quhat was best to be done. 1727 E. ERSKINE *Serm.* Wks. 1871 I. 295 They are in a hover and suspense. 1883 E. PENNELL-ELMHIRST *Cream Leicestersh.* 136 Without even a hover of hesitation.
3. Any overhanging stone or bank under which a fish can hide; also any kind of overhanging shelter, especially a hollow in the side of a hedge; a shelter used in the brooding of chickens. (Elworthy *W. Som. Word-bk.*) Chiefly *south. dial.*
1602 CAREW *Cornwall* 105 (R.) Boughs of trees..were cast in thither to serue as a houer for the fish. 1858 E. W. L. DAVIES in *Dartmoor Days* (1863) 137 Every holt and hover which could harbour a fox or an otter. 1863 KINGSLEY *Water-Bab.* iii. 116 Dark hovers under swirling banks, from which great trout rushed out. 1886 R. C. LESLIE *Sea-painter's Log* 207 The confidence of the trout in the security of his haunt or hover. 1907 *Elem. Sch. Teacher* Mar. 410 A hover which was made of felt was hung in the brooder. 1936 *Nature* 3 Oct. 583/1 The merits of the various systems of hovers and battery brooders are discussed.
4. 'A floating island, or bed of reeds' (E.D.D.). Chiefly Norfolk *dial.*
1892 P. H. EMERSON *Son of Fens* xiv. 120 'Have you got enough damming boards for another dam?' 'Yes... We shan't want many; there's a hover there.' 1893 H. COZENS-HARDY *Broad Norfolk* 77 *Hover*, a floating island. 1955 *Times* 3 Aug. 10/2 Now the lesser bulrush which grows on the 'hover' (excellent word to denote a table of floating vegetation) round the edge of the open water is all a-quiver.
5. *Comb.* hover-fly, a dipterous insect of the order *Bombyliidæ*, which hovers over flowers without settling.
a 1887 JEFFERIES *Field & Hedgerow* (1889) 14 Countless.. hosts of the yellow-barred hover-flies come to them.

hover ('hɒvə(r)), *a.* (*sb.*) *dial.* [perh. related to HOVE *v.*[2]] Of loose texture or composition; in Kent, said of hops loosely packed. b. as *sb.* Light loose soil.
1669 WORLIDGE *Syst. Agric.* (1681) 327 *Hover-ground*, Light-ground. 1674 in Ray *S. & E.C. Words* 68. 1703 T. N. *City & C. Purchaser* 189 To draw all the loose and hover Sand..into the empty part of the Mold. 1848 RUTLEY in *Jrnl. R. Agric. Soc.* IX. II. 547 The hops were generally small, loose, and hover. 1851 *Ibid.* XII. II. 487 Black light mould (provincially *black hover*). 1887 *Kent. Gloss.*, *Hover*, light; puffy; raised; shivery; hunched-up. Hence, poorly, unwell.

hover ('hɒvə(r), 'hʌvə(r)), *v.*[1] Also 6 hoover. [Not known bef. 1400, and app. not much used bef. 16th c., when it took, in sense 1, the place of HOVE *v.*[1] Of this it may have been an iterative derivative (cf. *flutter, shatter*, etc.), esp. if the historical pronunciation is ('hʌvə(r)).]
I. *intr.* 1. a. Of a winged creature: To hang or remain suspended in the air *over* or *about* a particular spot, as by flapping the wings (to which action the word is sometimes restricted by naturalists: cf. 4), esp. when preparing to dart or swoop in some direction. Also with *indirect passive.*
c 1400 MAUNDEV. (Roxb.) xxxiv. 153 Fewles..commez þider and houers abouue þam. 1530 PALSGR. 588/1, I hover, I flyker..This hauke hovereth to longe above, she is nat disposed to stoupe. 1585 T. WASHINGTON tr. *Nicholay's Voy.* Ep. Ded. ¶ij b, At one time or other it is meete to hoover with the winges. 1597 SHAKS. *Lover's Compl.* 319 The tempter..like a cherubin above them hover'd [*rime* cover'd]. 1665 BOYLE *Occas. Refl.* IV. ii. (1848) 174 Larks .. hovering and singing a while over our Heads. 1745 *De Foe's Eng. Tradesman* (1841) II. li. 237 Like bees unhived, they hovered about. 1847 LYTTON *Lucretia* I. i. 31 The dragon-fly darted and hovered in the air. 1871 B. TAYLOR *Faust* (1875) I. xxi. 180 Nearer hover Jay and screech owl, and the plover. 1885 STEVENSON *Dynamiter* 171 Rocky islets, hovered about by an innumerable cloud of sea-fowl. 1894 [see HOVERING *vbl. sb.* a].
b. Said of clouds, etc., that float or remain suspended in air or on water.
1578 BANISTER *Hist. Man* I. 30 Nature caused the same Processe of the viij bone, to hang, and hover inwardly like a seeled vawlte. 1600 J. PORY tr. *Leo's Africa* I. 3 Cloudes alwaies hovering about the tops thereof. 1664 POWER *Exp. Philos.* III. 163 The smallest Mote or Atom, which we see to hover and play in the Sun's beams. 1718 *Freethinker* No. 16 ¶4 The Bowl would stop in the Current, and hover over the Dead Body. 1818 M. G. LEWIS *Jrnl. W. Ind.* (1834) 297 The waves..hovering for a while over the ship, and then coming down upon us. 1877 BLACK *Green Past.* xl, Large schooners ..hovering in the white light.
c. Of a helicopter or other aircraft: to remain stationary in the air, relative to the ground.
1892 *Railroad & Engin. Jrnl.* Nov. 508/2 With 60 turns of the rubber the apparatus would just hold its own—i.e., hover in the same spot, against a wind of 9 ft. per second. 1926 J. L. PRITCHARD *Bk. Aeroplane* ix. 177 It had distinct possibilities of achieving what the helicopter sets out to achieve, rising, descending vertically in still air and hovering. 1935 P. H. SUMNER *Aircraft* II. 63 To be of any practical use the helicopter aircraft must be capable of forward motion in addition to rising vertically and hovering. 1972 *Daily Tel.* 3 July 2 (*caption*) A Sea King helicopter.. hovering over Rockall in the Atlantic.
d. Of a hovercraft: to be supported on its air-cushion, esp. while stationary; also *transf.*, to travel in a hovercraft.
1962 *Hovering Craft & Hydrofoil* Aug.–Sept. 20/1 Hovering at speeds below 10 knots..over water, the depression in the water surface beneath the craft gives a measure of 'keel' effect. 1962 *Air-Cushion Vehicles* Oct. 81/2 The rudder, however, is ineffective at low speeds or while hovering. 1967 *Jane's Surface Skimmer Systems 1967–68* 31/2 Echo sounding transducers..will remain immersed whether the craft is 'hovering' or underway. 1968 *Nature* 10 Aug. 549/1 (*heading*) Hover over from Dover. 1970 *Motoring Which?* July 111/2 A control stick adjusted the airflow from the fan, to make the craft hover or go forwards.
2. *transf.* and *fig.* To keep hanging or lingering *about* (a person or place), to wait near at hand, move to and fro near or around, as if waiting to land or alight; also said of things intangible (where the idea is sometimes nearer to 1).
1581 SAVILE *Tacitus' Hist.* II. xiv. (1591) 60 The fleete.. lay houering and ready to assaile the prouince of Narbon. 1602 MARSTON *Ant. & Mel.* IV. Wks. 1856 I. 44 His spirit hovers in Piero's court. 1686 LUTTRELL *Brief Rel.* (1857) I. 376 The French..lie hovering before Cadiz, Gibralter, and those parts. 1748 *Anson's Voy.* II. viii. 222 We were obliged to keep hovering about the Island. *a* 1754 J. MCLAURIN *Serm. & Ess.* 77 Vengeance was hovering over their guilty heads. 1803 JANE PORTER *Thaddeus* viii. (1831) 75 His thoughts continually hovered about his mother. 1838 THIRLWALL *Greece* III. 297 Leaving a small part of their force to hover on the rear of the Greeks. 1863 GEO. ELIOT *Romola* III. x, Pestilence was hovering in the track of famine.
3. †a. To remain waiting; to tarry, linger; to hesitate before taking action. *Obs.* b. To continue in a state of suspense or indecision; to waver as in an indeterminate or irresolute state; hence, to hang or remain *on the verge of* (a condition, etc.).
c 1440 *York Myst.* ix. 252 A twelmo[n]the bott xij weke Have we be houerand here. *Ibid.* xi. 352 It may not helpe to hover na hone. *c* 1475 *Rauf Coilȝear* 417 He huit and he houerit quhill midmorne and mair. 1573–80 BARET *Alv.* H 674 To houer over a thing to buy it, *emptioni imminere.* *c* 1620 A. HUME *Brit. Tongue* (1865) 2 Quhil I thus hovered betueen hope and despare. 1651 CLEVELAND *Poems, Senses Festivall*, When Bodies whine, and victory hovers Twixt the equal fluttering Lovers. 1712 ADDISON *Spect.* No. 441 ¶9 When the Soul is hovering in the last Moments of its Separation. 1872 BLACK *Adv. Phaeton* iii, He even hovered on the verge of rudeness. 1874 L. MORRIS *Organ-boy* 75 Sweet music hovering 'Twixt pain and 'twixt pleasure. *Mod.* A mind hovering on the verge of madness.
II. *trans.* †4. Of a bird, etc.: To flap or flutter (the wings) so as to maintain itself in the air. *Obs.*
1591 SYLVESTER *Du Bartas* I. v. 1054 Somtimes her wings she hovers. 1687 MRS. BEHN *Lucky Chance* I. i, Some blest sun-shine to warm me..and make me hover my flagging wings.
5. To brood over; to cover (the young) with wings and body: cf. HOVERING *vbl. sb.* b.
1776 G. WHITE *Selborne* xxxiii. (1875) 230 Capons.. hover chickens like hens. 1895 in *Daily News* 23 July 6/1 Cholera, that foe we have so often to face in India, hovered the ridge.
6. To maintain in a hovering state.
1967 B. W. MCCORMICK *Aerodynamics of V/Stol Flight* v. 162 The gross weight that can be hovered at the power available is found by correcting the thrust for download.. and for overlap. 1969 *Aeroplane* LXXIII. 708/2 In the case of the rescue system preferred by the USA Coast Guard.. the helicopter is hovered in contact with the water and a working platform is extended from the craft.

'**hover**, *v.*[2] [f. HOVER *a.*] *dial.* (See quots.)
1847–78 HALLIWELL, *Hover*..(2) To pack hops lightly, in order to defraud the measure. *Kent.* 1887 *Kent. Gloss.* s.v., One of the pickers..then comes to hover the hops; this is done by putting both hands down to the bottom of the great basket..as soon as they [the hops] reach the top, they are quickly shot out into the green bag before they have time to sag or sink;..hovering is nothing more than a recognized system of fraud. 1897 *Jrnl. R. Agric. Soc.* Mar. 63 The practice of hovering and turning is..most objectionable.

hover- ('hɒvə(r)), the first element of HOVERCRAFT, prefixed to other sbs. to denote things of a similar form or serving a similar purpose to the thing denoted by the sb., but having some connection with hovercraft or their principle of operation. a. Used to form the names of vehicles and other things that utilize an air-cushion as a means of support, as ***hoverbus***, ***-car***, ***-ferry***, ***-kiln***, ***-liner***, ***-pallet***, ***-ship***, ***-train***, ***-truck***, ***-vehicle***.
1962 *Daily Tel.* 1 Mar. 17/1 (*heading*) Hover-buses planned for south coast. 1961 *New Scientist* 31 Aug. 503 What they have in mind is a streamlined hovercar, seating 100 or more, travelling on..an elevated concrete track at speeds of around 300 m.p.h. 1970 *Nature* 17 Jan. 214/2 In the British design, the hovercar straddles a concrete beam of box-shaped cross-section. 1961 *New Scientist* 29 June 785/2 Denny's..hope by next year to produce an actual passenger-carrying hover-ferry... They ultimately envisage a hovercraft capable of carrying 50 to 70 passengers at about 20 knots. 1970 *Ibid.* 11 June 528/2 Both the hoverferry and the general purpose version have been subjected to an engineering modification programme. 1965 *Ibid.* 2 Dec. 633/1 The hoverkiln relies upon air pads to lubricate the pallets on which pottery is slowly conveyed through the baking kilns. 1962 *Listener* 16 Aug. 258/3 Plans for atomic-powered hoverliners. 1970 *New Scientist* 11 June 528/2 The original dreams of large hoverliners seem to have been shelved. 1966 *Times* 14 Oct. 11/7 The Ulster Prince, a 4,600-ton drive-on ferry.., will be equipped with 'hoverpallets'. 1967 *Jane's Surface Skimmer Systems 1967–68* 21/2 Palletised loads can be 'floated' in on hover-pallets, supplied with air from the main compressor. 1961 *Guardian* 23 June 10 The passenger-carrying 'hovership'.. is a substantial advance towards bringing these curious vessels that are neither of the sea nor of the air into practical, everyday use. 1971 *Country Life* 8 Apr. 830/2 In *The Future of Ships*..D. Phillips-Birt looks at projects for 4,000 and 5,000-ton hovership freighters. 1961 *New Statesman* 14 July 67/1 The possibility of hovertrains. 1971 *Daily Tel.* 16 Apr. 6/7 A French demonstration hovertrain has been running for 18 months on an 11-mile stretch of elevated monorail outside Orléans. 1960 *Daily Tel.* 12 Aug. 11/7 A series of Hovertrucks. 1963 *Guardian* 6 June 3/3 The 'hover truck', a development from the Hovercraft which some farmers in East Anglia regard as an essential farm implement of the future. 1962 *Daily Tel.* 6 June 22/3 What we have in mind is that hover vehicles, vehicles designed to be supported on a cushion of air, shall be considered as motor vehicles whether or not adapted for use on the roads.
b. Used to form the names of things related to the operation and requirements of hovercraft, as ***hoverport***, ***-rail***, ***-track***, ***-way*** [after *motorway*].
1967 *Guardian* 6 Feb. 3/2 A British hoverport in the south. 1967 *Jane's Surface Skimmer Systems 1967–68* 16/2 The route will be between a new hoverport in Pegwell Bay area and a French terminal..east of Calais harbour. 1962 *Engineering* 5 Jan. 6/2 A high-speed hover-rail system.. could also be cheaper than motorways. 1965 *New Scientist* 5 Aug. 318/3 The hovertrack, of concrete, would be elevated, and on it would run a 'train' probably capable of carrying several passengers at 100 miles an hour. 1973 *Daily Tel.* 7 Sept. 18/2 The strong constituency interest in the future of the hovertrack centre. 1960 *Times* 12 Aug. 6/4 They will be capable of operating over land, water, marsh, or broken ice, or along rough bulldozed 'hoverways' in undeveloped areas. 1962 *Hovering Craft & Hydrofoil* May–June 15/1 It is desirable that definite 'hoverways' be established and shown on charts, especially where these traverse commercial routes where the density of shipping is high.

hovercraft ('hɒvəkrɑːft, -æ-). Also Hovercraft. Pl. -craft. [f. HOVER *v.*[1] + CRAFT *sb.*[1]] A vehicle or craft that can be supported by a cushion of air ejected downwards against a surface close below it, and can in principle travel over any relatively smooth surface (as a body of water, marshland, gently sloping land) while having no significant contact with it.
For some years from 1961 registered as a proprietary term but now in the public domain.
1959 [see *ground effect* s.v. GROUND *sb.* 17 d]. 1959 *Daily Mail* 6 Apr. 5/2 The sea-saucer has been offically christened the Hovercraft. 1960 A. CROOME *Hover Craft* iv. 60/1 When the 455 h.p. engine is started the air-cushion quickly builds up underneath and the Hovercraft rises off the ground (or water) and hovers there very steadily. 1961 C. S. COCKERELL in *Hovering Craft & Hydrofoil* Oct. 8 My wife and I tried to find a name and settled for the not altogether appropriate word 'Hovercraft'. 1962 *Daily Tel.* 12 Mar. 13 British United Airways intends..to start the first Hovercraft service in the world this summer. 1965 *Guardian* 5 Jan. 3/3

Air cushion vehicles——or hovercraft, if you prefer the term. **1967** *Jane's Surface Skimmer Systems 1967–68* 24/2 Designed initially for military logistic-support duties, the BH. 8 is a twin-engined, 80 ton, open-water hovercraft with bow and stern loading doors. **1972** *Drive* Spring 75/2 From the attractive cliff gardens there are exciting views of modern hovercraft roaring in and out of Pegwell Bay.

† **'hovered**, *a. Obs.* [OE. *hoferede* (= OHG. *hovarohti*, MHG. *hoveroht*), f. *hofer* hump, swelling = OHG. *hovar*, *hover*.] Hump-backed.

c **897** K. ÆLFRED *Gregory's Past.* xi. 66 Se ðonne bið hoferede se þe sio byrðen of ðryceð ðisse eorðlican ȝewilnunge. *c* **1000** *Sax. Leechd.* III. 144 þonne ȝelimpeð hit hwilum þurh þæt þæt þæt cild bið hoforode and healede. *a* **1100** *Ags. Voc.* in Wr.-Wülcker 337/36 *Gybberosus uel strumosus*, hoferede. *a* **1225** *St. Marher.* 20 Nowther halt ne houeret. *a* **1225** *Leg. Kath.* 1063 þe dumbe, & te deaue.. halte & houerede.

hoverer ('hɒv-, 'hʌvərə(r)). [f. HOVER *v.*[1]] An animal or thing that hovers, esp. in the air.

1615 CHAPMAN *Odyss.* XI. (R.), Hurling round his frowne, At those vext houerers, aiming at them still. *a* **1821** KEATS *Sleep & Poetry* 13 Light hoverer around our happy pillows! **1880** *Libr. Univ. Knowl.* X. 496 Classification [of birds] by Cuvier.. Swimmers: *a.* Divers, *b.* Hoverers, *c.* Waddlers. **1897** P. ROBINSON in *Contemp. Rev.* Mar. 395 Like the hoverers with the big eyes and the blue-bottle.

'hover-height. Also **hoverheight.** [f. HOVER *v.*[1] + HEIGHT *sb.*] The distance separating the underside of a hovercraft (either stationary or in motion) from the surface below it when the vehicle is supported on its air-cushion.

1959 *Times* 2 Sept. 11/6 Even quite small Hovercraft can have a hover-height of several feet. **1961** *New Scientist* 2 Feb. 266/3 The installation of the second engine.. reduced the 'hoverheight' by 2½ inches to 8 inches. **1962** *Hovering Craft & Hydrofoil* Oct. 13/1 In rough conditions, speed can be reduced and the hover-height increased to give adequate wave clearance. **1967** *Jane's Surface Skimmer Systems 1967–68* 44/1 Its hover height can be varied to a maximum of three feet, depending on loading.

hovering ('hɒv-, 'hʌvərɪŋ), *vbl. sb.* [f. HOVER *v.*[1] + -ING[1].] The action of the vb. HOVER.

a. Suspension or poising in the air on fluttering or outstretched wings; lingering about or around, moving to and fro about a person or place. (See also HOVER *v.*[1] 1 c, d.)

1727 DE FOE *Hist. Appar.* ix. 178 The hovering or wandering in the air. **1802** *Act 42 Geo. III*, c. 82 Liable to Forfeiture for hovering, or being found or discovered to have been, within Four Leagues of the Coast. **1886** R. C. LESLIE *Sea-painter's Log* 211 The hovering in the sun of those bright-coloured two-winged flies we sometimes call drones. **1894** J. LE CONTE in *Pop. Sci. Monthly* XLIV. 746 *Hovering*.. always refers to a maintenance of a body in one position in the air..—either by vigorous flapping of the wings, or else.. with no motion of the wings at all. I shall.. confine the term *hovering* to the former. **1916** M. A. S. RIACH *Air-Screws* ix. 113 The value of (V) is zero, and the machine remains stationary. This is the condition already established for 'hovering' flight. **1960** HOUGHTON & BROCK *Aerodynamics* viii. 179 In steady hovering, the weight is balanced by the jet thrust and the force due to the 'cushion' of air below the craft. **1962** *Daily Tel.* 4 Sept. 17/1 Their hovering manœuvres,.. and the transformation in the air to 'normal' fast flying fighter planes, marked a new era in the development of aircraft.

(ii) Motion of a hovercraft while it is supported on an air-cushion: see HOVER *v.*[1] 1 d.

1967 *Hovercraft World* Jan.–Apr. 14/1 We waved good-bye.. at 10.15 hours heading for Wexford, 75 miles away. The fog soon lifted and this leg was a straightforward piece of 'hovering'.

† **b.** Brooding, incubation. *Obs.*

1671 GREW *Anat. Plants* vi. §13 What the Hen by Incubation or Hovering is to the Egg or Chick. **1677** HALE *Prim. Orig. Man.* III. vi. 280 Many Birds stand in need of the hovering of their Dams Wings.. after they are hatched.

c. Hesitation, wavering, suspense.

1679 OATES *Narr. Popish Plot* Ded. A, The Arts and Hoverings.. used in vain.. to suppress and traduce the Evidence. **1827** LYTTON *Pelham* (L.), A new play had just been acted, and the conversation, after a few preliminary hoverings, settled upon it.

hovering, *ppl. a.* [f. HOVER *v.*[1] + -ING[2].] That hovers: **a.** That hangs poised in the air; that floats or hangs about a particular spot.

1630 DRAYTON *Noah's Flood* (R.), The soaring kite.. to the ark the hovering castril brings. **1756** MASON *Odes* vii. (R.), He, too, perchance, when these poor limbs are laid, Will heave one tuneful sigh, and sooth my hov'ring shade. **1865** LONGF. *Divina Comm.* iii, The hovering echoes fly from tomb to tomb. **1875** SEARS *Serm. Chr. Life* 8 Hovering and protecting wings.

b. Hesitating, wavering; uncertain.

1611 SHAKS. *Wint. T.* II. ii. 302 A houering Temporizer. **1635** SIR H. WOTTON in *Lismore Papers* Ser. II. (1888) III. 220 We have stoode.. in a kinde of hovering conceypt that your Lordship would be shortly heere in person.

Hence **'hoveringly** *adv.*

1818 KEATS *Endym.* II. 819 Let the sounds Of our close voices marry at their birth; Let us entwine hoveringly! **1892** *Blackw. Mag.* CLI. 390/1 Her little white feet skimmed so hoveringly over the floor.

† **'hoverly**, *adv.* (*a.*) *Obs.* [? f. HOVER *a.* + -LY.] Lightly; slightly.

1549 COVERDALE, etc. *Erasm. Par. Rom.* vii. (R.), My mynde was but houerly and faintlye moued to synne. *c* **1555** HARPSFIELD *Divorce Hen. VIII* (Camden) 170 Two other special points.. the one which the said patrons of the University hoverly touched. *a* **1557** MRS. BASSET tr. *More's Treat. on Passion* M.'s Wks. 1358/2 Not with reuerence attentiuely to praye to hym, but like carelesse and slepy wretches hoverly to talk with him. *a* **1640** W. FENNER *2nd Pt. Christ's Alarm* (1657) 35 They do it lothly and hoverly, even so, so, they do not do it roundly and throughly.

b. *adj.* Light, slight, touching the surface.

1633 ROGERS *Treat. Sacram.* II. 25 It must be very inquisitive and narrow; not hoverly and superficial.

hove-to: see HEAVE *v.* 20 c.

hoving ('həʊvɪŋ), *vbl. sb.* Also **hooving.** [HOVE *v.*[2]] Swelling (of cheese).

1743 W. ELLIS *Mod. Husbandman* May vii. 93 Others to prevent the Cheese's Hoving, will mix skim and new milk together. **1811** AITON *Agric. Ayrsh.* 456 Hoving or fire-forging is so seldom met with in the sweet milk cheese of that county. **1858** C. L. FLINT *Milch Cows* 265 Heat would make them [*sc.* cheeses] sweat.. which extracts the fat, and tends to induce hooving.

Hovis ('həʊvɪs). The registered trade mark of a brand of flour; also, a loaf of brown bread made from this flour. Also *attrib.*

1890 *Trade Marks Jrnl.* 16 Nov. 1137/2 *Hovis.* Flour and Articles of Food, made partly or wholly of Flour, Richard Smith, Corn Flour Mills, Macclesfield, Cheshire. **1895** G. B. SHAW *Let.* 23 Dec. (1965) 584 Eat stewed fruit and hovis. **1898** *Christian World* 3 Feb. 4/5 Our representative was told that 'Hovis' was the concoction of a Cambridge undergraduate, being compounded of 'hominis' and 'vis,' 'strength of man'. **1907** *Yesterday's Shopping* (1969) 510/3 Hovis Food——No. 1, for infants... No. 2, for children and invalids. **1930** S. BECKETT *Whoroscope* 3 So we drink Him and eat Him And the watery Beaune and the stale cubes of Hovis. **1932** DYLAN THOMAS *Let.* (1966) 5 Give me a half-pint, a Hovis. **1962** L. DEIGHTON *Ipcress File* i. 10 He had a long thin nose, a moustache like flock wallpaper, sparse, carefully combed hair, and complexion of a Hovis loaf. **1967** A. LASKI *Seven Other Years* iii. 32 She liked the shapes of bread, and the different colours.. some, Hovises and wholemeals, dark and interesting.

† **how, howe**, *sb.*[1] *Obs.* exc. *dial.* Forms: 1 hoȝu, 3–4 hoȝe, howe, 4–5 how; 6–9 (see HOE *sb.*[3]). [OE. *hoȝu* str. f., a parallel formation to OHG. *hugu*, *hugi* (MHG. *hüge*), OS. *hugi* (MDu. *höghe*, Du. *heug*), ON. *hugr*, Goth. *hugs* thought:—pre-Teut. *kuk-*; cf. Skr. *çuk*, whence *çūk* heat, sorrow, grief.] Care, anxiety, trouble, sorrow.

c **1000** ÆLFRIC *Hom.* I. 132 He næfð nan andȝit ne hoȝa embe Godes beboda. *Ibid.* 446 Habbon hi hoȝe. *a* **1250** *Owl & Night.* 701 The nihtegale al hire hoȝe Mid rede hadde wel bitoȝe. **1297** R. GLOUC. (Rolls) 9466 þo þis bataile was ido, & hii were al out of howe [*rime* of bristowe]. **13..** *Sir Beues* 4507 (MS. A.) What for care and for howe, He lenede to his sadelbowe. *c* **1380** *Sir Ferumb.* 4539 Ac for þat strok had he non hoȝe [*rime* toȝe]. *c* **1420** *Chron. Vilod.* st. 230 And haue gret how bothe day and nyȝt How þey myȝt best bryng hit to anynde. **1567–1875** [see HOE *sb.*[3]].

how, howe (haʊ), *sb.*[2] *northern.* Also 7 hough, 9 houe. [a. ON. *haug-r* mound, cairn, app. related to OTeut. *hauh-* high.]

1. A hill, hillock: now only in some local names in the north of England, as Great How, Silver How, Brant How, How Hill (near Ripon), etc.

a **1340** HAMPOLE *Psalter* lxxi. 3 Howys [*montes*] take pees til þe folke: and hilles rightwisnes. *Ibid.* lxxix. 11 þe shadow of it couyrd howis [*montes*]: and the trese cedirs of god. *a* **1400–50** *Alexander* 3486 Be hiȝe hillis & howis & be holuȝe dounnes. **1628** COKE *On Litt.* I. i. §1 Howe also signifieth a Hill. **1800** WORDSW. *Rural Archit.* 4 To the top of Great How did it please them to climb.

2. An artificial mound, tumulus, or barrow.

(Also in local names, as *Maeshow*, at Stennis, Orkney.)
1669 W. SIMPSON *Hydrol. Chym.* 89 This patient.. sometimes did work in an Hough (as the country-people call it) of Blacomoore, for some suppos'd.. treasure deeply lodg'd in the earth. **1788** W. MARSHALL *Yorksh.* Gloss. (E.D.S.), *How*, a round hillock; perhaps sometimes a natural knoll; but generally of factitious origin. The Moreland swells abound with hows. **1855** ROBINSON *Whitby Gloss.*, *Houe* or *Barrow*, the tumuli which abound in the neighbourhood of Whitby, as the burial mounds of the ancient Britons. **1866** EDMONSTON *Gloss. Orkney & Shetl.* 50 *Howie*, a mound, a tumulus, a knoll. **1877** GREENWELL *Brit. Barrows* 2 They.. are known as barrows.. and cairns.. and popularly in some parts of England as lows, houes, and tumps. **1947** *Proc. Prehist. Soc.* XIII. 33 When we reach the 10th century there were brochs in Caithness and Orkney.. deemed eligible burial howes. **1963** *Field Archaeol.* (Ordnance Survey) (ed. 4) 45 Round burial mounds.. are the commonest objects of antiquity met with in the field. They are called by different names in different parts of the country.. barrow, low, howe, cairn. **1968** G. JONES *Hist. Vikings* II. iii. 117 The mightiest of all northern howes, Raknehaugen.., over a hundred metres in diameter and some eighteen metres high, is an empty cenotaph. **1971** G. M. BROWN *Fishermen with Ploughs* 7 Lust builds a howe over the burning ghost.

how (haʊ), *adv.* (*sb.*[3]) Forms: 1 hú, 2–4 hu, (3 hv, hwu, wu, quhu, qu(u)ow, heu, ou, heou, 3–4 hw, 4 (w)houȝ, whou, hwou, w, *Kent.* hue), 3–6 hou, 4– how, (4–5 hov, 4–6 whow, *Sc.* quhou, quhow, 5 howghe, owe, hough(e, who, 5–7 howe, 6 whoe). [OE. *hú*:—**hwô*, corresp. to OFris. *hû*, *hô*, OS. *hwô*, *hwuo*, *wô* (MDu. *hoe* (*ho*, *hou*), Du. *hoe*, MLG. *woe*), OHG. (Tatian) *wuo*:—OTeut. **hwô*, an adverbial formation from the interrog. pron. stem *hwa-* who? Parallel to MDu. *hû*, and to Goth. *hwaiwa*, OHG. *hweo*, *weo*, *wio*, G. *wie*, with different suffixes.]

A. *adv.* An adverb primarily interrogative, used also in exclamations, and in conjunctive and relative constructions: cf. WHEN, WHERE, WHY.

I. In direct questions.

1. a. Qualifying a verb: In what way or manner? By what means?

a **1000** *Cædmon's Gen.* 802 Hu sculon wit nu libban? *c* **1000** *Ags. Gosp.* Matt. xii. 29 Hu mæȝ man ingan in stranges hus? *c* **1200** *Trin. Coll. Hom.* 97 Hwu come þu [h]ider in? *c* **1300** *Havelok* 2753 Hw mithe he don him shame more? *c* **1315** SHOREHAM 16 Hou his hit ther bethe so fele? **1382** WYCLIF *1 Cor.* xv. 35 How schulen deede men ryse aȝen? *c* **1394** *P. Pl. Crede* 42 Whouȝ schulde þei techen þe God þat con not hemselue? *Ibid.* 141 Whow myȝt-tou in thine broþer eiȝe a bare mote loken? *c* **1440** *Promp. Parv.* 249/2 Howe.. [*S.* howȝ or qwow], *quomodo, qualiter.* **1590** SPENSER *F.Q.* III. iii. 25 How shall she know, how shall she finde the man? **1610** SHAKS. *Temp.* III. ii. 159 How came we a shore? **1676** HOBBES *Iliad* Pref. (1686) 2 How is it possible .. to please them all? **1776** *Trial Nundocomar* 23/2 How can I tell who has seen him? **1836** J. H. NEWMAN *Par. Serm.* (1837) III. x. 149 This marvellous benefit.. how was it to be attained?

b. With intensive additions, as *the devil*, *a fire*, *in the world*, etc. (see DEVIL, etc.).

c **1489** CAXTON *Sonnes of Aymon* xix. 408 How the devyll dare ye thus speke? **1694** ECHARD *Plautus* 19 How a fire cou'd he see all this? **1772** FLETCHER *Logica Genev.* 165 How in the world can he know.. whether he is in the faith or not? **1889** BOLDREWOOD *Robbery under Arms* xlix, How in the world did ever she get there?

† **c.** In pregnant use = How is it that? How comes it that? Why? *Obs.*

1340 *Ayenb.* 47 Hue is hit uoul dede zeþþe hit is kendelich? *c* **1380** WYCLIF *Serm.* Sel. Wks. I. 60 Hou shulde sich sense be error in man? *a* **1400–50** *Alexander* 459 How þat ȝe ga sa grete, gud dame? *Ibid.* 4345 Howe durst any be so bald to blemysche.. þe hand-werke of þat hiȝe gode? **1606** BIRNIE *Kirk-Buriall* xi, If thou be to ly at the Altar, how wantst thou a Priest to say thy soule Masse? **1611** BIBLE *Gen.* xxvi. 9 How saidst thou, She is my sister?

d. *ellipt.* (*a*) With ellipsis of the rest of the question, which, if expressed in full, would reflect the form of a previous statement or question; also ***as how?*** see AS *adv.* 30. (*b*) In '***How if...?***' 'How will (would) it be if...?'

1579, 1636 [see AS *adv.* 30]. **1590** SHAKS. *Com. Err.* II. i. 30 How if your husband start some other where? **1592** —— *Rom. & Jul.* IV. iii. 30 How, if when I am laid into the Tombe, I wake before the time? **1762** FOOTE *Lyar* I. i, This disguise procures me many resources.. As how?.. Why, at a pinch, Sir, I am either a teacher of tongues.. or a dancing-master. **1875** JOWETT *Plato* III. 355 Is such an order of things possible, and how, if at all?

2. a. In what condition or state? ***how are you?***: (in quot. 1918) used ironically in sense 'indeed!' ***how do you do?*** (formerly ***how do you?***): common phrases used in inquiring as to a person's health. See also HOW-DO-YE, HOW-DO-YOU-DO. Also, ***how goes it?*** = HOW-DO-YOU-DO 1; ***how's*** (or ***how are***) ***things*** (or, orig. Austral. and N.Z., ***tricks?***); ***how do?***: = HOW-DO-YOU-DO.

a **1300** *Cursor M.* 20089 'Alas! alas! alas!' said sco, 'How mai i liue, how mai i be!' *c* **1460** *Towneley Myst.* viii. 333 How do thay in gessen? *c* **1481** CAXTON *Dialogues* (E.E.T.S.) 4/36 What do ye? how is it with you? **1583** HOLLYBAND *Campo di Fior* 35 How doest thou my heart? **1592** SHAKS. *Ven. & Ad.* 249 How doth she now for wits? **1598** FLORIO *Worlde of Wordes* 41/1 How now? how goes it? go to, it is well. **1603** SHAKS. *Meas. for M.* II. ii. 75 How would you be, If he.. should But iudge you, as you are? **1764** [see GO *v.* 18]. **1799** [see DO *v.* 19]. *a* **1822** SHELLEY *Magn. Lady* v, How feel you now? **1837** DICKENS *Pickw.* vii, Several dozen of 'How-are-you's?' hailed the old gentleman's arrival. **1847** MARRYAT *Childr. N. Forest* xi, Well, Master Andrew, how fare you? **1848** THACKERAY *Van. Fair* xiv, How's little Miss Sharp? **1850** TENNYSON *In Mem.* iv, O heart, how fares it with thee now? **1886** H. BAUMANN *Londinismen* 79/2 *How-do*, how d'you do? **1892** I. ZANGWILL *Childr. Ghetto* I. 147 'Well, how goes it, Reb Moshé?' said Reb Shemuel with his cheery smile. **1918** JOYCE *Exiles* I. 2 *Beatrice.* Did he practise the piano while I was away? *Brigid.* Practise, how are you! **1926** K. S. PRICHARD *Working Bullocks* viii. 86 They halloed and yelled to him: 'H'lo, Red!' 'How's things?' **1928** H. CRANE *Let.* 27 Mar. (1965) 321 How goes it with your translations..? *a* **1930** D. H. LAWRENCE *Mod. Lover* (1934) 192 Hello, you two. How's things? **1934** *Passing Show* 27 Jan. 5/4 Hey, Morrison, old socks. How's things? **1939** C. BELTON *Outside Law in N.Z.* xxv. 129 'Hallo. How are things?' I greeted him. **1940** H. G. WELLS *Babes in Darkling Wood* I. iv. 90 'How do, Father?' said Gemini. **1941** *Coast to Coast 1941* 195 'G'day,' he said. 'How's tricks?' **1949** D. M. DAVIN *Roads from Home* I. iii. 49 How's things?.. How's tricks with you? **1971** B. MALAMUD *Tenants* 149 'I won't be coming around to say howdo this Friday, Irene,' Bill said tonelessly. **1973** L. MEYNELL *Thirteen Trumpeters* xiv. 211 'How's tricks?' he enquired. 'I'm fine. I slept like a top.'

b. ***how's that?*** in *Cricket*, an appeal to the umpire to give his decision whether a batsman is 'out' or not.

1833 *New Sporting Mag.* V. 325 'Well thrown by Huddleston!'—'How's that?' 'Run out!' **1891** GRACE *Cricket* xi. 379 'How's that, umpire?' 'Not out', said he. **1927** G. A. TERRILL *Out in Glare* iv. 62 The ball swerved——pitched; the inner edge of his bat grazed it. 'Rap!' it had got him on the pad. ''s *that?*' cried Verlenden, unaware of the graze. **1973** A. MANN *Tiara* ii. 13 The sharp click of bat on ball, and un-Italian cries of 'Owzat'.. showed that cricket was well underway.

3. To what effect? With what meaning? Also, By what name? *arch.* (The mod. Eng. equivalent is 'What?')

1382 WYCLIF *Luke* x. 26 What is writun in the lawe? hou redist thou? *c* **1460** *Towneley Myst.* viii. 398. *c* **1566** J. ALDAY tr. *Boaystuau's Theat. World* C iv, How is theyr maner when they would cove? **1582** N. LICHEFIELD tr. *Castanheda's Conq. E. Ind.* v. 13 b, How say you sir, heere is an other kinde of people. **1593** SHAKS. *2 Hen. VI*, v. i. 73 How art thou call'd? **1596** —— *Tam. Shr.* IV. iii. 20 How say you to a fat Tripe finely broyl'd? **1605** —— *Macb.* III. iv. 128 How say'st thou, that Macduff denies his person At our great bidding? **1777** SHERIDAN *Sch. Scand.* III. iii, *Sir O.* Is there nothing you could dispose of? *Ch.* How do you mean? **1820** SCOTT *Ivanhoe* ii, How call'd you your franklin, Prior Aymer? **1849** THACKERAY *Pendennis* lxxiv, 'Will you join us in a little conspiracy?' 'How do you mean conspiracy, young man?'

4. a. *ellipt.* for 'How is it?' or 'How say you?' and used interjectionally, the mod. equivalent being 'What?' or 'What!' (= F. *quoi!*) *arch.* (exc. in ***how about...?***). In U.S. colloq. speech 'How?' is used in asking for the repetition of something not quite understood (= F. *comment?*).

In OE. *hú* was prefixed to a negative question.

c **1000** *Ags. Gosp.* Matt. vi. 26 Hu ne synt ȝe selran þonne hiȝ? *c* **1250** *Gen. & Ex.* 3077 Hu! haue ȝe wrong. **1589** R. HARVEY *Pl. Perc.* (1860) 11 Whow? I go about to disgrace thee? **1603** SHAKS. *Meas. for M.* II. i. 71 *Elb.* My wife Sir? whom I detest before heauen, and your honour. *Esc.* How? thy wife? *Elb.* I sir. **1722** DE FOE *Col. Jack* (1840) 306 How! signior.. have you not authority? **1766** GOLDSM. *Vic. W.* xi, 'How', cried I, 'relinquish the cause of truth?' **1846** O. W. HOLMES *Rhymed Lesson* 506 Don't say 'How?' for 'What?' **1858** —— *Aut. Breakf.-t.* iv, I was thinking,—he said indistinctly. How? What is't?—said our landlady. **18..** EMERSON in *Harper's Mag.* (1884) Feb. 460/1 How about Matthew Arnold?

b. ***how now?*** ellipt. for 'How is it now?' Often used interjectionally. *arch.*

c **1380** *Sir Ferumb.* 3779 'What how now'.. 'Haþ Clarioun my cosyn aslawe þe man?' **1480** CAXTON *Chron. Eng.* cxlix. 129 What how nowe.. manace ye me? **1610** SHAKS. *Temp.* I. ii. 244 How now? moodie? *c* **1704** PRIOR *Merry Andrew* 10 Why how now, Andrew!.. To-day's conceit, methinks, is something dull. **1841** DICKENS *Barn. Rudge* xlviii, How now! he cried.. Why, where have you been hiding? **1878** BROWNING *Poets Croisic* xli, How now? My Duke's crown wrecked?

c. ***how much***: used in humorous colloq. requests for the repetition of something not heard or not understood. Also, ***how much?*** = what? eh? (Cf. *what price* so-and-so?)

1852 F. E. SMEDLEY *Lewis Arundel* xxxiv. 292 'Then my answer must mainly depend on the exact height of the principles.' 'On the how much?' inquired Frere, considerably mystified. **1914** C. MACKENZIE *Sinister St.* II. III. i. 509 'I've got to get.. a picture of Mona Lisa.' 'Mona how much?' said Alan. 'La Gioconda, you ass.' **1927** E. BOWEN *Hotel* ii. 11 'She is a Hedonist.' 'A *how*-much?' 'A Hedonist.' **1928** [see GAWD]. **1934** T. S. ELIOT *Rock* i. 12 *Ethelbert*: Ain't you ever 'eard me speak o' the principles of Social Credit Reform? *Alfred*: 'Ow much? *Ethelbert*: What Major Douglas 'as to say about banks. **1938** E. BOWEN *Death of Heart* II. iv. 243 'A friend of mine—could he ever come and stay here?'.. 'Could he how much?' said Daphne. **1949** WODEHOUSE *Uncle Dynamite* ii. 23 'You're like me, a gentle coffee-caddy.' 'A how much?'

d. ***and how!***: excl. used to indicate that the effect of something is difficult to describe = and no mistake, very much so! orig. *U.S.*

1865 B. TAYLOR *Let.* 16 June in M. H. Taylor *Life & Lett. Bayard Taylor* (1884) II. xviii. 434, I finished an article for the 'Atlantic' that day. As if I were not 'a tool of the elements!' 'And how?' as the Germans say (Americanicé—— 'You'd better believe it!'). **1932** J. W. DRAWBELL *Good Time!* xvii. §3 'How's that for your orders from a typical American woman?' 'You mean it, Peggy?' 'And how!' 'Baby!' **1932** T. E. LAWRENCE *Lett.* (1938) 752, I want to meet Yeats and Epstein and Eliot some day and how. **1933** E. E. CUMMINGS *eimi* 83, I have fallen, fallen And How; tumbled into exactly 180 minuteless minutes of 'materialist dialectic'. **1948** 'N. SHUTE' *No Highway* ii. 37 'Did Mr. Honey take it seriously?' she asked. 'And how!' I said. **1963** V. NABOKOV *Gift* iii. 175 One foot is buried in rich mud, the other is about to kick—and how!—the hideous, tar-black ball. **1965** *Listener* 25 Nov. 874/1 'Alas,' wrote Harrington, 'all earthly things do fail to mortals in enjoyment.' And how.

e. ***how about that?***: Isn't that good, pleasing, surprising, etc.? *colloq.* (orig. *U.S.*).

1939 *Time* 25 Sept. 8/3 How about that? **1966** *Word Study* Dec. 2/2 How bout that.

f. ***how's about?*** = how about? (sense 4 a). *colloq.* (chiefly *U.S.*).

1952 *Holiday* Jan. 41/1 How's about a drink? **1961** PARTRIDGE *Dict. Slang* (ed. 5) Suppl. 1184/1 How's about having a drink?

5. Chiefly qualifying an adj. or adv.: To what extent? In what degree? (Also with the vb. *like*, or an equivalent.)

c **1000** *Ags. Gosp.* Matt. xvii. 17 Hu lange for-bere ic eow? *Ibid.* Luke xvi. 5 Hu mycel scealt þu minum hlaforde? *a* **1300** *Cursor M.* 10437 Hu lang sal þou þus-gat be wroth? **1382** WYCLIF *Mark* ix. 21 Hou long is it sith this hath falle to hym? **1573–80** BARET *Alv.* H 686 How old, or what age are you? **1596** SHAKS. *Tam. Shr.* v. ii. 38 How likes Gremio these quicke witted folkes? **1602** *2nd Pt. Return fr. Parnass.* III. i. 1119 How many miles from Waltham to London? **1738** SWIFT *Pol. Conversat.* 147 Well, Colonel, how do you like that Wine? **1798** WORDSW. *We are seven* iv, Sisters and brothers, little Maid, How many may you be? **1857** HUGHES *Tom Brown* II. viii, How many runs?

6. At what rate or price?

1597 SHAKS. *2 Hen. IV*, III. ii. 54 *Shal.* How a score of Ewes now? *Sil.*... A score of good Ewes may be worth tenne pounds. **1606** —— *Tr. & Cr.* IV. ii. 23 How now, how now? how goe maiden-heads? *Mod.* How did things go at the auction? How do you sell the plums?

II. In direct exclamations.

7. a. In what a way! to what an extent or degree!

a **900** CYNEWULF *Crist* 216 Crist æl-mihtiȝ hu þu ær wære eallum ȝeworden.. mid þinne wuldor-fæder cild acenned þurh his cræft and meaht! *c* **1000** *Ags. Ps.* (Th.) lxxii[i]. 1 Hu god is ece God! **1340** *Ayenb.* 89 Hou hy byeþ uer uram þise heȝnesse. **1382** WYCLIF *Lam.* i. 1 Hou sitteth alone the cite ful of puple! *c* **1450** tr. *De Imitatione* I. xxii. 28 O hov gode a lif þat man haþ, hov grete, hov riche, hov miȝty, hov hye he is! *c* **1485** *Digby Myst.* (1882) III. 555 A! how I tremyl and trott for ȝese tydynges! **1513** DOUGLAS *Æneis* IV. Prol. 231 How [*ed.* **1553** quhou] schort quhile dois his fals plesance remane! **1583** HOLLYBAND *Campo di Fior* 307 O how sweet it smelleth. **1611** BIBLE *2 Sam.* i. 19 How are the mightie fallen! **1707** WATTS *Hymn*, My God, how endless is thy love! **1808** SCOTT *Marm.* III. vi, How pale his cheek, his eye how bright! *Mod. colloq.* How you do like to tease one!

b. ***how —— can you get?***: see GET *v.* 33 b.

III. In dependent questions and exclamations.

8. Qualifying a verb: In what way, manner, condition, etc.; by what means. (Formerly often followed by *that.*) **a.** in dependence on verbs of telling, asking, thinking, perceiving, etc.

a **1000** *Cædmon's Gen.* 431 Hycgað.. hu ȝe hi beswicen. *c* **1000** ÆLFRIC *Hom.* II. 310 Þa axode se casere þone ænne preost hu his nama wære. *c* **1050** *Byrhtferth's Handboc* in *Anglia* VIII. 312 Hwanon he cymð and hu he byð. *a* **1225** *Ancr. R.* 218 Nimeð nu ȝeme hwu hit fareð. *c* **1325** *Maximon* i. in *Rel. Ant.* I. 119 Nou herkne hou it wes. *c* **1440** *Gesta Rom.* lxv. 284 (Harl. MS.) He.. tolde his wife, Howe þat þe stiwarde saide. **1458** AGNES PASTON in *P. Lett.* No. 311 I. 422 Send me.. word.. who Clement Paston hath do his dever in lernyng. **1535** COVERDALE *Esther* ii. 11 Yᵗ he might knowe how Hester dyd. **1556** LAUDER *Tractate* 277 Attend heirfor, quhow ȝe sulde chuse ȝour Pastoris. **1600** E. BLOUNT tr. *Conestaggio* 117 About ten of the clocke hee demaunded howe the time went. **1766** GOLDSM. *Vic. W.* xvi, How we all came to disregard so material a point is inconceivable. **1875** JOWETT *Plato* (ed. 2) III. 147 Shakespeare has taught us how great men should speak and act.

b. In dependence on sbs. like *heed*, *caution*, and adjs. of kindred meaning.

[*c* **1000** *Ags. Gosp.* Luke viii. 18 Warniað hu ȝe ȝe-hyran.] **1526** TINDALE *Ibid.*, Take hede therfore how ye heare. **1573** TUSSER *Husb.* lxxxi. (1878) 172 Take heede how thou laiest the bane for the rats. **1718** *Freethinker* No. 24 ¶6 Let us be cautious how we innovate too much. **1848** THACKERAY *Van. Fair* xviii, Be wary how you engage. **1861** MAYHEW *Lond. Labour* (1865) II. 62/1 The hawkers.. are wary how they buy an animal suspected to be stolen.

c. In dependence on a preposition.

1827 SOUTHEY *Hist. Penins. War* II. 300 [They] began to think only of how to secure the booty. **1884** CHURCH *Bacon* ix. 214 The force and clearness of what was said depended so much on how it was said.

9. Followed by an infinitive: In what way; by what means. ***how to do*** = the way in which one should (or may) do; also *ellipt.*, as ***how to***, and often used *attrib.*, as '***how-to' discourse***, '***how-to-do-it' manual***, etc.; also (in titles of books, etc.) followed by a verb.

a **1300** *Cursor M.* 3751 Consail me, fader, how to liue [*Gött.* hu i sal liue]. **1390** GOWER *Conf.* II. 367 [He] wiste nought how for to rise. **1548** HALL *Chron.*, *Hen. VIII* 56 Thomas Wolsey.. studyed daye and night how to be a Cardinal. **1553** T. WILSON *Rhet.* (1580) 160 What should a manne doe with a weapon, that knoweth not how to use it? **1678** LADY CHAWORTH in *12th Rep. Hist. MSS. Comm.* App. v. 46 The House is.. consulting how to raise this vast some of monies. **1751** JOHNSON *Rambler* No. 174 ¶5 A set of companions who knew how to laugh. **1838** H. MARTINEAU (*title*) How to observe: morals and manners. **1847–9** HELPS *Friends in C.* Ser. I. (1851) II. 97 There is something I wanted to say.. but I did not see how to bring it in. **1857** (*title*) How to publish: a manual for authors. **1880** C. R. MARKHAM *Peruv. Bark* 272, I am at a loss how to express my feeling of admiration. **1895** *Law Times* XCIX. 546/1 What books to read, and how to read them. **1897** *Cavalry Tactics* Introd. 3 There is no better lesson how not to do it. **1922** JOYCE *Ulysses* 634 You had to come back.. to show the understudy in the title rôle how to. **1923** A. BENNETT (*title*) How to make the best of life. **1941** BEALS & BRODY *Lit. Adult Educ.* 453 Nearly all councils also make some provision for supplying information, such as distributing manuals of the 'how-to-do-it' variety. **1942** H. HAYCRAFT *Murder for Pleasure* p. vii, One or two 'how-to-write-it' manuals. **1946** C. MORRIS *Signs, Lang. & Behavior* v. x. 143 It is 'how to' discourse: discourse informing one how to rivet, how to play the flute. **1959** *Times Lit. Suppl.* 6 Nov. p. xxxviii/4 Light fiction, popular uplift, or how-to-do-it-books. **1960** *Farmer & Stockbreeder* 19 Jan. 43/1 A how-to-cook-turkey booklet! **1968** *Sat Rev.* 27 July 26/3 Most of the how-to books at this time of year are busy with water sports. **1972** T. P. MCMAHON *Issue of Bishop's Blood* (1973) xii. 176 She had washed her face, and though it doesn't say so in the women's how-to-books, there are some women who look great that way.

10. With weakened meaning, introducing an indirect statement, after verbs of saying, perceiving, and the like: = That. Formerly freq. ***how that***, and in mod. dialect speech ***as how*** (see AS *adv.* 28).

see how still more or less calls attention to the manner.

c **1000** ÆLFRIC *Josh.* ii. 10 We ȝehirdon.. hu ȝe ofsloȝon.. Seon and Og. *c* **1250** *Gen. & Ex.* 2732 We witen wel quat is bi-tid, Quuow ȝister-dai was slaȝen and hid. **13..** *K. Alis.* 1565 He.. saide to the kyng, How his fadir hette Felip. *c* **1386** CHAUCER *Knt.'s T.* 526 Hym thoughte how that the wynged god Mercurie Biforn hym stood. **1548** HALL *Chron.*, *Hen. VIII* 57 A letter was brought.. certefiyng him how he was elected to be a Cardinal. **1571** *Satir. Poems Reform.* xxix. 3 Seing quhow all erdly thingis wor subiect to mutatioun. **1611** BIBLE *Ruth* i. 6 Shee had heard.. how that the Lord had visited his people. **1707** WATTS *Hymn*, '*Now for a tune of lofty praise*', Sing how he left the worlds of light. **1748** SMOLLETT *Rod. Rand.* iii, He was well informed as how Rory was the best scholar of his age. **1801** *Monthly Rev.* XXXV. 358 'If people knew as how they could talk, they would be obliged to work also.' **1844** DICKENS *Christmas Carol* iii, Bob Cratchit told them how he had a situation in his eye for Master Peter.

11. Chiefly qualifying an adj. or adv. (also with verb *like*, etc.): To what extent; in what degree.

c **1000** *Ags. Gosp.* Matt. xxvii. 13 Ne ȝehyrst þu hu fela saȝena hiȝ onȝen þe secgeað? *c* **1175** *Lamb. Hom.* 5 Ȝe hi hered hu muchel edmodnesce ure drihten dude for us. *c* **1300** *Havelok* 287 Quanne the Erl.. herde.. hw wel she ferde, Hw wis sho was, w chaste, hw fayr. *c* **1400** MAUNDEV. (Roxb.) xxxiv. 153 Seez how gude a man þis was. **1563** WINȜET *Wks.* (1890) II. 21 It is.. furthschawin, quhoumekle calamitie is inbrocht. *a* **1632** T. TAYLOR *God's Judgem.* I. I. xi. (1642) 31 All which declareth.. upon how fickle ground all their Religion standeth. **1891** E. PEACOCK *N. Brendon* I. 11 You know how small my estate is. *Mod.* I do not know how she will take it.

12. With ellipsis of the rest of the clause introduced by *how*, or of part of it.

c **1200** *Trin. Coll. Hom.* 159 Lusteð nu.. hwo hire ledde and wu and hwider. **1390** GOWER *Conf.* I. 47 Say forth, quod she, and telle me how. **1471** SIR J. PASTON in *P. Lett.* No. 675 III. 15 [He] browt me word.. that he hathe sped well, but howghe, that wot I nott. **1548** HALL *Chron.*, *Hen. VIII* 52 Borowed.. golde and sylver, but howe muche I am not sure. **1634** SIR T. HERBERT *Trav.* 25 The Ocean was as white as snow, but how caused I am ignorant. **1821** BYRON *Sardan.* III. i. 178 He has wound About my heart, I know not how nor why. **1893** *Bookman* June 82/2 Nobody writes moral-allegorical tales now, because nobody knows how.

IV. Introducing a relative clause.

13. In what way, manner, condition, etc.; by what means; in the way that; however; as. (Formerly also ***how that.***) † ***how were it***, pa. t. of HOWBEIT. (Cf. HOWEVER.)

a **1400** *Pistill of Susan* 202 We schul presenten þis pleint, hou þou euer be paied. **1427** *Rolls Parlt.* IV. 326/2 Howe were it, þat it be not þought, þat any such þing wetyngly proceded of your entent. *c* **1475** *Partenay* 3207 Hou were it that ioy of hys fader had, And of Melusine his moders welfaire. **1596** SHAKS. *1 Hen. IV*, v. ii. 12 Looke how we can.. Interpretation will misquote our lookes. **1663** BUTLER *Hud.* I. iii. 955 That what she had atchiev'd.. She should dispose of how she pleas'd. **1695** WOODWARD *Nat. Hist. Earth* I. (1723) 61 Be that how it will. **1719** DE FOE *Crusoe* II. xiii, He would go as a merchant, or how I pleased to order him. **1837** J. H. NEWMAN *Proph. Office Ch.* 105 He left them to gather the great truth for themselves how they could. **1869** FREEMAN *Norm. Conq.* III. xii. 176 Others strove to escape how they might among the ditches.

† **14. a.** Qualifying an adj. or adv.: To what extent, in what degree (that); HOWEVER. ***how well (that)***: although, albeit; cf. Du. *hoewel*. *Obs.*

1481 CAXTON *Reynard* (Arb.) 38 How wel that he had supposed that he had made al faste I was not so moche a fool but that I fonde the hole wel. **1485** —— *Paris & V.* 45 How cruel that he be.. hys hert shal not suffre to do you ony harme. *c* **1500** *Melusine* xxiv. 182 To.. acquere thordre of knyghthode, as our bretheren.. haue don, how wel we be nat worthy to receuye it so nobly.. as they haue doo. ? *c* **1530** *Crt. of Love* 207 Aftir this shall be myne hole entent To serve and please, how dere that love be bought. **1602** *Narcissus* (1893) 687 How deepe I dive, yet thee I cannott find.

† **b.** = As ... as; ***how soon (that)*** = as soon as (F. *aussitôt que*). *Obs.* Chiefly *Sc.*

c **1449** PECOCK *Repr.* III. xvii. 394 Thei ben stabili endewid, how stabili a perpetual chauntry preest is endewid. **1582–8** *Hist. Jas. VI* (1804) 209 Sa that howsoone he espyit Sir James to be remouit from the hous, he then immediately approached with his souldiours. *a* **1639** SPOTTISWOOD *Hist. Ch. Scot.* I. (1677) 8 How long Hildebert lived he aboad in his company. **1754** W. GOODALL in J. Campbell *Love Lett. Mary Q. Scots* (1824) 192 Cecil.. had all in readiness to be published how soon the Duke should be beheaded.

† **c.** Correlative to *so* qualifying an adj. or adv. (sometimes omitted): To what extent; in what degree; as ... as. ***by how much... by so much*** = L. *quantum ... tantum*. (A Latinism.) *Obs.*

1382 WYCLIF *Eccl.* ii. 13 So myche wisdam wente beforn folie, hou myche [1388 as muche as] liȝt is in difference fro dercnesses. *c* **1450** tr. *De Imitatione* III. lv. 133 Hov muche þat euery man is in þin eyen, lorde, so muche he is & no more. **1535** COVERDALE *Jer.* ii. 28 How many cities thou hast (o Iuda) so many goddes hast thou also. **1600** J. PORY tr. *Leo's Africa* II. 378 They worship also serpents.. and the more they feare and reverence them, by how much the more deformed and monstrous they are. **1620** VENNER *Via Recta* iii. 47 By how much the younger they are, by so much the moyster they are. **1703** *Moderation a Virtue* 13 So much the more Amiable, by how much the less it has of humane Mixtures. **1879** E. ARNOLD *Lt. Asia* VIII. (1881) 233 By howsomuch the householder Purgeth himself of self.. By so much happier comes he to next stage.

† **15.** With sb. as antecedent (esp. with *manner*, *way*, etc.): In which (way); by which (name). *Obs.*

c **1400** MAUNDEV. (1839) v. 53 The names how thei clepen hem. **1548** HALL *Chron.*, *Hen. VII* 50 An hundred wayes.. how.. to deliver or convey them out of pryson. *c* **1680** BEVERIDGE *Serm.* (1729) I. 539, I see no way how it is possible. **1690** LOCKE *Hum. Und.* IV. xvi. §12 We perceive not the ways and manner how they are produc'd.

V. 16. With indef. adj. (or adv.): In (some, any) way or manner. *rare.* Cf. ANYHOW, SOMEHOW.

c **1000** *Eccl. Inst.* xxi. in Thorpe *Laws* II. 418 Ðæt se lareow þe him tela tæce him sylf elles-hu do. *c* **1000** in Cockayne *Shrine* 195 Ne meȝ nu hu ælles beon. **1671**

Milton *Samson* 604 To prosecute the means of thy deliverance By ransom or how else. **1719** De Foe *Crusoe* II. xiii, He found means, some how or other, to go. **1858** Hawthorne *Ancestral Footstep* (1883) 514 The old Hospitaller must die in his bed, or some other how.

VI. Phrases. **17. how so?**

a. *Interrogative*: How is it so? How is that?

a **1300** *Cursor M.* 5207 How sua, es þar na noþer king? *c* **1350** *Will. Palerne* 980 'Þis man..þat neȝh is driue to þe deþ al for youre sake!' 'How so for my sake?' *c* **1450** *Erle Tolous* 847 A, devyll! he seyde, how soo? **1598** Shaks. *Merry W.* III. v. 69 How so sir, did she change her determination? **1632** Sherwood, How so? *Puis, et puis? comment cela?*

†**b.** *Relative*: In whatever way, howsoever.

c **1205** Lay. 25703 Þat we hine læteð ane faren heu swa he wule. **1377** Langl. *P. Pl.* B. xvii. 183 Vnfolden or folden my fuste & myn paume, Al is but an hande how so I torne it. *c* **1586** C'tess Pembroke *Ps.* li. viii, O Lord, how soe I stand or fall, Leave not thy loved Sion to embrace.

†**c.** However much; notwithstanding that, although. *Obs.*

c **1330** R. Brunne *Chron. Wace* (Rolls) 16305 Ȝit wot non how hit wyl bynde [*v.r.* ende]; Hou so bitwyxt hem be strif or stresse. *c* **1460** Fortescue *Abs. & Lim. Mon.* iii. (1885) 113 How so be it that þe Ffrenche kynge reignith vppon is peple *dominio regali*, yet [etc.]. *Ibid.* iv. 116 How so be it þat thai do so ayenst thar willes. **1597** Daniel *Civ. Wars* II. (R.), Welcome home, howso unfortunate. **1614** J. Norden *Custom* in Farr *S. P. Jas. I* (1848) 310 [They] shall never fall, howso they seeme to slide.

18. †***how and about***: with reference to, (all) about. ***here's how!*** a formula used in drinking healths. †***how chance***: see chance *v.* 5. ***how, when, and where***: a game of guessing, in which the guesser asks the questions 'How do you like it? When do you like it?' etc., of each of the other players.

1754 Richardson *Grandison* (1766) V. 46 Emily wrote you all how-and-about it. *Ibid.* (1812) VI. 63 (D.) Be good, and write me everything how and about it. **1844** Dickens *Christmas Carol* iii, At the game of How, When, and Where, she was very great. **1896** R. Kipling *Seven Seas* 99 A health to ourselves ere we scatter..Here's how! **1925** [see bung-ho *int.*]. **1951** J. B. Priestley *Festival at Farbridge* II. i. 152 'Well,' said Mr. Hull, holding up his glass,..'here's how!' **1959** E. Burgess *Divided we Fall* xi. 132 Martin was clasping a tumbler half filled with whisky. 'Here's how,' said the fat man.

19. how come? *colloq.* (orig. *U.S.*) phr.: how did (or does) it come about (that)? Cf. come *v.* 21.

1848 Bartlett *Dict. Amer.*, *How-come?* rapidly pronounced huc-cum, in Virginia. Doubtless an English phrase, brought over by the original settlers, and propagated even among the negro slaves. The meaning is, How did what you tell me happen? How came it? **1897** R. M. Stuart *In Simpkinsville* 230 She heard Miss Euphemia wonderin' the other day how come the right shoulder of her black silk dress to wear out. **1930** *Sat. Even. Post* 8 Mar. 12/1 These firms assert blandly to..journalists who ring them up, wishful to know how come, they have nothing against women. **1932** T. S. Eliot *Sweeney Agonistes* 17 Hello Doris! Hello Dusty! How do you do! How come? how come? will you permit me——. **1938** M. K. Rawlings *Yearling* iv. 34 That's how come him to have appetite for a nip o' pore old Betsy. **1957** *New Yorker* 13 July 19/1 These days, the sensation of the stamp-collecting world is United Nations commemorative stamps. How come? **1958** G. Mitchell *Spotted Hemlock* xviii. 210 How come *they* didn't spot her? **1959** H. Hobson *Mission House Murder* xviii. 122 'How come you make it murder?' he asked. **1969** in Halpert & Story *Christmas Mumming in Newfoundland* 213 How come you ain't got Wallace with you tonight? **1971** *Black World* Oct. 62/1 So that's how come I asked My Man Bovanne to dance. **1973** T. Allbeury *Choice of Enemies* iv. 16 'Well, we are getting a bit like the Krauts, you know.' 'How come?'

B. *sb.*³ (often in collocation with *why*).

1. A question or query as to the way or manner. ***hows and whys*** (quot. 1730), doubts.

1533 More *Answ. Poysoned Bk.* Wks. 1061/2 He left their question & their how vnsoyled. *Ibid.*, Lette vs neuer in such high thinges either speake or thynke that same howe. **1577** Fulke *Confut. Purg.* 456 To all the other howes and whyes I aunswere with one word, he had no warrant..in the law of God. **1730** T. Boston *Mem.* App. 35 How difficult to get our hows and whys crucified. *Mod.* Bother your hows and whys!

2. The way or manner (in which).

1551 Bp. Gardiner *Pres. in Sacram.* 55 (R.) The (howe) and maner whereof, God knoweth. **1666** W. Boghurst *Loimographia* (1894) 75 Wee are not soe ignorant in the matter as the method, in the what, as the how. **1701** Norris *Ideal World* I. v. 226 In most things the how is more difficult than the whether, and our philosophy can prove a great deal more than it can explain. **1845** W. G. Simms *Wigwam & Cabin* 1st Ser. 7 You joined the army again, and come in with Greene? Was that the how? **1847** Longf. *Ev.* I. iii. 31 Must we in all things look for the how, and the why, and the wherefore? **1865** Mrs. Carlyle *Lett.* III. 284 Write distinctly the when, and the how, of your home-coming. **1878** J. H. Beadle *Western Wilds* ii. 27 Daddy went off at last, and that was the how of my first trip. **1916** 'B. M. Bower' *Phantom Herd* xvi. 272, I calc'late that's about the how of it. **1949** *Amer. Speech* XXIV. 39 In recent years *method*, *explanation*, and *the how*..promise to force *modus operandi* into the archives.

how, howe, *int.*¹ (*sb.*⁴) *Obs.* or *dial.* Also 6 **hoaw**, 7 **whowe**. [A natural utterance; it is probable that the different uses are independent in origin, and properly different words.]

1. An exclamation to attract attention, etc.; = ho *int.*¹ Also *sb.*, as name for this.

1377 Langl. *P. Pl.* B. vi. 118 [They] hulpen erie his half acre with 'how! trolli-lolli!' *c* **1386** Chaucer *Miller's T.* 391 'Thanne wol I clepe, how Alison! how John! Be myrie for the flood wol passe anon. *a* **1400** *Sir Perc.* 661 He cryed, 'How, mane, on thi mere, Bryng agayne the kynges gere'. **14..** Audelay in *MS. Douce* 302 lf. 34/1 Thai halowyd here howndys with how, In holtis herde I never soche hew. *c* **1485** *Digby Myst.* (1882) II. 85 How, hosteler, how, a peck of otys and a botell of haye. **1535** Lyndesay *Satyre* 602 Mak roume, sirs, hoaw! that I may rin! **1579** *Epit.* in Miller *Hist. Doncaster*, Howe, Howe, who is heare? I Robin of Doncastere and Magaret my feare. **1600** W. Watson *Decachordon* IX. viii. (1602) 327 With hallowes and how-bubs, with whowbes, whowes, and outcries. **1804** *Bob Cranky's 'Size Sunday* (Northmbld. Gloss.), Ki Geordy, how, where are ye gannin'? **1825** Brockett, *How 'way*, come away;..very common in Newcastle.

2. A cry of sailors in heaving the anchor up, etc.: usually with *hale*, *heave* (cf. heave ho, hey ho). Also *sb.*, as name for this.

c **1450** *Pilgr. Sea Voy.* 13 in *Stac. Rome* etc. 37 To dresse hem sone about the mast, Theyr takelyng to make With 'howe! hissa!' **1470–85** Malory *Arthur* VII. xv, Mariners noyse with hale and how. **1471**, **1475**, etc. [see hey-ho]. **1513** Douglas *Æneis* III. ii. 120 Mony marynair Besy at thair werk..with mony heis and how. *a* **1529** Skelton *E. Rummyng* 289 Wyth, Hey, and wyth howe, Sit we down arow. **1647** N. Bacon *Disc. Govt. Eng.* I. x. (1739) 18 Like a great Hoe in a ship-yard at the stirring of a little log. **1867** Morris *Jason* x. 587 And so drew Argo up, with hale and how, On the grass.

3. A cry of pain or grief. In *Sc.* (hou).

1575–6 *Durham Depos.* (Surtees) 271 [He] was so sore vexed with siknes that he raved and showtyd, cryinge 'howe'. *c* **1750** *Mary Hamilton* xi. in Child *Ballads* (1889) III. 392 Monie a lady fair Siching and crying, Och how!

how (haʊ), *sb.*⁵ Colloq. abbreviation of howitzer.

1915 *Times* 14 Apr. 7 The boom in the distance from one of our 'hows'. **1919** C. P. Thompson *Cocktails* 133 A couple of batteries of heavy Hows.

how (haʊ), *int.*² [Cf. Sioux *háo*, Omaha *hau*.] An ejaculation, orig. used by Indians of north-eastern North America in a variety of applications. Also repeated.

First noticed in the early 17th century by the French missionary Jean de Brébeuf, describing Huron oratory as he had observed it in Ontario. The Hurons showed their approval of a speech by a shouted *haau* (Jesuit Relations, documents pertaining to 1636, Thwaites, Vol. X, p. 259).

1817 J. Bradbury *Trav. Interior Amer.* 95 We were interrupted by one of the chiefs crying 'How', signifying amongst the Indians 'Come on', or 'let us begin'. **1841** G. Catlin *Lett. on N. Amer. Indians* II. 172 'How! how!' vociferated all of them, thereby approving what was said, giving assent by the word *how*, which is their word for yes. **1868** *Harper's Mag.* Feb. 301/2 The Indians..complimented 'Little Bill' with a succession of how-how-hows! **1911** *N.Y. Even. Post* 28 Jan. (Suppl.) 3 The expression 'How', used by army men in giving a toast, is equivalent to the expression, 'Here's to your health'. Some think it is merely the Indian corruption of 'How d'ye do?' abbreviated by the Indian to 'How'. Others believe the expression is derived from the Indian language direct. **1962** *Alberta Hist. Rev.* Autumn 11/1 The Blackfoot Indians usually greet a white man with 'How, How!' sometimes, 'How wa-pe'.

†**how, howe**, *v.*¹ *Obs.* Forms: 1 **hoȝian**, (**huȝian**), 2–3 **hoȝe**, 3 **heoȝe**, 4 **howe**; 8–9 (see ho *v.*³). [OE. *hoȝian*, a later modification of *hycgan* = OS. *huggjan*, OHG. *hucken*, ON. *hyggja*, Goth. *hugjan*, to think, f. Goth. *hug-s* thought: see how *sb.*¹ Cf. Du. *heugen* to remember.] *intr.* To be anxious, think, consider, purpose, intend.

Beowulf (Z.) 633 Ic þæt hoȝode..þæt ic anunga eowra leoda willan ȝeworhte. *c* **1000** *Ags. Gosp.* Matt. vi. 34 Ne beo ȝe na hoȝiende ymb þa morȝenlican neode. *c* **1175** *Lamb. Hom.* 113 Ȝif he hit betan mei, and umbe þe bota [ne] hoȝað. *c* **1205** Lay. 13417 Al þe king bilufde swa Fortiger hoȝede. *a* **1250** *Owl & Night.* 455 Hwane mon hoȝeþ of his scheve..Ich fare hom. *a* **1250** *Prov. Ælfred* 135 in *O.E. Misc.* 110 Ne scolde neuer yongmon howyen to swiþe. *a* **1310** in Wright *Lyric P.* 23 His hap he deth ful harde on hete, aȝeynz he howeth henne.

how, howe, *v.*² *Obs.* or *dial.* [f. how *int.*¹]

1. To cry *how!* to shout as sailors.

1508–16 *Promp. Parv.* 251/2 (edd. J. Notary and W. de W.) Howen, *celeumo* [*c* **1440** Howtyn, or cryen as shepmenn].

2. To cry *how!* with pain or grief.

c **1750** *Mary Hamilton* xiii. in Child *Ballads* (1889) III. 392 What need ye hech and how, ladies? What need ye how for me?

how: see hough, houve, howe.

how, obs. or dial. f. who.

howardite (ˈhaʊədaɪt). [f. the name of Edward *Howard* (fl. 1802), English chemist: see -ite¹.]

1. *Min.* A supposed silicate of iron and magnesium found in some meteorites.

1848 C. U. Shepard in *Amer. Jrnl. Sci.* VI. 253 The earthy constituent of this stone, like that of the Iowa meteorite..appears to be a tersilicate of the protoxyd of iron and magnesia, a mineral which though frequent in meteoric stones, has never yet been distinctly recognized, and which in a future paper on American Meteorites, I shall more particularly describe under the name of *Howardite*, after the Hon. Mr. Howard, that celebrated chemist, who was the first British writer whose labors contributed to elucidate the history of these extra-terrestrial bodies. **1955** M. H. Hey *Index Min. Species* (ed. 2) 127 Howardite (of Shepard). A doubtful meteoritic silicate of Fe and Mg.

2. *Astr.* [ad. G. *howardit* (G. Rose 1863, in *Physikal. Abhandl. d. K. Akad. d. Wiss. zu Berlin* 29).] Any of a group of achondritic meteorites principally composed of hypersthene and anorthite.

1881 L. Fletcher *Guide Coll. Meteorites* (Brit. Mus.) 17 Perhaps for those aerolites which contain little or no nickel-iron the division into Howardites, Eukrites, Chladnites, Chassignites, Shalkites, and Carbonaceous is the most convenient. **1915** O. C. Farrington *Meteorites* iii. 35 Of a total of nine meteorites belonging to the class of howardites, five have fallen in Russia. **1916** *Mineral. Mag.* XVIII. 36 The angrites, nakhlites, howardites, eucrites, and sherghottites..are richer in lime..than chondritic stones generally. **1971** B. Mason in I. G. Gass et al. *Understanding Earth* viii. 117 (*table*) [Achondrites are] sometimes divided into calcium-poor achondrites (aubrites, diogenites, chassignite, ureilite) and calcium-rich achondrites (angrite, nakhlite, howardites, eucrites).

howball: see hoball.

howbeit (haʊˈbiːɪt), *adv.* and *conj.* [Originally three words *how be it*, with pa. t. *how were it* (= however it were): see how *adv.* 13.]

A. *adv.* However it may be; be that as it may; nevertheless; however. *arch.*

1470–85 Malory *Arthur* x. i, How be hit I wyl not fayle you. **1511** in W. H. Turner *Select. Rec. Oxford* 5 How-behyt hit was not my desyre. *a* **1533** Ld. Berners *Huon* xlviii. 162 How be it, he was sory by cause one of them..skapyd away. **1612** Davies *Why Ireland* etc. (1747) 24 Howbeit in the meanetime, the english adventurers..did winne much ground. **1850** Mrs. Browning *Prometh. Bound* 17, I lack your daring..Howbeit necessity compels me so That I must dare it. **1887** Ruskin *Præterita* II. i. 8 How-beit, afterwards, the coins of Cnossus..became intelligible to me as to few.

†**B.** *conj.* or *conj. adv.* (orig. with *that*, which was the actual conjunctive element). Though, although. *Obs.*

1398 Trevisa *Barth. De P.R.* I. (1495) 6 How be it that this dyuyne essence..maye not be perfyghtly knowen..yet there is not any mortall persone but that he woll confesse there is a god. **1503** *Act 19 Hen. VII*, c. 5 Half Groats..being Silver (howbeit they be cracked, shall in likewise go and be current. **1570** *Satir. Poems Reform.* x. 108 Bot than, allace, he did sum thing without vs, Howbeit that all his lyfetyme he did dout vs. **1634** Sir T. Herbert *Trav.* 206 They..say the vertue of the Adamant was first by them discovered, how beit to this day they have but eight points unto their compasse. **1634** Rutherford *Lett.* (1862) I. 110, I..would fain have access and presence to The King..euen howbeit I should break up iron doors.

howbub, how-bub, obs. ff. hubbub.

how-come-ye-so, *adj. phr. archaic dial.* or *slang.* Tipsy.

1816 *Monthly Mag.* 1 July 494/2 [Degrees of intoxication.] How came you so. **1824** T. Hook *Sayings & Doings* III. (Merton) xiii. 89. She used to be—'Lord, how come ye so!' every night. **1827** J. F. Cooper *Red Rover* I. x. 258 It is quite in reason to believe your husband was..a little of what I call how-come-ye-so. **1843** *Knickerbocker* XXII. 366 We were never 'groggy', 'intoxicated',..'how-came-ye-so'..or 'tight', but once. **1904** J. C. Lincoln *Cap'n Eri* xii. 223 Drank rum by the hogshead... Well, one evenin' Labe was comin' home pretty how-come-you-so, and he fell into Jonadab Wixon's well.

‖**howdah** (ˈhaʊdə). *East Indies.* Also **houda, howda, houdah, houdar, -er.** [Pers. and Urdū *haudah*, modified from Arab. *haudaj*, a litter carried by a camel or an elephant.]

A seat to contain two or more persons, usually fitted with a railing and a canopy, erected on the back of an elephant.

1774 *Ann. Reg.* 211 Where proudly plac'd the regal Houdah stands. **1775–6** Carracciolli *Life Clive* III. 133 (Y.) Colonel Smith..reviewed his troops from the houdar of his elephant. **1800** *Asiat. Ann. Reg.*, *Misc. Tr.* 195/1 Two elephants caparisoned with scarlet howders. **1816** 'Quiz' *Grand Master* I. 14 A gorgeous howda deck'd the beast. **1882** B. D. W. Ramsay *Recoll. Mil. Serv.* I. v. 103, I sat in the same howdah with the Resident on his elephant.

Hence **ˈhowdahed** *a.*, bearing a howdah; **ˈhowdahful**, as many as a howdah will hold.

1804 W. Tennant *Ind. Recreat.* (ed. 2) II. 383 Howdahed elephants. **1892** *Strand Mag.* IV. 15 [An elephant] with a howdahful of children.

how-do-ye, how-d'ye, howdy, *phr.* and *sb.* Now *obs.* or *dial.* Forms: 6 **howedye, how dee**, 6–9 **how-do-you**, 7 **how d'ee**, 7–8 **how-do-ye**, 8 **how(-)dee**, 9 **how de**, 7– **howdy**, 8– **how d'ye**.

1. The phrase ***how do ye? how do you?*** (cf. next) = how are you? how fare you?: see do *v.* 19. Freq. in colloq. phr. ***to tell*** (a person) ***howdy***.

1563–87 How do you? [see do *v.* 19]. *c* **1828** T. O. Larkin in *Calif. Hist. Soc. Q.* (1937) XVI. 25 They (Southerners) often correct Yankees in their speaking... In those words they are right, but not in..how de for how do you do. **1837** A. Wetmore *Gaz. Missouri* 287 With a smile of welcome as she gave her hand, said, 'Howdy, Joseph.' **1850** J. Price *Let.* 17 Apr. in *Mississippi Valley Hist. Rev.* (1924) XI. 241 Tell Mother and the doctor Howdy. **1856** A. J. Hoole *Let.* 8 June in *Kansas Hist. Q.* (1934) III. 56 Give my love to..all enquiring friends; tell..all the negroes howdie for me. **1887** E. Eggleston *Graysons* i. (1888) 5 'Howdy, Rachel!' said Henry Miller..and 'Howdy! Howdy!' came from the two sisters, to which Rachel answered with a cordial 'Howdy! Come in!' **1917** J. M. Grider *War Birds* 20 Sept. (1927) 10 All the soldiers in the harbor came over to tell us howdy. **1928** L. North *Parasites* i. 30 Mr. Ashton greeted Henry a

trifle more warmly... 'Howdy,' he said. **1973** J. Mann *Only Security* ii. 16, I ought really to go in and say howdy to her.

2. *sb.* A message or salutation containing an inquiry as to the health of a person; = next 2.

1575 G. Harvey *Letter-bk.* (Camden) 90 To requite your gallonde of godbwyes, I regive you a pottle of howedyes. *a* **1652** Brome *Love-sick Court* ii. i. Wks. 1873 II. 107 My great Lords Howdies are upon the entry. **1670** Cotton *Espernon* iii. x. 510 Had the Bishop sent to him by the way of a simple How d'ee only. **1697** Vanbrugh *Relapse* ii. Wks. (Rtldg.) 309/1 He has already sent how-do-ye's to all the town. **1743** *Annesley Ejectm. Trial* in Howell *St. Trials* (1813) XVII. 1166 He was sent.. with messages and how-do-yous, to know how their child did. **1894** *Daily News* 28 Apr. 8/2 A missionary meeting.. at Kingston when the coloured children sent their 'howdies',.. which was short for 'how do you do', to the white children of Britain.

3. *attrib.* or *adj.*

c **1600** Norden *Spec. Brit., Cornw.* (1728) 58 The next day this potentate becometh 'How dee neighbour' agayne. **1654** Gayton *Pleas. Notes* iv. vi–vii. 212 His how d'you man comes every day to know how I slept last night. **1797** Mrs. A. M. Bennett *Beggar Girl* (1813) II. 130 The how-d'ye cards of all the lords, ladies [etc.]. **1806** Wolcott *Wks.* (1812) V. 297 No how-d'ye visits, my cool Neighbours make. **1931** *Times* 5 Nov. 13/4 The howdy folk of Kentucky may bring forth their best. **1932** E. Wallace *When Gangs came to London* xxiii. 224 It seems that this guy has been on howdy terms with the Big Boy ever since he came to town.

how-do-you-do, how-d'ye-do, *phr.* and *sb.* Also 7 **howdee do,** 9 **how-d'y-do, how-de-do, how d'you do.**

1. A phrase inquiring after the health or welfare of the person addressed: see do *v.* 19.

1697 Vanbrugh *Æsop* ii. i, There, how d'ye do now? **1738** Swift *Pol. Conversat.* i How do you do, Tom? **1882** J. Hawthorne *Fort. Fool* i. xxx, I looked in to say how-d'ye-do, but it isn't a serious call.

2. *sb.* Used as a name for the inquiry (which is often used as a mere greeting or salutation); = prec. 2. (In quot. 1632 applied to the inquirer.)

1632 Brome *North. Lasse* i. vi. Wks. 1873 III. 15 This Howdee do I mean with a cast Gown to put in apparel, and make my Gentleman Usher. **1797** Burke *Regic. Peace* iii. Wks. VIII. 301 The pacifick bearer of your 'how do you does'. **1824** Miss Mitford *Village* Ser. i. (1863) 121 Welcomes and how-d'ye-dos were pouring both at once on either side. **1832** J. R. Underwood *Jrnl.* in *Filson Club Hist. Q.* (1941) XV. 43 Joel Yancey.. was always ready with a *how d'ye do.* **1928** D. H. Larwence *Let.* 27 Mar. (1962) II. 1049 Goethe *began* millions of intimacies, and never got beyond the how-do-you-do stage. **1938** J. Cary *Castle Corner* iv. 213 When he came.. to make love as carelessly as how d'you do, he felt betrayed and lost.

3. A 'business'; an embarrassing or awkward state of things. [Cf. do *sb.*, *to do* sb. (do *v.* 33 b).]

1835 Haliburton *Clockm.* Ser. i. xxvi. (1837) 280 Thinks I, here's a pretty how do you do; I'm in for it now, that's a fact. **1885** Gilbert *Mikado* ii. in *Orig. Comic Operas* (1886) 31 Here's a pretty state of things! Here's a pretty how-de-do! **1890** *Harper's Weekly* 24 May 406/2 Here was a pretty how-d'ye-do! Going off with a silver spoon in his pocket.

Hence **how-d'ye do** *v.*, to say 'How d'ye do?' to.

1797–1802 G. Colman *Br. Grins, Knt. & Friar* i. xxxv, She met them every day, 'Good morninging' and 'how d'ye doing'. **1811** W. R. Spencer *Poems* 143 One half in How-d'y-doing goes. **1831** Lady Granville *Lett.* (1894) II. 89 [She] Bon jours and how-d'ye-does all the visitors much more audibly and busily than I do myself.

howdy, -ie ('haʊdɪ). *Sc.* and *north. dial.*, *vulgar.* [Origin uncertain.] A midwife.

1725 Ramsay *Gentle Sheph.* ii. iii, When Mungo's mare stood still and swat wi' fright, When he brought east the howdy under night. **1815** Scott *Guy M.* i, The laird's servant.. rade express by this e'en to fetch the houdie. **1830** Galt *Lawrie T.* ix. i. (1849) 404 She was determined to have at the occasion a howdie instead of an accoucheur. **1832** *Blackw. Mag.* XXXII. 853 The most illustrious man-howdie.

[*Note.* The conjectured derivation from the phrase *how d'ye?* is impossible, since the Sc. form would then have been (huːdɪ). On the analogy of Sc. *gowdie* = *goldy*, *howdy* might go back to *holdie*, an appellative (like *brownie*, etc.) from *hold*, friendly, benevolent, kind: cf. F. *sage-femme*.]

howdy: see how-do-ye.

howe, how (haʊ, hou), *sb.* *Sc.* and *north. dial.* [Sc. repr. of ME. holl *sb.*: cf. Sc. *bow(e*, *know(e*, *pow*, *row(e*, *scrow*, = *boll*, *knoll*, *poll*, *roll*, *scroll*.]

†**1.** A hole. *Obs. rare.*

1375 Barbour *Bruce* xi. 153 Howis in haill clath sall be rent.

†**2.** The hold of a ship. *Obs.*

1513 Douglas *Æneis* v. xii. 33 The hait fyre consumis fast the how; Our all the schip discendis the peralus low. **1536** Bellenden *Cron. Scot.* (1821) II. 52 The voce wes hard of ane woman, in the how of the schip. **1570** *Henry's Wallace* x. 825 Her is men off mar waill To saill thi schip; tharfor in how [*c* **1470** holl] thow ga.

3. A hollow place or depression; esp. a hollow on the surface of the earth, a basin or valley.

Frequent in place-names in Scotland, as *Habbie's How*, *the Howe of the Mearns*, *of the Merse*, etc.

1585 Jas. I *Ess. Poesie* (Arb.) 70 Thy thundring voice sone made them flie Ower hiddeous hills and howes. **1596** Dalrymple tr. *Leslie's Hist. Scot.* vi. 320 Donald now lyand vndir how in the Hilandis. **1724** Ramsay *Tea-t. Misc.* (1733) I. 90 Gibbie That won in the how of the hill. **1795** Burns *On Destr. Drumlanrig Woods* 3, I.. traced its bonie howes and haughs, Where linties sang and lambkins play'd. **1886** Stevenson *Kidnapped* xxii, We sat down.. in a howe of the hill-side till the mist should have risen. **1893** *Northumbld. Gloss.*, *How*, a hollow, a depression. The *how* of the neck.

b. The depth or middle (of winter, night, etc.).

1818 Hogg *Brownie of B.* I. 9 (Jam.) Ye ken fu' weel, gudeman, ye courtit me i' the howe o' the night yoursel'. **1825** Jamieson, *How o' Winter*, the middle or depth of winter. **1849** C. Bronte *Shirley* xxxii, Laid down in their hall in the 'howe of the night'. *Mod. Sc.* In the howe o' the year.

howe, how (haʊ, hou), *a.*[1] (*adv.*) *Sc.* and *north. dial.* Also **hou, hough.** [Sc. form of holl *a.*: see howe *sb.*] Hollow, concave; deep, low. In quot. 1536 ***how tide*** = low tide.

c **1450** Henryson *Test. Cres.* 157 His ene drowpit, how, sonkin in his heid. *a* **1500** P. Johnston *Thre Deid Powis* iii, Full laithly thus sall ly thy lusty heid, Holkit and how. **1536** *Reg. Mag. Sig.* 1513–1546 No. 1598 Descendentes ad aquam de Annand, et ab aqua de Annand ad aquam de Edin in lie howtide. **1552** Lyndesay *Monarche* 5491 Crepand furth of howe Cauernis. **16..** *Confess.* in Glanvill *Sadducismus* (1726) 393 (Jam.) The black man's voice was hough and goustie. **1828** *Craven Dial.*, *How gait*, a hollow gait or way. *Ibid.*, *How-rush*, a hollow rush. **1893** *Northumbld. Gloss.*, *How*, *hough*, *hogh*, hollow, deep.. *How-drill*, the hollow between two drills in a field.

b. *Comb.*, as ***how(e)-backed*** adj.

1786 Burns *To auld mare* i, Tho' thou's howe-backit.. an' knaggie. **1893** *Northumbld. Gloss.* s.v. *How*, *How-backt*, sunken in the back.

c. *adv.*

1535 Stewart *Cron. Scot.* II. 395 Ane grit horne, that borit wes all throw, Quhair[in] tha spak richt hideuslie and how. **1785** Burns *Death & Dr. Hornbook* ix, It spak right howe—'My name is Death'.

Hence **howness**, hollowness, concavity, depth.

a **1605** Montgomerie *Flyting w. Polwart* 417 Be the hight of the heauens, and be the hownesse of hell.

†**howe,** *a.*[2] *Obs.* Forms: 1 **hoȝa,** 3–4 ***hoȝe,** 4 **howe.** [OE. *hoȝa*, f. root of how *sb.*[1], *v.*[1]] Prudent.

a **950** *Durham Ritual* (Surtees) 105/1 Hoȝa bilwitnise [*prudens modestia*]. *c* **950** *Lindisf. Gosp.* Matt. xxiv. 45 Hwa .. is ȝeleafful þeȝn and hoȝa? *c* **1330** *Arth. & Merl.* 38 The howe wiif anon it fett.

howe, obs. f. hove, how, hue, owe.

howeid: see hoy *v.*

Howeitat (həʊweɪ'tɑːt). Also **Haueytat, Howeïtat, Huwaitat, Huweitat.** [Arab. (*al-*) *Huwaytāt*, Arab tribes in north-western Saudi Arabia.] **A.** *sb.* (A member of) a Bedouin tribe of northern Saudi Arabia. **B.** *adj.* Of or pertaining to this people.

a **1817** J. L. Burckhardt *Notes on Bedouins* (1831) I. 29 El Haueytat.. are about three hundred horsemen, but can furnish a large body of armed camel-drivers... In seasons of drought the Haueytat approach Gaza or Hebron. **1838** J. R. Wellsted *Trav. Arabia* II. ix. 167 The Howeïtát Bedowins occupy the coast from Magnah to Jebel 'Antar. **1917** T. E. Lawrence *Let.* 10 July (1938) 225 Sherif Nasir stayed in Kaf to enrol Rualla, Shererat and Huweitat for the Akaba expedition. **1926** —— *Seven Pillars* (1935) iii. xxx. 173 With his [*sc.* Feisal's] northern neighbours, the coastal Howeitat, he had already made a beginning. **1957** H. St. J. Philby *Forty Years in Wilderness* v. 99 The tribes mentioned were Huwaitat.. and some others.

howel ('haʊəl), *sb.* [prob. of LG. derivation: cf. MHG. *hovel*, *hobel*, Ger. *hobel*, dial. *hofel*, MLG. *hövel*, Da. *hövl*, Sw. *hyfvel* a plane.] A plane with a convex sole, used by coopers for smoothing the insides of casks, etc.

1846 Worcester cites Proctor. **1864** in Webster. **1875** in Knight *Dict. Mech.* I. 1138.

howel ('haʊəl), *v.* [f. prec.: cf. Ger. *hobeln*, Da. *hövle*, Sw. *hyfla* to plane, smooth, polish.] *trans.* To plane or smooth with a howel.

1864 in Webster. **1883** *Fisheries Exhib. Catal.* 83 Machine for chiming, crozing and howelling casks.

hower(e, obs. forms of hour.

howes, -ys, howse, var. of hoise, *v.*, to hoist.

c **1515** *Cocke Lorell's B.* (Percy Soc.) 12 Some howysed the mayne sayle. *Ibid.*, Some to howes the tope sayle dyde entre.

however (haʊ'ɛvə(r)); contr. **howe'er** (haʊ'ɛə(r)), *adv.* [f. how *adv.* + ever *adv.* 8 e.

In senses 2 and 3, *however* is the relic of an original subordinate clause (like those of sense 1), such as 'however this may be'.]

1. Introducing a subordinate clause, sometimes with *yet* in the principal clause:

a. qualifying a verb: In whatever manner, by whatever means.

c **1380** Wyclif *Wks.* (1880) 330 Hou-euer antecrist glauer, he letteþ not god to do his wille. *a* **1440** *Sir Degrev.* 864, I shal juste with that duke, Or I gete a rebuke, How ever that hyt be! **1605** Shaks. *Macb.* iv. i. 51, I coniure you.. (How ere you come to know it) answer me. **1709** Addison *Tatler* No. 119 ¶1, I am still in Doubt, whether it passed in my sleeping or waking Thoughts. However it was, I fancied that my good Genius stood at my Bed's-Head. **1875** Jowett *Plato* (ed. 2) I. 213 Men of Chios, Thurii, or however and whatever you call yourselves.

b. qualifying an adj. (or pa. pple.) or adv.: To whatever extent. Hence often used ellipt. with an adj. or adv. alone.

c **1400** *Apol. Loll.* 7 A bodily þing of how euer litil price howiþ not to be bout, but wiþ þis wisdam. *c* **1586** C'tess Pembroke *Ps.* lxxvi. iv, The most ragefull.. thou, how ever furious Shalt oft restraine. **1605** Shaks. *Lear* ii. i. 118, I shall serue you Sir truely, how euer else. **1707** Freind *Peterborow's Cond. Sp.* 230 He wou'd yet endeavour, however our circumstances seem'd desperate, to secure the kingdom of Valencia. **1766** Goldsm. *Vic. W.* vi, However dark the habitation of the mole to our eyes, yet the animal itself finds the apartment sufficiently lightsome. **1845** M. Pattison *Ess.* (1889) I. 25 His innocence, however manifest, could not save him. **1885** *Times* 25 May 9 Trawlers will, of course, protest against any interference, however slight.

c. However much; notwithstanding that; although. *Obs.* or *arch.*

1591 Spenser *Teares Muses* 523 How ever yet they mee despise and spight, I feede on sweet contentment of my thought. **1605** Shaks. *Lear* iv. ii. 67 Howe'er thou art a fiend, A woman's shape doth shield thee. **1690** Locke *Hum. Und.* ii. viii. §3 The Idea of Black is no less positive in his Mind, than that of White, however the Cause of that Colour in the external Object may be only a Privation. **1751** Johnson *Rambler* No. 175 ¶4 However those who have passed through half the life of man, may now wonder [etc.]. **1846** Trench *Huls. Lect.* Ser. ii. iii. 189 Humanity, however it craved a God for its deliverer, yet craved just as earnestly a man.

†**2.** In any case, at all events, at any rate. *Obs.* (Now merged in 3.)

1591 Shaks. *Two Gent.* i. i. 34 If hap'ly won, perhaps a haplesse gaine; If lost, why then a grieuous labour won; How euer: but a folly bought with wit. *a* **1616** Beaum. & Fl. *Bonduca* v. iii, A child that must have died however. **1736** Butler *Anal.* i. iv. 109 Till we know the Whole, or, however, much more of the Case. **1790** Paley *Horæ Paul.* Rom. i. 11 At the same time with, or soon however following, the contribution.. made in Achaia.

3. Qualifying a sentence or clause as a whole: For all that, nevertheless, notwithstanding; yet; = *but* at the beginning of the sentence.

1613 Shaks. *Hen. VIII*, iv. i. 106 All the Land knowes that: How euer, yet there is no great breach. **1671** Milton *Samson* 601, I, however, Must not omit a father's timely care. **1766** Goldsm. *Vic. W.* x, This curiosity of theirs, however, was attended with very serious effects. **1790** Burke *Fr. Rev.* 27 However, they did not think such bold changes within their commission. **1861** M. Pattison *Ess.* (1889) I. 47 It has been even said that this church was built by the Germans, which however was not the case. **1865** Lubbock *Preh. Times* 19 Bronze arrows, however, are not very common in Northern Europe.

†**4.** In any way whatsoever; at all. *Obs.*

1673 Marvell *Reh. Transp.* II. 139 All Laws however are but Probationers of time. **1740** J. Clarke *Educ. Youth* (ed. 3) 60, I cannot but be much of Mr. Locke's Mind with respect to versifying however.

5. Interrogative (and conjunctive): How, in any circumstances or way whatever? (See ever *adv.* 8 d.) *colloq.*

[**1607** R. C. tr. *Estienne's World Wonders* 240, I shal desire him to consider how ever it was possible.] **1871** B. Taylor *Faust* (1875) I. xiii. 147 However is it, such A man can think and know so much? *Mod.* However do you manage that?

6. Used by itself, or followed by points of suspension, as an interjection, or as a formula concluding, introducing, or modifying an utterance in some contextual way.

1876 Geo. Eliot *Dan. Der.* II. iv. xxxii. 319, I have not yet written a word... And I told the girls to leave it to me. However! **1901** Beerbohm *Variety of Things* (1928) 217 [I] doubt whether my creative power in caricature can be quite so strong as I had supposed. However... **1936** 'N. Blake' *Thou Shell of Death* viii. 137 Comes of givin' a vote to every hayseed and short-weight grocer in the —— However, hrrumph, where was I? **1964** D. Warner *Death of Dreamer* i. i. 9 We don't want to know where the stuff comes from but where it goes *to.* However!.. **1966** I. Jefferies *House Surgeon* i. 11, I.. said, 'However. Not to interrupt what you were asking me.' **1968** M. Woodhouse *Rock Baby* vii. 66 'Our component reliability was very high indeed during trials. However.' 'Go on,' I said.

howff (haʊf, hɒʊf). *Sc.* Also **houf(f, howf, hauf.** [Known from 16th c.: origin uncertain.

Howff is the name of the chief burial ground at Dundee, originally the garden or orchard of the Franciscan Friary, which was granted to the town as a burial ground by Queen Mary on 11 Sept. 1564, and was also for more than two centuries the meeting-place of the Trades. The name *Houf* appears as early as 1565, but it is not certain whether this arose from its use as 'a place of resort', or was the orig. name, connected with Du. and Ger. *hof*, court, yard. In the latter case the general Scotch use has to be accounted for.

1565 (Apr. 13) *Burgh Recds.* in Maxwell *Old Dundee* 179 Ordainit that what person that ever beis apprehendit louping in our the dykes of the Houf sal pay.. eight shillings. **1884** Maxwell *Hist. Old Dundee* 208 In 1611 the word was adopted in the Council register, and the gathering place of the crafts is subsequently denominated 'the Howff' instead of 'the common burial'.]

A place of resort; a haunt, a resort.

1711 Ramsay *Maggy Johnstoun* vii, When we were weary'd at the gowff, Then Maggy Johnstoun's was our howff. **1776** C. Keith *Farmer's Ha'* in Chambers *Pop. Hum. Scot. Poems* (1862) 34 This is the houff of ane and a'. **1796** Burns *Lett. to Thomson* Apr. Wks. (Globe) 562 The Globe Tavern here.. for these many years has been my howff. **1813** Hogg *Queen's Wake, Kilmeny* xxiv, The corby left her houf in the rock. **1862** Burton *Bk. Hunter* (1863) 60 Those who frequented this howf, being generally elderly men. **1950** *John o' London's* 24 Nov. 617/1 He was just seventeen .., when he began to haunt the howffs (drinking-places) of Edinburgh's underworld. **1957** Clark & Pyatt *Mountaineering in Brit.* ii. xi. 196 The crags were still relatively inaccessible—in spite of the use of boat and motor-car in conjunction with tents, howffs, or bivouacs.

Hence **howff** *v. intr.*, to have one's haunt.

1808–18 Jamieson, *To houff*, to take shelter. **1818** Scott *Hrt. Midl.* xvii, Where was't that Robertson and you were used to howff thegither?

howfing. *Sc.* 'A clumsy, awkward, senseless person' (Jam.). Also *attrib.*

1500–20 Dunbar *Poems* lxxv. 24 My new spanit howffing [*Bannatyne MS.* howphyn] fra the sowk. **1583** *Leg. Bp. St. Androis* 586 Alace! that Scotland had no schame, To send sic howfing carles from hame! **1871** W. Alexander *Johnny Gibb* xii, That aul', greedy, sneeshinie howffin.

† **'howful, houghful,** *a. Obs.* Forms: 1 **hoȝful,** 1–3 **hohful,** 3 **hoȝhefull, houhful, howful;** see also hoful. [OE. *hoȝful*, f. *hoȝu* thought, care, how *sb.*^{1} + -ful.] Careful; anxious, sorrowful.

970 in Thorpe *Dipl. Angl. Ævi Sax.* 240 Hohful embe ðæt hu ic his lof araere. *a* **1050** *Liber Scintill.* ix. (1889) 43 Æmtiȝ wamb & gyrla hohfull. *c* **1200** Ormin 8953 Ne þatt me birrþ beon hoȝhefull Abutenn hise þingess. *a* **1250** *Owl & Night.* 1292 Þe nihtegale sat and sihte And hohful was.

Hence † **howfully** *adv.*, carefully, anxiously.

1565 T. Stapleton *Fortr. Faith* 6 What is more howfully to be sought for, more charely to be kept?

† **howgate, -s,** *adv. Obs.* [f. how *adv.* + gate *sb.*^{2} 'way' (with genitival *-s*).] In direct and indirect questions: In what way; how.

a **1300** *Cursor M.* 6547 (Cott.) Hugat dele yee now? *Ibid.* 7118 Noght he did þam vnderstand Hugat [*v. rr.* hougat, howgate] he þat hony faand. **1375** Barbour *Bruce* ii. 156 And tauld him..als how-gate The Clyffurd held his heritage. *c* **1375** *Sc. Leg. Saints, George* 587 Þane dacyane wist nocht hou-gat To do.

β. *a* **1300** *Cursor M.* 5589 (Gött.), I sal tell you..hougatis he cam first in place. *c* **1440** *York Myst.* xxvi. 227 Howe gates bought schall he be? **1570** Levins *Manip.* 39/45 Hoggates, how? *quomodo*? Howgates, *idem*.

howge, obs. f. huge.

how(g)h, obs. ff. hough.

howghe, obs. f. how *adv.*

how go, obs. f. hogo.

howgozit (haʊ'gəʊzɪt). *Aeronaut.* orig. *U.S.* [Corruption of *how goes it?* (see how *adv.* 2 a).] A graph which essentially represents the amount of fuel remaining in an aircraft in relation to that needed to complete a journey or return to the point of departure. Also *attrib.*

1941 *Jrnl. R. Aeronaut. Soc.* XLV. 308 The 'Howgozit Curve' was developed by our ocean captains... Its purpose is to present..a continuous flow of information as to the fuel reserve remaining aboard the aircraft and the fuel required for completion of the flight to destination, or back to the point of departure. **1945** H. E. Benham *Aerial Navigation* iv. 92 In flight the actual progress of the aircraft..is plotted on the 'howgozit' for comparison with the forecasted data. The slope of the actual progress line as compared with the forecasted line and its tendency toward destination or dry tanks provides a vivid picture of the flight's progress. **1960** *Aeroplane* XCVIII. 98/2 An auto-landing indicator..will provide 'howgozit' information about the progress of the final approach.

howine, -yn, obs. ff. *hoven*, pa. pple. of heave.

† **howish** ('haʊɪʃ), *a. colloq. Obs.* [f. how *adv.* + -ish.] Perh. short for the earlier ***I-don't-know-howish, how-howish***: Having a vague sense of illness or indisposition; 'all-overish'.

1694 Dryden *Love Triumph.* v. Wks. 1884 VIII. 462, I am —I know not howish. **1708** Motteux *Rabelais* iv. lxiii. (1737) 257 We were..off the Hinges, and I don't know howish. **1746** in *Leisure Hour* (1880) 119 He is a little how-howish to-day, occasioned by a merry-making. **1787** *Minor* 39 [She] feels, as she says, quite howish and vapourish. **1802** Beddoes *Hygëia* viii. 47 Cachectic, or, as some familiar writer terms it, I don't-know-howish.

† **howitz, haubitz.** *Obs.* Forms: *α.* 8 **hau-, hawbitz, hob(b)its.** *β.* 7 **howitts,** 8 **hau-, howitz.** [a. Ger. *haubitze*, in 15th c. *haufnitz, haufenitz*, ad. Boh. *houfnice* stone-sling, catapult. (Introduced into German during the Hussite wars.) From the Ger., also 17th c. It. *obiza, obice*, F. *obus* bomb-shell.] = next. (Usually with pl. the same as the sing.: cf. cannon *sb.*^{1} 2 b.)

α. **1700** S. L. tr. *Fryke's Voy. E. Ind.* 61 Small Vessels which fetch'd us some Haubitzes (which is a kind of Field-Piece to load with small Shot). **1709** *Lond. Gaz.* No. 4590/3 Haubitz for sixteen Pound Ball, two. **1710** J. Harris *Lex. Techn.* II, *Hobits* are a sort of small Mortars from 6 to 8 Inches Diameter. Their Carriages are like those of Guns, only much shorter. **1729** Shelvocke *Artillery* v. 377 Little Hobbits charged with the various kinds of Fire-Balls. **1743–5** Tindal *Contin. Rapin* xxvi. i. (1745) III. 562 Sixty two cannon, eight mortars and hawbitz.

β. **1687** J. Richards *Jrnl. Siege Buda* 17 These Howitts are mounted on Carriages somwhat resembling those of Cannon. **1709** *Lond. Gaz.* No. 4556/2 Forty Mortars, and sixty Hauwitz. **1781** in Sparks *Corr. Amer. Rev.* (1853) III. 488 Two field-pieces, some howitz, and perhaps a mortar.

howitzer ('haʊɪtsə(r)). Forms: *α.* 8 **hau-, haw-, hobitzer.** *β.* 7 **hauwitzer,** 8 **hawitzer,** 8– **howitzer.** [A deriv. of prec.; the same suffix appears in Du. *houwitser* (in 1663 *houvietser*), Fr. *obusier* for earlier *obus* (see Hatz.-Darm.).] A short piece of ordnance, usually of light weight, specially designed for the horizontal firing of shells with small charges, and adapted for use in a mountainous country.

α. **1703** *Lond. Gaz.* No. 3941/2 A Battery of two Mortars and 4 Haubitzers. **1736** Lediard *Life Marlborough* III. 138, 12 Hawbitzers, or little Mortars. **1760** *Hist. Europe* in *Ann. Reg.* 14/1 The signal.. was given by four hawbitzers fired in the air.

β. **1695** *Lond. Gaz.* No. 3106/3, 40 Mortars and Hauwitzers. **1704** *Ibid.* No. 4059/3, 2 Hawitzers, and 100 Hand-Mortars. **1812** *Examiner* 14 Sept. 581/1 We drove the enemy from..the town by howitzers. **1884** J. Colborne *Hicks Pasha* 158 At each corner..were placed..the rifled howitzers.

† **b.** The shell thrown by this piece of ordnance.

1761 *Brit. Mag.* II. 442 A..body of Russians..had begun to throw some howitzers into that town, with an intention to set the magazines on fire.

c. *Comb.*, as ***howitzer-boat*** (cf. *gunboat*).

1801 Nelson 15 Aug. in Nicolas *Disp.* (1845) IV. 463 Captain Coun who commands the Division of Howitzer-Boats..is to open his fire from the Howitzers upon the batteries and camp. **1844** W. Siborne *Waterloo* I. x. 386 (Stanf.) Major Bull's British howitzer horse-battery.

howk, obs. f. hook; var. form of holk.

howk, *v.*: see holk, howk *v.*

howker, var. hooker^{2}, a sailing vessel.

howl (haʊl), *v.* Forms: (? 3 **hulen**), 4–6 **houle,** (5 **whoule**), 5–7 **howle,** (6 **owle**), 6– **howl.** [ME. ?*hulen, houlen* = MDu. *hûlen*, Du. *huilen*, MHG. *hûlen, hiulen*, Ger. *heulen*: of echoic origin. Cf. Gr. *ὑλάειν*, L. *ululāre*, It. *urlare*, OF. *uller, urler*, F. *hurler* to howl.]

1. *intr.* To utter a prolonged, loud, and doleful cry, in which the sound of *u* (*ū*) prevails. Said of dogs, wolves, and various wild animals; formerly also of the owl (now said to *screech* or *hoot*).

1390 Gower *Conf.* II. 265 The horned oule The which men here on nightes houle. *c* **1440** *Promp. Parv.* 250/1 Howlyn as beestys, *ululo*. **1484** Caxton *Fables of Æsop* v. xii, The dogges herd the voys [of the wulf] wherfore they beganne to barke and to howle. **1549–62** Sternhold & H. *Ps.* lix. (1566) 139 As houndes they houle and grenne. **1613** Purchas *Pilgrimage* (1614) 741 They heard Dogges howle on the shore. *c* **1705** Berkeley *Cave Dunmore* Wks. 1871 IV. 507 Two or three dogs..set themselves to howl with all their might. **1842** Prichard *Nat. Hist. Man* 36 Like other uncultivated breeds of dogs they only howl.

2. Of a human being: To utter a similar sound; to utter loud and doleful inarticulate cries; to wail, lament, esp. with pain. In modern use often somewhat contemptuously applied to any cry of pain or distress.

(Quot. 1220 is very uncertain; the word may be corrupt.)

[*c* **1220** *Bestiary* 396 Man hire [ðe fox] hatieð, hatien and hulen boðe men and fules.] *c* **1386** Chaucer *Knt.'s T.* 1959 Shrighte Emelye and howleth Palamon. *c* **1450** tr. *De Imitatione* i. xxiv. 33 Þe enviouse shul whoule for sorowe as wode houndes. **1526** Tindale *Jas.* v. 1 Goo to nowe ye Ryche men. Wepe and howle on youre wretchednes that shall come apon you. **1597** Shaks. *2 Hen. IV*, ii. iv. 374 There is another Indictment vpon thee..for the which I thinke thou wilt howle. **1682** N. O. *Boileau's Lutrin* ii. 140 My Angry Ghost shall haunt thy Conscious Soul, I'le Ring thee such a Peal, shall make thee Howl. **1805** Scott *Let. to Ballantyne* 12 Apr. in *Lockhart*, He still howls about the expense of printing, but I think we shall finally settle. **1885** *L'pool Daily Post* 7 May 4/9 Under these circumstances it will do the Conservatives very little good to howl.

b. ***howl at, howl upon***, to assail or address with howling. With *indirect pass.*

1647 A. Ross *Myst. Poet.* viii. (1675) 152 She [Hecate] was howled or called upon in the night by her Priests.

c. *trans.* To drive *into* a state by howling. ***howl down***, to reduce to silence by howls of obloquy.

1872 Bagehot *Physics & Pol.* (1876) 164 Any one who hears anything he does not like, tries to howl it down. **1885** *Manch. Exam.* 20 May 4/7 Mr. Gladstone was almost howled down in attempting to reply. **1892** *Argosy* Oct. 315 They have whirled or howled themselves into a mad delirium.

3. *trans.* To utter with howling. Also ***howl out***.

1530 Tindale *Expos. & Notes* (1849) 286 But the blind owls care not what they howl, seeing..that no man can spy them. **1605** Shaks. *Macb.* iv. iii. 194 But I haue words That would be howl'd out in the desert ayre, Where hearing should not latch them. **1613** Purchas *Pilgrimage* (1614) 307 Singing, or rather howling certaine Psalmes or Prayers. **1700** T. Brown tr. *Fresny's Amusem. Ser. & Com.* 21 And Howls out, Buy my Flawnders. **1816** J. Wilson *City of Plague* ii. iii. 198 To howl my dying curses in his ear.

4. *intr.* Of inanimate agents, esp. the wind or a storm: to make a prolonged wailing noise. Of an organ: to cipher.

1687 [see howling *vbl. sb.* 1]. **1728** Pope *Dunc.* i. 35 Keen, hollow winds howl thro' the bleak recess, Emblem of Music caus'd by Emptiness. **1742** R. Blair *Grave* 32 The wind is up: hark! how it howls! **1819** Shelley *Prometh. Unb.* i. 434 How fearfully God's thunder howls behind! **1852** Seidel *Organ* 46 This is a very good contrivance..if one of the reed pipes should howl. **1875** J. H. Bennet *Winter Medit.* i. x. (ed. 5) 303 The wind was howling in the mountains. **1886** R. C. Leslie *Sea-painter's Log* 148 Dozens of great steamers go howling through the Downs every day.

5. (See quot.)

1704 J. Harris *Lex. Techn.* s.v., When the Foot-hooks of a Ship are scarfed into the Ground-Timbers, and boulted, and then the Plank laid on them up to the Orlop, the Carpenters say, they begin to make the Ship Howle.

howl (haʊl), *sb.* [f. howl *v.*]

1. a. The prolonged and mournful cry of a dog, wolf, etc., which dwells upon the vowel *u* or some kindred sound; the similar sound of the wind or other inanimate agent.

1605 Shaks. *Macb.* ii. i. 54 The Wolfe, Whose howle's his Watch. *c* **1605** Middleton *Witch* iii. iii, No howls of wolves, no yelps of hounds. **1724** Swift *Drapier's Lett.* iv. Wks. 1778 II. 412 The last howls of a dog dissected alive. **1814** Scott *Ld. of Isles* iii. xxvi, Till sung his midnight hymn the owl, Answer'd the dog-fox with his howl. **1865** Kingsley *Herew.* xiii, She expected him at every howl of the wind.

b. A howling noise produced in a loud-speaker as a result of electrical or acoustic feedback; howling.

1921 *Wireless World* 10 Dec. 568/1 Ear-splitting howls associated with valve reception. **1928** L. S. Palmer *Wireless Princ. & Pract.* x. 374 The typical 'howl' to which low-frequency amplifiers are subject. **1939** H. J. Hicks *Princ. & Pract. Radio Servicing* xiii. 228 If the resistance-capacity filter in the a.v.c. line loses its effectiveness, a howl will result. **1962** E. E. Ecklund *Repairing Home Audio Systems* xiii, 246 Rumble, feedback, and howl are caused by mechanical vibrations being transmitted to the pickup.

2. A loud wail or outcry of pain or anguish; a savage yell of rage or disappointment. (Often used contemptuously.)

1599 Shaks. *Hen. V*, iii. iii. 39 Your naked Infants spitted vpon Pykes, Whiles the mad Mothers, with their howles confus'd, Doe breake the Clouds. **1697** Dryden *Eneid* vii. 527 She..fills with horrid howls the publick place. **1776** Twiss *Tour Irel.* 131 The Irish howl, which was made by the bellowing of a herd of men, women, and children, who attended the burial. **1833** L. Ritchie *Wand. by Loire* 100 Foulque uttered a howl of despair. **1858** Bright *Sp. Glasgow* 21 Dec. (1868) 307/2 You remember the howl of astonishment which arose. **1862** Ld. Brougham *Brit. Const.* App. ii. 421 His sufferings are exacerbated by the howl of popular execration or scorn.

howl, -e, var. holl.

† **howle.** *Obs.* A variant of owl, perh. influenced by howlet or by howl *v.*

c **1430** Lydg. *Chorle & Byrde* in *Min. Poems* (1840) 192 As goode an howle as a popingaye. **1500–20** Dunbar *Poems* xxxiii. 74 Wend he had bene the hornit howle.

howler ('haʊlə(r)). [f. howl *v.* + -er^{1}.]

1. a. An animal that howls.

1859 Thomson *Land & Bk.* i. viii. (1872) 94 To be torn ..and dragged about by these hideous howlers [jackals].

b. In full, ***howler monkey***. A South American monkey of the genus *Alouatta*.

1800 G. Shaw *Gen. Zool.* I. i. 72 The Allouates, or Howlers, inhabit the moist forests, in the neighbourhood of waters and marshes. **1840** *Penny Cycl.* XVI. 37/1 The species are, as the name [Mycetes] implies, Howlers, and the horrible yells sent forth by these animals..are described.. as surpassingly distressing and unearthly. **1865** *Reader* No. 121. 457/1 Numerous spider-monkeys, the red howlers. **1879** *Cassell's Techn. Educ.* i. 5 The chief monkey-furs imported are those obtained from the howlers. **1906** E. Ingersoll *Life Anim.: Mammals* 43 The howlers, arguatos, or alluates are the largest and most powerful of South American apes and the dullest, and are peculiar in having no thumb or only a rudimentary one, and in having the hyoid bones in the throat (of the males only) widely enlarged and cavernous, so as to form a curious hollow organ, by which their voice is so increased as to be audible two miles. **1932** S. Zuckerman *Soc. Life Monkeys* xi. 192 The well-known howler monkeys (genus *Alouatta*) of the forests of the northern half of South America are usually found in small parties. **1958** J. Carew *Black Midas* ii. 26 A big white devil does sit on a treetop roarin' like a howler baboon. **1964** *Listener* 5 Nov. 710/2 Fighting is rare in wild gibbons and apparently absent in wild howler monkeys. **1967** S. A. Altmann *Social Communication among Primates* xvii, 329 Other groups of howlers avoid areas from which such calls come.

2. a. A person hired to wail at a funeral or the bedside of the dying. **b.** A wassailer (see quot. 1875). *dial.*

1844 Kinglake *Eothen* xviii. (1878) 249 The funerals.. are attended by howlers. **1875** *Sussex Gloss.*, *Howlers*, boys who in former times went round wassailing the orchards. **1883** *Pall Mall G.* 25 July 2/1 When a man was dying (if his means allowed) professional howlers were employed.

3. *slang.* Something 'crying', 'clamant', or excessive; *spec.* a glaring blunder, esp. in an examination, etc. Cf. howling *ppl. a.* 3.

1872 W. F. Butler *Gt. Lone Land* xix. (1878) 300 If the hood was fastened down by frozen breath to the opening, then it must be a howler outside. **1875** *Punch* 2 Oct. 136/1 John..having come a howler over the Leger, is stumped. **1882** H. C. Merivale *Faucit of B.* II. ii. ii. 161 He's gone no end of a howler on the turf since. **1890** *Athenæum* 1 Mar. 275/1 In no examination papers..has any examiner met with more monstrous 'howlers' than crowd these pages. **1894** *Month* Apr. 464 The specimens of schoolboy blunders which, under the head of 'Howlers', are so popular in our journals.

† **4.** *Telephony.* A device (used by the exchange) for producing a howling noise in a receiver in order to attract the subscriber's attention. *Obs.*

1886 *Jrnl. Soc. Telegr. Engin.* XV. 322 We supply what we call a 'howler', and whenever a subscriber leaves his tubes hanging this howler is at once put on. **1917** G. D. Shepardson *Telephone Apparatus* viii. 137 For reminding

careless subscribers who neglect even to hang up the receiver..the operator..may send out a strong current of comparatively high frequency from the 'howler'.

howlet ('haʊlɪt, *Sc.* 'hulət). *dial.* Forms: 5 howlott, -lat, 6- **howlet**. (Also 6 hulet, 7 houlet, 9 *dial.* hoolet, hulote, hullat, -et, ullet.) See also OWLET. [app. a. F. *hulotte*, in 16th c. *hulote*, a word of diminutive form, of which the stem appears to be the same as in Ger. *eule*, MLG. *ûle*, perh. altered under the influence of *huer* to hoot: cf. the synonym *huette*.] An owl, owlet.

c **1450** HOLLAND *Howlat* 48, I sawe ane Howlat, in haist, vndir ane holyne. *c* **1450** *Cov. Myst.* (Shaks. Soc.) 179 Do howlott howtyn hoberd and heyn, Whan here barnys blede undyr credyl bende. **1513** DOUGLAS *Æneis* XII. xiii. 168 Quhilk we a litil howlet cleip, or owle. **1549** CHEKE *Hurt Sedit.* (1641) 5 Why, be yee Howlets and Bats, that yee cannot look on the light? **1570** LEVINS *Manip.* 88/15 An Hulet or oule, *vlula.* **1601** HOLLAND *Pliny* I. 156 Eies they haue red like the houlets. **1684** BUNYAN *Pilgr.* II. 189, I am also as poor as a Howlet. **1820** SCOTT *Ivanhoe* xxvii, That St. Withold's of Burton is a howlet's nest worth the harrying. **1828** *Craven Dial., Hullet, Hullat*, an owl.

howliglasse, obs. var. of OWL-GLASS.

howling ('haʊlɪŋ), *vbl. sb.* [f. HOWL *v.* + -ING[1].]

1. a. The uttering of a prolonged wailing cry, as by the dog, wolf, or other animal; the production of a similar sound by the wind or other inanimate agent; the ciphering of an organ.

c **1440** *Promp. Parv.* 250/1 Howlynge of doggys. **1495** *Trevisa's Barth. De P.R.* XVIII. xxv. (W. de W.), Ticius Sabinus hounde..abode wyth the deed body wyth dolefull and sorowfull noyse and howlynge [*Bodl. MS.* ȝelling]. **1598** HAKLUYT *Voy.* I. 400 Two or three hundred foxes, which make a marueilous wawling or howling. **1687** A. LOVELL tr. *Thevenot's Trav.* I. 2 The Isle of Stromboli..I was told that they who were near it heard great howlings, which proceed not from Hell..but from the violence of the Winds. **1735** SOMERVILLE *Chase* IV. 225 His Tail incurv'd He drops, and with harsh broken Howlings rends The poison-tainted Air. **1852** SEIDEL *Organ* 45 To remedy the so-called *howling* or *sounding-on* of certain pipes, when their respective keys are not pressed down. **1875** [see CIPHERING *vbl. sb.* 3].

b. The emission of howls (HOWL *sb.* 1 b) by a loud-speaker; undesirable feedback at audio frequencies in an amplifier.

1920 *Radio Rev.* Apr. 356 The resistance R_3 and condenser C_3 connected to the grid of the selected valve are increased in value until maximum amplification is obtained without 'howling'. **1939** H. J. HICKS *Princ. & Pract. Radio Servicing* xiii. 228 Open by-pass condensers across any of the tube elements..will often cause howling. **1953** J. E. HAINES *Automatic Control of Heating* xiv. 340 The variation exhibits a definite rhythm—in a manner analogous to the howling of a telephone when the sound waves from the receiver are fed back to the transmitter. **1966** *McGraw-Hill Encycl. Sci & Technol.* I. 520/2 Suppression of the low frequencies..in rooms that are excessively reverberant..increases the intelligibility of the speech and reduces the possibility of acoustic feedback (howling).

2. A prolonged wailing outcry of human beings.

c **1489** CAXTON *Blanchardyn* xliii. 169 Grete crye, noyse, and houlyng made the sarasyns. **1592** SHAKS. *Rom. & Jul.* III. iii. 48 Banished? O Frier, the damned vse that word in hell: Howlings attends it. **1665** SIR T. HERBERT *Trav.* (1677) 257 But for the greater solemnity, for seven dayes a general howling..was made. **1725** DE FOE *Voy. round World* (1840) 87 A sad lamentation and howling. **1887** A. MÜLLER in *Encycl. Brit.* XXII. 663/1 The insane howlings *hu hu* ('he, he')..practised by the 'howling' Rifâ'iya [Dervishes].

'howling, *ppl. a.* [f. as prec. + -ING[2].]

1. That howls; that utters or produces a prolonged wailing sound. Spec. ***howling baboon, monkey*** = HOWLER 1 b.

a **1605** POLWART *Flyting w. Montgomerie* 195 Where howlring howlets aye doth hant. **1668** H. MORE *Div. Dial.* III. xix. (1713) 217, I believe you mean the howling Quakers, as uncivil as they are. **1769** E. BANCROFT *Ess. Nat. Hist. Guiana* ii. 133 The Howling Baboons, as they are here called, seem to be the animals which are here described by Marcgrave, and which are called by the natives of Brasil, Guereba. *Ibid.* 135 There is another Monkey, somewhat larger than the howling Monkey, which is covered with long reddish hair. **1802** [see MONKEY *sb.* 1 b]. **1839** T. BEALE *Sperm Whale* 285 Peals of thunder..followed by a howling blast of wind. **1847** CARPENTER *Zool.* §159 The Myceti, or Howling Monkeys. **1863** H. W. BATES *Naturalist on River Amazons* I. ii. 72 Morning and evening the howling monkeys make a most fearful and harrowing noise. **1877** [see DERVISH]. **1887** J. G. WOOD *Illustr. Nat. Hist. for Young People* 15 The Howling Monkeys are larger and not so agile as the Spider Monkeys. **1924** C. W. DOMVILLE-FIFE *Among Wild Tribes of Amazons* viii. 121 On reaching camp..in the half light it was just possible to see the huddled and impaled body of a furry guaribas, or howling monkey (*simia mycetes*). **1959** *Jrnl. Mammalogy* XL. 317 (*title*) Field observations on a howling monkey society.

2. Characterized by, or filled with, howling, as of wild beasts or of the wind; dreary. In the Biblical ***howling wilderness***, and derived phrases, the word tends to become merely intensive.

1611 BIBLE *Deut.* xxxii. 10 He found him in a desert land, and in the waste howling wildernesse. **1696** tr. *Du Mont's Voy. Levant* 222 The very Sight of those howling Desarts deterr me. **1728-46** THOMSON *Spring* 13 His blasts obey, and quit the howling hill. **1847** EMERSON *Poems, Monadnoc* Wks. (Bohn) I. 435 Fit the bleak and howling place For gardens of a finer race. **1848** DICKENS *Dombey* iv. (C. D. ed.) 22 Going regularly aloft to bed..in a howling garret remote from the lodgers. **1857** THOREAU *Maine W.* (1894) 300 Generally speaking, a howling wilderness does not howl; it is the imagination of the traveler that does the howling.

3. *fig.* (chiefly *slang.*) Glaring, very pronounced, 'screaming': cf. HOWLER 3. Also, extreme, great (*colloq.*).

1865 SALA in *Daily Tel.* 25 Nov. 6/6 To risk a very vulgar phrase, a Nawab is 'a howling swell' in the East. **1884** *Nonconf. & Indep.* 7 Aug. 766/3 Those mistakes which are sometimes called 'howling' blunders. **1884** 'MARK TWAIN' *Huck. Finn* xliii. 437 Le's all three slide out of here, one of these nights, and get an outfit, and go for howling adventures amongst the Injuns. **1908** *Magnet* I. 1, 'You howling ass!' shouted Bulstrode. ' I tell you he's busted my two-guinea camera.' **1933** *Times Lit. Suppl.* 27 Apr. 283/4 If his book is not a big, a very big, a 'howling' success..but I need offer no 'if's'.

4. As *adv.* In the highest degree. (Cf. *screamingly.*) *colloq.*

1895 *Century Mag.* Sept. 678/2 It's howling lonesome at the Mule Deer. **1899** KIPLING *Stalky & Co.* 45 He'll be howling drunk to-night. **1928** *Sat. Even. Post* 4 Feb. 100/4 Glad! You're howling right I'm glad.

Hence **'howlingly** *adv.*

1593 NASHE *Christs T.* (1613) 52 The Owle on the house-top, euer-more howlingly, cals for some Corse.

howlite ('haʊlaɪt). *Min.* [f. the name of Henry *How* (d. 1879), mineralogist of Nova Scotia, who first described it: see -LITE.] A hydrated calcium borosilicate, $Ca_2B_5SiO_9(OH)_5$, that typically occurs as white nodules forming compact structureless masses resembling unglazed porcelain.

1868 J. D. DANA *Syst. Min.* (ed. 5) 598 *Howlite.* Silico-borocalcite *H. How*... 1868. Howlite *Dana.* In small rounded imbedded nodules. Texture compact, without cleavage; also chalk-like or earthy. **1917** *Amer. Mineralogist* II. 1 Not all fine grained, compact hydrous calcium borate is priceite; a number of such specimens from California localities..have been examined microscopically and all proved to be howlite. **1957** *Ibid.* XLII. 521 The mineral howlite, $H_5Ca_2SiB_5O_{14}$, has been recorded from a number of localities in California and elsewhere..and microscopic crystals have been described.., but in general the mineral is massive and very fine granular.

howlk, -e, obs. ff. HULK.

howlsom, var. HOLSOM.

howm, Sc. f. HOLM[1].

†**howne**, *sb.* or ? *a. Obs. rare.* (Meaning unknown.)

c **1374** CHAUCER *Troylus* IV. 182 (210) But Antenor, he shal com hom to towne, And she shal out; þus seyden here and howne [*MS. Gg.* 4. 27 hounne].

hownyd, obs. f. HONEYED.

howp, obs. f. HOOP, Sc. f. HOPE.

howr(e, obs. ff. HOUR, OUR, WHORE.

hows(e, howsel, obs. ff. HOUSE, HOUSEL.

howsband, obs. f. HUSBAND.

Howship ('haʊʃɪp). *Anat.* The name of John *Howship* (1781-1841), English surgeon, used in **Howship's lacuna** (earlier ***lacuna of Howship***): one of the numerous microscopic depressions or pits, irregular in shape and usually containing osteoclasts, that are found on the surface of bones and bony tissue where resorption is occurring.

1876 C. S. TOMES *Man. Dental Anat.* v. 175 Microscopic examination of the bone at this point shows that the lacunae of Howship..abundantly cover its surface. **1911** T. W. WIDDOWSON *Notes on Dental Anat.* viii. 44 Upon any part of the roots of the temporary teeth, undergoing absorption, cup-shaped depressions, Howship's lacunae, occur. **1970** J. M. VAUGHAN *Physiol. Bone* ii. 43 They [*sc.* osteoclasts] may be found closely applied to bone in Howship's lacunae.

howsoever (,haʊsəʊ'ɛvə(r)). *arch.* [f. HOW *adv.* + SO *adv.* + EVER *adv.* In the same sense the simple *how so* goes back to *c* 1200, *howsomever* to *c* 1300, and *howeger* to *c* 1400; *howsoever* appears to have been a later formation from *how so* or *however*, modelled on *howsomever*.]

1. In what manner soever; = HOWEVER 1. (Sometimes with ellipsis.) *arch.*

c **1430** *Pistell of Susan* 202 (MS. Cott. Calig.) We schulle present þe pleynte, how so euer þou be payde. **1534** ELYOT *Doctr. Princes* 4 Thei thinke it better..to liue in any other maner, how so ever it be. **1592** GREENE *Upst. Courtier* in *Harl. Misc.* (Malh.) II. 232 Howsoeuer right be, might carries away the verdict. **1741** MIDDLETON *Cicero* I. v. 349 Howsoever this may color, it cannot justify Cato's conduct. **1882-3** SCHAFF *Encycl. Relig. Knowl.* 547 As a mere rival to Rome, Constantinople has been of invaluable service to the Christian Church, howsoever her direct influence may be considered.

†**b.** Notwithstanding that, albeit; = HOWEVER 1 c. *Obs.*

1599 H. BUTTES *Dyets drie Dinner* I viij, It is a most.. innocent Animall, howsoever nature..hath armed it most magnificently. **1674** PLAYFORD *Skill Mus.* III. 1 The Parts of Musick are in all but four, howsoever some skilful Musicians have composed songs of twenty..parts.

2. With adj. or adv.: To what extent or in what degree soever. **a.** With tmesis: ***how...soever***.

1557 NORTH *Gueuara's Diall Pr.* (1619) 718/1 How great a friend or neere kinsman soeuer he be to them. **1588** SHAKS. *L.L.L.* I. i. 194 How low soeuer the matter, I hope in God for high words. **1647** CLARENDON *Hist. Reb.* I. §25 The Treaty..how well soever received, and how much soever desired by the King. **1769** ROBERTSON *Chas. V*, III. VIII. 105 [They] durst not refuse their consent, how unwilling soever to grant it. **1861** MAINE *Anc. Law* vii. (1876) 286 A right, how long soever neglected. **1874** CARPENTER *Ment. Phys.* I. vi. §2 (1879) 262 A summary expression of the entire process—how simple or how complex soever.

b. Also without tmesis.

1696 TATE & BRADY *Ps.* xc. 6 But howsoever fresh and fair. *a* **1751** BOLINGBROKE *Fragm.* (R.), Howsoever well instructed he might be in them himself and howsoever useful to government he might think them.

†**3.** In any case, at any rate: = HOWEVER 2. *Obs.*

1586 A. DAY *Eng. Secretary* I. (1625) 42 Die wheresoever and whensoever, yet howsoever honourably. **1590** SHAKS. *Mids. N.* V. i. 27 Something of great constancie; But howsoeuer, strange, and admirable. *a* **1613** OVERBURY *A Wife* (1638) 79 His boy is bound to admire him howsoever. **1663** *Flagellum, or O. Cromwell* (1672) 48 If the Scots as was hoped howsoever, would have proved honest.

†**4.** Nevertheless; yet: = HOWEVER 3. *Obs.*

1602 R. DOLMAN tr. *Primaudaye's Fr. Acad.* (1618) III. lx. 777 But howsoeuer, it is certaine that pilots..doe direct [etc.]. **1631** HEYWOOD *Eng. Eliz.* (1641) 83 It bred in her howsoever no small amazement. **1709** STRYPE *Ann. Ref.* I. xxxix. 404 But this passage, howsoever, was illy taken by some of the Oxonians.

howsomever (,haʊsə'mɛvə(r)), *adv.* Now *dial.* or *vulgar.* Also, *south. dial.* **howsomdever.** [A parallel formation to *howsoever*, of earlier appearance, with the conj. *sum, som* (= Da., Sw. *som*, ON. *sem* as, that) instead of *so.*]

†**1. a.** Introducing a subordinate clause: In whatever manner; = HOWEVER 1. **b.** Although; = HOWEVER 1 c. *Obs.*

a **1300** *Cursor M.* 2339 Nu at þe erth nu at þe lift, or hu sumeuer [*v.rr.* hou sum euir, how sim euer] þou will þe scift. *c* **1420** *Avow. Arth.* xxiv, Then to-gedur schulle we goe How-sumeuyr hit cheuis. *c* **1489** CAXTON *Sonnes of Aymon* x. 270 How somever the game gooth. **1560** DAUS tr. *Sleidane's Comm.* 297 How someuer the matter was. **1601** SHAKS. *All's Well* I. iii. 56 How somere their hearts are seuer'd in Religion, their heads are both one.

2. Nevertheless; yet: = HOWEVER 3. Now chiefly *U.S. colloq.*

1562 TURNER *Herbal* II. 70b, It is playn that he had Dioscorides howsomeuer. **1728** VANBR. & CIB. *Prov. Husb.* II. 27 But howsomdever, we'st ta' the best care we can. **1741** RICHARDSON *Pamela* (1824) I. 64 Howsomever, it will do you no good to make this known. **1822** SCOTT *Pirate* xxxiv, Howsomdever, I object nothing to Captain Cleveland. **1852** C. W. H[OSKINS] *Talpa* 135, I shall keep you to your promise, Sir, howsomever. **1861** HUGHES *Tom Brown at Oxf.* xliv, Howsumdever, as your countrymen say, I shall have a shy at him. **1896** 'M. RUTHERFORD' *Clara Hopgood* xxiii. 215 He allus begins to argue with me. Howsomever, arguing isn't everything. **1929** H. W. ODUM in A. Dundes *Mother Wit* (1973) 183 Howsomever, hard times in American camps whut I'm talkin' about. **1933** E. E. CUMMINGS *Let.* 26 May (1969) 123, I fear that naught will compare with domesticity, howsomeever. **1939** *Amer. Speech* XIV. 128 The great drive for 'correctness' of the later eighteenth and early nineteenth did succeed in branding as 'vulgarisms' such hitherto acceptable forms as ..*howsomever, mought, sarvent*, [etc.].

howsour, obs. f. HOUSER[2]; var. of HOUSSOUR. *Obs.*

†**howster**, *v. Obs. rare*$^{-1}$. ? To oust.

1642 ROGERS *Naaman* 348 Howster out such vermine (O ye Church officers, if ye serve for oughts) out of their kennells!

howt, obs. form of HOOT.

howtowdie (haʊ'taʊdɪ). *Sc.* Also **howtoudie, how-towdy.** ['Not recorded in O.Sc. but appar. O.Fr. *hétoudeau, estaudeau*, a fat young chicken for the pot' (*S.N.D.*).] A dish whose main ingredient is a chicken (see quot. 1951).

1728 A. RAMSAY *Poems* II. 230 They all, in an united Body, Declar'd it a fine fat How-towdy. **1759** E. CLELAND *New & Easy Method Cookery* (ed. 2) iv. 91 You may do Howtoudies, or any white Fowl, the same Way. **1901** *Daily Chron.* 17 Aug. 8 Howtowdie is another old Scotch dish. **1951** *Good Housek. Home Encycl.* 513/1 *Howtowdie*, a Scottish dish consisting of boiled chicken with poached eggs and spinach. **1970** SIMON & HOWE *Dict. Gastron.* 222/2 *Howtowdie*, Scots for pullet, possibly related to the old French *hutaudeau*... Eggs are poached in gravy or broth and placed around the bird on the carving dish, each on a pat of spinach.

howve: see HOVE.

howylle, obs. f. OWL.

howyne, Sc. f. *hovin*, obs. pa. pple. of HEAVE.

hox, hoxter, obs. ff. OX, HUCKSTER.

†**hox**, *sb. Obs. rare.* [app. shortened from a fuller form **hoxen* (retained in HOCKSHIN, *huckson*, HUXEN), repr. OE. *hóhsinu*, pl. *hóhsina*, HOUGH-SINEW, and corresp. to ON. *hásin*,

OFris. *hôxene*, *hoxne*, OHG. **hâhsina*, *hâhsna*, MDu. *haessene*, *haasen* (Kilian *haessen*), Du. *haassen*, *haasse*, *haas*, in Groningen *haoks*, in same sense. Cf. HOXEN *v.*

The final *-en* of **hox-en* may have been taken in ME. as a pl. ending (the OE. pl. *hôhsina* would give ME. **hoȝsin*, **hoxen*), and a sing. *hox* deduced from it (cf. CHICK).]

A hamstring.

c **1440** *Wyclif's Bible* 2 Sam. viii. 4 Dauid kitte the hoxes of alle the beestis drawynge.

†**hox**, *v.* *Obs.* or *dial.* Also 4 hoxe, 7–8 hocks. [Shortened from HOXEN *v.*, (?) under influence of HOX *sb.* Cf. Ger. dial. *hächsen*, *hessen*, *häsen* = Ger. *hechsnen*, in same sense.] *trans.* To hough, to hamstring.

1388 WYCLIF *Josh.* xi. 6 Thou schalt hoxe the horsis of hem. —— *1 Chron.* xviii. 4 He hoxide alle the horsis of charis [**1382** He kutte the knee senewis]. **1594** LYLY *Moth. Bomb.* III. iv. 113, I thrust my hand into my pocket for a knife, thinking to hox him. **1611** SHAKS. *Wint. T.* I. ii. 244 Thou art a Coward, Which hoxes honestie behind, restrayning From Course requir'd. **1699** DAMPIER *Voy.* II. ii. 97 Neither he nor any other Spaniard ever came hither afterward to hocks Cattle. **1718** *Entertainer* 280 They not only fired his Stacks of Corn and Hay, but hox'd and stabb'd his Cattel. **1756** FOOTE *Eng. fr. Paris* II. Wks. (1788) 35 Hocks the Heels.

Hence †**hoxing**, **hocksing** *vbl. sb.* (also *attrib.*); also †'**hockser**, one who houghs or hamstrings.

1598 MANWOOD *Forest Laws* xvi. §12. 100b, That..the old Forresters were wont to call *Hamling*, or *Hoxing*, and of some *Hocksynewing*. **1699** DAMPIER *Voy.* II. II. 97 The Hockser is mounted on a good Horse, bred up to the sport. *Ibid.*, His Arms is a Hocksing Iron, which is made in the shape of a Half Moon. *Ibid.* 98 The right Ear of the Hocksing-Horse, by the weight of the Pole..hangs down always.

†**hoxen**, *v.* *Obs. rare.* [f. **hoxen*, HOX *sb.*; corresp. to OHG. *hâhsinôn*, MHG. *hahsenen*, mod.G. *hächsnen*, *hechsnen*, MDu. *haessen-en*, *hesen-en* in same sense (f. OHG. **háhsina*, MDu. *haessene* hough-sinew).] *trans.* To hough, to hamstring; = HOUGH-SINEW *v.* (More frequently shortened to HOX *v.*, q.v.)

1387 TREVISA *Higden* (Rolls) VII. 139 Sche putte hir nurri ..for to fiȝte aȝenst þe accuser..whiche þoruȝ Goddes grace, þe hamme i-kut and hoxened, overcome þe accusour.

Hoxnian ('hɒksnɪən), *a.* [f. *Hoxne*, name of the village in Suffolk where the type site is situated: see -IAN.] Epithet of the second (penultimate) interglacial in Britain (identified with the Mindel-Riss interglacial of continental Europe), and of a stage of the middle Pleistocene; hence, of or contemporaneous with this interglacial or stage. Also *absol.* as *sb.*, the Hoxnian interglacial or the Hoxnian stage.

1956 WEST & DONNER in *Q. Jrnl. Geol. Soc.* (1957) CXII. 86 Hoxnian Interglacial. [*Note*] A general name suggested for this interglacial period. **1963** R. G. WEST in *Proc. Geologists' Assoc.* LXXIV. 171 Evidence for sea-levels during the Hoxnian Stage is summarized in Fig. 9. **1964** K. P. OAKLEY *Frameworks for dating Fossil Man* iii. 29 In Britain the silver fir (*Abies*) is absent from Cromerian diagrams, abundant in the Late Temperate phase of the Hoxnian. **1968** R. G. WEST *Pleistocene Geol. & Biol.* xii. 276 Often they are overlain by interglacial or Flandrian beach gravels, and..they are probably mostly Hoxnian or older. **1969** *Proc. Geol. Soc.* Aug. 152 It is recommended that for the Pleistocene and Holocene of the British Isles the following ages/stages be adopted as a regional scale... Pleistocene:..Wolstonian, Hoxnian, Anglian, Cromerian, [etc.]. **1970** *Phil. Trans. R. Soc.* B. CCLVII. 414 *Buxus* pollen has been found in the Hoxnian deposits at Birmingham. **1970** *Times* 10 Mar. 16/6 In the closing stage of the Hoxnian, the pine became the dominant forest tree.

Hoxtonian (hɒk'stəʊnɪən), *sb.* [f. *Hoxton*, the name of part of the borough of Shoreditch in London + -IAN.] A native or inhabitant of Hoxton; the variety of English spoken in Hoxton.

a **1935** T. E. LAWRENCE *Mint* (1950) II. xxii. 159 Adam and Eve on a raft (Hoxtonian for fried eggs on toast). **1935** G. INGRAM *Cockney Cavalcade* xii. 197 The West End—a place entirely foreign to most Hoxtonians.

hoy (hɔɪ), *sb.*[1] Also 6–7 **hoie, hoye,** 7 **hoigh, huy.** [app. ad. MDu. *hoei*, pl. *hoeyen* (Verwijs and Verdam), var. of *hoede*, *heude*, *huede*, mod.Du. †*heude*, *heu*, whence also obs. F. *heu* (Jal). Ulterior origin unknown.] 'A small vessel, usually rigged as a sloop, and employed in carrying passengers and goods, particularly in short distances on the sea-coast' (Smyth *Sailor's Word-bk.*).

1495 *Paston Lett.* No. 937 III. 388 An hoye of Dorderyght. **1497** *Naval Acc. Hen. VII* (1896) 95 An hoy of Andwarpe. **1562** *Act 5 Eliz.* c. 5 §9 English Hoys and Plats may cross the Seas as far as Caen. **1605** B. JONSON *Volpone* IV. i, Your Hoigh Carries but three men in her, and a boy. **1624** CAPT. SMITH *Virginia* VI. 228 Holland and Zeland.. hath..twenty thousand saile of Ships and Hoies. **1661** PEPYS *Diary* 16 June, To hire a Margate Hoy. *a* **1693** URQUHART *Rabelais* III. lii. 429 Crears..Huys, Catches, Capers, and other Vessels. **1794** *Rigging & Seamanship* I. 227 *Hoys and Lighters* are vessels with one mast, and sometimes a bowsprit; abaft the mast is a gaff-mainsail, before it a fore-sail, and a jib upon the bowsprit. **1806–7** J. BERESFORD *Miseries Hum. Life* (1826) XVIII. xxiii. 173 A coach as long and as crowded as the Margate Hoy. **1867** SMYTH *Sailor's Word-bk.* s.v., In the naval service there are gun-hoy, powder-hoy, provision-hoy, anchor-hoy, all rigged sloop-fashion.

†**b.** *jocularly.* A heavy or clumsy person. *Obs.*

1607 DEKKER & WEBSTER *North-w. Hoe* II. i, I heare trampling: 'tis my Flemish Hoy.

c. *Comb.* (See also HOYMAN.)

1612 DEKKER *If it be not good* Wks. 1873 III. 358 A whole Hoy-full are Landed. *a* **1618** RALEIGH *Observ.* in *Rem.* (1661) 167 They [the Dutch] have..Ships called Boyers, Hoybarks, Hoyes, and others. **1714** MANDEVILLE *Fab. Bees* (1725) I. 321 Low conversation in hoy-boats and stage-coaches. **1757** W. THOMPSON *R.N. Advoc.* 48 A Hoy Load of..Flags was sent.

hoy (hɔɪ), *int.* (*sb.*[2]) Also 6 **hoyghe,** 7– **hoi,** 8– **hoay.** [A natural exclamation.]

A. *int.* A cry used to call attention; also to incite or drive beasts, esp. hogs. In nautical language (also written *hoay*) used in hailing or calling aloft. (Cf. AHOY.)

1393 LANGL. *P. Pl.* C. IX. 123 And holpen to erie þis half acre with 'hoy! troly! lolly' [*A.* VII. 109 Hey! trolly-lolly! *B.* VI. 118 how! trolli-lolli!]. **1553** T. WILSON *Rhet.* (1580) 176 Wordes..derived from the nature of thynges. As..when one would seme galant, to crie hoigh, whereby also is declared courage. *a* **1605** MONTGOMERIE *Flyting w. Polwart* 121 Hoy, hurson, to hell. **1617** MINSHEU *Ductor*, *Hoi*, a word vsed in driuing hogges. **1620** BP. HALL *Hon. Mar. Clergy* II. ii. Wks. (1648) 721 Away nasty C. E. transformed by Circe! Hoy! back to her Styes, yea thine! **1769** FALCONER *Dict. Marine* s.v. *Holloa*, If the master intends to give any order to the people in the main-top, he calls, Main-top, hoay! To which they answer, Holloa! **1810** *Sporting Mag.* XXXV. 213 He hallooed, hoy, stop! **1862** TOTTEN *Naval Text Bk.* (N.Y.) 340 *Hoay*, an exclamation, to call attention, as 'Ship-hoay!'

B. as *sb.* **1.** A call of 'hoy!'

1641 BROME *Joviall Crew* IV. ii, Here's a Wedding with a witnesse, and a Holy-day with a hoigh. **1850** W. JAMIE *Stray Effus.* 76 The fisher's 'Hoy' was heard afar. **1865** DICKENS *Mut. Fr.* I. viii, I see your young man..chopping at the flies on the window-sill..and I give him a Hoy!

2. *Austral.* A gambling game, resembling lotto, in which playing-cards are used. Also *attrib.*

1965 *Courier-Mail* (Brisbane) 2 Mar. 15 A hoy evening which the Royal Society of St. George planned to hold at St. George House. **1969** *Ibid.* 25 Feb. 6/10 Juliet Jones couldn't object to a few games of hoy. **1969** *Sunday Mail* (Brisbane) 24 Aug. 3/3 Police said that bingo, or hoy, which was played in the same way, was illegal in Queensland. **1971** *Tel.* (Brisbane) 3 Nov. 4/2, I have been advised that the radio competition is above board, but have had no ruling on the game hoy.

hoy, *v.* [f. HOY *int.*]

1. *trans.* To urge on or incite with cries of 'hoy!'; to drive or convoy with shouts.

c **1536** LYNDESAY *Compl. Bagsche* 144, I gat none vther recompence Bot hoyit, & houndit of the toun. **1573** TUSSER *Husb.* lvii. (1878) 130 Hoy out (sir carter) the hog fro thy wheele. *c* **1590** D. MOYSIE *Mem. Affairs Scotl.* (1830) 37 He wes oppinlie onbeset by..rascalis of the toun, and howeid out of the toun by flinging of stones at him. *a* **1605** MONTGOMERIE *Dev. Poems* vi. 70 The hevy saulis ar had to hevin; The light, alace, ar hoyde to hell. **1785** BURNS *Halloween* xxiii, They hoy't out Will, wi' sair advice.

2. *intr.* To call 'hoy!'

1836–9 DICKENS *Sk. Boz, Mr. Watkins Tottle* ii, Quite hoarse with hoi-ing and imprecating.

hoy, obs. form of HUE.

‖**hoya** ('hɔɪə), *Bot.* [mod.Bot.L., from the name of Thomas Hoy, an English gardener (died 1821).] A large genus of climbing herbaceous plants (N.O. *Asclepiadaceæ*), bearing dense umbels of fleshy or waxen flowers, pink, white, or yellow; commonly known as *honey-plants*, *wax-plants*, or *wax-flowers*. They are natives of southern Asia, the Malay archipelago, and Australia, and are cultivated in greenhouses for their beauty.

[**1816** J. MAHER in *Trans. Hortic. Soc.* II. 197 (*heading*) On a remarkable property of the Hoya Carnosa.] **1851** *Illustr. Catal. Gt. Exhib.* 972 Hoya, or wax flower. **1881** MRS. C. PRAED *Policy & P.* I. 111 Native jessamine and waxen hoya shed their fragrance in the air. **1894** BLACKMORE *Perlycross* 446, I have almost spoiled that truss of Hoya.

hoybuck, corrupt form of HAUTBOY, HOBOY.

1588 PARKE tr. *Mendoza's Hist. China* (1854) II. 47 The instruments which they commonly do vse are hoybuckes, cornets, trompets, lutes.

hoyda, -day, obs. forms of HEY-DAY *int.*

†**hoyde.** *Obs.* Abbrev. of, or error for, HOYDEN.

1636 HEYWOOD *Love's Mistr.* II. Wks. 1874 V. 112 Harken oh you hoydes, and listen oh you Illiterates.

hoyden ('hɔɪdən), *sb.* (*a.*) Also 6–8 **hoydon,** 7–8 **hoidon,** 7–9 **hoiden.** [Found *c* 1600 (not in Shaks.); origin uncertain. ? Connected with HOIT *v.*

Skinner's conjectured derivation from Ger. and Du. *heide* heath, Du. *heiden*, in Kilian '*heyden*, homo agrestis et incultus', is perh. not impossible; but evidence is wanting.]

†**1.** A rude, ignorant, or awkward fellow; a clown, boor. *Obs.*

1593 NASHE *4 Lett. Confut.* 58 The hoyden and pointing stock of recreation of Trinitie hall. **1597** *1st Pt. Return fr. Parnass.* II. i. 833 I'le make every hoydon bestowe a fairinge on his dore, his wall, his windowe. *c* **1600** DAY *Begg. Bednall Gr.* II. ii. (1881) 40 A sort of Momes and Hoydons that know not chalke from cheese. **1611** COTGR., *Badault*, a foole, dolt, sot..gaping hoydon. **1645** MILTON *Colast.* Wks. (1851) 364 Shall I argue of conversation with this hoyd'n? **1708** MOTTEUX *Rabelais* IV. xlvi, The poor Devil..was made a common Laughing-Stock by the gaping Hoydons.

2. A rude, or ill-bred girl (or woman); a boisterous noisy girl, a romp.

1676 WYCHERLEY *Pl. Dealer* II. Wks. (Rtldg.) 113/2 Then Mrs. Hoyden, that calls all People by their surnames. **1706** PHILLIPS (ed. Kersey), *Hoidon*, a clownish ill-bred Wench. **1709** STEELE *Tatler* No. 13 ¶1 She was so ungainly in her Behaviour, and such a laughing Hoyden. **1744** MRS. DELANY in *Life & Corr.* 323 She is daughter to my lord Tyrone, such another slatternly ignorant hoyden I never saw. **1809** PINKNEY *Trav. France* 183 An elegant fashionable girl, and as far removed from a romp and a hoyden as it is possible to conceive. **1876** GREEN *Stray Stud.* 170 Hoydens covered with sand and seaweed.

B. *attrib.* or *adj.* Belonging to, of the character of, or resembling a hoyden; inelegant in deportment, roystering, hoydenish.

1728 YOUNG *Love Fame* v. 477 They throw their persons with a hoyden air Across the room, and toss into the chair. **1792** MARY WOLLSTONECR. *Rights Wom.* vii. 290 The jokes and hoiden tricks which knots of young women indulged themselves in. **1861** TULLOCH *Eng. Purit.* ii. 253 The wilful and hoyden blood of their mother.

Hence '**hoydenhood**, the condition of a hoyden; '**hoydenism**, the character or manners of a hoyden, hoydenishness.

1824 SCOTT *St. Ronan's* vi, In her maiden state of hoydenhood. **1886** MRS. HUNGERFORD *Green Pleas. & Grey Grief* I. iv. 71 A fatal tendency towards hoydenism.

'**hoyden**, *v.* [f. prec. sb.] *intr.* To play the hoyden. Hence **hoydening** *vbl. sb.* and *ppl. a.*

1709 *Brit. Apollo* II. No. 12. 3/1 A Strong dock'd Bucksome Quean, Who Hoidons over Parson's-Green. **1748** RICHARDSON *Clarissa* (1811) IV. 221 Did she never from girlhood to now, hoyden? **1758** GRAY *Let. to Stonhewer* in Mason *Mem.* (1807) II. 124 Primness and affectation.. has turned to hoydening and rude familiarity. **1806–7** J. BERESFORD *Mis. Hum. Life* (1826) v. xviii, Hoydening abbesses.

hoydenish ('hɔɪdənɪʃ), *a.* [f. as prec. + -ISH.] Having the character or manners of a hoyden; belonging to, or characteristic of a hoyden.

1780 MAD. D'ARBLAY *Diary* Apr., The young lady..half tonish, and half hoydenish. **1815** W. IRVING in *Life & Lett.* (1864) I. 343 Mrs. Mardyn..vulgar without humor, and hoydenish without real whim and vivacity. **1861** WHYTE MELVILLE *Good for Nothing* II. xlii. 195 Her somewhat hoydenish manner had acquired repose and dignity.

Hence '**hoydenishness**.

1858 MISS MULOCK *Th. ab. Wom.* 22 Tacitly suggestive of hoydenishness. **1863** HOLME LEE *A. Warleigh* III. 253 Her Mamma quite openly deplored her hoydenishness.

hoyes, obs. Sc. f. OYEZ.

hoyffer, obs. f. HEIFER.

hoyke, obs. f. HUKE.

†**hoyle**[1]. *Archery. Obs.* A mark made use of by archers when shooting at ROVERS.

1614 C. BROOKE *Ghost Rich. III*, F ivb, Gold sets vp markes, Hoyles, pricks for any Ayme. **1622** DRAYTON *Poly-olb.* xxvi. 334 [Robin Hood and his men] At long-buts, short, and hoyles, each one could cleave the pin. **1801** T. ROBERTS *Eng. Bowman* 226 *Hoyle.* **1845** *Anecd. Archery*, Glossary 388 *Hoyle*, a short moving mark.

Hence **hoyling** *vbl. sb.* or *ppl. a.*

1590 *Lanc. Wills* (Chetham Soc.) III. 68 My vewe bowe wth the redd handle and all my hoyling arrowes.

Hoyle[2] (hɔɪl). The name of Edmond *Hoyle* (1672–1769), author of several works on card-games (the earliest, on whist, dated 1742): often cited typically for an authority on card-playing. Phr. ***according to Hoyle***, according to the highest authority, in accordance with strict rules.

1906 'O. HENRY' *Four Million* (1916) 14 The financial loss of a dollar sixty-five, all so far fulfilled according to Hoyle. **1945** A. A. OSTROW *Compl. Card Player* p. vii, It has been the custom to call books of rules on card and board games 'Hoyles', so that 'according to Hoyle' has come to mean 'according to accepted rules'. **1962** R. BARKER *Clue for Murder* v. 38 This one [*sc.* murder]'s right out of the book —strictly according to Hoyle. **1965** J. M. CAIN *Magician's Wife* (1966) xix. 147, I want our marriage to be strictly on the beam—the way it is in the books, absolutely according to Hoyle. **1971** *Melody Maker* 21 Aug. 34/7 If everything goes according to Hoyle, I'll go into semi-retirement there.

hoylle, obs. north. form of WHOLE.

hoyman ('hɔɪmən). [f. HOY *sb.*[1] + MAN.] A man in charge of a hoy; the master of a hoy.

1666 PEPYS *Diary* 13 June, A hoyman's daughter. **1781** SIR W. JONES *Bailments* Wks. 1799 VI. 669 It soon became necessary for the Courts to declare, as they did in the reign of James I, that a common hoyman, like a common waggoner, is responsible for goods committed to his custody. **1885** *Law Times* LXXX. 128/2 The defendant was simply a hoyman, unprotected by bill of lading or charter-party.

hoyne, var. HONE *sb.* and *v.*; obs. Sc. f. OVEN.

hoys, obs. f. WHOSE.

hoys(e, hoyss, obs. ff. HOSE.

hoyst, rare obs. var. HOAST.

hoystings, obs. f. HUSTINGS.

hoystyr, obs. f. OYSTER.

hoyt, var. HOIT.

hoze, hozier, obs. ff. HOSE, HOSIER.

hr-, a frequent consonant combination in OE. [:—OTeut. *hr-*:—Aryan *kr-*]. In initial *hr-*, the *h* was lost in the transition to ME., in which and in modern Eng. the words begin with R: e.g. OE. *hræfn*, *hréod*, *hring*, *hróf*, *hrung*, *hrycg*, now RAVEN, REED, RING, ROOF, RUNG, RIDGE.

hsien, var. HIEN.

H-test: see H III.

hu, obs. f. HOW, HUE.

hua, obs. f. WHO.

huaca (ˈwɑːkə). [ad. Sp. *huacca*, *guaca*, from Quechua.] **a.** The name for the all-pervading spirit thought by the Peruvian Indians to be disseminated through the whole world; also, any material object thought to be the abode of such a spirit. **b.** A prehistoric Peruvian tomb or temple, usually a truncated pyramid of stone, and often of immense size.

1847 W. H. PRESCOTT *Hist. Conquest Peru* I. I. iii. 93 The subjects of the Incas enrolled among their inferior deities many objects in nature, as the elements,..great mountains and rivers... These consecrated objects were termed *huacas*,—a word of most prolific import; since it signified a temple, a tomb, any natural object remarkable for its size or shape, in short, a cloud of meanings. **1860** W. BOLLAERT *Antiquarian, Ethnol. Res. Chile* 161 A huaca was discovered, in 1830, at the entrance of the valley of Taparapacá; it was surrounded with stones. **1862** D. WILSON *Prehist. Man* I. ix. 298 The huacas or tombs of the Incas. **1875** *Encycl. Brit.* II. 452/2 The most interesting remains in Peru are those called *Huacas*; but whether they were forts, or palaces, or tombs, is not as yet clearly ascertained. **1901** A. H. KEANE *Central & S. Amer.* I. 208 Of these ruins the largest, as well as the most characteristic, are the truncated pyramids here [*sc.* Peru] called *huacas*, or burying-places. **1902** *Encycl. Brit.* XXV. 380/1 The most prolific source of Peruvian relics is the sepulchres or huacas. **1960** M. SAVILL tr. *Leicht's Pre-Inca Art & Culture* iv. 74 The ancestral worship in the land expressed itself most vividly in the veneration of the so-called Huacas, a word which signifies not only the large temples and pyramids but a host of small and insignificant objects sacred to the Indians.

huaco (ˈwɑːkəʊ). Also **guaco**. [See quot. 1931[1].] In Peru, Bolivia, and Chile, ancient pottery and other Indian antiquities.

1931 *Connoisseur* Feb. 95 The term *huaco* is derived from the Indian word, *huaca*, meaning 'a holy place', and refers to the cemeteries and tombs from which, with few exceptions, all the examples of pre-Incaic art are obtained. *Ibid.* 97 The linear decoration of the stirrup *huacos* tend [*sic*] to portray some form of action... In the static *huacos* the legs are almost invariably crossed. **1933** *Burlington Mag.* Aug. p. xii (Advt.), The pottery includes six rare Huacos from Paracas, with green colouring. **1959** G. WOODCOCK *Incas & Other Men* IV. iv. 229 The Mochica pots—..called *huacos* by the modern Peruvians—were made specifically as grave furniture, intended to hold food and chicha for the dead.

huam, obs. f. WHOM.

huanaco, var. GUANACO.

huarache (waˈrɑːtʃiː). Also **guaracha, guarache, guarachi, huaracho**. [Mex.-Sp.] A leather-thonged sandal, orig. worn by Mexican Indians.

1887 F. C. GOOCH *Face to Face with Mexicans* xii. 433 Leathern aprons and sandals of the same, called *guarachi*. **1892** *Dialect Notes* I. 190 *Huaracho, -s*, a kind of sandals worn by Indians and the lower classes generally. Used generally in the plural only. **1909** *Cent. Dict.* Suppl., Guaracha. **1926** D. H. LAWRENCE *Plumed Serp.* viii. 130 The dark feet in the glare of the torch looked almost black, in huaraches that had red thongs. **1928** *Funk's Stand. Dict.*, *Guaracha*, a Mexican-Indian sandal. **1943** *N. & Q.* 24 Apr. 262/1 The Mexican Indian uses a leather-thonged sandal, which he calls guarache. **1957** J. KEROUAC *On Road* (1958) I. ii. 13 My shoes..were Mexican huaraches, plantlike sieves not fit for the rainy night of America. **1963** C. BEALS *Latin Amer.* (1964) i. 11 *Guarache* sandals shuffled like a storm of autumn leaves.

huas, obs. f. WHOSE.

Huastec (ˈwɑːstɛk). Also **Huasteca, Huastek, Huaxtec, Huaxteca**. [ad. Sp. *huasteco*, *huaxteco*.] **a.** An Indian people inhabiting parts of Mexico; a member of this people. **b.** The language of the Huastecs.

1845 *Trans. Amer. Ethnol. Soc.* I. 4 A comparison of near three hundred words of the Mexican, Otomi, and Huasteca, exhibits but very few, and perhaps accidental, coincidences. **1875** H. H. BANCROFT *Native Races Pacific States* I. vi. 674 The Huastecs, Huaxtecs, Guastecs, or Cuextecas inhabit portions of the states of Vera Cruz and Tamaulipas. **1914** T. A. JOYCE *Mexican Archæol.* vii. 196 The presence of a spout distinguishes Huaxtec pottery from Mexican. **1931** T. GANN in Gann & Thompson *Hist. Maya* i. 11 The Huaxtecas..were evidently a section of the people left behind in their old home. **1946** S. G. MORLEY *Anc. Maya* iii. 39 The Maya-speaking, Maya-appearing Huasteca never shared with the Maya of the Yucatan Peninsula the latter's unique culture. **1948** D. DIRINGER *Alphabet* I. vii. 123 The Huastec..already separated from the main stock in ancient times. **1955** *Amer. Speech* XXX. 126 Huastek.

hub[1] (hʌb). Forms: 6 hubbe, 8 hubb, 7– hub. [Origin unascertained.

Skeat would identify with HOB *sb.*[2] If the various senses belong to the same word, the common notion would appear to be 'boss', '(rounded) protuberance'.]

†**1.** The HOB of a fire-place. *Obs.*

1511, 1600, *a* **1825** [see HOB *sb.*[2] 1].

2. a. The central solid part of a wheel from which the spokes radiate, and which rotates on (or with) the axle; the nave.

Although used by Blithe in 1649, and (from him) by several 17th c. writers, and in Bradley's *Fam. Dict.* 1725 (s.v. *Elm*), this word appears to have been merely dialectal, being unrecognized by the Dictionaries till the 19th c., when it appears first in the American Webster (1828) and Worcester (1846). It has received literary currency mainly from O. W. Holmes, and has recently become generally known in connexion with bicycles. Forby gives under *hob, hub* (besides the entry cited below) the alleged meaning 'the hilt or guard of a weapon', with which he connects ***up to the hub***, 'as far as possible'; this phrase is in American use associated with the hub of a wheel, as implying 'deeply, to a great extent, inextricably involved'.

1649 BLITHE *Eng. Improv. Impr.* (1652) 167 [The Elm] the best wood in England, for Wheelwrights Nathes or Hubs for wheels. **1675** GREW *Anat. Plants* (1682) 287 The particles ..of Salt stick in them, as the Spokes do in the Hub of a Wheel, or as the Quills in the Skin of a Porcupine. **1800** *Aurora* (Philadelphia) 23 May (Th.), 'This is not a half measure—I like to do things by the lump—and this bill you will allow is up to the hub.' Those who are acquainted with the slang language of the American Caucuses will be able to explain what is meant by up to the hub. **1815** D. HUMPHREYS *Yankey in Eng.* 33 I've bin up to the hub, and didn't flinch..nor won't back out now. *a* **1825** FORBY *Voc. E. Anglia, Hob, Hub*, the nave of a wheel. **1828** WEBSTER, *Hob, hub*, the nave of a wheel (citing Washington). **1831** in *Harper's Mag.* (1884) July 277/1 [They] talked..of being 'up to the hub'..for General Jackson. **1854** CAROLINE THOMAS *Formingdale* 81 The mud's up to the hubs in some spots. **1870** *Eng. Mech.* 7 Jan. 414/1, I do not..see what prevents the whole head, sails, hub, tail and all from being blown..off [the windmill]. **1882** *Bazaar Exch. & M.* 15 Feb. 174 Spokes, rim, and hub are all one. **1897** *Westm. Gaz.* 22 Nov. 7/3 It..prevents the back wheel from getting out of line, as so frequently happens with most of the hubs now in use.

†**b.** The centre or boss of a target; *fig.* a mark.

a **1657** R. LOVEDAY *Lett.* (1663) 221 The Proverb says, The blind man sometimes hits a Crow; but *ad januam virtutis excubant labor & sudor*; and that's the hubbe I aim at.

3. *transf.* and *fig.* That which occupies a position analogous to the hub of a wheel; a central point of revolution, activity, life, interest, etc.

Applied to Boston, U.S., and playfully to other places.

1858 O. W. HOLMES *Aut. Breakf.-t.* vi, Boston State-House is the hub of the solar system. You couldn't pry that out of a Boston man, if you had the tire of all creation straightened out for a crow-bar. **1863** KINGSLEY *Water-Bab.* viii. 299 Next he came to the centre of creation (the *hub*, they call it there), which lies in latitude 42·21 south, and longitude 108·56 east. **1869** *Boston Herald* Dec. (Farmer), He is to have a quintette club of amateurs with him, from the Hub. **1876** *Daily News* 18 Jan. (Farmer), Calcutta swaggers as if it were the hub of the universe. **1884** J. COLBORNE *Hicks Pasha* 9 This is the hub, so to speak, of what Canon Farrar calls the three great volcanic centres of religion—Sinai, Jerusalem, and Mecca. **1894** *Westm. Gaz.* 19 Oct. 3/2 This idea is the hub of the piece. **1897** *Strand Mag.* Sept. 293/2 The spider..sits unconcerned but watchful in the centre or hub of her snare.

4. Technical and local uses:

a. *Die-sinking.* A cylindrical piece of steel on which the design for a coin is engraved in relief. **b.** *Plumbing.* A short piece of pipe with a bell at each end, used for joining pipes in line or at an angle. **c.** An abruptly raised piece of ground, a stumbling-block. **d.** A thick sod. **e.** A block for stopping the wheel of a vehicle. **f.** A small stack of hay (*Craven Dial.* 1828).

a. 1851 *Illustr. Catal. Gt. Exhib.* 628 The making of a 'hub' or copy of the die in steel..used for the correction of duplicate copies of the die. **1875** KNIGHT *Dict. Mech.*, *Hub* ..2. (*Die-sinking.*) After hardening, the hub is used to make matrixes, from which are made punches which impress the dies used in coining. **1879** H. PHILLIPS *Addit. Notes Coins* 1 Upon the hub the portrait is cut in alto relievo by a machine.

c. 1669 BUNYAN *Holy City* (ed. Offor) III. 421 There shall be a smooth face upon the whole earth, all..hubs, and hills, and holes, shall now be taken away. **1828** *Craven Dial.*, *Hub*, an uneven piece of ground in a wood. **1864** WEBSTER, *Hub*.. a rough protuberance or projecting obstruction; as, a hub in the road (*U.S.*).

d. 1828 *Craven Dial.*, *Hub*, a thick square sod, pared off the surface of a peat bog, when digging for peats. This is sometimes dried for fuel, but it is inferior to the peat.

e. 1856 S. C. BREES *Gloss. Terms, Hub*, a block of wood of great service upon railways, and employed to stop the wheels of carriages.

5. *attrib.* and *Comb.*, as (sense 1) *hub-end*; (sense 2) *hub-borer*, *-flange*, *-sprocket*, etc.; ***hub-deep*** adj., adv.; **hub-band**, a metal band to reinforce a wooden hub of a wheel; **hub brake**, a brake that acts on the hub of a (cycle) wheel; so **hub-braking**; **hub-cap**, a covering for the hub of a wheel of a vehicle.

1851 *Illustr. Catal. Gt. Exhib.* 1458 The rims of the *hub-bands represent a wreath in silver. **1895** *Cassell's Techn. Educ.* V. 199/1 Bronze hub-bands with speech-holes were used by the Romans. **1883** H. STURMEY *Tricyclists' Indispensable Ann.* (ed. 3) 94 There are three great classes of brakes now in use, viz.:—Tyre, ground, and *hub brakes. **1936** F. J. CAMM *Every Cyclist's Handbk.* xvii. 108 The cyclist should..take great care to prevent oil entering the shell of a hub brake. **1973** *Sci. Amer.* Mar. 90/2 Two other types of brake made their appearance later. One is the coaster brake, or back-pedaling brake, which is particularly popular in the U.S. The other is the hub brake, or drum brake, of the type used in automobiles and motorcycles. **1909** *Daily Chron.* 20 Mar. 8/5 It combines hand control and *hub braking. **1913** *Collier's* 11 Jan. II. 7/1 Their wheels, perhaps, have plain *hub caps. **1954** A. HUXLEY *Let.* 5 Dec. (1969) 716 One would like to find out..why..so many cubists..used forms which are identical with those obtained by photographing reflections in curved surfaces. Did the suggestion actually come from hub caps and the backs of spoons? **1957** L. DURRELL *Justine* 27 The great silver Rolls with the daffodil hub-caps. **1959** *Times* 9 Jan. 12/6, I looked forward to removing the hub-cap. **1972** J. BROWN *Chancer* xiv. 188 You name it, we found it. All this and neat little packets of H. in the hub-caps. **1897** H. PORTER *Campaigning with Grant* xxvi. 415 The mud was nearly *hub-deep. **1870** *Swaledale Gloss.*, *Hub-end, the hob at the end of a fire-place. **1875** KNIGHT *Dict. Mech.* s.v., The inner ends of the spokes are secured in a mortised flange-ring, between which and the *hub-flanges are anti-friction rollers. **1895** *Daily News* 23 Nov. 3/6 These studs..play no part in driving the enlarged *hub-sprocket, at which point they run smoothly over an inner grooved pulley.

Hence (with ref. to Boston, U.S.: see 3, quot. 1858) **ˈHubbite, Huˈbbopolis, Huˈbbopolite**, etc. *nonce-words.*

1868 W. BOYD in *Cambridge* (Mass.) *Press*, Expressive as the face of a Hubbopolitan graduate-maiden. **1877** *Congregationalist* (U.S.) 28 Apr. (Cent.), As wide awake as a veritable New Englander, and as a native-born Hubbite.

hub[2]. A playful abbreviation of *husband*: cf. HUBBY.

1812 COMBE *Picturesque* IX, All that's passing, and has past, Since your dear Hub beheld it last. *a* **1845** HOOD *Clubs* i, My female friends they all agree They hardly know their hubs.

hub a dub. [Echoic. Cf. *dub-a-dub*, *rub-a-dub*.] The noise made by the beating of a drum.

1777 MAD. D'ARBLAY *Early Diary* 7 Apr., There was an immense hub a dub, with drums and trumpets..to proclaim his approach.

hubara, var. HOUBARA.

hubbaboo: see HUBBUBOO.

hubba-hubba (ˈhʌbəˈhʌbə), *int.* *U.S. slang.* Also **haba-haba**. [Origin unknown.] Used to express approval, excitement, or enthusiasm. Also as *sb.*, nonsense; ballyhoo.

1944 in *Amer. Speech* (1947) XXII. 35 The inevitable fact is that the cry 'Haba-Haba' is spreading like a scourge through the land. **1945** *Amer. Speech* XX. 261 *Hubba-hubba*, originally gibberish, now means the spirit of double-time and eagerness; it is a verb, adjective or noun, an imprecation, warning or insult. **1946** 'S. STERLING' *Where there's Smoke* iv. 36, I suppose you think that's a lot of hubba-hubba. **1970** C. MAJOR *Dict. Afro-Amer. Slang* 68 *Hubba hubba*, expression of approval.

Hubbard (ˈhʌbəd). Chiefly *N. Amer.* In full, ***Hubbard squash***: a variety of *Cucurbita maxima* yielding large green or yellow fruits.

1868 *Mich. Agric. Rep.* VII. 349 Thos. Smith, Hamtramck [exhibited] 8 Hubbard squashes. **1898** E. N. WESTCOTT *David Harum* xxiii, Turnips, Hubbard squash, succotash. **1921** *Daily Colonist* (Victoria, B.C.) 20 Oct. 7/4 Hubbard Squash, today's selling per lb. 4c. **1925** *Brit. Weekly* 26 Feb. 520/5 It was truly an old-fashioned Thanksgiving dinner. We had..celery, onions, and hubbard squash. **1963** J. ORGAN *Gourds* xii. 121 *C. maxima* is best represented in commerce by such popular varieties as the Hubbards, Boston Marrow and Delicious. **1971** *Rand Daily Mail* 27 Mar. 22/2 Hubbard Squash (sugar pockets). Good demand. 140 c to 200 c.

hubber de hoy, obs. var. HOBBLEDEHOY.

Hubble (hʌb(ə)l). *Astr.* The name of Edwin P. *Hubble* (1889–1953), U.S. astronomer, used in the possessive and *attrib.* to designate concepts arising out of his work, as **Hubble('s) constant** (or †**factor**), the ratio of the recessional speed of a galaxy to its distance, usu. expressed in km. per second per megaparsec; also, the reciprocal of this, usu. expressed in years and capable of being interpreted as the time that has elapsed since the galaxies first began to recede (at constant speeds) from a single point; **Hubble('s) law**, the red shifts of the spectra of distant galaxies (and hence their speeds of recession) are proportional, on average, to their distances.

1933 *Monthly Notices R. Astron. Soc.* XCIV. 159 We can consider a possible extension of Hubble's Law, and it will be seen that this may lead to a method for determining the cosmical constant and the sign of curvature in the generally accepted form of space-time. **1938** *Physical Rev.* LIII. 207/1 We can also derive a relation between *f* and Hubble's factor *u*.... *u* is about 500 km per sec. per mega-parsec. or $1{\cdot}6 \times 10^{-17}$ sec.$^{-1}$. **1952** H. BONDI *Cosmol.* v. 39 The relation may be written $V = r/T$ where *T* is a constant.. depending..on the average intrinsic luminosity of a nebula. On this interpretation the radial velocity of a nebula is proportional to its distance... The reciprocal of the

constant T is known as Hubble's constant and may be evaluated to be about 540 km./sec./megaparsec. This value leads to $T = 1{\cdot}8 \times 10^9$ years. **1957** *Encycl. Brit.* VI. 502B/2 A better appreciation of the meaning of this number, H, which came to be called Hubble's constant, is given by its reciprocal $1/H$ = 5,400,000,000 years. **1971** D. W. Sciama *Mod. Cosmol.* iii. 45 (*caption*) The expansion of the Universe as seen from another galaxy. The recession velocity is still proportional to the distance. Thus Hubble's law does not favour the Milky Way. *Ibid.* 46 Hubble's constant is now believed to be about 10 million years. *Ibid.* 48 Any systematic evolution in the intrinsic properties of the galaxies would contribute to the observed deviation from the simple Hubble law. **1972** *Sci. Amer.* Feb. 41/2 The new value of the Hubble constant is 53 ± 5 kilometers per second per megaparsec, or almost exactly one-tenth of Hubble's original value. **1973** *Physics Bull.* Nov. 652/1 Present estimates of the Hubble constant yield a value of R/R in a range (1–2) × 10^{10} years.

hubble-bubble (ˈhʌb(ə)lbʌb(ə)l). [Redupl. from bubble, as suggestive of the sound.]

1. A rudimentary form of the oriental hookah in which the smoke bubbles through a coco-nut shell half-filled with water.

Also applied to similar pipes, made of clay, glass, silver, etc.

1634 Sir T. Herbert *Trav.* 24 They esteeme much of Tobacco, and drinke it in long canes or pipes, called *hubble bubbles*. **1697** in J. T. Wheeler *Madras in Old. Time* (1861) I. 318 Each of whom sent two bottles of Rose-water, and a glass Hubble-bubble, with a compliment. **1840** *New Monthly Mag.* LX. 59 The use of an hubble-bubble, which, for continuance and monotony, comes as near to human garrulity as can be expected of anything mechanical. **1879** R. H. Elliot *Written on Foreheads* I. 160 The hubble-bubble passed from mouth to mouth.

2. A representation of a bubbling sound; also of confused talk.

1740 Dyche & Pardon *Dict.* (ed. 3), *Hubble-Bubble*, a confused noise made by a talkative person, who speaks so quick, that it is difficult to understand what he says or means. **1815** *Edin. Rev.* XXV. 533 Reprinting the whole of that hubble-bubble of words. **1853** De Quincey *Autobiog. Sk.* Wks. I. 68 My brother's wrath had boiled over in such a hubble-bubble of epithets. **1885** Lady Brassey *The Trades* 290 There was a considerable roll and hubble-bubble of the tides as we rounded the point. **1892** J. Payn *Mod. Whittington* I. 33 The monotonous hubble-bubble of the instrument [the water-receptacle of the hookah].

†**3.** A piece of empty tattle. *Obs.*

1720 T. Gordon *Lett. Auth. Indep. Whig* in *Cordial for low Spirits* (1751) II. 62 We may very well rank it among one of the Dr.'s Hubble-Bubbles, and no one will deny him the amiable Character of a Publisher of Scandal.

4. Turmoil, confusion (Grose *Dict. Vulg. T.* 1796).

5. *attrib.*

1796 Grose *Dict. Vulg. T.* s.v., A hubble-bubble fellow; a man of confused ideas, or one thick of speech. **1827** Bentham *Wks.* (1838–43) X. 323 A very hubble-bubble, trumpery creature. **1851** *Illustr. Catal. Gt. Exhib.* 687 Figures of.. a hubble-bubble smoker, and a faquir. **1893** W. B. Harris *Journ. Yemen* ii. i. 149 A group of Arabs.. chatting over a hubble-bubble pipe.

hubbleshow, -shew, -shoo (ˈhʌb(ə)lʃaʊ, -ʃuː). *Sc.* and *north. Eng.* Also 6 **hoble-shew**, 8–9 **hobbleshow, -shaw**. [Etymology obscure.

The first element and the sense as a whole suggest those of early mod.Flem. *hobbel-tobbel* or *hobbel-sobbel*, explained by Kilian (1599) as 'tumultuously, confusedly, in an uproar, promiscuously', and *hobbelen-tobbelen* 'to be in an uproar, rouse a tumult'. *Hubble* is also given by Jamieson, as used in some parts of Scotland in the sense 'uproar, tumult'; but we have no evidence carrying this back to 1515, when *hubbilschow* is found.]

A tumult, disturbance, commotion, uproar, hubbub.

a **1515** *Interlud of Droichis* in *Dunbar's Poems* (1893) 314 Hiry, hary, hubbilschow! Se ȝe not quha is cum now. **1570** Levins *Manip.* 180/23 An Hubbleshowe, *tumultus*. **1573** *Satir. Poems Reform.* xlii. 754 Quhat hubbilschow thair maist haue bene For the displacing of ane Pastour. **1583** *Inquisition* in T. West *Antiq. Furness* xvii. (1805) 227 That no assaulte, nor hubleshow, be made, sub pena iiis. iiij*d*. **1725** Ramsay *Gentle Sheph.* v. i, That gars me think this hobleshew that's past Will end in nothing but a joke at last. **1820** *Blackw. Mag.* VII. 268 The coachman was so extortionate, that another hobbleshaw arose. **1824** Miss Ferrier *Inher.* xl, What a pleasant thing for a few friends to meet this way, instead of these great hubbleshews of people one sits down with now. **1893** *Northumbld. Gloss.*, *Hublyshew, -shoo*, a tumult, a crowd of disorderly persons.

†**hubble-shubble**. *Obs. rare.* = prec.

c **1550** *Doctour Doubble Ale* 178 in Hazl. *E.P.P.* III. 312 All was on a hubble shubble: There was drawing and dragging, There was lugging and latching.

hubbub (ˈhʌbʌb). Forms: 6 **hooboube, -boobe, hoeboube**, 6–7 **who-, hu-, hobub**, 7 **whoo-bub, whoopubb, hoobub, howbub, how-bub, hub hub**, 7– **hubbub**. [In 16th c. *hooboube, -boobe*, often referred to as an Irish outcry, and prob. representing some Irish expression. Cf. Gaelic *ub! ub! ubub!* an interj. of aversion or contempt; *abu!* the war-cry of the ancient Irish.

Connexion with *hoop, whoop*, has been suggested by Richardson; but this was app. only a later association.]

1. A confused noise of a multitude shouting or yelling; esp. the confused shouting of a battle-cry or 'hue and cry' by wild or savage races.

With *Irish hubbub* cf. hubbuboo. The Welsh hubbub seems to have been (see quot. 1645) a 'hue and cry' only.

1555 W. Watreman *Fardle Facions* i. vi. 103 Thei [Ichthiophagi of Afrike] flocke together to go drincke.. shouting as they go with an yrishe whobub. **1581** J. Bell *Haddon's Answ. Osor.* 326b, Mightier is the force of the Veritie.. then that it can be dasht out of countenaunce with Irishe hooboobbes. **1586** J. Hooker *Girald. Irel.* in *Holinshed* II. 156 According to the custome of the countrie, the hobub or the hue and crie was raised. **1590** Spenser *F.Q.* iii. x. 43 They heard a noyse of many bagpipes shrill, And shrieking hububs them approaching nere. **1600** W. Watson *Decachordon* ix. viii. (1602) 327 With hallowes and howbubs, with whowbes, whowes, and outcries against all. **1611** Shaks. *Wint. T.* iv. iv. 629 Had not the old-man come in with a Whoo-bub against his Daughter. **1612** T. James *Jesuits Downf.* 53 Hissed out the College with whouts and hobubs. *c* **1613** Spelman *Relat. Virginia* 24 in *Capt. J. Smith's Wks.* (Arb.) p. cv, A great number Indians.. began with an oulis and whoopubb. **1622** R. Hawkins *Voy. S. Sea* xxvii. 58 Wee.. gaue them the Hubbub, after the manner of the Indians, and assaulted them. **1645** *Mercurius Civicus* 28 Aug., Whereupon an hubbub is raised, and 5000 together by the next morning [in Glamorganshire]. **1667** Milton *P.L.* ii. 951 A universal hubbub wilde Of stunning sounds and voices all confus'd. **1680** *Life Edw. II* in *Harl. Misc.* I. 87 The bruit of this novelty, like a Welch hubbub, had quickly overtaken the willing ears of the displeased Commons. **1871** L. Stephen *Playgr. Europe* i. (1894) 19 There issued.. a confused hubbub as of human voices.

b. In milder sense: The mingled din of a crowd, or of a multitude of speakers heard at once.

1779 Mad. D'Arblay *Diary* Jan., I felt myself already in Drury Lane [Theatre], amidst the hubbub of a first night. **1849** Macaulay *Hist. Eng.* ix. II. 415 Its Exchange resounding with the endless hubbub of all the languages spoken by civilised men. **1878** Seeley *Stein* II. 451 The hubbub, so new in Prussia, of Parliamentary discussion.

2. Noisy turmoil; confusion, disturbance; an instance of this; a tumultuous assembly or demonstration; a riot, 'row'.

1619 Fletcher *M. Thomas* iv. ii, All the chambermaids in such a whobub. **1659** D. Pell *Impr. Sea* 181 *note*, Diogenes .. in his Tub, tumbled it up and down.. when the greatest, and best of Citizens were in an Hubbub and in Arms. **1682** Bunyan *Holy War* iii, They asked the reason of the hubbub and tumult. **1836** W. Irving *Astoria* II. 14 A sudden uproar and hubbub ensued that defies description. **1874** Miss Braddon *Taken at Flood* i. 15 The place will be in a fine hubbub, I suppose.

3. A name given by the New England colonists to a noisy game of the Indians.

It was played with a platter and five small bones, with loud cries of *hub, hub, hub*. See *N. & Q.* Ser. 7, III. 472.

1634 Wood *New Engl. Prospects* II. xiv. 85. **1760** T. Hutchinson *Hist. Mass. Bay* v. (ed. 2) 470 Another game they called hubbub, the same the French called jeu de plat, the game of the dish among the Hurons.

4. *attrib.* and *Comb.*

1646 *New Letanie* (B. M.), From Irish Rebells, and Welsh hubbub-men, From Independents and their Tubmen. **1868** Browning *Ring & Bk.* xi. 1193 There follows noise enough: from hubbub mouths.

Hence **hubbub** *v.*, **hubbubish** *a. nonce-wds.*

1812 H. & J. Smith *Rej. Addr.*, *Rebuilding*, Better remain by rubbish guarded, Than thus hubbubish groan placarded. **1831** *Blackw. Mag.* XXX. 881 Huddled and hubbubbed into one chaotic sentence.

hubbuboo, -aboo (ˈhʌbəˌbuː). Forms: 6 **hubba-, hubbobowe**, 9– **hubbub(b)oo, hub(b)aboo**; also 8 **ho-bo-bo-boo**, 9 **hubbubbubboo**. [App. of same origin as prec.: cf. Irish *abu!* the war-cry of the ancient Irish.] A confused crying or yelling; esp. as a savage war-cry; hence, a tumult, turmoil.

1596 Spenser *State Irel.* Wks. (Globe) 632/1 They come running with a terrible yell and hubbabowe, as yf heaven and earth would have gone together, which is the very image of the Irish hubbabowe, which theyr kerne use at theyr first encounter. *c* **1730** Burt *Lett. N. Scotl.* xxiii. (1754) II. 210 Every now and then [they] break out into a hideous Howl and Ho-bo-bo-boo. **1830** *Examiner* 353/1 The speech.. is like an Irish row.. It is a hubaboo, an affair of noise and blows. **1874** Lisle Carr *Jud. Gwynne* I. vii. 210 What a hubbuboo arose! **1892** E. Lawless *Grania* II. viii. 151 Och, Mary Queen of Heaven, but that was a hubbuboo!

hubby (ˈhʌbɪ), *sb.* [f. hub *sb.*² + -y: cf. *baby*.] A familiar colloquialism for husband.

1688 E. Ravenscroft *London Cuckolds* 28 Oh my hubby, dear, dear, dear hubby. **1798** Morton *Secr. worth knowing* Epil. (Farmer), The wife, poor thing.. Scarce knows again her lover in her hubby. **1803** *True Briton* in *Spirit Pub. Jrnls.* (1804) VII. 274 My dear Hubbey, this can't make me sick. **1887** *Pall Mall G.* 23 July 11 In disputes between a hubby and his better half.

hubby, *a. U.S.* [f. hub *sb.*¹ 4c + -y.] 'Full of hubs or projecting protuberances; as, a road that has been frozen while muddy is hubby' (Webster 1864).

1860 in Bartlett *Dict. Amer.*

huberate, -ertie, obs. ff. uberate, uberty.

hubless (ˈhʌblɪs), *a.* [f. hub¹ + -less.] Without a hub.

1970 *Official Jrnl.* (*Patents*) 31 Dec. 4577/1 Circumferentially loaded and snubbered hubless wheel surface locomotion apparatus. **1971** *New Scientist* 10 June 632/2 A load belt is wrapped round both the hubless rollers and the load hub in a tortuous path so as to apply any load from above as a circumferential load on the hubless wheels. **1971** *Daily Tel.* (Colour Suppl.) 8 Oct. 16 (Advt.), Hubless 5½" sport wheels. Radial-ply tyres.

hübnerite (ˈhybnəraɪt). *Min.* [Named 1865, after Hübner, who analysed it.] Tungstate of manganese, found in reddish-brown bladed crystals.

1867 *Amer. Jrnl. Sc.* Ser. ii. XLIII. 123. **1868** Dana *Min.* §611.

‖**hubris** (ˈhjuːbrɪs). [a. Gr. ὕβρις (cf. hybris).] Presumption, orig. towards the gods; pride, excessive self-confidence.

1884 *Daily News* 28 Oct. (Ware), Boys of good family, who have always been toadied, and never been checked, who are full of health and high spirits, develop what Academic slang knows as *hubris*, a kind of high-flown insolence. **1923** J. M. Murry *Pencillings* 272 So confident indeed did I become that I began to join in the scholarly chuckle at the vainglorious and foolhardy man—was ever a purer case of *hubris*? **1924** G. B. Shaw *Saint Joan* v. 60 You have stained yourself with the sin of pride. The old Greek tragedy is rising among us. It is the chastisement of hubris. **1950** A. Huxley *Themes & Variations* 259 The Greeks.. knew very well that hubris against the essentially divine order of Nature would be followed by its appropriate nemesis. *a* **1963** C. S. Lewis *Poems* (1964) 3 Walk carefully, do not wake the envy of the happy gods, Shun Hubris. **1965** *Listener* 23 Sept. 449/2 There they learned morality and conduct; the virtues of nobility and the golden mean and the menace of *hubris*. **1971** *Country Life* 11 Mar. 541/1 Not much in the way of punishment for *hubris* will be seen falling on the heads of the publicity-maniacs.

hubristic (hjuːˈbrɪstɪk), *a.* [irreg. (for *hybristic*) ad. Gr. ὑβριστικός insolent, wanton, f. ὕβρις outrage, contempt.] Insolent, contemptuous. Also **huˈbristical**.

1831 *Let.* in Russell *Gladstone* (1891) i. 17 The hubristic qualities of the tufted race. **1893** *National Observer* 30 Sept. 508/2 If it is contemptuous.. to ignore the spoken word, why is it less hubristic to turn your back on the formal composition? **1904** *Westm. Gaz.* 6 May 2/1 These Chamberlainites are very hubristic. **1923** J. M. Murry *Pencillings* 272, I was feeling at my ease, perhaps even a little hubristical myself. **1930** *Punch* 1 Oct. 381/2 This deleterious and delirious Dean, Who of the fount of Hippocrene Drank in a manner most hubristic. **1961** *Times* 18 May 17/2 It was hubristic of the band to play the National Anthem in an eighteenth century version.

hubristically (hjuːˈbrɪstɪkəlɪ), *adv.* [See -ly².] With hubris; in a presumptuous manner.

1907 *Athenæum* 19 Oct. 473/1 He was.. rather inclined to treat cavalierly, not to say hubristically, the quiet people who [etc.].

Hubshee (ˈhʌbʃiː), *sb.* and *a.* Also 7 **Abbasie, Hobsy**, 8 **Hobshy, -ee, Habashi**, 9 **Haffshee, Hubshi**. [Pers. *ḥabšī*, Arab. *ḥabašī*, of or belonging to Habesh or Abyssinia.] **A.** *sb.* An Ethiopian, an Abyssinian. **B.** *adj.* Ethiopian, Abyssinian. In Anglo-Indian usage both *sb.* and *adj.* may be loosely applied to an African Negro (see quot. 1901).

1601 J. Sanderson *Trav. Levant* (1931) 108 Abbasies of Ethiopia. **1698** J. Fryer *New Acct. E.-India & Persia* 147 They speak of his *Hobsies* after this manner, That with their Swords they are able to cut down Man and Horse. *Ibid.* 168 He being from an *Hobsy Cophir* made a free Denizen. **1757** J. H. Grose *Voy. E.-Indies* 238 The Moors are also fond of having Abyssinian slaves known in India by the name of Hobshee Coffrees. **1789** *Seir Mutaqherin* III. 36 (Y.), In India Negroes, *Habissinians*, *Nobis* (*i.e.* Nubians), &c. &c. are promiscuously called Habashies or *Habissians*, although the two latter are no Negroes. **1834** J. Forbes *Oriental Mem.* (ed. 2) II. 473 The master of a family adopts a slave, frequently a Haffshee Abyssinian, of the darkest hue, for his heir. **1888** *Contemp. Rev.* Feb. 167 'Hubshees', who looked, though they were not, Negroes, have in India carved out thrones. **1901** Kipling *Kim* vii. 179, I would not appear to her as a *hubshi* (nigger). **1932** —— *Limits & Renewals* 214 Whether he had been General or Sweeper—Sahib—Mussulman—Yahudi—Hubashi—or heathen.

huc(c)h(e, huchette, obs. ff. hutch, -et.

huchen (ˈhuːkən, ˈhuːxən). Also **hucho**. [G.] A large salmonid fish, *Hucho hucho*, native to the Danube and its tributaries.

a **1829** H. Davy *Consolations in Travel* (1830) iv. 204 The trout, salmon, hucho and others of the salmo genus. **1897** *Encycl. Sport* I. 14/1 Mahseer in India, the hucho in Bavaria, the monster trout of the Canadian lakes.. are alike taken by the spinning rod. **1905** *Westm. Gaz.* 2/2 The huchen is excellent food. *Ibid.* 7/3 The Committee have proceeded with the experiment of attempting the introduction into the river [*sc.* the Thames] of the huchen, the non-migratory salmon. **1962** D. W. Tucker tr. *Sterba's Freshwater Fishes of World* 56 Huchen do very well in captivity. **1971** B. J. Muus *Freshwater Fish Brit. & Europe* 62/1 The huchen is found in the Danube and part of its tributaries, and only exceptionally in lakes.

huck (hʌk), *sb.*¹ *Obs.* exc. *dial.* Forms: 5 **hoke(bone)**, 6 **huc(bone), huke(bane)**, 7 **huck(bone)**, 8 **huke**, 9 *dial.* **hug, heuk, huck**. [Etymology uncertain: see *Note* below.] The hip, the haunch.

1788 W. Marshall *Yorksh. Gloss.*, *Huke*, the huckle, or hip. **1877** *N.W. Linc. Gloss.* s.v., I was wounded i' th' huck. **1880** Tennyson *Northern Cobbler* iv, Once of a frosty night I slither'd an' hurted my huck.

b. huck-bone (ˈhʌkbəʊn), the hip-bone or haunch-bone; = huckle-bone 1.

c **1440** *Partonope* 4166 The lyoun.. That flesch and skyn of hys hokebone Wyth his pawe did arace. **1508** Dunbar *Flyting w. Kennedie* 181 Thy hanchis hirklis, with huke-

banis harth and haw. **1523** FITZHERB. *Husb.* §57 Se that they [fatte oxen] be soft.. vpon the hindermost-rybbe, and vpon the hucbone, and the nache by the tayle. **1657** W. COLES *Adam in Eden* cix, Good for the pains in the Hips or Huck-bones, called the Hip-gout. **1828** *Craven Dial.*, *Hug-baan*, the hip bone. **1870** *Swaledale Gloss.*, *Heuk-beean*, the hip-joint.

c. *Comb.* **huck-backed** († *huckt-backt*), **huck-shouldered** *adjs.*, hump-backed, crump-shouldered.

1631 HEYWOOD *1st Pt. Fair Maid of West* II. i. 14 A little wee-man, and somewhat huckt-backt. **1847–78** HALLIWELL, *Huck-shouldered*, hump-backed.

[*Note.* The origin of *huck* is obscure, and the chronological evidence leaves its historical relation to *huck-bone, huck-back, huckle, huckle-bone, huckle-back*, far from clear. For, while the compound *huck-bone* is found in 1440, *huck* itself is not cited till late in the 18th c.; on the other hand, the apparent diminutive *huckle*, and its compound *huckle-bone*, are found soon after 1500. The two earliest examples, ME. *hoke-bone* and Sc. *huke-bane*, answer exactly in form to *hook-bone*; but identity of *huck* with HOOK *sb.*¹, though not impossible, is not greatly favoured by the sense or phonology of the group as a whole. It is possible that the origin is to be sought in the Teutonic root *huk-, hūk-, hukk-*, to be bent, whence MDu. *huken* and *hukken*, MLG. *hûken*, ON. *húka*, to crouch, sit bent, sit on the haunches. When the body is bent, the hip-joints play the chief part.]

huck, *sb.*² A commercial shortening of HUCKABACK, q.v.

1851 *Illustr. Catal. Gt. Exhib.* 513 Various samples of huck, dowlas, ticks, diaper, huck and twill dusters [etc.].

huck (hʌk), *v. Obs.* exc. *dial.* Forms: 5 **huk, hukke, 6–7 hucke, 6– huck.** [In form, the base of HUCKSTER (q.v.), but the chronological evidence makes their actual relations difficult to determine.

Huck has iterative derivatives, HUCKER and HUCKLE, which favours its being an old word; it agrees also in form and sense with Ger. dial. *hocken, höcken, hucken* to huckster: see Grimm.]

intr. To higgle in trading; to haggle over a bargain; to chaffer, bargain. Also *fig.* To haggle over terms, to stickle.

14.. *Voc.* in Wr.-Wülcker 566/36 *Auccionor*, to hukke. **1468** *Medulla* in *Promp. Parv.* 252 *note*, *Auccionor*, to merchaunt, and huk. *a* **1529** SKELTON *Poems*, Now adayes as hucksters they hucke and they styck. **1530** PALSGR. 588/2, I love nat to sell my ware to you, you hucke so sore. **1586** EARL LEICESTER *Lett.* (Camden) 323 It is noe reason for me to stand hucking with them for myself. *a* **1592** H. SMITH *Serm.* (1637) 128 As Christ said to the woman of Samaria, when she huckt to give him water. **1642** BP. REYNOLDS *Israel's Petit.* 17 Thus men huck, and stand upon abatements with Christ in the Bargaine of Salvation. **1658** MANTON *Exp. Jude* 2 As Pharaoh stood hucking with Moses and Aaron. **1895** *Gloucestersh. Gloss.*, *Huck*, to bargain, chaffer.

b. quasi-*trans.*

1606 WARNER *Alb. Eng.* XV. xcviii. (1612) 388 Whose holy Noses ouer-hang at Markets, Staules, and Sacks, There hucking cheapth, here hearkening dearth, to set abroach their Stacks.

Hence **ˈhucking** *vbl. sb.* and *ppl. a.*

1551 in Tytler *Hist. Scot.* (1864) III. 385 Marry, the hucking is about money matters. **1599** MINSHEU *Sp. Dict.*, *Recaton*, a pinching or hucking fellow in buying or selling. *a* **1656** HALES *Gold. Rem.* (1673) III. 20 A near, and hard, and hucking chapman shall never buy good flesh.

huckaback (ˈhʌkəbæk). Also 8 **hucca-, hukka-, hugaback, hag-a-bag, hagabag,** 9 **huggaback, huck-a-back.** [Origin unknown.

Prof. Skeat has pointed out the close resemblance of the word to LG. *hukkebak*, Ger. *huckepack*, adv., in *huckepack tragen* to carry on the back, to carry (a child) pick-a-back, suggesting that it may have originally meant goods carried on the back, 'pedlar's ware'. But there is no trace of the English sense in German, nor of the continental origin of the material, which was in 17th c. a noted product of the North of England; so that connexion cannot at present be assumed.]

A stout linen fabric, with the weft threads thrown alternately up so as to form a rough surface, used for towelling and the like.

1690 J. F. *Merchant's Ware-ho.* 12 A sort of Diaper made in England, and is very strong, called Huckaback. **1721** *New General Atlas* 230 Darlington..has a considerable Manufacture in Linen and the best Hugabacks. **1725** RAMSAY *Gentle Sheph.* I. ii, Clean hag-a-bag I'll spread upon his board. **1758** JOHNSON *Idler* No. 13 ⁋11 That they may spin hukkaback for the servants table. **1769** *De Foe's Tour Gt. Brit.* III. 162 Darlington..particularly excels in Huckabacks of ten Quarters wide, which are made no-where else in England. **1778** *Eng. Gazetteer* (ed. 2), *Warrington*.. has a particular market every week for the linen called huckaback, the manufacture of its neighbourhood. **1795** J. AIKIN *Manchester* 349 The weaving of sheeting, hagabag, window-sash and curtain line. **1876** MISS BRADDON *J. Haggard's Dau.* I. 6 With face smarting from the vigorous application of mottled soap and coarsest huckaback.

b. *attrib.*

1707 *Lond. Gaz.* No. 4379/4 One Huckaback Table Cloth. **1823** SCOTT *Peveril* xxi, The table was covered with a clean huckaback napkin. **1851** *Illustr. Catal. Gt. Exhib.* 512 Tape and damask-bordered huckaback towels.

c. as *adj. fig.* That will stand wear and tear.

1759 H. WALPOLE *Let. to E. Strafford* 30 Oct., All their good qualities are huckaback. **1765** —— *Let. to Cole* 9 Mar., As that furniture will not last above a fortnight..I shall prefer something more huckaback.

huck-backed, -bone: see HUCK *sb.*¹ b and c.

†**ˈhucker,** *sb. Obs. rare.* In 5 **hukker.** [f. HUCK *v.* + -ER¹, or back-formation from HUCKSTER, q.v. (Perh. only a glossarist's word.)] A petty dealer; one who bargains or haggles.

14.. *Voc.* in Wr.-Wülcker 566/37 *Auccionator et Auccionatrix*, an hukker & an hukkester.

†**ˈhucker,** *v. Obs. rare.* [Iterative of HUCK *v.*] *intr.* To chaffer.

1548 FORREST *Pleas. Poesye* 87 For his pryuate wealthe so daylye too hucker.

hucker-mucker, var. f. HUGGER-MUGGER.

†**huckery.** *Obs.* In 4 **hukkerye, hockerye, hokkerye, hukrie.** [f. HUCKER *sb.* or HUCK *v.*: see -ERY. Cf. also HUCKSTERY.] The business of a huckster.

1377 LANGL. *P. Pl.* B. v. 227 She hath holden hokkerye [*v. rr.* hukkerye, hukrie; *C.* hockerye, *also* huckerstrye; *A.* hoxterye] al hire lyf tyme.

huckle (ˈhʌk(ə)l), *sb.* Forms: 6 **hokyll-, hocle-, hokkel-, huckel-, hockle-(bone), houkel, 6– huckle.** [In form, a dim. of HUCK *sb.*¹ Cf. the combinations *huckle-back*, HUCKLE-BONE, with the synonymous *huck-back, huck-bone.*]

1. The hip or haunch. (See also quot. 1855.)

a **1529** SKELTON *E. Rummyng* 45 The bones of her huckles, Like as they were with buckels Togyther made fast. **1541** R. COPLAND *Guydon's Quest. Chirurg.* I iij b, How many bones ar in yᵉ huckles? Answere. After the veryte there is but one, howbeit after dyuers partyes of it there are thre. **1561** HOLLYBUSH *Hom. Apoth.* 7 If the disease were in ether of the houkels or shoulders. **1663** BUTLER *Hud.* I. ii. 925 Getting up on Stump and Huckle, He with the Foe began to buckle. **1708** *Lond. Gaz.* No. 4402/4 A black Mare..branded TM. below the Huckle on the near Side. **1711** E. WARD *Quix.* I. 295 Tho' he hurt her Haunch and Huckle. *a* **1825** FORBY *Voc. E. Anglia*, *Huckles*, the hips. **1855** RAMSBOTHAM *Obstetr. Med.* 10 The Coccyx is called vernacularly the huckle or knuckle.

†**2.** ? The hock of a quadruped. *Obs.*

1607 TOPSELL *Four-f. Beasts* (1658) 459 In the middle of the horns there is a little branch standeth out like a knob, or as a huckle in the hinder-part of a Beasts leg.

3. *Comb.* **huckle-back,** a hump-back; **huckle-backed** *a.*, hump-backed.

a **1652** BROME *Eng. Moor* III. iii. Wks. 1873 II. 48 Of all Features and shapes, from the huckle-back'd Bum-creeper To the streight spiny Shop-maid in St. Martins. **1764** T. BRYDGES *Homer Travest.* (1797) I. 72 Ulysses..drove his broomstick with a thwack Upon Thersites' huckle-back. **1851** S. JUDD *Margaret* xvii. (1871) 147 Diversities..that gave a wavy huckle-backed character to the entire field.

†**huckle,** *v.*¹ *Obs.* [f. HUCK *v.* + -LE iterative suffix.] *intr.* To haggle in bargaining.

c **1620** Z. BOYD *Zion's Flowers* (1855) 53 They will him sell, and I'le not huckling stand. **1644** BULWER *Chirol.* 161 After much base huckling, and rising by little and little. **1655** GURNALL *Chr. in Arm.* I. v. 220 Wilt thou stand..[and] huckle with him for a penny?

huckle, *v.*² *dial.* [f. HUCKLE *sb.*] To bend the body, to stoop: see quots.

1840 SPURDENS *Suppl. Forby* (E.D.S.), *Huckle*, to bend down with pain. **1854** W. GASKELL *Lect. Lanc. Dial.* 13 In Lancashire, a person who stoops is said to 'huckle'.

huckleberry (ˈhʌk(ə)lbɛrɪ). *U.S.* [Conjectured to be a corruption of HURTLEBERRY, WHORTLEBERRY.] **1. a.** The fruit and plant of species of *Gaylussacia* (N.O. *Vacciniaceæ*), low berry-bearing shrubs, common in North America. Also applied to N. American species of the closely allied *Vaccinium*, more properly called *blueberry*.

1670 D. DENTON *Descr. New York* (1845) 3 The Fruits natural to the Island are Mulberries, Posimons, Grapes great and small, Huckelberries. **1796** *Ned Evans* II. 118 The chief dish is broth made of bears' flesh, dogs, and huckleberries. **1837** HAWTHORNE *Twice-told T.* (1851) I. xvi. 249 To peddle out a lot of huckleberries. **1858** O. W. HOLMES *Aut. Breakf.-t.* 357 A small heap of solemn black huckleberries. **1897** WILLIS *Flower. Pl.* II. 384 The *Vaccinium pennsylvanicum*..is called the blue huckleberry.

b. *attrib.* and *Comb.*, esp. as ***huckleberry pie.***

1751 J. BARTRAM *Observ. Trav. Pennsylv.* etc. 13 The land hereabouts is middling white oak and huckleberry land. **1775** P. V. FITHIAN *Jrnl.* (1934) II. 68 We have..boil'd potatoes & huckleberry-pie. **1851** THOREAU *Autumn* (1894) 8 The huckleberry bushes on Conantum are all turned red. **1854** LOWELL *Cambridge 30 Yrs. Ago* Pr. Wks. 1890 I. 70 The greater part of what is now Cambridgeport was then (in the native dialect) a 'huckleberry pastur'. *a* **1862** THOREAU *Cape Cod* vii. (1894) 155 That kind of gall called Huckleberry-apple. **1865** WHITTIER *Snow-Bound* 479 Dread Olympus at his will Became a huckleberry hill. **1869** [see *cranberry pie*]. **1947** *Mazama* Sept. 1/1 Smell that turkey, those roasting ears, and the huckleberry pies? **1972** *Punch* 1 Mar. 292/3 A sliver of freeze-dried huckleberry pie with apple pandowdy and French fries.

2. *U.S. colloq.* A small amount, degree, or extent.

1832 J. K. PAULDING *Westward Ho!* I. 182 [I once got] within a huckleberry of being smothered to death. **1920** E. BOK *Americanization of Edward Bok* 165 He always kept 'a huckleberry or two' ahead of his readers.

3. A person, *spec.* (*derog.*) a person of little consequence.

[**1835** *Gent's. Vade-Mecum* (Philadelphia) 22 Aug. 2/4 Orson, the wild man of the woods is nothing to him—not a circumstance—not a huckleberry.] **1868** *New Eng. Base Ballist* 3 Sept. 17/1 Now then, my huckleberry, look sharp! you're wrong! **1889** 'MARK TWAIN' *Connecticut Yankee* 338 The Saracen..is no huckleberry.

4. In various phrases: ***to be someone's huckleberry***: to be someone's sweetheart, friend, or partner; ***to be a huckleberry to*** (or ***over***) ***someone's persimmon***: a proverbial phrase (see quots.).

1832 J. K. PAULDING *Westward Ho!* I. ix. 80 If the [broad-]horn gets broadside to the current, I wouldn't risk a huckleberry to a persimmon that we don't every soul get treed, and sink to the bottom. **1834** D. CROCKETT *Narr. Life* ix. 70 But to do this, and write the warrants too, was at least a huckleberry over my persimmon. **1856** W. G. SIMMS *Eutaw* 553 My larning ain't a huckleberry to your persimmon. **1880** A. A. HAYES *New Colorado* (1881) v. 68 The first words that we heard him speak settled his nationality, for..he sententiously remarked, 'Hi'm 'is 'uckleberry.' **1885** D. D. PORTER *Incidents Civil War* 204 'I am the fleet-surgeon of the Mississippi squadron!'..'I'm a huckleberry above that persimmon, 'cause I'm the chief cook.' **1889** [see PERSIMMON 3]. **1926** N. N. PUCKETT in A. Dundes *Mother Wit* (1973) 8/2 Sir, you is a huckleberry beyon' my persimmon. **1936** J. TULLY *Bruiser* (1946) 37 Well, I'm your huckleberry, Mr. Haney. **1951** *Publ. Amer. Dial. Soc.* xv. 56 I'll be your huckleberry.

Hence **ˈhuckleˌberrying** *vbl. sb.*, gathering huckleberries.

1721–2 in Temple & Sheldon *Hist. Northfield, Mass.* (1875) 160 By horse to go huckle-berrying o o 6. **1883** *Leisure Hour* 702/2, I have joined children in huckleberrying, thimbleberrying..and bilberrying.

huckle-bone (ˈhʌk(ə)lbəʊn). [See HUCKLE *sb.*]

1. The hip- or haunch-bone of man or beast; the ischium or whole *os innominatum.* (Rarely the head of the thigh-bone which turns in the hip-joint.)

1529 *Malory's Arthur* XII. iii. (W. de W.), The bore roue hym on the brawne of the thyghe vp to the huckle bone [*ed.* **1485** hough-bone]. **1545** RAYNOLD *Byrth Mankynde* (1564) 44 The knitting togeather of the hocle bone with the lowest turning ioynt of the loynes. **1547** BOORDE *Brev. Health* cccxv. 102 b, This infirmitie [Sciatica] doth come of hard lyenge on the hokyll bones. **1565–73** COOPER *Thesaurus*, *Acetabula*,..the hollownesse wherein the huckle bone turneth. **1580** HOLLYBAND *Treas. Fr. Tong*, *La boiste de os*, the pan wherein the huckle bone falleth. **1615** CROOKE *Body of Man* 807 The Thigh is that part which is betwixt the ioynt of the huckle bone and the knee. **1676** HOBBES *Iliad* (1677) 67 Tydides..hit him on the huckle bone, wherein Into the hip inserted is the thigh. *a* **1722** LISLE *Husb.* (1752) 264 A beast should be wide between its huckle bones. **1846** J. BAXTER *Libr. Pract. Agric.* (ed. 4) II. 90 The hip or huckle bones should be wide apart, coming upon a level with the chine.

2. The astragalus or small bone which joints with the tibia, in the hock joint of a quadruped; the knuckle-bone.

1542 UDALL *Erasm. Apoph.* 163 b, Ἀστράγαλος is in Latin *talus*, and it is the little square huccle bone in the ancle place of the hinder legge in all beastes, sauing man. **1613** T. GODWIN *Rom. Antiq.* (1625) 113 *Talus*, an huckle-bone, such wherewith children play Cockall. **1652** A. ROSS *Hist. World* I. ii. 6 The King presents him with some golden dice, or huckle bones to play withall. **1871** TYLOR *Prim. Cult.* I. 74 Hucklebones or astragali were used in divination in ancient Rome. **1877** *N.W. Linc. Gl.*, *Huckle-bone*, the astragalus, a small bone of a sheep, used for playing a game called..'dibs'. The floors of summer-houses used frequently to be paved with huckle-bones.

Hence **huckle-boned** *a.* [see -ED²].

1683 *Lond. Gaz.* No. 1850/8 A black Gelding..high Huckle-bon'd.

huckled (ˈhʌk(ə)ld), *a.* [cf. HUCKLE *sb.*]

†**a.** (?) Jointed. *Obs.*

1614 MARKHAM *Cheap Husb.* II. i. (1668) 70 They [bulls] are..big, round, and well huckled together in every member.

b. Hunched, having outstanding joints.

1893 *National Observer* 25 Mar. 468/1 The looseness [of the gown] made her shoulders seem huckled.

†**huckler.** *Obs.* Name of a kind of dance.

1617 ASSHETON *Jrnl.* (Chetham Soc.) 45 A maske of noblemen, knights, gentlemen, and courtiers afore the king ..dancing the Huckler, Tom Bedlo, and the Cowp Justice of Peace.

ˈhuckmuck. *local.* Also 5 **huk-,** 6 **-mock.** 'A strainer used in brewing. It consists of a bundle of twigs, generally part of an old broom, placed at the bottom of the mashing-keeve or vat, to prevent the grains running out when the wort is drawn off' (Elworthy *W. Som. Word-bk.* 1886).

1472 *Yatton Churchw. Acc.* (Som. Rec. Soc.), For iiij hukmuckes vjd, for hopyng iiid. **1517** *Ibid.* 135 Payd for huckmocks vjd. **1825** BRITTON *Wiltsh. Gloss.* (E.D.S.), *Huckmuck*, a kind of strainer used in brewing.

hucksheen, -shin, -son, var. of HOCKSHIN, HUXEN.

huckster (ˈhʌkstə(r)), *sb.* Forms: 3 *Orm.* **huccster,** 4–5 **hukstar,** 4– **huckster;** also 4–5 **hok(e)ster(e, hoxter,** 5 **howkster, hukstere, hukkester, huk-, hwkstare, (hoggester),** 5–6 **hook-, hukster,** 5–7 **hucster,** 5–9 **huxter,** 6 **hocster, houkester, huckester, huckstar,** 9 *dial.* **huikster.** [See HUCK *v.* Although the series *huck, hucker,*

huckster, corresponds formally with *bake*, *baker*, *baxter*, *brew*, *brewer*, *brewster*, etc., in which the verb is the starting-point, the late date of *huck* as compared with *huckster*, and the continental parallels of the latter, make difficulties. MDu. had *hokester*, *hoekster*, early mod.Du. *heukster*, 'huckster' fem.; also MDu. *hoeker*, early mod.Du. *heuker* masc. = MLG. *hoker*, mod.Ger. *höker*, 'higgler, hawker, retailer, market-man, costermonger'; none of these, however, appear to be known as early as our *huckster*.

The origin of the Du. and Ger. words themselves is unsettled; Ger., besides *höker*, has *höke*, *höcke*, MHG. *hucke*, MLG. *hoke*, to be referred, according to Kluge, prob. to *hocken* to squat, sit on the 'hunkers'; but Verwijs and Verdam state grounds for connecting MDu. *hoeker*, *hoekster* rather with Du. *hoek* a corner. The history is thus altogether obscure.]

1. A retailer of small goods, in a petty shop or booth, or at a stall; a pedlar, a hawker.

a. Applied to a woman.

a **1300** *Sat. People Kildare* xviii. in *E.E.P.* (1862) 155 Hail be ȝe hokesters dun bi þe lake.. He is sori of his lif þat is fast to such a wif. **14..** *Nom.* in Wr.-Wülcker 692/42 *Hec auxiatrix*, a huxter. *c* **1475** *Pict. Voc.* Ibid. 793/29 *Hec aucionatrix*, a hoxter. **1851** MAYNE REID *Scalp Hunt.* ix. 70 The women, light-hearted hucksters.

b. Without distinction of sex. (The ordinary use.) *locally* in specific senses: see quots. 1858–77.

c **1200** ORMIN 15817 Forr þatt teȝȝ turrndenn Godess hus Inntill huccsteress boþe. **1387** TREVISA *Higden* I. lx. (Rolls) II. 171 þey beeþ..in gaderyne of catel hoksters [*v.r.* hucksters] and tauerners. *c* **1440** *Promp. Parv.* 252/2 Hwkstare,.. *auxionator*, *auxionatrix*. **1483** *Gild Bakers Exeter* in *Eng. Gilds* 337 To make serche.. att all hoggesters houses with-yn the Juris-diccion of the said Cite. **1534** MORE *Treat. on Passion* Wks. 1304/1 A substanciall merchaunt and not an hukster. **1591** PERCIVALL *Sp. Dict.*, *Regatonear*, to sell pedlerie ware, to play the hucster. **1641** BEST *Farm. Bks.* (Surtees) 29 Wee buy our molten tallowe.. of the hucksters and tripe-wives. **1705** HICKERINGILL *Priest-cr.* II. vi. 62 The throwing down of a Hucksters Apples by a Fisher-Boy. **1858** SIMMONDS *Dict. Trade*, *Huckster*, an inferior dealer or minor trader; a hawker or itinerant vendor of goods with a pack, box, or tray. **1877** *Holderness Gloss.*, *Hucksthers*, dealers in farm produce, who attend the markets to purchase from the producers for the purpose of retailing it out again to small customers. **1889** *Spectator* 28 Dec., From the great shops in Regent Street and Bond Street to the smallest huxters' in the slums, there are Christmas presents in the windows.

c. As term of reproach: A regrater, an engrosser of corn, etc.; a broker, a middleman.

[*a* **1400** *Burgh Laws* lxvi. in *Sc. Stat.* I. 346/1 Hukstaris þat byis and sellis agane to wynning sal nocht by ony thing before þat undern be rungyn in wynter and mydmorne in somer.]

1573–80 BARET *Alv.* H 707 An Huckster: a regrater: a seller by retaile: a wifler, *propola*. **1580** HOLLYBAND *Treas. Fr. Tong*, *Dardanier*, an huckester, he that kepeth corne till it be deare. **1595** DUNCAN *App. Etymol.* (E.D.S.), *Mango*, interpolator, a hukster, a regrator. **1612** T. TAYLOR *Comm. Titus* i. 11 Such as by fraud and base arts play the hucksters to enhanse the price. **1630** LENNARD tr. *Charron's Wisd.* (1658) 49 It is the great Intermedler and Huckster, by which we traffick. **1700** T. BROWN tr. *Fresny's Amusem. Ser. & Com.* 78 Marriage Hucksters, or Wife-Brokers.

2. a. *trans.* and *fig.* A person ready to make his profit of anything in a mean or petty way; one who basely barters his services, etc., for gain; a mercenary; an overreacher of others.

1553 GRIMALDE *Cicero's Offices* I. (1558) 18 No hucsters of warre warremen as we bee. **1645** MILTON *Colast.* Wks. (1851) 350 Wee have it..as good cheap, as any hucster at law, newly set up, can possibly afford. **1673** *Vain Insolency Rome* 5 With what craft, and artifice, the Romish Hucksters endeavour to seduce the people of our Church of England.. to the Communion of Rome. **1842** ROGERS *Introd. Burke's Wks.* (1842) I. 9 Mr. Hamilton, who managed the whole matter in the true spirit of a political huckster, had the meanness to accept this offer. **1868** MISS BRADDON *Charlotte's Inher.* I. i. 7, I am no huckster, to sell my daughter to the best bidder.

b. An advertising agent chiefly concerned with the preparation of advertising programmes for radio broadcasting.

1946 F. WAKEMAN (*title*) The hucksters. **1947** *Britannica Bk. of Year* 840/2 *Huckster*, a radio advertising man. **1965** *English Studies* XLVI. 464 *Huckster*, broker... Also used colloquially of an advertisement copy writer.

† **3.** Phrase. ***in huckster's hands (handling)***: in a position in which it is likely to be roughly used or lost; beyond the likelihood of recovery. *Obs.*

1581 RICH *Farewell* D iv b, We will returne to his wife, who was lefte in hucsters handelyng (as you haue heard). *a* **1592** GREENE *Alphonsus* I. Wks. (Rtldg.) 226/2 The crown is lost, and now in hucksters' hands. **1687** R. L'ESTRANGE *Answ. Diss.* 21 They are gotten into Hucksters Hands, and there's No coming off without a Scratch'd Face. *a* **1700** B. E. *Dict. Cant. Crew* s.v., *In Huckster's Hands*, at a desperate Pass, or Condition, or in a fair way to be lost. **1738** SWIFT *Pol. Conversat.* 68 Madam, he shall ne'er have it [a Handkerchief] again; 'tis in Huckster's Hands.

4. *Comb.*, as ***huckster-booth***; ***huckster-like*** adj., adv.

1591 SPENSER *M. Hubberd* 925 The Ape wanting his huckster man, That wont provide his necessaries. **1665** GLANVILL *Scepsis Sci.* Pref. (R.), Nor will I huckster-like discredit any man's ware, to recommend mine own. **1866** BLACKIE *Homer & Iliad* I. 101 The huckster-booths of the Lawnmarket. **1870** *Standard* 13 Dec., He only mulcted nations, and did not hucksterlike fine every little open town he came across.

Hence **hucksterdom**, *nonce-wd.* [see -DOM]; **'hucksterism**, the theory or practice of being a huckster (usu. disparaging).

1886 *Pall Mall Budget* 8 July 28/2 From the hucksterdom of his environment. **1951** *Newsweek* 27 Aug. 80 Robert Saudek, a three-time Peabody Award winner for documentaries. Saudek, a soft-spoken man without a hint of hucksterism. **1957** *N.Y. Times* 6 Jan. E 11/4 An attack on Southern schools of journalism for 'kicking the humanities around' while emphasizing 'hucksterism' and 'quick turnover' in education. **1960** *Encounter* XV. 27 One can find 'hucksterism'..among academic people in search of reputations. **1972** *Village Voice* (N.Y.) 1 June 26/2 What particularly appeals to me about the 'Jack La Lanne Show' is its serious, heart-felt hucksterism. **1973** *Observer* 2 Dec. 7/3 This high-pressure hucksterism, backed by the multi-billion investment.., has failed to impress many scientists.

'huckster, *v.* [f. HUCKSTER *sb.*]

1. *intr.* To bargain, haggle. *lit.* and *fig.*

1592 [see HUCKSTERING *ppl. a.*]. *a* **1665** J. GOODWIN *Filled w. the Spirit* (1867) 319 Be ingenuous and noble towards God, and not stand picking and huckstering with your hearts to know how you must do to escape hell fire. **1775** BURKE *Sp. Conc. Amer.* Wks. III. 57 Despotism itself is obliged to truck and huckster. **1855** MOTLEY *Dutch Rep.* IV. i. II. 522 The estates..irritated the Prince of Orange by huckstering about subsidies. **1861** SALA *Dutch Pict.* xxi. 336 A dunghill of vanity for chapmen to huckster over.

2. *trans.* To traffic in, in a petty way; to retail or expose for sale (esp. in small quantities); to bargain over. Also, to adulterate. *lit.* and *fig.*

1642 T. HILL *Trade of Truth* 37 This graduall Huckstering up the purity of truth. **1670** MILTON *Hist. Eng.* III. Wks. (1847) 502/2 Some who had been called from shops and ware-houses..to sit in supreme councils and committees..fell to huckster the commonwealth. **1677** GALE *Crt. Gentiles* III. 19 Such as hucstered and made merchandise of Christ. **1770** BURKE *Pres. Discont.* Wks. 1842 I. 129 The sealed fountain of royal bounty, which had been infamously monopolized and huckstered. **1879** FARRAR *St. Paul* (1883) 541 The deceitful workers who had huckstered and adulterated the word of God. **1898** *Humanitarian* XI. 357 A man..huckstering cheap lollypops to the small fry of the Board Schools.

† **'hucksterage**. *Obs. rare*[−1]. [See -AGE.] Huckstering, bargaining, trafficking.

1641 MILTON *Reform.* II. (1851) 68 The gentle and benevolent mediocritie of Church-maintenance, without the ignoble Hucsterage of pidling Tithes.

'hucksterer. [f. HUCKSTER *v.* + -ER[1].] One who hucksters; a retail dealer, a petty trafficker.

1724 SWIFT *Consid.* etc. in *Fraud Detected* (1725) 161 Those Hucksterers, or Money-jobbers, will be found necessary if this Brass Money is made current. **1862** T. C. GRATTAN *Beaten Paths* II. 146 They become mere hucksterers of wit, the retail dealers in a commodity for which there are few wholesale houses. **1874** MOTLEY *Barneveld* II. xvi. 192 A venal hucksterer of his country's liberties.

'hucksteress, -tress. [f. HUCKSTER *sb.* + -ESS.] A female huckster or petty trafficker.

1611 COTGR., *Regratiere*, an Huckseresse; also a Regrateresse. **1811** *Morning Post* 30 Aug. in *Spirit Pub. Jrnls.* (1812) XV. 312 The huckstress..threw one arm franticly over Mr. B.'s head. **1851** HAWTHORNE *Ho. Sev. Gables* ii. (1883) 56 The immemorial lady..reduced now, in that very house, to be the hucksteress of a cent-shop.

huckstering ('hʌkstərɪŋ), *vbl. sb.* [f. HUCKSTER *v.* + -ING[1].] The action of the verb HUCKSTER; petty trafficking; sordid dealing; haggling.

1647 TRAPP *Comm. Matt.* xxi. 13 Base huckstering of holy things. **1797** BURKE *Regic. Peace* iii. Wks. VIII. 335 The spirit of huckstering and barter. **1858** FROUDE *Hist. Eng.* III. xiii. 89 From the wholesale purchases of the corndealer to the huckstering of the wandering pedlar. **1883** *Manch. Exam.* 27 Nov. 5/2 The process of diplomatic huckstering by correspondence.

'huckstering, *ppl. a.* [f. as prec. + -ING[2].] That hucksters; trafficking, hawking, haggling.

1592 G. HARVEY *Pierce's Super.* 175 A broking and huckstering penne. *a* **1661** FULLER *Worthies*, *Northumbld.* II. 308 Huckstering Husbandmen, who properly may be termed Knaves in grain. **1808** COBBETT *Pol. Reg.* XIII. vi. 202 We know you to be a huckstering nation. **1858** HUGHES *Scouring White Horse* 106 Half way up..I found an old huckstering woman and a boy in great trouble.

† **'hucksterize**, *v. Obs. rare.* [f. HUCKSTER *sb.* + -IZE.] **a.** *trans.* To deal with as a huckster; to adulterate. **b.** *intr.* To play the huckster.

1646 S. BOLTON *Arraignm. Err.* 21 There are such who hucsterise the word, adulterate, sophisticate the word. **1660** FISHER *Rusticks Alarm* Wks. (1679) 614 Hirelings that hucksterize and deal deceitfully about the Word of God.

huckstery ('hʌkstərɪ). Forms: see HUCKSTER. [f. HUCKSTER *sb.* + -Y.]

1. The trade or business of a huckster; the place in which he carries on his trade; *plur.* the goods dealt in by him (cf. *groceries*).

1362 LANGL. *P. Pl.* A. v. 141 Heo haþ holden hoxterye [*C.* VII. 233 huckustrye] þis Elleuene wynter. **1611** COTGR., *Regratement*, a..mending, or tricking vp of old things for sale; hucksterie. **1826** *Blackw. Mag.* XIX. Pref. 20 In the very shops and huxteries of our remotest towns and villages. **1833** *Fraser's Mag.* VIII. 280 A dealer in various articles, which..we shall call huxteries.

2. Petty bargaining, haggling; stickling.

1662 J. CHANDLER *Van Helmont's Oriat.* 243 A more slow and delicate digestion doth loath all things, as it were with much huckstery. *Ibid.* 308 Great eaters, and those who are brought up with dainty huckstery, are..notably lean.

3. *attrib.*

1824 GALT *Rothelan* I. I. vi. 55 Under the pent-house of a huxtry shop. **1897** *Westm. Gaz.* 12 June 4/3 The huckstery scheme of the Indian Government, spoken of as the Durand Treaty.

huckt-backt: see HUCK *sb.*[1]

hud (hʌd), *sb.*[1] *Obs.* exc. *dial.* Also 5–6 ? hudd(e, pl. **huddes**. [Origin uncertain.

It has been conjectured to be a dial. form of HOOD, corresp. to the current pronunc. of *blood*, *flood*, and Sc. *wud* = *wood*; but against this there are many considerations, connected with the age, use, and locality of the word, its non-interchange with *hood* in other senses, etc. If it was an (unrecorded) old word, it might be a deriv. of the Teut. root *hud-*, *hūd-*, to cover, whence *hide* vb., *hut*, and perh. *house*, *husk*. In sense *hud* is identical with MDu. *houde* 'tunica, concha, cortex, siliqua, calyx, et spica', cf. *boon-houde* bean-hull (Kilian); but this is a deriv. of *houden*, to HOLD.]

The husk or sheath of a seed; the hull or shell of a fruit; a pod or seed-vessel; †*fig.* an empty person who has 'nothing in him'. (See also quot. 1893.)

1398 TREVISA *Barth. De P.R.* XVII. lxv. (Tollem. MS.), þe stalke [of wheat] is biclippid with leues and huddes [*ed.* **1535** hulles]. **1549** LATIMER *3rd Serm. bef. Edw. VI* (Arb.) 84 Ye hoddy peckes, Ye doddye poulles, ye huddes, do ye beleue hym? **1578** LYTE *Dodoens* VI. xli. 711 Almondes..blanched or made cleane from their skinnes or huddes. **1622** R. HAWKINS *Voy. S. Sea* (1847) 87 They have hudds as our beans. *a* **1722** LISLE *Husb.* (1757) 126 (E.D.S.) *Hood*, the outer coat of a seed. **1790** GROSE *Provinc. Gloss.* (ed. 2), *Hud*, the husk of a nut or walnut. *Glouc.* **1876** *Oxfordsh. Gloss.*, *Hud*, a pea-shell. **1882** JAGO *Cornish Gloss.*, *Hud*, or *hull*, a shell, as of a nut. **1893** *Wiltsh. Gloss.*, *Hud* (1) The husk of a walnut, skin of a gooseberry, shell of a pea or bean, etc... (3) A finger-stall or finger of a glove.

Hence **hud** *v. dial. trans.*, to shell.

1790 GROSE *Provinc. Gloss.* (ed. 2), *To hud*, to take off the husk. *Glouc.* **1890** *Berksh. Gloss.* s.v., Get them warnuts hudded. **1893** *S.E. Worc. Gloss.* s.v., I a bin a 'uddin some bannits.

hud, hood (hʌd, hʊd), *sb.*[2] *north. dial.* Also 7 hudd(e, 8 hod. [Of uncertain origin and history. It is not certain that senses 1 and 2 are the same word.

Evidently distinct from HUD *sb.*[1] *Hude*, in sense 1, quot. 1483, might be, as to form, northern for HOOD, with which also Kennett and *Craven Dial.* identify sense 2; but it is difficult to see any connexion of sense.]

† **1.** A log placed at the back of the fire-place to keep the fire in by night; = HEAD-BLOCK 1. *Obs.*

1483 *Cath. Angl.* 191/1 An Hude..*repofocilium*. *a* **1500** *Ortus Voc.*, *Repofocilium*, *id est quod tegit ignem in nocte*, a hudde.

2. The place behind, or at the back of, a fire-place of the old fashion; the back of the chimney or grate; also = *hud-end* (see 3).

1641 BEST *Farm. Bks.* (Surtees) 122 [To beek or dry osiers] they take the stickes and sette them up an ende, slanttinge them against the hudde, and keepe a good fire under them. **1658** *Burgery Sheffield* (1898) 168 For making two hudds and materialls therto 2*s.* 6*d.* *a* **1728** KENNETT in *Laud MS.* 1033 lf. 190 [184] Ye Hod or hood, the back of the Chimney Box called the Hob in Chesh. **1791** *Statist. Acc. Scotl.* II. 289 (Jam.) A species of clay..of which the country people make what they call, Hudds, to set in their chimnies behind their fires. **1825** BROCKETT, *Hud*, the side of the fire place within the chimney. **1828** *Craven Dial.*, *Hood*, *Hud*, the place behind the fire.

3. *Comb.* **hud-end (hood-end)**, each of the two raised flat surfaces of stone or iron at the sides of an old-fashioned fire-place; a hob; **hud-stone**, the stone of which the hud-end is the upper surface, the hob-stone.

1828 *Craven Dial.*, **Hood-end*, corners near the fire, either of stone or iron. **1863** MRS. TOOGOOD *Yorks. Dial.*, Take the kettle off the fire and put it on the hood-end. **1697** *Vestry Bks.* (Surtees) 343 For setting up barrs and *hudstones in the vestery. **1825** BROCKETT s.v. *Hud*, Pans not in use are placed on the 'hud-stane'. **1883** *Almondbury Gloss.*, *Hudstone*, the hob, or hobstone, of the fireplace.

hud(de, obs. pa. t. and pple. of HIDE *v.*[1]; obs. f. HOOD.

† **hudder-mudder**, *sb. Obs.* Also 5–6 **hoder-moder**, 6 **hudder-mother**, **hudther-mudther**, **hudder-mutter**, **hutter-mutter**, **huther-muther**. [A reduplicated compound of which the first element appears to be related to HODER *v.* to huddle; the second is obscure, but in part, at least, onomatopœic: cf. HUGGER-MUGGER.] Concealment, secrecy, privacy; chiefly in phr. ***in hudder-mudder***.

1461 J. PASTON in *P. Lett.* No. 402 II. 28 He and hys wyfe and other have blaveryd here of my kynred in hoder-moder [*printed* hedermoder]. *a* **1529** SKELTON *Col. Clout* 69 Alas, they make me shoder! For in hoder moder The Churche is put in faute. **1545** ASCHAM *Toxoph.* I. (Arb.) 36 It hydes it not, it lurkes not in corners and hudder-mother. **1563–87** FOXE *A. & M.* (1596) 245/2 These things thus in hudder mutter among themselues concluded. **1579** GOSSON *Apol. Sch. Abuse* (Arb.) 74, I know not yet because it is doone in hudder mudder. **1583** GOLDING *Calvin on Deut.* vii. 39 The miracles..were not darksome nor done in hudther mudther, but so openly and apparantly.

Hence †**hudder-mudder, huther-muther** *v. trans.*, to huddle up, conceal, keep close. *Obs.*
1544 PHAER *Regim. Lyfe* (1560) A iij, What reason is it, y^t we shulde huther muther here amonge a fewe, the thing that was made to be common unto al?

huddle ('hʌd(ə)l), *v.* Also 6 huddel, 6–7 hudle, 8 hudell. [*Huddle* vb. and sb. are known only from the second half of the 16th c.; the vb., which prob. preceded the sb., has the form of a diminutive and iterative, perh. ultimately from the Teut. root *hud-*, *hūd-* to cover (see HUD *sb.*¹); cf. HODER *v.*, HUDDER-MUDDER, also LG. *hudern* to cherish, shelter, as a hen her chickens, iterative of LG. *hûden* to hide. Senses 4 b, c, come close to dialectal senses of Ger. *hudeln* to do (work) hastily and carelessly, to scamp; cf. *hudelei* slovenly work, scamping. But no satisfactory theory of relationship with these words can at present be offered.
The history and order of the senses is in many respects obscure; see esp. the early quots. under HUDDLE *adv.* and HUDDLING *ppl. a.*]

I. *trans.* †**1.** To put or keep out of sight; to conceal or hide, as among a crowd or under a heap; to hush *up*. *Obs.*
1581 J. BELL *Haddon's Answ. Osor.* 12 b, To chop of the head of the sentence, and slyly huddle the rest [*orig.* qui sententiæ caput abscindens astute reliqua subtices]. **1581** MULCASTER *Positions* xxvi. (1887) 103 They..neither can of them selues, neither ought at my hand to be hudled vp in silence. **1591** HARINGTON *Orl. Fur.* xxxv. xix, Time there doth all in dark oblivion huddle. **1653** A. WILSON *Jas. I* 285 (N.) The matter was hudled up, and little spoken of it. **1680** OTWAY *Orphan* III. i, I do not like this marriage, Huddled i' the dark, and done at too much venture. **1750** JOHNSON *Rambler* No. 2 ¶15 His merit may pass without notice, huddled in the variety of things. **1795** WOLCOTT (P. Pindar) *Wks.* (1812) III. 329 Huddle up the News.

2. To pile or heap up confusedly; to crowd together closely and unceremoniously. (In earlier use the sense was sometimes simply, To jumble, mix up in confusion.)
1599 SHAKS. *Much Ado* II. i. 252 Shee told mee..that I was duller then a great thaw, hudling iest vpon iest. **1623** tr. *Favine's Theat. Hon.* VII. xi. 252 This Genealogie is in this partie much hudled. **1706** PHILLIPS (ed. Kersey), *To Huddle*, to confound or mingle things together, after a confused manner. **1897** HALL CAINE *Christian* x, The furniture was huddled about in disorder.

b. Also with *together*, *up*.
1579 TOMSON *Calvin's Serm. Tim.* 63/1 That matters might not be huddeled and scuffled vppe together confusedly, and without order. **1581** W. CHARKE in *Confer.* IV. (1584) Ee iij b, You confound and huddle them together. **1650** FULLER *Pisgah* I. vi. 15 A heap of wildernesses hudled up together. **1658** W. BURTON *Itin. Anton.* 74 Those.. Writers..huddle together what ever they meet with in former Authors. **1759** ROBERTSON *Hist. Scot.* I. v. 376 The matter would seem to be huddled up in this manner merely to suppress discoveries. **1774** GOLDSM. *Nat. Hist.* (1776) VI. 122 A bullet might easily reach them, if huddled together in a flock. **1875** MᶜLAREN *Serm.* Ser. II. xii. 211 Huddling together in grotesque chaos things which are utterly diverse.

c. To contract or draw (oneself) together 'all of a heap'; to coil *up* unceremoniously.
1755 SMOLLETT *Quix.* (1803) IV. 264 He chose his ground, on which he huddled himself up, and enjoyed a most profound sleep. **1861** PEARSON *Early & Mid. Ages Eng.* 104 That at least he might not die huddled up like a cow. **1886** STEVENSON *Kidnapped* iv, He lay as he had fallen, all huddled.

3. To push or thrust in a disorderly mass or heap, *into*, *out of* (etc.) some place.
1655 FULLER *Ch. Hist.* IV. ii. §20 The obscurity of his burial (huddled into his grave at Langley). **1807–8** W. IRVING *Salmag.* (1824) 367 To whitewash my room and put things in order; a phrase which..means little else than huddling every thing into holes and corners. **1833** MARRYAT *P. Simple* xix, We were huddled out like a flock of sheep, by a file of soldiers with loaded muskets. **1840** THACKERAY *Paris Sk.-bk.* (1869) 296 They huddled the king's body into a postchaise. **1871** BLACKIE *Four Phases* i. 47 Reform bills.. are huddled or juggled through a House of fretful or feverish senators.

b. with *on*: To put on (clothes) hurriedly and 'all of a heap'.
1697 VANBRUGH *Relapse* II. Wks. (Rtldg.) 309/2, I.. huddle on my clothes and get dressed by one. **1709** PRIOR *Hans Carvel* 34 At Twelve She rose, with much ado Her Cloaths were huddl'd on by Two. **1820** SCOTT *Ivanhoe* xxxiii, The Friar..had huddled a friar's frock over his green cassock. **1824** —— *St. Ronan's* xxii, You must positively go back into your dressing room and huddle your things on as fast as you can. **1868** HELPS *Realmah* xv. (1876) 395 His clothes seem to be huddled on anyhow.

4. To drive or push hurriedly, and without order or ceremony; to hurry (a person or thing). ? *Obs.*
1649 MILTON *Eikon.* xxiv, I shall huddle him as he does Prayers. *a* **1661** FULLER *Worthies* (1840) I. xxv. 101 You have huddled your book too soon to the press. **1685** ROCHESTER *Valentin.* III. iii, Trembling through Terror lest he come too late They huddle his Dispatch while at the Gate. **1697** DRYDEN *Virg. Georg.* I. 353 Let him forecast his Work with timely care, Which else is huddled, when the Skies are fair.

b. with *over*, *through*: To hurry through, run over, or perform in a hurried slovenly way.
1648 GAGE *West Ind.* 102 To continue in the Church while a Masse is briefly hudled over. **1696** tr. *Duquesne's Voy. E. Ind.* 167 We presently huddled over a few prayers, according to custom. **1799** T. JEFFERSON *Writ.* (1859) IV. 261, I have suffered the post hour to come so nearly on me, that I must huddle over what I have more than appears in the public papers. **1885** *Manch. Exam.* 6 Mar. 5/4 The solemnities had to be huddled through at express speed.

c. with *up*: To hurry the completion of; to work up, finish up, or compile, in haste and without proper care; to botch up hastily.
1579 G. HARVEY *Letter-bk.* (Camden) 59 They were hudlid and as you know bunglid upp in more haste then good speede. **1581** SAVILE *Tacitus, Hist.* III. lv. (1591) 147 Him-selfe [Vitellius]..hudled up the election of officers [L. *festinare comitia*]. **1692** RAY *Dissol. World* Pref. (1732) 15 Too hasty in huddling up and tumbling out of Books. **1721** SWIFT *Corr.* Wks. 1841 II. 556, I was in fear lest the post should be gone, and so..huddled up without thinking of the date. **1784** COWPER *Task* II. 412 And reading..Just fifteen minutes, huddle up their work, And with a well-bred whisper close the scene. **1839** MACAULAY *Ess., Gladstone* (1860) II. 440 She sprang from a compromise huddled up between the eager zeal of reformers and the selfishness of greedy, ambitious, and time-serving politicians.

5. To hug. Now *dial.*
a **1650** *Ld. Barnard & Lit. Musgrave* 24 in Furniv. *Percy Folio* I. 121 But lie still, lie still, litle Musgreue, and huddle me from the cold. *c* **1665** *Roxb. Ball.* (1891) VII. 366 But huddle and cuddle, wee'l toy and wee'l kiss. **1811** WILLAN *W. Riding Gloss.* (E.D.S.), *Huddle*, to embrace. **1869** *Lonsdale Gloss., Huddle*, (1) to embrace, to squeeze, to hug, to cuddle.

II. *intr.* **6.** To gather or flock in a congested mass; to crowd together unceremoniously; to nestle closely in a heap. Also with *together*, *up*.
1596 SHAKS. *Merch. V.* IV. i. 28 Glancing an eye of pitty on his losses That haue of late so hudled on his backe. **1646** SIR T. BROWNE *Pseud. Ep.* VI. v. 292 Different seasons would have hudled upon each other. *a* **1656** USSHER *Ann.* (1658) 515 The people came huddling out of the severall Cities..to salute him. **1821** BYRON *Vis. Judgm.* xxvi, The very cherubs huddled all together. **1850** TENNYSON *In Mem.* xv, The cattle huddled on the lea. **1854** MARY HOWITT *Pict. Calendar* 528 The owl sits huddling by himself, The cold has pierced his body through. **1883** *Century Mag.* Aug. 487/2 Cozily huddling up to one another.

†**7.** To hurry in disorder or confusion. *Obs.*
1646 SIR T. BROWNE *Pseud. Ep.* III. xviii. 152 They will runne against things, and hudling forwards fall from high places. **1667** DRYDEN & NEWCASTLE *Sir Martin Mar-all* Epil., As country vicars, when the sermon's done, Run huddling to the benediction. **1707** ROWE *Gold. Verses Pythag.* (R.), Fools huddle on, and always are in haste, Act without thought, and thoughtless words they waste. *a* **1734** NORTH *Examen* III. vii. (1740) 522 That the Judges..might huddle in giving their Judgments, and so the Cause look more foul on their Side. **1766** [ANSTEY] *Bath Guide* xiii. 45 How the Misses did huddle, and scuddle, and run.

†**8.** Formerly, in the University of Cambridge, To go through in a hurried and slovenly way certain formal exercises in lieu of those regularly required for a degree. *Obs.*
1798 A. WALL *Senate-ho. Cerem.* 112 If he has not kept the requisite exercises, (viz. two acts and two opponencies) he goes to the sophs' schools, and huddles for that part which he has not kept. At the huddleing the father of the college, a bachelor, and a soph, attend. **1841** G. PEACOCK *Stat. Cambridge* 73 The term *huddling* not unhappily expressed the indecent accumulation of the..exercises which the candidates..were anciently required to perform.

huddle ('hʌd(ə)l), *sb.* [app. f. HUDDLE *v.*]
1. a. A mass of things crowded together in hurried confusion; a conglomeration.
1586 J. HOOKER *Girald. Irel.* in *Holinshed* II. 24/1 Ill haps come by heapes and by huddels. **1633** ROWLEY *Match Midnt.* IV. in Hazl. *Dodsley* XIII. 73 Randals fortunes comes tumbling in like lawyers' fees, huddle upon huddle. **1714** MACKY *Journ. thro' Eng.* (1723) (N.), The famous Stonehenge, one of the wonders of England..is a great huddle of large stones, placed in a circular form. **1841** *Blackw. Mag.* L. 156 A mere huddle and conglomeration of chances. **1876** LOWELL *Among my Bks.* Ser. II. 1 It gradually grew from a huddle of booths to a town. **1906** *Daily Chron.* 5 Mar. 6/6 A really fine organic city and not a mere gigantic huddle of apartment dwellings.

b. A confused crowd of persons or animals.
1642 *Vind. King* p. v, A seditious huddle of indigent people. *a* **1674** CLARENDON *Hist. Reb.* XVI. §132 In such a huddle and mixture of loose People of all conditions. **1742** FIELDING *J. Andrews* IV. xi, It frighted the women, who were all got in a huddle together, out of their wits. **1820** L. HUNT *Indicator* No. 64 (1822) II. 94 The Walruses..which lie in gigantic huddles upon the ice fields. **1924** W. M. RAINE *Troubled Waters* viii. 79 Beyond the post office a great huddle of sheep was being driven forward. **1959** *Listener* 26 Feb. 384/3 Stanley Spencer's 'Temptation of St. Anthony', with its huddle of precisely drawn nudes.

2. a. Confusion, disorder; confused utterance.
b. Disorderly or indecent haste, hurry, bustle.
1606 CHAPMAN *Gentlem. Usher* Plays 1873 I. 271 O noble Crone, Now such a huddle and kettle neuer was. *Ibid.* 288 Nay, he speakes huddles still, lets slit his tongue. **1692** tr. *Sallust* 149 The next day, the opinions of the Council being demanded in a huddle, and over-rul'd by the Consul. *a* **1734** NORTH *Lives* I. 296 The service was performed..with more harmony and less huddle than I have known it. **1840** THACKERAY *Crit. Rev.* Wks. 1886 XXIII. 160 Introduced.. not..for mere picturesque effect or ornamental huddle.

†**c.** A term at shovel-board: see quot. *Obs.*
1586 J. HOOKER *Girald. Irel.* in *Holinshed* II. 87/1 When the lieutenant and he [the earl] for their disport were plaieng at slidgrote or shoofleboord..By saint Bride lieutenant (quoth he) there is some mad game in that scroll; but fall how it will, this throw is for an huddle.

†**3.** A miserly old person; a hunks. *Obs.*
1579 LYLY *Euphues* (Arb.) 44 So these old huddles hauing ouercharged their gorges with fancie, accompt al honest recreation meere folly. *Ibid.* 106 Though Curio be olde huddle and twang, ipse. *Ibid.* 133 God shield aunswered this olde huddle, I can haue two seruaunts of yat price. **1604** MARSTON *Malcontent* (Mason), How does thy young wife, old huddle?

4. A close or secret conference; esp. in phr. *to go into a huddle*, to hold a secret conference, to consult specially (about something). *colloq.*
1929 E. LOOKER *White House Gang* i. 13 The Gang was recruited, and..it went into a huddle, to confound all rules of deportment in high places. **1932** *Harper's Mag.* Apr. 600 'When an agent comes,' explains René, 'we have a little *conférence*. We go into what you call a huddle, yes?' **1934** E. LINKLATER *Magnus Merriman* xi. 128 Your girl-friends'll need to go into a huddle to think up something to beat that one. **1938** F. SCOTT FITZGERALD *Let.* 5 Sept. (1964) 93 I'm going into a huddle on this script and probably won't be able to write you again at length before Vassar starts. **1947** J. BERTRAM *Shadow of War* 318 He went into a huddle with one of his minions. **1959** 'A. GILBERT' *Third Crime Lucky* iii. 49 If he writes in he wants to make some of what he never earned over to us there'll be a huddle. **1972** M. YORKE *Silent Witness* v. 121 Then she got scared when he was missing and that's why she and Roy were in a worried huddle this morning.

5. *Bridge.* A period of meditation during which a player considers his next call or play.
1934 *Amer. Speech* IX. 11/1 A *huddle* is a session of silent thought indulged in by a player either during the bidding or during play. **1964** *Official Encycl. Bridge* 248/1 If the huddle is followed by a positive action, usually no harm is done to the opponents.

†'**huddle**, *a.* and *adv.* *Obs.* [f. HUDDLE *sb.* or *v.*]
A. *adj.* Huddled, confused, congested.
1601 HOLLAND *Pliny* I. 162 Mowing with his mouth when hee spake,..in his huddle and thicke speech. **1698** *Revengeful Queen* (N.), A suddain, huddle, indigested thought Rowls in my brain. **1713** STEELE *Guardian* No. 21 ¶6 The huddle group of those who stand most distant.

B. *adv.* Confusedly; in a crowding mass; in disorderly haste.
1564 COVERDALE *Lett. Martyrs* 77 Al that was.. tumultuously spoken, and..obiected of so many, whiche spake oftentimes hudle, so that one could not well heare an other. **1566** DRANT *Horace Sat.* IV. B vij b, He..woulde not move his foote withall, but huddle he would roule. *c* **1580** J. JEFFERIE *Bugbears* I. ii. in *Archiv Stud. Neu. Spr.* (1897) 308 Old men speake hudell many times on that note [cuckold]. **1600** HOLLAND *Livy* XXVII. xl. 658 All dangers come huddle together. **1601** —— *Pliny* 81 Then no order forward can be kept: the rest thereof shall be set downe huddle by heapes. **1606** *Wily Beguiled* E ij b, I have suitors come huddle, twoes upon twoes.

huddled ('hʌd(ə)ld), *ppl. a.* [f. HUDDLE *v.*] Crowded together without order; all in a heap.
1643 MILTON *Divorce* II. xv. (1851) 99 The extreme shift of a huddl'd exposition. **1683** T. HOY *Agathocles* 6 A numerous huddled Concourse fill'd the place. **1712** STEELE *Spect.* No. 302 ¶11 That huddled Oeconomy of Dress which passes under the general Name of a Mob. **1809** PINKNEY *Trav. France* 141 The streets..are very narrow, and the houses mean, low, and huddled. **1870–4** J. THOMSON *City Dreadf. Nt.* II. ii, The huddled stones of grave and tomb: Some old God's-acre. **1888** TH. WATTS in *Athenæum* 18 Aug. 225/2 He drives the wing—a huddled throng—Back on the centre ships, that steer for flight.

huddledom ('hʌd(ə)ldəm). [f. HUDDLE *sb.* + -DOM.] A state or condition of confusion and disorder.
1923 *Glasgow Herald* 24 May 9 The huddledoms of haunting disease, poverty, and overcrowding. *Ibid.* 31 May 6 Into this huddledom..came a youth, David Watt Torrance.

†'**huddle-'duddle.** *Obs. rare*⁻¹. [Cf. HUDDLE *sb.* 3.] A decrepit old man.
1599 NASHE *Lenten Stuffe* 3 Those gray beard huddle-duddles and crusty cum-twangs were strooke with such stinging remorse.

'**huddlement.** [f. HUDDLE *v.* + -MENT.] Huddled condition, huddling.
1859 *Out of the Depths* 188 Writhing about in the close huddlement in which they had lain all night. **1898** *Echo* 5 Jan. 2/3 Their rule means the grinding of the faces of the poor, and huddlement in slumdom.

'**huddler.** *rare.* [f. HUDDLE *v.* + -ER¹.] One who huddles.
1611 COTGR., *Brouilleur*, a confounder, iumbler, hudler, disorderly shuffler, or mingler of things together.

'**huddling,** *vbl. sb.* [f. HUDDLE *v.* + -ING¹.] The action of the vb. HUDDLE, in various senses: esp. a confused or disorderly crowding together.
1581 LAMBARDE *Eiren.* I. ix. (1602) 41 By the vntoward huddeling of things together, which were at strife the one with the other of them. **1638** WILKINS *New World* II. (1707) 12 What a huddling and confusion must there be, if there were two Places of Gravity. **1841** [see HUDDLE *v.* 8]. **1869** *Lonsdale Gloss., Huddlin(g)*, an embracing, a cuddling.

'**huddling,** *ppl. a.* [f. HUDDLE *v.* + -ING².] That huddles: in various senses of the verb.
(Drant's use is perh. founded on the literal sense assigned to L. *satira* of 'hotch-potch, medley'.)
1566 DRANT *Horace Sat.* A, Next hudling Horace braue in Satyres grace. **1583** BABINGTON *Commandm.* iii. (1637) 26 It should be an offence very fearefull if..Judges, Justices, &c. should minister oaths..in such hudling, posting, and unreverent manner, as that a man can scarce tell what he saith. **1634** MILTON *Comus* 495 Thyrsis! whose artful strains have oft delayed The huddling brook to hear his madrigal. **1816** SCOTT *Antiq.* xvii, The lake discharged itself into the huddling and tumultuous brook. **1871** R. ELLIS *Catullus* lxiii. 28 On a sudden yell'd in huddling agitation every tongue.

Hence **'huddlingly** *adv.*, in confused haste.

1615 CROOKE *Body of Man* 42 The property of heate, is to confound and make a medley of all things, shuffling in one thing hudlingly vpon another.

†**huddon.** *Sc.* and *north. Obs.* Also 4 **hodon.** A whale, or large kind of whale.

? *c* **1370** *John of Bridlington* in *Pol. Poems* (Rolls) I. 196 Et grandia cete, Anglice hodones [*printed* hodoves]. **1513** DOUGLAS *Æneis* III. vi. 137 Hir hynd partis ar als grete, wele nere, As bene ane heiddyous huddoun, or a quhale. *Ibid.* x. iv. 132 The remanent straucht like a fischis taill, In simylitude of huddoun or a quhaill.

†**'huddron.** *Sc. Obs.* Also 7 **hudderon.** According to Jamieson, A young heifer; in quot. app. the skin of one.

1592 *Sc. Acts Jas. VI*, c. 155 Transporting and carrying foorth of this Realme, of Calue-skinnes, huddrounes, and Kid-skinnes [Skene 1609 quotes as 'Hudderons'].

huddroun, *a. Sc.* ? *Obs.* Also 8 **huderon.** According to Jamieson, Slovenly. Hence perh. ***belly huddroun***, 'slow-belly', sluggard, in Dunbar.

1500-20 DUNBAR *Poems* xxvi. 70 Mony sweir bumbard belly huddroun. *Ibid.* lxxv. 38 My belly huddrun, my swete hurle bawsy. **1721** KELLY *Sc. Prov.* 14 (Jam.) A morning-sleep is worth a foldful of sheep to a huderon duderon Daw.

huddypeke, var. HODDYPEAK, *Obs.*

hude, obs. form of HIDE, HOOD, HUED.

hudegeld, var. of HIDEGILD[2], *Obs.*

c **1290** FLETA I. xlvii. §20 Hudegeld [significat] quietantiam transgressionis illatæ in servum transgredientem.

huder, hudge, obs. ff. HITHER, HUGE.

Hudibrastic (hju:dɪ'bræstɪk), *a.* (*sb.*) [f. *Hudibras*, after such words as *fantastic*, *periphrastic*.] In the metre or after the manner of *Hudibras*, the celebrated mock-heroic satirical poem of Samuel Butler published in 1663–78; burlesque-heroic.

1712 *Lond. Gaz.* No. 4939/3 Merrily translated into Hudibrastick Verse. **1833** COLERIDGE *Table-t.* 1 July, There is great Hudibrastic vigour in these lines. **1879** B. TAYLOR *Stud. Germ. Lit.* 147 A didactic poem of a Hudibrastic character, full of shrewd and pithy phrases.

b. *absol.* or as *sb.* Hudibrastic language, verse, or style.

1758 J. ELLIS (*title*) The canto added by Maphaeus To Virgil's twelve books of Æneas... Done in English Hudibrastic. **1775** J. JEKYLL *Corr.* (1894) 56 He must indite Hudibrastics to Onslow.

Hence **Hudi'brastically** *adv.*

1873 MASSON *Drumm. of Hawth.* xvii. 388 The Anti-Covenanters or Malignants are described, Hudibrastically.

hudous, obs. form of HIDEOUS.

Hudson Bay ('hʌdsən beɪ). The name of a body of water in northern Canada (also with the possessive form *Hudson's*, from the name of the trading company, the Hudson's Bay Company), used in numerous phraseological combinations (see esp. Avis et al. *Dict. Canadianisms*), e.g. **Hudson('s) Bay blanket, Hudson's Bay tea.**

1900 J. LONDON *Son of Wolf* 181 Prince wrapped a Hudson Bay blanket about her with a mock reverence. **1912** 'R. CONNOR' *Corporal Cameron* 438 Tall, she looked.. lithe and strong, her close-fitting Hudson Bay blanket coat revealing the swelling lines of her budding womanhood. **1920** A. STRINGER *Prairie Mother* 263, I sat there wrapped up in one of Dinky-Dunk's four-point Hudson-Bays. **1943** R. E. & D. SWANSON *Rhymes Haywire Hooker* (1953) 51 The stranger smiles and then he says: 'Why, them is four point Hudson Bays!' **1948** *Beaver* Mar. 14 A tea used to be made from Hudson's Bay tea or Labrador tea. **1955** W. G. HARDY *Alberta Golden Jubilee Anthol.* 85 In his last days, the old warrior was a familiar sight in his Hudson Bay blanket coat. **1961** E. E. RICH *Hudson's Bay Company* III. xxvi. 738 In 1849–50 the American government had bought some Hudson's Bay blankets to distribute as gifts to the Indians. **1968** L. J. BRAUN *Cat who turned on & Off* (1969) iii. 25 One man in a Hudson Bay blanket coat carried a small dog dressed to match. **1970** *Beaver* Winter 22 Labrador tea, also known as Hudson's Bay tea across much of Northern Canada, is a pretty evergreen shrub whose robustly aromatic leaves make it one of the most famous teas of the north country.

Hudsonian (hʌd'səʊnɪən), *a.* [f. the name of an English navigator, Henry *Hudson* (died *c* 1611), discoverer of the North American bay, river, and strait which bear his name: see -IAN.] Of or pertaining to Hudson Bay and the surrounding land, *esp.* in the names of animals and the territory from Labrador to Alaska, as far south as the tree line, classified as the Hudsonian biogeographical zone.

1835 J. J. AUDUBON *Ornith. Biogr.* III. 727 The Hudsonian Godwit, *Limosa Hudsonica*.. is scarcely ever found farther south along the coast than the State of Maryland. **1858** S. F. BAIRD in *Rep. Explor. Route to Pacific* (U.S. War Dept.) IX. 744 *Numenius Hudsonicus.* Short-billed or Hudsonian Curlew... Atlantic and Pacific Coasts of North America. **1871** *Bull. Mus. Compar. Zool. Harvard* II. 401 The Hudsonian Fauna doubtless embraces outlying islands of the Canadian Fauna, as the upper part of the White Mountains, and the summits of the higher peaks in the Adirondacks. **1939** *Beaver* June 48/1 The Hudsonian chickadees and Canada jays would come near, making life a bit more cheerful. **1947** R. T. PETERSON *Field Guide Birds* (ed. 2) 266 *Parus hudsonicus*: (1) Hudsonian Brown-capped Chickadee, *P. h. hudsonicus.* **1948** A. L. RAND *Mammals E. Rockies* 15 The Hudsonian zone in Alberta is poorly characterized by mammals. **1952** T. M. STANWELL-FLETCHER *Tundra World* 42, I was startled by a series of loud, wild 'tit-tit-tit-tit-tit' notes from a big brown bird which leapt into the air a few feet in front. A Hudsonian curlew of course. **1952** D. F. PUTNAM *Canad. Regions* 139/1 The Hudsonian Life Zone.. extends from the timber limit to the south of James Bay, Lake Mistassini and Pointe des Monts on the North Shore. **1964** A. L. THOMSON *New Dict. Birds* 713/2 The smaller Whimbrel *N[umenius] phaeopus* is Holarctic (its American race being sometimes called 'Hudsonian Curlew'). *Ibid.* 715/1 The Hudsonian Godwit *L[imosa] haemastica* migrates from North America to South America.

'hudsonite. *Min.* [Named, 1842, from the Hudson River, near which it is found.] A black variety of pyroxene, containing much iron.

1842 BECK *Min. N. York* 405 Hudsonite.. was found by Dr. Horton in a vein of quartz. **1868** DANA *Min.* (ed. 5) 216 Aluminous Iron-Lime Pyroxene; Hudsonite.

Hudson seal. [f. the name of Henry *Hudson* (see HUDSONIAN *a.*) + SEAL *sb.*[1]] Musk-rat fur that has been plucked and dyed to give the appearance of seal fur. Also **Hudson Bay seal.**

1914 J. W. JONES *Fur-Farming in Canada* (ed. 2) 7 When the furdressers and dyers produced a clipped and dyed muskrat skin that resembled sealskin almost perfectly, it was found that it would not sell under its own name.. [the] high-priced fur is now sold as 'Hudson Bay seal'. **1920** *Eye Opener* (Calgary) 11 Sept. 1/4 The jackpot is to be the real thing in Hudson seal coats this coming winter. **1921** *Daily Colonist* (Victoria, B.C.) 2 Oct. 8/5 First Quality Hudson Seal Coat, fancy silk lined; extra large collar and cuffs of Alaska sable. **1936** D. MCCOWAN *Animals Canad. Rockies* xv. 134 When a muskrat skin has been tanned and the coarse outer hair removed the remaining soft silky undercoat is known to furriers as Hudson seal. **1945** H. MACLENNAN *Two Solitudes* (1946) II. 219 Paul looked out the window and saw ..women in black Hudson seal coats with their hands in black muffs, men with fur caps.

hue (hju:), *sb.*[1] Forms: 1 **híew, híw,** 1–2 **híow, héo,** 1–3 **hiu, heow,** (2–3 **hou**), 3 **heou, heouwe, heuwe, hiev,** (**howe, ewe, euhe**), 3–6 **hewe,** 3–7 **hew,** (**heu**), 4 **hu,** 4 **heuh, heuȝ, huee, hywe,** 4–5 **hwe, hye,** 4–6 **hiewe,** (5 **huwe, whew**), 6–7 **hiew,** (7 **hieu, heiw**), 6– **hue.** [OE. *híew, híw,* dial. *híow, híu, héo* (infl. *híewes*, etc.):—WGer. *hiuwj-* = Goth. *hiwi* form, appearance, show, Sw. *hý* skin, complexion (:—*hiuj-*):— OTeut. **hiwjo*[m]. Cf. Skr. *chawi* hide, skin, complexion, colour, beauty, splendour.]

†**1. a.** Form, shape, figure; appearance, aspect; species. *Obs.*

a **900** CYNEWULF *Crist* 721 in *Exeter Bk.*, He..þær mennisc hiw onfeng. **971** *Blickl. Hom.* 197 Heo [the church of St. Michael] is eac on onsyne utan yfeles heowes. *c* **1000** ÆLFRIC *Gen.* i. 12 Æfter his hiwe [*secundum speciem suam*]. *c* **1000** *Ags. Gosp.* Matt. xvi. 3 Nu cunne ȝe tocnawan heofones hiw. *a* **1100** *Ags. Voc.* in Wr.-Wülcker 317/37 *Forma*, hiw. *a* **1175** *Cott. Hom.* 223 He com þa a nedren hiwe. *c* **1200** ORMIN 12605 Godess Gast Inn aness cullfress heowe. *a* **1300** *Cursor M.* 4225 For þi suettnes and þi fair heu. *c* **1386** CHAUCER *Pard. T.* 93 (Harl.) Thus put I out my venym vnder hiewe Of holynes. **1398** TREVISA *Barth. De P.R.* VIII. xv. (Tollem. MS.), A fayre persone, fayre yȝen, fayre face and semely hye. *c* **1470** HENRY *Wallace* II. 398 [He] Hynt out his suerd, that was of nobill hew. **1590** GREENE *Orl. Fur.* Wks. (Rtldg.) 106/2 Thrice hath Cynthia chang'd her hue. **1653** H. MORE *Conject. Cabbal.* Wks. (1713) 187 In that squallid and horrid hew he sets out this Hyle or First Matter, in the First Day's Creation.

†**b.** *concretely.* An apparition, a phantasm. *Obs.*

a **1000** *Ags. Gloss.* in Wr.-Wülcker 236/8 *Fantasia*, ..*fantasma*, scinlac, *uel* hiw. *c* **1420** LYDG. *Assembly Gods* 2049 When I sy hit, hit was but a whew, A dreme, a fantasy, and a thing of nought. **1603** *Philotus* cxxii. E ij b, I conjure the.. Be Sanctis of Heuin and hewis of Hell.

2. External appearance of the face and skin, complexion. Also *transf.* (In late use passing into 3.) ***hide and*** (*or*) ***hue***: see HIDE *sb.*[1] 2 b.

c **1205** LAY. 24644 Wimmen wunliche on heowen. *c* **1250** *Gen. & Ex.* 3051 Wimmen.. Faiȝer on siȝte.. And briȝte on hewe. ? *a* **1366** CHAUCER *Rom. Rose* 1213 She was not broun ne dun of hewe. *c* **1440** *Generydes* 1677 How fayre of hewe and womanly she was. *c* **1560** A. SCOTT *Poems* (S.T.S.) vii. 33 Ȝe ladeis cleir of hew. **1600** J. PORY tr. *Leo's Africa* II. 25 The women..contenting themselves only with their naturall hiew. **1777** SHERIDAN *Sch. Scand.* Portrait 104 The tender hue of female doubt. **1836** HOR. SMITH *Tin Trump.* (1876) 78 Our mental hue depends as completely on the social atmosphere in which we move as our complexion upon the climate in which we live.

3. a. Colour.

Down to the 16th c. app. exactly synonymous with 'colour'; but it appears to have become archaic in prose use about 1600, for it is included by Bullokar, Cockeram, etc., in their collections of 'Hard Words', and explained as = 'colour'. In modern use it is either a poetic and rhetorical synonym of 'colour', or a vaguer term, including quality, shade or tinge of colour, tint, and applicable to any mixture of colours as well as to a primary or simple colour.

971 *Blickl. Hom.* 73 Seo [smerenes] is brunes heowes & godes stences. *c* **1050** *Byrhtferth's Handboc* in *Anglia* VIII. 322 Hyt sceal beon hwites hiwes. *a* **1225** *Ancr. R.* 150 Grene ouer alle heowes froureð mest eien. *c* **1375** *Sc. Leg. Saints*, *Bertholomeus* 56 Sete with stanis of purpure hew. *c* **1450** HOLLAND *Howlat* 431 The colour of asure, ane hevinliche hewe. **1576** FLEMING *Panopl. Epist.* Ded. ¶iij, With leaves and blossoms of glorious hewe. **1616** BULLOKAR, *Hew*, colour. **1694** ADDISON *Poems, Virgil*, The flower it self is of a golden hue. **1791** MRS. RADCLIFFE *Rom. Forest* ii, In the east, the hues became more vivid. **1808** SCOTT *Marm.* VI. xiv, On the Earl's cheek the flush of rage O'ercame the ashen hue of age. **1836** W. IRVING *Astoria* I. 169 Wild flowers of every hue. **1844-57** G. BIRD *Urin. Deposits* (ed. 5) 233 The urine is of a fine amber hue, often darker than in health. **1859** W. S. COLEMAN *Woodlands* (1866) 23 The autumnal hues of the Beech are rich and glowing in the extreme. **1880** *Daily News* 7 Dec. 5/2 The hue of health will instantly revisit his sunburnt cheek.

b. *Chromatics.* Variety of any colour, caused by approach to or slight admixture of another; tint or quality of a particular colour.

1857 WILLMOTT *Pleas. Lit.* xi. 43 A phrase or an epithet in a book is a particular hue or shade of a picture. **1861** *Chem. News* IV. 187 Crimson..and..scarlet. The first is a red with a violet hue, and the second is a red with an orange hue. **1874** R. TYRWHITT *Sketch. Club* 32 Hue [means] variety of colour. **1891** HELEN B. HARRIS *Apol. Aristides* ii. 19 The green of its garden with the contrasted hues of the almond and the cypress. **1898** *Westm. Gaz.* 19 May 3/2 Between tone and hue there is sometimes confusion; a colour has both tones and hues. There are, for example, a turquoise hue of blue and a cornflower hue of blue.. the first having been influenced by the addition of green, and the second by that of white or black... There may be many hues of a colour and many tones of each hue.

c. That attribute of a colour by which it is recognized as a red, a purple, a green, etc., and which approximately corresponds to its dominant wavelength (or to that of its complementary colour); it constitutes, along with saturation ('tint', purity, intensity) and lightness ('shade'), one of the three attributes required for the complete specification of any colour.

In this sense hue is the quality in which different 'hues' (as distinct from 'tints' and 'shades': see SHADE *sb.* 4) differ; cf. quot. 1835 below and quot. 1859 s.v. TINT *sb.*[1] 2 a.

[**1835** G. FIELD *Chromatography* iii. 28 By mixing his colours with white, the artist obtains..tints; by mixing colours with colours, he obtains compound colours, or hues; finally, by mixing colours or tints with black, he gets.. shades.] **1855** J. C. MAXWELL in *Trans. R. Scottish Soc. Arts* IV. 395 There will be two things on which the nature of each ray will depend:—(1.) its intensity or brightness; (2.) its hue, which may be estimated by its position in the spectrum, and measured by its wave length. *Ibid.* 396 Colours differ not only in intensity and hue, but also in tint; that is, they are more or less pure. **1872** —— in *Not. Proc. R. Inst. Gt. Brit.* VI. 263 Colour may vary in hue, tint, and shade... A difference in hue may be illustrated by the difference between adjoining colours in the spectrum. **1900** G. H. HURST *Colour* i. 13 The hue of a colour is that constant which is commonly denominated by the term colour, as blue, or green, or red. **1936** A. B. KLEIN *Colour Cinematogr.* i. 89 There are about 130 steps of just distinguishable difference in hue in the spectrum. **1939** M. LUCKIESH *Colour* 39 The names of colors are often taken from the hue and usually imply it. **1955** P. D. TREVOR-ROPER *Ophthalm.* x. 137 Mono-chromatic light may alter its apparent hue as it becomes more unsaturated, red turning to pink, orange to yellow. **1960** G. M. WYBURN *Nervous Syst.* vi. 83 Colour or hue, which is our interpretation of variations in light wave-length is comparable to the pitch of sound. **1966** R. R. COUPE *Sci. of Printing Technol.* ix. 209 To describe completely a colour, we must take into account three different properties, namely hue, saturation and lightness.

†**hue,** *sb.*[2] Also 4–5 **hu,** 4–6 **hew,** 4, 7 **heu,** 5 **hewe, hui(e,** 6–7 **huy,** (6 *Sc.* **hoy**). [a. OF. *hu, hui, huy, heu,* outcry, noise, war-cry, hunting-cry, n. of action to *huer* to hoot, cry, shout, HUE *v.*[2]] Outcry, shouting, clamour, esp. that raised by a multitude in war or the chase. *Obs.* exc. in HUE AND CRY, q.v.

c **1330** R. BRUNNE *Chron. Wace* (Rolls) 6089 Þe Wa[l]ssche and Scottes wyþal þer here Comen wyþ gret noise & hew [*v.r.* hu]. *Ibid.* 11984 Þey..tok þer weye toward Moungu Wyþ mykel noyse & cry & heu [*v.r.* hu]. **13..** *E.E. Allit. P.* A. 872 A hue fro heuen I herde þoo. **1423** *Rolls Parlt.* IV. 198/2 Wyth outen hewe or cry. **1565-73** COOPER *Thesaurus*, *Acclamatio*,..an hue or crie. **1576** TURBERV. *Venerie* 136 Why dost thou..me pursue with cry of hounds, with blast of horne, with hallow, and with hue? **1603** DRAYTON *Bar. Wars* II. liii, Like as a Heard of over-heated Deere.. With Hues and Hounds recou'red eu'ry where. **1779** *Gentl. Mag.* XLIX. 253 As soon as M. Lally appeared, a hue was set up by the whole assembly, hisses, pointing, threats and every abusive name.

hue ('hu:eɪ), *sb.*[3] *N.Z.* [Maori.] A local name for the bottle gourd, *Lagenaria vulgaris.*

1843 E. DIEFFENBACH *Trav. N.Z.* II. iv. 49 The calabashes (hue) were.. the next addition to their stock of eatables. **1868** W. COLENSO in *Trans. N.Z. Inst.* I. III. Essay. 36 The Hue, or gourd, (a species of *Cucurbitæ*), gave useful Calabashes, and vessels of several kinds and sizes, from a gill to three gallons. **1905** W. B. *Where White Man Treads* 15 Besides being a succulent delicacy when young, the matured vegetable hue, with its strong, horny rind, could be put to the uses of many utensils, as drinking cups, bowls, etc., and, most important of all, water and oil flasks. **1921** H. GUTHRIE-SMITH *Tutira* viii. 55 The land [was] usually too poor for the cultivation on a great scale of such exotics as.. the *hue* (*Lagenaria vulgaris*). **1949** P. BUCK *Coming of Maori* (1950) II. i. 91 The gourd (*hue*) was grown principally to provide containers for water and for preserved birds.

hue (hju:), *v.*[1] [OE. *híwian*, f. *híw*, HUE *sb.*[1]]

1. *trans.* To form, fashion, figure, give an external appearance to; esp. (in later use) to colour. †In early use sometimes, To fashion

falsely, feign, pretend. Chiefly in pa. pple.: see HUED *ppl. a.*

c **1000** ÆLFRIC *Hom.* I. 484 Herodes hiwode hine sylfne unrotne. c **1050** *Supp. Ælfric's Voc.* in Wr.-Wülcker 178/39 *Colorare*, hiwian. c **1050** *Ags. Gloss.* Ibid. 408/26 *Fingo*, ic hiwiȝe. a **1300** *Cursor M.* 28013 Yee leuedis..studis hu your hare to heu, hu to dub and hu to paynt. **1830** TENNYSON *Poems* 39 All that blue heaven which hues and paves The other. **1839** J. E. READE *Deluge* etc. 4 We..watched The sunset hueing the rich clouds.

b. *fig.* To tinge.

1576 FLEMING *Panopl. Epist.* 315 My mynde being surprised with sorrow, and hewed with heavinesse.

†**2.** To depict, describe vividly. *Obs.*

c **1450** HOLLAND *Howlat* 424 Part of the principale..I sall haist me to hewe hartlie but hyre.

†**3.** *intr.* To take a colour; to become coloured.

1682 J. COLLINS *Salt & Fishery* 51 The Liquor begins to hew, and is ready to kern or granulate.

hue, *v.*² Now *local.* Also 4 huw, 6 hew(e. [app. a. F. *hue-r* to shout as in war or the chase, to hoot: app. of onomatopœic origin. The Cornish use may be an independent onomatopœia.]

1. *intr.* To shout, make an outcry; *spec.* in hunting, and now in the Cornish sea fisheries. Cf. HUER.

a **1250** [see HUING *vbl. sb.*]. **13..** *Guy Warw.* (A.) 6728 Þe wisest hunt folweþ fast, Huweþ & gredeþ wiþ gret blast. **1799** *Naval Chron.* I. 475 By the 1st of James I. c. 23, fishermen are empowered to go on the grounds of others to *hue*. **1864** MRS. LLOYD *Ladies Polc.* 39 Do 'ee 'hue' to the ladies for the life of 'ee. Look to that ground swell.

2. *trans.* To assail, drive, or guide with shouts.

1590 COKAINE *Treat. Hunting* B ij b, Euery Huntsman..is to hew him or backe him into the Couert againe. *Ibid.*, To hewe the Roe bucke in, both with voyce and horne. **1603–4** *Act 1 James I*, c. 23 §1 It shall..be lawfull..for euery such Watchmen, Balcors, Huors, Condors, Directors and Guidors..to enter..any Landes..and there to watch..and to Balke, Hue, Conde, Direct and Guide the Fisher-men which shall be vpon the said Sea and Sea Coasts. **1676** HOBBES *Iliad* (1677) 163 As when a lion, coming from the wood..Is hu'd by dogs and pesants in the night. *Ibid.* 259 Dogs and herds-men looking on And hueing him.

hue, var. HEO, HI *pron.* she, they.

hue, var. HOEY, society of Chinese.

1882 DE WINDT *Equator* 29 Members of a 'Hue', or Chinese secret society.

hue and cry, *sb.* Also 6–7 hu(e)-on-cry, 7 huoncry, 8 hewing cry. (Often hyphened.) [Anglo-Norman *hu e cri*, the two words HUE *sb.*² and CRY *sb.*, combined in a legal phrase, which was sometimes even treated as one word.

(There is some ground to think that *hue* as distinct from *cry* originally meant inarticulate sound, including that of a horn or trumpet as well as of the voice: cf. quot. 1769 in 2, and Du Cange s.v. *Huesium*; also HORNING.)]

1. *Law.* Outcry calling for the pursuit of a felon, raised by the party aggrieved, by a constable, etc.

[**1292** *Year-bk. 20–21 Edw. I* (Rolls) 339 Les presentors de la vyle de Hulle aveyt concele Hu e cry e sanck espandu. **1292** BRITTON I. vi. §4 Ou homme serra trové occys..ne heu ne cri ne avera levé.] **1502** ARNOLDE *Chron.* (1811) 90 Ony persone..that wyll not helpe constable, sergeauntis and other officers..when hue and crye is made. **1555** in Strype *Eccl. Mem.* (1721) III. xxvii. 213 For keeping the statutes of hue and cry. c **1575** *Balfour's Practicks* (1754) 512 The finder sall raise the hoy and cry. **1589** *Pappe w. Hatchet* (1844) 29 Martin, wee are now following after thee with hue and crie, and are hard at thy heeles. **1598** SYLVESTER *Du Bartas* II. i. II. *Imposture* 345 He flies, And still looks back for fear of Hu-on-cries. **1609** SKENE tr. *Sc. Acts Malc. II*, c. 15 §1 [To be] followed, with huy and cry. **1668** *Lond. Gaz.* No. 324/3 That Huy and Cry be immediately raised and pursued with diligence. a **1680** BUTLER *Rem.* (1759) II. 454 He..flies beyond Persuit of Huon-cries. **1782** COWPER *Gilpin* 236 Six gentlemen upon the road..They raised the hue and cry:—'Stop thief! stop thief!—a highwayman!' **1838** DICKENS *O. Twist* x, But the old gentleman was not the only person who raised the hue-and-cry.

b. A proclamation for the capture of a criminal or the finding of stolen goods.

1601 *Nottingham Rec.* IV. 256 Searchinge for suspected persons vpon huy and crye. **1657** W. MORICE *Coena quasi Κοινὴ* Def. xxi. 180 If a hue and cry should issue for such persons as carry the marks of Diotrephes. **1685** *Col. Rec. Pennsylv.* I. 147 Wm. Haigue Request yᵉ Secretry that a hue and Cry from East Jersie..might have some force and authority to pass this Province..; the Secretary Indorsed it and Sealed it with yᵉ Seal of yᵉ Province. **1720** in *Rutland Gloss.* (E.D.S.) s.v. *Hewing cry*, For a hewing cry, 2*d.* **1834** MEDWIN *Angler in Wales* I. 151 No Hue-and-Cry was published, no means taken for my re-apprehension.

c. An official gazette in which particulars about offences committed, offenders 'wanted', etc. are published for the information of the authorities.

In the English *Police Gazette* the phrase ceased to form part of the title on March 30, 1839, but it is still (1898) so used in that of the Royal Irish Constabulary.

1825 J. WILSON *Noct. Ambr.* Wks. 1855 I. 279 Men literally without a name, except it be recorded in the *Hue-and-Cry*. **1838** DICKENS *O. Twist* xv, Deeply absorbed in the interesting pages of the *Hue-and-Cry*. **1898** (*title*) The Police Gazette, or Hue-and-Cry. Published (by Authority) for Ireland on every Tuesday and Friday.

2. The pursuit of a felon with such outcry.

1648 MAYNE *Amorous War* I. i, A Hue and Crye of fourty thousand. **1722** DE FOE *Moll Flanders* (1840) 326 The hue and cry was stopped, and the high constable went back again. **1769** BLACKSTONE *Comm.* IV. xxi. (1809) 293 An hue ..and cry, *hutesium et clamor*, is the old common law process of pursuing, with horn and with voice, all felons.

3. *generally.* A clamour or shout of pursuit or assault; a cry of alarm or opposition; outcry.

1584 POWEL *Lloyd's Cambria* 152 Set vpon them with great hew and crie. a **1619** FOTHERBY *Atheom.* I. x. §4 (1622) 105 Whom the Heathens haue pursued with such an Hue-and-Crie for most damnable Atheists. **1697** COLLIER *Ess. Mor. Subj.* II. 133 Prosecuted by Apparitions, and pursued by Hue and Crys from the other World. **1846** RUSKIN *Mod. Paint.* I. I. I. i. (1848) 3 *note*, The public took up the hue and cry conscientiously enough. **1871** SMILES *Character* v. (1876) 126 When the 'Novum Organon' appeared, a hue-and-cry was raised against it.

attrib. **1870** EMERSON *Soc. & Solit.* iv. 60 With his..hue-and-cry style of harangue.

Hence **hue-and-cry** *v.*, to raise the hue and cry, make an outcry; to pursue with hue and cry.

a **1734** NORTH *Exam.* (1740) 233 We may hue and cry all over his Book, and hear no Tidings of them. **1830** *Gentl. Mag.* Nov. 432/1 The Hedge Hog, hue-and-cried, like a felon.

hued (hjuːd), *ppl. a.* Forms: 1 (ȝe)híwod, 2–3 ihewed, 4–7 hewed, (5 huet), 7– hued. [f. HUE *v.* or *sb.* + -ED.] Having a hue, coloured. †In early use in a wider sense: Figured, formed, fashioned in outward appearance, including but not confined to colour; also sometimes, Falsely fashioned, feigned, simulated, apparent.

c **1000** ÆLFRIC *Hom.* II. 240 Swa micel is betwux þære ȝehiwodan anlicnysse and ðam soðan ðinge. c **1175** *Lamb. Hom.* 25 He..bið al swa is an eppel iheoweð, he bið wið-uten feire and frakel wið-innen. ? a **1366** CHAUCER *Rom. Rose* 213 So grene as ony leek, So yvel hewed was hir colour. c **1400** *Destr. Troy* 3899 Here huet on his hede as haspis of silke. c **1425** WYNTOUN *Cron.* VII. v. 192 (Jam.) Chanownys quhyt, For swa hewyd is thare habyt. **1508** DUNBAR *Flyting w. Kennedie* 171 Skin, hewd lyk ane saffrone bag. **1615** MARKHAM *Eng. Housew.* (1660) 113 Malmseys be full Wines, pleasant, well hewed and fine. **1877** L. MORRIS *Epic Hades* II. 228 Till all the sordid Earth Was hued like heaven. **1890** *Spectator* 15 Mar., What richly hued birds.

hued, obs. f. *hewed*, pa. pple. of HEW.

hueholl: see HICKWALL.

huel: see WHALE, WHEAL.

hueld, obs. pa. t. of HOLD *v.*

hueless ('hjuːlɪs), *a.* [f. HUE *sb.*¹ + -LESS.]

†**1.** (In OE. and ME.) Formless, shapeless.

a **1100** *Ags. Voc.* in Wr.-Wülcker 318/24 *Deformis*, hiwleas. a **1200** Ibid. 538/1 *Deformis*, heowleas.

2. Colourless, pallid.

c **1000** *Sax. Leechd.* II. 242 Hu hiwlease hie beoð. c **1380** *Sir Ferumb.* 923 Olyuer..þat hewles was of semblant; for he bar many a wounde. **1601** R. JOHNSON *Kingd. & Commw.* (1603) 65 The Empire resembled a bloodlesse, yea a huelesse bodie. **1817** COLERIDGE *Sibyll. Leaves* Poems 1828 II. 325 Thin and hueless as a ghost. c **1865** E. DICKINSON *Poems* (1955) II. 737, I sight the Aprils—Hueless to me until thou come. **1932** CHESTERTON *Chaucer* viii. 264 The sort of harsh and hueless light that can be seen in the black engravings in the old Family Bibles.

Hence **'huelessness**, absence of colour.

1861 W. BARNES in *Macm. Mag.* June 130/2 Huelessness, which is called black.

huelp, obs. pa. t. of HELP *v.*

huemul, var. GUEMAL.

huer ('hjuːə(r)). Now *local.* [f. HUE *v.*² + -ER¹: cf. F. *hueur.*]

†**1.** *Hunting.* One who is employed to rouse or drive deer with noise and shouting. *Obs.*

1530 PALSGR. 231/1 Hewar that fetteth the wyndelesse in huntyng, *hveur.* **1674** N. COX *Gentl. Recreat.* (1677) 125 Hewers set round the Coverts to make a noise on every side.

2. *Fishing.* One who directs seine-fishing from high ground by the sea. Chiefly used in the Cornish pilchard fishery. Cf. BALKER².

1602 CAREW *Cornwall* 32 b, They..are directed in their worke, by a Balker or Huer, who standeth on the Cliff-side, and from thence discerneth the..course of the pilchard. **1603** [see HUE *v.*² 2]. **1616** SIR R. BOYLE *Diary* in *Lismore Papers* (1886) I. 135 Agreed with yong davies..to be our hewer there the next seazon..if God bless me wᵗʰ a plentefull ffyshing he is to be further considered. **1774** GOLDSM. *Nat. Hist.* (1862) II. III. ii. 313 Men..called *huers*, who, with brooms in their hands, gave signals where the nets were to be extended. **1864** MRS. LLOYD *Ladies Polc.* 7 Watching the movements of the 'Huer' who was signalling, with green branches in his hands, to the off shore fleet of boats. **1883** *Times* 18 May 7 Another relic..is..an ancient horn blown by the 'huers' when the pilchards were first sighted.

huer, obs. f. WHERE.

huerds: see HURDS.

huere, var. HER *pron. Obs.*, their.

huermyde, var. WHEREMID *Obs.*, wherewith.

hueroppe, var. WHEREUP *Obs.*

huerta ('(h)wɛətə). [Sp.] A piece of irrigated land in Spain or in the Spanish-speaking areas of Latin America; also, an orchard.

1838 A. GANIHL *Mexico vs. Texas* i. 13 He was resting himself, and enjoying the cool of the evening breeze, under a spreading orange tree, in his *huerta*. **1841** BORROW *Zincali* I. II. iv. 287 The justicia will compel us to restore the ass; we have, however, already removed her to our huerta out of the town. **1859** T. R. WARREN *Dust & Foam* viii. 225 In each of these huertas is a reservoir, built of masonry, through which water is constantly flowing. **1924** *Glasgow Herald* 28 July 5 The huertas merge into a delicious confusion of flower and fruit. **1934** M. R. SHACKLETON *Europe* vii. 89 From the Ebro delta to Cape de la Nao in Valencia, the irrigated districts ('huertas', from Lat. *hortus* = a garden) are practically continuous along the coast. **1958** FISHER & BOWEN-JONES *Spain* iv. 52 Originally developed by the Moslems, the 'huertas' are small, highly cultivated plots which depend on irrigation water brought by an intricate system of channels, aqueducts and lifts.

huet, obs. f. WHAT.

huf(e, huff(e: see HOOF, HOVE.

huff (hʌf), *v.* [*Huff* vb. and sb. appear late in the 16th c.; the vb. being somewhat the earlier. The formation was evidently imitative of the sound of a blast of air through an orifice: cf. the earlier use of HUFF *int.*, and the parallel *puff*.

In Preston's *Cambyses* (c 1570), *Huff*, *Ruff*, and *Snuff* are the names of three ruffians; connected possibly with sense 4 of the vb., 3, 4 of the sb. See also HUFF-SNUFF. HUFF-NOSED appears to be an early derivative.]

†**1.** *intr.* To blow, puff. *Obs.* exc. *dial.* and in phr. *to huff and puff* (in some contexts not distinguishable from sense 4).

1583 STANYHURST *Æneis* III. (Arb.) 86 Too se in what quarter yt huffeth: How stands thee wind blast..he marcketh. **1592** WYRLEY *Armorie, Ld. Chandos* 83 So Æolus huffs, so billowes big arise. **1624** MIDDLETON *Game at Chess* IV. ii, My conscience is becalm'd rather. I'm sure there is a whirlwind huffs in mine, sir. **1706** DE FOE *Jure Div.* I. 9 His stormy Godship [Æolus] Huffs about the Skies With Two and Thirty pointed Deities. **1881** *Isle of Wight Gloss.*, *Hough*, to breathe hard. 'Gwine up-hill makes me huff.' **1890** J. JACOBS *Eng. Fairy Tales* xiv. 69 Then I'll huff, and I'll puff, and I'll blow your house in. **1959** *Times* 11 Nov. 13/6 But it would be unrealistic to think that by huffing and puffing at him..the General can be made to change his mind. **1963** *Guardian* 1 Oct. 8/6 Mr. Liukov may huff and puff..about pernicious Western influences..but the Bulgarians..are discovering..a sense of humour. **1967** *Listener* 13 July 57/2 Sarah [Churchill] herself never mastered the techniques of politics; she huffed and she puffed but at the end of it all few houses had been blown down. **1971** *Daily Tel.* 13 Jan. 1 Ministers were undisturbed by all the huffing and puffing against the Industrial Relations Bill at the Albert Hall last night.

†**2.** *trans.* To blow; esp. to blow or puff *up*; to inflate, cause to swell; to raise or erect by inflating or the like. Also *fig. Obs.* Cf. HUFF-CAP.

1601 HOLLAND *Pliny* I. 39 The said winde within the earth, able to huffe vp the ground. **1613** SYLVESTER *Elegie Sir M. D. Hill* 138 Lest I, Too-puft with knowledge, should be huft too-hie. **1649** G. DANIEL *Trinarch., Hen. V*, cccxviii, Barmye Brains huffs vp the rotten Paist Made apt to mould. **1670** COVEL *Diary* (Hakluyt Soc.) 256 A sheet of fire, which ..huft my hat and vest like a mighty gust of wind. **1677** GILPIN *Demonol.* (1867) 77 Huffing them up with a confidence that they are above the temptation. **1718** BP. HUTCHINSON *Witchcraft* 9 They can huff up their Bellies, that they may seem much swell'd. **1719** D'URFEY *Pills* V. 269, I Will that Butchers Huff their Meat.

†**3. a.** *intr.* To swell, swell up. *Obs.* exc. *dial.*

1656 W. D. *Gate Lang. Unl.* xxiii. §285 A wart, a wen.. a bunch huffing up. **1670–98** LASSELS *Voy. Italy* II. 117 A world of shirt huffing about his wrist. a **1680** BUTLER *Rem.* (1759) I. 168 They huff and swell, Like Pilferers full of what they steal. **1693** SIR T. P. BLOUNT *Nat. Hist.* 79 Cochinele ..being held..in the Flame of a Candle..huffs and swells. **1868** ATKINSON *Cleveland Gloss.*, *Huff*, to become swollen and puffy, as the flesh where a blow has been received.

†**b.** To effervesce. *Obs.*

1707 SLOANE *Jamaica* I. p. xxviii, Syder, Beer, and Ale do not keep well here; they huff and fly in this strange climate.

†**4.** *intr.* To puff or swell with pride or arrogance; to speak arrogantly or insolently; to storm, bluster, 'talk big'; to 'bluff'. Also *to huff it. to huff and ding*: see DING *v.* 5. *Obs.*

1591 HORSEY *Trav.* (Hakluyt Soc.) 238 The burger-meister..hufft therat, saienge they would pass with their shippinge in spight of the Quen of Englands power. **1598** FLORIO, *Scorrubbiare*, to chafe..to huffe and snuffe. **1677** *Govt. Venice* 300 After they had baul'd and huffed a good while one against another, they fell at length to Cuffs. **1678** R. L'ESTRANGE *Seneca's Mor.* (1702) 257 A Man may..Huff it out, and yet be rotten at Heart. **1682** BUNYAN *Holy War* 109 He refused, and huffed as well as he could, but in heart he was afraid. **1719** D'URFEY *Pills* (1872) VI. 249 The Pedlar began to huff, And said his Measure was good. a **1734** NORTH *Exam.* II. iv. (1740) 264 He..walked about well-dressed, huffing and swaggering.

5. *intr.* To swell with anger or irritation; to get out of temper, take offence. Also † *to huff it.*

1598 B. JONSON *Ev. Man in Hum.* I. ii, And still you huffe it, with a kind of carriage As void of wit, as of humanitie. **1611** *Coryat's Crudities* Panegyr. Verses, For which let not our carping Criticks huff. **1678** RYMER *Tragedies* 12 Did ever man huff with such a parenthesis? a **1703** BURKITT *On N.T.*, *Acts* viii. 31 Some would have huffed at it as a rude affront. **1840** MARRYAT *Olla Podr.* (Rtldg.) 323 The.. woman has huffed, and won't trust me.

6. a. *trans.* To hector, bully; to scold, chide, storm at. (Cf. mod. colloq. 'to blow up'.)

1674 S. VINCENT *Yng. Gallant's Acad.* 79 If he cannot have as much as he demands, presently huffs the good-natured man his Father. **1741** RICHARDSON *Pamela* I. 144 And she has huffed poor Mr. Williams all to-pieces for pleading for me. a **1784** MRS. PIOZZI in Boswell *Johnson*

(1848) 160/2 *note*, I asked him, if he ever huffed his wife about his dinner? **1822** W. Irving *Braceb. Hall* (1845) 60 Quarrelling with his bread and butter and huffing the waiter. **1862** Mrs. Sewell *Patience Hart* xxii. 151 It seemed no use to huff him; he only got the bolder.

b. To drive *to, into, off*, do *out of*, etc. by huffing or hectoring.

1681 in *Select. fr. Harl. Misc.* (1793) 461 They can huff and over-awe him to things most opposite to his judgment. **1685** H. More *Paralip. Prophet.* 370 As for that gross Arianism..it was hufft off the Stage betimes. **1692** Sir T. P. Blount *Ess.* 150 No man cares to be Huff'd and Hector'd out of it. **1709** Mrs. Manley *Secr. Mem.* (1736) IV. 215 If ..Cæsar [was to be] huffed into Compliance!

c. To treat with arrogance or contempt.

1676 D'Urfey *Mad. Fickle* v. ii, You shall be hufft and cufft, and flip'd and kick'd, Sirra, if you talk of private Rooms. **1786** Burns *Twa Dogs* 88 How huff'd, and cuff'd, and disrespeckit! **1859** J. C. Fairbairn *Hymns & Poems* 92 Alcmena's son advanced, the beast in scorn Huffed the uplifted club and brandished spear. **1882** Spurgeon *Serm.* XXVIII. 123 Pilate had huffed it off with the pert question [etc.].

7. To offend the dignity of, as by discourtesy or want of attention; to cause to take offence, put into a huff. Chiefly in passive.

1793 M. Rishton *Let.* 12 Aug. in F. Burney *Jrnls. & Lett.* (1972) II. 185, I am a horrid Coward and get huffed every time we drive out. **1800** *Aurora* (Philadelphia) 18 Dec. (Th.), The Philadelphia Gazette is huffed at our stating a fact. **1814** Mad. D'Arblay *Wanderer* III. 190 Which huffed me a little, I own. **1825** Brockett, *Huff*, to offend. 'She's easily huffed.' **1858** Carlyle *Fredk. Gt.* iv. x. I. 495 Serene Highness of Heidelberg was much huffed; Kaiser dreadfully so. **1864** Mary Eyre *Lady's Walks S. France* xvii. (1865) 193 She felt huffed at my supposing anything so vulgar. **1887** *Times* 31 Aug. 5/1 The Prince contrived to huff M. Stambouloff in his second interview with him. **1906** J. M. Synge *Lett. to Molly* (1971) 50 Dont imagine I'm huffed or anything, little heart, I'm only weary. **1969** *Listener* 17 Apr. 535/2, I don't know whether to be huffed or pleased about it.

8. *Draughts.* To remove (an opponent's man) from the board as a forfeit for deliberately or neglectfully failing to take with it a piece that is *en prise*. The removal was (and is still sometimes) marked by blowing on the piece. (Called in Sc. *to blaw* or *blow*, in Ger. *blasen*, F. *souffler une dame*.)

R. Holme uses 'huff' for the taking of the men at draughts in the ordinary progress of the game; Halliwell has also 'In Chess, to remove a conquered man from the board'. Evidence for these uses has not been found, but Du. *blazen* 'to blow' is used in chess, draughts and backgammon.

1688 R. Holme *Armoury* iii. 264/2 If a Man [at Draughts] may leap over his Adversaries Man's Head to a Void square, that Man is Huffed, that is he taken up as a slain Man. **1706** Phillips (ed. Kersey) s.v., At..Draughts to Huff is to take up and blow off a Man, that the Adversary by oversight let slip from taking another. **1812** *Sporting Mag.* XXXIX. 74 You may decline huffing an adversary's piece. **1857** *Chambers' Inform. People* II. 710/2 If a player omit to take a man when it is in his power to do so, his adversary can huff or blow him—that is, either take the man, or insist upon his own being taken.

9. *slang.* (See quot.)

1832 *Examiner* 845/1 Johnson huffed, as it is called, the murdered man; that is, threw his arms over his victim's shoulders, and took the money from his pockets..Johnson huffed and Fare robbed the deceased.

†**10.** To scare *away* by calling *huff!* [huff *int.*]

1621 Ainsworth *Annot. Gen.* (1639) 58 The fowles came downe upon the carkeises: and Abraham huffed them away. **1650** Trapp *Comm. Gen.* xv. 10 The fowls that came down upon them..Abrams huffing of them away.

11. *Mil. slang.* To kill.

1919 *Athenæum* 23 May 360/2 Unmitigated slang, like ..'to huff' for 'to kill'. **1925** Fraser & Gibbons *Soldier & Sailor Words* 122 *To be huffed*, to be killed. **1933** Partridge *Words, Words, Words!* iii. 197 The English synonyms for death..*huffed*; *out of mess*, dead.

Hence **huffed** *ppl. a.*

1591 Sylvester *Du Bartas* i. ii. 949 Thy huff'd, puff'd, painted, curl'd, purl'd, wanton Pride. **1871** *Daily News* 21 Sept., The Generals who blunder..should be scored off and placed aside, like the huffed pieces of the draftboard.

huff (hʌf), *sb.* [See huff *v.*]

†**1.** A puff of wind; a slight blast. *Obs.* exc. in phr. ***huff and puff*** (in some contexts influenced by sense 2).

1600 *Maides Metam.* ii. in Bullen *O. Pl.* I. 126 This takes fier like touch powder, and goes off with a huffe. **1668** H. More *Div. Dial.* v. xxix. (1713) 496 An Huff of Phancy, which ignorant giddy Men may call the Spirit. **1725** Bradley *Fam. Dict.* s.v. *Pigeon*, The little huff of wind thrown in from the Powter [pigeon] gives them heat and mirth. **1961** *John o' London's* 9 Nov. 517/3 Nor do I really fancy Papermac's huff-and-puff. **1962** *Listener* 19 July 112/2 It seems a pity that this new era in telecommunications should be accompanied by an international huff-and-puff over priorities which at its worst comes perilously near to sub-lunar soap-opera. **1966** *Listener* 26 May 772/3 Even Ernesto is essentially a pallid version of those huff-and-puff baritones of Donizettian melodrama. **1967** G. Sims *Last Best Friend* ix. 82 '—ing old woman,' Spiegl said. 'All huff and puff.' **1973** *Times* 16 Mar. 14/4 We are going through a period of a great deal of huff and puff generated by consumer organizations.

fig. **1679** Dryden *Troilus* Pref., If they be in a calm, 'tis in vain for him to be in a huff.

2. a. A gust or sudden swell *of* anger or arrogance.

1599 Sandys *Europæ Spec.* (1632) 47 Some of the ministers of Spaine in the huffe of their pride have not beene able to hold in. *a* **1716** South *Serm.* (1737) VII. xii. (R.), An anger that is but as the spleen of a wasp, a short phester and huff of passion. **1858** Carlyle *Fredk. Gt.* vi. ii. II. 15 Early in the Spring, a difficult huff of quarrel..had fallen-out with his neighbour of Saxony.

b. A fit of petulance or offended dignity caused by an affront, real or supposed; esp. in phr. ***in a huff, to take huff.***

(The quots. before 1757 are doubtful and may belong to prec.: this sense is not in J.)

[**1684** *Roxb. Ball.* (1886) VI. 171 Jockey he wondred at Moggie's strange huff; But Moggy was jealous, and that was enough. **1694** De la Pryme *Diary* (Surtees) 45 Upon which, in a great huff, he left the college.] **1757** Washington *Lett.* Writ. 1889 I. 426 Every petty person must..be caressed or otherwise takes huff, thinks his merit and wisdom slighted. **1778** Miss Burney *Evelina* xxiv, She went out of the room quite in a huff. **1836** T. Hook *G. Gurney* I. 4 Sir Charles having taken huff at my not being named after him. **1855** Browning *Fra Lippo* 338 You'll not mistake an idle word Spoke in a huff by a poor monk. **1869** C. Gibbon *R. Gray* xxxi, I wish..I hadna been sae ready to take the huff at him on Saturday.

†**c.** (?) A hectoring, a bullying. *Obs.*

1773 N. Frowde *Life* etc. 13 Many a sour Look from my Uncle, and many a Huff and Blow from his Wife.

†**3.** Inflated opinion of oneself, and its display; arrogance, bluster, bounce, brag. *Obs.*

1611 Cotgr., *Palmer les cheveux des orgueilleux*, to quell or abate, the huffe of the prowd. **1658** J. Harrington *Prerog. Pop. Govt.* (1700) 231 Away with..this huff of Wisdom maintain'd by making faces. **1694** R. L'Estrange *Fables* cxviii. (1714) 135 A Spaniard was Wonderfully upon the Huff about his Extraction. **1697** Creech *Manilius* ii. 73 The School's simplicity, the Court's Address, The Souldier's Huff.

†**4.** One puffed up with conceit of his own importance, valour, etc.; one who blusters or swaggers; a hector, a bully. *Obs.*

1667 South *Serm.* (1823) I. 374 A company of lewd, shallow brain'd huffs. **1674** S. Vincent *Yng. Gallant's Acad.* 91 No man is Valianter than our Huff in civil Company, and where he thinks no danger may come of it. **1678** *Advice to Soldier* in *Harl. Misc.* I. 479 To receive the laws of honour from the hectors and huffs of the town. **1700** T. Brown tr. *Fresny's Amusem. Ser. & Com.* 130 Every Silly Huff [is call'd] a Captain. **1713** Darrell *Gentlem. Instructed* Suppl. to 1st Pt. viii. §6. 91 This young Huff commanded a Sergeant to pay him Respect.

†**5.** A puffing up or artificial raising. *Obs.*

1630 *R. Johnson's Kingd. & C.* 51 A better purchase than the Italian huffe of the shoulder [cf. *huff-shoulders* in 9].

6. *local.* (See quots.)

1787 Grose *Prov. Gloss.*, *Huff*, light paste enclosing fruit or meat whilst stewing, so called from its huffing or puffing up in the operation. Generally made with yeast. *Glouc.* **1890** *Gloucester Gloss.*, *Huff*, light pastry, or pie crust.

7. *Draughts.* An act of 'huffing': see prec. 8.

1870 Hardy & Ware *Mod. Hoyle, Draughts* 110 The act of 'huffing' is not reckoned as a move; a 'huff and a move' go together. *Ibid.*, It is called 'standing the huff' when a player instead of taking the man which is *en prise*, makes some other move. **1893** *Northumb. Gloss.* s.v., A huff is still accompanied by a blow on the piece.

8. = huff-cap B. 1. *dial.*

1790 Grose *Provinc. Gloss.* (ed. 2), *Huff*, in Wiltshire it signifies strong beer. **1866** R. B. Mansfield *School Life Winchester Coll.* 180 (Farmer) Washed down by libations of huff. **1891** Wrench *Winchester Word-bk.*, *Huff*, the strong beer brewed in College.

9. *Comb.* †**huff-cod**, a kind of pea, ? one with a swollen pod; †**huff-gale**, a strong wind; †**huff-shoulders**, elevated shoulders (cf. 5); so †**huff-shouldered** *a.*, having such shoulders.

c **1680** *Enquiries* 2/2 The Rose Pea, the Horn Pea, large *Huffcods. **1583** Stanyhurst *Æneis* iv. (Arb.) 110 Too stay for a better passadge, for a prosperus *hufgale. **1650** Bulwer *Anthropomet.* xvi. 162 In the Island Tapobrana, High *huff-shoulders are in fashion. **1590** [Tarlton] *News Purgat.* (1844) 119 *Huffe shouldred and of a wrinckled visage. **1598** Hakluyt *Voy.* I. 21 Rough and huf-shouldred.

†**huff**, *a. rare.* [perh. for *huft, huffed*, f. huff *v.*] Offended, out of temper; huffed.

1714 C. Johnson *Country Lasses* v. i, This little huff-bluff Hector will let no body lie with your family but himself. **1727-38** Gay *Fables* ii. i. 87 Reynard grew huff. Says he, This sneer From you I little thought to hear.

†**huff**, *int. Obs.* [Of same origin as huff *v.*]

1. A sound to scare away birds, etc.: = *shoo!*

1486 *Bk. St. Albans* D j b, Cry huff, huff, huff, and make the fowle to spryng.

2. An exclamation attributed to a swaggerer or bully, esp. when introduced on the stage.

c **1485** *Digby Myst.* (1882) iii. 491 Her xal entyr a galavnt þus seyyng: Hof hof hof, a frysch new galavnt! *c* **1530** *Hickscorner* in Hazl. *Dodsley* I. 188 Huff, huff, huff! who sent after me? I am Imagination, full of jollity. **1586** R. W. *3 Ladies Lond.* ii. in Hazl. *Dodsley* VI. 254 Huff! once aloft, and if I may hit in the right vein.

huff, obs. form of hove *v.*[1] and [2].

†**huffa**, *int. Obs.* = huff *int.* 2.

1519 *Interl. 4 Elem.* B ij, Make rome syrs and let vs be mery With huffa galand synge tyrll on the bery. **1526** Skelton *Magnyf.* 754 *Hic ingrediatur Courtly Abusyon cantando.* Huffa, huffa, taunderum, taunderum, tayne, huffa, huffa! *Cl. Col.* This was properly prated, syrs! what sayda? *Court. Ab.* Rutty bully, ioly rutterkyn, heyda! **1610** *Histrio-m.* ii. in Simpson *Sch. Shaks.* II. 32 Huffa, huffa, who calls for me? I play the Prodigall child in jollytie.

huff-cap ('hʌfkæp), *a.* and *sb. Obs.* or *arch.* [f. huff *v.* + cap *sb.*, i.e., 'that huffs or raises the cap'.]

A. *adj.* **1.** Of liquor: That goes to the head, heady, strong. *Obs.* exc. *Hist.*

1599 Nashe *Lenten Stuffe* 74 The huffe-cappest drink in that house you shal be sure of alwayes. **1630** J. Taylor (Water P.) *Satyre* Wks. ii. 261/2 Sale of hufcap liquor. **1635** —— *Parr* in *Harl. Misc.* (Malh.) IV. 212 At the alehouse, huff-cap ale to taste.

2. Blustering, swaggering. *arch.*

1597 Bp. Hall *Sat.* i. iii, Graced with huff-cap terms and thundring threats. **1737** Ozell *Rabelais* i. liv, No huff-cap Squire, or Brother of the Blade. **1889** Swinburne *Study B. Jonson*, A huffcap hero as ever mouthed and strutted out his hour on the stage.

B. *sb.* **1.** Strong and heady ale; also, a composite drink made from it. *Obs.* exc. *Hist.*

1577 Harrison *England* ii. xviii. (1877) i. 295 There is such headie ale and beere in most of them, as for the mightinesse thereof, among such as seeke it out, is commonlie called huffecap, the mad dog, father whoresonne, angels food, dragons milke. **1594** Greene & Lodge *Looking Glasse* G.'s Wks. (Rtldg.) 127/2 [The] ale is strong ale, 'tis huffcap. **1630** T. Westcote *View Devonshire* v. x. (1845) 393 This [the nappiest ale that can be drunk] being made into a huff-cap is held to be meat, drink, and cloth for warmth. **1884** Black *Jud. Shaks.* xxi, The rascal brewers..put all manner of abominations into their huff-cap.

†**2.** A swaggering or hectoring blade; a swashbuckler. *Obs.*

1600 Dekker *Gentle Craft* Wks. 1873 I. 70, I am with child till I behold this huffecap..when we come in presence His madnesse will be dasht cleane out of countenance. **1687** M. Clifford *Notes Dryden* ii. 7 Was not this Huff-cap once the Indian Emperour, and at another time did not he call himself Maximine? **1706** Farquhar *Recruit. Officer* v. v, You have made a fine speech, good Captain Huff-cap!

huff-duff ('hʌfdʌf). [Representing the pronunc. as a word of the initials *h. f. d. f.*, for *h*igh-*f*requency *d*irection-*f*inder.] A device for determining the direction of incoming high-frequency radio signals, enabling their source to be located when bearings are obtained by two or more such devices.

1946 *N.Y. Herald-Tribune* 16 Jan. 22/1 'Huff duff', with a range that makes it possible to detect and plot radio signals of as little as fifteen seconds' duration emitted halfway around the globe from plotting stations. **1955** C. S. Forester *Good Shepherd* ii. 39 Huff-Duff reports foreign transmission. **1962** L. Farago *Tenth Fleet* viii. 162 They used decoy subs to befuddle the Huffduff.

†'**huffer.** *Obs.* [f. huff *v.* + -er[1].] A boastful, swaggering, hectoring person.

1664 Butler *Hud.* ii. iii. 1034 To be expos'd, i' th' end, to suffer By such a braggadocio huffer. **1664** Cotton *Poet. Wks.* (1765) 9 Because he knew them Huffers. **1694** Strype *Cranmer* iii. xxxvi. 453 He was no Huffer nor Contender, but of an exceeding peaceable and amicable Spirit. *a* **1797** Mason *Ode to Pinchback* (R.), No longer, England, shalt thou dread Such Presbyterian huffers. **1808** E. S. Barrett *Miss-led General* 118 When our generals play the..cowards, as the greatest huffers among them will do at times.

†**b.** A quadruped: ? a kind of skunk. *Obs.*

1729 *Wood's Voy.* 96 A little creature with a bushy tail, which we called a Huffer, because when he sets sight on you he stands vapouring and patting with his fore feet upon the ground.

huffily ('hʌfɪlɪ), *adv.* [f. huffy *a.* + -ly[2].] In a huffy or petulant manner; huffingly.

1861 G. Meredith *E. Harrington* I. xiii. 240 The landlady turned from him huffily. **1880** Mrs. Parr *Adam & Eve* x. 140, 'I shan't forget Mr. Adam's opinion of me for one while', said Eve, huffily.

huffiness ('hʌfɪnɪs). [f. as prec. + -ness.] The quality of being huffy: †**a.** Boastfulness, blustering, arrogance. **b.** Readiness to take offence or show oneself offended.

1678 H. More in *Glanvill's Sadducismus* (1727) 463 Their understandings being but creatural huffiness of mind. **1695** J. Sage *Cyprianic Age* (1847) II. 76 A reconciliation between ..huffyness and humility. **1858** Lytton *What will he do?* iv. xi, That degree of polite culture which gives dignity and cures huffiness. **1883** Ld. R. Gower *My Remin.* II. xxvii. 230 He is an amiable youth, but has some..brusquerie of manner and huffiness.

huffing ('hʌfɪŋ), *vbl. sb.* [f. huff *v.* + -ing[1].] The action of the verb huff.

†**1.** Inflating with wind; swelling. *Obs.*

1583 Stanyhurst *Æneis* iii. (Arb.) 85 And winds vaunce fully thy sayls with prosperus huffing. **1608** Heywood *Rape Lucr.* Wks. 1874 V. 200 The seas have left their rowling, The waves their huffing, the winds their puffing.

2. Blustering, hectoring, bullying.

1600 Dekker *Fortunatus* Wks. 1873 I. 124 He scornd all Famagosta when he was in his huffing. **1672** Wycherley *Love in Wood* ii. i, Coyness in a woman is as little sign of true modesty as huffing in a man is of true courage. **1729** Gay *Polly* i. xii, When kings by their huffing Have blown up a squabble. **1828** Miss Mitford *Village* Ser. iii. (1863) 468 All his huffings and cuffings from master and mistress.

3. *Draughts.* See huff *v.* 8.

1865 Dickens *Mut. Fr.* i. iv, The huffing of Miss Bella and the loss of three of her men at a swoop.

'**huffing**, *ppl. a.* [f. huff *v.* + -ing[2].] That huffs: in various senses of the vb.

†**1.** Blowing; puffing; inflating; swelling. *Obs.*

1591 Sylvester *Du Bartas* i. v. 109 Th' Ork, Whirl-poole Whale or huffing Physeter. **1614-15** —— *Panaretus* 708 If the puffing gales Into the Deep transport her huffing sails. **1650** Bulwer *Anthropomet.* Pref., High huffing-Shoulders here the Gallants weare. **1670** Lassels *Voy. Italy* I. 96 Vertigals of whale-bone..bear out her coats in such a

huffing manner, that she appears to be as broad as long. *a* **1687** COTTON *Winter* iii, Æol's huffing brood. **1835** I. TAYLOR *Spir. Despot.* VI. 280 The huffing gusts of the coming tempest.

2. Puffed up, conceited, boastful; blustering, swaggering, hectoring, bullying.

1602 *How Man may Chuse gd. Wife* IV. iii, A huffing wench ..whose ruffling silks Make, with their motion, music unto love. **1609** HOLLAND *Amm. Marcell.* XIV. x. 22 The huffing puffes of stoutness and pride. **1735** POPE *Donne Sat.* IV. 201 Huffing, braggart, puff'd Nobility. **1831** *Blackw. Mag.* XXIX. 516 The..huffing, hectoring, basket-hilted adventurer. **1866** WHIPPLE *Char. & Charac. Men* 186 The bluff, huffing, swearing imperiousness of Thurlow.

'huffingly, *adv.* [f. prec. + -LY².] In a huffing manner: **a.** Arrogantly. **b.** In an offended way, petulantly.

1611 COTGR., *Guinguois, de guinguois,* huffingly, swaggeringly, aswash. **1693** *Apol. Clergy Scot.* 54 He would treat us very huffingly. **1851** I. TAYLOR *Wesley* (1852) 30 When we deal with occult folk..huffingly and disrespectfully. **1864** CARLYLE *Fredk. Gt.* XVI. vi. IV. 323 Leave was at once granted him, almost huffingly.

huffish ('hʌfɪʃ), *a.* [f. HUFF *sb.* + -ISH.] **a.** Arrogant, insolent. **b.** Petulant.

1755 JOHNSON, *Huffish,* arrogant, insolent, hectoring. **1796** MRS. MARY ROBINSON *Angelina* II. 61 If any body has a right to be huffish, 't is I. **1848** DICKENS *Dombey* 430 To return..a huffish answer. **1885** *Punch* 13 June, It's no use to turn huffish or moody.

Hence **'huffishly** *adv.*, **'huffishness.**

1755 JOHNSON, *Huffishly,* with arrogant petulance; with bullying bluster. *Huffishness,* petulance; arrogance; noisy bluster. **1825** MOORE *Mem.* 26 Oct. (1853) IV. 329 'Is she indeed?' answered Piozzi huffishly, 'then pray tell her I can be as indifferent as she', and walked away. **1841** *Tait's Mag.* VIII. 275 The heady huffishness and shifting desperation of foiled ecclesiastics.

huffkin ('hʌfkɪn). *local.* Also **uffkin.** [Origin unknown.] A kind of tea-cake made chiefly in Kent.

1790 in *Eng. Dial. Dict.* **1869** *N. & Q.* 4th Ser. IV. 76/1 Most people know what muffins and crumpets are, but in East Kent the former..are known as *uffkins.* **1887** PARISH & SHAW *Dict. Kentish Dial., Huffkin, hufkin,* a kind of bun or light cake, which is cut open, buttered, and so eaten. **1928** *Daily Express* 14 Mar. 5/4 Our merry teas after net-ball, cricket, or football, without huffkins would be very 'dry'. **1952** F. WHITE *Good Eng. Food* v. iv. 199 This quantity makes 10 huffkins weighing 2½ oz. each.

huffle ('hʌf(ə)l), *v. Obs.* exc. *dial.* [dim. and freq. of HUFF *v.*: see -LE.]

1. a. *trans.* To blow; to fan (a fire); to inflate.

1583 STANYHURST *Æneis* I. (Arb.) 39 Whereby hee..with gyfts might carrye the Princesse Too braynesick loouefits, to her boans fire smouldered huffling. **1657** R. LIGON *Barbadoes* (1673) 39 Jerkin Beef, which is hufled, and slashed through, hung up and dryed in the Sun.

†**b.** To raise in relief, emboss. *Obs.*

1638 *Patent* No. 118. 17 July, Ymbroidering or hufling of guilded leather..fitt for hangings.

c. Of the wind: to make a sound as of blowing in gusts. So **'huffle** *sb.*, a sudden gust of wind, or the sound made by this.

1862 W. BARNES *Poems Rural Life* 3rd Coll. 122 Where sharp-leav'd ashes' heads did twist In hufflèn wind, an' driftèn mist. **1878** HARDY *Ret. Native* I. I. iii. 70 The winds do huffle queerer to-night than ever I heard 'em afore. **1889** S. BARING-GOULD et al. *Songs of West* 9 At the huffle of the gale, Here I toss and cannot sleep. **1891** 'L. MALET' *Wages of Sin* III. VI. ii. 82 A huffle of wind, hot with the festering reek of the streets away across the river, fluttered the leaves. .. The wind huffled again.

†**2. a.** *trans.* To puff up, inflate, or elevate with pride. **b.** *intr.* To puff, bluster. *Obs.*

a **1652** BROME *Damoiselle* III. ii. Wks. 1873 I. 426 Let not your fine French Frippery..Huffle you up to Soveraignty. **1673** DK. LAUDERDALE in *L. Papers* (Camden) III. xii. 14 Another who is about you who yow know hath long huffled at me. *Ibid.* 17 But now he is huffled up that he must appeare a considerable man.

Hence **'huffling** *vbl. sb.* and *ppl. a.*, blowing, blustering, swelling.

1583 STANYHURST *Æneis* I. (Arb.) 19 Auctoritye..Too swage seas surging, or raise by blusterus huffling. *Ibid.* III. 93 Scaped from rough tempestuus huffling. *a* **1657** LOVELACE *Poems* (1864) 225 When to our huffling Henry there complain'd A grieved earl. **1689** *State Europe* in *Harl. Misc.* I. 200 Her huffling and prosperous condition may be rendered languishing enough. **1847** C. A. JOHNS *Forest Trees Gt. Brit.* I. 357 The huffling winds which we often experience in summer.

huffler ('hʌflə(r)). [Origin obscure: cf. HOVELLER.] (See quots.) Still used of bargemen.

1723 J. LEWIS *Hist. Thanet* 23 *Huffler,* one that carrys off fresh provisions, and refreshments to Ships. **1808** *Athenæum* III. 115 Until very lately the hufflers, or pilots of Heligoland were under no sort of subordination. **1824** *Gentl. Mag.* Aug. 111/2 We have a class of people in these parts called *Ufflers,* i.e. men in the barging line out of employ, who attend as extra help to get the craft home in our inland navigation. **1918** *Chambers's Jrnl.* Feb. 109/1 Here it is that the barge skippers and the barge mates and the river 'hufflers' congregate. **1927** *Daily News* 27 May 6/6 If it is necessary to take on a third hand, he is generally regarded as being quite an inferior person, and is known as a 'huffler'. **1948** H. BENHAM *Last Stronghold of Sail* ii. 29 There were 'hufflers' in plenty in those days to come aboard and lend a hand.

†**huff-muff.** *Obs.* [f. HUFF *v.* + MUFF.] ? A braggart, a blusterer. Also *attrib.*

1600 WATSON *Decacordon* IX. v. (1602) 307 Austrian.. Netherlandian, and such like Germaine bred huff muff forces. *Ibid.* IX. viii. 328 Maugre all the Iesuites Spaniards and huff muffes in the world.

†**'huff-ˌnosed.** *Obs. rare.* [app. f. HUFF *int.*, *v.*, or *sb.* + NOSE.] ? That turns up the nose; scornful.

? *a* **1550** BECON *Nosegay* Wks. (1560-3) I. 103 The proude Pharises the galaunt Byshops, the huffe nosed priestes.

†**'huff-puff,** *a. nonce-wd.* [f. HUFF + PUFF.] Moved with every puff of wind.

1583 STANYHURST *Æneis* IV. (Arb.) 115 A wind fane changabil huf puffe Always is a woomman.

†**'huff-pufft,** *a. Obs.* Inflated, puffed up.

1608 SYLVESTER *Du Bartas* II. iv. v. *Bartas* 12 Huff-puft Ambition, Tinder-box of War. **1618** *Barnevelt's Apol.* B ij b, A matter of import no doubt, Which huff-puft lungs thus belches out. *c* **1620** Z. BOYD *Zion's Flowers* (1855) 82 Huff-puft some are thus in their proud ambition.

†**huff-snuff,** *sb.* (*a.*) *Obs.* [f. HUFF *v.* + SNUFF, in the sense 'offence, resentment'; but largely suggested by the riming of the two words, as in reduplicated formations: see HUFF *v.*]

A conceited fellow who gives himself airs and is quick to take offence; a braggart, hector.

1583 STANYHURST *Æneis* etc. (Arb.) 143 A loftye Thrasonical huf snuffe: In gate al on typstau's stalcking. **1591** GREENE *Disc. Coosnage* (1859) 43 Seeing such a terrible huffe snuffe swering with his dagger in his hand. **1598** FLORIO, *Risentito,*..a huffe snuffe, one that will soone take pepper in the nose. **1611** COTGR. s.v. *Ferré, Mangeur de charrettes ferrées,* a terrible huffsnuffe, scarre-crow, braggadochio. **1653** URQUHART *Rabelais* II. ii. 12 Part of the Heavens, which the Philosophers call *via lactea,* and the Huffsnuffs, St. James his way.

b. *attrib.* or *adj.* Arrogant, hectoring, vapouring.

a **1693** URQUHART *Rabelais* III. xlii. 349 The huff, snuff, honder-sponder, swash-buckling High Germans.

huffy ('hʌfɪ), *a.* [f. HUFF *sb.* + -Y.]

†**1.** Windy, effervescent, puffy. *Obs.* or *dial.*

1765 BROWNRIGG in *Phil. Trans.* LV. 227 Like the air of beer, cyder, champaign, and other huffy liquors. **1890** *Gloucester Gloss., Huffy,* puffy, not firm.

†**2.** *fig.* Airy, unsubstantial. *Obs.*

1678 CUDWORTH *Intell. Syst.* I. i. § 44. 53 The way of physiologizing by matter, forms, and qualities, is a more huffie and phanciful thing. **1681** H. MORE *Exp. Dan.* Pref. 74 This Spirit of Charity being an huffy blast of crude Enthusiasm.

†**3.** Puffed up with pride, conceit, or self-esteem; haughty; blustering. *Obs.*

1677 *Govt. Venice* 259 Those..who before the danger are most huffy and high, as were the Venetians. **1678** EARL MURRAY in *Lauderdale Papers* (Camden) III. lxxxvii. 151 Lord Cochrane and his brother Sr Johne talked mor huffey then the rest. **1691** tr. *Emilianne's Frauds Rom. Monks* 107 Whether the Church of Rome has reason to be so huffy and proud of her Pilgrims and Hospitals.

4. †**a.** Arrogant, choleric. **b.** Ready to take 'huff' or offence; touchy, pettish.

1680 BUNYAN *Life Badman* (ed. Virtue) 524 His natural temper was to be surly, huffy, and rugged, and worse. **1693** *Apol. Clergy Scot.* 35 There is no necessity to appear huffy and out of humour. **1803** JANE PORTER *Thaddeus* xv. (1831) 133 It does not become a person in your situation to be so huffy. **1890** JESSOPP *Trials Country Parson* ii. 79 He is apt to be stuck up, and she is very apt to be huffy.

hufil, dial. name of the Green Woodpecker: see HICKWALL.

†**'hufty.** *Obs.* or *dial.* [Cf. next and HUFF *sb.*] **a.** Swagger; = next B. **b.** (?) A swaggerer.

1620 MELTON *Astrologaster* 52 (N.) Cut their meat after an Italian fashion, weare their hat and feather after a Germaine hufty. **1847-78** HALLIW., *Hufty,* a swaggerer, *Yorksh.*

†**'hufty-'tufty,** *a.* and *sb. Obs.* [A riming compound, f. HUFF *sb.* and TUFT *sb.* (perh. in reference to tufts of feathers worn as 'bravery' or finery) + -Y.]

A. *adj.* Swaggering, bragging.

1596 NASHE *Saffron Walden* L iv b, Gabriell..came ruffling it out huffty tuffty in his suite of veluet. **1599** —— *Lenten Stuffe* (1871) 32 Hufty-tufty youthful ruffling comrades, wearing every one three yards of feather in his cap for his mistress's favour.

B. *sb.* **a.** Swagger. **b.** 'Bravery', finery.

1603 BRETON *Packet Mad Lett.* I. xxii, Master Wyldgoose, it is not your huftie tuftie can make mee afraid of your bigge lookes. *a* **1652** BROME *Damoiselle* III. ii, This is my Wife.. You have lost yours, you say: Perhaps for want Of Hufty-tufties [*printed* tusties], and of Gorgets gay.

hug (hʌg), *v.* Also 6-7 **hugge.** [Appears late in 16th c.: origin unknown.

Not to be confounded with HUGGE *v.* to dread, shudder, shrink with fear or cold. Not connected with Sw. *huka,* Da. *sidde paa huk* to squat. In some shades of meaning it approaches Ger. *hegen* to foster, cherish, orig. to enclose or encompass with a hedge; but it is difficult to see how they can be connected.]

I. 1. *trans.* To clasp or squeeze tightly in the arms: usually with affection = embrace; but also said of a bear squeezing a man, dog, etc., between its forelegs.

1567 DRANT *Horace, Art Poetry* (R.), And hugge, and busse, and culle, and cusse thy darling apishe fruite. **1589** *Pappe w. Hatchet* (1844) 39 Like an olde Ape, hugges the vrchin so in his Conceipt [etc.]. **1594** SHAKS. *Rich. III,* I. iv. 252 He bewept my Fortune, And hugg'd me in his armes. **1661** LOVELL *Hist. Anim.* Introd., The love of apes is such towards their young, that they often kill them by hugging them. *c* **1705** POPE *Jan. & May* 813 He hugg'd her close, and kiss'd her o'er and o'er. **1786** COWPER *Lett.* 4-5 June, I could have hugged him for his liberality and freedom from bigotry. **1841** DICKENS *Barn. Rudge* xli, Dolly..threw her arms round her old father's neck and hugged him tight. **1865** BARING-GOULD *Werewolves* x. 165 Bruin turned suddenly on him and hugged him to death.

b. *transf.* and *fig.* ***to hug one's chains,*** to delight in bondage.

1588 SHAKS. *Tit. A.* III. i. 214 Staine the Sun with fogge as somtime cloudes, When they do hug him in their melting bosomes. *a* **1661** FULLER *Worthies* (1840) I. ii. 8 Were many English plants as rare as they are useful, we would hug in our hands what we now trample under our feet. **1719** YOUNG *Busiris* V. i, Now, from my soul, I hug these welcome chains Which shew you all Busiris. **1769** GRAY *Ode for Music* 6 Servitude that hugs her chain. **1835** WILLIS *Melanie* 60 As the miser hugs his treasure.

c. *fig.* To exhibit fondness for; *spec.* to caress or court, in order to get favour or patronage.

1622 MASSINGER & DEKKER *Virg. Mart.* II. D.'s Wks. 1873 IV. 30, I do hug thee, For drilling thy quick brains in this rich plot. **1634** MILTON *Comus* 164, I..Wind me into the easy-hearted man, And hug him into snares. **1712** ARBUTHNOT *John Bull* III. i, He..hugged the authors as his bosom friends. **1832** AUSTIN *Jurispr.* (1879) I. v. 194 The general opinion of barristers condemns the sordid practice of hugging or caressing attorneys. **1836** MACAULAY in Trevelyan *Life* I. 451 Mr. Longueville Clarke refused to fight, on the ground that his opponent had been guilty of hugging attorneys [cf. HUGGERY].

d. *fig.* To cherish or cling to (an opinion, belief, etc.) with fervour or fondness.

1649 JER. TAYLOR *Gt. Exemp.* Ep. Ded. 1 While all strive for truth, they hug their own opinions dressed up in her imagery. *a* **1718** ROWE (J.), Mark with what joy he hugs the dear discovery! **1817** MOORE *Lalla R., Veiled Prophet,* Faith, fanatic Faith, once wedded fast To some dear false-hood, hugs it to the last. **1856** EMERSON *Eng. Traits, Race* Wks. (Bohn) II. 23 The Briton in the blood hugs the homestead still. **1862** GOULBURN *Pers. Relig.* V. II. (1873) 84 There are some, who..hug a sort of spiritual selfishness.

2. *refl.* †**a.** To cherish oneself; to keep or make oneself snug. *Obs.*

1642 FULLER *Holy & Prof. St.* V. xviii. 429 Here Andronicus hugg'd himself in his privacie. **1745** *Proj. Manning Navy* 10 We hug our Selves over a Glass of Wine, and a good Fire, in a Tavern. **1757** W. THOMPSON *R.N. Advoc.* 33 With a Salary of 150*l.* per Ann...to..hug himself comfortably at Night in his own House with his Bottle.

b. *fig.* To congratulate or felicitate oneself.

1622 MASSINGER & DEKKER *Virg. Mart.* V. D.'s Wks. 1873 IV. 77 As a curious Painter, When he has made some admirable piece, Stands off..and then hugs Himself for his rare workmanship. **1650** FULLER *Pisgah* II. xiv. 301 Herod.. hugs himself that he had fitted their new King with a short reign. **1731** SWIFT *On his Death* 115 They hug themselves, and reason thus; It is not yet so bad with us. **1843** LE FEVRE *Life Trav. Phys.* I. I. x. 238 We hugged ourselves with the idea that we had done right. **1863** MRS. CLARKE *Shaks. Char.* viii. 206 He hugs himself upon his power over her. **1895** F. HALL *Two Trifles* 32 You..hug yourself as a good patriot for holding it in detestation.

3. *absol.* (also in reciprocal sense). **b.** *intr.* To lie close, cuddle.

1595 SHAKS. *John* V. ii. 142 To hug with swine, to seeke sweet safety out In vaults and prisons. **1687** *Good Advice* 39 Now Ridly and Hooper hug, and are the dearest Brethren.. in the World. **1695** CONGREVE *Love for L.* III. v, I love to see 'em hug and cotton together like down upon a thistle. **1733** POPE *Hor. Sat.* II. i. 87 Tis a Bear's talent not to kick but hug.

4. *trans.* (orig. *Naut.*) To keep as close as possible to (the shore, etc.); to 'cling to'.

1824 HEBER *Narr. Journ.* (1828) I. 167 The naval tactics of Bengal..always incline to hug the shore as much as possible. **1829** MARRYAT *F. Mildmay* v, Hugging the Spanish coast. **1856** KANE *Arct. Expl.* II. xv. 155 It was a lofty headland, and the land-ice which hugged its base was covered with rocks. **1861** HUGHES *Tom Brown at Oxf.* ii, He was hugging the Berkshire side himself, as the other skiff passed him. **1873** BROWNING *Red Cott. Nt.-cap* 26 Be sure I keep the path that hugs the wall. **1882** B. D. W. RAMSAY *Recoll. Mil. Serv.* II. xiii. 24 We hugged the land as we rounded, and dropped anchor outside the bay. **1898** *Daily News* 27 June 4/6 There was no panic, no hugging of cover, such as overtook the troops at Bull Run.

II. *north. dial.* [It is not clear that this is the same word.] **5.** *trans.* To carry.

1788 W. MARSHALL *Yorksh.* II. Gloss. (E.D.S.), *Hug,* to carry; especially a cumbrous load. **1825** BROCKETT, *Hug,* to carry, especially if difficult. **1891** ATKINSON *Last Giant-Killers* 60 Pokes big enough to hold two or three pigs each, to 'hug' them in. **1893** SNOWDEN *Tales Yorksh. Wolds* 135, I hugged her box up fro' t' station.

(In most dialect glossaries from Northumberland to Lincolnshire: not in Sc.)

Hence **hugged, 'hugging** *ppl. adjs.*; also **'huggingly** *adv.*

1841 DICKENS *Barn. Rudge* lix, Who could look on..and not desire to be..either the hugging or the hugged? **1870** W. MORRIS *Earthly Par.* IV. 25 Into..a hugging bear He turned him. **1879** S. LANIER *Poems* (1884) 41 The hugged delusion drear. **1891** G. MEREDITH *One of our Conq.* I. xii. 234 There was an obstacle to his being huggingly genial, even candidly genial with her.

hug (hʌg), *sb.* [f. prec. vb.]

1. A strong clasp with the arms; an embrace of affection; also, a close or rough grasp; the clasp or squeeze of a bear.

1659 *Lady Alimony* II. Prol. in Hazl. *Dodsley* XIV. 288 Apt for a spousal hug. **1727** BAILEY vol. II, *A Hugg*, an Embrace. *a* **1732** GAY (J.), Why these close hugs? I owe my shame to him. **1773** GARRICK in Boswell *Johnson* Apr., Johnson gives you a forcible hug, and shakes laughter out of you, whether you will or no. **1828** SCOTT *F. M. Perth* vi, Keep at arm's-length, then.. I will have no more close hugs. **1839–40** W. IRVING *Wolfert's R.* (1855) 201 Bruin raised one arm, and gave the dog a hug that crushed his ribs. **1880** MISS BRADDON *Just as I am* xxxi, She gave his lordship a hug.

2. A squeezing grip in wrestling; esp. ***Cornish*** **(†*Devonshire*)** ***hug***, a special 'lock' of Cornish wrestlers; hence *fig.* (see quot. 1661).

1617 MIDDLETON & ROWLEY *Fair Quarrel* II. ii, I'll show her the Cornish hug. *c* **1626** *Dick of Devon.* IV. iii. in Bullen *O. Pl.* II. 80 Onely a Devonshire hugg, sir. *a* **1661** FULLER *Worthies, Cornwall* I. (1662) 197 The Cornish are Masters of the Art of Wrestling.. Their Hugg is a cunning close with their fellow-combatant, the fruits whereof is his fair fall, or foil at the least. It is figuratively appliable to the deceitfull dealing of such, who secretly design their overthrow, whom they openly embrace. **1705** *Char. Sneaker* in *Harl. Misc.* (1808) XI. 29 His St. Maw's Muse has given the French troops a Cornish hug, and flung them all upon their backs. **1754** FOOTE *Knights* I. Wks. 1799 I. 67 We don't wrestle after your fashion.. we all go upon close hugs or the flying mare. **1827** HONE *Every-day Bk.* II. 1009 In the 'Cornish hug', Mr. Polwhele perceived the Greek palæstral attitudes.

hugaboo ('hʌgə,buː). [Fanciful, prob. infl. by BUGABOO, HULLABALOO, etc.] Portentousness, pomposity.

1930 *Eng. Rev.* Feb. 140 The silly hugaboo of minutes and protocols. **1932** S. GIBBONS *Cold Comfort Farm* i. 9 Marriages.. should take place in churches, with all the usual paraphernalia and hugaboo.

huge (hjuːdʒ), *a.* (*adv.*) Forms: 3– huge; also 4–5 **hoge, heug(e,** 5–6 **houge,** 5–7 **hudge,** (4 **hogge, hug, hughe,** 5 **hugge, howge, hogh(e, hoege,** 6 **houdge, hewge, hoouge**). [ME. *huge, hoge,* app. aphetic f. OF. *ahuge, ahoge, ahoege,* in same sense, of unknown origin.

It is, however, noteworthy that no connecting link in the form of *huge* in OFr., or *ahuge* in early ME., has as yet been found.]

1. Very great, large, or big; immense, enormous, vast. **a.** Of things material or of spatial extent.

a **1275** *Prov. Ælfred* 709 in *O.E. Misc.* 138 þuru þis lore and genteleri he amendit huge companie. *c* **1330** R. BRUNNE *Chron.* (1810) 31 He brouht with him a deuelle, a hogge Geant. **13..** *Gaw. & Gr. Knt.* 743 Of hore okez ful hoge a hundreth to-geder. **1390** GOWER *Conf.* I. 236 He.. made an hughe fire. **1480** CAXTON *Chron. Eng.* ccxxvi. 231 A ful houge and boystous meyne of dyuerse nacions. **1581** MARBECK *Bk. of Notes* 343 The waues of the hudge floude. **1634** SIR T. HERBERT *Trav.* 212 Fishes are in huge numbers here. **1791** COWPER *Iliad* VII. 246 So moved huge Ajax to the fight. **1832** G. DOWNES *Lett. Cont. Countries* I. 373 Naples is huge, and populous. **1890** SWINBURNE *Stud. Prose & Poetry* 221 The huge fireplace with its dragon-like dogs.

b. Of things immaterial.

13.. *E.E. Allit. P.* B. 1659 He hade so huge an insyȝt to his aune dedes. *c* **1375** *Sc. Leg. Saints, Margaret* 671 A gret hug thonir com but bad. **1377** LANGL. *P. Pl.* B. XI. 242 Martha on Marye magdeleyne an huge pleynte she made. *c* **1450** *Mirour Saluacioun* 346 For hoege luf yᵗ he shuld noght hire greue. **1529** MORE *Comf. agst. Trib.* III. Wks. 1259/1 How woonderfull houge and gret those spirituall heauenly ioyes are. **1680** ALLEN *Peace & Unity* Pref. 3 The Peace.. of the Church is a matter of that huge moment, that [etc.]. **1834** MEDWIN *Angler in Wales* I. 143 [He] took a huge fancy to the wench. **1877** DOWDEN *Shaks. Prim.* vi. 135 His affliction serves as a measure of the huger affliction of the King.

c. *transf.* Of persons in reference to their actions or attributes: Of very great power, rank, possessions, capabilities, etc.

c **1400** *Destr. Troy* 3924 Hoger of hert and of her wille, He demenyt well his maners, & be mesure wroght. **1430–40** LYDG. *Bochas* VI. iii. (1554) 150b, The great Duke so mightie and so huge. *c* **1470** HENRY *Wallace* XI. 29 Off Glosyster that huge lord and her. **1858** CARLYLE *Fredk. Gt.* II. xi. I. 116 An only child, the last of a line: hugest Heiress now going.

†2. Very great in number, very numerous. *rare.*

1570 *Satir. Poems Reform.* xix. 89 Hudge is ȝour fais within this fals Regioun.

†3. Phr. ***in huge***: hugely, vastly, extensively. (Cf. *at large.*) *Obs. rare.*

1584 HUDSON *Du Bartas' Judith.* I. 101 More than euer Rome could comprehend, In huge of learned books that they ypend.

4. *Comb.* Parasynthetic, as ***huge-armed, -bellied, -bodied, -boned, -built, -grown, -horned, -limbed, -proportioned, -tongued,*** etc. adjs.

1599 MARSTON *Sco. Villanie* II. vi. 201 Huge-tongu'd Pigmy brats. **1612** DRAYTON *Poly-olbion* xiii. (R.), Many a huge-grown wood. **1624** MILTON *Paraphr. Ps.* cxiv. 11 The high hugebellied mountains skip like rams. **1808** SCOTT *Marm.* V. xv, Huge-boned, and tall and grim, and gaunt. **1877** BRYANT *Lit. People of Snow* 122 Huge-limbed men.

†B. *adv.* Hugely, immensely. *Obs.*

1450–70 *Golagros & Gaw.* 498 Yone house is sa huge hie. **1631** WEEVER *Anc. Fun. Mon.* 11 Tombes are made so huge great, that they take vp the Church. **1674** N. FAIRFAX *Bulk & Selv.* To Rdr., Lessenings of them, who have done huge well. **1679** PULLER *Moder. Ch. Eng.* (1843) 290 Many are huge concerned to shift off the conviction of this truth.

†hugeful, *a. Obs.* [f. prec. + -FUL.] Huge.

1413 *Pilgr. Sowle* (Caxton) IV. xxxviii. (1859) 65 Hugefull peyne, and laboure.

hügelite ('hʏgəlaɪt). *Min.* [ad. G. *hügelit* (V. Dürrfeld 1914, in *Zeitschr. f. Kryst. u. Min.* LIII. 183), f. the Ger. family name von *Hügel*: see -ITE¹.] A yellow or brown mineral originally described as a hydrated vanadate of lead and zinc but later shown to be a hydrated arsenate of lead and uranium.

1914 *Chem. Abstr.* VIII. 310 The name hügelite is suggested for the vanadate previously described. **1916** *Mineral Mag.* XVII. 352 Hügelite... A hydrated vanadate of lead and zinc occurring as yellow monoclinic needles on corroded galena at Reichenbach, Baden. **1962** *Amer. Mineralogist* XLVII. 418 Hügelite was described by Dürrfeld (1913) as a hydrous lead zinc vanadate... Transparent to translucent crystals are brown to orange-yellow... Microchemical tests showed Pb, U and As as main components, but no Zn, V or P... The formula is proposed as $Pb_2(UO_2)_3(AsO_4)_2(OH)_4.3H_2O$.

hugely ('hjuːdʒlɪ), *adv.* [f. HUGE *a.* + -LY².] In a huge manner; very greatly, extremely; immensely, vastly, enormously.

c **1380** *Antecrist* in Todd *Three Treat. Wyclif* (1851) 134 þei weren hugely comfortid whom Crist come unto. **1382** WYCLIF *Gen.* xvii. 2, I shal multiplye thee ful hugeli. **1422** tr. *Secreta Secret., Priv. Priv.* (E.E.T.S.) 192 Mariage.. is hugeli pleasant to god. **1530** RASTELL *Bk. Purgat.* II. xviii, When any member of the bodye is vehemently and hougly styred. **1651** JER. TAYLOR *Serm. for Year* I. ii. 19 The man was hugely rich. **1710** STEELE *Tatler* No. 266 ¶2 They love one another hugely. *a* **1839** PRAED *Poems* (1864) II. 121, I like him hugely! **1858** CARLYLE *Fredk. Gt.* I. iv. I. 33 A.. hugely ingenious old gentleman. **1871** R. ELLIS *Catullus* x. 12 Our prætor.. could hugely Mulct his company.

hugeness ('hjuːdʒnɪs). [f. HUGE *a.* + -NESS.] The quality or condition of being huge; extraordinary greatness of bulk; immensity, vastness.

c **1380** *Sir Ferumb.* 52 Of such anoþer herde ȝe nere, nowar þar ȝe han gone, Of Strengþe, of schap, of hugenys. **1398** TREVISA *Barth. De P.R.* XIII. xxvi. (Bodl. MS.), þe whale is icleped Cete for hougenes of his bodie. **1579** E. K. *Spenser's Sheph. Cal.* Apr. (Emblem), The hugenesse of his imagination. **1616** SURFL. & MARKH. *Country Farme* 649 Yet is the oake accounted the King of the forrest.. in respect of his largenesse and hudgenesse. **1753** HOGARTH *Anal. Beauty* vi. 29 The hugeness of its few distinct parts strikes the eye with uncommon grandeur. **1818** KEATS *Endym.* III. 346 A dread waterspout had rear'd aloft Its hungry hugeness.

hugeous ('hjuːdʒəs), *a.* (*adv.*) [f. HUGE *a.* + -OUS.] = HUGE.

a **1529** SKELTON *Ware the Hauke* 48 He made his hawke to fly, With hogeous showte and cry. **1555** EDEN *Decades* To Rdr. (Arb.) 49 The hugious heapes of stones of the Pyramides of Egypt. **1656** DAVENANT *Siege Rhodes* I. (1673) 27 Then the hug'ous great Turk Came to make us more work. **1754** RICHARDSON *Grandison* (1781) VI. liii. 342 They should all have taken it as a hugeous favour. **1826** SCOTT *Woodst.* xiv, My master is close by.. beside the hugeous oak. **1885** DOBSON *Sign of Lyre* 125 The Squire in transport slapped his knee At this most hugeous pleasantry.

†b. as *adv.* Hugely, immensely. *Obs.*

1673 WYCHERLEY *Gentlem. Dancing-Master* IV. Wks. (Rtldg.) 56/2, I am hugeous glad.

Hence '**hugeously** *adv.*, hugely; '**hugeousness**, hugeness.

a **1643** W. CARTWRIGHT *Ordinary* III. v, I love these ballads hugeously. **1752** FIELDING *Amelia* Wks. 1775 X. 75 My mind misgives me hugeously. **1785** SARAH FIELDING *Ophelia* II. vi, He will have fretted hugeously. **1859** G. MEREDITH *R. Feverel* xxi, His hugeousness seemed to increase.

[**hugesome,** *a.*, erroneous alteration of UGSOME, horrible, dreadful. [Cf. HUGGE *v.*]

a **1568** COVERDALE *Hope Faithf.* xxvi. (Parker Soc. II. 205), No tongue is able to express the terrible and hugesome [*orig. ed.* ugsome] pain and punishment thereof.]

huggaback, obs. form of HUCKABACK.

huggable ('hʌgəb(ə)l), *a.* [f. HUG *v.* + -ABLE.] Such as invites hugging.

1898 D. C. MURRAY *Tales* 205 Eminently kissable little face; eminently huggable little figure. **1908** *Daily Chron.* 5 Nov. 7/5 The 'Teddy' Bear is such a huggable creature that ..he almost compels a caress. **1928** L. ROSSITER *Sex Age* viii. §5 Sorry, Jacko. But you do look so huggable tonight. **1970** *Daily Tel.* 16 Dec. 11 Huggable rag doll.. with removable dress.

†hugge, *v. Obs.* [A variant of UGGE.] **a.** *intr.* To shudder, shrink, shiver, or shake with fear or with cold. **b.** *trans.* To abhor, abominate.

1483 *Cath. Angl.* 191/1 To Huge.. *abhominari, detestari* [etc.]. **1530** PALSGR. 588/2, I hugge, I shrinke me in my bed. It is a good sporte to se this lytle boye hugge in his bedde for colde. **1570** LEVINS *Manip.* 184/26 To Hugge, *horrescere.*

Hence **†hugged** *ppl. a.*, abhorred; abominable, ugly.

c **1530** LD. BERNERS *Arth. Lyt. Bryt.* (1814) 138 The stroke lyght on the grete deuyll, soo that hys hugged and foule heed flewe to the earth.

hugge, obs. form of HUGE.

hugger ('hʌgə(r)), *sb.*¹ [f. HUG *v.* + -ER¹.] One who hugs. **b.** *dial.* A porter or carrier (*Whitby Gloss.* 1876).

1682 OTWAY *Venice Pres.* II. i, *Bedamore.* Pierre! I must embrace him. My heart beats to this man as if it knew him. *Renault.* I never lov'd these Huggers! **1894** *Nation* (N.Y.) 13 Sept. 204/2 Not only are they [serpents] carried in such a way as to prevent their striking, but the 'hugger', as the attendant priest is called, is always present with his whip to guard against an accident.

†'hugger, *sb.*² *Obs.* [Cf. HUGGER *v.*] Concealment; = HUGGER-MUGGER *sb.* 1.

1576 FLEMING *Panopl. Epist.* 250 Hee counselleth.. to keepe them no longer in hugger, but to let them.. shewe themselves abroade.

hugger, *sb.*³ Var. HOGGER, a footless stocking.

1791 NEWTE *Tour Eng. & Scot.* 50 Others.. wear what they call huggers, and in the Northern parts of Scotland hugger-muggans, that is, stockings with the feet either worn away by long and hard service, or cut from them on purpose. **1827** J. WILSON *Noct. Ambr.* Wks. 1855 I. 287 A lassie frae Yarrow or Ettrick, in worsted huggers.

hugger ('hʌgə(r)), *v. Obs.* exc. *dial.* [prob. short for HUGGER-MUGGER *v.* (But possibly the source of the first element of the compound.)]

†1. *intr.* To be concealed; to lie in ambush. *Obs.*

1567 HARMAN *Caveat* (1869) 43–4 Such a one they saw there lyrkinge and huggeringe two houres before.

2. *trans.* To conceal, keep secret; to wrap *up.*

1600 BRETON *Pasquil's Message* (1626) E, Tell Trueth for Shame and Hugger up no ill. **1876** *Whitby Gloss.* s.v., 'Hugger 't up onny hoo, I's clash'd for time', wrap it up in any shape, I am in a hurry.

†3. *intr.* To become confused or disorderly; to get into confusion. *Obs.*

c **1520** SKELTON *Vox Populi* 603 By Godes blessed mother, Or thei begynne to hugger, For Godes sake looke aboute.

†hugger-mug. *Obs.* = next A. 1.

1654 E. JOHNSON *Wond. wrkg. Provid.* 206 They have taken up a desolate Wilderness to be their habitation, and not deluded any by keeping their possession in huggermug.

hugger-mugger ('hʌgə'mʌgə(r)), *sb.*, *a.*, and *adv.* Forms: 6 **hukermoker, hoker moker, hocker-mocker,** (also 9 *dial.*) **huckermucker, hugger mucker,** 6–7 **hucker mucker,** 6– **hugger mugger, hugger-mugger, huggermugger.** [This is the commonest of a group of reduplicated words of parallel forms and nearly synonymous meaning, including *hudder-mudder*, Sc. *hudge-mudge*, and obs. *hody-moke.* Nothing definite appears as to their derivation or origin, and it is not unlikely that they came from different sources, and influenced each other. An early form, more usual in 16th c., was *hucker-mucker* (*hoker-moker*), the second element of which may have been the ME. vb. *mukre, mokere-n* to hoard up, conceal, whence *mukrere, mokerere* hoarder, miser (cf. sense 1 b). Whether *hucker* had an independent existence (cf. the prec. words), or was merely a riming variation, cannot at present be determined. The change to *hugger-mugger* was phonetically easy and natural, but may have been helped by the influence of *hudder-mudder*, which was app. of different origin.]

A. *sb.*

1. Concealment, secrecy; *esp.* in phr. ***in hugger-mugger***: in secret, secretly, clandestinely. Formerly in ordinary literary use, now archaic or vulgar.

1529 MORE *Dyaloge* II. 52 b/2 He wolde haue hys faythe dyuulged and spredde abrode openly, not alwaye whyspered in hukermoker. *Ibid.* IV. 121 b/1 Suche thyngys.. these heretyques teche in hucker mucker. **1539** TAVERNER *Gard. Wysed.* I. 26 a, It shal be done moche better in open courte, and in the face of al the world, then in hugger mugger. **1553** BECON *Reliques of Rome* (1563) 129 The wordes of the Lordes Supper.. were not spoken in hocker mocker.. but playnely, openlye and distinctly. *c* **1590** in *Acc. & Pap. relating to Mary Q. of Scots* (Camden) 114 Secreatlie demeasned, or handled in hugger mucker, or rufflid up in hast. **1601** HOLLAND *Pliny* II. 563 Say that this is done in secret and hucker mucker. **1602** SHAKS. *Ham.* IV. v. 84. **1633** FORD *'Tis Pity* III. i, There is no way but to clap up the marriage in hugger-mugger. **1678** BUTLER *Hud.* III. iii. 123 In Hugger-mugger hid. *a* **1734** NORTH *Lives* III. 314 The good old lady.. took him into hugger-mugger in her closet, where she usually had some good pye or plumb cake. **1836** GEN. P. THOMPSON *Exerc.* (1842) IV. 91 The resolution that the voting in Committee shall take place in 'hugger-mugger'. **1874** MOTLEY *Barneveld* I. iv. 226 The trial was all mystery, hugger-mugger, horror.

b. One who keeps things hidden or in secret; a hoarder or miser. (? *erroneous use.*)

1862 TROLLOPE *N. Amer.* I. 289 Nor is the New Yorker a hugger-mugger with his money. He does not hide up his dollars in old stockings, and keep rolls of gold in hidden pots.

2. Disorder, confusion; a medley, muddle.

1674 N. FAIRFAX *Bulk & Selv.* 74 An hugger-mugger of meddlesom beings all at jars. **1867** CARLYLE *Remin.* II. 174 Huggermugger was the type of his [L. Hunt's] economics. **1871** SMILES *Charac.* ii. (1876) 54 Muddle flies before it, and hugger-mugger becomes a thing unknown. **1887** *S. Chesh. Gloss.* s.v., My pleeces bin aw i sich a huckermucker I'm.. asheemed o' annybody gooin' in 'em.

B. *adj.* **1.** Secret; clandestine.

1692 tr. *Sallust* 330 What hugger mugger Funerals of Citizens, what sudden Massacres committed in the very Arms of Parents and Children. **1754** RICHARDSON *Grandison* xliv. (1781) VI. 282 No hugger mugger doings! Let private weddings be for doubtful happiness! **1796** MRS. M. ROBINSON *Angelina* II. 127 No hugger-mugger doings for me!

2. Rough and disorderly, confused, makeshift.

1840 MRS. F. TROLLOPE *Widow Married* xix, I'd rather, ten times over, live hugger-mugger fashion, as we are now. **1853** JERDAN *Autobiog.* IV. xii. 213 You find matters..so clumsily set out, that you fare in the style called hugger-mugger. **1866** CARLYLE *Remin.* (1881) I. 203 In a kindly and polite yet very huggermugger cottage. **1883** S. C. HALL *Retrospect* II. 315 The household was supplied in a hugger-mugger fashion.

C. *adv.*

1. Secretly, clandestinely; 'in hugger-mugger'.

1526 SKELTON *Magnyf.* 392 Thus is the talkyng of one and of oder As men dare speke it hugger-mugger. *a* **1700** B. E. *Dict. Cant. Crew, Hugger-mugger*, Closely or by Stealth, Under board.

2. In rough disorder or confusion; in a muddle.

1880 TENNYSON *Village Wife* xviii, Hugger-mugger they lived, but they wasn't that eäsy to pleäse. **1894** *Daily Graphic* 3 May 7 The Reformation..left our Church system, as regards the appointment of the clergy, all hugger mugger.

hugger-mugger, *v.* [f. prec.]

1. *trans.* To keep secret or concealed; to hush *up*.

1803 MARY CHARLTON *Wife & Mistress* IV. 25 His uncle ..had saved a mort of money..and behold, it was all hugger muggered away. **1862** *N.Y. Tribune* 1 June (Bartlett), That is a venial offence, to be hugger-muggered up. **1891** ATKINSON *Last Giant-killers* 105 That..plunder..which.. you keep hugger-muggered up in..your cave. **1898** *Daily News* 5 Apr. 3/1 For two years the City Corporation tried to hugger-mugger this nasty little incident out of sight.

2. *intr.* **a.** To proceed in a secret or clandestine manner; *esp.* to meet or assemble in this manner. **b.** To go *on* in a confused or muddled way.

1805 *Morn. Herald* in *Spirit Pub. Jrnls.* (1806) IX. 356 It's a shame to hugger-mugger on without making a little figure now and then. **1862** *N.Y. Tribune* 25 Feb. (Bartlett), Listening to key-hole revelations, and hugger-muggering with disappointed politicians. **1879** MCCARTHY *Donna Quixote* III. vii, She won't stand much more of you and me hugger-muggering together. **1887** M. BETHAM-EDWARDS *Next of Kin Wanted* I. viii. 110 Let the whole lot hugger-mugger together—old maids, Jesuits, saints, sinners.

huggery ('hʌgərɪ). [f. HUG *v.*, HUGGER *sb.*[1]: see -ERY.] The action or practice of hugging; *esp.* the practice of courting an attorney, etc. with the view of obtaining professional employment.

1804 L. T. REDE *Ess. Exam. Laws Eng.* (ed. 2) I. 65 The barrier [of etiquette] is now removed by the eagerness of barristers to procure business by flattering and courting attornies who have the distribution of it—this is distinguished by the curious appellation of huggery. **1810** LD. CAMPBELL in *Life* (1881) I. 249 We lived together very amicably, not-withstanding a few jealousies and rumours of huggery. **1827** *Blackw. Mag.* XXII. 511 With the most ludicrous exultation and self-huggery. **1854** *Fraser's Mag.* L. 269 Though huggery and undue familiarity with attorneys are forbidden by the etiquette of the Bar, yet there is no canon of the profession against huggery of parliamentary agents.

'huggin. *dial.* Also **huggan, -on.** [cf. HUCK *sb.*[1], HUCK-BONE.] The hip-bone, esp. of a horse or cow.

1737 BRACKEN *Farriery Impr.* (1757) II. 28 His Ribs elevate and round near the Huggon or Haunch-Bones. **1829** *Glover's Hist. Derby* I. 205 From his huggin or hip bone to the root of his tail, 2 ft. 1 in. **1869** *Lonsdale Gloss., Huggan*, the hipbone of a horse or cow. **1877** *Holderness Gloss., Huggon*, the hip-bone of a horse. **1886** *S.W. Linc. Gloss., Huggin*, the hip. I was always a poor shortwaisted thing, my huggins come up so high.

hugging ('hʌgɪŋ), *vbl. sb.* [f. HUG *v.* + -ING[1].] The action of the verb HUG.

1615 CHAPMAN *Odyss.* XXII. (R.), They..pour'd a flame Of loue, about their lord: with welcomes home, With huggings of his hands. **1639** DU VERGER tr. *Camus' Admir. Events* 55 They were Apes huggings, which smother with their imbracings. **1810** *Sporting Mag.* XXXV. 193 After a hugging battle of forty minutes. **1897** W. H. THORNTON *Remin. W.C. Clergyman* iv. 125 There was..no hugging of children, no hand-shaking with friends.

hugging *ppl. a.*, **huggingly** *adv.*: see HUG *v.*

huggle ('hʌg(ə)l), *v.* Now *dial.* [? iterative of HUG *v.*] To hug.

1583 STUBBES *Anat. Abus.* I. (1879) 97 So he haue his pretie pussie to huggle withall, it forceth not. **1603** HOLLAND *Plutarch's Mor.* 221 She taketh it into her armes, she hugleth it in her bosome, and kisseth it. **1675** TEONGE *Diary* (1825) 10 The women..huggling the water-men about the necks. **1835** *Tait's Mag.* II. 513 Putting out his arms to huggle the old lady round the neck. **1881** *Leicestersh. Gloss., Huggle*, to hug, embrace. **1886** in *S.W. Linc. Gloss.*

Hence †**huggle-my-buff**, cant name of some drink. Cf. HUGMATEE.

1756 W. TOLDERVY *Two Orphans* IV. 79 Dry gin..in every dose of huggle-my-buff, or hot-pot.

huggo, obs. f. HOGO.

hughe, hughely, obs. ff. HUGE, UGLY.

Hughie ('hju:ɪ). *Austral.* and *N.Z. slang.* Also **Huey.** [Diminutive of the name *Hugh*: see -IE, -Y[6].] The 'god' of weather, especially in phr. ***send her down, Hughie!***

1937 PARTRIDGE *Dict. Slang* 209/1 New Zealanders and Australians say *send her down, Hughie!* **1958** *Tararua* XII. 27 The derisive phrases, 'Send it down, Hughie' and 'Let it come down, Hughie', go back to early in this century and are variants of the British military catch-phrase 'Send it down, David'... St. Hugh has long been associated with rain. **1962** *Austral. Women's Wkly.* Suppl. 24 Oct. 3/2 Come on, Huey, send the waves up. **1967** J. CLEARY *Long Pursuit* vii. 151 'Good on you, Hughie,' he said gratefully and with true religion... Hughie was the Australian working man's vernacular for the Lord. **1971** *N.Z. Listener* 19 Apr. 57/1 Well, that night Hughie sent it down, a nor' wester followed by a southerly buster.

huginess: see under HUGY.

hugly, obs. f. UGLY.

†**hugmatee.** *Obs.* [? from phrase *hug-me-t'ye.*] Cant name of a kind of ale.

1699 BENTLEY *Phal.* Pref. 33 He is better skill'd in the Catalogues of Ales, his Humty Dumty, Hugmatee, Three-Threads, and the rest of that glorious List, than in the Catalogues of MSS. *a* **1704** T. BROWN *Wks.* (1760) IV. 218 (D.) No hugmatee nor flip my grief can smother.

hug-me-tight ('hʌgmi:taɪt). [f. the phr. *hug me tight.*]

1. A woman's short close-fitting jacket, usu. made of wool. orig. *U.S.*

1860 *Godey's Lady's Bk.* Dec. 544 Hug me tight. A garment to be worn under a cloak. **1869** L. M. ALCOTT *Little Women* II. v. 68 She..made him..demand fiercely the meaning of a 'hug-me-tight'. **1910** *N.Y. Even. Post* 24 Dec., Suppl. 3 Hug-me-tights and mittens, all knit at home by grandmother. **1924** *Mod. Draper* II. 94 Articles, such as spencers, hug-me-tights, etc., which are worn above the undergarment, and under the outer garment. **1934** E. BOWEN *Cat Jumps* 130 Mrs. Archworth sat propped up in bed in a hug-me-tight trimmed with marabout. **1959** *Guardian* 25 Nov. 6/4 For that extra degree of warmth.. over the shoulders..this cuffed hug-me-tight of the same tweed as the dress. **1972** F. B. MAYNARD *Raisins & Almonds* 45 A variety of cozy garments called hug-me-tights.

2. A type of buggy. Also *attrib. U.S. Hist.*

1901 W. N. HARBEN *Westerfelt* i, I seed 'em takin' a ride in his new hug-me-tight buggy yesterday. **1902** —— *Abner Daniel* v, He's got a new buggy—a regular hug-me-tight. **1948** *Jrnl. Amer. Folk-Lore* Apr.-June 212 Those roads were so bad..that they kept making the buggies narrower and narrower... Some of them got so narrow they used to call them 'Hug-Me-Tights'.

Hugoesque (hju:gəʊ'ɛsk), *a.* [f. the name of Victor M. *Hugo* (1802–1885), French author + -ESQUE.] Resembling the character or style of V. Hugo. Also subst. with *the*.

1893 E. SALTUS *Madam Sapphira* xiii. 164 That would be mediæval. I mean nothing so Hugoesque. **1904** *Daily Chron.* 3 Mar. 3/2 There is a touch of the Hugoesque in Rodwell. **1960** J. LODWICK *Asparagus Trench* 20 Almost Hugoesque in his unflagging pursuit of maids.

hugsome ('hʌgsəm), *a.* [f. HUG *v.* + -SOME[1].] Such as invites hugging, huggable (see also quot. 1893).

1893 FARMER & HENLEY *Slang* III. 375/2 *Hugsome adj.* (colloquial), carnally attractive; fuckable. **1894** *Outing* (U.S.) XXIV. 417/1 A [bear's] long, straining, hugsome hug, which breaks the dog's ribs. **1942** BERREY & VAN DEN BARK *Amer. Thes. Slang* §427.1 Hotsy-totsy, hugsome hussy, humdinger, irresistibelle.

hugsome, var. UGSOME.

Huguenot ('hju:gənɒt, -nəʊ), *sb.* (*a.*) Also (6 huge-, 7 hague-, hugunot), 7–8 hugonet(t, 7–9 hugonot. [a. F. *Huguenot*, a word of disputed origin; according to Hatz.-Darm. (who cites the form *eiguenots* from *Chron. de Genève* of 1550), a popular alteration of Ger. *eidgenosz* (Du. *eedgenoot*), confederate, under the influence of the personal name *Hugues*, Hugh.] A member of the Calvinistic or Reformed communion of France in the 16th and 17th c.; a French Protestant. In French, orig. a nickname, said to have been imported from Geneva; in English, chiefly a historical term.

1565 T. STAPLETON *Fortr. Faith* 72 Except a number of rebellious hugenots. *c* **1592** MARLOWE *Massacre Paris* Wks. (Rtldg.) 234/2 There are a hundred Huguenots and more Which in the woods do hold their synagogue. **1630** *R. Johnson's Kingd. & Commw.* 89 For in Paris they..call any Prince Hugonet, who dares onely say, That Nostre Dame is but a darke melancholike Church. **1759** ROBERTSON *Hist. Scot.* (1761) I. 496 The French King had lately obtained.. advantages over the Hugonots. **1845** M. PATTISON *Ess.* (1889) I. 12 The Huguenots had pillaged the shrine; the Revolution swept it away altogether. **1846** HARE *Mission Comf.* (1850) 359 Some..took part in the massacre of the Hugonots. **1867** SMILES *Huguenots Eng.* i. (1880) 21 Mahn ..gives no fewer than fifteen supposed derivations of the word Huguenot.

B. *adj.* (or *attrib.*) Of or belonging to the Huguenots.

1682 *News fr. France* 10 The King is resolved to make his Hugonot Subjects grow weary either of their lives, or of their Religion. **1683** LOCKE in Ld. King *Life* (1830) II. 202 A man may be saved in the Presbyterian, Independent, or Hugonot Church. **1873** SMILES *Huguenots Fr.* Pref. (1881) 5 A Huguenot engineer directed the operations at the siege of Namur. **1896** *Prospectus of Huguenot Society of London*, Founded in 1885..Objects..2. To form a bond of fellowship among some of those who desire to perpetuate the memory of their Huguenot ancestors.

Hence **Huguenotic** (-'ɒtɪk) *a.*, of or pertaining to the Huguenots; **'Huguenotism**, the religious system or doctrine of the Huguenots; Calvinism.

1611 COTGR., *Huguenotterie*, Huguenotisme, Caluinisme. **1859** tr. *Lamartine's Mary Stuart* App. 150 Huguenotism was drowned in blood. **1897** *Saga-Bk. Viking Club* Jan. 272 He questioned whether some of the brachycephalic skulls [in Denmark] were not Huguenotic.

†**'hugy**, *a. Obs.* Forms: 5 hogy, 5–7 hugy, 6–7 -ie, 6 hougy, -ie, hudgy, 8 hugey. [f. HUGE *a.* + -Y. Cf. *dusk, dusky, murk, murky.*] = HUGE.

c **1420** LYDG. *Assembly of Gods* 1095 An hogy myghty hoost. **1422** tr. *Secreta Secret., Priv. Priv.* (E.E.T.S.) 174 An hugy ryuer rennynge by the Cite wallis. **1579** TWYNE *Phisicke agst. Fort.* I. lxxxvii. 109 b, Whence this roaring of the hougy waues? **1697** DRYDEN *Virg. Æneid* v. 113 His hugy bulk on sev'n high volumes roll'd. **1728** VANBR. & CIB. *Prov. Husb.* I. i, He has hugey business with you.

Hence †**'huginess**, hugeness.

1559 W. CUNNINGHAM *Cosmogr. Glasse* 169 The hougieness of the labor. **1608** SYLVESTER *Du Bartas* II. iv. IV. *Schism* 1016 This mighty Fish, of Whale-like huginess.

huh (hʌ), *int.* A natural utterance, expressing some suppressed feeling. Also as an expression of interrogation.

1608 MIDDLETON *Mad World* III. ii, There's gold for thee! huh, let her want for nothing, master doctor. **1732** FIELDING *Miser* IV. xiii, Huh! now would some lovers think themselves very unhappy. **1814** *Manœuvering* I. i, Married! huh —is it marriage you're talking of? **1890** 'O. THANET' *Expiation* ix. 166 A loud snort of contempt from the gallery betrayed that Hizzie had heard. 'Huh!' she bawled, 'you yent gwine get killed up, not long's ye kin *run!*' **1924** *Dialect Notes* V. 270 *Huh* (surp., disg., enquiry). **1937** L. B. MURPHY *Social Behavior & Child Personality* ii. 53 Agatha said, 'Want to play in the sand box, Theodore, huh? Do you?' **1940** R. CHANDLER *Farewell, My Lovely* xxi. 169 Pretty trivial in my case, huh? **1948** F. & R. LOCKRIDGE *Pinch of Poison* xvi. 151 'Listen, Mullins,' Weigand pleaded. 'Don't think, huh?' **1953** *Manch. Guardian Weekly* 20 Aug. 7/2 'I could go back there, I mean some other time.' 'But not now, huh?' **1969** K. AMIS *Green Man* iv. 182 God's purpose. Huh. I'm no more qualified than the next man to tell you what that is. **1970** *Washington Post* 30 Sept. D 4/2 'Oh boy that's just what he needs,' he said, cheerlessly. 'Tell him to take it easy, huh?' **1971** *Black World* Apr. 59 Hell, its all my fault, huh? **1972** *Canad. Jrnl. Ling.* XVII. 94 Whatever its origin and history, *huh?* is currently in widespread use in the United States. **1972** *Southerly* XXXII. 54 Because the fun part is over. They think. Huh! **1973** A. PRICE *October Men* IX. 126 'Huh!' Macready snorted derisively.

hühnerkobelite (hʏnə'kəʊbəlaɪt). *Min.* [f. *Hühnerkobel*, name of a hill near Lam in eastern Bavaria, Germany: see -ITE[1].] An olive-green phosphate of sodium, calcium, bivalent iron, and bivalent manganese, (Na, Ca) $(Fe^{++}, Mn^{++})_2 (PO_4)_2$, in which iron predominates over manganese.

1950 M. L. LINDBERG in *Amer. Mineralogist* XXXV. 75 It is here proposed to give the name hühnerkobelite to the material from Hühnerkobel and from Norrö, not isostructural with true arrojadite. **1965** *Amer. Mineralogist* L. 713 (*heading*) Hühnerkobelite crystals from the Palermo No. 1 pegmatite, North Groton, New Hampshire.

huhu ('hu:hu:). *N.Z.* [Maori.] The beetle *Prionoplus reticularis*, or its larva (in full ***huhu grub***), found in decayed timber.

1848 R. TAYLOR *Leaf from Nat. Hist. N.Z.* 5/1 Insects.. Huhu, a grub which bores into wood. **1926** R. J. TILLYARD *Insects Austral. & N.Z.* xx. 232 *Prionoplus reticularis* Wh., the largest of all New Zealand beetles, measures up to two inches in length and is dark brown..; it is very common and flies to light. The larva, called 'Hu-hu' by the Maoris, is eaten as a delicacy; it bores into fallen forest timber. **1949** F. SARGESON *I saw in My Dream* I. vii. 52 The children.. looked for wetas and huhus. **1956** T. SUTHERLAND *Green Kiwi* ii. 45 The timber tunnelled by the mokoroa or huhu grubs. **1960** B. CRUMP *Good Keen Man* 45 My next mate was a Maori... I once found him tearing a rotten log to pieces, scattering powdery wood all over the place as he searched for huhus. When he found one he'd pick the butter-coloured grub out with his fingers and eat it as it was. **1966** *Encycl. N.Z.* I. 187/2 Among the more conspicuous New Zealand beetles are the 'Huhu' (*Prionoplus reticularis*), a large dead-wood borer of the family Cerambycidae, [etc.].

huh-uh ('ʌʌ), *int. U.S.* An expression of negation. Cf. UH-HUH, UH-UH.

1948 F. & R. LOCKRIDGE *Pinch of Poison* xvi. 152 Mullins shook his head. 'Huh-uh,' he said. 'She ain't the type.' **1962** *Amer. Speech* XXXVII. 230 Foreign visitors to the United States, who have learned the proper affirmative and negative responses of *yes* and *no*, are often bewildered by the widespread colloquial use of *uh-huh* and *huh-uh*.

‖**hui** ('hu:ɪ). [Maori and Hawaiian.] In New Zealand, a large social or ceremonial gathering; in Hawaii, a formal club or association.

1858 J. MORGAN *Let.* 21 June in *Richmond-Atkinson Papers* (1960) I. 408 The *hui* at Rangiaohia to promote the Maori King movement broke up. **1898** M. H. KROUT *Hawaii* 18 Those present, with forty members of a royalist society called *Hui Kalaiaina*, marched to the palace. **1921** H. GUTHRIE-SMITH *Tutira* x. 81 The large *huis*—gatherings —of the Heretaunga people. **1948** KUYKENDALL & DAY *Hawaii* xxv. 274 The enterprise of oriental business men was strengthened by the local practice of forming a *hui*, the

Hawaiian name for an informal syndicate which enables Chinese or Japanese members to take great advantage of a business opportunity. **1954** J. SHERIDAN in *Ellery Queen's Mystery Mag.* Oct. 15/2 Our fishing *hui's* beginning to pay. **1959** M. SHADBOLT *New Zealanders* 20, I mean it's common knowledge about what happens at the pa when there's a big hui. There's always too much liquor there, and the boys and girls mix freely. **1960** N. HILLIARD *Maori Girl* III. vii. 220 We'll have fowls. Go to all the *huis*. **1973** *Parade* (Austral.) Sept. 11/1 The Maori custom of steeping the grain in water until it was half-rotten, and then serving it up as a special dish at a tribal hui.

‖**huia** ('hu:ɪə). Also hui ('hu:ɪ). [Native Maori name derived from the bird's peculiar whistle.] A New Zealand bird, *Heteralocha acutirostris*, the tail feathers of which are highly prized by the Maoris as ornaments.

1845 E. J. WAKEFIELD *Adv. New Zealand* I. 91 (Morris) The huia is a black bird about as large as a thrush, with long thin legs and a slender semi-circular beak. **1883** RENWICK *Betrayed* 36 One snow-tipped hui feather graced his hair. **1898** *Daily News* 29 Mar. 5/2 The 3*d*. stamp [of New Zealand] bears specimens of the great huia, a bird whose feathers are worn by Maori chiefs, as a sign of rank.

Huichol (wi:'tʃəʊl). [Sp., from the native name.] **A.** *sb.* **a.** A people of Mexican Indians; a member of this people. **b.** The language of this people. **B.** *adj.* Of or pertaining to this people or their language.

1900 *Mem. Amer. Mus. Nat. Hist.* III. I. i. 22 According to the Huichol myths, corn was once deer, the deer having been the chief source of food in earliest times. *Ibid.* vi. 154 With the Huichol, the 'eye' is the symbol of the power of seeing and understanding unknown things. *Ibid.* ix. 185 Peculiar to certain rain-making feasts are a stick and a dried armadillo, which form the paraphernalia of the clown.., called in Huichol Sikwaiki. **1903** C. LUMHOLTZ *Unknown Mexico* II. v. 91 The Huichols occasionally made comments that betrayed very fair reasoning powers. **1964** E. A. NIDA *Toward Sci. Transl.* x. 228 'Glorified God' (Mark 2:12) becomes in Huichol 'said to God: You are of good heart.' **1972** *Language* XXXVIII. 847 Hockett adds Huichol which has '/i / instead of /ü/'.

huid, Sc. f. HOOD.

huide, obs. f. HIDE *v.*[1]

huif, Sc. f. HOOF; obs. pa. t. of HEAVE; obs. f. HOVE *v.*[1]

†**huik**, *v. Sc. Obs.* [Used in Sc. bef. 1600. The phonology is somewhat difficult, but the sense appears to connect it with the family of OE. *hycgan*, Goth. *hugjan*, ON. *huga*, to employ the mind, take thought, consider.] *trans.* (with *simple obj.* or *obj. clause*) To regard, consider, give thought to.

1570 *Satir. Poems Reform.* xviii. 92 Huiking na harme sa thay may be possest In warldlie welth. *Ibid.* xxi. 13 Ȝour siluer beis na langer huikit. **1573** DAVIDSONE *Commend. Vprichtnes, Disc. Estaitis* (Jam.), Lament sen he is gone, That huikit nathing for thy health. **1597** MONTGOMERIE *Cherrie & Slae* 419 Quha huikis not, nor luikis not Quhat eftirward may cum. *Ibid.* 1132 Promitting, unwitting, Ȝour hechts ȝou neuir huiked.

huikstery, var. HUCKSTERY.

huill, obs. Sc. f. HULL.

huing ('hju:ɪŋ), *vbl. sb.* [f. HUE *v.*[2] + -ING[1].] Shouting, hooting; *spec.* the rousing of a deer from its lair, or driving it with shouts towards the huntsman or a net. Also the directing of fishermen. See HUER.

a **1250** *Owl & Night.* 1264 Huan ich min huing to heom sende. **1530** PALSGR. 231/1 Hewyng of a dere, *hvee*. **1575** LANEHAM *Let.* (1871) 13 The galloping of horsez, the blasting of hornz, the halloing and hewing of the huntsmen. **1616** SIR R. BOYLE *Diary* in *Lismore Papers* (1886) I. 151 Of his 20[li] for this seazons hewing he is paid vij[li] ster.

huir, obs. Sc. f. WHORE.

huird, Sc. var. HOARD.

huire, obs. f. HIRE.

†**huisher**, **husher**, now as Fr. ‖**huissier** (ɥisje), *sb.* Forms: 4–5 **huscher**, 5 **hoschere**, 5–6 **huissher(e**, **hussher(e**, 6–7 **husher**, **huisher**, 7 **hushier**, 7– **huissier**. See also USHER. [a. OF. *huisier*, *huscier*, mod.F. *huissier*, f. *h)uis* door:—pop. L. **ūstium* for *ostium* door.]

= USHER.

13.. *Sir Tristr.* 632 Þe huscher bad him fle. *c* **1400** *Apol. Loll.* 36 Þei schal be huscheris & portars. **1426** LYDG. *Pilgr. Life Man* (E.E.T.S.) 2809 That I myghte ben an huissher, Or at the gate a porter. **1464** *Mann. & Househ. Exp.* (Roxb.) 277 To ij. of the gentelmen hoscheres. **1502** *Privy Purse Exp. Eliz. of York* (1830) 71 Arnolde Chollerton yeoman huisshere. **1571** *Lett. Lit. Men* (Camden) 65 Ryc' Marlow.. will not tary here as hussher and teache wrytinge. **1600** HOLLAND *Livy* XXIV. xliv. 539 His sergeants or huishers [*lictores*] marching afore. *c* **1611** BEAUM. & FL. *4 Plays in One* Induct., Prologues are hushiers bare before the wise. **1627** R. ASHLEY *Almansor* 10 An Huissier of his Chamber. **1649** JER. TAYLOR *Gt. Exemp.* I. v. 153 When..hatred of idolatry is the huisher of Sacriledge. **1653** H. COGAN tr. *Pinto's Trav.* xliv. 173 Four Hushers..with Battouns headed with iron went before him. **1837** J. F. COOPER *Europe* II. 185 (Stanf.) The *huissier*..announced the wife of an ambassador. **1849** J. A. CARLYLE *Dante, Inferno* 70 *note*, The Huissiers which Benvenuto Cellini heard.

Hence †**huisher** *v. trans.*, to usher, precede.

1606 HOLLAND *Sueton.* 8 A public officer called Accensus should huisher him before and the Serjeants or Lictours follow after behinde.

†**huisht**, *a.* Obs. var. of HUSHT or WHISHT, silent. (Cf. HUSHT *int.*[1])

1576 FLEMING *Panopl. Epist.* 248 He y[t] might by authoritie, commaunde al men to be huisht and silent.

Hence †**huishtly** *adv.*

1548 UDALL, etc. *Erasm. Par. John* xvi. (R.), I shal then speake vnto you huishtlie and without woordes.

huit, obs. form of HOOT, WHITE.

‖**huitain** (wɪ'teɪn). Also 6 **huiteine**. [a. F. *huitain* (15–16th c. in Hatz.-Darm.), f. *huit* eight.] A set or series of eight lines of verse.

1589 PUTTENHAM *Eng. Poesie* II. x[i]. (Arb.) 102 In a huiteine he that putteth foure verses in one concord and foure in another concord [etc.]. **1881** SAINTSBURY in *Academy* 15 Jan. 40 The tendency of a sonnet is to split into a huitain and a sixain.

Huk (hʌk). [Abbrev. of Tagalog *Hukbalahap*, f. initial syllables of *hukbó* army + *bayan* people, country + *la*ban against + *hap*an Japanese (i.e. *hukbó ng bayan laban sa hapon* people's army against the Japanese).] A guerrilla movement in the Philippines, orig. against the Japanese in World War II, later popularly identified with communism. Also *attrib.*

1947 *Britannica Bk. of Year* 840/2 *Huks*, shortening of Hukbalahaps, a Tagalog word meaning 'armed peasants', 'people's army'. **1951** H. MACINNES *Neither Five nor Three* xv. 209, I read the article..about the Philippines. It seems that the Huks have nothing to do with Communism. **1966** *Economist* 22 Oct. 359/2 Killings and ambushes by Huk guerrillas..have recently been common in central Luzon. **1967** *Ibid.* 4 Feb. 414/2 The Huks, who began as anti-Japanese guerrillas, carried on an armed rural rebellion from 1950 to 1954. **1971** W. LAQUEUR *Dict. Politics* 403 Since 1965 there has been a revival of *Huk* activity. **1972** *Times* 30 Sept. 15/4 The Huks are well-educated, ideologically-motivated men.

huke (hju:k), *sb. Obs.* exc. *Hist.* Forms: 5 **huyke**, 5–6 **hewk(e**, 5–7 **huk**, 5– **huke**; also 6–7 **huik**, 7 **huicke**, **huyck**, **hoyke**, 9 *Hist.* **huque**. [a. OF. *huque*, *heuque* a kind of cape with a hood; in med.L. *huca* (13th c. in Du Cange), MDu. *hûke*, *hôike*, *heuke*, Du. *huik*, MLG. *hoike*, LG. *hoike*, *heuke*, *heike*, *hokke*, *hök*, E.Fris. *heike*, *heik'*, *haike*, *hoike*. Ulterior origin obscure. See also HAIK[1].]

A kind of cape or cloak with a hood; 'an outer garment or mantle worn by women and afterwards by men; also subsequently applied to a tight-fitting dress worn by both sexes' (Fairholt *Costume*).

1415 in Nicolas *Test. Vetust.* I. 187, I will that all my hopolands [and] huykes not furred, be divided among the servants. **1418** *E.E. Wills* (1882) 37 Also a Hewk of grene and other melly parted. **1423** JAS. I *Kingis Q.* xlix, An huke sche had vpon hir tissew quhite. *c* **1440** [see HAIK *sb.*[1]]. *a* **1529** SKELTON *E. Rummyng* 56 Her huke of Lyncole grene. **1530** PALSGR. 231/1 Hewke a garment for a woman, *surquayne, froc. Ibid.* 233/1 Huke. **1616** BULLOKAR, *Huke*, a Dutch attire couering the head, face, and all the body. *a* **1626** BACON *New Atl.* (1627) 24 A messenger, in a rich Huke. *a* **1657** LOVELACE *Poems* (1864) 210 Like dames i' th land of Luyck, He wears his everlasting huyck. **1694** *Dunton's Ladies Dict.* (N.), The German virgins..put on a streight or plain garment, such a one as they in some places call a huk. **1834** PLANCHÉ *Brit. Costume* 181. **1852** MISS YONGE *Cameos* (1877) II. xxxvi. 370 When not in armour, she wore a huque, or close-fitting gown.

b. Applied to the Arab. *haïk*: see HAIK[2].

1630 J. TAYLOR (Water P.) *Wks.* (N.), The richer sort [of women] doe weare a huicke, which is a rob of cloth or stuffe plated, and the upper part of it is gathered and sowed together in the forme of an English potlid, with a tassell on the top. **1660** F. BROOKE tr. *Le Blanc's Trav.* 269 (Cairo) They [ladies] go all as 'twere masked and covered with an Huke that hides their face.

Hence †**huke** *v. trans.*, to cover with or as with a huke; to veil, cloak.

1613 H. KING *Halfe-pennyw. Wit* (ed. 3) Ded. (N.), I will ..throw some light vaile of spotlesse pretended well-meaning over it, to huke and mask it from publicke shame.

huke, obs. form of HOOK, HUCK.

‖**hukilau** (hu:kɪ'laʊ). [Hawaiian, f. *huki* to pull + *lau* net.] An Hawaiian fishing party usually involving many people and much revelry.

1954 J. SHERIDAN in *Ellery Queen's Mystery Mag.* Oct. 20/1 Oh, we're going to a hukilau. *Ibid.* 21/2 We're about ready for the hukilau... He led us seaward, explaining to Bill that *huki* means pull and *lau* means leaf, from the *ti* leaves which are used to frighten fish into the net. **1972** *New Yorker* 8 Apr. 84/1 (Advt.), Come to a hukilau,..a sort of Polynesian fish-in.

huk(k)ah, var. of HOOKAH.

hukm, var. HOOKUM.

hul, obs. form of HILL, HULL.

hula ('hu:lə). Also †**hura**; **hula-hula**. [Hawaiian.] **a.** An Hawaiian dance, with six basic steps, which portrays through symbolic and imitative gestures natural phenomena, sports, and historical or mythological subjects. Also *attrib.* Hence as *vb.*, to dance the hula.

1825 W. ELLIS *Jrnl. Tour Hawaii* 59 At 4 p.m. the musicians from Kau again collected on the beach, and the dancers commenced a *hura*. *c* **1835** LOWELL SMITH in M. D. Frear *Lowell & Abigail* (1934) 102 [The public disturbance of] perpetual hulas, drumming and dancing accompanied by howling and intonations. **1851** F. A. BUCK *Yankee Trader in Gold Rush* (1930) 81 They also take advantage of this to have a grand Hoolah Hoolah, or native dance. **1853** *Putnam's Mag.* II. 21/1 And now the floor was cleared, and preparation made for the great feature of the evening, viz., the *Hula-hula*. **1866** 'MARK TWAIN' *Lett. fr. Hawaii* (1967) 70 The girls danced the lascivious hula-hula—a dance that is said to exhibit the very perfection of educated motion. *Ibid.* 170 The flower and evergreen trumpery worn by the hula girls. **1868** *Daily Territorial Enterprise* (Virginia City, Nevada) 29 Aug. 3/1 We have borne ourselves with calm fortitude at a Sandwich Island *hula-hula*. **1892** STEVENSON & OSBOURNE *Wrecker* xvii. 259, I was entertained to a sea-bathe, indiscriminate cocktails, a dinner, a *hula-hula*. **1898** [see *grass skirt* (GRASS *sb.*[1] 14)]. **1899** W. C. MORROW *Bohemian Paris* 96 The hula-hula of the Hawaiian women lacks the grace, dash and abandon of the Turkish dance. **1919** F. O'BRIEN *White Shadows South Seas* 4 Kelly began 'Tome! Tome!' a Hawaiian hula. **1927** [see EMPENNAGE]. **1928** L. NORTH *Parasites* 14 It appeared that you could buy anything from a home to a Hula-skirt on time-payment. **1954** 'N. BLAKE' *Whisper in Gloom* I. iii. 49 A dusky maiden in hula-hula skirt, brassiere, and little else. **1954** *Ellery Queen's Mystery Mag.* Oct. 30/1 Her *hula* was very good. *Ibid.* 31/1 David was the one who taught me to swim and to *hula*. **1956** 'N. SHUTE' *Beyond Black Stump* viii. 236 With straw hula skirts..for sale in one corner among the picture postcards. **1970** *Observer* (Colour Suppl.) 15 Feb. 26/2 An ability to hula well does not..appear to be a quality inherent in every Tahitian.

b. ***hula hoop***, a tubular, plastic hoop (HOOP *sb.*[1] 3) used for spinning round the body with movements akin to those of the hula; hence ***hula hoop*** v. intr., ***hula-hooping*** vbl. sb. and ppl. adj.

1958 *Economist* 11 Oct. 144/2 In a manner reminiscent of a primitive tribal ritual, the Hula Hoop..can be made to spin round the torso, or arm or leg or neck, by a broad swaying motion resembling the hip swinging of a Hawaiian hula dancer. **1958** *Observer* 9 Nov. 10/4 Hula-hooping children. **1958** *Times Lit. Suppl.* 21 Nov. p. xxix/3 Hoops, also of ancient origin, had virtually disappeared from shops and streets, until the sudden recent craze for 'hula' hoops brought them out in a new form. **1958** *Times* 19 Dec. 12/5 If she had been a little younger he would have asked her if she had been hula-hooping the previous day. **1959** *Times* 3 Jan. 10/4 As training they are advocating two hours of 'hula-hooping' every morning. **1969** *Official Gaz.* (U.S. Patent Office) 1 July TM16/2 Wham-O Mfg. Co., San Gabriel, Calif... Junior Hula Hoop... For plastic toy hoops. **1970** *Which?* Sept. 288/2 Remember hula-hoops and dislocated hips? **1973** *Daily Tel.* (Colour Suppl.) 6 Apr. 27/2 Few 'craze' toys have as long a life as the yo-yo: the hula-hoop and the late, unlamented 'clacker-balls' are examples which had success but were soon forgotten.

hulan, obs. var. of UHLAN, a (Polish) lancer.

†**hulch**, *sb.* and *a. Obs.* [Origin obscure.

The identity of meaning between *hulch*, *hulch-back*, *hulch-backed*, and *hunch*, *hunch-back*, *hunch-backed*, suggests that the two groups are connected; but the relations between them are at present undetermined. That they are mere phonetic variants seems to be negatived by the chronology; for while all the members of the *hulch* group are in Cotgr. 1611, only *hunch-backed* is known to be possibly of similar age, *hunch-back* being of the 18th, and *hunch* of the 19th c. (See HUNCH *v.*) Cf. also *huck-backed*, s.v. HUCK *sb.*[1]; *huckle-backed*, s.v. HUCKLE *sb.*; *hulch-backed* below.]

A. *sb.* A hump. Hence **hulched** *a.*, humped.

1611 COTGR., *Bosse*,..also, a hulch in the backe. *Bossé*, swollen, risen, bunchie, hulched, puffed vp. *Ibid.*, *Gibbasse* ..a great bunch, or hulch-like swelling. *Gibbe*, a bunch, or swelling; a hulch; any thing that stands poking out.

B. *adj.* or *attrib.* Hunched. Also in comb. **hulch-backed** *a.*, hunch-backed, hump-backed; also *transf.* of round-backed tools.

1611 COTGR., *Gibbar*, a kind of slender, and long-nosed Whale, that hath a hulch backe. *Ibid.*, *Gibbeux*, hulch, bunched, much swelling, imbossed. *Ibid.* s.v. *Pacquet*, *Il porte son pacquet*..(said of one that is hulch-backt). **1653** URQUHART *Rabelais* I. xxvii. 130 Little hulchback't demi-knives. **1685** COTTON tr. *Montaigne* III. 243 A man with a hulch back. **1688** R. HOLME *Armoury* III. vii. 315/1 The other [is] an Hulch or round Backed Cleaver. **1708** MOTTEUX *Rabelais* v. Prol. (1737) p. lxii, Little hulch-back'd Æsop.

Hence †**hulch** *v. trans.*, to make 'hulch' or humped; to 'bundle' *up*.

1676 ETHEREDGE *Man of Mode* III. iii, I hate to be hulched up in a coach; walking is much better.

†'**hulchy**, *a. Obs.* or *dial.* Also 8 **hulgy**. [f. HULCH *sb.* + -Y.] Humpy, hump-backed.

1632 SHERWOOD, Hulchie, *gibbeux*. *a* **1693** URQUHART *Rabelais* III. xvii. 142 The uneven shrugging of her hulchy Shoulders. **1768** ROSS *Helenore* 35 (Jam.) An ugly hulgie-backed, cankered wasp. *Ibid.* 78 And of a worldly hulgy-back get free.

†**hulck-backed**, *a. Obs. rare*$^{-1}$. [perh. an error for *hulch-backed*; but cf. *huck-backed*, s.v. HUCK *sb.*[1]; also HULK *sb.*[2] 4.] = HULCH-BACKED.

1656 W. D. tr. *Comenius' Gate Lat. Unl.* §289. 79 They that are bottle-nosed: also the hulck-backed, swoln-throated.

huld(e: see HILD *v.*, HOLD *a.* and *v.*

‖**huldee, huldi** ('hʌldi:). *East Ind.* [Hindī, etc.] The name in various East Indian vernaculars of the plant *Curcuma longa*, the tubers of which yield turmeric; also of the powdered turmeric itself.

1832 G. A. HERKLOTS tr. *Customs Moosulmans India* 97 A day or two..before the application of *huldee* to the bride-groom. 1834 MEDWIN *Angler in Wales* II. 335 Hindus, who besmear their persons and clothes with a red dye called Huldee. 1851 *Illustr. Catal. Gt. Exhib.* 905 A compound made with huldee, soap, etc.

†**hulder.** *Obs. rare.* Ger. †*hulder, holder* is 'elder'; but Ascham mentions *elder* as another tree; it is possible therefore that *hulder* is a misprint for *hulver* holly; others suggest *alder*, dial. *ouller*.

1545 ASCHAM *Toxoph.* II. (Arb.) 125 Hulder, black thorne, Serues tree, Beche, Elder, Aspe, and Salowe, eyther for theyr wekenes or lyghtenesse, make holow, starting, studding, gaddynge shaftes.

hule, ME. dial. f. HILL *v.*, to cover, hide.

*c*1350 *Will. Palerne* 97 Hov hertily the herdes wif hules þat child. *c*1450 MYRC 1872 Wyth þre towayles and no lasse Hule þyn auter at thy masse.

hule ('u:lı). Also ule, ulé, ulli. [Mexican Sp. *(h)ule*, Nahuatl *ulli* or *olli* caoutchouc.] A Central American tree of the genus *Castilloa* (formerly *Castilla*), or the crude rubber obtained from it. So **hu'lero, u'lero**, a collector of rubber.

1846 J. LINDLEY *Veget. Kingd.* 271 The tree Ule of Papantla, from which caoutchouc is obtained in that country. 1874 T. BELT *Naturalist in Nicaragua* 33 The Mexicans played with balls made from it, and it still bears its Aztec name of *Ulli*, from which the Spaniards call the collectors of it *Ulleros*. 1880 *Encycl. Brit.* XII. 835/2 Torquemada mentions..that an oil was extracted from the 'ulli', or rubber, by heat, possessing soft and lubricous properties... Even at that early date the Spaniards used the juice of the ulé tree to waterproof their cloaks. 1894 *Outing* XXIII. 353/1 Curious tales the huleros tell of carved rocks hidden in those fastnesses. *Ibid.*, This home of the gatherer of *hule*. 1920 *Edin. Rev.* Oct. 356 The garments he wears are splashed with ulli. 1959 J. C. T. UPHOF *Dict. Economic Plants* 79/2 *Castilla costaricana* Liebm. Hule (Moraceae). —Tree. Costa Rica. Latex from stem is source of a good rubber.

huler, -our, variants of HOLOUR *Obs.*

hulfer, obs. f. HULVER, holly.

hulgy, var. HULCHY.

†**hulk** (hʌlk), *sb.*[1] *Obs.* or *dial.* Forms: 1 hulc, 4– hulk; also 4 helk, 4–6 hulke, 5 hollek. [OE. *hulc* hut, prob. going back to an earlier **huluc*, a dim. formation from ablaut stem *hul-* of *helan* to cover; cf. HULL *sb.*[1], HOLE, HOLL.]

1. A hut, shed, hovel. *Obs.* or *dial.*

*a*1000 *Laws of Ethelred* II. c. 3 §2 Gyf he..hæbbe oððon hulc ȝeworhtne, oððon ȝeteld ȝeslaȝen. *c*1000 ÆLFRIC *Hom.* I. 336 He wolde ȝenealæcan his hulce. *c*1050 *Suppl. Ælfric's Gloss.* in Wr.-Wülcker 185/13 *Tugurium*, hulc. 1388 WYCLIF *Isa.* i. 8 As an hulke in a place where gourdis wexen. 1388 —— *Wisd.* xi. 2 Thei maden litle housis [*v.rr.* housis, ether hulkis; housis, either helkis] in desert places. 1391 in Foxe *A. & M.* (1570) 559/1 In a chappel not hallowed, but accurset sheperds hulke. 14.. *Nom.* in Wr.-Wülcker 726/23 *Hoc tugurrium*, a hollek. 1827 CLARE *Sheph. Cal.* 32 Shepherds, that within their hulks remain.

†2. A hiding-place; or ? hiding, concealment.

*c*1330 R. BRUNNE *Chron. Wace* (Rolls) 8288 Hengist..had don hem skulke In wodes, in hilles, to crepe in hulke.

3. A hull or husk (of fruit, grain, etc.); an outer covering or shell. *Obs.* or *dial.*

1398 TREVISA *Barth. De P.R.* XVII. cxxxv. (Bodl. MS.), þe schale [of an acorn] wiþ þe curnel and þe hulke. 1688 R. HOLME *Armoury* II. 85/1 The Hulk, hull, or pill is..any covering of fruit that is thin skinned or easily cut. 1707 J. STEVENS tr. *Quevedo's Com. Wks.* (1709) 223 Blown Bladders, nothing but Hulk and Air. *a*1796 PEGGE *Derbicisms, Hulk*, a hull, or husk.

hulk (hʌlk), *sb.*[2] Forms: 1 hulc, 5–7 hulke, (6 *Sc.* houk), 7– hulk, (7 hulck, 9 *dial.* helk). [OE. *hulc*, corresp. to med.L. *hulcus, -um, -a*; ME. *hulke*, corresp. to OF. *hulke, hulque, houlque, hurque, hourque* (fem.), a flat-bottomed transport-ship with prow and poop rounded (Godef.); MDu. *hulc, hulke*, mod.Du. *hulk*, MLG. *hulk, holk, holke*, OHG. *holcho*, MHG. *holche, hülk*, mod.G. *holk, hülk, hulk*: a word of early diffusion among the maritime peoples of Western Europe, of uncertain origin, conjecturally referred to Gr. ὁλκάς a ship that is towed, hence a ship of burthen, a trading vessel, merchantman.]

1. A ship. In an OE. glossary = L. *liburna*, a light, fast-sailing vessel. But usually, in ME. and later, A large ship of burden or transport, often associated with the carrack. Now *arch.* and in vague sense = 'big, unwieldy vessel'.

?*c*1000 *Latin Laws of Ethelred, De Inst. Lond.* c. 2 (13th c.) in Schmid *Gesetze* 218 Si adveniat ceol vel hulcus. *c*1050 *Suppl. Ælfric's Gloss.* in Wr.-Wülcker 181/28 *Liburna*, hulc. *c*1420 LYDG. *Assembly Gods* 88 No shyp..keruell, boot ner barge, Gret karyk, nor hulke. *c*1440 *Promp. Parv.* 252/2 Hulke, shype, *hulcus*. 1480 CAXTON *Chron. Eng.* ccxliv. (1482) 302 Grete carikkes, hulkes, galeyes and shippes. 1513 DOUGLAS *Æneis* X. v. 123 The mekle houk hym bayr was Tryton callit. 1558 W. TOWRSON in Hakluyt *Voy.* (1589) 120 Two hulkes of Dantzich, the one..a shippe of 400 tunnes. 1611 COTGR., *Hourque*, a Hulke, or huge Fly-boat. *Ibid.*, *Oulque*, a Hulke. *c*1620 Z. BOYD *Zion's Flowers* (1855) 22 Eight persons were in Noah's hulk together. 1670 COTTON *Espernon* III. IX. 441 One might..have call'd these prodigious Hulks (which were each of them of two thousand Tun) floating Cities, rather than Ships. 1730–46 THOMSON *Autumn* 126 The sooty hulk Steered sluggish on. 1885 RUNCIMAN *Skippers & Sh.* 91 A vast gloomy hulk hove up on his port bow.

fig. 1637 GILLESPIE *Eng. Pop. Cerem.* Ep. A iv, These are the best wares which the bigge hulke of Conformity..hath imported amongst us.

†2. The HULL of a ship. *Obs.*

1632 J. HAYWARD tr. *Biondi's Eromena* 39 The Galley.. her hulke painted over with sparkling vermilion. 1687 A. LOVELL tr. *Thevenot's Trav.* I. 110 These Saiques are like great Barks, having a round hulk. 1829 *Nat. Philos.* Prelim. Treat. 38 (U.K.S.) The back of its shell resembles the hulk of a ship.

3. The body of a dismantled ship (worn out and unfit for sea service) retained in use as a store-vessel, for the temporary housing of crews, for quarantine or other purposes; also applied to vessels specially built for such purposes. (See also SHEER-HULK.)

1671 DRYDEN *Even. Love* Pref., The hulk of Sir Francis Drake. 1681 COTTON *Wond. Peak* 75 Moor'd up with a Chain, Like Drake's old Hulk at Deptford. 1682 *Lond. Gaz.* No. 1756/1 The Hulk rides very securely within, and is.. employed in Careening one of His Majesties Ships. 1694 *Ibid.* No. 3017/3 Yesterday was Launched..a new Hulk named the Chatham Hulk, which exceeds all that has been before built of that kind. 1727–41 CHAMBERS *Cycl., Hulks*, are large vessels, having their gun-decks from 113 to 150 feet long, and from 31 to 40 feet broad;..Their chief use is for setting masts into ships, and the like. 1776 L. MCINTOSH in Sparks *Corr. Amer. Rev.* (1853) I. 163 We sunk a hulk in the channel of the river. 1817 J. EVANS *Excurs. Windsor* etc. 467 Those vast ponderous Hulks devoted to the purposes of quarantine.

fig. 1883 STEVENSON *Treas. Isl.* I. iii, I'm a poor old hulk on a lee shore.

b. A vessel of this kind formerly used as a prison. Usually *pl.* (See quot. 1864.)

1797 *Sporting Mag.* IX. 284 Major Semple..and another convict..were lodged on board the hulks at Portsmouth. 1834 MEDWIN *Angler in Wales* I. 151 The sentence of death ..would be commuted for—the hulks. 1864 *Chambers' Bk. of Days* II. 67/2 It was as a means of devising a severe mode of punishment short of death that the Hulks on the Thames were introduced, in 1776... These prison-ships have sometimes been constructed for this special purpose, and yet the term 'hulk' remains in use as a short and easy designation. 1887 *Times* 26 Aug. 7/5 Prison life..was very unlike what it now is;..the hulks were sinks of iniquity.

attrib. 1897 P. WARUNG *Old Regime* 60 In the moment which succeeded the hulk-warder's words. *Ibid.* Achieving ..a very bad 'hulk report' for himself.

4. *transf.* and *fig.* a. A big, unwieldy person.

1597 SHAKS. *2 Hen. IV*, I. i. 19 Harrie Monmouth's Brawne (the Hulke Sir Iohn). *a*1656 BP. HALL *Rem. Wks.* (1660) 22 The hulck of a tall Brabanter, behinde whom I stood..shadowed me from notice. 1828 *Craven Dial., Helk*, a large, heavy person. 1859 G. MEREDITH *R. Feverel* xl, There is something impressive in a great human hulk. 1894 CROCKETT *Raiders* 58 Think shame o' yersel', ye great hulk.

b. A bulky or unwieldy mass (of anything).

1818 SCOTT *Fam. Lett.* 17 Jan. (1894) II. xiv. 11 The wind has not stirred a stone of the ugly hulk of stone and lime. 1828 *Craven Dial., Helks*, large white clouds, indicative of a thunder-storm. 1853 KANE *Grinnell Exp.* (1856) 546 These huge ice hulks.

hulk, *sb.*[3] *local. Mining.* [Goes with HULK *v.*[2]] An excavation made in removing the 'gouge', etc.

1847–78 HALLIW., *Hulk*, an old excavated working. *Derb.*

†**hulk**, *v.*[1] *Obs. rare.* [? f. HULK *sb.*[1] 2.] *intr.* To hide, lie concealed.

*c*1330 R. BRUNNE *Chron. Wace* (Rolls) 15888 Al þat ilke day he sculked, Among þe pouere men he hulked.

hulk (hʌlk), *v.*[2] [app. a variant of HOLK *v.* to hollow out.]

†1. *trans.* To disembowel. *Obs.* or *dial.*

*a*1611 BEAUM. & FL. *Philaster* V. ii, And with this swashing blow..I could hulk your Grace, and hang you up cross-leg'd, Like a Hare at a Poulters. 1688 R. HOLME *Armoury* II. ix. 188/1 [To] *Hulk*, or *Paunch*, is to open the Hare, and take out her Garbage. 1741 *Compl. Fam. Piece* II. i. 302 Take up the Hare, and hulk her. *a*1825 FORBY *Voc. E. Anglia.* 1854 MISS BAKER *Northampt. Gloss., Hulk*, to take out the entrails of a hare or rabbit.

2. *Mining.* To remove the 'gouge' or softer part of a lode before blasting or breaking down the harder part.

1881 RAYMOND *Mining Gloss., Dzhu*, to cut ahead on one side of a face, so as to increase the efficacy of blasting on the remainder..Also called *to hulk*.

hulk (hʌlk), *v.*[3] [f. HULK *sb.*[2]]

I. 1. *trans.* †a. To condemn to 'the hulks' (see HULK *sb.*[2] 3b). b. To lodge (sailors, etc.) temporarily in a hulk.

1827 *Blackw. Mag.* XXII. 453 The poacher was taken, tried, hulked. 1836 E. HOWARD *R. Reefer* xxix, They were hulked on board of the Pegasus. 1859 *All Year Round* No. 17. 390/2 The Cherbourg authorities don't 'hulk' their seamen as we do in narrow, dirty, old-fashioned hulks.

II. 2. *intr.* To act, hang about, or go in a clumsy, unwieldy, or lazy manner. *dial.*

*c*1793 *Spirit Pub. Jrnls.* (1799) I. 76 Before I'd dance attendance upon you..till four or five o'clock in the after-noon, while you lie hulking in bed. *a*1825 FORBY *Voc. E. Anglia* s.v., It is said of a lazy lout, who has nothing to do, and desires to have nothing, that he goes *hulking* about from place to place, seemingly watching for opportunities to pilfer.

3. (With *up.*) To rise bulkily or massively.

1880 BLACKMORE *Mary Anerley* I. vi. 65 This is the chump of the spine of the Wolds, which hulks up at last into Flamborough Head. 1892 *Daily News* 17 Sept. 5/4 The working man is getting his body back again into good condition..He is hulking-up, as we say.

hulkage. *dial.* [f. HULK *sb.*[1] + -AGE.] Hulks, hull or husk collectively; bran.

1869 BLACKMORE *Lorna Doone* xxxii, She..pointed to the great bock of wash, and riddlings, and brown hulkage (for we ground our own corn always).

hulking ('hʌlkıŋ), *a. colloq.* [f. HULK *sb.*[2] 4 + -ING[2].] Bulky, unwieldy; clumsy or ungainly on account of great bulk.

1698 E. WARD *Lond. Spy* XIV. 324 (Farmer) Up in the Chimney Corner sat a great Hulking Fellow. 1767 H. BROOKE *Fool of Qual.* (1859) II. 165 You are grown a huge hulking fellow since I saw you last. 1806–7 J. BERESFORD *Miseries Hum. Life* (1826) XVI. 97 Rummaging over the two hulking volumes. 1854 H. MILLER *Sch. & Schm.* xvi. (1857) 351 He could scarce make himself heard over half the area of his large, hulking chapel. 1875 JOWETT *Plato* (ed. 2) III. 108 A great hulking son ought not to be a burden on his parents.

'**hulkish**, *a. rare.* [f. HULK *sb.*[2] + -ISH.] Pertaining to the hulks: see HULK *sb.*[2] 3b.

1800 *Morn. Chron.* in *Spirit Pub. Jrnls.* (1801) IV. 14 By this plan felons may be moralized..better, than by the hulkish scheme of reformation so long practised.

hulky ('hʌlkı), *a. colloq.* [f. HULK *sb.*[2] 4 + -Y.] Like or of the nature of a hulk; bulky, unwieldy, hulking.

1785 GROSE *Dict. Vulg. T.* s.v., A great hulkey fellow, an overgrown clumsey lout. 1827 *Blackw. Mag.* XXI. 789 That he may place his huge hulky heels on your fender. 1872 GEO. ELIOT *Middlem.* lvi, I want to go first and have a round with that hulky fellow who turned to challenge me.

hull (hʌl), *sb.*[1] Forms: α. 1 hulu, ? 2–3 *hule, (? 3) 4–6 hul, 4– hull, (4 hulle, 5 holl). β. 4–5 hole, 5 hoole, 8– hool, *Sc.* 8–9 huil, hule (ü). [OE. *hulu* husk, from ablaut grade *hul-* of *helan* to cover: cf. OHG. *hulla*, Ger. *hülle* covering, cloak, etc.:—**hulja*, and OHG. *hulsa*, Ger. *hülse* (:—**hulisi*, **hulusi*), hull of beans or pease. The normal Eng. descendant of OE. *hulu* is *hull*; but dialectally the *u* was lengthened in ME. to *ō* (see Luick *Engl. Lautgesch.* §§506, 536) giving *hoole*, mod. dial. *hool*, Sc. *huil, hule* (Y).]

1. The shell, pod, or husk of pease and beans; the outer covering or rind of any fruit or seed.

α. *c*1000 ÆLFRIC *Gloss.* in Wr.-Wülcker *Voc.* 127/38 *Culliola*, hnutehula. *c*1380 WYCLIF *Serm.* Sel. Wks. II. 71 Man coveitiþ to be fild wiþ þes hulis [*v.r.* holis]. 1495 *Trevisa's Barth. De P.R.* XVII. lxiv. (W. de W.), Beenys ete wyth the hullys [*Bodl. MS.* holes] ben harde to defye, but.. whan the hull is awaye it clensyth. 1589 COGAN *Haven Health* x. (1636) 34 Take..Jorden Almonds, and beate them in a Morter with the huls and all on. *a*1693 URQUHART *Rabelais* III. xviii. 145 The Bean is not seen till..its swad or hull be shaled. 1847 O. BROWNSON *Two Brothers* Wks. VI. 327 The mere hull without the kernel. 1853 MORFIT *Tanning & Currying* 75 The horse-chestnut. The hulls, as well as the young fruit, also contain tannin.

β. *c*1380 WYCLIF *Serm.* Sel. Wks. II. 69 þis sone coveitide to fille his beli wiþ þese holes. 1398 TREVISA *Barth. De P.R.* XVII. lxxx. (Bodl. MS.), Some greyne and sede..is ingendred in coddes and holes as it fareþ in benes. *c*1440 *Promp. Parv.* 242/2 Hoole, or huske (*S.* hole, *P.* holl), *siliqua*. 1724 RAMSAY *Tea-t. Misc.* (1733) I. 115 Ilk kind of corn it has it's hool. *Mod. Sc.* Pea-huils, bean-huils, grosel huils.

b. *collectively.* The cuticle of grain; bran.

*c*1450 *Two Cookery-bks.* 105 Take w[h]ete, and bray it in a morter, that al þe hole holl be awey. 1798 *Trans. Soc. Arts* XVI. 206, I take all the hull or bran out of the flour.

2. a. The core of an apple. b. The encompassing calyx of certain fruits.

1883 MRS. ROLLINS *New Eng. Bygones* 180 Others [apples], mild and fine-grained, were relishable close up to the hulls. 1883 *Evang. Mag.* Oct. 461 We miss the hollow, thimble-like cavity which is seen on turning a raspberry upside-down after pulling it from its 'hull'.

3. *transf.* and *fig.* Something that encases or encloses; a covering, envelope; the case of a chrysalis; *pl.* clothes, garments.

α. 1831 CARLYLE *Sart. Res.* I. ix, What hadst thou been without thy blankets, and bibs, and other nameless hulls? 1845 —— *Cromwell* IX. cciii. (1871) IV. 136 No hulls, leathern or other, can entirely hide it. 1850 —— *Latter-d. Pamph.* iii. (1872) 90 They, across such hulls of abject ignorance, have seen into the heart of the matter. 1878

Emerson *Sovereignty Ethics* in *N. Amer. Rev.* CXXVI. 405 The poor grub..casts its filthy hull, expands into a beautiful form with rainbow wings.

β. **1718** Ramsay *Christ's Kirk Gr.* III. xvi, I'se rive frae off ye'r hips the hool. *Mod. Sc.* (Mother undressing child) Now, out o' your huils!

b. The encompassing membrane of the heart; the pericardium.

a **1605** Montgomerie *Misc. Poems* xxviii. 18 Hope micht ..fray ane hairt..out of his huill. **1725** Ramsay *Gentle Sheph.* v. i, My heart out of its hool was like to loup. **1785** Burns *Halloween* xxvi, Poor Leezie's heart maist lap the hool.

4. †**a.** A hut or hovel. *Obs.* **b.** A sty or pen for animals. *north. dial.* (Cf. HULK *sb.*^{1} 1.)

a **1225** *Ancr. R.* 100 Leswe þine ticchenes bi heordmonne hulen of ris & of leaues. **1570** Levins *Manip.* 185/19 An Hul for hogs, *porcile*. **1637** in *Sheffield Gloss.* s.v., Tho. Hartley holdeth a cottage at will and a swine hull next the Church lane. *a* **1804** J. Mather *Songs* (1862) 42 (ibid.) Two steps there go up to his hull. **1825** Brockett, *Hull*, a place in which fowls, etc. are confined for the purpose of fattening. **1888** *Sheffield Gloss.* s.v., Pig-*hull*, rabbit-*hull*.

5. 'The house or building of a grinding wheel' (*Sheffield Gloss.*).

1831 J. Holland *Manuf. Metal* I. 289 Internally the building is divided into hulls, and these into troughs. **1884** *Harper's Mag.* June 75/1 In the dust of a 'hull' of grinding 'troughs'. **1885** *St. James's Gaz.* 2 Jan. 6/1 Many protective 'hulls' are necessary to this handicraft.

hull (hʌl), *sb.*^{2} [Of obscure origin: not known before *c* 1550; possibly the same word as HULL *sb.*^{1}, but decisive evidence is wanting.

It has been conjectured by some to be identical with the 15–16th c. HOLL (*sb.* 2), corrupted as early as 1591 to HOLD (*sb.*^{2}); but, beside the phonetic difficulty, this appears nearly always to mean the internal cavity of the ship (so Du. *scheepshol*; cf. HOLE *sb.* 6), and not to be applied like *hull* to the external framework. There is an equivalent sense of HULK *sb.*^{2}, which, however, is not known before *c* 1630, and thus does not help the explanation of *hull*. The following is app. the only quot. which favours the connexion of the word with *holl, hole, hold*.

c **1440** *Promp. Parv.* 243/1 Hoole of a schyppe (*K., P.* holle), *carina*.]

1. a. The body or frame of a ship, apart from the masts, sails, and rigging. Also of an airship, flying boat, etc.

1571 Digges *Pantom.* I. xxi. G j a, Till suche time as ye can see the shippe, or rather the very hull next to the water. **1627** Capt. Smith *Seaman's Gram.* ii. 4 By the hull is meant, the full bulke or body of a ship without masts or any rigging from the stem to the sterne. **1676** tr. *Guillatiere's Voy. Athens* 14 We discovered by her Hull she was a Christian Frigot. **1742** Woodroofe in Hanway *Trav.* (1762) I. II. xvii. 77 The russian government build hulls after the dutch manner fit for shoal water. **1869** Sir E. Reed *Our Iron-Clad Ships* ii. 24 Modes of..disposing the armour upon the hulls of our iron-clad ships. **1918** *Aviation* 15 Mar. 231/1 A hull for flying boats having its elevational aspect determined by lines rounding off rearwardly. **1923** *Gloss. Aeronaut. Terms* (*B.S.I.*) iv. 35 *Hull*, the main flotation body of a boat sea plane. **1923** Glazebrook *Dict. Appl. Physics* V. 128/2 The curves may be taken as representing the type of distribution which had been found for models of airship hulls. **1936** [see *air stewardess* (AIR *sb.*^{1} III. 4)]. **1950** *Gloss. Aeronaut. Terms* (*B.S.I.*) I. 37 *Hull*, the main structural and flotation body of a flying boat or boat amphibian. **1951** *Oxf. Jun. Encycl.* IV. 396/2 The hull of a flying boat has a planing bottom like a speedboat.

†**b.** A dismantled vessel; = HULK *sb.*^{2} 3. *Obs.*

1582 N. Lichefield tr. *Castanheda's Conq. E. Ind.* lxxv. 154 A certaine ship..Afterward that he had taken the spoyle of the same, hee lefte the Hull in keepinge. **1666** *Lond. Gaz.* No. 59/3 We saw the Admiral made a Hull, and three of the Enemy were fired.

2. Phrases. **a.** ***to lie at*** (†*a, on, to*) ***hull*** (cf. A-HULL): = HULL *v.*^{2} 1. Also ***to lie hull, try a hull, strike*** (*a*) ***hull***, in kindred sense. **b.** ***hull down***: so far away that the hull is invisible, being below the horizon; also *attrib.* and *fig.* Used also of a tank (see quot. 1948^2). So ***hull out***: with the hull above the horizon. **c.** ***hull-to*** = A-HULL.

a. **1556** W. Towrson in Hakluyt *Voy.* (1589) 98 We lay at hull about an hour after. **1582** N. Lichefield tr. *Castanheda's Conq. E. Ind.* xxix. 73 All this time the shippes laye a hull. **1597** J. Payne *Royal Exch.* 33 The ship on hull, the helme on lee. **1634** Brereton *Trav.* (Chetham Soc.) I. 12 In stormy weather they take down their masts, and fish, the vessel lying at hull. **1635** *Voy. Foxe & James to N. West* (Hakluyt Soc.) I. 181 He strooke sayle and lay to hulle. **1727–41** Chambers *Cycl.* s.v., To strike a Hull, is to lie closely or obscurely in the sea in a storm. **1773** N. Frowde *Life* etc. 122 Let the Ship drive with the Tempest, and at length, to try a Hull. **1828** *J. H. Moore's Pract. Navig.* (ed. 20) 184 When she lies hull, that is, with all her sails furled. **1867** Smyth *Sailor's Word-bk.* s.v., *To strike hull* in a storm, is to take in her sails and lash the helm on the lee side of the ship, which is termed *to lie a-hull*.

b. **1775** Dalrymple in *Phil. Trans.* LXVIII. 395 The vessel was hull down when they came aboard. **1804** *Naval Chron.* XII. 318 As soon as she was hull out I made sail. **1839** T. Beale *Sperm Whale* 283 Exclaimed, 'She is hull down', meaning that..the convexity of the sea between us and the ship was greater than the height of the body of the vessel. **1883** Stevenson *Silverado Sq.* 180 They were hull-down for us behind life's ocean, and we but hailed their topsails on the line. **1899** *Westm. Gaz.* 29 Nov. 1/3 He shook his fist at the hull-down coasting schooner. **1905** J. C. Lincoln *Partners of Tide* xiv. 264 You've got me beat, hull down. **1933** 'L. Luard' *All Hands* 132 We was goin' to see our Mary [Pickford]. Don't alf 'old with 'er. She's got the rest of 'em 'ull down. **1944** *Return to Attack* (Army Board, N.Z.) 18/1 Using the slight undulations of the desert to get hull down and so present the smallest target, they manœuvred for position. **1948** C. Day Lewis *Poems 1943–47* 29 Alas, hull-down upon hope's ashen verge Hastens the vessel that our joined hands launched. **1948** Partridge *Dict. Forces' Slang* 96 *Hull down*, a position for tanks and self-propelled guns where only the turret was visible, the rest being protected by a bank or fold in the ground. **1953** C. Day Lewis *Italian Visit* iv. 51 A cloud vibrating In the wash of the hull-down sun. **1960** C. S. Lewis *Studies in Words* iv. 105 But ten years later he and Cowley are leagues apart, each 'hull down' to the other.

c. **1744** *Lond. Mag.* 142 Some of the Weathermost Ships were, at Night, Hull-to. **1794** *Rigging & Seamanship* II. 252* *Hull-to*, the situation of a ship when she lies with all her sails furled; as in trying.

†**hull**, *sb.*^{3} *Obs.* [cf. HULVER.] Holly.

1557 Tusser *100 Points Husb.* xlii, Get Iuye and hull, woman deck vp thyne house. **1573** —— *Husb.* xviii. (1878) 46 To plots not full ad bremble and hull. **1586** W. Webbe *Eng. Poetrie* (Arb.) 74 Oft did a left hand crow foretell these things in her hull tree.

hull (hʌl), *v.*^{1} Forms: see HULL *sb.*^{1} [f. HULL *sb.*^{1}] *trans.* To remove the hull, shell, or husk of; to strip of the outer covering.

1398 Trevisa *Barth. De P.R.* XVII. lxvii. (Bodl. MS.), Pollenta is corne isode ipeled and holed [*ed.* **1495** hullyd] and ischeled wiþ frotinge of handes. *c* **1430** *Two Cookery-bks.* 33 Take Whyte Pesyn, and hoole hem in þe maner as men don Caboges. **1544** Phaer *Regim. Lyfe* (1553) D vij b, To eate barly hulled. **1612** Woodall *Surg. Mate* Wks. (1653) 346 Take..good Bay-berries, hulled well. **1662** H. Stubbe *Ind. Nectar* ii. 14 They cannot afford to pick or hull their nuts. **1781–5** Latham *Gen. Synopsis Birds* I. 310 (T.) The male will hull the seeds for his consort with his bill. **1880** *Jamieson's Dict.* s.v. *Hule*, To hule peas. **1890** *Spectator* 1 Nov., Two contrivances, one for irrigating, the other for hulling rice.

b. *transf.* †(*a*) To shed (teeth). (*b*) To pick (fruit) from the encompassing calyx.

1708 *Lond. Gaz.* No. 4442/4 A yellow Dun Stone-horse.. now hulling his Teeth. **1884** Roe *Nat. Ser. Story* viii, He brought the strawberries to Amy..and stood near while she ..hulled them.

†**c.** *intr.* (for *refl.*) To lose the hulls. *Obs.*

c **1430** *Two Cookery-bks.* 7 Take whete..an stampe with a pestel tyl it hole.

Hence **hulling** *vbl. sb.*, also *Comb.* in ***hulling-machine, -mill***.

hull (hʌl), *v.*^{2} [f. HULL *sb.*^{2}]

†**1.** *intr. Naut.* Of a ship: To float or be driven by the force of the wind or current on the hull alone; to drift to the wind with sails furled; to lie a-hull. *Obs.*

1558 W. Towrson in Hakluyt *Voy.* (1589) 130 We lost our maine saile, foresaile, and spreetsaile, and were forced to lye a hulling. **1594** Shaks. *Rich. III*, IV. iv. 438 There they hull, expecting but the aide Of Buckingham, to welcome them ashore. **1627** Capt. Smith *Seaman's Gram.* ix. 40 If that split..then hull, which is to beare no saile. *Ibid.*, They call it hulling also in a calme swelling Sea, which is commonly before a storme, when they strike their sailes lest she should beat them in peeces against the mast by Rowling. **1687** B. Randolph *Archipelago* 100 We were forced to.. hull (lye with our head to the wind without any saile). **1708** Motteux *Rabelais* IV. xxi. (1737) 92 What a devilish Sea there Runs? She'll neither try, nor hull.

†**b.** *transf.* and *fig. Obs.*

1599 B. Jonson *Ev. Man out of Hum.* II. ii. Wks. (Rtldg.) 45/2 He may hull up and down in the humorous World a little longer. **1601** Holland *Pliny* IX. viii. 239 The fish.. hulled too and fro with the waves, as if it had beene halfe dead.

2. *trans.* To strike (a ship) in the hull with cannon shot.

1726 Shelvocke *Voy. round World* (1757) 203 We had not a man killed or wounded, although the enemy often hulled us. **1776** W. Heath in Sparks *Corr. Amer. Rev.* (1853) I. 277 The Phœnix was thrice hulled by our shot. **1894** Clark Russell *Good Ship Mohock* II. 128, I did not know but that the Mohock had been hulled and was sinking. **1898** *Westm. Gaz.* 23 May 6/3 The Spaniards say that the hulling of the vessel was accidental.

hull, obs. form of HILL *v.*^{1}, to cover.

hullabaloo (ˌhʌləbəˈluː), *sb.* (*int.*) Also 8 **hollo-ballo**, 9 **halloo-, halla-, holla-, hulla-balloo, -boloo, halli(e)-, holliballoo, hille-, hilli-, hally-, hurla-, hulabaloo, hilliebalow**. [The form remained unsettled until the early 20th c.; it appears first in Sc. and north. Eng. writers and vocabularies.

It is app. the interj. *halloo, hullo, hilloa*, with riming reduplication, thus, *halloo-baloo!* The conjecture has been made, but without any evidence, that it was orig. a wolf-hunting cry, and contained the French words *bas le loup!* (Cf. BALOW, BALOO.)]

Tumultuous noise or clamour; uproar; clamorous confusion. Also *fig.*

1762 Smollett *Sir L. Greaves* vii, I would there was a blister on this plaguy tongue of mine for making such a hollo-ballo. **1800** Southey in C. C. Southey *Life* II. 81 One day there was a hallaballoo (I never saw that word in a dictionary..) in the stables. **1804** —— *Lett.* (1856) I. 260 You must come as soon as our hullabaloo is over. **1818** Cobbett *Pol. Reg.* XXXIII. 597 Those 'Cheap Publications', about which they have made such a halloobaloo. **1825–80** Jamieson, *Halloo-balloo, hallie-balloo*, a great noise and uproar. *Renfr.*; *Hilliebalow* Roxb.; *Hillie-bulloo* Angus; *Hillie-bullow* Fife. **1825** Brockett, *Hallabaloo, Hillebaloo*, a noise, an uproar. **1841** R. Oastler *Fleet Papers* I. xiii. 100 What a halloo-bo-loo the hunters sometimes caused! **1844** Disraeli *Coningsby* VIII. vi, The truth of all this hullaballoo was that Rigby had a sly pension. **1862** Mrs. H. Wood *Mrs. Hallib.* II. xxii. (1888) 265 There's no knowing what hullabaloo they might make! **1898** J. Arch *Story of Life* xiii. 312 When the movement started, there was a terrible hullaboloo.

b. as *int.*

a **1845** [see HULLOO]. **1887** R. Abbay *White Mare Whitestonecliff* 147 That lazy crew..Would sleep till the porter cried 'Hullaballoo, Hullaballoo, The abbot is waiting in chapel for you'.

Hence **hullabaˈloo** *v. intr.*, to make a hullabaloo; also *trans.*; **hullabaˈlooing** *ppl. a.*

1867 Miss Broughton *Cometh up as a Fl.* I. v. 54 When I die there'll be a great splash of tears and hullaballooing. **1936** M. Franklin *All that Swagger* x. 93 On harvest days they were hullabalooed from bed before dawn. **1952** Dylan Thomas *Coll. Poems* p. ix, Ho, hullaballoing clan Agape, with woe In your beaks, on the gabbing capes!

hullar, var. HOLOUR *Obs.*

hulled (hʌld), *a.* [f. HULL *sb.*^{1} and ^{2} + -ED^2.]

1. Having a hull or husk (of a particular kind).

1577 B. Googe *Heresbach's Husb.* I. (1586) 28 b, Barley.. yf it be Winter seede it is harder hulled.

2. Of a ship: Having a hull or body (of a particular kind).

1893 *Daily News* 1 May 4/4 The gracefully hulled three and four-masted schooners.

hulled (hʌld), *ppl. a.* [f. HULL *v.*^{1}] Stripped of the hull or husk.

1382 Wyclif *Prov.* xxvii. 22 If thou bete togidere a fool in a morter, as hoolid barli smytende there vp on the pestel. **1656** Ridgley *Pract. Physick* 58 Decoction of hulled barley. **1851** *Illustr. Catal. Gt. Exhib.* 1224 Oats and barley deprived of their first pellicle, and known under the name of groats and of hulled barley.

huller (ˈhʌlə(r)). [f. HULL *v.*^{1} + -ER^1.] One who or that which hulls; *spec.* a machine for separating the hulls from seeds.

1864 in Webster. **1875** in Knight *Dict. Mech.*

hulling (ˈhʌlɪŋ). [f. HULL *sb.*^{1} + -ING^1.] Outer covering; an outer garment (cf. HILLING).

1434 in *Priv. Purse Exp. Eliz. of York* (1830) 242/2 Her hullyng of black, red and green. **1708** Motteux *Rabelais* v. xvi, The Husks, and Hullings. **1847–78** Halliwell, *Hullings*, husks, or shells; chaff. Also, hillings or coverlets.

hullo, hulloa (həˈləʊ), *int.* [Cf. HALLO, HILLO, HOLLO.] A call used to hail a person or to excite his attention. Also used in response to a telephone call and (freq. repeated) to express surprise. Cf. HALLO *int.*, HELLO *int.* b.

1857 Hughes *Tom Brown* I. ix, Hullo, who's there? **1882** Mrs. Riddell *Daisies & B.* III. 57 Hulloa, you sir! **1900** C. H. Chambers *Tyranny of Tears* 3 [Goes to telephone.] Hullo! hullo! [Gives them a ring up.] Are you there? **1906** *Daily Chron.* 31 May 4/7 The telephone..we both begin with the same word: 'Hullo!' **1931** D. L. Sayers *Five Red Herrings* xix. 193 'Hullo-ullo-ullo!' he said. 'So here we are again.' **1959** *Listener* 13 Aug. 248/2 If, when you take off the receiver, you say 'Hullo!' just think how absurd that is. Why, you might be saying 'Hullo!' to a total stranger. **1972** N. Marsh *Tied up in Tinsel* viii. 198 Hullo-ullo! I thought there was something there.

†**hullock** (ˈhʌlək). *Naut. Obs.* [Origin unascertained.] A small part of a sail let out in a gale to keep the ship's head to the sea.

1553 Willoughby in Hakluyt *Voy.* (1589) 269 Then we spred an hullocke of our foresaile, and bare roome with her. **1627** Capt. Smith *Seaman's Gram.* ix. 41 Seeing the storm decreaseth, let vs trie if she will endure the Hullocke of a Saile, which sometimes is a peece of the mizen saile or some other little saile, part opned to keepe her head to the sea. **1708** Motteux *Rabelais* IV. xxii. (1737) 94 She'll bear the Hullock of a Sail.

hullok, obs. form of HILLOCK.

c **1430** *Pilgr. Lyf Manhode* II. cxlv. (1869) 133 Toward an hullok.

hulloo (həˈluː), *int.* A variant of HALLOO.

1707 Hickeringill *Priest-cr.* II. v. 53 Hulloo then, go on, run on; Hulloo! See who cares first, you or I. *a* **1845** Hood *Forge* II. xxiii, Hulloo! Hulloo! And Hullabaloo!

hull(o)ur, -owre, var. HOLOUR. *Obs.*

hully (ˈhʌlɪ), *a. rare*$^{-0}$. [f. HULL *sb.*^{1} + -Y^1.] Having or abounding in hulls or husks.

1727 Bailey vol. II, *Hully*, full of hulls. In Ainsworth, Johnson, and in mod. Dicts.

hully gee (ˈhʌlɪ ˈdʒiː), *int.* Chiefly *U.S.* Also **holly gee**. [Corruption of *Holy Jesus*.] An exclamation of delight or surprise.

1895 E. W. Townsend *Chimmie Fadden Explains* 58 And holly gee! I never knowed de Duckess could do it! *Ibid.* 69 'Holly gee!' says de mug, 'don't do dat,' he says, and slips me a fiver. **1898** 'O. Thanet' *Heart of Toil* 76 Hully gee, Michael, but you are just *there*, and don't you forget it. **1907** F. H. Burnett *Shuttle* xxiii. 238 To be treated as a gentleman by a gentleman—by 'a fine old swell like this—Hully gee!' **1936** F. Clune *Roaming round Darling* i. 3 We picked up a pair of wire-strainers, his leather coat, and a typewriter: then hully-gee! we were off again over the hideous Pyrmont Bridge. **1945** Mencken *Amer. Lang. Suppl.* I. 664 *Hully gee* (for *Holy Jesus*) was introduced by Edward W. Townsend's Chimmie Fadden and Major Max (New York, 1895), but it disappeared with the decay of the Bowery boy as an American comic type.

hully gully (ˈhʌlɪ ˈgʌlɪ). [Etym. unknown.] A dance that is a modification of the frug.

1964 *Cambr. Rev.* 10 Oct. 1/2 Two or three hours of the Hully-Gully. **1966** *Amer. Speech* XLI. 143 Mee, Charles

L., Jr. Discotheque Man... [Names and briefly describes current dances: the Hully-Gully, the Frug, La Bostella, the Jerk.] **1968** D. HALLIDAY *Dolly & Singing Bird* ii. 23 We danced a Hully Gully. And then..Johnson performed a frenzied Watusi. **1969** N. COHN *AWopBopaLooBop* (1970) ix. 85 Dance-crazes bossed pop right up until the Beatles broke. There was the Hully Gully, the Madison, [etc.].

huloist, hulotheism: see HYLOIST, -THEISM.

hulpe, obs. pa. t. and pple. of HELP *v.*

†**huls**, *v. Obs. rare*⁻¹. ?
c **1420** *Pallad. on Husb.* VII. 56 And euery puls, Ther lond is cold, is heruest now to huls [*cum strepitu metere*].

hulsite (ˈhʌlsaɪt). *Min.* [f. the name of Alfred *Hulse* Brooks (1871-1924), American geologist: see -ITE¹.] A black borate of bivalent and trivalent iron, magnesium, and calcium in which there is some substitution of tin for trivalent iron, known only from an Alaskan locality.
1908 KNOPF & SCHALLER in *Amer. Jrnl. Sci.* CLXXV. 323 Examination of this deposit showed that an unknown mineral..was present in considerable abundance. We propose for it the name *hulsite*, in honor of Mr. Alfred Hulse Brooks, geologist in charge of the Division of Alaskan Mineral Resources. **1954** *Amer. Mineralogist* XXXIX. 524 X-ray powder photographs of ludwigite, paigeite, pinakiolite, hulsite, warwickite, sussexite, and camsellite were taken.

hulster (ˈhʌlstə(r)), *sb. dial.* Also **holster.** [Cf. OE. *heolstor*, f. *hel-an* to cover, conceal, and see HOLSTER *sb.*] A hiding-place, a retreat.
[*a* **1000** *Satan* 101 Naȝan we þæs heolstres þæt we us ȝehydan maȝon.] **1880** *W. Cornwall Gloss., Hulster*,..a hold or retreat. 'This rubbish is only a hulster for snails'. T. Q. Couch. **1882** JAGO *Cornwall Gloss., Holt*, or *Holster*, a lurking place, a place of concealment.

†ˈ**hulster,** *v. Obs.* [f. prec.] *trans.* To hide.
c **1400** *Rom. Rose* 6146 There I hope best to hulstred be And certeynly sikerest hidyng Is vndirnethe humblest clothing. [**1616** BULLOKAR, *Hulstred*, hidden.]

hult, obs. form of HILT *sb.*

†**hulve.** *Obs.* (See quot.)
1764 *G. Jacob's Compl. Crt.-keeper* (ed. 6) 114 The Trunk or Hulve [to] convey the Water in the Common Sewer.

hulver (ˈhʌlvə(r)). *Obs.* exc. *dial.* Also 5 **holvyr, hulfere, -wur, -uyr,** 6 **-war.** [In late ME. *hulfere*, app. the same as ON. *hulfr*, which is explained by Vigf. as 'dogwood'. The ulterior history of the word, and the question of its relation to *holly* or *holm*, are undetermined.]
Holly. ***knee hulver***, Butcher's Broom, *Ruscus aculeatus*. ***sea hulver***, Sea Holly, Eryngo.
c **1430** LYDG. *Compl. Bl. Knt.* 129 Betwix an hulfere and a wodebinde. **14..** *Songs & Carols* (Percy Soc.) xl, Holvyr and Heyvy mad a gret party, Ho xuld have the maystri. *c* **1440** *Promp. Parv.* 253/1 Hulwur, tre (*K., P.* huluyr), *hulmus*. **1578** LYTE *Dodoens* IV. lviii. 519 Sea Holme, or Huluer, and Sea Holly. *Ibid.* VI. xxxiv. 701 In Englishe it is called Holme, Holly, and Huluer. **1819** H. BUSK *Vestriad* IV. 719 The skirt of hulver and the screen of spruce. *a* **1825** FORBY *Voc. E. Anglia, Hulver*, holly. **1859** *All Year Round* No. 36. 225/1 The holly..in Norfolk..called hulver.
b. *attrib.* and *Comb.*, as ***hulver bush, tree***; **hulver-head, -headed** *a.* (see quots.); **hulver oak**, the holm-oak.
1538 TURNER *Libellus, Ruscus*,..an Huluar tre. **1597** GERARDE *Herbal* III. xxx. 1159 The..Ilex..might be called Holme Oke, Huluer Oke, or Holly Oke. **1601** HOLLAND *Pliny* XXIV. xiii. (R.), Touching the Holly, or Hulver-tree. *a* **1700** B. E. *Dict. Cant. Crew, Hulver-head*, a silly foolish Fellow. **1785** GROSE *Dict. Vulg. T., Hulver-headed*, silly, puzzle-pated. *a* **1825** FORBY *Voc. E. Anglia, Hulver-headed*, stupid; muddled; confused; as if the head were enveloped in a hulver bush.

hulwa (ˈhʌlwə). Also 7 **helwa, holway.** [a. Urdu and Arab. *ḥalwā* sweetmeat.] A kind of sweetmeat in India, Persia, etc.; = HALVA. Cf. HALAWI.
1662 J. DAVIES tr. *Olearius's Voy. Ambass.* 311 At Tabris, they make a certain Conserve of it [*sc.* duschab], which they call Helwa. **1698** J. FRYER *New Acct. E.-India & Persia* 358 Every Friday Night, at the Sacrament of *Holway*, (or Wafer made up in Sweetmeats). **1884** *Times* 30 May 8 Provisions ran short and the voyagers had to live on hulwa, a glutinous sweetmeat.

†**hulwort.** *Herb. Obs.* The name of a plant.
c **1265** *Voc. Names Pl.* in Wr.-Wülcker 555/1 *Pulegium*, puliol, hulwurt. **1597** GERARDE *Herbal* App., Hulwort is *Polium*. **1884** MILLER *Plant-n., Teucrium Polium*, Cat-Thyme, Hul-wort, Poly Germander.

huly, var. HOOLY, *Sc.*, gently, tardily.

hum (hʌm), *v.*¹ Also 4-7 **humme,** 5 **home,** 6 **homme.** [Known from end of 14th c.; echoic; cf. MHG. *hummen*, mod.G. dial. *hummen, hommen*, early mod.Du. (Kilian) *hummen* = *hemmen* to hem, emit voice; also BUM *v.*, and Ger. *summen, brummen*, Du. *brommen*, expressing the same or similar sounds, all with the characteristic labial-nasal *m*. See also HUMBLE *v.*²]
1. *intr.* To make a low continuous murmuring sound or note, as a bee or other insect; also said of a top or wheel in rapid rotation, a bell vibrating after being struck, etc.
c **1420** *Pallad. on Husb.* VII. 124 Yf that they [bees] humme. **1573-80** BARET *Alv.* H 717 To Humme like a Bee, *bombilo*. **1644** DIGBY *Nat. Bodies* xxviii. (1645) 310 Trembling bells..hum a great while longer then others. **1774** GOLDSM. *Nat. Hist.* (1776) VIII. 157 The gnat..is sometimes heard to hum about our beds at night. **1783** CRABBE *Village* I, The dull wheel hums doleful through the day. **1887** BOWEN *Virg. Eclog.* VII. 13 Bees cluster and hum. **1924** *Foundry* (Cleveland) 1 Apr. 63 (Advt.), The wheels surely are humming in the foundries. **1937** WODEHOUSE *Lord Emsworth & Others* ix. 299 We buzzed on through the pleasant countryside... The engine of the two-seater hummed smoothly. **1972** *Daily Tel.* 23 Mar. 21/2 Computers hummed and slide rules flashed as City analysts tried to come to grips with the new corporation tax yesterday.
2. a. *intr.* To make a low inarticulate vocal sound; *esp.* to utter such a sound in expression of dissent or dissatisfaction, or †of approbation or applause.
13.. *Erkenwald* 281 in Horstmann *Altengl. Leg.* (1881) 272 þen hummyd he þat þer lay..And gefe a gronynge. *c* **1532** DEWES *Introd. Fr.* in *Palsgr.* 917 A chorle hommeth or grudgeth. **1605** SHAKS. *Macb.* III. vi. 42 The clowdy Messenger..hums; as who should say, you'l rue the time That clogges me with this Answer. **1687** *Magd. Coll. & Jas. II* (O. Hist. Soc.) vi. 142 Upon which the Rabble hummed. **1779-81** JOHNSON *L.P., Sprat* Wks. III. 11 When the preacher touched any favourite topick in a manner that delighted his audience, their approbation was expressed by a loud hum, continued in proportion to their zeal or pleasure. When Burnet preached, part of his congregation hummed so loudly and so long, that he sat down to enjoy it. **1893** J. S. WINTER *Aunt Johnnie* II. 93 He hum'd at the cutlets and he pshaw'd at the salad.
b. To sing with closed lips without articulation.
c **1485** *Digby Myst.* (1882) III. 1226, I home and I hast, I do þat I may, With mery tvne þe trebyll to syng. *c* **1640** F. HAWKINS *Youth's Behav.* (1663) 1 Sing not within thy mouth, humming to thy self, unless thou be alone. *Mod.* She was singing, or rather humming, in a low tone.
c. To make an inarticulate murmur in a pause of speaking, from hesitation, embarrassment, etc. Usually in phr. ***to hum and ha*** (***haw***): see HA *v.*, HAW *v.*¹
c **1374** CHAUCER *Troylus* II. 1150 (1199) Al rosy hewed tho woxe she, And gan to hum. **1530** PALSGR. 588/2 He hummeth and haeth and wyll nat come out withall. **1606** SHAKS. *Tr. & Cr.* I. iii. 165 Hum and stroke thy Beard. **1632** MASSINGER & FIELD *Fatal Dowry* IV. i, Do you stand Humming and hahing now? **1749** FIELDING *Tom Jones* VIII. xi, Don't stand humming and hawing, but speak out. **1865** CARLYLE *Fredk. Gt.* XIII. ii. V. 30 Robinson apologetically hums and hahs.
trans. **1678** BUTLER *Hud.* III. ii. 1161 [You] never hum'd and hah'd Sedition. *a* **1680** —— *Rem.* (1759) II. 103 A fifth-monarchy man..humms and hahs high Treason.
3. To give forth an indistinct sound by the blending of many voices, etc.; hence (*colloq.*) to be in a condition of busy activity, to be all astir. Phr. ***to make things*** (or something specified) ***hum***: to bring to such a condition, to liven things up.
1726-46 THOMSON *Winter* 632 The city swarms intense. The public haunt..warm with mixed discourse, Hums indistinct. **1814** BYRON *Corsair* III. xviii, The haven hums with many a cheering sound. **1842** TENNYSON *St. Sim. Styl.* 37, I scarce can hear the people hum About the column's base. **1884** 'MARK TWAIN' *Huck. Finn* 224 He lit into that horse with his whip and made him fairly hum. **1887** M. ROBERTS *Western Avernus* iii. 34 The owner of the farm..came home, and, in American parlance, 'fairly made things hum'. **1889** *Pall Mall G.* 15 July 1/3 [In] the expressive nomenclature of the Far West, Hong-kong 'just hums' all the time. **1893** R. KIPLING *Many Invent.* 29 The whole country was humming with dacoits. **1898** *Daily News* 11 Jan. 5/1 The report that he had plenty of money, and would make things hum at the club. **1902** E. BANKS *Autobiogr. Newspaper Girl* xviii. 205 We took you on this paper to help us make things hum! I understand you made things hum over in England. **1906** *Nation* (N.Y.) 18 Jan. 44 The colleges are making athletic reform hum, as if to make up for lost time. **1911** E. M. CLOWES *On Wallaby* x. 265 But still things are, as the American would express it, 'beginning to hum' in the irrigation line. **1914** G. ATHERTON *Perch of Devil* I. xxx, I want money to spend in Butte,..and make things hum. **1922** H. S. WALPOLE *Cathedral* I. vii. 135, I hardly need to tell you that he's not quite the man to make things hum. **1966** 'J. HACKSTON' *Father clears Out* 107 By gum! Wouldn't it just make things hum? **1973** *Times* 16 Jan. 17/7 Our view is that if you get the logistics right and do get concentration of the best modern equipment you can really get something humming in the 1974 period.
4. a. *trans.* To utter with humming; to sing with closed lips and without articulation.
1602 MARSTON *Antonio's Rev.* V. iii, One gives nods and hums what he would speake. **1710** ADDISON *Tatler* No. 157 ¶7 Then [she] would hum over Two or Three Notes. **1808** SCOTT *Marm.* I. ii, Low humming..Some ancient Border gathering song. **1840** DICKENS *Old C. Shop* xv, The bees..hummed forth their drowsy satisfaction.
b. *to hum and ha*: see after 2 c.
†**5.** To greet with a hum; to ***hum up, down***, to express approval or disapproval of, by humming.
1642 MILTON *Apol. Smect.* viii, Such as are most humm'd and applauded there. **1682** *New News fr. Bedlam* 43 By canting and ranting I'le hum all their Gigs. **1692** tr. *Sallust* 42 All humm'd him down and call'd him Enemy and Parricide. **1733** *Revolution Politicks* III. 55 Here the whole Council humm'd him up, and approved of the same.
6. To bring (into a specified state) by humming.
1821 CLARE *Vill. Minstr.* II. 181 The busy bee hath humm'd himself to rest. **1871** J. C. JEAFFRESON *Ann. Oxford* II. iii. 24 Such 'hummers', as those who hummed James the First into good contentment with himself.
Hence **hummed** (hʌmd), *ppl. a.* (in sense 4).
1849 H. MAYO *Pop. Superst.* (1851) 156 Singing the words to M. de Puységur's mentally hummed air. **1898** *Blackw. Mag.* Mar. 338/2 A hummed song of the country.

hum, *v.*² *arch.* [Short for HUMBUG *v.*]
1. *trans.* To impose upon, hoax, take in, humbug. (*slang* or *colloq.*)
1751 *Student* II. 288 How were people of learning and good understanding *hum'd* out of their money and judgment. *Ibid.* 290 Pray let them be *hum'd* if you please. **1765** *Meritriciad* 26 She hums by turns, the Vet'ran, and the Fop. **1782** MAD. D'ARBLAY *Lett. to S. Crisp* Aug., You and I know better than to hum or be hummed in that manner. **1805** W. HUNTER in *Naval Chron.* XIII. 24 Admiral Saunders had *hummed* me about my promotion. *a* **1845** HOOD *Spring* i, How couldst thou thus poor human nature hum?
2. *trans.* and *intr.* To borrow (without any intention of returning); to scrounge. *Austral. slang.*
1918 *Aussie* Sept. 4/2 Don't *shout* cigarettes, *hum* them. **1925** FRASER & GIBBONS *Soldier & Sailor Words* 122 *To hum*, to cadge. **1935** *Bulletin* (Sydney) 30 Jan. 21/4 Where other 'Bidgee whalers 'hummed' a town for booze, Mick 'hummed' it for tea, going from house to house with his plea: 'Missus, could y' spring a cup o' tea?' **1938** X. HERBERT *Capricornia* (1939) xviii. 234 Gertch—you old blowbag! You're only humming for a drink. Nick off home.
Hence ˈ**humming** *vbl. sb.*
1807 M. PENNINGTON *Life Eliz. Carter* I. 32 That species of false wit which is now called quizzing and was formerly known by the equally barbarous term of humming.

hum (hʌm), *v.*³ *slang. intr.* To smell disagreeably. Hence **hum** *sb.*³, a disagreeable smell.
1902 C. H. E. BROOKFIELD *Random Reminisc.* xi. 200 The burglar..finds a piece of Camembert cheese in the buffet, and exclaims: 'Lor'! it do 'um!' **1906** E. DYSON *Fact'ry 'Ands* xv. 197 Ther hum iv it was so fearful.. Killin' cats is rotten luck. **1927** W. E. COLLINSON *Contemp. Eng.* 23 Things didn't smell, but ponged, niffed or hummed. *Ibid.*, An awful pong or hum. **1946** I. L. IDRIESS *In Crocodile Land* xvi. 111 The abos certainly did 'hum'. **1970** *Daily Tel.* 31 Oct. 1/3 When the wind drops this stuff really hums.

hum (hʌm), *sb.*¹ Also 6-7 **humme,** 8 **humm.** [Cognate with HUM *v.*¹ It is doubtful whether sense 3 belongs here.]
I. 1. a. A low continuous sound made by a bee or other insect, also, by a spinning top, machinery in motion, etc. (Distinguished from a *buzz* by not being sibilant.)
1601 HOLLAND *Pliny* XI. x. (R.), One of them [bees] raiseth all the rest with two or three big hums or buzzes. **1698** FRYER *Acc. E. India & P.* 189 The Mosquito..not only wheals, but domineers by its continual Hums. **1786** tr. *Beckford's Vathek* (1868) 44 The sullen hum of those nocturnal insects. **1856** EMERSON *Eng. Traits, Relig.* Wks. (Bohn) II. 100 The hum of the mill. **1893** PEEL *Spen Valley* 156 The busy hum of the spinning-wheel.
b. The indistinct sound produced by the blending of distant voices or noises; a murmur; in quot. 1625, a 'buzz' of rumour.
1599 SHAKS. *Hen. V*, IV. Prol. 5 From Camp to Camp.. The Humme of eyther Army stilly sounds. **1625** B. JONSON *Staple of N.* V. i, The last hum that it made, was, that your Father, And Picklocke are fall'n out. **1797** MRS. RADCLIFFE *Italian* xxvi, A busy hum of voices from the tribunal. **1856** FROUDE *Hist. Eng.* (1858) I. iii. 189 The hum of expectation sounding louder and louder.
c. *Med.* In full ***venous hum***. A continuous humming sound sometimes heard during auscultation in the upper chest and the sides of the neck, esp. in children and in cases of anæmia, and attributed to the turbulence of the flow of venous blood.
1839 J. HOPE *Treatise Dis. Heart* (ed. 3) I. iv. 118 By the adroit management of the stethoscope..the venous murmur may often be raised, by a gradual swell, into a more or less musical hum, such as is yielded by a child's humming-top. I propose to denominate this the Venous Hum; for..this is ..more intelligible than *noise of the devil*, by which term, derived from a plaything known to few, M. Bouillaud has designated the hum in question. **1876, 1891** [see VENOUS *a.* 2]. **1907** H. S. ANDERS *Physical Diagnosis* xiv. 346 The venous hum or *bruit de diable* heard over the jugulars. **1960** J. S. BUTTERWORTH et al. *Cardiac Auscultation* (ed. 2) ix. 81 The venous hum is usually heard only in the upright position. *Ibid.*, The hum will disappear with finger compression of the jugular veins.
d. *Electronics.* (Usu. without *a* or *pl.*) Unwanted low-frequency variations in current or voltage (the cause of which is usually the alternating frequency of the mains) which will give rise in a loudspeaker to a steady humming sound; the sound so produced.
1929 K. HENNEY *Princ. Radio* xvi. 406 A hum output of 44 millivolts. **1934** J. H. REYNER *Television* viii. 90 The hum appears as a series of black bands moving slowly across the screen. **1950** A. MARCUS *Radio Servicing* xv. 714 An antenna that is too close and parallel to a power line may pick up hum by induction. **1966** R. KING *Electrical Noise* i. 3 Mains hum ..may be generated from cathodes of thermionic valves heated by alternating current or by electromagnetic

induction from near by mains frequency transformers and chokes.

2. a. An inarticulate vocal murmur uttered with closed lips in a pause of speaking, from hesitation, embarrassment, or affectation. (Usually in phr. ***hums and ha's*** (***haws***): see HA *sb.*^{2}, HAW *sb.*^{4})

1469 J. Paston in *P. Lett.* No. 607 II. 347 He wold have gotyn it aweye by humys and by hays, but I wold not so be answeryd. **1611** Shaks. *Wint. T.* II. i. 74 These Shrugs, these Hum's, and Ha's. **1711** Steele *Spect.* No. 32 ¶1 There were many very proper Hums and Pauses in his Harangue. **1749** Fielding *Tom Jones* VIII. v, After some hesitation, and many hums and ha's. **1852** R. S. Surtees *Sponge's Sp. Tour* (1893) 141 After sundry 'hums', 'indeeds', 'sos', etc.

b. A similar sound uttered as an expression of applause or approbation, or of mild surprise or dissent.

1653 *Noctes Hibernæ* I. 8 The greatest praise unto the Preacher comes From the Attentive Hearer's tears, not humnes. **1687** *Magd. Coll. & Jas. II* (Oxf. Hist. S.) vi. 134 Whereupon there was a tumultuous hum, or acclamation, made by the bystanders. *a* **1859** Macaulay *Hist. Eng.* xxiii. (1871) II. 641 The hum with which William's speech had been received, and the hiss which had drowned the voice of Seymour. **1877** T. A. Trollope *A Peep behind Scenes* xix. 277 There arose a little hum of approbation from all present.

c. A singing in a low tone with the lips closed, without articulation; an indistinct murmur.

1630 B. Jonson *New Inn* III. ii, *Lord B.* Would I could charm her! *Host.* Trundle will do it with his hum. **1711** E. Ward *Quix.* I. 381 No sooner did the Goat-herds find, Antonio by his Hum inclin'd To sing a Song. **1778** *Eng. Gazetteer* (ed. 2) s.v. *Elmhurst*, An eccho, which returns a hum, or clap with the hands..10 or 12 times.

II. †**3.** A kind of liquor; strong or double ale. *Obs.* (Cf. HUMMING *ppl. a.* 2 b.)

1616 B. Jonson *Devil an Ass* I. i, Strong-waters, Hum, Meath, and Obarni. *a* **1621** Fletcher *Wild Goose Chase* II. iii, Would I had some hum. **1670** Cotton *Voy. Irel.*, The best Cheshire hum he e'er drank in his life. *a* **1700** B. E. *Dict. Cant. Crew, Hum, or Humming Liquor*, Double Ale, Stout, Pharoah. **1719** D'Urfey *Pills* (1872) I. 311 To get us stout hum, when Christmas is come.

attrib. **1629** Shirley *Wedding* II. (N.), Sold For physic in hum-glasses and thimbles.

III. *Comb.* **hum-bucking coil** *Electronics* [BUCK *v.*^{6}], a coil arranged so as to cancel the hum in another coil by providing a signal of the opposite phase; †**hum-cap** = sense 3 (cf. HUFF-CAP); **hum-note**, a musical note of the character of a hum.

a **1700** B. E. *Dict. Cant. Crew*, *Hum-cap*, old, mellow and very strong Beer. **1896** *Pall Mall Mag.* Sept. 155 The hum-note of this great bell was too deep for a scientific test. **1940** *Chambers's Techn. Dict.* 425/1 Hum-bucking coil. **1950** A. Marcus *Radio Servicing* xv. 715 Some loudspeakers, especially of the electrodynamic type, have hum-bucking coils. **1967** P. Spring *Tape Recorders* vii. 90 The hum-bucking coil..picks up hum in opposite phase to the hum picked up by the head and of such magnitude that the two hum signals cancel.

hum, *sb.*^{2} [Short for HUMBUG *sb.*] **1.** A piece of humbug; an imposition, a hoax. (*slang* or *colloq.*)

1751 *Student* II. 288 What a delightful *Hum* had we about a poor man's getting into a quart bottle. **1753** Garrick in *Scots Mag.* Oct. 517/2 'Twas all a hum. **1799** Coleridge *Lett.* (1895) 270 The Bristol Library is a hum, and will do us little service. **1841** *Blackw. Mag.* L. 415 Is Homer a hum, and the Iliad a hoax? **1885** *Punch* 5 Sept. 114/2 Political honesty's all a big hum.

2. A persistent borrower, a scrounger. *Austral. slang.*

1919 V. Marshall *World of Living Dead*, The 'hum', the unskilled derelict or derelict-to-be who stands upon the 'pub' corner kerb, 'bites' all and sundry, and, at regular intervals, succeeds in getting lumbered for 'vag'. **1953** Caddie *Sydney Barmaid* xxxiii. 183 The speciality of the hum is the lone drunk.

hum, *sb.*^{3}: see HUM *v.*^{3}

hum (hjuːm), *sb.*^{4} *Physical Geogr.* [Serbo-Croat, = hill.] A small, usually conical, hill characteristic of karst topography.

1921 *Geogr. Rev.* XI. 602 (*caption*) General view of a polje strewn with hums. *Ibid.* 604 The former limestone mass being represented by isolated fragments which Cvijic calls 'hums'. **1937** Wooldridge & Morgan *Physical Basis Geogr.* xix. 289 Residual limestone masses or hummocks rising above polje floors are called 'hums'. **1971** B. W. Sparks *Rocks & Relief* v. 204 The interfluvial areas are finally reduced to little hillocks known as hums.

hum (həm), *int.* An inarticulate exclamation uttered with the lips closed, either in a pause of hesitation or embarrassment, or as expressing slight dissatisfaction, dissent, etc. (Cf. HEM, H'M, UM.)

1596 Shaks. *1 Hen. IV*, III. i. 158, I cry'd hum..But mark'd him not a word. **1598** —— *Merry W.* III. v. 141 Hum: ha? Is this a vision? **1847** Lytton *Lucretia* I. Prol., Hum! do you still miss your mother? **1855** Dickens *Dorrit* I. xxxi, I have a—hum—a spirit, sir, that will not endure it.

huma ('huːmə). Also **Huma, Ûma**. [Hind., a. Pers. *humā* phœnix.] A fabulous bird of the east, said to be a restless wanderer but to bring luck to any person over whom it hovers.

1841 R. C. Wellesley *Primitiæ et Reliquiæ* 104 (*heading*) The Ûma, or Indian Eagle, the bird of prosperous empire. *Ibid.* 105 The throne of the Sultan of Mysore..was surmounted by a representation of the Ûma, which is now deposited at Windsor Castle. *Ibid.* 106 A bird called by the natives the Ûma and which bore the appearance of a small eagle or vulture, built its nest..in the garden of Mr. Petrie, where Lord Wellesley resided while at Madras... The natives superstitiously ascribed much of the success of the war to the influence of the Ûma. **1858** O. W. Holmes *Autocrat of Breakfast-Table* i. 8, I am like the Huma, the bird that never lights, being always in the cars, as he is always on the wing. **1905** *Spectator* 14 Jan. 47/2 The legendary 'huma' of Eastern tradition.

human ('hjuːmən), *a.* (*sb.*) Forms: 5–6 **humayn(e**, 5–7 **humain(e**, 6–8 **humane**, 8– **human**. [a. F. *humain* (12th c. in Hatz.-Darm.) = It. *umano*, Sp., Pg. *humano*:—L. *hūmān-us* of or belonging to man, human, a derivative of the same root as *homo, homin-em* man. The stress was orig. as in OF. on the last syllable, but, in accordance with Eng. usage, was at an early date shifted to the first. The spelling *humane* remained, however, down to the beginning of the 18th c. (in Dicts. to *c* 1730), when *human* (of which isolated examples occur in 17th c.) was substituted in the senses following, leaving HUMANE with distinctive pronunciation as a distinct word. Cf. the history of DIVERS, DIVERSE.]

A. *adj.* **1.** Of, belonging to, or characteristic of mankind, distinguished from animals by superior mental development, power of articulate speech, and upright posture.

α. **1398** Trevisa *Barth. De P.R.* I. (1495) 6 This creatour thenne made man, and nature humayne comune. *c* **1475** *Partenay* 951 Neuer humain ey saw to it egal! *c* **1566** J. Alday tr. *Boaystuau's Theat. World* B, Others have bewailed..the humaine calamities. **1613** Purchas *Pilgrimage* (1614) 762 They thinke that all the gods are of humane shape. **1657** W. Coles *Adam in Eden* To Rdr., Our humane frailties. **1710** Steele *Tatler* No. 120 ¶1 The Contemplation of Humane Life. **1758** S. Hayward *Serm.* xiii. 370 The devil..knows humane nature.

β. **1697** Dryden *Virg. Georg.* IV. 604 Conceal'd from Human Eyes. **1736** Butler *Anal.* Introd. 5 The Structure of the human Body. **1799** Wordsw. *Lucy Gray* ii, Beside a human door. **1814** Byron *Lara* II. xxii, Is human love the growth of human will? **1878** Morley *Crit. Misc.* Ser. I. *Carlyle* 202 Human nature is not led for so long by lies.

2. a. Of the nature of humans; that is human or consists of human beings.

1484 Caxton *Fables of Æsop* VI. xii, Iupyter loued the humayn lygnage. *c* **1500** *Melusine* i. 15 Thou shalt..dey as a naturel & humayn woman. *c* **1566** J. Alday tr. *Boaystuau's Theat. World* B iv, All humaine creatures. **1613** Purchas *Pilgrimage* (1614) 320 Humane Sacrifices were offered to Diana. **1728–46** Thomson *Spring* 1146 By degrees, The human blossom blows. **1804** *Med. Jrnl.* XII. 340 The calamities of the human race. **1807** *Ibid.* XVII. 553 To make a mere experiment on a human subject. **1858** Kingsley *Lett.* (1878) II. 54 Wherever human beings are concerned.

b. *Astrol.* Applied to those signs of the zodiac, or constellations in general, which are figured in the form of men or women.

1658 in Phillips. **1679** Moxon *Math. Dict.*, *Humane Signs*,..those Signs of the Zodiack, which have, as it were, the form of Man, as Gemini, Virgo, Aquarius, and the first half of Sagittarius;..also such Asterisms without the Zodiack, as are usually represented in humane shape, as Perseus, Andromeda, Cassiopœa, Cepheus, Orion, etc... Ptolomy [says]..Whoever has neither the Lords of his Geniture, nor the Ascendent, in Humane Signs, will himself be a stranger to Humanity, or of churlish savage behaviour. **1819** Wilson *Compl. Dict. Astrol.* s.v., The lord of an eclipse being in any human sign, its evil effects will fall on mankind.

3. a. Belonging or relative to human beings as distinguished from God or superhuman beings; pertaining to the sphere or faculties of mankind (with implication of limitation or inferiority); mundane; secular. (Often opposed to *divine*.)

α. *a* **1533** Ld. Berners *Gold. Bk. M. Aurel.* (1546) B vj b, I haue vsed in this wrytyng, the whiche is humayne, that that diuers tymes hath bene vsed in diuinitie. **1590** Shaks. *Com. Err.* V. i. 189 Past thought of humane reason. **1600** J. Pory tr. *Leo's Africa* II. 392 There are two natures in Christ, one divine..the other humane. **1613** Purchas *Pilgrimage* (1614) 320 Humane and Divine learning. **1709** Pope *Ess. Crit.* 527 To err is humane, to forgive divine.

β. **1639** T. Brugis tr. *Camus' Mor. Relat.* 183 The divine disposings agree not alwayes with human purposes. **1712** W. Rogers *Voy.* 255 In all human probability. **1860** Motley *Netherl.* (1868) I. i. 1 An authority which seemed more than human. **1878** Browning *La Saisiaz* 154 To.. Pass off human lisp as echo of the Sphere-song out of reach.

b. Belonging or relative to humans, relating to or characteristic of activities, relationships, etc., which are observable in mankind, as distinguished from (*a*) the lower animals; (*b*) machinery or the mechanical element; (*c*) mere objects or events, as ***human affairs***, ***angle***, ***chain***, ***condition***, ***document***, ***element***, ***factor***, ***fly***, ***interest***, ***note***, ***period***, ***relations***, ***rights***, ***situation***, ***story***, ***torch***, ***torpedo***. Also **human engineering** orig. *U.S.*, the scientific study of the interaction of human beings and their working environment and the exploitation of this interaction in the interests of efficiency; the application of the human sciences to the design of machines; so **human engineer**; **human equation**: see EQUATION 3 b; **human-factors engineering** = *human engineering*; so **human-factors engineer**; **human resources** *sb. pl.* (orig. *U.S.*), people (esp. personnel or workers) considered as a significant asset of a business or other organization, as opp. to material resources, etc.; manpower; freq. *attrib.* (also in *sing.*); **human sciences** *sb. pl.* [cf. G. *geisteswissenschaften*, W. Dilthey (1883)], the sciences that treat of mankind, esp. those concerned with historical or social factors, as religion, the social sciences, literature, etc. (as opp. to *natural* and *physical sciences*).

1741 Hume *Ess. Moral & Pol.* I. 176 Such mighty Revolutions have happened in human Affairs..as are sufficient to beget the Suspicion of still farther Changes. **1798** Human affairs [see AFFAIR *sb.* 2 a.]. **1877** L. H. Morgan *Anc. Society* III. i. 399 From its limited prevalence it made but little impression upon human affairs. **1949** W. L. Warner in M. Fortes *Social Struct.* 2 Current procedures for class stratification..require too large a field staff of experts, often making it impossible for the interested student of human affairs to use a knowledge of social class to understand his particular problem. **1941** *Ann. Reg. 1940* 317 The Press mirrored the age, copying from America tabloid news, the 'human angle', and..illustrations. **1908** *Pop. Mechanics* Jan. 15/2, 50 men formed a human chain and pulled him out. **1926** B. A. McKelvie *Huldowget* iii. 40 Every male in the village was a link in the human chain. **1963** Human chain [see CHAIN *sb.* 5 f]. **1814** *Edin. Rev.* XXII. 199 The means of bettering the human condition. **1957** P. Coveney *Poor Monkey* xii. 276 Lawrence's perception of the 'human condition'. **1960** C. Day Lewis *Buried Day* v. 87, I could not myself opt out of the human condition, as to some degree the pacifist must do. **1892** W. H. Mallock (*title*) A human document. **1896** *Badminton Mag.* 195 Regarded as a human document my guide looked dog-eared, thumbed and a trifle mildewed. **1938** *Ann Reg. 1937* 320 Dr. Roberts' book is a 'human document' of great value. **1887** *Scribner's Mag.* I. 93/2 He managed, with masterly ingenuity, so to leave out the *human* element..that he gave hardly a glimpse of what it really is. **1897** *Trans. Inst. Naval Architects* 111 It is all very well to say the men are careless, but the human element has to be reckoned with. **1907** R. Herriot (*title*) The human element. A novel. **1908** *Modern Business* Aug. 65/1 System and organisation may be perfect on paper..but this does not necessarily lead to..efficiency. There is another element—the human element. **1913** *Pall Mall Mag.* July 46/2 You must remember that in regard to the human element, we are..behind Germany. The point is that they have the human element—a large body of pilots, observers, artisans, trained during the last sixteen years. **1944** *Electronic Engin.* XVI. 334 The additional errors due to the human element (observation and reaction times) can be eliminated. **1957** Goode & Machol *System Engin.* xxx. 500 Selection and training of operators..come within the province of the human engineer. **1934** Webster, Human engineering. **1944** *Amer. N. & Q.* June 48 Los Angeles..has more than its quota of 'spiritual engineers'..not to mention a 'School of Human Engineering' in a college curriculum... Such an academic unit might legitimately concern itself with anything..from anatomy and physiology to sociology. **1950** *Lancet* 1 Apr. 645/2 The field which has variously been described as 'fitting the machine to the man', human engineering, that part of industrial psychology not concerned with vocational guidance, etc. **1957** Goode & Machol *System Engin.* xxx. 481 The primary object of attention in human engineering is the man-machine link. **1970** *New Scientist* 23 July 199/3 Human engineering.. involves a careful moulding of an educational system to nurture what is most useful and beneficial in each individual. **1921** B. S. Rowntree (*title*) The human factor in business. **1943** J. B. Priestley *Daylight on Saturday* x. 65 He was worried about his production figures... In the last resort it was the human factor that counted. **1967** L. B. Archer in Wills & Yearsley *Handbk. Managem. Technol.* 130 In the U.S.A. the subject [ergonomics] is called 'human engineering' or 'human factors engineering' and the man may be described as a human factors engineer. **1969** *New Yorker* 56/2 A group of engineers called human-factors engineers has had as much to do as anybody else with making the astronauts seem like black boxes. **1964** E. J. McCormick (*title*) Human factors engineering. **1919** *Alameda* (Calif.) *Times-Star* 11 Jan. 1/3 Besides being a 'Human Fly', Williams has other unusual accomplishments. **1960** *Observer* 25 Dec. 7/6 The climber..is likely to be agile and athletic, but there is generally no need for him to be what the Press calls a cat burglar or human fly. **1824** Byron in T. Medwin *Conversations Lord Byron* 237 There was another objection: all the human interest would have been destroyed, which I have even endeavoured to give my Angels. **1860** Dickens in *All Year Round* 28 Jan. 321/1 Figuratively speaking, I travel for the great house of Human Interest Brothers. **1912** *Collier's* 21 Sept. 21/3 Fu, not understanding the American newspaper idea of 'human interest', elected to think I had written a eulogy of him deliberately. **1913** E. C. Bentley *Trent's Last Case* ii. 23 'Prostrated by the shock,' hinted the reporter, '..human interest.' **1915** W. P. Livingstone *Mary Slessor* (1916) II. vii. 46 Her simple but vivid style, the human interest of her story..made so great an impression that the ladies of Glasgow besought the Committee to retain her for a time. **1930** Wodehouse *Very Good, Jeeves!* x. 263 Just one of those human-interest stories, if you know what I mean. **1933** Leavis & Thompson *Culture & Environment* 141 What do you understand by the phrase 'human interest', and what.. is vicious in the journalistic practice it derives from? **1970** *Times* 27 Feb. 13/4 What about that boy with blood pouring from his eye, who has now become an extra in a 'human interest' story? **1920** Fairgrieve & Young *Brit. Isles* p. vi, This series of elementary books is just what its name denotes —human. Everywhere the human note is predominant and the relation of man to his environment insisted upon. **1882** A. Geikie *Text-bk. Geol.* 901 The long succession of Pleistocene ages shaded without abrupt change of any kind into what is termed the Human or Recent Period. *Ibid.* 902 The Human Period is above all distinguished by the presence and influence of man. **1916** G. B. Shaw *Overruled* 57 Spontaneous human relations..on the one hand and the property relation..on the other. **1926** B. Webb *My*

Apprenticeship i. 52 A poisonous cynicism about human relations. **1954** D. Riesman *Individualism Reconsidered* iv. xiv. 222 Men who take courses [in] human relations in order . . [to] get along with their colleagues in the office. **1967** M. Argyle *Psychol. Interpersonal Behaviour* x. 198 Experience with management training shows that lectures on 'human relations' are often very popular. *Ibid.* 199 Follow-up studies show that lectures on human relations lead to improved scores on questionnaires. **1961** *Act for Internat. Devel.: Summary Presentation* (U.S. President's Task Force) (Dept. of State Publ. No. 7205) The decade can bring significant progress in launching the slow process of developing their human resources and their basic services. **1966** *N.Y. Times* 12 Aug. 1/5 Mayor Lindsay will issue an executive order setting up the powerful Human Resources Administration. **1972** *Accountant* 28 Sept. 386/2 The popular vogue of 'manpower planning' (here, for obvious reasons termed 'human resource' planning) must be more competently compiled where new relevant facts and figures are fed back from the human resource accounting system. **1978** *Times* 2 Feb. 19/1 James F. Scull . . has had a meteoric rise through the corporation over the last 14 years, latterly as vice-president for human resources (personnel, I suppose we would call it). **1985** W. Safire in *N.Y. Times Mag.* 26 May 10/4 In the business-administration courses, the phrase *manpower development* was deemed outside the pale: in the Government's sexlesspeak, the acceptable version is *human resource development*. **1791** T. Paine *Rights of Man* 110 The representatives of the people of France . . considering that ignorance, neglect, or comtempt of human rights, are the sole causes of public misfortunes . . have resolved to set forth . . these natural, imprescriptible, and unalienable rights. **1877** *Independent* (N.Y.) 18 Jan. 2/2 'What does that little rat know about human rights?' Pack said. **1941** 'G. Orwell' in *Horizon* Aug. 134 An attempted definition of fundamental human rights. **1945** *Charter of United Nations* Art. 1 par. 3, To achieve international cooperation . . in promoting and encouraging respect for human rights. **1969** *New Yorker* 14 June 78/2 More middle-class blacks will become involved in human rights. **1943** Lasswell & McDougal in *Yale Law Jrnl.* LII. 214 The great contribution of modern specialists on the human sciences is less in the realm of general theory than in the perfecting of method by which ancient speculations can be confirmed, modified or rejected. **1979** H.-G. Gadamer in J. Sallis *Stud. in Phenomenol. & Human Sci.* 74 It is evident that the expression 'human sciences' is problematic for us today and that we must come to the conclusion that science should be defined by us in another way than it is for modern times. **1961** J. B. Wilson *Reason & Morals* ii. 46 The tragedy of the human situation (itself a Freudian phrase). **1872** B. Jerrold *London* iii. 28 The sad human stories that crowd the emigrant vessel. **1945** E. Waugh *Brideshead Revisited* ii. ii. 233 A woman reporter . . had come . . to get a 'human story' of the dangers of my journey. **1959** *Times Lit. Suppl.* 27 Mar. 173/3 The 'human story' and even the characters are but adjuncts of the whirling selling machine. **1969** *Guardian* 21 Jan. 1/1 Two more 'human torch' protests. . . A second Czechoslovak has tried to take his life as a political protest by setting fire to himself. **1944** *Hutchinson's Pict. Hist. War* 12 Apr.–26 Sept. 21/2 A new and devastating weapon called the 'human torpedo'. It can be likened to a miniature submarine. **1953** *Jane's Fighting Ships 1953–54* 151 Damaged in Northern waters in 1944 and repaired and reconstructed as 'Kaitan' (Human Torpedo) carrier.

c. As a subdivision of a science: that branch of the science which is concerned with the study of mankind, as ***human ecology***, ***geography***, ***psychology***.

1933 Human ecology [see ecology]. **1957** [see *bio-ecology* (bio-)]. **1965** *New Scientist* 28 Jan. 208/3 The tag for the necessary science is 'human ecology'— the comprehensive investigation of the effects of our environment on our well-being. **1919** Fairgrieve & Young (*title*) Human geographies. **1936** *Discovery* Feb. 56/2 This map is a valuable contribution to human geography. **1959** *Listener* 6 Aug. 219/3 Endless information about the human geography of England at the end of the eleventh century. **1961** L. D. Stamp *Gloss. Geogr. Terms* 242/1 Human geography, the geographical study (the complement of physical geography) of those features, objects and phenomena of the Earth's surface which relate directly, or are due, to man and his activities. **1924** R. M. Ogden tr. *Koffka's Growth of Mind* 16 To bridge the gap between human and animal-psychology.

4. Having or showing the qualities or attributes proper to or distinctive of humans. (In quot. 1727 = humane.)

1727 A. Hamilton *New Acc. E. Ind.* II. lii. 260 He was very human, and sent the poor Seamen Presents. **1837** Ht. Martineau *Soc. Amer.* III. 184 Every prison visitor has been conscious, on first conversing privately with a criminal, of a feeling of surprise at finding him so human. **1855** Longf. *Hiaw.* Introd. 91 Ye . . Who believe, that in all ages Every human heart is human. **1883** Fairbairn *City of God* ii. i. v. (1886) 140 The coming of a diviner faith made worship humaner and more spiritual. *Ibid.* iii. i. 230 The ideal of manhood He [Christ] created . . remains the regnant ideal of man, the humanest men being the men who realize it.

5. *Comb.* **a.** with another adj., denoting a combination of qualities, as ***human-angelic*** (of the nature of a human 'angel'). **b.** parasynthetic, as ***human-bounded***, ***-figured***, ***-headed***, ***-hearted*** (sense 4; hence ***-heartedness***), ***-sized***, ***-tainted*** adjs.

a **1711** Ken *Hymnotheo* Poet. Wks. 1721 III. 256 No Human-bounded Mind Can comprehend Love unconfin'd. **1749** Fielding *Tom Jones* ix. ii, The human-angelic species. **1768** *Woman of Honor* III. 196 A human-figured stick. **1850** Tennyson *In Mem.* xiii, The human-hearted man I loved. **1857** Birch *Anc. Pottery* (1858) I. 343 Human-headed birds. **1870** W. Graham *Lect. Ephes.* 246 The humanheartedness of the Father. **1880** Vern. Lee *Belcaro* ii. 33 This Niobe group, twice human-sized. **1929** D. H. Lawrence *Pansies* 73 Communion with the Godhead, they used to say in the past. But even that is human-tainted now, Tainted with the ego and the personality.

B. *sb.* **1.** A human being, a member of the human race.

a **1533** Ld. Berners *Gold. Bk. M. Aurel.* (1546) Gg vij b, No man among men, nor humain amonge the humains. *c* **1611** Chapman *Iliad* v. 441 Mars . . smear'd with the dust and bloud Of humanes, and their ruin'd wals. **1652** Kirkman *Clerio & Lozia* 83 Among you earthly humanes. **1832** F. Trollope *Dom. Manners Amer.* I. 70, I expect the sun will rise and set a hundred times before I shall see another human that does not belong to the family. **1839** Marryat *Diary Amer.* Ser. i. II. 211 Of all the humans, you're the one I most wish to see. **1878** Besant & Rice *Celia's Arb.* I. iii. 31 They [rooks] are not mere theorists, like poor humans, but simply investigators of fact. **1879** G. Macdonald *Sir Gibbie* ix. 54 Gibbie fell to . . hugging him [the dog] as if he had been a human. **1898** H. S. Canfield *Maid of Frontier* i. 18 A man could ride from here to forty-mile the other side of Edwardsville and never see a human. **1902** O. Wister *Virginian* iv. 56 'They are just like humans,' the Virginian concluded. **1905** A. Conan Doyle *Return of Sherlock Holmes* 27 You will see it often in humans. **1909** H. G. Wells *Ann Veronica* ii. 43 In all the species of animals the females are more important than the males; the males have to please them. Look . . at the competition there is everywhere, except among humans. **1922** Joyce *Ulysses* 501, I always understood that the act so performed by skittish humans with glimpses of lingerie appealed to you in virtue of its exhibitionististicicity. **1971** *Physics Bull.* Jan. 49/1 A third hailed him, as a great scientist and a superb human.

2. With *the*: (*a*) the human race, humanity; (*b*) that which is human, that which relates to mankind or humanity.

1841 E. B. Browning *Let.* 28 Aug. (1897) I. 88, I may say so now—as far as the human may say 'yes' or 'no' of their futurity. **1844** —— *Poems* I. 109 While the human in the minor Makes the harmony diviner. **1919** M. K. Bradby *Psycho-Analysis* 205 The distinctively animal gives way in order to express the distinctively human.

† **'humanate**, *a.* *Obs. rare.* [ad. med.L. *hūmānāt-us*, pa. pple. of *hūmānāre* to make human, f. *hūmān-us* human.] Made human; converted into human flesh.

1551 Cranmer *Answ. Gardiner* 369 That the breade is humanate or incarnate.

So † **huma'nation**, incarnation.

1651 Howell *Venice* 185* The humanation of our Saviour. **1659** H. L'Estrange *Alliance Div. Off.* 179.

humane (hjuː'meɪn), *a.* [A common earlier spelling of human, which became restricted after 1700 to a particular group of senses; the form and mod. stress seem to show more immediate association with L. *hūmānus*: cf. *germane*.]

1. Characterized by such behaviour or disposition towards others as befits a human being.

† **a.** Gentle or kindly in demeanour or action; civil, courteous, friendly, obliging. *Obs.* (passing gradually into b.)

c **1500** *Melusine* xx. 111 Be meke, humble, swete, curtoys & humayne, both vnto grete & lesse. **1530** Palsgr. 316/1 Humayne, courtoyse or belongyng to the nature of a man, *humayn*. **1555** Eden *Decades* 149 Thinhabitauntes enterteined them very frendly [*margin* Humane people]. **1632** Lithgow *Trav.* ix. 387 The people are very humane, ingenious, eloquent and pleasant. **1675** Marvell *Corr.* Wks. 1872–5 II. 489 Humane civility. **1784** Cowper *Task* v. 469 That humane address And sweetness.

b. Marked by sympathy with and consideration for the needs and distresses of others; feeling or showing compassion and tenderness towards human beings and the lower animals; kind, benevolent. (In early use not clearly distinguishable from a.)

1603 Holland *Plutarch's Mor.* 1270 As his martiall valour is humane [φιλάνθρωπον], so his humanitie is valorous. *a* **1774** Pearce *Serm.* IV. xiv. (R.), Christianity (the most compassionate and humane religion in the world). **1802** Mar. Edgeworth *Moral T.* I. xv. 124 The humane spirit of the law, which supposes every man . . innocent till proved . . guilty. **1814** D. H. O'Brian *Captiv. & Escape* 79 The jailer here . . was the most humane man in that situation I ever knew. **1841** Trench *Parables* viii. (1877) 159 It is just in man to be merciful . . to be humane is human. **1857** Buckle *Civiliz.* I. viii. 480 The humane and enlightened measures of Henry IV.

c. ***Humane Society***: title of a society for the rescue of drowning persons.

The Royal Humane Society was founded in 1774.

1776 *Minutes Soc. Recov. Persons app. drowned* 8 May, That this Society in future be distinguished by the name of 'The Humane Society'. **1782** R. A. Bromley (*title*) Sermon for the benefit of the Humane Society, on Luke viii. 52. **1784–95** W. Hawes (*title*) The Transactions of the Royal Humane Society, from 1774 to 1784, with an Appendix. **1819** Byron *Juan* i. cxxx, The apparatus Of the Humane Society's beginning. **1834** Medwin *Angler in Wales* I. 219 The men of the Humane Society . . came hurrying, with their apparatus for resuscitation. **1896** Violet Hunt in *Cosmopolis* Sept. 617, 'I chose the darkest place, farthest from the Humane Society's drags'.

d. Applied to certain weapons or implements which inflict less pain than others of their kind, *spec.* applied to an implement for the painless slaughtering of cattle.

1904 *Daily Chron.* 24 May 5/3 The doctors style the bullets 'humane'. **1920** *Act 10 & 11 Geo. V* c. 43 §(8) (*h*) Any . . butcher . . having in his possession . . any humane killer for the purpose of such business. **1927** *Daily Express* 6 Aug. 7/3 That the humane killer was a dangerous instrument to those who used it. **1973** *Times* 11 Jan. 2/6 Three veterinary surgeons . . had thought he must be put down. This was done . . using a humane killer.

2. Applied to those branches of study or literature (*literæ humaniores*) which tend to humanize or refine, as the ancient classics, rhetoric, and poetry; hence, elegant, polite. (See humanity 4.)

1691 Wood *Ath. Oxon.* I. 269 Edward Grant . . the most noted Latinist and Grecian of his time. He was well skill'd in all kind of humane literature. **1701** tr. *Le Clerc's Prim. Fathers* (1702) 174 To learn Humane Learning; that is to say, to understand the Greek Poets and Orators and to write well in that Tongue. **1712** Henley *Spect.* No. 396 ¶2 An uncommon Mastery in the more humane and polite Part of Letters. **1843** Lytton *Last Bar.* iv. v, Thou art acquainted, doubtless . . with the Humaner Letters. **1877** Symonds *Renaiss. in Italy, Reviv. Learning* ii. 71 *note*, The word Humanism has a German sound, and is in fact modern. Yet the generic phrase *umanità* for humanistic culture, and the name *umanista* for a professor of humane studies, are both pure Italian.

humanely (hjuː'meɪnlɪ), *adv.* [f. prec. + -ly².] In a humane manner; †courteously (*obs.*); kindly, compassionately, benevolently.

1596 Dalrymple tr. *Leslie's Hist. Scot.* viii. 139 The king humainlie receives him . . and honorablie sendis him hame. **1607** Shaks. *Cor.* i. i. 19 If they would yeelde vs but the superfluitie . . wee might guesse they releeued vs humanely. *a* **1677** Barrow *Serm.* Wks. 1686 III. xxviii. 313 We shall herein act humanely, and like good friends. **1725** Pope *Odyss.* xxiv. 311 Humanely hear, and answer my demand. **1828** *Life Planter Jamaica* (ed. 2) 287 Show the British people that you are equally humanely disposed with themselves.

(See also humanly.)

humaneness (hjuː'meɪnnɪs). [f. as prec. + -ness.] The quality of being humane.

1809 W. Taylor in *Monthly Mag.* XXVII. 455 So much forbearance and humaneness. **1878** Morley *Crit. Misc.*, *Vauvenargues* 25 The large and rational humaneness of the new time.

'humanhood. *rare.* [See -hood.] Human character or position in the scale of being.

1847 W. Maccall *Elem. Individualism* ix. 90 To benefit humanity by being faithful to his humanhood. **1894** *Church Union* (N.Y.) Mar., Oh, for a Christly humanhood that will relegate sexhood to its legitimate sphere.

hu'manics. *rare.* [irreg. f. human + -ics pl. suffix.] The subject or study of human affairs.

a **1864** Collins is cited by Webster. **1937** R. S. Morton *Woman Surgeon* xxxi. 351 The business side of practice is necessary, but its art and humanics are what carry us on. **1952** *King Geo. VI & Industry: a Tribute* (Industr. Welfare Soc.) p. ii, We give ungrudging honour to these pioneer students of the new science of what has been termed 'Industrial Humanics'. **1958** *Progress* Autumn 266/2 But, to British eyes, the American method looks superficial; it seems to rest on two doubtful assumptions. . . The second is that what Americans have called the 'humanics' of the subject can be reduced wholly to its 'mechanics'.

humaniform (hjuː'mænɪfɔːm), *a.* [ad. L. type **hūmāniform-is*, f. *hūmānus* human: see -form.] Of human form, anthropomorphous; in quot. Attributing human form to the Deity, anthropomorphic. So † **humani'formian**, one who attributes human form to God, an anthropomorphite.

1550 Hutchinson *Wks.* (Parker Soc.) 164 This image is in our souls, not in our bodies: as I have proved in my confutation of the Anthropomorphites, or humaniformians. **1624** F. White *Reply Fisher* 277 The errour of the Humaniformians. **1889** *Amer. Antiquarian* Jan. 11 All religion being more or less anthropomorphic, or humaniform.

humanify (hjuː'mænɪfaɪ), *v.* [f. human *a.* + -fy.] *trans.* To make human. Hence **hu,manifi'cation**, a making, or representing as, human.

1629 T. Adams *Medit. Creed* Pract. Wks. 1861–2 III. 211 For His own Son to be humanified, and being man to be crucified. **1860** H. B. Wilson in *Ess. & Rev.* 186 The humanifying of the Divine Word. **1874** H. R. Reynolds *John Bapt.* viii. 490 The humanification of the physical forces.

'humanish, *a.* *rare.* [f. as prec. + -ish.] Somewhat human or human-looking.

1837 L. Hunt in *New Monthly Mag.* XLIX. 511 It had a humanish kind of head and body. *a* **1843** Southey *Comm.-pl. Bk.* IV. 490 Cæsar's horse with humanish feet.

humanism ('hjuːmənɪz(ə)m). [f. human *a.* + -ism, after *humanist*. Cf. Ger. *humanismus*.]

† **1.** Belief in the mere humanity of Christ: cf. humanitarian *sb.* 1 a. *Obs.*

1812 Coleridge *Omniana* in *Lit. Rem.* (1836) I. 377 A man who has passed from orthodoxy to the loosest Arminianism, and thence to Arianism, and thence to direct Humanism.

2. The character or quality of being human; devotion to human interests.

1836 Hor. Smith *Tin Trump.* (1876) 241 More consonant . . to truth, as well as to an enlightened spirit of humanism. **1850** Gladstone *Homer* II. 242 The Homeric Mercury . . exceeds in humanism . . the other Olympian gods. **1875** Browning *Aristoph. Apol.* 119 With kindly humanism they countenanced Our emulation of divine escapes Thro' sense and soul. **1888** *Amer. Anthropol.* Jan. 12 According as he

[man] raises his intellectual and moral nature to the levels of a higher and higher humanism.

3. Any system of thought or action which is concerned with merely human interests (as distinguished from divine), or with those of the human race in general (as distinguished from individual); the 'Religion of Humanity'.

1860 J. GARDNER *Faiths World* II. 76/2 The Philanthropic Humanism soon gave place to a higher Humanism, which began to spring out of the ardent study of the ancient classics. **1876** GLADSTONE in *Contemp. Rev.* June 25 Comtism or Positivism, or, as it might be called, Humanism. **1877** W. K. CLIFFORD *Lect.* (1879) II. 249, I neither admit the moral influence of theism in the past, nor look forward to the moral influence of humanism in the future. **1883** A. BARRATT *Phys. Metempiric* 128 Altruism..overshadows the Egoism on which rests the morality of individual men, and already shows occasional symptoms of fading into a higher Humanism. **1887** *Spectator* 25 June 853/1 From the strictest Roman Catholicism to the nakedest humanism.

4. Devotion to those studies which promote human culture; literary culture; *esp.* the system of the Humanists, the study of the Roman and Greek classics which came into vogue at the Renascence.

1832 SIR W. HAMILTON *Discuss.* (1853) 276 *note, Die Gelehrten Schulen*, etc., i.e. Learned Schools, according to the principles of a genuine humanism. **1877** J. E. CARPENTER tr. *Tiele's Hist. Relig.* 91 Greek humanism and Greek philosophy. **1881** GARDINER & MULLINGER *Introd. Eng. Hist.* vii. 105 When the Middle Ages drew to a close with the humanism of Italy. **1882** M. ARNOLD in *19th Cent.* Aug. 220 We talk of knowing Greek and Roman antiquity.. which is what people have called humanism. **1885** SYMONDS in *Encycl. Brit.* XVIII. 709/2 Petrarch..was even less eminent as an Italian poet than as the founder of Humanism, the inaugurator of the Renaissance in Italy. **1885** *Academy* 5 Sept. 144/1 The humanism of Erasmus and More, once planted in England, grew there as it did abroad. **1897** DOWDEN *Fr. Lit.* I. iii. §2. 46 The early humanism of France was clouded and lost in the tempests of the Hundred Years' War.

5. *Philos.* A pragmatic system of thought introduced by F. C. S. Schiller and William James which emphasizes that man can only comprehend and investigate what is with the resources of the human mind, and discounts abstract theorizing; so, more generally, implying that technological advance must be guided by awareness of widely understood human needs.

1903 F. C. S. SCHILLER *Humanism* p. xvi, I propose..to convert to the use of philosophic terminology a word which has long been famed in history and literature, and to denominate Humanism the attitude of thought which I know to be habitual in William James and in myself. **1904** W. JAMES *Coll. Ess. & Rev.* (1920) xxxii. 450 No one can ever foresee what terms will succeed in the struggle to gain currency... 'Humanism' is perhaps too 'whole-hearted' for the use of philosophers, who are a bloodless breed; but, save for that objection, one might back it, for it expresses the essence of the new way of thought, which is, that it is impossible to strip the human element out from even our most abstract theorizing. **1907** F. C. S. SCHILLER *Studies in Humanism* 12 Humanism..is merely the perception that the philosophic problem concerns human beings striving to comprehend a world of human experience by the resources of human minds. **1945** E. A. BURTT in *Humanist* V. III. 108 It may seem presumptuous, if not paradoxical, to suggest that a movement claiming the name 'humanism', and emphasizing rational comprehension as the foundation of every good achievement, might fail lamentably in its understanding of man. **1959** P. TILLICH *Theology of Culture* II. viii. 121 He [*sc.* Sartre] calls his existentialism humanism. But if he calls it humanism, that means he has an idea of what man essentially is. **1961** O. REISER in J. S. Huxley *Humanist Frame* 240 A major objective of a scientific Humanism is the organization of human knowledge for the purpose of human progress. **1966** C. H. D. CLARK *Scientist & Supernatural* v. 174 Humanism glorifies science without telling us how the laws of science arose nor how they are to save us from our innate selfishness. **1969** K. KAUNDA *Towards Complete Independence* 43 Our philosophy of Humanism stresses above all the importance of man as an individual.

humanist ('hjuːmənɪst). [ad. F. *humaniste* (1539 in Hatz.-Darm.), ad. It. *umanista* (Ariosto *Sat.* vii): see HUMAN and -IST.]

1. A student of human affairs, or of human nature; formerly, sometimes, †a secular writer (as distinguished from a *divine*).

1617 MORYSON *Itin.* III. 11 The Humanist, I meane him that affects the knowledge of State affaires, Histories [etc.]. *a* **1734** NORTH *Exam.* III. vi. §36 (1740) 449 What a Discovery is it..that Vice raged at Court? Is it not the Hackney Observation of all Humanists? **1863** MRS. C. CLARKE *Shaks. Char.* ix. 215 The ample wisdom and bland morality of such a humanist as Shakespeare.

2. One devoted to or versed in the literary studies called 'the humanities'; a classical scholar; esp. a Latinist, a professor or teacher of Latin. *arch.* (Sometimes by early writers opposed to 'divine'.)

1589 FLEMING *Virg. Georg.* To Rdr., Considering the expositors drift to consist in deliuering a direct order of construction for the releefe of weake Grammatists, not in attempting by curious deuise and disposition, to content courtly Humanists. **1596** HARINGTON *Metam. Ajax* 74, I might repute him as a good humanist, but I should ever doubt him for a good devine. **1605** BACON *Adv. Learn.* II. x. §2 Antiquaries, Poets, Humanists, States-men, Merchants, Diuines. **1610** HEALEY *Vives' Comm. St. Aug. Citie of God* (1620) 512 The humanists cannot agree about the first city-founder. **1676** W. ROW *Contn. Blair's Autobiog.* xii. (1848) 397 One Mr. Andrew Bruce, humanist in the Old College. **1691** WOOD *Ath. Oxon.* II. 283 Jeremy Taylor..was a rare Humanist. **1755** JOHNSON, *Humanist*, a philologer; a grammarian: a term used in the schools of Scotland. **1817** J. BROWN *Gospel Truth Stated* (1831) 70 What he was for a humanist..his translation of his own work..into good Roman Latin will abundantly testify. **1876** GRANT *Burgh Sch. Scotl.* II. xiii. 366 In 1620 he [the Master of the grammar School]..was nominated grammarian or humanist in King's college.

3. *Literary Hist.* One of the scholars who, at the Revival of Learning in the fourteenth, fifteenth, and sixteenth centuries, devoted themselves to the study of the language, literature, and antiquities of Rome, and afterwards of Greece; hence, applied to later disciples of the same culture.

1670 LASSELS *Voy. Italy* II. 361 Of this town was Cælius Rhodiginus.. and Bonifacius Bonifacii, another learned humanist. **1764** GIBBON *Misc. Wks.* (1814) V. 455 The humanists of the fifteenth century revived the knowledge of the ancients. **1870** SEELEY *Lect. & Ess.* 135 Milton lived in antiquity as much as any fifteenth-century humanist. **1876** FAIRBAIRN *Strauss* II. in *Contemp. Rev.* June 140 Hutten had united in him the culture of the humanist and the energy of the enthusiast. **1879** M. ARNOLD *Mixed Ess., Equality* 80 Milton was born a humanist, but the Puritan temper mastered him. **1895** *Dublin Rev.* Oct. 318 A society of heathen-minded Humanists under the presidency of.. Pomponius Laetus.

attrib. **1881** G. W. KITCHIN in *Encycl. Brit.* XII. 412/2 Italy, that holy land of Humanist enthusiasm. **1882–3** SCHAFF *Encycl. Relig. Knowl.* III. 2033 Among the humanist predecessors of the Reformation. **1887** J. C. MORISON *Service of Man* (1889) 152 His superior culture and humanist sense of the 'becoming'.

4. *Theol. Hist.* (See quot.)

1860 J. GARDNER *Faiths World* II. 76 *Humanists*, a class of thinkers which arose in Germany towards the end of the eighteenth century, originating chiefly from the diffusion of the writings of Rousseau..Their system..usually called *Humanism*..sought to level all family distinctions, all differences of rank, all nationality, all positive moral obligation, all positive religion, and to train mankind to be men, as..the highest accomplishment.

5. *Philos.* One whose beliefs are in accordance with HUMANISM 5. Also *attrib.*

1903 F. C. S. SCHILLER *Humanism* p. xxi, A *humanist* philosopher is sure to be keenly interested in the rich variety of human thought and sentiment, and unwilling to ignore the actual facts for the sake of bolstering up the narrow abstractions of some *a priori* theory of what 'all men must' think and feel... The humanist, accordingly, will tend to grow *humane*, and tolerant of the divergences of attitude which must inevitably spring from the divergent idiosyncrasies of men. **1904** W. JAMES in *Mind* XIII. 462 Bergson in France, and his disciples the physicists Wilbois and Leroy, are thorough-going humanists in the sense defined. **1949** J. GUTMAN in P. A. Schilpp *Philos. Ernst Cassirer* II. xiii. 464 Thus as an historian and as a humanist Cassirer once again raised the standard of self-knowledge, [and] reaffirmed the doctrine that the unexamined life is no life for man. **1961** L. ELVIN in J. S. Huxley *Humanist Frame* 272 The Humanist is content to leave it to the free play of thought, so long as thought *is* kept free. **1963** J. S. HUXLEY *Human Crisis* 19 Today, the new humanist vision is giving us the key idea of man as the agent for the whole future of evolution on this planet. **1966** C. H. D. CLARK *Scientist & Supernatural* v. 175 The humanist trust in reason alone is actually unreasonable, since logic would suggest that affluence and scientific advancement ought to be accompanied by increasing mental satisfaction. **1968** A. J. AYER *Humanist Outlook* 4 Present-day humanists are in fact the intellectual heirs of those nineteenth-century free-thinkers.

huma'nistic, *a.* (*sb.*) [f. prec. + -IC.]

A. *adj.* **1.** Pertaining to or characteristic of the humanists or classical scholars of the Renascence; classical.

1845 S. AUSTIN *Ranke's Hist. Ref.* I. 287 A collision between the new and humanistic method [of instruction].. and the old modes, was inevitable. **1882–3** SCHAFF *Encycl. Relig. Knowl.* 753 Erasmus, the most brilliant representative of humanistic culture at the beginning of the sixteenth century. **1885** PATER *Marius* II. 128 The Church was becoming [in the latter part of second century] humanistic, in a best and earliest Renaissance. **1896** E. GOSSE *Crit. Kit-Kats* 252 With the accession of humanistic ideas, he [Pater] had gradually lost all belief in the Christian religion.

2. Pertaining to or characteristic of humanism. (Cf. HUMANISM 5.)

1904 W. JAMES *Coll. Ess. & Rev.* (1920) xxxii. 451 But humanistic empiricism will have many other steps forward to make before it conquers all antagonisms. **1923** B. RUSSELL *Prospects Industr. Civilization* II. xiii. 266 The distinction between the mechanistic and the humanistic conceptions of excellence is the most fundamental of all distinctions between rival sets of ideals. *Ibid.*, The humanistic conception..regards the good as something existing in the lives of individuals, and conceives social co-operation as only valuable in so far as it ministers to the welfare of the several citizens. **1932** C. K. OGDEN *Jeremy Bentham* 9 It was to French influences, to Fénélon, to Helvétius and to Voltaire,..that Bentham owed his first humanistic stimulus. **1961** B. WOOTTON in J. S. Huxley *Humanist Frame* 350 Plainly, what is actually happening in the world is the result of the accommodation of religions to evolving humanistic ideas and not *vice versa*. **1968** H. J. EYSENCK in A. J. Ayer *Humanist Outlook* 271 The future of humanistic thought on this subject is completely bound up with the growth of psychological knowledge—without this it must remain nothing more than an alternative superstition.

B. *sb. pl.* **humanistics**: Humanistic or classical studies or writings.

1716 M. DAVIES *Athen. Brit.* III. *Crit. Hist.* 2 Pomey's Onomasticks, and Tachard's Lexographicks, and Rapin's Critical Humanisticks..are far surpass'd by our Oxford Grammar. **1952** KOESTLER *Arrow in Blue* xxvi. 240, I would shift the emphasis in popular education from stale humanistics to a lively comprehension of the mysteries of the universe and life.

huma'nistical, *a.* [f. as prec. + -AL[1].] = HUMANISTIC 1; pertaining to classical studies.

1716 M. DAVIES *Athen. Brit.* I. 70 His [Sir Thomas More's] Humanistical Pamphlets. *Ibid.* II. To Rdr. 49 Their [Jesuits'] boasting Monopoly and bragging Tyrrany over Humanistical Schools. *Ibid.* III. *Crit. Hist.* 107 Master of Rhetorick and Poetry in the famous Trivial School of Humanistical Studies at Jena.

Hence **huma'nistically** *adv.*, in relation to humanism or classical studies; from the point of view of the humanist; also in relation to HUMANISM 5.

1886 A. SETH in *Encycl. Brit.* XXI. 423/2 The teaching of the school of Chartres, humanistically nourished on the study of the ancients. **1890** *Athenæum* 26 July 117/3 This may be humanistically true. **1904** W. JAMES *Coll. Ess. & Rev.* (1920) xxxii. 451 'Radium', for example; humanistically, both the *that* and the *what* of it are creations of yesterday. But we believe that ultra-humanistically they existed ages before their gifted discoverers were born. In what shape? There's the rub! for we have no non-humanistic categories to think in. **1909** —— *Meaning of Truth* iii. 79 The reader would conceive the knowing humanistically. **1944** *Scrutiny* XII. III. 210 The brilliant vitality of the keyboard writing..itself tends to render this passion more directly and humanistically dramatic than the more religious (if no less intense) keyboard style of Gibbons.

humanitarian (hjuːmænɪ'tɛərɪən), *sb.* and *a.* [f. HUMANITY, after *unitarian, trinitarian.*]

A. *sb.* **1.** *Theol.* **a.** One who affirms the humanity (but denies the divinity) of Christ.

1819 MOORE *Diary* 30 Jan., The sect of the Humanitarians. Parr..more shocked as a grammarian at the word than as a divine at the sect. **1819** M. STUART *Lett. to W. E. Channing* 144 Now [in New England]..there are scarcely any of the younger preachers of Unitarian sentiments who are not simple Humanitarians.

b. An anthropomorphite: see quot.

a **1844** R. BALMER *Lect. & Disc.* (1845) I. 193 The opinion of the humanitarians or anthropomorphites as they are called..that the Deity possesses a material body.

2. One who professes the 'Religion of Humanity', holding that mankind's duty is chiefly or wholly comprised in the advancement of the welfare of the human race: applied to various schools of thought and practice.

1831 *Fraser's Mag.* IV. 54 Herder..in his work, entitled, the *History of Humanity*, is merely what may be termed a Humanitarian. **1844** *Blackw. Mag.* LVI. 589 M. Pierre Leroux, most distinguished of the Humanitarians, the last sect which figures on the scene, bidding for disciples. **1876** C. M. DAVIES *Unorth. Lond.* (ed. 2) 400 The fifteen rules or doctrines of the Humanitarians. **1882–3** SCHAFF *Encycl. Relig. Knowl.* II. 1038/1 *Humanitarian*, a name applied..to such parties as profess the 'religion of humanity'..the spontaneous perfectibility of the human race.

3. One who advocates or practises humanity or humane action; one who devotes himself to the welfare of mankind at large; a philanthropist. Nearly always *contemptuous*, connoting one who goes to excess in his humane principles.

1844 LD. ASHBURTON in *Croker Papers* (1884) III. xxiii. 18 The most mischievous men of our day are our conceited political economists and our ultra humanitarians. **1851** GALLENGA *Italy* II. i. 20 The patriot merged into the humanitarian. **1861** GEN. P. THOMPSON *Audi Alt.* III. clxxvii. 213 Who can stand being called 'humanitarian and abolitionist'? **1891** H. S. CONSTABLE *Horses, Sport & War* 84 A man cannot be too really humane, but the typical humanitarian is only sentimental.

B. *adj.* **1.** Holding the views or doctrines of humanitarians; held or practised by humanitarians (in the senses, A 1, 2).

1846 WORCESTER cites *Church Observer*. **1876** C. M. DAVIES *Unorth. Lond.* (ed. 2) 413 The Humanitarian Solemnization of Matrimony. **1886** *Dict. Nat. Biog.* V. 180/2 The original Calvinism of the race had changed to Arianism, and he himself became humanitarian in his Christology.

2. Devoted to humanity or the human race as an object of worship.

1861 GOLDW. SMITH *Lect. Progr.* 4, I am not aware that so much as the rudiment of a new religion has yet been actually produced, unless it be the Humanitarian religion of M. Comte.

3. Having regard to the interests of humanity or mankind at large; relating to, advocating, or practising humanity or humane action; broadly philanthropic. Often *contemptuous* or *hostile*.

1855 MOTLEY *Dutch Rep.* (1861) I. 219 However open to criticism upon broad humanitarian grounds. **1882** A. W. WARD *Dickens* iii. 58 Pecksniff presents himself as a humanitarian philosopher. **1894** *Westm. Gaz.* 10 Feb. 2/3 These are the aims of the Humanitarian Movement, and with their realisation will come the regeneration of the race. **1897** F. N. MAUDE *Volunt. v. Compuls. Service* 33 All the nonsense of humanitarian sentimentalists.

Hence **humani'tarianism**, the system, principles, or practice of humanitarians (in any of the senses above); **humani'tarianize** *v. trans.*, to make humanitarian.

1833 J. MARTINEAU *Ess.* (1890) I. 11 His [Priestley's] transition from Low Arianism to Humanitarianism. **1850** *Tait's Mag.* XVII. 84 The puerile whimperings of an effeminate humanitarianism. **1857** TOULM. SMITH *Parish* 364 Specious but most mischievous humanitarianism, and

self-exalting but hollow philanthropy. **1865** Gladstone *Farew. Addr. Edinboro' Univ.* 27 A still deeper trace of humanitarianism lay in the transportation of the family order into heaven. **1895** *Columbus* (Ohio) *Disp.* 10 July 10/4 Persons who desire to humanitarianize capital punishment.

humanitary (hjuːˈmænɪtərɪ), *a. rare.* [f. as prec. + -ARY. Cf. F. *humanitaire.*]

1. Of or relating to humanity or the human race.

1857–8 Sears *Athan.* III. viii. 323 Individual and humanitary regeneration.

2. Of or relating to humanity or humane action; philanthropic, humanitarian.

1886 H. James *Bostonians* I. I. iv. 40 After fifty years of humanitary zeal.

‖**humanitas** (hjuːˈmænɪtæs). [L.] = HUMANITY.

1944 *Atlantic Monthly* Nov. 73 Philosophers of the ancient world would consider these to be strange limitations . . upon the spiritual jurisdiction of a school which concerns itself with *humanitas.* **1948** E. Pound *Pisan Cantos* lxxxiv. 117 Yin had these three men full of humanitas (manhood). **1964** *Economist* 4 Jan. 37/3 The fundamental *humanitas* of the author. **1964** L. Hjelmslev in R. H. Robins *Gen. Ling.* i. 10 Linguistic theory is led by an inner necessity to recognize . . man and human society behind language. . . At that point linguistic theory has reached its prescribed goal: *humanitas et universitas.* **1970** *Times Lit. Suppl.* 23 Apr. 442/4 The concern for a conception of society, life and *humanitas* that doesn't eliminate the depth in time.

†**humanitian** (-ˈɪʃən). *Obs.* Also 6 -ician. [irreg. f. HUMANITY + -AN, by association with *logician*, etc.] One versed in the 'humanities'; a classical scholar; = HUMANIST 2.

1577–87 Holinshed *Chron.* II. 40/2 Oliver Eustace, a student of the civill and canon law, a good humanician, and a proper philosopher. **1599** B. Jonson *Cynthia's Rev.* III. iii, I have read history, I am a little humanitian. **1606** Holland *Sueton.* Annot. 18 A deep Scholler and great Humanitian as we speake, and whom the Greekes call Philologon. **1691** Wood *Ath. Oxon.* I. 103 The said Robertson was an exact Grammarian and Humanitian.

humanity (hjuːˈmænɪtɪ). [a. F. *humanité* (older forms *humeinete, humanitet*, 12th c. in Littré), ad. L. *hūmānitāt-em*, f. *hūmānus* HUMAN.]

I. Connected with *human.*

1. The quality or condition of being human, manhood; the human faculties or attributes collectively; human nature; man in the abstract.

c**1430** Lydg. *Hors, Shepe, & G.* (Roxb.) 15 Whan he [Christ] . . Toke the clothyng of oure humanyte. **1526** *Pilgr. Perf.* (W. de W. 1531) 3 b, The humanite or manhed of our lorde. **1602** Shaks. *Ham.* III. ii. 39, I haue thought some of Natures Iouerney-men had made men, and not made them well, they imitated Humanity so abhominably. **1604** —— *Oth.* I. iii. 317, I would change my Humanity with a Baboone. **1710** Berkeley *Princ. Hum. Knowl.* Introd. §9 The abstract idea of man, or, if you please, humanity, or human nature. **1773** Ld. Monboddo *Lang.* (1774) I. Introd. 2 Without the use of reason and speech, we have no pretensions to humanity. **1834** *W. India Sketch Bk.* I. 23 One of the numerous specimens of rough-spun humanity peculiar to the sea-coast. **1875** E. White *Life in Christ* III. xvii. (1878) 206 A . . regenerative process . . which contemplates the whole humanity, body as well as soul. **1898** *New York Voice* 5 May 6/3 They denounced slavery as a sin, asserted the humanity of the blacks.

b. *pl.* Human attributes; traits or touches of human nature or feeling; points that concern mankind, or appeal to human sensibilities.

1800 Coleridge *Piccolom.* II. iv. 124 The fair humanities of old religion. **1837** Southey *Doctor* IV. cxix. 178 In the exercise of their calling, the distinctions of society disappear, and poor human nature is stript to its humanities. **1882** M. Arnold *Irish Ess.* 122 Individuals with a happy nature and an instinct for the humanities of life.

2. The human race; mankind; human beings collectively.

1579 Lyly *Euphues* (Arb.) 42 Vnlesse he be false, or that he be an enimye to humanitie. **1664** Power *Exp. Philos.* III. 184 The greatest part of Humanity is lost in Earth, and their Souls so fixed in that grosser moity of themselves (their Bodies). **1774** Pennant *Tour Scotl. in 1772.* 271 Each shore appeared pleasing to humanity. **1874** Bancroft *Footpr. Time* i. 59 Their Services to humanity are very great. **1892** Westcott *Gospel of Life* 109 Each nation contributes something to the fulness of the life of humanity. **1897** Mary Kingsley *W. Africa* 247 The inhabitants . . came—a brown mass of naked humanity—down the steep cliff path.

II. Connected with *humane.*

3. The character or quality of being humane; behaviour or disposition towards others such as befits a human being. †a. Civility, courtesy, politeness, good behaviour; kindness as shown in courteous or friendly acts, obligingness. (Cf. HUMANE 1 a.)

1382 Wyclif *2 Macc.* iv. 11 Bi cause of humanytee or curtasie. **1464** *Paston Lett.* No. 483 II. 147, I beseche you, schew the brynger of this letter sum humanite and worsschipe. c**1530** H. Rhodes *Bk. Nurture* 138 in *Babees Bk.* 86 To prate in thy maysters presence, it is no humanitye. **1664** Evelyn *Diary* 21 July, I din'd with my L. Treasurer . . where his Lordship used me with singular humanitie. **1694** Strype *Cranmer* (1848) I. Pref. 31 William Petyt of the Inner-Temple . . did with great humanity communicate unto me his collection of excellent papers. **1794** Godwin *Cal. Williams* xxvi. 198 The keeper . . with his former unconstitutional and ambiguous humanity.

b. Disposition to treat human beings and animals with consideration and compassion, and to relieve their distresses; kindness, benevolence; = HUMANENESS. (In earlier use not clearly separable from a.)

c**1386** Chaucer *Clerk's T.* 36 O noble Markys, youre humanitee Asseureth vs to yeue vs hardinesse. **1531** Elyot *Gov.* II. viii, Humanitie . . is a generall name to those vertues, in whome semeth to be a mutuall concorde and loue, in the nature of man. **1571** Golding *Calvin on Ps.* xxxvii. 21 Ther is commended humanitie, for that they are redy to releeve the want of their brethren. a**1639** W. Whateley *Prototypes* II. xxvi. (1640) 76 The vertue of humanity, that is, of being ready to shew love to man, as he is man. **1732** Lediard *Sethos* II. vii. 97 Treat the prisoners . . with humanity. **1791** Burke *App. Whigs* Wks. 1842 I. 501 Great tenderness of heart, and humanity of disposition. **1855** Macaulay *Hist. Eng.* xii. III. 224 The English laws against Popery . . were so much mitigated by the prudence and humanity of the Government.

c. *pl.* Instances or acts of humanity; †courtesies (*obs.*); kindnesses, tendernesses.

1577–87 Holinshed *Scot. Chron.* (1805) II. 51 Though thou seemed as enemie . . ȝit we found mair humanities and plaisures than damage by thy cumming. **1827** Hood *Mids. Fairies* lxviii, So are our gentle natures intertwined With sweet humanities. **1832** Southey *Hist. Penins. War* III. 925 All the courtesies and humanities of generous warfare. **1852** Robertson *Serm.* Ser. III. xv. 188 Blended graces and beauties, and humanities which are found . . in all churches, but not in each separate man.

4. Learning or literature concerned with human culture: a term including the various branches of polite scholarship, as grammar, rhetoric, poetry, and esp. the study of the ancient Latin and Greek classics. a. *sing.* (Still used in the Scottish Universities, in the sense of 'the study of the Latin language and literature'.)

This (= 15–16th c. It. *umanità*, F. *humanité*) appears to have represented L. *humanitas* in its sense of 'mental cultivation befitting a man, liberal education', as used by Aulus Gellius, Cicero, and others; hence, taken as = 'literary culture, polite literature, *literæ humaniores*'; but it was very often, in scholastic and academic use, opposed to *divinity*, as if = secular learning.

1483 Caxton *Gold. Leg.* 121 a/2 He floured in double science . . that is to saye dyuynyte and humanyte. **1555** Eden *Decades* 255 Hauynge . . sum knowleage of letters of humanitie. **1577** Hanmer *Anc. Eccl. Hist.* (1619) 97 By reason of prophane literature and humanity opposite unto sacred letters. **1605** Bacon *Adv. Learn.* II. v. §2. 20 There doe arise three knowledges, Divine Philosophy, Natural Philosophy, and Humane Philosophy, or Humanitie. **1679** Prance *Addit. Narr. Pop. Plot* 43 He . . went to Lisbone, and taught Humanity in the English Colledge there. **1737** *J. Chamberlayne's St. Gt. Brit.* II. III. x. 440 In this University [Edinburgh] are taught Divinity, Philosophy . . Oratory, Humanity. **1774** Warton *Hist. Eng. Poetry* xxxv. (1840) II. 547 Nicholas the fifth . . established public rewards at Rome for composition in the learned languages, appointed professors in humanity. *Ibid.* 550 Rodolphus Langius . . a tolerable Latin poet . . opened a school of humanity at Munster: which supplied his countrymen with every species of elegant learning. **1837–9** Hallam *Hist. Lit.* I. v. I. §27. 348 Lectures in humanity, that is, in classical literature, were, in 1535, established in all colleges of the University of Oxford. **1864** Burton *Scot Abr.* I. v. 269 The 'Professor of Humanity' has his place in . . official lists as if there were nothing antiquated or peculiar in the term. **1865** Gladstone *Glean.* (1879) VII. 10 The study, of which Greek learning is the main . . as well as the most arduous part, made its way, under the well-deserved name of Humanity, to the very head of the Faculty of Arts. **1869** Sir A. Grant *Address Students Univ. Edin.* 2 Nov., Latin, not altogether without reason called 'Humanity' in this University, is the greatest of all keys to the history, the thoughts, and the mind itself of civilized man. **1893** Fowler *Hist. C.C.C.* ii. 58 (O.H.S.) The first Professor of Humanity [in C.C.C., Oxford] was Ludovicus Vivès, the celebrated Spanish humanist.

b. *pl.* (Usually with *the*; = Fr. *les humanités.*)

1702 Woodroffe *Daniel's 70 Weeks* Ep. A iij b, What Philosophy, what Humanities, what Law, what Divinity did not his Discourses still infuse? **1828** Scott *F.M. Perth* vii, I have been bred in Paris, and learned my humanities and my *cursus medendi.* **1856** Emerson *Eng. Traits, Universities* Wks. (Bohn) II. 92 An Eton captain . . critically learned in all the humanities. **1886** Sir F. Pollock *Oxford Lect.* iv. (1890) 108 Neither would I have you neglect the humanities. I could wish that every one of you . . could enjoy in the originals Homer, and Virgil, and Dante, and Rabelais, and Goethe. **1886** Lowell *Wks.* (1890) VI. 147 The teaching of the Humanities and of the Hebrew.

5. *attrib.* and *Comb.* a. in sense 4.

1565 Harding in Jewel *Def. Apol.* (1611) 496 Some out of the Canonists, some out of the Schoolmen . . most of all out of Humanity Bookes, wherein you be pretily seene. . . As for Diuinity, there appeareth no great knowledge in you. a**1688** Fulman in Fowler *Hist. C.C.C.* (O.H.S.) 381 *note*, Ludovicus Vivès lodged in C.C.C., and, by Tradition, was Humanitie Reader to the Coll. **1695** Sibbald *Autobiog.* (1834) 129, I was a yeer at the Humanity classe.

b. in sense 3 b.

1823 in Cobbett *Rur. Rides* (1885) I. 384 To tell the humanity-men to look at home for slaves to free. *Ibid.*, Colonel Wodehouse . . opposed this humanity-scheme. **1829** Southey *Sir T. More* I. 109 The humanity-mongers, who deny the necessity and lawfulness of inflicting capital punishment.

humanization (ˌhjuːmənaɪˈzeɪʃən). [f. next + -ATION.]

The action or process of humanizing, or condition of being humanized: a. in sense 1 of the vb.

1836 Cdl. Wiseman *Sc. & Relig.* I. iii. 184 Advancing . . in this road to humanization . . their jabbering resolved itself into articulate sounds. **1858** J. Martineau *Stud. Chr.* 100 This degrading humanization of the Deity. **1883** *Century Mag.* XXVII. 113/2 The complete humanization of nature.

b. in sense 2 of the vb.

1783 W. F. Martyn *Geog. Mag.* II. 93 Learning and humanization quickly followed. **1788** Priestley *Lect. Hist.* v. lv. 427 Those diversions . . which . . promote the humanization of our manners. **1876** Maudsley *Phys. Mind* vi. 366 There is not a being born into the world who does not carry in his nature the cultivation of his epoch, marking, so to speak, its stage of humanization. **1879** M. Arnold *Mixed Ess., Equality* 65 Great elements in our humanisation.

c. The treatment of cow's milk to render it suitable for consumption by infants.

1905 F. L. Dodd *Municipal Milk* 14 The humanization adapts the milk to infants' digestive processes. **1932** V. E. M. Bennett *Welfare Infant & Child* v. 70 When cows' milk is to be used for feeding the infant two modifications are always requisite. . . These two processes are known respectively as Humanization and Pasteurization.

humanize (ˈhjuːmənaɪz), *v.* [ad. F. *humanise-r* (16th c. in Littré), f. *hūmān-us*: see -IZE.]

1. *trans.* To make or render human; to give a human character to, imbue with human qualities; to turn into, or represent in, the form of man; to conform to human nature or use.

1603 Holland *Plutarch's Mor.* 1210 Socrates . . hath humanized as I may so say, Philosophy, and attributed it to humaine reason. **1614** Earl Stirling *Domes-day* v. (R.), When humaniz'd our Saviour did remaine. **1756** Burke *Subl. & B.* II. v, Before the Christian religion had, as it were, humanized the idea of the Divinity. **1855** Milman *Lat. Chr.* xiv. x. (1864) IX. 338 The cloister . . must humanise itself that it may represent man. **1895** *Pop. Sci. Monthly* Sept. 671 It is clear that the Fijians humanized their gods.

2. To make humane; to civilize, soften, refine; to imbue with gentleness or tenderness.

1647 W. Browne tr. *Gomberville's Polexander* II–IV. 235 The wilder people . . were somewhat humaniz'd by our conversation. **1670** Walton *Lives* II. 132 My faithful Tears . . shall flow To humanize the Flints on which I tread. **1696** Phillips (ed. 5), *To Humanize*, to make gentle, tractable and familiar. **1790** J. B. Moreton *Mann. W. Ind.* 164 If blacks were humanized, instructed in arts and sciences, husbandry and commerce. **1867** Freeman *Norm. Conq.* I. ii. 33 The Evangelical precepts . . distinctly humanized the way in which war was carried on.

†3. *intr.* To act as a human being. *Obs. rare.*

1655 tr. *Gracian's Courtiers Orac.* 163 By Divinizing one gets Respect; by Humanizing, Contempt.

4. *intr.* for *pass.* To become humanized, to grow humane.

a**1790** Franklin (Webster 1864), Humanizing by degrees, it [the law of nations] admitted slavery instead of death [as a punishment]. **1862** Marg. Goodman *Exper. Eng. Sister Mercy* 28 Some few of them [boys] were observed to humanise considerably under the intercourse.

5. To treat (cow's milk) in order to make it more closely resemble human milk and suitable for consumption by infants.

1897 *Amer. Jrnl. Med. Sci.* CXIII. 374 Dufour . . describes a rather simple method of humanizing cow's milk. **1970** *Pharmaceutical Handbk.* (Pharm. Soc. Gt. Brit.) 379 In 'humanising' cow's milk, extra cane sugar or glucose is added because human milk contains more lactose than cow's milk.

Hence ˈ**humanizing** *vbl. sb.* and *ppl. a.*

1655 [see 3]. **1816** Southey *Pilgr. Waterloo* II. xvii, The love of peace and humanizing art. **1850** Kingsley *Alt. Locke* xxxi, A fresh centre of instruction, humanizing, disciplining . . to hundreds of little savage spirits. **1875** Jowett *Plato* (ed. 2) III. 145 Love . . has exercised a humanizing if not a strengthening influence on the world.

humanized (-aɪzd), *ppl. a.* [f. prec. + -ED[1].]

1. Made or represented as human (see prec. 1).

humanized lymph or ***virus***: vaccine lymph or virus modified by being communicated to a human being in vaccination.

1818 R. P. Knight *Symbolic Lang.* (1876) 19 The humanised head being sometimes bearded, and sometimes not. **1873** Symonds *Grk. Poets* x. 322 The humanized aspects of the external world. **1880** Dr. Cameron in Parlt. 11 June, Guarantee against the propagation of those human diseases occasionally invaccinated with humanised lymph.

2. Made humane; civilized, refined (see prec. 2).

1771 Burke *Corr.* (1844) I. 298, I live . . in liberal and humanized company. **1851** Gallenga *Italy* 331 Notions . . no longer suitable to our refined and humanized age.

3. Of milk (see HUMANIZE *v.* 5).

1888 *Baby* Dec. 15/1 This humanised cow's milk is the only natural food for artificially feeding infants, and the weakest of them thrive on it as on breast milk. **1901** *Westm. Gaz.* 19 Oct. 5/3 The Borough Council of Battersea has determined to undertake the supply of sterilised and humanised milk. **1947** A. B. Meering *Handbk. Nursery Nurses* xxii. 202 Humanised dried milk is fresh cows' milk, dried, and the content rendered as near as possible to human milk. **1955** Wohl & Goodhart *Mod. Nutrition* xxxiv. 919 'Humanized milks' . . imitate to a greater or lesser extent the caloric proportions, the mineral content or the fat of breast milk. *Ibid.*, The need for the humanized products is . . questionable.

ˈ**humanizer.** [f. as prec. + -ER[1].] One who or that which humanizes.

1776 Burney *Hist. Mus.* I. 324 Orpheus . . the . . humanizer of the . . savage Thracians. **1858** J. Martineau *Stud. Chr.* 36 The first humanizer of men was their worship.

humankind (ˈhjuːmənˈkaɪnd). [Properly two words, *human kind*; now commonly written as one, after *mankind*.] The human race; mankind.

c**1645** Cowley *To Sir W. Davenant* 16 So much more thanks from humane kind does merit The Poets Fury than

the Zealots Spirit. **1709** POPE *Ess. Crit.* 640 A knowledge both of books and human kind. **1728** YOUNG *Love Fame* VII. (1757) 162 The world their field, and humankind their prey. **1860** FARRAR *Orig. Lang.* xi. 222 All humankind will be gathered hereafter into one universal empire.

human-like, *a.* [f. HUMAN + LIKE *a.*] Like that which is human, resembling the human; like a human being, man-like.

1774 GOLDSM. *Nat. Hist.* IV. vii. 239 The human-like figure of their hands and feet. **1813** SOUTHEY *Life of Nelson* I. 15 No other animal has so humanlike an expression in its countenance. **1839** BAILEY *Festus* xix. (1848) 198 Their natives are, some human-like, and some Of great gigantic grace. **1851** MAYNE REID *Scalp Hunt.* xxiii. 172 The mare uttered a sort of human-like scream.

humanly (ˈhjuːmənlɪ), *adv.* In 5–8 also **humanely**. [f. HUMAN *a.* + -LY².]

1. After the manner of mankind, in accordance with human nature; by human means, by man.

1613 PURCHAS *Pilgrimage* (1614) 14 Thou shouldest rather thinke Divinely of Man, then Humanely of God. **1680** BAXTER *Cath. Commun.* (1684) 4 Humanly Instituted and Determined. **1824** LAMB *Lett.* (1837) II. 155 Is Sunday, not divinely speaking, but humanly . . a blessing? **1867** J. B. ROSE tr. *Virgil's Æneid* 83 So that I perish humanly 'twill please Me humanly to die. **1886** *Law Times* LXXX. 318/1 Judges are humanly fallible and subject to prejudice.

2. Within the range of human experience or power; from the standpoint of mankind.

1581 PETTIE *Guazzo's Civ. Conv.* I. (1586) 4 The true pleasure (to speak humanelie) is yᵗ which naturallie giveth pleasure to all persons. **1649** MILTON *Eikon.* xxvi, Every accident . . that may happ'n humanly to the affaires of men. **1707** FREIND *Peterborow's Cond. Sp.* 55 [The deed] was thought humanely impossible. **1716** ADDISON *Free-holder* No. 55 ¶8 There is no Question, humanly speaking, but these great Ends will be brought about. **1883–4** J. G. BUTLER *Bible-Work* II. 54 Under circumstances never humanly matched.

3. With the feelings distinctive or worthy of man; with human kindness. (In earlier use, Courteously, in a friendly manner: cf. HUMANE I a.)

c **1485** *Songs & Carols* (1847) 64 The gowdwyff ful humanly to hyr spowse gave gownys. **1596** DALRYMPLE tr. *Leslie's Hist. Scot.* VIII. 79 The king of Jngland . . prayes him to desist and to returne . . The Scotis king returnes . . humanlie and gentillie, confideng in his promises. **1709** POPE *Ess. Crit.* III. 77 Modestly bold, and humanly severe. *a* **1845** HOOD *Bridge of Sighs* iv, Think of her . . Gently and humanly. **1876** LOWELL *Among my Bks.* Ser. II. 93 If he had not felt intensely and humanly.

humanness (ˈhjuːmənnɪs). [f. as prec. + -NESS.] Human quality: = HUMANITY I.

1727 in BAILEY vol. II. **1802** COLERIDGE *Lett.* (1895) 400 It leaves all the echoes . . far behind, in number, distinctness, and humanness of voice. **1871** H. B. FORMAN *Living Poets* 226 The naïve innocence of the child's untainted humanness. **1889** J. M. ROBERTSON *Ess. Crit. Meth.* 78 Faces drop humanness without becoming recognizably bestial.

humano-, used as combining form of L. *hūmānus* HUMAN: = 'humanly . . .', 'human and . . .', as ***humano-solar***, ***-taurine***.

1816 G. S. FABER *Orig. Pagan Idol.* I. 350 The cherub, or humano-taurine apparition. **1828** —— *Sacr. Cal. Proph.* (1844) II. 14 The great humano-solar divinity of Paganism.

humanoid (ˈhjuːmənɔɪd), *a.* and *sb.* [f. HUMAN *a.* (*sb.*) + -OID.] **A.** *adj.* Of human form or character; man-like; *spec.* (*a*) distinguished from anthropoid as being more human in character (cf. HOMINOID *a.* and *sb.*); (*b*) as a term in Science Fiction.

1918 MRS. D. G. RITCHIE *New Warden* xvi. 186 Religion . . had its origin in the funk and cunning of the humanoid ape. **1922** *Glasgow Herald* 23 Dec. 4 Then came the separating off of the larger Anthropoid Apes, leaving the main stem humanoid. **1936** C. J. WARDEN *Emergence Human Culture* iii. 87 The humanoid stock must become specialized along human lines or forever perish from the earth. **1952** V. NABOKOV *Nabokov's Dozen* (1959) 207 Inhabitants of foreign planets, 'intelligent' beings, humanoid or of various mythic makes. **1965** *Punch* 7 Apr. 525/3 Ruined machinery . . leads our heroes to a planet revolving around Altair, where they meet a humanoid race. **1966** L. COHEN *Beautiful Losers* (1970) I. 96 It was just a shape of Edith: then it was just a humanoid shape: then it was just a shape.

B. *sb.* A humanoid animal or being.

1925 J. A. THOMSON *Concerning Evolution* iii. 210 The humanoids and the anthropoids parting company between a million and two million years ago. **1936** C. J. WARDEN *Emergence Human Culture* iii. 87 The humanoids that managed to survive from age to age became less ape-like and more man-like as time went on. **1958** *Manch. Guardian* 26 Sept. 4/3 The humanoids who are accidentally brought to earth by these means inevitably turn out to be superior to us. **1965** *Listener* 14 Jan. 56/2 The culmination is reached when peaceful humanoids are ruled by vicious insects or lizards.

humantin (hjuːˈmæntɪn). *Zool.* [a. Fr. *humantin* (G. Rondelet *Histoire des Poissons* (1558) XIII. viii. 301), of uncertain origin.] A spiny shark, *Oxynotus centrina*, of the family Oxynotidæ, found in the Mediterranean Sea and off the coast of Portugal.

Gamillscheg's suggestion that it is perhaps f. Fr. *humer* 'to inhale' arbitrarily modelled on Fr. *lamantin* LAMANTIN is chronologically inconclusive. The word is also sometimes identified with L. *humus* 'humus, soil', from the habit that the humantin has of lying in the mud on the sea-bed, but the connection remains uncertain.

[**1862** T. GILL in *Ann. Lyceum Nat. Hist. N.Y.* VII. 376 Cuvier, in his Regne Animal, proposed the following division . . Les Humantins (Centrina Cuv.). **1880–84** F. DAY *Fishes Gt. Brit. & Ireland* II. 319 *Centrina salviani* . . . Name.—La Humantin, French. Habits.—Is supposed to inhabit great depths.] **1925** J. T. JENKINS *Fishes Brit. Isles* 320 *The Humantin* (*Centrina salviani*). In this shark each dorsal fin has a strong spine. **1959** A. HARDY *Fish & Fisheries* ix. 181 The humantin, *Oxynotus centrina*, an even rarer straggler to our waters from the coasts of Portugal, is noteworthy for its peculiar spines situated within its large dorsal fins.

humate (ˈhjuːmət), *sb. Chem.* [f. HUM-IC + -ATE⁴.] A salt of humic acid.

1844 PETZHOLDT *Lect. Farmers* 93 Salts, denominated humates. **1857** BERKELEY *Cryptog. Bot.* §227. 237 From the solution of humates or ulmates contained in the soil.

†'**humate**, *ppl. a. Obs.* [ad. L. *humāt-us*, pa. pple. of *humāre* to bury.] Buried, interred.

1511 *Test. Ebor.* (Surtees) V. 24 That my body be humate byfore the v tapurs under the crucifix. **1518** *Will of Hopkinson* (Somerset Ho.), My body to be humate & berid.

†**hu'mation**. *Obs.* [ad. L. *humātiōn-em*, f. *humāre* to bury.] Burial, interment; inhumation.

1635 HEYWOOD *Hierarch.* III. 137 Giue them Humation Build them a Monument. *a* **1661** FULLER *Worthies, Lanc.* II. (1662) 117 Lancashire gave me Breath, And Cambridge Education. Middlesex gave me Death, And this Church my Humation.

humayn(e, obs. ff. HUMAN, HUMANE.

humber, obs. f. HUMMER, var. UMBER, the grayling.

†**hum-bird**. *Obs.* [f. HUM *sb.* or *vb.-stem* + BIRD *sb.*] = HUMMING-BIRD.

1634 W. WOOD *New Eng. Prosp.* (1865) 31 As shee flies, she makes a little humming noise like a Humble-bee: wherefore shee is called the Humbird. **1646** SIR T. BROWNE *Pseud. Ep.* VI. viii. 315 The Humbird, not much exceeding a Beetle. **1698** B. BULLIVANT in *Phil. Trans.* XX. 168 The Hum-bird I have shot with Sand. **1819** J. R. DRAKE *Culprit Fay* iv, Some from the hum-bird's downy nest. **1834** C. A. DAVIS *Lett. Jack Downing* 6 They both came within a humbird's eye of it. **1872** SCHELE DE VERE *Americanisms* 377 The tiny *Mango* Hummingbird (*Trochilus colubris*) . . is known familiarly . . as *Humbird* or *Hummer* simply. **1891** R. T. COOKE *Huckleberries* (1896) 167, I never see a humbird fuller o' buzz than little Prudy.

humble (ˈhʌmb(ə)l), *a.*¹ Forms: 3–6 umble, 4– humble, (4–5 humbyll, 5 oumbbylle, 6 humbul). See also HUMIL(E. [a. OF. *umble, humble* (12th c. in Littré):—L. *humil-em* low, lowly, small, slight, mean, insignificant, base, f. *humus* ground, earth. The *h* was originally mute as in F.; the pronunciation (ˈʌmb(ə)l) has prevailed down to the 19th c. See also the doublet HUMIL(E.]

1. Having a low estimate of one's importance, worthiness, or merits; marked by the absence of self-assertion or self-exaltation; lowly: the opposite of *proud*. **a.** Of persons.

c **1250** *Old Kent. Serm.* in *O.E. Misc.* 30 Ure lord god almichti . . þurch his grace maked of þo euele manne good man, of þe orgeilus umble. *c* **1386** CHAUCER *Pars. T.* ¶686 Humble folk been cristes freendes. *c* **1430** LYDG. *Hors, Shepe, & G.* 79 Vnto the wolffe contrarye of nature . . is this oumbbylle best [sheep]. **1548** HALL *Chron., Edw. IV* 194 b, Neither to wanton nor to humble. **1607** SHAKS. *Timon* III. v. 7, I am an humble Sutor to your Vertues. **1640** J. DYKE *Worthy Commun.* 130 Christ was humble, they are proud. *c* **1718** PRIOR *Solomon* III. 875 Thy sum of duty let two words contain . . Be humble, and be just. **1852** ROBERTSON *Serm.* Ser. III. xviii. (1882) 241 God . . places the humble consistent follower and the broken-hearted sinner on a level. *Mod.* A humble follower of the Master.

b. Of qualities, attributes, actions, etc.

c **1374** CHAUCER *Troylus* I. 68 (124) She hym thonkyd oft in humble chere. **1390** GOWER *Conf.* I. 64 There ben louers of such a sort, That feignen hem an humble port. **1509** HAWES *Past. Pleas.* XXXI. 130 (1845) 154 His umble service we pray you alow. **1552** *Bk. Com. Prayer, Morn. Pr.*, I praye and beseche you . . to accompany me wyth a pure heart and humble voyce. **1662** *Ibid.*, *Gen. Thanksgiving*, We thine unworthy servants do give thee most humble and hearty thanks. **1727** SWIFT *Gulliver* III. i, I . . spoke in the humblest accent. **1818** B. O'REILLY *Greenland* 95 There can be . . in my humble opinion, no doubt on the subject. **1841** ELPHINSTONE *Hist. Ind.* II. 475 He . . made the humblest professions of fidelity.

c. Used formally, esp. in subscriptions to letters, in addressing a person regarded as one's superior. ***your humble***: used ellipt. for 'your humble servant'.

c **1386** CHAUCER *Clerk's T.* 768, I neuere heeld me lady ne maistresse But humble seruant to youre worthynesse. **1414** *Rolls Parlt.* IV. 22/2 Oure soverain Lord, youre humble and trewe lieges that ben come for the Co[mmun]e of youre lond. **1450** *Paston Lett.* No. 76 I. 99 Sheweth and piteuously compleyneth youre humble trewe obeisantes Comunes. **1471** *Ibid.* No. 670 III. 8 Your humbylest servaunt, J. of Gelston. **1649** *Nicholas Papers* (Camden) 169 Your Majesties most faithfull and most humble subject and servant, Ormonde. **1653** WALTON *Angler* Ep. Ded. 6, I am really, Sir, Your most affectionate Friend, and most humble Servant, Iz. Wa. **1709** STEELE *Tatler* No. 118 ¶8 The humble Petition of Penelope Prim, Widow. **1765** FOOTE *Commissary* II. Wks. 1799 II. 32 Madam Mechlin, your humble. **1806** SURR *Winter in Lond.* (ed. 3) III. 117 His coldness has driven them from his mansion to that of your humble servant. **1808** in *Sir J. Sinclair's Corr.* (1831) II. 55, I have the honour to be, Dear Sir, your faithful humble servant, Wm. Pinkney. **1835** DICKENS *Let.* 2 May (1965) I. 58 The next stage, your humble, caught them before they had changed. **1926** D. H. LAWRENCE *Let.* 4 Jan. (1962) II. 875 As for your humble, he says his say in bits. **1929** KIPLING *Limits & Renewals* (1932) 359 'And where *does* he get his champagne?' 'From grateful appendices—same as your bloody 'umble,' said Scree.

2. a. Of lowly condition, rank, or estate; of modest dimensions; modest, unpretentious.

c **1386** Humble bed [see HUMBLEHEDE]. *c* **1400** *Rom. Rose* 6148 Sikerest hyding Is undirneth humblest clothing. **1548** HALL *Chron., Rich. III* 46 An humble page. **1601** SHAKS. *All's Well* I. iii. 162, I am from humble, he from honored name. **1621** T. WILLIAMSON tr. *Goulart's Wise Vieillard* A iij, A man of an obscure and humble condition. **1791** MRS. RADCLIFFE *Rom. Forest* ix, She retired to her humble bed. **1852** G. LONG *Pref. Caesar's Comm.* 9 An humble friend, a man unknown to fame. **1894** J. T. FOWLER *Adamnan* Introd. 38 A church or oratory of humble character. *Mod.* The duties of a humble station.

†**b.** Of local situation: Low-lying, not elevated.

1579 SPENSER *Sheph. Cal.* July 13 In humble dales is footing fast, the trode is not so tickle. **1681** COTTON *Wond. Peak* 82 Upon a Terrass, as most Houses high, Though from this prospect humble to your eye. **1729** S. SWITZER *Hydrost. & Hydraul.* 40 The Rivers Rea and Isis, which break out . . in the County of Oxon . . draw their original from so humble a Plain, that there is scarce any Declivity sufficient for their Current. *Ibid.* 75 Water is conveyed with more Ease into the humble Plains below.

c. Of plants: Low-growing. (Now often with some fig. notion of a.)

1658 WILLSFORD *Secrets Nat.* 53 These Dews . . being observed much more . . upon the humble shrub, then upon trees. **1796** WITHERING *Brit. Plants* (ed. 3) III. 601 It is a smaller and more humble plant than the *G. sanguineum*. **1860** RUSKIN *Mod. Paint.* V. VI. x. §24. 102 Lichen, and mosses (. . for the most part humblest of the green things that live). *Mod.* The species are mostly of humble growth.

d. ***humble plant***: the common Sensitive plant.

1664 POWER *Exp. Philos.* 80 That all Vegetables (as well as the Sensitive and humble Plants) have this latter kind of Sensation, as well as Animals. **1688** R. HOLME *Armoury* II. 114/1 The Humble Plant will fall of its own accord, when you come near it. **1796** MARSHALL *Garden.* xix. (1813) 341 Humble plant is one of the sensitives, the property of which is to close its leaves or drop them upon being touched. **1884** MILLER *Plant-n.*, Humble Plant, *Mimosa pudica*.

3. *Comb.* parasynthetic, as ***humble-hearted***, ***-minded***, ***-mouthed***, ***-spirited***, ***-visaged*** adjs.; whence ***humble-mindedness***, etc.; quasi-advb. in ***humble-acting*** adj.

1573 *New Custom* I. ii. in Hazl. *Dodsley* III. 16 The humble-spirited is termed a fool or a lout. **1580** SIDNEY *Arcadia* (1622) 136 Humble-heartednes and harty earnestnesse. **1580** T. POUNDE in H. Foley *Jesuits in Conflict* (1873) 109 That might soe be amonge the humble-minded. **1588** SHAKS. *L.L.L.* II. i. 34 Like humble visag'd suters. **1613** —— *Hen. VIII*, II. iv. 107 Y'are meek, and humble-mouth'd. **1712** STEELE *Spect.* No. 442 ¶3 Whether the Ambitious or Humble-minded. **1738** WESLEY *Wks.* (1872) XII. 34 A serious humble-acting Christian. **1893** *Athenæum* 24 June 790/2 His truthfulness was not less conspicuous than the humblemindedness of which it was the parent. **1905** W. JAMES *Mem. & Stud.* (1911) v. 77 It must be confessed that T. D. never was exactly humble-minded. **1961** NEW ENG. BIBLE *Matt.* xi. 29 Bend your necks to my yoke, and learn from me, for I am gentle and humble-hearted. —— *1 Pet.* iii. 8 Be full of brotherly affection, kindly and humble-minded.

humble, *a.*²: see HUMMEL *a.*

humble, *v.*¹ [f. HUMBLE *a.*]

1. *trans.* To render humble or meek in spirit; to cause to think more lowly of oneself.

1591 SHAKS. *Two Gent.* II. iv. 137 Loue's a mighty Lord, And hath so humbled me. **1659** HAMMOND *On Ps.* cii. 14 If they shall be truly sensible of thy punishments, and humbled for their sins. **1774** GOLDSM. *Nat. Hist.* (1776) II. 39 An account of the lowliness of our own origin, if it cannot amuse, will at least serve to humble us. **1879** CHR. ROSSETTI *Seek & F.* 161 When we ask to be humbled, we must not recoil from being humiliated.

2. To lower in dignity, position, condition, or degree; to bring low, abase.

1484 CAXTON *Fables of Æsop* IV. xx, The prowde shall be allway humbled. **1588** SHAKS. *Tit. A.* I. i. 472 All humbled on your knees. **1611** BIBLE *Deut.* xxii. 24 Because he hath humbled his neighbours wife. *a* **1661** FULLER *Worthies* (1840) II. 311 Though the purity therof is much subject to be humbled. **1692** RAY *Dissol. World* II. v. (1732) 245 The highest Mountains may be humbled into Valleys. **1759** ROBERTSON *Hist. Scot.* I. VI. 478 To humble the Church was the king's next step. **1816** KEATINGE *Trav.* (1817) I. 34 A French soldier is not to be humbled in the opinion of his countrymen or of himself. **1874** GREEN *Short Hist.* viii. §5 The Catholic League [was] humbled in the dust.

3. *refl.* To render oneself humble; to assume a humble attitude; to do obeisance, bow. *arch.*

[Cf. med.L. *se humiliare*, per adorationem inclinare se, genua flectere (Du Cange).]

c **1380** *Sir Ferumb.* 4965 Toward Mahoun he humblede him þan. **1390** GOWER *Conf.* I. 111 Our king hath . . humbled him in such a wise To hem that were of none emprise. **1483** CAXTON *G. de la Tour* A viij b, A grete lady tooke of her hood and humbled herself to a taylour. **1548** HALL *Chron., Hen. VII* 24 b, The army . . humbled them selfes mekely before the crosse. **1613** PURCHAS *Pilgrimage* (1614) 807 All the people did humble themselves, laying earth upon their heads. **1756–7** tr. *Keysler's Trav.* (1760) III. 254 *margin*, How far Charles V. humbled himself to the

pope. **1865** KINGSLEY *Herew.* xix, Let us humble ourselves under God's hand.

†**b.** *intr.* for *refl. Obs.* or *dial.*

c **1590** GREENE *Fr. Bacon* xvi. 2 Great potentates..Think that Prince Edward humbles at your feet. **1635** *Tom a Lincolne* in Thoms *Prose Rom.* (1858) II. 236, I..have made princes stoope and kings to humble when I have frownde. **1891** *Daily News* 17 Oct. 3/2 The charities..in many cases do not go to the most needy, 'who will not humble to ask for them'.

†**4.** *trans.* To offer humbly. *Obs. nonce-use.*

1624 FORD *Sun's Darling* IV. i, Let us attend to humble our best thanks For these high favours.

Hence **humbled** ('hʌmb(ə)ld) *ppl. a.*; **'humbling** *vbl. sb.* and *ppl. a.*, whence **'humblingly** *adv.*, in a humbling or humiliating manner.

1549 COVERDALE, etc. *Erasm. Par. Eph.* iv. (R.), Throughe lowlinesse are humbleyng of hymselfe. **1600** SHAKS. *A. Y. L.* III. v. 5 The common executioner..Falls not the axe vpon the humbled neck, But first begs pardon. *a* **1655** VINES *Lord's Supp.* (1677) 317 Of melting humblings. *a* **1732** T. BOSTON *Crook in Lot* (1805) 145 The prayers and cries of his humbled people in their humbling circumstances. **1813** L. HUNT in *Examiner* 1 Mar. 129/2 They should meet with no whining self-humblings. **1837** HT. MARTINEAU *Soc. Amer.* (1839) II. 310 Selfishly timid, humblingly dependent. **1861** GEN. P. THOMPSON *Audi Alt.* III. clxxviii. 215 On this occasion the English government and public have made a humbling spectacle.

†**humble,** *v.*^{2} *Obs.* [app. of same origin as MHG., LG. and mod.Ger. *hummelen, hummeln*, 'bombilare', mod.Du. *hommelen* to hum, buzz, 'bombilare, bombum edere, ut fucus, apis, etc.' (Kilian.) Cf. HUMBLE-BEE.] *intr.* To rumble; to mumble; to hum or buzz as a bee. Exemplified chiefly in **humbling** *vbl. sb.*^{2}

c **1384** CHAUCER *H. Fame* II. 531 Lyke the last humblynge After a clappe of oo thundringe. **1552** LATIMER *Serm.* (Parker Soc.) 144 It is better to say it sententiously one time, than to run it over an hundred times with humbling and mumbling. **1583** STANYHURST *Æneis* I. (Arb.) 19 A great hurly burlye the wyndblasts Would keepe..wyth woonderus humbling. *Ibid.* 31 Lyke bees..That flirt in soonbeams, and toyle with mutterus humbling. **1617** MINSHEU *Ductor*, To Humble or humme like a Bee.

humble, *v.*^{3}: see HUMMEL.

humble, *sb. Obs.* Only in *pl.* **humbles.** An occasional spelling of UMBLES (itself a later form of NUMBLES, OF. *nombles*), the inwards of a deer or other beast.

c **1590** GREENE *Fr. Bacon* xiv. 106, *Lacy.* What haue you fit for breakefast? *Margret.* Butter and cheese, and humbles of a Deere. **1637** T. MORTON *New Eng. Canaan* (1883) 203 The humbles was ever my dogges fee, which by the wesell was hanged on the barre in the chimney, for his diet only. **1709** STEELE *Tatler* No. 76 ¶1 Without telling..who has the Humbles, who the Haunch, and who the Legs of the last Stag.

†**humble,** app. a popular corruption of HOMILY.

1550 LEVER *Serm.* (Arb.) 65 He..slubbers vp his seruice, and he can not reade the humbles.

humble, obs. form of HUMBLY.

humble-bee ('hʌmb(ə)l,bi:). Also 5 **humbul-, -yl-.** [Known only from the 15th c.; but possibly an old word, representing an OE. **humbol-béo*: cf. OHG. *humbal, humpal*, MHG. *humbel, hummel* (masc.), Ger. *hummel* fem., *hummelbiene*, the large wild-bee, MLG. *homele, hummelbe, homelbe*, MDu. *hommel* (m. and f.), Kilian *hommel, bommel*, 'bombilius, fucus, et crabro', Du. *hommel* masc. a drone-bee, Da. *humlebi*, Sw. *humla* (from LG.).

The *b* in OHG. and MHG. makes it somewhat doubtful whether the sb. was orig. derived from the root of *hummen* to HUM; but there can be little doubt of the subsequent association of *hummel* with the dim. vb. *hummeln*, or of *humble-bee* with HUMBLE *v.*^{2}]

A large wild bee, of the genus *Bombus*, which makes a loud humming sound; a bumble-bee.

a **1450** *Fysshynge w. angle* (1883) 26 In Juyll the greshop & the humbylbee in the medow. *c* **1470** in *Rel. Ant.* I. 86 The humbul-be [*v.r.* hombull-be] haundylt a horne-pype. *c* **1475** *Pict. Voc.* in Wr.-Wülcker 767/20 *Hic tabanus*, a humbylbee. **1547** BOORDE *Introd. Knowl.* ii. (1870) 126 Lyke the hussyng of a homble be. **1590** SHAKS. *Mids. N.* III. i. 171 The honie-bags steale from the humble Bees. **1781** S. PETERS *Hist. Connecticut* 260 The Humble-bee is almost as large as the humming-bird. **1859** DARWIN *Orig. Spec.* iii. (1873) 57 Humble-bees alone visit red clover, as other bees cannot reach the nectar.

b. *attrib.* †**humble-bee orchis,** the Bee Orchis.

1597 GERARDE *Herbal* I. ci. §3. 163 The Humble Bee Orchis hath a fewe small weake and shorte leaues.

†**'humbledory.** *Obs.* [Cf. *humble-bee, drumble-dore, -drone*, Du. *hommel* a drone, and DOR *sb.*^{1}] A drone.

1555 in Strype *Eccl. Mem.* (1721) III. App. xlviii. 153 Not to lye in corners lyke humbledoryes, eatyng up the honey of the bees.

humblefi'cation. *nonce-wd.* [f. HUMBLE *a.*^{1} + -FICATION.] A making (oneself) humble.

1809 SOUTHEY *Lett.* (1856) II. 120 The Prospectus..has about it a sort of unmanly humblefication.

[**humblehede,** a reading in some Chaucer MSS. for *humble bed.*

c **1386** CHAUCER *Monk's T.* 682 (Ellesm. MS.) From humble bed to roial magestee Up roos he Iulius the Conquerour. (So *Harl., Hengw., Camb. MSS.; Corp., Petw., Lans.* Fro humblehede and fro Roial Maieste.)]

'humble-'jumble. *rare.* [A riming formation on JUMBLE.] A confused jumble. Also **'humble-'jumbled** *ppl. a.*

1550 CRANMER *Answ. to Gardiner* v. (1551) 361 A confusion, an humble iomble or hotch potch. **1929** H. S. WALPOLE *Hans Frost* I. ix. 98 The ironic disappointment of fixing pretty sentences together, all, humble-jumble, on the table of his mind. **1940** *Horizon* Jan. 61 It is the Big Bed of Ware combined with the Procrustean bed, in which, humble-jumbled or stretched or curtailed to fit, they all lie most curiously together.

humblely, obs. form of HUMBLY.

'humblement. *nonce-wd.* [f. HUMBLE *v.*^{1} + -MENT.] Humiliation.

1839 BAILEY *Festus* xix. (1854) 293 In whom was perfected all sacrifice, All penalty, all humblement, all death.

humbleness ('hʌmb(ə)lnɪs). [f. HUMBLE *a.* + -NESS.] The quality of being humble.

1. Meekness, lowliness, humility.

1388 WYCLIF *Heb.* Prol., He knowynge her pride, and schewinge his owene humblenesse [*later MSS.* humelnesse]. **1494** FABYAN *Chron.* IV. lxxv. 54, I here with al humblenesse salute her. **1535** COVERDALE *Acts* viii. 33 In his humblenesse is his judgment exalted. **1596** SHAKS. *Merch. V.* I. iii. 125 With bated breath, and whispring humblenesse. **1683** *Lond. Gaz.* No. 1864/3 With all humbleness and Duty we desire..to approach the Throne of your Sacred Majesty. **1823** MOORE *Loves Angels* III. 208 Thus in humbleness they trod, Abashed, but pure before their God. **1843** J. MARTINEAU *Chr. Life* (1867) 448 Hence the humbleness there always is in Christian dignity.

2. Unpretentiousness, modest character.

1802 COLERIDGE *Lett.* (1895) 386 A daring humbleness of language and versification. **1812** SHELLEY in Hogg *Life* (1858) II. 140 If the humbleness of their quality is no objection. **1814** BYRON *Corsair* I. ii, Earth's coarsest bread, the garden's homeliest roots..His short repast in humbleness supply.

humble pie.

†**1.** = UMBLE PIE, a pie made of the 'umbles' or inwards of a deer (or other animal). *Obs.*

a **1648** DIGBY *Closet Open.* (1677) 203 To season Humble-Pyes. [**1822** T. L. PEACOCK *Maid Marian* 241 Robin helped him largely to numble-pie..and the other dainties of his table.]

2. *to eat humble pie*: to be very submissive; to apologize humbly; to submit to humiliation.

[From HUMBLE *a.*, perh. with jocular reference to sense 1 here. Cf. *to eat rue-pie* (Lincolnsh.) to rue, repent.]

1830 *Forby's Voc. E. Anglia* App. 432 'To make one eat humble pie'—i.e. To make him lower his tone, and be submissive. It may possibly be derived from the *umbles* of the deer, which were the perquisite of the huntsman; and if so, it should be written *umble-pie*, the food of inferiors. **1847–78** HALLIWELL s.v., *To eat humble pie*, to be very submissive, *var. dial.* **1855** THACKERAY *Newcomes* I. xiv. 136 You must get up and eat humble pie this morning, my boy. **1863** READE *Hard Cash* xlii, 'The scornful Dog', had to eat wormwood pudding and humble pie. **1871** J. C. JEAFFRESON *Ann. Oxford* I. xiv. 224 The town had..to eat a considerable amount of humble pie. **1883** HOWELLS *Register* ii, Trying to think what was the very humblest pie I could eat.

b. In other analogous expressions.

1862 SALA *Seven Sons* II. ix. 217 The staple in the bill of fare was Humble Pie. **1895** *Times* 9 Jan. 4/1 To sue for peace when further resistance becomes hopeless is a kind of 'humble pie' that fate has condemned all vanquished nations to swallow from time immemorial.

humbler ('hʌmblə(r)). [f. HUMBLE *v.*^{1} + -ER^1.] One who or that which humbles.

1611 COTGR., *Abbaisseur*, an abaser,..humbler, bringer downe of. **1645** J. BOND *Occasus Occid.* 35 It is also an humbler for sinne. **1832** *Examiner* 293/1 Such a doughty humbler of the pride of the insolent nobles.

†**humblesse.** *Obs.* Also 4 **umblesse,** 5 **humbles, -is(se.** [a. OF. *(h)umblesse*, f. *humble*: see HUMBLE *a.*^{1} and -ESS^2. In ME. stressed on second syllable; by Spenser on first: cf. *richesse, riches.*] Humbleness, humility.

c **1374** CHAUCER *Former Age* 55 Vmblesse and pes good feith the emperice. *c* **1374** —— *Boeth.* III. pr. viii. 63 (Camb. MS.) Thow shal defowle thy-self thorw humblesse of axynge. *c* **1430** *Pilgr. Lyf Manhode* I. iv. (1869) 3 Wher inne weren stikked twelue degrees of humblisse. **1590** SPENSER *F.Q.* I. iii. 26 And with faire fearefull humblesse towards him shee came. **1610** G. FLETCHER *Christ's Vict.* I. lxxv, And with prone humblesse her feet's dust doth sweep. **1736** W. THOMPSON *Nativ.* IV. 2 The strawy bed Where Mary, queen of Heaven, in humbless lay.

†**hum'blesso.** *Obs.* [An affected nonce-formation on prec., after such It. or Sp. forms as *capriccio, capricho.*] An obeisance; a show of humility.

1599 NASHE *Lenten Stuffe* 55 He kissed his hand thrice, and made as many Humblessos ere hee would finger it.

†**humblete,** obs. by-form of HUMILITY.

c **1400–30** *Chaucer's Pars. T.* ¶35 (Harl. MS.) In werkyng of alle maner humblete [6 *texts* humylite(e].

humbling: see under HUMBLE *v.*^{1} and ^{2}.

humblok, obs. form of HEMLOCK *sb.*

humbly ('hʌmblɪ), *adv.* Also 4–6 **-umb, -liche, -li, -le, -lie.** See also HUMILY. [f. HUMBLE *a.* + -LY^2: cf. *simple, simply*, etc.]

1. In a humble manner; with humility, meekly.

c **1374** CHAUCER *Troylus* II. 1670 (1719) Loke þat ye þonke humbely [*v.rr.* humblely, vmbely] Hem alle þre. *c* **1380** *Sir Ferumb.* 1041 Oppon ys arm ys heued a layde, & humbliche ansuered þe kyng. *c* **1400** *Destr. Troy* 1837 The Troiane full umbly tolde hym anone. **1485** CAXTON *Paris & V.* (1868) 34 Thene sayd parys moche humbly with grete shamefastnes. *a* **1500** *Flower & Leaf* 345 With greet reverence and that ful humblely. **1535** COVERDALE *Mal.* iii. 14 Walkinge humbly before the Lorde. **1617** MORYSON *Itin.* II. 279 Tyrone..kneeled at the doore humbly on his knees for a long space. **1718** ROWE tr. *Lucan* v. (R.), Oft he is heard to threat, and humbly oft to pray. **1846** RUSKIN *Mod. Paint.* (1851) I. Pref. 39 He who walks humbly with Nature will seldom be in danger of losing sight of Art.

b. Used formally in addressing a superior.

1483 *Plumpton Corr.* (Camden) 44 Humble praying your good mastership to take no displeasure with me. **1548** HALL *Chron., Edw. IV* 230 Moste humbly besechyng your highnes..that I maie have a sure saufe conduite. **1639** MARQ. HAMILTON in *H. Papers* (Camden) 58, I shall humbly craue leiue to ade this to your self. **1711** STEELE *Spect.* No. 258 ¶2, I do humbly propose..that another..be erected.

2. In a low or lowly position or condition; modestly; unpretentiously.

1746 *Tom Thumb's Trav. Eng.* 105 Near an Acre of Pasture Ground..sunk gently down for several Hours, till at last it humbly settled about seventeen Yards below. **1855** MACAULAY *Hist. Eng.* xix. IV. 292 John Bart, humbly born, and scarcely able to sign his name.

3. *Comb.*

1654 GATAKER *Disc. Apol.* 97 As..humblie minded and demeaned a Gentlewoman, as I have ever [known]. **1892** D. A. CLARKE in A. E. Lee *Hist. Columbus* (Ohio) II. 668 The meek and humbly-clad Sisters of St. Francis.

Humboldtian (hʊm'bəʊltɪən), *a.* [f. name of K. Wilhelm von *Humboldt*, German philologist (1767–1835) + -IAN.] Of, pertaining to, or characteristic of Humboldt or his work.

1901 H. OERTEL *Lect. Study of Lang.* i. 45 Entirely Humboldtian in conception is James Byrne's General Principles of the Structure of Language (1885). **1907** E. SAPIR in *Mod. Philology* V. i. 141 Steinthal, himself an enthusiastic follower and developer of Humboldtian views, most emphatically denies any indebtedness on Humboldt's part to Herder. **1964** R. H. ROBINS *Gen. Ling.* viii. 335 Within typological comparison, the Humboldtian tripartite division, properly understood, may be said to be a more significant system of classification than some others. **1965** N. CHOMSKY *Aspects of Theory of Syntax* 199 It seems to me that 'deep structure' and 'surface structure', in the sense in which these terms will be used here, do correspond quite closely to Humboldtian 'inner form' and 'outer form'. **1967** R. L. BROWN tr. *W. von Humboldt's Conception Ling. Relativity* 15 Boas also came under Humboldtian influence in another way.

humboldtilite (hʊm'bəʊltɪlaɪt). *Min.* [Named 1825 after F. H. Alexander von Humboldt, a famous German traveller (1769–1859): see -LITE.] A variety of melilite, often found in large crystals.

1826 *Amer. Jrnl. Sc.* II. 251. **1835** SHEPARD *Min.* 325 Humboldtilite, in right-square prisms. **1868** DANA *Min.* (ed. 5) 280 Humboldtilite occurs in cavernous blocks of Somma.

humboldtine ('hʊmbəʊltaɪn). *Min.* [f. (1821) as prec.: see -INE.] Hydrous oxalate of iron, found usually in capillary crystals.

1822 *Amer. Jrnl. Sc.* V. 193 A new mineral, discovered..near Bilin in Bohemia has been named Humboldtine. **1852** SHEPARD *Min.* 76 Humboldtine..blackens in the flame of a candle.

humboldtite ('hʊmbəʊltaɪt). *Min.* [f. as prec.: see -ITE.] **1.** = prec.

†**2.** A synonym of datolite. *Obs.*

1823 in *Thomson's Ann. Philos.* Ser. II. V. 134, I would propose to call it Humboldtite after that eminent philosopher, to whom natural science is so much indebted. **1843** E. J. CHAPMAN *Min.* 28 Humboldtite; oxalate of iron.

humbug ('hʌmbʌg), *sb.* (*a.*) *colloq.* [A slang or cant word which came into vogue *c* 1750.

(An earlier date has been given in several Dictionaries, on the ground of the occurrence of the word in the title of F. Killigrew's *Universal Jester*, which the *Slang Dictionary* dates 'about 1735–40'. But the earliest ed. of that work is dated by Lowndes 1754; see below.)

Many guesses at the possible derivation of *humbug* have been made; but as with other and more recent words of similar introduction, the facts as to its origin appear to have been lost, even before the word became common enough to excite attention. Cf. the following:

1751 (Jan.) *Student* II. 41 There is a word very much in vogue with the people of taste and fashion, which though it has not even the 'penumbra' of a meaning, yet makes up the sum total of the wit, sense and judgement of the aforesaid people of taste and fashion!..I will venture to affirm that this Humbug is neither an English word, nor a derivative from any other language. It is indeed a blackguard sound, made use of by most people of distinction! It is a fine, make-weight in conversation, and some great men deceive themselves so egregiously as to think they mean something by it!]

†**1.** A hoax; a jesting or befooling trick; an imposition. *Obs.*

1751 *Student* II. 129 That exalted species of wit which is now practised by gentlemen of the brightest parts under the elegant denomination of a Humbug. *Ibid.* 287 (*article*) Of the Superlative Advantages arising from the use of the new-invented Science, called the Humbug. **1754** EARL ORRERY *Let.* in *Connoisseur* No. 14 ¶3 Single words, indeed, now and then broke forth; such as *odious, horrible, detestable, shocking, Humbug*. This last new-coined expression, which is only to be found in the nonsensical vocabulary, sounds absurd and disagreeable, whenever it is pronounced. **1754** *Ibid.* No. 42 ¶4 Our pretenders to wit.. When they talk of Humbug, etc. they seem to be jabbering in the uncouth dialect of the Huns. ?**1754** F. KILLIGREW (*title*) The Universal Jester; or a pocket companion for the Wits; being a choice collection of merry conceits, facetious drolleries, etc., clenchers, closers, closures, bon-mots, and humbugs. **1755** J. SHEBBEARE *Lydia* (1769) I. 333 He delighted greatly in the humbug, a species of wit that was then newly produced in this enlightened age. **1776** R. GRAVES *Euphrosyne* I. 108 Sprightly Humbugs and practical Jokes. *a***1799** TWEDDELL *Rem.* xxxi. (1815) 167 (Jod.) It was, to be sure, a very facetious humbug.

2. A thing which is not really what it pretends to be; an imposture, a deception, fraud, sham.

1751 *Student* II. 41 This peace will prove a confounded humbug upon the nation. **1831** *Cat's Tail* 20 A mere catch-penny humbug. **1884** LD. R. CHURCHILL in *West. Daily Press* 11 July 3/4 The whole legislature of the Government had been a gigantic humbug, a stupendous imposture, and a prodigious fraud.

3. Deception, pretence, sham; used interjectionally = 'stuff and nonsense!'.

1825 J. GEORGE *View Law Joint Stock Comp.* 58 The writer would have thought it the acmé of humbug. **1828** DE QUINCEY *Rhetoric* Wks. XI. 53 In fact, to borrow a coarse word, the mere impersonation of humbug. **1844** DISRAELI *Coningsby* II. iv, A government of statesmen or of clerks? Of Humbug or of Humdrum? **1860** TYNDALL *Glac.* I. xxii. 160, I believe a notion is growing prevalent that half what is said and written about the dangers of the Alps is mere humbug. **1880** MRS. FORRESTER *Roy & V.* II. 209 Humbug! come along! It's a shame to leave such claret as that.

4. A person that practises deception; an impostor, a 'fraud'.

[**1763** in Mackenzie *Royal Masonic Cycl.* s.v., The brethren of the Venerable Society of Humbugs met at brother Hallam's, in Goodman's Fields from 1763.] **1804** J. LARWOOD *No Gun Boats* 7 So essential a Familiar as the Humbug. **1807** in *Sheridaniana* 211, I think, father, said he, that many men who are called great patriots in the House of Commons, are great humbugs. **1857** DICKENS *Lett.* (1880) II. 9, I denounce the race as humbugs. **1860** L. STEPHEN *Vac. Tour* 272, I boldly informed my companions, and tried to persuade myself, that another half-hour would take us to the top; but I secretly felt that I was a humbug. **1875** LOWELL *Spenser* Pr. Wks. 1890 IV. 300 He is at least a man among men, and not a humbug among humbugs.

5. A kind of sweetmeat.

1825 [Remembered in common use in Gloucestershire]. **1847–78** HALLIWELL, *Humbug*,..also applied to a kind of sweetmeat. **1863** MRS. GASKELL *Sylvia's L.* xliii, He had provided himself with a paper of humbugs for the child—'humbugs' being the north-country term for certain lumps of toffy, well-flavoured with peppermint. **1877** *N.W. Linc. Gloss.* **1936** J. L. HODSON *Our Two Englands* vii. 115 A middle-aged member of the [Bradford Wool] Exchange moved about offering a paper bag of sweets; cheeks became swollen with humbugs. **1959** I. & P. OPIE *Lore & Lang. Schoolch.* ix. 166 'Lollies' is also becoming a general term, and so is 'gob-stoppers' for 'any sweet difficult to chew', as humbugs, large aniseed balls, and fruit drops.

6. (See quot.)

1850 [In use in Norfolk for holding cows or horses]. **1875** KNIGHT *Dict. Mech.*, *Humbug* (*Manege*), a nippers for grasping the cartilage of the nose. Used with bulls and other refractory bovines. **1896** *N. & Q.* 8th Ser. IX. 328, 412, 458.

7. *attrib.* or *adj.* Of the nature of or characterized by humbug or imposture; humbugging.

1812 COMBE *Picturesque* XXVI, A pun I do detest, 'Tis such a paltry, humbug jest. **1841** LEVER *C. O'Malley* lxxxviii, No humbug sort of devil-may-care and bad-luck-to-you kind of chaps.

humbug ('hʌmbʌg), *v.* [f. HUMBUG *sb.* In 18th c., and still dialectally, stressed *hum'bug*.]

1. a. *trans.* To practise humbug upon; to trick and make a jest of; to impose upon, hoax, delude.

1751 *Student* II. 41 'Did you observe how the Colonel Humbug'd his Grace last night?' 'These theatrical managers humbug the town damnably!' **1754** F. WEBBER *Def. Rector Exeter Coll.* 45 Thus had the poor Rector the Mortification to find himself, in the modern Phrase, humbugg'd, that is, if I understand the Word, trick'd and made a Jest of. **1762–97** T. BRYDGES *Homer Travest.* I. 85 Now we're humbugg'd, you plainly see. **1813** SIR R. WILSON *Priv. Diary* II. 182 John Bull loves to be humbugged, and they are enemies to themselves who write, speak, or seek truth. **1841** DE QUINCEY *Homer* Wks. VI. 298 Even we have been humbugged by this Pagan rascal. **1885** F. ANSTEY *Tinted Venus* i. 4 That isn't it... Don't try and humbug me.

b. To hoax or cajole *into* (doing something); to cheat out *of* (something).

1761 *Meretriciad* (1765) 21 What could a knight see in thy ugly face To be humbug'd of fifty pounds of lace? **1813** *Sporting Mag.* 218 The gentle reader humbugged into the belief. **1882** *Mrs. Raven's Tempt.* I. 346 Does she humbug herself into that belief, as neatly as she humbugs you?

c. To change or transfer by trickery.

1821 COMBE *Wife* III. 354 Your tricks..never cease To humbug health into disease. **1895** *Forum* (N.Y.) Jan. 561 The good things they have humbugged out of the charities.

2. *intr.* To practise humbug; to be a humbug; 'to fool *about*'. Also const. *about*: to make less progress than expected, to flounder *about*, to wallow (*local U.S.*).

1753 HAWKESWORTH *Adventurer* No. 100 ¶7 I..could..humbug with so much skill as..to take-in a knowing one. **1778** H. BROOKE *Epil. Humbugging* 6 Of worth and of wisdom the trial and test Is—mark ye, my friends!— who shall humbug the best. **1840** R. H. DANA *Two Yrs. before Mast* xxxiv. 433 For several days we lay 'humbugging about' in the Horse latitudes, with all sorts of wind and weather. **1861** H. KINGSLEY *Ravenshoe* xliii. (Farmer), She was always ready to help him, provided, as she told him, 'he didn't humbug'. **1879** F. W. ROBINSON *Coward Consc.* II. vi, Where are we? We're humbugging about..getting a bit nearer the town. **1882** FREEMAN in *Life & Lett.* (1895) II. 259 Why do we go humbugging, and bothering, and asking him to help us? **1908** G. S. WASSON *Home from Sea* vi. 189 We pitch-poled and humbugged about in them latitudes till the Cap'n..was sick and tired of the whole business. **1933** P. A. EADDY *Hull Down* x. 214 For several days we were kept humbugging about with light variable breezes.

Hence **humbugging** *vbl. sb.* and *ppl. a.* Also **humbuggable** *a.*, capable of being humbugged, gullible; whence **humbuggability**. **humbugger**, one who humbugs or practises imposture; a humbug, impostor. **hum'buggery**, **humbuggism**, the action or practice of humbugging; humbug, imposture.

1798 in *Spirit Pub. Jrnls.* (1799) II. 361 A learned dissertation on the *humbugability of its inhabitants. **1825** SOUTHEY *Lett.* (1856) III. 488 That any reasonable man (*humbuggable as the animal is) can have been so humbugged. **1853** *Fraser's Mag.* XLVII. 581 The easiest, most good-natured and most humbuggable of all two-legged animals. **1752** A. MURPHY *Gray's Inn Jrnl.* No. 11 All the Wit..and all the Fun of all the *Humbuggers of the Age. **1767** G. CANNING *Poems* 56 Such is the heart our Humbugger conceals. **1842** S. LOVER *Handy Andy* xviii. 157 I'll strangle you..you humbugger. **1831** J. MORISON in *Morisoniana* 386 The Jennerian vaccinic scheme..should counteract the virulence..which the past inoculating *humbuggery had failed to effect. **1892** *Voice* (N.Y.) 25 Feb., Hypocrisy and humbuggery are openly declared to be the only traits that entitle a man to political support. **1752** A. MURPHY *Gray's Inn Jrnl.* No. 11 ¶6 The never enough to be admired Art of *Humbugging came into Vogue. **1793** 'A. PASQUIN' *Life Earl Barrymore* 67 Lord Barrymore was the most apt and successful person in beginning and pursuing a social species of imposition called humbugging, I ever sat with or observed. **1864** BURTON *Scot Abr.* II. i. 22 A kind of calm insolence essential to great success in the function called humbugging. **1803** *Morn. Herald* in *Spirit Pub. Jrnls.* (1804) VII. 276 In hopes the Town Will gulp him down With good *humbugging sauce, Sir! **1870** BLAINE *Encycl. Rur. Sports* (ed. 3) §4064 There were then no skulkers, no humbugging apologies. **1842** MOORE in *Mem.* (1856) VII. 311 By dint of sheer *humbuggism.

'hum,buzz. *dial.* [f. HUM *v.* + BUZZ *v.*]

1. A local name of the cockchafer.

1756 TOLDERVY *Two Orphans* I. 124 What are there called humbuzes, by the Londoners cock-chafers. *c* **1820** MRS. SHERWOOD *May-bee* 13 William had caught another may-bee, or cockchafer, or humbuzz (for so that insect is called in different places).

2. A thin piece of wood with a notched edge which is swung round rapidly by a string, and emits a loud humming sound, like the flight of a cockchafer; a bull-roarer.

1847–78 in HALLIWELL.

humdinger (,hʌm'dɪŋə(r)). [Origin unknown.]

1. A remarkable or outstanding person or thing, anything of notable excellence. *slang* (orig. *U.S.*).

1905 *Dialect Notes* III. 62 *Hum-dinger*, term of admiration. 'She's a humdinger.' **1916** 'B. M. BOWER' *Phantom Herd* vi. 100 That pit'cher's a humdinger! **1926** *Brit. Weekly* 12 Aug. 399/1 They showed me a new game. I tell you Red, it's a humdinger. *Ibid.* 2 Sept. 456/3 She was a humdinger. She even puts a brand on Brangwyn, and she's no slouch. **1935** *Punch* 10 Apr. 399/2 Say, she knew her own mind, did that jane. A regular humdinger of a dame. **1937** N. MARSH *Vintage Murder* vii. 72, I reckon he's all right. Gosh, I reckon he's a humdinger. **1943** HUNT & PRINGLE *Service Slang* 40 *A humdinger*, any fast aircraft or vehicle; any engine which runs really well. **1958** *Times* 16 June 4/4 The last set was a humdinger, to use a transatlantic expression.

2. *Electronics.* A voltage divider connected across the heater circuit of a valve with the variable tap connected to a source of fixed potential, so that the hum introduced by the heater can be reduced by suitably biasing it with respect to the cathode.

1938 *Admiralty Handbk. Wireless Telegr.* II. Index, Humdinger. **1947** *Electronic Engin.* XIX. 82/3 It is..suggested that the centre point on the 'humdinger' be returned to a suitable tapping on the cathode bias battery. **1967** P. SPRING *Tape Recorders* vii. 90 It is customary to have a centre-tapped heater winding, or better still, a humdinger. This is adjusted until the hum level is at a minimum.

humdrum ('hʌm'drʌm), *a.* and *sb.* Also 6 **humtrum**. [Found *c* 1550: app. a reduplicating formation from HUM *v.*; it is doubtful whether the second element had any distinct connexion with DRUM *sb.*]

A. *adj.* **1.** Lacking variety; of a routine character; commonplace; monotonous; dull.

1553 BALE *Gardiner's De Vera Obed.* Dvj, Because I rather vse a newe makinge of distinccion, than yᵉ old accustumed Humtrum distinccion. **1702** VANBRUGH *False Friend* II. Wks. (Rtldg.) 400/2 A very hum-drum marriage this. **1711** ADDISON *Spect.* No. 9 ¶6 The *Hum-Drum* Club ..was made up of very honest Gentlemen, of peaceable Dispositions, that used to sit together, smoak their Pipes, and say nothing 'till Mid-night. **1782** MAD. D'ARBLAY *Diary* 30 Dec., We had rather a hum-drum evening. **1823** W. IRVING in *Life & Lett.* (1864) II. 158, I am writing in a sad, humdrum vein. **1864** J. H. NEWMAN *Apol.* Note C (1873) 313 A plain humdrum Sermon.

†**2.** (*adj.* or *adv.*) Without decision or distinction; undecided. *Obs.*

1660 R. COKE *Power & Subj.* 132 He..divides *Jus* into *Jus naturale*, and *voluntarium*; which may signifie either of them, or both together hum drum. **1663** BUTLER *Hud.* I. iii. 112 Shall we (quoth she) stand still hum drum, And see stout Bruin all alone By numbers basely overthrown? **1710** *Brit. Apollo* III. No. 58. 3/1 Your Wiser Rival..Ne'er stood Hum Drum, with Shilly Shally.

B. *sb.* **1.** A humdrum person; a dull, monotonous, commonplace fellow.

1598 B. JONSON *Ev. Man in Hum.* I. i, By gadslid I scorne it, I, so I doe, to be a consort for euery hum-drum. **1710** *Brit. Apollo* III. No. 66. 2/2 A Plodding Hum-Drum, A Schollar that's Grum. **1812** *Religionism* 59 Heed not the lazy beneficed hum-drums. **1894** BLACKMORE *Perlycross* 158 There are none but hum-drums, and jog-trots.

2. Dullness, commonplaceness, monotony; dull monotonous talk; with *a* and *pl.*, A humdrum saying, conversation, debate, etc.

1727 *Art Speaking in Publick* 71 (Jod.) Still in the same key to the tune of humdrum without either division or variety. **1748** RICHARDSON *Clarissa* (1811) III. xxxii. 191, I am frequently forced to go to my harpsichord and silence his humdrum. **1840** MRS. F. TROLLOPE *Widow Married* xxiii, To stand listening for an hour together to mamma's humdrums. **1854** W. CORY *Lett. & Jrnls.* (1897) 62, I have been to hear a debate, or a hum-drum, in the House of Lords. **1876** GEO. ELIOT *Dan. Der.* ii, She was living with some intensity, and escaping humdrum.

†**b.** in *pl.* Dullness; = DOLDRUMS 2. *Obs.*

1757 MRS. GRIFFITH *Lett. Henry & Frances* (1867) I. 140, I fear my epistle will..give you the hum-drums.

Hence **hum'drummery**, **hum'drumminess**, **hum'drumness**, the quality or state of being humdrum; humdrum action. **hum'drummish** *a.*, characterized by humdrum, monotony, or dullness; whence **hum'drummishness**.

1732 MRS. DELANY in *Life & Corr.* I. 385 Their two eldest daughters are beauties..but not entertaining, so we passed that day hum-drumish. **1830** *Blackw. Mag.* XXVII. 414 His 'discretion and taste'..mean humdrumishness and humbug. **1831** *Fraser's Mag.* IV. 52 The deity still that illumed my humdrummery, My Magnus Apollo was Robert Montgomery. **1886** *Daily Tel.* 23 Apr. 2/3 A sort of humdrumness that seemed to steal into the ship's inner life. **1889** *Spectator* 9 Nov. 626/2 Plain men, of..fair capacities, and an unsurpassable humdrumminess of nature and deportment. **1893** LELAND *Mem.* II. 72 To break out of orthodox humdrumness.

,hum'drum, *v.* [f. prec. sb.] *intr.* To proceed in a humdrum, monotonous, or undecided fashion. Also *to humdrum it*.

1733 SWIFT *Let. to Sheridan* 27 Mar., I humdrum it on.. endeavouring to write, but write nothing, merely out of indolence and want of spirits. **1825** T. L. PEACOCK *Wks.* (1875) III. 223 If you stand hum-drumming [etc.]. **1862** MOTLEY *Corr.* (1880) II. 108 We are humdrumming on as usual. **1894** A. D'HERISTAL *Discord. Life* xii. 99, I cannot humdrum with him in the Darby and Joan style.

Hence **hum'drumming** *ppl. a.*, monotonous, commonplace.

1698 F. B. *Modest Censure* 14 He is none of those hum-drumming Authors. **1894** F. S. ELLIS *Reynard the Fox* 189 To the humdrumming round, Wherein most men are bound, He furnishes pleasant variety.

humdudgeon (,hʌm'dʌdʒən). Also **humdurgeon**. [Cf. HUM *sb.*[2] and DUDGEON *sb.*[2]] (See quot. 1785.)

1785 GROSE *Dict. Vulg. T.*, *Hum Durgeon*, an imaginary illness; he has got the hum durgeon..nothing ails him except low spirits. **1815** SCOTT *Guy M.* xxiii, I would never be making a hum-dudgeon about a scart on the pow. **1827** —— *Two Drovers* ii, I maun down to the Clachan to see if the lad Harry Waakfelt is out of his humdudgeons yet. **1827** LYTTON *Pelham* lxxx, His ravings and humdurgeon will unman all our youngsters.

Humean, Humian ('hju:mɪən), *a.* and *sb.* Also **Hu'meian**. [f. personal name *Hume*: see -AN.] Of or pertaining to the philosophical system or doctrine of David Hume (1711–76). Also as *sb.* So **'Humism**, the philosophy of David Hume; **'Humist**, an adherent of this.

1800 LAMB *Lett.* (1888) I. 115 The cursed philosophical *Humeian indifference. **1866** *Reader* 24 Mar. 296 The old Humean dogma, that 'no amount of testimony can render a miracle credible'. **1884** J. H. STIRLING in *Mind* Oct. 540 Its general nature is understood, and the peculiar Humian point of it seen into. **1890** W. JAMES *Princ. Psychol.* I. x. 330 And if, with the *Humians, one deny such a principle and say that the stream of passing thoughts is all, one runs against the entire common-sense of mankind. **1960** *Guardian* 2 Mar. 7/2 Most unbelievers in our society are Humeans; and one can be a Humean in this sense without ever having heard of Hume. **1858** W. R. PIRIE *Inq. Human Mind* II. iv. 209 It is substantively *Humeism though the conclusion may be somewhat differently argued out. **1884** *Athenæum* 4 Oct. 425/3 The expansion of Humism by the Mills and their school. *Ibid.* 20 Dec. 800/1 The influence of the encyclopædists in France and of the *Humists in England.

humect (hju:'mɛkt), *v.* Now *rare.* [ad. L. *hūmectāre* (more correctly *ūm-*), f. *(h)ūmectus* moist, wet, f. *(h)ūmē-re* to be moist: see HUMID, HUMOUR. Cf. F. *humecter* (16th c., Rabelais).]

1. *trans.* To moisten, wet.

1531 ELYOT *Gov.* I. xi, It humecteth the body, or maketh it moyster and hotter. **1599** A. M. tr. *Gabelhouer's Bk. Physicke* 48/1 Humect an other peece of clothe in rayne water. **1670–98** LASSELS *Voy. Italy* I. 94 Many springs humect it from the Apennine hills. **1765** *Nat. Hist.* in *Ann. Reg.* 107/2 On the falling of rain that humects the earth, there arises a grateful smell. **1853** SOYER *Pantroph.* 139 The other half of this seasoning serves to humect the quenelles which you have taken beforehand. **1923** E. POUND *Let.* 16 Jan. (1971) 184 Jock Hielandman..ran Unto the river Liffey, Peeled off his breeches and jumped in, Humecting thus his hairy skin.

2. *intr.* To become humid or moist.

1686 W. HARRIS tr. *Lemery's Chym.* (ed. 3) 613 This Salt ..easily humects, and dissolves into a liquor.

Hence **hu'mecting** *ppl. a.*, moistening.

1612 *Ench. Med.* 57 Neither oile nor any other humecting thing. **1756** C. LUCAS *Ess. Waters* I. 42 By its general humecting quality, water is distinguished from *aqua philosophorum.*

humectant (hju:'mɛktənt), *a.* and *sb.* [ad. L. *hūmectānt-em*, pres. pple. of *hūmectāre* to HUMECT.]

A. *adj.* 1. ? *Obs.* Moistening, wetting.

1659 H. MORE *Immort. Soul* III. iv. (1662) 162 Which Fumes, if they be grosser and humectant, may raise [etc.].

2. Moisture-retaining.

1953 *Manuf. Chemist* May 202/2 The humectant action is provided by a combination of glycerin and propylene glycol. **1960** *McGraw-Hill Encycl. Sci. & Technol.* VI. 221/1 Because of its humectant properties, it is sprayed on tobacco before it is processed to prevent crumbling.

B. *sb.* 1. *Med.* A diluent.

1822–34 *Good's Study Med.* (ed. 4) I. 562 Those medicines..supposed capable of dissolving that tenacity.. denominated Diluents, Humectants, and Attenuants.

2. A substance used to reduce the loss of moisture; *spec.* a food additive that does this.

1854–67 C. A. HARRIS *Dict. Med. Terminol.*, *Humectant.* .. In surgery, the substance for retaining moisture in a water dressing. **1951** M. B. JACOBS *Chem. & Technol. Food & Food Products* (ed. 2) III. xxxvii. 1979 Substances which retain moisture are known as humectants. They..prevent loss of moisture when incorporated into the foodstuff. **1954** *Chem. & Engin. News* 15 Feb. 685/2 The product can be used as..a humectant for cellulose and paper products, polishes, and tobacco. **1963** *Residue Rev.* II. 54 Some humectants have been used experimentally to reduce evaporation under conditions of low humidity... Rain can, of course, wash the chemical from the leaf surface. **1972** *Sci. Amer.* Mar. 19/3 Humectants, which are hygroscopic, offset changes in the humidity of the environment to which food is exposed.

†**hu'mectate**, *ppl. a. Obs.* [ad. L. *hūmectāt-us*, pa. pple. of *hūmectāre.*] Moistened, wetted.

1432–50 tr. *Higden* (Rolls) I. 267 The white neckes schalle be humectate or made weiete with golde.

humectate (hju:'mɛkteɪt), *v.* Now *rare.* [f. L. *hūmectāt-*, ppl. stem of *hūmectāre* to HUMECT.] = HUMECT 1. Hence **hu'mectating** *ppl. a.*

1640 HOWELL *Dodona's Gr.* 13 Divided into sluces, to humectat the bordering soyle. **1644** DIGBY *Nat. Bodies* I. xxxv. (1645) 370 When we eate, nature draweth a moysture into our mouth, to humectate our meate. **1727–41** CHAMBERS *Cycl.* s.v. *Copal*, A warming, resolving, and humectating power. [**1855** *Househ. Words* XII. 449 To humectate the evening breeze on the Pincian Hill.]

humectation (hju:mɛk'teɪʃən). [a. F. *humectation* (14th c. in Littré) or ad. late L. *(h)ūmectātiōn-em*, n. of action f. *(h)ūmectāre* to HUMECT.]

1. The action or process of moistening or wetting; irrigation; the condition of being moistened or wet.

1544 PHAER *Pestilence* (1553) L ij b, Ther vpon folowed the excessiue humectacyon or moisting of mans body. **1610** BARROUGH *Meth. Physick* VI. iii. (1639) 363 The Humectation or moistnes of the uvula. **1773** *Phil. Trans.* LXIII. 407 If..the humectation exceeds the evaporation, the body at length wets through. **1849** CDL. WISEMAN *Ess.*, *Sense v. Science* (1853) III. 589 The requisite degree of humectation.

b. *Old Chemistry.* (See quot.)

1706 PHILLIPS (ed. Kersey), *Humectation*,...in Pharmacy and Chymistry, the moistening of a mixt Body in order to prepare it for some Operation, or for the more easy drawing out of its best or finest Parts.

c. *Path.* (See quot.)

1886 *Syd. Soc. Lex.*, *Humectation*,.. The term has been applied in the same sense as œdema or serous infiltration.

†2. Liquefaction. *Obs.*

1477 NORTON *Ord. Alch.* vi. in Ashm. (1652) 95 Vessells broade for Humectation. **1656** STANLEY *Hist. Philos.* VI. (1701) 255/1 Humectation..is the concretion of a vapour into water, or liquefaction of a solid Body, as Metal.

†**hu'mectative**, *a. Obs.* [f. L. *hūmectāt-*, ppl. stem of *hūmectāre* to HUMECT + -IVE.] Tending to moisten.

1640 *Erotomania* 321 The..Diet..ought to be somewhat more Humectative, and lesse Refrigerative. **1657** TOMLINSON *Renou's Disp.* 181 Lubricated with humectative aliments.

†**humec'tator.** *Obs.* [f. HUMECTATE *v.*: see -OR.] One who or that which moistens; a moistener.

1669 M. N. *Med. Medicinae* 283 Their Humectators and Coolers in Hecticks.

hu'mective, *a.* and *sb. rare.* [irreg. f. HUMECT *v.* + -IVE. Cf. *adaptive.*] A. *adj.* = HUMECTATIVE. B. *sb.* = HUMECTANT *sb.* 1.

1633 A. H. *Parthenia Sacra* 218 (T.) These fountain-waters have an humective and vegetative virtue within them. **1828** *Blackw. Mag.* XXIII. 593 Emollients, aperitives,..humectives, and absorbents.

humefy, var. HUMIFY (after L. *hūmefacere*).

humelich, -lie, -ly, var. HUMILY, humbly.

humeral ('hju:mərəl), *a.* and *sb.* [ad. late L. **humerāl-is*, used as sb. neut. *(h)umerāle* covering for the shoulders, f. *(h)umerus* shoulder. Cf. F. *huméral* (1541 in Hatz.-Darm.).]

A. *adj.* 1. *Anat.* Of or pertaining to the humerus or upper arm in man, or to the homogenetic bone in other vertebrates.

e.g. ***humeral artery, muscle, vein. humeral cincture***, a belt of bones bearing the pectoral fin of a fish, by some considered homogenetic with the humerus.

1615 CROOKE *Body of Man* 901 It lyeth vnder the foresaide humerall veyne where the Median or Common veyne ariseth thereout. **1650** BULWER *Anthropomet.* 162 Humeral or Shoulder-affectations. **1696** PHILLIPS (ed. 5), *Humeral Muscle*, the Muscle that moves the Arm at the upper End. **1760** WHITE in *Phil. Trans.* LI. 659 The danger of wounding the humeral artery. **1854** OWEN *Skel. & Teeth* in *Circ. Sc.*, *Organ. Nat.* I. 190 The scapula..divides at its humeral end into an acromial and coracoid process.

2. Of or pertaining to the shoulder or shoulders.

humeral veil (*Eccl.*): an oblong vestment of silk worn round the shoulders in various rites and enveloping the hands when holding sacred vessels.

1853 DALE tr. *Baldeschi's Ceremonial* 71 On the credence he will place the humeral veil. **1885** *Catholic Dict.* (ed. 3) 415/2 The use of the humeral veil at Benediction is strictly prescribed in several decrees of the Congregation of Rites.

3. Of or belonging to the part called HUMERUS in insects or other invertebrates.

a. Belonging to the humerus or femur of the fore-leg of an insect, or to the second joint of the pedipalp of a spider. b. Belonging to the anterior corner of the thorax in *Diptera*. c. Pertaining to the exterior front angle of the elytrum in *Coleoptera*.

1819 SAMOUELLE *Entomol. Compend.* 169 Humeral spot on the elytra. **1826** KIRBY & SP. *Entomol.* III. xxxv. 620 In the Homopterous Hemiptera the three axes may be readily traced, but the humeral plate..is more irregular in shape. *Ibid.* IV. xlvi. 333 Humeral Angle (*Angulus Humeralis*), the exterior basal angle. **1880** CAMPBELL *Jrnl. Linn. Soc.* XV. No. 83. 154 The humeral joint of each palpus.

B. *sb.*

1. *Eccl.* †a. A part of the Jewish sacerdotal vestment, worn on the shoulder. *Obs.* b. = *humeral veil* (A. 2).

1641 TRAPP *Comm. Exod.* xxviii. 14 These chains wherewith the breast-plate and humeral were tied.

2. The second joint, counting from the base, of the pedipalp of a spider (*Cent. Dict.*).

humero- ('hju:mərəʊ), used as combining form of L. *humerus* shoulder, in the sense 'pertaining to the humerus and (some other part)', as ***humero-abdominal, -cubital, -digital, -dorsal, -metacarpal, -olecranal, -radial.***

1884 FLOWER in *Jrnl. Anthropol. Inst.* Nov. 17 The humero-radial index which forms one of the most important differences between the skeleton of the Andamanese and the European. **1886** *Syd. Soc. Lex.*, *Humero-cubital*, relating to the upper arm and the forearm. *Humero-cubita, articulation*, the elbow-joint. *Ibid.*, *Humero-olecranal*, relating to the humerus and the olecranon.

†**'humerous**, *a. Obs. rare*⁻⁰. [ad. L. type **humerōsus*, f. *humerus* shoulder.] 'That hath great shoulders' (Blount *Glossogr.* 1656).

‖**humerus** ('hju:mərəs). *Anat.* Pl. -i. [L. (more correctly *umerus*) = shoulder, (rarely) upper arm.] The bone of the upper arm, extending from the shoulder-joint to the elbow-joint; the homogenetic bone in other vertebrates.

[**1578** BANISTER *Hist. Man* IV. 51 b, The same bone in Latin is called *Humerus*, which in English is shoulder.] **1706** PHILLIPS (ed. Kersey), *Humerus*, the Shoulder; the Shoulder-bone or first Bone of the Arm. **1727–41** CHAMBERS *Cycl.* s.v., At the lower end of the humerus are two processes, covered each with a cartilage. **1851** RICHARDSON *Geol.* viii. 295 Sockets for lodging the round head of the arm-bones, the humeri. **1875** BLAKE *Zool.* 89 The humerus is cylindrical, longest in Pelicans.

b. Applied by Cuvier to the proscapula, by Owen to the mesocoracoid, of fishes.

1854 OWEN in *Circle Sc.*, *Org. Nat.* I. 176 In the salmon ..The radius, after expanding to unite with the humerus, the ulna, and the radial carpals, sends a long and broad process downwards and inwards.

c. The third joint of the anterior pair of legs of insects.

1826 KIRBY & SP. *Entomol.* III. 369 *Humerus*, the third and elongated joint of the Brachium, answering to the Femur in the legs.

d. A corneous plate on the exterior front angle of the elytrum in *Coleoptera*.

1826 KIRBY & SP. *Entomol.* III. xxxv. 619 If you carefully extract one [wing] from the stag-beetle..the first thing that will strike you, upon examining the base, will be the plate.. called by Chabrier the *humerus*.

e. Applied by some to the anterior corner of the thorax, the 'shoulder', of an insect; by Walker, to the subcostal or submarginal vein of the forewing of certain *Hymenoptera.* (*Cent. Dict.*)

humest, var. UMEST, *Obs.*, uppermost.

†**humet**, *sb.*¹ *Her. Obs.* Also 6 h(e)umette. (See also HAWMED.) [? a. OF. **heaumet* dim. of *heaume* the bar of the helm or rudder.] A fess or bar so couped that its extremities do not touch the sides of the shield.

1572 BOSSEWELL *Armorie* II. 121 The fielde is d'Ermine, iij Humettes gules..The Heumettes borne in the armes before descried. **1586** FERNE *Blaz. Gentrie* 172 That tearme Humet is very new. **1592** WYRLEY *Armorie* 86 In Ermins sheild three hamets red he bare.

†**humet**, *sb.*² *Obs.* [? f. L. *hum-us* ground; or ? the same as prec. which is figured as a long rectangle.] A slab of stone, as a tombstone, placed upon the ground.

a **1645** HABINGTON *Survey Worc.* in *Worc. Hist. Soc. Proc.* III. 482 On a humet or ground tombe. **1688** R. HOLME *Armoury* III. iii. 94/1 A Taylor sitting upon a square Table (Stone or Humett, as some term it).

†**humet**, *a. Obs.* Also erron. **humid** (cf. HAWMED). An abbrev. of HUMETTY.

1661 MORGAN *Sph. Gentry* II. v. 47 This is called Humet by reason it is severed from the sides of the Escocheon. **1704** J. HARRIS *Lex. Techn.* s.v., Bloom, in his Heraldry, gives you a Fesse of this Form, which he calls, *Fesse Humid.* **1766** [see HUMETTY].

†**humetted**, *a. Her. Obs.* = next.

1586 FERNE *Blaz. Gentrie* 183 Cheuerons are borne crenelly, quarterly, counterly or transmuted, humetted, or truncked.

humetty (hju:'mɛtɪ), *a. Her.* Also -é, -ee. [f. HUMET + -Y = Fr. *-é.*] Said of an ordinary (as a cross, fesse, chevron, etc.) of which the extremities are couped or cut off so as not to reach the sides of the escutcheon.

1572 BOSSEWELL *Armorie* III. 1 b, Thys Crosse..beyng humette and ragueled. **1766** PORNY *Heraldry* Dict., *Humet* or *Humetty.* **1809** *Naval Chron.* XXI. 189 Azure a cheveron, humetty between three covered cups or. **1868–82** CUSSANS *Her.* iv. (ed. 3) 61 The Cross humetté, or couped, as its name implies, has its extremities cut off.

humgruffin (hʌm'grʌfɪn). [A made-up word, from *hum, gruff, griffin.*] 'A terrible or repulsive person' (Davies). Also **humgruffian**.

1825 J. K. PAULDING *John Bull in Amer.* iv. 29 Another declared she would not give a pin to save such a rude humgruffian from starvation. **1842** BARHAM *Ingol. Leg.* Ser. II. *St. Cuthbert*, One horrid Humgruffin, who seem'd by his talk, And the airs he assumed, to be cock of the walk.

†**humh**, *int. Obs.* [An inarticulate sound, more exactly *h'mh* (with aspirated *m*).] = HUMPH *int.*

1603 DEKKER *Wonderfull Yeare* E iij, Hee only shooke his head at this, and cried humh!

humhum. *Hist.* Also 7 **hammome, hummum,** 8 **hump-hump.** [Origin obscure.] A coarse Indian cotton cloth.

1620 in W. Foster *Eng. Factories India 1618–21* (1906) 193 Of sahannes and hammomes thiere are but fewe at presant in towne. **1687** *London Gaz.* No. 2269/2, 4172 pieces of Hummums. **1695** J. F. *Merch. Wareho. laid Open* 22, I shall begin with a Callico called Hummums. **1745** in J. F. Watson *Ann. Philad.* (1830) 179 Quilted humhums, turkettees, grassetts, [etc.]. **1801** in C. Cist *Cincinnati in 1841* (1841) 179 Among other goods..hum-hums. **1809** P. FRENEAU *Poems* I. 31 Hum-hums are here—and muslins—what you please. **1820** *Massachusetts Spy* 5 Jan. (Th.), The bleach rotted linen..or the sleazy humhum. **1894** A. M. EARLE *Costume Colonial Times* 142 *Hum-hum*, a plain coarse-meshed Indian fabric made of cotton, much advertised in the middle of the [18th] century. We read of 'blue Hum-hums' and 'Hump-humps for Sacks' for sale in various Boston newspapers, from 1750 to 1770. **1952** *Brewer's Dict. Phr. & Fable* (rev. ed.) 477/1 Humhum (U.S.A.), a thin cambric material.

Humian: see HUMEAN.

humic ('hju:mɪk), *a.* [f. L. *humus* ground, mould + -IC.] Of or pertaining to humus or mould; present in or of the nature of humus; rich in humus; also, formed or derived from plant remains. ***humic acid***, an acid found in humus or derived from it by boiling with an alkali.

1844 PETZHOLDT *Lect. Farmers Agric. Chem.* 93 A substance..which has been called humic acid. **1863** LYELL *Antiq. Man* viii. (ed. 3) 148 Mr. Staring..has attributed the general scarcity of human bones in Dutch peat..to the power of the humic and sulphuric acids to dissolve bones. **1891** *Chem. News* 22 May 248/2 The part played by humic matters in the fixation of nitrogen. **1918** STOPES & WHEELER *Monogr. Constit. Coal* 19/2 Potonié's separation of coals into two main groups, sapropelic and humic, is now widely adopted... But the use of the phrase 'humic coals' is much

in want of elucidation, as it, too, is given different meanings by different authors. As used by Potonié and most palæontologists, it means that the coal was formed from 'humic débris', or the various largely undecayed accumulations of mixed organs of plants... When the word 'humic' is applied to coals by chemists.. it may convey the implication that 'humic acid' exists in the substance of the coal. **1936** S. A. WAKSMAN *Humus* iii. 62 One may.. feel justified in abandoning without reservation the whole nomenclature of 'humic acids'. **1954** W. FRANCIS *Coal* v. 245 Humic substances are the major constituents of all normal coals. **1957** G. E. HUTCHINSON *Treat. Limnol.* I. ix. 609 The peaty sediments (*dy*) of brown humic lakes. **1960** N. POLUNIN *Introd. Plant Geogr.* xv. 497 Humic matter in solution may result in a browning of waters coming in from leached soils. **1966** B. SIMPSON *Rocks & Minerals* xx. 234 The first group is the Humic Coals in which woody tissue is of paramount importance in the composition... The second group, the Sapropelic Coals, have little woody tissue in their composition. **1971** *Nature* 19 Nov. 150/2 They are usually found in moist, humic soil, often near water.

humicubation (hjuːmɪkjuːˈbeɪʃən). [ad. L. type **humicubātiōn-em*, f. *humī* on the ground + *cubātio*, f. *cubāre* to lie down.] Lying down on the ground, esp. as a sign of penitence or humiliation.

1656 BRAMHALL in Hobbes *Lib., Necess., & Chance* 145 Fasting and Sackcloth, and Ashes, and Tears, and Humicubations, used to be companions of Repentance. **1662** GUNNING *Lent Fast* 195 That fasting be not divorc'd from its primitive society of watchings, humicubations, sorrowings. **1833** J. H. NEWMAN *Ch. of Fathers* (1842) 255 Frequent watchings, humicubations, and the like.

humid (ˈhjuːmɪd), *a.* Also 6–7 **humide**. [a. F. *humide* (15th c. in Hatz.-Darm.) or ad. L. *hūmid-us*, more correctly *ūmid-us*, f. *ūmēre* to be moist.] Slightly wet as with steam, suspended vapour, or mist; moist, damp.

1549 *Compl. Scot.* vi. 58 The rane.. is ane exalatione of humid vapours. **1632** J. HAYWARD tr. *Biondi's Eromena* 54 Such musicke, as.. drew humid lamentations from the driest eyes. **1667** MILTON *P.L.* IX. 193 The humid Flours, that breathd Thir morning Incense. **1766** GOLDSM. *Vic. W.* xxiii, Those mouldering walls and humid floor. **1870** YEATS *Nat. Hist. Comm.* 14 Ireland is more humid than England.

b. In mediæval physiology, said of elements, humours, etc.

1604 JAS. I. *Counterbl.* (Arb.) 102 Because the Braines are colde and humide. **1637** GILLESPIE *Eng. Pop. Cerem.* III. ix. 200 The complexion of a woman.. is more humide then the complexion of a man. **1809** *Med. Jrnl.* XXI. 199 When the choleric, phlegmatic, sanguine, and melancholic temperaments, are said to be occasioned by a humid and dry, hot and cold constitution.

c. Said of a chemical process in which liquid is used.

1800 tr. *Lagrange's Chem.* I. 411 It is a reduction in the humid way. **1816** J. SMITH *Panorama Sc. & Art* II. 480 Crystallization is of two kinds, the dry and the humid;.. the humid crystallization refers to fluids and gases holding solids in solution. **1838** T. THOMSON *Chem. Org. Bodies* 373 Iodine does not act sensibly in the humid way.

d. Of diseases: Marked by a moist discharge.

1813 J. THOMSON *Lect. Inflam.* 507 The French [usually express this difference] by those of humid and dry gangrenes. **1822–34** *Good's Study Med.* (ed. 4) IV. 484 Laminated Humid Scall.

Hence **humidly** *adv.*; **humidness**, moistness.

1727 BAILEY vol. II, *Humidness*, moisture. **1886** C. GIBBON *Clare of Claresmede* II. xi. 172 There was.. fear in her humidly bright eyes.

† **ˈhumidate**, *v. Obs.* [f. L. *hūmidāt-*, ppl. stem of *hūmidāre*, f. *hūmidus* HUMID.] *trans.* To make humid or moist; to moisten.

c **1540** BOORDE *The Boke for to Lerne* C iij b, Immoderat slepe and sluggyshnes doth humi[d]ate and make lyght the brayne. **1656** BLOUNT *Glossogr.*, *Humidate*, to moisten.

humidification (hjuːˌmɪdɪfɪˈkeɪʃən). [f. HUMIDIFY *v.*: see -FICATION.] The process of making moist or humid; *esp.* the process of rendering the air humid by means of special apparatus or techniques.

1890 J. NASMITH *Mod. Cotton Spinning Machinery* 10 The [spinning] rooms.. should be heated to a certain temperature. Closely allied to this question is that of humidification. It is not only essential to have heat, but that must be accompanied by.. moisture. **1940** A. C. Noé tr. *Stutzer's Geol. Coal* viii. 307 A peculiar case of weathering and humidification of coal is found in karst districts, producing a sooty material... The sootiness is caused by the access of karst water. **1945** *Times* 31 Aug. 2/3 Air-conditioning with humidification and cleaning by electrical filtration. **1970** D. KUT *Warm Air Heating* viii. 124 Humidification of the air prevents the build-up of static electricity.

humidify (hjuːˈmɪdɪfaɪ), *v.* [f. HUMID *a.* + -FY.] *trans.* To render humid or moist; to moisten, damp. Hence **huˈmidified** *ppl. a.*; **huˈmidifier**, an apparatus for rendering the atmosphere moist.

1884 *Health Exhib. Catal.* 109/1 Lacy's Patent Humidifier. **1885** J. J. MANLEY *Brit. Almanac Comp.* 25 Air-heating, cooling, and humidifying apparatus for workshops. **1898** *Pop. Sci. Monthly* LII. 470 Potted plants.. sufficed to humidify the air. **1921** C. V. EKROTH in A. Rogers *Industr. Chem.* (ed. 3) li. 1164 Humidified air keeps the exposed surfaces of the food soft and permeable. **1956** H. WILLIAMSON *Methods Bk. Design* xxii. 358 Specially humidified paper will have to be wrapped in waterproof material. **1971** *Nature* 24 Dec. 471/2 They.. are maintained at 36° C in a humidified atmosphere of 5% CO_2 in air.

† **huˈmidious**, *a. rare*⁻¹. [irreg. f. L. *humid-us* HUMID + -(I)OUS.] Moist, wet, watery.

1630 J. TAYLOR (Water P.) *World's Eighth Wond.* 45 Wks. II. 62/1 The great humidious Monarch tells him plaine 'Twere best he iogd from his commanding Maine.

humidistat (hjuːˈmɪdɪstæt). Also **humidostat**. [f. HUMIDI(TY (or HUMID *a.* + -O) + -STAT.]

1. (See quot.) *rare.* ? *Obs.*

1909 *Cent. Dict.* Suppl., *Humidostat*, a small chest or cabinet lined with sheet-metal and fitted with some device for holding a damp sponge or piece of felt: used to keep cigars moist.

2. An automatic apparatus for regulating the humidity of the air in a room or building; also called a *hygrostat*.

1918 ALLEN & WALKER *Heating & Ventilation* xvi. 248 In a compressed-air system of control, a diaphragm valve.. may be operated by means of a 'hygrostat' or 'humidostat', which corresponds to the thermostat of a temperature control system. **1936** *Archit. Rev.* LXXX. p. lxviii/1 The control consists of a thermostat, a humidistat and a change-over rotary switch which together control the supply of hot or cold humidified or dehumidified air as required. **1970** I. G. WALLS *Greenhouse Gardening* viii. 55 Humidistats can be used.. to put into operation mist nozzles in an air stream.

humidity (hjuːˈmɪdɪtɪ). Also 5 **humedite, vmydite, humidyte**, 5–6 **humidite(e**, etc. [a. F. *humidité* (14th c. in Hatz.-Darm.), ad. L. *hūmiditāt-em*, f. *hūmidus* HUMID.]

1. The quality or condition of being humid; moistness, dampness.

relative humidity (of the atmosphere) in *Meteorol.*, the amount of moisture which it contains as compared with that of complete saturation at the given temperature.

c **1450** BURGH *Secrees* 1906 Ffor Chaung of Complexioun by drynesse or humydite. **1542** BOORDE *Dyetary* xviii. (1870) 277 All maner of flesshe the whiche is inclyned to humydyte. **1615** G. SANDYS *Trav.* 129 By reason of the humidity of the Northerne wind, which here is the moystest. **1729** S. SWITZER *Hydrost. & Hydraul.* 207 This Hygrometer.. the use whereof is to find out precisely the Humidity and Siccity of the Air. **1820** SCORESBY *Acc. Arctic Reg.* I. 380 The relative humidity of the atmosphere, as indicated by a hygrometer. **1871** TYNDALL *Fragm. Sc.* (1879) I. ii. 58 A day of average humidity in England.

2. *concr.* Fluid matter that makes a body humid; moisture (diffused through a gas as vapour or through a solid substance, or condensed upon a surface); damp.

1412–20 LYDG. *Chron. Troy* I. vi. (MS. Digby 230), After þat ver haþ made out of þe roote The humydite kyndely to ascende. **1528** PAYNEL *Salerne's Regim.* A iv b, Blud.. is very nere like humidite whiche is as fundation of lyfe. **1656** STANLEY *Hist. Philos.* VI. (1701) 260/1 Death.. cometh.. when through want of Refrigeration the Radical Humidity is consumed and dried up. **1727** BRADLEY *Fam. Dict.* s.v. *Guaiacum*, The watery Humidity call'd Phlegm. **1893** SIR R. BALL *In High Heavens* 277 When the heat was greatest.. the air was.. largely charged with humidity.

b. *pl.* The humours and juices of animals and plants. (Cf. HUMOUR *sb.* 2.)

c **1400** *Lanfranc's Cirurg.* 28 Anoþer maner fleisch þer is þat is glandelose.. & his Iuuament is þat he turne humedites [*B.* vmydites], þat is to seie moistnes to her heete. **1691** WOOD *Ath. Oxon.* (R.), Imbibing the superfluous humidities of the body. **1725** BRADLEY *Fam. Dict.* s.v. *Pomegranate-tree*, This Mould.. and its Salts.. will.. penetrate the Roots of the Pomegranate-Trees, by Means of the Humidities which draw them thither.

humidor (ˈhjuːmɪdɔː(r)). [f. HUMID *a.*, after *cuspidor*.] A box, cabinet, or room in which cigars or tobacco are kept moist; also, any apparatus, such as damp sponges, for keeping cigars, the atmosphere, etc., moist.

1903 *Sun* (N.Y.) 4 Mar. 6/3 (Funk), A humidor as large as a small cottage occupies most of the ground floor. **1922** *Detective Mag.* Nov. 100 The cigar was soft and fresh from the humidor. **1927** P. MARKS *Lord of Himself* 198 Take a cigarette out of that humidor. **1955** STURDEVANT & BRAUER in J. C. Brauer *Dental Asst.* xx. 287 The impression should be stored in a humidor in order to minimize dimensional change. **1963** *Punch* 8 May 669/1 Champagne coolers and waste-paper baskets, to say nothing of door-stops and humidors. **1973** R. HAYES *Hungarian Game* viii. 61, I fumbled with the F.O.'s humidor for a Havanna.

† **huˈmiferous**, *a. Obs. rare*⁻⁰. [f. L. *(h)ūmifer* containing moisture, f. stem of *(h)ūm-ēre*, *(h)ūm-idus*, *(h)ūm-or*: see -FEROUS.] 'Waterish, that brings moisture' (Blount *Glossogr.* 1656).

† **humific** (hjuːˈmɪfɪk), *a. rare*⁻⁰. [ad. late L. *(h)ūmific-us* moistening, f. as prec. + *-fic-us* -FIC.] 'Causing moisture' (Bailey, vol. II. 1727).

humifuse (ˈhjuːmɪfjuːs), *a. Bot.* [ad. mod.L. *humīfūsus*, f. *humī* on the ground + *fūsus*, pa. pple. of *fundĕre* to pour, extend, spread.] (See quot.)

1854 MAYNE *Expos. Lex.*, *Humifusus*, applied to the stalk of vegetables when it runs or stretches along the surface of the ground, but without sending out roots: humifuse. **1866** *Treas. Bot.*

humify (ˈhjuːmɪfaɪ), *v.*¹ *rare.* Also 8 **humefy**. [ad. late L. *(h)ūmificāre*, f. *(h)ūmificus* moistening (see HUMIFIC and -FY).] *trans.* To render humid; to moisten. So **humifiˈcation**¹, moistening.

1651 BIGGS *New Disp.* ¶ 229 To refresh the thirst a little by the dregs of humification. **1658** R. WHITE tr. *Digby's Powd. Symp.* (1660) 22 The earth, which is humified either by rain, or the dew. **1774** GOLDSM. *Nat. Hist.* (1790) I. ix. 89 Marcasites and pyrites.. by being humefied with water or air, contract this heat.

humify (ˈhjuːmɪfaɪ), *v.*² [f. HUM(US + -IFY.]

a. *trans.* To convert (plant remains) into humus. **b.** *intr.* To undergo humification. So **ˈhumified** *ppl. a.*

1906 E. W. HILGARD *Soils* (1930) viii. 132 Excluding the unhumified while fully dissolving the humified matter. *Ibid.* viii. 139 Snyder.. caused various substances to humify by mixing the pulverized material intimately with a soil poor in humus. **1926** *Technol. Rep. Tôhoku Imp. Univ.* VI. I. 10 As humification advances more and more, the cell walls are quite humified. **1936** S. A. WAKSMAN *Humus* iv. 64 Plant material added to the soil has first to be 'humified' before the nutrient elements contained therein become available for plant growth. **1948** G. W. LEEPER *Introd. Soil Sci.* xi. 136 Residues of plants are said to be humified when they lose their structure and identity in the soil.

So **humifiˈcation**², the process by which plant remains are converted into humus; the state of being humified that results.

1897 *Minnesota Agric. Exper. Station Bull.* No. 53. 13 Analyses were made of both the soil, and the material used for humus production. After the humification process had been carried on for a year the material was weighed and analyzed. **1926** [see above]. **1958** F. E. ZEUNER *Dating Past* (ed. 4) iii. 64 A change in the rate of peat-growth from a slow one (allowing humification to begin in the layers near the surface), [etc.]. **1968** R. G. WEST *Pleistocene Geol. & Biol.* iv. 54 The amount of humification may be measured in the field by adding a little sediment to a few ml of dilute KOH.

† **humil, -ile**, *a. Obs.* Chiefly *Sc.* Also 5 **-yll**, 6 **-yle, -ill**. [ad. L. *humil-is* humble; in 16th c. F. also *humile*, 12th c. *humele*.] Humble.

c **1470** HENRY *Wallace* IV. 1, September, the humyll moneth suette, Quhen passyt by the hycht was off the hette. **1500–20** DUNBAR *Poems* ix. 4, I repent my synnys with humill hairt contreit. **1533** GAU *Richt Vay* 24 He that hes perfit lwiff in hime [God] he is humil, and redy to serwe euerie man. **1542** BOORDE *Dyetary* x. (1870) 225 Andrew Borde.. doth surrender humyle commendacyon. **1567** *Gude & Godlie B.* (S.T.S.) 96 Humill men sall inhereit the eird.

b. Of a plant: Of lowly growth.

1567 MAPLET *Gr. Forest* 32 The Balme tree.. his lowe and humile kinde of growth.

† **humile, humily**, *v. Obs.* Also 6 **-yle, -yll, -ill**. [In 15th c. *humilye*, a. F. *humilier*, ad. L. *humiliāre* to humble (see HUMILIATE); in 16th c. usually *humil, -ile*, after prec. adj.] *trans.* To humble, to humiliate.

1491 CAXTON *Vitas Patr.* (W. de W. 1495) II. 226 b/1 The herte contryte and humylyed. **1502** *Ord. Crysten Men* (W. de W. 1506) IV. i. 167 He is excessyuely humylyed. *Ibid.* IV. xxi. 260 Therfore they ought to fere & them humyle before god. **1523** LD. BERNERS *Froiss.* I. ccxi. 255 A care that greatly humiled the kynges courage. **1533** GAU *Richt Vay* 43 Quhow the sone of God humilit hime of his hie maieste. **1562** WINJET *Cert. Tractates* Wks. 1888 I. 33 The potent Spirit of God mot humyll ȝour hertis.

humiliant (hjuːˈmɪlɪənt), *a. rare.* [ad. L. *humiliānt-em*, pres. pple. of *humiliāre* to HUMILIATE.] Humiliating.

1844 MRS. BROWNING *Drama of Exile* iii, By my percipiency of sin and fall And melancholy of humiliant thoughts.

humiliate (hjuːˈmɪlɪeɪt), *v.* [f. *humiliāt-*, ppl. stem of late L. *humiliāre*, f. *humili-s* HUMBLE *a.*¹ Cf. F. *humilier*.]

† **1.** *trans.* To make low or humble in position, condition, or feeling; to humble. *refl.* To humble or abase oneself, to stoop; sometimes, to prostrate oneself, to bow. *Obs.*

1533–4 in *Suppression Monasteries* (Camden) 22 We be.. set in comforte to humyliate our selfes as prostrate afore your highnes. **1577** tr. *Fisher's Treat. Prayer* (R.), For God his wyll is, that we should humiliate and deiect our selues in the sight of his maiestie. **1601–2** FULBECKE *1st Pt. Parall.* 20 Such a religious man may not.. humiliate him-selfe to execute the rite of homage. **1621** BURTON *Anat. Mel.* I. iii. I. iv. (1676) 121 How much we ought to.. examine and humiliate our selves, seek to God, and call to him for mercy. **1656** BLOUNT, *Humiliate*, to make low or humble. **1656** B. HARRIS *Parival's Iron Age* I. xvii. 128 They might well fear, lest all the States of Germany humiliated, or joyned to those of the Emperour, he might come and re-demand some Towns amongst them. **1776** S. J. PRATT *Pupil of Pleas.* II. 17 He whom indigence and the strokes of ill-fortune have not.. humiliated.

2. To lower or depress the dignity or self-respect of; to subject to humiliation; to mortify.

1757 [see HUMILIATING *ppl. a.*]. **1796** W. TAYLOR in *Monthly Rev.* XX. 570 The luxury of individuals often.. humiliates those who miss its delights. **1817** SOUTHEY *Lett.* (1856) III. 66, I have.. to complain of my counsel.. for humiliating me. **1824** W. IRVING *T. Trav.* I. 113 Mere donations.. humiliate as much as they relieve. **1874** GREEN *Short Hist.* vii. §3. 362 The country was humiliated by defeat. **1879** CHR. ROSSETTI *Seek & F.* 161 When we ask to be humbled, we must not recoil from being humiliated.

Hence **huˈmiliated** *ppl. a.*

1782 MRS. E. BLOWER *Geo. Bateman* I. 81 Bateman was at that period in a humiliated state of mind. **1810** SOUTHEY *Ess.* (1832) I. 25 What a spirit would be kindled throughout

groaning and humiliated Europe! **1886** W. J. TUCKER *E. Europe* 280 The humiliated tillers of the soil.

humiliate, *a.* and *sb.* [ad. late L. *humiliāt-us*, pa. pple. of *humiliāre* (see prec.).]

A. *adj.* †a. Humiliated, humbled (*obs.*). b. Belonging to the order of Humiliates.

1593 NASHE *Christ's T.* (1613) 81 They would be more humiliate and deiected. **1880** *Libr. Univ. Knowl.* (N.Y.) VII. 689 A female order of Benedictines, known as humiliate nuns, or nuns of Blassoni.

†B. *sb.* (*With capital H.*) One of an order of monks and nuns who affected great humility in dress, behaviour, and occupation. *Obs.*

1611 SPEED *Hist. Gt. Brit.* IX. viii. (1632) 554 Nor were those wylie Humiliates regardlesse of choosing a delicate plot.. where hee built a goodly Abbey of their Order. **1656** BLOUNT *Glossogr.*, *Humiliates*, a Religious Order, instituted about the year 1166 by certain persons exiled by Fredericus Barbarossa.

humiliating (hjuːˈmɪlɪeɪtɪŋ), *ppl. a.* [f. HUMILIATE *v.* + -ING^1.] That humiliates; that lowers one's dignity or self-respect; abasing, mortifying.

1757 *Herald* I. ix. 147 To have demanded so humiliating a sacrifice of decorum. **1776** ADAM SMITH *W.N.* II. iii. (1869) I. 345 Bankruptcy is perhaps the greatest and most humiliating calamity which can befal an innocent man. **1834** MACAULAY *Ess.*, *Pitt* (1887) 320 The most humiliating of these events was the loss of Minorca. **1871** L. STEPHEN *Playgr. Europe* v. (1894) 127 A retreat.. would have been.. humiliating.

Hence **huˈmiliatingly** *adv.*, in a way that humiliates.

1782 H. ELLIOT *Let.* in *Life* viii. (1868) 250, I was very humiliatingly treated. **1842** R. ANDERSON *Regeneration* (1871) 99 How humiliatingly and sharply it convicts and reproves!

humiliation (ˌhjuːmɪlɪˈeɪʃən). [a. F. *humiliation* (14th c. in Hatz.-Darm.), ad. late L. *humiliātiōn-em*, n. of action from *humiliāre* to HUMILIATE.] The action of humiliating or condition of being humiliated; humbling, abasement. Formerly often = humbled or humble condition, humility.

c **1386** CHAUCER *Pars. T.* ¶406 The ferthe [manere of humylitee] is whan he nys nat sory of his humiliacion. **1490** CAXTON *Eneydos* iv. 18 Eneas knelyd doun on bothe his knees, bi grete humylyacyon of herte. **1552** ABP. HAMILTON *Catech.* (1884) 16 Tha war ordanit also for owr humiliatioun, instructioun and spiritual exercitioun. **1613** PURCHAS *Pilgrimage* (1614) 110 Receiving penitents.. having first before this washing testified their humiliation by fasting and prayer. **1648** *Shorter Catech. Westm. Assemb.* (1718) §23 Christ, as our Redeemer, executeth the offices of a Prophet, of a Priest, and of a King, both in his estate of humiliation and exaltation. **1678** BUNYAN *Pilgr.* I. 65 Yes, said Prudence,.. it is an hard matter for a man to go down into the valley of Humiliation, as thou art now, and to catch no slip by the way. **1700** S. L. tr. *Fryke's Voy. E. Ind.* 353 On the 10th, We kept a day of Fasting and Humiliation. **1771** *Junius Lett.* xlii. 221 Where will the humiliation of this country end? **1848** R. I. WILBERFORCE *Incarnation* vi. (1852) 162 As His Incarnation was the humiliation of His Godhead, so was His death the humiliation of His earthly nature. **1866** G. MACDONALD *Ann. Q. Neighb.* xiii. (1878) 273, I think 'humiliation' is a very different condition of mind from humility. 'Humiliation' no man can desire; it is shame and torture.

b. with *a* and *pl.*

1526 *Pilgr. Perf.* (W. de W. 1531) 79 Many voluntary humiliacyons in yᵉ waye to perfyte mekenes. **1751** SMOLLETT *Per. Pic.* (1779) I. xiv. 123 Nor would he pay the least regard to the humiliations and supplications of some among them. **1837** MACAULAY *Ess.*, *Bacon* (1887) 383 Incensed by multiplied wrongs and humiliations.

humiliative (hjuːˈmɪlɪətɪv), *a.* [f. L. *humiliāt-*, ppl. stem of *humiliāre* to HUMILIATE + -IVE.] Having a humiliating quality.

1810 BENTHAM *Packing* (1821) 23 Of these two.. the first mentioned may be termed the depressive or humiliative.

humiliator (hjuːˈmɪlɪeɪtə(r)). [Agent-n. in L. form, from *humiliāre*.] One who humiliates.

1850 H. H. WILSON tr. *Rig-veda* I. 135 The humiliator of his enemies. **1890** in *Daily News* 25 Jan. 5/6 That he was 'a grovelling humiliator of his distinguished race'.

huˈmiliatory, *a.* [f. as HUMILIAT-IVE + -ORY.] That tends to humiliate.

1872 RUSKIN *Aratra Pentilici* iii. 80 Of the impotence, take but this one, utterly humiliatory, and.. ghastly example.

humilific (hjuːmɪˈlɪfɪk), *a.* (*sb.*) Now *rare* or ? *Obs.* [f. L. *humilis* HUMBLE + -FIC.] Humiliating, self-depreciating, that humiliates or tends to humble; also as *sb.*, a humble expression. (Opp. to *honorific*.)

1892 *Spectator* 13 Feb. 244/1 Among the Chinese and Japanese.. merely honorific and humilific expressions. **1904** V. V. BANFORD in J. E. Hand *Ideals of Sci. & Faith* 120 The distinction between honorific and humilific occupations. **1905** D. SLADEN *Playing Game* I. vii, That conversation.., so full of the 'unfortunate mistake' vein, so burdened down with Japanese 'humilifics'.

†**humilist**. *Obs. rare*$^{-0}$. [f. L. *humil-is* HUMBLE + -IST.] = HUMILIATE *sb.*

1611 COTGR., *Humiliez*, the Humilists; Gray Friers of the Order of St. Bennet.

†**huˈmilitude**. *Obs. rare.* [f. L. *humili-s* HUMBLE + -TUDE.] Humility.

a **1586** SIR H. SIDNEY in *Lett. Abp. Ussher* (1686) App. 26 High Humilitudes take such deep root in the minds of the Multitude. **1702** C. MATHER *Magn. Chr.* II. iv. (1852) 127 With a sagacious humilitude he consented.

humility (hjuːˈmɪlɪtɪ). [a. F. *humilité* (earlier *umilitet*, 11th c. in Hatz.-Darm.), ad. L. *humilitāt-em*, f. *humilis* HUMBLE.]

1. The quality of being humble or having a lowly opinion of oneself; meekness, lowliness, humbleness: the opposite of *pride* or *haughtiness*.

c **1315** SHOREHAM 117 Thorȝ clennesse and humylyte. **1390** GOWER *Conf.* III. 200 And with full great humilite He suffreth his adversite. **1419** R. HOLME in Ellis *Orig. Lett.* Ser. II. I. 65 With all subjection and humilitee We recomend us to ȝoure roial Majestee. **1500–20** DUNBAR *Poems* lxx. 4 Thow that.. Gabriell send.. On-to the mayd of maist humilite. **1607** SHAKS. *Cor.* II. iii. 43 *stage direct.*, Enter Coriolanus in a gowne of Humility, with Menenius. *a* **1639** W. WHATELEY *Prototypes* I. xi. (1640) 99 That is true humility to have a meane esteeme of himselfe out of a true apprehension of Gods greatnesse. **1757** HUME *Ess.*, *Passions* (1817) II. 175 Humility.. is a dissatisfaction with ourselves on account of some defect or infirmity. **1873** HAMERTON *Intell. Life* II. i. (1876) 52 The humility which acknowledges present insufficiency.

b. with *pl.* An act of humility or self-abasement.

1612 DAVIES *Why Ireland* etc. (1747) 51 With these humilities.. they satisfied the young king. **1809–10** COLERIDGE *Friend* (1818) I. 32 All the tricksy humilities of the ambitious candidates for the favorable suffrages of the judicious Public.

2. Humble or low condition, rank, or estate; unpretentiousness, humbleness.

1623 COCKERAM, *Humilitie*, low estate, basenesse. **1757** FOOTE *Author* I. 8 But how will a Person of his Pride and Pedigree, relish the Humility of this Apartment? **1831** LAMB *Elia* Ser. II. *Ellistoniana*, I made a sort of apology for the humility of the fare. *c* **1838** DE QUINCEY *Shaks.* Wks. 1863 XV. 37 His course lay.. through the humilities of absolute poverty.

3. A local name of several N. American birds of the family *Scolopacidæ*.

1634 W. WOOD *New Eng. Prosp.* I. viii. (1865) 34 The Humilities or Simplicities (as I may rather call them) bee of two sorts, the biggest being as big as a greene Plover, the other as big as birds we call Knots in England. **1678** PHILLIPS (ed. 4), *Humility*, otherwise called Simplicity, a sort of Bird in New England. **1781** S. PETERS *Hist. Connecticut* 256 The Humility is so called because it speaks the word humility, and seldom mounts high in the air.

†**ˈhumilness**. *Obs.* Chiefly *Sc.* [f. HUMIL *a.* + -NESS.] Humbleness, humility.

1423 JAS. I *Kingis Q.* cxxvi, With dredefull humylnesse. *c* **1485** *Digby Myst.* (1882) IV. 479, I shall assiste you with all humylnesse. **1567** *Gude & Godlie B.* (S.T.S.) 75 Hartlie thankfulnes.. We offer the, Lord, with lawlie humilnes.

†**humily**, *adv. Obs.* Forms: 4 **humelich, -ili, -yly, -ely**, 4–6 **humly**, 5 **hummylly, homeliche, homly**, 6 **hum(e)lie, humilye**. [f. HUMIL(E *a.* + -LY^2. In 16th c. only *Sc.* It was united with the form *humbly* by the intermediate *humly*.] = HUMBLY.

1375 BARBOUR *Bruce* I. 578 He him thankit humyly. *c* **1380** *Sir Ferumb.* 2050 þe duk aunswerede þat mayde free, humelich & fayre. *a* **1400** *Pistill of Susan* 200 Homliche on hir heued heor hondus þei leyed. **1500–20** DUNBAR *Poems* x. 20 For he.. is cumin full humly. **1513** DOUGLAS *Æneis* XII. xiv. 121 Streik furth my handis humelie. **1552** LYNDESAY *Monarche* 6096 Full humilye he techeit ws. **1567** *Gude & Godlie B.* (S.T.S.) 104 Humlie I the exhort.

humin (ˈhjuːmɪn). *Chem.* [f. HUMUS + -IN.] A neutral substance existing, according to Mulder, in black humus.

1844 PETZHOLDT *Lect. Farmers Agric. Chem.* 93 To this the name *humine* or humus coal has been applied. **1869** E. A. PARKES *Pract. Hygiene* (ed. 3) 20 The organic vegetable matter consists of humin and ulmin, and of acids derived from humus. **1886** *Syd. Soc. Lex.*, *Humin*,.. the material in turf which is neither acid nor alkaline.

†**humiˈserpent**, *a. Obs. rare*$^{-1}$. [f. L. *humī* on the ground + *serpent-em*, pr. pple. of *serpĕre* to crawl.] Crawling on the ground.

1641 R. BROOKE *Eng. Episc.* I. ii. 3 He is *ex fæce plebis*, humi-serpent; of the lowest of the people.

Humism, -ist: see under HUMEAN.

humistratous (hjuːmɪˈstreɪtəs), *a. Bot.* [f. mod.L. *humīstrāt-us* (f. *humī* on the ground + *strātus* spread) + -OUS.] 'Spread over the surface of the ground' (Gray).

1880 GRAY *Struct. Bot.* (ed. 6) 415. **1886** *Syd. Soc. Lex.*

humite (ˈhjuːmaɪt). *Min.* [Named, 1813, after Sir Abraham Hume, of London.] A fluo-silicate of magnesium, long considered a variety of chondrodite, but now, on crystallographical grounds, made a distinct species.

1814 T. ALLAN *Min. Nomen.* 45 *Humite*, is a substance mentioned by Bournon. **1852** BROOKE & MILLER *Phillips' Min.* 353 Humite has been described.. as belonging to the prismatic system. **1895** STORY-MASKELYNE *Crystallogr.* §317 Twins of humite occur, twinned in two ways.

humlie, humblie. *Sc.* [f. HUMMEL *a.* + -Y.] A hummel or polled cow. Also *attrib.*, as ***humlie-cow***. In quots. 1818, 1825–80 *transf.*

1813 J. HEADRICK *Agric. Surv. Forfarsh.* 439 (Jam.) A great proportion of the permanent stock are humlies, that is, they have no horns. **1816** SCOTT *Old Mort.* iv, I gat the humlie-cow, that's the best in the byre.. for ten pund Scots. **1818** *E. Burt's Lett. N. Scotl.* II. 104 *note*, In the days of our grand-fathers the lower class of Highlanders, were.. denominated *humblies* from their wearing no covering on their head but their hair. **1825–80** JAMIESON, *Humlock, Humlie*, 'a polled cow; also a person whose head has been shaved, or hair cut'.

humlock, variant of HEMLOCK *sb.*

hummable (ˈhʌməb(ə)l), *a.* [f. HUM *v.*^{1} + -ABLE.] That may be hummed; apt for humming.

1941 *Time* 10 Nov. 54 Cole Porter's score, though never haunting, is often hummable. **1966** *New Statesman* 8 Apr. 512/2 Georges Delerue's music is a hummable element. **1970** *Daily Tel.* 19 Nov. 14/5 The soloist starts off with a most poetical and, what's more, hummable eleven note row. **1972** *Guardian* 11 Jan. 8/6 The hummable simplicity of Rome's melodies.

hummaul, hummaum: see HAMMAL, HAMMAM.

†**ˈhummel**, *sb. Sc. Obs.* [= MLG. and mod.G. *hummel* wild bee, drone, Du. *hommel* drone, = *humble* in HUMBLE-BEE.] A drone; a lazy fellow.

1500–20 DUNBAR *Poems* lx. 18 Wyld haschbaldis, haggarbaldis, and hummellis.

hummel (ˈhʌm(ə)l), **humble** (ˈhʌmb(ə)l), *a. Sc.* and *north. dial.* Forms: α. 5 **hommyl**, 6 **homill, hommil**, 8– **hummel**, (8 **hummle**). β. 7 **humbell**, 6– **humble**. [Corresponds to LGer. *hummel, hommel* hornless beast (hence draught-ox); cf. *hummelbock, hummelgeisz* a hornless goat, *humlich*, dial. *hommlich* hornless, Bav. *humlet* hornless. The earlier history of the word has not been traced: there may be radical connexion with HAMBLE to mutilate.]

1. a. Of cattle: Hornless, 'dodded'.

1536 BELLENDEN *Cron. Scot.* (1821) II. 164 Quhen uncouth ky fechtis amang thaimself, gif ane of thaim happenis to be slane, and uncertane quhat kow maid the slauchter, the kow that is homill sall beir the wyte. **1584** J. CARMICHAEL *Let.* in *Wodr. Soc. Misc.* (1844) 438 When we got it, it was but a Dun humble kow. **1775** JOHNSON *Journ. West. Isles, Ostig* Wks. X. 415 Of their black cattle, some are without horns, called by the Scots, humble cows.

transf. **1887** *Amer. Naturalist* Oct. 886 The lop-ear [in the zebu] is a decidedly 'hummel' characteristic.

b. Applied to a hornless stag. Also *absol.*

1907 *Spectator* 5 Jan. 11/1 The 'hummel' stag—that ungainly beast with no horns at all—is a better fighter than the 'switch-horn'. *Ibid.* 11/2 The supremacy of the 'hummels' and 'switch-horns' in battles with their own kind. **1925** J. BUCHAN *John Macnab* iv, A hummel, a great fellow of fully twenty stone. **1964** G. K. WHITEHEAD *Deer Gt. Brit. & Ireland* vii. 156 Some stags never grow any antlers at all and are known as hummels. These beasts would appear to be just as capable of breeding as their antlered brethren. **1972** *Country Life* 17 Feb. 424/3 The hummel or antlerless stag is not welcome on the purely sporting estate.

2. Of corn or grain: Awnless. ***hummel corn***, 'a term applied to the lighter grain of any kind, or that which falls from the rest when it is fanned' (Jam.); hence used attrib. 'mean, poor'.

1474 *Acta Audit.* (1839) 35/2, vii chalder of hommyll corne. *a* **1605** BIRREL *Diary* in Dalyell *Fragm. Scot. Hist.* (1798) 36 The ait maill 10 lib. the boll, the humbell corne 7 lib. the boll. **1792** *Statist. Acc. Scotl., Berwicksh.* IV. 386 The.. hinds.. receive 10 bolls oats, 2 bolls barley, and 1 boll peas, which two last articles are called hummel corn. **1870** RAMSAY *Remin.* (ed. 18) 87 A hummelcorn discourse.

†3. Broken, chapped, kibed. *Obs.*

1601 HOLLAND *Pliny* II. 128 In case of humble-heels he applied it sodden in oile.

hummel, humble, *v. Sc.* and *north. dial.* Also 9 homil, humel. [f. prec. adj.]

1. *trans.* To deprive of the horns: see HUMMELLED.

2. To remove the awns from (barley). See also quot. 1893.

? *a* **1800** *MS. Poem* (Jam.), Thair's bear tae hummil. **1822** HOGG *Perils of Man* II. 30 (Jam.) My heart dunt—duntit like a man humblin bear. **1893** *Northumbld. Gloss.*, *Homil*, to humble or remove the awns from barley... In breaking stones for macadamised roads, to *humel* means to break the lumps into smaller sizes preparatory to their being made the requisite size by a smaller hammer.

Hence **ˈhummelling, -eling** *vbl. sb.*

1835 *Penny Cycl.* III. 465/2 Barley requires care in thrashing, to break off all the awns close to the grain... It is often necessary.. to effect this by another operation.. called *hummeling*. **1851** *Illustr. Catal. Gt. Exhib.* 386 A barley aveller or hummelling machine.. for the purpose of rubbing the horns or avels off barley.. leaving the kernels clean.

†**hummel-bummel**. *Obs.* [Cf. HUMBLE *v.*^{2} and BUMBLE.] An imitation of mumbling.

1537–41 LYNDESAY *Kitteis Confess.* 44 And mekle Latyne he did mummill, I hard na thing but hummill bummill.

hummelled, -eled ('hʌm(ə)ld), **humbled** ('hʌmb(ə)ld), *a. north. dial.* Also 9 homilt, humelt. [f. HUMMEL *v.* + -ED^{1}.]

1. Of cattle: Hornless, 'dodded'.

1788 W. MARSHALL *Yorksh.* Gloss. (E.D.S.), *Humbled*, hornless; spoken of cattle and sheep. **1863** MRS. TOOGOOD *Yorksh. Dial.*, Some of his cows are Hummeld. **1880** *Echo* 4 Oct. 4/1 Mr. Horatio Ross killed what is called a 'hummelled' stag, a very remarkable rarity—that is, being full-grown without horns.

2. Of barley: Deprived of the awns.

†**3.** Broken, chapped, kibed. *Obs.*

1597 GERARDE *Herbal* I. xxxi. §10. 42 To heale kibed or humbled heeles. **1601** HOLLAND *Pliny* II. 38 If one lay them very hot to kibed or humbled heeles, they wil cure them.

hummeller, -eler ('hʌm(ə)lə(r)). [f. HUMMEL *v.* + -ER^{1}.] One who or that which hummels; *spec.* a machine for removing the awns from barley.

1842 C. W. JOHNSON *Farmer's Cycl.*, *Barley Hummeller*, an instrument for separating the awns of the barley plant from the seed. **1849** H. STEPHENS *Bk. Farm* (ed. 2) I. 421/2 In some cases the thrashing-machine itself is made the hummeller, by employing an iron fluted cover to the drum. **1862** J. WILSON *Farming* 161 When barley is thrashed, it is first carried by a separate set of elevators .. into a hummeller, in which it is freed from the awns.

hummer ('hʌmə(r)), *sb.*^{1} Also 7 humber. [f. HUM *v.*^{1} + -ER^{1}.] A thing or person that hums.

1. An insect that hums; also, a humming-bird.

1605 SYLVESTER *Du Bartas* II. iii. I. *Abraham* 606 The Swallow's silent, and the lowdest Humber, Leaning upon the earth, now seems to slumber. *a* **1694** M. ROBINSON *Autobiog.* (Mayor 1856) 7 Swarms of night enemies, the gnats, and hummers. **1796** MORSE *Amer. Geog.* I. 737 The hummer is a night bird, peculiar to the mountainous deserts of Peru, .. a strange humming [is] made in the air by the rapidity of their flight. **1816** KIRBY & SP. *Entomol.* (1818) II. xxiv. 379 The wasp and hornet .. are strenuous hummers. **1870** J. ORTON *Andes & Amazons* vi. (1876) 105 Save the hummers, beautiful plumage is rare.

2. A person that hums; one that utters 'hum!'

1771 *Contemplative Man* I. 107 Tho' he never sung in Form .. he was, nevertheless, a great Hummer. **1820** [see HAWER]. **1885** G. MEREDITH *Diana* I. 279 To vindicate Diana's name from the hummers and hawers.

3. a. A person or thing characterized by extreme activity, energy, etc.; see HUM *v.* 3, and cf. *bouncer, thumper*. (*colloq.* or *slang.*)

1681 OTWAY *Soldier's Fort.* I. i, She's a Hummer, such a Bona Roba, ha, ha, ha. **1701** CIBBER *Love makes Man* IV. ii, Odd! she's a Hummer! **1888** *Columbus* (Ohio) *Evening Disp.* 18 Dec., The Franklin county divorce court is a hummer, but it cannot compete with the similar court in Chicago, where a record of six cases an hour has just been made. **1892** *Current Lit.* (U.S.) Apr. 577 The woman of to-day is what is tritely known as a 'hummer'.

b. A person or thing of extraordinary excellence. *colloq.*

1907 C. E. MULFORD *Bar-20* (1914) xxiv. 229 She's a hummer—stands two hands under him, and is a whole lot prettier than that picture Cowan has got over his bar. **1919** WODEHOUSE *Damsel in Distress* (1920) xx. 235 Well, you can't get there quicker than in my car. She's a hummer. **1920** C. E. MULFORD *Johnny Nelson* (1921) xvii. 186, I claim I was justified—an' I'll leave it to you if th' joke on Wolf wasn't a hummer? **1934** N. SCANLAN *Winds of Heaven* xvi. 150 When the new car was swung out on to the wharf, Mike walked round it and touched it lovingly. 'She's a hummer, Dad.' **1945** BAKER *Austral. Lang.* II. xvi. 286 A *wow* or *hummer* [to an American] is a *bonzer* or *big twist* [to an Australian].

4. *slang.* †**a.** (See quot.) *Obs.*

a **1700** B. E. *Dict. Cant. Crew*, *Hummer*, a loud Lie, a Rapper. [Cf. 'a humming lie' in HUMMING *ppl. a.* 2.]

b. False or mistaken arrest (see quot. 1963).

1932 *Evening Sun* (Baltimore) 9 Dec. 31/4 *Hummer*, false arrest. **1961** RIGNEY & SMITH *Real Bohemia* p. xv, *Hummer*, an arrest which accidentally leads to a more serious charge. **1963** MENCKEN *Amer. Lang.* xi. 730 *Hummer*, any kind of charge placed against a suspect so that he can be held although there is insufficient evidence to hold him on the charge for which he is really wanted.

hummer, *sb.*^{2} [f. HUM *v.*^{2} + -ER^{1}.] †**1.** One who 'hums' or hoaxes; a humbugger. *Obs.*

1763 *Brit. Mag.* IV. 261 The hummer when he hath told a lye with a grave face. **1778** H. BROOKE *Epil. Humbugging* 17 Our hummers in state, physic, learning, and law.

2. A scrounger. *Austral. colloq.*

1919 W. H. DOWNING *Digger Dial.* 29 *Hummer*, a cadger. **1945** BAKER *Austral. Lang.* II. v. 108 *Hummer*, *poler* and *bot-fly* are additional synonyms for a cadger.

hummer ('hʌmə(r)), *v. dial.* Also 7 **humber**. [Iterative of HUM *v.*^{1}: cf. *batter, twitter.*] *intr.* To make a low humming or murmuring sound: see quots. **b.** *trans.* To murmur, mutter. Hence **hummering** *vbl. sb.* and *ppl. a.*

1629 LOWTHER in *13th Rep. Hist. MSS. Comm.* App. VII, Through Scotland the people in church .. use a hummering kind of lamentation for their sins. **1637** G. DANIEL *Genius of this Isle* 632 The hummering of Gnats. **1674–91** RAY *S. & E.C. Words* 103 *To Hummer*, to begin to neigh. **1684** *Last Speech of J. Semple* in *Cloud Witnesses* (1810) 282 He never opened his mouth more but humbred and rose up and went his way. **1781** J. HUTTON *Tour to Caves* Gloss., *Hummer*, to make a low rumbling noise. *a* **1825** FORBY *Voc. E. Anglia*, *Hummer*, .. in our use .. means the gentle and pleasing sound which a horse utters when he hears the corn shaken in the sieve. *a* **1860** J. YOUNGER *Autobiog.* xix. (1881) 227 Jamie hummered some sort of assent. **1884** *Chamb. Jrnl.* 9 Feb. 86/1 That pretty low 'hummering' sound so common with pet horses.

'hummie. *Dockers' colloq.* [? Related to *hummock* or *hump*.] See quot.

1887 *19th Cent.* XXII. 486 (*Dock Life of East Lond.*) With timber, a growth on the back of the neck called a 'hummie', the result of long friction, is needful to enable a man to balance a plank [in discharging cargoes] with any degree of comfort.

humming ('hʌmɪŋ), *vbl. sb.*^{1} [f. HUM *v.*^{1} + -ING^{1}.] The action of the verb HUM, q.v.

c **1440** *Promp. Parv.* 253/1 Hummynge (*S.* hunnynge), *reuma*. **1539** KYNGYSMYLL *Let.* 15 Apr. (MS. in P.R.O., *S. P. Hen. VIII*, §150. 138 b), The hummynge hacking and darke setting furthe of Gods word. **1577** B. GOOGE *Heresbach's Husb* IV. (1586) 176 b, At the doore of the Hyve .. you heare a great huzzing and humming within. **1660** *Trial Regic.* 49 b, Gentlemen, This Humming is not at all becoming the Gravity of this Court. It is more fitting for a Stage-Play, then for a Court of Justice. **1711** STEELE *Spect.* No. 148 ¶1 The Gentleman .. has .. practised Minuet-steps to his own Humming. *a* **1839** PRAED *Poems* (1864) II. 129 The drowsy humming of the bees.

humming, *vbl. sb.*^{2}: see HUM *v.*^{2}

humming, *ppl. a.* [f. as prec. + -ING^{2}.]

1. a. That hums; that makes or gives forth a low murmuring sound; †that hums approbation.

1606 SYLVESTER *Du Bartas* II. iv. I. *Trophies* 349 With sudden flerk the fatall hemp lets goe The humming Flint. **1681** HICKERINGILL *Wks.* (1716) I. 195 That .. endeavour at Wit, Pun, or Quibble, so much admir'd by the Humming Tribe. **1703** J. PHILIPS *Splendid Shilling* (R.), The humming prey, Regardless of their fate, rush on the toils Inextricable. **1827** *Blackw. Mag.* XXI. 504 The vernal balminess of the humming Sycamore.

b. Said of sounds.

1578 LYTE *Dodoens* III. l. 390 Grounde Iuie .. put into the eares, taketh away the humming noyse .. of the same. **1637** B. JONSON *Sad Sheph.* II. ii, The scalie beetles .. That make a humming murmur as they flie. **1692** LUTTRELL *Brief Rel.* (1857) II. 539 The earth swelled with a dismal humming noise. **1790** J. B. MORETON *Mann. W. Ind.* 17 The musquittoes .. Their humming songs kept me in dread.

c. Sometimes hyphened to its noun, forming a quasi-compound denoting a particular kind of the thing in question, as ***humming-bee, -top, -wheel***.

1660 BOYLE *New Exp. Phys. Mech.* xl. 326 We .. shut into a great Receiver a Humming Bee. **1819** KEATS *Let.* 27 Sept. (1958) II. 216, I shall .. make his little Boy a present of a humming top. **1837** HOOD *Ode to my Son* ii, Thou human humming-bee, extracting honey From ev'ry blossom. **1837** *London Med. Gaz.* 1 Apr. 8/1 He compares it to the sound of a humming-top, or some such toy, called a '*diable*' in French. **1847** EMERSON *Poems* (1857) 123 The Parcae .. at their humming-wheel. **1851** D. JERROLD *St. Giles* 18 Battledores, humming-tops.

2. a. Of extraordinary activity, intensity, or magnitude; brisk, vigorous, energetic, 'booming'; very large; 'thumping', 'stunning'. *slang* or *colloq.*

(In some cases, referring to the hum which accompanies busy activity; but it is doubtful if this is the origin in all.)

1654 GAYTON *Pleas. Notes* IV. iii. 183 Caught in a humming lie. **1684** J. H. *Epil. Lacy's Sir H. Buffoon*, With such, Ben. Johnson's humming Plays prevail. **1732** FIELDING *Mock Doctor* Epil., He'd have a humming chance. **1733** —— *Quixote in Eng.* III. iv, You seem to drive a humming trade here. *c* **1777** H. WALPOLE *Marg. Notes Chesterf. Wks.* in *Trans. Philobib. Soc.* (1867–8) XI. 59 *Humming* is a cant word for vast. A person meaning to describe a very large bird said, It was a *Humming* Bird. **1865** DICKENS *Mut. Fr.* III. vii, He received a humming knock on the back of his head. **1896** LD. ROSEBERY in *Daily News* 22 July 5/4 In the humming city, in the backwoods, in the swamps where the sentinel walked his lonely round .. the thoughts .. of men were that day directed to Robert Burns.

b. Of liquor: Strong; ? causing a humming in the head; ? effervescing, frothing. *colloq.* (Cf. HUM *sb.*^{1} 3.)

1675 DUFFETT *Mock Tempest* I. ii, A Tub of humming stuff would make a Cat speak. **1732** FIELDING *Covent Gard.* Wks. 1784 II. 315 A bowl of humming punch. **1894** BARING-GOULD *Queen of L.* II. 48 My humming brown ale.

advb. **1701** FARQUHAR *Sir H. Wildair* IV. ii, The wine was humming strong.

humming-bird. Any bird of the large family *Trochilidæ*, the species of which make a humming sound by the rapid vibration of their wings.

They are all of very small size, and are usually brilliantly coloured. They are peculiar to America, ranging from Alaska to Patagonia, but most frequent within the tropics.

1637 T. MORTON *New Eng. Canaan* (1883) 198 There is a curious bird to see to, called a humming bird, no bigger then a great Beetle. **1657** R. LIGON *Barbadoes* (1673) 60 That which we call the humming bird, much less than a Wren, not much bigger than an humble Bee, .. never sitting, but purring with her wings, all the time she stayes with the flower. **1742** POPE *Dunc.* IV. 446 Yet by some object ev'ry brain is stirr'd; The dull may waken to a humming-bird. **1769** E. BANCROFT *Guiana* 166 The Black Trochilus, or Humming Bird, is the smallest of the whole tribe, being not bigger than the top of a man's finger. **1877** BRYANT *May Even.* iv, The humming-bird, that, in the sun, Wandered from bloom to bloom.

b. *attrib.* **humming-bird bush**, *Æschynomene montevidensis*, a South American leguminous shrub much frequented by humming-birds (*Treas. Bot.* 1866); **humming-bird flower**, name for various flowers frequented by humming-birds; **humming-bird hawk-moth (sphinx)**, a species of hawk-moth (*Macroglossa stellatarum*), whose flight resembles that of a humming-bird.

1698 J. PETIVER in *Phil. Trans.* XX. 405 *Digitalis Mariana Persicæ folio*, This I take to be the Humming Bird Tree. **1819** G. SAMOUELLE *Entomol. Compend.* 244 Humming-bird hawk-moth. **1834** SELBY in *Proc. Berw. Nat. Club* I. No. 2. 40 A large moth hovering, in the manner of the Humming-bird Sphinx, in front of the flowers. **1863** BATES *Nat. Amazon* v. (1864) 115 Several times I shot by mistake a hummingbird-hawk-moth, instead of a bird. **1897** WILLIS *Flower. Pl.* I. 103 Passiflora sp., Abutilon sp. and many more are 'humming-bird flowers'.

hummingly ('hʌmɪŋlɪ), *adv.* [See -LY^{2}.] With a humming sound.

1908 *Daily Chron.* 21 Jan. 6/5 He .. endeavours to follow the service and join hummingly in the hymns. **1923** *Daily Mail* 6 Aug. 6 However warm the sun and hummingly populous the air, they [*sc.* the swifts] will go.

hummock ('hʌmək). Forms: α. 6 **hammok**, 6–9 **hammock**. β. 6 **hommoke, hoommocke**, 8 **hommock**. γ. 7 **hummack, humock**, 8 **hummoc**, 7– **hummock**, (9 **-uck**). δ. 7–8 **hommac(c)o**. [Orig. a nautical term: source obscure.

The ending in *-ock* suggests a dim. like *hillock*. But the stem *ham-, hom-, hum-*, remains unexplained. Assuming it to be *hum-*, it may be compared with HUMMIE, LG. *humpel, hümpel, hümmel*, a small height or eminence, a hump, Sc. dial. *humplock* 'little rising ground', and Eng. *hump*. But *hummock* could not be derived from *hump*, since the latter does not appear till 140 years later. The earliest form recalls another nautical word HAMMOCK; but comparison of the two words will show that neither form- nor sense-history favours any connexion (exc. perh. that the factitious *homacco*, hummock, may have been in imitation of *hamacco*, hammock).]

1. A protuberance or boss of earth, rock, etc., usually conical or dome-shaped, rising above the general level of a surface; a low hillock or knoll.

a. *orig.* 'A name given by mariners to a hillock, or small eminence of land resembling the figure of a cone, and appearing on the sea-coast of any country' (Falconer *Marine Dict.*, 1769, s.v. *Hommoc*).

α. **1556** W. TOWRSON in Hakluyt *Voy.* (1589) 104 Right above that into the land a round hammock and greene which we took to be trees. **1599** HAKLUYT *Voy.* II. II. 58 The sayd land seemed vnto vs as if it had bene a great number of shippes vnder saile, being in deed nothing els but the land which was full of Hammoks, some high some lowe, with high trees on them. **1622** R. HAWKINS *Voy. S. Sea* (1847) 180 Wee came to an anchor in the bay of Atacames, which on the wester part hath a round hammock.

β. **1555** R. GAINSH in Eden *Decades* 351 Vppon the mayne are foure or fyue hygh hylles rysynge .. lyke round hoommockes or hyllockes. **1556** W. TOWRSON in Hakluyt *Voy.* (1589) 105 A round green hommoke which commeth out of the maine. **1645** G. BOATE *Irel. Nat. Hist.* (1652) 38 Horn-head, being a Hill with two hommocks at the top, in fashion somewhat like unto two horns.

γ. **1608** W. HAWKINS in *Hawkins' Voy.* (1878) 378 A hummocke .. boare of us N.E. **1622** R. HAWKINS *Voy. S. Sea* (1847) 238 This iland .. is a round humock, conteyning not a league of ground, but most fertile. **1748** *Anson's Voy.* II. ix. 228 On this land we observed two remarkable hummocks, such as are usually called paps. **1834** M. SCOTT *Cruise Midge* (1863) 110 Do you see your marks now? Yes, I have the two trees on with the hummock. **1840** F. D. BENNETT *Whaling Voy.* I. 295 *note*, This island has the appearance of a very lofty .. rock .. with a hummock on each side of its base.

δ. **1670** NARBOROUGH *Jrnl.* in *Acc. Sev. Late Voy.* I. (1711) 114 These Islands made in four Hommaccoes, like Hay-cocks, when I saw them. **1743** BULKELEY & CUMMINS *Voy. S. Seas* 15 High Land, with Hillocks, and one remarkable Hommacoe like a Sugar-loaf.

b. (In Colonial and U.S. use.) A piece of more or less elevated ground, esp. in a swamp or marsh; *spec.* in the southern U.S., an elevation rising above a plain or swamp and often densely covered with hardwood trees; a clump of such trees on a knoll.

The local form in Florida and adjacent states is *hammock*.

α. **1765** J. BARTRAM *Jrnl.* 28 Dec. in Stork *Acc. E. Florida* (1766) 13 The hammocks of live-oaks and palmettos are generally surrounded either with swamp or marsh. **1766** *Ibid.* 24 Jan. 49 We observed on the north-end of the lake a hammock of oak. **1775** ROMANS *Florida* 283 A few spots of hammock or upland, are found on this island. **1884** *Times* 15 Apr. 8 Florida lands are ordinarily classified as pine lands, hammocks (lands covered with hard woods), and swamp lands.

β. **1636** *Boston Rec.* (1877) II. 9 A parcell of marsh land in which there stands 3 homocks, with Pyne trees upon the south side of the marsh neare the water. **1775** ROMANS *Florida* 229 *note*, Excepting the few hommocks near the sea, which are oak land. **1791** W. BARTRAM *Carolina* 117 Twenty miles of these green fields, interspersed with hommocks or islets of evergreen trees. **1839–40** W. IRVING *Wolfert's R.* (1855) 220 When Florida was ceded by the Spaniards .. the Indians .. retired .. [into the] intricate swamps and hommocks, and vast savannahs of the interior.

γ. **1650** R. WILLIAMS *Lett.* (1874) 195 A moose which was killed upon one of your hummocks by Fisher's Island. **1681** R. KNOX *Hist. Ceylon* (1817) 25 By marks of great trees, hummacks, or rocks, each man knows his own. **1766** H. LAURENS in Darlington *Mem.* (1849) 438, I thrice visited the River St. John .. exploring the swamps and hummocks, pine barrens, and sand barrens. **1775** ROMANS *Florida* App. 12 The island Amelia, which is .. to be known by a detached hummock of trees on the south side. **1869** in Coues *Birds N.W.* 478 The nest was a simple hollow in the ground, in a grassy hummock, in the centre of a marshy spot. **1872** C. J.

MAYNARD *Birds Florida* 29, I was walking in a narrow path through a hummock, which lies back of the old fort at Miami [Florida].

c. A sand hill on the sea shore.

1793 SMEATON *Edystone L.* 197 In 1773 the..boundary of the Sand Hommacks remained nearly the same..but now..the sand hommacks had established themselves. **1819** REES *Cycl., Hommacks*, in Engineery, are used by Mr. Smeaton to denote sand hills thrown up by the tide. **1888** *Boston* (Mass.) *Transcript* 7 July 5/5 This chart gives height of sand hills [on Sable Island] as 150 feet, when in no instance could Mr. Macdonald find a hummock having an elevation of eighty feet.

d. *Geol.* An elevated or detached boss of rock.

'Navigators use the word hummock to express circular and elevated mounts, appearing at a distance; I adopt the word from them' (Richardson, 1808, as below).

1808 RICHARDSON in *Phil. Trans.* XCVIII. 218 To these may be compared the stratified basaltic hummocks so profusely scattered over our area. *Ibid.* 221 It will hardly be asserted that these hummocks were originally formed solitary and separate as they now stand. **1829** *Glover's Hist. Derby* I. 51 Detached portions or hummocks of coal measures. **1839** MURCHISON *Silur. Syst.* I. xxxvi. 500 The trap..reappearing here and there in hummocks. **1878** HUXLEY *Physiogr.* 162 The flat-domed hummocks of rock, produced in this way are termed sheep-backs.

e. 'A protuberance raised upon any plane of ice above the common level' (Scoresby); 'a lump, thrown up by some pressure or force, on an ice field or floe' (Sir J. Ross).

1818 *Edin. Rev.* XXX. 17 A portion of ice rising above the common level, is termed a hummock. **1823** SCORESBY *Whale Fishery* 51 Many of the hummocks of the ice were at least twenty feet high..Some of these hummocks seemed to be of recent production. **1835** SIR J. ROSS *Arctic Exp.* xxix. 404 We proceeded over the level of the sea of ice, and, passing some hummocks, arrived at the desired cape. **1853** KANE *Grinnell Exp.* x. (1856) 74 At the margins of the floes, where their ragged edges have come into grinding contact, the ice is piled up into ridges... These are the 'hummocks'. **1878** A. H. MARKHAM *Gt. Frozen Sea* xxii. 308 The hummocks proved most formidable impediments to our advance.

f. *gen.* A boss-like protuberance rising irregularly from any surface; a knoll, hillock, or small piece rising abruptly above the general level, and causing inequality of the surface.

1845 DARWIN *Voy. Nat.* xxi. (1873) 493 The lava streams are covered with hummocks. **1854** THOREAU *Walden, Spring* (1863) 339 Jumping from hummock to hummock. **1859** TENNENT *Ceylon* IX. v. II. 503 The ground..was thrown into hummocks like great molehills. **1867** MUSGRAVE *Nooks Old France* I. vii. 255 Hummocks of hard earth varying between two and three feet in height.

g. *transf.* A hummock-like mass or lump.

1864 LOWELL *Fireside Trav.* 186 One of those yellow hummocks [polar bears] goes slumping up and down his cage.

2. *attrib.*, as ***hummock-land*** (see 1 b *a*, quot. 1884, and HUMMOCKY 1, quot. 1766), ***-ridge***, ***-soil***, etc.

1775 ROMANS *Florida* 15, I shall then treat of them by the names of pine land, Hammock land, savannahs, swamps, marshes, and bay, or cypress galls. *Ibid.* 17 The hammock land so called from its appearing in tufts among the lofty pines. *Ibid.*, The true hammock soil is a mixture of clay and a blackish sand, and in some spots a kind of ochre. **1856** KANE *Arct. Expl.* I. xxii. 274 To avoid the accumulation of snows and hummock-ridges. *Ibid.* xxvi. 338 Such ice I have seen 36 feet in height; and when subjected..to hummock-squeezing, 60 and 70 feet. *Ibid.* II. i. 16 Under the hospitable lee of an inclined hummock-slab.

Hence **'hummocked** ('hʌmәkt) *ppl. a.*, thrown into hummocks; hummocky, uneven. **'hummocking**, the forming of hummocks on an ice field.

1853 KANE *Grinnell Exp.* xvi. (1856) 122 The elastic material corrugated before the enormous pressure: then cracked, then crumbled, and at last rose... This imposing process of dynamics is called 'Hummocking'. **1856** —— *Arct. Expl.* I. xxxii. 447 It is a rugged, hummocked drive.

hummocky ('hʌmәkɪ), *a.* Also 8 **hammocky, hommocky.** [f. prec. + -Y.]

1. Abounding in or characterized by hummocks; having the surface rising irregularly in hummocks.

1766 J. BARTRAM *Jrnl.* in Stork *Acc. E. Florida* 69 That which is called hammocky land is generally full of large evergreen and water-oaks, mixed with red-bay and magnolia. **1791** W. BARTRAM *Carolina* 211 East Florida..being such a swampy hommocky country. **1817** SCORESBY in *Ann. Reg., Chron.* 536 Such fields as exhibit a rugged, hummocky surface. **1835** SIR J. ROSS *Narr. 2nd Voy.* Explan. Terms p. xvi, *Hummocky ice*, ice so uneven and rough as to be impassable or nearly so on foot. **1867** MUSGRAVE *Nooks Old France* I. vii. 256 This rugged and hummocky road.

b. *fig.* Uneven like hummocky ground.

1867 A. J. ELLIS *E.E. Pronunc.* I. iv. 410 The verse is so 'hummocky' that no conclusions could be drawn from it respecting the number of syllables in a word.

2. Of the form or nature of a hummock or boss-like eminence.

1791 W. BARTRAM *Carolina* 193 The opposite point of the crescent, gradually retires with hommocky projecting points, indenting the grassy marshes. **1823** SCORESBY *Whale Fishery* 71 Innumerable hummocky peaks [of ice] were on every hand, some of them reared to the height of 30 or 40 feet. **1873** J. GEIKIE *Gt. Ice Age* ii. 21 Even the projecting masses of rock..present a rounded hummocky aspect. **1882** *Pall Mall G.* 10 July 5/1 A firth winding among hummocky hills. **1894** *Field* 1 Dec. 838/1 These grayling lie..sometimes..in the hummocky waves above sunken rocks.

‖**hummum** ('hʌmʌm). [Corruption of Arab. *ḥammām* hot bath (HAMMAM). (Arab. *ḥammam*, *ḥummum* means 'coal, fuel, ashes'.)] An Oriental bathing establishment; a Turkish bath; a HAMMAM.

A bathing establishment called 'the Hummums' is said to have been established in Covent Garden in 1631; it subsequently became a hotel.

1634 SIR T. HERBERT *Trav.* 35 Found them in an Evening, bathing themselves in a secure Hummum. **1688** SIR J. BRAMSTON *Autobiog.* (Camden) 368 Sir Charles Scarborow ..aduised takinge the Northhall waters..bleedinge in the arme, and the hummums, which are bathing or swettinge. **1701** *Postman* 15 Nov. Advt., The Hummums in Covent Garden having..been neglected..whereby several Persons of Quality have been disgusted and have left off coming thither to sweat and bathe. **1712** BUDGELL *Spect.* No. 347 ¶10 It is also our Imperial Will and Pleasure, that our good Subjects the Sweaters do establish their Hummums in such close Places. **1778** JOHNSON in *Boswell* 12 May, My wife went to the Hummums (it is a place where people get themselves cupped). **1792** WOLCOTT (P. Pindar) *Odes of Codol* Wks. 1812 III. 100 In Convent Garden, at the Hummums, now I sit. **1856** *Househ. Words* XIII. 98 A complete hummums, or pile of buildings devoted to hot and cold baths. **1861** DICKENS *Gt. Expect.* xlv, I..got a late hackney chariot and drove to the Hummums in Covent Garden.

hummus ('hʊmәs). Also **hoummos.** [ad. Turk. *humus* mashed chick-peas.] In Middle Eastern countries (and also, more recently, elsewhere) an hors d'œuvre made from ground chick-peas and sesame oil flavoured with lemon and garlic.

1955 E. DAVID *Bk. Mediterranean Food* 158 Hummus... Cook the chick peas..pound them, [etc.]. **1967** *Guardian* 8 Dec. 6/4 Order the paste of ground chick peas, oil, and lemon which is called hummus. **1969** M. J. PHILIPPOU *101 Arabian Delights* 48 Hoummos ib bandora. Chick peas in tomato sauce... Hoummos ib Taheeneh. Chick peas in Taheeneh. **1970** SIMON & HOWE *Dict. Gastron.* 223/1 *Hummus bi Tahina*, a widely known, traditional..Arab dish of cooked, puréed chick peas... It is served as a *mezze* or appetizer in Arab countries. **1973** *Nation Rev.* (Melbourne) III. 31 Aug. 1460/4 Passing up the usual *hummus* as a starter.

hummyl, -ly, obs. ff. HUMIL, -LY.

humoral ('hju:mәrәl), *a.* Also 8–9 **humoural.** [a. F. *humoral* (14th c. in Littré), ad. L. type **hūmōrāl-is*, f. *hūmor* HUMOUR: see -AL¹.]

1. a. *Med.* Of or belonging to, consisting of, or containing, any of the humours or fluids of the body. Also in mod. use, contained in or involving the blood or other body fluid; involving or consisting of a chemical agent, esp. one present in the blood (such as hormones or ions).

humoral theory: (*a*) the theory that immunity is due to the presence of bactericidal substances in the blood (rather than the action of whole cells); (*b*) the theory that the transmission of nerve impulses at a synapse or a neuromuscular junction involves a chemical (rather than an electrical) agent. (See also sense 1 c.)

1543 TRAHERON *Vigo's Chirurg.* II. viii. iii. 80 Apostemes engendred in the knees, hote, and colde,..wyndy, and humorall, or full of water. **1665** G. HARVEY *Advice agst. Plague* 2 Pestilential Miasms, insinuating into the humoral and consistent parts of the Body. **1758** J. S. *Le Dran's Observ. Surg.* (1771) 20, I found this Tumour not to be humoral. **1878** T. BRYANT *Pract. Surg.* I. 15 Products which emanate from textural and humoral waste. **1898** W. S. L. BARLOW *Man. Gen. Path.* ix. 408 It was obvious..that a purely humoral theory..is insufficient, that natural immunity cannot be explained by the presence of 'alexins' in the blood. **1924** E. D. ADRIAN in *Brain* XLVII. 400 The 'inhibiting substance' theory (and the 'humoral' theory of Loewi and others) derives all its evidence from the peripheral inhibition of cardiac or plain muscle. **1935** O. LOEWI in *Proc. R. Soc.* B. CXVIII. 302 Some important investigations..suggest the possibility that the stimulation also of spinal nerves is transmitted by humoral means, namely, by liberation of acetylcholine. **1950** G. P. WRIGHT *Introd. Path.* vii. 113 The early history of immunology contains many vigorous controversies which arose from the sharp division of opinion between the so-called 'cellular' and 'humoral' schools. **1952** W. E. LE GROS CLARK *Tissues of Body* (ed. 3) xiii. 356 The conception of chemical (or humoral) transmitters [of nerve impulses] suggests an alternative explanation. **1968** PASSMORE & ROBSON *Compan. Med. Studies* I. xxvii. 2/1 The immune response can be purely humoral, mediated by circulating antibodies, or cellular, mediated by small lymphocytes, but often mixtures of both mechanisms are found. **1971** A. C. GUYTON *Textbk. Med. Physiol.* (ed. 4) xxv. 284/2 Superimposed onto the intrinsic regulations of the circulation..are two additional types of regulation: (1) nervous and (2) humoral. **1971** *Nature* 26 Feb. 593/1 Human breast cancer..may well be initiated by a virus but promoted by humoral factors, in particular sex hormones.

b. Of diseases: Caused by (or attributed to) a disordered state of the humours.

1547 BOORDE *Brev. Health* cxlii. 52 b, The putrifyed or humorall fever. **1655** MOUFET & BENNET *Health's Improv.* (1746) 86 Their old Men..subject to Palsies..and humoral Diseases. **1727** BRADLEY *Fam. Dict.* s.v. *Flux*, The humoral Flux or Diarrhœa. **1822–34** *Good's Study Med.* (ed. 4) IV. 44 In hysteria, and humoral asthma.

c. Relating to the bodily humours; applied esp. to the ancient medical doctrine (which continued in vogue till the 18th c.), that all diseases were due to the disordered state of the humours.

1793 BEDDOES *Lett. Darwin* 119 The loose analogies of the humoral pathology. **1809** PEARSON in *Phil. Trans.* XCIX. 313 Groundless hypotheses, originating in the humoural doctrines of Galen. **1825** COLERIDGE *Aids Refl.* (1848) I. 68 Terms and phrases from the humoral physiology long exploded. **1858** WHEWELL *Hist. Sci. Ideas* IX. ii. §2 (ed. 3) II. 179 The humoral pathology of the ancients.

†**2.** *gen.* Of the nature of, or containing, 'humour' or moisture; humid; fluid. *Obs.*

1605 TIMME *Quersit.* III. 162 That moyst euaporation taken from the more waterie part of humoral or mercurial things.

†**3.** Full of humours or fancies; whimsical: = HUMOROUS 3. *Obs.*

1591 UNTON *Corr.* (Roxb.) 84 Certeyne idle brayned humorall persons.

Hence **'humoralism**, humoral pathology (see 1 c); **'humoralist**, a believer in humoral pathology; **humora'listic** *a.*, of or belonging to the humoralists.

1846 WORCESTER cites CALDWELL for *Humoralism*. **1847** CRAIG, *Humoralism Humoralist*. **1864** W. T. FOX *Skin Dis.* 11 On the one hand the humoralist, on the other the neuropathist. **1875** H. C. WOOD *Therap.* (1879) 371 The term 'purifying the blood'..is sufficiently suggestive of their function as viewed from the pathological stand-point of the old humoralist. *Ibid.*, As the accepted pathology has been humoralistic or otherwise.

humoresque (hju:mә'rɛsk), *sb. Mus.* [ad. Ger. *humoreske*, f. L. *hūmor* HUMOUR: see -ESQUE.] A composition of a humorous or capricious character.

[**1880** GROVE *Dict. Mus.* I. 758 *Humoreske*, a title adopted by Schumann for his Op. 20 and Op. 88, No. 2... Heller and Grieg have also used the term for pianoforte pieces... There is nothing obviously 'humorous' in any of these, and the term 'caprice' might equally well be applied to them. Rubinstein also entitles his Don Quixote 'Humoreske', but the 'humour' is there of a much more obvious and boisterous kind.] **1889** GRIEG in *Pall Mall G.* 20 Mar. 3/1 One of my earliest works..a Humoresque in four parts.

humo'resque, *a.* [f. HUMOUR *sb.* + ESQUE.] Of a humorous style.

1896 E. GOSSE *Crit. Kit-Kats* 149 The..few purely fantastic poems of recent times which have..kept up the old tradition of humoresque literature.

humoric (hju:'mɒrɪk), *a. Med.* [f. L. *hūmŏr*- HUMOUR + -IC. Cf. F. *humorique.*] Belonging or relating to a fluid or 'humour', as in ***humoric bruit, sound*** (*Syd. Soc. Lex.*).

1854 MAYNE *Expos. Lex., Humoric*..has been applied to the sound produced by percussion on the stomach when distended with air and fluid.

humorific (hju:mә'rɪfɪk), *a.* [f. as prec. + -FIC.] Producing humour.

1818 COLERIDGE *Lit. Rem.* I. 136 Is there some one humorific point common to all that can be called humourous?

humorism ('hju:mәrɪz(ә)m). [f. L. *hūmor* HUMOUR, after *humorist*. In mod.F. *humorisme*.]

1. *Med.* The doctrine of the four bodily 'humours' (see HUMOUR *sb.* 2 b), and their relation to 'temperaments' and to diseases.

1832 *Edin. Rev.* LV. 468 Sometimes Humorism..seems to be favoured. **1832** SIR W. HAMILTON *Discuss.* (1852) 246 By Galen, Humorism was first formally expounded... Four elementary fluids..sufficed to explain the varieties of natural temperament, and the causes of disease. **1887** *Sat. Rev.* 13 Aug. 218/1 The dusty old lumber of the temperaments theory—the Humourism of the past.

2. a. The characteristics of a humorist (see HUMORIST 2); humorous style or manner.

1831 COLERIDGE *Table-t.* 30 July, The very soul of Swift —an intense half self-deceived humorism.

b. A humorous saying or remark.

1897 'MARK TWAIN' *Notebook* (1935) 335 In a dream I have at last encountered a humorism that actually remained one after waking. **1902** *Sat. Rev.* 15 Nov. 620/1 The most sparkling witticisms and the most obvious humourisms have fallen flat. **1907** *Daily Chron.* 26 June 7/5 His eloquent remarks were snatched up by the people he met and mistaken for brilliant humorisms. **1920** D. H. LAWRENCE *Women in Love* (1921) ii. 34 Gerald smiled grimly at this humorism.

humorist, humourist ('hju:mәrɪst). [a. F. *humoriste* (16th c. in Hatz.-Darm.), ad. med.L. and It. *humorista*, f. L. *hūmor* HUMOUR: see -IST.]

†**1.** A person subject to 'humours' or fancies (see HUMOUR *sb.* 6); a fantastical or whimsical person; a faddist. *Obs.*

1596 FITZ-GEFFRAY *Sir F. Drake* (1881) 31 Some base humorists. **1627–77** FELTHAM *Resolves* II. lxxxi. 332 Turbulent and contentious humorists. **1640** BP. HALL *Episc.* III. v. 242 Our late humorists give power of excommunication..to every Parish-Presbytery. **1712** ADDISON *Spect.* No. 477 ¶1, I am..looked upon as an Humorist in Gardening. I have several Acres about my House, which I call my Garden, and which a skilful Gardener would not know what to call. **1718** OCKLEY *Saracens* II. Introd. 7 All Humourists, Bigots and Enthusiasts. **1741** WATTS *Improv. Mind* I. i. §12 A humourist is one that is greatly pleased, or greatly displeased with little things, who sets his heart much upon matters of very small importance. **1830** MACKINTOSH *Eth. Philos.* Wks. 1846 I. 175 Indulging his own tastes and fancies..he became..a sort of humourist.

2. A facetious or comical person, a wag; a humorous talker, actor, or writer; in mod. use

esp. one skilled in the literary or artistic expression of humour. (See HUMOUR *sb.* 7.)

1599 B. JONSON *Ev. Man out of Hum.*, *The Stage*, To turn an actor, and a Humorist. **1707** *Reflex. upon Ridicule* II. 203 Men love to be Merry..and prefer the Character of Humourists before that of the Serious. **1850** MAURICE *Mor. & Met. Philos.* (ed. 2) 114 The Athenians liked a humorist, and a humorist Socrates..showed himself to be. **1871** *Athenæum* 24 June 775 Swift was an inimitable humourist.. Pope a consummate wit. **1874** L. STEPHEN *Hours in Library* (1892) II. iv. 110 Delight in blending the pathetic with the ludicrous is the characteristic of the true humorist.

b. *fig.*; also *attrib.*

1853 RUSKIN *Stones Ven.* III. iii. §34. 133 The pinnacled roofs set with their small humourist double windows, as if with so many ears and eyes, of Northern France. **1860** HAWTHORNE *Marb. Faun* xxxii, Those old humorists with gnarled trunks and twisted boughs, the olives.

†**3.** One given to humouring or indulging. *Obs.*

1601 DEACON & WALKER *Spirits & Divels* 349 You may be supposed..to be rather their humorist in an onely respect of their hier, then anie their approoued martialist to mannage these matters, in any right reuerend regard of their honours. **1686** W. DE BRITAINE *Hum. Prud.* vi. 28 Man is the greatest Humorist and Flatterer of himself.

4. = HUMORALIST.

1846 in WORCESTER. **1886** in *Syd. Soc. Lex.*

humoristic (hjuːmə'rɪstɪk), *a.* [f. prec. + -IC.]

1. Belonging to, characteristic of, or of the nature of a humorist: see prec. 2. (Sometimes *loosely* = HUMOROUS 4; F. *humoristique*, Ger. *humoristik.*)

1818 COLERIDGE in *Rem.* (1836) I. 147 By right of humoristic universality each part [in Rabelais and Sterne] is essentially a whole in itself. **1847** LOWELL *Lett.* I. 131 Dickens seems to me..to be rather a sketcher of humoristic characters..than himself a humorist. **1878** MORLEY *Crit. Misc.* Ser. I. *Carlyle* 195 The universal tone of humouristic cynicism.

b. as *sb.* (*pl.*) Humorous writings. (*nonce-use.*)

1886 TUPPER *My Life as A.* 30 Of..schoolboy literaria.. let me save here..one or two of my trivial humoristics.

2. = HUMORALISTIC: cf. prec. 4.

humorize ('hjuːməraɪz), *v.* [f. HUMOUR (or L. *hūmor*) + -IZE.]

†**1.** *intr.* To agree or comply with the humour of a person or thing. *Obs.*

1598 MARSTON *Pygmal.* III. 148 His clothes doe sympathize, And with his inward spirit humorize.

2. To speak or think humorously; to make humorous remarks or reflections.

1609 SIR E. HOBY *Let. to Mr. T. H.* 24 Euerie iching-eared congregation will..be serued with an humorizing Discourser. **1884** *Art Mag.* Mar. (Cent.), He had a little 'mental twist' which caused him to moralize and humorize over life in a fashion quite his own.

3. *trans.* To make humorous.

1893 W. B. YEATS *Celtic Twilight* 195 Our tales.. hopelessly humorize the creatures [*sc.* water-goblins and water-monsters].

humorology (hjuːmə'rɒlədʒɪ). *nonce-wd.* [f. L. *hūmor* HUMOUR + -(O)LOGY.] The doctrine of the humours.

1835 SOUTHEY *Doctor* III. Interch. xiii. 340 Oh men ignorant of humorology! more ignorant of psychology! and most ignorant of Pantagruelism. **1837** *Fraser's Mag.* XVI. 664/1 Of humorology, psychology, Pantagruelism..we shall dissertate hereafter.

humorous ('hjuːmərəs), *a.* Also 6–8 **humerous**, 7 **humurous**, 7–9 **humourous**. [In sense 1, perh. a. obs. F. *humereux* damp, full of sap (16th c. in Godef.), ad. late L. (*h*)*ūmōrōs-us* moist, wet, f. *hūmor* moisture, etc. In other senses, from Engl. senses of HUMOUR. For the spelling and pronunciation see HUMOUR *sb.*]

†**1.** Moist, humid, damp: see HUMOUR *sb.* 1. *Obs.*

(In first quot. with play on sense 3.)

1592 SHAKS. *Rom. & Jul.* II. i. 31 He hath hid himselfe among these Trees To be consorted with the Humerous night. **1603** DRAYTON *Bar. Wars* I. xlvii, The hum'rous Fogges. *c* **1611** CHAPMAN *Iliad* XXI. 186 All founts, wells, all deeps humorous. **1612** DRAYTON *Poly-olb.* XIII. 214 Every lofty top, which late the humorous night Bespangled had with pearle.

†**2.** Pertaining to the bodily humours (see HUMOUR *sb.* 2); of diseases, Caused by a disordered state of the humours: = HUMORAL 1. *Obs.*

1578 BURGHLEY *Let. to Hatton* 21 Apr., in Ld. Campbell *Chancellors* (1857) II. xlv. 268 Only the withdrawing of some one tooth that is touched with some humorous cause. **1697** R. PEIRCE *Bath Mem.* II. ii. 268 In all the three Degrees of Difficulty in Breathing..some Humerous, some Nervous, some mix'd. **1733** CHEYNE *Eng. Malady* I. vi. §10 (1734) 60 Other chronical and humorous Distempers. **1831** J. MORISON in *Morisoniana* 382 Small Pox Virus, inherent.. in proportion to the state of your own humourous affections.

†**3.** Subject to, influenced by, or dependent on humour or mood; full of humours or fancies; fanciful, capricious, whimsical, humoursome; odd, fantastic. (Of persons, actions, etc.) *Obs.* or *arch.*

1588 SHAKS. *L.L.L.* III. i. 177, I that haue beene loues whip? A verie Beadle to a humerous sigh. **1602** KYD *Sp. Trag.* I, You know that women oft are humurous. **1632** LITHGOW *Trav.* II. 71 The fluctuary motions of the humerous multitude. **1653** GAUDEN *Hierasp.* 151 Built upon the sands of humerous novelty, not on the rock of holy antiquity. **1709** STEELE *Tatler* No. 54 ⁋1 Pall'd Appetite is humorous, and must be gratify'd with Sauces rather than Food. **1823** *Valperga* III. 42, I am self-willed, sullen, and humourous.

†**b.** Moody, peevish, ill-humoured, out of humour.

1600 SHAKS. *A.Y.L.* I. ii. 278 The Duke is humorous. **1640** QUARLES *Enchirid.* III. 10 Be not Angry with him..too often, lest he count thee humorous. **1670** BAXTER *Cure Ch. Div.* 250 Those that are of uncharitable, humerous, peevish, contentious and fiery spirits. **1693** PENN *Fruits Solitude* (ed. 2) §18. 9 He is humorous to his Wife, he beats his Children. **1842** MISS MITFORD in L'Estrange *Life* (1870) III. ix. 142 Mr. Roebuck..is as cantankerous and humorous (in the old Shakesperian sense) as Cassius himself.

4. Full of, characterized by, or showing humour or drollery (see HUMOUR *sb.* 7); facetious, jocular, comical, funny. (Of persons, actions, etc.)

1705 ADDISON *Italy* (J.), Others [tell us] that this..alludes to the story of the satyr Marsyas..which I think is more humorous. **1738** SWIFT *Pol. Conversat.* p. xiv, Whatever Person would aspire to be completely witty, smart, humourous, and polite. **1756–7** tr. *Keysler's Trav.* (1760) I. 216 Mr. du Vernet..drew up the following humorous letter ..to the Moon, desiring her not to shew herself next Monday. **1861** WRIGHT *Ess. Archæol.* II. xxiii. 230 A taste for the humorous is..independent of national difference. **1876** BESANT & RICE *Gold. Butterfly* Prol. ii, The Western American is always humorous.

'humorously, *adv.* [f. prec. + -LY[2].] In a humorous manner. **a.** Capriciously, fantastically; peevishly. *arch.* **b.** Facetiously, jocosely.

1603 CHETTLE *Eng. Mourn Garm.* B iij, Too humorously affected to the Roman gouernement. **1611** COTGR., *Bigearrement*, odly, humorously, fantastically. *a* **1686** CALAMY (J.), We resolve rashly, sillily, or humorously, upon no reasons that will hold. **1751** EARL ORRERY *Remarks Swift* (1752) 127 Then follows the procession, most humourously described. **1882** PEBODY *Eng. Journalism* xxiii. 180 His humorously plaintive laments. **1895** R. F. HORTON *Teaching of Jesus* 40 How humorously perverse the human mind is in arguing against its chief good.

'humorousness. [f. as prec. + -NESS.] The quality of being humorous. **a.** Fancifulness, whimsicality. *arch.* **b.** Facetiousness, jocularity.

1611 COTGR., *Bizarrerie*, fantasticalnesse, toyishnesse, humorousnesse. **1684** J. GOODMAN *Winter Even. Confer.* III. (1705) 91 It must be extream humorousness to deny a Providence in them. **1727** BAILEY vol. II, *Humorousness*, comicalness, fulness of pleasantry, fantasticalness. **1768–74** TUCKER *Lt. Nat.* (1852) I. 456 There was..such a good-natured humourousness, in his countenance. **1861** SMILES *Engineers* II. 333 He had not lost the humorousness which had procured for him the sobriquet of 'Laughing Tam'.

humour, humor ('hjuːmə(r), 'juːmə(r)), *sb.* Also 4 **umour, -or**, 4–6 **humure**, 5 **-ore**, 5–6 **-oure**. [a. AF. (*h*)*umour*, F. (*h*)*umor*, *-ur*, mod.F. *humeur* (= It. *umore*, Sp., Pg. *humor*):—L. *hūmōrem*, more properly *ūmōr-em* fluid, moisture.

For the spelling cf. HONOUR; *humour* is now usual in Great Britain, *humor* in U.S. The English formations, *humoured*, *humourless*, *humoursome*, are here spelt like the sb. and vb.; but the derivatives formed on a Latin type, as *humoral*, *humorist*, *humorous*, are spelt *humor-* as in L. *humōrōsus*, etc. (This agrees with Johnson's use.) The pronunciation of the initial *h* is only of recent date, and is sometimes omitted, esp. in the senses under II: see H (the letter).]

I. Physical senses.

†**1.** Moisture; damp exhalation; vapour. *Obs.*

1382 WYCLIF *Jer.* xvii. 8 As a tree, that is ouer plauntide vp on watris, that at the humour [L. *ad humorem*, **1388** moisture] sendith his rootes. —— *Ecclus.* xxxviii. 29 The humour [L. *vapor*] of the fyr brenneth his flesh. *c* **1420** *Pallad. on Husb.* I. 790 That diche wol drie vp humours of thy londe. **1599** CHAPMAN *Hum. Dayes Myrth* Plays 1873 I. 52 The skie hangs full of humour and I thinke we shall haue raine. **1601** SHAKS. *Jul. C.* II. i. 262 To walke vnbraced, and sucke vp the humours Of the danke Morning. **1670** in *Evelyn's Mem.* (1857) III. 228 At Christmas last we could hardly find humour enough in the ground to plant. **1697** DRYDEN *Virg. Georg.* I. 129 Redundant Humours thro' the Pores expire.

2. Any fluid or juice of an animal or plant, either natural or morbid. (Chiefly in mediæval physiology; now *rare* or *arch.*)

1340 *Ayenb.* 132 He yuelþ þe kueade humours ine þe bodye. *c* **1386** CHAUCER *Nun's Pr. T.* 105 Whan humours been to habundant in a wight. **1489** CAXTON *Faytes of A.* II. xxxviii. 160 Nother in marche nor in aperyll the trees that thenne haue habondaunce of humore ought not to be felde a doune. **1553** EDEN *Treat. Newe Ind.* (Arb.) 34 The humoure or ioyse which droppeth out of the braunches of the date trees. **1610** GUILLIM *Heraldry* III. xi. (1660) 149 Either true and natural blood, or..some kind of hot humour that is to it instead of blood. **1704** J. HARRIS *Lex. Techn.* s.v. *Aspera*, The Wind-pipe..being besmear'd with a fattish and mucous Humour..to make the Voice smoother. **1727–41** CHAMBERS *Cycl.* s.v. *Mistletoe*, A flattish seed.. enclosed with a viscid, glutinous humour. **1789** W. BUCHAN *Dom. Med.* (1790) 639 The cold bath..occasions an excessive flux of humours towards the head. **1833** I. TAYLOR *Fanat.* vi. 198 Cold as marble:..solid as iron..because there are no humours or lymph in their constitutions.

b. *spec.* In ancient and mediæval physiology, one of the four chief fluids (***cardinal humours***) of the body (blood, phlegm, choler, and melancholy or black choler), by the relative proportions of which a person's physical and mental qualities and disposition were held to be determined: cf. 4, and see TEMPERAMENT. *Obs.* exc. *Hist.*

†***black humour***, black choler or melancholy (*obs.*).

c **1380** WYCLIF *Serm.* Sel. Wks. II. 169 Blood is moost kyndely umour, answeringe to þe love of God, þre oþere umors in man answeren to þree oþer loves. **1398** TREVISA *Barth. De P.R.* IV. vi. (Add. MS. 27944), þere beþ foure humours, Blood, Flewme, Colera and Melencolia. **1581** W. STAFFORD *Exam. Compl.* iii. (1876) 84 He answered me that choler was the cause of my sicknes, and that hee gaue me those purgations to auoyde this humour. **1588** SHAKS. *L.L.L.* I. i. 235 Besieged with sable coloured melancholie, I did commend the blacke oppressing humour to the most wholesome Physicke of thy health-giuing ayre. **1618** *Demeanour Sir W. Raleigh* 52 Two Physitions..being come, could tell nothing of what humor the said sicknesse was composed. *a* **1695** MARQ. HALIFAX *Lady's N. Year's Gift* (1756) 37 If your Husband should be really sullen..let the Black Humour begin to spend itself, before you come in. **1881** R. ROUTLEDGE *Science* I. 32 According to Hippocrates, the human body contained four humours; blood, phlegm, yellow bile, and black bile.

c. With allusion to the mental qualities or disposition held to arise from these 'humours'.

1604 SHAKS. *Oth.* III. iv. 31 *Æmil.* Is he not iealous? *Des.* Who, he? I thinke the sun where he was borne, Drew all such humors from him. **1844** MRS. BROWNING *Vis. Poets* ccxi, One that drew Sour humours from his mother.

†**d.** Used for the peculiar constitution or quality (e.g. saltness, sourness) of a material substance. *Obs.*

1661 J. CHILDREY *Brit. Bacon.* 166 Along the Sea side.. lye heaps of Sand, upon which the people pour water till it contract a saltish humour from the sand. **1729** S. SWITZER *Hydrost. & Hydraul.* 72 To wonder how Sea-Water shall be thus stripped of its pristine Humour.

3. One of the transparent fluid or semi-fluid parts of the eye, viz. the ***aqueous humour*** in front of the iris, and the ***vitreous humour***, which fills most of the space between the iris and the retina; formerly including also the denser *crystalline lens.*

1398–1615 [see CRYSTALLINE *a.* 6]. **1643** [see AQUEOUS 1 b]. **1710** J. CLARKE *Rohault's Nat. Phil.* (1729) I. xxx. 239 [The ray] falling..upon the Superficies of the Vitreous Humour. **1831** BREWSTER *Optics* xxxv. §166. 286 The..globe of the eye consists of four coats..these coats enclose three humours. **1861** HULME tr. *Moquin-Tandon* II. I. 50 A perfect dioptric apparatus. This consists of the aqueous humour, the crystalline humour or lens, and the vitreous humour. **1872** HUXLEY *Phys.* ix. 227 The two humours are separated by the..crystalline lens, denser..than either of the humours.

II. Senses denoting mental quality or condition.

4. Mental disposition (orig. as determined by the proportion of the bodily 'humours': see 2 b); constitutional or habitual tendency; temperament.

c **1475** in *Pol. Rel. & L. Poems* 154 In my loue was neuere desaite, Alle myn humours y haue opened hir to. **1596** SHAKS. *Tam. Shr.* IV. i. 212 Thus Ile curbe her mad and headstrong humor. **1639** T. BRUGIS tr. *Camus' Mor. Relat.* 156 You know the severe humour of my Lord. **1654** tr. *Martini's Conq. China* 222 Being of a bold and couragious humour. **1676** tr. *Guillatiere's Voy. Athens* 220 Having found our humours to be inquisitive and generous, he studied all ways of gratifying them. **1775** SHERIDAN *St. Patr. Day* I. i, The corporal is the lieutenant's countryman and knows his humour. **1861** TULLOCH *Eng. Purit.* I. i. 56 A fine old country gentleman..with the genuine hearty humour of the race.

†**b.** *transf.* Character, style, 'vein'; sentiment, spirit (of a writing, musical composition, etc.).

1599 *Broughton's Lett.* iv. 14 Of the like Lunaticall humour are your epistles. **1674** PLAYFORD *Skill Mus.* I. xi. 40 The understanding of the conceit and the humour of the words. **1686** *Lond. Gaz.* No. 2119/4 Several Overtures or Sonatta's, containing Variety of Humors, as Grave Aires, Minuetts, Borees, &c. **1717** tr. *Frezier's Voy.* 256 The Bass is made in France, to the Humour of the Harp.

5. Temporary state of mind or feeling; mood, temper.

1525 in Thoms *Anecd. E. Eng. Hist.* (Camden) 11 Hacklewitt and another..in a madde humour..coyted him downe to the bottome of the stayres. **1594** SHAKS. *Rich. III*, I. ii. 229 Was euer woman in this humour woo'd? Was euer woman in this humour wonne? **1596** SPENSER *F.Q.* IV. x. 50 With smyles that all sad humors chaced. **1676** tr. *Guillatiere's Voy. Athens* 97 The whole Company was in a very good humour. **1679** PENN *Addr. Prot.* I. ii. (1692) 4, I do not wrong the present Humor of too many in this Nation. **1711** ADDISON *Spect.* No. 26 ⁋1 When I am in a serious Humour. **1773** JOHNSON *Lett. to Mrs. Thrale* 21 Sept., We were by this time weary and disgusted, nor was our humour much mended by our inn. **1884** PAE *Eustace* 33 That's why you are in such a bad humour.

†**b.** Mood natural to one's temperament; habitual frame of mind. *Obs.*

1598 B. JONSON (*title*) Every Man in his Humour. **1599** —— (*title*) Every Man out of his Humour. **1676** D'URFEY *Mad. Fickle* III. i, Every man in his humor, and let the World rub.

c. An excited state of public feeling. Now *rare.*

1600 E. BLOUNT tr. *Conestaggio* 99 It was not fitte to stirre up humours in Spaine. **1633** T. STAFFORD *Pac. Hib.* I. iii. (1810) 46 The taking of this great Lord breeds unsetled humors in these parts. **1659** *Burton's Diary* (1828) IV. 423 These tymes, and the affairs transacted in them, give motion to all sorts of humours in the nation. **1761** HUME *Hist. Eng.* xxi. II. 27 The humours of the people, set afloat by the parliamentary impeachment..broke out in various

commotions. **1865** CARLYLE *Fredk. Gt.* XV. vi. VI. 21 Friedrich is deeply unaware of the humour he has raised against himself.

6. A particular disposition, inclination, or liking, *esp.* one having no apparent ground or reason; mere fancy, whim, caprice, freak, vagary.

(In this sense very frequent in late 16th and early 17th c., and ridiculed by Shakspere and Ben Jonson.)

1565 CALFHILL *Answ. Martiall's Treat. Cross* 94 They neded no more for hallowing of a Church, but a sermon, and prayers, in which peraduenture (that I may feede your humor) they made the signe of a crosse with their finger. **1588** SHAKS. *L.L.L.* III. i. 23 These are complements, these are humours. **1598** B. JONSON *Ev. Man in Hum.* III. iv, *Cob.* What is that humour? *Cas.* It is a gentleman-like monster, bred, in the speciall gallantrie of our time, by affectation; and fed by folly. **1611** [TARLTON] *Jests* (1844) 45 How now, dog, saies Tarlton, are you in your humours? and many daies after it was a by-word to a man being drunke. that he was in his humours. **1634** LAUD *Wks.* (1853) V. 324 The humours of those men that do not conform. **1675** TRAHERNE *Chr. Ethics* xxii. 334 A wise man discards the predominancy of all humors..for he is to live the life of reason, not of humor. **1715** DE FOE *Fam. Instruct.* I. iv. (1841) I. 88 And have you really burnt all your plays to please a humour? **1770** BURKE *Pres. Discont.* Wks. 1842 I. 129 All which had been done.. was the effect not of humour, but of system. **1822** W. IRVING *Braceb. Hall* xi. 91 The Squire receives great sympathy..in his antiquated humours, from the parson.

b. An inclination or disposition for some specified action, etc.; a fancy (*to do* something); a mood or state of mind characterized by such inclination. Const. †*of* (*obs.*), *for*, or infin. with *to*.

1590 SHAKS. *Mids. N.* I. ii. 30 My chiefe humour is for a tyrant. **1598** —— *Merry W.* II. i. 133-4 And this is true: I like not the humor of lying: hee hath wronged mee in some humors. **1599** —— *Hen. V*, II. i. 63, I haue an humor to knocke you indifferently well..and that's the humor of it. **1660** WYCHERLEY *Gentlem. Dancing-mast.* IV. Wks. (Rtldg.) 59/2, I am in a pretty humour to dance. **1709** STEELE *Tatler* No. 2 ¶1, I am not in Humour for telling a Tale. **1752** HUME *Pol. Disc.* x. 261 The humour of blaming the present, and admiring the past. **1802** MAR. EDGEWORTH *Moral T.* (1816) I. 205, I am in no humour to reason. **1833** LAMB *Elia* Ser. II. *Barrenness Imag. Faculty Mod. Art*, Since the humour of exhibiting began. **1863** GEO. ELIOT *Romola* II. xxi, People very stongly in the humour for fighting.

c. *pl.* Moods or fancies exhibited in action; vagaries; fantastic, whimsical, odd, quaint, or humorous traits. (Now associated with sense 7.)

1566 R. COX (*title*) Acteon and Diana; with a Pastoral Story of the Nymph Oenone, followed by the several conceited humours of Bumpkin, the huntsman, Bobbinall, the shepheard [etc.]. **1667** PEPYS *Diary* 9 Sept., The sport very good, and various humours to be seen among the rabble. **1674** S. VINCENT *Yng. Gallant's Acad.* Ded. A iv, To shew the Apish Fashions, and ridiculous Humors and Conversations of some of our Town-Gallants. *a* **1763** SHENSTONE *Ess.* (1765) 208 Observe the humours of a Country-Christening, and you will find no Court in Christendom so ceremonious. **1822** LAMB *Elia* Ser. I. *Praise Chimney-sweepers*, Rochester..could not have done the humours of the scene with more spirit than my friend. **1850** HAWTHORNE *Scarlet L.* xxi. (1879) 263 Mariners..who had come ashore to see the humors of Election Day.

7. a. That quality of action, speech, or writing, which excites amusement; oddity, jocularity, facetiousness, comicality, fun. **b.** The faculty of perceiving what is ludicrous or amusing, or of expressing it in speech, writing, or other composition; jocose imagination or treatment of a subject.

Distinguished from *wit* as being less purely intellectual, and as having a sympathetic quality in virtue of which it often becomes allied to pathos.

1682 tr. *Glanius' Voy. Bengala* 142 The Cup was so closed, that 'twas a difficult matter for us to open it, and therefore the General gave it us on purpose, to divert himself with the humour of it. **1709** SHAFTESB. (*title*) Essay on the Freedom of Wit and Humour. **1712** HUGHES *Spect.* No. 525 ¶3 Writings which once prevail'd among us under the Notion of Humour. **1727** SWIFT *To Earl of Oxford*, The priest.. shew'd some humour in his face. **1728** —— *Intelligencer* No. 3 Humour..in its perfection is allowed to be much preferable to wit, if it be not rather the most useful and agreeable species of it. **1759** GOLDSM. *Pol. Learn* ix, Wit raises human nature above its level; humour acts a contrary part, and equally depresses it. *a* **1854** H. REED *Lect. Eng. Lit.* ii. (1855) 63 The happy compound of pathos and playfulness, which we style by that untranslateable term humour. **1870** LOWELL *Stud. Wind.* 132 Humor in its first analysis is a perception of the incongruous. **1874** GREEN *Short Hist.* viii. §10. 585 The strange deficiency of humour which Milton shared with the Puritans generally. **1887** LOWELL *Democr.* 3 That modulating and restraining balance-wheel which we call a sense of humor.

III. 8. Phrases.

a. *out of humour*: displeased, vexed, in an ill humour; out of conceit or satisfaction *with*. (Cf. *out of temper*.) So † *in humour* (*obs.*).

1660 WYCHERLEY *Gentlem. Dancing-m.* IV. Wks. (Rtldg.) 59/2 *Don.* You seem to be out of humour... *Hip.* For my sake be in humour. **1683** D. A. *Art Converse* 23 The fall of ..a Glass, or some like accident, puts them in, or rather quite out of humour. **1709** ADDISON *Tatler* No. 108 ¶2 Out of Humour with my self, and at every Thing about me. **1729** BUTLER *Serm.*, *Self-Deceit* Wks. 1874 II. 481 Who would choose to be put out of humour with himself? **1842** LYTTON *Zanoni* 24 The Cardinal is observed to be out of humour.

b. GOOD HUMOUR, ILL HUMOUR: see these and their derivatives in their alphabetical places.

IV. 9. *Comb.*, as †*humour-brethren* (sense 2 b); *humour-blind* (sense 2), *humour-loving* (sense 7) adjs.

a **1618** SYLVESTER *Paradox agst. Libertie* 465 Then th' humor-brethren all, hot, cold, and wet, and dry, Falne out among themselves, augment his miserie. **1813** *Sporting Mag.* XLII. 54 Humour-blind, greasy-heeled, and broken-winded horses. **1897** *Daily News* 29 Sept. 6/4 A light heart and a humour-loving imagination.

humour, humor, *v.* [f. HUMOUR *sb.*]

1. *trans.* To comply with the humour of; to soothe or gratify by compliance; to indulge.

1588 SHAKS. *L.L.L.* IV. ii. 52 To humour the ignorant call I the Deare the Princesse kill'd a Pricket. **1590** —— *Com. Err.* IV. iv. 84 The fellow finds his vaine, And yeelding to him, humors well his frensie. *a* **1656** BP. HALL *Rem. Wks.* (1660) 302 Humouring our taste with dainties. **1689** WOOD *Life* 31 Aug. (O.H.S) III. 309 The quakers..have been since humour'd in their nonsense, excused from oathes [etc.]. **1790** J. B. MORETON *Mann. W. Ind.* 131 If you please and humour her properly, she will make and mend all your clothes. **1828** D'ISRAELI *Chas. I*, I. xi. 314 Acquiring popularity by humouring the present temper of the nation.

2. *fig.* To comply with the peculiar nature or exigencies of (something); to adapt or accommodate oneself to; to act in compliance or agreement with; to fit, suit (*with* something).

1588 SHAKS. *L.L.L.* III. i. 13 To ligge off a tune at the tongues end, canarie to it with the feete, humour it with turning vp your eie. **1648** MILTON *Sonn. to Lawes*, The man That with smooth air couldst humour best our tongue. **1712** ADDISON *Spect.* No. 414 ¶5 Our British Gardeners.. instead of humouring Nature, love to deviate from it as much as possible. **1779** J. MOORE *View Soc. Fr.* (1789) I. xxiv. 188 The path is continually winding to humour the position of the mountains. **1845** GRAVES *Rom. Law* in *Encycl. Metrop.* 758/1 The dunces, with simple credulity, would swallow all this; the smarter freshmen, tittering, would humour the joke. **1851** WILLMOTT *Pleas. Lit.* xv. (1857) 81 In reading this stanza we ought to humour it with a corresponding tone of voice.

†**3.** *intr.* ? To exercise one's humour or fancy; to imagine, devise. *Obs.*

1605 *Lond. Prodigal* III. ii, All the day he humours up and down How he the next day may deceive his friend.

†**4.** ? To imitate a person's humour. *Obs.*

1699 BENTLEY *Phal.* Introd. 17 [He] had not so bad a hand at Humouring and Personating, that several believed, it was the Tyrant himself.

†**5.** *trans.* ? To give a particular character or style to (cf. prec. 4 b). *Obs.*

1653 WALTON *Angler* iv. 123 This Song was well humor'd by the maker, and well remembred and sung by you.

b. To give a particular turn or slight direction to.

1885 *Athenæum* 1 Aug. 136/3 To let the stream bear them [flies] on..without that..undefinable humouring of them which an angler occasionally gives. **1893** STEVENSON *Catriona* 263 The patroon humoured his boat nearer in.

†'**humourable,** *a. Obs. rare.* [f. HUMOUR *sb.* + -ABLE: cf. *fashionable*.] Pertaining to or depending on the humours (see HUMOUR *sb.* 2).

1662 J. CHANDLER *Van Helmont's Oriat.* 297 That humourable and occasional cause in the Spleen.

humoural: see HUMORAL.

humoured, humored ('hju:məd, 'ju:məd), *a.* [f. HUMOUR *sb.* and *v.* + -ED.]

1. Having a (specified) humour or disposition. (Now only in comb., as GOOD-HUMOURED, etc.)

1598 BARRET *Theor. Warres* I. i. 6 Some men (being naturally humoured thereunto) do prooue better souldiers. **1621** BURTON *Anat. Mel.* I. ii. IV. iv. (1651) 150 He that mads others, if he were so humored, would be as mad himself. **1751** EARL ORRERY *Remarks Swift* (1752) 103 The free humoured Rabelais.

†**2.** Fancied, imaginary (cf. HUMOUR *v.* 3). *Obs.*

1613 PURCHAS *Pilgrimage* (1614) 462 Another (transported by this humoured Charon)..trembles at his supposed sights of the Divell.

3. Complied with, indulged.

1649 MILTON *Eikon.* xi, The breeding of most Kings hath been ever sensual and most humour'd. **1711** SHAFTESB. *Charac.* II. II. i. (1737) II. 117 The most humour'd and indulg'd State.

'**humourish,** *a. Obs. rare.* [f. HUMOUR *sb.* + -ISH.] Liable to humours; fanciful, fantastic.

1667 L. STUCLEY *Gospel-Glass* xxxiv. (1670) 365 Humourish, pievish lovers.

humourist, -ous: see HUMORIST, -OUS.

'**humourless, -orless,** *a.* [f. HUMOUR *sb.* + -LESS.] Devoid of humour. Hence '**humourlessness.**

1847 CRAIG, *Humorless.* **1875** *N. Amer. Rev.* CXX. 279 One of these humorless sublime utopias. **1890** *Sat. Rev.* 13 Sept. 308/2 That total inability to see yourself as others see you..the child of humourlessness.

humoursome, humorsome ('hju:məsəm), *a.* Also 7-8 hu*mersom*(*e*. [f. as prec. + -SOME.]

1. Subject to or full of humours; fanciful, capricious, fantastic; peevish, ill-humoured: = HUMOROUS 3.

1656 H. MORE *Enthus. Tri.* To Rdr. A iv a, Confusion of so great seriousnesse with so humoursome mirth. **1678** CUDWORTH *Intell. Syst.* Contents I. iv. §24 The Divine Will ..not a meer arbitrary, Humoursome, and Fortuitous thing, but Decency and Fitness it self. **1707** *Reflex. upon Ridicule* II. 130 Abundance of People think to distinguish themselves by humoursome Singularities. **1742** RICHARDSON *Pamela* III. 267 This Gentleman is very particularly odd and humoursome. **1823** DE QUINCEY *Dice* Wks. XI. 294 Every day he grew more fretful and humoursome. **1850** HAWTHORNE *Scarlet L.* vi. (1879) 112 With the humorsome gesticulation of a little imp. **1863** E. J. MAY *Stronges of Netherstronge* viii. 76 Well, there, women are, forsooth, humoursome beings.

2. Disposed to humour or indulge any one; indulgent. (*nonce-use.*)

a **1876** T. EDWARD in Smiles *Sc. Natur.* xiii. 275 He seemed to be most friendly..and humoursome to the little rabbit.

'**humoursomely,** *adv.* [f. prec. + -LY².] In a humoursome manner: see prec. 1.

1653 H. MORE *Antid. Ath.* I. viii. (1662) 25 Humoursomely and foolishly done. **1678** CUDWORTH *Intell. Syst.* I. iii. §4. 107 A thing intelligible, but humoursomely expressed. **1748** RICHARDSON *Clarissa* (1811) V. xvii. 183 To trifle thus humoursomely with such a gentleman's moments.

'**humoursomeness.** [f. as prec. + -NESS.] The quality or character of being humoursome; capriciousness of humour.

1653 H. MORE *Antid. Ath.* I. viii. (1662) 22 (*heading*) The factious Humoursomeness of the Atheist. **1750-1** MRS. DELANY in *Life & Corr.* III. 24 Nothing will so effectually ..get the better of any humoursomeness (a strange word) as in the discipline of a school. **1754** RICHARDSON *Grandison* (1781) IV. iv. 25, I never blame a Lady for her humoursomeness, so much, as..I blame her Mother. **1832** J. C. HARE in *Philol. Museum* I. 445 All the weaknesses, humoursomenesses, and contradictions which are presumed in the situations.

humous ('hju:məs), *a.* [f. HUM(US + -OUS.] Present in or of the nature of humus; rich in humus. Cf. HUMIC *a.*

1866 H. WATTS tr. *Gmelin's Hand-bk. Chem.* XVII. 473 Hermann..distinguishes eleven different humous substances. **1902** *Jrnl. Chem. Soc.* LXXXII. II. 521 Oats and soy beans..were grown in humous soil. **1909** GROOM & BALFOUR tr. *Warming's Oecol. Plants* xlvi. 195 The weightiest cause of the physiological dryness of the soil probably lies in the presence of free humous acids. **1968** R. G. WEST *Pleistocene Geol. & Biol.* iv. 55 Humous substances.

hump (hʌmp), *sb.* [This word, with its whole family, is of late appearance, and seems to have taken, *c* 1680–1720, the place of the earlier *crump* (CRUMP *a.*¹, *sb.*¹). It is first exemplified, 1681, in the comb. *hump-backed* = the earlier *crump-backed.* So *hump-back*, *hump-shoulder*, *-shouldered*, corresponding to earlier forms with *crump-*, are known before HUMP *sb.*, which is not in Phillips-Kersey 1706, Bailey 1721–53. HUMP *v.* is of much later appearance.

(*Humpish* in H. CROSSE *Vertues Commw.* (1603) L ij b, is an evident misprint for *lumpish*.)

Hump agrees in form with LG. *hump*, *humpe* portion, piece, hunk (of anything), Du. *homp* lump, hunch, thick piece, early mod.Du. *hompe* fem. 'pars abscissa', *hompe broods* 'cuneus panis' (Kilian 1599). But these words always mean a hunch, hunk, lump, or thick piece, cut or broken off something, not a protuberance upon it like 'hump'. Cf. however LG. *humpel*, *hümpel*, height, knoll, knob, hump of a camel, etc. The late appearance of the words in all the langs. leaves the question of their origin and relationship undetermined. See Kluge, s.v. *Humpe*, Franck, s.v. *Homp.* The English *hump-backed* in 1681 might be taken as a mixed form uniting *hunch-backed* and *crump-backed*, since these were both in earlier use. (Cf. HUNCH.)]

1. a. A protuberance on the back or other part of the body, formed by a curved spine or a fleshy excrescence, and occurring as a normal feature in certain animals, as the camel and bison, or as a deformity in man. Also applied to other kinds of protuberances in animal and plant life.

1709 *Tatler* No. 75 ¶6 The eldest Son of Philip..being born with an Hump-back and very high Nose..These several Defects were mended by succeeding Matches; the Eyes were open'd in the next Generation, and the Hump fell in a Century and half. **1728** MORGAN *Algiers* I. iv. 100 The rider sits behind the bunch or hump. *a* **1764** LLOYD *Cobbler Cripplegate's Let.* (R.), Tight stays they find oft end in humps. **1774** GOLDSM. *Nat. Hist.* (1776) III. 20 The breed of the urus, or those without an hump..the breed of the bison, or the animal with an hump. *a* **1839** PRAED *Poems* (1864) I. 199 With a gash beneath his clotted hair, And a hump upon his shoulder. **1839** T. BEALE *Sperm Whale* 24 At this point [the sperm whale has] a large prominence of a pyramidal form called the 'hump'. **1875** BENNETT & DYER *Sachs' Bot.* 20 The thickenings which project outwardly may appear in the form of knots, humps, spines, or ridges.

b. A hump-backed person. *nonce-use.*

1708 MOTTEUX *Rabelais* IV. xlviii. 137, I saw a little Hump [*petit bossu*] with long Fingers. **1871** R. ELLIS *Catullus* lii. 2 In the curule chair a hump sits, Nonius.

c. The flesh of a bison's hump used as food. Also, the flesh of the hump of other animals.

1805 M. LEWIS *Jrnl.* 13 June in *Orig. Jrnls. Lewis & Clark Expedition* (1904) II. 151 My fare is really sumptuous this evening; buffaloe's humps, tongues and marrow-bones. **1807** in *Spirit Pub. Jrnls.* (1808) XI. 41 Humps have long been a favourite dish at the splendid entertainments of the great Lords..in India. **1823** J. FRANKLIN *Narr. Journey Shores Polar Sea* 115 The meat [of the buffalo] which covers the spinal processes themselves, after the wig is removed, is next in esteem for its flavour and juiciness, and is more

extensively termed the hump by the hunters. **1851** MAYNE REID *Scalp Hunt.* iv, 'Yonder!' cried St. Vrain; 'fresh hump for supper!' **1861** C. J. ANDERSSON *Okavango River* 130 Rhinoceros hump was..a frequent and favourite dish of mine. **1863** Rhinoceros hump [see RHINOCEROS 3]. **1909** *Daily Chron.* 5 Jan. 4/7 'Humps have arrived.' So runs the legend in an old-established shop in Green-street, Leicester-square. *Ibid.*, A beef hump. **1913** C. PETTMAN *Africanderisms, Hump*... A favourite piece with South African housewives for salting.

d. *to live on one's hump*: to be self-sufficient, to operate from resources accumulated earlier: with reference to the camel's hump as a reserve of nourishment.

1909 *Westm. Gaz.* 11 Sept. 7/2 During nearly three weeks in this glorious place I have lived on my own hump.

2. *transf.* **a.** A rounded boss of earth, rock, etc.; a hummock.

1838 THIRLWALL *Greece* III. 409 The Athenian troops.. mounted Epipolæ, and reached the top, where it rises into a rocky hump called Euryelus. **1860** TYNDALL *Glac.* I. viii. 58 Climbing vast humps of ice. **1871** L. STEPHEN *Playgr. Europe* vii. (1894) 158 The rounded dome..forms the southern hump of the Viescherhorn.

b. A mound in a railway yard up which vehicles are pushed by an engine and down the other side of which they run by gravity and are switched to the proper track.

1901 *Railroad Gaz.* 4 Jan. 2/1 All that was necessary to take advantage of this mode of distributing cars, was to put a 'hump' in the switching track. **1911** *Encycl. Brit.* XXII. 842/1 Another method [of shunting], which was introduced into America from Europe about 1890, is that of the summit or 'hump'. **1921** *Daily Mail Yr. Bk.* 112/1 The London and South-Western Company has constructed at Feltham a new 'hump' marshalling yard. **1955** *Times* 12 July 3/4 They had approved new works at Perth, including the construction of a fully mechanized hump marshalling yard. **1958** *Times* 11 Feb. 15/3 We have carried out development on equipment ..for assisting the automatic operation of hump sorting yards. **1971** D. J. SMITH *Discovering Railwayana* x. 56 *Hump yard*, goods yards or sidings worked by gravity shunting methods.

c. A mountain barrier high enough to make both land and air travel difficult. Chiefly *U.S.*

1914 *Sat. Even. Post* 4 Apr. 10/2 There ain't a kid like him this side of the Hump [*sc.* mountain range in west of N. America]—nor t'other side either. **1931** 'D. STIFF' *Milk & Honey Route* 208 'Over the hump' means to cross the mountains to the West Coast. **1936** K. MACKENZIE *Living Rough* xv. 216 We're sure a pair of nuts riding the outside over the hump this time of the year. **1944** *Time* 26 June 52/1 They're flying it over 'The Hump'—the towering Himalayas between India and China. **1970** 'B. MATHER' *Break in Line* v. 64 'I think he'll be making for Rangoon, then over the bloody hills to China.'..'You really expect me to walk over the Hump?'

d. *transf.* and *fig.* The critical point (in an undertaking, ordeal, the ascent of a seaplane, etc.), esp. in the phr. *over the hump*, over the worst, well begun. (Cf. 2c.) Also, the high point, peak (of a graph, etc.).

1914 JACKSON & HELLYER *Vocab. Criminal Slang* 46 *Hump*,..the half-way point in a prison sentence. Example: 'How long have you got yet on your bit? I'm just over the hump.' **1914** *Techn. Rep. Advisory Comm. Aeronaut. 1912–13* 244 The floats of the flaring bow type require only about half the E.H.P. to surmount the hump. **1922** W. R. INGE *Lay Thoughts* (1926) II. i. 89 If we look at a chart of the births and deaths in Germany..each war is marked by a peak in the line showing the death rate and a ravine in the line showing the birth rate. But the ravine is followed by a hump..making good the numbers lost. **1929** D. HAMMETT *Dain Curse* (1930) xxii. 253 Today won't be like yesterday. You're over the hump, and the rest of it's downhill going. **1935** P. W. F. MILLS *Elem. Pract. Flying* v. 71 In rising from the normal semi-submerged state there is a critical point known as passing the hump, before the reaching of which point the floats are definitely water-bound. After passing the hump the floats very nearly emerge from the water and commence to hydroplane. The time taken to reach the 'hump' and the ease with which it is passed, vary greatly. **1938** *Amer. Speech* XIII. 188/2 Once a cocaine addict is *over the hump* he says he is *coasting* or *in high*. **1952** *Economist* 27 Sept. 771/1 The machine tool industry is probably 'over the hump' of its..task. **1959** *Listener* 19 Feb. 316/2 Things were very difficult with us that year, and the Americans helped *us* over the hump. **1960** *Economist* 8 Oct. 135/1 The 'hump' in imports that was desired has turned into a steady climb. **1965** *Listener* 16 Dec. 985/1 East German farming is getting over the hump.

3. a. A fit of ill humour or vexation; sulks. Esp. in phr. *to give* (a person) *the hump*. *slang*.

(Cf. HUMP *v.* 1. Quot. 1727 is of doubtful meaning.)

1727 DE FOE *Protest. Monast.* 4 Under many Hardships and Restrictions, many Humps and Grumps. **1873** *Slang Dict.* s.v., A costermonger who was annoyed or distressed about anything would describe himself as having 'the hump'. **1887** F. GALE *Game of Cricket* viii. 187 So let's alter the law, Without any more jaw, Or you'll give an old buffer the hump. **1897** *Westm. Gaz.* 18 Feb. 1/3 Well, my boy, you've evidently got the hump..but you must give up that sort of thing when I'm here. **1910** E. M. FORSTER *Howards End* vi. 51 That tune fairly gives me the hump. **1939** T. S. ELIOT *Family Reunion* 18 You seem to be wanting to give us all the hump. I must say, this isn't cheerful for Amy's birthday.

b. A walk or hike with a load on one's back. (Cf. HUMP *v.* 2.) *Austral.* and *N.Z. slang*.

1863 J. G. WALKER *Jrnl.* 7 Jan. (MS.) 4 It was a precious hump [over the hill for provisions]. **1890** 'R. BOLDREWOOD' *Miner's Right* v, We get a fair share of exercise without a twenty-mile hump on Sundays.

4. *to get a hump on*, to hurry. (Cf. HUMP *v.* 3.) *U.S. colloq.*

1892 *Harper's Mag.* Feb. 487/2 'We went fast enough then.' 'We do seem to be gittin' a lettle less hump on oursel's than we did then.' **1940** W. E. WILSON *Wabash* 231 'Let's git a hump on, Allen,' Abe said; and the two boys dipped their oars deeper into the brown water.

5. Sexual intercourse; hence, a woman who makes herself available for sexual intercourse. *coarse slang*.

1931 G. IRWIN *Amer. Tramp & Underworld Slang* 105 *Hump*,..sexual intercourse. **1969** E. R. JOHNSON *Mongo's back in Town* (1970) ii. 18 It might be a good idea to line up a Christmas hump for himself. **1969** P. ROTH *Portnoy's Complaint* 134 Now you want to treat me like I'm nothing but some hump. **1970** 'D. CRAIG' *Young Men may Die* vi. 48 It was hard to believe she could be more than an ad hoc hump for Lamartine.

6. *attrib.* and *Comb.*, as ***hump-curer, meat, rib***; ***hump-shaped*** adj. **hump speed** *Aeronaut.*, the speed of a seaplane or hovercraft at which the drag due to the water is a maximum (cf. quots. 1914[2], 1935 in sense 2 d). See also HUMP-BACK, -BACKED, -SHOULDER, -ED.

1807 in *Spirit Pub. Jrnls.* (1808) XI. 42 A mandate to Calcutta, enjoining the principal hump-curer..to buy up all the humps that could be had. **1834** in *Oreg. Hist. Soc. Q.* (1916) XVII. 126 The tongue, the heart, the marrow bones and the hump ribs is all they use when meat is plenty. **1836** W. IRVING *Astoria* III. 98 The hump meat afforded them a repast fit for an epicure. **1839** J. K. TOWNSEND *Narr. Rocky Mts.* iii. 164 They..appeared to be surveying, with the keenness of morning appetite, the fine 'hump ribs' which were roasting before them. **1861** G. F. BERKELEY *Sportsm. W. Prairies* xiv. 262, I found that it was the 'hump-rib'. **1886** *Pall Mall G.* 28 Aug. 13/2 The water is collected on a hump-shaped hill called the Knoll, and descends..to the village. **1915** *Techn. Rep. Advisory Comm. Aeronaut. 1913–14* 369 It was not practicable to fit air-holes to the second step, but it is probable that a slight reduction of power at the 'hump' speed could be obtained by this means in smooth water. **1938** *Jrnl. R. Aeronaut. Soc.* XLII. 559 The relative distance and time required to reach hump speed depend largely on the value of the accelerating force at high speeds. **1962** *New Scientist* 24 May 388/1 As a hovercraft accelerates from rest there is a so-called 'hump-speed' (about 14–18 knots) above which the drag suddenly drops.

hump, *v.* [f. HUMP *sb.*]

1. a. *trans.* To make humped or hump-shaped; to hunch. (Also with *up.*) *to hump the back* (fig.), to show vexation or sulkiness.

1840 MARRYAT *Poor Jack* xxii, It got into a dark corner, growling and humping its back. **1881** MISS YONGE *Lads & Lasses Langley* ii. 67 Frank had been used to hump up his back, and put his head on his arms and be comfortable. **1884** BOURKE *Snake Dance Moquis* xxvi. 288 The cats humped themselves in readiness for hostilities. **1889** *Spectator* 14 Dec. 851/1 She..tumbles her ringlets over her eyes, humps her back, and makes her shoulders look sulky. **1895** CROCKETT *Cleg Kelly* xxiii, Sal humped up the shoulder.. and turned sharply away from him.

b. *absol.*

1884 STOCKTON *Lady or Tiger?* etc. 108 He [the racoon].. come a humpin' inter the house. **1885** G. MEREDITH *Diana* III. iv. 79 Danvers humped, femininely injured by the notice of it.

c. *trans.* To round (a surface).

1878 J. PATON in *Encycl. Brit.* VI. 734/2 The 'humping' or rounding of scissors.

d. *transf.* of inanimate things.

1901 'LINESMAN' *Words by Eyewitness* (1902) 168 With the berg humping its mighty shoulders far behind them.

2. To hoist or carry (a bundle) upon the back: chiefly ***to hump one's swag*** (***bluey, drum***), to shoulder one's bundle. Also more generally, to carry or shift (a heavy object), not necessarily upon the back, and ***to hump it***. See also BLUEY *sb.* Chiefly *Austral.* and *N.Z. slang*.

1853 W. HOWITT *Two Years Victoria* xiii. (1855) I. 226 He 'humped his swag', in diggers' phrase, that is, shouldered his pack. **1863** J. GOLDIE *3rd Diary* 19 Feb. in J. H. Beattie *Pioneers explore Otago* (1947) 147 Digger custom, we humped our swag containing our house, our bed, our grub. **1863** J. G. WALKER *Jrnl.* Mar. (MS.) 4 Humping it over from the Tiviot on our backs would not do as it was too hard work. **1864** J. C. RICHMOND *Let.* 12 May in *Richmond-Atkinson Pap.* II. 111 It is very hard work humping your blankets and tucker. **1865** E. R. CHUDLEIGH *Diary* 16 July (1950) 193 Humping all their belonging with them. **1866** B. L. FARJEON *Shadows on Snow* 66 [Diggers]. The best thing we can do..is to try and hump it back again tomorrow. **1888** BOLDREWOOD *Robbery under Arms* I. xi. 142 We put it up roughly..with pine saplings. The drawing in was the worst, for we had to 'hump' the most of them ourselves. **1897** *Westm. Gaz.* 7 Aug. 1/3 He humped his load up country a bit. **1916** 'TAFFRAIL' *Pincher Martin* xii. 218 We'll have to hump the whole bloomin' lot out again, damn an' blast him! **1922** T. E. LAWRENCE *Let.* 7 Sept. (1938) 365, I went off to hump their swill to the camp pigs. **1924** —— *Let.* 20 Jan. (1938) 456 If it is the best I can do with a pen, then it's better for me to hump a rifle or spade about. **1925** FRASER & GIBBONS *Soldier & Sailor Words* 122 *To hump*, to lift, to carry. *Ibid.*, *To hump it*, to march with full kit, to tramp on foot. **1955** M. GILBERT *Sky High* viii. 112 Couldn't you hump around the heavy lectern vases. **1960** *Sunday Express* 6 Mar. 8/4 He..tugged out a suitcase containing his full-dress uniform, humped it across the pavement. **1971** B. W. ALDISS *Soldier Erect* 78, I followed behind him, humping the wireless set. **1971** *N.Z. Listener* 22 Mar. 13/1 He's humpin' a haversack. **1973** C. BONINGTON *Next Horizon* xii. 171 John and Dougal took the lead, while Layton and I followed, humping loads... I humped my big rucksack, taking the occasional photograph.

3. a. *refl.* To gather oneself together for an effort; to exert oneself, make an effort; to hurry; also, to pride or fancy oneself. Also *intr.* (for *refl.*) orig. and chiefly *U.S. slang*.

1835 in W. T. PORTER *Big Bear* etc. (1847) 126 (Farmer) He was breathin' sorter hard, his eye set on the Governor, humpin' himself on politics. **1883** *Philad. Times* 15 Aug. (Cent.), Col. Burns said, 'Now you all watch that critter hump himself'. **1884** 'MARK TWAIN' *Huck. Finn* xxix. 307, I never hunted for no back streets, but humped it straight through the main one. **1895** *Daily News* 26 Sept. 4/7 When the weather of St. Andrews 'humps itself' it can equal the feats of the weather in Montana. **1897** *Chicago Advance* 25 Feb. 263/1 Grit makes the man, the lack of it the chump; Therefore, young man, take hold, hang on and hump. **1906** D. COKE *Bending of Twig* iv. 71 'We shall have to hump ourselves for call-over,' he said..as they dashed up the hill. **1908** G. H. LORIMER *Jack Spurlock* i. 9 He..said to the cop on guard, 'One of them Ha'voids [= Harvard students],' and to me, 'Hump yourself.' **1928** 'SAPPER' *Female of Species* ii, Peter—your Sunbeam, and hump yourself. *Ibid.* xiv, That finger will connect with the trigger and the result will connect with you. So, hump yourself. **1968** M. WOODHOUSE *Rock Baby* vi. 48, I..humped myself into my coat.

b. In extended use.

1905 *Smart Set* Sept. 117/1 You'll have to get this machine to hump it all she knows. **1929** J. B. PRIESTLEY *Good Companions* I. i. 3 As you look down on Bruddersford, you feel..that it is only biding its time, that it will hump its way through somehow.

4. *trans.* To give (one) 'the hump': see prec. 3.

1840 THACKERAY *Paris Sketch-bk.*, *On some fashionable French novels* (ed. 2) I. 177 Did he not hump me prodigiously, by letting fall a goblet, after Cellini? **1898** A. BEARDSLEY *Let.* 16 Jan. (1971) 427 Letter writing humps me dreadfully.

5. *trans.* and *intr.* To have sexual intercourse (with). *coarse slang*.

1785 GROSE *Dict. Vulgar T.*, *Hump*, to hump, once a fashionable word for copulation. **1931** G. IRWIN *Amer. Tramp & Underworld Slang* 105 *Hump*, to have intercourse. *Ibid.* 263 In 1914–1918..*hump* and *niggle* were used of both sexes, *screw* and *shag* were operatively male. **1961** J. HELLER *Catch-22* (1962) xiii. 131 The girls had shelter and food for as long as they wanted to stay. All they had to do in return was hump any of the men who asked them to. **1962** J. BALDWIN *Another Country* (1963) I. i. 14 A nigger..lives his whole life, lives and dies according to a beat... He humps to that beat and the baby he throws up in there..comes out nine months later like a goddamn tambourine. **1965** M. BRADBURY *Stepping Westward* vii. 345 Story is he humped the faculty wives in alphabetical order. **1971** W. HANLEY *Blue Dreams* vii. 90 Gazing at her, the hem of her skirt pushed by the attitude of her dazzling legs far back along her thighs, he thought, Jesus, what would it be like to hump her?

Hence **humping** (ˈhʌmpɪŋ).

1878 [see 1 c]. **1896** SIR E. M. THOMPSON in *Proc. Soc. Antiq.* Ser. II. XVI. 215 A humping of the shoulders or back to a degree that almost amounts to deformity.

ˈhumpback, hump-back, *sb.* (*a.*) [See HUMP *sb.* In this combination, as in *hump shoulder*, *hump* may be taken as an adj.: cf. the earlier *crump-back*, under CRUMP *a.*]

A. *sb.* **1.** (ˌ*hump-ˈback.*) A back having a hump; a humped back.

1697 VANBRUGH *Æsop* II. Wks. (Rtldg.) 373/1 Who'd think that little hump-back of his should have so much brains in't? **1709** [see HUMP *sb.* 1]. **1731** MEDLEY *Kolben's Cape G. Hope* II. 64, I have never met with one, Bull, Ox, or Cow..with a high Hump-back. **1840** F. D. BENNETT *Whaling Voy.* I. 118 Those who are deformed with hump-backs bear the greatest share of reputation.

2. (ˈ*humpback.*) A person with a humped back; a hunchback.

1712 tr. *Arab. Nts.* xcix. (ed. 2) III. 125 He march'd along as they did and follow'd Humpback. **1715** *Ibid.* clxxxiv. (ed. 3) V. 67 That Hump-back is not dead. **1852** MOTLEY *Corr.* (1889) I. v. 139 Humpbacks and cripples. **1860** GEO. ELIOT *Mill on Fl.* II. iii, An ill-natured humpback.

3. = *humpback salmon, sucker, whale*: see B.

1725 DUDLEY in *Phil. Trans.* XXXIII. 258 Both the Finbacks and Humpbacks are shaped in Reeves longitudinal from Head to Tail on their Bellies and their Sides. **1840** F. D. BENNETT *Whaling Voy.* II. 232 The Humpback is seldom molested by whalers. **1881** *Amer. Naturalist* XV. 182 The hump-back, taken in salt water about Seattle, shows the same peculiarities. **1913** *Chambers's Jrnl.* Oct. 729/1 The 'steel-head', the 'dog-salmon', and the 'humpback'. **1955** [see CHINOOK b]. **1963** *Vancouver Sun* 13 Aug. 14/1 Humpback is the old and still popular name for the pink salmon. **1965** A. J. MCCLANE *Standard Fishing Encycl.* 411/1 The humpback [sucker] prefers the slow-moving parts of larger streams.

B. *attrib.* or as *adj.* (ˈ*humpback*). Having a hump on the back; hump-backed. **humpback salmon** = GORBUSCHA, HADDO; **humpback sucker** *U.S.*, *Xyrauchen texanus*, a freshwater fish of the Colorado basin; **humpback whale**, a whale of the genus *Megaptera*, so called because the low dorsal fin forms a characteristic hump on the back.

1725 DUDLEY in *Phil. Trans.* XXXIII. 258 The Bunch or humpback Whale, is distinguished from the right Whale, by having a Bunch standing in the Place where the Fin does in the Finback. **1860** *Merc. Marine Mag.* VII. 211 Whales of the 'humpback' species. **1869** *Mainland Guardian* (New Westminster, B.C.) 25 Sept. 2/1 The Oleys or Hones appear every alternate year; they are known as the Humpback salmon. **1881** *Amer. Naturalist* XV. 177 The fact that the hump-back salmon runs only on alternate years in Puget sound..is well attested. **1891** [see GORBUSCHA]. **1965** A. J. MCCLANE *Standard Fishing Encycl.* 410/2 Humpback sucker *Xyrauchen texanus*. **1971** B. MUUS *Freshwater Fish Brit. & Europe* 64/2 The humpback salmon is distinguished from other Pacific salmon by its short, 2-year life-cycle.

hump-backed, *a.* [See HUMP *sb.* This is the first exemplified word of the *hump* group: cf. the earlier *crump-backed.* The stress shifts according to construction.] Having a humped or crooked back; hunched, *esp.* in the names of fishes; cf. HUMPBACK *sb.* (*a.*). Also *transf.*
1681 *Lond. Gaz.* No. 1649/8 She has been formerly much galled under the Saddle, hump-backed under the Pillion-place. **1762** HUME *Hist. Eng.* II. xxiii. 439 This prince [Richard III] was of a small stature, hump-backed. **1769** MAD. D'ARBLAY *Early Diary*, He..has the misfortune to be hump-back'd. **1807** tr. *Garytschev's Voy.* 28 We managed.. to lay in a stock for ourselves of the hump-backed salmon, and other such fish. **1842** TENNYSON *Walking to Mail* 23 There by the humpback'd willow. **1884** G. B. GOODE *Fisheries U.S.: Nat. Hist. Aquatic Animals* 323 It is a frequent summer visitor all along the coast as far north as Wood's Holl, Massachusetts, where it has a peculiar name, the people there calling it the 'Hump-backed Butterfish'. **1886** J. K. JEROME *Idle Thoughts* (1889) 56 It might be hump-backed Vulcan. **1896** JORDAN & EVERMANN *Check-List Fishes N. & Mid. Amer.* 241 *Xyrauchen cypho.* Razor-back Sucker; Hump-backed Sucker. **1902** *Encycl. Brit.* XXVI. 391/1 The dog-salmon and the humpbacked have no commercial value. **1973** *Times* 10 Jan. 7/2 He watched two fishing boats return fully laden with hump-backed salmon.

humped (hʌmpt), *a.* [f. HUMP *sb.* + -ED².] Having a hump (or humps); hump-backed, hunch-backed; having the back or shoulders rounded (in a huddled or cramped posture). Also ***humped-up***.
1713 ADDISON *Guardian* No. 102 ¶3 A straight-shouldered man as one would desire to see, but a little unfortunate in a humpt back. **1756** BURKE *Subl. & B.* III. v, If the back be humped, the man is deformed. **1836** *Penny Cycl.* V. 241 Thorax convex above, the anterior part humped. **1876** G. MEREDITH *Beauch. Career* III. ii. 28 He wanted an audience as hotly as the humped Richard a horse. **1885** T. ROOSEVELT *Hunting Trips* iv. 104 The cattle.. standing humped up in the bushes. **1886** *Art Age* IV. 40 Its gables and humped roof are picturesque enough to please any artistic mind. **1895** K. GRAHAME *Gold. Age* 45 The drowsing peacock squatted humped on the lawn. **1906** W. S. MAUGHAM *Bishop's Apron* v. 71 The coachman..sat on his box in a slovenly, humped-up fashion. **1931** G. O. RUSSELL *Speech & Voice* xiv. 137 The high-arching and humped-up-rounding position of the tongue.

humpenscrump ('hʌmpənskrʌmp). [*dial.* (not in *E.D.D.*), perh. f. HUMP *sb.* + (*Old Father*) *Scrump*, a freq. appellation of Big Head in traditional English folk-plays; cf. HUMSTRUM and SCRUMP.] A musical instrument of rude construction; a hurdy-gurdy (sense 1 a).
[**1923** R. J. E. TIDDY *Mummers' Play* 172, I old father scrump with a bell on my rump... A man..kicked a hump up on to my shoulder and there remains the hump now.] *Ibid.* 173 [*stage directions*] Instruments Tin whistle. Jew's Harp. Father Scrump carries the humpenscrump made with a tin with wires across and bridge and a stick with notches for a bow. **1933** E. K. CHAMBERS *Eng. Folk-Play* 70 The musical instrument is generally a fiddle, or a rustic substitute called a hurdy-gurdy or humpen-scrump. **1954** L. MACNEICE *Autumn Sequel* 142 The humpenscrump that charmed some forebear's ear Now makes the roast pigs caper in Cockayne.

humper ('hʌmpə(r)). [f. HUMP *v.* + -ER¹.] Something or someone that humps, in the senses of the verb. (For quot. 1895 cf. HUMP *v.* 3.)
1895 *Columbus* (Ohio) *Dispatch* 27 Mar. 1/3 We were coming along on time. Engine 586 is a humper, and Rankin, my fireman, was keeping her hot. **1897** KIPLING *Capt. Cour.* vii. 142 Hark to her [*sc.* a ship]! She's a humper! **1961** *Spectator* 7 Apr. 471 The carrying of a second man, or 'humper', on newspaper delivery vans in London. **1967** *Times Rev. Industry* Feb. 35/2 Worked in the Smithfield meat market..earning 30s. as a humper.

humph (hʌmf), *int.* (and *sb.*) Also 7 **hemph**. The inarticulate syllable 'h'mf!', used:
†**a.** app. as a signal: cf. HUMPH *v.* 1. *Obs.*
1681 OTWAY *Soldier's Fort.* IV. i, Truly a good Conscience is a great Happiness; and so I'll pledge you, hemph, hemph.
b. as an expression of doubt or dissatisfaction. Also *sb.*, as a name for this utterance.
1815 *Sixteen & Sixty* I. ii, Humph!..her lips are of the brightest. **1824** SCOTT *Redgauntlet* Let. ii, A half articulated 'humph!' which seemed to convey a doubt. **1840** HOOD *Up the Rhine* 75 My Uncle received this intelligence with a 'Humph'. **1865** KINGSLEY *Herew.* iv, 'Humph!' says the eagle. **1872** DARWIN *Emotions* iv. 86 His humph of assent was rendered by a slight modulation strongly emphatic.

humph, *v.* [f. prec.] *intr.* To utter an inarticulate 'h'mf!'.
†**a.** as a signal. *Obs.*
1681 OTWAY *Soldier's Fort.* II. i, I desire you to humph.. and look back at me.
b. as an expression of doubt or dissatisfaction.
1814 JANE AUSTEN *Mansf. Park* xlv, After humphing and considering over a particular paragraph. **1834** L. RITCHIE *Wand. by Seine* 70 Some of the polite Frenchmen humphed, and shrugged their shoulders.

Humphrey. *to dine with Duke H.*: see DINE *v.* 1 b. So ***to have Duke H. as host.***
1693 *Humours of Town* 29 To make the World think he has been at a good Meal, when Duke Humphrey was his Host.

humpiness: see HUMPY *a.*

humpish ('hʌmpɪʃ), *a.* [f. HUMP *sb.* + -ISH¹ 2.] Somewhat like a hump, somewhat squat and dumpy.
1936 W. HOLTBY *South Riding* II. v. 130 Lydia stood up, a humpish stocky schoolgirl. **1939** R. FRY *Last Lectures* v. 68 They are squat and humpish renderings, often of seated forms.

humpless ('hʌmplɪs), *a.* [f. HUMP *sb.* + -LESS.] Having no hump.
1868 DARWIN *Anim. & Pl.* I. iii. 80 Blyth sums up emphatically that the humped and humpless cattle must be considered as distinct species. **1890** H. M. STANLEY *Darkest Africa* II. xxxiii. 363 The cattle..are mostly of a hornless and humpless breed.

†**hump-shoulder.** *Obs.* [See HUMP *sb.* Here, as in *hump-back*, *hump* may be taken as an adj. Cf. the earlier ***crump shoulder***, ***-shouldered***, under CRUMP *a.*¹] A shoulder raised into a hump. So †**hump-shouldered** *a.*, having a hump-shoulder, round-shouldered, 'crump-shouldered'.
a **1704** T. BROWN in *Collect. Poems* (1705) 40 The Duke of Luxemburg, who was Hump-Shoulder'd. **1704** SWIFT *Batt. Bks.* (1750) 27 His crooked Leg and hump Shoulder.

humpty ('hʌm(p)tɪ), *a.* and *sb.* [app. f. HUMP *sb.*, or *humpt*, HUMPED, but the formation is anomalous, and may have arisen out of next word.] **A.** *adj.* Humped, hump-backed. *Comb.*, as ***humpty-backed*** adj.
a **1825** FORBY *Voc. E. Anglia*, *Humpty*, hunch-backed. **1889** H. M. STANLEY in *Daily News* 26 Nov. 5/8 The humpty western flank [of a mountain] dipped down..into lands that we knew not by name as yet. **1898** *Daily News* 2 May 6/5 Humpty backed (as they call it in that region).
B. *sb.* A low padded cushion seat, a dumpty.
1924 *Drapery Sale Catal.*, Humptys and Cushions. **1926** *Brit. Weekly* 18 Mar. 600/2 The ladies of the village are busy making 'humpties', soft cushion seats to pull up on the rug before the peat fire. **1928** *Daily Express* 23 Jan. 5/2 Home-made Humpty.

humpty-dumpty ('hʌm(p)tɪ 'dʌm(p)tɪ), *sb.* and *a.* Also 7 **humtee dumtee, -y.** [It is doubtful whether the word is the same in senses 1 and 2: in sense 1 the name may have been concocted out of HUM *sb.*¹ 3; in sense 2 it is evidently formed from *hump* and *dump*, though this would naturally give *humpy-dumpy* (cf. HUMPY *a.*), and the intrusive *t* is not clearly accounted for.]
A. *sb.* **1.** A drink made with 'ale boiled with brandy' (B.E. *Dict. Cant. Crew*, *a* 1700).
1698 W. KING tr. *Sorbière's Journ. Lond.* 135 (Farmer) He answer'd me that he had a thousand such sort of liquors, as Humtie Dumtie, Three Threads. **1699** [see HUGMATEE]. **1837** DISRAELI *Venetia* I. xiv, They drank humpty-dumpty, which is ale boiled with brandy.
2. A short, dumpy, hump-shouldered person. In the well-known nursery rime or riddle (quoted below) commonly explained as signifying an egg (in reference to its shape); thence allusively used of persons or things which when once overthrown or shattered cannot be restored.
1785 GROSE *Dict. Vulg. T.*, *Humpty-Dumpty*, a little humpty dumpty man or woman; a short clumsey person of either sex. **1810** *Gammer Gurton's Garland* Part III. 36 [Not in Ritson's ed. *c* 1760, nor in the reprint of that in 1810] Humpty dumpty sate on a wall, Humpti dumpti had a great fall; Threescore men and threescore more, Cannot place Humpty dumpty as he was before. **1843** HALLIWELL *Nursery Rhymes Eng.* 113 [giving prec. version adds] *Note.* Sometimes the last two lines run as follows: All the king's horses and all the king's men, Could not set Humpty Dumpty up again. **1848** *Blackw. Mag.* July 39 To try the game of Humpty-Dumpty and to fall. **1872** 'L. CARROLL' *Thro' Looking-Gl.* vi. 114 'It's very provoking', Humpty Dumpty said,..'to be called an egg—very!' **1883** J. W. SHERER *At Home & in India* 193 She..could not, by all the miracles of millinery, be made other than a humpty-dumpty. **1896** *Westm. Gaz.* 26 June 3/1 Now that the Education Humpty-Dumpty has tumbled off the wall, and is hopelessly poached for the present year, and all the king's horses and all the king's men can't set him up again, the life has gone out of Parliament.
(In the nursery rime or riddle there are numerous variations of the last two lines, e.g. 'Not all the king's horses and all the king's men Could [can] set [put] Humpty Dumpty up again [in his place again, together again]'.)
B. *adj.* Short and fat. Also allusively referring to the Humpty-Dumpty of the nursery rime.
1785 [see A. 2]. **1828** *Craven Dial.*, *Humpty-dumpty*, short and broad, 'He's a lile humpty-dumpty fellow'. **1898** *Westm. Gaz.* 9 July 6/3 To set the humpty-dumpty conversion firmly on its legs.
b. Applied to a mechanical rhythm, as in the nursery rime.
1887 SAINTSBURY *Hist. Elizab. Lit.* iv. (1890) 128 The same humpty-dumpty measure of eights and sixes.

humpy ('hʌmpɪ), *sb.*¹ *Austral.* Also **humpey, humpie.** [ad. native Austral. *oompi*, to which 'has been given an English look, the appearance of the huts [of the aborigines] suggesting the English word *hump*' (Morris, *Austral Eng.*).] A native Australian hut. Hence, applied to a very small and primitive house, or hut such as is put up by a settler.
[**1846** C. P. HODGSON *Remin. Australia* 228 (Morris) A 'gunyia' or 'umpee'.] **1873** J. B. STEPHENS *Black Gin* 16 Lo, by the 'humpy' door, a smockless Venus! **1877** *Rep. Secretary Pub. Instruct. Queensland for 1876.* 64 The school building [at Mount Brisbane] is a slab humpy. **1890** BOLDREWOOD *Squatter's Dream* xx. 247 He's in bed in the humpy. **1911** *Chambers's Jrnl.* Sept. 591/2, I knew where this humpie was. **1927** M. TERRY *Through Land of Promise* xiii. 161 The manager's house..had been a small humpie consisting of four stone walls capped by a tin roof. **1928** 'BRENT OF BIN BIN' *Up Country* viii. 130 They are big tents or humpeys of bark, with flags on top to show if they are English or Russian or some other nation. **1942** C. BARRETT *On Wallaby* i. 14 The old fossicker was..seated outside a bark humpy. **1953** 'N. SHUTE' *In Wet* x. 348 His camp consisted of a tent for himself and his wife, and a humpy shelter made of gum tree boughs for his white ringer, Phil Fleming. **1969** *Australian* 7 June 16/1 There's a drawing in Petty's Australia Fair that shows an Aboriginal urchin in front of his family's humpy in the carcass of a Holden. **1971** *World Archaeol.* III. 168 Structures (termed 'humpies' by Europeans) which are the year-round type of dwelling used by mission-dwelling Aborigines.

humpy ('hʌmpɪ), *sb.*² *Austral. slang.* Also **humpie.** [f. HUMP *sb.* 1 + -Y⁶.] A camel.
1934 A. RUSSELL *Tramp-Royal in Wild Australia* i. 19 There's a spare riding camel in my outfit you can have... Only you'll have to rough it..rough it hard, too..same as me. But the humpie's there if you want it. *Ibid.* iii. 29 He is the despised 'humpie', the 'filthy camel'. **1945** BAKER *Austral. Lang.* 214 A camel is an *oont* or a *humpy*.

humpy ('hʌmpɪ), *a.* [f. HUMP *sb.* + -Y.]
a. Having or characterized by humps; marked by protuberances; humped; hump-like.
1708 MOTTEUX *Rabelais* v. iv. (1737) 12 This Isle Bossart (or Humpy Island). **1811** W. R. SPENCER *Poems* 207 Your genius is humpy, decrepid, and hagged. **1886** R. F. BURTON *Arab. Nts.* (abridged ed.) I. Foreword 8 The bellowing of the humpy herds. **1888** *Co-operat. News* 4 Aug. 783 As the cars ascend and descend the humpy road. **1895** W. R. W. STEPHENS *Life Freeman* I. 249 Round humpy hills rising abruptly out of it.
b. Out of humour; melancholy, sad. Cf. HUMP *sb.* 3.
1889 J. K. JEROME *Three Men in Boat* i. 10 Harris said he thought it would be humpy. He said he knew the sort of place I meant; where everybody went to bed at eight o'clock, and you..had to walk ten miles to get your baccy. **1911** 'IAN HAY' *Safety Match* xii. 194, I have got into the way of bringing you my little troubles, and turning to you generally if I felt dismal or humpy. **1920** *Glasgow Herald* 29 July 4, I mention these facts so that readers may be reassured if they are inclined to be 'humpy'... Many among us..are never so happy as when they are making themselves miserable by looking at the black side of things. **1941** 'R. WEST' *Black Lamb* I. 71 He had found himself tired and wounded and humpy and alone after a day's hunting.
Hence '**humpiness**, humpy condition.
1888 in *Chicago Advance* 16 Aug., Its back presented the odd look of 'humpiness' or 'a row of lumps' along its length. **1896** *Daily News* 12 June 5/1 Sleeves which, for humpiness and volume, excel even modern absurdity.

†**humster.** *Obs.* [f. HUM *v.*¹ + -STER.] One who expresses approval by humming (see HUM *v.*¹ 2).
1670 EACHARD *Cont. Clergy* 34 To have the right knack of letting off a joque, and of pleasing the humsters.

humstrum ('hʌm'strʌm). [f. HUM *v.*¹ + STRUM *v.*, the comb. being favoured by the jingling effect of the whole: cf. *helter-skelter*, *hurry-scurry*.]
1. A musical instrument of rude construction or out of tune; a hurdy-gurdy.
1739 GRAY *Let. to R. West* in Mason *Mem.* (1807) I. 185 Cracked voices..accompanied by an orchestra of humstrums. **1763** B. THORNTON in *Ann. Reg.* 245 *note*, This instrument [hurdy-gurdy] is sometimes called a hum-strum. **1779** WEDGWOOD in Smiles *Life* xviii. (1894) 232 My girl is quite tired out with her miserable hum-strum [spinet]. **1821** COL. HAWKER *Diary* (1893) I. 246, I..sat at my old humstrum, and boggled through a given number of Bach's fugues.
2. 'Music, esp. indifferently played music' (Ogilvie 1882).

hum-trum: see HUMDRUM.

humulene ('hju:mju:li:n). *Chem.* [f. mod.L. *humul-us* (in *Humulus lupulus*, taxonomic name of the hop) + -ENE.] A colourless liquid sesquiterpene, $C_{15}H_{24}$, identical with α-caryophyllene and forming the principal constituent of oil of hops.
1895 A. C. CHAPMAN in *Jrnl. Chem. Soc.* LXVII. 62 The evidence I have given as to its chemical individuality justifies me, I think, in adding to this list the sesquiterpene of the essential oil of hops, for which I venture to propose the name humulene. **1951** *Jrnl. Chem. Soc.* 22 Humulene ($C_{15}H_{24}$), the chief sesquiterpene constituent of hop oil and a minor constituent of the high-boiling terpene fraction of clove oil, has been shown to be present in the essential oil of Egyptian hashish.

humulin ('hju:mju:lɪn). *Chem.* [f. Bot. L. *Humul-us* (*lupulus*), the hop.] The bitter aromatic principle of the hop; lupulin.
1854 in MAYNE *Expos. Lex.*

humulone ('hju:mju:ləʊn). *Chem.* Also **-on** (-ɒn). [ad. G. *humulon* (I. W. Wöllmer 1916, in

Ber. d. Deut. Chem. Ges. XLIX. 780), f. as HUMULENE + -ONE.] A bitter, yellow, crystalline, cyclic ketone, $C_{21}H_{30}O_5$, that is an important constituent of hops and has strong antibiotic activity.

1916 *Jrnl. Chem. Soc.* CX. I. 494 A contribution to the chemistry of 'humulon' or 'a-hop bitter acid' or 'lupulic acid'. **1937** HOPKINS & KRAUSE *Biochem. appl. to Malting & Brewing* IV. 221 Both humulon and lupulon are secreted in the hop cone during growth and become more or less resinified. **1964** KIRK & OTHMER *Encycl. Chem. Technol.* (ed. 2) III. 302 By far the most important constituents of the hops are the bitter substances, humulone, lupulone, and their transition products, which give beer its characteristic taste. **1967** E. PARYSKI tr. *Korzybski's Antibiotics* II. vi. 1447 Lupulon and humulon strongly inhibit the growth of gram-positive micro-organisms and acid-fast bacilli.

humure, obs. form of HUMOUR.

‖**humus** ('hju:məs). [L., = mould, ground, soil.] Vegetable mould; the dark-brown or black substance resulting from the slow decomposition and oxidization of organic matter on or near the surface of the earth, which, with the products of the decomposition of various rocks, forms the soil in which plants grow.

1796 H. HUNTER tr. *St.-Pierre's Stud. Nat.* (1799) I. 474 That stratum called *humus*, which..serves as a basis to the vegetable kingdom. **1846** J. BAXTER *Libr. Pract. Agric.* (ed. 4) I. 15 It was usual, formerly, to attribute the carbon or charcoal of plants to their absorption of the humus existing in the ground. **1881** DARWIN *Earthworms* Introd. 5 Year after year the thrown-up castings cover the dead leaves, the result being a rich humus of great thickness.

b. *attrib.*, as ***humus acid, soil.***

1881 DARWIN *Veg. Mould* v. 242 The several humus-acids, which appear..to be generated within the bodies of worms during the digestive process. **1892** *Blackw. Mag.* July 99 The species of Palaquium require a humus soil.

humyle, -yll, -yly, obs. ff. HUMBLE, HUMBLY.

Hun (hʌn), *sb.* [OE. *Húne, Húnas,* = ON. *Húnar,* MHG. *Hünen, Hiunen,* Ger. *Hunnen,* med.L. *Hunni* (*Chunni, Chuni*), believed to represent the native name of the people, who were known to the Chinese as *Hiong-nu*, and also *Han.*]

1. One of an Asiatic race of warlike nomads, who invaded Europe *c* A.D. 375, and in the middle of the 5th c., under their famous king Attila (styled *Flagellum Dei*, the scourge of God), overran and ravaged a great part of this continent.

a **900** CYNEWULF *Elene* 21 (Gr.) Werod samnodan Huna leode and Hreðgotan, foron fyrdhwate Francan and Hunas. *Ibid.* 32 Huna cyning. **1607** TOPSELL *Four-f. Beasts* (1658) 226 The Companies or Armies of Huns, wandering up and down with most swift Horses, filled all things with slaughter and terrour. **1728** POPE *Dunciad* III. 90 The North..Great nurse of Goths, of Alans, and of Huns. **1838** *Penny Cycl.* XII. 346/2 Under Heraclius [610–641] many of the Huns embraced Christianity. After that period their name is no longer mentioned in History. **1851** RUSKIN *Stones Ven.* I. i. (1874) 16 Like the Huns, as scourges only.

2. *poet.* (and in U.S. vulgarly) A Hungarian.

1802 CAMPBELL *Hohenlinden* vi, Where furious Frank, and fiery Hun, Shout in their sulphurous canopy. **1890** *Daily News* 28 June 5/4 The Huns who are here [Pennsylvania] said to be creating a widespread dissatisfaction. They are engaged chiefly as labourers in the mines and ironworks.

3. *transf.* A reckless or wilful destroyer of the beauties of nature or art: an uncultured devastator: cf. 'Goth', 'Vandal'.

1806–7 J. BERESFORD *Miseries Hum. Life* (1826) VI. xxxii, Visiting an awful Ruin in the company of a Romp of one sex or a Hun of the other. **1892** *Pall Mall G.* 3 May 2/2 The marauding Huns whose delight it is to trample on flowers, burn the underwood, and kill the birds and beasts.

4. a. *gen.* A person of brutal conduct or character; *esp.* during and since the war of 1914–18 applied, often without animus, to the Germans (or their allies); a German. Also *attrib.*

[The immediate source of the application of *Hun* to the Germans was the speech delivered by Wilhelm II to the German troops about to sail for China on 27 July 1900. See the following examples:

1900 *Times* 30 July 5/3 According to the Bremen *Weser Zeitung* the Emperor said [27 July at Bremerhaven]:—'..No quarter will be given, no prisoners will be taken. Let all who fall into your hands be at your mercy. Just as the Huns a thousand years ago, under the leadership of Etzel (Attila) gained a reputation in virtue of which they still live in historical tradition, so may the name of Germany become known in such a manner in China that no Chinaman will ever again even dare to look askance at a German.' **1900** *Daily News* 20 Nov. 5/3 Herr Bebel [in the Reichstag] dwelt ..at some length on the so-called Hun letters, and stigmatized the cruel and barbarous methods of European warfare in China. **1900** *Times* 21 Nov. 5/2 A great portion of the speech of the Socialist leader [Bebel] was devoted to the so-called 'Letters from the Huns' (*Hunnenbriefe*)—epistles from German soldiers in China to their relatives at home giving an account of the cruelties which have been perpetrated by the army of occupation.]

1784–5 in *Publ. Navy Rec. Soc.* (1906) XXXI. 55 Andrew Duff, Midshipman. Dead. A drunken Hun. **1862** H. TIMROD *Poems* (1901) 143 Shout! let it reach the startled Huns! And roar with all thy festal guns! It is the answer of thy sons, Carolina! **1902** KIPLING in *Times* 22 Dec. 9/5 In sight of Peace.. With a cheated crew, to league anew With the Goth and the shameless Hun! **1914** —— in *Queen* 5 Sept. 388/2 Stand up and meet the war. The Hun is at the gate! **1915** E. CANDLER in *Daily Mail* 5 Apr. 4/3 She [*sc.* a Norfolk girl] told me how the eldest [brother 'at the front'] had held up three 'Huns' in a mill... She used the word 'Hun' quite naturally, with no hint of contempt or bitterness. **1916** 'BOYD CABLE' *Action Front* 133 Do you suppose our friend the Flighty Hun won't have a peep at us to-morrow morning? **1916** 'TAFFRAIL' *Pincher Martin* xiv. 269, I suppose you know Peter,.. that we were bang on the top of a Hun minefield. *a* **1918** [see CRASH *v.* 6 a]. **1918** *Times* 12 Dec. 9/4 'Supposed' statements ..of American 'advisers'..simply smell of Hun propaganda. **1932** [see BIT *sb.*² 4 h]. **1941** [see *crash-land* v.]. **1942** *Tee Emm* (Air Ministry) II. 63 The squadron has, after those months of inaction, started to bag Huns. **1945** [see ABROAD C *sb.*]. **1958** P. KEMP *No Colours or Crest* VI. 104 They ambushed a cartload of Huns the other day.

b. A flying cadet: see quots. *Air Force slang* (in the war of 1914–18).

1916 H. BARBER *Aeroplane Speaks* 36 The Aeroplane.. remonstrates... 'See the Medical Officer, you young Hun.' **1918** E. M. ROBERTS *Flying Fighter* 233 An aeroplane..was flying over the street, but I don't know what the couple of British Huns in it were trying to do. *Ibid.* 336 Every pilot is a Hun until he has received his wings. **1925** FRASER & GIBBONS *Soldier & Sailor Words* 123 The word 'Hun'..was used..for a newly-joined young officer qualifying for his 'wings', in consequence of the destructive effect of the instructional aeroplanes which young officers while learning to fly usually had.

5. *Comb.*, as ***Hun-folk, -hater, -land, -talk; Hun-eating, -hunting, -pinching.***

1928 *Manch. Guardian Weekly* 2 Nov. 350/2 There were two Englands—(a) the impossible Hun-eating England and (b) the better England. **1923** KIPLING *Irish Guards in Gt. War* I. 343 The Battalion..watched about them..the muddy-faced Hun-folk. **1920** R. MACAULAY *Potterism* II. i. 58 He would have to include among his jingoes and Hun-haters some fighting men too. **1925** FRASER & GIBBONS *Soldier & Sailor Words* 123 *Hun hunting*, an Airman's phrase for going out to look for, or chase, the enemy. **1916** *Daily Mirror* 1 Nov. 4/4 Gott strafe England.., the recognised toast throughout Hunland. **1918** [see EGG *sb.* 3 d]. **1920** *Glasgow Herald* 20 Nov. 5 No such sentiments could be admitted in Hunland. **1925** FRASER & GIBBONS *Soldier & Sailor Words* 124 *Hunland*, a term generally used in the War by Airmen for the country behind enemy lines, wherever it might be. **1917** A. G. EMPEY *Over Top* 295 '*Hun pinching*', raiding German trenches for prisoners. **1959** P. MOYES *Dead Men don't Ski* iii. 34 You ask her, Roger... You're the expert in Hun-talk.

Hence (esp. in sense 4) '**Hundom**, the state of being a 'Hun'; '**Hunless** *a.*, lacking Germans, '**Hun-like** *a.*, like a Hun, impiously destructive; '**Hunnian**, '**Hunnic**, '**Hunnican**, '**Hunnish** *adjs.*, of, pertaining to, or like the Huns; '**Hunnish** *a.*, whence '**Hunnishness**.

1607 TOPSELL *Four-f. Beasts* (1658) 226 These Hunnian horses elsewhere he calleth them Hunnican horses. **1820** BYRON *Mar. Fal.* IV. ii. 143 Dyed..With Genoese, Saracen, and Hunnish gore. **1865** J. BALLANTINE *Poems* 139 A thousand Hun-like hands are On her Ark of glory. **1875** *Encycl. Brit.* III. 62/1 Attila is described as having been of true Hunnish type. **1882** *Ibid.* XIV. 60/1 A Hunnic party. **1916** F. LAWRENCE *Mem. & Corr.* (1961) 211, I saw you being martyred on account of my Hundom! **1918** *Punch* 27 Mar. 207/2 The Hunnish conduct of the German officer who egged on the natives. **1920** *Blackw. Mag.* Feb. 154/1 The islands were entirely Hunless. **1924** C. J. TOLLEY *Mod. Golfer* 7 The only piece of Hunnishness we ever encountered at Heidelberg was at the hands of an appalling doctor, who..thought fit to inoculate us against every known disease. **1928** *Manch. Guardian Weekly* 2 Nov. 350/2 Once give the better England clear evidence that Hunnishness is not the sole attribute of the German spirit, and [etc.].

hun, colloq. abbrev. of HONEY 5 b.

1896 ADE *Artie* xiv. 126 'Look at the new hat on her.'.. 'It's a hun,' remarked Artie.

hun, var. HOON *sb.*[1]

Hunanese (hu:nə'ni:z), *a.* and *sb.* [f. *Hunan*, name of a province of southern China + -ESE.]

A. *adj.* Of, pertaining to, or characteristic of Hunan or of the Chinese spoken there. **B.** *sb.* **a.** An inhabitant of Hunan. **b.** The dialect of Hunan.

1937 J. R. FIRTH *Papers in Ling. 1934–51* (1957) vii. 80 It will be found convenient to regard the Hunanese monosyllable as having one, two, or perhaps three places in which the phonetic diacritica may be said to occur. **1937** E. SNOW *Red Star over China* II. iii. 65 Li Chiang-lin was a Hunanese. **1948** J. R. FIRTH *Papers in Ling. 1934–51* (1957) ix. 127 With the help of Mr. K. H. Hu, of Chang-sha, I studied the pronunciation and phonology of his dialect of Hunanese. **1957** *Times Lit. Suppl.* 8 Nov. 677/1 The structural analysis of an element in a Hunanese dialect. **1964** L. MITCHISON *Gillian Lo* v. 54 Ai-yang was clucking with excitement, her Hunanese accent..strong. **1967** *Everyman's Encycl.* VI. 643/2 Since the time of the Taiping rebellion..the Hunanese have been noted for their pride and obstinacy in admitting outside control. **1972** *N.Y. Times* 3 Nov. 24/6 It is probably correct to say that there are tricky but fruitful points of similarity between Hunanese food and the food of southern France. **1972** 'M. HEBDEN' *Killer for Chairman* II. iv. 162 There was a variety of dialects among the crowd from Chekiangese and Hunanese to the difficult Szechwanese.

hunch (hʌn(t)ʃ), *v.* Also 7 **hunsh**. [Of obscure origin: but cf. HINCH *v.* If sense 3 belongs to the same word as 1 and 2 (which is doubtful), the sense-development may have been 'to thrust or shoot out', 'to cause to stick out', and hence 'to form a projection or protuberance'.

It is noteworthy that the first trace of sense 3 appears, not in the simple *hunch* vb or sb., but in the comb. *hunch-backed* substituted in the 2nd Quarto of Shakspere's *Richard III* (1598) IV. iv. 81, for the earlier and ordinary 16–17th c. word *bunch-backed*, which the 1st Quarto and all the Folios have here, and which all the Quartos and all the Folios have in the parallel passage I. iii. 246. This substitution of *hunch-backed* in the one passage might be thought to be a mere misprint of the 2nd Qo., but it is retained in all the five subsequent Quartos 1602–1634; and the word appears again in 1635, and becomes frequent after 1675. Then we have *huncht back* 1656, *to hunch the back* 1678, *hunchback* 1712, *hunch back* 1718, and finally, *hunch* sb. *c* 1800. Johnson 1755–87 knew only *hunch* vb. (in our senses 2 and 3) and *hunch-backed*. With these words must be considered *hulch* sb., *hulch back*, and *hulch-backed*, in the same senses, given by Cotgr. 1611, which are thus earlier than the *hunch* group, except for *hunch-backed* in the Shaks. Qos.; also the forms *hutch back*, *hutch-back'd*, *hutch-shouldered*, found 1624–1667. We have further to compare the somewhat similar case of HUMP, where *hump-backed* is known earlier than *hump* sb. or vb., or *hump-back*.]

I. †**1.** *intr.* To push, thrust, shove. Also *fig.* to 'kick against' a thing; to show reluctance; to spurn. *Obs.*

1581 R. V. *Caluine on Gal.* IV. 30. 112 The heritage is saued for vs, howsoeuer bragly they hunche at vs for a time. **1598** R. BERNARD tr. *Terence, Heautont.* IV. v. (1607) 215, I will doe thee some good turne..without any hunching [*ac lubens*]. **1619** J. DYKE *Caveat* (1620) 17 Would we then hunch at a litle bodily paines? **1621** BP. MOUNTAGU *Diatribæ* 52 God..will send such curst Cowes short hornes, and keepe them from hurting, though they hunsh. **1658** GURNALL *Chr. in Arm.* verse 15. ix. §3 (1669) 145/1 Conscience is as much huncht at, and spighted among sinners, as Joseph was among the Patriarchs.

2. a. *trans.* To push, shove, thrust. *Obs.* exc. *dial.*

1659 in *Sussex Archæol. Collect.* (1864) XVI. 77 [Her husband] Did so hunch and Pincht her, that she Could not Lift her armes to her head. **1668** R. L'ESTRANGE *Vis. Quev.* (1708) 148 Hunching and Justling one another. **1670** COVEL *Diary* (Hakluyt Soc.) 204, I have been caryed in when Turkes have been huncht away. **1706** PHILLIPS (ed. Kersey), *To Hunch one*, to give him a thrust with the Elbow. **1712** ARBUTHNOT *John Bull* III. iii, Then Jack's friends begun to hunch and push one another. 'Why don't you go and cut the poor fellow down?' **1715** LADY COWPER *Diary* (1864) 43 A world of shouldering and hunching People. **1748** RICHARDSON *Clarissa* (1811) II. i. 8 A great overgrown ..boy, who would be hunched and punched by everybody. **1755** JOHNSON, *Hunch*, to strike or punch with the fist. **1806–7** J. BERESFORD *Miseries Hum. Life* XVIII. xii. 136 You are stoutly hunched aside, by the huge carcase of a panting fellow. *a* **1825** FORBY *Voc. E. Anglia, Hunch*, to shove; to heave up. **1891** 'J. S. WINTER' *Lumley the Painter* xi. 79 [The dog] hunching his large person heavily against her.

b. To nudge (a person) so as to direct attention to someone. Also *fig.* *U.S.*

a **1852** F. M. WHITCHER *Widow Bedott Papers* (1883) 76 She kept a hunchin' Miss Coon and grinnin'. **1884** 'MARK TWAIN' *Huck. Finn* xxv. 246 Then the king he hunched the duke, private. **1906** *Life* 1 Feb. 147 Soon some fellow hunched the Legislature, and then there had to be more or less investigating done.

c. *intr.* To push or lunge forward. *U.S.*

1911 S. E. WHITE *Bobby Orde* (1916) xvii. 196 Bending to his task the pusher at the rear dug his toes in, while the others hunched. **1913** G. S. PORTER *Laddie* viii. 232 She sat astride the foot log, and hunched along with her hands. **1925** C. E. MULFORD *Cottonwood Gulch* xix. 259 They hunched closer, hugging knees under chin.

II. 3. a. *trans.* To thrust *out* or *up*, or bend, so as to form a 'hunch' or hump; to compress, bend, or arch convexly. Also without *up*.

1678 DRYDEN & LEE *Œdipus* I. 6 Thy crooked mind within hunch'd out thy back. **1738** SWIFT *Pol. Conversat.* 70, I was hunch'd up in a Hackney-Coach with Three Country Acquaintances. **1858** HUGHES *Scouring White Horse* iv. 62 Peter..kept pulling away at his forelock, and hunching up his shoulders. **1863** W. E. FORSTER in T. W. Reid *Life* (1888) I. 215 Shutting his eyes and hunching himself up on the seat with hands clenched. **1892** EMILY LAWLESS *Grania* II. 7 He sat..hunched up, with his knees and his chin together. **1906** U. SINCLAIR *Jungle* xviii, Hiding his hands in his pockets and hunching his shoulders together. **1906** 'K. HOWARD' *Old Game* II. i. 54 She merely hunched her shoulders, swung on her heel, and marched off.

b. *intr.* ? To 'set one's back up'.

1873 MISS THACKERAY *Old Kensington* xv. 126 'Nonsense', said G., hunching up sulkily.

hunch (hʌn(t)ʃ), *sb.* [In sense 1 from HUNCH *v.*; in sense 2 app. deduced from *hunch-backed*. Sense 3 may belong to a distinct word; this, although known only from 1790, is found in vulgar use before 1830 in southern and northern dialects, in the West Indies, and in New England. Cf. also HUNK in same sense, exemplified from 1813.]

1. a. The act of 'hunching' or pushing; a push, thrust, shove. *Obs.* exc. *dial.*

1630 J. TAYLOR (Water P.) *Wks.* (N.), When he quaffing doth his entrailes wash, 'Tis call'd a hunch, a thrust, a whiffe, a flash. **1768–74** TUCKER *Lt. Nat.* (1852) I. 473 Suppose..you should give him a good hunch with your foot. *a* **1825** FORBY *Voc. E. Anglia, Hunch*, a lift, or shove.

b. A hint, 'tip'. (Cf. prec. 2 b.)

1849 T. M. GARRETT in *Amer. Speech* (1951) XXVI. 183/1 Another piece [of writing] gave a few hunches to the inexperienced freshman. **1901** 'H. MCHUGH' *John Henry* 57 The reason it's so good is because I took my hunch from Rud. Kipling's style. **1922** Z. GREY *To Last Man* ii. 36 All

shootin' arms an' such are at a premium in the Tonto... An' I was givin' you a hunch to come loaded.

2. A protuberance; a hump. (As to the late appearance of this see note to HUNCH *v.*)

1804 W. TENNANT *Ind. Recreat.* (ed. 2) II. 103 The common draught cattle of India are distinguished by..a large hunch, or protuberance, above the shoulders. **1823** SCORESBY *Whale Fishery* 36 His back carried a huge hunch. **1828** STARK *Elem. Nat. Hist.* I. 144 Camelus,..back with fleshy hunches. **1833** J. HODGSON in Raine *Mem.* (1858) II. 306 The old birches have on their crooked stems great hunches and wens.

3. A thick or clumsy piece, a lump, a hunk.

1790 GROSE *Provinc. Gloss.* (ed. 2), *Hunch*, a great hunch; a piece of bread. *South.* **1818** M. G. LEWIS *Jrnl. W. Ind.* (1834) 359 Another bit of cold ham..I ordered Cabina to give her a great hunch of it. **1823** E. MOORE *Suffolk Words* 180 *Hunch*, a good big slice, or lump, of bread or meat. **1828** *Craven Dial.*, *Hunch*, a large slice of any thing, as bread and cheese. **1828** WEBSTER, *Hunch*,..2. A lump..as, a hunch of bread; a word in common vulgar use in New-England. **1849** JAMES *Woodman* xxiii, A hunch of ewe-milk cheese.

4. A premonition or intuitive feeling that something will happen or may be the case; a presentiment.

1904 S. E. WHITE *Silent Places* xviii. 200 'I hope your hunch is a good one,' replied Dick. **1907** R. W. SERVICE *Songs of Sourdough* (1908) 52 Then you've a haunch [*sic*] what the music meant. **1918** E. M. ROBERTS *Flying Fighter* 62 This particular night Fritz had a hunch that somebody was going to pass the place behind the screen. **1926** G. D. H. & M. COLE *Blatchington Tangle* xiii. 97, I had an awful hunch what it was. **1938** *Brit. Jrnl. Psychol.* July 7, I relied not so much on conscious thought, as on what Americans call a 'hunch'. **1955** *Times* 9 May 5/2 A churchwarden's 'hunch' could never be a wholly satisfactory substitute for professional knowledge in regard to the care of churches. **1960** M. SPARK *Ballad of Peckham Rye* ii. 14 'Only a hunch,' said Dougal. 'I may be wrong.' **1973** 'H. HOWARD' *Highway to Murder* viii. 89 My sixth sense told me I'd got myself an extra shadow. That hunch was all I had to go on.

hunch, *a. dial.* [? f. HUNCH *v.*] That shrivels or pinches (with cold).

a **1825** FORBY *Voc. E. Anglia*, *Hunch-weather*, cold weather, which makes men hunch up their shoulders, and animals contract their limbs, and look as if they were hunch-backed. **1897** R. E. G. COLE *Hist. Doddington* 149 They [hops]..suffered from the 'cold hunch springs'.

hunchback, hunch-back. [f. HUNCH *sb.* + BACK *sb.*]

1. ('hʌnʃ'bæk) A hunched back.

1718 BP. HUTCHINSON *Witchcraft* 248 A Man with a Hunch-back higher than his Head. **1837** CARLYLE *Fr. Rev.* II. III. iii, One Lautrec, a man with hunchback, or natural deformity.

2. ('hʌnʃbæk) = HUMPBACK *sb.* 2.

1712 tr. *Arab. Nts.* cxxiii. (ed. 2) IV. 35 The Story of the little Hunch-back. **1818** B. O'REILLY *Greenland* 186 A hunch-back..about fourteen years of age. **1870** L'ESTRANGE *Miss Mitford* I. vii. 240 The only bearable hunch-back of my acquaintance is Richard the Third.

3. *attrib.* Hump-backed.

1850 W. B. CLARKE *Wreck Favorite* 181 The hump-back or hunch-back whale..with a larger hump than the sperm whale.

hunchbacked ('hʌnʃbækt), *a.* [See HUNCH *v.*] Having a protuberant or crooked back.

1598 SHAKS. *Rich. III*, IV. iv. 81 (2nd Qo.) That foule hunch-back'd [*Fols. and 1st Qo.* bunch-back'd] Toad. **1635** J. HAYWARD tr. *Biondi's Banish'd Virg.* 145 The babe..was now growne hunch-back'd. **1678** DRYDEN & LEE *Œdipus* III. i, To take that hunch-backed monster to my arms! **1711** DENNIS *Refl. Ess. Crit.* (R.), As stupid and as venomous as a hunch-back'd toad. **1809** *Med. Jrnl.* XXI. 283 A third.. is very much hunchbacked. **1855** MACAULAY *Hist. Eng.* xix. IV. 410 The hunchbacked dwarf who urged forward the fiery onset of France.

hunched (hʌnʃt), *a.* Also **huncht**. [f. HUNCH *sb.* or *v.* + -ED.] Having or bowed into a hump; hump-backed; *fig.* apt to 'set one's back up', 'stuck-up'. Also with advbs.

1656 *Choice Drolleries* 51, I love thee for thy huncht back, 'Tis bow'd although not broken. **1769** PENNANT *Zool.* III. 213 A very singular variety of perch: the back is quite hunched. **1804-6** SYD. SMITH *Elem. Sk. Mor. Philos.* (1850) 141 Imitating a drunken man, or a clown, or a person with a hunched back. **1859** TENNYSON *Guinevere* 41 If a man were halt or hunch'd, in him..Scorn was allow'd as part of his defect. **1870** E. PEACOCK *Ralf Skirl.* I. 146 They do say ..that they're strange, and huncht, and proud. **1883** STEVENSON *Treas. Isl.* I. iii, He was hunched, as if with age or weakness. **1910** W. DE LA MARE *Three Mulla-Mulgars* x. 144 His little hunched-up friend. **1920** *Chambers's Jrnl.* 110/1 A long..sinuous beast that hopped in a series of hunched-up bounds. **1921** C. E. MULFORD *Bar-20 Three* xxi. 267 He..clawed himself into a saddle..and rode for safety, hunched over and but half conscious.

'**hunchet.** [f. HUNCH *sb.* 3 + -ET[1].] A small 'hunch' or lump.

1790 GROSE *Provinc. Gloss.* (ed. 2), *Hunchet*, a diminutive of hunch. **1892** MRS. CROSSE *Red-letter Days* I. 89 A hunchet of cheese.

hunchy ('hʌn(t)ʃɪ), *a.* [f. HUNCH *sb.* + -Y.] Having a hunch; humped, humpy.

1840 DICKENS *Old C. Shop* v, I'm a little hunchy villain and a monster, am I? **1881** R. B. WATSON in *Jrnl. Linn. Soc.* XV. 404 Eleven..strong, but narrow hunchy ribs.

†**hund**, *sb.* and *a. Obs.* [OE. *hund* sb. neut. = OS. *hund*, OHG. *hunt*, Goth. (*hund*), pl. *hunda*, the original Teut. word for 100:—pre-Teut. **kmtó-m*, Skr. *çatám* Gr. (ἑ)κατόν, L. *centum*, OWelsh *cant* (mod. *cynt*), OIr. *cét*, Lith. *szimtas*, OSlav. *sŭto*, Russ. *sto*. In Gothic this primary form is found only in the plural *twa hunda*, *þrija hunda*, etc., which is also its ordinary use in OHG. *zwei hunt*. *drî hunt*, though *ein hunt* occurs late. In OE. *hund* was common in the sing. as well as the pl. In ME., *hund* appears to have become obsolete early in 13th c.]

1. = HUNDRED (OE. and early ME.).

c **893** K. ÆLFRED *Oros.* II. iv. §4 Senatum ðæt wæs an hund monna, þeh heora æfter fyr[s]te wære þreo hund. *c* **950** *Lindisf. Gosp.* Mark. vi. 37 Mið penningum tuæm hundum [*Ags. G.* mid twam hundred penegon]. *c* **1000** *Ags. Gosp.* Luke xvi. 6 Hund sestra eles. *Ibid.* 7 Hund mittena hwætes. *c* **1050** *Byrhtferth's Handboc* in *Anglia* VIII. 298 On þrim hund dagum & fif & syxtigum dagum. *c* **1175** *Lamb. Hom.* 5 Ysaias..iwitegede ueale hund wintra er þis were. *Ibid.* 93 þet weren twa hun manna. *c* **1205** LAY. 83 For hire weoren on ane daȝe hund þousunt deade.

2. The element *hund-* was also prefixed in OE. to the numerals from 70 to 120, in OE. *hund-seofontiȝ*, *hund-eahtatiȝ*, *hund-niȝontiȝ*, *hund-téontiȝ*, *hund-endlyftiȝ* (*-ælleftiȝ*), *hund-twelftiȝ*, some of which are also found in early ME.

[No certain explanation can be offered of this *hund-*, which appears in OS. as *ant-*, Du. *t-* in *tachtig*, and may be compared with *-hund* in Goth. *sibuntê-hund*, etc., and Gr. *-κοντα*.]

c **893** K. ÆLFRED *Oros.* I. x. §1, IIII hu[n]de wintrum ond hundeahtatigum. *a* **1000** *Cædmon's Gen.* 1741 Wærfæst hæle wintra hæfde twa hundteontiȝ..and fife eac. *c* **1000** ÆLFRIC *Hom.* I. 92 Hund-teontiȝ geara wæs Abraham. *c* **1000** in Cockayne *Shrine* 85 Hundteontiȝ and twentiȝ. *c* **1000** *Ags. Gosp.* Matt. xviii. 12 Hu ne forlæt he þa niȝon and hundniȝontiȝ on þam muntum? *c* **1160** *Hatton Gosp.* Matt. xviii. 22 Oððe seofen hundseofentiȝ siðan. *c* **1200** *Trin. Coll. Hom.* 51 On þralshipe hie wuneden two and sixti wintre, and sume hund seuenti wintre fulle.

hund, obs. form of HOUND.

†'**hundfold**, *a.*, *adv.*, and *sb. Obs.* Also **hunfold**. [f. HUND + *-feald*, *-fald*, -FOLD.] = HUNDREDFOLD.

c **1000** ÆLFRIC *Hom.* I. 338 Hundfeald ȝetel is fulfremed. *c* **1175** *Lamb. Hom.* 21 Hunfold mare is cristes eie. *Ibid.* 147 Heo sculen underfon hundfalde mede.

hundi ('hʊndɪ). *India.* Also **hoondee, hoondi, hoondy.** [Hind. *huṇḍī* (Skr. *huṇḍikā* bill of exchange).] A negotiable instrument, such as a bill of exchange or promissory note, used by native bankers in India and worded in the vernacular; also, money remitted by such an instrument.

1619 in W. Foster *Eng. Factories India 1618–21* (1906) 85 [They advise the dispatch of bills of exchange for rupees] hundies [17,100]. **1620** *Ibid.* 182 The exchange of rup[ees] secaus for hundies. **1810** T. WILLIAMSON *East India Vade Mecum* II. 330 Hoondies (i.e. bankers' drafts) would be of no use whatever to them. **1913** J. M. KEYNES *Indian Currency & Finance* vi. 197 The *hoondees* they buy and sell to each other..are chiefly the traders' *hoondees* bearing the shroffs' own endorsements. **1930** *Economist* 12 Apr. 820/1 Bills (hundis) of the native type. **1963** *Times* 18 May 8/4 It is thought that gold smuggling gangs obtain funds by operating the 'Hundi' system among Pakistani immigrants in Britain. **1969** *Commerce* (Bombay) 26 July 150/2 Apprehensions..may push up the rate of interest in the free market from 15–18 per cent to 20–24 per cent against the hundies, promissory notes and short loans.

hundred ('hʌndrəd), *sb.* and *a.* Forms: α. 1– **hundred**, 1 **-ræd**, 3 *Orm.* **hunndredd**, 3–5 **hondred**, 3–7 **hundered**, 4 **houndred**, 4–6 **hundrid(e, -ryd**, 5–6 **hondered, -ryd**; 3–4 **hund-, hond-, houndret**, 4 **hunderet, -it**, 4 **hund-, hondird, hundyrd**, 4–8 **hundered**, 5 **-urd, -yrt, honderd, -ert(e.** β. 1 **hundrað, -reð**, 4 **-reþ(e, (-richt)**, 4–5 **-rith**, 4–7 **-reth, houndreth**, 5 **hundrethe**, 5–6 **-ryth(e**, 6 **hundereth, honderyth, -dreth**; 6 (9 *dial.*) **hunderth**. γ. (Chiefly *Sc.*) 3–5 **hundre**, 4 **hondre**, 4– **hunder**, 5–6 **hundir, -yr**, 9 *dial.* **hunner**. [OE. *hundred*, pl. *-red*, *-redu*, neut., = OFris. *hundred*, *-erd*, *hondert*, OS. *hunderod* (MLG. *hundert*, MDu. *hondert(d)*, Du. *honderd*), late OHG. (MHG., Ger.) *hundert*, ON. *hundrað* (pl. *-oð*) (Sw. *hundra*, Da. *hundrede*), corresp. to a Gothic type **hunda-raþ*, lit. the tale or number of 100 (*-raþ*, *-rôþ*, related to *raþjan* to reckon, tell, *raþjô* reckoning, number). Other OE. words for 'hundred' were HUND (q.v.), and *hund-téontiȝ* = ON. *tío teger*, OHG. *zehanzug*, *zehanzô*, Gothic *taihuntêhund*, *taihuntaihund*. The word *hundrað* in ON. orig. meant 120; later, 120 and 100 were distinguished as *hundrað tolfrǿtt* 'duodecimal hundred' and *hundrað tírǿtt* 'decimal hundred'. In English the word has been usually applied to the decimal hundred, but remnants of the older usage remain: see sense 3. The *hundrath*, *-reth* forms are from ON., as are prob. *hundre*, *hunder*, etc.: cf. Sw. *hundra*.]

1. The cardinal number equal to ten times ten, or five score: denoted by the symbols 100 or C.

a. As *sb.* or quasi-*sb.*, with plural.

(*a*) In singular. Usually ***a*** (arch. ***an***) ***hundred***, emphatically ***one hundred***; in phrases expressing rate, ***the hundred***.

in (†***upon***, †***at***, †***for***) ***the hundred*** (in reckoning interest, etc.); now usually expressed by 'per cent.'

The construction (when there is any) is in OE. with gen. pl., later with *of* and a pl. noun. In mod.Eng. this is limited to *definite* things (e.g. *a hundred of the men*, *of those men*, *of them*); except in the case of measures of quantity, e.g. *a hundred of bricks*, we do not now use this constr. before a noun standing alone (e.g. *a hundred of men*), but substitute the constr. in b. But *a hundred* is construed with a plural verb, e.g. a hundred of my friends were chosen; a second hundred were then enrolled.

c **950** *Lindisf. Gosp.* Matt. xviii. 28 Hundrað scillinga [*Rushw. G.* hundred denera; *Ags. Gosp.* an hund peneȝa]. *c* **1000** *Ags. Ps.* (Th.) lxxxix. [xc.] 10 þeah þe heora hundred seo. *c* **1200** ORMIN 6078 All swa summ illc an hunndredd iss Full tale. *a* **1300** *Cursor M.* 6977 It was na folk þam moght wit-stand, þat an hundreth moght for-chace. **1450–1530** *Myrr. our Ladye* 309 Twyes syxe tymes ten, that ys to a hundereth and twenty. *c* **1540** *Pilgr. T.* 50 in *Thynne's Animadv.* (1865) App. i. 78 A-mongst an hundreth..of thes religyuse brethren. **1553** GRESHAM in Burgon *Life* (1839) I. 132 To lett upon interest for a xii monthes daye, after xiii upon the hundred. **1575–85** ABP. SANDYS *Serm.* (Parker Soc.) 203 The lender not content to receive less advantage than thirty at the hundred. **1617** MORYSON *Itin.* III. 91 For gaine of fifty in the hundred. **1648** NETHERSOLE *Self-condemned* I. A ij b, Not one of an hundred of them could tell. **1663** GERBIER *Counsel* D iv b, About one hundred of Leagues. **1692** BENTLEY *Boyle Lect.* 159 'Tis above a hundred to one against any particular throw..with four cubical dice. **1737** POPE *Hor. Ep.* I. vi. 75 Add one round hundred. **1885** *Times* (weekly ed.) 17 Apr. 9/4 Tickets fabricated by the hundred.

(*b*) In plural: *hundreds*. [OE. *hundred*, *-u*, neuter, ME. *hundredes*.]

In *Arith.* often *ellipt.* for the digits denoting the number of hundreds: cf. *units*, *tens*.

c **1000** *Ags. Gosp.* Mark vi. 40 Hi ða sæton hundredon and fiftiȝon. *c* **1050** *Suppl. Ælfric's Gloss.* in Wr.-Wülcker 176/26 *Centurias*, ȝetalu, *uel* heapas, *uel* hundredu. *c* **1275** LAY. 27830 Of alle þan hundredes þat to-hewe were. *a* **1300** *Cursor M.* 8886 O quens had he [Solomon] hundrets seuen. *c* **1380** WYCLIF *Last Age Chirche* in Todd *Three Treat.* p. xxvi, Two and twenty hundriddis of ȝeeris. *c* **1425** *Craft Nombrynge* (E.E.T.S.) 28 So mony hundrythes ben in þe nounbre þat schal come of þe multiplicacioun of þe ylke 2 articuls. **1542** RECORDE *Gr. Artes* 118 a, His place is the voyde space next aboue hundredes. **1613** PURCHAS *Pilgrimage* (1614) 110 Governours of thousands, hundreths, fifties and tens. **1617** MORYSON *Itin.* III. 78 Great store of red Deare..which the Princes kill by hundreds at a time. **1859** DARWIN *Orig. Spec.* iii. (1878) 52 One fly deposits hundreds of eggs. **1876** DIGBY *Real Prop.* i. 3 The body of invaders is a regular army..divided into 'hundreds' of warriors. *Mod.* Some hundreds of men were present.

(*c*) After a numeral adjective, *hundred* is commonly used as a collective plural, with the same construction as in (a). (Cf. *dozen.*)

c **1050** *Byrhtferth's Handboc* in *Anglia* VIII. 303 þrittiȝ siðon seofon beoð twa hundred & tyn. *a* **1100** *O.E. Chron.* (Laud MS.) an. 656 ⁊ 11 Seox hundred wintra. *c* **1200** ORMIN 6071 þurrh tale off fowwerr hunndredd. *c* **1205** LAY. 613 Six hundred of his cnihten. *c* **1340** *Cursor M.* 13345 (Fairf.) þe folk him folowed..be many hundre & thousande. *c* **1460** *Battle of Otterbourne* 260 Of nyne thowsand Ynglyssh men Fyve hondert cam awaye. **1668** HALE *Pref. Rolle's Abridgm.* 3 These many hundred of years. **1719** J. T. PHILIPPS tr. *Thirty Four Confer.* 105 He deluded many hundred of Women [*mod.* many hundred w., *or* hundreds of w.] **1782** COWPER *Loss of Royal George* ii, Eight hundred of the brave. *Mod.* He lost several hundred of his men in crossing the river.

b. As *adj.* or quasi-*adj.*, followed immediately by a plural (or collective) noun.

In OE. sometimes used as a true adjective, either invariable (like other cardinal numbers above *three*), or declined in concord with its sb. The use in later times may be regarded either as a continuation of this, or as an ellipsis of *of* before the noun. The word retains its substantival character so far as to be always preceded by *a* or some adjective (numeral, demonstrative, possessive, relative, or interrogative). Either the sing. or the collective pl. is used, as in a (a), (c). Cf. *dozen*, which has precisely parallel constructions.

c **975** *Rushw. Gosp.* Mark vi. 37 Mið peningum twæm hundreðum. *c* **1000** *Ags. Gosp.* ibid., Mid twam hundred peneȝon. *c* **1200** *Vices & Virtues* 113 Swo maniȝe hundred wintre. **1297** R. GLOUC. (Rolls) 2342 An hondred kniȝtes. *a* **1300** *Cursor M.* 22747 þe hundret and þe þusand knightes. *c* **1340** *Ibid.* 10399 (Fairf.) These hundird shepe that were ther. *c* **1420** *Sir Amadace* (Camden) xii, Thre hundrythe pownde Of redy monay. *c* **1470** HENRY *Wallace* I. 126 Scwne ..Quhar kingis was cround viij hundyr ȝer and mar. **1568** GRAFTON *Chron.* II. 83 Nine hundreth thousande poundes. **1579** FULKE *Heskins' Parl.* 256 A whole hundreth Popes in a rowe. **1611** BIBLE *Transl. Pref.* 5 Within a few hundreth yeeres after Christ. **1665** HOOKE *Microgr.* 216 A hundred and twenty five thousand times bigger. **1782** COWPER *Loss of Royal George* vi, With twice four hundred men. **1818** SHELLEY *Rev. Islam* IV. xxxii, Many a mountain chain which rears Its hundred crests aloft. **1864** BOWEN *Logic* x. 325 After one hundred millions of favourable instances..the hundred-million-and-first instance should be an exception. *Mod.* The hundred and one odd chances.

(*b*) Phrase. ***the Hundred Days*** [the immediate source of the phrase is the speech delivered by Louis de Chabrol de Volvic, prefect of Paris, to Louis XVIII in 1815 ('Cent jours se sont écoulés depuis le moment fatal où votre majesté

quitta sa capitale')], the period of the restoration of Napoleon Bonaparte, after his escape from Elba, ending with his abdication on 22 June 1815. Also *transf.*

1827 SCOTT *Life Napoleon Buonaparte* IX. i. 33 Here, therefore, ended that short space..that period of an Hundred Days, in which the events of a century seem to be contained. **1862** C. KNIGHT *Popular Hist. Eng.* VIII. ii. 21 This landing in the Gulf of St. Juan on the 1st of March was the introductory scene to the great drama called 'The Hundred Days'. **1887** O. W. HOLMES (*title*) Our hundred days in Europe. **1956** J. M. BURNS *Roosevelt* ix. 169 The President asked for quick authorization of a civilian conservation corps... This bill interested Roosevelt himself as much as any single measure of the Hundred Days. **1965** T. C. SORENSEN *Kennedy* ix. 242 'I'm sick of reading how we're planning another "hundred days" of miracles,' he [*sc.* J. F. Kennedy] said, 'and I'd like to know who on the staff is talking that up. Let's put in that this won't all be finished in a hundred days or a thousand.' **1965** MRS. L. B. JOHNSON *White House Diary* 10 Apr. (1970) 257 Lyndon talked of the harvest of legislation. He said that never has there been such a hundred days. **1966** H. WILSON *Purpose in Power* I. 1 (*heading*) The first hundred days.

(*c*) ***Hundred Years War***, the intermittent war between England and France from 1337 to 1453, arising out of the claim of the English kings to the French crown.

1874 J. R. GREEN *Short Hist. Eng. People* 275 The Hundred Years' War had ended. **1959** M. MCKISACK *14th Cent.* 127 Like the second world war of the twentieth century, the Hundred Years War gathered momentum slowly. Gascony was declared confiscate in May 1337 and in October Edward laid his claim to the French Crown; but there was no organized campaigning for another two years. **1961** E. F. JACOB *15th Cent.* 505 In the spring of 1453 Charles VII opened the last campaign of the Hundred Years War in overwhelming force.

(*d*) Phr., ***the Hundred Flowers***: name given to a period of approximately six weeks in the summer of 1957 when certain elements of the Chinese population were invited to criticize the political system then obtaining in Communist China. (See quot. 1958[2].)

1958 L. F. EDWARDS tr. *Fauré's Serpent & Tortoise* xiv. 121 In the intellectual China of the Hundred Flowers, no one has the right to be a counter-revolutionary, but one has, to a certain extent, the right to be an idealist. **1958** *Listener* 6 Nov. 718/1 The campaign for free speech [in China] that followed the encouraging words of Mao Tsetung—'let a hundred flowers bloom'—was evidently designed as an operation to find out what precisely were the prevailing criticisms of policy. **1959** *Ibid.* 5 Feb. 255/1 The intellectuals [in China] who blossomed with criticism during the brief Hundred Flowers Movement. **1973** *Ibid.* 2 Aug. 147/3 The humiliations which the Party had suffered during the so-called Hundred Flowers period.

c. The cardinal form *hundred* is also used as an ordinal when followed by other numbers, the last of which alone takes the ordinal form: e.g. 'the hundred-and-first', 'the hundred-and-twentieth', 'the six-hundred-and-fortieth part of a square mile'.

d. After a numeral, used to express the two noughts in the figure representing the number of hours since midnight. Cf. HOUR 1 b.

1953 P. C. BERG *Dict. New Words* 95/1 *Hundred*, the two noughts in the numerical symbols of full hours; e.g. we will meet at nine hundred hours [= 9.00 a.m.]. **1967** B. KNOX *Blacklight* vi. 135 'What's the time?'..'Coming up for seven-forty-five sir.' 'Let's be formal and say near enough to twenty hundred hours... Wait till twenty-two hundred, mister.' **1973** A. HUNTER *Gently French* i. 13, I got back to Elphinstone Road at about oh-one hundred hours.

2. a. Often used indefinitely or hyperbolically for a large number: cf. *thousand*. (With various constructions, as in 1.)

a **1300** *Cursor M.* 17031 He has a hundret sith Dublid þis ilk pain. **1362** LANGL. *P. Pl.* A. VI. 11 An hundred of ampolles on his hat seeten. *a* **1450** *Knt. de la Tour* (1868) 131 God rewardithe her in this worldely lyff, hundred sithe more after the departinge oute of this world. **1513** DOUGLAS *Æneis* II. iv. [v.] 2 A fer gretar wondir And mair dreidfull to cativis be sic hundir. **1573** J. SANFORD *Hours Recreat.* (1576) 12 That one growing misorder breed not an hundred. **1638** F. JUNIUS *Paint. of Ancients* 66 Altered into a hundred severall fashions and shapes. **1738** SWIFT *Pol. Conversat.* p. xlvi, How can she acquire those hundreds of Graces and Motions, and Airs? **1848** THACKERAY *Van. Fair* xiii, You and Mr. Sedley made the match a hundred years ago. **1885** *Times* 20 Feb. 5/1 The hundred and one forms of small craft used by the Chinese to gain an honest livelihood.

b. Phrases: ***not a hundred miles from***; ***within a hundred miles of***: near, close to, in or at; also *fig.*; (***all the same in***) ***a hundred years*** (***hence***) (and similar expressions): gnomic formulas of consolation for present adversity; ***a hundred of bricks***: see BRICK *sb.*[1] 5; ***a hundred to one***: a hundred chances to one; hence, an expression indicating very *slight* probability (implying 'a hundred to one against') or very *strong* probability ('a hundred to one in favour of').

1647 M. VERNEY in F. P. Verney *Mem.* (1892) II. xiv. 370 'Tis a hundred to one pegg's husband turns them out of his house again within a fortnight. **1675** T. JORDAN *Triumphs of London* 21 Though now she be pleasant and sweet to the sense, Will be damnably mouldy a hundred year hence. **1760** STERNE *Tristram Shandy* II. IV. ix. 72 What a chapter of chances, said my father... 'Twas a hundred to one—cried my uncle *Toby*. **1783** in J. Ritson *Select Coll. Eng. Songs* II. 14 We shall be nothing An hundred years hence. **1821** *Kaleidoscope* 27 Feb. 277/3 A sporting gentleman passing by a house, not a hundred miles from —— street. **1827** P. EGAN *Anecdotes of Turf* 270 Within one hundred miles of the great Chancery shop of the kingdom. **1838** DICKENS *Nickleby* (1839) ix. 76 As she frequently remarked when she made any such mistake, it would be all the same a hundred years hence. **1852** *Leisure Hour* I. 52/2 Scandalous transactions said to have transpired between two 'well-known' individuals 'not a hundred miles off'. **1874** L. TROUBRIDGE *Life amongst Troubridges* (1966) ix. 75 Let's look cheerful—it will be all the same a hundred years hence. **1888** 'R. BOLDREWOOD' *Robbery under Arms* III. iv. 50 If he gets clear off..you're right. But it's a hundred to one against it. **1891** KIPLING *Life's Handicap* 171 Did you ever know old Hummy behave like that before or within a hundred miles of it? **1895** A. W. PINERO *Benefit of Doubt* II. 109 Don't fret; it'll be all the same a hundred years hence. **1903** J. M'GOVAN *Brought to Bay* 74 This retreat, he admitted, was not a hundred miles from the spot where they were at that moment seated. **1914** C. MACKENZIE *Sinister St.* II. IV. ix. 1105 'Oh, well, it'll be all the same in a hundred years.' She picked up her white gloves, and swaggered across the crowded beerhall. **1925** W. S. MAUGHAM *Painted Veil* i. 11, I say, you must pull yourself together. It's a hundred to one it wasn't Walter. **1955** D. GARNETT *Aspects of Love* I. 27 Of course it is a hundred to one that the girl is just a tart he has picked up in Montpellier. **1968** C. WATSON *Charity ends at Home* vi. 69 Certain information has reached me privately concerning the disposal of funds raised not a hundred miles from here in the name of so-called 'charity'. **1971** G. HOUSEHOLD *Doom's Caravan* iv. 174 All the same a hundred years hence, as my Nanny used to say. **1973** M. WOODHOUSE *Blue Bone* xvi. 174, I don't want you, Rodway, or you, Quickie, within a hundred miles of me, ever.

c. ***a*** or ***one hundred per cent***: used adjectivally or adverbially with the meaning 'entire(ly), complete(ly)'. Hence ***hundred-per-center***, ***hundred-per-centism***. orig. *U.S.*

1911 H. S. HARRISON *Queed* vii. 90 You do more work in twenty-four hours than you're doing now, besides feelin' one hundred per cent. better all the time. **1918** T. ROOSEVELT in *N.Y. Times* 19 July 6/6 There can be no fifty-fifty Americanism in this country. There is room here for only 100 per cent. Americanism... No man who is not 100 per cent. American is entitled to the support of any party. **1923** *Westm. Gaz.* 1 Jan., An administrator is 100 per cent. successful only when he gets every individual in the factory ..working as enthusiastically as if he were working for himself on his own job. *Ibid.* 9 Feb., Under a hundred per cent. disability. **1923** *Smart Set* Feb. 30 (*title*) Diary of a 100% American. **1926** W. R. INGE *Lay Thoughts* 135 Such detachment would not be possible to a 'hundred per cent. American'. *a* **1927** W. W. WOOLLCOTT (*title of poem*) I am a one hundred percent. American. **1928** *Publishers' Weekly* 26 May 2164/2, I have frequently encountered excellent accounting systems which were 100 per cent. useless. **1928** *Observer* 4 Mar. 13/2 Perhaps New York is not the place for the Hundred-per-centers. I certainly never met any. *Ibid.* 8 Apr. 8/2 He is really another victim of hundred-per-centism. **1931** G. B. SHAW *Platform & Pulpit* (1962) 232 The first thing that would occur to a real hundred per cent. American in Russia is that..it must be a splendid country to make money in. **1931** *Times Lit. Suppl.* 29 Jan. 76/3 The inevitable 'honest-to-God' hundred-per-cent. American young man..besieges and wins Valerie's heart. **1931** G. D. H. COLE in W. Rose *Outl. Mod. Knowl.* 666, I see no sign of the actual approach of this hundred per cent. American paradise. **1946** *Amer. Speech* XXI. 34/1 *Hundred per center*, ..one who observes all customs and traditions without demur. **1946** *R.A.F. Jrnl.* May 169 The bomber crews had to make 100 per cent. certain of putting their H.E. loads right on the objective. **1968** M. WOODHOUSE *Rock Baby* xxiv. 233 You're one hundred per cent sure they'll never make any sort of bang, then?

d. ***a hundred per cent***: fit, well, recovered. Freq. in negative contexts.

1960 N. MITFORD *Don't tell Alfred* xiv. 155, I don't feel a hundred per cent. **1965** V. CANNING *Whip Hand* xi. 131 How's the arm?' 'It wasn't broken... It's almost a hundred per cent now.' **1965** N. FREELING *Criminal Conversation* I. viii. 52, I wasn't quite well, not ill but not quite a hundred per cent, and he did make me better. **1967** I. HAMILTON *Man with Brown Paper Face* xv. 214 Actually, I'm not completely one hundred per cent. **1973** 'D. CRAIG' *Bolthole* ii. 30 He's been, well, off colour, yes. Not ill, but not a hundred per cent.

3. In the sale of various commodities, often used for a definite number greater than five score; see quots.: esp. ***great*** or ***long hundred***, usually = six score, or a hundred and twenty.

1469 *Househ. Ord.* (1790) 102 Salt fishe for Lent..at 204 [*sic*, but ? error] to the hundred. **1533-4** *Act 25 Hen. VIII*, c. 13 §12 The nomber of the C. of shepe..in some countrey the great C where .vj. Score is accompted for the C. **1601** F. TATE *Househ. Ord. Edw. II* (1876) 61 Of somme manner of fish the hundred containeth six score, and of some other sort, nine score. **1688** R. HOLME *Armoury* III. v. 260/2 Ling, Cod, or Haberdine, have 124 to the Hundred. **1727-41** CHAMBERS *Cycl.* s.v., Deal boards are sixscore to the hundred, called the long hundred. **1813** *Q. Rev.* IX. 279 To take from ten to twenty thousand mackerel a-day at a price not exceeding ten shillings the hundred of six score, or a penny a-piece. **1859** SALA *Tw. round Clock* (1861) 16 Fresh herrings are sold from the vessel by the long hundred (130). **1886** *Glasgow Her.* 13 Sept. 4/2 A mease [of herring] ..is five hundreds of 120 each.

4. Elliptical uses. **a.** = HUNDREDWEIGHT.

1542 RECORDE *Gr. Artes* (1575) 203 An hundred is not just 100, but is 112 pounde. **1743** *Lond. & Country Brew.* IV. (ed. 2) 322 Three hundred Weight of Coals make but a hundred of Coaks. **1776** G. SEMPLE *Building in Water* 37 This Ram is only four hundred and a half. **1838** *Knickerbocker* XI. 15 When requested..to say how much flour she should make into bread, at their first baking, she answered..'I suppose about a quarter of a hundred.' **1852** *Trans. Mich. Agric. Soc.* III. 332 To dispose of the compound of acorns, ground nuts and carrion for $2 per hundred. **1861** *Trans. Ill. Agric. Soc.* IV. 373 We want a horse sixteen hands high, that will weigh fifteen hundred.

b. A hundred of some other weight, measure, or quantity.

1538 *Yatton Churchw. Acc.* (Som. Rec. Soc.) 152 Payd for ij hundryth of bords to make yᵉ Church coffur .iiijˢ. viijᵈ. **1703** MOXON *Mech. Exerc.* 258 An Hundred of Lime, being 25 Bushels, or an hundred Pecks. **1703** T. N. *City & C. Purchaser* 214 Oak is worth sawing 2s. 8d. per hundred,.. That is the hundred Superficial Feet. **1875** BEDFORD *Sailor's Pocket Bk.* x. (ed. 2) 367 Books of gold leaf contain twenty-five leaves. Gilders estimate their work by the number of 'hundreds' it will take (meaning one hundred leaves) instead of the number of books.

c. A hundred pounds (of money).

1543 BECON *Polecy of Warre* Wks. (1560-3) I. 139 The preste..maye dispende hondreds yearely, and do nought for it. **1599** B. JONSON *Ev. Man out of Hum.* II. iii, [He] may dispend some seven or eight hundred a year. **1728-49** [see COOL *a.* 7]. **1771** SMOLLETT *Humph. Cl.* 11 June, I'll bet a cool hundred he swings before Christmas. **1806** SURR *Winter in Lond.* (ed. 3) II. 150 It..contained three bank-notes for one hundred each. **1855** *Cornwall* 257 Laying out a few hundreds. **1876** T. HARDY *Ethelberta* (1890) 411 Faith and I have three hundred a year between us.

d. A hundred years, a century. *Obs.* exc. *dial.*

a **1656** BP. HALL *Rem. Wks.* (1660) 298 Even in the second hundred (so antient..this festivity is). **1883** *Longm. Mag.* Oct. 638 Since the last year of the last 'hunner'.

5. a. In England (and subseq. in Ireland): A subdivision of a county or shire, having its own court; also formerly applied to the court itself: cf. COUNTY[1] 4. ***Chiltern Hundreds***: see CHILTERN.

Most of the English counties were divided into hundreds; but in some counties *wapentakes*, and in others *wards*, appear as divisions of a similar kind. The origin of the division into hundreds, which appears already in OE. times, is exceedingly obscure, and very diverse opinions have been given as to its origin. 'It has been regarded as denoting simply a division of a hundred hides of land; as the district which furnished a hundred warriors to the host; as representing the original settlement of the hundred warriors; or as composed of a hundred hides, each of which furnished a single warrior' (Stubbs *Const. Hist.* I. v. §45). 'It is certain that in some instances the hundred was deemed to contain exactly 100 hides of land' (F. W. Maitland). The hundred, OHG. (Alemannisch) *huntari*, *huntre*, was a subdivision of the *gau* in Ancient Germany; but connexion between this and the English *hundred* is not clearly made out.

c **1000** *Laws of Edgar* I. (*title*) Þis is seo ʒerædnyss, hu mon þæt hundred healdan sceal. *Ibid.* c. 3 And se man þe þis forsitte, and þæs hundredes dom forsace..ʒesylle man þam hundrede xxx peninga, and æt þam æfteran cyrre syxtiʒ peneʒa, half þam hundrede, half þam hlaforde. *c* **1000** *Laws of Ethelred* I. c. i. §2 Nime se hlaford tweʒen ʒetreowe þeʒenas innan þam hundrede. ? *a* **1143** WILL. MALMESB. *Gesta Reg.* II §122 Centurias quas dicunt hundrez, et decimas quas thethingas vocant instituit [Elfredus]. **1292** BRITTON I. i. §13 En counteez et hundrez et en Court de chescun fraunc tenaunt. *Ibid.* iii. §7 De amercier nul homme en court de baroun ne en hundred. *c* **1325** *Poem Times Edw. II* 469 in *Pol. Songs* (Camden) 344 And thise assisours, that comen to shire and to hundred Damneth men for silver. **1450** J. PASTON *Petit.* in *P. Lett.* No. 77 I. 107 In the courtes of the hundred. **1465** MARG. PASTON *Ibid.* No. 510 II. 201 Endytyd..by the enquest of Fourhoo hunder. **1480** CAXTON *Descr. Brit.* 20 In Yorkshire ben xxij hondredis. **1559** in Strype *Ann. Ref.* (1824) I. II. App. vii. 409 There is..in every houndrethe one head counstable. **1588** FRAUNCE *Lawiers Log.* I. xii. 52. **1632** MASSINGER *City Madam* I. ii, Thy sire, constable Of the hundred. **1656** EVELYN *Mem.* 8 July, [Dedham] a clothing town, as most are in Essex, but lies in the unwholesome hundreds. **1748** *De Foe's Tour Gt. Brit.* I. 7 (D.) From hence [Tilbury Fort] there is nothing for many miles together remarkable but a continued level of unhealthy marshes called The Three Hundreds, till we come before Leigh. **1765** BLACKSTONE *Comm.* Introd. iv. 115 As ten families of freeholders made up a town or tithing, so ten tithings composed a superior division, called a hundred, as consisting of ten times ten families. **1806-7** J. BERESFORD *Miseries Hum. Life* (1826) II. xxx, On a visit in the Hundreds of Essex. **1874** STUBBS *Const. Hist.* I. v. 96 The union of a number of townships for the purpose of judicial administration, peace, and defence, formed what is known as the *hundred* or *wapentake*. **1876** DIGBY *Real Prop.* i. 3 It is impossible to trace the exact links of connexion between the hundreds of warriors who constituted the sub-divisions of the Teutonic army and the territorial hundred of later times; there can however be no question that the two are connected. **1886** *Act 49 & 50 Vict.* c. 38 Whereas by law the inhabitants of the hundred or other area in which property is damaged by persons riotously and tumultuously assembled together are liable in certain cases to pay compensation for such damage, and it is expedient to make other provision [etc.]..§5..the amount required to meet the said payments shall be raised as part of the police rate. **1888** *Act 51 & 52 Vict.* c. 41 §3 There shall be transferred to the council of each county..The making, assessing, and levying of county, police, hundred, and all rates. *Ibid.* §100 The expression 'division of a county', in.. this Act..includes any hundred, lathe, wapentake, or other like division.

b. A division of a county in the British American colonies or provinces of Virginia, Maryland, Delaware, and Pennsylvania, which still exists in the State of Delaware.

1621 *Ordin. Virginia* 24 July in Stith *Hist. Virginia* App. iv. 33 The other council..shall consist for the present, of the said council of state, and of two burgesses out of every town, hundred, or other particular plantation. **1637-8** in *Archives of Maryland* III. 59 Whereas the west side of St. Georges river is now..thought fit to be erected into a hundred by the name of St. Georges hundred. **1683** *Col. Rec. Pennsylv.* I. 21 Power to Divide the said Countrey and Islands, into Townes, Hundreds and Counties. **1888** BRYCE *Amer. Commw.* II. xlviii. 224 *note*, In Maryland *hundreds*, which still exist in Delaware, were for a long time the chief administrative divisions. **1896** P. A. BRUCE *Econ. Hist. Virginia* I. 210 At certain intervals..houses were put up, the

occupants of which formed a guard . . for the population of the Hundreds.

†**c.** Proverb. *Obs.*

1546 J. HEYWOOD *Prov.* (1867) 76 What ye wan in the hundred ye lost in the sheere. **1625** BACON *Ess., Empire* (Arb.) 307 Taxes, and Imposts vpon them [merchants] doe seldome good to the Kings Reuenew; For that that he winnes in the Hundred, he leeseth in the Shire. **1682** BUNYAN *Holy War* (R.T.S.) 297 They are Mr. Penny Wise-pound-foolish, and Mr. Get-i' th' Hundred-and-lose-i-the-Shire.

†**6.** A game at cards. *Obs.* (Cf. CENT^{2}.)

1636 DAVENANT *Wits* I. ii, Their glad sons are left seven for their chance, At hazard, hundred, and all made at sent. **1652** URQUHART *Jewel* Wks. (1834) 277 As we do of card kings in playing at the hundred.

7. ***hundreds and thousands***: a name for very small comfits.

c **1830** [Remembered in use]. **1894** G. EGERTON *Keynotes* 137 Little cakes with hundreds and thousands on top. **1922** G. K. CHESTERTON in *Illustr. London News* 12 Aug. 234/1 There ought not to be anything but a plural for . . the sweets called hundreds and thousands. **1932** A. CHRISTIE *Thirteen Problems* i. 22 'Cooks nearly always put hundreds and thousands on trifle, dear,' she said. 'Those little pink and white sugar things.' **1953** DYLAN THOMAS *Under Milk Wood* (1954) 60 Brandyballs, winegums, hundreds and thousands, liquorice sweet as sick. **1967** N. FREELING *Strike Out* 87 Little sugary pellets like hundreds and thousands.

8. *Comb.* **a.** In sense 1 (or 2). (*a*) attrib., as **hundred-work**, sawyers' work paid for by the hundred (square feet); (*b*) in adj. relation with a noun in the plural, as **hundred-eyes**, name for the plant Periwinkle (*Vinca*); **hundred-legs**, a centipede; also with a noun in the singular, forming adjectival compounds, in sense Having, containing, measuring, etc. a hundred (of what is denoted by the second element), as ***hundred-foot***, ***-franc***, ***-leaf***, ***-mesh***, ***-mile***, ***-petal***, ***-pound*** (e.g. *a hundred-franc piece*, *a hundred-pound note*); so **hundred-pounder**, a cannon firing shot weighing a hundred pounds each (see POUNDER); (*c*) parasynthetic, as ***hundred-citied***, ***-footed***, ***-gated***, ***-handed***, ***-headed***, ***-hued***, ***leaved***, ***-throated***, etc., adjs.

1855 KINGSLEY *Heroes, Theseus* II. 237 Minos, the King of *hundred-citied Crete. **1882** *Rep. to Ho. Repr. Prec. Met. U.S.* 264 A *100-foot shaft. **1646** SIR T. BROWNE *Pseud. Ep.* III. xv. 142 The Scolopendra or *hundred footed insect. **1742** YOUNG *Nt. Th.* IX. 922 Thy *hundred-gated Capitals. **1876** GEO. ELIOT *Dan. Der.* III. xxxviii. 131 The hundred-gated Thebes. **1805** W. TAYLOR in *Ann. Rev.* III. 266 The *hundred-handed Briareus. **1591** PERCIVALL *Sp. Dict., Cien cabeças*, *hundred headed thistle. **1601** HOLLAND *Pliny* II. 83 To bring forth these *hundred-leafe Roses. **1811** A. T. THOMSON *Lond. Disp.* (1818) 345 The petals of the *Hundred-leaved Rose. **1808** BENTHAM *Sc. Reform* 50 A bone breaking *hundred mile road. **1692** *Lond. Gaz.* No. 2831/4 Lost . . an *Hundred Pound Bag. **1684** J. PETER *Siege Vienna* 109 Mortar-piece, a *hundred pounder. **1842** TENNYSON *Vis. of Sin* 27 As 'twere a *hundred-throated nightingale. **1703** T. N. *City & C. Purchaser* 239 Some Sawyers claim it as a Custom, to have half Breaking-work, and the other half *Hundred-work.

b. In sense 5. **hundred-court**, in *Eng. Hist.* the court having civil and criminal jurisdiction within a territorial hundred; †**hundred-man**, OE. *hundredes-man*, the constable or officer of the hundred, = HUNDREDER 1; †**hundred-mote**, the assembly of the hundred, the hundred-court; †**hundred-penny**, a tax or payment anciently levied in a hundred.

1671 F. PHILLIPS *Reg. Necess.* 508 Unless he could not in the Century, or *Hundred-Court obtain any Remedy. **1789** W. HUTTON (*title*) History of the Hundred Court. **1874** STUBBS *Const. Hist.* I. v. 104 The hundred court was entitled to declare folk right in every suit. *a* **1000** *Laws of Edgar* I. c. 2 Gyf neod on handa stande, cyðe hit man þam *hundredes-men, and he syððan þam teoðing-mannum. *Ibid.* c. 4 Buton he hæbbe þæs hundredes mann[es] ȝewitnyssa, oððe þæs teoðingmannes. **1235–52** *Rentalia Glaston.* (Som. Rec. Soc.) 210 Et namiat cum hundredmanno in hundredo. **1874** STUBBS *Const. Hist.* I. v. 102 On analogy . . we may fairly maintain that the original hundred-man or hundredes-ealdor was an elected officer, and the convener and constituting functionary of the court which he held. **1839** KEIGHTLEY *Hist. Eng.* I. 77 The Hundred also had its Court, named the *Hundred or Folc-Mote. **1874** GREEN *Short Hist.* iii. §3. 125 The Charter was . . sworn to at every hundred-mote. **1189–95** *Charter* in *Wetherhal Register* (1897) 30 Et omnes terræ ad eam pertinentes . . sint quiete . . de *hundredpeni et de thethingepeni et de legerwite. **1293** *Rolls Parlt.* I. 115/1 Liberi et quieti ab omni Scotto . . et de Hidagio . . Hundredespeny, Borchafpeny, Thethyngpeny.

hundred (as ordinal): see HUNDREDTH.

†**hundredaghte.** *Obs. rare.* In 4 **hondredaȝte.** [app. an analogical formation after *þrittaȝte*, *zixtiaȝte*, for OE. *þritiȝoðe*, *sixtiȝoðe.*] Hundredth; hundredfold.

1340 *Ayenb.* 234 Þo þet byeþ ine spoushod . . habbeþ þet þrittaȝte frut. Þo þet byeþ in wodewe-hod habbeþ þet zixtiaȝte frut. Þo þet lokeþ maydenhod habbeþ þet hondredaȝte frut. . . Þet zed þet vil into þe guode londe fructefide of one half to þe þrittaȝte, of oþer half to zixtiaȝte and of þe þridde half to þe hondredaȝte.

hundredal ('hʌndrədəl), *a.* [f. HUNDRED 5 + -AL^{1}.] Of or pertaining to a territorial hundred.

1862 *Collect. Archæol.* I. 12 Single manors having a hundredal franchise were often called hundreds. **1875** STUBBS *Const. Hist.* III. xxi. 564 The ancient towns in demesne of the Crown . . possessed a hundredal jurisdiction. **1897** MAITLAND *Domesday & Beyond* 93 The relation of the manorial to the hundredal Courts is curious.

hundredary ('hʌndrədərɪ). [ad. med.L. *hundredārius*: see next and -ARY.] = HUNDREDER 1.

1700 SIR H. CHAUNCY *Hertfords.* (1826) I. 15 The Chief of them [Freemen] were Sheriffs, Hundredaries, and other Judges and Ministerial Officers in their several Counties. **1818** HALLAM *Mid. Ages* (1872) I. ii. II. §5. 238 Next in order was the Centenarius or Hundredary, whose name expresses the extent of his jurisdiction. **1850** *Fraser's Mag.* XLI. 343 Every county had still its shire-mote, every hundred its hundredary, every tything and parish its wardens.

hundreder, -or ('hʌndrədə(r)). Also 5–6 **hundrythar, hundredour, hunderder.** [f. HUNDRED 5 + -ER^{2}: in med.L. *hundredārius.* Cf. *centenarius*, *centener*, CENTENIER.]

1. The bailiff or chief officer of a hundred; the hundred-man.

[**1285** *Act 13 Edw. I*, c. 38 Quia etiam vicecomites hundredarii et ballivi libertatum consueverunt gravare subditos suos. **1315** *Rolls Parlt.* I. 343/2 Qe les Executions de Brefs qe vendront as Viscontes soient faites par les Hundreders, conuz & jurez en plein Conte.] **1455** *Paston Lett.* No. 239 I. 330 The Kyng [Hen. VI.] beyng then in the place of Edmond Westley, hunderdere of the seyd toun of Seynt Albones. **1591** LAMBARDE *Archeion* (1635) 38 That Sheriffes, Coroners, Hundreders, Burgesses, Serjeants, and Beadles, have their Courts within every their particular limits. **1607** COWEL *Interpr.* (1672), *Hundreder*, . . signifies also him that hath the Jurisdiction of a Hundred, and holdeth the hundred Court . . and sometimes it is used for the Bayliff of an Hundred. **1761** HUME *Hist. Eng.* I. ii. 50 Twelve freeholders were chosen; who, having sworn, together with the hundreder, or presiding magistrate of that division, to administer impartial justice, proceeded to the examination of that cause. **1874** *Act 37 & 38 Vict.* c. 45 §38 Nothing in this Act shall take away . . any right or privilege of the hundredor or hereditary sheriff of the hundred of Cashio.

2. An inhabitant of a hundred, especially one liable to be impanelled on a jury.

1501 *Plumpton Corr.* (Camden) 159 All these that is at the end of the names ar Hundrythars. **1543–4** *Act 35 Hen. VIII*, c. 6 §3 The shireffe . . shall returne in euery suche panell . . six sufficient hundredours at the least. **1628** COKE *On Litt.* 157a, In a plea personall, if two hundredors appear, it sufficeth. **1647** N. BACON *Disc. Govt. Eng.* I. xxv. (1739) 42 In raising of Forces one hundred were selected *ex singulis Pagis*, which first were called Centennarii, or Hundreders, from their number. **1768** BLACKSTONE *Comm.* III. ix. 161 To oblige the hundredors to make hue and cry after the felon. **1818–48** HALLAM *Mid. Ages* (1872) II. viii. 406 *note*, The trial by a jury . . replaced that by the body of hundredors. **1897** MAITLAND *Domesday & Beyond* 288 In order that all the hundredors may have an interest in the pursuit of thieves, it is otherwise decreed. Half shall go to the hundred.

†**3.** A centurion. *Obs.*

c **1550** CHEKE *Matt.* viii. 8 As Jesus cam into Capernaum, yeer cam an hunderder vnto him and sued vnto him.

hundredfold ('hʌndrədfəʊld), *a.*, *adv.*, and *sb.* Forms: see HUNDRED; also 2–4 **-fald**, 3 **-feald**, 3–4 **-feld(e**, 4 **-foold**, **-uald**, 4–6 **-folde**. [f. HUNDRED + -FOLD. Cf. ON. *hundrað-falda*, MHG. *hundertvalt*, Ger. *hundertfalt*, *-fältig*. OE. had *hundfeald.*]

A. *adj.* A hundred times as much or as many.

c **1200** *Trin. Coll. Hom.* 203 He shal fon þer-to-yenes hundredfeld mede. *c* **1200** ORMIN 19903 He wollde . . Hiss mede ȝeldenn hunndreddfald Forr hise gode dedess. **1552** HULOET, Hundreth folde, *centuplex*.

B. *adv.* A hundred times (in amount).

a **1200** *Moral Ode* 54 He hit scal finden eft þer and hundred fald mare. *Ibid.* 247 Þer is fur þet is undret fald hattre þene bo ure.

b. Now always ***a*** (***an***) ***hundredfold.***

c **1320** *Cast. Love* 1189 He that alle thyng may welde, Dowbled his peyne an hondred felde. **1340** *Ayenb.* 191 Þet god wolde yelde an hondreduald al þet me yeaue. *c* **1400** MAUNDEV. (Roxb.) xxiv. 112 Mare acceptable . . þan if he gafe him a hundreth falde so mykill. **1797** GODWIN *Enquirer* I. ix. 82 It diminishes them a hundred fold. **1840** MACAULAY *Ess., Ranke* (1854) II. 135 Armies which out-numbered them a hundredfold.

C. *sb.* **1.** A hundred times the amount or number.

c **1175** *Lamb. Hom.* 137 Eower weldede scal eft beon imeten eower mede, and bi hunderfalde mare. *a* **1300** *Cursor M.* 17055 (Cott.) But o ioi an hundret fald, he dublid þe þi sang. **1382** WYCLIF *Gen.* xxvi. 12 Isaac . . sowide in that loond, and he fonde that ȝeer the hundryd foold. **1393** LANGL. *P. Pl.* C. XIII. 158 He shal haue an hundred-folde of heuene-ryche blisse. **1526** TINDALE *Matt.* xiii. 8 Some an hundred fold, some fifty fold, some thyrty folde. **1655** MILTON *Sonn., Massacre Piedmont*, That from these may grow A hundredfold, who . . Early may fly the Babylonian woe. **1747** CHESTERF. *Let. to Prior* 6 May, Seed . . which indeed produced one hundred fold.

2. A local name for Lady's Bedstraw, *Galium verum*, from its numerous crowded blossoms.

1853 G. JOHNSTON *Nat. Hist. E. Bord.* I. 100 As the flowers are exceedingly numerous and clustered, our common people call the plant *A Hundred-fald.*

hundredth ('hʌndrədθ), *a.* and *sb.* (Also 4–6 **hundreth**, 4 **hundret**, **-re**, **-ride**, 5 **hondred**, 7 **hundred**). [f. HUNDRED + -TH^{1}. Of late formation: OE. had no ordinal from *hund* or *hundred*; ME. sometimes used forms identical with the cardinal, as is still done dialectally.] The ordinal numeral belonging to the cardinal HUNDRED.

A. *adj.* **1.** Coming last in order of a hundred successive individuals.

1483 *Cath. Angl.* 192/1 Hundreth, *centum*, *centenus . . cente[s]imus*. **1570** LEVINS *Manip.* 88/44 Ye Hundreth, *centesimus*. **1630** DRAYTON *Noah's Flood* (R.), On the six hundredth year of that just man, The second month, the seventeenth day began That horrid deluge. **1631** R. BYFIELD *Doctr. Sabb.* 14 The one hundred generation. **1841** W. SPALDING *Italy & It. Isl.* I. 103 Extending to the hundredth milestone.

2. ***hundredth part***: one of a hundred equal parts into which a whole is or may be divided.

a **1300** *Cursor M.* 23140 Þe hundret [*Gött.* hundreth, *F.* hundre, *Tr.* hundride] part i mai noght mele. **1413** *Pilgr. Sowle* (Caxton) v. i. (1859) 71, I sawe therof not the hondred part. *a* **1600** HOOKER (J.), We shall not need to use the hundredth part of that time. **1665** HOOKE *Microgr.* 213 Not above a four or five hundredth part of a well grown Mite. **1790** BURKE *Fr. Rev.* Wks. V. 111 [He] has not power left . . by the hundredth part sufficient to hold together this collection of republicks. **1833** N. ARNOTT *Physics* I. 39 Compressed . . so as to have bulk about a hundredth part less.

B. *sb.* **1.** A hundredth part.

1774 C. J. PHIPPS *Voy. N. Pole* 124 Divided . . by a Vernier division into hundredths of an inch. **1800** YOUNG in *Phil. Trans.* XCI. 40 We will therefore call this distance 12 hundredths. **1861** MILL *Utilit.* ii. 26 Ninety-nine hundredths of all our actions are done from other motives.

2. ***Old Hundredth***, a hymn tune which first appeared in the Geneva psalter of 1551 and was later set to Psalm 100 in the 'old' metrical version of the Geneva Psalter (hymn 166 in 'Hymns Ancient and Modern'); the psalm itself. Also *attrib.*

[**1790** BRADY & TATE *New Version Psalms* 240 The Psalms in this Version of four Lines in a single Stanza . . may properly be sung as the old 100 Psalm.] **1837** T. BACON *First Impr. Hindostan* I. vi. 153, I have often . . heard the organ pealing forth the solemn notes of the old hundredth psalm. **1837** DICKENS *Pickw.* xxxii. 349 Brother Mordlin had adapted the beautiful words of 'Who hasn't heard of a Jolly Young Waterman?' to the tune of the Old Hundredth. **1840** —— *Old C. Shop* xviii. 192 The dog . . ground hard at the organ . . and applied himself . . to the Old Hundredth. **1853** MRS. GASKELL *Cranford* xv. 298, I found out from the words, far more than from the attempt at the tune, that it was the Old Hundredth she was crooning to herself. **1934** R. FERGUSON *Celebrated Sequels* 25 Our vicar's wife says that on the whole we had better stick to the Old Hundredth. **1955** M. GILBERT *Sky High* i. 7 'What's the last hymn next Sunday . . ?' 'Hundred and Sixty-six. Old Hundredth. You all know *that.*'

hundredweight ('hʌndrədweɪt). [f. HUNDRED + WEIGHT. The plural is unchanged after a numeral or an adj. expressing plurality, as *many.*] An avoirdupois weight equal to 112 pounds; prob. originally to a hundred pounds, whence the name. Abbreviated cwt. (formerly C.).

Locally it has varied from 100 to 120 lb.; 'in the United States a hundredweight is now commonly understood as 100 pounds' (*Cent. Dict.*).

[**1542** see HUNDRED 4 a.] **1577** HARRISON *England* III. i. (1877) II. 4 Such [horses] as are kept also for burden, will carie foure hundred weight commonlie. **1672** PETTY *Pol. Anat.* (1691) 53 The said quantity of Milk will make 2½ C. of Raw-Milk-Cheese, and 1 C. of Whey-Butter. **1700** T. BROWN tr. *Fresny's Amusem. Ser. & Com.* 65 [She] could as soon fly with a Hundred Weight of Lead at her Heels. **1858** GREENER *Gunnery* 303 An anchor-shank weighing some hundredweights. **1862** ANSTED *Channel Isl.* IV. App. A (ed. 2) 564 The Jersey local hundred weight consists of 104 Jersey pounds, and the Guernsey hundred weight of 100 Guernsey pounds. **1895** *Times* 6 Mar. 10/6 The hundred-weight of certain kinds of cheese was 112 lb. and of others 120 lb.

attrib. **1883** P. S. ROBINSON *Saints & Sinners* 253 Hundredweight blocks of silver bullion.

†**hune.** *Naut. Obs.* Also 7 *Sc.* **huin.** [In Layamon, app. a. ON. *hún-n* knob at the masthead; in later use prob. a. F. *hune* (from Norse) in same sense. Cf. HOUND *sb.*^{2}] = HOUND *sb.*^{2} 1.

c **1205** LAY. 28978 Seil heo droȝen to hune. *a* **1605** MONTGOMERIE *Misc. Poems* xlviii. 93 Vp uent our saillis, tauntit to the huins. **1764** VEICHT in *Phil. Trans.* LIV. 286 The main-top-mast had great pieces carried from it, from the hunes down to the cap, at the head of the main-mast.

hune, var. of HONE *sb.*^{2} *Obs.*, delay.

hunframe, var. UNFRAME *Obs.*, evil, disadvantage.

hunfysh, obs. f. HOUNDFISH.

hung (hʌŋ), *ppl. a.* [pa. pple. of HANG *v.*]

1. a. Suspended, attached so as to hang down, etc.; see the vb. Often with qualification, as *well*, *ill*.

1663 F. HAWKINS *Youth's Behav.* 97 Annulet, a thing hung about the neck. **1678** *Quack's Acad.* 6 A Tongue well hung. **1771** SMOLLETT *Humph. Cl.* 26 June, The carriage is . . well hung. **1894** *Athenæum* 22 Sept. 393/2 In all hung window sashes means should be adopted to permit both the sashes being removed.

b. Of meat: Suspended in the air to be cured by drying, or (in the case of game) to become 'high'.

1655 MOUFET & BENNET *Health's Improv.* (1746) 349 Country-labourers, accustomed to feed usually upon hung Beef. **1772** NUGENT tr. *Hist. Fr. Gerund* I. 106 Old ewe-mutton, hung-meat, and household bread. **1833** MARRYAT *P. Simple* xxiii, A piece of hung beef, and six loaves. **1863** *Morn. Star* 1 Jan. 5, I have heard Dr. Hill's evidence as to hung game being unwholesome and unfit for food.

2. a. Furnished or decorated *with* hanging things.

1648 GAGE *West Ind.* 16 All her masts and tacklings hung with paper Lanthornes. **1791** *Trans. Soc. Arts* IX. 33 They [peas] grew rapidly and were very well hung. **1849** MACAULAY *Hist. Eng.* iii. I. 385 At the larger houses of entertainment were to be found beds hung with silk.

†**b.** Having pendent organs. *Obs.*

1641 BEST *Farm. Bks.* (Surtees) 1 Hunge tuppes are such as have both the stones in the codde. *c* **1645** HOWELL *Lett.* (1650) I. 32 They cut off his genitories, (and they say he was hung like an ass). **1685** *Lond. Gaz.* No. 1998/4 A large Hound Bitch..pretty well hung, all white. **1785** GROSE *Dict. Vulg. T.*, *Well-hung*.

3. a. Of a jury: unable to agree. Cf. HANG *v.* 6 b, 17 c. *U.S.*

1848 E. BRYANT *California* (1849) xxvi. 291 The jury.. were what is called 'hung'; they could not agree, and the matters in issue, therefore, remained exactly where they were. **1962** *Listener* 10 May 799/1 No one would deny that a deadlocked jury—what the Americans call a hung jury—is a bad thing. **1965** J. PORTER *Dover Two* v. 63 What with hung juries, appeals and pleas for mercy, they'd had it [*sc.* the story] on ice for a long time.

b. Of an elected body: in which no political party has an overall majority.

1974 *Economist* 3 Aug. 13/2 This Parliament has been called many names: the hung, the cynical, the shiftless, the cowed. **1978** *Times* 22 May 2 He saw all the pointers to another hung parliament. **1979** *Economist* 12 May 24/3 A hung parliament..helped to produce these hung councils. **1983** *Listener* 14 Apr. 4/3 We must not expect politicians to say anything sensible about their intentions in a hung Parliament until the results are known. **1985** *Abingdon Herald* 21 Feb. 6/4 There could be a 'hung' council, probably with the Tories being the largest group but unable to form an administration without the support of one of the other parties.

4. *slang.* Suffering from excess of liquor (or drugs). Also **hung-over** (cf. HANG-OVER 2), having or affected by a hang-over.

1950 R. STARNES *And when she was Bad* (1953) xvi. 76 Brafferton just came in, looking as hung over as you can get. **1952** J. VAN DRUTEN *I am a Camera* (1954) 90 Enters.. wearing a dressing gown and looks hung-over. 'I say, you don't look too well this morning.' 'I've got a terrible hangover.' **1958** *Amer. Speech* XXXIII. 225 Drunks are *hung*, too. **1960** *Homes & Gardens* Aug. 70/2 It is said to have therapeutic qualities on hungover mornings. **1960** I. SHAW *Two Weeks in another Town* x. 125 He awoke late, feeling headachy and hung-over from the liquor of the night before. **1962** K. ORVIS *Damned & Destroyed* vii. 48 A score or more of addicts—all hungover. **1963** H. SLESAR *Bridge of Lions* i. 7, I know you're hung, Mr. Drew. **1968** J. HUDSON *Case of Need* vi. 126, I was hung over from a party after the game. Really hung. Too hung. **1972** C. DRUMMOND *Death at Bar* v. 139 Christ! You look hung over!.. What about drinks all round?

hung (hʌŋ), pa. t. and pple. of HANG *v.*

hungal, var. HANGUL[1].

†**'Hungar.** *Obs.* [a. Ger. *Ungar*, med.L. *Hungarus* Hungarian.]

1. A Hungarian.

1606 G. W[OODCOCKE] tr. *Hist. Ivstine* Ii vj a, A while after, himself was ouercome by the said Hungars.

2. A gold coin of Hungary. Also ***Hungar-dollar***.

1650 FULLER *Pisgah* IV. ii. 29 Hungar-dollars, which are refined to the standard of Hungarian gold. **1684** T. SMITH *Acc. City Prusa* in *Phil. Trans.* XIV. 442 Zecchines and Hungars for Gold, and Spanish Dollars and Zalotts for Silver..pass current among them. **1756** ROLT *Dict. Trade*, *Hungar*, or *Hongre*, a gold coin struck in Hungary; and also a money of accompt, worth about a crown sterling.

Hungarian (hʌŋ'gɛərɪən), *a.* and *sb.* [f. med.L. *Hungaria* HUNGARY.] **A.** *adj.*

1. a. Of, belonging to, or native of Hungary. Applied to things orig. made or reared in Hungary, as ***Hungarian horse***, ***H. leather***; ***Hungarian balsam***, the resinous product of the Carpathian pine, *Pinus Mugho* or *Pumilio*; ***Hungarian bonnet*** or ***cap***, the shell of a marine gastropod mollusc, *Capulus ungaricus*; ***Hungarian bowls***, a kind of amalgamating machine, orig. used in the gold mines of Schemnitz; ***Hungarian grass*** *U.S.* (*obs.*), the forage grass, foxtail millet, *Setaria italica*; ***Hungarian machine***, a hydraulic machine on the principle of Hero's fountain: see quot.; ***Hungarian water***, Hungary water.

1600 J. PORY tr. *Leo's Africa* II. 48 The Hungarian coine is round. **1632** LITHGOW *Trav.* IX. 415 The Hungarian miles are the longest upon earth. *a* **1688** VILLIERS (Dk. Buckhm.) *Ep. To Julian* Wks. 1705 II. 92 Such Carbuncles..As no Hungarian Water can Redress. **1829** *Nat. Philos.*, *Hydraulics* ii. 17 (U.K.S.) The Hungarian machine, so called from its having been employed in draining a mine at Chemnitz, in Hungary, produces its action by the condensation of a confined portion of air produced by the descent of a high Column of water contained in a pipe. **1845** *Encycl. Metrop.* VII. 288/2 In the Hungarian Bonnet, *Pileopsis Ungarica*, the tip of the shell seems to drop backwards and downwards. **1854** P. H. GOSSE *Nat. Hist. Mollusca* 212 The only British species [of *Pileopsis*] is commonly known by the appellation of Torbay Bonnet..; it also bears the names of Fools-cap Limpet, Cap of Liberty, and Hungarian Bonnet. **1859** *Guide Illinois Central Railroad Lands* 34 *Hungarian Grass.* This cereal, first introduced by the Hungarian exiles, is becoming a favorite with the farmers. **1882** *Garden* 13 May 322/1 Hungarian Lilac will shortly be in bloom. **1883** *Rep. Indian Affairs* 23 About 12 acres were planted with Hungarian grass. **1901** E. STEP *Shell Life* 220 The Hungarian Cap or Cap of Liberty (*Capulus hungaricus*) is shaped much like the cap of Liberty, the beak or apex being spirally curved back. **1971** S. P. DANCE *Seashells* 103/2 A thick periostracum is a characteristic feature of some cap shells and is well seen in the Hungarian Cap.

b. Pertaining to Hungary, as ***Hungarian band***, a band specializing in the performance of Hungarian music; ***Hungarian point***, ***stitch*** (see quot. 1934).

1882 B. POTTER *Jrnl.* 2 July (1966) 19 Mr. Edwin Lawrence had the Hungarian Band last week... They are mostly string instruments. **1894** G. DU MAURIER *Trilby* III. VIII. 133 A large photograph..of Svengali, in the military uniform of his own Hungarian band. **1907** *Yesterday's Shopping* (1969) 1055 Blue Hungarian Band... Handsome National Uniforms... Any number from 4 to 30 may be engaged. **1921** A. G. I. CHRISTIE *Samplers & Stitches* vii. 99 *Hungarian stitch*... The stitch illustrated in the diagram is often seen in canvas embroidery, used for filling in a background whilst, perhaps, Tent or Cross stitch works out the intricacies of the pattern. **1932** D. C. MINTER *Mod. Needlecraft* 60/1 Some geometric all-over pattern, such as Hungarian stitch. **1934** M. THOMAS *Dict. Embroidery Stitches* 125 *Hungarian stitch*, a Canvas Stitch which produces a most attractive pattern, and may be worked either all in one colour or in contrasting shades. **1972** *Country Life* 8 June (Suppl.) 50 Queen Anne walnut wing-chair..covered in its original Hungarian point needlework.

†**2.** Thievish, marauding; needy, beggarly (with play on *hungry*: cf. B. 2; see Nares). *Obs. slang.*

1598 SHAKS. *Merry W.* I. iii. 23 O base hungarian wight: wilt yᵘ the spigot wield? **1608** *Merry Devil Edmonton* (1617) D iv b, Come yee Hungarian pilchers, we are once more come under the zona torrida of the forest.

B. *sb.*

1. A native or inhabitant of Hungary, a Magyar; a Hungarian horse; the language of Hungary.

1553 (*title*) A dialoge of comfort against tribulacion, made by Syr Thomas More Knyght, and set foorth by the name of an Hungarien. **1615** in Devon *Iss. Excheq. Jas. I* (1836) 318 One other gray gelding, instead of one of the Hungarians given to the Queen. **1668** WILKINS *Real Char.* I. i. §3. 4 The Hungarian [language], used in the greatest part of that Kingdom. **1841** W. SPALDING *Italy & It. Isl.* II. 83 Fresh invasions of the Saracens, to whom were now added the Hungarians from the north.

†**2.** (With play on *hunger*.) A hungry person, a great eater: cf. A. 2. *Obs. slang.*

1600–12 ROWLANDS *Four Knaves* (Percy Soc.) 110 A monstrous eater..Invited..unto a gentleman, Who long'd to see the same hungarian, And note his feeding. **1608** *Merry Devil Edmonton* (1617) C ij, Away, I..must tend the Hungarions. **1632** D. LUPTON *London* iii. 12 The middle Ile [of St. Paul's] is much frequented at noone with a Company of Hungarians, not walking so much for Recreation, as neede.

†**Hungaric** (hʌŋ'gærɪk), *a.* *Obs.* [ad. med.L. *Hungaric-us*: cf. HUNGARY.] = HUNGARIAN *a.* 1. ***Hungaric fever***: an old name for typhus fever.

1661 LOVELL *Hist. Anim. & Min.* 327 Hungarick feaver, which is..malignant and contagious. **1694** SALMON *Bates' Disp.* (1713) 473/2 It is good against a Hungarick Fever, which is a kind of sweating Sickness.

†**Hungarish**, *a.* *Obs. rare.* [f. next + -ISH.] = HUNGARIAN.

1606 G. W[OODCOCKE] tr. *Hist. Ivstine* Ll ij a, By his wife of the Hungarish race hee had one sonne.

Hungary ('hʌŋgərɪ). [ad. med.L. *Hungaria* (F. *Hongrie*), f. *Hungari*, *Ungari*, *Ungri*, *Ugri* (cf. UGRIAN), med.Gr. *Οὔγγροι*, Ger. *Ungar-n*, names applied to the Hungarians, who call themselves Magyars.] The name of a country of central Europe, formerly a kingdom forming, with several dependent provinces, the eastern or trans-Leithan division of the Austro-Hungarian monarchy. Used *attrib.* as in ***Hungary water***: see quots.

1698 VANBRUGH *Prov. Wife* v. vi, Your bottle of Hungary water to your lady. **1706** PHILLIPS (ed. Kersey), *Queen of Hungry Water*, a Spirit of Wine fill'd with the more essential part of Rosemary-flowers. **1727–41** CHAMBERS *Cycl.*, *Hungary Water*,..a distilled water, denominated from a queen of Hungary, for whose use it was first prepared;.. made of rosemary flowers infused in rectified spirit of wine, and thus distilled. **1813** *Sporting Mag.* XLII. 129 Hungary waters..were brought to recover the gentleman.

hungary, obs. form of HUNGRY.

hunger ('hʌŋgə(r)), *sb.* Forms: 1 hungor, 1–5 hungur, 1– hunger; (also 3 hounguer, (*Orm.*) hunngerr, 3–5 unger, 4 hungire, -yr, honggir, houngur, 4–5 hongur, -yr(e, 4–6 hungre, -ir, honger, hounger, 5– hongre, -ir). [OE. *hungor*, *-ur* = OS. *hungar*, MDu. *hongher* (Du. *honger*), OHG. *hungar*, (MHG., Ger. *hunger*), ON. *hungr*, (Sw., Da. *hunger*):—OTeut. **huŋgru-s*; cf. Goth. *huggrjan* to hunger: the actual Goth. sb. was *hûhrus*, corresp. to an OTeut. **huŋhru-s*; these imply pre-Teutonic **kuŋkru-*, **kŋkrú-*. Cf. Lith. *kankà* torment, *keñkti* to ache, Gr. (gloss) *κέγκει* = *πεινᾷ*: see Kluge, and Zupitza *German. Gutturale*.]

1. a. The uneasy or painful sensation caused by want of food; craving appetite. Also, the exhausted condition caused by want of food.

c **825** *Vesp. Psalter* lviii. 15 [lix. 14] Hungur ðrowiað. *a* **900** CYNEWULF *Crist* 1660 in *Exeter Bk.*, Nis þær hungor ne þurst slæp ne swar leȝer. *c* **1050** *Suppl. Ælfric's Gloss.* in Wr.-Wülcker 172/3 *Fames, uel popina*, hunger. **1154** *O.E. Chron.* an. 1137 ⁊3 Wrecce men sturuen of hungær. *a* **1200** *Moral Ode* 231 On helle is vnger & þerst. *c* **1290** *S. Eng. Leg.* I. 2/54 For strong hounguer he criede loude. *c* **1375** *Sc. Leg. Saints*, *Petrus* 88 Till ner for hungyre þe gaste he ȝalde. *a* **1400–50** *Alexander* 4608 Ȝe bot fede ȝow with frute at flyes noȝt ȝoure hongir. **1526** *Pilgr. Perf.* (W. de W. 1531) 8 What nedeth meet there where shall be no hunger? **1568** GRAFTON *Chron.* II. 35 After that he would never eate nor drinke, but pyned away for hunger and sorow. **1613** PURCHAS *Pilgrimage* (1614) 836 Very patient of labour and hunger, feasting if they have where-with..and fasting other-whiles. **1791** MRS. RADCLIFFE *Rom. Forest* ii, A repast which hunger and fatigue made delicious. **1858** LYTTON *What will he do* I. iii, I have the hunger of a wolf.

b. personified or represented as an agent.

c **1000** *Andreas* 1089 (Gr.) Hungres on wenum blates beodgæstes. **1362** LANGL. *P. Pl.* A. VII. 288 Fedde hunger ȝeorne With good Ale. **1393** *Ibid.* C. IX. 177 Honger have mercy of hem, and lete me geve hem benes. **1613** PURCHAS *Pilgrimage* (1614) 862 Some perishing in the devouring jawes of the Ocean, and others in their selfe-devouring Mawes of Hunger. **1774** GOLDSM. *Nat. Hist.* (1776) II. 125 Hunger is a much more powerful enemy to man than watchfulness, and kills him much sooner. **1894** H. DRUMMOND *Ascent Man* 251 The parent of all industries is Hunger.

c. Proverbs.

1546 J. HEYWOOD *Prov.* (1867) 39 Some saie, and I feele, hunger perceth stone wall. **1555** EDEN *Decades* 62 *marg.*, Hunger is the best sauce. **1607** SHAKS. *Cor.* I. i. 210. **1608** TOPSELL *Serpents* (1658) 780 Hunger breaketh stone-walls, and hard need makes the old wife trot. **1634** SIR T. HERBERT *Trav.* 12 Had they not so good a sauce as hunger. **1719** DE FOE *Crusoe* II. ii, Hunger knows no friend.

2. Want or scarcity of food in a country, etc.; dearth; famine. *Obs.* or *arch.*

c **1000** ÆLFRIC *Gen.* xli. 30 Hunger fondeþ ealle eorþan. *c* **1000** *Ags. Gosp.* Matt. xxiv. 7 Mann-cwealmas beoð and hungras..and eorþan styrunga. *a* **1046** *O.E. Chron.* (MS. C) an. 976 On þys ȝeare wæs se miccla hungor on Angel cynne. *c* **1250** *Gen. & Ex.* 2150 Ghe ðer him two childer bar, Or men wurð of ðat hunger war. **1387** TREVISA *Higden* (Rolls) II. 441 In his dayes fil a greet honger in þe lond of Israel. **1480** CAXTON *Chron. Eng.* cii. (1482) 83 The englyssh peple that were escaped the grete honger and mortalyte. **1559** *Homilies* I. *Swearing* II. (1859) 78 God..sent an universal hunger upon the whole country. **1600** HOLLAND *Livy* IV. 147 These calamities began with hunger. **1847** W. E. FORSTER in T. W. Reid *Life* (1888) I. vi. 196 When we entered a village [in Ireland] our first question was, 'How many deaths?' 'The hunger has been there', was everywhere the cry.

3. *transf.* and *fig.* Strong desire or craving.

1548 HALL *Chron.*, *Rich. III* 45 b, That cursed hungre of golde and execrable thirst of lucre. **1656–9** B. HARRIS *Parival's Iron Age* 4 The insatiable hunger of mony hath vayled..their understanding. **1860** GEO. ELIOT *Mill on Fl.* I. v, This need of love—this hunger of the heart. **1880** TENNYSON *Battle Brunanburh* xv, Earls that were lured by the Hunger of glory. **1889** RUSKIN *Præterita* III. 43 A fit took me of hunger for city life again. **1897** *Daily News* 24 Sept. 8/3 This so-called 'land hunger' might prevail in parts of Ireland where the possession of a small piece of land was absolutely necessary.

¶ *erroneously* for *hungri*, HUNGRY.

a **1300** *Cursor M.* 5094 (Cott.) Fiue yeir o þis hunger tide [*other MSS.* hungre, -ry, -ery]. *c* **1300** *Ibid.* 20121 (Edin.) Nakid and hunger [*other MSS.* hungry, hongry] sco clad and fed. *c* **1485** *Digby Myst.* (1882) III. 1934 þe hungor and þe thorsty.

4. *attrib.* and *Comb.* **a.** Of, belonging to, connected with, or characteristic of hunger, as ***hunger-den***, ***-pain***, ***-pinch***, ***-wolf***, ***-world***. **b.** instrumental, as ***hunger-beaten***, ***-driven***, ***-greedy***, ***-mad***, ***-pinched***, ***-pressed***, ***-stricken***, ***-stung***, ***-worn*** adjs.; ***hunger-pine*** vb. **c.** objective, as ***hunger-giving***. **d.** parasynthetic, as ***hunger-gutted***, ***-paunched*** adjs.

1606 J. RAYNOLDS *Dolarney's Prim.* (1880) 87 Because, that I was *hunger-beaten, I chaw'd a bit. **1843** CARLYLE *Past & Pr.* III. ii, The Atheist world, from its utmost summits of Heaven and Westminster Hall..down to the lowest cellars and neglected *hunger-dens of it, is very wretched. *a* **1618** SYLVESTER *Hymn St. Lewis the King* 489 In rags, and *hunger-driven. **1895** *Westm. Gaz.* 11 Feb. 5/2 The fearlessness of the hunger-driven birds. **1607** TOPSELL *Four-f. Beasts* (1658) 373 Satisfying his *hunger-greedy appetite. **1647** R. STAPYLTON *Juvenal* 67 Art thou with th' injury of a meale so tooke? So *hunger-gutted? **1805** CARY *Dante, Inferno* I. 44 With his head held aloft and *hunger-mad. **1820** KEATS *Isabella* lix, Seldom felt she any *hunger-pain. **1598** ROWLANDS *Betraying Christ* 11 Like *hunger-paunched wolues prone to deuour The lambe. **1855** BROWNING *Fra Lippo* 127 Admonition from the *hunger-pinch. **1639** FULLER *Holy War* I. viii. (1647) 11 Being well *hunger-pincht..[he] ran away from the rest of the Christians. **1610** *Chester's Tri.*, *Envie* 28 A rich man *hunger-pin'd with want. *a* **1756** COLLINS *Ode Pop. Superst. Highl.* 164 *Hunger-prest Along th' Atlantick rock undreading climb. **1614** T. ADAMS *Fatal Banquet* i. Wks. 1861 I. 161 Hath any gentleman the *hunger-worm of covetousness? **1838** DICKENS *O. Twist* xxiii, Many *hunger-worn outcasts close their eyes in our bare streets.

e. Special combs.: †**hunger-bane**, death by hunger, starvation; so †**hunger-baned** *a.*,

starved; †**hunger-bedrip**, a kind of BEDRIP or harvest service at which the lord gave the tenants food; **hunger-belt**, a belt worn round the abdomen, and continually tightened to alleviate the pangs of hunger; †**hunger-bond**, necessity arising from famine; **hunger-flower**, a species of Whitlow-grass, *Draba incana*, so called because it grows in 'hungry' soils (*Cent. Dict.*); **hunger-grass**, the grass *Alopecurus agrestis*: see *hunger-weed*; **hunger-house**, a place in which cattle are kept for some time before being slaughtered; a pining-house; **hunger-march**, a march, undertaken usually by the unemployed, in order to call attention to their needs and claims; so **hunger-marcher**; **hunger-pain**, pain due to hunger; also *Path.* (see quot. 1905); **hunger-rot**, †(*a*) a disease in cattle resulting from scanty feeding; (*b*) a miserly wretch (*dial.*); **hunger strike**, the action of a person, esp. a prisoner, who refuses food in order to induce someone to yield to his demands; so **hunger-strike** *v. intr.*, to go on hunger-strike; **hunger-striker**, **hunger-striking** *vbl. sb.*; **hunger swarm**, the swarming of bees caused by lack of food; **hunger-trace**, a flaw in the feathers of a hawk caused by improper or scanty feeding while the feathers are growing; **hunger-weed**, a name for *Ranunculus arvensis* and *Alopecurus agrestis*, corn-field weeds, found especially on clayey soil.

1617 MARKHAM *Caval.* I. 3 Nor..that they..for lacke of strength die with *hunger-bane. **1549** COVERDALE, etc. *Erasm. Par.* 1 *Cor.* 12 We beyng there were *hunger-baned and famyshed. *c* **1300** *Custumals Battle-Abbey* (Camden) 54 Ad quartam precariam, quod vocatur *Hunger-bedrip. **1846** STOKES *Discov. Australia* II. xii. 395 Mr. Pasco..had obtained from them a *hunger belt, composed of wallaby furs. **1865** *Daily Tel.* 21 Dec. 7/1 'Tis a device of savages to cheat an empty stomach, and is called 'the hunger belt'. *c* **1250** *Gen. & Ex.* 763 Ðeden for he, for *hunger bond, feȝer ut into egipte lond. **1839** G. TAYLOR *Mem. Surtees* in *Surtees' Durham* IV. 69 He went instantly to the *hunger-house, and set it at liberty. **1893** *Whitby Gaz.* 3 Nov. 3/6 In two instances the pining-lairs or hunger-houses are within the shops or open directly into them. **1908** *Westm. Gaz.* 16 July 10/3 A statement of the purpose of the '*Hunger March'. **1939** N. MONSARRAT *This is Schoolroom* I. 33 Hunger-marches, May Day processions..they were all new. **1972** M. JONES *Life on Dole* I. i. 11 Among the older people, there was grave talk of the days of mass unemployment and the Hunger Marches. **1908** *Westm. Gaz.* 16 July 10/3 He had no knowledge the '*Hunger Marchers' were coming there that day. **1922** *Ibid.* 29 Dec., Unemployed hunger marchers are persisting in their determination to see the Prime Minister. **1950** KOESTLER *God that Failed* I. 28 Europe trembled under the torn boots of hunger-marchers. **1820** *Hunger-pain [see HUNGER *sb.* 4a]. **1905** B. G. A. MOYNIHAN in *Lancet* 11 Feb. 341/1 If the pain does not come on for from two to four hours after a meal..the patient will often complain of what I have been accustomed to call 'hunger pain'. **1943** E. BOWEN *Seven Winters* 25 The vacuum, the hunger-pain, set up in me from being unable to read. **1523** FITZHERB. *Husb.* §54 Also *hunger rotte is the worst rotte that can be..and..cometh for lacke of meate, and so for hunger they eate suche as they can fynde. **1577** B. GOOGE *Heresbach's Husb.* III. (1586) 140 Against the Winter rotte, or hunger rotte, you must provide to feede them at home in Cratches. **1828** *Craven Dial.*, *Hunger-rot*, a penurious, griping wretch. **1889** *Century Mag.* Nov. 107/2 Here I heard..the narrative of the *hunger-strike of the four women in the prison of Irkutsk. **1903** H. CHISHOLM tr. *L. Deutsch's Sixteen Yrs. in Siberia* 78 Upon these conditions I consented not to prolong my 'hunger-strike'. **1908** *Westm. Gaz.* 18 Mar. 5/1 The Central Prisons Administration has circularised the provincial Governors regarding the so-called 'hunger strikes', which are a characteristic feature of Russian prison life. **1914** E. PANKHURST *My Own Story* III. v. 292 She has hunger-struck in prison. She submitted herself for more than five weeks to the horrible ordeal of feeding by force. **1916** W. J. LOCKE *Wonderful Year* xvii. 247 'I've been to prison.' Martin.. asked if she hunger-struck. **1937** KOESTLER *Spanish Testament* II. 333, I had intended to stop my hunger strike as soon as my letter to the Consul had been sent off. **1970** *Times* 11 May 8/4 In February Feron went on hunger strike in protest but was taken ill and for a month existed only on drugs. **1973** *Jewish Chron.* 19 Jan. 44/5 He will stage a 48-hour hunger strike outside the Soviet Embassy. **1922** *Blackw. Mag.* Aug. 146/1 He gave his orders for the release of the *hunger-strikers. **1972** *Guardian* 1 Dec. 12/1 Already the names of McSwiney and MacCaughey, hunger-strikers of an earlier era, are being conjured up. **1916** W. J. LOCKE *Wonderful Year* xxiii. 329 Her duties involved incendiarism, imprisonment, and *hunger-striking. **1870** A. PETTIGREW *Handy Bk. Bees* 150 We have known swarms starved out of their hives. Having made a few pieces of comb, and being without food, no eggs were set in them and the bees, through sheer want, cast themselves on the wide world. These are called '*hunger-swarms'. **1886** F. R. CHESHIRE *Bees* II. iv. 168 Bees sometimes abscond because their stores have run out, and circumstances are desperate. Such have usually been called 'hunger' or 'vagabond' swarms. **1928** C. WILLIAMS *Story of Hive* iii. 22 Bees on the point of starvation will, in a spirit of desperation, leave their hive in a body. This exodus is known as 'a hunger swarm'. **1954** C. G. BUTLER *World of Honeybee* xiii. 154 Another type of honeybee swarm is sometimes recognisable, the type which in Europe is usually known as a 'hunger' swarm, and which occurs when a colony is starving. **1828** SIR J. S. SEBRIGHT *Observ. Hawking* 7 Young hawks should be plentifully fed, for if they are left one day without food, the *hunger-traces will appear. **1852** R. F. BURTON *Falconry Valley Indus* iv. 42 *note*, The plumage will bear..'hunger-traces', a flaw on the shaft and web of every feather in the body, especially the wings and tail, often occasioning them to break off at the place injured. **1793** MARTYN *Flora Rust.* II. 56 It [Corn Crowfoot] has the name of *Hungerweed. **1894** *Times* 21 May 12/1 That most pestilent of weeds, the slender foxtail, blackbent, or hungerweed, *alopecurus agrestis*, is already in ear and flower in corn-fields.

hunger ('hʌŋgə(r)), *v.* Forms: 1 **hyngran, hingrian, (hyncgrian)**, 3–5 **hungre-n** (4 **hongre-, hengren**, 5 **hungyr**, 6 **houngir, -re, hungre**), 4– **hunger**. [OE. *hyngran* (later *hingrian*) = OS. *gihungrjan*, Goth. *huggrjan*, f. *hungr-*, HUNGER *sb.* Cf. also OHG. *hungaran, -arôn*, MHG. and Ger. *hungern*, MLG., MDu. *hungeren*, MD. and Du. *hongeren*; OFris. *hungera*; ON. *hungra*, Da. *hungre*, with a different verbal form. The normal mod. repr. of OE. *hyngr(i)an* would be *hinger*; in ME. this was assimilated to the sb. *hunger*.]

†**1.** *impers.* as in ***it hungers me*** (= Goth. *huggreiþ mik*, ON. *mik hungrar*, OHG. *mih hungrit*): 'there is hunger to me', I am hungry. (In OE. with accus. or dat.) *Obs.*

950 *Lindisf. Gosp.* John vi. 35 Seðe cymes to me ne hyncgreð hine. *c* **1000** *Ags. Gosp.* ibid., Ne hingrað þone þe to me cymð. *c* **1000** ÆLFRIC *Hom.* I. 166 Ac siððan him hingrode. *a* **1225** *Ancr. R.* 214 Ou schal euer hungren. *c* **1300** *Havelok* 654 Him hungrede swithe sore. **1375** BARBOUR *Bruce* XIV. 432 Thame hungerit alsua weill sar. **1393** LANGL. *P. Pl.* C. XVI. 252 Eet this when þe hungreþ.

2. *intr.* To feel or suffer hunger, be hungry.

a **900** CYNEWULF *Crist* 1354 in *Exeter Bk.*, þonne ȝe ..ȝefon hingrendum hlaf. *c* **1000** *Ags. Gosp.* Luke vi. 21 Eadiȝe synd ȝe ðe hingriað nu. *a* **1300** *Cursor M.* 12943, I wat at þou has fasted lang and hungres [*Trin.* hongrest] nu. *a* **1310** in Wright *Lyric P.* x. 37 Thenne mihti hengren on heowe. **1340** HAMPOLE *Pr. Consc.* 6151, I hungerd and yhe me fedde. **1382** WYCLIF *Luke* vi. 3 This, that Dauith dide, whanne he hungride. *c* **1440** *Promp. Parv.* 253/1 Hungryn, or waxyn hungry.., *esurio.* **1546** J. HEYWOOD *Prov.* (1867) 28 They must hunger in frost, that will not woorke in heete. *a* **1612** DONNE *Βιαθανατος* (1644) 129 If he had not hungred till then, his fasting had had no vertue. **1783–94** BLAKE *Songs Exper.*, *Holy Thursday* 15 Babe can never hunger there. **1881** N.T. (R.V.) *Matt.* iv. 2 When he had fasted forty days and forty nights, he afterward hungered [**1611** was..an hungred].

3. *transf.* and *fig.* To have a longing or craving; to long *for*; to hanker *after*. (With *indirect pass.*)

c **1440** *Jacob's Well* (E.E.T.S.) 113 þin eyȝin gredyly hungryn to se vanytees. **1526** TINDALE *Matt.* v. 6 Blessed are they which honger and thurst for [**1539** after] rightewesnes. **1563** WINȜET *Wks.* (1890) II. 12 The peple houngerit throw inlake of the heuinlie and necessare fuid of Godis Word. **1700** FARQUHAR *Constant Couple* IV. iii, Hell hungers not more for wretched souls, than he for ill-got pelf. **1737** WATERLAND *Rev. Doctr. Eucharist* vi. 161 The Word was made Flesh; which consequently is to be hungred after for the sake of Life. **1856** MRS. BROWNING *Aur. Leigh* VI. 455 Whom still I've hungered after more than bread. **1873** HELPS *Anim. & Mast.* vi. (1875) 143 If, over and above this necessary repute, you hunger for praise.

†**4.** *trans.* To have a hunger or craving for; to desire with longing; to hunger after. *Obs.*

c **1000** *Ags. Gosp.* Matt. v. 6 Eadiȝe synt þa ðe rihtwisnesse hingriað [*esuriunt iustitiam*] and þyrstað. **1382** WYCLIF *ibid.*, Blessid be þei þat hungren and þristun riȝt-wisnesse. *c* **1440** *Jacob's Well* (E.E.T.S.) 113 þi mowth hungreth gredyly delycacyes..þin erys hungryn gredyly newe tydynges. **1563** *Homilies* II. *Sacrament* I. (1859) 444 Spiritually they hungred it, spiritually they tasted it.

5. To subject to hunger; to starve, famish; to drive or force by hunger (*to, into, out*, etc.).

1575 GASCOIGNE *Dulce Bellum* cxxxii, The Prince to Zeland came himselfe To hunger Middleburgh. **1596** DALRYMPLE tr. *Leslie's Hist. Scot.* x. 313 It culd not be won be na force except thay war hungret out. **1641** BEST *Farm. Bks.* (Surtees) 119 Theire pasture will hunger our beasts that are used to better keepinge. **1727** P. WALKER *Life Peden* 56 (Jam.) Christ minds only to diet you, and not hunger you. **1803** S. PEGGE *Anecd. Eng. Lang.* 58 *note*, In the north they say of one who keeps his servants on short commons that he hungers them. **1858** KINGSLEY *Ode to N. East Wind*, Hunger into madness Every plunging pike. **1884** *Daily Tel.* 12 May 5/7 The Mahdi spent five months in hungering out Obeid.

b. *transf.* To deprive of strength by want of any kind; to 'starve'. ? *Obs.*

14.. *Iter Camerar.* c. 23 in *Scott. Stat.* (1844) 700/2 (*red*) [Skinners] hunger þer lethir in defaut of graith þat js to say alum eggis and oþir thingis.

'**hunger-bit**, *a.* = next.

1549–62 STERNHOLD & H. *Ps.* xxxiv. 10 The Lions shall be hungerbit, and pinde with famine much. **1671** MILTON *P.R.* II. 417 Lost in a Desert here and hunger-bit. *a* **1711** KEN *Psyche* Poet. Wks. 1721 IV. 201 Furious Panthers..hunger-bitt.

'**hunger-bitten**, *a.* 'Bitten' or pinched with hunger; famished, starved.

1549 CHEKE *Hurt Sedit.* (1641) 34 When every man for lack is hungerbitten. **1615** J. STEPHENS *Satyr. Ess.* 12 The hunger-bitten Client to distresse. **1816–17** COLERIDGE *Lay Serm.* 322 A hunger-bitten and idealess philosophy.

hungered ('hʌŋgəd), *a.* [Partly aphetic form of A-HUNGERED, partly pa. pple. of HUNGER *v.* 5.] Hungry; famished, starved.

c **1425** *Eng. Conq. Irel.* xlvi. 116 Beseged & hungrod. **1477** EARL RIVERS (Caxton) *Dictes* 21 a, He ete whansomeuer he was hungered. **1573** *Satir. Poems Reform.* xlii. 636 The pepill salbe houngerit haill Of Spirituall fude. **1790** J. WILLIAMS *Shrove Tuesday* (1794) 21 The courier..bid the hunger'd eat. **1837** LYTTON *E. Maltrav.* I. i. 4 To get food when I'm hungered. **1871** TENNYSON *Last Tournam.* 713, I am hunger'd and half-anger'd. *Mod.Sc.* A puir hungert creatur.

¶ ***a hungered, an hungered***: improperly divided forms of A-HUNGERED, ANHUNGERED, q.v.

1398, etc. [see A-HUNGERED, ANHUNGERED]. **1577** B. GOOGE *Heresbach's Husb.* IV. (1586) 164 Nor..let them goe a hungerd into the Pastures. **1841** JAMES *Brigand* xxiii, I trust that supper is ready, for I am an hungered.

hungerer ('hʌŋgərə(r)). [f. HUNGER *v.* + -ER[1].] One who suffers hunger; one who longs or craves.

1382 WYCLIF *Isa.* xxxii. 6 And voide he shal make the soule of the hungrere. **1784** R. BAGE *Barham Downs* II. 6 A hungerer after loaves and fishes. **1821** LAMB *Elia* Ser. I. *Grace before Meat*, Nothing in Milton is finelier fancied than these temperate dreams of the divine Hungerer. **1842** CROLY *Hist. Sk.* 90 The thwarted hungerer for office takes up the miserable commonplaces of politics; and is the radical.

hungering ('hʌŋgərɪŋ), *vbl. sb.* [f. HUNGER *v.* + -ING[1].] The action of the verb HUNGER; craving, longing.

1638 WILKINS *New World* I. (1707) 1 An Earnestness and Hungering after Novelty. **1678** BUNYAN *Pilgr.* I. 115 He findeth hungrings and thirstings after him. **1837** CARLYLE *Fr. Rev.* I. VI. iv, France has begun her long Curriculum of Hungering. **1891** *Athenæum* 10 Jan. 51/1 The insane hungering after quarterings.

'**hungering**, *ppl. a.* [f. as prec. + -ING[2].] That hungers; hungry.

971 *Blickl. Hom.* 5 þa hingriȝendan he ȝefylleþ mid godum. *a* **1300** *E.E. Psalter* cvi[i]. 9 Hungrand saule he filled with gode. *a* **1340** HAMPOLE *Psalter* cxlv. 5 He gifis mete til hungirand. *a* **1882** ROSSETTI *House of Life* vi, The half-drawn hungering face.

Hence '**hungeringly** *adv.*, hungrily, longingly.

1884 ARCH. FORBES in *Eng. Illustr. Mag.* I. 456 Tidings which peoples awaited hungeringly or tremblingly.

†**Hungerland.** *Obs.* [perh. = Hungary: cf. also HUNGERLIN.] In quot. *attrib.*

1632 MASSINGER *City Madam* IV. iv, Your Hungerland bands, and Spanish quellio ruffs.

'**hungerless**, *a. rare.* [f. HUNGER *sb.* + -LESS.] Free from hunger.

1620 SHELTON *Quix.* III. xxi. 148 Sad and sorrowful tho' hungerless.

†**Hungerlin.** *Obs.* [? A corruption of HUNGERLAND.] 'A sort of short furred robe, so named from having been derived from Hungary' (Nares).

c **1645** HOWELL *Lett.* I. I. i, It was a quaint difference the Ancients did put 'twixt a Letter and an Oration, that the one should be attir'd like a Woman, the other like a Man..A Letter or Epistle should be short-coated and closely couchd: a Hungerlin becomes a Letter more hansomely then a gown. **1658** BURBURY *Hist. Chr. Alessandra* 212 The Cardinal followed her Majesty, who had on a man's Hungerlin of plain black Velvet with a band, and an upper safegard for women of a dark grey colour, without which she would have lookt like a man.

hungerly ('hʌŋgəlɪ), *a. Obs.* or *arch.* [f. HUNGER *sb.* + -LY[1].] Hungry-looking; having a hungry, starved, or famished look.

1393 LANGL. *P. Pl.* C. VII. 197 Ich can nat hym discryue, So hongerliche and so holwe heruy hym-self lokede. **1555** EDEN *Decades* 99 Owre men were enforced to departe from thense more hungerly then theye came. **1596** SHAKS. *Tam. Shr.* III. ii. 177 His beard grew thinne and hungerly. **1846** MRS. GORE *Eng. Char.* (1852) 55 The linkmen of London.. are poor, lean, hungerly, brisk, and knowing.

'**hungerly**, *adv. Obs.* or *arch.* [f. HUNGER *sb.* + -LY[2]: in use a variant of HUNGRILY. Very frequent 1550–1650.] Hungrily; greedily.

1557 BURROUGH in Hakluyt *Voy.* (1886) III. 156, I sawe them eate rocke weedes as hungerly, as a cowe doeth grasse when shee is hungrie. **1607** SHAKS. *Timon* I. i. 262, I feed Most hungerly on your sight. **1653** HOLCROFT *Procopius, Vandal Wars* II. 36 The Vandale boy caught it first, and hungerly thrust it hot into his mouth. **1861** LD. LYTTON & FANE *Tannhäuser* 36 Hungerly our ears Wait the melodious murmurs of a harp.

†'**hunger-starve**, *v. Obs.* [f. HUNGER *sb.* + STARVE *v.*] *trans.* 'To starve with hunger': formerly in regular use where the simple 'starve' is now usual.

1390 GOWER *Conf.* III. 28 Min eye wolde..Ben hunger storven also faste, Till eft ayein that he her see. **1576** FLEMING *Panopl. Epist.* 351 If it were not..should not all kinde of cattell..perishe, and be hunger starved? **1587** GOLDING *De Mornay* xxxi. 499 It is written..I will hunger-starue all the Gods of the Gentiles. **1610** *Histrio-m.* VI. G iv b, Though Famine hungerstarue yet heauen saues.

So **hunger-starved**, †**-starven** *ppl. a.*; †**hunger-starving** *vbl. sb.* and *ppl. a.*

a **1533** LD. BERNERS *Gold. Bk. M. Aurel.* Ii iij b, Accompaignied with hunger staruen trewandes. **1578** J. STOCKWOOD *Serm. 24 Aug.* 17 The vnmercifull and hunger-staruen Souldiers. **1592** DEE *Comp. Rehears.* (Chetham Soc.) 35 To save us from hunger starving. **1597–8** BP. HALL *Sat.* I. i. 13 Such hunger-starven trencher poetrie. **1632** LITHGOW *Trav.* III. 100, I in that hunger-starving feare, fed upon the expectation of my doubtfull reliefe. **1647** TRAPP *Comm. Matt.* XV. 27 Those that are hunger-starved are glad

to feed upon hedge-fruit. **1692** DRYDEN *Eleonora* 47 The Hunger-starv'd, the Naked, and the Lame. **1725** DE FOE *Voy. round World* (1840) 345 They were indeed hunger-starved. **1728** MORGAN *Algiers* I. iv. 123 This tattered, and seemingly hunger-starved, Body of Cavalry. *a***1879** J. S. BREWER *Eng. Stud.* (1881) 434 Wolves and foxes..hunger-starved, swept down from the neighbouring forest.

hungery, obs. form of HUNGRY.

†**hungil, -ill.** *Obs. local.* [In 1450 *houndgilt*:—OE. type **hundgild* 'dog-payment'.] A payment under the Forest Laws on account of dogs.

In quot. 1621 app. a fine for not expeditating them, = FOOT-GILD; but otherwise explained by Marshall.

1450 *Rolls Parlt.* V. 195/1 Thomas Cateby..hath..lxs. of houndgilt silver yerly..by the hands of oure Receivour of oure Duchie of Lancastre. **1621** *N. Riding Rec.* (1894) I. 38 As towchinge the expeditating of doggs they saye that the laste yeare there was about the summe of xiij[li] x[s] collected within the said libertie by the graves of Pickeringe, for hungill. **1788** W. MARSHALL *Yorksh.* Gloss. (E.D.S.), *Horsam, Hungil-Money*, a small tax which is still paid (though the intention of it has long ceased) by the townships on the north side of the Vale, and within the lathe or weapontake of Pickering, for horsemen and hounds kept for the purpose of driving off the deer of the forest of Pickering from the corn-fields which bordered upon it.

hung-over: see HUNG *ppl. a.* 4.

hungre, obs. form of HUNGER, HUNGRY.

hungrify ('hʌŋgrɪfaɪ), *v. nonce-wd.* [f. HUNGRY *a.* + -FY.] *trans.* To make hungry. So '**hungrifying** *ppl. a.*, appetizing.

1881 BLACKMORE *Christowell* xxxii, The hungry and hungrifying potato. **1887** —— *Springhaven* xv, There was Mr. Cheeseman..amid a presence of hungrifying goods.

hungrily ('hʌŋgrɪlɪ), *adv.* [f. HUNGRY *a.* + -LY[2].] In a hungry manner; with hunger or craving; longingly; greedily.

1377 LANGL. *P. Pl.* B. xx. 122 Thanne cam coueityse.. And armed hym in auarice and hungriliche lyued. **1693** DRYDEN, junr. in *Dryden's Juvenal* xiv. (1697) 357 When on harsh Acorns hungrily they fed. **1791** WOLCOTT (P. Pindar) *Loyal Odes* viii. 42 So hungrily you every thing devour. **1887** BARING-GOULD *Gaverocks* xiv, He..ate hungrily.

hungriness ('hʌŋgrɪnɪs). [f. as prec. + -NESS.] The quality or condition of being hungry; greediness; longing.

1530 PALSGR. 232/1 Hongrynesse, *fayn, appetit a manger.* **1577** DEE *Relat. Spir.* I. (1659) 186 That her wormes might eat and forget their hungrynesse. **1661** J. CHILDREY *Brit. Bacon.* 118 Some Rivers overflowing their banks enrich more, and others less, according to the fatness or hungryness of their water. **1837** HOWITT *Rur. Life* VI. xiv. (1862) 561 A determined expression of fresh-air hungriness.

†'**hungriousness.** *Obs. rare*[−1]. [f. **hungrious* adj. (f. HUNGRY *a.* + -OUS) + -NESS.] = prec.

1549 COVERDALE, etc. *Erasm. Par. Eph.* Prol., Whan was excessyve riotous bankettyng..more outragiously vsed, and the pores hungriousnes lesse refreshed, than nowe?

hungry ('hʌŋgrɪ), *a.* Forms: 1 hungriʒ, 1–6 hungri, 3 (*Orm.*) hunngriȝ, 3–6 houngrie, 4–6 hungre, hongry, 4–7 hungery, 5 hongarye, 5–6 hungary, 6 hongrye, -ie, 6–7 hungrie, 4– hungry. [OE. *hungriʒ, -reʒ* = OFris. *hungerig, hongerig* (MDu. *hongerich*, MLG. *hungerich*, Du. *hongerig*), OHG. *hungerag, -ereg* (MHG. *hungerc*, Ger. *hung(e)rig*):—WGer. type **hungrag-*, f. *hungr-* HUNGER *sb.*: see -Y.]

1. a. Having the sensation of hunger; feeling pain or uneasiness from want of food; having a keen appetite.

*c***950** *Lindisf. Gosp.* Matt. xxv. 37 Huoenne ðec we seʒon hungriʒ *vel* hyngrende? [*Ags. Gosp.* hingriʒendne.] *a***1000** *Guthlac* 737 in *Exeter Bk.*, Oft he him æte heold þonne hy him hungriʒe ymb hond fluʒon. *c***1200** ORMIN 6162 þe birrþ fedenn hunngriȝ mann. *a***1300** *Cursor M.* 23084, I was hungre, yee gaf me fode. **1382** WYCLIF *Luke* i. 53 He hath fillid hungry men with goode thingis, and he hath left ryche men voyde [**1526** TINDALE, He hath filled the hongry with goode thinges]. **1480** CAXTON *Chron. Eng.* cxcvii. 175 An hungary wolfe. **1546** J. HEYWOOD *Prov.* vi, Hungry dogs will eat dirty puddings. *Ibid.* (1867) 75 Hungry flies byte sore. **1570** *Satir. Poems Reform.* xiii. 139 As houngrie tykis ȝe thristit for his blude. **1637** MILTON *Lycidas* 125 The hungry sheep look up, and are not fed. **1650** TRAPP *Comm. Lev.* xvii. 13 Though hee bee as hungrie as a hunter. **1774** GOLDSM. *Nat. Hist.* (1776) V. 89 How hungry soever he may be, he never stoops to carrion. **1855** LONGF. *Hiaw.* viii. 227 The hungry sea-gulls..Clamorous for the morning banquet.

b. Said of the belly or stomach.

1484 CAXTON *Fable of Æsop* III. xvi, When the bely was empty and sore hongry. **1526** *Pilgr. Perf.* (W. de W. 1531) 82 b, Scarcite in meate, and the bely alway somwhat hungry. **1573–80** BARET *Alv.* H 734 Bread and salt asswageth an hungrie stomach. **1630** *R. Johnson's Kingd. & Commw.* 87 A hungry belly may call for more meat.

c. *transf.* Indicating, characteristic of, or characterized by hunger; belonging to a hungry person.

1600 J. PORY. tr. *Leo's Africa* II. 266 Certaine Arabians lead here a miserable and hungrie life. **1601** SHAKS. *Jul. C.* I. ii. 194 Yond Cassius has a leane and hungry looke. **1818** SHELLEY *Rev. Islam* X. xv, The..flocks and herds Who had survived the wild beasts' hungry chase. **1865** DICKENS *Mut. Fr.* I. i, His shining eyes darted a hungry look. **1880** *Antrim & Down Gloss.* s.v., A hungry eye sees far.

2. a. Of times or places: Marked by famine or scarcity of food; famine-stricken. ***the hungry forties***, the decade beginning in 1840, characterized in the British Isles by much poverty and unemployment.

*c***1250** *Gen. & Ex.* 2136 Quan ðo hungri ȝere ben forðcumen. *a***1300** *Cursor M.* 5094 (Gött.) Fiue ȝere of þis hungery tyde. *c***1374** CHAUCER *Boeth.* I. pr. iv. 9 (Camb. MS.) In the sowre hungry tyme. **1393** LANGL. *P. Pl.* C. x. 206 Helden [ful] hungry hous and hadde much defaute. **1607** ROWLANDS *Diog. Lanth.* 29 When thou art hording vp thy foode, Against these hungry dayes. **1905** MRS. C. UNWIN *(title)* The hungry forties. **1910** A. BAKER *Poor against Rich* 34, I mention the Hungry Forties, because a lot of poor people have allowed themselves to be misled during the last election, by the fear of dear food. **1920** J. COLLINGS in J. L. Green *Life Jesse Collings* I. iv. 29 During the 'hungry forties' eggs were sold twenty for a shilling. **1958** *Spectator* 20 June 792/1 During the famine in Ireland at the end of the Hungry Forties, it was not uncommon [etc.].

b. Of food: Eaten with hunger or keen appetite. Now *rare* or *Obs.*

1552 HULOET, Hungry meale, *peredia.* **1653** WALTON *Angler* iv. 104 We shall..make a good honest, wholsome, hungry Breakfast. **1871** R. ELLIS *Catullus* cviii. 4 First should a tongue..Fall extruded, of each vulture a hungry regale.

3. a. Of food, etc.: That does not satisfy one's hunger; that leaves one hungry. Hence *fig.* Unsatisfying, insufficient. Now *rare.*

1561 T. NORTON *Calvin's Inst.* III. 234 Y[t] wil not be content with a hungry supper. **1597** HOOKER *Eccl. Pol.* v. lxvii. §12 Their discourses are hungrie and vnpleasant. **1617** MORYSON *Itin.* II. 260 To feed upon their owne hungery store. **1699** DAMPIER *Voy.* II. II. 128 Shrimps..tho' but a hungry sort of Food, they are mightily esteemed. **1865** *Pall Mall G.* 8 Aug. 10 In Lucian's time they found it rather hungry fare.

b. Causing or inducing hunger; appetizing. *rare.*

1611 CORYAT *(title)* Crudities hastily gobled vp in five Moneths Trauells..newly digested in the hungry aire of Odcombe, in the County of Somerset. **1681** PENN *Acc. Pennsylv.* in R. Burton *Eng. Emp. Amer.* vii. 109 A skie as clear as in Summer, and the Air dry, cold, piercing, and hungry. **1852** THACKERAY *Esmond* II. vii, There are woodcocks for supper..It was such a hungry sermon. *Mod.* We found it a very hungry place; the children had their appetites wonderfully sharpened.

4. In special collocations.

† ***hungry evil*** (***sickness***), a disease in horses characterized by insatiable hunger. † ***hungry gut***, (*a*) the *intestinum jejunum*, the part of the small intestine between the duodenum and the ileum, so called because it is supposed to be usually found empty after death; also *fig.*; (*b*) in quot. 1552, a person with hungry guts, a glutton. ***hungry rice***, a grain allied to millet, *Paspalum exile*, much cultivated in West Africa. † ***hungry worm*** (see quot. 1737).

1552 HULOET, Hungry gutte, *esurio. Ibid.*, Hungry sicnes, *bulima, bulimia.* **1570–6** LAMBARDE *Peramb. Kent* (1826) 184 To satisfie the hungrie gut of their ravenous appetite. **1598** FLORIO, *Digiuno*,..a gut in mans bodie called the hungrie gut, because it is alwayes emptie. **1607** TOPSELL *Four-f. Beasts* (1658) 296 The Hungry Evill..is a very great desire to eat, following some great emptiness or lack of meat. **1737** BRACKEN *Farriery Impr.* (1757) II. 101 The common People imagine them troubled with what they call the Hungry Worm under the Tongue... There is no such Thing as the Worm under a Dog's Tongue. **1858** HOGG *Veg. Kingd.* 818 *Paspalum exile* is a native of Sierra Leone..cultivated..for its small seeds, and called *Fundi* or *Fundungi*, which signifies *Hungry Rice*. **1887** MOLONEY *Forestry W. Afr.* 526 Fundi, fundungi, hungry rice, Sierra Leone millet.

5. *transf.* and *fig.* Having or characterized by a strong desire or craving (*for*, †*after*, †*of* anything); eager; greedy; avaricious.

a. of persons, their attributes, etc.

*c***1200** *Trin. Coll. Hom.* 215 De hodede..sholde..fede mid godes worde þe hungrie soule. *a***1325** *Prose Psalter* cvi[i]. 9 He..fulfild hungri soules of godes. **1393** LANGL. *P. Pl.* C. II. 188 Aren none hardur ne hongryour þan men of holy churche. **1548** UDALL *Erasm. Par.* Pref. 14 Hongrie of ferther Knoweladge. **1590** SIR J. SMYTH *Disc. Weapons* 6 Hungrie after charge, spoyle and gaine. **1748** *Anson's Voy.* III. vii. 357 A hungry and tyrannical Magistrate. **1813** SHELLEY *Q. Mab* vi. 137 That..the exulting cries..Might sate thine hungry ear. **1889** JESSOPP *Coming of Friars* vi. 266 Classes of eager youths hungry for intellectual food.

b. of things.

1650 COTGR. (ed. Howell) Of Fr. Lett., The French is a hungry language, for it devours more consonants than any other. **1725** POPE *Odyss.* XII. 18 The hungry flame devours the silent dead. **1845** HOOD *Mermaid Margate* xxx, He was saved from the hungry deep by a boat. **1886** TRAILL *Shaftesbury* iv. (1888) 52 The conveyance of prize-money.. into Charles's always hungry pocket. **1898** *Westm. Gaz.* 20 Apr. 5/1 Now and again a column of flame shot out..and stretched a hungry arm at the building.

6. a. Lacking elements which are needful or desirable, and therefore capable of absorbing these to a great extent; 'more disposed to draw from other substances than to impart to them' (J.); esp. of land, etc.: Not rich or fertile, poor; of rivers: Not supplying food for fish. †Applied formerly also to 'hard' waters and acrid liquids, wines, etc.

1577 B. GOOGE *Heresbach's Husb.* I. (1586) 24 The land.. which is nought and yeeldes not his fruite, is called leane, barren, hungry. **1626** BACON *Sylva* §395 The more Fat Water will beare Soape best; For the Hungry Water doth kill the vnctuous Nature of the Soape. **1649** BLITHE *Eng. Improv. Impr.* (1653) 157 Thy Sets may neither root in stiffe-binding Clay: nor hungry Sand. **1703** *Art of Vintners & Wine-C.* 17 To meliorate the taste of hungry and too eager White Wines. **1787** BEST *Angling* (ed. 2) 6 Carps in all hungry springing waters being fed at certain times will come up, and take their meat almost from your hand. **1816** KEATINGE *Trav.* (1817) I. 9 Flat tracts of hungry pasture ground. **1890** *Whitby Gaz.* 24 Jan. 3/3 Food was not plentiful in the river anywhere, and Goathland beck was certainly the hungriest part of the stream.

b. *fig.* Jejune; barren, sterile.

1571 GOLDING *Calvin on Ps.* xxv. 8 A cold and hungery imaginacion.

c. *Min.* 'A term applied to hard barren vein-matter, such as white quartz (not discolored with iron oxide)' (Raymond *Mining Gloss.* 1881).

7. *Comb.* † ***hungry-looked, -looking*** adjs.

1713 STEELE *Guardian* No. 54 ¶12 A lean hungry-looked rascal.

hung up ('hʌŋʌp), *a.* and *adj. phr.* Also **hung-up.** [f. vbl. phr. *to hang up* (HANG *v.* 29 d).]

1. Put into abeyance, delayed.

1878 *Lumberman's Gaz.* 18 Dec. 426 Others..find..their logs 'hung up' for want of water to float them.

2. Confused, bewildered, mixed-up. Also ***hung-up on***, obsessed with, preoccupied with (cf. also quot. 1961). *slang.*

[**1909** J. R. WARE *Passing Eng.* 156/1 *Hung up*, from the American—where personal catastrophe is referred to by this phrase.] **1945** L. SHELLY *Jive Talk Dict.* 21/1 *All hung up*, completely bewildered. **1957** [see DADDY 3]. **1958** *New Statesman* 6 Sept. 294/2 Helping each other in those phases in which they are 'hung up'. **1961** RIGNEY & SMITH *Real Bohemia* p. xv, *Hung up, to be*, one's behavior is 'stuck' in one pattern. **1966** *Sunday Times* (Colour Suppl.) 13 Feb. 35/4 *Hung up*, obsessed, cf. 'he is hung up on that girl'. **1966** *New Statesman* 1 Apr. 458/3 The U.S. is 'hung up', paralysed into inaction because it cannot reconcile the political goal of uniting Germany with the ideological necessity of maintaining Western Europe as an anti-communist fortress. **1968** *Word Study* Feb. 5/2 American students of poetry have been hung up on the lines ever since. **1969** *It* 11–24 Apr. 13/4 How we manage to generate so many good things on this hung-up, repressed little island I simply don't know. **1970** *Daily Tel.* 26 Nov. 9/2 You get so hung-up with the place you feel like going out and smashing something. **1971** *New Scientist* 4 Mar. 485/2 Roszak is very hung up on the power that science grants. **1971** B. MALAMUD *Tenants* 54 He was more than a little hung up, stupid from lack of sleep, worried about his work.

hunh (hʌ̃). *U.S. dial.* (esp. in *Black English*). Used as an intensifier after a question.

1935 in Z. N. Hurston *Mules & Men* (1970) I. x. 206 You got mo' poison in yuh than dat snake dat wuz so poison tell he bit de railroad track and killed de train, hunh? **1955** W. GADDIS *Recognitions* I. iv. 155 Hunh? What do you think of that, hunh? **1970** D. L. LEE in S. Henderson *Understanding New Black Poetry* (1973) III. 341 Can u do it, hunh? i say hunh, can u stop moving like a drunk gorilla? **1973** *Black World* Apr. 60 How about one more..for ol' times, hunh?

hunk (hʌŋk), *sb.*[1] [Known only since the 19th c., and not frequent in literature before 1850. It is identical in form and sense with West Flem. *hunke* (*een hunke brood of vleesch* a hunk of bread or meat; *eene hunke aan den bedelaar geven* to give a hunk to the beggar: De Bo *Westvl. Idiotikon* 1892). Franck would connect this with Du. *honk*, HUNK[2]; but the connexion of sense is not obvious.]

1. a. A large piece cut off (e.g. from a loaf, cheese, etc.); a thick or clumsy piece, a lump; a hunch.

*a***1813** A. WILSON *Foresters* Poet. Wks. (1846) 42 Hunks of bacon all around were spread. **1826** *Corresp. fr. Wiltshire* in Hone *Every-day Bk.* II. 1117 Cottage children..munching their 'hunks' of bread, smeared with butter. **1841** J. T. HEWLETT *Parish Clerk* I. 94 Munching two enormous hunks ..of cold meat and bread. **1861** SALA *Dutch Pict.* xv. 232 A leg [of mutton] cut up in hunks and handed round. **1891** RASHDALL in *Colleges Oxf.* 156 It became usual for men to go to the buttery for a hunk of bread and a pot of beer.

b. A large man or woman.

[**1823** in *Dialect Notes* (1913) IV. 47 *Hunk*, bulk. A large body.] **1941** BAKER *Dict. Austral. Slang* 37 *Hunk*, a large man. **1945** L. SHELLY *Jive Talk Dict.* 13/1 *Hunk*, stalwart male. **1946** B. TREADWELL *Big Book of Swing* 124/2 *Hunk*, very masculine male. **1957** J. KEROUAC *On Road* (1958) 62, I looked at Lee Ann. She was a fetching hunk, a honey-colored creature.

2. (*Sc. dial.*) A sluttish, indolent woman; as a 'nasty hunk', a 'lazy hunk' (Jamieson 1825).

[Possibly a distinct word; Jam. suggests connexion with HUNKER *v.*]

Hence **hunker**, a cutter of hunks. (*nonce-wd.*)

1864 SALA in *Daily Tel.* 27 Sept., The butchers..seem to have been taking lessons from the live-collop hunkers of Abyssinia.

hunk, *sb.*[2] and *a. U.S.* [a. Du. *honk* goal, home, in a game; of Frisian origin: cf. WFris. *honcke*, *honck* 'house, place of refuge or safe abode' (Japix); EFris. *hunk* 'corner, nook, retreat, home in a game' (Doornkaat-Koolman).]

A. *sb.* (*local, New York*) In children's games: The goal, home, or den; as 'to reach hunk'; 'to be on hunk', contr. 'to be hunk' (*Cent. Dict.*).

'A word descended from the Dutch children, and much used by New York boys in their play' (Bartlett 1860).

B. *adj.* **a.** In a safe or good position or condition, all right.

1856 *N.Y. Tribune* 30 Dec. (Bartlett), Now he felt himself all hunk, and wanted to get this enormous sum out of the city. **1860** Bartlett *Dict. Amer.* (ed. 3) s.v., *To be hunk* or *all hunk* is to have reached the goal or place of meeting without being intercepted by one of the opposite party, to be all safe.

b. Colloq. phr. *to get hunk* (*with*): to get even (with). Also const. *on*.

1845 *Spirit of Times* 24 May 146 Those who lost their money on Fashion had two or three chances to 'get hunk', especially on the last day. **1903** A. H. Lewis *Boss* vii. 93 No, I don't blame Sheeny Joe... Still, while I don't blame him, it's up to us to get hunk an' even on th' play. **1949** *Boston Globe* (Fiction Mag.) 12 June 2/4 Suppose I show you how to get hunk with the cheapskates? **1950** in H. E. Goldin *Dict. Amer. Underworld Lingo* 79/1 That fink (informer) tried to get hunk on me for glomming (stealing) his broad (girl) by belching (informing) on me.

hunk (hʌŋk), *sb.*³ *N. Amer. slang.* Also **hunkey, hunkie, hunky.** [Cf. bohunk.] A nickname applied, usually disparagingly, to immigrants to the U.S.A. from east-central Europe. Also *attrib.* Cf. honky.

1896 *N.Y. Herald* 13 Jan. 3/4 The average Pennsylvanian contemptuously refers to these immigrants as 'Hikes' and 'Hunks'. The 'Hikes' are Italians and Sicilians. 'Hunks' is a corruption for Huns, but under this title the Pennsylvanian includes Hungarians, Lithuanians, Slavs, Poles, Magyars and Tyroleans. **1910** *Sat. Even. Post* 3 Sept. 18/1 Almost every.. Hunky or Dutchman who lands in New York has in his 'kick' or wallet, the written address of some boarding house. **1914** Jackson & Hellyer *Vocab. Criminal Slang* 47 *Hunkie*, current in localities where North European laborers abound. A corruption of Hungarian, but employed to signify a Continental European who is unwashed and unnaturalized. **1928** S. Lewis *Man who knew Coolidge* i. 53 Too many foreigners—fellows with Wop names and Hunky names. **1929** *Amer. Speech* June 372 *Hunkey*, same as Bohunk. **1932** [see goof *v.* 1 a]. **1934** J. O'Hara *Appointment in Samarra* (1935) i. v. 83 The hunkeys, the schwackies..—regional names for non-Latin foreigners—probably were inside getting drunk. **1936** *Scrutiny* V. 1/5 The twelve-hour day kept the myriads of 'hunkies' who toiled in Mellon mills out of brawls and brothels. **1939** *Archit. Rev.* LXXXV. 219/2 It has to be close to the town because most of the workmen are foreign-born hunkies and do not readily adapt themselves to living conditions in Lyndora. **1962** C. L. Barnhart in Householder & Saporta *Probl. Lexicogr.* 178 Greaser, guinea, hunky, Jap, kike. **1971** *Maclean's Mag.* Oct. 78/1, I don't know if I should get mad if someone insults the Irish, or makes cracks about Polacks or Hunkies.

†**hunker** (ˈhʌŋkə(r)), *sb. U.S. ? Obs.* [app. f. hunks *sb.* + -er.

Remembered by Mr. W. J. Stillman as familiarly used *c* 1840 at Schenectady N.Y., 'to designate a surly, crusty, or stingy old fellow, a curmudgeon'. But some would refer it to hunk *sb.*² as 'one who sticks to his post, or home'.]

In U.S. politics: A conservative, one opposed to innovation or change; a nickname first used in the State of New York about 1845.

1849 *N.Y. Evening Post* 11 July (Bartlett), He is now the leader of the hunkers of Missouri. **1856** *Househ. Words* 9 Aug. 86/1 *Hunker* is derived from a popular nickname for a self-satisfied, surly rich man; a descendant of Old Hunks in fact. **1859** W. Phillips *Speeches* 268 Egypt, the hunker conservative of antiquity. **1864** *Boston Commonw.* 3 June, The judge, a white-haired old man, well preserved, and a stickler for law and precedent and a 'hunker'.

Hence ˈ**hunkerism.**

1845 R. Tyler *Let.* 19 Apr. in L. G. Tyler *Lett. & Times Tylers* (1896) III. 161 Every appointment made for New York or Pennsylvania or Maryland is a restoration of *Hunkerism*. **1848** C. A. Loomis *Let.* 23 Jan. in *Mich. Hist. Mag.* (1926) X. 216 Old Hunkerism is predominant, but it is hunkerism without brains. **1863** W. Phillips *Speeches* 365 All this fossil hunkerism is to linger thirty or forty years. *Ibid.* 528, I resolve hunkerism into indolence and cowardice, too lazy to think, and too timid to think. **1906** *Springfield* (Mass.) *Weekly Republ.* 6 Dec. 8 The old republican hunkerism.

hunker (ˈhʌŋkə(r)), *v.* orig. *Sc.* [Origin obscure: it has the form of an iterative from a stem *hunk-*. Cf. MDu. *hucken, huken* (Verwijs and Verdam), MLG. *hûken*, Du. *huiken* (Franck), ON. *húka*, mod.G. *hocken* (Kluge) to sit on the hams or heels, to squat. These words point to an original ablaut series *heuk-, hûk, huk-* (*hok-*); from this *hunk-er*, might perh. be a nasalized derivative. ON. *hok-ra* to crouch may be a parallel form; Du. *hunkeren* to hanker, is not connected.]

a. *intr.* To squat, with the haunches, knees, and ankles acutely bent, so as to bring the hams near the heels, and throw the whole weight upon the fore part of the feet.

1720 A. Pennecuik *Streams from Helicon* i. 80 And hunk'ring down upon the cald Grass. **1768** Ross *Helenore* ii. 81 Upo' the ground they hunker'd down a' three. **1789** D. Davidson *Seasons* 179 Tir'd wi' the steep, an' something dizzy, I hunker'd down. *a* **1801** R. Gall *Tint Quey* 177 Then hunkering down upo' her knees, Poor Hornie o' her milk to ease. **1897** Crockett *Lads' Love* iii, He appeared.. with his hands on his knees 'hunkering' a little. **1902** *Dialect Notes* II. 237 (Pioneer dialect of S. Illinois.) *Hunker down.* 1. To crouch in sitting. 2. To kneel. **1907** Kipling *Actions & Reactions* (1909) 187 We heard Imam Din hunker down on the floor. One gets little out of the East at attention. **1928** Barrie *Peter Pan* ii, in *Plays* 39 Hunkering on the ground ..the six are not unlike village gossips gathered round the pump. **1945** J. Steinbeck *Cannery Row* vii. 26 Mack and the boys sat on the floor, played cards hunkered down. **1946** K. Tennant *Lost Haven* (1947) ix. 129 Kelly got up, came out, and hunkered down by the sunny office wall. George hunkered down beside him. **1962** *Coast to Coast 1961–62* 85 The old woman had hunkered down, poking intently at an *hibachi*, some embers glowing darkly beneath. **1973** *N.Y. Times* 14 Aug. 34/3 One 14-year-old boy sat on a hornet when he hunkered down to get a better view of the green.

b. *transf.* To cower or squat in a lowly manner.

1790 A. Wilson *Poems* 210 A wee bit Cot, Bare, hunkerin' on some lanely spot.

hunkerish (ˈhʌŋkərɪʃ), *a. U.S. colloq.* [f. hunker *sb.* + -ish¹.] Conservative, old-fashioned.

1857 *Lawrence* (Kansas) *Republ.* 2 July 3 This has in times past, been considered rather a hunkerish neighbourhood. **1888** W. Lawrence *Life Amos A. Lawrence* 139 His Kansas experience did not move Mr. Lawrence from his hunkerish sympathies in politics. **1905** *Springfield* (Mass.) *Weekly Republ.* 8 Sept. 1 The hunkerish conservatism which Mr. Cannon and the Senate stand for.

hunkers (ˈhʌŋkəz), *sb. pl.* orig. *Sc.* [Connected with hunker *v.*: cf. the Du. phrases *op de hukken* or *hurken gaan zitten* (Verwijs and Verdam), Ger. *in der hocke sitzen* to squat, which have a similar relation to the verbs *hukken, hurken, hocken.*] In the phrase *on one's hunkers*, in a squatting position, as defined under hunker *v.*

1756 M. Calderwood *Journey in Eng. & Low Countries* (1842) 164 It goes down with a step, which makes the door so low, that if any body from without speaks to you, they must sit down on their hungkers. **1785** Burns *Jolly Beggars* Recit. vi. iii, Wi' ghastly ee, poor Tweedle-dee Upon his hunkers bended. **1808** A. Scott *Poems* 48 Twa paddocks sat, Exchanging words in social chat; Cock't on their hunkers, facin' ither. **1831** S. Lover *Legends & Stories of Ireland* 200 Up sits the fox on his hunkers. **1882** Stevenson *Merry Men* ii, I got a glisk o' him mysel', sittin' on his hunkers in a hag. **1888** in W. B. Yeats *Fairy & Folk Tales* 109, I seen an ould woman sittin' on her hunkers. **1896** *Dialect Notes* I. 419, I had to sit on my *hunkers*. Myersville, Md., and Tannersville, Pa. **1898** *Pall Mall Mag.* July 337 'We cannot set king Charles back on his throne.. by sitting here on our hunkers admiring the sea views.' **1935** A. J. Cronin *Stars look Down* i. ii. 17 Some colliers..squatted upon their hunkers against the wall. **1947** T. H. White *Elephant & Kangaroo* (1948) xx. 160 Mr. White seized Brownie by the tail—she had been sitting on her hunkers beside him.

hunkey, hunkie, hunky, varr. hunk *sb.*³

hunks (hʌŋks), *sb.* Also **hunx.** [Known soon after 1600; but not in Dicts. before Kersey's ed. of Phillips, 1706. Origin unknown: it has the appearance of a quasi proper name of nickname, like *Old Grumbles, Bags, Boots*, and the like. (An Icel. *hunskur* cited by Lye is imaginary.)]

A term of obloquy for a surly, crusty, cross-grained old person, a 'bear'; now, usually, a close-fisted, stingy man; a miser. (Generally with *close, covetous, niggardly*, or other uncomplimentary epithet.)

1602 Dekker *Satirom.* Wks. 1873 I. 201 *Blun.* Come you shall shake —— *Tucca.* Not handes with great Hunkes there, not hands. *a* **1627** Middleton *No Wit, no Help* v. ii, Now is Mercury going into the second house near unto Ursa Major, that great hunks. *a* **1634** Randolph *Muses' Looking-Glass* ii. iv, 'Twas to blind the eyes of the old huncks. *c* **1650** Brathwait *Barnabees Jrnl.* ii. (1818) 71 There the beares were come to town-a: Two rude hunks, 'tis troth I tell ye. **1676** Wycherley *Pl. Dealer* v. ii, [He] makes a very pretty show in the World, let me tell you; nay, a better than your close Hunks. **1681** Dryden *Sp. Friar* i. ii, A jealous, covetous, old hunks. **1706** Phillips (ed. Kersey), *Hunks*, as *a meer Hunks*, i.e. a base, covetous Wretch, a pitiful, niggardly Fellow. **1728** Young *Love Fame* iv. 224 The veriest Hunks in Lombard-street. *c* **1730** *Royal Remarks* 2 The Antediluvian Gentry, or the old Hunxes their Descendants. **1756** Earl Orrery in *Connoisseur* No. 129 ¶2 They all think me a close old hunks. **1821** Lamb *Elia* Ser. i. *Old Benchers I.T.*, C. was a close hunks—a hoarder rather than a miser. **1831** Trelawney *Adv. Younger Son* I. 53 To say nothing of the old hunkses about the past. **1857** Kingsley *Two Y. Ago* III. 190 One fellow comes and borrows my money, and goes out and calls me a stingy old hunks because I won't let him cheat me.

hunkster. *rare.* [f. hunks + -ster, in *huckster*, etc.] = prec.

1847 J. Wilson *Chr. North* (1857) I. 143 As if you were the greatest of hunksters and never gave but unavoidable dinners.

hunky (ˈhʌŋkɪ), *a.*¹ *U.S. slang.* [f. hunk *sb.*² and *a.* + -y¹.] In good condition; safe and sound; all right: = hunk *a.*

1861 'A. Ward' in *Vanity Fair* (N.Y.) 15 June 273/1 He (Moses) folded her to his hart, with the remark that he was 'a hunkey boy'. **1878** B. Harte *Man on Beach* 47 She's all hunky, and has an appetite. **1889** K. Munroe *Golden Days* xii. 125 If I'd took good care of that map..we'd been all hunky at this minute. **1907** C. E. Mulford *Bar-20* ix. 105 That was all hunky for a while. **1926** *Bulletin* 21 Oct. 4/2 I'll be all hunky. Nurse Dainton tends me like I was made of glass.

So ˌ**hunky-ˈdory, -ˈdorey** [second element of unknown origin] *a.*, satisfactory, fine.

1866 *Galaxy* 1 Oct. 275, I cannot conceive on any theory of etymology..why anything that is 'hunkee doree'..should be so admirable. **1868** in G. C. D. Odell *Ann. N.Y. Stage* (1936) VIII. 390 [Even Samuel Slater admitted that Tostee, when and if she sang, was] hunky-dory. **1907** N. Munro *Daft Days* xxi, Before one marries it's hunky-dory—it's fairy all the time. **1907** M. C. Harris *Tents of Wickedness* iv. ii. 341 I've had my luncheon, and I feel better already. Oh, it's all hunky-dory. **1943** N. Balchin *Small Back Room* 172 Well, unless the electricity they taught me is all wrong, that ought to be hunky-dory. **1956** D. M. Davin *Sullen Bell* iii. iv. 233, I thought everything was hunkydory and you were well on the way to being a big executive. **1969** J. Gardner *Founder Member* ii. 17 Everythink's 'unkey dorey 'ere. No problem.

hunky (ˈhʌŋkɪ), *a.*² [f. hunk *sb.*¹ + -y¹.] Thick-set, solidly built.

1911 E. Ferber *Dawn O'Hara* vii. 89 Rather be hunky and healthy than skinny and sick. **1959** *Listener* 23 Apr. 733/1 A vast, hunky, surly man.

hunne, var. unne *v.*, to grant.

hunne, -en, var. hen *adv.*, hence.

hunner, Sc. f. hundred.

Hunnian, Hunnic, etc.: see Hun.

hunny, hunsh, obs. ff. honey, hunch *v.*

hunsup, corrupt form of hunt's-up.

†**hunt,** *sb.*¹ *Obs.* Forms: 1 **hunta,** 2–6 **hunte,** 4–5 **honte,** 4–6 **hunt.** [OE. *hunta* hunter, huntsman (also hunting-spider) agent-n.:—OTeut. type **hunton-*, app. from a weak-grade of the same root as hent (:—**hantjan*), not exactly represented in the other Teut. langs. From its form, *hunta* is an old word, not a derivative of *huntian* hunt *v.*, but app. rather its source.

The ablaut-stem **hent-*, **hant-*, **hunt-* is identical in sense, and in origin evidently closely akin to *henþ-, hanþ-, hunþ-*, in Gothic *hinþan* to seize, capture, *fra-hunþans* captive, *hunþs* captivity, and OHG. *hunda*, OE. *húð* booty. But the interchange of *þ* and *t* (:— pre-Teut. *t* and *d*) is difficult to account for. On an apparent pre-Teut. change of *nt* to *nd* in these and some other words, see Prof. Napier in *Mod. Quart. Lang. & Lit.* July 1898, 130; cf. Brugmann *Grundr.* ed. 2, I. §701.]

A hunter; a huntsman. (In quot. 1000, a hunting-spider.) *Common Hunt*: see quot. 1707.

c **1000** *Sax. Leechd.* II. 144 Wiþ huntan bite, blace snegլas on hattre pannan ʒehyrste. *c* **1131** *O.E. Chron.* an. 1127 Ða huntes wæron swarte..& here hundes ealle swarte..& hi ridone on swarte hors. *c* **1200** *Trin. Coll. Hom.* 209 þe deuel ..henteð us alse hunte driueð deor to grune. **1387** Trevisa *Higden* (Rolls) VII. 357 Alle þe hontes schulde come wiþ her houndes. *c* **1450** *Bk. Curtasye* 629 in *Babees Bk.* 320 A halpeny þo hunte takes on þe day For euery hounde, þo sothe to say. **1566** Drant *Horace, Sat.* i. i. Aiij, The hungrye hunts muste haue it all. **1575** Turbervile *Bk. of Venerie* 127 Then the chiefe hunte shall take his knyfe and cut off the deares ryght foote. **1700** T. Brown tr. *Fresny's Amusem. Ser. & Com.* 30 Would you buy the Common Hunt, the Common Cryers, the Bridge-Master's.. Places? **1707** Chamberlayne *Pres. State Eng.* 357 He [the Lord Mayor] hath four Officers that wait on him, who are reputed Esquires by their Places; that is, The Sword-Bearer. The Common-Hunt, who keepeth a good Kennel of Hounds for the Lord-Mayor's Recreation abroad. The Common Cryer. The Water Bailiff. **1807** Dec. 17 *Journal* 84, *Common Council of London*, fol. 135 b, Motion thereupon made that the Office of Common Hunt be abolished, and eventually carried.

hunt (hʌnt), *sb.*² [f. hunt *v.*]

1. The act of hunting. **a.** The act of chasing wild animals for the purpose of catching or killing them; the chase.

c **1375** *Sc. Leg. Saints, Julian* 236 In ȝouthhede..he a day til hwntis ȝede. *c* **1386** Chaucer *Knt.'s T.* 1770 Ther nas no Tygre in the vale of Galgopheye..So crueel on the hunte. **1537** [see hunt's up]. **1588** Shaks. *Tit. A.* ii. ii. 1 The hunt is vp, the morne is bright and gray. *Ibid.* ii. iii. 19 Eccho mock's the Hounds,..As if a double hunt were heard at once. **1781** W. Blane *Ess. Hunt.* (1788) 133 Why a Hare, towards the end of the hunt, is often difficult to be killed. **1869** Trollope *He knew* etc. i. 5 [He] could not have ridden a hunt to save either his government or his credit.

b. *fig.* and *gen.* Pursuit, as of a wild animal; the act of strenuously seeking or endeavouring to find something; a search, esp. a diligent search. Also with *adv.*, as *a hunt-up*.

1605 Shaks. *Lear* ii. iii. 3, I heard my selfe proclaim'd, And by the happy hollow of a Tree, Escap'd the hunt. **1697** tr. *C'tess D'Aunoy's Trav.* (1706) 52 They were now upon the Hunt for him. **1764** Foote *Patron* ii. Wks. 1799 I. 347 It is three months ago since I got the first scent of it, and I have been ever since on the hunt. **1818** Jas. Mill *Brit. India* II. v. viii. 659 On the hunt for appearances of guilt. **1852** Mrs. Carlyle *Lett.* II. 194, I went off then on a new hunt for lodgings.

2. *concr.* **a.** A body of persons (which may include also horses and dogs) engaged in, or associated for the purpose of, hunting with a pack of hounds; also, a hunting association.

1579 Spenser *Sheph. Cal.* Sept. 159 For feare of raungers, and the great hunt. **1687** Dryden *Hind & P.* i. 27 The common hunt, though from their rage restrain'd..Grinn'd as they pass'd. **1762** in Eg.-Warburton *Hunt. Songs* (1883) Introd. 14 The Orders of the Tarporley Hunt, November yᵉ 14th, 1762. **1787** Burns *Poems* Ded., To the Noblemen and Gentlemen of the Caledonian Hunt. **1791** 'G. Gambado' *Ann. Horsemen* Pref. (1809) 55 They might ere now have belonged to the first hunts in the country. **1812** *Sporting Mag.* XXXIX. 134 Foxes..have been poisoned..to the great annoyance of the hunts established in that county. **1887** Sir R. H. Roberts *In the Shires* i. 7 She..is looked

upon as a privileged person, a pet of the hunt. **1889** *Repent. P. Wentworth* I. 56 To withdraw his subscription to the Hunt.

†**b.** That which is hunted; game killed in hunting: = CHASE *sb.*[1] 4. *Obs.*

1588 R. PARKE tr. *Mendoza's Hist. China* 17 In the which ..is great quantitie of hunt and flying foules. **1611** SHAKS. *Cymb.* III. vi. 90 Boyes wee'l go dresse our hunt.

c. The district over which a pack of hounds hunts. (Cf. CHASE *sb.*[1] 3.)

1857 in *Art Taming Horses* xi. (1859) 178 The celebrated 'Haycock' [inn].., standing..in the middle of the Fitzwilliam Hunt. **1882** *Field* 28 Jan. 100/3 Every landowner within the hunt should be careful to preserve foxes. *Mod.* The property is situated within the Heythrop hunt.

3. *Change-ringing.* (See quot. and cf. HUNT *v.* 7.)

1684 R. H. *School of Recreation* 93 In all Peals upon five Bells there are two Hunts, to wit, a whole and an half-Hunt. **1688** R. HOLME *Armoury* III. 462/2 The First, or Treble Bell, it is termed the Hunt, and the Second Bell the half Hunt, because they run from the round Ringing, through all the change of Bells backwards and forewards, before they come to round Ringing againe.

4. A hunting or oscillatory motion (see HUNT *v.* 7 b, HUNTING *vbl. sb.* 1 f).

1920 *Nature* 11 Mar. 46/1 It moves backwards and forwards very slightly, and this motion we term the 'hunt'. **1934** *Brit. Jrnl. Psychol.* XXIV. 399 The 'angle of hunt', i.e. the angle of oscillation about the mean radial velocity, cannot exceed 360/*N* degrees, where *N* is the number of segments in the armature. **1937** *Jrnl. R. Aeronaut. Soc.* XLI. 410 The well behaved short period oscillation develops into an irritating hunt. **1952** A. TUSTIN *Automatic & Manual Control* 280 If the amplitude is not too large, and ..we know how to reduce the amplitude by increasing the hunt frequency, it is possible to check a mean position of the system.

5. *Telephony.* An operation of hunting by a selector or switch (see HUNTING *vbl. sb.* 1 g).

1927 W. E. HUDSON *Director Syst. Autom. Telephony* ii. 42 Relay C..is used to determine when the impulse train is finished so as to allow the automatic hunt to start. **1966** RUBIN & HALLER *Communication Switching Syst.* i. 31 The hunt motion is a vertical move of the wipers along the contact bank.

6. *attrib.* and *Comb.*, as ***hunt-breakfast***, ***-button***, ***-dinner***, ***-servant***; ***hunt-weary*** adj.; **hunt ball**, a ball given by members of a hunt; †**hunt-beast**, a beast of the chase; **hunt-sergeant**, an officer of Massachusetts in the colonial and provincial period, who had charge of the hunts (carried on with hounds) for hostile Indians; †**hunt-spear**, a hunting-spear.

1807 *Sporting Mag.* XXXI. 40/1 The annual *Hunt Ball took place at Chepstow. **1853** MRS. GASKELL *Ruth* I. i. 13 The annual hunt-ball was to take place. **1933** A. POWELL *From View to Death* iv. 113 Ungainly young men who had had a glass too much of champagne at hunt-ball suppers. **1968** A. DIMENT *Bang Bang Birds* x. 193 Penny told us about a hunt ball she had attended recently. **1973** K. GILES *File on Death* iv. 90 'E provides the catering for the 'unt ball at seven guineas the ticket. **1535** STEWART *Cron. Scot.* I. 480 He ordanit..That na *hunt beist with schutting sould be slane. **1877** TROLLOPE *Amer. Senator* II. xxiv. 254 That old farmer at the *hunt breakfast. **1897** *Daily Tel.* 23 Nov. 9/3 A hunt-breakfast was given to the followers of the East Kent foxhounds. **1973** K. GILES *File on Death* v. 133 The other one..kept pawing the ladies..and falling off his horse after the Hunt Breakfast. **1859** *Art Taming Horses* xi. 183 Scarlet-coated, many with the Brocklesby *hunt button. **1844** DISRAELI *Coningsby* III. v, It was at the *Hunt dinner. **1706–7** *Acts Prov. Mass. Bay* (ed. Goodell) I. 599 Persons who shall..have them [hounds] at all times in readiness to attend the *hunt serjeant. **1894** ASTLEY *50 Years Life* II. 5 Horses, hounds, and *hunt-servants have never been better turned out. **1594** MARLOWE & NASHE *Dido* III. M.'s Wks. (Rtldg.) 263/2 Ascanius..Bearing his *hunt-spear bravely in his hand. *a* **1831** CLOUGH *Ess. Class. Metres, Actaeon* 4 Artemis..alone, *hunt-weary, Unto a dell..her foot unerring Had guided.

hunt (hʌnt), *v.* Forms: 1 **huntian**, 2–3 **huntien**, **hunten**, 3–7 **hunte**, 4– **hunt**; (also 3–4 **hont(e**, **hounte**, 4 **hownte**, *Sc.* **hwnt**, 4–6 **hount**, 5 **honte**). [OE. *huntian*:—OTeut. type **huntôjan*, stem of f. **hunton-*, OE. *hunta*, HUNT *sb.*[1]]

I. 1. a. *intr.* To go in pursuit of wild animals or game; to engage in the chase. Also of animals: To pursue their prey.

c **1000** ÆLFRIC *Colloq.* in Wr.-Wülcker 92/11 Ne canst þu huntian buton mid nettum. *c* **1000** *Sax. Leechd.* III. 172 Gif him þince þæt he huntige, beorge him ȝeorne wið his fynd. *c* **1131** *O.E. Chron.* an. 1127 Þa sæȝon & herdon fela men feole huntes hunten. *c* **1205** LAY. 1432 Ȝe huntieð i þes kinges friðe. *c* **1290** *S. Eng. Leg.* I. 256/5 Ase he hountede In a dai In Iolifte j-nouȝ. *a* **1300** *Cursor M.* 3519 Esau went for till hunt. **1398** TREVISA *Barth. De P.R.* XVIII. i. (Bodl. MS.), Some [beasts] hunteþ by nyȝt. *a* **1400** *Octouian* 891 To hounty yn ech mannys boundes Hyt was hys wone. **1513** MORE *Rich. III* (1883) 3 [He] sente for the Mayre and Aldermenne of London to hym..too haue them hunte and bee mery with hym. **1665** HOOKE *Microgr.* 201, I have beheld them instructing their young ones, how to hunt. **1774** GOLDSM. *Nat. Hist.* (1776) III. 270 The dog kinds.. love to hunt in company. **1841** LANE *Arab. Nts.* I. 91 One day the son went forth to hunt.

b. With prepositions (*after*, †*to*, †*at*, *for*). (Now blending with 3 a.)

c **1200** ORMIN 13467 Þatt teȝȝ sholldenn hunntenn Acc nohht wiþþ hundess affterr der Acc affterr menn wiþþ spelless. *c* **1385** CHAUCER *L.G.W.* 981 *Dido*, Ony wilde bor ..That they han huntid to in this foreste. *c* **1400** MAUNDEV. (Roxb.) xiv. 63 Grete plentee of wylde bestes for to hunt at. *c* **1450** *Merlin* 183 Yo do nought elles..but hunte after the hare thourgh the feldes. **1486** *Bk. St. Albans* E ij b, When ye hunt at the Roo. **1697** DAMPIER *Voy.* I. i. 9 Walks out into the Woods, and hunts about for Pecary, Warree..or Deer. **1774** GOLDSM. *Nat. Hist.* (1776) IV. 156 Training them up to hunt for fish.

fig. **1567** *Gude & Godlie B.* (S.T.S.) 184 Sa thay think to bleir ȝour E, And syne at ȝow to hount.

2. *trans.* To pursue (wild animals or game) for the purpose of catching or killing; to chase for food or sport; often *spec.* to pursue with hounds or other tracking beasts. Also said of animals chasing their prey.

c **1000** ÆLFRIC *Hom.* I. 576 Ic asende..mine huntan, and hi huntiað hi of ælcere dune and of ælcere hylle. *c* **1275** LAY. 1423 Corineus was to wode ivare for hunti deor wilde. *c* **1375** *Sc. Leg. Saints, Placidas* 86 He went to hont þe auld bestis, as he wes wont. **1398** TREVISA *Barth. De P.R.* XII. vi. (Bodl. MS.), Scheo [the owl] hunteþ and eeteþ myes and reremyesse. *Ibid.* xiii, Swalewes þat fleeþ in þe aiere hunteþ flies. **1486** *Bk. St. Albans* E iv a, All other beestys that huntid shall be. **1588** SHAKS. *L.L.L.* IV. iii. 1 The King he is hunting the Deare. **1697** DRYDEN *Virg. Georg.* I. 414 The proper Time..T'inclose the Stags in Toyls, and Hunt the Hare. **1788** W. BLANE *Hunt. Excurs.* 16 The hunting the wild buffaloe is also performed by shooting him from elephants. **1837** W. IRVING *Capt. Bonneville* III. 45 To hunt the elk, deer, and ahsahta or bighorn. **1859** *Art Taming Horses* xii. 203 When the hounds hunt anything beside fox the word is 'Ware Riot'.

3. *fig.* and *gen.* **a.** *intr.* To search, seek (*after* or *for* anything), esp. with eagerness and exertion.

c **1200** [see 1 b]. *a* **1225** *Ancr. R.* 66 Heo hunteð efter pris. *a* **1240** *Ureisun* in *Cott. Hom.* 203 Hwuder schal ich fleon hwon þe deouel hunteð efter me. *c* **1305** *St. Lucy* 119 in *E.E.P.* (1862) 104 Hit is al for noȝt þat þu huntest aboute. **1526** *Pilgr. Perf.* (W. de W. 1531) 60 Sathanas & his mynysters, whiche dayly hunteth to take thy soule. **1549** COVERDALE, etc. *Erasm. Par. Thess.* 3 We hunted so litell for rewarde at your handes. **1722** WOLLASTON *Relig. Nat.* ix. 211 Hunting after knowledge which must perish with them. **1830** DE QUINCEY *Bentley* Wks. VI. 171 Hunting backward, upon the dimmest traces, into the aboriginal condition of things. **1862** MRS. WOOD *Mrs. Hallib.* I. iii. 15 Spending all his superfluous minutes hunting for a house. **1895** *Law Times* C. 3/1 The judge and Master Macdonell hunted through the White Book, and unearthed a rule sufficiently elastic.

b. *trans.* To go eagerly in search of, search for, seek (esp. with desire and diligence); to endeavour to capture, obtain, or find.

c **1375** *Sc. Leg. Saints, Placidas* 126 And þi gud dedis causis me, As þou me huntis, to hont þe. **1573** *Satir. Poems Reform.* xli. 19 He neuer huntit benefice, Nor catchit was with Couatice. **1648** J. BEAUMONT *Psyche* I. ccxxxv, He therefore through close paths of wary hast Hunts his escape. **1753** J. BARTRAM in Darlington *Mem.* (1849) 195 Next morning..we hunted plants till breakfast. **1818** E. P. FORDHAM *Pers. Narr. Trav.* (1906) 221 The next day I shall cross the Little Wabash to 'hunt land'. **1834** *Visit to Texas* i. 10 An old Tennessean and his wife with their sons were going 'to hunt land'. *Ibid.* xiii. 122 He sometimes sends out three or four men to collect and mark them. This is called hunting cattle. **1891** M. E. RYAN *Told in Hills* IV. iii. 309 All were sleepy enough to hunt beds early. **1894** BARING-GOULD *Deserts S. France* I. 140 It [the truffle] is hunted regularly by trained dogs. **1903** A. ADAMS *Log of Cowboy* iii. 38 Flood..suggested that all hands hunt their blankets and turn in for the night.

c. To follow (as a hound does); to track.

1579 E. K. *Ep. Spenser's Sheph. Cal.*, In regard wherof, I scorne and spue out the rakehellye route of our ragged rymers (for so themselues vse to hunt the letter). **1590** SPENSER *F.Q.* I. i. 11 That path..Which when by tract they hunted had throughout At length it brought them to a hollowe cave. **1847** TENNYSON *Princ.* II. 368 'They hunt old trails' said Cyril 'very well; But when did woman ever yet invent?' **1860** TYNDALL *Glac.* II. xxxii. 417, I hunted the seams still farther up the glacier.

4. a. *trans.* To pursue with force, violence, or hostility; to chase and drive before one; to put to flight; to chase or drive *away* or *out*. (See HUNTAWAY *sb.*)

c **1340** *Cursor M.* 13658 (Trin.) Þei huntid him as a dogge Riȝt out of her synagogge. *c* **1385** CHAUCER *L.G.W.* 2414 *Phyllis*, So huntith hym the tempest to and fro. **1484** CAXTON *Curiall* 3 She is by force hunted away. **1535** COVERDALE *Ps.* cxxxix. [cxl.] 11 A malicious and wicked person shal be hunted awaye and destroyed. **1582** N. LICHEFIELD tr. *Castanheda's Conq. E. Ind.* li. 110 To hunt them foorth lyke theeues. **1642** ROGERS *Naaman* 31 The Lord would hunt her out of it. **1808** SCOTT *Life Dryden* iv, He might lay his account with being hunted out of society. **1886** R. C. LESLIE *Sea-painter's Log* 25 They are hunted by 'the bobby' from place to place.

b. *fig.* To pursue with injury or annoyance; to persecute, pester, worry.

1583 HOLLYBAND *Campo di Fior* 387 But hunger hunteth me. **1678** OTWAY *Friendship in F.* II. i, He hunts and kisses you when he is drunk. **1807–8** W. IRVING *Salmag.* (1824) 38 When..I choose to hunt a Monsieur for my own particular amusement. **1860** HAWTHORNE *Marb. Faun* (1879) II. viii. 90 These pests..had hunted the two travellers at every stage of their journey.

5. To scour (a district) in pursuit of game; *spec.* to make (a district) the field of fox-hunting; hence, *fig.* to search (a place) thoroughly and keenly for something which one hopes to find there; to examine every nook and cranny of.

a **1440** *Sir Degrev.* 174, I wulle ffore thy lordes tene, Honte hys fforesstus and grene. **1568** GRAFTON *Chron.* II. 121 The Citizens have free libertie of hunting a certeyne circuite aboute London. **1712** SWIFT *Let.* 28 Oct., I must now go hunt those dry letters for materials. **1834** MEDWIN *Angler in Wales* I. 101 Let us hunt the waterfalls higher up. **1875** WHYTE-MELVILLE *Riding Recoll.* i. (1879) 9 When he [Sir R. Sutton] hunted the Cottesmore country. *Mod.* I have hunted the house for it, but cannot lay my hands on it.

6. To use or employ in hunting; to ride (a horse), direct or manage (hounds), in the chase.

1607 TOPSELL *Four-f. Beasts* (1658) 117 The time of teaching a Gray-hound..Some hunt them at ten months, if they be males, and at eight months, if they be female. **1708** *Lond. Gaz.* No. 4465/6 The Owner..to certify, that his Horse was constantly Hunted the last Season. **1735** SOMERVILLE *Chase* I. 83 To rear, feed, hunt, and discipline the Pack. **1857** LD. MALMESBURY *Mem. Ex-minister* (1884) II. 80 In consequence of his always hunting his pointers down wind. **1875** WHYTE-MELVILLE *Riding Recoll.* i. (1879) 6 He hunts one pack of his own hounds in Northamptonshire. **1889** in *Horse & Hound* 24 Aug. 516/2 Horses described as 'hunters'..must have been hunted, and be capable of being hunted.

7. a. *Change-ringing.* To alter the position of (a bell) in successive changes so as to shift it by degrees from the first place to the last (***hunting up***), or from the last to the first (***hunting down***). Also *absol.* or *intr.*

1684 R. H. *School Recreat.* 92 So by turns, 'till every Bell being hunted up and down, comes into its proper Place again. *Ibid.* 96 Whatsoever Bells you follow when you Hunt up, the same Bells in the same order you must follow in Hunting down. **1880** C. A. W. TROYTE in Grove *Dict. Mus.* I. 334 The bells work in regular order from being first bell to being last, striking two blows as first and two as last: this is called by ringers 'hunting up and down'.

b. *intr.* Of a governor, a synchronous electric motor or generator, etc.: to run alternately faster and more slowly than the desired speed. Hence more widely of other machines, systems, etc.: to oscillate *about* a desired speed, position, or state to an undesirable extent, to jump backwards and forwards.

1877 *Proc. Inst. Mech. Engin.* 273 Siemens' interesting governor..had..a great tendency to 'hunt',..if it was first left a little behind, and then got an excess of force, it would be constantly 'hunting' or oscillating about a mean position. **1894** *Rep. Brit. Assoc. Adv. Sci.* 759 A Watt governor..does not hunt if designed for stability. **1902** *Trans. Amer. Inst. Electr. Engin.* XVIII. 374/2 The motors attempt to follow the generator exactly. If the latter pulsates, the motors pulsate also; they vibrate about a mean position, 'hunting' or pumping. **1921** M. WALKER *Diagn. Troubles Electr. Machines* vi. 239 In the case of steam turbines and steam engines, it is possible for the governor to hunt in a perfectly periodic manner. **1951** S. DEUTSCH *Theory & Design Television Receivers* xiii. 431 If the feedback loop is underdamped, the oscillator frequency will swing below 15,750 cycles per second, whereupon the correcting voltage causes a swing above 15,750 cycles per second, etc. In other words, the oscillator will 'hunt' about the correct frequency. **1953** *Electronic Engin.* XXV. 156/1 Since the torque balance has an on-off action..it has a tendency to hunt. **1969** *Daily Tel.* 10 Jan. 26/4 The British train will be able to use existing railway tracks because of a new type of suspension... This will stop the train 'hunting' sideways. **1969** J. ARGENTI *Managem. Techniques* 99 If the action is too late or too weak, control will be inadequate, if too early or too strong the system will 'hunt'—i.e. swing violently above and below the standard. **1970** 'J. EARL' *Tuners & Amplifiers* iii. 74 On weak stereo signals this circuit can 'hunt' over mono and stereo in a very disconcerting manner, switching to stereo as the signal rises and back to mono as it falls.

8. To call upon (a person) to fill up or drink off his glass: CHASE *v.*[1] 4.

1780 BANNATYNE in *Mirror* No. 76 ¶11 Umphraville received a slap on the shoulder from one of the company, who at the same time reminded him that he was *hunted*. My friend..thanked the gentleman..for his attention, and drank off his bumper.

9. *Telephony.* Of a selector or switch: to carry out the operation of hunting (HUNTING *vbl. sb.* 1 g). Const. *for*, *over*.

1924 W. AITKEN *Autom. Telephone Syst.* III. LVI. 275 Dialling O..results in the starting of a free-trunk finder, which automatically hunts for the calling line. **1924** H. H. HARRISON *Introd. Strowger Syst. Autom. Telephony* i. 26 The preselector or line switch..hunts to find one of ten or more idle group selectors. **1933** K. B. MILLER *Telephone Theory & Pract.* III. v. 250 It is usual to adjust the speed to permit the selector to hunt over a group of 30 trunks in 1 second. **1961** *Proc. Inst. Electr. Engin.* CVII. B. Suppl. 161/2 A maximum of 1·8 millisec is required to select a channel,.. and a further period of 900 microsec to hunt for a free channel.

II. Phrases.

10. ***hunt down***. **a.** To chase (an animal) until caught or killed; to run to earth, to bring to bay; *fig.* to pursue and overcome or destroy; also, to pursue until one gets possession or mastery of. (See also 7.)

a **1719** ADDISON (J.), We should single every criminal out of the herd, and hunt him down. **1816** KEATINGE *Trav.* (1817) I. 291 Errors, popular or not, are lawful game, and free to every one to hunt down. **1849** MACAULAY *Hist. Eng.* vii. II. 217 Refusing to spy out and hunt down little congregations of Nonconformists. **1877** E. R. CONDER *Bas. Faith* iv. 150 Let us..try to hunt down this fugitive question.

b. *N.Z.* (See quot. 1933.)

1933 L. G. D. ACLAND in *Press* (Christchurch, N.Z.) 28 Oct. 17/7 *Hunt down*, to hunt the sheep off the higher parts of their winter country on to lower, safer spurs when snow is expected; e.g., 'We hunted down every day for a week, but no snow came.' **1961** B. CRUMP *Hang on a Minute* 85, I want you blokes to go round to the Snow Hut and hunt the sheep down into the valley from the open spur.

11. ***hunt out***: to expel or drive from cover or shelter by hunting or persistent search; to track out; to arrive at or discover by investigation.

1576 FLEMING *Panopl. Epist.* 128 Except he hath taken flight into Dalmatia, from whence (notwithstanding he lurk for a season) we intend to hunt him out. **1596** SPENSER *State Irel.* Wks. (Globe) 626/1 Not certaynly affirming any thing, but by conferring of times, languages, monumentes, and such like, I doe hunte out a probabilitye. **1781** W. BLANE *Ess. Hunt.* (1788) 15 Or Spaniel, which will hunt out their master, or their master's horse distinctly from all others. **1881** J. TAYLOR *Scot. Covenant.* (Cassell) 128 To assist the soldiers in hunting out and butchering the hapless fugitives.

12. ***hunt up***: to prosecute the search for, until one finds; to pursue with eager investigation; to 'look up' (what is not found without energetic search). (See also 7.)

1791 W. BARTRAM *Carolina* 488 They enter..with a view of chasing the roebuck, and hunting up the sturdy bear. **1817** J. BRADBURY *Trav. Amer.* 265 If he finds them within three or four miles of his house, he thinks himself fortunate; but it sometimes happens that he is two days in 'hunting them up', as they term it. **1844** ALB. SMITH *Adv. Mr. Ledbury* vii. (1886) 20 [He] employed his time in hunting up all the old students that he had known formerly. **1884** J. A. H. MURRAY in *13th Addr. Philol. Soc.* 20 In..hunting up earlier quotations for recent words.

13. *to hunt* CHANGE (*sb.* 9), *to h.* COUNTER (*adv.* 1), *to h. in* COUPLES (*sb.* 1 b), *to h. the* FOIL (*sb.*[4]), *to h. at* FORCE (*sb.*[1] 22 a), *to h.* RIOT, *to h. at the* VIEW: see these words.

1630 J. TAYLOR (Water P.) *Navy Land Ships, Huntsmanship* Wks. I. 93/1 Allaye, Relaye, Foreloyning, Hunt-cownter, Hunt-change, Quarry, Reward, and a thousand more such Utopian fragments of confused Gibberish.

III. 14. a. *Comb.* **†hunt-counter**, (in Shaks. Folio) app. taken as one who hunts counter or traces the scent backward: but the Qos. have 'you hunt counter', i.e. you are on the wrong scent, you are off the track, which Nares and Schmidt accept; **†hunt-smock**, one who 'runs after' women.

1597 SHAKS. *2 Hen. IV*, I. ii. 102 You *Hunt-counter, hence: Auant. [**1765** JOHNSON *Note*, Hunt-counter, that is blunderer.] **1623** MASSINGER *Bondman* II. i, Your rambling *hunt-smock feels strange alterations.

b. In names of various games, as **hunt the fox, hunt the hare** = *fox and hounds, hare and hounds* (cf. FOX *sb.* 16 d, HARE *sb.* 3 b); **hunt the slipper**, a parlour game in which all the players but one sit in a ring and pass a slipper covertly from one to another, the remaining player standing in the middle and seeking to get hold of it; **hunt the squirrel**, an outdoor game in which one player is chased by another who must follow all his windings in and out of a ring formed by the remaining players; also called *cat and mouse*; **hunt the whistle**, a game resembling *hunt the slipper*, in which the seeker is blindfolded and has a whistle fastened to his dress, which the other players blow at intervals.

1762 in W. L. C. *Etoniana* xii. (1865) 179 [A list of Games popular at Eton in 1762 comprises] *Hunt the dark lanthorn [known also at Harrow]. *a* **1600** in Strutt *Sports & Past.* IV. iv. 487 When we play and *hunt the fox, I outrun all the boys in the schoole. **1825** BROCKETT, **Hunt-the-hare*, a game among children—played on the ice as well as in the fields. **1766** GOLDSM. *Vic. W.* xi, Last of all, they sat down to *hunt the slipper. **1885** *Athenæum* 16 May 635/3 The courtiers, playing at 'hunt the slipper' in a very decorous manner. **1897** *Daily News* 5 May 5/3 When the game of hunt the slipper was broken off for the day, the Committee..took the evidence of Mr. Lionel Phillips. **1742** H. WALPOLE *Lett. to H. Mann* 8 Oct., The raising of the siege of Prague, and Prince Charles and Marechal Maillebois playing at *hunt the squirrel, have disgusted me. **1883** NEWELL *Games Amer. Childr.* cxvii. (Cent). **1757** FOOTE *Author* II. Wks. 1799 I. 148 We ben't enough for *hunt the whistle, nor blind-man's buff.

huntable ('hʌntəb(ə)l), *a.* [f. HUNT *v.* + -ABLE.] Capable of being hunted.

1857 KINGSLEY *Two Y. Ago* I. i. 27 I've shot and hunted every beast, I think, shootable and huntable, from a humming bird to an elephant. **1895** *Daily News* 8 Apr. 7/4 Every huntable stream in the kingdom is repeatedly visited by [otter] hounds during the summer.

huntaway ('hʌntəweɪ), *sb.* [f. vbl. phr. *to hunt away* (HUNT *v.* 4), which is further illustrated below.] **a.** *Austral.* and *N.Z.* (See quot. 1933.)

1913 [see HEADING *vbl. sb.* 4 b]. **1933** L. G. D. ACLAND in *Press* (Christchurch, N.Z.) 28 Oct. 17/7 *Huntaway*, a dog whose work is to drive sheep forward when mustering. As a verb the word is used in two senses, illustrated in the sentences: 'That dog hunts away well' and 'I hunt away with that dog'. **1934** *Bulletin* (Sydney) 16 May 38/3 Rock, the kelpie leading-dog, and Bruce, the nondescript little huntaway, had never possessed any aspirations towards leadership. **1954** *Landfall* VIII. 221 Couple of times someone offered him big money for two good huntaways. **1961** B. CRUMP *Hang on a Minute* 74 They sold..two huntaway pups. **1966** BAKER *Austral. Lang.* (ed. 2) iii. 73 A huntaway is sometimes known as a forcing dog. **1968** *N.Z. News* 28 Aug. 16/1 The huntaway barks loudly to shift sheep.

b. Nelson huntaway (see quots.). *N.Z.*

1941 BAKER *N.Z. Slang* vi. 59 *Nelson huntaway*, a stone rolled down a hillside to move stock below instead of sending a dog out. **1949** P. NEWTON *High Country Days* 29 Brownie sent a boulder hurtling down the face—a 'Nelson huntaway'.

Also as *vb.* (*huntaway* or *hunt away*).

1931 T. A. HARPER *Windy Island* (1934) III. iii. 217 Vixen had turned her mob neatly over to Rough, who was hunting them away down the mountainside. **1933** [see sense a of the sb.]. **1934** J. LILICO *Sheep Dog Mem.* 27 The dogs would head, lead, huntaway, force and back.

hunted ('hʌntɪd), *ppl. a.* [f. HUNT *v.* + -ED[1].] Chased, pursued: see the verb.

1633 P. FLETCHER *Purple Isl.* XI. xxxi, A hunted Stag, now welnigh tir'd. **1810** SCOTT *Lady of L.* II. xxix, There, like the hunted quarry, dwell. **1882** OUIDA *Maremma* I. 121 She had sympathy with the hunted, not with the hunters.

hunter ('hʌntə(r)). [f. HUNT *v.* + -ER[1].]

1. A man who hunts. **a.** One engaged in the chase of wild animals; a huntsman.

c **1250** *Gen. & Ex.* 1481 Esau wilde man huntere, And Iacob tame man tiliere. *c* **1386** CHAUCER *Knt.'s T.* 780 The hunters in the regne of Trace. *c* **1420** *Anturs of Arth.* v, The hunteres thay haulen, by hurstes and by hoes. **1486** *Bk. St. Albans* E iij b, The hunter shall rewarde hem then with the hede. **1590** SPENSER *F.Q.* II. iii. 21 A goodly Ladie clad in hunters weed. **1692** LUTTRELL *Brief Rel.* (1857) II. 639 Last Satturday 9 highwaymen mett and robb'd 7 hunters, near Ingerstone, in Essex. **1735** SOMERVILLE *Chase* I. 37 When Nimrod bold, That mighty Hunter, first made War on Beasts. **1865** LUBBOCK *Preh. Times* xvi. (1869) 581 In a population which lives on the produce of the chase, each hunter requires on an average 50,000 acres.

b. *fig.* and *gen.* One who hunts or searches eagerly for something; a seeker. (Most freq. in comb., as ***fortune-hunter, place-hunter***.)

c **1374** CHAUCER *Boeth.* I. pr. iii. 12 (Add. MS.) We scorne swiche rauiners and honters [*Camb. MS.* henters] of foulest[e] þinges. **1526** *Pilgr. Perf.* (W. de W. 1531) 74 b, The hunter of mannes soule. **1542–5** BRINKLOW *Lament.* 6 b, Whore hounters and robbers of Goddes glorie. **1796** BURKE *Let. Noble Ld.* Wks. VIII. 52 They are the duke of Bedford's natural hunters; and he is their natural game. **1811** MISS MITFORD in L'Estrange *Life* (1870) I. v. 157 Are you a good motto hunter?

c. *Mil.* (tr. Ger. *jäger*, Fr. *chasseur*.)

1753 HANWAY *Trav.* (1762) I. VII. xciii. 428 Besides the hussars, the king has a small body of men whom they call hunters, who are reputed the most faithful couriers in his army. **1761** *Brit. Mag.* II. 443 Lieutenant-colonel de Stockhausen had..posted himself in the Solling with his hunters and cannon.

2. a. A horse used, or adapted for use, in hunting.

1687 *Lond. Gaz.* No. 2296/4 A milk white Mare above 14 hands..a very good Hunter. **1786** MRS. PIOZZI *Anecd. Johnson* in *Boswell* (1831) I. 512 He certainly rode on Mr. Thrale's old hunter. **1882** PEBODY *Eng. Journalism* xvi. 120 The dash and decision with which, upon a thorough-bred hunter, he rode to hounds.

b. A dog used in or adapted for hunting.

1605 SHAKS. *Macb.* III. i. 97 The valued file Distinguishes the swift, the slow, the subtle, The House-keeper, the Hunter. **1685** *Lond. Gaz.* No. 2037/4 To be sold 14 Couple of Harriers, very good Hunters, and have good Mouths. **1898** *Daily News* 5 Oct. 6/6 A very close hunter, and a fine hound to boot.

3. An animal that hunts or chases its prey; *spec.* **a.** = *hunting-spider* (see HUNTING *ppl. a.* b); **b.** The Jamaican cuckoo, *Hyetornis pluvialis.*

1658 ROWLAND *Moufet's Theat. Ins.* 1058 Spiders..others live in the open air, and from their greediness are called hunters or wolves. **1667** MILTON *P.L.* XI. 188 The Beast that reigns in Woods, First Hunter then. **1847** GOSSE & HILL *Birds Jamaica* 277 *Hunter.* Old Man.—Rainbird... The appellation of Rainbird is indiscriminately applied to both this and the preceding [sc. *Saurothera vetula*], as is, in a lesser degree, that of Old Man. I use a term by which I have heard it distinguished,..perhaps derived from the perseverance with which it hunts..for its prey. **1885** LADY BRASSEY *The Trades* 133 The most formidable of these insects appears to be the 'hunter ant'. **1960** J. BOND *Birds W. Indies* 116 Chestnut-bellied cuckoo. *Hyetornis pluvialis.* Local names: Old Man Bird; Hunter; Rain Bird.

4. = *hunting-watch*: see HUNTING *vbl. sb.* 3 b.

1851 *Illustr. Catal. Gt. Exhib.* 1268 A hunter, engraved, enamel dial, 1½ inches diameter. **1884** F. J. BRITTEN *Watch & Clockm.* 122 Hunter..[is] a watch case that has a metal cover over the dial.

5. *attrib.* and *Comb.* **a.** in sense 1, as ***hunter-boy, -craft, -crew, -goddess, -spear, -train, -troop, -warrior; hunter-like, -seeming*** adjs.; **b.** in sense 2, as ***hunter action, -breeder, -breeding, -fancier, -horse, -steed***; **c.** in sense 3, as ***hunter ant***; **hunter-spider** = sense 3 a.

1823 in Joanna Baillie *Collect. Poems* 15 A *hunter-boy blew horn beneath it. **1856** H. H. DIXON *Post & Paddock* i. 2 An old *hunter-breeder's confession. *Ibid.* 7 The Shropshire men..are more careful, both as to pedigree and style, in their *hunter-breeding. **1851** MAYNE REID *Scalp Hunt.* v, Different tricks known in *hunter-craft. **1838** MISS PARDOE *River & Desert* II. 53 Dedicated to the *Hunter-Goddess. **1735** SOMERVILLE *Chase* IV. 240 The *Hunter-Horse, Once kind Associate of his sylvan Toils. **1555–8** PHAER *Æneid* I. B j, *Hunterlyke her bow she bare, her lockes went with the wynd. **1483** *Cath. Angl.* 192/2 An *Hunter spere, *venabulum.* **1867** *Amer. Naturalist* I. 409 This very large *hunter-spider [*sc.* the tarantula] makes its appearance in Texas some years as early as the twenty-fifth of May. **1863** LYELL *Antiq. Man* 23 When the habits of the *hunter state predominated over those of the pastoral, venison was more eaten than the flesh of..sheep. **1697** DRYDEN *Æneid* XI. 1003 Young Ornitus bestrode a *hunter steed. **1735** SOMERVILLE *Chase* II. 357 The busy *Hunter-Train mark out the Ground.

d. Combinations with *hunter's*, in specialized senses: as **hunter's beef, pudding** (see quots.); **hunter's green** (see quot. 1957); **†hunter's mass** (cf. Ger. *jägermesse*), 'a short mass said in great haste for hunters who were eager to start for the chase' (Nares); **hunter's moon**, a name for the full moon next after the HARVEST MOON (q.v.).

1879 MRS. A. E. JAMES *Ind. Househ. Managem.* 55 A hump of beef is..best spiced and cured, as *hunter's beef is made at home. **1872** *Young Englishwoman* Nov. 599/1 Sombre greens,..*chasseur*, or *hunter's-green, myrtle, cypress. **1957** M. B. PICKEN *Fashion Dict.* 181/2 *Hunter's green*, dark, slightly yellowish green. **1595** COPLEY *Wits, Fits, & Fancies* 60 A Gentleman pray'd him to say a *Hunters Masse (meaning a briefe Masse). **1710** *Brit. Apollo* III. No. 70. 2/1 The Country People call this the *Hunters-Moon. **1854** TOMLINSON *Arago's Astron.* 171 There can, therefore, be but two full moons in the year which rise during a week almost at the same time as the sun sets; the former, occurring in September, is called the Harvest-Moon; and the latter, in the month of October, being in a similar predicament, is termed the Hunter's Moon. **1815** SIMOND *Tour Gt. Brit.* I. 45 This plum-pudding..This precious faculty of not losing anything from waiting, has made it be named emphatically *Hunter's Pudding, *Pudding de Chasseur.*

e. hunter-killer *a.*, designating a naval vessel or group of vessels equipped to locate and destroy enemy vessels, esp. submarines. Also as *sb.*

1948 *U.S. Naval Inst. Proc.* LXXIV. 505/2 The other two will be classified as 'hunter-killers'—destroyers with the prime purpose of tracking down submarines, instead of operating on convoy duty. **1950** *Jane's Fighting Ships 1950–51* 7 A new anti-submarine type of light cruiser, known as a hunter-killer ship, will be completed in 1951. **1957** *Times Lit. Suppl.* 20 Dec. 771/3 The escort carrier Guadalcanal and her 'hunter-killer' group of four escort destroyers. **1962** *Daily Tel.* 10 Dec. 18/4 Britain's first nuclear hunter-killer submarine, is expected to leave the..yard of her builders,..on Wednesday or Thursday for sea-trials. **1972** *Sci. Amer.* July 16/3 A hunter-killer submarine is large enough to carry an array of hydrophones to produce a narrow listening beam for long-range detection.

Hunterian (hʌn'tɪərɪən), *a.* [f. proper name *Hunter* + -IAN.] Of or belonging to John Hunter (1728–1793), a famous Scottish surgeon and physiologist, or his elder brother William Hunter (1718–1783), an anatomist and obstetric surgeon; esp. in ***Hunterian*** (also ***Hunter's***) ***canal***, ***Hunterian chancre*** (see quots.), investigated by John Hunter.

1807–26 S. COOPER *First Lines Surg.* (ed. 5) 224 That most of the Hunterian theories about it were always false. **1824** WATT *Bibl. Brit.* III. s.v., Hunterian Museum,..consisting principally of Collections in Natural History, the Fine Arts, and Antiquities, now the property of the Glasgow University. **1875** EMERSON *Lett. & Soc. Aims* ix. 220 The Hunterian law of arrested developement is not confined to vegetable and animal structure. **1881** *Syd. Soc. Lex.* s.v. *Chancre*, The Hunterian or hard chancre being the local manifestation of syphilis. **1886** *Ibid.*, *Hunter's canal*, a triangular canal giving passage to the femoral artery and vein and the internal saphenous nerve.

hunterite ('hʌntəraɪt). *Min.* [Named, 1859, after Rev. R. Hunter of Nagpore: see -ITE.] A synonym of CIMOLITE.

1859 HAUGHTON in *Phil. Mag.* IV. xvii. 18. **1868** DANA *Min.* (ed. 5) 457.

hunterman ('hʌntəmən). [f. HUNTER + MAN *sb.*[1]] Used widely outside the British Isles as a local term for 'hunter, huntsman'.

1891 'MARK TWAIN' tr. *Hoffmann's Slovenly Peter* (1935), Behold the dreadful hunterman In all his fateful glory stand. **1907** W. JEKYLL *Jamaican Song & Story* 137 Dory Dunn is a hunterman. **1913** *Chambers's Jrnl.* 22 Feb. 184/1 Nearly every village has its professional 'hunterman', whose duty it is to kill the larger game which do damage to the crops. **1922** H. B. HERMON-HODGE *Up against it in Nigeria* iv. 55 Huntermen are for the most part undependable. **1930** 'GREENHORN' *Tinker, Tailor* xi. 272 His hunterman came back to look for him and shot the python. **1933** *Amer. Speech* VIII. I. 50/1 *Hunterman*, hunter. One often sees this in country newspapers [of Ozarks]. **1954** G. DURRELL *Bafut Beagles* vi. 116, I tink dis hunter man be best for all.

†'hunteth. *Obs.* Forms: 1 huntoþ, -aþ, 3 hunteþ, honteþ. [OE. *huntoð* masc. f. *hunt-ian* to hunt + suffix *-oð*:—OTeut. *-ôþuz* = L. *-ātus* (*vēnātus*).] Hunting; the chase.

c **900** *Charter of Denewulf* in Kemble *Cod. Dipl.* V. 162 His men beon ʒearuwe, ʒe to ripe, ʒe to huntoðe. *c* **1000** ÆLFRIC *Gen.* xxv. 28 Isaac lufode Esau for his huntoþe. *c* **1000** *Sax. Leechd.* III. 212 Huntað don ʒestreon ʒetacnað. *c* **1200** *Trin. Coll. Hom.* 209 Ure fo fareð on hunteð. **1297** R. GLOUC. 8639 Vor to wende an honteþ in þe nywe forest.

huntilite ('hʌntɪlaɪt). *Min.* [Named after T. S. Hunt, an American scientist + -LITE.] Native arsenide of silver, from Silver Islet, Lake Superior.

hunting ('hʌntɪŋ), *vbl. sb.* [f. HUNT *v.* + -ING[1].]

1. The action of the verb HUNT. **a.** The action or practice of chasing game or other wild animals, either for profit or sport; the chase; venery.

c **1000** ÆLFRIC *Colloq.* in Wright *Voc.* 5 Hwæt dest þu be þinre huntunge? *c* **1205** LAY. 21342 He hafeð bihalues Baðen his huntinge bilæfued. *c* **1290** *S. Eng. Leg.* I. 349/148 þat þis child scholde wende An hontingue. *c* **1375** *Sc. Leg. Saints, Blasius* 60 þe president Til huntyne has his knychtis sent. **1484** CAXTON *Fables of Poge* (1889) 4 The studye of the huntynge and hawkynge is a slouful cure. **1548** HALL *Chron., Edw. IV* 194 b, The king being on huntyng in the

forest of Wychwod. 1696 tr. *Duquesne's Voy. E. Ind.* 134 No other Island..has better hunting. 1781 GIBBON *Decl. & F.* II. 112 Constans..was pursuing in the adjacent forest his favourite amusement of hunting. 1781 BECKFORD (*title*) Essays on Hunting. 1879 SIR G. CAMPBELL *White & Black* 330 What they call 'hunting' in America is not hunting in our sense, but shooting; either ordinary shooting, or drives for big game.

b. With *a* and *pl.* A hunt, a chase.

*a*950 *Rit. Eccl. Dunelm.* (Surtees) 118 Of hvntvngvm. *c*1420 *Anturs of Arth.* lv, Suche a hunting in a holt, aw noȝte to be hidde. 15.. *Chevy Chase* i, A woeful hunting once there did In Chevy-chase befall. 1611 SPEED *Hist. Gt. Brit.* VIII. iii. (1632) 399 That vpon the Lords Sabbath, publike Faires..Huntings, and all secular actions should not be exercised. 1727 A. HAMILTON *New Acc. E. Ind.* I. xxii. 263, I saw, in one of these Huntings, above a Dozen of Deer killed. 1871 FREEMAN *Norm. Conq.* IV. xx. 609 Services to be rendered in the royal huntings.

c. The chasing of their prey by animals.

1382 WYCLIF *1 Macc.* iii. 4 As whelp of lyoun rorynge in his huntyng. 1665 HOOKE *Microgr.* 202 These Spiders..are nothing so eager of hunting as they are in Italy.

d. The action of chasing, pursuing or searching; a pursuit or search. Also with *adv.* as ***hunting-up, -down.***

1542-5 BRINKLOW *Lament.* 4a, Then will they ronne..a whore hountinge after their false prophetes. 1589 L. WRIGHT (*title*) The Hunting of Antichrist. 1651 HOBBES *Leviath.* I. iii. 10 A hunting out of the causes. *a*1700 B. E. *Dict. Cant. Crew, Hunting*, decoying, or drawing others into Play. 1796 COLQUHOUN *Police Metrop.* 403 The driving of Cattle improperly, usually termed *bullock-hunting*. 1876 MISS YONGE *Womankind* xxiv. 204 A hunting-up of faults. 1901 *Westm. Gaz.* 7 Sept. 5/1 Sweeping movements will give place to hunting-down tactics where the country favours the latter. 1945 *Tribune* 9 Nov. 11/1 The hunting-down of war criminals.

e. *Change-ringing.* (See HUNT *v.* 7.)

f. The action of a machine, instrument, system, etc., that is hunting (see HUNT *v.* 7b); an undesirable oscillation about an equilibrium speed, position, or state.

1880 R. E. CROMPTON *Electr. Light for Industr. Use* 21 This causes a swinging or, as it is called by engine men, a 'hunting' action of the governor. 1894 *Rep. Brit. Assoc. Adv. Sci.* 759 If the isochronous governor works a slow-acting relay the hunting may be so serious that the steam supply alternates between complete cut-off and full supply. 1920 *Whittaker's Electr. Engineer's Pocket-bk.* (ed. 4) 223 If the damping is very small, oscillations or hunting may go on for a considerable time before the machine finally rotates steadily. 1932 *Discovery* Oct. 331/1 There was no suggestion of 'hunting' and the image remained exactly central in the [television] screen for the whole half hour. 1942 *Rev. Sci. Instruments* XIII. 218 The recording is easily accomplished at pen speeds of 12·7 cm per second across 25 cm of chart without 'hunting' taking place. 1943 *Electronic Engin.* XV. 438/2 A method for the determination of the power angle oscillations of a synchronous motor during hunting is described. 1950 *Gloss. Aeronaut. Terms* (*B.S.I.*) 8 *Hunting*, an uncontrolled oscillation about the flight path, the amplitude of which remains approximately constant. *Ibid.* 45 *Hunting*, angular oscillation of a [rotor] blade about the drag hinge. 1951 *Engineering* 6 Apr. 401/3 The train was derailed..because of a slight but periodic variation in the cant of the track which synchronised with the hunting periodicity of the engine. 1951 S. DEUTSCH *Theory & Design Television Receivers* xiii. 431 Hunting is revealed by a horizontal weaving or vibration of the picture. 1959 *Times* 27 Apr. (Rubber Industry Suppl.) p. vi/5 The control of the side-to-side swaying known to railway engineers as 'hunting'. 1968 *Practical Motorist* Dec. 459/1 *Hunting*, a rhythmical increase and decrease in the idling speed of an engine, caused by an over-rich mixture. 1971 *Nature* 2 Apr. 283/1 Society, regarded as a non-linear feedback system, is showing the signs of oscillation ('hunting') which one expects.

g. *Telephony.* An operation in which a selector or switch automatically goes through a group of lines until it reaches a free one and makes connection with it; now used esp. of the connection of a calling line with one of a group of outgoing lines.

1912 J. POOLE *Pract. Telephone Handbk.* (ed. 5) xxxii. 528 There is no 'hunting' for disengaged lines as in the case of selectors. 1933 K. B. MILLER *Telephone Theory & Pract.* III. v. 263 Automatic trunk hunting may be necessary to find an idle line. 1966 RUBIN & HALLER *Communication Switching Syst.* i. 31 In the Ericsson 500-line switch..the select motion is a rotation and the hunting action is radially outward to a free trunk.

†**2.** *concr.* Game killed in hunting. (Cf. VENISON.) *Obs.*

*c*1460 *Towneley Myst.* v. 19 Haue, ete, fader, of myn huntyng. 1608 TOPSELL *Serpents* (1658) 709 Pindus..did daily give unto him the greatest part of his hunting.

3. *attrib.* and *Comb.* **a.** General: Of, belonging to, used or worn in, adapted for, or engaged in hunting, as ***hunting-bit, boat, -boot, -bout, bridle, -cap, carpet, -clothes, -coat, -country, -craft, -cry, -day, -dress, -excursion, -frock, -gear, -habit, -hat, -horse, -javelin, -knife, -language, -nag, -net, -party, path, -place, -pole, pony, print, rifle, -saddle, -season, -skirt, -spear, -spur, -staff, -sword, -term, -tide, tie, -toil, -voyage, -whip***; for the accommodation of huntsmen, as ***hunting-camp, -house, -lodge, tower***, or of horses used in hunting, as ***hunting-stable***.

1696 *Lond. Gaz.* No. 3217/4 A white Leather Side Saddle, and *Hunting-Bit. 1828 *Western Monthly Rev.* I. 577 The passengers of the *hunting boats..saw him. 1894 Hunting boat [see BIDARKA]. 1895 *Montgomery Ward Catal.* 521/1 Men's black English grain leather '*hunting boots', double sole, laced leg and instep. 1928 S. SASSOON *Mem. Fox-Hunting Man* 143, I was going to try on my new hunting clothes and my new hunting boots. 1957 M. B. PICKEN *Fashion Dict.* 181/2 *Hunting boot*, high, laced boot with waterproof sole. 1715 LEONI *Palladio's Archit.* (1742) II. 83 Beasts..either for public *Hunting-bouts, or for the Shows in the Amphitheatres. 1939-40 *Army & Navy Stores Catal.* p. xxxix, *Hunting bridles. 1963 BLOODGOOD & SANTINI *Horseman's Dict.* 111 *Hunting bridle*, any bridle suitable for hunting. 1963 E. H. EDWARDS *Saddlery* iii. 32 Hunting bridles should be made of leather having plenty of substance and the width of the cheek will probably be ⅝ in. with the rein. 1770 WASHINGTON *Writ.* (1889) II. 310 The Indians..have their *hunting-camps and cabins all along the river. 1814 J. MAYNE *Jrnl.* (1909) 184 The postilions..do not, like our royal drivers, wear *hunting-caps. 1946 M. C. SELF *Horseman's Encycl.* 219 *Hunting cap*, the velvet cap worn by farmers, Masters and Servants of the hunt. 1931 A. U. DILLEY *Oriental Rugs & Carpets* Pl. 9 (*caption*), Finest Extant *Hunting Carpet, Middle Sixteenth Century. 1960 H. HAYWARD *Antique Coll.* 146/1 *Hunting carpets*, Persian carpets with elaborate hunting scenes, realistically depicted. 1625 K. LONG tr. *Barclay's Argenis* IV. xiii. 282 Comming in his *hunting-clothes. 1789 R. F. GREVILLE *Diary* 16 Jan. (1930) 171 Asked Me if I had my *Hunting Coat with Me. 1909 *Westm. Gaz.* 9 Oct. 15/1 Ladies..may always choose a little, short coat, known to French tailors as a hunting coat. 1921 *Daily Colonist* (Victoria, B.C.) 15 Oct. 10/1 (Advt.), Pheasant Shooting Begins..Hunting Coats, with front and rear game pockets, £8.75. 1928 S. SASSOON *Mem. Fox-Hunting Man.* 136 Stephen, who was wearing a pink silk cap and a long-skirted black hunting-coat, silently received from the groom the saddle and weight-cloth. 1708 *Lond. Gaz.* No. 4439/4 An Estate..situated..in..a good *Hunting Country. 1946 M. C. SELF *Horseman's Encycl.* 219 Nothing even faintly resembling the English hunting country exists in North America. 1808 SCOTT *Marm.* I. viii, Each..Knew *hunting-craft by lake and wood. 1864 TENNYSON *Aylmer's Field* (ed. 1) ad. fin., There the thin weasel with faint *hunting-cry Follows the mouse. 1859 —— *Enid* 165 Wearing neither *hunting-dress Nor weapon. 1801 A. MACKENZIE *Voy. from Montreal* 113 The Indians went on an *hunting excursion. 1856 M. J. HOLMES *'Lena Rivers* xxvi. 282 He had gone off on a hunting excursion. *c*1450 *R. Gloucester's Chron.* (1724) 482/2 (MS. Coll. Arms) Ofte holdeth he an honde swerdes, bowes, and *huntyngere. 1711 *Hunting-habit [see HABIT *sb.* 3]. 1881 MRS. O'DONOGHUE *Ladies on Horseback* III. vi. 83 If a hunting-habit be properly cut it will require no shotting. *Ibid.* 253 That *hunting-hats frequently fall off. 1565-73 COOPER *Thesaurus* s.v. *Equus, Venator equus*, a *hunting horse. 1686 *Lond. Gaz.* No. 2187/4 The keeping of Hunting-Horses. 1686 J. DUNTON *Lett. fr. New-Eng.* (1867) 277 Guides who will..oftentimes find out *Hunting-Houses, and other Lodgings at night. 1625 K. LONG tr. *Barclay's Argenis* IV. xiii. 282 In his hand he held his *hunting-javelin. 1803 in *Minnesota Hist.* (1940) XXI. 126 When the defendant came to pierce his tent with his *hunting knife..the larger part of the goods had already been moved to the spot agreed upon. 1842 MRS. GORE *Fascin.* 92 His girdle was garnished with horn-handled hunting-knives. 1933 B. WILLOUGHBY *Alaskans All* 3 His flannel shirt, high laced boots, the hunting-knife in his belt..made it difficult for me to realize he was a priest. 1949 *Chicago Tribune* 22 June II. 1/4 A policeman took a 6 inch hunting knife from the waist of one of the white boys. 1809 A. HENRY *Trav.* 6 A solitary Indian *hunting-lodge, built with branches of trees. 1826 MISS MITFORD *Village* Ser. II. (1863) 253 The old manorial Hall ..is cut down into a villa, or a hunting-lodge. *a*1680 BUTLER *Rem.* (1759) II. 81 Like a *Hunting-nag, [he] leaps over what he cannot get through. 1788 W. BLANE *Hunt. Excurs.* 3 His annual *hunting party. 1820 in *Minnesota Hist.* (1942) XXIII. 249 We found a *hunting path which..led directly to Sandy Lake. 1821 T. NUTTALL *Jrnl. Trav. Arkansa 1819* 167 We here crossed by a hunting path. 1730 A. GORDON *Maffei's Amphith.* 96 Buildings into which Beasts were brought, which they called *Hunting-Places. 1886 *Outing* Apr. 7/1, I was riding a well-trained *hunting pony. 1967 N. FREELING *Strike Out* 72 He makes these series of kind of *huntin' prints. 1973 M. MACKINTOSH *King & Two Queens* v. 76 Eighteenth-century English hunting prints hung on the pine-panelled walls. 1856 in *Kansas State Hist. Soc. Trans.* (1890) IV. 504 The marauders were well armed with muskets,..*hunting rifles,..bowie-knives, etc. 1886 *Outing* Mar. 615 No hunting-rifles in the world possess greater accuracy. 1956 'E. MCBAIN' *Cop Hater* (1963) xix. 143 He said he'd shot himself while cleaning his hunting rifle. 1678 *Lond. Gaz.* No. 1274/4 A Black Gelding..having on him a *hunting Saddle, and a blew Saddle-Cloth. 1730 A. GORDON *Maffei's Amphith.* 96 In the Canons of the Synod called *Quinisestus*, the *Hunting-Shews were prohibited. 1810 SCOTT *Lady of L.* I. xxvii, A battle-axe, a *hunting-spear. 1480 *Wardr. Acc. Edw. IV* (1830) 148 A paire of *hunting spurres parcelle gilt. *a*1649 DRUMM. OF HAWTH. *Hist. Jas. III* Wks. (1711) 42 Sir Alexander Boyd..struck the reverend governour with a *hunting-staff upon the head. 1869 TENNYSON *Pelleas* 359 That all the old echoes hidden in the wall Rang out like hollow woods at *hunting-tide. *c*1840 LADY WILTON *Art of Needlework* xiii. 189 The Hibernian Tie: The Eastern Tie: *The Hunting Tie: The Yankee Tie. 1907 *Yesterday's Shopping* (1969) p. xxxix, Hunting ties, ladies'. 1753 *De Foe's Tour Gt. Brit.* I. ii. 113 An Eminence, where now stands an *Hunting-tower of Brick. 1683 *Lond. Gaz.* No. 1842/8 A long *Hunting-Whip, with an Ivory handle. 1859 *Art Taming Horses* ix. 149 Every hunting-whip should have a lash, but it need not be long.

b. Special Combs.: **hunting-box**, a small house for occupation during the hunting season (see BOX *sb.*² 14); **hunting-case**, a watch-case with a hinged cover to protect the glass (orig. against accidents in hunting); **hunting-coal** (see quot.); **hunting-crop**, a straight whipstock with a leather loop for insertion of a thong or lash (CROP *sb.* 7c); **hunting-field**, the field or ground on which a hunt, esp. a fox-hunt, is going on; also, the body of mounted huntsmen following the hounds; **hunting-flask**, a flask for liquor, carried during hunting; **hunting-jug**, a jug adorned with figures of huntsmen, horses, dogs, stags, etc.; **hunting leopard**, the Cheetah (*Felis jubata*), which is tamed and used in hunting in India; †**hunting mass** = *hunter's mass* (see HUNTER 5d); †**hunting-match**, a hunt taken part in by a number of persons; †**hunting oath**, a bold or outspoken oath such as a huntsman might utter; **hunting-piece**, a picture representing a hunting scene; **hunting-pudding** = *hunter's pudding* (see HUNTER 5d); **hunting-seat**, a country-house reserved for occupation during the hunting season; **hunting-shirt** *U.S.*, 'a blowse or shirt originally made of deerskin and highly ornamented, worn by trappers, hunters and travellers on the Western frontier' (Bartlett *Dict. Amer.*); **hunting-song**, a song sung during a hunt, or relating to hunting, usually characterized by melodic phrases imitating the sound of a hunting-horn; also applied to an instrumental composition of the same character; †**hunting tail**, a horse's tail cut in the manner practised with horses used for hunting; **hunting tartan** (see quot. 1959); so ***hunting Stewart tartan***, etc.; **hunting-watch**, a watch having a *hunting-case* to protect the glass.

1799 *Times* 1 June 4/3 A Family Cottage, or *Hunting Box, pleasantly situate in a sporting part of the country. 1814 JANE AUSTEN *Mansf. Park* III. x. 208 Some small hunting-box in the vicinity of every thing so dear. 1821 BYRON *Juan* v. lx, Babel was Nimrod's hunting-box. 1838 LYTTON *Alice* 131 The old admiral has a hunting-box in the neighbourhood. 1883 *Standard* 16 Jan. 2/4 *Hunting coal was what was left after general workings. 1857 *Hunting-crop [see CROP *sb.* 7c]. 1881 MRS. O'DONOGHUE *Ladies on Horseback* 218 A short hunting-crop without a lash would do. 1890 BOLDREWOOD *Col. Reformer* (1891) 217 Light hunting crops having slender thongs. *c*1680 DK. YORK in J. Taylor *Scot. Covenant.* (Cassell) 117 There would never be peace in Scotland till the whole of the country south of the Forth was turned into a *hunting-field. 1846-83 EG.-WARBURTON *Hunt. Songs* lxxxi. (ed. 7) 218 Each in turn first and foremost the hunting field led. 1859 *Art Taming Horses* i. 22 [His] equestrian performances on the course and in the hunting-field. *a*1899 *Mod.* He lost his life accidentally in the hunting-field. 1824 SCOTT *St. Ronan's* vii, He has a *hunting-flask usually about him, which contains as good medicine as yours to the full. 1781 *Phil. Trans.* LXXI. 2 The *hunting Leopard, or Indian Chittah. 1881 HUNTER *Gaz. Ind.* IV. 619 The cheetah or hunting leopard must be carefully distinguished from the leopard proper. 1597 JAS. I. *Demonol.* I. v. 18 Like a Papist Priest, dispatching a *hunting Masse. 1845 NEALE *Mirror Faith* 15 King Oswald heareth hunting-mass. *a*1637 B. JONSON *Discov., Socrates* Wks. (Rtldg.) 764/2 What neede wee know any thing..more then a horse-race, or a *hunting-match. 1708 SWIFT *Predict.*, Not daring to propose a hunting-match. 1563-87 FOXE *A. & M.* (1631) III. x. 106/1 Swearing and raging with an *hunting oath or two. 1765 H. WALPOLE in *Lett. C'tess Suffolk* (1824) II. 314 Huge *hunting-pieces in frames of all-coloured golds. 1785 MRS. A. M. BENNETT *Juv. Indiscretions* (1786) IV. 26 She was famous for making *hunting puddings. 1716 ADDISON *Freeholder* No. 22 ¶2 A Traveller..who had..lost his *Hunting-Seat. 1740 GRAY *Let.* Poems (1775) 79 A house built by one of the Grand Dukes for a hunting-seat. 1775 J. TRUMBULL in Sparks *Corr. Amer. Rev.* (1853) I. 32, I have ordered our Commissaries..to send to your camp all the *hunting-shirts they can procure. 1876 BANCROFT *Hist. U.S.* IV. xv. 419 The hardy backwoodsman, clad in a hunting-shirt and deerskin leggins. 1727 SOMERVILLE *Poems* (1790) I. 254 *Hunting-song. 1846-83 EG.-WARBURTON *Hunt. Songs* (ed. 7) Introd. 9 An inappropriate introduction to a new edition of these Hunting Songs. 1686 *Lond. Gaz.* No. 2163/4 A brown bay Mare..with a *Hunting-Tail. 1855 A. STANLEY *Let.* 8 Sept. (1927) iii. 74 The carpets are Royal Stewart Tartan and green *Hunting Stewart [tartan]. 1864 QUEEN VICTORIA *Let.* 26 Mar. in R. Fulford *Dearest Mama* (1968) 312 What is Anna's dress made of? I am going to send her a Hunting Stewart velvet. 1871 *Monthly Packet* Oct. 396 Their new winter frocks of Hunting Stewart tartan. 1959 BAIN & MACDOUGALL *Clans & Tartans* (ed. 4) 28 Hunting tartans are worn for sport and outdoor activities. Brown or some other dark hue is the predominant colour. When a Clan possessed a brightly coloured tartan it was unsuitable for hunting purposes, and hunting setts [patterns] were devised to make the wearer less conspicuous. The colours were arranged so that, when concealed in the heather, the tartan blended with the surroundings. 1969 O. HESKY *Sequin Syndicate* x. 102 A kimono in the colours of the Royal Stuart hunting tartan. 1844 DICKENS *Mart. Chuz.* xiii, A gold *hunting-watch..capped and jewelled in four holes.

ˈ**hunting**, *ppl. a.* [f. HUNT *v.* + -ING².] **a.** That hunts: see the verb. (In quot. 1340 *absol.* as *sb.*)

*a*1340 HAMPOLE *Psalter* cxxiii. 6 Fra þe snare of huntand. 1682 T. A. *Carolina* 21 One hunting Indian. 1859 *Art Taming Horses* viii. 134 Hunting farmers and hunting country surgeons. *Ibid.* ix. 148 The 'Napoleons' of hunting ladies. 1887 ABBAY *White Mare Whitestonecliff* 173 The huntingest squire In the huntingest shire.

b. In special collocations (often hyphened): as **hunting-cog** (see COG *sb.*² 1); **hunting-man**, a man addicted to hunting; **hunting spider**, a spider that hunts its prey instead of lying in wait for it; **hunting wasp**, a wasp that preys upon other insects.

1665 HOOKE *Microgr.* 199 Not unlike a hunting Spider. 1812-16 J. SMITH *Panorama Sc. & Art* I. 352 It is a useful precaution..to give the wheel what is called a *hunting-cog*; that is, one cog more than what will answer to an exact division of the wheel by the trundle. This being done, every cog..will take the next staff or round behind the one which

it took in the former revolution. **1859** *Art Taming Horses* i. 21 Almost every distinguished horseman and hunting-man in the three kingdoms. **1885** *New Bk. Sports* 1 As well as a hunting-man knows his country. **1916** A. T. DE MATTOS tr. J. H. Fabre (*title*) The hunting wasp. **1925** R. W. G. HINGSTON in E. F. Norton *Fight for Everest, 1924* 287 Beetles and hunting-spiders found a shelter on it [*sc.* a moraine]. **1928** —— *Problems of Instinct* 100 Hunting wasps ..sting their victims with surgical precision. **1941** W. S. BRISTOWE *Comity of Spiders* II. v. 230 Some of these hunting spiders seek their prey by day and others by night. **1948** 'J. CROMPTON' *Hunting Wasp* i. 17 A large number of the hunting wasps sing at their work. **1964** V. B. WIGGLESWORTH *Life of Insects* xiii. 227 The hunting wasp *Philanthus* stocks its solitary nest solely with honey-bees. **1966** E. PALMER *Plains of Camdeboo* xiv. 233 On the farm we know most of the diurnal species as jagspinnekoppe or hunting spiders.

hunting dog, hunting-dog. [f. HUNTING *vbl. sb.* and *ppl. a.*]

1. A dog used for hunting game. ***Hunting Dogs***, a northern constellation, *Canes Venatici*.

1863 LYELL *Antiq. Man* 25 The people of the bronze age possessed a larger hunting-dog. **1868** LOCKYER *Guillemin's Heavens* (ed. 3) 326 We must notice the Hunting Dogs, above Berenice's Hair. **1886** *Pall Mall G.* 27 Aug. 5/1 Our old friend the hunting dog.

2. A name for two animals of the dog tribe which hunt their prey in packs. **a.** The Hyena-dog or Painted Hyena (*Lycaon*) of South Africa. **b.** The Dhole or wild dog of India.

1838 *Penny Cycl.* XII. 371/1 The animal..he describes under the name of *Lycaon, the Hunting Dog.* **1866** WOOD *Pop. Nat. Hist.* I. 89 The latter animal [Dhole]..is sometimes termed the Hunting Dog in compliment to its powers. **1883** W. H. FLOWER in *Encycl. Brit.* XV. 439/1 *Lycaon pictus*, the Cape Hunting Dog..is very distinct externally from all the other Canidæ.

Huntingdon (ˈhʌntɪŋdən). The title of Selina, Countess of *Huntingdon* (1707–91), used in (***Lady*** or ***Countess of***) ***Huntingdon('s) Connection*** to designate a Calvinistic Methodist sect founded by her. So **Huntingˈdonian** *a.* and *sb.*

[**1773** J. WESLEY *Let.* 22 Oct. (1931) VI. 51, I am afraid Lady Huntingdon's preachers will do little good wherever they go. They are wholly swallowed up in that detestable doctrine of Predestination, and can talk of nothing else.] *a* **1800** M. ROBINSON *Mem.* (1803) I. 90 Though Mr Harris was not a disciple of the Huntingdonian School, he was a constant church visitor on every Sunday. **1874** J. H. BLUNT *Dict. Sects* 205/1 *Huntingdon Connexion*, a sect of Calvinistic Methodists... Its history dates from the year 1748. **1884** *Encycl. Dict.* IV. 241/2 The denomination which rose out of his zealous labours was generally called..the Countess of Huntingdon's Connexion... Called also Lady Huntingdon's Connexion and Huntingdonians. **1970** *Brewer's Dict. Phr. & Fable* (rev. ed.) 556/2 *Huntingdonians*, members of 'the Countess of Huntingdon's Connexion', a sect of Calvinistic Methodists founded in 1748... The churches founded by the countess..are mostly affiliated with the Congregational Union.

ˈhunting-ground. [f. HUNTING *vbl. sb.*] **a.** A district or tract of country adapted for hunting, or in which hunting is practised.

1777 ROBERTSON *Hist. Amer.* (1783) II. 61 Tribes seated on..hunting-grounds abounding so much with game, that they have a regular and plentiful supply of nourishment with little labour. **1837** W. IRVING *Capt. Bonneville* II. 18 All the fastnesses, defiles, and favourable hunting grounds of the country. **1874** GREEN *Short Hist.* ii. §4. 72 Thousands of Hampshire peasants were driven from their homes to make him a hunting-ground.

b. *fig.* A place (book, etc.) made the scene of any kind of hunt or search, or containing a supply of something for which one hunts.

1877 LADY C. SCHREIBER *Jrnl.* 22 Mar. (1911) I. 6 Our favourite hunting-ground, Holland, appeared particularly fruitful. **1880** *Academy* 21 Aug. 133/3 The *Moyen de Parvenir* was a favourite hunting-ground of the author of *Tristram Shandy*. **1888** *Daily News* 15 Sept. 2/5 The hunting ground of pickpockets.

c. ***happy hunting-ground(s***: those expected by the American Indians in the world to come; hence, the future state. Also *fig.* a favourable place for hunting, collecting, or making acquisitions.

1826 J. F. COOPER *Last of Mohicans* (1831) 400 A young man has gone to the happy hunting grounds. **1836** W. IRVING *Astoria* (1849) 249 They will see the happy hunting-grounds, with the souls of the brave and good living in tents in green meadows. **1890** GUNTER *Miss Nobody* v, That he may send them to the happy hunting grounds also. **1894** MASKELYNE *Sharps & Flats* i. 6 At the present moment England is the happy hunting-ground of the swindling fraternity. **1938** D. DU MAURIER *Rebecca* ii. 13 My faithful Jasper has gone to the happy hunting grounds. **1972** *Nature* 17 Mar. 98/1 The effect of liquid sodium on other metals has been a particularly happy hunting ground for chemists.

hunting-horn.

1. A horn or bugle on which signals are blown in hunting.

1694 LD. MOLESWORTH *Acc. Denmark* 160 The Huntsmen..having their great Brass Hunting-horns about their Necks. **1846–83** EG.-WARBURTON *Hunt. Songs* lxxiii. (ed. 7) 206 Diana it proved, who her hunting horn blew. **1879** W. H. STONE in Grove *Dict. Mus.* I. 748/1 The hunting horn finally adopted differs from the orchestral horn in consisting of an unbroken spiral of three turns.

2. On a side-saddle, the second pommel on the near side, against which the left knee presses; first introduced for use in hunting; the leaping-head. (See HORN *sb.* 22 b.) Also ***hunting-horn crutch, leaping-horn.***

1854 *Art Taming Horses* viii. 117 The third or hunting-horn pommel must be fitted to the rider. *Ibid.* ix. 143 With the hunting-horn crutch the seat of a woman is stronger than that of a man, for she presses her right leg down over the upright pommel, and the left leg up against the hunting-horn. *Ibid.* 144 Ladies' saddles ought invariably to be made with what is called the hunting-horn, or crutch, at the left side.

Huntingtonian (hʌntɪŋˈtəʊnɪən). [f. the name of William *Huntington* (1745–1813), an Antinomian preacher.] An adherent of the teachings of William Huntington.

1815 J. BLACKNER *Hist. Nottingham* iv. 114 Bethel chapel is now called Providence chapel; and is occupied by an inconsiderable party of Huntingtonians, without a regular preacher, they being adherents to the tenets of the late William Huntington, of coal-heaving celebriety [*sic*]. **1921** M. A. CANNEY *Encycl. Relig.* 184/2 *Huntingtonians*, the followers of William Huntington (1745–1813).

Huntington's chorea. *Med.* [f. the name of George *Huntington* (1851–1916), American neurologist, who described it in 1872 + CHOREA.] A rare hereditary disease of the brain manifested in middle age and characterized by irregular body movements, disturbance of speech, and progressive dementia. Also ***Huntington's disease.***

1889 *Jrnl. Nerv. & Mental Dis.* XVI. 69 To Huntington has generally been accorded the credit of first describing hereditary chorea, and writers even speak of the affection as 'Huntington's chorea'. **1892** *Jrnl. Mental Sci.* XXXVIII. 560 Cases of hereditary chorea (Huntington's disease). **1969** *New Scientist* 10 July 80/2 The onset of Huntington's chorea usually occurs rather late in reproductive life, at around 40 years of age. **1972** *New Yorker* 29 Jan. 30/3 Woody Guthrie ..died, in 1967, after a fifteen-year battle with Huntington's disease.

huntite (ˈhʌntaɪt). *Min.* [f. the name of Walter Frederick *Hunt* (b. 1882), American mineralogist + -ITE¹.] A white carbonate of magnesium and calcium, $CaMg_3(CO_3)_4$.

1953 G. T. FAUST in *Amer. Mineralogist* XXXVIII. 4 (*heading*) Huntite, $Mg_3Ca(CO_3)_4$, a new mineral. **1968** *Nature* 28 Dec. 1309/2 Investigations of sediments from the hypersaline environment of the Tuz Gölü, a seasonal salt lake in Central Anatolia, Turkey.., showed that huntite, $CaMg_3(CO_3)_4$, dolomite and magnesite are often present in the playa muds. **1973** *Nature* 5 Jan. 17/2 In next Monday's *Nature Physical Science* (January 8), Veen and Arndt describe for the first time the occurrence in soils of the mineral huntite, $CaMg_3(CO_3)_4$. *Ibid.* 17/3 Alias pahn-jahn, huntite powder is a white pigment which the Aborigines prefer to kaolin-based paint for personal and other decorative purposes.

huntress (ˈhʌntrɪs). [f. HUNTER + -ESS.] A female hunter.

1. A woman (or goddess) who hunts or engages in the chase.

c **1386** CHAUCER *Knt.'s T.* 1489 And ther with al Dyane gan appeere With bowe in honde right as an hunteress. **1470–85** MALORY *Arthur* XVIII. xxi, A lady dwell'd in that forest, and she was a grete huntresse. **1590** SPENSER *F.Q.* III. v. 27 In those same woods ye well remember may How that a noble hunteresse did wonne..Belphœbe was her name. **1703** ROWE *Ulyss.* II. i. 544 The Huntress Cynthia and her Train. **1709** STEELE *Tatler* No. 37 ¶2 Mrs. Alse Copswood, the Yorkshire Huntress. **1884** SYMONDS *Shaks. Predec.* x. §11. 405 His sweetheart..became Maid Marian, and dwelt a virgin huntress in his company.

b. *transf.* and *fig.* (of women and animals).

1604 DEKKER *2nd Pt. Honest Wh.* Wks. 1873 II. 127 Y'are a good Huntresse, Lady, you ha found your Game already. **1665** HOOKE *Microgr.* 201 But, if the capricious Fly took wing, and pitch'd upon another place behind our Huntress, then would the Spider [etc.]. **1894** SIR E. SULLIVAN *Woman* 11 Every woman is, by nature and instinct, more or less a huntress of men.

2. A mare used or adapted for hunting.

1858 TROLLOPE *Dr. Thorne* iv, If you insist on calling the old pony a huntress. **1885** *Bazaar* 30 Mar. 1270/1 Brown cob, pretty, quiet to ride or drive, good huntress.

3. *attrib.* and *Comb.*, as ***huntress fashion, guise, -maid, -queen, -wise***; ***huntress-like*** adj.

1573 TWYNE *Æneid* XI. (1584) S ij b, In Thracian huntres-wise. **1725** POPE *Odyss.* VI. 119 A sylvan train the huntress-queen surrounds. **1788** I. RITSON *Homer's Hymn Venus* 7 Whether Latona, or the huntress-maid. **1887** BOWEN *Virg. Æneid* I. 318 See! from her shoulder slung in a huntress fashion the bow.

huntsman (ˈhʌntsmən). [f. *hunt's* genitive of HUNT *sb.* + -MAN. Cf. *craftsman.*]

1. A man who hunts, a hunter.

1567 MAPLET *Gr. Forest* 49 The one which the Huntesman vseth. **1590** SHAKS. *Mids. N.* IV. i. 145 Goe bid the huntsmen wake them with their hornes. **1666** J. DAVIES *Hist. Caribby Isls* 32 The Indians and Huntsmen, who have no setled habitation. **1697** DRYDEN *Virg. Georg.* III. 570 The dext'rous Huntsman wounds not these afar, With Shafts. **1796** SCOTT *Wild Huntsman* vii, He waved his huntsman's cap on high.

fig. **1808** SCOTT *Hunting Song* iv, Time, stern huntsman! who can baulk?

2. *spec.* **a.** The manager of a hunt; a man whose business is to take charge of the hounds and direct the pursuit of game; esp. the man in charge of a pack of hounds for fox-hunting.

1596 SHAKS. *Tam. Shr.* I. Induct. i. 16 Huntsman I charge thee, tender wel my hounds. **1616** SURFL. & MARKH. *Country Farme* 700 Now if it fall out that the hunts-man haue not earth dogs readie taught, hee may traine them in this manner. **1725** DE FOE *Voy. round World* (1840) 274 Just as a huntsman casts off his hounds. **1735** SOMERVILLE *Chase* II. 111 Huntsman, lead on! behind, the clust'ring Pack Submiss attend. **1812** *Sporting Mag.* XXXIX. 133 Dick Knight, the late crack huntsman of Lord Spencer. **1883** EG.-WARBURTON *Hunt. Songs* (ed. 7) 230 *note*, Joe Maiden was Huntsman to the Cheshire Hounds.

b. (See quot.)

1810 *Ann. Reg.* 620 Each gang of slaves [in Honduras] has one belonging to it, who is styled the huntsman..His chief occupation is to search the woods..to find employment for the whole.

3. *Comb.*, as ***huntsmanlike*** adj.; also **huntsman's cup**, *Sarracenia purpurea*, and **huntsman's horn**, *S. flava*, North American plants so called from their pitcher-shaped leaves; the latter also applied to the leaves themselves (Miller *Plant-n.*); **huntsman spider**, a spider of the family Sparassidæ, which is widely distributed in warm regions.

1848 A. GRAY *Man. Bot.* 25 S[arracenia] purpurea, L. (Sidesaddle-flower. Huntsman's Cup.) **1864** E. W. PAIGE *Catal. Flowering Plants Schenectady County* 7 Sarracenia Purpurea. Common Huntsman's Horn. **1865** *Dublin Univ. Mag.* II. 20 At every fence the leading pair pop over in huntsmanlike fashion. **1936** K. C. MCKEOWN *Spider Wonders Austral.* v. 79 The Huntsman Spiders, or, as they are more popularly known, Triantelopes, do not seem to fear man. **1945** C. H. CURRAN *Insects of Pacific World* xi. 293 The huntsman-spiders of the tropics include as one of their best known members the domestic *Heteropoda venatoria*. **1954** C. J. HYLANDER *Macmillan Wild Flower Bk.* 149 Common Pitcher-plant. *Sarracenia purpurea*. This species is also known in various parts of its range as Sidesaddle Flower and Huntsman's Cup. *Ibid.*, Trumpets. *Sarracenia flava*. The tubular insect-catching leaves of this species are longer and more slender, looking more like horns than pitchers. (In fact, another common name is Huntsman's Horn.) **1967** *Sunday Mail Mag.* (Brisbane) 9 Apr. 2/5 There was the Huntsman spider who adopted us and took up residence behind a painting in the living-room.

ˈhuntsmanship. Also 7 huntmanship. [f. prec. + -SHIP.] The position, office, or business of a huntsman; the art of hunting.

a **1631** DONNE *Love's Exch.* Poems (1633) 224 At court your fellows every day Give th' art of rhyming, huntmanship, or play, For them, which were their own before. **1636** MASSINGER *Gt. Dk. Florence* III. i, This..must force him to forsake the groves And Dian's huntmanship. *a* **1646** J. GREGORY *Posthum.* (1650) 228 To beetoken his Huntsmanship, hee holdeth in his hand the skin of a wilde Beast.

†**ˈhunts,master.** *Obs.* [f. *hunt's* + MASTER, rendering Ger. *jägermeister*.] The master of the hunt; an officer who directs a hunt.

1691 *Lond. Gaz.* No. 2727/2 Prince Maximilian continues under his Confinement, and the Hunts-master the Sieur de Molke, with his Brother..under a close Imprisonment.

hunt's-up. Also 7 (9 *dial.*) hunsup. Orig. ***the hunt is up***, name of an old song and its tune, sung or played to awaken huntsmen in the morning, and also used as a dance. Hence allusively: **a.** A song sung or tune played to rouse any one; an early morning song.

1537 *Lett. & Papers Hen. VIII* (1890) XII. I. 206 In formation against John Hogon, who, going about the country with a 'crowde' or a fiddle..sang a song with these words, 'The hunt is up', etc. **1549** *Compl. Scot.* vi. 66 Thai dancit al cristyn mennis dance, the northt of scotland, huntis vp, the comount entray [etc.]. *c* **1560** A. SCOTT *Poems* (S.T.S.) v. 13 With 'Hunts vp', every morning plaid. **1574** RICH *Dial. Mercury & Sold.* I ij b, Unlesse you some times arise to geve your parramours the *hunte is up* under the windowes. **1592** SHAKS. *Rom. & Jul.* III. iv. 34 Hunting thee hence, with Hunts-vp to the day. *a* **1625** FLETCHER *False One* IV. ii, They came to play you and your love a huntsup. **1674** PLAYFORD *Skill Mus.* I. 61 The Pythagorean Huntsup, or Morning Musick, which wakened and roused their dull Spirits. **1888** LOWELL *To a Lady playing on Cithern*, The horns of Oberon Blow their faint Hunt's-up from the good-time gone.

†**b.** In phrases denoting speech or action calculated to rouse or disturb a person's feelings (cf. *to lead one a dance*); hence, a disturbance, uproar. *Obs.* or *dial.*

1619 FLETCHER *M. Thomas* III. i, My spightful Dame, I'le pipe ye such a hunsup Shall make ye dance a tipvaes. *a* **1625** —— *Woman's Prize* III. iii, I would..in her hearing Begin her such a huntes-up. **1664** COTTON *Scarron.* Poet. Wks. (1765) 11 I'll play these Rake-hells such a Hunts-up. **1828** *Craven Dial., Hunsup*, a clamour, a turbulent outcry.

ˈhuntswoman. [Cf. HUNTSMAN.] A huntress; a woman who rides to hounds.

1621 LADY WROTH *Urania* 470 An excellent hors-woman, and hunts-woman she was. **1780** MAD. D'ARBLAY *Diary & Lett.* (1842) I. 302.

hunx, obs. f. HUNKS.

huny, obs. f. HONEY.

hunyak (ˈhʌnjæk). *U.S.* Also honyock, -er. [f. HUNGARIAN *a.* and *sb.* after POLACK.] = HUNK *sb.*³ (See also quot. 1941.)

Only in disparaging use.

1911 W. P. DILLINGHAM *Dict. Races* 92 *Magyar*, Hungarrian Hun, or Hunyak in popular language. **1919** S.

Lewis *Free Air* (1924) ix. 94, I could buy out half these Honyockers! **1938** 'E. Queen' *Four of Hearts* (1939) 17 Tossing away the stockholders' dough like a hunyak on Saturday night. **1941** *Sat. Even. Post* 7 June 29/1 'Honyocks', the Yankee neighbors called them [*sc.* immigrants from Central Europe]. 'Honyocker' came to be ..generally applied to any farmer who tries to raise grain and livestock in the high prairies of the Northwest. **1943** H. A. Smith *Life in Putty Knife Factory* xii. 185 Speaking as a pure-bred honyock out of the Middle West. **1957** P. Frank *Seven Days to Never* vii. 201 She cooked a Hungarian goulash better than any he'd tasted at a hunyak table. **1958** H. B. Allen in *Publ. Amer. Dial. Soc.* xxx. 8 *Honyock*..a boorish and uncouth farmer of foreign background. *Honyocker* (rarely *honyock*) was applied, on the contrary, to anyone who fenced in the open range. **1965** P. De Vries *Let me count the Ways* xii. 160 It was a kind of protest—the passionate outcry of honyocks everywhere.

hunyn, obs. f. ONION.

huo, obs. f. WHO.

Huon pine ('hju:ən paɪn). [Named from the river Huon in the south of Tasmania.] A large evergreen coniferous tree (*Dacrydium Franklinii*) found in Tasmania; also its timber.

1820 C. Jeffreys *Van Diemen's Land* 28 (Morris) On the banks of these..rivers, and the harbour, grows the Huon Pine (so called from the river of that name, where it was first found). **1832** Bischoff *Van Diemen's Land* II. 23 Huon pine is by far the most beautiful wood found in the island. **1851** *Illustr. Catal. Gt. Exhib.* 992.

huor, huork, obs. forms of HUER, WARK.

hup, hupp (hʌp), *int.* A call to a horse: **a.** to quicken his pace; **b.** (*Sc.* and *north.*) to turn to the right or away from the driver: the opposite of *hie*.

1733 Fielding *Don Quix. Eng.* II. xii, Gee, gee, boys, hup! **1825–80** Jamieson, *Hup*, used to a horse in order to make him quicken his pace. **1851** H. Stephens *Bk. Farm* (ed. 2) I. 160/1 *To go from you. Hup* is the counterpart to *hie* in the southern counties..in towns *Haap* is used where *wynd* is heard, and *Hip* bears a similar relation to *vane*. **1859** J. Brown *Rab & F.* (ed. Alden) 4 'Hupp!' and a stroke of the whip were given to Jess.

Hence **hup** *v.*, (*a*) *intr.*, to shout *hup!*, to urge on a horse; (*b*) *trans.*, to direct or turn (a horse) to the right; = HAP *v.*[4]

1824 Scott *St. Ronan's* xvii, Touchwood was soon heard 'hupping' and 'geeing' to the cart. **1851** H. Stephens *Bk. Farm* (ed. 2) I. 180/1 The horses are then hupped sharp round from you. *Ibid.* 181/2 [see HIE *v.*[2]]. **1851** *Jrnl. R. Agric. Soc.* XII. I. 125 To lay two 12-yard ridges together, by hupping, or turning to the right hand at the ends.

Hupa ('hu:pə, 'hu:pɔ:). Also 9 **Hoopah, Hoopa.** [Yurok *hupǭ* Hupa (i.e. from the name for this people in the language of their neighbours, the Yurok). The *-p-* is a glottalized consonant (Dr. Sturtevant).] An Athapascan Indian people in California; a member of this people; also their language. Also *attrib.* or as *adj.*

1853 H. R. Schoolcraft *Hist. & Stat. Information Indian Tribes* III. 139 The lower Trinity tribe is, as well as the river itself, known to the Klamaths by the name of Hoopah. **1872** *Overland Monthly* Aug. 157/1 The Hoopas closely resemble the Cahrocs in *physique*. **1885** *Rep. Indian Affairs* (U.S.) 6 It would be a benefit not only to the Government but to the Hoopa Indians, if their reservation were abandoned. **1903** G. W. James *Indian Basketry* (ed. 3) 53 On the lower Trinity River are the Hupas, the main reservation being in the Hoopa valley. **1921** [see APACHE 1]. **1936** J. Kantor *Objective Psychol. Gram.* xvii. 244 In Athapascan (Hupa) the prefix *neen* denotes past time in both substantives and verbs. **1965** *Canad. Jrnl. Ling.* Spring 132 The Wailaki and Hupa correspondent forms.

hupaithric, for *hypæthric* = HYPÆTHRAL.

1818 Shelley *Rev. Islam* VII. xii, That spacious cell Like an hupaithric temple wide and high.

hupe, huppe, obs. ff. HIP *sb.*[1] and *v.*[1] (= hop), HOOP *sb.*[1]

hupostasis, for HYPOSTASIS.

huppil, hupple, obs. ff. HIPPLE, little heap.

hur, obs. f. or var. HER *pron.*; var. HURR; obs. f. WHORE.

huracano, obs. f. HURRICANE.

hur-bur: see HURR-BURR.

hurburlie, obs. f. HURLY-BURLY.

hurcheon ('hɜ:tʃən). Now *Sc.* and *north. dial.* Forms: 4 **hircho(u)n**, 5 **hurchon, -yn, hyrchoun**, 6 **hurcheoun, hyrchen**, 6– **hurcheon**, 8–9 **hurchin**, 9 **-ent**. [a. ONF. *herichon*, OF. *heriçun* (12th c. in Littré), mod.F. *hérisson* (in Hainault *hirchon, hurchon*, Picard *hérichon, irechon*):—pop. L. **hēriciōn-em*, f. *hēricius*, late form of *ēricius* hedgehog. See also URCHIN.]

1. A hedgehog.

c **1325** *Gloss W. de Biblesw.* in Wright *Voc.* 165 *Yriȝoun*, an hirchoun. **1398** Trevisa *Barth. De P.R.* XIV. lvii. (Tollem. MS.), Also hirchonis [**1535** yrchins] and hares flew to holow stones. *c* **1425** *Voc.* in Wr.-Wülcker 639/11 *Hic erinacius*, hurchon. **1597** Montgomerie *Cherrie & Slae* 15, I saw the hurcheoun and the hair..Wer happing to and fro. *a* **1605** —— *Flyting w. Polwart* 336 With hurcheons eatand hips and hawes. **1883** *Huddersf. Gloss.*, Hurchent, Hurchin. **1893** Heslop *Northumbld. Gloss.*, *Hurchin, Hurcheon*, the hedge hog.

transf. **1508** Dunbar *Flyting w. Kennedie* 179 Hard hurcheoun, hirpland, hippit as ane harrow. **1894** Crockett *Lilac Sunbonnet* 55 The wizened auld hurcheon.

attrib. **1508** Dunbar *Tua mariit wemen* 107 With his hard hurcheone skyn sa heklis he my chekis. **1790** Burns *Elegy Capt. Henderson* i, The meikle devil..Haurl thee hame to his black smiddie, O'er hurcheon hides.

2. A mischievous person; an urchin.

1785 Burns *Jolly Beggars* Recit. VII. ii, Hurchin Cupid shot a shaft That play'd a dame a shavie.

hurc(k)le, var. HURKLE.

hurd, -e, obs. ff. HERD, HOARD.

hurdace, -as, -eys, -ice: see HURDIS.

hurden: see HARDEN.

'hurdies, *sb. pl. Sc.* [Origin unknown.] The buttocks; the hips. Also *fig.* the rump, the end or 'tail' of anything.

1535 Lyndesay *Satyre* 4363 Of hir hurdies scho had na hauld. **1623** *Elgin Session Rec.* in *Scotsman* (1898) 31 Jan. 2/7 There was litile justice in Elgin that suffered them [two witches] to leve so lang unhet baith their hurdies. **1786** Burns *Twa Dogs* 36 His gawcy tail..Hung o'er his hurdies wi' a swirl. **1894** Crockett *Raiders* 163 The long rows of cow's hurdies. **1895** —— *Men of Moss Hags* xl. 290 He was sitting on his hurdies in the shallows.

†**'hurdis, 'hurdice.** *Obs.* Also 4–5 **-ys(e**, 5 **-as, -ace, -eys, -yce, -esse**, 5 **hourdeys**; (4 **hardes**). [ME. *hurdis*, etc., a. OF. *hourdeis, -is*, earlier *hordeis, -is*, mod.F. *hourdis* (med.L. *hurdicium, hordecium* Du Cange):—L. type **hurdātīcium*, f. OF. *hurder, horder, hourder* (late L. *hurdāre*), f. OF. *hurt, hourt, hourd* palisade, a. OHG. *hurt* (pl. *hurdī*), Ger. *hürde* hurdle, cogn. w. ON. *hurð*, Goth. *haurds* door: see next.]

A palisade, orig. of hurdles or wicker-work.

13.. *Coer de L.* 3969 The Sarezynes, armyd, forth lepe Upon the walles the toun to kepe, Stout in touret, and in hurdys [*rime* vys]. *Ibid.* 6127 Her houses brende and her hurdys: Gret smok ther aros, I wis. *a* **1352** Minot *Poems* (ed. Hall) x. 14 þaire hurdis, þaire ankers, hanged þai on here. *c* **1400** *Melayne* 1600 A nobill hurdas ther was graythede. **1412–20** Lydg. *Chron. Troy* II. xviii, They.. Sette their bastyles and their hurdeys eke, Rounde about to the harde wall. **1447** Bokenham *Seyntys* (Roxb.) 169 Thai lyin in ful sympyl hurdeys And lykly for to be deed for cold. **1489** Caxton *Faytes of A.* II. xiv. 118 They made hourdeys or obstacles full thykke of thornes.

Hence †**'hurdised (hurdeysed)** *ppl. a.*, palisaded.

c **1450** *Merlin* 604 With-ynne the bailie were v. toures.. the fifthe was gret and high, and well hurdeysed a-boute with-ynne and with-oute.

hurdle ('hɜ:d(ə)l), *sb.* Forms: α. 1 **hyrdel, (hyrþil)**, 3 **herdel**, 4–5 **hirdel**, 4–6 **-dle**, 4–7 **hurdel, -ell**, 5 **herd-, hyrd-, hirdyl, -yll(e, -el, -ill, hurdull**, 5–6 **hyrd-, herdell, hirdil(l, herdyl, -le, (horthell)**, 6– **hurdle**. β. 5–6 **hardyll**, 6 **-yll, -ell**, 6–7 **hardel**, 6–8 **-le**. [OE. *hyrdel*:—OTeut. type **hurdilo-z*, deriv. of a primitive represented by Goth. *haurds*, ON. *hurð* door, OHG. *hurt* (MHG. *hurt*, pl. *hürte, hürde*, Ger. *hürde*, MDu., Du. *horde*), wickerwork, hurdle:—OTeut. **hurdí-s*, pre-Teut. **kr̥tís*: cf. L. *crātis* hurdle, Gr. *κυρτία* wickerwork, *κύρτη, κύρτος* fishing-creel, cage, Skr. *kr̥t* to spin, *cr̥t* to fasten together.]

1. a. A portable rectangular frame, orig. having horizontal bars interwoven or wattled with withes of hazel, willow, etc.: = wattle; but now often an open frame with light horizontal bars crossed by uprights, and strengthened by a diagonal bar, like a field gate: used chiefly to form temporary fences, sheep-pens, etc.

c **725** *Corpus Gloss.* 600 *Cratem*, flecta *vel* hyrþil. *c* **1000** Ælfric *Hom.* I. 430 þa forlet se wælhreowa casere ðone halgan lichaman uppon ðam isenan hyrdle. *c* **1050** *Voc.* in Wr.-Wülcker 371/30 *Crates*, hyrdlas. **1297** R. Glouc. (Rolls) 4788 Mid hor owe honde hii rerede verst an chirche Of herdles and of ȝerden as hii couþe wurche. **1462** Marg. Paston in *P. Lett.* No. 436 II. 85 He schall mak yow as many hyrdyllys as ye nede for yowyr fold. **1521** in *Archæologia* (1834) XXV. 437 Pd. to the said Thomas for v dussen hardylls vjs. viijd. **1572** Mascall *Plant. & Graff.* (1592) 70 Ye shail drie them on hurdells of Oziars made like Lettice windowes. **1669** Worlidge *Syst. Agric.* (1681) 327 Hurdles, made in form of Gates, either of spleeted Timber or of Hazle Rods..either serve for gates in Enclosures or to make Sheepfolds or the like. **1745** Pococke *Trav.* II. I. ix. 129 The houses of the village..are made of hurdles, covered with clay. **1794** T. Davis *Agric. Wilts* in *Archæol. Rev.* Mar. (1888), *Hurdles*..six feet long, three and a half feet high, made of hazel-rods closely-wreathed, the upright rods called sails and the long rods wreaths. **1880** H. Stewart *Shepherd's Man.* 27 As the crop is eaten, the line of hurdles is moved along the field until the whole is consumed.

b. A frame of this kind used as a barrier to be cleared in races. Also *pl.*, an athletic event consisting of a hurdle-race.

1833 [see 3, *hurdle sweepstake*]. **1870** Blaine *Encycl. Rur. Sports* (ed. 3) §1284 The hurdles were stout black wattles, which will bend but not break; and were placed, the first near the distance post [etc.]. **1887** T. B. Reed *Fifth Form St. Dominic's* i. 8 He is certain..to win the mile and the 'hurdles' at the Athletic Sports. **1897** *Isis* (Oxf.) 13 Nov. 63/1 Three events..: hundred yards, broad jump, and hurdles. **1905** *Athlete* Aug. 80/1 R. S. Stromach retained his title in the hurdles. **1930** *Daily Express* 8 Sept. 9/5 In the 80 metres hurdles. **1948** [see CLOCK *v.*[1] 1 b]. **1973** *Country Life* 13 Sept. 693/2 The first peak for the British crowd was the 400 metres hurdles.

c. A kind of frame or sledge on which traitors used to be drawn through the streets to execution.

(This remained part of the legal punishment for high treason till 1870, when it was abolished by Act 33 & 34 Vict. c. 23 §31.)

1412–20 Lydg. *Chron. Troy* V. xxxvi, (MS. Digby 230), Egistus was..dempt..On an hirdel naked to be drawe Thoruȝoute þe toun..And aftir ful hiȝe enhonged on a tree. **1450** in Ellis *Orig. Lett.* Ser. II. I. 115 To do drawe the body of a grete traytour..uppon an hurdull by the stretes of your Citee of London. **1577** Harrison *England* II. xi. (1877) I. 222 Drawing from the prison to the place of execution vpon an hardle or sled. **1634** Ford *P. Warbeck* III. i, Let false Audley Be drawn upon an hurdle from the Newgate To Tower-hill. **1769** Blackstone *Comm.* IV. vi. 92 Usually (by connivance, at length ripened by humanity into law) a sledge or hurdle is allowed to preserve the offender from the extreme torment of being dragged on the ground or pavement. **1777** Sheridan *Sch. Scand.* II. i, Many a wretch has rid on a hurdle who has done less mischief. **1859** Dickens *T. Two Cities* II. ii, He'll be drawn on a hurdle to be half hanged.

d. *Fortif.*, etc. A wattled hurdle, used to lay upon marshy ground or across a ditch to provide a firm passage, etc., or, often covered with earth, to stop up a breach, to strengthen a battery, or to protect a work or position from the enemy's fire.

13.. *K. Alis.* 6104 [6088] (Bodl. MS.) Of hirdles & brigges hy maden flores And so hy wenten in to þe mores. **1440** J. Shirley *Dethe K. James* (1818) 15 He laid certayne plaunckes and hurdelles over the diches. **1489** Caxton *Faytes of A.* II. xxiv. 137 The trestelles muste be garnissed with hirdellis for to make the aleies and weies to go ouere. **1555** Eden *Decades* 97 Theye made a greate trenshe.. coueringe the same with hurdels..the dogge tyger chaunsed fyrste into this pitfaul. **1704** J. Harris *Lex. Techn.*, *Hurdles*, or Clays, in Fortification, are made of..Twigs of Willows, or Osiers, being 5 or 6 Foot high, and from 3 to 4 Foot broad. They are interwoven very close together, and usually laden with Earth,..to render Batteries firm. **1853** Stocqueler *Milit. Encycl.* s.v., Hurdles are constructed in nearly the same manner as gabions, excepting that the picquets are placed in a straight line instead of a circle.

e. *fig.* An obstacle or difficulty.

1924 R. Campbell *Flaming Terrapin* ii. 34 Their slim keels like horses bounded free To leap the foamy hurdles of the sea. **1928** —— *Wayzgoose* i. 28 O'er lingual hurdles coax your tongues to prance. **1966** *Listener* 6 Jan. 13/2 Family planning has some major..hurdles to overcome. **1969** *Radio Times* 24 July 23/5 Andrew Cooper describes the hurdles to be cleared by business men eager to win the prize of a seat on the Board of Directors. **1971** *Nature* 11 June 346/2 The shuttle's hardest hurdle, however, is in the Senate.

2. Applied to various things formed, like a hurdle, of crossing bars or grating.

†**a.** A sieve, strainer, or colander. †**b.** Applied to a snowshoe. **c.** *Hat-making.* 'A grid of wood or wire, on which a bunch of felting hair is laid for bowing' (Knight *Dict. Mech.* 1875). **d.** *Salt-making.* (See quot. 1886.) **e.** The stick used in the game of lacrosse.

1725 Bradley *Fam. Dict.* s.v. *Paste*, To be drained upon a Hurdle or Grate, and passed through the Hair-Sieve. **1727** *Ibid.* s.v. *Cedre*, To be taken out, and drain'd in a Cullender or Hurdle. **1726** Leoni *Alberti's Archit.* I. 39/1 Those who walk over the Snow..wear upon their Feet hurdles made of Twigs and small Ropes.., the broadness of which keeps them from sinking in the Snow. **1837** Whittock *Bk. Trades* (1842) 293 (*Hatter*) When the workman is bowing he works at a 'hurdle', or thin boarded bench with several longitudinal chinks to suffer the dust, &c. to pass through. **1886** *Cheshire Gloss.*, *Hurdle*, salt-making term. A table or platform of wood planks running along each side of the pans, for the purpose of receiving the salt when drawn out of the pans. **1887** *Cornh. Mag.* Mar. 258 (*Lacrosse*) The 'stick', or 'hurdle',..consists of a piece of white ash.

3. *attrib.* and *Comb.*, as (sense 1) ***hurdle-fence, -maker, -rod, -stake, -wall, -work***; ***hurdle-wise*** adv.; (sense 1 b) ***hurdle-jumping, -leaping***; (sense 1 d) ***hurdle-revetment, -work***; **hurdle-house**, a wattle house; **hurdle-man**, (*a*) a man who looks after hurdled sheep or lambs (see quot. 1880); (*b*) a man who runs in hurdle-races; **hurdle-race**, a race in which the contestants have to jump over hurdles; so ***h. racer, h. racing, h. handicap***; **hurdle-wood**, wood used for wattling or making hurdles.

1609 Holland *Amm. Marcell.* XX. xi. 160 The *hurdle fences of oysiers. **1805** R. W. Dickson *Pract. Agric.* (1807) I. 160 A moveable hurdle-fence. **1890** *Daily News* 8 Jan. 3/6 The Thames *Hurdle Handicap. *a* **1879** J. S. Brewer *Eng. Stud.* (1881) 445 London..is still [9th c.] the old town of *hurdle-houses and whitewash. **1883** *Standard* 12 Feb. 2/6 Prudhomme has taken kindly to *hurdle jumping. **1894** *Times* 11 Sept. 16/7 Wire netting has taken the place of sheep hurdles. I have not made a hurdle for quite 15 years, and..the race of *hurdlemakers is as extinct as the race of sawyers. **1880** A. C. Grant *Bush Life Queensland* 459 'Toothless, ragged, old grannies', muttered the *hurdleman. **1892** *Pall Mall G.* 18 May 3/1 H. W. Batger is our hurdle man, and he won the 120 yards hurdle championship first in 1888. **1836** W. Dyott *Diary* 23 Mar. (1907) II. 228 Lichfield March races;..a *hurdle race, a new-fashioned sport much in vogue with the fox-hunters. **1848** Thackeray *Bk. Snobs* xiv, Lord Glenlivat..broke his neck at a hurdle-

race. **1897** M. H. HAYES *Points of the Horse* (ed. 2) xxv. 247 She [a mare] showed herself to be the best chaser and *hurdle-racer of her time. **1840–70** BLAINE *Encycl. Rur. Sports* (ed. 3) §1282 *Hurdle racing came into vogue above fifty years ago.. We by no means assert that hurdle leaping, as an organised sport, had not before been practised. **1821** in Cobbett *Rur. Rides* I. 50 The bricks, *hurdlerods and earth say..'Here dwell vanity and poverty'. **1887** H. R. HAWEIS *Light of Ages* i. 10 Hindu villages with their *hurdle-surrounded houses. **1833** *Sporting Mag.* Dec., *Hurdle sweepstakes of 5 guineas each, for horses not thorough-bred. **1611** COTGR., *Hourdé*,..couered with hurdles, or with reed wrought *hurdle-wise. **1649** BLITHE *Eng. Improv. Impr.* (1653) 160 In four or five years..the Willow rises to gallant *Hurdle-wood. **1851** J. S. MACAULAY *Field Fortif.* 127 To form a species of *hurdle-work above the fascines. **1866** *Reader* 22 Sept. 307 Huts..having a framework of piles and stakes, with wattle or hurdle-work of small branches woven between the upright piles.

ˈhurdle, *v.* [f. prec. sb.]

† **1.** *trans.* To construct like a hurdle; to wattle.

1598 FLORIO, *Aggratticcare*,..to make grater-wise, to make like a hurdle, to hurdle.

2. To enclose or mark *off* with hurdles. Also with *out, up, round.*

1632 SHERWOOD, To hurdle, make vp, hedge, close with hurdles. **1770–4** A. YOUNG in A. Hunter *Georg. Ess.* (1803) III. 145 They are usually hurdled off in the same manner as turnips. **1789** *Trans. Soc. Arts* (ed. 2) II. 107 A field of rape, hurdled out. **1894** *Times* 6 Mar. 4/1 To hurdle off a fresh portion [of meadow] for the ewes every day.

† **3.** To bush-harrow. *Obs.*

1733 TULL *Horse-hoeing Husb.* ix. 42 A yet worse Contrivance it was, to Till Land with a Hurdle made of Vine Twigs [Virg. *Georg.* I. 95 Vimineasque trahit crates]..This Harrowing and Hurdling.

4. *intr.* To run a hurdle-race; to jump over an obstacle, as in a hurdle-race. Also *fig.* Hence **ˈhurdling** *vbl. sb.*; also *attrib.*

1896 ADE *Artie* vii. 60 Artie did not know the tune or the words, so he merely whistled it on speculation, and when he came to the doubtful parts he hurdled. **1897** *Encycl. Sport* I. 52/2 Few good sprinters will take to hurdling, as there is little doubt that the mechanical and artificial action necessary in hurdling interferes with speed on the flat. *Ibid.* 53/1 Hurdling and long jumping ability often go together. **1912** [see *field events* (FIELD *sb.* 21)]. **1923** R. D. PAINE *Comrades of Rolling Ocean* xv. 256 He hurdled aboard this True American steamer as soon as he hit New York. **1928** *Daily Mail* 31 July 11/5 When Lord Burghley hurdled easily to victory. **1955** *Times* 13 Aug. 4/2 Higham hurdled with great élan.

hurdled (ˈhɜːd(ə)ld), *ppl. a.* Also 6 **hartheled**. [f. HURDLE *sb.* or *v.* + -ED[1] or [2].]

1. Constructed of or with hurdles; wattled.

1556 WITHALS *Dict.* (1568) 39b/2 A hartheled wall, or ratheled..*paries craticius.* **1652** BENLOWES *Theoph.* XIII. lxxxiii, The folded flocks are pent In hurdled grates. **1667** MILTON *P.L.* IV. 186 Shepherds pen thir Flocks at eeve In hurdl'd Cotes. **1746–7** HERVEY *Medit.* (1818) 265 As he tends his fleecy charge, or late consigns them to their hurdled cots! **1832** J. BREE *St. Herbert's Isle* 79 A hurdled panoply his front displays.

2. Enclosed with hurdles.

1632 SHERWOOD, Hurdled, hedged, made vp or covered with hurdles, *clée, hourdé.* **1830** MARRYAT *King's Own* xxxv, Sheep, dragged from the hurdled crowd. **1880** *Daily News* 18 Oct. 3/1 Clover, aftermath, or hurdled vetches.

hurdler (ˈhɜːdlə(r)). [f. HURDLE *sb.* + -ER[1].]

1. One who constructs hurdles; a hurdle-maker.

1874 T. HARDY *Far fr. mad. Crowd* II. i. 1 A thriving hurdler and cattle-crib-maker.

2. One who runs in hurdle races.

1884 *Pall Mall G.* 7 Apr. 3/2 The hurdles are more likely to fall to Cambridge, whose representative, Pollock, is now, perhaps..the best hurdler in the country. **1894** *Times* 16 July 7/4 The Yale hurdlers seem more quick and active than their English rivals.

hurdom, obs. form of WHOREDOM.

hurdpenny, obs. form of HEARTHPENNY.

hurds: see HARDS.

hurdy-gurdy (ˈhɜːdɪˈgɜːdɪ). [app. a riming combination suggested by the sound of the instrument. Cf. HIRDY-GIRDY, uproar, disorderly noise.]

1. a. A musical instrument of rustic origin resembling the lute or guitar, and having strings (two or more of which are tuned so as to produce a drone), which are sounded by the revolution of a rosined wheel turned by the left hand, the notes of the melody being obtained by the action of keys which 'stop' the strings and are played by the right hand; thus combining the characteristics of instruments of the bowed and the clavier kinds. **b.** In recent times, applied popularly to any instrument having a droning sound and played by turning a handle, as the barrel-organ.

1749 LADY LUXBOROUGH *Lett. to Shenstone* 10 Dec., Receive this incorrect epistle..not for its wit or its beauty: for it has no more pretence to either than a hurdy gurdy has to harmony. **1764** O'HARA *Midas* I. 7 A sightly clown!—and sturdy! Hum!—plays, I see, upon the hurdy-gurdy. **1770** MAD. D'ARBLAY *Early Diary* 10 Jan., Hetty went as a Savoyard, with a hurdy gurdy fastened round her waist. **1785–96** GROSE *Dict. Vulg. T.*, *Hurdy gourdy*, a kind of fiddle ..at present it is confounded with the humstrum. **1807** T. YOUNG *Course Lect. Nat. Philos.* I. xxxiv. 399 The vielle, or monochord, commonly called the hurdy gurdy, has frets which are raised by the action of the fingers on a row of keys. **1851** THACKERAY *Eng. Hum.* iv. (1876) 261 A Savoyard boy ..with a hurdy-gurdy and a monkey. **1879** A. J. HIPKINS in Grove *Dict. Mus.* I. 759/2 The Hurdy Gurdy was the prototype of the Piano Violin, and all similar *sostenente* instruments.

transf. and *fig.* **1863** LONGF. *Wayside Inn, Birds Killingworth* xviii, And hear the locust and the grass-hopper Their melancholy hurdy-gurdies play. **1871** SMILES *Charac.* i. (1876) 27 Perpetual grinding at the hurdy-gurdy of long-dead grievances.

2. (More fully ***hurdy-gurdy wheel.***) An impact wheel driven by a tangential jet of water which issues under pressure from a nozzle and strikes a series of buckets on the periphery. *U.S.*

1868 *Rep. J. Ross Brown on Min. Resources west of Rocky Mts.* (U.S. Treasury Dept.) 101 In 1866 they struck into pay and erected a 10-stamp mill, which is driven by a hurdy-gurdy wheel. **1872** RAYMOND *Statist. Mines & Mining* 86 An eight-stamp mill, run by a 'hurdy-gurdy' wheel 8 feet in diameter, using 75 inches of water under a pressure of 75 feet. **1882** *Rep. to Ho. Represent. Prec. Metals U.S.* 628 The actuating power of the derrick is, generally, a hurdy-gurdy. This is a peculiar kind of impact wheel made to utilize water under high pressures.

3. A crank or windlass used for hauling trawls in deep-sea fishing.

1883 *Fisheries Exhib. Catal.* 196 Trawl-winch or hurdy-gurdy.

4. a. *attrib.* and *Comb.*

1861 SALA *Dutch Pict.* i. 8 Airs..such as the hurdy-gurdy players..grind so piteously before cottage doors. **1891** DK. ARGYLL in *19th Cent.* Jan. 12 The famous formula that geology saw 'no trace of a beginning, no symptom of an end' ..may be called the great hurdy-gurdy theory.

b. Special comb. **hurdy-gurdy girl** *N. Amer. Hist.*, a dance hostess in a hurdy-gurdy house; **hurdy-gurdy house** *N. Amer. Hist.*, a disreputable type of cheap dance-hall.

[**1860** C. E. DE LONG in *Calif. Hist. Soc. Q.* (1931) X. 256 Rode over to young Hill's to see Tom Smith married to a hurdy gurdy.] **1865** *Harper's Mag.* June 4/1 *Hurdy-gurdy girls are singing bacchanalian songs. **1958** P. BERTON *Klondike* 6 A circus parade of camp-followers crowded in upon them, saloon-keepers, and hurdy-gurdy girls. **1973** *Islander* (Victoria, B.C.) 18 Nov. 12/3 A dance with a 'hurdy-gurdy' girl cost £10 a whirl! **1866** *Beadle's Monthly* Oct. 280/1 *Hurdy-gurdy houses, with dancing-girls, music, and long bars. **1874** T. B. ALDRICH *Prudence Palfrey* vii. 115 At sundown the dance-house would open,—the Hurdy-Gurdy House, as it was called. **1955** P. F. SHARP *Whoop-up Country* 192 The saloons and hurdy-gurdy houses of Benton, Macleod, and Calgary.

Hence **hurdy-ˈgurdyist**, a hurdy-gurdy player.

a **1845** HOOD *Town & Country* viii, Two hurdigurdists, and a poor Street-Handel grinding at my door. **1862** MISS MULOCK *Domestic Stor.* 335 He made friendships with blind pipers, Italian hurdy gurdyists.

ˈhurdy-ˈgurdyish, *a.* Resembling the sound of a hurdy-gurdy; also *fig.*

1923 *Daily Mail* 22 June 6 The concertina or harmonium music is too hurdy-gurdyish. **1931** *Observer* 27 Sept. 10 A cheap, hurdy-gurdyish fellow.

† **hure**, *sb. Obs.* Also 3 **huyre**, 5 **hwyr, hvyr, huwyr, huer.** [a. OF. *hure* hair of the head, head of man or beast (12th c. in Littré), in mod.F. a dishevelled head of hair, head of certain animals; cf. med.L. *hūra* 'pileus villosus' (Du Cange), early mod.Du. *hure* 'caput apri aut cerui' (Kilian), OSp. *hura*; for conjectures as to the origin, see Diez.]

1. A cap.

c **1290** *Beket* 2075 in *S. Eng. Leg.* I. 166 þare wende forth on of heom and is huyre [*v.r.* hure] of him drouȝ And is mantel a-non after-ward. *c* **1305** *Pol. Songs* (Camden) 156 Ther sit an old cherl in a blake hure. *c* **1400** A. DAVY *Dreams* 59 Vpon his heuede sat an gray hure. *c* **1440** *Promp. Parv.* 252/2 Hwyr, cappe (*v.rr.* hvyr, hure; *tena.* *c* **1460** J. RUSSELL *Bk. Nurture* 376 Y hed leuer þe sight of that than A Scarlet hure. **1482** [see HURRER].

2. The head of a boar, wolf, or bear.

[**1828** BERRY *Encycl. Herald.* Gloss., *Hure* is the French term for the head of a wild boar, bear, wolf, or other such like wild animal; but not for those of lions, or other creatures said to be noble.] **1844** *Camp of Refuge* I. 65 Of the wild boars..only the hure or head was served up. **1861–2** THACKERAY *Philip* I. xiii. 289 You never knew that you yourself had tusks, little eyes in your hure; a bristly mane to cut into tooth-brushes.

† **hure**, *adv. Obs.* Also 2 **hwure, hur.** [OE. *huru*, of obscure origin. Cf. Sw. *huru* how.] **a.** At least, least of all; anyhow; at any rate; with a negative: Even. **b.** Certainly, especially.

c **893** K. ÆLFRED *Oros.* I. i. §20 Se Estmere is huru fiftene mila brad. *c* **1000** *Laws of Ethelred* VIII. c. 9 (Schmid) Be emnihte oððe huru be Ealra Halȝena mæssan. *c* **1175** *Lamb. Hom.* 45 þet þu heom ȝefe rest la hwure þen sunne dei. *Ibid.* 131 Ne prophete ne patriarche ne hure Sancte iohannes baptiste. *c* **1230** *Hali Meid.* 41 Ne kepeð he wið na mon & hure wið his famon.

c. Often doubled, ***hure and hure*** (*hurend h.*).

a **1175** *Coll. Hom.* 237 þes lare and laȝe swiðe acolede þurh manifea[l]d senne and hur and hur þurh false godes. *c* **1200** *Trin. Coll. Hom.* 49 Habbe we hurend hure mildshipe of duue. *a* **1250** *Owl & Night.* 11 And hure and hure of oþres songe Hi heolde plaiding swiþe stronge.

hure: see EURE, EWER[2], HER *prons.*, HIRE, HOUR, OUR, WHORE.

hureaulite (ˈhyrəʊlaɪt). *Min.* [Named, 1825, from *Hureaux* in France: see -LITE.] Hydrous phosphate of manganese and iron, occurring in minute red crystals; found at Hureaux near Limoges in France, and at Branchville in Connecticut.

1831 *Amer. Jrnl. Sc.* XIX. 371 The Hureaulite..is in minute crystals the size of a pin-head. **1868** DANA *Min.* (ed. 5) 561.

hurican, -ano, obs. forms of HURRICANE.

hurin (ˈhjʊərɪn). *Chem.* [f. mod.L. *Hura*, the name of a genus of tropical American plants + -IN.] 'A crystallizable substance, insoluble in water, found in the juice of *Hura crepitans* or Sand-box tree' (*Syd. Soc. Lex.* 1886).

[**1838** T. THOMSON *Chem. Org. Bodies* 292 Of Hurina.]

† **hurk.** *Obs. rare*$^{-0}$. [a. OF. *hurque, hourque*, var. of *hulque* HULK[2].] = HULK *sb.*[2]

1598 FLORIO, *Vurchio*, a hulke, a hurk, a crayer, a lyter.

hurkaru, hurkorah, var. HIRCARRA.

hurkle (ˈhɜːk(ə)l), *v.* Now *dial.* Forms: 4 **hurkel**, 5 **-kil, -cle**, 6– **hurkle**, (6 **hirkle, hurkul**, 7 **hurckle**, 9 *dial.* **hircle**). *β.* 8–9 *dial.* **hurple, hirple, hurtle.** [app. closely related to MLG., LG., and Du. *hurken* to squat, held by Dutch etymologists to be an intensive formation with *-k* suffix from MHG. *hûren*, dial. Ger. *hauern, hûren* to squat, sit bowed together; cf. also Fris. *horcken* 'contrahere membra ut calefiant'. The Eng. verb has an additional dim. or intensive suffix *-le*. The dialect forms in *β* appear to be phonetic variants; yet those in *hurp-, hirp-* suggest connexion with ON. *herpa-st* to be contracted with cramp: see HIRPLED.]

1. *intr.* To draw the limbs and parts of the body closely together, esp. with pain or cold; to contract the body like a beast in a storm; to cower, crouch, squat; to shrink, shudder. Said also of the limbs: To be contracted or drawn together.

13.. *E.E. Allit. P.* B. 150 þat oþer burne watz abayst of his broþe wordez & hurkelez doun with his hede. *Ibid.* 406 Cubites fyftene Ouer þe hyȝest hylle þat hurkled on erþe. *a* **1400–50** *Alexander* 504 A litill brid, in-to his arme floȝe, And þar hurkils and hydis as scho were hand-tame. **1486** *Bk. St. Albans* E viij a, The haare..hurcles vppon hir houghis ay. **1607** WALKINGTON *Opt. Glass* xiii. 135 Hurckling with his heade to his shouldiers. **1611** COTGR., *Enchafouiné*..one that, through cold, hurkles like a cat. **1687** A. LOVELL tr. *Thevenot's Trav.* III. 78 Sometimes she hurkled down upon her Heels, nay, and sat down. *a* **1790** *Song* in *Scot. Ballads* (1790) II. 47 While I set hurklen in the ase. **1821** CLARE *Vill. Minstr.* II. 23 The hare..'Hind the dead thistle hurkles from the view. **1881** *Leicestersh. Gloss.*, *Hircle*, to crouch; contract the body; nestle up close. **1883** *Almondbury Gloss.*, *Hurcle*, to cower down, to squat..In some parts the word is hurple, or hirple.

β. **1788** W. MARSHALL *Yorksh.* Gloss. (E.D.S.), *Hurple*, to stick up the back, as cattle under a hedge in cold weather. **1811** WILLAN *W. Riding Gloss.* (E.D.S.), *Hurtle*, to contract the body into a round form, as through pain, severe cold, etc. **1868** ATKINSON *Cleveland Gloss.*, *Hirple*, to shrug or stick up the back as an animal does in inclement weather when standing under a hedge... Written also *Hurple, hurkle, hurtle.*

† **2.** *trans.* To crouch down upon; to brood over. *Obs. rare.*

1640 G. ABBOTT *Job Paraphr.* 249 Covering them [eggs] with a little sand or dust to cause them keepe their naturall heate, instead of hatching and hurkling them.

Hence **ˈhurkled** *ppl. a.*, contracted or drawn together, bowed together. **ˈhurkling** *ppl. a.*, contracting, crouching.

1508 DUNBAR *Flyting w. Kennedie* 186 With hurkland banis, holkand throw thy hyd. **1567** *Gude & Godlie B.* (S.T.S.) 105 With hurklit hude ouer a weill nureist neck. **1863** MRS. TOOGOOD *Yorksh. Dial.*, Fetch the cattle up. They look hurkled.

hurl (hɜːl), *v.* Also 4–5 **hourle**, 4–6 **horle**, (9 *dial.* **horl, hull**). [Akin in form and (in branch 1) in sense, to LG. *hurreln* to toss, sling, throw, precipitate, thrust, push, dash: cf. also mod.Du. *horrel* a push, a jog. The connexion of the other senses is doubtful; but sense 10 agrees with mod.E.Fris. *hurreln* to roar or bluster as the wind; cf. Upper Ger. dial. *hurlen* to roll, rumble as thunder. None of these continental words can be traced back even to the Middle period; and they are generally connected with the onomatopœic *hurr* expressing rapid motion. In early ME. there appears to have been frequent confusion of *hurl* and *hurtle*, partly scribal, but largely through contact of sense in the notion 'dash'; similarly also of *hurl* and *harl* to drag; in later times there seems to have been association with *whirl*, esp. in *hurlpit, hurlpool, hurlwind.*]

I. Referring to motion.

1. *intr.* To move, or be carried or driven with violence or impetuosity; to rush impetuously; to dash. *Obs.* or *arch.*

(The first quot. is doubtful; it may be *hurt* or *hurtle.*)

[*a* **1225** *Ancr. R.* 166 Iðe worldes þrunge, mid a lutel hurlunge [*MS. T.* hurtlinge] ȝe muhten al uor-leosen, ase þeo wrecches iðe worlde, þet hurleð togederes & to-brekeð hore uetles, & schedeð hore clennesse.] *a* **1300** *Curson M.* 23932 Þi leme leuedi vs light emell, Þat he mot haueles hurl to hell. **13..** *E.E. Allit. P.* B. 376 Water..wonez þat stryede, Hurled in-to vch hous. **1382** WYCLIF *1 Sam.* xxi. 13 He..hurlide hidir and thider bitwix the hoondis of hem. —— *Matt.* vii. 25 Flodis camen, and wyndis blewen and rusheden [*v.r.* hurliden] in to that hous. *c* **1400** *Destr. Troy* 1365 Maydons for mornyng hade þere mynde loste, Hurlet out of houses. **1513** DOUGLAS *Æneis* III. x. 39 A huge peple we se Of Ciclopes cum hurland to the port. **1585** JAS. I *Ess. Poesie* (Arb.) 62 Zour wordis to be cuttit short, and hurland ouer heuch. **1669** STURMY *Mariner's Mag.* I. ii. 20 We rolling climbe, then hurling fall beneath. **1728–46** THOMSON *Summer* 450 The very streams..impatient, seem To hurl into the covert of the grove. **1816** SCOTT *Antiq.* xvii, Its waters were seen hurling clear and rapid under their silvan canopy.

†**b.** app. identified or confused with *hurtle.*

c **1400** *Destr. Troy* 1198 When helmes and hard stele hurlet to-gedur. *Ibid.* 6638 Mony hurlit doun hedstoupis to þe hard vrthe! **1470–85** MALORY *Arthur* X. ii, He hurled vnto sir Tristram, & smote hym clene from his sadel. **1609** *Spenser's F.Q.* I. iv. 16 Suddaine vpriseth..The royall dame, and for her coche doth call: All hurlen [*ed.* **1590** hurtlen] forth, and she with princely pase, As faire Aurora in her purple pall.

†**c.** app. associated or confused with *whirl.*

13.. *E.E. Allit. P.* C. 271 He [Jonas] glydez in by þe giles ..Ay hele ouer hed, hourlande aboute. **1632** LITHGOW *Trav.* I. 21 Mens mindes..They hurling come and goe, like fish at baits.

2. *trans.* To drive or impel with impetuous force or violence. (In early use the passive was = sense 1.)

c **1305** *Judas Iscar.* 25 in *E.E.P.* (1862) 108 Þe see him hurlede vp and doun: as a liþer clot. *c* **1386** CHAUCER *Man of Law's T.* 199 O firste moeuyng crueel firmament With thy diurnal sweigh that..hurlest al from Est to Occident. **1535** COVERDALE *Jonah* i. 4 The Lorde hurled a greate wynde in to the see. **1688** S. SEWALL *Diary* 28 Nov. (1878) I. 237 Scarce any sleeping all night, things in the Cabbin were so hurled to and again. **1735** POPE *Prol. Sat.* 87 Pit, Box, and gall'ry in convulsions hurl'd. **1884** A. J. BUTLER *Coptic Ch. Egypt* I. 179 Amr hurled his troops and his engines in vain against the solid walls of Babylon.

b. *refl.* To throw oneself impetuously; = 1.

c **1400** *Destr. Troy* 10680 Þai hurlet hom full hard with hor hoge dynttes. **1886** STOKES *Celtic Ch.* (1888) 251 The Scandinavians hurled themselves..upon England.

†**c.** app. identified with *hurtle* and *whirl. Obs.*

1382 WYCLIF *Luke* vi. 49 Flood was hurtlid to that hous.. His hous..in to which the flood was hurlid [*v.r.* hurtlid]. **1590** SPENSER *F.Q.* I. i. 16 [The monster Error] hurling her hideous taile About her cursed head. **1617** MARKHAM *Caval.* III. 76 When you come euen to the brim of the ditch, you shall hurle your horse suddainly vpon that side which is from your aduersary.

3. *trans.* To throw or cast with violence (from some position); to precipitate, throw down, overthrow. *lit.* and *fig.*

c **1350** *Will. Palerne* 1243 Hetterly boþe hors & man he hurled to þe grounde. *c* **1400** *Destr. Troy* 10208 He hurlit of helmys, hedis within. *c* **1400** *York Myst.* xxx. 222 He bese hurled for [? fro] þe highnes he haunted. *c* **1485** *Digby Myst.* (1882) III. 142, I xal hovrle of yower hedes. *c* **1585** R. BROWNE *Answ. Cartwright* 1 Let vs shortly gather vp his vntrueths..and hurle them out by manifest and knowen markes. **1613** PURCHAS *Pilgrimage* (1614) 532 An Earthquake, that hurled downe Temples and Pallaces. **1757** GRAY *Desc. Odin* 93 Till wrap'd in flames, in ruin hurl'd, Sinks the fabric of the world. **1805** A. DUNCAN *Mariner's Chron.* IV. 63 One of those by the pump was suddenly torn away by a breaker..and hurled into the abyss. **1821** BYRON *Heav. & Earth* iii. 668 The first..hath been hurl'd From his once archangelic throne. **1849** MACAULAY *Hist. Eng.* v. I. 632 Raised to power and hurled from it. **1855** *Ibid.* xvi. III. 674 A mine exploded, and hurled a fine German battalion into the air.

refl. **1613** PURCHAS *Pilgrimage* (1614) 529 Hanging a great stone about their neckes..[they] hurle themselves into the Sea. **1871** L. STEPHEN *Playgr. Europe* viii. (1894) 186 The grand glacier..hurled itself madly downwards.

4. To throw or cast (a missile, projectile, or the like); to project; to fling.

a **1400–50** *Alexander* 2224 Oure pepill..hurled out arowis. **1530** PALSGR. 588/1, I horle, I throwe a thynge..I holde the a peny that I hurle this stone over yonder house. **1663** CHARLETON *Chor. Gigant.* 46 Profaning the Lord's Day with hurling the Ball. *a* **1735** LD. LANSDOWNE *Beauty & Law* 47 The Sire Omnipotent prepares the brand..Then flaming hurls it hissing from above. **1874** BOUTELL *Arms & Arm.* ii. 21 Hector and Ajax hurl their lances at each other. **1874** GREEN *Short Hist.* i. §3. 20 Leaping on horse-back, he hurled his spear into the sacred temple.

†**b.** *generally.* To throw, cast, toss; to 'throw' in wrestling. *Obs.*

1563–87 FOXE *A. & M.* (1684) III. 679 Here is a Testament in my hand, if I hurl him in the Fire and burn him, have I burned Gods Word, or not? *c* **1611** CHAPMAN *Iliad* XIV. 150 A heavenly veil she hurls On her white shoulders. **1611** BEAUM. & FL. *Knt. Burn. Pestle* III. ii, Why, Nell, I saw him wrestle with the great Dutchman, and hurl him. **1613** PURCHAS *Pilgrimage* (1614) 539 Flesh-pottage, which they hurle by handfuls into their mouthes. **1615** MARKHAM *Eng. Housew.* (1660) 92 Pull it all in pieces, and hurl in a good quantity of currants. **1659** D. PELL *Impr. Sea* 148 Though hee hurl the rod into the fire after all is done.

c. *absol.*

1530 PALSGR. 588/2 He can hurle as far by hande as some man can do with a slynge. **1611** BIBLE *Num.* xxxv. 20 If he ..hurle at him by laying of waite that he die.

d. *spec.* To play the game of 'hurling'.

1766 MRS. GRIFFITH *Lett. Henry & Frances* IV. 285 The Mob used to hurle there on every St. James's Fair-day. **1780** A. YOUNG *Tour Irel.* I. 365 Sometimes one barony hurls against another, but a marriageable girl is always the prize. **1836** W. H. MAXWELL *Capt. Blake* I. xi, I..danced, hurled, and was happy. *a* **1843** SOUTHEY *Comm.-pl. Bk.* IV. 563 The Irish custom of horsing a girl, and then hurling for her, that the winner may marry her. **1857** TRENCH *Proverbs* ii. (ed. 4) 34 *note*, 'The man on the dyke always hurls well;' the looker-on at a game of hurling, seated indolently on the wall, always imagines that he could improve on the strokes of the actual players.

5. *transf.* and *fig.* To throw out or forth with force; to utter (words, threats, etc.) with vehemence; to dart (rays, a glance, etc.).

1590 SPENSER *F.Q.* I. ii. 29 For golden Phoebus..From fiery wheeles of his faire chariot Hurled his beame. **1602** MARSTON *Ant. & Mel.* IV. Wks. 1856 I. 44 His spirit hovers in Piero's court, Hurling about his agill faculties, To apprehend the sight of Mellida. *c* **1611** CHAPMAN *Iliad* IV. 86 Jove, brandishing a star, which men a comet call, Hurls out his curled hair abroad. **1667** MILTON *P.L.* I. 669 Hurling defiance toward the vault of Heav'n. **1792** J. BARLOW *Conspir. Kings* 86 Truth's blest banners, o'er the regions hurl'd. **1858** CARLYLE *Fredk. Gt.* VI. ix. II. 221 Hurling a glance at Grumkow. **1875** MANNING *Mission H. Ghost* vii. 189 The accusations that may be hurled at you.

†**6.** To drag or pull with violence; = HARL *v.*[1] 1. (Also *absol.*) *Obs.*

c **1305** *Pol. Songs* (Camden) 211 Whan menne horlith ham here and there, *Nego* savith ham fram care. *c* **1400** *Destr. Troy* 10311 He..Festnyt hym..by his fete euyn, Hard by the here of his horse tayle, And hurlit hym with hethyng þurgh þe hoole ost. *c* **1420** *Anturs of Arth.* (Douce MS.) 187 Þey hurle [*Irel. MS.* hurlun, *Thornt. MS.* harle] me vnhendely. **1500–20** DUNBAR *Poems* lxxii. 20 In yre thai hurlit him heir and thair. **1663** R. BLAIR *Autobiog.* ii. (1848) 22 The new creature was assaulted, hurled and holed as a captive.

†**7.** To jostle; = HURTLE *v. Obs.*

1388 WYCLIF *Ezek.* xxxiv. 21 For that that ȝe hurliden [**1382** punchiden, *Vulg.* impingebatis] with sidis, and schuldris..alle sike beestis.

8. To wheel or drive (a vehicle, or in a vehicle, esp. one that goes heavily). (Also *intr.*) *Sc.* and *north.*

a **1745** MESTON *Poems* (1767) 126 Ne'er hackney hurl'd On better wheels in the wide world. **1786** BURNS '*Sir, Yours this moment*', If on a beastie I can speel Or hurl in a cartie. **1795** *Fortnight's Ramble* 18 Their shopmen..are hurling their whiskies along the villages. *a* **1810** TANNAHILL *Poems* (1846) 16 Now and then we'll hurl in a coach. **1893** *Northumbld. Gloss.*, *Horl*,..to wheel, to trundle. 'Where ye gan ti horl yor gords' (i.e. hoops)?

†**II. 9.** *intr.* To strive, contend: see HURLING *vbl. sb.* 3. *Obs.*

c **1440** *Promp. Parv.* 253/2 Hurlyn, or debatyn, *incursor.*

†**III. 10.** *intr.* To roar or bluster as the wind; to howl: see HURLING *vbl. sb.* 4. *Obs.*

1530 PALSGR. 589/1, I Hurle, I make a noyse as the wynde dothe, *je bruys. Ibid.*, The wynde hurled so sore that none of us coulde nat here an other. *c* **1535** *Hye Way Spyttel Hous* 101 in Hazl. *E.P.P.* IV. 27 The sharp north wynd hurled bytterly. **1598** DRAYTON *Heroic. Ep.* xxi. 76 The shrugging Ayre about thy Temples hurles.

IV. 11. *dial.* (*intr.*) To be chill, to be pinched with cold (*Craven Dial.* 1828).

Hence **hurled** *ppl. a.*

1638 F. JUNIUS *Paint. of Ancients* 231 When..finding of fault begins to interrupt our worke, it is impossible that the force of our hurled invention should keepe her course.

hurl (hɜːl), *sb.* [f. HURL *v.* Various groups of senses have arisen independently from different senses of the vb., and are practically distinct words.]

I. 1. The action or an act of hurling; a forcible or violent cast or throw.

1530 PALSGR. 233/1 Hurle or throwe with a stone, *coup de pierre.* *a* **1693** URQUHART *Rabelais* III. xii. 93 The darting Hurls, or slinging Casts of the Vulcanian Thunderbolts. **1695** CONGREVE *Taking of Namur* viii, Beholding Mountain on Mountain thrown! With threatening hurl! that shook th' Æthereal Firmament. **1813** LD. THURLOW *Poems* 24 With weak and idle hurl Their darts had sped.

2. The stick or club used in the game of hurling; in quot. 1791, a lacrosse-stick.

1791 W. BARTRAM *Carolina* 370 A company of young fellows..came in..with rackets or hurls in one hand. *Ibid.* 508 Each person having a racquet or hurl, which is an implement..somewhat resembling a laddle or scoop-net, with a handle near three feet in length, the hoop and handle of wood, and the netting of thongs of raw hide, or tendons of an animal. **1858** O'CURRY *Mann. Anc. Irish* (1873) II. 359 He would give his ball a stroke of his hurl..he would throw his hurl at it.

II. 3. ? The rush (of water); swirl. *rare.*

13.. *E.E. Allit. P.* C. 319 Þe pure poplande hourle playes on my heued. *a* **1400–50** *Alexander* 1154 Þe wawis of þe wild see apon þe wallis betis, Þe pure populande hurle [*v.r.* perle] passis it vmby. **1890** CLARK RUSSELL *Ocean Trag.* II. xviii. 109 A sea that had..lost the early snappish and worrying hurl put into it by the first of the dark blast.

4. A downward rush; esp. a violent and noisy rush of stones, etc. down a steep slope. *Sc.*

1549 *Compl. Scot.* vi. 39, I herd mony hurlis of stannirs & stanis that tumlit doune vitht the land rusche. **1632** LITHGOW *Trav.* VI. 262 Distempred feare brought him downe upon me with a rushling hurle. **1866** W. GREGOR *Banffsh. Gloss.*, *Hurl* (1) a quantity of any hard material thrown down, or falling down in confusion and accompanied with noise; as 'A hurl o' stanes cam doon on's back'... *In a hurl*, means in a confused mass, accompanied with noise. (2) The noise caused by any hard material thrown down, or falling down of itself.

†**5.** Diarrhœa. *Sc. Obs.*

1508 DUNBAR *Flyting w. Kennedie* 194 It is wittin..thow hes the hurle behind.

III. 6. A ride in a cart or other wheeled vehicle, a drive. *Sc.*

1822 CARLYLE *Early Lett.* (Norton) II. 144 We will not let you want a *hurl* up and down in the coach. **1826** J. WILSON *Noct. Ambr.* Wks. 1855 I. 236 I'll take a hurl wi' ye as far as the Harrow.

IV. †**7.** Strife, contention; commotion, tumult.

c **1440** *Promp. Parv.* 253/2 Hurl, or debate, *sedicio.* **1553** GRIMALDE *Cicero's Offices* I. (1558) 36 Making a hurle [*tumultuante*] to be thrust from his place. **1587** FLEMING *Contn. Holinshed* III. 1028/1 About the same time that this rebellion..began in the west, the like disordered hurles were attempted in Oxfordshire, and Buckinghamshire. **1603** KNOLLES *Hist. Turks* (1621) 358 In this hurle a great part of the Christian armie..was speedily transported over the river. **1653** URQUHART *Rabelais* I. iv. 23 They all went out in a hurle.

8. *Sc.* 'The act of scolding; sometimes expressed, *a hurl of a flyte*' (Jam.).

? *a* **1800** *H. Blyd's Contract* 6 (Jam.) She ga' me sic a hurl I never gat the like o't.

hurl, var. of HARL *sb.*[1]

'hurlbarrow. *Sc.* and *north. dial.* [f. HURL *v.* 8 + BARROW *sb.*[3]] A wheelbarrow.

1680 FR. SEMPILL *Banishm. Poverty* 86 My guts rumbl'd like a hurle-barrow. **1737** RAMSAY *Scot. Prov.* (1750) 60 It is kittle for the cheeks when the hurl-barrow gaes o'er the brig of the nose. **1819** W. TENNANT *Papistry Storm'd* III. (1827) 114 Hurlbarrows, filled..Wi' saxpence laifs. **1893** *Northumbld. Gloss.*, *Horl-barra.*

'hurlbat. Also 5–6 hurlebatte, 7 whorlebat, 7–8 whirl-bat. [app. f. HURL *v.* + BAT *sb.*[2] The earlier instances are mostly in translations, in which it is used to render two quite different words, *aclys* and *cæstus*, the latter app. through doubt as to its meaning. Cf. the following:

1696 KENNETT *Rom. Antiq.* (1713) 255 The cestus were either a sort of leathern guards for the hands, compos'd of thongs and commonly filled with lead or iron to add force and weight to the blow: Or, according to others, a kind of whirlbats or bludgeons of wood.]

†**1.** A weapon, ? some form of club; in 16th c. Lat.-Eng. Dictionaries, glossing L. *aclys* (*aclis*) a small javelin. *Obs.*

c **1440** *Jacob's Well* (E.E.T.S.) 105 Pleying at þe two hande swerd, at swerd & bokelere, & at two pyked staf, at þe hurlebatte. **1496** *Dives & Paup.* (W. de W.) v. xviii. 220/1 In playes of hethen men..as in playnge at the swerde & bokeler, at the staffe twohandswerde hurlebat in tourmentes. **1548** ELYOT *Dict.*, *Aclis*, a kynde of weapon, vsed in olde tyme, as it wer an hurlebatte. **1565–73** COOPER *Thesaurus*, *Aclis*, a kinde of weapon tyed by a string, much lyke a hurlebatte. *Ibid.*, *Adides* [i.e. *aclides*], short battes of a cubit long and a halfe, with pykes of yron, and were tied to a line, that when they were throwne, one might plucke them againe: Hurlebattes. **1634** *Withal's Dict.* 377/2 Hurlebats having pikes of yron in the end, *adides.* **1656** BLOUNT, *Hurlebats* (*adides*). See *Whorlebats.*

†**2.** Used to render L. *cæstus* CESTUS[2], partly through misapprehension of its meaning: see quot. in etym. *Obs.*

1603 HOLLAND *Plutarch's Mor.* v. iv. 773 Flinging the coit of brasse; yea, and as some say, at hurl-bats and fist-fight. **1609** —— *Amm. Marcell.* XXX. ix. 392 The moving of his armes, laying about him as if they had beene fighting at hurlebats [*velut cæstibus dimicantium*]. **1621** G. SANDYS *Ovid's Met.* v. (1626) 91 Inuincible with hurle-bats [*cæstibus invicti*]. **1634** *Withal's Dict.* 265/2 A whorle-bat, an Instrument of Leather covered with lead, to buffet one another, *cæstus.* **1700** DRYDEN *Fables* Pref. Wks. (Globe) 506 He rejected them, as Dares did the whirlbats of Eryx, when they were thrown before him by Entellus [*Æneid* v. 400–420]. **1791** COWPER *Iliad* VII. 167 Where him his royal whirl-bat nought avail'd.

3. The bat or stick used in the Irish game of hurling; = HURL *sb.* 2.

1820–29 CALLANAN *Convict of Clonmell* in Hayes *Ballads Irel.* I. 347 At my bed-foot decaying My hurlbat is lying.

Hence **hurlbatting**, (†**whirlbatting**), contending with hurlbats.

1744 J. PATERSON *Comm. Milton's P.L.* 208 The valient youths exercised themselves, at running, whirlbating, quoiting, jumping and wrestling.

hurl-bone, a late var. WHIRL-BONE.

hurlbutite ('hɜːlbʌtaɪt). *Min.* [f. the name of Cornelius Searle *Hurlbut* (b. 1906), American mineralogist + -ITE[1].] A colourless or greenish-white phosphate of calcium and beryllium, $Be_2Ca(PO_4)_2$.

1952 M. E. MROSE in *Amer. Mineralogist* XXXVII. 931 The mineral here described as hurlbutite was first found as a large broken crystal on the dump at the pegmatite known as the Smith mine. **1961** *Soviet Physics—Doklady* V. 1143 The structures of danburite $CaB_2Si_2O_8$ and hurlbutite are similar to the structure of the feldspars, in particular to anorthite $CaAl_2Si_2O_8$. **1968** I. KOSTOV *Mineral.* 449 Faheyite is hexagonal, occurring in acicular crystals, babefphite tetragonal.., hurlbutite orthorhombic.

hurlecan, -cano, obs. ff. HURRICANE.

†**hurled,** *a. Obs.* [Cf. HURL-FOOTED.] Deformed or distorted, as a club-foot.

c **1460** *Towneley Myst.* xxx. 315 His hede is like a stowke, hurlyd as hoggys. **1642** FULLER *Holy & Prof. St.* IV. v. 264 Statesmen sometimes must use crooked shoes, to fit hurl'd feet. **1647** —— *Good Th. in Worse T.* x. (1841) 119 He himself had hurled or crooked feet.

†**hurlement.** *Obs.* Also 7 hurli-. [f. HURL *v.* + -MENT.] Rush, violence; confusion, disturbance.

1585 T. WASHINGTON tr. *Nicholay's Voy.* II. xiii. 48 b, The Infidelles..with a greate hurlement and fury entred into the Citie. **1612** HAYWARD *Ann. Eliz.* (Camden) 63 In the very heat of these hurliments, the Englishe burnt one of the milles beyond the water. **1613–18** DANIEL *Coll. Hist. Eng.* (1621) 200 King Edward..discovering both this accident, and the hurlement made by the change of place, slackes not to take advantage thereof.

hurler[1] ('hɜːlə(r)). [f. HURL *v.* + -ER[1].]

1. One who hurls or throws with violence.

1532 MORE *Confut. Barnes* VIII. Wks. 768/1 Bi and by one hurled at him again. And anone as he saw that, what horsons (quoth he)..I se wel ye be hurlers or of counsaile with yᵉ hurlers al the wole maynye of you. **1579–80** NORTH *Plutarch* (1676) 461 Darters, Bow-men, and Hurlers with Slings. **1642** MILTON *Apol. Smect.* Wks. (1851) 276 This cursing Shimei a hurler of stones. **1873** SYMONDS *Grk. Poets* vi. 168 Supreme hurler of the thunderbolt.

2. *spec.* **a.** One who plays either game of HURLING.

1602 CAREW *Cornwall* 74 The Hurlers are bound to the observation of many lawes. **1850** 'BAT' *Crick. Man.* 25 A player..ran with [the ball], followed by the whole pack of hurlers.

b. (See quots.)

1607 CAMDEN *Brit.* 139 (Cornwall) Saxa..equibus septem vel octo æqua inter se distantia..*Hurlers* vicini vocant. **1610** HOLLAND *Camden's Brit.* I. 192 The neighbour Inhabitants terme them Hurlers..perswaded, they had beene men sometimes transformed into Stones, for profaning the Lord's Day, with hurling the Ball. **1797** MATON *West. Count.* I. 269 The Hurlers are three singular and large circles of stones. **1827** G. HIGGINS *Celtic Druids* Pref. 54 In the Parish of St. Clare in Cornwall, are three circles of stone called the Hurlers.

3. One who contends or strives; one who creates a disturbance.

c **1440** *Promp. Parv.* 253/2 Hvrlere, or debate maker.

4. One who wheels a barrow or cart. *Sc.*

1802 FINDLATER *Agric. Surv. Peeblesh.* 209 [The peat] is taken up by the women wheelers (*hurlers*)..Two hurlers commonly suffice to spread the peat dug by one man.

5. A pitcher at baseball. *N. Amer. slang.*

1926 *Daily Colonist* (Victoria, B.C.) 22 July 12/3 Fifty-six runs were scored in a Three-I League baseball game yesterday in which Springfield defeated Peoria... Thirteen hurlers appeared. **1965** O. NASH in *Times Lit. Suppl.* 25 Nov. 1036/5 When I am told that the hurler kicks, rocks, and either deals or delivers. **1968** *Globe & Mail* (Toronto) 10 July 26/5 But in a season dominated by pitchers, the hurlers once again reigned supreme.

Hurler[2] ('hɜːlə(r)). The name of Gertrud *Hurler*, German pædiatrician (qualified 1894), used in the possessive (and also *attrib.*) in ***Hurler('s) disease, syndrome*** = GARGOYLISM 2.

1937 W. R. ASHBY et al. in *Brain* LX. 175 We share the dislike of many workers for eponymous titles, but since the other four diseases in this group have..been designated by the names of those writers who have contributed largely to their elucidation, we consider that at this juncture it would be inadvisable to depart from this practice. We suggest, therefore, in place of the title 'Gargoylism' the title 'Hurler's disease'. **1938** *Jrnl. Pediatrics* XII. 579 (*heading*) Hurler's syndrome (gargoylism). **1970** COHEN & CATHCART in Keefer & Wilkins *Medicine* xxxv. 687 (*heading*) Hurler syndrome (gargoylism). *Ibid.*, The two clinical forms of Hurler's disease (one an autosomal recessive and the other a sex-linked recessive) are currently being related more specifically to these mucopolysaccharide abnormalities.

hurlet. *rare.* [?f. HURL *sb.* 2, or = HURLEY 2.] ?A small hurlbat.

1825 T. C. CROKER *Fairy Leg. S. Irel.* I. 305 The hurley, or hurlet, being an effective and desperate weapon. **1865** tr. *Senchus Mor* in *Anc. Laws Irel.* I. 139 The toys of children must be restored in one day, viz.,..hurlets, balls, and hoops.

†'**hurlewayn.** *Obs.* Also 7 helwayne, hellwain. In ***hurlewaynes kin, meyne***, supposed to be the same as F. *maisnie Hellequin*, med.L. *familia Harlequini* (see HARLEQUIN): The name of a rural sprite or hobgoblin formerly supposed to haunt hedges, etc.

1399 LANGL. *Rich. Redeles* I. 90 Oþer hobbis ȝe hadden of hurlewaynis kynne, Reffusynge the reule of realles kynde. *c* **1400** *Beryn* 8 Leyd wit & lustis all, to suche nyce Iapis As Hurlewaynes meyne in every hegg that capes. **1603** HARSNET *Pop. Impost.* 135 Ware where you walke for feare of bull-beggers..helwayne, the fire-drake..Tom thumbe, hobgoblin..and the rest. *c* **1605** MIDDLETON *Witch* II. ii, Why, Hoppo, and Stadlin, Hellwain and Puckle!

hurley ('hɜːlɪ). Also hurly. [f. HURL *v.*]

1. The Irish game of 'hurling'; hockey.

1841 S. C. HALL *Ireland* I. 256 The great game in Kerry, and indeed throughout the south, is the game of 'Hurley'. *Ibid.* I. 194 Playing 'hurly' on the surface of the waters. **1861** N. A. WOODS *Pr. Wales Canada* 129 La Crosse, a species of hurley, except that to the end of the stick is attached a small purse net, in which the ball may be caught, and so carried to the goal. **1893** [see HURLING *vbl. sb.* 2 b].

2. The stick or club used in this game; a hockey-stick; a club or cudgel of the same shape.

1825 [see HURLET]. **1841** S. C. HALL *Ireland* I. 257 The players..are arranged..in two opposing ranks, with their hurleys crossed, to await the tossing up of the ball. **1887** *Standard* 19 Sept. 3/6 'Hurleys' are made of ash, and are used for playing the national game of that name. **1891** *Pall Mall G.* 29 Oct. 5/1 Mr. Dillon was welcomed by a numerous concourse of Nationalists, carrying torches and hurleys.

3. The ball used in 'hurling'.

1856 KANE *Arct. Expl.* II. xxi. 206 They were contending to drive a hurley, made out of the round knob of a flopper-joint.

†**hurley-hacket.** *Sc. Obs.* Also 6 hurly hakkat. [Cf. HURL *v.*, HURLY[2].]

1. A sport consisting in sliding down a steep place in a trough or sledge, as in the modern tobogganing.

1529 LYNDESAY *Complaynt* 176 Sum gart hym raiffell at the rakkat: sum harld hym to the hurly hakkat. **1810** SCOTT *Lady of L.* v. note ix. (ed. 2) 411 The boys of Edinburgh, about twenty years ago, used to play at the hurly-hacket on the Calton-hill, using for their seat a horse's scull.

attrib. *a* **1861** R. RAE in Hunter *Biggar & Ho. Fleming* iii. 21 Fancy leads me back to some..Tremendous hurley-hacket rowe.

2. Applied contemptuously to an ill-hung carriage.

1824 SCOTT *St. Ronan's* xv, I never thought to have entered ane o' their hurley-hackets.

'**hurley-house.** *Sc.* [Cf. HURL *sb.* 4.] 'A large house fallen into disrepair or nearly in ruins' (Jam.).

1814 SCOTT *Wav.* lxvii, I now wish that I could have left Rose the auld hurley-house and the riggs belanging to it.

'**hurl-footed,** *a.* ? *dial.* [Cf. HURLED *a.*, and mod.Du. *horrel-voet* club-foot.] Club-footed.

1749 *Phil. Trans.* XLVI. 240 We..do well remember, that Nicolas Reeks..was born hurl-footed in both Feet, and a Cripple.

hurling ('hɜːlɪŋ), *vbl. sb.* [f. HURL *v.* + -ING[1].] The action of the verb HURL.

1. Throwing, casting: esp. with violence.

1388 WYCLIF *Baruch* iv. 33 Babiloyne made ioie in thi hurlyng doun, and was glad in thi fal. **1484** CAXTON *Fables of Poge* (1889) 5 By hurlynge and drawynge of stones. **1573–80** BARET *Alv.* H 743 A dart more vehement by the stroke and hurling. **1641** HINDE *J. Bruen* xxxviii. 120 The play at Dice, the property whereof is, by casting and hurling here and there.

2. a. A game, once very popular in Cornwall, played by two parties whose object is to hurl or carry a ball to a distant goal or to their own part of the country; the same as the Welsh *Knappan*, and closely akin to Hand-ball.

c **1600** NORDEN *Spec. Brit., Cornw.* 291 The Cornish men as they are stronge, hardeye and nymble, so are their exercises violent, two especially, wrastling and hurling. **1602** CAREW *Cornwall* 73 b, Hurling taketh his denomination from throwing of the ball. **1603** OWEN *Pembrokesh.* (1892) 279 This plaie is vsed in Wales, and the balle is called *Knappan*,..and our ancient cozens the Cornishmen haue the selfe same exercise among them yet obserued, wᶜʰ they call hurlinge. **1648** *Hamilton Papers* (Camden) 171 The 2 Counties of Devon and Cornewall are on Munday next to meet at a hurling (a sport they haue with a ball). **1781** WESLEY *Wks.* (1872) XIII. 314 Hurling, their favourite diversion, at which limbs were usually broke..is now hardly heard of [in Cornwall]. **1826** in Hone *Every-day Bk.* II. 1008 Cornish Hurling..is now scarcely ever practised.

b. A form of hockey played in Ireland.

1527 *Galway Stat.* in *10th Rep. Hist. MSS. Comm.* App. v. 402 The horlinge of the litill balle with hockie stickes. **1780** A. YOUNG *Tour Irel.* 365 Hurling is a sort of cricket, but instead of throwing the ball in order to knock down a wicket, the aim is to pass it through a bent stick, the ends stuck in the ground. **1893** LE FANU *70 Years Irish Life* 129 'Hurling', or 'hurley', as it is now called, was formerly the chief game in Ireland.

c. *attrib.*, as ***hurling ball, match, tournament.***

1780 *New Ann. Reg., Manners Nations* 64 All will pay her a visit after mass for a hurling match. **1825** T. C. CROKER *Fairy Leg. S. Irel.* I. 306 Hurling-balls. **1888** *Pall Mall G.* 24 Apr. 6/2 Returning from a hurling tournament near Ennis.

†**3.** Strife; commotion, disturbance, tumult. *Obs.*

1387 TREVISA *Higden* (Rolls) VIII. 231 Kyng Henry and þe chapitre of Caunterbury was rebel aȝenst hym. In þat horlynge he made it as þey he knewe it not. *c* **1440** *Promp. Parv.* 253/2 Hurlynge, or stryfe, *incurcio*. *c* **1440** *Partonope* 2000 And in this hurlyng Partanope With hys swerde a stroke smote he. **1570–6** LAMBARDE *Peramb. Kent* (1826) 406 That Taxe of money whereof I have before spoken:..the onely cause and fountaine of all that hurling, as they termed it.

†**b.** ***hurling time***, a time of tumult or commotion: applied by the old chroniclers to Wat Tyler's rebellion in the reign of Richard II. *Obs.*

1480 CAXTON *Chron. Eng.* ccxxxix. 264 In the iiij yere of kyng Richardes regne the comunes arisen vp in dyuerse partyes of the reame..the whiche they callyd the hurlyng time. **1494** FABYAN *Chron.* VII. 531 In this season also, called the hurlynge tyme, the Commons of Norfolke & Suffolke came vnto yᵉ Abbey of Bury, & there slewe one of yᵉ Kyngis iustycis, callyd Iohn Caundysshe. **1658** GURNALL *Chr. in Arm.* II. 233 There are great complaints of what men have lost in these hurling times.

†**4.** The violent rushing of wind; the sound of this, roaring or blustering (of the wind); rolling of thunder; grumbling or rumbling of the bowels.

1398 TREVISA *Barth. De P.R.* XVII. clxviii. (1495) 712 Newe whete..bredyth swellynge and ventosytee and hurlynge and kurlynge in the wombe. *a* **1400–50** *Alexander* 4794 Þare was hurling on hiȝe as it in hell ware. **1519** HORMAN *Vulg.* 46 Yf the herynge place be hurte..than comme the deffenesse, or it semeth hyssynge, hurrelynge, syngeynge, or suche other. **1583** STANYHURST *Æneis* II. (Arb.) 53 In corneshocks sindged with blasterus hurling Of Southwynd whizeling. **1585** JAS. I *Ess. Poesie* (Arb.) 15 They heare the whiddering Boreas bolde, With hiddeous hurling, rolling Rocks from hie. **1668** GLANVILL *Blow at Mod. Sadduc.* 99 The sign of its approach was an hurling in the Air over the House.

5. The wheeling of a barrow; driving in a cart. *Sc.*

hurling, *ppl. a.* [f. HURL *v.* + -ING[2].]

1. Rushing, impetuous, violent: sometimes esp. referring to sound; sometimes associated with *whirling*.

13.. *E.E. Allit. P.* B. 413 Þe arc houen watz on hyȝe with hurlande gotez. *c* **1555** HARPSFIELD *Divorce Hen. VIII* (Camden) 277 God did send a tempestuous hurling wind. *c* **1566** J. ALDAY tr. *Boaystuau's Theat. World* G viij, By the which meanes groweth such a hurling noyse. **1602** SHAKS. *Ham.* I. v. 133 These are but wild and hurling [*Qos.* whirling] words, my Lord. **1790** A. WILSON *Discons. Wren* Poet. Wks. (1846) 98 Some dreadfu' hurling noise I heard.

†**2.** Struggling, conflicting. *Obs.*

1528 PAYNEL *Salerne's Regim.* P b, The one labourethe to be losed and to go out: the other withstandeth and byndeth..Wherfore a hurlynge mouynge is caused in the bodye inducynge gnawynge and inflasion in the bealy.

hurlock ('hɜːlək). *local.* Also 9 hurluk. A hard kind of chalk.

1598 NORDEN *Spec. Brit., Msex.* II. 18 About the towne is a kinde of chalke, which they call Hurlocke, a stonie Marle, more fit to make lime then to soyle the grounde. **1847–78** HALLIWELL, *Hurluk*, hard chalk. *Beds.* **1892** J. LUCAS *Kalm's Eng.* 340 The harder kind of chalk which is here called Hurlock.

†**hurlpit,** var. f. WHIRLPIT *Obs.* = whirlpool.

1600 HOLLAND *Livy* XXIX. xxxii. 734 Two of them [horses]..were swallowed up of the deepe hurlpits.

†'**hurlpool.** *Obs.* [Cf. HURLWIND.]

1. An obs. variant of WHIRLPOOL.

1551 T. WILSON *Logike* (1564) 48 b, Against Cardinall Poule, and beyng vehement..saied thus in the middest of his heate, o Poule, o hurle Poule, as though his name declared his euil nature.

2. A whale or sea-monster: = WHIRLPOOL 2.

1556 WITHALS *Dict.* (1568) 8 b/2 A hurlpoole, *pistrix*. **1570** LEVINS *Manip.* 160/42 A Thirlepoole, *balena*. A Hurlepoole, *idem*. **1598** FLORIO, *Capidio, Capidolio*, a kinde of great whalefish, or hurlepoole.

†**hurlwind.** *Obs.* [From a confusion of HURL *v.* and WHIRL *v.*] = WHIRLWIND.

1509 BARCLAY *Shyp of Folys* 51 b, As coy and styll As the horle wynde [**1570** whirle winde] or clapper of a mylle. **1573** G. HARVEY *Letter-bk.* (Camden) 102 In a hurlewind of conceit. **1609** BIBLE (Douay) *2 Kings* ii. 1 When our Lord would take up Elias by a hurle winde into heaven. **1640** G. SANDYS *Crucif.* (1649) 13 No sudden hurl-windes shall your bodies cast On trembling Earth.

hurly[1] ('hɜːlɪ). [f. HURL *v.*: cf. HURLING *vbl. sb.* 3.] Commotion, tumult, uproar; strife.

1596 SHAKS. *Tam. Shr.* IV. i. 206 Amid this hurlie I intend That all is done in reuerend care for her. **1600** HOLLAND *Livy* VIII. xxvii. 301 In this hurlie and uprore [*tumultu*]. **1603** KNOLLES *Hist. Turks* (1621) 844 All things being thus in a hurley and out of order. **1806** J. GRAHAME *Birds Scotl.* 74 Oft in the hurly of the winter storm. **1855** SINGLETON *Virgil* II. 16 Amid the hurly and the din. **1888** *Harper's Mag.* Jan. 203/1 The wind screamed..Pokeberry squatted ignominiously in the fierce hurly.

hurly[2] ('hɜːlɪ). *Sc.* and *dial.* [f. HURL *v.*] A porter's barrow, a hand-cart.

1866 GREGOR *Banffsh. Gloss.*, *Hurly*, a large kind of wheel-barrow used by porters. **1880** *Antrim & Down Gloss.*, *Hurly* ..(2) a long, low cart with two wheels. **1892** G. TRAVERS *Mona Maclean* (1893) II. 10 Bill had a lot of luggage on a hurley.

hurly-burly ('hɜːlɪ'bɜːlɪ), *sb.*, *a.*, and *adv.* Also (with or without hyphen) 6 howrley burlei, horl(e)y borl(e)y, hurly burle, hurlei burley, whorle borle, whourliburly, 6–7 hurli(e) burli(e), -ly(e, -ley, 6– hurley burley. [Known from *c* 1540. The phrase *hurling and burling* occurs somewhat earlier. In this, the first word is HURLING *vbl. sb.*, sense 3, 'commotion', and *burling* seems to have been merely an initially-varied repetition of it, as in other 'reduplicated' combinations and phrases which express non-uniform repetition or alternation of action. *Hurly-burly* holds the same relation to *hurling and burling*, that the simple HURLY[1] holds to HURLING *vbl. sb.* 3.

But *hurly-burly* cannot, with present evidence, be considered a direct formation from *hurly*, since the latter has not been found before 1596. It is difficult to establish any historical contact with Fr. *hurluberlu* a heedless, hasty person (Rabelais *a* 1535), or the Ger. *hurliburli* adv., precipitately, with headlong haste (see Littré and Grimm).]

A. *sb.* Commotion, tumult, strife, uproar, turmoil, confusion. (Formerly a more dignified word than now.)

[*c* **1530** LD. BERNERS *Arth. Lyt. Bryt.* (1814) 240 Than the archbysshop answered hym agayne right sharplye; and so there began muche hurlynge and burlynge in the courte.] **1539** TAVERNER *Gard. Wysed.* II. Eijb, Hys comons, whome..he perceuyed in a hurly burly..and ready to make an insurrection. **1545** *Primer Hen. VIII* Prayers (1848) 506 For thy sake suffer I all this hurly-burly. **1548** HALL *Chron., Hen. VIII* 231 In this tyme of insurrection, and in the rage of horley borley. **1552** T. BARNABE in Ellis *Orig. Lett.* Ser. II. II. 201 This whorle borle of takinge of our shippes. **1571** GOLDING *Calvin on Ps.* ix. 14 Such as are desperate doo rage with more hurlyburly and greater headynesse. **1580** BARET *Alv.* B 1346 Whourliburly that riseth of a soudain and great feare. **1605** SHAKS. *Macb.* I. i. 3 When the Hurley-burley's done, When the Battaile's lost, and wonne. **1678** CUDWORTH *Intell. Syst.* I. ii. §18. 81 Nor could such a Deity ever have any quiet enjoyment of himself, being perpetually filled with tumult and Hurliburly. **1764** O'HARA *Midas* I. 5 What can this hurly-burly, this helter-skelter mean? Jove looks confounded surly!—Chaos is come again. **1824** L. MURRAY *Eng. Gram.* (ed. 5) I. 429 Avoid *low expressions*: such as 'Topsy turvy, hurly burly, pellmell'. **1830** DE QUINCEY *Bentley* Wks. 1863 VI. 43 In the very uttermost hurly-burly of the storm. **1888** BURGON *Lives 12 Gd. Men* I. II. 158 The voices which make themselves heard above the 'hurley burley'.

b. with *a* and *pl.* An instance of this.

1548 UDALL, etc. *Erasm. Par. Matt.* x. 63 These hurly burlyes the deuill shall rayse agaynste the gospell. **1575** *Brieff Disc. Troub. Franckford* (1846) 67 By occasion of our striffes and hurley burlies. **1600** HOLLAND *Livy* II. xxix. 63 These so great sturres and mutinous hurliburlies [*tantum concitum turbarum*]. **1657** J. SMITH *Myst. Rhet.* 73 English Examples of Onomatopeia..By imitation of sound, as to say, a hurliburly, signifying a tumult or uproar. **1764** MRS. DELANY in *Life & Corr.* Ser. II. I. 40, I have..given up all public hurley-burleys, but enjoy the recital of them very well. **1866** CARLYLE *Remin.* I. 114 Those Rector hurries and hurlyburlies, now so sad to me.

B. *adj.* Characterized by or attended with commotion, tumult, or disturbance; tumultuous.

1596 SHAKS. *1 Hen. IV*, v. i. 78 Newes Of hurly burly Innouation. **1648** *Persecutio Undecima* 11 In the hurlyburly days of queen Elizabeth. **1761** STERNE *Tr. Shandy* III. v, What has *con furia—con strepito*—or any other hurlyburly word whatever to do with harmony? **1815** SCOTT *Fam. Lett.* 28 Nov. (1894) I. xi. 350 A hurly-burly sort of performance.

†**C.** *adv.* In commotion, tumultuously; in confusion; confusedly. *Obs.*

a **1563** BECON *Flower godly Prayers* Wks. (1563) II. 186 b, Albeit the powers of this world..come together hurly burly ..against the Lorde and his annoynted. ? *c* **1600** *Distracted Emp.* II. i. in Bullen *O. Pl.* III. 187 Offices are like huntinge breakfasts gott Hurlye burlye, snatcht with like greedynes. **1615** J. TAYLOR (Water P.) *Siege Jerus.* 37 Wks. (1630) 14/1 They hurly burly all things overturn'd. **1704** J. PITTS *Acc. Mahometans* 106 We set out..without any Order at all, all hurly burly.

hurly-burly, *v. Obs.* or *arch.* [f. prec.]

†**1.** *trans.* **a.** To hurl or bandy about. **b.** To throw into confusion or uproar. *Obs.*

1550 BALE *Apol.* 48, I approve..the grounde of a vow.. and not the name of it, as it hath been hurly-burlyed in Antichristes kyngdom. **1678** *Pol. Ballads* (1860) I. 214 This hurly-burlies all the town, Makes Smith and Harris prattle.

2. *intr.* To make a hurly-burly or uproar.

1598 FLORIO, *Garbugliare*, to garboile, to hurli-burlie, to turmoile. **1614** T. FREEMAN *Runne & great Cast* i. F iv, Still more and more conceits come flocking in And in my braines do Hurly-burly it. **1884** G. ALLEN *Philistia* III. 13 The red-haired hurlyburlying Scotch professor.

hurmon, obs. form of HIREMAN.

hurn, obs. and s.w. dial. f. RUN *v.*

Huron ('hjʊərən). Also 7 **Hiroon.** [Fr., f. earlier *hure*, rough hair of the head.] A confederation of five Iroquoian peoples formerly inhabiting a region adjacent to Lake Huron; a member of one of these peoples; also their language. Also *attrib.* or as *adj.*

1658 F. GORGES in *Maine Hist. Soc. Coll.* (1847) II. 67 The Hiroons, who being neuters are friends both to the one [*sc.* the Iroquois] and the other [*sc.* the French]. **1756** A. BUTLER *Lives Saints* II. 650 The saint wrote earnestly to the general of the Society, desiring to be employed on a mission to the barbarous Hurons and Iroquois in Canada. **1782** 'J. H. ST. JOHN DE CRÈVECŒUR' *Lett. from Amer. Farmer* (1783) iv. 90 The Nattic, like the Huron, in the north-western parts of this continent, must have been the most prevailing one [*sc.* language] in this region. **1786** *Mem. Amer. Acad. Arts & Sci.* II. I. 125 The Huron, or Wyandot language having no affinity to the Shawanese, Delawares, and other nations. **1789** [see *Five Nations*]. **1823** J. S. MILL *Autobiogr.* (1924) 267 No one, I apprehend, would insult the understanding of this Society..by maintaining..that the Hurons and the Iroquois are the happiest and the most enlightened of mankind. **1832** 'M. DOYLE' *Hints on Emigration to Upper Canada* (ed. 2) 17 The soil in the Huron territory is a rich sandy loam. **1845** [see BUCKLE *sb.* 1 e]. **1880** A. H. SAYCE *Introd. Sci. of Lang.* II. ix. 291 The Hurons of North America believe that the souls of the departed turn into turtle-doves. **1933** L. BLOOMFIELD *Lang.* iv. 72 The Iroquoian family..includes, among others, the Huron (or Wyandot) language. **1959** *Listener* 9 July 75/2 He [*sc.* the American writer] can always feel himself to be a noble savage, a Huron, confronted by the degenerate, corrupt, or over-sophisticated stock from which he sprang. **1973** *Ibid.* 25 Oct. 549/1 The Jesuits..negotiated with the Hurons and Iroquois, as they treated with the *daimyos.*

huron, obs. var. of HERN *poss. pron.*[1]

Huronian (hjʊ'rəʊnɪən), *a. Geol.* [f. *Huron* + -IAN.] Of or belonging to Lake Huron in North America; a term applied by Sir W. Logan to a division of the archæan series of rocks as found in Canada; but now abandoned by most geologists.

1862 DANA *Man. Geol.* 142 The Azoic rocks of Canada are divided by Logan into the Laurentian..and the Huronian, comprising a narrow band on the borders of Lake Superior and Lake Huron. **1885** *Lyell's Elem. Geol.* xxviii. (ed. 4) 458 The strata called the Huronian by Sir W. Logan are of vast thickness.

huronite ('hjʊərənaɪt). *Min.* [f. as prec. + -ITE.] An impure felspar found in spherical masses in the vicinity of Lake Huron.

1836 T. THOMSON *Min.* I. 384. **1868** DANA *Min.* 485.

hurpeny, obs. form of HEARTHPENNY.

hurr (hɜː(r), hʌrr), *v. Obs.* exc. *dial.* [Echoic: cf. HARR.] *intr.* To make or utter a dull sound of vibration or trilling; to buzz as an insect; to snarl as a dog; to pronounce a trilled *r*.

1398 TREVISA *Barth. De P. R.* XII. xii. (Tollem. MS.), By continuall flappynge of wynges he [the gnat] makeþ noyse in þe eyer, as þouȝe he hurred [*quasi stridet*]. *c* **1440** *Promp. Parv.* 254/1 Hurron, or bombon as bees..(*K.* hurryn, or bumbyn as ben)..*bombizo.* **1636** B. JONSON *Eng. Gram.* (1640) 47 R is the Dogs Letter, and hurreth in the sound. **1638** H. ADAMSON *Muses Threnodie* (1774) 72 And, where no hope of gain is, huffe and hur, And bark against the moon, as doth a cur. **1882** *Lanc. Gloss.*, *Hurr*, to snarl like a dog.

Hence **hurring** *vbl. sb.* and *ppl. a.*

1583 STANYHURST *Æneis* II. (Arb.) 47 Thee skyes lowd rumbled with ringing thunderus hurring. **1599** T. M[OUFET] *Silkwormes* 73 Heare eke their hurring and their churring song. **1603** FLORIO *Montaigne* II. xxxi. (1632) 402 A fagot flame with hurring sounds.

†**hurr**, *sb. Obs.* [f. prec. vb.] 'A thin flat piece of wood, tied to a string and whirled round in the air' (Halliwell). Also called **hurre-bone.**

1483 *Cath. Angl.* 192/2 An Hurre bone (*A.* A Hurre), *giraculum.* **1500** *Ortus Voc.* ibid., *Giraculum*, a chylde's whyrle, or a hurre.

hurr, obs. var. HER *pron.*

hurrah (hʊ'rɑː, hə'rɑː), **hurray** (hʊ'reɪ, hə'reɪ), *int.* and *sb.* Also 7– **hurra**, 8 **hurrea**, **whurra**, 9 **hooray**, (**hooroar**), ‖**hourra.** [A later substitute for HUZZA (not in Johnson, Ash, Walker; in Todd 1818), perh. merely due to onomatopœic modification, but possibly influenced by some foreign shouts: cf. Sw., Da., LG. *hurra!*, Du. *hoera!*, Russ. *urá!* whence F. *houra*; F. *hourra* is from Eng. MHG. had *hurr, hurrâ*, as interjections representing rapid whirring motion (cf. *hurren* to rush), whence also a shout used in chasing. According to Moriz Heyne in Grimm, *hurrah* was the battle-cry of the Prussian soldiers in the War of Liberation (1812–13), and has since been a favourite cry of soldiers and sailors, and of exultation. In English the form *hurrah* is literary and dignified; *hooray* is usual in popular acclamation.]

A. *int.* A shout expressive of approbation, encouragement, or exultation; used esp. as a 'cheer' at public assemblies or the like.

1716 ADDISON *Drummer* v. i, *Coach.* The same good man that ever he was. *Gard.* Whurra. **1773** GOLDSM. *Stoops to Conq.* I. ii, Hurrea, hurrea, bravo! **1845** HIRST *Com. Mammoth* etc. 89 Hurrah for brown Autumn! hurrah! hurrah! **1855** THACKERAY *Rose & Ring* xiv, Captain Hedzoff flung up his helmet, and cried, 'Hurray! Hurray! Long live King Giglio!' **1865** DICKENS *Mut. Fr.* III. xi, 'Hooroar!' cried the man. **1888** J. PAYN *Myst. Mirbridge* I. xxii, There goes the gong..Hooray!

B. *sb.* **1.** A name for this shout.

1686 J. DUNTON *Lett. fr. New-Eng.* (1867) 301 Our Capt. ordered all his Guns to fire; at which they all of them (which were about twenty) fil'd the very Heavens with Hurras and Shouts. **1694** in Wood *Life* 1 Nov. (O.H.S.) III. 472 The prisoners in Lancashire are discharg'd..a great hurray followed. **1813** SCOTT *Trierm.* III. xxiii, Wild jubilee and loud hurra Pursued him on his venturous way. **1841** MACAULAY *Ess.*, *W. Hastings* (1887) 636 An European warrior who rushes on a battery of cannon with a loud hurrah. **1870** EMERSON *Soc. & Solit.*, *Courage* Wks. (Bohn) III. 106 They can do the hurras, the placarding, the flags —and the voting, if it is a fair day.

‖**2.** Representing F. *houra*, Russian *urá*: The shout of attack of the Cossacks; whence, by extension, an attack.

[**1827** SCOTT *Napoleon* V. 383 Platow with his Cossacks made a charge, or, in their phrase, a hourra, upon the French. *Ibid.* lxxv. Wks. 1870 XV. 113 The enemy had made a hourra upon Marmont.] **1841** GEN. P. THOMPSON *Exerc.* (1842) VI. 77 The best way they have of making a 'hurra' upon their enemies. *Ibid.* 375, I think we could get up such a 'hurrah' of water-borne Cossacks.

3. ***hurrah's nest***: a confused or disorderly mass; a state of confusion or disorder. *U.S.*

1829 LONGF. in *Life* (1891) I. 164 A queer looking Dutchman, with a head like a 'hurra's nest'. **1840** R. H. DANA *Two Years bef. Mast* ii, Everything was pitched about in grand confusion. There was a complete hurrah's nest. **1860** BARTLETT *Dict. Amer.*, *Hurra's Nest*, a state of confusion. A woman's word. **1889** S. W. MITCHELL in *Century Mag.* Aug. 503/1 The old lumberman pointed..to a 'hurrah's nest' (a mass of leaves left by a freshet in the crotch of the divergent branches of a bush) half-way up the slope—on it was coiled a large rattlesnake.

4. *attrib.* or *adj.* in various *slang* or *colloq.* uses = shouting hurrah, uproarious, blindly enthusiastic; joyous, 'glad'.

1835 *Franklin Repos.* (Chambersburg, Pa.) 2 June 2/3 The New York delegation cared nothing for principles! To them ..the men who could secure for the ticket and for *Martin Van Buren* the *hurra boys* was every thing! **1836** *Congress. Globe* 17 Feb., App. 115 [Some have declared] that his election had been brought about by the 'hurrah boys', and those who knew just enough to shout 'hurrah for Jackson!' **1903** *N.Y. Even. Post.* 30 Oct. 16 Added to this solid element is the hurrah crowd whose enthusiasm has a venal tone. **1907** N. MUNRO *Daft Days* xii. 102 'And what are you doing with your hurrah clothes on?' 'I like to put on my Sunday clothes when I'm writing Charles.' **1909** *Daily Chron.* 20 July 1/2 'Hurrah-boats', as the bluejacket aptly calls excursion steamers. **1925** FRASER & GIBBONS *Soldier & Sailor Words* 124 *Hurrah boats*, a Navy term for the pleasure steamers of touring trippers that go round the Fleet at Naval Reviews, usually cheering as they pass ships. **1926** *Flynn's* 16 Jan. 640/1, I had many a pal among th' touts and hurrah boys. **1928** *Daily Express* 4 Dec. 10/3 'Hurrah boys' are college students. **1964** N. FREELING *Double-Barrel* v. 176 We seem to have got quite a hurrah letter from the burgomaster. And there was a hint that I may be promoted.

hu'rrah, hu'rray, *v.* [f. prec.]

1. *intr.* To shout 'hurrah!'

1798 BERESFORD in *Ld. Auckland's Corr.* (1862) III. 443 Lord Edward heard the noise and the mob hurraying. **1868** KINGLAKE *Crimea* (1877) III. i. 252 The Grenadiers were hurrahing on their left. **1883** BESANT *All in Gard. Fair* II. i, The people would crowd to look upon him and to hooray.

2. *trans.* To receive or encourage with shouts of 'hurrah!'; to 'cheer', as at a public gathering.

1832 J. W. CROKER in *Diary* 12 May (1884), He had been hurrahed by the mob. **1856** LEVER *Martins of Cro' M.* 592 He stood upon an old wall, and hurrahed the people on.

Hence **hu'rrahing, hu'rraying** *vbl. sb.* and *ppl. a.*

1813 L. HUNT in *Examiner* 26 Apr. 257/2 Such a man is.. fond of hurrayings and shoutings. **1837** CARLYLE *Fr. Rev.* II. VI. iv, Through hurrahing streets. **1878** H. SMART *Play or Pay* xi. (ed. 3) 241 If there is no hurrahing, there is much jubilation.

'hurr-burr. [perh. for *hoar-bur*; cf. HARDOCK.] A local name for the Burdock.

1796 WITHERING *Brit. Plants* (ed. 3) III. 694 *Arctium Lappa*..Burdock, Common Burr, Clott-burr, Hurr-burr. **1861** MISS PRATT *Flower. Pl.* III. 224.

hurre, obs. f. HER *pron.*

[**hurre**, error for HURL *sb.* and *v.*]

hurrea, obs. f. HURRAH.

hurrelynge, obs. f. HURLING.

†**hurrer.** *Obs.* Also 5 **hurer**, 6 **-ar**, 8 **hurrier.** [f. HURE *sb.* cap + -ER[1].] A maker of, or dealer in, hats and caps; = HABERDASHER a.

1403 *Close Roll 4 Hen. IV* b, Johannes Spark, hurer. **1482** *Rolls Parlt.* VI. 223/2 No..Hurer, Capper or other..put.. eny Huers, Bonettes or Cappes..to be fulled or thikked at eny suche Mille. **1598** STOW *Surv.* xxxiii. (1603) 301 Hat Marchantes or Hurrers. **1657** HOWELL *Londinop.* 304 The Cappers, and Hat-Merchants, or Hurrers, being one Company of Haberdashers. **1766** ENTICK *London* IV. 127 The haberdashers..were anciently known by the name of hurriers and milleners.

Hurrian ('hʊrɪən), *sb.* and *a.* Also **Harrian**; (less freq.) **Harri, Hurri; Kharri, Khurri, -ian.** [f. Hittite and Assyrian *Ḫar·ri, Ḫur·ri* + -AN.]

A. *sb.* **a.** Name of a widespread non-Semitic people in the Middle East during the second and third millennia B.C., sometimes identified with the Horites. Also, a member of this people. **b.** The language (written in cuneiform) of this people, not known to be related to any other language. **B.** *adj.* Of or pertaining to the Hurrians or their language. Hence **'Hurrianize** *v. trans.*, to make Hurrian in form or character.

1911 *Encycl. Brit.* XVIII. 182/2 It is clear that Mesopotamia had now a further new element in its population, bearing apparently the name Kharri. **1928** C. DAWSON *Age of Gods* 302 Harrian is practically identical with the language of the people of Mitanni. *Ibid.*, The dominant element in Mitanni was..Indo-Iranian, in origin, but there is no trace of this in the Harrian language. **1929** J. GARSTANG *Hittite Empire* ii. 34 North of it[*sc.* Assyria]..was Alshe, a Harrian dependency; while..eastern Taurus was apparently wholly in possession of the Harrians, whose seat must probably be sought in Armenia itself, possibly in the neighbourhood of Lake Van. **1930** *Dublin Rev.* Jan. 9 Hurrian was one of the languages of the eastern part of the Hittite Empire. *Ibid.* 11 Nahmaulel..may be either Hurrianized Semitic, or wholly 'foreign'—*i.e.*, presumably Caucasian or Hurrian. **1939** L. H. GRAY *Foundations of Lang.* 380 Khurrian (or Kharrian). **1944** I. J. GELB *Hurrians & Subarians* i. 1 Both Hurrians and Subarians, their lands and their languages, are mentioned frequently in the cuneiform inscriptions discovered in the early 19th century during the British excavations at Kuyunjik. **1948** A. L. KROEBER *Anthropol.* (rev. ed.) xvii. 713 Soon after 1500 the Harri established themselves for a few brief centuries in Mitanni on the upper Euphrates. **1949** W. F. ALBRIGHT *Archaeol. of Palestine* viii. 183 The Hurrian language was a complex agglutinative tongue, resembling Sumerian or Turkish more closely in structure than either Semitic or Indo-European, but not related to any of them. **1952** O. R.

GURNEY *Hittites* i. 26 In 1457 B.C. the Hurrian domination was brought to an end by the victories of Tuthmosis III in his eighth campaign. **1957** *Chambers's Encycl.* VII. 156/1 The foundation of strong Amorite kingdoms..was followed by the establishment of Hurrian states on the upper Euphrates. *Ibid.*, The Hittites..took little part at first in the struggle in Syria between Egypt and the Hurrians. **1960** K. M. KENYON *Archaeol. in Holy Land* vii. 182 There are the Ḫurri, who seem to have established themselves on the middle Euphrates at the beginning of the millennium. **1972** *Times* 31 Aug. 12/6 David Willstar..succeeded in deciphering the musical notation of Hurrian hymns found on pieces of clay in the French dig at Rash-ash-shamra, dating from 1300 B.C.

hurricane (ˈhʌrɪkeɪn, -kən). Forms: α. 6 furacane, furicano(e, 6–7 furacana, 7 foracan(e, furicane. β. 6 haurachana, 6–7 (9) hurricano, 7 harau-, harou-, haracana; her(r)i-, hery-, hira-, hire-, hyrra-, hyrri-, (hurle-, hurli-), (h)uracano. γ. 6–7 uracan, 7 heri-, huri-, (hurle-, oran-), urycan; harau-, haura-, heri-, heuri-, herocane, harrycain, 7–9 hurrican, 7– hurricane. [a. Sp. *huracan*, OSp. **furacan*, Pg. *furacão*, from the Carib word given by Oviedo as *huracan*, by Peter Martyr (as transl. by R. Eden) as *furacan*. Thence also It. *uracano* (Diez), F. *ouragan*, Du. *orkaan*, Ger., Da., Sw. *orkan*. The earlier Eng. forms reflect all the varieties of the Sp. and Pg., with numerous popular perversions, *hurricane* being itself one, which became frequent after 1650, and was established from 1688. Earlier use favoured forms in final *-ana*, *-ano*, perh. deduced from the Sp. pl. *huracanes* (but words from Sp. were frequently assumed to end in *-o*).]

1. A name given primarily to the violent wind-storms of the West Indies, which are cyclones of diameter of from 50 to 1000 miles, wherein the air moves with a velocity of from 80 to 130 miles an hour round a central calm space, which with the whole system advances in a straight or curved track; hence, any storm or tempest in which the wind blows with terrific violence.

α. **1555** EDEN *Decades* 21 These tempestes of the ayer (which the Grecians caule *Tiphones*..) they caule *Furacanes*..violent and furious Furacanes, that plucked vppe greate trees. **1587** HAKLUYT *J. Hawkins' 3rd Voy.* (1878) 73 Their stormes..the which they call Furicanos. **1596** NASHE *Saffron Walden* To Rdr., Stormes in the West Indies cald the Furicanoes. **1632** HEYWOOD *2nd Pt. Iron Age* IV. Wks. 1873 IV. 405 With the tempests, gusts, and Furicanes, The warring windes, the billowes, rocks, and fires.

β. **1555** EDEN *Decades* 183 (*tr.* Oviedo) Great tempestes which they caule Furacanas or Haurachanas..ouerthrowe many howses and great trees. **1613** PURCHAS *Pilgrimage* (1614) 758 *note*, A Catch perished at Sea in a Herycano. *Ibid.* 903 Jamaica..is extremely subject to the Uracani,..terrible gusts of Winde. *Ibid.* 910 Oviedo reporteth of a Huricano or Tempest. **1617** RALEIGH *2nd Voy. Guiana* in *Discov. Guiana* (Hakluyt Soc.) 187 That night..a hurlecano fell vppon vs. **1642** FULLER *Holy & Prof. St.* II. xx. 130 The winds are..stark mad in an herricano. **1643** HOWELL *Parables* 15 An Haraucana, that Indian gust. *a* **1649** WINTHROP *New Eng.* (1853) I. 337 Cast away..in a great hyrracano. **1656** BLOUNT *Glossogr.*, *Haracana* or *Herocane*,..an impetuous kind of Whirlewind. **1670** R. COKE *Disc. Trade* 76 Plagues, Fires, and Hyrricanoes. **1684** T. BURNET *Th. Earth* II. (1690) 109 A storm or hurricano..makes a strange havock where it comes. **1816** J. WILSON *City of Plague* II. iii. 108 All at once the hurricano ceased.

γ. **1588** PARKE tr. *Mendoza's Hist. China* 313 [1854, II. 220] This word Vracan, in the Indian tongue of those Ilands, is as much to say, as the ioyning of all the foure principall winds togither. *a* **1613** OVERBURY *A Wife* etc. (1638) 159 The Hurican of the Sea. **1617** RALEIGH *2nd Voy. Guiana* in *Discov. Guiana* (Hakluyt Soc.) 187 Not half a quarter of an hower before the hurlecan. **1634** SIR T. HERBERT *Trav.* 26 Wee doubted a Hero-cane, a Tempest of thirtie dayes continuance. *c* **1645** HOWELL *Lett.* (1650) II. 22 The devill, whom they call 'Tantara',..appears often unto them specially in a haraucane. **1651** BIGGS *New Disp.* ⁋ 144 It's feared as a Harry-Cain. **1651** OGILBY *Æsop* (1665) 169 Bright Zephyre..Did bring a Heuricane To rend her. **1665** SIR T. HERBERT *Trav.* (1677) 374 Prodigious stormes called Tuffons or Hurricanes. **1682** WOOD *Life* 31 May (O.H.S.) III. 17 A prodigious hericane that broke bows and armes of trees. **1697** DAMPIER *Voy.* I. v. 94 No Tempests, no Tornados, or Hurricans. **1699** *Ibid.* II. III. 65 Hurricanes had never been known at Jamaica when I was there. **1788** *Gentl. Mag.* LVIII. I. 74/1 At eight the sky became obscured, and it blew a hurricane. **1860** MAURY *Phys. Geog. Sea* xix. §807, I have never seen a typhoon or hurricane so severe.

2. *transf.* and *fig.* **a.** A violent rush or commotion bringing with it destruction or confusion; a storm or tempest of words, noise, cheers, etc.

1639 MASSINGER *Unnat. Combat* v. ii, Each guilty thought to me is A dreadful hurricano. **1662** GURNALL *Chr. in Arm.* verse 18. xx. (1669) 480/2 This short Calm went before a sudden Hericano of Persecution. **1677** *Cleveland's Poems* Ep. Ded., He with Hurricanos of wit stormeth the sense. **1687** T. BROWN *Saints in Uproar* Wks. 1730 I. 74 Don't you hear what a cursed hurricane they make? **1763** C. JOHNSTON *Reverie* I. 25 Such an hurricane of riot and debauchery. **1775** JOHNSON *Tax. no Tyr.* 79 The loud hurricane of Pennsylvanian eloquence. **1882** *Daily News* 7 Mar. 5/4 A hurricane of cheers burst forth from the excited crowd.

†**b.** A large and crowded assembly of fashionable people at a private house, of a kind common during part of the 18th century. (Cf. DRUM *sb.*[1] 10, ROUT.) *Obs.*

1746 R. WHATLEY *Christian* p. vii. *note*, A confused meeting of Company of both Sexes on Sundays is called a Hurricane. **1746–7** MRS. DELANY in *Life & Corr.* 447 Tomorrow I go to St. James's..and finish at the duchess of Queensberry's, who is to have a hurricane. **1779** MRS. BARBAULD *Wks.* (1825) II. 22 There is a squeeze, a fuss, a drum, a rout, and lastly a hurricane, when the whole house is full from top to bottom. **1805** E. DE ACTON *Nuns of Desert* II. 271 Entirely absconded from plays, balls, routs, drums, hurricanes.

c. A space from which trees, etc., have been cleared by the force of a hurricane. (Earlier *hurricane ground*: see 3.) *U.S.*

1735 J. HEMPSTEAD *Diary* (1901) 291 The Stack..was made in the Hurrycane this Side the Swamp. **1833** [see DRIVE *sb.* 1 c]. **1891** W. F. SWASEY *Early Days & Men Calif.* 15 In Missouri, cause and effect had been blended in the common designation of 'hurricane'.

3. a. *attrib.* and *Comb.* 'Of or belonging to a hurricane', as ***hurricane cloud, force, month, season, violence***; 'that has been visited by a hurricane', as ***hurricane ground, tree***; **hurricane-bird**, the frigate-bird; **hurricane-deck**, a light upper deck or platform in some steamers; so **hurricane-decked** *a.*, having a hurricane-deck; **hurricane-house**, a shelter at the mast-head for the look-out man, sometimes made with a cask, a 'crow's nest'; also, a kind of round-house built on the deck; **hurricane-lamp**, a lamp so constructed that it will not be extinguished by violent wind; **hurricane-lantern** = *hurricane-lamp*; **hurricane roof** = *hurricane-deck*; **hurricane wind**, a very strong wind associated with a tropical cyclone or hurricane; also, any wind of hurricane force. **b.** Instrumental, as ***hurricane-swept*** adj.

1879 *Encycl. Brit.* IX. 786/1 Before gales Frigate-Birds are said often to fly low, and their appearance near or over land..is supposed to portend a hurricane. *Note*, Hence another of the names, '*Hurricane-Bird'. **1823** SCORESBY *Whale Fishery* 378 The *hurricane character of the gale began to change. **1833** *Niles' Reg.* XLIV. 261/1 The hull of the boat sunk, leaving a part of the *hurricane deck..floating on the surface. **1842** DICKENS *Amer. Notes* (1868) 46 The promenade or hurricane-deck. **1882** NARES *Seamanship* (ed. 6) 97 They are..stowed..on the hurricane deck. **1891** *Pall Mall G.* 19 Oct. 4/2 The wind blew from the west with *hurricane force. **1775** ROMANS *Florida* 307 We..travelled chiefly through pine land, and some *hurricane ground. *Note*, Tracts of wood formerly destroyed by hurricanes are so called. **1818** B. O'REILLY *Greenland* 122 To the main-mast is attached..about 100 feet above the deck, a structure resembling a water cask, called a *hurricane house. **1853** KANE *Grinnell Exp.* ii. (1856) 20 A little hurricane-house amidships contained the one galley that cooked for all hands. **1894** *Daily News* 24 Nov. 7/1 A *hurricane lamp was swinging in the corridor. **1903** *Motoring Ann.* 306 A *hurricane-lantern, the highly inflammable vapour of petrol, and a 'flash-back', resulted in the total destruction of the car. **1954** G. DURRELL *Bafut Beagles* ix. 166 In among the twinkling hurricane lanterns they were all dancing the polka. **1662** GERBIER *Princ.* 9 The West-Indian *Herican-like-windes. **1745** R. AUCHMUTY *Import. Cape Breton* 5 A safe retreat..in the *hurricane months. **1839** *Picayune* (New Orleans) 29 Mar. 2/2 The snag went through the guards, cabin and *hurricane roofs. **1883** *Century Mag.* June 222/1 The..steamers..hidden to their hurricane roofs in cargoes of cotton bales. **1740** W. STEPHENS *Jrnl.* 26 Oct. in *Colonial Rec. Georgia* (1908) IV. Suppl. 18 The two Frigates..being apprehensive of the *hurricane Season, retired into a safe Harbour at Charles-Town. **1812** J. JAY *Corr.* (1893) IV. 364 Those who sail in hurrican seasons and latitudes. **1775** ADAIR *Amer. Ind.* 337 They had passed over a boggy place..upon an old *hurricane-tree. **1887** *Daily News* 31 Oct. 3/8 Soon the wind was blowing with *hurricane violence. **1921** J. W. REDWAY *Handbk. Meteorol.* xiii. 156 *Hurricane winds at Galveston were estimated to have a velocity of 125 miles per hour. **1923** [see GALE *sb.*[3] 1 a]. **1954** G. T. TREWARTHA *Introd. Climate* (ed. 3) v. 209 In large storms in the western North Atlantic, the diameter of the hurricane winds may exceed 100 miles.

Hence **hurricane** *v.*, (*a*) *intr.* to make a 'hurricane' or commotion; (*b*) *trans.*, to blow upon as a hurricane; also, to spend in a 'hurricane' (sense 2 b). **ˈhurricanize** *v. intr.*, = prec. a. †**hurriˈcanious** *a. nonce-wd.*, hurricane-like.

1682 BUNYAN *Holy War* 319 They..fall forthwith to hurricaning in Man Soul, as if nothing but whirlwind and tempest should be there. **1698** FRYER *Acc. E. India & P.* 318 The Ambient Air from the high Tops..hurricanes us with such dismal chilling Gusts. **1706** VANBRUGH *Mistake* IV. Wks. (Rtldg.) 452/1 A sort of convulsive—yes,—hurricanious—um,—like, in short a woman is like the Devil. **1746** R. WHATLEY *Christian* p. vii, The idlest Day of the Seven, to be slept, debaucht, or journeyed, or hurricaned away. **1833** *Blackw. Mag.* XXXIV. 529 Storm-demon, that would otherwise hurricanize over the world.

†**hurriˈcano**, *sb. Obs.* [See HURRICANE.]

1. An early form of HURRICANE (q.v., 1 β).

2. Applied by Shakspere and Drayton to a waterspout.

1605 SHAKS. *Lear* III. ii. 2 Rage, blow You Cataracts, and Hyrricano's spout. **1606** —— *Tr. & Cr.* v. ii. 172 The dreadfull spout, Which Shipmen doe the Hurricano call. **1627** DRAYTON *Agincourt* etc. 167 Downe the shower impetuously doth fall, Like that which men the Hurricano call.

hurricano (hʌrɪˈkeɪnəʊ), *v. rare.* [f. prec.] *trans.* To whirl or drive as a hurricane.

1702 C. MATHER *Magn. Chr.* III. Introd. (1852) 237 After the persecution which then hurricanoed such as were nonconformists unto that establishment. **1868** LONGF. *G. Corey* I. ii, Ah, poor New England! He who hurricanoed The house of Jacob is making now on thee One last assault.

hurried (ˈhʌrɪd), *ppl. a.* [f. HURRY *v.* + -ED[1].] Driven or carried along, done or performed, with a rapidity due to pressure or want of time; characterized by hurry or excited haste; full of haste; hasty.

1667 MILTON *P.L.* v. 778 All this haste Of midnight march, and hurried meeting here. **1711** *Swift's Lett.* (1767) III. 191 One cannot see him otherwise here, he is so hurried. **1725** POPE *Odyss.* x. 52 Snatched in the whirl, the hurried navy flew. **1801** *Med. Jrnl.* V. 558 The patient lay with a short, hurried, and rattling respiration. **1829** D'ISRAELI 6 July in *Croker Papers* (1884), I seize a hurried moment to acknowledge the receipt of your two notes. **1855** MACAULAY *Hist. Eng.* xx. IV. 406 A hurried embrace was exchanged.

Hence **ˈhurriedly** *adv.*, in a hurried manner, hastily; **ˈhurriedness**, hurried condition.

1816 BYRON *Siege Cor.* xix, Oft his beating fingers went Hurriedly as you may see Your own run over the ivory key. **1863** GEO. ELIOT *Romola* I. xx, He could not speak harshly, but he spoke hurriedly. *a* **1832** SCOTT cited in Worcester for *hurriedness*.

hurrier (ˈhʌrɪə(r)). [f. HURRY *v.* + -ER[1].]

1. One who hurries (in various senses).

1611 COTGR., *Tracasseur*, a restlesse trotter, or hurrier vp and downe; a fond busie bodie. *c* **1611** CHAPMAN *Iliad* XVII. 346 Mars..(That horrid hurrier of men). **1866** ALGER *Solit. Nat. & Man* II. 72 A world of capricious external hurriers.

2. *Coal-mining.* A workman engaged in conveying the corves of coal from the face of the working to the bottom of the shaft.

1825 *Chron.* in *Ann. Reg.* 4 The corves..were drawn to the shaft of the pit by several other men called hurriers. **1862** SMILES *Engineers* III. 127 The men..were all supplied with safety-lamps—the hewers with Stephenson's, and the hurriers with Davy's. **1893** *Daily News* 5 July 5/7, 78 miners, 45 hurriers, 20 pony drivers, and four hangers on.

ˈhurrish (ˈhʌrɪʃ), **huˈr(r)oosh** (hʌˈruːʃ), *v.* Also hooroosh. *trans.* To drive with the cry 'hurrish!' or 'hurroosh!' Also *absol.*

1839 J. D. HOOKER *Jrnl.* in L. Huxley *Life* (1918) I. iv. 91 He used..to start up, take his stick, shout, hooroosh..and scare the poor little snips out of their senses. **1864** MRS. H. WOOD *Trev. Hold* II. xviii. 264 When he was put to hurrish the crows away from the land. **1884** *Upton Gloss.* (E. D. S.), *Hurrish*, to drive cattle. **1895** JANE BARLOW *Strangers at Lisconnel* 41 You might as well try to huroosh one chicken off a rafter and not scare the couple that were huddled beside it.

So **huˈrroosh** *sb.*

1836 *Knickerbocker* VIII. 208 When they were all free, they began to sky-lark and kick up a hooroosh in all quarters. **1851** H. MELVILLE *Moby Dick* III. xxxiv. 208 What a hooroosh aloft there! **1888** R. KIPLING *Plain T. fr. Hills* (1891) 31 There was a wild hurroosh at the Club. **1959** *News Chron.* 21 Oct. 6/5 Sex hormones..went off with a great hooroosh. Both breeders and butchers are now..having second thoughts.

hurrisome (ˈhʌrɪsəm), *a. dial.* [f. HURRY *v.* + -SOME.] Inclined to hurry; hasty.

1847–78 HALLIWELL, *Hurrisome*, hasty; passionate. *Devon.* **1884** JESSOP in *19th Cent.* Mar. 404 You gentlemen of the towns are too hurrisome as we say, for us lumbering swains. **1888** MRS. NOTLEY *Power of Hand* II. xxvi. 60 Don't be too hurrysome, Mr. Olver; let me go on quiet-like.

hurrock (ˈhʌrək). *Obs.* exc. *dial.* Also **-ack**. The part of a boat between the sternmost seat and the stern.

13.. *E.E. Allit. P.* C. 185 He [Jonah] watz flowen..In-to þe boþem of þe bot, & on a brede lyggede, On helde by þe hurrok. **1460** CAPGRAVE *Chron.* (Camden) 234 O boy, that fled to on of the Flemysch shippis, and hid him in the horrok [*MS. C.C.C.* hurrok]. **1866** T. EDMONSTON *Shetland & Orkney Gloss.*, *Hurrack*, that part of a boat between the after-thoft and the stern.

hurroo (hʌˈruː), *int.* (*sb.*)

1. A cry expressive of triumph or exultant excitement.

1824 MACTAGGART *Gallovid. Encycl.*, *Hurroo*, a halloa. **1891** E. L. WAKEMAN in *Columbus* (O.) *Dispatch* Oct. 29 They came with wild whoop and hurroo carrying their prize on their shoulders.

2. *Austral.* (Also hooroo and other variants.) = HOORAY *int.*

1913 J. STEPHENS *Here are Ladies* 102 [He] called hurroo to the boys and sauntered out of the place with a great deal of dignity and one week's wages in cash. **1941** BAKER *Dict. Austral. Slang* 36 Hooroo. **1942** E. LANGLEY *Pea Pickers* II. viii. 171 'Hurrooo!' Off he went, through the dead gums, to catch the boat to Bairnsdale. **1945**, **1963** Aroo [see HOORAY *int.*] **1969** *Coast to Coast 1967–68* 74 The others have, one by one,..lurched off—'Hooroo!' 'Seeya, mate!'

hur(r)oosh, *v.*: see HURRISH *v.*

hurry (ˈhʌrɪ), *sb.* Also 6–7 hurrey, -ie. [*Hurry* sb. and vb., with the exception of a doubtful ME. instance of the latter, are known only from end of 16th c.; it is uncertain which of them has priority etymologically, and the order of sense-development is not clear. In the earliest cited instances the sb. is identical in sense with HURLY[1]; so *hurry-burry* with *hurly-burly*. With

these cf. also mod.Du. *herrie*, *hurrie*, agitation, bustle, disorder, tumult. The earliest cited instances of the vb., on the other hand, go with branch II of the sb., and point to more immediate onomatopœic origin, the element *hurr* being naturally used in various languages to express the sound of rapid vibration, and the rapid motion which it accompanies. Thus MHG. and Ger. *hurren* to whir, Sw. and Norw. dial. *hurra* to whir, whizz, whirl round, Da. *hurre* to whir, Icel. *hurr* hurly-burly, noise.]

I. †**1. a.** Commotion or agitation, physical, social, or political; disturbance, tumult. (With or without *a* and *pl.*) *Obs.*

1600 HOLLAND *Livy* xxxviii. 1003 The tumult still encreased, and the multitude was all up on a hurrey. **1607** SHAKS. *Cor.* IV. vi. 4 The present peace, And quietnesse of the people, which before Were in wilde hurry. **1625** FLETCHER & SHIRLEY *Nt. Walker* II. ii, What thousand noises pass through all the rooms? What cryes and hurries? **1659** D. PELL *Impr. Sea* Ep. Ded. C, In a turbulent Sea, where there is nothing but a Chaos of hurry, and confusion. **1762** WESLEY *Jrnl.* 6 Sept., A poor man began to make some tumult. But many cried out, 'Constables, take him away'. They did so, and the hurry was over. **1843** R. R. MADDEN *United Irishmen* Ser. II. II. xx. 433 In the south of Ireland, the rebellion of 1798 is designated by a term..indicative of the confusion attendant on an insurrection. The people call it 'the hurry'.

†**b.** *concr.* A confused crowd, a mob. *Obs. rare.*

1620 SHELTON *Quix.* (1896) III. 54 For all your Pharaos, your Ptolomies..your Caesars..with all the hurrie (if I may so terme them) of your infinite Princes, Monarchs, Lords, Medes,..Persians, Grecians, and Barbarians. **1714** GAY *Trivia* III. 30 The Pavement sounds with trampling Feet, And the mixt Hurry barricades the Street.

†**2.** Mental agitation or disturbance; excitement; perturbation. (Also with *pl.*) *Obs.*

1600 HOLLAND *Livy* IX. xxiv. 331, I will for my part set all presently in a hurrie [*terrore implebo*]. **1682** NORRIS *Hierocles* 162 Void of all material passions, and terrestrial hurries. **1704** F. FULLER *Med. Gymn.* (1711) 146 There is nothing like Hurrying the Body, to divert the Hurry of the Mind. **1754** RICHARDSON *Grandison* V. ii. 10 They thought it adviseable that I should not be admitted into her presence, till the hurries she was in had subsided. **1789** MAD. D'ARBLAY *Diary* 18 Feb., He found nothing now remaining of the disorder, but too much hurry of spirits.

II. 3. a. Excited, hasty, or impetuous motion; rush. Now *rare* or *Obs.*

1659 STANLEY *Hist. Philos.* XIII. (1701) 596/2 The motion of the Heaven, or of the Stars..might in the first case..both have begun, and be continued by the hurry of some Air. **1696** WHISTON *Th. Earth* II. (1722) 74 Strange uncertain Hurries of Opake Masses hither and thither. **1709** MRS. MANLEY *Secr. Mem.* (1736) I. 125 My Heart is upon the Hurry. **1805** *Med. Jrnl.* XIV. 530 The hurry and vigour of circulation [of the blood] are greater than at any future period. **1860** LONGF. *Wayside Inn, Paul Revere* 73 A hurry of hoofs in a village street.

†**b.** A strong impulse. *Obs. rare.*

1693 C. MATHER *Invis. World* (1862) 188 Grievous and Pulling Hurries to Self-Murder are none of the smallest outrages, which the Devil in his Temptations commits upon us.

4. a. Action accelerated by some pressure of circumstances, excitement, or agitation; undue or immoderate haste; the condition of being obliged to act quickly through having little time; eagerness to get something done quickly. (See also 5.)

1692 DRYDEN *St. Euremont's Ess.* 77 To enjoy themselves equally in the hurry of Business, and the Repose of a Private Life. **1700** T. BROWN tr. *Fresny's Amusem. Ser. & Com.* 23 With what Hurry and Swiftness is the Circulation of London perform'd? **1769** *Junius Lett.* xxxv. 156 The imprudent hurry with which the first overtures from France were accepted. **1803** *Med. Jrnl.* X. 101 Much hurry of business prevents R. S. from entering further into the other queries. **1833** N. ARNOTT *Physics* I. 370 Surprised at the extent and hurry of the preparations. **1879** FARRAR *St. Paul* (1883) 188 There is no hurry in the designs of God.

b. Qualified by *no* or *any* (with negative implication): Need or occasion for hurry.

1849 MACAULAY *Hist. Eng.* iv. I. 434 Sometimes he said that there was no hurry, and sometimes that he was too weak. *Mod.* Is there any hurry?

5. Phrases (from 4). **a.** ***in a hurry***: In haste due to pressure, want of time, or excitement; in urgent haste.

1700 S. L. tr. *Fryke's Voy. E. Ind.* 42 The other had no sooner got his Gun, but in a hurry he fires upon him; but not taking good aim, did not do any execution. **1726** SHELVOCKE *Voy. round World* (1757) 202 He was in a great hurry to get his sprit-sail-yard fore and aft. *a* **1773** CHESTERF. in J. Trusler *Princ. Politeness* (1790) 61 A man of sense may be in haste, but he is never in a hurry... To be in a hurry is a proof that the business we embark in is too great for us. **1774** C. J. PHIPPS *Voy. N. Pole* 129 This instrument, though far from complete, having been constructed in a hurry for the purpose of a first experiment. **1805** *Med. Jrnl.* XIV. 124, I drew it up in a hurry, intending to transcribe it. **1872** RAYMOND *Statist. Mines & Mining* 114 While the sun shines, such an enterprise must make hay in a hurry. **1884** F. M. CRAWFORD *Rom. Singer* I. 53 What a hurry you are in!

b. ***not..in a hurry***, not very soon; ***to be in no hurry***, to have plenty of time, to take one's time. (*colloq.*)

1778 F. BURNEY *Evelina* II. xiii. 102 He won't put his tricks upon me again, in a hurry. **1812** LADY LYTTELTON *Let.* 28 Apr. in *Corr.* (1912) 132 That, you see, is very neat, and sounds as if it would not be forgotten in a hurry. **1837** GORING & PRITCHARD *Microgr.* 109 The late Mr. T...whose like we shall not see again in a hurry. **1858** BUCKLE *Civiliz.* (1873) II. viii. 595 Believing that little can be done they are in no hurry to do it. **1865** W. G. PALGRAVE *Arabia* I. 110 Not yet liberated, nor likely to be so in a hurry.

6. Technical and specific uses.

a. A small load of hay or corn. *dial.* (cf. HURRY *v.* 6). **b.** One of the 'spouts' which allow coal to rush down from cars (running on a timber framework) into the hold of a ship; *pl.* the whole framework or 'stathe'. **c.** *Dramatic Music.* A tremolo passage played on the violin or other instrument to accompany an exciting scene. **d.** Dr. Lodge's proposed term for a unit of acceleration (in *Physics*), i.e. an acceleration of one foot per second in a second.

1659 *Dedham Rec.* (1894) IV. 5 No Inhabitant of this Towne shall..cutt any grasse in any of the Comon meadows ..vpon the penaltie of forfieting tenn shillings for euery Loade or hurry of haye so cutt. **1787** W. MARSHALL *Norfolk* (1795) II. Gloss. (E.D.S.), *Hurry*, a small load of hay or corn. **1794** *Nat. Hist.* in *Ann. Reg.* 329 In this staith are fixed five hurries or spouts..the hurries or spouts lie with an inclining slope of about forty-five degrees. **1836–9** DICKENS *Sk. Boz* xii. 70/1 Then the wrongful heir comes in to two bars of quick music, (technically called 'a hurry'). **1879** LODGE *Elem. Mech.* 21 *note*, Suppose..we..call the unit of velocity a 'speed'... If a name were..wanted for the unit of acceleration, or one speed per second, it might perhaps be called a 'hurry'. **1888** STAINER & BARRETT *Dict. Mus. T.* 231 The 'hurry' is generally played as a preparation for the culminating point of a dramatic incident..during stage struggles or like exciting actions.

7. Used *adverbially*: With hurry.

1796 SCOTT *Will. & Helen* xxxvii, And, hurry! hurry! off they rode.

8. *Comb.* (from sense 1). Also **hurry call** (orig. *U.S.*), a call for immediate help in an emergency; a request for immediate action.

1650 TRAPP *Comm. Lev.* xxvi. 8 Those..that heard an hurrie-nois in the aër (made by the Angels likely). **1901** *Munsey's Mag.* XXIV. 798/1 If it was a hurry call, she would send them to Gilchrist. **1908** G. H. LORIMER *Jack Spurlock* i. 11 In answer to a hurry-call from his wife to get rich. **1915** WODEHOUSE *Something Fresh* iii. 73 His friends..send in a hurry-call to police headquarters. **1938** F. D. SHARPE *Sharpe of Flying Squad* v. 63 A wireless 'hurry call' was flashed out from the Yard and a Flying Squad car raced to the house. **1964** WODEHOUSE *Frozen Assets* ix. 160 Percy would be sending out hurry calls for the police.

hurry ('hʌrɪ), *v.* Also ? 4 horye(n. [See HURRY *sb.* (The order of senses is uncertain: possibly sense 3 was the earliest, as app. in the sb.)]

1. *trans.* To carry, convey, or cause to go with excessive haste, under the influence of external pressure or of excitement. Frequently with *along*, *away*, *down*, *up*, *in*, *out*, etc.

(It is not certain that the first quot. belongs to this word.)

[**13..** *E.E. Allit. P.* B. 883 Þe ȝonge men..by þe hondez hym hent & horyed him with-inne.]

1592 SHAKS. *Ven. & Ad.* 904 A second fear..Which madly hurries her she knows not whither. **1601** WEEVER *Mirr. Mart.*, *Sir J. Oldcastle* E viij b, To Thickets feeld then was Oldcastle hurried. **1676** tr. *Guillatiere's Voy. Athens* 289 Caverns, into which the poor Shepheards hurry their Flocks upon any alarm. **1760** C. JOHNSTON *Chrysal* (1822) II. 214 My master was seized and hurried away to a prison. **1834** MEDWIN *Angler in Wales* I. 148, I rushed out of the house, not knowing whither my steps were hurrying me. **1874** L. STEPHEN *Hours in Library* (1892) II. i. 6 We commonplace beings are hurried along in the crowd.

b. To carry or drive with impetuosity or without deliberation to some action, conduct, or condition of mind.

1595 SHAKS. *John* v. i. 35 Wilde amazement hurries vp and downe The little number of your doubtfull friends. **1621** T. WILLIAMSON tr. *Goulart's Wise Vieillard* 104 Those raging and unruly passions, which hurry the wicked up and downe. **1647** CLARENDON *Hist. Reb.* I. §2 The poor People..are furiously hurried into actions..destroying all foundations of Law and Liberty. **1704** J. PITTS *Acc. Mahometans* 18 Drinking hurries Men on to the worst of Vices. **1838** THIRLWALL *Greece* III. 97 To hurry you into an act of unjust aggression.

†**c.** To drive (anything) with rapid or impetuous motion. *Obs.*

1615 G. SANDYS *Trav.* 278 Exhalations..hurried about with a most violent motion. **1696** WHISTON *The. Earth* IV. (1722) 370 A Comet's Atmosphere is a very stormy Fluid wherein Masses of Opake Matter are continually hurried about.

2. *intr.* To move or act with excited haste, or with an evident or apparent effort at speed; to press on without leisure or with great or undue haste. With advbs. as in 1. ***hurry up!*** make haste, increase your speed (*colloq.*).

1590 SHAKS. *Com. Err.* v. i. 140 Desp'rately he hurried through the streete. **1591** —— *1 Hen. VI*, IV. iii. 53 Liues, Honours, Lands, and all, hurrie to losse. **1602** MARSTON *Ant. & Mel.* III. Wks. 1856 I. 32 Gastly amazement..Shall hurry on before, and usher us. **1700** S. L. tr. *Fryke's Voy. E. Ind.* 74 Near enough to hear them..and to see their Troops hurry from one place to another. **1816** KEATINGE *Trav.* (1817) I. 49 At sun-set all must hurry inside the gates. **1837** W. IRVING *Capt. Bonneville* II. 47 They hurried off to obtain relief. **1871** H. MACMILLAN *True Vine* vi. (1872) 259 Nature never hurries, never takes leaps, never wearies. **1878** HUXLEY *Physiogr.* 74 The fresh water hurrying onward to the sea. **1890** *Acrobats & Mountebanks* 72 'Walk in, walk in! ladies and gentlemen', cries the showman... 'Walk in, walk in! Hurry up!'

†**3.** *trans.* To agitate, disturb, excite; to molest, harass, worry. *Obs.* exc. *dial.* Cf. HURRY *sb.* 1.

1611 COTGR., *Harassé*,..harried, molested, hurried. **1613** T. MILLES tr. *Mexia's, etc. Treas. Anc. & Mod. T.* I. 17/1 Then must the conscience be hurried with her owne piercings. **1683** TRYON *Way to Health* 380 As those savage Beasts do delight to kill, hurry, oppress, tear and eat the Blood of their fellow Creatures. **1829** I. TAYLOR *Enthus.* ix. 232 So under the influence of the imagination as to have their sleep hurried with visions. **1832** HT. MARTINEAU *Ireland* iv. 63 Her form wasted, her spirits were hurried. **1848** A. B. EVANS *Leicestersh. Words* s.v., I've been very much hurried this morning; for I've just heard of the death of my old friend T——.

4. To urge or excite to greater speed; to hasten the action, motion, or progress of; often, to hasten unduly.

1713 ADDISON *Guardian* No. 154 ¶2, I hurried my habit, and got it ready a week before the time. **1761** HUME *Hist. Eng.* III. liv. 175 The Commons..now hurried on as much as they formerly delayed, the disbanding of the armies. **1836** *Westm. Rev.* Apr. 176 Indeed, the conclusion [of the drama] appears to be somewhat hurried up. **1845** FORD *Handbk. Spain* I. 55 Nor is there any good to be got in trying to hurry man or beast in Spain. **1889** MRS. WALFORD *Stiff-necked Generat.* 190 Shall I ring and hurry up the tea?

refl. **1838** DICKENS *Nich. Nick.* v, You needn't hurry yourself. **1877** M. M. GRANT *Sun-Maid* i, There was no reason why the express should hurry itself.

5. To put *away*, *on*, *out*, *forth*, etc., hurriedly or hastily.

1806 SURR *Winter in Lond.* (ed. 3) I. 208 Lady Roseville hurried away a tear that would start unbidden. **1807** SIR R. WILSON *Jrnl.* 9 June in *Life* (1862) II. viii. 256 Hurrying on my clothes. **1810** SCOTT *Lady of L.* II. xxxii, Ere His tongue could hurry forth his fear. **1833** N. ARNOTT *Physics* (ed. 5) I. 650 When the glottis is once opened,..the stutterer..is glad to hurry out as many words as he can.

6. *north. dial.* To transport or convey (= DRIVE *v.* 5 b; *e.g.*, to drive a cart, drive coal). *spec.* in *Coal-mining*, To transport (the coal) from the face of the working to the bottom of the shaft (see HURRIER 2); also *absol.*

1847–78 HALLIWELL, *Hurry* (1) to bear, lead, or carry anything away. *North.* **1883** *Almondbury & Huddersf. Gloss.*, *Hurry*, to draw or move a cart. A horse hurries coals, &c. **1898** *Cleckheaton Guardian* 21 Oct., Joel B——, son of the deceased, said he hurried for his father.

'hurry-'burry, *sb.* (*adv.*) *Sc.* [Reduplicated extension of HURRY: cf. HURLY-BURLY.] Tumult, confusion or bustle caused by excitement, hurly-burly. **b.** as *adv.* Tumultuously.

1791 A. WILSON *Laurel Disputed* Poet. Wks. (1846) 127 To read the King's Birth-day's fell hurry-burry. ? *a* **1800** *Christmas Ba'ing* in J. Skinner *Misc. Poet.* (1809) 125 (Jam). The hurry-burry [that] now began..Wi' routs and raps frae man to man. **1813** D. ANDERSON *Poems* 116 (Jam.) Hurry burry runnin' loupin'. **1832–53** A. RODGER in *Whistle-Binkie* (Sc. Songs) Ser. III. 65 I'll just tak' ye at your word, An' end this hurry-burry.

†**hurry-curry.** *Obs.* ? *nonce-wd.* [A jingling formation from *hurry* (see esp. HURRY *v.* 6); perh. with reference to L. *currus* chariot. Cf. also HARRY-CARRY.] ? A swift car or curricle.

1599 NASHE *Lenten Stuffe* 45 The sunne was so in his mumps vppon it..that hee had thought to haue topled his burning carre or Hurrie currie into the sea.

†**hurry-durry**, *sb. rare.* = HURRY-BURRY.

1732 MRS. DELANY in *Life & Corr.* (1861) I. 389 Mrs. Clayton designs having her assembly..so we must prepare for hurry-durry; but as it will be the only agreeable crowd, I think it may be borne once a week. **1774** *Ibid.* Ser. II. II. 41 Whilst we are enjoying sweet peace in this delightful place, the world is in a hurry-durry.

†**'hurry-'durry**, *a. Obs.* [Cf. HURRY *sb.* 1.] A sailor's epithet applied to rough, boisterous, foul weather. Hence *fig.* in quot. 1676.

1672 *State Papers, Domest.* (P.R.O.) CCCXIV. No. 90 The wind was at east and blew hard and, as the seamen terme it, was thick hurry durry weather, which is wind and raine. **1676** WYCHERLEY *Pl. Dealer* I. Wks. (Rtldg.) 105/2 1 *Sail.* Nay, there's no more dealing with him, than with the land in a storm, no near — 2 *Sail.* 'Tis a hurry-durry blade. Dost thou remember..when I welcomed him ashore, he gave me a box on the ear, and called me fawning water-dog? **1693** R. GRIFFITHS *Let. to Sir J. Trenchard* (P.R.O.), We have mett with very foule hurry-durry weather and much raine.

†**hurry-durry**, *int. Obs.* An exclamation of impatience or indignation.

1682 OTWAY *Venice Pres.* III. i, I will not stir from the door, that I resolve—hurry durry, what, shut me out. *Ibid.*, Hurry durry—good for nothing! **1682** MRS. BEHN *Roundheads* III, How dost do, Nacky? hurry durry! I am come, little Nacky. *Ibid.* IV. ii, What my Nicky Nacky! Hurry Durry! Nicky Nacky in the Plot?

hurrygraph ('hʌrɪgrɑːf, -græf). *U.S.* [f. HURRY *sb.* + -GRAPH after PHOTOGRAPH *sb.*] Something done, produced, or experienced in a hurry, esp. a hasty glance or fleeting impression.

1851 *Oquawka* (Ill.) *Spectator* 3 June 1/1 Just as we are 'putting up' this hurry graph a flat boat is passing up First street laden with several hundred sacks of grain. **1886** *Cassell's Family Mag.* June 417/1 Idyllic countryside stations,..the town-tired traveller catches 'hurry-graphs' of them sufficiently tempting for him to wish that the 'limited mail' were a City omnibus. **1887** J. J. HISSEY *Holiday on Road* 331 The traveller by rail..notices only its beauty[i.e.

of the country] from the 'hurrygraphs' he gets. **1918** *Hist. Amer. Lit.* I. iii. 242 Fleeting impressions, 'dashes at life', ephemera, 'hurrygraphs' were his forte.

hurrying ('hʌrɪɪŋ), *vbl. sb.* [f. HURRY *v.* + -ING¹.] The action of the vb. HURRY: †**a.** Harassing, disturbance, molestation, worrying (*obs.*). **b.** Hastening under excitement or pressure.

1653 H. MORE *Antid. Ath.* III. vii. (1712) 108 Under most grievous hurryings and tortures of the body. **1674** N. FAIRFAX *Bulk & Selv.* (Contents), The nimbleness of Ghosts in their hurryings of Body. **1683** TRYON *Way to Health* 343 For all Hurrying, Hunting, Oppressing and Killing. **1816** BYRON *Ch. Har.* III. xxiv, Ah! then and there was hurrying to and fro.

'hurrying, *ppl. a.* [f. as prec. + -ING².] That hurries; that hastens under pressure or excitement; moving with excited haste.

1751 EARL ORRERY *Remarks Swift* (1752) 183 They were written in a careless, hurrying manner. **1801** *Med. Jrnl.* V. 164 A hurrying message was brought, requiring Mr. C.'s attendance to a young man. **1849** MACAULAY *Hist. Eng.* iii. I. 352 Courts and alleys..alive with hurrying feet and anxious faces. **1873** BLACK *Pr. Thule* vii, The clouded and hurrying sky.

Hence **'hurryingly** *adv.*

1748 RICHARDSON *Clarissa* (1811) II. xxxv. 257 Going out of one apartment, hurryingly, as I may say, into another. **1818** KEATS *Endym.* III. 729 They went till unobscur'd the porches shone; Which hurryingly they gain'd, and enter'd straight.

hurry-scurry ('hʌrɪ'skʌrɪ), *adv.*, *a.*, and *sb. colloq.* Also **hurry-skurry.** [f. HURRY *v.* + SCURRY *v.*: the jingling combination has the effect of a reduplicative formation; cf. *helter-skelter*.]

A. *adv.* With the hurry and confusion of persons, etc., running in diverse directions; in disorderly haste, pell-mell.

1750 GRAY *Long Story* 63 Each hole and cupboard they explore..Run hurry-skurry round the floor. **1798** COLERIDGE *Poems, Mad Ox* xiv, The victor ox scoured down the street, The mob fled hurry-scurry. **1833** LONGF. *Outre-Mer* Pr. Wks. 1886 I. 125 Away went horse and rider at full speed,—hurry-scurry,—up hill and down. **1883** E. PENNELL-ELMHIRST *Cream Leicestersh.* 138 A whistling coal train drove these horsemen hurry-scurry out of its way.

B. *adj.* Characterized by hurry and commotion.

1732 E. FORREST *Hogarth's Tour* 4 We made a hurry-scurry dinner at the Smack at the ten-gun battery. **1789** MAD. D'ARBLAY *Diary* Dec., It must be a mighty hurry-skurry life! **1836** DISRAELI *Lett. Runnymede* 154 That volatile effusion which is the hurry-skurry offspring of ignorance and guile. **1863** *Bradford Advertiser* 18 July 5/2 Then hurry-skurry retreat; men tumbling over one another for fear.

C. *sb.* Hurry and confusion; the hurrying and disorderly rushing of a number; a 'rush'.

1754 RICHARDSON *Grandison* (1781) VI. xlvii. 296 Why should not we women, after all, contrive to make hurry-skurries? **1797** MAD. D'ARBLAY *Let. to Burney* 20 July, The close of the season is always hurry-scurry. **1800** A. CARLYLE *Autobiog.* 134 While our dinner was preparing, an alarm was beat in the camp, which occasioned a great hurry-scurry in the courtyard. **1852** R. S. SURTEES *Sponge's Sp. Tour* lxvi. 371 All was now commotion and hurry-scurry inside and out. **1862** SHIRLEY *Nugæ Crit.* xi. 488 This is the age of progress. No,..it is the age of hurry-skurry. We have all run ourselves out of breath.

'hurry-'scurry, *v.* [f. prec.]

1. *intr.* To move or proceed with hurry-scurry; to run or rush in confused and undignified haste.

1771 FOOTE *Maid of B.* III. Wks. 1799 II. 227 Out bolted the Squire, and hurry-scurried away. **1812** COMBE *Picturesque* I. (Chandos) 6 She was among those busy wives, Who hurry-scurry through their lives. **1896** *Daily News* 4 Dec. 7/4 Having to hurry-scurry about the platform in search of a vacant seat.

2. *trans.* (*nonce-use.*)

1896 *Westm. Gaz.* 20 Mar. 2/1 The paste is hurry-skurried into pie, pudding, or tart.

'hurry-up. *colloq.* [f. vbl. phr. *to hurry up*, HURRY *v.* 2.] **1.** Used *attrib.*: involving or requiring haste; completed in a hurry. **hurry-up wagon,** one equipped to act in an emergency; a police van. *U.S.*

1893 W. K. POST *Harvard Stories* 118 The manager..told him to send for a hurry-up wagon, and run us all in. **1902** H. L. WILSON *Spenders* 466 He would not be compelled to seek one of those 'hurry-up' lunch places with its clamour and crowd. **1907** *Putnam's Monthly* July 487/1 A hurry-up telegram. **1916** B. HALL *Diary* 23 Sept. in Hall & Niles *One Man's War* (1929) xxiv. 191 He had to..wait for some hurry-up repairs. **1930** *Dixon* (Ill.) *Evening Telegraph* 24 Sept. 2/2 It is hoped there will be a large attendance at the 'hurry-up' meeting this evening. **1943** *Copper Camp* 191 A frantic bartender called the police and Callahan was once more looking out of the hurry-up wagon on his way to the City Hall. **1949** *Sunday World-Herald Mag.* (Omaha) 13 Feb. 5/2 It is often necessary to make a hurry-up call to a registered donor who is known to have the right type of blood.

2. Used as simple *sb.*: an encouragement or demand to hurry up.

1944 J. H. FULLARTON *Troop Target* I. vii. 61 Let's give 'em a bit of a hurry up, Jock. **1952** S. KAUFFMANN *Philanderer* (1953) xi. 186 Ordinarily he would have been irritated to learn that Benjamin (and therefore Tappan) had not yet looked at his material—especially after the big hurry-up they'd given him. **1956** H. GOLD *Man who was not with It* (1965) iv. 32 The hurry-up which the sight of death gives us. **1966** BAKER *Austral. Lang.* (ed. 2) x. 218 *Give* (someone) *a bit of hurry up*, to demand or encourage prompt action.

hurse-skin, var. or erron. f. *huss-skin*: see HUSS *sb.*

hurson, obs. Sc. f. WHORESON.

hurst (hɜːst). Forms: 1 **hyrst,** 3– **hurst,** (4 **hurste,** 5 **hirste,** 6 **hyrst,** 6– **hirst**). [OE. *hyrst*:—OTeut. type **hursti-z*, whence OHG., MHG. *hurst*, G. dial. *horst* 'heap, cluster, thicket, top of rock, sandbank' (Flügel); MLG. *horst* hill, wooded or bushy eminence, small wood, LG. *horst, host*, a bushy piece of land surrounded with marsh, a wooded eminence, EFris. *hörst, horst, höst*, thicket, copse, sandy eminence (prob. formerly overgrown with brushwood); MDu. *horst* (Kilian *horscht, horst*) thicket of brushwood. In the forms *-hurst, -hirst, -herst*, a frequent element in place-names, as in *Hawkhurst, Chislehurst, Ferniehirst, Amherst.* (So *-horst* in Du. and LG.)

Icel. *hrjóstr* rough place, barren rocky place, Norw. dial. *rust, ryst*, little wood, thicket, clump of alders and dwarf birch, wooded tract on a mountain, lateral ridge of a mountain, Færöese *rust* ridge, show similarity of sense, but are difficult to connect phonologically.]

I. 1. An eminence, hillock, knoll, or bank, esp. one of a sandy nature.

a **1000** *Riddles* xli. 61 (Gr.) Swylce ic eom wraðre þonne wermod sy þe her on hyrstum heasewe stondeð. *c* **1290** *S. Eng. Leg.* I. 300/18 Opon þe hexte hurste of al þe hulle atþe laste he him fond. *Ibid.* 473/378 Huy lokeden heom bi-side and seiȝen an heiȝh hurst Swiþe feor in þe se. **1387** TREVISA *Higden* (Rolls) I. 419 At Nemyn in Norþ Wales A litel ilond þere is, þat hatte Bardeseie..Men lyueþ so longe in þat hurste, þat þe eldest deiȝeþ furst. **1513** DOUGLAS *Æneis* XI. vii. 56 Thai hard hillis hirstis for to eir [*colles, atque horum asperrima pascunt*]. **1781** J. HUTTON *Tour to Caves* Gloss., *Hirst*, a bank or sudden rising of the ground. **1814** SCOTT *Wav.* xxxviii. *note*, We are bound to drive the bullocks, All by hollows, hirsts, and hillocks.

b. A sandbank in the sea or a river; a ford made by a bed of sand or shingle.

1398 TREVISA *Barth. De P.R.* XVI. i. (Tollem. MS.), It is harde and most perel to falle and smyte on hurstes of grauel [*arenarum obstaculis*] hid in þe see under water. **1576** in W. H. Turner *Select. Rec. Oxford* 384 The..Cytie dothe suffer the Thames to geather a great hurst or banck. **1805** *State, Fraser of Fraserfield* 192 (Jam.) If..there would be a ford or hirst in the water. **1820** J. CLELAND *Glasgow* 113 To remove the ford at Dambuck and some other prominent hirsts. **1879** MISS JACKSON *Shropsh. Word-bk.* s.v., A bed of shingle in the Severn is called a *hurst.*

2. A grove of trees; a copse; a wood; a wooded eminence. (The last variety of sense, found in mod. dialects, may be the primary one.)

The OE. quots. are of uncertain sense.

822 *Charter* in *O.E. Texts* 458 Iu hyrst, sciofingden, snad-hyrst. **858** *Ibid.* 438 Stanehtan denn, et illa silva, sand-hyrst nominatur quae pertinet to wassingwellan. ? *a* **1400** *Morte Arth.* 3370 Brawnches so heghe..they heldede to hir heste alle holly at ones, The hegheste of iche a hirste. **1612** DRAYTON *Poly-olb.* ii. 27 Each rising hurst Where many a goodlie oake had carefullie been nurst. **1628** COKE *On Litt.* 4 b, *Hurst* or *hirst* signifieth a wood. **1825** BROCKETT, *Hirst, Hurst*, a woody bank. **1827** J. HODGSON *Northumbld.* II. I. 100 *note*, Scraggy hirsts of hazel. **1871** R. ELLIS *Catullus* lxiii. 72 In hursts that house the boar.

b. *Her.* 'A charge representing a small group of trees, generally borne upon a mount or base' (Cassell).

1889 ELVIN *Dict. Her.*, *Hurst*, a wood, or thicket of trees.

II. Technical senses. (The connexion of these with the prec. is doubtful.)

3. The frame of a pair of millstones.

1710 RUDDIMAN *Gloss. Douglas* s.v., Miln-hirst, is the place on which the Cribs or Crubs (as they call them) ly, within which the mil-stone hirsts, or hirsills. **1764** CROKER, etc. *Dict. Arts & Sc.* s.v. *Mill*, The hurst or round frame..containing the lower mill-stone..and the upper one. **1884** KNIGHT *Dict. Mech.* Suppl., *Hurst*, the frame on which a run of millstones is placed. A husk.

4. The ring of the helve of a trip- or tilt-hammer, which bears the trunnions.

1825 J. NICHOLSON *Operat. Mechanic* 336 The centre..or axis of the hammer, is supported in a cast-iron frame..called the hirst. **1875** KNIGHT *Dict. Mech.*, Hurst.

III. 5. *Comb.* **hurst-beech,** the Hornbeam; **hurst-frame** = sense 4.

1825 J. NICHOLSON *Operat. Mechanic* 336 To form a pillar of solid timber; on the top of which the hirst-frame..is placed, and firmly held down by the four bolts, which descend through all the platforms, and have secure fastenings in the solid masonry beneath. **1866** *Treas. Bot.*, Hurstbeech, *Carpinus Betulus.* **1879** PRIOR *Plant-n.*, *Hurst-* or *Horst-* or *Horse-beech*, the hornbeam.

hurt (hɜːt), *sb.*¹ Forms: 2–7 **hurte,** 4 **hirt, hourte,** 5 **hort, hurth,** 5–6 **hurtt(e,** 4– **hurt.** [app. a. OF. *hurte* (mod.F. *heurte*) shock of collision, stroke, blow, f. *hurter, heurter*: see HURT *v.* Cf. also later F. *heurt* 'shocke, push, or dash; violent meeting or conflict; a knock or knocking together' (Cotgr.), It. *urto* a push, thrust, shock; also (from French) MHG. *hurt* and *hurte* shock of encounter, MDu., Du. *hort* thrust, push, shove. The sense 'injury' is a purely Eng. development: see HURT *v.*]

†**1.** A knock, blow, or stroke causing a wound or damage. *Obs.*

c **1205** LAY. 1837 Heo leopen to Brutus folke, þer heo hurtes duden. *a* **1240** *Lofsong* in *Cott. Hom.* 207 Ich bide þe ..bi þe herde hurtes and þe unwurðe wowes ðet he for us ..þolede. *c* **1330** R. BRUNNE *Chron. Wace* (Rolls) 12401 He ne lefte for swerd ne oþer hirt þat he vntil Arthur stirt. *c* **1400** *Destr. Troy* 6526 He..Gird hom to ground with mony grym hurt. **1590** SIR J. SMYTH *Disc. Weapons* 23 b, Of the great disordering of horses with the hurts of our English arrowes. **1653** HOLCROFT *Procopius, Goth. Wars* II. iv. 43 Synthues by a hurt of a Lance upon his right hand, was disabled. **1841–4** EMERSON *Ess., Circles* Wks. (Bohn) I. 126 You admire this tower of granite, weathering the hurts of so many ages.

2. Bodily or material injury, esp. that caused by a blow or stroke; a wound; a lesion; damage.

c **1205** LAY. 8178 þa wes his hurte æðe. *a* **1225** *Ancr. R.* 112 A lutel ihurt i þen eie dereð more þen deð a muchel iðe hele. *c* **1375** *Sir Beues* (MS. E) 1691 + 5 He was so ffeynt ffor hys hurte. *c* **1375** *Sc. Leg. Saints, Laurentius* 357 A fare ȝung man..Clengeand þi hortis þat are sare. *c* **1386** CHAUCER *Sqr.'s T.* 463 Herbes..To heele with youre hurtes hastily. **1474** CAXTON *Chesse* 100 Instrumentis..for to serche woundes and hurtes. **1563** W. FULKE *Meteors* (1640) 30 b, Sometime it killeth a man, and there appeareth no wound without, neither any hurt within. **1592** SHAKS. *Rom. & Jul.* III. i. 115 My very Friend hath got his mortall hurt In my behalfe. **1658** A. FOX *Wurtz' Surg.* III. xvi. 267 A Gentlemans child..had a hurt on the ancle, wherein a callus was grown. **1704** J. HARRIS *Lex. Techn.* s.v. *Bolts*, Fender-Bolts..are struck into the uttermost Bends or Wales of a Ship to save her Sides from Bruises and Hurts. **1794** LD. HOOD 12 July in Nicolas *Disp. Nelson* (1845) I. 436 *note*, I am truly sorry to hear you have received a hurt, and hope..it is not much. **1855** MACAULAY *Hist. Eng.* xvi. (1871) II. 193 He ordered his own surgeon to look to the hurts of the captive.

3. *gen.* Injury of any kind inflicted or suffered; harm, wrong, damage, detriment.

(In first quot. *fig.* from 2.)

a **1225** *Ancr. R.* 282 þi salue hit is, ȝif þu hit luuest, aȝean soule hurtes. *c* **1460** FORTESCUE *Abs. & Lim. Mon.* xviii. (1885) 154 To þe kynges gret harme and hurt off his said seruantes. **1526** *Pilgr. Perf.* (W. de W. 1531) 4 b, That..causeth heresyes & errours, and so is great hurte to fayth. **1586** J. HOOKER *Girald. Irel.* in *Holinshed* II. 150/1 Sir Nicholas Bagnoll was called to answer such hurts as were obiected against him. **1588** J. UDALL *Diotrephes* (Arb.) 11 They do euer with their preaching, more hurte than good. **1666** PEPYS *Diary* 7 Oct., But [I] do not think that all this will redound to my hurt. **1702** *Eng. Theophrast.* 123 It is safer to do some men hurt, than to do them too much good. **1865** DICKENS *Mut. Fr.* I. i, What hurt can it do you?

†**4.** Hurtful or noxious quality or action. *Obs.*

1608 TOPSELL *Serpents* (1658) 786 At what time they are very swift, quick, nimble, and of most certain hurt, more dangerous and more venemous in their bitings.

hurt (hɜːt), *sb.*² *Her.* Also **hurte, heurte.** [a. F. *heurte* (*a* 1558 in Godef.): '*heurtes*, small Azure balls, tearmed (in Heraldry) hurts on men, and tongue-moles on women' (Cotgr.). Cf. F. *heurt* mark left by a blow, and quot. 1572.

The English heraldic writers generally identify this with HURT *sb.*³, a bilberry; but (since the bilberry is not known as *heurt* or *heurte* in French) it is evident that this can be correct only if *hurt* and *hurtleberry* took their names from the heraldic word (or from the blue mark of a blow).]

A roundel azure: usually held to represent a hurtleberry.

1572 BOSSEWELL *Armorie* 10 Seuen signes, or tokens whiche are figured in Armes round..4. Is of Azure, and is termed a *Hurte.* 7. Is of Purpre, and is to be called a *Wounde.* **1610** GUILLIM *Heraldry* III. viii. (1660) 138 These appeare light-blew..they are indeed a kind of fruit or small round berry, of Colour betwixt Black and Blew..In some places they are called..Hurts or Hurtle-berries. *Ibid.* IV. xix. 352 If they [Roundles] be Light-blew then we call them Hurts. **1766** PORNY *Heraldry* Gloss., *Hurts* or *Huerts*, roundelets of the Azure Colour, so termed by none but English Heralds..These being blue, some will have them to signify Bruises or Contusions in the Flesh, which often turn to that colour. **1882** CUSSANS *Her.* iv. (ed. 3) 73 Roundles..are distinguished..by their several Tinctures,—they are..The Heurte, *az.*

hurt (hɜːt), *sb.*³ Now *dial.* Also 6 **hurte,** 7 **heurt.** See also WHORT. [Known to us from 16th c., but the fuller name *hurtleberry* appears *c* 1450; the relation between these, and the origin of both, are uncertain; no cognate name appears in other langs. See prec.] = HURTLEBERRY.

1542 BOORDE *Dyetary* xiii. (1870) 267 Rawe crayme..eaten with strawberyes or hurtes. **1610** [see HURT *sb.*²]. **1624** CAPT. SMITH *Virginia* II. 26 During Sommer there are either Strawberries..or Mulberries..Raspises, hurts. **1671** NARBOROUGH *Jrnl.* in *Acc. Sev. Late Voy.* I. (1694) 121 Small red Berries, much like Hurts. **1705** BEVERLEY *Virginia* II. ¶13 (1722) 113 There are three Sorts of Hurts, or Huckleberries, upon Bushes, from two to ten Foot high. **1883** *Leisure Hour* 572/2 Vendors of wild strawberries, and 'hurts'.

b. *Comb.*, as ***hurt-gatherer.***

1887 *Pall Mall G.* 29 July 5/2 The true region of heath and hurtle-berries, and here you will find the hurt-gatherers busily engaged in small groups and parties.

hurt (hɜːt), *v.* Pa. t. and pple. **hurt.** Forms: 2 (3rd sing.) **hert,** 3 (*Orm.*) **hirrtenn,** 3–6 **hurte,** (3–4 **horte,** 4–5 **hirte**); 5– **hurt.** Pa. t. 3–4 **hurte,** (4 **herte, hirte,** *Sc.* **hwrte**), 5– **hurt;** also *β.* 4 **hirtide,** 5 **hurtid,** 5–8 (9 *dial.*) **hurted.** Pa. pple. 3 **hird,** 3–5 **i-, yhurt,** 4 **hirt, yhert,** 4–6 **hurte,** 4– **hurt;** also *β.*

5 hurtyd, 5–9 hurted. [app. a. OF. *hurte-r* (now *heurter*) to bring into violent collision, 'to knocke, push, jarre, joult, strike, dash, or hit violently against' (Cotgr.). The phonology is not altogether clear; but app. the word was adopted early enough for OF. *u* to be treated as OE. *y*, becoming *i* in north and midl., and in the south remaining *ü*, which later became *ŭ* as in *hurst*, OE. *hyrst*; the variants in *-er*, *-or*, are mainly due to the disturbing influence of *r* upon the preceding vowel: cf. the historical forms of *dirt*, *first*, *gird*, *third*, *worse*, etc.

OF. *hurter* = Pr. *urtar*, It. *urtare*, is of obscure origin; in Darmesteter's opinion 'probably Germanic'. As, however, no corresponding Germanic word is known, Diez suggested a possible derivation from Celtic, comparing Welsh *hwrdd* ram, push, *hyrddu*, *hyrddio* to push; but see Thurneysen *Keltoromanisches* 81. MHG. and MLG. *hurten* to rush into collision, MDu. *hurten*, *horten*, Du. *horten* to jolt, jostle, push, are from French, and were orig. words of the tournament.]

I. Transitive uses.

†**1.** To knock, strike, dash (a thing against something else, or two things together); in quot. 1400, to run (a ship) aground. (= HURTLE *v.* 1.) *Obs.*

c **1200** ORMIN 11370 Swa þatt tu nohht ne shallt tin fot Uppo þe staness hirrtenn. *c* **1205** LAY. 1878 Heo hurten heora hafden. *a* **1400** *Wyclif's Bible* Acts xxvii. 41 (MS. Banister) Whanne we felden into a place of grauel..thei hurten the schippe. **1483** *Cath. Angl.* 192/2 To Hurte, *allidere, col-, elidere, illidere.* ?*a* **1500** *Chester Pl.* xii. 118 That thou hurt nether foot nor knee. **15..** *Miller of Abington* in Wright *Anecd. Literaria* (1844) 110 Against a fourme he hurte his shin. **1634** WINTHROP *New Eng.* (1825) I. 136 The Elizabeth Dorcas..being hurt upon a rock at Scilly..lost sixty passengers at sea.

†**2.** To knock, strike, give a blow to (so as to wound or injure). *Obs.* (In later instances blending with sense 3.)

13.. *Coer de L.* 4715 Stones and stokkes they threw doun; Some off the Crystenes they herte. *c* **1374** CHAUCER *Troylus* v. 1045 Whan þurgh þe body hurte was Diomede. *c* **1400** *Destr. Troy* 10387 þen þe kyng at hym caupit with a kene speire, Hurt hym full hidusly, harmyt hym sore. *c* **1489** CAXTON *Sonnes of Aymon* xxvi. 560 Thone hurted the other soo harde that thei felle doun almoost bothe to the erthe. **1525** LD. BERNERS *Froiss.* II. lxxii. [lxvi.] 216 They dyd let fly theyr quarelles, wherwith they hurted many. **1662** J. DAVIES tr. *Olearius' Voy. Ambass.* 280 [He] fell upon him, got him down, and having hurt him in several places, thrust him out of Doors.

3. a. To cause bodily injury to (by a blow or otherwise); to wound; to give bodily pain to.

1297 R. GLOUC. (Rolls) 5833 Hii velle & to brusede some anon to deþe, & some ymaymed, & some yhurt. *a* **1300** *Cursor M.* 3940 Iacob was þan hurt wel sare þe maister sinu of his the. *c* **1375** *Sc. Leg. Saints, Marcus* 82 He hwrte rycht sare his hand. **1470–85** MALORY *Arthur* IV. xii, I haue foughten with a knyght..I am sore hurte and he bothe. *c* **1566** J. ALDAY tr. *Boaystuau's Theat. World* K v, My shooe is newe, faire and well made, but you know not where about it doeth hurt and grieve me. **1654** WHITLOCK *Zootomia* 39 Hee that striketh a Wall may hurt his Knuckles. **1748** SMOLLETT *Rod. Rand.* (1812) I. 7, I have been found guilty of killing cats I never hurted. **1841** LYTTON *Nt. & Morn.* I. iv, No more hurt in the loins than I am. **1885** TENNYSON *North. Cobbler* iv, Once of a frosty night I slither'd an' hurted my huck.

b. To injure (a thing) physically; to do harm to, damage.

1382 WYCLIF *Rev.* ix. 4 It is comaundid to hem, that thei shulden not hirte hay of the erthe. **1481** CAXTON *Godefroy* clxxxiii. 269 They mocqued oure peple..and more asprely defended them self and hurted thengyns. **1577** B. GOOGE *Heresbach's Husb.* I. (1586) 44 b, Hurle out all the stones and suche thinges as may hurt the Sythe. **1645** BOATE *Irel. Nat. Hist.* (1652) 167 It is a common saying in Ireland, that the very dryest Summers there never hurt the land. **1727** DE FOE *Syst. Magic* I. iv, Which shall greatly hurt the fruits of the earth.

c. Of an injured limb, etc.: to be the source of pain to (one). (Cf. the corresponding intr. sense 8.)

1850 F. E. SMEDLEY *Frank Fairleigh* xxxiv. 280, I gave that [*sc.* the ankle] a twist somehow, and it hurts me dreadfully. **1871** *Two Little Bruces* viii. 76 My arm hurts me most. **1911** G. B. SHAW *Doctor's Dilemma* I. 12 Sometimes I think it's my heart: sometimes I suspect my spine. It doesnt exactly hurt me; but it unsettles me completely.

4. *gen.* To injure, do harm or mischief to; to affect injuriously, be prejudicial or detrimental to; to wrong, inflict injury upon.

c **1200** *Vices & Virtues* 45 He tobrekð, ʒif he ani god wille hafð, forðan he hert his gode wille. *a* **1225** *Ancr. R.* 98 Hwo haueð ihurt te, mi deore? *a* **1300** *Cursor M.* 28197 Wit flitt, wit brixil, striue and sturt, Myn euen-cristen haue i hurt. *c* **1385** CHAUCER *L.G.W.* Prol. 424 That ye hym nevere hurte in al his lyve. *c* **1400** *Apol. Loll.* 22 Vnleful curse hirtiþ not him þat is notid þer wiþ. *c* **1489** CAXTON *Sonnes of Aymon* iii. 78 It is the man among all oure enmyes, that..more hath hurted vs. **1533** in Picton *L'pool Munic. Rec.* (1883) I. 25 To be thus prejudiced and hurted of our said toll. **1671** MILTON *Samson* 1676 Among them he a spirit of phrenzie sent, Who hurt their minds. **1726–31** TINDAL *Rapin's Hist. Eng.* XVII. (1743) II. 96 Both parties equally hurted her. **1821** SCOTT *Kenilw.* xxii, Tressilian..had much hurt his interest with her. **1894** SIR E. SULLIVAN *Woman* 9 Innocent delusion, it amuses you and it doesn't hurt us.

5. To give mental pain to; to grieve, distress, vex, offend.

1526 TINDALE *Matt.* xi. 6 Happy is he thatt is noott hurte by me. —— *Mark* xiv. 27 All ye shalbe hurtt thorowe me thys nyght. **1756** BURKE *Subl. & B.* III. v, When we are thrown out of this state, or deprived of any thing requisite to maintain us in it..we are always hurt. **1777** SHERIDAN *Sch. Scand.* I. i, I own I was hurt to hear it. **1815** WELLINGTON *Let. to Ld. Hill* 9 May in Gurw. *Desp.* XII. 368, I consider the transactions too recent..to write a true history without hurting the feelings of nations, and of some individuals. **1879** MISS BATES *Egypt. Bonds* I. ix. 221 How mortified and 'hurt' poor Fred would have looked.

II. Intransitive and absolute uses.

†**6.** *intr.* To strike, dash (*on* or *against* something); to come into collision. In first quot. *fig.* To come or hit upon a thing; in quot. *c* 1500, To make a rush at a person. *Obs.*

a **1225** *Ancr. R.* 176 Nu we hurteð [*v.r.* hitte], leoue sustren, to the ueorðe dole. *Ibid.* 186 A child, ʒif hit spurneð o summe þing..me bet þet þing þet hit hurteð on. *c* **1330** R. BRUNNE *Chron. Wace* (Rolls) 4626 Schipes..þat on vn-to toþer hurte. **1382** WYCLIF *John* xi. 9 If ony man schal wandre in the day, he hirtith not. **1388** —— *Jer.* xiii. 16 Bifor that ʒoure feet hirte at derk hillis. **1483** CAXTON *Gold Leg.* 430 b/2 The Shyppe where the kyng was in hurted and smote twyes ageynst the roche. *c* **1500** *Melusine* v. 25 Whan Raymondyn cam ayenst the said bore..the bore anoone hurted to hym. **1622** R. HAWKINS *Voy. S. Sea* xli. 99 Arrowes..headed with a flint stone, which is loose, and hurting, the head remaineth in the wound.

7. *absol.* To cause injury, do harm (physical or otherwise); to cause or inflict pain.

1390 GOWER *Conf.* III. 367 Cupide, which maie hurt and hele In loves cause. **1500–20** DUNBAR *Poems* lxii. 13 It micht hurt in no degre. **1611** BIBLE *Isa.* xi. 9 They shall not hurt nor destroy in all my holy mountaine. **1651** HOBBES *Leviath.* II. xix. 97 Orators..though they have great power to hurt, have little to save. **1844** MRS. BROWNING *Fourfold Aspect* ii, How that true wife said to Pœtus..'Sweet, it hurts not!'

8. *intr.* for *pass.* To suffer injury or pain. (Now only *colloq.*)

a **1300** *E.E. Psalter* xxxvi[i]. 24 When rightwise falles, hortes na lime. **1545** ASCHAM *Toxoph.* II. (Arb.) 109 If that wylle not serue, but yet youre finger hurteth, you must take [etc.]. *a* 1899 *Mod.* Does your hand still hurt? **1902** *Dialect Notes* II. 237 *Hurt*, v.i., to ache; to pain. **1970** J. HANSEN *Fadeout* (1972) x. 83 I'm sorry you're hurting... But I'm glad I found you. **1972** *N.Y. Times* 4 June 4/5 When I heard that first lap time..I thought I'd be hurting.

hurt (hɜːt), *ppl. a.* [Pa. pple. of HURT *v.*]

a. Injured, wounded, etc.: see the verb.

c **1400** *Destr. Troy* 7166 The Troiens..Helit þere hurt men þurgh helpis of leches. *c* **1420** *Pallad. on Husb.* I. 287 The hole is saaf, the hurte is forto cure. **1541** R. COPLAND *Guydon's Quest. Chirurg.*, The wounde is bounde.. begynnynge fro the party opposite to the hurt place. **1617** SIR R. BOYLE in *Lismore Papers* (1886) I. 178 For curing my hurt leg. **1790** BURKE *Fr. Rev.* Wks. V. 140 The balm of hurt minds. **1887** R. N. CAREY *Uncle Max* xxviii. 220 In rather a hurt voice.

†**b.** *hurt majesty*: = LESE-MAJESTY. *Sc. Obs.*

c **1375** *Sc. Leg. Saints, Paulus* 159 Paule, as for hurte maieste, [Nero] Syne eftir bad hedit suld be. **1488** *Sc. Acts Jas. IV* (1597) §4 They that..committis the crime of hurt-majestie against his Hienesse.

c. Of an inanimate thing: injured, damaged. *U.S. colloq.*

1930 *Publishers' Weekly* 15 Feb. 863 The annual 'hurt book' sales.

†'**hurtberry.** *Obs. rare*⁻¹. [f. HURT *sb.*[3] + BERRY.] = HURTLEBERRY.

a **1661** FULLER *Worthies* I. (1662) 246 Hurtberries: In Latine Vaccinia, most wholsome to the Stomack, but of a very astringent Nature.

hurted ('hɜːtɪd), *ppl. a.* Now *dial.* [f. HURT *v.* + -ED[1].] = HURT *ppl. a.*

1643 I. STEER tr. *Exper. Chyrurg.* vi. 26 Lest they should flow to the hurted part. **1727** BRADLEY *Fam. Dict.* s.v. *Burn*, Apply it to the hurted Part.

hurter[1] ('hɜːtə(r)). [f. HURT *v.* + -ER[1].] One who or that which hurts or injures.

1552 ABP. HAMILTON *Catech.* (1884) 10 Hurtaris of the common weil. **1597** in Row *Hist. Kirk* (Wodrow Soc.) 181 Hurters and mutilaters of ministers. **1611** BEAUM. & FL. *King & no King* v. i. I shall not be a hurter if no helper. **1834** A. W. HARE *Serm.* II. xvii. 319 The great and fatal hurter, Death.

hurter[2] ('hɜːtə(r)). Forms: 4–5 **hurtour, -ur(e, hortour,** 6 **horter,** 8– **hurter.** [ad. F. *hurtoir*, in 1375 *hurtouoir* (Godef.), f. *hurter* to strike, HURT *v.*]

1. The shoulder of an axle, against which the nave of the wheel strikes; also, a strengthening piece on the shoulder of an axle.

1300–1 *Durham MS. Burs. Roll*, Sellis, hurtur', buklis, cingulis novis empt. *c* **1310** *Ibid.*, xvj Cluttis et j Hortour empt. pro Carect. Prioris, xiiijd. **1349–50** *Ibid.*, viij Hurtours pro Carectis..de proprio ferro faciendis. **1404** *Durham MS. Sacr. Roll*, j hurtour. **1600** *Vestry Bks.* (Surtees) 48 To the Smith of Pittington for makeinge a claspe and a horter to the great bell. **1788** *Chambers' Cycl.*, *Hurter*, in Artillery, a flatted iron fixed against the body of an axle tree, with straps to take off the friction of the naves of wheels against the body. **1825** BROCKETT, *Hurter*, the shoulder of the axle against which the nave of the wheel knocks. **1875** KNIGHT *Dict. Mech.*, *Hurter*..2. (*Vehicles.*) A butting-piece on an axle.

2. a. A beam fixed on a gun-platform, to stop the wheels of the gun-carriage from injuring the parapet. **b.** A wooden or iron piece fastened to the top rails of the lower gun-carriage or chassis, either in front or behind (*counter-hurter*), to check the motion of the gun.

1828 J. M. SPEARMAN *Brit. Gunner* (ed. 2) 326 Platforms ..Sleepers, Hurters, Planks, Pickets. **1851** J. S. MACAULAY *Field Fortif.* 80 In laying a gun-platform the first thing to be done is to fix the hurter, which may be a piece of timber 7 or 8 feet long, and 7 inches square, or a strong fascine may be used..The hurter should be placed perpendicular to the axis or central line of the embrasure. **1884** *Mil. Engineering* (ed. 3) I. II. 56 Two short hurters, each 3 feet × 6 inches × 6 inches, are also provided to prevent the gun carriage running up too far.

hurter[3]. *local.* [f. HURT *sb.*[3]] A gatherer of hurtleberries. (Common in Surrey.)

†'**hurtfoot.** *Obs. nonce-wd.* [f. HURT *v.* + FOOT *sb.*] That which hurts the foot.

1567 MAPLET *Gr. Forest* Pref., The common Stone hath his name and vocable (if I may so say) hurtfoote, for that it is in mouing..and iourneying the footes pain and griefe.

hurtful ('hɜːtfʊl), *a.* [f. HURT *sb.*[1] + -FUL.] Having the quality of causing hurt or injury; harmful, injurious, detrimental, prejudicial, pernicious, mischievous, noxious, noisome.

1526 *Pilgr. Perf.* (W. de. W. 1531) 150 b, The beestes.. not noysom or hurtfull. **1563** W. FULKE *Meteors* (1640) 27 b, The most dangerous, violent and hurtfull kind of lightning is called Fulmen. **1586** T. B. *La Primaud. Fr. Acad.* I. (1589) 62 Thales called vice the hurtfullest thing in the world, bicause that..it marreth and destroieth all. **1651** HOBBES *Leviath.* II. xxviii. 162 To certain actions, there be annexed by Nature, divers hurtful consequences. **1718** *Freethinker* No. 87 ¶5 It is..Advantageous to Many, and Hurtful to None. **1862** LD. BROUGHAM *Brit. Const.* xvii. 272 *note*, The vulgar and hurtful error of considering the Church as a corporation.

hurtfully ('hɜːtfʊlɪ), *adv.* [f. prec. + -LY[2].] In a hurtful manner; injuriously.

1552 HULOET, Hurtfullye, *nociue.* **1580** HOLLYBAND *Treas. Fr. Tong*, *Malicieusement*,..hurtfully. **1685** BOYLE *Salub. Air* 40 There are ways of making common water violently and hurtfully operative upon Humane Bodies. **1868** KINGLAKE *Crimea* (1877) III. ii. 328 The sight was of a kind to press hurtfully upon the imagination.

hurtfulness ('hɜːtfəlnɪs). [f. as prec. + -NESS.] The quality of being hurtful, injuriousness.

1611 COTGR., *Mauvaistié*,..shrewdnesse, curstnesse, hurtfulnesse. **1634** T. JOHNSON *Parey's Chirurg.* XI. (1678) 271 The hurtfulness of Thunder. **1651** BAXTER *Inf. Bapt.* Apol. 6 Sensible of the vanity and hurtfulness of filling the world with too many Books. **1870–4** ANDERSON *Missions Amer. Bd.* IV. 260 The folly and hurtfulness of the proposal.

hurting ('hɜːtɪŋ), *vbl. sb.*[1] [f. HURT *v.*]

1. The action of the verb HURT; injury, damage, hurt. (Now usually gerundial.)

a **1225** *Ancr. R.* 344 Of keorfunge, oðer of hurtunge. *a* **1340** HAMPOLE *Psalter* xxvi. 9 He hild me fra hortynge. **1382** WYCLIF *Dan.* vi. 23 Noon hirtyng is founden in hym. *a* **1568** ASCHAM *Scholem.* I. (Arb.) 77 Malice in hurting without cause. **1653** WALTON *Angler* vii. 150 With as little bruising or hurting the fish as.. diligence will enable you to do. **1759** ADAM SMITH *Mor. Sent.* II. ii. 203 If by hurting be understood the doing mischief wantonly.

†**2.** Stumbling; also *concr.* a stumbling-block.

1382 WYCLIF *Ezek.* iii. 20 Y shal putte an hirtynge before hym. **14..** in *Rel. Ant.* I. 41 God wole sende to the aungels to kepe the fro hirtynge.

hurting, *vbl. sb.*[2] *dial.* [f. HURT *sb.*[3] + -ING[1].] Gathering of 'hurts' or hurtleberries.

1884 JEFFERIES *Red Deer* x. 204 Among the labouring people..to go gathering whortleberries is to go 'a-hurting'. **1887** *Pall Mall G.* 29 July 5/1 'Hurting' is a process which involves nothing worse than the picking of the hurt, otherwhere known as the hurtle-berry,..or common bilberry.

hurting, *ppl. a.* [f. HURT *v.* + -ING[2].] That hurts; injurious.

1681 FLAVEL *Meth. Grace* xviii. 328 Its hurting and terrifying power. **1894** *Westm. Gaz.* 3 May 3/2 Dignity and self-respect, without any hurting haughtiness.

†**hurtle,** *sb.*[1] *Obs.* or *dial.* [? related to HURT *sb.*[1], or to F. *heurt* a blow, the mark of a blow: see HURT *sb.*[2]] A swelling upon the skin.

1599 T. M[OUFET] *Silkwormes* 74 Vpon whose palmes such warts and hurtells rise As may in poulder grate a nutmegge thick. *c* **1720** W. GIBSON *Farrier's Guide* II. v. (1738) 188 A vast number of Tubercles and little Hurdles. **1847–78** HALLIWELL, *Hurtle*, a spot. *Heref.*

†**hurtle,** *sb.*[2] *Obs. rare.* = HURT *sb.*[3], HURTLEBERRY: see also WHORTLE. *Comb.* **hurtle-tree,** the dwarf shrub that bears the hurtleberry.

1597 GERARDE *Herbal* 1229 *Vaccinia nigra* the blacke Whortle or Hurtle is a base and lowe tree or woodie plant. *a* **1630** in Risdon *Surv. Devon* §312 (1810) 322 Taw..Whose sides are stor'd with many a hurtle tree.

hurtle ('hɜːt(ə)l), *sb.*[3] *poet.* and *rhet.* [f. HURTLE *v.*] The action or an act of hurtling; dashing together, collision, conflict; clashing sound.

1773 J. ROSS *Fratricide* v. 10 (MS.) The elements..had wag'd Tremendous hurtle. **1856** MRS. BROWNING *Aur. Leigh* IX. 835, I flung closer to his breast..And, in that hurtle of united souls [etc.]. **1867** MUSGRAVE *Nooks Old France* II. x. 310 The hurtle of the arrows.

hurtle ('hɜːt(ə)l), *v.* Now only *literary* or *arch.* Also 4 **hortel,** 4–7 **hurtel,** 5 **hurtul.** [app. a

diminutive and iterative of HURT *v.*, in its original sense of 'strike with a shock'.

Palsgrave (1530) and Cotgrave (1611) give a F. *hurteller* 'to trample on with the feet', which corresponds in form; but this appears to be a late formation.

Sometimes confused with *hurl*; but the essential notion in *hurtle* is that of forcible collision, in *hurl* that of forcible projection; if, however, I *hurl* a javelin at a shield and strike it, I also *hurtle* the one against the other; hence the contact of sense.]

I. Transitive senses.

1. To strike, dash, or knock (something against something else, or two things together); †to knock or thrust *down* with force or violence; †to run (a ship) aground.

a **1225** [see HURTLING *vbl. sb.*]. *a* **1325** [see *hurtled* below]. **1382** WYCLIF *Gen.* xxv. 22 But the litil children..weren hurtlid togidere. —— *Acts* xxvii. 41 Whanne we felden into a place of grauel..thei hurtliden [*v.r.* hurten, **1388** *v.r.* hurliden, Vulg. *impegerunt*] the schipp. *c* **1386** CHAUCER *Knt.'s T.* 1758 He foyneth on his feet with his tronchon And he hym hurtleth [so *Cambr.* and *Harl. MSS.*; *other* 4 *MSS.* hurteth] with his hors adoun. **1388** WYCLIF *Mark* ix. 17 Where euer he takith hym, he hurtlith [**1382** hirtith, *v.r.* hurtlith] hym doun. **1470–85** MALORY *Arthur* x. lxviii, There he..pulled awey theire sheldes and hurtled doun many knyghtes. **1884** CHILD *Ballads* II. xli. 378 *note*, The horse was not sure-footed and hurtled his rider against a tree.

2. To strike or dash against; to come into collision with.

c **1430** *Syr Gener.* (Roxb.) 5789 Eithir hors hurtled othir. *c* **1430** *Pilgr. Lyf Manhode* IV. xix. (1869) 185 We..committe þee þat..þou hurtle alle þilke so cruelliche. **1848** LYTTON *Harold* IX. vi, His emotions..so hurtling one the other. **1881** JUDD *Volcanoes* iv. 68 The ragged cindery masses hurtling one another in the atmosphere.

b. *fig.* To assail, attack (in words).

c **1374** CHAUCER *Boeth.* II. pr. i. 20 (Camb. MS.) Thow weere wont to hurtelyn and despysen hir with manly wordes [*virilibus incessere verbis*]. **1804** W. TAYLOR in Robberds *Mem.* (1843) I. 519 Not the theologian whom Gregory Blunt hurtles.

3. To drive violently or swiftly; to dash, dart, shoot, fling, cast. App. often confounded with *hurl*. By Spenser, *erroneously*, To brandish, wave.

[**1590** SPENSER *F.Q.* II. vii. 42 His harmefull club he gan to hurtle hye.] *a* **1678** MARVELL *Verses* iii, An arrow, hurtel'd ere so high. **1833** MRS. BROWNING *Prometh. Bound* Poems 1850 I. 190 Such a curse on my head..From the hand of your Zeus has been hurtled along. **1851** C. L. SMITH tr. *Tasso* IV. ix, Whom grand mischance..Down to this horrible den has hurtled forth. **1881** *Boy's Own Paper* 17 Dec. 184 Pieces of ice are being belched forth or hurtled into the air with a continued noise.

II. Intransitive senses.

4. To strike *together* or *against* something, esp. with violence or noise; to come into collision; to dash, clash, impinge; to meet in shock and encounter. (Also *fig.*)

1340 HAMPOLE *Pr. Consc.* 4787 Hard roches and stanes Sal strik togyder, alle attanes..And ilkan agayn other hortel fast. *c* **1374** CHAUCER *Boeth.* V. met. iv. 130 (Camb. MS.) Ryht so as voys or sown hurtelith to the Eeres and commoeueth hem to herkne. **1388** WYCLIF *Jer.* xlvi. 12 A strong man hurtlide aȝens a strong man, and bothe fellen doun togidere. **1413** *Pilgr. Sowle* (Caxton 1483) III. viii. 55 Twoo fendes..maden them for to hurtlen ageyn a pyler. *c* **1450** *Merlin* 155 Thei hurtled togeder with their bodyes and sheldes and helmes. *c* **1477** CAXTON *Jason* 57 The ship ..hurtlyd again the grounde in suche a random and force that hit was all to broken. *c* **1540** tr. *Pol. Verg. Eng. Hist.* (Camden) I. 55 To traine his enemie farder from the sea beefore they hurteled together in fighte. **1600** FAIRFAX *Tasso* VI. xli. 101 Together hurtled both their steedes, and brake Each others necke, the riders lay on ground. **1833–42** ALISON *Europe* lxxxviii. §14 (1849–50) XIII. 122 His strength was unequal to hurtling against their immense masses. **1874** GREEN *Short Hist.* vii. §7. 415 Its fauns dancing on the sward where knights have hurtled together.

5. To emit a sound of collision; to clatter: said esp. of the clatter, rattle, or rustle of a shower of missiles, or things in motion; hence, to move with clattering or clashing; to come with a crash.

1509 BARCLAY *Shyp of Folys* (1874) II. 115 Thy throte hurtlyth, thy wordes, and thy syght Theyr naturall offyce shall vnto the denye. **1601** SHAKS. *Jul. C.* II. ii. 22 The noise of Battel hurtled in the Ayre. **1761** GRAY *Fatal Sisters* i, Iron-sleet of arrowy shower Hurtles in the darken'd air. **1814** SOUTHEY *Roderick* xxv. 166 The arrows hissed—the javelins hurtled by. **1826** E. IRVING *Babylon* I. III. 248 The sixth thunder already hurtles in the heavens. **1880** JEFFERIES *Hodge & M.* II. v. 118 The rain hurtles through the branches. **1888** BRYCE *Amer. Commw.* II. lxxii. 589 The tempest of invective and calumny which hurtles round the head of a presidential candidate.

6. To dash, rush, hurry; esp. with noise.

1509 HAWES *Past. Pleas.* XXXV. xiii, He hurtled aboute, and kest his shelde afore. **1590** SPENSER *F.Q.* I. iv. 16 All hurtlen [*ed.* **1609** hurlen] forth. *Ibid.* viii. 17 The Gyaunt.. Came hurtling in full fiers, and forst the knight retyre. **1599** NASHE *Lenten Stuffe* (1871) 16 Gangs of good fellows that hurtled and bustled thither. **1852** HAWTHORNE *Wonder Bk.*, *Gorgon's Head* (1879) 43 They hurtled upward into the air. **1873** in *Mem. Alice Cary* 240 Pell mell the men came hurtling out. **1893** *Northumbld. Gloss.*, *Hirtle*, to hurry. 'The clud's gan hirtlin alang the hill side.'

Hence **hurtled** *ppl. a.*

a **1325** *Prose Psalter* cxliv. 15 [cxlv. 14] Our Lord.. drescep vp alle þe hurteled. **1833** MRS. BROWNING *Prometh. Bound* Poems 1850 I. 146 Shake The hurtled chains wherein I hang. **1850** BLACKIE *Æschylus* II. 118 With one acclaim, a forest of right hands Rose through the hurtled air.

hurtleberry ('hɜːt(ə)lbɛrɪ). Also 5 hurtil-, 6 hurtel-, hirtle-, 7 heurtle-; see also WHORTLEBERRY. [app. a derivative of HURT *sb.*³, q.v.]

The fruit of *Vaccinium Myrtillus*, or the shrub itself; the whortleberry or bilberry; also applied to other species of *Vaccinium*, and to the allied American genus *Gaylussacia* (HUCKLEBERRY).

c **1460** J. RUSSELL *Bk. Nurture* 82 Of Strawberies & hurtilberyes with the cold Ioncate. **1513** *Bk. Keruynge* A ij a in *Babees Bk.* 266 After mete, peres, nottes, strawberyes, hurtel-beryes, & hard chese. **1562** TURNER *Herbal* II. 61 a, Ble-berries or hurtel berries. **1634** W. WOOD *New Eng. Prosp.* (1865) 15 In other seasons there bee Gooseberries, Bilberies,..Hurtleberries, Currants. **1716** B. CHURCH *Hist. Philip's War* (1865) I. 114 He perceived they were gathering of Hurtle-Berries. **1772–84** COOK *Voy.* (1790) V. 1879 The berries found here were hurtle-berries, heath-berries, partridge-berries. **1884** *Health Exhib. Catal.* 157/2 Preserved Lingon, a genus of Hurtleberry found in Sweden.

b. Comb., as *hurtleberry-tree*.

1589 FLEMING *Virg.*, *Ecl.* II. 32 You O baytrees will I crop, and hirtleberrie trees.

hurtless ('hɜːtlɪs), *a.* [f. HURT *sb.*¹ + -LESS.]

1. Free from hurt; unhurt.

a **1400–50** *Alexander* 102 Ert þ ou noȝt hurtles and hale? *c* **1586** C'TESS PEMBROKE *Ps.* XCI. vi, On lionet shalt hurtlesse soe, And on the dragon tread. **1681** W. ROBERTSON *Phraseol. Gen.* (1693) 750 Hurtless or not hurt, *illaesus.* **1876** G. MACDONALD *T. Wingfield* iv. 34, I shall be hurtless, nor here, nor there.

2. Causing no hurt or injury; harmless.

1549 COVERDALE, etc. *Erasm. Par. Rom.* Argt., The boucherye of hurtles beastes. **1580** SIDNEY *Ps* XXIV. ii, He that hath hurtles hands. **1605** B. JONSON *Volpone* II. ii, They had neuer..Beene murderers of so much paper, Or wasted many a hurtlesse taper. **1697** DRYDEN *Æneid* IX. 1101 Hurtless blows he makes. **1775** SHERIDAN *Rivals* V. iii, Modest hurtless flowers. **1881** G. MACDONALD *Mary Marston* III. xiii. 236 The beads came pelting down in a cataract of hurtless hail.

Hence **'hurtlessly** *adv.*, without hurt, harmlessly; **'hurtlessness**, harmlessness, innocence.

1580 HOLLYBAND *Treas. Fr. Tong*, *Innocence*, hurtlesnesse. **1580** SIDNEY *Arcadia* I. (1622) 12 Your neighbours haue found you so hurtelesly strong. *Ibid.* III. 235 Hoping that the goodnes of their intention, and the hurtlesnesse of their sexe shall excuse the breach of the commandement. **1611** MARKHAM *Countr. Content.* I. ix. (1668) 47 The Art of Angling..having ever been most hurtlesly necessary, hath been the sport or Recreation of Gods Saints.

hurtling ('hɜːtlɪŋ), *vbl. sb.* [f. HURTLE *v.* + -ING¹.] The action of the verb HURTLE; clashing, collision, conflict; †a charge, onset; dashing, rushing, darting, etc.: see the verb.

a **1225** *Ancr. R.* 166 Mid a lutel hurlunge [*MS. T.* hurtlinge] ȝe muhten al uor leosen. *a* **1300** *Cursor M.* 27931 Hurtling o sculder. **1387** TREVISA *Higden* (Rolls) IV. 153 Noyse and hurtlynge to gidre of armure was i-herd. **1413** *Pilgr. Sowle* (Caxton 1483) III. viii. 55 At the hurtlynge hit semed as theyr brayne sturt oute. **1600** SHAKS. *A. Y. L.* IV. iii. 132 Kindnesse..Made him giue battell to the Lyonnesse: Who quickly fell before him, in which hurtling From miserable slumber I awaked. **1670** MILTON *Hist. Eng.* II. Wks. (1851) 33 Amaz'd at the strangeness of those new Sea Castles..the hurtling of Oares, the battring of fierce Engines. **1814** CARY *Dante*, *Inf.* XXIV. 146 Sharp and eager driveth on the storm With arrowy hurtling o'er Piceno's field. **1892** *Pall Mall G.* 11 Oct. 2/2 Useful points in his letter..obscured in the hurtling of his abusive rhetoric.

'hurtling, *ppl. a.* [f. as prec. + -ING².] That hurtles: see the verb.

1832 L. HUNT *Poems, Gentle Armour* ii. 45 Clatt'ring shields, and helms, and hurtling steeds. **1851–5** BRIMLEY *Ess.*, *Tennyson* 41 A hurtling storm of multitudinous arrowy rounds. **1897** *Fortn. Rev.* July 139 Devoutly crossing themselves as every hurtling shell burst near.

Hence **'hurtlingly** *adv.*

1882 FARRAR *Early Chr.* I. x. 217 The day of the Lord.. in which the heavens shall pass hurtlingly away.

hurtness ('hɜːtnɪs). [f. HURT *ppl. a.* + -NESS.] The state of being hurt.

1909 *Daily Chron.* 12 Oct. 7/3 Her voice conveyed the gentlest intimation of hurtness. **1922** JOYCE *Ulysses* 341 She kissed away the hurtness.

'hurt-sickle. [tr. med.L. *blaptisecula*, f. Gr. βλάπτ-ειν to hurt + L. *secula* sickle.] A name for the Corn Bluebottle (*Centaurea Cyanus*), which grows among corn, and is apt to injure the edge of the sickle with its hard tough stem.

[**1551** TURNER *Herbal* I. N iv a, Blew bottell..Sume herbaries call it baptisecula, or blaptisecula: because it hurteth sicles, whiche were ones called of olde wryters seculae.] **1578** LYTE *Dodoens* II. xii. 161 This floure..may also be called Hurte Sicle. **1597** GERARDE *Herbal* II. ccxl. 594 In English it is called blewe Bottle..and hurt sickle. **1598** FLORIO, *Barbarauoce*, blew bottle, corne floure, or hurtsickle. **1829** *Glover's Hist. Derby* I. 124 *Centaurea Cyanus*..blue bottle, knapweed, hurt sickle or corn flower.

'hurtsome, *a.* Chiefly *Sc.* [f. HURT *sb.*¹ + -SOME.] Hurtful, injurious.

a **1699** A. SHIELDS *Faithful Contend.* (1780) 108 (Jam.) Their entry was hurtsome to the cause. **1887** *North Star* 26 May 3/4 The letter..in your issue of yesterday, is likely to prove hurtsome to the subscription list.

hurty ('hɜːtɪ), *a. Her.* [f. HURT *sb.*² + -Y.] Charged with (an indefinite number of) hurts; semé of hurts.

1828 BERRY *Encycl. Herald.* Gloss., *Hurty*, charged with hurts, or semée of hurts, that is, strewed over with hurts.

hus, obs. form of HOUSE, US, USE.

husband ('hʌzbənd), *sb.* Forms: 1 húsbonda, -bunda, 2 husbonde, -bunde, 3 husebande, houssebonde, 3–4 husebonde, (4 -boonde), 3–5 hosebonde, (3 -baunde, 4 -bounde), 4 hos(e)band(e, housebonde, -bounde, 4–5 hosbond(e, 4–6 husbond(e, housbond(e, housband(e, 4–7 husbande, 5 housbounde, (hosbon), 6 huszbande, 6–7 houseband(e, (7 hisband), 4– husband. [Late OE. *húsbonda*, *-bunda*, f. *hús* house + late OE. ? *bónda, bonda, bunda*, a. ON. *bóndi*, peasant owning his own house and land, freeholder, franklin, yeoman; earlier *búandi, bóandi*, orig. pres. pple. of *búa*, *bóa* to dwell, have a household; but the OE. use answered immediately to ON. *húsbóndi*, a man of this rank in his capacity as head or master of the household. In ME. often with connective *e*, as in *husewif*, HOUSEWIFE.]

I. †**1.** The master of a house, the male head of a household. *Obs.*

c **1000** *Ags. Gosp.* Matt. xx. 28 Ne sitte ȝe on þam fyrmestan setlum þe læs þe..se husbonda [*Hatton MS.* husbunde] hate þe arisan. *a* **1100** *O.E. Chron.* an. 1048 An his manna wolde wician æt anes bundan huse his unðances and ȝewundode þone husbundon and se husbunda ofsloh þone oðerne. *c* **1200** *Trin. Coll. Hom.* 165 Nis þe gist siker of þe husebonde, ne noðer of oðer. *a* **1240** *Sawles Warde* in *Cott. Hom.* 247 Þe husebonde, þat is wit, warneð his hus.

2. a. A man joined to a woman by marriage. Correlative of *wife*.

c **1290** *Beket* 193 in *S. Eng. Leg.* I. 112 Is wif gret Ioie made with hire housebonde. *a* **1300** *Cursor M.* 10158 Anna ..ioachim had til husband. **1382** WYCLIF *Matt.* i. 16 Joseph, the husbond of Marie. *c* **1450** *Merlin* 20 Thyn hosbonde and thow were at debate. **1548–9** (Mar.) *Bk. Com. Prayer*, *Matrimony*, Wilt thou haue this man to thy wedded houseband? **1590** SHAKS. *Com. Err.* III. ii. 68 Thou hast no husband yet, nor I no wife: Giue me thy hand. **1631–5** W. SALTONSTALL *Picturæ Loquentes* F vij, Her mouth is drawne into so narrow a compasse that she will not speake a broad word, but calls her husband hisband. **1638** FORD *Fancies* V. ii, Hisband, stand to thy tackling, hisband like a man of mettle. **1765** BLACKSTONE *Comm.* I. xv. (1809) 442 By marriage, the husband and wife are one person in law. **1842** TENNYSON *Locksley Hall* 47 As the husband is, the wife is.

b. *transf.* The male of a pair of the lower animals; a male animal kept for breeding.

1607 TOPSELL *Four-f. Beasts* (1658) 47 A Bull is the husband of a Cow, and ring-leader of the herd. **1697** DRYDEN *Virg. Georg.* III. 253 Whom to reserve for Husband of the Herd. **1894** H. DRUMMOND *Ascent Man* 379 The apathy and estrangement between husband and wife in the animal world.

†**c.** Applied to the male in diœcious plants; also to a tree forming the prop or support of a vine. *Obs.*

1553 T. WILSON *Rhet.* (1567) 24 a, Of trees, wherin.. there is found Mariage, with some manifeste difference of bothe kyndes, that excepte the housebande Tree, doe leane ..vpon the women Trees..Thei would elles..waxe barraine. **1796** PEGGE *Anonym.* (1809) 59 The husband, as we may call it, being a tree of some kind, and I suppose the elm chiefly, the grape could never ripen kindly.

II. †**3. a.** One who tills and cultivates the soil; a cultivator, tiller, farmer, husbandman. In early northern use, app. applied spec. to a manorial tenant, the *villanus* or villein of other districts. Cf. HUSBANDLAND. *Obs.*

c **1220** *Bestiary* 388 Fox is hire to name..husebondes hire haten, for hire harm dedes. [**1239** *Cart. Mon. de Rameseia* I. 426 Gilbertus Copsi..dat domino Abbati dimidiam marcam, ut Henricus Koc filius suus fiat housebonde de sex acris terrae..Abbatis in Depedale.] *c* **1290** *Beket* 2428 in *S. Eng. Leg.* I. 176 Of seriaunz and of squiers and oþere housebondes i-nowe; And þe simple men of þe londe. *c* **1330** R. BRUNNE *Chron.* (1810) 168 Do com..burgeis & merchant, & knyght & squiere..hosbond & sergant, & tak of þam homage. *c* **1375** *Sc. Leg. Saints*, *Julian* 127 A housband agane our lay Telyt his land one sownday. **1494** FABYAN *Chron.* VII. 421 In this yere..fell so excedynge rayne in the monethes of Iulii & August, that husbondys myght not brynge in theyr lytle store of corne. **1513** DOUGLAS *Æneis* X. vi. 53 The routis of the lauboreris Or rurell husbandis. **1532–3** *Act 24 Hen. VIII*, c. 10 Preamb., All the Tillers, Husbondes and Sowers of the Erthe. **1697** DRYDEN *Virg. Georg.* II. 578 When Husbands have survey'd the last Degree, And utmost Files of Plants, and order'd ev'ry Tree.

†**b.** In later times esp. with qualifying epithet as in 5. *Obs.*

c **1380** WYCLIF *Serm.* Sel. Wks. I. 98 Þe kyngdom of hevene, seiþ Crist is lyke to a good huseboonde. **1540–1** ELYOT *Image Gov.* (1556) 153 b, The Romaines beeyng good husbondes..overseeyng theyr tyllage and husbondry. **1613–16** W. BROWNE *Brit. Past.* I. iii. Wks. 1772 I. 81 With shrubs that cloy ill husband's meadow-ground. **1723** *Carew's Cornwall* Life (1769) p. xvi, He was accounted..the greatest Husband, and most excellent Manager of Bees in Cornwall. **1733** TULL *Horse-Hoing Husb.* Pref. 5 The Proverb..That once in seven Years, the worst Husbands have the best Corn.

4. a. The manager of a household or establishment; a housekeeper; a steward. Also a

title of various public functionaries: see quots. *Obs.* exc. in spec. applications.

c 1450 *Bk. Curtasye* 574 in *Babees Bk.*, Now speke y wylle of tresurere, Husbonde and houswyf he is in fere. **1475** Sir J. Paston (to his Mother) in *P. Lett.* No. 762 III. 139, I purpose to leeffe alle heer, and come home to yow, and be yowr hosbonde and balyff. a **1483** *Liber Niger* in *Househ. Ord.* (1790) 69 This hathe bene proved by many olde yeres husbandes and yett myght there be made alweyes of a busshell xxix loves. **1613** Sir H. Finch *Law* (1636) 240 The King hath a proper Court..for all things touching his reuenues, called the Exchequer. The Judges whereof are called Barons, or housebands for the Kings Reuenue. **1695** *Act 7 & 8 Will. III*, c. 13 §2 It shall..be Lawful for the Royal African Company of England, to bring to His Majesties Tower of London..such Gold as shall be Imported by them, the Husband of the said Company first making Oath before the Warden [etc.]. **1737** *List Govt. Officers* in *Chamberlayne's St. Gt. Brit.* II. 65 Officers.. belonging to the Custom-House..The Husband for receiving and taking up all Goods consign'd from the Plantations on Account of the Duty of 4 and half per Cent. **1833** *Rep. Sel. Committee Munic. Corporat.* 319 Is there any other fee paid to you as town's husband [at Hull]? [**1886** *Times* 3 Aug. 6/3 'Husband to the East India Company', a functionary whose duty seems to have been to look after the interests of his employers in their relations with the Custom House.]

b. ***ship's husband***: an agent appointed by the owners to attend to the business of a ship while in port, esp. to attend to her stores, equipment, and repairs, and see that the ship is in all respects well found. Now little used, the duties being generally performed by a 'Marine Superintendent'.

1730–6 Bailey (folio), *Husband of a Ship*, a Person whose Office it is to see a Ship's Cargoe entered, landed, laid up in Warehouses, etc. for the Merchants. **1756** Rolt *Dict. Trade, Husband of a ship*, or the ship's husband. **1774** Colman *Man of Business* III. 159 The Ship's husband desires to speak with him. **1800** Colquhoun *Comm. Thames* 629 To furnish an exact statement of disbursements to the Ship's Husband. **1839** *36 Years Seaf. Life* 44 One of the brothers, who acted the part of working partner, or as it was called ship's husband. **1858** Simmonds *Dict. Trade, Ship's husband*, a part owner, or other person appointed as a manager to look after and provide stores, provisions, or assistance for a ship when in port. **1878** Sir F. Kelly in *Law Rep.* 4 Exch. Div. 22 A ship's husband has the authority of the ship's owners to procure a charter party, and to make contracts for their benefit.

5. a. With qualifying epithet: One who manages his household, or his affairs or business in general, well or ill, profitably or wastefully, etc. Most commonly ***good husband***: One who manages his affairs with skill and thrift; a saving, frugal, or provident man; an economist. (Cf. HOUSEWIFE.) Now *rare* or *arch.*

c **1510** *Robin Hood* I. 180 Or elles thou hast ben a sorry housband. **1553** T. Wilson *Rhet.* 67 When I call..a pynche penye, a good husbande, a thriftye man. **1597–8** Bacon *Ess., Honour* (Arb.) 68 A man is an ill husband of his Honour that entereth into any action, the failing where-in may disgrace him more than the carrying of it through can Honour him. **1656** Jer. Taylor *Let.* in *Evelyn's Mem.* (1857) III. 79 You see what a good husband I am of my paper and ink. **1719** De Foe *Crusoe* I. xvi, I had been so good a husband of my rum, that I had a great deal left. **1895** M. R. James *Abbey St. Edmund at Bury* 119 The next abbot was a bad husband to the Abbey.

†**b.** *absol.* = *good husband* in prec. *Obs.*

c **1400** *Gamelyn* 13 He had ben wide-where but non husbonde he was. **1530** Palsgr. 233/1 Husbande, a thrivyng man, *mesnagier*. **1577** Fenton *Gold. Ep.* 129 If hee bee a husbande of that hee hath, they will say hee is couetous.

6. *attrib.* and *Comb.* **a.** in sense 2; (*a*) appositive, as ***husband-lover***, ***-soldier***, ***-tree***; (*b*) objective and obj. gen., as ***husband-beater***, ***-catching***, ***-hunter***, ***-hunting***, ***-seeking***, ***-slayer***; (*c*) **husband-ripe** *a.*, ripe for a husband, of marriageable age. **b.** in sense 3, as **husband-field**, a cultivated field; † **husband-town**, a farm; † **husband weed**, agricultural or rustic clothing. See also HUSBANDLAND, -LIKE, -MAN.

1892 *Daily News* 2 May 2/4 The en-tout-cas is..not quite so large this year as it has been in some previous seasons, and the long handles facetiously called '*husband-beaters', have quite disappeared. **1899** *Daily News* 26 Sept. 7/5 One of the greatest reasons of my contempt for them is their *husband-catching propensities. **1949** M. Mead *Male & Female* i. 7 In some societies it is girls for whom parents must collect a dowry or make husband-catching magic. **1811** Scott *Don Roderick* xxxix, The sable land-flood from some swamp obscure, That poisons the glad *husband-field with dearth. **1905** *To-Day* 8 Mar. 173/1 She will demand a better article than the mere *husband-hunter has been able to stand out for. **1932** *Times Lit. Suppl.* 21 Jan. 40/4 Arabella Trefoil is a husband-hunter of shameless duplicity and greed. **1771** Smollett *Humph. Cl.* 15 July, I must make you acquainted with my sister Tabby's progress in *husband-hunting. **1823** Byron *Juan* XI. lxxxix, Some sage husband-hunting countess. **1682** Mrs. Behn *City-Heiress* 20 Oh hideous, a *Husband-Lover! **1557–8** Phaer *Æneid* VII. S iij b, One doughter..Now *husbandripe, now wedlockable ful, of lawful yeeres. **1899** *Daily News* 26 Sept. 7/5 Their object in life is..plain—*husband seeking. **1897** *Edin. Rev.* Apr. 458 The Danaides, spring-nymphs as well as *husband-slayers. c **1375** *Sc. Leg. Saints, Ninian* 867 þe knycht..In til a *housband ton þat nycht To slepe and ese hyme can dycht. c **1470** Harding *Chron.* ccxl. *note* (Harl. MS.) Many goode villages and husbonde townys. **1553** *Housebande tree [see 2 c]. c **1475** *Rauf Coilyear* 593 Ane man in *husband weid.

c. Combinations with *husbands'*, in specialized senses: as **husbands' boat, train**, etc., in former times a means of transport run chiefly for the convenience of men wishing to join their wives on holiday, esp. applied to ships, etc., run on Saturday; **husband's tea** *colloq.*, very weak tea.

1869 *Porcupine* XI. 172/2 Passengers by the 'husbands' boat' are more heavily laden with provisions. **1870** *London Soc.* XVIII. 170 The Husbands' boat can carry lovers too! **1909** *Daily Chron.* 24 July 8/6 The New Palace Steamers announce that their p.s. Koh-i-noor will be making the 'husband's boat' trip to-day as usual. **1874** Hotten *Slang Dict.* s.v. *Water-bewitched*, Sometimes very weak tea is called 'husband's tea'. **1886** A. Hornblow tr. *Normand's Splashes from Parisian Ink-Pot* 163 A special train, the husband's train, would permit him to arrive at Tréport the same night.

d. husband-wife *a.*, pertaining to or involving a husband and his wife.

1956 J. M. Mogey *Family & Neighbourhood* 61 'My wife trusts me' indicates excellent husband-wife adjustment. **1959** *Encounter* July 73/1 [This book] is by a husband-wife duet of French journalists. **1960** *Guardian* 14 Apr. 8/6 The quintessential husband-wife relationship. **1965** *Language* XLI. 124 The husband-wife team of Pavle and Milka Ivić.

husband ('hʌzbənd), *v.* [f. prec. sb.]

I. 1. *trans.* To till (the ground), to dress or tend (trees and plants), to manage as a husbandman; to cultivate.

c **1420** [see HUSBANDING *vbl. sb.* 1]. **1545** Ascham *Toxoph.* I. (Arb.) 93 A good grounde..well husbanded bringeth out great plentie of byg eared corn. **1590** R. Payne *Descr. Irel.* (1841) 9 To husband this farme, your tenaunt must keepe viii persons. **1652–62** Heylin *Cosmogr.* IV. (1682) 33 Husbanding the Vallies which lie nearest to them. **1737** Bracken *Farriery Impr.* (1756) I. 25 Till such Time as the Ground be dug up and husbanded. **1876** L. Morris *Epic Hades* II. (1877) 96 The grain scarce husbanded by toiling hands Upon the sunlit plain.

b. *fig.* To cultivate (the mind, etc.).

1639 T. Brugis tr. *Camus' Mor. Relat.* 197 So dexterously to husband the minde of Rogat, that he will worke him to condescend unto his desires. *Ibid.* 271 Whether it were that he ill husbanded the mind of [him] or whether this woman changed it.

2. To administer as a good householder or steward; to manage with thrift and prudence; to use, spend, or apply economically; to make the most of; to economize; also, to save, lay by a store of. **a.** material things.

c **1440** *Promp. Parv.* 254/1 Husbondyn, or wysely dyspendyn worldely goodys. **1574** Hellowes *Gueuara's Fam. Ep.* (1577) 312 The office of the husband is, to husband yᵉ goods and of the wife to gouerne the familie. **1586** J. Hooker *Girald. Irel.* in *Holinshed* II. 135/1 That his majesties..revenues [be] well husbanded and looked unto. **1613–18** Daniel *Coll. Hist. Eng.* (1626) 106 This Archbishop so husbanded the Kings businesse, that..hee yeelded an account vnto him, that [etc.]. **1687** A. Lovell tr. *Thevenot's Trav.* I. 166 A Jar of Brandy, which we husbanded as well as we could. **1748** *Anson's Voy.* III. ii. 309 We were obliged to husband our ammunition. **1857** C. Bronte *Professor* I. ii. 36 Husbanding my monthly allowance.

b. immaterial things.

1605 Bp. Hall *Medit. & Vows* I. §59, I will labour so to husband the stock that God hath left in my hands, that I may returne my soule better then I received it. **1639** Fuller *Holy War* I. vii. (1647) 7 If they had husbanded this occasion. **1742** Young *Nt. Th.* I. 105 For human Weal, Heav'n husbands all Events. **1836** *Johnsoniana* 246 Garrick husbanded his fame.

c. with *out*: to economize (a thing) so that it may last out; to eke out.

1760–2 Goldsm. *Cit. W.* xviii, The Dutch frugally husband out their pleasures. **1770** —— *Des. Vill.* 87 To husband out life's taper at the close.

†**3.** ***to husband it***: to do household or farm work. *rare. Obs.*

1597–8 Bp. Hall *Sat.* III. i. 74 Good Saturne selfe..was not so clad of yore..Husbanding it in work-day yeomanrie.

II. 4. *trans.* To provide or match with a husband; to mate.

1565 [see HUSBANDING *vbl. sb.* 3]. **1602** Rowlands *Gossips* (1609) 4, I am husbanded with such a Clowne, 'Twould pul a merrier heart then mine is downe. **1608** Day *Hum. out of Br.* I. i. (1860) 6 Wiue it for them, you shall not husband me. a **1845** Hood *To Sylv. Urban* vii, Parishioners,—hatched,—husbanded,—and wived. **1875** Tennyson *Q. Mary* II. ii, I am not..so amorous That I must needs be husbanded.

5. To act the part of a husband to; to become the husband of, to marry.

1601 Shaks. *All's Well* V. iii. 126 You shall as easie Proue that I husbanded her bed in Florence, Where yet she neuer was. **1605** —— *Lear* V. iii. 70 That were the most if he should husband you. **1843** *Tait's Mag.* X. 139 Husbanding his means, with the hope of ultimately husbanding a wife. **1880** G. Meredith *Tragic Com.* (1881) 248 He had been ready to perform the duty of husbanding a woman.

b. *fig.* To 'espouse' (an opinion).

1883 H. H. Bancroft *Centr. Amer.* vi. I. 318 *note*, Nor should I deem it wise in me to husband a doctrine on this or any other palpably unprovable proposition.

6. ***to husband it***: to act or play the husband.

1608 Day *Hum. out of Br.* II. ii, Say, we desire to husband it with you.

'husbandable, *a. rare.* [f. prec. + -ABLE.]

a. Capable of being economically used. **b.** Fit for husbandry or cultivation, cultivable.

1611 Cotgr., *Mesnageable*, husbandable. **1619** *Time's Storehouse* 12 (L.) Neither were they permitted to tarry longer then a yeare in a place to till or make it husbandable.

'husbandage. [f. HUSBAND *sb.* + -AGE.] The commission or allowance paid to a 'ship's husband': see HUSBAND *sb.* 4 b.

1809 R. Langford *Introd. Trade* 132, *Husbandage*, the managing owners allowance or commission.

'husbanded, *ppl. a.* [f. HUSBAND *v.* (or *sb.*)]

1. Cultivated; tilled.

1578 Lyte *Dodoens* III. lix. 399 The husbanded Hoppe beareth his flowers or knoppes ful of scales. **1616** Surfl. & Markh. *Country Farme* 294 The husbanded or tame figge-tree. **1636** Featly *Clavis Myst.* v. 56 Better husbanded land. **1657** W. Coles *Adam in Eden* lii, In Gardens, Vineyards, Orchards, and other like husbanded grounds.

2. Carefully managed, used sparingly, economized.

1677 Gilpin *Demonol.* (1867) 394 A better husbanded strength might be truly more advantageous.

3. Provided or matched with a husband, mated.

1601 Shaks. *Jul. C.* II. i. 297 Thinke you, I am no stronger then my Sex, Being so Father'd, and so Husbanded? **1654** Whitlock *Zootomia* 61 The ill Wived, or ill Husbanded Wretches might here be comforted.

'husbander. [f. as prec. + -ER[1].] One who husbands, economizes, or saves up.

1897 Max Pemberton in *Windsor Mag.* Jan. 267/1 Wonderful men are these cooks, the husbanders of wonderful fortunes.

'husbandhood. [f. HUSBAND *sb.* + -HOOD.] The position or relation of a husband.

1888 Mrs. H. Ward *R. Elsmere* xii, Husbandhood, fatherhood, and all the sacred education that flows from human joy. **1894** *Woman's Signal* II. No. 27. 5/1 The commonest feelings of humanity, of husbandhood and of fatherhood.

†**hus'bandically**, *adv. Obs. nonce-wd.* Economically: cf. HUSBAND *sb.* 5.

1654 Gayton *Pleas. Notes* II. iv. 50 Husbandically provided.

husbanding, *vbl. sb.* [f. HUSBAND *v.*]

1. Cultivation, culture, tillage (of soil or plants).

c **1420** *Pallad. on Husb.* I. 469 Oon good poynt of husbondyng. **1587** Golding *De Mornay* xii. (1617) 188 Land which for want of tillage and husbanding brought forth briars and thistles. **1616** Surfl. & Markh. *Country Farme* 153 Describing the manner of husbanding and tilling of the Earth. **1665** *Sir. T. Roe's Voy. E. Ind.* in G. Havers *P. della Valle's Trav. E. India* 330 Salads, which the soyl brings forth without husbanding. **1703** Maundrell *Journ. Jerus.* (1732) 65 For the husbanding of these Mountains, their manner was, [etc.]. **1898** *Westm. Gaz.* 31 Mar. 5/1 Waiting for the produce of their husbanding.

2. Economical and thrifty use (of anything); the action of saving or storing up.

c **1420** [see 1]. **1597** *1st Pt. Return fr. Parnass.* I. i. 205 For the husbanding of my witt I put it out to interest, and make it returne twoo phamphlets a weeke. **1601** R. Johnson *Kingd. & Commw.* (1603) 17 The riches of a prince consist not in the abundance of revenues, but in the thriftie husbanding therof. **1708** *Royal Proclam.* in *Lond. Gaz.* No. 4452/1 The Curing, Salting, Drying and Husbanding of their Fish. c **1842** Lance *Cottage Farmer* 7 For the husbanding of manures and their increase. **1872** *Globe* 5 Aug., A careful husbanding of the elements of wealth.

3. Mating with a husband.

1565 Golding *Ovid's Met.* x. (1593) 251 O Atalanta, thou at all of husband hast no need, Shun husbanding.

husbanding, *ppl. a.* [f. as prec. + -ING[2].] That husbands; sparing, economical, parsimonious.

1811 Southey in *Q. Rev.* VI. 275 The husbanding politicians and peace-praters.

†**'husbandize**, *v. Obs. rare*[−1]. [f. HUSBAND + -IZE.] *trans.* To administer as a steward, to economize; = HUSBAND *v.* 2. (Cf. *husbandrize*, *husbandry* vb., also used by Blithe.)

1649 Blithe *Eng. Improv.* i. 4 He also made..all the creatures subservient to man, and man to husbandize the fruits of the earth, and dresse, and keepe them for the use of the Creature.

'husbandland. [f. HUSBAND *sb.* or ON. *húsbóndi* in its sense of 'freeholder' + LAND.] An old Northumbrian and Lowland Scotch term for the holding of a 'husband' or manorial tenant, = yardland, virgate; the land occupied and tilled by the tenants of a manor, in contradistinction to the demesne lands.

As this holding normally consisted of two bovates or ox-gangs, the word was sometimes taken as = this quantity of arable land.

[c **1290** *Liber de Calchou* (1846) 461 Habent villam de bolden in qua sunt viginti octo terre husbandorum, quarum quelibet solebat reddere per annum vj*s.* et viij*d.*..et faciendo talia seruicia [etc.] **1321** *Merton Coll. Rec.* No. 6186 Willelmus Alsilwyr pro i. toft' et i. bovett' de terra dominici et ij. bovett' de terra husband' reddit iiij. li.] **1414** *Newminster Cartul.* (Surtees) 264 Unam terram vocatam Husbondeland. **1567** *Surv. Long Houghton* in Bateson *Hist. Northumbld.* II. 370 Before the partition of this towne, every tenant had, besyd his husband lande, certayne parte of the demayne lands; every husband lande was at the yearly rent of xxij*s*. **15..** *Acts Parlt. Scotl.* I. 198 Item xiij akker of land is callit ane ox gang. Tua ox gang is ane husband land. **1633** *Sc. Acts Chas. I*, c. 5 To set downe ane stent upon everie Plough or Husband Land, according to the worth, for maintenance..of the said Schools. **1860** C. Innes *Scot. in Mid. Ages* iv. 139 Each tenant of a husbandland kept two

oxen. **1883** SEEBOHM *Eng. Vill. Commun.* 61 In the district of the old Northumbria, virgates and half-virgates were still the usual holdings, but they were called 'husband-lands'. **1892** F. W. DENDY *Farms Northumbld.* in *Archæol. Æliana* XVI. 127 The full number of strips in the open arable fields which belonged to each customary homestead in the village, with the meadow and common rights also appurtenant to it, was called throughout England a 'yardland', . . in the North of England and in Scotland a 'husband land', or a 'whole tenement', and in Northumberland and in the North of Durham a 'farm' or 'farmhold'. **1894** EARL PERCY *Ibid.* XVII. 10 An area equal to the size of an average husbandland was in the hands of the cottagers. *Ibid.*, Hitherto these holdings have been entered as 'husbandlands'. Here [survey of Lesbury, 1616] for the first time they are called 'farms'. **1895** BATESON *Hist. Northumbld.* II. 424 These husbandlands or farms contained on an average 31½ acres of arable land, 3 acres of meadow, and 4 acres of pasture.

'husbandless, *a.* [f. HUSBAND *sb.* + -LESS.] Having no husband; unwedded; bereaved of a husband, widowed.

1546 BALE *Eng. Votaries* I. (1550) 4 Their vowed wyuelesse and husbandelesse chastyte is altogyther of the deuyll. **1641** EARL STRAFFORD 12 May in Rushw. *Hist. Coll.* (1721) III. I. 269 One Stroke will make my Wife Husbandless. **1790** SOUTHEY *Lett.* (1856) I. 2 Till husbandless, houseless, without wealth or land, Poor Sentiment closes by walking the Strand. **1850** BLACKIE *Æschylus* II. 246 Sonless mothers thou hast left us, Weeping wives and husbandless.

husbandlike ('hʌzbəndlaɪk), *a.* and *adv.* [f. as prec. + LIKE *a.* and *adv.*]

A. *adj.* Like or after the manner of a husband (in various senses).

1542 UDALL *Erasm. Apoph.* I. 3 That, that is aboue good housbandlyke clenlynes, we would bestowe in almes vppon our Christian brethren. *a* **1722** LISLE *Husb.* (1752) 101, I ploughed and sowed the corn in the most husbandlike manner I could. **1845** POLSON *Eng. Law* in *Encycl. Metrop.* 829/1 In the case of a farm, a promise is implied on the part of a yearly tenant, that he will use it in a husbandlike manner, and cultivate the lands according to the custom of the country. **1898** *Daily News* 21 July 8/6 Mr. Calvert suggested that the plaintiff could have . . left his wife at Ostend. The Deputy Judge did not think that would have been very husbandlike.

B. *adv.* After the manner of a husband.

1748 RICHARDSON *Clarissa* (1811) III. 100 The man . . husband-like, will let nobody insult you but himself.

husbandly ('hʌzbəndlɪ), *a.* [f. HUSBAND *sb.* + -LY[1].]

1. Belonging to or befitting a husband; having the character proper to a husband; marital.

1581 J. BELL *Haddon's Answ. Osor.* 353 He loveth his Church, with more then an husbandly love. **1679** SHADWELL *True Widow* v, I will lead a solid, sober, husbandly life, if you will marry me. **1769** *Oxford Mag.* II. 142/2 The timid offspring of husbandly authority. **1882** MASSON *Carlyle* in *Macm. Mag.* XLV. 248 How husbandly [he would be] in his looks round to his wife when she interjected one of her bright and witty remarks.

2. Pertaining or appropriate to a husbandman or to husbandry. ? *Obs.*

1573 TUSSER *Husb.* xlvi. (1878) 101 Though neuer so much a good huswife doth care, that such as doe labour haue husbandlie fare. **1610** W. FOLKINGHAM *Art of Survey* III. vi. 75 The performance of certaine inferiour and husbandly seruices vnto the Lord of the Fee. **1649** BLITHE *Eng. Improv.* To Rdr., As our English climate and best husbandly experience will admit. **1791** PENNANT in *Phil. Trans.* LXXX. 80 Old Tusser, in his Account of the Christmas Husbandlie Fare.

†**b.** Of plants: Cultivated, domestic; trimmed.

1546 J. HEYWOOD *Prov.* (1867) 78 Ye will as soone stop gaps with rushes, As with any husbandly handsome bushes. **1578** LYTE *Dodoens* IV. xviii. 473 The domesticall, or husbandly beanes, do growe in feeldes and gardens.

†**3.** Thrifty, saving, frugal, economical. *Obs.*

1593 NASHE *Christ's T.* (1613) 94 He is very thrifty, and husbandly. **1617** MARKHAM *Caval.* I. 7 The course I haue formerly prescribed, I hold most Husbandly for his profit. *a* **1716** BLACKALL *Wks.* (1723) I. 17 He . . is nevertheless oblig'd to be frugal and husbandly, and not to lavish . . what he has. *a* **1734** NORTH *Lives* I. 413 Lord Rochester . . was working the husbandly point to save the pension.

'husbandly, *adv.* ? *Obs.* [f. as prec. + -LY[2].] In the manner of a good 'husband' (see HUSBAND *sb.* 5); thriftily, frugally, economically.

a **1483** *Liber Niger* in *Househ. Ord.* (1790) 75 To knowe howe honorablye & husbandlye the officers handle & minister the kinge's goodes. **1573** TUSSER *Husb.* viii. (1878) 16 Some husbandlie thrieuth that neuer had wife, yet scarce a good husband in goodnes of life. **1671** *N. Riding Rec.* VI. 161 Two gentlemen named to see the money husbandly employed. *a* **1734** NORTH *Lives* I. 37 However moderately and husbandly the cause was managed.

husbandman ('hʌzbəndmən). Pl. **-men.** Forms: see HUSBAND *sb.* (In early use often two words.) [f. HUSBAND *sb.* + MAN: cf. *masterman, merchantman.*]

1. A man who tills or cultivates the soil; a farmer. In earlier northern use, app., the holder of a *husbandland*: cf. HUSBAND *sb.* 3.

c **1330** R. BRUNNE *Chron. Wace* (Rolls) 6608 Husbondemen þat tyled lond, & werkmen. **1497** *Naval Acc. Hen. VII* (1896) 291 Thomas Jourde of Crofton in Hampeshyre husbandman. **1530** PALSGR. 233/1 Husbandeman, *labourevr de uilage, agricole, paisant.* **1583** STUBBES *Anat. Abus.* II. (1882) 44 Be there husbandmen there and such others as manure and till the ground? **1670** D. DENTON *Descr. New York* (1845) 7 They live principally by Hunting, Fowling, and Fishing: their Wives being the Husbandmen to till the Land, and plant their corn. *a* **1713** ELLWOOD *Autobiog.* (1714) 8 An Husband-Man, who was at Plow not far off. **1828** TYTLER *Hist. Scot.* (1864) I. 237 In the village of Bolden . . there were twenty-eight husbandmen, who possessed each a husbandland, with common pasture. **1834** *Brit. Husb.* I. viii. 179 After . . the adoption of turnips, potatoes, and other esculent roots, into field culture, a new era dawned upon the husbandman. **1885** J. C. ATKINSON in *N. & Q.* 6th Ser. XII. 363 Proof that . . down to the first half of the seventeenth century, the appellation husband-man still distinguished the man of the class next below the yeoman, and that he was literally the holder of the orthodox husband-land consisting of two oxgangs.

fig. **1641** HINDE *J. Bruen* xxvii. 83 Such as did sowe and plant (as Gods husbandmen) the seeds and roots of grace and truth amongst them. **1838** LYTTON *Alice* 174 We are better husbandmen than you who sow the wind and reap the whirlwind.

†**b.** *husbandman's dial*: the marigold. *Obs.*

1563 HYLL *Art Garden.* (1593) 93 This floure [marigold] also of certaine, is named the Husbandmans Diall, for that the same so aptly declareth the houres of morning and euening, by the opening and shutting of it.

†**2.** A man who is the head of a household; the 'goodman' of the house; the householder: = HUSBAND *sb.* 1. *Obs.*

1382 WYCLIF *Matt.* xxiv. 43 3if the housbonde man wiste in what houre the theef were to cumme. **1400–30** *Chaucer's Sompn.* T. 60 (Harl. MS.) Syk lay þe housbond man [6 *texts* good man, bond man] whos þat þe place is. **1432–50** tr. *Higden* (Rolls) I. 35 A howsebonde man in a howse . . a contemplatif man in the chirche.

†**b.** A married man: = HUSBAND *sb.* 2. *rare.*

1430–40 LYDG. *Bochas* III. v. (MS. Bodl. 263) lf. 161/1 Husbondmen, in soth, ar most to blame . . I trowe ther wyues may hem inouh suffise.

†**3.** A thrifty man, an economist; = HUSBAND *sb.* 5. *Obs. rare.*

1711 STEELE *Spect.* No. 109 ¶7 He was an excellent Husbandman, but had resolved not to exceed such a Degree of Wealth.

4. *Comb.*, as ***husbandman-like*** adj.

1789 *Trans. Soc. Arts* VII. 25 The work was done in a husbandmanlike manner. **1841** W. SPALDING *Italy & It. Isl.* I. 324 The husbandman-soldier of Rome, with his rude and stern partriotism.

husbandom ('hʌzbəndəm). *rare.* [f. HUSBAND *sb.* + -DOM.] The position or condition of a husband, married state (of a man).

1895 HARDY *Jude* III. ix. 236 'Wifedom has not yet annihilated you.' . . 'Nor has husbandom you, so far as I can see!' **1926** *New Republic* 12 May 358 If husbandom and fatherhood are still being practiced when he comes to maturity.

'husbandress. *rare.* [f. HUSBANDER + -ESS.] A woman who husbands or saves up.

1895 W. WRIGHT *Palmyra & Zenobia* xii. 132 She was a husbandress of wealth more than is the custom with women.

†**'husbandrize,** *v. Obs. rare.* [f. HUSBANDRY + -IZE.] *trans.* To treat in the way of husbandry, to cultivate, till. (Cf. *husbandize, husbandry* vb., also used by Blithe.)

1653 BLITHE *Eng. Improv. Impr.* (ed. 3) 58 There will be enough for many years of the other two sorts [of land] remain to husbandrize, and toss and tumble up and down.

husbandry ('hʌzbəndrɪ), *sb.* Forms: see HUSBAND; also 3 **housebondrie,** 4 **hosboundrie, hosebounderye,** 5 **husbandery,** 6 **howsbondry.** [f. HUSBAND *sb.* + -RY.]

†**1.** The administration and management of a household; domestic economy. *Obs.* (Cf. HOUSEWIFERY 1.)

c **1290** *S. Eng. Leg.* I. 463/56 Of oþur þingus ne tok he no ȝeme, ne to housebondrie. **1332** *Literæ Cantuarienses* (Rolls) I. 356 Poy avoms entremys de hosebounderye. **1425** *Ord. Whittington's Alms-house* in Entick *London* (1766) IV. 354 The office and charge of him shal be . . the husbandry of the same house, in as much as he may goodly oversee. **1596** SHAKS. *Merch. V.* III. iv. 25 Lorenso I commit into your hands, The husbandry and mannage of my house. **1629** N. C[ARPENTER] *Achitophel* 53 The generall administration of a family, which wee may call husbandry.

†**b.** *transf.* and *fig.* Management, economical administration, ordering (as of a household). *Obs.*

1536 *Lisle Papers* XII. 70 (P.R.O.), I think you never ware better [velvet]; but I will see the cutting out and husbandry thereof myself. **1635** PAGITT *Christianogr.* I. ii. (1636) 86 West India, which hath long inioyed the husbandrie of Ministers. **1658** *Whole Duty Man* vii. §12. 63 There is a husbandry of the soul, as well as of the estate.

2. The business or occupation of a husbandman or farmer; tillage or cultivation of the soil (including also the rearing of live stock and poultry, and sometimes extended to that of bees, silkworms, etc.); agriculture, farming.

c **1380** WYCLIF *Wks.* (1880) 387 Merchandise & hosbondrie & oþer craftis. *c* **1460** FORTESCUE *Abs. & Lim. Mon.* xiii. (1885) 141 The new husbondry þat is done þer, namely in grobbyng and stokkyng off treis, busses, and groves. **1534** FITZHERB. (*title*) The Boke of Hvsbandry. **1535** COVERDALE *2 Chron.* xxvi. 10 He delyted in husybandrye. **1577** B. GOOGE *Heresbach's Husb.* II. (1586) 78 b, The vine requireth great husbandry about it. **1581** W. STAFFORD *Exam. Compl.* I. (1876) 19 Those sheepe is the cause of all these mischieues, for they haue driuen husbandry out of the countrey. **1660** SHARROCK *Vegetables* 98 The husbandry of sowing clover grass . . will here come in most properly. **1767** A. YOUNG *Farmer's Lett. People* 128 There is not a more dubious point in agriculture than the difference between the Old and the New husbandry. **1806** *Gazetteer Scotl.* s.v. *Yarrow*, The chief branch of husbandry is the rearing of sheep. **1849** COBDEN *Speeches* 51 In 1790 the price of iron and implements of husbandry was double what it is now.

fig. **1675** TRAHERNE *Chr. Ethics* xxx. 483 The heart . . prepared to receive it by the husbandry of Providence.

†**b.** Industrial occupation in general. *Obs.*

1604 DEKKER *King's Entert.* D iv, Dutch countrey people toyling at their Husbandrie; women carding of their Hemp, the men beating it. *a* **1639** W. WHATELEY *Prototypes* II. xxvi. (1640) 21 Live as Abraham and Jacob did, not as Esau, follow some study, follow some good husbandry.

†**3.** *concr.* (from 1 and 2). **a.** Household goods. **b.** Agricultural produce, cultivated crops. **c.** Land under cultivation; an agricultural holding. **d.** The body of husbandmen on an estate; the farm tenantry. *Obs.*

c **1386** CHAUCER *Wife's Prol.* 288 Spoones and stooles, and al swich housbondrye. **1526** TINDALE *1 Cor.* iii. 9 Ye are goddis husbandrye, ye are goddis byldynge. **1599** SHAKS. *Hen. V*, v. ii. 39 All her Husbandry doth lye on heapes, Corrupting in it owne fertilitie. *a* **1628** PRESTON *Breastpl. Love* (1631) 205 How goodly a sight is it when a man looks into the husbandrie, to see the vine full of clusters, to see the furrowes full of corne. **1675** *Phil. Trans.* X. 321 Sir Hugh Plat had a long and tedious task . . before the Husbandry would stirr. **1697** A. DE LA PRYME *Diary* (Surtees) 159 The lord or steward of this mannour of Broughton . . had also a capon of every husbandry, and a hen of a whole cottagry, and a chicken of a half cottagry. . . To this day some of the chief husbandry fetches their coals and wood.

4. a. With qualifying epithet (*good* or *ill*): Management (profitable or wasteful) of a household or of resources; (good or bad) economy.

1540–1 ELYOT *Image Gov.* (1556) 122 By negligence or lacke of good housbandrie. **1573** *New Custom* I. ii. in Hazl. *Dodsley* III. 16 Covetousness they call Good husbandry, when one man would fain have all. **1649** N. BACON *Disc. Govt. Eng.* I. lxiv. (1739) 134 Wars . . occasioning much waste of Treasure, put the King to the utmost pitch of good Husbandry. **1665** MANLEY *Grotius' Low C. Warres* 355 That old negligence, and ill husbandry in the disposing of mony. **1735** BOLINGBROKE *Lett. Study Hist.* ii. (1752) 38 The excessive ill husbandry practised from the very beginning of King William's reign. **1745** *De Foe's Eng. Trades-man* (1841) I. x. 75 Good husbandry and frugality are quite out of fashion.

b. Hence *absol.*: Careful management; employment of a thing sparingly and to the best advantage; economy, thrift, profit. (Cf. HOUSEWIFERY 1 b.)

1362 LANGL. *P. Pl.* A. I. 55 Husbondrie and he holden togedere. **14..** *MS. Cotton. Cleop. E. iv.* lf. 35 in *P. Pl. Crede* Notes 38 Also to the buttrey dore ther be xij. sundrye keyes in xij. hands, wherein symythe to be small husbandrye. **1552** HULOET, Husbandrye or profite, *vtilitas.* **1663** PEPYS *Diary* 6 June, Every thing [is] managed there by their builders with such husbandry as is not imaginable. **1712** STEELE *Spect.* No. 428 ¶1 The Ways of Gain, Husbandry, and Thrift. **1841** EMERSON *Lect.*, *Conservative* Wks. (Bohn) II. 265 Reform has no gratitude, no prudence, no husbandry.

5. *attrib.* and *Comb.*

1624 CAPT. SMITH *Virginia* v. 185 In such husbandry qualities he well deserued great commendations. **1795** J. PHILLIPS *Hist. Inland Navig.* Addenda 143 Pleasure and husbandry boats. **1796** MORSE *Amer. Geog.* I. 684 Obliged to manufacture . . most of their husbandry tools. **1843** J. SMITH *Forest Trees* 5 No part of husbandry-labour can be carried on without it [timber].

Hence †**husbandry** *v. trans.*, to apply husbandry to; to till, cultivate. *Obs. rare.*

1649 BLITHE *Eng. Improv.* xii. 71 One Acre of well Manured and Husbandryed Land. *Ibid.*, Consider the vast advantage there will be by Husbandring a little well. . . One Acre Manured, Plowed, and Husbandred in season, may and doth usually beare as much Corne as two or three ill Husbandred.

'husbandship. [f. HUSBAND *sb.* + -SHIP.] The action or office of husband.

1784 R. BAGE *Barham Downs* II. 314 Such a loving piece of good husband-ship as a letter. **1881** *Academy* 2 July 3/3 There was no better portion for his [Arnold's] daughter than the neighbouring convent or the husbandship of one Lorenzo da Fiori. **1892** MRS. CROSSE *Red-letter Days* I. 237, I never heard of his being remarkable for anything in the world except for husbandship of the authoress.

huscarle: see HOUSECARL.

husche, obs. f. HUTCH *sb.*

huse, anglicized f. HUSO, sturgeon.

†**huseau.** *Obs.* [a. obs. F. *houseau* (Cotgr.) 'a course drawer worne ouer a Stocking instead of a Boot' (cf. OF. *housel* in Godef.), dim. of OF. (and F. dial.) *house, heuse, husse* boot.] Some kind of boot or legging.

Husens in the first quot. is app. an error for *huseus* = *huseaus*, for which *huseans* in Cowell is again an error, copied by Minsheu and Phillips. But cf. Sc. HUSHION.

1464–5 *Act 4 Edw. IV*, c. 7 Qe nulle persone Cordewaner . . face . . ascuns solers galoges ou husens oveque ascun pike ou polein qe passera la longeur . . de deux poutz. *Ibid.*, Ascuns solers husens ou galoges [*Rolls Parlt.* V. 566/2 Shoes, Galoges or Botes . . Shoes, Botes or Galoges]. **1607** COWELL *Interpr.*, *Huseans*, commeth of the French (*houseaux*) i. *ocrea*, a boote. It is vsed in the Statute, an. 4 Ed. 4. ca. 7. **1706** PHILLIPS (ed. Kersey), *Huseans* (old Word), a kind of Boot or Spatterdash of course Cloth. **1720** STRYPE

Stow's Surv. II. v. xii. 212/2 (tr. Act 1464-5) Any Shoes, Galoshes, or Huseaus.

husel, hushel, obs. ff. HOUSEL.

husewif, husfrey, obs. ff. HOUSEWIFE, -RY.

hush (hʌʃ), *sb.*[1] A local Sc. name for the Lumpfish (*Cyclopterus lumpus*). Also **hush-bagaty, hush-padle** (cf. COCK-PADDLE).

a **1605** POLWART *Flyting w. Montgomerie* 746 Hush padle, lick ladle. **1808-18** JAMIESON, *Hush*, the Lump, a fish.

hush (hʌʃ), *sb.*[2] [f. HUSH *v.*[1] Rare before the 19th c., but then (perhaps following Byron) in extensive use in prose and poetry.]

1. a. Suppression of sound, imposed or enforced; silence (where noise has been or might be); stillness, quiet.

1689 in *Magd. Coll. & Jas. II* (O.H.S.) 274 At the very instant was a hush. **1724** RAMSAY *Tea-t. Misc.* (1733) III. 285 Where the shrill trumpets never sound, But one eternal hush goes round. **1816** BYRON *Ch. Har.* III. lxxxvi, It is the hush of night. **1835** LYTTON *Rienzi* x. v, A dead hush lay like a heavy air over the multitude. **1870** DICKENS *E. Drood* xii, A certain awful hush pervades the ancient pile, the cloisters, and the churchyard. **1877** BLACK *Green Past.* xxvi, The hush of evening had fallen over the birds. **1897** *Westm. Gaz.* 24 Dec. 3/1 There are moments of solemn hush between the verses of the hymn.

b. Suppression of discussion; the hushing-up of a scandal, etc. Also *attrib.* and *Comb.*

1898 *Daily News* 1 Feb. 3/5 The distinguishing feature of the Board was a policy of 'Hush'. **1917** T. E. LAWRENCE *Home Lett.* (1954) 336, I wonder what the censor will make of this letter?.. There is a 'Hush' policy over the Red Sea and Arabia. **1917** H. G. WELLS *Let.* Nov. in *Exper. Autobiogr.* (1934) II. ix. 711 In Britain and France 'hush' in the interests of diplomacy is being organized with increasing violence. **1919** H. F. B. WHEELER *War in Underseas* 317 Mighty 'hush' ships which lived and moved.. on the surface of great waters. **1920** *Argus* (Melbourne) 29 May 6 Time seems to have left.. no surviving link between the frigate of Trafalgar and the 'hush-boat' of to-day. **1930** *Publishers' Weekly* 31 May 2735/2 Youngsters that are reared on the 'hush plan'. **1968** *Guardian* 31 July 6/6 It's still a source of Labour amazement that the Harry Nicholas scheme didn't leak in advance of the coup. Nicholas ringleaders maintained unique hush, and may do so again.

2. An utterance of 'hush!'

1871 L. STEPHEN *Playgr. Europe* xii. (1894) 282 A scarce audible hush seems to be whispered throughout the region.

3. *Phonetics.* The sibilant (ʃ) or (ʒ). Also *attrib.* and *Comb.*

1933 L. BLOOMFIELD *Lang.* vi. 100 These hushes or abnormal sibilants are separate phonemes [š, ž], as in *shin* [šin], *vision* ['vižn]. **1953** *Archivum Linguisticum* V. II. 68 The distinction between hiss- (Fr. *sifflantes*) and hush-sibilants (Fr. *chuintantes*) emerges.. between the 'complementary' Indo-European types Latvian and Lithuanian. **1964** E. PALMER tr. *Martinet's Elem. Gen. Ling.* iii. 64 We obtain the following classes:.. 'apical' t d n; 'hiss' s z; 'hush' š ž.

hush (hʌʃ), *sb.*[3] *north. dial.* [Echoic. Goes with HUSH *v.*[3] Cf. Ger. *husch* sudden or swift motion, sudden shower of rain.]

1. The sound made by water flowing swiftly but smoothly.

1868 G. MACDONALD *R. Falconer* I. 242 In his ears was the hush rather than rush of the water over the dam.

2. A gush or rush of water; *spec.* in *Lead mining*, an artificial rush of water from a dam, to wash away the surface, etc.: see HUSH *v.*[3] Hence **hush-dam, hush-gutter**: see quot. 1821.

1821 W. FORSTER *Treat. Strata Newcastle to Cross Fell* (ed. 2) 283 Where the sloping ground to be hushed, is of any considerable length, from the hush-dam down to the bottom of the slope, the reservoir must contain a considerable quantity of water.. to carry down the great quantity of rubbish which the water will raise in a long hush-gutter. **1825-80** JAMIESON, *Hush*, a sudden bursting out of water, a gush. Ettr. For. **1861** *Durham Chron.* 13 Sept., The 'hushes' from the lead mines, which had done so much harm to the fish. **1893** HESLOP *Northumbld. Gloss.*, *Hush*, a great rush of water. This is produced artificially.. so as to bare the surface of the rock in order to discover indications of ore in the face of a hill side.

hush (hʌʃ), *a.* [A later modification of HUSHT *a.*, after the introduction of HUSH *v.*[1] and *int.*]

a. Silent, still, quiet, hushed. *arch.*

1602 SHAKS. *Ham.* II. ii. 508 The bold windes speechlesse, and the Orbe below As hush as death. **1607** ROWLANDS *Diog. Lanth.* 22 At night when all was hush. **1666** PEPYS *Diary* 22 July, Walked through the House, where most people mighty hush, and, methinks, melancholy. **1702** *Mouse grown a Rat* 31 You.. are hush in his Cause, that you may be able to speak in your own. **1813** SCOTT *Rokeby* VI. iii, The owl has seen him, and is hush. **1841** LONGF. *Frithiof's Homestead* 29 Hush sat the listening bench.

b. Secret. Cf. HUSH-HUSH.

This use merges with HUSH *sb.*[2] 1 b *attrib.*

1944 H. CROOME *You've gone Astray* xxii. 218 A tremendous journalistic job.. something important and hush. **1945** N. STREATFEILD *Saplings* i. 10 'I've got some new gadgets to make...' 'What sort of things?' 'It's all a bit hush.' **1957** 'J. WYNDHAM' *Midwich Cuckoos* vi. 50, I don't know what goes on at The Grange, but I do know that it is very hush. **1966** *Economist* 9 July p. xxvi/1 Volkswagen.. is keeping very hush about its solution to the pollution problem.

hush (hʌʃ), *v.*[1] Also 7 **whosh.** [Found first in 16th c.; app. in its origin a back-formation from HUSHT *a.*, which was in much earlier use, and appears to have been, from its final *t*, at length treated as a pa. pple.: see HUSHED. A verb HUSHT (q.v.) of the same form as the adjective is recorded in 16th c. dicts.]

1. a. *trans.* To make silent, still, or quiet; to impose silence upon; to silence, quiet.

1546 *Supplic. Poore Commons* in 4 *Supplic.* (E.E.T.S.) 83 Yf they were of God, they woulde.. not be hushed wyth an acte in parliament. **1601** SHAKS. *Twel. N.* v. i. 110 My dutie hushes me. **1643** MILTON *Divorce* II. xvii, Which.. (like the Word of God) in one instant hushes outrageous tempests into a sudden stillness and peaceful calm. **1725** POPE *Odyss.* XIII. 3 A pause of silence hush'd the shady rooms. **1794** MRS. RADCLIFFE *Myst. Udolpho* xv, To.. hush the sailor's fearful groan. **1832** W. IRVING *Alhambra* II. 152 The very birds.. hushing their own strains, listened in charmed silence. **1852** DICKENS *Bleak Ho.* xxxi, The little child awoke.. Charley.. began to walk about hushing it. **1883** STEVENSON *Silverado Sq.* 35 Hushing their talk.

b. with *up*, *down*, as intensive additions.

1682 BUNYAN *Holy War* (ed. Cassell) 21 Thus would Diabolus hush up and quiet the town of Mansoul. **1858** FROUDE *Hist. Eng.* xii. III. 4 If he would hush down the waves of heresy as he had restored peace to the waters of the Mediterranean. **1870** ROSSETTI *Poems, Dante at Verona* xiv, Pages hushed their laughter down.

c. *to hush one's mouth*: to be quiet, stop talking; so ***hush my mouth!***, used as an exclamation of surprise. *U.S. dial.*

1903 *Dialect Notes* II. 317 'Hesh your mouth,' i.e. stop talking. **1931** *Amer. Speech* VII. 29 Hush mah mouf. **1972** G. BAXT *Burning Sappho* ii. 42 Pat.. glared at him. 'You hush your mouth Malcolm.'

2. *transf.* and *fig.* To reduce to tranquillity, to suppress (anything disturbing or disquieting); to allay, lull, pacify. Also with *up*.

1632 J. HAYWARD tr. *Biondi's Eromena* 178 The matter was whosht up with the conclusion of the marriage. **1682** OTWAY *Venice Pres.* I. i, Wilt thou then Hush my cares thus? **1784** MANN in *Lett. Lit. Men* (Camden) 427, I do sincerely congratulate you, that the disturbance is hushed. **1819** BYRON *Juan* I. lviii, There's a rumour which I fain would hush. **1874** GREEN *Short Hist.* v. §3. 233 The quarrel between the baronage and the Church.. was hushed in the presence of a common danger.

3. Usually in phr. ***to hush up.*** To suppress talk, mention, or discussion of; to procure silence concerning; to keep from getting known.

1632 J. HAYWARD tr. *Biondi's Eromena* 125 Resolved to have all things husht up. **1709** STEELE *Tatler* No. 59 ¶5 It had indeed cost him a Hundred Pounds to hush the Affair. **1727** SWIFT *Gulliver* II. v, The thing was hushed up, and never known at court. **1798** T. JEFFERSON *Writ.* (1859) IV. 207 Either the Envoys have not written.. or their communications are hushed up. **1812** *Sporting Mag.* XL. 165 What is vulgarly called hushing the transaction. **1893** *Law Times* XCV. 225/2 Opportunities for a suspicious matter being improperly hushed up.

4. *intr.* To become or be silent, quiet, or still. Also *colloq.* with *up*.

1561 [see HUSHING *ppl. a.*]. **1580** SIDNEY *Ps.* XXXIX. v, But I doe hush, why do I say thus much? *a* **1634** RANDOLPH *Amyntas* III. ii. Wks. (1875) 318 All hush to bed. **18..** LOWELL *Sonnets* xx, Let praise hush. **1855** LYNCH *Rivulet* XVII. iv, O, let us hush and hear His holy word. **1860** BARTLETT *Dict. Amer.*, *To hush up*, to cease speaking, to be silent, to hush. **1895** *Westm. Gaz.* 17 Feb. 3/3 Mr. Gladstone rose as Leader of the House, and everyone hushed to hear his decision.

Hence **husher** (in 7 **whoosher**), one who hushes or quiets.

1659 TORRIANO, *Ninnatrice*, a rocker, a stiller, a luller, a whoosher or a dandler of children asleep.

hush, *v.*[2] Now *dial.* [A modification of the natural utterance *sh!*: cf. SHOO. Cf. Ger. *huschen* in same sense.] *trans.* To scare or drive off (birds, etc.) with cries of 'hush!' or 'sh!'.

1613-16 W. BROWNE *Brit. Past.* II. iii, She husht him thence, he sung no more, But.. flew tow'rds the shore. **1675** BROOKS *Gold. Key* Wks. 1867 V. 409 Whilst David was hunted up and down like a partridge, and hushed out of every bush. **1880** *Antrim & Down Gloss.*, *Hush*, to drive a flock of fowl, saying at the same time, 'Hush, hush'. Sometimes *Whush*, or *Wheeshoo*.

hush, *v.*[3] *north. dial.* [Echoic. Cf. HUSH *sb.*[3]] *trans.* To send or let forth (water) with a rush; *spec.* in *Lead mining*, to send a rush of water over a sloping surface, in order to uncover ore, and separate it from the earth and stones in which it is embedded, or for similar purposes. Hence **hushing** *vbl. sb.*, also *attrib.*

1750 *Phil. Trans.* XLVI. 364 Which gives it [the River] the Colour of Water hushed from Lead-mines. **1799** *Mining lease* in Barnewall & Cressw. *King's B. Rep.* IX. 507 With full power.. to do all other things (hushing only excepted) as might be necessary. **1821** W. FORSTER *Treat. Strata Newcastle to Cross Fell* (ed. 2) 282 *note*, Considerable quantities of float ore have been procured at Greengill mine, in Alston-moor by Hushing. **1828** *Craven Dial.*, *Hush*, to detach, by force of a running stream, earthy particles from minerals. **1878** *Cumberld. Gloss.*, *Hush*,.. to wash away soil from mines or quarries by a rush of water. **1886** W. M. EGGLESTONE *Weardale Names* 73 The earliest method of searching for lead ore was by collecting the water in dams and hushing the surface of the ground where metalliferous veins existed. **1887** *North Star* 28 Oct., [He] had promised ..that he would have a stop put to the hushing process.

hush (hʌʃ), *int.* [app. a later form of HUSHT *int.*[1]: cf. SH! It might also be taken as imperative of HUSH *v.*[1]] A command to be silent or quiet; silence! = *Sc.* whisht!

1604 R. CAWDREY *Table Alph.*, *Hush, Husht*, peace, or be still. **1611** SHAKS. *Cymb.* v. iv. 94 No more you petty Spirits of Region low Offend our hearing: hush. **1700** T. BROWN tr. *Fresny's Amusem. Ser. & Com.* 125 'They employ'd themselves while the Bills were reading, about—' 'Hush, hush'. **1797** MRS. RADCLIFFE *Italian* xii, 'Hush, they are pilgrims', whispered Viraldi. **1873** SYMONDS *Grk. Poets* vii. 225 Silence! Hush! what noise was this?

hushaby ('hʌʃəbaɪ), *int.*, *v.*, and *a. dial.* [f. HUSH *v.*[1] or *int.* + *by* in *by-by*, BYE-BYE[1], child's name for 'sleep' or 'bed': cf. also *lullaby*, *rockaby*.]

A. *int.* (or imperative of vb.) Hush! and go to sleep; a word used in lulling a child.

1796 *Mother Goose's Melody* 15 Hush-a-by baby On the tree top, When the wind blows The cradle will rock. **1824** MACTAGGART *Gallovid. Encycl.*, *Hushie-baw-Babbie*, the cradle-song to babes. **1864** MISS YONGE *Trial* I. 66 'It is one constant hush, hushaby', he said; 'it would make one sleep pleasantly'.

B. *vb. trans.* To lull to sleep with 'hushaby'. Also, to speak softly (*nonce-use*).

1848 MRS. GASKELL *M. Barton* ix. (1882) 23/2 Hushabying a babby as wouldn't be hushabied. **1934** S. BECKETT *More Pricks than Kicks* 85 'Too good of you to come' she hushabied.

C. *adj.* 'Tending to quiet or lull' (*Eclectic Rev.* cited in Worcester 1846).

hushed (hʌʃt), *ppl. a.* Also 7-8 **hush'd.** See also HUSHT. [Historically a continuation of the earlier adj. HUSHT, but treated as the pa. pple. of HUSH *v.*[1], after the appearance of the latter.]

Reduced to silence; silenced, stilled, quieted.

1602 MARSTON *Ant. & Mel.* I. Wks. 1856 I. 15 Vouchsafe me, then, your hush'd observances. **1670** DRYDEN *Conq. Granada* I. i, No more; but hush'd as Midnight Silence go. **1709** STEELE *Tatler* No. 8 ¶7 The Air was hushed, the Multitude attentive. **1877** MRS. OLIPHANT *Makers Flor.* vii. 183 No brethren of Saint Dominic inhabit the hushed and empty cells. **1898** *Daily News* 8 Mar. 3/6 All spoke in hushed whispers.

Hence **hushedly** ('hʌʃɪdlɪ) *adv.*, in a hushed manner.

1851 G. MEREDITH *Poems, Song*, Hushedly, mournfully, mistily up to the shore. **1892** LE GALLIENNE *Love's Worship*, In morning meadows I have knelt to thee, In noontide woodlands hearkened hushedly.

husher = *usher*: see HUISHER.

hushful ('hʌʃfʊl), *a. rare.* [f. HUSH *sb.*[1] + -FUL.] Full of or pervaded by silence or stillness; tending to hush to rest. Hence **'hushfully** *adv.*, with suppression of noise, silently.

a **1861** D. GRAY *Poet. Wks.* (1874) 7 Hushfully falls the soft, white, windless snow. **1884** W. SHARP in *Harper's Mag.* June 117 The tide's faint ripples creep Along the brown sands hushfully. **1889** M. CAIRD *Wing of Azrael* I. vii. 110 Harry found himself alone in the hushful twilight.

'hush-hire. *rare.* = HUSH-MONEY.

1811 W. TAYLOR in *Monthly Mag.* XXXI. 426 Their noble disinterest rejected all hush-hire.

hush-hush. Reduplicated form of HUSH *int.*, used *attrib.* or as *adj.* to denote any object of manufacture, process, plan, or policy, the details or existence of which are kept secret; *occas.* a person engaged in such matters; also, secrecy.

1916 H. YOXALL *Let.* 22 Sept. in *Fashion of Life* (1966) iv. 32 The hush-hush Tanks were splendid. **1919** C. P. THOMPSON *Cocktails* 133 The Flying Tank fixed the job without calling on that elaborate organisation for anything more hush-hush than a couple of batteries of heavy Hows. **1920** *Glasgow Herald* 3 May 8 The dramatic arrival at Baku in July, 1918, of General Dunsterville's 'hush-hush' force after its splendidly adventurous march through Persia. *Ibid.* 12 Aug. 4 Minute accounts of the hush-hush birth of this new monster of war. **1922** *Ibid.* 30 Aug. 9 A 'hush-hush' Bristol monoplane. **1927** A. E. W. MASON *No Other Tiger* i. 11 He had never been able to take the hush-hush men seriously. **1927** LLOYD GEORGE *Slings & Arrows* (1929) 184 That 'hush, hush' policy which prevailed before the war. **1931** *Morning Post* 5 June 12/4 Italian 'hush hush' car in Irish race. **1937** A. CHRISTIE *Murder in Mews* vi. 127 'A burglary? What was taken?' 'Oh, I don't know. It's all very hush-hush.' **1942** [see CAKE *sb.* 7c]. **1955** [see *closed door*]. **1955** *Times* 26 May 4/3 In each party the idea of a broadsheet was the secret of a few. It was intended to be the 'hush-hush' weapon. **1970** *Private Eye* May 20 A hush hush top-level inquiry. **1973** A. CHRISTIE *Postern of Fate* III. xvii. 249 The present trend of political thinking is that hush-hush, necessary as it is at certain times, should not be preserved indefinitely.

hush-hush, *v.* [Reduplicated form of HUSH *v.*[1]] *trans.* To say 'hush, hush' to; to quiet, silence.

1861 *New Monthly Mag.* Feb. 151, I don't feel the zest now that I used to feel cutting through the water with.. that merry, wicked little dog, Phil Hervey, for coxswain; he's a bishop now, and hush-hushes you. **1883** G. MEREDITH *Poems & Lyrics* 49 Not the pines with the faint airs afloat, Hush-hushing the nested dove. **1928** *Daily Express* 12 June 10/4 She might have done it long ago if she had not been firmly hush-hushed by men.

hushing ('hʌʃɪŋ), *vbl. sb.*[1] [f. HUSH *v.*[1] + -ING[1].] The action of HUSH *v.*[1]; the action of rendering

still, silent, or quiet; the whispering of *sh!* as in enjoining silence. ***hushing up***: see HUSH *v.*[1] 3.

1813 L. HUNT *Poems, To T—— B—— Esq.*, With thousand tiny hushings, like the swarm Of atom bees. **1831** [POTE] *Assassins Paradise* 41 But whisper'd hushings checked the words that broke. **1849** MRS. PEABODY in *Hawthorne & Wife* (1885) I. 338 She believed that it was better for all, even for the criminals, that there should be no hushings-up.

hushing, *vbl. sb.*[2]: see HUSH *v.*[3]

hushing, *ppl. a.* [f. HUSH *v.*[1] + -ING[2].] That hushes: see the verb.

1561 T. HOBY tr. *Castiglione's Courtyer* (1577) Y iij b, The tunable notes of the prety birds among the hushyng woodes of the hilles. **1800** L. HUNT *Robin Hood* Poems 141 The coffin was stript of it's hiding pall, Amidst the hushing choirs. **1820** KEATS *Hyperion* II. 119 When a God gives sign, With hushing finger. **1870** MORRIS *Earthly Par.* II. III. 183 More vocal through the hushing night.

Hence **'hushingly** *adv.*, in a hushing manner; with the sound *sh!* as in enjoining silence.

1833 RITCHIE *Wand. by Loire* 10 The echo of our measured, tiptoe tread ran hushingly round the vault. **1841** HOR. SMITH *Moneyed Man* III. i. 6 The waves..laid themselves hushingly upon the sands, as if to caution us to silence.

hushion ('hʌʃən). *Sc.* Also **hoeshin, hoshen.** [Possibly a popular formation from HUSEAU.] A stocking without a foot; a hogger, hugger.

1789 D. DAVIDSON *Seasons* 118 Some wi' wallets, some wi' weghts, An' some wi' hoshens caprin Right heigh. **1792** BURNS *Willie's Wife* iv, She dights her grunzie wi' a hushion. **1890** *Songs of Nursery* in *Whistle-Binkie* (Sc. Songs) II. 121 Hushions on her bare legs.

hush-money. [See HUSH *v.*[1] 3.] Money paid to prevent disclosure or exposure, or to hush up a crime or discreditable transaction.

1709 STEELE *Tatler* No. 26 ¶9, I expect Hush-Money to be regularly sent for every Folly or Vice any one commits in this whole Town. **1731** SWIFT *Poems, To Gay* 107 A dext'rous Steward, when his Tricks are found, Hush-money sends to all the Neighbours round. **1845** (16 Apr.) BRIGHT *Sp. Ireland* (1868) 150 This bill..is hush-money given that they may not proclaim to the whole country..the sufferings of the population. **1849** MACAULAY *Hist. Eng.* vii. II. 214 He had been forced to pay hushmoney to informers. **1953** H. MILLER *Plexus* (1963) x. 352 The cops will be sitting on our necks... The natural thing, under the circumstances, would be to put something aside for hush money. **1957** *Economist* 9 Nov. Suppl. 11/2 She would write her memoirs and include in them faithful records of her association with every noble lord who failed to pay hush money to the tune of two hundred pounds.

hush puppy, hush-puppy ('hʌʃ 'pʌpɪ). [f. HUSH *v.*[1] + PUPPY *sb.*] **1.** *U.S.* (See quots.)

1918 *Dialect Notes* V. 18 *Hushpuppy*, a sort of bread prepared very quickly and without salt. **1942** M. K. RAWLINGS *Cross Creek Cookery* 28 Fresh-caught fried fish without hush puppies are as men without women. **1947** *This Week Mag.* (U.S.) 4 Oct. 27/1 What's a hush puppy? You mean you don't know that Southern fried bread like a miniature corn pone—but glorified? It's made of the white cornmeal of the South, smooth and fine as face powder. **1960** *Harper's Bazaar* July 48 Crisp, brown 'hush puppies', crunchy morsels of deep-fried cornmeal batter. **1964** *Cookbk.* (Amer. Heritage) (1967) 220 Hush Puppies are usually served with fried fish. **1967** *Daily News* (N.Y.) 5 Mar. II. 4 I'm going to eat hush-puppies, wear a snuffler and every night sing 'Silent Night'.

2. The proprietary name (*Hush Puppy*) of a lightweight soft shoe. Also *attrib.*

1961 *Trade Marks Jrnl.* 15 Nov. 1616/1 Hush Puppies. Shoes. Wolverine Shoe and Tanning Corporation. **1963** *Observer* 13 Oct. 9/1 Abbott makes 'Hush Puppies', the lightweight..shoes. **1965** *Amer. Speech* XL. 249 Hush puppies, a brand of nationally advertised shoes for men and women. **1966** 'O. MILLS' *Enemies of Bride* xxiii. 196 An intelligent..woman in..Hush-puppy shoes. **1969** P. DICKINSON *Pride of Heroes* 38 Mr. Singleton wore rubber-soled Hush-Puppies which went squeak-squeak on the shiny surface.

hush-shop. *local.* [f. HUSH *v.*[1] or *a.*, in reference to the quietness of its operations.] A house for the clandestine sale of drink; an unlicensed drink-shop. (See quot. 1865.)

1844 S. BAMFORD *Life of Radical* 108 In short, it was a hush-shop. **1854** *Fraser's Mag.* L. 287 The Sunday is spent ..in the beer-shop, or gin-shop, or hush-shop. **1865** B. BRIERLEY *Irkdale* I. 15 *note*, The term 'Hush Shop'..'hush' signifying that the company frequenting such places were expected to conduct themselves as orderly as possible, that no alarm might be given to parties in authority.

husht (hʌʃt), *int.*[1] Now *dial.* Also 6 **hui(s)sht.** [app. a variant of HUST *int.*, q.v.] = HUSH *int.*

1387-8 (ed. 1531) T. USK *Test. Love* I. v. (ed. Skeat I. 90), Thus, after jangling wordes, cometh huissht! pees! and be stille! **1565-73** COOPER *Thesaurus, Bat*, a worde of reproche: as tush: tut. Sometyme of silence, as husht. **1598** FLORIO, *Citto*, a word to bid children holde their peace, as we say whusht, husht. **1611** COTGR., *Houische*,.. husht, whist, ist, not a word for your life. **1845** CARLYLE *Cromwell* (1871) V. 155 Husht, poor weeping Mary. **1887** *S. Chesh. Gloss.*, *Husht*, hush!

husht, *int.*[2] [Cf. HIST *int.* 2.] A cry to frighten off or drive away an animal.

1853 W. B. BARKER *Lares & Penates* 285 As soon as the dog seizes the bird, the master calls out, *Husht! Husht!* throwing a stone or anything he can at him to make him let go the bird.

husht (hʌʃt), *a. arch.* Also 5 **hussht, hushte, hoscht.** See also HUSHED. [In 15th c. texts, *hussht, hushte*, varies with HUST, *huyst*, and WHIST, derived from the corresponding interjectional forms, to express the state which these enjoin or produce. As an adj., *husht* gave rise to a vb. and sb. of the same form; but it appears to have been at length felt as a pa. pple., as if *hush-t*, from which feeling there arose a new verb HUSH; under the influence of this, the original adj. itself passed into the pa. pple. *hush'd*, HUSHED, of which it is now treated as a variant spelling.] Silent, still, quiet; later, Reduced to silence, rendered silent.

1400-30 *Chaucer's Knt.'s T.* 2123 (Harl. MS.) Whan þey were sette and hussht [*Six-text*, hust, huyst] was al þe place. *c* **1440** *Bone Flor.* 813 All was hoscht and stylle. **1530** PALSGR. 589/1, I can make my chylde hushte whan me lyst, though he krye never so fast. **1592** SHAKS. *Ven. & Ad.* 458 Euen as the wind is husht before it raineth. **1697** DRYDEN *Virg. Past.* IX. 80 Husht Winds the topmost Branches scarcely bend. **1812** J. WILSON *Isle of Palms* I. 72 The husht billow.

†**husht**, *v. Obs. rare*[−0]. Also 6 **whosht.** [f. HUSHT *int.*[1] or *a.*: cf. HUST, WHIST, WHISHT *vbs.*, and see HUSH *v.*] **a.** *trans.* To still, to hush. **b.** *intr.* To be still or silent.

1530 PALSGR. 589/1, I huste, I styll, *je repayse* and *je recoyse*. Declared in 'I husht'. **1552** HULOET, Husht or kepe silence, *reticeo..sileo.* **1598** FLORIO, *Tasentare*, to whosht, to still, to put to silence, to hould ones peace.

husht, *sb.* [f. HUSHT *int.* or *a.*: cf. HUSH *sb.*[2]] Silence, quiet, hush.

1566 DRANT *Wail. Hierim.* K vj b, He that was proude and bare him hye muste syt in hushte alone. **1602** MARSTON *Antonio's Rev.* I. i, Even in the husht of night.

†**hushtness.** *Obs.* [f. HUSHT *a.* + -NESS.] Silence, stillness.

1609 HEYWOOD *Brit. Troy* (N.), A generall hushtnesse hath the world possest.

hushy ('hʌʃɪ), *a.* [f. HUSH *sb.*[3] + -Y.] That is characterized by the sound *hush*.

1803 MISS ANNA SEWARD *Lett.* (1811) VI. 97 The hushy sound (if I may be allowed to coin that epithet) of the sea-shore.

husi, var. JUSI.

husk (hʌsk), *sb.*[1] [Late ME. *huske*, of uncertain origin.

A common word since *c* 1400, of which no earlier trace has been found. Conjectures have been offered of its relationship to Ger. *hülse*, Du. *hulze, huls*, which (notwithstanding the identity of sense) appear to be historically and phonetically untenable, and of its ultimate derivation from *hús* 'house', which is perhaps possible: cf. for the form, *chink, dalk, halk, holk, polk, stalk* (and see Kluge, *Stammbildung*. §61); for the sense, LG. *hûske* = Ger. *häuschen*, 'little house', in E. Fris. also 'core (of an apple)', 'case' (e.g. spectacle-case), 'paper bag'; also MDu. *huuskijn, huusken*, Du. *huisken*, 'little house', core (of an apple); Ger. *gehäuse*, 'case, capsule', etc. The connexion of Norwegian *husk* 'piece of leather used to enlarge a shoe-last', is quite uncertain.]

1. a. The dry outer integument of certain fruits and seeds; *esp.* the hard fibrous sheath of grain, nuts, etc.; a glume or rind; *spec.* in *U.S.*, the outer covering of an ear of maize or Indian corn.

1398 TREVISA *Barth. De P.R.* XVII. cliv. (1495), Codde and an huske hyght Siliqua. *c* **1400** MAUNDEV. xxi. (1839) 188 As the Note of the Haselle hathe an Husk with outen. *Ibid.* (Roxb.) 94 þe macez er þe huskes of þe nutemuge. *c* **1440** *Promp. Parv.* 254/2 Huske of frute, or oþer lyke, *corticillus.* **1474** CAXTON *Chesse* 81 The huske whiche is about the grayn. **1548** UDALL *Erasm. Par. Luke* xv. (R.), To fil his bealie..with the verai huskes and coddes, wherwith the hogges were fedde. **1557** N. T. (Genev.) *Luke* xv. 16 The huskes [WYCL., TIND., COVERD. coddis, coddes] that the swyne ate. **1631** WIDDOWES *Nat. Philos.* (ed. 2) 36 The Chesnut..is covered with a sharpe huske, and within it hath a red huske. **1665** HOOKE *Microgr.* 156 Carret seeds are like a cleft of a Coco-Nut Husk. **1704** J. HARRIS *Lex. Techn.* s.v. *Verdegrease*, The Husks of pressed Grapes. **1830** M. DONOVAN *Dom. Econ.* I. 87 The malt is parched until it has acquired a slight tinge of yellowness on the husk. **1855** LONGF. *Hiaw.* xiii. 29 The women who in Autumn Stripped the yellow husks of harvest.

†**b.** The calyx or involucre of a flower. *Obs.*

1450-1530 *Myrr. our Ladye* 210 Whyche floure yf he se yt not yet sprynge oute of the huske. **1727-41** CHAMBERS *Cycl.*, *Husks*, among botanists, the part which a flower grows out of ..Of these there are several kinds, as bulbous or round husks, bottle husks, middle husks, foot husks, hose husks.

c. Husks collectively, husky matter.

1883 C. J. WILLS *Mod. Persia* 233 By about the twenty-fourth day the wine was ready for clearing of the husk. *Ibid.* 234 The sweet wine had already no husk in it.

2. Applied to animal coverings or shells: †**a.** The coriaceous wing-case of an insect; an elytron. *Obs.* **b.** The shell or case of a chrysalis; a cocoon. ? *arch.* **c.** In Georgia, U.S., an oyster shell.

1552 HULOET, Byttel flye with a blacke huske. **1616** SURFL. & MARKH. *Country Farme* 488 Euerie one [silkworm] shutting vp himselfe in his scale or huske, which they make and build vp in two daies. **1653** WALTON *Angler* xii. 226 A good bait is the young brood of Wasps or Bees, baked or hardned in their husks. **1665** HOOKE *Microgr.* 187 Several of them flew away in Gnats, leaving their husks behind them in the water floating under the surface. *Ibid.* 215 They seem cover'd, upon the upper side of them, with a small husk, not unlike the scale, or shell of a Wood-louse. **1802** PALEY *Nat. Theol.* xix. (1830) 228 This [chrysalis] also in its turn dies; its dead and brittle husk falls to pieces, and makes way for the appearance of the fly or moth. **1842** TENNYSON *Two Voices* II, I saw the dragon-fly Come from the wells where he did lie. An inner impulse rent the veil Of his old husk.

3. *techn.* Applied to a frame of various kinds: see quots.

1688 R. HOLME *Armoury* III. 100/2 *Husk* is a square Frame of Moulding..set over the Mantle Tree of a Chimney between two Pillasters. **1873** KNIGHT *Dict. Mech.*, *Husk*, the supporting frame of a run of millstones.

4. *transf.* and *fig.* **a.** The outside or external part of anything; mostly in depreciatory sense, the mere rough or worthless exterior, as contrasted with the substantial inner part or essence.

1547-64 BAULDWIN *Mor. Philos.* (Palfr.) 98 That..the bitternesse & hardnesse of his [Death's] rough huske should hinder vs from the sweet taste of such a comfortable kirnell. **1644** HUNTON *Vind. Treat. Monarchy* iii. 10 A few huskes of reason. **1652** L. S. *People's Liberty* xvi. 39 Their acquiescing in God's choice should be the pith and kernel of the precept, and the setting up of a King onely the husk and shell of it. **1841-4** EMERSON *Ess., Friendship* Wks. (Bohn) I. 85 Bashfulness and apathy are a tough husk, in which a delicate organization is protected from premature ripening. **1861-8** LOWELL *Emerson* Pr. Wks. 1890 I. 355 He..gave us ravishing glimpses of an ideal under the dry husk of our New England. **1887** W. H. STONE *Harveian Oration* 21 The mere reproduction of the dry husks of thought termed words.

b. Applied to the human body.

a **1677** BARROW *Serm.* Wks. 1716 I. 62 May not our soul.. challenge a good share of our time..or shall this mortal husk engross it all? **1818** M. G. LEWIS *Jrnl. W. Ind.* (1834) 102 It is a matter of perfect indifference to me what becomes of this little ugly husk of mine, when once I shall have 'shuffled off this mortal coil'.

†**c.** Applied to a person. *Obs.*

1601 ? MARSTON *Pasquil & Kath.* I. 76 in Simpson *Sch. Shaks.* (1878) II. 138 You keepe too great a house..Yon same drie throated huskes Will sucke you vp. *Ibid.* IV. 39 *Ibid.* 183 *Bra. Iu.* How like you the new Poet Mellidus? *Bra. Sig.* A slight bubling spirit, a Corke, a Huske.

d. A figure or ornament somewhat resembling a husk.

1934 *Burlington Mag.* Oct. p. xv/2 The tablet is carved with festoons, and the frieze and jambs inlaid with festoons and pendants of husks and coloured marble. **1955** R. FASTNEDGE *Eng. Furnit. Styles* 285 *Husk*, with 'honeysuckle' 'wheat-ear' a favourite ornament on furniture of the Adam and Hepplewhite periods. **1971** *Country Life* 3 June 1356/3 The ground paint was decorated with motifs such as festoons of drapery and husks, interlacing hearts, urn patterns, and so on.

5. *attrib.* and *Comb.* (from 1), as ***husk-porridge***; ***husk-like*** adj.; 'in the husk', as ***husk corn, nut***; (from 4 d) ***husk design, festoon, ornament, pattern***; **husk-hackler**, 'a machine for tearing corn-husks into shreds for stuffing for mattresses, pillows, cushions, etc.' (Knight *Dict. Mech.* 1875).

1687 S. SEWALL *Diary* 3 Oct. (1878) I. 191 *Husk Corn. **1904** P. MACQUOID *Hist. Eng. Furnit.* vii. 191 The sides are inlaid with the..*husk design so popular at this time. **1973** *Country Life* 31 May 1567 Chestnut wood window seats.. the..legs..faced by well carved husk design. **1770** J. WEDGWOOD *Let.* 20 Aug. (1965) 94 First, his Majesty approved of the *husk festoons in particular, and I think more so than the desert pattern. **1796** WITHERING *Brit. Plants* (ed. 3) II. 60 Flowers with valves like grasses, and *husk-like calyxes. **1888** *Pall Mall G.* 24 Jan. 5/2 The *husk nuts piled on the top. **1934** *Burlington Mag.* Oct. 165/1 The back shows the honeysuckle, *husk or catkin ornament. **1960** H. HAYWARD *Antique Coll.* 146/2 *Husk ornament*, an ornamental motif resembling the husk of a wheat ear used continually by architects and craftsmen during the Adam period. **1876** C. SCHREIBER *Jrnl.* 14 Nov. (1911) I. 485 A good set of Wedgewood, *husk pattern. **1851** MRS. BROWNING *Casa Guidi Wind.* I. 1003 To see the people swallow hot *Husk-porridge which his chartered churchmen stir.

husk (hʌsk), *sb.*[2] [In sense 1 of uncertain origin; possibly from HUSK *sb.*[1]: cf. also HUSK *v.*[2]; in sense 2 app. a back-formation from HUSKY *a.* 4.]

1. A disease affecting cattle: see quots.

a **1722** LISLE *Husb.* in *O.C. & F. Wds.* (E.D.S.) 62 *Hassacks*, a disease affecting the throat. The result of worms in the bronchial tubes; called also *Husk, Hosk*, and *Hoose.* **1755** NICHOLLS in *Phil. Trans.* XLIX. 247 The husk..is a disease, to which bullocks are very subject, while young... The creature is seized with a short dry cough, by which he is perpetually teized. **1787** WINTER *Syst. Husb.* 230 Some of my hogs..were affected with a violent cough vulgarly called the husk. **1828** *Sporting Mag.* XXII. 210 In oxen, sheep and swine, the disorders called the foul, the rot, and the husk will be perpetuated from generation to generation. **1892** *Wiltsh. Co. Mirror* 5 Aug. 1/6 Mixture for Pigs..intended to cure Colds, Lameness, Husk, Worms.

2. Huskiness.

1816 T. L. PEACOCK *Headlong Hall* 4 Clearing the husk in his throat with two or three hems. **1887** *Daily News* 23 July 6/7 [It] brings a husk to the father's voice as they shake hands in a last 'good-bye'.

†**husk**, *sb.*[3] *Obs.*, the dog-fish: see HUSS.

husk (hʌsk), *a. dial.* [app. a back-formation from *husky*: but cf. HASK *a.*] Dry, parched, HUSKY. Also comb., ***husk-voiced*** *adj.*

1847-78 HALLIWELL, *Husk*..(3) Dry; parched. *Linc.* **1876** LANIER *Poems, Clover* 24 Nor Dick husk-voiced upbraids The sway-back'd roan.

husk (hʌsk), *v.*[1] [f. HUSK *sb.*[1]] *trans.* To remove the husk from, to deprive of the husk. Also *transf.* and *fig.*

1562 TURNER *Herbal* II. 57b, The germanes husk millet and eat it with milk. **1601** HOLLAND *Pliny* I. 567 Pistores were those..who husked and cleansed the bearded red wheat. **1698** FRYER *Acc. E. India & P.* 53 Pepper..when dried it is black, and husked white. **1737** EDWARDS *Wks.* (1834) I. 363/1 The children were..husking Indian corn. **1856** OLMSTED *Slave States* 42 The maize is afterwards husked in the field, at leisure. **1878** B. F. TAYLOR *Between Gates* 182 The rough dresses of the men..out of which they husk themselves. **1880** MISS BIRD *Japan* I. 138 They are husking rice, a very laborious process. **1892** KIPLING *Barrack-Room Ballads* 199 Go husk this whimpering thief ..: Winnow him out 'twixt star and star. **1910** C. E. MULFORD *Hopalong Cassidy* xviii. 110 He determined to husk Meeker's body from its immortal soul.

husk (hʌsk), *v.*[2] [Goes with HUSK *sb.*[2]] **1.** *intr.* Of cattle: To cough as when suffering from the 'husk'. Hence **husking** *vbl. sb. local.*

1577 B. GOOGE *Heresbach's Husb.* III. (1586) 135 Sicknes of the Loongs is..a short husking, and thrusting out of the toong withall. **1848** *Jrnl. R. Agric. Soc.* IX. II. 354 They [bullocks] were all observed to husk soon after being purchased.

2. *intr.* Of the voice: to be or to become husky.

1922 H. TITUS *Timber* xxix. 254 Her voice husked for the first time. **1958** *Sunday Times* 29 June 11/1 The birds sing louder than the crooner husking from the loudspeaker.

huskanaw, -oy (ˈhʌskənɔː, -ɔɪ). [American Indian.] The ceremony or ordeal, formerly in use among the Indians of Virginia, of preparing young men for the duties of manhood by means of solitary confinement and the use of narcotics. So **huskanaw, -oy** *v.*, to subject to this treatment.

1705 R. B. BEVERLEY *Virginia* III. ¶32 (1722) 177 The Solemnity of Huskanawing is commonly practis'd once every fourteen or sixteen Years... The choicest and briskest young Men..are chosen out by the Rulers to be Huskanawed. *Ibid.* 179 The Appamattucks, formerly a great Nation, tho' now an inconsiderable People, made an Huskanaw in the Year 1690. **1730–6** BAILEY (folio), *Huskanawing*, a Solemnity practised by the Virginian Indians... It is an Institution or Discipline that all young Men must pass under before they can be admitted to be of the Number of Great Men, Officers, or Cockarouses of the nation. **1788** T. JEFFERSON *Writ.* (1859) II. 444 So much out of his element that he has the air of one huskanoyed.

†**huske.** *Obs.* According to Strutt, An old name for a 'company' of hares.

1801 STRUTT *Sports & Past.* I. i. (1876) 80 A huske or a down of hares; a nest of rabbits; a clowder of cats.

husked (hʌskt), *a.* [f. HUSK *sb.*[1] and *v.*[1]]

†**1.** Furnished or covered with a husk. *Obs.*

1583 STANYHURST *Æneis*, etc. *Epit. Ld. Offalye* (Arb.) 152 Thee soundest wheatcorne with chaffy filthod is husked. **1624** CAPT. SMITH *Virginia* II. 26 A small fruit..husked like a Chesnut. **1638** *Hist. Albino & Bellama* (N.), Like Jupiter huskt in a female skin. **1686** PLOT *Staffordsh.* 205 Though the Corn be like Wheat, and not husked, as all Spelt is.

†**b.** Having husks (to feed on). *Obs.*

(Referring to the parable of the prodigal son, *Luke* xv.)
1604 PARSONS *3rd Pt. Three Convers. Eng.* 3 Lead by Iohn Fox into this wyld hogge-field of his husked Saincts.

2. Stripped of the husk; hulled.

1607 TOPSELL *Four-f. Beasts* (1658) 199 Let her seethe husked Barley and Scallions, and the fat of a male Goat. **1682** WHELER *Journ. Greece* IV. 329 Rice which they sell ready husked. *a* **1868** MEADE *New Zealand* (1870) 332 Cocoa-nuts, husked and opened.

ˈ**husken,** *a.* [f. HUSK *sb.*[1] + -EN[4].] Of the nature of a husk.

1635 SWAN *Spec. M.* viii. §2 (1643) 419 When these daintie creatures [silkworms] have made them little husken houses.

husker (ˈhʌskə(r)). [f. HUSK *v.* + -ER[1].] **a.** One who husks; one who removes the husk of corn; *U.S.*, one who takes part in a husking-bee.

1780 E. PARKMAN *Diary* (1899) 279 Breck was very generous in treating ye huskers with Liquor. **1793** J. BARLOW *Hasty Pudding* III, When to the board the thronging huskers pour. **1850** WHITTIER *Huskers* 10 From many a brown old farm-house..the merry huskers came.

b. A machine for removing husks.

1874 KNIGHT *Dict. Mech.*, *Corn-husker.* **1880** MISS BIRD *Japan* I. 365 The automatic rice-husker.

huskily (ˈhʌskɪlɪ), *adv.* [f. HUSKY *a.* 4 + -LY[2].] In a husky manner; with a husky voice.

1858 CARLYLE *Fredk. Gt.* VII. viii. (1872) II. 337 The ruggedest of human creatures..growling huskily something which we perceive is real prayer.

†**Huskin.** *Obs. rare.* [f. *Huss* (see HUSSITE) + dim. suffix -KIN.] A Hussite.

1532 MORE *Confut. Tindale* Wks. 716/1 The Huskins and Swinglianes pursue the Lutheranes. **1533** —— *Answ. Poysoned Bk.* ibid. 1051/2 These Lutherane heretikes, these Huskins, Swinglians: and Tyndalins.

huskiness (ˈhʌskɪnɪs). [f. HUSKY *a.* + -NESS.] The quality or condition of being husky, esp. of having a husky voice, etc.

1793 BEDDOES *Catarrh* 156 The huskiness of the bronchiæ. **1861** GEO. ELIOT *Silas M.* vi, 'I tell no lies', said the butcher, with the same mild huskiness as before. **1871** NAPHEYS *Prev. & Cure Dis.* III. vii. 893 The patient is warned by the huskiness of his throat.

husking (ˈhʌskɪŋ), *vbl. sb.*[1] [f. HUSK *v.*[1] + -ING[1].] The action of HUSK *v.*[1]; the removal of the husk. *spec.* in *U.S.*, the removal of the husk from Indian corn; hence, a party or gathering of the neighbours and friends of a farmer to assist him in husking his corn, usually enlivened with festivities; called also *husking-bee* (see b).

1721 B. LYNDE *Diary* (1880) 132 Fair day; husking at Colo's. **1787** T. JEFFERSON *Writ.* (1859) II. 195 A..machine for husking. **1793** J. BARLOW *Hasty Pudding* III, The invited neighbors to the husking come. **1848** LOWELL *Fable for Critics* 1099 A tight, buxom girl..Who can sing at a husking or romp at a shearing. **1882** H. E. SCUDDER *Noah Webster* i. 15 Huskings and spinning bees made work and play shade into each other.

b. *attrib.*, as ***husking-ballad, -bee*** (see BEE[1] 4), ***party***; **husking-glove, -peg, -pin**, articles used in husking Indian corn.

1800 ADDISON *Amer. Law Rep.* 156 The prisoner and the deceased were at a husking frolic. **1809** Husking-bee [see BEE[1] 4]. **1850** WHITTIER *Huskers* 13 The master of the village school..a husking-ballad sung. **1854** LOWELL *Jrnl. in Italy* Pr. Wks. 1890 I. 186 The..husking-bee, where the lads and lassies sit round laughingly busy under the swinging lantern.

husking, *vbl. sb.*[2]: see HUSK *v.*[2]

†ˈ**husking,** *a. Obs. rare*$^{-1}$. [Cf. HUSK *sb.*[2] and HUSKY *a.* 4.] Of a cough: Husky, dry, rough.

a **1707** BP. PATRICK *Autobiog.* (1839) 19 He had a husking cough, and frequently spit up stones. So I call them, for they resembled cherry-stones.

†ˈ**huskish,** *a.*[1] *Obs. rare*$^{-1}$. [f. HUSK *sb.*[1] + -ISH.] Of the nature of husks.

1631 R. H. *Arraignm. Whole Creature* xv. §1. 251 All these huskish Vanities, on which our Prodigall eates.

†ˈ**huskish,** *a.*[2] *Obs. rare*$^{-1}$. [f. HUSK *sb.*[2] (or ? HUSK *a.*) + -ISH.] Somewhat husky.

1718 BATES in *Phil. Trans.* XXX. 873 They [cows] first refused their Food; the next Day had Huskish Coughs.

husky (ˈhʌskɪ), *sb.*[1] Also -ey, -ie. [Supposed to be a corrupted contraction of Eskimo.] **a.** An Eskimo. Also *attrib.* **b.** The Eskimo language.

[**1743** J. ISHAM *Obs. Hudson's Bay* (1949) 155 Among'st the Northward Indians, and Ehuskemay's they have neither of these beasts.] **1830** in K. G. Davies *N. Quebec & Labrador Jrnl. & Corr.* (1963) 115 There was a cry that the river was full of *Hoskies* (Esquimaux). **1864** C. F. HALL *Life among Esquimaux* I. 66 Carl Petersen no speak Husky.. quick. **1889** *Pall Mall G.* 25 Apr. 6/3 The Indians were terribly afraid of the Esquimaux, who up there are called Huskeys. **1922** *19th Cent.* Feb. 274 As a seamstress the 'husky' woman has no equal.

c. An Eskimo dog. Also ***husky dog***.

1852 R. COLLINSON *Jrnl. H.M.S. Enterprise 1850–55* (1889) 218 On his way to the ship [the dog] was kidnapped by the natives, and not being of a pure huski breed, would most likely be prized by them. **1872** *Canadian Monthly* Oct. 307/1 The 'huskie' or Esquimaux dogs..are only fed once a day. **1878** *Sask. Herald* (Battleford, N.W.T.) 18 Nov. 3/1, I had with me a 'Huskie' dog. **1886** *Colonial & Indian Exhib. Rep. Col. Sect.* 75 The original Husky has always been an animal requiring firm treatment. **1896** *Blackw. Mag.* May 682 The original Newfoundland was but little removed from the native 'huskie', and therefore from the timber-wolf of North America. **1947** *New Biol.* III. 152 The most widely used type of sleigh dog is the huskie, employed mainly by Eskimos. **1970** *Islander* (Victoria, B.C.) 22 Feb. 5/1 We now had about 30 husky dogs on deck, and the noise they made when they all howled together was blood-curdling.

husky (ˈhʌskɪ), *sb.*[2] *U.S.* [f. HUSKY *a.* 1 b.] A strong, stoutly-built person; one whose appearance suggests strength and force.

1864 *Old Piute* (Virginia, Nev.) 17 May, He demanded to see the Charter of the concern, which was read by the Rev. Geo. Birdsall, in his usual impressive manner, and the 'husky' accepted the apology. **1884** 'MARK TWAIN' *Huck. Finn* xxix. 305 It was a beautiful time to give the crowd the slip; but that big husky had me by the wrist. **1916** C. SANDBURG *Chicago Poems* 60 The real huskies that are doing the work of the world. **1929** W. HEYLIGER *Builder of Dam* v. 46 You're going to need muscle, and he's a husky. **1945** *Jefferson Co. Republican* (Golden, Colo.) 26 Sept. 1/3 One faculty member who strayed too close to the Washington Avenue bridge was picked up bodily by ten huskies and tossed in the murky waters below.

husky (ˈhʌskɪ), *a.* [f. HUSK *sb.*[1] + -Y.]

1. a. Full of, containing, or consisting of husks; of the nature of a husk.

1552 HULOET, Huskye, or ful of huskes, *siliquosus.* **1697** DRYDEN *Virg. Georg.* I. 315 Most have found A husky Harvest, from the grudging Ground. **1711** E. WARD *Quix.* I. 70 And made the husky Food go down. **1794** T. STONE *Agric. Surv. Linc.* 74 (E.D.S.) Large ant-hills, producing sour, coarse, husky sedge, or sword-grass. **1819** H. BUSK *Vestriad* IV. 147 Browsing the jagged leaf or husky ear. **1905** *Daily Chron.* 14 Sept. 3/6, I have always understood that brown bread is far superior to white bead in muscle-making power and (unless very husky) in digestibility.

b. Tough and strong (like a corn-husk); big, strong, and vigorous. Also *transf.* *N. Amer.*

1869 MRS. STOWE *Oldtown Folks* xvii. 191 Them wild Injuns..they're so kind o' wild, and birchy, and husky as a body may say. **1889** *Kansas City* (Missouri) *Times & Star* 1 Apr., Mike Burnett, the husky ex-fire chief. **1894** *Outing* XXIV. 447/1 He lit out of the country soon as he got husky enough to travel. **1897** *Ibid.* XXX. 364/2 A husky run down old Ontario in a gale from the West brought *Nox* into Charlotte harbor. **1906** *Eye Opener* (Calgary) Aug. 1/6 Watty himself is a husky all-round athlete. **1909** S. E. WHITE *Rules of Game* I. ix. 51 Good food and leisure and heredity gave me a husky build. **1932** J. DOS PASSOS *1919* 263 Husky looking young men in khaki. **1958** *Times* 29 Nov. 9/3 If something more husky is preferred, one can camp or stay in one of the small uninhabited cabins which are to be found throughout Lapland.

†**2.** Having or consisting of a chrysalis case. (Cf. HUSK *sb.*[1] 2 b.) *Obs.*

1655 G. S. in Hartlib *Ref. Commw. Bees* 22 Wormes.. which after turn into Flies, and so again into other husky Wormes without motion, and from them to other flying Insects. **1734** WATTS *Reliq. Juv., Medit. 1st May*, Other families of them have forsaken their husky beds, and exult, and glitter in the warm sun-beams.

3. Dry, as a husk; without natural moisture, arid. *lit.* and *fig.*

1599 *Soliman & Perseda* I. A ij a, A tale wherein she lately hath bestowed, The huskie humor of her bloudy quill. *c* **1694** ADDISON *Virg., Georg.* IV. (R.), Cut their dry and husky wax away. *a* **1722** LISLE *Husb.* (1752) 152 We had also for the most part very dry husky winds. **1729** SWITZER *Hydrost. & Hydraul.* 132 Grounds..of a dry, gravelly, husky Nature. **1826** DISRAELI *Viv. Grey* IV. i, His translation is hard, dry, and husky, as the outside of a cocoa-nut. **1846** *Jrnl. R. Agric. Soc.* VII. II. 523 The soil becomes dusty, or husky..that is, like a dry sponge. **1896** P. A. BRUCE *Econ. Hist. Virginia* I. 441 There was also a possibility that it [tobacco] would become husky from repeated sweatings.

4. Of persons and their voice: Dry in the throat, so that the timbre of the voice is lost, and its sound approaches more or less a hoarse whisper. (An effect of continued speaking, laryngeal inflammation, or violent emotion.)

a **1722** LISLE *Husb.* 343 (E.D.S.) They have in Wilts a disease on their cows, which they call a hask or husky cough. **1740** DYCHE & PARDON, *Husky*,..spoken of a person that has phlegm sticking in his throat, which occasions him to speak imperfectly. **1770** FOOTE *Lame Lover* I. 12 Weezy (who, between ourselves, is as husky as hell). **1831** J. MORISON in *Morisoniana* 420 A deep husky cough. **1858** LONGF. *M. Standish* IV. 122 His voice was husky with anger.

husling: see HUSTLING *vbl. sb.*[2]

‖ˈ**huso.** Also anglicized huse. [med.L. *hūso*, a. OHG. *hûso* = MHG. *hûse*, mod.Ger. *hausen*, early mod.Du. *huys*: cf. HAUSEN.] The great sturgeon, *Acipenser huso*, found esp. in the Black and Caspian Seas.

1706 PHILLIPS (ed. Kersey), *Huso*, the Hausen or Lask, a Fish of a prodigious Bigness, so as it can scarce be drawn with a Team of three or four Horses. **1708** KERSEY, *Huse, Huso.* **1721** BAILEY, *Huse*, a Fish, of which is made the white Glew called Ising-Glass. **1774** GOLDSM. *Nat. Hist.* VI. 282 The Huso, or Isinglass Fish. **1835** KIRBY *Hab. & Inst. Anim.* I. ii. 107 There are two noted species of this fish;..the one is called the sturgeon by way of eminence, and the other the huso.

huspil, -el (ˈhʌsp(ə)l), *v. Obs.* exc. *dial.* [a. F. *houspiller* (15th c. in Littré) to maltreat by dragging about and shaking, altered from *hous-*, *houssepigner* (13th c.), f. *housse* (see HOUSE *sb.*[2]) + *pigner*, *peigner* to comb, and therefore properly = 'peigner le manteau, battre' (Hatz.-Darm.).] *trans.* To treat with violence; to maltreat; to despoil; to harass.

c **1440** *Promp. Parv.* 255/1 Huspylyn, or spoylyn..*spolio, dispolio.* **1658** BROMHALL *Treat. Specters* I. 38 When they are most terrified and huspil'd by these Ghosts. **1663** P. HENRY *Diaries* (1882) 143 Yᵉ quarter Sessions at Clanroost where yᵉ Conventiclers, so called, were huspeld. **1873** in Miss Jackson *Shropsh. Word-bk.* s.v. *Huspel*, 'I'll 'uspel yo' childern off that causey.'

†**huss,** *sb.* Also 5 husk(e; 9 hurse. [Deriv. unascertained: the change of *husk* to *huss* appears to be as in Sc. *busk*, *buss*, etc.] The dog-fish, the skin of which was much used by fletchers for smoothing and polishing arrows; the lesser or greater spotted dogfish, *Scyliorhinus caniculus* or *S. stellaris.* Also *attrib.*, as ***huss skin*** (***huskyn, hurse-skin***).

c **1440** *Promp. Parv.* 254/2 Huske, fyshe (*K.*,*H.*, husk, fishe)..., *squamus.* **1530** PALSGR. 233/2 Husse a fyshe, *rousette.* **1550–1600** *Customs Duties* (B.M. Addit. MS. 25097), Huskyns for Fletchers, The skyn vj*d.* **1612** *Rates of Customs* in *Halyburton's Ledger* (1867) 328 Skins called.. Husse skins for fletchers the skin..vis. **1662** *Stat. Irel.* (1765) II. 415 Huss skins for fletchers, the skin 6*d.* **1721** C. KING *Brit. Merch.* I. 286 Buck dress'd..Calf..Huss.. Sheep and Lamb Skins. **1858** SIMMONDS *Dict. Trade*, *Hurse-skin*, the hard tuberculated skin of a fish, from which shagreen is made. **1963** *Newnes Encycl. Angling* 232/2 Until recently, dogfish have been sold in the shops under the more glamorous name of rock salmon... Today, the recommended names in the retail shops are huss, flake, and rig. **1965** S. NORTON-BRACY in *Newnes Compl. Guide Sea Angling* 117/2 The lesser spotted dogfish (*Scyliorhinus canicula*), a smaller edition of the greater spotted, is also known by many names, probably the best known of them being robin huss... Many anglers seem to think it should have been 'robbing' huss, due to its habit of nipping off the bait. **1967** R. ARNOLD *Anglers' Handbk.* xv. 161 The most popular dogfish, from the angler's standpoint, is the bull huss, or large spotted dog, or nurse hound. **1972** A. WRANGLES *Inshore Sport Fishing* v. 117 Lesser spotted dogfish... Local names. Sandy dog, dogger, rough hound, blind Jimmy, huss, etc. *Ibid.* 118 Greater spotted dogfish... Local names. Bull huss, nurse hound, etc.

†**huss**, *v.* *Obs.* [An echoic word, parallel to HUZZ. Cf. HOSS.] *intr.* To buzz.

1530 PALSGR. 589/1, I husse, I bomme or make a noyse, as a flye dothe.. Declared in 'I hosse'. **1547** BOORDE *Introd. Knowl.* ii. (1870) 126 Muche lyke the hussyng of a homble be. **1577** DEE *Relat. Spir.* I. (1659) 67, I feel a hussing thing go from my head. **1699** DAMPIER *Voy.* II. III. 38 We find such a hussing Breez, that sometimes we are not able to ply against it.

hussa(h, obs. forms of HUZZA.

hussar (hʊ'zɑː(r)), *sb.* Also 6 **hussayre, -are,** 7 **husare, (vs(s)aron)**. [a. Hungarian *huszar*, orig. 'freebooter, free-lance', later 'light horseman', ad. OServian *husar*, also *gusar*, *hursar*, *gursar*, *kursar* pirate, robber, freebooter, ad. It. *corsaro*, *corsare*, CORSAIR.

In the time of King Matthias Hunyady, in the second half of the 15th century, the word became applied to the Hungarian light horsemen, in which application it became known and used in the Western European languages: cf. Pol., Ger. *husar*, F. *hussard*, in 18th c. *houssard*, *housard*.
In a Latin deed of armistice *c* 1450, mention is made of 'prædones aut Hwzarij hungari', and in other Latin documents of the 15th c. they are called *huzarones*, *hussarones* after *prædones*), whence occasionally *vs(s)arons* in English. (Before the history was known, the word was fancifully derived from Magyar *husz* twenty: see *Magyar Nyelvör* (Budapest) VI. 24, and Miklosich.)]

1. a. One of a body of light horsemen organized in Hungary in the 15th c., and long confined to the Hungarian army; hence, the name of light cavalry regiments formed in imitation of these, which were subsequently introduced, and still exist, in most European armies, including that of Great Britain.

The dress of the Hungarian force set the type for that of the hussars of other nations, these being distinguished by uniforms of brilliant colours and elaborate ornament, two special characteristics being the dolman and busby (the former of which is now abandoned in the British army).

1532 R. COPLAND *Vict. agst. Turks* in *Ames' Typogr. Antiq.* (1816) III. 117 The capitayn generall..came..into yᵉ towne..with..xv. hondred hussayres, lyght horses. **1560** DAUS tr. *Sleidane's Comm.* 269 The horsmen of Hongary are commonly called Hussares, an exceadyng rauenous and cruell kynde of men. **1603** KNOLLES *Hist. Turks* (1610) 739 Hungarian horsemen, such as in time of peace liued by robbing, and are by an infamous name called 'Vsarons'. **1656-9** B. HARRIS *Parival's Iron Age* 321 The Bashaw himself..being pursued by a Hussar, was taken hold of by him. **1688** *Lond. Gaz.* No. 2349/3 The Regiment of Hussars, which the Elector of Bavaria resolved to raise..is now compleat: They are cloathed in Red, having Caps with Feathers on their Heads, and Wolfs Skins on their left Shoulders. **1711** *Vind. Sacheverell* 20 He appears to me more like a forraging Hussar. **1799** CAMPBELL *Pleas. Hope* I. 352 Her whisker'd pandoors and her fierce hussars. **1802-16** C. JAMES *Milit. Dict.* s.v., There are also several regiments of hussars in the British service. **1847** GLEIG *Waterloo* II. xxiv, The bold front presented by Vivian's hussars. **1851** GALLENGA *Italy* 471 Squadrons of hussars and Hulans were scouring the plain in every direction.

b. ***Black*** or ***Death Hussar***, one of the 'Black Brunswickers' (hussars with black uniform) who, in the war with France, 1809–13, neither gave nor received quarter; hence *fig.*

1815 SIR C. BELL *Let. to G. J. Bell* 2 July in Lockhart *Scott*, This was a Brunswicker, of the Black or Death Hussars. **1816** SCOTT *Let. to Jas. Ballantyne* ibid., I belong to the Black Hussars of Literature, who neither give nor receive criticism.

2. *transf.* and *fig.* A skirmisher; a free-lance in literature or debate.

1768-74 TUCKER *Lt. Nat.* (1852) I. 473 Your infinitely-infinite monades in infinitely-never single bodies..cannot get the better even of my light armature, my skipping scampering hussars. **1800** A. CARLYLE *Autobiog.* 432 He was a mere hussar, who had no steady views to direct him.

3. *attrib.* and *Comb.*, as ***hussar blue, boot, broth, cap, jacket, livery, regiment, saddle, waistcoat, war***, etc.; ***hussar-like*** adj. and adv.

1748 SMOLLETT *Rod. Rand.* xi. (1760) I. 67 An Hussar waist-coat, scarlet breeches. **1762** STERNE *Tr. Shandy* VI. xi, Hussar-like, they skirmish lightly and out of all order. **1774** J. COLLIER *Mus. Trav.* (1775) 60 A pair of hussar boots laced at the seams. **1834** MEDWIN *Angler in Wales* II. 211 He wore a deep green hussar jacket. **1846** *Knickerbocker* XXVII. 287 [He had] a smart hussar cap of green chestnut burrs. **1851** *Illustr. Catal. Gt. Exhib.* 521 Hussar saddle, with holsters and furniture. **1854** B. F. TAYLOR *Jan. & June* 85 Hens with hussar caps. **1861** WHYTE MELVILLE *Tilbury Nogo* 189 'Hussar broth', red herrings fried in gin. **1895** SIR E. WOOD *Cavalry in Waterloo Camp.* iv. 81 The Brunswick Hussar regiment was now ordered forward from Quatre Bras. **1896** *Daily News* 10 Oct. 6/3 Hussar blue is in much demand.

Hence (*nonce-wds.*) **hu'ssar** *v. intr.*, to carry on light warfare like a hussar. **hussared** (hʊ'zɑːd) *a.*, made or ornamented like that of a hussar.

†**hu'ssarian**, ? a Hungarian hussar.

1760 FOOTE *Minor* I. Wks. 1799 I. 241 Amongst his countrymen, the High-dutchians and Hussarians. **1774** *Westm. Mag.* II. 111 Sattin or silk waistcoats, huzzar'd. **1864** CARLYLE *Fredk. Gt.* XVIII. xiv. (1872) VIII. 82 A Daun Detachment, hussaring about in those parts.

hussaw, hussel, obs. ff. HUZZA, HUSTLE.

Husserlian (hʊ'sɜːlɪən), *a.* [f. name of Edmund *Husserl*, German philosopher (1859–1938) + -IAN.] Of, pertaining to, or characteristic of Husserl or his work.

1932 *Mind* XLI. 247 Coming from the same Husserlian school. **1939** E. WELCH *Edmund Husserl's Phenomenology* II. ii. 78 All of these theories, on Husserlian grounds, are based on nothing but pure prejudice. **1950** *Mind* LIX. 127 As it is we have Hegelian and Husserlian phenomenology on one hand and Kierkegaardian preaching on the other. **1965** *Language* XLI. 492 It is therefore a transcendental English, an English idealized out of controllable experience, an English known only to Husserlian pure egos.

hussher, var. HUISHER.

hussif, dial. f. HOUSEWIFE.

hussilling: see HUSTLING *vbl. sb.*²

Hussite ('hʌsaɪt, 'hʊsaɪt). *Eccl. Hist.* [ad. mod.L. *Hussīta* (usu. pl.), f. the surname of John Huss, or Hus (an abbreviation of the name of his native village *Husinec*, lit. 'goose-pen', in Bohemia).] A follower of John Huss, the Bohemian religious reformer of the 15th century.

1532 MORE *Confut. Tindale* Wks. 352/2 In Boheme the Hussites, in England the wicliffystes. **1621** J. TAYLOR (Water P.) *Motto* 31 Wks. (1630) II. 45/1 Of Romish Catholike, or Protestant: Of Brownist, Hussite or of Caluinist. **1641** MILTON *Ch. Govt.* I. vi, As at first by those of your tribe they were call'd Lollards and Hussites, so now by you be term'd Puritans and Brownists. **1838** *Penny Cycl.* XII. 361/1 There are a few Hussites now in Bohemia.

b. *attrib.* or *adj.*

1838 *Penny Cycl.* XII. 361/1 The Emperor Sigismund.. agreed that the Hussite priests should be tolerated, even at court. **1883** *Athenæum* 17 Nov. 631/1 In the fifteenth century we find traces of Hussite teaching and Hussite communities scattered throughout the whole of the land.

Hence **'Hussitism**.

1884 *Brit. & For. Evang. Rev.* Oct. 620 The new doctrine was known as Wyclifism, a term which was only gradually abandoned in favour of Hussitism after the year 1420.

hussive, hussle, obs. ff. HOUSEWIFE, HUSTLE.

hussy, huzzy ('hʌzɪ), *sb.* Also 7 **hussie, huzzie**, 8–9 **hussey**, *Sc.* **hizzie**. [A phonetic reduction of HOUSEWIFE, q.v.]

†**1.** The mistress of a household; a thrifty woman: = HOUSEWIFE 1. *Obs.*

1530 *Edin. Burgh Rec.* (1871) 30 Na seruandis [shall] tak vther clathis than thar masteris and husseis and thar houshaldis clathis to wesche. **15..** SIR J. MOFFAT *Wife of Auchtermuchty* iii, Dame, ye maun to the pleugh the morn, I sall be hussy, gif I may. **1722** DE FOE *Col. Jack* (1840) 245 Her being so good a hussy of what money I had left her. **1800** HURDIS *Fav. Village* 98 His loud hussey, in her cobbled suit..Screams through the village.

2. A rustic, rude, opprobrious, or playfully rude mode of addressing a woman.

1650 B. *Discolliminium* 7 [To a mare] You are mistaken Hussy. **1676** HOBBES *Iliad* (1677) 47 Then Venus vext, 'Hussie!' said she, 'no more Provoke my anger'. **1684** OTWAY *Atheist* v, Yes, huzzy, and you shall be serviceable to me in the matter. **1749** FIELDING *Tom Jones* VII. viii, Hussy, ..I will make such a saucy trollop as yourself know, that I am not a proper subject of your discourse. **1853** READE *Chr. Johnstone* 235 Meg, ye idle hizzy..your pat is no on yet.

3. In some rural districts a mere equivalent of Woman, lass; hence, A strong country woman, a female of the lower orders; a woman of low or improper behaviour, or of light or worthless character; an ill-behaved, pert, or mischievous girl; a jade, minx. Also jocularly or in raillery.

The bad sense was at first mostly with qualification (*light*, etc.), or contextual.

1647 TRAPP *Comm. Matt.* xiv. 8 Such another hussy as this was dame Alice Pierce, a concubine to our Edward III. **1648** BP. HALL *Sel. Thoughts* §96 The light hussy 'wipes her mouth' and [says] it was not she. **1685** CROWNE *Sir C. Nice* I. 8 You talk of paltry husses. **1711** STEELE *Spect.* No. 242 ¶3 The young Husseys would persuade me, that to believe one's Eyes is a sure way to be deceived. **1738** SWIFT *Pol. Conversat.* 56 No, Miss; you are very light; but I don't say, you are a light Hussy. **1741** RICHARDSON *Pamela* II. 117, I, like a little proud Hussy, looked in the Glass and thought myself a Gentlewoman. **1775** MAD. D'ARBLAY *Let.* 24 Apr. in *Early Diary*, He..patted my cheek, and genteely called me a little hussey. **1786** BURNS *Twa Dogs* 85 Buirdly chiels, an' clever hizzies. **1795** WASHINGTON *Let.* Writ. 1892 XIII. 158 A more..impudent huzzy, is not to be found in the United States. **1859** GEO. ELIOT *A. Bede* 70 The naughtier the little huzzy behaved the prettier she looked. **1889** H. F. WOOD *Englishman Rue Caïn* x, That bonnetless, bold hussey round that corner.

†**4.** A case for needles, thread, etc.: = HOUSEWIFE 3. *Obs.*

1741 RICHARDSON *Pamela* I. 159 So I..dropt purposely my Hussey. **1824** SCOTT *Redgauntlet* ch. xxii, A better rope than the string of a lady's hussy.

5. *Comb.*, as †**hussy-case** = sense 4; †**hussy make** (cf. *housewife's cloth* s.v. HOUSEWIFE *sb.* 1 b).

15.. *Aberd. Reg.* V. 16 (Jam.) Ane pair of schetis of ten elne of hussy mak. **1818** SCOTT *Hrt. Midl.* xxxix, I have seen the Queen, which gave me a hussy-case out of her own hand.

Hence **'hussy** *v. trans.*, to call 'hussy'; **'hussydom**, the realm or aggregate of hussies; **'hussyness**, the character of a hussy.

1694 CROWNE *Married Beau* IV. Dram. Wks. 1874 IV. 309 *Mrs. Lo.* Begone! *Lio.* Begone? I won't be so snapp'd. *Mrs. Lo.* You won't, hussy? *Lio.* I won't be hussied neither. **1865** *Athenæum* No. 1981. 499/1 The blackguardism and hussydom of London. **1881** DORAN *Drury Lane* II. 147 The leaders of fashion and the gaudiest flowers of husseydom.

hussyf-, hussyskep, Sc. ff. HOUSEWIFESHIP.

†**hust**, *int.* *Obs.* [A natural utterance or 'vocal gesture', enjoining silence. It varies with *husht*, *huisht*, *whisht*, *whist*, and *hist*, all having the characteristic element *'st! 'sht!* preceded by the whispered consonant *h* or *hw*, with the connecting vowel *i*, or *u* (*ui*). See HIST.

As an interjection of command it is in effect identical with a verb in the imperative; nearly all the above variants were so treated, and in course of time developed verbs of the same form. The forms *husht*, *whist* were also in early use as adjs. of condition; thence, by further development, came the vb. *hush*, followed by adj. and int. of the same form.]

A sharp whispered sound enjoining silence: = HIST! ST! HUSH!

c **1386** CHAUCER *Miller's T.* 536 (only in Ellesm. MS.), Vn to Nicholas she seyde stille Now hust and thou shalt laughen al thy fille.

†**hust**, *a.* *Obs.* [app. an adjectival use of HUST *int.*, as expressing the state which the int. produces: cf. HUSHT *a.*; also WHIST, WHISHT *adjs.*] Silent, quiet, hushed.

c **1374** CHAUCER *Troylus* II. 866 (915) Whan al was hust þanne lay she stille and þoughte. —— *Boeth.* II. met. v. 35 (Camb. MS.) Tho weeryn þᵉ crwel claryouns ful hust [*Addit. MS.* whist] and ful stylle. *c* **1385** —— *L.G.W.* 2682 *Hypermnestra*, And hust [*Fairf.* hushst, *Tanner* houste, *Thynne* hushte] were alle In argon that cete. *c* **1386** —— *Knt.'s T.* 2123 Whan they were set and hust [3 *MSS.* huyst, *Harl.* hussht] was al the place.

†**hust**, *v.* *Obs.* *rare*⁻⁰. [app. derived from HUST *int.*, which can also be taken as a vb. in the imperative.] **a.** *trans.* To reduce to silence, to hush. **b.** *intr.* To be silent.

1530 PALSGR. 589/1, I huste, I styll, *je repayse* and *je recoyse*. **1570** LEVINS *Manip.* 194/23 Huste, *silére*.

husting ('hʌstɪŋ). Usually in pl. **hustings**. Forms: 1, 3 (9 *Hist.*) **husting**, 3 **-eng(e**; *pl.* 3–4 **hustingis**, 6 **-es, hoysting(e)s**, 6–7 **hoistings**, 5– **hustings**. [OE. *hústing*, a. ON. *hús-þing*, house-assembly, a council held by a king, earl, or other leader, and attended by his immediate followers, retainers, etc., in distinction from the ordinary *þing* or general assembly of the people (the OE. *folcȝemót*, FOLKMOOT).

The *t* is probably due to weakening of the stress on the second syllable; cf. *nostril* from older *nos-þril*. The change may conceivably have already taken place in Danish, as in ON. *estu* for *es þu*.
The form *hoistings* found in 16–17th c. may have been due to association with HOIST *v.*; but there is no evidence that the word was taken to mean 'platform' before 1682; Blount (1656), who suggests a derivation from F. *haulser* (*hausser*) to raise, does so on the ground that it is 'the principal and highest court in London'.]

* In form *husting*.

1. An assembly for deliberative purposes, esp. one summoned by a king or other leader; a council. *rare* (in general sense). *Obs.* exc. *Hist.*

a **1030** *O.E. Chron.* (MS. C) an. 1012 Hi [the Danes] ȝenamon þa ðone biscop [Ælfeah], læddon hine to hiora hustinge [*Laud MS.* heora hustinga]. *c* **1205** LAY. 4766 Belin in Euerewic huld eorlene husting. *Ibid.* 11544 Octaues ure king i Lundene heold his husting. Þat hustinge was god; hit wes witene-imot. *Ibid.* 12988 Þa comen to Lundenne al þis leodisce folc to heore hustinge [*c* 1275 to one speking]. **1861** PEARSON *Early & Mid. Ages Eng.* 149 Ælfeg.. proceeded to preach to the hus-ting. **1864** KINGSLEY *Rom. & Teut.* viii. (1875) 202 They might drag him out into their husting, and threaten him with torture.

** In form *husting*, pl. *hustings*.

2. A court held in the Guildhall of London by the Lord Mayor, Recorder, and Sheriffs (or Aldermen), long the supreme court of the city.

The early history of this is in many points obscure. The mention of 'husting's weight' in the charter of Cnut (see 5) suggests that the *husting* had already then become a permanent institution for the transaction of civic business.
The ***Hustings*** or ***Court of Hustings*** was formerly a court of common pleas, of probate, of appeal against decisions of the sheriffs, a court of record for the formal conveyance of property, etc.; but it is now convoked only for the purpose of considering and registering gifts made to the City. In the Calendar for 1898 'Hustings' were set down for 31 Tuesdays during the year, although there had been only one meeting since 1885.

a. singular *husting*. *Obs.* exc. *Hist.*

c **1100** *Carta civibus London.* §9 in Schmid *Gesetze* 435 Et amplius non sit miskenninga in hustenge, neque in folkesmote..Et husting sedeat semel in ebdomada, videlicet die lunæ. ?*c* **1140** *Docmt. of Sale* in Spelman *Gloss.* s.v., Wlfnothus de Walebroc de London vendidit..quandam suam terram..coram omni Hustingo de London, in domo Alfwini. ?**12..** *Lois de la cite de Lond.* (B.M. Addit. MS. 14252) (Godef.), En la cort le rei, ço est a saveir el husteng. **1237** in A. Thierry *Mon. inéd. du Tiers Etat* I. 805 (ibid.) Donné en pleyn hustenge de Londres, devant Andreu Bekerel, adonk meyre de Londres. **1289-90** in Madox *Hist. Exch.* xx. 553 Rex..vult quod Scaccarium suum usque Hustengum Londoniæ transferatur. **1368** *Charter* in Madox *Formul. Angl.* (1702) 200 In pleno Hustingo Londoniæ de Communibus placitis. [**1865** KINGSLEY *Herew.* xx, We will give you your lands in full husting. **1888** *Athenæum* 27 Oct., Session of the Court of Husting.]

β. plural *hustings* in same sense as the sing.

c **1462** *Plumpton Corr.* 5 He haith taken his *exigi facias de novo* & is with us called in the hustings. **1494** *Act 11 Hen. VII*, c. 21 §2 The Hustynges of London holden for Comen Plees before the Maire and Aldermen. **1513** More *Rich. III* Wks. 61/1 In the east ende of the hall where the maire kepeth the hustinges [**1568** Grafton, where the hoystinges be kept]. **1613** Sir H. Finch *Law* (1636) 349 In London, where their hustings are as the Countie Courts. **1704** J. Harris *Lex. Techn.* s.v. *Inrolment*, Entring of any Lawful Act in the Rolls of the Chancery..or in the Hustings of London, or by the Clerk of the Peace in any County. **1707** J. Chamberlayne *St. Gt. Brit.* iii. xi. 355 The highest and most ancient Court, is that called the Hustings..which doth preserve the Laws, Rights, Franchises, and Customs of the City. **1768** Blackstone *Comm.* III. vi. (1809) 89 *note*, The sheriffs' courts..from which a writ of error lies to the court of hustings, before the mayor, recorder, and sheriffs. **1818** Cruise *Digest* (ed. 2) I. 206 Enrolled in the court of hustings. **1863** H. Cox *Instit.* ii. xi. 585 The Hustings is the supreme Court of London. **1890** Gross *Gild Merch.* I. 125 An alien was to be admitted to the freedom only at the Hustings. *fig.* **1883** *Standard* 24 Sept. 5/2 Determined to have their differences out while science is in full hustings.

†**b.** According to Cowell, a similar court anciently held in other cities: but it is doubtful whether this is the meaning of the passage in *Fleta*. For a hustings court, *curia hustengorum*, in Oxford, see Wood's *Life and Times* (O.H.S.) IV. 183-4.

1607 Cowell *Interpr.*, *Hustings*,..Other Cities and towns also haue had a court of the same name, as Winchester, Lincolne, Yorke, and Sheppey, and others [*Fleta* ii. lv, Habet etiam Rex curiam suam in civitatibus..et locis..sicut in Hustengis Londoñ Wintoñ Lincolñ Ebor' & apud Shepey & alibi], where the Barons or Citizens haue a record of such things as are determinable before them.

*** In form *hustings*, now usually constr. as *sing*.

†**3.** The upper end of the Guildhall, where this Court was held; the platform on which the Mayor and Aldermen took their seats. *Obs.*

[**1682** *Lond. Gaz.* No. 1738/3 The Common-Hall met..where the Lord Mayor and Aldermen being come down to the Hustings, etc.] *a* **1734** North *Exam.* iii. viii. §22 (1740) 598 When..the Lord-Mayor and Court of Aldermen are come upon the Suggestum, called the Hustings [etc.]. **1761** *Brit. Mag.* II. 603 The royal family returned into the hall, and were conducted to the upper end of it, called the Hustings; where a table was provided for them.

4. The temporary platform from which, previous to the Ballot Act of 1872, the nomination of candidates for Parliament was made, and on which these stood while addressing the electors. Hence, contextually, the proceedings at a parliamentary election.

1719 D'Urfey *Pills* (1872) II. 242 What tricks on the Hustings Fanatics would play. **1774** Burke *Sp. Electors Bristol* Wks. III. 14, I stood on the hustings..less like a candidate, than an unconcerned spectator of a publick proceeding. **1796** Coleridge *Lett.* (1895) 164 In the market place stands the hustings. **1850** Carlyle *Latter-d. Pamph.* vi. (1872) 204 One thing the stupidest multitude at a hustings can do. **1850** Ht. Martineau *Hist. Peace* II. v. ii. 231 The Church question was the leading one on the hustings. **1883** S. C. Hall *Retrospect* I. 23 An unpopular candidate had frequently to beat a hasty retreat from the hustings.

5. *attrib.*, as ***husting-court***, ***-day***; ***hustings-cry***, ***-movement***, ***-orator***, ***-topic***; **hustings court** = sense 2; also, a court of local jurisdiction in Richmond and other cities of Virginia, U.S.; **hustings-weight** (in OE. *hustinges ȝewiht*), a standard weight for precious metals in the 11th c. (cf. *hustinum pondus* in Du Cange).

[*c* **1000** in Thorpe *Dipl. Angl. Ævi Sax.* (1865) 533 Duos cyphos argenteos de xij marcis ad pondus Hustingie Londonensis.] **1032** *Charter of Cnut* in Kemble *Cod. Dipl.* IV. 37 Mid hundeahtiȝum marcan hwites seolfres be hustinges ȝewihte. **1598** Stow *Surv.* v. xxvii. (1754) II. 467/1 Troy weight, was, in the time of the Saxons called the Hustings-weight of London. **1671** F. Phillips *Reg. Necess.* 281 Some Courts or Husting dayes. **1675** Ogilby *Brit.* Introd. 4 The High and Antient Hustings-Court for Preservation of the Laws. **1837** Disraeli *Let.* 21 Nov. in *Corr. w. Sister* (1886) 75 A second-rate hustings orator. **1844** —— *Coningsby* ii. i, The hustings-cry at the end of 1832. **1889** *Academy* 1 June 374/3 A husting court was held in 1885, and again in 1888 [for the enrolment of deeds relating to benefactions to the City of London School]. **1898** E. W. James *Let. to Editor*, In Richmond and other cities the Corporation Courts, frequently called Hustings Courts, exercise both civil and criminal jurisdiction. The Hustings Court of Richmond has appellate jurisdiction in small civil matters coming from the police courts or justices' courts.

hustle ('hʌs(ə)l), *v.* Also 8 **hussell**, 8–9 **hussle**. [ad. Du. *husselen*, *hutselen*, to shake, to toss, MDu. *hutselen* to shake the money in the game of hustle-cap, EFris. *hütseln*, to toss about, to move hither and thither, a frequentative of Du. *hutsen*, MHG. *hutzen*; cf. Du. *hotsen*, G. (dial.) *hotzen*, *hotzeln* of similar meaning (see hotch). The stems *hot-*, *hut-* appear in a number of formations in both High and Low German dialects, all implying a shaking movement. The development of sense 2 is exclusively English.]

†**1. a.** *trans.* To shake to and fro, toss (money in a hat or cap, in the game of hustle-cap). Also *absol.* *Obs.*

1684 Otway *Atheist* i. i, As the boys do by their farthings, hustle them in a hat together, and go to heads or tails for them. **1736** Fielding *Pasquin* v, Places, requiring learning and great parts, Henceforth shall all be husled in a hat, And drawn by men deficient in them both. **1755** Johnson, *To Hustle*, to shake together in confusion. **1801** Strutt *Sports & Past.* iii. vii. §15 When they hustle, all the half-pence pitched at the mark are thrown into a hat held by the player who claims the first chance.

b. To shake about.

1851 S. Judd *Margaret* i. ii, She saw a blue-jay washing itself..and hustling the water with its wings.

2. a. To push or knock (a person) about roughly or unceremoniously; to jostle in a rough or violent fashion; said esp. of a number who subject an individual to this treatment as a method of assaulting or robbing him.

1751 Smollett *Per. Pic.* (1779) I. ii. 21, I was hussled by those rebellious rapscallions. **1798** *Ann. Reg.* 56 Mrs. Dearling..was hustled by a gang of pickpockets. **1844** Alb. Smith *Adv. Mr. Ledbury* x. (1886) 31 Two or three..gathered round the fresh comers..apparently with the intention of hustling them. **1879** Sala *Paris herself again* (1880) II. xi. 164 The business of the bludgeon men was to hustle and maltreat people.

fig. **1796** Burke *Regic. Peace* ii. Wks. VIII. 234 The proposed fraternity is hustled in the crowd of those treaties. **1883** *Fortn. Rev.* June 784 Liking nothing better than hustling a Dissenter in print.

b. *with complement*: To push, thrust, force in such a way *into* or *out of* a certain position or *through* a certain space. Also *transf.* of the action of the wind, tide, etc.

1755 *Man* No. 21. 3 When the clergyman ended his discourse, the people..directly hussell'd the freethinker into my cart. **1768** J. Byron *Narr. Patagonia* (ed. 2) 243 The ship had been hustled through the Granadillos in the night. **1824** *Mechanic's Mag.* No. 36. 126 The tide sometimes runs so rapidly, as to hustle the ship on shore, before the sails can be made to act. **1840** Dickens *Old C. Shop* xxvi, Mr. Chuckster was pushed and hustled to the office again. **1841** Catlin *N. Amer. Ind.* (1844) II. xxxvi. 30 My packages..and Indian articles, minerals, fossils..I shall hustle them altogether. **1883** *Pall Mall G.* 27 Dec. 3/1 The enormous Budget for 1884 is being successfully hustled through the French Senate. **1889** Jessopp *Coming of Friars* v. 242 The husband who had just been hustled into his grave.

c. To urge, impel, push forward (into some action) in a rough unfastidious fashion.

1887 Sir R. H. Roberts *In the Shires* ii. 28 He hustles the cob into a canter, and makes for the nearest ford. **1890** *Spectator* 4 Jan., Women hustled into speech on all sorts of subjects, are like flowers planted in water-glasses with their roots exposed to the light.

d. *U.S. colloq.* To obtain, produce, or serve by hustle or pushing activity. Also with *up*.

In some contexts spec. = 'to steal' (cf. sense 2 a).

1840 *Southern Lit. Messenger* VI. 414/2 Can't you go out to the woodpile and hustle me up a few chips to start this fire? **1908** *Grand* Dec. 614 Anita was really hungry and hustled up the luncheon in..an unromantic, business-like sort of way. **1914** R. Grau *Theatre of Science* 80 He had to write his own scenarios, direct the productions and 'hustle props'. **1926** J. Black *You can't Win* vi. 65 Don't think because you couldn't hustle a can that you ain't entitled to your coffee. **1940** S. Lewis *Bethel Merriday* iii. 35 When you grow up..you try to squirm into prison, or get a nice job hustling hash..anything to avoid going on the stage. **1950** [see fix *sb.* 5]. **1953** W. Burroughs *Junkie* (1972) ix. 86 'Do you want to score?' he asked. 'I'm due to score in a few minutes. I've been trying to hustle the dough.' **1957** P. Mansfield *Final Exposure* ix. 134 Perhaps they can hustle up some coffee. **1967** M. M. Glatt et al. *Drug Scene* iii. 34 Hustling is a generic term which usually refers to any number of strategies addicts may use to obtain drugs. **1970** H. E. Roberts *Third Ear* 8/2 *Hustle, hustling*, to be aggressively, actively engaged in the acquisition of goods and money.

e. To sell or serve (goods, etc.), esp. in an aggressive, pushing manner. *N. Amer. slang.*

1887 *Grip* (Toronto) 5 Mar. 6/2 She hustled the hash at Gilhooley's on Blank St. **1894** T. R. Dewar *Ramble round Globe* 84 Almost every second man you meet..is now either 'hustling lumber' or farming at four or five dollars a week. **1973** *Black World* Aug. 56/2 He hustled the watch to a barber for 35 bills.

3. a. *intr.* To push roughly *against*. Also *absol.* To crowd together, jostling each other.

1823 Byron *Juan* ix. lxxxii, Ambassadors began as 't were to hustle Round the young man. **1837** Lytton *Athens* II. 180 Their tall vessels..driven and hustling the one against the other. **1897** Mary Kingsley *W. Africa* 497 The woman will accuse some man of having hustled against her.

b. *intr.* To push or elbow one's way.

1855 Thackeray *Newcomes* I. xxxv. 346 The..society..that hustles into the churches on public festivals. **1857** Mrs. Gatty *Par. fr. Nat.* Ser. ii. (1868) 98 The tortoise began to hustle under the leaves and rubbish again.

4. *intr.* To move hastily, to hurry, to bustle; to work busily, push one's way actively, 'make a push'.

1821 Clare *Vill. Minstr.* II. 84 Haymakers, hustling from the rain to hide. **1826** Scott *Woodst.* xxii, The King..had hustled along the floor. *c* **1867** Edison in *Temple Mag.* (1897) Sept. 885/1 I've got so much to do, and life is so short, that I am going to hustle. **1903** *Westm. Gaz.* 25 Feb. 5/2 The 'Decapod' will 'hustle' in true American fashion. **1906** 'O. Henry' *Four Million* 62 Do you think I'm going to let you hustle for wages while I philander in the regions of high art? **1908** G. H. Lorimer *Jack Spurlock* v. 87, I decided that..I'd hustle over to the nearest trust company.

5. *intr.* To engage in prostitution. *slang.*

In quot. 1954 used transitively in sense 'to "work" an area, soliciting as a prostitute'.

1930 J. Dos Passos *42nd Parallel* v. 411 She showed him a snapshot of her steady... I don't hustle when he's in town. **1954** J. Steinbeck *Sweet Thursday* i. 4 If you were hustling a state you should do honour to that state. **1957** C. MacInnes *City of Spades* ii. ii. 117 'You're positive she's not hustling?' 'Muriel..is no harlot.' *Ibid.* 120 Hustling with Jumble queers. **1959** *Listener* 10 Dec. 1048/1 She..revolted in revenge against her family, 'hustled' in Piccadilly, hated men as clients, took a ponce. **1960** *Guardian* 23 Sept. 26/7 Several clubs have been threatened with proceedings for keeping a brothel if they allow prostitutes to hustle on the premises. **1970** *Daily Colonist* (Victoria, B.C.) 8 Feb. 11/1 To put it bluntly, she was hustling, and liked the rewards in the shape of cash and jewelry.

hustle ('hʌs(ə)l), *sb.* [f. hustle *v.*] The act of hustling.

1. The act of shaking together: in pitch and hustle = hustle-cap, pitch-and-toss.

1715 *State Quacks* 24 Playing at Pitch and Huzle. **1801** Strutt *Sports & Past.* iii. viii. §15 Pitch and Hustle.

2. The act of pushing or jostling roughly.

1803 W. Taylor in *Ann. Rev.* I. 351 The hustle of anarchy. **1837** Carlyle *Fr. Rev.* II. v. iii, A thousand-handed hustle and jostle. **1837** Mrs. Sherwood *Henry Milner* iii. xi. 216 They clung fast to him, and it would have been impossible for him to have extricated himself without coming to a downright hustle.

3. *U.S.* Pushing activity; 'push'. Also with *a.* (Cf. move *sb.* 6.)

1892 *Home Missionary* (N.Y.) July 120 The hustle and stir of our day. **1898** *Daily Chron.* 3 Dec. 5/1 With characteristic 'hustle', excursions in the United States have already been organised to Hawaii. **1902** W. N. Harben *Abner Daniel* ii. 19, I..told 'em to git a hustle on the'rse'ves. **1908** [see drive *sb.* 1 i]. **1968** *Globe & Mail* (Toronto) 15 Jan. 21/1 Earl Balfour is a veteran hockey player who well remembers the secret to success—hustle.

4. A swindle, racket; a means of deception or fraud; a source of income; a paid job. *slang* (orig. *U.S.*).

1963 R. I. McDavid *Mencken's Amer. Lang.* 729 *Hustle*, a racket which one pushes to get his bread. **1965** 'Malcolm X' *Autobiogr.* vi. 87 Each of the military services had their civilian-dress eyes and ears picking up anything of interest to them, such as hustles being used to avoid the draft..or hustles that were being worked on servicemen. **1969** R. Pharr in A. Chapman *New Black Voices* (1972) 63, I got me a good hustle. I write over $200 worth of numbers a day, which gives me a cool 40 bucks. **1972** *Observer* 20 Aug. 7/4, I was stark broke..from the horses..and the cards. It didn't really matter because I was on a hustle.

hustle-bustle. *rare*⁻¹. [Cf. hustle and bustle.] A bustle in which there is much hustling or jostling: in quot. *attrib.*

1836 T. Hook *G. Gurney* III. 35 A sort of hustle-bustle kind of confusion.

hustle-cap ('hʌs(ə)l,kæp). ? *Obs.* Also **hussel-cap.** [f. hustle *v.* (sense 1) + cap *sb.* Cf. MLG. *hutseken*, *hütschen*, MDu. *hutssecruyssen* as names of similar games.] A form of pitch-and-toss, in which the coins were 'hustled' or shaken together in a cap before being tossed.

1709 *Brit. Apollo* II. No. 2. 1/2 If He delight at Hustle-Cap to play. **1751** Smollett *Per. Pic.* ii, An excellent hand at a song, hussle-cap, and chuck-farthing. **1809** W. Irving *Knickerb.* (1849) 167 Youngsters who..squandered what little money they could procure at hustle-cap and chuck-farthing. **1881** Besant & Rice *Chapl. of Fleet* I. 232 We played all night at brag, all-fours, teetotum, hussle-cap.

hustlement ('hʌs(ə)lmənt). *Obs.* exc. *dial.* Forms: 4 **ostel(e)-**, 4–5 **ostil-**, 4–5 **hustil-**, **-yl-**, 5 **(hostilia-)**, 6 **hostil(e)-**, **hustel-**, **ustyl(l)-**, **hussel-**, 7 **husle-**, 7–9 **hustlement**, *dial.* **husslement.** [a. OF. *(h)ostillement*, *(h)oust-*, *(h)ust-*, later *out-* (13th c. in Godef.), furniture, f. *(h)ostiller*, mod.F. *outiller*, to furnish, equip, fit out with tools, f. OF. *(h)ostil*, *(h)oustil*, mod.F. *outil* tool, and *(h)ostille* apparatus, utensil, tool.

M. Paul Meyer holds the OF. word to belong to *h)ostel*, L. *hospitāle*: cf. med.L. *hostilia* house, dwelling (1265 in Du Cange). Conjectures of derivation from L. *ūtilis*, *ūsus*, are nugatory; though the accidental resemblance of later F. *outil* to *ūtilis* has probably affected the later F. sense, 'utensil, tool'.]

1. Household furniture; chiefly *pl.* articles of furniture, household goods.

c **1374** Chaucer *Boeth.* ii. pr. v. 33 (Camb. MS.) It nedeth of ful manye helpynges to kepyn the diuersyte of presyos ostelementus [*Addit. MS.* ostelmentz, *ed.* **1560** hostilements]. **1418** *E. E. Wills* (1882) 35 Alle the hustilmentis of Beddyng. **1463** *Bury Wills* (Camden) 25 Pewter vessell, cofferys, and tubbes, wid alle othir ostilmentys generally. **1548** *Richmond. Wills* (Surtees) 61 All the ustylment within the hows. **1599** *Acc.-Bk. W. Wray* in *Antiquary* XXXII. 244 One stee wth all other husselment. **1877** *N.W. Linc. Gloss.*, *Husslement*, household goods.

2. *transf.* Lumber; odds and ends, a miscellaneous collection. [? associated with *hustle*.]

1664 Power *Exp. Philos.* Pref. A iij b, Described as being the disregarded pieces and huslement of the Creation. **1773** *Inventory* in *Cheshire Gloss.* 418 In Lumber or Hustlements 2*s.* 6*d.* **1876** *Mid-Yorksh. Gloss.*, *Hustlement*, a mixed gathering of persons or things.

hustler ('hʌslə(r)). [f. hustle *v.* + -er¹.]

1. One who takes part in hustling a person; one of a gang of pickpockets who work on this plan. Also, a thief, a criminal; one who makes his living dishonestly or by begging; a pimp. *slang.*

1825 Knapp & Baldw. *Newgate Cal.* IV. 295/2 Known as a hustler. **1914** Jackson & Hellyer *Vocab. Criminal Slang* 47 *Hustler*,..a grafter; a pimp who steals betimes. The

genteel thief is designated a 'hustler'. **1926** *Clues* Nov. 161/2 *Hustler*, members of the underworld in general. **1953** W. BURROUGHS *Junkie* (1972) 158 *Pop corn*, someone with a legitimate job, as opposed to a 'hustler' or thief. **1957** C. MACINNES *City of Spades* II. ix. 164 They's wreckage of jazz musicians.., ponces, and other hustlers like myself... I pimp around the town, picking the pounds up where I can. **1972** *Observer* 20 Aug. 7/4 Once, the hustler was the odd man out.

2. a. orig. *U.S.* An extremely energetic or 'pushing' person. Also, a salesman, esp. one who is energetic or aggressive. **b.** *U.S.* A 'hustling' storm.

1882 T. G. BOWLES *Flotsam & Jetsam* (1883) 245 The sky ..had that dull, leaden, greasy look which usually portends a real good hustler. **1886** *Publishers' Weekly* 18 Dec. 965/1 Young man, a 'hustler' in every respect, wants a strictly first-class position with a 'live' book house. **1890** *Pall Mall G.* 5 Mar. 7/2 They have a word here to describe the typical New York man. They say he is a hustler. It..means a person in a condition of nervous hurry, and they are all hustlers here. **1891** *Grip* (Toronto) 18 Mar. 254/1 An enterprising down East Hustler lately conceived the idea of crowding the 'Best Fifty Books' into one volume, and selling the same by subscription. **1907** F. H. BURNETT *Shuttle* xxiii. 235 I'm not passing myself off as anything but an ordinary business hustler..—just under salesman to a typewriter concern. **1907** *Westm. Gaz.* 6 Sept. 4/1 His proper title is The Hustler, and his real business is to hustle from morning till night every man and woman..connected with the business. **1926** *Daily Colonist* (Victoria, B.C.) 10 Jan. 32/3 (Advt.), Hustler wanted, 25 years or older, to sell a high-grade appliance. **1954** A. M. BEZANSON *Sodbusters invade Peace* 194 Chris was a hustler, and brought to our partnership a type of aggressiveness I lacked. **1971** *Black World* Apr. 38/1 He pulls in £1,500 some weeks, and he's a *small-time* hustler.

c. A prostitute. *slang.*

1924 G. C. HENDERSON *Keys to Crookdom* 408 *Hustler*, prostitute. **1929** D. HAMMETT *Red Harvest* iii. 27 'Who is this Dinah Brand?'..'A soiled dove..a de luxe hustler, a big-league gold-digger.' **1952** J. STEINBECK *East of Eden* 436 They would think she was just a buzzed old hustler. **1960** P. GOODMAN *Growing up Absurd* (1961) ix. 194 The juvenile delinquents, like the hustlers (male prostitutes), fancy themselves as movie heroes in sports cars. **1970** *Women Speaking* Apr. 4/2 Man keeps her on the defensive by a constant barrage of insulting words that describe her in sexual terms:..hustler, slut.

hustling ('hʌslɪŋ), *vbl. sb.*[1] [f. HUSTLE *v.* + -ING[1].] **a.** The action of the verb HUSTLE in various senses.

1760 J. ADAMS *Diary* 2 June Wks. 1850 II. 86, I had no.. companions for pleasure, either in walking, riding, drinking, hustling, or any thing else. **1797** *Sporting Mag.* X. 198 Amusing himself with pricking in the belt, hustling in the hat, &c. **1890** BOLDREWOOD *Col. Reformer* (1891) 154 It [a horse] took a little hustling to prevent his being distanced. **1897** *Daily News* 30 July 7/1 The first woman to cross over the divide..She did much 'hustling' in the winter, and she showed a noble pair of moose antlers as a trophy of her skill with the rifle.

b. Robbery, esp. with violence.

1823 'J. BEE' *Slang* 102 *Hustling*, forcible robbery, by two or more thieves seizing their victim round the body, or at the collar. **1826** *New Newgate Calendar* V. 337 Transported for hustling. **1972** *Observer* 20 Aug. 7/4 'Hustling' has been growing steadily for years... By 1968,.. of 150 cases of bag-snatching, 87 were alleged to have been committed by black youths.

c. Prostitution, soliciting as a prostitute.

1924 G. C. HENDERSON *Keys to Crookdom* 408 *Hustling*, streetwalking. **1938** 'M. BENNEY' *Scapegoat Dances* vi. 77 Bond Street might be better. There's good 'ustling there. **1959** ANON. *Streetwalker* iv. 85, I had to use the flat for hustling. **1969** *Jeremy* I. III. 22/2 *Hustling*, working as a male prostitute.

†**hustling**, *vbl. sb.*[2] *Obs. rare*[−1]. [? Echoic: cf. *rustle.*] Clashing, hurtling; ? rustling.

1513 DOUGLAS *Æneis* XII. xii. 7 The husling in [*ed.* **1553** hussilling of] his armour dyd rebund And kest a terribill or a feirfull sound [Virgil, *horrendumque intonat armis*].

hustling ('hʌslɪŋ), *ppl. a.* [f. HUSTLE *v.* + -ING[2].] That hustles, pushing.

1871 PALGRAVE *Lyr. Poems* 11 The low bee-hive bench, the trough Of hustling swine. **1896** *Boston* (Mass.) *Jrnl.* 4 Jan. 10/5 It..is more like the hustling United States dailies than the other Mexican dailies.

huswife, etc.: see HOUSEWIFE, etc.

hut (hʌt), *sb.* Also 7–9 **hutt.** [First in 17th c.; a. F. *hutte* (16–17th c. D'Aubigné in Hatz.-Darm., 1611 in Cotgr.), a. MHG., Ger. *hütte*, OHG. *hutta, huttea*, hut, perh.:—OTeut. **hudjā*, f. root *hud-*, *hūd-* of OE. *hýdan* to hide. A specific HG. word which has passed into LG., Du., and Swedish, as well as the Romanic langs. and Eng.; perh. as a word of the camp: cf. sense 1 b.]

1. a. A dwelling of ruder and meaner construction and (usually) smaller size than a house, often of branches, turf, or mud, such as is inhabited in primitive societies, or constructed for temporary use by shepherds, workmen, or travellers. In Australia, applied to the cottages of stock-men: cf. *hut-keeper* in 4.

1658 EVELYN *Fr. Gard.* (1675) 100 A small hutt of fern or straw. **1669** WORLIDGE *Syst. Agric.* (1681) 327 *Hut*, a small Hovel or Cottage. **1697** DAMPIER *Voy.* I. ii. 16 The next night came on before we could build more Hutts, so we lay straggling in the Woods. **1717** LADY M. W. MONTAGU *Let. to Abbé Conti* 1 Apr., Their houses are nothing but little huts, raised of dirt baked in the sun. **1726–46** THOMSON *Winter* 337 How many shrink into the sordid hut Of cheerless Poverty! **1775** JOHNSON *Journ. West. Isl.*, *Ostig* Wks. X. 439 By a *house* I mean a building with one story over another: by a *hut*, a dwelling with only one floor. **1837** W. IRVING *Capt. Bonneville* II. 219 They proceeded until they came to some Indian huts. **1844** *Port Phillip Patriot* 11 July 1/3 At head station are a three-roomed hut, large kitchen, wool shed [etc.]. **1893** *Bookman* June 86/1 Dining off black bread..in a Swiss peasant's hut.

b. *Milit.* A wooden structure for the temporary housing of troops. (App. the earlier use.)

1545 *State Papers, Hen. VIII* X. 609 The French armey ..having broken up their campe and brent all their huittes, removed..towardes Arde. **1665** SIR T. HERBERT *Trav.* (1677) 120 Within the Fort are many small houses or huts which lodge the Souldiers. *a* **1674** CLARENDON *Hist. Reb.* ix. §63 Above a thousand Deal-boards, to make huts for the Soldiers. **1704** J. HARRIS *Lex. Techn.*, *Barack*, is an Hutt like a little Cottage, for Soldiers to lie in, in the Camp: Formerly those for the Horse were called *Baracks*, and those for the Foot *Hutts.* **1706** PHILLIPS (ed. Kersey), *Hut*,..a Soldier's Lodge in the Field. **1882** MRS. EWING *Story Short Life* ii, The huts for married men and officers were of varying degrees of comfort and homeliness, but those for single men were like toy-boxes of wooden soldiers.

†**c.** A beaver's 'lodge'. *Obs.*

1722 D. COXE *Carolina* 48 Most Parts of North-America have Beavours; you shall scarce meet with a Lake, where there are not some of their Dams and Hutts.

†**2.** *transf.* The shell of a tortoise. *Obs.*

1698 FRYER *Acc. E. India & P.* 122 The Tortoise..the Neck reaching as far as the Hut, soft and undefensible. *Ibid.* Index Explanatory, *Callipat*, the Hut of the Tortoise.

3. The back end or body of the breech-pin of a musket.

1867 SMYTH *Sailor's Word-bk.*, *Hutt*, the breech-pin of a gun. **1868** *Act 31 & 32 Vict.* c. xiii. Sched. B, The Barrels ..shall be smoothed in the finished State, with the Breeches in the percussioned State, Huts filled up.

4. *attrib.* and *Comb.*, *as* ***hut-building***, ***-circle***, ***-door***, ***-life***, ***-tax***, ***-village***; ***hut-shaped*** adj.; **hut circle** *Archæol.*, a circle of earth or stones indicating the circumference of a previously existing hut; **hut-hold**, the inmates of a hut; so **hut-holder**, the occupant of a hut (after *household*, *-er*); **hut-keeper**, one who keeps or guards a hut; *esp.*, in Australia, one who looks after the huts on a station while the occupants are away at work; hence **hut-keep** *v.*, **hut-keeping** *vbl. sb.*; **hut-shooter**, one who shoots from a hut; **hut-urn**, a cinerary urn of the shape of a hut.

1807 P. GASS *Jrnl.* 174 We continued at our *hut-building. **1865** LUBBOCK *Preh. Times* 63 There are..other remains of great interest, such, for example, as..the '*Hut-circles'. **1913** *Rep. Brit. Assoc. Adv. Sci.* 205 The district is rich in prehistoric remains, including some hut circles. **1963** W. F. GRIMES in Foster & Alcock *Culture & Environment* v. 105 There is the likelihood of confusion with hut-circles or barrow-rings, or even with small defensive earthworks. **1906** *Macmillan's Mag.* Nov. 13 He went back to the fire, drawing the *hut-door close. **1866** CARLYLE *Remin.* (1881) I. 126 Boatman and *huthold were in bed. **1886** *Belgravia* Feb. 417 Each *hutholder..sweeps up and burns all the *débris* that may have accumulated during the day. **1897** MARY KINGSLEY *W. Africa* 112 We made for a group of *hut-homesteads and chatted with the inhabitants. **1865** S. SIDNEY *Three Colonies Australia* (ed. 2) 380 (Morris) At every other station I have called at, a woman '*hut-keeps', while the husband is minding the sheep. **1794** G. THOMPSON *Slavery & Famine* (1947) 37 The women [convicts] have a more comfortable life than the men; those who are not fortunate enough to be selected for wives..are made *hut-keepers. **1802** BARRINGTON *Hist. N.S. Wales* x. 390 Hut-keepers to remain at home and prevent robbery, while the other inhabitants of the hut were at labour. **1911** C. E. W. BEAN *'Dreadnought' of Darling* xi. 98 In the early days in Australia..they used to have shepherds..men living out in lonely huts twenty miles back on the run, generally with a hutkeeper to mind their little log 'humpy'. **1890** *Melbourne Argus* 14 June 4/2 Did I go *hutkeeping? Did you ever know a hutkeeper cook for sixty shearers? **1882** MRS. EWING *Story Short Life* ii, Simple and sociable ways of living, necessitated by *hut-life in common. **1857** BIRCH *Anc. Pottery* (1858) II. 145 The old *hut-shaped vases of the Alban lake. **1855** J. W. COLENSO *Ten Weeks in Natal* p. xxviii, This *hut-tax was first sanctioned by Earl Grey in 1848. **1884** *Nonconf. & Indep.* 28 Feb. 213/2 The cost.. being defrayed by a hut-tax. **1935** G. GREENE *Basement Room* 120 Chief say no white man been here long time.. since he pay hut tax. **1969** *Tanzania Notes & Records* July 10 Every adult male native not liable to hut-tax..had to pay 1–3 rupees a year. **1865** LUBBOCK *Preh. Times* ii. (1878) 53 '*Hut-urns'..or urns in the form of huts.

hut (hʌt), *v.* [a. F. *hutter* refl., to make a hut for one's lodging, f. *hutte*: see prec. sb.]

1. *trans.* To place in a hut or huts; to furnish with a hut or huts; to place (troops, etc.) in huts, esp. for winter quarters.

1652 COTTERELL *Cassandra* III. III. (1676) 272 Souldiers, who made an end of hutting themselves. **1758** SMOLLETT *Hist. E.* (1841) III. xxvi. 300 They were obliged to hut their camp, and remain in the open fields till January. **1834** *Blackw. Mag.* XXXV. 758 We might have..been hutted.. in some deplorable inn. **1865** CARLYLE *Fredk. Gt.* XVIII. xiv. VIII. 63 He makes his people hut themselves (weather wet and bad). **1879** DIXON *Brit. Cyprus* xiii. 124 Some of the men are hutted, but the officers are still in tents. **1894** J. WINSOR *Cartier to Frontenac* 288 In the neighborhood there were a few New England Indians hutted for the winter.

b. *trans.* 'To put up (grain) in the field in a small stack' (Jam.).

1805 R. W. DICKSON *Pract. Agric.* (1807) II. 286 The hutting of grain in the field is mostly had recourse to in late wet harvests. *Ibid.* 794 Gaiting and hutting corn.

2. *intr.* To lodge or take shelter in a hut or huts; to go into winter quarters.

1807 WILKINSON in Pike *SourcesIssiss.* II. (1810) App. 29 The men solicited me to hut. **1849** SIR C. J. NAPIER in *Life* (1859) 148 Gough may hut, yet that will hardly do I fear. **1881** *Mem. G. Thomson* ix. 126 At the end of the hamlet where we hutted, I observed a neat little fence.

Hence **'hutting** *vbl. sb.*

1805 [see 1 b]. **1869** E. A. PARKES *Pract. Hygiene* (ed. 3) 526 Not merely trench work, but hutting, cooking, washing. **1898** *Daily News* 14 Mar. 5/6 The troops are engaged in hutting with grass from the west bank. **1937** *Discovery* Mar. 70/1 The irregularities of the hutting area. **1945** W. S. CHURCHILL *Victory* (1946) 108 Full hutting..is nearing completion.

hut (hʌt), *int.* A call to a horse (see quots.).

1856 *N. & Q.* 2nd Ser. I. 395 When a horse forgets what he is doing, and becomes careless, he is reminded of his duty by a sharp *hut.* **1899** *Pall Mall Mag.* Feb. 262 'Hut, you beast!' he added, as Englishmen do, when the mare nuzzled into his neck.

hut, obs. 3rd sing. pres. ind. of HIDE *v.*[1]

hut(t: see HOT *sb.*[1] 3, a roll for a cock's spur.

hutch (hʌtʃ), *sb.* Forms: 4–6 **huche,** (4 **houche,** 4–5 **hucch(e, hoche,** 5 **husche, huch),** 5–7 **hutche,** (6 **hotche),** 5– **hutch.** [ME. *huche, hucche*, a. F. *huche* (13th c. in Littré; also *huge* 12–13th c. in Hatz.-Darm.):—med.L. *hūtica* ('cista vulgo *Hutica* dicta', 11th c. in Du Cange): ulterior etymology obscure, referred by some to Ger. *hut*, OHG. *huota* care, keeping, *hüten* to watch, guard (see HEED). In ME., *hucche* ran together more or less with *whucche, whicche*:—OE. *hwicce* in same sense: see WHITCH *sb.*]

1. a. A chest or coffer, in which things are stored.

1303 R. BRUNNE *Handl. Synne* 6230 To ley hyt vp..Oþer yn cofre, oþer yn hucche. *c* **1440** *Promp. Parv.* 242/1 Hoche, or whyche (*S.* husch, *H., P.*, hoche, hutche), *cista, archa.* **1455** *Paston Lett.* No. 257 I. 351 His menye robbe his chambre, and ryfled his huches. **1495** *Trevisa's Barth. De P.R.* XVIII. cv. (W. de W.), Leues of the Lauri tree of Cedres and of Cipresse..put amonge clothes in hutches [*Bodl. MS.* whucches] saue the clothes..fro corrupcyon and etynge of moughtes. **1536** *Rem. Sedition* 22 a, To gyue him money out of the comune hutche, to bye hym botis and showes. **1593** NASHE *Christ's T.* 85 a, An old Vsurer..rakes vp thirty or forty thousande pounds together in a hutch. **1642** J. LANGTON in *Lismore Papers* Ser. II. (1888) V. 48 Some money was founde..hidd in the hutches of Otmeale. **1742** *Lond. & Country Brew.* I. (ed. 4) 5 From the Cistern, it [the malt] is put into a square Hutch or Couch, where it must lie thirty Hours. **1789** BRAND *Hist. Newcastle* I. 421 *note*, Amongst the writings in the town's hutch. **1872** RILEY in *3rd Rep. Hist. MSS. Comm.* 341/2 The various documents ..from the various lockers, and the ancient hutch, or chest in which they are preserved.

fig. **1585** ABP. SANDYS *Serm.* xiv. §28 All knowledge is shut vp..in the hutch of his breast.

†**b.** Applied to the 'ark of God'. *Obs.*

c **1315** SHOREHAM 51 Ine the ealde lawe beren hy The hoche of holy crefte. *a* **1340** HAMPOLE *Psalter* cxxxi. 8 þou & þe huche of þi halighynge. *c* **1400** MAUNDEV. (1839) viii. 85 That Arke or Hucche, with the Relikes, Tytus ledde with hym to Rome.

2. a. A box or box-like pen or 'house' in which an animal is confined, as a *rabbit-hutch.*

1607 TOPSELL *Four-f. Beasts* (1658) 171 These Ferrets are kept in little hutches, in houses. **1666** J. DAVIES *Hist. Caribby Isls* 139 They retreat, as the Conies do into their Clappers or Hutches. **1803** J. KENNY *Society* 152 A rabbit who had all his life been pent within a hutch. **1879** J. WRIGHTSON in *Cassell's Techn. Educ.* IV. 70/2 Immediately the calf is born, it is removed to a suitable hutch or crib.

b. A small confined place or compartment occupied by a human being; applied contemptuously to a hut or cabin, or humorously to a small house.

1607 TOPSELL *Four-f Beasts* (1658) 372 In a very spacious field there are little hutches built of that height as a man may stand upright in them: every one of these is shut with a little gate. **1719** DE FOE *Crusoe* I. viii, I cannot express what a satisfaction it was to me to come into my old hutch. **1880** KINGLAKE *Crimea* VI. vi. 140 The French army..mainly used the 'tente d'abri', a low canvas hutch which was a miserable substitute for the ordinary tent. **1893** *Westm. Gaz.* 4 July 5/1 It is probably cheaper to have such a private 'hutch' than to pay for five or six seats in the legitimate stands.

3. Technical. **a.** A salmon coop, crib, or cruive. **b.** Short for *bolting-hutch* (see BOLTING *vbl. sb.*[1] 3). **c.** A kneading trough. **d.** A box trap. **e.** A box for washing ore. **f.** A box-like carriage, wagon, truck, etc., used for transport purposes in agriculture, mining, etc. **g.** As a measure: see quots.

a. 1602 CAREW *Cornwall* 28 b, The Sammons principall accesse is betweene Michaelmas and Christmas..The.. more profitable meanes of their taking, is by hutches.

b. 1619 B. JONSON *Pleas. reconciled to Virtue*, The plough and the flail, the mill and the hopper, The hutch and the boulter, the furnace and copper. **1875** KNIGHT *Dict. Mech.*, *Hutch*..2. (*Milling.*) The case of a flour bolt.

c. 1658 tr. *Porta's Nat. Mag.* IV. xix. 146 The next day cast it [dough] into a Hutch, and adde more meal to it.

d. 1669 WORLIDGE *Syst. Agric.* (1681) 329 *Hutch*..also a trap made hollow for the taking of Weasels, or such like

Vermin alive. **1772** T. SIMPSON *Vermin Killer* 4 Some make vse..of wooden traps, called hutches.

e. **1881** RAYMOND *Mining Gloss.*, *Hutch*..2. A cistern or box for washing ore. *Cornw.*

f. **1744–50** W. ELLIS *Mod. Husbandm.* IV. III. 42 [They] carry [pease] home in a hutch-waggon, as they call it here [Sandwich, Kent]. **1792** A. YOUNG *Trav. France* (1794) I. I. 84 Driving a one-horse booby hutch about the streets. **1796** J. BOYS *Agric. Kent* (1813) 54 The carriages used for carrying corn to market, &c. are called hutches, drawn by four horses..They are thirteen feet long..generally three feet wide before, and four behind at the bottom..and twenty [inches] deep. **1825–80** JAMIESON, *Hutch*, the kind of basket or small waggon, in which coals are brought from the mine. *Lanarks.*, *Renfr.* **1891** *Labour Commission Gloss.*, *Hutches or Tubs*, small waggons into which the miner loads his coal.

g. **1802** C. FINDLATER *Agric. Surv. Peebles* 140 Dung is..emptied from carts into every third furrow, in small heaps (or *hutches*), five or six of such hutches being contained in a single-horse cart. **1812** J. WILSON *Agric. Surv. Renfr.* 26 The price of these pyrites or copperas stones, by old contract, was 2½*d.* per hutch, of two hundred weight. **1825–80** JAMIESON s.v., The coal hutch is two Winchester bushels. **1858** SIMMONDS *Dict. Trade* s.v., Six hutches of coal make a cart-load of about 14 cwt.

4. *attrib.*, as ***hutch box*** (see 3 a), ***trap*** (see 3 d); **hutch table** *N. Amer.* (see quot. 1961).

1744–50 [see 3 f]. **1846** J. BAXTER *Libr. Pract. Agric.* (ed. 4) II. 371 The common or hutch trap may be used with effect..where but a few vermin prevail. *Ibid.* 372 The weasel..may be readily caught by hutch or box traps. **1868** *Law Rep.* Q. Bench Div. III. 288 A hutch-box, crib, or enclosed place in connection with a fishing mill-dam. **1928** W. NUTTING *Furnit. Treas.* Illustration 1770 (*caption*) Pine Chair Table. More Properly Hutch Table on Shoes..18th Century. **1961** WEBSTER, *Hutch table*, a combination table and chest whose top can be tilted back to convert the unit into a chair or settee. **1970** *Globe & Mail* (Toronto) 25 Sept. 37/3 (Advt.), Genuine antique Canadiana pine turn-over hutch table, oval 72″.

†**hutch**, *a.* *Obs.* [app. a phonetic variant of HULCH *a.*; but cf. also HUCK-.] Hunched, humped, gibbous: chiefly in ***hutch back***. Also in *comb.* in ***hutch-back'd***, hump-backed, ***hutch-shouldered***, hump-shouldered.

1624 HEYWOOD *Gunaik.* II. 115 Some..with crooked legges, and hutch-backes, rather like monsters than men. —— *Captives* II. ii. in Bullen *O. Pl.* IV, An ould bald fellowe, hutch-shoolderd. **1632** —— *1st Pt. Iron Age* III. i. Fijb, What if Thersites..striu'd to hide his hutch-backe. **1668** H. MORE *Div. Dial.* II. xiii. 249 The Acephali..might be nothing but some strong hutch-back'd People.

hutch, *v.* Also 6 huch. [f. prec. sb.]

1. a. *trans.* To put or lay up in a hutch or chest. Also *fig.*

1574 HELLOWES *Gueuara's Fam. Ep.* (1584) 254 To huch up double Ducates, to tell golde. **1634** MILTON *Comus* 719 In her own loins She hutched the all-worshipped ore, and precious gems To store her children with. **1863** LD. LYTTON *Ring Amasis* II. 213 Hutched among the gray and dewy slabs, in the bloomy bottom of the glen, the old brown mill was crouching by his spectral wheel.

b. *intr.* To crouch or squat. Also *trans.*, with *body* (or the like) as object. Freq. as *pa. pple.* or *ppl. a.*

In restricted regional use.

1874 E. WAUGH *Chimney Corner* (1879) 151, I wonder how thou can for shame..sit keawerin' theer, hutch't of a lump, like garden-twod. **1892** MRS. H. WARD *Hist. David Grieve* vi. 139 Hutched thegither like an owd man o' seventy. **1894** J. T. CLEGG *David's Loom* v. 58 Fortin' hutches at mi feet! **1898** —— *Works* II. 302 So poor Ab were as ill off as afore, an' hutcht into his corner in a face as long as a bass fiddle. **1905** W. B. *Where White Man Treads* 76 He will..hutch on his heels and watch, and comment. *Ibid.* 161 When we arrived, Taupoki hutched down on his heels without greeting, and fixed his eyes on George's boot-trees. **1918** D. H. LAWRENCE *New Poems* 35 Sleep-suave limbs of a youth with long smooth thighs Hutched-up for warmth. **1956** W. GOLDING *Pincher Martin* 7 He hutched his body towards the place where air had been but now it was gone. **1959** —— *Free Fall* ix. 170 Busily I hutched along the walls, knees down, hands against concrete.

2. To wash (ore) in a hutch (HUTCH *sb.* 3 e).

In recent Dicts.

†**hutchet**. *Her. Obs.* [ad. F. *huchet* (15th c. in Godef.), f. *hucher* to call or summon.] A hunter's horn; a bugle.

1572 BOSSEWELL *Armorie* II. 36 Beareth Sable, a Cheuron betwene three Huchettes D'argent. **1610** GUILLIM *Heraldry* VI. i. (1660) 384 A Hutchet or Hunters horn Argent. **1611** COTGR., *Cornette*, a Bugle, Hutchet, or little Horne. *a* **1661** FULLER *Worthies*, *Yorksh.* III. (1662) 224 A Hutchet or Bugle Argent.

Hutchinson ('hʌtʃɪnsən). The name of Sir Jonathan *Hutchinson* (1828–1913), English surgeon, used in the possessive (and also *attrib.*) to designate various diseases, diagnostic signs, etc., as **Hutchinson('s) tooth** (the condition of having) a permanent incisor tooth, often in the middle of the upper set, with a narrow, notched biting edge, found chiefly in children with congenital syphilis; usu. *pl.*; **Hutchinson('s) triad**, a rare triad comprising Hutchinson's teeth, interstitial keratitis, and eighth-nerve deafness, diagnostic of congenital syphilis.

1890 BILLINGS *Med. Dict.* I. 656/1 Hutchinson's teeth. **1906** *Dental Rev.* Jan. 12, I have seen several cases of typical Hutchinson teeth that were certainly in no way connected with a syphilitic taint. **1908** *Practitioner* Jan. 5 He had well-marked Hutchinson's teeth. **1908** E. L. KEYES *Syphilis* xxxvi. 533 Hutchinson's triad, consisting of dental, ocular, and auditory stigmata. **1949** H. T. KARSNER *Human Path.* (ed. 7) xvi. 547/2 The Hutchinson tooth has normal width at the gum line with sides tapering to an incisal edge of diminished mesiodistal dimensions. **1968** A. J. ROOK *Textbk. Dermatol.* I. xxii. 704/2 Interstitial keratitis, Hutchinson's teeth and eighth-nerve deafness form 'Hutchinson's triad'.

Hutchinsonian (hʌtʃɪn'səʊnɪən), *a.* and *sb.* [See -IAN.]

A. *adj.* **1. a.** Of or pertaining to John Hutchinson (died 1737), a writer on natural philosophy, who interpreted the Bible mystically, and opposed the Newtonian philosophy. **b.** Of or according to Anne Hutchinson (died 1643), an antinomian teacher in New England.

1765 WESLEY *Jrnl.* 9 Oct., Mr. Jones..seems to have totally overthrown the Newtonian Principles. But whether he can establish the Hutchinsonian, is another Question. **1844** W. H. MILL *Serm. Tempt. Christ* Notes 155 The doctrine of the Hutchinsonian School..which presumes..to teach that the relations of Father, Son, and Holy Ghost, are merely official in the œconomy of redemption. **1894** W. WALKER *Hist. Congreg. Ch. U.S.A.* 215 The Hutchinsonian dispute, in the early days of Massachusetts.

2. (Also ***hutchinsonian.***) *Med.* Of an incisor tooth: having the characteristic appearance described s.v. *Hutchinson('s) tooth* (see prec.).

1900 C. H. MAY *Man. Dis. Eye* viii. 126 These changes are especially marked in the upper central incisor teeth (Hutchinsonian teeth). **1930** JEANS & COOKE *Prepubescent Syphilis* x. 220 The typical hutchinsonian teeth may be associated with a syphilitic lesion in the premaxillae. **1957** S. L. ROBBINS *Textbk. Path.* xx. 698/2 The following may occur singly or together in congenital syphilis: the Hutchinsonian incisor..and the 'mulberry molar'.

B. *sb.* An adherent of either of the above (sense A. 1).

1753 *Scots Mag.* Oct. 528/2 It appears to be written by an Hutchinsonian. **1770** WESLEY *Jrnl.* 30 Aug., Both of those are Hutchinsonians. **1882–3** SCHAFF *Encycl. Relig. Knowl.* III. 2058 A Hutchinsonian in science and learning, he was, nevertheless, chosen professor of astronomy in Gresham College.

Hence **Hutchin'sonianism**.

1860 J. GARDNER *Faiths World* II. 95/2 Mr. Catcott of Bristol..wrote a defence of Hutchinsonianism in Latin.

hutchinsonite ('hʌtʃɪnsənaɪt). *Min.* [f. the name of Arthur *Hutchinson* (1866–1937), English mineralogist + -ITE[1].] A sulpharsenite of lead and thallium $(Tl, Pb)_2As_5S_9$, often with some copper and silver, that occurs as small red orthorhombic crystals.

1905 R. H. SOLLY in *Mineral. Mag.* XIV. 72 Hutchinsonite usually occurs as very small crystals in the white dolomite, or is closely associated with sartorite and rathite. **1954** *Mineral Abstr.* XII. 452 Hutchinsonite..is now described from the Segen Gottes Pb-Zn mine at Wiesloch, where it occurs as minute (usually 1μ) needles embedded in calcite, blende, pyrite, &c., with associated Pb sulpharsenites.

†**hute**. *Obs. rare.* [A variant of HUE *sb.*[2] The inserted *t* is found also in AFr. *huteys* and the AngloL. *hutesium* = *huesium*, OF. *hueis*, *hueys* outcry: its origin is obscure.] Outcry; = HUE *sb.*[2]

[**1276** *Act 4 Edw. I* (Office of Coroner) Similiter de omnibus homicidiis..levetur Hutesium. **1292** BRITTON I. xxx. §3 Il porount enquere..de huteys a tort levé.] **1534** *Act 26 Hen. VIII*, c. 5 §1 Any outcrie, hute, or fresshe suite of or for anie felonie.

huther-muther, var. of HUDDER-MUDDER.

hutia (hu:'ti:ə). Also **houtia**, **jutia**, **utia**. [a. Sp. *hutía*, f. Taino *huti*, *cuti*.] Any of several rodents of the family Capromyidæ, including *Capromys* and closely related genera, native to Cuba, the West Indies, and northern South America.

[**1793** B. EDWARDS *Hist. Brit. Colonies W. Indies* I. I. 90 The *agouti* is sometimes called *couti*, and *coati*. It was corrupted into *uti* and *utia*, by the Spaniards.] **1834** H. MCMURTRIE tr. *Cuvier's Animal Kingdom* 84 The Houtias have four molars. **1839** *Penny Cycl.* XV. 509/2 According to Bomare, the Utias is a species of rabbit of the size of a rat, which inhabits the West Indies. **1851** P. H. GOSSE *Naturalist's Sojourn Jamaica* 468 (*heading*) The Utia, or Indian Cony. *Ibid.* 469 A few years ago M. Fournier brought to Europe specimens of the animal which still bears in Cuba the name of Utia. **1877** *Encycl. Brit.* VI. 680/2 The only peculiar quadruped known in the island [of Cuba] is the *jutia* or *hutia*. **1939** *Geogr. Jrnl.* XCIII. 275 There exists on this island [*sc.* Swan Island] the hutia or capromys, a curious guinea-pig-like rodent of which only some four species are known. **1971** L. MATTHEWS *Life of Mammals* II. vii. 213 The family Capromyidae contains the coypu and the hutias, the latter name spelt 'jutia' in Spanish. *Ibid.* 214 Hutias are stout bodied, short limbed, rat-like rodents.

†**hutit**, *ppl. a.* *Sc. Obs.* Also 6 **huttit**. [See HOOT *v.* 2.] Execrated, execrable, abominable.

c **1500** *Roull's Cursing* 47 in Laing *Sel. Rem. Pop. Poetry Scot.*, Ffluxis, hyvis, or huttit ill, Hoist, heidwark, or fawin ill. **1513** DOUGLAS *Æneis* VII. x. 65 This hutit Goddes [*invisum numen*]. *Ibid.* VIII. iv. 33 Onto this hutit monstre, this Cacus.

hutment ('hʌtmənt). [f. HUT *v.* + -MENT.] Accommodation or lodging in huts; a hutted encampment.

1889 *Lancet* 30 Mar. 650/1 £14,230 for hutment for increased garrison at Malta. **1895** *Times* 9 Mar. 7/5 A company of infantry from the North Front hutments [Gibraltar]. **1898** *Daily News* 25 Aug. 5/2 A sea of white tents, brown blanket shelters, and nondescript grass hutments.

hutt, obs. form of HOT *sb.*[1] (sense 3), HUT.

†**hutte**. *Obs.* [Variant of HOT *sb.*[1]]

1. A clod (of earth).

c **1420** *Pallad. on Husb.* II. 188 With a shelle or hutte [*gleba*] adoun hem presse.

2. The mass of foam on a boiling surface.

? *c* **1390** *Form of Cury* in Warner *Antiq. Culin.* (1791) 13 Set it over the fire and boile it; and when the hutte arisith to goon over, take it adoun and kele it.

hutted ('hʌtɪd), *a.* [f. HUT *v.* or *sb.* + -ED.] Furnished with or consisting of huts.

1778 *Hist. Europe* in *Ann. Reg.* 212*/1 Enduring all the necessities of the season, under a hutted camp in the open field. **1885** R. HARTMANN *Anthrop. Apes* 294 A hutted encampment of the Obongo or the Doko. **1948** *Sci. News* VII. 45 A hutted laboratory has been established, as a centre for field studies at Rossdhu, Loch Lomond. **1955** *Times* 3 June 2/6 The transfer, from a hutted class-room overshadowed by the science block, has been entirely a matter of self-help. **1973** *Times* 11 Jan. 15/3 Charing Cross Hospital is certainly not a hutted structure.

Hutterite ('hʌtəraɪt), *sb.* (*a.*). [f. the name of Jacob *Hutter* (d. 1536), a Moravian Anabaptist + -ITE[1].] A member of an Anabaptist sect established by Jacob Hutter in Moravia, or of immigrant communities in North America having similar beliefs. Also **'Hutite**, **Huttite**. **b.** *attrib.* or as *adj.* Of, pertaining to, or holding the doctrines of, the Hutterites. Also **Hu't(t)erian** *a.*, esp. ***Hutterian Brethren***.

1645 E. PAGITT *Heresiography* (ed. 2) 33 Hutites, who boast themselves to be the only children of God, and heires of heaven. **1897** J. L. & E. G. MULLIKEN tr. *Kautsky's Communism in Cent. Europe* v. 214 The community of the Huterites in Moravia has the greatest significance in the history of socialism. **1924** *Jrnl. Pol. Econ.* XXXII. 472 Huterian communities were established all over Moravia. **1931** J. HORSCH *Hutterian Brethren* i. 10 In the matter of the toleration of the Hutterian brethren there was a great principle at stake. *Ibid.* iii. 65 He warned the nobility who still had Hutterites in their service of the consequences, threatening them with imperial disfavor. **1935** R. J. SMITHSON *Anabaptists* xi. 205 The Anabaptists of the Reformation period survive to the present day not only in the Hutterites but also in the Mennonites. **1953** R. MOON *This is Saskatchewan* 75 To the northwest of Shaunavon are Hutterite communities. **1957** *Encycl. Brit.* IX. 90/2 The Hutterite Brethren, about 300 of whom settled in South Dakota in 1875–77 in three [farm] colonies, grew in size to 93 colonies in 1951. *Ibid.*, The Hutterites support themselves through diversified farming and stock raising. **1959** *Listener* 11 June 1039/1 The bizarre setting of a Hutterite community in Alberta. **1969** *Times* 9 Jan. 4/4 Today's 15,000 Hutterites, a Protestant sect descended from 440 pioneers who emigrated to North America in the 1870s, are expected to number more than 55 million by A.D. 2168 if the present rate of growth continues.

huttock, obs. and dial. var. HATTOCK.

Huttonian (hʌ'təʊnɪən), *a.* [See -IAN.]

A. *adj.* Of or relating to James Hutton the geologist (1726–1796), who maintained against Werner the igneous or 'plutonic' origin of unstratified rocks, as basalt, granite, etc.

1802 *Edin. Rev.* I. 206 Deducible from the..Huttonian hypothesis. **1802** PLAYFAIR (*title*) Illustrations of the Huttonian Theory. **1852** TH. ROSS *Humboldt's Trav.* I. xiv. 457 The partisans of the Huttonian or volcanic theory. **1859** J. HAMILTON *Mem. J. Wilson* i. 12 The discussion..between Wernerian and Huttonian theorists.

B. *sb.* An adherent of the geological principles advocated by Hutton.

1802 *Edin. Rev.* I. 202 The leading positions..of the Huttonians. **1815** W. PHILLIPS *Outl. Min. & Geol.* (1818) 196 These two parties are termed volcanists and neptunists: or more familiarly by geologists, Huttonians and Wernerians. **1876** PAGE *Adv. Text-bk. Geol.* vi. 113 The Huttonians or Vulcanists..advocated an igneous and eruptive origin for the traps, basalts, greenstones, and granites.

Hence **Hu'ttonianism**, the theory of Hutton.

1892 *Athenæum* 6 Aug. 181/3 Playfair constituted himself the apostle of Huttonianism.

huttonite ('hʌtənaɪt). *Min.* [f. the name of Colin Osborne *Hutton* (b. 1910), the American mineralogist born in New Zealand + -ITE[1].] A silicate of thorium, $ThSiO_4$, that occurs as colourless or very pale cream monoclinic crystals.

1950 A. PABST in *Nature* 22 July 157/2 The name 'huttonite' is proposed for a newly recognized monoclinic mineral of the composition $ThSiO_4$. **1957** *Amer. Mineralogist* XLII. 764 We also have synthesized huttonite hydro-thermally. **1968** I. KOSTOV *Mineral.* 294 Huttonite is monoclinic.., isostructural with monazite $CePO_4$, and is dimorphous with thorite.

Hutu ('hu:tu:). Also **BaHutu**, **Bahutu**. [Bantu name. *Ba* is a plural prefix.] The name of a Bantu people which forms the majority of the population of Rwanda and of Burundi; one of these people. Also *attrib.* or as *adj.*

1959 *Times* 9 Nov. 8/6 The Bahutu were reported to be attacking houses and villages. **1964** H. J. DE BLIJ *Geogr. Subsaharan Afr.* xiv. 280/1 The BaHutu comprise perhaps 84 per cent of the total population of the combined countries, but they have been the serfs of the WaTusi. **1965** *Observer* 17 Jan. 2/1 As a Hutu, the Prime Minister tried to discourage the extremist Tutsis who..try to overthrow the Hutu Government of Rwanda. **1973** 'S. HARVESTER' *Corner of Playground* II. v. 109 Tutsi, known to Whitey as Watutsi, once overlords of Rwanda, whose ancestors..enslaved the Hutu people.

‖**hutung** ('hutuŋ). [Chin.] In northern Chinese cities: a narrow side-street, an alley.

1922 *Blackw. Mag.* Dec. 730/2 Old Sung, the curio-dealer of the Soochow *hutung*. **1923** *Ibid.* Dec. 726/2, I sat and listened to Pang the Soochow *hutung* dealer. **1960** *Times* 17 May 9/4 These hutungs—the lanes off Peking's still unkept main streets—are scarcely changed either. **1972** *Times* 6 Dec. 18/1 Modern buildings..provide a front for the old hutungs (side streets). *Ibid.* 18/2 In places the hutungs are only just wide enough for a man to pass.

huus, obs. f. HOUSE.

huve, var. HOUVE, HOVE.

huwe, obs. f. HEUGH, HOVE *v.*, HUE *sb.*[1]

huwyr, var. HURE, *Obs.*

†**hux.** *Obs. rare.* Also 1 husc. [OE. *hux*, *husc* = OS., OHG. *hosc*, of like meaning.] Mockery, scorn, derision. (Only OE. and early ME.)

a **1000** *Cædmon's Gen.* 2382 (Gr.) Heo..þone hleoðorcwyde husce belexde. *c* **1000** *Gloss.* in Wr.-Wülcker 513/11 *Per hironiam*, þurh hucx. *c* **1205** LAY. 28865 Hux and hoker me warp him on. *Ibid.* 29798 Hu Bruttissce biscopes hine grætte mid huxes.

b. *Comb.*, as *hux-word*. (Cf. OS. *hoscword.*)

a **1000** *Andreas* 669 (Gr.) Huscworde hyspan. *c* **1205** LAY. 21682 Mid heore hux worden [*c* **1275** hokere wordes].

†**huxen, huxon.** [Another form of *hoxen, HOX *sb.*, and HOCKSHIN, repr. OE. *hóhsinu* HOUGH-SINEW.] The hough or hock of a quadruped; the hough of a man.

1681 *Lond. Gaz.* No. 1677/4 A dapple Grey Gelding..a white spot above the Huxen of his further Leg behind. **1736–46** PEGGE *Kenticisms* (E.D.S.), *Huxon*, the same as Somers[et] *hucksheens*, i.e. the hocks or hams.

Huxham ('hʌksəm). The name of John *Huxham* (1692–1768), English physician, used in the possessive in **Huxham's tincture (of bark)**, compound tincture of cinchona bark, first described in Huxham's *Essay on Fevers* (1750) and formerly used as a bitter tonic and febrifuge; also *ellipt.* as **Huxham**.

1788 T. HEALDE tr. *New Pharmacopoeia R. Coll. Physicians London* 192 Tinctura corticis Peruviani composita... This medicine has been celebrated under the name of Huxham's Tincture. It is given as a corroborant and stomachic..to convalescents after long fevers; and sometimes, in larger doses, for the cure of agues in persons averse to taking Bark in substance. **1808** JANE AUSTEN *Let.* 15 June (1952) 190, I hope Huxham is a comfort to you; I am glad you are taking it. **1901** S. O. L. POTTER *Handbk. Materia Medica* (ed. 8) 271 Huxham's Tincture of Bark, 1788 (Unofficial), is still used. **1952** *Martindale's Extra Pharmacopœia* (ed. 23) I. 364 Tinctura Cinchonæ Composita (B.P.C.) *Syn.* Huxham's Tincture of Bark.

'**huxing.** [Derivation uncertain; in form a vbl. sb. of a vb. *hux, the existence of which is assumed by Ash, and in later Dicts.] A method of catching pike, by means of hooks suspended by lines from bladders.

1708–15 KERSEY, *Huxing of the Pike*, a particular way of taking that sort of Fish. **1727–41** in CHAMBERS *Cycl.* **1787** BEST *Angling* (ed. 2) 46 There is also a method to take pikes with, called Huxing. Take thirty or forty bladders, blow them up, and tie them close and strong; and at the mouth of each, tie a line..at the end of the lines, let hooks be armed ..the pike having taken the bait, will bounce about with the bladder, to the infinite diversion of all the spectators; when he is almost spent take him up.

Huxley ('hʌksli). The name of T. H. *Huxley* (1825–95), English biologist, used in the possessive in **Huxley's layer**, a layer, one or more cells thick, of horny flattened nucleated cells lying inside Henle's layer in the inner root-sheath of the hair follicle, described by him in 1845.

1853 BUSK & HUXLEY tr. *Kölliker's Man. Human Histol.* I. 187 These [cells] which form a simple or a double layer (*Huxley's* layer) are constantly situated internal to the common, and as far as I have seen, always single, fenestrated layer of cells. **1890** *Gray's Anat.* (ed. 12) 61 The inner root-sheath consists of a delicate cuticle next the hair; then of one or two layers of horny, flattened, nucleated cells, known as Huxley's layer, and finally of a single layer of non-nucleated, horny, cubical cells, called Henle's layer. **1954** *Physiol. Rev.* XXXIV. 115 Above the lower bulb region [of the hair follicle], immediately central to the external sheath, is Henle's layer of the internal sheath. Huxley's layer and the cuticle are next in order.

Huxleyan, Huxleian ('hʌksliən), *a.* [f. the name *Huxley* (see below) + -AN.] **a.** Of, pertaining to, or characteristic of T. H. Huxley (see prec.), or his work. Also as *sb.*

1889 E. DOWSON *Let.* 26 May (1967) 81 A reasonable Huxleian agnosticism is logical & consistent. **1901** *Science* 22 Mar. 453/2 Yet it is worth while, now and then, to take stock of advances subsequent to, and largely consequent on, the Huxleian declaration. **1907** W. JAMES *Meaning of Truth* (1909) vi. 154 Your genuine truth-lover must discourse in huxleyan heroics, and feel as if truth, to be real truth, ought to bring eventual messages of death to all our satisfactions. **1909** —— *Mem. & Stud.* (1911) viii. 186 The major premise is: 'Any spirit-revelation must be romantic.' The minor of the spiritist is: 'This *is* romantic'; that of the Huxleyan is: 'this is dingy twaddle.' **1939** *Jrnl. R. Anthrop. Inst.* LXIX. 148, I have descanted long enough on my Huxleian text, and hardly know whether I have vindicated or contravened its essential purport. **1973** *Nature* 22 June 436/1 The result is a true Huxleian tragedy—a beautiful and virtuous hypothesis butchered by a gang of ugly facts.

b. Of, pertaining to, or characteristic of Aldous Huxley, English novelist (1894–1963), or his work.

1934 *Punch* 9 May 531/1 It [*sc.* the travel book] opens..on a cruising liner, with some acid and Huxleyan comments on the people who frequent these modern portents. **1961** *Times* 11 Dec. 13/6 An Orwellian or Huxleian world, isolated, stream-lined, packaged. **1971** *Daily Tel.* (Colour Suppl.) 19 Mar. 39 His first 'serious' book, a futurist, slightly Huxleyan novel about life in 1980.

huxter, etc., obs. forms of HUCKSTER, etc.

huy, var. HI *pron.*; obs. f. HOY *sb.*, HUE *sb.*[2]

huyd, obs. pa. pple. of HIDE *v.*[1]

huydalgo, obs. f. HIDALGO.

huyde, obs. f. HIDE.

huydels, var. HIDELS, *Obs.*

huyfe, var. HOVE *sb.*[3] *Obs.*

Huygens ('haɪgənz). Also (erron.) **Huyghens**. The name of Christiaan *Huygens* (see HUYGHENIAN *a.*), used, chiefly in the possessive, to designate inventions, principles, etc., devised or enunciated by him, as **Huygens' construction**, the geometrical construction for finding the position of a wave front by using Huygens' principle; **Huygens' eyepiece**, a Huygenian eyepiece (see HUYGHENIAN *a.*); **Huygens' principle**, a principle of wave propagation, according to which each point on a wave front may be regarded as a source of new secondary waves, and the resultant effect of all these waves constitutes the propagation of the wave front, their envelope at a later time representing a new position of it.

[**1835** *Rep. Brit. Assoc. Adv. Sci. 1834* 308 The composition of the grand, or primary wave, by the union of the several secondary or partial waves, in this demonstration, has been denominated the principle of Huygens.] **1840** *Phil. Mag.* XVII. 243 (*heading*) On the application of Huyghens's principle in physical optics. **1899** W. WATSON *Text-bk. Physics* III. i. 353 The construction for finding the position..of the wave-front, at a time *t* by means of the tangent to a series of circles, the radius of each of which is equal to the space passed over by the wave in a time *t*, is due to Huyghens, and is known as Huyghens's construction for the wave-front. **1900** J. C. P. ALDOUS *Elem. Course Physics* x. 577 The chief negative eye-piece is Huyghens' eye-piece. **1957** *Encycl. Brit.* XV. 439/1 The Huygens eyepiece..is the most common type used with the microscope. **1959** BORN & WOLF *Princ. Optics* viii. 370 Fresnel was able to account for diffraction by supplementing Huygens' construction with the postulate that the secondary wavelets mutually interfere. **1970** M. V. KLEIN *Optics* i. 20 To follow the propagation of the optical disturbance..we have, in theory, only to make repeated applications of Huygens' principle. *Ibid.* 21 The Huygens construction.

Huyghenian (haɪ'giːnɪən), *a.* [f. *Huyghen-s* (see prec.) + -IAN.] Of or pertaining to Christiaan Huygens, a Dutch mathematician and astronomer (1629–95).

Huyghenian eyepiece, a negative eyepiece of an optical instrument invented by Huygens, consisting of two plano-convex lenses, with their plane sides towards the eye.

1704 J. HARRIS *Lex. Techn.* s.v. *Satellites*, The.. Hugenian Satellite, as 'tis called, because discovered first by Mr. Hugens, revolves round Saturn, in about 16 Days. **1837** GORING & PRITCHARD *Microgr.* 95 The pictures formed by deep achromatic triplet object-glasses acting with Huyghenian eye-pieces. **1867** J. HOGG *Microsc.* I. ii. 50 The Huyghenian eye-piece..is the best for merely optical purposes.

huyr(e, obs. ff. HIRE; var. HURE, *Obs.*, a cap.

huyssenite ('haɪsənaɪt). *Min.* [Named after Huyssen, its discoverer.] A greenish grey mineral, a borate of manganese and iron, from the salt mine at Stassfurt.

1863 DANA *Min.* (ed. 5) Suppl. 799.

huyst, obs. f. HUST, WHIST.

huyt, obs. f. HUED.

huyte, obs. f. WHITE.

huz, north. dial. f. US.

huzoor (hə'zʊə(r)). Also 8 huzzoor, huzur. [a. Arab. *hudūr* (pronounced in India as *huzūr*) presence (employed as a title), f. *hadara* to be present.] An Indian potentate; often used as a title of respect.

1776 *Trial of Joseph Fowke* Depositions 17/2[They] endeavour to lay their complaints before the Huzzoor. **1843** C. J. C. DAVIDSON *Diary Trav. Upper India* I. 77 The huzoor's countenance..is as immovably tranquil as that of Boodh. **1898** *Longman's Mag.* May 80 What pleasure hath this slave in life, save to do the Huzoor's will? **1899** KIPLING *Land & Sea Tales* (1923) 229 'Huzoor! (Your Highness!)' said Imam Din, stooping low. **1957** M. M. KAYE *Shadow of Moon* xxx. 438 'Be swift, my father,' said Niaz pleasantly. 'Do not keep the Huzoor waiting.'

huzz, *sb.* ? *Obs.* [Origin obscure. In the northern glossary to J. Hutton's 'Tour to the Caves' 1781, is '*Huzzin*, an husk'.] (See quot.)

1747 *Gentl. Mag.* 310 The smaller hulls, chaff and huzzes, that is, grains of corn in their hulls, passed thro' this wide wire grate.

huzz (hʌz), *int.* [Echoic.] A buzz.

1827 HARDMAN *Waterloo* 20 The sprouts of this twig will rustle out Huzz! While their verdant branch lies buried in the fuzz.

huzz (hʌz), *v.* Also 6 husz. [Echoic; see prec.: cf. *whizz.*] *intr.* (rarely *trans.*) To buzz. Hence '**huzzing** *vbl. sb.* and *ppl. a.*

1555 W. WATREMAN *Fardle Facions* I. vi. 94 Gnattes.. driue the Lions with their stingyng and terrible huszyng, cleane out of that quartre. **1557–8** PHAER *Æneid* VI. Riij b, As bees..With huzzing feruent noyse. **1616** SURFL. & MARKH. *Country Farme* 320 Whether you heare a great noise and huzzing within [the hive]. **1664** ETHEREDGE *Love in Tub* I. ii, Mrs. Graciana has flung a Squib into his bosom, where the Wild-fire will huzz for a time, and then, crack, it flies out. **1682** OTWAY *Venice Pres.* V. i. 67 The waves Huzzing and booming round my sinking head. **1747** *Gentl. Mag.* 381 Let not your vessel be..stopped close, until, by drawing it off, it be made to leave huzzing and sputtering. **1864** TENNYSON *North. Farmer (O.S.)* xvi, Wi' 'is kittle o' steäm Huzzin' an' maäzin' the blessed feälds wi' the Divil's oän teäm. **1894** F. S. ELLIS *Reynard* 70 Just as a big dragon fly Was huzzing-buzzing in his eye.

huzza (hʌ'zɑː, hʊ'zɑː), *int.* and *sb.* Also 6–8 **hussa**, 7 **hussaw**, 7– **huzzah**, **huzzay** (hʌ'zeɪ). [app. a mere exclamation, the first syllable being a preparation for, and a means of securing simultaneous utterance of the final (ɑː).

It is mentioned by many 17–18th c. writers as being originally a sailor's cheer or salute: 'It was derived from the marine and the shouts the seamen make when friends come aboard or go off' (North *Exam.* (1740) 617). It may therefore be the same as *heisau! hissa!* originally hauling or hoisting cries: see HEEZE *v.* quot. 1549 and HISSA. (German has also '*hussa* as a cry of hunting and pursuit, and, subsequently, of exultation.)]

A. *int.* A shout of exultation, encouragement, or applause; a cheer uttered by a number in unison; a hurrah.

1682 N. O. *Boileau's Lutrin* III. 33 Oh see (says Night) these Rogues sing Huzza! proud Of sure success, under my favouring Shroud. **1706** FARQUHAR *Recruit. Officer* I. i, Huzza then! huzza for the queen, and the honour of Shropshire! **1830** C. WORDSWORTH *Jrnl.* in Overton *Life* (1888) 50 Winchester beat Eton by sixty runs, huzza. **1855** THACKERAY *Rose & Ring* xix, Everybody was shouting, 'Huzzay! huzzay!.. Long live the King and Queen!'

B. *sb.* The shout of huzza; a shout of exultation or applause; a hurrah.

1573 G. HARVEY *Scholar's Love* in *Letter-bk.* (Camden) 115 Whattes now..My youthfulliste hollaes, hussaes, and sahoes, But wretchid allasses, godhelpes, and woes? **1665** EVELYN *Diary* 1 July, Went on board the Prince..she had 700 men. They made a great huzza or shout at our approch, 3 times. **1679** *Lond. Gaz.* No. 1372/4 At his passing over the Bridge, the Castle saluted him with five great Guns, and closed the farewel with three Hussaws, Seamen like. **1686** S. SEWALL *Diary* 25 Sept., Queen's birth-day..made a great fire in the evening, many hussas. **1688** WOOD *Life* 16 Dec. (O.H.S.) III. 289 Followed with a numerous company, with loud huzzaies. **1712** W. ROGERS *Voy.* 220 We saluted each of the other Ships with 3 Huzzas from on board her. **1734** POPE *Ess. Man* IV. 256 One self-approving hour whole years outweighs Of stupid starers and of loud huzzas. **1838** *Hist. Rec. 2nd Regt. Foot* 65 The battalion advanced with a British Huzza, and the enemy abandoned the redoubt and fled. **1858** THACKERAY *Virgin.* xxxix, The chaplain slapped down his cards with a huzzay. **1880** E. KIRKE *Garfield* 16 The wild huzza of victory.

†**b.** *allusively.* One given to noisy or riotous conduct: a rake, a gallant. Also *huzza-woman.*

1660–73 WYCHERLEY *Gentl. Dancing-Mast.* I. ii, We are for the brisk huzzas of seventeen or eighteen. *Ibid.*, Tearing midnight ramblers, or huzza-women.

c. **huzza-men**, men hired to shout 'huzza'.

1715 *Flying Post* 27 Jan., For scores of huzza-men..£40.

huzza (hʌ'zɑː, hʊ'zɑː), *v.* Also 9 **huzzah, huzzay** (hʌ'zeɪ). [f. HUZZA *int.*]

1. *intr.* To shout huzza. Constr. *at*, *for*.

1683 TRYON *Way to Health* 510 They are Carouzing and Huzzaing like mad Devils with their roaring Companions. **1705** HICKERINGILL *Priest-cr.* II. iv. 42 They drink a Health—Huzzah—to the Prosperity of the Highflown.. Ceremony-Monger. **1768** BOSWELL *Corsica* iii. (ed. 2) 228 He immediately sets fire to it, huzzas at the explosion. **1802** HOME *Hist. Reb.* v, The populace..who huzza for any thing that brings them together, huzzaed. *a* **1845** HOOD *Pub. Dinner* ii, Hip, hip! and huzzaing, And singing and saying. **1856** WHYTE MELVILLE *Kate Cov.* ix, The rustics huzzaed for their landlord. **1860** THACKERAY *Round. Papers, Ribbons*, I huzzay respectfully when they pass in procession.

2. *trans.* To acclaim with huzzas.

1688 in Gutch *Coll. Cur.* I. 381 They huzza'd and humm'd them in great abundance. **1710** STEELE *Tatler* No. 193 ¶5, I..have yet Lungs enough to huzza their Victories. **1710** HEARNE *Collect.* (O.H.S.) II. 339 Some Persons were so impudent (to speak in the canting phrase) as to huzza him. **1813** SCOTT *Rokeby* VI. xxvi, The brute crowd, whose envious zeal Huzzas each turn of Fortune's wheel. **1855** THACKERAY *Newcomes* I. v. 49 The way of the world, which huzzays all prosperity.

Hence **hu'zzaing** *vbl. sb.* and *ppl. a.*; **hu'zzaer**, one who shouts huzza.

1708 W. KING *Cookery* (R.), A caldron of fat beef and stoop of ale On the huzzaing mob shall more prevail. *a* **1734** NORTH *Exam.* III. viii. §44 (1740) 617 At merry Meetings, good Fellowship in Way of Healths, run into some Extravagance and Noise, as that which they called Huzzaing, an Usage then at its Perfection. **1805** *Naval Chron.* XIV. 384 The huzzaing multitude. **1838** *Tait's Mag.* V. 426 Shouters, or singers, or huzzaers. **1862** GEN. P. THOMPSON in *Bradford Advertiser* 15 Feb. 6/1 A vulgar huzzaer in the mob. **1862** CARLYLE *Fredk. Gt.* x. viii. (1872) III. 298 'These huzzahings only tell me what I have lost!' said the new King.

huzzard. ? *Obs.* [? f. HUZZ *v.* + -ARD. Cf. BUZZARD *sb.*[2], and *huzz-buzz* cockchafer (Chester and Shropsh.).] A species of fly used in angling.

1799 G. SMITH *Laboratory* II. 299 *Huzzard*..This fly is little known..It is larger than the green-drake, of a beautiful lemon-colour, both body and wings. **1829** GLOVER *Hist. Derby* I. 177 Well known to the expert angler..harry long-legs fly, hawthorn fly, huzzard fly.

huzzie, huzzy: see HUSSY.

hv-, a rare ME. spelling of *hu-*, as in *hv* = *hu*, HOW; *hvnt* = HUNT; *hvyr* = *huir*, HURE.

hw-, a frequent OE. initial element (:—OTeut. *hw-*, pre-Teut. *kw-*), for which *wh-* was afterwards substituted; e.g. OE. *hwá*, *hwelp*, *hwistle*, *hwý*, *hwylc* (early ME. *hwuch*), now WHO, WHELP, WHISTLE, WHY, WHICH. All OE. and early ME. words in *hw-* included in this dictionary will be found under WH-.

hw- also occurs, esp. in early Sc. works, for *huu-* and *hu-*: e.g. **hw** = *hu*, HOW; **hwe** = HUE; **hwgsom** = UGSOME; **hwick** = *huik*, HOOK; **hwid** = *huid*, HOOD; **hwide** = *huide*, HIDE; **hwmble** = HUMBLE; **hwnt** = HUNT; **hwou, hwu** = HOW; **hwre** = *hure*, WHORE; **hws, hwsz** = *huus*, *hus*, HOUSE; **hwyd** = *huyd*, HID; etc.

hwyl ('hu:ɪl). Also (erron.) **hwyll.** [W.] An emotional quality which inspires and sustains impassioned eloquence; also, the fervour of emotion characteristic of gatherings of Welsh people.

1899 *Daily News* 1 Mar. 7/5 What is termed the Welsh 'hwyl', a form of eloquence which seems to exert remarkable influence on the hearers. **1928** *Observer* 15 July 11/3 The National Eisteddfod is a microcosm of Wales. There you may see preacher and ploughman, collier and clerk, all rubbing shoulders and all under the influence of the intangible and untranslatable 'hwyl' of the Eisteddfod. **1959** W. GOLDING *Free Fall* ii. 57 Father Anselm..was not emotional, no Welsh hwyll for him. **1970** *Daily Tel.* 16 June 7 Plaid Cymru, full of 'hwyl' and hope, are making an all out effort to repeat in Cardigan the success they achieved..in Carmarthen. **1973** *Ibid.* 13 Jan. 16 There should be a considerable degree of hwyl on board HMS Glamorgan today when 20 members of the London Glamorgan Society are entertained to lunch.

hwyr, var. HURE.

hy, var. HEO, HI *prons.*; obs. f. HIE, HIGH, I.

hyacine, corrupt f. HYACINTH (sense 1).

1590 SPENSER *F.Q.* II. xii. 54 Some deep empurpled as the Hyacine [so *ed.* 1611; *ed.* 1590 *mispr.* Hyacint; *rimes* vine, wine, incline] Some as the Rubine laughing sweetly red.

hyacinth ('haɪəsɪnθ). Also 6 **hiacinthe, hyacint,** 6–7 **hiacynth, hyacinthe,** 7 **hiacint**; see also JACINTH. [Ultimately ad. Gr. ὑάκινθος hyacinth (flower and gem), of unknown origin, explained in Greek myth as the name of a youth beloved by Apollo: see sense 2. The earliest forms in English were *jacincte*, *jacynct*, *jacynth*, a. OF. *jacincte*, mod.F. *jacinthe* (see JACINTH); the more classical form (after L. *hyacinthus*) was introduced in the 16th c. (so also F. *hyacinthe*, now antiquated, acc. to Hatz.-Darm.). In modern usage the gem is called *jacinth* and *hyacinth*, but the latter is the exclusive form for the flower.]

1. A precious stone. **a.** Rendering or representing Gr. ὑάκινθος, L. *hyacinthus*, ancient name of a precious stone of a blue colour, probably the sapphire. **b.** In modern use, a reddish-orange variety of zircon; also applied to varieties of garnet and topaz of similar colour.

[**1230**, etc. see JACINTH.] **1553** EDEN *Treat. Newe Ind.* (Arb.) 20 Rubines, Hiacinthes, Saphyres, Topases. **1610** B. JONSON *Alch.* II. ii. Wks. (Rtldg.) 246/1 Dishes of agate, set in gold, and studded, With emeralds, saphyres, hiacynths, and rubies. **1727–41** CHAMBERS *Cycl.* s.v., *Confection of Hyacinth*, is a thin cordial electuary, composed of divers kinds of precious stones, particularly of that whose denomination it bears. **1782–3** W. F. MARTYN *Geog. Mag.* I. 709 A stone, through which many beautiful hyacinths are..dispersed. **1850** LEITCH tr. *C. O. Müller's Anc. Art* §207 (ed. 2) 199 Claudian describes the court dress of Honorius as sparkling with amethysts and hyacinths. **1879** ROSCOE & SCHORLEMMER *Treat. Chem.* II. ii. 267 Zircon and hyacinth possess the formula $ZrSiO_4$.

c. *Her.* In blazoning by precious stones, the name for the colour *tenné* or tawny.

[**1688** R. HOLME *Armoury* I. ii. 12/2 Jacynthe.] **1704** J. HARRIS *Lex. Techn.*, *Tenny* or *Tawney*, the Heralds term for a bright Colour, made of Red and Yellow mixed;..in the Coats..of nobles 'tis called Hyacinth.

†**d.** A blue or purple fabric: = JACINTH 1 c. *Obs.*

1609 BIBLE (Douay) *Eccles.* xlv. 12 An holie robe, of gold: and hyacinthe [**1388** WYCLIF iacynct], and purple.

2. A plant. **a.** Rendering or representing Gr. ὑάκινθος, L. *hyacinthus*, a name among the ancients for some flower; according to Ovid a deep red or 'purple' lily (? *Lilium Martagon*), but variously taken by authors as a gladiolus, iris, or larkspur. (See Bubani *Flora Virgil.* 63.) Now only *Hist.* or *poetic*.

In ancient mythology the flower is said to have sprung up from the blood of the slain youth Hyacinthus, and the ancients thought they could decipher on the petals the letters AI, or AIAI, exclamation of grief (cf. Moschus III. 6, Ovid. *Met.* x. 211). Hence many literary allusions; also Linnæus's specific name for the Wild Hyacinth or Bluebell, *Hyacinthus non-scriptus*.

1578 LYTE *Dodoens* II. xliii. 202 Of the redde Lillie Ouide wryteth this, that it came of the bloud of the Boy Hyacinthus ..And for a perpetuall memorie of the Boy Hyacinthus, Apollo named these floures Hyacinthes. **1595** DANIEL *Sonn.* xxxiv, You are changed, but not t' a hyacint; I fear your eye hath turned your heart to flint. *a* **1649** DRUMM. OF HAWTH. *Poems* Wks. (1711) 16 O hyacinths! for ay your AI keep still, Nay, with more marks of woe your leaves now fill. **1837** WHEWELL *Hist. Induct. Sc.* (1857) III. 220 The hyacinth on whose petals the notes of grief were traced.

b. In modern use, the English name of the genus *Hyacinthus* (N.O. *Liliaceæ*), consisting of bulbous plants with bell-shaped six-parted flowers, of various colours, usually drooping, arranged in a loose upright spike; esp. *H. orientalis*, a native of the Levant, of which numerous varieties are cultivated for the beauty and fragrance of their flowers. Also applied, with or without qualification, to various allied plants of similar habit, as species of *Scilla*, *Muscari*, etc.

Californian h., the genus *Brodiæa*. **Cape h.**, a plant of the genus *Galtonia*, esp. *G. candicans*; **feathered h.**, *Muscari comosum monstrosum*. **grape h.**, the genus *Muscari*, esp. *M. botryoides*. **lily h.**, *Scilla Lilio-Hyacinthus*. **Missouri h.**, the genera *Brodiæa* and *Hesperoscordum* (*Hesperanthus*). **Peruvian h.**, *Scilla peruviana*; **Roman h.**, an early-flowering variety, bred from *Hyacinthus orientalis* var. *albulus*. **star h.**, *Scilla amœna*. **starch h.**, *Muscari racemosum*. **tassel h.**, *Muscari comosum*. **water h.**, a name of *Pontederia crassipes*, a water plant of Florida, etc., with clusters of light-blue or violet flowers. **wild** or **wood h.** (of Britain), *Scilla nutans* (= BLUEBELL 2); (of N. America), *Scilla* or *Camassia Fraseri*. (See *Treas. Bot.* and Miller *Plant-n.*)

1578 LYTE *Dodoens* II. xlviii. 205 There be two sortes of Hyacinthes, yet ouer and aboue diuers others whiche are also counted Hyacinthes. *Ibid.* 206 In Englishe also Hyacinthe or Crowtoes. [**1629** J. PARKINSON *Parad.* xi. 126 The Starry Iacinth of Peru, being thought to have grown in Peru, a Province of the West Indies, but he that gave that name first unto it, eyther knew not his naturall place, or willingly imposed that name, to conceale it, or to make it the better esteemed.] **1659** T. HANMER *Garden Bk.* (1933) 36 The Branch'd Hyacinths of Peru,..very rare here. **1664** EVELYN *Kal. Hort.* (1729) 198 Tuberous Iris, Hyacinth Zeboin. **1673** J. RAY *Observations Journey Low-Countries* 250 In the ditches by the wayside, I observed growing wild ..the lesser Grape Hyacinth, and Hepatica. **1728–46** THOMSON *Spring* 546 Hyacinths, of purest virgin white. **1731** P. MILLER *Gardener's Dict.* s.v. *Hyacinthus*. The Hyacinth of Peru may also be rais'd from Seeds in the same manner as the common Hyacinths. *Ibid.*, Another Hyacinth ..is now preserved in curious Collections of Exotick Plants; it was originally brought from the Cape of Good Hope. **1741** *Compl. Fam.-Piece* II. iii. 353 Beds of Ranunculus, Hyacinth, and Anemonies. **1820** SHELLEY *Sensit. Pl.* I. vii, The hyacinth, purple, and white, and blue, Which flung from its bells a sweet peal anew. **1851** LONGF. *Gold. Leg.* IV. *Convent Hirschau* 74 A delicious fragrance..as of hyacinths. **1859** TENNYSON *Guinevere* 386 Sheets of hyacinth That seem'd the heavens upbreaking thro' the earth. **1877** [see ROMAN *a.*[1] 14 b]. **1882** *Garden* 11 Feb. 90/1 Spare bulbs of Grape Hyacinths..might be naturalised in the Grass. **1897** *Daily News* 30 June 8/1 Sir Herbert Maxwell objects to the southron use of the name bluebells, as applied to the flowers that he prefers to call wood hyacinths. **1897** H. J. WEBBER in *Bulletin U.S. Dep. Agric., Bot.* No. 18 (*title*) The Water Hyacinth, and its relation to navigation in Florida. **1911** J. WEATHERS *Bulb Bk.* 282/1 There is a blue Roman Hyacinth that flowers somewhat later than the white form. **1917** L. H. BAILEY *Stand. Cycl. Hort.* VI. 3117/2 [*Scilla*] *Peruviana*.. Cuban Lily. Peruvian Jacinth. Hyacinth of Peru. *Ibid.* 3118/1 The Hyacinth of Peru is not hardy in Mass[achusetts]. **1924** J. WEATHERS *My Garden Bk.* xx. 348/1 Galtonia (after the S. African explorer, Francis Galton). Cape Hyacinth. **1936** T. S. ELIOT *Coll. Poems* 127 Lord, the Roman hyacinths are blooming in bowls. **1956** A. M. COATS *Flowers & their Histories* I. 122 The Spire Lily or Cape Hyacinth..is on the other hand not a true hyacinth, although closely related to the family; it has therefore been renamed *Galtonia candicans*. **1961** P. M. SYNGE *Collins Guide to Bulbs* 162 The Roman Hyacinths tend to flower among the earliest and the spikes are rather looser and more delicate.

c. *fig.* (*pl.*). Hyacinthine locks. (See HYACINTHINE 1.)

1768 SIR W. JONES *Solima* 5 in *Poems*, etc. (1777) 1 The fragrant hyacinths of Azza's hair.

d. A purplish blue colour resembling that of a common variety of the flower (see b).

1891 *Daily News* 24 Feb. 5/8 The new spring colour is called 'hyacinth' and is exactly that of the purple-blue hyacinth.

3. a. A bird; a kind of water-hen with purple plumage, as the genera *Ionornis* and *Porphyrio*.

b. A variety of pigeon, characterized by its blue-black colour and white markings.

1855 *Poultry Chron.* III. 9/1 Those pretty spangled Toys ..known by various names, as Porcelains, Hyacinths, Ermines, &c. **1879** L. WRIGHT *Pract. Pigeon Keeper* 208 Victorias are simply Hyacinths of a lighter shade. **1935** R. MANNERING *Lyell's Pigeon-Keeping for Amateurs* (ed. 4) 107 The Hyacinth is among those breeds which do not reveal their true colouration and markings until after the first moult. **1965** W. M. LEVI *Encycl. Pigeon Breeds* 189 The Hyacinth appears to have much in common with the Suabian, and they are probably related.

4. *attrib.* and *Comb.* **a.** as *hyacinth-like* adj.; **hyacinth-glass**, a glass vessel for the water-culture of a hyacinth-bulb; **hyacinth-stone** = sense 1.

1836–9 DICKENS *Sk. Boz* ix, The hyacinth-glasses in the parlour-window. *a* **1849** MANGAN *Poems* (1859) 61 A price less hyacinth-stone. **1859** W. S. COLEMAN *Woodlands* (1866) 71 Delicate white blossoms..arrayed in a hyacinth-like form. **1887** *Pall Mall G.* 15 Oct. 11/1 In 1730 the hyacinth trade experienced its greatest prosperity.

b. esp. in reference to the reddish-orange colour of the gem (1 b), or the blue or purple colour of the flower (2).

1694 SALMON *Bates' Disp.* (1713) 381/1 The Odoriferous yellow or Hyacinth Oil. **1796** KIRWAN *Elem. Min.* (ed. 2) I. 29 Hyacinth red—high red with a shade of brown. **1876** OUIDA *Winter City* x. 299 The hyacinth-hued hills. **1898** *Daily News* 9 Apr. 6/3 The favourite colour..the hyacinth blue, so called by the milliners, notwithstanding the fact that it is more mauve than blue.

hyacinthian (haɪə'sɪnθɪən), *a.* [f. L. *hyacinth-us* + -IAN.] Of or pertaining to the hyacinth (sense 1 or 2), hyacinthine.

1714 EUSDEN *Crt. of Love* in *Steele's Poet. Misc.* 102 Proud Columns..That hewn from Hyacinthian Quarries came. **1794** MRS. A. M. BENNETT *Ellen* I. 5 A profusion of white waving locks..conveyed some idea of their hyacinthian beauty, before age had silvered them over. **1858** CASWALL *Poems* 93 Hyacinthian blue.

hyacinthine (haɪə'sɪnθɪn, -aɪn), *a.* Also 7–8 -in. [ad. L. *hyacinthin-us*, a. Gr. ὑακίνθιν-ος, f. ὑάκινθος HYACINTH: see -INE.]

1. Of the colour of a hyacinth (either the gem (1 a) or the flower). (Chiefly as a poetic or rhetorical epithet of hair, after *Hom. Od.* VI. 231, κόμας ὑακινθίνῳ ἄνθει ὁμοίας, 'locks like the hyacinthine flower', which in the next line seem to be compared to gold.)

1656 BLOUNT *Glossogr.*, *Hyacinthine*, of Violet or Purple colour. **1667** MILTON *P.L.* IV. 301 Hyacinthin locks Round from his parted forelock manly hung Clustring. **1725** POPE *Odyss.* VI. 274 His hyacinthine locks descend in wavy curls. **1791** PEARSON in *Phil. Trans.* LXXXI. 363 Argentine flowers of anitmony, hyacinthine glass of antimony. **1863** BATES *Nat. Amazon* iv. (1864) 80 The splendid Hyacinthine Macaw (*Macrocercus Hyacinthinus*)..is entirely of a soft hyacinthine blue colour, except round the eyes. **1874** LOWELL *Agassiz* Poet. Wks. 1890 IV. 112 Shaking with burly mirth his hyacinthine hair. **1874** H. D. WESTROPP *Man. Precious Stones* 74 Many fine engravings, and also camei, occur in the essonite, and the hyacinthine garnet. *Ibid.* 93 The hyacinthine sard is..a rich..variety of this stone which possesses the orange-red tint.

2. Of, made of, or adorned with hyacinths.

1675 HOBBES *Odyssey* (1677) 73 From his hair the colour gray she [Pallas] took, And made it like the hyacinthine flower. **1760** FAWKES tr. *Anacreon* xlii. (R.), With hyacinthine chaplet crown'd. **1791** COWPER *Odyssey* VI. 286 His curling locks like hyacinthine flowers. **1822** 'B. CORNWALL' *Sonn. to Skylark*, Hyacinthine bowers.

3. Like the boy Hyacinthus of Greek mythology.

1847 EMERSON *Poems*, *Threnody*, The hyacinthine boy, for whom Morn well might break and April bloom.

‖**Hyades** ('haɪədi:z), *sb. pl.* *Astron.* Rarely anglicized **Hyads.** [a. Gr. ὑάδες, fem. pl., in popular etymology connected with ὕειν to rain (their heliacal rising being supposed to prognosticate rain), but perhaps f. ὗς, ὑός swine, the L. name being *suculæ* little pigs. With the anglicized *Hyads* cf. F. *Hyades*.] A group of stars near the Pleiades, in the head of the constellation Taurus, the chief of which is the bright red star Aldebaran.

1398 TREVISA *Barth. De P.R.* VIII. xxv. (Bodl. MS.), Hyades..bene reyny sterres, for in þe risynge of them falleþ moche rayne. **1513** DOUGLAS *Æneis* III. viii. 21 Of every sterne the twinkilling notis he..Arthuris huyfe, and Hyades. **1587** GOLDING *De Mornay* xiii. 192 The Pleiads and Hiads make the Seasons, the Dogstarre maketh the heat of the Sommer. **1637** HEYWOOD *Royal Ship* 27 Shining like five of the seven Hyades. **1842** *Penny Cycl.* XXIV. 104/2 Aldebaran and the Hyades form the forehead and eye. **1854** KEIGHTLEY *Mythol. Anc. Greece* (ed. 3) 413 The Pleiads, Hyads, and Orion's strength.

hyæna, variant of HYENA.

‖**hya-hya** ('haɪə'haɪə). [Native name.] The Cow-tree of Guyana (formerly British Guiana) (*Tabernæmontana utilis*): see COW-TREE 2.

1842 *Penny Cycl.* XXIII. 494/1 The milk-tree, or Hya-hya of Demerara. *a* **1882** SIR R. CHRISTISON *Autobiog.* (1885) I. 390, I examined in 1830 the juice obtained by incision into the trunk of the Hya-hya tree.

hyalescent (haɪə'lɛsənt), *a.* [f. Gr. ὕαλ-ος glass + -ESCENT.] Becoming hyaline or glassy. So **hya'lescence**, the process of becoming or condition of being hyaline.

1864 WEBSTER, *Hyalescence.*

hyalin ('haɪəlɪn). [f. Gr. ὕαλ-ος glass (see next) + -IN.] **a.** *Physiol.* 'The pellucid point which is the first stage of developement of the nucleolus of Schleiden' (Mayne). **b.** *Path.* Recklinghausen's term for the translucent substance found in tubercle; called by Langhans 'canalised fibrin' (*Syd. Soc. Lex.*). **c.** An opalescent substance resembling chitin, which is the chief constituent of the wall of a hydatid cyst. (So called by Hoppe-Seyler.)

1854 in MAYNE *Expos. Lex.*

hyaline ('haɪəlɪn, -aɪn), *a.* and *sb.* [ad. L. *hyalinus*, a. Gr. ὑάλινος of glass or crystal, f. ὕαλος, ὕελος glass (said to be originally an Egyptian word). Cf. F. *hyalin* (OF. *ialin*).]

A. *adj.* Resembling glass, transparent as glass, glassy, crystalline, vitreous. (Chiefly *technical.*) ***hyaline cartilage***, ordinary cartilage, as distinguished from fibro-cartilage or other varieties; ***hyaline cast***, a more or less transparent urinary cast composed mainly of precipitated protein; ***hyaline cell***, (*a*) *Bot.*, a cell without chlorophyll, found in the leaves and stem of certain mosses; †(*b*) *Med.* (also ***hyaline leucocyte***), a type of white blood-cell; = MONOCYTE (*obs.*); ***hyaline degeneration***, a form of degeneration of various tissues in which they assume a glassy appearance; ***hyaline membrane disease*** (or ***syndrome***), a condition in some newborn (esp. premature) babies in which the lung spaces are lined with a hyaline membrane, causing severe dyspnœa and often early death.

a **1661** HOLYDAY *Juvenal* (1673) 174 Sprinkled over with hyaline or glass-colour'd dust. **1791** E. DARWIN *Bot. Gard.* I. 117 As below she braids her hyaline hair. **1828** STARK *Elem. Nat. Hist.* II. 118 Body oblong, depressed..tunic whitish, hyaline. **1855** HOLDEN *Hum. Osteol.* (1878) 24 The ..skeleton of the foetus..consists at first of hyaline cartilage. **1867** H. MACMILLAN *Bible Teach.* ii. (1870) 30 Like the hyaline pavement which John saw in vision. **1870** *Jrnl. Bot.* VIII. 229 In neither [species of *Dicranum*] do I find the beautiful chlorophyllose contents observable in the Finland specimens..nor are the longitudinal rows of hyaline cells, in the centre of the basal wing, so well defined. **1880** W. B. CARPENTER in *19th Cent.* April 613 Near the surface of the water..the inter-spaces [of the iceberg] lose their dead whiteness, and become hyaline or bluish. **1881** *Practitioner* Oct. 243 The urine contained red corpuscles, albumin, and hyaline casts. **1894** KANTHACK & HARDY in *Jrnl. Physiol.* XVII. 96 The hyaline cell occurs both in blood and in the extra-vascular spaces. **1896** H. N. DIXON *Student's Handbk. Brit. Mosses* 9 The pores in the hyaline cells of the branch leaves [of *Sphagnum* species] are.. occasionally found on the face of the hyaline cells. **1897** ALLBUTT *Syst. Med.* II. 698 These hyaline or hyaloid degenerations are found..in aged dogs. **1906** *Jrnl. Pathol. & Bacteriol.* XI. 67 The immature hyaline cell is an evenly round or oval cell. *Ibid.* 79 Others consider that the lymphocytes are the young forms of hyaline leucocytes. **1929** *Encycl. Brit.* III. 742/1 The large hyaline cell may really include two quite different cells of similar appearance. **1931** A. PINEY *Recent Adv. Hæmatol.* (ed. 3) ii. 18 The large hyaline leucocyte or monocyte is not easy to place with complete certainty in either the group of granulocytes or of lymphocytes. **1938** G. M. SMITH *Cryptogamic Bot.* II. iv. 87 The hyaline cells of leaves and similar cells in the cortex of a stem play an important role in the absorption and retention of water. **1953** *Adv. Pediatrics* VI. 173 If an infant does not exhibit respiratory difficulty within the first 12 hours of life I do not believe it will die of hyaline membrane disease. **1955** *Jrnl. Pediatrics* XLVII. 40/1 The triad of pathologic changes in the lungs of infants who die with the pulmonary hyaline membrane syndrome consists of atelectasis, vascular engorgement, and an eosinophilic hyaline-like membrane which lines alveolar ducts and alveoli. **1958** *New Biol.* XXVI. 102 The leaves [of *Sphagnum*] are composed of large empty 'hyaline' cells, with narrow green cells between them. **1966** *Lancet* 24 Dec. 1384/2 Mid-stream urine showed small numbers of hyaline and granular casts. **1973** *Sci. Amer.* Apr. 75/1 In the past some infants with hyaline membrane disease recovered spontaneously. Many became exhausted and died.

B. *sb.* **1.** 'A sea of glass like unto crystal' (θάλασσα ὑαλίνη, Rev. iv. 6); hence a poetic term for the smooth sea, the clear sky, or any transparent substance.

1667 MILTON *P.L.* VII. 619 On the cleer Hyaline, the Glassie Sea. **1827** MONTGOMERY *Pelican Isl.* I. 162 Through the clear hyaline the Ship of Heaven Came sailing. **1876** M. COLLINS *Fr. Midn. to M.* II. Pref. Poem 186 Like halcyon brooding on the hyaline. **1876** BLACKMORE *Cripps* II. xiv. 215 Meadows..fluttered with the pearly hyaline of dew.

2. *Anat.* and *Biol.* **a.** The HYALOID membrane of the eye. **b.** Hyaline cartilage (see A). **c.** = HYALOPLASM.

1864 WEBSTER, *Hyaline*,..the pellucid substance in cells in process of development.

hyalinization (ˌhaɪəlɪnaɪ'zeɪʃən). *Med.* [f. HYALIN(E *a.* and *sb.* + -IZATION.] A change of tissue into a homogeneous, translucent, often firm, mass somewhat resembling glass under the microscope; hyaline degeneration.

1919 *Amer. Jrnl. Med. Sci.* CLVII. 673 Undoubtedly there are other factors [affecting malignancy and benignancy] such as lymphocytic infiltration, fibrosis, hyalinization, [etc.]. **1926** *Arch. Path.* II. 338 The muscle lesion usually consists of hyaline degeneration of the contractile substance of the fibers... The hyalinization of the muscle may result in rupture with subsequent hemorrhage. **1961** *Lancet* 22 July 182/2 Histologically the aneurysmal sac was composed of dense fibrous tissue showing hyalinisation. **1963** WALTER & ISRAEL *Gen. Path.* v. 71 Hyalinisation of the walls of many small arterioles may occur as part of the aging process.

So **'hyalinized** *ppl. a.*, having the appearance that results from hyalinization.

1929 *Arch. Path.* VIII. 906 The corpus fibrosum.. consists of irregularly outlined and more or less thoroughly hyalinized fibrous tissue. **1962** *Lancet* 27 Jan. 191/1 This exudate becomes hyalinised to form membranes, lining the sacs, and dense plugs in the alveolar ducts.

‖**hyali'nosis.** *Path.* [See -OSIS.] Hyaline degeneration: see HYALINE *a.*

1876 tr. *Wagner's Gen. Pathol.* 325 Hyaloid degeneration, or hyalinosis.

hyalite ('haɪəlaɪt). *Min.* [f. Gr. ὕαλ-ος glass + -ITE (F. *hyalite*): named by Werner 1794.] A colourless variety of opal, occurring in globular concretions.

1794 KIRWAN *Elem. Min.* (ed. 2) I. 297 Hyalite, Müller's Glass, of the Germans. **1852** TH. ROSS *Humboldt's Trav.* I. i. 36 Known by the names of volcanic glass, glass of Muller, or hyalite. **1868** DANA *Min.* (ed. 5) 201 Hyalite occurs in amygdaloid.

‖**hyalitis** (haɪə'laɪtɪs). *Path.* [f. Gr. ὕαλ-ος glass + -ITIS.] Inflammation of the vitreous humour of the eye.

1847 in CRAIG. **1875** H. WALTON *Dis. Eye* (ed. 3) 975 Hyalitis is not excited by wounds.

hyalo- (haɪələʊ), combining form of Gr. ὕαλ-ος glass, used in various modern terms, chiefly scientific and technical: as **'hyaloclast** (-klɑːst, -æ-) *nonce-wd.* [after *iconoclast*], a glass-breaker; **'hyalograph** (-grɑːf, -æ-) [Gr. -γραφος that writes], 'an instrument for etching on a transparent surface'; so **hyalography** (-'ɒgrəfɪ) [Gr. -γραφια writing], 'the art of writing or engraving on glass' (Webster 1864); †**hya'lomelan(e**, *Min.* [Gr. μελαν- black], a name formerly given to glassy varieties of basalt; **'hyalomere** *Cytol.* [-MERE], the lightly staining ground-substance of a blood platelet; **'hyalomicte** (-mɪkt), *Min.* [Fr. *hyalomicte*, f. Gr. μικτός mixed], a mixture of quartz and mica, of granulated texture; ˌ**hyalo-o'phitic** *a. Petrol.* [ad. G. *hyaloophitisch* (B. Polenov 1899, in *Trav. de la Soc. Impér. des Naturalistes, St. Pétersbourg* XXVII. 473)] (see quot. 1920); **'hyalophane** (-feɪn), *Min.* [Gr. -φανης appearing], a barium feldspar, found in transparent crystals; ˌ**hyalopi'litic** (-paɪ'lɪtɪk) *a. Petrol.* [ad. G. *hyalopilitisch* (H. Rosenbusch *Mikrosk. Physiogr. d. Min. u. Gesteine* (ed. 2, 1887) II. 466), f. Gr. πῖλ-ος felt + *-itic* (see -ITE[1])], characterized by or having needle-like microlites embedded in a glassy ground-mass; **'hyaloplasm** (-plæz(ə)m), *Biol.* [Gr. πλάσμα moulding, formation], transparent homogeneous protoplasm; hence **hyalo'plasmic** *a.*, pertaining to or of the nature of hyaloplasm; **hyalopterous** (-'ɒptərəs), *a. Entom.* [Gr. πτέρον wing], having transparent wings (Mayne *Expos. Lex.* 1854); **hyalosiderite** (-'sɪdəraɪt), *Min.* [Gr. σιδηρίτης of iron: see SIDERITE], a very ferruginous variety of chrysolite, occurring in large glassy crystals; **'hyalosome** *Cytol.* [ad. G. *hyalosom* (S. M. Lukjanow 1887, in *Arch. f. mikrosk. Anat.* XXX. 551): see -SOME[4]], a lightly staining cell structure resembling the nucleolus; **hyalospermous** (-'spɜːməs), *a. Bot.* [Gr. σπέρμα seed], having transparent seeds (Mayne 1854); **hyalotekite** (-'tiːkaɪt), *Min.* [Gr. τήκειν to melt: see -ITE], a silicate of lead with barium and calcium, which fuses to a clear glass; †**hyalotype** (see quot.).

18.. MOORE *Devil among Schol.* 106 That redoubted *Hyaloclast, Who still contrived, by dint of throttle, Where'er he went to crack a bottle! **1879** RUTLEY *Study Rocks* xi. 199 He subdivides them into tachylites, or those which are soluble in acids, and *hyalomelanes or those which are insoluble in acids. **1936** P. E. SMITH et al. *Bailey's Text-bk. Histol.* (ed. 9) vi. 150 Structurally they [*sc.* blood platelets] consist of a central granular mass (chromomere).. and a peripheral hyaline zone *(hyalomere). **1969** A. W. HAM *Histol.* (ed. 6) xiv. 303/1 Most of a platelet appears to consist of a fairly clear ground substance which is colored only a very pale blue with a blood stain and is called its hyalomere. **1853** TH. ROSS *Humboldt's Trav.* III. xxv. 65 Analogous to the stanniferous granites, the *hyalomictes, and the pegmatites. **1855** *Amer. Jrnl. Sc.* Ser. II. XIX. 362 *Hyalophan..occurs..in the dolomite of the Binnen valley. **1868** DANA *Min.* (ed. 5) 346 Hyalophane..fuses with difficulty to a blebby glass. **1920** A. HOLMES *Nomencl. Petrol.* 120 **Hyalo-ophitic texture*, Polenov, 1899, a texture resembling ophitic texture, in which the spaces of an open network of felspar laths are occupied by glass; a limiting case of intersertal texture. **1954** H. WILLIAMS et al. *Petrogr.* ii. 20 Where glass takes the place of pyroxene, the texture is called hyaloophitic. **1888** J. J. H. TEALL *Brit. Petrogr.* 443 The normal structure of the andesites is the *hyalopilitic. **1959** W. W. MOORHOUSE *Study of Rocks in Thin Section* v. 159 Hyalopilitic lavas are glassy with felted microlites. **1886** DALLINGER in *Jrnl. R. Microsc. Soc.* Apr. 199 A distinct granular condition becomes apparent in what was the homogeneous *hyaloplasm. **1824** *Phil. Mag.* LXIII. 182 *Hyalosiderite occurs for the most part in crystals. **1889** *Q. Jrnl. Microsc. Sci.* XXX. 168 They are therefore distinguished..as (a) 'karyosomes'..; (b) 'plasmasomes'..; (c) *'hyalosomes', which are not stained (vide Lukjanow). **1851** R. HUNT *Photogr.* ix. 102 Specimens, which they term *Hyalotypes. These are positive pictures, copied on glass from negatives obtained upon the same material. Their peculiarity is the adaptation of them for magic-lantern slides.

hyaloid ('haɪəlɔɪd), *a.* and *sb.* [a. F. *hyaloïde*, or ad. L. *hyaloïdes*, a. Gr. ὑαλοειδής like glass, glassy, f. ὕαλος glass: see HYALINE.]

A. *adj.* (Chiefly *Anat.*) **a.** Glassy, hyaline. ***hyaloid coat*** or ***membrane***, a thin transparent membrane enveloping the vitreous humour of the eye. ***hyaloid body***, ***humour***, ***substance***: names for the vitreous humour (*Syd. Soc. Lex.*). **b.** Connected with the hyaloid membrane, as ***hyaloid artery***, ***canal***, ***vein*** (ibid.).

1835–6 TODD *Cycl. Anat.* I. 306/1 The outer capsule formed by the hyaloid membrane. *Ibid.* 553/1 The hyaloid coat..is perfectly transparent. **1838** *Penny Cycl.* X. 139/1 There can be no doubt that the vitreous humour is secreted by the surfaces of the hyaloid cells. **1877** HUXLEY *Anat. Inv. Anim.* viii. 527 Covered by a thick hyaloid membrane.

B. *sb.*

1. *Anat.* The hyaloid membrane: see A. a.

[**1670** *Phil. Trans.* V. 1025 The *Hyaloeides*, which invelopes the Vitreous humour, is perfectly transparent.] **1838** *Penny Cycl.* X. 138/2 The pigment left by the ciliary body, which..rests upon that portion of the surface of the hyaloid. **1869** *Eng. Mech.* 3 Dec. 272/2 Beyond this hyaloid ..is the retina.

2. = HYALINE B. 1.

1844 *Blackw. Mag.* LVI. 31 A picturesque rock, immersed up to its shoulders in a green hyaloid.

‖**hyaloiditis** (-'aɪtɪs). [f. prec. + -ITIS.] Inflammation of the hyaloid membrane.

1854 in MAYNE *Expos. Lex.*

‖**hyalonema** (haɪələʊ'niːmə). [mod.L., f. Gr. ὕαλο-ς glass + νῆμα thread.] The glass-rope sponge, which roots itself to the sea-bed by a long stem twisted of fine siliceous threads. Hence **hyalo'nemid**, a sponge of this family (*Hyalonemidæ*).

1855 KINGSLEY *Glaucus* (1878) 86 The Hyalonemas, or glass-rope sponges. **1876** *Beneden's Anim. Parasites* 64 In the sea of Japan is found a very remarkable sponge, generally known by the name of Hyalonema.

hyalose ('haɪələʊs). *Chem.* [f. as HYALIN + -OSE.] A dextro-rotatory sugar obtained from the hyalin of a hydatid cyst.

1886 in *Syd. Soc. Lex.*

hyaluronic (ˌhaɪəljʊ'rɒnɪk), *a. Biochem.* [f. HYAL(OID *a.* (from its first being isolated from the hyaloid or vitreous humour of the eye) + URONIC *a.*] ***hyaluronic acid***: a viscous mucopolysaccharide composed of acetylglucosamine and glucuronic acid units, widely found in animal tissues (e.g. in synovial fluid, in the ground-substance of connective tissue, and in the vitreous humour of the eye) as well as in bacterial capsules.

1934 MEYER & PALMER in *Jrnl. Biol. Chem.* CVII. 631 Data on the preparations of this acid for which we propose ..the name 'hyaluronic acid', from hyaloid (vitreous) + uronic acid. **1957** *Sci. News* XLV. 85 *In vivo*, hyaluronic acid has the important function of offering resistance to penetration by foreign matter, including agents of infectious disease. **1969** *New Scientist* 24 Apr. 167/2 Dr W. C. McCutchen..was adamant that if the hyaluronic acid is removed from synovial fluid, it still lubricates efficiently.

Hence **hya'luronate**, a salt of hyaluronic acid.

1946 *Biochem. Jrnl.* XL. 583 (*heading*) The influence of hydrolysates of hyaluronate upon hyaluronidase production by micro-organisms. **1970** R. W. MCGILVERY *Biochem.* xxiv. 585 Solutions of hyaluronate have a high viscosity, and it is especially concentrated in the synovial fluid of the joints.

hyaluronidase (ˌhaɪəljʊ'rɒnɪdeɪz, -eɪs). *Biochem.* [f. *hyaluronid-* (f. HYALURON(IC *a.* + -ASE.] Any of the enzymes which catalyse the depolymerization of hyaluronic acid, thereby

reducing its viscosity and rendering tissue containing it more permeable.

1940 CHAIN & DUTHIE in *Brit. Jrnl. Exper. Path.* XXI. 325 Hyaluronic acid is the substrate for the 'mucolytic' enzyme in spreading factor solution which accordingly is termed 'hyaluronidase'. **1951** A. GROLLMAN *Pharmacol. & Therapeutics* xxix. 652 To accelerate the rate of absorption from the skin and subcutaneous tissues, hyaluronidase may be added to the infusion. **1967** *Martindale's Extra Pharmacopoeia* (ed. 25) 886/1 The diffusion of local anaesthetics is accelerated by the injection of 1000 units of hyaluronidase to each 20 ml. of the anaesthetic solution. **1970** AMBROSE & EASTY *Cell Biol.* xii. 391 The sperm acrosome secretes enzymes (including hyaluronidase) which assist penetration [of the ovum].

hyan ('haɪən). *local.* Also **hyant, hyen, hyon.** [Origin unknown.] An acute, usually fatal, infectious disease of cattle or, occasionally, sheep, caused by the bacterium *Clostridium chauvœi*; = *black quarter* (s.v. BLACK *a.* 19), BLACKLEG 1, SPEED *sb.* 11 a.

1789 *Trans. Soc. Arts* VII. 73, I..should annually have attempted to rear one hundred [calves], were it not for the disorder called here [*sc.* Scarisbrook] the *Hyon.* **1795** J. AIKIN *Descr. Country round Manchester* 325 Great numbers of calves having been taken off by a disease here called the *hyon.* **1801** *Sporting Mag.* XVII. 153 Drinks to be given to young calves for striking of the *Hyen.* **1881** [see SPEED *sb.* 11 a].

hyawa ('haɪəwə). Also **haiowa, hayawa, hiawa, hyawai.** [Arawak (Makuchi) *haijawa*. In Du. *hajawa* (1770).] One of several balsam-bearing trees or shrubs of Guyana, esp. *Protium heptaphyllum*. Also *attrib.*

1825 C. WATERTON *Wanderings S. Amer.* 190 They paint themselves with the Roucou, sweetly perfumed with Hayawa. **1840** R. SCHOMBURGK *Descr. Brit. Guiana* 98 The latter tree [sc. *Amyris ambrosiaca*], called *Haiowa* or *Sepou* by the Indians, is most abundant. **1851** *Illustr. Catal. Gt. Exhib.* IV. 980/1 Hyawai gum or incense, from the River Demerara. **1887** *Colonial & Indian Exhib. Rep. Col. Sect.* 295 Hyawa gum..is very fragrant when burnt. **1899** J. RODWAY *In Guiana Wilds* 208 Then it struck him that a torch would be useful, as he saw a hyawa bush growing near. **1924** RECORD & MELL *Timbers Trop. Amer.* 335 The bastard cedar, incense tree, or 'hiawá' of British Guiana is *P[rotium] heptaphyllum* March.

hyawaballi (ˌhaɪəwə'bælɪ). Also **haiariballi, hiawaballi, haiowaballi.** [Arawak (Makuchi) *hyawaballi*, f. HYAWA + *-balli* resembling.] A timber tree of Guyana, *Tetragastris panamensis*.

1851 *Illustr. Catal. Gt. Exhib.* IV. 985/1 Transverse and vertical sections of the hyawaballi tree, from the River Demerara. **1887** *Colonial & Indian Exhib. Rep. Col. Sect.* 451 Hiawa-Balli. **1917** *Timehri* IV. 260 Hiawa-balli... Hard, heavy, compact, fine grain. **1943** RECORD & HESS *Timbers of New World* 109/2 The Haiowaballi of British Guiana is *T[etragastris] panamensis.* **1952** D. B. FANSHAWE *Vegetation Brit. Guiana* 60 *Tetragastris* sp. (Haiawaballi) community. **1956** *Handbk. Hardwoods* (Forest Prod. Res. Lab.) 107 Haiariballi is a timber of British Guiana. Material received at the Laboratory showed the timber to be worthless for commercial sawing.

hybern-, incorrect spelling of HIBERN-.

Hyblæan (haɪ'bliːən), *a.* Also **Hyblean.** [f. L. *Hyblæ-us* (f. *Hybla*, Gr. Ὕβλη) + -AN.] Of or pertaining to the town of Hybla in Sicily, celebrated for the honey produced on the neighbouring hills; hence *poet.*, honied, sweet, mellifluous.

1614 T. ADAMS *Devil's Banquet* 17 Not the Hyblaean Nectar of heauen, whereof, he that drinkes, shall neuer thirst againe. **1682** TATE *Abs. & Achit.* II. 1123 Thronging and busy as Hyblæan swarms. **1742** YOUNG *Nt. Th.* II. 536 From friendship..The Wise extract Earth's most Hyblean Bliss. **1880** SWINBURNE *Study Shaks.* 201 Golden and Hyblæan elequence!

Hyblan ('haɪblən), *a. rare*⁻¹. = prec.

1856 MRS. BROWNING *Aur. Leigh* v. 190 She'll hear the softest hum of Hyblan bee.

hybodont ('hɪbəʊdɒnt), *sb.* and *a.* [f. Gr. ὕβος hump, ὑβός hump-backed + ὀδούς, ὀδοντ- tooth.]

A. *sb.* A shark of the extinct genus *Hybodon* or family *Hybodontidæ*, with conical compressed teeth.

1847 CARPENTER *Zool.* §589 Intermediate between these [Cestracionts] and the ordinary Sharks was another family, to which the name of Hybodonts has been given. **1862** DANA *Man. Geol.* 278 *note.* **1877** LE CONTE *Elem. Geol.* (1879) 388.

B. *adj.* Belonging to this family of fishes.

1872 NICHOLSON *Palæont.* 339 The teeth are of what is called the 'Hybodont' form, having a general conical shape.

Hy Brasil, Hy-Brazil (haɪ brə'zɪl). Also 9 **Brasil Rock, O'Brazil.** [Cf. BRAZIL¹.] Name originally applied to one of the larger islands of the Azores; subsequently and chiefly to a legendary island located off the west coast of Ireland.

[**1436** A. BIANCO *Atlas* (1869) (*caption*) Y de borzil.] **1812** J. PURDY *Mem. N. Atlantic Ocean* IV. i. 128 *Brasil Rock*, in lat. 51° 10', and long. 15° 58'..although its existence has been doubted..it was, however, seen in the year 1791. **1843** G. GRIFFIN *Works* VIII. 210 On the ocean that hollows the rocks where ye dwell, A shadowy land has appeared as they tell; Men thought it a region of sunshine and rest, And they called it O'Brazil—the isle of the blest. **1899** KIPLING *Stalky & Co.* p. vii, Far and sure our bands have gone—Hy-Brasil or Babylon. **1906** —— *Puck of Pook's Hill* 14 Sir Huon.. setting off from Tintagel Castle for Hy-Brasil. **1948** L. MACNEICE *Holes in Sky* 30 Both myth and seismic history have been long suppressed Which made and unmade Hy Brazil. **1967** V. GIELGUD *Conduct of Member* xviii. 139 Want to go a long way..Cipangu—or better, Hy-Brazil. The world was more fun when its countries had names like these.

hybrid ('haɪbrɪd, 'hɪbrɪd), *sb.* and *a.* Also 7 **hi-, hybride.** [f. L. *hybrida*, more correctly *hibrida* (*ibrida*), offspring of a tame sow and wild boar; hence, of human parents of different races, half-breed. Cf. F. *hybride* (1798 in Hatz.-Darm.).

A few examples of this word occur early in 17th c.; but it was scarcely in use till the 19th. The only member of the group given by Johnson is HYBRIDOUS *a.*; Ash and Todd have also *hybrid* adj., to which Webster 1828 adds *hybrid* sb. As to the ultimate etym. of L. *hybrida* see Prof. Minton Warren in *Amer. Jrnl. Philol.* V. No. 4.]

A. *sb.*

1. The offspring of two animals or plants of different species, or (less strictly) varieties; a half-breed, cross-breed, or mongrel.

reciprocal hybrids, hybrids produced from the same two species A and B, where in the one case A is male and B female, in the other B is male and A female; *e.g.* the mule and the hinny.

a. of animals. (In 17th c. only as in original L.)

1601 HOLLAND *Pliny* II. 231 There is no creature ingenders so soon with wild of the kind, as doth swine: and verily such hogs in old time they called Hybrides, as a man would say, halfe wild. **1623** COCKERAM, *Hibride*, a Hog ingendred betweene a wilde Boare and a tame Sow. **1828** WEBSTER, *Hybrid*, a mongrel or mule; an animal or plant, produced from the mixture of two species. **1851** D. WILSON *Preh. Ann.* (1863) II. IV. ii. 232 Grotesque hybrids, half-bird, half-beast. **1859** DARWIN *Orig. Spec.* i. 26 The hybrids or mongrels from between all the breeds of the pigeon are perfectly fertile. **1862** HUXLEY *Lect. Wrkg. Men* 112 There is a great difference between 'Mongrels' which are crosses between distinct races and 'hybrids' which are crosses between distinct species.

b. of human beings.

1630 B. JONSON *New Inn* II. ii, She's a wild Irish born, sir, and a hybride. **1861** J. CRAWFURD in *Trans. Ethnol. Soc.* (N.S.) I. 357 At the best we [English] are but hybrids, yet, probably, not the worse for that. **1878** BOSW. SMITH *Carthage* 434 Negroes from the Soudan, not such sickly.. hybrids as you see in Oxford Street..but real down-right Negroes halfnaked, black as ebony.

c. of plants.

[**1788** J. LEE *Introd. Bot.* (ed. 4) Gloss., *Hybrida*, a Bastard, a monstrous Production of two Plants of different Species.] **1828** [see a]. **1845** LINDLEY *Sch. Bot.* x. (1858) 167 No hybrids but such as are of a woody perennial character can be perpetuated with certainty. **1846** J. BAXTER *Libr. Pract. Agric.* (ed. 4) II. 358 Swedes are generally sown first. Hybrids..are usually sown next, and white turnips the last. **1867** DARWIN in *Life & Lett.* (1887) III. 306 The common Oxlip found everywhere..in England, is certainly a hybrid between the primrose and cowslip.

2. *transf.* and *fig.* **a.** Anything derived from heterogeneous sources, or composed of different or incongruous elements; in *Philol.* a composite word formed of elements belonging to different languages.

1850 H. ROGERS *Ess.* II. iv. 213 A free resort to grotesque compounds..favours the multiplication of yet more grotesque hybrids. **1860** DARWIN in *Life & Lett.* (1887) II. 338, I will tell you what you are, a hybrid, a complex cross of lawyer, poet, naturalist, and theologian! **1874** LISLE CARR *Jud. Gwynne* II. vii. 163 A remarkable hybrid between a frank..bumpkin, and a used up exquisite. **1879** MORRIS *Eng. Accid.* 39 Sometimes we find English and Romance elements compounded. These are termed *Hybrids.* **1895** F. HALL *Two Trifles* 28 The ancient Romans would not have endured *scientistes* or *scientista*, as a new type of hybrid.

b. *Petrol.* A hybrid rock (see sense B. 2 b below).

1918 *Q. Jrnl. Geol. Soc.* LXXIV. 129 Compared with the Potter-Fell type..they would be hybrids, the former are transitional varieties. **1934** *Ibid.* XC. 599 The hybrid or its parent magma rose along the bedding-planes of the sediments. **1950** E. E. WAHLSTROM *Introd. Theor. Igneous Petrol.* x. 234 The products of intermingling of these magmas originally were called hybrids, a term which..has come to have a broader meaning and now includes all rocks resulting from the assimilation or melting of solid igneous rocks by later intrusions from the same source.

c. *Physical Chem.* A hybrid orbital (see sense B. 2 d below).

1932 *Physical Rev.* XL. 62 A hybrid of 3*d*, 4*s*, and 4*p* electrons. **1962** P. J. & B. DURRANT *Introd. Adv. Inorg. Chem.* v. 144 The bond angles, at a given atom, are determined by the angles between its σ hybrids. **1968** K. F. REID *Prop. & React. Bonds in Org. Molecules* iii. 43 The second kind of hybridized orbital, termed the trigonal hybrid, arises through the hybridization of one *s* and two *p* A[tomic] O[rbital]s.

B. *adj.*

1. a. Produced by the inter-breeding of two different species or varieties of animals or plants; mongrel, cross-bred, half-bred.

1775 ASH, *Hybrid*, begotten between animals of different species, produced from plants of different kinds. **1789** E. DARWIN *Bot. Gard.* 149 *note*, Many hybrid plants described. **1823** J. BADCOCK *Dom. Amusem.* 47 These hybrid, or mule productions. **1857** DARWIN in *Life & Lett.* (1887) II. 96, I think there is rather better evidence on the sterility of hybrid animals than you seem to admit. **1865** PALGRAVE *Arabia* II. 211 The town inhabitants..are at present a very hybrid race, yet fused into a general..type.

b. As the first element in the names of varieties of rose, esp. **hybrid China**, a variety produced by crossing *Rosa chinensis* and *R. semperflorens*, characterized by a long flowering period; **hybrid perpetual**, a cross between *Rosa damascena* and a hybrid China rose; **hybrid polyantha** = FLORIBUNDA; **hybrid tea**, a cross between a hybrid perpetual and a tea-scented rose (*Rosa odorata*).

1837 T. RIVERS *Rose Amateur's Guide* I. 20 Perhaps no plant presents such a mass of beauty as a finely grown hybrid China rose in full bloom. **1848** W. PAUL *Rose Garden* II. 121 The Bourbon Perpetual..is a division embracing the varieties of Hybrid Perpetual, in which the characters of the Bourbon Rose are strikingly developed. **1859, 1890**, [see PERPETUAL *sb.* 1 b]. **1890** *Gardeners' Chron.* 1 Feb. 132/1 Primrose Dame and Vicomtesse Folkestone are also included with hybrid Teas. **1931** M. GRIEVE *Mod. Herbal* II. 688/1 The most suitable are the so-called Hybrid Perpetuals, flowering from June to October. **1945, 1956** [see FLORIBUNDA]. **1951** *Dict. Gardening* (R. Hort. Soc.) IV. 1824/1 Hybrid Perpetual Roses..originated in the crossing of the Damask Rose with the Hybrid China varieties. **1968** A. CHRISTIE *By Pricking of Thumbs.* vi. 82 Got some old-fashioned roses here... Better than them new-fashioned Hybrid Teas. **1970** [see FLORIBUNDA]. **1973** *Rose Ann.* 37 The first of the new race to bear the characteristics of the hybrid tea was 'Victor Verdier' (1859), although some may claim that 'La France' (1867) was the first true hybrid tea rose.

2. *transf.* and *fig.* **a.** Derived from heterogeneous or incongruous sources; having a mixed character; composed of two diverse elements; mongrel.

hybrid bill, a bill in Parliament combining the characteristics of a public and private bill, which is referred to a ***hybrid committee***, i.e. a committee nominated partly (as in a public bill) by the House of Commons and partly (as in a private bill) by the Committee of Selection.

a **1716** SOUTH *Serm.* (1737) V. xii. 118 As Saint Paul..did [deal] with those judaizing hybrid Christians. **1805** *Med. Jrnl.* XIV. 309 Incomplete vaccination..again followed by a sort of hybrid result or modified variolæ. **1837–9** HALLAM *Hist. Lit.* I. i. I. §87. 79 The historians use a hybrid jargon intermixed with modern words. **1859** ERSKINE MAY *Law of Parl.* (ed. 4) xxiv. 613 Established by a public bill, brought in by the government, but otherwise treated as a private or 'hybrid' bill. **1864** BOWEN *Logic* v. 120 As well executed as such a hybrid scheme can be. **1887** SKEAT *Princ. Eng. Etymol.* I. 430 English abounds with Hybrid compounds.. words made up from different languages. **1888** BRYCE *Amer. Commw.* I. xiii. 185 *note*, In England..Hybrid committees are appointed partly by the House and partly by the Committee of Selection. **1893** *May's Law of Parl.* (ed. 10) 444 Public bills which affect private rights..are termed in practice 'hybrid bills'.

b. *Petrol.* Of rock: formed by the mixing of two different magmas or by the incorporation into an intruding magma of adjacent solid rock (esp. rock of the same origin as the magma).

1904 A. HARKER *Tertiary Igneous Rocks Skye* xi. 183 The processes..were of a less simple kind, mere admixture being supplemented by diffusion. The resulting hybrid rocks.. are thus only in a general sense intermediate in composition between the two parent rocks, and may be abnormal in comparison with any ordinary igneous rocks formed from a single magma. **1954** H. WILLIAMS et al. *Petrogr.* vi. 110 Most diorites..are probably hybrid rocks, and many contain xenoliths that exhibit various stages of magmatic reaction.

c. *Computers.* Utilizing or involving both analogue and digital methods.

1959 E. M. GRABBE et al. *Handbk. Automation, Computation, & Control* II. xxix. 4 The purpose of the hybrid system..is to combine the advantages noted above for each of the two types of conventional computer, while at the same time obviating the disadvantages. **1964** *Ann. N.Y. Acad. Sci.* CXV. 573 More complex operations such as multiplication are not as critical to most hybrid operations and can be slower. **1968** *Brit. Med. Bull.* XXIV. 193/1 The limited accuracy of analogue computers..can be overcome by using 'hybrid' computers in which certain elements..are digitally designed to preserve accuracy.

d. *Physical Chem.* Applied to a bond or valence orbital obtained by the linear combination of two or more different atomic orbitals.

1939 L. PAULING *Nature Chem. Bond* iii. 82 The strength of the best *s–p* hybrid bond orbital. **1960** J. W. LINNETT *Wave Mech. & Valency* viii. 128 The appropriate hybrid orbitals are the most successful for indicating the spatial distribution of the electrons. **1968** K. F. REID *Prop. & React. Bonds in Org. Molecules* iii. 42 The 2*s* and the three 2*p* orbitals of the excited atom are treated in such a way that.. they combine to produce four equivalent orbitals, each termed a tetrahedral or sp^3-hybrid orbital, which have their axes directed towards the four corners of a regular tetrahedron.

3. Special Combs.: **hybrid coil** *Electr.*, a type of transformer used in two-wire telephone circuits when amplification in both directions is required, having four pairs of terminals so arranged that if the impedances connected to two pairs balance, a voltage applied to a third pair divides equally between them without inducing a voltage in the fourth pair; also called a ***hybrid transformer***; **hybrid swarm** *Ecol.*, a variable population caused by the hybridization of neighbouring species; **hybrid vigour** = HETEROSIS 3.

1925 C. A. WRIGHT *Telephone Communication* x. 244 Conjugate alternating-current bridges or hybrid coils..are generally used in repeater and multiplex telephone lines. **1959** K. HENNEY *Radio Engin. Handbk.* (ed. 5) xxviii. 33

Instead of connecting the respective input of one amplifier and output of the other amplifier directly to a line circuit, there is introduced a balancing coil or so-called hybrid coil. **1926** *Nature* 30 Oct. 623/2 (*heading*) The naming of wild hybrid swarms. *Ibid.* 624 Nor do the 'Rules' have in view the existence of the highly polymorphic hybrid swarms—in no few cases hundreds or probably thousands of distinct individuals—that are known to exist. **1947** *New Phytologist* XLVI. 229 The Oxlip is confined in Britain to a small area in East Anglia, and at the edges of this area Oxlip-Primrose hybrid populations are found; such well-defined hybrid swarms are not common amongst British plants. **1963** E. MAYR *Animal Species & Evol.* vi. 118 The barrier between two sympatric species sometimes breaks down so completely, locally or over wide areas, that the two parental species are replaced by a hybrid swarm that serves as a continuous bridge between the two parental extremes. **1969** BRIGGS & WALTERS *Plant Variation & Evol.* xi. 186 Hybrid swarms are found in which there is a remarkable range of variation. **1941** *Stand. Handbk. Electr. Engin.* (ed. 7) xxii. 2055 (*caption*) Principle of hybrid transformer. **1962** *Newnes Conc. Encycl. Electr. Engin.* 379/1 A separating device consisting of a pair of matched 'hybrid' transformers is a common method of securing two-way amplification. [**1909** E. M. EAST in *Amer. Naturalist* XLIII. 179 In every case an increase in vigor over the parents [*sc.* maize plants] was shown by the crosses.] **1918** BABCOCK & CLAUSEN *Genetics Rel. Agric.* xii. 230 Not all species hybrids, however, display hybrid vigor. **1949** C. C. LINDEGREN *Yeast Cell* xxvii. 2 The degeneration or 'running out' of hybrids showing heterosis has been one of the principal problems of hybrid vigor. **1970** *Watsonia* VIII. 131 Its robust growth, vigorous vegetative spread and large fronds..suggest hybrid vigour.

So † **'hybridal**, † **'hybridan** *adjs.* = HYBRID *a.*

1623 COCKERAM, *Hybridan*, whose parents are of diuers and sundry Nations. **1801** T. JEFFERSON *Writ.* (ed. Ford) VIII. 16, I am persuaded the squash..is a hybridal plant.

hybridation (-'eɪʃən). [a. F. *hybridation*, f. *hybride* HYBRID: see -ATION.] = HYBRIDIZATION 1 a.

1879 tr. *De Quatrefages' Hum. Spec.* 69 Finally, crossing between species, or hybridation, is extremely exceptional among plants and animals when left to themselves. **1882** *American* V. 88 The rejection of the theory of hybridation advocated by some ostreiculturists.

hybridism ('haɪbrɪdɪz(ə)m, 'hɪb-). [f. HYBRID + -ISM: cf. F. *hybridisme.*]

1. The fact or condition of being hybrid; the hybrid condition in plants or animals as a biological phenomenon.

1846 in WORCESTER. **1857** DARWIN in *Life & Lett.* (1887) II. 110, I have now been three whole months on one chapter [of 'Origin of Species'] on Hybridism. **1862** HUXLEY *Lect. Wrkg. Men* 147 Here are the phenomena of Hybridism staring you in the face.

b. The production of hybrids; cross-breeding.

1845 LINDLEY *Sch. Bot.* x. (1858) 169 Recourse is had to hybridism, when a wild insipid fruit may be possibly improved. **1863** DICEY *Federal St.* I. 208 It is, in fact, the instinct of self-preservation, which revolts at hybridism. **1883** H. DRUMMOND *Nat. Law in Spir. W.* Pref. (1884) 13 Inappropriate hybridism is checked by the Law of Sterility.

2. *Philol.* The formation of a word from elements belonging to different languages.

1862 LATHAM *Eng. Lang.* (ed. 5) 480 In seamstress and songstress we find instances of hybridism.

'hybridist. [f. as prec. + -IST.] = HYBRIDIZER.

1849 *Florist* 223 By the acquisition of this species, a new field for the hybridist is thrown open. **1850** *Ibid.* 80 Of late the skill of hybridists has been misdirected to the production of size of blossom and novelty of colour. **1882** *Garden* 25 Feb. 123/1 Old Hybridisers had not, however, the material to work upon which modern Hybridists possess.

hybridity (haɪ'brɪdɪtɪ, hɪb-). [f. as prec. + -ITY: cf. F. *hybridité.*] Hybrid condition.

1837 DARWIN in *Life & Lett.* (1887) II. 8 It would lead to closest examination of hybridity. **1842** PRICHARD *Nat. Hist. Man* 12 Briefly surveying the phenomena of hybridity. **1890** STUART GLENNIE in *Nature* 2 Oct., The Aryan languages present such indications of hybridity as would correspond with such racial intermixture.

'hybriˌdizable, *a.* [f. as next + -ABLE.] Capable of hybridization.

a **1864** J. D. HOOKER (W.), Hybridizable genera are rarer than is generally supposed. **1871** W. T. DYER in *Jrnl. Bot.* IX. 304 Willows are hybridizable. **1893** ROMANES *Let.* in *Life* iv. (1895) 332 Its constituent species being freely hybridisable.

ˌhybridi'zation. [f. HYBRIDIZE + -ATION.]

1. a. The formation of hybrids; cross-breeding between parents of different species.

1851 *Illustr. Catal. Gt. Exhib.* 205 In the hybridization of plants experiments are always of much interest. **1883** G. ALLEN in *Longm. Mag.* July 314 The possibility of fertile hybridisation in such a manner shows that the plants have not long diverged from the common central stock.

b. *Petrol.* The formation of a hybrid rock.

1926 G. W. TYRRELL *Princ. Petrol.* ii. 31 There is a good deal of commingling of the magmas, with enclosure of fragments and hybridisation, along the interior contacts. **1968** B. BAYLY *Introd. Petrol.* ix. 100 At the interface between a magma and a solid rock, the possibility of interpenetration exists... Where the environment is solidified magma from an earlier stage of the same magmatic event, the process is called hybridization; when, as is more common, the environment is some independent solid, the process is contamination.

c. *Physical Chem.* The mathematical combination of atomic orbitals to form a hybrid orbital.

1932 *Physical Rev.* XL. 1037, sp^3 hybridization is encountered only when the repulsions between the four electrons of the H atoms are included. **1962** P. J. & B. DURRANT *Introd. Adv. Inorg. Chem.* v. 145 Table 5.1 shows some of the valence states of atoms which can be produced by the hybridisation of atomic orbitals. **1968** [see HYBRID *sb.* and *a.* A. 2 c].

d. *Biochem.* The formation of a hybrid macromolecule by artificially recombining complementary subunits (single polynucleotide strands in the case of nucleic acids and individual polypeptide chains in the case of proteins) obtained from slightly different varieties of the same molecular species or (in the case of RNA-DNA hybrids) of similar molecular species.

1959 WOLSTENHOLME & O'CONNOR *Biochem. Human Genetics* (Ciba Found. Symp.) 123 Vinograd, Schroeder and Hutchinson (1959) have shown by an ingenious 'hybridization' experiment involving haemoglobin labelled with ^{14}C that the α chains of haemoglobins A and S are interchangeable and therefore similar. **1962** *Science* 21 Dec. 1329/1 It is perhaps not surprising that s-RNA is resistant to hybridization since x-ray analysis..suggests that s-RNA is a hairpin structure kept together by a highly regular system of hydrogen bonding. Until this secondary structure is disrupted there is no opportunity for pairing between s-RNA molecules and complementary sequences in the DNA. **1965** *Jrnl. Molecular Biol.* XII. 830 Hybridization in solution has one obvious disadvantage, stemming from the fact that RNA-DNA formation must compete with the re-formation of the DNA-DNA complexes. **1966** LEHMANN & HUNTSMAN *Man's Haemoglobins* xxi. 224 (*heading*) Hybridisation of abnormal human haemoglobin variants. **1968** W. A. SCHROEDER *Primary Struct. Proteins* 206/1 (*index*) Hybridization of ribonuclease. **1972** *Arch. Biochem. & Biophysics* CL. 407 (*title*) Hybridization of rabbit muscle and liver phosphofructokinases. **1972** W. V. BROWN *Textbk. Cytogenetics* ii. 13/1 The biochemical techniques of nucleic acid hybridization, either DNA-DNA or RNA-DNA.., have recently been providing new and unexpected understanding about the DNA sequences in the nucleus.

e. *Cytology.* The fusion, by artificial means or in artificial cultures, of two somatic cells of different karyotypes to form a hybrid cell containing the nuclear material of both.

1961 *Nature* 13 May 653/2 (*heading*) Karyological demonstration of hybridization of mammalian cells *in vitro.* **1965** *Proc. Nat. Acad. Sci.* LIII. 1040 Hybridization of somatic cells *in vitro*..has since been shown to occur in mixed cultures of many different pairs of cultured mouse cells. **1970** *Nature* 18 Apr. 280/2 Somatic cell hybridization is a potentially useful technique for the introduction of genetic variability into plant species. **1970** *McGraw-Hill Yearbk. Sci. & Technol.* 214/2 Whereas these first experiments involved two closely related transformed mouse cell lines,..somatic hybridization can occur between cells derived from different species, such as mouse and man.

2. *fig.*

1960 E. R. GOODMAN in J. A. Fishman *Readings Sociol. of Lang.* (1968) 733 One should add that the idea of 'hybridization' or fusion of languages, which Stalin continued to use, was Marrist in origin. **1964** M. MCLUHAN *Understanding Media* v. 48 The crossings or hybridizations of the media release great new force and energy as by fission or fusion. **1971** *Farmer & Stockbreeder* 23 Feb. 3/1 We shall be the old Stockbreeder Redivivus: not dead, not reborn, just rejuvenated. Or, if you prefer it, reinvigorated by hybridization; for we join forces with the *British Farmer*, the journal of the NFU.

hybridize ('haɪbrɪdaɪz, hɪb-), *v.* [f. HYBRID + -IZE.]

1. a. *trans.* To subject (species or varieties of plants or animals) to cross-breeding; to cause to interbreed and thus to produce hybrids.

1845 *Florist's Jrnl.* 258 Suited to the purposes of hybridising. **1849** *Florist* 201 This [sameness] led enterprising cultivators to hybridise the sorts they possessed. **1861** DELAMER *Fl. Gard.* 53 The produce therefrom [a large bed] is completely hybridized by the agency of the wind and of bees.

b. To form or construct (words) in a hybrid manner (*Cent. Dict.*).

c. *Physical Chem.* To combine (atomic orbitals) mathematically so as to obtain hybrid orbitals.

1933 [implied in HYBRIDIZED *ppl. a.*]. **1939** L. PAULING *Nature Chem. Bond* iii. 96 It is found on hybridizing these orbitals that four strong bonds directed to the corners of a square can be formed. **1962** COTTON & WILKINSON *Adv. Inorg. Chem.* iii. 67 The *s* and the three *p* orbitals are hybridized to produce four sp^3 hybrids.

d. *Biochem.* To cause (a subunit of a macromolecule) to combine *with*, or become attached *to*, a complementary subunit of the same or a very similar molecular species from a different source; to cause (two such subunits) to combine together.

1959 *Jrnl. Amer. Chem. Soc.* LXXXI. 3169/1 When labelled and unlabelled hemoglobins are hybridized, the hybrids contain both labelled and unlabelled chains. **1965** *Jrnl. Molecular Biol.* XII. 829 The procedure involves immobilizing denatured DNA on nitrocellulose membrane filters, hybridizing complementary RNA to the membrane-fixed DNA, and eliminating RNA 'noise'. **1966** LEHMANN & HUNTSMAN *Man's Haemoglobins* xxi. 226 When canine haemoglobin and human haemoglobin are hybridised together, the new hybrids that result differ considerably in their mobility. **1969** *Nature* 10 May 573/1, 100 μg of RNA was hybridized with 50 μg of DNA. **1972** *Arch. Biochem. & Biophysics* CL. 407 Phosphofructokinases from rabbit muscle and rabbit liver were hybridized by dissociation at low pH followed by recombination at neutrality. **1972** S. L. WOLFE *Biol. Cell* ix. 199/1 The best evidence that transcription is asymmetric comes from experiments in which RNA is hybridized with its DNA template... The RNA will form hybrid double helices with no more than 50 percent of its template DNA... Thus the RNA is complementary to only one of the two DNA strands, and only one..serves as a template for RNA transcription.

2. *intr.* **a.** To produce a hybrid or hybrids between two distinct species or varieties.

1853 *Blackw. Mag.* LXXIII. 131 He grafted, and budded, and hybridised, and experimented. **1885** *Manch. Exam.* 23 Feb. 5/4 His attempts to hybridise with the other tuberous species have failed.

b. Of an animal or plant: To produce hybrid offspring by crossing *with* another species or variety; to cross or interbreed.

1862 *Proc. Amer. Phil. Soc.* IX. 119 [Sorghum] Its disposition to hybridize with broom-corn. **1880** *Chamb. Encycl.* s.v. *Canary*, The canary hybridizes readily with some other species of finch.

c. *Biochem.* Of a protein or nucleic acid: to exchange complementary subunits in hybridization (sense 1 d). Const. *with* (or *to*).

1962 *Science* 21 Dec. 1331/2 Their sequences are unique, since they hybridize readily only to homologous DNA. **1965** *Jrnl. Molecular Biol.* XII. 830 RNA molecules possessing an extensive secondary structure will not hybridize until their own melting temperature is approached. **1969** *Times* 16 May 14/7 Each kind of RNA chemically recombines or hybridizes with the DNA segment off which it was copied. **1971** *Biochemistry* (Easton, Pa.) X. 3509/2 Hexokinases A and B can hybridize in 0·1 M sodium phosphate solution at pH values near 8. **1972** S. L. WOLFE *Biol. Cell* ix. 206/2 For example, rRNA from *Drosophila* will hybridize to some degree with chick DNA or vice versa, even though there are wide differences in base composition of the total DNA complement from the two species.

3. *fig.* (*trans.*).

1964 M. MCLUHAN *Understanding Media* v. 50 With literacy now about to hybridize the cultures of the Chinese, the Indians, and the Africans. **1971** *Nature* 24 Sept. 241/2 In the more remote future it may well be, when further improvements in the combustion intensity of low grade fuel mixtures are required, that they will be achieved by hybridizing the high and low temperature branches.

hybridized ('haɪbrɪdaɪzd), *ppl. a.* [f. prec. + -ED[1].] Obtained by hybridization; hybrid (in various senses).

1859 DARWIN *Orig. Spec.* ix. (1872) 249 Hybridised embryos probably often perish in like manner. **1926** G. W. TYRRELL *Princ. Petrol.* viii. 165 Wholesale enclosure of Dalradian quartzites and mica-schists within a large mass of norite..has led to the formation of a zone of hybridised or contaminated rocks, full of xenoliths in all stages of digestion. **1933** *Jrnl. Chem. Physics* I. 502 The valence orbital..could be of the strongly hybridized type. **1955** [see FINE ART 2]. **1959** G. E. W. WOLSTENHOLME et al. *Significant Trends Med. Res.* (Ciba Found. Symp.) 7 The N-terminal residues of the hybridized hemoglobin S were labelled with Sanger's reagent. **1968** [see HYBRID *sb.* and *a.* A. 2 c]. **1969** *Nature* 10 May 573/2 The rat from which the hybridized RNA was obtained.

'hybridizer. [f. HYBRIDIZE *v.* + -ER[1].] One who produces hybrids by crossing different species or varieties of animals or plants.

1849 *Florist* 223 These difficulties..every hybridiser must make up his mind to encounter and surmount. **1859** DARWIN *Orig. Spec.* iv. (1872) 76 Every hybridizer knows how unfavourable exposure to wet is to the fertilisation of a flower. **1882** [see HYBRIDIST].

'hybridous, *a.* Now *rare* or *Obs.* [f. L. *hybrida* + -OUS. (The only word of the group in Johnson.)] = HYBRID *a.*; of hybrid character.

1691 RAY *Creation* II. (1692) 69 Why such different Species should not only mingle together, but also generate an Animal, and yet that that hybridous Production should not again generate, and so a new Race be carried on. **1714** L. MILBOURNE *Traitor's Rew.* Pref., The phrase was hybridous, and therefore inelegant. **1771** *Misc.* in *Ann. Reg.* 172/2 Botanists..have produced hybridous plants. **1794** MARTYN *Rousseau's Bot.* xxvi. 390 It proved to be a hybridous plant or mule. **1803** S. PEGGE *Anecd. Eng. Lang.* 192 Elizabeth R., which is a glaring hybridous mixture of English and Latin. **1885** W. MCDONALD IN *N. Amer. Rev.* Sept. 290 No hybridous architecture.

hybris ('haɪbrɪs). [ad. Gr. ὕβρις.] = HUBRIS.

1920 *Public Opinion* 27 Aug. 195/2 During one of these the oppressor, possessed of place and power, imagined in his hybris, that he might extend his arm across the ocean. **1929** *Encycl. Brit.* XXII. 53/1 Themis is the servant or companion of Zeus... Her opposite is Hybris (ὕβρις), insolent encroachment upon the rights of others. **1949** *Horizon* Aug. 87 Hybris means believing that you *are* a god, i.e., that you cannot suffer; pride means a defiant attempt to *become* a god. **1969** *Commonweal* 22 Aug. 524 America, like all earlier empires, is going to march to the brink of *hybris* and plunge in.

hyce, hycht, obs. ff. HOISE, HEIGHT.

hyd: see HIDE *sb.*[1] and *v.*[1]

hydage, obs. f. HIDAGE.

hydantoic (haɪdæn'təʊɪk), *a. Chem.* [Arbitrary formation from Gr. ὑδ-ωρ water + (ALL)ANTOIC.] = Glycoluric. So **hydantoate** (haɪ'dæntəʊət) [see -ATE[1] 1 c]; **hy'dantoïn** = Glycolylurea.

1866 ODLING *Anim. Chem.* 127 Schlieper added the leucoturic, allituric, dilituric, hydantoic, hydurilic, and allanturic or lantanuric acids. *Ibid.* 135 Hydantoine. **1872**

WATTS *Dict. Chem.* VI. 702 Hydantoic acid . . crystallizes in large, transparent, colourless . . prisms. *Ibid.*, All the hydantoates . . are easily soluble in water. *Ibid.*, The hydantoïn separates in colourless specular crystals.

hydathode ('haɪdəθəʊd). *Bot.* [a. G. *hydathode* (G. Haberlandt 1894, in *Sitzungsber. Akad. Wiss. Wien* CIII. I. 494), f. Gr. ὑδατ-, ὕδωρ water + ὁδός way, path.] A pore or gland which discharges water from the leaf of a plant.

1895 *Jrnl. R. Microsc. Soc.* 333 Under the name *hydathode*, Prof. G. Haberlandt designates those organs, which are frequently found in the leaves of tropical and other plants, especially designed for the storing up or excretion of water. *Ibid.*, A very simple type of hydathode occurs in the leaves of grasses. **1897** J. C. WILLIS *Man. Flowering Plants* I. 116 Water-pores or hydathodes are openings, resembling stomata, upon leaves or elsewhere, through which the plant excretes water. **1914** M. DRUMMOND tr. *Haberlandt's Physiol. Plant Anat.* x. 487 Many of our native plants are provided with organs which secrete water in the liquid form. Such hydathodes are even more widely distributed among plants inhabiting the humid tropics. **1931** E. C. MILLER *Plant Physiol.* vii. 390 The physiological significance of the hydathodes and of the loss of water by guttation is not definitely known. **1953** K. ESAU *Plant Anat.* xvi. 433 Hydathodes are structures that discharge water from the interior of the leaf to its surface. **1967** C. D. SCULTHORPE *Biol. Aquatic Vasc. Plants* iv. 90 The possibility remains that the hydathodes [of water plants] are functionless relict structures.

hydatic (haɪ'dætɪk), *a.* [ad. Gr. ὑδατικ-ός watery, f. ὑδατ- water. Cf. F. *hydatique.*] Pertaining to or of the nature of a hydatid; watery. So †**hy'datical** *a.*

1710 DOUGLAS in *Phil. Trans.* XXVII. 34 A large hydatical or watery Tumor. **1872** PEASLEE *Ovar. Tumours* 42 The hydatic [cyst], with contents clear as spring water.

hydatid ('haɪdətɪd, 'hɪd-), *sb.* (*a.*) *Path.* Chiefly in *pl.*; formerly in Lat. form **hydatides** (hɪ'dætɪdiːz). [ad. Gr. ὑδατίς, ὑδατιδ- a drop of water, watery vesicle. Cf. F. *hydatide.*] A cyst containing a clear watery fluid, occurring as a morbid formation in the tissues of animal bodies; *esp.* one formed by and containing the larva of a tapeworm; hence, the larva of a tapeworm (esp. of *Tænia echinococcus*) in its encysted state.

α. **1683** *Phil. Trans.* XIII. 284 Some . . by no means will admit of Egs, but will have them all to be Hydatides. **1687** *Ibid.* XVI. 506 That Hydatides often met with in morbid Animal Bodies, are a Species of Worms, or Imperfect Animals. **1762** R. GUY *Pract. Obs. Cancers* 91 A great quantity of Hydatides, or small connected Bladders of clear water.

β. **1782** H. WATSON in *Med. Commun.* I. 90 The kidnies were . . filled with hydatids. **1794–6** E. DARWIN *Zoon.* (1801) III. 236 Calves, which have an hydatide with insects inclosed in it in the frontal sinus. **1851** H. STEPHENS *Bk. Farm* (ed. 2) II. 163/1 The disease ['the sturdy'] is caused by a living animal in the brain, the Many-headed hydatid. **1880** MAC CORMAC *Antisept. Surg.* 218 An operation planned and carried out . . for the radical cure of cases of hydatid of the liver.

b. ***hydatid of Morgagni***, a small body of which one or more are often found attached to the epididymis or to the Fallopian tube; formerly supposed to be a hydatid, now generally held to be the remnant of the Müllerian duct.

1886 in *Syd. Soc. Lex.* s.v. *Morgagni.*

B. *attrib.* or *adj.* Of or belonging to hydatids; of the nature of a hydatid; containing or affected with hydatids.

1807–26 S. COOPER *First Lines Surg.* (ed. 5) 203 The hydatid tumour of the breast . . so named from its containing cysts of the nature of hydatids. **1829** SIR A. COOPER *Illust. Dis. Breast* I. iii. 20 On the Hydatid Disease of the Breast. The term Hydatid might be applied to every watery tumour, and it may therefore here with propriety be employed. **1845** BUDD *Dis. Liver* 341 The hydatid cyst. **1861** HULME tr. *Moquin-Tandon* II. VII. xiii. 391 The old writers gave them the name of Hydatids, or Hydatid Worms. **1897** ALLBUTT *Syst. Med.* II. 1116 One hydatid patient for every sixty-five admitted. *Ibid.* 1134 Percussion seldom yields the hydatid thrill.

Hence **hyda'tidiform** (also contr. '**hydatiform**) [cf. F. *hydatiforme*] *a.*, having the form or character of a hydatid; ***hydatidiform mole***, a uterine mole (MOLE *sb.*[5]) formed by the proliferation and distension of the chorionic villi; also, the condition of having such a mole in the uterus; **hyda'tidinous** *a.*, of the nature of a hydatid; containing hydatids; **hyda'tigenous** *a.*, producing hydatids.

1859 *Lancet* 15 Oct. 397/2 A case in which a specimen of the *hydatidiform mole was expelled from the uterus seven months after the birth of a first child. **1860** TANNER *Pregnancy* v. 238 Vesicular or hydatidiform disease of the chorion. **1971** T. J. DEELEY *Gynaecol. Cancer* XV. 228 The incidence of hydatidiform mole is about 1:700 - 1:3,000 known pregnancies. **1855** RAMSBOTHAM *Obstetr. Med.* 78 Solid tumours . . are found imbedded in the mass, and occasionally, but very rarely, it is *hydatidinous. **1854** MAYNE *Expos. Lex.*, *Hydatiform. **1876** HARLEY *Mat. Med.* (ed. 6) 368 Hydatiform and polypoid tumors of the uterus. **1854** MAYNE *Expos. Lex.*, *Hydatigenous. **1889** J. M. DUNCAN *Lect. Dis. Wom.* vii. (ed. 4) 37 Hydatigenous degeneration of the ovum is an objectionable name.

hydatidosis (haɪdətɪ'dəʊsɪs). *Path.* [f. HYDATID *sb.* (*a.*) + -OSIS.] A pathological condition resulting from infestation with tapeworm hydatids.

1925 *Med. Jrnl. Austral.* 24 Oct. 502/1 The whole abdominal cavity may be packed with cysts of all sizes—a condition which has been called hydatidosis. **1966** *Lancet* 24 Dec. 1422/1 Subjects with pulmonary hydatidosis . . were tested.

hydatism ('haɪdətɪz(ə)m, 'hɪd-). *Med.* [ad. Gr. ὑδατισμ-ός, f. *ὑδατίζειν to be watery, f. ὑδατ- water. Cf. F. *hydatisme.*] A sound produced by motion of effused fluid in a cavity of the body.

1753 in CHAMBERS *Cycl. Supp.* **1847** in CRAIG. **1854** in MAYNE *Expos. Lex.*

hydatoid ('haɪdətɔɪd, 'hɪd-), *a.* and *sb.* [ad. mod.L. *hydatoīdēs*, a. Gr. ὑδατοειδ-ής like water, watery (f. ὑδατο- water + εἶδος form); τὸ ὑδατοειδές the aqueous humour of the eye. Cf. F. *hydatoïde.*]

A. *adj.* Resembling water, watery, aqueous. **B.** *sb.* The aqueous humour of the eye; also, the investing membrane of the aqueous humour (Webster 1864). (Cf. HYALOID.)

[**1706** PHILLIPS (ed. Kersey), *Hydatoides*, the aqueous or watery Humour of the Eye.] **1886** *Syd. Soc. Lex.*, *Hydatoid fluid*, the aqueous humour of the eye. *H. membrane*, the membrane of Descemet.

hy-day-gies, hydegy: see HAY *sb.*[4] 2.

hydd, obs. f. HIDE *sb.*[1]

hydder, -ir, obs. ff. HITHER.

hyde, obs. f. HIDE; obs. pa. t. and pple. of HIE.

Hyde (haɪd). Name of the evil personality assumed by Dr. Jekyll in R. L. Stevenson's story, 'Strange Case of Dr. Jekyll and Mr. Hyde' (1886): used allusively in reference to the evil side of a person's character. (Cf. JEKYLL.)

1887 *Puck* (U.S.) XXII. 188 Is that you, Livingston? . . No, m'dearsh, it'sh Doct' Hyde. **1915** 'I. HAY' *First Hundred Thousand* xiv. 192 But we encountered surprisingly few Hydes. Nearly all were Jekylls. **1960** *Encounter* Sept. 9/1 Normally we let Hyde loose only when for some reason he is socially acceptable. The Saturnalia existed to satisfy his demands. **1967** V. NABOKOV *Speak, Memory* (ed. 2) viii. 165 One ribald and agile boy (could it be I after all—the Hyde of my Jekyll?) managed to silhouette his foot.

hydel, -les, hyddillis, hydles, var. HIDEL, HIDELS.

Hyde Park ('haɪd 'pɑːk). The name of a park in central London, of which a part (known as Speakers' Corner) is traditionally the scene of 'soap-box' oratory, used allusively (freq. *attrib.*) of the type of speaker, oratory, etc., found there. So **Hyde 'Parkian** *a.*, having the quality (of voice) of a Hyde Park orator.

1892 G. B. SHAW *Let.* 21 Apr. (1965) 337 Her voice has become much more powerful—quite Hyde Parkian in its pedal notes. **1897** *London Handbk.* 143/1 They [*sc.* 'contentious Jews'] pose as martyrs in the cause of liberty, and certainly any man well deserves such an honourable title who will listen unflinchingly to two hours of Hyde Park oratory. **1912** C. MACKENZIE *Carnival* xii. 132 Love . . was as incredible to her as . . to a Hyde Park materialist. **1914** 'I. HAY' *Knight on Wheels* (ed. 2) xix. 186 This is a peculiarity of the Hyde Park orator. Set him on his legs, and in ten minutes he has wandered . . from the point. **1934** 'G. ORWELL' *Burmese Days* xvii. 245 He told Flory 'not to start talking like a damned Hyde Park agitator', and then read him a snappish little sermon. **1937** *Discovery* Aug. 254/1 Each having something to say like so many Hyde Park orators. **1965** C. FREMLIN *Jealous One* xi. 85 Everyone . . competing, like Hyde Park orators, for an audience for their particular problem. **1966** *Listener* 24 Feb. 287/2 A few jibes against the Christian Church more reminiscent of Hyde Park oratory than of Voltaire and Gibbon. **1972** 'E. LATHEN' *The Longer the Thread* xi. 106 A small Hyde Park seemed to have sprung up on the green. A whole medley of impassioned orators was in full voice.

hyder, obs. f. HITHER, HYDRA.

hydious, obs. f. HIDEOUS.

hydnocarpic (hɪdnəʊ'kɑːpɪk), *a. Chem.* [f. next + -IC.] ***hydnocarpic acid***: a crystalline alicyclic acid, $C_5H_7 \cdot (CH_2)_{10} \cdot COOH$, which in the form of its glycerides is one of the chief constituents of chaulmoogra oil and hydnocarpus oil.

1905 POWER & BARROWCLIFF in *Jrnl. Chem. Soc.* LXXXVII. I. 885 The acids obtained from the respective Hydnocarpus oils consist chiefly of chaulmoogric acid and a lower homologue of the same series, the latter having been isolated . . also from chaulmoogra oil. This new acid has the formula $C_{16}H_{28}O_2$, and is designated hydnocarpic acid. **1960** K. S. MARKLEY *Fatty Acids* (ed. 2) I. ii. 215 All these oils contain one or more fatty acids having a terminal cyclopentenyl ring, especially chaulmoogric, hydnocarpic, and gorlic acid, which account for 80 to 90% or more of the total fatty acids of these oils. *Ibid.* 217 *dl*-Hydnocarpic acid has been synthesized.

Hence **hydno'carpate**, a salt or ester of hydnocarpic acid.

1905 *Jrnl. Chem. Soc.* LXXVII. I. 890 Ethyl Hydnocarpate, $C_{15}H_{27} \cdot CO_2Et$. **1927** *Proc. R. Soc. Med.* XX. 999 The veins become blocked by sodium hydnocarpate in some cases. **1953** R. A. RAPHAEL in E. H. Rodd *Chem. Carbon Compounds* IIA. iv. 119 When ethyl hydnocarpate is reduced by the Bouveault-Blanc process, an alcohol is obtained which can be converted . . to chaulmoogric acid.

hydnocarpus (hɪdnəʊ'kɑːpəs). *Bot.* [mod.L. (J. Gaertner *De Fructibus et Seminibus Plantarum* (1788) I. 288), f. Gr. ὕδνον truffle + καρπός fruit, from the resemblance of the fruit to a truffle.]

a. A tree of the genus so called, belonging to the family Flacourtiaceæ and native to tropical Asia.

1928 *Daily Express* 20 Feb. 2/1 Hydnocarpus oil is obtained from the dried fruit of the hydnocarpus tree. **1953** N. L. BOR *Man. Indian Forest Bot.* 145 In *Hydnocarpus* the fruits are produced on the branches.

b. *attrib.*, as ***hydnocarpus therapy***; **hydnocarpus oil**, a yellowish oil or soft cream-coloured fat obtained from the seeds of trees of the genus *Hydnocarpus*, esp. *H. wightiana* and *H. anthelminthica*, and used, formerly extensively, in the treatment of leprosy.

1905 Hydnocarpus oils [see HYDNOCARPIC *a.*]. **1927** *Proc. R. Soc. Med.* XX. 1011 Since early in 1921 we have used the preparations of chaulmoogra and hydnocarpus oils in our Hospital for Lepers, at Dichpalli, Hyderabad State. **1967** *Martindale's Extra Pharmacopoeia* (ed. 25) 494/2 Although largely replaced by the sulphones, hydnocarpus oil is still employed in the treatment of leprosy, especially in endemic areas in the East where it is cheap and readily available. **1964** R. G. COCHRANE *Leprosy* (ed. 2) xxi. 377, I do not hold with many workers that the day of hydnocarpus therapy has disappeared.

hydnoid ('hɪdnɔɪd), *a. Bot.* [See -OID.] Resembling or allied to the genus *Hydnum* of fungi.

hydose, -ous, etc., obs. ff. HIDEOUS.

hydour(e, hydowse, var. HIDOUR, HIDOUS, *Obs.*

hydr-, the usual form of HYDRO- bef. a vowel.

hydra ('haɪdrə). Forms: α. 4–6 **ydre**, 5 **ydres**, 6–7 **hydre, hyder.** β. 4 **idra**, 6–7 **hidra**, 6– **hydra.** [a. L. *hydra*, a. Gr. ὕδρα, water-serpent; spec. as in sense 1. Some of the earlier forms are a. OF. *idres, ydre* (mod.F. *hydre*).]

I. 1. *Gr. Myth.* The fabulous many-headed snake of the marshes of Lerna, whose heads grew again as fast as they were cut off: said to have been at length killed by Hercules.

α. *c* **1374** CHAUCER *Boeth.* IV. pr. vi. 104 (Camb. MS.) Whan o dowte is determyned and kut awey, ther wexen oother dowtes with-owte nowmbyr ryht as the heuedes wexen of ydre the serpent þat Ercules slowh. **1460** CAPGRAVE *Chron.* (Rolls) 33 The VII. [labour of Hercules], killyng of the grete serpent cleped Ydres. **1509** HAWES *Past. Pleas.* XI. xix, How redoubted Hercules . . Fought with an ydre. **1590** SPENSER *F.Q.* II. xii. 23 Spring-headed Hydres; and sea-shouldring Whales.

β. **1398** TREVISA *Barth. De P.R.* XVIII. ix. (Bodl. MS.), Ydra is a serpente wiþ many hedes . . and it is seide that ȝif one hed is smyte of þree hedes growiþ aȝen. **1596** SPENSER *F.Q.* VI. xii. 32 Like the hell-borne Hydra, which they faine That great Alcides whilome overthrew. **1604** SHAKS. *Oth.* II. iii. 308 Had I as many mouthes as Hydra, such an answer would stop them all. **1667** MILTON *P.L.* II. 628 Worse Than Fables yet have feign'd, or fear conceiv'd, Gorgons and Hydra's, and Chimera's dire. **1780** HARRIS *Philol. Enq.* Wks. (1841) 463 When Alexander the Great died, many tyrants, like many hydras, immediately sprung up. **1879** GLADSTONE in *Lib. Mag.* I. No. 6. 663 The Eastern question has as many heads as the hydra.

2. *transf.* and *fig.* A thing, person, or body of persons compared to the Lernæan hydra in its baneful or destructive character, its multifarious aspects, or the difficulty of its extirpation.

1494 FABYAN *Chron.* VI. cciv. 215 The serpent Idre of enuy and false conspyracy, whiche euer burned in the harte of Edricus. **1546** BALE *Eng. Votaries* II. (1550) 118 b, That odyouse hydre and hissinge serpent of Rome. **1586** T. B. *La Primaud. Fr. Acad.* I. (1589) 378 They minister life and nourishment . . to this monstrous Hydra of covetousnes and lucre. **1592** DANIEL *Sonn. Delia* xv. (R.), And yet the hydra of my cares renews Still new born sorrows of her fresh disdain. **1726** AMHERST *Terræ Fil.* ix. 41 The hydra is not to be destroy'd, unless you strike off all the heads at once; . . if you were to turn out one jacobite head of a college, another as bad is ready to step in his room. **1809** HAN. MORE *Cœlebs* I. 387 Selfishness . . is the hydra we are perpetually combating. **1850** MERIVALE *Rom. Emp.* (1865) II. xii. 59 The hydra of revolt lay stunned and prostrate.

3. A rhetorical term for any terrific serpent or reptile; a 'dragon'.

1546 BALE *Eng. Votaries* I. (1560) 98 b, As greate honoure . . it was to Saint George that noble Captaine, to slea the great hydre or Dragon at Silena. **1613** PURCHAS *Pilgrimage* VI. i. 467 The Deserts of Lybia have in them many Hydras. **1851–78** C. L. SMITH tr. *Tasso* IV. v, Hydras hiss, and Pythons whistling wail.

4. A water-snake; esp. one of the venomous sea-snakes of the Indian and Pacific Oceans.

1608 TOPSELL *Serpents* (1658) 759 All Water-serpents, as well of the fresh, salt, and sweet waters may be called Hyders, or Snakes. **1814** CARY *Dante, Inf.* IX. 41 Around them greenest hydras twisting roll'd Their volumes. **1855**

EMERSON *Misc., Sov. Ethics* Wks. (Bohn) III. 374 Her interiors are terrific, full of hydras and crocodiles.

5. *Astron.* An ancient southern constellation, represented as a water-snake or sea-serpent. Its chief star is Alphard or Cor Hydræ, of the second magnitude.

1559 W. CUNNINGHAM *Cosmogr. Glasse* 27 A Table of many notable fixed Sterres with their longitude.. Brightest in Hydra. **1674** MOXON *Tutor Astron.* (ed. 3) 221 *Hydra,* the Hydre. **1838** *Penny Cycl.* XII. 379/2 *Hydra,* the Water-snake, one of the old constellations. **1870** PROCTOR *Other Worlds* xii. 293 The very existence of such a stream as Eridanus or Hydra.. implies.. such a process of segregation.

II. 6. *Zool.* **a.** (pl. usually **hydræ**.) A genus of Hydrozoa, consisting of fresh-water polyps of very simple structure, the body having the form of a cylindrical tube, with a mouth surrounded by a ring of tentacles with stinging thread-cells.

The name was given to it by Linnæus (1756), in allusion to the fact that cutting it in pieces only multiplies its numbers.

1798 F. KANMACHER *G. Adams' Ess. Microscope* (ed. 2) title-p., An account of the.. singular properties of the Hydræ and Verticellæ. **1835-6** TODD *Cycl. Anat.* I. 609/1 The Hydra.. is the largest.. of the Fresh-water Polypi. **1847** CARPENTER *Zool.* § 1050 If cut transversely into several segments, each will in time become a perfect animal, so that thirty or forty Hydræ may thus be produced by the section of one. **1861** J. R. GREENE *Man. Anim. Kingd., Cœlent.* 20 The Hydra possesses a gelatinous, sub-cylindrical body.. having one end expanded into an adherent disc, or foot, a mouth being situated at its opposite extremity.

b. The sexual bud or medusa of any hydroid hydrozoan; so called from its resemblance to an individual of the genus Hydra.

1865 E. & A. AGASSIZ *Seaside Stud. Nat. Hist.* 23 The whole mass of the coral is porous, and the cavities occupied by the Hydrae are sunk perpendicularly to the surface within the rock.

c. ***hydra tuba***: a larval or non-sexual form of hydroid in certain Hydrozoa, of a trumpet-like form.

1847 SIR J. G. DALYELL *Rare Animals Scotl.* I. 76 *Hydra tuba,* the Trumpet Polypus. **1858** HUXLEY *Oceanic Hydrozoa* 7 The like structure is observable in the 'Hydra tuba', the larval form of the Lucernarian Medusæ. **1870** H. A. NICHOLSON *Man. Zool.* I. 101 The Hydra-tuba, as the young organism at this stage of its career has been termed by Sir J. G. Dalyell. **1888** ROLLESTON & JACKSON *Anim. Life* 780 The non-sexual Hydroid form of the Acraspeda, the *Scyphistoma* or *Hydra tuba.*

III. 7. *attrib.* and *Comb.* **a.** *attrib.* (*a*) in senses 1 and 2: Of or belonging to a hydra, hydra-like; having as many heads, or as difficult to extirpate, as the Lernæan hydra.

1586 T. B. *La Primaud. Fr. Acad.* I. (1589) 430 Protectors of this Hydra Ignorance. **1597** SHAKS. *2 Hen. IV,* IV. ii. 38 Whereon this Hydra-Sonne of Warre is borne. **1683** T. HOY *Agathocles* 16 Poor Men! our Fruitful Hydra-Ills encrease, For One Head lost, an Hundred in the Place. **1708** OZELL tr. *Boileau's Lutrin* VI. 113 Tyranny Erects her Hydra-head. **1742** YOUNG *Nt. Th.* IV. 837 Dark Dæmons I discharge, and Hydra-stings. **1797** MARY ROBINSON *Walsingham* I. 7 They are the hydra assailants which return with every hour. **1813** SIR R. WILSON *Priv. Diary* II. 444 If there is a fight.. you will then hear what a hydra force sprouted out for the occasion.

(*b*) in sense 6: Belonging to or resembling the genus *Hydra* of polyps.

1878 E. CLARK *Visit S. Amer.* 45 This singular organism the physalia belongs to the hydra family, and is in every respect a jelly fish. **1880** E. R. LANKESTER in *Nature* XXI. 413 The sperms from which a new generation of hydra-forms will spring.

b. similative or parasynthetic, as ***hydra-headed***, ***-kinded***, ***-necked*** adjs.; also ***hydra-like*** adj.

1589 WARNER *Alb. Eng.* V. xxviii. 126 (Stanf.) Those Hydra-kinded warres. **1599** SHAKS. *Hen. V,* I. i. 35 Nor neuer Hidra-headed Wilfulnesse So soone did loose his Seat; and all at once; As in this King. **1666** DRYDEN *Ann. Mirab.* ccxlix, Hydra-like, the fire Lifts up his hundred heads to aim his way. **1798** MALTHUS *Popul.* (1878) 50 This hydra-headed monster rose again after a few years. **1842** *Ainsworth's Mag.* II. 43 The Puff Literary is hydra-headed. **1875** JOWETT *Plato* (ed. 2) III. 49 Fancying that they can cut off at a blow the Hydra-like rogueries of mankind. **1899** *Daily News* 8 Feb. 7/5 The hydra-headed leadership of the Irish party. **1963** *Daily Tel.* 20 Nov. 14/2 The hydra-headed challenge of London's mounting traffic congestion.

hydracid (haɪˈdræsɪd). *Chem.* [f. HYDR(O- d + ACID. Cf. F. *hydracide,* and HYDRO-ACID.] A term applied to an acid containing hydrogen, to distinguish it from an *oxyacid,* or *oxacid,* containing oxygen; now esp. to the halogen acids, or simple compounds of hydrogen with chlorine, bromine, iodine, fluorine, or cyanogen.

1826 HENRY *Elem. Chem.* I. 374 These results are calculated on the supposition that hypo-phosphorous or per-phosphorous acid is a binary compound of oxygen and phosphorus; but it is doubtful whether it may not be a triple compound of oxygen, phosphorus, and hydrogen, or a hydracid. **1831** T. P. JONES *Convers. Chem.* xxiii. 231 There are several.. acids in which hydrogen performs the office once supposed to belong exclusively to oxygen.. Acids of this kind are called hydracids. **1854** J. SCOFFERN in *Orr's Circ. Sc., Chem.* 351 Hydrosulphuric acid is the first hydrogen acid, or *hydr-acid,* that has.. come under our notice. **1864-72** WATTS *Dict. Chem.* II. 669 Ampère, in 1810, suggested that it (HF) was a hydracid analogous to hydrochloric acid; and this.. was.. confirmed by Davy. **1889** MUIR & MORLEY *Watts' Dict. Chem.* II. 702/1 The name [hydracid] is more particularly applied when it is desired to distinguish between two classes of compounds of the same element,.. thus we speak of the oxy-acids and the hydracids of the halogen elements.

b. *attrib.* or *adj.* Of or belonging to a hydracid.

1854 J. SCOFFERN in *Circ. Sc., Chem.* 352 The attempt to assimilate oxyacid salts with the type of hydracid salts.

hydracrylic (haɪdrəˈkrɪlɪk), *a. Chem.* [f. HYDR(O- d + ACRYLIC.] In ***hydracrylic acid*** $C_3H_6O_3$, a monobasic lactic acid, which exists as a thick uncrystallizable syrup, and decomposes on heating into acrylic acid ($C_3H_4O_2$) and water (H_2O). Hence **hydracrylate**, a salt of this acid.

1877 WATTS *Fownes' Organ. Chem.* 328 Ethene-lactic or hydracrylic acid. *Ibid.,* The metallic hydracrylates are crystallisable.

hydradephagous (haɪdrəˈdɛfəgəs), *a. Entom.* [f. mod.L. *Hydradephaga* (f. Gr. ὕδωρ, ὑδρ- water + ἀδηφάγος voracious: see ADEPHAGA.] Belonging to the *Hydradephaga* or aquatic carnivorous beetles.

1840 SWAINSON & SHUCKARD *Hist. & Nat. Arrangem. Insects* II. v. 195 Some few [predaceous beetles].. live in fresh water; from which circumstance they have been named Hydrodephagous.

‖**hydræmia** (haɪˈdriːmɪə). *Path.* Also **hydremia**. [f. HYDR(O- b + Gr. -αιμία (as in ἀναιμία ANÆMIA), f. αἷμα blood. Cf. F. *hydrémie.*] A watery condition of the blood.

1845 G. E. DAY tr. *Simon's Anim. Chem.* I. 308 In hydræmia, the serum.. is usually transparent. **1880** A. FLINT *Princ. Med.* (ed. 5) 62 Hydraemia or diminution of the solid ingredients of the plasma, especially the albumen, is also an element in most forms of anaemia.

Hence **hyˈdræmic, -emic**, *a.*, of the nature of or affected with hydræmia.

1876 tr. *Wagner's Gen. Pathol.* 541 Cachectic or hydræmic dropsy. **1897** ALLBUTT *Syst. Med.* II. 729 The blood is hydræmic.

hydraform, erroneous var. of HYDRIFORM.

†**hydragogal** (haɪdrəˈgəʊgəl), *a. Obs.* [f. as HYDRAGOGUE + -AL[1].]

1. = HYDRAGOGUE *a.*

1652 FRENCH *Yorksh. Spa* x. 91 Hiera picra, with Jollap, Mechoacan, or the like hydragogal medicaments.

2. Serving for the conveyance of water.

1669 W. SIMPSON *Hydrol. Chym.* 311 Driving up the waters.. by hydragogal syphons.

hydragogic (haɪdrəˈgɒdʒɪk), *a.* [f. Gr. ὑδραγωγ-ός HYDRAGOGUE + -IC.] = HYDRAGOGUE *a.*

1712 tr. *Pomet's Hist. Drugs* I. 179 The hydragogick Electuary. **1830** LINDLEY *Nat. Syst. Bot.* 68 A purgative hydragogic property.

†**hydraˈgogical**, *a. Obs.* [f. as prec. + -AL[1].]

1. = prec.

1675 E. WILSON *Spadacr. Dunelm.* 83 You must.. use some hydragogical Medicine.

2. = HYDRAGOGAL 2.

1675 E. WILSON *Spadacr. Dunelm.* 31 The subterraneal correspondence this Lake hath with the Ocean through hydragogical conveyances.

Hence **hydraˈgogically** *adv.*, in the manner of a hydragogue.

c **1700** D. G. *Harangues Quack Doct.* 15 It affecteth the Cure either Hypnotically, Hydrotically.. Hydrogogically.

hydragogue (ˈhaɪdrəgɒg), *a.* and *sb.* [a. F. *hydragogue,* or ad. L. *hydragōg-us,* ad. Gr. ὑδραγωγ-ός conveying water, f. ὑδρ- water (see HYDRO-) + ἄγειν to lead; ὑδραγωγὰ φάρμακα (Galen), medicines which remove water from the body.]

A. *adj.* Of medicines: Having the property of removing accumulations of water or serum, or of causing watery evacuations.

1638 VENNER *Censure* in *Via Recta* (1650) 391 A fitting hydragog medicine to evacuate the reliques of the water. **1710** T. FULLER *Pharm. Extemp.* 104 An Hydragogue Draught. **1855** GARROD *Mat. Med.* (ed. 6) 222 Gamboge acts as a drastic and hydragogue purgative.

B. *sb.* A hydragogue medicine or drug.

1658 PHILLIPS s.v. *Hydragogy,* Hydragogues are Medicines that are prepared to draw forth the Water from any Hydropical parts. **1727-41** CHAMBERS *Cycl.* s.v., All sudorific, aperitive, and diuretic medicines, are hydragogues. **1831** J. DAVIES *Manual Mat. Med.* 361 It was formerly employed as a hydragogue in passive dropsies.

†**ˈhydragogy.** *Obs.* Also *erron.* hydro-. [ad. Gr. ὑδραγωγία the conveying of water (also, an aqueduct, canal, etc.): see prec.] The conveyance of water by an artificial channel or aqueduct.

1570 DEE *Math. Pref.* d j b, Hydragogie, demonstrateth the possible leading of Water.. from any head (being a Spring, standing, or running Water) to any other place. **1656** in BLOUNT *Glossogr.* **1658** in PHILLIPS.

hydral (ˈhaɪdrəl), *a. Bot.* [f. Gr. ὕδωρ, ὑδρ-, water + -AL[1].] Epithet of Lindley's alliance of Endogens containing *Hydrocharidaceæ* and kindred orders of aquatic plants.

1866 *Treas. Bot.* 775 *Naiadaceæ,* a natural order.. belonging to Lindley's hydral alliance of Endogens, consisting of plants living in fresh or salt water.

hydralizine (haɪˈdræləziːn). *Pharm.* Also **hydrallazine.** [f. hydra*zinophthal*azine, f. HYDRAZINO- + PHTHALAZINE.] A sympatholytic drug, $C_8H_5N_2{\cdot}NH{\cdot}NH_2$, used in the form of the hydrochloride, a white crystalline powder, in the treatment of hypertension.

1952 *Jrnl. Amer. Med. Assoc.* 1 Nov. 861/2 Hydrallazine Hydrochloride for 1-hydrazinophthalazine hydrochloride. **1953** *Jrnl. Pharmacol. & Exper. Therap.* CIX. 182 Hydrallazine.. stimulates the heart and increases cardiac output. **1963** *Brit. Pharmacopœia* p. xxviii, British Pharmacopœia... Hydrallazine hydrochloride. International Pharmacopoeia... Hydralazine hydrochloride. **1970** A. GOTH *Med. Pharmacol.* (ed. 5) xiv. 157 Hydralizine (1-hydrazinophthalazine; Apresoline) is a potent antihypertensive drug, but it can produce serious toxic reactions.

hydramide (ˈhaɪdrəmaɪd), *Chem.* [f. HYDR(O- d + AMIDE.] A tertiary diomide formed by the action of ammonia on certain aldehydes, chiefly aromatic, as benzoic aldehyde.

1865-72 WATTS *Dict. Chem.* III. 178 The hydramides are crystalline solids, insoluble in water.. not possessing alkaline properties. *Ibid.,* Some hydramides, e.g. hydrobenzamide and hydrosalicylamide, are decomposed by acids, yielding ammonia and the corresponding aldehydes.

hydramine (ˈhaɪdrəmaɪn). *Chem.* [f. HYDR(O- d + AMINE.] An oxethene base; an amine containing hydroxyl substitution compounds of ethyl.

1877 WATTS *Fownes' Organ. Chem.* 222 When ethene-oxide, C_2H_4O.. is treated with aqueous ammonia, 1, 2, or 3 molecules of the oxide unite with 1 mol. ammonia, producing.. Ethene-hydramine, Diethene-hydramine, Triethene-hydramine.. They are viscid, alkaline liquids, decomposed by distillation.

hydramnios (haɪˈdræmnɪəs). *Path.* Also **hydramnion.** [f. HYDR- + AMNIOS, AMNION.] Excessive accumulation of amniotic fluid during pregnancy.

1838 F. CHURCHILL *Outl. Princ. Dis. Females* 145 'Hydramnios', or excess of liquor amnii.., is said to result from a general serous diathesis. **1885** W. T. LUSK *Sci. & Art Midwifery* (ed. 3) xv. 288 The causes of hydramnion are hardly to be found in a single morbid condition. **1961** *Lancet* 30 Sept. 742/2 She came into hospital three times during her eighth pregnancy with.. mild hydramnios.

hydrangea (haɪˈdreɪndʒ(ɪ)ə, haɪˈdrændʒiːə). [mod.L. *Hydrangēa* (Linnæus), f. Gr. ὕδωρ, ὑδρ- water + ἄγγος vessel (in allusion to the cup-like form of the seed-capsule). Cf. F. *hydrangée.*] A genus of shrubs (N.O. *Saxifragaceæ*), natives of the temperate regions of Asia and America, with white, blue, or pink flowers in large globular clusters; esp. the Chinese species *H. hortensis,* commonly cultivated in Britain.

1753 in CHAMBERS *Cycl. Supp.* **1797** MRS. BURTON *Laura* I. 198, I should like to make.. a sonnet upon the lasting bloom of a hydrainger. **1803** *J. Abercrombie's Ev. Man his own Gardener* (ed. 17) 197 Pots of.. flowering plants.. such as pinks, hydrangea, roses. **1861** DELAMER *Fl. Gard.* 121 In the Channel Islands, and in Normandy, there are Hydrangeas eight feet high, or more, with balls of flowers bigger than a man's head.

hydrant (ˈhaɪdrənt). [Irregularly formed from Gr. ὕδωρ, ὑδρ- water + -ANT[1]. Of U.S. origin.] An apparatus for drawing water directly from a main, esp. in a street, consisting of a pipe with one or more nozzles to which the hose of a fire-engine, etc. may be attached, or with a spout or the like.

1828 in WEBSTER. **1839** MARRYAT *Diary Amer.* Ser. I. I. 286 Some black fellow.. brings out the leather hose, attached to the hydrants, as they term them here. **1847** EMERSON *Repr. Men, Swedenborg* Wks. (Bohn) I. 324 In the transmission of the heavenly waters, every hose fits every hydrant. **1851** *Illustr. Catal. Gt. Exhib.* 651 Hydrant, or fire-cock with stand pipe. **1871** *Daily News* 28 Dec., There should be a hydrant in every hundred yards of street, to which nothing but a hose need be attached in order to throw a stream of water over the highest building near it.

hydranth (ˈhaɪdrænθ). *Zool.* [f. HYDRA (sense 6) + Gr. ἄνθ-ος flower.] One of the non-sexual zooids, typically nutritive in function, occurring in colonial Hydrozoa, usually on the branches of the cœnosarc (like flowers on a plant). Sometimes extended to any hydroid (free or colonial).

1874 LUBBOCK *Orig. & Met. Ins.* iii. 49 Every branchlet crowned by its graceful hydranth. **1877** HUXLEY *Anat. Inv. Anim.* iii. 128 In an early stage of its existence every hydrozoon is represented by a single hydranth. **1888** ROLLESTON & JACKSON *Anim. Life* 245 The hydrosome [of *Sertularia*] consists of a number of hydranths or nutritive zooids collectively forming the trophosome and connected to one another by a branching cœnosarc.

hydrapulper ('haɪdrəpʌlpə(r)). *Paper-making.* Also Hydrapulper. [Irreg. f. Gr. ὑδρ(ο-, combining form of ὕδωρ water + PULPER.] A large vessel with a set of motor-driven rotating vanes at the bottom, designed to break up the fibres of wood pulp or other paper stock in water.

1941 *Techn. Pap. Addr. Techn. Assoc. Pulp Pap. Ind.* XXIV. 384/2 The hydrapulper is simply a cylindrical open-top tank with a dished bottom at the center of which is a heavy impeller. **1951** J. N. STEPHENSON *Pulp & Paper Manuf.* II. i. 67 Straw bales.. are fed as rapidly as possible into a Hydrapulper.. containing the required amount of chemical in hot water. **1966** *Paper Technology* VII. II. 135 These rejects are in a suspension and could possibly be extracted from the bottom of the hydrapulper tub. **1967** E. CHAMBERS *Photolitho-Offset* xvi. 244 This acidity in uncoated paper can be traced to aluminium sulphate, which is added in the beater or hydrapulper during paper manufacture.

hydrarch ('haɪdrɑːk), *a. Ecol.* [f. Gr. ὕδωρ, ὑδρ- water + ἀρχή beginning.] Of a succession of plant communities: having its origin in a watery habitat.

1913 W. S. COOPER in *Bot. Gaz.* LV. 11 The terms xerarch and hydrarch are here used for the first time, for the purpose of indicating a natural and important classification of plant successions. The former is applied to those successions which, having their origin in xerophytic habitats, such as rock shores, beaches, and cliffs, become more and more mesophytic in their successive stages; the latter to those which, originating in hydrophytic habitats such as lakes and ponds, also progress towards mesophytism. **1929** WEAVER & CLEMENTS *Plant Ecol.* iv. 55 Successions beginning in ponds, lakes, marshes, or elsewhere in water are termed hydrarch. **1960** N. POLUNIN *Introd. Plant Geogr.* xi. 324 They [*sc.* the seres] are distinguished as 'hydrarch', 'mesarch', or 'xerarch', according to whether their initiation is under damp, median, or dry conditions.

†**hydrarchy.** *Obs. rare*⁻¹. [f. Gr. ὕδωρ, ὑδρ- water + -αρχία rule, sovereignty.] The watery realm or domain.

1631 BRATHWAIT *Whimzies, Sayler* 89 Agents of maine importance in that hydrarchy wherin they live.

hydrargillite (haɪ'drɑːdʒɪlaɪt). *Min.* [Named, 1805, f. Gr. ὕδωρ, ὑδρ- water + ἄργιλλος clay, in reference to its composition.] A synonym of WAVELLITE.

1805 DAVY in *Phil. Trans.* XCV. 162 If a name founded upon its chemical composition be preferred, it may be denominated Hydrargillite. **1868** DANA *Min.* (ed. 5) 178. **1879** RUTLEY *Study Rocks* xiv. 298 The rock contains as accessories.. asbestus, hydrargillite,.. etc.

‖**hydrargyrum** (haɪ'drɑːdʒɪrəm). Formerly also **hydrargyre** (-gire, -girie). [mod.L. *hydrargyrum*, altered (on the analogy of other names of metals, as *aurum*, *argentum*) from L. *hydrargyrus*, a. Gr. ὑδράργυρος artificial quicksilver, f. ὑδρ- (HYDRO-) + ἄργυρος silver. *Hydrargyre* was from Fr.] Quicksilver, mercury. (The name in medical and chemical Latin, whence the symbol Hg.)

1563 T. GALE *Treat. Gonneshot* 9b (Stanf. s.v. *Guiacan*), Vnguentes receyuing into there composition Hydrargyron. **1706** PHILLIPS (ed. Kersey), *Hydrargyrum*, quick-silver. **1861–2** THACKERAY *Philip* (1887) I. ii. 26 He will prescribe taraxacum for you, or pil: hydrarg:.

β. **1569** J. SANFORD tr. *Agrippa's Van. Artes* 157b, That they will get greater riches in Hydrargirie, then nature geueth in golde. **1598** SYLVESTER *Du Bartas* II. i. III. *Furies* 67 The Steel and Load-stone, Hydrargire and Gold. **1696** PHILLIPS (ed. 5), *Hydrargyre*, a Name which the Chymists give to Mercury.

Hence **hy'drargyral**, **hy'drargyrate**, **hydrar'gyric**, **hy'drargyrous** *adjs.*, of or relating to quicksilver, mercurial. ‖**hydrar'gyria**, ‖**hydrargy'riasis**, **hy'drargyrism** (erron. **hydrargysm**), ‖**hydrargy'rosis**, a morbid condition caused by the introduction of mercury into the system, mercurial poisoning (see also quot. 1753).

1664 POWER *Exp. Philos.* 96 *Hydrargyral emanations. *Ibid.* 107 Our Hydrargyral Experiments. **1864** WEBSTER, **Hydrargyrate.* **1810** SIR G. ALLEY (*title*) Observations on the *Hydrargyria, or that Vesicular Disease arising from the Exhibition of Mercury. **1875** H. C. WOOD *Therap.* (1879) 389 The altered blood of chronic hydrargyria. **1854** MAYNE *Expos. Lex.*, *Hydrargyriasis. *Ibid.*, *Hydrargyric. **1753** CHAMBERS *Cycl. Supp.*, **Hydrargyrosis*, a term used by the chirurgical writers to express the anointing the body with a mercurial unction, in order to the raising a salivation. **1646** SIR T. BROWNE *Pseud. Ep.* 90 Containing also a salt, and *hydrargyrus mixtion.

‖**hydrarthrosis** (haɪdrɑː'θrəʊsɪs). *Path.* [f. HYDR(O- b + ARTHROSIS.] Dropsy of the joints.

1861 BUMSTEAD *Ven. Dis.* (1879) 233 Gonorrhoeal rheumatism is essentially an hydrarthrosis. **1879** *St. George's Hosp. Rep.* IX. 769 A patient whose knee had been laid open for chronic hydrarthrosis.

hydrase ('haɪdreɪz, -eɪs). *Biochem.* [f. HYDR- + -ASE.] Any enzyme which catalyses an addition reaction between water and a substrate or the reverse process.

1943 SUMNER & SOMERS *Chem. & Methods of Enzymes* IV. xvii. 296 The hydrases add water to organic compounds without causing a splitting. **1961** P. D. BOYER et al. *Enzymes* (ed. 2) V. xxviii. 455 Among enzymes catalyzing the addition of groups to double bonds (and the reverse reaction), the hydrases (or dehydrases) form the largest group.

hydrastine (haɪ'dræstaɪn). [f. mod.L. *Hydrastis* (see def.) + -INE.] **a.** An alkaloid obtained from the root of *Hydrastis Canadensis*, a North American ranunculaceous plant. **b.** A medicine used by eclectic physicians, consisting of this alkaloid mixed with berberine and resin.

1876 HARLEY *Mat. Med.* (ed. 6) 781 It contains.. an active principle called hydrastin. **1876** BARTHOLOW *Mat. Med.* (1879) 142 Hydrastine, the alkaloid, should not be confounded with the eclectic preparation, hydrastin, which is composed chiefly of berberine.

hydrastinine (haɪ'dræstɪniːn). *Chem.* [ad. G. *hydrastinin* (Freund & Will 1887, in *Ber. d. Deut. Chem. Ges.* XX. 88), f. HYDRASTIN(E + -INE⁵.] A synthetic alkaloid, $C_{11}H_{13}NO_3$, derived from hydrastine and sometimes employed in the form of the hydrochloride to control uterine bleeding.

1887 *Jrnl. Chem. Soc.* LII. I. 383 [Freund and Will] have examined the base hydrastinine, $C_{11}H_{11}NO_2 + H_2O$, obtained together with opianic acid where hydrastine is treated with oxidising agents. **1929** *Encycl. Brit.* XI. 961/1 The hydrolytic product, hydrastinine, is an important drug, being used as an internal styptic. **1970** S. W. PELLETIER *Chem. Alkaloids* iii. 65 Oxidative hydrolysis of hydrastine with dilute nitric acid results in the formation of two fragments, opianic acid and hydrastinine.

hydrastis (haɪ'dræstɪs). [mod.L. (J. Ellis in Linnæus *Systema Naturæ* (ed. 10, 1759) II. 1088): etym. unkn.] The dried rhizome and roots of the herb golden seal or yellow root (*Hydrastis canadensis*), or an extract or tincture of them, formerly used medicinally as a bitter stomachic and to control uterine bleeding.

1865 WOOD & BACHE *Dispensatory U.S.A.* (ed. 12) 459 Hydrastis might probably be advantageously prepared in the form of a fluid extract. **1882** R. BENTLEY *Man. Bot.* (ed. 4) 425 Hydrastis is.. used by the Indians of the Western States of North America to dye various shades of yellow. **1908** *Practitioner* Jan. 96 Styptol and hydrastis.. are recommended for arresting haemorrhage from the non-pregnant organ. **1951** A. GROLLMAN *Pharmacol. & Therapeutics* 757 Color may also be imparted by the addition of.. Hydrastis Tincture (N.F.) which.. is soluble in alcohol and hydro-alcoholic preparations giving a yellow color. **1967** *Martindale's Extra Pharmacopoeia* (ed. 25) 592 Hydrastis.. in the treatment of post-partum haemorrhage.. is much inferior to ergot.

hydratable (haɪ'dreɪtəb(ə)l), *a.* [f. HYDRAT(E *v.* + -ABLE.] Capable of becoming hydrated.

1953 J. DAVIDSOHN et al. *Soap Manuf.* I. xiii. 220 Animal fats.. are for the most part substantially free of phosphatides or other hydratable substances. **1956** *Soil Sci.* LXXXII. 198 Hydratable products may be formed as the clay minerals decompose.

hydratase ('haɪdrəteɪz, -eɪs). *Biochem.* [f. HYDRAT(E *v.* + -ASE.] = HYDRASE.

1922 *Chem. Abstr.* XVI. 936 The enzymes can be divided into hydratases, hydrolases and oxido-reductases. **1953** *Adv. Enzymol.* XIV. 237 Hence the enzyme hitherto called 'fumarase' should be renamed fumaric hydratase.

hydratation (haɪdrə'teɪʃən). *Chem.* [Cf. F. *hydratation.*] = HYDRATION.

1876 tr. *Schützenberger's Ferment.* 32 The hydratation.. is effected under the influence of acids.

hydrate ('haɪdrət), *sb. Chem.* Also **hydrat.** [f. Gr. ὕδωρ, ὑδρ- water + -ATE¹ 1 c. Cf. F. *hydrate.*] A compound of water with another compound or an element, e.g. hydrate of chlorine. Formerly, and still by some, applied also to a HYDROXIDE, e.g. KOH, potassium hydrate; NH_4OH, ammonium hydrate.

1802 SMITHSON in *Phil. Trans.* XCIII. 23 A peculiar compound of zinc and water, which may be named hydrate of zinc. **1807** T. THOMSON *Chem.* (ed. 3) II. 104 The attention of chemists was drawn to them by Mr Proust, who has given to such combinations the name of hydrates. **1822** IMISON *Sc. & Art* II. 20 An oxide combined with water is called a hydrat. **1871** TYNDALL *Fragm. Sc.* (1879) I. xviii. 459 Faraday analysed the hydrate of chlorine. **1876** HARLEY *Mat. Med.* (ed. 6) 171 Hydrate of lime is formed whenever water is sprinkled upon caustic lime. **1889** MUIR & MORLEY *Watts' Dict. Chem.* II. 703/2 The compound Cl_5H_2O is a hydrate of Cl, i.e. it is a compound of Cl with water. *Ibid.*, Another way of stating the theoretical difference between hydrates and hydroxides is to say that hydrates contain water as such, and that hydroxides contain the elements of water.

hydrate ('haɪdreɪt), *v.* [f. prec. Cf. F. *hydrater.*]

a. *trans.* To combine chemically with water; to convert into a hydrate.

1850 DAUBENY *Atom. The.* viii. (ed. 2) 252 Acidified by 3 atoms of oxygen, and hydrated by the addition to each of 1 atom of water. **1897** ALLBUTT *Syst. Med.* II. 814 The gland cells manufacture a ferment—pepsine or trypsine—which.. hydrates the albumins, forming albumoses.

b. *intr.* To undergo hydration, to become combined with water.

1909 in WEBSTER. **1921** J. R. PARTINGTON *Text-bk. Inorg. Chem.* xl. 846 The residue of anhydrous $CaSO_4$ rapidly takes up water, but if the heating has been more intense the residue hydrates only very slowly. **1947** R. H. BOGUE *Chem. Portland Cement* xxv. 435 Complete hydration.. was obtained by mixing the compounds with water to form a plastic paste, allowing the pastes to hydrate in sealed containers for a month, [etc.]. **1962** HARRIS & GRUBER in A. Pirie *Lens Metabolism Rel. Cataract* 382 If the block is sufficient, more sodium is gained than potassium lost and the lens hydrates in a predictable manner.

hydrated ('haɪdreɪtɪd), *a.* [f. prec. sb. or vb. + -ED.] Chemically combined with water or its elements; formed into a hydrate.

1809 DAVY in *Phil. Trans.* XCIX. 465 Hydrated sulphur was instantly formed. **1826** HENRY *Elem. Chem.* II. 99 A combination of peroxide of copper with water, or a hydrated peroxide of copper. **1851** *Illustr. Catal. Gt. Exhib.* 1449 Steatite.. is a hydrated silicate of magnesia and alumina. **1885** MUIR & WILSON *Thermal Chem.* iv. 149 Most hydrated salts dissolve in water with absorption of heat. **1889** MUIR & MORLEY *Watts' Dict. Chem.* II. 704/1 Caustic baryta combines with water to form a compound $BaO_2H_2.8H_2O$; this compound is said to be a hydrated hydroxide.

hydration (haɪ'dreɪʃən). [f. HYDRATE: see -ATION.] The action of hydrating or condition of being hydrated; combination with water.

1854 J. SCOFFERN in *Circ. Sc., Chem.* 452 In both conditions of hydration the crystals of sulphate of nickel are very beautiful. **1876** J. FOWLER in *Archæologia* XLVI. 128 *note*, The hydration of lime in badly tempered mortar. **1878** KINGZETT *Anim. Chem.* iii. 36 The chemical decompositions for ever occurring in the living body are all included in two processes, viz., those of hydration and oxidation. **1880** [see HYDROLYSIS]. **1889** MUIR & MORLEY *Watts' Dict. Chem.* II. 703/2 Another form of words.. is to speak of *water of hydration*, or *water of crystallisation* and to contrast these with *water of constitution*.

hydratuba (ˌhaɪdrə'tjuːbə). [f. HYDRA II. 6 + TUBA¹, formerly *Hydra tuba*, when the organism was thought to be a species of *Hydra*; in reference to the shape of the larva.] The polyp-like larval stage of a jellyfish of the class Scyphozoa; a scyphistoma.

1847 J. G. DALYELL *Rare & Remarkable Animals Scotl.* I. iii. 76 (*heading*) Hydra tuba, the Trumpet Polypus. *Ibid.* 77 The body of the *hydra tuba* is a hollow cone five lines in length, thick and fleshy. **1898** A. SEDGWICK *Student's Text-bk. Zool.* I. iv. 159 In the *Ephyronina* the development is generally accompanied by an alternation of generations; the asexual generations being represented by the *Scyphistoma* (*Hydra tuba*) and *Strobila*; but in exceptional cases it is direct (*Pelagia*). **1901** SHIPLEY & MACBRIDE *Zool.* iii. 64 Each [planula] fixes itself and develops into a little polyp, called a Hydratuba, not unlike a *Hydra* in appearance. **1927** *Glasgow Herald* 5 Nov. 6/2 This [*sc.* the larva] settles as a polyp-like form, the hydratuba, and this, by a kind of budding, gives origin to little saucer-like discs which grow into medusæ. **1932** BORRADAILE & POTTS *Invertebrata* v. 155 At certain seasons the whole hydratuba is segmented by transverse horizontal furrows. **1951** *Microscope* VIII. 193 (*title*) Planula, hydratuba and ephyra stages of the common jellyfish.

hydraulic (haɪ'drɔːlɪk, -'drɒlɪk), *a.* and *sb.* [ad. L. *hydraulic-us*, a. Gr. ὑδραυλικ-ός, f. ὕδωρ, ὑδρ- water + αὐλός pipe. In Greek ὑδραυλικὸν ὄργανον denoted a kind of musical instrument played by means of water (also called ὕδραυλις, ὕδραυλος); the extension of the word to other kinds of water-engines is first found in Latin authors (*hydraulicae machinae* in Vitruvius). Cf. F. *hydraulique.*]

A. *adj.*

1. a. Pertaining or relating to water (or other liquid) as conveyed through pipes or channels, esp. by mechanical means; belonging to hydraulics.

1661 *Humane Industry* 37 Birds on the tops of Trees, which by Hydraulic art and secret conveyances of water.. are made to sing. **1729** SWITZER *Hydrost. & Hydraul.* 69 Nero Alexandrinus, and other Hydraulick Writers. **1851** *Illustr. Catal. Gt. Exhib.* 1364 A shaft moved by hydraulic power. **1860** *All Year Round* No. 52. 35 A bale of dry goods.. packed by hydraulic pressure. **1898** *Times* 22 Aug. 6/3 Hydraulic pressure exerted against the deposits by what are known as.. 'Monitors', huge squirts... These huge jets of water strike against the mass of gravels with a force of many thousand horse-power.

b. Special collocations.

hydraulic engineering (see quots); so ***hydraulic engineer***; ***hydraulic gradient***: (a line representing) the variation along a pipe or channel of the head due to elevation and pressure in a liquid flowing along it; ***hydraulic jump***: an abrupt change from a fast, shallow flow to a slower, deeper flow at some point in a liquid flowing in an open channel; ***hydraulic mining***: a method of mining in which the force of a powerful jet of water is used to wear down a bed of auriferous gravel or earth, and to carry the debris to the sluices where the particles of gold are separated; ***hydraulic radius*** or ***mean depth***: a length equal to the cross-sectional area of the liquid in a channel or pipe divided by the length of the wetted perimeter.

1838 *Penny Cycl.* XII. 382/1 Besides the construction of harbours for ships, the formation of the aqueducts which supplied the cities with water must have constituted an important part of the duties of the hydraulic engineer among the antients. **1916** J. PARK *Textbk. Pract. Hydraulics* p. x, A valuable work of reference for all hydraulic engineers. **1835** *Rep. Brit. Assoc. Adv. Sci. 1834* 473 Practical works in hydraulic engineering of great magnitude and extent have been carried on in England. **1858** G. R. BURNELL *Rudiments Hydraulic Engin.* I. i. 1 Hydraulic Engineering will be considered to include.. questions connected with building

in water. *Ibid.* 2 Hydraulic engineering is principally confined to the operations in which water acts as an incompressible fluid. **1940** *Chambers's Techn. Dict.* 427/1 *Hydraulic engineering*, that branch of engineering chiefly concerned in the design and production of hydraulic machinery, pumping plants, pipelines, etc. **1956** A. H. COMPTON *Atomic Quest* II. 106 His..degree in hydraulic engineering at the University of Iowa. **1881** *Encycl. Brit.* XII. 484/2 Hence [the line] CD is termed the virtual slope or hydraulic gradient of the pipe. **1935** A. J. MARTIN *Work of Sanitary Engin.* viii. 92 If a series of open-ended vertical pipes were carried up from the main at intervals, the water would rise in each of them up to the line of the hydraulic gradient. **1951** W. L. RUSSELL *Princ. Petroleum Geol.* xii. 212 By using..high hydraulic gradients, oil globules and gas bubbles may be forced through these sandstones. **1922** H. E. BABBITT *Sewerage* iv. 74 The hydraulic jump will occur when a high velocity of flow is interrupted by an obstruction in the channel, by a change in grade of the invert, or the approach of the velocity to the 'critical' velocity. **1969** CHIA-SHUN YIH *Fluid Mech.* v. 226 Tidal bores observed in estuaries are hydraulic jumps propagating against flowing water. **1797** *Encycl. Brit.* XVIII. 891/1 Column 1..contains the hydraulic mean depths of any conduit in inches... The column is continued to 100 inches, which is fully equal to the hydraulic mean depth of any canal. **1829** *Nat. Philos.* (Libr. Useful Knowl.) I. vi. 5/2 Suppose the whole quantity of water to be spread on a horizontal surface, equal in extent to the bottom and sides of the river, when the height at which the water would so stand is called the hydraulic mean depth. **1930** *Engineering* 7 Feb. 180/1 By means of the following table, maximum scour can be calculated from calculated values of the hydraulic mean depth. **1873** RAYMOND *Statist. Mines & Mining* xvii. 390 Hydraulic mining in California —The origin of this branch of mining dates back as far as the spring of 1852. **1876** L. D'A. JACKSON tr. *Kutter's Mean Velocity of Discharge of Rivers* i. 2, *r* is the mean hydraulic radius, or the quotient of the water section by the wetted perimeter. **1948** D. W. TAYLOR *Fund. Soil Mech.* vi. 109 The ratio of volume to surface area of flow channel may be used as an alternative definition of hydraulic radius.

2. a. Applied to various mechanical contrivances operated by water-power, or in which water is conveyed through pipes; e.g. a ***hydraulic crane, engine, machine, motor.*** Also used in connection with liquids other than water.

hydraulic belt, an endless woollen band passing over rollers for raising water by absorption and compression. ***hydraulic block*** (*Shipbuilding*), a hydraulic lifting-press made to occupy the place of a building-block beneath the keel of a vessel in a repairing-dock, so as to raise the vessel when needed. ***hydraulic brush***, a brush with a hose connexion through its handle whereby it discharges water upon the surface scrubbed. ***hydraulic buffer***, a device for checking the recoil of a mounted gun, consisting of a piston in a cylinder filled with liquid. ***hydraulic condenser*** (see CONDENSER 4c.) the chamber in which gas is cooled. ***hydraulic dock***, a floating dock (see DOCK 4), on which a vessel is raised for examination and repairs. ***hydraulic elevator***, or ***lift***, a lift or hoist worked by hydraulic power. ***hydraulic indicator***, a gauge indicating hydraulic pressure. ***hydraulic intensifier***, a device for obtaining an increase in pressure in a hydraulic system, usu. comprising two cylinders of different diameters containing pistons that are joined to one another. ***hydraulic main***, in gas-works, a large pipe containing water, and receiving the pipes from the several retorts, which dip below the surface of the water so that the raw gas passes through the water and is partly purified on its way to the condenser. ***hydraulic organ***, an ancient musical instrument in which water was used in some way, prob. to regulate the pressure of the air. ***hydraulic press*** = HYDROSTATIC *press.* ***hydraulic ram***, an automatic pump in which the kinetic energy of a descending column of water in a pipe is used to raise some of the water to a height above that of its original source; also applied to the lifting piston of a hydrostatic press. ***hydraulic valve***, a valve formed by an inverted cup placed with its edge under water over the upturned open end of a pipe, so as to close the pipe against the passage of air. ***hydraulic wheel***, a wheel for raising water by applied power.

1656 BLOUNT *Glossogr.*, *Hydraulick*, pertaining to Organs, or to an Instrument to draw water. **1659** LEAK *Waterwks.* 30 The Pipes of the Organs in Hydraulique [*mispr.* Hydrautique] Instruments. **1704** J. HARRIS *Lex. Techn.* s.v. *Hydraulo-Pneumatical*, A Description of the Common Hydraulick Engine used to Quench Fire. **1808** YOUNG in *Phil. Trans.* XCIX. 22 As a stream of water strikes on the valve of the hydraulic ram. **1838** *Penny Cycl.* XI. 87/1 A much larger pipe, technically called the hydraulic main, which..receives the gas produced from all the retorts. **1851** *Illustr. Catal. Gt. Exhib.* 210 Hydraulic presses of various kinds..among them the vast machine which was employed to lift the Brittannia tube into its place. *Ibid.* 236 Hydraulic lifting jack for railway engines and carriages. *Ibid.* 1194 Hydraulic crane. *Ibid.* 1228 Hydraulic clock..by keeping up a constant flow of water, the clock will never require winding up. **1856** S. C. BREES *Gloss. Terms, Hydraulic belt*, an endless double band, formed of woollen cloth, for raising water. **1871** G. E. VOYLE *Dict. Artillery Terms* (ed. 2) 45/1 The Hydraulic Buffer. **1876** VOYLE & STEVENSON *Mil. Dict.* (ed. 3) 54/2 Where guns are mounted on carriages and platforms fitted for hydraulic buffers, the buffer will invariably be kept on the platform filled with the proper quantity of oil. **1899** G. D. HISCOX *Mech. Movements* VII. 153 Hydraulic intensifier.—High pressure obtained from low pressure by differential pistons. **1959** *Chambers's Encycl.* VI. 646/1 A hydraulic buffer or brake consists of a cylinder filled with liquid, a piston and a piston rod. **1962** WALSHAW & JOBSON *Mech. Fluids* ii. 32 A 100 ton press with a 12 in. stroke is to be operated from a main in which the pressure is 40 lbf/in^2 gauge, via a hydraulic intensifier with a 4 ft stroke.

b. ***hydraulic brake***: (*a*) a brake that utilizes the resistance to motion experienced by a piston or rotor in a chamber full of liquid; also, a hydraulic buffer; (*b*) a brake that operates by means of friction but is actuated hydraulically; (*c*) a dynamometer that works on the principle of the hydraulic brake (sense (*a*)).

(*a*) **1874** *Engineering* 11 Sept. 194/3 (*heading*) Hydraulic brakes. **1894** J. A. EWING *Steam-Engine* ix. 269 Many governors are furnished with a dash-pot, which is a hydraulic or pneumatic brake, consisting of a piston connected to the governor, working loosely in a cylinder which is filled with oil or with water. **1902** *Encycl. Brit.* XXXI. 897/1 The buffer-stop to be seen in terminal railway stations, and the hydraulic brakes of quick-firing guns, are examples. **1959** [see sense 2 above]. **1962** D. J. MYATT *Machine Design* i. 151 Because braking torque is a function of speed of rotation of the brake rotor, electric and hydraulic brakes should not be depended upon to hold a load stationary. (*b*) **1875** *Engineering* 8 Jan. 29/1 The hydraulic brake comprises a pump, a cistern, and an accumulator for collecting and storing the power, a regulator, and apparatus for applying that power in retarding the speed of the train. **1876** J. W. BARRY *Railway Appliances* vii. 286 In the hydraulic break the pressure on the pistons is derived from the pressure of a small hydraulic accumulator. **1924** WRIGHT & SMITH *Automotive Construction & Operation* xiv. 331 Several cars have adopted the hydraulic-brake system for all four wheels. **1963** D. V. W. FRANCIS *Morris Minor* i. 11/1 Lockheed hydraulic brakes operate on 7-in. brake drums. (*c*) **1890** *Min. Proc. Inst. Civil Engin.* XCIX. 169 At the same meeting, Mr. William Froude gave an account of his hydraulic brake, for measuring the power of large engines. **1925** A. W. JUDGE *Automobile Engines* I. vi. 170 The Froude hydraulic brake..is now largely employed for automobile engine tests. In this case the power is absorbed by hydraulic resistance.

c. Of a liquid: used, or suitable for use, in hydraulic brakes or other hydraulic equipment. (Not used predicatively.)

1941 E. MOLLOY *Hydraulic Equipment* 86 A valve on the master-brake cylinder..allows the hydraulic fluid to escape, under pressure, to the brake cylinder in the wheel. **1951** *Adv. Chem. Ser.* V. 241 Hydraulic fluids..include those made from petroleum, synthetic oils, and aqueous solutions containing antifreeze and rust inhibitors. **1967** E. R. BRAITHWAITE *Lubrication* iii. 161 Fire-resistant hydraulic oils represent a class of lubricants in which there is increasing interest. **1971** *Drive* New Year 33/2 It is advisable to change hydraulic fluid every eighteen months or 24,000 miles.

3. Applied to substances which harden under water and so become impervious to it; as ***hydraulic cement, lime, mortar.***

1829 *Arcana of Sci. & Art* 246 When the bridge of Louis XVI was constructed, much advantage was derived from mixing with the hydraulic mortar which was used, a portion of the clinkers..which had passed through the grates of the glass bottle furnace, at Meudon. **1843** *Civil Engin. & Arch. Jrnl.* VI. 157/2 Hydraulic lime will harden in a very short time. *Ibid.*, Roman cement, the most hydraulic of all mortars. **1851** *Illustr. Catal. Gt. Exhib.* 135 Silica is an essential element in the formation of a good hydraulic cement. *Ibid.* 1114 Hydraulic chalk cement, hardening under water in a few minutes. **1863** A. C. RAMSAY *Phys. Geog.* xii. (1878) 167 Blue argillaceous limestone, largely quarried..for hydraulic lime. **1871** ROSCOE *Elem. Chem.* 218 Hydraulic mortars, which harden under water.

B. *sb.* **†1.** A hydraulic organ: see A. 2. *Obs.*

1626 BACON *Sylva* §102 The Sounds that produce Tones ..such are the Percussions of Mettall, as in Bels;..And of Water, as in the Nightingals Pipes of Regalls, or Organs, and other Hydraulicks; which the Ancients had..but are now lost. **1661** *Humane Industry* 109 He used onely warm water to give them motion and sound. Such Hydraulics are frequent in Italy.

2. a. Short for *hydraulic engine, press*, etc. (see A. 2). **b.** Applied hydraulic force.

1729 SWITZER *Hydrost. & Hydraul.* 347 The Hydraulick or Engine before mentioned, and its Effects, being thus explain'd. **1890** W. J. GORDON *Foundry* 63 Great is the power of hydraulic! Here is a hole..squeezed out of a slab of steel with no more fuss than if the steel were piecrust! *Ibid.* 157 The hydraulic is again brought into play, and with a pair of huge pincers the rivets are nipped and finished.

hydraulic (haɪˈdrɔːlɪk, -ˈdrɒlɪk), *v. U.S.* [f. *hydraulic* in *hydraulic mining*.] *trans.* To work or obtain by the methods of hydraulic mining. Hence **hyˈdraulic(k)ing** *vbl. sb.*

1868 *Rep. J. Ross Browne Mineral Resources* (U.S. Treas. Dept.) 94 They can hydraulic away about 300 feet along the face of their Claim, but beyond that the hill is too deep to pay for piping. **1880** G. T. INGHAM *Digging Gold* ix. 243 Two steam pumps have been..forcing water from French Creek up to these dry diggings for hydraulicing. **1892** C. F. LUMMIS *Tramp across Continent* viii. 122 To run a fifteen-mile pipe-line from the Sandias to Golden, and thus bring water to hydraulic the enormous areas of gold-bearing gravel. **1904** J. LYNCH *Three Yrs. Klondike* (1967) ix. 127 Those grounds can only be dredged or hydraulicked. **1908** W. R. CRANE *Gold & Silver* v. 379 In 1903 the Crown Mountain Mining Company..hydrauliced the material in sluices to a 60-stamp mill. **1928** W. A. CHALFANT *Outposts Civilization* 42 From which it was said the owner hydraulicked $90,000 worth of gold. **1965** *Mineral Facts & Problems* (U.S. Bureau of Mines) 231 Some kaolin deposits are mined by hydraulicking.

†hyˈdraulical, *a. Obs.* [f. as HYDRAULIC *a.* and *sb.* + -AL[1].] = HYDRAULIC *a.* A.

1664 POWER *Exp. Philos.* II. 88 These Physico-Mechanical Experiments are of four sorts, Hydrargyral, Hydraulical, Pneumatical, and Mixt. **1713** DERHAM *Phys.-Theol.* 11 *note*, Pumps..and divers other Hydraulical Engines. **1792** J. TOWNSEND *Journ. Spain* I. 79 Gardens watered by hydraulical machines.

hyˈdraulically, *adv.* [f. prec. + -LY[2].] By means of hydraulic power or appliances.

1890 W. J. GORDON *Foundry* 48 The work was all bolted into position and riveted hydraulically. **1892** *Daily News* 21 Sept. 2/3 A swing bridge..worked hydraulically. **1893** G. ALLEN *Scallywag* I. 18 Calling out..to the boy at the lift, [he] mounted hydraulically..to the second story.

hydraulician (haɪdrɒˈlɪʃən). [ad. F. *hydraulicien*; cf. *mechanician*, etc.] One versed in hydraulics; a hydraulic engineer.

1882 *Nature* XXV. 351/1 The system of dredging introduced by M. Bazin, the celebrated hydraulician, on the rivers of France. **1894** *Athenæum* 19 May 648/2 The formulæ [for the flow of water] drawn up by various hydraulicians.

hydraulicity (-ˈlɪsɪtɪ). [ad. F. *hydraulicité*: see HYDRAULIC and -ITY.] The property or quality of being hydraulic (sense 3).

1843 *Civil Engin. & Arch. Jrnl.* VI. 157/2 In constructions of this kind..the lime should possess some degree of hydraulicity, in order that it may harden before the injurious action of frost comes upon it. **1902** J. BLACK *Illustr. Carpenter & Builder Ser.: Plastering* iii. 46 The hydraulicity is greatest when the limestone contains thirty per cent. of clay. **1959** *Chambers's Encycl.* III. 320/2 The calcium oxide..retains all these impurities and the proportion in which they are present greatly affects the properties of the lime, notably its hydraulicity.

hydraulicking (haɪˈdrɔːlɪkɪŋ, -ˈdrɒl-), *vbl. sb. U.S.* Also **-icing.** [f. HYDRAULIC + -ING[1] (with insertion of *k* as in *frolicking, trafficking*, etc.).] Hydraulic mining.

1880 R. H. PATTERSON in *Fortn. Rev.* Sept. 341 That [form of gold-seeking] which is termed 'hydraulicking'. **1882** *Rep. to Ho. Repr. Prec. Met. U.S.* 105 The Russian Company..are well rigged for hydraulicking, but lack a constant supply of water. *Ibid.* 636 Where a sufficient head of water..can be had, hydraulicing is the method of working employed. **1898** *Westm. Gaz.* 27 Sept. 8/1 It is open to grave doubt whether hydraulicking will be possible.

hydraulico-, combining form of Gr. ὑδραυλικός HYDRAULIC, as in **†hyˌdraulico-pneuˈmatical** *a.* = HYDRAULO-PNEUMATICAL; **†hyˌdraulico-ˈstatics** (see quot.).

1688 BOYLE *Final Causes Nat. Things* iv. 225, I take the body of a living man to be a very compounded engine, such as mechanicians would call Hydraulico-Pneumatical. **1807** T. YOUNG *Lect. Nat. Philos.* I. xxv. 300 The mutual effects of fluids and moveable solids..have been considered by Bernoulli..under the name of hydraulicostatics.

‖**hyˈdraulicon.** Pl. **-a.** [a. Gr. ὑδραυλικὸν (ὄργανον): see HYDRAULIC.] = *hydraulic organ*: see HYDRAULIC *a.* A. 2.

1570 DEE *Math. Pref.* 35 *Hydraulica*, Organes goyng by water. **1776** BURNEY *Hist. Mus.* (1789) I. viii. 111 The hydraulicon or water-organ. **1881** EDWARDS *Organs* 4 Archimedes has had the credit of advancing the hydraulicon.

hydraulics (haɪˈdrɔːlɪks, -ˈdrɒlɪks). [Plural of HYDRAULIC, after earlier names of sciences in -ICS, q.v.] That department of science which deals with the conveyance of water or other liquids through pipes or other artificial channels, and with the various mechanical applications of the force exerted by moving liquids. Often used in a wider sense, corresponding to what is now expressed by *hydrokinetics* or *hydrodynamics*.

1671 BOYLE *Usefulness Exp. Philos.* II. ii. I. ii, Hydrostaticks and hydraulicks, that teach us to make engines and contrivances for the lifting up, and for the conveying of water. **1729** SWITZER *Hydrost. & Hydraul.* Ded. A ij, I present this Volume of Hydrostaticks and Hydraulicks to your Patronage. **1794** SULLIVAN *View Nat.* I. 338 From what level, upon any principle of hydraulics, can these waters be supposed to be deduced? **1806** HUTTON *Course Math.* II. 221 Hydraulics is the science which treats of the motion of fluids, and the forces with which they act upon bodies. **1839** HALLAM *Hist. Lit.* II. viii. IV. 43 The more difficult science of hydraulics was entirely created by two disciples of Galileo, Castellio and Torricelli. **1855** EMERSON *Misc., Fort. Repub.* Wks. III. 387 It is a rule..in economy as well as in hydraulics, that you must have a source higher than your tap.

hyˈdraulist. [f. HYDRAUL-IC + -IST; cf. F. *hydrauliste* (1836).] One skilled in hydraulics; a hydraulician.

1847 LEITCH tr. *C. O. Müller's Anc. Art* 72 Meton (the astronomer and hydraulist).

†hyˈdraulo-pneuˈmatical, *a. Obs.* [f. *hydraulo-* combining form of Gr. ὕδραυλος (see HYDRAULIC) + PNEUMATICAL.] Relating to hydraulics and pneumatics: see quots. So **†hyˈdraulo-pneuˈmatic** *a.* in same sense; **†hyˈdraulo-pneuˈmatics**, the combination of hydraulics and pneumatics.

1669 BOYLE *Contn. New Exp.* I. 13 A new Hydraulo-pneumatical Fountain..with the uses to be made of it, as in Hydraulo-pneumaticks. **1685** —— *Enq. Notion Nat.* 310, I look..on a Human Body..as an Hydraulical, or rather Hydraulo-pneumatical Engine. **1730–6** BAILEY (folio), *Hydraulopneumatick* Engine. **1741** *Phil. Trans.* XLI. 821 Hydraulo-pneumatical and other Engines, for raising Water.

hydraulus (haɪ'drɔːləs). *Mus.* Also **hydraulis.** [L., f. Gr. ὕδραυλος hydraulic organ (cf. αὐλός pipe).] A type of water organ popular in classical times; = *hydraulic organ* (HYDRAULIC *a.* 2).

1874 W. CHAPPELL *Hist. Mus.* I. xiii. 328 Philōn defines.. a kind of 'syrinx played by the hands, which we call hydraulis'. **1903** C. F. A. WILLIAMS *Story of Organ* ii. 35 Sylvester made an organ that was played by 'warm water'; this was.. the hydraulus. **1934** *Times Educ. Suppl.* 27 Jan. p. iv/2 [The Albert Hall organ] has.. been heard as an accompaniment to choral singing, and, like the hydraulus in the Roman amphitheatres of old, to gladiatorial spectacles. **1970** *Oxf. Compan. Mus.* (ed. 10) 496/2 Hydraulus, hydraulis, or water organ. This is the most ancient form of organ known. *Ibid.*, In general appearance the hydraulus is like any small organ of today.

hydrazide ('haɪdrəzaɪd). *Chem.* [f. HYDRAZ(INE + -IDE.] Any compound which may be represented as $R{\cdot}CO{\cdot}NH{\cdot}NH_2$; also, any derivative of such a compound in which univalent radicals replace one or more of the hydrogen atoms.

1888 *Jrnl. Chem. Soc.* LIV. 686 Malonyl hydrazide, $CH_2(CO{\cdot}NH{\cdot}NHPh)_2$,.. crystallises.. in white leaflets. **1955** Z. E. JOLLES in E. H. Rodd *Chem. Carbon Compounds* IIIA. vi. 320 Hydrazo compounds and hydrazides yield the corresponding azo derivatives by oxidation.

hydrazine ('haɪdrəziːn, formerly -aɪn). *Chem.* [mod. f. HYDR(OGEN) + AZO- (for *azote*) + -INE.] A colourless stable gas, with strong alkaline reaction, also called DIAMIDOGEN, N_2H_4; now used esp. in rocket fuels. Also extended to a class of compounds in which one or more of the Hydrogen atoms in this are replaced by a univalent radical, as ***ethyl hydrazine*** $N_2H_3.C_2H_5$.

1887 *Athenæum* 9 July 57/2 Curtius describes the preparation of a new compound of nitrogen and hydrogen. .. He terms it hydrazine or diamidogen. **1950** *Sci. News* XV. 77 One class [of propellants], called hypergols, react as soon as they come together... Such pairs are.. hydrazine hydrate and hydrogen peroxide. **1955** *Sci. News Let.* 1 Oct. 212/1 Monopropellants, whose chemical structures carry both fuel and oxidizer, were listed by him as ethylene oxide, hydrazine, hydrogen peroxide and nitromethane. **1960** *Aeroplane* XCIX. 638/2 Achieving a lunar orbit would depend largely on the hydrazine engine which has yet to be tested in flight. **1969** *Times* 3 June (Suppl.) p. iii/7 Aerozine 50—an equal blend of hydrazine and unsymmetrical dimethyl hydrazine.

hydrazinium (haɪdrə'zɪnɪəm). *Chem.* [f. HYDRAZIN(E + -IUM b.] **a.** The ion $H_2N-NH_3{}^+$ derived from hydrazine (or a substituted ion derived from this in which univalent radicals replace one or more of the hydrogen atoms). Usu. *attrib.* **b.** The less common ion $H_3N^+-NH_3{}^+$ (or a substituted ion derived from this in which univalent radicals replace one or more of the hydrogen atoms). Usu. *attrib.*

The application of the terms *hydrazinium* and *hydrazonium* has been inconsistent. Some authors have favoured using one or other of them (with or without a distinguishing numeral) for both ions, whilst some prefer *hydrazinium* for $N_2H_6{}^{++}$ and *hydrazonium* for $N_2H_5{}^+$; others would abandon the names entirely. The International Union of Pure and Applied Chemistry recommends *hydrazinium*(1+), *hydrazinium*(2+), respectively, for the two ions (*Nomencl. Inorg. Chem.* (ed. 2, 1971), Rule 3.17).

1927 *Chem. Abstr.* XXI. 2672 These 'acid products' really contain hydrazinium salts. **1936** *Jrnl. Amer. Chem. Soc.* LVIII. 1606/2 The ionization constants for the hydrazinium ion as an acid and hydrazinium hydroxide as a base have been determined. **1949, 1954** [see HYDRAZONIUM a, b.]. **1955** *Chem. & Engin. News* 3 Jan. 70/3 A.C. Nixon.. suggests that ' hydrazonium' be retained for $H_2NONH_3{}^+$ [*sic*] and 'hydrazinium' be applied to $^+H_3N{\cdot}NH_3{}^+$. **1957, 1966** [see HYDRAZONIUM c]. **1964** J. W. LINNETT *Electronic Struct. Molecules* iv. 64 The NN bond-length in hydrazine, H_2N-NH_2, is 1·47 Å whereas that in the hydrazinium ion, $H_3\overset{+}{N}-\overset{+}{N}H_3$, is 1·40 Å. **1966** COTTON & WILKINSON *Adv. Inorg. Chem.* (ed. 2) xii. 335 Two series of hydrazinium salts are obtainable, those of $N_2H_5{}^+$ and those of $N_2H_6{}^{2+}$.

hydrazino(-) (haɪdrə'ziːnəʊ). *Chem.* A combining form of HYDRAZINE, denoting the univalent radical $-NH{\cdot}NH_2$ (or a substituted radical derived from this in which univalent radicals replace one or more of the hydrogen atoms); also used *attrib.* as an independent word.

1907 *Jrnl. Chem. Soc.* XCII. I. 880 The present work was undertaken to determine the conditions under which the hydroxyls of phenols can be displaced similarly by the hydrazino-group $\cdot NH{\cdot}NH_2$. **1919** *Chem. Abstr.* XIII. 1304 (*heading*) Hydrazino acids. *Ibid.*, Dihydrazine hydrazinodimalonic acid. **1952** E. H. RODD *Chem. Carbon Compounds* I. xii. 841 Hydrazinoacetic acid, $NH_2NHCH_2CO_2H$. **1953** C. C. CLARK *Hydrazine* iii. 35 Hydrogenation of hydrazones and azines to hydrazino compounds is possible in many cases. *Ibid.* 36 (*heading*) Hydrazino acids and esters.

hydrazo(-) ('haɪdrəzəʊ). *Chem.* A combining form of HYDRAZINE, denoting the bivalent radical $-NH{\cdot}NH-$ (not linked to the same atom) or a substituted radical derived from this in which univalent radicals replace one or both of the hydrogen atoms; also used *attrib.* as an independent word.

1872 *Jrnl. Chem. Soc.* XXV. 694 It also unites with hydrogen, giving rise to hydrazophenylene, $C_{12}H_{10}N_2$. **1877** *Ibid.* I. 307 On boiling the hydrazo-compound with hydrochloric acid, the isomeric dibromobenzidine.. is obtained. **1907** *Chem. Abstr.* I. 498 (*heading*) Hydrazo derivatives. **1955** [see HYDRAZIDE]. **1958** PACKER & VAUGHAN *Mod. Approach Org. Chem.* xviii. 608 Azoxybenzene gives hydrazobenzene but not azobenzene with alkaline reducing agents.

Hydrazoa, erron. form of HYDROZOA.

hydrazoate (haɪdrə'zəʊeɪt). *Chem.* [f. HYDRAZO(IC *a.* + -ATE[4].] = AZIDE.

1910 [see AZIDE]. **1938** *Van Nostrand's Sci. Encycl.* 583/2 Hydrazoic acid reacts.. with metals.. to form azides or hydrazoates (or trinitrides).

hydrazoic (haɪdrə'zəʊɪk), *a. Chem.* [f. HYDR(O- d + AZO- (for *azote*) + -IC.] In ***hydrazoic acid***, a compound of nitrogen and hydrogen (N_3H), as yet obtained only in solution, resembling hydrochloric acid, and forming explosive salts. Also called *azoimide.*

1894 ROSCOE & SCHORLEMMER *Chem.* I. 472 Azoimide or Hydrazoic Acid.

hydrazone ('haɪdrəzəʊn). *Chem.* [ad. G. *hydrazon* (E. Fischer 1888, in *Ber. d. Deut. Chem. Ges.* XXI. 984), f. HYDRAZ(INE + -ONE.] Any compound which contains the group $=N{\cdot}NH_2$ (attached to a single carbon atom) and which is thus a condensation product of an aldehyde or ketone with hydrazine; also, any substituted derivative, $=N{\cdot}NHR$ or $=N{\cdot}NRR'$, of such a compound.

1888 *Jrnl. Chem. Soc.* LIV. 590 The name hydrazone is proposed for the compounds of hydrazine with aldehydes and ketones. **1938** ALLEN & BLATT in H. Gilman *Org. Chem.* I. vi. 569 Oximes, hydrazones, and phenylhydrazones are utilized primarily for isolating and identifying carbonyl compounds. **1970** *Nature* 5 Sept. 1048/1 Experiments.. suggested that the hydrazone side-chain of rifampicin was essential for its antiviral activity.

hydrazonium (haɪdrə'zəʊnɪəm). *Chem.* [f. HYDRAZ(INE + -ONIUM.] **a.** = HYDRAZINIUM a. **b.** = HYDRAZINIUM b.

See the note s.v. HYDRAZINIUM.

[**1876** *Jrnl. Chem. Soc.* II. 528 The author [*sc.* E. Fischer] has isolated a body of the formula $C_6H_5.N_2H_2(C_2H_5)(C_2H_5Br)$, which he names phenyldiethylhydrazoniumbromide.] **1949** *Chem. & Industry* 26 Feb. 134/2 The ions derived from hydrazine are also troublesome. The one most commonly encountered, $N_2H_5{}^+$, is called hydrazinium in the 1940 Rules but hydrazonium in Chemical Abstracts (1945). Since the ion is essentially a substituted ammonium, the latter is strictly the more correct, but neither affords a means of distinguishing $N_2H_5{}^+$ from $N_2H_6{}^{++}$, which occurs in a few compounds. The two names could be used in fact for this purpose, but the distinction is best achieved, without confusion, by writing

$N_2H_5{}^+$ Hydrazonium (I) or (+1)
$N_2H_6{}^{++}$ Hydrazonium (II) or (+2).

1953 C. C. CLARK *Hydrazine* iii. 36 The asymmetric dialkyl hydrazines are also strong bases. They react quantitatively with active alkyl chlorides to form water soluble hydrazonium salts: $R_2NNH_2 + R'X \rightarrow R_2NNH_2.R'X$. **1954** *Chem. & Engin. News* 6 Sept. 3548/3 As a name for the ion $H_2N.NH_3{}^+$ there has been some division of usage between 'hydrazonium' and 'hydrazinium'; and some have applied one or other of these names to the ion $^+H_3N.NH_3{}^+$ as well as to the ion of single charge. The newly revised inorganic rules propose to settle the question by naming $N_2H_5{}^+$ 'hydrazinium (1+)' and $N_2H_6{}^{2+}$ 'hydrazinium (2+)'. This does not seem to us an ideal solution, to give two different ions (which are not isomers) the same name except for an affixed numeral. Might not the name 'hydrazinium' be retained for $N_2H_5{}^+$ and some such name as 'hydrazidiinium' coined for $N_2H_6{}^{2+}$? **1955** [see HYDRAZINIUM]. **1957** [see sense c].

c. [Cf. HYDRAZONE.] The ion $R=N{\cdot}NH_3{}^+$ that results from the addition of a proton to a hydrazone; also, any substituted ion derived from this in which univalent radicals replace one or more of the hydrogen atoms.

1957 *Chem. Rev.* LVII. 1022 The cation having the formula $R_3\overset{+}{N}NR_2$ has been given many names. Emil Fischer called the first known representative of this type a 'hydrazonium bromide' but later referred to the same compound as an 'azonium bromide'. *Chemical Abstracts* has used the names 'azinium', 'azonium', 'hydrazinium', and, most commonly of late, 'hydrazonium' for the same type. As a logical extension of the recommendations recently made for naming $[H_3NNH_2]^+$, it is suggested that the name 'hydrazinium' be adopted... It is suggested here that the name 'hydrazonium' be restricted to salts of hydrazones (including quaternary salts). **1966** P. A. S. SMITH *Chem. Open-Chain Org. Nitrogen Compounds* II. ix. 149 Quaternary hydrazinium salts can also be obtained by the hydrolysis of quaternary hydrazonium salts ($R_3\overset{+}{N}-N=CR_2X^-$).

† **hydre.** *Obs.* In 3 ydre. [a. OF. *ydre, ydrie*, ad. L. HYDRIA.] A water-pot.

c **1250** *Kent Serm.* in *O.E. Misc.* 29 þer were. vi. Ydres of stone.

hydre, obs. form of HYDRA.

‖ **hydre'læon, -um.** Also corruptly **hydræleum, -lon, -olean, hydroleon,** etc. [Gr. ὑδρέλαιον (ἔλαιον oil). Cf. F. *hydréléon.*] A mixture of water and oil, formerly used medicinally.

c **1550** LLOYD *Treas. Health* (1585) L v, Hydroleon and Allegant dronke is wonderful good also. **1657** TOMLINSON *Renou's Disp.* 39 It leaves an impression much like to that of Hydræolean. **1727–41** CHAMBERS *Cycl.* s.v., The Hydrelaeon was taken internally, to excite vomiting.

† **hy'drelic,** *a.* and *sb. Obs. rare.* [f. Gr. ὑδρηλ-ός watery, moist + -IC.] (See quots.)

1612 STURTEVANT *Metallica* (1854) 42 Hydrelica is an Ignick inuention, for the cheaper making of all kinde of hotte liquids or liquoures, by the meanes of metallicall instruments, whereupon the materialls made by this art are called Hydrelicks. **1665** J. WILSON *Project.* I. Dram. Wks. (1874) 226 An ignick, hydrelick, hydroterrick invention, consisting of heat without fire or smoke!

hydremia, -ic: see HYDRÆMIA, -IC.

hydrencephal, -ic, -oid, -on, -us. [f. HYDRO- b + Gr. ἐγκέφαλος brain]: see HYDROCEPHALE, etc.

1847 CRAIG, *Hydrencephalic.. Hydrencephalus.* **1866–80** A. FLINT *Princ. Med.* (ed. 5) 704 The so-called hydrencephaloid affection incident, in children, to exhaustion from diarrhoea.

hydrencephalocele (haɪdrɛn'sɛfələʊsiːl). *Path.* [f. HYDR(O- b + ENCEPHALOCELE.] An encephalocele containing serous liquid.

1854 MAYNE *Expos. Lex.*, *Hydrencephalocele*, term for hydrocephalic tumour or hernia. **1878** T. BRYANT *Pract. Surg.* I. 239 In a hydrencephalocele.. there will be a portion of one or both of the ventricles filled with fluid.

hydrenterocele (haɪ'drɛntərəʊsiːl). *Path.* [f. HYDR(O- b + ENTEROCELE.] Intestinal hernia the sac of which contains water.

1706 in PHILLIPS (ed. Kersey). **1727–41** in CHAMBERS *Cycl.* **1811** in HOOPER *Med. Dict.* **1847** in CRAIG, and in mod. Dicts.

† **'hydret.** *Chem. Obs.* [Cf. *sulphuret.*] An early term for *hydruret, hydride.*

1838 T. THOMSON *Chem. Org. Bodies* 46 Oil of cinnamon is a hydret of that base, or $C_{18}H_7O_2 + H$.

‖ **hydria** ('haɪdrɪə, 'hɪdrɪə). Pl. -æ. [L. *hydria*, a. Gr. ὑδρία a water-pot, f. ὕδωρ, ὑδρ- water. Cf. HYDRE.] A water-pot; in *Archæol.* a large Greek jar or pitcher for carrying water, with two or three handles.

1398 TREVISA *Barth. De P.R.* XIX. cxxviii. (1495), Ydria is a water vessel. **1850** LEITCH tr *C. O. Müller's Anc. Art* § 299 (ed. 2) 338 The Corinthian hydriæ had two handles at the top. **1851** C. NEWTON in Ruskin *Stones Ven.* I. App. xxi. 408 A stork seated on a hydria, or pitcher, from which water is flowing.

hydriad ('haɪdrɪæd). [a. Gr. ὑδριάς, ὑδριαδ- (νύμφη), f. ὕδωρ water.] A water-nymph.

1864 in WEBSTER.

hydriatric (haɪdrɪ'ætrɪk), *a. rare.* (*erron.* hydriatic). [mod. f. Gr. ὑδρ- water + ἰατρός physician, ἰατρεία healing, ἰατρικός medical. Cf. F. *hydriatrie.*] Of or pertaining to the water-cure; hydropathic. So **hy'driatrist,** a hydropathist; **hy'driatry,** hydropathy.

1843 T. J. GRAHAM *Cold-Water System* (ed. 2) Contents xvii, Hydriatic measures ought not to be pushed too far. **1843** ABDY *Water Cure* 157 Hahn.. and his two sons were zealous hydriatists. **1843** *Tait's Mag.* Apr. 271/2 The hydriatic method of treatment. **1886** *Syd. Soc. Lex.*, Hydriatric.. *Hydriatry*, same as *Hydrotherapy*.

hydric ('haɪdrɪk), *a.*[1] *Chem.* [f. HYDR(OGEN) + -IC. Cf. F. *hydrique.*] Of hydrogen, containing hydrogen in chemical combination; as in ***hydric chloride*** = *hydrogen chloride* or *hydrochloric acid.*

1854 MAYNE *Expos. Lex.*, *Hydricus*, of or belonging to water; applied to the compounds of a simple body with hydrogen: hydric. **1870** *Eng. Mech.* 18 Feb. 565/3 Aqueous hydric-chloride. **1876** HARLEY *Mat. Med.* (ed. 6) 101 Hydric Cyanide was called Prussic acid.

hydric ('haɪdrɪk), *a.*[2] *Ecol.* [f. Gr. ὕδωρ, ὑδρ- water + -IC.] Of a habitat: having a plentiful supply of water.

1926 COOPER & WEESE in *Ecology* VII. 390 In order.. to provide terms which shall be applicable to both plants and animals, we suggest that the adjectives 'xerophytic', 'hydrophytic' and 'mesophytic' be entirely abandoned as useless and misleading. In their place we offer the terms 'xeric', 'hydric' and 'mesic', to be defined as follows: Xeric (hydric, mesic): characterized by or pertaining to conditions of scanty (abundant, medium) moisture supply. **1947** R. F. DAUBENMIRE *Plants & Environment* iii. 148 Hydric, xeric, and mesic are commonly encountered in ecologic literature. .. These adjectives, if used, should be applied only to habitats. **1960** N. POLUNIN *Introd. Plant Geogr.* xi. 328 Typically this mean [between two seres] is inhabited by mesophytes and is said to be 'mesic', though relatively xeric (dry) and hydric (damp) exceptions exist. **1968** R. F. DAUBENMIRE *Plant Communities* iii. 116 Bare areas may be classified according to their characteristic water relations: wet or hydric, as a pond bottom; dry or xeric, as a rock

surface exposed to the sun; or intermediate mesic, as a glacial moraine.

hydrid (ˈhaɪdrɪd). *Zool.* [f. mod.L. *Hydridæ* sb. pl., f. *Hydra*.] A hydrozoan of the family *Hydridæ*, typified by the genus *Hydra* (see HYDRA 6).

hydride (ˈhaɪdraɪd). *Chem.* [f. HYDRO- d + -IDE.] † **a.** Formerly, A substance formed by the combination of water with a radical; = HYDRATE in the earlier sense. **b.** Now, A substance formed by the union of hydrogen with an element or a radical.

1849 D. CAMPBELL *Inorg. Chem.* 20 Water combines with acids and oxides, forming hydrides. *Ibid.* 55 It is no longer SO_3, but HO,SO_3—a hydride of sulphuric acid. *Ibid.* 56 In the processes throughout this book, when sulphuric acid is mentioned it is this hydride which is meant. **1869** ROSCOE *Elem. Chem.* 273 Each of these bodies is therefore termed the hydride of a radical. **1877** ROSCOE & SCHORLEMMER *Treat. Chem.* I. 90 The compounds of Hydrogen form Hydrides.

hydridic (haɪˈdraɪdɪk), *a. Chem.* [f. HYDRID(E + -IC.] Of an atom of hydrogen: having a negative charge (like the hydrogen in ionic hydrides).

1966 PHILLIPS & WILLIAMS *Inorg. Chem.* II. xxxiii. 565 Boron-hydrogen bonds generally react with Grignard reagents as if they contained hydridic hydrogen. **1966** K. M. MACKAY *Hydrogen Compounds Metallic Elem.* v. 155 The behaviour of hydrogen in the hydride complexes reflects a change from acidic hydrogen in the carbonyl hydrides to basic, hydridic, hydrogen in the other compounds. **1968** *Inorg. Chem.* VII. 1952/2 The nature of the hydrogens in boron hydrides varies from hydridic (or negative) in diborane(6) to protonic (or positive) in the moderately strong acid decaborane(14).

hydriform (ˈhaɪdrɪfɔːm), *a.* Also *erron.* **hydraform.** [f. L. type *hydriformis: see HYDRA + -FORM.] Hydra-shaped.

1. Of the form of the Lernæan Hydra.

1822 *New Monthly Mag.* V. 110 Dividing their discourses into heads—Cerberean, Polypean, and Hydraform.

2. Having the form of the hydra polyp.

1847 CARPENTER *Zool.* § 1044 The arms [of the Hydra] are destitute of cilia; and this is an important character, by which all the Polypes of the Hydra-form kind may be at once distinguished from those of a higher group. **1847–9** TODD *Cycl. Anat.* IV. 20/1 Polypes hydriform. **1874** LUBBOCK *Orig. & Met. Ins.* iii. 49 Distinguished by the absence of a hydriform stage.

† **hydriodate** (haɪˈdraɪəʊdət). *Chem. Obs.* [f. as next + -ATE[1] 1 c.] An old name for an iodide, as a salt of hydriodic acid; also, a hydriodide.

1823 CRABB *Technol. Dict.* s.v., The Hydriodate of ammonia, of potash, of soda, or barytes, etc. **1826** HENRY *Elem. Chem.* I. 537 Iodate and Hydriodate of Potassa. **1851** *Illustr. Catal. Gt. Exhib.* 190 Hydriodate of quinine.

hydriodic (haɪdraɪˈɒdɪk), *a. Chem.* [f. HYDR(OGEN) + IOD(INE) + -IC. Cf. F. *hydriodique*.] Containing hydrogen and iodine in chemical combination. *hydriodic acid*, the simple combination of hydrogen and iodine, also called *hydrogen iodide* (HI), a colourless very soluble gas, of strongly acid properties and suffocating odour.

1819 J. G. CHILDREN *Chem. Anal.* 110 Hydriodic acid is formed of one volume of the vapour of iodine and one volume of hydrogen. **1849** D. CAMPBELL *Inorg. Chem.* 91 Hydriodic acid gas very much resembles hydrochloric acid gas. **1859** *Fownes' Chem.* 372 Iodide of ethyl; hydriodic ether. **1869** ROSCOE *Elem. Chem.* 299 Olefiant gas.. combines with hydriodic acid to form ethyl iodide.

So **hydriodide** (haɪˈdraɪəʊdaɪd), a compound formed by the combination of hydriodic acid with an organic radical (or, formerly, with an element).

1823 FARADAY *Exp. Res.* xvii. 81 Hydriodide of carbon.

hydrion (ˈhaɪdraɪən, ˈhaɪdrɪɒn). *Chem.* [Contraction of *hydr(ogen) ion*: see -ION[3].] The hydrogen ion or proton.

1901 J. WALKER in *Chem. News* 4 Oct. 162 The proposals which I make for naming the positive and negative radicals of salts, acids, and bases considered as ions are as follows:—. .. If we use with Ostwald a dot to express unit positive charge, we have for some typical kations:—Hydrion..H·. Sodion..Na·. **1921** *Phil. Mag.* XLII. 455 There are only two elements, Sir Ernest Rutherford's proton (hydrion) and electron. **1930** *Nature* 20 Sept. 434/2 The hydrion concentration (*p*H) of the rain has been recorded. **1943** *Thorpe's Dict. Appl. Chem.* (ed. 4) VI. 381/2 There is a great excess of hydroxyl ions over hydrions. **1968** PASSMORE & ROBSON *Compan. Med. Stud.* I. p. xxxii (Index), Hydrion excretion, by kidney.

hydro[1] (ˈhaɪdrəʊ). Short for HYDROPATHIC *sb.*

1882 *Brit. Med. Jrnl. Advert.* 9 Dec., Visitors will find the 'Hydro' a pleasant Home during their residence in Bournemouth. **1894** *Advt.*, Buxton, The Peak Thermal Establishment. The best Hydro in district. Mineral water and other baths. **1898** *Navy & Army Illustr.* 23 July p. vii, Palatial establishments..all..modestly calling themselves Hydros.

hydro[2] (ˈhaɪdrəʊ). Short for HYDRO-ELECTRIC (*power, plant*). Also *attrib.* In Canada also = *hydro-electric power supply*. Cf. HYDRO-POWER.

1916 A. BRIDLE *Sons of Canada* 185 The product of Niagara..is Hydro-Electric—familiarly abbreviated to Hydro. **1925** *Rep. Brit. Assoc. Adv. Sci. 1924* 43 Various hydro systems were formed as circumstances dictated. **1938** 'R. HYDE' *Nor Years Condemn* x. 200 Did I ever tell you about that hydro I was on, a bit South? **1939** F. P. GROVE *Two Generations* 230 The telephone and hydro wires are down. **1947** E. A. MCCOURT *Music at Close* 71 There was talk of water works, a hydro plant, a newspaper, paved streets. **1949** L. PETERSON *Chipmunk* 149 Claude wrote out the address..on the envelope of the hydro bill he'd forgotten to pay. **1952** D. F. PUTNAM *Canad. Regions* xvii. 387/2 The cities of Alberta, also, have good sources of power including coal, natural gas and hydro. **1958** *New Statesman* 11 Oct. 480/1 Geological reserves of coal are estimated to constitute about four-fifths of all Russia's coal deposits, and much of this coal lies on the surface and this favours the development of thermal-power stations to supplement the hydro-stations of the River Angara. **1962** R. F. LEGGET *Geol. & Engin.* (ed. 2) x. 354 Across the Niagara River is the ..Niagara power project of the Power Authority of the State of New York, constructed a few years after the Ontario hydro project. **1963** *B.S.I. News* Feb. 14/2 The hydro developments in Scotland really got under way in the early 1950s. **1970** *Globe & Mail* (Toronto) 26 Sept. 47/2 (Advt.), T.V. outlets in each room, drapes and hydro included.

hydro- (haɪdrəʊ), before a vowel also **hydr-**, = Gr. ὑδρ(ο-, combining form of ὕδωρ water, employed in many compounds adopted or formed from Greek.

Of the numerous compounds in Greek some were adopted in Latin, whence they passed into English either directly or through French: the earliest of these are *hydropic, hydropsy, hydromancy*, and *hydromel*, found in the 13th and 14th c. A few others were added to the language during the 16th and 17th c., as *hydrocele, hydrographer, -graphy, hydrology, hydrophobia, hydrostatic*; but the greater number of the words now in use belong to the common scientific vocabulary of the 19th c. (including the end of the 18th c.).

The words so formed may be thus classed:

a. Miscellaneous terms, in which *hydro-* has the sense of 'water', as in *hydrography, hydrometer, hydropathy, hydrostatics*. These pass into terms in which *hydro-* is used in more or less loose combination, as *hydrogeology, hydro-galvanic, hydro-electricity, hydro-extractor, hydro-propulsion*.

b. In medical and pathological terminology, *hydro-* is extensively used to form names of diseases (chiefly in Latin or Greek form), being prefixed (*a*) to names of parts of the body, to denote that such part is dropsical or affected with an accumulation of serous fluid, as in ***hydroabdomen*** (dropsy of the abdomen, ascites), ***hydroblepharon (-um)*** [Gr. βλέφαρον eyelid], ***hydrocardia*** [Gr. καρδία heart], ***-cranium, -derma, -gaster*** [Gr. γαστήρ belly], ***-gastria, -hystera*** [Gr. ὑστέρα womb], ***hydromphalum (-us)*** [Gr. ὀμφαλός navel], ***hydromyelus, -myelia*** [Gr. μυελός marrow, used for 'spinal cord'], ***-nephros*** [Gr. νεφρός kidney], ***hydro-ovarium*** [see OVARY], ***-pericardium, -peritonæum, hydrorrhachis*** [Gr. ῥάχις spine], ***hydrosalpinx*** [Gr. σάλπιγξ trumpet, used for 'Fallopian tube'], ***hydrothorax***; also, in the combination *hydropneumo-*, to express the presence of water and air, as in ***hydropneumopericardium, hydropneumothorax***; (*b*) to names of diseases or diseased formations, denoting the accompaniment of dropsy or of an accumulation of serous fluid, as ***hydrocachexia, -y*** [see CACHEXY], ***-diarrhœa, -hæmothorax, -meningitis, -pericarditis, -peritonitis, hydrorrhachitis***, etc.; ***hydrocirsocele, hydr(o)enterocele, hydromeningocele, -myelocele, -physocele, -sarcocele, hydroscheocele***, etc.

c. Prefixed to names of minerals, *hydro-* denotes a hydrous compound, or the addition of water or its constituents to the elements of the primary mineral.

d. (*a*) In modern chemical terms (the earliest of which were formed in French), the prefix *hydro-* originally meant combination with *water*. In many cases however this really amounted to combination with the hydrogen supplied by the water; so that *hydr(o-* has become the regular combining form of *hydrogen*, like *oxy-* for *oxygen*, *nitro-* for *nitrogen*, *cyano-* for *cyanogen*.

1822 IMISON *Sc. & Art* II. 21 To distinguish the acids formed by hydrogen, from those formed by oxygen, the former are designated by the word *hydro*, as the hydro-chloric acid. **1853** W. GREGORY *Inorg. Chem.* (ed. 3) 4 If composed of oxygen united to a metalloid, such as carbon, or a metal..the acid is simply named from the metalloid or metal, as carbonic acid, chromic acid. But if the acid contains hydrogen united to a metalloid, the word 'hydro' is prefixed; as hydro-chloric acid (hydrogen and chlorine), hydro-sulphuric acid (hydrogen and sulphur), &c.

(*b*) Prefixed to the name of a compound substance, *hydro-* usually means the addition or substitution of hydrogen in its constitution, e.g. *benzoin* $C_{14}H_{12}O_2$, *hydrobenzoin* $C_{14}H_{14}O_2$; so *cinchonine, hydrocinchonine, cellulose, hydrocellulose*, etc.

e. In modern zoological terminology, *hydro-* is used in the nomenclature relating to members of the class HYDROZOA and their characteristic organs or parts. Strictly speaking, *hydro-* is here a combining form of the generic name HYDRA; but this is itself a derivative of Gr. ὕδωρ, ὑδρ(ο- water, so that, as being ultimately from the same source, these terms may be classed with the other *hydro-* formations.

f. Derivatives of Gr. ἱδρώς 'sweat' have been erroneously written *hydro-* instead of *hidro-* (the error being encouraged by the fact that sweat is a form of water), e.g. ***hydroadenitis*** inflammation of the sweat glands, ***hydrocritics, hydropyretic***.

The more important words in all these groups appear in their alphabetical order in the main series; others of less importance follow here.

hydroaeric (ˌhaɪdrəʊeɪˈɛrɪk) *a.* (see quot.); **ˌhydro-alcoˈholic** *a.*, in or consisting of a mixture of an alcohol and water; **hydroˈapatite** *Min.*, hydrous apatite, a milk-white subtransparent mineral; **ˌhydro-aroˈmatic** *a. Chem.*, having one or more benzene rings which are partially or completely hydrogenated (reduced); also as *sb.*, a hydro-aromatic compound; **hydrobaˈrometer**, an instrument for determining the depth of the ocean from the pressure of the superincumbent water (Webster 1864); **hydroˈbenzoin** *Chem.*, a crystalline substance, $C_{14}H_{14}O_2$, obtained by the action of nascent hydrogen on oil of bitter almonds; **ˌhydro-biˈology**, the biology of aquatic plants and animals; hence **hydrobioˈlogical** *a.*, **hydro-biˈologist**, one engaged in the study of hydrobiology; ‖**hydrobiosis** (-baɪˈəʊsɪs) *Zool.* [Gr. βίωσις way of life], the development of living organisms, as bacteria, in fluid media; the conditions of life of such organisms; **hydroˈbiotite** *Min.*, (*a*) a hydrated variety of biotite; (*b*) any clay composed of an intimate mixture of biotite and vermiculite; **hydroˈboracite** *Min.* [named 1834], hydrous borate of calcium and magnesium, resembling gypsum; **ˈhydrobranch** (-bræŋk) *Zool.* [Gr. βράγχια gills], a member of the *Hydrobranchiata*, a division of gastropods in Lamarck's classification, containing species which breathe water only; so **hydrobranchiate** (-ˈbræŋkɪət) *a.*, pertaining to the *Hydrobranchiata* (Mayne *Expos. Lex.* 1855); **hydroˈcalcite** *Min.* [named 1846], a hydrous carbonate of calcium (Dana *Min.* (1850) 212); **hydroˈcalumite** *Min.* [f. blend of CAL(CIUM + ALUM(INATE], a transparent, colourless to light green hydrated hydroxide of calcium and aluminium, $Ca_2Al(OH)_7.3H_2O$; ‖**hydroˈcardia** *Path.*, dropsy of the heart (see b above); **ˈhydrocast** *Oceanography* [contraction of *hydrographic cast* (CAST *sb.* 5)], a long cable having sampling bottles attached at intervals along it; also, a sampling operation in which this is used; **hydrocauline** (-ˈkɔːlaɪn) *a. Zool.* [Gr. καυλός stem], pertaining to or characteristic of the ‖**hydroˈcaulus** or main stem of the cœnosarc of a hydrozoan; **hydroˈcellulose** *Chem.* [a. F. *hydro-cellulose* (A. Giraud 1875, in *Compt. Rend.* LXXXI. 1106)], any of the chemically heterogeneous substances produced by the partial hydrolysis of cellulosic material; ‖**hydrocephalis** (-ˈsɛfəlɪs) [Gr. κεφαλή head], the oral and stomachal regions of a hydroid; **hydro-ceˈramic** *a.*, designating porous, unglazed pottery used for cooling or filtering; **hydroˈcerussite** *Min.*, a variety of basic lead carbonate; † **hydroˈchinone** *Chem.* = HYDROQUINONE; **ˈhydro-chore** [Gr. χωρεῖν to spread], a plant whose seeds are dispersed by water; hence **hydro-ˈchoric, -ous** *adjs.*, **ˈhydrochory**, the dissemination of seeds by water; **hydroˈcinchonine** *Chem.*, an alkaloid ($C_{20}H_{26}N_2O$) obtained by heating cinchonine ($C_{20}H_{24}N_2O$) with $KMnO_4$; **hydroˈcirsocele** *Path.* [CIRSOCELE], hydrocele complicated with a varicose state of the spermatic cord (*Syd. Soc. Lex.*(1886); **ˈhydroclone** [CY)CLONE] = *hydrocyclone*; **ˈhydrocœl(e)** (-siːl) *Zool.* [Gr. κοιλία cavity of the body], the water-vascular system of an echinoderm; also **-cele**; ‖**hydroˈcœlia** (-ˈsiːlɪə) *Path.* [Gr. κοιλία belly], dropsy of the abdomen, ascites; **hyˈdroconite** *Min.* [named, 1847, f. Gr. κονία lime], hydrous calcium carbonate (Dana *Min.* (1892) 303); **ˈhydrocope** (ˈhaɪdrəʊkəʊp) *Zool.* [Gr. κώπη shaft], the peduncle of a hydroid; **hydrocoralline** (-ˈkɒrəlaɪn) *Zool.* [CORALLINE]

a., pertaining to the *Hydrocorallinæ*, an order or sub-order of *Hydroidea*, the coral-making hydroid hydrozoa; *sb.* one of this order of Hydrozoa; **hydroco'tarnia, -co'tarnine** (-aın) *Chem.*, a crystalline alkaloid existing in opium, and containing two atoms of hydrogen more than cotarnine; **hydrocou'maric** *a. Chem.*, in ***h. acid*** = melilotic acid; † **hydro'critics** (erron. for *hidrocritics*): see quot; **'hydrocycle** [CYCLE *sb.* 11], a velocipede adapted for propulsion on the surface of water; hence **hydro'cyclist**, one who propels a hydrocycle; **hydrocyst** ('haıdrəʊsıst) *Zool.* [Gr. κύστις bladder, CYST], one of the tentacles or feelers, resembling immature polypites, attached to the cœnosarc in certain Hydrozoa, as in the family *Physophoridæ*; hence **hydro'cystic** *a.*; **hydro-'cyclone**, a device in which centrifugation in a conical vessel is employed to remove or separate particles in suspension in a flow of liquid; **hydro'dolomite** *Min.*, hydrous carbonate of calcium and magnesium, a yellowish-white, greyish, or greenish mineral; **'hydrodrill**, a device for injecting water or fertilizers near the roots of plants; also as *v. trans.*; **hydrœcial** (haı'dri:sıəl) *a.*, pertaining to the ‖ **hydrœcium** (-'i:sıəm) [Gr. οἰκίον, f. οἶκος house], a sac into which the cœnosarc can be retracted in certain Hydrozoa, as the *Calycophoridæ*; **'hydro-extract** *v. trans.* [back-formation from *hydro-extractor*], to dry by means of a hydro-extractor; so ***hydro-extracting*** vbl. sb.; also **'hydro-extraction**; **hydro-extractor** [F. *hydro-extracteur*], a centrifugal machine for drying clothes and other articles; **hydroferricy'anic, -ferridcyanic**, *a. Chem.*, in ***h. acid*** = hydrogen ferricyanide, $H_6Fe_2Cy_{12}$; hence **hydroferri(d)'cyanate**, a salt of this acid; **hydroferrocy'anic** *a. Chem.* in ***h. acid*** = hydrogen ferrocyanide, H_4FeCy_6; hence **hydroferro'cyanate**, a salt of this acid; **,hydroformy'lation** *Chem.*, the catalytic addition of both carbon monoxide and hydrogen to an olefin to produce an aldehyde; **hydrofuge** ('haıdrəʊfju:dʒ) [see -FUGE F. *hydrofuge*] *a.*, impervious to water, as the plumage of ducks, the pubescence of many insects, etc.; *sb.* a substance which is impervious to or resists the action of water; **hydrogal'vanic** *a.* [GALVANIC], pertaining to the production of galvanic electricity by means of liquids (Webster 1864); **hydro'garnet** *Min.*, any mineral whose formula is that of a garnet in which water molecules replace some or all of the silicate groups; **'hydroglider**, a form of craft designed to glide on the surface of water (see also quot. 1961); † **hy'drognosy** [Gr. -γνωσια knowledge], a history and description of the waters of the earth (Mayne *Expos. Lex.* 1855); **hydro'grossular** *Min.*, a calcium aluminosilicate with a composition varying between that of hibschite and that of grossular (see quot. 1966); **hydro'hæmatite, -hematite** *Min.*, a hydrated sesquioxide of iron, resembling hæmatite, also called *turgite*; **hydrohalite** (-'hælaıt) *Min.* [ad. G. *hydrohalit* (J. F. L. Hausmann *Handbuch d. Mineralogie* (ed. 2, 1847) II. 1458)], a hydrated chloride of sodium, $NaCl.2H_2O$; **,hydrohetærolite** (-hɛ'tıərəʊlaıt) *Min.*, a hydrous oxide of zinc and manganese similar to hetærolite; **hydrohy'steric** *a. Path.*, pertaining to *hydrohystera*, an accumulation of water in the womb; **hydroi'odic** = HYDRIODIC; **hydro'kineter** (also *-ki'neter*) [Gr. κινητής, -ήρ one that sets going], a device for heating water at the bottom of large boilers by injecting surplus steam; **hydro'laccolith** *Physical Geogr.* [from its resemblance to a LACCOLITH], an underground mass of ice in a region of permafrost which tends to increase in size and thrust up the overlying soil forming a mound; a mound so formed, esp. a pingo; so **,hydrolacco'lithic** *a.*; **'hydrolite** *Min.* [-LITE], the zeolitic mineral GMELINITE; **hydro'magnesite** *Min.* [named 1827], hydrous carbonate of magnesium, found in white silky crystals or earthy crusts; **hydromedusan** (-mı'dju:sən) [MEDUSA] *a.*, belonging or relating to the *Hydromedusæ*, now a sub-class of Hydrozoa (called also *Craspedota*), formerly a synonym of Hydrozoa; *sb.* a member of this subclass; **hydrome'dusoid** *a.* [see -OID], of the form of or resembling the *Hydromedusæ* (Cent. Dict.); ‖ **hydromenin'gitis** *Path.*, inflammation of the cerebral membranes with serous effusion; **hydrome'ningocele** (see b, and MENINGOCELE); **,hydrometa'llurgical** *a.*, of or pertaining to hydrometallurgy; **hydrome'tallurgy** [METALLURGY], 'the act or process of assaying or reducing ores in the wet way, or by means of liquid re-agents' (Webster 1864); **hydro-meta'morphism** *Geol.*, a kind of METAMORPHISM of igneous rocks effected by means of water; so **hydro-meta'morphic** *a.*, pertaining or relating to this; **hydro'meteor** [see METEOR: cf. F. *hydrométéore*], an atmospheric phenomenon which depends on the vapour of water, as rain, hail, and snow; hence **,hydrometeoro'logical** *a.*, pertaining to **,hydrometeo'rology**, that part of meteorology which deals with atmospheric phenomena depending on the vapour of water (Webster 1864); **hydro'mica** *Min.*, a variety of potash mica containing more water than ordinary muscovite; hence **hydromi'caceous** *a.* **hydro'morphic, -'morphous** *adjs. Soil Sci.*, (of a soil) developed and maintained in contact with a high water-table; (of a soil-forming process) acting in conjunction with a high water-table; **hydro'motor**, a kind of motor for the propulsion of vessels, the propelling power being produced by jets of water ejected from the sides or the stern; **hydro-'muscovite** *Min.*, a variety of muscovite containing more water and less potassium than that mineral; **hydromyd** ('haıdrəʊmıd) *Zool.* [Gr. μῦς mouse], a rodent of the genus *Hydromys*, comprising the water-rats and beaver-rats of the Australian region (*Cent. Dict.*); ‖ **hydromy'elia**, ‖ **-'myelus, hydro'myelocele** *Path.* (see b above, and quots.); **hydro'nephelite** *Min.*, a hydrous silicate of aluminium and sodium, derived from nephelite; † **hydro'nitric** *a. Chem.*, containing hydrogen and nitrogen in combination; ***hydronitric acid***, an old name of nitric acid or hydrogen nitrate; ‖ **hydro-o'varium** *Path.* (see b above and quot.); † **hydro-oxide** *Chem.* = HYDROXIDE; † **hydro-oxygen** *Chem.* = OXYHYDROGEN; **hydro'parastates** *sb. pl.*, *Eccl. Hist.* [ad. Gr. pl. ὑδροπαραστάται, f. παραστάτης comrade] (see quots.); ‖ **hydroperi'cardium, hydroperito'næum** *Path.* (see b above and quots.); **'hydrophid** *Zool.* [Gr. ὄφις serpent], a venomous sea-snake of genus *Hydrophis* or family *Hydrophidæ*, found in the Indian Ocean; **hy'drophilid**, a water-beetle of the family Hydrophilidæ; also as *adj.*, of or pertaining to an insect of this type; **'hydrophite** *Min.*, a hydrous silicate of iron and magnesium, allied to serpentine (ophite); **hydroph'thalic** *a. Chem.* (see d above and quot.); **'hydrophyll** (-fıl) *Bot.*, Lindley's name for plants of N.O. *Hydrophyllaceæ*, of which the typical genus is *Hydrophyllum*, the Waterleaf of N. America; **hydrophylliaceous** (-fılı'eıʃ(ı)əs) *a.* [see -ACEOUS], having the characters of the ‖ **hydrophyllium** (-'fılıəm) [Gr. φύλλιον leaflet], one of the protective zooids, of a laminar or leaf-like character, attached either to the cœnosarc or to the pedicles of the polypites in certain oceanic hydrozoa; = BRACT 2; **hydro'physocele** *Path.* (see b above, and quot.); **'hydro-plant**, plant for generating hydro-electric power; a hydro-electric generating station; ‖ **hydroplanula** (-'plænjʊlə) [PLANULA], the transitional stage of a hydrozoan intermediate between the planula and the tentaculated actinula (*Cent. Dict.*); **hydroplu'tonic** *a. Geol.* (see quot.); **hydro'polyp** [POLYP], a hydrozoan as distinguished from an actinozoan polyp; **hydropo'tassic** *a. Chem.*, containing hydrogen and potassium in combination, as ***hydropotassic sulphate***, a double sulphate of H and K, $K_2SO_4.H_2SO_4$, commonly called bisulphate of potash; **hydropro'pulsion**, propulsion by means of a hydromotor (*Cent. Dict.*); **hydropult** ('haıdrəʊpʌlt) [f. *-pult* in CATAPULT *sb.*], a force-pump worked by hand; a garden-pump; hence **hydro'pultic** *a.*; **hydropy'retic** *a.*, erron. for *hidropyretic*, pertaining to *Hidropyretos* or sweating sickness (Mayne *Expos. Lex.* 1855); ‖ **hydrorachis, -orrhachis** (haı'drɒrəkıs) *Path.* (see b above, and quot.); **hydrorenal** (-'ri:nəl) *a.* [L. *rēn-es* kidneys: see RENAL], characterized by a dropsical condition of the kidney; ‖ **hydrorhiza** (-'raızə) [Gr. ῥίζα root], the root-stock or rooting fibres by which a colony of Hydrozoa is attached to some foreign object; hence **hydrorhizal** (-'raızəl) *a.*; ‖ **hydro'salpinx** *Path.* (see b above, and quot.); **hydro'sarcocele** *Path.* (see b above, and SARCOCELE); **hydroscheocele** (haı'drɒskiːəʊsiːl) *Path.*, dropsical oscheocele or scrotal hernia; **hydrose'lenic** *a. Chem.*, consisting of hydrogen and selenium in combination; ***h. acid***, another name for hydrogen selenide or seleniuretted hydrogen, H_2Se, an offensive gas; hence **hydro'selenate, -se'lenuret; hydrosere** *Ecol.*, a plant succession having its origin in a wet habitat; **hydro'silicate** *Min.*, a silicate containing water, a hydrous silicate; **'hydro-ski** *Aeronaut.*, a hydrofoil on a seaplane or amphibious aircraft that skims the surface of the water and provides hydrodynamic lift; **hydro'sodic** (-'səʊdık) *a. Chem.*, containing hydrogen and sodium in combination, as ***hydrosodic sulphate***, a double sulphate of hydrogen and sodium, $Na_2SO_4.H_2SO_4$, commonly called *hydrated bisulphate of soda*; **'hydrospace**, the underwater realms; **hydro-'sphygmograph**, a kind of sphygmograph in which the variation in the quantity of blood in a part is measured by the pressure on a fluid contained in a closed chamber or vessel (*Syd. Soc. Lex.* 1886); **hydrospire** ('haıdrəʊspaıə(r)) *Zool.* [Gr. σπεῖρα coil, SPIRE], one of the system of lamellar tubes lying between and below the ambulacra in blastoids, supposed to have been respiratory in function; **hydro'tachylite, -lyte** *Min.*, a hydrous variety of tachylite; **hydro'talcite** *Min.* [TALC], a hydrous oxide of aluminium and magnesium, a fibrous white mineral of pearly lustre and greasy feel; **hydro'technic** *a.* [Gr. τεχνή art: F. *hydrotechnique*], relating to or dealing with the technical management or utilization of water; **hydrote'lluric** *a. Chem.*, formed by hydrogen and tellurium in chemical combination; ***h. acid***, another name for telluretted hydrogen, H_2Te, an offensive gas; its salts are **hydro'tellurates**; ‖ **hydrotheca** (-'θi:kə) *Zool.* [L. *thēca*, Gr. θήκη receptacle], one of the perisarcal cups or calycles in which the polypites in certain Hydrozoa (as the *Sertularidæ*) are lodged; hence **hydrothecal** (-'θi:kəl) *a.* † **hydro'thion** [Gr. θεῖον sulphur], an old name of hydrogen sulphide or sulphuretted hydrogen, also called † **hydrothi'onic** ***acid***; hence † **hydro'thionate**, a salt of this acid, a sulphydrate; so † **hydro'thionous** = hydrosulphurous; † **hydrothionite**, a salt of hydrosulphurous acid; ‖ **hydro,thio'næmia** *Path.* [Gr. αἷμα blood], blood-poisoning with sulphuretted hydrogen; **hydrotroilite** (-'trəʊılaıt, -'trɔılaıt) *Min.* [ad. Russ. *gidrotroilit* (M. Sidorenko 1901, in *Mém. Soc. Naturalistes Nouv.-Russie* XXIV. 1. 119)], a black hydrated ferrous sulphide, $FeS.nH_2O$, occurring in the mud of lakes and inland seas; **hydro'tungstite** *Min.*, a hydrated tungstic acid, $H_2WO_4.H_2O$, occurring as minute green tabular crystals; **'hydrowire** *Oceanography* [contraction of *hydrographic wire*], a cable used for hydro-casts; **hydro'zincite, -kite** *Min.*, hydrous carbonate of zinc, also called zinc bloom (Dana *Min.* 1854).

1886 *Syd. Soc. Lex.*, **Hydroaeric sound*, the percussion note produced over a cavity containing both water and air. Also, the sounds heard on auscultating a similar cavity. **1887** A. M. BROWN *Contrib. Animal Alkaloids* 46 The *hydro-alcoholic solution of the alkaloid was injected hypodermically into a dog of medium size. **1951** Hydro-alcoholic [see HYDRASTIS]. **1969** *Biochim. & Biophys. Acta* CXCIV. 265 (*heading*) Optical rotatory dispersion of polyglutamic and polyuridylic acids at low temperatures in fluid hydro-alcoholic solvents. **1858** *Amer. Jrnl. Sc.* Ser. II. XXV. 408 *Hydroapatite is a hydrous apatite. **1900** E. F. SMITH tr. *V. von Richter's Org. Chem.* (ed. 3) II. 290 Hexahydrobenzene is the parent hydrocarbon of the *hydroaromatic substances. **1940** *Industr. & Engin. Chem.* Apr. 528/2 The cyclization of paraffins to hydroaromatics is preceded by dehydrogenation. **1951** I. L. FINAR *Org. Chem.* xix. 390 Many benzene derivatives may be reduced to the corresponding cyclohexane compounds, and because of this, cyclohexane and its derivatives are known as the hydroaromatic compounds. The cyclic terpenes are hydroaromatic compounds. **1877** WATTS *Fownes' Chem.* (ed. 12) II. 571 Benzoin .. converted .. by heating with alcoholic potash into *hydrobenzoïn and benzile. **1933** *Geogr. Jrnl.* LXXXI. 533 It [*sc.* the Arctic Institute of the U.S.S.R.] .. carries on geological, geomorphological, hydrological and *hydrobiological investigations. **1932** *Ecology* XIII. 110 The fresh water *hydrobiologists, especially the limnologists, have developed a third type of nomenclature based more upon the habitat than on the biotic communities. **1938** Hydro-biologist [see HYDROLOGIST]. **1964** *Oceanogr. & Marine Biol.* II. 379 The three large brackish water lagoons on the continental coast of the Baltic .. have long attracted the interest of hydrobiologists. **1972** *Nature* 28 July 194/1 It is hoped that the committee will be able to produce a register of hydrobiologists working in Britain. **1928** K. E. CARPENTER *Life Inland Waters* p. viii, The life of the ocean [has] .. engrossed the energies even of followers of the new tradition in *Hydrobiology. **1941** J. G. NEEDHAM in *Symposium Hydrobiol.* 3 Hydrobiology is an offshoot from the old maternal rootstock of natural history. **1965** *Math. in Biol. & Med.* (Med. Res. Council) 309 His [*sc.* Antonio Moroni's] main interests are human population

genetics and hydrobiology. **1880** H. C. Lewis in *Proc. Acad. Nat. Sci. Philadelphia* 319 Such mica exfoliates slightly when heated, is uniaxial, fusible with difficulty, and might be called *Hydrobiotite for convenience. **1892** E. S. Dana *Dana's Syst. Min.* (ed. 6) 632 Hydrobiotite *H. C. Lewis.* A hydrated biotite. The name has been similarly but more definitely used by Schrauf. **1934** J. W. Gruner in *Amer. Mineralogist* XIX. 558 Specimens 9 and 10 belong to a species for which the name *hydrobiotite* is proposed. This name was used long ago by Schrauf and others to designate biotite-like material high in water. *Ibid.* 575 X-ray diagrams are necessary to distinguish vermiculite from hydrobiotite. **1962** W. A. Deer et al. *Rock-Forming Min.* III. 251 Mixed layer clays with vermiculite as a constituent are not uncommon, the most well known being 'hydrobiotite', a random mixture of vermiculite and biotite. **1835** C. U. Shepard *Min.* II. 326 *Hydroboracite. **1868** Dana *Min.* (ed. 5) 595 Hydroboracite.. resembles fibrous and foliated gypsum. **1934** C. E. Tilley in *Mineral. Mag.* XXIII. 607 In allusion to its composition as an hydrated calcium aluminate ($4CaO.Al_2O_3.12H_2O$) the name *hydrocalumite is proposed. **1968** I. Kostov *Mineral.* 215 Apart from hydrocalumite, which is rather soft.., the other minerals are hard. **1753** Chambers *Cycl. Supp.*, **Hydrocardia*, a term invented by Hildanus to express a serous, sanious, or purulent tumour of the pericardium. **1960** *McGraw-Hill Encycl. Sci. & Technol.* IX. 267/1 Such a laboratory is located near the winches used for running out and retrieving a long string of water-sample bottles *(hydrocasts). **1968** D. F. Martin *Marine Chem.* I. i. 8 The vessel must be stationary for the time needed to complete the hydrocast. **1971** *Nature* 7 May 37/1 In 1966, one hydrocast in this narrow and steep-sided deep revealed a temperature of 29·07°C and a salinity of 74·2‰. Attempts to place a hydrocast in the Chain deep on this cruise failed because of high winds and consequent ship drift. **1869** Nicholson *Zool.* 77 The cœnosarc generally consists of a main stem—or '*hydro-caulus'—with many branches. **1876** *Jrnl. Chem. Soc.* I. 696 Hydrocellulose is also formed when cellulose is impregnated with dilute acid and submitted to a temperature of about 100°. **1920** E. Sutermeister *Chem. Pulp & Paper Making* i. 9 The formation of friable hydrocelluloses by acids is of great importance industrially for upon it is based the carbonization process for separating cotton from wool. **1956** *Nature* 18 Feb. 319/2 The hydrocelluloses produced by the action of mineral acids on cotton and wood. **1888** Rolleston & Jackson *Anim. Life* 246 The hydranth resembles Hydra in all essentials... Like that organism it consists of a **hydrocephalis* (= oral and stomachal regions) and a peduncle or hydrocope which is very short. **1883** J. W. Mollett *Illustr. Dict. Art & Archæol.* 174/1 **Hydro-ceramic* (vessels), Gr., vessels made of a porous clay, in which liquids were put for the purpose of cooling them; they were a kind of *alcarazas*. **1940** *Chambers's Techn. Dict.* 428/2 *Hydroceramic*, porous unglazed pottery, used for filters and for cooling vessels. **1905** F. E. Clements *Res. Methods Ecol.* iv. 216 *Hydrochores.. comprise all plants distributed exclusively by water, whether the latter acts as ocean currents, tides, streams, or surface run-off. *Ibid.* 218 Most hydrophytes are hydrochorous. **1940** *Chambers's Techn. Dict.* 428/2 *Hydrochoric*, dispersed by water. **1969** L. van der Pijl *Princ. Dispersal Higher Plants* v. 61 It is difficult to describe concisely the structural modifications of hydrochory. *Ibid.*, Many hydrochores bend their fruit stalks down.. whereas in *Nuphar* (not purely hydrochorous) the seeds mature above water. **1965** D. Bradley *Hydrocyclone* i. 1 'Hydraulic cyclone' has been abbreviated to 'hydrocyclone' and even '*hydroclone'. **1967** Whistler & Paschall *Starch* II. i. 46 The starch stream.. must be further purified by passing.. through hydroclones to reduce the protein content. **1888** *Phil. Trans. R. Soc.* B. CLXXIX. 266 After separating from the *hydrocele the anterior body-cavity grows towards the ectoderm on the right side. **1900** E. R. Lankester *Treat. Zool.* III. viii. 23 Whatever may be the homologies of the hydrocoel, there is.. no nephridial or other excretory system in Echinoderma. **1962** D. Nichols *Echinoderms* x. 121 This [sac] is called the left axohydrocoel, the anterior part being the axocoel.. and the posterior the hydrocoel. **1873** *Fownes' Chem.* (ed. 11) 824 *Hydro-coumaric Acid exists in the yellow melilot. **1721** Bailey, **Hydrocriticks* [**1706** Phillips (ed. Kersey), *Hydrocritica*], critical Judgment of Distempers taken from Sweating. **1893** *Westm. Gaz.* 5 Apr. 4/3 The '*hydro-cycle'—hitherto regarded as more or less a mechanical monstrosity—has at length proved its speed and capabilities... The '*hydro-cyclists' finished in good condition. **1898** *River & Coast* 9 July 13/1 One of the most interesting items was the Hydrocycle *versus* Skiff Race. **1952** *Chem. Abstr.* XLVI. 1668 Data are presented on *hydrocyclones used as thickeners in starch processing, as classifiers for highly viscous and non-Newtonian liquids and as washers in ore prepn. **1962** *Engineering* 3 Aug. 146/1 The cone-shaped nozzle at the bottom of the hydrocyclones used by the National Coal Board..(for the separation and thickening of coal and shale fines from water). **1869** Nicholson *Zool.* 82 There occur also in the Physophoridæ certain peculiar bodies, termed *hydrocysts or 'feelers'. **1888** Rolleston & Jackson *Anim. Life* 770 Hydrocysts or feelers.. are polypites in which the distal or oral extremity is imperforate and usually armed with cnidoblasts. **1850** Dana *Min.* (ed. 3) 213 *Hydrodolomite.. has the composition of the magnesia alba of the shops. **1962** *New Scientist* 4 Oct. 31/3 They are using a specially-designed '*hydrodrill' to inject relatively small amounts of water into the soil, placing it directly in the plant's root zone. *Ibid.*, The vine cuttings are simply dropped into holes which have been hydrodrilled. **1861** J. R. Greene *Man. Anim. Kingd., Cœlent.* 99 Praya, Hippopodius, and Vogtia have 'incomplete' *hydrœcia. **1869** Nicholson *Zool.* 80 This chamber, which is present.. in all the genera, is termed the 'hydrœcium'. **1858** Huxley *Oceanic Hydrozoa* 39 The lateral walls of the hydrœcial canal of the distal nectocalyx. **1928** C. E. Mullin *Acetate Silk* xxxviii. 437 Yarns or loosely knit fabrics which are not liable to crease may be *hydroextracted in the ordinary rotating cage or drum machine. **1952** E. Kornreich *Introd. Fibres & Fabrics* viii. 143 Fabrics can also be hydroextracted by winding them on a perforated beam which is then inserted in a suitable whizzer. **1882** *Spon's Encycl. Industr. Arts* v. 1839 Centrifugal hydro-extracting machines.. have been tried for separating beet-juice from the pulp. **1895** *Trans. Soc. Engin.* 1894 227 (*heading*) The principles and practice of hydro-extraction. **1912** H. H. Hodgson tr. *Masselon's Celluloid* v. 71, 100 kilogrammes of bleached pulp after hydro-extraction should weigh 60 kilogrammes. **1963** A. J. Hall *Textile Sci.* ii. 53 The water in wet viscose rayon materials is best removed by hydro-extraction. **1851** *Illustr. Catal. Gt. Exhib.* 1199 *Hydro-extractor.. capable of revolving 2,000 times a minute... It will dress.. all kinds of materials, cloths, felts [etc.]. **1890** W. J. Gordon *Foundry* 165 The hydro-extractor, in which the yarn is dried like clothes in a laundry, being thrown into a horizontal drum and spun round at lightning speed. **1849** D. Campbell *Inorg. Chem.* Index 376 *Hydroferridcyanic acid, or ferridcyanide of hydrogen. *Hydroferrocyanic acid, or ferrocyanide of hydrogen. **1868–72** Watts *Dict. Chem.* V. 20 The *hydroferrocyanate [of quinine], $C_{20}H_{24}N_2O_2.H_4FeCy_6.2H_2O$, is an orange-yellow crystalline precipitate, obtained on mixing the alcoholic solutions of quinine and hydroferrocyanic acid. **1949** *Jrnl. Amer. Chem. Soc.* LXXI. 3051 (*heading*) *Hydroformylation of unsaturated compounds with a cobalt carbonyl catalyst. **1969** S. A. Miller *Ethylene* xiv. 1169 The *OXO* reaction or 'hydroformylation' is now an important industrial process. **1886** Hamerton in *Longm. Mag.* VII. 375 The efficacy of resinous solutions, as *hydrofuges. **1941** E. P. Flint et al. in *Jrnl. Res. Nat. Bureau of Standards* (U.S.) XXVI. 14 An extension of the study revealed that silica could replace water in both $3CaO.Al_2O_3.6H_2O$ and $3CaO.Fe_2O_3.6H_2O$, and that the end products of these substitutions are grossularite garnet, $3CaO.Al_2O_3.3SiO_2$, and andradite garnet, $3CaO.Fe_2O_3.3SiO_2$, respectively... The hydrous members of the series may be termed '*hydrogarnets' to indicate their relationship to the naturally occurring garnets. **1966** W. A. Deer et al. *Introd. Rock-Forming Min.* 23 In the hydrogarnets there is replacement of SiO_2 by $2H_2O$, with vacant Si spaces in the structure. **1921** *Glasgow Herald* 23 July 7/2 The idea of using *hydrogliders for passengers and for mail purposes on the lochs in the outlying districts of Scotland. **1927** *Ibid.* 26 July 9 The hydroglider which has been constructed.. to accomplish the crossing of the Atlantic from Cherbourg to New York. **1961** F. H. Burgess *Dict. Sailing* 119 *Hydroglider*, a type of boat that is designed with air-screws as its main means of propulsion. **1943** C. O. Hutton in *Trans. & Proc. R. Soc. N.Z.* LXXIII. 174 (*heading*) *Hydrogrossular, a new mineral of the garnet-hydrogarnet series. *Ibid.*, All of the isomorphous mixtures between plazolite and grossularite are termed by the writer, hydrogrossular. **1966** W. A. Deer et al. *Introd. Rock-Forming Min.* 26 Hydrogrossular has been taken as the name for members of the series $3CaO.Al_2O_3.3SiO_2$—$3CaO.Al_2O_3.6H_2O$ with a composition between grossular and hibschite (plazolite), $3CaO.Al_2O_3.2SiO_2 2H_2O$. **1861** H. W. Bristow *Gloss. Mineral.* 185/1 **Hydrohalite*... A hydrous chloride of sodium. **1949** *Mineral. Abstr.* X. 459 A drop of sea-water.. evaporated at a low temperature.. yields hexagonal flakes (½ mm.) of hydrohalite, $NaCl.2H_2O$. **1928** C. Palache in *Amer. Mineralogist* XIII. 308 The following data establish the characters of unaltered hetaerolite. For the partly hydrated mineral hitherto described, the name *hydrohetaerolite may well be employed. **1942** [see hetærolite]. **1955** *Amer. Mineralogist* XL. 350 Hydrohetaerolite has the same structure as hausmannite, except that one sixth of the trivalent manganese occupying the octahedral sites are randomly absent, and the balance of charge is supplied by hydrogen bonds. **1890** Abney *Treat. Photogr.* (ed. 6) 24 It.. produces *hydroiodic acid (HI). **1883** A. E. Seaton *Man. Marine Engin.* xx. 376 (*heading*) Weir's *hydrokineter. *Ibid.* 377 There are many other ways of promoting the circulation when steam is up, but none do this so efficiently during the time of raising steam as the hydrokineter. **1951** *Engineering* 20 Apr. 483/3 Surplus steam from the waste-heat boiler will be used.. to keep the Scotch boilers warm and ready for service, Weir hydrokineters being fitted to the Scotch boilers to maintain a circulation. **1955** M. Hollander tr. *Kuenen's Realms of Water* v. 220 (*caption*) *Hydro-laccolith or hummock caused when ground-water under artesian pressure is checked by formation of layers of ice. **1961** L. D. Stamp *Gloss. Geogr. Terms* 244/2 The pingos in East Greenland but not those in the Mackenzie delta are hydrolaccoliths. **1968** R. W. Fairbridge *Encycl. Geomorphol.* 845/2 The genetic term *hydrolaccolith*, which applies to all ice-intrusions, is not just synonymous with pingo. **1970** E. Watson tr. *Tricart's Geomorphol. Cold Environments* II. i. 78 These ice masses and the hills which they raise are called hydrolaccoliths. **1963** D. W. & E. E. Humphries tr. *Termier's Erosion & Sedimentation* 412 An arctic soil phenomenon.. formed in the permafrost by a hydrolaccolithic process. **1843** Portlock *Geol.* 221 *Hydrolite occurs in abundance at Island Magee, in beautifully marked crystals. **1837** Dana *Min.* 199 *Hydromagnesite.. occurs in crusts; also as a white powder. **1888** Rolleston & Jackson *Anim. Life* 745 There are two principal types of the Hydroid. One, the *Hydromedusan or Craspedote type, consists typically of an oral and stomachal region (hydrocephalis), with or without tentacles, borne upon a peduncle (hydrocope). **1890** Webster, *Hydrometallurgical. **1929** *Encycl. Brit.* VI. 406/1 Hydro-metallurgical treatment.. is eminently suited for low grade ores. **1959** J. Newton *Extractive Metall.* vii. 436 Hydrometallurgical methods are widely employed today in the treatment of low-grade oxidized uranium ores. **1879** Rutley *Study Rocks* xii. 208 To admit for granite what may be called *hydro-metamorphic origin. *Ibid.*, *Hydro-metamorphism, by which rocks, originally fused, and when in liquid fusion, poured into veins and dykes in pre-existing rocks, are subsequently altered in specific gravity and arrangement of minerals, by the action of water. **1857** J. P. Nichol *Cycl. Phys. Sci.*, **Hydrometeors*. The whole aqueous phenomena of the Atmosphere... The chief specific Hydrometeors, viz. *Clouds, Dew, Fogs, Snow*, and *Rain*. **1885** C. H. Hitchcock in *Amer. Jrnl. Sc.* Oct. 282 *Hydromicaceous and argillaceous schists. **1938** M. Baldwin et al. in *U.S. Dept. Agric. Yearbk.* 991 The terms 'halomorphic', '*hydromorphic', and 'calomorphic' are not entirely satisfactory, since soil genetics rather than soil characteristics are implied. **1970** E. M. Bridges *World Soils* iii. 25/1 These poorly drained or hydromorphic soils frequently occur in the lower parts of the landscape. **1927** *Russian Pedol. Investigations* v. 26 Recently a single group has been formed which is.. known by the name.. of '*hydromorphous' soils (Neustruev). **1932** G. W. Robinson *Soils* xv. 301 Hydromorphous processes are those which take place under the influence of ground-water. **1886** *Sci. Amer.* 24 July 47/1 The little vessel supplied with the *hydromotor met with a fair degree of success. **1889** A. Johnstone in *Q. Jrnl. Geol. Soc.* XLV. 364 Margarodite, gilbertite, damourite, and sericite are mineralogists' names for varieties possessing the same composition as muscovite, differing from the latter mineral merely in containing at least about 5 per cent. of water. All of these varieties.. ought to be known under one term. The common name proposed for them by the Author is *hydromuscovite. **1966** W. A. Deer et al. *Introd. Rock-Forming Min.* 202 Hydromuscovites have high H_2O and low K_2O content. **1866–80** A. Flint *Princ. Med.* (ed. 5) 716 A tumor, consisting of the serous accumulation with its enveloping membranes (*hydromyelocele), protrudes through the fissure, most frequently in the sacral or dorsal regions. *Ibid.* 759 Dilatation of the central canal is called *hydromyelus, and is generally congenital. **1826** Henry *Elem. Chem.* I. 328 *Hydro-nitric acid is perfectly limpid and colourless, and emits white fumes when exposed to the air. **1872** Peaslee *Ovar. Tumours* 28 'Ovarian dropsy', or '*hydro-ovarium'. **1826** Henry *Elem. Chem.* II. 25 There appear to be two hydrates or *hydro-oxides. **1834** Medwin *Angler in Wales* I. 95 Vermicular monsters exhibited in the *hydro-oxygen microscope. **1838** *Proc. Amer. Phil. Soc.* I. 14 Platinum fused by his hydro-oxygen blowpipe. **1854** J. Scoffern in *Orr's Circ. Sc., Chem.* 298 Gurney's hydro-oxygen blowpipe is made in conformity. **1730–6** Bailey (folio), **Hydroparastates*, a Sect; a Branch of the Manichees, whose distinguishing Tenet was, That Water should be used in the Sacrament instead of Wine. **1853** M. Kelly tr. *Gosselin's Power Pope Mid. Ages* I. 79 Manicheans who disguised themselves under the names of Encratides, Saccophori, and Hydroparastates. **1834** J. Forbes *Laennec's Dis. Chest* (ed. 4) 537 The lower extremities are œdematous... The same state exists in the serous membranes, whence arise ascites, hydrothorax, and *hydropericardium. **1877** Roberts *Handbk. Med.* (ed. 3) II. 36 Hydropericardium generally follows hydrothorax. **1866–80** A. Flint *Princ. Med.* (ed. 5) 596 The term *hydro-peritoneum or ascites denotes peritoneal dropsy. **1864** Webster, **Hydrophid*, a species of ophidian, including the water-snake. **1899** D. Sharp in *Cambr. Nat. Hist.* VI. v. 219 The pupae of *Hydrophilides repose on the dorsal surface. **1958** F. Balfour-Browne *Brit. Water Beetles* III. 3 The mandibles of *Hydrophilus* also differ from.. those of all our other Hydrophilids. **1964** R. M. & J. W. Fox *Introd. Compar. Ent.* iii. 73 The hindleg of the hydrophilid beetle is provided with a fringe of hairs. **1873** *Fownes' Chem.* (ed. 11) 826 *Hydrophthalic Acid is produced by the action of nascent hydrogen on phthalic acid. **1861** J. R. Greene *Man. Anim. Kingd., Cœlent.* 101 Groups of organs became detached from the cœnosarc, each group consisting of a *hydrophyllium, polypites, tentacles, and gonophores. **1753** Chambers *Cycl. Supp.*, **Hydrophysocele*, a term used by some authors for a sort of hernia, or rupture, occasioned by a mixture of water and flatulencies. **1927** J. G. Tarboux *Electr. Power Equipm.* ii. 31 High-voltage transmission lines must be used to connect the *hydro plant to the load center. **1966** *McGraw-Hill Encycl. Sci. & Technol.* XIV. 399/2 Installed capacity of hydroplants cannot be counted upon for perpetuity because of the gradual filling of reservoirs with sediment. **1878** Lawrence tr. *Cotta's Rocks Class.* 380 Plutonic processes do not exclude the combined action of water as an auxiliary agent; and thus may deserve the name of *Hydroplutonic. **1876** Harley *Mat. Med.* (ed. 6) 316 *Hydropotassic Oxalate is the form in which oxalic acid exists in the acid species of Oxalis, Rumex, Rheum, Geranium [etc.]. **1866** Blackmore *C. Nowell* li, A sail which they wetted with a *hydro-pult. **1879** W. L. Lindsay *Mind in Lower Anim.* 462 The elephant makes a similar use of his trunk as a syringe or hydropult, and of water as a projectile. **1866** Blackmore *C. Nowell* lxiii, He had not acquired the delightful *hydro-pultic art, so dear to the nation. **1866–80** A. Flint *Princ. Med.* (ed. 5) 716 Extensive serous accumulation within the spinal canal is called *hydrorrachis. **1886** *Syd. Soc. Lex.*, **Hydrorenal distension*, same as Hydronephrosis. **1861** J. R. Greene *Man. Anim. Kingd., Cœlent.* 29 In Hydra, and a few of the simpler forms of Corynidæ, the proximal end of the polypite is closed by the *hydrorhiza. **1870** Rolleston *Anim. Life* 253 The animal is.. attached by its hydrorhiza to a piece of weed. **1887** *Lancet* 11 June 1200/2 Dr. Schlesinger concludes that in *hydrosalpinx, or hæmatosalpinx, laparotomy is the only.. resource. **1767** *Phil. Trans.* LVII. 293 An Account of an Hydro-enterocele, appearing like an *Hydro-sarcocele. **1854** J. Scoffern in *Orr's Circ. Sc., Chem.* 354 So does *hydroselenic acid afford parallel results. **1826** Henry *Elem. Chem.* I. 449 A *hydro-selenuret of potassa of a deep ale colour. **1926** Tansley & Chipp *Study of Vegetation* ii. 19 The earlier stages of a prisere are altogether different, according to whether the succession begins on a wet or a dry habitat... Such successions may be conveniently called **hydroseres* and *xeroseres* respectively. **1952** P. W. Richards *Tropical Rain Forest* xiii. 283 During the course of the hydrosere there is a gradual change from open water to relatively dry conditions. **1967** C. D. Sculthorpe *Biol. Aquatic Vasc. Plants* xii. 417 In the ultimate stages of the hydroseres plant debris is less and less completely decomposed. **1850** Daubeny *Atom. The.* xii. 409 The silicates that contain water may be divided, into those in which the water is simply united to the silicic combination.. called *hydrosilicates. **1952** *Jrnl. R. Aeronaut. Soc.* LVI. 334/2 Somewhat allied to the hydrofoil is the *hydro-ski. These obtain their lift from the water pressure on their lower surface in a similar manner to the planing lift of the [flying] boat planing bottom. **1954** *Flight* 17 Sept. 433 The Sea Dart hydro-ski fighter.. which is land-based, but which uses water (or snow or ice) for take-off and landing. **1960** K. C. Barnaby *Basic Naval Archit.* (ed. 3) 448 Modifications of the submerged type consist in replacing the forward hydrofoils by partly submerged planing surfaces or 'hydroskis'. **1964** *Adv. Hydro-science* I. 2 The use of acoustic energy to perform all those functions in *hydrospace for which electromagnetic energy is employed in aerospace. **1966** *New Scientist* 22 Dec. 691/1 Other categories of plot [in science fiction] include a growing preoccupation with 'inner space' or 'hydrospace'. **1890** H. Ellis *Criminal* iii. 122 With the sphygmograph (or, rather the *hydrosphygmograph) he observed the degree of excitement produced on various individuals. **1869** E. Billings in *Amer. Jrnl. Sci.* XCVIII. 76 In order to avoid the use of double terms, I propose to call them '*hydrospires'. *Ibid.* 77 In *Caryocrinus ornatus* there are thirty hydrospires. **1888** Rolleston & Jackson *Anim. Life* 577 (Class Blastoidea), The pores lead to a cleft (*hydrospire

cleft)..and the cleft in its turn to an underlying hydrospire canal, into which open a system of interradial lamellar tubes, the hydrospires. *Ibid.* 578 The genital ducts probably opened into some portion of the hydrospires. **1879** RUTLEY *Study Rocks* xiii. 270 To them..may be added chromic iron ..*hydrotalcite, native copper, copper pyrites. **1893** *Times* 6 Oct., The most famous *hydrotechnic authorities of our time have found no other method of overcoming the obstruction to navigation caused by the Iron Gate than the identical one adopted by the Romans. **1847** CRAIG, **Hydrotellurates*, a genus of salts. **1864** WEBSTER, **Hydrotelluric*. **1873** *Fownes' Chem.* (ed. 11) 215 Hydrotelluric acid is a gas, resembling sulphuretted and selenietted hydrogen. **1872** NICHOLSON *Palæont.* 77 Polypites are also protected within '*hydrothecæ', or little cup-like expansions derived from the polypary. **1877** HUXLEY *Anat. Inv. Anim.* iii. 129 A hard, chitinous, cuticular skeleton..which frequently gives rise to hydrothecae, into which the hydranths can be retracted. **1876** tr. *Wagner's Gen. Pathol.* 576 *Hydrothionæmia.. consists in the entrance into the blood of sulphuretted hydrogen. **1807** T. THOMSON *Chem.* (ed. 3) II. 328 The Germans have given it [sulphuretted hydrogen] the name of *hydrothionic acid. **1913** *Mineral. Mag.* XVI. 362 *Hydrotroilite. **1957** G. E. HUTCHINSON *Treat. Limnol.* I. xi. 723 The rather poorly characterized ferrous sulfide of lake sediments, supposedly FeS, has received the name hydrotroilite. **1940** KERR & YOUNG in *Program & Abstr. 21st Ann. Meeting Min. Soc. Amer.* 9 Since this mineral appears to be an intermediate product in the alteration of ferberite to tungstite and since it resembles tungstite in many of its physical properties, the name *hydrotungstite is suggested. **1963** *Amer. Mineralogist* XLVIII. 935 A similarity between the *x*-ray patterns for hydrotungstite (tungstic acid, $H_2WO_4.H_2O$) and molybdic acid ($H_2MoO_4.H_2O$). **1955** *Deep-Sea Research* III. (Suppl.) 170 A jelly bottle..will remain uncongealed long enough to permit slope determinations to be made of *hydrowires. **1969** R. LANGE *Chem. Oceanogr.* v. 80 The sampler is attached to the hydrowire with a screw clamp and a snap clamp.

†**hydro-'acid.** *Chem. Obs.* = HYDRACID.

1845 TODD & BOWMAN *Phys. Anat.* I. 5 Hydrogen would be [united] to a simple or compound radicle (chlorine or cyanogen), to form a hydro-acid. *c* **1865** G. GORE in *Circ. Sc.* I. 226/2 The hydro-acids—hydrochloric acid, for example.

†**hydro-aeroplane** (ˌhaɪdrəʊ'ɛərəpleɪn). *Obs.* Also (*U.S.*) **hydro-airplane.** [f. HYDRO- + AEROPLANE *sb.*, AIRPLANE.] An aircraft designed to land on and take off from the water; a seaplane.

1909 *Westm. Gaz.* 7 Jan. 4/2 Before the present year expires the hydro-aeroplane will be an accomplished fact. **1914** *Scotsman* 21 Dec. 8/2 A German hydro-aeroplane threw two bombs on Calais this afternoon. **1922** *Encycl. Brit.* XXX. 49/2 Its performance as a hydro-aeroplane suffered from the extra weight and resistance of the floats. **1930** *Flight* 25 July 837/1 You [*sc.* G. H. Curtiss] invented the hydroaeroplane and the flying-boat and thus opened the way for trans-Atlantic flight. **1932** CHATFIELD & TAYLOR *Airplane & its Engine* (ed. 2) xiv. 316 The term *seaplane*.. is synonymous with *hydroairplane*, a word too clumsy ever to have come into common use.

hydroborane (haɪdrəʊ'bɔəreɪn). *Chem.* Also **-boran.** [ad. G. *hydroboran* (A. Stock 1926, in *Ber. d. Deut. Chem. Ges.* LIX. 2229): cf. BORANE.] The name used by A. Stock for any of the hydrides or boron that are richer in hydrogen than others with the same number of boron atoms.

1927 *Chem. Abstr.* XXI. 541 When all of the B atoms are tervalent..the names should be 'diboran', 'triboran', 'decaboran', etc., for B_2H_4, B_3H_5, $B_{10}H_{12}$, etc. The names for the hydroborans [*printed* hydroborons] are illustrated by the following: B_2H_6 = dihydro-diboran, B_5H_9 = dihydro-pentaboran, B_5H_{11} = tetrahydropentaboran, etc. **1933** A. STOCK *Hydrides of Boron & Silicon* i. 18 The less stable hydrides, which are richer in hydrogen, should be called 'hydroboranes', e.g. dihydrotetraborane (B_4H_{10}).

hydroborate (haɪdrəʊ'bɔəreɪt), *sb.* *Chem.* [f. HYDRO- + BORATE.] = BOROHYDRIDE.

1950 *Chem. Abstr.* XLIV. 12392/1 (Index), *Hydroborates.* See such headings as *Aluminium borohydride* and *Lithium borohydride.* **1963** *Jrnl. Amer. Chem. Soc.* LXXXV. 2725/1 Among the numerous derivatives of boranes and hydroborate ions known there are no compounds reported to date containing an NO group directly attached to one of the boron atoms. **1964** R. M. ADAMS *Boron* vi. 373 While the latter name [*sc.* borohydride] belongs to the ferrocyanide type which has long been disapproved by the IUPAC, it has become so firmly established in American usage that it will be used interchangeably with hydroborate in this chapter.

hydroborate (haɪdrəʊ'bɔəreɪt), *v.* *Chem.* [Back-formation from next.] *trans.* To add a borane or other boron compound to (another compound) by hydroboration.

1961 *Jrnl. Amer. Chem. Soc.* LXXXIII. 2550/1 β-Pinene ..was hydroborated internally in diglyme with sodium borohydride and boron trifluoride etherate. **1964** KIRK & OTHMER *Encycl. Chem. Technol.* (ed. 2) III. 709 Dienes can be hydroborated utilizing diisoamylborane and diphenyldiborane.

Hence ˌ**hydrobo'rating** *vbl. sb.*

1962 H. C. BROWN *Hydroboration* i. 28 The treatment of internal acetylenes, such as 3-hexyne, with the theoretical quantity of hydroborating agent results in the formation of the corresponding trivinylborane.

hydroboration (ˌhaɪdrəʊbɔə'reɪʃən). *Chem.* [f. HYDRO- + BOR(ON + -ATION.] The addition of a linked boron–hydrogen pair of atoms in a molecule across a double or triple bond between a carbon atom and another atom; for example,

$$\begin{array}{c} \quad\ \ |\quad\ | \qquad\quad\ \ |\quad\ | \\ =\mathrm{B}-\mathrm{H} + \mathrm{C}=\mathrm{C} \rightarrow =\mathrm{B}-\mathrm{C}-\mathrm{CH}. \\ \quad\ \ |\quad\ | \qquad\quad\ \ |\quad\ | \end{array}$$

1957 BROWN & RAO in *Jrnl. Org. Chem.* XXII. 1136/2 (*heading*) Hydroboration of olefins. A remarkably fast room-temperature addition reaction of diborane to olefins. *Ibid.* 1138/2 The hydroboration reaction should provide a useful and convenient synthetic route for the transformation of olefins into organoboranes, alcohols, and other functional derivatives. **1966** STEINBERG & BROTHERTON *Organoboron Chem.* II. viii. 225 The reaction sequence can be formulated to involve hydroboration of the carbon–nitrogen triple bond followed by a hydrogen shift and final cyclization. **1971** *Nature* 20 Aug. 536/2 Many related organic syntheses depend on the hydroboration of acetylenes or dienes as the first step.

†**hydro'bromate.** *Chem. Obs.* [f. as next + -ATE[1] 1 c.] An old name for a bromide, viewed as a salt of hydrobromic acid; also, for a hydrobromide.

1836 J. M. GULLY *Magendie's Formul.* (ed. 2) 124 Hydrobromic acid..affords various salts with bases; these are hydrobromates or bromurets. **1876** HARLEY *Mat. Med.* 86 Bromine..forms with ammonia a colourless hydrobromate.

hydrobromic (haɪdrəʊ'brəʊmɪk), *a.* *Chem.* [f. HYDRO- d + BROMIC. In F. *hydrobromique.*] Containing hydrogen and bromine in chemical combination. ***hydrobromic acid,*** also called *hydrogen bromide* (HBr), a colourless gas with a pungent odour and strongly acid taste, fuming in the atmosphere and very soluble in water.

1836 [see prec.] **1838** T. THOMSON *Chem. Org. Bodies* 308 Neither hydrobromic nor muriatic acid decompose bromide of aldehyden. **1873** *Fownes' Chem.* (ed. 11) 190 Hydrogen Bromide, or Hydrobromic Acid, bears the closest resemblance to hydriodic acid.

So **hydrobromide** (haɪdrəʊ'brəʊmaɪd), a compound formed by the combination of hydrobromic acid with an organic radical.

1877 WATTS *Fownes' Chem.* (ed. 12) II. 61 **1880** CLEMINSHAW *Wurtz' Atom. The.* 111 Amylene hydrobromide cannot possess several vapour densities.

†**hydro'carbide.** *Chem. Obs.* [f. HYDRO- d + CARB(ON + -IDE.] = next.

1884 *Athenæum* 13 Dec. 776/1 Hydrocarbides, which undergo decomposition by electric discharges with formation of carbonic acid, are added to the atmosphere from a variety of sources.

hydrocarbon (haɪdrəʊ'kɑːbən). *Chem.* [f. HYDRO- d + CARBON *sb.*] **a.** A chemical compound of hydrogen and carbon.

These compounds, of which there are at least twelve series, the chief of them being the *paraffins, olefines, acetylenes,* and *benzenes,* are very numerous and important, and, with their derivatives, constitute the subject-matter of organic chemistry.

1826 FARADAY *Exp. Res.* xxxii. (1859) 183 The peculiar hydro-carbons forming the subject of that paper. **1842** PARNELL *Chem. Anal.* (1845) 269 Contraction and formation of oily drops show the presence of olefiant gas, or vapours of hydrocarbons. **1863** TYNDALL *Heat* iii. 62 Coal-gas is what we call a hydro-carbon. **1865–72** WATTS *Dict. Chem.* III. 186 The most fruitful source of hydrocarbons is the dry or destructive distillation of organic bodies.

b. *attrib.*, as ***hydrocarbon radical, series,*** etc. **hydrocarbon gas**, any gaseous hydrocarbon; **hydrocarbon oil**, any oil consisting chiefly of hydrocarbons.

1864 *Mechanics' Mag.* 22 Jan. 55/3 (*heading*) Petroleum and hydro-carbon oils for generating steam. *c* **1865** LETHEBY in *Circ. Sc.* I. 123/2 *Hydro-carbon Gas*, this name is given to the mixed gases which are generated from water, together with substances that are rich in hydro-carbons, as tar, resin, fats, oils, and the better kinds of cannel coal. **1873** RALFE *Phys. Chem.* 45 The homologous series of hydro-carbon radicals. **1880** RICHARDSON in *Med. Temp. Jrnl.* 67 Alcohol is..a chemical of the hydro-carbon series. **1904** G. H. HURST *Textile Soaps & Oils* iv. 115 The cheapest oils are the so-called mineral or hydrocarbon oils. **1942** *Progress Appl. Chem.* XXVII. 82 The analysis of hydrocarbon oils is a valuable aid in the control of refinery processes such as cracking.

hydrocarbonaceous (ˌhaɪdrəʊkɑːbə'neɪʃəs), *a.* *Chem.* [f. prec. + -ACEOUS.] Pertaining to, of the nature of, or containing a hydrocarbon.

1851 *Illustr. Catal. Gt. Exhib.* 144 The tar yields.. paraffine..light hydro-carbonaceous oil. **1874** tr. *Lommel's Light* 5 In order to obtain the highest illuminating power of a flame in which hydro-carbonaceous compounds are undergoing combustion, the regulation of the supply of air is essential.

hydrocarbonate (-'kɑːbənət). *Chem.* Also **-at.** [f. HYDRO(GEN + CARBONATE (in sense 1 used for 'product of combination with carbon', thus *lit.* 'carbonated or carburetted hydrogen').]

1. An early name for a hydrocarbon; †formerly, a name of carburetted hydrogen (CH_4), the chief constituent of coal-gas.

1800 HOWARD in *Phil. Trans.* XC. 228 It burns like hydrocarbonate, but with a bluish green flame. *Ibid.*, Should this inflammable gas prove not to be a hydrocarbonate. **1819** *Pantologia* s.v., There are different species of Hydro-carbonats, depending on the proportion of their constituents..commonly distinguished into heavy and light Hydro-carbonats. **1896** *Daily News* 26 Mar. 5/1 The Italian workman has too much hydrocarbonate for dinner, and too little albuminoid.

2. 'A term applied by Berzelius to a double salt resulting from the combination of a carbonate with a hydrate; by Beudant to the combination of a carbonate and water' (Mayne).

1843 PORTLOCK *Geol.* 214 Associated with the hydro-carbonate of magnesia, and lime. **1851** *Illustr. Catal. Gt. Exhib.* 193 The hydro-carbonate much used in Pharmacy (*magnesia alba*). **1854** J. SCOFFERN in *Orr's Circ. Sc., Chem.* 490 Two hydrocarbonates of copper occur native: one, malachite..has a composition represented by the formula $CuO.CO_2$ + CuO.HO; a second..having the composition $2CuO.CO_2$ + CuO.HO.

hydrocarbonic (-kɑː'bɒnɪk), *a.* *Chem.* [f. HYDROCARBON + -IC.] Relating to, or of the nature of, a hydrocarbon; in quot., obtained from carburetted hydrogen: see prec. 1.

1807 F. A. WINSOR in *Standard* (1883) 19 July 5/6 His grand discovery of the Hydrocarbonic Lights.

hydrocarbonous (-'kɑːbənəs), *a.* *Chem.* [f. HYDRO(GEN + CARBONOUS.] Of the nature of a hydrocarbon.

1804 *Edin. Rev.* IV. 129 These gasses are not carbureted hydrogen..but..they are hydro-carbonous oxides. **1845** GROVE *Contrib. Sc.* in *Corr. Phys. Forces* (1874) 295 Enough was ascertained to lead me to believe that it [the gas] was hydrocarbonous.

†**hydrocarburet** (-'kɑːbjʊərət). *Chem. Obs.* [f. HYDRO- d + CARBURET; F. *hydrocarbure.*] A compound of hydrogen and carbon, a hydrocarbon; *spec.* carburetted hydrogen gas.

1815 HENRY *Elem. Chem.* (ed. 7) I. 371 Mixtures of hydrocarburet and oxygen gases. **1838** *Penny Cycl.* XII. 396/2 Liquid Hydrocarburet..was obtained by Mr. Faraday, after separating solid bicarburet of hydrogen from the fluid procured by pressure upon oil gas, at a temperature of 0°. **1850** DAUBENY *Atom. The.* (ed. 2) Gloss., *Hydrocarburet*, a compound of hydrogen and carbon in any proportion whatsoever.

†**hydrocarburetted** (-'kɑːbjʊərɛtɪd), *a.* *Chem. Obs.* [f. as prec. + CARBURETTED.] Formed by the combination of hydrogen and carbon.

1809 HENRY in *Phil. Trans.* XCIX. 448 Hydro-carburetted gases, like ammonia, are separated by electrization into their elements. **1842** PARNELL *Chem. Anal.* (1845) 270 Analysis of Coal-Gas..The determination of the hydro-carburetted vapours may be accurately effected..by means of oil of vitriol.

hydrocele ('haɪdrəʊsiːl). *Path.* [a. L. *hydrocēlē*, a. Gr. ὑδροκήλη, f. ὑδρο- water + κήλη tumour. Cf. F. *hydrocèle* (Paré, 16th c.).] A tumour with a collection of serous fluid; *spec.* a tumour of this kind in the cavity of the *tunica vaginalis* of the testis; dropsy of the testicle or of the scrotum.

1597 A. M. tr. *Guillemeau's Fr. Chirurg.* 21 a/2 The Scrotum commeth to swel, which tumefactione of the Greeks is called Hydrocele. **1607** TOPSELL *Four-f. Beasts* (1658) 307 Called of the Physitians Hydrocele, that is to say, Water-bursten. **1727–41** CHAMBERS *Cycl.* s.v., Youth is most exposed to the hydrocele. **1878** T. BRYANT *Pract. Surg.* I. 103 When seen in the neck they are described as hydroceles of the neck.

hydrocele, var. *hydrocœl(e)* (s.v. HYDRO-).

†**hydrocephale.** *Obs. rare.* [a. F. *hydrocéphale* (Paré, 16th c.).] = HYDROCEPHALUS.

a **1648** LD. HERBERT in *Life* (1770) 33 My cousin..having an hydrocephale also in that extremity that his eyes began to start out of his head.

hydrocephalic (ˌhaɪdrəʊsɪ'fælɪk), *a.* and *sb.* [f. HYDROCEPHAL-US + -IC.] **A.** *adj.* Pertaining to, or characteristic of, hydrocephalus; affected with hydrocephalus; hence *transf.* big-headed.

1815 *Edin. Rev.* XXV. 262 Hydrocephalic patients. **1833–58** COPLAND *Dict. Pract. Med.* (L.), Liable to hydrocephalic and convulsive diseases. **1860** *All Year Round* No. 38. 283 With..enormous head and hydrocephalic prominency of brain.

B. *sb.* A person affected with hydrocephalus.

1908 A. F. TREDGOLD *Mental Deficiency* (*caption* to Plate xix), Male hydrocephalic. **1930** D. PATERSON *Sick Children* xii. 331 Fifty per cent. of all hydrocephalics suffer from convulsions. **1971** *Nature* 17 Sept. 171/1 Medicine is keeping alive idiots, hydrocephalics and cases of spina bifida.

hydro'cephalocele. *Path.* [f. as prec.: see CEPHALOCELE.] = HYDRENCEPHALOCELE.

hydrocephaloid (-'sɛfəlɔɪd), *a.* *Path.* [f. as next + -OID.] Resembling hydrocephalus. ***h. disease***, a term applied by Marshall Hall to a condition of coma incident to young children and resulting apparently from cerebral anæmia.

1842 M. HALL *Gulston. Lect.* ii. 62 The hydrocephaloid disease in children. Its designation announces its similarity to hydrocephalus. But its nature, origin, and treatment are opposite. **1878** A. M. HAMILTON *Nerv. Dis.* 115.

hydrocephalous (-'sɛfələs), *a.* *Path.* [f. next + -OUS.] Affected with hydrocephalus.

1860 PITT BYRNE *Undercurrents Overlooked* II. 273 Epileptic or hydrocephalous children. **1879** GEO. ELIOT *Theo. Such* xvii. 307 A scanty hydrocephalous offspring.

hydrocephalous (-ˈsɛfələs), *a. Path.* [f. next + -OUS.] Affected with hydrocephalus.

1860 PITT BYRNE *Undercurrents Overlooked* II. 273 Epileptic or hydrocephalous children. **1879** GEO. ELIOT *Theo. Such* xvii. 307 A scanty hydrocephalous offspring.

‖**hydrocephalus** (haɪdrəʊˈsɛfələs). *Path.* [Medical L., ad. Gr. ὑδροκέφαλον, f. ὑδρο- water + κεφαλή head.] A disease of the brain especially incident to young children, consisting in an accumulation of serous fluid in the cavity of the cranium, resulting in gradual expansion of the skull, and finally inducing general weakness, with failure of the memory and mental faculties; water on the brain.

1670 *Phil. Trans.* V. 2080 A child, one year old, so diseased with the *Hydrocephalus*, that when open'd, there were taken out of his Head 36 ounces of clear, but saltish, water. **1727–41** CHAMBERS *Cycl.* s.v., Children are more liable to hydrocephali, than adults. **1756** *Gentl. Mag.* XXVI. 516 [He] laboured under a hydrocephalus. **1866–80** A. FLINT *Princ. Med.* (ed. 5) 716 By the term hydrocephalus .. is understood an excessive accumulation of serous fluid in the ventricles of the brain, particularly the lateral ventricles.

hydroˈcephaly. [f. prec. + -Y. Cf. F. *hydrocéphalie.*] = prec.

1882 *Athenæum* 16 Dec. 817/2 A case of hydrocephaly from the Trou Rosette, Belgium.

†**hydrochlorate** (haɪdrəʊˈklɔərət). *Chem. Obs.* [f. as next + -ATE[1] 1 c.] An old name for a chloride, viewed as a salt of hydrochloric acid (formerly also called *muriate*); also for a hydrochloride.

1819 J. G. CHILDREN *Chem. Anal.* 269 Dr. Murray.. conceives the carbonates to arise from the decomposition of the hydrochlorates of lime and magnesia, in the process of evaporation to dryness. **1880** J. W. LEGG *Bile* 11 A precipitate.. consisting of hydrochlorate of glycocoll. **1898** *Rev. Brit. Pharm.* 13 The hydrochlorates are now all called hydrochlorides.

hydrochloric (haɪdrəʊˈklɔərɪk), *a. Chem.* [f. HYDRO- d + CHLORIC. F. *hydrochlorique.*] Containing hydrogen and chlorine in chemical combination. ***hydrochloric acid***, called also *hydrogen chloride* (HCl), a colourless gas of strongly acid taste and pungent irritating odour, extremely soluble in water. (Earlier names were *muriatic acid, spirit of salt, chlorhydric acid.*)

1817 A. URE in Thomson *Ann. Philos.* X. 203 On the Quantity of Real Acid in Liquid Hydrochloric. **1831** J. DAVIES *Manual Mat. Med.* 143 The hydro-chloric acid of the shops is a saturated solution of this gas in water. **1863** TYNDALL *Heat* vii. 188 One volume of chlorine combines with one volume of hydrogen, to form two volumes of hydrochloric acid. **1878** HUXLEY *Physiogr.* vii. (ed. 2) 109 Chlorine eagerly seizes on the hydrogen to form a compound known as hydrochloric acid gas.

hydrochloride (haɪdrəʊˈklɔəraɪd). *Chem.* [f. HYDRO- d + CHLORIDE.] A compound formed by the combination of hydrochloric acid with an organic radical (formerly, also, with an element).

1826 HENRY *Elem. Chem.* I. 427 It is constituted of two atoms of olefiant gas + 1 atom of chlorine. It has been called by Dr. Thomson *chloric ether*; but a more appropriate name would be *hydro-chloride of carbon.* **1880** CLEMINSHAW tr. *Wurtz' Atom. The.* 111 Amylene hydrochloride. **1890** ROSCOE *Elem. Chem.* xxxix. 393 When a solution of naphthylamine hydrochloride is mixed with solution of potassium nitrite, the hydrochloride of diazonaphthalene is formed.

hydrochlorothiazide (ˌhaɪdrəʊklɔərəʊˈθaɪəzaɪd). *Pharm.* [f. HYDRO- + CHLOROTHIAZIDE.] A white crystalline powder which is a diuretic and saluretic sulphonamide drug, $C_7H_8ClN_3O_4S_2$, analogous to chlorothiazide, and which is given orally in the treatment of œdema and as an adjuvant in the treatment of hypertension.

1958 *Experientia* XIV. 458/1 Hydrochlorothiazide is the generic name of a new diuretic agent manufactured by CIBA. **1959** *Lancet* 13 June 1221/2 Hydrochlorothiazide promotes less bicarbonate excretion than chlorothiazide, but the loss of potassium after the two drugs is not significantly different. **1965** J. POLLITT *Depression & its Treatment* v. 72 In mild cases [of premenstrual depression] ..Hydrochlorothiazide with potassium chloride (Hydrosaluric K) 25–75 mg. daily or on alternate days from 7–10 days premenstrually is effective. **1968** J. H. BURN *Lect. Notes Pharmacol.* (ed. 9) 105 Hydrochlorothiazide and hydroflumethiazide are ten times stronger than chlorothiazide.

†**hydroˈchloruret.** *Chem. Obs.* [f. HYDRO- d + CHLORURET.] An old synonym of HYDROCHLORIDE.

1822–34 *Good's Study Med.* (ed. 4) I. 713 The preparation called hydrochloruret of lime is recommended..as an internal remedy, in certain stages of fever and dysentery.

hydrocolloid (haɪdrəʊˈkɒlɔɪd). Also (with hyphen) hydro-colloid. [f. HYDRO- + COLLOID *a.* and *sb.*] Any substance that will form a gel on the addition of water; a gel so produced. Also *attrib.* or as *adj.*

1926 *Brit. Pat.* 271,306, The subject matter of the present invention is a reversible hydro-colloid mass which may serve for..enabling castings to be taken from the oral cavity for dental purposes. **1946** C. K. TSENG in J. Alexander *Colloid Chem., Theoret. & Appl.* VI. xxxi. 717 Agar is a reversible hydrocolloid and materials made with it must be warmed to a solution and cooled to a gel. **1954** *Adv. Chem. Ser.* XI. 92 Irish moss extractive, also known as carrageenin, ..is a hydrocolloid gum. **1955** STURDEVANT & BRAUER in J. C. Brauer *Dental Asst.* xx. 287 The reversible hydrocolloids are used for tray impressions to form casts of the teeth and jaws.

Hence ˌ**hydrocoˈlloidal** *a.*

1928 *Chem. Abstr.* XXII. 1659 A mixt. of rubber, fatty substances and resins is incorporated, in fine distribution, in a hydrocolloidal mucilaginous basic substance such as sea weeds or algaceous plants. **1947** J. C. RICH *Materials & Methods Sculpture* v. 96 Commercial hydrocolloidal compositions. **1956** J. N. ANDERSON *Appl. Dental Materials* xx. 240 All hydrocolloidal gels consist largely of water enclosed rather loosely within the gel fibrils.

ˈ**hydro-ˌcooler.** orig. *U.S.* [See next and -ER[1].] An apparatus for hydro-cooling, usually consisting of a water tank with cooling equipment and a conveyer.

1947 *Ice & Refrigeration* Nov. 33/2 Hydro-coolers are used commercially today to pre-cool celery, asparagus, peas, ..and carrots. **1958** *Agriculture* LXV. 133 Small-scale tests were made with a small and simple hydrocooler consisting of two tanks, one containing blocks of ice and water and the other for submersion of the watercress. **1964** A. E. CANHAM *Electr. Hort.* xiii. 137 The capacity of hydro-coolers varies from the large 2000 crate-per-day unit down to the 200 crate-per-day packaged unit.

ˈ**hydro-ˌcooling,** *vbl. sb.* orig. *U.S.* [HYDRO- a.] A method of preserving the freshness of vegetables or fruit after harvesting and packing by immersing them for a time in chilled water (or, sometimes, by spraying them).

1942 *Ice & Refrigeration* Nov. 302/2 The hydro-cooling machine takes 130 boxes of asparagus at a time. *Ibid.*, After this hydro-cooling the produce is loaded into trucks. **1955** WORK & CAREW *Veg. Prod. & Marketing* (ed. 2) iv. 62 Dipping in very cold water (hydrocooling) is much more rapid. **1964** A. E. CANHAM *Electr. Hort.* xiii. 135 Hydro-cooling provides an excellent simple, effective and rapid method of cooling produce which is not seriously affected by the presence of moisture.

Hence (as a back-formation) ˈ**hydrocool** *v. trans.*, to chill by this method; ˈ**hydrocooled** *ppl. a.*

1945 *Refrig. Engin.* Apr. 275/3 Test boxes of..Bing cherries were handled in the following manner:..(3) hydrocooled for 7 min. in a water bath of melting ice at 32°. **1945** *Proc. Amer. Soc. Hort. Sci.* XLVI. 196 As far as cracking and decay in storage are concerned, it apparently made little difference whether the hydrocooled fruit was packaged wet or dry. **1958** *Agriculture* LXV. 133 Comparison was made between the behaviour of samples hydrocooled to 34–35°F and control samples which had received no cooling.

hydrocortisone (haɪdrəʊˈkɔːtɪzəʊn). *Biochem.* and *Pharm.* [f. HYDRO- + CORTISONE.] A steroid hormone, $C_{21}H_{30}O_5$, which is produced by the adrenal cortex and involved in the regulation of carbohydrate metabolism, and which is prepared synthetically for use as an anti-inflammatory and anti-allergic agent.

1951 *Jrnl. Amer. Med. Assoc.* 22 Dec. 1631 Hydro-cortisone acetate had a constant anti-inflammatory effect on the rheumatoid arthritic joint when administered locally. **1952** *Ibid.* 27 Dec. 1664/2 One eye was treated with cortisone while the more severely involved eye was treated with hydrocortisone. **1953** *Jrnl. Amer. Chem. Soc.* LXXV. 5369/1 We have isolated a fungus..which converts Compound S directly to the biologically active steroid, 17α-hydroxycorticosterone (Kendall's Compound F, hydrocortisone, Reichstein's Compound M). **1963** *Lancet* 19 Jan. 142/1 Hydrocortisone has revolutionised the treatment of itching skin diseases. **1965** *New Scientist* 1 July 32/3 The glucocorticoids, of which cortisone and hydrocortisone (cortisol) are the principal members, are.. mainly concerned with carbohydrate metabolism. **1967** *Martindale's Extra Pharmacopoeia* (ed. 25) 448 Hydro-cortisone is administered by mouth and by intramuscular injection and it is applied externally in ointments, creams, and lotions. **1970** R. W. MCGILVERY *Biochem.* xxiii. 565 The most active of the glucocorticoids in humans is cortisol, or hydrocortisone.

hydrocracking (ˈhaɪdrəʊˌkrækɪŋ), *vbl. sb.* [f. HYDRO- + *cracking* vbl. sb. (see CRACK *v.* 23).] The catalytic cracking of crude petroleum or a heavy distillate by subjecting it to the action of gaseous hydrogen at a high temperature and pressure, so that long-chain paraffins and other hydrocarbons undergo hydrogenolysis; also called *hydrogenation cracking.*

1940 *Jrnl. Soc. Chem. Industry Japan* (Suppl. binding) XLIII. 363/1 The 'Hydro-Cracking' is a method of cracking in which mineral oil is decomposed in the presence of high pressure hydrogen. **1955** V. HAENSEL in B. T. Brooks et al. *Chem. Petroleum Hydrocarbons* II. xxix. 205 Hydrocracking produces lower boiling hydro-carbons which have higher octane numbers and lower densities than the parent hydrocarbons. **1970** *Adv. Chem. Ser.* CIII. vi. 113 When the modern version of hydro-cracking was announced in 1959, capacity was 1000 barrels per day. As the decade ended capacity..was approaching 1,000,000 barrels per day.

Hence (as a back-formation) ˈ**hydrocrack** *v. trans.*, to subject to, or convert by means of, hydrocracking; ˈ**hydrocracked** *ppl. a.*, obtained by hydrocracking. Also ˈ**hydro-cracker**, an apparatus or plant where hydro-cracking is carried out.

1940 *Jrnl. Soc. Chem. Industry Japan* (Suppl. binding) XLIII. 363/1 The hydro-cracked gasoline is reputed to be of superior quality. **1959** R. J. HENGSTEBECK *Petroleum Processing* xii. 274 Any heavy petroleum stock can be hydrocracked. **1965** *Chem. & Engin. News* 29 Mar. 32/2 (*heading*) Gulf adds hydrocracker at Port Arthur refinery. **1970** *Adv. Chem. Ser.* CIII. vi. 119 The feed is hydro-cracked efficiently to jet fuel with minimum formation of lighter products. *Ibid.* 120 The hydrocracker should be operated to give maximum liquid yields.

†**hydrocyanate** (haɪdrəʊˈsaɪənət). *Chem. Obs.* [f. as next + -ATE[1] 1 c.] An old name for a cyanide, considered as a salt of hydrocyanic acid.

1818 HENRY *Elem. Chem.* (ed. 8) II. 342 This base, like chlorine and iodine, is acidified by hydrogen, and the proper appellation for the prussic acid Gay Lussac conceives to be hydro-cyanic acid, and for its compounds hydro-cyanates. **1819** J. G. CHILDREN *Chem. Anal.* 320 The hydrocyanate of potassa..is not identical with the salt commonly known by the name of prussiate of potash. **1854** SCOFFERN in *Circ. Sc., Chem.* 440 Cyanogen..unites with certain metals, forming compounds which..must be regarded as cyanides, and not hydro-cyanates, seeing that they contain neither oxygen nor hydrogen.

hydrocyanic (haɪdrəʊsaɪˈænɪk), *a. Chem.* [f. HYDRO- d + CYANIC. Cf. F. *hydrocyanique.*] Containing hydrogen and cyanogen in chemical combination. ***hydrocyanic acid***, or *hydrogen cyanide* (HCN or HCy), the combination of hydrogen with cyanogen (CN or Cy), an extremely poisonous volatile liquid with an odour like that of bitter almonds, the solution in water being known as ***prussic acid***; it occurs in bitter almonds and other kernels, in cherry and laurel leaves, etc.

1818 HENRY *Elem. Chem.* (ed. 8) II. 342 As muriatic acid is decomposed by the black oxide of manganese, so is hydrocyanic vapour by peroxide of copper. **1819** J. G. CHILDREN *Chem. Anal.* 317 Hydrocyanic or Prussic Acid. **1830** LINDLEY *Nat. Syst. Bot.* 82 Amygdaleæ..are particularly characterised by their..hydrocyanic juice. **1896** REMSEN *Organic Chem.* vi. 80 Hydrocyanic acid can be detected by the fact that when its solution is saturated with caustic potash, and a solution containing a ferrous and a ferric salt is added, a precipitate of Prussian blue is formed.

hydrocyanite (haɪdrəʊˈsaɪənaɪt). *Min.* [Named 1870, f. Gr. ὕδωρ, ὑδρο- water + κύανος blue: see -ITE.] Anhydrous sulphate of copper occurring in pale green crystals, which, when exposed to the air, absorb water and become bright blue.

1875 DANA *Min.* App. ii. 29.

ˌ**hydrodeˌsulphuriˈzation.** Also (*U.S.*) -sulfur-. [f. HYDRO- + DE- II. 1 + SULPHUR + -IZATION.] The removal (as hydrogen sulphide) of sulphur from crude petroleum or a petroleum product by the action of a catalyst and gaseous hydrogen at a moderately high temperature and pressure.

1950 *Industr. & Engin. Chem.* Sept. 1882/2 Several high sulfur gas oils were reduced in sulfur contents to those of gas oils from sweet crudes by hydrodesulfurization..at 750°F., 300 pounds per square inch pressure,..and 1000 cubic feet of hydrogen per barrel of charge. **1967** *Proc. 7th World Petroleum Congr.* IV. 167/2 Hydrodesulphurization has long been recognized as a means of removing sulfur [from] residual oils and asphalts.

Hence (as a back-formation) ˌ**hydrodeˈsulphurize** *v. trans.*, to subject to hydrodesulphurization; ˌ**hydrodeˈsulphurized** *ppl. a.*, **-deˈsulphurizing** *vbl. sb.* Also ˌ**hydrodeˈsulphurizer**, an apparatus in which this process is carried out.

1950 *Industr. & Engin. Chem.* Sept. 1881/1 Instead of processing the gas oil, it is possible to hydrodesulfurize the entire crude. **1955** *Industr. Chemist* XXXI. 351/1 The first commercial hydrodesulphurizer applying the Shell trickle technique was recently started up. **1960** *Times Rev. Industry* Jan. 31/1 The regeneration of hydrodesulphurising catalysts for further use. **1967** *Proc. 7th World Petroleum Congr.* IV. 168/2 The hydrodesulfurized product tends to be relatively rich in nickel.

hydrodictyon (ˌhaɪdrəʊˈdɪktɪən). *Bot.* [mod.L. (A. W. Roth *Catalecta Botanica* (1800) II. 237), f. HYDRO- + Gr. δίκτυον net.] A green freshwater alga of the genus so called; = *water-net* (WATER *sb.* 31).

1841 W. H. HARVEY *Man. Brit. Algæ* p. viii, Among British Algæ, the only structure analogous to these exists in *Hydrodictyon*, which grows in the form of a perfect net, with regular meshes. **1872** H. C. WOOD *Contrib. Hist. Fresh-Water Algæ N. Amer.* 94 When the hydrodictyon disappear in the fall it is months before they reappear in the spring. **1927** WEST & FRITSCH *Treat. Brit. Freshwater Algae* 101 A new *Hydrodictyon*-net or *Pediastrum*-plate is formed..by the asexual method. **1967** I. MORRIS *Introd. Algae* iv. 50 *Hydrodictyon* colonies consist of large numbers of cylindrical cells joined terminally with two others to form an open net-like structure.

hydrodynamic (ˌhaɪdrəʊdaɪ-, -dɪˈnæmɪk), *a.* [ad. mod.L. *hydrodynamic-us*: see HYDRODYNAMICS and DYNAMIC.] = next.

1828 in WEBSTER. **1855** MAYNE *Expos. Lex.*, *Hydrodynamic*, of or belonging to the power of water, or other fluids, at rest, or in motion. **1891** *Brit. Med. Jrnl.* 29 Aug. 482/1 To bring the whole organ [brain] to rest, a certain degree of peripheral hydrodynamic compression is required.

hydrodynamical (-daɪ-, dɪˈnæmɪkəl), *a.* [f. as prec. + -AL[1].] Pertaining or relating to the forces acting upon or exerted by water or other liquids; belonging to HYDRODYNAMICS.

1830 HERSCHEL *Stud. Nat. Phil.* §189 Newton himself.. laid the foundation of hydrodynamical science. **1837** BREWSTER *Magnet.* 15 In his electrical, magnetical, and hydrodynamical researches. **1843** *Rep. Brit. Assoc.* 109 It depended on the hydrodynamical fact, that if a reservoir be filled with water to a certain height, the water will flow from an orifice at the bottom with a velocity proportionate to the height.

ˌhydrodyˈnamically, *adv.* [f. HYDRODYNAMIC, -DYNAMICAL *adjs.*: see -ICALLY.] From the point of view of hydrodynamics.

1957 G. E. HUTCHINSON *Treat. Limnol.* I. i. 156 Schriever (1955) concludes that Croke's final theory is hydrodynamically impossible. **1971** *Nature* 11 June 383/2 The turbulent boundary layer found near the sediment water interface may be described hydrodynamically in one of three ways.

hydrodynamicist (ˌhaɪdrəʊdaɪˈnæmɪsɪst). [f. HYDRODYNAMIC(S + -IST.] An expert in or a student of hydrodynamics.

1961 *Aeroplane* CI. 553/2 Hydrodynamicists.. were less interested in ships travelling in shallow water at a particular speed.. than in sea-going ships or river-going ships at any speed. **1970** N. DE NEVERS *Fluid Mech.* x. 324 By 1900 the two schools had gone their separate ways, the hydrodynamicists publishing learned mathematical papers with little bearing on engineering problems and the hydraulicians solving engineering problems by trial and error.

hydrodynamics (ˌhɔɪdrəʊdaɪ-, -dɪˈnæmɪks). [ad. mod.L. *hydrodynamica*: see HYDRO- a and DYNAMICS. Cf. F. *hydrodynamique*.

The Lat. word appears in a treatise by Daniel Bernoulli, 1738, entitled 'Hydrodynamica, sive de viribus et motibus fluidorum commentarii'.]

The branch of Physics which treats of the forces acting upon or exerted by liquids. In earlier use = HYDROKINETICS; now usually taken in a comprehensive sense to include Hydrokinetics and Hydrostatics; but the earlier usage is still retained by some physicists. (Cf. DYNAMICS.)

1779 MANN in *Phil. Trans.* LXIX. 596 The certain principles of hydrodynamics laid down in this essay. **1794** G. ADAMS *Nat. & Exp. Philos.* III. xxxiii. 338 The science describing the mechanical affection of fluids.. is properly and usually called by foreign writers *hydrodynamics*. **1812** PLAYFAIR *Nat. Phil.* (1819) I. 17 When the bodies to which motion is communicated are fluid, another modification of the principles of dynamics takes place, which consititutes the science of hydrodynamics. **1829** *Nat. Phil.* I. *Hydrost.* i. 1 (U.K.S.) The whole science of liquids, or watery fluids, comprehending both Hydrostatics and Hydraulics, is sometimes called *Hydrodynamics*. **1881** SIR W. THOMSON in *Nature* No. 619.434 Some of the finest principles of mathematical hydrodynamics have.. been put in requisition for perfecting the theory of hydraulic mechanism.

hydrodynamometer (-daɪnəˈmɒmɪtə(r)). [f. HYDRO- a + DYNAMOMETER.] An instrument for measuring the force exerted by a liquid in motion.

1890 in *Cent. Dict.*

hydro-eˈlectric, *a.* Also hydroelectric. [f. HYDRO- a + ELECTRIC.]

†**1.** Of or pertaining to hydro-electricity; galvanic. *Obs.*

1827 J. CUMMING *Man. Electro Dynamics* IV. 115 Retaining the name *Hydro-electric*, for current produced by the intervention of fluids. **1832** *Nat. Philos., Electro-Magnet.* xiii. §305. 93 (U.K.S.) The electrical current thus excited has been termed Thermo-electric, in order to distinguish it from the common galvanic current, which, as it requires the intervention of a fluid element as one of its essential components, was denominated a Hydro-electric current. **1851** *Illustr. Catal. Gt. Exhib.* 1027 The powers of nature, as steam, the moving power, lightning, the hydro-electric fluid, and light. *Ibid.* 1102 Engraving on a tin plate, produced by the action of the hydro-electric current. **1855** MAYNE *Expos. Lex.*, *Hydro-Electricus*, applied to the phenomena which produce the voltaic pile, because the presence of water is the condition of their full development: hydro-electric.

2. Effecting the development of electricity by the friction of water or steam: as in Armstrong's hydro-electric machine.

1844 *Rep. Brit. Assoc. Adv. Sci. 1843* 39 (*heading*) On the electricity of high-pressure steam, and a description of a hydro-electric machine. **1863-72** WATTS *Dict. Chem.* II. 408 The electric excitement resulting from the friction of water is applied to the construction of an electrical machine of great power, called the Hydro-electric machine. **1881** JUDD *Volcanoes* ii. 29 Every volcano in violent eruption is a very efficient hydro-electric machine.

3. Generating electricity by utilizing the motive power of water; generated by, or relating to generation by, such means.

1884 *Engineering* 11 Jan. 38/3 A Hydro-Electric Syphon. .. A most ingenious scheme for draining the valley of the city of Mexico by means of electrical power generated by the fall of water raised by electrically driven pumps. **1899** *Min. Proc. Inst. Civil Engin.* CXXXVI. 433 (heading) Hydro-electric installation at Mont-Dore. **1904** *Electrical Mag.* I. 592/1 On the river Ain.. near Lake Geneva, a hydro-electric plant has recently been completed. **1905** *Daily Chron.* 18 Sept. 4/5 Abundant hydro-electric power. **1927** CREAGER & JUSTIN *Hydro-Electric Handbk.* xxxv. 874 Hydro-electric plants are much more reliable than steam plants. **1951** T. H. CARR *Electric Power Stations* (ed. 3) II. xxiv. 579 Hydro-electric stations are usually located in wild, mountainous districts. **1955** *Bull. Atomic Sci.* Oct. 281/2 Hydroelectric power is never likely to contribute more than a small fraction of the total energy consumption of the world, since the total potential capacity is relatively limited. **1963** W. E. BALLARD *Metal Spraying* (ed. 4) xiv. 479 In hydro-electric schemes, metal spraying has often been used for the protection of the large pipes bringing the water down from a high altitude to the turbines. **1972** *Daily Tel.* 11 Apr. 13/6 Brazil wants to build a huge hydro-electric dam on the upper reaches of the River Parana.

ˌhydro-eˈlectrical, *a.* [f. prec. + -AL[1].] = HYDRO-ELECTRIC *a.* 3.

1925 *Trans. Soc. Engin.* 127 In New Zealand the largest hydro-electrical power scheme.. is controlled by the Christchurch County Council. **1930** BAKER & CONKLING *Water Supply & Utilization* i. 17 (*heading*) Recent growth of hydroelectrical development in the United States.

ˌhydro-elecˈtricity. [f. HYDRO- + ELECTRICITY.]

1. The electricity of the galvanic battery.

1828 F. WATKINS *Pop. Sk. Electro-Magnetism* 61 The term hydro-electricity, applied to that which emanates from a voltaic combination. **1851** J. GRAHAM in *Illustr. Catal. Gt. Exhib.* 1052 Hydro-electricity, which is the grand agent in operations of this kind, is different in the phenomena it exhibits from that of dry electricity, or that shown by an electrical machine. For.. the electricity of the galvanic battery is scarcely perceptible, unless that which is called the circuit be complete.

2. Electricity generated by utilizing the motive power of water.

1904 *Electrical Mag.* I. 378/1 (*heading*) Hydro-electricity in California. *Ibid.* 592/1 (*heading*) Hydro electricity for small French factories. **1959** *Petroleum Handbk.* (Shell Internat. Petroleum Co.) (ed. 4) 19 There are.. limitations to the future growth of hydro-electricity. **1972** *Sci. Amer.* Dec. 13/2 With ample supplies of coal and hydroelectricity China should be able to devote much of the oil.. to a petrochemical industry.

hydrofining (ˈhaɪdrəʊfaɪnɪŋ), *vbl. sb.* [f. HYDRO- + RE)FINING *vbl. sb.*] A catalytic process in which a petroleum product is stabilized and its sulphur content reduced by treatment with gaseous hydrogen under relatively mild conditions, so that unsaturated hydro-carbons and sulphur compounds undergo selective hydrogenation.

1931 C. ELLIS *Hydrogenation Org. Subst.* xlviii. 578 The term *hydrofining* is best applied to those treatments by hydrogen which are carried out at temperatures in the lower ranges,.. where no extensive alteration of the carbon-containing molecule occurs. On the other hand, where great disturbance of carbon structure results the process is better denominated *hydroforming*. **1955** *Petroleum Refiner* May 154/1 Hydrofining was found to.. improve the burning quality of West Texas No. 1 fuel oil. **1970** J. R. HUGHES *Storage & Handling Petroleum Liquids* (ed. 2) 5 Hydrofining and autofining aim to remove or reduce the content of unwanted sulphur compounds.

So **ˈhydrofined** *ppl. a.*, obtained by hydrofining.

1931 C. ELLIS *Hydrogenation Org. Subst.* xlviii. 577 The hydrofined lubricating oils are not as readily oxidized as the untreated oils. **1955** *Petroleum Refiner* May 153/2 The quality of the raw and hydrofined distillates was determined by inspection tests, measurement of hydrogen content, and burning-quality tests.

†**hydroˈfluate.** *Chem. Obs.* [f. HYDRO- d + FLUATE.] An old name for a fluoride viewed as a salt of hydrofluoric acid; also for a hydrofluoride, as in ***hydrofluate of ammonia*** = hydrogen ammonium fluoride, fluoride of ammonium and hydrogen, or acid fluoride of ammonium ($NH_4F.HF$).

1841 BRANDE *Chem.* 1031 Hydrofluate of ammonia remains in solution.

hydroflumethiazide (ˌhaɪdrəʊfluːmɛˈθaɪəzaɪd). *Pharm.* [f. HYDRO- + *flumeth-* (f. FLU(ORO- + METH(YL + CHLOROTH)IAZIDE.] A white crystalline compound, $C_8H_8F_3N_3O_4S_2$, analogous to hydrochlorothiazide and having similar effects and uses.

1959 *Lancet* 12 Sept. 303/2 Two substances related to chlorothiazide—hydroflumethiazide and hydrochlorothiazide—have recently been produced, and are effective in much smaller quantity. **1964** A. GOTH *Med. Pharmacol.* (ed. 2) xxix. 358 Hydroflumethiazide (Saluron) has the same structural formula as hydrochlorothiazide, except that F_3C replaces Cl. **1968** [see HYDROCHLOROTHIAZIDE].

hydrofluoboric (ˌhaɪdrəʊfluːəʊˈbɔərɪk), *a.* *Chem.* [f. HYDRO- d + FLUO- + BORIC.] In ***hydrofluoboric acid*** ($BF_3.HF$), or ***hydrogen borofluoride***, a compound obtained by passing gaseous boron fluoride into water: also called *borofluorhydric acid.*

1849 D. CAMPBELL *Inorg. Chem.* 95 A new acid named hydrofluoboric acid ($3HF + 2BF_3$). **1863-72** WATTS *Dict. Chem.* I. 634 Distilled with sulphuric acid, they [borofluorides] give off gaseous fluoride of boron and aqueous hydrofluoboric acid.

hydrofluoric (haɪdrəʊfluːˈɒrɪk), *a.* *Chem.* [f. HYDRO- d + FLUORIC. Cf. F. *hydrofluorique*.] Containing hydrogen and fluorine in chemical combination. ***hydrofluoric acid***, or ***hydrogen fluoride*** (HF), a colourless gas, fuming in moist air and rapidly absorbed by water.

1822 IMISON *Sc. & Art* II. 91 No acid can act upon it, except the hydro-fluoric, which dissolves it. **1863-72** WATTS *Dict. Chem.* II. 670 Etching with hydrofluoric acid vapour is the best mode of marking scales of equal parts on glass tubes and jars.

hydrofluosilicic (ˌhaɪdrəʊfluːəʊsɪˈlɪsɪk), *a.* *Chem.* [f. HYDRO- d + FLUO- + SILICIC.] Containing hydrogen, fluorine, and silicon in chemical combination. ***hydrofluosilicic acid*** (H_2SiF_6), or ***hydrogen silicofluoride***, a fuming liquid which gradually attacks glass, esp. on heating.

1842 PARNELL *Chem. Anal.* (1845) 315 Strontian and barytes are separated from each other, when in solution, by hydrofluosilicic acid, which precipitates barytes.. but not strontian. **1853** GREGORY *Inorg. Chem.* (ed. 3) 191 Hydrofluosilicic acid is the only test that forms a precipitate in cold and pretty strong solutions of soda salts.

So **hydrofluoˈsilicate**, a salt formed by the union of hydrofluosilicic acid with a base; a silicofluoride.

1847 in CRAIG.

hydrofoil (ˈhaɪdrəfɔɪl). [f. HYDRO- + FOIL *sb.*[1], after *aerofoil.*] **1.** A plane designed to give rise to a force (other than drag) when moving through a liquid; *spec.* (*a*) a plane (usually one of two or more) attached to a vessel by means of which the hull is lifted clear of the water at speed; (*b*) one attached to a seaplane to facilitate take-off by increasing the hydrodynamic lift; (*c*) one attached at the side of a ship to act as a stabilizer.

1920 *Chambers's Jrnl.* 28 Feb. 207/2 [A boat.] Under each wing at its forward end is a series of narrow steel planes known as hydrofoils. **1933** *Aeroplane* 24 May 945/1 The possibility of using hydrofoils to cure porpoising and to revolutionise the design of flying-boats. **1939** *Jrnl. R. Aeronaut. Soc.* XLIII. 552 A special landing and take-off gear in the form of hydrofoils which will be retracted in flight. **1958** *New Scientist* 27 Feb. 15/3 The aerofoils of the sails and the hydrofoil of the keel are separated by the hull of the yacht. **1966** *McGraw-Hill Encycl. Sci. & Technol.* XIII. 212/1 Diving planes [on a submarine] are pairs of hydrofoils which extend from the sides of the ship. **1968** J. E. PLAPP *Engin. Fluid Mech.* xii. 486 The hydrofoil.. is a wing designed to operate in water instead of air. **1972** *Daily Tel.* 28 Sept. 6/5 The mono hull has surface-piercing hydrofoils which lift the craft out of the water. **1973** *Nature* 12 Jan. 114/2 The use of hydrofoils for a wide variety of purposes such as propeller blades on boats, as sailboat keels, ship rudders, submarine and torpedo fins, lifting surfaces of hydrofoil boats, and shroud ring stabilizers for missiles, has prompted efforts to increase the lift-to-drag ratio.

2. A vessel fitted with hydrofoils for raising it clear of the water.

1959 *Times Rev. Industry* Nov. 41/1 This speed.. will be valuable for work on high speed motor boats or hydrofoils. **1962** *Daily Tel.* 12 Feb. 16/8 The United States Maritime Administration.. believes there is a big future for hydrofoils as passenger vessels. **1968** [see FOIL-BORNE *a.*]. **1969** *N.Z. Listener* 12 Dec. 19/1 Jaunting up Auckland Harbour on the hydrofoil. **1970** R. C. DORF *Mod. Control Syst.* x. 351 The Denison is an 80-ton hydrofoil capable of operating in seas ranging to 9 ft in amplitude at a speed of 60 knots. **1972** *Guardian* 27 May 5/3 The Thames's first modern commuter service—by Italian hydrofoil—opened yesterday.

3. *attrib.*, as ***hydrofoil boat, craft, service, ship.***

1950 *Electronic Engin.* XXII. 205 A hydrofoil boat—one which has wings extending into the water to support it in motion so that the hull is out of the water—has speed and stability advantages. **1960** *Times* 19 Jan. 10/7 The United States Government has awarded a contract for the construction of a hydrofoil ship capable of carrying 100 passengers at speeds up to 90 miles an hour. **1960** *New Scientist* 15 Sept. 703/2 The hydrofoil craft is particularly suited for river work. **1964** *Weekly News* (Auckland) 8 July 30 The beginning of the hydrofoil service to Waiheke Island ..means that island residents..can now make the trip between Auckland and Matiatia in 20 minutes. **1973** *Cook's Continental Timetable* June 456 Hydrofoil Services. Journey 35 minutes [from Naples] to Capri.

hydroformate (ˈhaɪdrəʊˈfɔːmeɪt). [f. as next + *-ate*, after *filtrate, precipitate*, etc.] A product obtained by hydroforming.

1953 A. A. DRAEGER et al. in *Sci. Petroleum* V. ii. 266/2 For the production of high purity aromatic chemicals, however, additional processing of the hydroformate is required. **1969** KIRK & OTHMER *Encycl. Chem. Technol.* (ed. 2) XX. 538 Then the.. light hydrocarbons are removed by distillation in a 'product stabilizer'; the undistilled portion constitutes the product or 'stabilized hydroformate'.

hydroformer ('haɪdrəʊ'fɔːmə(r)). [f. next + -ER[1].] In an oil refinery, an apparatus or plant where hydroforming is carried out.

1941 *Refiner & Natural Gas Manuf.* May 66/2 The potential toluene production of the hydroformer amounts to about 5,000,000 gallons per year. **1959** *Times Rev. Industry* Nov. 72/3 To achieve petrol of a higher octane number a powerformer in place of the traditional hydroformer is to be employed.

hydroforming ('haɪdrəʊfɔːmɪŋ), *vbl. sb.* [f. HYDRO- + *-forming*, after REFORMING *vbl. sb.*] In the petroleum industry, a catalytic reforming process that converts the paraffins and alicyclic compounds in low-octane petroleum naphtha to aromatic compounds by dehydrogenation at a high temperature and moderate pressure in the presence of gaseous hydrogen. Freq. *attrib.*

1931 [see HYDROFINING *vbl. sb.*]. **1941** *Oil & Gas Jrnl.* 27 Mar. 87/1 The first commercial hydroforming plant was placed in operation recently. **1953** A. A. DRAEGER et al. in *Sci. Petroleum* V. II. 266/2 The hydroforming process is employed by the petroleum refining industry both to elevate the anti-knock quality of petroleum naphthas..for inclusion in premium quality gasolines and to produce aromatic compounds of high purity for specialized uses. **1959** *Times Rev. Industry* Aug. 112/2 Examples of..new knowledge include the technique of making high octane gasoline by hydroforming and fluid catalytic cracking. **1969** KIRK & OTHMER *Encycl. Chem. Technol.* (ed. 2) XX. 534 Toluene is produced principally from petroleum by the hydroforming of selected petroleum naphthas..which are rich in naphthenic hydrocarbons.

Hence (as a back-formation) **'hydroform** *v. trans.*, to subject to hydroforming; **'hydroformed** *ppl. a.*, produced by hydroforming.

1941 *Nat. Petroleum News* 2 Apr. R-102/1 The anti-knock quality of hydroformed gasoline has not yet been thoroughly evaluated. **1949** P. C. CARMAN *Chem. Constitution & Properties Engin. Materials* xxvii. 824 A low octane feed boiling 90°–200°C. can be hydro-formed at 480°–540°C. and 100–300 p.s.i. to give an aromatised motor fuel with an octane rating of 80. **1953** A. A. DRAEGER et al. in *Sci. Petroleum* V. II. 274/1 These factors..make it a desirable procedure to hydroform cracked naphthas in admixture with virgin naphthas.

hydrogasification (ˌhaɪdrəʊgæsɪfɪ'keɪʃən). [f. HYDRO- + GASIFICATION.] The production of methane directly from coal by treatment with hydrogen (or hydrogen and steam) at a high temperature and pressure.

1954 *Proc. Amer. Gas Assoc.* 644/2 Pressure hydrogasification produces high-Btu oil gases with satisfactory combustion characteristics. **1963** H. H. LOWRY *Chem. Coal Utilization* Suppl. xx. 996/1 The hydrogasification of coal to produce methane has an inherent thermo-chemical advantage. **1967** *McGraw-Hill Yearbk. Sci. & Technol.* 139/2 Up to 70% of the hydrogen needed for hydrogasification is made in place by reaction of steam with carbon. **1968** *Chem. & Engin. News* 29 July 12/3 Coal hydrogasification has reached the pilot-plant stage.

So **hydro'gasifier**, an apparatus in which hydrogasification is carried out.

1966 *Chem. & Engin. News* 18 Apr. 70/1 There is a net heat of reaction and this serves to supply the necessary heat for the hydrogasifier..to operate adiabatically.

hydrogel ('haɪdrədʒɛl). [f. HYDRO- + GEL(ATIN.] A gel or gelatinous precipitate in which the liquid constituent is water.

1864 [see ALCOSOL]. **1895** THOMSON & BLOXAM *Bloxam's Chem.* (ed. 8) 123 Colloids..can generally exist in solution (the hydrosol form), but are apt to separate as a jelly (the hydrogel form) from such solutions. **1938** R. G. TORRENS *Dental Dis.* vi. 90 Gelatine is a hydrosol when warm and a hydrogel when cold. **1972** *Physics Bull.* June 336/1 Probably a wide range of factors can precipitate the clotting process including..surface texture and surface wettability as relating to hydrogel formation.

hydrogen ('haɪdrədʒən). *Chem.* Also 8–9 **hydrogene.** [a. F. *hydrogène*, f. Gr. ὕδωρ, ὑδρ- water: see -GEN I.]

1. a. One of the elements; a colourless, invisible, odourless gas; it burns with a pale-blue flame, whence its former name of *inflammable air*. It is the lightest substance known, having a specific gravity of about one-fourteenth of that of air. Symbol H; atomic weight 1.

It occurs free in nature in small quantities in certain volcanic gases, and is an essential constituent of all animal and vegetable matter. It forms two-thirds in volume and one-ninth in weight of water (H_2O), which is the sole product of the combustion of hydrogen in ordinary air. It is a constituent of all acids, in which it can be replaced by bases to form salts.

antimoniuretted, arseniuretted, carburetted, phosphoretted, seleniuretted, sulphuretted, telluretted hydrogen, early names sometimes still used for gaseous combinations of hydrogen with antimony, arsenic, carbon, phosphorus, selenium, sulphur, tellurium.

1791 E. DARWIN *Bot. Gard.* I. 132 *note*, Mr. Lavoisier and others of the French School have most ingeniously endeavoured to shew that water consists of pure air, called by them oxygene, and of inflammable air, called hydrogene. **1794** G. ADAMS *Nat. & Exp. Philos.* I. xii. 493 Inflammable air may be obtained in great purity by decomposing water, of which it is a constituent part. The French writers term it hydrogene, that is generator of water. **1794** PEARSON in *Phil. Trans.* LXXXIV. 391 A mixture of carbonic acid, hydrogen, and nitrogen gaz. **1799** W. TOOKE *View Russian Emp.* I. 283 Hepatic air or sulphurated hydrogene gas. **1820** SHELLEY *Œdipus* I. 188 As full of blood as that of hydrogene. **1833** N. ARNOTT *Physics* (ed. 5) I. 421 The carburetted hydrogen..is generally employed for filling balloons. **1875** BENNETT & DYER *Sachs' Bot.* 620 Hydrogen is present, equally with carbon, in every organic compound. **1878** HUXLEY *Physiogr.* 111 Most of our ordinary combustibles..are rich in hydrogen. **1893** SIR R. BALL *In High Heav.* vii. 157 Dr. Huggins..succeeded in establishing the existence of hydrogen in these remote regions of space.

b. An atom of hydrogen.

1920 *Jrnl. Amer. Chem. Soc.* XLII. 1431 A free pair of electrons on one water molecule might be able to exert sufficient force on a hydrogen held by a pair of electrons on another water molecule to bind the two molecules together. **1957** G. E. HUTCHINSON *Treat. Limnol.* I. iii. 196 The hydrogens, owing to their capacity to form hydrogen bonds.., will act as if they had unsatisfied single valencies.

2. *attrib.* **a.** ***hydrogen harmonicon, lamp, line, spectrum; hydrogen*** (*sc.* hydrogen bomb) ***warhead***; **hydrogen acid** = HYDRACID; †**hydrogen air**, an old name for hydrogen, freq. also called **hydrogen gas** (cf. F. *gaz hydrogène*); **hydrogen bomb**, an immensely powerful bomb in which the energy released is derived from the fusion of hydrogen nuclei in an uncontrolled self-sustaining reaction initiated by a fission bomb; **hydrogen bond**, a weak bond between a strongly electronegative atom with a lone pair of electrons in one molecule and a hydrogen atom covalently bonded to another strongly electronegative atom or group in the same or a different molecule; hence ***hydrogen-bonded*** pa. pple. and ppl. adj., ***-bonding*** vbl. sb.; **hydrogen (gas) electrode**, an electrode (usu. of platinum coated with platinum black) partially immersed in a solution that contains hydrogen ions and hydrogen gas, so that an equilibrium between the ions and the molecules is established on the surface of the electrode enabling it to be used as a standard of zero potential (e.g. in measurements of other electrode potentials and of *p*H); **hydrogen ion**, the positive ion H^+ (the proton) derived from a hydrogen atom by the loss of its electron; a solvated form of this in a solution, esp. the hydrated form H_3O^+ (cf. HYDRONIUM).

1866 S. MACADAM *G. Wilson's Inorg. Chem.* Index, *Hydrogen acids, or hydracids. **1793** BEDDOES *Calculus* 212 Arterial blood exposed to the contact of hydrogene air loses its vermilion colour. **1947** *N.Y. Times* 13 Apr. IV. 9/5 *Hydrogen bomb. New and improved atomic bombs were discussed at the recently held forum of the Northern California Association of Scientists. **1948** *Sci. News Let.* 17 July 35/1 This is the 'hydrogen bomb' that certain high officials in past months have vaguely..hinted may be made. **1951** C. ROBERTS *Terrace in Sun* i. 12 Would the hydrogen bomb that could reduce New York to a tangled skeleton penetrate thus far? **1954** W. S. CHURCHILL in *Hansard Commons* 30 Mar. 1840 The development of the hydrogen bomb raises strategic and political issues. **1972** *Sci. Amer.* Dec. 13/3 China exploded a fission device in 1964 and a fusion device in 1967, and it has tested several hydrogen bombs since that date. **1923** G. N. LEWIS *Valence* ix. 109 The hydrogen atom can form a loose attachment to another pair of electrons, thus forming the *hydrogen bond. **1939** L. PAULING *Nature Chem. Bond* ix. 264 Although the hydrogen bond is not a strong bond..it has great significance in determining the properties of substances. **1966** *McGraw-Hill Encycl. Sci. & Technol.* XIV. 387/2 Ordinary ice consists of water molecules joined together by hydrogen bonds in a regular arrangement. **1970** AMBROSE & EASTY *Cell Biol.* iii. 110 When double-stranded DNA is heated to near 100°C, the hydrogen bonds between the two chains break and the strands separate. **1950** *Jrnl. Amer. Chem. Soc.* LXXII. 5349/2 Each residue is hydrogen-bonded to the third residue from it in each direction along the chain. *Ibid.*, The second hydrogen-bonded spiral is the five-residue spiral. **1936** *Ibid.* LVIII. 1903/2 One isomer should show complete hydrogen bonding detectable by appropriate physical methods. **1898** *Jrnl. Chem. Soc.* LXXIV. II. 89 A similar method may be used in the titration of acids and bases, if a *hydrogen electrode be employed..being made of gold electrolytically coated with palladium. **1942** GLASSTONE *Introd. Electrochem.* x. 352 The hydrogen gas electrode cannot be employed in solutions containing oxidizing agents. **1964** R. G. BATES *Determination of pH* ix. 230 The hydrogen electrode is the ultimate standard for the determination of pH values, but..other electrodes reversible to hydrogen ion are commonly employed for routine pH measurements. **1802–12** BENTHAM *Ration. Judic. Evid.* (1827) III. 315 An air-balloon, on the *hydrogen gas principle. **1805** W. NISBET *Dict. Chem.*, *Hydrogen Gas*, sometimes termed inflammable gas, is formed by the union of hydrogen with caloric. It was discovered by Mr. Cavendish. **1866** S. MACADAM *G. Wilson's Inorg. Chem.* 93 This arrangement has been called the *hydrogen harmonicon; but any of the combustible gases will produce musical notes if burned in the same way. **1896** *Jrnl. Chem. Soc.* LXX. II. 638 Etherification occurring, with or without the addition of a catalysing acid, is primarily caused by the activity of the *hydrogen ions present. **1935** *Discovery* Nov. 322/1 Every process of manufacture is subject to constant scientific control, regulating temperature, humidity,..hydrogen-ion concentration. **1939** L. PAULING *Nature Chem. Bond* ix. 266 The positive hydrogen ion is a bare proton. **1942** GLASSTONE *Introd. Electrochem.* ix. 308 The hydrogen ion in solution is not to be regarded as a bare proton, but as a combination of a proton with, at least, one molecule of solvent. **1968** M. S. LIVINGSTON *Particle Physics* vi. 120 Experiments on the deflection of hydrogen-ion beams in electric and magnetic fields. **1893** SIR R. BALL *In High Heav.* vii. 160 The spectrum of the star in the vicinity of the line G... The *hydrogen line in that neighbourhood. *Ibid.* xv. 366 A bright line, such as one of those of which the *hydrogen spectrum is composed. **1954** in *Amer. Speech* (1957) XXXII. 137 That missile, or I.B.M. as the experts call it, will be an accurately guided rocket..capable of carrying a *hydrogen warhead over a range of 4000 to 5000 miles.

b. In systematic names of chemical compounds of hydrogen with an element or radical = 'of hydrogen': as ***hydrogen bromide*** HBr, ***h. chloride*** HCl, ***h. iodide*** HI (also called hydrobromic, hydrochloric, and hydriodic acids); ***hydrogen monoxide*** or ***protoxide*** H_2O (water), ***hydrogen dioxide*** H_2O_2 (oxygenated water); ***hydrogen arsenide*** H_3As, ***h. selenide*** H_2Se, ***h. sulphide*** H_2S (also arseniuretted, seleniuretted, sulphuretted h.); ***hydrogen disulphide*** H_2S_2, ***hydrogen potassium carbonate*** $HKCO_3$, ***hydrogen sodium arsenate*** $HNa.AsO_4 + 12H_2O$. On the analogy of hydrogen chloride, etc., acids are often named as salts of hydrogen, e.g. ***hydrogen acetate*** $C_2H_3O_2.H$, ***h. chlorate*** $HClO_3$, ***h. chlorite*** $HClO_2$, ***h. nitrate*** HNO_3, ***h. sulphate*** H_2SO_4, ***h. sulphite*** H_2SO_3 (= acetic, chloric, chlorous, nitric, sulphuric, sulphurous acids); **hydrogen cyanide**, the more usual term in modern usage for hydrocyanic acid; **hydrogen peroxide**, a colourless, viscous, somewhat unstable liquid, H_2O_2, which can act as an oxidizing and a reducing agent, is usu. prepared as an aqueous solution, and is used esp. as an oxidizing and bleaching agent, in the manufacture of peroxides and organic compounds, as a weak antiseptic, and (in concentrated form) as a rocket propellant.

1869 ROSCOE *Elem. Chem.* 105 Hydrochloric Acid or Hydrogen Chloride. *Ibid.* 197 Hydrogen Sodium Carbonate or Bicarbonate of Soda..is a white crystalline powder which on heating is readily converted into sodium carbonate. *Ibid.* 320 Acetic acid..hydrogen acetate. **1872** *Jrnl. Chem. Soc.* XXV. 922 (*heading*) Determination of nitrates, nitrites, and hydrogen peroxide by solution of indigo. **1873** *Fownes' Chem.* (ed. 11) 193 Hydrogen Iodate, or Iodic Acid. *Ibid.* 206 Hydrogen sulphide is a colourless gas, having the odour of putrid eggs. *Ibid.* 215 Hydrogen Telluride is a gas, resembling sulphuretted and selenietted hydrogen. **1877** ROSCOE & SCHORLEMMER *Treat. Chem.* I. 519 In order to prepare the hydrogen arsenide in the pure state. **1882** *Jrnl. Chem. Soc. Index of Subjects 1873–1882* 215/2 Hydrogen cyanide. **1907** G. S. NEWTH *Text-bk. Inorg. Chem.* (ed. 12) II. iii. 226 When such a discoloured picture [in oils] is washed over with dilute hydrogen peroxide, the black sulphide is oxidised into the white lead sulphate. **1948** *New Biol.* IV. 71 The most common fumigants in use in this country are hydrogen cyanide;..methyl bromide; [etc.]. **1951** A. GROLLMAN *Pharmacol. & Therapeutics* xxv. 514 Hydrogen peroxide solution differs from most other disinfectants in the short duration of the action, which passes off as soon as all the oxygen is liberated. **1962** J. GLENN in *Into Orbit* 192 The hydrogen peroxide jets began to turn the capsule round to orbital attitude.

c. In journalistic and colloquial use: of the age, era, etc., marked by the advent of the hydrogen bomb.

1953 *Ann. Reg. 1952* 403 [Pres. Truman's] references to the bomb..firmly dated the beginning of the 'hydrogen era' as occurring in the period of the Truman Administration. **1954** *Commonweal* 10 Dec. 279/2 An unexpected wind shift and fallout of radioactive ashes made some unfortunate Japanese fishermen..the first public victims of the hydrogen age. **1959** *Times Lit. Suppl.* 29 May 315/1 His naval reforms..seem unimportant..in the hydrogen age.

3. *Comb.* **hydrogen-like** *a. Physics*, consisting (like the hydrogen atom) of a nucleus to which is bound a single negatively charged particle; characteristic of such an atom.

1927 E. N. DA C. ANDRADE *Struct. Atom* (ed. 3) ix. 190 An atom of helium from which one electron has been altogether removed, and an atom of lithium from which two electrons have been altogether removed, constitute similar systems, and may be called hydrogen-like. **1927** J. FISHER tr. *Born's Mech. Atom* iii. 155 The orbit of the radiating electron was hydrogen-like for large values of *k*, since it is situated in an approximately Coulomb field of force. **1951** S. DUSHMAN *Fund. Atomic Physics* ix. 131 A hydrogenlike atom, having a nucleus of charge *Ze* and one electron revolving about this nucleus in a circular orbit. **1969** K. ZIOCK *Basic Quantum Mech.* v. 89 Muonic atoms have hydrogen-like spectra.

hydrogenase (haɪ'drɒdʒəneɪz, -eɪs). *Biochem.* [ad. F. *hydrogénase* (J. de Rey-Pailhade 1900, in *Bull. de la Soc. chim. de Paris* XXIII. 668), f. HYDROGEN + -ASE.] Any enzyme which catalyses the addition of hydrogen to an organic substrate.

1900 *Jrnl. Chem. Soc.* LXXVIII. II. 678 The evolution of gas [from the yeast] is almost immediately arrested by the addition of sulphur, a fact which suggests that the ferments in question are closely related to philothion or hydrogenase. **1943** *Jrnl. Biol. Chem.* CLI. 384 Hydrogenase is closely related to the nitrogen-fixing system in *Azotobacter*. **1965** A. H. ROSE *Chem. Microbiol.* vii. 142 There exists a close relationship between the ability of organisms..to fix nitrogen, and the presence in the organisms of the enzyme hydrogenase. **1966** FRENKEL & COST in Florkin & Stotz *Comprehensive Biochem.* XIV. viii. 417 Hydrogenase activity can also be observed in certain algae which can carry out photoreduction of CO_2 with molecular hydrogen.

hydrogenate ('haɪdrəʊdʒəneɪt, haɪ'drɒdʒəneɪt), *v. Chem.* [f. HYDROGEN + -ATE[3]. Cf. F. *hydrogéner.*] *trans.* To charge, or cause to combine, with hydrogen; to hydrogenize. Hence **hydrogenated, -ating** *ppl. adjs.*; also **hydroge'nation.**

1809 DAVY in *Phil. Trans.* XCIX. 464 Analogous to the hydrogenated sulphur of Berthollet. **1819** *Pantologia, Hydrogurets,*..in the writings of Berthollet, they are denominated Hydrogenated sulphurets. **1819** H. BUSK *Dessert* Notes 95 The excessive hydrogenation of the system. **1826** HENRY *Elem. Chem.* I. 158 De-oxidizing or hydrogenating rays. **1866** ODLING *Anim. Chem.* 89 Oxidation tends to the separation, hydrogenation to the conjunction of carbon atoms.

hydrogenator (haɪ'drɒdʒəneɪtə(r)). [f. HYDROGENAT(E *v.* + -OR.] A vessel or apparatus in which hydrogenation is carried out.

1914 C. ELLIS *Hydrogenation of Oils* xi. 192 The contents are thoroughly agitated and transferred to the hydrogenator where the actual hydrogenation takes place. **1963** *Times* 17 Jan. 7/1 The revolutionary feature of the gas recycle hydrogenator..is that it can produce high quality town gas solely from light petroleum distillate.

†**hydrogenetted** ('haɪdrəʊdʒəˌnɛtɪd), *a. Chem. Obs.* [f. HYDROGEN after *sulphuretted.*] Hydrogenated, hydrogenized.

1866 ODLING *Anim. Chem.* 114 Ammonia is the most thoroughly deoxidised, or rather hydrogenetted, compound of nitrogen.

hydrogenic (-'dʒɛnɪk), *a.* [f. as prec. + -IC.]

a. = HYDROGENOUS. *rare.*

1866 LAWRENCE tr. *Cotta's Rocks Class.* I. i. 63 Hematite ..is sometimes possibly a direct hydrogenic formation.

b. *Physics.* = *hydrogen-like* adj.

1935 CONDON & SHORTLEY *Theory Atomic Spectra* v. 137 Energy levels in hydrogenic atoms. **1960** J. C. SLATER *Quantum Theory of Atomic Struct.* I. viii. 190 The wave function of an electron in such a spherical field is very similar to the hydrogenic function given in Eq. (7-31). **1970** G. K. WOODGATE *Elem. Atomic Struct.* ii. 20 The equation therefore applies to all the hydrogenic atoms hydrogen, deuterium, tritium, muonium, positronium, etc.

hydrogeniferous (ˌhaɪdrəʊdʒə'nɪfərəs), *a. rare.* [f. as prec. + -(I)FEROUS.] (See quot.)

1855 MAYNE *Expos. Lex., Hydrogeniferus,* containing hydrogen; applied by Tondi to the sublimed sulphur of thermal springs; hydrogeniferous. **1886** in *Syd. Soc. Lex.*

hydrogenite (haɪ'drɒdʒənaɪt). [ad. F. *hydrogénite* (P. Mauricheau-Beaupré 1908, in *Compt. Rend.* CXLVII. 310), f. HYDROGEN + -ITE[1] 4 a.] Either of two powders formulated to provide a convenient and portable means of generating hydrogen: (*a*) a mixture of aluminium filings, mercuric chloride, and potassium cyanide; (*b*) a mixture of ferrosilicon, sodium hydroxide, and usually also calcium hydroxide.

1908 *Jrnl. Chem. Soc.* XCIV. II. 829 Aluminium filings are mixed with a small quantity of mercuric chloride and potassium cyanide in powder. The product, to which the name 'hydrogenite' is given, has D = 1·42. **1911** *Chem. Abstr.* V. 1499'Hydrogenite' is a compressible powder consisting of an alloy of Si and a base of soda lime, and when ignited by a suitable 'match' it reacts spontaneously..with the evolution of H. **1922** J. W. MELLOR *Comprehensive Treat. Inorg. & Theoret. Chem.* I. vii. 285 A mixture, devised by G. F. Jaubert (1910), containing 25 parts of 90–95 per cent. ferrosilicon or manganosilicon, 60 of sodium hydroxide, and 20 slaked lime, is commercially known as hydrogenite. **1963** G. S. BRADY *Materials Handbk.* (ed. 9) 678 A mixture of ferrosilicon and sodium hydroxide, called hydrogenite, which yields hydrogen gas when water is added, is used for filling balloons.

hydrogenium (haɪdrəʊ'dʒiːnɪəm). *Chem.* [f. as HYDROGEN + -IUM in names of new metals.] Hydrogen regarded as a metal, and, as such, capable of being absorbed or occluded by certain metals.

1868 T. GRAHAM in *Proc. Royal Soc.* (1869) XVII. 212 On the Relation of Hydrogen to Palladium. Examination of the properties of what, assuming its metallic character, would have to be named Hydrogenium. *Ibid.* 213 The density of hydrogenium then, appears to approach that of magnesium 1·743 by this first experiment. **1871** ROSCOE *Elem. Chem.* 186 Metallic palladium takes up no less than 982 volumes of hydrogen gas, forming a veritable alloy of the metal with hydrogenium, or hydrogen in its solid form.

hydrogenize ('haɪdrəʊdʒəˌnaɪz), *v. Chem.* [f. as prec. + -IZE.] *trans.* To charge, or combine with hydrogen. Hence '**hydrogenized** *ppl. a.*; '**hydrogenizing** *vbl. sb.* and *ppl. a.*

1802 HOWARD in *Phil. Trans.* XCII. 194 The oxide of nickel was precipitated by hydrogenized sulphuret of ammonia. **1866** ODLING *Anim. Chem.* 91 Alcohol is also procurable from acetic acid by the hydrogenising processes of Wurtz and Mendius. *Ibid.* 130 By hydrogenising alloxan we obtain dialuric acid. **1870** *Eng. Mech.* 25 Feb. 591/2 Coal or other hydrogenised gases.

hydrogenolysis (ˌhaɪdrədʒə'nɒlɪsɪs). *Chem.* [f. HYDROGEN + -O + LYSIS, after *hydrolysis.*] The splitting of a bond accompanied by the addition of an atom of hydrogen to the atoms originally bonded (one or both of these being carbon atoms).

1931 C. ELLIS *Hydrogenation Org. Subst.* xlv. 522 For reasons of convenience we shall use 'hydrogenolysis' for all processes in which fuel material is treated with hydrogen at high pressures and high temperatures... Another general term frequently used..is 'destructive hydrogenation'. **1932** *Jrnl. Amer. Chem. Soc.* LIV. 4685 The hydrogenolysis of carbon-carbon linkages. **1971** ANDERSON & BAKER in J. R. Anderson *Chemisorption & Reactions Metallic Films* II. viii. 189 The overall hydrogenolysis and disproportionation reactions may be represented by $CH_3NH_2 + H_2 \rightarrow CH_4 + NH_3$; $2CH_3NH_2 \rightarrow (CH_3)_2NH + NH_3$.

hydrogenous (haɪ'drɒdʒənəs), *a. Chem.* [f. HYDROGEN + -OUS.] Of, pertaining to, or consisting of hydrogen.

†*hydrogenous gas*, an early name for hydrogen; †*carbonated hydrogenous gas* = carburetted hydrogen; †*hydrogenous sulphurated gas* = sulphuretted hydrogen.

1791 HAMILTON *Berthollet's Dyeing* I. I. I. v. 81 Dr. Priestley obtained inflammable air, or hydrogenous gas. **1800** HENRY *Epit. Chem.* (1808) 321 Sulphuretted hydrogenous waters. **1802** *Med. Jrnl.* VIII. 522 That an animal died immediately on inspiring hydrogenous sulphurated gas. **1848** GROVE *Contrib. Sc.* in *Corr. Phys. Forces* 349 The differences between the hydrogenous and the other gases. **1878** NEWCOMB *Pop. Astron.* III. ii. 267 The structure of the hydrogenous protuberances.

hydrogeologist (ˌhaɪdrəʊdʒiː'ɒlədʒɪst). [f. HYDROGEOLOG(Y + -IST.] An expert in, or student of, hydrogeology.

1935 *Geogr. Jrnl.* LXXXV. 551, I might indicate a few lines of research which..require the services of hydrogeologists. **1964** *Discovery* Oct. 7/3 An FAO hydrogeologist..has put the importance of groundwater very high.

hydrogeology (ˌhaɪdrəʊdʒiː'ɒlədʒɪ). [mod. f. HYDRO- a + GEOLOGY: cf. F. *hydrogéologie.*] That part of geology which treats of the relations of water on or below the surface of the earth. Hence **hydrogeo'logical** *a.*, relating to this.

1824 R. WATT *Bibl. Brit.* III, Hydrogeology [referring to Lamarcke's *Hydrogéologie*]. **1855** MAYNE *Expos. Lex., Hydrogeologia,*..a branch of general physics which treats of the waters spread upon the surface of the earth: hydrogeology. **1877** *Academy* 3 Nov. 434/2 Hydrogeology is a term which Mr. J. Lucas has introduced to denote the relation of geological science to the important subject of water-supply. A hydrogeological survey would..examine into all facts which relate to the form, the position, and the capacity of subterranean water-systems. **1881** J. SOLLAS in *Nature* XXIV. 474 Physiological geology..includes Meteorology, hydro-geology.

hydrogogue, erroneous form of HYDRAGOGUE.

hydrograph ('haɪdrəgrɑːf, -æ-). [f. HYDRO- + -GRAPH.] †**1.** An instrument for transmitting sound under water and recording messages so received. *Obs. rare.*

1893 *Westm. Gaz.* 19 Oct. 7/3 (*heading*) Talking through the water. The wonders of the hydrograph.

2. A graph showing the variation of level, speed of flow, or another quantity at some point on a river. orig. *U.S.*

1897 *Monthly Weather Rev.* (U.S.) XXV. 129/1 Hydrographs for typical points on seven principal rivers are shown on Chart VI. **1936** *Water-Supply Paper U.S. Geol. Survey* No. 771. 71 Among the graphic devices that have been widely used in the study of stream-flow data is the hydrograph of discharge, which depicts the average flows by days,..years, or other time intervals. **1969** *Stud. & Rep. Hydrol.* I. 125 A linear distributed-system model..predicts a flood hydrograph from rainfall information and catchment characteristics.

hydrographer (haɪ'drɒgrəfə(r)). [This and the following words are 16th c. formations on Gr. ὕδωρ, ὑδρο- water, on the pattern of the corresponding *geographer, -graphic, -graphical, -graphy,* which came down through L. from actual Gr. formations. The immediate precursors of the English words were the Fr. *hydrographe* (1548), *hydrographique, -graphie* (1551).]

One skilled or practised in hydrography; *spec.* one whose business it is to make hydrographic surveys and to construct charts of the sea, its currents, etc., as the ***Hydrographer to the Admiralty***.

The first Hydrographer to the Navy was appointed in 1795.

1559 W. CUNNINGHAM *Cosmogr. Glasse* Table T ij, Shipmans compasse unknowne to the olde Hydrographers. **1570** DEE *Math. Pref.* 18 What way, the Tides and Ebbes, come and go, the Hydrographer ought to recorde. *c* **1675** J. SELLER *Coasting Pilot* title-p., Collected and Published by John Seller, Hydrographer in Ordinary to the King. **1697** DAMPIER *Voy.* (1729) I. 288 The South Sea must be of a greater breadth..than it's commonly reckoned by Hydrographers. **1795** *Admiralty Ord. in Council* 12 Aug. I. 124 We would humbly propose to Your Majesty that a proper person should be fixed upon to be appointed Hydrographer to this Board. **1835** SIR J. ROSS *Narr. 2nd Voy.* ii. 9 Captain Beaufort, the Admiralty hydrographer. **1880** W. B. CARPENTER in *19th Cent.* 609 All the best hydrographers..agree..that the Florida current dies out in the mid-Atlantic.

hydrographic (haɪdrəʊ'græfɪk), *a.* [See prec.] = next. ***Hydrographic Department*** (or ***Office***), the office of the Hydrographer to the Admiralty in Great Britain, and of the Navy Department in U.S.

In Great Britain the style *Hydrographic Department* has been used in the official Navy List since 1854, while in other official documents the title is *Hydrographical*.

1665 SIR T. HERBERT *Trav.* (1677) 24 Those dreadful flats of Death, where notwithstanding our Hydrographic cards.. we had doubtless been cast away. **1762** FALCONER *Shipwr.* II. 574 The..traverses..He on the hydrographic circle laid. **1854** *Navy List* 187 Hydrographic and Harbour Department, Rear Admiral Sir Francis Beaufort. **1860** MAURY *Phys. Geog. Sea* v. 106 These three rivers should all be regarded as belonging to one hydrographic basin. **1877** W. THOMSON *Voy. Challenger* I. i. 11 The Chart-room.. with ranges of shelves stocked with charts and hydrographic, magnetic, and meteorological instruments.

hydrographical (haɪdrəʊ'græfɪkəl), *a.* [See HYDROGRAPHER.] Pertaining or relating to hydrography. ***Hydrographical Department***: see prec.

1570 DEE *Math. Pref.* 23 The Heauenly Globe, may..be duely described vpon the Geographicall, and Hydrographicall Globe. **1610** HOLLAND *Camden's Brit.* II. 226 As we may see in their Hydrographicall Cards. **1680** MORDEN *Geog. Rect.* (1682) To Rdr. 2, Charts, Maps, Globes and all other Hydrographical and Geographical Descriptions. **1830** LYELL *Princ. Geol.* I. 185 The hydrographical basin of the Mississippi displays, on the grandest scale, the action of running water on the surface of a vast continent. **1862** *Admiralty Ord. in Council* 19 July II. 3 In the Chart Branch of the Hydrographical Department of Your Majesty's Navy. **1863** A. C. RAMSAY *Phys. Geog.* xi. (1878) 164 During the hydrographical survey of the Ægean Sea.

Hence **hydro'graphically** *adv. rare.*

1727 BAILEY vol. II, *Hydrographically*, by the Art of Hydrography.

hydrography (haɪ'drɒgrəfɪ). Also 6 hidro-. [See HYDROGRAPHER.]

1. The science which has for its object the description of the waters of the earth's surface, the sea, lakes, rivers, etc., comprising the study and mapping of their forms and physical features, of the contour of the sea-bottom, shallows, etc., and of winds, tides, currents, and the like. (In earlier use, including the principles of Navigation.) Also a treatise on this science, a scientific description of the waters of the earth.

1559 W. CUNNINGHAM (*title*) The Cosmographical Glasse, conteyning the pleasant Principles of Cosmographie, Geographie, Hydrographie or Nauigation. **1594** J. DAVIS *Seaman's Secr.* (1607) 47 Hidrography is the description of the Ocean Sea, with all Iles, bancks, rocks and sands therein contained. **1671** R. BOHUN *Wind* 260 Fournier (who is..skilfull in what relates to Hydrography) mentions an Inundation on the Coasts of America. *a* **1687** PETTY *Pol. Arith.* (1690) 62 Fournier in..his Hydrography hath laboured to prove the contrary of all this. **1727–41** CHAMBERS *Cycl.* s.v., Some of the best authors use the term in a more extensive sense; so as to denote the same with navigation. In this sense hydrography includes the doctrine of sailing; the art of making sea-charts, with the uses thereof [etc.]. **1772–84** COOK *Voy.* (1790) VI. 1973 He compleated the hydrography of the habitable globe. **1851–9** BEECHEY in *Man. Sci. Enq.* 17 Other curious and important facts in physical hydrography have been ascertained. **1898** *Pop. Sci. Monthly* LII. 552 The body of the work, to which the title of hydrography is applied, consists in the determination of existing water supply.

2. The subject-matter of this science; the hydrographical features of the globe or part of it; the distribution of water on the earth's surface.

1852 EARP *Gold Col. Austr.* 33 Capt. Stokes has added immensely to our knowledge of the hydrography of tropical Australia. **1882** *Times* 21 Sept. 3 The geography and hydrography of the ground must be studied.

†**3.** [Gr. γραφή, -γραφία writing.] Writing with water. (In quots. *fig.* with reference to tears.) *Obs.*

1649 G. DANIEL *Trinarch., Hen. V,* cxliii, More then a Man, and Mightier then a King; A Text of Honour, weak Hydrographie. *a* **1659** CLEVELAND *Wks.* (1687) 61 Whose Fate we see Thus copyed out in Grief's Hydrography.

†**hy'droguret.** *Chem. Obs.* [f. HYDROG-EN + -URET (after *sulphuret*).] A compound of hydrogen with another element; a hydruret or hydride.

1819 *Pantologia, Hydrogurets*, substances formed by the union of hydrogen gas with such combustible bodies as were deemed simple when the name was imposed. **1886** *Syd. Soc. Lex.* s.v., A hydroguret is usually designated by a name taken from the other substance of the combination, as the hydroguret of carbon is called *Carburetted hydrogen*.

So †**hy'droguretted** *a.*, chemically combined with hydrogen.

1806 DAVY in *Phil. Trans.* XCVII. 37 Solutions of hydroguretted sulphurets. **1826** HENRY *Elem. Chem.* I. 549 Hydrogureted sulphuret of potassa may be formed by boiling flowers of sulphur in liquid hydrate of potassa, or by digesting sulphur with the liquid hydro-sulphuret.

‖**hydrohæmia** (haɪdrəʊ'hiːmɪə). *Path.* [f. HYDRO- b + Gr. αἷμα blood.] = HYDRÆMIA.

1840 ANCELL *Lect. Blood* xix. in *Lancet* 1 Aug. 667/1 We may take another view of poverty of blood or hydrohæmia. *Ibid.*, In hydrohæmia the serum is in general transparent.

Hence **hydro'hæmic, -hemic** *a.* = HYDRÆMIC; also †**'hydrohemy** = hydrohæmia (Mayne *Expos. Lex.* 1855).

hydroid ('haɪdrɔɪd), *a.*, *sb.* [f. HYDRA 6 + -OID.] **A.** *adj. Zool.* Resembling or allied to the genus HYDRA of Hydrozoa. **a.** Belonging to the order or subclass *Hydroidea*, of which *Hydra* is the typical genus. **b.** Of the nature of a hydroid (see B. b): opposed to *medusoid*.

1864 in WEBSTER. **1867** J. HOGG *Microsc.* I. iii. 227 Hydroid zoophytes with expanded tentacles. **1877** HUXLEY *Anat. Inv. Anim.* iii. 132 Some medusoids..the hydroid stages of which are not..known. **1888** ROLLESTON & JACKSON *Anim. Life* 746 Colonies containing polymorphic hydroid individuals, and generally medusoid as well.

B. *sb.* **1.** *Zool.* **a.** A Hydrozoan belonging to the *Hydroidea*. **b.** One of the two forms of zooids occurring in Hydrozoa, resembling *Hydra* in structure, but typically asexual: opposed to *Medusa*.

1865 E. & A. AGASSIZ *Seaside Stud. Nat. Hist.* 21 Below these [Ctenophorae and Discophorae] come the Hydroids, embracing the most minute..of all these animals. **1880** *Libr. Univ. Knowl.* I. 332 The fixed hydroids and swimming jelly-fishes are alternate forms assumed by the successive generations of the same animal. **1888** ROLLESTON & JACKSON *Anim. Life* 745 The Hydroid is (1) a permanent locomotor sexual form, multiplying by gemmation, but only temporarily colonial,—*Hydra*: (2) a larval form which passes by a metamorphosis into a Medusa: (3) a non-sexual but permanent form, sometimes solitary, usually however multiplying by gemmation..giving origin to colonies: (4) a locomotor sexual form..never multiplying by gemmation.

2. *Bot.* [a. G. *hydroid* (H. Potonié 1883, in *Jahrb. K. Bot. Gartens Berlin* II. 243).] An element forming part of the HYDROME tissue of a plant.

1887 W. HILLHOUSE tr. *Strasburger's Handbk. Pract. Bot.* v. 58 The perfect wood-cells..consist only of dead cell-walls, and, as..they simulate the tracheæ, i.e. vessels, they are known as tracheïdes, more recently as hydroïdes. **1968** BELL & WOODCOCK *Diversity Green Plants* iv. 126 Surrounding a core of tracheid-like cells (sclereids), containing scattered thin-walled cells (hydroids), is a zone of cells conspicuously large in transverse section. **1971** E. V. WATSON *Struct. & Life Bryophytes* (ed. 3) ix. 126 Collectively these tissues are known as hadrom and leptom (analogues respectively of xylem and phloem) but the constituent elements are conveniently termed hydroids and leptoids.

hy'droidean. *Zool.* [f. mod.L. *Hydroidea* (see prec.) + -AN.] = HYDROID B. a.

1888 ROLLESTON & JACKSON *Anim. Life* 747 The existence of a free sexual Hydroidean—*Hydra*.

hydrokinetic (-kaɪ'nɛtɪk), *a.* [f. HYDRO- a + KINETIC.] Relating to the motion of liquids. So **hydroki'netical** *a.* in same sense; **hydroki'netics**, the kinetics of liquids; that branch of hydrodynamics (in the wider sense) which deals with the motion of liquids.

1873 MAXWELL *Electr. & Magn.* I. 367 The case of images in hydrokinetics when the fluid is bounded by a rigid plane surface. **1876** STEWART & TAIT *Unseen Univ.* 139 The hydrokinetic researches of Helmholtz.

hydrol ('haɪdrɒl). [f. HYDR- + -OL.] **1.** *Chem.* [f. BENZ)HYDROL.] Any substituted derivative of benzhydrol (diphenylcarbinol), $(C_6H_5)_2$ CHOH; *esp.* Michler's hydrol (see MICHLER).

1897 *Jrnl. Chem. Soc.* LXXII. I. 353 (*heading*) Condensation of hydrols with aromatic amines in presence of sulphuric acid. **1937** F. C. WHITMORE *Org. Chem.* 833 The dye intermediate, Michler's hydrol, is *pp'*-$(Me_2N)_2$-benzhydrol. **1956** E. H. RODD *Chem. Carbon Compounds* IIIB. xvii. 106 They are too unstable and reactive to be used as dyes but some of the hydrols are intermediates for the synthesis of triarylmethane dyes. **1971** R. L. M. ALLEN *Colour Chem.* viii. 111 The formaldehyde then condenses with two molecules of unchanged dimethylaniline, giving 4,4'bis(dimethylamino) diphenylmethane, and this is oxidised to the corresponding hydrol.

2. *Chem.* A name suggested for the simple water molecule, H_2O, as a basis for the systematic nomenclature of its polymers, $(H_2O)_n$.

1900 W. SUTHERLAND in *Phil. Mag.* L. 460, I propose for international convenience to call H_2O hydrol, $(H_2O)_2$ dihydrol, and $(H_2O)_3$ trihydrol. Steam is hydrol, ice is trihydrol, and water a mixture of dihydrol and trihydrol. **1915** W. M. BAYLISS *Princ. Gen. Physiol.* viii. 234 It is to be supposed that the molecular forces, which permit the molecules of hydrol to press unusually closely together [in water], disappear when the new group constituting ice is formed, so that the latter occupies the greater volume. **1957** G. E. HUTCHINSON *Treat. Limnol.* I. iii. 196 Sutherland (1900)..supposed liquid water to consist of dihydrol H_4O_2 with trihydrol H_6O_3 in solution... Other workers believed that hydrol H_2O was also present, at least near the boiling point.

3. [perh. f. HYDROL(YSIS.] A dark viscous liquid of unpleasant taste left as a mother liquor when starch is subjected to acid hydrolysis and dextrose is allowed to crystallize out.

1926 *Jrnl. Amer. Chem. Soc.* XLVIII. 2627 The fermentable part of 'hydrol' is chiefly *d*-glucose. **1953** *Jrnl. Assoc. Official Agric. Chemists* XXXVI. 457 Hydrol, or corn sugar molasses, is obtained as a by-product in the manufacture of dextrose from starch. **1954** I. A. PREECE *Biochem. Brewing* xi. 327 In badly attenuated beers there may be a notable amount of maltotriose present.., whilst if such material as hydrol is used as a sugar adjunct it may be expected to find some gentiobiose.

hydrolase ('haɪdrəleɪz, -eɪs). *Biochem.* [a. F. *hydrolase* (Battelli & Stern 1921, in *Arch. internat. de Physiol.* XVIII. 413), f. HYDROL(YSIS + -ASE.] Any enzyme which catalyses the hydrolysis of a substrate.

1922 *Jrnl. Chem. Soc.* CXXII. I. 1077 Ferments are divided into three groups..namely hydratases..; hydrolases producing esterification or hydrolysis; and oxydo-reductases. **1955** NEILANDS & STUMPF *Outl. Enzyme Chem.* xvi. 188 Lipases and phosphatases, being hydrolytic enzymes, logically fall into the group of hydrolases. **1970** W. H. FISHMAN *Metabolic Conjugation & Metabolic Hydrolysis* 373 The demonstration of the existence of latent hydrolases in the tadpole tail.

hydrolith ('haɪdrəʊlɪθ). [ad. F. *hydrolithe* (G. F. Jaubert), f. HYDRO- + Gr. λίθος stone.] A commercial name for calcium hydride as used as a convenient source of hydrogen (evolved when water is added).

1906 *Chambers's Jrnl.* 28 July 558/1 A new chemical compound somewhat akin to the calcium carbide familiar as a generator of acetylene gas has been placed on the market recently under the name of hydrolithe. **1967** G. D. PARKES *Mellor's Mod. Inorg. Chem.* xxx. 697 Calcium hydride..is a colourless, crystalline compound which has been used under the name of hydrolith for making hydrogen.

hydrologic (haɪdrəʊ'lɒdʒɪk), *a.* [f. mod.L. *hydrologia* (see HYDROLOGY) + -IC. Cf. F. *hydrologique*.] = next.

1887 B. E. FERNOW in *Pop. Sci. Monthly* Dec. 226 We.. consider the forests..as regulators of hydrologic conditions, influencing the waterflow in springs, brooks, and rivers.

hydrological (haɪdrəʊ'lɒdʒɪkəl), *a.* [f. as prec. + -AL[1].] Pertaining or relating to hydrology (senses 1, 2); relating to the properties of water, its distribution over the earth's surface, etc.

1670 W. SIMPSON (*title*) Hydrological Essayes; or a Vindication of Hydrologia Chymica, being a Further Discovery of the Scarborough Spaw, and the right use thereof. **1716** M. DAVIES *Athen. Brit.* III. Dissert. Physick 56 The Astrological and Hydrological Branches of Physick. **1828** in WEBSTER. **1882** *Edin. Rev.* Oct. 451 The summer and winter flow and other hydrological peculiarities of the English rivers. **1913** R. F. FOX *Princ. & Pract. Med. Hydrol.* p. xi, Several chapters are devoted to a discussion of the *indications* for hydrological treatment in different chronic ailments and diseases. *Ibid.* x. 106 A cardinal fact in hydrological medicine. **1921** *Oxf. Index Therap.* 452 It is convenient to consider hydrological treatment from two points of view. **1957** G. E. HUTCHINSON *Treat. Limnol.* I. iv. 221 (*heading*) The hydrological cycle and the water balance of lakes.

hydrology (haɪ'drɒlədʒɪ). [ad. mod.L. *hydrologia*, f. Gr. ὑδρο- water: see -LOGY. Cf. F. *hydrologie*.] **1.** The science which treats of water, its properties and laws, its distribution over the earth's surface, etc.

1762 tr. *Busching's Syst. Geog.* I. 49 Wallerius was the first who made accurate enquiries into the Aqueous Kingdom, or Hydrology. **1796** HUTTON *Math. Dict.*, *Hydrology*, is that part of natural history which examines and explains the nature and properties of water in general. **1866** *Proc. Amer. Phil. Soc.* X. 209 Mr. Blackwell's memoir entitled 'The Hydrology of the St. Laurence'. **1895** *Westm. Gaz.* 11 Sept. 7/2 The whole science of hydrology..depends on the study of rainfall.

2. *Med.* The branch of medicine concerned with treatment by baths and waters. *rare.*

[Cf. quots. 1670, 1716 s.v. HYDROLOGICAL *a.*] **1850** J. BELL (*title*) Dietetical and medical hydrology. A treatise on baths; ..with a description of bathing in ancient and modern times. **1913** R. F. FOX (*title*) The principles and practice of medical hydrology being the science of treatment by waters and baths.

Hence **hy'drologist** [cf. F. *hydrologue*], one skilled in hydrology.

1830 in MAUNDER *Dict. Eng. Lang.* **1938** *Times* 19 Feb. 13/2 With Papanin..on Franz Josef Land..were P. P. Shirshoff, a hydrologist and hydrobiologist, E. K. Federoff, [etc.]. **1971** *Nature* 30 July 301/1 Flood, erosion, drought and pollution..are also the chief problems facing the hydrologist.

hydrolube ('haɪdrəʊl(j)uːb). [f. HYDRO- + *lube*, repr. first syllable of *lubricant*.] Any of various non-flammable hydraulic fluids having water and a glycol as the principal constituents.

1944 *U.S. Naval Res. Lab. Rep.* P-2273. 23 Sprays of 'Hydrolube' fluids made from a polymer thickened mixture of ethylene glycol and water required over 80% oxygen to propagate a flame. **1947** *Ibid.* P-3020. 3 The name 'Hydrolube' was selected by this laboratory early in the war ..for any hydraulic fluid consisting of a polymer-thickened, corrosion-inhibited, aqueous solution having one or more glycols as major organic components. **1956** *Chem. & Engin. News* 3 Sept. 4245/3 The Navy..uses 'hydrolubes' in aircraft carrier catapult systems.

hydrolysable ('haɪdrəʊlaɪzəb(ə)l). *Chem.* Also (chiefly *U.S.*) -lyzable. [f. HYDROLYS(E *v.* + -ABLE.] Capable of being hydrolysed.

1908 *Jrnl. Chem. Soc.* XCIV. I. 199 (*heading*) Cacao butter, especially its non-hydrolysable constituents. **1913** *Jrnl. Amer. Chem. Soc.* XXXV. 629 Those esters which are most easily hydrolyzable with excess of alkali. **1946** L. E. WISE *Wood Chem.* vi. 150 The disaccharide..must be hydrolyzable by alkali. **1965** PHILLIPS & WILLIAMS *Inorg. Chem.* I. xiv. 522 The metals with basic oxides do not give readily hydrolysable salts.

hydrolysate (haɪ'drɒlɪseɪt). *Chem.* Also (chiefly *U.S.*) -lyzate. [f. HYDROLYS(E *v.* + *-ate*, after *filtrate*, *precipitate*, etc.] A product of, or preparation obtained by, hydrolysis.

1915 *Jrnl. Amer. Chem. Soc.* XXXVII. 1634 The hydrolysate in this instance was jet-black. **1944** L. F. & M. FIESER *Org. Chem.* xvi. 408 The determination of the proportion of the different amino acids present in a given protein hydrolyzate. **1964** *Oceanogr. & Marine Biol.* II. 149 Paper chromatography is a useful tool to establish the presence or absence of amino acids and other substances in hydrolysates and tissue extracts.

hydrolyse ('haɪdrəʊlaɪz), *v. Chem.* Also (chiefly *U.S.*) -lyze. [f. HYDROLYSIS, after *analyse*, *analysis*.] **1.** *trans.* To subject to hydrolysis; to decompose by hydrolysis.

1880 H. E. ARMSTRONG *Introd. Study Org. Chem.* (ed. 2) 190 *note*, The substance hydrolysed is the *hydrolyte*. **1902** *Westm. Gaz.* 6 Jan. 2/1 Grape sugar is formed by hydrolysing cellulose with acids. **1944** L. F. & M. FIESER *Org. Chem.* xvi. 404 Proteins are hydrolyzed by acid or alkali and by enzymes, and in the case of the simple, nonconjugated proteins, the products consist of mixtures of amino acids. **1955** *Sci. Amer.* May 37/1 When a peptide or protein is hydrolyzed—treated chemically so that the elements of water are introduced at the peptide bonds—it breaks down into amino acids. **1968** C. A. HAMPEL *Encycl. Chem. Elem.* 567/1 The trivalent praseodymium ion occurs as $[Pr(H_2O)n]^{3+}$ and is only weakly hydrolyzed in aqueous solutions. **1971** *Nature* 17 Sept. 209/1 Crude starfish extracts were hydrolysed with hydrochloric acid.

2. *intr.* To undergo hydrolysis.

1920 *Jrnl. Biol. Chem.* XLIII. 173 The gum hydrolyzes quantitatively into levulose. **1931** LEVENE & BASS *Nucleic Acids* vii. 195 Embden and Schmidt..compared the rates of hydrolysis of the three substances and found that the muscle adenylic and inosinic acids hydrolyze at about the same rate, whereas the other adenylic acid hydrolyzes much faster. **1951** C. R. NOLLER *Textbk. Org. Chem.* v. 79 Although highly toxic to animals, it hydrolyzes rapidly to harmless phosphoric acid and ethyl alcohol when exposed to moist air. **1964** N. G. CLARK *Mod. Org. Chem.* viii. 131 Tertiary halides hydrolyse most easily and primary halides are most resistant.

Hence **'hydrolysed** *ppl. a.*, **'hydrolysing** *vbl. sb.* and *ppl. a.*

1900 PERKIN & KIPPING *Org. Chem.* (rev. ed.) x. 188 The rapidity with which hydrolysis takes place depends..on the nature of the ethereal salt and of the hydrolysing agent. **1912** *Jrnl. Biol. Chem.* XII. 297 Osborne and Guest..obtained 59·2 per cent nitrogen in amino form in completely hydrolyzed gliadin. **1935** R. H. A. PLIMMER in Harrow & Sherwin *Textbk. Biochem.* v. 157 Arginine may be directly precipitated from the hydrolyzed solution of the protein. **1943** *Thorpe's Dict. Appl. Chem.* (ed. 4) VI. 388/2 An alcoholic solution of potassium hydroxide is sometimes used for hydrolysing purposes. **1973** *Daily Tel.* 16 Feb. 17/3 In a world of monosodium glutamate and hydrolised protein, her work is a living testimonial of a fine palate.

hydrolysis (haɪ'drɒlɪsɪs). [f. Gr. ὕδωρ, ὑδρο- water + λύσις dissolving, f. λύειν to dissolve.] Any reaction in which a bond is broken by the agency of water and the hydrogen and hydroxyl of the water become independently attached to the two atoms previously linked; the decomposition or splitting of a compound in this way. Also applied to the analogous decomposition of an organic compound by the action of an acid or alkali, and to any reaction between a water molecule and an ion that produces a hydrogen or hydroxyl ion.

1880 H. E. ARMSTRONG *Introd. Study Org. Chem.* (ed. 2) 190 *note*, Decompositions like those of starch into dextrose, of cane-sugar into dextrose and levulose..which involve the fixation of the elements of water, may all be said to be the result of *hydrolysis*, and those substances which, like sulphuric acid, diastase, emulsin, etc., induce hydrolysis, may be termed hydrolytic agents or *hydrolysts*. The substance hydrolysed is the *hydrolyte*. The mere fixation of the elements of water unaccompanied by decomposition.. may be termed *hydration* in contradistinction. **1890** *Athenæum* 27 Dec. 893/1 Other processes..already in constant use on very large scales..[are] bromination and chlorination, nitration, sulphonation with its concomitant hydrolysis. **1894** McGOWAN tr. *Bernthsen's Org. Chem.* 84 By saponification or hydrolysis of their ethers. **1900** PERKIN & KIPPING *Org. Chem.* (rev. ed.) x. 188 All ethereal salts are decomposed by water, mineral acids, and alkalies, the change..being spoken of as hydrolysis... $CH_3{\cdot}COOC_3H_7 + KOH = CH_3{\cdot}COOK + C_3H_7{\cdot}OH$. **1935** R. H. A. PLIMMER in Harrow & Sherwin *Textbk. Biochem.* v. 155 Hydrolysis of proteins to the amino acids is effected by boiling with acids, or alkalis, or by the action of the enzyme trypsin. **1938** C. D. HURD in H. Gilman *Org. Chem.* I. vii. 617 In reactions in which the C—N bond is severed by hydrolysis, it is universally characteristic for the nitrogen to attract the hydrogen of water, and carbon the oxygen or hydroxyl. **1948** GLASSTONE *Textbk. Physical Chem.* (ed. 2) xii. 986 The hydrolysis must then be represented by $M(H_2O)n^+ + H_2O \rightleftharpoons H_3O^+ + M(H_2O)n_{-1}OH$. **1950** P. J. DURRANT *Org. Chem.* xxix. 447 Many of the chemical reactions occurring in fermentation and in the metabolism of living organisms are hydrolyses. **1951** KIRK & OTHMER *Encycl. Chem. Technol.* VII. 741 The reaction of a nitrile with water to form an amide $CH_3CN + H_2O \rightarrow CH_3CONH_2$ is thought of as a hydrolysis, although it is also a hydration. **1964** N. G. CLARK *Mod. Inorg. Chem.* xi. 201 Hydrolysis [of nitriles] may be effected either by hot mineral acids..or by hot alkali... $CH_3{\cdot}CN + 2H_2O + HCl \rightarrow CH_3{\cdot}COOH +$

NH_4Cl... $CH_3{\cdot}CN + H_2O + NaOH \rightarrow CH_3{\cdot}COONa + NH_3$.

So **'hydrolyst** [cf. *analyst*], a hydrolytic agent; **hydrolyte** [Gr. λυτός that may be dissolved], a body subjected to hydrolysis.

See quot. 1880 above.

hydrolytic (haɪdrəʊ'lɪtɪk), *a.* [f. as prec. + λυτικ-ός having the property of dissolving; see prec.] Of or pertaining to hydrolysis.

1875 A. GAMGEE tr. *Hermann's Hum. Phys.* (1878) 224 The products of the hydrolytic decomposition of all the essential constituents of the body. **1878** FOSTER *Phys.* II. i. 186 The action.. is of such a kind as is effected by the agents called catalytic, and by that particular class of catalytic agents called hydrolytic. **1896** ALLBUTT *Syst. Med.* I. 520 Fermentation, like putrefaction, is a hydrolytic process.

hydro'lytically, *adv. Chem.* [f. HYDROLYTIC *a.*: see -ICALLY.] By means of hydrolysis; as regards hydrolysis.

1928 *Chem. Abstr.* XXII. 200 (*heading*) Ion exchange of zeolitic silicates with hydrolytically dissociated salts. **1963** F. M. DEAN *Naturally Occurring Oxygen Ring Compounds* v. 135 The furan ring can sometimes be opened hydrolytically. **1969** *Jrnl. Materials Sci.* IV. 432/2 These groups must be bonded to the silicon in a hydrolytically and thermally stable manner.

hydromagnetic (ˌhaɪdrəʊmæg'nɛtɪk), *a.* [f. HYDRO- (in *hydrodynamic*) + MAGNETIC *a.* (in *electromagnetic*).] Of, relating to, or involving an electrically conducting fluid (as a plasma or molten metal) acted on by a magnetic field.

1943 H. ALFVÉN in *Ark. f. Matem., Astr. och Fysik* XXIXB. II. 7 As the term 'electromagnetic-hydrodynamic waves' is somewhat complicated, it may be convenient to call the phenomenon 'magneto-hydrodynamic' waves. (The term 'hydromagnetic' is still shorter but not quite adequate.) **1955** *Proc. R. Soc.* A. CCXXXIII. 310 Hydromagnetic waves in rare ionized gases are of interest in connexion with galactic magnetic fields, the heating of the corona and other astrophysical problems. **1963** ALFVÉN & FÄLTHAMMAR *Cosmical Electrodynamics* (ed. 2) iii. 73 In the sun all phenomena which are large enough to be observed visually from the earth are hydromagnetic, and the same holds for interstellar clouds. **1966** FERRARO & PLUMPTON *Introd. Magneto-Fluid Mech.* (ed. 2) i. 13 It is this coupling between the electromagnetic and mechanical forces which characterizes hydromagnetic phenomena. **1973** *Nature* 9 Nov. 58/2 Nobody can yet give a hydromagnetic description of the process by which the neutron star captures the plasma.

Hence ˌ**hydromag'netically** *adv.*, from the point of view of hydromagnetics.

1970 *Nature* 4 Apr. 48/1 Warm plasmas are considered hydromagnetically.

hydromagnetics (ˌhaɪdrəʊmæg'nɛtɪks), *sb. pl.* (const. as *sing.*). [f. prec.: see -IC 2.] The branch of physics concerned with hydromagnetic phenomena; = MAGNETOHYDRODYNAMICS.

1953 T. G. COWLING in G. P. Kuiper *Sun* viii. 532 The subject of hydromagnetics is a new one. **1958** *New Scientist* 27 Feb. 12 The theory of an interaction like this, between a fluid and a magnetic field, is a central problem of the new science of hydromagnetics.

† **hydro'mance**. *Obs. rare*$^{-1}$. In 4 **ydromaunce**. [a. OF. *ydromance.*] = HYDROMANCY.

1390 GOWER *Conf.* III. 45 And of the flood his ydromaunce And of the fire the piromaunce.

† **'hydromancer**. *Obs.* [f. HYDROMANC-Y + -ER[1].] One who practises hydromancy.

c **1400** *Apol. Loll.* 96 þus are callid geomanceris, þat werkun bi þe ȝerþ. And idromauncers, þat þus wirkun bi þe watir. **1692** in COLES. Hence **1775** in ASH.

hydromancy ('haɪdrəʊmænsɪ). Also 5 **ydro-**, 6 **hidromancy**, 6–7 **hydromantie**, 7 **-ty**. [a. F. *hydromancie*, or ad. late L. *hydromantīa*, a. Gr. *ὑδρομαντεία, f. ὑδρο- water + μαντεία divination: see -MANCY.] Divination by means of signs derived from water, its tides and ebbs, etc., or the pretended appearance of spirits therein.

c **1400** MAUNDEV. (1839) xxii. 234 Pyromancye, Ydromancye.. and many other scyences. **1496** *Dives & Paup.* (W. de W.) I. xxxvi. 77/2 Ydromancye, that is wytchecrafte done in the water. **1594** R. ASHLEY tr. *Loys le Roy's Interchang. Var. Things* 50 a, Necromantie, Geomantie, Hydromantie. **1601** HOLLAND *Pliny* II. 631 As for Ananchitis, it is said, That spirits may be raised by it in the skill of Hydromantie. **1610** HEALEY *St. Aug. Citie of God* 293 Numa him-selfe.. was faine to fall to Hydromancie. **1777** BRAND *Pop. Antiq.* (1849) II. 377 A species of hydromancy appears to have been practised at wells. **1877** W. JONES *Finger-ring* 112 The 'suspended ring'.. is.. described by Peucer among various modes of hydromancy.

hydromania (haɪdrəʊ'meɪnɪə). [f. HYDRO- + MANIA; cf. F. *hydromanie.*] A mania or craze for water; *Path.* an excessive craving for water or liquids.

1793 SOUTHEY *Lett.* (1856) I. 17, I.. have discovered that the hydromania is almost as bad as the hydrophobia. **1835** *New Monthly Mag.* XLIV. 9, I have a hydromania in the way of lakes, rivers, and waterfalls. **1897** ALLBUTT *Syst. Med.* III. 248 In view of the almost insane craving ('hydromania') for fluid.. the question has been considered whether the diuresis could be controlled by placing limits on the amount of fluid ingested.

Hence **hydro'maniac**, a person affected with hydromania; **hydroma'niacal** *a.*, affected with hydromania.

1855 MAYNE *Expos. Lex.*, *Hydromaniacus*,.. hydromaniacal. **1860** PIESSE *Lab. Chem. Wonders* 54 Liable to be drowned in a flood of watery effusions from the modern hydromaniacs.

hydromantic (haɪdrəʊ'mæntɪk), *a.* and *sb.* [ad. med.L. *hydromantic-us*, f. Gr. ὑδρο- water + μαντικός prophetic: see -MANTIC. Cf. F. *hydromantique.*]

A. *adj.* Of or pertaining to hydromancy. ***hydromantic machine, vessel***: see quot. 1741.

1651 BIGGS *New Disp.* ¶ 157 Its own hydromantick vehicle. **1741** CHAMBERS *Cycl.* s.v., The writers in optics furnish us with divers hydromantic machines, vessels, etc. .. To make a hydromantic vessel, which shall exhibit the images of external objects, as if swimming in water.

† **B.** *sb. Obs.* **1.** = HYDROMANCY.

c **1590** GREENE *Fr. Bacon* ii. 16 To tell by thadroma[n]ticke, ebbes and tides.

2. One skilled or practised in hydromancy.

1638 SIR T. HERBERT *Trav.* (ed. 2) 215 Sorcerers, Inchanters, Hydro- and Pyro-mantiques.

So **hydro'mantical** *a.*, **hydro'mantically** *adv.*

1727 BAILEY vol. II, *Hydromantically*, by Hydromancy.

hydrome, hydrom ('haɪdrəʊm). *Bot.* [ad. G. *hydrom* (H. Potonié 1883, in *Jahrb. K. Bot. Gartens Berlin* II. 243), f. HYDRO- + *-ome* as in *rhizome*, etc.] The water-conducting section of a vascular bundle.

1900 B. D. JACKSON *Gloss. Bot. Terms* 273/1 Tracheome, stated by Potonié not to be the tracheal, but the hydral system of the bundle, he therefore names it Hydrome. **1911** J. M. COULTER et al. *Textbk. Bot.* II. iii. 682 The conductive portion of the xylem is known as *hadrome* (or *hydrome*). **1929** *Encycl. Brit.* XVII. 6/1 The hydrom strand is either slightly developed or altogether absent. **1969** K. ESAU *Phloem* viii. 268 The corresponding conducting cells are hydroids (from hydrom, part of hadrom consisting of conducting cells only).

hydromechanics (ˌhaɪdrəʊmɪ'kænɪks). [f. HYDRO- a + MECHANICS.] The mechanics of liquids; hydrodynamics (in its wider sense); esp. in relation to its application to mechanical contrivances.

1851 *Illustr. Catal. Gt. Exhib.* 94 Hydro-Mechanics, as Instruments to illustrate the Motion and Impinging Force of Waves, &c. **1884** *Science* 18 Jan. 78/2 The important place which.. hydromechanics has occupied in modern mathematical physics since the labors of Helmholtz, Maxwell, and Thomson, in reducing the mathematical treatment of electricity and magnetism to that of the motion of incompressible fluids.

So **hydrome'chanical** *a.*, of or pertaining to hydromechanics; relating to the employment of water in mechanical contrivances.

1825 J. NICHOLSON *Operat. Mechanic* 293 A hydro-mechanical engine, whereby a weight amounting to 2304 tons can be raised by a simple lever, through equal space, in much less time than could be done by any apparatus constructed on the known principles of mechanics. **1881** *Athenæum* 5 Mar. 339/1 Dr. O. J. Lodge showed two hydromechanical analogies of electricity.

hydromel ('haɪdrəʊmɛl). Also 5 **ydromel(le**, 6 **hydromell**, 7 **hidromel**. [a. L. *hydromel*, ad. Gr. ὑδρόμελι, f. ὑδρο- water + μέλι honey. With the earliest forms cf. OF. *ydromelle.*] A liquor consisting of a mixture of honey and water, which when fermented is called *vinous hydromel* or *mead*.

c **1400** *Lanfranc's Cirurg.* 83 A stynkynge wounde is heelid in remeuynge awey þe stinche & þe rotenes; & þerto is myche worþ a waischinge of ydromel: þat is hony & watir soden togidere wiþ mirre. **1563** T. GALE *Treat. Gonneshot* 2 b (Stanf.), Nitrum helpeth the Collicke if it bee taken with cummyne in hydromell. *c* **1645** HOWELL *Lett.* (1650) I. 367 In Russia, Moscovy and Tartary, they use Mead,.. this is that which the antients called hydromel. **1839** E. D. CLARKE *Trav. Russia* 18/1 The young man used to drink the Russian beverage of hydromel, a kind of mead. **1861** LD. LYTTON & FANE *Tannhäuser* 42 A fountain!—yea, but flowing deep With nectar and with hydromel.

hydrometer (haɪ'drɒmɪtə(r)). [mod. f. Gr. ὑδρο- water + -METER.

F. *hydromètre* (first recorded 1768) was app. adopted from English, but has commonly the sense 'rain-gauge', the hydrometer being called in F. *aréomètre*, ARÆOMETER.]

1. An instrument for determining the specific gravity of liquids, or sometimes (as in *Nicholson's Hydrometer*) for finding the specific gravity of either liquids or solids.

The common type consists of a graduated stem having a hollow bulb and a weight at its lower end, so as to float with the stem upright in a liquid, the specific gravity of which is indicated by the depth to which the stem is immersed. Special names are given to it as constructed for particular liquids, as *alcoholometer*, *acidimeter*, *lactometer*, etc.

Nicholson's Hydrometer consists of a brass cylinder having a small pan supported on a stem above the water and another pan dependent below in the water; the specific gravity of a solid body is calculated from the difference of its weights in air and in water, as determined by weighing it in the upper and lower pans respectively.

1675 BOYLE in *Phil. Trans.* Abr. II. 214 A New Easy Instrument (a Hydrometer). **1766** SMOLLETT *Trav.* xl. II. 245, I had neither hydrometer nor thermometer to ascertain the weight and warmth of this water. **1819** *Pantologia* s.v., Mr. Nicholson has made an improvement by which the hydrometer is adapted to the general purpose of finding the specific gravity both of solids and fluids. **1860** MAURY *Phys. Geog. Sea* v. §285 The hydrometer.. shows that the water of the North Atlantic is, parallel for parallel, lighter than water in the Southern Ocean. **1875** KNIGHT *Dict. Mech.* s.v., The most familiar hydrometer, to many, is a hen's egg, used by a farmer's wife to test the strength of lye for making soap.

2. An instrument used to determine the velocity or force of a current; a current-gauge.

1727–41 CHAMBERS *Cycl.*, *Hydrometer*, an instrument wherewith to measure the gravity, density, velocity, force, or other properties, of water. **1864** WEBSTER, *Hydrometer*,.. called by various specific names, according to its construction or use, as *tachometer*, *rheometer*, *hydrometric pendulum*, *Woltmann's mill*, etc.

‖ **hydrometra** (haɪdrəʊ'miːtrə). *Path.* [mod.L., f. Gr. ὑδρο- water + μήτρα womb. Cf. F. *hydromètre.*] An accumulation of watery mucous fluid in the cavity of the womb; dropsy of the uterus.

1811 in HOOPER *Med. Dict.* **1819** in *Pantologia.* **1872** F. G. THOMAS *Dis. Women* 256 A closure of the os internum uteri having been effected by adhesion, hydrometra exists.

hydrometric (haɪdrəʊ'mɛtrɪk), *a.* [f. as HYDROMETRY + -IC. Cf. F. *hydrométrique.*]

1. Of or pertaining to hydrometry, or to the determination of specific gravity by the hydrometer.

1828 in WEBSTER. **1860** MAURY *Phys. Geog. Sea* ix. §447 In order to weigh the seas in this manner, it is necessary that the little hydrometric balance by which it is to be done should be well and truly adjusted.

2. Relating to the measurement of the velocity and force of currents.

'***Hydrometric pendulum***, a current-gage. An instrument consisting of a ball suspended from the center of a graduated quadrant, and held in a stream to mark by its deflection the rate of motion of the water' (Knight *Dict. Mech.* 1875).

1864 in WEBSTER.

So **hydro'metrical** *a.* = prec.

1779 MANN in *Phil. Trans.* LXIX. 654 The hydrometrical principles laid down in this essay. **1807** P. JONAS (*title*) A Complete Set of Hydrometrical Tables.

hydrometry (haɪ'drɒmɪtrɪ). [ad. mod.L. *hydrometria*, f. Gr. ὑδρο- water + -μετρία measuring; cf. F. *hydrométrie.*] The determination of specific gravity by means of the hydrometer; hence, that part of hydrostatics which deals with this.

In early use the term seems to have been co-extensive with 'hydrodynamics' (in the mod. sense).

[**1727–41** CHAMBERS *Cycl.* s.v., Hydrometria includes both hydrostatics, and hydraulics.] *Ibid.*, In the year 1694.. a new chair, or professorship, of hydrometry, was founded in the university of Boulogna. **1796** HUTTON *Math. Dict.*, *Hydrometria*, *Hydrometry*, the mensuration of water and other fluid bodies, their gravity, force, velocity, quantity, etc.; including both hydrostatics and hydraulics. **1847** CRESY *Encycl. Civ. Engin.* I. iv. 207 A new chair was created for him [Dominico Guglielmini], under the title of that of Hydrometry, which, from that period, was accounted deserving of being ranked among the cultivated sciences.

‖ **hydronephrosis** (ˌhaɪdrəʊnɪ'frəʊsɪs). *Path.* [mod. f. Gr. ὑδρο- water + νεφρ-ός kidney + -OSIS.] A distended condition of the ureter, the pelvis, and the renal calices caused by an obstruction of the outflow of urine; dropsy of the kidney.

1847–9 TODD *Cycl. Anat.* IV. 81/2 Atrophy of the kidney with.. hydronephrosis. **1890** *Brit. Med. Jrnl.* 1299/1 Hydronephrosis in former times was treated by tapping.

So **hydronephrotic** (-nɪ'frɒtɪk) [f. prec.: cf. *amaurosis*, *amaurotic*] *a.*, relating to, characteristic of, or affected with hydronephrosis.

1866–80 A. FLINT *Princ. Med.* (ed. 5) 901 A very large hydronephrotic sac sometimes consists of a single cavity. **1891** *Lancet* 18 Apr. 885/1 Specimens of hydronephrotic kidneys.

hydronium (haɪ'drəʊnɪəm). *Chem.* [a. G. *hydronium* (A. Hantzsch 1907, in *Zeitschr. f. phys. Chemie* LXI. 306), contraction of HYDR(OX)ONIUM.] A name for the hydrated hydrogen ion (usu. represented as H_3O^+).

1908 *Jrnl. Chem. Soc.* XCIV. II. 15 Just as a molecule of ammonia may attach itself to a hydrogen ion, forming the ammonium ion NH_4, so it is supposed that a molecule of water may similarly attach itself, forming the 'hydronium' ion H_3O, so that a solution of a little water in sulphuric acid is a dissociated solution of hydronium sulphate. **1937** F. C. WHITMORE *Org. Chem.* 341 The effective catalyst is the hydronium ion, $(H_3O)^+$. **1940** *Jrnl. Chem. Soc.* 1410 When the hydrogen ion is considered to occur (in aqueous solution or in a compound) in the form $[H_3O]^+$, it is advisable to call it the hydronium ion (not hydroxonium ion). **1956** *Jrnl. Amer. Chem. Soc.* LXXVIII. 5999 (*heading*) The vibrational spectrum of the hydronium ion in hydronium perchlorate. **1959** *Nomencl. Inorg. Chem.* (*I.U.P.A.C.*) 26 The ion H_3O^+.. is to be known as the oxonium ion when it is believed to have this constitution, as for example in $H_3O^+ClO_4^-$, oxonium perchlorate. The widely used term hydronium should be kept for the cases where it is wished to denote an indefinite degree of hydration of the proton, as, for example, in aqueous solution. [*The latter sentence is dropped in ed. 2 (1971).*] **1966** *Mineral. Mag.* XXXV. 1071 The existence of the individual H_3O^+ pyramidal complex,

called the hydronium ion, or sometimes the hydroxonium or oxonium ion, in crystalline substances is a well-established fact.

hydropath (ˈhaɪdrəʊpæθ). [mod. (= G. *hydropath*, F. *hydropathe*) f. HYDROPATHY (cf. *allopath*, etc.).] = HYDROPATHIST.

1842 ABDY *Water Cure* (1843) 146 How different would have been my lot in this world, if this distinguished physician had been an hydropath himself thirty years ago! **1843** T. J. GRAHAM *Cold-Water System* (ed. 2) 5 There are not a few diseases in which the skilful physician will be far more successful by the use of medicine, and his other ordinary means, than the most perfect hydropath.

hydropathic (haɪdrəʊˈpæθɪk), *a.* (*sb.*) [f. HYDROPATH-Y + -IC.] Of, pertaining to, or of the nature of hydropathy; practising hydropathy.

1843 *Tait's Mag.* Apr. 271/1 When the cold-water cure was first heard of in this country, we prophesied.. that there would forthwith be numerous Hydropathic Establishments in England. **1851** *Illustr. Catal. Gt. Exhib.* 784 Hydropathic bandages. **1869** CLARIDGE *Cold Water Cure* Pref. 4 Hydropathic establishments are now to be found in England, Ireland, and Scotland, and in America. **1876** DARWIN in *Life & Lett.* (1887) I. ii. 81, I went in 1848 for some months to Malvern for hydropathic treatment.

B. *sb.* Short for *hydropathic establishment.*

1887 MISS BRADDON *Like & Unlike* xxiii, To go to a Hydropathic in the wilds of Scotland or Ireland. **1895** A. STODDART *J. S. Blackie* x. 240 Dull with villa lodgings and hideous hydropathics.

So **hydroˈpathical** *a.* = prec.

1844 DICKENS in Forster *Life* IV. i. 137, I had withdrawn from Public Life..to pass the evening of my days in hydropathical pursuits and the contemplation of virtue.

hydropathist (haɪˈdrɒpəθɪst). [f. as prec. + -IST.] One who practises or advocates hydropathy.

1847 (*title*) Hints to the Sick, the Lame, and Lazy, or Passages in the Life of a Hydropathist, by a Veteran. **1853** *Fraser's Mag.* XLVIII. 287 The family doctor—he was an hydropathist. **1885** *Manch. Exam.* 18 Feb. 3/2 Treatment.. proved serviceable and sanative by practical hydropathists.

hydropathize (haɪˈdrɒpəθaɪz), *v.* [f. as prec. + -IZE.] *intr.* To practise hydropathy.

1855 GEO. ELIOT *Ess.* (1884) 319 People who only allow themselves to be idle under the pretext of hydropathising. **1859** DARWIN in *Life & Lett.* (1887) II. 172, I am here hydropathising and coming to life again.

hydropathy (haɪˈdrɒpəθɪ). [mod. (= G. *hydropathie*), f. HYDRO-, on analogy of *allopathy*, *homœopathy*, the second element of these words having been vaguely apprehended as = 'treatment' or 'cure' of disease.] A kind of medical treatment, originated in 1825 by Vincenz Preissnitz at Gräfenberg in Germany, consisting in the external and internal application of water; the water-cure.

1843 SIR C. SCUDAMORE *Med. Visit Gräfenberg* 1 On hydropathy, or the water-cure treatment. **1858** DARWIN in *Life & Lett.* (1887) II. 112 On Tuesday I go for a fortnight's hydropathy. **1869** CLARIDGE *Cold Water Cure* Pref. 3 Hydropathy was practised at Gräfenberg..twenty years before it was known in England.

hydrophane (ˈhaɪdrəfeɪn). *Min.* [mod. f. Gr. ὑδρο- water + -φανής apparent, φανός bright, clear, f. φαίνειν to show.] A variety of opaque or partly translucent opal which absorbs water upon immersion and becomes transparent.

1784 KIRWAN *Elem. Min.* 114 Opals and chalcedonies, which by admitting water within their pores, are called hydrophanes. **1833** N. ARNOTT *Physics* (ed. 5) I. 36 The stone called hydrophane (agate) is opaque, until dipped into water, when it absorbs..one sixth of its weight of the water, and..gives passage to light. **1875** BLACKMORE *Alice Lorraine* III. xxiii. 306 Changed its dullness (like a hydrophane immersed) into glancing and reflecting play of tender light and life.

hydrophanous (haɪˈdrɒfənəs), *a. Min.* [f. prec. + -OUS: cf. *diaphanous.*] Having the property of becoming transparent by immersion in water, as certain opals.

1794 SULLIVAN *View Nat.* I. 362 The *oculus mundi*, or hydrophanous stone, steeped in water..will..become by that means more transparent than otherwise. **1831** BREWSTER *Newton* (1855) I. viii. 185 The colours of Labrador felspar, and of precious and hydrophanous opal, which we have shewn to be produced by thin plates and minute pores and tubes.

†**hydroˈphantic.** *Obs. rare.* [f. Gr. ὑδροφαντικ-ή discovery of water, f. ὑδρο- water + -φαντης manifester, f. φαίνειν to show.] A water-finder.

1729 SWITZER *Hydrost. & Hydraul.* 79 Hydrophanticks, or Dicoverers of Water.

hydrophil (ˈhaɪdrəfɪl), **-phile** (-faɪl), *a.* [f. HYDRO- + -PHIL.] = HYDROPHILIC *a.*

1903 *Electrician* 30 Oct. 42/1 He applied two electrodes.., contact being made by means of hydrophil cotton impregnated with a 1 per cent solution of zinc chloride. **1915** W. W. TAYLOR *Chem. Colloids* i. 7 The term lyophile has been applied to those systems in which there is marked affinity between the phases, and lyophobe to the others. When water is the dispersion medium the terms hydrophile and hydrophobe are commonly used. **1930** J. ALEXANDER *Colloid Chem., an Introd.* (ed. 3) iii. 39 Colloids of the reversible type are..said to be hydrophile or lyophile, while the irreversible colloids are hydrophobe or lyophobe. **1963** A. J. HALL *Textile Sci.* i. 10 Synthetic fibres are made from organic hydrophobic (water-repellent) polymers—the natural fibres are hydrophile (water-attractive). *Ibid.* 13 The hydrophile fibre wool..contains about 18% of moisture in its ordinary air-dry state. **1971** *Nature* 12 Feb. 489/2 The outer walls of the respiratory trumpets of mosquito pupae are hydrophil while the inner lining is hydrophuge.

hydrophilia (haɪdrəˈfɪlɪə). *rare.* [f. HYDRO- + Gr. φιλία fondness.] A love of being near water.

1904 G. S. HALL *Adolescence* II. xii. 195 Others..can sit by the hour, seeing and hearing the movements of water in sea or stream. The best demonstration of the fact of this hydrophilia is the amount of cold..that it will overcome. **1959** *Times Lit. Suppl.* 31 July 450/4 A symptom of the derangement of sober, law-abiding citizens succumbing to hydrophilia is public confession... These very readable confessions can infect hardened land-lubbers with sea fever.

hydrophilic (haɪdrəˈfɪlɪk), *a.* [f. HYDRO- + Gr. φίλ-ος loving + -IC.] **a.** Having an affinity for water, readily absorbing water; relating to such an affinity.

1901 *Buck's Handbk. Med. Sci.* (ed. 2) III. 694/1 The ear should be very carefully dried out, as of course the effectiveness of this solution depends upon the hydrophilic properties of the materials employed. **1954** KIRK & OTHMER *Encycl. Chem. Technol.* XIII. 919 The hydrophilic fibers can absorb and transfer water, and as such they are not naturally water-repellent. **1963** R. R. A. HIGHAM *Handbk. Papermaking* ii. 37 Because of the natural affinity of cellulose for water, paper is termed hydrophilic (water-receptive). **1971** *Nature* 19 Nov. 126/3 Attached to their hydrocarbon tails phospholipid molecules also..have hydrophilic head groups.

b. *spec.* in *Physical Chem.* [after Fr. *hydrophile* (J. Perrin 1905, in *Jrnl. de Chim. phys.* III. 85)]: applied to a hydrosol that does not readily form a precipitate, and to a gel that readily forms a sol on the addition of water or on being warmed.

1915 M. H. FISCHER tr. *Ostwald's Handbk. Colloid-Chem.* ii. 50 Different names are employed in the literature for these two sets of colloids... J. Perrin [calls them] 'hydrophilic' and 'hydrophobic' colloids. **1936** J. H. PARSONS *Dis. Eye* (ed. 8) xvi. 322 It has all the properties of a hydrophilic gel, undergoing turgescence in an alkaline, deturgescence in an acid aqueous medium. **1948** GLASSTONE *Textbk. Physical Chem.* (ed. 2) xiv. 1235 Sols of gums, starches, proteins and soaps, provide instances of hydrophilic systems. **1967** M. E. HALE *Biol. Lichens* iv. 53 The imbibition of water by a hydrophilic gel.

Hence **hydrophiˈlicity**, hydrophilic quality.

1953 *Chem. Abstr.* XLVII. 9035 'Hydrophil[ic]ity' is defined as the ratio, by wt. of the hydrophilic to hydrophobic groups in the same mol. **1970** R. D. SWISHER *Surfactant Biodegradation* ii. 32 The nonionic hydrophilic groups have a multiplicity of elements..which have a cumulative effect; increasing their numbers in the group increases the hydrophilicity of the aggregate.

hydrophilite (haɪˈdrɒfɪlaɪt). *Min.* [Named 1869 from Gr. ὑδρο- + φίλ-ος loving + -ITE: from its affinity for water.] Native calcium chloride; chlorocalcite.

1875 in DANA *Min.* App. ii.

hydrophilous (haɪˈdrɒfɪləs), *a.* [f. as prec. + -OUS.] Water-loving. **a.** Applied to certain insects.

1855 MAYNE *Expos. Lex.*, *Hydrophilus*,..applied by Moehring to a Family (*Hydrophilæ*) corresponding to those which Illiger names *Hygrobatæ*; loving or frequenting water: hydrophilous.

b. *nonce-wd.* Fond of a watering-place.

1855 *Fraser's Mag.* LI. 259 The crowded rendezvous of fastidious fashionables and hydrophilous ennui.

c. *Bot.* Of plants, dependent upon water as the agency of pollination or dissemination of seeds; formerly = *hydrophytic* (see quot. 1898).

1883 D. W. THOMPSON tr. *Müller's Fertilisation of Flowers* III. 567 The plants of this order [*sc.* Naiadaceæ] are anemophilous or hydrophilous. **1898** POUND & CLEMENTS *Phytogeogr. Nebraska* I. iii. 67 Hydrophilous fungi..are algae-like aquatic fungi. **1902** *Encycl. Brit.* XXV. 437/1 Dissemination is effected by the agency of water, of air, of animals—and fruits and seeds are therefore grouped in respect of this as hydrophilous, anemophilous, and zooidophilous. **1920** A. ARBER *Water Plants* xviii. 235 Certain plants, however, present transitional methods of pollination, which without being actually hydrophilous, show approaches to this state. **1967** C. D. SCULTHORPE *Biol. Aquatic Vasc. Plants* ix. 248 The ultimate adaptation to aquatic life is the formation of wholly submerged hydrophilous flowers. **1973** PROCTOR & YEO *Pollination of Flowers* viii. 283 Among the most specialised of all hydrophilous species are the Eelgrasses (*Zostera*).

hydrophily (haɪˈdrɒfɪlɪ). *Bot.* [f. HYDRO- + Gr. φιλία friendship.] Pollination by the agency of water.

1920 A. ARBER *Water Plants* xviii. 236 The family Hydrocharitaceae..includes within itself all stages in the transition from entomophily to hydrophily. **1967** C. D. SCULTHORPE *Biol. Aquatic Vasc. Plants* ix. 249 The probable affinities of these few specialised plants support the belief that hydrophily and marine life are both recently acquired habits. **1973** PROCTOR & YEO *Pollination of Flowers* viii. 277 The adaptations to pollination by water (*hydrophily*) are diverse, so that it is hardly possible to speak of a syndrome of hydrophily.

hydrophobe (ˈhaɪdrəfəʊb), *sb.* and *a.* [a. F. *hydrophobe*, ad. L. *hydrophob-us*, Gr. ὑδροφόβος having a horror of water, f. ὑδρο- water + φόβος fear, dread.] **A.** *sb.* **1.** One suffering from, or affected with, hydrophobia.

2. A hydrophobic substance.

1924 H. FREUNDLICH in R. H. Bogue *Theory & Applic. Colloidal Behavior* I. xii. 320 The dyestuff sols..are so little affected by alkali salts that they cannot be classed as true hydrophobes. **1970** R. D. SWISHER *Surfactant Biodegradation* ii. 31 As an example of hydrophobes which are not derived from hydrocarbons we can cite the polyoxypropylenes.

B. *adj.* = HYDROPHOBIC *a.* 2.

1915, 1930 [see HYDROPHIL, -PHILE *a.*]. **1970** R. D. SWISHER *Surfactant Biodegradation* vi. 207 Increased distance between the sulfonate group and the far end of the hydrophobe group increases the speed of primary biodegradation of ABS and possibly of other surfactant types.

hydrophobia (haɪdrəˈfəʊbɪə). In 6 *erron.* **hidroforbia**, and anglicized 7–8 **hydrophoby** (haɪˈdrɒfəbɪ). [a. L. *hydrophobia* (Cælius Aurelianus *c* 420), a. Gr. ὑδροφοβία (in Celsus, A.D. 50) horror of water, rabid disease, f. ὑδροφόβος (see prec.).]

1. *Path.* A symptom of rabies or canine madness when transmitted to man, consisting in an aversion to water or other liquids, and difficulty in swallowing them; hence the disease of rabies, esp. in human beings.

1547 BOORDE *Brev. Health* 122 *Hidroforbia* or abhorynge of water... This impediment doth come..of a melancoly humour. **1621** BURTON *Anat. Mel.* I. i. I. iv, The most knowne are these, *Lycanthropia, Hydrophobia, Chorus sancti viti.* **1646** SIR T. BROWNE *Pseud. Ep.* IV. xiii. 231 *margin*, Upon the biting of a mad dog there ensues an hydrophobia or fear of water. **1752** *Phil. Trans.* XLVII. 412 Isaac Cranfield..was received into the infirmary..with an hydrophobia upon him. **1837** M. DONOVAN *Dom. Econ.* II. 95 Its [Mus giganteus] bite is dangerous, and sometimes produces hydrophobia. **1838** *Penny Cycl.* XII. 399/2 *Hydrophobia*,..is the disease caused by inoculation with the saliva of a rabid animal, and is so called from the violent and suffocating spasms of the throat which occur when the patient attempts to drink. **1893** H. DALZIEL *Dis. Dogs* (ed. 3) 96 Man inoculated by the rabie virus of a mad dog suffers from the terrible disease called popularly hydrophobia, from a dread of water and inability to swallow liquids being a main feature of the malady, but more accurately the disease is known in man also as rabies.

β. **1601** HOLLAND *Pliny* II. 322 That symptome of hydrophobie or fearing water, incident to those that be bitten with a mad dog. *a* **1711** KEN *Anodynes* Poet. Wks. 1721 III. 432 He whom Hydrophoby infests, Fair Water of all things detests. **1767** GOOCH *Treat. Wounds* I. 199 Before the appearance of the Hydrophoby or other symptoms of madness.

2. In etymological sense: Dread or horror of water. Also *fig.* madness.

1759 STERNE *Tr. Shandy* II. ix, What then..must the terror and hydrophobia of Dr. Slop have been! *a* **1772** HUME *Let.* in Haldane *Life Adam Smith* (1887) iii. 34, I am mortally sick at sea, and regard with..a kind of hydrophobia the great gulf that lies between us. **1802** *Morning Post* in *Spirit Pub. Jrnls.* (1803) VI. 161, I'm raving with a French hydrophoby. **1816** COLERIDGE *Lay Serm.* 317 The hydrophobia of a wild and homeless scepticism. **1834** MEDWIN *Angler in Wales* I. 86 For my part I have a hydrophobia: you will scarcely get me to wet my feet.

3. The property of a substance of being hydrophobic.

1956 *Soil Sci.* LXXXII. 163 All treated powdered clays had to overcome an initial hydrophobia which took place during the first few minutes of contact with water. **1958** J. J. BIKERMAN *Surface Chem.* (ed. 2) iii. 239 At a first approximation, hydrophoby may mean good miscibility with benzene and poor miscibility with water.

Hence **hydroˈphobial, -ˈphobious** *adjs.*, hydrophobic; **hydroˈphobiac, -ˈphobian**, one suffering from hydrophobia.

1662 J. CHANDLER *Van Helmont's Oriat.* 280 One..said, that old man was now Hydrophobial or had the Disease causing the fear of water, and to have been lately bitten by a mad dog. *Ibid.* 282 The madness..doth forthwith arise, and the Hydrophobians are left without hope. **1800** *Med. Jrnl.* IV. 58 Hydrophobial patients..generally die in strong convulsions. **1843** *Fraser's Mag.* XXVII. 177 Poodle-dogs in the highest state of hydrophobious fury. **1883** L. WINGFIELD *A. Rowe* II. vii. 176 What a pity he might not smother her like a hydrophobiac!

hydrophobic (haɪdrəˈfɒbɪk, -ˈfəʊbɪk), *a.* (*sb.*) [ad. L. *hydrophobic-us*, a. Gr. ὑδροφοβικ-ός: see prec. and -IC. Cf. F. *hydrophobique* (OF. *ydroforbique*)] **A.** *adj.* **1.** Of or pertaining to hydrophobia; suffering from or affected with hydrophobia.

1807 *Med. Jrnl.* XVII. 348 Out of these eleven, five died hydrophobic. *a* **1815** A. FULLER in Spurgeon *Treas. Dav.* Ps. cxxxix. 14 The hydrophobic saliva. **1887** *19th Cent.* Aug. 200 The number of hydrophobic deaths.

2. a. Tending to repel, or not to absorb, water; pertaining to such a lack of affinity.

1938 A. D. WHITEHEAD tr. *Jordan's Technol. Solvents* i. 13 This group have a pronounced solvent power for non-polar or weakly polar, that is hydrophobic, materials. **1947** *Jrnl. Res. Nat. Bureau of Standards* (U.S.) XXXVIII. 106/1 It is common practice..to treat fabrics intended to be water repellent with various hydrophobic compounds. **1954** KIRK & OTHMER *Encycl. Chem. Technol.* XIII. 919 With hydrophobic fibers, fabric structure to a large degree will control water repellency. **1963** [see HYDROPHIL, -PHILE *a.*]. **1967** E. CHAMBERS *Photolitho-Offset* xiv. 205 The image is oleophilic (ink-accepting) and hydrophobic (water-

rejecting), making an excellent imaging material for an offset lithographic plate.

b. *spec.* in *Physical Chem.*: applied to a hydrosol that readily forms a precipitate and on evaporation or cooling gives a solid that cannot readily be converted back into a sol.

1915 [see HYDROPHILIC *a.* b]. **1948** GLASSTONE *Textbk. Physical Chem.* (ed. 2) xiv. 1235 Typical examples of hydrophobic sols are those of metals, sulfur, sulfides and sulfur halides.

B. *sb.* One affected with hydrophobia.

1864 *Daily Tel.* 3 Aug., The cruel superstition that a human hydrophobic can legally be smothered.

So **hydro'phobical** *a.* = prec.; **hydropho'bicity**, hydrophobic quality.

1650 W. CHARLETON *Ternary of Paradoxes* cxlviii. 77 The primitive and genuine Phansy of all the blood in the wounded body.. compulsively assumes the Hydrophobicall phansy of the Exotick Tincture. **1656** BLOUNT *Glossogr.*, *Hydrophobical.* **1947** *Jrnl. Res. Nat. Bureau of Standards* (U.S.) XXXVIII. 105/1 The difference between these two energies will depend upon the relative humidity, the hydrophobicity of the surface,..etc. **1963** A. J. HALL *Textile Sci.* ii. 63 These newer fibres have several different and useful properties which are associated with their increased hydrophobicity. **1969** *Nature* 15 Feb. 637/2 A quantitative treatment for comparing the average hydrophobicities of proteins.

hydrophobist (haɪ'drɒfəbɪst). [f. HYDROPHOBIA + -IST.]

1. One who treats cases of hydrophobia.

1855 W. WHITE *Suffolk Direct.* 740 Underwood Dan, Farmer and Hydrophobist.

2. One who has a dread of or aversion to water.

1840 *Blackw. Mag.* XLVIII. 215 A learned hydrophobist addressing himself to those whom he styles the Antichristian Sect, vulgarly and illiterately calling themselves tea-totalers. **1898** *Voice* (N.Y.) 31 Mar. 4/1 The hydrophobists who hurled whisky bottles against the sides of the Kentucky, as she was launcht.

hydrophobous (haɪ'drɒfəbəs), *a.* [f. L. *hydrophob-us* (see HYDROPHOBE) + -OUS.]

1. = HYDROPHOBIC.

1684 tr. *Bonet's Merc. Compit.* VIII. 262 The canine madness quickly shews it self in the Hydrophobous. **1789** MRS. PIOZZI *Journ. France* II. 309 Smothered up in down.. like an hydrophobous patient. **1842** DE QUINCEY *Mod. Greece* Wks. 1890 VII. 339 If we should suddenly prove hydrophobous in the middle of this paper.

2. Having a dread of water. (Cf. HYDROPHOBIA 2.)

1748 tr. *V. Renatus' Distemp. Horses* 298 Sometimes Horses are afraid of Water, and such are said to be Hydrophobous.

†**hy'drophoby.** *Obs.* Anglicized form of HYDROPHOBIA, q.v.

hydrophone ('haɪdrəfəʊn). [f. HYDRO- a + Gr. -φωνος, f. φωνή voice, sound, on analogy of *microphone*, etc.] An instrument for the detection of sound by water; also of water, or of something in water, by sound. **a.** A bag containing water, placed between the stethoscope and the chest, to intensify the sounds heard in auscultation. **b.** (See quot. 1887.) **c.** An instrument devised to give warning by electricity to a port or fleet of the approach of a hostile vessel.

1860 *N. Syd. Soc. Year Bk. Med.* 59 A water-bag increases the impression conveyed to the ear by the wooden stethoscope if it be placed between the flat ear-piece and the external ear. The name of hydrophone has been given to it. **1862** H. W. FULLER *Dis. Lungs* 76 Another form of instrument, introduced by Dr. Scott Alison, and termed by him a 'hydrophone'. **1887** *Engineering* 29 July 131 The hydrophone.. is a clever little instrument devised to detect any water escapes from the mains or service pipes, cocks or closets. **1893** *Daily News* 8 June 5/8 Captain McEvoy's hydrophone.. in connection with a new instrument named a kinesiscope.. has for its object the prevention of surprise attacks from torpedo boats, or other hostile vessels, approaching anchorages or mine fields.

hydrophoran (haɪ'drɒfərən), *a.* and *sb.* *Zool.* [f. mod.L. *Hydrophor-a* (f. HYDRA + Gr. -φόρος bearing) + -AN.]

A. *adj.* Belonging to the *Hydrophora*, one of the three sub-classes of Hydrozoa, comprising *Hydra* and compound forms bearing zooids similar to Hydra. **B.** *sb.* One of the *Hydrophora*. So **hy'drophorous** *a.*, related to the *Hydrophora*.

hydrophore ('haɪdrəʊfɔə(r)). [ad. Gr. ὑδροφόρ-ος water-carrying.] An instrument for procuring specimens of water from any desired depth, in a river, lake, or ocean.

1842 D. STEVENSON *Marine Surveying & Hydrometry*, An apparatus, (to which I have applied the name of the hydrophore). **1842** *Mech. Mag.* XXXVI. 307 When the hydrophore is to be used, it is lowered to the required depth by the pole, which is fixed to its side. **1864** in WEBSTER.

‖**hydrophthalmia** (ˌhaɪdrɒf'θælmɪə). *Path.* Also (anglicized) '**hydrophˌthalmy**. [f. HYDRO- b + OPHTHALMIA.] 'Expansion of the whole eye with increase of its fluid contents' (*Syd. Soc. Lex.*). Hence **hydroph'thalmic** *a.*, 'of or belonging to hydrophthalmia' (Mayne *Expos. Lex.* 1855).

1706 PHILLIPS (ed. Kersey), *Hydrophthalmy*, a Disease of the Eye, when it grows to a wonderful bigness, and starts almost out of the Head. **1784** E. FORD in *Med. Commun.* I. 409 Cases of hydrophthalmia.

hydrophyte ('haɪdrəfaɪt). *Bot.* [ad. Da. *hydrophyt*, mod.L. *hydrophyta* (J. F. Schouw *Grundtræk til en almindelig Plantegeographie* (1822) 132), f. Gr. ὑδρο- water + φυτόν plant.] An aquatic plant, or one needing a waterlogged environment for its growth.

1832 LYELL *Princ. Geol.* II. 72 The number of hydrophytes, as they are termed, is very considerable. **1857** BERKELEY *Cryptog. Bot.* §63. 81, I shall.. consider Algals, or Hydrophytes, as forming the first grand group. **1858** A. GRAY *Introd. Struct. & Syst. Bot.* 536 *Hydrophyte*: a water-plant. **1880** GRAY *Struct. Bot.* (ed. 6) 415/2 Hydrophytes.. Water-plants. **1894** F. W. OLIVER et al. tr. *Kerner's Nat. Hist. Plants* I. 75 It is usual to designate all plants that grow in water as hydrophytes or water-plants. **1920** A. ARBER *Water Plants* i. 3 The ultimate term in the acceptance of aquatic conditions is reached in certain hydrophytes with submerged flowers, in which even the pollination is aquatic. **1967** C. D. SCULTHORPE *Biol. Aquatic Vasc. Plants* v. 147 Experimental data on the water relations of submerged hydrophytes do not lend themselves to generalisation.

Hence **hydro'phytic** *a.*; **hydrophy'tography**, the description of aquatic plants; **hydrophy'tology**, the branch of botany which deals with aquatic plants.

1847 CRAIG, *Hydrophytology.* **1855** MAYNE *Expos. Lex.*, *Hydrophytography.* **1905** F. E. CLEMENTS *Res. Methods Ecol.* iv. 209 The effect of these conditions is to produce a plant xerophytic as to its aerial parts, and mesophytic or even hydrophytic as to subterranean parts. **1934** *Discovery* XV. 11/1 Suitable protection [for mosquitoes] may be furnished by grass or other hydrophytic vegetation. **1955** G. M. SMITH *Cryptogamic Bot.* (ed. 2) II. v. 97 As the mat [of vegetation] becomes drier.. the *Sphagnum* eventually disappears and the hydrophytic angiosperms are replaced by those of a more mesophytic type. **1973** *Nature* 12 Jan. 88/2 A halophytic vegetation covered the basin during the past century with a hydrophytic woodland forming in the first quarter of the present century.

‖**hydrophyton** (haɪ'drɒfɪtɒn). *Zool.* [f. as prec.] The branched plant-like structure supporting the zooids in certain colonial Hydrozoa.

1885 *Athenæum* 28 Mar. 412/1 In this [*Thuiaria heteromorpha*] are found combined on the same hydrophyton no fewer than three morphological types which, if occurring separately, would be justly regarded as representing three genera. **1888** ROLLESTON & JACKSON *Anim. Life* 245 The hydranths are lodged in perisarcal cups or *hydrothecæ* (= *calycles*) and are borne by a supporting plant-like structure or *hydrophyton*. This hydrophyton.. is divisible into a system of stems with branches, the *hydrocaulus*, and of rooting fibres, the *hydrorhiza*, by which the colony is attached to some foreign object.

Hence **hy'drophytous** *a.*, having the character of a hydrophyton.

hydropic (haɪ'drɒpɪk), *a.* and *sb.* Forms: 4–6 **ydropike**, 5 **ydropycke**, **idropik**, 6 **-ique**, **edrop(p)ic**, 6–8 **hydropick**, 7– **hydropic**. [ME. a. OF. *ydropique*, *-ike* (12th c.), ad. L. *hydrōpic-us*, a. Gr. ὑδρωπικ-ός, f. ὕδρωψ, ὑδρωπ- HYDROPS. In 16th c. conformed to the L.: so F. *hydropique*.]

A. *adj.* **1.** = DROPSICAL 1, 2.

1483 CAXTON *Gold. Leg.* 428b/1 One parfytelye ydropycke or fylled with dropsy. **1536** BELLENDEN *Cron. Scot.* (1821) II. 109 His wambe.. wes swolin, as he had been edroppic [*printed* edroppit]. **1589** PUTTENHAM *Eng. Poesie* III. xxv. (Arb.) 306 The hydropick and swelling gowte. **1651** CLEVELAND *Poems* 49 Like an Hydropick body ful of Rhewms. **1752** BERKELEY *Further Th. Tar-water* Wks. III. 505 This medicine.. is to hydropic patients a strong purge. **1784** JOHNSON *Let.* 9 Sept. in *Boswell*, Of the hydropick tumour there is now very little appearance. **1802** *Med. Jrnl.* VIII. 354 Some hydropic symptoms appeared, which gradually increasing in the form of an ascites or hydrothorax [etc.]. **1822–34** *Good's Study Med.* (ed. 4) III. 327 When the general hydropic enlargement.. began to increase.

†**2.** Having an insatiable thirst, like a dropsical person; hence *fig.* *Obs.*

13.. *E.E. Allit. P.* B. 1096 Drye folk & ydropike. **1430–40** LYDG. *Bochas* VII. viii. (Bodl. MS. 263) lf. 354b/2 This excessif Glotoun Moste Idropik drank ofte ageyn lust; The mor he drank, the mor he was athrust. **1648** *Eikon Bas.* vi. (1824) 39 If some mens hydropick insatiablenesse had not learned to thirst the more by how much more they drank. *a* **1763** SHENSTONE *Econ.* I. 172 Thy voice, hydropic fancy! calls aloud For costly draughts.

3. Charged or swollen with water; swollen.

1651 JER. TAYLOR *Serm. for Year* I. xxvii. 349 It.. swels like an hydropick cloud. **1651** OGILBY *Æsop* (1665) 33 The Hydropic Kingdoms of the Bog. **1695** BLACKMORE *Pr. Arth.* x. 439 Dark Clouds.. hang their deep Hydropick Bellies down. **1880** GUNTHER *Fishes* 122 The young.. remain in an undeveloped condition, assuming an hydropic appearance.

†**4.** Tending to cause dropsy. *Obs. rare.*

1657 R. LIGON *Barbadoes* (1673) 32 So unwholsome and Hydropick he conceived this drink to be.

†**5.** Having the quality of curing dropsy. *Obs.*

1684 tr. *Bonet's Merc. Compit.* VIII. 299 Astringents and Strengthners are always mixt with Hydropick Medicines. **1710** T. FULLER *Pharm. Extemp.* 13 Hydropic Ale.

B. *sb.* **1.** A dropsical person. Now *rare.*

1549 *Compl. Scot.* xv. 126 Thai may be comparit to the edropic, the quhilk the mair that he drynk the mair he hes desire to drynk. *a* **1655** VINES *Lord's Supp.* (1677) 221 No physician would reach water to an hydropick that earnestly thirsts for it. **1755** *Phil. Trans.* XLIX. 47 This recovery was much talked of, and set all the hydropics a rubbing. **1891** C. E. NORTON tr. *Dante, Hell* xxx. 166 And the hydropic, 'Thou sayest true in this'.

2. A medicine for the cure of dropsy.

1694 SALMON *Bates' Disp.* I. (1713) 61/1 It is a Diuretick Medicament, and a specifick Hidropick. **1721** BAILEY, *Hydropicks*, Medicines which expel watery Humours in the Dropsy.

hydropical (haɪ'drɒpɪkəl), *a.* Now *rare.* (Very common in 17th c.) [f. L. *hydropic-us* (see prec.) + -AL[1].]

1. = prec. A 1.

c **1550** LLOYD *Treas. Health* (1585) M vij, Wyne that Isope hath sodden in being dronke, burneth yᵉ hydropical humors. **1612** WOODALL *Surg. Mate* Wks. (1653) 172 An Hydropicall inflation of the whole body. **1670** MAYNWARING *Vita Sana* vi. 81 One puffs up, fills, and grows hydropical. **1748** HARTLEY *Observ. Man* I. i. 47 It.. may arise from a hydropical Disposition.

2. = prec. A 2.

1656 PRYNNE *Demurrer Jews' Remitter* 23 An Hydropical thirster after gold. **1799** *Ann. Reg.* 113 A hydropical increase of avarice.

b. Of thirst: Unquenchable.

1607 WALKINGTON *Opt. Glass* xi. (1664) 120 A Saltish Nature.. in the Ventricle, causeth an Hydropical thirst. **1791** NEWTE *Tour Eng. & Scot.* 385 This hydropical hunger and thirst after the earth.

3. = prec. A 3.

1649 J. TAYLOR (Water P.) *Wand.* 7 Mine Host often did visit me with most delightfull and hydropicall non-sense. **1658** SIR T. BROWNE *Hydriot.* iii. 44 Who would expect a quick flame from Hydropicall Heraclitus? **1684** *Phil. Trans.* XIV. 769 Filled with too great a quantity of aqueous and undigested sap, as it were hydropical.

Hence **hy'dropically** *adv.*, with or as with dropsy; dropsically.

1646 SIR T. BROWNE *Pseud. Ep.* II. iii. 73 Such as be hydropically disposed. **1663** BP. PATRICK *Parab. Pilgr.* xxxv. (1668) 437 All Histories.. are so hydropically swollen with lying Legends.

hydropisy, obs. form of HYDROPSY.

hydroplane ('haɪdrəpleɪn), *sb.* [f. HYDRO- + PLANE *sb.*[3] (in sense 2, after *aeroplane*).]

1. A movable horizontal plane (usually one of several) projecting from the side of a submarine and used to control movement in a vertical plane and to provide stability during motion under water.

1901 *Submarine Torpedo Boats* (Lake Torpedo Boat Company) 19 The depth of submergence beneath the surface is maintained nearly constant by hydroplanes, one or more on each side of the vessel. **1902** *Sci. Amer.* 22 Nov. 346/2 While submerged.. the boat has a reserve buoyancy, and in order to totally submerge it is necessary to employ the hydroplanes. **1907** S. LAKE in *Trans. Inst. Naval Archit.* XLIX. 39 The practicability of navigating on the bottom and of opening a door for the purpose of conducting mining operations, &c, together with the hydroplanes, were the features most questioned in connection with my plans for a submarine torpedo-boat submitted to the U.S. Government in 1893. **1911** *Encycl. Brit.* XXIV. 921/1 Another technical point in the design of submarines.. is the desirability or otherwise of 'bow-rudders' or 'hydroplanes'. **1919** *Jane's Fighting Ships* 118 They.. have large rudder and hydroplane areas and small reserve of buoyancy for quick diving and rapid handling. **1954** K. C. BARNABY *Basic Naval Archit.* (ed. 2) vi. 93 In the submerged condition, there usually remains a small excess of buoyancy... This is overcome by means of the horizontal diving rudders or 'hydroplanes'.

2. A motor boat designed to skim the surface of the water by means of a bottom that consists in part of one or more flat surfaces sloping upwards towards the bow. Also ***hydroplane boat***.

1904 *Sci. Amer.* 8 Oct. 250/3 Hydroplanes—new forms of gliding boats. This name, formed on the analogy of aeroplane, is suggested for vessels which, instead of floating in water, glide over its surface as sleighs glide over ice. **1907** *Engineering* 4 Oct. 457/2 (*heading*) The Crocco and Ricaldoni hydroplane boat. **1909** *Westm. Gaz.* 5 Jan. 4/2 We have exhibited marked enterprise in regard to the hydroplane. **1909** *Ibid.* 9 Mar. 4/1 The Alla-Va, a hydroplane boat having more than ordinary pretensions to speed, has been placed in the unrestricted racer class. **1913** W. OWEN *Let.* 28 Sept. (1967) 199 Hydroplanes are in the habit of planing over the [River] Garonne. **1936** E. G. BARRILLON in W. F. Durand *Aerodynamic Theory* VI. 137 In a hydroplane in motion, the water does not act by static pressure alone, but also by a.. dynamic force analogous to that on the wings of an airplane. **1957** *Times* 8 Nov. 10/3 [Mr. Donald Campbell's] hydroplane Bluebird, which is powered by a Metropolitan-Vickers jet engine, was timed over the measured kilometre at 260·107 m.p.h. **1965** R. SHECKLEY *Game of X* (1966) xviii. 127 The hydroplane climbed out of the water, balancing on her two sponsons.

†**3.** = HYDRO-AEROPLANE, SEAPLANE. *Obs.* exc. *Hist.*

1911 *Daily Colonist* (Victoria, B.C.) 9 Apr. 1/1 Glenn Curtiss, the aviator, gave a successful exhibition of his new hydroplane on the surface of Salt Lake this afternoon, ascending from and descending upon the water. **1913** W. S. CHURCHILL in *Hansard Commons* 17 July 1501 We have decided to call the naval hydroplane a seaplane, and the ordinary aeroplane or school machine, which we use in the Navy, simply a plane. **1913** *Q. Rev.* Apr. 471 For reconnaissance, the work is better done by hydroplanes costing a few hundreds apiece. **1914** *Daily Express* 19 Sept. 3/4 His flights in a hydroplane attracted the attention of the King at Weymouth a couple of years ago. **1969** K. MUNSON *Pioneer Aircraft 1903–14* 161/2 Two other intermediate designs of 1907 were another airship, the No. 16, and a

wingless hydroplane, the No. 18, which underwent taxying tests on the Seine.

hydroplane (ˈhaɪdrəpleɪn), *v.* [f. prec. sb.] *intr.*
1. a. To travel in a hydroplane boat.
1909, 1918 [see *hydroplaning* vbl. sb. below].
b. To skim the surface of the water by the use of hydroplanes.
1914 *Techn. Rep. Advisory Comm. Aeronaut. 1912–13* 237 The machine at once hydroplaned on leaving its shed. **1928** C. F. S. GAMBLE *Story N. Sea Air Station* i. 32 Having succeeded in making his machine hydroplane on her floats. **1936** J. GRIERSON *High Failure* v. 91 Once one is hydroplaning it is much easier to go on accelerating until flying-speed is gained. **1938** C. WINCHESTER *Wonders World Aviation* I. 39 When the seaplane has gathered sufficient speed it climbs over its own wave and so hydroplanes or skims along the surface.
2. Of a motor vehicle, etc.: to aquaplane. Chiefly *U.S.*
1962 *Daily Tel.* 17 May 17/5 Flooding on the Kingston by-pass caused a car travelling at speed to 'hydroplane' and ..turn completely round. **1969** C. CAMPBELL *Sports Car* (ed. 3) vii. 179 Aquaplaning (hydroplaning in America)..is in effect a high-speed skating of the tyre on a film of water when travelling on wet roads. **1973** R. HAYES *Hungarian Game* xxviii. 164 The 707 skipped once as its wheels hydroplaned on the wet runway.
So **ˈhydroplaning** *vbl. sb.*
1909 *Westm. Gaz.* 5 Jan. 4/3 It is due entirely to its performance at Southampton that hydroplaning has gained recognition in this country. **1918** *Chambers's Jrnl.* 20 July 541/1 The water..provides the finest possible field for motor-boating in small craft, and, I should imagine, for hydroplaning. **1922** *Encycl. Brit.* XXX. 50/2 Hydroplaning efficiency..could be sacrificed for sea-worthiness. **1938** C. WINCHESTER *Wonders World Aviation* I. 37 Running on the step is the expression used to describe the hydroplaning of a seaplane on the surface of the water. **1969** [see sense 2 above].

hydro-pneumatic (ˌhaɪdrəʊnjuːˈmætɪk), *a.* (*sb.*) [f. HYDRO- a + PNEUMATIC: in F. *hydro-pneumatique*.] Pertaining to water and air or gas; applied to apparatus involving the combined action of water and air.
Originally applied to the method of collecting and retaining gas over water in the pneumatic trough, invented by Cavendish about 1765.
1794 PEARSON in *Phil. Trans.* LXXXIV. 399 In close vessels, with the hydro-pneumatic apparatus affixed. **1812** SIR H. DAVY *Chem. Philos.* 35 Mr. Cavendish, about 1765, invented an apparatus for examining elastic fluids confined by water, which has been since called the hydro-pneumatic apparatus. **1815** W. CONGREVE (*title*) A Description of the Construction and Properties of the Hydro-Pneumatic Lock. **1816** J. TILLEY in *Philos. Mag.* XLIII. 280 Description of a Hydro-Pneumatic Blow-pipe for the use of Chemists [etc.]. **1851** *Illustr. Catal. Gt. Exhib.* 222 New hydro-pneumatic engine. The..water pressure to drive the piston..in one direction, and a vacuum being produced, to make.. atmospheric pressure to drive it in an opposite direction. *Ibid.* 311 Hydro-pneumatic lift, for canal locks. Hydro-pneumatic elevators. **1884** *Mil. Engineering* (ed. 3) I. II. 40 Guns mounted on hydro-pneumatic (disappearing) carriages.
B. *sb. pl.* Hydro-pneumatic appliances.
1887 *Pall Mall G.* 27 Dec. 11/2 The application of hydro-pneumatics in substitution for counterweights was protected by letters patent, granted to Col. Moncrieff in 1869.

hydropneumonia (ˌhaɪdrəʊnjuːˈməʊnɪə). *Path.* [f. HYDRO- b + PNEUMONIA.] Dropsy or œdema of the lungs.
1886 in *Syd. Soc. Lex.*

hydroponics (ˌhaɪdrəʊˈpɒnɪks). [f. HYDRO- + Gr. πόνος work: see -IC 2.] The process of growing plants without soil, in beds of sand, gravel, or similar supporting material flooded with nutrient solutions. Hence **hydroˈponic** *a.*, **hydroˈponically** *adv.*; **hydroˈponicist**, one who practises hydroponics; **hydroˈponicum**, the building or garden in which hydroponics is practised.
1937 W. F. GERICKE in *Science* 12 Feb. 178/1 'Hydroponics', which was suggested by Dr. W. A. Setchell, of the University of California, appears to convey the desired meaning better than any of a number of words considered. **1938** *California Monthly* Feb. 13/2 My first planting..was set in the hydroponicum on September 18, 1936. *Ibid.* 40/3 The important factors..must be understood by the hydroponicist, as they must be understood by the successful gardener. **1940** *Times* 20 Apr. 1 (Advt.), Hydroponics (crops without soil)..easy if you use Gromost hydroponic mixture. **1940** *Manch. Guardian Weekly* 17 May 394/4 Hydroponics received a great impetus in the United States shortly after the trans-Pacific air line was established. **1951** A. C. CLARKE *Sands of Mars* viii. 94 The local brew..was completely synthetic—the joint offspring of hydroponic farm and chemical laboratory. **1951** J. S. DOUGLAS *Hydroponics* iii. 30 A farm or garden devoted to soilless cultivation is usually called a hydroponicum. **1955** *Sci. News Let.* 30 Apr. 282/3 Chemical gardening or hydroponics makes a favorite exhibit. **1956** *Jrnl. Brit. Interplanetary Soc.* XV. 20 As hydroponicists have pointed out, soil is in no way a perfect medium. **1961** *Astronautica Acta* VII. 134 Men have survived over extended periods on hydroponically produced plant food. **1967** *Technology Week* 23 Jan. 48/1 Water and minerals from the Moon can be used to grow food hydroponically. **1970** *New Scientist* 5 Feb. 259/3 The potential of hydroponics..is only just beginning to be tapped. **1971** *Daily Colonist* (Victoria, B.C.) 13 May 1/4 Hydroponic grass has produced encouraging results with dairy herds, increasing their milk yield. **1973** *Listener* 13 Sept. 338/2 Growing vegetables like aubergines and sweet corn and green peppers hydroponically—that is, without soil.

hydropot (ˈhaɪdrəʊpɒt). [ad. mod.L. *hydropota*, ad. Gr. ὑδροπότης water-drinker: in mod.F. *hydropote*.] A water-drinker; an abstainer from alcoholic drinks.
[**1727–41** CHAMBERS *Cycl.*, *Hydropota*, in medicine, a person who drinks nothing but water.] **1727** BAILEY Vol. II, *Hydropote*, a Water-Drinker. **1885** *Pall Mall G.* 19 Dec. 3 The momentous change from 'taking wine as an article of food', and becoming a hydropot.
So †**hydroˈpotic, -ˈopotist** *Obs. rare*⁻⁰, in same sense.
1623 COCKERAM, *Hydropoticke*, one that still drinkes water. **1678** PHILLIPS (ed. 4) *List Barbarous Words, Hydropotist*, a water-drinker.

hydropower (ˈhaɪdrəʊpaʊə(r)). Also **hydro-power** (with hyphen) and as two words. [f. HYDRO- (in *hydro-electric*) + POWER *sb.*[1]] Hydro-electric power.
1933 F. F. FOWLE *Stand. Handbk. Electr. Engineers* (ed. 6) xiii. 1295 (*heading*) Steam power and its relation to hydro power. **1946** *Nature* 3 Aug. 160/1 The inexhaustible nature of hydro-power. **1969** *New Scientist* 18 Sept. 565/1 In the north western states..fossil fuel is expensive and nearly all potential hydropower sites have already been exploited. **1971** *Sci. Amer.* Sept. 157/3 Tidal energy and other forms of hydropower.

‖**hydrops** (ˈhaɪdrɒps). Now only *Path.* Also 4 **ydrope.** [L. *hydrōps, hydrōp-em*, a. Gr. ὕδρωψ dropsy, a derivative of ὕδωρ, ὑδρ- water. With *ydrope*, cf. OF. *idropie*.] Dropsy.
c **1375** *Sc. Leg. Saints, Alexis* 523 Of ydrope of parlesy he heylyt syndry. **1706** PHILLIPS (ed. Kersey), *Hydrops*, the Dropsie. **1771** J. FOOT *Penseroso* III. 116 High-floated by the hydrops ceas'd to breathe. **1866–80** A. FLINT *Princ. Med.* (ed. 5) 34 The term hydrops signifies a serous effusion, usually in a cavity. **1878** T. BRYANT *Pract. Surg.* I. 542 Hydrops antri..is characterised by a gradual painless expansion of the bone.

hydropsy (ˈhaɪdrɒpsɪ). Forms: 4–5 **id-, ydropisie, -esie, -esy(e, ydropsi(e, -cy,** 5–6 **hidropsie, -ecye, (ydropsi, 6 idropisé, -ycé, -esie; hie-, hyedropsy),** 6–7 **hydropsie, (7 -pisie),** 6– **hydropsy.** [ME., a. OF. *idro-, ydropisie* (12th c.), = Sp. *hidropesia*, It. *idropesia*, med.L. (*h*)*ydrōpisīa* (*ydropicia* in Simon Januensis, *c*1300) for L. *hydrōpisis* (Pliny), a. Gr. *ὑδρώπισις, f. ὕδρωψ, ὑδρωπ-, HYDROPS. Formerly stressed *hyˈdropesie, hyˈdropsy* (not yet obs.) whence the aphetic *dropesie*, DROPSY, found from the first appearance of the word in Eng., and perh. due in part to coalescence of the initial short vowel with *the* in *þe ydropesie, th' idropesie, the dropesie*.]
Dropsy.
a **1300** *Cursor M.* 11829 Ydropsi [*Fairf.* dropecy, *Trin.* dropesy] held him sua in threst, þat him thoght his bodi suld brest. *c* **1380** WYCLIF *Serm.* Sel. Wks. I. 42 Ydropesie is an yvel of fals gretenesse of mennys lymes. *c* **1400** *Lanfranc's Cirurg.* 84 An yuel disposicioun of al þe bodi as ydropisie [*B.* dropsye]. **1542** BOORDE *Dyetary* xxxviii. (1870) 299 The more a man doth drynke that hath the Idropise, the more he is a thurst. **1552** LYNDESAY *Monarche* 5109 Sum fallis in to frynasie, Sum deis in Idropesie. **1578** LYTE *Dodoens* II. lxvii. 234 Such as begin to fall into the Hydropsie. **1665** *Lond. Gaz.* No. 1/2 An Hydropsie attended with a Flux. **1748** THOMSON *Cast. Indol.* I. lxxv, Of limbs enormous, but, withal unsound, Soft-swoln and pale, here lay the Hydropsy. **1826** SCOTT *Jrnl.* 19 Mar., Her asthmatic complaints are fast terminating in hydropsy. **1879** *St. George's Hosp. Rep.* IX. 769 Operative measures in hydropsies.
Hence †**hyˈdropsic** *a. Obs. rare*, hydropic, dropsical.
1649 JER. TAYLOR *Gt. Exemp.* II. Ad § 12. 51 Like drinke to an hydropsick person.

hydroptic (haɪˈdrɒptɪk), *a. Obs.* exc. *arch.* [Erroneously f. HYDROPSY, after such pairs as *epilepsy, epileptic*.] = HYDROPIC, dropsical.
a **1631** DONNE *Lett.* (1651) 51 An hydroptique immoderate desire of humane learning and languages. **1640** BP. REYNOLDS *Passions* xl. 520 The distemper of an Hydropticke Body. **1661** *Sir A. Haslerig's Last Will* 2 My hydroptick Thirst is quenched. **1855** BROWNING *Grammar. Fun.* 95 Soul-hydroptic with a sacred thirst.
So †**hyˈdroptical** *a. Obs.*, in same sense.
1640 BP. REYNOLDS *Passions* xvii. 187 These Desires are Hidropticall. **1657** TOMLINSON *Renou's Disp.* 202 To help the Hydroptical..Patients.

hydroquinone (haɪdrəʊˈkwaɪnəʊn). *Chem.* Also **-chinon(e, -kinone.** [f. HYDRO(GEN + QUINONE.] A diatomic phenol, $C_6H_4(OH)_2$, prepared from quinone, $C_6H_4O_2$, by reduction with sulphurous acid, crystallizing from water in colourless rhombic prisms. Now used as a developer in photography.
1865–72 WATTS *Dict. Chem.* III. 213 *Hydroquinone, Hydrochinone, Hydrokinone*... Colourless Hydroquinone (Pyroquinole), $C_6H_6O_2$..is the chief product of the dry distillation of quinic, carbohydroquinonic, and oxysalicylic acids. *Ibid.*, Green Hydroquinone or Quinhydrone.. $C_6H_6O_2.C_6H_4O_2$,..may be regarded..as a compound of quinone and colourless hydroquinone. **1889** *Anthony's Photogr. Bull.* II. 171 Hydroquinone, or more shortly quinol, will be the developer of the future. **1893** *Brit. Jrnl. Photog.* XL. 795 The development was effected with hydroquinone, as giving a blacker tone.

hydrorrhœa, -rhea (haɪdrəʊˈriːə). *Path.* [mod. ad. Gr. ὑδρόρροια flow of water, water-course.] A copious watery discharge.
1857 BULLOCK *Cazeaux' Midwif.* 306.

†**hydrosacre.** *Obs.* In 5 **ydro-.** [ad. (through OF.) med.L. *hydrosaccharum*, f. Gr. ὕδωρ, ὑδρο- water + σάκχαρον sugar.] A syrup made of sugar and water.
c **1400** *Lanfranc's Cirurg.* 139 (MS. B.) Y gaf hym to drynke hot ydrosacre, þat ys y-mad of sugre & of watyre.

hydroscope (ˈhaɪdrəʊskəʊp). [mod. ad. Gr. ὑδροσκόπ-ος (f. ὑδρο- water + -σκοπος -SCOPE) water-seeker, well-sinker, and ὑδροσκόπιον water-clock (Synesius). In F. *hydroscope* water-searcher.]
†**1.** An instrument for the detection of moisture in the air; a hygroscope. *Obs.*
1678 PHILLIPS (ed. 4), *Hydroscope*, a certain Instrument.. for discerning of the Watry volatil streams in the Air. **1721** in BAILEY. Hence in Mod. Dicts.
2. A kind of water-clock. *Hist.*
It consisted of a cylindrical graduated tube, filled with water, which trickled through an aperture in the conical bottom, and marked by its subsidence the successive hours.
1727–41 in CHAMBERS *Cycl.* **1809** *Naval Chron.* XXI. 375 The chief part of this machine is a hydroscope.

hydroscopist (haɪˈdrɒskəpɪst). [f. as prec. + -IST: in F. *hydroscope* (1798 in *Dict. Acad.*).] A water-diviner; a dowser.
1885 *Eng. Mech.* 20 Nov. 232 The..mystery which appertains to the general run of hydroscopists and workers with the divining rod.

hydroskimmer (ˈhaɪdrəʊˌskɪmə(r)). [f. HYDRO- + SKIMMER *sb.* 7.] An amphibious air-cushion vehicle, supported by peripheral jet-generated air. Orig., the name assigned by the Bureau of Ships to an experimental craft of the U.S. Navy.
1960 *Bureau of Ships Jrnl.* Feb. 22 Hydro-skimmer Model A David Taylor Model Basin. **1962** *Ibid.* Apr. 27/2 The Bureau of Ships has awarded a contract..for the design and construction of a 22-ton hydroskimmer research craft, designated SKMR-1... The craft will have four cushion fans..which will provide the lift needed. **1965** *Naval Engineers Jrnl.* June 364/1 Ground effect machines are very much in the picture of the Amphibious Force of the future. One such machine is the hydroskimmer which rides free of the surface on an air cushion... They will skim over land, sand bars, marshes, mud flats and open water with equal ease. **1970** M. W. CAGLE *Flying Ships* i. 1 One of our first tasks..is to straighten out the varied and confusing terminology which surrounds words like 'hovercraft', 'PAK-V' and 'hydroskimmer', and cryptic initials like ACV, GEM, TAC, CAB, SEV, and SES.

hydrosol (ˈhaɪdrəsɒl). [f. HYDRO- + SOL(UTION.] A sol in which the liquid constituent is water.
1864 [see ALCOSOL]. **1895, 1938** [see HYDROGEL]. **1937** *Industr. & Engin. Chem.* (News Ed.) 10 Mar. 104/2 Gold hydrosols nearly always contain unreduced gold compounds, which are fully reduced to metal hydrosols under suitable conditions. **1954** R. L. PARKER tr. *Niggli's Rocks & Min. Deposits* xi. 463 In mineralogy the hydrosols —i.e., the colloidal solutions with water as the dispersing medium—are almost the only sols of any importance.

hydrosome (ˈhaɪdrəʊsəʊm). *Zool.* Also in Lat. form **hydrosoma.** [ad. mod.L. *hydrosōma*, f. HYDRA + Gr. σῶμα body.] The entire body of any hydrozoan, esp. that of a colonial hydrozoan consisting of a number of zooids connected by a cœnosarc.
1861 J. R. GREENE *Man. Anim. Kingd., Cœlent.* 57 The branching hydrosoma of the complete organism, with its crowded assemblage of polypites. **1871** T. R. JONES *Anim. Kingd.* (ed. 4) 62 Minute gemmules or buds are developed from the common substance of the body (*hydrosome*). **1877** HUXLEY *Anat. Inv. Anim.* iii. 129 The Hydrophora are, in all cases but that of Hydra, fixed ramified hydrosomes, on which many hydranths and gonophores are developed.
Hence **hydroˈsomal, hydroˈsomatous** *adjs.*, of or belonging to a hydrosome.
1877 HUXLEY *Anat. Inv. Anim.* iii. 166 The first formed hydrosomal expansion is completed.

hydrosphere (ˈhaɪdrəʊsfɪə(r)). [mod. f. HYDRO- a + SPHERE, after *atmosphere*.] **a.** The waters of the earth's surface collectively. **b.** By some used to designate the moisture contained in the air enveloping the earth's surface (*Cent. Dict.*).
1887 H. J. KINDER in *Times* 6 Sept. 11/3 A descriptive analysis of the Earth's surface, including in that term the atmosphere, the hydrosphere, the form of the lithosphere and the material of its surface. **1889** *Nature* 21 Mar. 490 The sea, or hydrosphere of the earth. *Ibid.* 491 Swedenborg's ancient idea that a change in the rotation of the earth caused a change in the form of the hydrosphere.

†**hyˈdrostasy.** *Obs. rare.* In 8 **-stacy.** [f. Gr. στάσις setting, weighing.] = HYDROSTATICS.
1729 SWITZER *Hydrost. & Hydraul.* Pref. p. viii, The stated Laws of Hydrostacy. *Ibid.* 14 Take a view..of the

new Lake at Blenheim..see to what a Pitch practical Hydrostacy is arriving.

hydrostat ('haɪdrəʊstæt). [f. HYDRO- a + *-stat* as in AEROSTAT; cf. Gr. *ὑδροστάτης* hydrostatic balance.]

1. An apparatus for preventing the explosion of steam-boilers.

1858 in SIMMONDS *Dict. Trade.* **1864** in WEBSTER, etc.

2. An electrical device for detecting the presence of water.

1871 A. M. HAMMOND *Nerv. Dis.* p. xxix, The hydrostat overcomes the great difficulty hitherto experienced with all electric machines in which liquids are used. **1888** L. WEIL in *Jrnl. Franklin Inst.* Oct. 331 The first hydrostat I constructed consisted of two sets of conductors running at angles to each other, and separated by a material which would act as an insulator when dry and become a conductor when wet.

hydrostatic (haɪdrəʊ'stætɪk), *a.* [Ultimately f. Gr. *ὑδρο-* water + *στατικ-ός* making to stand, balancing, weighing (see STATIC); but prob. proximately f. Gr. *ὑδροστάτης* a hydrostatic balance, in med.Gr. a fire-engine, which prob. originated mod.L. *hydrostaticus*, F. *hydrostatique*.]

1. Relating to the equilibrium of liquids, and the pressure exerted by liquids at rest; belonging to hydrostatics.

hydrostatic paradox: the principle (depending on the law of uniform pressure of liquids) that any quantity of a perfect liquid, however small, may be made to balance any quantity (or any weight), however great. (Cf. *hydrostatic bellows* in 2.) ***hydrostatic arch***: see quot. 1858.

1671 R. BOHUN *Wind* 258 Illustrated from Hydrostatique experiments. **1729** SWITZER *Hydrost. & Hydraul.* 207 Hydrostatick Instruments. **1797** Hydrostatic paradox [see 2]. **1858** RANKINE *Applied Mechanics* §183 The Hydrostatic Arch is a linear arch suited for sustaining normal pressure at each point proportional, like that of a liquid in repose, to the depth below a given horizontal plane. **1860** HARTWIG *Sea & Wond.* i. 16 The mixture of the water of rivers with that of the sea presents some hydrostatic phenomena which it is curious enough to observe. **1871** B. STEWART *Heat* §23 The hydrostatic pressure of the column of mercury.

2. Used to denominate various instruments and appliances involving the pressure of water or other liquid as a source of power or otherwise.

hydrostatic balance: a balance for ascertaining the specific gravity of substances by weighing them in water. ***hydrostatic bed***: a bed consisting of an india-rubber bag filled with water; a water-bed. ***hydrostatic bellows***: a contrivance for illustrating the law of uniform distribution of pressure in liquids; it consists of a bellows-like chamber, into which water, being introduced by a narrow vertical tube, supports a weight placed on the upper board of the bellows, the upward pressure on this being that of the column of water in the tube multiplied in proportion to the area of the bellows. ***hydrostatic joint***: a joint used in large water-mains, in which a ring of sheet-lead is made fast by the pressure of a liquid (usually tar) in an annular space within the bell of the pipe. ***hydrostatic press***: a machine (having various practical applications) in which the pressure of a body of water (produced either by the weight of the water itself, or by a piston or other mechanical means) is transmitted from a cylinder of small sectional area to one of greater, and thus multiplied in accordance with the law of hydrostatic pressure. Also called *hydraulic press* or *Bramah's press*. ***hydrostatic weighing-machine***: a machine of similar construction to the hydrostatic bellows, in which the weight of a body is indicated by the height of the column of water which supports it.

1755 J. SHEBBEARE *Lydia* (1769) II. 87 It was impossible by the nicest hydrostatic-balance to decide which had the preference in her mind. **1797** *Nicholson's Jrnl.* Apr. 29 [(*Heading*), A New Press operating by the Action of Water, on the Principle of the Hydrostatic Paradox. Invented by Joseph Bramah, Engineer.] (*Page heading*) Description of a New Hydrostatic Press [Bramah's]. **1799** G. SMITH *Laboratory* I. 77 It [silver] loses in the hydrostatic balance about an eleventh part of its weight. **1822** IMISON *Sc. & Art* I. 111 The hydrostatic bellows is perhaps the best machine for demonstrating the upward pressure of fluids. **1833** N. ARNOTT *Physics* (ed. 5) I. 589 In the hydrostatic bed, there is no tense surface or web at all: the patient is floating upon the water. **1898** *Daily News* 5 Sept. 2/2 The use of 'hydrostatic vans' is now a luxury unknown in this arid portion of the town [*i.e.* East end of London during the 'Water-famine'].

3. Used of or in reference to certain aquatic animals having air-bladders which enable them to float on the surface of the water.

1840 F. D. BENNETT *Whaling Voy.* II. 295 One of the many hydrostatic univalve shells which float upon the surface of the ocean. *Ibid.* 317 Air, in the form of small bubbles..fully accounts for the hydrostatic power the animal possesses. **1870** ROLLESTON *Anim. Life* Introd. 75 The air-bladder of an ordinary Teleostean Fish..is..all but exclusively hydrostatic.

hydro'statical, *a.* [f. as prec. + -AL[1]: cf. *statical*.] Dealing with or referring to hydrostatics; also = prec.

1666 BOYLE (*title*) Hydrostatical Paradoxes. **1704** J. HARRIS *Lex. Techn.* s.v., Such useful Propositions as those given us by Hydrostatical Writers. **1796** HUTTON *Math. Dict.* s.v., Another machine which may be substituted instead of this common Hydrostatical bellows. **1833** N. ARNOTT *Physics* (ed. 5) I. 557 The hydrostatical truth, that pressure in a fluid operates equally in all directions.

hydro'statically, *adv.* [f. prec. + -LY[2].] In accordance with, or by means of hydrostatics.

1666 BOYLE in *Phil. Trans.* I. 237 To discover Hydrostatically..the bigness of the Buble. **1770** WATSON *ibid.* LX. 337 The specific gravities which have been determined..hydrostatically. *c* **1790** IMISON *Sch. Art* I. 152 The relative weight is found by weighing it hydrostatically in water. **1875** CROLL *Climate & T.* vi. 100 Hydrostatically, the ocean, considered as a mass, will then be in a state of equilibrium.

hydrostatician (ˌhaɪdrəʊstə'tɪʃən). [f. HYDROSTATIC + -IAN; cf. *physician*, etc.] One versed in hydrostatics.

1690 BOYLE *Med. Hydrost.* xv. §2 It is known to hydrostaticians that..the weight of a body..may be gathered from the weight of the water..equal in magnitude to that part of the body that is immersed. **1729** SWITZER *Hydrost. & Hydraul.* 69 Our learned and curious Hydrostatician.

hydrostatics (haɪdrəʊ'stætɪks). [In form pl. of HYDROSTATIC, in conformity with other names of sciences in *-ics*, L. *-ica*, Gr. *-ικά* pl. and *-ική* sing. Cf. STATICS. In F. *hydrostatique* (1695 in Hatz.-Darm.).] That department of Physics which treats of the pressure and equilibrium of liquids at rest; the statics of liquids: a branch of *Hydrodynamics* in the wider sense.

1660 BOYLE *New Exp. Phys. Mech.* xxxiv. 258 Those that are conversant in the Hydrostaticks. **1753** *Phil. Trans.* XLVIII. 75 In the case of the denser fluids being nearer to the center, as hydrostatics require. **1837** WHEWELL *Hist. Induct. Sc.* (1857) I. 74 Archimedes..solved the principal problem of Hydrostatics, or the statics of Fluids; namely the conditions of the floating of bodies. **1857** BUCKLE *Civiliz.* I. vii. 337 It is also to Boyle, more than to any other Englishman, that we owe the science of hydrostatics in the state in which we now possess it.

†**hydrosulphate** (haɪdrəʊ'sʌlfət). *Chem. Obs.* [mod. f. HYDRO(GEN + SULPHATE.] An earlier term for a salt of hydrosulphuric acid, now called a *hydrosulphide* or *sulphydrate*.

1828 WEBSTER, *Hydrosulphate*, the same as hydrosulphuret. **1842** PARNELL *Chem. Anal.* (1845) 88 Hydrosulphate of ammonia..when added to such an alkaline solution, produces a brown precipitate of sulphuret of copper. **1854** J. SCOFFERN in *Orr's Circ. Sc., Chem.* 452 With..the hydrosulphates..a black precipitate is furnished. **1863-72** WATTS *Dict. Chem.* I. 194 Sulphydrate or Hydrosulphate [of Ammonium] $NH_4.H.S$, obtained by mixing dry hydrosulphuric acid and ammonia..It is a combination of the two gases in equal volumes.

hydrosulphide (haɪdrəʊ'sʌlfaɪd). *Chem.* [f. HYDRO(GEN + SULPHIDE.] A compound obtained by the union of hydrogen sulphide (sulphuretted hydrogen) with a metal or radical; a sulphydrate.

1849 D. CAMPBELL *Inorg. Chem.* 46 Metallic oxides, capable of precipitation by sulphide of hydrogen or hydrosulphide of ammonium, in acid, neutral, or alkaline solutions. **1871** ROSCOE *Elem. Chem.* 215 At the ordinary temperature the sulphide loses NH_3, and is converted into a crystalline mass of the hydrosulphide NH_4HS, a very volatile body, which decomposes above 50° into ammonia and sulphuretted hydrogen.

hydrosulphocar'bonic, -cy'anic, *Chem.*, earlier equivalents of *sulphocarbonic, -cyanic*.

†**hydro'sulphurated**, *a. Chem.* Obs. var. of HYDROSULPHURETTED.

1802 *Nicholson's Jrnl.* Feb. 113 Hydro-sulphurated water.

†**hydrosulphuret** (-'sʌlfjʊrɛt). *Chem. Obs.* [f. HYDRO(GEN + SULPHURET.] An old name for a compound formed by the union of sulphuretted hydrogen with a base; a hydrosulphide or sulphydrate. ***hydrosulphuret of potassa***, hydrogen potassium sulphide, HKS.

1800 tr. *Lagrange's Chem.* I. 199 To prepare hydrosulphuret of lime, mix lime in distilled water, and impregnate it with water charged with sulphurated hydrogen. **1826** HENRY *Elem. Chem.* I. 549 Hydrosulphuret of Potassa may be formed by transmitting a current of sulphureted hydrogen gas through liquid hydrate of potassa.

hydrosulphuretted (-'sʌlfjʊrɛtɪd), *a. Chem.* [f. as prec. + SULPHURETTED.] Charged or combined with sulphuretted hydrogen.

1828 in WEBSTER. **1870** *Eng. Mech.* 18 Mar. 651/2 The action of the hydro-sulphuretted vapours.

†**hydrosulphuric** (-sʌl'fjʊərɪk), *a. Chem. Obs.* [mod. f. HYDRO(GEN + SULPHURIC.] Containing or consisting of hydrogen and sulphur only. ***hydrosulphuric acid***, an old name for sulphuretted hydrogen gas or hydrogen sulphide (H_2S), also called sulphydric acid.

1823 CRABB *Technol. Dict.*, *Hydrosulphuric Acid*, another name for sulphureted hydrogen. **1854** J. SCOFFERN in *Orr's Circ. Sc., Chem.* 348 By the evidence of hydrosulphuric acid the analytical chemist gleans a vast amount of information. .. An unknown solution..yields a precipitate with hydrosulphuric acid, and, *therefore*, contains a metal. **1872** WATTS *Dict. Chem.* Suppl. VI. 721 *Hydrogen Sulphide*, H_2S, Hydrosulphuric or Sulphydric acid.

†**hydrosulphurous** (-'sʌlfjʊrəs), *a. Chem. Obs.* [f. as prec. + SULPHUROUS.] In ***hydrosulphurous acid***, a name given first to dithionic acid; afterwards to hyposulphurous acid, or hydrogen hyposulphite, $H_2S_2O_4$.

1855 in MAYNE *Expos. Lex.* **1872-94** [see HYPOSULPHUROUS].

hydrotherapeutic (ˌhaɪdrəʊθɛrə'pjuːtɪk), *a.* [f. HYDRO- b + THERAPEUTIC. Cf. F. *hydrothérapeutique*.] Pertaining to or connected with hydrotherapeutics; hydropathic.

1885 *Athenæum* 10 Oct. 477/3 The Artemisium Nemorense was not only a place of worship and pilgrimage, but also an hydro-therapeutic establishment.

hydrotherapeutics (ˌhaɪdrəʊθɛrə'pjuːtɪks). [Plural of prec. adj.: see -ICS.] That part of medicine which treats of the therapeutical application of water; the practice of this; water-cure.

1842 ABDY *Water Cure* (1843) 49 One of the most powerful and beneficial instruments in hydrotherapeutics.. the sitting bath. **1896** *Pop. Sci. Monthly* Apr. 780 Recent developments of the science of hydrotherapeutics.

hydrotherapy (haɪdrəʊ'θɛrəpɪ). [f. Gr. *ὑδρο-* water + *θεραπεία* healing. Cf. F. *hydrothérapie*.] = prec. Hence **hydrothe'rapic** *a.*, hydropathic.

1876 BARTHOLOW *Mat. Med.* (1879) 60 Alterations of sensibility..analgesia,..hyperaesthesia, are often relieved by hydrotherapy—by the wet-pack, by ice, by local hot and cold effusion. **1894** *Daily News* 5 May 7/2 The Congress of Hydrotherapy and the International Sanitary and Health Exhibition which are to take place at Boulogne..on the occasion of the opening of the very extensive hydrotherapic establishment recently constructed.

hydrothermal (haɪdrəʊ'θɜːməl), *a. Geol.* [mod. f. Gr. *ὑδρο-* water + *θερμός* hot: see THERMAL.] Of or relating to heated water; *spec.* applied to the action of heated water in bringing about changes in the earth's crust.

1849 MURCHISON *Siluria* xix. 459 By igneous or hydrothermal action from beneath. **1863** A. C. RAMSAY *Phys. Geog.* iv. (1878) 48 Hydrothermal action due to the presence of heated alkaline waters deep beneath the surface.

hydrothermally (haɪdrəʊ'θɜːməlɪ), *adv.* [f. HYDROTHERMAL *a.* + -LY[2].] By hydrothermal action.

1941 *Ecology* Oct. 448/2 The hydrothermally altered andesites and basalts of parts of the Great Basin. **1957** [see HUTTONITE]. **1962** W. A. DEER et al. *Rock-Forming Min.* V. 329 Pure hydroxyapatite crystals up to 0·3 mm. in length have been synthesized hydrothermally by the hydrolysis of monetite..at 300°C. and 1250 lb./in.[2] saturated steam pressure. **1965** G. J. WILLIAMS *Econ. Geol. N.Z.* vi. 61/1 All writers presumed the gold to have been derived hydrothermally from granitic sources.

‖**hydrothorax** (haɪdrəʊ'θɔəræks). *Path.* [Medical L., f. Gr. *ὑδρο-* HYDRO- b + *θώραξ* chest. F. *hydrothorax*.] A disease characterized by an effusion of serous fluid into one or both of the pleural cavities; dropsy of the chest.

1793 BEDDOES *Let. Darwin* 56 [This] may be employed with probable advantage..in Anasarca and Hydrothorax, after the evacuation of the water. **1807** M. BAILLIE *Morb. Anat.* (ed. 7) 55 A watery fluid is not uncommonly found in one or both cavities of the chest, forming the disease called hydrothorax. **1876** tr. *Wagner's Gen. Pathol.* 225 Hydrothorax, dropsy of the thoracic cavity.

Hence **hydrotho'racic** *a.* (Mayne 1855).

hydrotic (haɪ'drɒtɪk), *a.* and *sb. Path.* [Erroneously for HIDROTIC, sudorific, ad. Gr. *ἱδρωτικός*, f. *ἱδρώς* sweat, through confusion with the better-known derivatives of *ὑδρο-* HYDRO-; the mis-spelling has to some extent influenced the sense. Cf. F. *hydrotique* ('mot barbare et qui mérite d'être effacé' Littré).] **A.** *adj.* Sudorific; also sometimes in wider sense, from the erroneous spelling, Causing a discharge of water. **B.** *sb.* A sudorific medicine, or in wider sense, a hydragogue.

1671 SALMON *Syn. Med.* III. xxii. 423 Sneezewort..is Diuretick, Hydrotick and Anodyne. **1681** tr. *Willis' Rem. Med. Wks.* Vocab., *Hydrotic*, a medicine evacuating watery humors. **1705** [see HIDROTIC B].

So **hy'drotical** *a.* = prec.; **hy'drotically** *adv.*

1616 tr. *Fernelius & Riolanus* in *Two Treat. Eye-sight* (1633) 21 The same Hydroticall Decoction of the infusion of Tutia. *c* **1700** Hydrotically [see HYDRAGOGICALLY]. **1864** WEBSTER, *Hydrotical*.

hydrotimeter (haɪdrəʊ'tɪmɪtə(r)). [= F. *hydrotimètre*, app. f. Gr. *ὑδρότης* moisture + *μέτρον* measure.] An apparatus for testing the hardness of water, consisting of a graduated tube to measure the water to be tested, and a tubular graduated burette containing a standard soap-solution, with which the test is made.

1886 in *Syd. Soc. Lex.* **1890** *Cent. Dict.* s.v., In saying that 'the water does not exceed 8 degrees hydrotimeter', it is meant that not more than 8 divisions of the standard soap-solution delivered from the hydrotimeter is necessary to make a permanent lather with 40 cubic centimeters of the water in question.

So **hydroti'metric** *a.*, relating to **hydro'timetry** (see quot.).

1886 *Syd. Soc. Lex.*, *H[ydrotimetric] fluid*, the test-solution used in Hydrotimetry.. *Hydrotimetry*, the process of testing the properties of water,.. based on Clarke's soap test for the hardness of water.

hydrotropic (haɪdrəʊ'trɒpɪk), *a.* [f. Gr. ὑδρο- water + -τροπος turning + -IC. Cf. HELIOTROPIC.] **1.** *Bot.* Turning towards or under the influence of water; affected by hydrotropism.

2. *Physical Chem.* [f. HYDROTROPY.] Of, pertaining to, or produced by hydrotropy; causing a substance that is otherwise only slightly soluble in water to dissolve readily.

1916 *Jrnl. Chem. Soc.* CX. II. 555 (*heading*) Hydrotropic phenomena. **1946** *Industr. & Engin. Chem.* Apr. 382/2 Most hydrotropic solutions precipitate the solute on dilution with water. **1954** P. A. WINSOR *Solvent Properties Amphiphilic Compounds* v. 123 The reduction in solvent action on dilution.. is very great with hydrotropic salts of lower molecular weight.

hydrotropically (haɪdrəʊ'trɒpɪkəlɪ), *adv.* [f. prec.: see -ICALLY.] **1.** *Bot.* In a manner that results in a movement towards water.

1915 *Ann. Bot.* XXIX. 281 A disturbance of the equilibrium within the cells would thus be effected in exactly the same way as by the difference of osmotic pressure in hydrotropically stimulated roots.

2. *Physical Chem.* As regards hydrotropy.

1928 *Chem. Abstr.* XXII. 770 Hydrotropically active salts. **1951** E. HÄGGLUND *Chem. Wood* iv. 261 The extracted lignin can be precipitated from the solution by diluting the latter to a lower concentration of the hydrotropically active salt.

hydrotropism (haɪ'drɒtrəpɪz(ə)m). *Bot.* [f. as HYDROTROPIC *a.* + -ISM.] The property, exhibited by the growing parts (esp. the roots) of plants, of bending or turning under the influence of moisture. Cf. HELIOTROPISM.

1882 F. DARWIN in *Nature* 27 Apr. 600 *Hydrotropism*,—Roots have the power of bending towards a wet surface. **1897** WILLIS *Flower. Pl.* I. 21 The root will be deflected toward the damp side, or.. will exhibit positive hydrotropism.

hydrotropy (haɪ'drɒtrəpɪ). *Physical Chem.* [ad. G. *hydrotropie* (C. Neuberg 1916, in *Biochem. Zeitschr.* LXXVI. 107), f. HYDRO- + Gk. τροπή turn, turning.] The phenomenon whereby a substance that is only slightly soluble in water will readily dissolve in certain aqueous solutions.

1928 *Chem. Abstr.* XXII. 770 (*heading*) The applicability of Traube's rule to the phenomenon of hydrotropy. **1950** J. W. MCBAIN *Colloid Sci.* xvii. 268 Hydrotropy occurs in concentrated solutions of salts or of colloidal electrolytes. **1954** P. A. WINSOR *Solvent Properties Amphiphilic Compounds* i. 5 With the amphiphilic salts of short chain length (e.g. C_3-C_8) the 'solubilization' effect becomes marked only with their rather concentrated aqueous solutions and has, in this case, been termed 'hydrotropy'.

hydrous ('haɪdrəs), *a.* *Chem.* and *Min.* [f. Gr. ὕδωρ, ὑδρο- water + -OUS. Cf. ANHYDROUS.] Containing water, as an additional chemical or mineralogical constituent.

1826 HENRY *Elem. Chem.* I. 283 Capable of existing either in solution, or in the state of hydrous salts. **1851** *Illustr. Catal. Gt. Exhib.* 1131 Hydrous oxide of iron, brown haematite. **1876** PAGE *Adv. Text-bk. Geol.* v. 101 Fullers'.. earth is a hydrous silicate of alumina. **1894** *Harper's Mag.* Jan. 410 A hydrous hematite.. that is a hematite which has absorbed a particle of water.

hydrovane ('haɪdrəveɪn). [f. HYDRO- + VANE.] **a.** = HYDROPLANE *sb.* I.

1919 *Times* 22 Mar. 8/1 The submarine commander.. could do a 'crash dive', that is, go under with full weight on, hydrovanes set hard down, and taking in water ballast. **1940** 'N. SHUTE' *Landfall* ii. 49 British submarines carried identification marks upon the hydrovanes.

b. = HYDROFOIL I.

1920 *Glasgow Herald* 27 Apr. 7 The possibilities of the large flying boat are very great... Hydrovanes may be found .. to give good results for reducing landing shocks and increasing the 'getting off' efficiency. **1936** *Jrnl. R. Aeronaut. Soc.* XL. 476 A combination of ship and hydrovane can only reduce the overall resistance to propulsion. **1939** *Ibid.* XLIII. 402 It is proposed to provide flying boats with hydrovanes. **1967** *New Scientist* 9 Mar. 460/3 The special type of hydrofoil anchor designed by Kingston.. has hydro-vanes rigged in such a way as to be self-reversing in tidal currents.

hydroxamic (haɪdrɒk'sæmɪk), *a.* *Chem.* [tr. G. *hydroxamsäure* hydroxamic acid (H. Lossen 1869, in *Ann. d. Chem. u. Pharm.* CL. 315), f. *hydrox(ylamin* HYDROXYLAMINE + *am(id* AMIDE: see -IC.] *hydroxamic acid*: any of the acyl derivatives, R·CO· NHOH or $(R{\cdot}CO)_2NHOH$, of hydroxylamine (see quot. 1966).

1875 *Jrnl. Chem. Soc.* XXVIII. 751 (*heading*) Distillation of hydroxamic acids. *Ibid.* 766 The ethers of aromatic hydroxamic acids. **1926** *Biochem. Jrnl.* XX. 1362 The hydroxy-acids present in rape oil give hydroxamic acids whose sodium salts are soluble in alcohol. **1966** MILLAR & SPRINGALL *Sidgwick's Org. Chem. Nitrogen* (ed. 3) ix. 333 The mono N-acyl derivatives of hydroxylamine are usually referred to as hydroxamic acids, a name which strictly refers to structure (I). They can clearly have the alternative structure (II) which should be called a hydroximic acid. In no case are the two isomers known as separate compounds: (I) R·C=O (II) R·COH and a compound of this class.. can
| ‖
NHOH NOH
react as if it had either structure. Commonly the term hydroxamic is used to imply either of these structures.

hydroxide (haɪ'drɒksaɪd). *Chem.* [mod. f. HYDRO- d + OXIDE.] **1.** A compound of an element or radical with oxygen and hydrogen, not with water; by some chemists restricted to compounds whose reactions indicate the presence of the group hydroxyl (OH).

†Formerly used interchangeably with HYDRATE.

1851 *Illustr. Catal. Gt. Exhib.* 1327 Hydroxide of iron, from San Claudio. **1869** ROSCOE *Elem. Chem.* xvii. 175 If only a portion of the hydrogen of water is replaced by metal, the resulting compound is termed a *Hydroxide*: thus, by the action of potassium on water, hydrogen is liberated and caustic potash KHO, potassium hydroxide, is formed. **1877** ROSCOE & SCHORLEMMER *Treat. Chem.* I. 193 The basic oxides.. form in combination with water a class of compounds termed Hydroxides or hydrated oxides. **1890** MORLEY & MUIR *Watts' Dict. Chem.* II. 703/2 Compounds formed by the union of molecules of H_2O with other molecules or atoms, without a rearrangement of the atoms of the group H_2O, are called hydrates; compounds formed by a reaction of molecules of H_2O with other molecules or atoms, such that the group H_2O is separated into its constituent atoms, which are rearranged in the new molecule, are called hydroxides. But it is often impossible to tell whether a given compound is an hydrate or an hydroxide.

2. *attrib.*, as ***hydroxide ion***.

1955 *Chem. & Engin. News* 1 Aug. 3190/3 The name 'hydroxyl' has long denoted the group OH. In organic contexts it is undoubtedly correct; but the expression 'hydroxyl ion' is very frequently used, although possibly less logical than 'hydroxide ion'. **1959** *Nomencl. Inorg. Chem.* (I.U.P.A.C.) 30 Certain polyatomic anions have names ending in -ide. These are: OH – hydroxide ion [etc.]... The OH – ion should not be called the hydroxyl ion. The name hydroxyl is reserved for the OH group when neutral or positively charged.

Hence **hy'droxidated** *a.*, converted into a hydrated oxide.

1851 *Illustr. Catal. Gt. Exhib.* 1326 Galenas.. mixed with pyritic iron and hydroxidated iron.

hydroxo- (haɪ'drɒksəʊ). *Chem.* A combining form of HYDROXYL, denoting a coordinated hydroxyl group; also used *attrib.* as an independent word.

1907 *Jrnl. Chem. Soc.* XCII. II. 560 This salt and others of the same series are classified by the author [*sc.* A. Werner] as hydroxonitrosotetra-ammineruthenium salts. *Ibid.*, Precipitates of the neutral hydroxo-salts. **1940** *Jrnl. Chem. Soc.* 1411 When the hydroxyl group is bound in a complex, Werner's system of notation should be used, according to which the hydroxyl groups are designated *hydroxo-* or *ol-*groups. **1965** PHILLIPS & WILLIAMS *Inorg. Chem.* I. xiv. 532 Examples include.. the formation in alkaline solution of the polynuclear cationic hydroxo-complexes of the cobalt(III) ion, e.g. $[Co(en)_2(OH)]^{4+}_2$ where en is ethylenediamine.

hydroxocobalamin (haɪˌdrɒksəʊkəʊ'bɒləmɪn). *Biochem.* [f. HYDROXO- + COBALAMIN.] An analogue of cyanocobalamin (vitamin B_{12}) in which the cyanide ion is replaced by a hydroxide (OH –) ion.

1950 [see COBALAMIN]. **1961** *Lancet* 26 Aug. 483/1 For the treatment of pernicious anæmia hydroxocobalamin appears to be equal in activity to cyanocobalamin and is better retained. **1970** *Times* 24 Jan. 7/3 The condition can be successfully treated by injection of hydroxocobalamin, a special form of vitamin B_{12}.

hydroxonium (ˌhaɪdrɒk'səʊniːəm). *Chem.* [a. G. *hydroxonium* (A. Hantzsch 1907, in *Zeitschr. f. phys. Chemie* LXI. 306), f. HYDR- + OXONIUM.] = HYDRONIUM.

1925 *Chem. Abstr.* XIX. 2309 (*heading*) Action of ammonium chloride vapor on metals and similarity of ammonium salts and hydroxonium salts as acids. *Ibid.* 2310 This expt. provides an important confirmation of Hantzsch's hydroxonium theory. **1940**, **1966** [see HYDRONIUM]. **1956** *Jrnl. Chem. Soc.* 2913 (*heading*) Raman spectra and constitution of solid hydrates. Hydroxonium perchlorate, nitrate, hydrogen sulphate, and sulphate. **1957** G. E. HUTCHINSON *Treat. Limnol.* I. iii. 197 Three of the hydrogen atoms could be at 0·99 A. and one at 1·77 A., corresponding to the hydroxonium ion H_3O^+.

†**hy'droxure.** *Chem.* Obs. synonym of HYDROXIDE.

1826 HENRY *Elem. Chem.* I. 496 The compounds of oxides and water, in which the water exists in a condensed state, are termed Hydrates, or Hydro-oxides, or Hydroxures.

hydroxy- (haɪ'drɒksɪ). *Chem.* Before a vowel hydrox-. [f. HYDRO(GEN + OXY(GEN.]

1. An element in names of chemical compounds, signifying the addition or substitution of oxygen and hydrogen or the radical hydroxyl.

1872 WATTS *Dict. Chem.* Suppl. VI. 722 *Hydroxybenzyluric acid*, $C_{16}H_{21}NO_5$.. An acid produced by oxidation of hydrobenzyluric acid, when an alkaline solution of the latter is exposed to the air. *Ibid.*, *Hydroxethylene-triethylammonium*... The chloride.. is obtained by heating hydroxychloride of ethylene with triethylamine. **1887** *Athenæum* 11 June 770/1 The outer coating of walnuts contains a crystalline substance termed nucin or juglone, which has been found to be a hydroxynaphthaquinone.

2. *spec.* Used as a prefix in the names of acids of the series having the general formula $C_nH_{2n}O_3$ which differ from the corresponding fatty acids (*oxy-acids*) by containing one more atom of oxygen, or by having one hydroxyl in place of one hydrogen; as ***hydroxy-formic acid*** $(HO.CO_2H)$, corresp. to *formic acid* $(H.CO_2H)$.

1888 REMSEN *Organ. Chem.* 169 A hydroxy-succinic acid. **1896** *Ibid.* x. 155 Hydroxy-acids.. may be regarded either as monobasic acids into which one alcoholic hydroxyl has been introduced, or as monacid alcohols into which one carboxyl has been introduced.

3. Special Combs.: **hyˌdroxyam'phetamine** *Pharm.*, a sympathomimetic amine that is a hydroxy derivative of amphetamine but lacks its stimulant effect on the central nervous system, and is used (as a solution of the hydrobromide) as a nasal decongestant and a mydriatic; methyl tyramine, $HO{\cdot}C_6H_4{\cdot}CH_2CH(NH_2)CH_3$; **hyˌdroxyben'zoic** *a.*, in ***hydroxybenzoic acid***, any of three derivatives, $HO{\cdot}C_6H_4{\cdot}COOH$, of benzoic acid having a ring-substituted hydroxyl group; *spec.* the *ortho* isomer, salicylic acid; **hyˌdroxybu'tyric** *a.*, in ***hydroxybutyric acid***, any monohydroxy derivative of a butyric acid; *spec.* the acid $CH_3CHOHCH_2COOH$, one of the 'ketone bodies'; **hyˌdroxycitro'nellal**, a monohydroxy derivative, $C_{10}H_{20}O_2$, of citronellal, prepared synthetically and used extensively in perfumery to give the odour of lily of the valley; **17-hyˌdroxycortico'steroid** *Biochem.*, any corticosteroid that has a hydroxyl group attached at position 17 of the steroid nucleus; **hyˌdroxycortico'sterone** *Biochem.* = HYDROCORTISONE; **hyˌdroxy'lysine**, an amino-acid, $H_2N{\cdot}CH_2CHOH(CH_2)_2CH(NH_2)COOH$, found principally in collagen; **hyˌdroxy'methyl**, the univalent radical $-CH_2OH$, in which a hydroxyl group replaces one of the hydrogen atoms of a methyl group; **hyˌdroxymethy'lation**, the introduction of a hydroxymethyl group into a compound; **hyˌdroxymethyl'cytosine**, a pyrimidine base, $C_4H_4N_3O{\cdot}CH_2OH$, that is present in place of cytosine in the DNA of certain bacteriophages; **hyˌdroxy'proline**, any of the monohydroxy derivatives, $C_5H_9NO_3$, of proline; *esp.* 4-hydroxyproline, the lævorotatory form of which is a non-essential amino-acid (strictly, an imino-acid) that is an important constituent of collagen and elastin; **hyˌdroxy'tryptamine**, any of the ring-substituted monohydroxy derivatives, $C_{10}H_{16}N_2O$, of tryptamine, esp. SEROTONIN (5-hydroxytryptamine).

1948 *Arch. Otolaryngol.* XLVIII. 659 The product used .. provides.. 800 units of penicillin per cubic centimeter in a 1 per cent solution of hydroxyamphetamine hydrobromide (paredrine hydrobromide). **1876** *Jrnl. Chem. Soc.* II. 85 (*heading*) A new hydroxybenzoic acid. **1888** BLOXAM *Chem.* (ed. 6) 524 Salicylic or hydroxybenzoic acid, $C_6H_4.HO.CO_2H$, is prepared artificially by combining phenol with soda, and heating the product in carbonic acid gas. **1958** PACKER & VAUGHAN *Mod. Approach Org. Chem.* xxiv. 796 The most important hydroxy-benzoic acid is salicylic acid (*o*-hydroxybenzoic acid). **1879** *Jrnl. Chem. Soc.* XXXVI. 615 (*heading*) Hydroxybutyric acid, $C_4H_8O_3$. **1970** W. S. HOFFMAN *Biochem. Clin. Med.* (ed. 4) iv. 149 The so-called ketone bodies, namely, acetoacetic acid, β-hydroxybutyric acid, and acetone.. are formed during the oxidation of fatty acids. **1929** *Chem. Abstr.* XXIII. 95 Pure rhodinal.. was prepd. by vacuum distn. of hydroxycitronellal. **1951** P. Z. BEDOUKIAN *Perfumery Synthetics & Isolates* 231 Hydroxycitronellal has not been found in nature and is entirely a development of the laboratory. **1951** *Jrnl. Clin. Endocrinol. & Metabolism* XI. 1029 Treatment with adrenocorticotropic hormone led to an increase in concentration of the 17-hydroxycorticosteroids. **1968** *Brit. Med. Bull.* XXIV. 225/2 Simple steroid screening tests such as single determinations of 17-hydroxycorticosteroid in plasma or in collections of urine. **1943** REICHSTEIN & SHOPPEE in *Vitamins & Hormones* I. 356 17-Hydroxycorticosterone... Isolated and described as 'Substance M' by Reichstein (55) and by Kendall et al. (54), who called it 'Compound F'. **1961** *Lancet* 7 Oct. 796/1 Further reports on the urinary levels of 17-hydroxycorticosterone.. of such patients will be awaited with interest. **1925** *Chem. Abstr.* XIX. 2347 Hydroxylysine does not occur in casein or ovalbumin. **1969** *New Scientist* 3 July 11/1 One [family] excreted excessive quantities of hydroxylysine. **1937** *Chem. Abstr.* XXXI. 9888/3 (Index), Hydroxy-methyl group, detn. in resol. **1964** G. H. HAGGIS et al. *Introd. Molecular Biol.* ix. 218 In 5-hydroxy-methyl-cytosine, a hydroxy-methyl ($-CH_2OH$) group replaces the hydrogen at position 5. **1948** H. WYNBERG tr. *Theilheimer's Synthetic Methods Org. Chem.* I. 147 (*heading*) Hydroxymethylation of phenols with formaldehyde. **1968** H. V. APOSHIAN in H. Fraenkel-Conrat *Molecular Basis Virol.* v. 504 Shortly after infection with a T-even phage, a new enzyme is produced which catalyzes the hydroxymethylation of dCMP at the 5 carbon atom. **1952** WYATT & COHEN in *Nature* 20 Dec. 1072/1 We have now resolved this discrepancy by isolation from *T*-even bacteriophages of a new pyrimidine base, identified as 5-hydroxymethylcytosine. **1968** H. V. APOSHIAN in H. Fraenkel-Conrat *Molecular Basis Virol.* v. 499 The unusual base, 5-hydroxymethylcytosine, is not found in uninfected

E. coli. **1905** *Jrnl. Chem. Soc.* LXXXVIII. I. 545 *(heading)* Synthesis of hydroxypyrrolidinecarboxylic acids (hydroxyprolines). **1965** A. Meister *Biochem. Amino Acids* (ed. 2) I. i. 87 3-Hydroxyproline was first obtained from cattle Achilles' tendon collagen. **1967** *New Scientist* 24 Aug. 375/1 In fish from cold water the precise proportion of the imino-acid hydroxyproline in the important protein collagen..was lower than that in fish from warm water. **1949** *Jrnl. Biol. Chem.* CLXXX. 968 Tentatively, then, the constitutional formula of 5-hydroxytryptamine..may be assigned to this vasoconstrictor principle. **1956** *Nature* 18 Feb. 332/2 The pharmacologically active substance 5-hydroxytryptamine is known to be liberated from platelets during clotting. **1956** *Chem. Abstr.* L. 5630 *(heading)* A new synthesis of bufotenine and related hydroxytryptamines. *Ibid.* 5631 6-Hydroxytryptamine.

hydroxyapatite (haɪˌdrɒksɪ'æpətaɪt). [f. HYDROXY- + APATITE.] Calcium phosphate hydroxide, ideally $[Ca_3(PO_4)_2]_3.Ca(OH)_2$, which occurs as a rare mineral of the apatite group (in which hydroxyl replaces all or most of the fluorine of the commoner fluorapatite), and which is the principal inorganic constituent of tooth enamel and bone.

1912 *Bull. U.S. Geol. Surv.* No. 509. 100 The three formulas developed are repeated here... To the list are added those of apatite, both the fluorapatite and the hypothetical hydroxyapatite... Hydroxyapatite, $9CaO.3P_2O_5.CaO.H_2O$. **1917** *Jrnl. Chem. Soc.* CXI. 638 The mineral constituents of bone consist in the main of hydroxyapatite, $(Ca_3P_2O_8)_3Ca(OH)_2$, mixed with a certain amount of calcium carbonate. **1962** W. A. Deer et al. *Rock-Forming Min.* V. 333 The hydroxyapatite..in talc schist and the fluor-hydroxyapatite in chlorite schist, both from a serpentinite near Holly Springs, Georgia, are considered to be metamorphic in origin. **1964** A. White et al. *Princ. Biochem.* (ed. 3) xli. 781 It seems likely that in bone, divalent cations other than Ca^{++} can replace Ca^{++} in the hydroxyapatite crystal lattice, whereas anions other than phosphate and hydroxyl may be adsorbed on the vast areas of surface offered by the minute crystals. **1971** *Physics Bull.* July 411/1 The enamel of a tooth is composed of hydroxyapatite crystals in prismatic form.

hydroxyl (haɪ'drɒksɪl). *Chem.* [f. HYDR(OGEN + OXY(GEN) + -YL, repr. Gr. ὕλη matter, stuff.] The monad radical HO or OH, consisting of an atom of hydrogen in combination with an atom of oxygen, which is a constituent of a vast number of chemical compounds.

1869 Roscoe *Elem. Chem.* xxix. 292 In the foregoing class of primary alcohols the group OH, hydroxyl, is attached to a carbon atom at the end of the chain. **1871** *Ibid.* 139 One atom of chlorine [is] substituted for the group of atoms OH (termed the radical *hydroxyl*). **1880** Cleminshaw *Wurtz' Atom. The.* 263 Hydroxyl does not exist; combined with itself it constitutes hydrogen peroxide. **1890** Roscoe *Elem. Chem.* 159 All the oxy-acids and also the hydroxides.. contain the group OH (water minus 1 atom of hydrogen); this group may be considered as a monad radical, and has received the name of Hydroxyl. **1896** Remsen *Organ. Chem.* x. 156 This instability is generally met with in compounds containing two hydroxyls in combination with one carbon atom.

b. *attrib.*, as ***hydroxyl group***; **hydroxyl acid** = hydroxy-acid.

1881 *Athenæum* 26 Feb. 303/1 This author..has thus disproved the conclusion that the two hydroxyl groups had different functions. **1886** *Syd. Soc. Lex.* s.v., Monobasic acids of the series, $C_nH_{2n}O_3$, or lactic series..are called hydroxyl acids because they can be simply and easily obtained by replacing the halogen in the mono-substituted fatty acids by hydroxyl. **1896** *Liv. Top. Cycl.* I. 412 Gun-cotton..is made from the best white cotton by treatment with nitric acid, three hydroxyl groups being replaced by three NO_3 groups.

c. in *Comb.* indicating the addition or substitution of the group OH in the compound, as ***hydroxyl-benzol***, ***hydroxylcarbamide*** or ***hydroxylurea***.

1872 Watts *Dict. Chem.* Suppl. VI. 725 Hydroxyl-urea is decomposed by boiling potash-ley, with evolution of ammonia. **1877** —— *Fownes' Chem.* (ed. 12) II. 394 Hydroxylcarbamide or hydroxyl-urea, $CH_4N_2O_2$,..is prepared by adding a strong solution of potassium cyanate to a solution of hydroxylamine nitrate cooled to -10°. **1893** *Brit. Jrnl. Photog.* XL. 818 Hydroxyl-monohydride is simply..common water.

hydroxylamine (haɪ'drɒksɪləˌmaɪn). *Chem.* [f. prec. + AMINE.] A basic substance, NH_2OH, allied to ammonia, which combines with acids to form a well-defined series of salts. Discovered in 1865 by Lossen, but until 1891 known only in its salts or in aqueous solution.

1869 Roscoe *Elem. Chem.* 216 Hydroxylamine has not been isolated in the pure state, but its aqueous solution has been prepared. **1889** *Anthony's Photogr. Bull.* II. 329 In these times of hydroquinone and hydroxylamine developers. **1894** Roscoe & Schorlemmer *Chem.* I. 475 Hydroxylamine forms white inodorous scales or hard needles, has a sp. gr. of about 1·3.

hydroxylapatite (haɪˌdrɒksɪl'æpətaɪt). [f. HYDROXYL + APATITE.] = HYDROXYAPATITE.

1927 N. H. & A. N. Winchell *Elem. Optical Mineral.* (ed. 2) II. viii. 128 The following formulas and names are tentatively assigned to minerals closely related to apatite... Hydroxylapatite (unknown alone) $3Ca_3P_2O_8.Ca(OH)_2$. **1946** *Nature* 6 Apr. 453/1 It is generally believed that bone salts are constituted either of hydroxylapatite which has absorbed calcium carbonate or of carbonato-apatite. **1951** C. Palache et al. *Dana's Syst. Min.* (ed. 7) II. 882 Fluorapatite, chlorapatite, and hydroxylapatite conform to the formula $Ca_5(PO_4)_3(F,Cl,OH)$. **1962** Waley & van Heyningen in A. Pirie *Lens Metabolism Rel. Cataract* 343 Chromatography on a column of calcium phosphate (hydroxylapatite).

hydroxylase (haɪ'drɒksɪleɪz, -eɪs). *Biochem.* [f. HYDROXYL + -ASE.] Any enzyme which catalyses the hydroxylation of a compound.

1953 *Jrnl. Biol. Chem.* CCI. 187 The authors propose.. the term 11β-hydroxylase..for the enzyme whose function and properties have been described here. **1970** E. Heftmann *Steroid Biochem.* vii. 64 Animal tissues contain hydroxylases that mediate the introduction of oxygen into specific positions of steroids to produce α- or β-oriented hydroxyl groups.

hydroxylate (haɪ'drɒksɪleɪt), *v.* *Chem.* [f. HYDROXYL + -ATE[3].] **a.** *trans.* To introduce a hydroxyl group into (a molecule or compound). **b.** *intr.* To accept a hydroxyl group.

1951 P. Z. Bedoukian *Perfumery Synthetics & Isolates* 232 The tertiary carbon atom hydroxylates with greater ease than the secondary carbon atom. **1954** G. M. Badger *Struct. & Reactions Aromatic Compounds* vii. 308 Such a reaction mixture also hydroxylates aromatic compounds. **1970** E. Heftmann *Steroid Biochem.* x. 97 Either pregnenolone or progesterone may be hydroxylated at C-17 by an enzyme.

So **hy'droxylated, hy'droxylating** *ppl. adjs.*

1900 *Rep. Brit. Assoc. Adv. Sci.* 298 The hydroxylated nucleus of the tribromonaphthol. **1930** *Chem. Abstr.* XXIV. 2988 $H_2S_2O_8$ may be used as a hydroxylating agent. **1954** G. M. Badger *Struct. & Reactions Aromatic Compounds* vii. 308 Hydrogen peroxide becomes a very effective hydroxylating agent in the presence of mineral acid. **1961** *Engineering* 31 Mar. 462/2 Hydroxylated carboxylic acids.

hydroxylation (haɪdrɒksɪ'leɪʃən). *Chem.* [f. HYDROXYL + -ATION.] The introduction of a hydroxyl group into a molecule or compound.

1879 *Jrnl. Chem. Soc.* XXXVI. 139 *(heading)* Hydroxylation by direct oxidation. **1962** H. Heath in A. Pirie *Lens Metabolism Rel. Cataract* 364 Ascorbic acid is an essential cofactor for the hydroxylation of tryptophan to 5-hydroxytryptophan.

hydroxylic (haɪdrɒk'sɪlɪk), *a.* *Chem.* [f. HYDROXYL + -IC.] Of or containing a hydroxyl group.

1898 *Jrnl. Chem. Soc.* LXXIII. 997 The substance is therefore an anhydride of nitrocamphor,..but it must necessarily be derived from a hydroxylic modification. **1948** Glasstone *Textbk. Physical Chem.* (ed. 2) ix. 680 Hydroxylic solvents, e.g., water and alcohols. **1950** *Symposium Hydrogen Bond 1949* (R. Inst. Chem.) 4 The oxygen atom of one molecule coordinates with the hydroxylic hydrogen atom of another, thus forming the weak intermolecular bond responsible for molecular association. **1963** C. N. R. Rao *Chem. Applications Infrared Spectroscopy* iii. 175 The important bond in hydroxylic compounds arises from the O-H stretching vibration.

hydroxyprogesterone (haɪˌdrɒksɪprəʊ'dʒɛstərəʊn). *Biochem.* and *Pharm.* [f. HYDROXY- + PROGESTERONE.] Any of several synthetic derivatives of progesterone that have a hydroxyl group in place of one of the hydrogen atoms of the steroid nucleus; *esp.* the derivative in which the hydroxyl group is at position 17, used (chiefly as the caproate ester) as a long-acting progestational compound in cases of *corpus luteum* deficiency.

1941 *Jrnl. Biol. Chem.* CXXXIX. 855 It was found to be the hitherto unknown steroid..17-hydroxyprogesterone.., a position isomer of desoxycorticosterone. **1948** W. H. Pearlman in Pincus & Thimann *Hormones* I. xi. 441 Erhart and co-workers..described the preparation of 12(α)-hydroxyprogesterone..from desoxycholic acid..; the substance was found to be lacking in physiological activity. **1954** *Nature* 30 Oct. 839/2 Various derivatives of progesterone by oxidation at C_{11} such as.. 11-α-hydroxyprogesterone and 11-β-hydroxyprogesterone ..have been found to be only about 3-10 per cent as progestational as progesterone. **1962** N. Applezweig *Steroid Drugs* v. 100 When administered to pregnant women for the prevention of habitual abortion, Norlutin and 17α-hydroxyprogesterone caproate have been shown on occasion to cause masculinization of the female fetus. **1968** J. H. Burn *Lect. Notes Pharmacol.* (ed. 9) 93 The progestogen [in contraceptive pills] is either a 19-norsteroid derivative..or a 17-hydroxy-progesterone derivative.

hydroxyquinoline (haɪˌdrɒksɪ'kwɪnəliːn). *Chem.* [f. HYDROXY- + QUINOLINE.] Any of the seven monohydroxy derivatives, C_9H_7NO, of quinoline, esp. OXINE (8-hydroxyquinoline).

1881 *Jrnl. Chem. Soc.* XL. 613 An excellent yield of hydroxyquinoline is obtained by fusing the sulphonic acid with three times its weight of soda. **1925** *Chem. Abstr.* XIX. 1572 The formation of 4-hydroxyquinoline is suspected. **1937** A. W. Groves *Silicate Analysis* vi. 131 The perfection of the separation of aluminium, iron, titanium, and zirconium from beryllium by means of 8-hydroxyquinoline now affords the improved method for the determination of beryllia which is adopted here. **1947** *Biochem. Jrnl.* XLI. 544/2 It was found that oxine alone of the seven isomeric hydroxyquinolines had chelating ability. **1970** *Watsonia* VIII. 23 Root tips..were given a pretreatment in a 0·002M solution of 8-hydroxyquinoline.

hydroxyzine (haɪ'drɒksɪziːn). *Pharm.* [f. HYDROXY- + PIPERA)ZINE.] A tranquillizing drug which is usu. administered as the hydrochloride, a white bitter-tasting powder, and is a complex derivative of piperazine.

1956 *Jrnl. Amer. Med. Assoc.* 16 June 604/1 Hydroxyzine (Atarax) hydrochloride is a new tranquilizing drug that is currently under clinical investigation. **1968** J. H. Burn *Lect. Notes Pharmacol.* (ed. 9) 59 Hydroxyzine appears to relieve anxiety without impairing critical faculties.

‖**Hydrozoa** (haɪdrəʊ'zəʊə), *sb. pl.* *Zool.* [mod.L. (Owen 1843), f. HYDRO- e, as combining form of HYDRA 6 + Gr. ζῷον animal.] A class of Cœlenterate animals, chiefly marine, simple or more frequently compound, found in all parts of the world, and differing widely in form and complexity of structure; the individual zooid consists of a soft gelatinous sac composed of an outer and inner layer of cells (ectoderm and endoderm), and usually with tentacles surrounding the mouth. Familiar examples are the fresh-water Hydra, and the various organisms called Acalephs, Medusæ, or Jelly-fishes. Also in sing. **hydrozoon** (-'zəʊɒn), an animal of this class.

1843 Owen *Invert. Anim.* vii. 82 The first and lowest organised class [of *Radiata*], which I have called *Hydrozoa.* *Ibid.* Gloss., *Hydrozoa*, the class of Polypi organised like the Hydra. **1858** Huxley *(title)* Monograph of the Oceanic Hydrozoa. **1870** Nicholson *Man. Zool.* 67 The Hydrozoa are all aquatic, and the great majority are marine. **1877** Huxley *Anat. Inv. Anim.* iii. 111 The embryo sponge is.. similar to the corresponding stage of a hydrozoon, and is totally unlike any known condition of a protozoon.

Hence **hydro'zoal, hydro'zoan, hydro'zoic** *adjs.*, of or belonging to the class Hydrozoa. **hydro'zoan** *sb.*, an animal of this class.

1869 Huxley *Crit. & Addr.* (1873) 315 The formation of a radiate Medusa upon a Hydrozoic stock. **1870** Nicholson *Man. Zool.* I. 96 There are no fossil remains which would be universally conceded to be of a Hydrozoal nature. **1877** Le Conte *Elem. Geol.* II. (1879) 244 A compound Hydrozoan allied to Sertularia. **1880** *Libr. Univ. Knowl.* II. 563 The equivalent of the individual *comatula* is the hydrozoic stock *plus* all the Medusae which proceed from it.

hydruret ('haɪdrʊrɛt). *Chem.* [f. HYDR(OGEN + -URET (taken from *sulphuret*).] A compound of hydrogen with a metal or organic radical; a hydride.

1812 Sir H. Davy *Chem. Philos.* 411 A solid combination of hydrogene and tellurium..was first observed by M. Ritter in 1808. The composition of the solid hydruret of tellurium has not been yet ascertained. **1822** Imison *Sc. & Art* II. 21 Products not acid, formed by hydrogen, and a simple substance, if solid, are called hydrurets. **1850** Daubeny *Atom. The.* vii. (ed. 2) 216 The highly poisonous principle, hydruret of benzoyle, which is found in the essential oil of bitter almonds. **1854** J. Scoffern in *Orr's Circ. Sc., Chem.* 491 Hydruret of Copper. *a* **1864** Gesner *Coal, Petrol.*, etc. (1865) 128 The hydruret of salicile, or oil of spirea.

Hence **'hydruretted** *a.*, combined with hydrogen.

1819 J. G. Children *Chem. Anal.* 46 Detonate in the mercurial eudiometer, one volume of hydruretted carbon, with five volumes of oxygen, the result will be carbonic acid and water. **1886** in *Syd. Soc. Lex.*

‖**hydruria** (haɪ'drʊərɪə). *Path.* [mod.L., f. Gr. ὕδωρ, ὑδρ- water + -ουρία, f. οὖρον urine.] An excessive flow of watery urine; similar to *Diabetes insipidus.*

1876 tr. *Wagner's Gen. Pathol.* 580 Hydruria of short duration, combined with diabetes, is produced by injury or irritation of the second lobe of the vermis of the cerebellum. **1897** Allbutt *Syst. Med.* III. 235 Hydruria, according to hospital statistics, is a somewhat rare disease.

Hence **hydruric** (haɪ'drʊərɪk) *a.*, of, pertaining to, or subject to hydruria.

1897 Allbutt *Syst. Med.* III. 237 Symptoms of the hydruric form of diabetes insipidus.

‖**Hydrus** ('haɪdrəs). [L., ad. Gr. ὕδρος water-snake; cf. HYDRA.]

1. A fabulous water-snake or sea-serpent.

1667 Milton *P.L.* x. 525 The Hall, thick swarming now With complicated monsters, head and tail,..Cerastes hornd. Hydrus, and Ellops drear.

b. A former name for a genus of venomous sea-snakes, now called *Hydrophis.*

[**1601** Holland *Pliny* II. 258 The goodliest and fairest snakes to see too, are those which live in the water, and are called Hydri, water-snakes.] **1838** *Penny Cycl.* XII. 405/1 *Hydrus.* The serpents of this genus have the posterior part of the body and the tail very much compressed and elevated vertically, so as to give them a facility of swimming.

2. *Astron.* One of the southern constellations, introduced by La Caille in the 18th c.

1796 Hutton *Math. Dict.*, *Hydrus*, or Water Serpent, one of the few southern constellations, including only ten stars. **1868** Lockyer *Guillemin's Heavens* (ed. 3) 423 These half-stellar, half-nebulous systems..are situated, one between the Pole and Canopus..the other..in Hydrus, between Achernar and the Pole.

hyduous, -dus, -dws, -dwis, obs. ff. HIDEOUS.

hydurilic (haɪdjʊ'rɪlɪk), *a.* *Chem.* [f. HYDRO- d + URIC, with arbitrary modifications.] In ***hydurilic acid***, $C_8H_6N_4O_6$, a body belonging to the uric acid group, obtained by heating hydrated alloxantin to 338° Fahr.; it crystallizes in small four-sided prisms. So **hy'durilate**, a salt of this.

1865–72 Watts *Dict. Chem.* III. 220 *Hydurilic acid*.. discovered by Schlieper. *Ibid.* 221 *Hydurilates*: Hydurilic acid is dibasic, yielding both acid and neutral salts.

hye, obs. f. EYE, HE, HEO, HI *prons.*, HIE, HIGH, HUE.

hyealde, obs. (Kentish) f. HOLD *v.*

hyech, obs. Sc. f. HIGH.

hyemal, etc., var. of HIEMAL, etc.

†**'hyemnal**, *a. Obs.* [Erroneous f. = HIEMAL: ? after *autumnal.*]
1674 MOXON *Tutor Astron.* II. (ed. 3) 69 The Equinoctial between the Hyemnal and Solstitial Colures. **1792** SIBLY *Occult Sc.* I. 23 The cold blasts of the hyemnal air.

hyena, hyæna (haɪ'iːnə). Forms: α. 4 **hiene, hyene, -ane,** (7 **hyen**); β. 4–7 **hiena,** 6– **hyæna, hyena,** (7 **hyenna**). [a. L. *hyæna*, a. Gr. ὕαινα, app. a feminine (cf. λέαινα), f. ὗς, ὑ- pig. The earlier forms were a. OF. *hiene, hyene* (mod.F. *hyène*).]
1. A carnivorous quadruped of a family *Hyænidæ* allied to the Dog-tribe, though in the skull approaching the *Felidæ* or Cat-kind; having powerful jaws, neck, and shoulders, but the hind quarters low and comparatively poorly developed.
There are three extant species, the ***striped hyena*** (*Hyæna striata*), inhabiting northern Africa and much of Asia; the ***brown h.*** (*H. brunnea*), and ***spotted h.*** or tiger-wolf (*H. crocuta*) natives of southern Africa. Closely allied to the last was the extinct ***cave h.*** (*H. spelæa*) the remains of which occur in caverns in many parts of the Old World. The name ***laughing hyena*** was originally applied to the striped h., but is considered by some to be more appropriate to the spotted h.
α. **1340** *Ayenb.* 61 Þet is þe felliste best þet me clepeþ hyane, þet ondelfþ þe bodies of dyademen and hise eteþ. *c* **1398** CHAUCER *Fortune* 35 The nedeth nat the galle of no hyene. **1600** SHAKS. *A.Y.L.* IV. i. 156, I will laugh like a Hyen, and that when thou art inclin'd to sleepe.
β. **1398** TREVISA *Barth. De P.R.* XVIII. lxi. (W. de W.), Hiena is a cruell beest lyke to the wulfe in deuouryng and gloteny, and diggeth buryels and graues and etith the flesshe of dede bodyes. **1560** BIBLE (Genev.) *Ecclus.* xiii. 19 What felowship hathe hyena [*marg.* Which is a wilde beaste that counterfaiteth the voyce of men, and so entiseth them out of their houses and deuoureth them] with a dogge? **1581** MARBECK *Bk. of Notes* 488 Hiena is a wilde beast that counterfaiteth the voice of men. **1600** TOURNEUR *Transf. Metamorph.* li, At length Malvortio..Heard of the harme wrought by Hyenna's spight. **1696** PHILLIPS (ed. 5), *Hyena*, or *Hyæna*, a Wild Beast, which is said to be Male one Year, and Female another, and to counterfeit Humane Voice. **1727–46** THOMSON *Summer* 921 And, scorning all the taming arts of man, The keen hyæna, fellest of the fell. **1834** MEDWIN *Angler in Wales* I. 194 These two shikkaries told us they had discovered the den of a hyena. **1834** PRINGLE *African Sketches* iv. 186 The laughing-hyæna heard near the folds last night. The sound truly horrible. **1881** *Encycl. Brit.* XII. 421/1 The Striped Hyæna..Its unearthly howling.. when the animal is excited, changes into what has been compared to demoniac laughter, and hence the name of 'laughing hyæna', by which it is also known.
2. *transf.* Applied to a cruel, treacherous, and rapacious person; one that resembles the hyena in some of its repulsive habits.
1671 MILTON *Samson* 748 Out, out, hyena! these are thy wonted arts, And arts of every woman false like thee. **1821** SHELLEY *Hellas* 403 The base hyenas of the battle That feed upon the dead and fly the living. **1888** J. INGLIS *Tent Life Tigerland* 188 Done to death..by the false oaths and lying testimony of a pack of ruthless human hyenas.
3. a. A name of the Thylacine or Tasmanian Tiger, the most formidable of Australasian animals.
[**1813** *Hist. N.S. Wales* (1818) 430 (Morris) About Port Dalrymple an animal was discovered which bore some resemblance to the hyena both in shape and fierceness.] **1832** ROSS *Hobart Town Almanack* 85 During our stay a native tiger or hyena bounded from its lair beneath the rocks. **1851** *Illustr. Catal. Gt. Exhib.* 996 The Thylacine or 'pouched hyæna' of the Tasmanian colonists is the largest.. carnivorous species of that order..(*Marsupialia*).
b. ***painted hyena*** = HYENA-DOG I.
†**4.** A fabulous stone said to be taken from the eye of the hyena; also called *hyæneum. Obs.*
1607 TOPSELL *Four-f. Beasts* (1658) 339 The skilful Lapidarists of Germany affirm that this beast hath a stone in his eyes (or rather in his head) called Hyæna or Hyænius. **1750** tr. *Leonardus' Mirr. Stones* 109 *Hyena*, is a precious Stone and worthy to be preserved. It is denominated from the Beast of its own Name, in whose Eyes it is found. **1855** SMEDLEY *Occult Sc.* 355 *Hyena*, a many-coloured stone, taken from the eye of the animal so called.
†**5.** An ancient name for some ravenous fish. *Obs.*
1607 TOPSELL *Four-f. Beasts* 435 The like is attributed to a Sea-calf, and the fish Hyæna.
6. *attrib.* and *Comb.*, as ***hyena foeman, laughter***; also ***hyena-like*** adj.
1818 BYRON *Ch. Har.* IV. lviii, Even his tomb Uptorn, must bear the hyæna bigot's wrong. **1819** —— *Juan* II. lxxix, They..Went raging mad..And, with hyæna-laughter, died despairing. **1820** KEATS *Eve St. Agnes* x, Hyena foemen, and hot-blooded lords. **1837** *Penny Cycl.* IX. 57/1 Dogs with hyæna-like feet. **1840** HOOD *Up the Rhine* 158 After a long hyena-like grin at the receeding object of his aversion.
Hence, chiefly *nonce-wds.*, **hy'enaish, hye'nesque, hy'enic** (-'iːnɪk), **hyenine** (haɪ'iːnaɪn) *adjs.*, like or characteristic of a hyena; **hy'eniform, hy'enoid** *adjs.*, shaped like a hyena, hyena-like; **hy'enaism**, action characteristic of a hyena.
1833 *Blackw. Mag.* XXXIV. 464 A hyaena in the fleecy hosiery of a lamb!.. The devil incarnate of hyaenaism in shape! **1884** *Ibid.* Aug. 210 The evils of political hyenaism. **1868** F. E. PAGET *Lucretia* xxxv. 185 [With a sound] more howling, caterwauling, and hyenaish. **1884–5** *Stand. Nat. Hist.* V. 435 The hyenine habit of walking or crawling upon wrist and ankle-joints when fighting. **1885** *Illustr. Lond. News.* Christm. No. 6/3 Laugh, perhaps is the word, unless you interpret it in a hyaenesque sense. **1885** ROBERTSON SMITH *Kinship & Marr.* vii. 203 The Arabs..call certain men hyaenic, and believe that there is an irresistible affinity between them and the hyaena. **1945** G. G. SIMPSON *Princ. Class. & Class. Mammals* III. 224/1 The genera here set aside..are large, later Tertiary canids with heavy jaws, rather distantly convergent toward the hyenas, and so sometimes called 'hyænoid dogs'.

'hyena-dog.
1. A South African canine quadruped (*Lycaon pictus*), having a superficial likeness to the hyenas.
1837 *Penny Cycl.* IX. 57/1 The hyæna-dog, *Canis pictus*. **1838** *Ibid.* XII. 371/1 In the number and form of its teeth the Hyæna-Dog agrees with the dogs, as well as in its general osteological structure.
†**2.** The AARD-WOLF of South Africa. *Obs.*
1838 *Penny Cycl.* XII. 371/1 Mr. Swainson gives the name of Hyæna-Dog as the English synonym of *Proteles*.

hyer, hyere, obs. forms of HIRE, HEAR, HERE.

hyera, obs. form of *hiera*, for HIERA PICRA.
c **1550** LLOYD *Treas. Health* (1585) C v, The infusion of hyera healeth the melancholike paynes of the head.

hyerþe: see HEARTH *sb.*[2]

hyetal ('haɪətəl), *a. rare.* [f. Gr. ὑετ-ός rain (f. ὕειν to send rain, to rain) + -AL[1].] Of or belonging to rain (Webster 1864).

hyethe, obs. form of HEIGHT.

hyeto- (haɪətəʊ), comb. form of Gr. ὑετός rain; as in **'hyetograph**, a chart showing the rainfall (*Syd. Soc. Lex.* 1886); hence **hyeto'graphic, -ical** adjs.; **hyeto'graphically** *adv.*; **hye'tography**, the branch of meteorology that deals with the distribution and mapping of the rainfall. **hyeto'logical** *a.*, of or pertaining to **hye'tology**, the branch of meteorology that treats of rain. **hye'tometer**, a rain-gauge. **hyeto'metrograph**, an automatic instrument for registering the amount of rainfall during successive periods.
1849 *Blackw. Mag.* LXV. 414 The *Hyetographic or rain chart of this volume gives a most complete and minute detail of a most important subject. **1858** MAURY *Phys. Geog. Sea* xiv. §781 The trade-wind zones may be described, in a hyetographic sense, as the evaporating regions. **1878** HUXLEY *Physiogr.* 46 Such maps [shaded to shew the rain-fall] are generally called **Hyetographical* or **Hyetological* maps. **1858** MAURY *Phys. Geog. Sea* vi. §335 *Hyetographically it is also different, being dryer, and possessing a purer atmosphere. **1849** D. P. THOMSON *Introd. Meteorol.* (L.), The rain-gauge..one of the most important instruments in *hyetography. **1730** *Phil. Trans.* XXXVI. 250 The Author..gives a Description of the particular Sort of..Hygrometer, and *Hyetometer, which he made use of in the subsequent Observations. **1886** H. R. MILL in *Encycl. Brit.* XX. 257/1 In Hermann's '*hyetometrograph', 1789, a fixed funnel conducts the rain into one of twelve glasses placed on the circumference of a horizontal wheel, which is turned by clockwork, so that each glass remains under the funnel for one hour.

hygeen, hajeen (hɪ'dʒiːn, hə'dʒiːn). Also 6 **hugiun,** 8 **hajan,** etc., **hyghgeen,** 9 **hadjeen, hejeen, hejin.** [Arab. *hajīn* dromedary, pronounced in Egypt *hagīn* (cf. Syriac *haginā, hugānā*, in the Talmud *hōgnā*). Ult. origin uncertain.] A riding dromedary.
1600 J. PORY tr. *Leo's Geographical Hist. Afr.* IX. 338 Of camels there are three kinds; whereof the first being called Hugiun [orig. *quarum primi Hugiun nuncupati*] are grosse, and of a tall stature. **1713** *Guardian* No. 124 There has not been a Tyger, Leopard, Elephant or Hyghgeen, for some Years past, in this Nation, but I have taken their particular Dimensions. **1790** J. BRUCE *Trav.* IV. 332 If..there was danger, [he] should return..mount a hajan or dromedary, and [etc.]. **1803** W. WITTMAN *Trav. in Turkey* 216 A smaller and more slender species of the camel, called *hedgin*, is mounted by the natives and others, and is capable of making a greater progress, on a journey, than a horse. **1830** [see DELOUL]. **1864** J. A. GRANT *Walk across Afr.* 419 A 'Hadjeen', or riding camel, is indispensable to comfort. **1865** W. G. PALGRAVE *Narr. Journey through Arabia* I. 325 The dromedary is the race-horse of his species, thin, elegant,..light of step, easy of pace,..though yet more often the dromedary enjoys his special title of 'hejeen' or 'delool'. **1875** [see DELOUL]. **1890** S. W. BAKER *Wild Beasts* II. 374 As a general rule, the hygeens are not so powerfully proportioned as those which carry baggage. **1908** *Animal Managem.* 276 The riding camel (..Hagheen, Egypt).

‖**Hygeia** (haɪ'dʒiːə). Also rarely **Hygiea, Hygea.** [a. Gr. ὑγεῖᾱ, late and non-Attic form of ὑγίεια health, Ὑγίεια the goddess of health, f. ὑγιής sound, healthy. From the same Gr. form were late L. *Hygēa* and *Hygīa* (cf. *Darēus* and *Darīus* = Gr. Δαρεῖος). The rare variant *Hygiea* represents Gr. ὑγίεια.]
1. In *Gr. Mythol.* the goddess of health, daughter of Æsculapius; health personified; *transf.* a system of sanitation or medical practice. (In quot. 1816, a statue of Hygeia.)
[**1615** G. SANDYS *Trav.* 29 Another daughter of hers by Æsculapius called Higia. **1706** PHILLIPS (ed. Kersey), *Hygiea*, health.] **1737** M. GREEN *Spleen* 73 Hygea's sons with hound and horn, And jovial cry awake the morn. **1781** SHERIDAN *Critic* I. ii, The temple of Hygeia. **1789** E. DARWIN *Bot. Gard.* 75 Divine Hygiea! on thy votaries bend Thy angel-looks, oh, hear us, and defend! **1802–3** T. BEDDOES (*title*) Hygëia; or Essays Moral and Medical. *Ibid.* I. 73 So entirely does Hygeia disdain to become the slave of Plutus. **1816** J. DALLAWAY *Of Stat. & Sculpt.* vi. 314 He had an Hygeia about 2 feet high. **1841–4** EMERSON *Ess., Nom. & Real.* Wks. (Bohn) I. 251 Criticism on the hygeia or medical practice of the time.
2. *Astron.* Name of the 10th asteroid, discovered by Gasparis in 1849.

hygeian (haɪ'dʒiːən), *a.* Also **hygean,** and (in mod. Dicts.) **hygiean.** [f. prec. + -AN.] Pertaining to Hygeia, or to health; healthy; relating to hygiene or medical science, sanitary.
1766 MRS. E. GRIFFITH *Lett. Henry & Frances* III. 149, I know no Hygean Spring which can effect their cure. **1825** J. MORISON in *Morisoniana* (1831) 194 The Hygeian Art. **1868** W. RITCHIE *Script. Test. agst. Intox. Wines* VIII. iv. 182 The manifest object of this ministry of love is soothing and hygean. **1879** G. MACDONALD *P. Faber* III. i. 14 Saving the world by science, education, hygeian and other economics.

hygeiolatry (haɪdʒiː'ɒlətrɪ). *rare.* [f. Gr. ὑγεία (see HYGEIA) + λατρεία worship.] Worship of health; excessive devotion to hygiene.
1882 MISS COBBE *Peak of Darien* 81 (heading) Hygeiolatry. **1882** *Christian Life* 30 Sept. 468/2 'Hygeiolatry' is the latest invention in words. It is meant to indicate an excessive devotion to one's health. **1887** MISS COBBE in *Contemp. Rev.* June 804 His [Kingsley's] voice.. would have been loudest in the denunciation of that hygeiolatry which threatens to become our only religion.

hygeist ('haɪdʒiːɪst). Also (in mod. Dicts.) **hygieist.** [f. Gr. ὑγεία, ὑγίεια (see HYGEIA) + -IST.] One versed in hygiene; a sanitarian.
Assumed as a title by James Morison, the maker of certain 'vegetable medicines' formerly in vogue.
1716 M. DAVIES *Ath. Brit.* III. *Dissert. on Physick* 12 Magists, Magirists..Geoponists, Hygeists, Prophylactists, Remedists. **1825** J. MORISON in *Morisoniana* (1831) 195 The Hygeist, viewing all disease in its..natural light. **1839** *New Monthly Mag.* LV. 310 More precipitation than is consistent with the rules of hygeists. **1841** GEN. P. THOMPSON *Exerc.* (1842) VI. 4 The real Hygeist Morison contending with the pseudo-doctor Gordon for the only Vegetable Pills. **1891** *Spectator* 24 Jan., The increased survival of the unfittest which is the grand present result of the successful labours of modern hygeists.
Hence **hyge'istic** *a.*, sanitary, medicinal.
1836 *Fraser's Mag.* XIII. 343 The peasants..deem the herbs to possess sundry Hygeistic virtues.

hygeology, var. form of HYGIOLOGY.

hygh(e, hyȝ(e, obs. ff. HIE, HIGH, EYE.

hyght, hyghth, hyȝt, obs. ff. HEIGHT, HIGHT.

hygi'antic, *a. rare.* [f. Gr. ὑγιαντ-ός curable + -IC.] = next. So **hygi'antics** = HYGIASTICS.
1816 BENTHAM *Chrestom.* 44 *Hygiastics* or *Hygiantics*,.. the branches of art and science, which appertain to health. *Ibid.* 45 Sound hygiantic instruction. **1824** *Westm. Rev.* I. 62 Hygiantics or Hygiastics.

hygiastic (haɪ-, hɪdʒɪ'æstɪk), *a.* [ad. Gr. ὑγιαστικ-ός curative, f. ὑγιάζειν to heal, f. ὑγιής healthy.] Relating to health; sanitary, hygienic.
1670 MAYNWARING *Vita Sana* Pref. 3 The Hygiastick Laws and Rules hereafter prescribed. **1855** MAYNE *Expos. Lex.*, Having power to heal: hygieastic. **1884** *Health Exhib. Catal.* 72/2 Improved Hygiastic Ventilating Grate.
So **hygi'astics** *sb.*, the science of health, hygiene.
1816 [see HYGIANTIC]. **1855** MAYNE *Expos. Lex.*, *Hygieastica*,..hygieastics.

hygiean, hygieist: see HYGEIAN, HYGEIST.

hygienal (haɪ-, hɪdʒɪ'iːnəl), *a.* ? *Obs.* In 7 **hygieinal.** [f. as HYGIENE + -AL[1].] Relating to hygiene, hygienic.
1663 BOYLE *Usefulness Nat. Phil.* IV. (*heading*), The Hygieinal Part of Physick.

hygiene ('haɪdʒiːn, 'haɪ-, 'hɪdʒiːn). [a. F. *hygiène* (*Dict. Acad.* 1762, in 16th c. *hygiaine* Paré), in mod.L. *hygieina*, ad. Gr. ὑγιεινή (τέχνη art), fem. of ὑγιεινός healthful, f. ὑγιής healthy. Formerly used in Lat. or Gr. form.] That department of knowledge or practice which relates to the maintenance of health; a system of principles or rules for preserving or promoting health; sanitary science.
[**1597** A. M. tr. *Guillemeau's Fr. Chirurg.* 1 b/1 *Hygiena*,.. which instructeth how we shoulde continuallye preserve our presente health. **1671** SALMON *Syn. Med.* III. i. 322* The Speculative part of Medicine is threefold: to wit, in Physiologia, Hygiene, and Pathologia. **1704** J. HARRIS *Lex. Techn.* s.v. *Analepticks*, A part of Hygieina, or the Art of preserving Health. **1727–41** CHAMBERS *Cycl.*, *Hygieine*, that branch of medicine which considers health.] **1796** SOUTHEY *Lett. Journ. Spain* (1799) 470 The second [Professorship] shall be of Physiology and *Higiene*. *Note*, I do not

understand this word; perhaps it means the doctrine of health. **1811** HOOPER *Med. Dict.*, *Hygiene*, modern physicians have applied this term to that division of *therapia* which treats of the diet of the sick. **1861** M. ARNOLD *Pop. Educ. France* 132 Extending only to matters of what our [French] neighbours call 'hygiene, salubrity, and morality'. **1864** E. A. PARKES *Pract. Hygiene* (1869) 1 Hygiene is the art of preserving health. **1874** MAHAFFY *Soc. Life Greece* ix. 274 Greek medicine rather started from hygiene than from pathology. **1898** *Times* 25 Aug. 5/6 The improved hygiene of dwellings and workshops.

hygienic (haɪ'dʒiːnɪk, haɪ-, hɪdʒɪ'ɛnɪk, -'iːnɪk), *a.* [f. prec. + -IC. Cf. F. *hygiénique* (1812 in Hatz.-Darm.).] Belonging or relating to hygiene; sanitary.

1833 DUNGLISON cited in Worcester 1846. **1842** PEREIRA *Elem. Mat. Med.* (ed. 2) I. 46 Air, Aliment, Exercise, Excretions, Sleep.. are now denominated *Hygienic Agents*. **1860** *New Syd. Soc. Year-bk.* 471 The hygienic rules given by the Medical Council of Prussia. **1877** ROBERTS *Handbk. Med.* (ed. 3) I. 31 Unfavourable hygienic conditions. **1898** F. J. GOULD in *Lit. Guide* 1 Oct. 154/2 The mere bending over printed volumes is neither hygienic nor aesthetic.

So **hy'gienical** *a.* = prec.; hence **hy'gienically** *adv.*, in a hygienic manner, in relation to hygiene.

1872 W. R. GREG *Enigmas* iii. 123 Those who morally and hygienically are fittest to perpetuate it [the race]. **1876** BARTHOLOW *Mat. Med.* (1879) 66 Various hygienical relations of the subject are also therapeutical.

hy'gienics. [Plural of prec., after earlier names of sciences in -ICS, q.v.] Hygienic subjects or matters; = HYGIENE.

1855 MISS COBBE *Intuit. Mor.* 159 Like one who observes the rules of hygienics not to preserve his health, but for the sake of avarice. **1885** *Manch. Exam.* 18 Feb. 3/2 Practical hygienics.

†**'hygienism.** *Obs.* = HYGIENE.

1864 in WEBSTER.

hygienist (haɪ'dʒiːnɪst, 'haɪ-, 'hɪdʒɪɪnɪst). [f. as prec. + -IST. Cf. F. *hygiéniste.*] One versed in hygiene. Also *attrib.*

1844 DUNGLISON *Human Health* (ed. 2) Pref. 4 Researches of distinguished hygienists. **1867** SIR J. Y. SIMPSON in *Trans. Soc. Sci. Assoc.* 109 We have the whole story vividly painted by one of our best hygienist poets. **1871** *Echo* 6 Jan., The French hygienists are strong in the belief of the sustaining power of their wine. **1897** *Sat. Rev.* 19 June 675/2 No one was ever a better hygienist than Moses.

hygiology (haɪ-, hɪdʒiː'ɒlədʒɪ). Also hygie-, hygeology. [f. Gr. ὑγεία (see HYGEIA) + -(O)LOGY.] The science of health; hygiene.

1855 MAYNE *Expos. Lex.*, *Hygieologia*.. hygieology. **1885** *Science* 11 Dec. 512/2 The word 'hygiology' was a far better term than 'sanitation', or than 'sanitary science'.

†**hy'graulic**, *a. Obs. rare.* [f. Gr. ὑγρός moist, after *hydraulic.*] = HYDRAULIC.

1730–6 BAILEY (folio), *Hygraulic*,.. of or pertaining to Pipes or Conveyances for Water. **1756** C. LUCAS *Ess. Waters* I. 2 The animal.. is an hygraulic body.

hygre ('haɪgə(r)), var. form of EAGRE.

hygric ('haɪgrɪk), *a. rare.* [f. Gr. ὑγρός moist, wet + -IC.] Relating to water or moisture.

1902 *Jrnl. Nerv. & Mental Dis.* XXIX. 751 Various deviations from the normal in the hippocampal convolution contribute.. support to the hypothesis that hygric illusions may be referred to that area. **1907** *Trans. Med. Soc. London* XXX. 371 The patient has complained of..'hygric sensibility', that is to say.. whatever she touches with her hands.. feels wet to her.

hygrine ('hɪgraɪn). *Chem.* [f. Gr. ὑγρός moist + -INE.] An alkaloid obtained from coca-leaves in the form of a thick pale yellow oil of a burning taste.

1865–72 WATTS *Dict. Chem.* III. 222.

hygro- ('haɪgrəʊ), before a vowel also **hygr-**, repr. Gr. ὑγρο-, ὑγρ-, combining form of ὑγρός wet, moist, fluid: extensively employed in Greek; the English compounds are mostly scientific terms of recent formation. The chief of these are HYGROMETER and HYGROSCOPE, with their derivatives. Other words in *hygro-* are the following:

(The υ in Gr. is short, and the etymological pronunciation would be (hɪg-); but the tendency to take *y* as long *i*, has in this, as in other cases, prevailed against the etymology.)

†**hygro'baroscope** [see BAROSCOPE], an instrument for measuring the specific gravity of liquids; a hydrometer. **hygroblepharic** (-blɪ'færɪk) *a.* [Gr. βλέφαρον eyelid], moistening the eyelid; applied to the lachrymal duct. †**hygrocirsocele** (-'sɜːsəʊsiːl), a CIRSOCELE accompanied with dropsy of the scrotum. **'hygrodeik** (-daɪk) [Gr. δεικνύναι to show], a form of hygrometer consisting of a wet-bulb and a dry-bulb thermometer together with a scale on which the degree of humidity is shown by an index whose position depends on the height of the mercurial column in each. **'hygrograph** (-grɑːf, -græf) [Gr. γραφος- writing], an instrument for registering automatically the variations in the humidity of the air (Webster, 1864). **hygrophanous** (-'ɒfənəs) *a. Bot.* [Gr. ὑγροφανής], of moist appearance; also, appearing translucent when moist and opaque when dry (*Syd. Soc. Lex.* 1886). **'hygroplasm** (-plæz(ə)m) *Biol.* [Gr. πλάσμα a thing moulded], 'Nägeli's term for the fluid part of protoplasm' (*Syd. Soc. Lex.*). †**hygrostatics** (-'stætɪks) [see STATICS], 'the art of finding the specific weights of moist bodies' (Bailey, 1731). **hygrothermal** (-'θɜːməl) *a.* [Gr. θερμός warm], relating to moisture and heat. **hygro'thermograph**, an instrument that records the temperature and humidity of the air on a single chart.

1696 WOODWARD *Instruct. making Observ.* 18 The *hygrobaroscope.. serving to try and compare the specific gravity of liquids. [**1855** MAYNE *Expos. Lex.*, *Hygroblepharicus.*] **1886** *Syd. Soc. Lex.*, **Hygroblepharic*. **1706** PHILLIPS (ed. Kersey), **Hygrocyrsocele*. **1855** MAYNE *Expos. Lex.*, *Hygrocirsocele*, old term used by Galen for a species of hernia. **1867** O. W. HOLMES *Guard. Angel* xiii. (1891) 157 The dry and wet bulbs of the ingenious '*Hygrodeik'. **1871** COOKE *Brit. Fungi* 145 Pileus *hygrophanous.. smooth. **1679** EVELYN *Sylva* (ed. 3) To Rdr. Aiij, Hydro- and *Hygrostaticks, divers Engines, Powers and Automata. **1895** *Athenæum* 10 Aug. 195/3 A general view of the climatological conditions of Africa, which he divided into *hygrothermal regions. **1929** WEAVER & CLEMENTS *Plant Ecol.* xi. 264 It is convenient for comparison to record both humidity and air temperature upon the same record sheet... Such an instrument is called a *hygrothermograph. **1969** *Ecology* L. 742/1 Hygrothermograph readings were taken.. at three elevations above ground and four exposures.

hygrology (haɪ'grɒlədʒɪ). [mod. f. HYGRO- + -LOGY; prob. ad. F. *hygrologie.*] That department of physics which relates to the humidity of the atmosphere or other bodies.

1790 DE LUC in *Phil. Trans.* LXXXI. 7 Anomalies.. of no consequence for the great objects of hygrology and meteorology. **1792** *Ibid.* LXXXII. 400 An inquiry into the cause of evaporation belongs more to hygrology than to hygrometry. **1849** HERSCHEL in *Man. Sci. Enq.* ix. 268 [On the sea] we approach the chief problems of hygrology in their least involved and complicated form.

¶ Erroneously explained in mod. Dicts.

1819 *Pantologia*, *Hygrology*,.. the doctrine of the fluids. **1842** BRANDE *Dict. Sci.*, etc., *Hygrology*, a medical term, implying the doctrine of the humours or fluids of the body. [Hence in WORCESTER and later Dicts.]

‖**hygroma** (haɪ'grəʊmə). *Path.* [medical L., a. Gr. *ὕγρωμα, f. ὑγρός moist: see HYGRO-. Cf. F. *hygroma, hygrome.*] 'A tumour containing serum or other morbid fluid, but not pus; a serous cyst' (*Syd. Soc. Lex.*).

1819 in *Pantologia*. **1846** G. E. DAY tr. *Simon's Anim. Chem.* II. 489, I have examined the fluid of an hygroma situated on the lower jaw of a horse.

Hence **hy'gromatous** *a.*, of the nature of or pertaining to a hygroma.

1819 *Pantologia* s.v. *Hygroma*, Hygromatous tumours.

hygrometer (haɪ'grɒmɪtə(r)). [mod. f. Gr. ὑγρο- HYGRO- + -METER; prob. ad. F. *hygromètre* (1666 in Hatz.-Darm.).] An instrument for measuring the humidity of the air or a gas, or the ratio of the amount of moisture actually present in it to that required for saturation. (Formerly often applied to a contrivance for simply indicating the comparative humidity, to which the name HYGROSCOPE is more properly given.)

1670 E. TONGE in *Phil. Trans.* V. 1199, I want a good Thermometer, Barometer, and Hygro-meter. **1725** BRADLEY *Fam. Dict.* s.v. *Oat*, Wild.. Oats is distinguished by a Beard that is made use of to make Hygrometers. **1729** SWITZER *Hydrost. & Hydraul.* 207 The Hygrometer, a Specimen of which we have lately had in the Toy wherein the Man comes out.. in wet Weather and the Woman in dry. **1791** E. DARWIN *Bot. Gard.* I. Notes 172 Mr. Saussure observed in placing his hygrometer in a receiver of an air-pump that.. the hair of his hygrometer contracted. **1845** DARWIN *Voy. Nat.* i. 4 The hygrometer gave a difference of 29·6 degrees, between the temperature of the air, and the point at which dew was precipitated.

hygrometric (haɪgrəʊ'mɛtrɪk), *a.* [f. mod.L. *hygrometric-us*: see -IC; in F. *hygrométrique.*]

1. Belonging to hygrometry; measuring, or relating to, the degree of humidity of the atmosphere or other bodies.

1819 *Pantologia* s.v. *Hygrometer*, The grass is superior to any other substance.. for hygrometric purposes. **1851** *Illustr. Catal. Gt. Exhib.* 641 Shallow pans of water placed over the stove may keep the air in its proper hygrometric state. **1852** TH. ROSS *Humboldt's Trav.* II. xvi. 10 Hygrometric observations made at different hours.

2. = HYGROSCOPIC 2.

1794 MARTYN *Rousseau's Bot.* xxxii. 494 One species of Mnium whose filaments.. are so sensible of Moisture, that it has obtained the name of hygrometric. **1796** WITHERING *Brit. Plants* (ed. 3) III. 835 When the Bryum flexuosum is moist, the capsules lie concealed amongst the leaves by a singular hygrometric quality in the fruit-stalk; but, as the moisture exhales, they become nearly upright. **1851** *Illustr. Catal. Gt. Exhib.* 208 This starch.. being less hygrometric than wheat starch, retains a more permanent.. glaze. **1862** DARWIN *Fertil. Orchids* v. 190 The contraction and consequent movement is hygrometric in its nature.

3. Said of water or moisture so diffused as to be apparent only by the humidity that it imparts.

a **1835** J. MACCULLOCH *Attrib. God* (1837) III. xlii. 94 The dissolved or hygrometric water. *c* **1865** J. WYLDE in *Circ. Sc.* I. 410/1 Absence of hygrometric moisture.

hygro'metrical, *a.* [see -AL[1].] = prec.

1773 DE LUC in *Phil. Trans.* LXIII. 409 The basis.. of my hygrometrical scale was to be the soaking power of melting ice. **1830** LINDLEY *Nat. Syst. Bot.* 331 The variable hygrometrical state of the atmosphere. **1861** H. MACMILLAN *Footnotes Page Nat.* 50 These hairs or filaments are.. highly elastic and hygrometrical.

hygro'metrically, *adv.* [f. prec. + -LY[2].] In a hygrometric manner; in relation to hygrometry, or to the degree of moisture in the air.

1808 DAVY in *Phil. Trans.* XCIX. 62 Sulphur.. burned in oxygene gas hygrometrically dry. **1860** MAURY *Phys. Geog. Sea* (Low) xii. §554 The climate of the Dead Sea must have been hygrometrically very different.

hygrometry (haɪ'grɒmɪtrɪ). [mod. f. Gr. ὑγρο- HYGRO- + -μετρία measurement; prob. ad. F. *hygrométrie.*] That branch of physics which relates to the measurement of the humidity of the air.

1783 DE SAUSSURE (*title*) Essays on Hygrometry. **1871** B. STEWART *Heat* §150 Hygrometry is that branch of science which treats of the state of the air with regard to moisture.

hygrophilous (haɪ'grɒfɪləs), *a. Ecol.* [ad. Fr. *hygrophile* (J. Thurmann *Essai de Phytostatique* (1849) I. 268), f. HYGRO- + Gr. φίλος loving.] Of plants: growing in a moist environment. Also **'hygrophile** *sb.*, a plant of this type.

1863 J. G. BAKER *N. Yorksh.* 189 Characteristically hygrophilous plants in the floras of the drainage districts. **1878** A. HENFREY *Elem. Bot.* (ed. 3) IV. i. 661 Plants are divided into *Xerophiles*, or those capable of existing in very dry climates; *Hygrophiles*, or those which can only exist in the presence of abundant moisture. **1883** F. TOWNSEND *Flora Hampsh.* 497 Hygrophilous or moisture-loving plants thrive on eugeogenous soils. **1903** W. R. FISHER tr. *Schimper's Plant-Geogr.* I. iii. 260 The Rain-forest is evergreen, hygrophilous in character, at least thirty meters high. **1914** M. DRUMMOND tr. *Haberlandt's Physiol. Plant Anat.* viii. 439 The degree of development of this tissue.. at once shows whether any given plant is distinctly hygrophilous or xerophilous in character. **1934** H. GILBERT-CARTER tr. *Raunkiaer's Life Forms of Plants* viii. 321 More or less hygrophilous communities are succeeded by mesophilous woods of oak and beech. **1957** P. DANSEREAU *Biogeogr.* iv. 206 Hygrophilous plants are 'moisture-loving'.

hygrophyte ('haɪgrəʊfaɪt). *Bot.* [f. HYGRO- + Gr. φυτόν plant.] A plant that grows in a moist habitat. Hence **hygro'phytic** *a.*

1903 W. R. FISHER tr. *Schimper's Plant-Geogr.* I. 17 Typical hygrophytes have weakly developed roots, elongated axes, and large thin leaf-blades. **1932** FULLER & CONARD tr. *Braun-Blanquet's Plant Sociol.* v. 126 Hygrophytes, moisture-loving species with favourable water economy,.. have morphological devices that permit the free loss of water. **1936** M. I. NEWBIGIN *Plant & Animal Geogr.* vii. 126 The actual appearance of the forests in any area depends on the competition between the hygrophytic species proper and those adapted to withstand seasonal drought. **1952** J. CLEGG *Freshwater Life* 50 The plants in the marshy area surrounding the pond are.. not truly aquatic... They are usually referred to as hygrophytes.., in contrast to the true water-plants, which are called hydrophytes. **1960** N. POLUNIN *Introd. Plant Geogr.* xi. 325 With further rising in level of the soil surface and relative depression of the water-table, shrubs and ultimately trees enter and in time give rise to a hygrophytic woodland. **1965** BELL & COOMBE tr. *Strasburger's Textbk. Bot.* 177 In the hygrophytes we find large, thin, delicate laminae, rich in sap.

hygroscope ('haɪgrəskəʊp). [mod. f. Gr. ὑγρο- HYGRO- + -σκοπος observing. F. *hygroscope.*] An instrument which indicates (without accurately measuring) the degree of humidity of the air.

Usually a device in which a vegetable or animal fibre (in *Saussure's h.*, a human hair) which contracts with moisture, is made to move an index round a graduated scale as in the wheel barometer, or, in a familiar form, to make a small male or female figure emerge from a toy house.

1665 *Phil. Trans.* I. 31 A Hygroscope, or an Instrument, whereby the Watery steams, volatile in the Air, are discerned. **1665** HOOKE *Microgr.* Table 252 Of a wild Oat.. and.. the manner of making an Hygroscope with it. **1679** MOXON *Math. Dict.*, *Hygrometer*, an Instrument to measure the Moisture of the Air, it is also called by the Name of Hygroscope. **1790** DE LUC in *Phil. Trans.* LXXXI. 11, I made two hygroscopes of different elastic animal substances. **1801** *Monthly Rev.* XXXV. 456 The hair hygrometer, or rather hygroscope. **1878** HUXLEY *Physiogr.* 70 The instrument.. simply indicates the presence of moisture without accurately measuring its amount; it is in truth, a hygroscope rather than a hygrometer.

hygroscopic (haɪgrəʊ'skɒpɪk), *a.* [f. as prec. + -IC. Cf. F. *hygroscopique.*]

1. Pertaining to the hygroscope or hygroscopy; relating to the degree of humidity of the air, hygrometric.

1775 ASH, *Hygroscopic*, belonging to the hygroscope. **1836** MACGILLIVRAY tr. *Humboldt's Trav.* xxiii. 332 Experiments on the constitution of the air,—its elasticity, its electrical, magnetic, and hygroscopic qualities.

2. *spec.* Said of bodies which readily absorb moisture from the air, so as to swell up, contract in length, or change form or consistence, and

thus indicate roughly the presence or absence of humidity; sensitive to moisture.

1790 De Luc in *Phil. Trans.* LXXXI. 2 An hygroscopic body, which is not brought into contact with any other body drier than itself, cannot lose any part of its moisture but by evaporation. **1875** H. C. Wood *Therap.* (1879) 583 Glycerine..is very hygroscopic, and absorbs water from the air. **1880** C. & F. Darwin *Movem. Pl.* 489 The hygroscopic movements of plants.

3. = hygrometric 3.

1862 *Lond. Rev.* 26 July 85 Moisture, but not in the form of rain..aqueous vapour in the air, and hygroscopic moisture in the soil. **1885** Goodale *Physiol. Bot.* (1892) 242 Water..which adheres to the particles of an air-dry soil and which does not affect at all the appearance of the particles..has been called..hygroscopic water.

hygro'scopical, *a.* [f. as prec. + -al[1].] = prec. Hence **hygro'scopically** *adv.*

1775 Ash, *Hygroscopical*, belonging to the hygroscope. **1796** Hutton *Math. Dict.* I. 614/1 A series of Hygroscopical observations. **1818** H. T. Colebrooke, Hygroscopically (F. Hall). **1869** E. A. Parkes *Pract. Hygiene* (ed. 3) 407 This property of hygroscopically absorbing water.

hygroscopicity (ˌhaɪgrəʊskəʊ'pɪsɪtɪ). [f. hygroscopic + -ity. In mod.F. *hygroscopicité*.] Hygroscopic quality.

1847 *Nat. Cycl.* XI. 492 The hygroscopicity of vegetable tissue. **1860** *All Year Round* 389/2 The rotifers..are preserved..by the help of the hygroscopicity of the sand.

hygroscopy (haɪ'grɒskəpɪ). [f. Gr. ὑγρο- hygro- + -σκοπία observation. In mod.F. *hygroscopie*.] The observation of the humidity of the air or other substance.

1855 Mayne *Expos. Lex.*, *Hygroscopy*, a synonymous term for..*Hygrometry*.

hygrostat ('haɪgrəʊstæt). [f. hygro- + -stat.] = humidistat 2.

1915 R. C. Carpenter *Heating & Ventilating Buildings* (ed. 6) xx. 525 Some form of differential hygrostat..controls the wet bulb temperature with respect to the dry bulb temperature so as to maintain a constant relative humidity. **1918** [see humidistat 2]. **1937** *Archit. Rev.* LXXXI. p. lxxii/1 Heating and humidifying equipment are incorporated in each unit, the desired temperature and humidity being automatically controlled by thermostats and hygrostats. **1965** *Bull. Entomol. Res.* LVI. 265 Kitchen & Gall (1953) describe a modified Friez hair hygrostat which they used to control a humidifier for an insect breeding room.

hygtaper, obs. form of hag-taper.

1597 Gerarde *Herbal* II. cclvii. §4. 632 Common Mullein or Hygtaper.

hyh(e, obs. forms of hie, high.

hyher, hyheyr, obs. forms of hire.

hying ('haɪɪŋ), *vbl. sb. arch.* Forms: see hie *v.*[1] [f. hie *v.*[1] + -ing[1].] The action of the verb hie; hastening; haste, speed. (Cf. hie *sb.*)

c **1205** Lay. 9330 Mid muchelen hiȝinge he leup [*v.r.* leop] to þan dæde kinge. *c* **1275** *Passion our Lord* 467 in *O.E. Misc.* 50 Pilates wrot him seolf a wryt al on hying. *c* **1350** *Will. Palerne* 2440 What of here hard heiȝing, and of þe hote weder, Meliors was al mat. *c* **1460** *Emare* 511 He wrowghte hit yu hyghynge.

†**hyingly**, *adv. Obs.* [f. *hying*, pres. pple. of hie *v.*[1] + -ly[2].] With haste or speed, quickly.

c **1205** Lay. 1071 Þu swiðe hiendliche [*c* **1275** hiȝenliche] scild þe wið dæðe. *a* **1225** *Juliana* 69 Hihendliche iher me. **1382** Wyclif *2 Sam.* xvii. 20 Thei wenten hiyngli.

hyke, obs. form of haik[2], huke.

hyke (haɪk), *int.* ? *Obs.* [Cf. hey ('hey go bet') and hi, used in the same sense.] A call to incite dogs to the chase. Hence **hyke** *v.*, *nonce-wd.*

1764 T. Brydges *Homer Travest.* (1797) I. 86 If thats the case, I know you'll say Tis time indeed to hyke away. **1823** Scott *Quentin D.* xxxiii, Uncouple the hounds! Hyke a Talbot! hyke a Beaumont!

Hyksos ('hɪksəʊs), *sb. pl.* Also 7-8 **Hicsos, Hycsos.** [ad. Gr. Ὑκσώς interpreted by Manetho either as 'shepherd kings' or as 'captive shepherds', ad. Egyptian *heqa khoswe* chief of foreign lands.] A people of mixed Semitic-Asiatic stock, probably including a proportion of Habiru, who gave their name to the fifteenth Egyptian Dynasty (1650–1558 B.C.) which ruled the eastern delta. Also *attrib.* or as *adj.*

1602 T. Lodge tr. *Josephus' Works* 769 This nation was called Hicsos, which signifieth Kings shepheards,..but in other coppies I find that *Hicsos*, is not interpreted kings shepheards, but shepheards that were captiues. **1743** W. Stukeley *Abury* xiii. 78 The shepherds who quitted Egypt, under the conduct of our Hercules, call'd themselves Hycsi, as Manethon informs us in Josephus & Eusebius in chronol. The word imports royal shepherds, valiant, freemen, heroes. **1788** Gibbon *Decl. & F.* V. l. 184 Under the name of Hycsos, the shepherd kings, they had formerly subdued Egypt. **1877** *Encycl. Brit.* VII. 735/1 The invasion and conquest, at least in part, of Egypt by the Hyksos..is undoubtedly the chief cause of the obscurity of this age. **1899** A. H. Sayce *Early Israel* Introd. p. xxv, A Hyksos Pharaoh and his Hebrew vizier. **1931** J. G. Duncan *Digging up Biblical Hist.* II. 163 Hyksos pottery. **1931** M. M. Green tr. *Schneider's Hist. World Civilization* I. II. 42 Aahmes took the capital of the Hyksos in the Delta about 1580 B.C. **1955** E. Pound *Section: Rock-Drill* xciii. 83 Where the spirit is clear in the stone as against Filth of the Hyksos, butchers of lesser cattle. **1957** [see *dark ages*]. **1960** K. M. Kenyon *Archaeol. in Holy Land* vii. 184 At the period at which the Hyksos appear in Palestine and Egypt, we have on the move groups of Hurrians and Habiru, and the most probable explanation of the Hyksos is that they were recruited from such bands. **1971** *Encycl. Judaica* VIII. 1142 The Hyksos..attempted to Egyptianize and assimilate Egyptian culture. This synthesis is attested by the Hyksos religion.

hyl, obs. form of hill *sb.*, ill *a.*

‖**hyla** ('haɪlə). [mod.L., adopted as generic name by Laurenti (1768), ad. Gr. ὕλη wood, forest.] A tree-frog or tree-toad, as *Hyla pickeringi* of the United States.

a **1842** W. E. Channing in Salt *Thoreau* (1890) 130 Each clear hyla trilling the new spring. **1859** Tennent *Ceylon* II. IX. iv. 477 The incessant metallic chirp of the hyla.

hyla, var. of hyle.

hylactic (hɪ'læktɪk), *a. rare.* [ad. Gr. ὑλακτικ-ός given to barking.] Of the nature of barking.

1861 T. L. Peacock *Gryll Gr.* vii. 52 Lawyers barking at each other in that peculiar style of hylactic delivery which is called forensic eloquence.

So **hy'lactism**, barking.

1818 Shelley *Lett.* Pr. Wks. 1888 II. 245 Two or three dogs, who bark with a sharp hylactism.

‖**hylæosaurus** (haɪliːəʊ'sɔːrəs). *Palæont.* Also **hy'læosaur.** [mod.L. (Mantell, 1832), f. Gr. ὑλαῖος belonging to forests (f. ὕλη wood) + σαῦρος lizard.] A gigantic fossil saurian, found in the Wealden formation of Tilgate forest, chiefly characterized by a dermal ridge of large bony spines.

1833 Sir C. Bell *Hand* (1834) 119 The Hylæosaurus..is estimated to have been about thirty feet in length. **1877** Le Conte *Elem. Geol.* II. (1879) 434 The Hylæosaur was another huge reptile of the same [Mesozoic] period.

hylair, var. hilaire *a. Obs.*, cheerful.

†**hy'larchic**, *a. Obs.* [ad. Gr. *ὑλαρχικ-ός = ὑλάρχιος, f. ὕλη matter + ἄρχειν to rule. Cf. F. *hylarchique*.] Ruling over matter.

1676 H. More *Remarks* Contents b vij b, Water is..suspended in Pumps..by Gravitation upwards, more expresly here explained, and at last resolved into the Hylarchick Principle. *Ibid.* 186 The Hylarchick Spirit of the world holds strong and entire still. **1713** Berkeley *Hylas & Phil.* III. Wks. 1871 I. 355 What difficulties concerning entity in abstract, substantial forms, hylarchic principles.

So †**hy'larchical** *a. Obs.*

1676 [see hylostatical]. **1678** Cudworth *Intell. Syst.* I. v. 668 Some other substance besides Body, such as is self active and hylarchical, or hath a natural power of ruling over matter. **1681** Hallywell *Melampron.* 70 (T.) This hylarchical principle, or plastick nature.

‖**hy'lasmus.** *Obs. rare.* [mod.L., repr. a Gr. type *ὑλασμός, f. ὕλη matter.] Materialization; presentation under a material form.

1664 H. More *Myst. Iniq.* 217 Hylasmus is a Prophetick Scheme bearing strongly upon the Phancy by exhibiting crass and palpable Objects, such as in Logick would bear the Notion of Subject or Matter. **1680** —— *Apocal. Apoc.* 189 All this may be nothing else but a Prophetick Hylasmus.

So †**hy'lastic** *a.*, materialistic; also †**hy'lastically** *adv.*, materialistically.

1639 Wm. Sclater *Worthy Commun.* 46 As men dye but once for all, no more is Christ offered up..but once for all, hylastically and in propitiation. **1664** H. More *Myst. Iniq.*, *Synopsis Proph.* 217 This City so Hylastically set out has a most Spiritual meaning. **1684** —— *Answer* 241 He in this Hylastick and Israelistick way prophesies of..the new Jerusalem.

hyld, hyllde, obs. ff. *held*, pa. t. of hold *v.*

hylde, obs. f. hield *v.*, var. hild *v. Obs.*

hylding, var. hilding, *Obs.*

‖**hyle** ('haɪliː). *Obs.* Also 4-5 **yle**, 6 **hile**, (7 **hyla**). [med.L. *hȳlē*, a. Gr. ὕλη wood, timber, material, by Aristotle and in later Gr. 'matter'.] Matter, substance; the first matter of the universe.

[**1390** Gower *Conf.* III. 91 That matere universall, Which hight Ylem in speciall.] *c* **1400** tr. *Secreta Secret.*, *Gov. Lordsh.* (E.E.T.S.) 94 Of þe saule commys anoþer substance, þat ys clepyd þe yle. **1569** J. Sanford tr. *Agrippa's Van. Artes* 70 b, Of the undiuisible partes, of *Hile*, of matiers. **1619** Purchas *Microcosm.* lviii. 564 Vncreated Chaos, or Hyla, or first Matter. *a* **1652** J. Smith *Sel. Disc.* iv. 118 This hyle or matter..is indeed nothing else but the soul's potentiality. *a* **1687** H. More *App. to De Philos. Cabbal.* viii. (1713) 182 That Hyle or first Matter is mere Possibility of Being, according to Aristotle. **1768–74** Tucker *Lt. Nat.* (1852) I. 464 Jove produced the two first numbers, the mundane soul and hyle: he made hyle inert and stupid, but to the mundane soul he gave activity and understanding.

hyleg ('haɪlɛg). *Astrol.* Also 7 **hilege, hylech.** [Of obscure origin. In Pers. (and Turkish) *hailāj*, 'a calculation of astrologers by which they obtain evidence of the length of an infant's life', 'a nativity'; said by the Persian lexicographers to be a Greek word, meaning originally 'fountain of life'. The Pers. equivalent is given as *kadbānū*, lit. 'mistress of the house'. In OF. *yleg*, *ilech* (Oresme, 14th c.).] Ruling planet of a nativity; apheta (cf. quot. 1706).

a **1625** Beaumont & Fl. *Bloody Brother* IV. ii, Mars out of the self sam house..Looks at the Hilege with a quartile ruling. **1647** Lilly *Chr. Astrol.* civ. 527 Of the Prorogator of Life, called Hylech, or Hyleg, or Apheta. **1668** Dryden *Even. Love* II. i, What think you, sir, of the taking Hyleg? or of the best way of the rectification for a nativity? **1706** Phillips (ed. Kersey), *Hyleg*, or *Hylech*..a Planet or part of Heaven, which in a Man's Nativity becomes the Moderator and Significator of his Life. **1819** Wilson *Dict. Astrol.* s.v. *Apheta*, If by day the Sun be in an Aphetic place, he becomes Hyleg in preference to all others. **1881** Shorthouse *J. Inglesant* (1882) I. xv. 281 The significator being combust..and the hyleg afflicted by evil planets.

†**hyle'giacal**, *a.* (*sb.*) *Obs.* [f. prec.]

A. *adj.* Of or pertaining to the hyleg.

1647 Lilly *Chr. Astrol.* xliv. 255 When the five Hylegiacall places at the hour of Birth..are oppressed, judge death immediatly to follow. **1674** Moxon *Tutor Astron.* IV. Prob. viii. (ed. 3) 134 Turn about the Globe till the Promittor come to the Hylegiacal point. **1706** Phillips (ed. Kersey), *Hylegiacal Places* are..reckon'd to be five in number, viz. the Ascendant, the Mid-Heaven, the 7th House, the 9th and the 11th.

B. *sb.* = Hylegiacal place.

1668 Dryden *Even. Love* III. i, The five Hylegiacalls; the Ascendant, *Medium Cœli*, Sun, Moon and Stars.

†**hy'legial**, *a. Obs.* [see -ial.] = prec.

1652 Gaule *Magastrom.* 141 They have..found all the hylegiall places strong and well constituted. **1727–41** Chambers *Cycl.*, *Hylegial Places*..are those wherein a planet being found, is qualified to have the government of life attributed to it.

hylic ('haɪlɪk), *a.* [ad. med.L. *hȳlic-us* (Du Cange), a. Gr. ὑλικ-ός material, f. ὕλη hyle.] Pertaining to matter, material. (In Gnostic theology opposed to *psychic* and *pneumatic*.)

1853 W. E. Tayler *Hippolytus* II. ii. 86 They regarded Cain as the representative of the Hylic, Abel of the Psychical and Seth of the Pneumatic principle. **1860** J. Gardner *Faiths World* II. 97/1 The Gnostic notion that a class of men..suffered themselves to be so captivated by the inferior world as to live only a hylic, or material life.

So †'**hylical** *a.* = hylic; '**hylicism**, materialism; '**hylicist**, a materialist.

1708 H. Dodwell *Nat. Mort. Hum. Souls* 6 He supposes them..to be Hylical and Choical, not Cœlestial. **1880** Webster Supp., *Hylicist*. **1893** *Athenæum* 12 Aug. 220/3 The 'Ionian hylicists', Descartes, Kant, and Mr. Spencer, all resemble one another in this respect.

hylien, obs. f. hill *v.*[1], to cover.

1377 Langl. *P. Pl.* B. XII. 231 And tauȝte hym and Eue to hylien hem with leues.

hylism ('haɪlɪz(ə)m). [f. hyle + -ism.] = hylicism.

In mod. Dicts.

hyll, rare var. of hull *sb.*[1], husk.

[? an error, or assimilated to *hyll*, hill, *v.*[1] to cover.] **1495** *Trevisa's Barth. De P.R.* (W. de W.) XVII. cxii. 675 Oyle is the Juys of beryes of oliue..And the more slyly that it comyth oute of the hylles: the better it is.

hyll, obs. f. hill *sb.*, ill; var. hill *v.*[1]

hyllor, obs. form of elder *sb.*[1]

hylo- (haɪləʊ) = Gr. ὑλο-(ῡ), combining form of ὕλη wood, material, matter (see hyle). The modern formations are either technical terms of natural history (with *hylo-* = 'wood', 'forest') or of philosophy (with *hylo-* = 'matter').

'**hylobate** [ad. mod.L. *Hylobatēs* (Illiger, 1811), a. Gr. ὑλοβάτης, f. -βατης walker], a long-armed ape or gibbon. **hy'lobatine** *a.* [-ine], belonging to, or characteristic of, the *Hylobatinæ*, or anthropoid apes allied to *Hylobates*. †**hy'lobian** [Gr. ὑλόβι-ος (f. βίος life)] (see quot.). **hylo-'genesis** [genesis], the origin or formation of matter (*Syd. Soc. Lex.* 1886); so **hy'logeny** [cf. F. *hylogénie*]. ˌ**hylo-i'deal** *a.*, pertaining to hylo-idealism. ˌ**hylo-i'dealism**, the doctrine of R. Lewins that reality belongs to the immediate object of belief as such; material or somatic idealism, sensuous subjectivism; hence ˌ**hylo-i'dealist**, one who holds this. **hy'lology** [-logy], a doctrine or theory concerning matter. †**hylo'mania** [mania], excessive tendency towards materialism. **hylo-'morphic, hylo'morphical** *adjs.*, pertaining to **hylo'morphism** [Gr. μορφή form], the doctrine that primordial matter is the First Cause of the universe; so **hylo'morphist**, a believer in hylomorphism. †**hylo'morphous** *a.*, having a material form. †**hylopa'thetic** *a.* = *hylopathic*. †**hylo'pathian** *a.* [see *hylopathy*], pertaining to, or holding, the view that all things are affections of matter; also as *sb.* one who holds this view. †**hylo'pathic** *a.*, capable of affecting or being affected by matter. **hy'lopathism**, the doctrine that matter is sentient; hence **hy'lopathist**, a believer in hylopathism. †**hy'lopathy** [Gr. πάθος, -πάθεια affection], a

spirit's power of affecting matter. **hy'lophagous** *a.* [f. Gr. ὑλοφάγ-ος (f. -φαγος eating)], wood-eating (said of certain beetles) (*Syd. Soc. Lex.*). **ˌhylo-phe'nomenal** *a.* = *hylo-ideal*; hence **ˌhylo-phe'nomenalism.** **† hylo'static, -ical** *adjs.* [Gr. στατικός causing to stand, STATIC], that places or arranges matter. **'hylotheism** [THEISM], the doctrine that God and matter or the material universe are identical; material pantheism; hence **'hylotheist**, a believer in hylotheism; **ˌhylothe'istic** *a.*, pertaining to hylotheism. **hy'lotomous** *a.* [f. Gr. ὑλοτόμ-ος (f. τέμνειν to cut) + -OUS], wood-cutting (said of certain insects).

[**1871** DARWIN *Desc. Man* I. vi. 196 The anthropomorphous apes, namely the gorilla, chimpanzee, orang, and *hylobates.] **1727-41** CHAMBERS *Cycl.*, *Hylobii*, or **Hylobians*, a sect of Indian philosophers, thus denominated..in regard they retired to forests, to be more at leisure for the contemplation of nature. **1864** H. SPENCER *Illustr. Univ. Progr.* 125 *Hylogeny: Gravity, Matter, Ether. .. He [Oken] explains that.. Hylogeny [is the doctrine of] material totalities. **1883** CONSTANCE NADEN in *Jrnl. Science* Mar. 127 Many a cherished illusion must fall when the ..'*Hylo-Ideal' theory is finally established. **1884** *Cassell's Encycl. Dict.* s.v., The central insistence of the hylo-ideal philosophy is that man is, for man, the measure of the universe. **1883** C. NADEN in *Jrnl. Science* Mar. 122 The standpoint of *hylo-idealism. **1891** R. W. DALE in *Contemp. Rev.* Apr. 520 The philosophical creed which, under Dr. Lewins's teaching, Miss Naden accepted, is called 'Hylo-Idealism'. **1856** F. HALL *Sánkhya-pravachanabháshya* Pref. 7 The puerile *hylology of the Nyáya. **1711** SHAFTESB. *Charac.* Misc. II. ii. (1737) III. 65 Being acted..at the same time, with an *Hylomania, whereby they madly dote upon Matter. **1881** *Dublin Rev.* Ser. III. V. 236 He..establishes the *hylo-morphical system held by St. Thomas. **1888** J. MARTINEAU *Study Relig.* I. II. i. 324 No biomorphic or *hylomorphic doctrine can raise its head against the decree of Kant. *Ibid.* 337 To mark the differentia of these three theories we may call them respectively Anthropomorphism, Biomorphism, and *Hylomorphism. **1897** *Month* Sept. 332 The scholastic doctrine of hylomorphism. **1888** J. MARTINEAU *Study Relig.* II. III. i. 142 'Matter', construed by the *hylomorphists, declares itself competent to all. **1895** F. HALL *Two Trifles* 27 Solidiform spirits, whether *hylomorphous or otherwise, are an object of rational curiosity. **1655-87** H. MORE *App. Antid.* (1712) 228 Whether in mere Spirits themselves any arbitrary impenetrability cannot be a part of this *Hylopathetick faculty, I leave others to discuss. **1678** CUDWORTH *Intell. Syst.* Pref. 9 The eduction of all things, even life and understanding it self, out of matter, in the way of qualities, or as the passions and affections thereof, generable and corruptible; which form of atheism is styled by us..'*hylopathian'. *Ibid.* I. v. 759 This was the Subterfuge of the Old Hylopathian Atheists. *c* **1800** R. CUMBERLAND *John de Lancaster* (1809) I. 269 Thales, the hylopathian, whose principle of things was water. **1682** H. MORE *Annot. Glanvill's Lux O.* 217 A kind of *Hylo-pathick disposition of Impenetrability. **1864** WEBSTER, **Hylopathism*, **Hylopathist*. [**1655-87** H. MORE *App. Antid.* iii. (1712) 189 This affection of a Spirit we will make bold to call..by one Greek term ὑλοπάθεια which..we will as plainly as we can define thus, A power in a Spirit..of becoming.. so firmly and closely united to a Body, as both to actuate, and to be acted upon, to affect, and be affected thereby.] *Ibid.* 228 The voluntary exertion of this *Hylopathy. **1891** *Daily News* 3 Apr. 5/2 The *Hylo-Phenomenal theorem of existence. **1884** *Cassell's Encycl. Dict.*, *Hylo-idealism*, ..is sometimes called *hylo-phenomenalism. **1676** H. MORE *Remarks* 141 That matter is misplaced, and the *Hylostatick Spirit of the Universe would dispose of it better. *Ibid.* 118 That which I call the Hylarchical or *Hylostatical Spirit of the world. **1828** WEBSTER, **Hulotheism*, the doctrine or belief that matter is God, or that there is no God, except matter and the universe. **1847** in CRAIG. **1864** WEBSTER, *Hulotheism*, Hylotheism. **1881** *Jrnl. Science* Jan. 50 All adoration therefore 'becomes pure Hylo-theism and self-worship'. **1859** F. HALL *Contrib. towards Index* 1 Aphorisms of the *hylotheistic theory.

‖**hylodes** (haɪ'ləʊdiːz). *Zool.* [mod.L. (1826) a. Gr. ὑλώδης woody.] A genus of American toads; an animal of this genus.

1858 THOREAU *Maine W.* (1894) 183 We also heard the hylodes and tree-toads.

hyloid ('haɪlɔɪd), *a.* and *sb.* *Zool.* [f. HYLA + -OID.] **a.** *adj.* Of or pertaining to the *Hylidæ* or tree-frogs. **b.** *sb.* One of the *Hylidæ*.

hyloist ('haɪləʊɪst). Also **huloist**. [erron. for *hylist*, f. Gr. ὕλη matter.] (See quot. 1847.)

1818 T. L. PEACOCK *Nightmare Abb.* (1875) 340 Leaving ..the materialists, hyloists, and antihyloists to settle this point among them. **1847** CRAIG, *Huloist*, one who affirms that matter is God. **1864** WEBSTER, *Huloist*, the same as Hyloist.

hylote, obs. form of HELOT.

hylozoic (haɪləʊ'zəʊɪk), *a.* [f. HYLO- + Gr. ζω-ή life + -IC.] Of or pertaining to hylozoism; believing in hylozoism; materialistic.

1678 CUDWORTH *Intell. Syst.* I. ii. §3. 62 These atheists may be also called 'Hylozoick'..because they derive all things in the whole universe..from the life of the Matter. **1837-9** HALLAM *Hist. Lit.* (1847) III. iii. §8. 305 Hylozoic atheism which accounts the universe to be animated in all its parts. **1888** J. MARTINEAU *Study Relig.* II. III. i. 160 Hylozoic systems that stop with plant life as a type.

So **† hylo'zoical** *a.* = prec.

1678 CUDWORTH *Intell. Syst.* I. iii. §1. 105 Another form of Atheism, called by us hylozoical.

hylozoism (haɪləʊ'zəʊɪz(ə)m). [f. as prec. + -ISM. Cf. F. *hylozoïsme*.] The theory that matter is endowed with life, or that life is merely a property of matter.

1678 CUDWORTH *Intell. Syst.* I. iii. §1. 105 Hylozoism.. makes all Body, as such, and therefore every smallest Atom of it, to have Life Essentially belonging to it. **1817** COLERIDGE *Biog. Lit.* 63 The hypothesis of Hylozoism..is the death of all rational physiology, and indeed of all physical science. **1887** R. D. HICKS in *Encycl. Brit.* XXII. 563/2 To Cleanthes and Chrysippus..there was no real difference between matter and its cause..they have reached the final result of unveiled hylozoism.

hylozoist (haɪləʊ'zəʊɪst). [f. as prec. + -IST.] A believer in hylozoism; a materialist.

1678 CUDWORTH *Intell. Syst.* I. iii. §2. 105 As every Atomist is not therefore necessarily an Atheist, so neither must every Hylozoist needs be accounted such. **1768-74** TUCKER *Lt. Nat.* (1852) I. 299 The ancient hylozoists, as we learn from Cudworth, ascribed an imperfect perception to their atoms. **1869** MOZLEY *Ess.*, *Argt. Design* (1878) II. 370 The ancient Hylozoists and Kosmoplastic philosophers.

Hence **hylozo'istic** *a.*, materialistic; **hylozo'istically** *adv.*

1869 BARING-GOULD *Orig. Relig. Belief* I. 296 This infinite substance [matter] was, he said, immortal and imperishable, and he designated it hylozoistically the Deity. **1885** *Sat. Rev.* 14 Nov. 654/1 The doctrine termed technically hylozoistic. **1890** J. F. SMITH tr. *Pfleiderer's Develop. Theol.* IV. i. 338 His agnostic evolutionism is only a disguised materialistic (hylozoistic) pantheism.

hylp, obs. f. HELP.

hylt, obs. f. HILT *sb.*

hylte, pa. t. of HILD *v.* *Obs.*

hyly, obs. f. HIGHLY *adv.*

hylyn, obs. f. ISLAND.

hym, obs. form of HIM, HEM, *pron.*

Hymen^{1} ('haɪmən). [a. L. *Hymen*, a. Gr. Ὑμήν, in mythology the god of marriage; also in later Greek = ὑμέναιος a wedding hymn.]

1. In Greek and Roman mythology: The god of marriage, represented as a young man carrying a torch and veil. ***Hymen's band***, etc., marriage, wedlock. ***Hymen's temple, fane***, etc., the church at which a marriage is solemnized.

1590 MARLOWE *Edw. II*, I. iv. 174 Would..That..at the marriage-day The cup of Hymen had been full of poison. **1600** SHAKS. *A. Y. L.* V. iv. 135 Here's eight that must take hands, To ioyne in Hymens bands. **1789** E. DARWIN *Bot. Gard.* 164 To Hymen's fane the bright procession moves. *a* **1839** PRAED *Poems* (1864) II. 404 Oh! why should Hymen ever blight The roses Cupid wore? **1883** MISS BRADDON *Gold. Calf* I. ix. 268 It was an awful business, this marriage, when she came to the very threshold of Hymen's temple.

2. Marriage; wedlock; wedding, nuptials. Now *rare*.

1608 D. T. *Ess. Pol. & Mor.* 109 a, The bond of an honorable and lawfull Hymen. **1624** MASSINGER *Renegado* V. iii, To whose bounty Owe we our thanks for gracing thus our hymen? **1697** DRYDEN *Æneid* VII. 769 A bloody Hymen shall th' alliance join Betwixt the Trojan and Ausonian line. **1788** LADY HAWKE *Julia de Gramont* II. 203 On your propitious hymen may smiling peace..for ever wait! **1838** LYTTON *Alice* III. viii, 'These are the feelings for a prudent Hymen', said Vargrave.

3. A wedding-hymn, hymeneal song. *rare*.

1613 R. CAWDREY *Table Alph.* (ed. 3), *Hymen*, songs sung at marriages. **1633** P. FLETCHER *Purple Isl.* XII. lxxvii, Heaven's winged shoals..Attune their higher notes, and hymens sing. **1807** ROBINSON *Archæol. Græca* V. xi. 460 Many hymens sang.

4. *attrib.*, as ***Hymen-bed, -wings***.

1597-8 BP. HALL *Sat.* IV. i. 129 And give him hansell of his Hymen-bed.

hymen^{2} ('haɪmən). [a. Gr. ὑμήν, ὑμένος thin skin, membrane. Cf. F. *hymen* (Paré 16th c.).]

1. *Anat.* The virginal membrane, a fold of mucous membrane stretched across and partially closing the external orifice of the vagina.

1615 CROOKE *Body of Man* 235 Let vs set downe..the true History of the Hymen. **1704** J. HARRIS *Lex. Techn.*, *Hymen*, is a circular Folding of the inner Membrane of the Vagina. **1789** BAILLIE in *Phil. Trans.* LXXIX. 76 The existence of the hymen..becomes a collateral confirmation of the same opinion. **1807** M. BAILLIE *Morb. Anat.* (ed. 7) 392 The hymen was perfect; and the uterus had not received that increase of bulk which is usual at puberty.

† 2. *Bot.* (See quot.) *Obs.*

1727-41 CHAMBERS *Cycl.*, *Hymen* is..used by botanists for a fine delicate skin, wherewith flowers are inclosed while in the bud, and which bursts as the flower blows or opens. **1730-6** in BAILEY (folio). **1818** in TODD; and in later dicts.

3. *Conch.* The ligament between the opposite valves of a bivalve shell.

4. *Comb.*, as ***hymen-like*** adj.

1889 J. M. DUNCAN *Lect. Dis. Wom.* XV. (ed. 4) 108 A diaphragm or hymen-like membranous dissepiment.

hymen, var. HEMEN *pron.*, *Obs.*, them.

Hymenaic (haɪmə'neɪɪk), *a.* *rare*. [ad. L. *hymenaicum*, f. Gr. ὑμέναι-ος, f. Ὑμήν HYMEN^{1}.] *lit.* Of or pertaining to Hymen; used to invoke Hymen. ***Hymenaic dimeter*** (L. *hymenaicum dimetrum*), a dactylic dimeter acatalectic (–◡◡–◡◡).

(Described by the Latin grammarian Marius Plotius, who exemplifies it by the two Sapphic lines Ὑμεν' Ὑμήναον, ὦ τὸν Ἀδώνιον, and the L. 'mens sibi conscia'.)

hymenal ('haɪmənəl), *a.* [f. HYMEN^{2} + -AL^{1}.] Of or relating to the hymen, as in *hymenal caruncles*.

1886 in *Syd. Soc. Lex.*

hymeneal (haɪmə'niːəl), *a.* and *sb.* Forms: 7 **hymniall, himeneall, hymeneall, -æall,** 8–9 **-æal,** 7– **-eal.** [f. L. *hymenæ-us* (also *hymenēius*), a. Gr. ὑμέναιος belonging to wedlock, also as sb. a wedding, wedding-song (see HYMEN^{1}) + -AL^{1}.]

A. *adj.* Pertaining to marriage.

1602 MARSTON *Antonio's Rev.* III. v. F iv b, Disloyal to our hymniall rites. **1654** WHITLOCK *Zootomia* 522 Martyrs.. who lookt on flaming Faggots, but as Hymenæall, and Nuptiall Torches. **1792** MAD. D'ARBLAY *Lett. to J. Bryant* 7 Aug., Views of hymeneal connexions. **1838** JAS. GRANT *Sk. Lond.* 165 The 'lovely bride', about to be led to the hymeneal altar.

B. *sb.* **1.** A wedding-hymn.

1717 POPE *Eloisa* 220 For her white virgins Hymenæals sing. **1719** *Freethinker* No. 140 ¶5 The Birds warbled out their Hymeneals. **1871** R. ELLIS *Catullus* lxi. 4 Now doth a virgin approach, now soundeth a glad hymeneal.

2. *pl.* A wedding, nuptials.

1655 *Theophania* 112 All in general expected either with envy or desire the consummation of their hymeneals. **1744** H. WALPOLE *Lett. H. Mann* (1834) I. ci. 340, I will not talk any more politically but turn to hymeneals. **1809** MAR. EDGEWORTH *Manœuvring* xvi, All the pride, pomp, and circumstance of these glorious hymeneals appeared to them but as a dream.

Hence **hyme'neally** *adv.*

1839 T. HOOK in *New Monthly Mag.* LV. 443 The 'roseate bands', which sound so harmoniously and so hymeneally, had not been sufficiently strong. **1841** ORDERSON *Creol.* xv. 167 Our hymeneally addicted isle.

hymenean (haɪmə'niːən), *a.* and *sb.* Also 7 **hymenæan**. [f. as prec. + -AN.]

A. *adj.* = HYMENEAL *a.* Now *rare*.

1606 WARNER *Alb. Eng.* XVI. cv. 410 To haue but strict-confined loue in Hymænean bownes? *a* **1649** DRUMM. OF HAWTH. *Poems* Wks. (1711) 40 The hymenean bed fair brood shall grace. **1799** CAMPBELL *Pleas. Hope* I. 202 The sacred home of Hymenean joy.

† B. *sb.* = HYMENEAL *sb.* 1. *Obs.*

1667 MILTON *P.L.* IV. 711 Here..Eve deckt first her Nuptial Bed, And heav'nly Quires the Hymenæan sung.

hymenectomy (haɪmə'nɛktəmɪ). *Surg.* [f. HYMEN^{2} + -ECTOMY.] Excision of the hymen.

1931 in R. J. E. SCOTT *Gould's Med. Dict.* (ed. 3). **1962** *Lancet* 26 May 1117/2 After consulting a gynæcologist she underwent an operation for a hymenectomy 8 days before the hearing of the petition.

hymenial (haɪ'miːnɪəl), *a.*^{1} *Bot.* [f. HYMENI-UM + -AL^{1}.] Pertaining to the hymenium.

hymenial layer (of lichens): the layer of the thallus which is composed of paraphyses and asci (*Syd. Soc. Lex.*).

1874 COOKE *Fungi* 40 Smaller and younger spores pushing up from the hymenial cells. **1875** BENNETT & DYER *Sachs' Bot.* 240 The hymenial surfaces are greatly extended.

hy'menial *a.*^{2}, erroneous var. of HYMENEAL.

1710 *Brit. Apollo* III. No. 48. 3/1, I shall link her in th' Hymenial Tye. **1835** MISS SEDGWICK *Linwoods* (1873) II. 266 It must have been compounded by some good hymenial genius.

hymenic (haɪ'mɛnɪk), *a.* [f. HYMEN^{2} + -IC.] Pertaining to the hymen: membranous.

1855 in MAYNE *Expos. Lex.* **1886** in *Syd. Soc. Lex.*

hymenicolar (haɪmə'nɪkələ(r)), *a.* *Bot.* [f. HYMENI-UM + L. *cola* inhabitant + -AR.] Inhabiting the hymenium of fungi.

1886 in *Syd. Soc. Lex.*

hymeniferous (haɪmə'nɪfərəs), *a.* *Bot.* [f. as prec. + -FEROUS.] Provided with a hymenium.

1890 in *Cent. Dict.*

hymeniophore (haɪ'miːnɪəʊfɔə(r)). *Bot.* [f. *hymenio-* HYMENIUM + Gr. -φόρος carrying.] = HYMENOPHORE.

1890 in *Cent. Dict.*

hymenitis (haɪmə'naɪtɪs). *Path.* [f. HYMEN^{2} + -ITIS.] Inflammation of the hymen.

1855 in MAYNE *Expos. Lex.* **1886** in *Syd. Soc. Lex.* **1889** J. M. DUNCAN *Lect. Dis. Wom.* XX. (ed. 4) 162 Other remote causes..such as..hymenitis, vestibulitis.

‖**hymenium** (haɪ'miːnɪəm). *Bot.* Pl. **hymenia**. [mod.L., ad. Gr. ὑμένιον, dim. of ὑμήν HYMEN^{2}.] The spore-bearing surface in fungi. In the common mushroom the hymenium covers the gills.

1830 LINDLEY *Nat. Syst. Bot.* 334 The hymenium, in which the sporules are deposited. **1858** CARPENTER *Veg. Phys.* §778 This..pileus, or cap, is composed of two membranes, of which the upper and outer is simple and imperforate, like the cortical layer of lichens; whilst the inner bears the fructification, and is termed the hymenium. **1882** VINES *Sachs' Bot.* 311 Small stalked cups, the flattened cavity of which bears a hymenium in which ascospores are formed.

b. *attrib.* and *Comb.*

1875 BENNETT & DYER *Sachs' Bot.* 240 The hymenium-bearing body itself may be the product of a sexual process.

hymeno- (ˌhaɪmənəʊ), repr. Gr. ὑμενο-, combining form of ὑμήν, ὑμένος (ῠ) membrane, HYMEN², as in ὑμενόπτερος HYMENOPTEROUS. The other compounds now in use are technical terms of recent formation.

hymenodictyonine (-ˈdɪktɪəʊnaɪn) [Gr. δίκτυον net + -INE], an alkaloid obtained from *Hymenodictyon excelsum*, an East Indian shrub. **hymeˈnogeny** [-GENY], the production of membranes by the simple contact of two liquids. **hymeˈnography** [-GRAPHY], a description of the membranes of animal bodies (Mayne, 1855). **hymenolichen** (ˌhaɪmənəʊˈlaɪkən), a lichen having features in common with hymenomycetal fungi. **hymeˈnology** [-LOGY] (see quot. 1855); hence **ˌhymenoˈlogical** *a.* **hymenomycete** (ˌhaɪmənəʊmaɪˈsiːt) [ad. mod.L. *hymenomycētēs* pl., f. Gr. μύκητες, pl. of μύκης mushroom], one of the *Hymenomycetes*, an order of fungi in which the hymenium is on the exposed surface of the sporophore; hence **ˌhymenomyˈcetal**, **ˌhymenomyˈcetous** *adjs.*, belonging to or having the nature of a hymenomycete; **ˌhymenomyˈcetoid** *a.* [-OID], resembling a hymenomycete. **ˈhymenophore**, ‖**hymeˈnophorum** [Gr. -φόρος carrying], the part of a fungus which supports the hymenium (cf. HYMENIOPHORE). **ˌhymenophyˈllaceous** *a.* [Gr. φύλλ-ον leaf], belonging to, or having the characters of, the *Hymenophyllaceæ*, or film-ferns, a family of ferns with delicately membranous and pellucid fronds, including *Hymenophyllum* and *Trichomanes*. **hymeˈnotomy** [Gr. -τομία, τομή cutting], dissection of animal membranes (Mayne 1855); incision of the hymen (*Syd. Soc. Lex.* 1886).

1884 *Times* 14 Aug. 3 There is a close analogy in chemical properties between nicotine and *hymenodictyonine. **1884** *Cassell's Encycl. Dict.* (quoting DUNGLISON), **Hymenogeny.* **1890** *Athenæum* 5 Apr. 439/2 Specimens of a new British *hymeno-lichen, *Cyconema interruptum.* **1847** CRAIG, **Hymenology.* **1855** MAYNE *Expos. Lex.*, *Hymenology*, term for that branch [of anatomy] which treats of the nature and structure of membranes. **1874** COOKE *Fungi* 50 Such *hymenomycetal forms as Clavaria and Pterula. **1884** *Athenæum* 26 Jan. 124/1 Structurally it [*Sphæria pocula*] is hymenomycetal and not ascomycetal. **1887** GARNSEY tr. *De Bary's Fungi* v. §88. 302 The sporophore would be thought at first sight to belong to a Peziza rather than to a *Hymenomycete. **1857** BERKELEY *Cryptog. Bot.* §410. 374 Other *hymenomycetoid expansions. **1866** *Treas. Bot.* 608/1 *Hymenophorum*, the cellular or filamentous structure in *hymenomycetous fungi, on which the hymenium or fructifying surface is spread like wax upon a mould. **1874** COOKE *Fungi* 18 The stem and cap or pileus, which together constitute what is called the *hymenophore.

hymenoid (ˈhaɪmənɔɪd), *a. Bot.* [ad. Gr. ὑμενοειδής membranous: see HYMEN² and -OID.] Resembling a membrane; having a membranous structure.

1886 in *Syd. Soc. Lex.*

hymenopter (haɪməˈnɒptə(r)). [ad. F. *hyménoptère*: see next.] A hymenopterous insect.

1828 in WEBSTER. **1859** R. F. BURTON *Centr. Afr.* in *Jrnl. Geog. Soc.* XXIX. 135 *note*, This large hymenopter is of several varieties. **1881** —— in *Academy* 21 May 366/3 That 'terrible hymenopter', the Quissonde ant.

‖**Hymenoptera** (haɪməˈnɒptərə), *sb. pl. Zool.* [mod.L. (Linnæus, 1748), a. Gr. ὑμενόπτερα, neut. pl. of ὑμενόπτερος; see HYMENOPTEROUS.] A large and important order of insects (including the ants, wasps, bees, etc.), having four membranous wings (which are, however, sometimes caducous or absent); the females have an ovipositor, which may also serve as a sting.

1773 T. P. YEATS *Instit. Entom.* 19 *Hymenoptera*..have four membranaceous naked wings..[and] the abdomen armed with a sting. **1802** KIRBY *Monogr. Apium Ang.* title-p., Some Introductory Remarks upon the Class Hymenoptera. **1834** MEDWIN *Angler in Wales* I. 163 Like other hymenoptera, during the period of generation..they have wings.

Hence **hymeˈnopteral** *a.* = HYMENOPTEROUS; **hymeˈnopteran**, a member of the order Hymenoptera; **hymeˈnopterist**, an entomologist whose special study is Hymenoptera.

1828 WEBSTER, *Hymenopteral*, having four membranous wings. **1842** BRANDE *Dict. Sc.*, etc., *Hymenopterans.* **1877** HUXLEY *Anat. Inv. Anim.* vii. 450 The female..never leaves the body of the Hymenopteran in which she is parasitic. **1881** *Pennsylv. Sch. Jrnl.* XXX. 125 Prof. Henri de Saussen, a distinguished hymenopterist, of Geneva.

hymenopterology (ˌhaɪmənɒptəˈrɒlədʒɪ). [f. prec. + -(O)LOGY.] The branch of Entomology that deals with the Hymenoptera. Hence **hymenopteˈrologist** = HYMENOPTERIST; **hymenopteroˈlogical** *a.*, belonging to hymenopterology.

1855 MAYNE *Expos. Lex.*, Hymenopterology, Hymenopterological. **1875** LUBBOCK *Orig. Civiliz.* App. 480 Our most learned hymenopterologist.

hymenopterous (haɪməˈnɒptərəs), *a.* [f. mod.L. *hymenopter-us*, a. Gr. ὑμενόπτερος (f. ὑμενο- membrane, HYMENO- + πτερόν wing) + -OUS.] Having membranous wings; belonging to the Hymenoptera.

1813 BINGLEY *Anim. Biog.* (ed. 4) I. 48 Hymenopterous insects..have generally four membranaceous naked wings. **1816** KIRBY & SP. *Entomol.* (1843) I. 88 The sting of hymenopterous insects. **1874** LUBBOCK *Orig. & Met. Ins.* ii. 33 The ordinary type of Hymenopterous larva..is a fleshy apod grub.

Hymettian (haɪˈmɛtɪən), *a.* [f. L. *Hymettius* (f. *Hymettus*, Gr. Ὑμηττός) + -IAN.] Of or belonging to Mount Hymettus in Attica, famous in antiquity for its honey and marble; hence *poet.* honeyed, sweet (cf. HYBLÆAN).

1601 HOLLAND tr. *Pliny's Nat. Hist.* XVII. i. 499 Foure goodly pillars of Hymettian Marble. **1658** J. ROWLAND tr. *Moufet's Theater of Insects* 908 He that will make a good mixture of wine and honey, must mingle with new Hymettian Honey, old Falernian Wine. **1795** COLERIDGE *To R. B. Sheridan* in *Poetical Works* (1912) I. 88 Thy temples with Hymettian flow'rets wreath'd.

hymn (hɪm), *sb.* Forms: 1 ymen, ymmon, hymen, 3–6 ymne, (3–5 imne, 4–5 impne), 4–6 ympne, (4 ymyn, 5 umne), 5–6 hympne, (6 ime, imme, himme), 6–7 hymme, hymne, 6– hymn. [f. L. *hymnus*, a. Gr. ὕμνος a song or ode in praise of gods or heroes, taken by the LXX to render various Heb. words, meaning a song of praise to God; hence in N.T. (Eph. v. 19, Col. iii. 16), and in the Latin Vulgate and Christian writers from Augustine. Late eccl. L. *ymnus* was adopted in OE. as *ymen*, pl. *ymenas*, *ymnas*; but the ME. forms repr. OF. *ymne*, often modified after contemporary L. *ympnus*, *hympnus*, and at length under classical influence to *hymn* (mod.F. *hymne*). The earliest evidence for the non-pronunciation of final *-n* is app. Palsgrave's *imme.*]

1. A song of praise to God; any composition in praise of God which is adapted to be chanted or sung; spec. a metrical composition adapted to be sung in a religious service; sometimes distinguished from *psalm* or *anthem*, as not being part of the text of the Bible.

c **825** *Vesp. Psalter* cxxxvi. 3 Hymen singað us of songum Sione. **971** *Blickl. Hom.* 147 He [Michael] wæs ymen singende mid eallum þæm englum. *c* **1000** *Ags. Ps.* (Th.) cxviii. [cxix.] 171 Nu mine weleras ðe wordum belcettað ymnas elne. *a* **1225** *Ancr. R.* 20 To [ðe] laste uers of euerich imne. *Ibid.* 158 Vor so hit is in his ymne: 'antra deserti teneris sub annis'. *a* **1300** *E.E. Psalter* xcix. [c.] 4 In schrift his porches þat be, In ympnes to him schrive yhe. **1382** WYCLIF *Col.* iii. 16 In salmes, and ymnes and spiritual songis. *c* **1420** *Pallad. on Husb.* VII. 260 (148) Saluz, blisse, ymne, honour..Iesu, be to The. **1483** *Cath. Angl.* 186/1 To synge Hympnes, *himpnizare.* **1526** *Pilgr. Perf.* (W. de W. 1531) 215 b, As the chirche syngeth in the ymne Aue Maris stella. **1530** PALSGR. 231/2 Hymme that is song in the churche, *hymne. Ibid.* 234/1 Imme that is songe, *hymne.* **1624** SANDERSON *12 Serm.* (1632) 458 His disciples sang an hymme. **1738** WESLEY *Hymn, Lift up your Heads* iii, To Psalms and Hymns we may aspire, If Anthems are too high. **1856** STANLEY *Sinai & Pal.* iii. (1858) 192 The earliest hymn of Christian devotion, burst forth from the multitude, Hosanna to the Son of David.

2. a. An ode or song of praise in honour of a deity, a country, etc.

1513 DOUGLAS *Æneis* VI. x. 70 Hympnis of price, trivmphe, and victory All singand. **1613** PURCHAS *Pilgrimage* (1614) 457 Every noone-tide they sing Hymnes to the Sunne. **1697** DRYDEN *Virg. Georg.* II. 535 In jolly Hymns they praise the God of Wine. **1796** H. HUNTER tr. *St. Pierre's Stud. Nat.* (1799) III. 254 This hymn will stand a comparison with the finest odes of Horace. **1843** *Penny Cycl.* XXVI. 171/2 The names of the authors of the hymns of the Rigveda have been handed down with the Veda itself. **1871** R. ELLIS *Catullus* lxi. 12 Chant in melody musical Hymns of bridal. **1880** *Grove's Dict. Mus.* II. 219/2 (*La Marseillaise*) The words and music of this popular French hymn are the composition of Claude Joseph Rouget de Lisle [24 Apr. 1792].

b. hymn of hate, the *Hassgesang* of the German poet Ernst Lissauer (1882–1937), an anti-British song; freq. *transf.*

1914 [see HATE *sb.*[1] 1 c]. **1915** A. HUXLEY *Let.* 26 Apr. (1969) 70 We're losing our heads and our senses of humour—and soon we shall be reduced to writing Hymns of Hate—then we're lost. **1916** *Anzac Book* 44 No 'Hymn of Hate' has yet been composed which would give expression to the hatred which has possessed me. **1918** G. B. SHAW *Pen Portraits* (1932) 40 Mr Chesterton, in his wildest hymns of hate, will break into a joke on his top note. **1945** H. G. WELLS *Happy Turning* viii. 31 (*heading*) A hymn of hate against sycamores. **1963** E. HYAMS *New Statesmanship* 8 This must not also entail blinking the facts about the Germans even if one did not join in the hymn of hate. **1966** B. KIMENYE *Kalasanda Revisited* 67 She boarded the bus whilst still employed on her hymn of hate.

3. *attrib.* and *Comb.*, as ***hymn-maker***, ***-singer***, ***-singing***, ***-tune***, ***-writer***, ***-writing***; ***hymn-quoting*** adj., ***hymn-wise*** adv.

1483 *Cath. Angl.* 186/1 An Himpne maker, *hympnista.* **1653** ASHWELL *Fides Apost.* 263 His Creed..sung hymne-wise in the Church-service. **1768–74** TUCKER *Lt. Nat.* (1852) II. 234 Pathetic lectures, long prayers, and incessant hymn-singings. *a* **1835** MRS. HEMANS *Poems, View from Castri*, The pine-woods, their choral hymn-notes sending. **1879** WHITNEY *Sanskrit Gram.* p. xiv, It is the most interesting of all, after the Rig-Veda, because it contains the largest amount of hymn-material.

hymn (hɪm), *v.* [f. prec. sb.]

1. *trans.* To worship or praise in song; to sing hymns to.

1667 MILTON *P. L.* VI. 96 As sons of one great Sire Hymning th' Eternal Father. **1733** POPE *Ess. Man* III. 156 In the same temple..All vocal beings hymn'd their equal God. **1796–7** COLERIDGE *Poems* (1862) 21 Therefore oft I hymn thy name. **1830** SIR R. GRANT *Hymn, 'Oh Worship the King'* vi, While angels delight to hymn thee above. **1874** PUSEY *Lent. Serm.* 453 Evening by evening, as they came to the setting sun, they hymned Father, Son, and Holy Ghost.

2. To sing as a hymn; to express in a hymn or song of praise.

1727 POPE *Mary Gulliver to Capt. Gulliver* 106 To hymn harmonious Houyhnhnm through the nose. **1794** COLERIDGE *Relig. Musings* 6 The heavenly multitude, Who hymned the song of peace o'er Bethlehem's fields. **1813** H. & J. SMITH *Rej. Addr., Rebuilding*, The spheres hymn music. **1875** JOWETT *Plato* (ed. 2) III. 451 They hymn their praises and call them by sweet names.

3. *absol.* To sing hymns.

1715–20 POPE *Iliad* XXIV. 83 Where this minstrel-god..amid the quire Stood proud to hymn, and tune his youthful lyre. **1778** *Sk. Tabernacle Frames* 28 Then, as they're hymning, checks 'em with a Gag. **1804** J. GRAHAME *Sabbath* 122 Thus reading, hymning, all alone, unseen, The shepherd-boy the Sabbath holy keeps. **1827** POLLOK *Course T.* VII, The thrush Concerting with the lark that hymned on high.

Hence **hymning** (ˈhɪmɪŋ) *vbl. sb.* and *ppl. a.*

1667 MILTON *P.L.* III. 417 Thus they in Heav'n..Thir happie hours in joy and hymning spent. **1674** DRYDEN *State Innoc.* IV. i, None of all his hymning guards are nigh. **1874** FARRAR *Christ* (1894) 118 Some band of hymning angels.

hymnal (ˈhɪmnəl), *a.* and *sb.* [f. L. *hymn-us* + -AL[1]. The sb. use represents a med.L. *hymnāle* occurring as *imnale* in Wr.-Wülcker 589/1.]

A. *adj.* Of or pertaining to a hymn or hymns.

1644 SIR E. DERING *Prop. Sacr.* C iij b, Use of Musick in the hymnall part of Service. **1763** J. BROWN *Poetry & Mus.* vi. 102 We find many of the elder Poets of Greece mixing the hymnal and enthusiastic with the historic or narrative Species. **1887** SIR T. MARTIN in *Blackw. Mag.* Nov. 689 They begin the awful Hymnal lay.

B. *sb.* A collection of hymns for use in divine worship; a hymn-book.

14.. *Voc.* in Wr.-Wülcker 588/6 *Hymnare* [*in later hand*] a hymnale. **1537** in Glasscock *Rec. St. Michael's, Bp. Stortford* (1882) 127 *Item* an Imnall prynted and iiij pr[oc]essionals of parchement. **1543** *Churchw. Acc. St. Giles, Reading* 67 Paid for an Imnenall xiiij[d]. **1554** in *Antiquary* (1894) Nov. 187 For ij hymnalls iiijs. **1846** MASKELL *Mon. Rit.* I. p. xcvi, It cannot be doubted that S. Augustine, with the breviary and missal recommended by S. Gregory, introduced also the hymnal then used at Rome. **1887** (*title*) Congregational Church Hymnal.

hymnar, var. HYMNARY, HYMNER[1].

1853 ROCK *Ch. of Fathers* III. II. 13 One of Ælfric's enactments requiring each clerk to have..a hymnar.

hymnarium (hɪmˈnɛərɪəm). Pl. **-ia.** [med.L.] = HYMNARY.

1924 *Glasgow Herald* 7 June 4 The extensive hymnaria attributed to the famous Bishop of Milan [St. Ambrose].

hymnary (ˈhɪmnərɪ). [ad. med.L. *hymnārium*, f. *hymn-us*: see -ARY.] A collection of hymns; a hymnal.

1888 E. H. PLUMPTRE in *Contemp. Rev.* Jan. 59 They [the vicars] were required to learn by heart..their Psalter, their Hymnary [*ympnario*], and their Anthem-book. **1898** (*title*) The Church Hymnary. Authorised for use in Public Worship by the Church of Scotland, the Free Church of Scotland, the United Presbyterian Church [etc.].

hymn-book (ˈhɪmbʊk). A book containing a collection of hymns.

c **900** tr. *Bæda's Hist.* V. xxii[i.]. (Concl.), Ymenbec misenlice metre. **1779** WESLEY *Hymns* Pref. 4, I am persuaded no such Hymn-book..has yet been published. **1854** EMERSON *Lett. & Soc. Aims, Eloquence* Wks. (Bohn) III. 190, I call him only a good reader who can read sense and poetry into any hymn in the hymn-book.

†**ˈhymner**[1]. *Obs.* Forms: 1 ymener, hymner, ymner, 5 i-, ymner(e, hympner. [ad. eccl. L. *hymnārium*, *hymnārius* (later also *hymnāre*, *ym(p)nāre*, etc.), a hymnal; cf. OF. *(h)ymnier*, mod.F. *hymnaire.*] A book of hymns; a hymnal or hymnary.

c **900** in Raine *Fabric Rolls York Mins.* (Surtees) 147 Twa Cristes bec..and j. mæssboc and j. ymener and j. salter. *a* **1100** *Charter of Leofric* in Kemble *Cod. Dipl.* IV. 275 .II. ymneras and .I. deorwyrðe bletsingboc and .III. oðre. ?*c* **1450** in Wr.-Wülcker 589/1 *Imnale et Imnarium*, an ymnere. **1483** *Cath. Angl.* 186/1 an Hympner..*himpnarium.*

hymner[2] (ˈhɪmə(r), ˈhɪmnə(r)). [f. HYMN *v.* + -ER[1].] One who hymns; a singer of hymns.

1816 W. TAYLOR in *Monthly Rev.* LXXX. 358 These hymners of idolatry. **1848** LYTTON *K. Arthur* VIII. cxxi, Nature, thou..never-silent Hymner unto God. **1857** H. H. WILSON tr. *Rig-veda* III. 53 Hymner, we hear thy words, that thou hast come from afar.

hymnic ('hɪmnɪk), *a.* (*sb.*) [f. HYMN *sb.* + -IC; cf. F. *hymnique*.] Of, pertaining to, of the nature of, a hymn or hymns.

1589 PUTTENHAM *Eng. Poesie* III. vi. (Arb.) 164 The Poets Hymnick and historicall who be occupied either in diuine laudes, or in heroicall reports. **1615** SYLVESTER *St. Lewis* 592 To whom wee pay Heroick Duties in this Hymnik Lay. *a* **1631** DONNE *Poems* (1650) 255 He rounds the aire, and breaks the hymnique notes In birds, Heavens choristers, organique throates. **1830** H. N. COLERIDGE *Grk. Poets* (1834) 197 Callimachus, as in hymnic duty bound, bitterly reviles Euhemerus. **1882–3** in Schaff *Encycl. Relig. Knowl.* III. 2589/2 Several cases in which very moderate poetic talents have produced eminent hymnic benefactions.

B. *sb.* A composition of the nature of a hymn.

a **1834** LAMB *Misc. Wks.* (1871) 451 The more modern or Wattsian hymnics.

'hymnicide. *nonce-wd.* [f. as next + -CIDE 2.] The 'murdering' of a hymn, i.e. by alterations.

1862 *Evangel. Christendom* July 355 We have here a new illustration of the unhappy practice of hymnicide, which is as unjust to the authors of hymns, as it is generally detrimental to poetry.

†**hym'niferous,** *a. rare*$^{-0}$. [f. L. *hymn-us* HYMN *sb.* + -FEROUS.] 'Bringing or producing hymns' (Bailey, 1721).

hymnifi'cation. *nonce-wd.* [f. as prec. + -FICATION.] The making of hymns.

1891 G. MEREDITH *One of our Conq.* III. ix. 173 The hideousness of our hymnification.

†**'hymnish,** *a. Obs.* [f. HYMN *sb.* + -ISH.] Like a hymn.

1583 STANYHURST *Æneis* II. (Arb.) 51 Sonnets are carroled hymnish By lads and maydens.

hymnist ('hɪmnɪst). [f. L. *hymn-us*, Gr. *ὕμν-ος*, HYMN *sb.* + -IST: cf. *psalmist*.] A composer of hymns.

1621 G. SANDYS *Ovid's Met.* XI. (1626) 217 A Dragon.. gaping to deuoure the Hymnists face. **1813** T. JEFFERSON *Writ.* (1830) IV. 225, I have no hesitation in giving him the palm over all the hymnists of every language. **1858** BAILEY *The Age* 104 The awful hymnist Orpheus, bard of fable.

hymnless ('hɪmlɪs), *a.* [f. HYMN *sb.* + -LESS.] Without a hymn.

1822 MILMAN *Martyr of Antioch* 166 And mute as sepulchres the hymnless temples stand. **1873** W. TAYLOR in Spurgeon *Treas. Dav.* Ps. cxlix. 6 The man who has a dumb spirit and a hymnless heart.

hymnodist ('hɪmnədɪst). [f. next + -IST.] One skilled in hymnody; a hymnist.

a **1711** KEN *Hymns Evang.* Poet. Wks. 1721 I. 197 For their Divines their Hymnodists they own'd, Who while they prais'd a God, that God aton'd. **1883** *Ch. Times* 25 May 372 St. Joseph the Hymnographer.. was the most prolific hymnodist of the Eastern church.

hymnody ('hɪmnədɪ). [ad. med.L. *hymnōdia*, a. Gr. *ὑμνῳδία* singing of hymns, f. *ὕμνος* HYMN + *ἀείδειν* to sing, *ᾠδή* song, ODE. Cf. PSALMODY.]

1. The singing of hymns or sacred songs; the composition of hymns for singing.

a **1711** KEN *Urania* Poet. Wks. 1721 IV. 448 For as thy Temple-Offrings fall or rise, Hymnody chills or fires, Religion lives or dies. **1838** THIRLWALL *Greece* II. xii. 124 The epos.. appears to have adhered to the model of the ancient hymnody. **1862** MERIVALE *Rom. Emp.* (1865) III. xxiii. 86 The poet has strictly preserved the proper form of hymnody. **1876** C. M. DAVIES *Unorth. Lond.* (ed. 2) 151, I had been prepared for the Moravians being great in hymnody.

2. Hymns collectively; the body of hymns belonging to any age, country, church, etc.

1864 in WEBSTER. **1882–3** SCHAFF *Encycl. Relig. Knowl.* II. 1654 Among the jewels of German hymnody.

hymnographer (hɪm'nɒgrəfə(r)). [f. Gr. *ὑμνογράφ-ος* hymn-writer (f. *ὕμνο-ς* HYMN + *-γραφος* writing, writer) + -ER[1].] A composer of hymns.

a **1619** FOTHERBY *Atheom.* Pref. (1622) 4 There could none haue any cause to insult ouer another: not the Hymnographer ouer the Historiographer. [**1656** BLOUNT *Glossogr.*, *Hymnigrapher*, a Writer of Hymns. **1721** in BAILEY.] **1841** CDL. WISEMAN *Rem. Let. Rev. W. Palmer* 56 St. Prudentius, the Christian hymnographer. **1846** GROTE *Greece* I. i. (1854) I. 46 The hymnographer describes him [Dionysos] as standing on the sea-shore. **1864** *Sat. Rev.* 488 To bring before us the character of Hermes as conceived by the so-called Homeric hymnographer.

hymnography (hɪm'nɒgrəfɪ). [f. as prec. + -GRAPHY.] The literary history and bibliography of hymns.

1864 in WEBSTER. **1886** *American* XII. 154 Hymnography has become a distinct branch of literature within the last forty years.

hymnologic (hɪmnəʊ'lɒdʒɪk), *a.* [f. late Gr. *ὑμνολογικ-ός*, f. *ὑμνολόγος*: see HYMNOLOGY and -IC.] Of or pertaining to hymnology.

1883 *Homilet. Monthly* Dec. 159 The best hymnologic results of that country.

So **hymno'logical** *a.* = prec.; **hymno'logically** *adv.*, in relation to hymnology.

1882 SALA *Amer. Revis.* (1885) 392 It was something of a hymnological melody with a comic flavour. **1888** *Literary World* 10 Aug. 115/2 The lines, which recent hymnological controversy has made famous. **1892** *Sat. Rev.* 23 Apr. 485/1 Hymnologically worthless.

hymnologist (hɪm'nɒlədʒɪst). [f. Gr. *ὑμνολόγ-ος* (see next) + -IST.] **a.** A composer of hymns, a hymnist. **b.** One who studies or is versed in hymnology.

1796 C. BURNEY *Mem. Metastasio* I. 42 If Metastasio had been a mere psalmodist, or hymnologist. **1882–3** in Schaff *Encycl. Relig. Knowl.* II. 1054 Professor F. M. Bird, the hymnologist, has said that his [T. H. Gill's] hymns were destined to a long life. **1889** J. W. ROGAN in *Homilet. Rev.* Mar. 207 (Funk) Cowper.. took his place in the world as.. one of the sweetest of hymnologists and the most popular poet of his generation.

hymnology (hɪm'nɒlədʒɪ). [Originally ad. Gr. *ὑμνολογία* the singing of hymns (f. *ὑμνολόγος* hymn-singing; cf. L. *hymnologus* a singer of hymns); but in modern usage app. taken as f. HYMN *sb.* + -(O)LOGY. Cf. F. *hymnologie*, the singing of hymns, a treatise on hymns.]

†**1.** The singing of hymns. *Obs.*

a **1638** MEDE *Diat.* 56 (T.) That hymnologie which the Primitive Church used at the offering of bread and wine for the Eucharist. **1727** BAILEY vol. II, *Hymnology*, a singing of Hymns or Psalms. **1775** in ASH. **1855** MILMAN *Lat. Chr.* IX. viii. (1864) V. 385 The Chanting and Psalmody of the Church he would perhaps replace.. by a more simple and passionate hymnology.

2. The composition of hymns.

1839 STONEHOUSE *Axholme* 222 With reference to hymnology, he [Charles Wesley] was a poet of very considerable talents. **1879** FARRAR *St. Paul* II. 463 *note*, Christian hymnology began very early, though the hymns were not necessarily metrical.

3. The study of hymns, their history, use, etc.; also, the subject of this study, hymns collectively or as a form of literary composition.

1818 TODD, *Hymnology*, a collection of hymns. **1828** *Q. Rev.* July 17 We shall enter into a preliminary historical sketch of the psalmody, and what we shall take the liberty of calling the hymnology, of the Christian Church. **1855** MILMAN *Lat. Chr.* XIV. iv. (1864) IX. 174 In fact, all Hymnology, vernacular as well as Latin, is poetry only to predisposed or habituated ears. **1880** *Manch. Guard.* 24 Dec., The most comprehensive and trustworthy handbook of hymnology in the language. **1892** J. JULIAN (*title*) A Dictionary of Hymnology.

hympe, hympe halt: see HIMP.

hyn, obs. f. HIN *pron.*, HYNE, INN.

hynch, obs. f. HINCH.

hynd, obs. f. HEND *a.*

hynd, hyne, obs. ff. HIND.

hynd-, hynmast, -mest, obs. ff. HINDMOST.

hynder, obs. f. HINDER *a.*, *v.*

hyne (haɪn), *adv. Obs.* exc. *dial.* Also 4–5 **hyn, hyene, heyn(n)e, heine,** 5 **hien,** 5–7 **hine,** (8 **hind**). [A northern (chiefly Sc.) word, synonymous with southern ME. HEN, HENNE, 'hence', but app. of different origin, as OE. *hionan, heonan* would not normally be represented by *hyne*. The ordinary northern word for 'hence' was HETHEN, of which *hyne* was perh. a contraction, as also *whyne, thyne* = ME. *hweðen, þeðen*, whence, thence. Cf. also SYNE:—*siðen* (ON. *síðan*).]

1. Hence; from this place; away; departed. ***is (gone) hyne***, is departed, is no more. *dial.*

c **1375** *Sc. Leg. Saints, Paulus* 1162 þu wekit spryt, ga hyne þe way! *c* **1440** *York Myst.* xxxvi. 272 Lede we her heyne [*rimes* pyne, tyne]. *c* **1460** *Towneley Myst.* xviii. 216 We haue nede for to go hien [*rimes* myne, tyne, fyne]. *c* **1470** HENRY *Wallace* x. 514 All the men, hyn till [the] orient. *c* **1475** *Rauf Coilȝear* 49 Hine ouir seuin mylis I dwell. **1508** DUNBAR *Gold. Targe* 233 Sudaynly in the space of a luke, All was hyne went. *c* **1560** A. SCOTT *Poems* (S.T.S.) xvi. 39 All the blythenes, joy, and bliss, The lusty, wantoun lyfe, I wiss, Of lufe is hyne. **1674–91** RAY *N.C. Words* 37 *Hine*, Hence. *Cumb.* **1724** RAMSAY *Tea-t. Misc.* (1733) I. 86 Far hind out o'er the lee. **1813** W. BEATTIE *Fruits Time Parings* (1871) 32 Hyne o'er ayont the mill-stane craigs. **1871** W. ALEXANDER *Johnny Gibb* ii, They're maybe hyne awa'.

†**2.** From this world; out of this life. ***(baith) heir and hyne***, both in this world and the next. *Obs.*

c **1375** *Sc. Leg. Saints, Symon & Judas* xi. 96 Eftyr Ihesu vpraisit wes fra hyne to hewyne. *a* **1400–50** *Alexander* 799 þou must rewle all my realm qwen I am raght hyne. **1560** ROLLAND *Crt. Venus* I. 442 God ordanit lufe to be baith heir and hine. **1567** *Gude & Godlie B.* (S.T.S.) 235 Confes thy sinnis les and maer, Vnto thy God, or thow hyne wend.

†**3.** From this time; hereafter. *Obs. rare.*

c **1460** *Towneley Myst.* xvii. 90 Well is me that I shall dre Tyll I haue sene hym with myn ee, And no longer hyne. **1674–91** RAY *N.C. Words* 37 *Hine of a while*; ere long.

Hence **hyneforth**, henceforth; **hyne'forward**, henceforward (also ***fra hyne forward***); **'hyneward**, hence.

a **1400–50** *Alexander* 734 Hy þe hyneward. *c* **1400** MAUNDEV. (Roxb.) xxvi. 125 Fra heyne forward my worde sall be of als grete strenth.. as my swerde. **1434** MISYN *Mending Life* xi. 123 Heynforward, swettist lorde, go not fro me. **1570** *Henry's Wallace* I. 19 Hyne furth now [*c* **1470** hensfurth] I will my proces hald.

hyney, hynny, obs. ff. HINNY *v.*

hyng, -e, obs. ff. HANG *v.*, HINGE.

hyngel, obs. f. HINGLE.

hynt, var. HENT *v. Obs.*

hynward, obs. form of HINDWARD *adv.*

c **1440** HYLTON *Scala Perf.* (W. de W. 1494) I. xiii, Hynwarde are all bodely thynges, fforwarde are goostly thynges.

hyo- (haɪəʊ). [f. Gr. *ὑο-* in *ὑο-ειδής*: see HYOID.] A formative element employed in various modern scientific terms, chiefly anatomical, referring to the hyoid bone in connexion with adjoining parts of the body.

1811 HOOPER *Med. Dict.*, *Hyo*, names compounded of this word belong to muscles which originate from, or are inserted into, or connected with the *os hyoides*, as *Hyo-glossus, Hyo-pharyngeus, Genio-hyo-glossus*, etc.

hyo'branchial *a.*, pertaining to the hyoid bone and the branchiæ. **'hyodont, hyo'dontid** [Gr. *ὀδούς, ὀδοντ-* tooth], one of the *Hyodontidæ* or toothed herrings, a family of fresh-water fishes having teeth on the hyoid bone, found in the rivers and lakes of North America. **,hyo-epi'glottic, ,hyo-epiglo'ttidean** *adjs.*, connecting the hyoid bone with the epiglottis. **hyo'ganoid, ,hyoga'noidean** *adjs.* [GANOID], belonging to, or characteristic of, the *Hyoganoidei*, a sub-class of ganoid fishes, having the hyoid apparatus like those of the teleosts. **hyo'glossal, hyo'glossian** *adjs.* [Gr. *γλῶσσα* tongue], connected with the hyoid bone and the tongue. ‖**hyo'glossus**, a muscle of the hyoid bone and tongue. **hyo'mental** *a.* [L. *mentum* chin], pertaining to the hyoid bone together with the chin. ‖**hyo'plastron** [PLASTRON] = HYOSTERNAL *sb.*; hence **hyo'plastral** *a.*, belonging to the hyoplastron. **hyo'scapular** *a.*, pertaining to the hyoid bone and the scapula. **hyo'thyroid** *a.*, pertaining to the hyoid bone and the thyroid cartilage; also as *sb.* = hyothyroid muscle.

1848 *Hyo-branchial [see HYPOBRANCHIAL]. **1865** *Reader* No. 153. 631/3 The hyo-branchial apparatus. **1886** *Syd. Soc. Lex.*, *Hyobranchial cleft*, a cleft or fissure situated in the embryo of Vertebrata between the hyoid arch in front and the.. first true branchial arch behind. **1847** CRAIG, **Hyo-epiglottic*. **1886** *Syd. Soc. Lex.*, *Hyo-epiglottic ligament*, extending from the upper border of the hyoid bone to the epiglottis. **1881** MIVART *Cat* 230 The *hyo-epiglottidean muscles are very small ones. **1886** *Syd. Soc. Lex.*, **Hyoglossal membrane*, a fibrous layer, connecting the under surface of the base of the tongue with the body of the hyoid bone. *Ibid.*, **Hyoglossian nerve*, another term for the hypoglossal nerve. **1811** HOOPER *Med. Dict.*, **Hyo-glossus*. **1842** E. WILSON *Anat. Vade M.* 273 The posterior border of the hyo-glossus muscle. **1872** MIVART *Elem. Anat.* 287 The hyo-glossus is a flat muscle, passing from the cornua of the hyoid upwards to the side of the tongue. **1871** HUXLEY *Anat. Vert.* v. 202 In the Turtle the plastron consists of nine pieces ..the second, *hyoplastron. **1844** J. G. WILKINSON *Swedenborg's Anim. Kingd.* II. ii. 40 The *hyo-thyroid elevates the larynx, and closes the glottis.

hyocholic (haɪəʊ'kɒlɪk), *a. Chem.* [f. Gr. *ὗς, ὑο-* swine + *χολή* bile: see CHOLIC *a.*] In ***hyocholic acid***, formerly a synonym of hyoglycocholic acid, now applied to an acid ($C_{25}H_{40}O_4$) derived from this by the action of acids and alkalies.

1859 *Fownes' Chem.* 565 Hyocholic acid contains $C_{54}H_{43}NO_{10}$. **1865–72** WATTS *Dict. Chem.* III. 234 *Hyocholic acid*, $C_{25}H_{40}O_4$, an acid obtained, together with glycocine, by the action of potash on hyoglycocholic acid. **1873** RALFE *Phys. Chem.* 58 Pig's bile contains hyo-cholic acid.. conjugated with glycocin and taurin.

hyoglycocholic (,haɪəʊglɪkəʊ'kɒlɪk), *a. Chem.* [f. Gr. *ὗς, ὑο-* pig + *γλυκύς* sweet + *χολή* bile: see GLYCOCHOLIC.] In ***hyoglycocholic acid***, an acid ($C_{27}H_{43}NO_5$) which, in the form of a sodium salt, is the chief constituent in the bile of pigs. Hence **hyogly'cocholate**, a salt of this acid.

1865–72 WATTS *Dict. Chem.* III. 235 Hyoglycocholic acid is monobasic, the hyoglycocholates in the dry state containing $C_{27}H_{42}MNO_5$.

hyoid ('haɪɔɪd), *a.* and *sb. Anat.* [ad. F. *hyoïde* (16th c. in Paré), ad. mod.L. *hyoïdes*, Gr. *ὑοειδής*, shaped like the letter *υ*; *ὀστοῦν ὑοειδές* (also *ὑψιλοειδές*), the hyoid bone. Cf. HYO-.]

A. *adj.* **1.** ***hyoid bone***: the tongue-bone or *os linguæ*, situated between the chin and the thyroid cartilage. In man it is a horseshoe-shaped or U-shaped bone (whence the name) imbedded horizontally in the root of the tongue, with its convexity pointing forwards, and held in place by several ligaments.

In most mammals it is comparatively larger than in man, and is a more complicated and important structure, consisting of several distinct pieces.

1811 HOOPER *Med. Dict.* 394/2 Hyoid bone. **1830** R. KNOX *Béclard's Anat.* 35 This aperture is.. furnished with a branchial membrane supported by rays from the hyoid

bone, and an osseous operculum. **1880** M. MACKENZIE *Dis. Throat & Nose* I. 4 The cornua of the hyoid bone.

2. Pertaining to the hyoid bone.

hyoid arch, hyoid apparatus, the second visceral arch in Vertebrates, lying between the hyomandibular and hyobranchial clefts.

1842 E. WILSON *Anat. Vade M.* 271 The Hyoid branch passes forwards beneath the thyro-hyoideus. **1854** OWEN *Skel. & Teeth* in *Circ. Sc., Organ. Nat.* I. 185 The hyoid arch is the chief support of the branchial arches and gills. **1870** ROLLESTON *Anim. Life* Introd. 71 Fish have no salivary gland, and the tongue is only moveable as a part of the hyoid apparatus upon which it is carried.

B. *sb.* **1.** The hyoid bone: see A. 1.

[**1706** PHILLIPS (ed. Kersey), *Hyoides*, a Bone at the root of the Tongue. **1727-41** CHAMBERS *Cycl.* s.v., The basis of the hyoides is about a thumb's breadth long on the outer side.] **1872** MIVART *Elem. Anat.* xii. 490 His hyoid is a small structure with one pair of cornua, instead of several branchial arches. **1888** ROLLESTON & JACKSON *Anim. Life* 18 The greater cornu of the hyoid.

2. The hyoid artery.

1883 *H. Gray's Anat.* (ed. 10) 340 The hyoid runs along the upper border of the hyoid bone, supplying the muscles attached to it.

Hence **hy'oidal, hy'oidan** *adjs.* = next.

1852 TH. ROSS *Humboldt's Trav.* II. xvii. 70 The bony drum of the hyoidal bone of the araguato. **1888** ROLLESTON & JACKSON *Anim. Life* 93 The embryonic hyoidan cartilage.

hyoidean (haɪ'ɔɪdiːən), *a. Anat.* [f. mod.L. *hyoidē-us* (f. *hyoīdēs*, HYOID B) + -AN. F. has *hyoïdien*.] Of or belonging to the hyoid (bone).

1835-6 TODD *Cycl. Anat.* I. 279/2 The hyoidean furrows being separated at first by the cerebellic protuberance. **1854** OWEN *Skel. & Teeth* in *Circ. Sc., Organ. Nat.* I. 177 The hæmal arch is called the 'hyoidean arch', in reference to its supporting the movements of the tongue. **1888** ROLLESTON & JACKSON *Anim. Life* 88 The hyoidean artery.

hyomandibular (ˌhaɪəʊmæn'dɪbjʊlə(r)), *a.* and *sb. Anat.* [f. HYO- + MANDIBULAR.]

A. *adj.* Pertaining to the hyoid bone and the mandible or lower jaw.

hyomandibular bone, in fishes, the bone of the suspensorium which articulates with the cranium. ***hyomandibular cartilage***, the dorsal segment or the upper end of the hyoid arch. ***hyomandibular cleft***, the cleft between the mandibular and hyoid arches in the embryo of Vertebrates.

1875 HUXLEY in *Encycl. Brit.* I. 765/2 A hyomandibular artery..appears to represent the remains of the hyoidean and mandibular aortic arches. **1877** —— *Anat. Inv. Anim.* i. 67 The hyomandibular cleft and its boundary walls. **1888** ROLLESTON & JACKSON *Anim. Life* 93 The hyomandibular and symplectic bones.

B. *sb.* The hyomandibular bone.

1872 MIVART *Elem. Anat.* 121 In the last-named group the lower jaw is suspended from elements of the ear capsule by a bone called the Hyomandibular. **1878** BELL *Gegenbaur's Comp. Anat.* p. xii, The incus is developed from the uppermost extremity of the second or hyoid arch, and corresponds to the hyomandibular of fishes.

hy'ometer. [Short for HYETOMETER.] A rain gauge.

1886 in *Syd. Soc. Lex.*

hyon, var. of HYAN.

hyoscine ('haɪəʊsaɪn). *Chem.* [Arbitrarily f. HYOS(CYAMUS) + -INE.] An amorphous alkaloid isomerous with hyoscyamine. (The name was first given by Reichardt to a body which proved to be tropine.)

1872 WATTS *Dict. Chem.* Suppl. VI. 726 Hyoscine was obtained as an oily liquid having a strong alkaline reaction. **1897** ALLBUTT *Syst. Med.* II. 858 The hypodermic injection of $\frac{1}{100}$ grain of hyoscine has been recommended.

So †**hyoscinic** (haɪəʊ'sɪnɪk) *a.*, in ***hyoscinic acid*** ($C_9H_{10}O_3$), Reichardt's name for tropic acid.

‖**hyoscyamia** (ˌhaɪəʊsaɪ'eɪmɪə). *Chem.* [mod.L., f. as next, with ending of *ammonia*.] = next.

1823 URE *Dict. Chem.* (ed. 2) 503/1 *Hyosciama* [sic], a new vegetable alkali, extracted..from the hyosciamus nigra. **1875** H. C. WOOD *Therap.* (1879) 269 Hyoscyamia has a very similar, if not identical, action with atropia.

hyoscyamine (haɪəʊ'saɪəmaɪn). *Chem.* [f. next + -INE.] An extremely poisonous alkaloid ($C_{17}H_{23}NO_3$), obtained from the seeds of *Hyoscyamus niger* and some other *Solanaceæ*, isomerous with atropine; used in medicine as a sedative.

1858 HOGG *Veg. Kingd.* 553 The seeds [of henbane]..contain an alkaline principle, called *hyoscyamine*. **1865-72** WATTS *Dict. Chem.* III. 236 Hyoscyamine neutralises acids completely. **1875** *Ibid.* Suppl. VII. 664 Hyoscyamine sulphate..crystallises over sulphuric acid in radiate groups of white shining needles.

‖**hyoscyamus** (haɪəʊ'saɪəməs). *Bot.* [ad. Gr. ὑοσκύαμος (f. ὑός, gen. of ὗς pig + κύαμος bean), in Palladius written *iusquiamus*, whence JUSQUIAM.]

A genus of plants belonging to the N.O. *Solanaceæ*; the British species is *Hyoscyamus niger*, HENBANE. **b.** The narcotic extract or tincture of henbane.

[**1706** PHILLIPS (ed. Kersey), *Hyoscyamos*, the Herb Henbane.] **1799** *Med. Jrnl.* I. 285 Hyoscyamus boiled in milk, to be applied to the eyes. **1838** *Penny Cycl.* XII. 410/1 Hyoscyamus, when taken by a person in health, produces disorder of the nervous system. **1878** A. M. HAMILTON *Nerv. Dis.* 203 Hyoscyamus and belladonna also do good.

hyosternal (haɪəʊ'stɜːnəl), *a.* and *sb. Anat.* [f. HYO- + STERNAL.] **a.** *adj.* Pertaining to the hyoid apparatus together with the sternum or breast-bone. **b.** *sb.* The second pair of plates in the plastron of a turtle, also called the hyoplastron.

1835-6 TODD *Cycl. Anat.* I. 284/1 Two anterior lateral pieces, the hyosternals. **1839-47** *Ibid.* III. 838/1 This central piece is bounded..posteriorly by another pair named the hyosternal. **1870** ROLLESTON *Anim. Life* 28 The hyosternal processes are continued.

‖**hyosternum** (haɪəʊ'stɜːnəm). *Anat.* [f. HYO- + STERNUM.] = HYOSTERNAL *sb.*

hyostylic (haɪəʊ'staɪlɪk), *a. Anat.* [f. HYO- + Gr. στῦλ-ος pillar + -IC.] Having the lower jaw suspended from the cranium by a hyomandibular bone (opposed to *autostylic* and *amphistylic*, q.v.). Also said of the lower jaw itself.

1880 GÜNTHER *Fishes* 74 The Ganoid fishes with persistent notochord, but with a hyostylic skull. **1888** ROLLESTON & JACKSON *Anim. Life* 96 When the lower jaw is connected to the cranium solely by a hyomandibular element derived from the hyoid arch..it is said to be hyostylic.

hyp (hɪp). Also *pl.* **hyps.** *colloq.* ? *Obs.* [Abbreviation of HYPOCHONDRIA. See HIP *sb.*[3] and HYPO.] Usually ***the hyp, the hyps***: hypochondria, morbid depression of spirits.

c **1705** BERKELEY in Fraser *Life* (1871) 422 Hyps and such like unaccountable things. **1712** THORESBY *Diary* (ed. Hunter) II. 120 So overrun with the hyps, that he told me he thought he should not live till night. **1731** SWIFT *Cassinus & Peter* 35 Heav'n send thou hast not got the hyps! **1736** GRAY *Lett.* Wks. 1884 II. 5 If the default of your spirits and nerves be nothing but the effect of the hyp, I have no more to say. **1738** SWIFT *Pol. Conversat.* Introd. 51 Some Abbreviations exquisitely refined; as..Hypps, or Hippo, for Hypochondriacks. **1806-7** J. BERESFORD *Miseries Hum. Life* (1826) Post. Groans v, An unconquerable fit of sullenness, indolence, the hyp, or the head-ache. **1825** R. P. WARD *Tremaine* II. i. 2 Belmont was a melancholy place, and I was dying there of hyp!

attrib. **1731** *Lett. fr. Fog's Jrnl.* (1732) II. 236 As to..your Hyp-Doctors..and your Country Parsons, let him leave all these Fellows to my Management.

hyp, obs. form of HIP.

hyp, var. HYPE *sb.*[1]

hyp-, the form of HYPO- used before a vowel: see the words below.

hypabyssal (haɪpə'bɪsəl), *a. Petrol.* [ad. G. *hypabyssisch* (attributed by H. Rosenbusch 1891, in *Tschermak's min. u. petrogr. Mittheil.* XII. 386, and by W. C. Brögger *Die Eruptivgesteine des Kristianiagebietes* (1894) iii. 123, to Brögger, 1886): see HYPO- 4.] Of igneous rock: formed from magma which has intruded into and solidified among other rocks; intermediate between plutonic and volcanic.

1895 *Mineral. Mag.* XI. 115 It [*sc.* sölvsbergite] is a true dyke-rock ('hypabyssal' rock). **1896** *Science Progress* IV. 476 Brögger has insisted on the necessity of a division intermediate between the plutonic and the volcanic, which he terms 'hypabyssal'. **1896** *Q. Jrnl. Geol. Soc.* LII. 613 The laccolitic rocks..would seem to belong to what Prof. Brögger calls hypabyssal. **1926** G. W. TYRRELL *Princ. Petrol.* vi. 106 The hypabyssal group includes the rocks of dykes, sills, and small laccoliths, etc., which occupy an intermediate position in the crust between the deepseated plutonic bodies, and the surficial lava flows. **1951** TURNER & VERHOOGEN *Ign. & Metamorphic Petrol.* iii. 51 Some writers recognize an intermediate (hypabyssal) class to include rocks that have crystallized at moderate depth. **1969** BENNISON & WRIGHT *Geol. Hist. Brit. Isles* x. 251 The Great Whin Sill is the largest hypabyssal intrusion in Britain.

hypactic (hɪ'pæktɪk), *a.* and *sb. Med.* [ad. Gr. ὑπακτικ-ός, f. ὑπάγειν to carry off below, f. ὑπό HYPO- 1 + ἄγειν to lead, carry.] Purgative. Also as *sb.* (see quot. 1823).

1753 CHAMBERS *Cycl. Supp.*, *Hypactic medicines*, a term used by some authors for cathartic medicines. **1823** CRABB *Technol. Dict.*, *Hypactics*, medicines which serve to evacuate the fæces. **1886** in *Syd. Soc. Lex.*

hypacusis (haɪpə'k(j)uːsɪs). *Med.* Also **-acousis, -acusia, -akusis.** [mod.L., f. HYP- + Gr. ἄκουσις hearing (ἀκούειν to hear).] Diminished acuteness of hearing. Cf. HYPERACUSIS.

1886 *Syd. Soc. Lex.*, Hypacusia. *Ibid.*, Hypacusis. *Ibid.*, Hypakusis. **1895** T. B. HYSLOP *Mental Physiol.* ix. 273 Hypakusis—diminution of sense of hearing, seen in various forms of insanity. **1967** A. B. GRAHAM *Sensorineural Hearing Processes* xii. 143 Some patients with hypacusis as against normal-hearing patients.

‖**hypæsthesia** (hɪpɪs'θiːsɪə). *Path.* [mod.L., f. HYPO- 4 + Gr. -αισθησία, αἴσθησις sensation, ÆSTHESIS.] Diminished capacity for sensation; dulled sensitiveness.

1886 in *Syd. Soc. Lex.*

Hence **hypæs'thesic** *a.*, of or belonging to hypæsthesia.

hypæthral, -ethral (hɪp-, haɪ'piːθrəl), *a.* [f. L. *hypæthr-us, hypæthr-os*, adj. and sb., ad. Gr. ὕπαιθρος under the sky, in the open air (f. ὑπό HYPO- 1 + αἰθήρ air, ETHER) + -AL[1].]

1. Open to the sky; having no roof.

In its application to buildings adopted from Vitruvius, who used it to designate a supposed type of Greek temple, in which the cella was left wholly or partly uncovered.

[**1715** LEONI *Palladio's Archit.* (1742) II. 9 All the space surrounded by the inner columns was open, whence the Prospect of such Temples was *Hypethros*, that is, uncover'd.] **1794** *Rudim. Anc. Archit.* (ed. 2) 107 The internal colonnade to the hypaethral temple is a peristyle. **1845** FORD *Handbk. Spain* I. 377/2 The Patio is an hypethral quadrilateral oblong of some 120 ft. by 60. **1871** M. COLLINS *Mrq. & Merch.* I. i. 1 The old Elizabethan house, built as an hypaethral quadrangle with cloisters, stands on a hill looking southward. *a* **1876** —— *Pen Sketches* (1879) I. 26 The builders of Stonehenge..sought to make their hypaethral temple sublime in its vastness.

2. Open-air. Also as *sb.* (nonce-use): One who lives in the open air.

1875 LOWELL *Lett.* (1894) II. 135 Being much of an hypaethral, I augured ill from it. **1879** RUSKIN *Arrows of Chace* (1880) I. 246 The Greek and Istrian marbles used at Venice are absolutely defiant of hypæthral influences. **1887** LOWELL *Democr.* 184 What a hypaethral story it is, how much of it passes in the open air!

hypalgesia, -ic: see HYPO-.

‖**hypalgia** (hɪ'pældʒɪə). *Path.* [mod.L., f. HYPO- 4 + Gr. -αλγία, ἄλγος pain; cf. Gr. ὑπαλγέειν to have a slight pain.] A slight feeling of pain; a decrease in pain. Hence **hy'palgic** *a.*

1855 in MAYNE *Expos. Lex.* **1886** in *Syd. Soc. Lex.*

hypa'llactic, *a. rare.* [ad. Gr. ὑπαλλακτικ-ός exchangeable.] Of the nature of hypallage.

1896 F. HALL in *Nation* (N.Y.) LXII. 342/1 This expression..in seemingly hypallactic constructions.

‖**hypallage** (hɪ'pælədʒiː, haɪp-). Also 6 **hipallage, hyppalage,** (7 **hypallagy**). [L. *hypallagē*, a. Gr. ὑπαλλαγή interchange, exchange, f. ὑπό HYPO- 1 + ἀλλάσσειν (stem ἀλλαγ-) to exchange. Cf. F. *hypallage* (16th c.).]

A figure of speech in which there is an interchange of two elements of a proposition, the natural relations of these being reversed.

Servius, in commenting on Virg. *Æn.* iii. 61, explains *dare classibus austros* as a hypallage for *dare classes austris*. In Quintilian (VIII. vi. 23) the word (written as Greek) has the sense of METONYMY, and English authors have sometimes applied it loosely or incorrectly to other variations from natural forms of expression, esp. to the transference of attributes from their proper subjects to others (cf. quot. 1586).

1586 A. DAY *Eng. Secretary* II. (1625) 83 *Hypallage*, when by change of property in application a thing is delivered, as to say..*the wicked wound thus given*, for, having thus wickedly wounded him. **1589** PUTTENHAM *Eng. Poesie* III. xv. (Arb.) 183 The Greekes call this figure (Hipallage)..we in our vulgar may call him the (vnderchange) but I had rather haue him called the (Changeling). **1654** VILVAIN *Theorem. Theol.* vi. 153 Names of Men may import Men of name, sith such Hypallages are usual in Scripture. **1789** MADAN *Persius* (1795) 66 *note*, Casaubon..says that this is an Hypallage. **1844** T. MITCHELL *Sophocles* I. 25 *note*, Hypallages of this kind abound in Sophocles. **1874** T. N. HARPER *Peace through Truth* Ser. II. I. 44 *note*, The phrase, 'you also are become dead to the law',..is a hypallage for 'the law has become dead to you'.

Hence **hy'pallagize** *v. intr.*, to use hypallage.

1896 F. HALL in *Nation* (N.Y.) LXII. 342/1 Here Shakespeare hypallagizes.

‖**hypanthium** (hɪ'pænθɪəm, haɪ'pænθɪəm). *Bot.* [mod.L., f. HYPO- 2 + Gr. ἄνθος flower.] = HYPANTHODIUM.

1855 MAYNE *Expos. Lex.*, *Hypanthium*, term given by Link to the inferior part of the calyx. **1866** LINDLEY & MOORE *Treas. Bot.* II. 611/2 Hypanthium. The fleshy enlarged hollow of the end of a flower-stalk, such as occurs in the rose, apple, or myrtle. **1880** GRAY *Struct. Bot.* (ed. 6) 415/2 *Hypanthium*, an enlargement or other development of the torus under the calyx. **1887** W. HILLHOUSE tr. *Strasburger's Handbk. Pract. Bot.* xxx. 349 The five-celled ovary is here [*sc.* in the apple] immersed in a hollowed flower-stalk, a so-called hypanthium. **1912** H. H. RUSBY *Man. Struct. Bot.* iii. 46 The enclosed portion of the calyx really is adherent, but it is not visible, since it is enclosed and concealed by the hollow torus, which is known as a Hypanthium. **1968** A. CRONQUIST *Evol. & Class. Flowering Plants* iii. 87 It is customary and convenient to define the hypanthium in terms of external descriptive morphology rather than on evolutionary homologies.

Hence **hy'panthial** *a.*, belonging to or of the nature of a hypanthium.

1880 GRAY *Struct. Bot.* (ed. 6) 214 A hypanthium or hypanthial receptacle is..a flower-axis or receptacle developed mainly under the calyx.

hypanthodium (haɪpæn'θəʊdɪəm). *Bot.* [mod.L. (H. F. Link *Elementa Philosophiae Botanicae* (1824) ix. 265), f. HYPO- + ANTHODIUM.] In certain plants, an enlargement

of the receptacle, sometimes becoming fleshy and surrounding the ovary.

1832 J. LINDLEY *Introd. Bot.* ii. 108 If the receptacle is fleshy, and is not enclosed within an involucrum, as in Dorstenia and Ficus, it is then called by Link Hypanthodium. **1861** R. BENTLEY *Man. Bot.* 204 The Hypanthodium.. is formed by a receptacle which is usually of a fleshy nature becoming more or less incurved.

‖**hypapante** (hɪpəˈpæntiː). *Gr. Ch.* [a. Gr. ὑπαπαντή, late form of ὑπαντή a coming to meet.] A festival commemorating the meeting of the infant Jesus and his mother with Simeon and Anna in the temple.

a **1646** J. GREGORY *Posthuma, Episc. Puerorum* (1649) 108 The Arabick Translation of this Constitution hath more Holiedaies than the Originall, and the Hypapante for one.

hypapophysis (hɪpəˈpɒfɪsɪs, haɪp-). *Anat.* Pl. -ses. [f. HYPO- 2 (*b*) + APOPHYSIS.] An APOPHYSIS or spinous process on the lower or ventral side of a vertebral centrum.

1854 OWEN *Skel. & Teeth* in *Circ. Sc., Organ. Nat.* I. 169 The exogenous parts are the.. parapophysis.. the metapophysis.. the hypapophysis. **1873** MIVART *Elem. Anat.* ii. 42 Processes which appear on the ventral aspect of the centrum in many animals, and which are termed hypapophyses.

Hence **hypapoˈphysial** *a.*, of or pertaining to a hypapophysis.

1854 OWEN *Skel. & Teeth* in *Circ. Sc., Organ. Nat.* I. 197 The hypapophysial part of the atlas. **1886** *Syd. Soc. Lex.*, *Hypapophysial arch*, a bony ring on the under surface of the vertebræ of some animals, constituted by the junction of two hypapophyses.

hypargyrite (hɪˈpɑːdʒɪraɪt). *Min.* [f. HYPO- 4 + ARGYRITE (f. Gr. ἄργυρος silver).] A silver ore, a massive variety of MIARGYRITE, from Clausthal in the Harz Mountains.

1868 DANA *Min.* (ed. 5) 89.

hyparterial (-ɑːˈtɪərɪəl), *a. Anat.* [f. HYP(O- 2 + ARTERIAL.] Situated below the pulmonary artery.

In mod. Dicts. **1882** *Quain's Elem. Anat.* (ed. 9) II. 511 From the continuation of the bronchus four dorsal and as many ventral hyparterial branches are given off in succession in each lung. **1921, 1962** [see EPARTERIAL *a.*].

‖**hyparxis** (hɪˈpɑːksɪs). *Philos. rare.* [a. Gr. ὕπαρξις existence, subsistence, f. ὑπάρχειν to begin to be, to exist, f. ὑπό HYPO- 1 + ἄρχειν to begin.] Being, essence.

1792 T. TAYLOR *Proclus* II. 361 Every thing subsists in its own order, according to hyparxis. **1797** —— in *Monthly Mag.* III. 511 They consider ideas, at one time, as the conceptions of the father; at another.. as the exempt hyparxes (or summits) of beings.

hypaspist (hɪˈpæspɪst, haɪp-). *Gr. Antiq.* [ad. Gr. ὑπασπιστής shield-bearer, f. ὑπό HYPO- 1 + ἀσπίς shield.] A shield-bearer; one of a distinguished body of troops (to which the foot-guards belonged) in the Macedonian army.

a **1827** W. MITFORD cited in Webster (1828). **1839** THIRLWALL *Greece* VI. 313 The king himself went up with 500 of the hypaspists to view the place. **1855** GROTE *Greece* II. xcii. XII. 82 Another description of infantry organized by Philip called the Hypaspists—shield bearers or Guards; originally few in number and employed for personal defence of the prince. *Ibid.* 83 The hypaspists are used also for assault of walled places, and for rapid night marches.

‖**hypate** (ˈhɪpətiː). *Anc. Gr. Music.* [L. *hypatē*, a. Gr. ὑπάτη (sc. χορδή CHORD) uppermost string, fem. of ὕπατος uppermost, last. Cf. F. *hypate.*] The name of the lowest tone in the lowest two tetrachords of ancient Greek music.

1603 HOLLAND *Plutarch's Mor.* 1254 It appeareth also manifestly, by the Hypates, that it was not for ignorance that in the Dorian tunes they forbade this Tetrachord. **1660** STANLEY *Hist. Philos.* IX. (1701) 386/1 The gravest sound in the diapason concord, is called Hypate; because ὕπατον signifieth highest.

hypaxial (hɪˈpæksɪəl, haɪp-), *a. Compar. Anat.* [f. HYPO- 2 + AXI-S + -AL[1]; cf. AXIAL.] Lying beneath, or on the ventral side of, the vertebral axis.

1872 MIVART *Elem. Anat.* 221 Hypaxial processes may also be developed beneath vertebræ to which complete paraxial arches are annexed.. in the thoracic region of many birds. **1886** *Syd. Soc. Lex.*, *Hypaxial arch*, the arch of bone formed by the hæmapophyses of a vertebra.

hyp'd, obs. form of HYPPED.

hype (haɪp), *sb.*[1] *slang* (orig. *U.S.*). Also **hyp.** [Abbrev. of HYPODERMIC.] **a.** A drug-addict. **b.** A hypodermic needle or syringe. **c.** A hypodermic injection. Cf. HYPO *sb.*[3]

1924 G. C. HENDERSON *Keys to Crookdom* xxiv. 306 Next down on the list is the 'hype' or morphine-user. Morphine is taken by hypodermic injections. **1929** [see BANG *sb.*[3]]. **1936** *Amer. Speech* XI. 122/2 *Hype*, the hypodermic needle used to inject narcotics. **1952** D. E. HULBURD *H is for Heroin* II. 52 They smoked two marijuana cigarettes apiece that an old addict—'an old hype'—had sold Hortense. **1955** *U.S. Senate Hearings* (1956) VIII. 4164 Terms for morphine addicts: 'Hype', 'Hygelo', 'Head', 'Fiend', 'Needle man', 'Junky', 'Junker'. **1963** *New Society* 7 Nov. 9/1 'Once a hype, always a hype,' the American narcotics addict says. **1972** J. WAMBAUGH *Blue Knight* (1973) i. 11 They were dumb strung-out hypes. *Ibid.*, The tall one is wearing a long-sleeved shirt buttoned at the cuff. To hide his hype marks.

hype (haɪp), *sb.*[2] *slang* (orig. *U.S.*). [Origin unknown.] **a.** An instance of short-changing; a person who does not give the correct amount of change. **b.** (The usual current sense.) Deception, cheating; a confidence trick, a racket, a swindle, a publicity stunt.

1926 *Clues* Nov. 161/2 *Hype*, short change artist. **1926** [see HYPE *v.*[1]]. **1935** A. J. POLLOCK *Underworld Speaks* 60/2 *Hype*, a short change artist. A person who does not give the correct amount of change to a customer. **1955** D. W. MAURER in *Publ. Amer. Dial. Soc.* XXIV. 85 Sometimes he has auxiliary *rackets*, such as the *hype* or some form of the *short con.* **1962** J. BALDWIN *Another Country* (1963) II. iv. 336 Life is a *bitch*, baby. It's the biggest hype going. **1966** C. HIMES *Heat's On* xxii. 173 That was how Gus got the money... That shocked her; she had believed Gus's hype about his wife leaving him a farm. **1967** N. MAILER *Cannibals & Christians* I. 29 The hype had made fifty million musical-comedy minds; now the hype could do anything. **1968** *Sunday Times* 11 Aug. 5/1 Hype is an American word for the gentle art of getting a tune into the pop charts without actually selling any records. Its methods are various: from the crudest bribery to devious techniques for upsetting the.. calculations of chart-compilers. **1969** *Listener* 25 Sept. 420/3 All the 'hype' and conning that goes into the establishing of every star. **1970** L. SANDERS *Anderson Tapes* li. 135 He's been on the con or hustling his ass or pulling paper hypes. **1972** *Publishers Weekly* 6 Mar. 2/2 They carried off the biggest money-making hype in sports history.

hype (haɪp), *v.*[1] *slang* (orig. *U.S.*). Also **hipe.** [Origin unknown.] To short-change, to cheat; to deceive, to con, esp. by false publicity. So **ˈhyping** *vbl. sb.* and *ppl. a.*

1926 MAINES & GRANT *Wise-Crack Dict.* 9/2 *Hype*, to overcharge. As, 'That place has a hype on this week.' **1931** G. IRWIN *Amer. Tramp & Underworld Slang* 99 *Hipe*, to cheat or short change... Perhaps connected with the North-England 'hipe', to find fault with, to slander; perhaps from 'high pressure'. **1945** L. SHELLY *Jive Talk Dict.* 13/1 *Hype* (v.), to try a trick. **1946** MEZZROW & WOLFE *Really Blues* 375 *Hype* v., to deliver a phony but convincing line. **1962** J. BALDWIN *Another Country* (1963) III. i. 402 He doesn't seem to be trying to hype me, not even when he talked about his wife and kids. **1968** *Sunday Times* 11 Aug. 5/1 The dominance of the charts over the pop music industry is such that many thousands of pounds may depend on these hyping operations. **1969** N. COHN *AWopBopaLooBop* (1970) v. 51 Hype is a crucial word. In theory it is short for hyperbole. In practice, though, it means to promote by hustle, pressure, even honest effort if necessary, and the idea is that you leave nothing to chance. Simply, you do everything possible. Hype has become such an integral part of pop that one hardly notices it any more. **1969** *Sat. Rev.* (U.S.) 27 Sept. 25/1 You can't hype kids into buying things they don't want. .. They hate hype. **1970** *It* 27 Feb.–13 Mar. 15/1 Paying.. lip-service to furiously hyping publicists. *Ibid.*, A lunchtime hyping session. **1971** *Listener* 15 Apr. 467/1 Bogus alternatives are hyped into prominence and fortune with appalling ease. **1971** *Bookseller* 23 Oct. 2053/2 In America a practice exists (known as 'hyping' in the record business) whereby a film company which has acquired the rights in a title forces it on to the bestseller list by sending young publicity men around armed with hundred-dollar bills and instructions to buy twenty or more copies from selected book shops.

hype (haɪp), *v.*[2] *U.S. slang.* [f. HYPE *sb.*[1]] Usu. as **hyped** *pa. pple.* or *ppl. a.* (const. *up*): stimulated, worked up (as if from the effects of a hypodermic injection).

1938 D. CASTLE *Do Your Own Time* xxi. 200 Y' gotta lay off the wimmin, an' don't hype y'rself up till y' goes out t' heist a joint. **1946** MEZZROW & WOLFE *Really Blues* iv. 54, I was so hyped-up I couldn't sit still. **1950** in WENTWORTH & FLEXNER *Dict. Amer. Slang* 278/2 No fireworks [in this movie], no fake suspense, no hyped-up glamour. **1970** V. JOHNSTON *Phantom Cottage* (1971) xxi. 165 If some hyped-up character goes past at seventy miles an hour, we'll take out after him. **1973** *Publishers Weekly* 12 Feb. 64/3 Witty, intellectual fun that keeps his readers hyped up and on their mettle. **1973** *Time* 25 June 16/2 As he works, Mitchell has at times been so hyped up that Martha once asked his doctor to prescribe medication to slow him down.

hype, obs. form of HIP *sb.*[1]

hypecacuana, obs. form of IPECACUANHA.

†**hyˈpenemy.** *Obs. rare.* [ad. L. *hypēnemium* (*ovum*), a. Gr. ὑπηνέμιον (ᾠόν) wind-egg, f. ὑπό beneath + ἄνεμος wind. Also used in L. form.] A wind-egg.

[**1646** SIR T. BROWNE *Pseud. Ep.* IV. vi. 194 Such as are addled swim, as do also those which are tearmed *hypenemia* or wind-egges.] **1668** H. MORE *Div. Dial.* Schol. (1713) 571 Provided that it be not a Hypenemy or Wind Egg.

So **hypeˈnemious** *a.* [Gr. ὑπηνέμιος], full of wind, windy; said of an egg.

1855 in MAYNE *Expos. Lex.* **1886** in *Syd. Soc. Lex.*

hyper[1] (ˈhaɪpə(r)), humorous or colloquial abbreviation (*a*) of *hypercritic*, (*b*) of *hyper-Calvinist*.

1689 PRIOR *Ep. to F. Shephard* 168 Criticks I read on other Men, And Hypers upon them again. **1856** SPURGEON *New Park St. Pulpit* No. 102 We are called Antinomians; we are cried down as *hypers.* **1863** CATER *Punch in Pulpit* xi. (ed. 3) 110, I call you, then, Mr. *Hyper*, not for the sake of giving you a nickname, but for the sake of distinguishing you from other religionists to whom you do not belong.. It is the well-known designation of those who go *beyond* Calvin.

hyper[2] (ˈhaɪpə(r)). *U.S. slang.* [Cf. HYPE *v.*[1]] (See quot. 1914.)

1914 JACKSON & HELLYER *Vocab. Criminal Slang* 47 *Hyper*, current amongst money-changers. A flim-flammer. **1931** G. IRWIN *Amer. Tramp & Underworld Slang* 106 *Hyper*, a 'short change' artist... The logical explanation.. is that the word came from 'hyp', a contraction of hypochondria.

hyper (ˈhaɪpə(r)), *a. slang* (orig. and chiefly *U.S.*). [Shortening of *hyperactive* s.v. HYPER- 4.] Hyperactive, excitable, highly-strung; extraordinarily energetic.

1942 BERREY & VAN DEN BARK *Amer. Thes. Slang* §274/6 Overzealous; fanatic. Bats, bugs, hipped, hippish, hyper, nuts. **1971** *Time* 8 Mar. 18/2 'I was definitely hyper,' said Calley. **1977** C. MCFADDEN *Serial* (1978) iv. 14/2 He couldn't stop.. rapping at her in this very hyper way. **1985** *Dirt Bike* Mar. 14/1 Andre Malherbe never hopped from sponsor to sponsor like a hyper bumblebee in search of a bit more honey. **1986** *Washington Post* 10 July B5/1 Lately he has become so nervous and hyper when he is disciplined that he beats himself on the head or throws himself on the ground to punish himself.

hyper- (haɪpə(r)), *prefix*, repr. Gr. ὑπερ- (ὑπέρ prep. and adv., 'over, beyond, over much, above measure'); in Gr. combined adverbially with verbs, in the local sense 'over, above, beyond', as ὑπερβαίνειν to step over, overstep, cross, ὑπερβάλλειν to throw over or beyond; and hence in the adjectives and substantives thence derived, as ὑπερβατός going across, transposed (cf. HYPERBATON), ὑπερβολή a throwing over or beyond, overshooting, excess, extravagance, HYPERBOLE, ὑπερβολικός HYPERBOLIC. Also with adjectives formed on substantive stems, implying that the thing or quality is present over or beyond the ordinary degree, as ὑπέρθυμος over-daring, high-spirited, ὑπέρβιος of overwhelming might; and later with ordinary adjectives with the sense 'exceedingly', as ὑπέρμεγας immensely great, ὑπέρκαλος exceedingly beautiful. In this sense also sometimes with verbs, as ὑπεραγαπᾶν to love exceedingly, ὑπερεχθαίρειν to hate exceedingly. Also combined prepositionally with sbs., forming adjs. with the sense of lying or going beyond, surpassing, as ὑπερβόρεος that is beyond the north wind, HYPERBOREAN, ὑπερόριος lying over the frontier, ὑπερουράνιος that is above the heavens, ὑπέρθεος more than divine, ὑπέρμετρος going beyond measure (or metre); whence also with sbs. from adjs., as ὑπερθύριον the lintel of a door, ὑπερμετρία a passing all measure.

Comparatively few of these have come down or been adopted in English, *hyperbole*, *hyperborean*, with their derivatives, being the chief; but from the 17th century *hyper-* has been extensively used, more or less on Greek analogies, in the formation of new compounds, and has even become a kind of living element, freely prefixed to adjectives and substantives, as in groups 1 and 4 below.

I. Formations in which, as in HYPERBOREAN, the prefix has the prepositional force of 'over, beyond, or above' (what is denoted by the second element).

1. General formations: **a.** adjectives, as ***hyper-angelical***, ***-archæological***, ***-archiepiscopal***, ***-barbarous***, ***-constitutional***, ***-creaturely***, ***-diabolical***, ***-equatorial***, ***-magical***, ***-magnetic***, ***-miraculous***, ***-pathetic***, ***-prophetical***, ***-stoic***, see also *hyperethical*, *hyperrational*, etc., below. **b.** Rarely in substantives (except abstracts from the adjs.), and verbs; e.g. *hyper-analysis*, *hypergoddess*, *hyperdeify*: see below.

1650 R. GELL *Serm.* 27 The divine, intellectual, *hyper-angelical world. **1882** H. GOODWIN in *Trans. Cumbld. & Westmld. Archæol. Soc.* VI. 234 A *hyper-archæological chapter in the history of the world. **1657** J. GOODWIN *Triers Tried* 25 Authority.. not so *hyper-archepiscopall, so super-metropolitan. **1831** T. L. PEACOCK *Crotchet Castle* ii. (1887) 27 A *hyperbarbarous technology, that no Athenian ear could have borne. **1827** HALLAM *Const. Hist.* (1876) III. xiv. 98 A kind of paramount, and what I may call *hyper-constitutional law. **1856** R. A. VAUGHAN *Mystics* (1860) I. 100 Virtues which are unhuman, anti-terrestrial, *hypercreaturely—forgive the word. **1641** J. JACKSON *True Evang. T.* III. 199 A hyperbolicall, diabolicall, nay *hyper-diabolicall plot. **1820** SHELLEY *Witch Atl.* Introd. vi, Scorched by Hell's *hyperequatorial climate. **1837** CARLYLE *Diam. Neckl.* xiv. Misc. Ess. 1872 V. 184 Such a *Hyper-magical is this our poor old Real world. **1680** R. FLEMING *Fulfill. Script.* (1801) II. iii. 179 By a touch of this *hyper-magnetic power. **1826** SOUTHEY *Vind. Eccl. Angl.* 483 Though introduced.. by such *hyper-miraculous miracles. **1866** *Lond. Rev.* 15 Sept. 288/2 That which is *hyper-pathetic, which is really too deep for tears. **1613** JACKSON *Creed* II. xxii. §4 His [Christ's] *hyperprophetical spirit. **1817** COLERIDGE *Biog. Lit.* I. ix. 48 A crude egoismus, a boastful and *hyperstoic hostility to nature. **1870** *Temple*

Bar Mag. Mar. 41 Listening to that *hyperterrestrial singing.

2. *Mus.* **a.** In the names of the musical modes ***hyperæolian***, ***-dorian***, ***-ionian***, ***-lydian***, ***-mixolydian***, ***-phrygian***, denoting either (*a*) the acute modes in ancient Greek music, which began at a definite interval above the ordinary *Æolian*, *Dorian*, etc., or (*b*) the 'authentic' modes in mediaeval music (the same as *Æolian*, *Dorian*, etc.) as contrasted with the 'plagal' modes *hypoæolian*, *-dorian*, etc. **b.** Also formerly in names of intervals measured upwards, as ***hyperdiapason***, ***hyperdiapente***, ***hyperdiatessaron***, ***hyperditone*** (see DIAPASON, etc.). (Cf. HYPO- 3.)

1761 STILES in *Phil. Trans. R. Soc. 1760* LI. 713 The modes being thus augmented to fifteen.. their meses will be found to stand.. in the following order. Hyperlydian, Hyperæolian, Hyperphrygian or Hypermixolydian. *Ibid.* 722 They placed the Hypermixolydian at a diapason from the Hypodorian, towards the acute, giving it that denomination from its position above the Mixolydian. **1867** MACFARREN *Harmony* i. 14 The fourth mode Ambrose selected is the Hyper-Lydian sometimes called Mixo-Lydian. **1873** H. C. BANISTER *Text-bk. Mus.* 31 The authentic modes were also called Hyper-Ionian, Hyper-Dorian, etc. **1922** JOYCE *Ulysses* 493 It is susceptible of nodes or modes as far apart as hyperphrygian and mixolydian.

3. a. In various terms of modern Mathematics, as *hyperconic*, *hypercycle*, etc. (see below); esp. in adjectives applied to functions, etc., related to or resembling those denoted by the simple adjectives, but involving some extension or complication, as ***hyper-complex***, ***-elliptic***, ***-geometric*** (***-ical***), ***-jacobian***, ***-spherical***. See also HYPERDETERMINANT.

1816 tr. *Lacroix's Diff. & Int. Calculus* 574 These series, in which the number of factors increases from term to term, have been designated by Euler.. hypergeometrical series. **1881** *Athenæum* 22 Jan. 136/1 'On the Periodicity of Hyper-elliptic Integrals of the First Class', by Mr. W. R. W. Roberts. *Ibid.*, The Differential Equation which is satisfied by the Hypergeometric Series. **1893** FORSYTH *The. Functions* 32 The hypergeometric series, together with all its derivatives, is holomorphic within a circle of radius unity and centre the origin.

b. In substantives in which *hyper-* has the sense 'the analogue in a space of four or more dimensions of (what is denoted by the second element) in ordinary three-dimensional space'; as ***hypercube***, ***-cylinder***, ***-plane***, ***-sphere***, ***-surface***.

1895 *Proc. R. Soc.* LVIII. p. xxxi, The manifoldness in this space.. is the quadri-quadric two-dimensional amplitude common to thirteen quadric hyper-cylinders. **1903** C. M. JESSOP *Treat. Line Complex* xiii. 244 Any linear equation of the form $\sum_1^5 a_i X_i = 0$ singles out ∞^3 points from S_4, which will then form a space of three dimensions; the locus of these ∞^3 points will be called a hyperplane. *Ibid.* 251 In four-dimensional space, the three-dimensional quadric spaces through the intersection of $S^2{}_3$ and $X_5 = 0$.. may be termed 'hyperspheres'. **1909** *Sci. Amer.* 3 July 6/2 Just as portions of our space are bounded by surfaces,.. so portions of hyperspace are bounded by hyper-surfaces (three-dimensional), i.e., flat or curved 3-spaces. *Ibid.* 6/3 Of these [regular hyper-solids], C_8 (or the hyper-cube) is the simplest, because, though with more bounding solids than C_5, it is right-angled throughout. **1955** O. KLEIN in W. Pauli *Niels Bohr* 100 Let.. x^1, x^2, x^3, x^4 be the four space-time coordinates regarded as *c*-numbers, x^1, x^2, x^3 forming a space-like hypersurface for any given value of the general time coordinate x^4. **1966** A. BATTERSBY *Math. in Managem.* v. 122 When the number of variables exceeds three.. we could represent the process of solution by a series of three-dimensional solid bodies showing successive cross-sections of the solution space when cut by the 'hyper-plane' of P. **1968** ROSENBERG & JOHNSON *Geom.* xiii. 520/2 If the solid cube moves in a direction 'perpendicular' to its original space, it may trace a solid hypercube. **1969** R. J. BUMCROT *Mod. Projective Geom.* ii. 30 Subspaces of dimensions 1, 2, *n*-1 are called, respectively, lines, planes, and hyperplanes. **1970** E. E. KRAMER *Nature & Growth Mod. Math.* vii. 160 To say that a relation like $x^2 + y^2 + z^2 + w^2 = 9$ is a hyper-sphere with radius 3 is so much easier than to state that the relation is the set of all ordered quadruples of real numbers such that the sum of the squares of these four numbers is always 9. **1972** *Computer Jrnl.* XV. 214/1 The problem of optimising a function globally over the vertices of a hypercube is encountered, for example, in hierarchical classification.

II. Formations in which, as in HYPERCRITICAL, HYPERCRITIC, the prefix has the adverbial sense of 'over much, to excess, exceedingly'.

4. General formations, comprising adjectives (with their adverbs), substantives, and (a few) verbs; often corresponding to one another in meaning.

a. adjectives (with corresponding adverbs): as ***hyperaccurate***, ***-acid***, ***-active***, ***-acute***, ***-archaic***, ***-brutal***, ***-carnal***, ***-civilized***, ***-classical***, ***-colloquial***, ***-composite***, ***-confident***, ***-conscientious***, ***-educated***, ***-elegant***, ***-excitable***, ***-excursive***, ***-fastidious***, ***-grammatical***, ***-hilarious***, ***-idealistic***, ***-latinistic***, ***-logical***, ***-lustrous***, ***-metaphorical***, ***-metaphysical***, ***-modest***, ***-moral***, ***-mystical***, ***-neurotic***, ***-obtrusive***, ***-orthodox***, ***-pure***, ***-ridiculous***, ***-saintly***, ***-sceptical***, ***-sentimental***, ***-speculative***, ***-superlative***, ***-torrid***, ***-tragical***, ***-transcendent***, ***-tropical***, ***-wrought***, etc. **b.** substantives, as ***hyperacidity***, ***-activity***, ***-acuteness***, ***-archaism***, ***-characterization***, ***-civilization***, ***-climax***, ***-conformist***, ***-conscientiousness***, ***-conservatism***, ***-determination***, ***-dialecticism***, ***-dialectism***, ***-division***, ***-exaltation***, ***-excitability***, ***-federalist***, ***-hypocrisy***, ***-orthodoxy***, ***-panegyric***, ***-paroxysm***, ***-pietist***, ***-plagiarism***, ***-ritualism***, ***-scrupulosity***, ***-sensibility***, ***-subtlety***, ***-vitalization***, etc. **c.** verbs, as ***hypercharacterize***, ***-emphasize***, ***-realize***, ***-vitalize***.

1893 SIR R. BALL *In High Heav.* iii. 60 The reader must not think that I am attempting to be *hyper-accurate in this definition of the North Pole. **1897** ALLBUTT *Syst. Med.* III. 525 A *hyperacid gastric juice is secreted. *Ibid.* II. 915 This [grinding] pain I believe to be due to *hyperacidity. **1867** ANSTIE in *Bienn. Retrosp. New Syd. Soc.* 89 The ..*hyperactive condition of the brain in acute mania. **1888** *Medical News* 2 June 608 Organs.. in a state of *hyper-activity. **1888** F. WINTERTON in *Mind* July 389 Subtlety and *hyperacuteness were the bane of Scholasticism. **1956** K. CLARK *Nude* 380 Considering that they were spoken of as '*hyper-archaic', his restorations were remarkably self-effacing. **1956** *Archivum Linguisticum* VIII. 124 Attributable to assimilation and *hyperarchaism. **1890** *Ch. Times* 17 Jan. 56/3 The *hyper-carnal views which predominated prior to the Reformation. **1957** *Archivum Linguisticum* IX. 79 If a given linguistic formation develops in such a way as to allow.. one of its distinctive features to stand out more sharply than at the immediately preceding stage, one may speak of *hypercharacterization (or hyperdetermination) of that feature, in the diachronic perspective. *Ibid.* 80 One may analyse Sp. dial. *Jesuso* and *Raquela* as *hypercharacterized, with respect to gender, in comparison with standard *Jesús* and *Raquel*. **1844** *Fraser's Mag.* XXIX. 52 The conventional trammels of *hyper-civilisation. **1915** *Times Lit. Suppl.* 13 May 160/3 Only in a *hyper-civilized and introspective society such themes would be possible. **1844** *Fraser's Mag.* XXIX. 55 The *hyper-classical may dispute as they will. **1817** COLERIDGE *Biog. Lit.* (1882) xxii. 212 His feelings are alternately startled by anticlimax and *hyper-climax. **1940** O. JESPERSEN *Mod. Eng. Gram.* V. xxiii. 437 It sounds *hyper-colloquial.. when too many *don't*, *isn't* are substituted for *do not*, *is not*, etc. in reading serious prose aloud. **1894** *Westm. Gaz.* 10 Jan. 3/2 The *hyper-confident tone in which the gentlemen referred to presume to lecture the executive. **1702** THORESBY *Diary* (ed. Hunter) I. 259 For fear the ..*Hyperconformists should.. prevail against the Bishops themselves and the moderate party. **1845** O. BROWNSON *Wks.* VI. 369 It seems that the sin of Rome is *hyperconservatism. **1960** T. B. W. REID *Historical Philol. & Ling. Sci.* 6 Reactions such as those known as hyper-urbanism and *hyperdialecticism. **1925** P. RADIN tr. *Vendryès's Lang.* I. ii. 50 There are many *hyper-dialectisms, for instance, in the Doric of the Pythagorean authors. **1838** *Blackw. Mag.* XLIII. 644 [He] falls into the easy error of *hyperdivision. **1914** J. JOYCE *Dubliners* 238 The generation which is now on the wane.. had certain qualities of hospitality, of humour, of humanity, which the new and very serious and *hypereducated generation.. seems to me to lack. **1893** *Bookseller's Catal.*, 'Ape' and 'Spy' have succeeded in *hyperemphasizing the peculiarities of manner, appearance and dress of all the leading men of the day. **1882** *Trans. Victoria Inst.* 177 A *hyper-exaltation of the tree of knowledge above the tree of life. **1875** H. C. WOOD *Therap.* (1879) 167 A stage of muscular *hyper-excitability. **1886** *Lancet* 13 Mar. 485/2 Even normal mental impulses may cause undue motorial demonstrations if the spinal centres are *hyper-excitable, as is seen in strychnine poisoning, hysteria, &c. **1972** *Nature* 10 Mar. 74/1 The animal became hyperexcitable with exaggerated startle response. **1849** POE *Marginalia* Wks. 1864 III. 538 The harum-scarum, *hyperexcursive mannerism. **1807** J. ADAMS *Wks.* (1854) IX. 592 The.. tories, and *hyperfederalists will rebellow their execrations against me. **1834** GEN. P. THOMPSON *Exerc.* (1842) III. 89 A few quakerly or *hypergrammatical individuals linger by the olden forms. **1839** J. ROGERS *Antipopopr.* xv. ii. 314 What hypocrisy! what *hyper-hypocrisy! **1884** *Athenæum* 27 Dec. 852/2 The *hyper-idealistic speculations of.. Ibsen. **1819** COLERIDGE in *Blackw. Mag.* VI. 197 [Sir Thos. Browne is] often truly great and magnificent in his style and diction, though,.. too often big, stiff, and *hyperlatinistic. **1883** *Edin. Rev.* Jan. 27 The *hyperlogical cerements that held his mind in bondage. **1831** CARLYLE *Sart. Res.* III. xii, This piebald, entangled, *hyper-metaphorical style of writing. **1668** H. MORE *Div. Dial.* II. 465 This is *Hypermetaphysical.. very highly turgent and mysterious. **1886** *Sat. Rev.* 25 Dec. 848/1 *Hypermystical solutions are avoided. **1829** E. H. BARKER *Parriana* II. 101 *note*, This *hyper-orthodox and ultra-Tory divine. **1800** W. TAYLOR in *Monthly Mag.* X. 319 Another fault or misfortune of Klopstock, is his *hyperorthodoxy. **1877** DAWSON *Orig. World* vi. 135 A piece of pedantic hyperorthodoxy. **1852** LYELL in *Life* II. 185 There was no *hyperpanegyric. **1801** W. TAYLOR in *Monthly Mag.* XII. 224 Sneezing indicates over-action, super-irritation, *hyper-paroxysm. **1804** SOUTHEY in *Ann. Rev.* II. 548 The whole volume is made up of these *hyper-plagiarisms, where the theft is not more daring. **1873** F. HALL *Mod. Eng.* 39 Masters of *hyperpolysyllabic sesquipedalianism. **1958** *Times Rev. Industry* June 26/2 Production of *hyper-pure silicon entails purifying the selected chemical to a very high degree. **1892** *Temple Bar Mag.* June 149 The Burgomasteress..*hyper-realised, perhaps, how much Elias was to blame. **1859** I. TAYLOR *Logic in Theol.* 224 The *hyper-reverential regard. **1882** T. MOZLEY *Remin.* I. xliv, There is not the slightest.. palliation of my little piece of *hyper-ritualism. **1874** FARRAR *Christ* (ed. 2) II. xliv. 117 *note*, The cold *hyper-saintly ones might say.. surely she might wait yet one day longer! **1638** CHILLINGW. *Relig. Prot.* I. vi. § 38. 357 If you will be so *hypersceptical as to perswade me, that I am not sure that I doe beleeve all this. **1881** BLACKIE *Lay Serm.* ix. 312 The *hyperscrupulosity of a verbal conscience. **1883** F. M. CRAWFORD *Dr. Claudius* iii, The blandishments and caressing *hypersensualism of Delmonico. **1868** MRS. WHITNEY *P. Strong* vii, 'One less little life in the world', said I, *hypersentimentally. **1859** DARWIN in *Life & Lett.* (1887) II. 144 The *hyperspeculative points we have been discussing. **1877** BLACK *Green Past.* xiv, *Hyper-subtleties of fancy. **1663** COWLEY *Verses & Ess., Liberty* (1669) 83 If the person be *Pan huper sebastus*, there's a *Hupersuperlative ceremony then of conducting him to the bottome of the stairs. **1825** SOUTHEY in *Q. Rev.* XXXII. 372 Souls in Purgatory, and even beyond it, in the *hyper-torrid Zone of the spiritual world. **1800** W. TAYLOR in *Monthly Mag.* X. 502/1 The two devils.. rant and roar somewhat *hypertragically. **1877** E. CAIRD *Philos. Kant* vi. 117 Such *hyper-transcendent conceptions. **1885** L. OLIPHANT *Sympneumata* 210 In this struggle for a curative *hypervitalisation. *Ibid.*, Those *hypervitalised vegetable and mineral substances. **1859** I. TAYLOR *Logic in Theol.* 319 A *hyper-wrought theology.

5. Specific and technical terms, esp. of Pathology and Physiology, as *hyperacuity*, *hyperalbuminosis*, etc.: see below. Also HYPERÆMIA, etc.

III. 6. Formations in which *hyper-* qualifies the second element adverbially or attributively, signifying that this is itself the higher in position of two or more, or the highest in serial order or degree; as in HYPERAPOPHYSIS, HYPERCORACOID, *hyperhypostasis*.

7. In Chemistry, *hyper-* denotes the highest in a series of oxygen compounds (cf. HYPO- 5), e.g. *hyperchloric*, *hyperiodic*, *hyperoxide*; but this is now more commonly expressed by PER-.

1795 PEARSON in *Phil. Trans.* LXXXV. 341 It may be called, according to the new nomenclature, hyper-carburet of iron. **1842** PARNELL *Chem. Anal.* (1845) 303 Treat the residue with alcohol, by which hyperchlorate of soda and the excess of hyperchlorate of barytes are dissolved. **1855** MAYNE *Expos. Lex.*, *Hypercarbonates*, a former term for the salts now called Bicarbonates. *Ibid.*, Hypersulphuret.

IV. The more important words belonging to all these groups appear in their alphabetical order as main words; others of less importance or less frequent use, and mostly of recent introduction, follow here. (For many of these no statement of derivation is needed, as they are simply formed by prefixing *hyper-* to another word, the etymology of which will be found in its place: e.g. *hyperacuity*, f. *hyper-* + ACUITY, q.v. In the following words *e* often replaces *æ*, *œ*, esp. in U.S. usage; the alternative spelling is not given for each word individually.)

hyperab'duction, extreme abduction (sense 3); so **hyperab'duct** *v. trans.*, **-ab'ducted** *ppl. a.*; **hypera'cuity**, excessive or morbid acuteness (of the bodily senses); ‖**hyperalbumi'nosis** *Path.*, excess of albumen in the blood; ˌ**hyperaldo'steronism** *Med.*, any condition characterized by excessive secretion of aldosterone; aldosteronism; ‖**hyperalgesia** (-æl'dʒiːsɪə), ‖**hyperalgia** (-'ældʒɪə) *Path.* [Gr. ὑπεραλγέ-ειν to be pained exceedingly, -αλγία, ἄλγος pain], excessive sensitiveness to painful impressions; hence **hyperalgesic** (-æl'dʒiːsɪk) *a.*, pertaining to or affected with hyperalgesia; **hyperalgic** (-'ældʒɪk) *a. Path.*, of, pertaining to, or affected with hyperalgia (hyperalgesia); **hyperanalysis**: (see quot.); **hyper'anarchy**, a condition beyond or worse than anarchy; **hyperaphic** (-'æfɪk) *a. Path.* [Gr. ἁφ-ή touch], excessively sensitive to touch (Mayne, 1855); **'hyperarchy** [Gr. ἀρχή, -αρχία rule], excess of government; **hyperas'thenia**, **-'astheny** *Path.* [ASTHENIA]: see quot; ˌ**hyperbilirubi'næmia** *Physiol.* [Gr. αἷμα blood], an abnormally high concentration of bilirubin in the blood; **hyperbrachycephalic** (-ˌbrækɪsɪ'fælɪk) *a. Craniol.*, extremely brachycephalic; applied to a skull of which the cranial index is over 85; so **hyperbrachycephaly** (-brækɪ'sɛfəlɪ), the condition of being hyperbrachycephalic; **hyper'branchial** *a. Zool.*, situated above the gills or branchiæ; **hypercalcæmia** (-kæl'siːmɪə) *Physiol.* [CALC(IUM + Gr. αἷμα blood], an abnormally high concentration of calcium in the blood; so **hypercal'cæmic** *a.*; **hypercalcuria** (-kæl'sjʊərɪə), **-calciuria** (-kælsɪ'jʊərɪə) *Physiol.* [-URIA], an abnormally high concentration of calcium in the urine; **hyper'capnia** *Physiol.* [Gr. καπνός smoke], an abnormally high concentration of carbon dioxide in the blood; so **hyper'capnial** (*rare*), **-'capnic** *adjs.*; ‖**hyper'cardia** *Path.* [Gr. καρδία heart], hypertrophy of the heart (*Syd. Soc. Lex.* 1886); **hyperca'thexis** (pl. **-exes**) *Psychol.*, an excessive degree of cathexis; ˌ**hypercellu'larity** *Path.*, an excess of cells at a site in the body; so **hyper'cellular** *a.*, containing more than the normal number of cells; ˌ**hyperchlo'ræmia** *Physiol.*, an abnormally high concentration of chlorides in the blood; ˌ**hyperchlor'hydria**

Physiol. [CHLORHYDR(IC *a.*], an abnormally high concentration of hydrochloric acid in the gastric juice; so **ˌhyperchlor'hydric** *a.*; **ˌhypercholeste'ræmia, -cholestero'læmia** *Physiol.* [Gr. *αἷμα* blood], an abnormally high concentration of cholesterol in the blood; so **ˌhypercholestero'læmic** *a.*; **hyperchromatism** (-'krəʊmətɪz(ə)m), abnormally intense coloration; **hyper'chromatopsy** (see quot., and *chromatopsy* s.v. CHROMATO-); **ˌhypercoagula'bility** *Med.*, an excessive tendency (of the blood) to coagulate; so **hyperco'agulable** *a.*; **hyper'conic** *a. Geom.*, relating to the intersection of two conicoids or surfaces of the second order; **hyper'cosmic** *a.*, above the world, supramundane; **'hypercycle** *Geom.* [a. F. *hypercycle*], name given by Laguerre to a class of curves comprising the hypocycloid with four cusps, the parabola, the anticaustics of the parabola, etc. (1882 *Comptes Rendus* XCIV. 778, etc.); **hyper'dactyly** *Zool.* [Gr. *δάκτυλ-ος* finger] = POLYDACTYLY; †**hyper'deify** *v. trans.*, to exalt above God; **hyperdi'stributive** *a.*, distributive in relation to more than one variable (see DISTRIBUTIVE *a.* 6); *sb.* a hyperdistributive function; **hyperdy'namic** *a.*, excessively violent or excited, as the vital powers in certain morbid conditions (Mayne, 1855); ‖**hyperemesis** (-'ɛmɪsɪs) *Path.*, excessive vomiting; so **hyperemetic** (-iː'mɛtɪk) *a.*, pertaining to or affected with hyperemesis (Mayne, 1855); **hypere'motional** *a.*, affected by or displaying an abnormal degree of emotion; hence **ˌhyperemotio'nality**, hyperemotional behaviour; **hyper'ethical** *a.*, beyond the sphere of ethics; **hypereu'tectic** *a.*, (of an alloy of iron) containing a higher proportion of carbon than the eutectic composition (i.e. more than about 4·3%); (in quot. 1902 = *hypereutectoid, eutectoid* itself not having been coined at that date); **hypereu'tectoid** *a.* (of steel) containing a higher proportion of carbon than the eutectoid composition (i.e. more than about 0·8%); **'hyperform** *Linguistics* [contraction of *hypercorrect form*], a hypercorrect spelling or pronunciation; **'hyperfragment** *Nuclear Physics* [HYPER(ON], a hypernucleus, esp. one produced by the breaking up of a heavier one (see quot. 1964); **hyper'function** *Med.*, over-activity or over-production (in a gland or other part of the body); so **hyper'functional** *a.*, **hyper'functioning** *vbl. sb.* and *ppl. a.*; **ˌhypergammaˌglobuli'næmia** *Physiol.* [Gr. *αἷμα* blood], an abnormally high concentration of gamma globulins in the blood; hence **ˌhypergammaˌglobuli'næmic** *a.*; ‖**hyper-genesis** (-'dʒɛnɪsɪs), excessive production or growth; so **hypergenetic** (-dʒɪ'nɛtɪk) *a.*, pertaining to or characterized by hypergenesis (Mayne, 1855); **hypergeusia** (-'gjuːzɪə) *Med.* [Gr. *γεῦσις* taste], excessive acuteness of the sense of taste; **ˌhyperglobuli'næmia** *Physiol.* [Gr. *αἷμα* blood], an abnormally high concentration of globulins in the blood; hence **ˌhyperglobuli'næmic** *a.*; **hypergly'cæmia** *Physiol.*, an abnormally high concentration of sugar in the blood; so **hypergly'cæmic** *a.*; **hyper'goddess**, a being of higher rank than a goddess, a supreme goddess; **hyperhi'drosis, -idrosis** (erron. *-hydrosis*) *Path.*, excessive sweating; **hyperhy'postasis**: see quot; †**hyperhyp'sistous** *a.* [Gr. *ὕψιστ-ος* highest], exalted above the highest; **hyperide'ation**, excessive flow of ideas, extreme mental activity, or restlessness; **hyperi'mmune** *a. Med.*, subjected to, resulting from, or produced by hyperimmunization; having a high concentration of antibody; **ˌhyper-immuni'zation** *Med.*, the production of a high concentration of antibody in the serum of an animal, esp. by the repeated injection of the same antigen; so **hyper'immunize** *v. trans.*, to produce such a condition in (an animal); **hyper'immunized** *ppl. a.*; **hyperin'fection** *Med.*, continued infection with parasitic worms owing to their larvæ developing into adult worms without leaving the body; so **hyperin'fective** *a.*, causing or characterized by hyperinfection; **hyperinflation** (also hyphened), an acute form of economic inflation; **ˌhyperinsuli'næmia** *Physiol.* [Gr. *αἷμα* blood], an abnormally high concentration of insulin in the blood; **hyper'insulinism** *Med.*, a condition in which the body produces excessive insulin, usu. as a result of a tumour of the islets of Langerhans in the pancreas; the presence of an excessive amount of insulin in the body; **ˌhyperirrita'bility** *Med.*, increased irritability; abnormally high responsiveness to stimuli; so **hyper'irritable** *a.*; **hyperkalæmia** (-kə'liːmɪə), **-kaliæmia** (-kælɪ'iːmɪə) *Physiol.* [mod.L. *kalium* potassium (see KALI) + Gr. *αἷμα* blood] = *hyperpotassæmia* below; hence **hyperka'læmic** *a.*; **ˌhyperkera'tosis** *Path.*, (*a*) (see quot. 1848); now *rare* or *Obs.*; (*b*) excessive development of the horny layer of the skin; **hyperki'nesia** *Path.* = *hyperkinesis* (s.v. HYPER- IV); ‖**hyperkinesis** (-kaɪ'niːsɪs) [Gr. *κίνησις* movement], abnormal amount of muscular movement, spasmodic action; so **hyperkinetic** (-kaɪ'nɛtɪk) *a.*, pertaining to or affected with hyperkinesis; **ˌhyperleucocy'tosis, -leukocy'tosis** *Path.* = LEUCOCYTOSIS; **hyperli'pæmia** *Physiol.*, an abnormally high concentration of fats (or lipids) in the blood; any condition characterized by this; **ˌhypermagne'sæmia** *Physiol.* [Gr. *αἷμα* blood], an abnormally high concentration of magnesium in the blood; **hyper'mania** *Psychiatry*, (*a*) sometimes used to mean a severe degree of mania with partial or complete disorientation, often accompanied by violent behaviour and forming a stage in manic-depressive illness; (*b*) used *erron.* for HYPOMANIA (quot. 1928: see also quot. 1956 for HYPERMANIC); hence **hyper'manic** *a.*; **hyperma'ture** *a. Ophthalm.*, applied to a cataract in its final stage (see quots.); so **hyperma'turity**; **hypermedi'cation**, excessive use of medicines; **hyperme'tabolism** *Physiol.*, metabolism at a high rate; so **ˌhypermeta'bolic** *a.*, of hypermetabolism; **hyper'mnesia** [Gr. *μνῆσις* remembrance], unusual power of memory; **hypermo'bility** *Med.*, abnormally great freedom of movement or flexibility in a joint; so **hyper'mobile** *a.*, characterized by or exhibiting hypermobility; **'hypermorph** *Genetics* [Gr. *μορφ-ή* form], any allele which is functionally more effective than the corresponding wild-type allele; so **hyper'morphic** *a.*; **hypermo'tility** *Med.*, excessive movement, esp. of the stomach and intestines; **hyperna'træmia** *Physiol.* [NATR(IUM + Gr. *αἷμα* blood], an abnormally high concentration of sodium in the blood; hence **hyperna'træmic** *a.*; **hypernatural** *a.*, beyond what is natural (in quot. as *sb.*); †**hyper'nephelist** [Gr. *ὑπερνέφελ-ος* above the clouds, *νεφέλη* cloud], one who goes above the clouds; **hyperne'phroma** *Path.* [NEPHR(O- + -OMA], a malignant tumour of the cortical parenchyma of the kidney; orig. such tumours were believed to derive from misplaced tissue of the suprarenal gland (whence the name) and were described in other tissues besides that of the kidney; so **ˌhyperne'phromatous** *a.*; **hyper'nomian** *a.* [Gr. *ὑπέρνομ-ος* transgressing the law, *νόμος* law], above or beyond the scope of law; **'hyperˌnote**, an additional or supplementary note; **hyper'nucleus** *Nuclear Physics* [HYPER(ON], a nucleus in which a hyperon replaces one of the nucleons; a composite particle in which a hyperon is bound to one or more nucleons; hence **hyper'nuclear** *a.*; **hypernu'trition**, excessive nutrition: = HYPERTROPHY; **hyperor'ganic** *a.*, beyond or independent of the organism; **hyperorthognathic** (-ɔːθəʊg'næθɪk) *a. Craniol.*, excessively orthognathic; applied to a skull in which the cranial index is over 91; so **hyperorthognathy** (-ɔː'θɒgnəθɪ), the condition of being hyperorthognathic; **hyperos'motic** *a. Physiol.* = HYPERTONIC *a.* 2; const. *to*; **hyperphagia** (-'feɪdʒ(ɪ)ə) *Med.* [Gr. *-φαγία* -PHAGY], an abnormally great desire for food; excessive eating; hence **hyperphagic** (-'fædʒɪk) *a.*, of or exhibiting hyperphagia; **hyperphalangia** (-fə'lændʒɪə), **-phalangism** (-fə'lændʒɪz(ə)m), **-phalangy** (-'fæləndʒɪ) *Med.* and *Zool.* [L. *phalang-*: see PHALANX], the condition of having more digital phalanges than normal, esp. in cases where polydactyly is absent; **hyperpha'ryngeal** *a. Zool.*, situated above the pharynx; ‖**hyperphasia** (-'feɪzɪə) *Path.* [Gr. *φάσις* speaking; after *aphasia*], excessive talking occasioned by a want of control over the vocal organs, due to cerebral affection (*Syd. Soc. Lex.* 1886); hence **hyperphasic** (-'fæzɪk) *a.*, affected with hyperphasia; **hyperphe'nomenal** *a.*, superior to what is phenomenal, noumenal, **hyper'phoria** *Ophthalm.*, latent strabismus in which there is a tendency for one eye to be directed above (or below) the line of sight of the other; so **hyper'phoric** *a.*; **ˌhyperphospha'tæmia** *Physiol.* [Gr. *αἷμα* blood], an abnormally high concentration of phosphates (or other phosphorus compounds) in the blood; so **ˌhyperphospha'tæmic** *a.*; **hyperpiesia** (-paɪ'iːzɪə), **-piesis** (-paɪ'iːsɪs, -'paɪəsɪs) *Med.* [Gr. *πίεσις* pressure], high blood pressure, hypertension, esp. when without evident cause (the two words were distinguished in meaning by Allbutt: see quots.); hence **hyperpi'etic** *a.*; **ˌhyperpigmen'tation** *Med.*, excessive pigmentation; so **ˌhyperpig'mented** *ppl. a.*, exhibiting hyperpigmentation; **hyper-pi'tuitarism** *Path.* [PITUITAR(Y *a.* + -ISM], increased hormone secretion by the pituitary body; hence **hyperpi'tuitary** *a.*, of, pertaining to, or affected with hyperpituitarism; **'hyperploid** *a. Genetics* [-PLOID], having one or a few extra chromosomes (orig. also chromosome fragments) in addition to a haploid, diploid, triploid, etc., set; containing such cells; also as *sb.*, a hyperploid cell or individual; so **'hyperploidy**, the condition of being hyperploid; **hyperpnœa** (haɪpə'niːə, -pniːə) *Physiol.* [Gr. *πνοή* breath, breathing], deep and rapid breathing; panting; so **hyper'pnœic** *a.*; **ˌhyperpota'ssæmia** *Physiol.* [Gr. *αἷμα* blood], an abnormally high concentration of potassium in the blood; so **ˌhyperpota'ssæmic** *a.*; **hyperpro'sexia** *Psychol.* [Gr. *προσέχ-ειν* to turn (one's attention) (*ἔχειν* to hold, possess mentally)], the concentration of attention on one stimulus to the exclusion of all others; **ˌhyperprotei'næmia** *Physiol.* [Gr. *αἷμα* blood], an abnormally high concentration of protein in the blood; **hyperpyretic** (-paɪ'rɛtɪk) *a. Path.* [Gr. *πυρετός* fever], pertaining to or affected with ‖**hyperpy'rexia**, a high or excessive degree of fever; whence **hyperpy'rexial, hyperpy'rexic** *adjs.* = *hyperpyretic*; **hyper'rational** *a.*, above or beyond the scope of reason; **hyper'reactive** *a. Med.*, reacting unusually strongly to certain stimuli; of or pertaining to this tendency; so **ˌhyperreac'tivity**; **hyper'realism** *Art* [a. F. *hyperréalisme*] = PHOTOREALISM; also *transf.*; hence **hyper'real** *a.*, **hyper'realist**; **hyper-'resonance**, excessive resonance of a part of the body on percussion; so **hyper-'resonant** *a.*; **hyper'rhythmical** *a.*, additional to the rhythm, hypermetrical; **hyper'saline** *a. Biol.*, (of naturally occurring water) more salty than typical sea water; hence **hypersa'linity**, the condition of being hypersaline; ‖**hypersar'coma, hypersar'cosis** *Path.*, proud or fungous flesh; **hyperse'cretion**, excessive secretion; **hyper'sensual** *a.*, above or beyond the scope of the senses, super-sensuous; **ˌhypersexu'ality**, a condition in which the sexual instinct is abnormally strong; **hyper'somnia** *Med.* [L. *somnus* sleep], a condition characterized by abnormally long or frequent periods, or abnormal depth, of sleep; hence **hyper'somnic** *a.*, of, exhibiting, or producing hypersomnia; **'hyperspace** *Geom.*, space of more than three dimensions; also, any non-Euclidean space; (esp. in *Science Fiction*) **hyper'spatial** *a.*, of or in hyperspace; **hypersper'matic** *a.* [Gr. *σπέρμα* seed], characterized by excess of semen; **hypersplenism** (-'splɛnɪz(ə)m) *Path.* [SPLEN-], over-activity of the spleen; *spec.* a condition characterized by a general destruction of blood cells, often associated with enlargement of the spleen but in which direct involvement of the spleen is now considered doubtful; so **hyper'splenic** *a.*; **hyper'static** *a. Engin.*, statically indeterminate, i.e. having more members or supports than the minimum required to render it stable (and therefore requiring more than considerations of equilibrium alone for the calculation of all the internal forces and moments); of or pertaining to such a structure; **hyper'stereograph** *Photogr.*, a picture or pair of photographs taken by hyperstereoscopy; **ˌhyperstere'oscopy** *Photogr.*, stereoscopic photography in which the separation of the two viewpoints is greater than the distance between the eyes, resulting in a greater stereoscopic effect or exaggerated perspective; hence **ˌhyperstereo'scopic** *a.* ; **hypersu'sceptible** *a. Med.* = HYPERSENSITIVE *a.*

2; so ˌ**hypersuscepti'bility**; **hyper'telorism** *Med.* [Gr. τῆλ-ε at a distance + ὁρίζειν to separate from: see -ISM], a condition in which the eyes are abnormally far apart, freq. found accompanying other congenital malformations of the face; **hyper'thermal**, *a.* [Gr. θερμός hot, THERMAL] characterized by excess of heat, of very high temperature; ‖**hypertrichosis** (-trɪ'kəʊsɪs) [Gr. τρίχωσις growth of hair, f. τριχ-, θρίξ hair], excessive growth of hair, locally or over the body generally; **hypertridi'mensional** *a. Geom.*, of or relating to more than three dimensions. **hyper'tropia** *Ophthalm.*, strabismus in which one eye is directed above the line of sight of the other; **hyper'typic, -ical** *a.*, surpassing what is typical; **hyperu'ranian** *a.* [Gr. ὑπερουράνι-ος], lying above the heavens, super-celestial; **hyperu'resis** [Gr. οὔρησις urination], excessive discharge of urine; ˌ**hyperuri'cæmia** (-jʊərɪ'siːmɪə) *Physiol.*, an abnormally high concentration of uric acid in the blood; = LITHÆMIA, URICÆMIA; hence ˌ**hyperuri'cæmic** *a.*; **hyper'vascular** *a.*, vascular to an abnormal degree; hence **hypervascu'larity**, hypervascular condition or quality; **hyperve'locity**, a speed that is (relatively) very high; usu. *attrib.*; ˌ**hypervitami'nosis** *Path.* [-OSIS], any condition caused by excessive intake of a vitamin, esp. over a prolonged period; **hypervo'læmia** *Physiol.* [VOL(UME *sb.* + Gr. αἷμα blood], an increased volume of circulating blood in the body; hence **hypervo'læmic** *a.*

1945 *Amer. Heart Jrnl.* XXIX. 7 The pulse in the left arm could be obliterated only by having the patient *hyperabduct his arm above a 150-degree angle. *Ibid.* 6 The habit of sleeping with the arms in the *hyperabducted position. **1905** GOULD *Dict. New Med. Terms* 299/2 *Hyperabduction. **1945** *Amer. Heart Jrnl.* XXIX. 4 The term 'hyperabduction' is used in this paper to mean that phase of circumduction which brings the arms together above the head... Actually, the term hyperabduction, although accepted in anatomic terminology, is not..an entirely logical term, for abduction is movement away from the median plane of the body, and beyond the 90° angle; the arm in so-called hyperabduction actually again approaches the median plane. **1966** J. E. FLYNN *Hand Surg.* xiv. 696/1 Hyperabduction of the arm alone could stretch the subclavian artery sufficiently to produce occlusion in certain persons. **1887** F. W. H. MYERS in *Mind* Jan. 154 Hypnotic *hyper-acuity of vision. **1866–80** A. FLINT *Princ. Med.* (ed. 5) 67 We know nothing of absolute *hyperalbuminosis as a morbid state of the blood. **1876** BARTHOLOW *Mat. Med.* (1879) 225 Lead may cause that condition of hyperalbuminosis which eventuates in albuminous urine. **1955** CONN & LOUIS in *Trans. Assoc. Amer. Physicians* LXVIII. 229 What is the relationship of *hyperaldosteronism to the production of renal arteriosclerosis? **1966** R. B. SCOTT *Price's Textbk. Pract. Med.* (ed. 10) vii. 436/2 Patients with hyperaldosteronism usually present in one of two ways, either with manifestations of hypertension or with muscular weakness and hyporeflexia sometimes sufficiently severe to cause episodic paralysis. *Ibid.* 437/1 Without treatment hyperaldosteronism is fatal, the patient usually dying of the hypertensive vascular complications. **1896** ALLBUTT *Syst. Med.* I. 665 Cutaneous *hyperalgesia is common. **1886** *Syd. Soc. Lex.*, **Hyperalgia.* **1946** *Nature* 10 Aug. 202/1 We obtained successful results with this substance in other *hyperalgic conditions, namely, cervical neuritis and trigeminal neuralgia. **1968** CAHN & HEROLD in A. Soulairac et al. *Pain* IV. 367 We have defined these changes as a hyperalgic state. **1942** C. S. LEWIS in *Essays & Stud.* XXVII. 18 This brings us to..the psycho-analysis of psycho-analysis itself. Such a *hyper-analysis..would not refer to 'really scientific people', but to the great mass of ordinary people who read psycho-analytic books with avidity and undergo their influence. **1806** W. TAYLOR in *Ann. Rev.* IV. 253 If Adam Smith's system tends somewhat to anarchy, Sir James Steuart's tends surely to *hyperanarchy. **1797** —— in *Monthly Rev.* XXIV. 532 *Hyperarchy, or excessive government, has ruined more empires than anarchy, or deficient government. **1855** MAYNE, **Hyperasthenia*, excessive debility: *hyperastheny. **1923** *Q. Jrnl. Med.* XVI. 409 These latter cases are on the border line between 'physiological *hyperbilirubinaemia' and the actual disease known as haemolytic (acholuric) jaundice. **1965** W. TAYLOR *Biliary Syst.* 647 (*heading*) Bilirubin excretion in congenital hyperbilirubinaemia. **1925** *Jrnl. Biol. Chem.* LXIII. 444 Dog 51 showed typical symptoms of *hyper-calcemia. **1970** C. N. GRAYMORE *Biochem. Eye* viii. 551 Hypercalcaemia results from vitamin D poisoning, hyperthyroidism and severe renal damage. **1932** *Physiol. Rev.* XII. 605 The occurrence of ..*hypercalcemic symptoms. **1930** *Jrnl. Biol. Chem.* LXXXVII. p. xv (*heading*), Calcium and phosphorus metabolism in relation to certain bone diseases. I. *Hypercalcuria. **1961** *Lancet* 26 Aug. 455/2, 10 of the 28 patients with hypercalciuria had no evidence of renal calcification. **1964** D. M. DUNLOP *Textbk. Med. Treatm.* (ed. 9) 757 A variety of disorders which are associated with hypercalciuria tend to cause stone formation. **1908** *Amer. Jrnl. Physiol.* XXI. 140 Hypo- and *hyper-capnia are abnormal conditions. **1962** *Lancet* 2 June 1183/2 The combination of hypoxia and hypercapnia is often lethal. **1908** *Amer. Jrnl. Physiol.* XXI. 141 An asphyxial (or *hyper-capnial) condition of the blood supply to the spinal bulb. **1955** *Jrnl. Physiol.* CXXIX. 405 The achievement of a steady state of *hyper-capnic ventilation. **1962** *Lancet* 8 Dec. 1224/2 When pH was kept normal by the infusion of this organic buffer..circulation was unaltered in the hypercapnic dog. **1923** FREUD in *Internat. Jrnl. Psycho-Anal.* IV. 6 Our consideration of the first case, the jealousy paranoia, led to a similar estimate of the importance of the quantitative factor, by showing that there also the abnormality essentially consisted in the *hyper-cathexis (over-investment) of the interpretations of another's unconscious behaviour. **1950** J. STRACHEY tr. *Freud's Totem & Taboo* iii. 89 The psychological results must be the same in both cases, whether the libidinal hypercathexis of thinking is an original one or has been produced by regression. **1968** D. RAPAPORT et al. *Diagn. Psychol. Testing* (rev. ed.) iii. 108 The drive cathexes are kept in balance and control, harmonizing with and not encroaching upon the ego's functions, nor demanding that it employ its hyper-cathexes to curb them. **1955** *Bull. N.Y. Acad. Med.* XXXI. 135 Under such circumstances the marrow is *hypercellular but the blood is cytopenic. **1967** J. METCOFF *Acute Glomerulonephritis* vi. 110 Some lobules may be quite hypercellular. **1908** *Lancet* 23 May 1467/2 In the older or quiescent stages [of carcinoma of the tongue] the *hypercellularity disappears. **1967** J. METCOFF *Acute Glomerulonephritis* vi. 110 Mitotic figures..are easy to find in areas of hypercellularity. **1921** *Endocrinology* V. 802 One or two days before the onset of menstruation..there is generally an absolute and relative *hyperchloremia. **1969** R. L. SEARCY *Diagn. Biochem.* i. 14/1 Treatment with ammonium chloride can lead to..hyperchloremia. **1891** F. P. FOSTER *Med. Dict.* III. 1938/2 *Hyperchlorhydria. **1893** *Med. Ann.* 169 Hyperchlorhydria and hypochlorhydria are not identical with hyperacidity and hypoacidity. **1957** I. AIRD *Compan. Surg. Stud.* (ed. 2) xxxiii. 710 *Hyperchlorhydria* is present in 90 per cent of duodenal ulcers. **1903** *Med. Rec.* 7 Feb. 229/2 In the last year the pain increased, and the disturbance was always of the *hyperchlorhydric type. On entrance to the hospital, a small, painless tumor was clearly felt in the region of the pylorus. **1926** J. A. RYLE *Gastric Function* 119 The fractional test-meal gives hyperchlorhydric curves. **1894** GOULD *Dict. Med.* 589/1 *Hypercholesteremia. **1916** *Physiol. Abstr.* I. 327 (*heading*) Experimental hypercholesteræmia. **1969** R. L. SEARCY *Diagn. Biochem.* xviii. 170/2 Hypercholesteremia usually..accompanies hypothyroidism. **1916** *Arch. Internal Med.* XVII. 768 In pregnancy *hypercholesterolemia occurs physiologically. **1970** *Nature* 31 Oct. 465/1 Growth hormone is as efficacious as thyroid hormone in preventing hypercholesterolaemia. **1916** *Arch. Internal Med.* XVII. 784 Cells which have been bathed in and irritated by *hypercholesterolemic blood. **1961** *Lancet* 7 Oct. 802/2 Cases of familial hyper-cholesterolæmic xanthomatosis. **1849–52** TODD *Cycl. Anat.* IV. 1462/1 The characteristic of *Hyperchromatopsy is that of attaching colours..to..objects which have no pretensions to them. **1934** WEBSTER, *Hyper-coagulability, -coagulable. **1962** *Lancet* 8 Dec. 1230/2 This permits one to anticipate the periods of blood hyper-coagulability and thus to prevent thromboembolism successfully. **1972** *Nature* 28 Apr. 452/1 All showed adverse changes which might lead to a hypercoagulable or hyperthrombotic state compared with the non-smoker. **1877** BOOTH *New Geom. Meth.* II. 2 To these curves may be given the appropriate name of *Hyperconic sections. **1877** BLACKIE *Wise Men* 339 Until they climb To *hyper-cosmic fields. **1902** WEBSTER Suppl., *Hyperdactyly. **1929** R. S. LULL *Org. Evol.* (ed. 2) xx. 297 As though extra toes over the normal five had been added (hyperdactyly). **1965** W. B. YAPP *Vertebrates* v. 93 The paired limbs show both more digits and more joints than usual—hyperdactyly and hyperphalangy. **1663** *Aron-bimn.* 76 They do *Hyper-deifie it, advance it above God. **1855** MAYNE *Expos. Lex.*, **Hyperemesis.* **1875** H. C. WOOD *Therap.* (1879) 429 Hyper-emesis may..be divided into.. such as is due to overdoses of depressing centric emetics;.. such as arises from irritation of the stomach. **1946** O. FENICHEL *Psychoanal. Theory of Neurosis* xx. 478 A 'generally frigid' person has forgotten childhood emotions; the *hyperemotional person is still a child. **1971** *Jrnl. Gen. Psychol.* LXXXIV. 245 Loud vocalization..is a prominent characteristic of vigorous fighting among rats and has been labelled..an index of hyperemotional behavior among normally silent species. **1958** *Science* 19 Sept. 655/2 These animals did show a gradual, but only partial, development of *hyperemotionality. **1972** *Nature* 25 Aug. 454/1 According to some reports, bulbectomy also induces irritability and hyper-emotionality resembling the classic septal 'rage' syndrome. **1882** J. MARTINEAU *Study Spinoza* 289 The boundary between the ethical and the *hyper-ethical. **1902** *Encycl. Brit.* XXIX. 573/2 The undisturbed slow cooling from the molten state of a *hyper-eutectic steel containing 1·00 per cent. of carbon. **1912** W. H. HATFIELD *Cast Iron* i. 13 Hypereutectic alloys deposit primary iron-carbide along the line B′C. **1959** A. G. GUY *Elem. Physical Metall.* (ed. 2) vi. 186 As the composition changes from hypoeutectic (less than eutectic) to hypereutectic (more than eutectic) in terms of metal *B*, the primary crystals change from alpha phase to beta phase. **1911** *Encycl. Brit.* XIV. 805/2 The large massive plates of cementite which form the network or skeleton in *hyper-eutectoid steels. **1966** A. PRINCE *Alloy Phase Equilibria* vi. 107 Hyper-eutectoid alloys on cooling from the austenite phase region deposit cementite over a range of temperature until *A* 1 is reached. As before, the remaining austenite then transforms to pearlite. **1933** L. BLOOMFIELD *Lang.* xxvii. 479 This may be disclosed by isolated relic forms, or by the characteristic phenomenon of *hyper-forms. **1937** *Amer. Speech* XII. iii. 168 Hyper-forms are by no means always attempts to imitate city pronunciation. **1964** H. KÖKERITZ in D. Abercrombie et al. *Daniel Jones* 141, I have heard the hyperform [həˌrɑs] from a colleague now deceased. **1955** W. F. FRY et al. in *Physical Rev.* XCIX. 1561 Following a suggestion of M. Goldhaber, we propose to call a nuclear fragment containing a bound hyperon or some other unstable particle, a *hyperfragment. **1963** K. NISHIJIMA *Fund. Particles* vi. 290 The study of hyperfragments offers almost the only source of getting information about the Λ-nucleon force. **1964** *Progress Nuclear Physics* IX. 172 The nucleus in which the capture occurs is usually broken up and the Λ^0-hyperon may be bound in one of the fragments that are emitted... Fragments such as these are referred to as hyperfragments. **1909** *Jrnl. Amer. Med. Assoc.* 24 July 252/2 Massalongo's supposition that the disease represents a condition of *hyper-function—hyperpituitarism—has been widely discredited. **1961** *Lancet* 16 Sept. 655/1 There was general agreement that the diagnosis of adrenocortical hyperfunction should be made preoperatively. **1962** *Circulation Res.* X. 250 (*heading*) Compensatory hyperfunction of the heart and cardiac insufficiency. **1934** WEBSTER, *Hyperfunctional. **1961** *Jrnl. Amer. Med. Ass.* 29 July 232/1 One hyper-functional nodule proved to contain a papillary carcinoma in an adenoma. **1970** N. SIMIONESCU *Histogenesis Thyroid Cancer* iv. 28 (*heading*) The hyperfunctional cell. **1918** *Endocrinology* II. 46 A *hyperfunctioning thyroid may be poor in colloids. **1926** Hyperfunctioning [see *hypofunctioning* s.v. HYPO- II]. **1954** A. WHITE et al. *Princ. Biochem.* xliii. 946 Hyperfunctioning of the adrenal cortex in man is seen as a result of tumors composed of cortical cells. **1961** *Lancet* 16 Sept. 655/2 There was disagreement..about whether adrenalectomy for patients with hyperplastic or hyperfunctioning glands should be total or subtotal. **1947** DORLAND & MILLER *Med. Dict.* (ed. 21), *Hypergammaglobulinemia. **1958** *Immunology* I. iii. 245 Hypergammaglobulinaemia was a feature of the acute phase when complement levels were very low. **1971** *Nature* 31 Dec. 558/2 We have obtained evidence in support of the idea that hypergammaglobulinaemia represents an immunological host response to tumour-associated antigen(s). *Ibid.* 559/1 A hundred instances of individual immunoglobulin increases occurred in the fifty hypergammaglobulinaemic mice. **1855** MAYNE *Expos. Lex.*, **Hypergenesis*,..a congenital excess or redundancy of parts. **1878** T. BRYANT *Pract. Surg.* I. 559 The hypergenesis of the pulp [of a tooth]. **1855** R. G. MAYNE *Expos. Lex. Med. Sci.* (1860) 480/1 *Hypergeusia. **1888** *Encycl. Brit.* XXIII. 80/2 Increase in the sense of taste is called hypergeusia, diminution of it hypogeusia, and entire loss ageusia. **1936** *Jrnl. Clin. Invest.* XV. 475 (*heading*) Acid-base equivalence of the blood in diseases associated with *hyperglobulinemia. **1966** *McGraw-Hill Encycl. Sci. & Technol.* VIII. 256/2 The diseases usually associated with hyperglobulinemia are multiple myeloma, kala-azar, Hodgkin's disease, [etc.]. **1958** DAMESHEK & GUNZ *Leukemia* viii. 187 *Hyperglobulinemic purpura. **1894** GOULD *Dict. Med.* 590/1 *Hyperglycemia. **1966** WRIGHT & SYMMERS *Systemic Path.* I. xxiii. 693/2 It has become obvious that diabetes mellitus is a syndrome and not a disease, and that a number of diverse factors may produce prolonged hyperglycaemia. **1903** *Med. Rec.* 24 Jan. 123/1 In coma diabeticum..it is likely that the *hyperglycæmic condition stands at the foundation of a diminished electrical conductivity of the serum. **1969** R. L. SEARCY *Diagn. Biochem.* liii. 461/2 This theory..could account for the hyperglycemic tendency. **1847** GROTE *Greece* II. xxxii. IV. 264 These supreme goddesses [the Mœræ]—or *hyper-goddesses, since the gods themselves must submit to them. **1854–67** C. A. HARRIS *Dict. Med. Terminol.*, **Hyperhidrosis.* **1876** DUHRING *Dis. Skin* 125 Hyperidrosis is a functional disorder of the sweat glands. **1874** MIVART *Evolution* in *Contemp. Rev.* Oct. 788 As if the term **hyperhypostasis* was not a familiar one to denote the absolute personality as distinguished from every dependent one. **1680** *Counterplots* 26 The Angels in their exalted nature, have they knees for this *hyperhypsistous Immanuel? **1927** *Lancet* 15 Jan. 117/2 Fluids from ten different *hyper-immune..rats. **1940** *Jrnl. Bacteriol.* XXXIX. 66 Mice born of hyperimmune mothers are themselves immune to intranasally administered virus. **1957** CUSHING & CAMPBELL *Princ. Immunol.* i. 24 For many laboratory procedures, or for the production of potent therapeutic serums, animals are injected for many weeks or even months. Such animals are often referred to as being hyperimmune. **1958** *Immunology* I. 82 Titres of hyper-immune sera. **1913** DORLAND *Med. Dict.* (ed. 7) 445/2 *Hyperimmunization. **1968** F. HAUROWITZ *Immunochem. & Biosynthesis Antibodies* x. 209 Hyperimmunization is the routine method used in the production of high antibody titers. **1905** *Rep. Brit. Assoc. Adv. Sci.* 553 Spreuill..by *hyper-immunising sheep with virulent blood has succeeded in producing a serum efficacious in cases of Blaauw tongue. **1968** GELL & COOMBS *Clin. Aspects Immunol.* (ed. 2) xlviii. 1278 It is even possible to hyper-immunize a horse with more than one major antigen at the same time. **1927** *Lancet* 15 Jan. 117/2 A *hyperimmunised rat. **1962** *Ibid.* 27 Jan. 208/2 They seem a likely source of the plasma cells which accumulate in the lung in hyper-immunised animals. **1931** E. C. FAUST in *Amer. Jrnl. Hygiene* XIV. 209 In addition to the direct and indirect types of Strongyloides..there is a distinct hyperinfective type..which is responsible for the so-called 'auto-infection' (i.e. '*hyperinfection') of individuals who have once become parasitized. **1943** CRAIG & FAUST *Clin. Parasitol.* (ed. 3) xiv. 249 In cases of hyperinfection, all or some of the rhabditoid larvæ in the lumen of the bowel metamorphose into dwarfed filariform larvæ *en transit* down the bowel, and..may produce reinfection. **1960** J. M. WATSON *Med. Helminthol.* xii. 116/2 The belief formerly held that the parasitic forms had a life-span of as much as fifteen years, based on the continuance of the infection in individuals removed from all possibility of external reinfection, did not take account of the possibility of auto-infection and hyper-infection. **1931** *Hyperinfective [see *hyperinfection* above]. **1936** A. C. CHANDLER *Introd. Human Parasitol.* (ed. 5) xvii. 359 The course of development of these larvae may follow any of three different lines..indirect, direct, and hyperinfective. **1930** F. D. GRAHAM (*title*) Exchange, prices and production in *hyper-inflation. **1952** P. EINZIG *Inflation* i. 23 When inflation has reached an extreme stage it may be described as 'hyper-inflation'. **1970** *Daily Tel.* 21 Dec. 3/7 The bulletin suggests a prices and incomes policy and a wealth tax, to deal with the emerging problem of hyper-inflation [in Australia]. **1924** *Jrnl. Amer. Med. Assoc.* 6 Sept. 729/2 Hypoglycemia is the result of *hyperinsulinemia. **1962** *Lancet* 12 May 1003/2 Either hyperplasia or tumour of the islet-cells of the pancreas, without evidence of hyper-insulinæmia. **1924** S. HARRIS in *Jrnl. Amer. Med. Assoc.* 6 Sept. 729/2 It was this line of reasoning that caused me to think that there may be such a condition as *hyper-insulinism. **1962** *Lancet* 13 Jan. 73/2 It seems reasonable to suppose that the characteristic hyperinsulinism immediately after these babies are born is the result of abnormal stimulation of the fœtal pancreas in utero by maternal hyperglycæmia and/or by some other factor. **1969** R. L. SEARCY *Diagn. Biochem.* xxxv. 322/1 Hyperinsulinism is now a well-characterized condition known to be caused by a functioning tumor termed an insulinoma or nesidio-blastoma. **1913** L. FORSTER tr. *Biedl's Internal Secretory Organs* II. 61 Rudinger's contention that the condition of *hyperirritability arises in the ganglion cells of the anterior cornua..did not survive the test of experiment. **1935** D. H. SHELLING *Parathyroids* vi. 115 In 1876, the older Chvostek described hyperirritability of the facial nerve as a sign of tetany. **1960** *Adv. Pediatrics* XI. 107 Symptoms of acute hypernatremia

are hyperirritability to stimuli despite extreme lethargy, coma, [etc.]. **1922** L. F. Barker et al. *Endocrinol. & Metabolism* I. I. 165 If the sympathetic nerve cells are *hyperirritable, sympathetic action predominates in the individual. **1954** *Pediatric Clinics N. Amer.* May 347 The infant was markedly dehydrated and alternately hyperirritable and drowsy. **1949** *New Gould Med. Dict.* 483 *Hyperkalemia. **1955** Elkinton & Danowski *Body Fluids* xxii. 483 Hyperkalemia is characteristic of adrenocortical insufficiency. **1961** *Lancet* 19 Aug. 399/2 Respiratory failure and hyperkalæmia are the main lethal factors. **1969** J. H. Green *Basic Clin. Physiol.* xvi. 89/1 This combination of a high blood potassium, with a high blood acid content, is termed *hyperkalaemic metabolic acidosis. **1972** *Lancet* 1 July 36/2 If..the patient still tends to be hyperkalæmic, exchange resins can be given orally once or twice a day. **1841** W. Lawrence *Treat. Dis. Eye* (ed. 2) xiv. 368 Conical Cornea. Synonymes:—Sugar-loaf cornea; *staphyloma conicum*..*hyperceratosis. **1848** Dunglison *Dict. Med. Sci.* (ed. 7) 442/2 *Hyperceratosis*, staphyloma of the cornea. **1907** W. A. Pusey *Princ. & Pract. Dermatol.* 88 The term hyperkeratosis is applied to those conditions of the stratum corneum in which there is an increased thickness of the horny layer with complete cornification of the cells. **1970** Jubb & Kennedy *Path. Domestic Animals* (ed. 2) II. x. 568/2 Hyperkeratosis may be..diffuse as in cattle poisoned with chlorinated naphthalenes. **1971** *Brit. Med. Bull.* XXVII. 29/2 The hyperkeratoses and pigmentation that accompanied the arsenical cancers of the hand. **1848** Dunglison *Dict. Med. Sci.* (ed. 7) 442/2 *Hypercinesia. **1875** R. Fowler *Med. Vocab.* (ed. 2) 245/1 Hyperkinesia. **1935** *Jrnl. Mental Sci.* LXXXI. 835 Articulatory and respiratory hyperkinesias were the pathological basis of the coprolalia. **1961** *Lancet* 23 Sept. 683/2 He was readmitted..with an acute choreiform illness, consisting of hyperkinesia and constant writhing movements. **1855** Mayne *Expos. Lex.*, **Hypercinesis*. **1878** A. M. Hamilton *Nerv. Dis.* 103 There is hyperkinesis, there being a tendency to muscular spasm. **1880** *Mind* V. 385 Hyperkinesis or super-abundant vivacity of movement. **1888** *Med. Chron.* VII. 391 (*heading*) The treatment of chorea and other *hyperkinetic diseases with physostigmine. **1935** *Jrnl. Mental Sci.* LXXXI. 834 The onset of a hyperkinetic encephalitis was associated with tics. **1966** *Med. Ann.* 308 The hyperkinetic syndrome in children is characterized by hyperactivity, short attention span, impulsivity..and poor social adjustment. **1972** *Village Voice* (N.Y.) 1 June 36/2 Court suits can also be of help in discovering the full extent of the drugging of so-called hyperactive or hyperkinetic children. **1897** *Lippincott's Med. Dict.* 493/2 *Hyperleucocytosis. **1898** *Allbutt's Syst. Med.* V. 420 In the second stage..a hyperleucocytosis occurs. **1951** *Jrnl. Clin. Endocrinol. & Metabolism* XI. 1027 Although her pneumonia was clearing..hyperleucocytosis, hypokaliemia, and the picture of metabolic alkalosis developed. **1894** Gould *Dict. Med.* 590/2 *Hyperlipemia. **1936** *Physiol. Abstr.* XX. 818 In the rabbit hyperlipæmia was obtained with olive oil. **1955** H. J. Deuel *Lipids* II. v. 349 A moderate hyperlipemia (increased blood fat level) may occur. **1966** *Lancet* 24 Dec. 1379/2 The recognition that some hyperlipæmias are 'carbohydrate-induced'..further suggests that dietary carbohydrate influences serum-triglyceride. **1933** *Hyper-magnesaemia [see *hypomagnesæmia* s.v. hypo- II]. **1955** Elkington & Danowski *Body Fluids* xxii. 482 Hypermagnesemia is present. **1928** *Daily Express* 10 May 7 'He is suffering from *hyper-mania, a state of unnatural excitement,' said Dr. Mould. **1945** W. S. Sadler *Mod. Psychiatry* xxxvii. 439 While three stages of mania are recognized—hypomania, acute mania, and hypermania—there is a fourth classification which has been denominated delirious mania. **1963** H. H. Kendler *Basic Psychol.* v. xiv. 510/1 A patient with hypermania, the more intense form, behaves like a raving maniac. **1956** W. H. Whyte *Organization Man* (1957) 408 A few mild neuroses conceded here and there won't give you too bad a score, and..you have the best margin for error if you err on the side of being *'hypermanic'—that is, too energetic and active. **1963** H. H. Kendler *Basic Psychol.* v. xiv. 510/1 A young soldier who exhibited at different times both hypomanic and hypermanic reactions. *Ibid.* 510/2 This hypermanic episode lasted about two weeks. **1897** *Lippincott's Med. Dict.* 494/1 **Hypermature cataract*, the final stage of progressive cataract, in which the lens substance breaks down, shrinking into a hard mass or becoming liquefied. **1962** D. G. Cogan in A. Pirie *Lens Metabolism Rel. Cataract* 294 When the entire cortex becomes liquefied the cataract is said to have become hypermature. **1904** L. W. Fox *Dis. Eye* xii. 309 The last stage is that of *hypermaturity or overripeness. **1964** S. Duke-Elder *Parsons' Dis. Eye* (ed. 14) xix. 271 If the process is allowed to go on uninterruptedly the stage of hypermaturity sets in when the cortex becomes disintegrated and transformed into a pultaceous mass. **1962** *Lancet* 22 Dec. 1317/2 There is no hint of an environmental factor which could have caused this very persistent *hypermetabolic state. **1971** N. R. Alpert *Cardiac Hypertrophy* 55 The particular factor that stimulates the growth of the heart acts upon the heart continuously during the hypermetabolic period. **1937** *Physiol. Abstr.* XXII. 528 It [*sc.* rectal temperature] may remain low during intense *hypermetabolism. **1958** Dameshek & Gunz *Leukemia* viii. 185 Occasional cases of chronic lymphocytic leukemia are associated with extraordinary degrees of hypermetabolism (+ 60 + 80 per cent). **1882** tr. *Ribot's Dis. Memory* iv. 174 Is this exaltation of memory, which physicians term **hypermnesia*, a morbid phenomenon? **1941** *Jrnl. Heredity* XXXII. 232 (*heading*) *Hypermobile joints in all descendants for two generations. **1967** *Ann. Rheumatic Dis.* XXVI. 423/2 Her mother had generalized osteo-arthritis and..was probably hypermobile. **1927** *Jrnl. Amer. Med. Assoc.* 28 May 1711/2 The father's feet were normal, except for the *hypermobility of the joints. **1941** *Jrnl. Heredity* XXXII. 232/2 All members of this generation show hypermobility, in varying degrees, of the joints of the fingers, thumbs, knees and elbows. **1967** *Ann. Rheumatic Dis.* XXVI. 423/2 The isolated joint hypermobility..is considered to be the result of generalized familial ligamentous laxity. **1949** Darlington & Mather *Elem. Genetics* vii. 152 The *hypermorph is more efficient than the wild-type gene... The wild-type gene is hypomorphic to its hypermorphic mutant and amorphic to its neomorphic mutant. **1932** H. J. Muller in *Proc. 6th Internat. Congr. Genetics* I. 242 Since it has been found that there are reverse mutations of hypomorphic genes.., we must regard the allelomorphs thereby resulting not as hypomorphic but as *hypermorphic to their immediate progenitor genes. **1966** E. A. Carlson *Gene* xiii. 112 Another type of activity exaggerated or increased the normal activity of genes; most reverse mutations would be examples of such hypermorphic activity. **1894** Gould *Dict. Med.* 590/2 *Hypermotility. **1926** J. A. Ryle *Gastric Function* 83 Abnormally rapid emptying or hypermotility [of the stomach]. **1949** Koestler *Insight & Outlook* vii. 107 Pathological laughter may thus be classed among other forms of hypermotility—epileptic attacks, tantrums, tics—caused by similar release phenomena. **1932** Dorland & Miller *Med. Dict.* (ed. 16) 605/2 *Hypernatremia. **1969** L. G. Wesson *Physiol. Human Kidney* xxvii. 552/1 Hypernatremia (plasma sodium concentration in excess of 150 mM/L) is observed in a variety of clinical situations. **1955** *Arch. Internal Med.* XCV. 21/1 A severe hyponatremic rather than *hypernatremic acidosis. **1854** S. Phillips *Ess. fr. Times* Ser. II. 324 There is Heep, articled clerk..him, too, we are inclined to put in the category of the *hypernaturals. **1708** Motteux *Rabelais, Pantagr. Prognost.* Prol., Whatever all the Astrophyles, *Hypernephelists..have thought. **1900** Dorland *Med. Dict.* 310/2 *Hypernephroma. **1912** *Q. Jrnl. Med.* V. 157 The objects of this paper are:—(1) To classify and describe the commoner adrenal tumours... (3) To present new reasons against the hypothesis that renal hypernephromata are derived from adrenal rests. **1916** E. H. Kettle *Path. Tumours* 132 The term hypernephroma is applied to a particular group of tumours, in the belief that they are derived from suprarenal tissue. **1921** *Jrnl. Obstetr. & Gynæcol.* XXVIII. 23 (*heading*) A comparison between ovarian 'hypernephroma' and luteoma and suprarenal hypernephroma. **1923** *Guy's Hosp. Rep.* LXXIII. 193 The hypernephromata of the kidneys arise in the renal epithelium. **1967** J. S. King *Renal Neoplasia* ii. 24 The patient..had a large renal tumor..which proved to be a hypernephroma when examined microscopically. **1946** *Jrnl. Urol.* LV. 18 (*heading*) Renal adenomas in *hypernephromatous kidneys: a study of their incidence, nature and relationship. **1841–4** Emerson *Ess., Experience* Wks. (Bohn) I. 188 The intellect..is antinomian or *hypernomian, and judges law as well as fact. **1758** *Monthly Rev.* 153 Notes which refer again to other notes, and *hypernotes or further quotations. **1962** *Sci. Amer.* Jan. 53/2 The discovery of hyperfragments led to a rapid development of a new field: *hypernuclear physics. **1971** *Nature* 28 May 226/2 Subjects of special interest in Poland include hypernuclear physics and strong interactions. **1957** *Ann. Rev. Nuclear Sci.* VII. 473 Nuclear matter can bind Λ to form systems stable for a time comparable with the Λ mean life. Such systems are well known and are called *hypernuclei or hyperfragments. **1965** R. H. Dalitz *Nuclear Interactions of Hyperons* ii. 5 The lightest Λ-hypernucleus known is $_{\Lambda}H^3$. *Ibid.* 14 Λ-Hypernuclei will generally have excited states, whose spectra will be of interest for hypernuclear physics. **1885** G. H. Taylor *Pelvic Therap.* 128 *Hypernutrition of nerve centres. **1841–2** Sir W. Hamilton in *Reid's Wks.* (1863) 864 The..purely mental act of will: what for distinction's sake I would call the **hyperorganic* volition. **1892** *Jrnl. Chem. Soc.* LXII. I 557 This flow may be counterbalanced by subjecting the *hyperosmotic solution to external pressure. **1903** *Med. Rec.* 24 Jan. 121/2 The crystalloid substances rapidly accumulate in the serum, causing it to be hyper-osmotic. **1905** W. H. Howell *Text-bk. Physiol.* 885 A hypertonic or hyperosmotic solution in one whose osmotic pressure exceeds that of serum. **1964** *Oceanogr. & Marine Biol.* II. 307 Their body fluids are hyperosmotic to the surrounding water. **1941** T. C. Ruch et al. in *Amer. Jrnl. Physiol.* CXXXIII. 434 Both monkeys exhibited some type of disturbance of the chewing mechanism and a striking *hyperphagia and adiposity. **1946** *Physiol. Rev.* XXVI. 549 The word hyperphagia was chosen because it does not have the subjective, psychological connotations of the terms 'hunger', 'appetite', 'satiety' and 'bulimia', and because the word 'polyphagia'..implies 'omnivorousness'... Hyperphagia is taken to mean simply, increased eating. **1969** W. Haymaker et al. *Hypothalamus* xv. 529/2 Hyperphagia and obesity have now been produced by bilateral destruction within or near the midregion of the hypothalamus in the monkey, dog, cat, rabbit, rat and mouse. **1943** *Yale Jrnl. Biol. & Med.* XV. 839 After 6 obese animals..had been completely fasted to return their weight to normal, they were again *hyperphagic and became obese a second time on re-feeding. **1972** *Science* 9 June 1124/1 A hyperphagic response occurs when calcium in excess of its normal concentration is perfused..in the ventromedial region. **1899** *Jrnl. Anat. & Physiol.* XXXIII. 213 Prof. Pfitzner..read papers on brachyphalangia, *hyperphalangia and on the inferior tibio-fibular joint. **1969** W. T. Mustard et al. *Pediatric Surgery* (ed. 2) II. lxxxiii. 1423 Hyperphalangia refers to an excessive number of phalanges in the longitudinal axis. **1891** Flower & Lydekker *Introd. Study Mammals* viii. 234 The Ichthyopterygia have been shown..to have gradually acquired their *hyperphalangism as an adaptive character. **1959** J. J. Byrne *Hand* xv. 273 Hyperphalangism consists of an excessive number of phalanges, the thumb being most commonly involved with three phalanges. **1898** *Jrnl. Anat. & Physiol.* XXXII. p. ii (*heading*) The ossification of the terminal phalanges of mammalian fingers, in relation to *hyperphalangy. **1946** R. R. Gates *Human Genetics* I. xi. 404 The fingers show considerable variation, including hyperphalangy (four joints instead of three). **1951** C. K. Weichert *Anat. Chordates* x. 485 The paddlelike limbs of plesiosaurs and ic[h]thyosaurs have a very large number of phalanges (hyperphalangy). **1887** A. E. Shipley in *Q. Jrnl. Micros. Sc.* Jan. 350 The *hyperpharyngeal groove of Amphioxus. **1882** A. C. Fraser in *Encycl. Brit.* XIV. 761/1 The *hyperphenomenal reality of our own existence. **1886** *Hyperphoria [see *exophoria* s.v. exo-]. **1964** S. Duke-Elder *Parsons' Dis. Eye* (ed. 14) xxx. 472 It is impossible to be sure whether there is absolute hyperphoria of one eye or hypophoria of the other, the condition being relative. **1887** *Arch. Ophthalm.* XVI. 163 Only a comparatively small proportion of *hyperphoric persons experience in marked degree this inability to see small objects well. **1970** *Jrnl. Gen. Psychol.* LXXXII. 111 The average period of perceived sweep..was not significantly affected by the hyper-phoric condition. **1926** *Amer. Jrnl. Physiol.* LXXVI. 472 Hypercalcemia, *hyperphosphatemia, cessation of kidney function and acidosis. **1969** R. L. Searcy *Diagn. Biochem.* xlvii. 418/1 Hyperphosphatemia has long been regarded as an early sign of kidney failure. **1955** H. J. Deuel *Lipids* II. iv. 324 A *hyperphosphatemic reaction does not occur in dogs whose bile ducts have been ligated and transected. **1915** C. Allbutt *Dis. Arteries* I. i. 10 Lately I have preferred the etymology of *hyperpiesia for the malady, and hyperpiesis for the hæmodynamic aspect of it. **1923** J. F. H. Dally *High Blood Pressure* v. 64 Hyperpiesia is the term applied by Sir Clifford Allbutt to a clinical morbid series characterised by persistently raised blood pressure (hyperpiesis) in association with hyper-trophy of the heart and changes in the vessels. **1927** *Physiol. Rev.* VII. 474 (*heading*) Hyperpiesia or essential hypertension. **1951** R. Hargreaves *This Happy Breed* vii. 77 He must 'wangle' an extra half bag of coal from the Q.M. stores without provoking in the presiding demi-god an advanced condition of hyperpiesia. **1895** C. Allbutt in *Abstr. Trans. Hunterian Soc.* (1896) LXXVII. 47 The symptoms of arterial *hyperpiesis are often of a functional nervous character. **1961** G. Pickering *Nature Essential Hypertension* ii. 5 His [*sc.* Allbutt's] term hyperpiesis, however, never became widely used. **1968** —— *High Blood Pressure* (ed. 2) i. 3 There remains a large residue in which no specific lesion can be found—hyperpiesis, primary hypertension, essential hypertension, high blood pressure without evident cause. **1915** C. Allbutt *Dis. Arteries* I. ix. 60 The following seemed to be a case of mixed senile and *hyperpietic disease. **1920** L. M. Warfield *Arteriosclerosis* (ed. 3) viii. 187 In the hyperpietic cases the arteries undergo a transient thickening. **1890** Billings *Med. Dict.* 669/2 *Hyperpigmentation. **1899** G. T. Jackson *Dis. Skin* (ed. 3) 394 Nævus Pigmentosus... A congenital, circumscribed hyper-pigmentation of the skin. **1956** D. M. Pillsbury et al. *Dermatol.* xxxviii. 868 Endocrine disturbances are..commonly associated with hyperpigmentation such as is seen..during pregnancy, and with exophthalmic goiter. *Ibid.* 873 These areas [of the skin] are whitish and often present a well defined hyperpigmented border. **1970** Jubb & Kennedy *Path. Domestic Animals* (ed. 2) II. x. 568/2 The production of pigment in the basal cells is..a common response to injury so that acanthotic areas may also be hyperpigmented. **1909** H. Cushing in *Jrnl. Amer. Med. Assoc.* 24 July 249/1 (*heading*) The hypophysis cerebri. Clinical aspects of *hyperpituitarism and of hypopituitarism. [*Note*] From an etymological point of view the terms *hyper-*, *hypo-*, *dys-*, and *a-pituitarism* are doubtless of badly mixed parentage, but there are certain obvious objections to such a combination as *hypohypophysism*. **1939** M. A. Goldzieher *Endocrine Glands* lvii. 341 The only condition to be distinguished from true gigantism, i.e. primary eosinophile hyperpituitarism, is the secondary hyperpituitarism attendant on primary insufficiency of the gonads. **1924** G. B. Shaw *St. Joan* p. xix, St Teresa's hormones had gone astray and left her incurably *hyperpituitary or hyperadrenal or hysteroid or epileptoid or anything but asteroid. **1954** K. E. Paschkis et al. *Clin. Endocrinol.* iii. 31 Hyperpituitary giants may develop acromegalic features in later life. **1930** *Jrnl. Genetics* XXII. 306 In generations subsequent to the breakage it is possible for some individuals—*'hyper-ploids'—to inherit the chromosome fragment (attached or unattached) in addition to two otherwise normal sets of chromosomes. *Ibid.* 329 Hypoploid and hyperploid individuals. **1957** C. P. Swanson *Cytol. & Cytogenetics* vi. 177 Individuals having irregular chromosome numbers are called aneuploids... The terms hyperploid and hypoploid have also been used, but less frequently. **1930** *Jrnl. Genetics* XXII. 309 Text-fig. 11 illustrates *hyperploidy of parts of the *X*-chromosome. **1969** N. S. Cohn *Elem. Cytol.* (ed. 2) xvi. 373 An addition or loss of less than an entire set of chromosomes..is called aneuploidy, and it subsumes two classes, hypoploidy and hyperploidy. **1860** R. Fowler *Med. Vocab.* 157/2 **Hyperpnœa*, excessive respiration—e.g. panting. **1877** M. Foster *Textbk. Physiol.* 260 Respiratory movements become deeper..and the rate of the rhythm is hurried... In this respect, dyspnœa, or hyperpnœa as this first stage has been called, contrasts very strongly with the peculiar respiratory condition caused by section of the vagi. **1904** *Jrnl. Physiol.* XXXI. p. xlv, The hyperpnœa of healthy men during exercise. **1962** *Lancet* 27 Jan. 172/1 Usually this significant hyperpnœa is coupled with a red suffusion of the face. **1909** *Jrnl. Physiol.* XXXVIII. 401 Where the subject had been made *hyperpnœic by want of oxygen, apnœa followed after a few breaths of normal air. **1961** *Lancet* 29 July 249/2 The blood-pressure rises in the hyperpnœic phase [of breathing]. **1932** Dorland & Miller *Med. Dict.* (ed. 16) 606/2 *Hyperpotassemia. **1963** J. H. Bland *Clin. Metabolism Body Water* xxi. 574/1 Muscle weakness and paralysis are commonly observed in both hypopotassemia and hyperpotassemia. **1953** *Lancet* 11 July 60/1 (*heading*) *Hyperpotassæmic paralysis. **1902** A. R. Defendorf *Clin. Psychiatry* 17 Distractibility is not to be confused with '*hyperprosexia', which consists in the total absorption of the attention by a single process. **1940** Henderson & Gillespie *Text-bk. Psychiatry* (ed. 5) v. 107 Increase of attention (hyperprosexia) is less common, and is sometimes associated with a sensory hyperaesthesia. **1948** Hyperprosexia [see aprosexia]. **1922** *Physiol. Abstr.* VII. 493 The *hyper-proteinæmia does not run parallel with precipitin formation. **1969** R. L. Searcy *Diagn. Biochem.* xvii. 154/1 Extreme degrees of hyperlipemia or hyperproteinemia may falsely lower serum electrolyte measurements. **1876** tr. *Wagner's Gen. Pathol.* 614 *Hyperpyretic temperatures are such as considerably exceed even the high-febrile. **1866–80** A. Flint *Princ. Med.* (ed. 5) 190 *Hyperpyrexia..is to be combated by the cold bath or by sponging the surface of the body. **1875** H. C. Wood *Therap.* (1879) 654 Good effects of the sudden withdrawal of heat in rheumatic hyperpyrexia. **1896** Allbutt *Syst. Med.* I. 500 *Hyperpyrexial symptoms. **1897** *Ibid.* III. 25 *Hyperpyrexic symptoms commenced on the seventh, eighth or ninth day. **1829** I. Taylor *Enthus.* ii. (1867) 27 The man of imaginative or *hyper-rational piety. **1940** *Amer. Heart Jrnl.* XIX. 408 The majority of individuals with essential hypertension..manifest..marked reactions of blood pressure to various internal and external stimuli. This suggests that the mechanism for regulating blood pressure..is *hyperreactive. **1955** *Sci. Amer.* Apr. 44/3 In this hyperreactive state the body responds with rapid formation of antibody to a second invasion, either by live or by killed virus. **1940** *Amer. Heart Jrnl.* XIX. 412 The vascular *hyperreactivity of some patients with essential hypertension is extreme. **1970** *Clin. Sci.* XXXIX. 793 (*heading*) Vascular hyper-reactivity with sodium loading and with desoxycorticosterone induced

hypertension in the rat. **1971** *Guardian Weekly* 6 Nov. 19/1 He created a prototype which spawned so many schools, from Surrealism to Pop, and most recently the *Hyperrealism of the Paris Biennale. **1972** *Ibid.* 10 July 8/4 The new wave of realists, Hyper-realists as they have been dubbed. **1973** *Art & Artists* Mar. 51 The hyperreal still remained obscured by a dream of contact, which was perhaps the message of the artists involved. **1973** *AA Internat.* Mar. 19/2 Brent Wong's work passes beyond the hyper-realism of the New Zealand hard edge school into a kind of surrealism. **1980** *San Francisco Bay Guardian* 16–23 Oct. 25/1 'Winterplay': the world premiere of Adele Edling Shank's hyperreal (defined by the theater as a style derived from the style of painting called photorealism) and humorous portrait of the modern American family on Christmas Day. **1985** *N.Y. Times* 17 Apr. C22/4 Whether hyperrealism can also be art may be an unanswerable question. **1879** *St. George's Hosp. Rep.* IX. 246 Acute pain in right chest..*Hyper-resonance on percussion. *Ibid.*, Upper two-thirds of right side of chest still *hyper-resonant. **1611** J. Hoskins in *Coryat's Crudities* sig. e6 Encomiological Antispasticks..rythmicall and *hyper-rythmicall. **1774** Mitford *Ess. Harmony Lang.* 203 Mr. Addison's periods mostly end with the *hyperrhythmical syllable. **1953** *Publ. Inst. Marine Sci.* III. 175 *Hyper-saline lagoons..occur in several parts of the world. **1964** *Oceanogr. & Marine Biol.* II. 283 Natural water containing dissolved solids in concentrations equivalent to salinities of 40 to 80‰ is referred to [in this review] as hypersaline water. **1971** D. S. McLusky *Ecol. of Estuaries* vi. 97 Hypersaline seas should not be confused with inland brines or salterns, such as the Utah Salt Lakes of America. **1957** *Publ. Inst. Marine Sci.* IV. 198 Fish have been killed by..*hypersalinity. **1970** B. H. McConnaughey *Introd. Marine Biol.* i. 24 Unusually high salinities (hypersalinity) are rare in marine environments. **1811** Hooper *Med. Lex.*, **Hypersarcoma*..A fleshy excrescence. **1847** Craig, *Hyper-sarcoma*, exuberant growth of granulations on a sore. **1706** Phillips (ed. Kersey), **Hypersarcosis*, a preternatural Excrescence, or growing out of Flesh in any part of the Body. **1864** W. T. Fox *Skin Dis.* 71 *Hypersecretion. **1876** Gross *Dis. Bladder* 44 Hypersecretion of mucus and pus. **1915** *Amer. Jrnl. Obstetr. & Dis. Women* LXXII. 279 In many cases where dementia precox develops, a previous attack of mental disturbance has existed and the patient is to a certain extent forced by the family into the marital state on account of *hypersexuality. **1964** C. W. Lloyd *Human Reprod.* xxv. 456 Temporal lobe lesions generally cause humans and monkeys to have decreased sexual responsiveness, but occasionally hypersexuality may develop. **1876** Dunglison *Dict. Med. Sci.* (rev. ed) 523/1 *Hypersomnia. **1910** *Lancet* 8 Oct. 1093/1 Dr. Albert Salmon..differentiates hypersomnia, which is an increase in normal sleep, from somnolence, apathy, and torpor,..and from the drowsiness which occurs in old people. **1939** N. Kleitman *Sleep & Wakefulness* xxv. 361 Cerebral neoplasms have been known to produce interference with the sleep—wakefulness rhythm mainly in the direction of hypersomnia. **1966** *McGraw-Hill Encycl. Sci. & Technol.* XII. 376/1 The best known cause of hypersomnia is epidemic or lethargic encephalitis. **1929** *Jrnl. Nerv. & Mental Dis.* LXIX. 5 It is unquestionably in infundibular tumors that one encounters..the *hypersomnic form of brain tumors. **1955** A. B. Baker *Clin. Neurol.* II. xxi. 1203 The hypersomnic patient closely resembles a normally sleeping individual. **1867** Cayley in *Math. Pap.* (1893) VI. 191 The quasi-geometrical representation of conditions by means of loci in *hyper-space. **1892** W. W. R. Ball *Math. Recreations & Problems* x. 191 The term *hyper-space was used originally of space of more than three dimensions but now it is often employed to denote any non-Euclidean space. *Ibid.* 201 Riemann has shown that there are three kinds of hyper-space of three dimensions. **1893** *Academy* 21 Oct. 345/3 Sometimes called pan-geometry, sometimes the geometry of hyper-space, and sometimes non-Euclidian geometry. **1947** I. Asimov in *Astounding Science Fiction* Mar. 117/2 Fooling around with hyper-space isn't fun... We run the risk continually of blowing a hole in normal space-time fabric. **1956** E. H. Hutten *Lang. Mod. Physics* v. 171 The propagation of the wave must be described as taking place, in most instances, in a multi-dimensional hyper-space, and not in ordinary space. **1961** *Times Lit. Suppl.* 1 Sept. 577/3 Time Travel, like hyperspace, is one of the classical Science-Fiction presumptions. **1973** *Publishers Weekly* 17 Sept. 58/3 The crew of the first interstellar voyage through hyperspace comes back as monsters. **1909** Webster, *Hyperspatial. **1919** R. T. Browne *Mystery of Space* viii. 263 This is undoubtedly the weakest point in the structure of the hyperspatial geometries. **1943** C. L. Hull *Princ. Behavior* xi. 181 It seems unlikely that the Fisher-design type of experiment will yield dependable indications of the complex hyperspatial curvatures which will almost certainly be found. **1811** W. Taylor in *Monthly Rev.* LXV. 9 Men..in the *hyperspermatic state are very subject to mental hallucination. **1946** *Blood* I. 28 Five cases of thrombocytopenia associated with well defined splenomegaly of nonleukemic and non-neoplastic origin ('symptomatic *hypersplenic thrombopenia'). **1949** Britton & Neumark tr. *Leitner's Bone Marrow Biopsy* viii. 151 Hypersplenic anæmias. **1963** Basu & Aikat *Trop. Splenomegaly* iii. 20 The clinical recognition of the hypersplenic state. **1914** *Arch. Internal Med.* XIV. 145 There may exist for the spleen conditions associated with a hyperactivity of some of its functions, let us say the function of influencing hemolysis. To such a condition the term "hypersplenism" may be applied. **1955** W. Dameshek in *Bull. N.Y. Acad. Med.* XXXI. 114 Who first used the term 'hypersplenism' is not accurately known, but it began to appear in Chauffard's writings from 1907 on and subsequently, and in those of Morawitz and Eppinger at a late date. **1963** Basu & Aikat *Trop. Splenomegaly* iii. 20 Hypersplenism..is a clinical term indicating non-specific overactive function of the spleen in a variety of clinical disorders. **1930** *Engineering* 3 Oct. 421/3 The method is used to solve problems arising in the design of *hyperstatic systems, such as arches and portal openings, with sufficient precision. **1959** J. A. L. Matheson et al. *Hyperstatic Struct.* I. vi. 320 The behaviour of multi-storey buildings..in terms of the composite action of the floors and walls with the frame..is essentially a very complicated hyperstatic problem. **1966** J. S. C. Browne *Basic Theory of Struct.* v. 100 Extra or redundant bars will produce a truss that is hyperstatic. **1952** E. F. Linssen *Stereo-Photography* x. 147 If we take a *hyperstereograph..of a mountain formation..which starts a kilometre away from us, we must beware not to include any trees or houses which are in our immediate neighbourhood. **1971** C. R. Arnold *Appl. Photogr.* xiii. 373 This tendency to produce a model effect is a well-known feature of hyperstereographs. **1939** Henney & Dudley *Handbk. Photogr.* xx. 588 The *hyper-stereoscopic effect..can add greatly to a stereograph's effectiveness by its strong emphasis of the depth quality. **1956** *Focal Encycl. Photogr.* 570/2 Consecutive photographs from an aerial survey series form hyperstereoscopic pairs. **1911** *Cassell's Cycl. Photogr.* 298/2 *Hyper-stereoscopy. **1926** A. W. Judge *Stereoscopic Photogr.* iii. 32 Hyper-stereoscopy is of much assistance in obtaining a true impression of distant hill or mountain scenery. **1958** *Newnes' Compl. Amat. Photogr.* xxvi. 231 If..we wish to take pictures of scenes such as distant mountains then, providing there are no objects in the foreground nearer than about 300 ft., we can use the long base separation method known as hyperstereoscopy. **1906** *Hyper-susceptibility [see hypersensitive *a.* 2]. **1924** *Jrnl. Immunol.* IX. 86 The production of skin hypersusceptibility without infection. **1914** *Q. Jrnl. Med.* VII. 273 The so-called anaphylactic or *hypersusceptible state. **1971** *Brit. Med. Bull.* XXVII. 57/1 Hypersusceptible individuals may still develop the disease despite the reduction of dust concentrations to a very low level. **1924** D. M. Greig in *Edin. Med. Jrnl.* XXXI. 560 The outstanding peculiarity of the cranial deformity for which I propose the name ocular hypertelorism, or briefly, *hypertelorism, is the great breadth between the eyes. **1957** *Arch. Ophthalm.* LVII. 607/2 This is an instance of hypertelorism associated with mental retardation. **1972** *Daily Tel.* (Colour Suppl.) 22 Sept. 21/4 Jeanine..was born 28 years ago with the fish eyes, one on each side of the face, and the monstrously deformed nose characteristic of hypertelorism (Grieg's Disease). **1886** *Syd. Soc. Lex.*, **Hyper-thermal*, of an insupportable heat. **1880** *Nature* 4 Mar. 424 Instances of *hypertrichosis in woman. **1875** Cayley in *Phil. Trans.* CLXV. 675 The language of *hypertridimensional geometry. **1897** *Hypertropia [see *exotropia* s.v. exo-]. **1950** F. H. Adler *Physiol. Eye* x. 406 In a case of right hypertropia..if the right superior oblique is a fault, the head will be strongly tilted toward the left shoulder. **1886** W. H. Flower in *Pop. Sci. Monthly* Jan. 318 [Oceanic negroes] are represented, in what may be called a *hypertypical form, by the extremely dolichocephalic Kai Colos. **1883** Symonds *Shaks. Predecess.* xv. 614 The poet moves in a *hyperuranian region. **1813** *Q. Rev.* IX. 470 Where there is *hyperuresis, he forbids fruit. **1894** Gould *Dict. Med.* 592/1 *Hyperuricemia. **1924** *Arch. Internal Med.* XXXIV. 504 Blood uric acid values of 3·5 mg. per hundred cubic centimeters..were considered as presenting a hyperuricemia. **1970** W. S. Hoffman *Biochem. Clin. Med.* (ed. 4) xv. 756 Hyperuricemia may be due either to overproduction of uric acid or to undersecretion. **1962** *Lancet* 15 Dec. 1273/1 My own experience with three *hyperuricæmic patients, two with a history of gout and one without,..lends support to Dr. Eidlitz's letter. **1876** *Trans. Clin. Soc.* IX. 49 The dura mater was not especially *hyper-vascular. *Ibid.* 50 There was..an outgrowth of cerebral substance..it presented marked *hyper-vascularity. **1955** A. E. Eggers et al. *Compar. Anal. Performance Long-Range Hypervelocity Vehicles* 24 Mar. (N.A.C.A. Rep. RM A54L10) 2 On the basis of equal ratios of mass at take-off to mass at the end of powered flight, the *hypervelocity vehicle compares favourably with the supersonic airplane. **1960** *Nature* 29 Oct. 353/2 If the fused earth were hurled in the manner that ejectamenta from hypervelocity impact[s] in stone are hurled, then the maximum entry velocity [etc.]. **1962** J. L. Potter et al. in F. R. Riddell *Hypersonic Flow Res.* 599 A small, low density, hypervelocity, continuous wind tunnel. **1964** *Bull. Amer. Physical Soc.* IX. 308/2 (*heading*) Attainability of fusion temperatures under high densities by impact shock waves of microscopic solid particles accelerated to hypervelocities. **1972** *Science* 2 June 979/2 Hypervelocity impact craters on the moon. **1928** *Biochem. Jrnl.* XXII. 1461 In the case of the fat-soluble vitamins..several instances of supposed *hypervitaminosis have been recorded. **1963** *Lancet* 5 Jan. 34/2 As in hypervitaminosis D, the increased intestinal absorption of calcium is probably responsible for the high urinary calcium. **1971** J. Z. Young *Introd. Study Man* xl. 582 A European would produce up to 800 000 I.U. [of vitamin D] per day in the tropics and might therefore suffer from hypervitaminosis, for the body has no way of detoxicating any excess. **1925** Brown & Rowntree in *Arch. Internal Med.* XXXV. 132 In view of..confusion,..terms as follows are suggested: (1) normovolemia for normal blood volume, (2) *hypervolemia for increased blood volume, and (3) hypovolemia for decreased blood volumes. These terms are self-explanatory and apply only to volume states. **1964** I. N. Kugelmass *Biochem. Clinics* IV. 270 Hypervolemia in acute and subacute glomerulonephritis with pulmonary edema increases with the duration of anuria. **1948** *Amer. Jrnl. Physiol.* CLV. 338 Table 1*A* shows the bilateral rises in auricular pressure of 4 *hypervolemic cats.

hyperacusis (-ə'k(j)uːsɪs). *Med.* Also -acousis, -acusia, -akusis. [mod.L., f. hyper- 5 + Gr. ἄκουσις hearing (ἀκούειν to hear), after F. *hypercousie* (J. M. G. Itard *Traité des Maladies de l'Oreille et de l'Audition* (1821) II. 4).] Abnormally acute hearing, often resulting in pain on hearing only moderately loud sounds.

1825 J. M. Good *Study of Med.* (ed. 2) IV. 245 Hearing painfully acute and intolerant of the lowest sounds... It is the hypercousis, or, as it should rather be, the hyperacusis of M. Itard. **1894** T. M. Hovell *Treat. Dis. Ear* xlv. 656 Hyperacusia, of a pathological kind, may be associated with increased power of other special senses. **1927** Lake & Peters *Handbk. Dis. Ear* (ed. 5) xiv. 267 Hyperacusis is usually found (as otalgia) in females. **1971** D. E. Rose *Audiol. Assessment* iii. 44 Other symptoms of disorders of the ear are ..increased aural sensitivity to sound (recruitment and hyperacusis).

‖**hyperæmia** (haɪpə'riːmɪə). *Path.* Also -hæmia, -emia. [mod.L., f. hyper- 5 + Gr. -αιμία (cf. *anæmia*, etc.), f. αἷμα blood. Cf. Gr. ὑπεραιμό-ειν to have excess of blood.] An excessive accumulation of blood in a particular part, arising either from increased flow through the arteries (*active* or *arterial h.*) or from obstruction in a vein (*passive* or *venous h.*); congestion.

1836–9 Todd *Cycl. Anat.* II. 826/2 Hyperæmia of one organ may give rise to anæmia of another. **1876** Duhring *Dis. Skin* 64 Cutaneous hyperæmia consists in an excessive amount of blood in the capillaries of the skin. **1878** Foster *Phys.* iii. v. §3. 487 Due to a one-sided hyperhæmia of the spinal cord.

Hence **hyperæmic, -emic** (haɪpə'riːmɪk) *a.*, of, pertaining to, or affected with hyperæmia.

1839–47 Todd *Cycl. Anat.* III. 62/2 The bones..were in an hyperæmic condition. **1897** Allbutt *Syst. Med.* III. 424 The mucous coat [of the stomach] is most frequently hyperæmic.

hyperæolian, *a. Anc. Mus.*: see hyper- 2.

‖**hyperæsthesia** (-ɛs-, -iːs'θiːsɪə). [mod.L., f. hyper- 5 + Gr. -αισθησία, αἴσθησις perception, feeling.] *Path.* Excessive and morbid sensitiveness of the nerves or nerve-centres.

1849–52 Todd *Cycl. Anat.* IV. 1184/2 In a case of Hyperæsthesia..the patient could perceive the distinctness of the two points on the foot. **1880** M. Mackenzie *Dis. Throat & Nose* I. 415 Hysterical persons, suffering from hyperaesthesia or paraesthesia of the larynx, often erroneously fancy that something is sticking in the part.

b. *transf.* Excessive sensibility or sensitiveness (in general).

1865 Lecky *Ration.* II. 103 *note*, In sleep, hyperæsthesia of the memory is very common. **1866** Alger *Solit. Nat. & Man* iv. 264 He suffered dreadfully from what may be called social hyperæsthesia, a morbid over-feeling of the relations between himself and others.

hyperæs'thesic, bad form for next.

1888 *Amer. Jrnl. Psychol.* Feb. 339 Hyperaesthesic states.

hyperæsthetic (-ɛs-, -iːs'θɛtɪk), *a.* Also -esthetic. [f. hyper- 4, 5 + Gr. αἰσθητικ-ός perceptive: see æsthetic.]

1. Affected with hyperæsthesia; excessively or morbidly sensitive.

1855 Mayne *Expos. Lex.*, Hyperesthetic. **1872** F. G. Thomas *Dis. Women* 116 The hyperæsthetic condition of the nerves. **1897** Allbutt *Syst. Med.* III. 872 In peritonitis the skin of the abdomen is hyperæsthetic.

2. (*hyper-æsthetic*). Excessively æsthetic.

1879 F. Harrison *Choice Bks.* (1886) 85 When one meets bevies of hyperæsthetic young maidens. **1896** *Advance* (Chicago) 25 June 918/2 Some hyper-esthetic people think that no good can come from a sermon whose divisions are marked by 'first', 'secondly', and 'thirdly'.

hyperapophysis (-ə'pɒfɪsɪs). *Anat.* [f. hyper- 6 + apophysis.] 'A process of bone extending backward from the neural spine of one vertebra to that of another, or developed from the post-zygapophysis' (*Syd. Soc. Lex.* 1886).

1872 Mivart *Elem. Anat.* ii. 45 It is possible..for the neural spine to send back a pair of processes (hyperapophyses), as in Galago.

Hence **hyperapo'physial** *a.*, of or pertaining to a hyperapophysis.

†**hyperaspist** (-'æspɪst). *Obs.* Also in Gr. form ‖**hypera'spistes**. [ad. Gr. ὑπερασπιστής protector, defender, f. ὑπερασπίζειν to hold a shield over, f. ἀσπίς shield.] A defender, champion.

1638 Chillingw. *Relig. Prot.* i. i. §5. 33, I appeal to any indifferent reader, whether C. M. be not by his Hyperaspist forsaken in the plain field. **1647** Jer. Taylor *Lib. Proph.* iii. 63 If it should meet with peevish opposites on one side, and confident Hyperaspists on the other. **1747** Warburton *Shaks., Macb.* iv. iv. 4 The allusion is to the Hyperaspists of the ancients, who bestrode their fellows faln in battle, and covered them with their shields.

hyperbaric (haɪpə'bærɪk), *a. Med.* [f. hyper- 5 + Gr. βαρύς heavy + -ic.] **a.** Of a solution for spinal anæsthesia: having a greater density than the cerebro-spinal fluid.

1930 W. H. Jones in *Brit. Jrnl. Anæsthesia* VII. 110, I shall use the terms hyper-, iso- and hypo-baric, to describe solutions which have specific gravities greater than, equal to, or less than that of the cerebro-spinal fluid. **1946** J. L. Southworth et al. *Pitkin's Conduction Anesthesia* xvii. 761/2 The anesthetist should know in advance whether the anesthetic solution is hypobaric, hyperbaric, or isobaric, so that the posture of the patient can be regulated accordingly. **1962** J. Adriani *Chem. & Phys. Anaesthesia* (ed. 2) xxxi. 652/2 Hyperbaric solutions gravitate caudad if the body is inclined in the head-up, supine position after injection, while hypobaric solutions migrate cephalad.

b. At a pressure greater than normal (often, greater than the partial pressure of the gas in the atmosphere); employing or pertaining to such gas.

1963 *Lancet* 16 Nov. 1022/1 It is our firm impression that hyperbaric oxygen is the most effective method of resuscitation yet devised for the severely asphyxiated newborn infant. **1965** *Economist* 20 Feb. 780/2 Hyperbaric oxygen chambers have been used increasingly in the treatment of diseases involving oxygen deficiency. **1966** *Lancet* 24 Dec. 1394/2 A hyperbaric chamber was made from a large domestic pressure cooker. **1968** *Sci. Jrnl.* Nov. 64/2 Some kidneys survived when hyperbaric nitrogen was employed. **1972** *Lancet* 22 Sept. 639/1 Patients with advanced growths are being given hyperbaric oxygen (3–4 atmospheres absolute) for a period immediately before and during irradiating. **1973** C. Bonington *Next Horizon* xiv.

199 The following six weeks passed .. in hospital, recovering from frost-bite. I spent much of the time as a guinea-pig for a new method of treatment called hyperbaric oxygen, which entailed hours spent lying in a cylinder filled with two atmospheres of oxygen. You had to wear a special anti-static tunic .. apparently, in oxygen so pure and concentrated, even the slightest static electricity could have caused a fire.

hyperbatic (haɪpəˈbætɪk), *a. Gram.* and *Rhet.* [ad. Gr. ὑπερβατικός, f. ὑπέρβατον HYPERBATON.] Pertaining to or of the nature of hyperbaton; transposed, inverted.

1847 in CRAIG.

Hence **hyperˈbatically** *adv.*, in the way of hyperbaton, by transposition or inversion.

‖**hyperbaton** (haɪˈpɜːbətɒn). *Gram.* and *Rhet.* Also 6 **hiper-**, **-tone**. [a. L. *hyperbaton*, a. Gr. ὑπέρβατον, literally 'overstepping', f. ὑπερβαίνειν (ὑπέρ over + βαίνειν to step, walk).]

A figure of speech in which the customary or logical order of words or phrases is inverted, esp. for the sake of emphasis. Also, an example of this figure.

(The substantive is first recorded in Latin authors (Quintilian and Pliny); but Plato and Aristotle use the verbal adj. ὑπερβατός with reference to transpositions in language.)

1579 E. K. *Gloss. Spenser's Sheph. Cal.* May, A patheticall parenthesis, to encrease a carefull Hyperbaton. **1599** THYNNE *Animadv.* (1875) 56 The sence .. ys 'the fende makethe this' for whiche Chaucer vsethe these wordes by Transpositione, (accordinge to the rethoricall figure Hiperbatone), 'This makethe the fende'. **1641** MILTON *Animadv.* v. (1851) 223 If your meaning be with a violent Hyperbaton to transpose the Text. **1727** H. HERBERT tr. *Fleury's Eccl. Hist.* I. 62 There are so many .. hyperbatons and transpositions, which render his stile difficult. **1776** G. CAMPBELL *Philos. Rhet.* (1801) II. 348 We have here a considerable hyperbaton .. there being no less than thirteen words interposed between the noun and the preposition. **1866** BAIN *Eng. Composit.* 38 The Hyperbaton .. is purposed inversion .. before announcing something of great emphasis and import, thus giving to a meditated expression the effect of an impromptu.

hyperbola (haɪˈpɜːbələ). *Geom.* [a. mod.L. *hyperbola*, ad. Gr. ὑπερβολή the name of the curve, lit. excess (cf. HYPERBOLE), f. ὑπερβάλλειν to exceed (ὑπέρ over + βάλλειν to throw). In F. *hyperbole*.

The hyperbola was so named either because the inclination of its plane to the base of the cone exceeds that of the side of the cone (see ELLIPSE), or because the side of the rectangle on the abscissa equal to the square of the ordinate is longer than the latus rectum.]

One of the conic sections; a plane curve consisting of two separate, equal and similar, infinite branches, formed by the intersection of a plane with both branches of a double cone (i.e. two similar cones on opposite sides of the same vertex). It may also be defined as a curve in which the focal distance of any point bears to its distance from the directrix a constant ratio greater than unity. It has two foci, one for each branch, and two asymptotes, which intersect in the centre of the curve, midway between the vertices of its two branches. (Often applied to one branch of the curve.)

1668 *Phil. Trans.* III. 643 The Area of one Hyperbola being computed, the Area of all others may be thence argued. **1692** BENTLEY *Boyle Lect.* viii. 267 They would not have moved in Hyperbola's, or in Ellipses very eccentric. **1706** W. JONES *Syn. Palmar. Matheseos* 256 The Sections of the opposite Cones will be equal Hyperbolas. **1728** PEMBERTON *Newton's Philos.* 232 With a velocity still greater the body will move in an hyperbola. **1828** HUTTON *Course Math.* II. 102 The section is an hyperbola, when the cutting plane makes a greater angle with the base than the side of the cone makes. **1885** GOODALE *Phys. Bot.* (1892) 381 *note*, If the outline of the growing plant is a hyperbola, the periclinals will be confocal hyperbolas, with the same axis but different parameter.

b. Extended (after Newton) to algebraic curves of higher degrees denoted by equations analogous to that of the common hyperbola.

1727-41 CHAMBERS *Cycl.* s.v., Infinite Hyperbola's, or Hyperbola's of the higher kinds, are those defined by the equation $ay^{m+n} = bx^m(a + x)^n$. *Ibid.*, As the hyperbola of the first kind or order has two asymptotes, that of the second kind or order has three, that of the third, four, etc. **1753** —— *Cycl. Supp.* s.v., Hyperbolas of all degrees may be expressed by the equation $x^m y^n = a^{m+n}$. **1852** [see HYPERBOLIC 2].

hyperbole (haɪˈpɜːbəliː). Also 6 **yperbole**, **hiperbole**. [a. Gr. ὑπερβολή excess (cf. HYPERBOLA), exaggeration; the latter sense is first found in Isocrates and Aristotle. Cf. F. *hyperbole* (earlier *yperbole*).]

1. *Rhet.* A figure of speech consisting in exaggerated or extravagant statement, used to express strong feeling or produce a strong impression, and not intended to be understood literally. **b.** With *a* and *pl.*, an instance of this figure.

1529 MORE *Dyaloge* IV. 110 b/1 By a maner of speking which is among lerned men called yperbole, for the more vehement expressyng of a mater. **1579** FULKE *Heskins' Parl.* 340 He must note an hyberbole or ouerreaching speach in this sentence. **1588** SHAKS. *L.L.L.* v. ii. 407 Three-pil'd Hyperboles, spruce affectation, Figures pedanticall. **1657** J. SMITH *Myst. Rhet.* 58 Scriptural Examples of Hyperbole .. Deut. 9. 4, Cities fenced up to heaven .. Joh. 21. 25, The whole world could not contain the books. **1726** GAY *Fables* I. xviii. 11 Hyperboles, tho' ne'er so great, Will still come short of self-conceit. **1824** L. MURRAY *Eng. Gram.* (ed. 5) I. 510 Hyperboles are of two kinds; either such as are employed in description, or such as are suggested by the warmth of passion. **1838** PRESCOTT *Ferd. & Is.* (1846) I. xi. 439 An Arabic interpreter expatiated, in florid hyperbole, on the magnanimity and princely qualities of the Spanish king.

b. *gen.* Excess, extravagance. *rare.*

1652 L. S. *People's Liberty* xviii. 45 [He] spared him out of an Hyperbole of clemency. **1678** NORRIS *Coll. Misc.* (1699) 6 Under the great Hyperbole of Pain He mourns. **1874** H. R. REYNOLDS *John Bapt.* iii. §2. 175 They agreed with the Pharisees in their extraordinary regard for the Sabbath, even pressing their rigour to an hyperbole.

†**2.** *Geom.* = HYPERBOLA. *Obs.*

(Perh. with *e* mute, as in F. *hyperbole*.)

1579 DIGGES *Stratiot.* 188 Whether .. the sayde Curue Arke, be not an Hyperbole. **1716** DOUGLASS in *Phil. Trans.* XXIX. 535 Within it hath an Angle or sharp Ridge which runs all along the Middle, at the Top of the Hyperbole [of its beak].

Hence **hyˈperbole** *v. intr.* (*nonce-wd.*), to use hyperbole, to exaggerate.

1698 LOCKE *Let. to E. Masham* 29 Apr. in Fox Bourne *Life* (1876) II. xv. 461 Your poor solitary verger who suffers here under the deep winter of frost and snow: I do not hyperbole in the case.

hyperbolic (haɪpəˈbɒlɪk), *a.* [ad. Gr. ὑπερβολικός extravagant, f. ὑπερβολή HYPERBOLE; in sense 2 used as the adj. of HYPERBOLA. So F. *hyperbolique* in both senses.]

1. *Rhet.* = HYPERBOLICAL 1.

1646 CHAS. I. *Let. to Henderson* (1649) 56 There are alwaies some flattering Fooles that can commend nothing but with hyperbolick expressions. **1748** RICHARDSON *Clarissa* (1811) II. xxx. 191 Eternal gratitude, is his word, among others still more hyperbolic. **1835** I. TAYLOR *Spir. Despot.* ii. 55 The claims of God's ministers will be asserted in a hyperbolic yet insidious style.

2. *Geom.* Of, belonging to, or of the form or nature of a hyperbola.

hyperbolic branch (of a curve): an infinite branch which, like the hyperbola, continually approaches an asymptote (opp. to *parabolic*). ***h. conoid***: a conoid of hyperbolic section, a hyperboloid of revolution. † ***h. cylindroid***: name given by Wren to the hyperboloid of revolution of one sheet. ***h. paraboloid***: see PARABOLOID.

1676 HALLEY in Rigaud *Corr. Sci. Men* (1841) I. 240 Foci and diameter describe that hyperbolic line, whose vertex is nearest to A. **1797** *Encycl. Brit.* VII. 687/2 When the vessel is a portion of a cone or hyperbolic conoid, the content by this method is found less than the truth. **1827** G. HIGGINS *Celtic Druids* 104 Their doctrine that comets were planets, which moved in hyperbolic curves. **1852** SALMON *Higher Plane Curves* v. (1879) 172 Cubics having three hyperbolic branches are called by Newton redundant hyperbolas.

b. Applied to functions, operations, etc., having some relation to the hyperbola.

hyperbolic curvature: the curvature of a surface whose indicatrix is a hyperbola; the same as ANTICLASTIC curvature. ***hyberbolic function***: a function having a relation to a rectangular hyperbola similar to that of the ordinary trigonometrical functions to a circle; as the ***hyperbolic sine***, ***cosine***, ***tangent***, etc. (abbrev. *sinh*, *cosh*, *tanh*, etc.). ***hyperbolic geometry***: the geometry of hyperbolic space. ***hyperbolic involution***: an involution of points (or lines) whose double points (or lines) are real (opp. to *elliptic involution*, where they are imaginary). ***hyperbolic logarithm***: a logarithm to the base *e* (2·71828 . .), a natural or Napierian logarithm; so called because proportional to a segment of the area between a hyperbola and its asymptote. ***hyperbolic navigation***: navigation that utilizes the difference in the times of arrival or the phases of signals transmitted in synchronism by two radio stations to determine a hyperbola on which the receiver must lie, two intersecting hyperbolas from two pairs of stations determining its position; so ***hyperbolic system***, etc. ***hyperbolic space***: (*a*) the space between a hyperbola and its asymptote or an ordinate; (*b*) name given by Klein to a space, of any number of dimensions, whose curvature is uniform and negative (see quot. 1872-3). ***hyperbolic spiral***: a spiral in which the radius vector varies inversely as the angle turned through by it; so called from the analogy of its polar equation ($r\theta$ = constant) to the Cartesian equation of the hyperbola (xy = constant). ***hyperbolic substitution***: term for a class of substitutions in the theory of homographic transformation.

1704 J. HARRIS *Lex. Techn.*, *Hyperbolick-Space*, is the Area or Space contained between the Curve of an Hyperbola, and the whole Ordinate. **1743** EMERSON *Fluxions* 97 The Fluxion of any Quantity divided by that Quantity is the Fluxion of the Hyperbolic Logarithm of that Quantity. *Ibid.*, The hyperbolic Space between the Assymptotes. **1816** tr. *Lacroix's Diff. & Int. Calculus* 129 An equation which belongs to the hyperbolic spiral. **1872-3** CLIFFORD *Math. Papers* (1882) 189 That geometry of three-dimensional space which assumes the Euclidian postulates has been called by Dr. Klein the *parabolic* geometry of space, to distinguish it from two other varieties which assume uniform positive and negative curvature respectively, and which he calls the *elliptic* and *hyperbolic* geometry of space. *Ibid.* 236 *note*, According to Dr. Klein's nomenclature, a space, every point of which can be uniquely represented by a set of values of *n* variables, is called elliptic, parabolic, or hyperbolic, when its curvature is uniform and positive, zero, or negative. **1880** CHRYSTAL *Non-Euclidean Geom.* 19 In hyperbolic space a straight line has two distinct real points at infinity. **1893** FORSYTH *The. Functions* 517 If the multiplier be a real positive quantity, the substitution is called hyperbolic. **1894** CHARLOTTE SCOTT *Mod. Anal. Geom.* 162 A hyperbolic involution is non-overlapping. **1945** *Electronics* Nov. 94/1 Loran .. is one of a family of systems known as 'hyperbolic navigation systems', which measure the relative time of arrival of two or more radio signals sent synchronously from known points. **1959** [see DECCA]. **1972** *Jrnl. Inst. Navigation* XXV. 308 The navigator has three main aids—d.f. using the world-wide chain of shore-based transmitter beacons, the short-range hyperbolic systems, mainly Decca, and his own radar.

hyperbolical (haɪpəˈbɒlɪkəl), *a.* Also 5 **iper-**, 6 **hiper-**. [f. as prec. + -AL[1].]

1. *Rhet.* Of the nature of, involving, or using hyperbole; exaggerated, extravagant (in language or expression).

1432-50 tr. *Higden* (Rolls) I. 77 Alexander seythe that not to be trawthe, but after a locucion iperbolicalle. **1581** J. BELL *Haddon's Answ. Osor.* 43 Your infamous, shame-lesse, and reprochfull Hiperbolicall speach. **1581** MARBECK *Bk. of Notes* 196 An Hiperboricall loquution, of which Chrisostome is full. *a* **1661** FULLER *Worthies* (1840) II. 438 He is too hyperbolical in praising his own country. **1774** WARTON *Hist. Eng. Poetry* iii. (1840) I. 113 A taste for hyperbolical description. **1820** HAZLITT *Lect. Dram. Lit.* 347 It embodies .. all the pomp of action in all the vehemence of hyperbolical declamation. **1872** GEO. ELIOT *Middlem.* xxii, I have a hyperbolical tongue: it catches fire as it goes.

†**b.** *gen.* Extravagant in character or behaviour; excessive, enormous. *Obs.*

1589 GREENE *Menaphon* (Arb.) 61 Being all plunged welnigh in a speachlesse astonishment .. Pleusidippus, not vsed to such hyperbolical spectators, broke off the silence by calling for his victualls. **1633** T. STAFFORD *Pac. Hib.* I. v. (1810) 62 These hyperbolical demands, were .. absolutely rejected. **1663** COWLEY *Verses & Ess.*, *Greatness* (1669) 121 This Hyperbolical Fop whom we stand amazed at. **1859** GEO. ELIOT *A. Bede* ix, The gardener .. was over head and ears in love with her, and had lately made unmistakeable avowals in luscious strawberries and hyperbolical peas.

2. *Geom.* = HYPERBOLIC 2.

1571 DIGGES *Pantom.* IV. Pref. Tj a, Conoydall, Parabollical, Hyperbollical and Ellepseycal circumscribed and inscribed bodies. **1669** WREN in *Phil. Trans.* IV. 961 The Generation of an Hyperbolical Cylindroid demonstrated and the Application thereof for Grinding Hyperbolical Glasses. **1716** DOUGLASS in *Phil. Trans.* XXIX. 535 The Figure of each Beak is truly Hyperbolical. **1822** IMISON *Sc. & Art* II. 359 Either an elliptical conoid or a hyperbolical conoid. **1871** tr. *Schellen's Spectr. Anal.* §69. 413 Thus its path may be elliptical, hyperbolical, or parabolical.

hyperˈbolically, *adv.* [f. prec. + -LY[2].]

1. In a hyperbolical manner; with hyperbole or exaggeration.

1555 EDEN *Decades* Pref. (Arb.) 51 Although .. it bee hyperboricallye wrytten that in the dayes of Salomon golde and syluer were in Hierusalem .. as plentiful as stones. **1579** FULKE *Heskins' Parl.* 244 Chrysostom doth hyperbolically amplifie the excellencie of the Ministers office. **1610** HEALEY *St. Aug. Citie of God* XVI. xxi. (1620) 562 Such a multitude as holy Writ thought to signifie hyperbolically by the sands of the earth. **1774** PENNANT *Tour Scotl. in 1772*, 220 The northern bards speak hyperbolically of the effect of the blast blown by the mouth of the heroes. **1842** DE QUINCEY *Cicero* Wks. VI. 224 Unless his income were hyperbolically vast.

2. 'In form of an hyperbola' (J.).

†**hyperˈbolicly**, *adv. Obs.* [f. HYPERBOLIC + -LY[2].] = prec. 1.

1596 DALRYMPLE tr. *Leslie's Hist. Scot.* I. 63 To speik hyperboliklie or abone my boundes. **1669** GALE *Crt. Gentiles* I. III. x. 109 What Cicero hyperbolicly affirmes of Thucydides, is no where to be found but in the Sacred Scriptures.

†**hyperboliform**, *a. Obs.* [f. HYPERBOLA + -FORM: cf. F. *hyperboliforme*.] Of the form of, or resembling, a hyperbola.

1727-41 CHAMBERS *Cycl.*, *Hyperboli-form Figures*, are such curves as approach, in their properties, to the nature of the hyperbola; called also hyperboloids. (In recent Dicts.)

hyperbolism (haɪˈpɜːbəlɪz(ə)m).

1. *Rhet.* [f. HYPERBOLE + -ISM; cf. F. *hyperbolisme*.] Use of or addiction to hyperbole; exaggerated style, or an instance of this.

1653 H. MORE *Antid. Ath.* Ep. Ded. (1712) 2 Nor is there anything here of Hyperbolism or high-flown Language. *a* **1806** HORSLEY *Serm.* I. v. (1811) 69 With all the allowances that can be made for the hyperbolisms of the oriental style. **1879** D. J. HILL *Bryant* 83 The mock-sentimental hyperbolism that has made Mark Twain's books so popular.

2. *Geom.* [ad. mod.L. *hyperbolismus* (Newton), f. HYPERBOLA.] A curve whose equation is derived from that of another curve by substituting xy for y, as that of the hyperbola is from that of the straight line.

[**1704** NEWTON *Lin. Tertii Ordinis* iv. §9 Hyperbolismus Hyperbolæ tres habet Asymptotos.] **1861** TALBOT tr. *Newton's Lines 3rd Order* 21 Of the four Hyperbolisms of the Hyperbola. Whenever .. both the terms ax^3 and bx^3 are deficient, the curve will be a hyperbolism of some conic section. *Ibid.* 23 A hyperbolism of the parabola is expressed by the equation $xy^2 + ey = d$, and has two asymptotes. **1873** G. SALMON *Higher Plane Curves* (ed. 2) 175 If $y = \phi(x)$ be the equation of any curve, Newton calls the curve $xy = \phi(x)$ a hyperbolism of that curve.

hyperbolist (haɪˈpɜːbəlɪst). [f. HYPERBOLE + -IST.]

1. One given to the use of hyperbole; one who uses exaggerated language or statements.

1661 BOYLE *Style of Script.* (1675) 253, I .. cease to think the Psalmist an hyperbolist, for comparing the transcendent sweetness of God's word to that inferiour one of honey. *a* **1734** NORTH *Exam.* III. viii. §79 Our ordinary Anecdotarians .. do not declaredly transcribe them [libels] into their Text, as our Hyperbolist hath done here. **1872** *Daily News* 2 Sept., Court hyperbolists and loyal dispatches

..had swelled his achievements to the proportions of matchless feats.

2. [*nonce-use*, f. HYPERBOLA.]

1831 I. TAYLOR in Edwards *Freed. Will* Introd. III. 55 The friends of the first of the curves would think themselves justified in denouncing the hyperbolists as extravagant heretics.

hyperbolize (haɪˈpɜːbəlaɪz), *v.* Now *rare.* [f. as prec. + -IZE. Cf. F. *hyperboliser.*]

1. *intr.* To use hyperbole; to exaggerate.

1599 *Broughton's Lett.* ii. 10 Will you hyperbolize aboue S. Gregorie, who is contented to marshall the foure generall Councels? **1632** G. HUGHES *Saints Losse* 52 If I should tell all, I should..seeme to hyperbolize. **1656** S. H. *Gold. Law* 90 God in Scripture allows of Titles;..nay, God doth hyperbolize it, and saith of al Powers, You are Gods. **1783** BLAIR *Rhet.* xvi. I. 321 The person..who was under the distracting agitations of grief, might be permitted to hyperbolize strongly.

2. *trans.* To express or represent hyperbolically; †to extol or praise extravagantly; to exaggerate.

1609 BP. W. BARLOW *Answ. Nameless Cath.* 41 Glosses hyperbolizing the flatteries of the Canonists. **1660** HICKERINGILL *Jamaica* (1661) 26 Of the Fruit or Nuts of these Trees is made the so fam'd Chocoletta, whose virtues are hiperboliz'd upon every post in London. **1797** *Monthly Mag.* III. 271 He has hyperbolized the Spanish hyperbolical salutation, 'May you live a thousand years!' **1814** *Edin. Rev.* XXIV. 40 Surprising events which were but moderately hyperbolized at the time.

Hence **hyˈperbolizing** *vbl. sb.* and *ppl. a.*

a **1619** FOTHERBY *Atheom.* II. vii. §6 (1622) 272 The rhetoricall amplification of hyperbolizing Orators. **1638** CHILLINGW. *Relig. Prot.* I. v. §89. 291 This had been without hyperbolizing, *Mundus contra Athanasium.* **1671** J. WEBSTER *Metallogr.* xv. 233 If I gave no credit to their hyberbolizing fancies.

hyˈperbolo-, combining form of HYPERBOLA, as in **hyˈperboloˌgraph** [Gr. -γραφος that writes or describes], an instrument for tracing hyperbolas; **hyˈperbolo-paraˈbolical** *a.*, partaking of the nature of the hyperbola and parabola.

1736 STONE in *Phil. Trans.* XLI. 319 The two species are to be reckoned amongst the Hyperbolo-parabolical Curves. **1876** *Catal. Sci. App. S. Kens.* §70 Hyperbolograph.

hyperboloid (haɪˈpɜːbəlɔɪd). *Geom.* [f. HYPERBOLA + -OID. Cf. F. *hyperboloïde.*]

†1. A hyperbola of a higher degree: = HYPERBOLA b. *Obs.*

1727-41 CHAMBERS *Cycl.*, *Hyperboloides*, are hyperbola's of the higher kind..expressed by this equation: $ay^{m+n} = bx^m (a + x)^n$. **1740** CHEYNE *Regimen* 326 Like the several Orders of the Hyperboloids, some of which meet the Asymptot infinitly sooner and faster than others, but through which all must pass sooner or later. **1796** in HUTTON *Math. Dict.*

2. A solid or surface of the second degree, some of whose plane sections are hyperbolas, the others being ellipses or circles. Formerly restricted to those of circular section, generated by the revolution of a hyperbola about one of its axes; now called ***hyperboloids of revolution***.

There are two kinds of hyperboloid: ***the hyperboloid of one sheet***, e.g. that generated by revolution about the conjugate axis (formerly called *hyperbolic cylindroid*), a figure resembling a cylinder but of continuously varying diameter, like a reel narrower in the middle than at the ends; and the ***hyperboloid of two sheets***, e.g. that generated by revolution about the transverse axis, consisting of two separate parts corresponding to the two branches of the hyperbola. The word is sometimes extended to analogous solids of higher degrees: cf. HYPERBOLA b.

1743 EMERSON *Fluxions* 210 The Hyperboloid is always between ½ and ⅓ the circumscribing Cylinder. **1828** HUTTON *Course Math.* II. 339 To find the surface of an hyperboloid. **1829** *Nat. Philos., Hydraulics* i. 4 (U.K.S.) Newton..found that the solid figure produced by the streams flowing from all parts to one common centre..was an Hyperboloid of the fourth order. **1840** LARDNER *Geom.* 286 If an hyperboloid of revolution be formed by the revolution of an hyperbola on its transverse axis. **1867** J. HOGG *Microsc.* I. ii. 24 If a plano-convex lens has its convex surface part of a hyperboloid. **1895** *Oracle Encycl.* III. 84/1 A point moving round a fixed point at a constant distance from it describes a circle, and a straight line rotating round a fixed line not in the same plane generates a hyperboloid.

hyperboˈloidal, *a.* [f. prec. + -AL[1].] Of the form of a hyperboloid.

1879 *Cassell's Techn. Educ.* IV. 300/1 Domes..the circular may be spherical..hyperboloidal [etc.].

†**hyˈperbolous**, *a. Obs. rare.* [f. HYPERBOLE + -OUS.] Involving hyperbole; hyperbolical.

1638 M. PARKER *Earthquake Calabria*, This wondrous palpitation of earth's frame Hath marvels wrought hyperbolous to name.

†**hyˈperboly.** *Obs.* [app. a modification of HYPERBOLE, after words in *-y*, as *monarchy*, etc. But cf. Gr. ὑπερβολία (Hesychius).] = HYPERBOLE I.

1598 DRAYTON *Heroic. Ep.* xii. 65 Although the envious English doe devise A thousand Jests of our Hyperbolies. **1658** OSBORN *Q. Eliz.* Wks. (1673) 464 Let the Proverb *As sure as Check* bayl me from the least suspicion of hyperboly. **1690** BOYLE *Chr. Virtuoso* II. 33 If it be said that these are very bold Hyperbolies, I hope the Texts..will keep them from seeming..groundless Conceits.

†**hyperˈboreal**, *a. Obs. rare.* [f. HYPER- 1 + BOREAL; cf. next.] = next A. 1.

1596 R. L[INCHE] *Diella* (1877) 80 Whiter then snow on Hyperboreall hyll. *c* **1790** A. BELL in Southey *Life* (1844) I. 122 In that cold climate, so congenial to my hyperboreal constitution.

hyperborean (haɪpəˈbɔəriːən), *a.* and *sb.* [ad. late L. *hyperboreān-us* = classical L. *hyperboreus*, ad. Gr. ὑπερβόρεος, -βόρειος (in early writers only in pl. Ὑπερβόρεοι, the Hyperboreans), f. ὑπερ- HYPER- 1 + βόρειος northern, βορέας the north wind, BOREAS. Cf. F. *hyperboréen, hyperborée*; the latter is found in the 14th c.]

A. *adj.* 1. Of, pertaining to, or characterizing the extreme north of the earth, or (*colloq.* or *humorously*) of a particular country; in ethnological use, cf. B.

1591 SYLVESTER *Du Bartas* I. v. 635 Gray-beard Boreas..Is prisoned close in th' Hyper-Borean Cave. **1633** C. BUTLER *Eng. Gram.* (L.), Northern Isles; as Groenland, Freesland, Iseland, etc., even to the hyperborean or frozen sea. *a* **1649** DRUMM. OF HAWTH. *Poems* Wks. (1711) 6 The hyperborean hills. **1740** J. WARTON *Virg. Georg.* IV. 618 The Hyperborean ice he wander'd o'er. **1860** MAURY *Phys. Geog. Sea* (Low) x. §488 This water then may go off as an under current freighted with heat to temper some hyperborean region. **1875** F. PARKMAN in *N. Amer. Rev.* CXX. 37 The first, or Hyperborean, group comprises the tribes of Alaska and a part of British America. **1885** *Manchester Exam.* 12 Jan. 6/1 We are held to dwell..in a hyperborean region, though we are only two hundred miles from London.

b. Of or pertaining to the fabled Hyperboreans.

1613 PURCHAS *Pilgrimage* (1614) 398 The Hyperborean [nation], which..dwell in an Iland in the Ocean neere unto the Pole. **1806** FELLOWES tr. *Milton's 2nd Def.* (1848) I. 272 Some hyperborean and fabled hero, decorated with all the shewy varnish of imposture.

2. (*nonce-use.*) Surpassing that of the north wind.

1859 THACKERAY *Virgin.* lxxix, He blew a hyperborean whistle, as if to blow his wrath away.

B. *sb.* An inhabitant of the extreme north of the earth; in *pl.* members of an ethnological group of Arctic races. *loosely* and *fig.* One who lives in a northerly clime.

In Greek legend the Hyperboreans were a happy people who lived in a land of perpetual sunshine and plenty beyond the north wind.

1601 HOLLAND *Pliny* I. 121 Certain people..not much vn- like in their maner of life to the Hyperboreans. **1613** PURCHAS *Pilgrimage* (1614) 395 Next to these both in place and credit, we may reckon the Hyperboreans. **1816** KEATINGE *Trav.* (1817) II. 138 At six in the morning the yokes of oxen were going to their work a field; and nearly three hours advantage..of active life is possessed [in France] over us Hyperboreans. **1856** KANE *Arct. Expl.* II. i. 24 Our party of American hyperboreans.

Hence **hyperˈboreanism** (*nonce-wd.*), an extreme northernism.

1824 DE QUINCEY *Goethe* Wks. 1863 XII. 207 *note*, 'Just' ..[in 'we must just put up with it'], is a Hyperboreanism, and still intelligible in some provinces.

†**hyperˈbyssal**, *a. nonce-wd.* [f. HYPER- 4 + Gr. βυσσός = βυθός depth (of the sea).] Of or belonging to surpassing depth or profundity.

1691 E. TAYLOR *Behmen's Theos. Philos.* 350 Sink down into the Hyperbyssal, Supersensual, Unsearchable, Eternal One.

Hyper-ˈCalvinism. *Theol.* Calvinistic doctrine which goes beyond that of Calvin himself; extreme Calvinism. So †**Hypercalˈvinian, Hyper-ˈCalvinist**, one who holds such doctrine; **Hyper-Calviˈnistic** *a.*, pertaining to Hyper-Calvinists or Hyper-Calvinism.

1674 HICKMAN *Quinquart. Hist.* (ed. 2) 68 Thomas Aquinas,..is rather an Hypercalvinian than not a Calvinist in this matter of the absolute Decree. **1856** R. A. VAUGHAN *Mystics* (1860) II. 93 Behmen argues against the Hyper-Calvinist. **1882-3** SCHAFF *Encycl. Relig. Knowl.* II. 874/1 [John Hill (1697-1771)] one of the leading advocates of his day of Hyper-Calvinism. **1892** B. TALBOT in A. E. Lee *Hist. Columbus* (Ohio) I. 831 A growing distaste for the extreme views of Hyper-Calvinists. **1896** D. L. LEONARD *Congregationalism in Ohio* 9 A hyper-Calvinistic system of theology, which landed not a few in formalism and fatalism.

hypercatalectic (-kætəˈlɛktɪk), *a. Pros.* [ad. late L. *hypercatalēctic-us* (Gr. ὑπερκατάληκτος is recorded); see HYPER- 1 and CATALECTIC.] Of a verse or colon: Having an extra syllable after the last complete dipody. Also applied to the syllable itself. †Formerly also = HYPERMETRIC.

Used occas. of Old English verse.

1704 J. HARRIS *Lex. Techn.* s.v. *Deposition*, Hypercatalectick, where a Syllable or two are Redundant. **1752** NEWTON *Milton, Mask* 631 Such redundant or hyper-catalectick verses sometimes occur in Milton. **1813** J. J. CONYBEARE in *Archæologia* (1814) XVII. 265 Of the Trochaic species, with the Hypercatalectic syllable, as, Ahte ic, ealdor, stol. **1886** J. B. MAYOR *Eng. Metre* i. 10 To state whether it is metrically complete, or incomplete, owing to final or initial truncation, or more than complete..in technical language, whether it is *acatalectic, catalectic* or *hypercatalectic.* **1894** *Trans. Philol. Soc.* *1891-4* 386 Expanded lines, called by German scholars *Schwell-verse* or *Streck-verse*, are hypercatalectic.

‖**hypercatharsis** (ˌhaɪpəkəˈθɑːsɪs). *Path.* [a. Gr. ὑπερκάθαρσις: see HYPER- 5 and CATHARSIS.] Excessive or violent purging, esp. as induced by the use of drugs.

1681 tr. *Willis' Rem. Med. Wks.* Vocab. **1684** tr. *Bonet's Merc. Compit.* VIII. 306 If..a Hypercatharsis follow Purging. **1710** T. FULLER *Pharm. Extemp.* 144 This Rosin.. will..cause sickness at Stomach..and Hypercatharsis. **1876** BARTHOLOW *Mat. Med.* (1879) 448 Occasionally profuse watery evacuations have been produced by it, and rarely severe hypercatharsis.

So **hypercaˈthartic** *a.*, causing hypercatharsis, violently cathartic; *sb.* a medicine of this nature.

[**1657** *Physical Dict.*, *Hypercathartica*, most violent purges: too purging.] **1706** PHILLIPS (ed. Kersey), *Hypercatharticks* (in Physic), purges that work too violently. **1855** MAYNE *Expos. Lex.*, *Hypercatharticus*,.. hypercathartic.

hypercharge (ˈhaɪpətʃɑːdʒ). *Nuclear Physics.* [f. *hyper(onic) charge*: see quot. 1956.] A property of hadrons that is conserved in strong interactions and is represented by a quantum number *Y* that is the same for all the particles of a charge multiplet (isospin multiplet), being equal to twice their average charge quantum number.

The hypercharge *Y* of a particle is related to its charge *Q* and the third component, I_3, of isospin by $Y = 2(Q - I_3)$; and to its strangeness *S* and baryon number *B* by $Y = S + B$.

1956 J. SCHWINGER in *Physical Rev.* CIV. 1164/2 It is now natural to suppose that the *K* meson, with isotopic spin ½, possesses a similar physical property [to the nucleonic charge] in the nature of a charge, which is also dynamically realized by a coupling with the π field. We shall term this new property hyper(onic) charge *Y*, with $Y = +1$ characterizing the K^+K^0 multiplet, and $Y = -1$ describing the antiparticles $\bar{K}^0K^-$. As the agent for the dynamical exhibition of nucleonic and hypercharge, the π field does not itself bear these charges. **1964** *New Scientist* 20 Feb. 460/3 According to the conservation of baryons and hypercharge, the omega-minus should be produced in collisions between K-minus mesons and protons and should decay (weakly, with a change of hypercharge) to a xi-particle and pion, or to a lambda-particle and K-minus. **1972** G. L. WICK *Elem. Particles* v. 92 All of the strongly interacting particles fall into families which are specified by three quantum numbers—hypercharge, isotopic spin and baryon number. *Ibid.*, In the final analysis, either strangeness or hypercharge will suffice as a quantum number. In practice experimenters prefer to use strangeness—largely for historical reasons... On the other hand, some theoreticians have adopted the new terminology as it is easier to manipulate in the equations.

hyperchromasia (ˌhaɪpəkrəʊˈmeɪzɪə). Also in anglicized form **hyperchromasy** (-ˈkrəʊməsɪ) (*rare*). [mod.L., f. HYPER- 5 + Gr. χρῶμα, χρώματ- colour (in sense 2 repr. CHROMATIN): see -IA[1].] 1. *Med.* a. Excessive coloration or pigmentation of the skin.

1889 *Cent. Dict.*, *Hyperchromasia*, a pathological condition marked by excess of pigment. **1908** *Practitioner* Aug. 349 A condition known as hyperchromasia, in contradistinction to achromasia, or leucodermia.

b. = HYPERCHROMIA.

1929 R. B. H. GRADWOHL tr. *Schilling's Blood Picture* II. 107 Special, generally designated erythrocytic blood pictures... Hyperchromasia: generally increased pigmentation. **1966** J. W. LINMAN *Princ. Hematol.* iii. 60 Large or excessively thick cells that stain more darkly than normal are described as being hyperchromatic or as displaying hyperchromasia.

2. *Cytology.* The condition, in a cell or nucleus, of having an abnormally large amount of chromatin.

1930 *Med. Jrnl. Austral.* 22 Feb. 244/1 A detailed examination of carcinoma cells shows that hyperchromasy is the dominant cytological feature of these components. **1948** *Amer. Jrnl. Path.* XXIV. 1200 Cytologic descriptions of tumors are limited to generalities such as..hyperchromasia of nucleus. **1971** *Nature* 31 Dec. 547/2 The individual tumour cells were more rounded with nuclear hyperchromasia.

hyperchromatic (haɪpəkrəʊˈmætɪk), *a.* [f. HYPER- 5 + CHROMATIC *a.* (in sense 2, CHROMAT(IN + -IC).] 1. *Med.* a. Of the skin: excessively pigmented.

1894 in GOULD *Dict. Med.* 589/2.

b. = HYPERCHROMIC *a.* 1.

1929 R. B. H. GRADWOHL tr. *Schilling's Blood Picture* II. 113 Single or many large hyperchromatic cells (megalocytes, occasional megaloblasts). **1966** [see HYPERCHROMASIA 1 b].

2. *Cytology.* Of a cell or nucleus: having an abnormally large amount of chromatin.

1896 E. B. WILSON *Cell* ii. 68 In many cancer-cells many of the nuclei are especially rich in chromatin (hyperchromatic cells). **1930** *Med. Jrnl. Austral.* 22 Feb. 244/1 Highly differentiated, hyperchromatic sarcoma cells. **1966** WRIGHT & SYMMERS *Systemic Path.* II. xxxii. 1128/1 Not infrequently the nucleus of the tumour cells varies considerably in size; it may be large and hyperchromatic.. or it may appear as a small, irregular, pyknotic structure.

hyperchromatosis (ˌhaɪpəkrəʊməˈtəʊsɪs). [mod.L., f. HYPER- 5 + CHROMAT(O-, CHROMAT(IN + -OSIS.] 1. *Med.* Excessive colouring or pigmentation, esp. of the skin.

1886 *Syd. Soc. Lex.*, *Hyperchromatosis*, Auspitz's term for an excessive deposit of pigment in the epidermis. **1919**

Encycl. Medica (ed. 2) VI. 272 *Hyperchromatosis*, excessive pigmentation, especially in certain skin diseases.

2. *Cytology*. [ad. G. *hyperchromatose* (R. Woltereck 1898, in *Zeitschr. f. wiss. Zool.* LXIV. 604).] An abnormally large number of chromosomes or amount of chromatin in a cell or nucleus.

1898 *Jrnl. R. Microsc. Soc.* 628 They are remarkable for their excess of chromosomes (hyperchromatosis), and for the tendency these have to group themselves in dyads and tetrads. **1913** J. Ritchie in Pembrey & Ritchie *Text-bk. Gen. Path.* viii. 240 In malignant tumours the division of the chromosomes between the poles is often unequal... This can be recognized by the existence of differences in size and staining qualities of the nuclei, and the two phenomena are sometimes referred to as hyperchromatosis and hypochromatosis. **1946** *Nature* 31 Aug. 304/1 A hyperchromatosis and pyknosis of the nucleus which has hitherto been wrongly interpreted as a degeneration.

hyperchromia (haɪpə'krəʊmɪə). *Med.* [f. as next + -IA[1].] A hyperchromic condition of the blood or of an erythrocyte (see HYPERCHROMIC *a.* 1).

1931 *Amer. Jrnl. Med. Sci.* CLXXXII. 521 There might be two types of pernicious anemia—the megaloblastic, associated with macrocytosis and hyperchromia, and the erythroblastic, associated with microcytosis and hypochromia. **1935** Whitby & Britton *Disorders of Blood* iii. 49 Hyperchromia is inevitably associated with macrocytosis. **1958** G. C. de Gruchy *Clin. Haematol.* ii. 43 Because it is now customary to describe the haemoglobin content of cells in terms of concentration rather than absolute amount, the term hyperchromia is best avoided.

hyperchromic (haɪpə'krəʊmɪk), *a.* [f. HYPER- 5 + Gr. χρῶμ-α colour + -IC.] **1.** *Med.* Characterized by or designating a colour index greater than one, or red blood cells that contain more hæmoglobin than normal and show little or no central pallor.

1924 T. R. Waugh in *Canad. Med. Assoc. Jrnl.* XLVII. 114/2 The color index is high, though total cell volume may be considerably reduced. Such a condition may be termed, therefore, hyperchromic. We find this type of anaemia.. especially in pernicious anaemia. **1935** Whitby & Britton *Disorders of Blood* vi. 116 The anæmia produced by a deficiency of the hæmopoietic principle is invariably macrocytic and almost always markedly hyperchromic. **1942** M. M. Wintrobe *Clin. Hematol.* vi. 225 It has been assumed that the red corpuscles in this condition [*sc.* pernicious anæmia] are 'hyperchromic' or supersaturated with hemoglobin. This is not true... The darker appearance of these corpuscles..is due to their increased thickness. **1960** C. H. Smith *Blood Dis. Infancy & Childhood* v. 62 Hyperchromic anemias identify conditions in which macrocytes prevail and in which the color index is greater than unity.

2. Characterized by or exhibiting an increase in the extent to which light (usually, ultra-violet radiation) is absorbed; chiefly in ***hyperchromic effect***.

1939 W. R. Brode *Chem. Spectroscopy* vii. 128 Ethylene.. has an absorption band at 1545 f (1950 A) in the extreme ultraviolet, but the conjugated coupling of two or more ethylene radicals together results in both hyperchromic and bathochromic effects. **1955** G. Schmidt in Chargaff & Davidson *Nucleic Acids* I. xv. 569 The quantitative degradation of PNA to mononucleotides by alkali is accompanied by an increase of approximately 20% in the absorption at 260 mμ (hyperchromic effect). **1958** *Nature* 29 Nov. 1503/2 The hyperchromic degradation of polymers. **1968** M. W. Strickberger *Genetics* v. 73 The double-stranded form [of DNA] is called hypochromic, and the loose, single-stranded form is called hyperchromic.

Hence ˌ**hyperchro'micity**, the property of absorbing more (ultra-violet) light.

1958 *Nature* 29 Nov. 1502/1 In view of the profound importance of the anomalous ultra-violet absorption characteristics of nucleic acids in relationship to the fine structure of the macromolecule, the hyperchromicity of a number of relatively simple polynucleotide derivatives was studied. **1968** M. W. Strickberger *Genetics* v. 73 Hyperchromicity [of DNA] can be induced by heating.

ˌ**hyperconju'gation**. *Physical Chem.* [f. HYPER- 1 b + CONJUGATION.] A direct interaction between the electrons of a methyl or substituted methyl group in a molecule and the electrons of an adjacent conjugated system, the former being attracted towards the latter.

1939 R. S. Mulliken in *Jrnl. Chem. Physics* VII. 340/2 In the cyclic dienes..there is interaction between this [pair of electrons] and the unsaturation orbitals, resulting in what may be called 'cyclic conjugation'. This phenomenon has been..discussed by Hückel, except for the case where A is CH_2. For this case we may introduce the term 'hyperconjugation', meaning an additional conjugation beyond that ordinarily recognized. [*Note*] The term..was suggested by Professor W. G. Brown, as an improvement on the term 'superconjugation' at first used by the writer. **1949** *Q. Rev.* III. 229 Delocalisation of this type is known as σ-hyperconjugation, and since σ electrons are relatively tightly bound, the resulting energy of delocalisation is likely to be very small. Consequently, σ-hyperconjugation is generally ignored. **1952** *Chem. & Engin. News* 17 Nov. 4881/2 Hyperconjugation denotes resonance interaction by alkyl, and particularly methyl, substituents in systems exemplified by

$$H_3 \equiv C - C = C \leftrightarrow H^{+} H_2C = C - C.$$

1962 M. J. S. Dewar *Hyperconjugation* i. 13 The evidence.. for the importance of hyperconjugation is much less conclusive than has been commonly supposed. **1965** Phillips & Williams *Inorg. Chem.* I. xi. 400 Hydrogen is also unable to act as a π-donor, except possibly to a small extent in groups of hydrogen atoms as in CH_3, the so-called hyperconjugation effect.

Hence **hyper'conjugated** *ppl. a.*, exhibiting hyperconjugation.

1949 *Q. Rev.* III. 233 The carbon-carbon distance in acetaldehyde is approximately 0·04 A. less than the normal value, and..the shortening has been attributed to hyperconjugated structures. **1959** E. S. Gould *Mechanism & Struct. Org. Chem.* ii. 49 Hyperconjugated structures in which a shift of electron density..has left the C–H bonds with partial no-bond character.

hypercoracoid (-'kɒrəkɔɪd). *Ichthyol.* [f. HYPER- 6 + CORACOID.] The upper of the two bones forming the shoulder-girdle in typical fishes, with which the fin-rays articulate; the *scapula*.

1876 *Johnson's New Univ. Cycl.* (N.Y.) II. 1079/1 *Hypercoracoid*..the upper bone opposed to the inner surface of the great scapular cincture of the typical fishes.

hyperco'rrect, *a.* *Linguistics.* Also **hyper-correct** (with hyphen). [f. HYPER- 4 a + CORRECT *a.*] Of a spelling, pronunciation, or construction: falsely modelled on an apparently analogous prestigeful form. Also of a speaker using such a form.

1922 O. Jespersen *Lang.* xv. 294 Such hypercorrect forms are closely related to those 'spelling pronunciations' which become frequent when there is much reading of a language whose spelling is not accurately phonetic. **1937** *Amer. Speech* XII. 167 When James the footman says *chicking* for 'chicken' he is being hypercorrect, leaning over backward to be correct. **1972** *Archivum Linguisticum* III. 4 Modern authors have focussed on the [French] imperfect subjunctive as a hypercorrect grammatical form and have used it to characterize or satirize the pedantic and the pretentious.

Hence **hyperco'rrection, -co'rrectness**.

1934 Webster, Hypercorrection, -ness. **1935** *Language* XI. 143 It is only by unceasing vigilance that hyper-correction can be avoided by one whose native dialect has this phonological feature and who wishes to correct it. **1955** *Archivum Linguisticum* VII. 142 Phonemic interference may be due to..phone substitution and hyper-correctness. **1959** M. Schlauch *Eng. Lang. in Mod. Times* vi. 167 The zeal of social inferiors for hyper-correctness. **1964** H. Kökeritz in D. Abercrombie et al. *Daniel Jones* 141 Salmon..tends to become ['sæmən] by hypercorrection. **1972** *Language* XLVIII. 484 Hyper-corrections like *tesk, mast* (for 'mask') seem to establish that *tes, mas* are full forms in NNE and not stylistic reductions.

hypercritic (haɪpə'krɪtɪk), *sb.* and *a.* [ad. 16th c. L. *hypercritic-us* (see HYPER- 4 + CRITIC), applied vituperatively to the younger Scaliger by the Italian R. Titius in 1589, and by Delrio in 1609. Cf. F. *hypercritique* (Boileau, 1703).]

A. *sb.* **1.** †A master critic (*obs.*); an extreme or severe critic; a hypercritical or over-critical person.

1633 T. Carew *Cœl. Brit.* Wks. (1824) 154 My offices and title are, supreme theomastix, hupercrittique of manners, protonotarie of abuses. **1647** Trapp *Comm. Matt.* vii. 2 Scaliger the hypercritic gives this absurd and unmannerly censure. **1656** Blount *Glossogr.*, *Hypercritick*,..a Master Critick. **1674** Dryden *State Innoc.* Apol., These hyper-critics of English poetry. *a* **1764** Lloyd *Ep. to J.B. Esq.*, Yet Hypercritics I disdain, A race of blockheads dull and vain. **1822** C. Butler *Remin.* (ed. 3) 329 An Italian hyper-critic would deny it to be music.

†**2.** Hypercriticism; also a minute criticism, a critique. *Obs.*

1618 Bolton *Florus* To Rdr., In mine Hypercriticks, concerning our countreys history, I have dealt freely. **1695** Bentley *Let. to Evelyn* 29 Jan. in *Corr.* (1842) 93 My Alterations..which I have done with so much freedom and simplicity; such seeming fastidiousness and Hypercritic.. that I should fear to send them, but that [etc.]. **1757** Mrs. Griffith *Lett. Henry & Frances* (1767) I. 257 My observations are mostly an hypercritick upon Lord Orrery.

B. *adj.* = next.

1820 Keats *Cap & Bells* xi, A long hypercritic howl Against the vicious manners of the age.

hyper'critical, *a.* [f. HYPER- 4 + CRITICAL.] Of the character of a hypercritic; extremely or unduly critical; addicted to excessive adverse criticism, esp. upon minute or trivial points.

1605 Camden *Rem.* (1637) 16 The hypercriticall controller of Poets, Julius Scaliger, doth so severely censure Nations, that he seemed to sit in the chaire of the scornfull. **1611** Coryat *Crudities* 515, I suppose that some hyper-criticall carpers will taxe me of vanity. **1738** Swift *Pol. Conversat.* Introd. 56, I..hope, that such Hypercritical Readers will please to consider [etc.]. **1863** Miss Braddon *Eleanor's Vict.* I. i. 3 It would have been hypercritical to have objected to the shortness of the skirt.

Hence **hyper'critically** *adv.*, in a hypercritical manner.

1715 M. Davies *Athen. Brit.* I. Contents at end Zzijb, Too Hipercritically lavishing of their Lashes and Encomiums upon Friend and Foe, Indiscriminatively, rather than impartially. **1867** Stubbs *Lect. Med. & Mod. Hist.* (1886) 13 God forbid that we should speak contemptuously or hypercritically of any honest worker.

hypercriticism (-'krɪtɪsɪz(ə)m). [f. HYPER- 4 + CRITICISM.] Excessive criticism; criticism that is unduly severe or minute.

1678 Phillips (ed. 4) App., *Hypercriticism*, an over exact or curious Judgment or Censure passed upon the works of any one. **1824** *Edin. Rev.* XL. 337 The details of an obnoxious hypercriticism. **1835** Mrs. Carlyle *Lett.* I. 43, I clean beautifully when you do not dishearten me with hyper-criticism. **1873** H. Spencer *Stud. Sociol.* Notes 414 Even were these hyper-criticisms, it might be said that they are rightly to be made on a passage which is considered a model of style.

hyper'criticize, *v.* [f. HYPER- 4 + CRITICIZE.] *trans.* To criticize excessively or unduly. **b.** *intr.* To be hypercritical.

1812 *Religionism* 55 What! hypercriticise the dead! for shame! **1835** *Fraser's Mag.* XII. 688 Those who hyper-criticised on the awkward terminations of some of his plots. **1863** Mrs. C. Clarke *Shaks. Char.* xvi. 406, I have no desire to hypercriticise, or to see more in our poet than he himself intended.

hyperde'terminant, *sb.* and *a.* *Math.* [See HYPER- 3.] **a.** *sb.* A determinant of operative symbols; a symbolic expression for an invariant or covariant: invented by Cayley. **b.** *adj.* Of the nature of a hyperdeterminant.

1845 Cayley in *Camb. Math. Jrnl.* IV. 195 The function *u* whose properties we proceed to investigate may be conveniently named a 'Hyperdeterminant'. *a* **1846** —— in *Camb. & Dublin Math. Jrnl.* I. 104 The question may be proposed 'To find all the derivatives of any number of functions, which have the property of preserving their form unaltered after any linear transformations of the variables'. .. I give the name of Hyperdeterminant Derivative, or simply of Hyperdeterminant, to those derivatives which have the property just enunciated. **1895** Elliott *Algebra Quantics* 161 Hyperdeterminants form a complete system of co-variants. *Ibid.*, The hyperdeterminant symbols.

hyperdiapason, -diapente, -diatessaron, -ditone *Mus.*: see HYPER- 2.

hyperdisyllable (-daɪ'sɪləb(ə)l). [ad. late Gr. ὑπερδισύλλαβος; see DISYLLABLE.] A word of more than two syllables. Also *attrib.* or *adj.* Of more than two syllables.

1678 Phillips (ed. 4), *Hyperdissyllable*. **1704** J. Harris *Lex. Techn.*, *Hyperdisyllable*. **1843** T. K. Arnold *Latin Prose Comp.* II. 13 *Esse* in compound infinitives very frequently precedes a hyperdissyllable participle. **1895** J. P. Postgate in *Class. Rev.* IX. 77 Hyperdisyllables at the end of the pentameter are ten times as rare as in the second book [of Tibullus].

hyperdorian, *Anc. Mus.*: see HYPER- 2.

hyperdrive ('haɪpədraɪv). *Science Fiction.* Also **hyper-drive**. [f. HYPER- + DRIVE *sb.*; perh. suggested by *hyperspace, overdrive*.] A fictitious device by which a spaceship is enabled to travel from one point to another in a shorter time than light would take (usually by passing out of ordinary space into 'hyperspace' for the journey); also, the state of so travelling.

1955 B. Davenport *Inquiry into Sci. Fiction* 11 A 'hyperdrive'..may be defined simply as something that *does* enable ships to travel faster than the speed of light, no matter what Einstein says. **1959** P. Anderson *Virgin Planet* (1966) iii. 20 The ship went into hyperdrive and outpaced light. **1960** K. Amis *New Maps of Hell* (1961) i. 20 The author will fabricate a way of getting around Einstein..[by] a device known typically as the space-warp or the hyper-drive. **1965** D. Morgan in J. Carnell *New Writings in S-F* III. 144 The jolt as he came out of hyper-drive..had confirmed what he had suspected for some months. **1968** M. S. Livingston *Particle Physics* i. 7 No responsible scientist would attempt to justify support for research in this field with prediction of an 'anti-matter engine'..or a 'hyper-drive' for spaceships.

‖**hyperdulia** (haɪpəduː'laɪə). Also 5 **-doulia**, 7 (anglicized) **hyperduly**. [a. med.L. *hyperdūlīa*; see HYPER- 4 and DULIA. Cf. F. *hyperdulie*.] The superior DULIA or veneration paid by Roman Catholics to the Virgin Mary. Hence **hyper'dulic, hyper'dulical** *adjs.*, of the nature of hyperdulia.

1530 Tindale *Answ. More* (1850) 57 As for hyperdoulia, I would fain wete where he readeth of it in all the scripture. **1625** Ussher *Answ. Jesuit* 429 From whom our Romanists did first learne their Hyperdulia, or that transcendent kinde of seruice, wherewith they worship the Virgin Mary. **1664** Jer. Taylor *Dissuas. Popery* II. II. §6 Be careful that if *dulia* only be due that your worship be not hyperdulical. **1674** Brevint *Saul at Endor* xvi. 352 Devotion..whether Duly or Hyperduly. **1846** G. S. Faber *Lett. Tractar. Secess. Popery* 91 The worship..of the Virgin Mary..the Papists distinguish by the name of Hyperdulia. *Ibid.* 101 *note*, The Hyperdulic Adoration of Mary. **1865** *Union Rev.* III. 404 The hyperdulia and dulia due respectively to our Blessed Lady and the Saints.

hyperelliptic, -geometric, -al, *Math.*: see HYPER- 3.

hyperemia, var. HYPERÆMIA.

hyperesthesia, var. HYPERÆSTHESIA.

hyperextend (haɪpərɪk'stɛnd), *v.* [f. HYPER- 4 c + EXTEND *v.*] *trans.* To extend, in the sense opp. to FLEX *v.*, (a joint, or a part of the body moving about a joint) so as to attain an abnormally great angle. So **hyperex'tended** *ppl. a.*

1883 *Brain* V. 348 The toes are spread out and hyper-extended. **1886** *Ibid.* IX. 169 Between this ridge and the toes there is a deep hollow, to which the hyperextended first phalanges form an almost perpendicular boundary. **1903** Tubby & Jones *Mod. Methods Surg. Paralyses* II. 218

Treatment should consist in rendering the forearm supine and hyperextending the wrist. **1927** *Jrnl. Amer. Med. Assoc.* 28 May 1711/1 The fingers could be hyperextended until they touched the dorsum of the wrist. **1963** *Lancet* 5 Jan. 6/1 An injury in which the neck has been forcibly hyperextended or flexed.

Also **hyperex'tension**, the state of being hyperextended.

1883 *Brain* V. 480 There is a slight hyper-extension at the torso-phalangeal, and flexion at the phalangeal joints. **1905** A. B. JACKSON *Influence Growth on Deformities* iv. 85 The best result after this affection is a knee ankylosed in extension or hyperextension. **1961** *Lancet* 5 Aug. 297/1 The common pattern of deformity was flexion . . and dislocation of the hip, with extension or hyperextension of the knee. **1968** J. WINEARLS *Mod. Dance* (ed. 2) ii. 48 In the case of the backwards contraction, the spine is really in hyper-extension.

hyperextensible (ˌhaɪpərɪk'stɛnsɪb(ə)l), *a.* [f. prec., after *extensible*.] Capable of being hyperextended. So ˌ**hyperextensi'bility**.

1946 R. R. GATES *Human Genetics* I. xi. 449 All the finger joints are hyperextensible. *Ibid.* 448 Hyperextensibility or doublejointedness of the thumbs may occur in the first joint or the second. **1961** *Lancet* 2 Sept. 526/2 There were obvious transverse palmar folds and hyperextensibility of the joints.

hyperfine ('haɪpəfaɪn), *a. Physics.* [tr. G. *hyperfeinstruktur* hyperfine structure (W. Pauli 1924, in *Naturwiss.* 12 Sept. 741/1), f. HYPER- + *feinstruktur* FINE STRUCTURE.] ***hyperfine structure***: (the presence of) multiplets of closely spaced lines in a spectrum that are closer together than those of fine structure; *esp.* multiplets that result from the further splitting of lines by the coupling between the magnetic moment (and higher multipole moments) of the atomic nucleus and the electromagnetic field of the electrons. Also (with ellipsis of *structure*), of or pertaining to this phenomenon.

1927 *Proc. Nat. Acad. Sci.* XIII. 430 The hyper-fine structure of λ 2537 of mercury has been shown . . to consist of five lines of very nearly equal intensity. *Ibid.* 431 Each of the five hyper-fine structure lines has a triplet Zeeman pattern. **1942** J. D. STRANATHAN *Particles of Mod. Physics* x. 400 Other details of characteristic line spectra, known as hyperfine structure, have made it necessary to assign also to the nuclei of atoms certain magnetic moments. **1950** D. HALLIDAY *Introd. Nucl. Physics* xiii. 479 Hyperfine studies of optical spectral lines. **1953** N. F. RAMSEY in E. Segrè *Exper. Nucl. Physics* I. III. i. 358 If this fine structure is examined more closely, it is often found that each line of the fine structure can in turn be resolved into further lines or 'hyperfine structure' with a separation of the order of 1 cm^{-1}. **1954** H. SEMAT *Introd. Atomic & Nucl. Physics* (ed. 3) viii. 273 Two distinct types of hyperfine structure have been observed. One type . . has been explained as due to the presence of two or more isotopes of the element. **1958** CONDON & ODISHAW *Handbk. Physics* VII. vi. 88/1 Nuclear electric quadrupole hyperfine structure in molecular spectra has yielded a number of nuclear spins and quadrupole moments. **1962** [see FINE STRUCTURE 1 a]. **1965** C. M. H. SMITH *Textbk. Nucl. Physics* viii. 229 If the number of hyperfine components can be counted, the nuclear spin *I* is obtained.

hyperfocal (haɪpə'fəʊkəl), *a.* [f. HYPER- 1 + FOCAL *a.*] Applied to the distance on which a camera must be focused to give the maximum depth of field (see quot. 1957), and to the object plane at this distance.

1905 WASTELL & BAYLEY *Hand Camera* viii. 96 The best position for the lens . . is sometimes called the 'hyperfocal distance'. . . By dividing the hyperfocal distance by two we get the distance beyond which everything is in focus. **1957** AMOS & BIRKINSHAW *Television Engin.* I. ix. 178 If a lens system is focused on infinity, the images are in focus . . for all objects lying between infinity and the hyperfocal distance. If, however, the lens system is focused on the hyperfocal distance, images are in focus for all objects lying between infinity and half the hyperfocal distance. **1961** G. MILLERSON *Technique Television Production* iii. 34 We can adjust any camera lens system so that it is focused on its hyperfocal plane.

hypergamy (haɪ'pɜːgəmɪ). *Anthrop.* [f. HYPER- + -GAMY.] A term first used by W. Coldstream, to denote the custom which forbids the marriage of a woman into a group of lower standing than her own; also *transf.*, of any marriage with a partner of higher social standing. Hence **hy'pergamous** *a.*, pertaining or relating to hypergamy.

1883 D. C. J. IBBETSON *Rep. Census Panjáb 17 Feb. 1881* I. 356 They [*sc.* the social rules] . . may be referred to two laws, which I shall call the laws of isogamy and hypergamy. . . Mr. Coldstream writes from Hushyárpur: . . For 12 years past certain classes of Khatris . . have been agitating to extend the principle of isogamy, and to free themselves from the rule of contracting hypergamous alliances for their daughters. **1903** RISLEY & GAIT *Rep. Census India 1901* §701 *Hypergamy*, or 'marrying up' is the custom which . . compels [a woman] to marry in a group equal or superior in rank. A hypergamous division, therefore, is a group forming part of a series governed by the foregoing rule. **1909** E. S. HARTLAND *Primitive Paternity* I. 266 The Brahmans everywhere follow a custom known as *hypergamy*, by which a man may marry or have sexual relations with a woman of lower rank, but no man of lower rank may marry into a caste above his own. **1921** *Nature* 13 Jan. 646/1 Dr. Rivers said that the term 'hypergamy' had been used loosely by both Sir Herbert Risley and Dr. W. Crooke to denote marriage between groups which differ in rank, but for the sake of clearness the term should be confined to those instances in which there was a characteristic difference between the marriage rules for the two sexes. **1929** *Encycl. Brit.* IV. 979/2 The ancient hypergamous rule which allowed a woman to be married to a man of higher class. **1951** *N. & Q. Anthropol.* (ed. 6) II. iii. 94 Sometimes there is a hypergamous system in which a socially inferior sub-caste can obtain wives from another and higher sub-caste on payment. **1957** *New Statesman* 4 May 566/2 The curse which is ruining, in fantasy if not in their own lives, these brilliant young men of working-class origin and welfare-state opportunity is what anthropologists have dubbed male hypergamy. **1966** *Ibid.* 15 Apr. 548/2 Hypergamous young men claim that the district [*sc.* Chelsea] offers more available classy girls than other art-school areas. *Ibid.* 2 Dec. 832/1 English women have long been able to go in for hypergamy.

hypergelast (haɪ'pɜːdʒiːlæst). [f. HYPER- 4 + Gr. γελαστής a laugher, f. γελᾶν to laugh; cf. GELASTIC *a.*] (See quot. 1877.)

1877 G. MEREDITH *Ess. Comedy* in *New Q. Mag.* VIII. 2 We have another class of men . . whom we may term hypergelasts; the excessive laughers. **1902** *Times Weekly Educ. Suppl.* 19 Dec. p. ii/2 As to the savage, he is a great laugher—a hypergelast, in fact. **1933** *Scrutiny* I. 356 Meredith's hypergelasts are enemies of the Comic spirit, but his ideal audience all laugh, in their polite drawing-room way. **1947** N. CARDUS *Autobiogr.* I. 47 The word 'hypergelast' . . denoting the loud vacant laughers.

hypergol ('haɪpəgɒl). *Astronaut.* [a. G. *hypergol* (one of a series of terms ending in *-ergol*), app. f. HYPER- + Gr. ἔργ-ον work + -OL 3.] A hypergolic rocket propellant.

1947 *Jrnl. Brit. Interplanetary Soc.* VI. 104 Fuels are broadly classified in three groups, monergols, hypergols and non-hypergols. *Ibid.* 105 The distinct property of hypergols is that the reaction is self-starting. **1950** [see HYDRAZINE]. **1969** R. T. HOLZMANN *Chemical Rockets* ii. 140 The use of hypergols is both simple and safe.

So **hyper'golic** *a.*, igniting spontaneously on contact with the oxidant or another propellant; also as *sb.*, a hypergol.

1947 *Jrnl. Brit. Interplanetary Soc.* VI. 106 A third method is to inject auxiliary fuels, hypergolic or self-igniting monergolic, into the chamber before the main fuels. **1965** *Ibid.* XX. 154/2 Ignition does not pose problems as the propellent is hypergolic. **1970** N. ARMSTRONG et al. *First on Moon* i. 28 During the second week of June it was time to start putting hypergolic propellants into the fuel tanks. *Ibid.* iv. 75 The self-igniting . . hypergolics which went into the separate control systems of the command and service module and the lunar module.

hyperhexapod (-'hɛksəpɒd). *Zool.* [f. mod.L. *Hyperhexapoda* sb. pl.; see HYPER- 1 and HEXAPOD.] An animal of the division *Hyperhexapoda* of arthropods, having more than six legs; comprising the classes *Crustacea*, *Arachnida*, and *Myriapoda*. So **hyperhexapodous** (-hɛk'sæpədəs) *a.*, belonging to the *Hyperhexapoda*; having more than six legs.

1855 MAYNE *Expos. Lex.*, Hyperhexapodous.

‖**hypericum** (haɪ'pɛrɪkəm, etymologically hɪpə'raɪkəm). Also 5-8 -on. [L. *hypericum*, *hypericon*, a Gr. ὑπέρεικον (ὑπέρῑκον), f. ὑπέρ over + ἐρείκη heath. Cf. F. *hypéricon*.]

1. *Bot.* A large genus of plants (herbs or shrubs), of very wide distribution, the type of the N.O. *Hypericaceæ*, having pentamerous yellow flowers, stamens arranged in from 3 to 5 clusters, and leaves usually marked with pellucid dots (specially conspicuous in the common species *H. perforatum*); commonly known as St. John's-worts.

1538 TURNER *Libellus, Hypericon*, . . uulgus appellat Saynt Iohns gyrs. **1578** LYTE *Dodoens* I. xliii. 64 S. Johns worte is called in Greeke ὑπερικόν: in Latine and in Shoppes *Hypericum*, and of some *Perforata*. **1646** SIR T. BROWNE *Pseud. Ep.* 41 That any vertue there is in Hipericon to make good the name of *fuga Demonis* . . it is not easie to beleeve. **1741** *Compl. Fam.-Piece* II. iii. 386 Other . . Shrubs . . now in Flower, . . Canary Hypericum, . . shrubby stinking Hypericum. **1784** COWPER *Task* VI. 165 Hypericum all bloom, so thick a swarm Of flow'rs, like flies clothing her slender rods, that scarce a leaf appears. **1842** G. TURNBULL in *Proc. Berw. Nat. Club* II. No. 10. 7 Wild geraniums, hypericums, and willow-herbs.

†**2.** *Pharm.* (in form **hypericon**). A drug prepared from a plant of this genus. Also *oil (of) hypericon*. *Obs.*

1471 RIPLEY *Comp. Alch.* Ep. in Ashm. (1652) 113 Use Hipericon Perforate with milke of Tithimall. **1543** TRAHERON *Vigo's Chirurg.* 94/1 Oyle of hypericon. **1691** J. WILSON *Belphegor* v. ii, I'll have ye burnt in effigy, with brimstone, galbanum, aristolochia, hypericon.

‖**hyperinosis** (ˌhaɪpərɪ'nəʊsɪs). *Path.* [f. HYPER- 5 + Gr. ἴς, ἰν-ός fibre + -OSIS. Cf. F. *hyperinose*.] A diseased state of the blood in which it contains an excessive amount of fibrin: opp. to HYPINOSIS.

1845 G. E. DAY tr. *Simon's Anim. Chem.* I. 280 The blood exhibits the characters of hyperinosis, for the quantity of fibrin is in one instance twice, and in the other thrice the normal amount. **1876** BARTHOLOW *Mat. Med.* (1879) 290 Measures to favor hyperinosis and the coagulation of the blood in the aneurismal sac.

Hence **hyperi'nosed**, **hyperi'notic** *adjs.*, affected with hyperinosis; having excess of fibrin.

1847-9 TODD *Cycl. Anat.* IV. 113/2 Hyperinotic blood. **1877** ROBERTS *Handbk. Med.* (ed. 3) I. 54 The blood is hyperinotic, containing excess of fibrin and coagulating firmly. **1878** A. M. HAMILTON *Nerv. Dis.* 141 Attended by a hyperinosed condition of the blood.

hyperionian, *Anc. Mus.*: see HYPER- 2.

hyperite ('haɪpəraɪt). *Min.* Also **hyperyte**. [? short for *hypersthenite*.] A name for various rocks allied to Diabase and to Diorite; sometimes = HYPERSTHENITE.

1862 DANA *Man. Geol.* II. 78 Hyperite—Granite like in texture . . consisting of cleavable labradorite . . and hypersthene. **1868** —— *Min.* (ed. 5) 210 Hypersthene . . is often associated with labradorite, constituting a dark-colored, granite-like rock, called *Hyperyte*. *Ibid.* 343 If the hornblendic constituent [of Labradorite] is a dark lamellar variety of either hornblende or pyroxene, or the species hypersthene, the rock is called *hyperyte* (or hypersthenyte).

hyperjacobian, *Math.*: see HYPER- 3.

†**hy'perlogism**. *Obs. rare*$^{-1}$. [f. HYPER- 4 + Gr. λογισμ-ός reckoning: formed after HYPOLOGISM.] (See quot.)

1656 tr. *Hobbes' Elem. Philos.* (1839) 147 When the proportion of the first antecedent to the first consequent is greater than that of the second antecedent to the second consequent, the four magnitudes, which are so to one another, may be called *hyperlogism*.

hyperlydian, *Anc. Mus.*: see HYPER- 2.

hypermarket ('haɪpəmɑːkɪt). [f. HYPER- + MARKET *sb.*, translating F. *hypermarché* (f. *marché* market, after *supermarché* SUPERMARKET).] A very large self-service store, usually situated outside a town, having an extensive car park and selling a wide range of goods.

1970 *Guardian* 1 Oct. 7/1 A proposed new 'hypermarket', a gigantic supermarket which could be the precursor of complete shops as big as whole villages. **1971** *Times* 14 July 19/4 The catalyst has been the imminent arrival in the United Kingdom of Carrefour hypermarkets. **1971** *Observer* 3 Oct. 15/2 Hypermarkets are like retail factories, vast warehouse-type buildings. **1972** *New Statesman* 28 Jan. 101/1 By 1966 four hypermarkets (i.e. units of over 25,000 sq. ft. of floor space) had been set up. These huge self-service stores have caught on in France more than in Britain —today there are 144 of them. **1972** *Daily Tel.* 23 May 22/7 Although only a quarter the size of the typical hypermarket, it has all the other ingredients—one-level parking, discount prices, a substantial non-food sector, and late opening.

hypermetamorphosis (ˌhaɪpəmɛtə'mɔːfəsɪs). *Entom.* [f. HYPER- 5 + METAMORPHOSIS.] An extreme form of metamorphosis occurring in certain insects (esp. in beetles of the family *Meloidæ*), in which the animal passes through two or more different larval stages. So **hypermeta'morphism**, the character of undergoing hypermetamorphosis; also **hypermeta'morphic**, **-mor'photic** *adjs.*, characterized by hypermetamorphism.

1875 W. HOUGHTON *Sk. Brit. Ins.* 155 Hypermetamorphosis of the larva, as in the Meloidæ. **1875** DARWIN *Anim. & Pl.* xxvii. (ed. 2) II. 363 Certain beetles . . undergo what has been called a hyper-metamorphosis—that is, they pass through an early stage wholly different from the ordinary grub-like larva. **1881** R. MCLACHLAN in *Encycl. Brit.* XIII. 147/1 'Hypermetamorphism' . . in which the larva at one period of its life assumes a very different form and habit from those of another period. *Ibid.* 149/1 The extraordinary genus *Sitaris* (equally hypermetamorphotic), a parasite in bees' nests. **1888** ROLLESTON & JACKSON *Anim. Life* 508 In a few instances (*Mantispa* among *Neuroptera*, *Meloidæ* among *Coleoptera*) there is a hyper-metamorphosis. The first larva is Campodeiform, the second more or less eruciform.

hypermeter (haɪ'pɜːmɪtə(r)). [ad. Gr. ὑπέρμετρ-ος, -ον, beyond measure, beyond metre, f. μέτρον measure. In mod.F. *hypermètre*.]

1. *Pros.* A hypermetric verse.

1656 BLOUNT *Glossogr.*, *Hypermeter*, a verse having a redundant syllable, or one syllable above measure; called by some a feminine Verse.

2. (*humorous nonce-use*.) A person above the ordinary stature.

1713 ADDISON *Guardian* No. 108 ¶3 When a man rises beyond six foot, he is an hypermeter, and may be admitted into the tall club.

hypermetric (haɪpə'mɛtrɪk), *a.* [f. Gr. ὑπέρμετρ-ος (see prec.) + -IC; cf. μετρικός METRIC.]

1. *Pros.* Of a 'verse' or line: Having one or more syllables beyond those normal to the metre; having a redundant syllable or syllables. Also said of the redundant syllable. Used esp. of Old English verse.

1865 *Athenæum* No. 1975. 302/3 Hypermetric lines. **1887** *Pall Mall G.* 29 Aug. 3/2 'While heav'n is silver o'er him, and underfoot', for example, is hypermetric. **1892** F. J. MATHER in *Mod. Lang. Notes* VII. 200 It will be well to note the occurrences of hypermetric lines in the different poems. **1906** G. P. KRAPP *Andreas* p. xlvii, *Beowulf* (which contains twelve hypermetric lines). **1958** A. J. BLISS *Metre of Beowulf* 96 The distribution of hypermetric verses varies from poem

to poem. **1970** M. SWANTON *Dream of Road* 61 Blocks of hypermetric verse used contrapuntally to accommodate significantly more complex thematic material.

2. *gen.* Beyond measure, excessive, immoderate.

1854 LADY LYTTON *Behind the Scenes* II. viii. II. 34 His sublimated hypermetric impudence.

hyper'metrical, *a. Pros.* [f. as prec. + -AL[1].] = prec. 1.

1751 JOHNSON *Rambler* No. 88 ¶15 Milton frequently uses..the hypermetrical or redundant line of eleven syllables. **1871** *Public Sch. Lat. Gram.* 466 Hypermetrical verses were introduced by Ennius, probably..from his misapprehending Homer. **1886** J. B. MAYOR *Eng. Metre* vi. 98 Verses with hypermetrical syllables. **1891** J. W. BRIGHT *Anglo-Saxon Reader* 238 These hypermetrical half-lines occur either singly or in groups, and usually add dignity to the sense and movement of the passage. **1922** F. KLAEBER *Beowulf* p. lxxi, Groups of emphatic hypermetrical types are introduced three times. **1935** A. C. BARTLETT *Larger Rhet. Patterns Anglo-Saxon Poetry* 70 The hypermetrical irregularities of the other Anglo-Saxon poems. **1958** A. J. BLISS *Metre of Beowulf* 88 It is common ground that the vast majority of hypermetrical verses end with a group of syllables which is exactly equivalent to an ordinary verse.

hypermetrope (haɪpə'mɛtrəʊp). *Path.* [mod. f. Gr. ὑπέρμετρ-ος beyond measure + ὤψ, ὠπ-α eye.] A person affected with hypermetropia.

1864 tr. *Donders' Accom. & Refr. Eye* 620 Hypermetropes ..lose for a time their asthenopia. **1875** H. WALTON *Dis. Eye* 345 The hypermetropes have a little more difficulty in seeing at all ranges. **1893** *Brit. Med. Jrnl.* 30 Sept. 732 The eye-strain necessary in hypermetropes and others to focus a clear image on the retina.

‖**hypermetropia** (ˌhaɪpəmɪ'trəʊpɪə). *Path.* Also in anglicized form **hypermetropy** (-'mɛtrəpɪ). [mod.L., f. as prec. + *-ia* -IA[1].] An affection of the eye, usually due to a flattened form of the eyeball, in which the focus of parallel rays lies behind instead of on the retina; 'long-sightedness'.

1868 DARWIN *Anim. & Pl.* xii. II. 8 Hypermetropia, or morbidly long sight: in this affection, the organ..is too flat from front to back. **1878** T. BRYANT *Pract. Surg.* I. 300 This anomaly is known as hypermetropia or far sight. **1880** LE CONTE *Sight* 51 Hypermetropy is the true opposite of Myopy.

hypermetropic (-'ɒpɪk), *a.* [f. as prec. + -IC.] Pertaining to or affected with hypermetropia; 'long-sighted'.

1864 tr. *Donders' Accom. & Refr. Eye* viii. 525 The compound hypermetropic astigmatism often keeps very close to the simple. **1870** *Pall Mall G.* 23 Feb. 3/3 Hypermetropic subjects are not, except in extreme cases, conscious that they see differently from others. **1876** LOWE in *Life* I. 5 The other [eye] was hypermetropic.

hypermixolydian, *Anc. Mus.*: see HYPER- 2.

hypermodern (haɪpə'mɒdən), *a.* [f. HYPER- 4 a. + MODERN *a.*] Excessively modern; *spec.* in Chess, of or pertaining to the strategy, first used in the early 20th cent., of controlling the centre of the board with pieces at a distance.

1923 *Brit. Chess Mag.* Sept. 338 What is claimed as hyper-modern turns out to be..respectably medieval. **1945** KOESTLER *Yogi & Commissar* III. i. 127 His flair for hyper-modern avant-garde methods in Economy,..and Warfare. **1951** 'ASSIAC' *Adventure in Chess* II. v. 75 This 'hypermodern' move has been all the rage during the last few years. **1966** G. N. LEECH *Eng. in Advertising* xxii. 196 These extra features..add animation to the language, imparting a racy, hyper-modern image of the product. **1970** A. SUNNUCKS *Encycl. Chess* 41 An exponent of the ideas of the hypermodern school of chess.

Hence **hyper'modern, hyper'modernist** *sbs.*; **hypermo'dernity**.

1923 J. HART tr. *Reti's Mod. Ideas in Chess* v. 122 The Hyper-moderns are the greatest opponents of routine play. **1925** *Brit. Chess Mag.* May 219 *Humpeldinck's opening*.. may be fairly described as the *dernier cri* of hypermodernity, the most up-to-date of the 'hypermodern' openings. **1959** B. J. HORTON *Dict. Mod. Chess* 89/2 The long-term plan of the hypermodernist was to allow the enemy to occupy the center and then to demolish him later.

hypernic ('haɪpənɪk, haɪ'pɜːnɪk). [f. HYPER- + *Nic(aragua.)*] A wood from one of several tropical American trees, esp. *Hæmatoxylon brasiletto*, or the red dye extracted from it. Also *attrib.*

1897 C. T. DAVIS *Manuf. Leather* (ed. 2) xlii. 567 Take 10 lbs. hypernic chips... Add the hypernic solution by degrees. **1924** RECORD & MELL *Timbers Tropical Amer.* 247 The wood [of *Haematoxylon brasiletto*] from Nicaragua is known..in the trade as Nicaragua wood or 'hypernic', the latter term coined to indicate a superlative quality of the wood from that country, but subsequently applied rather indiscriminately to any red dyewood or dyewood extract. **1971** R. J. ADROSKO *Nat. Dyes & Home Dyeing* 26 Besides being called by the other common names for brazil-wood, braziletto was also known as Nicaragua wood and hypernick.

†**hypero'chality.** *Obs. nonce-wd.* [f. Gr. ὑπέροχ-ος eminent, distinguished + -AL[1] + -ITY.] Eminence, distinguished position.

1637 BASTWICK *Litany* I. 21, I will..so plauge the Metropolicallity of Yorke and Canterbury, and the hyperocality of all the other Prelats, as I will neuer leaue them.

hyperon ('haɪpərɒn). *Nuclear Physics.* [app. f. HYPER- + -ON[1].] Any of a group of unstable sub-atomic particles that includes all the baryons apart from the proton and neutron; any strongly interacting particle with half-integral spin and a mass greater than that of the nucleons.

1953 *Compt. Rend. du 3me Congrès Internat. sur le Rayonnement Cosmique* 269 Nomenclature more frequently used during the conference... Groups of particles... H-particles (hyperons): symbol H: particles with mass intermediate between those of the neutron and the deuteron (this definition to be revised if 'fundamental' particles heavier than the deuteron are found). **1963** S. TOLANSKY *Introd. Atomic Physics* (ed. 5) xxiii. 391 The baryons..can best be subdivided into two groups namely (a) the familiar nucleons,..(b) the extremely unstable somewhat heavier particles, now called hyperons. **1965** *New Scientist* 18 Mar. 738/3 The SU(3) symmetry relates not just the proton and the neutron one to another, but includes also in one multiplet the six particles known as hyperons.

Hence **hype'ronic** *a.*

1956 [see HYPERCHARGE]. **1969** *Physical Rev. Lett.* XXII. 1238/1 Σ^- hyperons are formed in the targets through the reactions $K^- + p \to \Sigma^- + \pi^+$ and $K^- + n \to \Sigma^- + \pi^0$, and upon capture by target nuclei make hyperonic atoms. **1970** *Physics Lett.* XXXIII. B. 230/2 The capture of the Σ^- hyperons takes place in atomic levels with high main quantum number *n*... The typical pattern of the Σ hyperonic X-rays is determined by the fact that the Σ^- hyperon..is a strongly interacting particle.

‖**hyperoödon** (haɪpə'rəʊədɒn). *Zool.* [mod.L. (1803), f. Gr. ὑπερῷ-ος that is above, superior, or ὑπερῴ-η palate + ὀδούς, ὀδοντ- tooth.] A genus of Cetacea, containing the bottle-nosed whales.

1843 *Penny Cycl.* XXVII. 274/1 (Whales) The Hyperoodons, which only have a few teeth. **1854** OWEN in *Circ. Sc., Organ. Nat.* I. 278 The great bottle-nose or hyperoodon. **1876** tr. *Beneden's Anim. Parasites* 155 Among these skeletons there were several hyperoodons and other cetacea.

‖**hyperopia** (-'əʊpɪə). *Path.* [f. HYPER- 5 + Gr. ὤψ, ὠπ-α eye + *-ia* -IA[1].] = HYPERMETROPIA. So **hyperopic** (-'ɒpɪk) *a.* = HYPERMETROPIC.

1884 H. E. MITCHELL in *N. York Med. Jrnl.* 27 Dec. 720 The hyperopic or myopic astigmatism. **1886** *Syd. Soc. Lex., Hyperopia.* **1889** *Brit. Med. Jrnl.* 28 Sept. 702/2 The hyperopic eye.

hyperosmolality (ˌhaɪpərɒzməʊ'lælɪtɪ). *Med.* [f. HYPER- + OSMOLALITY.] = HYPEROSMOLARITY.

1959 *Pediatric Clinics N. Amer.* VI. 259 In severe hyperosmolality there may be a striking reduction of cerebro-spinal fluid pressure. **1963** *Amer. Jrnl. Cardiol.* XII. 654/2 Hypernatremia and hyperosmolality of serum result from loss of water without sodium. **1972** [see *hyperosmolar* adj.].

hyperosmolarity (ˌhaɪpərɒzməʊ'lærɪtɪ). *Med.* [f. HYPER- + OSMOLARITY.] The condition (in a bodily fluid, esp. serum) of having abnormally high osmotic pressure; also, the condition (in an individual) of having such serum.

1947 *Amer. Jrnl. Dis. Child.* LXXIV. 684 The less the ability of the kidney to excrete urine of high solute content, the more readily hyperosmolarity of the body fluid develops. **1958** *Jrnl. Chronic Dis.* VII. 1 The ultimate effect of hyperosmolarity of serum is dehydration of cells. **1963** *Lancet* 20 Apr. 891/1 We saw a patient with marked hyperosmolarity, due to an unusually high plasma-sodium, dehydration, and moderate ketonuria, but no loss of consciousness. **1965** *Neurology* XV. 205/1 Hyperosmolarity secondary to hypernatremia in various clinical states is known to be associated with severe neurological disturbances.

So **hyperos'molar** *a.*, of, exhibiting, or associated with hyperosmolarity.

1953 *Amer. Jrnl. Med.* XV. 185/1 After discontinuance of pitressin the hyperosmolar state promptly recurred. **1966** *Lancet* 26 Mar. 679/2 Eight patients with hyperosmolar non-ketoacidotic diabetic coma were new diabetics with an average age of 63 years. **1972** *Science* 19 May 815 Malone et al. stated that severe hyperosmolar dehydration could be responsible for the entire galactose toxicity syndrome. However, we have concluded..that hyperosmolality per se is not the major factor responsible.

‖**hyperostosis** (ˌhaɪpərɒ'stəʊsɪs). *Path.* and *Physiol.* Pl. **-oses**. [f. HYPER- 5 + Gr. ὀστέον, ὀστο- bone: see -OSIS.] An overgrowth or increase of bony tissue; hypertrophy of bone; an outgrowth of bone from a bone; exostosis.

1835–6 TODD *Cycl. Anat.* I. 745/2 Cases of hyperostosis in which there is a uniform deposit of bone. **1878** T. BRYANT *Pract. Surg.* I. 395 Hyperostosis of the bony meatus. **1897** ALLBUTT *Syst. Med.* III. 117 When the hyperostoses are large they remain in a modified form.

Hence **hyperostotic** (-'ɒtɪk) *a.*, affected with hyperostosis.

1867 J. B. DAVIS *Thes. Craniorum* 127 This..skull is heavy and hyperostotic, and connected with this state there is a premature closure of the sutures.

hyperoxidation (-ɒksɪ'deɪʃən). [f. HYPER- 4 + OXIDATION.] Excessive oxidation.

1876 HARLEY *Mat. Med.* (ed. 6) 164 Due to hyperoxydation of the blood.

hyperoxide (-'ɒksaɪd), *sb. Chem.* [f. HYPER- 7 + OXIDE.] = PEROXIDE.

1855 MAYNE *Expos. Lex., Hyperoxydum*, term employed by Berzelius..: a hyperoxide. **1879** G. PRESCOTT *Sp. Telephone* 38 Hyperoxide of lead..may be used.

†**hype'roxide,** *a. Obs.* [a. F. *hyperoxyde*, irreg. f. Gr. ὑπέροξυ-ς exceeding sharp.] Extremely sharp (in form, taste, etc.); very acute or acid.

1805–17 R. JAMESON *Char. Min.* (ed. 3) 209 Hyper-oxide ([Fr.] hyper-oxyde); that is to say, uncommonly acute, as in the variety of calcareous-spar, which consists of two rhomboids, of which the one is acute and inverted, and the other much more acute. **1855** MAYNE *Expos. Lex., Hyperoxys*,..superacute; superacid: hyperoxide.

hyperoxygenate (-'ɒksɪdʒɪneɪt), *v.* [f. HYPER- 4 + OXYGENATE.] *trans.* To impregnate or combine with an excess of oxygen; to supersaturate with oxygen. (Chiefly in pa. pple.)

1793 BEDDOES *Calculus* 223 By surcharging the blood with oxygene, by hyper-oxygenating it, if I may use the expression. *Ibid.* 264 An hyper-oxygenated atmosphere. **1803** *Ann. Rev.* I. 377/1 All those alkaline and earthy salts.. are shown..to be hyperoxygenated muriates. **1855** MAYNE *Expos. Lex., Hyperoxygenatus*,..hyperoxygenated.

b. (*humorous nonce-use*, with allusion to Gr. ὀξύς sharp, acid.) To impart excess of sourness to.

c **1811** SOUTHEY *Let. to J. Murray* in Smiles *Mem. J. Murray* (1891) I. 198 An old huckstering grocer..whose natural sourness..is hyperoxygenated by Methodism.

So **hyperoxyge'nation**, the action of hyperoxygenating or condition of being hyperoxygenated; **hype'roxygenize** *v. trans.* = HYPEROXYGENATE (chiefly in pa. pple.).

1793 E. DARWIN in Beddoes *Lett.* 61 Your..reasonings.. indicate..hyperoxygenation to be the cause of this fatal disease [consumption]. **1802** CHENEVIX in *Phil. Trans.* XCII. 126 Oxygenized and hyperoxygenized muriatic acids. **1811** *Edin. Rev.* XVII. 407 The acid supposed to be hyperoxygenized. **1875** H. C. WOOD *Therap.* (1879) 278 Dr. Colton..maintains the absurdity that nitrous oxide produces hyperoxygenation of the blood.

†**hyperoxymuriate** (ˌhaɪpərɒksɪ'mjʊərɪət). *Chem. Obs.* [f. HYPER- 7 + OXYMURIATE.] A salt of 'hyperoxymuriatic' (now called chloric) acid; a chlorate.

1794 G. ADAMS *Nat. & Exp. Philos.* I. App. 546 Hyper-oxymuriats—by heat converted to muriats. **1812** SIR H. DAVY *Chem. Philos.* 228 From any of the salts called hyper-oxymuriates, oxygene is procured by a dull red heat. 100 grams of the hyperoxymuriate of potassa afford about 114 cubical inches oxygene gas. **1823** [see CHLORATE]. **1854** J. SCOFFERN in *Orr's Circ. Sc., Chem.* 361 Salts..termed chlorates, but formerly hyper-oxy-muriates.

†**hyperoxymuri'atic,** *a. Chem. Obs.* [f. as prec. + OXYMURIATIC.] In *h. acid*, the old name of chloric acid $HClO_3$, as containing a larger amount of oxygen than an 'oxymuriatic' (chlorous) acid, $HClO_2$.

1794 G. ADAMS *Nat. & Exp. Philos.* I. App. 541 The oxymuriatic, the hyperoxymuriatic..acids. **1807** T. THOMSON *Chem.* (ed. 3) II. 237 Berthollet..concluded from them, that the oxymuriatic acid had been decomposed during the process; that..another portion combined with an additional dose of oxygen, and was converted into hyperoxymuriatic acid.

hyperparasite (-'pærəsaɪt). *Zool.* [f. HYPER- 1 + PARASITE.] An animal parasitic upon a parasite, as certain insects in the larval state. So **hyperpara'sitic** *a.*, parasitic on or in a parasite; **hyper'parasitism**, the condition of being hyperparasitic, as exemplified by certain *Ichneumonidæ* and *Chalcididæ*, the larvæ of which live in the bodies of other insect parasites.

1833 A. H. HALIDAY in *Entomol. Mag.* I. 482, I am not aware that any of them [*sc.* a group of ichneumons] are hyperparasitic. **1886** *Nature* 6 May 16/2 About 25 species of the various parasitic and hyper-parasitic groups [of ants]. **1889** *Cent. Dict.*, Hyperparasite, hyperparasitism. **1897** L. O. HOWARD *Study in Insect Parasitism* 14 Many parasites suffer..from the attacks of hyperparasites. **1906** J. W. FOLSOM *Entomol.* x. 312 (*heading*) Hyperparasitism. **1914** *Entomologist* XLVII. 77 C. W. Colthrup sent me..two females which he had captured with three specimens of the hyperparasite *Hemiteles areator*. **1932** E. STEP *Bees, Wasps, Ants* 185 These parasites [*sc.* Braconidæ]..are in turn attacked by still smaller species—hyperparasites. **1951** G. LAPAGE *Parasitic Animals* ix. 264 Many species of Hymenoptera implant their eggs inside the bodies of other parasitic insects, so that they provide good examples of hyperparasitism. **1952** A. LYSAGHT tr. *Caullery's Parasitism & Symbiosis* vi. 108 Sometimes, too, under new conditions, a parasite changes into a hyperparasite. **1964** T. C. CHENG *Biol. Animal Parasites* 143/1 Various species of *Nosema* and *Glugea* are capable of hyperparasitism in larval and adult helminths. *Ibid.*, One species of *Nosema*..is hyperparasitic in tapeworms.

ˌ**hyperpara'thyroidism.** *Med.* [f. HYPER- 5 + PARATHYROID + -ISM.] A condition in which there is an abnormally high level of parathyroid hormone in the blood, resulting in the loss of calcium from the bones, which become brittle.

1917 C. VOEGTLIN in *Surg., Gynecol. & Obstetr.* XXV. 249 A condition which might justly be termed hyperparathyroidism is unknown at the present time. **1948** ALBRIGHT & REIFENSTEIN *Parathyroid Glands* iii. 67 It is a

fact, however, that one may have severe hyperparathyroidism and show no clinical, roentgenological, or histological evidence of bone disease... For all practical purposes, it usually comes down to whether or not the patient drinks milk. **1966** WRIGHT & SYMMERS *Systemic Path.* II. xxxii. 1127/1 Secondary hyperparathyroidism occurs when more parathyroid hormone is required by the body than under normal circumstances. **1971** RIMOIN & SCHIMKE *Genetic Disorders Endocrine Glands* iv. 87 The symptoms of primary hyperparathyroidism are essentially those of hypercalcemia.

Hence ˌ**hyperparaˈthyroid** *a.*, of or having hyperparathyroidism.

1961 *Lancet* 16 Sept. 641/1 Hyperparathyroid bone disease was the first form of the disorder to be recognised. **1966** WRIGHT & SYMMERS *Systemic Path.* II. xxxii. 1130/1 'Parathyroid poisoning' is a term that has been applied to the sudden increase in the extent of metastatic calcification of organs..when a high calcium diet is forced on the hyperparathyroid patient.

hyperper (haɪˈpɜːpə(r)). *Numism.* [ad. med.L. *hyperperum, -pyrum*, ad. Gr. ὑπέρπυρον, f. ὑπέρ HYPER- + πῦρ fire: applied to gold highly refined by fire.] A Byzantine coin; the gold solidus (which at the cession of Crete was rather heavier than a half-sovereign). Cf. Du Cange *Dissert. de inf. ævi numismatibus* (Rome 1755) 123.

1598 HAKLUYT *Voy.* I. 94 For each carte loade they giue two webbes of cotton amounting to the value of half an yperpera. **1886** J. BURY in *Jrnl. Hellenic Stud.* VII. 312 By this compact Boniface ceded to Venice Crete and the sum of 100,000 hyperpers.

hyperphoric (haɪpəˈfɒrɪk), *a.* [f. HYPER- 1 + Gr. -φορικ-ός, f. -φέρειν to carry; cf. ὑπερφέρειν to carry over.] **1.** (See quot.)

1889 *Nature* 21 Nov. 49 Changes brought about by the introduction of a new, or the removal of an old mineral (e.g. dolomitization) are treated under the head of hyperphoric change.

2. *Ophthalm.* (See s.v. HYPER- IV.)

hyperphrygian, *Anc. Mus.*: see HYPER- 2.

hyperphysical (haɪpəˈfɪzɪkəl), *a.* [f. HYPER- 1 + PHYSICAL.] Above or beyond what is physical; supernatural.

1600 *Dr. Dodypoll* II. iii. in Bullen *O. Pl.* III. 121 Two sorts of dreams, One sort whereof are only phisicall,.. The other Hiperphisicall. **1686** GOAD *Celest. Bodies* II. xiv. 358 We don't introduce Hyperphysical Causes to defeat Natural, but only unite them, and make them agree. **1820** T. JEFFERSON *Writ.* (1830) IV. 332 Speculations hyperphysical and antiphysical. **1843** MILL *Logic* I. iii. §4 The existence of God, the soul, and other hyperphysical objects.

Hence **hyperˈphysically** *adv.*, in a hyperphysical manner.

1842 SIR W. HAMILTON in *Reid's Wks.* I. 210 *note*, Both the organic motions in the brain..and the representations in the mind itself, hyperphysically determined on occasion of those motions.

hyperˈphysics. [f. HYPER- 1 + PHYSICS.] The science or subject of supernatural things.

1855 in MAYNE *Expos. Lex.* **1878** F. FERGUSON *Life Christ* vi. 68 He called upon them to explain physics and metaphysics, hyperphysics and hypophysics.

‖**hyperplasia** (haɪpəˈpleɪzɪə). *Path.* [mod.L., f. HYPER- 5 + Gr. πλάσις formation, f. πλάσσειν to form. Cf. F. *hyperplasie*.] A form of hypertrophy consisting in abnormal multiplication of the cellular elements of a part or organ; excessive cell-formation.

1861 BUMSTEAD *Ven. Dis.* (1879) 593 In either case hyperplasia is the morbid process, but in scleroses the newly-formed cells persist..while in gummata they are eliminated. **1873** T. H. GREEN *Introd. Pathol.* 93 The increased nutritive activity of the elements, which leads to an increase in their *size*, leads also to an increase in their *number*, and to the formation of a new tissue, which is similar to that from which it originated:—this is termed numerical hypertrophy, or hyperplasia.

So ˈ**hyperplasm** = prec.; **hyperplasic** (-ˈplæzɪk), **hyperˈplastic** *adjs.*, of, pertaining to, or exhibiting hyperplasia.

1873 T. H. GREEN *Introd. Pathol.* 149 The new formation of lymphatic tissue is in the first place hyperplastic.. subsequently, however, it may become heteroplastic. *Ibid.* 258 As the fever subsides, the hyperæmia diminishes, the hyperplastic process ceases. **1876** GROSS *Dis. Bladder* 48 Epithelial hyperplasm, with epidermoid transformation. **1886** *Syd. Soc. Lex.*, *Hyperplasic*.

ˌ**hyperpolariˈzation.** *Physiol.* [f. HYPER- + POLARIZATION.] An increase in the potential difference across the membrane of a nerve fibre above the normal resting potential, so that the inside of the fibre becomes (or is) even more negative with respect to the outside.

1946 LORENTE DE NÓ & FENG in *Jrnl. Cellular & Compar. Physiol.* XXVIII. 412 This overshooting is analogous to the temporary hyperpolarization of the membrane (positive after-potential) which occurs after the end of tetani. **1955** *Acta Physiol. Scand.* XXXV. 12 The hyperpolarization usually amounts to 25–35 mV. *Ibid.*, The rate of hyperpolarization is about 150 mV/sec. **1966** C. F. STEVENS *Neurophysiol.* ii. 13 Any change which decreases the inside-outside potential difference is known as a depolarization, whereas an increase in the membrane potential is called a hyperpolarization. **1971** *Nature* 9 July 123/1 Lundberg inserted intracellular electrodes in secretory cells of this gland and observed a hyperpolarization of 5–20 mV with a latency of 200–400 ms after applying single shocks to the chorda tympani nerve.

So **hyperˈpolarize** *v. trans.*, to produce such a change in (a nerve fibre); *intr.*, to undergo such a change; **hyperˈpolarizing** *vbl. sb.*

1950 *Jrnl. Cellular & Compar. Physiol.* XXXV. Suppl. II. 105 It appears that presynaptic impulses may exert upon the ganglion cells a catelectrotonic (depolarizing) action as well as an anelectrotonic (hyperpolarizing) action. **1955** *Jrnl. Physiol.* CXXX. 394 On hyperpolarizing the motoneurone ..the amplitude of the e.p.s.p. was only slightly affected. **1971** *Nature* 23 July 269/2 In one pair of touch cells..a depolarizing or a hyperpolarizing synaptic potential was observed when the anterior or the posterior cell was stimulated. **1973** *Ibid.* 9 Mar. 102/1 Most of these cells only hyperpolarize in response to light.

hypersensitive (haɪpəˈsɛnsɪtɪv), *a.* [f. HYPER- 4a + SENSITIVE *a.*] **1.** Sensitive to an abnormal or excessive degree; over-sensitive.

1871 MISS BRADDON *Lovels* ix. 170 Apt to be hypersensitive, and easily disturbed about trifles. **1897** ALLBUTT *Syst. Med.* III. 111 In this condition the reflex apparatus of the glottis is so hypersensitive. **1892** *Jrnl. Mental Sci.* XXXVIII. 525 Charcot and his pupils..believe in the influence of the magnet in hysteria, where the nervous system is hyper-sensitive. **1912** D. H. LAWRENCE *Phoenix II* (1968) 269 This soldier poet is so straight, so free from the modern artist's hyper-sensitive self-consciousness, that we would have more of him. **1939** E. & C. PAUL tr. *Stekel's Technique Analytical Psychotherapy* xx. 283 A woman brought up on religious lines, morally hypersensitive, who pursues ideal aims. **1972** *Oxford Times* 19 May 7/1 Mr Francis Barnes, defending, described Jeffries as a 'retiring and hypersensitive' man who had lived as a semi-recluse for 17 years.

2. *spec.* in *Med.*: characterized by the fact that a marked adverse bodily response may be evoked by some specific substance or agent which (in similar amounts) has no such effect on most individuals. Const. *to*.

1899 E. O. JORDAN tr. *Hueppe's Princ. Bacteriol.* vi. 337 Behring has found that it is possible..to immunize animals so highly..that they..become hyper-sensitive to the toxin. **1906** *Jrnl. Amer. Med. Assoc.* 29 Sept. 1007/2 At first glance it would appear much more important for an organism to be hyposensitive than hypersensitive to infectious processes, but a closer study of the complex problems of immunity develops the curious fact that resistance to disease may be largely gained through a process of hypersusceptibility. **1922** *Jrnl. Immunol.* VII. 128 The similarity of symptoms of drug reactions with those of foreign proteins in specifically hypersensitive persons. **1935** N. P. SHERWOOD *Immunol.* xxiii. 465 One injection of a nontoxic dose of horse serum will render guinea pigs hypersensitive to a second injection of the antigen provided an interval of almost ten days is allowed to intervene. **1951** WHITBY & HYNES *Med. Bacteriol.* (ed. 5) vii. 95 Human idiosyncrasy..differs in some important respects from anaphylaxis. The exciting agent is not necessarily an antigen; patients may become hypersensitive, for example, to drugs with a very simple chemical structure. **1964** W. G. SMITH *Allergy & Tissue Metabolism* i. 7 In patients who are specifically hypersensitive to a single allergen, it is very likely that sensitisation has been brought about by a previous contact with the allergen. *Ibid.* 13 A vast literature exists on histamine..and leaves no doubt about its involvement in the hypersensitive state.

3. *Photogr.* Of a film or plate, or its emulsion: hypersensitized (see HYPERSENSITIZE *v.* b).

1937 *Discovery* May p. xliv (Advt.), Hypersensitive panchromatic roll film. **1965** M. J. LANGFORD *Basic Photogr.* x. 179 Red-pan or hypersensitive pan materials are.. sensitive to red and respond up to 6,800 Å.

hyperˈsensitiveness. [f. prec., after *sensitive, sensitiveness.*] = next. **a.** *gen.* **b.** *Med.* (See HYPERSENSITIVE *a.* 2.)

In medical use *hypersensitiveness* was at first commoner than *hypersensitivity*, but the latter is now more usual.

a. 1876 GEO. ELIOT *Dan. Der.* xxxvii, As private as the utmost hypersensitiveness could desire. **1898** W. SCHEPPEGRELL *Electr. in Dis. Nose, Throat & Ear* xxi. 218 In hyperesthetic rhinitis, Sajous recommends that each point of hypersensitiveness be destroyed by means of the electrocautery. **1917** GLUECK & LIND tr. *Adler's Neurotic Constitution* (1921) 164 Every one who has become acquainted with the hypersensitiveness of neurotic subjects knows with what slight cause they feel themselves to be undervalued. **1939** E. & C. PAUL tr. *Stekel's Technique Analytical Psychotherapy* xxi. 327 A persistent illusion of a bad smell, disturbances of taste,..may all be indications of an uneasy conscience; so may hypersensitiveness of certain areas of skin. **1951** I. COMPTON-BURNETT *Darkness & Day* 21 One feels that being alive to all the troubles about one is a sign of sensitiveness and feeling, when it may be hypersensitiveness and trying for other people.

b. 1906 *Jrnl. Amer. Med. Assoc.* 29 Sept. 1009/1 As far as we know, this is the first recorded instance in which hypersensitiveness, or anaphylaxis, has been experimentally shown to be transmitted from a mother to her young. **1922** *Jrnl. Immunol.* VII. 128 The condition now known as human hypersensitiveness or allergy. **1940** BECKER & OBERMAYER *Mod. Dermatol. & Syphilol.* vii. 75/2 The resulting inflammation is of the vesicular type, but a condition of hypersensitiveness does not have to be considered, since everyone's skin reacts to this solution. **1953** F. K. HANSEL *Clin. Allergy* iii. 58 The existence of an inherited predisposition is certainly not a prerequisite to the development of hypersensitiveness.

ˌ**hypersensiˈtivity.** [f. as prec., after *sensitivity*.] The state or fact of being hypersensitive. **a.** *Med.* (See HYPERSENSITIVE *a.* 2.) **b.** *gen.*

a. 1914 *Q. Jrnl. Med.* VII. 273 Richet, in 1902, introduced the term 'anaphylaxis' to explain certain phenomena of hypersensitivity. *Ibid.* 275 Before hypersensitivity can manifest itself a period of time must be allowed to elapse between the first and second injection. **1929** H. G. WELLS *Chem. Aspects Immunity* (ed. 2) ix. 225 One of the most spectacular phenomena discovered in immunity is that of hypersensitivity to foreign proteins. **1946** *Nature* 19 Oct. 554/2 Most human beings appear to give very similar results when subjected to the same degree of exposure [to insect bites], though special cases of hypersensitivity and severe allergy also occur. **1947** L. SCHWARTZ et al. *Occup. Dis. Skin* (ed. 2) iv. 43 The tendency to hypersensitivity may be inherited; it may be due to..a pigment deficiency causing hypersensitivity to light; or there may be a true allergy caused by exposure to an allergen. **1964** M. HYNES *Med. Bacteriol.* (ed. 8) viii. 104 Dermal hypersensitivity [ed. 5–7 (1951–61): hypersensitiveness] to dyes, solvents, etc., is most conveniently demonstrated by a patch test. **1970** PASSMORE & ROBSON *Compan. Med. Stud.* II. xxii. 19/1 It was soon found that hypersensitivity could be evoked also by intrinsically harmless substances such as..simple chemicals.

b. 1954 J. A. HADFIELD *Dreams & Nightmares* xi. 221 If that were so, hypersensitivity of hearing would be ruled out. **1956** I. MURDOCH *Flight from Enchanter* x. 140 It was as if Mischa were deliberately reducing him to a state of hypersensitivity and confusion. **1970** D. W. SWANSON et al. *Paranoid* iii. 61 The patient's hypersensitivity to others' feelings and failings can be disconcerting when focused on the interviewer. **1972** *Daily Colonist* (Victoria, B.C.) 27 Feb. 4/5 A hypersensitivity to criticism hangs them all up in time.

ˌ**hypersensitiˈzation.** [f. next + -ATION.] The action or process of hypersensitizing, or the state of being hypersensitized.

a. *Med.* **b.** *Photogr.*

a. 1908 *Jrnl. Amer. Med. Assoc.* 15 Feb. 528/1 The remarkable phenomenon of hypersensitization or anaphylaxis. **1947** L. SCHWARTZ et al. *Occup. Dis. Skin* (ed. 2) iv. 39 If such a worker is able to keep on working, the dermatitis clears up... In other words exposure first causes a hypersensitization, then further exposure causes a dermatitis, and still further exposure causes hyposensitization. **1959** *New England Jrnl. Med.* CCLX. 170/2 The use of human gamma globulin rather than that derived from animal plasma significantly diminishes the risk of hypersensitization to a foreign protein.

b. 1933 CARROLL & HUBBARD in *Bureau of Standards Jrnl. Res.* X. 212 We shall use the term 'hypersensitization' to cover any case in which increase in sensitization by a dye is produced by treatment with a material itself colorless or absorbing a spectral region different from that of the dye. *Ibid.* 213 In our experiments hypersensitization always involved an increase in relative sensitivity to the longer wave lengths. **1956** *Electronic Engin.* Feb. 78/1 The processes of hyper-sensitization (treatment before exposure) and latensification (treatment after exposure) may give an increase in relative speed of up to two or three times with normal development. **1964** J. ROUBIER *Odham's Pract. Photogr. & Film-Making* ii. 34 The effective speed of an emulsion can be raised by 100% or even 150% by hypersensitisation.

hypersensitize (haɪpəˈsɛnsɪtaɪz), *v.* [f. HYPER- 4c + SENSITIZE *v.*] *trans.* To render hypersensitive. *spec.* **a.** *Med.* (See HYPERSENSITIVE *a.* 2.) **b.** *Photogr.* To increase the speed of (a photographic film or plate, or its emulsion) by immersion in a special solution, exposure to light, or other means, usually before it is exposed in the taking of a photograph (cf. LATENSIFICATION). So **hyperˈsensitized** *ppl. a.*, **hyperˈsensitizing** *vbl. sb.*

1897 G. B. SHAW *Let.* 16 Apr. (1965) 746 Teddy, though hypersensitized..and petulated by more luxury than was good for him in the way of a mammy seems highly and nervously intelligent. **1914** *Q. Jrnl. Med.* VII. 277 In anaphylaxis the degree of specificity is difficult to determine, as a hypersensitized animal has an increased susceptibility to any toxin. *Ibid.* 280 A serum may have strong hypersensitizing power for passive anaphylaxis and yet have no precipitating power. **1917** E. POUND *Let.* 10 Nov. (1971) 123 Still, what the hell else are you? I mean apart from being a citizen, a good fellow.., a grouch, a slightly hypersensitized animal, etc.?? **1920** *Jrnl. Franklin Inst.* CLXXXIX. 25 (*heading*) Hypersensitizing commercial panchromatic plates. **1929** E. J. WALL *Pract. Color Photogr.* (ed. 2) xiii. 173 The exposure with these hypersensitized plates and the aesculin filter is about one-tenth of that required for the normal plate. **1954** tr. *L. P. Clerc's Photogr.* (ed. 3) viii. 178/2 The first exposure 'hypersensitizes' the material towards the second. **1969** M. J. LANGFORD *Adv. Photogr.* viii. 171 'Hypersensitizing' or increasing the speed of an emulsion *before* camera exposure can be carried out chemically or by means of light.

hypersonic (haɪpəˈsɒnɪk), *a.* [f. HYPER- + SONIC *a.*, after *supersonic, ultrasonic.*] **1.** Of, pertaining to, or designating sound waves or vibrations with a frequency greater than about 1000 million Hz. (Cf. ULTRASONIC *a.*)

1937 B. V. R. RAO in *Nature* 22 May 885/1 Spontaneously existing sound-waves of thermal origin of very high frequencies ('hyper-sonic waves'). **1938** —— in *Proc. Indian Acad. Sci.* A. VII. 163 It appears desirable to designate the portion of the acoustic spectrum having a frequency higher than a thousand mega-cycles per second as the 'hyper-sonic' region, while the 'ultra-sonic' region may be taken to extend from one to a thousand mega-cycles per second. **1948** *Rep. Progress Physics* XI. 205 Workers in India particularly have used *hypersonic* to denote ultrasonic phenomena (of thermal origin) at frequencies of the order of 1000 Mc/sec. or higher. **1960** *Physical Rev.* CXVII. 1248 The hypersonic absorption was studied for longitudinal and transverse waves at various frequencies up to 4000 Mc/s. **1963** J. BLITZ *Fund. Ultrasonics* vi. 167 Bömmel and Dransfeld measured the attenuation of both longitudinal and shear waves in quartz at frequencies ranging from 1,000 to 4,000 Mc/s using a hypersonic technique. **1971** *Nature* 24 Sept. 238/2 Mechanical surface waves can now be generated up to 10

GHz. Mechanical waves of these frequencies (up to 100 GHz) are often termed hypersonic.

2. Involving, pertaining to, capable of, or designating speeds greater than about five times the speed of sound. (Cf. SUPERSONIC *a.*)

1946 *Jrnl. Math. & Physics* XXV. 247 Hypersonic flows are flow fields where the fluid velocity is much larger than the velocity of propagation of small disturbances, the velocity of sound. **1958** *Engineering* 14 Mar. 347/2 Flow about bodies at subsonic, supersonic, and hypersonic speeds. **1958** *Times* 19 Dec. 11/7 Hypersonic travel is just possible in the foreseeable future. **1960** *New Scientist* 14 July 88/2 The hypersonic wind tunnel is almost more necessary than the supersonic... A tunnel capable of producing..air speeds between Mach 10 and Mach 27 (something near 18,000 m.p.h.) is now in daily use. **1960** *Nature* 6 Feb. 346/2 The transition from the supersonic to the hypersonic régime occurs at a Mach number of about 5, but all the characteristic features of the latter régime may only become well developed at a much higher Mach number of, say, 15. **1969** *Courier Mail* (Brisbane) 17 Apr. 2 The construction of a 500-seat hypersonic aircraft could cost as much as £4000 million.

hyperspherical, *Math.*: see HYPER- 3.

hypersthene ('haɪpəsθiːn). *Min.* Also **hyperstene.** [ad. F. *hyperstène* (named by Haüy in 1803), f. HYPER- 4 + Gr. σθένος strength; from its superior hardness as compared with hornblende, with which it was formerly confounded. The Eng. form is assimilated to the Greek.] A silicate of iron and magnesium, of the pyroxene group, a greenish-black or greenish-grey mineral, closely allied to hornblende, often exhibiting a peculiar metalloidal lustre.

1808 T. ALLAN *List Min.* 37 Hyperstene. **1821** R. JAMESON *Man. Min.* 132 Prismatoidal Schieler-Spar, or Hypersthene. **1849** DANA *Geol.* xvii. (1850) 632 The pearly crystallization of the light grayish-green hypersthene. **1862** ANSTED *Channel Isl.* II. x. (ed. 2) 259 Varieties of hornblende and hypersthene, with chlorites, serpentines and mica, all abound.

b. *attrib.*, esp. as ***hypersthene rock***: = HYPERSTHENITE.

1838 *Penny Cycl.* XII. 412/1 Dr. McCulloch..first noticed Hypersthene rocks in Skye and Ardnamurchan. **1869** *Contemp. Rev.* XI. 366 The hypersthene mountains are painted in their real blackness. **1886** *Pall Mall G.* 4 Sept. 4/2 The Cuchullins are quite unlike any other mountain group ..the coal-black 'hypersthene' rocks of which they are composed being only found in that district.

Hence **hypersthenic** (haɪpəs'θɛnɪk) *a.*[1], related to or containing hypersthene.

1838 *Penny Cycl.* XII. 412/1 A dyke of Hypersthenic trap was noticed in Radnorshire. *Ibid.*, Hypersthenic sienite. **1862** ANSTED *Channel Isl.* II. x. (ed. 2) 259 Most of the veins are filled up with hypersthenic rocks. **1876** PAGE *Adv. Text-bk. Geol.* vii. 127 The term hypersthenic granite is applied to an admixture of quartz and hypersthene, with scattered flakes of mica.

‖**hypersthenia** (haɪpə'sθiːnɪə). *Path.* [mod.L., f. HYPER- 5 + Gr. σθένος strength.] Extreme or morbid excitement of the vital powers; the opposite of *asthenia.*

1855 in MAYNE *Expos. Lex.* **1886** in *Syd. Soc. Lex.*

Hence **hyper'sthenic** *a.*[2], relating to, characterized by, or producing hypersthenia.

1886 in *Syd. Soc. Lex.*

hypersthenite (haɪpəs'θiːnaɪt). *Min.* [f. HYPERSTHENE + -ITE.] A dark granite-like aggregate of hypersthene and labradorite; also called HYPERITE and NORITE.

1849 MURCHISON *Siluria* App. C. 537 'Greenstones'..are different varieties of hypersthenite and gabbro. **1879** RUTLEY *Study Rocks* xiii. 249 The hypersthenites, or those rocks which consist of rhombic pyroxene in conjunction with triclinic felspar.

hypertely (haɪ'pɜːtɪlɪ, 'haɪpəˌtɛlɪ). *Zool.* [ad. G. *hypertelie* (C. Brunner 1873, in *Verh. Zool.-Bot. Ges. Wien* XXIII. 133), f. Gr. ὑπερτέλειος beyond completeness, f. τέλος end.] Extreme development of size, patterns of behaviour, mimetic coloration, etc. beyond the degree to which these characteristics are apparently useful. Also *fig.* Hence **hyper'telic** *a.*

1895 D. SHARP in *Cambr. Nat. Hist.* V. xiii. 323 Brunner ..came to the conclusion that they [*sc.* close resemblances] cannot be accounted for on the ground of mere utility, and proposed the term Hypertely to express the idea that in these cases the bounds of the useful are transcended. **1920** G. D. H. CARPENTER *Naturalist on Lake Victoria* x. 196 Special procryptic colouring never fails to arouse wonder from its extreme perfection... This complimentary [*sic*] doctrine has been termed Hypertely. **1936** *Nature* 10 Oct. 603/2 We find that intraspecific selection frequently leads to results which are mainly..useless to the species as a whole, including 'hypertelic' characters. **1937** A. HUXLEY *Ends & Means* xiv. 262 We are doing our best to develop a militaristic 'hypertely', to become, in other words, dangerously specialized in the art of killing our fellows. **1953** G. G. SIMPSON *Major Features of Evolution* ix. 282 Almost any case in which size, structure, or habit..is carried to extremes may be cited as hypertely. *Ibid.* 287 Many of the characters commonly designated as hypertelic are striking secondary sexual characters. **1965** B. E. FREEMAN tr. *Vandel's Biospeleol.* xi. 168 Hypertely represents the end of a long orthogenetic evolution.

hypertensin (haɪpə'tɛnsɪn). *Biochem.* [f. HYPERTENS(ION, -IVE *a.* + -IN[1].] Either of two polypeptides, of which one (***hypertensin I***) is formed in the blood by the action of renin on a protein (hypertensinogen), and the other (***hypertensin II***) is derived from it by the loss of two amino-acid residues, causes a rise in blood pressure, and stimulates the secretion of aldosterone; also, analogous polypeptides in animals. Now usually called *angiotensin.*

1939 J. M. MUÑOZ et al. in *Nature* 9 Dec. 980/1 This substance, which we name hypertensin, is different from adrenalin, tyramin, pitressin and urohypertensin. **1954** *Jrnl. Exper. Med.* XCIX. 282 Two types of hypertensin have been demonstrated... The first type..has been designated hypertensin I. It can be rapidly converted to a second, approximately equally pressor compound, hypertensin II. **1956** *Nature* 17 Mar. 527/2 The isolation and purification of a hypertensin peptide, resulting from the action of rabbit renin on ox serum. **1959** A. WHITE et al. *Princ. Biochem.* (ed. 2) xxx. 750 Hypertensin I preparations of slightly different composition have been described, depending on the sources of the renin and the substrate used. *Ibid.*, Hypertensin has also been called angiotonin. A uniform nomenclature has been proposed which would designate this compound as angiotensin.

Hence **ˌhyperten'sinogen** [ad. F. *hypertensinogène* (E. Braun-Menendez 1940, in *Compt. Rend. de la Soc. de Biol.* CXXXIV. 489): see -OGEN], a globulin produced by the liver and present in blood, from which hypertensin I may be liberated by renin.

1941 *Amer. Jrnl. Physiol.* CXXXV. 214 Braun-Menendez has preferred the term hypertensinogen, which implies that it is the substrate on which renin acts. **1965** *New Scientist* 25 Nov. 561/3 Kidney cells, in the presence of a poor blood flow .., secreted an enzyme called renin which converted a normal constituent of plasma (hypertensinogen) into a new substance (hypertensin).

hypertension (haɪpə'tɛnʃən). [f. HYPER- 5 + TENSION *sb.*] **1.** *Med.* Abnormally or excessively high 'tension' or pressure of a bodily fluid.

a. Of arterial blood; ***essential hypertension***, hypertension that has no apparent cause and cannot be explained as a consequence or symptom of some other lesion.

1893 *Brit. Med. Jrnl.* 4 Nov. 997/1 'Hypertension' and 'hypotension' are regarded not as indications, but as *mala in se.* **1927** *Physiol. Rev.* VII. 464 More recent writers have coined the name 'essential hypertension'. **1955** G. W. PICKERING *High Blood Pressure* vi. 130 By current practice which takes not a very high figure, such as 150/100, as the lower limit of hypertension, essential hypertension becomes by far the commonest form of hypertension. **1957** *New Scientist* 9 May 23/1 Hypertension causes one in every four deaths in the United States. **1966** WRIGHT & SYMMERS *Systemic Path.* I. iii. 106/1 The hypertension sometimes found in patients with hyperthyroidism is usually limited to elevation of the systolic pressure (systolic hypertension).

b. Of the intra-ocular fluid.

1918 R. H. ELLIOT *Glaucoma: Textbk. for Student* v. 303 The treatment of established glaucoma. In these cases the hypertension is commonly associated with evidence of ocular congestion. **1969** DUKE-ELDER & JAY in S. Duke-Elder *Syst. Ophthalm.* XI. ix. 630 In some cases the rise in the intra-ocular pressure has been slight and transient, to some extent possibly because the formation of aqueous may have been inhibited by the hypertension itself in a physiological compensatory mechanism.

2. A state of great (nervous or emotional) tension.

1936 *Times Educ. Suppl.* 28 Nov. 429/3 In every such case the nervous instability and hypertension should be treated by relaxation and psychological readjustment. **1947** *Year Bk. Arts in N.Z.* III. 152 Mind burst out... Man's understanding tangled, ripped. Extremes are too much with us and the hypertensions. **1953** J. MASTERS *Lotus & Wind* vii. 101 The opportunity for which she had been tensely waiting was upon her. In a few minutes, as this hypertension and ruthlessness faded in her, it would be gone. **1972** D. HASTON *In High Places* xii. 140 Flying out of Katmandu, I felt really pleased at having a chance to come back so quickly... There was friendliness all around; urgency to do things didn't seem to exist. None of the hypertensions of the West. A relaxing atmosphere.

hypertensive (haɪpə'tɛnsɪv), *a.* and *sb. Med.* [f. prec. + -IVE.] **A.** *adj.* Of, exhibiting, or associated with hypertension, esp. of the blood; tending to raise the blood pressure.

1904 T. C. JANEWAY *Clin. Study Blood-Pressure* vii. 221 The bath-treatment of typhoid fever seems to have as distinct an effect on the blood-pressure curve... I cannot but feel that this hypertensive effect is evidence of an action on the vaso-motor system. **1918** *Endocrinology* II. 94 In case of the more strongly hypertensive extracts, kidney dilation and diuresis, together with augmented blood pressure, occur as the primary reaction. **1939** D. M. DUNLOP *Textbk. Med. Treatm.* 654 Digitalis..does not raise blood pressure in the hypertensive patient. **1954** S. DUKE-ELDER *Parsons' Dis. Eye* (ed. 12) xiv. 212 This involves a rise determined.. by the difficulty experienced by the sticky albuminous aqueous in escaping through the filtration channels at the angle of the anterior chamber (hypertensive iridocyclitis). **1956** *Nature* 17 Mar. 523/2 These [compounds] are highly effective in lowering blood pressure and relieving certain hypertensive symptoms. **1971** *Brit. Med. Bull.* XXVII. 39/1 Hypertensive heart disease, diagnosed on electrocardiographic and radiographic criteria, is also more common among negroes.

B. *ellipt.* as *sb.* A person with arterial hypertension.

1939 D. M. DUNLOP *Textbk. Med. Treatm.* 652 Many hypertensives tend to over-eat. **1961** *Lancet* 2 Sept. 510/2 The systolic and diastolic blood-pressures were slightly higher in the hypertensives' sons. **1972** *Daily Tel.* 22 Nov. 13/8 In hypertensives, prostaglandins can lower the blood pressure.

hyperthermia (haɪpə'θɜːmɪə). *Med.* Also in anglicized form **hyperthermy** ('haɪpəθɜːmɪ) (*rare*). [f. HYPER- 5 + Gr. θέρμη heat + -IA[1].] The condition of having a body temperature substantially above the normal either as a result of natural causes or artificially induced (e.g. for therapeutic purposes).

1886 *Syd. Soc. Lex.*, Hyperthermy. **1887** A. M. BROWN *Contrib. Animal Alkaloids* 143 Intoxication by the extractive matters is accompanied by hyperthermia. **1898** *Nature* 24 Nov. 95 Researches on lesions of the nervous centres produced by hyperthermy. **1921** F. A. WELBY tr. *Luciani's Human Physiol.* V. ii. 82 Billroth..found that the temperature rose to 42·2° after fracture of the sixth cervical vertebra; in a similar case Simon observed a hyperthermia of 44°. **1935** *Jrnl. Amer. Med. Assoc.* 18 May 1788/2 As with all other forms of treatment for chronic infectious arthritis, the results of hyperthermia depend to a marked extent on the duration and activity of the disease. **1941** *Virginia Med. Monthly* Mar. 158/1 It was decided to give the patient another period of hyperthermy, but in view of the attack of substernal pain a medical check-up was requested. **1971** *New Scientist* 15 July 133/2 The gazelles..cannot withstand desiccation to the extent that camels do, and do not show the same degree of hyperthermia. **1971** L. B. ROWELL in E. Simonson *Physiol. Work Capacity & Fatigue* vii. 149 Hyperthermia will be accompanied by high rates of sweat loss and dehydration.

So **hyper'thermic** *a.* [cf. Gr. ὑπέρθερμος overwarm], of or exhibiting hyperthermia.

1896 ALLBUTT *Syst. Med.* I. 154 The 'hyperthermic' state produced by puncture [of the brain] is found to differ from true febrile pyrexia. **1898** W. S. L. BARLOW *Man. Gen. Path.* x. 434 The symptoms presented by a hyperthermic animal when its temperature is reaching a dangerous height are those of severe distress, respiration and pulse are accelerated, and the animal lies outstretched. **1948** [see HYPOTHERMIC *a.*].

hyperthesis (haɪ'pɜːθɪsɪs). [a. Gr. ὑπέρθεσις transposition, f. ὑπέρ HYPER- + θέσις placing.] Transposition, metathesis.

a. *Anc. Pros.* In a logaœdic series, the substitution, for a particular foot in one line, strophe, etc., of another foot in a corresponding line, strophe, etc., involving interchange or reversal of the quantities; e.g. the substitution of an iamb (⏑–) for a trochee (–⏑) or vice versa.

1890 in *Century Dict.*

b. *Philol.* Transposition or metathesis of a letter from a particular syllable to the preceding or following syllable, as in Gr. μέλαινα for *μελανια.

1882 in OGILVIE.

hyperthetic (haɪpə'θɛtɪk), *a.* [ad. Gr. ὑπερθετικός superlative.] Pertaining to or exhibiting hyperthesis.

†**hyper'thetical,** *a. Obs.* [f. as prec. + -AL[1].] Superlative.

*c*1611 CHAPMAN *Iliad* xv. Comm. (R.), These hyperthetical or superlative sort of expressions and illustrations.

hyper'thyroidism. *Med.* [f. HYPER- 5 + THYROID *a.* (*sb.*) + -ISM.] A condition in which the thyroid gland produces more hormone than normal, resulting in an increased rate of metabolism, often with wasting of muscle and loss of weight together with restlessness and emotional instability.

1900 DORLAND *Med. Dict.* 311/1 Hyperthyroidism. **1909** G. DOCK in Osler & McCrae *Syst. Med.* VI. xvii. 431 Hyperthyroidism..seems to be the cause of the exophthalmos. **1912** *Med. Ann.* 3 Sleeplessness following.. fevers, hyperthyroidism, and hysteria. **1961** L. MARTIN *Clinical Endocrinol.* (ed. 3) i. 22 A goitre and signs of mild hyperthyroidism are not uncommon [in gigantism]. **1970** S. GROLLMAN *Human Body* (ed. 2) xvi. 507 The most common form of hyperthyroidism, resulting from a diffuse increase in thyroid tissue, is known as exophthalmic goiter, Graves' disease, or Basedow's disease.

Hence **hyper'thyroid, -thy'roidic** *adjs.*

1916 *Internat. Jrnl. Surg.* XXIX. 312 (*heading*) The etiology of the exophthalmos in hyperthyroid goitre. **1916** *Med. Times* (N.Y.) 7 July 207/1 An impression is given by the hypothyroidic eye which is just the reverse of that made by the typical hyperthyroidic, or exophthalmic organ. **1968** *Listener* 18 July 70/1, I had recently been diagnosed as hyperthyroidic. **1971** N. R. ALPERT *Cardiac Hypertrophy* 55 The pumping function of the hyperthyroid heart.

hypertonia (haɪpə'təʊnɪə). *Med.* Also in anglicized form **hypertony** (haɪ'pɜːtənɪ) (*rare*). [mod.L., f. HYPER- 5 + Gr. τόν-ος TONE *sb.* + -IA[1].] The condition (in muscle or muscular tissue) of being hypertonic.

1842 DUNGLISON *Dict. Med. Sci.* (ed. 3) 368/1 Hypertonia. **1881** J. ROSS *Treat. Dis. Nervous Syst.* I. I. v. 178 The condition of motor excess, or of increased tonus, may be called hypertony. **1905** *Med.-Chir. Trans.* LXXXVIII. 212 The arterial hypertonia is to be regarded as a result of the greater strain thrown on the circulatory mechanism. **1914** A. MORISON *Sensory & Motor Disorders Heart* v. 203 Exaggerated tonic cardiac action tends to be

succeeded by..a minus quantity. Hypertonia necessarily yields to hypotonia. **1933** W. R. BRAIN *Dis. Nervous Syst.* i. 8 Not all muscle-groups exhibit hypertonia in equal degree in hemiplegia. **1962** *Lancet* 27 Jan. 222/1 She was re-examined..and found to have variable and bizarre hypertonia of the jaw, tongue, and neck muscles.

hypertonic (haɪpəˈtɒnɪk), *a.* [f. HYPER- 5 + TONIC *a.*] **1.** *Med.* Exhibiting or characterized by excessive tone or tension (in muscle or muscular tissue).

1855 R. G. MAYNE *Expos. Lex. Med. Sci.* (1860) 484/1 *Hypertonicus*, of or belonging to hypertonia: hypertonic. **1886** *Lancet* 13 Mar. 486/2 For convenience I describe the group of symptoms under the term 'hyper-tonic paresis', a symptomatic nomenclature which commits to no theory. **1907** W. RUSSELL *Arterial Hypertonus* i. 3 The degree of contraction may exceed the limits of normal variation, and when it does the term hypertonic contraction, or merely arterial contraction, will be used here. **1933** W. R. BRAIN *Dis. Nervous Syst.* i. 8 Immediately following a capsular haemorrhage the paralysed limbs are completely flaccid... After a variable interval..tone gradually returns to the affected muscles and they ultimately become hypertonic or 'spastic'. **1966** *McGraw-Hill Encycl. Sci. & Technol.* X. 528/1 When the stretch reflex is absent, the muscle is hypotonic or flaccid; when stretch reflexes are exaggerated ..the muscles are hypertonic or spastic.

2. *Physiol.* Of a solution: having a higher osmotic pressure than some particular solution (usually that in a cell, or a bodily fluid). Const. *to.*

1895 *Jrnl. Physiol.* XVIII. 107 None of the water is taken up from hypertonic or isotonic solutions. **1936** A. P. MATHEWS *Princ. Biochem.* xxxiv. 364 If the solution have an osmotic pressure greater than that of the blood, it is said to be hypertonic to the blood. **1951** WHITBY & HYNES *Med. Bacteriol.* (ed. 5) vi. 73 The optimum salt concentration is usually near the range of isotonicity to body cells; markedly hypertonic saline diminishes the reaction. **1970** A. F. BRADING in E. Bülbring et al. *Smooth Muscle* vi. 172 Tissues will swell in hypotonic solutions, and shrink in hypertonic ones.

hypertonicity (ˌhaɪpətəˈnɪsɪtɪ). [f. prec. + -ITY.] The condition of being hypertonic.

a. *Med.* Of muscle or muscular tissue (see HYPERTONIC *a.* 1); = HYPERTONIA.

1886 *Brain* IX. 231 A condition of extreme functional over-activity of the ganglion cells of the anterior cornua of the cord and medulla, causing hyper-tonicity of the entire muscular system. **1923** J. F. H. DALLY *High Blood Pressure* v. 64 Arterial hypertonicity, in larger or smaller areas, is met with in a host of disorders. **1949** *Jrnl. Neurophysiol.* XII. 371 Hypertonicity of muscles with hyperactive deep reflexes or clonus.

b. *Physiol.* Of a solution (see HYPERTONIC *a.* 2); the extent to which a solution has higher osmotic pressure than some other.

1896 T. L. STEDMAN *20th Cent. Pract.* VII. 284 The hypertonicity of the plasma is easily calculated. **1906** *Amer. Jrnl. Physiol.* XV. 359 When the hypertonicity is slight, the degree of recovery is relatively greater than in the case of the more concentrated solutions. **1963** E. ERNST *Biophysics Striated Muscle* (ed. 2) 131 The next experiments were planned in such a way that the loss of water [from the muscle] due to the hypertonicity of the medium should be balanced by water taken up by the swelling elicited by lactic acid.

hypertonus (haɪpəˈtəʊnəs). [f. HYPER- 5 + TONUS.] **1.** *Ophthalm.* A state of increased pressure of the intra-ocular fluid; = HYPERTENSION 1 b. Now *rare.*

1891 F. P. FOSTER *Med. Dict.* III. 1944/1 *Hypertonus*, that condition of the eye in which the intra-ocular tension is increased, sometimes without any organic disease being present. **1918** R. H. ELLIOT *Glaucoma: Textbk. for Student* v. 300 It would appear, then, that the thrombotic type of glaucoma possesses a very distinct inflammatory element; it thus comes into line with the hypertonus which we find secondary..to intra-ocular tumours.

2. *Med.* = HYPERTONIA.

1904 *Rev. Neurol. & Psychiatry* II. 775 The arms showed the typical muscular rigidity (hypertonus) of paralysis agitans, while the legs were markedly hypotonic. **1923** J. F. H. DALLY *High Blood Pressure* v. 65 To some extent raised blood pressure may be differentiated from arterial hypertonus by instrumental methods. **1924** *Brain* XLVII. 333 General hypertonus may, however, be inferred from a slight increase of the tendon reflexes. **1950** *Physiol. Rev.* XXX. 466 After the somnolence and plastic hypertonus had passed, marked poverty of movement still persisted. **1971** RASCH & BURKE *Kinesiology* (ed. 4) iv. 83 The limb is then said to be spastic. In man such hypertonus occurs only in the antigravity muscles.

hypertrophic (haɪpəˈtrɒfɪk), *a.* [f. HYPERTROPH-Y + -IC.] Of the nature of, affected with, or producing hypertrophy. (Also *fig.*)

1832 COLERIDGE in *Blackw. Mag.* XXXI. 956 The following Out-slough, or hypertrophic Stanza. **1839–47** TODD *Cycl. Anat.* III. 719/2 The anatomical characters of a hypertrophic brain. **1856** W. L. LINDSAY *Brit. Lichens* 41 Their hypertrophic or abnormal condition.

b. *Gram.* Characterized by excess of expression.

1874 T. H. KEY *Lang.* 271 In the Old German we find an abundant crop of hypertrophic comparatives from prepositions.

So **hyperˈtrophical**, *a.* (Craig 1847).

hypertrophied (haɪˈpɜːtrəfɪd), *a.* [f. HYPERTROPHY *sb.* or *v.* + -ED.] Affected with hypertrophy; enlarged by excessive growth.

1835–6 TODD *Cycl. Anat.* I. 240/2 This cellular substance seemed to be hypertrophied. **1857** BERKELEY *Cryptog. Bot.* §603. 532 The marginal sori being seated on the hypertrophied teeth. **1873** T. H. GREEN *Introd. Pathol.* 92 The kidney..may become hypertrophied, owing to the loss or incapacity of its fellow.

b. *fig.* Overgrown, excessive.

1879 ROMANES in *19th Cent.* Sept. 414 Such hypertrophied conservatism as this ought not to be allowed to obstruct progress. **1881** —— in *Nature* XXIII. 285 It is hard to be patient with such hypertrophied absurdity.

hypertrophous (haɪˈpɜːtrəfəs), *a.* [f. stem of HYPERTROPH-Y + -OUS.] Characterized by or affected with hypertrophy.

1836–9 TODD *Cycl. Anat.* II. 826/2 The hypertrophous condition. **1876** G. W. BALFOUR *Dis. Heart* ii. 60 The greatly dilated and hypertrophous left ventricle sends forward a wave of blood.

hypertrophy (haɪˈpɜːtrəfɪ), *sb.* [ad. mod.L. *hypertrophia*, f. Gr. ὑπέρ (see HYPER- 5) + -τροφία, τροφή nourishment: cf. ATROPHY.] *Physiol.* and *Path.* Enlargement of a part or organ of an animal or plant, produced by excessive nutrition; excessive growth or development. The opposite of ATROPHY.

1834 J. FORBES *Laennec's Dis. Chest* (ed. 4) 657 Hypertrophy or dilatation of the heart. **1844** *Blackw. Mag.* LVI. 21 We question..whether this hypertrophy of fruit or vegetables improves their flavour. **1866–80** A. FLINT *Princ. Med.* (ed. 5) 41 The term hypertrophy is applied to enlargement of a part from an increase of its normal constituents, the structure and arrangement remaining essentially unaltered. **1881** *Encycl. Brit.* XII. 597/2 In many cases hypertrophy cannot be regarded as a deviation from health, but rather on the contrary as indicative of a high degree of nutrition and physical power. **1884** BOWER & SCOTT *De Bary's Phaner.* 492 Accumulations of parenchymatous cells..constituting as it were local hypertrophies of the medullary rays.

b. *fig.* Overgrowth.

1856 *Chamb. Jrnl.* VI. 131 That hypertrophy of monarchism which grew up under Louis XIV, and in the end destroyed his dynasty. **1883** *Century Mag.* July 419/1 Nights of financial hypertrophy.

hyˈpertrophy, *v.* [f. prec. sb.; cf. ATROPHY *v.*] **1.** *trans.* To affect with hypertrophy.

1846 P. M. LATHAM *Lect. Clin. Med.* (ed. 2) xxxiv. 314 [The heart] is sooner hypertrophied, sooner attenuated. **1885** W. K. PARKER *Mammal. Desc.* iv. 101 The simple forms of its facial bones, not hypertrophied to make room for the teeth.

2. *intr.* To undergo hypertrophy.

1883 tr. *Ziegler's Pathol. Anat.* i. §72 (Cent.) When a tissue manifests an abnormal tendency to overgrowth, it is said to hypertrophy.

hyperˈurbanism. [f. HYPER- 5 + URBANISM.] Extreme urbanism; *spec.* in *Philol.*, the manner of speech arising from an effort to avoid provincialism; a hypercorrect form of speech or phrase resulting from this. So **hyperˈurban** *a.*, exhibiting hyperurbanism; **hyperˌurbaniˈzation** *sb.*

1925 P. RADIN tr. *Vendryès's Lang.* ii. 49 Hyper-urbanism consists in those excesses brought about by consideration for correct speech. *Ibid.*, *Plaustrum* for *plostrum*, *cauda* for *coda*... These are hyper-urbanisms. **1928** L. BLOOMFIELD in *Language* IV. iv. 286 Hyper-urban forms occur, e.g., *foot* pronounced as [fyːt] instead of [fuːt]. **1933** —— *Lang.* xviii. 309 We may take *cōda* to be the older of the two Latin forms, and *cauda* to be a hyper-urban (over-elegant) variant. *Ibid.* xix. 330 This flavor of the [yː]-variants appears strikingly in the shape of hyper-urbanisms: in using the elegant [yː], the speaker sometimes substitutes it where it is entirely out of place. **1935** *Language* XI. ii. 106 Social climbers betray themselves by hyper-urbanisms, such as [a] in *bass* or *lass.* **1937** *Amer. Speech* XII. 175 The women who wear gloves on the most informal occasions have probably acquired the habit of never forgetting them, and so-called hyper-urbanization in speech as well as in dress, often springs from ..a sense of social insecurity. **1940** C. C. FRIES *Amer. Eng. Grammar* vi. 94 There appeared in the Standard English materials some uses of *whom* which should probably be looked upon as hyperurbanisms. **1951** TRAGER & SMITH *Outl. Eng. Struct.* iii. 85 The hyperurbanism *Between you and I* for the standard *Between you and me.*

hyperventilate (haɪpəˈvɛntɪleɪt), *v. Physiol.* [f. HYPER- 5 + VENTILATE *v.*, or back-formation from next.] **a.** *intr.* To breathe deeply or rapidly.

1931 *Jrnl. Neurol. & Psychopath.* XII. 14 It is..of much interest to ascertain to which changes the epileptic organism reacts with a seizure when the patient hyperventilates. **1961** *Flight* LXXX. 760/1 An experienced pilot who had..been told..that he hyperventilated and should regulate his breathing. **1968** *Everybody's* (Austral.) 12 June 31/4 Ron Taylor, perhaps Australia's greatest underwater expert, advises: Don't hyperventilate to the stage where you become dizzy. **1970** *Sci. Amer.* Feb. 56/1 They do not need to hyperventilate as much as lowlanders do when the latter go to high altitudes.

b. *trans.* To produce hyperventilation in.

1931 *Jrnl. Neurol. & Psychopath.* XII. 15 Our method has been..to hyperventilate the person in question with two or three of the methods. **1953** *Physiol. Rev.* XXXIII. 447 Brown et al... hyperventilated subjects for 24 hours in a body respirator at rates just under those producing tetany. **1968** C. OSBORNE tr. *Stenuit's Dolphin* vii. 119 When a.. skin-diver hyperventilates his lungs by deep breathing.., he loads the haemoglobin of his blood with a reserve of oxygen.

ˌhyperventiˈlation. *Physiol.* [f. HYPER- 5 + VENTILATION.] An increased or excessive exposure of the lungs to oxygen, resulting in a more rapid loss of carbon dioxide from the blood; the action of bringing this about (in oneself, by deep or rapid breathing, or in another individual).

1928 *Canad. Med. Assoc. Jrnl.* LVIII. 210/2 Such a 'hyperventilation' tetany occurring under clinical conditions has been but seldom reported. **1932** *Arch. Neurol. & Psychiatry* XXVIII. 574 We injected into each animal 0·1 mg. of strychnine sulphate per kilogram of body weight and started hyperventilation after..twenty to thirty minutes. **1951** H. DAVSON *Textbk. Gen. Physiol.* vi. 124 Special mechanisms for heat dissipation such as sweating or hyperventilation of the lungs. **1961** *Lancet* 26 Aug. 474/2 Another cause of fainting, more often related to emotional than to physical states, is hyperventilation. **1965** *Handbk. Physiol.: Circulation* (Amer. Physiol. Soc.) III. liii. 1889/2 It is not at all difficult by hyperventilation to cause a severe gaseous alkalosis with dizziness, blurred vision, mental confusion, numbness of extremities,..and muscle spasm, rarely going on to..convulsions and unconsciousness. **1970** *Sci. Jrnl.* June 84/1 The noticeable hyperventilation (heavy breathing) which occurs at orgasm shows up clearly on the tracing.

hypethral, var. of HYPÆTHRAL.

‖**hypha** (ˈhaɪfə). *Bot.* Pl. **hyphæ** (-fiː). [mod.L. (C. L. Willdenow, 1810), ad. Gr. ὑφή web.] The structural element of the thallome of Fungi, consisting of long slender branched filaments, usually having transverse septa, and together constituting the *mycelium.*

1866 in *Treas. Bot.* **1874** COOKE *Fungi* 14 In Chionyphe Carteri the threads grow over the cysts exactly as the hypha of lichens is represented as growing over the gonidia. **1875** [see HYPHAL]. **1897** WILLIS *Flower. Pl.* I. 23 In most of our forest trees and in many other plants, the root-hairs are replaced by a fungus whose hyphæ absorb the products of decay in organic matter..in the same way.

‖**hyphæmia, -emia** (hɪf-, haɪˈfiːmɪə). *Path.* [f. Gr. ὑφ- = ὑπό under + αἷμα blood; cf. Gr. ὕφαιμος blood-shot. In mod.F. *hyphémie.*]

a. Deficiency of blood. **b.** Extravasation of blood.

1886 in *Syd. Soc. Lex.*

‖**hyphæne, -ene** (haɪˈfiːniː). *Bot.* [mod.L. (1801) arbitrarily f. Gr. ὑφαίν-ειν to weave.] A genus of palms with branching stems, found in Arabia, Africa, and Madagascar. One species, *H. Thebaica*, is the DOUM-palm. Also *attrib.*

1878 H. M. STANLEY *Dark Cont.* II. viii. 239 Hyphene palms. **1881** *Gd. Words* Jan. 37 Among other vegetable curiosities were the hyphæne—the only branching member of the palm family.

hyphæresis, -eresis (hɪ-, haɪˈfɪərɪsɪs). *Gram.* [a. Gr. ὑφαίρεσις a taking away from under, omission: cf. *aphæresis.*] The omission of a letter or syllable in the body of a word.

1890 *Cent. Dict.* s.v., Syllabic hyphæresis.

hyphal (ˈhaɪfəl), *a. Bot.* [f. HYPHA + -AL¹.] Of or pertaining to the hypha of a fungus.

1875 BENNETT & DYER *Sachs' Bot.* 267 In *Usnea barbata* the growth in length and thickness and the internal differentiation of the tissue depend entirely on the hyphæ, and..the gonidia behave like foreign bodies in the hyphal tissue. **1896** ALLBUTT *Syst. Med.* I. 90 The spores and developing hyphal filaments become surrounded by dense clusters of leucocytes.

†**ˈhyphear.** *Obs.* [a. L. *hyphear* (Pliny), a. Gr. (Arcadian) ὕφεαρ, a kind of mistletoe growing on pines or firs.] A kind of mistletoe.

1601 HOLLAND *Pliny* I. 496 A difference there is in the Hyphear and Misselto, on what tree soeuer they are found. **1613–16** W. BROWNE *Brit. Past.* I. i, Whose muting on those trees doth make to grow Rots curing hyphear, and the misseltoe.

†**hypheˈgetic,** *a. Obs.* [ad. Gr. ὑφηγητικός fitted for guiding (applied to Plato's expository dialogues).] Of guiding or directing nature.

1655 STANLEY *Hist. Philos.* v. (1701) 175/1 Of Platonick discourse there are two kinds, Hyphegetick, and Exegetick.

hyphen (ˈhaɪfən), *sb.* [a. late L. *hyphen*, a. late Gr. ἡ ὑφέν, subst. use of adv. ὑφέν together, in one, f. ὑφ', ὑπό under + ἕν one.

The hyphen of the Greek grammarians was the sign ◡, placed under a compound, to indicate that it was not to be read as two words: in this sense the word is sometimes used technically by Palæographers.]

1. A short dash or line (-) used to connect two words together as a compound; also, to join the separated syllables of a word, as at the end of a line; or to divide a word into parts for etymological or other purposes.

[**1603** HOLLAND *Plutarch's Mor.* 41 He would have us to reade these two last words in one, by way of ὑφέν, thus.] *c* **1620** A. HUME *Brit. Tongue* (1865) 23 Hyphen is, as it wer, a band uniting whol wordes joined in composition; as, a hand-maed [etc.]. **1636** B. JONSON *Discov.*, *Bellum Scribent.*, What a sight it is, to see writers committed together by the ears, for ceremonies, syllables, points, colons, commas,

hyphens, and the like? **1678** PHILLIPS (ed. 4), *Hyphen*..is used, either when two words are joyned together, for the more conciseness of expression, as *Self-interest*; or when one part of a word concludes the former Line, and the one begins the next. **1881** MASON *Eng. Gram.* §299 When the two elements of the compound are only partially blended, a hyphen is put between them.

b. Applied to the 'plus' sign (+).

1850 DAUBENY *Atomic The.* iii. (ed. 2) 105 In Berzelius's method..to express compound salts, the symbols for each were brought together by means of an hyphen +.

2. *transf.* **a.** A short pause between two syllables in speaking.

1868 GEO. ELIOT *Sp. Gipsy* I. 15 Whistles low notes or seems to thrum his lute As a mere hyphen 'twixt two syllables Of any steadier man. **1872** C. KING *Mountain. Sierra Nev.* x. 208 With hyphens of silence between each two syllables.

b. A small connecting link.

1868 G. DUFF *Pol. Surv.* 169 It was a bridge for migrations. It was a hyphen, connecting different races. **1881** *Daily Tel.* 21 June 6/8 M. de Lesseps, who is the sworn foe of all such geographical hyphens [isthmuses].

hyphen ('haɪfən), *v.* [f. prec. sb.] *trans.* To join by a hyphen; to write (a compound) with a hyphen.

1814 W. TAYLOR in *Monthly Rev.* LXXIV. 306 The Englishman imagines all words connected by apposition to be hyphened together, and inflects them as a single word. **1884** *New Eng. Dict.* Introd. 23 Many specialized combinations..are often not even hyphened. **1891** S. MOSTYN *Curatica* 128 The Joneses, when their father was induced to move from Shepherd's Bush to Kensington, showed their gratitude to their mother by hyphening her name with their own..'The Misses Robinson-Jones'. **1894** *Sunday Sch. Times* (Philad.) 3 Feb., On the principle that words should not be hyphened unless absolutely necessary.

hyphenate ('haɪfəneɪt), *v.* [f. HYPHEN *sb.* + -ATE[3].] *trans.* = HYPHEN *v.*

1892 *Guardian* 14 Sept. 1358 We ought to hyphenate 'noble-simple' [Shaks. *Cymb.* III. iv. 133]. Cloten is noble by rank, but 'simple', that is, a clown, by nature and habit.

Hence **hyphe'nation**, the action of joining by a hyphen.

1886 *19th Cent.* May 700 Arbitrary italicising, meaningless bracketing, and senseless hyphenation.

'hyphenate, *sb.* [f. HYPHENATED *a.* 2.] A hyphenated person.

1916 *Yorks. Post* 4 Mar. 6/7 The Hyphenates throughout the country are greatly excited. **1920** *Glasgow Herald* 27 Nov. 6 This political hyphenate or composite is desirous of running a Home Rule for Scotland campaign. **1922** *Contemp. Rev.* Dec. 693 The 'hyphenates'—Irish and Germans, Poles and Russians and Italians—..joined in the condemnation of Wilsonism.

hyphenated, *a.* **1.** Consisting of two (or more) parts joined by a hyphen.

1852 *N. & Q.* 1st Ser. V. 124/2 The Germans giving the hyphenated title thus. **1893** E. COUES *Exp. Lewis & Clark* I. 66 In the text..the name usually stands Council-bluff, in one hyphenated word.

2. Applied to persons (or, by extension, their activities) born in one country but naturalized citizens of another, their nationality being designated by a hyphenated form, e.g. *Anglo-American, Irish-American*; hence, to a person whose patriotic allegiance is assumed to be divided. Also in extended use. orig. *U.S.*

1893 FARMER & HENLEY *Slang* III. 386/2 *Hyphenated American*, a naturalised citizen, as German-Americans, Irish-Americans, and the like. **1900** *Daily News* 15 Aug. 3/1 My opponents were of the hyphenated variety—Dutch-Americans and Irish-Americans predominating. **1904** *Westm. Gaz.* 3 Jan. 3/2 American politics, where men who call themselves Irish-Americans, German-Americans, Dutch-Americans, and so on, are contemptuously referred to as 'hyphenated Americans'. **1907** *Nation* (N.Y.) 7 Nov. 410 Some of these hyphenated American journals. **1915** *Lit. Digest* 4 Sept. 462/1 Hyphenated residents will continue to insist that American newspapers should be strictly neutral. **1948** *Manch. Guardian Weekly* 3 June 7/1 'Hyphenated Americans'—undigested immigrant stock. **1965** B. SWEET-ESCOTT *Baker St. Irreg.* i. 37 It was thought that, with the whole of western Europe under Nazi domination, hyphenated Americans might provide recruits for work in occupied territory. **1973** *Times* 17 Oct. 6/8 This did not go down well with the Greek community here [*sc.* in the U.S.], or with other groups of 'hyphenated Americans'.

hyphenic (haɪ'fɛnɪk), *a.* [f. as HYPHENATE *v.* + -IC.] Of or pertaining to a hyphen.

1851 *N. & Q.* 1st Ser. IV. 204/1 The following I should call a hyphenic error.

hyphening ('haɪfənɪŋ), *vbl. sb.* [f. HYPHEN *v.* + -ING[1].] The action of the vb. HYPHEN.

1929 *Conc. Oxf. Dict.* p. ix, A consequence of this reformed hyphening is that the presence of a hyphen in such a compound [as *tipsy cake*] assures the reader that the word-stress falls on the first part.

hyphenism ('haɪfənɪz(ə)m). *U.S.* [f. HYPHEN + -ISM; cf. HYPHENATED *a.* 2.] The state of being a hyphenated American; the attitude or conduct involved or implied by this.

1930 P. W. SLOSSON *Great Crusade* (1931) xi. 288 The years..so marked by hyphenism and the echoes of Old World feuds.

hyphenize ('haɪfənaɪz), *v.* [f. HYPHEN *sb.* + -IZE.] *trans.* = HYPHEN *v.*

1869 *South. Rev.* July 59 A flood of absurdities, many of which are badly hyphenised elongations of existing vocables. **1879** *Daily News* 20 Nov. 4/6 The reconciliation of Austria and Hungary, and the predominance of the latter in a hyphenized monarchy.

Hence **hypheni'zation**, the action of joining or writing with a hyphen.

1851 *N. & Q.* 1st Ser. IV. 204/1 A neglect of mental hyphenization often leads to mistake as to an author's meaning. **1894** *Sunday Sch. Times* (Philad.) 3 Feb., No two writers, probably, would agree as to the hyphenization of any fifty words taken at random.

hyphomycetes (ˌhaɪfəʊmaɪ'siːtiːz, -ts), *sb. pl. Bot.* Also in *sing.* form **hyphomycete**. [mod.L. (E. M. Fries *Systema Mycologicum* (1821) I. p. xxx), f. Gr. ὑφή web + μύκητες fungi.] Imperfect fungi of the group Hyphomycetes; filamentous moulds bearing naked, asexual spores.

1836 M. J. BERKELEY in J. E. Smith *Eng. Flora* V. II. 328 Hyphomycetes... Sporidiferous flocci naked (not included in a uterus or seated on a proper receptacle). **1857** —— *Introd. Cryptogamic Bot.* 297 The species contained in the division *Hyphomycetes*, consist of Fungi which, like *Mucorini*, are known under the common name of moulds. **1887** H. E. F. GARNSEY tr. *A. de Bary's Compar. Morphol. & Biol. Fungi* i. 1 In the more simple Fungi the branched hypha alone constitutes the thallus; such forms are termed Hyphomycetes, Filamentous Fungi (Fadenpilze), or Haplomycetes. **1930** C. THOM *Penicillia* iv. 24 A hyphomycete genus such as Penicillium..is an aggregation of species with a common type of asexual fruiting. *Ibid.* xi. 147 Penicillium is characterized and discussed here as a 'form-genus' in the great aggregate of form genera commonly known as the Hyphomycetes. **1971** M. B. ELLIS *Dematiaceous Hyphomycetes* 7 About 50 per cent of the specimens sent to the Commonwealth Mycological Institute are hyphomycetes.

hyphomycetous (ˌhɪf-, ˌhaɪfəʊmaɪ'siːtəs), *a. Bot.* [f. prec. + -OUS.] Of or belonging to the *Hyphomycetes*, a group of fungi consisting simply of hyphæ (Martius *Flora Crypt. Erlang.* 1817).

1887 GARNSEY tr. *De Bary's Fungi* II. v. 172 The Entylomeae..are simple hyphomycetous forms.

hypidiomorphic (hɪˌpɪdɪəʊ'mɔːfɪk), *a. Min.* [mod. f. (Rosenbusch) *hyp-*, HYPO- 4 + IDIOMORPHIC.] Partially or incompletely idiomorphic.

1888 A. C. LAWSON in *Amer. Geologist* Apr. 204 The order being first plagioclase in more or less idiomorphic lath-shaped individuals, lying in all positions, then augite generally allotriomorphic, sometimes hypidiomorphic.

Hence **hypidio'morphically** *adv.*

1888 W. S. BAYLEY in *Amer. Naturalist* Mar. 209 The rock is hypidiomorphically granular.

hypinosis (hɪpɪ'nəʊsɪs). *Path.* [f. HYPO- 4 + Gr. ἴς, ἰν-ός tissue + -OSIS.] A diseased state of the blood in which the quantity of fibrin is below the normal; opp. to *hyperinosis*.

1845 G. E. DAY tr. *Simon's Anim. Chem.* I. 296 These researches exhibit less of the characters of hypinosis than those instituted on the blood at the commencement of continued fever. **1876** tr. *Wagner's Gen. Pathol.* 704 Hypinosis may be a result of hæmorrhage.

Hence **hypi'notic** *a.*, pertaining to hypinosis.

1855 in MAYNE *Expos. Lex.* **1886** in *Syd. Soc. Lex.*

hypiodic, -iodous, etc.: see HYPO-IODIC, etc.

hypish, obs. form of HYPPISH.

‖**hypnæsthesis** (hɪpnɪs'θiːsɪs). *Path.* [f. Gr. ὕπν-ος sleep + αἴσθησις perception, feeling.] Sleepy feeling; dulled sensibility; drowsiness.

1855 in MAYNE *Expos. Lex.*

Hence **hypnæs'thesic** *a.*, affected with hypnæsthesis.

1889 *Lancet* 28 Dec. 1331/1 Many of these pathological phenomena are simply the hypnæsthesic nerves picking up the physiological sights, sounds, and sensations.

hypnagogic (hɪpnə'gɒdʒɪk), *a.* Also **hypnogogic**. [ad. F. *hypnagogique*, f. Gr. ὕπν-ος sleep + ἀγωγός leading, f. ἄγειν to lead.] *Properly*, Inducing or leading to sleep; in quots. = that accompanies falling asleep.

1886 GURNEY *Phantasms of Living* I. 390 The 'hypnagogic' hallucination was as truly the projection of the percipient's own mind as the dream. **1895** *Q. Rev.* July 215 Hallucinations like the 'hypnagogic illusions' with which many people are familiar. **1906** E. SALTUS *Vanity Square* II. i. 154 The hypnogogic hallucinations continue. **1933** *Scrutiny* I. 380 In this hypnogogic state the mind makes no selection. **1962** *New Scientist* 2 Aug. 267/3 The next section contains a quantity of fascinating material on such topics as ..'night jerks', which occur in the hypnogogic state (his spelling 'hypn*a*gogic' is not a useful innovation). **1972** [see HYPNOPOMPIC *a.*].

hypna'gogically, *adv.* [f. HYPNAGOGIC *a.*: see -ICALLY.] In a hypnagogic manner.

1957 P. MCKELLAR *Imagination & Thinking* iii. 40 Confusion of hypnagogically imaged music with the noises of reality also occurred, and more than one of our subjects descended the stairs believing that the wireless had been left on.

‖**'hypnale**. *Obs.* [ad. late L. *hypnalē* (Solinus), a. Gr. ὑπναλέη, fem. of ὑπναλέος sending to sleep, f. ὕπνος sleep.] (See quots.)

1398 TREVISA *Barth. De P.R.* XVIII. x. (1495) 763 Ympnalis is a manere of adder that sleeth wyth slepe. **1613** PURCHAS *Pilgrimage* (1614) 560 The Dipsas killes those whom shee stingeth with thirst. The Hypanale with sleep, as befell to Cleopatra. **1635** SWAN *Spec. M.* (1670) 440 Those whom the Hypnale stingeth die with sleep.

hypnic ('hɪpnɪk), *a. rare.* [ad. Gr. ὑπνικ-ός, f. ὕπνος sleep.] Of, pertaining to, or inducing sleep.

1886 *Syd. Soc. Lex.*, *Hypnic*, having power to produce sleep.

hypno- ('hɪpnəʊ), before a vowel **hypn-**, combining form of Gr. ὕπνος sleep. The compounds in Greek were not numerous, and all those employed in English are new formations, and chiefly pathological terms.

'hypnobate [Gr. -βατης walker], a sleep-walker (*Cent. Dict.*). **hypnocyst** ('hɪpnəʊsɪst) *Biol.*, an encysted protozoan which remains quiescent and does not develop spores. **hypnodylic** (-'dɪlɪk) *a.* [ODYLIC], pertaining to an 'odylic force' producing the hypnotic state; so **hyp'nodylism**, the practice of using this force. **hypno'genesis, hyp'nogeny**, induction of the hypnotic state; so **hypnoge'netic, -'genic, hyp'nogenous** *adjs.*, producing the hypnotic state; *rarely*, producing sleep. **hypnoge'netically** *adv.*, by hypnogenesis. **hyp'nology** [cf. F. *hypnologie*], the part of physiological science which deals with the phenomena of sleep; hence **hypno'logic, -ical** *adjs.*, of or pertaining to hypnology. **hyp'nologist**, one versed in hypnology. **hypno'phobia, hyp'nophoby** [Gr. -φοβία, f. φόβος fear; cf. F. *hypnophobie*], a morbid dread of falling asleep (*Syd. Soc. Lex.* 1886); hence **hypno'phobic** *a.* (Mayne *Expos. Lex.* 1855). **'hypnoscope** [Gr. σκοπός see -SCOPE], an instrument used to ascertain if a person is a hypnotic subject. **hyp'nosophist**, an adept in **hyp'nosophy** [Gr. σοφία wisdom], knowledge of the phenomena of sleep. **'hypnosperm, -spore** *Bot.*, an oospore or zygospore (in the *Algæ*) which, after fertilization, passes through a period of rest before germinating; a resting cell or spore; so **'hypnospoˌrange, ˌhypnospo'rangium** *Bot.*, a sporangium containing hypnospores; **hypno'sporic** *a.*, of the nature of a hypnospore.

1885 E. R. LANKESTER in *Encycl. Brit.* XIX. 841/2 The sclerotia are similar in nature to the *hypnocysts of other Protozoa. **1888** ROLLESTON & JACKSON *Anim. Life* 258 The [Amœba] when in a state of repose..forms a spherical or oval ball... It sometimes occurs in this condition surrounded by a delicate membrane forming a 'hypnocyst'. It is then 'resting', owing to drought or plentiful nutrition. **1889** *Daily News* 24 Dec. 2/7 *Hypnodylic operators are born, not made. *Ibid.*, The phenomena of *hypnodylism in actual operation. *Ibid.*, The scope of hypnotism and odylism, the aspects of *hypnogenesis, the conditions of odylic force. **1887** E. GURNEY in *Mind* Apr. 214 Certain recent events, however, have given special importance to this topic of trance-induction or 'hypnogeny', and have raised..the question of the efficacy of psychical influence as a *hypnogenetic agent. **1888** *Science* 9 Nov. 222 Physical methods [of hypnotization], especially hypnogenetic zones, do not exist except as the results of suggestion. **1884** *Lond. Med. Rec.* Aug. 360 We call those substances *hypnogenic which, when administered, may cause sleep. **1887** *Fortn. Rev.* May 737 The so-called 'hysterogenic' and 'hypnogenic' pressure points. **1886** F. W. H. MYERS in *Proc. Soc. Psych. Res.* Oct. 127 No attempt..has been made to correlate this *hypnogenous force or suggestion at a distance with hypnogenous agencies employed in the subject's actual presence. *Ibid. note*, I must adopt from the French the word **hypnogeny* for the production of hypnotic states. **1886** *Syd. Soc. Lex.*, **Hypnologic*, of or belonging to hypnology. **1847** CRAIG, **Hypnological*. **1860** *New Syd. Soc. Year-bk.* 203 Azam has repeated Mr. Braid's hypnological experiments, and finds that catalepsy and anæsthesia can be obtained in the way he indicates. **1847–9** TODD *Cycl. Anat.* IV. 681/2 An advertising *hypnologist whom I allowed to try his art upon the sleepless individual. **1833** DUNGLISON (Worcester), *Hypnology. **1886** *Syd. Soc. Lex.*, *Hypnology*, the part of hygiene which treats of the doctrine of sleep. **1855** MAYNE *Expos. Lex.*, **Hypnophobia*, term for fear or dread of sleep; also a term for Ephialtes, or night-mare; *hypnophoby. **1885** *Athenæum* 3 Jan. 21/2 He [Dr. J. Ochorowicz] finds that by hanging a magnetic tube, which he calls a '*hypnoscope', from the index finger, sensations of a peculiar description are realized. **1885** *Pall Mall G.* 27 Feb. 3/2 Experiments have proved that about 30 per cent. of mankind can be subjected to mesmeric influences, while on the rest the hypnoscope has no effect. **1888** *Sat. Rev.* 18 Aug. 196/1 Every *hypnosophist..has his own little private dodge for smuggling himself over the frontier of the land of Nod. *Ibid.*, The term *hypnosophy is new, perhaps, but it looks rather neat and convenient. *Ibid.*, Hypnosophy stands to scientific discussion of the facts about sleep as theosophy stands to religion. **1889** BENNETT & MURRAY *Cryptog. Bot.* 266 It [the zygosperm] then remains dormant through the winter as a resting cell or *hypnosperm, germinating in the spring.

hypnoanalysis (hɪpnəʊə'nælɪsɪs). Also **hypno-analysis**. [f. HYPNO- (taken as combining form of *hypnosis*) + ANALYSIS.] Psychoanalysis performed while the subject is under hypnosis; psychotherapy that combines psychoanalysis with hypnosis.

1920 J. A. HADFIELD in H. C. Miller *Functional Nerve Dis.* v. 71 The method which I venture to name 'Hypno-analysis' consists simply in hypnotizing the patient and inducing him to speak of his troubles. **1949** KOESTLER *Insight & Outlook* x. 146 The less drastic forms of psychotherapy like psycho-, narco-, and hypnoanalysis..are all primarily means of releasing functional components of the psychoneural apparatus which had been repressed by faulty integration. **1963** W. S. KROGER *Clin. & Exper. Hypnosis* xlvii. 323/1 Hypnoanalysis is particularly indicated for psychoneurotics who do not respond to brief hypnotherapeutic procedures.

Hence **hypno'analyst**, one who uses hypnoanalysis; ˌ**hypnoana'lytic** *a.*, of or involving hypnoanalysis.

1922 *Jrnl. Abnormal Psychol.* XVI. 344 (*heading*) A hypnoanalytic study of two cases of war neurosis. **1945** *Diseases Nervous Syst.* VI. 374/1 The hypnoanalyst..is thrust into a form of relationship with his patient that transcends even the transference situation obtaining in routine psychoanalysis. **1947** LECRON & BORDEAUX *Hypnotism Today* xiii. 229 Basically, hypnoanalytic treatment is modified psychoanalysis with inclusion of hypnotism for brevity. **1960** I. BENNETT *Delinquent & Neurotic Children* iv. 124 Lindner (1944) undertook the hypno-analytic treatment of a criminal psychopath. **1963** W. S. KROGER *Clin. & Exper. Hypnosis* xlvii. 323/2 The process utilizes free associations, dreams, analyses and recollections, all of which are interpreted by the hypno-analyst.

hypnogogic, var. HYPNAGOGIC *a.*

hypnoid ('hɪpnɔɪd), *a.*[1] *Bot.* [f. HYPN-UM + -OID.] Belonging or akin to the genus *Hypnum*.

1852 TH. ROSS *Humboldt's Trav.* I. xv. 481 The surrounding rocks are covered with jungermannias and hypnoid mosses.

hypnoid ('hɪpnɔɪd), *a.*[2] *Psychol.* [a. G. *hypnoid* (Breuer & Freud 1893, in *Neurol. Centralblatt* XII. II. 43), f. Gr. ὕπν-ος sleep + -OID.] Applied to a state of consciousness characterized by heightened suggestibility or dissociation, such as occurs in hysterical conditions.

1898 B. SIDIS *Psychol. of Suggestion* xxiii. 234 By the term 'hypnoid' I indicate the coexistence of two or more fully independent functioning constellations of moments-consciousness, such as is presented in the phenomena of automatic writing and of hysteria. **1902** W. JAMES *Var. Relig. Exper.* xvi. 413 To the medical mind these ecstasies signify nothing but suggested and imitated hypnoid states. **1924** J. RIVIERE et al. tr. *Freud's Coll. Papers* I. 34 Splitting of consciousness..exists in a rudimentary fashion in every hysteria and..the tendency to this dissociation—and therewith to the production of abnormal states of consciousness, which may be included under the term 'hypnoid'—is a fundamental manifestation of this neurosis. **1951** R. BRUN *Gen. Theory Neuroses* III. 333 Fantasies in hypnoid conditions, such as constantly occur in hysteria, will even more readily produce regressive excitations in the most disparate organs.

Also **hyp'noidal** *a.*, in the same sense.

1898 B. SIDIS *Psychol. of Suggestion* xxiii. 239 In hypnoidal states past, outlived experiences heave up into the upper consciousness. **1921** *Discovery* Nov. 294/1 A similar [half-waking] state can be produced artificially and is called light hypnosis or the hypnoidal state. **1970** R. R. MONROE *Episodic Behavioral Disorders* ii. 45 Abrupt alteration in awareness, such as [is] seen in petit mal or hypnoidal states.

hypnone ('hɪpnəʊn). *Med.* [a. F. *hypnone*, f. Gr. ὕπν-ος sleep + -ONE.] A name given to acetophenone, $C_6H_5.CO.CH_3$, as a hypnotic.

1886 *Syd. Soc. Lex.*, *Hypnone*,.. Dujardin-Beaumetz's term for phenylmethyl-ketone or acetophenone. A colourless, very mobile liquid..obtained by distilling a mixture of calcium benzoate and acetate. **1888** *Medical News* (U.S.) 19 May 547/2 Various other hypnotics have been more recently proposed, such as..hypnone and methylal.

hypnopædia (hɪpnəʊ'piːdɪə). Also **-pedia**. [f. HYPNO- + Gr. παιδεία education.] The exposure of a sleeping subject to lessons played on a radio, tape recorder, etc.; teaching or learning by this method, 'sleep-learning'.

1932 A. HUXLEY *Brave New World* ii. 27 The principle of sleep-teaching, or hypnopædia, had been discovered. **1959** *Listener* 26 Feb. 385/1 Subliminal persuasion, hypnopaedia, brain-washing. **1969** *New Scientist* 30 Jan. 216/1 Sleep learning or hypnopedia, as its practitioners prefer to call it, is now acquiring a new status among Soviet teaching circles. **1971** *Nature* 24 Sept. 290/1 The opening chapters dispel misconceptions many people have about hypnopaedia.

Hence **hypno'pædic** *a.*, of or involving hypnopædia; **hypno'pædically** *adv.*

1932 A. HUXLEY *Brave New World* iv. 82 The sort of words that suddenly make you jump..they seem so new and exciting even though they're about something hypnopædically obvious. *Ibid.* x. 173 Listening unconsciously to hypnopædic lessons in hygiene and sociability. **1970** *Globe & Mail* (Toronto) 26 Sept. 7/1 The Russians are also learning..how to avoid the fatigue brought on by repeated hypnopedic sessions.

hypnophilous (hɪp'nɒfɪləs), *a.* [f. Gr. ὕπνο-ν HYPNUM + φίλος loving.] (See quot.)

1855 in MAYNE *Expos. Lex.* **1886** *Syd. Soc. Lex.*, *Hypnophilous*, growing among the mosses.

hypnopompic (hɪpnəʊ'pɒmpɪk), *a.* [f. HYPNO- + Gr. πομπ-ή sending away (f. πέμπειν to send) + -IC.] That accompanies the process of awakening from sleep.

a **1901** F. W. H. MYERS *Human Personality* (1903) I. p. xvii, To similar illusions accompanying the *departure* of sleep, as when a dream-figure persists for a few moments into waking life, I have given the name *hypnopompic*. *Ibid.* iv. 125 Equally remarkable are the hypnopompic pictures. **1925** *Proc. Soc. Psychical Res.* XXXV. 331 Of these four examples only the first is hypnagogic; Herschel's was a day-vision (at the breakfast-table), and the other two are hypnopompic. **1972** *Science* 16 June 1203/3 The ASC's [*sc.* altered states of consciousness] experienced by almost all ordinary people are dreaming states and the hypnogogic and hypnopompic states, the transitional states between sleeping and waking.

Hypnos ('hɪpnɒs). [Gr. Ὕπνος (ὕπνος sleep) (see below).] Name of the god of sleep in Greek mythology.

1906 T. E. LAWRENCE *Home Lett.* (1954) 40 It is eleven o'clock now and I ought to have thoughts on Hypnos. **1938** W. DE LA MARE *Memory* 38 What of the strange world that teems—Where brooding Hypnos reigns—with dreams? **1970** *Oxf. Classical Dict.* (ed. 2) 535/2 Throughout antiquity Hypnos was usually thought of as a winged youth who touches the foreheads of the tired with a branch..or pours sleep-inducing liquid from a horn.

hypnosis (hɪp'nəʊsɪs). *Phys.* [f. Gr. type *ὕπνωσις, n. of action f. ὑπνό-ειν to put to sleep. Cf. F. *hypnose* morbid sleep.]

1. 'The inducement or the gradual approach of sleep' (*Syd. Soc. Lex.* 1886).

1876 HARLEY *Mat. Med.* (ed. 6) 765 It invariably produced hypnosis and contraction of the pupil in him.

2. Artificially produced sleep: esp. that induced by hypnotism; the hypnotic state.

1882 *Quain's Dict. Med.* 973 The too ready adoption of hypnosis or Braidism may do harm rather than good. **1892** *Brit. Med. Jrnl.* 27 Aug. 459 The stages of hypnosis attained, varied from a slight degree of drowsiness to deep trance. **1893** *Pall Mall G.* 10 Jan. 2/1 The waking from hypnosis occurs through immediate action of the imagination, the command to wake up, or through sense [etc.]. **1898** *Times* 13 July 4/1 Any suggestion offered to a person during hypnosis has an exaggerated effect on his mind.

hypnotherapy (hɪpnəʊ'θɛrəpɪ). [f. HYPNO- (taken as combining form of *hypnosis*) + THERAPY.] Psychotherapy that involves the use of hypnotism.

1897 *Lippincott's Med. Dict.* 496/1 *Hypnotherapy*, the therapeutic use of hypnotism. **1907** *Alienist & Neurologist* XXVIII. 447 Constant current..cephalic galvanization..is a valuable addition to hypnotherapy, medical or otherwise, in psychiatry. **1931** A. EILOART tr. *Heyer's Hypnosis & Hypnotherapy* xiii. 204 Occasionally impotence or spasm of the vagina..are suitable subjects for hypnotherapy. **1947** LECRON & BORDEAUX *Hypnotism Today* xii. 196 Direct persuasive suggestion under hypnosis was the type of hypnotherapy used by the old medical practitioners of hypnotism. **1958** *Sunday Times* 17 Aug. 15/5 Hypnotherapy has a rightful place in medical treatment. **1960** *Spectator* 25 Nov. 838 Scientific training is attempted in the..two-year Hypnotherapy Centre course.

Hence **hypno'therapist**, one who employs hypnotherapy; ˌ**hypnothera'peutic** *a.*, of or involving hypnotherapy; ˌ**hypnothera'peutically** *adv.*

1892 *Jrnl. Mental Sci.* XXXVIII. 522 (*heading*) Hypno-therapeutic treatment. **1944** BRENMAN & GILL *Hypnotherapy* (1947) iv. 79 Erickson..who frequently collaborates with psychoanalysts in his hypnotherapeutic work, often utilizes the insights of psychoanalysis. **1958** *Spectator* 15 Aug. 236/1 Hypnotherapist and hypnoanalyst. **1963** Hypnotherapeutic [see HYPNOANALYSIS]. **1963** W. S. KROGER *Clin. & Exper. Hypnosis* xlvii. 323/2 Age-regression was hypnotherapeutically induced in several patients as an emergency measure to prevent suicide. **1970** *Daily Tel.* 8 June 11/4 Hypnotherapists have found that migraine has psychological causes.

hypnotic (hɪp'nɒtɪk), *a.* and *sb.* [ad. F. *hypnotique* (16th c. in Paré), ad. late L. *hypnōticus*, a. Gr. ὑπνωτικός inclined to sleep, sleepy; also, putting to sleep, narcotic, f. ὑπνόειν to put to sleep. In 2, short for *neuro-hypnotic*: see HYPNOTISM.]

A. *adj.* **1.** Inducing sleep; soporific.

1625 HART *Anat. Ur.* I. ii. 31 Not neglecting hypnoticke, cordiall, and deoppilatiue medicines. **1758** J. S. *Le Dran's Observ. Surg.* (1771) 300 Hypnotic Draughts constantly repeated. **1878** T. BRYANT *Pract. Surg.* I. 249 The hydrate of chloral is a drug of great value as possessing hypnotic qualities without the evils attendant on other drugs of this class.

2. Of, pertaining to, or of the nature of hypnotism or 'nervous sleep'; accompanied by hypnotism; producing hypnotism, hypnotizing.

1843 BRAID *Neurypnol.* 7 In respect to the Neuro-Hypnotic state induced by the method explained in this treatise. *Ibid.* 14 The method I now recommend for inducing the hypnotic condition. **1847–9** TODD *Cycl. Anat.* IV. 696/2 Some remarkable connection between the state of the eyes and condition of the brain and spinal cord, during the hypnotic state. **1874** MAUDSLEY *Respons. in Ment. Dis.* vii. 238 In the hypnotic or so-called mesmeric state. **1884** E. GURNEY in *Mind* Jan. 115 A gradual and continuous decline of hypnotic waking into hypnotic sleep. **1892** *19th Cent.* Jan. 24 To this day the..Fakirs of India throw themselves into a state of hypnotic ecstasy. **1898** *Times* 13 July 3/6 If they were going to suggest that the will had been obtained by hypnotic suggestion.

3. Susceptible to hypnotism; hypnotizable.

1881 *Standard* 29 Jan., The unfortunate young man was ..'hypnotic'. **1892** E. HART in *Brit. Med. Jrnl.* 3 Dec. 1220 The confirmed and trained hypnotic subject is a maimed individual in mind and body.

B. *sb.* **1.** An agent that produces sleep; a sedative or soporific drug.

1681 tr. *Willis' Rem. Med. Wks.* Vocab., *Hypnotic*, a medicine that causes sleep. **1684** tr. *Bonet's Merc. Compit.* XIV. 489 Hypnoticks are oft necessary in this Disease. **1787** BEST *Angling* (ed. 2) 70 Evident to all who know the nature and operation of hypnotics. **1874** CARPENTER *Ment. Phys.* II. xv. (1879) 576 The droning voice of a heavy reader on a dull subject, is often a most effectual hypnotic. **1876** HARLEY *Mat. Med.* (ed. 6) 344 In moderate doses chloral hydrate is a pure hypnotic.

2. A person under the influence of hypnotism.

1888 C. L. NORTON in *N. Amer. Rev.* June 705 It is a recognized fact that the senses of hypnotics fall completely under the control of the hypnotizer. **1893** E. HART in *Brit. Med. Jrnl.* 11 Feb. 302 The hypnotic under the influence of suggestion is capable of becoming a dangerous lunatic of a new kind.

†**hypnotical** (hɪp'nɒtɪkəl), *a. Obs.* [f. as prec. + -AL[1].] = prec. A. 1.

1657 TOMLINSON *Renou's Disp.* 112 Their similitude to Hypnoticall medicaments.

Hence **hyp'notically** *adv.*, in a hypnotic manner; by means of hypnotism.

c **1700** D. G. *Harangues Quack Doctors* 15 It affecteth the Cure..Hypnotically. **1883** *19th Cent.* Oct. 708 It would be a conceivable hypothesis that the trance condition is produced hypnotically. **1891** *Daily News* 31 Mar. 5/1 The Hypnotiser..hypnotically suggested her visions.

hypnotism ('hɪpnətɪz(ə)m). [f. HYPNOT-IC + -ISM. This word is due to Dr. James Braid of Manchester, who in 1842 introduced the term *neuro-hypnotism* for 'the state or condition of nervous sleep', and in 1843 used the shortened form *hypnotism*, when the context made the sense plain.]

1. The process of hypnotizing, or artificially producing a state in which the subject appears to be in a deep sleep, without any power of changing his mental or physical condition, except under the influence of some external suggestion or direction, to which he is involuntarily and unconsciously obedient. On recovering from this condition, the person has usually no remembrance of what he has said or done during the hypnotic state. The term is also applied to the branch of science which deals with the production of this state, and its causes and phenomena. See BRAIDISM, MESMERISM.

The usual way of inducing the state consists in causing a person to look fixedly, for several minutes, with complete concentration of the attention, at a bright or conspicuous object placed above and in front of the eyes at so short a distance that the convergence of the optic axes can only be accomplished with effort.

1842 BRAID in *Trans. Brit. Assoc.* (29 June), Practical Essay on the Curative Agency of Neuro-Hypnotism. **1843** —— *Neurypnol.* 13 By the term 'Neuro-Hypnotism' then, is to be understood 'nervous sleep'; and, for the sake of brevity, suppressing the prefix 'neuro', by the terms—*Hypnotic*, will be understood 'The state or condition of *nervous* sleep'; *Hypnotize*, 'To induce *nervous* sleep'; *Hypnotized*, 'One who has been put into the state of *nervous* sleep'; *Hypnotism*, '*Nervous* sleep'; *Hypnotist*, 'One who practises Neuro-Hypnotism'. **1847–9** TODD *Cycl. Anat.* IV. 695/2 Modes of inducing somnambulism..practised.. under the designation of hypnotism. **1852** BRAID (*title*) Magic, Witchcraft, Animal Magnetism, Hypnotism and Electro Biology (ed. 3). **1883** *19th Cent.* Oct. 696 Under the name of Hypnotism, the subject has after a long interval reappeared on the scientific horizon. **1892** *Brit. Med. Jrnl.* 27 Aug. 459 Hypnotism is an agent of great value in the treatment of chronic alcoholism. **1893** *Pall Mall G.* 10 Jan. 1/3 Hypnotism is the science which deals with the phenomena of a peculiar mental state produced by artificial means. **1898** *Times* 14 July 14/3 The habitual use of hypnotism on women is greatly injurious, both morally and intellectually.

2. The state thus induced: the hypnotized or hypnotic condition.

1843 [see sense 1]. **1847** *Nat. Encycl.* I. 760 This induced him [Braid] to give another name, Hypnotism, to the state in which persons are thus placed. **1860** *Illustr. Lond. News* 11 Feb. 139/2 Hypnotisme, or nervous sleep, now exciting so much attention in the French medical world. **1862** LYTTON *Str. Story* II. 215 The enchanters and magicians arrived.. at the faculty of..inducing fits of hypnotism, trance, mania. **1876** C. M. DAVIES *Unorth. Lond.* (ed. 2) 98 Swedenborg had the power of inducing, in his own case, a state clearly the same as what we now call mesmerism or hypnotism.

3. Sleepiness or sleep artificially induced by any means; also *fig.*

1860 I. TAYLOR *Spir. Hebr. Poetry* (1873) 27 He has fallen into a sort of Biblical hypnotism, or artificial slumber, under the influence of which the actual meaning of words and phrases fails to rouse attention. **1875** H. C. WOOD *Therap.* (1879) 23, I have given a hypodermic injection of a grain of morphia to a man, inducing a degree of hypnotism. **1885** *Times* 15 Dec. 9 The country will be the gainer by the hypnotism of the one party and the forbearance of the other.

hypnotist ('hɪpnətɪst). [f. as prec. + -IST.] One who studies or practises hypnotism; a hypnotizer. Also *attrib.*

1843 [see HYPNOTISM 1]. **1884** *Proc. Soc. Psych. Res.* I. v. 12 Results which.. indicate a special sympathy or 'rapport' between a hypnotist or mesmerist and a sensitive 'subject'. **1890** *Athenæum* 10 May 603/1 The cleverest hypnotists have recently told us that they cannot induce a victim to commit an act altogether repugnant to his or her moral character. **1893** E. Hart in *Brit. Med. Jrnl.* 18 Feb. 363 The hypnotist faith-curer of the hospital ward and the priestly faith-curer of the grotto are in truth utilising the same human elements.

Hence **hypno'tistic** *a.*, relating to hypnotists or hypnotism.

hypnotize ('hɪpnətaɪz), *v.* [f. as HYPNOT-IC + -IZE: in F. *hypnotiser.*] *trans.* To put into a hypnotic state; to place under the influence of hypnotism; to mesmerize. Also ***to hypnotize into*** (a state or belief). Also *absol.*

1843 [see HYPNOTISM 1]. **1847–9** Todd *Cycl. Anat.* IV. 703/1 Observations upon individuals hypnotised by Mr. Braid. **1880** *Brit. Med. Jrnl.* 4 Sept. 382 The natural normal state of those who may be readily hypnotised. **1892** *Daily News* 17 Dec. 5/5 They hypnotised themselves into believing in it. **1892** *Brit. Med. Jrnl.* 3 Dec. 1219 Anyone can hypnotise, and every one can hypnotise if he is patient enough, and either scientifically intelligent or ignorantly fanatic. **1896** *Voice* (N.Y.) 6 Feb. 2/4 Houses of Representatives have been hypnotized into subserviency.

Hence **'hypnotized** *ppl. a.*; **'hypnotizing** *vbl. sb.* and *ppl. a.* **'hypnotizable** *a.*, capable of being hypnotized. **hypnotizability** (,hɪpnətaɪzə'bɪlɪtɪ), capability of being hypnotized. **hypnoti'zation**, the action of hypnotizing, or condition of being hypnotized. **'hypnotizer**, one who hypnotizes.

1888 *Amer. Jrnl. Psychol.* May 520 To furnish a criterion of the *hypnotizability of the subject. **1885** *Eng. Mechanic* 13 Feb. 512 The number of *hypnotisable subjects. **1883** *Proc. Soc. Psych. Res.* I. v. 67 After a very short course of *hypnotisation. **1892** *Spectator* 2 Jan. 26/2 Horses are very susceptible to hypnotization. **1843** *Hypnotized [see HYPNOTISM 1]. **1880** Romanes in *19th Cent.* Sept. 475 When he clattered his teeth, the hypnotised patient repeated the movement. **1883** *Ibid.* Oct. 701 The 'subject' mimics or obeys his *hypnotiser in a quite mechanical way. **1889** *Athenæum* 25 May 661/1 He meets the monk Heliobas.. reputed hypnotizer and mesmerist. **1843** Braid *Neurypnol.* 7 It was alleged that my mode of *hypnotizing was no novelty. **1883** *Proc. Soc. Psych. Res.* I. v. 63 The hypnotising process may carry a 'sensitive' subject in a minute.. into hypnotic sleep.

hypnotoid ('hɪpnətɔɪd), *a.* [f. HYPNOT-IC + -OID.] Like or resembling the hypnotic state.

1887 E. Gurney in *Proc. Amer. Soc. Psych. Res.* Dec. 201 This young lady had a wonderful hypnotoid sensitiveness, by which she was sometimes able to make unconscious estimates.

‖**hypnum** ('hɪpnəm). *Bot.* Pl. **hypnums, hypna**. [mod.L., ad. Gr. ὕπνον (Theophr.) 'moss growing on trees'.] A large genus of pleurocarpous mosses; feather-moss.

1753 Chambers *Cycl. Supp.* s.v., The branches of the Hypnums are usually spread about upon the ground, and are perennial. *Ibid.*, The family of the Hypna is very numerous. **1837** Johnston in *Proc. Berw. Nat. Club* I. No. 5. 155 Amongst hypna in spongy places. **1857** Thoreau *Autumn* (1894) 138 One whole side, the upper, was covered with green hypnum.

hypo ('hɪpəʊ), *sb.*[1] ? *Obs.* Also 8 hippo, hyppo, 9 *pl.* (*rare*) **hypos**. [Abbreviation of HYPOCHONDRIA: cf. HYP.] Morbid depression of spirits.

1711 Mandeville (*title*) A Treatise of the Hypochondriack and Hysterick Passion vulgarly call'd the Hypo in Men and Vapours in Women. **1725** Bailey *Erasm. Colloq.* 163 When he's neither in a Passion, nor in the Hippo, nor in Liquor. **1738** [see HYP]. **1756–66** Amory *J. Buncle* (1770) III. 157 A chronic hyppo. **1851** H. Melville *Whale* i. 1 When my hypos get the upper hand of me. **1869** Mrs. Stowe *Oldtown F.* 333 Alleging as a reason that "t would bring on her hypos'.

hypo ('haɪpəʊ), *sb.*[2] *Photogr.* [Abbreviation of HYPOSULPHITE.] The salt formerly called hyposulphite, now thiosulphate, of soda, used for fixing photographic pictures. Also *attrib.*

1855 [see PRINT *sb.* 13]. **1861** *Photogr. News Alm.* in *Circ. Sc.* (*c* 1865) I. 155/1 A little will be lost in the hypo fixing bath. *Ibid.* 155/2 The proof assumes a disagreeable red hue after it is fixed with the hypo. **1889** *Anthony's Photogr. Bull.* II. 76 Hypo is cheap, and can be bought at nearly every drug store. *Ibid.* 274 The action of restrainers and retarders, of hypo-eliminators.

hypo ('haɪpəʊ), *sb.*[3] *slang.* [Abbrev. of HYPODERMIC.] A hypodermic needle or injection; a drug-addict.

1904 *San Francisco Chron. Suppl.* 30 Oct. 4 (caption to picture showing a morphine addict) The 'Hypo'. **1925** *Writer's Monthly* June 486/2 Hypo, a hypodermic syringe or a hypodermic needle. **1926** J. Black *You can't Win* xii. 159 'Vag these two hypos', said the cop to the desk man. **1936** G. K. Zipf *Psycho-Biol. of Lang.* ii. 31 *Hypo* may be a truncation of a *hypodermic injection*.. or it may be an abbreviation of '*hyposulfite of soda*'. **1942** *R.A.F. Jrnl.* 3 Oct. 30 Horrible rumours about the ease with which a hypo. needle will break. **1953** W. Burroughs *Junkie* (1972) ii. 21 An eyedropper is easier to use than a regular hypo, especially for giving yourself vein shots. **1956** H. Gold *Man who was not with It* (1965) ii. 18 He.. dragged his fingers along the little scabs from the hypo. **1973** J. Wainwright *Devil you Don't* 89 The night medic.. held the loaded hypo.

hypo ('haɪpəʊ), *v. slang.* [f. HYPO *sb.*[3]] To administer a hypodermic injection (to). Also *fig.* Hence **'hypoing** *vbl. sb.*

1925 *Flynn's* 7 Feb. 489/2 *Hypo*, to use a hypodermic syringe. **1945** *Variety* 24 Oct. 4/4 (*heading*) Many new pix to hypo bond preems [i.e. new pictures offered as inducements for bond premieres]. **1956** C. D. Simak *Strangers in Universe* (1958) 14 Apparently not too dangerous. Not with every single soul hypoed and immunized and hormoned to his eyebrows. **1960** *Time* (Dom. ed.) 25 Jan. 90/3 Because of continuing hypo-ing, his arms and legs become abscessed. **1968** *Listener* 31 Oct. 567/3 This impulse is very much hypo'd up during an election year.

hypo- (hɪpəʊ, haɪpəʊ), before vowels also **hyp-**, *prefix*, repr. Gr. ὑπο-, ὑπ- (f. ὑπό prep. and adv. 'under' = L. *sub*), largely employed in Greek in the formation of verbs, adjectives, and substantives.

With verbs, and their derivatives, ὑπο- had the senses 'under, beneath, down, from below; underhand, secretly; in a subordinate degree, slightly'. With adjectives and substantives, ὑπο- had the local sense 'beneath, under' in a prepositional relation to the substantive implied in the radical part, or the sense 'in a lower relation, in a lower degree, slightly, somewhat, a little' in an adverbial relation. Few Greek words containing the prefix came down through late L. and Fr. into English; the only ones of ME. age being the ecclesiastical words *hypocrite* and *hypocrisy*, found soon after 1200 (the derivatives, *hypocritic, -al*, etc. are later, of 16th c.). A few technical words, e.g. *hyposarca, hypostasis*, occur (though hardly as Eng.) in end of 14th c.; a considerable number, including *hypochonder, -chondria, hypostatic, hypotenuse, hypothec, hypothesis, hypotrachelium, hypotyposis*, appear in 16th c., and others, as *hypocaust, hypogaster, -gastrium, hypogæal*, in 17th c. But the great majority of the *hypo-* formations belong to the vocabulary of modern science, and have no actual Greek prototypes, but are formed (usually) on Greek elements, and more or less in accordance with Greek principles of word-formation. *Hypo-* has not, like *hyper-*, become a living element, capable of being prefixed at will to words of any origin.

The first vowel in Gr. ὑπο-, L. *hypo-*, is short, and all the early words in English were introduced with the *y* short, as in *hypocrite, hypocrisy*, etc. The *y* is marked as short in all compounds with *hypo-* in Pronouncing Dictionaries down to the middle of the 19th c. Some later Dictionaries, while retaining short *y* under stress, primary or secondary, as in *hypocaust, hypothetic*, make it long (aɪ) in unaccented syllables, as in *hypothesis, hypotenuse*. But the later tendency in the South of England has been to treat *y* in all positions except before two consonants as (aɪ), and, against etymology and history, to say *hȳposulphate, hȳpostatical*, etc.

I. 1. In words from Greek: the most important of these are *hypochondria, hypocrisy, hypocrite, hypotenuse, hypothec, hypothesis*, and their derivatives.

2. In modern formations, with sense 'under, beneath, below', of relative position; sometimes antithetical to terms in EPI- or HYPER-. In one set (*a*) *hypo-* has a prepositional relation governing the sb. occurring or implied in the following element, as in *hypobasal*, HYPOBRANCHIAL, HYPODERMIC, HYPOGLOSSAL; in another (*b*) *hypo-* qualifies the second element adverbially or attributively, signifying that this is itself the *nether* or *lower* of two (or more), as in HYPOBLAST, *hypomere, hypozoa* (animals low in the scale).

3. *Mus.* **a.** Prefixed to the names of musical modes in ***hypoæolian, -dorian, -ionian, -lydian, -mixolydian, -phrygian***, to denote either (*a*) the grave modes in Ancient Greek music, beginning at a definite interval below the ordinary *Æolian, Dorian*, etc. or (*b*) the 'plagal' modes in mediæval music, each of which has a compass a fourth below that of the corresponding 'authentic' mode. **b.** Also formerly in names of intervals measured downwards, as *hypodiapason, -diapente, -diatessaron, -ditone* (see DIAPASON, etc.). (Cf. HYPER- 2.)

1597 Morley *Introd. Mus.* 98 If the leading part were highest, then would they call it [a Fuge] in hypodiatessaron, which is the fourth beneath. **1651** J. F[reake] *Agrippa's Occ. Philos.* 260 Clio with the Moon move after the Hypo-dorian manner. *Ibid.* 261 Urania also doth the eight create And musick Hypo-Lydian elevate. **1760** Stiles *Anc. Greek Music* in *Phil. Trans.* LI. 712 We have already shown the Hypodorian mese to have been in *e*, the Hypophrygian in *f*♯, and the Hypolydian in *g*♯. *Ibid.*, The Hypoïonian mese was inserted in *f* natural, and the Hypo-æolian in *g* natural, at a fourth respectively from the Ionian and Æolian. **1844** Beck & Felton tr. *Munk's Metres* 290 The Mixolydian and Hypolydian were subordinate species of the Lydian [mood]. **1867** Macfarren *Harmony* i. 17. **1897** *Daily News* 19 Mar. 6/4 Much fun was made of a sailor's ditty said to be written in the hypomixolydian mode.

4. 'To some extent', 'slightly', 'somewhat', in many adjectives; similarly in substantives, with the sense 'slight' or 'deficient'. These words belong chiefly to pathology, and are the opposites of similar formations beginning with HYPER- II.

5. In Chemistry, *hypo-* (in contrast to HYPER- 7) is used to name an oxygen compound lower in the series than that having the simple name without *hypo-*; thus, *sulphurous acid* = H_2SO_3, *hyposulphurous acid* = H_2SO_2, *vanadic oxide* V_2O_5, *hypovanadic oxide* $V_2O_4(VO_2)$, *vanadious oxide* V_2O_3, *hypovanadious oxide* $V_2O_2(VO)$.

II. a. The more important words belonging to all these groups appear in their alphabetical order as main words; others of less importance or less frequent use follow here. (In many of these the immediate derivation is obvious, they being simply formed by prefixing *hypo-* to another word, the etymology of which will be found in its place: e.g. *hypoazotic*, f. *hypo-* + AZOTIC, etc. In the following words *e* often replaces *æ, œ*, esp. in U.S. usage; the alternative spelling is not given for each word individually.)

hypalgesia (-'dʒiːsɪə) *Med.* [Gr. ἄλγησις sense of pain], diminished sensitivity to pain, hypalgia; so **hypal'gesic** *a.*, exhibiting or tending to produce hypalgesia. **hypoa'cidity** *Physiol.*, a deficiency of acid constituents, esp. in the gastric juice. **hypoac'tivity** *Physiol.*, diminished activity, *esp.* diminished secretory activity of a gland. **hypoæsthesia** (,haɪpəʊɪs'θiːzɪə) *Path.* = HYPÆSTHESIA; hence **hypoæs'thetic** *a.* **,hypoalbumi'næmia** *Physiol.* [Gr. αἷμα blood], an abnormally low concentration of albumins in the blood. **hypoal'gesia** *Med.*, = *hypalgesia*. **hypoan'timonate** *Chem.*, a salt of antimony tetroxide. ‖**hypo'aria** *pl. Ichthyol.* [Gr. ᾠάριον little egg], a pair of protuberant oval ganglia developed beneath the optic lobes of osseous fishes; hence **hypo'arian** *a.* **hypoa'zotic** *a. Chem.* = HYPONITROUS; hence **hypoazotide** = hyponitrous acid, $H_2N_2O_2$ (*Syd. Soc. Lex.* 1886). **hypo'basal** *a. Bot.*, applied to the lower of the two cells or portions of the oospore of vascular cryptogams (cf. EPIBASAL). ‖**hypobole** (hɪ'pɒbəliː) *Rhet.* [Gr. ὑποβολή, f. ὑποβάλλειν to throw under, suggest], the mentioning and refuting of objections which might be brought against the speaker's case by an opponent. **hypocalcæmia** (-kæl'siːmɪə) *Physiol.* [CALC(IUM + Gr. αἷμα blood], an abnormally low concentration of calcium in the blood; hence **hypocal'cæmic** *a.* **hypo'capnia** *Physiol.* [Gr. καπνός smoke], an abnormally low concentration of carbon dioxide in the blood. ‖**hypoca'tharsis** *Med.* [CATHARSIS], a slight purging; so **hypoca'thartic** *a.* (*Syd. Soc. Lex.* 1886). **'hypochil** (-kɪl), ‖**hypochilium** (-'kaɪlɪəm) *Bot.* [Gr. χεῖλος lip], the basal portion of the labellum of an orchid (*Treas. Bot.* 1866). **,hypochlo'ræmia** *Physiol.*, an abnormally low concentration of chlorides in the blood. **,hypochlor'hydria** *Physiol.* [CHLORHYDR(IC *a.*], an abnormally low concentration of hydrochloric acid in the gastric juice; so **,hypochlor'hydric** *a.* **hypo'chlorin** *Chem.* [Gr. χλωρός green], Pringsheim's name for a substance found in every plant-cell which contains chlorophyll. **hypo'chordal** *a. Zool.* [CHORD *sb.*[1]], ventral to the notochord or spinal cord. ‖**hypoclidium** (-'klaɪdɪəm) *Ornith.* [Gr. κλείς, κλειδ- key], the interclavicular element of the clavicles of a bird, seen in the merrythought of a fowl; hence **hypo'clidian** *a.* †**hypo'colon**, a semicolon. **hypo'crystalline** *a. Min.*, consisting of crystals contained in a non-crystalline or massive mineral substance. **'hypocycle** *nonce-wd.* (see quot., and cf. EPICYCLE). ‖**hypo'dactylum** *Ornith.* [Gr. δάκτυλος finger], the lower surface of a bird's toe (Mayne, 1855). †**hypo'deacon** [Gr. ὑποδιάκονος under-servant], a subdeacon. **,hypoder'matomy** *Med.* [Gr. δέρμα skin + τομή cutting], incision of a subcutaneous part (*Syd. Soc. Lex.* 1886). **hypodermoclysis** (-də'mɒklɪsɪs) *Med.* [Gr. κλύσις a washing, drenching], the injection of nutrient fluids under the skin in the collapse from cholera or other exhausting diseases. ‖**hypodiastole** (-daɪ'æstəliː) *Gr. Gram.* [Gr. ὑποδιαστολή] = DIASTOLE 3 (q.v., quot. 1833). **hypodicrotous** (-'daɪkrətəs) *a. Phys.*, having a slight secondary wave in each pulse-beat. †**hypodi'dascal** [ad. Gr. ὑποδιδάσκαλος: see DIDASCALIC], an under-teacher, an usher. **,hypodig'matical** *a.* [Gr. ὑποδειγματικός], indicating by way of example or symbol. **'hypodrome** [med.L. *hypodromum* (see Du Cange), f. Gr. ὑπό under + δρόμος course], a roofed porch or colonnade. **hypody'namic** *a. Path.*, characterized by weakness or prostration (cf. ADYNAMIC). **hypo-e'llipsoid** *Geom.*, a curve traced by a point in the circumference of a circle

or ellipse rolling along the inside of an ellipse (cf. HYPOCYCLOID). **hypoesthesia**, var. *hypoæsthesia* above. **hypoeu'tectic** *a.*, (of an alloy of iron) containing a lower proportion of carbon than the eutectic composition (i.e. less than about 4·3%; (in quot. 1902 = *hypoeutectoid*, *eutectoid* itself not having been coined at that date). **hypoeu'tectoid** *a.*, (of steel) containing a lower proportion of carbon than the eutectoid composition (i.e. less than about 0·8%). **hypo'function** *Med.*, diminished or insufficient activity or production (in a gland or other part of the body); so **hypo'functional** *a.*; similarly **hypo'functioning** *vbl. sb.* **,hypogamma,globuli'næmia** *Path.* [Gr. αἷμα blood], an abnormally low concentration of gamma globulins in the blood; also, a disorder of which this condition is characteristic. **hypogæate** (-'dʒiːət) *Chem.*, a salt of hypogæic acid. **hypogæic** (-'dʒiːɪk) *a. Chem.* [f. mod.L. (*Arachis*) *hypogæa* the earth-nut; see HYPOGEAN], in ***hypogæic acid***: see quots. †**hypo'geiody** [f. Gr. ὑπόγειος underground, HYPOGEAN + ὁδός way], a branch of applied mathematics, by which subterranean distances and directions are ascertained; subterraneous surveying. **hypo'genitalism** *Path.*, hypogonadism; also, underdevelopment of the genitalia. **hypogenous** (-'ɒdʒɪnəs) *a. Bot.* [Gr. -γενής produced], (*a*) growing upon the under surface of leaves; (*b*) growing beneath the surface. **hypogeusia** (-'gjuːzɪə) *Med.* [Gr. γεῦσις taste], diminished acuteness of the sense of taste. **hypogly'cæmia** *Physiol.*, an abnormally low concentration of sugar in the blood; so **hypogly'cæmic** *a.*, of or exhibiting hypoglycæmia; tending to reduce the blood-sugar level. **hy'pognathism**, hypognathous conformation. **hy'pognathous** *a. Ornith.* [Gr. γνάθος jaw], having the under mandible longer than the upper. **hypo'gonadism** *Path.*, the reduction or absence of gonadal activity, esp. of hormone secretion; so **hypo'gonadal** *a.* †**'hypogram** [Gr. ὑπόγραμμα something written below] (see quot.). **hypo'hyal** *a. Anat.* [see HYO-, HYOID], forming the base of the hyoid arch; also as *sb.*, that part of the hyoid arch which lies between the stylohyal and basibranchial. **hypoischium** (-'ɪskɪəm) *Zool.* [ISCHIUM], a small cartilaginous or bony process that projects backwards from the ischial symphysis in the pelvic arch of many reptiles and some other vertebrates, supporting the ventral wall of the cloaca; hence **hypo'ischiac**, **-'ischial**, **-ischi'atic** *adjs.* **hypokalæmia** (-kə'liːmɪə), **-kaliæmia** (-kælɪ'iːmɪə) *Physiol.* [mod.L. *kalium* potassium (see KALI) + Gr. αἷμα blood], = *hypopotassæmia* below; hence **hypoka'læmic** *a.* **hypokeime'nometry** [Gr. ὑποκείμενον underlying substance or essence + -METRY] (see quot.). **hypoki'nesia**, **-ki'nesis** *Path.*, abnormally decreased muscular movement. **hypoki'netic** *a. Path.* [KINETIC], having defective muscular action (*Syd. Soc. Lex.* 1886). ‖**hypolem'niscus**, †**hypo'lemnisk** [Gr. ὑπολημνίσκος, f. λημνίσκος band, fillet], the critical mark ⁝. **,hypoleucocy'tosis**, **-leukocy'tosis** *Path.* = *leucopenia* (s.v. LEUCO-). **hypologism** (-'ɒlədʒɪz(ə)m) [Gr. ὑπολογισμός a ratio in which the antecedent is the smaller number] (see quot.). **,hypomagne'sæmia** *Physiol.* and *Vet. Sci.* [Gr. αἷμα blood], an abnormally low concentration of magnesium in the blood, important in cattle as the cause of grass tetany; hence **,hypomagne'sæmic** *a.* **hy'pomenous** *a. Bot.* [Gr. μένειν to remain] (see quot.). **'hypomere** *Biol.* [Gr. μέρος part], the lower half of certain sponges; hence **hy'pomeral** *a.*, pertaining to a hypomere. **hypome'tabolism** *Physiol.*, metabolism at a low rate. **hypomne'matic** *a.* [Gr. ὑπομνηματικός, f. ὑπόμνημα note, memorandum], having the form of memoranda or notes. **hypom'nestic** *a.* [Gr. ὑπομνηστικός suggestive to the memory], pertaining to or awakening recollection. **'hypomorph** *Genetics* [Gr. μορφ-ή form], any allele which is functionally less effective than the corresponding wild-type allele; so **hypo'morphic** *a.* **hypomo'tility** *Med.*, diminished movement, esp. of the stomach and intestines. **hypona'træmia** *Physiol.* [NATR(IUM + Gr. αἷμα blood], a lower than normal concentration of sodium in the blood; hence **hypona'træmic** *a.* ‖**hypo'neuria** *Path.* [Gr. νεῦρον nerve], deficient or diminished nervous power (*Syd. Soc. Lex.*). ‖**hypo'noia** [Gr. ὑπόνοια, f. ὑπονοέειν to suspect], underlying meaning. **'hyponome** ('hɪpəʊnəʊm) *Zool.* [Gr. ὑπονομή underground passage], the ambulatory pipe or fleshy funnel of a cephalopod. **hyponychial** (-'nɪkɪəl) *a.* [Gr. ὄνυξ, ὀνυχ- nail], seated under the nail (*Syd. Soc. Lex.* 1886). ‖**hy'ponychon**, **-chum** *Path.* [as prec.], an effusion of blood under a nail (*ibid.*). **hypo-'osmious** *a. Chem.* [OSMIUM], containing less oxygen than osmious compounds, as ***h. oxide*** = osmium monoxide OsO, ***h. sulphite*** $OsSO_3$. **,hypo-os'motic**, **hypos'motic** *adjs. Physiol.* = HYPOTONIC *a.* 1; const. *to*. **hypo'pepsy** *Path.* [Gr. πέψις digestion], defective digestion. **hypopetalous** (-'pɛtələs) *a. Bot.* (also †**-petaleous**, **-ious**), having the petals inserted beneath the ovary (Mayne 1855); belonging to the *Hypopetalæ* of Jussieu, a division of dicotyledonous polypetalous plants; hence **hypo'petaly**, hypopetalous condition (*Syd. Soc. Lex.* 1886). **hypophalangia** (-fə'lændʒɪə), **-phalangism** (-fə'lændʒɪz(ə)m), **-phalangy** (-'fæləndʒɪ) *Med.* [L. *phalang-*: see PHALANX], the congenital absence of one or more digital phalanges. **'hypophet** [Gr. ὑποφήτης], an interpreter, expounder. **hypophlœous** (-'fliːəs) *a. Bot.* [Gr. φλοιός bark], of lichens: growing under the outer layers of bark on trees, etc. (Mayne 1855); so also **hypo'phlœodal**, **hypophlœ'odic** *adjs.* **hypo'phoneme** [PHONEME] *Linguistics*, in the terminology of stratificational grammar, a phonological unit (see quots.); so **hypopho'nemic** *a.*, **hypopho'nemically** *adv.* **hypophonic** (-'fɒnɪk) *a.* [Gr. φωνή voice], serving as an accompaniment or response; so **hy'pophonous** *a.* ‖**hy'pophora** *Rhet.* [Gr. ὑποφορά], the statement of an opponent's probable objection to the speaker's argument (cf. *hypobole*). **hypo'phoria** *Ophthalm.*, latent strabismus in which there is a tendency for one eye to be directed below the line of sight of the other. **,hypophospha'tæmia** *Physiol.* [Gr. αἷμα blood], an abnormally low concentration of phosphates in the blood; so **,hypophospha'tæmic** *a.* **,hypophospha'tasia** *Path.*, a familial congenital disease associated with an abnormally low level of alkaline phosphatase in the body and defective bone development. ‖**hypo'phyllium** *Bot.* [Gr. φύλλιον little leaf] (see quot.). †**hypophyllo'spermous** *a. Bot.* [Gr. φύλλον leaf + σπέρμα seed] (see quot.) **hypophyllous** (-'fɪləs) *a. Bot.* [Gr. φύλλον leaf], growing under, or on the under side of, a leaf. **hypo'physical** *a.* [PHYSICAL], lying beneath or below the physical. **hypo'physics**, matters that lie beneath physics. **'hypopial** *a.*, pertaining to the hypopus. **hypopi'tuitarism** *Path.* [PITUITAR(Y *a.* + -ISM], diminished hormone secretion by the pituitary body; hence **hypopi'tuitary** *a.*, of, pertaining to, or affected with hypopituitarism. **hypo'plankton**, plankton found in the layer of water directly above the bottom of the ocean. ‖**hypo'plasia** *Path.* [Gr. -πλασία, πλάσις formation], defective growth of an organ or tissue. **hypo'plastral** *a.*, pertaining to the hypoplastron. ‖**hypo'plastron** *Zool.*, Huxley's name for the third lateral piece of the plastron of Chelonia = *hyposternal*. **'hypoplasty** *Path.* [Gr. πλαστός moulded, formed], 'a diminution of the fibrin in the blood; also, a diminution of the nutritive or generative activity' (*Syd. Soc. Lex.* 1886). **hypo'pleura**, **-'pleuron** *Ent.* (pl. **-pleura**), the region on the thorax of Diptera underneath the metapleuron and above the middle and posterior coxæ; so **hypo'pleural** *a.* **'hypoploid** *a. Genetics* [-PLOID], having one or a few chromosomes (orig. also chromosome fragments) missing from a haploid, diploid, triploid, etc., set; containing such cells; also as *sb.*, a hypoploid cell or individual; so **'hypoploidy**, the condition of being hypoploid. ‖**hypo'podium** *Bot.* [Gr. πούς, ποδ- foot], the stalk of the carpels (*Treas. Bot.* 1866). **,hypopota'ssæmia** *Physiol.* [Gr. αἷμα blood], an abnormally low concentration of potassium in the blood; so **,hypopota'ssæmic** *a.* **,hypoprotei'næmia** *Physiol.* [Gr. αἷμα blood], an abnormally low concentration of protein in the blood; so **,hypoprotei'næmic** *a.* **,hypoprothrombi'næmia** *Med.* [Gr. αἷμα blood], an abnormally low concentration of prothrombin in the blood; a disorder so characterized; so **,hypoprothrombi'næmic** *a.* **hy'popterate** *a. Bot.* [Gr. πτερόν wing], 'applied by Mirbel to a cupula when it is winged inferiorly' (Mayne 1855). ‖**hy'poptilum** *Ornith.* [Gr. πτίλον feather], the subsidiary shaft or plume of a feather, which springs from the main stem at the junction of quill and rachis; the after-shaft, the hyporachis; hence **hy'poptilar** *a.* ‖**hypopus** ('hɪpəʊpəs) *Zool.* [Gr. ὑπόπους having feet beneath], a heteromorphous nymphal form of certain acaroids. **hypopygial** (-'pɪdʒɪəl) *a.*, pertaining to the hypopygium; situated under the end of the abdomen. ‖**hypopygium** (-'pɪdʒɪəm) *Entom.* [Gr. ὑποπύγιον rump, tail, πυγή buttocks], (*a*) see quot.; (*b*) the clasping organ at the end of the abdomen of many male dipterous insects. **hypora'chidian (hyporrh-)** *a.*, of or pertaining to the hyporachis. ‖**hyporachis (hyporrhachis)** (-'pɒrəkɪs), *Ornith.* [Gr. ῥάχις spine], the accessory rachis or shaft of a bird's feather, the hypoptilum. **hypo'radial** *a.*, of or pertaining to the hyporadii of a feather. ‖**hypo'radius** *Ornith.*, one of the barbs of the after-shaft or hyporachis of a feather. ‖**hypor'chema**, **hyporcheme** ('hɪpɔːkiːm) [Gr. ὑπόρχημα, f. ὀρχέεσθαι to dance], a choral hymn to Apollo, accompanied by dancing and pantomimic action. **hyporchematic** (hɪpɔːkiː'mætɪk) *a.* [Gr. ὑπορχηματικός], accompanied by dancing. **'hyporrhined** *ppl. a. nonce-wd.* [Gr. ὑπόρρῑνος under the nose, ὑπορρίνιον moustache], moustached. **hyporrhythmic** (-'rɪθmɪk) *a.* [RHYTHMIC], deficient in rhythm; said of a heroic hexameter in which the cæsura is not observed (*Cent. Dict.*). **hyposcleral** (-'sklɪərəl) *a. Surg.* [see SCLEROTIC], performed beneath the sclerotic coat of the eye. **hyposclerite** (-'sklɪəraɪt) *Min.* [Gr. σκληρός hard], a blackish-green less hard variety of ALBITE (Dana *Min.* (1868) 350). **hypo'sclerous** *a.*, somewhat hard (*Syd. Soc. Lex.* 1886). **'hyposcope** *Mil.* [-SCOPE, after *periscope*], a form of periscope for attachment to a rifle or for use as a hand instrument. **hypose'cretion**, diminished secretion. **hypo'skeletal** *a. Anat.* [see SKELETON], developed below the endoskeleton; = HYPAXIAL (cf. EPISKELETAL). **hyposmotic**: see *hypoosmotic* above. †**hypo'sphagma**, **'hyposphagm** [Gr. ὑπόσφαγμα], a contusion; a blood-shot eye. **hyposphene** ('hɪpəʊsfiːn) *Comp. Anat.* [Gr. σφήν wedge], Cope's name for a wedge-shaped vertebral process situated on the neural arch below the postzygapophyses, in some extinct reptiles of the Permian period; hence **hypo'sphenal** *a.* ‖**hypospo'rangium** *Bot.* [SPORANGIUM], the indusium of a fern, when this grows from beneath the spore-case. **hypo'sternal** *a. Anat.* [Gr. ὑπόστερνος: see STERNUM], in ***hyposternal bone***, also ***hyposternal*** as *sb.*, St. Hilaire's name for the hypoplastron of a chelonian; also called ‖**hypo'sternum**. **hyposthenic** (-'sθɛnɪk) *a. Path.* [Gr. σθένος strength], of a medicine or disease: having power to lower or reduce strength (Mayne 1855). **,hyposthe'nuria** *Med.* [Gr. σθένος strength + -URIA], the secretion of urine of abnormally low specific gravity. **hypo'stigma** *Palæogr.* [Gr. ὑποστιγμή a comma], the comma, which in ancient punctuation had the form of a modern full stop. **hypo'stilbite** *Min.*, a hydrous silicate of alumina and lime allied to stilbite, with which it is often associated. **hypo'stomatous**, **hy'postomous** *a. Zool.* [Gr. στόμα, στοματ- mouth], having the mouth inferior, as certain fishes and infusoria (*Hypostomata*). ‖**hypo'stroma** *Bot.* [Gr. στρῶμα layer], Martius' name for the cellular layer supporting the stroma of fungi. ‖**hypostrophe** (hɪ-, haɪ'pɒstrəfɪ) [Gr. ὑποστροφή turning back], (*a*) *Path.* (i) a turning or tossing as of the sick in bed; (ii) a relapse, return of a disease; (iii) a falling back, as of the womb (Mayne 1855); (*b*) *Rhet.* reversion to a subject after a parenthesis. **hypostyle** ('hɪpəstaɪl) *a. Arch.* [Gr. ὑπόστυλος; see STYLE], having the roof supported on pillars. **hypo'styptic** *a. Med.* [see STYPTIC], slightly astringent (Mayne 1855). **hyposyllo'gistic** *a.*, having the value, but not the strict form, of a syllogism. **hypo'tactic** *a. Gram.* [Gr. ὑποτακτικός], dependent, subordinate in construction (cf. *hypotaxis*). ‖**hypo'tarsus** *Ornith.* [TARSUS], a process of the hinder part of the tarso-metatarsus of most birds; the talus or so-called calcaneum; hence **hypo'tarsal** *a.* **hypotaurine** (-'tɔːriːn) *Chem.* [a. F. *hypotaurine* (Chatagner & Bergeret 1951, in *Compt. Rend.*

CCXXXII. 450)], a pale yellow crystalline amino-acid, $NH_2(CH_2)_2SO_2H$, found in some higher organisms; 2-aminoethanesulphinic acid. ‖**hypo'taxis** *Gram.* [Gr. ὑπόταξις, f. τάσσειν to place], subordination, subordinate construction. ‖**hypothecium** (hɪpəʊ'θiːsɪəm) *Bot.* [Gr. θηκίον, dim. of θήκη case] (see quots.); hence **hypo'thecial** *a.* **hypothenar** (-'ɒθɪnə(r)) *a. Anat.* [Gr. ὑποθέναρ, f. θέναρ palm of the hand], of or pertaining to the eminence on the inner side of the palm, over the metacarpal bone of the little finger. **hypo'thermal, hypo'thermic** *adjs.* [Gr. ὑπόθερμος somewhat warm, f. θερμός warm, hot], (*a*) tepid; (*b*) relating to reduction of the heat of the body; (*c*) *Petrol.*, of, pertaining to, or designating mineral and ore deposits formed by hydrothermal action at relatively high temperature and pressure; so '**hypothermy**, 'the condition of being hypothermal' (*Syd. Soc. Lex.* 1886). **hypotrichosis** (-trɪ'kəʊsɪs) *Path.* [ad. G. *hypotrichose* (R. Bonnet 1892, in *Anat. Hefte* I. I. viii. 235), f. Gr. τρίχωσις growth of hair, f. τριχοῦν to cover with hair (θρίξ, τριχ- hair)], partial or complete absence of hair; hence **hypotri'chotic** *a.* **hypotrichous** (hɪp-, haɪ'pɒtrɪkəs) *a. Zool.* [Gr. θρίξ, τριχ- hair], of or pertaining to the *Hypotricha*, an order of the class *Ciliata* of *Protozoa*, having the locomotive cilia confined to the ventral surface. **hypotrophy** (-'ɒtrəfɪ) *Path.* [Gr. τροφή nourishment], a condition of an organ or part due to defective nourishment (Mayne 1855). **hypotym'panic** *a. Anat.* [see TYMPANUM], situated beneath the tympanum; applied esp. to the lower bone of the jaw-pier in osseous fishes; also as *sb.*, the quadrate. **hypo'typic, hypo'typical** *adjs.*, subtypical; not fully typical. **hypo'vanadate** *Chem.*, a salt of hypovanadic acid. **hypova'nadic** *a. Chem.*, containing less oxygen than a vanadic compound, as ***h. oxide*** = vanadium tetroxide, V_2O_4. **hypova'nadious** *a. Chem.*, containing less oxygen than a vanadous compound, as ***hypovanadious oxide*** = vanadium dioxide, V_2O_2. ˌ**hypovitami'nosis** *Path.* [-OSIS], any condition caused by vitamin deficiency. **hypovo'læmia** *Physiol.* [VOL(UME *sb.* + Gr. αἷμα blood], a decreased volume of circulating blood in the body; hence **hypovo'læmic** *a.* **hypoxæmia** (haɪpɒk'siːmɪə) *Med.* [ad. F. *hypoxémie* (P. A. Piorry *Traité de Méd. pratique* (1847) III. 123), f. *ox-ygène* + *-émie* (Gr. αἷμα blood)] = ANOXÆMIA. **hypoxia** (haɪ'pɒksɪə) *Med.* [OX(YGEN + -IA[1]] = ANOXIA; hence **hy'poxic** *a.*, of or pertaining to hypoxia; deficient in oxygen. **hypoxylous** (-'ɒksɪləs) *a. Bot.* [Gr. ξύλον wood], pertaining to ascomycetous fungi of the genus *Hypoxylon*, which grow on trees, decaying wood, etc. ‖**hypo'zeugma** *Gram.* [ZEUGMA], the combination of several subjects with a single verb or predicate. ‖**hypo'zeuxis** *Gram.* [Gr. ὑπόζευξις], the use of several parallel clauses, each having its own subject and verb. ‖**hypozoa** (hɪpəʊ'zəʊə) *Zool.* [Gr. ζῷον animal], a subdivision of the animal kingdom, including the lowest living forms; = PROTOZOA (*Syd. Soc. Lex.* 1886); hence **hypo'zoan** *a.* **hypo'zoic** *a.* (*a*) *Geol.*, lying beneath the strata which contain remains of living organisms; (*b*) *Zool.* of or pertaining to the *Hypozoa* (*Syd. Soc. Lex.* 1886).

1881 J. ROSS *Treat. Dis. Nervous Syst.* I. iii. 84 Eulenberg has proposed the term *hypalgesia or hypalgia, to indicate diminution of painful reaction, while limiting analgesia to its abolition. **1906** *Jrnl. Nerv. & Mental Dis.* XXXIII. 324 (*heading*) Hypesthesia and hypalgesia and their significance in functional nervous disturbances. **1971** P. C. LUND *Spinal Anesthesia* vii. 318 Sharp needles are..utilized to determine the level of hypalgesia which precedes the development of analgesia. **1911** STEDMAN *Med. Dict.* 405/2 *Hypalgesic. **1916** L. F. BARKER *Monographic Med.* IV. 137 The effect of summation of stimuli should..be noticed, by drawing a sharp needle lengthwise over an analgesic or hypalgesic area. **1935** *Discovery* Aug. 226/2 One very fortunate property which such a generator appears to possess is its pain-relieving virtue, or hypalgesic action, a very useful condition when treating post-operative cases. **1900** DORLAND *Med. Dict.* 311/2 *Hypoacidity. **1902** *Encycl. Brit.* XXXI. 551/2 Hyperacidity from lactic may obscure hypoacidity of hydrochloric acid. **1943** E. URBACH *Allergy* (1944) ii. 67 Gastric hypo- or anacidity is often observed. **1910** *Bull. Johns Hopkins Hosp.* XXI. 127/2 Conditions therefore simulating grades of *hypoactivity. **1914** *Arch. Internal Med.* XIV. 145 Hypo-activity of the thyroid and pituitary. **1965** B. E. FREEMAN tr. *Vandel's Biospeleol.* xxi. 351 The majority of the follicles of the thyroid..show signs of hypoactivity. **1906** *Jrnl. Nerv. & Mental Dis.* XXXIII. 324 *Hypoesthesia is the term heretofore employed to express this condition, but its awkward form at least excuses the employment of hypesthesia as a more euphonious and therefore more satisfactory expression. **1967** D. SINCLAIR *Cutaneous Sensation* viii. 148 'Hyperaesthesia' and 'hypoaesthesia' are similarly misused. **1909** *Jrnl. Physiol.* XXXVIII. 158 On a *hypoæsthetic area it may be that no sense of touch is elicited with a bristle of less than 3000 milligrammes pressure. **1940** *Lancet* 17 Feb. 303/2 Complete recovery [from frostbite] may apparently take place, but after a variable interval neuralgic pains may begin. The skin is usually hypoæsthetic. **1937** *Acta Med. Scand.* XCI. 336 A simple method for the determination of *hypoalbuminemia and hypoproteinemia..is afforded by the determination of the specific gravity of serum. **1962** *Lancet* 6 Jan. 52/1 This loss of protein may be significant in the pathogenesis of the hypoalbuminæmia of kwashiorkor. **1929** DORLAND & MILLER *Med. Dict.* (ed. 15) 584/1 *Hypoalgesia. **1945** *Jrnl. Clin. Invest.* XXIV. 505 A patient had 'hypoalgesia' to pin prick on parts of his left hand. **1968** A. SOULAIRAC et al. *Pain* 36 The marked hypoalgesia recorded in this animal was associated with a double right lesion. **1879** ROSCOE & SCHORLEMMER *Treat. Chem.* II. II. 313 Antimony tetroxide forms salts with basic oxides which have been termed *hypoantimonates. **1844–6** OWEN *Lect. Comp. Anat. Vert.* I. viii. 179–80 In most osseous fishes the corresponding fibres of the pre-pyramidal tracts swell out suddenly, beneath the optic lobes, into two protuberant well-defined oval ganglions ('*hypoaria'):..they are well developed in the common Cod, in which, as in some other fishes, they contain a cavity called '*hypoarian ventricle'. **1854** J. SCOFFERN in *Orr's Circ. Sc., Chem.* 326 *Hypo-azotic or hyponitric acid. **1883** *Athenæum* 6 Oct. 439/1 To cause the patient to inhale with prudence hypoazotic vapour mixed with air. **1882** VINES *Sachs' Bot.* 351 In the Marchantieæ and Anthoceroteæ the short seta of the sporogonium is developed from the lower or posterior (*hypobasal cell). *Ibid.* 426 The hypobasal half of the embryo [of a fern]. **1704** J. HARRIS *Lex. Techn.*, **Hypobole*, is a Figure in Rhetorick whereby we answer what we prevented to be objected against by an Adversary. **1925** *Jrnl. Biol. Chem.* LXVI. 345 *Hypocalcemia was produced..by thyroparathyroidectomy. **1960** *Farmer & Stockbreeder* 22 Mar. 135/2 What is the glucose dosage for young pigs with hypocalcæmia? **1962** A. SORSBY in A. Pirie *Lens Metabolism Rel. Cataract* 298 Congenital cataract..can be caused by such frankly environmental disturbances as..maternal hypocalcæmia. **1935** D. H. SHELLING *Parathyroids* vi. 148 Other means of demonstrating *hypocalcemic tetany are now available. **1908** *Hypocapnia [see *hypercapnia* s.v. HYPER- IV]. **1961** *Lancet* 26 Aug. 475/1 The combination of extreme hypoxia with hypocapnia may well be fatal. **1706** PHILLIPS (ed. Kersey), **Hypocatharsis*, gentle Purging. **1927** *Amer. Jrnl. Med. Sci.* CLXXIII. 649 (*heading*) Acute intestinal obstruction: mechanism and significance of *hypochloremia and other blood chemical changes. **1963** H. L. BOCKUS et al. *Gastroenterology* (ed. 2) I. xxviii. 646/2 If hypochloremia and alkalosis are present, gastric retention and vomiting have probably preceded the bout of bleeding. **1893** *Hypochlorhydria [see *hyperchlorhydria* s.v. HYPER- IV]. **1971** J. SONG *Path. Sickle Cell Dis.* xviii. 355 The usual hypochlorhydria present in this disease may account for some of the gastric manifestations. **1921** *Chem. Abstr.* XV. 894 When the concn. varies between 0.010 and 0.012 sp. gr. the indications are that it [*sc.* the stomach] contains dissolved alimentary residues and tends to be *hypochlorhydric. **1971** J. SONG *Path. Sickle Cell Dis.* xviii. 356 Many individuals present hypochlorhydric states of a like degree. **1881** *Nature* XXIII. 561 Professor Pringsheim ..announced the discovery in the chlorophyll-corpuscles of a substance called *Hypo-chlorin. **1901** *Gray's Anat.* (ed. 15) II. 96 The future vertibræ..are soon joined across the middle line on the ventral aspect of the notochord by a *hypochordal cartilaginous bar. **1962** M. JOLLIE *Chordate Morphol.* vi. 153 This splint is the ventral, perichondral ossification of the hypochordal cartilage. **1657** J. SERGEANT *Schism Dispach't* 249 He goes smothly..without the least rub so much as of an *hypo-colon to stop him. **1888** W. S. BAILEY in *Amer. Naturalist* Mar. 208 When [a rock].. contains crystals in a hyaline ground-mass, the structure is described as *hypocrystalline. **1716** M. DAVIES *Athen. Brit.* II. To Rdr. 45 The Heteroclit Dissenters..move in an Excentrical *Hypocycle. *a* **1529** SKELTON *Image Hypocrisy* 62 Subdeacons that be *ypo-deakons. **1884** *Pall Mall G.* 10 Oct. 10/2 Till a physician could be obtained to perform Pacini's operation of *hypodermoclysis. **1877** ROBERTS *Handbk. Med.* (ed. 3) II. 21 A minor degree of this variety is named *hypo- or sub-dicrotous. **1625** SHIRLEY *Sch. Complement* III. v, There is the starre of Eloquence, vnder whom I am an *Hypodidascall, in English, his Vsher. **1708** MOTTEUX *Rabelais* IV. xlviii. 137, I saw a little Hump..say to the Hypodidascal [etc.]. **1860** T. A. G. BALFOUR *Typ. Char. Nature* 64 The typical, or symbolical, or *hypodeigmatical character. **1820** T. MITCHELL *Aristoph.* I. p. lvi, The *hypodrome, or covered porch where the wrestlers practised their exercises in winter. **1846** G. E. DAY tr. *Simon's Anim. Chem.* II. 275 If the disease..should take a *hypodynamic character, the urine..will assume an alkaline reaction. **1854** MOSELEY *Astron.* lxi. (ed. 4) 183 This curve..being of the nature of an hypo-cycloid, or rather, an *hypo-ellipsoid. **1902** *Encycl. Brit.* XXIX. 572/2 They are called hyper-eutectic or *hypo-eutectic according as this excess is cementite or ferrite, i.e., according as their carbon-content is above or below the 0·90 per cent. which the eutectic itself contains. **1926** W. E. WOODWARD *Metallogr. Steel & Cast Iron* i. 27 In a 2·0% C steel 0·3% C (= 4·5% Fe_3C) will have been required to form the eutectic portion of the hypo-eutectic alloy. **1959** Hypoeutectic [see *hypereutectic* adj. s.v. HYPER- IV]. **1911** *Encycl. Brit.* XIV. 805/2 This ferrite flows around and immediately heals over any cracks which form in the small quantity of cementite interstratified with it in the pearlite of *hypo-eutectoid steels. **1966** A. PRINCE *Alloy Phase Equilibria* vi. 107 The structure of a hypo-eutectoid Fe—Fe_3C alloy is one of ferrite with pearlite, the latter appearing in characteristic form. **1905** GOULD *Dict. New Med. Terms* 303/2 *Hypofunction. **1913** L. FORSTER tr. *A. Biedl's Internal Secretory Organs* 53 Vassale thinks that the new formation of tissue points to a hyper-function of the gland, the wasting of the colloid to a hypo-function. **1920** *Endocrinology* IV. 344 Hypofunction of the thyroid. **1972** *Lancet* 12 Aug. 299/2 There was a high frequency of sexual hypofunction and testicular atrophy among male patients. **1933** A. W. ROWE *Differential Diagn. Endocrine Disorders* viii. 116 'Hyperfunction' indicates a condition..in direct antithesis to..the known *hypofunctional state. **1961** *Jrnl. Amer. Med. Assoc.* 29 July 232/2 Of 43 hypofunctional nodules, only 2 proved to be due to carcinoma. **1926** J. S. HUXLEY *Ess. Pop. Sci.* 291 Whenever we can trace the effect of a *hypo- or hyperfunctioning of one of these [ductless] glands, we find that it affects..a complex of characters.. related to the performance of a single function. **1954** A. WHITE et al. *Princ. Biochem.* xliii. 936 In circumstances of adrenal cortical hypofunctioning..there is a failure of normal renal tubular reabsorption of sodium. **1865–72** WATTS *Dict. Chem.* III. 239 *Hypogæate of Copper. *Ibid.* 238 **Hypogæic acid*, $C_{16}H_{30}O_2$..discovered in 1855..in oil of earthnut. **1955** *Jrnl. Amer. Med. Assoc.* 13 Aug. 1344 (*heading*) *Hypogammaglobulinemia associated with a severe wound infection. **1970** PASSMORE & ROBSON *Compan. Med. Stud.* II. xviii. 103/1 Individuals with hypogammaglobulinaemia..produce little or no detectable circulating antibody and are vulnerable to bacterial invasion, but are not so susceptible to viral infection. **1972** *Lancet* 27 May 1151/2 Patients with the common variable type of severe hypogammaglobulinæmia exhibit lymphocytes with surface immunoglobulins. **1570** DEE *Math. Pref.* d j b, *Hypogeiodie, is an Arte Mathematicall, demonstratyng, how, vnder the Sphæricall Superficies of the earth, at any depth, to any perpendicular line assigned.. certaine way may be præscribed and gone. **1917** STEDMAN *Med. Dict.* (ed. 4) 458/2 *Hypogenitalism. **1922** L. F. BARKER *Endocrinol. & Metabolism* I. 157 Obesity is a frequent manifestation of hypogenitalism, either the physiological hypogenitalism of the menopause or the acquired form due to disease or to the surgical removal of the ovaries. **1964** L. MARTIN *Clinical Endocrinol.* (ed. 4) vii. 222 Hypogenitalism [in males] means abnormally small size or underdevelopment of the male external genitalia which need not necessarily include testicular failure. **1871** COOKE *Brit. Fungi* 490 Brand-spores, *hypogenous, scattered over the leaves in minute tufts. **1888** *Hypogeusia [see *hypergeusia* s.v. HYPER- IV]. **1969** C. PFAFFMANN *Olfaction & Taste* 578 Treatment with D-penicillamine had produced hypogeusia (a decrease in taste acuity). **1894** GOULD *Dict. Med.* 594/2 *Hypoglycemia. **1911** *Jrnl. Biol. Chem.* X. 160 Recent investigations on the production of hypoglycaemia. **1960** *Farmer & Stockbreeder* 9 Feb. 102/1 Hypoglycæmia is a symptom rather than a disease on its own. **1923** *Jrnl. Physiol.* LVII. 318 The blood became *hypoglycæmic. **1965** J. POLLITT *Depression & its Treatment* vi. 78, 20–80 units of soluble insulin before breakfast may be necessary to produce a mild hypoglycæmic reaction. **1970** PASSMORE & ROBSON *Compan. Med. Stud.* II. vi. 18/1 Today, approximately one-third of the total diabetic population is being treated with an oral hypoglycaemic agent. **1872** COUES *Key N. Amer. Birds* 323 *Rhynchopinæ*, Skimmers. Bill *hypognathous. **1933** *Med. Jrnl. & Rec.* CXXXVII. 457/2 The vast majority of *hypogonadal patients were within normal weights. **1944** R. S. HOTCHKISS *Fertility in Men* iv. 90 Disproportional height span of legs and torso suggest the hypogonadal state. **1961** W. C. YOUNG *Sex & Internal Secretions* (ed. 3) I. v. 348 Hypogonadal disorders of man. **1918** STEDMAN *Med. Dict.* (ed. 5) 469/1 *Hypogonadism. **1933** *Jrnl. Amer. Med. Assoc.* 7 Jan. 70/2 A method for the assay of blood and urine for testicular hormone..has been used as a laboratory test for hypogonadism. **1966** R. B. SCOTT *Price's Textbk. Pract. Med.* (ed. 10) vii. 450/1 The term female hypogonadism implies a deficiency of both the ovulatory and hormone secretory functions of the ovary. **1970** PASSMORE & ROBSON *Compan. Med. Stud.* II. xii. 11/2 In children hypogonadism leads to delayed puberty. **1656** BLOUNT *Glossogr.*, **Hypogram*, a subscription, or that is subscribed. **1882** W. R. PARKER in *Trans. Linn. Soc.* II. III. 168 This bar..has its distal fourth segmented off to form a *hypohyal. **1894** *Athenæum* 17 Nov. 680/3 The basi- and hypo-hyal cartilages of the Elasmobranchii. **1951** C. K. WEICHERT *Anat. Chordates* x. 485 A posterior prolongation from the ischial symphysis in *Sphenodon* and in many lizards and turtles is called the *hypoischiac process, or cloacal bone. **1910** PARKER & HASWELL *Text-bk. Zool.* (ed. 2) II. 354 In the Chelonia..both pubes and ischia meet in ventral symphyses, and epipubic and *hypoischial cartilages may be present. **1959** W. MONTAGNA *Compar. Anat.* v. 116 In lizards an epipubic cartilage projects anteriorly and an hypoischial cartilage projects posteriorly from the symphysis. **1897** W. N. PARKER tr. *Wiedersheim's Compar. Anat. Vertebr.* (ed. 2) 117 In Hatteria there is a marked epipubis and a *hypoischiatic process continuous with the epipubic cartilage. *Ibid.* 118 A longitudinal fibro-cartilaginous ligament, continuous anteriorly with the plug-like epipubic cartilage and posteriorly with the *hypoischium. **1925** J. S. KINGSLEY *Vertebr. Skeleton* 265 Squamata... The hypoischium, usually movable, is well developed and may be cartilage or bone in the adult. **1949** *Jrnl. Clin. Invest.* XXVIII. 409 (*heading*) Some observations on the development of *hypokaliemia during therapy of diabetic acidosis. **1951** *Dorland's Med. Dict.* (ed. 22) 713/2 Hypokalemia, hypokaliemia. **1972** *Lancet* 1 July 36/2 Hypokalæmia may be seen in any stage of renal failure. **1953** *Jrnl. Clin. Invest.* XXXII. 538 (*heading*) The effect of potassium in nephrectomized rats with *hypokalemic alkalosis. **1962** *Lancet* 1 Dec. 1145/1 During this period the patient became hypokalæmic. **1882** J. MARTINEAU *Study Spinoza* II. i. 165 Spinoza..attempts to construct a *Hypokeimenometry—a science of Substance and its affections, whereby the constitution of the universe shall be deduced from its primary essence—the All out of the One. **1886** *Syd. Soc. Lex.*, *Hypokinesia. *Ibid.*, *Hypokinesis. **1927** I. S. WECHSLER *Clin. Neurol.* IV. 391 Instead of hypokinesis there may be *hyperkinetic phenomena. **1970** *Nature* 4 Apr. 21/1 Parkinsonism is..characterized by tremor, rigidity of the limbs and poverty of movement (hypokinesia). **1718** PRIDEAUX *Connect. O. & N. Test.* II. I. 55 The *Hypolemnisk, a straight line with one point under it (as thus ÷). **1849** W. FITZGERALD tr. *Whitaker's Disput.* 125 Origen marked these texts with various asterisks and obeli, lemnisci and hypolemnisci. **1897** *Lippincott's Med. Dict.* 498/1 *Hypoleucocytosis. **1898** [see *leucopenia* s.v. LEUCO-]. **1930** H. DOWNEY in E. T. Bell *Text-bk. Path.* xxviii. 599 In pernicious anemia we see an example of neutrophile hypoleukocytosis. **1656** tr. *Hobbes' Elem. Philos.* (1839) 147 When the proportion of the first antecedent to the first consequent is less than that of the second to the second, the four magnitudes may be called *hypologism. **1933** *Jrnl. Clin. Invest.* XII. 982 (*heading*) Clinical manifestations of *hypo- and hyper-magnesaemia. **1971** *Arable Farmer* Feb. 70/2 A high level of potash in the soil.. can lead to hypomagnesaemia (grass staggers) in dairy cows. **1960** *Times* 28 Nov. 16/5 *Hypomagnesaemic tetany was common on sheep that were rapidly transferred back from good pasture to poorer hill grazing. **1866** *Treas. Bot.*,

*Hypomenous, free, not adherent; arising from below an organ, without adhering to it. **1887** SOLLAS in *Encycl. Brit.* XXII. 415/2 The lower half [of a Rhagon], which consists of all three fundamental layers, may be called the *hypomere. **1932** DORLAND & MILLER *Med. Dict.* (ed. 16) 6111/2 *Hypometabolism. **1962** T. L. SOURKES *Biochem. Mental Dis.* xxiv. 302 This syndrome has been variously termed metabolic insufficiency, nonmyxedematous hypometabolism, and euthyroid hypometabolism. **1891** *Athenæum* 4 Apr. 435/2 The treatise [on 'The Constitution of Athens'] is '*hypomnematic' in a very literal sense, presupposing familiarity with an existing body of literature. **1659** STANLEY *Hist. Philos.* XII. (1701) 498/1 Of Signes.. some are according to them, *Hypomnestick, others Endictick. **1932** H. J. MULLER in *Proc. 6th Internat. Congr. Genetics* I. 235 Scute-1 is therefore a *hypomorph. **1946** *Nature* 12 Oct. 520/1 This mutant allele is therefore a hypomorph to the normal allele. **1962** I. H. HERSKOWITZ *Genetics* xxiv. 210/1 Mutants having a similar but lesser effect than the normal gene are called hypomorphs. **1932** H. J. MULLER in *Proc. 6th Internat. Congr. Genetics* I. 235 Apricot, like eosin, is a mutant gene which produces an effect similar to that of the normal allelomorph, but a lesser effect... It is..like a lesser-normal. I therefore call it a '*hypomorphic' mutant. **1962** I. H. HERSKOWITZ *Genetics* xxiv. 210/1 We can represent the relationship between the normal gene and its hypomorphic mutants diagrammatically. **1900** DORLAND *Med. Dict.* 312/2 *Hypomotility. **1914** C. G. STOCKTON *Dis. Stomach* ix. 183 (*heading*) Diminished gastric motion, hypomotility, gastric atony. **1970** *Radiology* XCIV. 303/2 An upper gastrointestinal examination..failed to show any abnormality, except for generalized hypomotility of the stomach and small intestine. **1935** DORLAND & MILLER *Med. Dict.* (ed. 17) 649/1 *Hyponatremia. **1969** L. G. WESSON *Physiol. Human Kidney* xxvii. 554/1 Hyponatremia may be defined somewhat arbitrarily as a plasma sodium concentraton less than 130 mM/L in man. **1955** *Arch. Internal Med.* XCV. 21/1 Infants who present *hyponatremic acidosis. **1897** *Edin. Rev.* Oct. 290 Those who have no great skill at deciphering the *Hyponoia, the underlying significance, of the Idylls. **1884** A. HYATT in *Science* 1 Feb. 123 The fleshy pipe is therefore an ambulatory pipe or *hyponome. **1873** *Fownes' Chem.* (ed. 11) 441 *Hypo-osmious sulphite, OsSO₃, is a black-blue salt. **1905** W. H. HOWELL *Text-bk. Physiol.* 885 A hypotonic or *hyposmotic solution is one whose osmotic pressure is less than that of serum. **1957** B. T. SCHEER et al. *Rec. Adv. Invertebr. Physiol.* 237 The antennal secretion of *P. crassipes* is slightly hypo-osmotic to the blood in 50% sea water. **1963** R. P. DALES *Annelids* v. 104 The ability to form a hyposmotic urine. **1971** W. J. MCCAULEY *Vertebr. Physiol.* i. 9 If it has a lower osmotic pressure, it is said to be a hyposmotic solution. **1897** ALLBUTT *Syst. Med.* II. 802 A marked degree of '*hypopepsy' due to catarrh. **1916** *Genetics* I. 90 Various types of developmental malformation of the hands and feet have been described under such terms as..*hypophalangia. **1911** STEDMAN *Med. Dict.* 411/2 *Hypophalangism. **1965** *Arch. Internal Med.* CXV. 581/2 The present family is unique in that hypophalangism is limited to the fourth digits and associated with symphalangism. **1929** R. R. GATES *Heredity in Man* viii. 154 Brachyphalangy combined with *hypophalangy (less than five fingers) was transmitted for six generations. *a***1843** SOUTHEY *Comm.-pl. Bk.* IV. 721 Greg. Nazianzen calls S. Basil..an interpreter of the Spirit. *Hypophet as distinguished from prophet. **1966** S. M. LAMB *Outl. Stratif. Gram.* 18 Such cases have particularly attracted the attention of linguists in *hypophonemic systems... The hypophonemic and hypersememic strata might be called the phonetic and semantic, respectively. *Ibid.* 19 The hypophonemic system appears not to have a sign pattern. *Ibid.* 28 The tactics of the hypophonemic stratum of a language specifies how *hypophonemes (i.e. phonological components) are arranged in segments and clusters. **1968** J. ALGEO in *South Atlantic Bull.* XXXIII. ii. 2 The distinctive features of sound, the hypophonemes in Lamb's terminology, and relatively easy to study because there are so few of them—only about twelve to fifteen in most languages. Sample hypophonemes are *plosion, spirancy, nasality, labiality,* and *unvoicing.* **1969** *Language* XLV. 303 Such alternations would be treated as alternate realizations of these phonons in terms of the units of the lower phonological stratum, the hypophonemes. *Ibid.* 307 In Figure 6 the first vowels of /glɒsɔ́/ and /dɔbɔ́/ would be treated as the same, as /Vo/ *hypophonemically... They would be the same only when viewed as hypophonemic signs, which include non-distinctive as well as phonemic elements. **1882-3** in Schaff *Encycl. Relig. Knowl.* III. 2554/2 The church-singing was at first only a sort of monotonous (*hypophonic) cantilation. **1860** BOMBERGER tr. *Kurtz's Ch. Hist.* I. §89. 232 The laity continued for a long time the practise of *hypophonous chants, which consisted of responses to the intonation [etc.]. **1657** J. SMITH *Myst. Rhet.* 127 *Hypophora.. is when the speaker makes answer unto his own demand: As,..Shall we continue in sin, that grace may abound? God forbid. **1932** L. C. MARTIN *Introd. Appl. Optics* II. iv. 143 In *hypophoria one eye turns downwards. **1964** [see *hyperphoria* s.v. HYPER- IV]. **1935** D. H. SHELLING *Parathyroids* vi. 138 Fish has found *hypophosphatemia as well as hypocalcemia. **1962** *Lancet* 2 June 1169/1 The other forms of rickets and osteomalacia are of the vitamin-D-resistant type, and are characterised by persistent hypophosphatæmia. **1946** M. R. EVERETT *Med. Biochem.* (ed. 2) viii. 628 The Fanconi syndrome (intractable *hypophosphatemic rachitis accompanied by acidosis and renal glycosuria). **1968** R. F. PITTS *Physiol. Kidney & Body Fluids* (ed. 2) xiii. 237/2 One or the other parent is hypophosphatemic. **1948** J. C. RATHBUN in *Amer. Jrnl. Dis. Children* LXXV. 831 It was therefore decided to call this disease '*hypophosphatasia' to single out the remarkably low alkaline phosphatase levels. **1957** *Amer. Jrnl. Med.* XXII. 730/1 There is now good evidence that hypophosphatasia is a specific genetically determined metabolic disease characterized by three salient features: (1) abnormal mineralization of bone, (2) diminished alkaline phosphatase activity, and (3) increased urinary excretion of phosphorylethanolamine. **1866** *Treas. Bot.,* *Hypophyllium, a small abortive leaf, like a scale, placed below a cluster of leaf-like branches, or leaves. **1704** J. HARRIS *Lex. Techn.,* *Hypophyllospermous-plants, are such as bear their Seeds on the Backsides of their Leaves; as the Capillaries. **1855** MAYNE *Expos. Lex.,* *Hypophyllous. **1857** BERKELEY

Cryptog. Bot. §570. 508 The circinate æstivation and hypophyllous fruit..at once establish their nature. **1871** COOKE *Brit. Fungi* 502 Brand-spores hypophyllous, blackish, surrounded by the ferruginous epidermis. *a***1834** COLERIDGE *Omniana* in *Lit. Rem.* I. 349 Holding the anti-moralism of Paley and the *hypophysics of Locke. **1878** Hypophysics [see HYPERPHYSICS]. **1884** D. M. ALBERT *Brit. Oribatidæ* 5 The Tyroglyphidæ are usually parasitic during the curious *hypopial stage. **1909** *Hypopituitarism [see *hyperpituitarism* s.v. HYPER- IV]. **1921** *Glasgow Herald* 10 Sept. 4/5 There were several causes of dwarfism; sometimes disorders of the thyroid gland were the cause, but other varieties were produced by hypo-pituitarism. **1961** *Lancet* 30 Sept. 760/2 Prof. H. L. Sheehan showed that, in severe postpartum hypopituitarism, patients who had occasional uterine bleeding had just as great a destruction of the anterior pituitary as those who had permanent amenorrhœa. **1921** *Endocrinology* V. 800 A presentation of five cases of preadolescent *hypopituitary infantilism. **1955** R. H. WILLIAMS *Textbk. Endocrinol.* (ed. 2) ix. 604 The hypopituitary dwarfs usually show marked retardation of their epiphysial development. **1902** *Encycl. Brit.* XXXIII. 933/2 It is possible that the plankton immediately over the bottom [of the ocean] may prove to be sufficiently distinct to be separately classed as *hypoplankton. **1903** *Nature* 5 Nov. 23/2 There is evidence that certain forms [of Copepoda] are confined to the bottom, and form part of a true hypoplankton. **1942** H. U. SVERDRUP et al. *Oceans* xvii. 814 The swimming powers of many animals put them midway between the plankton and the nekton, and many forms..live both on or near the bottom and are sometimes called hypoplankton. **1955** C. C. DAVIS *Marine & Fresh-Water Plankton* i. 28 The hypoplankton consists of plankters living near the bottom. **1889** J. M. DUNCAN *Lect. Dis. Wom.* xvii. (ed. 4) 131 In one of these which I examined, there was marked *hypoplasia of the decidua. **1871** HUXLEY *Anat. Vert.* v. 202 In the Turtle the plastron consists of nine pieces .. the third, *hypoplastron. **1884** *Trans. Entomol. Soc. Lond.* 503 *Hypopleura, a distinct piece above the two last pairs of coxæ, and behind the sternopleura, from which it is separated by a suture. **1951** COLYER & HAMMOND *Flies Brit. Isles* 24 Spiracles or apertures of the tracheae (breathing-tubes) are located before the mesopleuron and behind the hypopleuron respectively. **1951** L. S. WEST *Housefly* ii. 28 The hypopleura lies behind the middle coxa, the sternopleura just in front. **1884** *Trans. Entomol. Soc. Lond.* 511 *Hypopleural bristles. **1930** *Jrnl. Genetics* XXII. 306 Other individuals—'*hypoploids'—may fail to inherit the fragment. *Ibid.* 313 Viable heteroploid or hypoploid zygotes. **1957** Hypoploid [see *hyperploid* s.v. HYPER- IV]. **1930** *Jrnl. Genetics* XXII. 329 The phaenotypic effects of *hypoploidy and hyperploidy of every portion of the chromatin. **1969** Hypoploidy [see *hyperploidy* s.v. HYPER- IV]. **1932** DORLAND & MILLER *Med. Dict.* (ed. 16) 612/2 *Hypopotassemia. **1949** *Jrnl. Clin. Invest.* XXVIII. 409/1 Hypopotassemia may appear during therapy of diabetic acidosis or coma. **1963** Hypopotassemia [see *hyperpotassæmia* s.v. HYPER- IV]. **1950** *Jrnl. Amer. Med. Assoc.* 16 Dec. 1328 A resultant *hypopotassemic, hypochloremic alkalosis. **1953** *Lancet* 11 July 60/1 The more familiar hypopotassæmic paralysis. **1934** *Jrnl. Biol. Chem.* CV. 327 (*heading*) The effect of nutritional *hypoproteinemia on the electrolyte pattern and calcium concentration of serum. **1961** *Lancet* 5 Aug. 299/1 Hypoproteinæmia may be due to impaired synthesis of protein (especially albumin) in malnutrition or liver disease, or..to abnormal loss of protein in starvation, after injury, and from discharges. **1935** *Clin. Sci.* II. 60 *Hypoproteinæmic. **1942** *Jrnl. Amer. Med. Assoc.* 3 Jan. 22 The disturbed osmotic relations in the hypoproteinemic dog. **1966** J. W. LINMAN *Princ. Hematol.* v. 156 Hypoproteinemic dogs or rats. **1936** *Jrnl. Exper. Med.* LXIII. 798 Titration of prothrombin, however, revealed a very marked *hypoprothrombinemia. **1961** *Lancet* 19 Aug. 390/1 Subacute intestinal obstruction associated with excessive hypoprothrombinæmia due to oral anticoagulant therapy. **1962** *Ibid.* 27 Jan. 177/1 Two types of hereditary hypoprothrombinæmia are known to exist. **1942** *Chem. Abstr.* 20 Nov. 7087 The danger of the *hypoprothrombinemic haemorrhage was very slight. **1955** *Arch. Internal. Med.* XCV. 2/2 The opportunity to study various types of congenital hypothrombinemic states repeatedly over a period..has furnished data on their clinical course. **1884** MICHAEL in *Jrnl. Linn. Soc., Zool.* XVII. 379 The true *Hypopus is a heteromorphous nymphal form of *Tyroglyphus.* **1826** KIRBY & SP. *Entomol.* III. 390 *Hypopygium, the last ventral segment of the abdomen. *Ibid.* 707 In many other insects it [the podex] unites with the last ventral segment, the hypopygium, to form a tube for that organ (the ovipositor). **1886** NEWTON in *Encycl. Brit.* XX. 505/2 [The contour-feathers of the Rheas] want the *hyporrhachis or after-shaft that in the Emeus and Cassowaries is so long as to equal the main shaft. **1603** HOLLAND *Plutarch's Mor.* 801 Hee who hath proceeded well in these *Hyporchemata [etc.]. **1873** SYMONDS *Grk. Poets* v. 118 The choric hymn, called Hyporchem..originally formed a portion of the cult of Phoebus. **1850** LEITCH tr. *C. O. Müller's Anc. Art* (ed. 2) §77 The gymnopædic, *hyporchematic, and other kinds of orchestics were.. cultivated in a highly artistic manner. **1894** BLACKMORE *Perlycross* 405 A man.. *hyporrhined with a terse moustache. **1880** *Brit. Med. Jrnl.* 389 The operation of *hyposcleral cyclotomy cuts through the ciliary body. **1902** *Daily Chron.* 16 July 9/1 The '*Hyposcope' competition.. the peculiarity of which is that, by an optical contrivance, the marksman, completely under cover, may fire round a corner, so to speak, at an enemy. **1915** *Illustr. London News* 20 Feb. 236/1 A trench-periscope (or, to give it its correct name, a hyposcope)... The Hyposcope is on the principle of the camera-obscura. **1909** *Jrnl. Amer. Med. Assoc.* 24 July 251/2 A condition of *hyposecretion of this part of the gland. **1939** B. J. E. IHRE *Human Gastric Secretion* vii. 95 A reduced rate of secretion (hyposecretion). **1871** HUXLEY *Anat. Vert.* ii. 45 The *hyposkeletal muscles are separated from the episkeletal..by the ventral branches of the spinal nerves. **1614** J. DAY *Festivals* (1615) 310 Sicke of the disease the Phisitions call *Hyposphagma. **1659** STANLEY *Hist. Philos.* XII. (1701) 478/1 They who have a Hyposphagme in their Eyes. **1661** LOVELL *Hist. Anim. & Min.* 342 The hyposphagme, or contusion, being a red or livid spot, caused by bloud flowing out the veines opened. **1886** *Syd. Soc. Lex.,* *Hyposporangium, term used by Bernhardi for the indusium of ferns which bears the sporangium itself, as in

the Adiantum. **1835-6** TODD *Cycl. Anat.* I. 284/1 Two posterior lateral pieces [termed] the *hyposternals. **1855** OWEN *Skel. & Teeth* 57 The junction between the hyo- and hyposternals admits of some yielding moment. **1900** DORLAND *Med. Dict.* 313/2 *Hyposthenuria. **1909** J. B. HERRICK in Osler & McCrae *Syst. Med.* VI. vi. 126 Unless hyposthenuria be counteracted by polyuria, renal insufficiency must result. **1971** J. SONG *Path. Sickle Cell Dis.* xv. 284 Hyposthenuria in sickle cell anemia was considered a reversible renal defect by Keitel et al. **1868** DANA *Min.* (ed. 5) 442 *Hypostilbite occurs on the island of Faröe with stilbite and epistilbite. **1855** MAYNE *Expos. Lex.,* *Hypostroma. **1866** *Treas. Bot., Hypostroma,* the mycelium of certain fungals. **1831** *Westm. Rev.* XIV. 416 The *hypostyle hall, and some other additions that he made to the temple of Karnac. **1896** *Academy* 12 Sept. 186/2 In which the sentence is subordinated, both in meaning and in outward form, to another—in other words, is '*hypotactic'. **1951** *Chem. Abstr.* XLV. 6232, H₂N(CH₂)₂SO₂H, tentatively named *hypotaurine. **1965** A. MEISTER *Biochem. Amino Acids* (ed. 2) I. i. 75 This amino acid [sc. L-cysteinesulfinic acid], and the product of its decarboxylation, hypotaurine,.. have been found in the free state in rat brain. **1966** *Biochim. et Biophys. Acta* CXVII. 495 (*heading*) The occurrence of hypotaurine and other sulfur-containing amino acids in seminal plasma and spermatozoa of boar, bull and dog. **1883** B. L. GILDERSLEEVE in *Amer. Jrnl. Philol.* IV. 420 Now to make *hypotaxis out of parataxis we must have a joint. **1886** MEYER in *Philol. Soc. Proc.* 18 June p. xliv, The paratactical arrangement of sentences, in preference to hypotaxis. **1866** *Treas. Bot.,* *Hypothecium, the cellular stratum below the thalamium of lichenals. **1875** BENNETT & DYER *Sachs' Bot.* 269 The term *Hypothecium is given to the mass of fibres lying beneath the sub-hymenial layer. **1706** PHILLIPS (ed. Kersey), *Hypothenar (in Anat.), a Muscle which helps to draw the little Finger from the rest; also the space from the Fore-finger to the little Finger. **1836-9** TODD *Cycl. Anat.* II. 523/2 On the inner side of the palm is the hypothenar eminence. **1922** W. LINDGREN in *Econ. Geol.* XVII. 293 The terminology proposed..would be as follows:..A. Hydrothermal deposits. *a.* Epithermal. Formed by ascending hot waters near the surface in or near effusive rocks at relatively low temperature and pressure. *b.* Mesothermal. Formed by ascending hot waters in or near intrusive rocks at intermediate temperature and pressure. *c.* *Hypothermal. Formed by ascending hot water in or near intrusive rocks at high temperature and pressure... The prefix 'hypo' has been substituted for 'kata' to correspond with Ransome's now generally accepted terms of 'hypogene waters', the suggestion implied being that the hypogene waters are principally derived from the region of the hypothermal deposits. **1969** BENNISON & WRIGHT *Geol. Hist. Brit. Isles* x. 247 The latter [mineral veins] are of two phases, hypothermal and mesothermal, usually of different and characteristic trend. **1970** PARK & MACDIARMID *Ore Deposits* (ed. 2) xii. 294 Many minerals of the igneous metamorphic zone continue without interruption into the hypothermal zone. **1896** T. L. STEDMAN *20th Cent. Practice* V. 575 Bonnet.. suggests designating any lack of hair through error of development, *hypotrichosis. **1968** A. J. ROOK et al. *Textbk. Dermatol.* II. xlvi. 1377 Congenital hypotrichosis of sufficient degree to cause social embarrassment..is not uncommon. **1937** *Jrnl. Biol. Chem.* CXVIII. 627 The administration of cystine stimulated hair growth in the *hypotrichotic rat. **1885** RAY LANKESTER in *Encycl. Brit.* XIX. 862/2 One of the Hypotricha; lateral view of the animal when using its great *hypotrichous processes as ambulatory organs. **1848** OWEN *Homol. Skel.* 60 The homologue of the *hypotympanic of batrachians and fishes. **1880** GÜNTHER *Fishes* 55 The large triangular hypotympanic or quadrate has a large condyle for the mandibulary joint. **1855** MAYNE *Expos. Lex.,* *Hypovanadate. **1897** ROSCOE & SCHORLEMMER *Treat. Chem.* II. 745 The hypovanadates are all insoluble except those of the alkali metals. *Ibid.* 746 Silver hypovanadate, Ag₂V₂O₅, is a black crystalline powder. **1855** MAYNE *Expos. Lex.,* *Hypovanadic. **1879** ROSCOE & SCHORLEMMER *Treat. Chem.* II. 290 Thus vanadic salts are yellow; the hypovanadic salts blue; the vanadious salts green; and the hypovanadious salts lavender-coloured. *Ibid.* 289 The solution of *hypovanadious sulphate absorbs oxygen with such avidity as to bleach indigo. **1923** STEDMAN *Med. Dict.* (ed. 7), *Hypovitaminosis. **1946** *Nature* 7 Sept. 342/2 The excretion of aneurin was decreased on account of deficient renal function, a fact not signifying hypovitaminosis in this case. **1925** *Hypovolemia [see *hypervolæmia* s.v. HYPER- IV]. **1935** HARROW & SHERWIN *Textbk. Biochem.* xv. 413 Simple hypovolemia occurs in obesity and in certain types of renal edema. Polycythemic hypovolemia occurs in conditions of..water deprivation. **1965** R. P. MOREHEAD *Human Path.* xxi. 501/2 Deficient water absorption leads to hypovolemia, dehydration, or both. **1952** *Jrnl. Amer. Med. Assoc.* 6 Sept. 11 The question of whether the normovolemic or the *hypovolemic patient or animal should be used in evaluation of plasma expanders. **1961** A. C. GUYTON *Textbk. Med. Physiol.* (ed. 2) xxxvii. 482/2 One of the most common types of shock..is that caused by hemorrhage; this is called hemorrhagic shock and is a type of hypovolemic shock. **1886** *Syd. Soc. Lex.,* *Hypoxæmia. **1936** *Brain* LIX. 115 The hypoxaemia of arterial and of arm vein blood encountered in a large proportion of epileptics is an expression of the stagnant physical and mental state which so often accompanies epilepsy. **1971** PORTER & KNIGHT *High Altitude Physiol.* 36, 25 per cent of the reported cases of chronic mountain sickness have some type of pathology which *per se* produces hyperventilation and hypoxaemia. **1941** *Ann. Internal Med.* XIV. 1245 During *hypoxia..blood flow is increased. **1967** *New Scientist* 26 Jan. 195/1 Today, the single most important cause of perinatal deaths is intrauterine hypoxia, in which the foetus becomes starved of oxygen because of impaired metabolism in the placenta. **1970** *Sci. Amer.* Feb. 53/2 Life on the mountains is made rigorous not only by hypoxia but also by cold. **1958** C. C. ADAMS et al. *Space Flight* 243 The *hypoxic zone, less than three miles up, where the decreased oxygen pressure brings human psychological and physiological discomfort. **1966** *Lancet* 24 Dec. 1381/2 Polycythæmia secondary to hypoxic lung disease. **1970** *Sci. Amer.* Feb. 56/1 The mountain dwellers' metabolism also appears to be affected by the hypoxic conditions. **1589** PUTTENHAM *Eng. Poesie* III. xii. (Arb.) 176 If such supplie be placed after all the clauses.. then is he called by the Greeks *Hypozeugma. **1706** in PHILLIPS (ed.

Kersey); and in mod. dicts. **1589** Puttenham *Eng. Poesie* III. xii. (Arb.) 177 If this supplie be made to sundrie clauses, or to one clause sundrie times iterated . . then is it called by the Greekes *Hypozeuxis. **1887** Mivart in *Encycl. Brit.* XXII. 106 Those lowly organisms known as Protozoa or *Hypozoa. **1865** *Intell. Observ.* No. 40. 283 This approach to a *hypozoic zero. **1876** Page *Adv. Text-bk. Geol.* vi. 121 The term Hypozoic simply points out their position as lying under those systems which are decidedly fossiliferous.

hypoacusis (ˌhaɪpəʊə'k(j)uːsɪs). Also **-acousia, -acousis.** [f. hypo- 4: see hypacusis.]

= hypacusis.

1947 Ackerman & del Regato *Cancer* vii. 336 A unilateral diminution in the sense of hearing, hypoacousia, is very commonly found accompanying tumors of the nasopharynx. **1961** Stedman *Med. Dict.* (ed. 20) 740/2 Hypoacusis. **1969** *New Scientist* 10 July 53/2 Their ears have been done in by discotheques and it's not expressions of dumb insolence they're displaying but the symptoms of hypoacousis.

hypoæolian, *Anc. Mus.*: see hypo- 3.

hypo-allergenic (ˌhaɪpəʊælə'dʒɛnɪk), *a.* orig. *U.S.* Also **hypoallergenic.** [f. hypo- 4 + allergenic *a.*] Having little tendency to cause an allergic reaction; specially prepared or treated so as to cause no reaction in persons allergic to the normal product.

1953 *Jrnl. Soc. Cosmetic Chemists* Aug. p. x (Advt.), Investigations indicate that Modulan is hypo-allergenic. **1953** *Arch. Otolaryngol.* Nov. 541 The cosmetic-sensitive patient must mingle in society with persons who are not wearing hypoallergenic powder. **1957** S. Kramer in E. Sagarin *Cosmetics* xxxviii. 879 Hypo-allergenic cosmetics are an important contribution to the allergic woman in that they enable her to continue the use of cosmetics. **1962** L. H. Crisp *Clin. Immunol. & Allergy* 187 Hypo-allergenic milk . . is milk denatured by heating. **1972** *Times* 22 Aug. 6/5 Ashley clothes fit in with hypo-allergenic cosmetics, . . ethnic dress, conservation and home grown food.

hypobaric (haɪpəʊ'bærɪk), *a. Med.* [f. hypo- 4 + Gr. βαρ-ύς heavy + -ic.] Of a solution for spinal anæsthesia: having a lower density than the cerebro-spinal fluid.

1930, etc. [see hyperbaric *a.* a]. **1971** P. C. Lund *Princ. & Pract. Spinal Anesthesia* vii. 300 When administering hypobaric local anesthetic solutions in large volumes . . the rate of injection is relatively unimportant but the positioning very important.

hypoblast ('hɪpəʊ-, 'haɪpəʊblæst). [f. hypo- 2 + -blast. Cf. F. *hypoblaste.*]

1. *Bot.* The flat dorsal cotyledon of a grass. ? *Obs.*

[**1830** Lindley *Nat. Syst. Bot.* 296 Esenbeck . . seems to entertain the opinion that this cotyledon [of grasses] is a special organ, for which he retains Richard's name of hypoblastus. **1855** Mayne *Expos. Lex.*, *Hypoblastus.*] **1882** in Ogilvie (ed. Annandale). **1886** in *Syd. Soc. Lex.*

2. *Biol.* The inner layer of cells in the blastoderm.

1875 Huxley in *Encycl. Brit.* II. 51/1 In the embryo [of the Metazoa] the representatives of these two layers [ectoderm and endoderm] are the epiblast and hypoblast. **1877** —— *Anat. Inv. Anim.* i. 50 The inner wall of the sac is the hypoblast (endoderm of the adult), the outer the epiblast (ectoderm). **1897** Allbutt *Syst. Med.* I. 59 The endoderm or hypoblast, appears as a cul-de-sac.

Hence **hypoblastic** (hɪpəʊ-, haɪpəʊ'blæstɪk) *a.*, of or belonging to the hypoblast.

1877 Huxley *Anat. Inv. Anim.* xii. 663 The hypoblastic cells are invested by those of the epiblast. **1897** Allbutt *Syst. Med.* III. 680 The body cavity is the outgrowth from the primitive alimentary canal with the hypoblastic covering of which its lining membrane is continuous.

hypobranchial (hɪpəʊ-, haɪpəʊ'bræŋkɪəl), *a.* and *sb. Anat.* [f. hypo- 2 + branchial. Cf. F. *hypobranche.*] **a.** *adj.* Situated under the branchiae or gills. **b.** *sb. pl.* The lower portion of the branchial arch.

1848 Owen *Homol. Vertebr. Skel.* Table I. note 2 The metamorphoses of the hyo-branchial skeleton in the batrachian larvæ demonstrate the thyro-hyals to be special developments of the hypo-branchials. **1878** Bell *Gegenbaur's Comp. Anat.* 553 Mention has still to be made of the hypobranchial groove and its derivates. **1888** Rolleston & Jackson *Anim. Life* 474 The hypobranchial gland.

hypobranchiate (hɪpəʊ-, haɪpəʊ'bræŋkɪət), *a. Zool.* [f. mod.L. *Hypobranchiāta*: see hypo- 2 and branchiate.] Belonging to the *Hypobranchiata* (*Inferobranchiata*), gasteropod molluscs in which the branchiæ are situated beneath the body (Mayne, 1855).

hypobromite (hɪpəʊ-, haɪpəʊ'brəʊmaɪt). *Chem.* [f. hypo- 5 + bromite.] A salt of hypobromous acid.

1877 Roscoe & Schorlemmer *Treat. Chem.* I. 278 Hypobromous Acid . . with the salts, termed the *hypobromites*, are formed in a similar manner to hypochlorous acid. **1878** Kingzett *Anim. Chem.* 195 With alkaline hypochlorites and hypobromites, urea decomposes.

hypobromous (hɪpəʊ-, haɪpəʊ'brəʊməs), *a. Chem.* [f. hypo- 5 + brom-ine + -ous.] In ***hypobromous acid***, an acid (HBrO) derived from bromine, having strong oxidizing and bleaching properties.

1865–72 Watts *Dict. Chem.* III. 237 Half the bromine is precipitated as bromide of silver, while the other half remains in solution as hypobromous acid. **1877** Roscoe & Schorlemmer *Treat. Chem.* I. 278 Aqueous hypobromous acid is a light straw yellow coloured liquid, closely resembling in its properties hypochlorous acid.

hypocaust ('hɪpəkɔːst, 'haɪpəʊ-). *Rom. Antiq.* [ad. late L. *hypocaustum, -causton*, a. Gr. ὑπόκαυστον, *lit.* room or place 'heated from below', f. ὑπό hypo- 1 + καυ-, καίειν to burn.]

A hollow space extending under the floor of the *calidarium*, in which the heat from the furnace (*hypocausis*, ὑπόκαυσις) was accumulated for the heating of the house or of a bath.

It has been sometimes explained as 'a vaulted room heated by a furnace below' (which may have been the primary sense), and sometimes erroneously identified with the *hypocausis* or furnace itself.

1678 Phillips (ed. 4), *Hypocaust*, a Hot-house to sweat in, or a Stove. **1696** *Ibid.* (ed. 5), *Hypocaust*, a subterraneal Place, wherein there was a Furnace, which served to heat the Baths of the Ancients. **1774** Pennant *Tour Scotl. in 1772.* 70 A fine hypocaust or bath was discovered. **1851** D. Wilson *Preh. Ann.* (1863) II. iii. ii. 25 The Roman Mansion with its hypocaust. **1885** J. H. Middleton *Anc. Rome* 334 Vitruvius's description of the hypocausts or hollow floors used for heating the hot rooms (*calidaria*) agrees closely with many existing examples. **1887** *Encycl. Brit.* XXII. 579/1 In the remains of Roman Villas found in Britain the hypocaust is an invariable feature. **1890** *Smith's Dict. Gr. & Rom. Antiq.* I. 278/1 The passages from the furnace to the hypocaust and the flues in the walls appear to have been called *cuniculi.*

b. *transf.* A stove.

1829 Scott *Anne of G.* xix, The *stube* of a German inn derived its name from the great hypocaust, or stove, which is always strongly heated, to secure the warmth of the apartment in which it is placed.

Hence **'hypocausted** *ppl. a.*, furnished with a hypocaust or hypocausts.

1897 *Antiquary* Nov. 321 They found a large villa. It was very extensively hypocausted.

hypocentre ('haɪpəʊsɛntə(r)). Also (*U.S.*) **-center.** [f. hypo- 2 + centre *sb.*] **1.** The focus of an earthquake, the point within the earth where it originates.

1905 C. Davison *Study Rec. Earthquakes* i. 3 The region within which the displacement occurs is sometimes called the hypocentre, but more frequently the seismic focus, or simply the focus. **1938** [see centrum 2]. **1972** *Sci. Amer.* May 58 The first seismic waves to leave the region of the break (the hypocenter) are waves of alternate compression and rarefaction.

2. = *ground zero* (ground *sb.* 18).

1960 *Observer* 29 May 26/1 The Hiroshima survivors are unusual in having experienced a single whole-body exposure, the dose varying according to distance from the hypocentre (point directly beneath centre) of the explosion. **1962** J. F. Loutit *Irradiation* ii. 75 The incidence of leukemia . . is high for those who were exposed near to the hypocenter.

†**hypochloric** (hɪpəʊ-, haɪpəʊ'klɔərɪk), *a. Chem. Obs.* [f. hypo- 5 + chloric. Cf. F. *hypochlorique.*] In ***hypochloric acid***, an old name of chlorous acid.

1841 Brande *Chem.* 368 Hypochloric acid was discovered by Sir H. Davy in 1815. **1870** *Eng. Mech.* 18 Mar. 658/1 Hypochloric acid is a yellow gas, possessing a very peculiar odour.

hypochlorite (hɪpəʊ-, haɪpəʊ'klɔəraɪt). *Chem.* [f. hypo- 5 + chlorite. Cf. F. *hypochlorite.*] A salt of hypochlorous acid.

1849 D. Campbell *Inorg. Chem.* 75 *Hypochlorites* . . When the base is in excess, they are sufficiently stable . . but when neutral, they are decomposed into chlorides and chlorates. **1876** Harley *Mat. Med.* (ed. 6) 156 Hypochlorite of soda. **1877** Roscoe & Schorlemmer *Treat. Chem.* I. 267 The hypochlorites . . are unstable compounds, which in the pure state are almost unknown.

hypochlorous (hɪpəʊ-, haɪpəʊ'klɔərəs), *a. Chem.* [f. hypo- 5 + chlorous. Cf. F. *hypochloreux.*] ***hypochlorous acid***, an oxy-acid of chlorine (HClO), which in its aqueous form has a yellowish colour, acrid taste, and sweet smell, and possesses strong oxidizing and bleaching qualities. ***hypochlorous anhydride***, a gas (Cl_2O) of a pale reddish-yellow colour and powerful odour. Discovered by Balard in 1834.

1841 Brande *Chem.* 367 Balard . . has . . proposed to designate it hypochlorous acid. **1854** J. Scoffern in *Orr's Circ. Sc., Chem.* 360 Hypochlorous acid . . is an orange-coloured volatile liquid. **1865–72** Watts *Dict. Chem.* III. 907 Hypochlorous anhydride.

hypochonder, -chondre (hɪpəʊ'kɒndə(r)). ? *Obs.* Also 6 **hypocunder.** [a. F. *hypocondre* (16th c. in Paré): see next.] = hypochondrium. Also pl. = hypochondria 1.

1547 Boorde *Brev. Health* clxxxv. 65 Hipocondrion is the greke worde, . . in Englyshe it is named Hypocunder. **1657** W. Coles *Adam in Eden* cliv. 236 Obstructions of the Spleen, and Hypochonders. **1684** tr. *Bonet's Merc. Compit.* xi. 377 That the chief Cure [in Mania] be always directed to the Hypochondres. **1740** Mackarness in *Phil. Trans.* XLI. 502 A Swelling just above the Groin, in the Left Hypochondre. **1817** *Blackw. Mag.* I. 565/2 They were magnetised . . by the pressure of the fingers upon the hypochonders. **1834** J. Forbes *Laennec's Dis. Chest* (ed. 4) 15 This method . . consists in pressing forcibly upon the hypochondres from below upwards.

hypochondria (hɪpəʊ'kɒndrɪə, haɪpəʊ-). Also **hypocondria**, and 8 **hypocondrias.** [ad. late L. *hypochondria* pl. (Priscian), a. Gr. τὰ ὑποχόνδρια the soft parts of the body below the costal cartilages (rendered *præcordia* by Celsus), neut. pl. of ὑποχόνδριος, f. ὑπό hypo- 1 + χόνδρος gristle, cartilage, esp. that of the breast-bone (the 'ensiform cartilage'). See also prec. and hypochondrium.]

‖**1. a.** as *pl.* of hypochondrium. Those parts of the human abdomen which lie immediately under the ribs and on each side of the epigastric region. †**b.** The viscera situated in the hypochondria; the liver, gall-bladder, spleen, etc., formerly supposed to be the seat of melancholy and 'vapours'.

1563 T. Gale *Antidot.* ii. 39 It . . healeth flatulentnes of Hypochondria. *a* **1652** J. Smith *Sel. Disc.* iv. 127 If our spleen or hypochondria . . send up such melancholic fumes into our heads as move us to sadness and timorousness, we cannot justly call that vice. **1754–64** Smellie *Midwif.* III. 484 There was no hardness or inflammation about . . the hypochondria. **1835–6** Todd *Cycl. Anat.* I. 4/2 Between the hypochondria is the proper epigastric region.

†**c.** Erroneously as *sing.*, for hypochondrium.

1725 in G. Sheldon *Hist. Deerfield, Mass.* (1895) I. 448 The indians fired upon them, and woundd Deacon Samll Field, the ball passing through the right Hypocondria. **1727** De Foe *Syst. Magic* i. iv. (1840) 97 Thus raising the vapours in their hypocondrias, they were every night dreaming that they heard it thunder.

d. *Entom.* (See quot.)

1826 Kirby & Sp. *Entomol.* III. 388 *Hypochondria*, . . two portions of segments, one on each side; which in some genera (*Carabus* L., etc.) intervene between the first intire ventral segment and the posterior part of the Postpectus.

2. as *sing.* A morbid state of mind, characterized by general depression, melancholy, or low spirits, for which there is no real cause. Now identical in meaning with hypochondriasis (q.v.); it remains the commoner term among laymen.

This use of the word was app. developed in English, prob. on the supposition that it was an abstract feminine sb. Cf. F. *hypocondrie* which seems to be of late introduction (1812 in Hatz.-Darm.).

1668 Dryden *Even. Love* iv. ii, I know what you would say, that it is melancholy; a tincture of the hypochondria you mean. **1700** Astry tr. *Saavedra-Faxardo* II. 242 The Pannick Fears of that Hypochondria of State-Interest. **1710** *Tatler* No. 231 ¶4 Will Hazard was cured of his hypochondria by three glasses. **1830** Scott *Demonol.* i. 23 The symptom . . is . . equally connected with hypocondria. **1839** F. Winslow *Physic & Physicians* II. 155 Cowper's madness, most undoubtedly, originated from some bodily ailment. . . All through his disorder, the digestive organs were impaired. . . Such, indeed, was the true source of his hypochondria. **1853** C. Brontë *Villette* xx, There sat a silent sufferer—a nervous, melancholy man. Those eyes . . had long waited comings and goings of that strangest spectre, Hypochondria. **1899** J. Macpherson *Mental Affections* viii. 147 The two affections [*sc.* melancholia and hypochondria] are different in so far as the emotional depression, combined with the intellectual disturbance of melancholia, is not present in hypochondria. **1928** R. D. Gillespie in *Guy's Hosp. Rep.* LXXVIII. 409 The term hypochondria appears always to have referred to preoccupation with complaints of illness, and usually of bodily illness. **1955** *Times* 4 Nov. 5/4 The fantastic array of purges, nerve sedatives, tonics, . . processed this, irradiated that, and impregnated the other shows that hypochondria is widespread.

hypochondriac (hɪpəʊ'kɒndrɪæk, haɪpəʊ-), *a.* and *sb.* Also 7–9 **hypocondriac.** [a. F. *hypocondriaque* (16th c.) ad. med.L. *hypochondriac-us*, a. Gr. ὑποχονδριακ-ός affected in the hypochondria; see prec.]

A. *adj.* **1. a.** Of morbid states: Proceeding from, or having their origin in, the hypochondria, regarded as the seat of melancholy; hence, consisting in, or having the nature of, a settled depression of spirits.

1599 R. Surflet tr. *A. Du Laurens' Discourse Preservation of Sight* 125 The Hypochondriake disease . . [is] a drie and hote distemperature of Mesenterium, the liver and spleene. **1615** Crooke *Body of Man* 416 An honest Citizen . . was sicke or indisposed with a hypochondriake melancholy for 3. yeares. **1669** *Phil. Trans.* IV. 1089 The Causes of the Hysterick and Hypochondriack Passions. **1679** J. Goodman *Penitent Pardoned* iii. iii. (1713) 310 That hypochondriack sourness and austerity, which some place a great deal of religion in. **1794–6** E. Darwin *Zoon.* (1801) III. 209 The hypochondriac disease consists in indigestion and consequent flatulency, with anxiety or want of pleasurable sensation. **1822–34** *Good's Study Med.* (ed. 4) III. 66 Melancholy . . often assumes many of the symptoms that essentially appertain to the hypochondriac disease. **1965** W. G. Klopfer in B. B. Wolman *Handbk. Clin. Psychol.* 830/2 Hypochondriac symptoms commonly occur and may, if no discernible cause for the symptom is found, be due to exaggerated needs for attention and other psychological desires.

b. Of persons, their temperaments, looks, thoughts, etc.: Affected by hypochondria;

characterized by, or expressive of, a morbid melancholy.

1599 R. SURFLET tr. *A. Du Laurens' Discourse Preservation of Sight* 131, I have seene two Hypochondriake persons.. raging mad. **1641** J. JACKSON *True Evang. T.* III. 187 What is poore and silly man alone, but..a melancholick and hypochondriack creature? **1643** SIR T. BROWNE *Relig. Med.* II. §4 Democritus that thought to laugh the times into goodnesse, seems to me as deeply Hypochondriack, as Heraclitus that bewailed them. **1782** V. KNOX *Ess.* (1819) I. XXI. 124 Complaints founded only in an hypochondriac imagination. **1803** BEDDOES *Hygëia* ix. 184 The hysterical, the hypochondriac, very generally agree in complaining of a decrease of memory. **1856** MRS. STOWE *Dred* I. ii. 19 That occasional gleam of troubled wildness which betrays the hypochondriac temperament.

2. a. *Anat.* Situated in the hypochondria. ***hypochondriac region***, the part of the abdomen occupied by the hypochondria.

1727–41 CHAMBERS *Cycl.* s.v., The hypochondriac regions. **1793** BEDDOES *Sea Scurvy* 70 Pain in the breast and left hypochondriac region. **1879** *St. George's Hosp. Rep.* IX. 46 An exploratory puncture having been made into the hypochondriac swelling [etc.].

b. *Entom.* 'Of or pertaining to the hypochondria or basal ventral plates of the abdomen: as, the hypochondriac segment' (*Cent. Dict.*).

B. *sb.* **1.** A person affected with or subject to hypochondria.

1639 DU VERGER tr. *Camus' Admir. Events* 33 Those melancholly Hypochondriacks..whose fantasies, how extravagant soever..must never be opposed. **1676** D'URFEY *Mad. Fickle* I. i, Thou art a Melancholly Fellow, a kind of Hypocondriack, as I am told. **1791** BOSWELL *Johnson* (1831) I. 36 But let not little men triumph upon knowing that Johnson was an Hypochondriack. **1866–80** A. FLINT *Princ. Med.* (ed. 5) 854 The hypochondriac is the victim of a delusion with respect to his condition. **1888** R. ROOSE *Nerve Prostration* I. xv. 348 The hypochondriac is always dwelling upon his symptoms, and constantly talks about his health. **1916** M. H. FUSSELL *Monographic Med.* V. XII. 781 Hypochondria is more likely to be confounded with neurasthenia [than with hysteria], but as the hypochondriac believes he is ill and constantly talks about his symptoms, and hysteriacs also..complain of various symptoms there may be confusion. **1932** H. S. WALPOLE *Fortress* IV. v. 693 She was no hypochondriac, but from a kind of outside consideration she summoned her forces. Had she a headache? Did her eyes smart? How was her throat? **1955** *Sci. Amer.* Apr. 104/3 He was a hypochondriac and a crank, chronically dyspeptic and unamiable. **1973** *Times* 27 Sept. 15/1 George S. Kaufman..was..an obsessive card player, compulsive womanizer, necrophobe, hypochondriac.

†**2.** = The disease, HYPOCHONDRIA 2. *Obs.*

1599 R. SURFLET tr. *A. Du Laurens' Discourse Preservation of Sight* 126 The other part where the Hypochondriake breedeth, is the liver. **1652** CULPEPPER *Eng. Physic.* (1809) 109 The liver, gall and spleen, and the diseases that arise from them, as the jaundice and hypochondriac. **1681** tr. *Willis' Rem. Med. Wks.* Vocab., *Hypochondriac*, a windy melancholy bred in the hypochondria, from whence a black phlegm arises that infects and troubles the mind. **1698** W. CHILCOT *Evil Thoughts* iii. (1851) 24 By an hypocondriac, or some other disease. **1738** SWIFT *Pol. Conversat.* Introd. 51 Abbreviations exquisitely refined: as..Hypps, or Hippo, for Hypochondriacks. **1796** BURNEY *Mem. Metastasio* I. 383 This performer comes to entertain and solace me in my doleful hypochondriacs.

hypochondriacal (hɪpəʊkən'draɪəkəl, haɪpəʊ-), *a.* [f. as prec. + -AL[1].]

1. = HYPOCHONDRIAC A. 1 a.

1621 BURTON *Anat. Mel.* Democr. to Rdr. 70 That Hypocondriacall winde especially which proceedes from the short ribbes. **1748** HARTLEY *Observ. Man* I. iii. 397 Subject to low Spirits, and the Hypochondriacal Distemper. **1872** GEO. ELIOT *Middlem.* lxvii, A hypochondriacal tendency had shewn itself in the banker's constitution of late.

b. = HYPOCHONDRIAC A. 1 b.

1665 GLANVILL *Scepsis Sci.* xiii. 73 The wonders it works upon Hypochondriacal Imaginants. **1694** SALMON *Bates' Disp.* (1713) 199/2 There is a Preparation of the Crocus.. which..after an admirable Manner relieves the Hypochondriacal. **1832** MACAULAY *Ess., Ld. Mahon's Wars Success.* (1887) 262 He very soon became quite as hypochondriacal and eccentric [as his predecessor].

2. = HYPOCHONDRIAC A. 2 a. *rare.*

1727–41 CHAMBERS *Cycl.* s.v., Hypochondriacal regions.

Hence **hypochon'driacally** *adv.*

1822–56 DE QUINCEY *Confess.* (1862) 211, I should certainly have become hypochondriacally melancholy. **1863** FORBES WINSLOW *Obscure Dis. Brain & Mind* xii. (ed. 3) 265 The mind, hypochondriacally disposed.

hypochondriacism (hɪpəʊkən'draɪəsɪz(ə)m, haɪpəʊ-). [f. HYPOCHONDRIAC + -ISM.] The condition of a hypochondriac; = HYPOCHONDRIA 2.

1697 FLOYER *Cold Baths* I. iii. (1700) 75 Melancholies, Hypochondriacism. **1786** R. W. DARWIN in *Phil. Trans.* LXXVI. 320 The immediate consequence is indigestion and hypochondriacism. **1879** BEERBOHM *Patagonia* xviii. 291 Those who are inclined to hypochondriacism or obesity.

hypo'chondrial, *a.* [f. HYPOCHONDRIA + -AL[1].] Pertaining to the hypochondria; = HYPOCHONDRIAC A. 2 a; situated upon the flanks.

1601 HOLLAND *Pliny* Explan. Words of Art, *Hypochondriall* parts be the flanks or soft parts vnder the short ribs. **1607** TOPSELL *Four-f. Beasts* (1658) 503 Of it they make Plaisters to asswage the Hypochondrial inflamations and ventosity in the sides. **1837** MACGILLIVRAY *Hist. Brit. Birds* I. 89 The feathers covering the back are named dorsal; the breast, pectoral; the sides, hypochondrial or lateral.

‖**hypochondriasis** (ˌhɪpəʊkən'draɪəsɪs, haɪpəʊ-). *Path.* [f. as prec. + -ASIS. The formation is unusual, the suffix *-asis* being almost entirely limited to names of cutaneous diseases.]

Hypochondria in its pathological aspect: a disorder of the nervous system, generally accompanied by indigestion, but chiefly characterized by the patient's unfounded belief that he is suffering from some serious bodily disease. Now regarded as a condition characterized by a morbid preoccupation with one's bodily health together with unfounded beliefs and exaggerated anxieties about real or imagined ailments, usually the symptom of a neurotic disorder.

1766 SIR J. HILL (*title*) Hypochondriasis, a practical Treatise on the Nature and Cure of that Disorder; Commonly called the Hyp and Hypo. **1798** A. CRICHTON *Inquiry Mental Derangement* II. 339 Hypochondriasis, therefore, is chiefly characterized by erroneous notions relating to the patient's own frame, and by painful corporeal feeling. **1810** R. THOMAS *Pract. Phys.*, Hypochondriasis bears a strong resemblance to dyspepsia. **1855** *Asylum Jrnl.* I. 214/1 Hypochondriasis and melancholia monomania were not clearly distinguished by physicians until recent years. **1866–80** A. FLINT *Princ. Med.* (ed. 5) 854 The name hypochondriasis..has very little significance as indicating the character and seat of the affection. **1905** M. CRAIG *Psychol. Med.* vii. 114 Though hypochondriasis is usually found in patients in whom no known bodily disease can be diagnosed, it may be associated with organic disease, the hypochondriacal symptoms being..the patient's misinterpretation of true physical signs. **1956** H. P. LAUGHLIN *Neuroses Clin. Pract.* x. 451 Sigmund Freud very early included Neurasthenia, along with Anxiety Neurosis and Hypochondriasis, as the so-called 'actual neuroses'. *Ibid.* xi. 500 In some psychiatric quarters today Hypochondriasis is regarded simply as a symptom complex, or merely as a manifestation which is present as a part of many other emotional reactions, rather than as a separate diagnostic entity.

hypochondriasm (hɪpəʊ'kɒndrɪəz(ə)m, haɪpəʊ-). *rare.* [f. HYPOCHONDRIA, on analogy of *enthusiasm*, etc.] = prec.

1755 AMORY *Mem.* (1769) I. 8 The superstition and hypochondriasm of the prophet. **1836** *Blackw. Mag.* XL. 149 The infectious hypochondriasm of the tradesman who has nothing to do. **1841** D'ISRAELI *Amen. Lit.* (1867) 705 Aubrey has given a gossiper's account of this ludicrous hypochondriasm.

So **hypo'chondriast** = HYPOCHONDRIAC *sb.* 1.

1798 COLERIDGE *Satyrane's Lett.* in *Biog. Lit.* (1817) II. 222 The Miser, Hypochondriast..of Molière. **1825** —— *Aids Refl.* (1848) I. 103, I have not found it at all, except as a hypochondriast finds glass legs. **1834** *New Monthly Mag.* XLI. 487 The 'misanthrope' and 'hypochondriast' might hug Despair.

†**hypochondri'atic**, *a. Obs. rare*[−1]. [f. as prec. + -ATIC.] = HYPOCHONDRIAC *a.* 1.

1657 G. STARKEY *Helmont's Vind.* 332 Opium..is..an admirable remedy..against Hypochondriatick melancholy.

hypochondric (hɪpəʊ'kɒndrɪk, haɪpəʊ-), *a. rare.* [f. HYPOCHONDRIA + -IC: cf. *anæmia, anæmic.*] = HYPOCHONDRIAC *a.*

1681 HICKERINGILL *Vind. Naked Truth* II. Ep. 1 Windy and Hypochondrick Vapour. **1871** B. TAYLOR *Faust* (1875) I. Notes 239, I discarded all hypochondric distortions of fancy and determined to live.

So **hypo'chondrical** *a.*, **hypo'chondrism**, **hypo'chondrist**. *rare.*

1665 J. SPENCER *Vulg. Proph.* 130 Persons so extremely ignorant, vicious, vain or hypochondrical [etc.]. **1812** COLERIDGE in *Southey's Omniana* II. 15 An hypochondrist, to whom his limbs appear to be of glass. **1822–34** *Good's Study Med.* (ed. 4) III. 60 We shall have little scruple in assigning the origin of most cases of hypochondrism to a morbid condition of one or more of the digestive organs.

‖**hypochondrium** (hɪpəʊ'kɒndrɪəm). [mod.L., ad. Gr. ὑποχόνδριον (neut. sing.), as τὸ δεξιὸν ὑποχόνδριον the right hypochondrium (Hippocrates); see HYPOCHONDRIA.] Each of the two hypochondriac regions which are distinguished as 'right' and 'left'.

1696 PHILLIPS (ed. 5), *Hypochondrium*, the upper part of the Abdomen under the Cartilages of the Chest. **1727–41** CHAMBERS *Cycl.* s.v. *Hypochondriac*, A swelling or distension of the hypochondriums, or upper part of the belly. **1735** FERGUSON in *Phil. Trans.* XL. 426 A Skane or great Knife, which went through the muscular part of his Fore-Arm, and into the Left Hypochondrium. **1843** J. G. WILKINSON *Swedenborg's Anim. Kingd.* I. iv. 109 Placed, for the most part, in the left hypochondrium, immediately under the diaphragm.

b. The corresponding part of the body of lower animals; the iliac region.

†**hypo'chondry.** *Obs.* Also 7 -condry. [ad. L. *hypochondrium, -ia.* With sense 2 cf. F. *hypocondrie* (1812 in Hatz.-Darm.).]

1. = HYPOCHONDRIUM. Chiefly in pl., as ***hypochondries.***

1621 BURTON *Anat. Mel.* I. i. I. v. (1651) 13 His hypocondries misaffected. *Ibid.* I. iii. II. i. 198 Blood and hypocondries both are often affected even in head-melancholy. **1685** J. SCOTT *Chr. Life* (1698) IV. 220 Envy swells the hypochondries.

2. = HYPOCHONDRIA 2.

1669 PENN *No Cross* iii. §2 Stingy and singular Tempers, affected with the Hypocondry. **1820** LAMB *Elia* Ser. I. *South-sea Ho.*, As if he feared every one about him was a defaulter; in his hypochondry ready to imagine himself one. **1874** SIR G. W. DASENT *Half a Life* III. 322 He recovered him of his hypochondry as soon as ever he married.

hypochoristic (ˌhaɪpəʊkə'rɪstɪk), *a.* Erroneous (but increasingly used) form of HYPOCORISTIC *a.*

1931 G. STERN *Meaning & Change of Meaning* 262 Bob has been considered a hypochoristic shortening of *Robert*. **1933** L. BLOOMFIELD *Lang.* xxiii. 424 It seems..that forms like *Bob, Dick* existed as common nouns, perhaps with symbolic connotation, before they were specialized as hypochoristic forms of *Robert, Richard.* **1958** A. S. C. ROSS *Etymology* 167 The hypochoristic form..of a name..is the 'familiar' form, as MnE *Liz* for *Elizabeth*.

hypochromasia (ˌhaɪpəʊkrəʊ'meɪzɪə). *Med.* [mod.L., f. HYPO- 4 + Gr. χρῶμα, χρώματ- colour: see -IA[1].] = HYPOCHROMIA b.

1929 R. B. H. GRADWOHL tr. *Schilling's Blood Picture* III. 258 Regarding the color index, marked decrease is called hypochromasia. **1930** H. DOWNEY in E. T. Bell *Text-bk. Path.* xxviii. 586 In addition to hypochromasia, poikilocytosis may develop. **1942** M. M. WINTROBE *Clin. Hematol.* ii. 68 Hypochromia, hypochromasia or 'achromia' are terms used to describe cells in which this normal pallor is increased.

hypochromatic (haɪpəʊkrəʊ'mætɪk), *a. Med.* [f. HYPO- 4 + CHROMATIC *a.*] **a.** Of the skin: deficient in pigment.

1894 in GOULD *Dict. Med.* 593/2.

b. = HYPOCHROMIC *a.* 1.

1929 R. B. H. GRADWOHL tr. *Schilling's Blood Picture* II. 112 Remissions, often very extensive, are striking... The blood picture may appear normal again and may become temporarily hypochromatic. **1930** H. DOWNEY in E. T. Bell *Text-bk. Path.* xxviii. 585 In this type of anemia one may find all gradations from cases showing abundant signs of regeneration to the simple hypochromatic types. **1971** V. F. FAIRBANKS et al. *Clin. Dis. Iron Metabolism* (ed. 2) iii. 129 Hypochromatic changes in the erythrocyte..may occur in a variety of unrelated disorders including iron-deficiency anemia.

hypochromatosis (ˌhaɪpəʊkrəʊmə'təʊsɪs). *Cytology.* [mod.L., f. HYPO- 4 + CHROMAT(O-, CHROMAT(IN + -OSIS.] An abnormally small amount of chromatin or number of chromosomes in a cell or nucleus.

1913 [see HYPERCHROMATOSIS 2]. **1919** *Encycl. Medica* (ed. 2) VI. 311 Hypochromatosis is a deficiency in chromatin —thus nuclear hypochromatosis is the condition of the nucleus of a cell in which there is a reduction in the number of chromosomes.

hypochromia (haɪpə'krəʊmɪə). *Med.* [f. as next + -IA[1].] **a.** (See quot. 1890.)

1890 GOULD *New Med. Dict.* 201/2 *Hypochromia*, abnormal pallor or transparency of the skin, occurring in certain skin diseases. **1968** A. J. ROOK et al. *Textbk. Dermatol.* I. xxii. 724 The lesions always retain their tendency to merge together producing progressive atrophy of the skin with tendency to hypochromia and achromia.

b. A hypochromic condition of the blood or of a red blood cell (see HYPOCHROMIC *a.* 1).

1931 [see HYPERCHROMIA]. **1966** J. W. LINMAN *Princ. Hematol.* v. 177 Because of the clear-cut relationship between iron deficiency and hypochromia, it has often been assumed erroneously that this morphologic abnormality must be the result of iron lack or a block in iron incorporation. **1972** *Nature* 10 Mar. 71/2 Lead seems to affect red cells chiefly by..interfering with haemoglobin synthesis, as judged by..hypochromia of the red cells.

hypochromic (haɪpəʊ'krəʊmɪk), *a.* [f. HYPO- 4 + Gr. χρῶμ-α colour + -IC.] **1.** *Med.* Characterized by or designating a colour index less than one, or red blood cells that contain less hæmoglobin than normal and show an increased central pallor; esp. in ***hypochromic anæmia.***

1924 T. R. WAUGH in *Can. Med. Assoc. Jrnl.* XLVII. 114/1 Such anaemias consequently show considerable variation in their blood pictures. If the response is slight.. the red cells are small, and stain poorly,..and the color index is low. This type is therefore hypochromic. **1935** WHITBY & BRITTON *Disorders of Blood* vi. 126 Hypochromic anæmia, especially, is more often a symptom than a disease. **1958** G. C. DE GRUCHY *Clin. Haematol.* ii. 42 In the tail of the film the cells are often distorted and flattened, and hypochromic cells may actually appear normochromic. **1966** J. W. LINMAN *Princ. Hematol.* v. 157 Most hypochromic anemias are caused by iron lack.

2. Characterized by or exhibiting a decrease in the extent to which light (usually, ultra-violet radiation) is absorbed; chiefly in ***hypochromic effect.***

1946 *Ann. Rep. Progr. Chem.* XLII. 118 For substituents attached to the carbonyl group, the effects are quite different, both $\lambda_{max.}$ and $\epsilon_{max.}$ being usually decreased (hypso- and hypochromic effects). **1959** *Jrnl. Amer. Chem. Soc.* LXXXI. 6003/1 In general the oxidation of a methylthio group to a methyl sulfone involves a hypsochromic shift of from 10 to 40 mμ... This hypsochromic shift usually is accompanied by a definite hypochromic effect. **1968** [see HYPERCHROMIC *a.* 2].

Hence ˌ**hypochro'micity**, the property of absorbing less (ultra-violet) light.

1958 *Nature* 29 Nov. 1502/1 In view of the zero hyperchromicity of polyguanylic acids at alkaline *p*H's, the variation of hypochromicity with *p*H was examined for a number of derivatives. **1960** D. SHUGAR in Chargaff & Davidson *Nucleic Acids* III. xxx. 59 When the extinction of a given oligonucleotide is lower than that of its constituent

mononucleotides, it is 'hypochromic' or exhibits 'hypochromicity'.

†'**hypocist.** *Obs.* [Cf. F. *hypociste.*] = next.
1751 SIR J. HILL *Hist. Mat. Med.* 793 Hypocist is an Astringent, and that of considerable Power.

†**hypocistis** (hɪpəʊ'sɪstɪs). *Med. Obs.* Also 6 **ypoquistis,** 7 **hypoquistis.** [a. L. *hypocistis* (Pliny), a. Gr. *ὑποκιστίς* (see def.), f. *ὑπό* under + *κίστος* the plant Cistus. Cf. F. *hypociste.* (The early form *(h)ypoquistidos* represented the Gr. genitive.)] The solidified juice of *Cytinus hypocistis*, a parasitic plant of the South of Europe, growing on the roots of Cistus: it contains gallic acid and was formerly employed in medicine as a tonic and astringent.
c **1550** LLOYD *Treas. Health* (1585) Pj, Yarvine stampid wyth the water of the decoctyon of ypoquistidos. **1601** HOLLAND *Pliny* II. 326 Some there be who put Hypoquistis thereto. **1616** BULLOKAR s.v., A certaine Mushroome, which being bruised yieldeth a liquor, called by Apothecaries Hypoquistidos. **1658** ROWLAND *Moufet's Theat. Ins.* II. xxxiii. 1116 His stomach must be fomented with Acacia or Hypocistis with wine. **1751** SIR J. HILL *Hist. Mat. Med.* 792 Hypocistis is an inspissated Juice, much resembling the true Ægyptian Acacia.. It is considerably hard and heavy, of a fine shining black Colour.

hypocochoana, corrupt form of IPECACUANHA.

hypocolon, -cone, etc.: see HYPO- II.

hypocon, colloq. abbrev. of HYPOCHONDRIA.
a **1704** T. BROWN *Lett. fr. Dead* Wks. 1760 II. 223 'Tis as much as a plentiful dose of the best canary can do to remove the hypocon [*ed.* **1707** hyppocon] for a few minutes.

hypoconder, -condriac, etc., obs. ff. HYPOCHONDER, -CHONDRIAC.

hypocone ('haɪpəʊkəʊn). *Zool.* [f. HYPO- + CONE *sb.*^{1}] An external cusp on the inner back corner of a mammalian upper molar tooth.
1888 H. F. OSBORN in *Amer. Naturalist* XXII. 1072 The first 'secondary' cusps (hypocone—hypoconid), added to the upper and lower molars of the primitive triangle, modify the crown from a triangular to a quadrangular shape. **1891** FLOWER & LYDEKKER *Mammals* ii. §2. 33 Finally, in the bunodont series, the addition of a postero-internal cusp, termed the hypocone, forms the sex-tubercular molar. **1933** A. S. ROMER *Vertebr. Paleontol.* xii. 248 In the upper molars the tooth tends to square itself up usually by the additiion of a fourth cusp, the hypocone, at the inner back corner. **1968** R. ZANGERL tr. *Peyer's Compar. Odontol.* 187 In the upper jaw a talon formed in that a second lingual cusp developed next to the protocone, a so-called hypocone.

hypoconid (haɪpəʊ'kəʊnɪd). *Zool.* [f. HYPOCON(E + -ID^{5}.] A cusp on a mammalian lower molar tooth corresponding to the hypocone on an upper molar.
1888 H. F. OSBORN in *Amer. Naturalist* XXII. 1075 There is no evidence as to the origin of the hypoconid, which as a rule preceded the hypocone. **1919** J. H. MUMMERY *Microsc. Anat. Teeth* i. 36 In man the trigonid is represented by the protoconid and metaconid only,..and the five cusps are made up of these and three cusps of the talonid—the hypoconid, entoconid, and hypoconulid. **1968** R. ZANGERL tr. *Peyer's Compar. Odontol.* 187 In the lower jaw three cusps developed on the talonid: counting labio-lingually, hypoconid, hypoconulid, and entoconid. **1970** *Nature* 25 July 356/1 The crest connecting the entoconid and the hypoconid was continuous.

hypoconulid (haɪpəʊ'kəʊnjuːlɪd). *Zool.* [f. HYPOCON(E + *-ul-* + -ID^{5}.] An intermediate cusp between the principal ones on the heel of a mammalian lower molar tooth.
1897 H. F. OSBORN in *Amer. Naturalist* XXXI. 1002 The talonid widened into a basin-like shelf supporting an outer cusp, the 'hypoconid'; an intermediate cusp, the 'hypoconulid', and an inner cusp, the 'entoconid'. *Ibid.* 1003 Why notice such a detail as the posterior intermediate cusp or hypoconulid? **1933** A. S. ROMER *Vertebr. Paleontol.* xii. 248 A hypoconulid may also appear in the heel. **1972** *Nature* 24 Mar. 180/1 *Oligopithecus* as well as the other Fayum catarrhines share the distinct lingually placed and somewhat prominent hypoconulid.

hypocoracoid (hɪpəʊ-, haɪpəʊ'kɒrəkɔɪd). *Ichthyol.* [f. HYPO- 2 (*b*) + CORACOID.] The lower of the two bones forming the shoulder-girdle in typical fishes; also called simply *coracoid* (cf. HYPERCORACOID).

hypocorism (hɪp-, haɪ'pɒkərɪz(ə)m). *rare*$^{-1}$. [ad. Gr. *ὑποκόρισμα, -κορισμός* pet-name, f. *ὑποκορίζεσθαι* to play the child, use terms of endearment, f. *ὑπό* in sense 'somewhat, slightly' + *κόρος, κόρη* child, boy, girl.] A pet-name.
1850 *N. & Q.* 1st Ser. I. 242/1 'Polly' is one of those 'hypocorisms' or pet-names with which our language abounds.

hypocoristic (ˌhɪpəʊ-, ˌhaɪpəʊkə'rɪstɪk), *a.* (*sb.*) [ad. Gr. *ὑποκοριστικός*, in *ὄνομα ὑποκοριστικόν* pet-name, diminutive, f. *ὑποκορίζεσθαι*: see prec. Cf. F. *hypocoristique.*] Of the nature of a pet-name; pertaining to the habit of using endearing or euphemistic terms. Also as *sb.*
1796 PEGGE *Anonym.* (1809) 98 Harry..is the free or hypocoristic name for Henry. **1865** FARRAR *Chapt. Lang.* xxii. 282 Imagine the power and danger of this hypocoristic process in times when it was fashionable to fling a delicate covering over the naked hideousness of vice. **1889** in *Cent. Dict.* **1930** *Times Lit. Suppl.* 1 May 361/2 Mere riddles.. where there is no question of..stop-voicing of hypocoristics. **1953** K. JACKSON *Lang. & Hist. Early Brit.* II. 555 The AS. personal names *Cata, Ceatta*..are from Pr[imitive] W[elsh] hypocoristics. **1957** R. W. ZANDVOORT *Handbk. Eng. Gram.* IX. ii. 303 The technical term for attributive 'pet' is 'hypocoristic' (adj. and noun).
So †**hypoco'ristical** *a.*; **hypoco'ristically** *adv.*
1609 BP. W. BARLOW *Answ. Nameless Cath.* 20 An hypocoristicall alleuiation. **1652** URQUHART *Jewel* Wks. (1834) 292 With hyperbolical [expressions] either epitatically or hypocoristically, as the purpose required to be elated or extenuated.

hypocotyl (hɪpəʊ-, haɪpəʊ'kɒtɪl). *Bot.* See quot. 1880.
1880 C. & F. DARWIN *Movem. Pl.* 5 With seedlings, the stem..has been called by many botanists the hypocotyledonous stem, but for brevity sake we will speak of it merely as the *hypocotyl*. *Ibid.* 10 The radicles, hypocotyls, and cotyledons of seedling plants. **1882** *Nature* 23 Mar. 482 Buck-wheat plants grow from small seeds containing a small hypocotyl, that enlarges afterwards to an exceedingly long part.
Hence **hypo'cotylous** *a.*, of or pertaining to the hypocotyl.

hypocotyledonary (ˌhɪpəʊ-, ˌhaɪpəʊkɒtɪ'liːdənərɪ), *a.* [f. HYPO- 2 + COTYLEDON + -ARY.] Placed under, or supporting, the cotyledons. Cf. HYPOCOTYL. So **hypocoty'ledonous** *a.*
1875 BENNETT & DYER *Sach's Bot.* 559 The elongation of the hypocotyledonary portion of the axis. **1880** Hypocotyledonous [see HYPOCOTYL]. **1881** *Academy* 12 Feb. 120 Hypocotyls—an abbreviation for hypocotyledonary axes. **1885** GOODALE *Phys. Bot.* (1892) 361 The parenchyma of the hypocotyledonary stem.

hypocras, obs. form of HIPPOCRAS.

hypocrateriform (ˌhɪpəʊ-, ˌhaɪpəʊkrə'tɪərɪfɔːm), *a. Bot.* [f. Gr. *ὑποκρᾱτήρι-ον* the stand of a large mixing-bowl (f. *ὑπό* HYPO- 1 + *κρᾱτήρ* CRATER *sb.* 1) + -FORM.] Having the form of a salver raised on a support: said of a corolla in which the tube is long and cylindrical, with a flat spreading limb at right angles to it, as in the periwinkle and phlox.
[**1753** CHAMBERS *Cycl. Supp.*, *Hypocrateriformis*,..the name given by Mr. Tournefort to a peculiar sort of flowers.] **1788** J. LEE *Introd. Bot.* (ed. 4) 7 *Hypocrateriform*, salver-shaped, that is plain or flat, and standing on a Tube. **1830** LINDLEY *Nat. Syst. Bot.* 222 Corolla monopetalous,.. hypocrateriform, with from 5 to 8 divisions. **1847** W. E. STEELE *Field Bot.* 169 Perianth hypocrateriform..having a cup-shaped crown surrounding the top of the tube.
So **hypocra'terimorphous** *a.* [Gr. *μορφ-ή* shape, form + -OUS; cf. F. *hypocratérimorphe.*]
1880 GRAY *Struct. Bot.* vi. §5. 248 Hypocrateriform, or rather (not to mix Latin and Greek) Hypocraterimorphous, in English Salverform.

Hypocrates, -cratian, -cratic, obs. forms of HIPPOCRATES, etc.

Hypocrene, obs. form of HIPPOCRENE.

†**hy'pocrify,** *v. Obs. rare.* [f. *hypocri(te* + -FY.] *intr.* To play the hypocrite. *trans.* To imbue with hypocrisy.
1716 M. DAVIES *Athen. Brit.* II. 242 The modern Astrological Arius hypocrifies the very top of his Door with a Notorious Insolent Falsity. *Ibid.* III. 70 Since the Arians as well as the Papists hypocrifie and lye.

hypocrise ('hɪpəkraɪz), *v. rare.* [perh. ad. obs. F. *hypocriser* (Godefroy) or a back-formation from HYPOCRISY.] *intr.* To practise hypocrisy.
1680 G. KEITH *Rector Corrected* xii. 227 Here again thou Hypocrizest. **1711** *C. M. Lett. to Curate* 47 In K. Edward's time he Hypocris'd and comply'd with the Reformation. **1892** *Silver Domino* iii. (ed. 2) 55 We cannot possibly be 'in the swim' unless we are good hypocrites. Herein is my sore point. I am unable to hypocrise.

‖**hypocrisis** (hɪ'pɒkrɪsɪs). [L.: see HYPOCRISY.] Hypocrisy, dissembling, feigning; a false or deceitful show.
a **1225** *Ancr. R.* 198 Þe þridde hweolp is Ipocrisis; þet is þeo þet makeð hire betere þen heo beo. **1678** PHILLIPS (ed. 4), *Hypocrisis*, a feigning or dissembling, a Rhetorical figure called by Julius Russinianus,..*Pronunciatio*. **1850** CARLYLE *Latter-d. Pamph.* iv. 7 The miserable mortals, enacting their High Life Below Stairs, with faith only that this Universe may perhaps be all a phantasm and hypocrisis.

†'**hypocrism.** *Obs. rare*$^{-1}$. [An irreg. formation from *hypocrisy, hypocrite.*] = next.
1591 SYLVESTER *Du Bartas* I. ii. 938 Cloak'd Hypocrism.

hypocrisy (hɪ'pɒkrɪsɪ). Forms: 3–6 **ypo-, ipo-,** 3 **-crisi,** 4–6 **-crisie,** (4 **-crisye, -cricie, -cresye,** 4–5 **-crysie, -crysye, -cryse,** 4–6 **-cresie, -crisy, -crysy,** 5 **-cresy,** 6 **-cracy, -crasie, -chrisi),** 6 **hipocrisie, hypocresie,** 6–8 **hypocrisie,** 6– **hypocrisy.** [a. OF. *ypocrisie* (mod.F. *hypocrisie*), f. eccl. L. *hypocrisis*, a. Gr. *ὑπόκρισις*, the acting of a part on the stage, feigning, pretence, f. *ὑποκρίνεσθαι* to answer, to play a part, pretend, f. *ὑπό* HYPO- + *κρίν-ειν* to decide, determine, judge. The etymological spelling with *h* became current (as in French) in the 16th c.]
The assuming of a false appearance of virtue or goodness, with dissimulation of real character or inclinations, esp. in respect of religious life or beliefs; hence in general sense, dissimulation, pretence, sham. Also, an instance of this.
a **1225** *Ancr. R.* 342 Of alle kudde & kuðe sunnen, ase of prude..of ipocrisie. *a* **1300** *Cursor M.* 27598 O pride becums..Ypocrisi. **1340** *Ayenb.* 25 Ypocrisye..is a zenne þet makeþ to ssewy þe guod wyþ-oute þet ne is naȝt wyþ-inne. **1426** AUDELAY *Poems* 31 A prechur schuld lyve parfytly, And do as he techys truly, Ellys hit is ypocresy. *c* **1440** *Promp. Parv.* 266/1 Ipocrysye, *ipocrisis*. **1529** S. FISH *Supplic. Beggers* (E.E.T.S.) 11 By theyre cloked ypochrisi. **1555** HOOPER *Let.* in Coverdale *Lett. Mart.* (1564) 159 No coulor nor cloked hipocrisie. **1567** *Satir. Poems Reform.* v. 98 Purge vs from Ipocrasie. **1567** *Gude & Godlie B.* (S.T.S.) 183 Thair fals Hypocresie Throw all the warld is now out-cryit. **1612** T. TAYLOR *Titus* ii. 6 Those promises but hypocrisies, without any soundnesse. *a* **1704** T. BROWN *Sat. agst. Wom.* Wks. (1730) I. 56 Cruelty inconstancy and lies, Envy and malice, deep hypocrisies. **1876** MOZLEY *Univ. Serm.* ii. 40 It is the law of goodness to produce hypocrisy.

hypocrital (hɪ'pɒkrɪtəl), *a.* Now *rare.* [f. next + -AL^{1}.] = HYPOCRITICAL.
1658 BP. REYNOLDS *Rich Man's Charge* 42 Your Faith is Hypocrital, your Religion vain. **1683** CAVE *Ecclesiastici* App. 42 Looking upon his repentance as feign'd and hypocrital. **1784** *Laura & Aug.* II. 12 The hypocrital Boswell attempted to take my hand. **1820** *Examiner* No. 654. 674/1 Ignorant, hypocrital, and servile eyes. **1884** J. WEDGWOOD in *Brit. Q. Rev.* Apr. 290 The type of all in humanity that was weak, and hollow, and even hypocrital.

hypocrite ('hɪpəkrɪt). Forms: 3–6 **ypo-, ipocrite,** (4 **ypocrit),** 4–6 **ypocryte,** (5 **epocryte,** 6 **ypocreit, ipoc(h)ryte, -crit, ippo-, hippocrite),** 6–7 **hipocrit(e,** 6– **hypocrite.** [a. OF. *ypo-, ipocrite* (mod.F. *hypocrite*), ad. eccl. L. *hypocrita*, ad. Gr. *ὑποκριτής* an actor on the stage, pretender, dissembler, f. *ὑποκρίνεσθαι*: see HYPOCRISY.]
1. One who falsely professes to be virtuously or religiously inclined; one who pretends to have feelings or beliefs of a higher order than his real ones; hence generally, a dissembler, pretender.
a **1225** *Ancr. R.* 128 Þe valse ancre..is ipocrite & weneð forte gilen God. *a* **1300** *Cursor M.* 12205 Ypocrites! for yee ar sua. *c* **1375** *Sc. Leg. Saints, Eugenia* 379 He is wolf in lamskine hyd & ful verray ypocrite. **1382** WYCLIF *Matt.* xxiii. 13 Woo to ȝou, scribis and Pharisees, ypocritis. *c* **1386** CHAUCER *Sqr.'s T.* 512 Swich was the ypocrite bothe coold and hoot. **1426** AUDELAY *Poems* 15 Thay likon hym to a lossere, and to an epocryte. **1522** MORE *De Quat. Noviss.* Wks. 82 Ipocrites that faine to haue vertues that they lack. **1559** *Mirr. Mag., Warwick* xiii, I was no hippocrite. **1592** TIMME *Ten Eng. Lepers* E iv, These hypocrites are like unto glo-wormes, which although they shine in the night, yet in the day they are..vile wormes. *c* **1645** HOWELL *Lett.* (1655) IV. v. 13 This is not to keep Lent aright, But play the juggling Hypocrit. **1711** ADDISON *Spect.* No. 126 ¶3 Such infamous Hypocrites, that are for promoting their own Advantage, under Colour of the Publick Good. **1814** JANE AUSTEN *Mansf. Park* iii, Her cousins, seeing her with red eyes, set her down as a hypocrite. **1876** MOZLEY *Univ. Serm.* ii. 34 Who is to convert the hypocrite? He does not know he is a hypocrite..The greater hypocrite he is, the more sincere he must think himself.
2. *attrib.* or as *adj.* = HYPOCRITICAL.
c **1380** WYCLIF *Wks.* (1880) 89 On þis ypocrite manere þei seyn [etc.]. *c* **1400** *Apol. Loll.* 105 Swilk similitudis of religious efter habit, & ypocrit signis. **1530** LATIMER *Serm. & Rem.* (1845) 307 The hypocrite-wolves clad in sheep's clothing. **1691** BAXTER *Nat. Ch.* ii. 9 Nominal Hypocrite Christians. **1725** SWIFT *Riddle*, Hypocrite fanatics cry, I'm but an idol rais'd on high. **1875** L. MORRIS *Ode to Free Rome* 136 Nor dark deceit, Nor hypocrite pretence.
Hence †'**hypocritely** *a.* and *adv.*; †'**hypocriteness**; †'**hypocritess.** *rare.*
1541 BARNES *Wks.* (1573) 307/1 Peraduenture hee vseth them not so hipocritely agaynst God omnipotent as you doe. **1574** tr. *Marlorat's Apocalips* 39 The hipocritly Jewes.. stirred vp trouble on all sides. **1602** DEKKER *Satirom.* Wks. 1873 I. 226 When I pray to God, and desire in hipocritnes that bald Sir Adams were heer. **1605** SYLVESTER *Du Bartas* II. iii. III. 473 Like a stubborn Boy That plies his Lesson (hypocritely-coy). **1708** MOTTEUX *Rabelais* IV. lxiv, You may find these many goodly Hypocritesses, jolly spiritual Actresses..Women that have a plaguy deal of Religion.

hypocritic (hɪpəʊ'krɪtɪk), *a.* and *sb.* [ad. Gr. *ὑποκριτικ-ός* acting a part, dissembling (prob. through a med.L. **hypocriticus*): see HYPOCRISY.]
A. *adj.* = HYPOCRITICAL.
1540 *Act 32 Hen. VIII*, c. 24 Preamb., The hipocritike & superstiouse Religions within this Realme. **1638** SIR T. HERBERT *Trav.* (ed. 2) 267 Their rules are many and masqued under a serious (hypocritique) sanctitie. *a* **1680** BUTLER *Rem.* (1759) I. 184 And, like an hypocritic Brother, Profest one thing, and did another. **1764** CHURCHILL *Author* 371 His silken smiles, his hypocritic air. **1848** KINGSLEY *Saint's Trag.* III. ii. 211 All your selfish hypocritic pride.
B. *sb. rare.* **1.** = HYPOCRITE.
1818 HAZLITT *Eng. Poets* viii. (1870) 199 He plays the hypocritic on himself.
†**2.** The art of declamation with appropriate gestures (= Gr. *ἡ ὑποκριτική*, sc. *τέχνη*). *rare*$^{-1}$.
1776 BURNEY *Hist. Mus.* (1789) I. ix. 152 The term hypocritic..is used to express Gesture or theatrical action.

hypocritical (hɪpəʊ'krɪtɪkəl), *a.* [f. as prec. + -AL[1].] Of actions: Of the nature of, characterized by, hypocrisy. Of persons: Addicted to hypocrisy, having the character of hypocrites.

1561 tr. *Calvin's 4 Godly Serm.* C ij, As touching that same hypocriticall supper [etc.]. **1592** TIMME *Ten Eng. Lepers* E ij, The intention..is not good, but rather they doe it to an hypocriticall ende. **1613** PURCHAS *Pilgrimage* (1614) 524 They are exceedingly subtill, hypocriticall and double-dealing. **1790** J. B. MORETON *Mann. W. Ind.* 177 Numbers are daily ruined by such hypocritical villians [sharpers]. **1850** KINGSLEY *Alt. Locke* xiii, Useless formalism! which lets through..the hypocritical. **1867** FREEMAN *Norm. Conq.* I. vi. 480 These are surely no mere formal or hypocritical professions.

hypo'critically, *adv.* [f. prec. + -LY[2].] In the manner of a hypocrite; in a hypocritical fashion.

1548 HALL *Chron., Hen. VIII* 226 But very folishly and hipocritically knowledged their treason whiche maliciously thei avouched. **1550** BALE *Apol.* 84 b, That putteth he in here, vngroundedly, doubtfully, hypocritically. **1698** FRYER *Acc. E. India & P.* 418 So that the Ground of this Quarrel, however hypocritically gilded with an Holy War, is Love. **1867** SMILES *Huguenots Eng.* xii. (1880) 206 Their consciences would not allow them..hypocritically to conform to a Church which they detested.

†**hypo'critish**, *a. Obs.* [f. HYPOCRITE + -ISH.] = HYPOCRITICAL.

1530 TINDALE *Answ. More* in *More's Wks.* 686/2 The ypocretishe wolues. **1535** COVERDALE *Isa.* x. 6, I shal sende him amonge those ypocritish people. **1641** R. BAILLIE *Parallel Liturgy w. Mass-Bk.* Pref. 2 This is all the labour of his hypocritish emissary.

†**'hypocritize**, *v. Obs. rare*[−1]. [f. as prec. + -IZE.] *intr.* To act as a hypocrite; to hypocrise.

a **1734** NORTH *Autobiog.* xii. §204 in *Lives* (1890) III. 160 These fellows never thought fit to hypocritize in the matter.

hypocunder, obs. form of HYPOCHONDER.

hypocycloid (hɪpəʊ-, haɪpəʊ'saɪklɔɪd). *Geom.* [f. HYPO- 2 + CYCLOID. Cf. F. *hypocycloïde.*] A curve traced by a point in the circumference of a circle which rolls round the interior circumference of another circle (cf. EPICYCLOID).

1843 [see HYPOTROCHOID]. **1854** MOSELEY *Astron.* lxi. (ed. 4) 183 This curve..being of the nature of an hypocycloid. **1879** THOMSON & TAIT *Nat. Phil.* I. I. §94 The curve..is called an Epicycloid, or a Hypocycloid, as the rolling circle is without or within the fixed circle.

Hence **hypocy'cloidal** *a.*, of the nature or form of a hypocycloid.

1884 F. J. BRITTEN *Watch & Clockm.* 288 The pinion flanks should be hypocycloidal in form.

hypoderm ('hɪpəʊ-, 'haɪpəʊdɜːm). [ad. next. Cf. F. *hypoderme.*] = HYPODERMA I.

1855 in MAYNE *Expos. Lex.* **1878** BELL *Gegenbaur's Comp. Anat.* 264 In Arthropoda..The vitreous body, pigment cells, and 'retina' are therefore clearly continuous with the ectodermal layer (hypoderm), and are differentiations of it, just as the cornea-lens was formed from the cuticular layer, which again can be derived from the hypoderm.

‖**hypoderma** (hɪpəʊ-, haɪpəʊ'dɜːmə). Pl. -dermata, [mod.L., f. Gr. ὑπό under + δέρμα skin; cf. HYPODERMIS.]

1. *Zool.* A tissue or layer lying beneath the skin or outer integument: as the membrane that lines the under-side of the elytra of Coleoptera (*obs.*); 'the soft cellular layer lying under the carapace of the Arthropoda and the thick cuticle of Vermes and Nematoda'; 'the subcutaneous areolar tissue of the skin of mammals' (*Syd. Soc. Lex.* 1886).

1826 KIRBY & SP. *Entomol.* xxxiii. III. 373. *Ibid.* xxxv. 600 An oblong..spot, occasioned by the hypoderma in that part being particularly tense. *Ibid.* xlvii. IV. 413.

2. *Bot.* A layer of cells lying immediately under the epidermis of a leaf or stem.

1877 BENNETT tr. *Thomé's Struct. & Phys. Bot.* 58 In many cases, there lie beneath the epidermis, peculiar layers or strings of cells (the hypoderma). **1884** BOWER & SCOTT *De Bary's Phaner.* 404 In most cases..the outer cortex of the stem is built up of two more or less distinct parts; one, the Hypoderma, bordering directly on the epidermis..the other, a thinner-walled, internal mass of parenchyma. *Ibid.* 411 The cells in many-layered hypodermata increase in size towards the inside.

Hence **hypo'dermal** *a.*, of or pertaining to the hypoderma.

1854 OWEN *Skel. & Teeth* in *Circ. Sc., Organ. Nat.* I. 50 The hypodermal system in mammals. **1875** BENNETT & DYER *Sach's Bot.* 376 Bundles or layers of firm thick-walled cells (Hypodermal Tissue) are of common occurrence [in Equisetaceæ]. **1884** BOWER & SCOTT *De Bary's Phaner.* 225 A group of tissues bordering directly on the epidermis is called from its position hypodermal, while distinct hypodermal layers are indicated by the substantive hypoderma.

hypodermatic (ˌhɪpəʊ-, ˌhaɪpəʊdə'mætɪk), *a.* [f. HYPO- 2 + DERMATIC. (Cf. Gr. ὑποδερματῖτις name of a disease.)] = HYPODERMIC. Also as *sb.* = hypodermic injection.

1855 in MAYNE *Expos. Lex.* **1876** BARTHOLOW *Mat. Med.* (1879) 11 In practising the hypodermatic injection. **1888** *Med. News* (U.S.) 17 Mar. 293, I again administered the hypodermatic of morphia.

Hence **hypoder'matically** *adv.*

1888 *Med. News* (U.S.) 10 Mar. 273 It is..impossible to use the bichloride hypodermatically about the legs without producing abcesses.

hypodermatomy: see HYPO- II.

hypodermic (hɪpəʊ-, haɪpəʊ'dɜːmɪk), *a.* (*sb.*) [f. HYPODERM-A + -IC: cf. DERMIC. In mod.F. *hypodermique.*]

1. *Med.* **a.** Pertaining to the use of medical remedies introduced beneath the skin of the patient; esp. in ***hypodermic injection***, the introduction of drugs into the system in this manner.

1863 *Lancet* 17 Oct. 444/1 Many..speedily furnished the journals with their experience of the 'hypodermic treatment'. **1865** *Reader* No. 142. 316/1 The hypodermic treatment of neuralgic affections. **1880** *Chambers' Encycl.* x. 512/1 The hypodermic method, in which medicines are introduced into the subcutaneous cellular tissue by means of a very finely pointed syringe..[For this] the science of medicine is indebted to Dr. Alexander Wood of Edinburgh. **1882** *Standard* 18 Mar. 5/6 The use of morphia..by hypodermic or subcutaneous injection.

b. Used as *sb.*: A hypodermic remedy. Also, a hypodermic injection or syringe.

1875 H. C. WOOD *Therap.* (1879) 227 In cases of severe pain, hypodermics are invaluable. **1893** *Funk's Stand. Dict.*, *Hypodermic*, a hypodermic syringe or injection. **1907** I. MCISAAC *Primary Nursing Technique* vii. 104 Hypodermics are given in the chest or fleshy part of the arm or thigh. **1969** *Daily Tel.* 11 Apr. 28/5 He..preferred a hypodermic of nicotine to a cigarette inhaled. **1970** *Ibid.* (Colour Suppl.) 18 Sept. 18 Divers..began to use large hypodermics designed to inject a 10 c.c. dose of formalin, enough to kill a starfish within hours.

c. *fig.* (adj. and sb.).

1901 *Harper's Mag.* CII. 786/1 Novelty is at a ruinous premium, and amusement a hypodermic to be taken in large doses, ever increased. **1903** *Monthly Rev.* Jan. 44 The admission of clergymen to the schools at certain hours for the purpose of administering a sort of hypodermic injection of religion is futile. **1936** W. PLOMER *Visiting Caves* 46 The hypodermic steeple Ever ready to inject The opium of the people. **1959** *Listener* 12 Feb. 300/3 Admirers may find his appreciation of Waugh's more hypodermic humour respectful rather than hilarious. *Ibid.* 5 Nov. 796/1 The professional intimate, the confidential heart-worm with the hypodermic technique, is one of the horrors of television.

2. *Anat.* Lying under the skin; pertaining to the hypoderm.

1877 HUXLEY *Anat. Inv. Anim.* ix. 592 It remained hypodermic, spreading out between the ectoderm and the endoderm of the hydroid. **1878** BELL *Gegenbaur's Comp. Anat.* 263 The eye, which is formed from the hypodermic layer lies behind this lens. Around it the hypodermic cells elongate, and change their position; they become pigment cells.

Hence **hypo'dermically** *adv.*, subcutaneously.

1863 C. HUNTER in *Lancet* 17 Oct. 444/1 The alkaloids of belladonna, aconite, and other medicines were first employed hypodermically by myself. **1872** FAYRER *Thanatoph. India* 2 The secretion of the poison gland is hypodermically injected into the bitten animal. **1894** D. CHRISTIE *10 Years Manchuria* 79 Inject a little morphia hypodermically.

‖**hypodermis** (hɪpəʊ-, haɪpəʊ'dɜːmɪs). [f. HYPO- 2 + Gr. -δερμις, *-dermis* as in EPIDERMIS. (Gr. had ὑποδερμίς in special sense.)]

1. *Bot.* (See quot.)

1866 *Treas. Bot.* 614/1 *Hypodermis*, the inner layer of the spore-case of an urn-moss.

2. *Zool.* = HYPODERMA I.

1874 LUBBOCK *Orig. & Met. Ins.* ii. 36 But also the hypodermis and the muscles. **1888** ROLLESTON & JACKSON *Anim. Life* 491 Beneath the hypodermis a thin basement membrane is nearly always to be detected. *Ibid.* 579 The nervous system [of Vermes] may retain a position in the hypodermis.

hypodermoclysis: see HYPO- II.

hypodiapason, -diapente, -diatessaron, -ditone, -dorian. *Mus.*: See HYPO- I. 3.

hypodigm ('haɪpəʊdaɪm, -dɪm). *Taxonomy.* [ad. Gr. ὑπόδειγμα example.] The material on which the description of a species is based.

1940 G. G. SIMPSON in *Amer. Jrnl. Sci.* CCXXXVIII. 418, I therefore propose the term 'hypodigm' (pronounced hȳ·podim, from the Greek ὑπόδειγμα, 'token, example'). All the specimens used by the author of a species as his basis for inference, and this should mean all the specimens that he referred to the species, constitute his hypodigm of that species. *Ibid.*, The hypodigm, whether it include one specimen or a thousand, is a sample from which the characters of a population are to be inferred. **1953** E. MAYR et al. *Methods & Princ. Syst. Zool.* xii. 237 A hypodigm is all the available material of a species. This term is mentioned here because it is occasionally used in the paleontological literature. **1963** DAVIS & HEYWOOD *Princ. Angiosperm Taxon.* i. 11 The hypodigm changes with our knowledge of the species. **1972** *Nature* 24 Mar. 180/1 The sixteen teeth which make up the hypodigm of this taxon [sc. *Purgatorius unio*] have, however, been correctly allocated.

hypogæal, -gæous: see HYPOGEAL, etc.

hypogæic, etc.: see HYPO- II.

hypogamy (haɪ'pɒgəmɪ). *Anthrop.* [f. HYPO- + -GAMY.] The marriage of a woman into a lower caste or into a tribe of lower standing than her own. Hence **hy'pogamous** *a.*, pertaining or relating to hypogamy. Cf. HYPERGAMY.

1946 J. H. HUTTON *Caste in India* v. 48 Hypogamy, on the other hand, is associated with a bride-price. *Ibid.*, Hypogamous marriages..are *pratiloma*, against the grain, that is, against what is natural or proper, since the status of the bride is in this case higher than that of the bridegroom. **1949** R. K. MERTON *Social Theory* (1951) i. 60 This pattern, which we may call caste hypogamy, is not institutionalized, but it is persistent. **1956** R. PIERIS *Sinhalese Social Organization* v. i. 177 A very rare case of *hypogamy*, that is, women marrying *below* their caste. **1957** *New Statesman* 4 May 566/3 The fictions of D. H. Lawrence have several examples of the lady marrying downwards (hypogamy, in anthropological vocabulary).

†**hypogaster.** *Obs. rare*[−1]. [ad. F. *hypogastre.*] = HYPOGASTRIUM.

a **1693** URQUHART *Rabelais* III. xxxiv. 290, I will..grope her Pulse, and see the disposition of her *Hypogaster.*

†**hypo'gastrian.** *Obs. rare*[−1]. [f. HYPOGASTRI-UM + -AN.] = HYPOGASTRIC.

a **1693** URQUHART *Rabelais* III. xi. 90 The Hypogastrian Crany.

hypogastric (hɪpəʊ-, haɪpəʊ'gæstrɪk), *a.* and *sb.* Also 7 hyppo-, hipo-. [ad. F. *hypogastrique* (16th c. in Paré), f. *hypogastre* HYPOGASTRIUM.]

A. *adj.* Pertaining to, or situated in, the hypogastrium; ***hypogastric region*** = HYPOGASTRIUM.

1656 BLOUNT *Glossogr.*, *Hyppogastrick*,..belonging to that part of the belly, which reacheth from the Navel to the privy members. **1694** SALMON *Bates' Disp.* (1713) 207/2 Obstructions of the Mesentery, and hypogastrick Diseases. **1797** CRUIKSHANK in *Phil. Trans.* LXXXVII. 206 The spermatic and hypogastric arteries were divided. **1835-6** TODD *Cycl. Anat.* I. 181/1 The hypogastric plexus of nerves.

†**B.** *sb. pl.* The hypogastric arteries. *Obs. rare.*

1774 COOPER in *Phil. Trans.* LXV. 316 The blood passed ..through the hypogastrics and umbilicals to the placenta. **1797** CRUIKSHANK *ibid.* LXXXVII. 207 The spermatics and hypogastrics not cut through.

So †**hypo'gastrical** *a. Obs. rare*[−1].

1615 CROOKE *Body of Man* 232 The branches of this Hypogastricall veine..do mingle themselues with the vpper braunches proceeding from the spermaticall.

‖**hypogastrium** (hɪpəʊ-, haɪpəʊ'gæstrɪəm). [mod.L., ad. Gr. ὑπογάστριον, f. ὑπό HYPO- I + γαστήρ, γαστρ- belly. Cf. F. *hypogastre* (16th c. in Paré).] The lowest region of the abdomen; *spec.* the central part of this, lying between the iliac regions.

1681 tr. *Willis' Rem. Med. Wks.* Vocab., *Hypogastrium*, the lower part of the belly. **1727-41** in CHAMBERS *Cycl.* **1876** GROSS *Dis. Bladder* etc. 18 Contusions of the perineum and hypogastrium. **1879** *St. George's Hosp. Rep.* IX. 247 Great pain over pubes and hypogastrium.

hypogastrocele (hɪpəʊ-, haɪpəʊ'gæstrəʊsiːl). *Path.* [f. as prec. + Gr. κήλη tumour (CELE).] A hernia in the hypogastric region.

1811 in HOOPER *Med. Dict.* **1886** in *Syd. Soc. Lex.*

hypogeal (hɪpəʊ-, haɪpəʊ'dʒiːəl), *a.* Also -**gæal.** [f. as next + -AL[1]. The form *hypogæal* is perh. after late Attic ὑπόγαιος, f. γαῖα earth.] = HYPOGEAN, subterranean.

1686 PLOT *Staffordsh.* 80 Hypogeal heats or Estuaries. **1886** *Athenæum* 7 Aug. 182/3 This Roman site..is certain to reveal a rich hypogeal harvest. **1898** *Ibid.* 19 Feb. 252/1 The arrangement of the bundles in the fleshy hypogaeal cotyledons.

hypogean (hɪpəʊ-, haɪpəʊ'dʒiːən), *a.* [f. L. *hypoge-us*, ad. Gr. ὑπόγειος underground (f. γῆ earth) + -AN. Cf. F. *hypogé.*] Existing or growing beneath the surface of the ground; underground.

1852 BADHAM in *Fraser's Mag.* XLVI. 271 Fabricius minutely describes, as belonging to this hypogean race, a fish about one foot in length. **1855** MAYNE *Expos. Lex.*, *Hypogeus*, applied to certain cotyledons which..remain below the ground during germination: hypogean. **1880** C. & F. DARWIN *Movem. Pl.* 27 The cotyledons are hypogean, or never rise above the ground. **1885** *Science* 26 June 519/1 In any hypogean insect which continually uses its claws in burrowing, the need of shedding and renewal of these organs is apparent. *Ibid.*, The facts regarding the cicada's hypogean life.

‖**hypogee** ('hɪpəʊdʒiː). *rare.* Also 7 **hypoge.** [a. F. *hypogée* (16th c.) or ad. L. *hypogēum.*] = HYPOGEUM.

1656 BLOUNT *Glossogr.*, *Hypoge* (*hypogæum*), a vault or cellar, or such like underground room. **1847** LEITCH tr. *C. O. Müller's Anc. Art* §177 The painted hypogees [*ed.* **1850** hypogæa] of Etruria.

hypogene ('hɪpəʊ-, 'haɪpəʊdʒiːn), *a. Geol.* [f. HYPO- 2 + Gr. γεν- to produce, γίγνεσθαι to be born, to originate; prob. after F. *endogène, exogène* (see -GEN). Cf. F. *hypogène.*] Formed under the surface; applied to rocks otherwise called primary and metamorphic; also, subterranean, hypogean.

1833 LYELL *Princ. Geol.* III. 374 We propose the term 'hypogene'..a word implying the theory that granite and gneiss are both *nether-formed* rocks, or rocks which have not assumed their present form and structure at the surface.

1845 Newbold in *Jrnl. Asiat. Soc. Bengal* XIV. 282 The edge of the trap is seen reposing on the hypogene schists at the base of the trap hills. **1882** Geikie *Text-bk. Geol.* III. 196 Hypogene or Plutonic Action.

b. Relating to the subterranean origin of rocks.

1843 Portlock *Geol.* 175 The hypogene theory of Lyell.

Hence **hypo'genic** *a.*

1880 *Libr. Univ. Knowl.* VI. 572 In the great hypogenic laboratory of nature, rocks have been softened and fused. **1882** *Athenæum* 28 Oct. 566/3 The great changes which are being wrought upon the surface of the earth, partly by hypogenic agents acting from below.

hypogenous: see HYPO- II.

ˌ**hypogeo'carpous**, *a. rare.* [f. Gr. ὑπόγειος underground + καρπ-ός fruit + -OUS.]

1855 Mayne *Expos. Lex.*, *Hypogeocarpus*, having fruit under the surface of the earth; hypogeocarpous.

hypogeous (hɪpəʊ-, haɪpəʊ'dʒiːəs), *a.* Also **-gæous.** [f. as HYPOGE-AN + -OUS.] Underground; = HYPOGEAN.

1847 Craig, *Hypogæous.* **1857** Berkeley *Cryptog. Bot.* §274. 271 It is amongst the hypogeous species that the most beautiful.. fruit is produced. **1880** Gray *Struct. Bot.* (ed. 6) 19 This hypogaeous (i.e. underground) situation of the cotyledons throughout the germination.

‖**hypogeum** (hɪpəʊ'dʒiːəm, haɪpəʊ-). Also **-gæum.** Pl. **hypogea** (-'dʒiːə). [L. *hypogēum, hypogæum*, ad. Gr. ὑπόγειον, ὑπόγαιον neut. sing. of ὑπόγειος underground; see HYPOGEAN, and cf. HYPOGEE.] An underground chamber or vault.

1706 Phillips (ed. Kersey), *Hypogæum*, a Cellar or Vault arched over head, a Place under Ground. **1850** Leitch tr. *C. O. Müller's Anc. Art* (ed. 2) §177 The painted hypogæa of Etruria. *Ibid.* §319 The Etruscan hypogea. **1865** J. Fergusson *Hist. Archit.* I. I. iii. I. 99 The tombs of Beni Hassan.. are situated on the eastern side of the Nile, and are almost the only hypogea that are so placed in Egypt.

hypoglossal (hɪpəʊ-, haɪpəʊ'glɒsəl), *a.* [f. mod.L. HYPOGLOSS-US + -AL[1].] ***hypoglossal nerve***, the motor nerve of the tongue proceeding from the medulla oblongata and forming the twelfth or last pair of cranial nerves. Also *absol.* = HYPOGLOSSUS.

1831 R. Knox *Cloquet's Anat.* 475 The pneumo-gastric nerve is at first placed before the hypoglossal. **1848** Carpenter *Anim. Phys.* x. (1872) 372 The hypoglossal nerve which gives motion to the tongue. **1878** T. Bryant *Pract. Surg.* I. 213 Paralysis of the hypoglossal has also been observed.

hypoglossis, var. of HYPOGLOTTIS.

‖**hypoglossus** (hɪpəʊ'glɒsəs). *Anat.* [mod.L., f. Gr. ὑπό under + γλῶσσα tongue: cf. Gr. ὑπογλώσσιος, F. *hypoglosse.*] The hypoglossal nerve.

1811 Hooper *Med. Dict.*, *Hypoglossus*,.. a nerve which goes to the under part of the tongue. **1878** Bell *Gegenbaur's Comp. Anat.* 522 The hypoglossus, which supplies the muscles of the tongue.

†**hypo'glottian**, *a. Obs. rare*[−0]. [f. Gr. ὑπογλώττι-ος (f. ὑπό HYPO- I + γλῶττα tongue) + -AN.] (See quot.)

1678 Phillips (ed. 4), *Hypoglottian Medicines*, medicines that are to lie under the Tongue and melt.

hypoglottis (hɪpəʊ-, haɪpəʊ'glɒtɪs), **hypoglossis** (-'glɒsɪs). [a. Gr. ὑπογλωττίς, -γλωσσίς a swelling under the tongue, etc., f. γλῶττα, γλῶσσα tongue.]

1. *Anat.* and *Med.* (See quot.)

1706 Phillips (ed. Kersey), *Hypoglossis*, or *Hypoglottis*, a little piece of Flesh that joyns the Tongue to the nether part of the Mouth: Also an Inflammation or Ulcer under the Tongue;.. also a Medicine proper to lie and dissolve under the Tongue, to take away Roughness in the Throat. **1886** in *Syd. Soc. Lex.*

2. *Entom.* A sclerite occasionally present between the mentum and labium of certain Coleoptera, as in clavicorn and serricorn beetles.

Hence †**hypoglo'ttidian** *a.* = HYPOGLOTTIAN.

1657 Tomlinson *Renou's Disp.* 173 Pastilles.. called.. from the manner of their use Hypoglottidian.

hypognathism, etc.: see HYPO- II.

hypogriff, -gryph, obs. ff. HIPPOGRIFF.

hypogyn ('hɪpəʊ-, 'haɪpəʊdʒɪn). *Bot.* [ad. F. *hypogyne.*] A hypogynous plant.

1847 in Craig.

So **hypo'gynic** *a.* [F. *hypogynique.*] = next.

1886 in *Syd. Soc. Lex.*

hypogynous (hɪp-, haɪ'pɒdʒɪnəs), *a. Bot.* [f. Gr. ὑπό under + γυνή woman, wife, in Bot. taken as 'pistil' + -OUS.] Situated below the pistils or ovary; said of the stamens of a flower when these grow on the receptacle and are not united to any other organ; also of plants having the stamens so placed.

1821 S. F. Gray *Arrangem. Brit. Pl.* II. 708 Ranunculaceæ.. petals 5 to 10, hypogynous. **1845** Lindley *Sch. Bot.* i. (1858) 15 If the filaments grow from immediately below the pistil.. they are called *hypogynous.* **1866** *Treas. Bot.*, *Icacinaceæ*.. Lindley places the order under his berberal alliance of hypogynous Exogens. **1870** Hooker *Stud. Flora* 73 Filaments inserted on a hypogynous ring. **1881** *Science Gossip* No. 203. 248 The stamens or male organs of the plant are indefinite, polyadelphous and hypogynous.

So **hy'pogyny** [cf. F. *hypogynie*], the quality or state of being hypogynous.

1887 *Athenæum* 10 Dec. 787/3 The shortening of the axis within the flower itself, giving the transition from hypogyny through perigyny to epigyny.

hypoid ('haɪpɔɪd), *a.* and *sb. Mech.* [Said to be a contraction of *hyperboloid* or of *hyperbolic paraboloid* (in reference to the shape of the teeth on the wheel).] **A.** *adj.* **a.** Applied to a kind of gear similar to a spiral bevel gear but having the pinion offset from the centre-line of the wheel, so that it can be used to connect shafts whose axes do not intersect; it is commonly employed in motor vehicles to transmit the power from the propeller shaft to the axle.

1926 *Jrnl. Soc. Automotive Engin.* June 575/1 Hypoid-gears are tapered gears having offset axes. **1935** *Times* 2 Oct. 6/5 The rear axle is fully-floating, and final drive is by hypoid spiral bevel gears. **1937** *Jrnl. Applied Mech.* IV. A-31 The behavior of lubricants in the region of boundary lubrication has become of added importance due to the recent adoption of hypoid gears in automobiles. **1941** F. D. Jones *Engin. Encycl.* I. 676 The chief advantages of hypoid gears are noiseless operation, increased load-carrying capacity, the possibility of high reduction and low numbers of teeth, long life, and high efficiency. **1969** K. Ball *Rover 2000 1963–1969 Autobook* vii. 64/1 The unit contains a hypoid crownwheel and pinion for the final drive from the power input shaft to the half shafts.

b. Suitable for or employing a hypoid gear.

1937 *S.A.E. Jrnl.* (*Transactions*) XLI. 557/2 Six or seven months ago the lubrication of hypoid axles in the field was a much more serious problem than it is today. *Ibid.* 563/1 One lubricant submitted by a manufacturer as an extreme-pressure hypoid lubricant was found to be a 'straight' mineral oil when analyzed. **1963** *Times* 3 May 10/6 A four-speed, all synchromesh gearbox.. incorporates the hypoid final drive. **1969** G. M. Mitchell *Jowett Javelin, Jupiter 1947–1953 Autobook* vi. 65/1 For lubrication of this axle, hypoid lubricant only should be used.

B. *sb.* A hypoid gear.

1935 R. Trautschold *Stand. Gear Bk.* ix. 144 Hypoids are machined in practically the same manner as spiral gears. **1962** D. W. Dudley *Gear Handbk.* ii. 12 Sufficient offset of the hypoid permits straddle mounting of the pinion and the gear.

†**hypo-i'odic, hy'piodic**, *a. Chem, Obs.* [f. HYPO- 5 + IODIC.] In ***hypo-iodic acid***, an old name for periodic oxide.

1854 J. Scoffern in *Orr's Circ. Sc.*, *Chem.* 368 Hypoiodic acid.. IO_4. **1865–72** Watts *Dict. Chem.* III. 297 Periodic oxide (Millon's Hypo-iodic acid) IO_2 or I_2O_4.

hypo-'iodite, hy'piodite. *Chem.* [f. as next: see -ITE.] A salt of hypo-iodous acid.

1865–72 Watts *Dict. Chem.* III. 297 Hypo-iodite of ammonium is formed by the action of iodine on excess of ammonia. **1866** Odling *Anim. Chem.* 149 Free iodine or hypiodite of potassium, like peroxide of nitrogen, [is] a facile oxygenant. **1894** [see next].

hypo-iodous (hɪpəʊ-, haɪpəʊ'aɪədəs), **hypiodous** (hɪ'paɪədəs), *a. Chem.* [f. HYPO- 5 + *iodous* (f. IOD-INE + -OUS).] In ***hypo-iodous acid***, an oxyacid of iodine, HIO.

1865–72 Watts *Dict. Chem.* III. 297 Wöhler.. by distilling iodine with anhydrous peroxide of barium, obtained a yellow liquid which he regarded as hypo-iodous acid. **1894** *Brit. Jrnl. Photog.* XLI. 34 Hypoiodous acid and its salts, the hypoiodites.

hypo-ionian, -lydian, -mixolydian, *Anc. Mus.*: see HYPO- 3.

hypolimnion (haɪpəʊ'lɪmnɪən). Pl. **hypolimnia.** [f. HYPO- 2 + Gr. λιμνίον, dim. of λίμνη lake.] The lower, cooler layer of water below the thermocline in a stratified lake.

1910, 1936 [see EPILIMNION]. **1957** G. E. Hutchinson *Treat. Limnol.* I. v. 341 The hypolimnia of all lakes. **1960** *New Scientist* 31 Mar. 773/3 The hypolimnion.. has become deoxygenated as the vegetation decomposes and provides ideal living conditions for sulphate-reducing bacteria. **1971** *Nature* 26 Feb. 596/1 In summer months.. the upper layers warm up more quickly than the lower regions and a sharp division in temperature—a thermocline—is formed... The reservoir or lake becomes divided into a lower, anaerobic cool layer or hypolimnion and an upper, warm aerobic epilimnion.

Hence **hypolim'netic** [cf. Gr. λιμνήτης living in marshes], **hypo'limnial** *adjs.*, of or within the hypolimnion.

1928 *Proc. Linn. Soc.* CXL. 101 On account of the depth the hypolimnetic body of water is great compared with the epilimnetic. **1940** Hypolimnial [see EPILIMNION]. **1964** *Oceanogr. & Marine Biol.* II. 126 Alsterberg (1927) suggests that hypolimnetic (upper) water movements are confined to thin horizontal laminae, with currents in alternate directions.

hypomania (haɪpəʊ'meɪnɪə). *Psychiatry.* [mod.L., ad. G. *hypomanie* (E. Mendel *Die Manie* (1881) ii. 38): see HYPO- 4.] A minor form of mania, often part of the manic-depressive cycle, characterized by elation and a feeling of well-being together with quickness of thought.

1882 *Jrnl. Nerv. & Mental Dis.* IX. 432 This description.. belongs not to acute mania properly so-called, but to the hypomania of Mendel,.. or the so-called subacute mania of asylum reports. **1892** D. H. Tuke *Dict. Psychol. Med.* I. 618/2 *Hypomania*, a name given to subacute attacks of mania, which are marked by an initial melancholia, retardation of the flow of ideas, and consequently as incoherence, restlessness, increased self-consciousness with delusions of a grandiose character and perversion of sexual instincts. **1904** T. Johnstone tr. *Kraepelin's Lect. Clinical Psychiatry* vii. 60 This combination of symptoms.. we designate by the name of Mania, or, if the individual disturbances are only slightly developed,.. by that of Hypomania. **1912** B. Hollander *First Signs of Insanity* xviii. 225 The chief mental characteristic of this disease, known as hypomania, is a loss of mental inhibition and consequently a rapid, ill-regulated, and easily disconnected train of thought. **1927** Henderson & Gillespie *Text-bk. Psychiatry* vii. 121 While such conditions as hypomania, acute mania, and delirious mania can readily be recognised,.. the differentiation of these states is not by any means clean cut. **1963** N. H. Pronko *Textbk. Abnormal Psychol.* x. 367 The mildest degree of manic excitement is termed hypomania, and concerns essentially speed and direction of thought rather than thought content. **1971** *Brit. Med. Bull.* XXVII. 77/2 Is a mild hypomania, with some euphoria and flight of ideas, but no delusions or gross behavioural disturbance, to be called psychotic or not?

hypomaniac (haɪpəʊ'meɪnɪæk). [f. prec., after MANIAC *a.* and *sb.*] = HYPOMANIC *sb.*

1910 B. Hollander *Mental Symptoms Brain Dis.* iii. 25 The good spirits of the hypomaniac seem, excepting for occasional slight abatement, to be inexhaustible. **1965** Rosen & Gregory *Abnormal Psychol.* xiv. 291/2 Like simple depressives, many hypomaniacs receive no treatment.

hypomanic (haɪpəʊ'mænɪk), *a.* and *sb.* [f. as prec., after MANIC *a.* and *sb.*] **A.** *adj.* Of or affected with hypomania.

1927 Henderson & Gillespie *Text-bk. Psychiatry* vii. 126 The hypomanic elation showed the usual characteristics—overactivity (with erotic tendencies coming to the fore), an infectious and excessive gaiety, over-talkativeness.. and lack of sustained attention. **1941** S. H. Kraines *Therapy Neuroses & Psychoses* xv. 359 Early in the attack she appeared to the casual observer to be merely an active, vivacious girl;.. she was hypomanic only in relation to her accustomed and usual behavior. **1965** [see *cyclothymic* s.v. CYCLO-].

B. *sb.* A person affected with hypomania.

1932 *Brit. Jrnl. Psychol.* XXIII. 155 The expansive hypomanic greets us with the sunny smile of happiness. **1938** S. Beckett *Murphy* ix. 168 A hypomanic teaching slosh to a Korsakow's syndrome. **1954** W. Mayer-Gross et al. *Clin. Psychiatry* v. 196 Hypomanics are realistic, quick to grasp opportunities, versatile and often rather superficial.

Hence **hypo'manically** *adv.*

1958 M. Argyle *Relig. Behaviour* ix. 107 Hysterics tend to become hypomanically excited at revival meetings.

hypomere, -mnematic: see HYPO- II.

‖**hypomochlion** (hɪpəʊ'mɒklɪən). *rare.* [L. *hypomochlion* (Vitruvius), a. Gr. ὑπομόχλιον fulcrum of a lever, f. Gr. ὑπό under + μοχλός, μοχλίον lever.] = FULCRUM.

1665 Hooke *Microgr.* 199 The hypomochlion or centers on which the parts of the leggs move. **1729** Switzer *Hydrost. & Hydraul.* 283 A Cylinder.. sustain'd at each End with a Hypomochlion, Fulcrum, or Prop, call it which you will. **1825** Coleridge *Aids Refl.* (1858) I. App. C. 393 The hypomochlion of the lever is as good an illustration as any thing can be that is thought of mechanically only.

hyponastic (hɪpəʊ-, haɪpəʊ'næstɪk), *a. Bot.* [f. HYPONAST-Y + -IC.] Pertaining to, or characterized by, hyponasty.

1875 Bennett & Dyer *Sachs' Bot.* 767 As long as the organ grows most rapidly on the dorsal side, it may be termed, after de Vries, *hyponastic.* **1895** Vines *Stud. Text-bk.* 60 The leaves.. are hyponastic, that is.. the dorsal surface grows more rapidly at first than the ventral.

hyponasty ('hɪpəʊ-, 'haɪpəʊnæstɪ). *Bot.* [f. HYPO- 2 + Gr. ναστ-ός pressed (f. νάσσειν to press) + -Y. Cf. EPINASTY.

The current use of the terms *hyponasty* and *epinasty* originated with De Vries in *Arbeiten des Bot. Inst. in Würzburg* 1872 (Heft II. p. 252).]

A tendency in plant-organs to grow more rapidly on the under or dorsal side than on the upper or ventral.

1875 Bennett & Dyer *Sachs' Bot.* 768 The hyponasty of the axis often counterbalances the greater mass of the pendent parts. **1880** C. & F. Darwin *Movem. Pl.* 6 Hyponasty.. implies increased growth along the lower surface, causing the part to bend upwards.

†**hyponitric** (hɪpəʊ-, haɪpəʊ'naɪtrɪk), *a. Chem. Obs.* [f. HYPO- 5 + NITRIC.] In ***hyponitric acid***, an old name for tetroxide (or peroxide) of nitrogen, pernitric oxide, NO_2 or N_2O_4.

1854 [see *hypoazotic* s.v. HYPO-]. **1864** H. Spencer *Biol.* I. 8 Hypo-nitric acid is decomposed both by water and by contact with the various bases. **1876** tr. *Wagner's Gen. Pathol.* 560 The latter first takes oxygen from the blood, and forms hyponitric acid.

hyponitrite (hɪpəʊ-, haɪpəʊ'naɪtraɪt). *Chem.* [f. HYPO- 5 + NITRITE.] A salt of hyponitrous acid.

1846 *Penny Cycl.* Suppl. II. 67/2 Hyponitrites may.. be formed by moderately heating certain nitrates. **1873** *Fownes' Chem.* (ed. 11) 150 Salts called respectively hypo-nitrites,

nitrites, and nitrates. **1894** ROSCOE & SCHORLEMMER *Chem.* I. 504 The formation of hyponitrites from derivatives of hydroxylamine shows that in these salts the oxygen atom must be between the nitrogen atom and that of the metal: N.O.K.

hyponitrous (hɪpəʊ-, haɪpəʊˈnaɪtrəs), *a. Chem.* [f. HYPO- 5 + NITROUS. Cf. F. *hyponitreux.*] In ***hyponitrous acid***, an unstable acid, $(HNO)_2$, obtained in combination as a potassium salt.

1826 HENRY *Elem. Chem.* I. 319 It appears to me that there are sufficient grounds for admitting the existence of hyponitrous acid as a distinct compound. **1838** T. THOMSON *Chem. Org. Bodies* 101 Nitric and hyponitrous acid transform picrotoxin to oxalic acid. **1894** ROSCOE & SCHORLEMMER *Chem.* I. 505 Free hyponitrous acid has not been prepared, as when liberated from its salts, it very rapidly splits up into its anhydride (nitrous oxide) and water.

hyponym (ˈhaɪpəʊnɪm). [f. HYPO- + Gr. ὄνομα name.] **1.** *Taxonomy.* A name made invalid by the lack of adequate contemporary description of the taxon it was intended to designate.

1904 *Bull. Torrey Bot. Club* XXXI. 258 A specific or subspecific name is a hyponym when it has not been connected with a description identifiable by diagnostic characters or by reference to a type specimen, figure or locality. **1904** *Science* 25 Mar. 509/2 Some are hyponyms, never having been associated with a recognizable binomial species. **1946** D. B. SWINGLE *Textbk. Syst. Bot.* (ed. 3) ix. 225 A name not so described or identified is a hyponym and nonvalid for the group for which it was intended. *Ibid.* 226 Homonyms and hyponyms result in the formation of synonyms, for these names must be replaced by usable terms, leaving them as synonyms.

2. *Linguistics.* One of two or more words related by hyponymy.

1963 J. LYONS *Structural Semantics* iv. 69, I say that *scarlet* is a hyponym of, or is included in, *red.* **1965** *Language* XLI. 509 Hyponyms are placed under the head word.

hyponymy (haɪˈpɒnɪmɪ). *Linguistics.* [f. HYPO- + Gr. ὄνομα after SYNONYMY, etc.] (See quot. 1963.)

1955 C. E. BAZELL in *Litera* II. 34 There is a relation of hyponymy when one word may invariably be replaced by a second word, but not vice-versa, without change of meaning. **1962** F. W. HOUSEHOLDER in Householder & Saporta *Probl. in Lexicogr.* 280 Thorough investigation of semantic structure is desirable, and where we have already sufficient knowledge to indicate relationships of incompatibility, hyponymy.. etc., this should be done in the most economical way possible. **1963** J. LYONS *Structural Semantics* iv. 69 Hyponymy is the relation that holds, for instance, between *scarlet* and *red*, or between *tulip* and *flower*, in English... It may be defined in terms of unilateral implication. Thus, *X is scarlet* will be understood (generally) to imply *X is red*; but not conversely. **1970** A. CAMERON et al. *Computers & O.E. Concordances* 92, I would draw your attention to the sketchy attempt to state the sense-relations of Old English words in terms of .. hyponymy (or inclusion of sense: ⊂ sign).

ˌhypoparaˈthyroidism. *Med.* [f. HYPO- + PARATHYROID + -ISM.] A condition in which there is an abnormally low level of parathyroid hormone in the blood, resulting in hypocalcæmia and hyperphosphatæmia with consequent tetany and other signs of neuromuscular excitability.

1910 OCHSNER & THOMPSON *Surg. & Path. Thyroid & Parathyroid Glands* xx. 345 In a patient suffering greatly from subtetanic hypoparathyroidism.. tetany has for two years been averted. **1938** SMITH & GAULT *Ess. Path.* lx. 746/1 The relationship of tetany to hypoparathyroidism is dependent primarily upon a drop in blood calcium. **1966** WRIGHT & SYMMERS *Systemic Path.* II. xxxii. 1126/1 The commonest cause of hypoparathyroidism is, of course, accidental removal of the glands during thyroidectomy. **1970** *Med. Ann.* 199 The tragedy of hypoparathyroidism lies in the lifelong burden of its control.

Hence **ˌhypoparaˈthyroid** *a.*, of, resulting from, or having hypoparathyroidism.

1910 OCHSNER & THOMPSON *Surg. & Path. Thyroid & Parathyroid Glands* xii. 205 To the internist the question of a hypoparathyroid etiology in the various tetanies became of interest. **1950** COPE & HAMLIN in S. Soskin *Progr. Clin. Endocrinol.* ii. 110 Following operative correction of hyperparathyroidism, patients may have chronic tetany of continued hypoparathyroid origin. **1970** C. N. GRAYMORE *Biochem. Eye* iv. 309 Lens lesions indistinguishable from hypoparathyroid cataract.

hypopecouana, corrupt form of IPECACUANHA.

hypopepsy, -petalous, etc.: see HYPO- II.

hypopharyngeal (ˌhɪpəʊ-, ˌhaɪpəʊfəˈrɪndʒiːəl), *a.* [f. HYPOPHARYNX: see PHARYNGEAL.]

a. *Anat.* Situated beneath, or in the lower part of, the pharynx. **b.** *Entom.* Belonging to the hypopharynx.

1851-6 WOODWARD *Mollusca* 346 Branchiae consisting of two bands stretched across the interior, one above (*epi*) and one below (*hypopharyngeal*). **1871** HUXLEY *Anat. Vert.* 136 The posterior parts [of branchial arches] are single bones.. called hypopharyngeal bones. **1877** —— *Anat. Inv. Anim.* x. 602 The hypopharyngeal folds.

c. as *sb.* (*pl.*) = Hypopharyngeal bones.

hypopharynx (hɪpəʊ-, haɪpəʊˈfærɪŋks). [a. F. *hypopharynx*, f. HYPO- 2 + PHARYNX.]

1. *Entom.* A median projection from the internal surface of the lower lip in insects.

1826 KIRBY & SP. *Entomol.* III. 458 This cushion, I suppose, may be analogous to the 'hypopharynx' of M. Savigny. **1888** ROLLESTON & JACKSON *Anim. Life* 499 The oral surface of the base of the labium also bears an internal process or hypopharynx.

2. *Anat.* The lower, laryngeal part of the pharynx (into which the larynx opens), extending from the epiglottis to the top of the œsophagus.

1907 *Lancet* 25 May 1421/1, I propose to give a description of a new and excellent method of inspecting the laryngeal part of the pharynx, the hypopharynx as it is also called. **1954** W. H. HOLLINSHEAD *Anat. for Surgeons* I. viii. 405/2 The laryngeal pharynx or hypopharynx extends from just above the level of the hyoid bone superiorly to the cricoid cartilage inferiorly, narrowing rapidly to become continuous with the esophagus. **1962** *Lancet* 28 Apr. 901/2 The patients were placed in the lateral head-down position owing to bleeding from the hypopharynx.

hypophosphate (hɪpəʊ-, haɪpəʊˈfɒsfət). *Chem.* [f. HYPO- 5 + PHOSPHATE *sb.* So in F.] A salt of hypophosphoric acid.

1864 in WEBSTER. **1894** ROSCOE & SCHORLEMMER *Chem.* I. 586 On neutralizing with caustic soda, a slightly soluble salt, sodium hypophosphate, $H_2Na_2P_2O_6$, separates out.

hypophosphite (hɪpəʊ-, haɪpəʊˈfɒsfaɪt). *Chem.* [f. HYPO- 5 + PHOSPHITE. So in F.] A salt of hypophosphorous acid.

1818 HENRY *Elem. Chem.* (ed. 8) II. 13 The hypophosphites of potash, soda, and ammonia, are soluble.. in highly rectified alcohol. **1876** HARLEY *Mat. Med.* (ed. 6) 66 Hypophosphite salts are monobasic, soluble in water, and easily crystallisable. **1883-4** *Med. Annual* 34/1 While triturating a mixture of Hypophosphite of Lime three parts, and Hypophosphite of Soda one part, [he] was seriously injured by the compound exploding.

hypophosphoric (hɪpəʊ-, haɪpəʊfɒsˈfɒrɪk), *a. Chem.* [f. HYPO- 5 + PHOSPHORIC. So F. *hypophosphorique.*] In ***hypophosphoric acid***, $P_2O_2(OH)_4$, a tetrabasic acid, obtained as an odourless liquid.

1854 J. SCOFFERN in *Orr's Circ. Sc., Chem.* 376 This operation furnishes a.. solution of hypophosphoric acid. **1894** ROSCOE & SCHORLEMMER *Chem.* I. 586 Salzer has.. shown that in addition to phosphoric and phosphorous acids this liquid contains hypophosphoric acid.

hypophosphorous (hɪpəʊ-, haɪpəʊˈfɒsfərəs), *a. Chem.* [f. HYPO- 5 + PHOSPHOROUS. So F. *hypophosphoreux.*] In ***hypophosphorous acid***, an oxygen-acid of phosphorus, PH_3O_2.

1818 HENRY *Elem. Chem.* (ed. 8) II. 12 Hypophosphorous or Per-phosphorous Acid.. a viscous fluid, strongly acid and uncrystallizable. **1841** BRANDE *Chem.* 488 Hypophosphorous acid.. was discovered by Dulong in 1816. **1877** ROSCOE & SCHORLEMMER *Treat. Chem.* I. 487 On cooling the solution, the hypophosphorous acid is obtained in the form of a thick very acid liquid.

hypophrygian, *Anc. Mus.*: see HYPO- 3.

†hyˈpophysal, *a. Obs.* [f. HYPOPHYS(IS + -AL.] = HYPOPHYSIAL *a.*

1877 *Gray's Anat.* (ed. 8) p. cxxx, Others refer the hypophysal part of the pituitary body to epiblastic elements derived from the buccal part of the epiblast only. **1892** C. S. MINOT *Human Embryol.* (1897) xxvi. 574 The hypophysal diverticulum now elongates and its upper end expands to a considerable vesicle.

hypophyseal, var. HYPOPHYSIAL *a.*

hypophysectomy (ˌhaɪpəʊfɪˈsɛktəmɪ). *Surg.* [f. HYPOPHYS(IS + -ECTOMY.] Excision of the hypophysis.

1909 REFORD & CUSHING in *Bull. Johns Hopkins Hosp.* XX. 106/1 The effects of total canine hypophysectomy. **1939** M. A. GOLDZIEHER *Endocrine Glands* I. 270 Adult amphibia show atrophy of both ovaries and testes after hypophysectomy. **1962** *Lancet* 15 Dec. 1235/1 Women with advanced breast cancer who subsequently fail to respond to adrenalectomy or hypophysectomy excrete significantly smaller amounts of urinary 11-deoxy 17-oxosteroids than do women who respond. **1967** S. TAYLOR et al. *Short Textbk. Surg.* xv. 189 Adrenalectomy and hypophysectomy are being performed much less often now than a few years ago, because remissions are unpredictable and often short-lived.

Hence **ˌhypophyˈsectomize** *v. trans.*, to deprive of the hypophysis, perform hypophysectomy on; usu. as **ˌhypophyˈsectomized** *ppl. a.*

1910 *Bull. Johns Hopkins Hosp.* XXI. 131/1 Two of the partially hypophysectomized animals survived for 5 months. **1912** H. CUSHING *Pituitary Body & its Disorders* i. 11 Of a litter of three puppies.. one, the largest, was partially hypophysectomized, one was fed daily.. with powdered extract of the whole gland..: the third and smallest was kept as a control. **1934** C. J. WIGGERS *Physiol. Health & Dis.* (1935) lxvii. 1055 Hypophysectomized tadpoles neither grow nor metamorphose. **1936** *Jrnl. Path. & Bacteriol.* XLII. 403 A tendency to maintenance of body weight after grafting of pituitary cultures into hypophysectomised rats has been taken as evidence of replacement of pituitary function. **1966** W. S. HOAR in Harris & Donovan *Pituitary Gland* I. vi. 246 The Amphibians are relatively easy to hypophysectomize. **1970** *Nature* 31 Oct. 464/2 Administration of growth hormone to hypophysectomized rats essentially prevented the appearance of any hypercholesterolaemia.

hypophysial (haɪpəʊˈfɪzɪəl), *a.* Also **hypophyseal** (haɪpəʊˈfɪzɪəl, ˌhaɪpəʊfɪˈsiːəl) [f. HYPOPHYSI(S + -AL; *hypophyseal* by alteration of *hypophysial.*] Of or pertaining to the hypophysis.

1882 *Jrnl. Linn. Soc.* (*Zool.*) XVI. 133 In the Mammalian series I have to observe that, in the lower and smaller members, as the brain loses in relative size and complexity, the pineal or conarial and pituitary or hypophysial bodies and connections show a relatively larger size. **1893** *Jrnl. Path. & Bacteriol.* I. 360 In the dog there is a more or less symmetrical lateral arrangement of the hypophyseal fissures. **1909** H. CUSHING in *Jrnl. Amer. Med. Assoc.* 24 July 254/1 Symptoms of hypophyseal origin doubtless occur in association with many diseases in which they are overlooked. **1912** —— *Pituitary Body & its Disorders* III. 233 In clinical conditions of hypophyseal deficiency somnolence is a conspicuous feature. **1943** G. W. CORNER in *Science* 15 Jan. 68 In the 1864 revision of Webster.. epiphyseal appears before epiphysial; in the revision of 1909 apophyseal enters the lists; in the current (1934) revision hypophyseal appears, and the spelling with -eal is preferred in all three cases... Possibly 'epiphyseal' goes back to the days when the noun was often written 'epiphyse', or possibly some writers thought it was advisable to make the adjectives from the genitives of the Greek nouns (e.g., *epiphyseos, hypophyseos*). Much more likely, however, the spelling has been influenced by an American trend in the pronunciation... At the present time (and as far as my observation goes, for decades past) American speakers almost universally place the primary accent on the fourth syllable, e.g., hypophyséal. .. In spite of the fact that '-eal' is philologically irregular, I make bold to suggest that it be adopted as standard in American scientific writing,.. in conformity with our well-nigh general pronunciation of the three words in question. **1955** G. W. HARRIS *Neural Control Pituitary Gland* v. 124 The pathway by which a stimulus passes from the hypothalamus to the anterior pituitary appears to be by means of the hypophysial portal vessels. **1962** *Gray's Anat.* (ed. 33) 1038 The hypophysis receives its blood supply from the internal carotid artery through a superior and an inferior hypophyseal artery on each side.

hypophysiotrophic (ˌhaɪpəʊfɪzɪəʊˈtrəʊfɪk), **-tropic** (-ˈtrəʊpɪk, -ˈtrɒpɪk), *a. Physiol.* [f. HYPOPHYSI(S + -O + -TROPHIC, -TROPIC.] Regulating the activity of the hypophysis.

1962 B. HALÁSZ et al. in *Jrnl. Endocrinol.* XXV. 147 Histological and functional evidence has been obtained which defines what may be called the 'hypophysiotrophic' region of the hypothalamus. **1968** C. B. JØRGENSEN in Barrington & Jørgensen *Perspectives in Endocrinol.* viii. 489 The existence of more diffuse 'hypophysiotropic' regions within the hypothalamus has been supported by the results of recent studies. **1970** *Nature* 25 Apr. 322/2 These results allow us to claim the preparation, for the first time, of a hypothalamic hypophysiotropic releasing factor.

‖**hypophysis** (hɪp-, haɪˈpɒfɪsɪs). Pl. **hypophyses** (haɪˈpɒfɪsiːz). [a. Gr. ὑπόφυσις offshoot, outgrowth (cf. APOPHYSIS, EPIPHYSIS).]

†1. *Path.* Cataract in the eye. *Obs.*

1706 PHILLIPS (ed. Kersey), *Hypophysis*, a Fault in the Eye, the same as *Hypochyma.* **1886** in *Syd. Soc. Lex.*

2. *Bot.* **a.** A part of the embryo in angiosperms, from which the root and root-cap are developed.

1875 BENNETT & DYER *Sachs' Bot.* 515 A cell.. which arises between the end of the pro-embryo and the body of the embryo.. is especially to be noted. It is from this that the root is subsequently developed. Hanstein calls it and the tissue which proceeds from it the Hypophysis.

b. 'In mosses, an enlargement of the pedicel at the base of the capsule' (*Cent. Dict.*).

3. *Anat.* (In full ***hypophysis cerebri.***) [First used by S. T. Soemmerring (*De Corporis Humani Fabrica* (rev. ed., 1798) IV. 70).] The pituitary body of the brain. A small endocrine organ that is attached or adjacent to the hypothalamus in the brain of vertebrates, has two lobes distinct in origin, nature, and function (cf. ADENO- and NEUROHYPOPHYSIS), and produces a number of hormones, some of which regulate the activity of other endocrine organs; in man it lies within a cavity of the sphenoid bone under a covering of *dura mater* and is attached by the infundibulum to the undersurface of the brain.

The application of the term has varied. Some writers have restricted it to the anterior or the posterior lobe only (differentiating the hypophysis from the pituitary body); others have taken it to include not only the two lobes but also the infundibulum.

1825 A. MONRO *Elem. Anat. Human Body* II. VI. ii. 371 The Pituitary Gland, or Hypophysis, is a small oblong-shaped body, which is inclosed by the dura mater, and situated in the tela sphenoidalis. **1864** in WEBSTER. **1877** W. TURNER *Introd. Human Anat.* I. v. 213 This ventricle is prolonged downwards into a funnel-shaped process, the infundibulum, which is connected with the pituitary body, or hypophysis cerebri. **1898** W. H. HOWELL in *Jrnl. Exper. Med.* III. 246 The hypophysis cerebri is usually described as consisting of two lobes. One, the large anterior lobe, is distinctly a glandular structure... Properly speaking the term hypophysis cerebri should be restricted to this lobe, and this significance is now given to it by morphological writers, although in human anatomy it is still commonly employed to include the so-called posterior lobe as well. *Ibid.* 247 Extracts were made of both the hypophysis cerebri, or anterior lobe, and the infundibular body. **1899** F. H. GERRISH *Text-bk. Anat.* 534 The hypophysis has been found greatly enlarged in cases of giantism, and hence has been supposed to sustain a relation to the stature of the individual. **1906** J. P. MCMURRICH *Devel. Human Body* (ed. 2) xiv. 428 At its extremity the hypophysis comes in contact during the fifth week with the enlarged extremity of Rathke's pouch.. and applies itself closely to the posterior surface of this.. to form with it the pituitary body. **1915** A. M. PATERSON *Man. Embryol.* II. i. 110 The pituitary body

has a double origin... The tuber cinereum, infundibulum, and posterior lobe (hypophysis cerebri) are outgrowths from the ventral aspect of the diencephalon. The anterior lobe of the pituitary body is derived from Rathke's pouch. **1919** W. B. BELL *Pituitary* 2 The word 'hypophysis', strictly speaking, refers to the epithelial portions of the Pituitary—the pars anterior and the pars intermedia—and should only be used in this connexion. **1926** G. R. DE BEER *Compar. Anat. Pituitary Body* ii. 26 The term *pituitary body* should be used to denote the well-defined anatomical unit consisting of four parts—anterior, intermedia, nervosa, and tuberalis. Other structures, such as the infundibulum and the tuber cinereum, may be grouped with the pituitary body to form a functional unit, the pituitary complex. The term *hypophysis* is often loosely used as synonymous with pituitary body, but wrongly, since it definitely refers only to the epithelial constituent of the body. **1936** *Jrnl. Morphol.* LX. 127 A cytological study of the hypophyses of more than 100 female bats. **1940** *Res. Publ. Assoc. Res. Nerv. & Mental Dis.* XX. 22 The mammalian hypophysis consists of three major divisions: lobus glandularis, lobus nervosus and the infundibulum or neural stalk. This classification has been recommended by the International Commission on Anatomical Nomenclature (1935). **1944** E. T. BELL *Text-bk. Path.* (ed. 5) xxviii. 755 The hypophysis exercises a certain amount of control over the other glands of internal secretion and the growth and activity of various organs by means of specific hormones which it elaborates. **1954** A. WHITE et al. *Princ. Biochem.* xlv. 957 The hypophysis is one of the most important endocrine glands in the body, exerting a profound influence over other endocrine structures and thereby regulating a large portion of the endocrine activity of the organism. **1960** B. I. BALINSKY *Introd. Embryol.* xviii. 452 The agent necessary for activating the thyroid gland is produced in the anterior (epidermal) lobe of the hypophysis.

hypoplasia-hypopygium: see HYPO- II.

hypoplastic (haɪpəʊˈplæstɪk), *a. Med.* [f. *hypo-(plasia* (s.v. HYPO- II) + -PLASTIC.] Of an organ or tissue: undersized at maturity owing to insufficient growth; ***hypoplastic anæmia***, anæmia that is due to an insufficient production of red blood cells by the bone-marrow.

1877 tr. *H. von Ziemssen's Cycl. Pract. Med.* XVI. 543 The sexual organs will remain relatively hypoplastic, or will be late in arriving at functional maturity. **1906** C. P. EMERSON *Clin. Diagn.* v. 515 By hypoplastic anæmia is meant one due to insufficient blood formation. **1915** *Brit. Dental Jrnl.* XXXVI. 174 In studying the etiology of hypoplastic teeth, development and calcification may be divided into three distinct periods. **1918** *Amer. Jrnl. Med. Sci.* CLVI. 49 The aorta was described as hypoplastic in 101 cases... In 71 of these cases hypoplasia was determined by actual measurement of the relative width of the pulmonary artery and the aorta. **1938** DIAMOND & BLACKFAN in *Amer. Jrnl. Dis. Children* LVI. 464 In the past seven years we have had the opportunity to see an intermediate type of anemia—hypoplastic rather than completely aplastic. This condition has been characterized by slowly progressive anemia.. with the production of a small and inadequate number of reticulocytes from bone marrow which shows moderate hypoplasia. **1961** L. MARTIN *Clinical Endocrinol.* (ed. 3) vii. 199 The breasts were large but the nipples hypoplastic. **1963** M. C. G. ISRAËLS *Diagn. & Treatm. Blood Dis.* viii. 59 Senile hypoplastic anæmia is really a premature diminution of bone-marrow activity.

‖**hypopyon** (hɪˈpəʊpɪən). *Path.* Also erron. **-ion**. [a. Gr. ὑπόπυον an ulcer, neut. of ὑπόπυος tending to suppuration, f. πύον pus, matter.

The erroneous spelling *hypopion* was prob. due to the assumption that the word was a derivative of ὤψ, ὠπ- eye; cf. Gr. ὑπώπιον a black eye.]

A morbid accumulation of pus in the anterior chamber of the eye (cf. quots.).

[**1657** *Physical Dict.*, *Hypogion* [sic], or matter under the cornea, a great inflammation of the eyes with swellings.] **1706** PHILLIPS (ed. Kersey), *Hypopyon*, a gathering of Matter under the Horney Tunick of the Eye. **1807** *Med. Jrnl.* XVII. 80 Hypopion, or the occupation of one or both chambers of the eye, with a glutinous opake fluid, instead of the true transparent humours. **1878** T. BRYANT *Pract. Surg.* I. 19 The absorption of pus is constantly seen in the eye in hypopyon.

hypoquistis, obs. variant of HYPOCISTIS.

hyporachis, -radial, etc.: see HYPO- II.

‖**hyposarca** (hɪpəʊˈsɑːkə). *Path. rare.* [med.L. *hyposarca*, a. Gr. ὑπὸ σάρκα under the flesh.] A species of dropsy: = ANASARCA.

1398 TREVISA *Barth. De P. R.* VII. lii. (MS. Bodl.), þe furste dropesie hatte lentofleuma..þe secunde hatte yposarca oþer anasarca, and comeþ of distemperaunce of colde and drynes. **1704** J. HARRIS *Lex. Techn.*, *Hyposarca*, the same with Anasarca. **1876** tr. *Wagner's Gen. Pathol.* 225 If dropsy affect the parenchyma, it is called œdema, anasarca, or hyposarca.

‖**hyposcenium** (hɪpəʊˈsiːnɪəm, haɪpəʊ-). *Gr. Antiq.* [f. Gr. *ὑποσκήνιον (on analogy of προσκήνιον PROSCENIUM) = τὰ ὑποσκήνια the parts beneath the stage, f. σκήνη SCENE.] The low wall supporting the front of the stage in a Greek theatre.

[**1676** tr. *Guillatiere's Voy. Athens* 300 At the foot of the Logeon upon the Orchestra was a row of Pillars incompassing a place called the Hyposcenion.] **1753** CHAMBERS *Cycl. Supp.*, *Hyposcenium*,..a partition under the pulpit or logeum of the Greek theatre, appointed for the music. **1853** KINGSLEY *Hypatia* xxii, The hyposcenium had been painted to represent rocks.

hyposensitization (ˌhaɪpəʊsɛnsɪtaɪˈzeɪʃən). *Med.* [f. HYPO- 4 + SENSITIZATION, after *hypersensitization*.] The process of diminishing the sensitivity of a hypersensitive individual (as by the introduction of the allergen in a series of gradually increasing doses); a state of diminished sensitivity so produced.

1922 R. A. COOKE in *Jrnl. Immunol.* VII. 241 On account of the confusion that must result from the use of the well defined term 'desensitization' to designate clinically lessened sensitiveness in allergy it is suggested that the latter be referred to as a 'hyposensitization'. **1941** J. W. THOMAS *Allergy in Clin. Pract.* i. 11 When complete avoidance is impossible or impractical, hyposensitization with inhalants ..should be considered. **1953** F. K. HANSEL *Clin. Allergy* xxxix. 750 The terms desensitization and hyposensitization are used interchangeably to designate a lessening of sensitization or an increase of tolerance. **1971** O. SWINEFORD *Asthma* ix. 148 Treatment of allergic asthma by injecting extracts of allergens is called hyposensitization.

Hence **hypo'sensitize** *v. trans.*, to subject (an individual) to such a process; also *absol.*; **hypo'sensitized** *ppl. a.*

1931 W. T. VAUGHAN *Allergy & Appl. Immunol.* xx. 249 If contact with the allergen then produces no symptoms, he is..desensitized. If his symptoms are improved but not entirely relieved, he is hyposensitized. **1939** —— *Primer of Allergy* vii. 67 We can hyposensitize with practically any of the allergens which are inhaled (except chemicals). **1944** E. URBACH *Allergy* x. 249 Coca has succeeded in hyposensitizing a patient with turpentine allergy..by injecting turpentine dissolved in sterile almond oil every seven days. **1971** O. SWINEFORD *Asthma* ix. 148 How does one hyposensitize a patient?

‖**hypospadias** (hɪpəʊˈspeɪdɪəs, haɪpəʊ-). *Path.* [a. Gr. ὑποσπαδίας (Galen) one affected with hypospadias, app. f. ὑπό HYPO- 1 + σπάειν to draw.] A congenital malformation consisting in a fissure of the lower wall of the male urethra, the result of arrested development.

1855 in MAYNE *Expos. Lex.* **1874** VAN BUREN *Dis. Genit. Org.* 38 Hypospadias consists of an arrest of development of a portion of the lower wall of the urethra. **1884** *Athenæum* 17 May 636/1 He has recorded the occurrence of the malformation termed hypospadias in the males of six successive generations in one family.

Hence **hypo'spadiac**, **hypo'spadial**, **hypo'spadic** *adjs.*, of the nature of, pertaining to, or affected with hypospadias.

1836–9 TODD *Cycl. Anat.* II. 464/1 A man affected with hypospadiac malformation of the urethra. *Ibid.* 699/1 A hypospadiac male. **1874** VAN BUREN *Dis. Genit. Org.* 38 Lying between a hypospadial opening and the meatus.

hyposphagma, -sphene, etc.: see HYPO- II.

Hypospray (ˈhaɪpəʊspreɪ). Also **hypospray**. [f. HYPO(DERMIC *a.* + SPRAY *sb.*[2]] The proprietary name of a kind of jet injector (see JET *sb.*[3] 9).

1947 *Life* 24 Nov. 65/1 Known as the Hypospray, this new device 'blasts' a microscopically small jet of medicinal fluid into the body tissues. **1948** *U.S. Pat. Off. Gaz.* 7 Sept. 69/1 *Hypospray.* R. P. Scherer Corporation, Detroit, Mich... For Hypodermic Injection Devices. **1948** *Amer. Practitioner* III. 206/1 The Hypospray may be used to give either intramuscular or subcutaneous injections. **1956** *Ann. Rheumatic Dis.* XV. 231/2 A practical feature of the hypospray injection is the simplicity of the technique. The physician can inject several joints in a short time without the preliminary preparation required for needle injection. **1969** *Ibid.* XXVIII. 61/2 The Hypospray was considerably less painful and more acceptable to patients.

hypostase (ˈhɪpəʊsteɪs). *rare*[−1]. [ad. next, or a. F. *hypostase*.] (See quot.)

1867 *Eng. Leader* 15 June 326 In every process whatever ..the subject-matter, the hypostase, is not two instants in the same state.

hypostasis (hɪp-, haɪˈpɒstəsɪs). Pl. **hypostases** (-siːz). [a. late L. *hypostasis*, a. Gr. ὑπόστασις (f. ὑπό HYPO- 1 + στάσις standing, position, state), lit. that which stands under, hence, sediment; also, groundwork, foundation, subject-matter; later, substance, subsistence, existence, reality, essence, personality (see below).

The development of sense, esp. in Metaphysics and Theology, belongs to Neo-Platonic and Early Christian use; the English senses only reflect those established in late Greek. See Chambers *Cycl.* s.v.]

1. *Med.* **a.** Sediment, deposit; *spec.* that of urine.

[**1398** TREVISA *Barth. De P.R.* v. xlv. (Bodl. MS.), By substaunce and colour of vrine & namelich by diuers regions þereof þat physicians clepen ypostasym.] **1590** MARLOWE *2nd Pt. Tamburl.* v. iii, I view'd your urine, and the hypostasis, Thick and obscure, doth make your danger great. **1683** SALMON *Doron Med.* II. 433 Then put them into a cold place, that its hypostasis may appear. **1753** N. TORRIANO *Gangr. Sore Throat* 118 The Water..tended to deposit a laudable Hypostasis. **1855** in MAYNE *Expos. Lex.*

b. Hyperæmia in dependent organs of the body, caused by subsidence of the blood into these parts.

1855 in MAYNE *Expos. Lex.* **1866–80** A. FLINT *Princ. Med.* (ed. 5) 193 The prevention and removal of hypostasis in the dependent portions of the lungs. **1897** ALLBUTT *Syst. Med.* II. 961 The skin and internal organs..as well as any post-mortem hypostases, exhibit a bright red colour.

†**2.** Base, foundation, groundwork, prop, support.

1577 tr. *Bullinger's Decades* I. iv. 82 The substance, or *hypostasis*, is the foundation, or the unmoveable prop, which upholdeth us. **1621** S. WARD *Life of Faith* (1627) 46 And is not Faith an Hypostasis and euidence to thee of an infallible inheritance?

3. *Metaph.* That which subsists, or underlies anything; substance: (*a*) as opposed to qualities, attributes, or 'accidents'; (*b*) as distinguished from what is unsubstantial, as a shadow or reflection.

1605 TIMME *Quersit.* Ded. 1 That spirit of life..acteth in all creatures, giving them existence in three—to wit, salt, sulphure, and mercury, in one *hupostasis*. **1670** *Moral State Eng.* 43 It commonly turneth even the souls of its votaries into its own Hypostasis. **1720** WATERLAND *Eight Serm.* 155 The Ante-Nicene as well as Post-Nicene Writers understood the Phrases of Christ's being the Image of God, and express Image of his *Hypostasis*. **1817** COLERIDGE *Biog. Lit.* I. viii. 130 Either as a property or attribute or as an hypostasis or self-subsistence. **1870** *Outl. Hamilton's Philos.* 170 We cannot think a *quality existing absolutely*, in or of itself; we are constrained to think it as inhering in some basis, substratum, hypostasis, subject or substance.

4. Essence, principle, essential principle.

1678 CUDWORTH *Intell. Syst.* I. i. §22 That Plato and his followers held τρεῖς ἀρχικὰς ὑποστάσεις, Three Hypostases in the Deity, that were the first Principles of all things, is a thing very well known to all. **1685** CROWNE *Sir C. Nice* II. Dram. Wks. 1874 III. 276 A scholar..emptied by old suck-eggs of all that nature gave me, and crumbl'd full of essences, hypostases and other stuff o' their baking. **1688** NORRIS *Theory Love* I. ii. 7 We know Love is made the first Hypostasis in the Platonic Triad. **1702** tr. *Le Clerc's Prim. Fathers* 72 Three Hypostases, which are the Three Principles of all things. **1847** LEWES *Hist. Philos.* (1867) I. 392 God therefore in his absolute state—in his first and highest hypostasis—is neither Existence nor Thought, neither moved nor mutable.

5. *Theol.* Personality, personal existence, person: (*a*) distinguished from *nature*, as in the one 'hypostasis' of Christ as distinguished from his two *natures* (human and divine), (*b*) distinguished from *substance*, as in the three 'hypostases' or 'persons' of the Godhead, which are said to be the same in 'substance'.

[**1747** JOHNSON *Plan Eng. Dict.* Wks. 1787 IX. 170 Of those [words] which still continue in the state of aliens,.. some seem necessary to be retained..such are some terms of controversial divinity, as hypostasis.]

a **1529** SKELTON *Col. Clout* 534 And what ipostacis Of Christes manhode is. **1565** T. STAPLETON *Fortr. Faith* 148 b, Those busy heads would for thre persons, saie thre hipostases. **1600** J. PORY tr. *Leo's Africa* XVII. 391 The Cofti fearing, that to attribute two natures unto Christ, might be all one, as if they had assigned him two hypostases or persons, to avoid the heresie of the Nestorians, they became Eutichians. **1602** W. WATSON *Quodlibets* 49 (Stanf.) By reason of the hypostasis or hypostaticall vnion of his deitie to his humanity. **1620** T. GRANGER *Div. Logike* 43 The Brutall soule is materiall,..not subsisting by it selfe (therefore a beast is not hypostasis, *id est*, a person). **1651** JER. TAYLOR *Serm. for Year* I. i. 2 That two natures could be concentred into one hypostasis (or person). **1682** H. MORE *Annot. Glanvill's Lux O.* 95 There is no confusion of the Humane and Divine Nature in the Hypostasis of Christ. *a* **1716** SOUTH *Serm.* (1717) IV. 299 [It] is urged by some to relate ..to the three Hypostases of the Godhead. **1782** PRIESTLEY *Corrupt. Chr.* I. I. 103 The word hypostasis..we now render person. **1833** R. PINKERTON *Russia* 46 The eternal beginning of the hypostasis of the Holy Ghost.

6. *Bot.* (See quot.)

1866 *Treas. Bot.* 615/2 *Hypostasis*, the suspensor of an embryo.

7. *Genetics.* [Back-formation from HYPOSTATIC *a.* 3] The inhibition of the expression of one gene by the action of another non-allelic (epistatic) gene.

1917 *Genetics* II. 615/1 (Index), Hypostasis. **1962** I. H. HERSKOWITZ *Genetics* vii. 53/1 Genes whose detection is hampered by nonallelic genes are said to be hypostatic, i.e., to exhibit hypostasis. As dominance implies recessiveness, so epistasis implies hypostasis.

8. *Linguistics.* The citing of a word, word-element, etc., as an example, a model, etc. Also, a linguistic element thus referred to.

1933 L. BLOOMFIELD *Lang.* ix. 148 Hypostasis, the mention of a phonetically normal speech-form, as when we say, 'That is only an *if*', or 'There is always a *but*', or when we talk about 'the word *normalcy*' or 'the name *Smith*'. One may even speak of parts of words, as..'the suffix *-ish* in *boyish*'. **1940** *Language* XVI. 238 When the sign is combined with a morpheme or is used in another grammatical category (hypostasis)..it is said to be characterized or positivized. **1961** *Lingua* X. 175 All I want to say is that the subject of this paper is..how to analyse linguistic signs occurring in *suppositio materialis* or (as I shall henceforth say) in hypostasis. **1963** *Ibid.* XII. 211 Sometimes hypostasis forms are used in other syntactical functions than subject, object or part of an adverbial adjunct, but at least those three functions are the most frequent in English. **1967** K. L. PIKE *Lang. in Rel. Human Behavior* (ed. 2) 108 Spelling words aloud is a form of hypostasis. *Ibid.* 484 This is treating sentences in hypostasis.

hypostasize (hɪp-, haɪˈpɒstəsaɪz), *v.* [f. prec. + -IZE.] *trans.* To make into or regard as a self-existent substance or person; to embody, impersonate. Cf. HYPOSTATIZE.

1809–10 COLERIDGE *Friend* (1818) III. 90 The power and principle of acidification must be embodied and as it were impersonated and hypostasized in this gas. **1817** —— *Biog. Lit.* I. 98 The admission of the logos as hypostasized in no respect removed my doubts concerning the Incarnation and the Redemption by the cross. **1877** SYMONDS *Renaissance in Italy, Reviv. Learn.* 202 The products of speculative analysis are hypostasised as divine persons.

Hence **hypostasi'zation**, the action of hypostasizing, or regarding as a substance.

1884 *Athenæum* 19 Apr. 496/3 The second period [of Plato's philosophy] is marked by the hypostasization of universals.

†**hy'postasy.** *Obs. rare.* [Adapted form of HYPOSTASIS: cf. ECSTASY.]

1. = HYPOSTASIS 1.

1547 BOORDE *Brev. Health* lxxiii. 21 The hypostasy is the substance of the uryne. **1638** SHIRLEY *Mart. Soldier* III. iv. in Bullen *O. Pl.* I. 218 Doe but marke These black Hypostacies; it plainely shewes Mortification generally through the Spirits.

2. = HYPOSTASIS 5.

1551 BP. GARDINER *Explic. Cath. Faith* 117 Wheir as in that vnion the rest is an ineffable mysterie, the two natures in Christ to haue one subsistence called & termed an hypostasie. **1628** GAULE *Pract. The.* (1629) 58 O the vnsearchable depth of this speciall Hypostasie!

hypostatic (hɪpəʊ-, haɪpəʊ'stætɪk), *a.* [ad. Gr. ὑποστατικ-ός pertaining to substance, substantial, personal (f. ὑποστατός set under, supporting); used as adj. to ὑπόστασις HYPOSTASIS; but the medical sense of the English word is not found in Greek.]

1. *Theol.* Of or pertaining to substance, essence, or personality (see HYPOSTASIS). ***hypostatic union***: (*a*) the union of the divine and human natures in the 'hypostasis' of Christ; (*b*) the consubstantial union of the three 'hypostases' in the Godhead.

1678 CUDWORTH *Intell. Syst.* I. iv. §36. 566 The humane soul of our Saviour Christ Himself..being not partially appointed to that transcendent dignity of its hypostatick union, but by reason of its most faithful adherence to the divine word and wisdom in a pre-existent state. *a* **1711** KEN *Hymns Evang.* Poet. Wks. 1721 I. 25, I sing the Infinite and Finite join'd In Hypostatick Union for Mankind. **1827** HOOK in *Life* I. 118 To state and enforce the Catholic doctrine concerning the Third Person on Whit Sunday and that of the hypostatic union on the Sunday following. **1846** SIR J. STEPHEN *Eccl. Biog.* (1850) I. 85 He who first taught men to speak of an Hypostatic change beneath unchanging forms, may have taught them to use words without meaning. **1894** H. B. SWETE *Apost. Creed* i. 17 The doctrine of the hypostatic Trinity.

2. *Path.* Of the nature of hypostasis or excess of blood in dependent parts of the body.

1866–80 A. FLINT *Princ. Med.* (ed. 5) 192 Passive hyperæmia occurring in the dependent portions of the lungs is called hypostatic congestion. **1878** A. M. HAMILTON *Nerv. Dis.* 224 The long continuance of the erect position seems to favor the gravitation of blood, and hypostatic hyperæmia of the spine is thereby induced.

3. *Genetics.* Of, causing, or affected by hypostasis (sense 7). Const. *to.*

1907 [see EPISTATIC *a.*]. **1961** A. MÜNTZING *Genetic Res.* vi. 58/2 We may also say that B is hypostatic to A. **1965** J. A. SERRA *Mod. Genetics* I. iii. 62 The effect of one gene, the epistatic gene, is superimposed on the effect of another, the hypostatic gene, either by obscuring the phenotypic effect of the hypostatic gene, or by inhibiting its effect.

hypostatical (hɪpəʊ-, haɪpəʊ'stætɪkəl), *a.* [f. as prec. + -AL[1].]

1. = HYPOSTATIC 1.

1561 T. NORTON *Calvin's Inst.* II. 154 He being the Word ..did by hypostatical vnion take vpon hym the nature of man. **1616** BULLOKAR *Eng. Expos.*, *Hypostaticall*, belonging to substance; or that which consisteth in the substance of a thing. **1620** T. GRANGER *Div. Logike* 310 To the singular number (Jehovah) his essentiall name, noting the unity..is added the plurall (Elohim) his hypostaticall, or subsistentiall name, noting the Trinity. **1656** HOBBES *Answ. Bp. Bramhall* 434 (R.) But the word hypostatical..is properly used, as I have said before, of the union of the two natures of Christ in one person. **1674** HICKMAN *Quinquart. Hist.* Ep. (ed. 2) A iij b, I believe the Hypostatical Union, a Trinity of persons in the Unity of Essence. **1852** HOOK *Ch. Dict.* (1871) 377 The hypostatical union is the union of the human nature of our Lord with the divine, constituting two natures in one person.

†**2.** Of or pertaining to the essential principles or elements of bodies; elemental. *Obs.*

1661–80 BOYLE *Scept. Chym.* I. 80 They do not pretend by fire alone to separate out of all compound Bodies their Hypostatical Principles. **1676** —— *Hist. Colours* Exp. xv, Divers learned men, having adopted the three hypostaticall principles. **1706** PHILLIPS (ed. Kersey), *Hypostatical Principles*, a Title given by Paracelsus and his Followers to the three Chymical Principles, viz. Salt, Sulphur and Mercury.

Hence **hypo'statically** *adv.*, in a hypostatic manner; in actual substance or personality.

1593 T. BELL *Motives conc. Rom. Faith* (1605) 118 [He] affirmeth the substance of bread to be united to the body of Christ hipostatically. **1614** T. ADAMS *Devil's Banq.* 123 God ..is hypostatically in Christ: graciously in his Saints: gloriously in Heauen: powerfully in Hell. **1681–6** J. SCOTT *Chr. Life* (1747) III. 41 Our Ransom from eternal Punishment being paid with the Blood of one of our kind, hypostatically united to God. **1697** C. LESLIE *Snake in Grass* (ed. 2) 154 After a Soul is Hypostatically, that is, Personally united to a Body, their separation is call'd Death. **1883** *Catholic Dict.* (1885) 428/2 Sin was a physical impossibility in the human soul of Christ, because it was hypostatically united to the Divinity.

hypostatize (hɪp-, haɪ'pɒstətaɪz), *v.* [f. Gr. ὑποστατός (see HYPOSTATIC) + -IZE.] *trans.* To make into or treat as a substance; = HYPOSTASIZE.

1829 SIR W. HAMILTON *Discuss.* (1853) 17 These negations, hypostatised as positive, under the Platonic name of Ideas. **1872** *Contemp. Rev.* XX. 828 Neither Space nor Time..offer any reason for hypostatizing their reality as a real substratum, apart from the phenomena. **1877** E. CAIRD *Philos. Kant* II. xviii. 627 If thus we hypostatise this idea of the *ens realissimum*, and follow it to its legitimate development.

Hence **hy'postatized, -izing** *ppl. adjs.* Also **hypostati'zation** = HYPOSTASIZATION.

1869 J. MARTINEAU *Ess.* II. 141 The hypostatizing propensities of our natural faculties. **1870** HUXLEY *Lay Serm.* (1871) 329 The 'Absolute' and all the other hypostatized adjectives. *a* **1882** T. H. GREEN *Prol. Ethics* Introd. (1883) 8 What after all, it is asked, is any faculty but an hypostatised abstraction? **1886** A. SETH in *Encycl. Brit.* XXI. 421/2 To deny the hypostatization of an accident like colour or wisdom.

hyposternal, etc.: see HYPO- II.

†**hy'postle.** *nonce-wd.* [Formed after APOSTLE, from Gr. ὑποστολή drawing back (cf. *Hebrews* x. 38, 39).] One who draws back; an apostate.

a **1626** BP. ANDREWES *Serm.* ix. (1661) 454 They be Hypostles; so doth Saint Paul well term them.

hypostomatous, -stomous: see HYPO- II.

hypostome ('hɪpəʊstəʊm, 'haɪpəʊ-), Also in L. form **hy'postoma.** [ad. F. *hypostome*, mod.L. *hypostoma*, f. HYPO- 2 + Gr. στόμα mouth.] A part of the mouth in arthropods and some other invertebrate animals; e.g. the clypeus of dipterous insects, the labium or under lip of trilobites, the proboscis of Hydrozoa.

1862 DANA *Man. Geol.* 188 *note*, *Hypostome*, a prominent piece on the under surface of the head, covering the mouth. **1872** NICHOLSON *Palæont.* 147 The aperture of the mouth.. bounded in front by a plate, known as the 'labrum' or 'hypostoma'. **1888** ROLLESTON & JACKSON *Anim. Life* 246 The hypostome or oral cone [in hydranths] is conical.

hypostroma, -strophe, etc.: see HYPO- II.

†**hypo'sulphate.** *Chem. Obs.* [f. HYPO- 5 + SULPHATE.] A salt of hyposulphuric acid. (Now called a DITHIONATE.)

1819 J. G. CHILDREN *Chem. Anal.* 435 Hyposulphate of lime crystallizes in regular hexagonal plates. **1868–72** WATTS *Dict. Chem.* V. 637 Dithionates or Hyposulphates.

hyposulphite (hɪpəʊ-, haɪpəʊ'sʌlfaɪt). *Chem.* [ad. F. *hyposulfite*: see HYPO- 5 and SULPHITE.] A salt of hyposulphurous acid.

a. Originally (and still commercially) applied to the salts now called by chemists *thiosulphates*; as ***hyposulphate of soda*** = sodium thiosulphate.

1826 HENRY *Elem. Chem.* II. 136 Hypo-sulphite of silver may be formed by mixing hyposulphite of soda with dilute nitrate of silver, or by dissolving chloride of silver in any of the hypo-sulphites. Though formed of ingredients that have a metallic and very bitter taste, its flavour is intensely sweet. **1868–72** WATTS *Dict. Chem.* V. 540 Allied to the sulphates there is a group of salts called thiosulphates, or more frequently hyposulphites. **1894** ROSCOE & SCHORLEMMER *Chem.* I. 412 Thiosulphuric acid..forms a series of stable salts known as the thiosulphates (hyposulphites).

b. Now, with chemists, a salt of the acid $H_2S_2O_4$, formerly called a *hydrosulphite.*

1872 WATTS *Dict. Chem.* Suppl. VI. 1063 The formation of thiosulphates..is only a secondary reaction due to the slow and spontaneous decomposition of the hyposulphite. **1877** —— *Fownes' Chem.* (ed. 12) I. 213 The solution.. solidifies in a few hours to a mass of slender colourless needles, consisting of sodium hyposulphite. **1894** ROSCOE & SCHORLEMMER *Chem.* I. 409 Sodium hyposulphite ($Na_2S_2O_4$) is employed by the dyer and calico-printer for the reduction of indigo, as it possesses the same reducing properties as the free acid.

†**hyposul'phuric,** *a.* *Chem. Obs.* [ad. F. *hyposulphurique*; see HYPO- 5 and SULPHURIC.] In ***hyposulphuric acid***, old name of DITHIONIC acid.

1819 J. G. CHILDREN *Chem. Anal.* 433 The authors [Welter and Gay Lussac] propose to name this new acid, the hyposulphuric, by analogy with the hyposulphurous, to denote that it contains less oxygen than sulphuric acid, and more than sulphurous acid. **1894** ROSCOE & SCHORLEMMER *Chem.* I. 415 Dithionic Acid ($H_2S_2O_6$)..formerly called hyposulphuric acid, was discovered by Welter and Gay Lussac in 1819.

hyposulphurous (hɪpəʊ-, haɪpəʊ'sʌlfjʊərəs), *a.* *Chem.* [f. HYPO- 5 + SULPHUROUS.] In ***hyposulphurous acid***: †**a.** The name originally given to the acid $H_2S_2O_3$, now called *thiosulphuric acid.*

1817 T. THOMSON *Chem.* (ed. 5) II. 112 Besides the two acid compounds of sulphur and oxygen, (viz. sulphurous and sulphuric acids) we have the fullest evidence of the existence of a third..to which the name of hyposulphurous acid may be given. **1871** ROSCOE *Elem. Chem.* 138 Hyposulphurous Acid, or Hydrogen Hyposulphite is not known in the free state. **1894** ROSCOE & SCHORLEMMER *Chem.* I. 412 Thiosulphuric Acid ($H_2S_2O_3$). This compound is better known under its old name of 'hyposulphurous acid', with which name however we now designate the body obtained by the reduction of sulphurous acid.

b. Now applied to the acid $H_2S_2O_4$, containing one atom of oxygen less than sulphurous acid; formerly called *hydrosulphurous acid.*

1872 WATTS *Dict. Chem.* Suppl. VI. 1063 *Hyposulphurous Acid*, H_2SO_2 (*Hydrosulphurous Acid*, Schützenberger)..is produced by the action of zinc on aqueous sulphurous acid. *Ibid.* 1074 Schützenberger calls his acid *hydrosulphurous acid*; but it is more consistent with analogy to designate it as *hyposulphurous acid.* **1877** —— *Fownes' Chem.* (ed. 12) I. 213 Hyposulphurous acid is obtained, as a deep orange-coloured strongly bleaching liquid.

hypotactic, -tarsus, -taxis: see HYPO- II.

hypotension (haɪpəʊ'tɛnʃən). *Med.* [f. HYPO- 4 + TENSION *sb.*] Abnormally low 'tension' or pressure of a bodily fluid. **a.** Of arterial blood.

1893 [see HYPERTENSION 1 a]. **1938** *Lancet* 31 Dec. 1510/2 Hypotension is sometimes accompanied by..postural giddiness. **1966** WRIGHT & SYMMERS *Systemic Path.* I. iii. 110/1 Moderate degrees of hypotension may..occur in patients with chronic wasting diseases, especially when they are confined to bed for long periods.

b. Of the intra-ocular fluid.

1909 A. M. RAMSAY *Diathesis & Ocular Dis.* v. 46 The easiest..method..is to puncture the sclerotic with a broad needle... This causes immediate hypotension. **1969** DUKE-ELDER & JAY in S. Duke-Elder *Syst. Ophthalm.* XI. x. 724 The subject of ocular hypotension has excited much less interest and speculation than that of hypertension.

hypotensive (haɪpəʊ'tɛnsɪv), *a.* *Med.* [f. prec. + -IVE.] Of, exhibiting, or associated with hypotension, esp. of the blood; tending to lower the blood pressure.

1904 T. C. JANEWAY *Clin. Study Blood-Pressure* vi. 153 Typhoid fever is more frequently hypotensive in the average case than the other acute diseases, pneumonia least. **1927** *Medicine* VI. 147 It is also true that many hypotensive subjects possess great bodily vigor. **1951** A. GROLLMAN *Pharmacol. & Therapeutics* xi. 213 It is also used..to combat a drop in blood-pressure occurring during spinal anesthesia and in other acute hypotensive states due to vasomotor failure. **1961** *Lancet* 29 July 222/2 Patients with severe arterial hypertension were given hypotensive drugs only if they had been so treated previously. **1966** *Ibid.* 26 Mar. 677/1 A few hours after admission the patient became hypotensive and vasopressor drugs had to be used. **1973** *Times* 2 Oct. 15/2 One of the most common fatal side-effects is that it becomes hypotensive (low blood pressure).

hypotenusal (hɪp-, haɪpɒtə'njuːsəl), *a.* and *sb.* Also **hypothenusal.** [ad. late L. *hypotēnūsāl-is*, f. *hypotēnūsa* HYPOTENUSE.]

A. *adj.* Pertaining to, or of the nature of, a hypotenuse; forming a hypotenuse. Now *rare.*

1571 DIGGES *Pantom.* I. xxxi. Kj a, Fyrste I measure the Hypothenusall lyne. **1658** PHILLIPS, *Hypothenusal line*, a term in Geometry, it is that side of a right-angled triangle which is subtended or opposite to the right angle. **1785** ROY in *Phil. Trans.* LXXV. 420 The tops of the pickets, marking the hypothenusal distances, were the points on which the levelling rods were placed. **1831** G. B. AIRY *Math. Tracts* (1842) 293 Two glass prisms, right-angled or nearly so, are placed with their hypotenusal sides nearly in contact.

†**B.** *sb.* (sc. *line*) = HYPOTENUSE. *Obs.*

1641 WILKINS *Math. Magick* II. xv. (1648) 279 If the Hypotenusall, or Screw be 5, the perpendicular or elevation must be 3, and the basis 4. **1656** HOBBES *Six Less.* Wks. 1845 VII. 317 The hypotenusal of a rectangled triangle. **1661** S. PARTRIDGE *Double Scale Proport.* 136 In a right angled Triangle, the Angles and the Hypothenusal being given [etc.].

hypotenuse (hɪp-, haɪ'pɒtənjuːs). Forms: (6–7 **hypothenusa**, 7 **-tenusa, -tinusa**), 6 **hipothenuse**, 7– **hypotenuse, hypothenuse.** [ad. late L. *hypotēnūsa*, a. Gr. ὑποτείνουσα pr. pple. (fem.), 'stretching under, subtending' (the full expression being ἡ τὴν ὀρθὴν γωνίαν ὑποτείνουσα (sc. γραμμή or πλευρά), the line or side subtending the right angle), f. ὑπό under + τείνειν to stretch. In F. *hypoténuse.*

In the 16–17th c. the Latin form *hypotenusa* was commonly used. The erroneous spelling with *th* (cf. F. *ypothenuse*, 1520) was app. the more frequent in 19th-c. use.]

The side of a right-angled triangle which subtends, or is opposite to, the right angle.

1571 DIGGES *Pantom.* II. ii. Liv a, Yᵉ squares of the two contayning sides ioyned togither, are equall to the square of yᵉ Hypothenusa. **1594** BLUNDEVIL *Exerc.* II. (1636) 119 They cal the line Secant the Hipothenuse, because it subtendeth the right angle A. **1674** JEAKE *Arith.* (1696) 174 The Perpendicular, the Base, and the Hypotenusa. **1678** CUDWORTH *Intell. Syst.* I. v. 734 The Power of the Hypotenuse in a Rectangular Triangle is Equal to the Powers of both the Sides. **1704** J. HARRIS *Lex. Techn.* s.v. *Plain Sailing*, The Base of the Triangle represents the Departure; and the Hypothenuse the Distance Sailed. **1834** *Nat. Philos.* III. *Navigation* I. i. 2 (U.K.S.) The side AB, opposite to the right angle, is called the hypotenuse. **1878** H. S. WILSON *Alp. Ascents* iv. 117 The hypothenuse of the angles.

hypothalamo-hypophysial (haɪpəʊ,θæləməʊ-haɪpəʊ'fɪzɪəl), *a.* Also **-eal.** [f. HYPOTHALAM(US + -O + HYPOPHYSIAL *a.*] Of, pertaining to, or connecting the hypothalamus and the hypophysis; applied *spec.* to a tract of nerve fibres that runs from the hypothalamus to the neurohypophysis.

1934 *Arch. Neurol. & Psychiatry* (Chicago) XXXII. 217 The entity of the fibers traversing the infundibulum and entering the posterior lobe of the hypophysis is called the hypothalamo-hypophyseal fasciculus ('faisceau hypothalamo-hypophysaire'). **1950** G. W. HARRIS in *Jrnl. Physiol.* CXI. 347 The hypophysial stalk has two main component parts, the hypothalamo-hypophysial tract of nerve fibres associated with the neurohypophysis, and the hypophysial portal vessels associated with the

adenohypophysis. **1971** N. G. SUTTON *Anat. Brain & Spinal Medulla* v. 78 A series of hypothalamohypophyseal portal vessels descend in the form of numerous blood sinusoids to end among the cells of the adenohypophysis. **1972** *Nature* 5 May 15/1 These connexions.. may prove to be an important component of the pathways which subserve the marked effect of light on the hypothalamo-hypophysial activity.

Also **hypotha,lamico-hypo'physial, -eal** *a.*, in the same sense.

1934 *Trans. Coll. Phys. Philadelphia* II. 223 Diabetes insipidus and Fröhlich's syndrome are due to disturbances of this hypothalamico-hypophyseal mechanism. **1944** J. HOFFMAN *Female Endocrinol.* xv. 226 A neuro-endocrine unit which has recently attracted much attention is the so-called hypothalamico-hypophyseal system. **1961** *Lancet* 2 Sept. 522/2 Lesions have been found in the hypothalamicohypophyseal system in only a few cases of primary diabetes insipidus.

hypothalamus (haɪpəʊ'θæləməs). *Anat.* [mod.L. (W. His (at Waldeyer's suggestion) 1893, in *Arch. f. Anat. u. Physiol.* (*Anat. Abth.*) 159), f. HYPO- + THALAMUS.] The lower part of the diencephalon of the brain in vertebrates, lying below and in front of the thalamus and forming the floor and part of the wall of the third ventricle; in mammals it acts as the chief co-ordinating region of the autonomic nervous system and helps to regulate the hormonal activity of the adenohypophysis.

Writers vary in counting as part of the hypothalamus (*a*) the infundibulum and neurohypophysis, and (*b*) the subthalamic tegmental region.

1896 *Jrnl. Compar. Neurol.* VI. 309 (*in list of anatomical names*) Hypothalamus. **1899** L. F. BARKER *Nervous Syst.* xlvi. 666 These various fibres.. pass through the pedunculus cerebri.. to reach the diencephalon, where most of them in all probability terminate in the hypothalamus, in the thalamencephalon, or in the nucleus lentiformis. **1909** *Gray's Anat.* (ed. 17) 849 The hypothalamus.. includes the subthalamic tegmental region and the structures which form the greater part of the floor of the third ventricle, viz. the corpora mamillaria, tuber cinereum, infundibulum, pituitary body, and optic commissure. **1942** L. H. HYMAN *Compar. Vertebr. Anat.* (ed. 2) xiv. 434 The hypothalamus reaches its greatest development in fishes, where it is an important correlation center for olfactory, gustatory, and other sensory impulses. **1944** J. HOFFMAN *Female Endocrinol.* xv. 231 Proof that the hypothalamus regulates the gonadotropic function of the anterior hypophysis is still lacking. **1956** A. C. GUYTON *Textbk. Med. Physiol.* I. 633/1 When a surgeon operates in the region of the hypothalamus, simply tugging on the tissues is likely to cause such intense changes in heart rate, blood pressure, blood glucose level, body temperature, etc., that the operative mortality is approximately 40 per cent from these factors alone. **1962** T. W. TORREY *Morphogenesis Vertebr.* xviii. 510 In all vertebrates it is the hypothalamus which exercises control over such truly involuntary actions as temperature regulation, sexual reactions, breathing rate, emotional responses, and the rhythm of sleep. **1964** PARKER & HASWELL *Text-bk. Zool.* (ed. 7) II. 245 [In the dogfish, *Scyliorhinus*] the hypothalamus in the floor of the diencephalon is well-developed and may, as in 'higher' vertebrates, be concerned with the regulation of various unconditioned reflexes and visceral functions. **1968** A. VAN TIENHOVEN *Reprod. Physiol. Vertebr.* viii. 207/1 The hypothalamus thus performs the task of being an intermediary between the nervous system, of which it is part, and the endocrine system, to which it can send 'hormonal' information. **1968** *Times* 10 Oct. 8/5 One part of the brain which contains noradrenaline is the hypothalamus, which has the function of controlling body temperature by monitoring the temperature of the blood and directing the body systems to lose or conserve heat. **1972** *Sci. Amer.* Nov. 24/1 The pituitary gland is attached by a stalk to the region in the base of the brain known as the hypothalamus.

Hence **hypo'thalamic** *a.*, of or pertaining to the hypothalamus.

1899 L. F. BARKER *Nervous Syst.* xlvi. 683 In man the fibres of the main mass of white matter in the hypothalamic region.. do not pass through the hilus into the thalamus. **1938** J. BEATTIE in W. E. Le Gros Clark et al. *Hypothalamus* 100 Sleep.. is due to a damping-down of hypothalamic activity. **1942** O. LARSELL *Anat. Nerv. Syst.* iii. 28 The thalamus and hypothalamus are bounded from each other by the hypothalamic sulcus. **1954** T. L. PEELE *Neuroanat. Basis Clin. Neurol.* xiv. 310/2 Hypothalamic lesions.. have resulted in a loss of cyclical sexual activities and genital atrophy. **1968** A. VAN TIENHOVEN *Reprod. Physiol. Vertebr.* viii. 249/1 Some of the hypothalamic hormones, e.g. oxytocin and vasopressin, are stored in the neurohypophysis.

‖**hypothallus** (hɪpəʊ-, haɪpəʊ'θæləs). *Bot.* [mod.L., f. HYPO- 2 + THALLUS.] The fibrous or filamentary substratum on which the thallus of lichens is developed.

1855 MAYNE *Expos. Lex.*, *Hypothallus*, term given by Fries to the internal or inferior thallus or couch of the lichens. **1857** BERKELEY *Cryptog. Bot.* §410. 374 The inner [coat].. gives birth beneath to the fibres by which the plant is often attached to the surface (hypothallus). **1875** BENNETT & DYER *Sachs' Bot.* 268 Isolated scaly pieces of a true Lichen-thallus then arise on a fibrous substratum called the Hypothallus.

Hence **hypo'thalline** *a.*, pertaining to, or of the nature of, a hypothallus.

1855 in MAYNE *Expos. Lex.* **1856** W. L. LINDSAY *Brit. Lichens* 55 A pulverulent or persistent hypothalline type.

hypothec (hɪp-, haɪ'pɒθɪk). Also 7–8 **-eque**, 8 **-ic**; 6– **hypotheca** (hɪpəʊ'θiːkə). [a. F. *hypothèque* or ad. late L. *hypothēca*, ad. Gr. ὑποθήκη a deposit, pledge, mortgage, f. ὑποτιθέναι to deposit as a pledge (f. ὑπό down + τιθέναι to put, place). The Latin form is now used only in sense 1 a.]

1. 'A security established by law in favour of a creditor over a subject belonging to his debtor, while the subject continues in the debtor's possession' (*Bell's Dict. Law Scot.*).

a. In ancient Roman law.

1592 WEST *1st Pt. Symbol.* §18 C, An improper pledge is called *Hypotheca*, which is of a thing not deliuered, which is made and perfected by couenant onelie. **1726** AYLIFFE *Parergon* 272 A Man's Bed, Wearing Apparel and other Things of the like Kind, necessary to his daily Use.. do not pass under an Hypotheque. **1875** POSTE *Gaius* IV. (ed. 2) 642 In a hypotheca, that is, an agreement without delivery, the mortgagee acquired no possession. **1880** MUIRHEAD *Gaius* I. §199 *note*, A pledge or hypothec could not be accepted instead. **1883** MAINE *Early Law & Cust.* x. 357 Possession, Usucapion, Bonitarian ownership, and Hypothek occupy together a prodigious space in the Roman jurisprudence.

b. In Scots Law.

(*a*) The lien or prior claim of a landlord for his rent over the crop and stock of a tenant farmer (but see quot. 1880), and over the furniture and other effects of a tenant in urban property. (*b*) The lien which seamen, freighters, and repairers have over a ship for their wages, etc., and that which a ship-owner has over cargo for the freight. (*c*) The lien which a legal agent has for costs over costs recovered from the adverse party. Sometimes applied to the right to retain writs and title-deeds in security of a professional account.

c **1730** BURT *Lett. N. Scotl.* (1818) II. 57 The Landlord has, by law, an hypothic, a right of pledge, with respect to the corn for so much as the current year's rent. **1733** P. LINDSAY *Interest Scot.* 39 Their Hypotheck secures them absolutely against Loss by the Tenant. **1754** ERSKINE *Princ. Sc. Law* (1809) 291 Writers also, and agents, have a right of hypothec, or more properly of retention, on their constituent's writings, for their claim of pains and disbursements. **1816** SCOTT *Antiq.* xli, As we hold your rights, title-deeds, and documents in hypothec. **1854** H. MILLER *Sch. & Schm.* xi. (1857) 238 The cattle and horses of the farm—appropriated by the landlord, at the time under the law of hypothec. **1880** *Act 43 Vict.* c. 12 §1 The landlord's right of hypothec for the rent of land.. exceeding two acres.. let for agriculture or pasture, shall cease and determine.

c. In the Channel Islands.

(In Fr. form *hypothèque*.)

1682 WARBURTON *Hist. Guernsey* (1822) 106 An Hypothèque differs from a mortgage in England in this respect chiefly, that he who parts with his money can never call it in again. **1694** FALLE *Jersey* ii. 86 All Bonds are not Personal as in England, but real, and carry an express Hypotheca or Mortgage upon the Estate both real and personal of the Debtor.

2. ***the whole hypothec*** (*colloq. Sc.*), the whole stock or lot, the whole 'concern' or 'business', the whole of anything.

1871 W. ALEXANDER *Johnny Gibb* i. (1873) 13 Johnny Gibb stopped Jess, got the whole 'hypothec' into the cart, and then [etc.]. **1879** STEVENSON *Trav. Cevennes* 22 And at last.. saddle and all, the whole hypothec turned and grovelled in the dust below the donkey's belly.

hy'pothecal, *a.* ? *Obs.* [f. L. *hypothēca* (see prec.) + -AL[1].] = next.

1606 DANIEL *Queen's Arcadia* Wks. (1717) 184, I overwhelm My Practice with Darkness and Strange Words, With.. Acceptilations, Actions, Recissory, Noxal and Hypothecal. **1767** A. CAMPBELL *Lexiph.* (1774) 57 To deposite as a mode of hypothecal security.

hypothecary (hɪp-, haɪ'pɒθɪkərɪ), *a.* [ad. late L. *hypothēcārius*, f. *hypothēca* HYPOTHEC. Cf. F. *hypothecaire* (1316 in Hatz.-Darm.).] Of, pertaining to, of the nature of, an hypothec or mortgage.

1656 BLOUNT *Glossogr.*, *Hypothecary*, pertaining to a pledge or gage. **1827** CARLYLE *Germ. Rom.*, *Quintus Fixlein* III. 238 The Parson.. to whom no security but a hypothecary one appeared sufficient. **1855** LORENZ tr. *Van der Keessel's Select Theses* dccclxxiv, How can the hypothecary action against the same debtor remain for a period of forty years? **1875** POSTE *Gaius* III. (ed. 2) 352 Simple hypothecary creditors, who have priority according to the date of their mortgage.

So **hypothe'carious** *a. rare*[−1]. = prec.

1726 AYLIFFE *Parergon* 337 A Real or Hypothecarious Action does not lie against a Feudal Estate, yet a Personal Action lies.

hypothecate (hɪp-, haɪ'pɒθɪkeɪt), *v.* [f. *hypothēcāt-*, ppl. stem of med.L. *hypothēcāre*, f. *hypothēca* HYPOTHEC: see -ATE[3]. Cf. F. *hypothéquer*.

The pa. pple. in Sc. was formerly *hypothecat*(*e*: see -ATE[2].]

1. *trans.* To give or pledge as security; to pledge, pawn, mortgage.

1681 STAIR *Instit.* IV. xxv. §5 (1693) 619 The Fruits of the Ground.. which by the Law were Hypothecat for the Rents of the said year. **1754** ERSKINE *Princ. Sc. Law* (1809) 197 The whole cattle on the ground.. are hypothecated for a year's rent, one after another successively. **1755** MAGENS *Insurances* II. 55 We oblige ourselves and hypothecate, for the Security and Payment of the Sum of this Writing, the said Ship.. and we oblige ourselves not to dispose thereof in any manner, until the said Sum be entirely paid. And whatever is done to the contrary, let it be null, as a Thing done against an express Prohibition and Hypothecation. **1756** ROLT *Dict. Trade*, *Hypotheca*, among the moderns to hypothecate a ship, is to pawn or pledge the same for necessaries; and into whose hands soever the ship comes, it is liable. **1797** BURKE *Regic. Peace* III. Wks. VIII. 319 Whether they to whom this new pledge is hypothecated, have redeemed their own. **1827** SCOTT *Napoleon* (1834) I. vi. 206 The assembly adopted a system of paper money, called assignats, which were secured or hypothecated upon the church lands. **1855** MACAULAY *Hist. Eng.* xii. III. 148 He had no power to hypothecate any part of the public revenue.

2. *trans.* = HYPOTHESIZE *v.* 2.

1906 *Nature* 7 June 136/1 Mr. Cowell hypothecated a resisting medium through which the earth travels. **1912** R. FRY in *Gt. State* ix. 271 Mr. Wells's Modern Utopia.. hypothecates a vast superstructure of private trading. **1915** E. B. HOLT *Freudian Wish* i. 4 One will best.. not hypothecate to this end any such thing as 'psychic energy'. **1920** E. POUND *Let.* 12 Sept. (1971) 161 You are talking through your hat when you suggest that I.. was ever ass enough to have picked 'La Figlia' for the fantastic occasion you hypothecate. **1952** *Pediatrics* IX. 724 One had to hypothecate the existence of a mutation of organisms.

Hence **hy'pothecated** *ppl. a.*; also **hy'pothecator**, one who hypothecates or pledges something as security.

1779 SIR W. JONES *Comm. Isæus* Wks. 1799 IV. 205 The property.. was distinguished like all other hypothecated estates, by small columns, and inscriptions.. containing a specification of the sum for which they were pledged. **1828** WEBSTER cites Judge Johnson for *Hypothecator*. **1865** *Day of Rest* Oct. 574 The iron box in the back sitting room, containing the hypothecated jewels, had been rifled.

hypothecation (hɪp-, haɪpɒθɪ'keɪʃən). [n. of action f. prec.: see -ATION.] The act of pledging as security; pledging or pawning. In some legal systems applied only to a lien upon immovable property; in others to a lien on personal property, negotiable securities, etc.

1681 STAIR *Instit.* I. xiii. §15 (1693) 122 With us there remains the Tacit Hypothecation of the Fruits on the Ground.. belonging to the Possessor, for the Terms or the Years Rent. **1755** [see HYPOTHECATE]. **1756** ROLT *Dict. Trade* s.v. *Hypotheca*, It was held, that, by the maritime law, every contract of the master implies an hypothecation; but at common law it is not so. **1861** *Kent's Comm.* (1873) I. xvii. 378 The admiralty has cognizance of maritime hypothecations of vessels and goods in foreign ports. **1875** POSTE *Gaius* III. (ed. 2) 371 Hypothecation was effected by mere convention without delivery of possession.

hy'pothecative, *a. rare.* [f. HYPOTHECATE: see -IVE.] Characterized by hypothecating.

1856 *Leisure Hour* V. 11/2 A pawnbroker's side-door which admits the hypothecative philosopher.

So **hy'pothecatory** *a.*, of the nature of hypothecation.

hypothenusal, hypothenuse, erron. ff. HYPOTENUSAL, HYPOTENUSE.

hypothermia (haɪpəʊ'θɜːmɪə). *Med.* Also in anglicized form **hypothermy** ('haɪpəʊθɜːmɪ) (*rare*). [f. HYPO- 4 + Gr. θέρμ-η heat + -IA[1].] The condition of having a body temperature substantially below the normal, either as a result of natural causes or artificially induced (e.g. for cardiac surgery).

1886 in *Syd. Soc. Lex.* **1887** A. M. BROWN *Contrib. Animal Alkaloids* 143 Intoxication by animal alkaloids is accompanied by hypothermia. **1898** W. S. BARLOW *Man. Gen. Path.* x. 441 Emphysema and some other forms of pulmonary disease.. are associated with a slight degree of hypothermia. **1903** *Jrnl. Nerv. & Mental Dis.* XXX. 574 The same toxic agent which acts on the nervous system producing the condition of epilepsy may be the cause of the hypothermy in these cases. **1937** *Brit. Encycl. Med. Pract.* III. 499 The reduction of the metabolic processes in cretinism is shown, as in myxoedema, by hypothermia. **1955** *Sci. News Let.* 18 June 389/2 When patients are given 'frozen sleep', or hypothermia, for operations inside the heart, they can be quickly warmed to normal by diathermy. **1964** *Courier-Mail* (Brisbane) 18 July 2 His problem probably had been 'hypothermia'—low body temperature—quite common in cold weather in elderly people who do not keep themselves sufficiently warm. **1966** *New Statesman* 11 Nov. 697/1 The experts concluded that 'hypothermia is a serious though unspectacular condition with a very high mortality rate'.

So **hypo'thermic** *a.* [cf. Gr. ὑπόθερμος somewhat hot], of or exhibiting hypothermia.

1898 W. S. L. BARLOW *Man. Gen. Path.* x. 440 A general sluggishness of nerve and of muscle in hypothermic persons and animals is always noticeable. **1948** A. R. MORITZ in W. A. D. Anderson *Path.* vi. 143 The severity of injury caused at any given temperature tends to be proportional to the duration of the hypo- or hyperthermic episode. **1961** *Lancet* 2 Dec. 1216/2 The complete absence of residual signs of cerebral dysfunction was particularly noteworthy in one patient who remained hypothermic and unconscious for seven days.

hypothesis (hɪp-, haɪ'pɒθɪsɪs). Pl. **hypotheses** (-siːz). [a. Gr. ὑπόθεσις foundation, base; hence, basis of an argument, supposition, also, subject-matter, etc., f. ὑπό under + θέσις placing.]

†**1.** A subordinate particular thesis involved in a general thesis; a particular case of a general proposition. In quot. 1596, a particular or detailed statement. Cf. F. *hypothèse* (sense 3 in Littré). *Obs.*

1596 EARL OF ESSEX in Ellis *Orig. Lett.* Ser. III. IV. 137 If I be commaunded to sett doune the Hypothesis, or to descend into particulars. **1620** T. GRANGER *Div. Logike* 10 *note*, The compound Theme is also (*a*) speciall, or (*b*) generall: (*a*) Hypothesis; (*b*) Thesis. *Ibid.* 204 To amplifie a speciall or particular sentence, called hypothesis. **1638** BAKER tr. *Balzac's Lett.* (Vol. III.) 24 Without descending from the thesis to the hypothesis. *a* **1647** FILMER *Patriarcha* i. §1 (1884) 13 If the thesis be true, the hypothesis will

follow. *a* **1721** KEILL *Maupertius' Diss.* (1734) 49 Whence it is plain that there is no Hypothesis wherein the Spheroid is not flat at the Poles.

†**b.** A proposition laid down; a thesis. *Obs.*

1669 GALE *Crt. Gentiles* I. Introd. 1 Endeavoring to promote this Hypothesis. **1678** *Ibid.* III. Pref., It is.. impossible..demonstratively to discusse such an hypothesis without some opposition against such as defend the antithesis.

2. A proposition or principle put forth or stated (without any reference to its correspondence with fact) merely as a basis for reasoning or argument, or as a premiss from which to draw a conclusion; a supposition. In *Logic*, the supposition or condition forming the antecedent or protasis of a conjunctive or conditional proposition (e.g. *If A is B*, C is D): cf. HYPOTHETICAL 1 b.

1656 BLOUNT *Glossogr.*, *Hypothesis*, a supposition or condition; sometimes it is taken for a Position of something, as it were demonstrated, and granted by another. **1657** J. SMITH *Myst. Rhet.* 263 Hypothesis is an argument or matter whereon one may dispute; or it is a conditional proposition. **1660** BARROW *Euclid* I. xxvii. (1714) 23 Which being supposed, the outward angle AEF will be greater than the inward angle DFE, to which it was equal by Hypothesis. **1827** HUTTON *Course Math.* I. 3 An Hypothesis is a supposition assumed to be true, in order to argue from, or to found upon it the reasoning and demonstration of some proposition. **1837** BABBAGE *Bridgew. Treat.* App. E. 196 Collusion being, by hypothesis, out of the question. **1885** LEUDESDORF *Cremona's Proj. Geom.* 67 The hypothesis is satisfied in the particular case where the rays *a* and *a'* coincide.

b. An actual or possible condition or state of things considered or dealt with as a basis for action; one of several such possible conditions, a case or alternative (cf. 1).

1794 BURKE *Corr.* IV. 217 The other hypothesis, upon which the war ought 'to be carried on with vigour', though last put, must be preliminary to the other. **1803** WELLINGTON *Let. to Col. Stevenson* in Gurw. *Desp.* I. 545 In each of these last hypotheses, you will observe the necessity that we should be within reach of each other. **1876** MOZLEY *Univ. Serm.* v. 119 Christianity..only sanctions war..upon the hypothesis of a world at discord with herself.

3. A supposition or conjecture put forth to account for known facts; *esp.* in the sciences, a provisional supposition from which to draw conclusions that shall be in accordance with known facts, and which serves as a starting-point for further investigation by which it may be proved or disproved and the true theory arrived at.

1646 SIR T. BROWNE *Pseud. Ep.* II. ii. 60 Irons doe manifest a verticity not only upon refrigeration..but (what is wonderfull and advanceth the magneticall hypothesis) they evidence the same by meer position according as..their extreams [are] disposed..unto the earth. **1660** R. COKE *Power & Subj.* 265 By a perpetuall motion of the Earth from West to East according to the new Hypotheses in Astronomy, or of the Sun from East to West, after the former Hypotheses. **1664** POWER *Exp. Philos.* 82 To make good the Atomical Hypothesis. **1674** BOYLE *Excell. Theol.* I. v. 207 One of the conditions of a good hypothesis is, that it fairly comport..with all other phænomena of nature, as well as those 'tis framed to explicate. **1774** WARTON *Hist. Eng. Poetry* (1775) I. Diss. i. 22 A late ingenious critic has advanced an hypothesis, which assigns a new source, and a much earlier date, to these fictions. **1843** MILL *Logic* III. xiv. §4 It appears..to be a condition of a genuinely scientific hypothesis, that it be not destined always to remain an hypothesis, but be of such a nature as to be either proved or disproved by that comparison with observed facts which is termed Verification. **1862** HUXLEY *Lect. Wrkg. Men* 67 Do not allow yourselves to be misled by the common notion that a hypothesis is untrustworthy simply because it is a hypothesis. **1893** SIR R. BALL *In High Heav.* ix. 212 The celebrated nebular hypotheses of Herschel and of Laplace.

4. A supposition in general; something supposed or assumed to be true without proof or conclusive evidence; an assumption.

1654 H. L'ESTRANGE *Chas. I* (1655) 182 The Romanists.. began..to cry him [Laud] up for their Proselyte. Upon this hypothesis..they grew excessive proud and insolent. **1665** SIR T. HERBERT *Trav.* (1677) 352 That no other place in the East-Indies produces Gold..An Hypothesis found mistaken by such as drive a Trade for Gold..towards Cochin-China. **1827** JARMAN *Powell's Devises* II. 353 The gift should first be read on the supposition that it is intended to embrace legitimate children, and if there be nothing in the terms..or..context, incompatible with this hypothesis [etc.]. **1868** GLADSTONE *Juv. Mundi* iii. (1870) 76 The hypothesis that the Pelasgians were the base of the Greek nation.

b. Hence *spec.* A groundless or insufficiently grounded supposition; a mere assumption or guess.

1625 N. CARPENTER *Geog. Del.* I. iv. (1635) 87 Which later Astronomers..haue derided, or at least omitted as Hypotheses or suppositions. **1747** WESLEY *Prim. Physic* (1762) p. ix, To build Physick upon Hypotheses. **1827** SCOTT *Surg. Dau.* vii, Your reasoning..seems plausible; but still it is only hypothesis. **1865** SEELEY *Ecce Homo* v. (ed. 8) 46 The statement rests on no hypothesis or conjecture; his [Paul's] Epistles bear testimony to it. **1876** E. MELLOR *Priesth.* i. 14 This explanation of Bellarmine..is a pure hypothesis, for which there is not a shadow of evidence in the New Testament itself.

Hence **hy'pothesist**, one who forms a hypothesis.

1788 T. JEFFERSON *Writ.* (1859) II. 431 The blank..must remain for some happier hypothesist to fill up.

hypothesize (hɪp-, haɪ'pɒθɪsaɪz), *v.* [f. HYPOTHESIS + -IZE.]

1. *intr.* To frame a hypothesis or supposition.

1738 WARBURTON *Div. Legat.* I. 421 After the Greeks began to hypothesize. **1808** PIKE *Sources Mississ.* Ded., When I..presumed to hypothesize, I have merely suggested doubts without conclusions, which, if deemed worth, may hereafter be analyzed by men of genius and science. **1836** DARLEY *Introd. Beaum. & Fl.'s Wks.* I. 20 It is difficult to apportion their authorship..though easy enough to hypothesize.

2. *trans.* To make the hypothesis of; to assume.

1856 W. H. THOMPSON in *W. A. Butler's Hist. Anc. Philos.* I. 317 *note*, They hypothesize a vacuum through which the emanative particles pass. **1883** *Nature* XXVII. 355 Professor Quincke hypothesizes the presence..of a colourless iron-albumen. **1894** *Blackw. Mag.* Jan. 818 At all social gatherings there is an hypothesised equality of rank.

Hence **hypothesizer** = HYPOTHESIST.

1833 J. C. HARE in *Philol. Museum* II. 249 The slight difficulty attending such a hypothesis..the hypothesizer will reply, may be got over in two ways.

hypothetic (hɪp-, haɪpə'θɛtɪk), *a.* and *sb.* [ad. Gr. ὑποθετικ-ός, pertaining to ὑπόθεσις: see HYPOTHESIS. Cf. F. *hypothétique.*] **A.** *adj.* = next.

a **1680** BUTLER *Rem.* (1759) I. 66 On hypothetic Dreams and Visions Grounds everlasting Disquisitions. **1701** NORRIS *Ideal World* I. ii. 94 That which gives it the form of a hypothetic, and distinguishes it from a categoric proposition. **1813** SHELLEY *Notes Q. Mab* Poet. Wks. (1891) 47/1 Admitting the existence of this hypothetic being. **1876** R. NOEL in *Macm. Mag.* XXXIV. 334 How these hypothetic entities [atoms] pulsate and radiate, whirl and travel. **1897** ALLBUTT *Syst. Med.* II. 5 This effect was ascribed to the presence of a hypothetic body.

B. *sb.* †**1.** A hypothetical statement, a hypothesis; in *Logic*, a hypothetical proposition or syllogism (= next, B). *Obs.*

1698 FRYER *Acc. E. India & P.* 48 Modest Hypotheticks, not any ways informing the Understanding. **1701** NORRIS *Ideal World* I. ii. 122 This double hypothetic, that if the proposition be true the extremes do really exist, and..that unless the extremes do really exist the proposition cannot be true.

2. *sb. pl.* The making of hypotheses; hypothesizing.

1890 A. LANG *Life Sir Stafford Northcote* (ed. 2) II. xiii. 89 That belongs to the science of hypothetics, and anyone may sincerely believe that matters might have been kept quiet by a sagacious and well-informed policy. **1958** *New Biol.* XXV. 15 Perhaps we shall be helped to estimate its importance by an exercise in hypothetics.

hypothetical (hɪpəʊ'θɛtɪkəl, haɪpəʊ-), *a.* (*sb.*) [f. as prec. + -AL[1].]

A. *adj.* **1.** Involving or of the nature of hypothesis; conjectural.

1617 BACON *Sp. on taking his place in Chancery* in *Resuscitatio* (1661) 82, I must utterly discontinue the Making of an Hypotheticall, or Conditionall Order. **1663** BUTLER *Hud.* I. iii. 1322 Thy other arguments are all Supposures, Hypothetical. **1759** JOHNSON *Rasselas* xlvii, He that can set hypothetical possibility against acknowledged certainty, is not to be admitted among reasonable beings. **1893** SIR R. BALL *In High Heav.* ix. 196 The..line which divides the truths that have been established in astronomy from those parts of the science which..[are] more or less hypothetical.

b. *Logic.* Of a proposition: Involving a hypothesis or condition, conditional: opp. to CATEGORICAL. Of a syllogism: Having a hypothetical proposition for one of its premisses.

(By some logicians used to include all complex propositions and syllogisms, conjunctive and disjunctive; by others restricted to the conjunctive.)

[**1551** T. WILSON *Logike* (1580) 21 b, Propositio Hypothetica.] **1588** FRAUNCE *Lawiers Log.* II. v. 93 The woord, hypotheticall,..is neither proper nor fit..for, in absolute copulative and discretive axiomes there is no ὑπόθεσις, no condition at all. **1624** N. DE LAUNE tr. *Du Moulin's Logic* 155 Of compounded Enuntiations, some are Conditionall or Hypotheticall, and some Disjunctive. **1656** STANLEY *Hist. Philos.* v. (1701) 182/1 Of Propositions some are Categorical, some Hypothetical. **1837** WHEWELL *Hist. Induct. Sc.* IV. ii. §3 I. 271 Theophrastus stated..the rules of hypothetical syllogisms. **1860** ABP. THOMSON *Laws Th.* §73 (ed. 5) 120 The Hypothetical Judgment expresses seemingly a relation between two judgments, as cause and effect, as condition and conditioned.

c. Of a person: Dealing in hypotheses or groundless suppositions; fanciful. *rare.*

1748 *Anson's Voy.* III. vi. 349 The extravagant panegyrics, which many hypothetical writers have bestowed on the ingenuity and capacity of this Nation [the Chinese].

2. Depending on hypothesis; concerning which a hypothesis is made; supposed, assumed.

1665 HOOKE *Microgr.* 236 The hypothetical height and density of the Air. **1822** WELLINGTON in *Desp.* (1867) I. 293 It would be..impossible..to declare..what would be our conduct upon any hypothetical case. **1860** TYNDALL *Glac.* II. xxix. 401 Any other obstacle will produce the same effect as our hypothetical post. **1874** STUBBS *Const. Hist.* I. iv. 63 A hypothetical colony from a hypothetical settlement on the Littus Saxonicum of Gaul.

†**3.** *hypothetical necessity*: that kind of necessity which exists, not absolutely, but only on the supposition that something is or is to be: repr. Aristotle's ἀναγκαῖον ἐξ ὑποθέσεως, opp. to ἀναγκαῖον ἁπλῶς. *Obs.*

1615 CROOKE *Body of Man* 320 Hypotheticall or materiall necessitie. **1656** HOBBES *Lib., Necess. & Chance* (1841) 247 It is granted by all divines, that hypothetical necessity, or necessity upon a supposition, may consist with liberty. **1678** CUDWORTH *Intell. Syst.* I. iii. §33. 138 The necessity of a plastick life, which Aristotle calls an hypothetical necessity. **1685** BAXTER *Paraphr. N.T., Acts* i. 16 This must needs signifie no necessity or constraint put on Judas, but a necessity Hypothetical, and of consequence, that is, it cannot but be true which God foretelleth or foreseeth. **1717** S. CLARKE tr. *Leibnitz's 5th Paper* §5. 157 Hypothetical Necessity is that which the Supposition or Hypothesis of God's Foresight and Pre-ordination lays upon future Contingents.

B. as *sb.* A hypothetical proposition or syllogism: see A. 1 b.

1654 Z. COKE *Logick* (1657) 131 Let a compound or Hypothetical, never be put in the place of a conclusion, but only a Simple or Categorical. **1849** SIR W. HAMILTON *Logic* II. App. 378 Hypotheticals (Conjunctive and Disjunctive Syllogism). **1881** *Athenæum* 27 Aug. 269/2 As he used the logic of chance to elucidate the difficult subject of modals, so here he employs symbolic logic to cast light on hypotheticals. **1888** [see CONJUNCTIVE *a.* 4].

hypothetically, *adv.* [f. prec. + -LY[2].] In a hypothetical manner or form; by or upon a hypothesis or supposition; conjecturally, supposedly; conditionally.

1628 T. SPENCER *Logick* 298 How many wayes a Syllogisme is made Hypothetically. **1665** HOOKE *Microgr.* 67 Thus have I..endeavoured to explicate (Hypothetically at least) the causes of the Phænomena. **1698** NORRIS *Pract. Disc.* (1707) IV. 78 Both agree in this that God might Absolutely do it, and that Hypothetically he could not, i.e. supposing him to act consistently with the Moral Perfections of his Nature. **1789** BURKE *Corr.* (1844) III. 113 In my present want of information I must only speak hypothetically. **1864** BOWEN *Logic* viii. 266 Any Immediate Inference, also, may be stated hypothetically.

hypo,thetico-de'ductive, *a.* *Philos.* [f. HYPOTHETIC(AL *a.* + -O + DEDUCTIVE *a.*, prob. as ad. It. *ipotetico-deduttivo* hypothetical-deductive (M. Pieri 1900, in *Mem. d. R. Accad. d. Sci. di Torino* XLIX. 173).] Making use of or consisting in the testing of the consequences of hypotheses (i.e. seeing whether the consequences are consistent with observation) as a means of determining whether the hypotheses themselves are false or can be accepted.

1912 *Philos. Rev.* XXI. 642 The type of reasoning that takes place in the hypothetico-deductive fields of thought. **1929** H. A. WOLFSON *Crescas' Critique of Aristotle* i. 25 The Talmudic hypothetico-deductive method of text interpretation. **1949** tr. *H. Weyl's Philos. Math. & Nat. Sci.* I. i. 27 Pure mathematics, in the modern view, amounts to a general hypothetico-deductive theory of relations; it develops the theory of logical 'molds' without binding itself to one or the other among the possible concrete interpretations. **1952** J. O. WISDOM *Found. Inference Nat. Sci.* xxiv. 223 Many difficulties in the nature of the causal relation and inductive inference are obviated by using the scheme of explanation provided by the hypothetico-deductive system, according to which a hypothesis is accepted when it has been 'tempered' by severe testing and has not been falsified. **1953** R. B. BRAITHWAITE *Scientific Explanation* i. 9 It is this hypothetico-deductive method applied to empirical material which is the essential feature of a science. **1957** G. H. VON WRIGHT *Logical Probl. Induction* (ed. 2) 208 The theory of induction cannot, in the name of the hypothetico-deductive method, be banished from holding a prominent place within the methodology of science. **1963** *Listener* 12 Sept. 378/1 This alternative interpretation of the nature of the scientific process..is sometimes called the 'hypothetico-deductive' interpretation, and this is the view which Professor Karl Popper..has persuaded us is the correct one. **1971** J. Z. YOUNG *Introd. Study Man* xxi. 283 It is by adopting the 'hypothetico-deductive' system that men have been able to make forecasts much more far-reaching and reliable than those of any animal.

Hence **hypo,thetico-de'ductively** *adv.*, by the hypothetico-deductive method.

1953 R. B. BRAITHWAITE *Scientific Explanation* ix. 299 The latter of these propositions is establishable hypothetico-deductively without reference to the establishment of the former.

hypothetico-disjunctive, *a.* *Logic.*

a. Combining the 'hypothetical' (conjunctive) and disjunctive forms of statement: applied to a conditional proposition of which the consequent is disjunctive (e.g. If A is B, C is either D or E); also to that form of syllogism (the DILEMMA) in which one premiss is conjunctive and the other disjunctive. **b.** as *sb.* A proposition or syllogism of this kind.

1837-8 SIR W. HAMILTON *Logic* xviii. (1866) I. 351 An hypothetico-disjunctive syllogism is called the dilemma or horned syllogism. **1864** BOWEN *Logic* Contents 13 Dilemmas or Hypothetico-Disjunctives.

hy'pothetize, *v.* *rare.* [f. Gr. ὑπόθετ-ος, basis of ὑποθετικός HYPOTHETIC + -IZE.] = HYPOTHESIZE. So **hy'pothetist**, **hy'pothetizer** = HYPOTHESIST, HYPOTHESIZER.

1852 TREGELLES *Def. Authentic. Daniel* (1864) 225 The notion of objecting hypothetists..is singularly at variance with the facts of the case. **1891** *Pall Mall G.* 24 Nov. 2/3 The far-away folly of these two pedagogic hypothetizers. **1895** MACEWEN *Life Dr. Cairns* 161 Next appeared Fichte with his demolition of Kant's hypothetised world.

hypo'thyroidism. *Med.* [f. HYPO- 4 + THYROID *a.* (*sb.*) + -ISM.] A condition in which the level of thyroxine in the blood is abnormally low resulting in a decreased metabolic rate and which when severe causes cretinism (if the condition was congenital) and myxœdema (if acquired).

1905 GOULD *Dict. New Med. Terms* 304/1 Hypothyroidism. **1909** G. DOCK in Osler & McCrae *Syst. Med.* VI. xviii. 447 The known results of hypothyroidism or athyroidism are: 1. Congenital myxœdema... 2. Infantile myxœdema... 3. Spontaneous myxœdema of adults. **1955** *Sci. News Let.* 24 Sept. 207/3 The tragic effects of hypothyroidism in babies, such as dwarfing and mental retardation, may be prevented by early diagnosis and adequate treatment. **1961** L. MARTIN *Clin. Endocrinol.* (ed. 3) iii. 111 Transient neonatal hypothyroidism may also result from maternal overdosage with antithyroid drugs during pregnancy. **1966** WRIGHT & SYMMERS *Systemic Path.* II. xxxi. 1103/2 It is customary to refer to the milder forms as hypothyroidism and to reserve the term myxœdema for the severer clinical varieties.

Hence **hypo'thyroid, -thy'roidic** *adjs.*

1909 G. DOCK in Osler & McCrae *Syst. Med.* VI. xviii. 448 Many other conditions, especially certain forms of infantilism and obesity, are classed by some writers as hypothyroid states. *Ibid.* 455 Hypothyroid infants. **1916** *Med. Times* (N.Y.) 7 July 207/1 The hypothyroidic eye is *dull*, seemingly small, apparently sunken, expressionless, in short, featurally insignificant. **1968** PASSMORE & ROBSON *Compan. Med. Stud.* I. xxv. 18/2 The hypothyroid person is characteristically cold, sluggish and constipated and often has mild anaemia.

hypotonia (haɪpəʊ'təʊnɪə). Freq. in anglicized form **hypotony** (haɪ'pɒtənɪ). [mod.L., f. HYPO- 4 + Gr. τόν-ος TONE *sb.* + -IA[1].]

1. *Ophthalm.* A state of reduced pressure of the intra-ocular fluid.

1886 *Syd. Soc. Lex., Hypotony...* Applied by Nagel to the globe of the eye when less resistant than normal. **1892** A. DUANE tr. *Fuchs's Text-bk. Ophthalm.* II. vii. 360 Diminution of the intra-ocular pressure (hypotonia) is found in very diverse affections of the eyeball. **1951** H. S. SUGAR *Glaucomas* xxiv. 371 Hypotony, particularly after the trephining operation, may result from too rapid drainage into the conjunctiva. **1966** S. LERMAN *Basic Ophthalm.* iv. 246 Another major cause of postoperative hypotony..is a serous detachment of the ciliary body.

2. *Med.* The condition (in muscle or muscular tissue) of being hypotonic.

1886 *Syd. Soc. Lex., Hypotony*, defective tone of a part, or an organ, or a structure. **1907** *Practitioner* Oct. 547 Undue muscular strain on the ankle, knee, hip, and spine, which, together with hypotonia, tends to break down the long arch. **1914** [see HYPERTONIA]. **1933** W. R. BRAIN *Dis. Nervous Syst.* I. 12 A lesion of this path causes hypotonia, which is manifested in flaccidity and a diminished resistance to stretching of the affected muscles. **1962** *Lancet* 6 Jan. 22/1 Her growth was stunted and the muscles showed a marked hypotonia with genu recurvatum.

hypotonic (haɪpə'tɒnɪk), *a.* [f. HYPO- 4 + TONIC *a.*] **1. a.** *Physiol.* Of a solution: having a lower osmotic pressure than some particular solution (usually that in a cell, or a bodily fluid). Const. *to*.

1895 *Jrnl. Physiol.* XVIII. 114 The passage of a salt from a hypotonic fluid into the blood-plasma. **1946** *Nature* 9 Nov. 665/2 The fluid obtained in this way was hypotonic to the cœlomic fluid. **1951** H. DAVSON *Textbk. Gen. Physiol.* vii. 163 If the plasma surrounding the cells is steadily diluted (i.e., made hypotonic), the latter increase in volume until they finally burst. **1970** [see HYPERTONIC *a.* 2].

b. *Ophthalm.* Of the eye: having a reduced intra-ocular pressure.

1918 R. H. ELLIOT *Glaucoma: Textbk. for Student* ii. 19 The case of a hypotonic eye (with a Schiötz reading corresponding to a tension of 8 to 15 mm. of Hg.) such as may be met with after a trephining or other sclerectomy operation. **1966** S. LERMAN *Basic Ophthalm.* iv. 246 A hypotonic eye indicates that a leaking wound may be present.

2. *Med.* Exhibiting or characterized by diminished tone or tension (in muscle or muscular tissue).

1904 [see HYPERTONUS 2]. **1908** *Practitioner* Oct. 560 The lower extremities have been thin, powerless, and extraordinarily hypotonic. **1966** [see HYPERTONIC *a.* 1].

hypotonicity (ˌhaɪpəʊtə'nɪsɪtɪ). [f. prec. + -ITY.] The condition of being hypotonic.

a. *Physiol.* Of a solution (see HYPOTONIC *a.* 1 a): the extent to which a solution has a lower osmotic pressure than some other.

1906 *Amer. Jrnl. Physiol.* XV. 367 Osmotic changes in the direction of hypotonicity. **1939** A. KROGH *Osmotic Regulation Aquatic Animals* 66 Enid Edmonds..found a slight but definite hypotonicity, viz. ocean water 622 mM., blood of the crab 577 mM. **1972** *Lancet* 2 Dec. 1160/2 Hypotonicity of the plasma was observed only on the 3rd and 4th postoperative days, when the daily intake of isotonic dextrose exceeded 1500 ml.

b. *Med.* Of muscle or muscular tissue (see HYPOTONIC *a.* 2); = HYPOTONIA 2.

1910 A. ABRAMS *Diagn. Therapeutics* v. 711 This hypotonicity of the muscles..may also be noted in executing other unaccustomed movements of the muscles of the hand. **1934** C. J. WIGGERS *Physiol. Health & Dis.* (1935) xlix. 765 Gastric hypotonicity does not necessarily interfere with emptying the stomach, because the tone of the pyloric sphincter is also reduced, and consequently less intragastric pressure is required to expel the chyme. **1959** E. B. SMITH et al. *Princ. Human Path.* lv. 912/1 The hypercalcemia causes interesting clinical findings incident to.. hypotonicity of muscle.

hypotonus (haɪpə'təʊnəs). [f. HYPO- 4 + TONUS.] **1.** *Ophthalm.* = HYPOTONIA 1. Now *rare.*

1891 F. P. FOSTER *Med. Dict.* III. 1955/2 *Hypotonus*, that condition of the eye in which the intra-ocular tension is below normal, without being of necessity accompanied by any organic disease of the eyeball. **1918** R. H. ELLIOT *Glaucoma* ii. 22 If too large and too free a channel is cut in the ocular tunic, the escape of fluid is so rapid that a condition of hypotonus results.

2. *Med.* = HYPOTONIA 2.

1904 *Rev. Neurol. & Psychiatry* II. 776 The legs showed very marked hypotonus. **1928** J. F. H. DALLY *Low Blood Pressure* ii. 22 Hypotonia (vascular hypotonus) represents a dynamic and physical state of diminished tonus of the smooth muscle in the walls of arteries and veins. **1939** W. HAYMAKER tr. *Bing's Textbk. Nervous Dis.* xi. 318 Hypotonus of the quadriceps is sometimes so marked in tabes that the heel can be brought up to the buttock.

‖**hypotrachelium** (hɪpəʊtrə'kiːlɪəm). *Arch.* Also 7- **hypotrachelion.** [L. (Vitruvius), ad. Gr. ὑποτραχήλιον the lower part of the neck, f. ὑπό HYPO- 1 + τράχηλος neck. Cf. F. *hypotrachélion.*] The lower part or neck of the capital of a column; in the Doric order, the groove or sinking between the neck of the capital and the shaft.

1563 SHUTE *Archit.* C j a, The hedde or Capituli shalbe.. in height one Modulus,..that height you shall deuide into .3. partes, geue the one parte to Hypotrachelium. **1664** EVELYN tr. *Freart's Archit.* 126 Otherwhiles again it [the Astragal] is taken for the Cincture or Coller next the Hypotrachelium. **1704** J. HARRIS *Lex. Techn.*, *Hypotrachelion*, in Architecture, is the Top or Neck of a Pillar, or the most slender part of it which toucheth the Capital. It is taken by some, for that part of the Tuscan or Dorick Capitals, which lies between the Echinus and the Astragal, and is otherwise called, the Collar, Gorge, or Frize of the Chapiter. **1842–76** GWILT *Archit.* 814 Hypotrachelion. **1862** RICKMAN *Goth. Archit.* 17 He divides the capital into three parts, one for the hypotrachelium.

hypotrochoid (h(a)ɪpəʊ'trəʊkɔɪd, h(a)ɪ'pɒtrəʊkɔɪd). *Geom.* [f. HYPO- 2 + TROCHOID.] The curve described by a point rigidly connected with the centre of a circle which rolls on the inside of another circle.

1843 *Penny Cycl.* XXV. 282/1 A class [of curves] called.. hypotrochoids, of which one particular case is the hypocycloid. **1879** THOMSON & TAIT *Nat. Phil.* I. I. §94 When the tracing point is not in the circumference, we have Epitrochoids and Hypotrochoids.

Hence **hypotro'choidal** *a.*, of the form of, or pertaining to, a hypotrochoid.

1843 *Penny Cycl.* XXV. 283/1 When the convexities are opposed, the trochoidal system is called *epi*-trochoidal, and when concavity fits convexity, *hypo*-trochoidal.

‖**hypotyposis** (hɪpəʊt(a)ɪ'pəʊsɪs). *Rhet.* [a. Gr. ὑποτύπωσις sketch, outline, pattern, f. ὑποτυποῦν to sketch, f. τύπος impression, form, TYPE.] Vivid description of a scene, event, or situation, bringing it, as it were, before the eyes of the hearer or reader.

1583 FOXE *A. & M.* 839/2 Under which Hypotyposis or Poesie, who is so blind that seeth not by the Pellican, the doctrine of Christ: and of the Lollardes to be defended against the Church of Rome? *a* **1638** MEDE *Wks.* (1672) I. 32 A Poetical or Prophetical hypotyposis of the destruction or fall of Babylon. **1732** STACKHOUSE *Hist. Bible* Introd. (1767) 64 Above all other figures that whereon poets and orators love to dwell is the hypotyposis or lively description. **1897** *Dublin Rev.* Oct. 387 Simple and suitable language, the effective metaphor, 'the nervous hypotyposis' may be introduced.

hypovanadic, etc.: see HYPO- II.

ˌhypoventi'lation. *Physiol.* [f. HYPO- 4 + VENTILATION.] A diminished or insufficient exposure of the lungs to oxygen, resulting in a reduced oxygen content of the blood or an increased carbon dioxide content (or both).

1932 *Arch. Neurol. & Psychiatry* XXVIII. 580 To combat this physiologic hypoventilation, the animals were subjected to artificial respiration of normal frequency and depth. **1954** A. WHITE et al. *Princ. Biochem.* xxvii. 715 Hypoventilation of whatever origin (morphine poisoning, pneumonia, pulmonary edema, etc.) has the opposite effect and lowers extracellular pH. **1961** L. MARTIN *Clinical Endocrinol.* (ed. 3) ii. 55 A cardio-respiratory syndrome has been described by Berlyne (1958) in cases of extreme obesity, of which alveolar hypoventilation is the basic defect.

hypoxanthine (hɪp-, haɪpɒk'sænθaɪn). *Chem.* [f. HYPO- 5 + XANTHINE. Cf. F. *hypoxanthine.*] A nitrogenous substance, $C_5H_4N_4O$, found in the muscle, spleen, heart, etc. of vertebrates, and forming a white crystalline powder; also called SARCINE.

1844–57 G. BIRD *Urin. Deposits* (ed. 5) 46 This interesting body..bears so close a resemblance to xanthine or uric oxide, that Scherer has named it hypoxanthine.

attrib. **1873** RALFE *Phys. Chem.* 96 The precipitate consists of hypoxanthin nitrate and silver oxide; this is to be decomposed with sulphydric acid, and hypoxanthin is precipitated.

Hence **hypo'xanthic** *a.*, derived from, or of the nature of, hypoxanthine.

hypoxylous, hypozeugma, hypozoa, -zoic: see HYPO- II.

hyppe, obs. form of HIP.

hypped (hɪpt), *ppl. a.* Also 8 hyp'd, hypp'd, 8–9 **hypt.** Later HIPPED, q.v. [f. HYP + -ED.] Affected with hypochondria; morbidly depressed or low-spirited.

c **1710** J. EDWARDS in *Camb. Antiq. Soc. Com.* III. 130 Allmost half of them are Hypt (as they call it), that is, disordered in their brains. **1784** J. BELKNAP in *B. Papers* (1877) II. 178 It was the common opinion among his friends that he was hyp'd. **1799** COLERIDGE *Lett.* (1895) 296, I.. spent a day with them. They were melancholy and hypped. **1824** LAMB *Lett.* (1888) II. 101, I am much hypt. **1853** MRS. GASKELL *Ruth* Wks. 1863 VI. 200 On a dull Sunday, when people are apt to get hypped if not well amused.

hyppish ('hɪpɪʃ), *a.* Also 8 **hypish.** Later HIPPISH, q.v. [f. HYP + -ISH.] Somewhat depressed or low-spirited.

a **1732** GAY *On Wine* 34 In pensive hyppish mood. **1733** CHEYNE *Eng. Malady* III. iv. (1734) 335 The constant Complaints, common to Hypish People. **1823** C. WESTMACOTT *Points Misery* 16 The disturbed imagination of the hyppish man.

hyppo, obs. f. HYPO.

hyppocon: see HYPOCON.

hyps, pl. of HYP, hypochondria.

hypsi- ('hɪpsɪ), repr. Gr. ὕψι *adv.* on high, aloft, in comb. also = high, lofty. The English words are new formations with *hypsi-* in the latter sense. See also HYPSO-.

hypsibrachycephalic (ˌhɪpsɪbrækɪsɪ'fælɪk) *a. Ethnol.* [BRACHYCEPHALIC], characterized by having a high and broad skull; pertaining to *Hypsibrachycephali* or races of men so characterized, as the Malay inhabitants of Madura; so **hypsibrachy'cephalism**, the presence or prevalence of high broad skulls, the combination of brachycephaly with hypsicephaly. **hypsicephalic** (-sɪ'fælɪk) *a.* [Gr. κεφαλή head], characterized by having a high skull, *spec.* one of which the vertical index, or ratio of height to antero-posterior length, is over 75; hence **hypsi'cephaly**, the condition of being hypsicephalic. **'hypsiconch** (-kɒŋk), **hypsiconchic** (-'kɒŋkɪk), **-conchous** (-'kɒŋkəs) *adjs. Anthropol.* [Gr. κόγχ-ος eye-socket], having orbits that are high in relation to their width, with an orbital index of 89 (formerly, 85) or more; so **'hypsiconchy**, the condition of being hypsiconchic. **hypsilophodont** (-'lɒfədɒnt) *a. Zool.* [Gr. ὑψίλοφο-ς high-crested (λόφ-ος crest, ridge) + ὀδούς, ὀδοντ- tooth], having the dental characteristics of the genus *Hypsilophodon* of extinct dinosaurian reptiles. **hypsiprymnine** (-'prɪmnaɪn), **-prymnoid** (-'prɪmnɔɪd) *adjs.* [Gr. πρύμνα stern], pertaining to or characteristic of the Marsupial sub-family containing the Kangaroo Rat (*Hypsiprymnus*). **hypsistenocephalic** (-stɛnəʊsɪ'fælɪk) *a. Ethnol.* [Gr. στενό-ς narrow + κεφαλή head], characterized by the presence of a high and narrow skull; so **ˌhypsisteno'cephalism**, **ˌhypsisteno'cephaly**, hypsistenocephalic character or condition. **hypsi'thermal** *a. Geol.* [ad. It. *ipsotermico* (A. Chiarugi 1936, in *Nuovo giorn. bot. ital.* XLIII. 55)], designating that period of the geologically recent past (*c* 7000 to *c* 600 B.C.) when relatively warm conditions prevailed in the northern hemisphere; also *absol.*

1920 H. H. WILDER *Lab. Man. Anthropometry* 67 *Hypsiconch..[Orbital index of] 85 +. **1960** M. F. A. MONTAGU *Introd. Physical Anthropol.* (ed. 3) 606 Hypsiconch..[Orbital index of] 85·0 – ×. **1902** *Hypsiconchic [see *chamæcephalic* adj. s.v. CHAMÆ-]. **1960** J. COMAS *Man. Physical Anthropol.* vii. 409 Hypsiconchic ..[an orbital index of] 89·0 and over. **1885** *Jrnl. R. Anthropol. Inst.* XIV. 71 *Hypsikonchous..[Orbital index of] 85·1 and over. **1965** *Dorland's Med. Dict.* (ed. 24) 717/2 *Hypsiconchous*, having an orbital index over 85. **1902** *Biometrika* I. 460 In both sexes there is sensible correlation between the palate and orbital indices, *hypsiconchy being associated with brachystaphyline characters. **1871** HUXLEY *Anat. Vert.* v. 263 It remains to be seen how far the *hypsilophodont modification extended among the *Ornithoscelida.* **1870** —— *Crit. & Addr.* (1873) 199 As to the *Didelphia*,..a true *Hypsiprymnoid form existed at the epoch of the Trias, contemporaneously with a Carnivorous form. **1878** BARTLEY tr. *Topinard's Anthrop.* v. 177 Certain [skulls] of..New Guinea..are *hypsistenocephalic. **1881** *Academy* 29 Jan. 84 The Fijians are remarkable as the most dolichocephalic people in the world... The skulls are eminently hypsistenocephalic, to use Dr. B. Davis's term. **1881** *Nature* XXV. 144 Combinations of dolichocephaly and *hypsistenocephaly. **1957** *Bull. Geol. Soc. Amer.* LXVIII. 1895 The period from 7000 B.C. to 600 B.C. is now

known as the *hypsithermal interval, rather than by its former but less suitable designations (postglacial climatic optimum, thermal maximum). **1957** DEEVEY & FLINT in *Science* 1 Feb. 182/2 The long, warm interval spanned by Danish pollen zones V through VIII, which has been dated from approximately 7000 B.C. to approximately 600 B.C., we propose to call the *hypsithermal* interval. We have changed the spelling of Chiarugi's *ipsotermico* to conform with the English style of Greek adjectives and to express the customary distinction between *hypsi-*, high, and *hypso-*, a height. **1967** MARTIN & WRIGHT *Pleistocene Extinctions* 135 The onset of widespread aridity [in Australia], which Gill (1955) equates with the Climatic Optimum or Hypsithermal of the Northern Hemisphere. **1968** R. W. FAIRBRIDGE *Encycl. Geomorphol.* 1051/2 Modern deposits may have obtained their maximum growth during the hypsithermal phase of postglacial time.

hypsiloid (hɪp'saɪlɔɪd, 'hɪpsɪlɔɪd), *a.* [ad. Gr. ὑψιλοειδής, f. ὖ ψιλόν UPSILON: see -OID.] Shaped like the Greek letter upsilon, or its Roman equivalents; V-shaped, or U-shaped.

1886 in *Syd. Soc. Lex.* **1888** W. H. FLOWER in *Anthropol. Jrnl.* 14 Feb. 9 The palatal index of the male..is exceptionally low, viz. 103·8, the general form of the palate being remarkably hypsiloid.

Hypsistarian (hɪpsɪ'stɛərɪən), *a.* and *sb. Eccl. Hist.* [f. Gr. Ὑψιστάρι-ος (f. ὕψιστος highest; see def.) + -AN.] **a.** *adj.* Belonging to an eclectic sect of the 4th century, so called from worshipping God under the name of the Most High (ὕψιστος). **b.** *sb.* A member of this sect.

1705 W. WALL *Hist. Infant Bapt.* (1845) II. 77 St. Gregory Nazianzen's father was of the religion called Hypsistarian. **1727–41** CHAMBERS *Cycl.* s.v., The doctrine of the Hypsistarians, was an assemblage of Paganism, Judaism, and Christianity. **1882–3** SCHAFF *Encycl. Relig. Knowl.* II. 1055 *Hypsistarians*, a religious sect living in Cappadocia in the fourth century,..a singular mixture of Paganism and Judaism.

†**Hyp'sistary.** *Obs.* [ad. Gr. Ὑψιστάρι-ος: see prec.] = prec. sb.

c **1610** *Women Saints* 171 The professors of this base and abiect sect, arrogate..to themselues the name of Hypsistaries, that is, 'moste highe', and they worship onelie the omnipotent.

hypso- ('hɪpsəʊ), repr. rare Gr. ὑψο-, used with same force as ὑψι- HYPSI-; in modern use, sometimes taken as comb. form of ὕψος 'height'. Hence **hypsoce'phalic** *a.* = HYPSICEPHALIC; so **hypso'cephalous** *a.* and **hypso'cephaly** (*Syd. Soc. Lex.* 1886). **'hypsodont** *a.* [Gr. ὀδοντ- tooth], of teeth: having high or lengthened crowns with short roots. **hypsophonous** (hɪp'sɒfənəs) *a.* [Gr. ὑψόφωνος (φωνή voice)], 'having a high clear voice' (*Syd. Soc. Lex.* 1886). **hypsophyll** ('hɪpsəʊfɪl) *Bot.* [Gr. φύλλ-ον leaf: repr. Ger. *hochblatt*], a leaf of the inflorescence, a bract or bracteole; hence **hypso'phyllar, -'phyllary, -'phyllous** *adjs.*

1878 BARTLEY tr. *Topinard's Anthrop.* v. 176 *Hypsocephalic, elevated skull. **1883** W. H. FLOWER in *Encycl. Brit.* XV. 430/1 Modification of [the selenodont form] from a brachyodont to a *hypsodont type. [**1880** GRAY *Struct. Bot.* (ed. 6) 416/1 *Hypsophylla*, answers to the German 'Hochblätter', or high leaves, those of the inflorescence, i.e. bracts and the like.] **1895** VINES *Stud. Text-bk.* 76 There are two kinds [of leaves of the sporophore]; those which bear sporangia..termed sporophylls; those which do not bear sporangia, termed *hypsophylls. **1877** BENNETT tr. *Thomé's Struct. Bot.* 86 The bracts or *hypsophyllar leaves, i.e. those leaves, in the axils of which the flowers are placed. **1875** BENNETT & DYER *Sachs' Bot.* 546 The mode of insertion of the cataphyllary and foliage-leaves, and very often that of the *hypsophyllary leaves (as for instance that of the spathe)..is generally amplexicaul. **1880** GRAY *Struct. Bot.* (ed. 6) 6 *note*, *Hypsophyllous.

hypsochrome ('hɪpsəʊkrəʊm), *a.* and *sb.* [f. as next.] **A.** *adj.* = next.

1892 *Jrnl. Soc. Chem. Industry* 31 Oct. 807/2 Groups causing deepening are distinguished as 'bathochrome', whilst those to which heightening of the colour is due are termed 'hypsochrome'. **1908** *Jrnl. Chem. Soc.* XCIV. I. 477 (*heading*) Measurement of the effect of certain hypsochrome and bathochrome groups on the colour of azobenzene. **1917** FORT & LLOYD *Chem. Dyestuffs* xiv. 130 Acylation..always gives hypsochrome properties, whether acting upon amines or hydroxy groups.

B. *sb.* A hypsochromic atom or group.

1917 FORT & LLOYD *Chem. Dyestuffs* xiv. 130 Groups or atoms that cause an intensification of colour when introduced into compounds have been called Bathochromes, and those that decrease the colour of a compound Hypsochromes.

hypsochromic (hɪpsəʊ'krəʊmɪk), *a.* [ad. G. *hypsochrom* (M. Schütze 1892, in *Zeitschr. f. physik. Chem.* IX. 136), f. HYPSO- + Gr. χρῶμ-α colour: see -IC.] Causing or characterized by a lightening of colour, or a shift of the absorption spectrum towards shorter wavelengths.

1892 *Jrnl. Chem. Soc.* LXII. I. 562 Definite atoms or groups of atoms on entering a molecule cause..a characteristic rise [*read* fall] ('bathochromic groups'), or fall [*read* rise] ('hypsochromic groups'), of the tint. **1932** S. J. GREGG tr. *Eggert's Physical Chem.* 559 The hydrogen atom itself is hypsochromic in nature, for on removing the unsaturated character of a chromophoric group by adding hydrogen to it the absorption band migrates toward the ultra-violet. **1946** [see HYPOCHROMIC *a.* 2]. **1957** *Jrnl. Biol. Chem.* CCXXIX. 716 In addition to the reduction in extinction there is a hypsochromic shift of 2 to 3 mμ accompanying the formation of the polymers. **1972** RYS & ZOLLINGER *Fund. Chem. & Applic. Dyes* x. 153 As a rule, the vatting of indigo derivatives..produces a hypsochromic shift.

hypsograph ('hɪpsəʊgrɑːf, -æ-). [f. HYPSO- + -GRAPH.] = *hypsographic curve*.

1937 *Geogr. Jrnl.* XC. 60 The verticality in all the hypsographs at low elevations is explained by the high coastal cliffs and deep V-shaped valleys which prevail.

hypsography (hɪp'sɒgrəfɪ). [f. Gr. ὕψο-ς height (see HYPSO-) + -γραφια writing, sketching.] That department of geography which deals with the comparative altitude of places, or parts of the earth's surface.

1885 *Athenæum* 9 May 602/3 A further contribution towards the hypsography of Eastern Venetia, by Prof. Giovanni Marinelli. **1888** M. BAKER in *Science* 7 Dec. 280 'Hypsography' and 'topography' are each used for this purpose; but the first refers rather to elevation than to form.

Hence **hypso'graphic** *a.*, hypsographical; ***hypsographic curve***, a curve showing the area or proportion of the earth's (solid) surface, or of a part of it, above any given elevation or depth. **hypso'graphical** *a.*, of or pertaining to hypsography; ***hypsographical map***, a map specially designed to exhibit (whether by shading, by contour lines, or by an actual embossed surface) the comparative altitude of places or parts of the earth's surface.

1881 *Academy* No. 455. 65 The map..almost resembles a hypsographical one, for the Alps and other mountain regions, no less than the valley of the Rhine..form very conspicuous features upon it. **1881** *Athenæum* 30 July 149/1 We are thus presented with..a hypsographical map of Central Europe. **1895** *Geogr. Jrnl.* V. 577 The author points out how the generalized hypsographic curve of the Earth's surface defines the continental plateau. **1937** [see CLINOGRAPHIC *a.*]. **1971** *Nature* 16 July 181/2 Kuenen was able to show from the world hypsographic curve that under present conditions a eustatic rise of 100 m would flood about ¼ to ⅓ of the continents.

hypsometer (hɪp'sɒmɪtə(r)). [f. Gr. ὕψος height (see HYPSO-) + -METER. Cf. F. *hypsomètre*.] An instrument for measuring altitudes, consisting essentially of a delicate thermometer, by which the boiling point of water is observed at particular elevations.

1864 in WEBSTER. **1879** *Daily News* 23 Aug. 6/4 Major Pinto recommended the hypsometer and aneroids for altitudes. **1884** *Brit. Almanac* Companion 17 An instrument called the Hypsometer, whose business it is to determine the heights of mountains by means of the boiling-point of water.

hypsometric (hɪpsəʊ'mɛtrɪk), *a.* [f. prec. or HYPSOMETRY + -IC. Cf. F. *hypsométrique*.] = next. ***hypsometric curve*** = *hypsographic curve*.

1845 W. D. COOLEY tr. *Parrot's Ararat* 54 The foregoing is taken from the hypsometric tables of Lindenau, the accuracy of which however seems liable to some doubt. **1874** J. D. WHITNEY *Barometric Hypsometry* Pref., The accuracy of the barometer as a hypsometric instrument may be very considerably increased. **1924** J. G. A. SKERL tr. *Wegener's Orig. Continents & Oceans* ii. 28 If the whole earth be divided into square kilometres and these are arranged in a series according to their height above sea-level, the well-known..hypsometric curve of the earth's surface is obtained. **1954** W. D. THORNBURY *Princ. Geomorphol.* xxi. 531 A hypsometric curve obtained in this way permits comparison of forms of drainage basins of different sizes and altitudes.

hypso'metrical, *a.* [f. as prec. + -AL[1].] Pertaining to hypsometry or the hypsometer; relating to the measurement of altitudes.

1855 MAYNE *Expos. Lex.*, *Hypsometricus*,.. hypsometrical. **1880** C. R. MARKHAM *Peruv. Bark* xi. 99 Dr. Spruce..took meteorological and hypsometrical observations throughout the vast region he traversed. **1880** *Nature* XXI. 391 The hypsometrical distribution of the species is carefully given. **1884** *American* VIII. 379 Our hypsometrical knowledge of the..Catskill Mountain region.

Hence **hypso'metrically** *adv.*, by hypsometrical methods; with the hypsometer.

1849 MRS. SABINE tr. *Humboldt's Aspects Nat.* II. 320, I have constantly..urged, that the isthmus [of Panama] should be examined hypsometrically throughout its entire length, and more especially where..it joins the continent of South America. **1895** *Edin. Rev.* Oct. 503 Père Roblet..had ..surveyed astronomically and hypsometrically the whole of the interior highland province.

hypsometry (hɪp'sɒmɪtrɪ). [f. HYPSOMETER: see -METRY. Cf. F. *hypsométrie*.] The measuring of altitudes; the science which treats of this; also, the subject of this science, the condition of a part of the earth's surface in reference to height above (or depth below) the level of the sea.

1570 DEE *Math. Pref.* a iij b, How High or depe, aboue or vnder the leuel of the measurers standing, anything is.. called *Hypsometrie*. **1847** in CRAIG. **1860** MAURY *Phys. Geog. Sea* (Low) v. §283 That part of the extra-tropical North Atlantic..is peculiar as to its hypsometry. **1861–3** DE SCHLAGINTWEIT *Sci. Miss. Ind.* II. (*title*), General Hypsometry of India, the Himalaya, and Western Thibet. **1874** J. D. WHITNEY (*title*) Barometric Hypsometry.

hypt, obs. form of HYPPED.

hypural (hɪp-, haɪ'pjʊərəl), *a.* (*sb.*) [f. Gr. ὑπ(ό HYPO- 2 + οὐρά tail + -AL[1].] Situated beneath the tail; *spec.* in *Ichthyol.* applied to the bones beneath the axis of the tail, which support fin-rays. Also *absol.* as *sb.*

1871 HUXLEY *Anat. Vert.* i. 16 In most osseous fishes the hypural bones which support the fin-rays of the inferior division [of the tail] become much expanded. **1880** GÜNTHER *Fishes* 84 The hypural is but a union of modified hæmapophyses.

hyr, obs. form of HER *pron.*, HIRE.

hyraceum (haɪə'reɪsɪəm). Also **hyracium**. [f. mod.L. HYRAX, once used as the name of a genus including these animals.] A secretion produced by the African rock hyrax, *Procavia capensis*, formerly used as a fixative for perfume.

1866 BRANDE & COX *Dict. Sci., Lit. & Art* II. 182/1 Hyracium. An article imported, as a substitute for castor, from the Cape of Good Hope, and derived from one of the species of *Hyrax*. **1892** P. L. SIMMONDS *Commercial Dict. Trade Products* (rev. ed.) Suppl. 462/2 Hyraceum, a secretion of the Cape badger, at one time considered to have medicinal properties. **1923** W. A. POUCHER *Perfumes & Cosmetics* I. 3 Hyraceum is a secretion having a most disagreeable odour of excreta and urine, and is obtained from a species of monkey [*sic*]. It is occasionally used as a substitute for Castor... This material is not recommended. **1966** C. SWEENEY *Scurrying Bush* ii. 34 The faeces of the rock rabbit..contains a substance called hyraceum, which is ..incorporated in various perfumes. **1971** D. J. POTGIETER et al. *Animal Life S. Afr.* 394/1 These deposits [of the dried urine of the dassie] contain hyraceum, a valuable material used in perfumery.

hyraci-, hyraco- (before a vowel **hyrac-**), Lat. and Gr. comb. forms respectively of HYRAX. **hyraciform** (haɪ'ræsɪfɔːm) *a.* [see -FORM], resembling a hyrax; hyracoid. **hyracodont** (haɪ'rækədɒnt) *a.* [Gr. ὀδοντ- tooth], having the dentition characteristic of the genus *Hyrax*, and found also in the Rhinoceros and the extinct *Hyracodon*, a rhinoceros-like perissodactyl of the Lower Miocene of North America.

hyracid (haɪ'ræsɪd), *a.* [f. mod.L. *Hyracidæ*: see -ID.] Belonging to the family *Hyracidæ*, or its sole genus HYRAX.

hyracoid ('haɪərəkɔɪd), *a.* [f. *hyrac-*, stem of HYRAX + -OID.] Resembling a hyrax; pertaining to or characteristic of the order or sub-order *Hyracoidea*, containing the Hyrax and its congeners.

hyracotherium (ˌhaɪərəkəʊ'θɪərɪəm). Also **H-**. [mod.L., f. HYRACO- + Gr. θηρίον wild beast.] An extinct mammal of the genus so called; a primitive type of horse.

1840 R. OWEN in *Proc. Geol. Soc.* III. 163 The resemblance of the molar division..in the new genus, for which the name of Hyracotherium is proposed, and the Chæropotamus, is sufficiently close. *Ibid.*, The incisor teeth with the ossa intermaxillaria are wanting in the specimen of the Hyracotherium. **1851** RICHARDSON *Geol.* (1855) 324 Hyracotherium, so named in consequence of its structural affinities in the size of the orbits, &c., with the Hyrax, was found in the London clay and the lacustrine eocene sand at Kyson. **1904** *Daily Chron.* 4 Jan. 9/1 Illustrations were given of a four and a five-toed horse, the extinct hyracotherium, no bigger than a Newfoundland dog. **1931** *Discovery* XII. 32/1 The evolution of the horse from the little hyracotherium of the Eocene period—a creature not much larger than a cat—is admirably shown. **1955** *Sci. News Let.* 12 Feb. 104/1 The ancient horse, *Hyracotherium*, was not very much of a horse by modern standards. It was about the size of a shepherd dog and, unlike modern horses, it had four functional toes.

Hence **hyracotherian** (-'θɪərɪən), **-theriine** (-'θɪərɪaɪn) *adjs.*, belonging to the genus *Hyracotherium*.

1887 E. D. COPE in *Amer. Nat.* Nov. 994 It has been from the Hyracotheriine sub-family that the horse line was derived.

hyrald, -eild, var. HEREYELD, *Obs.*

‖**hyrax** ('haɪəræks). *Zool.* [mod.L., a. Gr. ὕραξ, ὕρακ- shrew-mouse.] A genus of small rabbit-like quadrupeds, containing the DAMAN, 'cony', or rock-rabbit of Syria, an Abyssinian species or sub-species, and the Cape Hyrax or rock-badger (*klipdas*) of South Africa.

The position of the Hyrax in zoological classification has been difficult to fix; it was formerly placed among *Rodentia*, subsequently among *Pachydermata*, and is now made the type of an order or sub-order *Hyracoidea*, which is sometimes associated with *Perissodactyla* (horse, hippopotamus, tapir) and *Proboscidea* (elephant) in an order *Ungulata*. The dentition combines characters of perissodactyls, esp. the rhinoceros, with some others belonging to rodents; and it is now generally regarded as the survivor of an ancient generalized type, to which ungulates, rodents, and insectivora are all related.

1832 *Proc. Sci. & Corresp. Comm. Zool. Soc.* II. 207 This muscle..occasions the peculiar fulness of the neck in the Hyrax. **1834** *Nat. Philos.* III. *Phys. Geog.* 55/2 (U.K.S.) The hyrax and the hog tribes do not extend into cold climates. **1891** *Daily News* 1 Jan. 5/5 The hyrax or coney, which looks like an agouti, or some other rodent... Its nearest living relations are the rhinoceroses; and it must be looked upon as a dwarf rhinoceros with a dash of rodent in

its composition, the result of this mixture being an animal which will not fit into any order, and therefore needs a special one all to itself.

Hyrcan ('hɜːkən), *sb.* and *a.* Also 6–7 Hircan, 6 Hyrcane. [ad. L. *Hyrcānus*, a. Gr. Ὑρκανός.] = next.

Hyrcan tiger, after L. *Hyrcanæ tigres* (Virgil *Æn.* IV. 367).

1567 W. Barker tr. *Xenophon's Discipline of Cyrus* IV. sig. O2ᵛ, Cyrus beholding the feates of the Medes and Hyrcanes, did as it were, rebuke him selfe. **1584** B. Rich *Second Tome Simonides* sig. C1, These Souldiers, like to Hircan Tigers, reuenge them selues on their owne bowelles. **1592** Daniel *Delia* xviii, But yet restore thy fearce and cruell minde, To Hyrcan tygers, and to ruthles Beares. **1602** T. Lodge tr. *Josephus' Workes* 755 Conspiring with the king of the Hyrcans to passe into Media. **1605** Shakes. *Macb.* III. iv. 101 The arm'd Rhinoceros, or th'Hircan Tiger. **1911** in W. James *Mem. & Stud.* xv. 395, I took the Hyrcan tiger by the scruff And tore him piecemeal.

Hyrcanian (hɜː'keɪnɪən), *sb.* and *a.* [f. L. *Hyrcānia* (Gr. Ὑρκανία) + -AN. Cf. prec.] **A.** *sb.* A native or inhabitant of Hyrcania, an ancient region on the Caspian Sea. **B.** *adj.* Of or pertaining to this region.

Hyrcania was the wild region *par excellence* to the ancients.

1567 W. Barker tr. *Xenophon's Discipline of Cyrus* VIII. sig. C8, Of the Hyrcanians, the Colonells son. **1596** Shakes. *Merch. V.* II. vii. 41 The Hircanion deserts. **1602** —— *Ham.* II. ii. 472 The rugged Pyrrhus like th'Hyrcanian Beast. **1607** [see Cimbrian *a.* and *sb.*]. **1671** Milton *P.R.* III. 317 The Hyrcanian cliffs Of Caucasus. **1777** J. Richardson *Dict. Persian, Arabic & Eng.* I. 1172/2 The red Hyrcanian or Tabristan willow. **1820** Shelley *Ode to Liberty* viii, in *Prometh. Unb.* 213 From what Hyrcanian glen or frozen hill, ..Didst thou lament the ruin of thy reign? **1824** Carlyle *Let.* 4 Dec. (1909) II. 44 Frightful as the Hyrcanian Tiger. **1838** *Penny Cycl.* XII. 419/2 Josephus..mentions a king of the Hyrcanians in the time of Vespasian. **1885** *Encycl. Brit.* XVIII. 603/1 In [A.D.] 59 the Hyrcanian ambassadors were able to return home. *Ibid.*, The Hyrcanians were still independent *c.* 155. **1973** R. L. Fox *Alexander the Great* ix. 141 In the Caicus valley..the colonists from distant Hyrcania..lived on in the land called the Hyrcanian Plain, where Cyrus had settled them two centuries earlier. *Ibid.* xi. 160 Medes, Armenians, Hyrcanians, North Africans and Persians themselves..fled through the stockade.

hyrchen, -oun, obs. forms of HURCHEON.

hyrd(e, obs. ff. HERD, var. HIRD *Obs.*

hyrdell, etc., obs. ff. HURDLE.

hyrdes, obs. f. *hurds*, HARDS.

hyre, obs. f. HAIR, HER *pron.*, HIRE.

hyrne, obs. f. HERN, corner.

hyrone, obs. f. IRON.

hyrra-, hyrricano, obs. ff. HURRICANE.

hyrse, obs. f. HIRSE.

hyrst: see HIRST, HURST.

hyrt, var. HIRD, *Obs.*, household.

hys, obs. f. HIS, HISS.

hyse, obs. f. HIS, HOISE, ICE.

hyse-hykylle, obs. f. ICICLE.

hyson ('haɪsən). [ad. Chinese *hsi-ch'un*, in Cantonese *hei-ch'un*, 'bright spring', the name of coarse green tea. *young hyson* is *Yü-ch'ien* = 'before the rains' (so called from the early picking of the leaf), whence a former trade-name *uchain*.] A species of green tea from China. ***young hyson***, a fine green tea (see above).

1740 R. Graves *Euphrosyne* (1776) I. 123 Nor Hyson yet, nor Gallic wines were known. **1756** Nugent *Gr. Tour* IV. 34 He will also buy you..good hyson tea for about 17 livres a pound. **1780** Sheridan *Camp* I. i, I'll give you a pound of smuggled hyson. **1832** *Veg. Subst. Food* 379 There are three kinds of green tea..one called hyson, hayssuen, is composed of leaves..carefully picked. **1852** Morfit *Tanning & Currying* (1853) 77 Schulong tea is the hyson aromatised with the leaves of the *olea fragrans* (fragrant olive).

hy-spy (haɪ spaɪ). Also **hi-spy, I spy**. A boy's game played in many parts of Great Britain and of the United States, in which a seeker, on discovering one of the hiders, cries 'hy spy!', or 'I spy (such a one)!', upon which all the seekers run back to 'den' pursued by the hider who has thus been 'spied', and who tries to capture one or more of them, so as to add them to the side of the hiders.

1777 Brand *Pop. Antiq.* (1870) II. 336, 'I spye', is the usual exclamation at a childish game called 'Hie, spy, hie'. **1815** Scott *Guy M.* lviii, I must come to play at Blind Harry and Hy Spy with them. **1821** Clare *Vill. Minstr.* I. 5 The 'I spy', 'halloo', and the marble-ring, And many a game that infancy employs. **1880** *Antrim & Down Gloss.*, *Hy spy*, a boy's game. **1876** 'Mark Twain' *Tom Sawyer* xxviii. 267 They had an exhausting good time playing 'hi-spy'. **1890** W. James *Princ. Psychol.* II. xxiv. 421 It is the same instinct which leads a boy playing 'I spy' to hold his breath when the seeker is near. **1906** *Folk-Lore* XVII. 97 *Key Hoy.* Possibly a modification of 'I Spy'. **1963** *Times* 13 May 15/7, I lament the passing of our daily games of catch-as-catch-can in the cupboards, hide-and-seek behind the wardrobe and I-spy under the piano!

hysse, obs. form of HISS, HOISE.

hyssop ('hɪsəp). Forms: 1 (h)ysope, ysopo, 3–7 ysope, 4 ysoop, 4–6 ysop, 4–7 isope, 5–6 isop(pe, 6 hisop, hissope, 6–7 hys(s)ope, 7–9 hysop, 6– hyssop. [ad. L. *hyssōpus, hyssōpum*, ad. Gr. ὕσσωπος, ὕσσωπον, app. an eastern word, being represented in Hebrew by *ēzōb*.

OE. had *(h)ysope*, weak fem., also *ysopo* indecl. or with *ysopon* in obl. cases. The ME. *ysope, isope*, are identical with the OFr. forms, and continued in use to *c* 1630; the spelling with *h* appears *c* 1550: cf. mod.F. *hysope, hyssope*.]

1. a. A small bushy aromatic herb of the genus *Hyssopus* (N.O. *Labiatæ*); *spec.* the common cultivated species *H. officinalis*, a native of Southern Europe, formerly much used medicinally, esp. in decoctions.

c **1000** *Sax. Leechd.* I. 254 Ðenim ðas ylcan wyrte & ysopan. *Ibid.* 374 Wið lungen adle, ȝenim..ysopo. **1398** Trevisa *Barth. De P.R.* XVII. lxxxv. (Tollem. MS.), Ysop is a litel schorte herbe, and groweþ amonge stones, and..is hoot and drye in þe þridde gre. *c* **1420** *Liber Cocorum* (1862) 23 Take persole and sawge and ysope bryȝt. **1542** Boorde *Dyetary* xx. (1870) 281 Isope clenseth viscus fleume. **1562** Turner *Herbal* II. 19 a, The brothe of Hysop. **1591** Spenser *Muiopot.* 190 Sharpe Isope, good for greene wounds remedies. **1597** Gerarde *Herbal* II. clxvii. 463 There be diuers sortes of Hyssope. **1747** Wesley *Prim. Physic* (1762) 48 Two or three sprigs of Hyssop. **1834** Lytton *Pompeii* IV. iii, Water with myrrh and hyssop for the finishing lavation.

b. Extended with various qualifications to other plants of the *Labiatæ* and allied orders.

anise hyssop, *Lophanthus anisatus*. **bastard hyssop**, *Teucrium Pseudo-hyssopus*. **giant hyssop**, species of *Lophanthus*. **hedge hyssop**, species of *Gratiola*, esp. *G. officinalis*. **water hyssop**, *Herpestis Monnieria*. **wild hyssop**, *Verbena hastata*. (Miller, *Plant-names*.)

1597 Gerarde *Herbal* II. clxviii. 467 Hedge Hyssope is called in Latine Gratiola..Hedge Hissope is hot and drie of temperature. **1661** J. Childrey *Brit. Bacon.* 10 Upon the Sea-cliffs in Cornwall grow wilde Hysope, Sage,..and other fragrant Herbs.

2. a. In Biblical translations and derived use: A plant, the twigs of which were used for sprinkling in Jewish rites; hence, a bunch of this plant used in ceremonial purification, and allusively.

Variously conjectured to be a species of *Satureia*, Marjoram (*Origanum*), or (with more probability) the Thorny Caper (*Capparis spinosa*).

c **825** *Vesp. Psalter* l. 9 [li. 7] Ðu onstrigdes mec mid ysopan and ic biom ȝeclasnad. *c* **1000** Ælfric *Exod.* xii. 22 Dyppaþ ysopan sceaft on þam blode..and sprengaþ on þæt oferslege and on æȝþer ȝedyre. *c* **1200** *Vices & Virtues* (E.E.T.S.) 83 Spræng me mid tare ysope of ðare holi rode. **1382** Wyclif *Ps.* l[i]. 7 Thou shal sprenge me, Lord, with isope, and I shal ben clensid. *c* **1586** C'tess Pembroke *Ps.* LI. iv, With hisop, Lord, thy hisop purge me soe. **1856** Stanley *Sinai & Pal.* i. (1858) 21 The caper plant, the bright green creeper which climbs out of the fissures of the rocks..has been identified..with the 'hyssop' or 'ezob' of Scripture.

b. Hence, A holy-water sprinkler; an aspergillum. (So med.L. *hyssōpus*.)

1838 Prescott *Ferd. & Is.* (1846) II. xvii. 132 The mop, or hyssop, with which the Roman Catholic missionaries were wont to scatter the holy drops.

c. With reference to 1 Kings iv. 33, *hyssop* stands as the type of a lowly plant; whence used *fig.*

1382 Wyclif *1 Kings* iv. 33 And he [Solomon] disputide vpon the trees, fro the cedar that is in Liban, vnto the ysoop that goth out of the wal. **1450–1530** *Myrr. our Ladye* 298 The hy ceder of the lybane is conformed to the ysop in oure vale. **1663** Cowley *Verses & Ess., Of myself* (1669) 144 That violent Publick storm which..rooted up every Plant, even from the Princely Cedars to Me, the Hyssop. **1781** Cowper *Hope* 287 Say, botanist, within whose province fall The cedar and the hyssop on the wall. **1878** Browning *Poets Croisic* xx, Tasting how it feels to turn Cedar from hyssop-on-the-wall.

3. Applied in the western U.S. to species of Artemisia (*A. arbuscula, tridentata, trifida*), also called *sage-bush* or *sage-brush*, which grow on the dry prairies.

1807 P. Gass *Jrnl.* 79 There is a great quantity of hysop in the vallies. **1812** Brackenridge *Views Louisiana* (1814) 29 There are other places..producing nothing but hyssop and prickly pears. **1817** J. Bradbury *Trav. Amer.* 116 A species of Artemisia, common on the prairies, and known to the hunters by the name of Hyssop.

4. *Comb.*, as ***hyssop-bunch, -sprinkler, -water, -wine; hyssop-heavy, -laden*** adjs.

1579 Langham *Gard. Health* (1633) 693 Ysope leaues stripped from the stalkes, may bee kept a yeare. **1601** Holland *Pliny* I. 421 After the same sort is Hyssop wine made, to wit of three ounces..of Cilician Hyssope cast whole as it is into two gallons of Must, and so let them worke together. **1647** Trapp *Comm. Hebr.* ix. 13 A hysop-bunch. *a* **1867** J. Hamilton *Moses* xvii. (1870) 272 Moses took a hyssop-sprinkler. **1881** O. Wilde *Poems* 229 No need have we of hyssop-laden rod. **1899** W. B. Yeats *Wind among Reeds* 52 The hyssop-heavy sponge, the flowers by Kidron stream.

Hence † **hy'ssopic** *a.* (see quot.).

1727–41 Chambers *Cycl.*, *Hyssopic Art*, a name which Paracelsus gave to chymistry, considered, as that art purifies metals, minerals, &c., in allusion to that text..'Purge me with hyssop, and I shall be clean'. **1775** in Ash.

hyst-: see HIST-.

‖**hysteralgia** (hɪstə'rældʒɪə). *Path.* Also anglicized **'hysteralgy**. [mod.L., f. Gr. ὑστέρα womb + -αλγία, f. ἄλγος pain. Cf. Gr. ὑστεραλγής causing pains in the womb. In F. *hystéralgie*.] Pain occurring in the womb; *esp.* neuralgia of the uterus.

1657 *Physical Dict.*, *Hysteralgia*, pain in the belly or womb. **1727–41** Chambers *Cycl.*, *Hysteralgy*, in medicine, a pain in the matrix or womb. **1808** *Med. Jrnl.* XIX. 550 History of a Case of Hysteralgia.

Hence **hyste'ralgic** *a.*

1855 in Mayne *Expos. Lex.* **1886** in *Syd. Soc. Lex.*

hysteranthous (hɪstə'rænθəs), *a. Bot.* [f. Gr. ὕστερ-ος later + ἄνθ-ος flower + -OUS. Cf. F. *hystéranthe*.] Of plants: Having the flowers appearing before the leaves.

(Etymologically the word should mean the reverse of this; the correct term would be *hysterophyllous*.)

1835 Lindley *Introd. Bot.* (1848) II. 368 *Hysteranthous*, when leaves appear after flowers. **1880** Gray *Struct. Bot.* (ed. 6) 416/1.

hysterectomy (hɪstə'rɛktəmɪ). *Surg.* [f. HYSTERO-[1] + Gr. ἐκτομ-ή excision (f. ἐκ out + τέμνειν to cut) + -Y.] Excision of the uterus.

1886 in *Syd. Soc. Lex.* **1889** J. M. Duncan *Lect. Dis. Wom.* xiii. (ed. 4) 94 The operation of hysterectomy. **1894** *Brit. Med. Jrnl.* 26 May 1120/3 Now hysterectomy is an accepted operation, the mortality following its performance is small.

‖**hysteresis** (hɪstə'riːsɪs). [a. Gr. ὑστέρησις a coming short, deficiency, f. ὑστερεῖν to be behind, come late, etc., f. ὕστερ-ος late.] **1. a.** A phenomenon observed in some physical systems, by which changes in a property (e.g. magnetization, or length) lag behind changes in an agent on which they depend (e.g. magnetizing force, or stress), so that the value of the former at any moment depends on the manner of the previous variation of the latter (e.g. whether it was increasing or decreasing in value); any dependence of the value of a property on the past history of the system to which it pertains.

1881 *Proc. Roy. Soc.* XXXIII. 22 The change of polarisation lags behind the change of torsion. To this action..the author [J. A. Ewing] now gives the name *Hysteresis*. *Ibid.*, The effects of hysteresis may be wiped out by subjecting the wire to mechanical vibration. **1882** J. A. Ewing in *Proc. R. Soc.* XXXIV. 40 All changes of magnetisation produced by slow or fast, continuous or discontinuous, changes of the magnetising force exhibit hysteresis. **1894–5** S. P. Thompson *Elem. Less. Electr. & Mag.* §368 Ewing has given the name of *Hysteresis* to the subject of the lag of magnetic effects behind their causes. *Ibid.*, Ewing has also shown that under constant magnetizing force the magnetism will go on slowly and slightly increasing for a long time: this is called magnetic *creeping*, or *viscous hysteresis*. **1903** *Nature* 17 Dec. 160/2 In the relationship of stress to strain, or twisting couple to twist produced, rocks exhibit a marked hysteresis. **1906** *Biochem. Jrnl.* II. 72 The slow change in osmotic pressure observed in colloidal solutions, such as that back to normal conditions in gelatine after a short period at a higher temperature,..indicates a kind of hysteresis in such solutions, or a very slow return to equilibrium after the state of aggregation has been disturbed. **1931** E. S. Hedges *Colloids* xv. 197 The hysteresis in the case of agar is..far more striking, gelation occurring at about 40° and melting at about 85°. **1939** L. F. Bates *Mod. Magnetism* ix. 279 Temperature hysteresis, i.e. the ferromagnetic loses its ferromagnetism at θf on heating and regains it at a temperature below θf on cooling. **1950** J. W. McBain *Colloid Sci.* xi. 166 There is a good deal of hysteresis, that is, a time lag between the cooling and the setting to be expected of the jelly. **1956** J. F. D. Smith in McPherson & Klemin *Engin. Uses of Rubber* v. 130 An inspection of load-deflection diagrams reveals that the loading line may not be the same as the unloading line, for hysteresis plays an important part in flexometers. **1965** A. P. Boresi *Elasticity Engin. Mech.* iv. 103 Whenever a body exhibits the phenomenon of hysteresis—that is, of returning to its original size and shape only slowly or not at all—its behavior is not perfectly elastic.

b. = *hysteresis loss.*

1896 *Min. Proc. Inst. Civil Engin.* CXXVI. 216 If B = 2,500 were taken as the limit of the cycle the hysteresis of this 'record' specimen would be only 0·16 watt per lb.

2. *Comb.*, as **hysteresis curve** = *hysteresis loop*; **hysteresis loop**, a graph showing how the value of some property of a hysteretic system varies as the agent causing it is varied from one value to another and back again, having the form of a closed curve whose area is a measure of the loss of energy in the cycle; **hysteresis loss**, the energy dissipated as heat in a system as a result of hysteresis.

1894 *Rep. Brit. Assoc. Adv. Sci.* 577 The three stages of magnetic displacement each have a sharply defined position on the hysteresis curve. **1954** C. Zwikker *Physical Prop. Solid Materials* xii. 208 Permanent magnet materials are chosen for having a large area of loop on the *B–H* hysteresis curve. **1896** F. Bedell *Princ. Transformer* iii. 32 Curves of magnetization for a complete cycle, or 'hysteresis loops', as they are called, are shown in Fig. 33. **1897** A. G. Webster *Theory Electr. & Magn.* ix. 394 The hysteresis-loop..has an important physical significance. **1946** *Rubber in Engin.* (H.M.S.O.) iv. 69 The stress–strain curve for rubber on retraction does not follow the same course as during

extension, but forms a hysteresis loop. **1966** McClintock & Argon *Mech. Behavior Materials* i. 6 Under cyclic straining, any kind of inelastic strain leads to a hysteresis loop on a stress-strain plot. **1893** *Proc. R. Soc.* LIV. 76 Great permeability does not necessarily imply small hysteresis losses. **1927** T. F. Wall *Applied Magnetism* xv. 233 A simple and rapid means for measuring the hysteresis loss in a transformer. **1962** A. Edwards in D. Hadfield *Permanent Magnets* vi. 294 If the flux density in a magnet continually increases and decreases in use, there is hysteresis loss at every cycle and some eddy-current loss.

Hence **hysteresial** (-ˈiːsɪəl) *a.*, of or pertaining to hysteresis.

1887 *Rep. Brit. Assoc. Adv. Sci. 1886* 551 The hysteresial dissipation of energy per unit volume of iron is the same whether the magnetic circuit be open or closed. **1894-5** S. P. Thompson *Elem. Less. Electr. & Mag.* §368 Mechanical agitation tends to help the magnetizing forces to act, and lessens all residual and hysteresial effects. **1971** J. A. C. Harwood in C. M. Blow *Rubber Technol. & Manuf.* iii. 69 Stress softening, a hysteresial phenomenon observed at moderate and high extensions, is probably also viscoelastic in origin.

hysteretic (hɪstəˈrɛtɪk), *a.* [Prob. f. hysteresis after such pairs as *synthesis, synthetic* and *prosthesis, prosthetic*; but cf. Gr. ὑστερητικός 'which comes on later'.] Of, pertaining to, or exhibiting hysteresis.

1892 *Trans. Amer. Inst. Electr. Engin.* XI. 25 Two other sets of determinations of the hysteretic loss of energy, for the frequency of 170 complete periods per second, were made on two laminated horse shoe magnets. *Ibid.* 43 This figure shows well the three characteristic forms of hysteretic curves. **1931** S. R. Williams *Magnetic Phenomena* i. 60, η is called the hysteretic constant or coefficient of hysteresis loss, which varies from one ferromagnetic body to another. **1958** C. L. Mantell *Engin. Materials Handbk.* xxxii. 10 Hysteretic properties of elastomers also affect their utility in applications where resilience is important. **1971** *Nature* 15 Jan. 155/3 A slow change in the concentration of a metabolite may still be rapid compared with the hysteretic adjustment of the activity of an enzyme that it controls.

Hence **hysteˈretically** *adv.*, by means of or as a result of hysteresis.

1904 *Electr. World & Engin.* 30 July 163/2 The actual condenser dissipates energy hysteretically in the dielectric. **1956** *Aeronaut. Q.* VII. 60 A general theory of small hysteretically damped vibration.

‖**hysteria** (hɪˈstɪərɪə). [mod. medical L., formed as abstract sb. to hysteric. Cf. F. *hystérie* (1812 in Hatz.-Darm.).]

1. *Path.* A functional disturbance of the nervous system, characterized by such disorders as anæsthesia, hyperæsthesia, convulsions, etc., and usually attended with emotional disturbances and enfeeblement or perversion of the moral and intellectual faculties. (Also called colloquially *hysterics.*)

Women being much more liable than men to this disorder, it was originally thought to be due to a disturbance of the uterus and its functions: cf. hysteric and the Ger. term *mutterweh*. Former names for the disease were *vapours* and *hysteric(al) passion*.

1801 *Med. Jrnl.* V. 14 Account of Diseases in an Eastern District of London... Chronic Diseases... Hysteria. **1811** Hooper *Med. Dict.* s.v., Hiccup is a symptom which attends, in some instances, on hysteria; and now and then it happens, that a fit of hysteria consists of this alone. **1866-80** A. Flint *Princ. Med.* (ed. 5) 832 The name hysteria, as commonly used, embraces a multiplicity of morbid phenomena. **1874** Carpenter *Ment. Phys.* i. ii. §75 (1879) 79 Hysteria; a state of the Nervous system which is characterized by its peculiar excitability, but in which there is no such fixed tendency to irregular action as would indicate any positive disease.

2. *transf.* and *fig.* Morbidly excited condition; unhealthy emotion or excitement.

1839 Poe *Wks.* (1884) I. 132 (Stanf.) An evidently restrained *hysteria* in his whole demeanour. **1877** Morley *Crit. Misc.* Ser. ii. 256 Those of us who dislike literary hysteria. **1897** F. N. Maude *Volunt. v. Compuls. Serv.* 119 A wave of humanitarian hysteria capable of wrecking any Government we have ever had.

hysteric (hɪˈstɛrɪk), *a.* and *sb.* Also 7-8 histeric(k. [ad. L. *hysteric-us*, ad. Gr. ὑστερικ-ός belonging to the womb, suffering in the womb, hysterical (f. ὑστέρα womb), esp. in ὑστερικὴ πνίξ, ὑστερικὰ πάθη, *hysterica passio* (see infra, 1). For the application of the word, see note to hysteria 1. Cf. F. *hystérique* (recorded 1568).]

A. *adj.*

1. = hysterical A. 1. *hysteric passion*: hysteria.

1657 Tomlinson *Renou's Disp.* 25 The Plague is a poyson .. which retained in Histerick women [etc.]. **1704** J. Harris *Lex. Techn.*, *Vapours*, .. the Disease called otherwise Hysterick, or Hypochondriack Fits, or Melancholy. **1732** Arbuthnot *Rules of Diet* 377 Such as are Hypochondriacal and Hysterick. **1822-34** *Good's Study Med.* (ed. 4) III. 401 Swediaur .. affirms that men may labour under the hysteric passion as well as women. **1850** Kingsley *Alt. Locke* xxxviii, An hysteric or paralytic patient.

2. = hysterical A. 2.

1751 Smollett *Per. Pic.* lxxvi, The united pangs .. produced a sort of hysteric laugh. **1779** Sheridan *Critic* i. i, Misses and Ma'ams piping hysteric changes on Juliets and Dorindas, Pollys and Ophelias. **1832** *Fair of May Fair* III. *Hearts & Diamonds* viii. 35 Her voice was broken by hysteric sobs. **1889** R. St. J. Tyrwhitt in *Univ. Rev.* 15 Feb. 251 Professor Ruskin curses all field sports .. with the hysteric passion of his later days.

†**3.** Of medicines: Having the property of curing hysteria; good for diseases of the uterus (see hysteria 1, *note*). *Obs.*

1694 Salmon *Bates' Disp.* (1713) 609/2 Any proper Hysterick or Cephalick Water, or Decoction. **1727-41** Chambers *Cycl.* s.v. *Waters*, *Hysteric-Waters*, are those proper to strengthen the matrix, or womb, and remedy the disorders that befal it. **1732** Arbuthnot *Rules of Diet* 257 Walnuts are cordial and hysterick, and gently sudorifick.

B. *sb.*

†**1.** A remedy for hysteria; a medicine efficacious in uterine disorders. *Obs.*

1684 tr. *Bonet's Merc. Compit.* iii. 92 We must first make use of aperient Hystericks. **1720** Blair in *Phil. Trans.* XXXI. 33 The Corymbiferous kind, are either Stomachicks, Hystericks, or Vermifuges. **1757** A. Cooper *Distiller* iii. xxvi. (1760) 189 This composition is .. excellently adapted to the Intention of an Hysteric.

2. One subject to hysteria.

1751 Bp. Lavington *Enthus. Meth. & Papists* (1754) II. iii. 100 Physicians have proved this to be the Case in common Hysterics and Epileptics. **1892** *Athenæum* 21 May 661/2 We have met the shepherdess of Domremy as strategist .. as saint, as hysteric, and lastly .. as spiritualistic medium.

3. *pl.* **hysterics** [= Gr. τὰ ὑστερικά] (also *sing.*). A familiar equivalent of hysteria, but chiefly = hysterical fits or convulsions; hence (β) in sing.: A convulsive fit of laughter or weeping.

1727 Swift *To a very young Lady*, Those wives, who, when their husbands are gone a journey, must have a letter every post upon pain of fits and hystericks. **1754** Richardson *Grandison* (1781) III. xiii. 101 The woman .. was taken out of the coach in violent hystericks. **1818** Byron *Juan* i. clxii, Sobs, And indications of hysterics.

β. **1776** S. J. Pratt *Pupil of Pleasure* II. 76, I found Harriet in a strong hysteric. **1835** Lytton *Rienzi* ix. iv, He was thought to weep from hypocrisy, when in truth it was the hysteric of over-wrought and irritable emotion. **1856** F. E. Paget *Owlet Owlst.* 145 To control a fit of nerves, or a rising hysteric. **1870** L'Estrange *Miss Mitford* I. vii. 245 The lowly Maria fell into a sort of hysteric of fright, lamentation, and anger because she was not suffered to wear a diamond necklace.

Hence **hystericism** (hɪˈstɛrɪsɪz(ə)m) [cf. F. *hystéricisme*], the state or condition of being hysterical; hysteria. **hystericize** (hɪˈstɛrɪsaɪz) *v. intr.*, to go into hysterics.

1710 T. Fuller *Pharm. Extemp.* 394 Why then must Hystericism and Hypochondriacism be confusedly jumbl'd together? **1855** Mayne *Expos. Lex.*, *Hystericismus*, .. the same as *Hysteria*: the presence or existence of hysterical affection: hystericism. **1894** *Westm. Gaz.* 5 Dec. 3/1 The Newest Woman queens it here In all her last uncomely guises; A screaming Sisterhood severe Hystericises.

hysterical (hɪˈstɛrɪkəl), *a.* and *sb.* [f. as prec. + -al¹.] **A.** *adj.*

1. Of, pertaining to, or characteristic of hysteria; affected with or suffering from hysteria. †*hysterical passion*: hysteria. *hysterical fever*: see quot. 1822-34.

1615 Crooke *Body of Man* 326 Hysterical women, that is, such as are in fits of the mother. **1704** J. Harris *Lex. Techn.* s.v. *Clavus*, Dr. Sydenham calls such a Pain in the top of the Head of Hysterical Persons, *Clavus Hystericus*. **1803** Beddoes *Hygëia* ix. 184 The epileptic, the hysterical, the hypochondriac. **1818** Scott *Hrt. Midl.* x, The unfortunate young woman .. finally fell into a hysterical fit. **1822-34** *Good's Study Med.* (ed. 4) I. 688 It [mild typhus] has sometimes been denominated *hysterical fever*. **1880** Beale *Slight Ailm.* 72 Hysterical girls are very apt to lose their appetite for a time.

2. *transf.* and *fig.* Characterized by convulsive emotion or excitement such as marks hysteria; morbidly emotional or excited. (Said freq. of convulsive fits of laughter or weeping.)

1704 F. Fuller *Med. Gymn.* (1711) 9 Those weaker Hysterical People whose Spirits are of so fine a Make. **1817** J. McLeod *Voy. Alceste* i. (ed. 3) 14 The men [of the Brazils], in their exterior appearance, are a squalid, hysterical, grim-looking tribe. **1865** Carlyle *Fredk. Gt.* xiii. vii. V. 83 This of Pisek was but one of the many unwise hysterical things poor Broglio did. **1897** F. N. Maude *Volunt. v. Compuls. Serv.* 125 A misdirected outbreak of hysterical humanitarianism.

B. *sb.* †**1.** = hysteric B. 1. *Obs.*

1649 Culpepper *Lond. Disp., Key Galen* ii. viii. (1653) 310 Such Medicines as provoke the Terms, or stop them when they flow immoderately, are properly Hystericals. **1671** Salmon *Syn. Med.* iii. xv. 359 Hystericals are such things as are appropriated to the Womb, and these are most of them Cephalicks.

2. *pl.* = hysteric B. 3. *rare.*

1834 *Blackw. Mag.* XXXVI. 472/1 Since Father O'Shauchnessy cured aunt Katey's old pig of the hystericals. **1857** Kingsley *Two Y. Ago* xxiv, Most astonished .. to see a lassie that never gave him a kind word in her life .. greet and greet at his going, till she vanished away into hystericals.

3. = hysteric *a.* and *sb.* B. 2.

1892 A. W. Pinero *Magistrate* iii. i. 136 (The sound of a shriek from Agatha and Charlotte.) *Lugg*... Don't notice them. They're hystericals. They're mild now to what they have been. **1922** M. Sadleir *Excursions in Victorian Bibliogr.* 2 This is a book about first editions, and will be read only by the initiate. If we be hystericals, we have at least our weakness in common. **1950** E. Hemingway *Across River* xxxix. 229 'I've stopped [crying],' she said. 'I'm not an hysterical.'

hysterically (hɪˈstɛrɪkəlɪ), *adv.* [f. prec. + -ly².] In a hysterical manner; in a fit of hysterics.

1710 T. Fuller *Pharm. Extemp.* 305 Whensoever the Spirits being Hysterically confined, do not flow in plentifully. **1834** Medwin *Angler in Wales* II. 78, I was laughing hysterically all the time. **1860** Froude *Hist. Eng.* V. 234 The Protector himself then addressed them wildly, passionately, hysterically. 'He would not fall alone', he said.

‖**hysterica passio** (hɪˈstɛrɪkə ˈpæsɪəʊ). [L., = 'hysteric passion'. See hysteric.] = hysteria 1.

1603 S. Harsnet *Declaration Popish Impostures* vi. 25 Maynie had a spice of the Hysterica passio, as seems from his youth. **1605** [see mother *sb.* 13]. **1934** W. B. Yeats *King of Gt. Clock Tower* 22 But popular rage *Hysterica passio* dragged this quarry down. **1963** *Listener* 17 Oct. 626/2 Before watching 'The Mersey Sound' .. I took tranquillizers to forestall a fit of *hysterica passio*.

hystericky (hɪˈstɛrɪkɪ), *a.* *U.S. colloq.* [f. hysteric + -y.] Inclined to, subject to, or characteristic of hysteria; hysterical.

1823 J. F. Cooper *Pilot* II. xiv. 239 In order that the women need not be 'stericky in squalls. **1867** O. W. Holmes *Guardian Angel* xi. (1891) 129 And that queer woman, the Deacon's mother,—there's where she gets that hystericky look. **1888** *N.Y. Herald* (in *Times* 1 Nov.), A Secretary of State who in an emergency scolds like an hystericky woman is not a safe man for any President.

hysteriform (hɪˈstɛrɪfɔːm), *a.*¹ *Path.* [f. hysteri-a + -form.] Resembling or having the aspect of hysteria.

1861 Bumstead *Ven. Dis.* (1879) 138 General nervous excitement which sometimes rises to the point of hysteriform spasm.

hysteriform (hɪˈstɛrɪfɔːm), *a.*² *Bot.* [f. *Hysterium* (see below), f. Gr. ὕστερος later: see -form.] Having the form or character of the genus *Hysterium* of ascomycetous fungi, growing on decayed wood, branches, leaves, etc.

1887 W. Phillips *Man. Brit. Discomycetes* 384 *Stictis hysterioides.* Desm. Immersed, closed, hysteriform, then erumpent. **1957** Snell & Dick *Gloss. Mycol.* 79/1 Hysteriform... Elongated, boat-shaped and cleft, resembling the sporocarps of the genus *Hysterium*.

‖**hysteritis** (hɪstəˈraɪtɪs). *Path.* [mod.L., f. Gr. ὑστέρ-α womb + -itis.] Inflammation of the uterus; metritis.

1803 *Med. Jrnl.* X. 12 That the appearances .. in cases of hysteritis and puerperal fever, are widely different.

hystero-¹ (ˈhɪstərəʊ), before a vowel **hyster-** (as in *hysteralgia*), combining form of Gr. ὑστέρα womb. Used in medical terms of recent formation with the senses: **a.** Of the womb, uterine, as in *hystero-colic*, *hystero-paralysis*, *-phthisis*. **b.** Accompanied or associated with hysteria, hysterical (see hysteria 1 *note*), as *hystero-catalepsy*, *-epilepsy* (whence *hystero-epileptic* adj.), etc.

hysterocele (ˈhɪstərəʊsiːl) *Path.* [Gr. κήλη tumour], a hernia containing the uterus or some part of it. **hysterocystic** (ˌhɪstərəʊˈsɪstɪk), *a.* *Path.* [Gr. κύστις bladder], pertaining to the uterus and the bladder. ‖**hysterodynia** (-ˈdaɪnɪə) *Path.* [Gr. ὀδύνη pain], pain of the womb (*Syd. Soc. Lex.* 1886). ˌ**hystero-ˈepilepsy**, a form of hysteria characterized by the occurrence of convulsions more or less resembling those of epilepsy; occurring chiefly among females, especially of the Latin races (*Syd. Soc. Lex.*); hence ˌ**hystero-epiˈleptic** *a.* and *sb.* ‖**hysteroˈmania** *Path.*, an old name for nymphomania; also = hysterical insanity (*Ibid.*). **hysterometer** (hɪstəˈrɒmɪtə(r)) *Surg.* [-meter], an instrument for ascertaining the size of the womb; a uterine sound (Mayne 1855); hence **hysteˈrometry**, the use of the hysterometer (*Syd. Soc. Lex.* 1886). **hysteropexy** (ˈhɪstərəʊˌpɛksɪ) *Surg.* [Gr. -πηξία fixing], the operation of supporting the womb in a case of prolapsus. **hysterophore** (ˈhɪstərəʊfɔə(r)) *Surg.* [Gr. -φορος bearing], a pessary for supporting the uterus. ‖**hysteropˈtosis** *Path.* [Gr. πτῶσις falling], falling of the womb, *prolapsus uteri* (*Syd. Soc. Lex.* 1886). **hysteˈrorrhaphy** *Surg.* [-rrhaphy] = *hysteropexy*.

1706 Phillips (ed. Kersey), *Hysterocele, the Rupture or falling down of the Womb. **1855** Mayne *Expos. Lex.*, *Hysterocystic. **1886** *Syd. Soc. Lex.*, *Hysterocystic retention*, retention of urine during pregnancy from pressure or stretching of the neck of the bladder by the enlarged womb. **1881** *Encycl. Brit.* XII. 601/1 *Hystero-epilepsy, a nervous disease of women. **1887** *Fortn. Rev.* May 734 The perfection of mimicry reached by the hypnotized *hystero-epileptic. **1894** *Westm. Gaz.* 21 July 5/2 The mortality from ovariotomy, hysterectomy, *hysteropexy, and exploratory incisions is high. **1887** H. A. Kelly in *Amer. Jrnl. Obstetr.* XX. 34 It is my purpose here formally to propose, and to formulate rules for the adoption of a new operative procedure in the treatment of .. intractable cases of retroflexion, and of prolapsus uteri... In accordance with

the principles here laid down, the term '*Hysterorrhaphy' is used to define the suspension by suture of a viciously posed uterus. **1953** R. W. TE LINDE *Oper. Gynecol.* (ed. 2) vi. 107 Ventrofixation, hysterorrhaphy and hysteropexy were terms applied to the earliest operation in which an attempt was made to suspend the retroplaced uterus. The chief interest of this operation is now historical.

hystero-^{2} ('hɪstərəʊ), combining form of Gr. *ὕστερος* later, latter, inferior, as in *hysterogenetic*, *hysterology*, etc.

hysterogenetic (ˌhɪstərəʊdʒɪ'nɛtɪk), *a. Bot.* [f. Gr. *ὑστερο-* HYSTERO-^{2} + GENETIC.] = next. (Opposed to *protogenetic*.)

1884 BOWER & SCOTT *De Bary's Phaner.* 201 Hysterogenetic reservoirs of this category arise in old masses of tissue. *Ibid.* 526 The spaces filled with resin.. are subsequent, hysterogenetic products of disorganization.

hysterogenic (ˌhɪstərəʊ'dʒɛnɪk), *a.*^{1} *Bot.* [f. as prec. + *-genic*; cf. *protogenic*, etc.] Of later origin or formation; applied to intercellular spaces formed in older tissues.

1885 GOODALE *Phys. Bot.* (1892) 99 *note*, Those [intercellular spaces] formed in older tissues [are called] hysterogenic.

hystero'genic, *a.*^{2} *Path.* [f. HYSTERO-^{1} + -GENIC.] Producing hysteria; relating to the production of hysteria. So **hyste'rogenous** *a.*, in same sense; **hyste'rogeny**, the production of hysteria.

1886 *Syd. Soc. Lex.*, *Hysterogenic*.. *Hysterogenous*. **1886** F. W. H. MYERS in *Proc. Soc. Psych. Res.* Oct. 127 *note*, I must adopt from the French the word.. *hysterogeny* for the production of hysterical states. **1887** *Fortn. Rev.* May 737 The so-called 'hysterogenic' and 'hypnogenic' pressure points. **1897** ALLBUTT *Syst. Med.* III. 532 The presence of other hysterical symptoms, such as hemi-anæsthesia.. hysterogenic zones, contraction in the field of vision.

hysteroid ('hɪstərɔɪd), *a.* [Irreg. f. HYSTER-IA + -OID.] Resembling or having the form of hysteria. So **hyste'roidal** *a.*

1855 DUNGLISON *Med. Lex.* (ed. 12), *Hysteroid*,.. resembling hysteria; as a hysteroid disease, symptom, &c. **1887** *Fortn. Rev.* May 738 The undoubted greater prevalence of hysteroid symptoms among the Latin.. races. **1887** *Med. News* (U.S.) 8 Jan. 37 Their value is much diminished by the unmistakable hysteroidal impress which they bear. **1891** *Lancet* 3 Oct. 756 No one who has not been to Paris, and seen the hysteroid condition in its extreme development, can realise fully this form of neurosis.

†**'hysterolite**. *Min. Obs.* Also *erron.* **hysterio-**. [f. Gr. *ὑστέρα* womb + *λίθος* stone, from its fancied appearance. Cf. F. *hystérolithe*.] A fossil shell: see quot. 1854.

[**1706** PHILLIPS (ed. Kersey), *Hysterolithus*, a sort of Stone.] **1799** KIRWAN *Geol. Ess.* v. 244 Petrifactions, as hysteriolites, mytilites, &c. are found in it [rubble stone]. **1854** WOODWARD *Mollusca* II. 229 Orthis Striatula: internal casts of this fossil were called *hysterolites* by old authors.

†**hyste'rology**^{1}. *Obs. Gram.*, etc. [ad. late L. *hysterologia*, a. Gr. *ὑστερολογία*, f. *ὑστερο-*, HYSTERO-^{2} + *λόγος* speech. Cf. F. *hystérologie*.] = HYSTERON PROTERON. (See also quot. 1842.)

1623 COCKERAM, *Historologie*, an altering of the order of speech, by placing that after that should be before. **1657** W. MORICE *Coena quasi Κοινὴ* Def. xi. 129 These Notes are.. never used to manifest an hysterology, or transposition of things. **1684** H. MORE *Answer* 156 Here therefore is an Hysterology in the Cortex. **1842** BRANDE *Dict. Sci*, etc. s.v., Some comprehend the figure usually called anti-climax.. under the name Hysterology.

hysterology^{2} (hɪstə'rɒlədʒɪ). *Med.* [f. HYSTERO-^{1} + -LOGY.] A treatise on the uterus.

1855 MAYNE *Expos. Lex.*, *Hysterologia*,.. term for a treatise or dissertation on the womb, its functions, etc.: hysterology. **1880** E. N. CHAPMAN (*title*) Hysterology, a Treatise, Descriptive and Clinical, on the Diseases and Displacements of the Uterus.

‖**hysteron proteron** ('hɪstərɒn 'prɒtərɒn), *sb.* (*a.* and *adv.*) [late L. (Servius), a. Gr. *ὕστερον πρότερον*, the latter (put as) the former; called also *πρωθύστερον* (f. *πρῶτος* first), and *ὑστερολογία* (see HYSTEROLOGY^{1}).]

1. *Gram.* and *Rhet.* A figure of speech in which the word or phrase that should properly come last is put first.

1565 JEWEL *Repl. Harding* 476 In these woordes, 'Take ye: Eate ye: This is my Bodie', They have founde a Figure called Hysteron Proteron. **1589** PUTTENHAM *Eng. Poesie* III. xii[i.] (Arb.) 181 Another manner of disordered speach.. we call it in English prouerbe, the cart before the horse, the Greeks call it *Histeron proteron*, we name it the Preposterous.. as he.. said: 'My dame that bred me vp and bare me in her wombe.' Whereas the bearing is before the bringing vp. **1706** PHILLIPS (ed. Kersey), *Hysteron Proteron*, a preposterous manner of speaking or writing, expressing that first which should be last. **1883** MARCH *A.S. Gram.* 141 Transposition.. of clauses [is called] hysteron-proteron.

†**2.** Inversion of the natural or logical order; as by placing the conclusion before the premisses, etc.

1620 GRANGER *Div. Logike* 318 Inverted Method, is when particulars are disposed before universals: also, when the parts.. are not handled after the same order, by which they were laid downe, which is called Hysteron Proteron.

3. *generally.* The position or arrangement of things in the reverse of their natural or rational order; 'putting the cart before the horse'; topsy-turvydom.

1589 COGAN *Haven Health* To Rdr. ¶¶iv, Contrariwise vsing Hysteron Proteron.. as I haue heard say of a gentleman who.. would not begin his meale with potage, but insteed of cheese would eat his potage last. **1648–99** J. BEAUMONT *Psyche* I. lxxxv, How wild A Hysteron Proteron's this, which Nature crosses, And far above the top the bottom tosses.

B. *attrib.* or *adj.*

1646 *Unhappy Game Scotch & Eng.* 14 Those jugling Husteron Proteron trickes. **1689** HICKERINGILL *Ceremony Monger* Wks. 1716 II. 418 Shall Christians be like that Histeron-Proteron-Herb, which Physicians as foolishly call *Filius ante Patrem*? *a* **1734** NORTH *Exam.* I. ii. (1740) 88 This *hysteron proteron* Stuff, Causes without Effects, and Effects before Causes.

†**C.** as *adv.* By or with an inversion of the natural order of things; topsy-turvy; vice versa.

1600 W. WATSON *Quodlibets Relig. & State* (1602) 47 The Catholicke religion will be vtterly extinguished and perish, and so by consequent all runne Hysteron Protheron. **1617** MIDDLETON & ROWLEY *Fair Quar.* I. i. Ciij, Wisemen begets fooles, and fooles are the fathers To many wise Children. Histeron, Proteron, A great scholler may beget an Ideot, And from the plow tayle may come a great scholler.

Hence **'hystero-'proterize** *v. intr.*, to use hysteron proteron.

a **1834** COLERIDGE in Southey *Life Wesley* (1846) I. 324 We must explain the force of the horse by the motion of the cart-wheels, and hystero-proterize with a vengeance!

hysterophytal (ˌhɪstə'rɒfɪtəl), *a. Bot.* [f. mod.L. *Hysterophyta* (see next) + -AL^{1}.] Of or pertaining to *Hysterophyta* or *Fungi*; fungal.

1857 BERKELEY *Cryptog. Bot.* §63. 81 Fungi may be defined as Hysterophytal or Epiphytal Mycetals, deriving nutriment, by means of a mycelium, from the matrix. **1874** COOKE *Fungi* 6.

hysterophyte ('hɪstərəfaɪt). *Bot.* [ad. mod. L. *hysterophytum*, pl. *-phyta* (Fries 1821), f. Gr. *ὑστέρα* womb + *φυτόν* plant: see quot. 1855.] A plant of the class *Hysterophyta* or *Fungi*; any fungus growing upon, and deriving its nourishment from, organic matter.

1855 MAYNE *Expos. Lex.*, *Hysterophytum*, applied by Fries to mushrooms.. because, according to him, they cannot grow but at the cost of some organized body living or dead, which serves them in some sort for a womb; a hysterophyte.

‖**hysterosis** (hɪstə'rəʊsɪs). *Gram.* and *Rhet.* [med. or mod.L., f. Gr. *ὕστερος* later, after such words as *anadiplosis*, etc.] = HYSTERON PROTERON.

1620 GRANGER *Div. Logike* 318 *note*, Hysteron Proteron, Hysterosis, Hysterologia. **1623** LISLE *Ælfric on O. & N. Test.* To Rdr. 15 He speakes by Hysterosis or Anachronisme (a figure much vsed in Historie, yea euen in the Bible). *a* **1658** J. DURHAM *Exp. Revelation* xxi. (1680) 641 There will hardly be found any such hysterosis or hysterologia in one and the same explicatory prophesie.

hysterotome ('hɪstərətəʊm). *Surg.* [f. HYSTERO-^{1} + Gr. *-τόμος* cutting, cutter. So mod.F. *hystérotome*.] An instrument for performing hysterotomy.

1851 *Illustr. Catal. Gt. Exhib.* 96 Hysterotomes and Instruments for Paracentesis Uteri. **1864** *Daily Tel.* 13 Aug., We will not fight with the pen against lancets, and probes, and hysterotomes, and the tremendous armoury of the surgical cutlers.

hysterotomy (hɪstə'rɒtəmɪ). *Surg.* [mod.L. *hysterotomi-a*, f. HYSTERO-^{1} + Gr. *-τομία* cutting. Cf. F. *hystérotomie*.] The operation of cutting into the uterus; the Cæsarean section; also excision, or dissection, of the uterus.

[**1706** PHILLIPS (ed. Kersey), *Hysterotomia*, an Anatomical Dissection of the Womb.] **1801** *Med. Jrnl.* V. 353 Hysterotomy, or the Cesarean Section was performed upon a woman at Rochdale. **1859** TODD *Cycl. Anat.* V. 206/1 Stark performed hysterotomy successfully for a tumour.

hystrichosphere ('hɪstrɪkəʊsfɪə(r)). *Palæont.* [ad. mod.L. *hystrichosphæra* (O. Wetzel 1933, in *Palaeontographica* A. LXXVIII. 32), f. Gr. *ὕστριξ, ὑστριχ-* porcupine + *σφαῖρα* ball.] Any of numerous kinds of microscopic planktonic fossil organisms characterized by a spherical or oval shape with numerous short thin projections.

1957 *Q. Jrnl. Geol. Soc.* CXII. 416 In the clays, dinoflagellates and hystrichospheres were abundant and formed a considerable proportion of the combustible organic matter. **1963** *Palaeontology* VI. 83 The hystrichospheres having spines closed distally exhibit an overall range in shell diameters from 5 μ to 240 μ.

‖**hystriciasis** (hɪstrɪ'saɪəsɪs). *Path.* [f. L. *hystric-em*, after *elephantiasis*: see -ASIS.] (See quot.)

1811 HOOPER *Med. Dict.*, *Hystriciasis*, a disease of the hairs, in which they stand erect, like porcupine quills. An account.. is to be seen in the *Philosophical Transactions*, No. 424 (1732).

hystricid (hɪ'strɪsɪd). *Zool.* [ad. mod.L. *Hystricid-æ*, f. *hystrix*, *hystric-em*, a. Gr. *ὕστριξ*, *ὕστριχ-*, porcupine: see -ID.] A rodent of the family *Hystricidæ*; a porcupine.

So **'hystricine** *a.*, pertaining to the sub-family *Hystricinæ*.

1883 W. H. FLOWER in *Encycl. Brit.* XV. 416/2 In the Sciurine and Hystricine Rodents the tibia and fibula are distinct.

hystricism ('hɪstrɪsɪz(ə)m). *Path.* [ad. mod.L. *hystricismus*, f. *hystrix* porcupine.] The porcupine disease, an extreme form of ichthyosis (*ichthyosis hystrix*), in which the epidermis is covered with horny prominences.

1886 in *Syd. Soc. Lex.* **1891** in F. P. FOSTER *Med. Dict.* 1960.

hystricomorph ('hɪstrɪkəʊmɔːf). *Zool.* [f. Gr. *ὕστριξ, ὕστριχ-*, L. *hystric-*, stem of *hystrix* (see HYSTRICID) + Gr. *-μορφος* shaped (*μορφή* form).] A member of the *Hystricomorpha*, a primary division of Rodents including the porcupine and its congeners. So ˌ**hystrico'morphic**, **-'morphine** *adjs.*, of, belonging to, or having the characters of the *Hystricomorpha*.

1882 *Pop. Sci. Monthly* XX. 423 The hystricomorphs (porcupines, Guinea-pigs and capybaras), which are now confined to the southern hemisphere. **1894** *Athenæum* 31 Mar. 415/3 A paper on the hystricomorphine and sciuromorphine rodents.

hyt, obs. form of HIT, IT.

hyte (haɪt), *a. Sc.* [Of obscure origin: cf. GYTE.] Crazy; mad.

1721 RAMSAY *Ep. to R.H.B.* iii, The cauldrife carlies.. gathering gear gang hyt and gare. **1786** BURNS *Ep. to Major Logan* x, The witching curs'd delicious blinkers Hae put me hyte.

hyte, obs. form of HAIT *int.*

hythe, variant spelling of HITHE, harbour.

hyther ('haɪθə(r)). [See quot. 1907.] A quantity determined from temperature and humidity and intended to represent the discomfort attributable to their combined effect; also, a unit on a scale of 0 to 10 expressing this.

1904 W. F. TYLER in *Jrnl. Balneology* VIII. 25 A number of persons.. were requested to estimate daily at noon the degree of 'hyther' on a scale of 0 to 10. This word hyther was introduced to indicate the sensation caused by a warm climate, and supposed to be due to the combined effect of heat and humidity. **1907** —— in *Monthly Weather Rev.* June 268/1, I consider the term 'sensible temperature' to be rather misleading, temperature being only one factor in the subjective effect. It was for this reason that.. I coined the word *hyther* from *hydro* and *thermos*. **1931** A. CASTELLANI *Climate & Acclimatization* ii. 39 It was observations like these that caused Tyler to attempt to correlate personal sensations with meteorological data, and to formulate his 'hyther' degrees, by which he meant the degree of discomfort caused by high air temperatures associated with high relative humidity. **1937** *Nature* 9 Jan. 79/1 Their sensations [of temperature] were recorded on an arbitrary scale extending from 1 to 10; the numbers on the scale have been called hythers, hyther 10 being taken to represent an 'unbearable condition'.

hyther, obs. f. HITHER.

hythergraph ('haɪθəgrɑːf, -æ-). *Climatology.* [f. Gr. *ὑ-ετός* rain + *θέρ-μη* heat + -GRAPH.] A climograph having temperature and either humidity or precipitation as coordinates; usu., one in which the mean monthly values of these coordinates are plotted for each month of the year, the plotted points for each successive month then being joined by straight lines.

1918 T. G. TAYLOR *Austral. Environment* viii. 30 The two chief controls.. are temperature and rainfall... To the graph representing these controls I have given the name *hythergraph*—from the Greek words for rain and heat. [*Note*] Tyler has used the word 'hyther' to express the joint effect of humidity and temperature. **1940** *Ecology* XXI. 189/1 Though shown.. as being an area of tall grass, the hythergraphs of stations in the area depart somewhat from the typical grassland figure and approach diagrams of the deciduous forest. **1950** CONRAD & POLLAK *Methods in Climatol.* (ed. 2) vii. 221 The annual variation of the combined rainfall-temperature element is represented by the graphs shown in Fig. 58. These curves are called hythergraphs.

hyve, obs. f. HIVE.

hywe, obs. form of HUE.

I

I (ai), the ninth letter and third vowel of the Roman alphabet, going back through the Greek *Iota* to the Semitic *Yod*. The simple form Ӏ of the character in Greek from about 500 B.C., and in the Roman alphabet, was reduced from a more complex Early Greek form ⟨, which originated in the Phœnician ⟨. The Semitic letter represents a consonant (= English Y in *yellow, yoke*, etc.), but this forms diphthongs with preceding *a* and *e*, and 'quiesces' in a preceding *i*, making long *ī*. It is thus, in the body or at the end of a word, often an indication of the vowel *ī*; and it was adopted as the symbol of the *i* vowel by the Greeks, who had no *y* consonant. In the Latin alphabet, on the other hand, it was used with both values, viz. that of *i* vowel (long and short), and *y* consonant, as in *ibidem, ibis; iacui, Iupiter, Iouis*. Even when the consonant passed in Romanic from the sound of Y to that of 'G soft' (Italian *gi-*, Eng. and OF. *j*), and subsequently, in some languages, to other sounds, it continued for many centuries to be expressed by the same letter as the vowel I, with which it had no longer phonetic relations. At length, after 1600 (in England chiefly 1630-1640), a differentiation was made, the consonant being expressed by the character J j, in its origin merely a variant form of I i, used in certain positions; for the history of which see the next letter J. The result is that, in the modern development of the Roman alphabet, the ninth letter has been split into two, I and J; and I remains only a vowel.

The original value of the Græco-Roman Ӏ vowel when long was that of the 'high-front-narrow' vowel of Bell's scale, which the letter still has in all the continental languages, and in some English words thence adopted, as *Louisa*, *machine*, *clique*, *casino*, a sound which in native English words is now normally represented by *ē*, *ee*, in *be, see, mete, meet*. The short *i* was doubtless originally the true 'short' of the same sound, the 'narrow' *i* in French *fini*, Italian *fortissimo*; but, in Teutonic, the short vowel represented by *i* has probably always been the corresponding 'wide' vowel (ɪ), as in English *finny, missing*. Thus, our current sound of short *i* in *him, it, has*, has, apparently, come down unchanged from OE. times. Long *ī*, on the other hand, has undergone a great change, having about the beginning of the modern period changed into a diphthong with *i* as its second element. This evidently arose from the practice of beginning the utterance of the long vowel before the vocal organs had quite attained the very close position of long (iː), so that the sound began with an opener and less definite vowel quality, which tended in use to become more and more distinct from the second element. The exact quality of the first element at present is difficult to fix: it varies greatly in different localities and in different individuals. 'We have symbolized the diphthong by (əi), taking the first element as the "mid-mixed-wide" vowel of Melville Bell's scale, the general "obscure vowel" of English; but some phoneticists take it as the "mid-back" or the "low-mixed" vowel, wide or narrow; and it may be heard locally as the "mid-front" and "low-front" wide or narrow.' (*N.E.D.*) This diphthongization of original long *ī* is not peculiar to English, but has taken place also in German and Dutch. The difference is that in English the old simple vowel symbol is retained for the new diphthong, while in German and Dutch this is expressed by the new diphthongal symbols *ei* and *ij* (formerly *y*): cf. OE., OHG., OLG. *mín* with Eng. *mine*, Ger. *mein*, Du. *mijn*, formerly *myn*.

In addition to the two normal modern English values (ɪ) and (ai), the letter *i* has others, due either to the disturbing influence of a following *r*, to the retention by foreign words of their foreign sounds, or to the obscuring effect of absence of stress in certain positions. The sounds that occur in stressed syllables are the following:

1. ɪ in h*i*t (hɪt).   4. ɜː in f*i*r (fɜː).
2. aɪ in *i*ce (aɪs).   5. iː in p*i*que (piːk).
3. aɪə in h*i*re (haɪə(r)).   6. ɪə in em*i*r (ɛˈmɪə(r)).

All these may occur also in unstressed syllables.

The combination *ie* has the value of No. 2 in *die, dies, died*, etc.; of Nos. 5 and 6 in *field, chief, grieve, pier*, grenad*ier*, etc.; exceptionally that of (ɛ) in fr*ie*nd, (ɪ) in s*ie*ve. Finally, and unstressed, it has that of simple (ɪ), as in a*e*r*ie*, cit*ie*s, pit*ie*d.

The combinations *ai, ei, oi* represent diphthongs in Is*ai*ah (aiˈzaiə), *ai*sle (ail), *ei*der (aidə(r)), *oi*l (ɔil), etc.; but *ai, ei* merely represent (ei), (ɛə), (iː) or (ɪə) in a*i*m (eim), a*i*r (ɛə(r)), r*ei*n (rein), f*ei*nt, h*ei*r (ɛə(r)), receive, receipt, Leith (liːθ), weir (wɪə(r)), etc.

Before another vowel in the suffixes *-ian, -ier, -ion, -ious*, etc., *i* has often the consonantal value of (j), or a value which readily passes into it: e.g. Chr*i*stian, cloth*i*er, court*i*er, mill*i*on, un*i*on, cop*i*ous, prev*i*ous; after certain consonants, this (j) value is merged in the consonant, which it palatalizes, as in spac*i*ous (ˈspeiʃəs), nat*i*on (ˈneiʃən), sold*i*er (ˈsəuldʒə(r)), fus*i*on (ˈfjuːʒən), Pers*i*a (pɜːʃə), hos*i*er (həuʒə(r)), fash*i*on (ˈfæʃən).

The minuscule or 'small letter' i is now surmounted by a dot. This is no original part of the letter, but is derived from a diacritic mark, like an acute accent, used to particularize the ɪ in positions in which it might have been taken merely for the stroke of another letter. It appears to have begun in Latin MSS. about the 11th c. with the *ii* in such words as *ingenii*, and to have been thence extended to *i* in contiguity with *m, n*, or *u*, and finally to have been used with *i* in all positions. The accent form of the mark, seen in Caxton's type and in modern German, was in 15th c. handwriting often developed into a long curved flourish; but in books printed in Roman type it was reduced to the round dot now in use. In chirography, the dot still largely serves its original purpose of indicating the *i*; hence the phrase *to dot the i's*.

The same cause that led to the dotting of *i* contributed largely to the formation of *j*, originally merely a lengthened or tailed i used finally as a more distinctive form, especially when two *i*'s came together, as in *ingenij*, or in the numerals ij, iij, viij, etc.; also to the substitution of *y* for *i*, especially in contiguity with *m, n, u*, etc., or when final. In English it became at length a kind of scribal canon that *i* must not be used as a final letter, but must in this position be changed to *y*; but in inflected forms, where the *i* was not final, it was retained; hence our current spellings, *city, cities; holy, holier, holiest; carry, carries, carried, carrier; weary, wearisome*, etc. In modern English no native word ends in *i*; in alien or adopted words so ending, the *i* is usually pronounced (ai) in *cirri, foci, magi*, and other Latin plurals, also in *Rabbi, Rabboni, Eli, Levi*, and other Hebrew names, but as (ɪ) in *Cadi, kohlrabi, Mahdi*, and other foreign words of recent adoption.

I. 1. Illustrations of the literary use of the letter: **a.** simply. (The plural appears as *Is, I's, is, i's*.) *I per se*, or *I per se I*, the letter *I* by itself forming a word, esp. the pronoun *I*. Also *fig.* esp. in *dot of* (on) *an* i, *to put the dots on the* i's, *to dot the* (one's) i's: see DOT *sb.*[1] 5 b, *v.*[1] 1 b.

c 1000 ÆLFRIC *Gram.* iii, Of þam [stafum] syndon fif vocales, þæt synd clypjendlice: *a, e, i, o, u. Ibid.*, Gyf þu cwyst nu *iudex*, ponne byð se *i* consonans. *c* 1450 *Poem agst. Friars* i. (*Rel. Antiq.* I. 322) With an I. and an O. thai praysen not Seynt Poule. *Ibid.* ii, With an O. and an I. men weven that thai wede. *c* 1532 DU WES *Introd. Fr.* (in Palsgr. 899), Ye shal pronounce . . your *i*, as sharpe as can be. 1552 HULOET Q iv, I Letter is as wel a consonante as a vowell. 1622 MABBE tr. *Aleman's Guzman* II. III. ii. II. 226, I only was compleat; I was *I per se I*; I was like a Rule, without exception. 1669 W. HOLDER *Elem. Speech* 95 Our vulgar (*i*) as in (*stile*) seems to be . . a Diphthong . . composed of *o* or *e, i*, and not a simple Original Vowel. 1711 J. GREENWOOD *Eng. Gram.* 240 No English Word ends in I, but has always an E after it, as *easie* . . tho' now *ie* is frequently changed into *y*. 1727-41 CHAMBERS *Cycl.* s.v., That verse in Virgil, *Accipiunt inimicum imbrem, rimisque fatiscunt*; which abounds in *i*'s. 1890 J. H. STIRLING *Gifford Lect.* xvi. 317 It is but a logical breathing: a logical dot on a logical *i*. 1892 BOWEN in *Law Rep.* 2 Ch. Div. 486 He must . . have full notice. But there is no regulation as to what t's are to be crossed or what i's are to be dotted in the notice to be given.

b. Representing Gr. *ὶῶτα*, IOTA: see JOT.

c 975 *Rushw. Gosp.* Matt. v. 18 Oþþæt ʒeleoreþ heofun and eorþe, an i [Vulg. *iota unum*] eþþa an holstæfes in ʒelioreþ from æ. *c* 1000 *Ags. Gosp. Ibid.*, in oððe an prica.

2. Comb. a. i-dot, the dot of an *i*; I-bar, I-beam, I-iron, I-rail, an iron bar, rail, etc., the section of which is like the letter I.

1875 KNIGHT *Dict. Mech.* s.v. *Angle-iron*, Other forms are known as Z-iron, I-iron, etc. *Ibid.* 1195, *I-rail*, a double-headed rail with flanges on each side above and below; on the foot and tread. 1890 GORDON *Foundry* 69 A ceaseless hoisting and swinging and lowering of angle-bar, I-bar, Z-bar, or other bar gliding into its appointed place. 1897 P. WARUNG *Tales Old Regime* 23 They were identical to . . the position of an i-dot.

b. i-mutation, i-umlaut (also *i/j-mutation*, etc.) *Philology*, the fronting influence of an **i* or **j* on the vowel of a preceding syllable in one and the same word; also, the result of this. So **i-mutated, i-umlauted** ppl. adjs.

1870 F. A. MARCH *Compar. Gram. Anglo-Saxon Lang.* 13 i-umlaut of *ō: fōt, fêt(e)*. 1891 A. L. MAYHEW *Synopsis Old Eng. Phonol.* 41 In North. and Mercian *oe = e*, the *i*-umlaut of *o*. 1906 H. C. WYLD *Hist. Study Mother Tongue* i. 10 This particular kind of change, known as *i*-mutation, occurs in hundreds of words in O.E., though, as a rule, the *i* or *j* which caused the fronting, disappeared. 1908 J. & E. M. WRIGHT *Old Eng. Gram.* iii. 28, *a* was the only vowel which underwent *i*-umlaut in OS. and OHG. 1927 *Englische Studien* 10 Nov. 81 There was, by the side of OE. *sceat* . . an i-mutated variant *sciete* or *scyte* with the same sense. 1927 E. V. GORDON *Introd. Old Norse* 246, ø₂ was the *w*-mutation of *ę* or (rarely) a late *i*-mutation of *o*. 1945 S. EINARSSON *Icelandic* I. v. 30 The I-Shift (. . *i*-umlaut, i-mutation) is so called because it was caused by an *i* or a *j*— now often lost —in the ending of a word. 1953 L. F. BROSNAHAN *Some Old Eng. Sound Changes* 63 The phenomenon of *i*- or *j*-mutation.

II. 3. Used, like other letters of the alphabet, to denote serial order; marking, e.g. the ninth sheet of a book, or quire of a MS., etc.

4. In *Logic*, the symbol of a particular affirmative.

1552 T. WILSON *Logike* 54 b, A dooeth affirme: E dooeth deny, whiche are bothe vniuersall: I dooth affirme, O dooth deny, whiche we particular call. 1620 T. GRANGER *Div. Log.* 262 The Vowels . . signifie the qualities, and quantities of the premisses. A. An vniuersall affirmative. E. An vniuersall negative. I. A particular affirmative. O. A particular negative. 1866 FOWLER *Deduct. Logic* (1869) 14 If I be false; A is false, E true, O true.

5. The Roman numeral symbol for One.

This was not originally the letter, but a single line denoting unity. It is repeated for the units up to 3 (II, III), formerly, as still on a dial-plate, to 4 (IIII). These are added to symbols of higher numbers, as VI = 6, XII = 12, XXIII = 23, LI = 51, CII = 102, etc. Prefixed to V and X, it diminishes them by 1: IV = 4, IX = 9. In ME. MSS. and early printed books these symbols are very frequent instead of the corresponding words, being usually written with a point before and after, thus, 'he hadde .IIII. c. knyghtes'.) 1450 W. SOMNER in *Four C. Eng. Lett.* 4 He, with ij or iij of his men. 1727-41 CHAMBERS *Cycl.* s.v., I, in the ordinary Roman way of numbering, signifies one; and when repeated, signifies as many units as it is repeated times.

6. Math. In Higher Algebra, *i* or *ι* is often used for the imaginary quantity $\sqrt{-1}$, square root of minus one. In Quaternions, *i, j, k* are symbols of vectors, as distinguished from scalars.

7. a. In *Physics I* (rarely *i*) is the symbol of the quantum number of nuclear spin. [Adopted by Back and Goudsmit 1928, in *Zeitschr. f. Physik* XLVII. 175.]

1930 PAULING & GOUDSMIT *Struct. Line Spectra* xi. 203, i is a new quantum number, the nuclear spin quantum number. 1932 BACHER & GOUDSMIT *Atomic Energy States* 20 The spectrum of bismuth, for which the nuclear moment I is $4\frac{1}{2}$, is an interesting example of this type of hyperfine structure. 1966 D. H. WHIFFEN *Spectroscopy* iii. 22 Intrinsic nuclear angular momenta are quantised and may be expressed as $I\hbar$ where I . . is called the spin quantum number. 1967 [see F III. 1 k].

b. Occas. used as the symbol of the quantum number of isospin (more commonly T).

1953 *Progress Theoret. Physics* IX. 420 In general, selection rules are intimately connected with the conservative quantities which we shall inquire for a system involving Fermions. Those are the total angular momentum J and the total isotopic spin I of the system. 1962 A. RAMAKRISHNAN *Elem. Particles & Cosmic Rays* i. 31 We use the symbol *t* for the isotopic spin operator of a system of particles and *τ* for a single particle, their eigenvalues being denoted by T and I respectively.

III. Abbreviations. (Abbreviations cited here with full stops are frequently used without them.) I. = various proper names, as Isaac, Isabella, India, etc.; formerly also = Jesus; I (*Zool.*) in dental formulæ = incisor; I., Intelligence (see also I.Q. below); I (*Chem.*) = Iodine; †i. the earlier equivalent of *i.e.* = *id est*; I.A.A., indoleacetic acid (indolylacetic acid); I.A.E.A., International Atomic Energy Agency; I.A.T.A., International Air Traffic (or Transport) Association; I.B.A., Independent Broadcasting Authority; I.B.M., (*a*) intercontinental ballistic missile; (*b*) International Business Machines (used to denote the computers made by this firm); I.C., (*a*) in charge, in command; (*b*) integrated circuit; (*c*) (*Linguistics*) immediate constituent; I.C.A., Institute of Contemporary Arts; I.C.A.O., International Civil Aviation Organization; I.C.B.M., intercontinental ballistic missile; I.C.E., internal combustion

engine; **I.C.F.T.U.**, International Confederation of Free Trade Unions; **I.C.I.**, Imperial Chemical Industries; **I.C.S.**, Indian Civil Service; **I.D.**, identification, identity (card); **I.D.A.**, International Development Association; **I.D.B.**, illicit diamond buyer, buying; **I.E.**, Indo-European; **i.e.**, *id est* (L.), that is (to say); **I.F.**, **i.f.**, intermediate frequency (see INTERMEDIATE *a.* and *sb.* A. 3); **I.F.F.**, Identification, Friend or Foe; **I.F.R.**, Instrument Flight Rules; **I.G.Y.**, International Geophysical Year; **i.h.p.** (*Mech.*) = indicated horse power; **I.L.O.**, International Labour Organization; **I.L.P.**, Independent Labour Party; **I.L.S.**, Instrument Landing System; **I.M.C.O.**, Intergovernmental Maritime Consultative Organization; **I.M.F.**, International Monetary Fund; **I/O** (*Computing*), input/output; **I.P.A.**, International Phonetic Alphabet (or Association); **i.p.s.**, inches per second; **I.Q.**, intelligence quotient (see INTELLIGENCE *sb.* 8); **I.R.**, infra-red; **I.R.A.**, (*a*) individual retirement account (*U.S.*); (*b*) Irish Republican Army; **I.R.B.M.**, intermediate range ballistic missile; **I.R.O.**, International Refugee Organization; **I.R.S.**, Internal Revenue Service (*U.S.*); **ISBN**, International Standard Book Number; cf. *SBN* s.v. S 4 a; **I.S.O.**, (*a*) Imperial Service Order; (*b*) International Organization for Standardization; **IT**, information technology; **I.T.A.**, Independent Television Authority; **I.T.A.**, **i.t.a.**, initial teaching alphabet; **I.T.U.**, International Telecommunication Union; **I.T.V.**, Independent Television; **I.U.**, **i.u.**, international unit; **I.U.(C.)D.**, intrauterine (contraceptive) device; **I.V.**, **i.v.**, intravenous(ly); also as *sb.*, an intravenous drip, injection, etc.; **I.W.W.**, Industrial Worker(s) of the World. See also IHS and IOU in their alphabetical places.

c **1265** *Voc. N. Plants* in Wr.-Wülcker 554/3 *Artimesie*, *i. mugwrt, *i.* merherbarum. **1641** FRENCH *Distillation* (1651) i. 40 Then invert it (*i*) turn it upside down. **1727–41** CHAMBERS *Cycl.* s.v., In abbreviatures and ciphers **I* frequently represents the whole word Jesus. **1917** 'CONTACT' *Airman's Outings* iv. 87 An air reconnaissance is essentially the observer's show; its main object being to supply the '*I' people at headquarters with private bulletins from the back of the German front. **1925** FRASER & GIBBONS *Soldier & Sailor Words* 125, *I*, the Service abbreviation for 'Intelligence', *i.e.* information of military value. **1972** G. LYALL *Blame the Dead* xiii. 86 'What were you in?' '"I" Corps.' **1947** *Jrnl. Biol. Chem.* CLXIX. 465 Indoleacetic acid (*IAA) tends to stimulate growth in the light. **1969** *New Scientist* 7 Aug. 272/1 Isolated bacteria were cultured and shown to form IAA from the amino acid tryptophan. **1958** *Times* 20 Jan. 6/4 Mr. Robert McKinney, United States member of the *I.A.E.A. board of governors. *Ibid.*, The United States last year already declared its intention to match all contributions of materials to the I.A.E.A. made by other countries up to June, 1960. **1958** P. NOEL-BAKER *Arms Race* p. xvii, IAEA, International Atomic Energy Agency (established in Vienna, October 1957). **1963** *Times* 28 Sept. 6/7 Sir Roger Makins, chairman of the British Atomic Energy Authority and chief delegate to I.A.E.A. **1931** *Flight* 20 Mar. 255/1, I..submitted therefore to the International Air Traffic Association, *IATA, a suggestion for organising, at the earliest possible moment, a general European air mail net. **1962** *Daily Tel.* 11 Sept. 12/3 The continuance of rate-cutting could not be tolerated if IATA was to continue its work. **1970** *Internat. & Compar. Law Q.* 4th Ser. XIX. I. 125 It is something of a surprise that the United States Government and the International Air Transport Association (IATA)..should be proposing a system of absolute liability. **1971** *Guardian* 12 Nov. 1/8 The Sound Broadcasting Bill..authorises the new stations under the control of the Independent Television Authority—renamed the Independent Broadcasting Authority... The *IBA could be advanced up to £2 millions to set up the services. **1971** *Times* 12 Nov. 8/5 The IBA would have the same obligation in radio to devote sufficient time to accurate and impartial news. **1954** *I.B.M. [see BALLISTIC *a.* d]. **1955** *Ann. Reg. 1954* 402 Reports from the United States referred to a rocket called I.B.M. (intercontinental ballistic missile), a wingless rocket-shaped device already perfected to travel 2,500 miles and expected to have a range of 5,000 miles in due course. **1955** R. J. SCHWARTZ *Compl. Dict. Abbrev.* 89 *I.B.M.*, International Business Machines. **1956** S. BELLOW *Seize the Day* (1957) ii. 42 When he saw the two sums punched out so neatly on the cards he cursed the company and its IBM equipment. **1956** A. HUXLEY *Adonis & Alphabet* 109 Thanks to finger-printing, punched cards and IBM machines, they know practically everything about practically everyone. **1963** I. FLEMING *On H.M. Secret Service* i. 16 Bond's mind ticked and whirred, selecting cards like an IBM machine. **1970** *Amer. Jrnl. Physics* XXXVIII. 1294/2 Computations on the *j*th particle velocity ..have been carried out on the Oberlin College IBM 360/44. **1928** T. E. LAWRENCE *Let.* 19 July (1938) IV. 615 No, I am not adjutant, to this camp. Just typist, and *i/c files, and duty rolls. **1958** *Spectator* 15 Aug. 219/1 If you were i/c security, it was obviously necessary to flush the lavatories of spies. **1962** L. DEIGHTON *Ipcress File* viii. 51 The above named article of War Department property.. should be returned to officer i.c. special issue room. **1965** *Listener* 11 Nov. 763/2 The commanding officer; the 2 I.C.; the adjutant. **1947** R. S. WELLS in *Language* XXIII. ii. 81 We aim in this paper to replace by a unified, systematic theory the heterogeneous and incomplete methods hitherto offered for determining immediate constituents (hereafter abbreviated *IC, plural ICs). **1953** *Language* XXIX. 88 Shannon has conducted experiments in ordinary English orthography, and the reviewer has conducted similar ones, with the proper audiences, in terms of phonemic notation, the results of which bear on the stated correlation between IC-analysis and information theory. **1962** B. M. H. STRANG *Mod. Eng. Struct.* vi. 79 They are immediate constituents (ICs), i.e. the forms that directly go to make up that which is under analysis. They themselves have ICs. **1965** *Canad. Jrnl. Ling.* Fall 45 Chomsky develops..IC analysis by his grammatical model of 'phrase structure + transforms'. **1971** D. CRYSTAL *Linguistics* iv. 212 In IC analysis, however, such disambiguation was impossible. **1966** *Electronics* 17 Oct. 87 The major problems in using *IC's. **1969** *New Scientist* 18 Dec. 601/3 The IC memory is three times faster than the conventional memory. **1970** 'J. EARL' *Tuners & Amplifiers* ii. 28 In a few years' time the majority of radio tuners will carry ICs as well as a few transistors and junction diodes. **1958** *Listener* 20 Nov. 842/1 At the *I.C.A. there is an exhibition of three collagists. **1969** *Ibid.* 27 Mar. 436/3 The ICA has taken us aback by giving some public performances of a radio work, reproducing it stereophonically in a darkened theatre. **1947** *Times* 17 May 3/5 (*headline*) Italy nominated for *I.C.A.O. **1955** *Sci. Amer.* Jan. 94/3 The specialized agencies of the United Nations..ICAO (International Civil Aviation Organization). **1963** *Thorn Electr. Industr. Group Profile* 25 The system has been approved..by the ICAO. **1955** *Newsweek* 30 May 13 The Air Force is now calling the Intercontinental Ballistic Missile the Italy nominated for *ICBM. **1956** *Spaceflight* Oct. 24/1 The relatively small margin in performance between the I.C.B.M. and a satellite vehicle suggests that great use will be made of it in the future. **1965** I. FLEMING *Man with Golden Gun* ii. 28 Their U-boat fleet and their ICBMs. **1950** *Chambers's Encycl.* XV. 586/2 *I.C.E.: *see* Internal Combustion Engine. **1958** *Listener* 20 Nov. 835/2 The present advanced state of the internal combustion engine, or 'I.C.E.' as my log-book calls it. **1968** *Economist* 25 May 45/3 But now a modern version of the steam engine has appeared as the major threat to the ICE. **1955** *Times* 30 May 4/4 First, the *I.C.F.T.U. will continue its fight to ensure that all workers' rights are respected. **1968** *Telegraph* (Brisbane) 18 Apr. 10/2 Mr Mick Jordan..represents the International Confederation of Free Trade Unions (ICFTU)—a world-wide anti-Communist union body. **1934** H. G. WELLS *Exper. Autobiogr.* II. viii. 638 Brunner Mond & Co. was only the embryo of *I.C.I. **1964** M. GOWING *Britain & Atomic Energy 1939–1945* ii. 75 I.C.I. offered to take over..the Halban and Kowarski research. **1931** *Times Lit. Suppl.* 14 May 390/3 The late Ross Scott, *I.C.S. **1957** J. MASTERS *Far, Far the Mountain Peak* iii. 27 If Peter has really made up his mind to go to the I.C.S.—it will be wonderful. **1971** *Shankar's Weekly* (Delhi) 18 Apr. 22/4 The Prime Minister called the ICS Secretaries of the Central Departments some weeks ago and admonished them. **1955** R. J. SCHWARTZ *Compl. Dict. Abbrev.* 90 **Id*, identification. **1963** T. PYNCHON *V.* xiii. 373 Pig was understandably nervous, trying simultaneously to salute, produce ID and liberty cards. **1965** *New Statesman* 3 Dec. 880/3 'ID's'..are pretty obscure to English readers as translations..of..*papiers* (identity documents). **1968** A. DIMENT *Bang Bang Birds* v. 75, I had the usual range of forged driver's licences, ID cards, credit chits. **1970** *Globe & Mail* (Toronto) 28 Sept. 7/1 Once inside I was forced to produce my driver's licence, draft card, student I.D. **1971** *Leader* (Durban) 7 May 1/1 The loss of the money was not important. I am more concerned about my ID card, as I am presently applying for a house in Unit 10. **1972** J. BALL *Five Pieces Jade* ii. 21 Tibbs was politely asked for his ID. He produced his police credentials. **1961** *Ann. Reg. 1960* 472 The major development among international agencies was the establishment of the International Development Association (*I.D.A.). **1965** *Economist* 26 June 1512/2 The World Bank's 'soft-loan' subsidiary, the International Development Association (IDA), already lends for up to fifty years. **1884** M. A. CAREY-HOBSON *At Home in Transvaal* II. xlii. 520 'The fellow had money there, with which he turned *I.D.B.' 'What's that?'..'Illicit diamond buyer.' **1886** W. M. KERR *Far Interior* I. i. 15 In spite of the vigilance of the detective department a great deal of illicit diamond buying is successfully carried on; hence the well-known 'IDB', which refers to the illegal trade. **1909** H. G. WELLS *Tono-Bungay* II. i. 122 Barmentrude..used to be an I.D.B.—an illicit diamond buyer. **1917** *New Statesman* 17 Nov. 150/1 To represent the typical Bolshevik as a German agent..is just as clever and fair as to try to make out that an I.D.B. from the Rand..is the type of a British Imperialist. **1972** P. DRISCOLL *Wilby Conspiracy* (1973) xiii. 163 He does a bit of IDB on the side. So what? He's a jeweller. **1662** STILLINGFL. *Orig. Sacr.* I. iii. §3. 45 He dwelt in Pethor by the river, *i.e. saith the Chaldee Paraphrast, in Peor of Syria by Euphrates. **1875** JOWETT *Plato* (ed. 2) III. 26 Under favourable conditions, i.e. in the perfect State. **1894** V. HENRY *Compar. Gram. Eng. & Ger.* v. 113 The greater part of such roots as began with the group in question exhibited already in the *I.-E. period a peculiar alternation. **1964** R. H. ROBINS *Gen. Ling.* viii. 307 The I-E language family is represented all over the world today. **1927** H. J. ROUND *Shielded Four-Electrode Valve* viii. 77 It should be possible to do with only one stage of intermediate frequency on account of the gain per stage in H.F. and *I.F. **1956** TIBBS & JOHNSTONE *Frequency Modulation Engin.* (ed. 2) ix. 387 Second channel interference can be avoided by choosing the i.f. to be greater than half the band of frequencies to be covered. **1963** J. A. WALSTON *Transistor Circuit Design* xxiii. 321 The difference frequency (IF frequency)..must be such that the transistor will function as an amplifier. **1945** *Electronic Engin.* XVII. 686 An *I.F.F. unit can be briefly described as being a transmitter-receiver device installed in friendly aircraft whose purpose is to reply to the interrogation of the friendly Radar station. **1961** *Listener* 30 Nov. 909/1 The I.F.F. radar identification sets in our bombers. **1948** *Jrnl. R. Aeronaut. Soc.* LII. 90/1 The biggest factor affecting reliable running is the time difference between operations under clear and low visibility conditions, C.F.R. (Contact Flight Rules) and *I.F.R. (Instrument Flight Rules) as they are called. **1964** *Times Rev. Industry* Apr. 40/3 Under IFR, electronic navigation equipment defines the position, and facilitates landing in bad weather or at night. **1955** *Sci. News Let.* 15 Jan. 42/1 Scientists from at least 39 countries, including Russia, are now making plans for coordinated research efforts during 1957–58 in a world-wide investigation of the earth, its seas and air. The many-pronged attack, aimed at a better understanding of the planet we live on, is known as the International Geophysical Year, or *IGY. **1964** *Economist* 11 Jan. 128/3 The IGY lasted 30 months. **1894** *Times* 20 Sept. 4/6 With an expenditure of 110 *i.h.p. **1924** B. WEBB *Diary* 8 Jan. (1956) I. 2 The P.M. to meet Thomas, the French head of the *I.L.O. at Geneva. **1969** *Listener* 1 May 614/3 We're going to give legislative backing to the ILO conventions on the right to join trade unions. **1893** G. B. SHAW *Let.* 24 Apr. (1965) 390 My remarks..were not levelled at the *I.L.P. **1917** A. HUXLEY *Let.* 12 Nov. (1969) 136, I suppose it would pain the poor Duke too much if he sat in Parliament as a member of the I.L.P. **1932** AUDEN *Orators* III. 104 The Simonites, the Mosleyites and the I.L.P. **1946** KOESTLER *Thieves in Night* ii. 91 Max, who has an enormous, sniffing tapir-nose and an unkempt I.L.P.-mane. **1959** *Listener* 22 Jan. 179/3 A number of intellectuals and I.L.P-ers. **1947** *Shell Aviation News* No. 108. 3/1 *I.L.S. (Instrument Landing System), G.C.A. (Ground Control Approach), ground radar and flight radar are all proven, available, and should be installed. **1966** *New Scientist* 13 Jan. 65/1 The special Trident has been trying the ILS of other airports,..and has actually made 'hands-off' landings at them. **1954** *Chambers's Encycl. World Survey* 42/2 The Intergovernmental Maritime Consultative Organization (*IMCO). **1970** *Globe & Mail* (Toronto) 28 Sept. 6/2 After the Torrey Canyon disaster the Intergovernmental Maritime Consultative Organization (IMCO) turned to the machinery of the international convention on safety of life at sea to try to establish rules that would ease the threat of pollution. **1948** G. CROWTHER *Outl. Money* (rev. ed.) ix. 330 The main purpose of the *I.M.F... is to provide countries that have deficits with the foreign currencies they require to cover those deficits. **1965** *New Statesman* 23 Apr. 632/2 A determination to invoke the scarce currency clause in the IMF agreement to legalise discrimination against chronically surplus countries. **1964** *CIS Gloss. Automated Typesetting* 19 *Input-output* (**I/O*), a general term for the equipment used to communicate with a computer and the data involved in the communication. **1977** *McGraw-Hill Yearbk. Sci. & Technol.* 42 The disparity in the speed of electromechanical I/O and electronic components resulted in ineffective use of the more expensive resources. **1985** *Personal Computer World* Feb. 163/1 It also includes 'I/O redirection' and 'pipes'. **1933** L. BLOOMFIELD *Lang.* vi. 103 There has arisen a convention of transcribing British English, not by the symbols..in accord with the principles of the *IPA alphabet. **1954** PEI & GAYNOR *Dict. Ling.* 105 *I.P.A.*, The International Phonetic Alphabet. **1961** *Amer. Speech* XXXVI. 201 The modified IPA symbols used in the [linguistic] Atlas. **1970** *Publ. Amer. Dial. Soc. 1968* L. 5 The phonetic notation used in transcribing the responses of the informants is..a finely graded phonetic alphabet based on that of the IPA. **1959** W. S. SHARPS *Dict. Cinematogr.* 104/2 **I.P.S.*, abbreviation for inches per second. **1968** *Times* 29 Nov. p. ii/1 The rise of the tape recorder was attested by the publication of commercial tapes at 7½ i.p.s. **1922** R. S. WOODWORTH *Psychol.* xii. 274 Brightness or dullness can also be measured by the intelligence quotient, which is employed so frequently that it is customarily abbreviated to '*I.Q.' **1948** A. HUXLEY *Let.* 3 June (1969) 582 Cecil Burt sees a drop in the average intelligence of the British population..of 5 IQ points before the end of the present century. **1959** N. MAILER *Advts. for Myself* (1961) 150 Any man in the infantry or cavalry who has a good I.Q. is sure to have his name turned up.. whenever a new typist is needed. **1968** *Scottish Daily Mail* 16 July 2/1 The questionnaire is a tongue-in-cheek parody of the IQ tests which the U.S. Government gives would-be employees. **1972** *Science* 20 Oct. 232/2 The IQ tests ignore much in us that is artistic, contemplative, and nonverbal. **1957** *Which?* Autumn 7/2 An investigation into the effects, on bottle-makers, of the infra-red and ultra-violet (often referred to as *I.R. and U.V.) radiations. **1967** *Electronics* XL. 127/1 A scope tracing that shows i-r energy as a curve derived from the video signal, with the amount of energy determining vertical deflection. **1921** G. B. SHAW *Matter with Ireland* (1962) 245 The *I.R.A. is flushed with success. **1932** *Morning Post* 23 Aug. 10/3 A force of 200 men of the I.R.A. have seized Donamon Castle. **1939** J. B. PRIESTLEY *Let People Sing* ii. 24 So they thought he was the I.R.A., eh? That explained the bomb, of course. **1959** *New Statesman* 7 Nov. 615/2 The IRA is now really discredited; young men in the dreary pubs which offer the only way out of the drearier provincial towns of Ireland must find other amusements than plotting. **1971** *Guardian* 11 Aug. 10/2 The IRA and the Provisionals use the South as a sanctuary. **1974** *Forbes* (N.Y.) 15 Nov. 139/1 Moneymen call these new pension plans *IRAs (individual retirement accounts). **1984** *Sun* (Gainsville, Florida) 3 Apr. 6B/3 It's been just two years since nearly everybody was invited to open an individual retirement account (IRA), but it's time to assess..how skillfully you're exploiting this tax shelter. **1957** *Economist* 30 Nov. 774/2 *IRBMs are to begin flowing to Europe by late 1958. **1960** *Ibid.* 30 July 460/3 In April the official defence policy was laid in ruins with the abandonment of Britain's IRBM, Blue Streak. **1947** *Times* 15 May 5/7 Resettlement will still remain one of the main features of the *I.R.O. **1948** *Hansard Commons* 11 Mar. 1531/1 I.R.O. consented to act as our agents. **1955** *Sci. Amer.* Jan. 95/1 IRO (International Refugee Organization). **1963** *Listener* 7 Mar. 412/1 The *I.R.S. takes good care that the United States citizen abroad knows just where he stands, taxwise. **1964** *Financial Times* 12 Mar. 24/3 The attitude of the I.R.S. in 1958, after they had caught up with Mr. Wilson, was to say: 'We're not concerned with your troubles.' **1972** *New York Law Jrnl.* 22 Aug. 4/4 (*heading*) IRS issues rulings on political dinners. **1969** *Proc. Internat. Assoc. Technol. Univ. Libraries* Dec. 51 Every book is labelled by an *ISBN and each edition, each binding..allotted its own ISBN. **1986** *Bookseller* 3 May 1776 (Advt.), Where to Fish..£11.95 net ..Printed case. ISBN 0-948807-00-8. Heavily illustrated. **1902** *Encycl. Brit.* XXXI. 340/1 The members of the order have the distinction of adding the letters *I.S.O. after their names. **1909** *Whitaker's Almanack* 118 Thos. H. Sanderson Sanderson, G.C.B., K.C.M.G., I.S.O. **1947** *N.Y. Times* 2 Nov. 22/6 Howard Coonley..has been elected president of the new International Organization for Standardization, formation of which has been completed by delegates from twenty-five nations meeting in London... Gustave L. Gerard..has been chosen vice president of the new organization which will be known informally as *ISO. **1969** *Jane's Freight Containers 1968–69* 400/1 The equipment

covered by this plan is standard ISO 20 ft steel containers with fork-lift pockets, and standard 40 ft ISO aluminium containers. **1982** *Times* 14 Jan. (Information Technol. Suppl.) p. iv/6 Teletext and personal computers are *IT, but Hollywood movies on a video machine are probably not. **1983** *Listener* 21 Apr. 38/1 IT includes banking and shopping via your television set. **1955** *Ann. Reg. 1954* 385 While viewing through *I.T.A. stations would not be possible for some time, competitive bidding for 'stars' went on actively. **1962** *Rep. Comm. Broadcasting 1960* 1 in *Parl. Papers 1961–2* (Cmnd. 1753) IX. 259 There is a distinction to be drawn.. between the ITA and independent television (ITV). The ITA is the Authority, the public corporation set up by the Television Act, 1954: independent television comprises not only the ITA but also the programme companies. **1965** *Guardian* 2 Feb. 3/8 Mr Gordon Walker .., adviser to the *ITA foundation,.. would have to learn more about the initial teaching alphabet. **1967** *New Statesman* 6 Oct., All the mothers know everything about O- and A-levels, have taken the measure of the 11-plus.., and some have heard of i.t.a. **1950** *Chambers's Encycl.* XI. 470/1 The International Telecommunations Union (*I.T.U.). **1962** *B.B.C. Handbk.* 113 The BBC also participates in the work of the International Telecommunication Union (ITU), a specialized agency of the United Nations with its headquarters in Geneva. **1958** 'A. Gilbert' *Death against Clock* 93 All they talk about is what they saw on *ITV last night. **1958** *Spectator* 27 June 827/3 As the General Election approaches, both BBC and ITV must know where they stand. **1969** *Listener* 24 Apr. 559/3 While shepherds washed their socks by night And turned on ITV, The Angel of the Lord came down And switched on BBC. **1950** *Chambers's Encycl.* XIV. 347/2 The League of Nations standard or requirement for vitamin B_1 is 300 *I.U. per day. **1951** *Good Housek. Home Encycl.* 339/1 The chief food value of apricots lies in their roughage and in their vitamin A content—approximately 1,000 i.u. per serving. **1962** *Lancet* 6 Jan. 12/1 A small bottle.. of some 60 ml. capacity, filled to the top with normal saline and containing 1000 I.U. of heparin. **1963** *New Scientist* 19 Dec. 716/3 A simple, cheap, safe and effective method of birth control.. known as IUCDs (intrauterine contraceptive devices). **1966** *New Statesman* 18 Mar. 370/1 The IUCD consists of a small loop or coil of plastic material which is inserted into the uterus. **1965** *New Scientist* 27 May 606/3 When as occasionally happens, conception occurs and gestation proceeds with the *IUD *in situ*, [etc.]. **1967** *Time* 7 Apr. 73 The IUD's underlying principle traces back to an old practice of Arab cameleers: putting a round, smooth stone in the womb of a female camel at the start of a long trade journey, to avoid the economic loss of having the animal get pregnant. **1973** *Guardian* 29 June 13/3 With the nationalisation of birth control virtually every GP in the country will be inserting IUDs. **1951** *Dorland's Med. Dict.* (ed. 22) 766/2 **I.V.*, abbreviation for intravenously (by intravenous injection). **1961** *Amer. Speech* XXXVI. 145 *I.V.*,.. an intravenous infusion. **1970** *New Yorker* 21 Nov. 64/2 One of the doctors from Surgery will be coming down soon to put in your I.V. and a stomach tube. **1971** *Guardian Weekly* 24 Apr. 5/1 The bedside IV feeding bottle. **1972** *Nature* 8 Dec. 351/1, 3 African green monkeys were inoculated i.c. (0·2 ml.) and i.v. (0·3 ml.). **1917** B. Hall *Diary* 25 July in Hall & Niles *One Man's War* (1929) 278 The Government had some trouble in Los Angeles with the *I.W.W. **1919** H. L. Wilson *Ma Pettengill* vii. 212 Even the youngest [girl].. had tenaciously held out for a grown man's pay, which made her something even worse than a Bolshevik; it made her an I.W.W. **1920** M. Beer *Hist. Brit. Socialism* II. iv. xviii. 356 Similiar views .. led in 1905 to the formation of the Industrial Workers of the World (I.W.W.). **1957** *Encounter* Apr. 65/1 That strange and unique contribution of America to anarcho-syndicalism, the 'Wobblies' (officially the Industrial Workers of the World, or IWW..) organised great masses of unskilled workers and led strikes.. that were as much social rebellions as economic conflicts. **1969** Taft & Ross in Graham & Gurr *Violence in Amer.* viii. 285 Unlike the other national federations.., the IWW advocated direct action and sabotage.

I (aɪ), *pers. pron.*, *1st sing. nom.* Forms: see below. [OE. *ic* = Goth., OFris., OLG. (Fris., LG., Du.) *ik*, OHG. *ih* (MHG., mod.G. *ich*), ON. *ek*, *eg* (Norw. *eg*, Sw. *jag*, Da. *jeg*):—OTeut. **ek*, *ik* = OSl. *azŭ*, Lith. *aż*, L. *ego*, Gr. ἐγώ(ν, Skr. *ahám*:—primitive type **egóm*, **egō*. The OTeut. *ik* is supposed to have originated as the unstressed or enclitic form of *ek*, and to have become at length the general form. Of *ic*, as of its cognates *ego*, etc., no inflexional forms are known; the oblique cases of the singular are supplied from a stem *me*- common to the whole Aryan family. The plural nom. *we* has a Germanic form **wî-z* (Goth. *weis*, OHG. *wîr*, ON. *vér*), from a primitive stem *wei-*, Skr. *vay-ám*; its oblique cases are from a stem *uns-* (:—**n̥s*), co-radicate with L. *nos*, Skr. *nas*. Thus the inflexion of the pronoun is supplied from four distinct roots. Besides the sing. and pl., OE. had also a dual = we two, us two, which survived into early ME. and was in use after 1200. The original accusative forms became obs. at an early date, so that in later OE., as in ME. and mod.Eng., this case was levelled with the dative. The OE. genitive case was also declined as an adj. (the possessive pronoun), and already in ME. *mīn* (*mī*) was confined to this use, while *ūre*, *our*(*e* retained certain genitival uses almost to the close of the ME. period: see our. The paradigm of the pronoun is thus as follows:

	Singular.	Dual.	Plural.
	Old English.		
Nom.	ic	wit	we, wē
Acc.	mec; me, mē	*uncit; unc	úsic; ús
Dat.	me, mē	unc	ús
Gen. / *Poss. Pron.*	mín	uncer	úser; úre
	Middle English.		
Nom.	ic, ich; i	wit (witt)	we (weo)
Dat. Acc.	me	unc (unnc)	us, ous
Gen.	[*not found*]	[*not found*]	ure, ur, oure, our
Poss. Pron.	min, mi	unker	ure, ur, oure, our
	Modern English.		
Nom.	I	[*obs.*]	we
Dat. Acc.	me	,,	us
Poss. Pron. *absol.*	mine	,,	ours
Poss. Pron. adj.	my	,,	our

OE. *ic* remained in ME. as *ic*, *ik* in the north; in midl. and south it was early palatalized to *ich* (ɪtʃ). In north and midl. the final consonant began by 12th c. to be dropped before a consonant, the pronoun being in this position reduced to *i*; in the 14th c. *ik* and *i* were still used before vowel and consonant respectively in the north, but *I* alone appears in north and midl. after *c* 1400. In the south, *ich* remained much longer, esp. before an initial vowel, in which position, also, it was in 16th c. commonly reduced to *ch*, in writing conjoined with the verb, as in *cham* I am, *chave* I have, *chill* I will, *chot* I wot (initial *h* and *w* being elided). Before a consonant, *ch* was sometimes extended to *che*, as in Shakspere's 'che vor' ye'; and, in the forms *ich*, *utch*, *ch-*, *che*, or *utchy*, the pronoun remained in s.w. dialects till the 18th or first half of the 19th c. The simple vowel *i*, to which the pronoun was elsewhere reduced, was in course of time diphthongized (as ɪi, əi, ɛɪ, or æɪ); at first prob. only when under stress, but at length when unstressed also; a relic of the earlier unstressed form remains in north Eng. dialects in the enclitic pronoun following a verb, which is still (ɪ) or (iː), as in *wad-I* 'would I', *did-I*, pronounced *waddy*, *diddy* ('wadɪ, 'dɪdɪ). In most northern dialects a new unstressed form originated from the diphthongal *I* by dropping the second element, and retaining the first (ə) as *eh*, *a*; by the lengthening of this again there has been developed a new stressed form (æː, ɑː, ɔː), written *ah*, *aa*, *aw*, *oa*, which is now the ordinary form of the pronoun in north Eng. and Sc. dialects.

The ME. *ic*, *ik*, *ich*, were also spelt *yk*, *ych*(*e*; *i* varied with *j* or *I* (the MS. character for these being often the same), also with *y*, *Y*, and finally at the introduction of printing settled down as *I*. Both *i* and *ich* were often written in combination with the verb, as in *idude* I did, *icham* I am, *ichill* I will; these last were often erroneously divided by later scribes and printers as *I cham*, *I chill* (also erratically spelt *c'ham*, *ch'am*, etc.).

The history and uses of the oblique forms will be found in the separate articles me, mine, my, our, ours, etc.]

A. I. 1. Illustration of Forms.

α. 1–4 **ic** (2–3 *Orm.* **icc**, 3 **ig**, 3–4 **hic**), 4 **ik** (**yk**, **ike**, **hyc**).

c **725** *Corpus Gloss.* 526 *Convenio*, ic groetu. *c* **1000** *Ags. Gosp.* John vii. 29 Ic hyne can, and ȝif ic secge þæt ic hine ne cunne, ic beo leas. *c* **1175** *Lamb. Hom.* 13 þenne sende ic eou rihte widerunge and ic eou wille ȝeuan wela. *c* **1200** Ormin Ded. 11 Icc hafe wennd inntill Ennglissh Godd-spelless hallȝhe lare. *c* **1250** *Gen. & Ex.* 315 Ic wene ðat ic and eue hise wif sulen adam bilirten. *Ibid.* 34 Queðer so hic rede or singe. *c* **1300** *Havelok* 304 For.. noble shrud, That hic haue youen hire to offte; Hic haue yemed hire to softe. *Ibid.* 686 For litel ig do the lede To the galues. *c* **1300** *Cursor M.* 23921 (Edin.) For med ik [*Cott.* ic] ask a litil bon þat ik [*Cott.* i] beseke wit wordis quon. *Ibid.* 24797 (Edin.) þis ilke tim þat ike [*Gött.* i] of sai. *c* **1310** in *Rel. Ant.* I. 146 The lif that hyc ledh. **1375** Barbour *Bruce* I. 384 As Ic hard say. **1377** Langl. *P. Pl.* B. v. 228 Ac I swere now, so the ik, þat synne wil I lete. *c* **1386** Chaucer *Reeve's Prol.* 13 But ik [*v.r.* yk] am oold, me list no pley for Age.

β. 2–6 **ich** (3 **hich**, 3–6 **ych**, 5 **yche**, 5–6 **iche**). β^{1}. 2–3 **ih**, **ihc**. β^{2}. *ich* was combined with its verb, with elision of *h* or *w*; e.g. *icham*, *ichave*, *ichill*, *ichot*; by later scribes often wrongly divided *i cham*, *i chill*, *y choulde*, etc. Also *so theech* = *so thee ich*, so may I thrive! β^{3}. Subsequently, in s.w. dial., initial *ich* became **ch** joined to a verb; e.g. 6–8 *cham*, *chwas*, *cha*, *chave*, *chad*, *chill*, *chould*, *chard* (= I heard): see ch, 'ch. β^{4}. Later, in s.w. dial., *ch'* became **che**.

β. *c* **1160** *Hatton Gosp.* John viii. 14 Ich wat hwanon ich com, and hwider ich ga. *a* **1225** *Ancr. R.* 8 þe þinges þet ich write her. *a* **1275** *Prov. Ælfred* 576 in *O.E. Misc.* 134 Hich þe wile sagen soþe þewes. *a* **1300** *Vox & Wolf* 36 in Hazl. *E.P.P.* I. 59 Be stille, ich hote, a Goddes nome! *c* **1386** Chaucer *Merch. T.* 916 Now wyf quod he, heere nys but thou and I.. Leuere ich hadde to dyen on a knyf Than thee offende, trewe deere wyf. **1393** Langl. *P. Pl.* C. I. 14 Esteward ich byhulde after þe sonne, And sawe a toure, as ich trowede. *c* **1420** *Chron. Vilod.* 1382 As yche vnderstonde. *c* **1450** Lonelich *Grail* lii. 692 Mochel lever hadde Ich here to dye. *c* **1460** *Towneley Myst.* xiii. 207, I must haue reuerence; why, who be ich? *a* **1529** Skelton *E. Rummyng* 219 Ich am not cast away. **1561** Awdelay *Frat. Vacab.* 8 My maysters, ich am an old man, and halfe blinde. **1568** T. Howell *Arb. Amitie* (1879) 89 With cap and knee, ich will serve thee, what should ich more declare. **1589** in Puttenham *Eng. Poesie* III. xix. (Arb.) 213 Iche pray you good mother tell our young dame, Whence I am come and what is my name. *c* **1645** T. Davies *Somersetsh. Man's Compl.* i. (E.D.S.), Dost thinke 'chill labor to be poore, No no, ich haue a-doe.. Ich will a plundring too. **1706** Phillips (ed. Kersey), *Ich*, a Word us'd for I in the Western Parts of England.

β^{1}. *c* **1175** *Lamb. Hom.* 75 Ih ileue gode.. ich ileue þet god is. *Ibid.* 77 þe worde þet ihc speke to ou of mine muþe. *a* **1250** *Owl & Night.* 866 Thar-to ich helpe, God hit wot! Ne singe ih hom no foliot. *a* **1300** *K. Horn* 981 Ihc habbe walke wide Bi þe se side. *c* **1300** *Havelok* 1377 Ihc haue ther offe douthe and kare.

β^{2}. *a* **1225** *Juliana* 12 Ichulle leoten deor to teoren ant to luken þe. **1297** R. Glouc. (Rolls) 8359 Ich.. abbe.. iholpe er ywis & ȝut icholle her after more. *c* **1300** *Harrow. Hell* 71 Wost thou never whet ycham? *a* **1327** *Death Edw. I* in *Pol. Songs* (Camden) 247 Ycholde, ȝef that y myhte. *c* **1330** *Amis & Amil.* 945 Yif y swere, icham forsworn. *c* **1386** Chaucer *Pard. T.* 619 Lat be, quod he, it schal not be, so theech [*v.rr.* thee ich, þeche, theche, þeiche]. *c* **1420** *Chron. Vilod.* 536 Cudberth of Dereham, he sayde, ychame. *a* **1529** Skelton *E. Rummyng* 1 Tell you I chyll, If that ye wyll. **1547** Boorde *Introd. Knowl.* i. (1870) 122 Iche cham a Cornyshe man. *c* **1566** *Merie Tales of Skelton* in *S.'s Wks.* (1843) I. p. lxvi, I cham sicke; I chill go home to bed. **1640** Brome *Sparagus Gard.* IV. xi, I chill look to you.

β^{3}. **1529–1746** [see ch *pron.*]. **1562** J. Heywood *Prov. & Epigr.* (1867) 108 By Iys cham a shamd. *Ibid.*, Cha forgote it quight. At shrift chad my *pater noster*. *Ibid.* 141 Chil ley my gowne. **1567** *Damon & Pythias* in Hazl. *Dodsley* IV. 72 Chill say no more, lest I offend. **1575** *Gammer Gurton* II. i. in Dodsley *O.P.* II. 25 And channot sumwhat to stop this gap, cham utterly undone. **1586** Ferne *Blaz. Gentrie* 459 By my vaye, chame more wearye.. than yif chad gone to plowe all this daye. **1605** Shaks. *Lear* IV. vi. 250 Chill picke your teeth Zir. *c* **1645** T. Davies *Somersetsh. Man's Compl.* ii. (E.D.S.), 'Chill sell my cart & eake my Plow. **1746** *Exmoor Scolding* (E.D.S.) 244 Chad et in my Meend, and zo chave still. Bet chawnt drow et out bevore tha begen'st agen, and than chell.

β^{4}. **1568**, **1594** [see che]. **1605** Shaks. *Lear* IV. vi. 246 Keepe out che vor'ye. ? **16..** *Plain Truth* in *Reliq. Anc. Eng. Poetry* (1823) III. 127 Ah! ah! che zmell the now, man; Che know well what thou art.

γ. 2–4 **i**, (3 **hi**, 3–4 **j**, **e**), 4–6 **y**, 5 **Y**, 4– **I**. γ^{1}. **i-** (**y-**), combined with following verb: formerly esp. frequent with contracted verbs, where an apostrophe is now inserted, as in **ide** = *I'd*, I had, **ild** = *I'd*, I would, **ile**, **yle** = *I'll*, I will, **ime** = *I'm*, I am, **ise**, **ice**, **i'sh** = *I s'*, I shall, **ive** = *I've*, I have. So Sc. *I'nk*, *aa'nk* = I think. γ^{2}. **-i**, **-y**, appended enclitically to verbs; e.g. *ami*, *cani*, *havy*, *haddy*; mod. dial. **-y** or **-ee**.

γ. **1154** *O.E. Chron.* an. 1137 §3, I ne can ne i ne mai tellen alle þe wunder. *a* **1240** *Ureisun* in *Cott. Hom.* 197 Hwar ich was and hwat i dude. *a* **1240** *Wohunge* ibid. 283 A hwat schal i nu don? *a* **1275** *Prov. Ælfred* 336 in *O.E. Misc.* 123 Hi ne sawe it nocht. *c* **1290** *S. Eng. Leg.* I. 110/139 Hire heþene name ne j nouȝt telle. *a* **1300** *Cursor M.* 25408 To þe mak j mi bon. *c* **1300** *St. Margarete* 107 For him ic wole þane deþ afonge: y nabbe þerof no doute. **1382** Wyclif *Matt.* xiv. 27 Haue ȝe trust, I [**1388** Y] am; nyl ȝe dreede [**1526** Tindale, It is y, be not a frayed]. *c* **1386** Chaucer *Prol.* 31 So hadde I spoken with hem euerychon That I was of hir felaweshipe anon. *c* **1399** *Pol. Poems* (Rolls) II. 9 Among the ten comandementz y rede. **1411** in *E.E. Wills* (1882) 19 Also y be-queyth to William my son an aburioun of stele. *a* **1450** *Knt. de la Tour* Prol. 1 But a litelle y reioysed me. **1509** Barclay *Shyp of Folys* (1570) 30 As I haue sayde (therfore) I say agayne. **1548** Hall *Chron., Hen. VIII* 51 b, I Charles went nexte to hym. **1611** Bible *Gen.* ix. 9, I, behold I, establish my covenant with you. **1653** W. Basse in *Walton's Angler* iii. 80, I care not, I, to fish in seas. **1719** De Foe *Crusoe* I. xviii. (1840) 320 They have all been as bad as I. **1722** —— *Col. Jack* (1840) 46, I could not tell money, not I. **1816** Scott *Antiq.* viii, 'I', 'And I', 'And I', answered many a ready voice.

γ^{1}. *c* **1200** *Moral Ode* 2 in *Trin. Coll. Hom.* 220 Ich wealde more þan idude. *Ibid.* 4 þeih ibie a winter eald. *a* **1240** *Lofsong* in *Cott. Hom.* 217 Ibileue on ðe holi goste. **1533** J. Heywood *Pard. & Frere* in Hazl. *Dodsley* I. 231 By Jis, I'sh lug thee by the sweet ears! *Ibid.* 232 I'sh knock thee on the costard. **1567** *Triall Treas.* (1850) 9 If you will giue me leaue, yle tell ye howe. *Ibid.* 14 Ise teache you to speake! **1592** Shaks. *Rom. & Jul.* I. iv. 38 Ile be a Candle-holder and looke on. **1598** —— *Merry W.* v. i. 1 Go, Ile hold. **1605** —— *Lear* IV. vi. 246 Ice try whither your Costard, or my Ballow be the harder. **16..** *Fair Rosamund* (in *Percy Reliq.*), Nay, death Ild rather chuse! **1657** Trapp *Comm. Ezra* x. 44 Ile meddle with none of them. **1742** Richardson *Pamela* III. 308 I'd a better Opinion of thy Spirit!

γ^{2}. *c* **1200** *Trin. Coll. Hom.* 129 Ne ami noht crist. *c* **1300** *Harrow. Hell* 43 Hard gates hauy gon. *a* **1310** in Wright *Lyric P.* x. 37 Navy the none harmes to hethe. *c* **1310** in *Rel. Ant.* I. 146 Fayrer ho [= on] lond hawy non syen.. Thar for amy cummen here. *Ibid.*, Wit my roc y me fede Cani do non othir dede. *c* **1330** R. Brunne *Chron. Wace* (Rolls) 14892 Seint Bede so herdy telle. *c* **1391** Chaucer *Astrol.* II. §1 Than haddy.. the ful experience. *Ibid.* §40 Thus hauy 2 degrees. **1790** Mrs. Wheeler *Westmld. Dial.* 55 Mun E maak a bit a Braad Mudder. **1828** *Craven Dial.*, *I* is sometimes pronounced like E, particularly when the pronoun follows the verb, as 'do-E', for I do.

B. Senses and constructions.

I. As pronoun.

1. a. The pronoun by which a speaker or writer denotes himself, in the nominative case, as the subject of predication, or in attributive or predicative agreement with that subject.

See examples above, under head A.

b. Sometimes = I, if I were you (he or she).

1846 G. E. Corrie 25 Mar. in M. Holroyd *Mem.* xi. (1890) 241, I should not be too strict about the 'artificial flowers'.

c. Sometimes qualified by an adj.

1588 SHAKS. *Tit. A.* II. iii. 171 Poore I was slaine, when Bassianus dy'd. **1687** *Death's Vis.* iii. (1713) 4 Alas! What shall poor I become? **1690** DRYDEN *Don Sebastian* Epil. 4 Poor I to be a nun, poor you a friar. **1693** —— *Roundelay* i, Wretched I, to love in vain!

2. Sometimes used for the objective after a verb or preposition, esp. when separated from the governing word by other words.

This was very frequent in end of 16th and in 17th c., but is now considered ungrammatical.

1596 SHAKS. *Merch. V.* III. ii. 321 All debts are cleerd betweene you and I. **1600** —— *A.Y.L.* I. ii. 18 My father hath no childe but I. *c* **1600** —— *Sonn.* lxxii, And hang more praise upon deceased I. **1598** B. JONSON *Ev. Man in Hum.* v. iii, Brayne-worme ha's beene with my cossen Edward and I, all this day. **1649** *Nicholas Papers* (Camden) 136 To give you and I a right understanding of those particulars. **1698** VANBRUGH *Prov. Wife* v. ii, It must all light upon Heartfree and I. *Ibid.*, Between you and I. **1710** MRS. CENTLIVRE *Bickerstaff's Burying* 14 Leave your Lady and I alone. **1744** J. STEUART *Letter-Bk.* (1915) 449 The postscript to your letter..gave my wife and I unexpressable joy. **1857** HUGHES *Tom Brown* I. iii, Let you and I cry quits. **1866** *Harper's Mag.* Jan. 162/2, I have heard him..make a bet that 'between you and I' is correct, and refuse to be convinced of his error. **1959** *N.Z. Listener* 25 Sept. 11/2, I have heard 'between you and I, old man', and 'people like you and I', from graduates in some arts other than the art of speech. **1971** *Guardian* 20 Aug. 24/4 'There were two grilles between Eugene and I, and we must have been about six feet apart,' she said. **1972** J. ROSSITER *Rope for General Dietz* ii. 24, I was sure they were looking for Michael and I. **1973** *Oxford Mail* 27 Aug. 4/4 After showing photographer Bill Radford and I her stitching skill she went back to the tea table.

3. In mod. s.w. dial. used as an emphatic objective.

a **1859** *Cupid's Garden* in Hughes *Scouring White Horse* vii. (1859) 180 Let thee and I go our own waay, And we'll let she go shis'n. **1859** BARNES *Hwomely Rhymes* 20 How you do muddle! Gi'e I the spade. **1863** —— *Dorset Gram.* (Philol. Soc.) 23 We should say unemphatically 'Gi'e me the pick'.. but emphatically 'Gi'e the money to *I*, not he'. **1877** ELWORTHY *W. Somerset Gram.* 35.

II. As substantive.

4. a. The pronoun regarded as a word.

1599 *Broughton's Let.* ii. 8 The Cleerer of *Diuinitie*, the *I per se I*, and the belweather of Diuines. **1722** WOLLASTON *Relig. Nat.* ix. 185 It would be the same as to say *the soul of the soul, or the body of the body, or the I of me.* **1859** HARE *Guesses* Ser. I. (ed. 5) 94 The proudest word in English, to judge by its way of carrying itself, is *I*. **1874** HELPS *Soc. Press.* v. (1875) 66 An 'egotistical fellow', as you call him.. presses forward with his 'I, I, I', simply because, perhaps unjustly, you do not recognise that 'I' sufficiently. **1883** WESTCOTT *Ep. John* (1886) 220 The unchanged and unchangeable 'I' of the Word.

b. ***another I*** = a second self.

1539 TAVERNER *Erasm. Prov.* (1545) 140 My frende is as who shuld say an other I. **1579** LYLY *Euphues* (Arb.) 48 At al times another I, in all places the expresse Image of myne owne person. **1614** SYLVESTER *Panaretus* Wks. (1621) 855 That same other I.

5. *Metaph.* The subject or object of self-consciousness; that which is conscious of itself, as thinking, feeling, and willing; the *ego*.

1710 BERKELEY *Princ. Hum. Knowl.* §139 What I am myself—that which I denote by the term I—is the same with what is meant by soul or spiritual substance. **1711** SHAFTESB. *Charac.* VI. IV. i. III. 193 The Question is, 'What constitutes the 'we' or '*I*?' and, 'Whether the *I* of this instant, be the same with that of any instant preceding, or to come'. **1764** REID *Inquiry* i. §3 How do I know that..the I of this moment is the very individual I of yesterday? **1829** CARLYLE *Misc.* (1857) II. 75 A Manifestation of Power from something which is *not I*. **1870** H. MACMILLAN *Bible Teach.* viii. 152 Man is not an independent unit; a self-centred, self-sustaining *I*. **1874** W. WALLACE *Logic Hegel* §20. 32 'I', in the abstract, as such, is the mere act of concentration or reference to self. **1891** E. B. BAX *Outlooks fr. New Standpoint* iii. 199 The *I* which we think of when we say *myself*..is not the true *I*, the *I* that is thinking, but merely a pseudo-*I*, a synthesis of thoughts and feelings reflected in this *I*, which are immediately or intuitively identified with that *I*.

6. The narrator of a work of fiction, appearing on his own account. Also *attrib.* or as *adj.*

1946 'G. ORWELL' in *Observer* 10 Feb. 3/3 The 'I' of the story describes himself as a Democrat. **1962** *John o' London's* 19 Apr. 372/1 The tendency for novelists to move away from the 'I' kind of storytelling. **1965** *English Studies* XLVI. 390 The point of view of the 'I' narrator is perfectly maintained throughout the tale. **1969** *Listener* 30 Jan. 151/3 The 'I' of David Martin's tense and elusive story.

III. Phrases containing *I* and its verb, taken substantively: ***I say***, a mere assertion; ***I will***, a formula of promise, e.g. in marriage; ***I know not what*** (= F. *je ne sais quoi*), the unknown, unintelligible, or inexpressible. **I AM**, the Lord Jehovah, the Self-existent. Also in weakened colloq. use: a (self-)important person.

1611 BIBLE *Exod.* iii. 14 And God saide vnto Moses, I am that I am: And he said, Thus shalt thou say vnto the children of Israel, I AM hath sent me vnto you. **1634** CANNE *Necess. Separ.* (1849) 241 His proofs are always beggarly, I says, or ifs, and may be sos. **1711** SHAFTESB. *Charac.* (1737) I. 332 Which the rest of mankind, feeling only by the effect,.. term the je-ne-scay-quoy, the unintelligible, or the *I know not what*. *Ibid.* II. 413 Whatever is commonly said of the unexpressible, the unintelligible, the *I-know-not-what* of beauty. **1772** T. OLIVERS *Hymn, 'The God of Abraham praise'* viii, Jehovah—Father—great I AM, We worship Thee. **1850** TENNYSON *In Mem.* Concl., Her sweet 'I will' has made you one. **1884** H. CONWAY in *Harper's Mag.* Dec. 147/2 Both bride and bridegroom said their 'I wills' in..low tones. **1915** D. H. LAWRENCE in *Signature* 18 Oct. 8 David dancing naked before the Ark, asserting the oneness, his own oneness, the one infinity, *himself*, the one God, I AM. **1926** S. T. WARNER *Lolly Willowes* III. 184 Jim thought himself quite a Great I AM. **1928** D. H. LAWRENCE *Lady Chatterley* x. 131, I am a cypher. You are the great I-am! as far as life goes. *a* **1940** F. SCOTT FITZGERALD *Last Tycoon* (1949) vi. 138 'Get one that can talk—tell him to bring one of his books along.' He spoke as if he wanted to meet a member of the 'I am' cult. **1954** W. FAULKNER *Fable* 57 Lifting its voice against the Absolute, the ultimate I-Am. **1965** N. GULBENKIAN *Pantaraxia* xi. 227 Cyril Radcliffe.. did not take the short-cut favoured by so many of his colleagues who say..: 'I am the great I am, Queen's Counsel.' **1970** D. FRANCIS *Rat Race* i. 13 He had none of the 'I am' aura which often clings around the notably successful.

Also ***I and Thou, I-and-Thou***. In the theology of M. Buber: describing a relationship between two people, as opposed to that between a person and an object. Also *attrib.*

1937 R. SMITH tr. *Buber's Ich-Du* (*title*) I and Thou. **1958** D. M. BAILLIE *Out of Nazareth* xxii. 157 Divine realities can only be known in a personal 'I-and-Thou' relationship. **1968** L. BERG *Risinghill* 64 Such teachers had never seen their pupils as fellow human beings before, as Martin Buber's 'I' and 'Thou'.

Hence **I-ety** *nonce-wd.*, **I-hood, I-ness, I-ship,** (*Metaph.*), conscious personality; **I-ism,** (*a*) *Metaph.*, the reference of all things to one's own consciousness, egoism; (*b*) *nonce-wd.*, the frequent use of 'I', egotism of style; **I-now** (*Metaph.*), the subject of present consciousness.

1835 MRS. CARLYLE in *Lett.* (1883) I. 18 In spite of the honestest efforts to annihilate my *I-ety. **1662** SPARROW tr. *Behme's Rem. Wks., Apol. conc. Perfection* 118 The Man Christ is..the First who in the Anointing dyed to the Humane *I-hood. *Ibid., 2nd Apol. to Tylcken* 17 He inclineth himself to my Minehood, and my Ihood inclineth it self up into him. **1871** MACMILLAN *True Vine* iii. (1872) 82 He has no *autarkia*, or self-sufficingness—no *ichheit*, or I-hood, as the Germans would say. **1840** *Fraser's Mag.* XXII. 620 The *oneism*, the **I-ism* of the German, making for each individual his own mind the centre of his universe. **1848** GEO. ELIOT in J. W. Cross *Life* (1885) I. 191 Your affectionate letter demanded some I-ism. **1886** *Illustr. Lond. News* 4 Dec. 598/2, I wonder whether any other writers.. often fall into the sin of 'I, I, I-ism'. **1891** E. B. BAX *Outlooks fr. New Standpoint* iii. 184 Being..is simply transfigured *I-ness. *Ibid.* 189 Both alike are modes of I-ness. *Ibid.* 200 This distinction is..traceable to that between the **I-now*, which thinks and presents, and the thing thought considered *per se*, that which is thought and presented in it... The thinking and presenting *I-now* may be regarded as the material. *a* **1834** COLERIDGE *Lit. Rem.* (1839) IV. 232 Who can comprehend his own..personeity, that is his *I-ship (*Ichheit*).

i, obs. f. AYE, yes, and of EYE; var. HI *Obs.*, they.

i', i, weakened form of IN *prep.* before a cons., as in *i' faith*: now *dial.* or *arch.*

†**i-**[1], ME. *prefix*, also written Y-, OE. *ȝe-* [= Goth. *ga-*, OHG. *ga-*, *ge-*, *gi-*, Ger., LG., Du. *ge-*] forming collective sbs., deriv. adjs., advbs., and vbs.; esp. used with the pa. pple. of verbs, and in southern ME. a normal prefix of the pa. pple. like mod.Ger. and Du. *ge-* in *gesehen*, *gezien*, ME. *i-sen*, *i-se*, *yseen*, *yse*.

In early ME., this prefix regularly appears as *i-*; words which did not survive to *c* 1340 have rarely any other form. Later, *y* became (for graphic reasons) more usual, and was the form in which the prefix was borrowed from Lydgate, etc., by the Spenserian archaists, as in *yclad*, *ycleped*, *ygo*, *ypent*, *ywis*, etc. In this Dictionary, the earlier words which are known only with the *i-* spelling, are entered under I; those which survived to have *y-*, and esp. the archaistic *yclad*, *yclept*, etc. appear under Y. In MSS., the *i* often stands separate from the rest of the word, or is united to it by a hyphen; the latter practice is frequently followed by editors, and it has been adopted here, in order to render the character and sense of these words more distinct to the eye.

i-[2], reduced form of the negative prefix IN-[3] (q.v.), used in some words of L. origin before *gn-* (later *n*), as *ignoble*, *ignominy*, *ignorant*.

-i, *suffix*[1]: the plural ending of Lat. 2nd decl. nouns in *-us* (*-er*), also of Ital. words in *-o*, *-e*, retained in English in the plurals of some words in learned or scientific use, as *cirri*, *foci*, *radii*, *banditti*, *dilettanti*, *literati*. In some words a learned or technical pl. in *-i* and a popular one in *-uses* are both in use, e.g. *foci*, *focuses*, *hippopotami*, *hippopotamuses*.

It is also frequent (without a singular) in mod.L. names of orders or other groups in Natural History, as *Acanthopterygii*, *Chondropterygii* (sc. *pisces*, fishes), *Acrocarpi*, *Cladocarpi* (sc. *musci*, mosses).

-i, *suffix*[2], a termination used in the names of certain Near-Eastern and Eastern peoples, as *Iraqi*, *Israeli*, *Pakistani*.

-i-, connective or quasi-connective L. *-i-*, being the stem-vowel, as in *omni-vorus*, or a weakened representative thereof, as in *grani-vorus* (*grano-*), or *herbi-vorus* (*herba-*), or merely connective, as in *gramin-i-vorus* (*gramin-*); so *uni-formis*, *auri-fer*, *terri-genus*, *pac-i-ficus*. So in many English words taken from L. directly or through French, and in modern words formed on their analogy, e.g. *amœbi-form*, *hydri-form* (erroneously *hydraform*, *hydræform*), *seti-form*, etc.

ia-: obs. spelling of JA-. (Cf. I the letter.)

-ia, *suffix*[1], a termination of L. and Gr. sbs. [= *i-*, ι-, stem or connective vowel + -A *suffix* 2], in Gr. esp. frequent as the ending of abstract sbs. from adjs. in -ος, etc. Many words so formed are in Eng. use, as *hydrophobia*, *mania*, *militia*; hence frequent in mod.Latin terms of Pathology (*cephalalgia*, *hæmaturia*, *hyperalgia*, *hysteria*); of Botany, in names of classes, orders, or other divisions, as *Monandria*, *Digynia*, *Cryptogamia*, and in generic names of plants, formed on personal names, or otherwise derived, as *Dahlia*, *Fuchsia*, *Lobelia*, *Wisteria*, *Woodsia*; *Calceolaria*, *Mantisia*, etc.; in names of countries, as *Australia*, *Tasmania*, *Rhodesia*; and in names of alkaloids (after *ammonia*), as *aconitia*, *atropia*, *conia*, *morphia*, *strychnia*, in which more recent nomenclature prefers the ending *-ine*. In Fr. *-ia* became *-ie*, whence ME. *-ie*, Eng. *-y*, in sbs. in *-ency*, *-ography*, *-ology*, etc.

-ia, *suffix*[2] [f. *-i-* stem or connective vowel + -A *suffix* 4], forming plurals of Lat. and Gr. sbs. in *-ium*, *-e* (*-i*), -ιον, some of which are in Eng. use, as *paraphernalia*, *regalia*, *saturnalia*; hence frequent in mod.L. names of classes, etc. in Zoology, as *Mammalia*, *Marsupialia*, *Reptilia*, *Amphibia*.

iacint, obs. f. JACINTH.

iacstro, obs. f. JACKSTRAW.

i-ærned, ME. pa. pple. of EARN *v.*

†**i-ahn(e,** *v. Obs.* [OE. *ȝeáȝnian*, f. *áȝnian* to OWN.] *trans.* To own, possess.

c **1000** ÆLFRIC *Hom.* II. 102 Hwi sceal he ðonne him anum ȝeaȝnian þæt him bam is forgifen? *c* **1000** ÆLFRIC *Gram.* xxvi. (Z.) 157 *Possideo*, ic ȝeaȝniȝe. *c* **1205** LAY. 1932 Nu wes al þis lond iahned a Brutus hond. *Ibid.* 3743 He wolde bi norðen iahnien þa londa.

-ial, *suffix*, repr. L. *-iālis*, *-iāle*, in adjs. formed from sb. stems in *-io-*, *-ia-*, as *cūriālis*, *tibiālis*; extensively used in med.L., Fr., and Eng. to form derivative adjs. from L. adjs. in *-is*, *-ius*, as *cælest-is*, *celest-i-al*, *terrestr-is*, *terrestr-i-al*, *dictātōr-i-us*, *dictator-i-al*. See -AL *suffix*[1] I.

iamb ('aɪæmb). *Pros.* [a. F. *iambe*, ad. L. *iamb-us*.] = IAMBUS.

1842 BRANDE *Dict. Sci.* etc. s.v. *Iambics*, To add three short syllables to the last iamb. **1847** SCHMITZ tr. *Zumpt's Lat. Gram.* App. i. 553 Two anapaests, according to the analogy of two iambs, make an anapaestic metre. **1894** *Athenæum* 24 Mar. 372/2 Using the phrase 'rising rhythm' to denote an iamb.

iambic (aɪ'æmbɪk), *a.* and *sb.* *Pros.* [a. F. *iambique* (1529 in Hatz.-Darm.) or ad. L. *iambic-us*, ad. Gr. ἰαμβικός, f. ἴαμβος IAMBUS.]

A. *adj.* **1.** Of a foot, verse, rhythm, etc.: Consisting of, characterized by, or based on iambuses.

iambic trimeter, a verse consisting of six iambuses (three dipodies) in the odd feet of which the iambus may be replaced by its metrical equivalent (the tribrach) or a spondee or its equivalent, the even feet being kept pure (though in Latin especially the licence of substitution was extended even to them).

1586 WEBBE *Eng. Poetrie* (Arb.) 62 Ye shall perceiue them to containe in sound ye very propertie of Iambick feete, as thus... 'Ĭ thăt mȳ slĕndĕr ōatĕn pīpe ĭn vĕrse wăs wōnt tŏ sōunde'. **1711** ADDISON *Spect.* No. 39 ¶5 Aristotle observes, that the Iambick Verse in the Greek Tongue was the most proper for Tragedy. **1755** JOHNSON *Gram. Eng. Tongue, Prosody*, The feet of our verses are either iambick, as 'aloft, create'; or trochaick, as 'holy, lofty'. **1789** TWINING *Aristotle's Treat. Poetry* (1812) II. 445 The hexameter is but one third longer than the Iambic trimeter. **1869** SEELEY *Lect. & Ess.* (1870) 176 The regular beat of the iambic cadence.

2. Of a poet: Employing iambic metres.

1581 SIDNEY *Apol. Poetrie* (Arb.) 28 These be subdiuided into..the Heroick, Lirick, Tragick, Comick, Satirick, Iambick, Elegiack, Pastorall, and certaine others. Some of these being termed according to the matter they deale with, some by the sorts of verses they liked best to write in. **1585** T. WASHINGTON tr. *Nicholay's Voy.* II. viii. 42 Hipponax the poet Iambique. **1633** P. FLETCHER *Purple Isl.* I. xx, O let th' Iambick Muse revenge that wrong.

B. *sb.* (Usually *pl.*) An iambic foot, verse, or poem. Also *transf.*, a piece of invective or satire in verse (cf. IAMBUS).

1575 G. HARVEY *Letter-bk.* (Camden) 100 In the nexte seate to thes hexameters, adonickes, and iambicks, I sett those that stand uppon the number, not in meter, such as my lorde of Surrey is sayde first to have putt forthe in prynte. **1651** CLEVELAND *Poems* 34 Come keen Iambicks, with your Badgers feet. **1671** MILTON *P.R.* IV. 262 What the lofty grave tragedians taught, In Chorus or Iambic. **1682**

DRYDEN *Mac Flecknoe* 204 Thy genius calls thee not to purchase fame In keen Iambics, but mild Anagram. **1809** COLERIDGE *Metr. Feet* 5 Iămbĭcs mărch frŏm shōrt tŏ lōng.

i'ambical, *a. rare* or *Obs.* [-AL¹.] = prec. adj.
1583 STANYHURST *Æneis* etc. (Arb.) 126 Too my seeming ..the Iambical quantitye relisheth soom what vnsauorlye in oure language. **1598** MERES *Paladis Tamia* 283 b, Two Iambical Poets, Gabriel Harvey, and Richard Stanyhurst.
Hence **i'ambically** *adv.*, 'in the manner of an iambic' (Worcester 1846, citing *Chr. Observer*).

iambist (aɪ'æmbɪst). [ad. Gr. ἰαμβιστ-ής, agent-n. f. ἰαμβίζειν to iambize.] A composer of iambic verse; a writer of iambics.
1839 TUFNEL & LEWIS tr. *C. O. Müller's Hist. Doric Race* II. 339 The Syracusan choruses of iambists were, without doubt, connected with this worship [of Demeter]. **1849** GROTE *Greece* II. lxvii VI. 33 With a malignity of personal slander not inferior to the Iambist Archilochus.

iambize (aɪ'æmbaɪz), *v. rare.* [ad. Gr. ἰαμβίζειν to assail in iambics, f. ἴαμβος: see IAMBUS and -IZE.] *trans.* To attack in iambic verse; hence *gen.* to satirize.
1789 T. TWINING tr. *Aristotle's Treat. Poetry* (1812) I. I. vi. 110 The Iambic..was the measure in which they used to iambize each other.

iambographer (aɪæm'bɒgrəfə(r)). [f. Gr. ἰαμβογράφ-ος (f. ἴαμβος IAMBUS + γράφος writing, writer) + -ER¹.] A writer of iambics.
1625-6 SHIRLEY *Maid's Rev.* I. ii, I am an iambographer ..One of the sourest versifiers that ever crept out of Parnassus. **1873** SYMONDS *Grk. Poets* iv. 107 Next in date to Simonides among the Iambographers ranks Hipponax of Ephesus, who flourished about 540 B.C.

‖**iambus** (aɪ'æmbəs). *Pros.* [L., a. Gr. ἴαμβος iambus, iambic verse or poem, lampoon, f. ἰάπτειν to assail (in words); the iambic trimeter being first used, according to tradition, by the Greek satiric writers Archilochus and Hipponax.] A metrical foot consisting of a short followed by a long syllable; in accentual verse, of an unaccented followed by an accented syllable.
The iambic rhythm, as being closest to that of ordinary speech, was employed in Greek and Latin as the common metre of dialogue; its earliest known use is as a vehicle of invective and satire. (Cf. etym. above.)
1586 W. WEBBE *Eng. Poetrie* (Arb.) 69 A myxt foote of 2 syllables..of one short and one long called Iambus as ◡ –. **1589** PUTTENHAM *Eng. Poesie* II. xiii. [xiv.] (Arb.) 135 Of all your words bissillables the most part naturally do make the foote Iambus, many the Trocheus, fewer the Spondeus, fewest of all the Pirrichius. **1603** HOLLAND *Plutarch's Mor.* 1257 The intension of Iambus unto Pæan Epibatos. **1823** J. B. SEALE *Anal. Grk. Metres* 3 In the Iambus and Trochee, the Arsis (or Ictus) is invariable, being upon the long Syllable of each. **1824** L. MURRAY *Eng. Gram.* (ed. 5) I. 374 The Alexandrine measure..consists of six Iambuses. 'Fŏr thōu ărt būt ŏf dūst; bĕ hūmblĕ ănd bĕ wīse'. **1833** *Edin. Rev.* LVI. 372 The Iambus, which in technical language is said to consist of *anacrusis* and *arsis*.

-ian, *suffix*. **1.** repr. L. *-iān-us*, i.e. an original or connective vowel *-i-*, with suffix *-ānus*: see -AN I, 'of or belonging to'. Formed by adding *-ānus* to stems ending in *-i*, as *Itali-a*, *Itali-ān-us*, *Fabi-us*, *Fabi-ān-us*, *Vergili-us*, *Vergili-ān-us*, *Christ-us*, *Christ-i-ān-us*. Hence, in many Eng. words adapted or formed from L., in which the suffix forms both adjs. and sbs., as *antediluvian*, *barbarian*, *historian*, *equestrian*, *patrician*, *saturnian*; and in modern formations from proper names, the number of which is without limit, as *Addisonian*, *Arminian*, *Arnoldian*, *Bodleian*, *Cameronian*, *Gladstonian*, *Hoadleian*, *Hugonian*, *Johnsonian*, *Morrisonian*, *Ruskinian*, *Salisburyian*, *Shavian*, *Sheldonian*, *Taylorian*, *Tennysonian*, *Wardian*, *Wellsian*, *Wordsworthian*; *Aberdonian*, *Bathonian*, *Bostonian*, *Bristolian*, *Cantabrigian*, *Cornubian*, *Devonian*, *Galwegian*, *Glasgowegian*, *Johnian*, *Oxonian*, *Parisian*, *Salopian*, *Sierra Leonian*. There are also sportive formations, as *any-lengthian*. See also -AN.
2. *Min.* [Abstracted from the adjs. *magnesian*, *manganesian*.] Used to form, from the (Eng. or L.) names of the elements, adjectives having the sense 'having a (small) proportion of a constituent element replaced by (the element concerned)' (see quot.).
1930 W. T. SCHALLER in *Amer. Mineralogist* XV. 568 Can a uniform, clearly understandable scheme of nomenclature be adopted to express a minor and variable isomorphous replacement of an essential chemical element of a mineral by another analogous element?.. The writer has concluded that the ending *ian*, or *oan* if it is desired to indicate a lower valency, is the most satisfactory, and its consistent use is here advocated... If the chemical element has only one valency or the author does not wish to bring up the question of valency, *ian* should be used.

-iana, *suffix*. Form of -ANA *suff.* added to nouns whose adjectival suffix is, or would be, -IAN.
1679 [see BIBLIOGRAPHICAL *a.*]. **1718** [see SHAKESPEARIANA]. **1728** J. SMEDLEY (*title*) Gulliveriana: or, a fourth volume of Miscellanies, being a sequel to the three volumes published by Pope and Swift. To which is added, Alexanderiana, etc. **1776** [see JOHNSONIANA]. **1800** (*title*) Walpoliana. **1838** (*title*) Railroadiana. A New History of England, or Picturesque..Sketches..Descriptive of the Vicinity of the Railroads. **1879** G. J. FINCH-HATTON *Voices through Many Years* III. 85 Gladstoniana. *Ibid.* 118 Grevilliana. **1890** *Century Mag.* Aug. 515/2 A number of these 'whaleiana' hang in the 'Captains' Room'. **1898** W. GRAHAM *Last Links with Byron* 120 Several writers of Keatsiana follow that most inaccurate of writers,..Leigh Hunt. **1902**, etc. [see EDWARDIANA *sb. pl.*]. **1929** *Daily Tel.* 22 Jan. 6/5 The personal papers of James Boswell..are being published... Sixteen or eighteen volumes will eventually be needed to hold all the new Boswelliana. **1952** J. CARTER *ABC for Bk.-Collectors* 19 Boswelliana, Railroadiana, Etoniana... Harveiana and Dickensiana.. Wiseiana. **1972** *Country Life* 17 Jan. 223/2 In his.. biography *William Butterfield*..Dr Paul Thompson has hauled in Butterfieldiana in shoals..churches, colleges, schools, hospitals, cottages.

ianthine (aɪ'ænθɪn), *a.* Also 7 -in. [ad. L. *ianthin-us*, ad. Gr. ἰάνθινος.] Violet-coloured; dyed of a violet colour. (See also quot. 1876.)
1609 BIBLE (Douay) *Exod.* xxv. 5 Rammes skinnes died redde, and ianthin skinnes [*pelles ianthinas*]. **1876** *Treas. Bot.* (Rev. ed.) 616/1 *Ianthine*, pure blue stained with red, so as to be intermediate between the two colours.

ianthinite (iː'æ-, aɪ'ænθɪnaɪt). *Min.* [ad. Du. *janthiniet* (A. Schoep 1926, in *Natuurwetenschappelijk Tijdschrift* VII. 97), f. Gr. ἰάνθῐν-ος violet-coloured: see -ITE¹.] A hydrated oxide of uranium found as orthorhombic crystals of a dark violet colour.
1927 *Mineral. Abstr.* III. 232 Small (to 2 mm.) black crystals with a violet tinge and semi-metallic lustre were found in veinlets in pitchblende from the Kasolo mine in Katanga, and are named ianthinite. **1954** *Amer. Mineralogist* XXXIX. 1018 Ianthinite reportedly contains only quadrivalent uranium and has a formula of $2UO_2.7H_2O$.

Iapygian (aɪə'pɪdʒɪən), *a.* and *sb.* [f. L. *Iāpygius*, f. *Iāpyx*, *-ygem*, a son of Dædalus said to have ruled over southern Italy: see -IAN.] **A.** *adj.* Of or pertaining to the ancient natives and district of Iapygia, the name given by the Greeks to the peninsula of Apulia in southern Italy. **B.** *sb.* **a.** A native of Iapygia. **b.** The language of the Iapygians; = MESSAPIAN *sb.* b.
1773 J. LANGHORNE tr. *Denina's Diss. Anc. Republics Italy* 26 The Iapygyans and Messapians [lost] fifty thousand infantry. **1864** P. SMITH *Hist. World* II. 138 It is here..that we find traces of the Iapygian race, in the peninsula called by the Greeks Messapia. **1880** *Encycl. Brit.* XIII. 443/2 The peninsula which stretches eastward towards Greece was inhabited by a people termed by the Greeks Messapians or Iapygians. **1882** *Ibid.* XIV. 327/1 Inscriptions have been found in considerable numbers, written in a language known as Iapygian or Messapian. **1888** KING & COOKSON *Princ. Sound & Inflexion Gr. & Latin* 30 Of the Iapygian in the extreme south and the Ligurian in the north, very little is known. **1959** *Chambers's Encycl.* VII. 778/1 In Apulia.. the Iapygian tribes of Messapii, Daunii and Peucetii established themselves.

iare, iarke, obs. ff. YARE, ready, YARK *v.*

iarfine ('iːəfɪnɪ). *Irish Hist.* [Ir., f. *iar* after + FINE *sb.*²] One of the four branches of the Irish clan structure comprising the men in the third grade of relationship to the chief. Cf. GEILFINE, INDFINE.
1875 H. S. MAINE *Lect. Early Hist. Inst.* 209 The eldest member of the Iarfine moved into the Indfine. **1879** *Anc. Laws Ireland* IV. p. xlix, In all the Brehon Law Tracts there are references to an existing organization, generally known as the Geilfine system, and to the four classes designated as the Geilfine, Deirbfhine, Iarfine, and Indfine. **1921** E. MACNEILL *Celtic Ireland* x. 162 If the *Iarfine* and the *Indfhine* existed as communal family groups,..the explanation is to be found in the reluctance to disturb the family holdings when the *Derbfhine* had run its course. **1967** F. J. BYRNE in Moody & Martin *Course Irish Hist.* iii. 49 The brehon lawyers drew up a very elaborate scheme of the different degrees of relationship. The *geilfhine*..was the normal family group... And the *iarfine* and *indfhine* the second and third cousins respectively.

i-armed, ME. pa. pple. of ARM *v.*

-iasis, *suffix*, the form in which -ASIS *suff.* always occurs as a living mod.L. suffix.

†**i-athel(e**, *v. Obs.* [OE. *ʒeæðelian* to ennoble, f. *æðelian*: see ATHEL(E *v.*]
1. *trans.* To make noble or renowned.
a **1000** *Hymns* vii. 26 (Gr.) Ðu eart ʒeæðelod ʒeond ealle world. *c* **1205** LAY. 22496 Þu hine scalt iæðelien, to cnihte hine dubben.
2. To elate, fill with joy.
c **1205** LAY. 3605 Sone werð þe alde king wunliche iæðeled.

Iatmul ('jætmʊl). [Native name.] A people of New Guinea, living near the Great Sepik River; their language. Also *attrib.* or as *adj.*
1932 G. BATESON in *Oceania* II. 245 (*title*) Social structure of the Iatmül people of the Sepik River. *Ibid.* 248 In the Iatmül language as in English, adjectival words precede the nouns which they qualify. In Iatmül there is no equivalent of the English conjunction 'and'. *Ibid.* 249, I have thought it most convenient to use the simple word Iatmül to denote that part of the linguistic group which lives on the banks and close to the Sepik river. **1943** S. W. REED *Making of Mod. New Guinea* i. 22 The Iatmul of the Middle Sepik River, who number approximately 10,000 persons, live in twenty-odd villages on either side of the river. *Ibid.* 23 In an isolated mountain enclave west of the Iatmul area and north of the Sepik River dwell the Kwoma. **1949** G. BATESON in M. Fortes *Social Struct.* 35 The sayings, actions, and organization of the Iatmul had certain characteristics. **1949** M. MEAD *Male & Female* iii. 52 A Iatmul head-hunter, calling in his age-grade to rape his recalcitrant wife into submission. *Ibid.* App. 403 We had to analyze the language ..and this was true also..of Mr. Bateson's original work in Iatmul. **1951** R. FIRTH *Elem. Social Organiz.* i. 22 The chronic state of the Iatmül culture.

iatraliptic (aɪætrə'lɪptɪk), *a.* and *sb. rare.* Also 8 *erron.* iatroleptic(k. [? ad. F. *iatraliptique* (Littré), ad. late L. **iatralipticus* (inferred from *iatraliptice*), ad. Gr. ἰατραλειπτικός, f. ἰατραλείπτης, f. ἰατρός physician + ἀλείπτης anointer.] **a.** *adj.* Relating to the cure of diseases by the use of unguents. **b.** *sb.* A physician who follows this method.
1656 BLOUNT *Glossogr.*, *Iatraliptick*, a Physitian or Surgeon that cureth only by outward applications of oyntments or frications. **1727-41** CHAMBERS *Cycl.* s.v., It was one Prodicus..who first instituted the iatraliptic art. **1755** JOHNSON, *Iatroleptick.* **1864** WEBSTER, *Iatraliptic.* **1886** *Syd. Soc. Lex.*, *Iatraleiptic*, *Iatraliptic.*

i'atrarchy. *nonce-wd.* [f. Gr. ἰατρός physician, after *hierarchy*.] The order of physicians.
a **1843** SOUTHEY *Doctor* (1847) VII. 498 The chiefs of the Hierarchy, the Iatrarchy, the Nomarchy, and the Hoplarchy.

iatric (aɪ'ætrɪk), *a. rare.* [ad. Gr. ἰατρικός, f. ἰατρός healer, physician, f. ἰᾶσθαι to heal: cf. obs. F. *iatrique*.] Belonging or relating to a physician or to medicine; medical; medicinal.
1851 BADHAM *Halieut.* (1854) 84 In an early age of the iatric art. **1853** *Ibid.* 346 The iatric liver of the cod. **1865** *Englishm. Mag.* Feb. 158 The iatric powers with which he [Æsculapius] is credited.

i'atrical, *a.* [f. as prec. + -AL¹.] Medical.
[**1716** M. DAVIES *Ath. Brit.* III. *Dissert. Physick* 14 Doctors of the same Panto-Jatrical Scriptures.] **1816** BYRON *Let. to Moore* 20 Feb., I..am..still under Iatrical advice.

iatro-, repr. Gr. ἰατρο-, combining form of ἰατρό-ς physician, used in Greek in ἰατρομαθηματικός IATRO-MATHEMATICAL; after which similar compounds have been formed in the mod. langs. generally.

†**iatro'chemic.** *Obs. rare*⁻⁰ [See IATRO- and CHEMIC *sb.* 2.] = iatrochemist.
[**1706** PHILLIPS, *Iatrochymicus*, a Chymical Physician.] **1721** BAILEY, *Iatrochymick*, a Chymical Physician.

iatro-chemical (aɪætrəʊ'kɛmɪkəl), *a.* [f. as prec. + -AL¹.] Relating to or holding the chemical theory of medicine and physiology adopted by Paracelsus and others: = CHEMIATRIC.
1832 SIR W. HAMILTON *Discuss.* (1853) 252 The crudities of the Iatro-mathematical and Iatro-chemical hypotheses. **1892** *Athenæum* 6 Aug. 197/2 The history of the iatro-chemical period.

iatrochemist (-'kɛmɪst). [f. as prec. + CHEMIST.] One belonging to the iatrochemical school; also *gen.* (quot. 1866), one who applies the knowledge of chemistry to medical practice.
1668 E. MAYNWARING *Medicus Absolutus* ix. 78 The Compleat Chymical Physitian. This Iatro-chymist and Hermetick Philosopher, is educated from his Youth in all necessary learning..that he may be introduced into the Medical Art legitimately. **1727** BAILEY vol. II, *Iatrochymist*, a Chymical Physician, or one who uses or prescribes chiefly Chymical Preparations. **1832** SIR W. HAMILTON *Discuss.* (1853) 260 In theory [he was]..Iatro-chemist. **1866** ODLING *Anim. Chem.* 4 Only the iatro-chemist, if I may so call him, can ever hope to understand the varied series of actions, healthy and morbid..in the living organism.

iatrochemistry (aɪætrəʊ'kɛmɪstrɪ). [f. IATRO- + CHEMISTRY, after the family of mod.L. words beginning *iatrochem-*, *iatrochym-* (cf. CHEMIC *a.* and *sb.*).
These words appear to have originated in the (translated) work of Paracelsus (d. 1541): **1573** I. DALHEMIUS tr. *Paracelsus' Chirurgia Magna* I. II. xiii. 21 Verum quia Iatrochymista [*so in* Opera Omnia (1658), *but here printed* latrochymista] sum: vtrumq3 enim scio & Medicinam & chemiam. They afterwards occur in medical works in L. by other writers, e.g. G. Phædro *Opuscula iatro-chemica quatuor* (1611); D. Burnet *Iatrochymicus, siue de præparatione et compositione medicamentorum chymicorum artificiosa* (1616).]
The theory or school of thought that existed in the 16th and 17th centuries and regarded medicine and physiology as subjects to be understood in terms of the chemistry of the time (see CHEMIATRIC *a.*).
1830 T. THOMSON *Hist. Chem.* I. v. 201 The most eminent of all the English supporters of iatro-chemistry was Thomas Willis, who was a contemporary of Sylvius. **1881** ROSCOE & SCHORLEMMER *Treat. Chem.* III. I. 4 Towards the sixteenth century, the cultivators of this science [*sc.* alchemy].. exhibited activity mainly in two directions, in the first place in the prosecution of the branch science of metallurgy, and secondly, in the development of iatrochemistry. **1909** P. J. HARTOG in *Dict. Nat. Biogr.* XIII. 176/2 Mayow stands immeasurably above such men as Willis and Sylvius, with

their medley of half-digested Cartesianism and iatrochemistry. **1958** L. THORNDIKE *Hist. Magic & Exper. Sci.* VIII. xxvii. 117 The alchemy and iatrochemistry and medicine of the late seventeenth century differed little from that of the early seventeenth century, especially in Germany.

iatrogenic (aɪˌætrəʊ'dʒɛnɪk), *a. Med.* [f. IATRO- + -GENIC.] Induced unintentionally by a physician through his diagnosis, manner, or treatment; of or pertaining to the induction of (mental or bodily) disorders, symptoms, etc., in this way.

1924 E. BLEULER tr. *Brill's Textbk. Psychiatry* xiii. 502 Not entirely unimportant, unfortunately, is the iatrogenic origin of neurotic manifestations. **1948** L. KANNER *Child Psychiatry* (ed. 2) ix. 143 Difficulties, arising from medical clumsiness in the handling of patients, are common enough to have originated the diagnosis of iatrogenic, or physician-determined, conditions of health. **1952** A. HUXLEY *Devils of Loudun* vii. 219 Like the sulpha poisoning and serum-fevers of the present, the Loudun epidemic was an 'iatrogenic disease', produced and fostered by the very physicians who were supposed to be restoring the patients to health. **1970** *Brit. Med. Bull.* XXVII. 13/2 The epidemic of iatrogenic deaths in asthmatic children shows the need for continuous monitoring of vital statistics. **1971** *Sci. Amer.* June 99/1 Although it is not common in this country, iatrogenic goiter—goiter caused by medical treatment—is becoming a more significant factor. Sulfonamides prescribed for urinary-tract infections.. and many iodine-containing compounds administered as expectorants in the treatment of asthma are potentially goitrogenic. **1973** *Guardian* 18 Jan. 12 Drug induced (iatrogenic) conditions are on the increase.

So **ia'trogeny**, the iatrogenic induction of a disorder.

1927 HENDERSON & GILLESPIE *Text-bk. Psychiatry* xiv. 416 Too often we find that in the causation of a psychoneurotic illness there has entered a very large element of 'iatrogeny'. **1940** HINSIE & SHATZKY *Psychiatric Dict.* 275/1 When the physician.. gives any diagnosis that serves as the nucleus around which the patient builds a neurosis or psychosis, the condition is known as iatrogeny. **1973** *Interfaces* May 45 The biographers of Alfred Nobel have not dealt satisfactorily with the question of his full grasp of the powers of iatrogeny (prize in physiology and medicine).

iatrology (aɪæ'trɒlədʒɪ). *rare*$^{-0}$ [ad. Gr. ἰατρολογία (Philo), f. ἶᾱτρό-ς physician: see -LOGY.] The science of, or a treatise on, medicine.

1855 in MAYNE *Expos. Lex.*

iatromathematical (-mæθɪ'mætɪkəl), *a.* [f. mod.L. *iatromathēmaticus* (Ampsingius, 1602), a. Gr. ἰατρομαθηματικός (Proclus), applied to 'those who practised medicine in conjunction with astrology', f. ἶᾱτρό-ς physician + μαθηματικ-ός mathematical: see -ICAL. Cf. F. *iatromathématique*.]

†**a.** Practising medicine in conjunction with astrology (quot. 1621). *Obs.* **b.** Relating to or holding a mathematical theory of medicine; applied to a school of physicians which arose in Italy in the 17th century, whose system of physiology and medicine was founded on the principles of mathematics and mechanics.

1621 BURTON *Anat. Mel.* II. i. IV. i. 298 Paracelsus.. will haue.. time of cure, of gathering of herbs.. Astrologically obserued, which Thurnesserus, and some Iatromathimatical professors, are too superstitious in my Iudgment. **1832** [see IATRO-CHEMICAL]. **1838–9** HALLAM *Hist. Lit.* IV. IV. viii. §38. 362 A second school of medicine.. the iatro-mathematical.

Hence **iˌatromathe'matically** *adv.* So also †**iˌatromathe'matic** *sb.* (see quot. 1656).

1603 SIR C. HEYDON *Jud. Astrol.* vi. 178 He neglecteth not the preceptes of Phisick, but Iatromathematicallie ioineth them together. **1656** BLOUNT *Glossogr.*, *Iatromathematique*.. may signifie a Physitian that is also a Mathematician, or one skild both in Physic, and the Mathematicks. **1889** H. E. HANDERSON tr. *Baas's Outl. Hist. Med.* 503 Edward Barry thought that the age of a man could be calculated Iatro-mathematically from the frequency of the pulse.

iatromathematician (-mæθɪmə'tɪʃən). [f. as prec., after *mathematician*: in F. *iatromathématicien*.] One belonging to the iatromathematical school.

1727 BAILEY vol. II, *Iatromathematician*, a Physician, who considers Diseases, and their Causes mathematically, and prescribes according to mathematical proportions. **1838–9** HALLAM *Hist. Lit.* IV. IV. viii. §38. 362 Pitcairn and Boerhaave were leaders of the iatro-mathematicians. **1858** WHEWELL *Hist. Sci. Ideas* IX. ii. §3 II. 185 Several of the iatromathematicians were at the same time teachers of engineering and of medicine.

iatromathematics. †**a.** A work on medicine and astrology. *Obs.*

1647 LILLY *Chr. Astrol.* xliv. 268, I have endeavoured to English the Iatromathematicks of Hermes. **1855** MAYNE *Expos. Lex.*, Iatromathematics.

b. The iatromathematical theory or school of thought.

1830 T. THOMSON *Hist. Chem.* I. v. 209 He was a zealous supporter of iatro-mathematics, and as such a professed antagonist of the iatro-chemists. **1889** H. E. HANDERSON tr. *Baas's Outl. Hist. Med.* 504 This was accomplished.. at a time when within its borders Iatro-chemistry and Iatro-mathematics were still in the perfection of their bloom. **1961** J. R. PARTINGTON *Hist. Chem.* II. xii. 442 Some steps in the direction of Iatromathematics (probably influenced by Galileo) were taken by Santorio Santorio (Sanctorius Sanctorius, 1561–1636),.. who discovered insensible perspiration.. by living on the platform of a large balance, on which he worked and took his meals.

iatromechanical (-mɪ'kænɪkəl), *a.* [See IATRO-.] = IATROMATHEMATICAL.

[**1801** K. SPRENGEL *Versuch einer pragm. Geschichte d. Arzneikunde* (ed. 2) IV. XIV. 500 Die Schule.. heisst die iatromathematische oder iatromechanische.] **1856** C. G. COMEGYS tr. *Renouard's Hist. Med.* VIII. x. 533 After the death of the celebrated professor of Leyden [*sc.* Boerhaave], the iatro-mechanical doctrine fell apart. **1881** HUXLEY in *Nature* No. 615. 345 This conclusion strikes at the root of the whole iatro-mechanical system. **1971** *Nature* 30 July 351/1 Long established Aristotelian doctrines began to crumble before the assault of Baconian empiricism and atomism modified by Descartes, Gassendi and Boyle: the emergence of the iatrochemical and iatromechanical 'schools' of medicine completed the rout.

iatromechanics (aɪætrəʊmɪ'kænɪks), *sb. pl.* (const. as *sing.*). [f. IATRO- + MECHANICS.] = IATROMATHEMATICS b.

1886 *Syd. Soc. Lex.*, *Iatromechanics*, the same as Iatromathematics. **1889** H. E. HANDERSON tr. *Baas's Outl. Hist. Med.* 496 Subsequently an effort was made to bring Iatro-chemistry into accord with Iatro-mechanics. **1926** C. G. CUMSTON *Introd. Hist. Med.* xvii. 274 Specificity.. was to end in a sort of Kabbalism or in union with chemistry or physics.., and, from the latter, were soon to develop the new systems of Iatro-chemistry and Iatro-mechanics. **1953** M. H. FISCH in E. A. Underwood *Sci., Med. & Hist.* I. IV. 546 It was perhaps on the strength of the Neapolitan edition of this his major work, a contribution to iatromechanics along Cartesian lines, that Santanelli became professor of medicine at Naples in 1708.

So **iatrome'chanic**, **-mecha'nician**, **-'mechanist**, one belonging to the iatromathematical school.

1856 C. G. COMEGYS tr. *Renouard's Hist. Med.* VIII. x. 548 The Iatro-chemists and the Iatro-mechanics had attempted in vain to explain the functions of organized bodies by the general laws of matter. *Ibid.* xi. 576 The essence of inflammation consists.. with the Iatromechanician, in the obstruction of the vessels. **1899** F. S. LEE tr. *Verworn's Gen. Physiol.* i. 18 The hopes of the iatromechanics and iatrochemists of being able completely to resolve vital phenomena into physics and chemistry were not fulfilled. **1926** C. G. CUMSTON *Introd. Hist. Med.* xix. 320 Lancisi, Hecquet and Baglivi.—These three names are those of the leaders of organicism at the beginning of the XVIIIth century. They were supposed to be Iatro-mechanicians with a smattering of Hippocraticism and Galenism. **1943** GARRISON & MORTON *Med. Bibliogr.* 6 Hoffmann of Halle was the most important of the Iatromechanists. He believed an ether-like 'vital fluid' to be present in the nervous system and to act upon the muscular system, giving them 'tonus'. **1955** E. H. ACKERKNECHT *Short Hist. Med.* x. 111 The iatrochemists were never accepted to the extent that the iatromechanists were.

iatromechanism (aɪætrəʊ'mɛkənɪz(ə)m). [f. IATRO- + MECHANISM.] = IATROMATHEMATICS b.

1885 *Index-Catal. Library Surg.-General's Office, U.S. Army* VI. 769 (*subject heading*) Iatro-mechanism. **1886** *Syd. Soc. Lex.*, *Iatromechanism*, the doctrine of the Iatromechanics. **1926** C. G. CUMSTON *Introd. Hist. Med.* xxi. 351 Towards the end of the XVIIth century Iatromechanism so completely counterbalanced Iatrochemistry that the mechanics of the living being rather than the composition of the humours became the object of study.

iatrophysical (aɪætrəʊ'fɪzɪkəl), *a.* [See IATRO-.] = IATROMATHEMATICAL *a.* b.

1883 *Encycl. Brit.* XV. 810/2 The iatro-physical school of medicine grew out of physiological theories. **1886** *Syd. Soc. Lex.*, *Iatrophysical*, of or belonging to what is medical and physical; anciently applied as an epithet of certain writings which treated of natural phenomena with relation to medicine. **1954** R. H. MAJOR *Hist. Med.* I. 506 Borelli was unquestionably the perhaps unwitting founder of a new school of medicine—the Iatro-physical School, whose most extreme advocates sought the explanation of all medicine in physics or in mechanics, just as the Iatro-chemists found the ultimate explanation in fermentation.

iatrophysicist (aɪætrəʊ'fɪzɪsɪst). [f. next, after *physics, physicist*.] = IATROMATHEMATICIAN.

1889 H. E. HANDERSON tr. *Baas's Outl. Hist. Med.* 497 In therapeutics the Iatro-physicists.. managed in accordance with the principles of genuine (Hippocratic) experience. **1917** A. H. BUCK *Growth of Med.* xxviii. 366 It became customary to employ the terms, 'iatrochemists' and 'iatrophysicists' in speaking of the partisans of the two schools of medicine (the iatrochemical and the iatrophysical or iatromechanical). **1957** *Encycl. Brit.* XV. 201/1 The language and the theories of the iatrophysicists, the iatrochemists and the vitalists.. have long been discarded.

iatrophysics (aɪætrəʊ'fɪzɪks), *sb. pl.* (const. as *sing.*). [f. IATRO- + PHYSICS.] = IATROMATHEMATICS b.

1886 in *Syd. Soc. Lex.* **1889** H. E. HANDERSON tr. *Baas's Outl. Hist. Med.* 501 William Cockburn (about 1696) too embraced Iatro-physics eclectically. **1928** C. SINGER *Short Hist. Med* iv. 127 Numerous fresh theories arose, of which the more important can be classed under the three headings Iatrophysics, Iatrochemistry, and Vitalism. **1945** D. GUTHRIE *Hist. Med.* xi. 204 Sydenham.. rejected entirely the ideas of iatro-physics or iatro-chemistry. **1961** J. R. PARTINGTON *Hist. Chem.* II. viii. 297 Domenico Sanguinetti and Joseph del Papa.. were practically the only Italian physicians of the time to oppose the chemical theory and prefer Iatrophysics.

i-attred, -et, ME. pa. pple. of ATTER *v.*, to poison.

ib., abbrev. of IBIDEM.

Iban ('iːbæn, iː'bæn), *sb.* and *a.* [Native name.] **A.** *sb.* A people of Sarawak, also known as the Sea Dyaks; a member of this people, and the name of their language. **B.** *adj.* Of or pertaining to this people.

1911 F. W. PAGE-TURNER in *Sarawak Mus. Jrnl.* I. 133 A child which they adopted and named Diang Idah who is the origin of the tribe called Iban. *Ibid.*, Tiang Laju is thus the origin of the Iban race as the grand-parents of Diang Idah came from there. **1960** *Guardian* 9 Nov. 10/3 The population includes Ibans (also known as Sea Dayaks). **1962** B. HARRISSON *Orang-Utan* ii. 53 An Iban Dayak from the Sebuyan area in the Second Division of Sarawak. **1967** B. SANDIN *Sea Dayaks of Borneo* p. xix, 'Iban' is a term of Kayan origin which did not come into general use until quite late in the nineteenth century, while the term 'Sea Dayak' was imposed by the Brookes... The Ibans originally had no term which recognised their indisputable ethnic unity. **1969** *Franciscan Missionary Herald* XXXIV. 35 Mother St. Robert and Sister Otteran speak Iban. *Ibid.* 36 The interior of an Iban Long-house.

Ibanag ('iːbənɑːg), *sb.* and *a.* [Native name.] **A.** *sb.* The name of one of the peoples inhabiting northern Luzon in the Republic of the Philippines, of a member of this people, and of their language. **B.** *adj.* Of or pertaining to this people.

1885 *Encycl. Brit.* XVIII. 753/1 The other tribes of the Philippines—the Ilocanes, Pampangos, Pangasinanes, Ibanags or Cagayans,.. &c. **1900** F. H. SAWYER *Inhabitants Philippines* 252 The Ibanags inhabit the Babuyanes and Batanes Islands. **1901** *Rep. Philippine Comm.* III. 405 In order to state very briefly how the remaining Philippine languages or dialects are related we select from among them some of the principal ones... These are the Ibanag and Ilocano, of North Luzon. **1924** D. P. BARROWS *Hist. Philippines* (rev. ed.) 11 The valley of the Cagayan [is inhabited] by a people commonly called Cagayanes, but whose dialect is Ibanag. **1937** *Publ. Inst. Nat. Lang.* (Manila) I. 3 The Institute.. has taken unto itself the task of studying as many.. languages as it could possibly manage, and has included.. Ibanag and Ivatan. **1942** J. R. HAYDEN *Philippines* 864 Ranging in number from between 700,000 and 800,000 to about 60,000 are the Bikol,.. Ibanag, and Sambal groups. **1958** G. F. ZAIDE *Hist. Filipino People* ii. 11 The Malayan Filipinos.. comprise the.. Ilokanos, Bikols, Kagayans (Ibanags), Pampangans.

i-banned, ME. pa. pple. of BAN *v.*

i-bannysshed, ME. pa. pple. of BANISH *v.*

i-baptized, ME. pa. pple. of BAPTIZE *v.*

c **1305** *St. Kath. 191* in *E.E.P.* (1862) 95 Tuo hondred knyȝtes ek ibaptized were.

i-barnd, ME. pa. pple. of BURN *v.*

1297 R. GLOUC. (Rolls) 9535 Wircestre was þus ibarnd.

†**i-be,** *v. Obs. rare.* [f. I- *pref.*[1], OE. *ʒe-* + BE *v.*] *intr.* To be.

a **1175** *Cott. Hom.* 235 Hwe seden ærst þat þes ærndraces wer isent of fif cheðen, swa ibeoð. *a* **1225** *Ancr. R.* 392 Hes deciples, þet schulden stonden bi him and ibeon his siden. *c* **1320** *Seuyn Sag.* (W.) 458, I thi soget wil ibe.

i-be, i-beo, i-ben, ME. pa. pple. of BE *v.*

i-beate(n, -bete(n, ME. pa. pple. of BEAT *v.*

†**i-bedde.** *Obs.* [OE. *ʒebedda, -e* (= OS. *gibeddio*, MHG. *gebette*), f. BED *sb.*] A bedfellow.

Beowulf (Z.) 655 Wolde wiʒfruma wealh-þeo secan cwen to ʒebeddan. *a* **1250** *Owl & Night.* 1570 þat [he].. hire sende betere ibedde. *Ibid.* 1490.

†**i-bede,** *v. Obs.* [OE. *ʒebéodan*, f. *béodan*: see BID *v.* A.] *trans.* To command, proclaim, offer.

a **800** *O.E. Chron.* an. 755 Hiera se æþeling ʒehwelcum feoh and feorh ʒebead. *c* **930** *Laws of Æthelst.* II. c. 20 Hit beo seofon nihtum ʒeboden. *a* **1300** *Floris & Bl.* 804 Ihc wulle ȝeue þe a kinedom, Also long and also brod Also eure ȝet þi fader ibod.

i-beft, ME. var. of BEFT *pa. pple.*, beaten.

c **1300** *Cursor M.* 20974 (Edin.) Anis was he I-beft a tuise.

i-bent, ME. pa. pple. of BEND *v.*

†**i-beot.** *Obs.* [OE. *ʒebéot*, f. *ʒe-* I- *pref.* + BEOT.] Threatening.

c **1000** ÆLFRIC *Hom.* I. 568 Alys us nu Drihten fram his ʒebeote. *c* **1205** LAY. 7682 Heo speken of þrætte & of prute ibeote. *Ibid.* 21029 þis was heore ibeot.

i-berded, southern ME. form of BEARDED.

1387 TREVISA *Higden* (Rolls) II. 195 A mayde.. i-chaunged and i-torned into a man, and was i-berded anon.

†**i-bere,** *sb. Obs.* [OE. *ʒebǽru, -e* bearing, f. *beran* to BEAR.] Bearing, comportment, conduct.

a **900** CYNEWULF *Elene* 659 (Gr.) We.. on ʒewritu setton þeoda ʒebæru. *a* **1250** in *O.E. Misc.* 100 Milde wes þat mayde.. And of fayre ibere. *a* **1250** *Owl & Night.* 222 Alle þat ihereth þine ibere.

†**i-bere,** *v.*[1] *Obs.* [OE. *ʒeberan* (= OS. and OHG. *giberan*, Goth. *gabairan*), f. *beran* to BEAR.] *trans.* To bear, bring forth.

c **893** K. ÆLFRED *Oros.* IV. i. §7 Ne mehton nanuht libbendes ʒeberan. *c* **1000** ÆLFRIC *Gen.* xxxv. 19 Rachel

..ȝebær..Beniamin. *c* **1205** LAY. 27850 Arður..þider iberen lette Luces þene kaisere. *a* **1225** *Ancr. R.* 194 Wel is þe moder þet ou iber. *c* **1275** *Pass. our Lord* 12 in *O.E. Misc.* 37 þrytty wyntre and more..Seoþþe þat Mayde hyre yber.

†**i-bere**, *v.*² *Obs.* [OE. *ȝebǽran* to comport oneself = OS. *gibârian*, MHG. *gebæren*: see BERE *v.*] *intr.* To conduct oneself.

c **897** K. ÆLFRED *Gregory's Past.* xlvi. 356 Ne scule [ȝe] wið hine ȝebæran swa swa wið feond. *c* **1205** LAY. 21010 þe mon þe swa ibereð. *Ibid.* 30288 Nu we maȝen wepen and wanliche iberen. *a* **1225** *Juliana* 52 He iberde as..ful wiht.

Iberian (aɪˈbɪərɪən), *a.* and *sb.* [f. L. *Ibēria* the country of the *Ibēri* or *Ibēres*, a. Gr. Ἴβηρες the Spaniards, also an Asiatic people near the Caucasus in modern Georgia. See -AN, -IAN.]

A. *adj.* **1.** Of or pertaining to ancient Iberia in Europe (comprising Spain and Portugal, the 'Iberian peninsula'), or its inhabitants; hence **a.** Basque; **b.** Of Spain and Portugal unitedly.

a **1618** SYLVESTER *Tobacco battered* 692 By This, th' Iberian Argonauts May be suppos'd..T' have kill'd more Men then by their Martyrdom, Or Massacre. **1634** MILTON *Comus* 60 Roving the Celtic and Iberian fields. **1828–32** THIRLWALL & HARE tr. *Niebuhr's Hist. Rome* (1851) I. 171 An Iberian colony at Nora. **1881** *Times* 21 Apr. 9/4 Whether this Iberian scheme has any chance of realization. **1898** J. HERON *Celtic Church* 7 There are reasons for believing that the Firbolgs contained an Iberian element.

2. Of or pertaining to ancient Iberia in Asia, nearly corresponding to modern Georgia.

1671 MILTON *P.R.* III. 318 The Hyrcanian cliffs Of Caucasus, and dark Iberian dales.

3. Pertaining to the Iberians of Britain (cf. B. *sb.* 3).

1880 *Encycl. Brit.* XII. 605/2 Extreme exponents of the theory do not hesitate to speak of the Iberian ancestors of the people of England. **1907** T. R. HOLMES *Anc. Brit.* 65 The race to which they [*sc.* neolithic inhabitants of Britain] belonged is often called the Iberian, though there is no reason to believe that its British representatives belonged to the Iberian rather than to some other branch of the Mediterranean stock.

B. *sb.* **1. a.** An inhabitant of ancient Iberia in Europe; hence (*a*) a Basque, (*b*) a Spaniard. **b.** The language of ancient Iberia, supposed to be represented by the modern Basque.

1623 COCKERAM, *Iberians*, Spaniards. **1632** MASSINGER *Maid of Hon.* I. i, When the Iberian quaked, her [England's] worthies named. **1842** PRICHARD *Nat. Hist. Man* xxiv. (1848) 256 The language of the ancient Iberians has survived..in the vernacular speech of the Biscayans in Spain and the Basques of France.

2. An inhabitant of ancient Iberia in Asia.

1601 HOLLAND *Pliny* I. 119 You enter..into the Iberians region, who are separated from the Albanois..by the riuer Alazon, which runneth downe from the Caucasian hills. **1613** PURCHAS *Pilgrimage* (1614) 43 The Iberians, saith Montanus, dwelt neare to Meotis: certaine Colonies of them inhabited Spaine, and called it Hiberia. **1635** PAGITT *Christianogr.* I. ii. (1636) 54 The Georgians are those people whom Cosmographers cal Iberians.

3. A neolithic inhabitant of Britain, considered as one of a branch of the continental Iberians.

1880 W. B. DAWKINS *Early Man in Brit.* 322 The Silures, identified by Tacitus with the Iberians, were left only in those fastnesses which were subsequently a refuge for the Welsh against the English invaders. **1900** W. A. DUTT *Norfolk* 7 The Iceni..were probably mentally as well as physically superior to the Iberians. **1920** H. F. HENDERSON *Relig. in Scotl.* i. 11 The Iberians absorbed the Celts without serious dilution of their original characteristics. **1957** G. ASHE *King Arthur's Avalon* i. 15 Throughout a long stretch of years the inhabitants of Britain were dark little Iberians.

Hence **I'berianism** (see quot.).

1880 *Literary World* 8 Oct. 234/2 Iberianism, the project of bringing Spain and Portugal together under a single crown.

Iberic (aɪˈbɛrɪk), *a.* [ad. L. *Ibēricus* (*Hi-*) Spanish, f. *Ibēri*: see prec.] = IBERIAN A. 1 b.

1881 *Times* 21 Apr. 4/1 A large stride towards the Iberic union.

iberis (aɪˈbɪərɪs). [mod.L. (J. J. Dillenius in Linnæus *Systema Naturæ* (1735)), prob. f. Gr. Ἴβηρες Iberians, as several species come from Spain, but cf. Gr. ἰβηρίς, L. *iberis* a kind of cress.] A low-growing herb or sub-shrub of the genus so called, native to southern Europe and western Asia, and bearing flattened heads of small white, pink, or purple flowers; = CANDYTUFT.

1768 P. MILLER *Gardeners Dict.* (ed. 8) s.v. Iberis 7, Iberis with roundish crenated leaves. **1788** MAWE & ABERCROMBIE *Every Man his Own Gardener* (ed. 12) 582/2 Round leaved alpine Iberis, Evergreen linear-leaved Cretan Iberis. **1871** W. ROBINSON *Hardy Flowers* viii. 25 How pretty and useful even as tiny evergreen shrubs, are the Iberisis! **1931** M. E. STEBBING *Hardy Flower Gardening* x. 170 Catmint, *Iberis*, and similiar half-shrubby plants should have each shoot pulled off with a downward jerk. **1971** A. SCOTT-JAMES *Down to Earth* xi. 128 Iberis (both annual and perennial), valerian,..polyanthus and sedum have all grown contentedly in my garden.

Iberism (ˈaɪbərɪz(ə)m). [f. as IBERIAN + -ISM.] (See quots.) So **'Iberist**, an advocate of 'Iberism'.

1881 *Sat. Rev.* 23 Apr. 519 Iberism..signifies the desire for a coalition of Spain and Portugal, in which Iberia is to be for the Iberians. *Ibid.*, The Iberist..would probably retort that England and Scotland got on very well together.

iberite (ˈaɪbəraɪt). *Min.* [f. L. *Ibēria* Spain + -ITE.] An altered form of iolite found at Toledo.

1868 DANA *Min.* (ed. 5) 301 *Weissite, iberite, huronite*, are ..supposed to be altered iolite.

Ibero- (aɪˈbɪərəʊ), combining form of IBERIAN *a.* and *sb.*, with the meaning 'Iberian and'.

1891 RHYS in *Academy* 26 Sept. 268/2, I believe Picts and Iberians to have belonged to one and the same family, which I have ventured to call Ibero-Pictish. **1896** A. H. KEANE *Ethnology* 378 *margin*, The Ibero-Berber problem. **1900** tr. *J. Deniker's Races of Man* 285 Tawny white skin, black hair. Short stature, dolicho-cephalic Ibero-insular. **1920** *Glasgow Herald* 24 Sept. 6 The Ibero-American Republics. **1927** [see GETULIAN A. *adj.* b]. **1955** *Proc. Prehist. Soc.* XXI. 50 As for the micro-burins of the Capsian and Iberomauretanian, it seems possible to relate them to ours. **1955** *Archivum Linguisticum* VII. 68 The immense resources of Ibero-Romance have rarely been tapped. **1963** *Economist* 7 Dec. 985/3 The new Ibero-French relationship. **1964** C. F. & F. M. VOEGELIN in *Anthropol. Ling.* Nov. VI. VIII. 1 (*title*) Languages of the world: Ibero-Caucasian and Pidgin-Creole. **1971** *Language* XLVII. 232 Klimov rejects the migrational theory for the Ibero-Caucasian languages, regarding them as autochthonous.

i-bet, ME. pa. pple. of BEET *v.*, to amend.

†**i-bete**, *v. Obs.* [OE. *ȝebétan*, f. *bétan* to make good, amend, BEET.] *trans.* To make good, amend, mend.

971 *Blickl. Hom.* 91 Đonne sceolan we..ȝebetan ealle þa we ær..ȝedydon. *c* **1175** *Lamb. Hom.* 35 Wa is me þet ic..heo ne ȝebette. *Ibid.* 149 If he ne mei..his neode ibete. *c* **1275** *Moral Ode* 234 Heo nolde..heore sinne ibete.

ibex (ˈaɪbɛks). Also 7 **ibecks**. Pl. **ibexes**, rarely **ibices** (ˈaɪbɪsiːz). [L. *ibex* (*ibic-em*) a kind of goat, a chamois.] A species of wild goat (*Capra ibex* or *Ibex ibex*) inhabiting the Alps and Apennines, the male of which has very large strongly ridged recurved diverging horns, and hair of a brownish or reddish grey becoming grey in winter; the female, shorter horns and grey hair; also called *bouquetin* and *steinbock*. Extended to other species of the same genus or subgenus, inhabiting mountain-ranges in Europe, Asia, and Africa.

1607 TOPSELL *Four-f. Beasts* (1658) 194 They inhabit..the Rocks or Mountains, but not the tops like the Ibecks. *Ibid.* 347 The Ibex..[some] take it to be a wilde Goat..these are bred in the Alpes, and are of an admirable celerity, although their heads be loaded with such horns, as no other Beasts of their stature beareth. **1671** J. WEBSTER *Metallogr.* ix. 140 Goats that are called Ibices. **1774** GOLDSM. *Nat. Hist.* II. 38 The ibex resembles the goat in..shape. **1776** PENNANT *Zool.* (ed. 4) I. 34 The origin of the domestick goat is the *Stein-boc, Ibex*, or wild goat. **1878** G. F. MACLEAR *Joshua* xv. (1880) 142 Numerous ibexes or Syrian chamois inhabit these cliffs.

Ibibio (ɪbɪˈbiːəʊ), *sb.* and *a.* [Native name.]

A. *sb.* A people of Southern Nigeria; a member of this people; their language. **B.** *adj.* Of or pertaining to this people.

1822 J. ADAMS *Sk. Voy. Afr.* v. 77 Three-fourths of all the negroes sold at Bonny were Heebos, the remaining fourth was composed of..the Ibbiby. **1862** H. GOLDIE *Dict. Efik Lang.* v. p. xlix, A few Ibibio words are inserted. **1890** —— *Calabar & its Mission* i. 13 By far the greater part of the oil exported is produced by the tribes behind, especially by Ibibio. **1905** C. PARTRIDGE *Cross River Natives* ii. 33 The district of Calabar is peopled by..the Efiks, the Ibibios, and the Ekois. *Ibid.* ii. 43 Most of the native labour is drawn from the Ibibio country. **1915** D. A. TALBOT *Woman's Mysteries of Primitive People* xv. 213 Among the Ibibios different funeral rites are prescribed according to age, position, and manner of death. **1919** H. H. JOHNSTON *Compar. Study Bantu & Semi-Bantu Lang.* I. 814 My information regarding..*Ibibiω*, and the allied *Kwō* dialect..has been chiefly obtained from the Rev. Hugh Goldie's *Dictionary of the Efik Language*. **1925** J. A. MACCULLOCH *Mythol. All Races* VII. 111 The head-pad..figures in some curious magical ceremonies of the Ibibio. **1932** *Africa* V. 503 One West African language, viz. Ibibio, spoken by about three-quarters of a million people in the Calabar province of Southern Nigeria. **1936** J. G. FRAZER *Aftermath: Suppl. Golden Bough* i. 18 Among the Ibibios of Southern Nigeria, 'old women may not touch soup made in deep pots, lest they receive too much nourishment therefrom, which will cause them to live beyond the allotted span'. **1958** J. S. COLEMAN *Nigeria* i. 31 The Ibo and Ibibio languages belong to different branches of the large Niger-Congo linguistic family. **1960** *Times* 5 Oct. 18/7 Astonishing..naturalism in the very large Ibibio mask in wood.

Ibicencan (ɪbɪˈθɛŋkən), *sb.* and *a.* Also Ibicenco, Ibizenco. [f. Sp. *ibicenca* native or inhabitant of Ibiza, *ibicenco* pertaining to Ibiza + -AN.] **A.** *sb.* A native or inhabitant of Ibiza, an island off the Mediterranean coast of Spain. **B.** *adj.* Of or pertaining to Ibiza, esp. in ***Ibicencan hound*** (= IVICENE *sb.*).

1911 J. E. C. FLITCH *Mediterranean Moods* ix. 188 The Ibicencos have never naturalised the guitar. *Ibid.* 199 They sang chiefly in Catalan, and the song had a different character from that of the Ibicenco peasants. **1952** E. WHELPTON *Balearics* xv. 189 The Ibicencans..were for centuries considered to be savage barbarians. **1959** *Encounter* Oct. 39 The Ibicencan hounds—pale rib-thin beasts. **1969** C. IRVING *Fake!* (1970) xii. 139 He liked the Ibizencos, too, a friendly and dignified island people. **1970** *Globe Mag.* (Toronto) 26 Sept. 12/1 There is a native strain of dogs on the island, the Ibicencan hounds, said to be descended from the hunting hounds of the ancient Egyptians. **1972** *Times* 3 Feb. 25/6 One of the most attractive apartment developments..in typical Ibicenco style.

†**i-bid**, *v. Obs.* [OE. *ȝebiddan* (= OS. *gebiddean*, Goth. *gabidjan*), f. *biddan*, BID *v.* B.] *intr.* To pray. (In OE. with refl. dative.)

971 *Blickl. Hom.* 139 Uton ȝebiddan us to urum Drihtne. *c* **1000** *Ags. Gosp.* Matt. vi. 5 Þonne ȝe eow ȝebiddon. *c* **1175** *Lamb. Hom.* 45 Ic ham ȝeue reste alswa þu ibeden hauest. *a* **1225** *Ancr. R.* 144 Wakieð & ibiddeð ou, & tet schal makien ou stonden. *a* **1300** *Vox & Wolf* 135 Ich hedde so ibede for the.

‖**ibidem** (ɪˈbaɪdɛm, ˈɪbɪdɛm). [L., = in the same place; f. *ibi* there + demonstr. suffix *-dem*, as in *idem, tandem*, etc.] In the same place; in the same book, chapter, passage, etc.: used to avoid the repetition of a reference. Abbreviated *ibid.* or *ib.*

1663 BOYLE *Exp. & Nat. Philos.* II. 415 Ad pag. 257..Ibid. Hæc, &c. *Ibid.* 416 Ad pag. 259 Ib. Cholera..is cured by the same Remedies. **1675** BAXTER *Cath. Theol.* I. I. 13 See more Ibid..to the same purpose. *Ibid.* II. VIII. 169, I find Dr. Twisse (*ibid.* and *alibi sæpe*) charging it on them [etc.]. **1762–71** H. WALPOLE *Vertue's Aneced. Paint.* (1786) I. 119 Ibidem, Adam and Eve, half figures. **1868** FURNIVALL *Forewords to Babees Bk.* 51 R. Whiston, *Cathedral Trusts*, p. 2–4. .. *Ibid.*, p. 10–12.

ibidine (ˈaɪbɪdaɪn), *a. Zool.* [f. L. *ībis, ībid-* (see IBIS) + -INE.] Related to the ibis.

1875 PARKER & NEWTON in *Encycl. Brit.* III. 713/1 In most of these Ciconian and Ibidine types the vomer is evidently azygous.

-ibility [F. *-ibilité*, L. *-ibilitātem, -tās*], termination of abstract sbs. from adjs. in -IBLE.

†**i-binde**, *v.* [OE. *ȝebindan* (= OS. *gibindan*, OHG. *gibintan*), f. BIND *v.*] *trans.* To bind.

c **1000** *Ags. Gosp.* Mark v. 3 Hine nan man..ne mihte ȝebindan. *a* **1175** *Cott. Hom.* 229 Þat þa wel reowen hine ȝenaman and ȝebunden. *c* **1205** LAY. 2487 Heo nom Æstrild & Abren & lette heom ibinden.

ibis (ˈaɪbɪs). Pl. ibises; also (now rarely) **ibides** (ˈaɪbɪdiːz), **ibes** (ˈaɪbiːz). [a. L. *ībis* (gen. *ībis, ībidis*, pl. *ībēs*), a. Gr. ἶβις (gen. ἴβιδος, ἴβεως) the ibis, an Egyptian bird. So in F., Sp., and Pg.; It. *ibi.*] **1.** A genus of large grallatorial birds of the family *Ibididæ*, allied to the stork and heron, comprising numerous species with long legs and long slender decurved bill, inhabiting lakes and swamps in warm climates; a bird of this genus, esp. (and originally) the Sacred Ibis of Egypt (*Ibis religiosa*), with white and black plumage, an object of veneration among the ancient Egyptians.

Other species are the Glossy Ibis (*Ibis* or *Plegadis falcinellus*), found widely in the Old World and occasionally in N. America; the White Ibis (*Eudocimus albus*) of the Southern U.S.; the Scarlet Ibis (*E. ruber*) of tropical and subtropical America, etc.

1382 WYCLIF *Deut.* xiv. 16 An ybyn [1388 a siconye], that is a foule of Nyle flood. *c* **1400** MAUNDEV. (Roxb.) vi. 23 Aboute þis ryuer er grete plentee of fewles þat er called in Latyne Ciconie or Ibices [*ed.* 1839, 45 Sikonyes that thei clepen Ibes]. **1588** GREENE *Pandosto* (1843) 51 Like the bird Ibys in Egipt, which hateth serpents yet feedeth on their egges. **1594**? GREENE *Selimus* Wks. 1881–3 XIV. 284 Those industrious birds, Those Ibides. *a* **1661** HOLYDAY *Juvenal* 271 They ador'd the bird ibis, for eating the eggs of serpents, which infest their countrey; and for destroying snakes. **1839–43** YARRELL *Hist. Brit. Birds* II. 506 The appearance of the Glossy Ibis [*Ibis falcinellus*] in this country, though not uncommon, is still accidental. **1874** COUES *Birds N.W.* 513 Ibises inhabit the warmer parts of both hemispheres. They are nearly related to Herons.

2. *Angling.* The name of a type of artificial fly; now more usu. applied to a sort of red-dyed feather used in making this type of fly.

1863 *Harper's Mag.* Oct. 691/2 He trailed his 'ibis' lightly across the dark eddy at the edge of the foam. **1931** *Hardy's Anglers' Guide* (ed. 53) 75 Wet flies for brook trout...Ibis. **1961** A. C. WILLIAMS *Dict. Trout Flies* (ed. 3) 294 Tail: Red ibis feather. *Ibid.* 299 Tag: Bright red wool, or scarlet ibis. **1973** *Country Life* 7 June 1585/3 The butcher is a well-tried trout fly... It is made from what is known as dyed ibis (a hen's feather, dyed bright red), silver tinsel, [etc.].

3. A fashion colour (see quot.).

1927 *Daily News* 9 May 2/3 A skirt of satin..in the new pale apricot known as 'ibis'.

4. *attrib.* and *Comb.*, as *ibis-headed, -red* adjs.

1910 *Daily Chron.* 19 Feb. 6/2 Thoth, god of wisdom, was ibis-headed. **1907** *Westm. Gaz.* 29 Oct. 4/3 A pretty blouse of white lace, so arranged with ibis-red velvet as to have the effect of a smart little bolero. **1909** *Ibid.* 21 June 5/2 An ibis-red coat and skirt.

Ibiza (ɪˈbiːθə, ɪˈviːθə). The name of one of the Balearic Islands, used esp. *attrib.* to denote a local breed of dog, the IVICENE.

1935 *Hutchinson's Dog Encycl.* II. 924/1 (*caption*) The Ibiza hound..is reputed to refuse to interbreed with any other type of dog. **1948** B. VESEY-FITZGERALD *Bk. Dog* I. 73 An Ibiza hound, one of the rarest breeds I know and found ..only in the Balearics. *Ibid.*, The Ibiza is not, at first sight, prepossessing.

Ibizan (ɪ'bi:θən, ɪ'vi:θən), *a.* [f. IBIZ(A + -AN.] = IBICENCAN *a.* **Ibizan hound** = IVICENE *sb.* Also as *sb.*, the language of Ibiza; an Ibizan hound.

1911 J. E. C. FLITCH *Mediterranean Moods* viii. 169 An Ibizan oasis. **1936** M. K. SHEPPARD *Cottage in Majorca* iii. 51 Their gold ornaments were similar to those of the Ibizan women. **1952** E. WHELPTON *Balearics* xv. 199 See the local dances and hear the strange Ibizan music. *Ibid.* xvi. 201 Ibizan, like Mallorquin, is based on Catalan. **1971** F. HAMILTON *World Encycl. Dogs* 371 As a hunter the Ibizan Hound is unequalled. **1972** *Country Life* 10 Feb. 329/2 When the sporting varieties were exhibited the classes were almost entirely filled with pharaoh hounds and Ibizan hounds. *Ibid.* Suppl. 17 Ibizans..Irish Terriers..Jack Russell Terriers. **1972** *Listener* 13 July 55/2 Irving, with help from another Ibizan writer, put together the book.

i-blamed, ME. pa. pple. of BLAME *v.*

-ible, the form of the suffix -BLE, representing L. *-ĭbilis*, formed from Latin consonantal stems (verbal or participial) and some *e*-stems, and *-ībilis* from *ī*-stems; as *leg-ible*, *poss-ible*, *vis-ible*, *flex-ible*, *permiss-ible*, *terr-ible*, *aud-ible*. Often displaced by *-able* in words that have come through French, or that are looked upon as formed immediately on an Eng. verb. as *refer-able*, *ten-able*, *readmitt-able*, *convert-able*, *divid-able*.

i-bleched, ME. pa. pple. of BLEACH *v.*

i-bled, ME. pa. pple. of BLEED *v.*

i-blend, i-blent, ME. pa. pple. of BLEND *v.*, to blind, etc.: see also YBLENT.

i-blessed, -et, ME. pa. pple. of BLESS *v.*

i-blowe(n, ME. pa. pple. of BLOW *v.*[1] and [2].

Ibo ('i:bəʊ), *a.* and *sb.* Also Ebo, Igbo. [Native name.] **A.** *adj.* Of or pertaining to the Ibos (see below). Cf. EBOE.

Some of the examples refer to Ibos in the U.S.A. and the West Indies.

1732 *South Carolina Gaz.* 20/1 Stolen..an old Ebo Negro Man;..had on a blue Negro Cloth Frock. **1774** E. LONG *Hist. Jamaica* II. III. ii. 403 The Ebo men are lazy, and averse to every laborious employment; the women performing almost all the work in their own country. **1799** [see NEGRO 3 a]. **1822** J. ADAMS *Sk. Voy. Afr.* iii. 41 Breeché, in the Heebo language, signifies gentleman. **1834** [see EBOE]. **1884** *Encycl. Brit.* XVII. 319/1 Soudan and Guinea. .. Ibo group. **1899** E. A. WISE in *Niger & Yoruba Notes* Nov. 37/1 We are morally pledged to do this by having a Mission in the Ibo country for over 40 years. **1950** D. JONES *Phoneme* 21 The Igbo language of Nigeria. **1951** R. FIRTH *Elem. Social Organiz.* v. 165 Some of the Ibo people of South-Eastern Nigeria construct elaborate series of clay figures. **1960** *Spectator* 31 Oct. 616 The squalor and nobility of life in an Ibo tribe. **1968** *Listener* 19 Sept. 353/1 The Ibo officer who had just murdered the Premier of the Northern Region. *Ibid.*, The Ibo leader, Ojukwu, and his five or six million Ibo are now concentrated within a narrowing portion of their former region.

B. *sb.* **1. a.** A Negro people of the lower Niger in Africa; also, a member of this people.

1757 *St Jago Intelligencer* 14 May, 1 Ebo, 1 Angola, 1 Mundingo. [**1789** O. EQUIANO *Life* I. i. 18 Mahogany-coloured men from the south west of us: we call them *Oye-Eboe*, which term signifies red men living at a distance.] **1822** J. ADAMS *Sk. Voy. Afr.* iii. 40 To this nation the Heebos express a strong aversion. *Ibid.* 41 The Heebos, in their persons, are tall and well-formed. **1822** *Amer. Beacon* (Norfolk, Va.) 3 Sept. 2/1 (Th. Suppl.), Monday Gell is an Ebo, and now in the prime of life. **1836** F. H. RANKIN *White Man's Grave* I. v. 106 Shortly after arriving, when Settlers and Maroons were to me as equally black and undistinguishable as Soosoos and Ibbos, I innocently inflicted deep injury on the sensitive mind of the laundress by inquiring why she had omitted to bring home some particular article of dress. **1911** *Encycl. Brit.* XIV. 223/2 The Ibo are a strong well-built Negro race. **1954** M. GLUCKMAN in *Institutions Primitive Soc.* vi. 70 In the past, an Ibo in Nigeria could only travel safely in distant parts to trade by following chains of relationship from place to place. **1960** *Guardian* 15 July 15/3 The Ibos (or better, the Igbos) live mainly in the Eastern Region [of Nigeria]. **1961** *Listener* 30 Nov. 901/2 The intensely individualistic and vital Ibo in the south-east [of Nigeria]. **1973** *Black World* Jan. 9/1 Another example is the figure of Ikenga—god of fortune among the Igbos—in whose left hand is a skull.

b. The language of this people, which constitutes one of the major language groups of Nigeria.

1880 MRS. G. STURGE tr. *Burdo's Niger & Benueh* viii. 141 'The King, our master,' one of them said to me in the language of Ebo. **1883** R. N. CUST *Sk. Mod. Lang. Afr.* I. xi. 223 Ibo or eboe: commences at the apex of the Delta of the Niger... There appear to be four dialects. **1950** FORDE & JONES *Ibo & Ibibio Speaking Peoples* 11 *Igbo* is one of the Kwa languages. **1955** [see FANTI *sb.* and *a.* a]. **1958** J. S. COLEMAN *Nigeria* i. 18 Before the British occupation..the present Eastern region consisted of small semiautonomous communities of Ibo- and Ibibio-speaking peoples. **1962** *Amer. Speech* XXXVII. 227 A case of disagreement taken from Ibo, a tone language. **1968** CHOMSKY & HALLE *Sound Pattern Eng.* 378 In a language such as Turkish there are four classes of harmonizing words, rather than two as in Nez Perce or Igbo.

i-bobbed, ME. pa. pple. of BOB *v.*

†**i-bod**, *sb.* *Obs.* [OE. *ȝebod* (= OS. *gibod*, OHG. *gabot*, *gibot*, Ger. *gebot*), f. OE. *béodan*, OTeut. **beudan* to command: see BID *v.* A.]

a. Command, order. **b.** Bid, offer.

c **888** K. ÆLFRED *Boeth.* xxxix. §13 Be þæs cyninges ȝebode. *c* **1205** LAY. 14611 Nulle we nauere mare þine iboden here. *Ibid.* 22524 Al þat he ȝirnde al he him ȝette, ȝisles and aðes, and alle his ibodes.

i-bod, ME. pa. t. of IBEDE *v.*, to offer.

i-boded, ME. pa. t. of BODE *v.*

i-boden, ME. pa. t. of *bede*, BID *v.* A.

†**i-boen, i-bon**, *ppl. a.* [f. I- (:—*ȝe-*) + ODa. *bóin* = ON. *búinn* pa. pple. of *bóa*, *búa* to make ready, etc.: cf. BOUND *ppl. a.*[1]] Made ready, prepared, attired, dressed.

c **1205** LAY. 14294 Heo weoren swiðe wel ibon. *a* **1300** *Siriz* 434 Ich am redi and iboen To don al that thou saie.

ibogaine (ɪ'bəʊgəi:n). *Chem.* [a. F. *ibogaïne* (Dybowski & Landrin 1901, in *Compt. Rend.* CXXXIII. 749), f. *iboga*, Congolese name and specific epithet (E. H. Baillon 1889, in *Bull. de la Soc. linn. de Paris* I. 782) of the shrub (see def.): see -INE[5].] The principal alkaloid, $C_{20}H_{26}N_2O$, of the shrub *Tabernanthe iboga* of equatorial Africa, a colourless crystalline compound that is a pentacyclic indole derivative and acts as a stimulant of the central nervous system when ingested, producing intoxication.

1902 *Jrnl. Chem. Soc.* LXXXII. I. 114 The active principle, ibogaine,..is present in the bark and wood and particularly in the roots of the plant. **1955** *Amer. Jrnl. Psychiatry* CXII. 467 Concerning ibogaine, the natives of French West Africa do not ascribe to it any hallucinogenic property. 'When questioned they insist that it has an action identical with that of alcohol without impairing the reason.' **1960** *Acta Crystallogr.* XIII. 553 Ibogaine, $C_{20}H_{26}N_2O$, is an alkaloid in which an indole ring system is attached to a seven-membered nitrogen containing ring, two sides of which form part of an adjoining tricyclic *iso*-quinuclidine ring system.

i-boghen, -boȝen, obs. pa. pple. of BOW *v.*

i-boght, -boht, -bought, obs. pa. pple. of BUY *v.*

i-bolȝe(n, var. of BOLGHEN, enraged.

i-boned, var. of BONED *a.*

ibony, obs. f. EBONY.

i-boren, ME. pa. pple. of BEAR *v.*

†**i-borenesse.** [f. *iboren* born + -NESS.] Birth.

a **1225** *Ancr. R.* 262 His iborenesse on eorðe of þe clene meidene. *a* **1240** *Lofsong* in *Cott. Hom.* 205 Ich bide þe and biseche þe..bi his iborenesse.

i-borghe(n, -borȝe(n, -borhe(n, -borewe(n, saved, delivered, preserved; ME. pa. pple. of BERGHE *v.*

i-borsten, ME. pa. pple. of BURST *v.*

c **1250** *Meid Maregrete* li, He is iborsten a two.

i-bosked, -et, ME. pa. pple. of BUSK *v.*

i-botened, ME. pa. pple. of BUTTON *v.*

i-bounde(n, i-bunde(n, ME. pa. pple. of BIND, I-BINDE *v.*

i-braced, ME. pa. pple. of BRACE *v.*

i-brad, ME. pa. pple. of BREDE *v.*[2], to broaden.

i-bred, ME. pa. pple. of BREDE *v.*[1], to roast.

i-brend, i-brent, ME. pa. pple. of BURN *v.*

i-brevet, ME. pa. pple. of BREVE *v.*

†**i-bringe**, *v.* *Obs.* [OE. *ȝebringan*, f. *bringan* to BRING.] *trans.* To bring. *lit.* and *fig.*

a **1000** *Sol. & Sat.* 87 (Gr.) He mæȝ ðone laðan gast.. fleonde ȝebrengan. *c* **1205** LAY. 26861 Feouwer eorles he hæhte forð heom ibringen. *a* **1250** *Owl & Night.* 1539 Nis nan mon þat ne mai ibringe His wif amis mid swuche þinge.

i-broched, ME. pa. pple. of BROACH *v.*[1]

i-broded, ME. pa. pple. of BROAD *v.*

i-broght, -broht, -brou(g)ht, ME. pa. pple. of BRING *v.*

i-broiden, ME. pa. pple. of BRAID *v.*: see BROIDEN.

†**i-broke, -en**, *pa. pple.* *Obs.* Broken. (See BREAK.)

c **900** tr. *Bæda's Hist.* v. vi. (1890) 400 Se ðuma ȝebrocen wæs. *c* **1175** *Lamb. Hom.* 83 Ȝef he hefde on his moder ibroken hire meidenhad. *a* **1225** *Juliana* 49 Ich habbe.. ibroken ham þe schuldren & te schonken. *c* **1290** *Beket* 1007 in *S. Eng. Leg.* I. 135 For he suor..and hath ibroke is oth. **1519** *Four Elem.* in Hazl. *Dodsley* I. 49 Jack boy, is thy bow i-broke?

†**i-brotheren, -thren**, *sb. pl.* *Obs.* [OE. *ȝebróðor*, *-ðru* (= OS. *gibrôðar*, OHG. *gabruoder*, Ger. *gebrüder*), collective pl. of *bróðor* BROTHER.] Brethren, brothers collectively (or mutually).

c **1000** *Ags. Gosp.* Matt. xxxix. 8 ȝe synt ealle ȝebroðru. *c* **1200** *Trin. Coll. Hom.* 219 For þi beð alle man ibroþren and isustren. *c* **1205** LAY. 3880 Beine iweren ibroðeren.

i-browe(n, ME. pa. pple. of BREW *v.*

Ibsenism ('ɪbsənɪz(ə)m). [f. the name of Henrik *Ibsen* (1828–1906), Norwegian dramatist and poet + -ISM.] The dramatic principles and aims characteristic of the writings of Ibsen and the Ibsenites, which examined and criticized social conventions. So **Ib's(c)ene, Ib's(c)enity** *nonce-wds.* (with play on *obscene*, *obscenity*); **Ibse'nesque, Ib'senian, 'Ibsenish** *adjs.*, of, pertaining to, or resembling the style or views of Ibsen; **'Ibsenist, 'Ibsenite**, an admirer or imitator of Ibsen; also as *adjs.* = *Ibsenian* adj.

1889 E. DOWSON in *Lett.* (1967) 432 The brave little band of Ibsenites. **1890** G. B. SHAW *London Music 1888–89* (1937) 283 A reprobate who greatly prefers Ibsenism to Walter Besantism. **1891** —— (*title*) The quintessence of Ibsenism. *Ibid.* 141 When one of the more specifically Ibsenian parts has to be filled, it is actually safer to entrust it to a novice than to a competent and experienced actor. *Ibid.* App. 158 Without being necessarily an Ibsenist, a critic may see at a glance that abuse of the sort quoted..is worthless. *Ibid.* 159 Mr William Archer expressly guards himself against being taken as an Ibsenist doctrinaire. **1892** *National Observer* 17 Dec. 107/1 When the din of political factions is silent, and Ibscenity has faded into a literary curiosity. **1893** *Ibid.* 7 Jan. 190/2 Her story is amateurish, sentimental, Ibsene. But Ibsenity is in the air. **1893** *Athenæum* 16 Dec. 857/3 The suicide of the woman..is nothing if not Ibsenish. It is unheroic, unromantic, ineffective, insignificant. **1895** G. B. SHAW in *Sat. Rev.* 9 Nov. 618/1 The material is what we now call Ibsenite: the technique is that of Scribe. **1902** CHESTERTON *Lunacy & Lett.* (1958) 39 The resistance of the conventional mind to Ibsenism..is fundamentally right. **1902** M. BEERBOHM in *Sat. Rev.* 24 May 644/2 Ellida..is the usual Ibsenist heroine, propounder of the regular Ibsenist ideas. **1902** W. B. YEATS *Let.* 4 Dec. (1954) 386 He [*sc.* Joyce]..did not knock at the gate with his old Ibsenite fury. **1905** *Daily Chron.* 7 July 8/4 She takes what might be called an Ibsenian view of humanity. **1906** M. BEERBOHM in *Sat. Rev.* 5 May 552/2 A strong-minded, Ibsenesque heroine, with a contempt for social conventions. **1906** W. STEVENS *Let.* 27 Apr. (1967) 91 You always were an Ibsenist, without knowing it. **1912** R. MACAULAY *Views & Vagabonds* vi. 112 She thinks they're Ibsenesque, but really they're like Miss Yonge in a fit of religious doubt. **1916** *Everyman* 5 May 54/2 Their passion for the erotic and Ibsene. **1916** T. MACDONAGH *Lit. in Ireland* 18 The drama of modern Ireland, in English, is..not free from the faults of impressionism, of quasi-scientific Ibsenism, of unreal gloom and of shallow cynicism. **1928** *Radio Times* 16 Mar. 564/2 Two distinguished Ibsenites..will be heard from London tonight. **1957** A. MILLER *Coll. Plays* (1958) Introd. 12 When *All My Sons* opened on Broadway it was called an Ibsenesque play. **1966** *Punch* 9 Feb. 206/1 The first love —for all her professed Ibsenist rationalism—won't let him go. **1970** *Daily Tel.* 30 Oct. 12/2 The play..remained Scandinavian in..its Ibsenite thesis that the truth is dangerous to man's precarious happiness. **1972** *Listener* 7 Sept. 310/1 The formation of the 'new woman' of the Ibsenite and Shavian period. **1973** *Times* 8 June 11/6 This meeting between Dr Miller and Charles Darwin, for example, had something unmistakably Ibsenish about it.

i-built, i-buld, i-bult, obs. forms of BUILT *pa. pple.*

a **1300** *Floriz & Bl.* 643 His palais þat was so faire ibuld. **1610** HOLLAND *Camden's Brit.* I. 367 The roufe aloft Ibuilt Of Geat.

†**i-bure**, *v.* *Obs.* [OE. *ȝebyrian* = OS. *giburian*, OHG. *gaburjan*, Ger. *gebühren*: see BIR *v.*] *intr.* To pertain, behove, be proper.

c **1000** ÆLFRIC *Gen.* xlviii. 18 Ne ȝebyraþ hit swa. *a* **1100** *O.E. Chron.* (MS. C.) an. 1036 Hine man byriȝde swa him wel ȝebyrede. *c* **1175** *Lamb. Hom.* 79 Nu hit iburd breke þas word. *a* **1250** *Prov. Ælfred* 75 þe eorl and þe eþelyng ibureþ vnder godne king þat lond to leden.

i-buried, ME. pa. pple. of BURY *v.*

†**i-burned**, *ppl. a.* *Obs.* [OE. *ȝebyrnod*, f. *byrne* BURNE, BRINIE.] Mailed.

c **1000** ÆLFRIC *Gram.* xliii. (Z.) 256 *Loricatus*, ȝebyrnod. *c* **1205** LAY. 26277 Gerin & Beof..iburned and ihelmed.

i-by, i-bye, been, ME. pa. pple. of BE *v.*

†**i-bye**, *v.* *Obs. rare.* [OE. *ȝebycgan*, f. *bycgan* to BUY.] *trans.* To purchase; to pay for, atone for.

10.. *OE. Chron.* anno 1016 Lundenwaru..him friþ ȝebohton. *c* **1435** *Torr. Portugal* 1222 þou shalt ibye it.

ic, obs. form of I, *pron.*

-ic (formerly -ick, ik(e, -ique), *suffix*, primarily forming adjs., many of which are used as sbs. The latter have also the form -ics: see 2.

1. In adjs., immediately representing F. *-ique*, ad. L. *-ic-us*, of Latin origin, as in *cīvic-us*, *classic-us*, *public-us*, *domestic-us*, *aquātic-us*, or ad. Gr. *-ικ-ός*, as in *κωμικ-ός cōmic-us*, *γραμματικ-ός grammatic-us*, *ποιητικ-ός poētic-us*. This was in Gr. one of the commonest of suffixes, forming adjs., with the sense 'after the manner of', 'of the nature of', 'pertaining to', 'of'. Its use in L. was

much more restricted, and it ceased to be a living formative, except in the compound suffix *-āticus* (see -ATIC, -AGE), and in words formed from Greek, or on Greek types. These were very numerous in late and med.L., whence they passed into the modern langs.; since the 16th c. they have been taken directly from Gr., or formed upon Gr. elements, and in some recent (esp. scientific) terms on words from L. or other sources, as *carbonic*, *oratoric*, *artistic*, *bardic*, *scaldic*, *felspathic*, *Icelandic*, *Byronic*. **b.** In *Chemistry*, the suffix *-ic* is specifically employed to form the names of oxygen acids and other compounds having a higher degree of oxidation than those whose names end in *-ous*; e.g. *chloric acid* HO_3Cl, *chlorous acid* HO_2Cl, *sulphuric acid* H_2SO_4, *sulphurous acid* H_2SO_3.

At the time when this nomenclature was introduced only two such compounds were provided for. In many cases other oxygen compounds have since been obtained, but the names in *-ic* and *-ous* have been retained in their original applications, and prefixes as *per-*, *hyper-*, *hypo-*, *sesqui-*, etc. prefixed to denominate the additional compounds.

1807 THOMSON *Chem.*. ii. 254 The French chemists.. made some of the names of the combustible acids end in *ic*, as if they were saturated with oxygen; and others in *ous*, as if they were capable of combining with an additional dose. The fact is, that none of them are, strictly speaking, saturated with oxygen; for all of them are capable of combining with more. **1849** D. CAMPBELL *Inorg. Chem.* 4 Acids formed by oxygen with another element, are distinguished by the termination *ous*, given to acids with a lesser quantity of oxygen, and *ic* to acids with a greater quantity.

2. Already in Gr., adjs. in *-ικός* were used absolutely as sbs., e.g. in sing. masc., as *Στωικ-ός* (man) of the porch, Stoic, *κριτικ-ός* (man) able to discern, critic, hence in L. *Stōicus*, *criticus*, etc.; also, in sing. fem., in names of arts (sc. *τέχνη*) or systems of thought, knowledge, or action (sc. *θεωρία*, *φιλοσοφία*), e.g. *ἡ μουσική* the art of the Muses, music, *ἡ ῥητορική* the oratorical art, rhetoric, *ἡ ἠθική* theory of morals, ethics, *ἡ ὀπτική* science of vision, optics; and in neuter pl., as expressions for the affairs or matters pertaining to some department, and hence as names of treatises on these subjects, as *τὰ οἰκονομικά* things pertaining to the management of a household, a treatise on this, economics. Sometimes both forms were in use with a distinction of sense; e.g. *ἡ πολιτική* the art of the statesman, political science, *τὰ πολιτικά* affairs of state, politics; this distinction tended however to become obliterated, as in *ἡ τακτική*, *τὰ τακτικά* tactics, *ἡ φυσική*, *τὰ φυσικά* physics. In pairs like *φυσική*, *φυσικά* both forms gave regularly a L. form in *-ica*, as *physica*, which might be taken as fem. sing. or neuter pl.; hence there was in med.L. considerable fluctuation in the grammatical treatment of these words. In the Romanic langs. (It., Sp. *-ica*, F. *-ique*), as also in Ger. (*-ik*), they were regularly treated as fem. sing.; though in French, from the 16th c., sometimes as plural (*les mathématiques*).

In English, such words of this class as were in use before 1500 had the singular form, and were usually written, after French, *-ique*, *-ike*, as *arsmetike*, *magike*, *musike*, *logike* (*-ique*), *retorique*, *mathematique* (*-ike*, *-ik*), *mechanique*, *economique*, *ethyque* (*-ik*); this form is retained in *arithmetic*, *logic*, *magic*, *music*, *rhetoric* (though *logics* has also been used). But, from the 15th c., forms in -ics (*-iques*) occur as names of treatises (repr. Gr. names in *-ικά* or their L. translations in *-ica*), e.g. *etiques* = *τὰ ἠθικά*; and in the second half of the 16th c. this form is found applied to the subject-matter of such treatises, in *mathematics*, *economics*, etc. From 1600 onward, this has been the accepted form with names of sciences, as *acoustics*, *conics*, *dynamics*, *ethics*, *linguistics*, *metaphysics*, *optics*, *statics*, or matters of practice, as *æsthetics*, *athletics*, *economics*, *georgics*, *gymnastics*, *politics*, *tactics*. The names of sciences, even though they have the form in *-ics*, are now construed as singular, as in 'mathematics *is* the science of quantity; *its* students are mathematicians'; in recent times some writers, following German or French usage, have preferred to use a form in *-ic*, as in *dialectic*, *dogmatic*, *ethic*, *metaphysic*, *static*, etc. Names of practical matters as *gymnastics*, *politics*, *tactics*, usually remain plural, in construction as well as in form.

3. Besides the preceding, there are many sbs. formed directly from adjectives in *-ic* taken absolutely, either after ancient models or on ancient analogies, as in names of medical agents, as *alexipharmic*, *emetic*, *cosmetic*, *hidrotic* (pl. *emetics*, etc.); in names of styles of poetry or metres, as *epic*, *lyric*, *Anacreontics*, *iambics*; and in words of various kinds, as *domestic*, *rustic*, *catholic*, *classic*, *mechanic*, *lunatic*.

Words in *-ic* from Gr. or L. have the stress regularly on the penult, e.g. *me'chanic*, *dra'matic*, *en'clitic*, *fa'natic*. The exceptions, as *a'rithmetic*, *'arsenic*, *'catholic*, *'heretic*, *'rhetoric*, *'lunatic*, are chiefly words taken directly from French, in which originally the final syllable had the main stress, and the antepenult a secondary stress (*ˌrheto'rique*), which afterwards became the primary in accordance with the regular treatment of French words (e.g. *ˌvani'te*, *ˌani'mal*), in English.

A few adjs. in *-ic* form advs. in *-icly*, as *publicly*, *franticly*, *heroicly*; but the adv. is usually in -ICALLY, from the secondary adj. in -ICAL. Derivative abstract sbs. are formed in -ICITY, as *domesticity*, *atomicity*, and agent nouns in -ICIAN as *arithmetician*, *musician*, *physician*.

i-cached, i-cakeled, ME. pa. pples. of CATCH, CACKLE *vbs.*

icacin: see under ICICA.

icaco (ɪ'kɑːkəʊ). [a. Sp. *icaco*, *hicaco*, f. Taino *hikako*.] A small tree, *Chrysobalanus icaco*, of the family Rosaceæ, native to tropical America and the West Indies; the fruit of this tree. Also called COCO-PLUM.

1752 P. MILLER *Gardeners Dict.* (ed. 6) s.v. Chrysobalanus. This Genus of Plants is titled by Father Plumier *Icaco* which is the Indian name of this Fruit. **1756** P. BROWNE *Civil & Nat. Hist. Jamaica* 250 *(heading)* Chrysobalanus... Icaco... The Cocco Plumb Tree. **1852** T. ROSS tr. *A. von Humboldt's Personal Narr. Trav. Amer.* II. xvii. 136 Hedges of bead-trees encircled groups of icacoes laden with fruit. **1887** C. A. MOLONEY *Sk. Forestry W. Africa* 347 Icaco or Cocoa Plum of the West Indies. **1943** RECORD & HESS *Timbers of New World* 454/2 The best known species [of *Chrysobalanus*] is the Coco Plum or *Icaco*, *C. icaco* L., which has a large edible fruit so wrinkled as to suggest the face of a monkey.

-ical, a compound *suffix*, f. -IC + -AL[1], sometimes forming an adj. from a sb. in *-ic*, as *music*, *musical*, but more frequently a secondary adj., as *comic*, *comical*, *historic*, *historical*. Its origin appears to have been the formation in late L. of adjs. in *-ālis* on sbs. in *-ic-us*, or in *-icē*, e.g. *grammatic-us* grammarian, *grammaticē* grammar, *grammatic-āl-is* grammatical, *clēricus* clergyman, clerk, *clērical-is* clerical. So in med.L., *chīrurgicāl-is*, *dominic-āl-is*, *medicāl-is*, *mūsicāl-is*, *physicāl-is*. In French, adjs. of this type are few, and mostly taken directly from L. formations, as *chirurgical*, *clérical*, *grammatical*, *médical*, etc. But in English they are exceedingly numerous, existing not only in all cases in which the term in *-ic* is a sb., but also as the direct representatives of L. adjs. in *-icus*, F. *-ique*. Thus we find before 1500 *canonical*, *chirurgical*, *domestical*, *musical*, *philosophical*, *physical*. Many adjs. have a form both in *-ic* and *-ical*, and in such cases that in *-ical* is usually the earlier and that more used. Often also the form in *-ic* is restricted to the sense 'of' or 'of the nature of' the subject in question, while that in *-ical* has wider or more transferred senses, including that of 'practically connected' or 'dealing with' the subject. Cf. '*economic* science', 'an *economical* wife', '*prophetic* words', '*prophetical* studies', 'a *comic* song', 'a *comical* incident', 'the *tragic* muse', 'his *tragical* fate'. A *historic* book is one mentioned or famous in history, a *historical* treatise contains or deals with history. But in many cases this distinction is, from the nature of the subject, difficult to maintain, or entirely inappreciable.

Adjectives of locality, nationality, and language, as *Baltic*, *Arabic*, *Teutonic*, and those of chemical and other technical nomenclature, as *oxalic*, *ferric*, *pelagic*, *dactylic*, *hypnotic*, *megalithic*, have usually no secondary form in *-al*.

Hence some derivative sbs. in *-icality*, as *technicality*.

i-called, ME. pa. pple. of CALL *v.*

-ically, advb. ending, f. -ICAL + -LY[2], forming advs. from adjs. in *-ical*, which are also used as the advs. from the corresponding adjs. in -IC. Thus *historic*, *historical*, adv. *historically*, *poetic*, *poetical*, adv. *poetically*. The adv. is almost always in *-ically* even when only the adj. in *-ic* is in current use, as in *athletically*, *hypnotically*, *phlegmatically*, *rustically*, *scenically*.

Icarian (aɪ'kɛərɪən), *a.*[1] Also 9 Icarean. [f. L. *Īcarius* = Gr. *'Ικάριος*, f. *Īcarus*, *'Ικαρος* the son of Daedalus, in Greek Mythology.]

Of, pertaining to, or characteristic of Icarus, fabled, in escaping from Crete, to have flown so high that the sun melted the wax with which his artificial wings were fastened on, so that he fell into the Ægean sea: hence, applied to ambitious or presumptuous acts which end in failure or ruin.

1595 *Polimanteia* (1881) 58, I feel my Icarian wings to melt with the heate of so bright a sunne. **1623** COCKERAM, *Icharian soaring*, Pride. **1639** G. DANIEL *Poems* Wks. 1878 II. 121 Mee better suits to Creepe Then with Icarian winge Contrive a scorned Ruine. *a* **1822** SHELLEY *Mann. Anc.* in *Ess. & Lett.* (Camelot) 43 Expectations are often exalted on Icarean wings, and fall. **1844** DISRAELI *Coningsby* VII. i, Your Icarian flight melts into a very grovelling existence. **1936** E. SITWELL *Sel. Poems* 249 Eagle-winged Icarian flights. **1972** *Daily Tel.* (Colour Suppl.) 1 Dec. 16/1 In the view of some social philosophers and historians, space flight is an Icarian venture at its best—and an extravagance at its worst.

Icarian (aɪ'kɛərɪən), *a.*[2] and *sb.* [f. *Icari-a* (see def.) + -AN.]

a. *adj.* Pertaining to or characteristic of Icaria, an ideal republic described in a work (*Voyage en Icarie*, 1840) by the French communist Étienne Cabet (1788–1856), afterwards taken as the name of several communistic settlements, established by Cabet at Nauvoo and elsewhere in U.S. **b.** *sb.* A follower or adherent of Cabet; a member of an Icarian community such as that at Nauvoo.

1865 *Athenæum* No. 1949. 309/1 A Phalansterian, perhaps an Icarian. **1875** NORDHOFF *Communistic Soc. U.S.* 387 The Icarians reject Christianity. *Ibid.* 393 The Icarian system is as nearly as possible a pure democracy.

Hence **I'carianism**, the communism of Cabet.

1883 R. T. ELY *Fr. & Germ. Socialism* iii. 50 The apostles of Icarianism should..convert the world by teaching, preaching..and by setting good examples.

i-caried, ME. pa. pple. of CARRY *v.*

Icarus ('ɪkərəs). *Gr. Myth.* The name of the son of Dædalus, who attempted to fly by means of artificial wings fastened with wax (see ICARIAN *a.*[1]): used allusively.

[**1589** GREENE *Menaphon* (Arb.) 53, I feare..in the height of my thoughts soaring too high, to fall with wofull repenting Icarus.] **1591** SHAKES. *1 Hen. VI*, IV. vi. 56 Then follow thou thy desp'rate Syre of Creet, Thou Icarus, thy Life to me is sweet. *Ibid.* vii. 16 There di'de My Icarus, my Blossome, in his pride. **1594** NASHE *Unfort. Trav.* I3[v], These insolent fancies are but Icarus feathers, whose wanton waxe melted against the sun. **1694** D'URFEY *Don Quix.* II. Ep. Ded. sig. A1[v], The roving Icarus in Poetry, By you is levell'd, when he soars too high. **1924** B. RUSSELL *(title)* Icarus, or, The future of science. **1931** *Times Lit. Suppl.* 24 Sept. 714/2 Much that he [*sc.* D'Annunzio] has given is not pure gold, but decorative lumber comparable to the ill-assorted trophies of the Vittoriale from which, an Icarus who has ceased to fly, he makes well-calculated sallies.

icary, var. of IKARY, caviare.

†**icasm.** *Obs. rare*[−1]. [ad. Gr. *εἴκασμα* comparison, simile, f. *εἰκάζειν* to make like, to depict.] A figurative expression. So †**i'castic** *a.* [ad. Gr. *εἰκαστικός*], figurative.

1664 H. MORE *Myst. Iniq.* II. i. ix. 259 The difficulty of understanding Prophecies is in a manner no greater, when once a man has taken notice of the settled meaning of the peculiar Icasms therein. *Ibid.*, These be the chief Icastick terms that occur in the Prophetick style.

i-cast, ME. pa. pple. of CAST *v.*

†**icche(n**, *v. Obs.* [Of obscure history; in meaning it agrees with the later forms HITCH, ITCH *v.*[2], but evidence of continuity is wanting.] *trans.* and *intr.* To move, stir.

c **1200** ORMIN 8123 He..icchedd himm a litell upp & wollde himm sellfenn mirrþrenn. *Ibid.* 11833 Uss birrþ..te mare uss godenn, & icchenn uppwarrd ass summ del Inn alle gode dedess. *c* **1305** *St. Lucy* 105 in *E.E.P.* (1862) 104 Hi ne miȝte hire a fot awinne, Ne make hire icche anne fot, of þe stede. *Ibid.* 132. 105 Hi gonne to drawe and tuicche, And euere lai þis maide stille, hi nemiȝte hire enes icche.

iccle, obs. form of ICKLE *sb.*, icicle.

iccol, dial. variant of HICKWALL.

ice (aɪs), *sb.* Forms: 1–3 *ís*, 3 *ys*, (*isse*), 3–6 *yse*, 4 *ijs*, *iys(e*, *yss*, 4–5 *ysz*, *yise*, 4–7 *ise*, (5 *hyse*, 6 *Sc.* *ische*), 5–7 *yce*, 5– *ice*. [Com. Teut.: OE. *ís*, OFris., OLG., OHG. (MDu., MHG.) *ís* (Du. *ijs*, Ger. *eis*), ON. *íss* (Sw., Da. *is*):—OTeut. **iso-*. There are no certain cognates outside Teutonic.]

I. 1. a. Frozen water; water rendered solid by exposure to a low temperature.

Beowulf (Z.) 1608 Hit eal ȝemealt ise ȝelicost. *a* **1000** *Boeth. Metr.* xxviii. 59 Hwa wundraþ þæs..hwy þæt is mæȝe weorðan of wætere. *c* **1000** *Ags. Ps.* (Th.) cxlviii. 8 Fyr, forst, hæȝel and ȝefeallen snaw, is and yste. *c* **1175** *Lamb. Hom.* 43 Þe forme wes swnan [? snaw], þat oðer is. *c* **1250** *Gen. & Ex.* 99 Ðe firmament..Of watres froren, of yses wal ðis middel werld it luket al; May no fir ȝet melten ðat ys. **1340** HAMPOLE *Pr. Consc.* 6644 It suld frese and turne al in-til yse þar. *c* **1400** MAUNDEV. (Roxb.) xiv. 65 Þe frost and þe ysz es mykill harder þare þan here. *c* **1440** *Promp. Parv.* 258/1 Ice, *glacies*. **1567** MAPLET *Gr. Forest* 5 b, Isidore saith, that it [Cristall] is nothing else then a congeled Ise. **1620** T. GRANGER *Div. Logike* 128 Colder then yce. **1774** GOLDSM. *Nat. Hist.* (1776) I. 180 Ice, which is water in another state, is very elastic. **1878** HUXLEY *Physiogr.* 62 Ice is in fact crystalline, while snow is crystallized. **1883** HOWELLS *Register* i, My feet are like ice.

b. With *pl.*: A mass or piece of ice.

c **900** tr. *Bæda's Hist.* v. xii[i]. (1890) 436 þæm sticcum halfbrocenra iisa. **1388** WYCLIF *Dan.* iii. 70 Yces and snowis

[L. *glacies et nives*] blesse ȝe the Lord. **1796** H. Hunter tr. *St.-Pierre's Stud. Nat.* (1799) I. p. xxviii, We shall treat . . of the sources of the Atlantic, of it's ices, . . of it's currents, of it's tides. **1823** Scoresby *Whale Fishery* 219 These ices or glaciers, evidently give rise to the numerous floating bergs. **1875** *Wond. Phys. World* II. iii. 246 Sometimes these ices offered but a level uniform sheet.

2. a. ***the ice***: the layer of ice on a river, lake, sea, etc.; the frozen surface of a body of water.

[*c* **900** tr. *Bæda's Hist.* III. i[i.]. (1890) 156 þa eode he sume neahte on ise unwærlice.] **1297** R. Glouc. (Rolls) 9511 Me miȝte boþe ride & go In Temese vpe þe yse. *c* **1394** *P. Pl. Crede* 436 His wyf walked him wiþ . . Barfote on þe bare ijs. **1473** Warkw. *Chron.* 3 Ther was ane fervent froste . . that menne myght goo overe the yise. **1535** Stewart *Cron. Scot.* II. 619 Or euir tha wist on Forres loch tha ran, Wnder the ische syne drownit thair ilkman. **1694** *Acc. Sev. Late Voy.* II. (1711) 42 In the Spring the Whales are in . . the West Ice, as they call it. **1820** Scoresby *Acc. Arctic Reg.* I. 266 Separation between the east or *whaling*, and west or *sealing* ice of the fishers. **1850** Lyell *Princ. Geol.* vii. (ed. 8) 99 Captain Cook was of opinion that the ice of the antarctic predominated over that of the arctic region.

b. ***to break the ice***: to make a passage for boats, etc. by breaking the frozen surface of a river, lake, etc.; *fig.* to make a beginning in some undertaking or enterprise (cf. *to break ground*); to prepare the way for others (cf. quot. 1590); in modern usage, to break through cold reserve or stiffness.

1579–80 North *Plutarch* (1676) 89 To be the first to break the Ice of the Enterprize. **1590** Swinburne *Testaments* Epil., The authour therefore in aduenturing to breake the yse to make the passage easie for his countrymen, failing sometimes of the fourd, and falling into the pit, may seeme worthie to be pitied. **1646** J. Cooke *Vind. Prof. Law* To Rdr., I have attempted to break the Ice in a subject concerning reformation in Courts of Justice. **1678** Butler *Hud.* III. ii. 494 The Oratour . . At last broke silence, and the Ice. **1741** Richardson *Pamela* (1824) I. ix. 246 You see . . that I break the ice, and begin first in the indispensably expected correspondence between us. **1823** Byron *Juan* XIII. xxxviii, And your cold people are beyond all price, When once you've broken their confounded ice. **1893** Earl Dunmore *Pamirs* I. 226 The ice being thus broken, Ching Dolai put aside the reserve habitual to all Celestials.

c. Phrases. ***on ice***: (*a*) kept out of the way until wanted, in reserve; in custody, in prison; (*b*) of a venture, game, etc.: sure of being achieved or won, a certainty; ***to cut no ice***: to carry no weight, to fail to impress; hence ***to cut ice***: to impress, to make an effect.

1890 A. C. Gunter *Miss Nobody* xx. 231 For Election. Gussie de P. Van Beekman. . . On ice! **1894** P. L. Ford *Hon. Peter Stirling* 328 They say she's never been able to find a man good enough for her, and so she's keeping herself on ice. **1895** J. S. Wood *Yale Yarns* 12 *Such* speeches! Eloquence cut no ice at *that* dinner. **1897** *Scribner's Mag.* Sept. 305/1 And it don't cut no ice with you whether folks call you inconsistent or not. **1916** J. Buchan *Greenmantle* ix. 117 Because the German mercantile marine was laid on ice till the end of the war, they had turned him on to this show. **1917** A. Conan Doyle *His Last Bow* 291 It cuts no ice with a British copper to tell him you're an American citizen. **1924** A. Huxley *Let.* 28 Oct. (1969) 235, I was very glad . . to hear that you liked *Those Barren Leaves.* It cuts more ice, I think, than the others and is more explicit and to the point. **1930** W. S. Maugham *Cakes & Ale* iv. 48 There was a softness in Roy's voice such as I imagined he would use if he were telling a prospective father that his wife was about to gratify his wishes. It cut no ice with me. **1930** G. B. Shaw *Apple Cart* I. 7 Oh, sit down, man, sit down. Youre in your own house: ceremony cuts no ice with me. **1931** *Sat. Rev. Lit.* (U.S.) 18 July 978/2 Among the words and phrases common among racketeers, not yet in general use . . there are the following: . . *on ice*, in the penitentiary. **1932** E. Bowen *To North* xxiii. 247 Sheer man-to-man envy of Markie for cutting so much ice. **1933** D. L. Sayers *Murder must Advertise* xix. 322 Their idea is to put you on ice quietly till they've had time to settle up their affairs. **1936** E. S. Gardner *Case of Sleepwalker's Niece* xiv. 131, I figured that and the record of the telephone call would be enough to put the case on ice. **1936** Wodehouse *Laughing Gas* xviii. 195 Take him back to his room and keep him there on ice till it's time to go to the studio. **1944** W. S. Maugham *Razor's Edge* vii. 276, I haven't signed on the dotted line yet, but it's on ice. The fella I'm going in with was a roommate of mine at college . . and I'm dead sure he wouldn't hand me a lemon. **1945** *Chicago Daily News* 4 Oct. 12/1 They . . accumulated enough runs in the first inning to put the game on ice. **1953** W. Burroughs *Junkie* (1972) x. 103 'I sent for the wagon,' said the guy with the pipe. 'We'll take them over to the third precinct and put them on ice.' **1954** Koestler *Invis. Writing* xxxiv. 369 He will for a considerable time be 'put on ice' . . isolated from any contact with other members. **1955** *Times* 12 May 14/5 Burns demanded that the purse be handed over before he entered the ring. He ended a bitter argument by declaring: 'That cuts no ice with me. I want the referee to hold the money.' **1957** A. Grimble *Return to Islands* 75 The problem that his resignation had left on ice, for whomever it might concern. **1965** *New Statesman* 14 May 771/2 Presumably the book, finished in 1957, was put on ice, for Mr Wood can hardly have hoped to get away in Beaverbrook's lifetime with much of the discussion of his 'brash brutality'. **1973** 'I. Drummond' *Jaws of Watchdog* xii. 154 Scotland Yard could not keep him on ice that long. He would have to be brought to a court to be charged. **1973** J. Porter *It's Murder with Dover* vii. 63 MacGregor remembered . . that logical argument didn't cut much ice with Dover and he abandoned it.

d. A piece or pieces of ice placed in a drink, or into which a bottle, etc., is placed to cool the contents.

1833 C. Redding *Hist. Mod. Wines* xiv. 316 Before drinking, the wine should be kept an hour in ice. **1846** A. Soyer *Gastronomic Regenerator* 701 When the syrup is a little cool, taste if palatable, place a little upon some ice, and if strong enough fill your mould, which place in ice. *a* **1922** T. S. Eliot *Waste Land Drafts* (1971) 61 Where's a cocktail shaker, Ben, here's plenty of cracked ice. **1927** E. Glyn '*It*' xii. 110 A perfect dinner had been ordered—the champagne was on ice.

3. In figurative expressions, with allusion to the slippery, cold, or brittle nature of ice.

a **1420** Hoccleve *De Reg. Princ.* 907 Beware, I rede; thow stondest on the yce. *c* **1560** A. Scott *Poems* (S.T.S.) xxii. 22, I seik the watter hett In vndir the cauld yce. **1594** Shaks. *Rich. III*, IV. ii. 22 Tut, tut, thou art all Ice. **1649** G. Daniel *Trinarch., Hen. IV*, cxxix, Soe Spirits bound vp in the Ice of feare Are thawed by Nobler Passions shineing there. **1749** Fielding *Tom Jones* VIII. iv, The bright eyes of our hero thawed all her ice in a moment. **1849** Macaulay *Hist. Eng.* vii. II. 170 Those who knew him well . . were aware that under all this ice a fierce fire was constantly burning. **1884** 'Mark Twain' *Huck. Finn* xxxii. 333 'How'd you get your breakfast so early on the boat?' It was kinder thin ice, but I says: 'The captain see me standing around.' **1892** Ouida in *Fortn. Rev.* LII. 785 The incessant, breathless round of intermingled sport and pleasure danced on the thin ice of debt. **1904** [see coin *sb.* 6]. **1938** E. Bowen *Death of Heart* III. ii. 343 The *idea* of her never leaves me quiet, and by coming into this room she drives me on to the ice. **1962** J. G. Bennett *Witness* xxii. 287 Thus, without knowing it, I was treading on very thin ice.

4. a. A congelation or crystalline appearance resembling ice.

1605 Bacon *Adv. Learn.* II. xxi. §5 Iewellers . . if there be a graine, or a cloude, or an ise which may be ground forth, without taking to much of the stone, they help it.

b. = *ice pigeon*.

1881 J. C. Lyell *Fancy Pigeons* 81 The smooth-legged chequered or spangled ones are known in this country as Ural ice, while the rough-legged spangled birds are called Siberian ice.

c. Diamonds; jewellery. *slang* (orig. *U.S.*).

1906 H. Green *At Actors' Boarding House* 26 Her in evenin' clothes and a bunch of ice on her hands. **1915** G. Bronson-Howard *God's Man* IV. iv. 281 Along comes a guy . . a piece of ice in his tie that made Tiffany's front window look like a hardware exhibit. **1924** Wodehouse *Leave it to Psmith* ix. 184 Diamonds, Eddie. A necklace. . . Some of the best ice I've saw in years. **1925**, **1942** [see hot *a.* 7 e]. **1936** J. G. Brandon *Pawnshop Murder* i. 2 The glitter of stolen 'ice' or other jewels spread out upon the table. **1942** M. Schlauch *Gift of Tongues* (1943) 269 Jewels become 'ice'. **1959** *Listener* 23 Apr. 706/2 'Shiners' and 'ice' to the light-fingered boys, the diamond is known to the gemmologist as the hardest . . of all minerals. **1961** Wodehouse *Ice in Bedroom* i. 11 Yes, someone got away with her bit of ice all right. **1972** 'H. Howard' *Nice Day for Funeral* i. 30 Prager caught sight of five hundred grand in cracked ice.

d. Profit from the illegal sale of theatre, cinema, etc., tickets. *U.S. slang*.

1927 *Theatre Mag.* Sept. 30/2 Thousands of tickets for special attractions in the large movie houses are sold over the box-office counter to speculators by the treasurers of the houses, their charge, or 'ice', running to as much as £1 a ticket on the 'sell-outs'. **1960** *Observer* 30 Oct. 1/17 'Ice' . . is the money from the sale of hot tickets . . and enables . . box office clerks to buy themselves Cadillacs. **1964** *Economist* 25 Jan. 313/2 Kick-backs—'ice' as it is called on Broadway—on theatre tickets whose prices are marked up illegally.

e. Protection money. *slang*.

1948 E. L. Johnson in E. L. Irey *Tax Dodgers* (1949) xiii. 229 Willie . . said, 'The extra hundred sixty is ice.' 'Ice' is argot for graft or protection fees. **1951** *Economist* 29 Sept. 747 Gross . . who had confessed to paying this sum in 'ice' for the protection that made it possible for him to earn $100,000 a year. **1951** E. Kefauver *Crime in Amer.* (1952) xvii. 186 When the combine's books finally were seized, examination disclosed recorded payments totalling $108,000 for the service known as 'juice', which is the California gambling profession's euphemism (in Florida the term is 'ice') for 'protection' money.

5. a. A frozen confection. Now with *an* and *pl.*: An ice-cream or water-ice.

(In French the pl. *glaces* in this sense was admitted by the Acad. in 1762; but as late as 1825 it was asserted to be incorrect to say *une glace*.)

[**1716** Lady M. W. Montagu *Let. to Lady X* —— 1 Oct., The company are entertained with ice in several forms, winter and summer.] **1773** Brydone *Sicily* xxxiii. (1809) 318 A free indulgence in the use of ices. **1831** Disraeli *Yng. Duke* xiii, The cakes and the confectionary, and the ices. **1848** Thackeray *Van. Fair* xiii, He went out and ate ices at a pastry-cook's shop. **1850** T. & J. M. Morton *All that Glitters* etc. II, Toby, take that load of pine apple ice into the ball-room, and present an ice to each lady.

b. = icing.

1723 J. Nott *Cook's & Confectioner's Dict.* sig. B4 Make Ice with the White of an Egg, powder'd Sugar, Orange or Lemon Flowers. **1725** Bradley *Fam. Dict.* s.v. *March pane*, You may also ice them . . and the Ice is to be bak'd with the Oven-lid. **1819** *Pantologia, Ice*, . . concreted sugar. **1885** C. M. Yonge *Nuttie's Father* II. v. 61 How dreadfully hard the ice on the wedding cake was, so that when Annaple tried to cut it the knife slipped.

II. *attrib.* and *Comb.*

6. *simple attrib.*

1744 (*title*) An Account of the Glacieres or Ice Alps in Savoy. **1813** Ellis *Brand's Pop. Antiq.* II. 319 *note*, The antient Northern Nations held annual Ice Fairs. See Olaus Magnus. We too have heard of Ice Fairs on the River Thames. **1884** *Bath Jrnl.* 16 Feb. 7/2 The ice carnival at Montreal opened on Monday. *Ibid.*, In the evening the Ice Palace was a wonderfully beautiful structure. **1895** *Westm. Gaz.* 31 Aug. 3/1 We are increasing our ice consumption at about the rate of five per cent. a year. **1898** *Ibid.* 31 Mar. 2/1 The crew will consist of twenty-four men, all of them experienced in ice navigation.

7. General combinations: **a.** *attrib.* Of or pertaining to ice, connected with, characterized by, occurring in, performed on, ice or the ice, as ***ice-battle***, ***-break***, ***-chart***, ***-clue***, ***-coldness***, ***-crack***, ***-crossing***, ***-dancer*** (so ***-dancing*** vbl. sb.), ***-fight***, ***-flower***, ***-fog***, ***-hole***, ***-marsh***, ***-measurement***, ***-melting***, ***-merchant***, ***-movement***, ***-pressure***, ***-range***, ***-ravine***, ***-road***, ***-shove***, ***-show***, ***-spot***, ***-storm***, ***-temper***, ***-track***, ***-tramp***, ***-travel***, ***-upheaval***, ***-voice***, ***-wagon***; ***-walk***; esp. in names of tools and implements used in the harvesting, carriage, and storage of ice for economic purposes, as ***ice-barge***, ***-basket***, ***-crusher***, ***-cutter***, ***-fork***, ***-leveller***, ***-mallet***, ***-marker***, ***-pick***, ***-preserver***, ***-scraper***, ***-shaver***, ***-spade***, ***-tongs***, ***-tool***. Also ***ice-clear*** adj.

1856 Kane *Arct. Expl.* II. xxix. 297 The scars which their own *ice-battles had impressed on the vessels. *Ibid.* I. xxiv. 314, I met my officers . . and showed them my *ice-charts. **1946** S. Spender *European Witness* II. iii. 146 The *ice-clear light of that part of Germany. **1948** C. Day Lewis *Poems 1943–1947* 87 Toward my expectation's bed They move in a hushed, ice-clear trance. **1970** R. Lowell *Notebk.* 204 Once or twice, blurt your ice-clear sentence. **1856** Kane *Arct. Expl.* I. xii. 133 On this return I had much less difficulty with the *ice-cracks. *Ibid.* II. xxvi. 267 The third [sledge] we had to reserve as essential to our *ice-crossings. **1883** *Fisheries Exhib. Catal.* 200 *Ice-crusher, ice-picks, and tools used in handling ice. **1791** J. Long *Voy. & Trav. Indian Trader* 120 The fishing party consisted of . . natives of Canada, who, being provided with axes, *ice-cutters . . set off. **1969** *New Scientist* 13 Mar. 574/2 A new type of ice-breaker is needed for breaking up solid ice. We have devised one and christened it an ice-cutter. **1925** E. Law *Dancing on Ice* iii. 24 To the question what should *ice-dancers do to acquit themselves properly, the obvious answer is, that they should first learn exactly what the valse-figure is. **1969** *Times* 15 Nov. 10/8 Only one skater now remains of that team of six brilliant ice dancers. **1925** E. Law *Dancing on Ice* v. 46 Invite the independent judgment of . . some one who knows and understands the whole theory and practice of *ice-dancing. **1969** *Times* 15 Nov. 10/8 The world ice dancing champions . . will not be competing. **1856** Kane *Arct. Expl.* I. iii. 32 One of those heavy *ice-fogs . . settled around us. **1853** —— *Grinnell Exp.* xii. (1856) 87 The *ice-hole of the Vituline seal. **1864** *Chambers's Jrnl.* 99/1 The men take the ice to *ice-merchants, who are ready to buy it in any quantity. **1973** *Post Office Telephone Directory Section 471, London Yellow Pages Classified* (*North*) 177/2 (*heading*) Ice and cold storage companies and ice merchants. **1856** Kane *Arct. Expl.* I. xxiv. 314 Knowledge of Lancaster Sound and its *ice-movements. **1896** Nansen in *Daily Chron.* 2 Nov. 4/1 The *ice-pressures began to be tremendous. **1884** S. E. Dawson *Handbk. Canada* 122 The *ice-roads [across the St. Lawrence] are always marked out by spruce-trees stuck in the snow. **1865** Parkman *Champlain* xi. (1875) 334 He built a wall of bricks . . in order to measure the destructive effects of the '*ice-shove' in the spring. **1950** *Oxf. Jun. Encycl.* IX. 432/2 Of recent years '*ice shows' have been made popular in the U.S.A. and Canada. **1966** *Listener* 29 Dec. 959/1 Original plays . . and an ice-show. **1858** Simmonds *Dict. Trade*, **Ice-tongs*, utensils for taking up ice at a table. **1875** Knight *Dict. Mech.*, *Ice-tongs*, grasping implements for carrying blocks of ice. **1856** Kane *Arct. Expl.* I. vi. 58 Nothing of *ice-upheaval has ever been described equal to this. **1865** J. D. Burn *Three Years among Working-Classes U.S.* 304 The *ice-waggons may be seen with their crystal loads flying about the towns in all directions from May to the end of September. **1898** J. London *Let.* 30 Nov. (1966) 6 Saturday I worked on an ice wagon. **1905** *Sketch* LI. 38/1 The earliest on his rounds was the man with the ice-waggon, who put down on the door-step of each house a block of ice. **1971** M. Tak *Truck Talk* 88 *Ice wagon*, a refrigerated trailer. **1972** *News & Observer* (Raleigh, N. Carolina) 30 Dec. 4/2 We don't hear much [nowadays] about . . ice wagons, branch-lines.

b. Composed or consisting of ice; as ***ice-barricade***, ***-barrier***, ***-bay***, ***-beach***, ***-bed***, ***-blockade***, ***-bridge***, ***-cake***, ***cascade***, ***-case***, ***-cataract***, ***-chain***, ***-cliff***, ***-cone***, ***-cover***, ***-crag***, ***-crystal***, ***-disc***, ***-dock***, ***-drift***, ***-drop***, ***-dust***, ***-edge***, ***-expanse***, ***-face***, ***-flake***, ***-float***, ***-fragment***, ***-fringe***, ***-growth***, ***-hummock***, ***-hump***, ***-lake***, ***-lump***, ***-margin***, ***-mass***, ***-neck***, ***-ocean***, ***-pearl***, ***-pile***, ***-plain***, ***-precipice***, ***-rain***, ***-ridge***, ***-roof***, ***-sea***, ***-shoal***, ***-slope***, ***-spicule***, ***-surface***, ***-table***, ***-torrent***, ***-trap***, ***-vault***, ***-wall***, ***-waste***, ***-wharf***.

1856 Kane *Arct. Expl.* I. xx. 248 Deep cavities filled with snow intervened between lines of *ice-barricades. **1874** G. Campbell *Let.* 14 Feb. in *Log Lett. from 'Challenger'* (1876) ii. 99 We had hoped to see the great *ice-barrier, that endless wall of ice two hundred feet in height which fringes the southern continent. **1934** I. W. Hutchison *North to Rime-Ringed Sun* x. 106 The ice-barrier was thickening fast, and as it seemed impenetrable under the westerly gale . . we cast the *Trader's* anchor. **1856** Kane *Arct. Expl.* xxxi. 421 A brig, high and dry, spending an Arctic winter over an Arctic *ice-bed. **1939** L. MacNeice *Autumn Jrnl.* xxiv. 95 The waters of life are free of the *ice-blockade of hunger. **1969** in Halpert & Story *Christmas Mumming in Newfoundland* 32 The winter ice-blockade which made the inshore fishery a limited seasonal operation. **1792** E. P. Simcoe *Diary* 15 Feb. (1911) vii. 77 Coll. Simcoe and I were going to walk on the *ice bridge. **1880** 'Mark Twain' *Tramp Abroad* II. xl. 115 A young porter . . started across an ice-bridge which spanned a crevasse. **1909** *Westm. Gaz.* 2 Sept. 9/2 After twenty days we found an ice-bridge over the water between the continental ice and the Polar ice. **1870** *Canad. Illustr. News* 26 Mar. 334/1 One *ice-cake after another struck her boat. **1923** R. Frost *New Hampshire* (1924) 65 The seal yelp On an ice cake. **1953** *Canad. Geogr. Jrnl.* July 150/1 A strip of open water stretched between shore and ice-cake which filled most of the bay. **1960** S. Plath *Colossus* (1967) 44 Farther out, the waves will be mouthing icecakes. **1966** T. Armstrong et al. *Illustr. Gloss. Snow & Ice* 21 *Ice cake*, a floe smaller than 10 m across. **1873** J. Geikie *Gt. Ice Age* (1894) 543 The glacier descends in a series of *ice-cataracts. **1860** Tyndall *Glac.* II. viii. 266 Such sand-layers give birth to *ice-cones. **1882** A. Geikie *Text-bk. Geol.* III. ii. 416 On the ice-worn surface of Norway singular cavities . . known as

'giants' kettles'..have had an origin under the massive *ice-cover which once spread over that peninsula. **1958** PRIEBSCH & COLLINSON *German Lang.* (ed. 4) ii. 22 The ice-cover made the whole of Scandinavia and Northern Germany uninhabitable. **1849** THOREAU *Week Concord Riv.* 394 It matters not through what *ice-crystals it is seen. **1919** D. H. LAWRENCE in *Eng. Rev.* June 485 Some, blonde, blue-eyed, northern, are evidently water-born, born along with the ice-crystals and blue, cold deeps. **1956** *Nature* 18 Feb. 321/2 Collisions occurring between ice crystals and small hailstones. **1856** KANE *Arct. Expl.* I. xxv. 327 The *ice-drift from the southern of these had now piled itself in our way. **1795-7** SOUTHEY *Juvenile & Minor Poems* Poet. Wks. II. 97 Blue-lipt, an *ice-drop at thy sharp blue nose. **1860** TYNDALL *Glac.* I. xviii. 124 An avalanche..came heralded by clouds of *ice-dust. **1947** G. RAWSON *Arctic Adventures* ix. 187 The cutter reached the *ice edge, and a man sprang out of it. **1966** T. ARMSTRONG et al. *Illustr. Gloss. Snow & Ice* 22 *Ice edge*, the boundary at any given time between open water and sea, river or lake ice of any kind, whether drifting or fast. **1856** E. K. KANE *Arctic Explorations* I. xvi. 187, I had to walk through the broken ice, which rose in toppling spires over my head, for nearly fifty yards, before I found an opening to the *ice-face, by which I was able to climb down to them. **1898** J. O. MAUND in W. A. Morgan *'House' on Sport* 276 Above the ice face snow slopes lying at a much less rapid angle led to the final rock peak. **1915** E. POUND *Cathay* 23 Hung with hard *ice-flakes, where hail-scur flew. **1937** *Discovery* July 220/1 Two of them..were the first to land on the ice-flake. **1774** GOLDSM. *Nat. Hist.* (1776) IV. 326 They [bears] are not only seen at land, but often on *ice-floats, several leagues at sea. **1902** *Spectator* 25 Oct. 604/1 Persecuted until they were practically driven off the seas, they took refuge furthest north along the *ice-fringe. **1966** T. ARMSTRONG et al. *Illustr. Gloss. Snow & Ice* 23 *Ice fringe*, a very narrow ice piedmont, extending less than about 1 km inland from the sea. **1897** *Edin. Rev.* Oct. 325 Among the *ice-hummocks off the southern shore of Franz Josef Land. **1910** W. DE LA MARE *Three Mulla-Mulgars* 67 Floating like a cork among the *ice-humps. **1961** *Times* 24 Apr. 14/7, I cannot tell whether an icehump is two inches high or a dangerous two feet. **1934** *Ice-lake [see GEOCHRONOLOGICAL *a.*]. **1957** G. E. HUTCHINSON *Treat. Limnol.* I. i. 8 The earliest postglacial Baltic was an ice lake. **1889** G. F. WRIGHT *Ice Age N. Amer.* xx. 482 The buried vegetable deposits under consideration do not mark a warm climate, but a climate much colder than the present—such a vegetation, in fact, as would naturally flourish near the *ice-margin. **1958** F. E. ZEUNER *Dating Past* (ed. 4) 22 As the ice-margin retreated the varves followed it. **1591** SYLVESTER *Yvry* 133 North-west winde..his volleys racqueted, Of bounding Balls of *Ice-pearl slippery shining. **1853** KANE *Grinnell Exp.* l. (1856) 485 The great *ice-plain formed one continuous sheet from the Greenland shore as far as the eye could reach. **1860** TYNDALL *Glac.* I. xi. 84 Breathing more freely after we had cleared the *ice-precipice. **1892** C. T. DENT et al. *Mountaineering* vi. 223 Nothing tends more to weary and render him [*sc.* a mountaineer] careless than some hours of step-cutting on an *ice-ridge. **1929** F. SMYTHE *Climbs & Ski Runs* xv. 288 We gained the foot of the rock pitch separating the third ice-ridge from the fourth. **1957** J. BLISH *Fallen Star* vii. 104 The ice-ridge on our left screamed, broke free and reared skyward. **1860** TYNDALL *Glac.* I. xxii. 152, I waited for him..and helped him down the *ice-slope. **1881** *Nature* 10 Feb. 338/2 The *ice-spicules are built up 'in the teeth' of this current. **1962** F. I. ORDWAY et al. *Basic Astronautics* iii. 90 Three in number, they [*sc.* the rings of Saturn] are very thin in comparison to their width, and are made up of millions upon millions of..particles, pebbles, grains of dust, and perhaps ice spicules. **1856** KANE *Arct. Expl.* I. vii. 71 We could see the strait growing still narrower, and the heavy *ice-tables grinding up. **1860** TYNDALL *Glac.* I. xxiv. 173, I visited the *ice-wall at the Tacul. **1905** *Westm. Gaz.* 9 Dec. 16/1 There is neither the sport nor the game that cheers the Northern *ice-wastes. **1964** F. WARNER *Early Poems* 80 Lonely ice-wastes.

c. instrumental, with passive participles, forming adjs., as ***ice-battered***, ***-bemarbled***, ***-born***, ***-built***, ***-capped***, ***-chained***, ***-checked***, ***-chocked***, ***-clad***, ***-clogged***, ***-clothed***, ***-coated***, ***-cooled***, ***-covered***, ***-crusted***, ***-cumbered***, ***-embossed***, ***-enveloped***, ***-fed***, ***-glazed***, ***-ground***, ***-imprisoned***, ***-laden***, ***-lined***, ***-locked***, ***-marked***, ***-polished***, ***-preserved***, ***-rubbed***, ***-sheltered***, ***-worn***. Also *ice-like*.

1856 KANE *Arct. Expl.* I. xxviii. 364 Ensconced in our *ice-battered citadel. **1757** GRAY *Progr. Poesy* II. ii, In climes beyond the solar road, Where shaggy forms o'er *ice-built mountains roam. **1799** CAMPBELL *Pleas. Hope* II. 122 The *ice-chain'd waters slumbering on the shore. **1880** A. R. WALLACE *Isl. Life* 154 Where the whole country is completely *ice-clad. **1853** KANE *Grinnell Exp.* x. (1856) 76 Through this *ice-clogged bay. **1880** 'MARK TWAIN' *Tramp Abroad* II. xxxiv. 32 They came to an *ice-coated ridge. **1928** *Observer* 15 July 22 Ice-coated ships. **1755** SMOLLETT *Quix.* (1803) IV. 167 Those savoury banquets, and *ice-cooled potations. *a* **1847** ELIZA COOK *Poems, Dog of Alps* i, The *ice-covered scalps..of the Alps. **1956** *Nature* 17 Mar. 508/1 The lofty ice-covered interior of Antarctica. **1856** KANE *Arct. Expl.* I. xiv. 156 Through the *ice-crusted window-panes of the cabin. **1798** SOTHEBY tr. *Wieland's Oberon* (1826) I. 97 Wedg'd in masses *ice-emboss'd. **1813** COLERIDGE *Remorse* II. i. 18 An *ice-glazed precipice. **1872** TYNDALL *Forms of Water* §365 The *ice-ground part of the mountains is clearly distinguished from the splintered crests. **1860** TYNDALL *Glac.* I. xvi. 107 Between us and the *ice-laden valley. **1860** GEN. P. THOMPSON *Audi Alt.* III. cxix. 60 On the supposed *ice-like plain. **1866** J. G. WHITTIER *Snow-Bound* 50 Wide swung again our *ice-locked door. **1907** *Westm. Gaz.* 21 Oct. 2/3 Ice-locked Polar snows. **1972** S. BURNFORD *One Woman's Arctic* i. 13 Now the strait was ice-locked. **1897** E. CONYBEARE *Cambridgesh.* 5 Travelled fragments of rock, usually *ice-marked. **1880** A. R. WALLACE *Isl. Life* 176 The *ice-preserved Arctic mammalia. **1860** G. H. K. *Vac. Tour.* 165 Smooth, grey, *ice-worn, gneiss banks. **1893** SIR H. H. HOWORTH *Glacial Nightmare* II. 704 The higher parts of the Dovrefelds..have not been ice-worn.

d. parasynthetic, as ***ice-bearded***, ***-belted***, ***-dammed*** (see sense 8 below), ***-hearted***, ***-helmed***, ***-pillared***, ***-ribbed*** adjs.

1591 SYLVESTER *Yvry* 174 *Ice-bearded Boreas. **1819** SHELLEY *Cenci* III. i. 153 Oh, *ice-hearted counsellor! **1950** G. BARKER *News of World* 49 Just as the ice-hearted stars Stand around like avatars. **1960** S. PLATH *Colossus* (1967) 23 At the source Of your ice-hearted calling—Drunkenness of the great depths. **1875** LONGF. *Pandora* vi. *Voices of the Waters*, The mountains, the giants, The *ice-helmed, the forest-belted. **1838** ELIZA COOK *Melaia, King of Wind* i, He burst through the *ice-pillar'd gates of the North. **1866** B. TAYLOR *Poems, The Harp*, The thunders of the *ice-ribbed ocean.

e. objective, as ***ice-blasting***, ***-breaking***, ***-cutting***, ***-haunting***, ***-loving***, ***-making***, sbs. and adjs.

1824 *Canad. Mag.* III. Dec. 541 He accosted us all gaily, without any of that long *ice-breaking conversation about the weather, which generally occupies the first half-hour of our stage-coach journeys. **1883** *Fisheries Exhib. Catal.* 362 Ice-breaking Boat..used in..sailing among the Ice. **1956** *Nature* 31 Mar. 600/2 The two expeditions will share a large ice-breaking sealer. **1970** *Daily Tel.* 21 Mar. 15 Canadian seal-hunting ships with ice-breaking capacity. **1854** THOREAU *Walden* 229 The only obvious employment, except wood-chopping, *ice-cutting, or the like business. **1908** *Westm Gaz.* 29 May 2/1 The ice-cutting looks so like harvesting or hay-making. **1960** J. J. ROWLANDS *Spindrift* 75 Few remember the days of ice-cutting. **1831** *Edin. Rev.* LIII. 343 *Ice-haunting..species. *Ibid.*, *Ice-loving and maritime species. **1864** *Chambers's Jrnl.* 13 Feb. 101/1 The attention of some millions of persons was attracted, in the International Exhibition of 1862, to two *ice-making machines of a very remarkable character. **1875** *Ure's Dict. Arts* II. 488 Harrison's ice-making machine..is a particular application of the exhausting air-pump. **1856** KANE *Arct. Expl.* I. vi. 64 A smart *ice-shattering breeze, to open a road for us.

8. Special Combinations: **ice-action**, the action of ice upon the surface of the earth, esp. during the glacial period; **ice-age**, the glacial period (see GLACIAL 3); also *fig.* and *Comb.*; **ice-anchor**, a grapnel for holding a ship to an ice-floe; **ice-apron**, (*a*) a pointed structure for protecting a bridge-pier from ice carried down by the stream; (*b*) (see quot. 1958); **ice-arm**, an arm or projecting portion of ice; **ice-auger**, an auger for boring large holes in ice, used in ice-fishing; **ice-axe**, (*a*) an axe used by Alpine climbers, for cutting steps in icy slopes; (*b*) an implement for cutting ice for domestic purposes; = *ice-pick* (*a*); **ice-bag**, an india-rubber bag filled with ice and applied to some part of the body for medical or surgical purposes; **ice-banner** (*U.S.*) = *ice-feathers* (*Cent. Dict.*); **ice-beam**, a beam placed at the stern or bow of a ship to resist the pressure of ice; **ice-bearer**, a frost-bearer or CRYOPHORUS; **ice-bed**, a stratified glacial deposit; **ice-belt**, the fringe of ice along an Arctic coast; = ICE-FOOT; **ice-block**, (*a*) a block of ice; also *fig.*; (*b*) Austral. = *ice-lolly*; **ice-blue**, a very pale blue; **ice-boulder**, a boulder conveyed by glacial action; **ice-box**, a box or compartment for holding ice, an ice-chest; or one that is kept cold by means of ice; also (*U.S.*), a refrigerator (see also quot. 1971); also *transf.*; **ice-bucket** = *ice-pail*; **ice-calk** = CALK *sb.*[1] 2 (Knight *Dict. Mech.* 1875); **ice-calorimeter**, an apparatus for determining specific heat by means of ice; **ice-canoe**, a canoe with iron runners for use on frozen lakes or rivers; **ice-capade** [jocular blend of ICE *sb.* + ESCAPADE], an event, show, etc., that takes place on ice; **ice-car**, a refrigerating van adapted for the transport of perishable goods; **ice-cart**, a cart in which ice is conveyed for delivery; **ice-cataplasm** = *ice-poultice* (*Syd. Soc. Lex.*); **ice-cave**, (*a*) a cave which contains ice even in summer; (*b*) a hollow in the ice at the lower end of a glacier; (*c*) a kind of small domestic refrigerator (*disused*); (*d*) a cave hollowed out of ice as a shelter; **ice-cellar** *N. Amer.*, a cellar kept cool by blocks of ice and used to preserve food; **ice-chair**, a chair fitted with runners so as to be propelled easily upon ice; a sledge-chair; **ice-chamber**, a compartment containing, or cooled by, ice; a refrigerating chamber; **ice-chest** (see quot.); **ice-chimney**, a chimney (CHIMNEY *sb.* 8) formed in ice; **ice-chisel**, a chisel used for cutting holes in ice, or splitting blocks of ice; **ice-claw**, an iron claw for grappling and lifting blocks of ice (Knight *Dict. Mech.* 1875); = CRAMPON *sb.* 3; **ice-closet**, an ice-chamber or ice-chest; **ice-clothes**, clothing suitable for wearing on the Arctic ice; **ice-cloud**, a cloud consisting of ice crystals; **ice colour**, any of a class of azo dyes which are insoluble in water, being formed directly on the fibre by impregnating it with one component of the dye (naphthol or a naphthol derivative) and then immersing it in a solution of the other (a diazo compound); so called because the solutions originally used needed to be kept ice-cold; **ice-compress** = *ice-poultice* (*Syd. Soc. Lex.* 1886); **ice contact** *Physical Geogr.*, a surface or deposit that was originally formed in contact with a body of ice; usu. *attrib.*, esp. in ***ice-contact slope***, a (usually steep) slope so formed; **ice-craft**, ability to deal with the ice in mountaineering or Arctic exploration; icemanship; **ice-creeper** = *ice-calk* (Knight *Dict. Mech.* 1875); **ice-crop**, the yield of ice in a single winter or from a certain place; **ice cube**, a small block of ice formed in a mould in a refrigerator and used to chill drinks; †**ice-dagger**, an icicle; **ice-dam**, a dam across a river formed by a glacier; so **ice-dammed** *a.*; **ice-drift**, drifted ice in the mass; **ice-drill** = *ice-auger*; **ice-drops**, in *Bot.*, transparent processes resembling icicles, as in the ice-plant (Webster 1864); **ice-dyke**, a narrow crevasse filled with ice columns; **ice-elevator**, a machine for lifting blocks of ice to a higher level; **ice-escape**, an apparatus for rescuing persons who have fallen through the ice; **ice-farm**, (*a*) a place where ice is formed by allowing water to freeze in specially hollowed-out beds, or in shallow earthenware pans; (*b*) a place where naturally frozen ice is stored; **ice-feathers**, feather-like forms assumed by ice exposed to wind, in mountainous parts of the United States (*Cent. Dict.*); **ice-fender**, a fender or guard to protect a vessel from being injured by ice (Ogilvie 1882); **ice-ferns**, the fern-like formations produced on the surface of glass by the action of frost; **ice-fish**, the caplin (Funk); **ice-fishing**, fishing in winter through holes made in the ice; see also quot. 1907; hence [as a back-formation] ***ice-fish*** v. intr.; ***ice-fisherman***; **ice-flow**, an ice-stream; **ice-flowers** = (*a*) *ice-ferns*; (*b*) (see quot. 1955), also in *sing.*; **ice-fox**, the Arctic fox; **ice-front**, the margin of a glacier, ice-shelf, or ice-sheet; **ice-glass** = *crackle-glass* (CRACKLE *sb.* 3); **ice-gorge** (*U.S.*), an accumulation of ice-blocks choking the bed of a river; **ice-green**, a very pale green; **ice guard**, (*a*) (see quot. 1905) *U.S.*; (*b*) *Aeronaut.* , a wire grid that may be fitted in the intake of an aero-engine, so that any ice forms on it rather than in the engine; **ice-gull**, a name given in N. America to the glaucous gull and the ivory gull; **ice-hammer** , (*a*) a hammer for breaking ice to be used in drinks; (*b*) a hammer used in mountaineering (see quot. 1932); **ice-harvest**, the ice-crop; the period during which the ice-crop is gathered; **ice hockey**, a game developed from field hockey but played on ice; also *attrib.*; **ice-jam**, the blocking of a channel with broken ice; the jam so formed; also *fig.*; **ice-ladder** = *ice-escape*; **ice-lane** (see quot.); **ice-leaf**, a local name of Mullein, *Verbascum Thapsus* (Britten & Holl.); **ice-ledge** = ICE-FOOT; **ice line**, in a phase diagram of water, a line representing the conditions of temperature and pressure at which ice and water will be in equilibrium in the absence of water vapour; **ice-lobe**, a portion of a continental ice-sheet that projects from the main area; **ice-lolly**, a water ice on a stick; **ice-loon**, the great northern diver (*U.S.*); **ice-machine**, a machine for the artificial production of ice; **ice-maiden** *colloq.*, a 'cold' or unresponsive woman; **ice-maker**, (*a*) one who manufactures artificial ice; (*b*) = *ice-machine*; **ice-mark**, a mark, scratch, or groove produced by ice-action, esp. by glacial action during the ice-age; †**ice-meer**, a cake of ground-ice; **ice-mill**, a spot where a glacier grinds out the underlying rock by the action of loose stones, a glacier-mill; **ice-mould**, a hollow utensil used in shaping ice; **ice-needle**, (*a*) a strong needle used to break up a lump of ice; (*b*) any elongated, needle-like ice crystal; **ice-pack**, (*a*) a body of separate pieces of drift-ice closely packed so as to form one great ice-field; (*b*) a pack (PACK *sb.*[1] 11) prepared with ice; **ice-pail**, a pail for holding ice, in which bottles of wine, etc. are plunged in order to cool the liquor; **ice-pan**, a small slab of floating ice; **ice-paper** [tr. F. *papier glacé*], transparent gelatine in thin sheets used in copying drawings (*Cent. Dict.*); **ice-period**, the glacial period of Geology, the ice-age; **ice-pick**, (*a*) a small domestic tool with a sharp spike designed for breaking up ice (e.g. for drinks); (*b*) in Mountaineering, a pick (PICK *sb.*[1]); **ice pigeon**, a breed of domestic pigeon whose prevailing colour is a pale bluish lavender; **ice-pit**, a pit in which ice is stored for preservation;

ice-pitcher, a pitcher with double sides, or of non-conducting material, for holding broken ice or iced water; **ice-piton**, a piton used to assist climbing on ice; **ice-plane** (see quots.); **ice-plate**, a small, usu. glass, plate on which ice-cream is served; **ice-point**, a temperature at which ice and water are in equilibrium; *spec.* the temperature (0°C.) at which ice is in equilibrium with water saturated with air and under standard atmospheric pressure, formerly taken as a primary fixed point but now replaced for this purpose by the triple point; **ice-pole** *Canad.*, a long pole used by seamen for levering against ice-floes, etc.; **ice-poultice**, a bag or bladder filled with pounded ice, for application to inflamed parts of the body (C. A. Harris *Dict. Med. Terminol.* 1854–67); **ice-pudding**, a frozen confection in the form of pudding; **ice-pulse**, the throbbing movement which precedes an ice-quake; **ice-push**, lateral pressure exerted on a shore as a sheet of floating ice expands following changes in temperature; also, an ice-rampart formed as a result; **ice-quake**, the convulsion which accompanies the break-up of an ice-field or ice-floe; **ice-raft**, a floating sheet of ice; **ice-ram**, a pointed projection from a ship's bows, to assist it in forcing its way through ice; **ice-rampart**, a ridge of beach material along a shore-line which has been forced up by the lateral movement of floating ice; **ice-rink** (see RINK *sb.*^{2} 3); **ice-river** = ICE-STREAM; **ice-room** = *ice-chamber*; **ice-run**, a stretch of ice prepared for tobogganing; also *fig.*; **ice-safe**, a meat-safe having chambers for containing ice; **Ice Saints** (see quot. 1922); **ice-sandal**, a sandal or golosh with spiked sole, worn on ice; **ice-saw**, a large saw employed by Arctic voyagers and in ice harvesting for cutting ice; **ice-scape** [after LANDSCAPE *sb.*], (a picture of) ice scenery; **ice-scour, -scouring**, the action of an ice-sheet or glacier in eroding the land and modifying and producing landforms; so **ice-scoured** *a.*; **ice-screw**, an ice-elevator having a spiral motion; also, an ice-piton (q.v.) which is screwed, rather than hammered, into the ice; **ice-shed**, a divide between two expanses of moving ice; **ice-shelf**, a floating sheet of ice permanently attached to a land mass; **ice-ship**, a ship specially built to resist ice-pressure; **ice-shoe**, a spiked shoe used for walking on ice; **ice-shop**, a shop where ice is sold; **ice-skate** = SKATE *sb.*^{2} 1; also as *vb.*; so ***ice-skater, ice-skating*** vbl. sb.; **ice-spirit**, frost as a nature-spirit; **ice sport**, a sport taking place on ice; **ice-spur**, a spur or spike fixed in the sole of a boot, to assist in walking on ice; **ice-station**, a station where ice is collected for storage; **ice step**, a step cut into ice; **ice-stick**, a stick with a spike at the end, used in walking on ice; **ice-storm**, a storm of freezing rain that leaves a deposit of ice on trees, etc.; **ice-striæ**, thin lines of scoring made in rocks by ice passing over them; **ice-system**, a connected system or group of glaciers; **ice-tongue**, any body of ice that projects from a glacier, iceberg, or ice-sheet, esp. one that is relatively long and narrow (see also quot. 1893); **ice-tray**, a tray used in a refrigerator for making ice cubes; **ice-wedge**, a vertical wedge-shaped mass of ice in the soil of a permafrost region; **ice-whale**, the great polar whale; **ice-white** *a.*, having a whiteness like that of ice; **ice wool** = EIS WOOL; **ice-yacht** = ICE-BOAT 1; hence **ice-yachting, -yachtsman**.

1863 Lyell *Antiq. Man* 308 Proof of a close connection between *ice-action and contorted stratification. **1873** J. Geikie (*title*) The Great *Ice Age. **1888** *Daily News* 17 Sept. 3/1 Geologists have lately been working out the facts of what is called the 'Glacial Period', or the 'Ice Age'. **1957** C. Day Lewis *Pegasus* 24 Cold chisels of wind, *ice-age-edged. **1966** *Listener* 10 Mar. 338/2 With..the certainty by 1950 that America and Russia both possessed atomic weapons, the world entered the new ice-age of the cold war between the big two. **1973** A. Price *October Men* ix. 122 The temperature was perhaps slightly less arctic now he had said his piece, but that was no sure sign that a second..ice age was not about to set in. **1774** C. J. Phipps *Voy. N. Pole* 59 The ice being all round us, we got out our *ice-anchors, and moored along-side a field. **1880** *Standard* 20 May 3 The vessel will..'hook on' with an S-shaped ice-anchor to the floe alongside. **1871** *Scribner's Monthly* II. 170 It [has been] necessary to construct enormous breakwaters, having *ice-aprons of strong oak timber. **1875** Knight *Dict. Mech.* 1161/1 The ice-aprons of the Eads's St. Louis Railway Bridge are 200 feet long and 60 feet wide. **1958** Armstrong & Roberts in *Polar Record* IX. LIX. 93 *Ice apron*, a thin mass of snow and ice adhering to a mountain side. **1928** *Daily Tel.* 4 Sept. 11/5 He..had mistaken the Frederikshaab ice arm for the Sukkertoppen *ice arm. **1820** Scoresby *Acc. Arctic Reg.* II. 349 *note*, The '*ice-axe', with which the hole is made... Sometimes an 'ice-drill'..is made use of for this purpose. **1894** Fenn *In Alpine Valley* I. 44 The ice-axes they carried. **1960** J. J. Rowlands *Spindrift* 69 It was the magic of his [*sc.* an ice-vendor's] skill in using an ice-axe that enthralled me. **1963** I. Deutscher *Prophet Outcast: Trotsky* v. 504 He [*sc.* Trotsky] grappled with the murderer, bit his hand, and wrenched the ice-axe from him. **1883** *Brit. Q. Rev.* July 15 The use of the spinal *ice-bags for sea-sickness. **1820** Scoresby *Acc. Arctic Reg.* II. 191 Oak-timbers, called *ice-beams, about 12 inches square and 25 feet in length are placed beneath the hold beams. **1842** Francis *Dict. Arts* etc., **Ice-Bearer*. **1885** Eliz. C. Agassiz *Louis Agassiz* I. 289 The ancient *ice-beds and moraines of England. **1856** Kane *Arct. Expl.* I. viii. 78 The little brig was fast to the *ice-belt which lined the bottom of the cliffs. **1853** —— *Grinnell Exp.* xxvi. (1856) 218 There it was, with the gangway stairs of *ice-block masonry. **1864** G. M. Hopkins *Notebks. & Papers* (1937) 27 Those wastes where the ice-blocks tilt and fret. **1957** J. Blish *Falling Star* ix. 120 We built Wentz's igloo with..the one Keystone ice-block at the summit. **1958** *Church Times* 3 Jan. 3/1 Hopes of some thaw in the international ice-block rose with the publication of warm greetings of peace and goodwill sent by the Russian leaders. **1962** J. R. Bernard in *Southerly* XXII. 97 Without loss we add to..the meaning of..ice-block that of frozen confection. **1966** Baker *Austral. Lang.* (ed. 2) xiii. 290 *Ice-block*, a small block of coloured and sweet-tasting ice on a stick. **1935** *N. & Q.* 5 Jan. 7/2 From a draper's catalogue for the coming winter sales, I cull a few names of colours to me at least new: *Ice-blue, [etc.]. **1952** 'J. Ross' *Yellow Drawing-Room* ix. 138 An ice-blue satin skirt. **1958** A. Wilson *Middle Age of Mrs Eliot* II. 219 The walls [were] distempered ice blue. **1970** W. Smith *Gold Mine* xxv. 57 His office was in white and ice-blue. **1846** *St. Louis Reveille* 9 Sept. 4/5 Everything requisite for funerals, such as Hearse, Carriages,..Ice, *Ice-boxes. **1875** Ice-box [see *ice-chest*]. **1877** [see BAVAROISE]. **1884** F. J. Britten *Watch & Clockm.* 65 The 'ice-box'..is also a metal chamber, with a receptacle for ice round the sides, and jacketed all over with a non-conductor. **1908** Wodehouse & Westbrook *Globe by the Way Bk.* 13/2 His brain worked like a buzz-saw in an ice-box. **1927** *Rev. Eng. Stud.* Oct. 435 This healthy linguistic instinct is seen in *e.g.* the substitution of *raincoat* for *mackintosh*, *ice-box* for *refrigerator*. **1938** D. Castle *Do Your Own Time* v. 45 Scavengers..cut down the hanged men, place them in cheap coffins, and cart them to the 'ice box', as the morgue is known in prison. **1943** Wyndham Lewis *Let.* 31 Mar. (1963) 352 We are freezing out here [*sc.* in Canada] slowly, in this icebox of a country. **1963** *Amer. Speech* XXXVIII. 173 *Icebox*, a co-ed engaged to a young man in a distant college who refuses to date at all while at college. **1971** M. Tak *Truck Talk* 87 *Ice box.* (1) A refrigerated trailer used for hauling produce and perishables. (2) The bunker for ice in a bunk-and-blower type cooling system in an insulated trailer. **1919** Barrie *Alice Sit-by-the-Fire* II. 61 Supper for two, champagne in an *ice-bucket. **1929** E. Hemingway *Farewell to Arms* xxv. 276 The champagne in the ice-bucket and our glasses on the table. **1939** N. Monsarrat *This is Schoolroom* II. vii. 176 A magnum of GH Mumm ready to hand in an ice-bucket. **1959** N. Marsh *False Scent* (1960) iv. 94 Gantry tipped some [water] out of the ice bucket. **1941** *Time* 10 Feb. 67/1 Another touring frostbite fiesta called **Ice-Capades of 1941*. **1963** *Times* 7 Mar. 3/6 Football..finally broke out of the strangling cocoon of snow, ice and mud to be rediscovered as a thing of excitement and calculated skill almost forgotten during the recent ice-capades. **1909** *Chambers's Jrnl.* Aug. 560/2 In Canada there is also a special *ice-car service for the carriage of butter to Montreal. **1842** *Knickerbocker* XX. 205 Before an omnibus or hotel or restaurant or *ice-cart had assumed its popular cognomen. **1864** T. L. Nichols *40 Yrs. Amer. Life* I. 247 Every morning the ice-cart comes round. **1873** *Young Englishwoman* July 334/1 Ice-carts call as regularly as does the baker. **1889** A. B. Marshall *Cookery Bk.* p. xx (Advt.), Marshall's patent *ice cave..will freeze a quantity of water placed in the inner cave into a solid mass. **1897** *Geogr. Jrnl.* June 670 The term 'ice-cave'..should especially apply to the hollows in the ice at the lower end of glaciers, whence the glacier waters make their exit. **1911** *Madame* 20 May 318/1 Various forms of iced pudding, which, even if you do not happen to possess one of A. B. Marshall's ice caves, are still quite possible to prepare with very little trouble. **1926–7** *Army & Navy Stores Catal.* 167/3 Ice caves with loose shelves. Japanned iron. **1930** F. Smythe *Kangchenjunga Adventure* ii. 45 In lieu of tents, ice caves were carved in the solid ice at Camps Eight and Nine, large enough to hold six to eight persons. **1933** J. Buchan *Prince of Captivity* I. iii. 95 He would draw terrible pictures of an ice-cave at Gundbjorns Fjord, and two dead men. **1950** *Chambers's Encycl.* VII. 359/1 The so-called ice caves (not to be confused with caves in glacier ice) are caves in solid rock which, although situated below the line of perpetual snow, nevertheless contain large deposits of ice. **1961** R. M. Patterson *Buffalo Head* iv. 136 We explored.. finding..mountain sheep, ice caves, the fairest of alpine rock gardens, [etc.]. **1771** J. R. Forster tr. *Kalm's Trav. N. Amer.* III. 232 Some of the people of quality make use of *ice-cellars, to keep beer cool. *Ibid.*, These ice-cellars are commonly built of stone, under the house. **1865** Milton & Cheadle *N.W. Passage by Land* vi. 82 They even went down into the ice-cellar, where the meat is kept. **1883** *Harper's Mag.* July 261, I visited one of the..largest beer factories, and took copious notes about..the ice cellars colder than Siberia ever dared to be. **1921** *Chambers's Jrnl.* 21 May 395/2 Seeds of maple and wheat have been observed growing into blocks of ice in an ice-cellar. **1875** Knight *Dict. Mech.*, *Ice-chest*, a form of domestic *ice-chamber having apartments for the ice and the provisions, the food-chamber being cooled by air..from the ice-box or by the cold side of the latter. **1893** Gladstone *Sp. Ho. Com.* 23 Feb., In the great sea-going steamers there is always an ice-chamber. **1841** C. Cist *Cincinnati in 1841* (Advt.), Manufacturer of packing-boxes, *ice-chests, trunk and segar boxes, &c. **1897** Hughes *Mediterranean Fever* v. 191 Milk..should be..kept in the ice-chest. **1935** 'J. Guthrie' *Little Country* xxiv. 359 Young Merryweather..thought the place like an ice chest. **1972** *Even. Telegram* (St. John's, Newfoundland) (Advt. Suppl.) 27 June 1 Foam plastic ice chest 99¢. **1929** F. Smythe *Climbs & Ski Runs* xv. 293 The *ice-chimney continued for some distance with great difficulty. **1934** *Discovery* Mar. 60/2 We were obliged to negotiate some ugly ice-chimneys. **1955** J. E. B. Wright *Technique Mountaineering* v. 97 Ice chimneys may be pitches in couloirs and icefalls. **1853** Kane *Grinnell Exp.* xlix. (1856) 468 While three men were out on a low berg..one of them ..struck his *ice-chisel against the mass. **1920** G. W. Young *Mountain Craft* vii. 286 Any man who wishes to make big ascents is well advised if he begins early to learn how to use *ice-claws (or crampons). **1954** W. Noyce *South Col* v. 79 Crampons or ice-claws are sets of metal spikes on frames tied to the feet to assist walking up ice. **1955** G. Band *Road to Rakaposhi* xii. 141 Climbers have managed for so long without these useful 'ice-claws' in the Himalayas. **1853** Kane *Grinnell Exp.* xxix. (1856) 249 The *ice-clothes ready for a jump. **1883** R. H. Scott *Elem. Meteorol.* 403 (Index), *Ice clouds. **1900** W. Allingham *Man. Marine Meteorol.* xvi. 154 Halos and other refraction phenomena afford proof that cirro-stratus is an ice cloud. **1963** D. Irving *Destruction of Dresden* III. i. 106 Ice clouds were blanketing Europe. **1903** C. Salter tr. *G. von Georgievics's Chem. Dye-Stuffs* 82 This method is employed to produce dyeings of considerable beauty and fastness, which now play a great part in dyeing cotton piece goods and in calico printing (*Ice colours). **1968** E. N. Abrahart *Dyes* vi. 161 A small range of Ice Colours, so called because the preparation of the diazo solutions by the dyer needed ice, was built up. **1896** *Amer. Geologist* XVIII. 152 The tracing on the ground of the *ice-contacts shows that other morainal belts come into the region about Wickford from the southeast. *Ibid.*, The accompanying map..exhibits by special designations the position of the ice-contact slopes or moraine terraces. **1968** R. W. Fairbridge *Encycl. Geomorphol.* 438/2 Ice contact deposits outline the holes and tunnels in the last wasting of the basal ice. **1970** C. A. Lewis *Glaciations Wales* ii. 29 The fresh ice-contact slopes (15°–20°) and re-entrant features noted on the inner flanks of the Cors Geirch terraces are present also on their eastern side. **1890** *Daily News* 5 Mar. 5/2 Proficiency in *ice-craft grows gradually. **1923** G. D. Abraham *First Steps to Climbing* iv. 45 We find the Mount Everest Expedition largely composed of rock-climbing specialists whose knowledge of snow and ice-craft is almost negligible. **1955** E. Hillary *High Adventure* 16 Harry was New Zealand's outstanding climber, with a tremendous reputation for brilliant ice-craft. **1889** *Montreal Daily Star, Carnival No.*, '*Ice Yatching*' 5/1 *Ice-creepers taking the place of wading-boots. **1853** A. Bunn *Old Eng. & New Eng.* I. ii. 31 Content ourselves by observing that the *ice-crop (as it is drolly called)..proved to be a fair average one. **1864** *Chambers's Jrnl.* 100/1 Producing an ice-crop which will pay all expenses and leave a profit. **1929** M. Lief *Hangover* vii. 128 She dashed into the kitchen and came back with a bowl of *ice-cubes and some more bottles. **1939** *Vogue's Cookery Book* 122 Ice cubes for summer drinks can be made decorative by freezing cherries..inside them. **1949** *Consumer Reports* June 250/1 Four medium-size ice-cube trays. **1962** J. Braine *Life at Top* iv. 71 She took out the ice cube tray. **1519** Horman *Vulg.* 103 b, A childe was slayne with an *yse dagger [*Paruulus stiria occisus est*]. **1883** *Proc. Amer. Assoc. Adv. Sci.* XXXII. 207 Among the most interesting results of the author's survey in Ohio, was the demonstration of the existence of an *ice-dam across the river at Cincinnati. **1935** W. J. Miller *Introd. Physical Geol.* (ed. 3) xiv. 396 Existing ice-dam lakes are not common, and few, if any of them, are large. During the Ice Age, however, thousands of them formed and lasted only as long as the ice dams existed. **1914** W. B. Wright *Quaternary Ice Age* iii. 71 Two main chains of *ice-dammed lakes in the Cleveland valleys to the north of Pickering are described by Professor Kendall. **1965** G. de Boer in A. Small *Fourth Viking Congress* 207 The whole flat floored, hill girt hollow, is readily seen for what it is, the bed of a former ice-dammed lake. **1867** Motley *Netherl.* xxxvi. III. 557 The strait was already filled with *ice-drift. **1820** *Ice-drill [see *ice-axe*]. **1905** W. H. Sherzer in *Smithsonian Misc. Coll.* XLVII. 468 *Ice dykes. These consist of narrow crevasses, two to fifteen inches across, completely filled with columnar ice. **1864** *Illustr. Lond. News* 9 Jan. 31/1 A number of sledge-chairs and an *ice-escape were conveyed to the place of amusement. **1889** *Pall Mall Gaz.* 6 Feb. 3/1 When the winter fairly sets in the scene on an *ice-farm is a busy one. **1908** *Sci. Amer.* 25 Jan. 58/2 Natural ice making in the tropics—the peculiar 'ice farms' of hot Bengal. **1864** Tennyson *Aylmer's F.* 222 Fine as *ice-ferns on January panes. **1963** *Brit. Columbia Digest* Nov.–Dec. 31 It'll be nothing less than wonderful if I manage to make one good steelhead trip and *icefish in three lakes all winter. **1960** M. Sharcott *Place of Many Winds* vii. 123 The *ice-fisherman ..earns a few extra cents a pound. **1963** *Times* 12 Mar. 9/6 In most cases, the ice fisherman will avail himself (at a modest fee) of the services of a resort owner who ploughs roads across the ice and clears sites for the ice houses. **1890** T. H. Bean in *Forest & Stream* XXXV. 417 (*title*) *Ice fishing in arctic Alaska. **1907** J. G. Millais *Newfoundland* i. 9 Twenty years at the 'ice fishing' (seal hunting)..will try the strongest man. **1970** *Globe & Mail* (Toronto) 25 Sept. 35/6 (Advt.), Sand beach, floating dock, very private, ice fishing. **1873** J. Geikie *Gt. Ice Age* (1894) 542, I may shortly describe one or two of the better known of the old *ice-flows. **1694** *Acc. Sev. Late Voy.* II. (1711) 41 Just as *Ice flowers on our Glass-windows, get all sorts of figures. **1909** E. Shackleton *Heart of Antarctic* II. 341 Ice-flowers occurred on freshwater ice at Clear Lake. **1911** J. Masefield *Jim Davis* iii. 26 The frost had covered the window with ice-flowers, so that we could not see through the glass. **1955** *Arctic Terms* 42/1 *Ice flower*, a delicate tuft of frost or rime, resembling a fern or flower, that occasionally forms on surface sea ice around a salt crystal nucleus. **1965** P. Wayre *Wind in Reeds* vi. 79 All along the tide mark the frost had formed delicate ice-flowers. **1890** *Bull. Geol. Soc. Amer.* I. 201 Further inland, where plains are found up to altitudes of a thousand or more feet above sea level, I think the water in which they accumulated was fresh water, temporarily ponded by the *ice front. **1957** G. E. Hutchinson *Treat. Limnol.* I. xv. 833 The receding ice front passed Hertford about 19,500 years ago. **1966** B. B. Baker et al. *Gloss. Oceanogr. Terms* (ed. 2) 83/1 *Ice front* (also called *front, ice cliff, ice face, ice wall*), (1) the seaward facing, cliff-like edge of an ice shelf (so called by the British Antarctic Place-names Committee), (2) any vertical wall of ice. **1862** *Congress. Globe* 2896/1 The island is..below the bend in the Delaware, and hence mainly out of danger from *ice gorges. **1884** W. H. Bishop in *Harper's Mag.* Mar. 514/2 An ice-gorge forming in the river..has smashed..whole fleets of them. **1925** E. Sitwell *Troy Park* 40 Leaves like a starry crown Are clear as the splintered star *ice-green That is a crown for a negro queen. **1934** L. B. Lyon *White Hare* 16 The washed sky opened like an arctic rose, ice-green. **1938** W. de la Mare *Memory* 62 Skies ice-green. **1905** *Forestry Bureau Bull.* (U.S.) No. 61, 40 **Ice guards*, heavy timbers fastened fan shaped about a cluster of boom piles at an angle

of approximately 30 degrees to the surface of the water. They prevent the destruction of the boom by ice, through forcing it to mount the guards and be broken up. **1947** *Jrnl. R. Aeronaut. Soc.* LI. 298/2 In the early stages of the war some Mosquitos had flown home from Sweden through bad icing weather. The machines had reached home, but there was a complaint that they had lost 2 lb. of boost because the ice guards had iced up completely. **1907** *Yesterday's Shopping* (1969) 599/4 Electro-plated ice tongs and *ice hammer. **1932** *Mountaineering Jrnl.* Dec. 100 The ice-hammer is used for chiselling steps and handholds as well as for driving in pitons. **1933** G. D. Abraham *Mod. Mountaineering* ix. 175 Young Continental experts..have evolved the ice hammer which is used for driving in the pitons. **1953** J. Hunt *Ascent Everest* I. iv. 38 The more familiar gear..rope and line, pitons, snaplinks, icehammers and axes. **1864** *Chambers's Jrnl.* 100/2 The season of the *ice-harvest being short and uncertain. **1884** *Longm. Mag.* Feb. 413 The ice harvest lasts about two months. **1904** *Westm. Gaz.* 17 Mar. 2/1 Men with horses were ploughing the ice-harvest of the river. **1883** *Boy's Own Paper* 13 Oct. 30/1 For *ice hockey the ball is from six to seven inches in circumference. **1898** *Daily News* 28 Nov. 8/7 The first ice hockey match at Niagara took place on Saturday. **1907** *Westm. Gaz.* 4 Dec. 7/2 An ice-hockey match at Prince's last night. **1909** *Ibid.* 18 Jan. 12/4 The great ice carnivals, skating championships, and ice-hockey matches. **1940** Auden *Another Time* 26 Superb at ice-hockey, a prince at the dance, He's fierce as the tigers, secretive as plants. **1970** *Guardian* 5 Jan. 14/5 Canada yesterday withdrew from this year's world ice hockey championships after losing their battle to allow professionals to take part. **1846** R. H. Bonnycastle *Canada & Canadians in 1846* II. 3, I have mentioned that, in the spring of 1845, an *ice-jam, as it is called here, occurred, which suddenly raised the level of the Niagara thirty and forty feet above its ordinary floods. **1863** Lyell *Antiq. Man* viii. (ed. 3) 139 When 'ice-jams' occur on the St. Lawrence. **1909** *Westm. Gaz.* 23 Apr. 8/2 The great ice-jam at Niagara. **1924** M. H. Mason *Arctic Forests* 246 In the depth of winter they travelled by dog-sled over the rough ice jams of Bear River. **1959** *Washington Post* 3 Feb. A.16/1 A willingness to explore new ideas could help break the East-West ice-jam. **1962** R. B. Fuller *Epic Poem on Industrialization* 158 The inevitable Social-economic ice jam. **1860** *All Year Round* No. 39. 293 The man with the *ice-ladder on wheels..cannot get any nearer to me. **1893** Kipling *Seven Seas* (1896) 29 Down a cruel *ice-lane, That opened as he sped, We saw dead Henry Hudson Steer, North by West, his dead. **1879** *Encycl. Brit.* VIII. 731/2 At this point the steam line, *ice line, and hoar-frost line intersect, and it has therefore been called the triple point. **1937** M. W. Zemansky *Heat & Thermodynamics* xi. 177 In investigating the ice line of water at very high temperatures, Bridgman and Tammann discovered four new modifications of ice. **1893** *Jrnl. Geol.* I. 131 Moraines formed by the Great Miami *ice lobe. **1954** W. D. Thornbury *Princ. Geomorphol.* xvi. 384 The edges of the ice caps were probably never straight for any great distance, but in addition to many minor reentrants and projections along their margins there were numerous larger protrusions or ice lobes down lowlands. **1949** *Ice Cream Topics* June 12 *Ice lollies or iced lollies..sell at 1d. or 2d. and capture the kiddy trade, being cheaper than cones and wafers filled with ice cream. **1957** *Times* 22 Aug. 8/6 They..drip ice-lollies on the desk. **1970** *Daily Tel.* (Colour Suppl.) 2 Jan. 24/4 Ishmahil licked at a spoon of caviar as if it were an ice-lolly. **1850** T. Masters *Short Treat. Production Ice* iii. 19 The patent *ice machine and its various modifications. Before giving a detailed description of the ice machine,..it will be as well to mention a few of the prominent advantages it possesses. **1873** C. M. Yonge *Pillars of House* II. xvii. 129 Is he awake? I have brought some more ice... I have a little ice-machine for Indian use. **1897** 'Mark Twain' *Following Equator* iii. 62 The ice-machine has traveled all over the world. **1973** *Country Life* 8 Feb. 345/1 There are enough hotels..to suit any pocket. And swimming pools, air-conditioning and ice-machines are usually included. **1953** Dylan Thomas *Under Milk Wood* (1954) 61 The butcher's unmelting *icemaiden daughter veiled for ever from the hungry hug of his eyes. **1968** V. Canning *Melting Man* v. 134 Now stop doing an ice-maiden act on me. Write it off to experience. **1970** B. Turner *Another Little Death* xx. 118 Her ice-maiden act was a cover for frustrated lust. **1775** Barker in *Phil. Trans.* LXV. 252 The *ice-maker belonging to me..made a sufficient quantity in the winter for the supply of the table during the summer season. **1792** Williams *ibid.* LXXXIII. 56 The ice-makers informed me the cold was most intense. **1927** *Daily Tel.* 11 May 18/3 New patent non-chemical refrigerator and ice-maker. **1969** K. Amis *Green Man* i. 12 The ice-maker had broken down. **1970** *Cape Times* 28 Oct. (S.A. Fishing Rev.) 6/6 (Advt.), South African Agents for Skokie international seawater ice makers. **1677** Plot *Oxfordsh.* 27 They [the Oxford watermen] frequently meet the *Ice-meers (for so they call the cakes of Ice thus coming from the bottom) in their very rise. **1891** *Pall Mall G.* 30 Nov. 3/1 A wedge of rounded rock, worn smooth by the vast *ice-mills of the glacial epoch. **1846** R. Ford *Gatherings from Spain* vii. 74 The leading animal is furnished with a copper bell with a wooden clapper ..which is shaped like an *ice-mould. **1864** *Chambers's Jrnl.* 101/1 A continuous current through the cistern containing the ice-moulds. **1873** *Young Englishwoman* July 334/1 We put in a block as large as the tin will hold, and then with an *ice-needle, price one shilling, break up the rest of the ice. **1928** *Funk's Stand. Dict.*, *Ice-needles*, n.pl., a deposit of ice, especially in gravelly soil, in the form of vertical needles. **1937** *Jrnl. R. Aeronaut. Soc.* XLI. 598 A further very rare case occurs when at a high altitude in the 'ice needle clouds' ..a light accretion of hoar frost..forms on the aeroplane. **1965** H. Riehl *Introd. Atmosphere* v. 100 Ice needles are long thin crystals forming on very cold winter days through sublimation... Floating leisurely in the air, they provide a magnificent spectacle when the sun is shining on them. **1970** R. J. Small *Study of Landforms* x. 323 Another process which leads to the upheaval of material in the active layer [of the soil] is the development of small localised ice-masses and ice-needles ('pipkraker'). **1853** Kane *Grinnell Exp.* xxviii. (1856) 234 Apprehensions of being frozen up in the heart of the *ice-pack. **1900** *Daily Chron.* 12 Nov. 5/6 The condition of Lord Roberts's daughter is somewhat serious. Ice-packs have been applied. **1926** *Daily Colonist* (Victoria, B.C.) 3 Jan. 3/3 The letter informed the President [Coolidge] that the [Detroit Aviation] society was about to join in an attempt to explore the ice pack between Point Barrow and the Ice Pole. **1930** *Times Educ. Suppl.* 25 Jan. p. iv/1 Rocky outcrops and ice-packs. **1955** *Sci. Amer.* Apr. 52/3 The Atka saw very little of the drifting ice pack that surrounds the continent. **1973** R. Ludlum *Matlock Paper* xiv. 129 There's a nurse in there with ice packs and stuff if localized pain bothers her. **1773** *Lond. Chron.* 7 Sept. 248/3 *Ice-pails. **1850** Lever *Martins of Cro' M.* 264 Four bottles.. rose from amidst the crystal ruins of a well-filled ice-pail. **1901** *Geogr. Jrnl.* July 40 The *ice-pans appear to drift capriciously backward and forward, and, without any apparent cause, they will select some unexpected course. **1926** *Blackw. Mag.* July 67/1 An awful journey through a country devoid of human beings, across treacherous moving ice-pans. **1934** I. W. Hutchison *North to Rime-Ringed Sun* xii. 120 Suddenly out of the mist, upon an ice-pan, stood the little shrivelled figure of an old Eskimo hunter of seals. **1963** *Calgary Herald* 20 Sept., Turquoise ice pans (last year's ice) cluttered the water just off shore. **1876** Agassiz *Geol. Sk.* Ser. II. 100 The vegetation which succeeded the *ice-period was of a different character. *a* **1877** Knight *Dict. Mech.* II. 1169/1 **Ice-pick* (Domestic), an awl-shaped tool to break ice into fragments. **1879** F. R. Stockton *Rudder Grange* i, It is not probable that I can sell that ice-pick after you have used it for ten years. **1883** [see *ice-crusher*, sense 7 a]. **1937** E. A. M. Wedderburn *Alpine Climbing* ii. 29 A Hammer for driving in ring-spikes may be combined with an ice-pick; this weapon is..useful for cutting steps..in very steep ice. **1953** E. S. Gardner *Case of Green-Eyed Sister* (1959) viii. 97 J. J. Fritch was killed by repeated stabs with an ice-pick. **1960** *News Chron.* 11 June 2/8 Jacques Mornard, ice-pick assassin of Leon Trotsky. **1881** J. C. Lyell *Fancy Pigeons* 81 The *Ice Pigeon. This variety derives its name from its beautiful lavender blue colour, considered by the German fanciers to resemble blue ice. **1969** C. R. Hill *Pet Library's Pigeon Guide* viii. 151 (*caption*) White barred blue Ice Pigeon, young cock. A German exhibition breed. *Ibid.* 152 Ice pigeon, blue spangled, old hen. **1865** *Nation* (N.Y.) 3 Aug. 159/3 (Advt.), At this season of the year nothing adds more to one's comfort than to drink freely of the contents of our new pattern richly double-plated *ice pitchers. **1883** 'Mark Twain' *Life on Mississippi* xviii. 221 Take that ice-pitcher down to the texas-tender. **1775** Barker in *Phil. Trans.* LXV. 255 In their..visits with me to the *ice-pits. **1932** *Mountaineering Jrnl.* Dec. 100 *Ice-pitons are made of wrought iron not too soft and not too brittle, 7 to 10 inches long and saw-toothed along both edges. **1954** W. Noyce *South Col* vi. 110 We then fixed the bridge and tied it down with ice pitons. **1956** C. Evans *On Climbing* vii. 114, I should be reluctant to trust a piton for this, since ice-pitons are less certain in their hold than rock-pitons. **1876** Lady C. Schreiber *Jrnl.* (1911) I. 443 Small *ice-plates have now become the object of our pursuit. **1902** H. James *Wings of Dove* v. x. 178 The very servant who came to receive Milly's empty ice-plate. **1907** *Yesterday's Shopping* (1969) 944 (*caption*) Ice plates. **1858** Simmonds *Dict. Trade*, **Ice-plane*, an instrument for smoothing away the rough surface of ice ..before cutting and carting it away for storage. **1875** Knight *Dict. Mech.*, *Ice-plane*,..2, an instrument for shaving off fragments of ice for cooling drinks. **1903** *Phil. Trans. R. Soc.* A. CC. 108 The Comité International adopted as the normal scale of temperature the scale of a constant-volume hydrogen thermometer, in which the pressure at the *ice-point was 1000 millims. of mercury. *Ibid.*, The coefficient for hydrogen, at a pressure of 100 millims. of mercury at the ice-point, is given..as 0·00366254. **1941** *Temperature* (Amer. Inst. Physics) i. 10 A limitation of this scale [*sc.* Kelvin's thermodynamic scale] is that if we make the fundamental interval from the ice point to the steam point 100 degrees, the actual temperature of the ice point is subject to experimental determination. **1966** *Units & Standards of Measurement: Temperature* (Nat. Physical Lab.) (ed. 2) 18 Changes made in 1960 to the text of the International Temperature Scale of 1948... The triple-point of water was given formal status as one of the defining fixed points of the scale... Its value was given as 0·01°C (Int. 1948) and the ice point appeared among the secondary fixed points with the value 0·000°C. **1851** W. P. Snow *Voy. 'Prince Albert'* 154 The slackest and thinnest part of the floe, or fragment, was cut into with the axes and chisels until some fortunate blow or prise of the *ice-pole rent and loosened it. **1906** J. Lumsden *Skipper Parson* 107 This useful instrument also serves as an ice pole, enabling the daring sealer..to leap from 'pan to pan'. **1970** *Globe & Mail* (Toronto) 28 Sept. 4/4 Men working on the ice.. should hold a boat-hook or small ice-pole in their hands. **1869** *Punch* 10 July 2/2 An *ice-pudding to follow turtle soup, or boiled mutton to be eaten after custard. **1888** J. Payn *Myst. Mirbridge* (Tauchn.) II. i. 8 From soup till ice-pudding time. **1911** *Jrnl. Geol.* XIX. 157 He has never detected any evidence of *ice push against shores as a result of expansion. **1939** P. G. Worcester *Textbk. Geomorphol.* xii. 383 Although unimportant on most sea shores, the shores of many lakes that freeze over in winter are profoundly affected by ice push. **1957** G. E. Hutchinson *Treat. Limnol.* I. vii. 532 This sheet may then exert pressure on the shore, forcing gravel and stones landward and building an ice push or ice rampart. **1969** J. L. Davies *Landforms Cold Climates* iv. 63 Seasonally frozen lakes in the tundra and elsewhere may form ice-push ramparts around their edges. **1853** Kane *Grinnell Exp.* xxxii. (1856) 279 The deep stillness..the mysterious *ice-pulse, as if the energies were gathering for another strife. **1891** *Dublin Rev.* Oct. 278 The perils of the awful *ice-quake in the convulsed and riven floe. **1856** Kane *Arct. Expl.* II. xxiii. 228 The transporting forces of the *ice-raft. **1873** J. Geikie *Gt. Ice Age* xxviii. 393 Fleets of icebergs and icerafts. **1895** *Westm. Gaz.* 3 Aug. 1/3 A barque-rigged sailing-ship..furnished with a double copper hull and *ice-ram. **1901** E. R. Buckley in *Trans. Wisc. Acad. Sci., Arts & Lett.* XIII. 142 The diurnal and weekly changes of temperature during the winter months cause a sufficient expansion and contraction of the ice covering the inland lakes of Wisconsin to shove up the sand, gravel, boulders, and sod along the shores into peculiar ridges, known as *ice ramparts. **1968** R. W. Fairbridge *Encycl. Geomorphol.* 546/1 Along the margins of ice-covered lakes and seas and the shores of the Arctic Ocean the effects of floating ice pressure (under wind stress) may be observed, leading to the building of large pressure-ridges in the beach gravels and other littoral deposits... The terms ice-shore ridges and ice ramparts are also sometimes used. **1886** *Field* 13 Mar. 310/1 Nor is it less strange that so few *ice rinks are found in England. **1930** *Daily Express* 16 Aug. 3/1 By the middle of October there will be at least nine ice-rinks in London alone. **1953** X. Fielding *Stronghold* 277 The surface of this winding watercourse was like that of a shattered ice-rink. **1872** Tyndall *Forms of Water* §364 It is indubitable that an *ice-river..once flowed through the vale of Hasli. **1900** *Daily News* 30 Nov. 5/2 The new *ice-run for tobogganers..is almost ready for use. **1910** H. G. Wells *Hist. Mr. Polly* vi, Mr. Polly swerved a little from the conversational ice-run upon which he had embarked. **1895** *Brewer's Dict. Phrase & Fable* (new ed.) 643/2 **Ice Saints*, those saints whose days fall in..'the black-thorn winter'. **1922** *Meteorol. Mag.* LVII. 177 The quasi-periodic occurrence of a cold spell lasting for a few days early in May is a well-known popular belief... On the Continent three 'Saint Days', those of St. Mamertius, St. Pancras and St. Gervais, falling on May 11th, 12th and 13th..are popularly known as the *Eisheiligen*, or 'Ice Saints'. **1936** *Times* 13 Feb. 14/1 May will be remembered mainly on account of the severe frost during the period 12th to 19th, an impressive vindication of the firmly rooted tradition of the 'Ice Saints'. **1969** *Guardian* 7 June 7/5 There was the normal cold iceburst in mid-May, but it came a week later than the proverbial 'Ice Saints' days on the Continent. **1842** Francis *Dict. Arts* etc., **Ice-saw*, a large saw used for cutting through the ice, for relieving ships when frozen up. **1878** A. H. Markham *Gt. Frozen Sea* iv. 49 Ice-saw crews were organized in readiness for cutting a dock. **1904** J. D. Hooker *Let.* 3 Dec. in L. Huxley *Life J. D. Hooker* (1918) II. 457 His landscapes, seascapes and *ice-scapes are most interesting. **1936** J. Grierson *High Failure* ix. 208, I had never before experienced the hypnotic splendour of the ice-scape. It seemed as though I were flying in a dream. **1969** *Sunday Times* 9 Feb. 6 The whole icescape was awash with light. **1936** Finch & Trewartha *Elem. Geogr.* xvii. 364 The surface configuration of plains where *ice scour was predominant is characterized by rounded rock hills and broad open valleys with comparatively low local relief. **1968** R. W. Fairbridge *Encycl. Geomorphol.* 502/2 The basins of the Great Lakes..were formed by a combination of stream erosion during Mesozoic to Pleistocene times and glacial ice scour in the Pleistocene. **1936** Finch & Trewartha *Elem. Geogr.* xvii. 364 The drift of *ice-scoured plains commonly is neither deep enough nor continuous enough to be tillable except in patches. **1954** W. D. Thornbury *Princ. Geomorphol.* xvi. 385 In areas where the surface over which the ice caps moved was mountainous..the result was not an ice-scoured plain, but a general smoothing off..of the topography. **1901** *Science* 5 Apr. 552/1 *Ice-scouring during maximum glaciation reached far up the mountain slopes above the trough walls. **1957** G. E. Hutchinson *Treat. Limnol.* I. i. 57 The Saint Gotthard lakes..are noted..as having been formed by ice-scouring. **1965** D. Bathgate in *Scottish Mountaineering Club Jrnl.* XXVIII. 109 At the shortest point I surmounted the steep part, fixed an *ice screw, and then traversed back across the centre of the ice to about twenty feet above the belay. **1968** P. Crew *Encycl. Dict. Mountaineering* 71/1 Ice-screws are very effective as they can be used on most types of ice..with a reasonable degree of security and they are very easy to remove after use. **1971** C. Bonington *Annapurna South Face* x. 116 It's difficult to get an ice-screw started, rather like an ordinary screw in hard wood—you first have to tap out a little hole to allow the thread to get a purchase. **1894** J. Geikie *Gt. Ice Age* (ed. 3) 830 The *ice-shed in Scandinavia did not coincide with the water-parting. **1932** E. G. Woods *Baltic Region* 159 When the ice-shed lay east of the watershed..a considerable amount of ice and also water flowed along the originally eastward-sloping valleys towards the west. **1957** J. K. Charlesworth *Quaternary Era* I. iv. 77 The iceshed, more than 1000 miles (1600 km) long, seems to lie behind South Victoria Land and Dronning Maud Mountains. **1914** T. W. E. David in *Geogr. Jrnl.* XLIII. 606 If the meaning of the term 'shelf' can be extended to include old pack ice, old bay ice, 'schollen-eis', piedmonts aground or afloat, glacier tongues, etc., it may be termed the *ice shelf coast, or, as it is hardly a true coast at all, simply ice shelf. **1940** *Beaver* June 22/1 The men worked with feverish energy to repair the damage caused by the treacherous ice shelf. **1958** *Times* 13 Jan. 9/6 We..made our very laborious way..on to the flat going of the Ross ice shelf itself. **1958** J. H. Zumberge *Elem. Geol.* x. 180 Masses of ice that break off from the edge of the various ice shelves form the huge tabular icebergs unique to the Antarctic region. **1885** Schley & Soley *Rescue of Greely* viii. 113 The first [*i.e.* sealers] are distinctively *ice-ships. **1824** *Blackw. Mag.* XV. 172/2 His one hand armed with a broom, and his other charged with the *ice-shoes, or tramps. **1875** Croll *Climate & T.* xxx. 510 Blocks of ice..in the windows of *ice-shops. **1897** *Sears, Roebuck Catal.* 97/2 *Ice skates. **1912** T. Dreiser *Financier* 36 He was an adept at turning all sorts of practical tricks, such as..taking the agency for the sale of a new kind of ice-skate from an ice-skate company. **1950** *Oxf. Jun. Encycl.* IX. 432 There are three principal kinds of ice skates: those for figure-skating, for hockey, and for racing. **1937** *Ice-skater [see audition *v.* 2]. **1948** *Evening News* 2 Jan. 2/6 Two nephews are down on the creek *ice-skating. **1957** *Encycl. Brit.* XX. 730/1 An additional valuable impetus in bringing figure skating before the public was the ice-skating carnival. **1973** E.-J. Bahr *Nice Neighbourhood* vi. 61 We told him about the museums, free exhibits, outdoor concerts, ice-skating, bicycling. **1897** E. L. Voynich *Gadfly* III. viii. 353 He might have recalled some splendid and fearful *ice-spirit of the mountains. **1900** *Month* Jan. 85, I took you for that evil thing, the ice-spirit, who freezes the limbs of our people. **1901** (*title*) *Ice sports. **1908** *Daily Chron.* 27 July 4/4 Boating in summer and ice sports in winter. **1617** Minsheu *Ductor*, **Ice-spurre*, a shooe driuen full of iron nailes pointed. **1642** Fuller *Holy & Prof. St.* IV. i. 240 He standeth but in a slippery place; and therefore needs constantly to wear ice-spurres, for he rather glides than goes. **1893** *Westm. Gaz.* 27 Mar. 4/2 The party had to unbuckle their shoes and climb, with the help of ice-spurs and axes. **1868** B. J. Lossing *Hudson* 304 Rockland Lake village..[is] the most extensive *ice-station on the river. **1898** J. O. Maund in W. A. Morgan *'House' on Sport* 276 It took but a moment before our *ice steps were filled with these hailstones. **1908** *Westm. Gaz.* 25 Jan. 14/1 We stood in the ice-steps. **1931** *Discovery* Feb. 41/1 To cut ice-steps all along so great a ridge will be an affair not of hours but of a day or two. **1876** 'Mark Twain' *Punch, Brothers, Punch!* (1878) 17 We have to credit the weather with..the *ice-storm. **1886** J. Geikie *Outl. Geol.* 50 By repeated thawings and regelations the branches and boughs are gradually

loaded with ice and snow, and becoming top-heavy, the trees are liable to fall, even when no wind is blowing. Should one be over-thrown, it collides against its neighbour, and this in turn falls upon another, until shortly the trees are seen crashing to the ground in all directions. This is what is known in North America as an ice-storm. **1899** *Daily News* 20 An 'ice storm' in Somerset..reminded me of a sudden hailstorm. **1921** R. Frost *Mountain Interval* 29 But swinging doesn't bend them down to stay. Ice-storms do that. **1965** *Kingston* (Ontario) *Whig-Standard* 13 Dec. 19/1 Nearly every cloud has a silver lining and Sunday's ice-storm was no exception. **1968** Ice storm [see freezing *ppl. a.* 1]. **1872** C. King *Mountaineer. Sierra Nev.* vii. 147, I found unmistakable **ice-striae*, showing that the glacier had actually poured over the brink. **1876** T. G. Bonney in *Proc. Geol. Soc.* No. 306 Wales, Scotland, and Scandinavia must have had their own *ice-systems. **1893** *Funk's Stand. Dict.*, **Ice-tongue*, a steep, narrow cliff of ice, rising high above glacial névé, and extending upward toward the higher mountain-peaks. **1896** *Amer. Geologist* XVIII. 155 Between the ice-tongue which filled the cove and the hills on the west, coarse gravels were deposited. **1919** E. Shackleton *South* viii. 129 At the head of an ice-tongue that nearly closed the gap through which we might enter the open space was a wave-worn berg. **1968** R. W. Fairbridge *Encycl. Geomorphol.* 673/1 Where the borders of these ice sheets roughly coincide with the coastal mountain ranges, the ice spills through them in the form of ice rivers called outlet glaciers or ice tongues. **1936** *New Yorker* 29 Feb. 37/2 (Advt.), Then think of *ice-trays—stacks of them. **1962** *Which?* June 176/2 We filled the ice trays with cold water.. and set the thermostats to coldest. **1965** M. Spark *Mandelbaum Gate* iv. 109 A scarred, lop-sided oil refrigerator..stood in the passage outside, from which anyone who wanted beer took it, depositing the money in the ice-tray. **1915** *Jrnl. Geol.* XXIII. 642 The constant association of *ice wedges with definite loci of frost cracks. **1970** C. A. Lewis *Glaciations Wales* ii. 29 Near Traian (328365) a large fossil ice-wedge..cuts the deposits in a small quarry. **1928** *Daily Express* 10 Oct. 3/3 Where an *ice-white salmon stream flows through a gorge. **1931** *Daily Tel.* 21 May 6/3 A gown of very heavy ice white satin. **1882** *Ice wool [see eis wool]. **1926** *Daily Colonist* (Victoria, B.C.) 10 Jan. 18/1 Ice Wool Scarves in a good assortment of colors, stripes or plain shades, with contrasting stripe borders. **1882** *Standard* 1 Dec. 5/4 The *ice yacht is really a skeleton boat mounted on gigantic runners. **1881** *Scribner's Mag.* XXII. 532/1 *Ice-yachting seems to be the acme of recklessness.

ice (aɪs), *v.* Also 5 yse, 7 yce. [f. the sb.]

1. *trans.* **a.** To cover with ice. (Also *to ice over*.) *to ice up*, to fill up with ice; also, to hold fast with ice. **b.** To convert into ice; to freeze, congeal.

a **1400-50** *Alexander* 2883 (Dublin MS.) To þe grete flode of gratun to-geder þai ryddyn, And fyndyn it frosyn þaim byfore, a fute-thyke ysyd. **1602** Marston *Antonio's Rev.* I. iii. Wks. 1856 I. 80 My trembling joynts (Iced quite over with a froz'd cold sweate). *a* **1639** Webster *Appius & Virginia* v. (1654) 59 This sight hath stiffned all my operant powers, ic'd all my blood, benum'd my motion quite. **1658** R. White tr. *Digby's Powd. Symp.* (1660) 147 When it is iced all ouer, he shall feel neither heat nor cold. **1829** *Examiner* 21/2 A frost that iced the spray of the sea as it fell on the deck. **1856** Kane *Arct. Expl.* I. xvii. 201 Icing up again the opening in the walls. **1899** C. J. C. Hyne *Further Adventures Capt. Kettle* xii, The boats are frozen on to the chocks... Did you never see a boat iced up before?

c. *fig.* To cause to become frigid or cold and reserved in manner; cf. *to break the ice*: ice *sb.* 2 b.

1741 Richardson *Pamela* (1824) I. xxix. 293 Laying myself open to too early a suspicion, I thought would but ice the girl over. **1748** —— *Clarissa* (1811) III. i. 3 Such a sudden transition must affect her; must ice her over.

2. a. To cover or garnish (cakes, etc.) with a concretion of sugar (cf. icing).

1602 Plat *Delightes for Ladies* xviii, To make Tumbolds ..when they are baked, yce them. **1725** Bradley *Fam. Dict.* s.v. *March pane*, To ice March-Panes. **1852** Mrs. Acton *Mod. Cookery* xvi. (ed. 11) 335 The best mode of icing fruit tarts..is to moisten the paste with cold water, sift sugar thickly upon it [etc.].

b. *fig.* To cover or surround as with ice.

1679 Puller *Mod. of the Ch. of Engl.* To Rdr. a iij, Noise and passion, and hardy confidence, iced over with some sanctimonious pretences. **1890** Clark Russell *Ocean Trag.* II. xxv. 281 The moon..was now icing her crimson visage with crystal.

3. To refrigerate with ice; to cool (esp. wine) by placing among ice.

1825 T. Cosnett *Footman's Direct.* 130 If you have ice-pails to ice the wine, let this be done. **1877** Mrs. Forrester *Mignon* I. 24 The champagne is iced. **1885** *Times* (weekly ed.) 18 Sept. 15/1 The fish are iced, packed in boxes.

4. a. To make cold; to freeze, chill. Chiefly *fig.*

1804 Anna Seward *Lett.* (1811) VI. 137 That unfortunate ..proneness to scepticism, which iced his affections. **1836** Dickens *Sk. Boz* (1837) I. iii. 24 Thus they vegetated—living in Polar harmony among themselves, and.. occasionally iceing the neighbours. **1845** Mrs. Hall *Whiteboy* vi. 52 Much trouble had iced her nature. **1873** M. Collins *Squire Silchester* III. iii. 26 Her very enthusiasms were cold; she iced you..by the tone of her conversation.

b. To kill. *U.S. slang.*

1969 *New Yorker* 15 Feb. 51 A friend of his had come to his apartment..in clothes that were spattered with blood, and announced, 'I just iced two girls.' **1973** *Guardian* 6 Mar. 14/3 A would-be assassin who considers it his mission to 'ice the fascist pig police'.

5. a. *intr.* To turn to ice; to freeze. Also *fig.*

1839 Bailey *Festus* xx. (1848) 266 Winter is when these we love have perished For the heart ices then. *Ibid.* xxviii. 336 When the poles Are icing.

b. Esp. of aircraft: to become covered with ice (and thus rendered ineffective). Const. *up.* Chiefly in *pass.*

1928 *Aviation* 16 Apr. 1032/2 Once a plane has become iced-up, two alternatives for clearing away the accumulation of glazing may be available. **1940** *Times* (Weekly ed.) 10 Jan. p. ii/4 During the operations a snowstorm was encountered and the aircraft became badly iced-up, in addition to being subjected to anti-aircraft fire. **1943** *Aeronautics* Mar. 60/1 The wings and controls may be iced up. **1947** *Sci. News* IV. 72 A ship has often been thoroughly de-greased by wind-swept rain and spray before it becomes iced-up. **1950** T. Longstaff *This my Voyage* ii. 24 By now we were all looking like Arctic travellers, well iced-up.

-ice, *suffix*[1], in ME. also -is(e, -ys(e, etc.

1. a. OF. *-ice* (*-ise*), of non-popular origin, ad. L. *-itia* (Sp. *-icia*, It. *-izia*), or *-itius*, *-itium* (Sp. *-icio*, It. *-izio*). Thus *avarice, justice, malice, notice* (ad. L. *avāritia, justitia, malitia, nōtitia*), the later *police* (ad. L. *politia* = *polītīa*), and the French formations *cowardice, jaundice.* The masc. and neut. are represented by *novice, precipice, service* (= L. *novitius, precipitium, servitium*).

L. *-itia* would normally have given OF. *-eise*, *-oise*, through common Romanic *-ẹtja*, *-ezja*, but in the literary language this was represented by *-ece*, *-esce* (as in *parece*, *pares-ce*:—L. *pigritia*; *haut-ece*, *haut-esce*:—L. *altitia*), subsequently assimilated to *-esse* from L. *-issa* (cf. mod.F. *noblesse, paresse, hautesse*).

2. The ending *-ice* has various other origins, partly through assimilation to the preceding; as in the words *(ac)complice, (ap)prentice, bodice, caprice, coppice, crevice, lattice, poultice, practice.*

-ice, -icè (ɪsiː), *suffix*[2], in med.L. forming adverbs from adjs., as Anglice, Gallice, *ironice*, Scotticè, Scoticè, and hence used occas. to form jocular nonce adverbs on English stems, as *golficè*.

1743 Pope *Dunciad* I (*footnote to l. 23*), *Ironicè*, alluding to Gulliver's representations of both. **1886** *Golficè* [see divot *sb.* 2].

iceberg (ˈaɪsbɜːg). Also 8 ice-burg. [Adapted form of the term employed in several of the cognate languages, MDu., Du. *ijsberg*, G. *eisberg*, Da. *isbjerg*, Sw. *isberg* (f. *is* ice + *berg* hill, mountain); prob. taken immediately from Du.]

†**1.** An Arctic glacier, which comes close to the coast, and is seen from the sea as a hill or 'hummock'. *Obs.* Cf. ice-hill, ice-mountain.

1774 *Jrnl. Voy. under Com. Phipps* 44 Of the ice-hills there are seven.. These are known by the name of the seven ice-burgs, and are thought to be the highest of the kind in the country [Spitzbergen]. **1774** C. J. Phipps *Voy. N. Pole* 70 Icebergs are large bodies of ice filling the vallies between the high mountains; the face towards the sea is nearly perpendicular. **1797** *Encycl. Brit.* s.v. **1820** Scoresby *Acc. Arctic Reg.* I. 101 The Iceberg..written Ysberg by the Dutch signifies ice-mountain. I speak not here of the islands of ice which are borne to southern climates on the bosom of the ocean, but of those prodigious lodgments of ice which occur in the valleys. *Ibid.* 108 Icebergs are as permanent as the rocks on which they rest.. In some places..the berg or glacier makes its way to a great extent into the sea..and then being capable of large dismemberments, gives rise to the kind of mountainous masses or icebergs, found afloat. **1821** Byron *Juan* iv. c, 'Tis as a snowball which derives assistance From every flake, and yet rolls on the same, Even till an iceberg it may chance to grow.

2. a. A detached portion of a glacier carried out to sea; a huge floating mass of ice, often rising to a great height above the water. Formerly also called *ice-island*, also *island* or *shoal of ice.*

1820 Scoresby *Acc. Arctic Reg.* I. 250 The term Ice-berg ..is also as commonly extended to the large peaks..or islets of ice, that are found floating in the sea. **1830** *Edin. Encycl.* XVII. 12/1 The floating iceberg remains to be considered. .. In many parts of the Antarctic regions, they are met with in vast numbers, and of a prodigious size. **1835** Sir J. Ross *Narr. 2nd Voy.* iv. 50 But one iceberg was seen to-day, and that a very small one. **1853** Kane *Grinnell Exp.* viii. (1856) 58 Ice-berg. [*Note*] This term is applied by many authors to ice masses either on shore or at sea. I restrict it to detached ice, in contradistinction to the glacier or ice *in situ.* **1878** Huxley *Physiogr.* 163 The icebergs, like glaciers, are laden with fragments of rock. **1961** A. Defant *Physical Oceanogr.* viii. 274 The flat-topped Antarctic icebergs immerse to greater depths.

b. *transf.* Used allusively with reference to the larger portion of an iceberg being unseen (and hence a largely unknown quantity, problem, etc.).

1961 in Webster. **1964** *Observer* 26 July 10/4 This.. situation is illustrated by what is..called the iceberg of disease. Above the surface is the illness we know about. **1965** *Listener* 21 Oct. 614/2 These were only the visible part of the iceberg. Most of the organs of the left..were greatly influenced. **1969** M. Gilbert *Etruscan Net* ii. ii. 109, I believe that Broke's been made the victim of an elaborate frame-up. I think, to employ a well-known metaphor, that all we can see at the moment is the tip of the iceberg, and that there is depth beyond depth below it. **1973** *Daily Tel.* 19 Feb. 2/1 They believe the number of prosecutions for such offences represent only 'the tip of the iceberg', and that many undischarged bankrupts..are violating the law undetected.

3. *fig.* A person compared to an iceberg, on account of his cold unemotional nature.

1840 Lady C. Bury *Hist. of Flirt* v, Captain Thelwal is a perfect iceberg. **1882** Spurgeon *Treas. Dav.* Ps. cxix. 79 We neither care for devout dunces nor for intellectual ice-bergs.

4. *Comb.*, as **iceberg-droppings**, boulders, gravel, clay, etc. dropped by melting icebergs; **iceberg-green**, a light green resembling that of an iceberg; **iceberg lettuce** *U.S.*, a crisp light-green lettuce.

1889 J. Geikie in *Nature* 19 Sept., The drifts of those regions are not iceberg-droppings..but true morainic matter and fluvio-glacial detritus. **1893** *Burpee's Farm Annual* 28 As long as our supply lasts we will send a sample packet of the iceberg lettuce free for trial. **1895** *Daily News* 19 Jan. 8/2 One of the Polish dresses is in iceberg green cloth. **1904** W. W. Tracy *Amer. Varieties Lettuce* 56 *Iceberg* [*lettuce*], a decidedly crisp variety, strictly cabbage-heading, large, late, slow to shoot to seed. **1933** F. M. Farmer *Boston Cooking-School Cook Bk.* (rev. ed.) xxviii. 420 Iceberg or California Lettuce. Cut in halves or quarters. Remove hard center. **1960** 'I. Devi' *Yoga for You* (1965) 189 One head romaine or any other green salad, except iceberg lettuce, which contains almost no chlorophyll. **1966** *McGraw-Hill Encycl. Sci. & Technol.* VII. 478/2 Crisphead or iceberg lettuce is the most widely grown type. **1970** 'J. Morris' *Candywine Devel.* xx. 223 He took a loaf of French bread, an iceberg lettuce and three onions from the refrigerator.

Hence ˈ**iceberger**, one who has had experience of icebergs; ˈ**icebergship**, coldness, indifference; ˈ**icebergy** *a.*, cold, icy.

1842 *United Service Mag.* II. 154 Many a fine fellow was doomed to fall, before official icebergship was thawed. **1861** L. L. Noble *Icebergs* 217 Captain Knight, an experienced iceberger. **1888** Mrs. Spender *Kept Secret* I. xi. 198, I was prepared with my most icebergy manner.

ˈ**ice-bird.** *Ornith.*

1. The little auk or sea-dove.

1620 J. Mason *New-found-land* (1867) A iv b, The sea fowles are Sea Pigeons, Ice Birds, Bottle noses. **1694** *Acc. Sev. Late Voy.* II. (1711) 78, I saw also..a very beautiful Ice-bird, which was so tame, that we might have taken him. **1777** G. Forster *Voy. round World* I. 110 A small black and white bird, which some called an ice-bird. **1802** G. Montagu *Ornith. Dict.* (1833) 267 *Ice-bird*, a name for the Rotche or Little Auk.

2. The Indian night-jar, *Caprimulgus asiaticus.*

1862 T. C. Jerdon *Birds India* I. §112. 197 Its usual note ..is like the sound of a stone scudding over ice (hence it is sometimes called the Ice-bird).

iceblink (ˈaɪsblɪŋk). [= Du. *ijsblink*, G. *eisblink*, Da. *iisblink*, *-blik*, Sw. *isblink*; f. ice *sb.* + blink *sb.*[2] 4.

The question of the original language, and history of this combination, is obscure. Sense 2 is the only meaning of *iisblink* in the Dictionary of the Danish Academy in 1820.]

1. A luminous appearance on the horizon, caused by the reflection of light from ice. See blink *sb.*[2] 4.

[**1772-1818**: see blink *sb.*[1] 4. **1774** C. J. Phipps *Voy. N. Pole* 71 A bright appearance near the horizon, which the pilots called the blink of the ice.] **1817** Scoresby in *Ann. Reg., Chron.* 555 The ice-blink consists in a stratum of a lucid whiteness, which appears in that part of the atmosphere next the horizon. **1847** Sir J. C. Ross *Voy. S. Seas* I. 171 The weather was beautifully clear, and a strong ice-blink in the sky. **1885** *Century Mag.* XXX. 78/2 Over it [the floe edge] hung the hazy gray of the 'ice-blink'.

2. The name of a range of lofty ice cliffs on the south-east coast of Greenland. Also generally: An ice-cliff, the sea-front of a glacier. ? *Obs.*

[**1796** Morse *Amer. Geog.* I. 132 The famous Ice-glance, called in some charts, Eis-blink. It is a large high field of ice.] **1819** Montgomery *Greenland* III. 63 O'er rocks, seas, islands, promontories spread, The Ice-Blink rears its undulated head. [*Note*] The most stupendous accumulation of ice in the known world, which has been long distinguished by this peculiar name by the Danish navigators. **1837** Macdougall tr. *Graah's E. Coast Greenland* (1839) 24 To such cliffs or barriers of ice I shall in the sequel give the name of ice-blink, or simply blink. The reflection of ice in the atmosphere, which is usually designated by that name, I shall, for distinction's sake, call 'sky-blink'. *Ibid.* 71 In the interior of the bay some four or five not inconsiderable ice-blinks protrude into the sea.

ˈ**ice-boat.**

1. A boat mounted on runners for propulsion on the ice; *spec.* a light triangular structure mounted on skate-runners, and fitted with a mast and sail, used as a pleasure-boat for traversing smooth ice.

1819 *Pantologia, Ice-boats*, boats so constructed as to sail upon ice.. They go with incredible swiftness, sometimes so quick as to affect the breath. **1868** Lossing *Hudson* 277 The river had offered good sport for skaters, and the navigators of ice-boats. **1875** Knight *Dict. Mech.* 1161/1 The ice-boats on the Maeze and Y, in Holland, consist of ordinary boats mounted on runners.

2. A boat or barge employed to break the ice in a river or canal.

1842 Francis *Dict. Arts* etc. s.v., The other kind of ice-boat is a heavily laden barge, drawn along a frozen canal by a number of horses, and in its passage breaking through the ice, and thus clearing the navigation. **1892** *Daily News* 31 Dec. 3/4 This was the ice-boat—a small barge, sharp in the bows, much like a tug steamer, and the greenish-grey sheet of ice heaved before the pressure of its coming.

3. A fishing-vessel equipped with facilities for the refrigeration of fish. *N. Amer.*

1878 *Saskatchewan Herald* (Battleford) 29 July 4/1 The crew of the Lady Ellen are building an ice-boat for the fishing trade this winter. **1941** E. J. Kammer *Socio-Econ. Survey Marshdwellers Louisiana* viii. 118 Ice boats are larger than the ordinary trawl boat and are used only for

transporting shrimp. **1970** *National Fisherman* Sept. 18-A/4 They were ice boats, designed for a 10-ton capacity.

Hence **'ice-,boating**, sailing in an ice-boat.

1885 *Pall Mall G.* 15 Apr. 4/2 Ice-boating is perhaps a more dangerous amusement than we are led to believe.. and ice-boat accidents are frequent. **1887** *Cornh. Mag.* Mar. 275 Ice-boating as a Canadian sport is most extensively practised near the cities and towns upon the great lakes of Erie, Huron, and Ontario.

'ice-bolt. [f. BOLT *sb.*[1]] A 'bolt' or dart of ice: hence *fig.* **a.** A cold piercing sensation; a sudden deadly chill. **b.** An avalanche.

1789 E. DARWIN *Bot. Gard.* II. (1791) 38 The keen ice-bolt trembles at her heart. **1829** MRS. SOUTHEY *Churchyards* I. 301 The sudden revulsion of feeling came upon Andrew like an ice-bolt. **1870** H. MACMILLAN *Bible Teach.* iv. 70 Protecting the inhabitants of the valley from the fearful ice-bolts of the mountain.

ice-bone ('aɪsbəʊn). Chiefly *dial.* Forms: 6- ise-, 7- ice-, 8 ize-, 9 isch-, ische-bone. [Known from 16th c.: corresponds to OLG. *îsbên*, MDu. *ise-been* (*ys-*, *ysch-*, *yse-been*), in Kilian *is-*, *isch-been*, MDu. *ijsbeen*; MLG. *îsch-*, *îsbên*, LG. *îsbên*, whence mod.G. *eisbein* (Henisch 1616), Da., Sw. *iisben*, *isben*; the os pubis or share-bone.

The OE. *ísbán*, cited in some Ger. and Du. Dictionaries, appears to be unverified; but the OLG. word is given from a Bodl. Virgil Gloss (10th c. MS.) by Gallée, *OS. Texts* 166: '*clunis* isben *uel* arsbelli'. Kilian explains Du. *isbeen*, *ischbeen* as 'ischia, coxendix, os inferius circa nates; *et* os pubis, os pectinis'.]

The share-bone (or perh. some other bone of the pelvis or haunch); in *Cookery*, the AITCH-BONE.

1576 *Exp. Queen's Table* in Nichols *Progr.* (1823) II. 8 Isebones..2 st...2 d. **1691** RAY *S. & E. Country Wds.*, *Ice-bone*, a rump of beef (*Norf.*). **1703** THORESBY *Let. to Ray*, *Ize-bone*, the huckle-bone, the coxa (*Yorksh.*). *c* **1818** *Yng. Woman's Compan.*, The hind quarter contains the sirloin.. and the ish, each, or ash-bone. *a* **1825** FORBY *Voc. E. Anglia*, *Ice-bone*, a part of the rump of beef. **1828** *Craven Dial.*, *Ice-bone*, the pelvis. This is also called the natch or aitch-bone, from which the *ice-bone* may be corrupted. **1875** PARISH *Sussex Gloss.*, *Ice-bone*, the edge-bone of beef.

ice-borne ('aɪsbɔən), *ppl. a.* [f. ICE *sb.* + BORNE *ppl. a.*] Borne by or on ice; transported (as a boulder) during the glacial epoch.

1850 LYELL *Princ. Geol.* (ed. 8) xvi. 231 The line of coast ..is strewed..with iceborne boulders, often 6 feet in diameter. **1859** DARWIN *Orig. Spec.* xi. (1860) 263, I suspected that these islands [the Azores] had been partly stocked by ice-borne seeds, during the Glacial epoch.

ice-bound ('aɪsbaʊnd), *ppl. a.* [f. ICE *sb.* + BOUND *ppl. a.*[2]] Held fast or confined by ice; frozen in; surrounded or hemmed in by ice.

a **1659** CLEVELAND *Poems, Content* 14 Some Ice-bound Wilderness. **1822** BYRON *Vis. Judgem.* xxvii, A new Aurora borealis..seen, when ice-bound, By Captain Parry's crew. **1887** BOWEN *Virg. Æneid* VI. 17 Dædalus..Sailed for the ice-bound north.

'ice-,breaker. [f. ICE *sb.* + BREAKER[1].]

1. Anything that breaks up moving ice, so as to diminish its impact; *spec.* a structure protecting the upper end of a bridge-pier (cf. *ice-apron*).

1819 D. THOMAS *Trav. Western Country* 247 Notwithstanding these precautions, and that of placing ice-breakers to the south, [the bridge] was only saved from destruction the ensuing winter by the intrepidity of..one of the proprietors. **1856** KANE *Arct. Expl.* I. vii. 68 Three heavy hawsers out to the rocks of our little ice-breaker [an islet that turned the moving ice]. **1875** KNIGHT *Dict. Mech.* 1721/2 A view of the Swing Bridge..shows the..ice-breakers in the stream.

2. a. A vessel specially adapted for breaking a channel through the ice: cf. ICE-BOAT 2.

1875 KNIGHT *Dict. Mech.* 1161/2 An ice-breaker for harbors is a steam-vessel provided with means for..keeping open a channel for ships. **1886** *Times* 9 Mar. 11/6 The Gothenburg icebreaker keeps the channel open. **1890** *Daily News* 23 Dec. 5/5 The Finnish Government has had an icebreaker constructed strong enough to force the severest of ice.

b. *transf.* Cf. *to break the ice* (ICE *sb.* 2 b).

1883 'MARK TWAIN' *Life on Mississippi* xxxix. 365 They closed up the inundation with a few words—having used it, evidently, as a mere ice-breaker and acquaintanceship-breeder—then they dropped into business. **1904** *Daily Chron.* 27 Feb. 4/6 If you must use an ice-breaker, the pianola is decidedly effective..as a cure for shyness. **1961** BOWMAN & BALL *Theatre Lang.* 178 *Icebreaker*, a fast song for chorus girls—Musical comedy. **1963** BARNARD & LAUWERYS *Handbk. Brit. Educ. Terms* 110 *Icebreaker*, a term used to describe a preliminary to a series of tests. It is designed to accustom the candidate to the experience which he is about to undergo, but its results are not counted in the ultimate assessment of the tests. **1963** M. MCCARTHY *Group* i. 19 The recipe was an icebreaker..everyone tasted it and agreed that it was the maple syrup that made all the difference. **1968** *Daily Tel.* 15 Nov. 16/7 Swearing, in addition to its cathartic effect and as a means of non-violent assault.., is also an ice-breaker. **1973** *Sun-Herald* (Sydney) 26 Aug. 80/3 Then they went on to 'icebreakers'—short talks about themselves, reading a message they'd selected from a book.

3. A machine or hand-tool for breaking ice for economic use.

Mod. The ice-house with the ice-breaker to be worked by a gas-engine.

4. A whaler's name for the Greenland whale.

'ice-cap.

1. A permanent cap or covering of ice over a tract of country, such as exists on high mountains, and on a large scale at either pole.

1875 CROLL *Climate & T.* App. 543 [To] cover the antarctic regions with an enormous ice-cap. **1880** A. R. WALLACE *Isl. Life* viii. 156 A similar ice-cap is..believed to exist on the Antarctic pole at the present day.

2. *Med.* A bladder or elastic bag containing pounded ice, for application to the head in congestion of the brain, etc.

1854-67 C. A. HARRIS *Dict. Med. Terminol.*, *Ice Cap*, a bladder filled with pulverized ice, and applied to the head.

'ice-cold, *a.* [f. COLD *a.* Cf. Du. *ijskoud*, G. *eiskalt*, ON. *ískaldr*.] As cold as ice.

a **1000** *Boeth. Metr.* xxvii. 3 Is-calde sæ. *a* **1000** *Seafarer* 19 Iscaldne wæᵹ. **1798** CT. RUMFORD in *Phil. Trans.* LXXXVIII. 94 The former quantity of ice-cold water. **1808** W. H. ELLA *Rosenberg* II. 123, I felt her ice-cold lips upon mine. **1887** BOWEN *Virg. Ecl.* VIII. 66 The passionless heart of this ice-cold lover of mine.

,ice-'cream. A compound of flavoured and sweetened cream or custard, congealed by being stirred or revolved in a vessel surrounded by a freezing mixture. (Earlier term, *iced cream*.)

1744 in *Pennsylvania Mag. Hist. & Biogr.* (1877) I. 126 Among the rarities..was some fine ice cream, which, with the strawberries and milk, eat most deliciously. **1751** H. GLASSE *Art of Cookery* (ed. 4) 333 (*heading*) To make Ice Cream..set it [*sc.* the cream] into the larger Bason. Fill it with Ice, and a Handful of Salt. **1769** MRS. RAFFALD *Eng. Housekpr.* (1778) 249 To make Ice Cream. **1789** MRS. PIOZZI *Journ. France* I. 181 The ice-creams melt with the room's excessive heat. **1841** EMERSON *Lect.*, *Man the Reformer* Wks. (Bohn) II. 242 We dare not trust our wit for making our house pleasant to our friend, and so we buy ice-creams. **1957** *Min. Agric. Food Standards Comm. Rep. Ice Cream* (H.M.S.O.) 4 The bulk of ice cream now produced in this country is made from margarine and other non-milk fats... We recommend that special provision should be made to reserve the description 'dairy ice cream'..for ice cream in which the fat content is wholly milk fat.

attrib. **1821** *National Advocate* (New York) 3 Aug. 2/2 Among the number of ice cream gardens in this city, there was none in which the sable race could find admission and refreshment. **1844** J. COWELL *30 Yrs. among Players* II. iii. 64/2 With the ice-cream profits, he purchased bricks and mortar, and built the *Chatham Theatre*. **1851** A. O. HALL *Manhattaner* 46 How the ice cream saloons resound with clattering spoons. **1854** *Rep. Trans. Pennsylvania State Agric. Soc.* 363 Three ice cream freezers. **1873** J. H. BEADLE *Undevel. West* xxviii. 623 Two months vigorous courting will cost more than that—particularly in the ice-cream season. **1878** N. A. DONNELLEY *Lakeside Cook Bk.* 30/2 Ice Cream Cake. **1880** E. W. WILCOX *Buckeye Cookery & Pract. Housek.* 83 Ice-cream cake... Make good sponge-cake... Fill with ice-cream just before serving. **1881** C. C. HARRISON *Woman's Handiwork* III. 223 Finger-bowls and ice-cream plates were ruby Bohemian glass. **1884** *Milnor* (Dakota) *Teller* 27 June, An ice cream parlor where the dudes and dudines sip..congealed milk and sugar. **1886** *Mobile* (Alabama) *Daily Reg.* 23 Apr. 2/3 (Advt.), Drink Ice Cream Soda. **1887** A. A. HAYES *Jesuit's Ring* 56 The days of bright summer, and lawn tennis..and ice-cream soda. **1889** A. T. PASK *Eyes Thames* 123 Three Italian ice-cream men, with their heavy barrows. **1893** *Critic* (U.S.) 8 Apr. 226/1 Our national beverage 'ice-cream soda'. **1904** *Proc. R. Soc.* LXXIII. 504 Using the modified ice-cream mixer described by Moody. **1905** Ice-cream cake [see *angel-cake*]. **1909** *Sat. Even. Post* 15 May 11/2 The remainder is about equally divided among popcorn, ice cream cones, and candy. **1934** *Archit. Rev.* LXXVI. 159/1 (*caption*) 40-gallon ice-cream fountain. **1947** *Ibid.* CI. 212/1 Across the road, though, competition has set in, not only from the tricycle ice-vendors but from the Ice Cream Parlours. **1950** G. GREENE *Third Man* ii. 16 The American zone, which you couldn't mistake because of the ice-cream parlours in every street. **1961** E. WILSON in R. Weaver *Canad. Short Stories* (1968) 2nd Ser. 14 How about an ice-cream cone? **1961** C. WILLOCK *Death in Covert* iii. 73 The liveried servants held flambeaux like ice-cream cornets. **1966** J. CLEARY *High Commissioner* i. 19 An ice-cream van went slowly by, its bell tinkling. *a* **1966** M. ALLINGHAM *Cargo of Eagles* (1968) xv. 162 An ice cream tricycle was already doing good business. **1968** P. JENNINGS *Living Village* 204 The dreadful hoarse tintinnabulations, as though a giant were banging a dulcimer, which herald the urban ice cream van. **1972** *Guardian* 2 Sept. 9/2 He fetched his mother an ice-cream cornet.

Hence **ice-'creamer**, an (Italian) ice-cream vendor; so (*derogatory*) an Italian.

1901 E. W. HORNUNG *Black Mask* 110 He had every low-down Neapolitan ice-creamer on my tracks. **1940** N. MITFORD *Pigeon Pie* iii. 41, I remembered that there are Chinks and Japs and Fuzzy Wuzzies and Ice Creamers and Dagos, and so on. **1949** L. P. HARTLEY *Boat* i. 3 Italians are not people according to our ideas... Ice-creamers, some call them, but it's too polite for them.

iced (aɪst), *ppl. a.* [f. ICE *sb.* or *v.* + -ED.]

1. Covered with ice; cooled by means of ice.

1673 J. RAY *Observations Journey Low-Countries* 267 Many..with a barrel at their backs and glasses in their hands, crying *Acqua ghiacciata*, or *Acqua nevata*. *i.e.* Snowed water or iced water. **1688** *Lond. Gaz.* No. 2383/2 All such Fruits, Iced Creams, and such other Varieties as the Season afforded. **1775** SIR E. BARRY *Observ. Wines* 174 Their tables were constantly supplied with iced Liquors. **1777** P. THICKNESSE *Year's Journey* I. xxviii. 240 Their chocolate, lemonade, iced water, fruits &c. are their chief luxuries. **1820** KEATS *St. Agnes* xxxii, Impossible to melt as iced stream. **1831** B. H. SMART *Outl. Sematology* iii. 237 The thirsty wight who, in a state of profuse perspiration, calls for a glass of iced-water, may know there is danger in the draught. **1848** Iced champagne [see *ball supper* s.v. BALL *sb.*[2] 4]. **1852** FORD in *Q. Rev.* Mar. 432 Iced puddings now-a-days assume the shape and seeming of hams. **1877** *Forest & Stream* VIII. 411/1 Courtney..became very sick immediately after taking a glass of iced tea after his dinner, and was unable to row. **1879** *St. George's Hosp. Rep.* IX. 800 Iced champagne, a little iced milk and soda-water. **1879** M. E. BRADDON *Vixen* III. vii. 187 Afternoon tea at Ashbourne included iced coffee. **1880** *Amer. Punch* Jan. 4/1 Some were talking of..the cooling and invigorating influences of 'iced tea'. **1893** LD. MEATH in *19th Cent.* Mar. 508 Of all the pleasant drinks..in hot weather recommend me to an iced-cream soda. **1902** H. JAMES *Wings of Dove* v. x. 172 The small cup of iced coffee she had vaguely accepted from somebody. **1913** W. STEVENS *Let.* 7 July (1967) 179 A spread of chicken salad,..watermelon, iced-tea etc. **1930** A. BENNETT *Imperial Palace* xvii. 109 The cocktail jugs, the iced-water jugs. **1952** W. M. MILLER *View from Stars* (1965) 42 She..drank a glass of iced tea. **1954** *Good Housek. Cookery Bk.* (rev. ed.) 453 (*heading*) Iced coffee. **1958** *Listener* 14 Aug. 229/1 Fifteen of the family hang over the back and laugh at you through their iced lollies. **1960** *News Chron.* 6 Aug. 1/1 Prince Charles bought an iced-lolly. **1972** H. OSBORNE *Pay-Day* IV. i. 163 Every year..another hotel with an iced-water tap rises out of the mud.

2. a. Of a cake, bun, etc.: covered with icing. Of preserved fruit: = GLACÉ *a.* 2.

1858 P. L. SIMMONDS *Dict. Trade Products*, *Iced*, cakes frosted with sugar. **1866** MRS. BEETON *Preserves & Confectionery* 5 Iced Apples, or Apple Hedgehog... Cover the apples very smoothly all over with the icing. *Ibid.* 89 Iced currants... Lay them to dry on paper, when the sugar will crystallize round each currant. **1892** *Encycl. Pract. Cookery* I. 240/1 Iced cake. **1973** *Fortnum & Mason Christmas Catal.* 4/2 Iced and decorated Christmas cake.

b. (See quots.) Cf. FROSTED *ppl. a.* 3 b.

1829 J. C. LOUDON *Encycl. Plants* 1100/1 Iced..covered with particles like icicles. **1900** B. D. JACKSON *Gloss. Bot. Terms*, *Iced*, having a glittering papillose surface, as *Mesembryanthemum crystallinum*.

'ice-fall. [After *waterfall*.]

1. A cataract of ice; a steep part of a glacier resembling a frozen waterfall.

1817 COLERIDGE *Sibyll. Leaves* Poet. Wks. (1862) 184 Ye ice-falls! ye that from the mountain's brow Adown enormous ravines slope amain. **1860** TYNDALL *Glac.* I. xv. 100 We were amid the wild chasms at the brow of the ice-fall. **1871** L. STEPHEN *Playgr. Europe* iv, We followed the usual track..as far as the top of the great icefall of the.. glacier.

2. The fall of a mass of ice, from an ice-cliff or iceberg.

1861 L. L. NOBLE *Icebergs* 261 Then the ice-fall, with its ringing, rumbling, crashing roar, and the heavy, explosion-like voice of the final plunge, followed by the wild, frantic dashing of the waters.

'ice-field. A wide flat expanse of ice, esp. of marine ice in the Polar regions.

1694 *Acc. Sev. Late Voy.* II. (1711) 40 Ice-fields, that are as the Meadows for the Seales. **1748** H. ELLIS *Hudson's Bay* 240 We saw vast numbers of Seals and Sea-Horses lying basking upon the Ice-Fields. **1860** TYNDALL *Glac.* I. xvi. 110 The ice-field before us was a most noble one. **1890** BOLDREWOOD *Col. Reformer* (1891) 175 A fresh blast had been unchained among the far south ice-fields.

ice-floe ('aɪsfləʊ). [See FLOE.] A large sheet of floating ice: sometimes several miles in extent (cf. quot. 1835).

1819 *Edin. Rev.* XXXI. 341 Jammed in between two ice-floes. **1835** LESLIE *Polar Seas* i. 43 The whale-fishers enumerate several varieties of the salt-water ice. A very wide expanse of it they call a field, and one of smaller dimensions a *floe*. **1882** H. LANSDELL *Through Siberia* I. 198 A dense mass of ice-floes and pack-ice rushed irresistibly up the Kureika.

'ice-foot. [According to quot. 1856, ad. Da. *isfod*, in same sense: the ice forms a foot or base to the cliff or high land.]

a. A belt or ledge of ice extending along the coast in Arctic regions (cf. *ice-belt*), caused by the shore-water being largely mixed with snow and so freezing at a higher temperature than the salter water of the deep sea. **b.** Also applied to the margin of an ice-floe: see quot. 1897.

1856 KANE *Arct. Expl.* I. xv. 175 The name is adopted.. from the Danish 'Eis-fod' to designate a zone of ice which extends along the shore from the untried North..almost to the Arctic circle. *Ibid.* II. App. ii. 303 The ledge of ice which, under the name of 'ice-foot', I have before described as clinging to the shore. **1877** A. H. GREEN *Phys. Geol.* iii. §2. 109 A belt of ice known as coast ice or the ice foot. **1882** GEIKIE *Text-bk. Geol.* III. II. ii. §6 This shelf, known as the ice-foot, serves as a platform on which the abundant débris ..gathers at the foot of the cliff. **1897** tr. *Nansen's Farthest North* II. ix. 452 *note*, The ice-foot is the part of a floe which often projects into the water under the surface. It is formed through the thawing of the upper part of the ice in the summer-time by the warmer surface layer of the sea.

'ice-free, *a.* [= Ger. *eisfrei*, Da. *iisfri*.] Free from ice; of a port: Not frozen up in winter.

1891 *Pall Mall G.* 13 Nov. 6/1 Russia, says Björnson, must sooner or later have an ice-free harbour on the Atlantic coast. **1897** *Daily News* 22 Dec. 4/7 Because Russia desires, and may be about to take an ice-free port in the Pacific. **1898** *Ibid.* 29 Sept. 1/2 After forty-eight hours' sailing we were once more in ice-free water.

'ice-hill.

1. A hill or mound of ice; an elevated glacier or hummock of ice; a slope covered with ice, used for sliding or tobogganing.

1694 *Acc. Sev. Late Voy.* II. (1711) 26 The Ice-Hills that fill up the Valleys. **1816** *Sporting Mag.* XLVIII. 244

Inclined planes to imitate the ice-hills of Russia. **1855** *Englishwoman in Russia* 215 The Russians are extremely fond of this amusement, and often have these ice-hills erected at some village at a little distance from the town. **1856** KANE *Arct. Expl.* I. xxxi. 427 Myouti..began climbing the dune-like summits of the ice-hills.

†**2.** A floating iceberg. *Obs.*

1694 *Acc. Sev. Late Voy.* II. (1711) 44 The great Ice-hills ..that drive up and down in the Sea. *Ibid.* 47 A great Ice-hill came driving towards our Ship.

ˈice-hook. †**a.** A species of boat-hook, used to push large flakes of ice away from a ship. †**b.** An ice-anchor. **c.** A hook employed in securing and hoisting ice for storage.

1694 *Acc. Sev. Late Voy.* II. (1711) 43 The Seamen hinder the pressing on of the Ice as much as in them lieth, with great Ice-hooks. *Ibid.*, Where there is pretty large Ice-fields, they joyn their Ships to them with great Ice-hooks, fastned to strong Cables. **1774** C. J. PHIPPS *Voy. N. Pole* 40 And stationed them to the ice hooks, poles, crabs.

ˈice-house. **1.** A structure, often partly or wholly underground, and with non-conducting walls, in which ice is stored in winter for use during the year. Often taken as the type of a frigid place.

1687 A. LOVELL tr. *Thevenot's Trav.* II. 96 The Persians make great use of Ice..; they make not their Ice-houses as in France. **1698** FROGER *Voy.* 35 Their Hutts..are of a round Figure, and cannot be better compar'd than to our Ice-Houses. **1772** BARRINGTON in *Phil. Trans.* LXII. 285 *note*, The very name of an ice-house almost strikes one with a chill. **1860** TYNDALL *Glac.* I. xiv. 301 When we fill an ice-house..we break the ice into very small fragments. **1892** *Daily News* 15 Mar. 7/2 It is absolutely impossible to sit here this cold weather..the place is like an ice-house.

2. A hut made of ice or snow.

1857 G. F. MCDOUGALL *Eventful Voy.* '*Resolute*' 426 The remains of two ice houses yet existed, but were rapidly thawing away, under the influence of the heat of the sun. **1958** *Listener* 25 Sept. 482/2 They sat marooned for four days in an icehouse 14,000 feet up.

ice-ickel, -icle, obs. forms of ICICLE.

ice-island. An insulated mass of floating ice; an island-like ice-field; an extensive iceberg.

1777 COOK *Voy. S. Pole* etc. Introd. 17 It is, therefore, very probable, that what Bouvet saw was nothing more than a large ice-island. **1820** SCORESBY *Acc. Arctic Reg.* I. 225 The stupendous masses, known by the name of ice-islands, or Ice-bergs..from their height..and the depth of water in which they ground. **1840** R. H. DANA *Bef. Mast* xxxi. 116 We saw thirty-four ice-islands of various sizes.

ˈice-isle. = prec.

1808 J. BARLOW *Columb.* I. 599 The loosen'd ice-isles o'er the main advance. **1839** BAILEY *Festus* xxvii. (1848) 322 Dark wretched thoughts like ice-isles in a stream Choke up my mind and clash.

iceland[1] (ˈaɪslænd). [f. ICE *sb.* + LAND *sb.*[1]] A country covered with ice; the realm of perpetual ice.

1842 LYTTON *Zanoni* IV. x, An oasis in the desert, a summer in the iceland. **1889** *Mag. Amer. Hist.* XXI. 217 Mackenzie had excluded from the unprofitable search another vast extent of that iceland.

Iceland[2] (ˈaɪslənd). Also 6 **Yselonde, Iseland,** 7 **Island, Isling.** [ME. *Island, Yslond*, etc., ad. ON. *Ísland*, f. *ís-s* ICE + *land* LAND.] The name of a large island lying on the border of the Arctic Ocean, between Norway and Greenland; used *attrib.* in the names of articles imported from or peculiar to that country, as ***Iceland clothes, fish, horse, pony, wool***; also **Iceland beer,** a fermented liquor made from *Arenaria peploides* (*Syd. Soc. Lex.*); **Iceland crystal** = *Iceland spar*; **Iceland cur, Iceland dog** (also short **Iceland**), a shaggy, sharp-eared white dog, formerly in favour as a lap-dog in England; **Iceland falcon,** *Falco rusticolus islandicus*, a variety of gyr-falcon native to Iceland; **Iceland gull,** *Larus glaucoides*, a grey and white Arctic gull, **Iceland lichen, Iceland moss,** a species of edible lichen, *Cetraria islandica*, having certain medicinal properties; hence ***Iceland moss jelly, starch*** (*Syd. Soc. Lex.*); **Iceland poppy,** a variety of *Papaver nudicaule*, the yellow Arctic poppy; **Iceland sea-grass,** *Ulva latissima* (*Syd. Soc. Lex.*); **Iceland spar,** a transparent variety of calcite, used in demonstrating the polarization of light.

c **1205** LAY. 22622 Gutlond & Irlond, Orcanie & Islond. **1297** R. GLOUC. (Rolls) 3734 Scotlonde & yslonde & orcadas. **1577–87** HOLINSHED *Scot. Chron.* (1805) I. 22 Island, that lieth in the cold frosty sea beyond the Artike circle toward the North pole. **1780** VON TROIL *Iceland* 63 Floke stayed here the whole winter, and..gave the name of Iceland to the country.

c **1420** *Durham Acc. Rolls* (Surtees) I. 58 In vj yslandfyss' xxj*d.* *c* **1430** *Ibid.* 60 Iselandfishs. **1541** *Will of Joyce Stingen* (Somerset Ho.), Yselonde clothe. **1547** BOORDE *Introd. Knowl.* vi. (1870) 147 They wyll sell there Iselond curres. **1576** FLEMING tr. *Caius' Eng. Dogs* v. (1880) 37 Iseland dogges, curled & rough al ouer,..greatly set by, esteemed, taken vp, and made of. **1599** SHAKS. *Hen. V*, II. i. 44. *c* **1618** FLETCHER *Q. Corinth* IV. i, Hang, hair, like hemp, or like the Isling curs. **1627** DRAYTON *Moon-calf* Wks. (1748) 174/1 Our water-dogs and islands here are shorn. **1659** *Lady Alimony* V. iii, Lies the fault there you Island Curre? **1771** SIR J. HILL *Fossils* 76 Iceland Spar. **1771** *Gentl. Mag.* XLVI. 297/1 The Iceland Falcon..is a noble and stately bird. **1797** BROUGHAM in *Phil. Trans.* LXXXVII. 379, I ground to an even and pretty sharp edge two pieces of Iceland crystal. **1805** R. REECE (*title*) Observations on the Anti-Phthisical Properties of the Lichen Islandicus or Iceland Moss. **1822** *Mem. Wernerian Nat. Hist. Soc.* IV. 181 They [*sc.* the Shetland fishermen] have distinguished this bird by the name of Iceland *Scorie*, (or the Young Iceland Gull); *Scorie* being the general Shetlandic appellation for the young of several species of the gull family. **1829** *Nat. Philos.* I. *Polaris. Light* Introd. 1 (U.K.S.) A substance called Iceland spar, calcareous spar, or carbonate of lime. **1842** BISCHOFF *Woollen Manuf.* II. 191 The last foreign wools I bought were a cargo of Iceland wools. **1843** W. YARRELL *Hist. Brit. Birds* I. 27 Those specimens obtained from Iceland were called exclusively Iceland Falcons. *Ibid.* III. 461 The Iceland Gull sometimes makes its appearance in winter at the mouth of the Elbe. **1884** *Gardening Illustrated* 8 Nov. 425/2 A hot summer.. seems to be particularly trying to these Iceland poppies. **1901** H. H. SLATER *Man. Birds Iceland* 31 The Iceland Falcon is a remarkably handsome bird. **1927** M. U. HACHISUKA *Handbk. Birds Iceland* 40 The Iceland Falcon is a national emblem. **1930** *Ibis* 415 The Iceland Gull apparently fills the same 'niche' in Godthaab Fiord as the Herring-Gull..in the British Isles. **1956** D. A. BANNERMAN *Birds Brit. Isles* V. 21 In Ireland the Iceland gyr-falcon has been recorded five times. *Ibid.* 22 The Iceland falcon was not nearly as uncommon as had been supposed. **1962** *Ibid.* XI. 334 In flight the Iceland gull looks more graceful and has more rapid wing-beats.

Icelander (ˈaɪsləndə(r)). [f. prec. + -ER[1] 1. Cf. Da. *Islænder*, G. *Eisländer*.]

1. An inhabitant or native of Iceland.

1613 PURCHAS *Pilgrimage* (1614) 744 Arngrin Jonas an Islander. **1674** tr. *Martiniere's Voy. N. Countries* title-p., A Description of the Manners [etc.] of the Norwegians, Laponians..and Islanders. **1742** BLAIR *Grave* 491 The shivering Icelander. **1876** BANCROFT *Hist. U.S.* I. i. 8 The remote discoveries which Icelanders had made in Greenland.

2. An Icelandic falcon; see GYRFALCON.

1828 SIR J. S. SEBRIGHT *Hawking* 44 The Icelander is the largest hawk that is known, and highly esteemed by falconers.

Icelandic (aɪˈslændɪk), *a.* and *sb.* [See -IC.]

A. *adj.* Pertaining to Iceland, or to the language in use there.

1674 tr. *Scheffer's Lapland* 4 In the old Gothick or Islandick language. **1770** T. PERCY tr. *Mallet's North. Antiq.* iii. (1847) 83 The Icelandic chronicles paint out Odin as the most persuasive of men. **1780** VON TROIL *Iceland* 326 Where less fish and sour whey are eaten, and more Icelandic moss. **1844** ANSTED *Geol.* II. 515 The best known of the Icelandic hot springs are called Geysers. **1850** LATHAM *Eng. Lang.* (ed. 3) 43 Of the Icelandic verbs the infinitives end in *-a.*

B. *sb.* The language of Iceland, which in all essential points retains the form of the tongue anciently spoken over the whole Scandinavian region (Old Norse).

1833 SOUTHEY *Lett.* (1856) IV. 352 Old Icelandic, like the old Anglo-Saxon..is so difficult as often to perplex the best scholars. **1850** LATHAM *Eng. Lang.* (ed. 3) 44 The characteristic..of the Icelandic..is the possession of a passive form.

So †**Iceˈlandian,** †**ˈIcelandish** [cf. Du. *ijslandsch*, Da. *islandsk*, Icel. *íslenzkr*], *adjs.*

1708 J. CHAMBERLAYNE *St. Gt. Brit.* II. I. ii. (1737) 328 Snorro Sturlison, the Islandish Historian. **1712** BLACKMORE *Creation* I. 367 A cold icelandian desart. **1807** W. TAYLOR in *Monthly Mag.* XXIV. 547 Corroborated by the analogy of the Iselandish language.

iceless (ˈaɪslɪs), *a.* [f. ICE *sb.* + -LESS.] Free from ice; not covered by ice.

1853 KANE *Grinnell Exp.* (1856) 544 The Polynya, or Iceless Sea. **1855** BAILEY *Mystic* 75 Many an iceless and unfathomed pool.

iceman, ice-man (ˈaɪsmæn).

1. A man skilled in traversing ice, either in Alpine or polar regions.

1851 W. P. SNOW *Voy. 'Prince Albert'* 302 Ten men formed the number of the working seamen; there were no 'icemasters', nor regular 'ice-men'; but most of the sailors were long accustomed to the ice. **1855** J. D. FORBES *Tour of Mont Blanc* ix. 117 It requires an expert iceman..to effect this passage. **1856** KANE *Arct. Expl.* I. xxix. 378 We knew as icemen that the access to the land-ice from the floe was.. both toilsome and dangerous. **1860** TYNDALL *Glac.* I. vii. 47 Found him so good an iceman.

2. A man appointed to look after the ice on a skating-pond and assist in cases of accident.

1845 *Times* 10 Feb. 5/4 The ice in the Serpentine yesterday was not above an inch thick, and through the exertions of the icemen of the Royal Humane Society, no persons ventured on except a few boys. **1860** *All Year Round* No. 39. 292 A rescue by the icemen belonging to the Royal Humane Society. **1894** *Daily News* 5 Jan. 5/4 A large staff of 'ice-men' to protect the ice on the forty lakes and ponds under the control of the Council.

3. One engaged in the ice trade, or in harvesting ice for storage and sale. Also, one who delivers ice for domestic use. (*U.S.*)

1844 *Maysville* (Kentucky) *Eagle* 7 Sept. 1/3, I do wish an ice man would come this morning. **1870** 'F. FERN' *Ginger-Snaps* 179 Let no grocer boy or ice-man fondly hope to retain the celestial spark, while he briefly deposits his wares in my kitchen. **1889** *Pall Mall G.* 6 Feb. 3/1 A rapid thaw will put a stop to the operations of the ice-man. **1959** N. MAILER *Advts. for Myself* (1961) 230 We played our games. I was the iceman and she was the housewife.

4. A maker of ices.

1882 *Daily Tel.* 11 Apr., An iceman..thoroughly proficient in all kinds of water and cream ices.

Hence **ˈicemanship,** skill in dealing with the ice in mountaineering, etc.; ice-craft.

1884 GRAHAM in *Pall Mall G.* 11 June 3 What I may venture to call icemanship is a fine art, only acquired by much experience... This art, which we call mountaineering, the use of ropes and ice-axes, and all that goes with them, does not yet exist in India.

ˈice-ˌmaster.

1. A pilot or sailing-master who has special experience in navigating vessels among ice-floes.

1851 [see ICEMAN 1]. **1853** KANE *Grinnell Exp.* xiii. (1856) 98 Much as I respect the ice-masters, the Greenland pilots as they are termed. **1883** *American* VI. 173 The expedition ..[had] two Norwegian ice-masters.

2. One in charge of the ice of a public pond.

1880 *Daily News* 28 Jan. 2/5 The park bailiff and ice-master considered the ice on the Serpentine about 3½ inches thick.

ˈice-ˌmountain. = ICEBERG 1 and 2. So also **ice-mount.**

1694 *Acc. Sev. Late Voy.* II. (1711) 22 There are seven large Ice-Mountains in a Line..which look of a glorious blew colour. *Ibid.* 46 These Ice-Mounts change their first colour in time by the Air. **1774** GOLDSM. *Nat. Hist.* I. 247 Thus are these amazing ice mountains launched forth to sea, and found floating in the waters round both the Poles. **1853** KANE *Grinnell Exp.* xiv. (1856) 104, I noticed very many ice-mountains traveling to the north in opposition to both wind and surface ice.

Icenian (aɪˈsiːnɪən), *sb.* and *a.* Also **Icenæan** (aɪsiːˈniːən). [See -IAN.] **A.** *sb.* A member of the Iceni, an ancient British tribe inhabiting the district roughly corresponding to modern Norfolk and Suffolk.

1598 R. GRENEWEY tr. *Tacitus' Annales* XIV. x. 209 The chiefest of the Icenians..were dispossessed of al their ancient inheritance. **1670** MILTON *Hist. Britain* II. 55 The Icenians, a stout people untouch'd yet by these Warrs. **1864** TENNYSON '*Boädicea*' in *Enoch Arden* 169 Hear Icenian, Catieuchlanian, hear Coritanian, Trinobant!

B. *adj.* **1.** Of or pertaining to the Iceni or the district they inhabited. Also **Iˈcenic** *a.*

1757 J. DYER *Fleece* III. 72 This method still Norvicum favours, and the Icenian towns. **1830** *Forby's Vocab. E. Anglia, Mem.* p. xxxix, With only one more extract I will close what remains to be said respecting the Icenian Glossary. *c* **1873** A. D. BAYNE *Royal Illustr. Hist. E. Eng.* I. 393 Some Icenic names are supposed to remain in several towns of Norfolk and Suffolk. *Ibid.* 395 There are thousands of pits in many places, and these are supposed to have been the foundations of Icenian huts. **1900** W. A. DUTT *Norfolk* 39 Some authorities have suggested that that important Icenic settlement was at Caistor. **1921** R. A. S. MACALISTER *Text-bk. Europ. Archæol.* I. 158 To this type of flint, or to the supposed industry which it represents, has been given the name *Icenian.* **1962** T. C. LETHBRIDGE *Witches* vii. 95 Hiccafrith becomes the Sun husband of the Icenaean moon and horse goddess, Ma Gog.

2. *Geol.* Applied to the Norwich Crag, Chillesford Beds, and Weybourne Crag of Norfolk and Suffolk (sometimes, to the Norwich Crag alone) and to the period when they were deposited, formerly regarded as late Pliocene but now held to be early Pleistocene; occas. used as the epithet of a stratigraphical stage in Britain. Also *absol.*

1896 *Q. Jrnl. Geol. Soc.* LII. 782 He [*sc.* H. B. Woodward] was..glad that Mr. Harmer now agreed that the beds belonged to one formation; and if it were desirable to use a term that should correspond with the other group-names used by the Author, he would suggest that the old term 'Icenian' be used for this Norwich Crag Series. **1900** F. W. HARMER in *Ibid.* LVI. 721 For the deposits hitherto known as Norwich Crag.., which extend..from Aldeburgh in Suffolk to Horstead and Burgh in Norfolk, a distance of more than 40 miles in one direction, and 20 miles, from Hoxne to Southwold, in another, I adopt the name Icenian, originally proposed for the Crag-formation generally by S. P. [*sic*] Woodward. *Ibid.*, The Icenian Period. **1931** GREGORY & BARRETT *Gen. Stratigr.* xvi. 228 The Sicilian Series is represented in England by the Norwich Crag, Chillesford Beds, and Weybourne Crags, which were grouped by Harmer as the Icenian. **1957** J. K. CHARLESWORTH *Quaternary Era* II. xxxii. 697 The impoverished state of many Icenian shells may (doubtfully) have been due to a freshened North Sea which resulted when the Scandinavian ice..blocked the northern outlet of that sea. **1968** R. G. WEST *Pleistocene Geol. & Biol.* xiii. 337 A major time of extinction [of species of mollusc] was after Icenian Crag times, and before the Hoxnian temperate stage.

ˈice-plant. A plant (*Mesembryanthemum crystallinum*), having leaves covered with pellucid watery vesicles looking like ice: a native of the Canary Islands, S. Africa, etc. Also used in Tasmania to refer to two species of *Tetragonia*.

1753 CHAMBERS *Cycl. Supp.*, *Ice-Plant*..is also commonly called with us the diamond-plant, and the frost-plant. **1767** ABERCROMBIE *Ev. Man his own Gard.* Apr. 113 The egg plant..like-wise, diamond ficoides, or ice plant. **1889** J. H. MAIDEN *Useful Native Plants Austral.* 63 *Tetragonia implixicona*... Called 'Ice Plant' in Tasmania. Baron Mueller suggests that this plant be cultivated for spinach. **1893** EARL DUNMORE *Pamirs* II. 275 On the top of the second Takka pass, I found the ice plant growing. **1898** E. E. MORRIS *Austral Eng.* 429/1 Spinach, New Zealand, *n.*

Tetragonia expansa Murr... called also *Iceplant*, in Tasmania. **1944** *Mod. Jun. Dict.* (Whitcombe & Tombs) 204 Ice plant... The Tasmanian name for a plant allied to 'New Zealand spinach', and to the mesembryanthemum or 'pig-face'.

ˈice-plough.
1. 'An instrument used in America for cutting grooves in the ice on ponds and lakes, to facilitate the removal of blocks of 1 or 2 cwt. which are stored for summer use' (Simmonds *Dict. Trade* 1858).
1884 *Cassell's Fam. Mag.* Feb. 188/1 The ice-area is.. then trenched or sawn by the ice-plough..a succession of curved blades like teeth attached to a long beam.
2. Applied to a glacier, from its action in furrowing rocks and scooping out valleys.
1881 *Rep. Geol. Explor. N. Zealand* 57 How potent has been, and still is, the great 'ice-plough'.

icer (ˈaɪsə(r)). [f. ICE *v.* + -ER¹.] One who ices; *spec.* a worker who prepares icing and applies it to the surface of cakes, pastry, etc.
1909 WEBSTER, *Icer*, one who ices. **1921** *Dict. Occup. Terms* (1927) §433.

ˈice-rock. A large solid mass of ice; an iceberg; an ice-clothed rock.
1817 T. L. PEACOCK *Melincourt* I. 105 We want no philosophical ice-rock towed into the Dead Sea of modern society to freeze that which is too cold already. *a* **1849** H. COLERIDGE *Ess.* (1851) I. 70 Now nothing remains to be discovered but the sandy deserts of Central Africa, and the inaccessible ice-rocks of the North Pole. **1861** L. L. NOBLE *Icebergs* 172 The danger of lying under the shadow of this great ice-rock.

ice-schokkill, -seekel, -shackle, obs. and dial. ff. ICICLE.

ˈice-sheet. A sheet or layer of ice covering an extensive tract of land; *spec.* that supposed to have covered a great part of the northern hemisphere during the glacial period.
1873 J. GEIKIE *Gt. Ice Age* (1894) 364 Long before the appearance of the ice-sheet. **1891** SIR R. BALL *Ice Age* 168 In future periods the ice-sheets will again return and desolate those regions which now contain the most civilized nations of the earth. **1897** *Daily News* 9 Nov. 6/6 Everywhere else, with the exception of a few low islands, the ice-sheet overran everything.

ice-shockle, -shog, -shog(g)le, -shoglin, -shokle, -sickel, obs. or dial. var. ICICLE.

ˈicespar. *Min.* [ad. Ger. *eisspath* (Werner 1812); from its appearance.] Glassy orthoclase, first found in the lava of Vesuvius.
1816 R. JAMESON *Syst. Min.* (ed. 2) I. 404 It was named.. Ice-Spar on account of its icy appearance. **1869** PHILLIPS *Vesuv.* x. 291 Nepheline found in ejected blocks on Somma, with icespar, garnet, and mica.

ˈice-stream.
1. A stream of ice-floes carried by the wind or a permanent current in a particular course. Chiefly applied to that which sweeps round Cape Farewell at the southern extremity of Greenland.
1878 NARES *Voy. Polar Sea* I. 8, I found that we had run deeper into the ice-stream than I had intended.
2. A term applied to a valley glacier in reference to its river-like course, and continuous downward movement.
1853 KANE *Grinnell Exp.* xviii. (1856) 138 Contributions from the ice-streams of several minor valleys. **1871** L. STEPHEN *Playgr. Europe* iii. (1894) 71 In the whole Alps there is no ice-stream to be compared to the noble Aletsch glacier.

ˈice-ˌwater. Water obtained from, or cooled by, ice; iced water.
1722 *Lond. Gaz.* No. 6035/1 The..Ladies were.. entertained with all sorts of..Chocolate, Ice-Waters, &c. **1773** BRYDONE *Sicily* xxxiii. (1809) 318 In a very violent heat, there is no such cordial to the spirits as ice, or a draught of ice-water. **1797** MRS. RADCLIFFE *Italian* vi, About noon.. the carriage stopped at a post-house, and ice-water was handed through the window. **1803** C. WILMOT *Let.* 6 Mar. in *Irish Peer* (1920) 160 Ice water is their [*sc.* the Neapolitans'] greatest luxury. **1846** *Knickerbocker* XXVIII. 187 They may pour in a large spoonful of that [*sc.* brandy], and then fill it up with ice-water. **1889** *Harper's Mag.* Sept. 560/1 Here were found..the huge brown hogsheads for ice-water. **1906** *N.Y. Even. Post* 25 July 4 A glass of ice-water placed before us the moment we sit down to breakfast;..a pitcher of ice-water sent to our bed-rooms. **1910** W. DE LA MARE *Three Mulla-Mulgars* xxi. 280 Colder than ice-water. **1969** *New Yorker* 6 Sept. 35/1 She will..arrange them, filling the Chinese bowl with ice water, carefully clipping the stems. **1972** *Straits Times* 25 Nov. 10/6 They were sitting at an ice water stall when they saw four men approaching them from the direction of Sembawang Circus.

ˈice-work.
1. Ornamentation executed in ice, or having the appearance of ice; frosted work.
1729 SAVAGE *Wanderer* I. 107 On this bleak Height tall Firs, with Ice-work crown'd, Bend, while their flaky Winter shades the Ground! **1790** W. WRIGHTE *Grotesque Archit.* 7 The walls should be lined with flints, decorated with ice-work.
2. *Geol.* Work done by glaciers or icebergs.
1843 DARWIN in *Life & Lett.* (1887) I. 333 My marine theory for these roads was..knocked on the head by Agassiz' ice-work. **1863** LYELL *Antiq. Man* 304 The ice-work done by the extinct glaciers, as contrasted with that performed by their dwarfed representatives of the present day.
3. *Mountaineering.* Climbing on icy surfaces; the techniques of such climbing.
1856 A. WILLS *Wanderings High Alps* xiv. 288 Our ice hatchet..was..better adapted to the mere ice-work we had then to perform. **1892** C. T. DENT et al. *Mountaineering* iv. 125 For a snow expedition—that is, one in which snow and ice work will probably form the chief difficulties—the numbers of a party may be largely increased even to eight or ten. **1940** F. S. CHAPMAN *Helvellyn to Himalaya* iv. 89, I was not much good on really difficult rock, my experience of step-cutting and ice-work was small. *Ibid.* v. 98 At last, in early September, by developing an entirely new technique of ice-work, the ridge was reached.

ice-worm (ˈaɪswɜːm). [f. ICE *sb.* + WORM *sb.*]
a. A small oligochaete worm, *Mesenchytræ us solifugus*, found in North American glaciers and ice fields; also called glacier-worm and snow-worm. **b.** *Canada.* An imaginary creature that first 'appeared' during the Klondike gold rush.
a. [**1885** J. LEIDY in *Proc. Acad. Nat. Sci. Philadelphia* 408 The little worms of the ice appear to be an undescribed species. **1886** *Bull. Washburn Coll. Lab. Nat. Hist.* I. 186 What was popularly supposed to be an Ice Worm was found in the ice used in Salina, Kansas, toward the latter part of the summer of 1885.] **1904** G. EISEN in C. H. Merriam *Harriman Alaska Exped.* XII. 61 It is not impossible that the various glaciers of Alaska contain several species of black ice worms. **1949** *Nature* 24 Dec. 1098/1, I found a considerable number of the oligochaetous annelids known as ice-worms. **1970** *Nature* 14 Feb. 587/1 During the day, ice worms, which are black and about three quarters of an inch long, were found clumped together 6–12 inches deep under the drainage furrows of the névé.
b. **1901** *Klondike Nugget* 10 Apr. 2/2 In a country where ice worms abound there is no telling but that deadly serpents may also be found. **1964** *Edmonton Jrnl.* 11 July 27/1 The Klondike ice worm, immortalized in Robert Service's The Ice Worm Cocktail, has been imported to Edmonton.

icey, iceycle, obs. forms of ICY, ICICLE.

ich, obs. form of I *pron.*, EACH.

Ichabod (ˈɪkəbɒd). Name given by Eli's daughter-in-law to her son, used as an exclamation of regret, in allusion to 1 Sam. iv. 21 (she named the child Ichabod, saying, 'The glory is departed from Israel').
1702 I. MATHER (*title*). Ichabod, or A discourse, shewing what cause there is to fear that the glory of the Lord, is departing from New-England. **1812** BOGUE & BENNETT *Hist. Dissenters* IV. vi. 383 The orthodox dissenter would inscribe, 'Ichabod, the glory is departed'. **1901** 'A. HOPE' *Tristram of Blent* xxi, 'Bring me some cold beef,' he commanded, and the waiter brought it with an air that said 'Ichabod' for the Imperium. **1904** 'H. S. MERRIMAN' *Last Hope* xxi, 'Ichabod,' he said, with a short laugh. **1915** *N. & Q.* 6 Feb. 110/1 At one time the Scriptural name Ichabod was used, presumably with a knowledge of its derivation, with the sense of alas! regretting the good old times. **1941** J. GORE *King George V* xi. 125 An income-tax, still adjusted from time to time in pennies below a shilling, left to the newly rich and the owners of ancient wealth, newly recruited, plenty over for luxurious living and only a scintilla of justification for crying *Ichabod.* **1957** A. MACNAB *Bulls of Iberia* xiii. 139 Belmonte—the first torero ever to wear a bowler hat, ichabod!
Hence **Ichaˈbodian** *a.*, regretful, lamenting.
1887 *Daily News* 1 Dec. 2/1 Dirges were sung with an Ichabodian refrain.

icham = *I am*: see I *pron.*

†iˈchane, *int. Sc. Obs.* [perh. for *ochane*: cf. Gael. *ochain* and *ochòin* oh! alas!] An exclamation of sorrow: alas!
1513 DOUGLAS *Æneis* IX. viii. 63 Ichane [*ed.* 1553 ythane], allace! intill ane vncouth land..thy fayr body..Sall ly as pray! [*Heu, terra ignota..jaces.*]

i-changed, ME. pa. pple. of CHANGE *v.*

i-chard, ME. pa. pple. of CHARE, I-CHERRE *v.*, to turn.

i-charged, ME. pa. pple. of CHARGE *v.*

i-chaste, ME. pa. pple. of CHASTE *v.*

Ich dien (ɪçˈdiːn). [a. G. *ich dien* = I serve.] Used as the motto of the Prince of Wales, adopted with the crest of ostrich feathers after the battle of Crécy (1346), from John of Luxembourg, King of Bohemia, who was killed in the battle. So *concr.* for the Prince of Wales himself, and allusively.
Spelt *ich diene* on the tomb of the Black Prince, Edward Prince of Wales, at the time of his burial at Canterbury in 1376.
a **1529** SKELTON *Sp. Parrot* in *Poetical Works* (1843) II. 5 *Ic dien* serueth for erstrych fether. **1545** in *Catal. Seals Dept. MSS. Brit. Mus.* (1892) II. 232 Henry VIII. Ich Dien. **1677** F. SANDFORD *Geneal. Hist. Kings Eng.* III. iv. 182 Prince Edward..deplumed his Casque of those Ostrich Feathers, which..became his Cognizance,..with Scroles containing this Motto, ICH DIEN, that is, *I serve.* **1780** H. WALPOLE *Let.* 23 Sept. (1858) VII. 441 If *Ich Dien* does not wear one, he at last,..boudes those who voted against the Admiral. **1923** D. H. LAWRENCE *Birds, Beasts & Flowers* 170 That pale fragment of a Prince up there, whose motto is *Ich dien.* *a* **1930** —— *Phoenix* (1936) 588 The whole world screams *Ich dien.*

iche: see EACH, ECHE *v.*, I *pron.*, ILK.

ichebo, -u, ichibo, -u, varr. ITZEBU.

†i-cheose, *v. Obs.* [OE. *ȝecéosan* (= OS. *gikiosan*, OHG. *gichiosan*), f. *céosan* to CHOOSE.] *trans.* To choose.
a **1000** *Cædmon's Gen.* 2722 Wuna mid usic and þe wic ȝeceos on þissum lande. *a* **1175** *Cott. Hom.* 227 He wolde of þise cynne hem moder ȝeceosen. *c* **1205** LAY. 6356 þes Damas..ane chiuese hem ichæs. *a* **1225** *Ancr. R.* 56 King & prophete echosen vt of alle. **13..** *E.E. Allit. P.* A. 903 To Krystez chambre þat art ichose.

†i-cherre, *v. Obs.* [OE. *ȝecerran, -cierran*, f. *cerran* to turn (see CHARE).] *intr.* To turn, return.
c **1000** *Ags. Gosp.* Matt. xii. 44 Ic ȝecyrre [*Hatton* ȝecherre] on min hus. *c* **1175** *Lamb. Hom.* 117 ȝif..he nule icherran from his sunnan. *c* **1275** LAY. 21053 þat Childrich were ichord [*c* 1205 iliðen] to his owe londe.

I Ching (iː ˈtʃɪŋ). [Chin., lit. = Book of Changes.] The name of an ancient Chinese divination manual, based on symbols known as the eight trigrams and sixty-four hexagrams.
1876 T. MCCLATCHIE tr. *Classic of Change* p. v, The mere translating of the Yih King is not without difficulties; but to decipher the *system* taught therein, is impossible without some knowledge of other pagan systems. **1952** *Musical Q.* XXXVIII. 128 Cage has often used the I-Ching, an old Chinese method of throwing coins or marked sticks for chance numbers, like our use of dice. **1957** *Encycl. Brit.* V. 519/2 Wên Wang..is said to have produced the *I Ching*, or *Canon of Changes*, a volume based upon the trigrams and later viewed with great veneration and incorporated into the Confucian canon. **1965** L. T. CULLING *Incredible I Ching* 8 There was no language attached to the I Ching of Fu Hsi —only eight figures, or Trigrams. **1968** *Listener* 19 Sept. 377/1 By means of chance operations—the use of the I-Ching, filling in imperfections in the manuscript paper, tossing coins—the parameters of pitch (and therefore form) were removed from the domains of the composer's will and taste. **1970** FENG & KIRK *Tai-Chi* 7/2 Although it was an ancient document when Confucius first encountered it, I Ching is traditionally awarded the status of a 'Confucian' classic. **1971** R. VAN OVER *I Ching* I. ii, The text of the *I Ching* was an early valuable reference for ministers and leaders in ancient China as well as the average citizen. **1972** *Last Whole Earth Catalog* (Portola Inst.) 433/3 And then, way back under the bed, face down on the floor, opened at the hexagram called Youthful Folly, D.R. found their *I Ching.* **1973** *Listener* 15 Feb. 209/1 Margaret is 'into' astrology, and consults the *I-Ching* each morning.

ichneumon (ɪkˈnjuːmən). (Also 6 **ichnewmon,** 7 **icnumon.**) [a. L. *ichneumōn*, a. Gr. ἰχνεύμων the ichneumon, also, a small kind of wasp that hunts spiders, lit. 'tracker', f. ἰχνεύειν to track or trace out, f. ἴχνος track, footstep. In F. *ichneumon* (16th c. in Hatz.-Darm.).]
1. A small brownish-coloured slender-bodied carnivorous quadruped, *Herpestes* (formerly *Viverra*) *ichneumon*, closely allied to the mongoose, and resembling the weasel tribe in form and habits. It is found in Egypt, where it feeds on small mammals and reptiles, but is especially noted for destroying the eggs of the crocodile, on which account it was held in veneration by the ancient Egyptians. (Also called *Pharaoh's Rat*, and formerly *Indian Mouse.*)
(With the early fabulous accounts cf. COCKATRICE, = *calcatrix*, in origin a L. translation of ἰχνεύμων.)
1572 BOSSEWELL *Armorie* III. 17b, Called a Mouse of Indie, otherwise Ichneumon, a beaste of Egypte of the greatnes of a Catte..who creepeth into the body of a Crocodyle, when in sleape he gapeth and eating his bowels, sleaeth him. **1579** GOSSON *Sch. Abuse* (Arb.) 38 Ichneumon a little worme, overcomes the Elephant. **1607** TOPSELL *Four-f. Beasts* (1658) 349 Marcellus and Solinus, do make question of this Beast (Ichneumon) to be a kinde of Otter, or the Otter a kinde of this Ichneumon,..it diligently searcheth out the seats of wilde Beasts, especially the Crocodile and the Asp, whose Eggs it destroyeth. **1615** G. SANDYS *Trav.* 101 As for the *Icnumon*, hee hath but onely changed his name; now called the Rat of Nilus. **1681** COLVIL *Whigs Supplic.* (1751) 34 If Ichneumon and Crocodile Do fight in Niger, as in Nile. **1734** tr. *Rollin's Anc. Hist.* (1827) I. II. 222 The ichneumon was adored because he prevented the too great increase of crocodiles. **1855** *Eng. Cycl., Nat. Hist.* III. 82 Lucan and Rumphius both notice the skill of the Ichneumon in seizing serpents by the throat so as to avoid injury.
2. A small parasitic hymenopterous insect (family *Ichneumonidæ*), which deposits its eggs in or on the larva of another insect; upon which its larvæ feed when hatched; an ichneumon-fly.
The name had been already applied by Aristotle to 'a small kind of wasp that hunts spiders'; partly from which, partly in reference to the old stories as to the entry of the mammalian ichneumon into the body of the crocodile, Linnæus applied it to the parasitic flies. The genus is now much restricted from its Linnæan extent.
1658 ROWLAND *Moufet's Theat. Ins.* 924 The Wasps called Ichneumones, are less than the rest: they kill Spiders called Phalangia, and after they have done they carry them into their nests, and dawb them over with dirt, and so sitting upon them do procreate their own species. **1671** F. WILLOUGHBY in *Phil. Trans.* VI. 2279 It is very surprizing to observe, that a great Caterpillar, instead of being changed

into a Butter-fly..should produce sometimes..a whole swarm of Ichneumones. **1753** CHAMBERS *Cycl. Supp.* s.v., Some of these Ichneumons make the bodies of other smaller flies the places of hatching their eggs. **1815** KIRBY & SP. *Entomol.* I. xi. 193 Some Ichneumons, instead of burying their eggs in the body of the larvæ..content themselves with gluing them to the skin of their prey. **1864** H. JONES *Holiday Papers* 149 On the cocoon which the caterpillar spins being opened, an ichneumon steps out, instead of a butterfly or a moth.

3. *attrib.* and *Comb.* **ichneumon-fly** = 2; †**ichneumon maggot**, the larva of the ichneumon-fly.

1671 F. WILLOUGHBY in *Phil. Trans.* VI. 2279 There come many of these Ichneumon maggots out of the body of the same Caterpillar. **1713** DERHAM *Phys.-Theol.* VIII. vi. (1727) 375 *note*, The Insects that infest Fruits are either of the Ichneumon-Fly kind, or Phalænæ. **1789** G. WHITE *Selborne* (1853) 377, I saw lately a small ichneumon fly attack a spider much larger than itself. **1883** WOOD in *Gd. Words* 763/1 The parasitic Ichneumon flies..are here in great force.

ichneumon-, combining stem of prec. (in sense 2), as in **ichneumonid** (ɪk'njuːmənɪd) = ICHNEUTIC *a.* sb. **ichneumonidan** (ɪknjuː'mɒnɪdən) *a.*, pertaining to the family *Ichneumonidæ* of hymenopterous insects, typified by the ichneumon-flies; *sb.* an insect of this family. **ichneumonideous** (ɪknjuːmə'nɪdɪəs), **ichneumonidian** (-'ɪdɪən) *adjs.* = prec. adj. **ichneumoniform** (-'mɒnɪfɔːm) *a.*, having the form or characters of an ichneumon-fly (Mayne *Expos. Lex.* 1855). **ichneumonize** (ɪk'njuːmənaɪz) *v. trans.*, to infest, as the ichneumon-fly, the bodies of other insects. **ich'neumonoid** *a.* and *sb.* = ICHNEUMONIDAN *a.* and *sb.* **ichneumo'nology**, the natural history of ichneumon-flies (*Cent. Dict.*).

1826 KIRBY & SP. *Entom.* IV. xliv. 218 Ichneumonidan devourers are kept in check by other Ichneumonidan devourers. **1843** *Ibid.* (ed. 6) I. ix. 226 Such is the activity and address of the Ichneumonidans. **1842** *Jrnl. R. Agric. Soc.* III. I. 37, I offered a conjecture, that those larvæ which entered the ground had been 'ichneumonized', whilst those which remained encased and in the ears would be found uninjured. **1852** T. THOMPSON *Ann. Influenza* 389 The Cecidomyia of wheat would produce a famine but for the ichneumonidian parasites. **1865** *Reader* No. 119. 406/1 A dipterous or ichneumonideous insect.

ichneumoned (ɪk'njuːmənd), *a.* [f. ICHNEUMON 2 + -ED².] Infested with parasitic ichneumon flies.

1897 W. F. KIRBY in R. Lydekker et al. *Conc. Knowledge Nat. Hist.* 576 Ichneumoned larvæ generally attain their full growth, and then die. **1944** W. J. STOKOE *Caterpillars Brit. Butterflies* 99 A very large proportion of any [Large Tortoiseshell caterpillars] collected are almost certain to be found 'ichneumoned'.

ichneutic (ɪk'njuːtɪk), *a. rare.* [ad. Gr. ἰχνευτικ-ός good at tracking, f. ἰχνευτής tracker, hunter, f. ἰχνεύειν to track.] Of or pertaining to a tracker or tracking.

1838 MAGINN in *Fraser's Mag.* XVII. 651 If Eustathius is right, when he, attributing to Argus powers of seeing, takes away from his ichneutic merits.

ichnite ('ɪknaɪt). *Geol.* [f. Gr. ἴχν-ος track, footprint + -ITE.] A fossil footprint; the footprint of an animal preserved in a rock.

1854 PAGE *Introd. Geol.* x. 88 These fossil footprints, termed ichnites..found at Corncockle Muir in Dumfriesshire, at Storeton in Cheshire..and many other places.

ichnographic (ɪknəʊ'græfɪk), *a.* [f. ICHNOGRAPHY + -IC. Cf. F. *ichnographique* (1752 in Hatz.-Darm.).] = next.

1695 ALINGHAM *Geom. Epit.* 35 The Ichnographick projection of any regular Fort. **1782** *Jesuits Perspective* 3 To project the ichnographic representation of any building is to draw the exact plot of the same building.

ichnographical (ɪknəʊ'græfɪkəl), *a.* [f. as prec. + -AL¹.] Pertaining or relating to ichnography.

1658 R. NEWCOURT *Title to Map of London*, A breife Ichnograficall discription of this famous & Honorable City of London. *a* **1706** EVELYN *Sylva* (1776) 351 Claudius Perrault has assisted the text with a figure or Ichnographical plot. **1762** tr. *Busching's Syst. Geog.* I. 8 Ichnographical descriptions of the Earth, which we call Maps. **1794** *Rudim. Anc. Archit.* (1810) Pref. 6 An accurate ichnographical description of the most celebrated Greek and Roman structures.

Hence **ichno'graphically** *adv.*, in an ichnographical way; by a ground-plan or map.

1658 R. NEWCOURT *Title to Map of London*, An Exact Delineation of the Cities of London and Westminster and the Svbvrbs Thereof... Composed by a Scale and Ichnographically described. **1675** OGILBY *Brit.* Pref. 4 Towns are describ'd Ichnographically.

ichnography (ɪk'nɒgrəfɪ). Also 7 *erron.* **igno-**. [a. F. *ichnographie* (1547 in Hatz.-Darm.), or ad. late L. *ichnographia*, a. Gr. ἰχνογραφία a tracing out, ground-plan, f. ἴχνος track, trace + -γραφία -GRAPHY.] A ground-plan; the representation of the horizontal section of a building or of part of it (or, rarely, of some object resting on the ground); also, the plan or map of a place.

The sense in the first quot. is doubtful; it may be 'section'.

1598 R. HAYDOCKE tr. *Lomatius* I. 111 The ichnographie of a mans head. *a* **1638** MEDE *Rem. Apoc.* iii. Wks. III. 589 The Ichnography and Platform of the Temple's Fabrick. **1691** WOOD *Ath. Oxon.* II. 704 While he continued in Oxon he drew an exact ichnography of the City of Oxon. **1703** MOXON *Mech. Exerc.* 252 The Ground Plat or Ichnography of each Floor or Story. **1782** *Jesuits Perspective* 3 The geometric ichnography of a column is a circle, of a pedestal is a square. **1865** MERIVALE *Rom. Emp.* VIII. lxvii. 266 The ichnography of the wall of Antoninus.

b. *transf.* and *fig.*

1637 GILLESPIE *Eng. Pop. Cerem.* Ep. A ij b, [He] taketh the patterne of his religion from the Court Ichnographie. *a* **1711** KEN *Hymnotheo* Poet. Wks. 1721 III. 274 The Serpent..In his own Slime the Ichnography drew, That all his Legions might the Work pursue. **1830** *Fraser's Mag.* I. 32 The theatre is, as it were, the ichnography (ground-plan) of a people.

ichnolite ('ɪknəlaɪt). *Geol.* [f. Gr. ἴχνο-ς footprint + λίθος stone, -LITE.] = ICHNITE. Hence **ichno'litic** (*Cent. Dict.*).

1846 WORCESTER cites Rogers. **1859** *Edin. Rev.* CX. 112 Of the peculiar animals of a quadrupedal nature which have left the impress of their footsteps on these ancient sandy coasts the only records are these ichnolites.

ichnolithology (ˌɪknəʊlɪ'θɒlədʒɪ). [f. Gr. ἴχνο-ς footprint + λίθο-ς stone + -λογία -LOGY.] = ICHNOLOGY. Hence **ˌichnolitho'logical** *a.* = ICHNOLOGICAL.

1882 in OGILVIE.

ichnology (ɪk'nɒlədʒɪ). [f. Gr. ἴχνο-ς footprint + -LOGY.] That part of palæontology which treats of fossil footprints. **b.** The ichnological characters or features of a district collectively.

1851 SIR W. JARDINE *Ichnol. Annandale* 7 Our knowledge of the footprints of recent animals, what may be termed modern Ichnology..is so limited. **1855** E. HITCHCOCK (*title*) Report to the Government of Massachusetts on the Ichnology of New England. **1864** *Proc. Amer. Phil. Soc.* IX. 445 Ichnology, as a science, began..with him [Dr. E. A. Hitchcock].

Hence **ichno'logical** *a.*, relating to ichnology (Worcester 1859).

ichnomancy ('ɪknəʊmænsɪ). [f. as prec. + Gr. μαντεία divination, -MANCY.] (See quot.)

1855 SMEDLEY *Occult Sci.* 296 Ichnomancy..is the art of finding out the figure, peculiarities, occupations, &c., of men or beasts by the traces of their posture, position and footsteps.

‖**ichoglan** ('ɪtʃəʊglæn). Also 8 **itcheoglan**. [obs. Turkish *ich oylān*, f. *ich* interior + *oylān* young man, page.] A page in waiting in the palace of the Sultan.

1677 J. PHILLIPS tr. *Tavernier's Grand Seignior's Serag.* 2 The *Ichoglans* are those, in whom, besides the accomplishments of the Body, they discover also a noble Genius, fit for a high Education, and such as may render them capable of serving their Prince. **1687** A. LOVELL tr. *Thevenot's Trav.* I. xviii. 24 The Eunuchs also have the charge of the *Ichnoglans*, or the Grand Signiors Pages. **1745** R. POCOCKE *Trav.* I. II. III. ii. 134 The education of the itcheoglans for the seraglio of the grand signor. **1846** THACKERAY *Journ. Cornhill to Cairo* vii, Ichoglans and pages, with lazy looks and shabby dresses.

ichon, *each one*: see EACH B, C. Cf. ILKANE.

ichor ('aɪkə(r), 'ɪkə(r), -ɔː). [a. Gr. ἰχώρ (in senses below). Cf. F. *ichor* (16th c. in Paré).]

1. *Gr. Myth.* The ethereal fluid supposed to flow like blood in the veins of the gods.

1676 HOBBES *Iliad* (1677) 68 From the wound out sprang the blood divine; Not such as men have in their veins, but ichor [*rime* liquor]. **1728** POPE *Dunc.* II. 92 Amus'd he reads, and then returns the bills Sign'd with that Ichor which from Gods distills. **1822** BYRON *Vis. Judgem.* xxv, Of course his perspiration was but ichor, Or some such other spiritual liquor. **1855** KINGSLEY *Heroes* II. v. (1856) 146 To live ever youthful like the Gods, who have ichor in their veins.

2. *transf.* and *fig.* Blood; a fluid, real or imaginary, likened to the blood of animals. †Formerly, the serum of the blood. Now chiefly *poet.*

1638 BURTON *Anat. Mel.* I. i. III. iii. (ed. 5) 34 Ichores and those serious matters being thickned become flegme. **1774** J. BRYANT *Mythol.* I. 343 The dog stained his mouth with the ichor of the fish. **1845** FORD *Handbk. Spain* I. 295/1 The azure ichor of this élite of the earth. **1880** HUXLEY *Crayfish* i. 31 The older Naturalists thought that the crayfish was devoid of blood, and had merely a sort of ichor in place of it. **1895** W. WATSON *Hymn to Sea*, Through the veins of the Earth, riots the ichor of spring. **1930** BLUNDEN *Poems* 128 Meanwhile the woods with ichor in their limbs Wake in a dance of slow religious love. **1960** S. PLATH *Colossus* (1967) 77 The ichor of the spring Proceeds clear as it ever did From the broken throat, the marshy lip. **1970** R. P. WARREN *Incarnations* 15 The great-gashed navel's cup Pours forth the ichor that had filled it up.

3. *Path.* A watery acrid discharge issuing from certain wounds and sores.

1651 BIGGS *New Disp.* ¶ 243 The Fontanel by reason of the more powerful hurt of digestion then is accustomed doth weep forth an Ichor. **1710** T. FULLER *Pharm. Extemp.* 51 A Balsamick Decoction..corrects acrid Ichor. *c* **1720** W. GIBSON *Farrier's Guide* II. li. (1738) 200 There is an Ichor and viscid Matter perpetually flowing from the Tendons. **1897** ALLBUTT *Syst. Med.* III. 158 Occasionally they [chalk stones] push through the cutaneous covering and form indolent ulcers..and discharge a purulent ichor.

4. *Geol.* A fluid or 'emanation' from a magma which is held to cause granitization of rock.

1926 J. J. SEDERHOLM in *Bull. de la Comm. Géol. de Finlande* XII. LXXVII. 89 The writer proposes to introduce, instead of the word granitic juices, the term granitic ichor, preliminarily with no more strictly defined signification than that possessed by the word juice. It will soon be possible..to give to the term a stricter definition. **1934** *N.Z. Jrnl. Sci. & Technol.* XV. 354 The minerals described..constitute an assemblage typical of an area mineralized by granitic ichor. **1965** A. HOLMES *Princ. Physical Geol.* (ed. 2) viii. 183 When he [*sc.* Sederholm] was urged to define his 'ichor' in more material terms, as he often was, he suggested 'a magma containing much water in a gaseous state'.

i-chord: see I-CHARD.

†**icho'rescent**, *a. Obs.* [f. prec. + -ESCENT.] Growing or becoming ichorous. So †**icho'rescence**, the fact of becoming ichorous; †**icho'rescency**.

1684 tr. *Bonet's Merc. Compit.* VII. 256 Fluxions and Ichorescency of the Seed. *Ibid.* VIII. 270 Things that incrassate..the ichorescent Bloud. *Ibid.* XVIII. 617 Alexipharmacks..hinder Ichorescence..and too great rarefaction of the Blood.

†**icho'rose**, *a. Obs.* [f. ICHOR + -OSE.] = next.

1710 T. FULLER *Pharm. Extemp.* 6 Of singular avail against..Ichorose Ulcers. **1739** HUXHAM in *Phil. Trans.* XLI. 669 Whence issued a very stinking ichorose Matter.

ichorous ('aɪkərəs), *a.* [f. ICHOR + -OUS. Cf. F. *ichoreux* (16th c. in Paré).] Of the nature or character of ichor; containing or discharging ichor.

1651 BIGGS *New Disp.* ¶ 243 The man should feel himself better, when the stream of ichorous matter flowes out, then when pus is made. **1755** PARSONS in *Phil. Trans.* XLIX. 43 Foul ichorous ulcers. **1878** T. BRYANT *Pract. Surg.* I. 127 They discharge a fetid ichorous pus.

‖**ichorrhæmia** (aɪkə'riːmɪə). *Path.* Also **-emia**. [f. Gr. ἰχώρ ICHOR + -αιμία, f. αἷμα blood.] See quots. Hence **icho'rrhæmic** (-ɛmɪc) *a.*, pertaining to ichorrhæmia.

1854–67 C. A. HARRIS *Dict. Med. Terminol.*, *Ichoræmia*..poisoning of the blood from the absorption of sanious matter. **1874** JONES & SIEV. *Pathol. Anat.* (ed. 2) 118 Ichorrhæmia..or putrid infection. **1876** tr. *Wagner's Gen. Pathol.* 587 Many make a distinction between septicæmia and ichorrhæmia. *Ibid.*, Ichorrhæmic infection.

i-chosen, ME. pa. pple. of CHOOSE, I-CHEOSE, *v.*

ichthammol ('ɪkθæmɒl). *Pharm.* Also †**ichthamol**. [f. ICHTH(Y)OL with insertion of AMM(ONIA.] Ichthyol (as defined).

1907 *Brit. Pharm. Codex* 89 Ammonii Ichthosulphonas. Ammonium Ichthosulphonate. Synonyms.—Ichthamol; Ammonium Sulpho-ichthyolate. Ammonium ichthosulphonate consists of the ammonium salts of the sulphonic acids prepared from ichthyol—the oily product of the destructive distillation of a greyish bituminous schist..found in the Karwendel Mountains. **1950** [see ICHTHYOL]. **1956** D. M. PILLSBURY et al. *Dermatol.* xxvi. 388 In a patient with atopic dermatitis..our own single preference for an initial ointment is one containing 2 to 3 per cent ichthammol in zinc oxide ointment USP. **1967** *Martindale's Extra Pharmacopoeia* (ed. 25) 1406/2 Ichthammol has occasionally been administered by mouth..as an expectorant and intestinal antiseptic but it is irritant to the gastric mucosa.

ichthyal ('ɪkθɪəl), *a.* [f. Gr. ἰχθύ-ς fish + -AL¹.] = ICHTHYIC.

1874 W. C. WILLIAMSON in *Owen's Coll. Ess.* vii. 222 The Ichthyal division of that kingdom.

ichthyarchy ('ɪkθɪɑːkɪ). *nonce-wd.* [f. ICHTHY(O- + Gr. -αρχία rule, government.] The domain of fishes; the fish-world in all its orders.

1853 BADHAM *Halieut.* (1854) 275 To back an Agnano..or Thrasymene 'tenca' against the whole of the Mediterranean ichthyarchy.

ichthyic ('ɪkθɪɪk), *a.* [ad. Gr. ἰχθυϊκός fishy, f. ἰχθύ-ς fish. Cf. F. *ichthyique*.] Of, pertaining to, or characteristic of fishes; having the zoological characters of a fish; piscine.

1844–6 OWEN *Comp. Anat. Vert.* I. iv. 83 This remarkable type of ichthyic organisation [the Lepidosiren]. **1858** GEIKIE *Hist. Boulder* vii. 128 Despite their seeming reptilian character, they were undoubtedly ichthyic. **1869** BRISTOW tr. *Figuier's World bef. Deluge* iv. 112 The first great ichthyic period of the Old Red-Sandstone.

ichthyo- ('ɪkθɪəʊ), before a vowel **ichthy-**, combining form of Gr. ἰχθύς, ἰχθύο-ς fish, entering into many scientific terms, of which the following are words of less frequent occurrence:

'**ichthydin**, '**ichthyin** (**-thin**), '**ichthylin** (**-ulin**), *Chem.*, names of albuminoid substances got from the egg-yolk of various fishes. **ichthyoacantho'toxism** (ˌɪkθɪəʊəˌkænθəʊ-) [Gr. ἀκανθο- thorn (f. ἀκή point) + TOX-¹], poisoning resulting from a venomous sting or bite by a fish. **ichthyobatrachian** (ˌɪkθɪəʊbə'treɪkɪən), *a.*, *Zool.* combining the characters of Fishes and Batrachia, as the Lepidosiren and Protopterus (*Syd. Soc. Lex.* 1886). **ichthyocephalous** (-'sɛfələs) *a. Ichthyol.* [Gr. κεφαλή head],

belonging to the *Ichthyocephali*, a group of fishes in Cope's classification (1870) including certain eels. **ichthyocoprolite** (-ˈkɒprəlaɪt) *Palæont.* [COPROLITE], the fossilized excrement of a fish; also *ichthyocoprus*. **ichthyocrinid** (ˌɪkθɪˈɒkrɪnɪd) *a. Palæont.* [see CRINOID], belonging to the extinct family *Ichthyocrinidæ* of articulate crinoids of Devonian age; so **ichthy'ocrinoid** *a.* and *sb.* **ichthyodont** (ˈɪkθɪəʊˌdɒnt) *Palæont.* [Gr. ὀδοντ- tooth], a fossil tooth of a fish. **ichthyo'fauna**, the fish fauna, or fish-life, of a sea or region. **ichthy'olatry** [-LATRY], fish-worship, the worship of a fish-god, as Dagon; hence **ichthyolatrous** (-ˈɒlətrəs) *a.* **ichthyomancy** (ˈɪkθɪəʊˌmænsɪ) [-MANCY], divination by means of the heads or entrails of fishes; so **ichthyo'mantic** *a.*, of or relating to ichthyomancy. **ichthyonomy** (ɪkθɪˈɒnəmɪ) [Gr. -νομία arrangement], arrangement or classification of fishes. **ichthyopatolite** (-ˈpætəlaɪt) *Palæont.* [Gr. πάτο-ς path + -LITE], a fossil imprint supposed to be that of the pectoral fin-rays of a fish, used in progression on damp surfaces. **ichthyophile** (ˈɪkθɪəʊfaɪl), **ichthy'ophilist** [Gr. φίλ-ος loving], a lover of fish or fishes. **ichthyophthiran** (-əʊfˈθaɪərən) *Zool.* [Gr. φθείρ louse] *a.*, belonging to the crustacean order *Ichthyophthira*, parasites upon fishes; *sb.* a crustacean of this order, a fish-louse. **ichthyopodolite** (-ˈpɒdəlaɪt) *Palæont.* [Gr. ποδ- foot + -LITE], a fossil imprint supposed to have been made by some fish (Buckland 1844). **ichthyopolism** (ɪkθɪˈɒpəlɪz(ə)m) [Gr. ἰχθυοπώλ-ης fishmonger, πώλης seller], the sale of fish; so **ichthy'opolist**, a seller of fish, a fishmonger. **ichthyosarcolite** (-ˈsɑːkəʊlaɪt) *Palæont.* [Gr. σάρξ, flesh + -LITE], a fossil bivalve shell of the genus *Caprinella*. **ˌichthyoˌsarco'toxism** [SARCO- + TOX-[1]], poisoning resulting from the ingestion of a fish whose flesh is poisonous. **ichthyotomist** (ɪkθɪˈɒtəmɪst) [Gr. -τομος cutting + -IST], a dissector or anatomist of fishes; so **ichthy'otomy**, dissection of fishes. **ichthyo'toxism** [TOX-[1]], poisoning resulting from the natural poison or venom of a fish. **ˌichthy'taxidermy**, the taxidermy or stuffing of the skins of fishes as zoological specimens.

1859 TODD *Cycl. Anat.* V. 141 Ichthine, Ichthidine, Ichthuline. **1953** B. W. HALSTEAD in *Copeia* I. 32/2 The following nomenclature and classification is proposed: Ichthyo-toxism is the general term which would be used to include the forms of intoxication resulting from contact with both 'poisonous' and 'venomous' fishes... Ichthyotoxism may be of two types: (a) Ichthyosarcotoxism... (b) *Ichthyoacanthotoxism. **1962** K. F. LAGLER et al. *Ichthyol.* iv. 131 The field of ichthyotoxism includes the various forms of intoxication resulting from eating poisonous fishes (ichthyosarcotoxism) or being stung by venomous fishes (ichthyoacanthotoxism). **1708** *Phil. Trans.* XXVI. 78 *Bufonites*, The Toad-stone, or Capsular *Ichthyodont. **1828** STARK *Elem. Nat. Hist.* I. 492 Fossil teeth or ichthyodontes occur in great quantity in Malta and Sicily. **1883** *Fisheries Exhib. Catal.* 283 The genus *Mugil* is richly represented in our *Ichthyo-fauna. **1853** W. B. BARKER *Lares & Penates* 224 The worship..was afterwards associated in one common form of *ichthyolatry, in Derceto or Atergates. **1656** BLOUNT *Glossogr.*, **Ichthyonomancy* [sic], a divination by fishes. *a* **1693** URQUHART *Rabelais* III. xxv. 209 Ichthiomancy, in ancient times so celebrated. **1847** CRAIG, *Ichthyomancy*. **1822** *Edin. Rev.* 49 Blainville next abuses Volta's *ichthyonomy. **1845** FORD *Handbk. Spain* I. 218 The fore-claws are titbits for the Andaluz *ichthyophile. **1852** BADHAM *Halieut.* (1854) 154 We..arrived..at the gate of the old *ichthyophylist. **1853** *Ibid.* 474 If we look back into the history of *ichthyopolism. *Ibid.*, He once beat an Irish *ichthyopolist..at her own weapons. **1953** *Ichthyosarcotoxism [see *ichthyoacanthotoxism* above]. **1960** Ichthyosarcotoxism [see CIGUATERA]. **1962** K. F. LAGLER et al. *Ichthyol.* v. 160 The strongest evidence as to the origin of ichthyosarcotoxism now points to the feeding habits of fishes. **1844–6** OWEN *Comp. Anat. Vert.* I. viii. 198 The first spinal nerve..is called 'hypoglossal nerve' by some *ichthyotomists. [**1898** V. C. VAUGHAN in T. L. Stedman *20th Cent. Pract.* XIII. 33 (*heading*) Fish poisoning (ichthyotoxismus).] **1900** DORLAND *Med. Dict.* 315/2 *Ichthyotoxism. **1922** *U.S. Naval Med. Bull.* XVII. 201 Poisoning by inherent fish poisons is called 'ichthyotoxism'. **1953** Ichthyotoxism [see above]. **1883** *Fisheries Exhib. Catal.* 220 Stuffed fishes, prepared by Davidson's method of *ichthytaxidermy.

‖**ichthyocolla** (ɪkθɪəʊˈkɒlə). [L., a. Gr. ἰχθυόκολλα, f. ἰχθυο- fish- + κόλλα glue.] Fish-glue, isinglass. Also *attrib.*

1601 HOLLAND *Pliny* II. 438 A fish there is named Ichthyocolla, which hath a glewish skin, and the very glue that is made thereof, is likewise called Ichthyocolla. **1678** PHILLIPS (ed. 4), *Ichthyocolla*, a kind of Glew made of the skin of Fishes, commonly called Isonglass. **1772** JACKSON in *Phil. Trans.* LXIII. 3 Processes for making ichthyocolla, fish-glue or isinglass.

ichthyodorylite, -dorulite (ɪkθɪəʊˈdɒrɪlaɪt, -ˈdɒr(j)ʊlaɪt). *Palæont.* [f. ICHTHYO- + Gr. δόρυ spear + λίθος stone (see -LITE). The etymological spelling is *-dorylite*: cf. F. *ichthyodorylithe.*] A fossil spine of a fish or fish-like vertebrate.

1837 BUCKLAND *Geol.* I. 287 Dorsal spines of Fishes.. have been named Ichthyodorulites. **1842** H. MILLER *O.R. Sandst.* viii. (ed. 2) 167 A bulky but very imperfectly-preserved ichthyodorulite. **1872** W. S. SYMONDS *Rec. Rocks* viii. 272, I saw a small ichthyodorulite in some silicious beds.

ichthy'ographer. [f. as prec. + Gr. -γραφος writing, writer + -ER[1].] A writer on fishes. So **ichthy'ography**, description of fishes; **ichthyo'graphic** *a.*, pertaining to ichthyography.

1677 PLOT *Oxfordsh.* 103 All the Pectines or Escallop-shells I could find in the Icthyographers. **1736** BAILEY (folio) Pref., *Ichthyography*,..a Discourse, or Description of Fishes. **1847** CRAIG, *Ichthyography*, a treatise on fishes.

ichthyoid (ˈɪkθɪɔɪd), *a.* and *sb.* [f. as prec. + -OID. Cf. Gr. ἰχθυώδης = ἰχθυοειδής.]

A. *adj.* Resembling or having the form or characteristics of a fish; fish-like.

1855 MAYNE *Expos. Lex.*, *Ichthyoides*, resembling a fish,.. ichthyoid. **1865** PAGE *Handbk. Geol.* s.v., The ichthyosaurus ..is partly ichthyoid and partly sauroid. **1870** RUSKIN *Wks.* (1872) III. 135 This ichthyoid, reptilian, or monochondyloid ideal of the self-made man.

B. *sb.* A vertebrate of the fish type; *spec.* = ICHTHYOPSID.

1863 HUXLEY *Comp. Anat.* (1864) v. 74 The classes of the Vertebrata are capable of being grouped into three provinces (I.) the Ichthyoids..(II.) the Sauroids..and (III.) the Mammals. **1866** —— in *Intell. Observ.* No. 56. 100 The Ichthyoids, comprising fishes and amphibia. **1870** ROLLESTON *Anim. Life* Introd. 67 Instances of larval Ichthyoids maturing sexual products are furnished to us by the immature Lamprey.

So **ichthy'oidal** *a.* = prec. A.

ichthyol (ˈɪkθɪɒl). *Med.* [f. ICHTHYO- + L. *oleum* oil. (But perh. suggested by *ichthyolite.*)] A brownish-yellow syrupy liquid of disagreeable odour, obtained by the dry distillation of bituminous rocks containing remains of fossil fishes; used as a remedy in skin diseases. Also, the dark, viscous liquid obtained by sulphonating the distillate and neutralizing the product with ammonia, in which form the substance has been most commonly employed (see quot. 1950). Hence **ichthy'olic** *a.*, pertaining or related to ichthyol.

Ichthyol has been registered as a proprietary name.

1884 *Trade Marks Jrnl.* 1 Oct. 908 Ichthyol... Ichthyol Gesellschaft Cordes, Hermanni & Co., Hamburg; merchants... Chemical substances prepared for use in medicine and pharmacy. **1885** *Lancet* 26 Sept. 577 The ammonium salt of sulpho-ichthyolic acid... The ichthyol salt may be taken indefinitely. **1898** *Voice* (N.Y.) 10 Feb. 5/2 Ichthyol and other similar agents..may be painted on the affected portions of the skin. **1900** A. R. CUSHNY *Text-bk. Pharmacol. & Therapeutics* II. 379 Ichthyol is the ammonia salt of a sulphonic acid derived from the tar of a bituminous shale which is found in the Tyrol. **1907** [see ICHTHAMMOL]. **1932** C. J. MILLER *Clin. Gynecol.* v. 105 Eroded and inflamed cervices are often temporarily improved by local applications of tincture of iodine..or some similar agent, after which tampons saturated with ichthyol and glycerine are inserted into the vagina. **1950** *Jrnl. Soc. Chem. Industry* LXIX. 107/1 There is confusion in the nomenclature: the British Pharmacopoeia defines ichthammol as 'the ammonium salts of sulphonic acids of an oily substance, prepared from a bituminous schist, together with ammonium sulphate and water'. The oily substance..is commonly known as ichthyol. The B.P.C. however, states that ichthyol is a proprietary name for a brand of ichthammol. Unna..urged the use of the unsulphonated oil and the restriction of the name ichthyol to this material... When [sulphonated and] neutralized with ammonia, the product was variously known as ammonium ichthyosulphonate, the original name of ichthyol, and finally as ichthammol: this is the ichthammol of the B.P. **1962** *Brit. Jrnl. Plastic Surg.* XV. 278 All burns have had the same basic treatment—exposure and regular painting of the burned areas and surrounding skin with glycerin and ichthyol.

ichthyolite (ˈɪkθɪəlaɪt). *Palæont.* [f. as prec. + Gr. λίθος stone: see -LITE. Cf. F. *icht(h)yolithe* (1762 in Hatz.-Darm.).] A fossil fish; any fossil of ichthyic origin.

1828 WEBSTER cites E. Hitchcock. **1842** H. MILLER *O.R. Sandst.* ix. (ed. 2) 193 The ichthyolites of the Old Red Sandstone. **1850** LYELL *Princ. Geol.* ix. (ed. 8) 134 Similar Ichthyolites have been met with in still older rocks. **1854** PAGE *Introd. Geol.* 112 The most common ichthyolites in the English tertiaries are the shark-like teeth of gigantic placoids which seem to have thronged these waters.

Hence **ichthyo'litic** *a.*, pertaining to, or characterized by containing, ichthyolites.

1850 H. MILLER *Footpr. Creat.* x. (1874) 192, I found it partially embedded..in an ichthyolitic deposit. **1854** —— *Sch. & Schm.* xx, The ichthyolitic formations of Moray.

ichthyologic (ɪkθɪəʊˈlɒdʒɪk), *a.* [f. ICHTHYOLOG-Y + -IC. Cf. F. *icht(h)yologique* (1770 in Hatz.-Darm.).] Of or belonging to ichthyology, ichthyic.

1853 BADHAM *Halieut.* (1854) 257 The ichthyologic section of Acanthopterygii. **1861** H. F. HORE in *Macm. Mag.* V. 53 The number of fish left to breed is but a decimal fraction of that algebraic, ichthyologic *x*, the unknown quantity of salmon which ought to be spared.

ichthyo'logical, *a.* [f. as prec. + -AL[1].] Of or pertaining to ichthyology; relating to or dealing with the natural history and classification of fishes; *loosely*, pertaining to fishes; ichthyic, piscine.

1716 M. DAVIES *Athen. Brit.* III. *Crit. Hist.* 104 In blazening those Ichthyological Medals. **1752** SIR J. HILL *Hist. Anim.* 297 All the Ichthyological writers have described it. **1837** WHEWELL *Hist. Induct. Sc.* III. XVI. vii. 368 Cuvier himself..attempted to improve the ichthyological arrangements. **1868** *Daily News* 24 July, Some very curious ichthyological phenomena have been noticed in Southampton Water this season.

Hence **ichthyo'logically** *adv.*, according to ichthyology; (in quot.) with reference to fishes.

1854 BADHAM *Halieut.* 189 'Apolecti',..applied ichthyologically to the thunny, and probably to young specimens.

ichthyologist (ɪkθɪˈɒlədʒɪst). [f. ICHTHYOLOGY + -IST.] One versed in ichthyology; a student of the natural history of fishes.

1727 in BAILEY vol. II. **1752** SIR J. HILL *Hist. Anim.* 224 The coryphaena..was well known to the Ichthyologists of all times. **1772** JACKSON in *Phil. Trans.* LXIII. 7 The anatomy and uses of the sound in fish seems not yet adjusted by ichthyologists. **1889** *Nature* 5 Dec. 101 The well-known Indian ichthyologist, Francis Day.

ichthyology (ɪkθɪˈɒlədʒɪ). [f. Gr. ἰχθύς, ἰχθυο- fish + -LOGY.] The natural history of fishes as a branch of zoology. **b.** The ichthyological features or characteristics (*of* a district), the fishes (*of* a region) as subjects of scientific study.

1646 SIR T. BROWNE *Pseud. Ep.* III. xxiv. 169 Some there are in the Land which were never maintained to be in the Sea..which carry no name in Icthyologie. **1772** JACKSON in *Phil. Trans.* LXIII. 8 The latest, and perhaps the most accurate author on icthyology. **1816** *Gentl. Mag.* LXXXVI. II. 616 The Ichthyology of these parts of North America. **1842** H. MILLER *O.R. Sandst.* ii. (ed. 2) 59 The labours of these two great men in fossil ichthyology. **1880** GÜNTHER *Fishes* 2 The commencement of the history of Ichthyology coincides with that of Zoology generally.

ichthyomorphic (ˌɪkθɪəʊˈmɔːfɪk), *a.* [f. ICHTHYO- + Gr. μορφ-ή shape + -IC.]

a. Having the form of a fish, as the fish-god Dagon. **b.** Possessing (all or some of) the zoological characters of fishes; ichthyoid.

1879 *Contemp. Rev.* 478 The ichthyomorphic nature belonging to this aspect of his personality. **1887** H. H. HOWORTH *Mammoth & Flood* 432 The legend..recalls the ichthyomorphic God Ea.

†**ichthy'ophagan.** *Obs. rare.* [f. L. *ichthyophag-us* (see next) + -AN.] A fish-eater.

1607 TOPSELL *Four-f. Beasts* (1658) 225 People of Arabia ..which some call Ichthyophagans, and Troglodytans.

‖**ichthyophagi** (ɪkθɪˈɒfədʒaɪ), *sb. pl.* [L., pl. of *ichthyophag-us* (usually in pl. as name of fish-eating races), a. Gr. ἰχθυοφάγος, f. Gr. ἰχθυο- fish- + -φάγος eating, f. φαγεῖν to eat.] Fish-eaters. (Rarely in sing. *ichthyophagus* = ICHTHYOPHAGIST.)

1555 W. WATREMAN *Fardle Facions* I. vi. 103 Ichthiophagi of Afrike. **1661** LOVELL *Hist. Anim. & Min.* 231 The Ichthyophagi made bread of their [whales'] flesh, and houses, &c. of their bones. **1777** G. FORSTER *Voy. round World* I. 143 We were now indeed become perfect ichthyophagi. **1855** MOTLEY *Dutch Rep.* Introd. i. (1866) 2 Here, within a half-submerged territory, a race of wretched ichthyophagi dwelt upon *terpen*, or mounds.

ichthyophagian (-ˈfeɪdʒ(ɪ)ən), *a.* [f. as prec. + -IAN.] Of or characteristic of *Ichthyophagi*; characterized by the eating of fish.

1852 BADHAM *Halieut.* (1854) 137 These ichthyophagian banquets.

ichthyophagist (ɪkθɪˈɒfədʒɪst). [f. as prec. + -IST.] A fish-eater; one whose food is fish.

1727 in BAILEY vol. II. **1819** W. LAWRENCE *Physiol.* (1848) 144 They are not, however, pure ichthyophagists. **1859** R. F. BURTON *Centr. Afr.* in *Jrnl. Geog. Soc.* XXIX. 242 The Lakists generally are..strong swimmers and fishermen, and vigorous ichthyophagists all.

So **ichthy'ophagite** = prec.; **ichthy'ophagize** *v.* (*nonce-wd.*) *intr.* to eat fish.

1835 KIRBY *Hab. & Inst. Anim.* I. ii. 117 One [tribe] were perfect Ichthyophagites, and would touch no other animal food. **1853** BADHAM *Halieut.* (1854) 346 This very important duty of ichthyophagizing dates some way back in ecclesiastical history.

ichthyophagous (ɪkθɪˈɒfəgəs), *a.* [f. L. *ichthyophag-us*, ad. Gr. ἰχθυοφάγος (see ICHTHYOPHAGI) + -OUS.] Fish-eating; that feeds on fish.

1828 in WEBSTER. **1831** CARLYLE *Sart. Res.* III. x, A few are Ichthyophagous, and use Salted Herrings. **1852** TH. ROSS *Humboldt's Trav.* II. xxiv. 455 The icthyophagous nations, that dwelt on the Persian Gulf and the shores of the Red Sea. **1897** ALLBUTT *Syst. Med.* II. 1018 Transferred in raw, smoked or imperfectly cured and cooked fish to the intestine of man, dog, cat or other ichthyophagous animal.

Hence **ichthy'ophagously** *adv.*, in reference to ichthyophagy.

1854 BADHAM *Halieut.* Advt., The Author's purport..is, to treat of fish ichthyophagously, not ichthyologically, and to give, not fish science, but fish tattle.

ichthyophagy (ɪkθɪ'ɒfədʒɪ). [a. F. *ichthyophagie* (16th c. in Hatz.-Darm.), ad. Gr. *ἰχθυοφαγία* fish diet, f. *ἰχθυοφάγος*: see prec.] The practice of eating fish.

1656 BLOUNT *Glossogr.*, *Ichthyophagie*, fish-eating. *a* **1693** URQUHART *Rabelais* III. xxii. 178 Poor Snakes, the very Extracts of Ichthyophagy. **1819** *Chron.* in *Ann. Reg.* 519, I ..am still almost at odds with ichthiophagy.

ichthyophthalmite (ɪkθɪɒf'θælmaɪt). *Min.* [f. Gr. *ἰχθύ-ς* fish + *ὀφθαλμ-ός* eye + -ITE, in reference to its appearance. (In 1801 called *ichthyophthalme*.)] A synonym of APOPHYLLITE.

[**1801** *Nicholson's Jrnl.* V. 195 With sulphate of lime (gypsum), the ichtyophtalme is infusible.] **1805** R. JAMESON *Syst. Min.* II. 601 Ichthyophthalmite, or Fish-eye-stone. **1883** *Encycl. Brit.* XVI. 421/1.

‖**ichthyopsida** (ɪkθɪ'ɒpsɪdə), *sb. pl.* *Zool.* [mod.L., f. ICHTHYO- + Gr. *ὄψις* appearance: see -ID.] The lowest of the three primary groups of *Vertebrata* in Huxley's classification, comprising the branchiate vertebrates, i.e. the amphibians or batrachians, the fishes, and fish-like vertebrates. Hence **ichthy'opsid, -'opsidan, -op'sidian** *adjs.*, of or belonging to the *Ichthyopsida*; *sbs.* a vertebrate of this group.

1871 HUXLEY *Anat. Vert.* ii. 75 The spinal accessory exists in no Ichthyopsid vertebrate. *Ibid.* iii. 112 The Vertebrata are divided into three primary groups or provinces: the Ichthyopsida, the Sauropsida, and the Mammalia. **1872** MIVART *Elem. Anat.* ii. 43 All Vertebrates above the Ichthyopsida. **1887** J. CLELAND in *Nature* 24 Feb. 391/1 There were two kinds of protovertebrates, namely, piscine and reptilian—or ichthyopsidan and sauropsidan, as Prof. Parker would probably prefer to call them. **1888** ROLLESTON & JACKSON *Anim. Life* 432 Class Cyclostomi..Elongated Eel-like Ichthyopsida, with the mouth not supported by jaws as in other Vertebrata.

ichthyopterygian (ˌɪkθɪəʊptə'rɪdʒɪən), *a.* and *sb.* *Palæont.* [f. Gr. *ἰχθυο-* (see ICHTHYO-) + *πτέρυξ*, *πτερυγ-* wing, *πτερύγι-ον* wing, fin + -AN.]

a. *adj.* Belonging to the *Ichthyopterygia*, an order of extinct marine reptiles in Owen's classification (1860, *Palæont.* 198–9), so named from the paddle- or fin-like character of the digits of the fore and hind limbs, the type of which is the ichthyosaurus; ichthyosaurian. **b.** *sb.* A reptile of this order; an ichthyosaurian.

‖**ichthyornis** (ɪkθɪ'ɔːnɪs). *Palæont.* [mod.L. (Marsh 1872), f. Gr. *ἰχθύ-ς* fish + *ὄρνις, ὄρνιθ-ος* bird.] An extinct genus of toothed birds (*Odontornithes*) belonging to the order or sub-class *Odontotormæ*, having socketed teeth and biconcave vertebræ, the remains of which occur in the cretaceous rocks of North America. Hence **ichthyornithic** (-ɔː'nɪθɪk) *a.*, belonging to this genus. **ichthy'ornithid**, a bird of the family *Ichthyornithidæ*.

1872 O. C. MARSH in *Amer. Jrnl. Sc. & Arts* 3rd Ser. IV. 344 Notice of a new and remarkable bird... This species may be called *Ichthyornis dispar*. **1873** *Ibid.* VI. 74 Notice of a new Species of Ichthyornis. **1884** G. ALLEN in *Longm. Mag.* Jan. 290 The ichthyornis has a row of teeth in each jaw. **1896** NEWTON *Dict. Birds* 954 The Teeth of Ichthyornis are..restricted to the mandibles and maxillæ; but they stand each in a separate socket.

ichthyosaur ('ɪkθɪəʊsɔː(r)). [ad. mod.L. *ichthyosaur-us*: see next.] = next, b.

1830 LYELL *Princ. Geol.* I. 123 The huge iguanodon might reappear in the woods, and the ichthyosaur in the sea. **1865** PAGE *Handbk. Geol.* 253 The ichthyosaurs..were the 'reptile whales' of their period—a period extending from the middle Trias..till near the close of the Chalk formation. **1876** tr. *Beneden's Anim. Parasites* Introd., The fishes and the crustaceans which were chased by the plesiosaurs and the ichthyosaurs.

‖**ichthyosaurus** (ˌɪkθɪəʊ'sɔːrəs). *Palæont.* Pl. -i. [mod.L., f. Gr. *ἰχθύ-ς, ἰχθύο-* fish + *σαῦρος* (= *σαύρα*) lizard.]

a. A genus of extinct marine animals, combining the characters of saurian reptiles and of fishes with some features of whales, and having an enormous head, a tapering body, four paddles, and a long tail. (Their remains are found chiefly in the Lias.) **b.** An animal of this genus.

1832 DE LA BECHE *Geol. Man.* (ed. 2) 385 Of the various reptiles of this period, the Ichthyosaurus..seems to have been best suited to rule in the waters. **1833** LYELL *Princ. Geol.* III. 172 Vertebræ of ichthyosauri. *Ibid.* Gloss. 71 *Ichthyosaurus*, a gigantic fossil marine reptile, intermediate between a crocodile and a fish. **1851** RICHARDSON *Geol.* (1855) 298 The Ichthyosaurus had the general contour of a dolphin, the head of a lizard, the teeth of a crocodile, the sternal arch of an ornithorhynchus, and the paddles of a whale. **1872** MIVART *Elem. Anat.* 37 In the extinct Ichthyosaurus the neural arch was permanently distinct from the centrum.

Hence **ichthyosaurian** (ɪkθɪəʊ'sɔːrɪən) *a.*, of or pertaining to the ichthyosaurus; belonging to the order *Ichthyosauria*; *sb.* an animal of this order. **ichthyo'saurid**, an animal of the Ichthyosaurus family, *Ichthyosauridæ*. **ichthyo'sauroid** *a.*, having the form or characters of an ichthyosaurus.

1854 HOOKER *Himal. Jrnls.* I. iii. 79 With his ichthyosaurian snout raised high above the water.

‖**ichthyosis** (ɪkθɪ'əʊsɪs). *Path.* [mod. medical L. (Willan 1801), f. Gr. *ἰχθύ-ς* fish + -OSIS. More etymologically called by Good (*Study Med.* 1822 IV. 597) *ichthy'iasis* (cf. *elephantiasis*), names in *-osis* being properly verbal sbs., from Gr. verbs in *-όειν*.] A congenital disease of the skin in which the epidermis becomes thickened and assumes a dry and horny appearance. (Also called *fish-skin disease* and *porcupine disease*.)

1815 R. BATEMAN *Delin. Cutaneous Dis.* Pref. 5 Exhibiting the disease *Ichthyosis*. **1864** W. T. FOX *Skin Dis.* 43 Ichthyosis is of two kinds, epithelial and sebaceous. **1876** DUHRING *Dis. Skin* 353 Ichthyosis is a congenital, chronic, hypertrophic disease..characterized by dryness and harshness of the skin, the formation of scales, and a variable amount of papillary growth. **1878** HABERSHON *Dis. Abdomen* 17 The morbid growth of epithelium..gives rise to an appearance which has been called 'ichthyosis of the tongue'.

Hence **ichthyotic** (ɪkθɪ'ɒtɪk) *a.*, subject to or affected with ichthyosis.

1876 DUHRING *Dis. Skin* 356 Ichthyotic persons are noted to perspire but very slightly. **1878** T. BRYANT *Pract. Surg.* I. 522 An ichthyotic tongue.

ichu ('iːtʃuː). Also **icho, ychu.** [Quechua.] An alpine grass, *Stipa ichu*, growing on the uplands of the Andes, where it is used for fodder and thatching.

[**1781** H. RUIZ *Relación del Viaje* (1931) 137 Se mantiene porción de ganado bacuno y carneros de Castilla con el Icho y con el corto, pero abundante pasto.] **1891** E. B. CLARK *Twelve Months Peru* 136 The coarse *ychu* grass, growing in tufts upon the mountain slopes. **1921** *Glasgow Herald* 23 Apr. 10/1 The great ichu-covered steppes of the plateau. **1950** T. H. GOODSPEED *Plant Hunters in Andes* iv. 119 Herds of llamas and alpacas graze the ichu. **1964** A. R. STEELE *Flowers for King* ii. 42 Other desired specimens rating special mention [in 1776] were cinchona, the source of quinine; *icho* grass from the high mountain plateaus, useful for matting and cordage. *Ibid.* vii. 99 The scientists..swung perilously upon a raw-hide rope bridge one cold midnight by the light of *icho* grass flares.

-ician (ɪʃən), a compound suffix, in F. *-icien*, consisting of -IAN (ME. and F. *-ien*), added to names of arts or sciences in L. *-ica*, F. *-ique*, Eng. -IC, -ICS, to denote a person skilled in the art or science; e.g. *arithmetic-ian, logic-ian, magic-ian, music-ian, physic-ian, rhetoric-ian*; *mathematic-ian, mechanic-ian, optic-ian, politic-ian, statistic-ian, tactic-ian*; sometimes formed by analogy on names not ending in *-ic* (though there may be an adj. in *-ic*), as *academ-ician, algebr-ician, geometr-ician, Hebr-ician*: cf. also *patrician*, f. L. *patrici-us*.

The termination goes back to 12th c. in OF. (where it was merely a case of the usual suffix *-ien* as in *astrolog-ien, astronom-ien*): thus 12th c. *physicien*, 13th c. *logicien*, 14th c. *mathematicien, musicien*. In Eng. *fisicien* is known *c* 1225, *magicyen c* 1380, *musicien, rethoricien c* 1425, *logycien c* 1475. Extended formations, with suffix *-er*, are *musician-er* (now obs. or vulgar), and *practition-er* for *practicianer* (F. *practicien*).

‖**icica** ('ɪsɪkə). *Bot.* [The native name in Guiana.] The name of a genus of S. American trees (N.O. *Burseraceæ*), of which *I. altissima* is the Cedar-wood and *I. heptaphylla* the Incense-wood of Guiana. **icica resin**, a fragrant resin obtained from the Incense-wood; hence **'icican**, also **'icacin**, a crystalline resin, obtained from this.

1865–72 WATTS *Dict. Chem.* III. 242 Another crystalline resin, icican, which has the same melting-point as brean. **1890** MUIR & MORLEY *Watts' Dict. Chem.* II. 746 Icacin is the crystalline resin of conima or Incense resin.

icicle ('aɪsɪk(ə)l). Forms: α. (1 **ises ȝicel**), 4 **ysse-ikkle, ysekele, isechele, isykle,** 5 **iseȝekille, izekelle, hyse-hykylle,** 6 **yse-yckel, ice-ickel,** 6–7 **ysicle, isikle, isicle,** 7 **ycicle, icikle, isickle, iceycle, -icle,** 7–8 **isecle,** 8– **icicle.** β. 6–7 **ice-sickle,** 7 **-sicle, -sickel, -seekel.** γ. 4 **ise-yokel**; *Sc.* and *dial.* 6 **isch(e-, yse-, ice-schokkill** (*pl.* **-schoklis**), 7 **ice-shokle,** 8 **-shogle,** 9 **-shockle, -shoggle, -shoglin, -shog, -shackle.** [OE. type **ís-ȝicel* (for which is actually found *íses ȝicel*), f. *ís* ICE + *ȝicel* ICKLE *sb.*; corresp. to MLG. *îs-jokel* (LG. *îs-jukel, -jäkel, -oekel*, EFris. *isjökel*), Da. *isjokkel*, dial. *iisegle* (but the usual Da. word is *istap*), Norw. *isjukel*. In English the second element has retained an independent stress only in some corrupt dialect forms; but the word was app. sometimes pronounced as a compound in the 17th c. Of the dialect γ-forms, the ME. *ise-yokel* corresponds to several continental forms with *jokel* instead of *ickle*; perhaps the *ice-schokle, isch-schokle* forms are to be referred to an earlier *isch-yokel* type. Thence arose further corruptions, *ice-shackle, -shoggle*, etc., and the second element came to be a separate word in Sc.; see SHOCKLE, SHOGGLE.]

1. A pendent ice-formation resembling a rod tapering downward to a point, produced by the freezing of successive drops of water falling or trickling from the point of attachment, as from the eaves of a house or other overhanging point.

α. *c* **1000** ÆLFRIC *Gloss.* in Wr.-Wülcker 117/14 *Stiria, stillicidia*, ises ȝicel. **13..** *Gaw. & Gr. Knt.* 732 Claterande fro the crest þe colde borne rennez & henged heȝe ouer his hede in hard ysse-ikkles. **1377** LANGL. *P. Pl.* B. XVII. 227 Ysekeles [*v.r.* iseyokels, *C.* isykles, isecheles] in eueses þorw hete of þe sonne Melteth in a mynut while to myst & to watre. **1483** *Cath. Angl.* 198/2 An Izekelle (*A.* Iseȝekille), *stirium, stiricus*. **1579** SPENSER *Sheph. Cal.* Jan. 36 Whose drops in drery ysicles remaine. **1624** CAPT. SMITH *Virginia* III. ii. 49 The boughs of a great tree loaded with Isickles. **1712** W. ROGERS *Voy.* 348 Pieces of Stone, resembling Salt, which congeal like Icecles, as the Water drops from the Rock. **1860** TYNDALL *Glac.* I. ii. 21 Eaves of snow, from which long icicles depended. **1887** R. BUCHANAN *Heir of Linne* vii, The girl was cold as an icicle.

β. **1514** BARCLAY *Cyt. & Uplondyshm.* (Percy Soc.) 3 The longe yse sycles at the hewsys honge. **1598** FLORIO, *Ghiacciuoli*, ise-sickles, dropping ises. **1605** TIMME *Quersit.* III. 155 Congealed..into ise-sickels. **1632** SHERWOOD, Ice-seekles, *gouttes gelees*. **1680** *Answ. Stillingfleet's Serm.* 28 We see what Icesicles are hanging on the Eves of the Parliament House at this Motion.

γ. **1377** [see α]. *c* **1480** HENRYSON *Test. Cres.* (1593) 160 The ice-schoklis that fra his hair doun hang Was wonder greit, and as ane speir als lang. **1513** DOUGLAS *Æneis* VII. Prol. 62 Gret isch schoklis lang as ony spere. **1630** DRUMM. OF HAWTH. *Poems, Shadow of Judgem.*, A mountain lifteth up his crested head: His locks are ice-shockles, his brows are snow. **1721** RAMSAY *I'll never leave thee* v, Bid iceshogles hammer red Gauds on the studdy. **1805** J. NICOL *Poems* II. 158 (Jam.) But wi' poortith, hearts het as a cinder Will cald as an ice-shogle turn. **1825** BROCKETT, *Ice-shoggle*, an icicle. **1828** *Craven Dial.*, *Ice-shackles*. **1855** ROBINSON *Whitby Gloss.*, *Ice Shoglins* or *Ickles*.

fig. **1812** *Let.* 2 June in *Daily News* (1898) 22 Jan. 6/1, I hope you don't make yourself unhappy about her. She is really an icicle. **1822** BYRON *Werner* II. ii. 240 Must I turn an icicle?

2. *transf.* A formation resembling an icicle; *esp.* **a.** a stalactite.

1644 DIGBY *Nat. Bodies* xxv. (1645) 285 Allom falleth down in lumps, Saltpeter in long icicles. **1695** WOODWARD *Nat. Hist. Earth* (1702) 177 The Sparry Striæ, or Iceycles called Stalactitæ: the Native Saline Iceycles, or Sal Stalacticum. **1792** *Massachusetts Mag.* Nov., Some of these stony isicles have at length reached the bottom of the cave.

b. A needle-shaped or acicular crystal.

1704 J. HARRIS *Lex. Techn.*, *Snow*..is an infinite Mass of Icicles regularly figured. *Ibid.*, The several Points of each Starry Icicle of Snow. *Ibid.*, The Icicles of Urine. **1715** *Pancirollus' Rerum Mem.* II. vi. 300 Iuices are mostly concreted into Globules or Icicles. **1737** BRACKEN *Farriery Impr.* (1757) II. 242 The Icicles of Nitre, if I may so call them.

c. In *Heraldry*: see quot.

1830 ROBSON *Brit. Herald* Gloss., *Icicles*, depicted in shape as guttées, but reversed; some authors call them clubs.

3. *Comb.*, as ***icicle-like*** adj.

1849–52 TODD *Cycl. Anat.* IV. 1189/1 Descending..in icicle-like projections.

icicled ('aɪsɪk(ə)ld), *a.* [f. prec. + -ED².] Overhung with icicles; also, †frozen, congealed.

a **1640** DAY *Parl. Bees* ix, My bloud's not boyl'd with fevers, nor..Is't isicled with cramps, or dropsie cold. **1652** BENLOWES *Theoph.* XIII. liii, When quivering winters dress Is icicled with hoary tresse. **1806** E. RUSHTON *Poems* 29 The thrush from the icicl'd bough, Gives his song to the winterly gale. **1831** PALGRAVE *Vis. Eng.*, *Sir H. Willoughby* vii, Giant beards of icicled cascade.

icily ('aɪsɪlɪ), *adv.* [f. ICY *a.* + -LY².] In an icy manner; coldly, freezingly. Also *fig.*

1848 E. BRONTË *Wuthering Heights* (1858) 4, I..shrunk icily into myself, like a snail. **1866** MRS. GASKELL *Wives & Dau.* I. 292 A tone which he meant to be icily indifferent. **1878** BOSW. SMITH *Carthage* 220 The wind blew icily cold.

iciness ('aɪsɪnɪs). [f. ICY + -NESS.] The quality of being icy; extreme coldness. Chiefly *fig.*

1579 TWYNE *Phisicke agst. Fort.* I. xxvii. 36 a, A colde ycinesse of sorowe and repentaunce. *a* **1652** J. SMITH *Sel. Disc.* vii. 372 Love..enough to thaw all the icyness of men's hearts which self-love had quite frozen up. **1814** BYRON *Lara* I. xxviii, O'er his brow the dampening heart-drops threw The sickening iciness of that cold dew. **1883** *Contemp. Rev.* Aug. 238 A most distressing and depressing iciness of tone and manner.

icing ('aɪsɪŋ), *vbl. sb.* [f. ICE *v.* + -ING¹.]

1. The process of encrusting or adorning with crystallizations of sugar; *concr.* an incrustation of white or coloured sugar applied in various ways to the surface of cakes, pastry, etc. Also *fig.* in phr. ***the icing on the cake***, the 'trimmings'.

1769 MRS. RAFFALD *Eng. Housekpr.* (1778) 144 Tarts that are iced require a slow oven, or the icing will be brown. **1774** WARTON *Hist. Eng. Poetry* lxi. (1840) III. 396 The splendid iceing of an immense historic plum-cake. **1845** ELIZA ACTON *Mod. Cookery* xvi. (ed. 2) 335 When a whiter icing is preferred, the pastry must be drawn from the oven..and brushed with white of egg..then well covered with sifted sugar. **1969** *Listener* 3 Apr. 468/3 All this theology is icing on the cake... '*Pas sérieuse*'..is an epithet I would apply to the whole book. **1970** *Globe & Mail* (Toronto) 26 Sept. 12/1 The missionaries have a dubious legacy, says Father Gallagher. 'We had been giving them the icing and not the cake, the Christian tools with which they need to meet the circumstances in life they face.' **1973** R. PERRY *Nowhere Man* v. 100 It was quite a neat ploy, the icing on the cake.

2. a. The process of cooling by means of ice. **1837** M. DONOVAN *Dom. Econ.* II. 378 Some kinds of bad port wine are improved by icing. **1864** SALA in *Daily Tel.* 20 July, Champagne—which, for all its deceptive iceing, is a very heating wine.

b. Preservation by means of ice; refrigeration with ice.

1883 R. F. WALSH *Irish Fisheries* (Fish. Exhib. Publ.) 17 A rate for fish carrying is then struck; this includes icing.

3. *Naut.* and *Aeronaut.* esp. with *up* (occas. *down*). The process of becoming covered with ice; the formation of ice on a vessel or an aircraft.

1881 tr. *Nordenskiöld's Voy. of 'Vega'* I. ix. 451 It is such a mist that causes the icing down of the rigging of vessels.. the tackling of the Vega was covered with pieces of ice so large, and layers so thick, that accidents might have happened by the falling of the ice on the deck. **1929** R. DUNCAN *Air Navigation & Meteorol.* (ed. 3) xii. 124 What goes on during the action known as icing-up, or the accumulating of ice-coats on the plane's surfaces. **1937** *Evening News* 29 Jan. 8/3 The latest theory connects the very fine rain with one of the most dangerous phenomena in flying: icing-up of the wings. **1945** *Tee Emm* (Air Ministry) V. 48 Icing-up caused him to lose control of the aircraft. *Ibid.* 53 Icing may occur, which requires hot air and.. reduces available engine power. **1955** *Times* 12 Aug. 5/1 The Hull Trawler Officers' Guild are meeting soon to discuss the icing up of trawlers, and it is expected that they will make recommendations to the trawler owners. **1957** *Economist* 21 Sept. 965/1 This warns pilots to fly no higher than 16,000 feet whenever they meet conditions likely to bring on the Britannia's particular form of icing trouble. **1958** 'N. SHUTE' *Rainbow & Rose* viii. 295 There was no icing on the aircraft. **1966** T. ARMSTRONG et al. *Illustr. Gloss. Snow & Ice* 27 *Icing*, the accumulation of a deposit of ice on exposed objects, e.g. aircraft, ships, aerials, instruments. Icing may be produced by the deposition of water vapour or by the freezing on impact of droplets in the air.

4. *icing sugar*: finely powered sugar.

1889 A. B. MARSHALL *Cookery Bk.* iii. 41 *Royal Icing.*—To two and a half pounds of icing sugar put seven or eight whites of fresh eggs and half a tablespoonful of lemon juice strained. **1896** J. T. LAW *Grocer's Manual* 232/1 Icing sugar is that [sugar] which is ground to a very fine, impalpable powder, resembling flour, and should consist of pure cane sugar; for beet sugar.. is not capable of high crystallisation. **1907** *Yesterday's Shopping* (1969) 42 Sugars... Loaf.. Granulated.. Icing. *c* **1938** *Fortnum & Mason Price List* 58/2 Icing sugar.. per tin 1/2. **1970** SIMON & HOWE *Dict. Gastron.* 365/1 Icing sugar.. is used to make icing.. and meringues. **1972** J. WILSON *Hide & Seek* i. 19 Where's the icing sugar?.. There's only the gran and castor there.

icinge: see YISSING.

icing-glass, obs. form of ISINGLASS.

-icity (ˈɪsɪtɪ), a compound suffix, a. F. *-icité*, ad. L. *-icitāt-em* (nom. *-icitās*), formed by the addition of the suffix *-tāt-* (see -TY) to adj. stems in *-ic(i)*, as *rusticitās*, *lubricitās*, f. *rustic-us*, *lubric-us*. On the analogy of these (perh. also influenced by sbs. like *simplicitās*, *felicitās* from *simplex*, *felix*), abstract sbs. in *-icité* in Fr. and *-icity* in Eng. are formed freely upon adjs. of any origin in *-ic*: e.g. *apostolicity*, *atomicity*, *authenticity*, *catholicity*, *domesticity*, *eccentricity*, *elasticity*, *electricity*, *publicity*.

icker (ˈɪkər). *Sc.* Forms: 6 echer, -ir, 8- icker. [The Sc. form of EAR *sb.*²; repr. the ONorthumb. form *eher*, *æhher*.] An ear of corn.

1513 DOUGLAS *Æneis* VII. xiii. 35 Or how feill echirris [*ed.* **1553** echeris] of corn thik growing.. dois hing On Hermy feildis. **1785** BURNS *To a Mouse* iii, A daimen icker in a thrave 'S a sma' request.

ickle (ˈɪk(ə)l), *sb. Obs.* exc. *dial.* Forms: α. 1 ȝecilæ, -e, ȝicel, 4 ychele, 5 ikyl, iekyll, 7 icle, 8 iccle, 6- ickle. β. 5 yokle. See also ICICLE. [OE. *ȝiecel (ȝicel, ȝycel), ȝecilæ, cognate with ON. *jǫkull* icicle, ice, glacier (mod.Icel. *jökull* glacier, Norw. dial. *jukel*, *jukul*, *jøkul* icicle):—OTeut. types **jekulo-z*, **jikilo-z*, f. OTeut. **jekon-*, in ON. *jaki* piece of ice: cf. OIr. *aig* ice.] = ICICLE. Also *transf.*

a **700** *Epinal Gloss.* 954 *Stiria*, ȝecilae [*Erfurt* ȝecile]. *a* **1000** (tr. *Bæda*) *Be Domes Dæge* 191 Se þrece ȝicela [WULFSTAN *Hom.* xxix. (Napier 138) ȝycela] swiðe hat and ceald. *c* **1000** [see ICICLE 1]. *c* **1325** *Gloss. W. de Biblesw.* in Wright *Voc.* 161 *Un esclarcyl*, an ychele. *c* **1440** *Promp. Parv.* 259/1 Ikyl (*W.* ickyll), *stiria*. **1500** *Ortus Voc.*, *Stiria*.. a ȝokyll. **1570** LEVINS *Manip.* 125/6 Ickles, *stiriæ*. **1676** HODGSON in *Phil. Trans.* XI. 766 From the roof of which hang large lumps of petrified water, like Icles,.. these icles are good Limestone. *a* **1687** COTTON *Joys of Marriage* 14 Be she constant, be she fickle, Be she fire, or be she ickle. **1828** *Craven Dial.*, *Ickles*, isicles; *water ickles*, stalactites. **1868** ATKINSON *Cleveland Gloss.*, *Ickles*, icicles.

ickle (ˈɪk(ə)l), *a.* A hypocoristic form of LITTLE *a.*: in childish use. Also **'ickly.**

1846 DICKENS *Dombey* (1848) i. 5, I came down from seeing dear Fanny, and that tiddy ickle sing. **1905** E. M. FORSTER *Where Angels fear to Tread* viii. 278 Good ickle quiet boysey, then. **1906** E. DYSON *Fact'ry 'Ands* xiv. 184 Oo's mummy's ickle sly-boots, oo is—*oo is*! Baby's a baddy baddy 'icky bubb-bubb. **1936** 'G. ORWELL' *Keep Aspidistra Flying* i. 26 A Peke, the ickle angel pet, wiv his gweat big Soulful eyes and his ickle black nosie—oh so ducky-duck! **1937** R. MACAULAY *I would be Private* I. i. 19 Was it a nice ickly boy, then? **1968** 'P. HOBSON' *Titty's Dead* xi. 121 She changed her role. Now she was Daddy's ickle girl.

ickle, ickwell: see HICKWALL.

icky, ikky (ˈɪkɪ), *a.* and *sb. colloq.* [Origin uncertain.] **A.** *adj.* **a.** *Jazz.* Ignorant (of true swinging jazz and liking the 'sweet' kind). *U.S.* **b.** Sweet, sickly, sentimental; hence a general term of disapproval: nasty, repulsive, sticky, etc.; also, ill, sick.

1935 *Vanity Fair* (N.Y.) Nov. 71/2 If the straight music is also oversweet, the term *icky* (a pseudo-baby-patter word, meaning 'little') is frequently employed to denote this. **1938** D. BAKER *Young Man with Horn* IV. vii. 277 Smoke Jordan tried hard to get him to.. maybe take a vacation, Florida's nice. 'Get yourself wheeled up and down like an icky banker?' **1939** JOYCE *Finnegans Wake* 555 His wrinkly waste of methylated spirits.. and pulverised rhubarbarorum, icky. **1942** D. POWELL *Time to be Born* (1943) x. 229 'A pet-shop on the first floor? But Miss Haven! Really!' gasped Miss Finkelstein. 'How *icky*!' **1945** L. SHELLY *Jive Talk Dict.* 26/2 *Icky vicki*, stupid gal. **1952** S. KAUFFMANN *Philanderer* (1953) 13 'It's just that—oh, I don't know—now everything's so icky.'.. Another of her dubious charms. The high-school words. **1959** S. BELLOW *Henderson Rain King* xiv. 200 Under the thickened rain clouds, a heated, darkened breeze sprang up.. choky, sultry, icky. **1964** C. CHAPLIN *Autobiogr.* xxi. 352 He must hide his blindness... His stumblings and bumpings into things make the little girl laugh joyously. But that was too 'icky'. **1964** *Harper's Bazaar* Nov. 110/2 Roast chestnuts or icky home-made fudge. **1967** H. HUNTER *Case for Punishment* vi. 108 She wears the most *fright*-ful cardigans. Always some sort of *ikky* colour—to go with everything, I suppose. **1968** J. HUDSON *Case of Need* IV. iii. 239 I'm not hungry... The food tastes icky. **1970** *New Yorker* 28 Nov. 122/2 We pick out the icky things in men and call them male, and then we say that the woman who has them.. we say she's a male-identifier. **1972** R. QUILTY *Tenth Session* 21 A group of ton-up boys dipped their icky fingers in the sugar bowls. **1972** M. WOODHOUSE *Mama Doll* ix. 117, *I* showed *him*.. lots of gore, you know, and he went all green and icky and dashed off.

B. *sb.* **1.** A person who is ignorant of true swinging jazz and likes the 'sweet' kind. *U.S.*

1937 *Amer. Speech* XII. 180 Musicians unable to swing, and who therefore can only play corn are called 'long hairs' and those who enjoy listening to their music are 'Ickies'. This term implies definite bovine qualities. **1938** *Better English* Nov. 51/2 *Icky*, one who is not hip but thinks he is. **1939** *Words* Oct. 108/1 *Ickies*.. are hicks who'll never be able to tell a sweet from a swing arrangement. **1955** L. FEATHER *Encycl. Jazz* x. 346 *Icky* (*Obsolete*), person with poor musical taste.

2. Something which is sickly, disagreeable; sickness.

1969 D. FRANCIS *Enquiry* vii. 88 Poppy's got the morning ickies again. I'll be glad when this lousy pregnancy's over.

Also in extended (and possibly unconnected) expressions, as **icky-boo** *a.*, ill (in quot. 1970² written *icky-poo*); **ickylickysticky** *a.* (nonce-wd.), unpleasantly sticky.

1920 'SAPPER' *Bull-Dog Drummond* ix. 234 Can it be that my little pet is feeling icky-boo? Face going green—slight perspiration—colour tight. **1922** JOYCE *Ulysses* 570 They blow ickylickysticky yumyum kisses. **1930** 'SAPPER' *Finger of Fate* 188 The jolly old tum-tum is not icky-boo or anything like that. **1970** 'B. MATHER' *Break in Line* v. 57 Call the airline office.. and tell 'em you're feeling an icksy bit icky-boo and want a stopover. **1970** *New Yorker* 14 Nov. 55 (*caption*) If any.. engine conkouts, or fires make you feel icky-poo, you just come and tell.

i-clad, var. of YCLAD *ppl. a.*, clad.

i-clensid, -clansid, ME. pa. pple. of CLEANSE.

i-cleped, i-cliped, etc., ME. pa. pple. of CLEPE *v.*: see YCLEPT.

i-closed, ME. pa. pple. of CLOSE *v.*

i-clothed, ME. pa. pple. of CLOTHE *v.*

i-clumben, ME. pa. pple. of CLIMB *v.*

i-clunge(n, ME. pa. pple. of CLING *v.*

i-clypt, -clupt, ME. pa. pple. of CLIP *v.*¹

i-cnawen, i-cnowen, ME. pa. pple. of KNOW *v.*; see also YKNOW.

i-cnouleche: see KNOWLEDGE *v.*

i-cnut, ME. pa. pple. of KNIT *v.*

i-cnutte: see I-KNIT *v.*

†**icod** (ɪˈkɒd), *int. Obs.* [A variant of ECOD, in origin the same as EGAD, AGAD.] An asseveration.

1697 VANBRUGH *Relapse* IV. i, I'cod, I don't care how often I'm married. **1749** FIELDING *Tom Jones* XVIII. viii, 'Icod! I shall lose two or three thousand pounds. **1790** *Bystander* 343 Icod, Sir, the back stairs has conveyed him to the cellar.

i-come(n, ME. pa. pple. of COME *v.*

icon (ˈaɪkɒn, ˈaɪkən). Also **ikon, eikon.** [a. late L. *īcōn* (Pliny), ad. Gr. εἰκών, εἰκον- likeness, image, portrait, semblance, similitude, simile, f. *εἴκ-ειν to be like.]

†**1. a.** An image, figure, or representation; a portrait; a picture, 'cut', or illustration in a book; esp. applied to the 'figures' of animals, plants, etc. in books of Natural History. *Obs.*

1572 BOSSEWELL *Armorie* III. 23 b, The Icon, or forme of the same birde, I haue caused thus to bee figured. **1611** SPEED *Hist. Gt. Brit.* V. vii. §2. 38 The two first ensuing Icones or Portraitures. **1646** SIR T. BROWNE *Pseud. Ep.* V. xvii. 258 He is set forth in the Icons or Cuts of Martyrs by Cevallerius. **1710** SALMON (*title*) Botanologia.. beautifully adorned with exquisite Icons or Figures of the most considerable Species. **1727** SWITZER *Pract. Gardiner* III. xxvii. 143 The same that the Herbals have left both the icons and description of.

b. An image in the solid; a monumental figure; a statue.

1577–87 HOLINSHED *Chron.* (1807–8) II. 147 The pope ment, by causing such ikons to be erected, to prefer Thomas as a perpetual saint to all posterities. **1638** SIR T. HERBERT *Trav.* (ed. 2) 225 Returne him in pure gold the Icon of an Elephant, Cammell, or Dromedary. **1885** *Athenæum* 4 Apr. 445 Otto of Brunswick in Hildesheim Church.. whose monumental icon is figured here. *Ibid.*, The monumental statues of Queen Eleanor of Castile wear the wimple exactly as this icon of Ingeborg wears it.

c. *Computing.* A small symbolic picture of a physical object on a VDU screen, esp. one that represents a particular option and can be selected to exercise that option.

1982 *Computerworld* 29 Sept. 70/2 Star's screen displays black characters on a white background. These are known as icons on the Star and are equivalent to the familiar physical object in an office. **1984** *Austral. Micro Computerworld* Feb. 13/2 The PCjr is menu-driven, using icons to identify the programs available. **1984** *Sounds* 1 Dec. 60/4 Once loaded, the program reveals its basic areas and functions. These are set out on the Control Screen as 'icons', or symbols that correspond to the five.. musical activities that the program will tackle. **1985** *Sci. Amer.* Sept. 13/2 Unfortunately bitblt in this form cannot use the solid crab icon produced by the pencil exercise described above.

2. *Eastern Church.* A representation of some sacred personage, in painting, bas-relief, or mosaic, itself regarded as sacred, and honoured with a relative worship or adoration.

1833 R. PINKERTON *Russia* 227 Behind them were carried .. six censers, and six sacred ikons. **1864** W. T. GREIVE *Servia* in *Vac. Tour.* 428 It is beneath the icon of the Blessed Virgin that women kneel during the office of Churching. **1877** D. M. WALLACE *Russia* iv. 98 Icons are pictorial half-length representations of the Saviour, of the Madonna, or of a saint, executed in archaic Byzantine style, on a yellow or gold ground... Very often the whole picture with the exception of the face and hands of the figure is covered with a metal *plaque* embossed so as to represent the form of the figure and the drapery. **1879** H. S. EDWARDS *Russians at Home* I. 90 The believer is expressly cautioned against such an abuse of the holy eikons.

†**3. a.** *Rhet.* A simile. *Obs.*

1589 PUTTENHAM *Eng. Poesie* III. xix. (Arb.) 250 Icon or Resemblance by imagerie. **1620** GRANGER *Div. Logike* 148 Metaphores are contracted similitudes. To which if the note be added, it is called Icon. **1676** HOBBES *Iliad* To Rdr., The perfection and curiosity of descriptions, which the ancient writers of eloquence call icones, that is images.

b. *Philos.* (See quot. 1934.) Also *transf.*

a **1914** C. S. PEIRCE *Coll. Papers* (1931) I. III. iii. 195 It has been found that there are three kinds of signs which are all indispensable in all reasoning; the first is the diagrammatic sign or *icon*, which exhibits a similarity or analogy to the subject of discourse. *Ibid.* 196 There may be a mere relation of reason between the sign and the thing signified; in that case, the sign is an *icon*. **1934** *Mind* XLIII. 497 An *icon* is a sign which represents its object by virtue of having some character in common with the object: the colour of a colour-card as representing the colour of the object which it resembles is an icon, and a map as representing spatial relations is an icon. **1949** *Poetry* (Chicago) Jan. 234 *Icons*, images, which are the aesthetic signs of the poem, analogous to the symbolic signs of scientific discourses; they have, as signs, semantic objects, or refer to objects, and, in addition, as iconic signs, resemble those objects. **1954** W. K. WIMSATT *Verbal Icon* (1967) p. x, The term *icon* is used today by semeiotic writers to refer to a verbal sign which *somehow* shares the properties of, or resembles, the objects which it denotes.

4. A realistic representation or description in writing. Now *rare* or *Obs.*

1579 E. K. *Gloss. Spenser's Sheph. Cal.* Feb. 102 This tale of the Oake and the Brere.. is very excellente for pleasaunt descriptions, being altogether a certaine Icon or Hypotyposis of disdainfull younkers. **1852** *Tait's Mag.* XIX. 592 A good book is a perfect icon, a faithful picture and representation of nature and human life.

5. *Comb.* **icon-stand** = ICONOSTASIS, q.v.

†**ˌiconantiˈdyptic**, *a. Obs.* [f. Gr. εἰκών ICON + ἀντί opposite to + δύπτ-ειν to dive, duck + -IC.] Applied to a kind of telescope (see quot.): cf. DIPLANTIDIAN.

1778 *Phil. Trans.* LXIX. 130 This Telescope is called the Iconantidiptic Heliometer, because it produces two images of the objects, the one in a direct position, and the other reversed.

i-confermed, ME. pa. pple. of CONFIRM.

Iconian (aɪˈkəʊnɪən), *a.* and *sb.* [-AN.] **A.** *adj.* Of or pertaining to Iconium (mod. Konya), a town in southern Asia Minor where St. Paul preached, or to the church established there (Acts xiii. 5, xiv. 1–7). **B.** *sb.* A native or inhabitant of Iconium.

1899 W. M. RAMSAY in *Expositor* Aug. 112 There were strife and wrangling and jealousy between the Antiochean Church and the Iconian Church about precedence and comparative dignity. **1911** —— *First Christ. Cent.* xxv. 168 St. Paul addressed the Iconian audiences in Greek. *Ibid.* 171 The Iconians clung to their Phrygian character as opposed to the Lycaonian.

iconic (aɪ'kɒnɪk), *a.* Also eiconic. [ad. late L. *iconic-us*, ad. Gr. *εἰκονικ-ός*, f. *εἰκών* ICON.] **a.** Of or pertaining to an icon, image, figure, or representation; of the nature of a portrait; *spec.* in *Art*, applied to the ancient portrait statues of victorious athletes commonly dedicated to divinities, and hence to memorial statues and busts executed according to a fixed or conventional type.

1656 BLOUNT *Glossogr.*, *Iconic*, belonging to an Image, also lively pictured. **1801** FUSELI in *Lect. Paint.* iii. (1848) 415 Iconic figures in metal began, says Pliny, to be the ornaments of every municipal forum. **1850** LEITCH tr. *C.O. Müller's Anc. Art* (ed. 2) §123 *note*, An iconic statue of Lysander in marble at Delphi. **1881** E. W. GOSSE in *Fortn. Rev.* June 703 In iconic sculpture the Royal Academy presents nothing so considerable as Mr. Boehm's.. bust of Mr. Gladstone. **1882** *Athenæum* 29 Apr. 543/2 Several heads appeared to be eiconic.

b. Of or pertaining to an image used in worship.

1890 *Sat. Rev.* 20 Sept. 348/1 Apparatus of the iconic character required by Roman Catholic devotion.

c. *Semiotics.* Pertaining to or resembling an icon (sense 3 b). Also *transf.*

1939 C. W. MORRIS in *Kenyon Rev.* I. IV. 415 The aesthetic sign..is an iconic sign (an 'image') in that it embodies these values in some medium where they may be directly inspected (in short, the aesthetic sign is an iconic sign whose designatum is a value). **1949** [see ICON 3 b]. **1956** E. H. HUTTEN *Lang. Mod. Physics* ii. 15 Sometimes, the sign is similar to the thing it stands for, in the manner in which a picture represents, and we have iconic signs. **1964** T. W. MCRAE *Impact of Computers on Accounting* v. 132 There are many kinds of model. The one described above is an *iconic* model, that is a physical representation of the original item. **1965** C. H. SPRINGER et al. *Adv. Methods and Models* i. 6 He might use..an *iconic* model, which doesn't *act* like the real thing (as the analog model does) but only *looks* like it. **1966** M. PEI *Gloss. Ling. Terminol.* 118 *Iconic*, characterized by a symbolism which purports to present an image of the object described (Chinese pictographs). **1970** *English Studies* LI. 279 Non-roman notations are generally 'iconic', i.e. 'the symbols are not arbitrary signs, but in some way resemble what they stand for'. **1971** *Language* XLVII. 416 There is.. growing evidence that language contains many elements which are iconic—that is, imitative of non-linguistic reality.

iconical (aɪ'kɒnɪkəl), *a. rare.* [f. as prec. + -AL[1].] Pertaining to an icon, iconic. †In quot. 1652, of the nature of a simile (see ICON 3); †in quot. 1776, consisting, or of the nature of, pictures or pictorial illustrations (see ICON 1).

1652 URQUHART *Jewel* Wks. (1834) 292 Figurative expressions..whether paradigmatical, iconical, symbolical. **1776** DA COSTA *Elem. Conchol.* 36 (Jod.) The work is entirely iconical, or consists only of figures without any letterpress, catchword, alphabet, or number to the pages.

i'conically, *adv.* [f. ICONIC *a.*: see -ICALLY.] In an iconic manner.

1946 C. MORRIS *Signs, Lang. & Behavior* 193 Such conflict is presented iconically in the music itself. **1973** *Times Lit. Suppl.* 5 Oct. 1188/4 The rhythm..depicts the distance iconically, since the farther away the goal, the fewer cycles of the dance occur in a given period.

iconicity (aɪkə'nɪsɪtɪ). [f. ICONIC *a.* + -ITY.] The quality or fact of being iconic (in various senses).

1946 C. MORRIS *Signs, Lang. & Behavior* 191 Spoken language contains some sounds which are clearly iconic ('onomatopoeic'); the extent of its iconicity is a difficult matter to determine. **1971** *Language* XLVII. 425 In some cases, there is iconicity between language and a non-human communication system. **1972** *Sci. Amer.* Sept. 91/2 The only element of genuine representation (also called iconicity) in such a case is the actual shape of the geographical features, although even these are normalized according to given rules of transformation to allow a part of the globe to be shown on a flat map.

'iconism. [ad. late L. *īconismus*, a. Gr. *εἰκονισμός* delineation, f. *εἰκονίζειν* to ICONIZE (cf. Gr. *εἰκόνισμα* copy, image).] †**a.** A representation by some image or figure; imagery; metaphor. *Obs.* **b.** *Semiotics.* The quality or fact of being an icon or intentional sign.

1656 BLOUNT *Glossogr.*, *Iconism*, a true and lively description. **1662** EVELYN *Chalcogr.* v. Misc. Writ. (1805) 321 The annexed Iconisme is thus explained. **1678** CUDWORTH *Intell. Syst.* I. iii. §8. 155 These..in Aristotle's judgment, would be fit iconisms or representations of the Plastick Nature. **1680** H. MORE *Apocal. Apoc.* 47 A Book.. which consists of Representations Symbolical or Hieroglyphical, of Iconismes or Images of things future. **1971** *Language* XLVII. 417 Among homotherms—that is, warm-blooded vertebrates, such as birds and mammals—iconism is less salient. Yet it seems to be present, at least latently, in the 'intention movements' exhibited..by herring gulls who are about to take flight and who seem, by spreading their wings, not only to be preparing for flight themselves but also to be inviting neighboring gulls to fly with them.

So †**ico'nistical** *a.*, metaphorical, figurative. Hence †**ico'nistically** *adv.*, by a figure.

1684 H. MORE *Answer* 86 Blasphemy being an Iconisme of Idolatry, that sense is more probable for its being Iconistical; the Genius of the Apocalyptick style being such as to signifie Iconistically rather than plainly.

†**'iconize,** *v. Obs.* [ad. Gr. *εἰκονίζειν*, f. *εἰκών*, *εἰκον-* ICON.] *trans.* To form into an image; to figure, to represent.

1678 CUDWORTH *Intell. Syst.* I. iv. §36. 572 This world is an image always iconized, or perpetually renewed (as the image in a glass is) of that First, second and third Principle, which are always standing.

i-conned, -con'd, obs. pa. pple. of CON *v.*[1]

icono-, Gr. *εἰκονο-*, combining form of *εἰκών* ICON, as in **icono'duly** [see DULIA], the worship or veneration of images; so **iconodulic** (*-doulic*), (aɪkənəʊ'duːlɪk), *a.*; **icono'dule, icono'dulist,** a worshipper or server of images. **iconomania** (ˌaɪkənəʊ'meɪnɪə) [MANIA], (*a*) an infatuated devotion to images; (*b*) a mania for collecting icons or portraits. **iconophile** ('aɪkənəʊfaɪl), **iconophilist** (-'ɒfɪlɪst) [Gr. *φίλος* loving], a connoisseur of pictures, engravings, book illustrations, and the like; hence **ico'nophilism, -phily,** the taste for these objects. **icono'phobia,** hatred of images; also **'iconophobe, icono'phobic** *adjs.*, of or pertaining to one who hates images. **iconoplast** (aɪ'kɒnəplæst) [Gr. *-πλάστης* moulder: after *iconoclast*], a fashioner or maker of images.

1893 *Funk's Stand. Dict.*, **Iconodule, iconodulist*, one who serves images; an image-worshipper; iconolater. **1900** 'ODYSSEUS' *Turkey in Europe* 230 The division of Asia representing Iconoclasts and Europe Iconodules is almost without exception. **1901** E. GOSSE in *Daily Chron.* 22 Nov. 3/3 The sentiment of the author is vehemently on the side of the Iconodules. **1939** A. TOYNBEE *Study of Hist.* IV. 595 The indomitable Iconodule Patriarch Germanus found a worthy successor in the reigning Patriarch Nicephorus. **1967** H. CHADWICK *Early Church* xviii. 283 The iconodules replied: (*a*) we venerate not the icons but those whom they depict [etc.]. **1893** W. M. RAMSAY *Ch. in Rom. Emp.* xvii. 441 The *iconodoulic tendency was already beginning in the Orthodox Church. **1716** M. DAVIES *Athen. Brit.* II. 232 *Iconodoulists or Iconolaters, join'd also with the Monks and Fryars. **1882–3** SCHAFF *Encycl. Relig. Knowl.* II. 1063 Leo's successor, Michael II..again yielded to the iconodulists, and allowed image-worship in private. **1640** R. BAILLIE *Canterb. Self-Convict.* 55 All their practice heere is but *iconoduly, not idolatrie. **1722** J. COVEL *Acc. Grk. Ch.* 395, I must call it *Iconomania, perfect Madness for Image Worship. **1770** W. COLE in *J. Granger's Lett.* (1805) 332 The Icomania you talk of is very ripe at Cambridge, where we have many collectors. **1881** *Athenæum* 30 July 145/2 'Le graveur de 1488', as *iconophiles designate [Duplessis], possesses at least the merit..of being one of the first artists who in France made use of metal as a means of reproduction. **1888** *N.Y. Tribune* 12 Feb. (Cent.), He instructs his customers in biblomania,..in *iconophilism, in the knowledge of art. **1884** *Sat. Rev.* 29 Mar. 420/1 It would have been an advantage to the *iconophilist. **1894** *Athenæum* 16 June 780/1 We explain this extraordinary development of *iconophily by the peculiarities of Egyptian religious beliefs. **1958** *Times Lit. Suppl.* 23 May 278/3 Saxl himself believed that such an approach to history was natural, and indeed inevitable, in an age of illustrated papers and the film and television; but the English are notoriously *iconophobe, and it may still be necessary to insist on this point. **1926** H. READ *Eng. Stained Glass* ii. 16/1 Free from the *iconophobia which infested Southern Christianity, the Romanesque builders freely developed the art of sculpture. **1963** AUDEN *Dyer's Hand* 359 The *Mayflower* carried *iconophobic dissenters. **1898** L. A. TOLLEMACHE in *Literature* 8 Jan. 24/2 He [Pattison] could not..be a thorough iconoclast, and yet delude himself into thinking that he was (if I may coin such a word) an *iconoplast all the time.

iconoclasm (aɪ'kɒnəklæz(ə)m). [f. Gr. *εἰκών* ICON + *κλάσμα* breaking, f. *κλᾶν* to break: after next.]

The breaking or destroying of images; *esp.* the destruction of images and pictures set up as objects of veneration (see ICONOCLAST 1); *transf.* and *fig.* the attacking or overthrow of venerated institutions and cherished beliefs, regarded as fallacious or superstitious.

1797 W. TAYLOR in *Monthly Rev.* XXIV. 512 That vulgar iconoclasm which has estranged until this day the fine arts from every Protestant community. **1858** FROUDE *Hist. Eng.* xii. III. 73 The stormy eloquence of Pole, the iconoclasm of Latimer, the superstitions of the complaining clergy. **1874** GREEN *Short Hist.* viii. §4. 497 In Edward's time iconoclasm had dashed the stained glass from its windows. **1882** FARRAR *Early Chr.* II. 163 The iconoclasm of the Jew made such places detestable to him.

iconoclast (aɪ'kɒnəklæst), *sb.* (*a.*). [ad. late L. *īconoclastēs*, a. late Gr. *εἰκονοκλάστης*, f. *εἰκών* ICON + *-κλάστης* breaker. Cf. F. *iconoclaste* (17th c. in Hatz.-Darm.).]

1. A breaker or destroyer of images; *spec.* (*Eccl. Hist.*) one who took part in or supported the movement in the 8th and 9th centuries, to put down the use of images or pictures in religious worship in the Christian churches of the East; hence, applied analogously to those Protestants of the 16th and 17th centuries who practised or countenanced a similar destruction of images in the churches.

[**1596** DALRYMPLE tr. *Leslie's Hist. Scot.* v. 269 A counsel of thrie hunder and fiftie Bischopis haldne at Nice against the secte of Jmagebrekeris, thair name Jconoclastæ.] **1641** HINDE *J. Bruen* xxvi. 80 So did Pope Gregory the third excommunicate the Emperour Leo, and stamped the name of Iconoclast in his forehead, for breaking downe of Images in the Churches. **1654** JER. TAYLOR *Real Pres.* xii. §28. 315, I remember only one thing objected to this testimony of so many bishops, that they were Iconoclasts, or breakers of images, and therefore not to be trusted in any other article. **1782** PRIESTLEY *Corrupt. Chr.* I. IV. 385 This new heresy was called that of the Iconoclasts. **1814** SOUTHEY in *Q. Rev.* XII. 74 When idolaters turn iconoclasts, they act as if the outrageousness of the one excess were to efface or atone for the folly of the other. **1840** CARLYLE *Heroes* VI. (1858) 338 The Puritans..seem mere savage Iconoclasts, fierce destroyers of Forms; but it were more just to call them haters of *untrue* Forms. **1882** E. C. BABER in *R. Geog. Soc. Suppl. Papers* I. I. 35 The second..is the famous iconoclast who melted down all the bronze idols he could lay hold of.

2. *transf.* and *fig.* One who assails or attacks cherished beliefs or venerated institutions on the ground that they are erroneous or pernicious.

1842 MRS. BROWNING *Grk. Chr. Poets* (1863) 177 An iconoclast of their idol rhyme. **1866** J. MARTINEAU *Ess.* I. 77 Kant was the great iconoclast. **1874** H. R. REYNOLDS *John Bapt.* viii. 514 Respectable vices, which take shelter under the eaves of the Church, need nothing so much as the stern iconoclast.

3. *attrib.* or *adj.* Of or relating to iconoclasts; iconoclastic.

1685 H. MORE *Illustration* 298 His excommunicating the Iconoclast Emperours. **1781** GIBBON *Decl. & F.* (1809) VII. 13 *note*, St. John Damascenus was already a monk before the Iconoclast dispute. **1845** S. AUSTIN *Ranke's Hist. Ref.* II. 25 An iconoclast riot now commenced... The images were torn from the altars, chopped in pieces and burnt. **1847** LD. LINDSAY *Chr. Art* I. 108 The iconoclast reform took place, statues and bas-reliefs were banished from the churches of Greece.

iconoclastic (aɪkɒnəʊ'klæstɪk), *a.* [f. prec. + -IC.] Of or pertaining to iconoclasts or iconoclasm.

1640 R. BAILLIE *Canterb. Self-Convict.* 53 Iconoclasticke and iconomachian hereticks. **1703** MAUNDRELL *Journ. Jerus.* (1721) 15 In testimony of their Iconoclastick principle. **1855** MILMAN *Lat. Chr.* XIV. ix. (1864) IX. 309 The Iconoclastic Emperors found statues..to war upon. **1867** SMILES *Huguenots Eng.* iii. (1880) 50 In their iconoclastic rage they hewed and broke the images..of the cathedrals.

Hence **icono'clastically** *adv.*, after the fashion of iconoclasts. **icono'clasticism,** the principles or practice of iconoclasts; iconoclasm.

1865 *Morn. Star* 29 Apr., Iconoclastically to demolish all it had previously revered. **1885** L. OLIPHANT *Haifa* (1887) 301 Modern iconoclasticism and love of truth have..proved too strong for..unfounded tradition.

†**iconograph**[1] (aɪ'kɒnəgrɑːf, -æ-). *Obs. rare.* [ad. Gr. *εἰκονογράφος* portrait-painter, f. *εἰκών* ICON + *-γράφος* writer, painter.]

= ICONOGRAPHER.

1804 *Monthly Mag.* XVIII. 291 The Iconographs are those who have published the figures of monuments, but without a detailed explanation.

i'conograph[2]. [f. as prec. + *-γραφος* written, *γραφή* writing.] A drawing, engraving, or illustration for a book: = ICON 1.

1884 *Science* 4 July 28/2 The illustrations have never been surpassed by the most expensive and careful iconographs.

iconographer (aɪkə'nɒgrəfə(r)). [f. as next + -ER[1]: cf. Gr. *εἰκονογράφ-ος* (see ICONOGRAPH).] One who makes figures or drawings of objects.

1888 *Athenæum* 7 Jan. 19/1 The lepidopteral iconographer. **1892** *Ibid.* 27 Aug. 291/2 Those gorgeous species beloved by the iconographer and chromo-lithographist.

iconographic (aɪkɒnəʊ'græfɪk, ˌaɪkənəʊ-), *a.* Also **ikon-**. [f. ICONOGRAPHY, or its source + -IC: cf. F. *iconographique*.] Of or pertaining to iconography; representing or describing by pictures, drawings, or engravings; also, pertaining to symbolic representation (cf. ICONOLOGY 2).

1855 MAYNE *Expos. Lex.*, *Iconographic.* **1861** BERESF. HOPE *Eng. Cathedr. 19th C.* v. 181 Covering the walls and the cupolas of this vast building with a complete iconographic epopee from the pencil of Schraudolph. **1877** W. JONES *Finger-ring* 266 Six rings, gold and silver, of the iconographic type. **1879** SIR G. SCOTT *Lect. Archit.* I. 309 You must study the object and meaning of everything.. whether ritual, iconographic, artistic, or simply utilitarian.

So **icono'graphical** *a.* **icono'graphically** *adv.*

1865 WRIGHT *Hist. Caricat.* iii. 48 This kind of iconographical ornamentation had been encroaching..on the old architectural purity. **1880** *Nature* 12 Feb. 357/2 A magnificently illustrated 'Iconographical History of the Orchid'. **1958** *Times Lit. Suppl.* 12 Dec. 716/3 The book is a *tour de force* in iconographical method. **1959** *Times* 17 Jan. 9/1 Iconographically they [paintings] are of great interest in relation to the usages of the Eastern Church. **1962** *Daily Tel.* 20 Nov. 17/4 The space between is filled entirely by Nicolas Untersteller's superb, sparkling glass, dark red and blue in patterns that are both good abstracts and also tell an iconographical story. **1962** *Listener* 27 Dec. 1087/1 Parallel with the abundance and high quality of abstract art is a great deal of what one may call iconographical art. Let me remind you of a few names: Bacon, Balthus, Giacometti, Dubuffet, Asger Jorn, de Kooning.

ico'nographist. *rare.* [f. next + -IST.] One skilled in iconography.

1850 *Ecclesiologist* X. 100 Gérente..was an artist, and he was also an iconographist.

iconography (aɪkə'nɒgrəfɪ). [ad. med.L. *īconographia*, ad. Gr. εἰκονογραφία sketch, description (Strabo), f. εἰκών ICON + -γραφία writing, -GRAPHY. Cf. F. *iconographie* (1701 in Furetière).]

†**1.** *concr.* A pictorial representation, delineation; a drawing or plan. *Obs.*

1628 BURTON *Anat. Mel.* II. ii. IV. (ed. 3) 269 Those curious Iconographies of Temples and pallaces. **1678** PHILLIPS (ed. 4), *Iconography*..is the platform or model of a House.

2. The description or illustration of any subject by means of drawings or figures; any book or work in which this is done; also, the branch of knowledge which deals with the representation of persons or objects by any application of the arts of design. Also *transf.*

1678 PHILLIPS (ed. 4), *Iconography*, a Description by Cuts, etc. **1809** KENDALL *Trav.* III. lxxviii. 213 An elaborate monument of some transaction of which no other trace remains to elucidate this imperfect iconography. **1851** E. J. MILLINGTON tr. *Didron* (*title*) Christian Iconography; or, the History of Christian Art in the Middle Ages. **1874** MICKLETHWAITE *Mod. Par. Churches* 131 The iconography of the altar-canopy. **1883** *Pall Mall G.* 20 Sept. 4/2 Expensive large iconographies like Couch's, Yarrell's or Day's. **1939** E. PANOFSKY *Stud. Iconology* i. 3 Iconography is that branch of the history of art which concerns itself with the subject matter or meaning of works of art, as opposed to their form. **1957** *Times Lit. Suppl.* 8 Nov. 680/1 The iconography of the watermark is a new aspect of the study of the migration of symbols at present so popular among art historians. **1960** *Listener* 8 Dec. 1041/2 The fashion of so-called 'iconography' at this moment has produced many cumbersome interpretations. **1962** *Ibid.* 27 Sept. 473/2 The iconography of a work of art is its dramatic structure seen in terms of characters, situations, and images that are related to a specific religious, social, or historical context. **1969** *Ibid.* 17 Apr. 533/2 Now people are interested in iconography, in saying what the subject represents, and offering infinitely ingenious interpretations of every picture. **1970** *Oxf. Compan. Art* 555/1 *Iconography*, a term in art history.. extended in the 20th c. to cover the whole descriptive investigation of the subject matter of the figurative arts... Iconography..studies the development of the themes which artists use, for instance the transformation of the images of planets in astrological manuscripts, the rise of genre painting, the origins of still life, and the use of political satire.

iconolater (aɪkə'nɒlətə(r)). [f. Gr. εἰκών image, ICON, after *idolater*. Cf. F. *iconolâtre*.] A worshipper of images.

1654 VILVAIN *Theorem. Theol.* vi. 160 He animated Iconolaters in the East. **1722** J. COVEL *Acc. Grk. Ch.* 396 How can the Iconoclaters [*sic*] justify their praying to a Cross or Crucifix? **1844** LINGARD *Anglo-Sax. Ch.* (1858) II. 381 Evasive language adopted for the defence of iconolaters.

iconolatry (aɪkə'nɒlətrɪ). [f. as prec., after *idolatry*, or ad. eccl. Gr. εἰκονολατρεία. Cf. F. *iconolâtrie* (Littré).] The worship of images.

1624 F. WHITE *Repl. Fisher* 270 Simon Maiolus, a most eagre defender of Iconolatrie. **1635** PAGITT *Christianogr.* II. vii. (1636) 66 Idolatrie and Iconolatrie, that is, Image worship. **1722** J. COVEL *Acc. Grk. Ch.* 400 The School-men and Patrons of Iconolatry. **1884** *Ch. Q. Rev.* July 451 Equally removed from the iconoclasm of 754 and the iconolatry of 787.

iconology (aɪkə'nɒlədʒɪ). [mod. f. Gr. εἰκών, εἰκονο- image: see -LOGY. Cf. Gr. εἰκονολογία figurative speaking, whence It. *iconologia* (1611 Cæsare Ripa), F. *iconologie* (1636 Baudouin), in titles of collections of pieces of rhetorical imagery (cf. quot. 1777); but this is distinct from the extant use.]

1. That branch of knowledge which deals with the subject of icons (in any sense of the word); also the subject-matter of this study, icons collectively, or as objects of investigation, etc.

1730–6 BAILEY (folio), *Iconology*, interpretation of ancient Images, Monuments, and Emblems. [**1777** G. RICHARDSON (*title*) Iconology; or, a Collection of emblematical Figures, moral and instructive, with Explanations from classical Authorities.] **1808** SIR R. PORTER *Trav. Sk. Russ. & Swed.* (1813) I. vi. 48 Professors of..mythology, and iconology. **1851** SIR C. EASTLAKE tr. *Kugler's Sch. Paint. Italy* I. I. 6 The violent aversion entertained by the Christians for the Iconology of Heathendom kept, as was natural, equal pace. **1939** M. PRAZ *Stud. 17th-Cent. Imagery* I. iv. 184 Iconology during the period of enlightenment in philosophy and in literature, takes the place held by emblematics during the age of the Jesuits and the Baroque. **1949** WELLEK & WARREN *Theory of Lit.* xi. 125 The conceptual and symbolic meanings of works of art ('Iconology'). **1956** E. PANOFSKY *Meaning in Visual Arts* 31 The discovery and interpretation of these 'symbolical' values (which are often unknown to the artist himself and may even emphatically differ from what he consciously intended to express) is the object of what we may call 'iconology' as opposed to 'iconography'. **1958** *Times Lit. Suppl.* 23 May 278/3 If the Institute were not called after its founder, *tout court*, and had to find a compendious title to describe its activities, it might surely best be called an Institute of Iconology, as being a body dedicated to the study and interpretation of historical processes through visual images.

2. Symbolical representation; symbolism.

1849 J. R. JACKSON *Lett. Minerals* 225 In the language of Iconology, the Diamond is the symbol of constancy, of strength, of innocence, and other heroic virtues. **1862** *Ecclesiologist* XXIII. 58 The iconology of these decorations is as follows:—Over the chancel arch is the Doom [etc.].

Hence **icono'logical** *a.*, of or relating to iconology. **ico'nologist**, one versed in iconology.

1851 E. J. MILLINGTON tr. *Didron's Chr. Iconogr.* I. 369 Jesus, to an Iconologist, is present in the cross as well as in the lamb, or the lion. **1854** *Ecclesiologist* XV. 25 This great iconological work. **1938** E. PANOFSKY in *Jrnl. Warburg Inst.* I. 23 From the purely iconological point of view the Ottawa picture may be compared to the two Cassone panels. **1958** *Times Lit. Suppl.* 23 May 278/3 On the contrary, the uniquely valuable and fruitful idea embodied in the Warburgian programme is the iconological idea; it is of universal application, and thus of service to all the special historical disciplines mentioned.

†**i'conomach.** *Obs. rare.* [ad. eccl. L. *iconomach-us*, a. eccl. Gr. εἰκονομάχος, f. εἰκών ICON + -μάχος fighting.] One who is hostile to images.

c **1552** PHILPOT *Exam. & Writ.* (Parker Soc.) 407 They were named Iconomaches, that is overthrowers of images.

†**ico'nomachal,** *a. Obs. rare.* Erron. **-mical.** [f. as prec. + -AL¹.] Hostile to images.

1646 SIR T. BROWNE *Pseud. Ep.* v. xxi. 269 We should be too Iconomicall to question the pictures of the winds, as commonly drawne in humane heads, and with their cheeks distended. [**1656** BLOUNT *Glossogr.*, *Iconomical*, belonging to Images, or after the manner of Images.]

iconomachy (aɪkə'nɒməkɪ). [ad. eccl. L. *iconomachia*, a. eccl. Gr. εἰκονομαχία, f. εἰκών ICON + -μαχία fighting.] A war against images; hostility or opposition to images, esp. to their use in connexion with worship.

1581 E. CAMPION in *Confer.* III. (1584) P, That of Constantinople, was not a generall nor lawfull Councill, but a certaine Iconomachy. **1650** R. STAPYLTON *Strada's Low C. Warres* v. 123 *margin*, A new Iconomachy at Antwerp. **1855** MOTLEY *Dutch Rep.* II. vii. I. 569 The celebrated iconomachy of the Netherlands. *Ibid.* VI. i. III. 383 Nothing more excited the indignation of the Prince of Orange than such senseless iconomachy.

Hence †**icono'machian,** †**icono'machical** *adjs.*, practising or advocating iconomachy. **ico'nomachist**, one who contends against the cultus of images.

a **1638** MEDE *Apost. Latter Times* xvii. Wks. III. 674 The Iconomachical Council of Constantinople. **1640** Iconomachian [see ICONOCLASTIC]. **1875** J. C. ROBERTSON *Hist. Chr. Ch.* III. 137 An anathema was pronounced against all opponents of images..with curses against iconomachists and heretics of every kind.

iconomatic (aɪkɒnə'mætɪk), *a.* Also **ikon-**. [contr. for *icononomatic*, f. Gr. εἰκών, εἰκονο- ICON + ὄνομα, ὀνοματ- name + -IC.] A word proposed to describe a stage intermediate between picture-writing and phonetic writing, in which pictures or representations of objects stand not for the objects themselves, but for their names considered merely as phonetic elements, as in a pictorial rebus, or the use made by the Chinese of the *sounds* of their characters to express the sound of a foreign word. Hence **icono'matically** *adv.*; **icono'maticism**; **iconoma'tography**.

1886 D. G. BRINTON *Ess. Americanist* (1890) 207–8 We have, so far as I am aware, no scientific term to express this manner of phonetic writing, and I propose for it therefore the adjective *ikonomatic*, from the Greek εἰκον, a figure or image, and ὄνομα..name, a writing by means of the names of the figures or images represented. The corresponding noun would be *ikonomatography*. **1887** *Sci. Amer.* 22 Jan. 56 Iconomatic writing..occupies an intermediate position, standing in some sense in relation to both letter and picture writing. *Ibid.*, How complete a system of iconomaticism they [Egyptian and Chinese writing] passed through is unknown. **1895** HOFFMANN *Begin. Writing* 70 Ikonomatically.

iconometer (aɪkə'nɒmɪtə(r)). *Photogr.* [f. ICONO- + -METER.] (See quots.)

1894 E. L. WILSON *Cycl. Photogr.* 194/1 *Iconometer*, view-meter; a pocket instrument which quickly indicates what kind of objective to use..from a given standpoint, or..the standpoint suitable for a view with a given objective. **1918** *Photo-Miniature* Mar. 25 *Iconometer*, a view-meter of 'direct-vision' pattern, i.e., consisting of an open frame with an eyehole or lens fixed behind it. **1919** *Brit. Jrnl. Photogr. Alm.* 244 A view-meter, or iconometer, is a separate accessory for ascertaining the picture produced by any given lens and size of plate.

iconometry (aɪkə'nɒmɪtrɪ). [ad. F. *iconométrie* (A. Laussedat 1892, in *Ann. du Conservatoire d. Arts et Métiers* IV. 374), f. Gr. εἰκονο- ICONO-: see -METRY.] The process of taking measurements from photographs of an area and using them to make a map or survey of it.

1898 *Ann. Rep. U.S. Coast & Geodetic Survey 1897* II. 628 Iconometry means the measuring of dimensions of objects from their perspectives ('Bildmesskunst'), and this term could well be applied to those graphic constructions which serve to convert perspectives into horizontal projections; iconometry is the reverse of perspective drawing. **1923** D. CLARK *Plane & Geodetic Surveying* II. vi. 244 In plotting the map, the distances and elevations required must be obtained from the perspective dimensions on the photographs. The process—termed iconometry—is therefore the reverse of perspective drawing. **1934** R. E. DAVIS et al. *Surveying* (ed. 2) xxvii. 787 The iconometry of aerial photographic surveying is much less accurate than that of terrestrial work.

Hence **icono'metric, -'metrical** *adjs.*, employing or forming part of this process; **icono'metrically** *adv.*, in or by means of iconometry.

1898 *Ann. Rep. U.S. Coast & Geodetic Surv. 1897* II. 631 The correct orientation of the picture traces forms the most important part of iconometric plotting. *Ibid.* 630 If..two different perspectives..of the same object..are given, the dimensions and the position of the object with reference to the two stations may be determined iconometrically. **1906** J. A. FLEMER *Elem. Treat. Phototopogr. Methods* i. 6 It is not easy to make free-hand sketches of landscapes geometrically accurate enough to be used iconometrically in place of the landscapes. *Ibid.* vi. 121 (*heading*) Graphical iconometrical plotting methods. **1934** R. E. DAVIS et al. *Surveying* (ed. 2) xxvii. 775 (*heading*) Iconometric interpretation of the stereoscopic view. **1944** A. L. HIGGINS *Higher Surveying* iii. 219 [Photogrammetry.] Office Work. Apart from the preparation of negatives and prints, this consists of (1) plotting the triangulation, (2) iconometrical plotting, and (3) topographical mapping.

†**ico'nomicar.** *Obs. rare*⁻¹. [erroneously f. L. *œconomic-us*, Gr. οἰκονομικ-ός (see ECONOMIC) + -AR.] A writer on husbandry.

1523 SKELTON *Garl. Laurel* 328 Esiodus, the iconomicar And Homerus, the fresshe historiar.

iconoscope (aɪ'kɒnəskəʊp). [f. ICONO- + -SCOPE.] †**1.** [a. F. *iconoscope* (E. Javal 1866, in *Compt. Rend.* LXIII. 927).] (See quot. 1890.) *Obs.*

1866 *Chem. News* 7 Dec. 273/2 (*heading*) On a new instrument, the iconoscope, intended to give relief to plain images examined with the two eyes. **1890** BILLINGS *Med. Dict.* 678/2 *Iconoscope*, an instrument for suppressing binocular parallax. It makes real objects appear flat like pictures, but..gives to flat pictures a relief like that obtained by a monocular view, by removing those binocular sensations that keep the observer reminded of the flatness of the picture. It may be described briefly as a small telestereoscope reversed. **1900** C. WEILAND tr. *Tscherning's Physiol. Optics* xxiii. 321 The iconoscope of Javal resembles somewhat an inverted telestereoscope. *Ibid.*, Looking through the iconoscope the relief is more marked than when simply closing one eye.

2. A kind of television camera tube (now little used) in which the target plate that receives the image consists of a mosaic of photoemissive material on an insulating sheet that is backed with a conducting sheet, the video signal being obtained from the variation in the current flowing to or from this latter sheet as the mosaic is scanned with an electron beam.

The term was registered in the U.S.A. as a trade name in 1935 but it is now a generic term in the public domain.

1933 V. K. ZWORYKIN in *Jrnl. Inst. Electr. Engin.* LXXIII. 437/1 The device has been named the 'iconoscope', and it consists of a vacuum tube containing an electron-emitting gun and a photo-sensitive surface of a unique type. This photo-sensitive surface is scanned by an electron beam from the gun, which serves as a type of inertialess commutator. **1935** [see DEFINITION 5 c]. **1953** AMOS & BIRKINSHAW *Television Engin.* I. iv. 68 Iconoscope camera tubes have given satisfactory results in television services over a number of years. **1961** G. MILLERSON *Technique Television Production* 50 A familiar effect with the iconoscope camera-tube, shading appears as gradual darkening or lightening over parts of the picture. **1966** *McGraw-Hill Encycl. Sci. & Technol.* XIII. 464/1 The iconoscope was used in early live television broadcasting but is now used only in motion picture reproduction... The vidicon is replacing the iconoscope as a film reproducer.

b. Applied to a modified form of the instrument intended as an infra-red telescope or detector.

1946 *Electronic Engin.* XVIII. 317 Another instrument used by the Germans was an infra-red iconoscope. It does not differ in general principle from the iconoscope used in television, the only difference being in the photosensitive layer. Whereas in television, a mosaic layer..is used, the infra-red instrument uses a semiconducting layer, the resistance of which changes on irradiation. **1949** A. R. WEYL *Guided Missiles* 97 The final installation would have been the 'Electric Eye' iconoscope target-finding device of Rambauske which was, however, not operationally developed when the War came to an end.

‖**iconostas** (aɪ'kɒnəʊstæs). *Eastern Ch.* [Russ. *ikonostás*, f. Gr. εἰκονόστασις: see next.] = next.

1833 R. PINKERTON *Russia* 268 On the ikonostas are hung the sacred pictures. **1877** THOROLD in *Gd. Words* XVIII. 17/2 The iconostas, or skreen, which in Greek churches separates the body of the church from the sanctuary. **1896** *Daily News* 20 May 7/6 A small oratory, including the iconostas, shrines, and innumerable icons, forms an ensemble which literally blazes with gold and gems.

‖**iconostasis** (aɪkə'nɒstəsɪs). *Eastern Church.* [eccl. L., a. eccl. Gr. εἰκονόστασις, f. εἰκών ICON + στάσις standing, position, station.] The screen which separates the sanctuary or 'bema' from the main body of the church, and on which the icons or sacred pictures are placed.

1833 R. PINKERTON *Russia* 211 The priest perfumes the worshippers, the iconostases, and the altar. **1849** CURZON *Visits Monast.* 293 The iconostasis, or screen before the altar is most beautifully carved. **1890** *Guardian* 18 June 970/1 The iconostasis is of white marble, on which, some 12 ft. from the ground (to avoid dangers of iconolatry), are the pictures. **1899** A. H. HORE *Grk. Church* 41 The Iconostasis or Iconstand, with the lighted tapers in front of it, is the most prominent object. On it Icons of our Saviour, the Virgin, the Apostles, and Saints are always painted.

iconotropy (aɪkə'nɒtrəpɪ). [f. Gr. εἰκών, εἰκον- ICON + τροπή a turn, turning: cf. TROPE.] The misinterpretation by one cult of the icons, etc., of another (earlier) cult, so as to bring the beliefs and myths depicted into accord with those of the later cult. Hence **icono'tropic** *a.*, of a myth, tradition, etc., suggestive of an origin in such a misinterpretation.

1946 R. GRAVES *King Jesus* 355 A similar technique of misinterpretation—let us call it iconotropy—was adopted in ancient Greece as a means of confirming Olympian religious myths at the expense of the Minoan ones which they superseded.. In iconotropy the icons are not defaced or altered, but merely interpreted in a sense hostile to the original cult. *Ibid.* 356 The story of Lot and the Sodomites suggests the same ancient icon from which Herodotus derived his iconotropic account of the sacking of the Temple of the Love-goddess Astarte at Ascalon by the Scythians. **1955** —— *Greek Myths* I. 21 If some myths are baffling at first sight, this is often because the mythographer has accidentally or deliberately misinterpreted a sacred picture or dramatic rite. I have called such a process 'iconotropy'... Greek myth teems with iconotropic instances. **1958** *Observer* 7 Sept. 18/8 Professor Webster appears to subscribe to Mr. Robert Graves's theory of iconotropy, or the misinterpretation of myths from visual sources.

iconymus: obs. form of ŒCONOMUS.

i-core(n, i-corn, ME. pa. pples. of CHOOSE, I-CHEOSE *v.*

i-corve(n, ME. pa. pple. of CARVE *v.*

icos-, icosa-, icosi-, repr. Gr. combining forms of εἴκοσι twenty, used in Eng. in several technical terms (see below); also in **icosacolic** (aɪkəʊsə'kəʊlɪk) *a. Anc. Pros.* [Gr. εἰκοσάκωλ-ος, f. κῶλον member, clause, COLON], consisting of twenty cola, or members. **icosasemic** (aɪkəʊsə'siːmɪk) *a. Anc. Pros.* [Gr. σῆμα mark, σημεῖον mark, mora], consisting of or containing twenty moræ or units of time, i.e. the equivalent of twenty short syllables. **icosian** (aɪ'kəʊsɪən) *a.*, of or pertaining to twenty.

b. In *Chem.* (usu. spelt eicos-) denoting the presence in a molecule of twenty atoms of some element (usu. carbon). [App. first so used in G. *eikosylen* (Lippmann and Hawliczek 1879, in *Ber. d. Deut. Chem. Ges.* XII. 72).] So **'eicosane** [-ANE 2b], a hydrocarbon, $C_{20}H_{42}$, of the paraffin (alkane) series, esp. the normal isomer; **eico'sanic** *a.*, in ***eicosanic acid***, = *eicosanoic* adj.; **eicosa'noic** *a.*, in ***eicosanoic acid***, a saturated fatty acid, $C_{19}H_{39}COOH$, of which the normal isomer (also called arachidic acid) is a waxy solid present in small amounts in many natural oils and fats; **eicosenic** (-'iːnɪk) *a.*, in ***eicosenic acid*** [tr. G. *eikosensäure* (M. Bodenstein 1894, in *Ber. d. Deut. Chem. Ges.* XXVIII. 3403)], = *eicosenoic* adj.; **eicose'noic** *a.*, in ***eicosenoic acid***, an unsaturated fatty acid, $C_{19}H_{37}COOH$, of which one isomer, 9-eicosenic acid (gadoleic acid), is a minor constituent of many fish oils and another, 11-eicosenic acid, occurs in the wax of certain plant seeds; **eico'soic** *a.*, in ***eicosoic acid***, = *eicosanoic* adj.

1889 G. MCGOWAN tr. *Bernthsen's Text-bk. Org. Chem.* 34 *(table)* $C_{20}H_{42}$. Eicosane. **1948** A. W. RALSTON *Fatty Acids* xi. 882 The following are the melting and boiling points which have been reported for the higher normal saturated hydrocarbons: nonadecane, $C_{19}H_{40}$, 32°, —; eicosane, $C_{20}H_{42}$, 38°, $b_{0.5}$ 148°; [etc.]. **1966** *Nomencl. Org. Chem.* (I.U.P.A.C.) (ed. 2) A. 6 The first four saturated unbranched acyclic hydrocarbons are called methane, ethane, propane and butane. Names of the higher members of this series consist of a numerical prefix and the termination '-ane'... Examples:..6 Hexane. 7 Heptane... 20 Eicosane. **1923** *Chem. Abstr.* XVII. 2560 Normal eicosanic acid is found in nature in the oil of *Nephelium lappaceum* J. as a glyceride. **1953** HEILBRON & BUNBURY *Dict. Org. Compounds* (rev. ed.) II. 464, *n*-Eicosanic Acid (Arachidic acid, *n*-nonadecane-1-carboxylic acid, eicosoic acid, eicosanoic acid). **1924** *Chem. Abstr.* XVIII. 4318/2 (Index), Eicosanoic acid. *See* Arachidic acid. **1948** A. W. RALSTON *Fatty Acids* i. 44 The vegetable oils generally contain less than 1% of eicosanoic acid. *Ibid.*, Coffee bean oil contains 2·11% of eicosanoic acid..and peanut oils from 3 to 4%. **1895** *Jrnl. Chem. Soc.* LXVIII. I. 127 Icosenic acid, $C_{20}H_{38}O_2$, is formed when behenolic acid is heated with fused caustic potash at 250–270°. **1953** HEILBRON & BUNBURY *Dict. Org. Compounds* (rev. ed.) II. 464 Δ^{10}-Eicosenic Acid (Eicosenoic acid). **1936** *Jrnl. Chem. Soc.* 1755 The fatty matter present in the seeds of *Simmondsia californica* Nutt...is a mixture of wax-esters, and not glycerides... The chief acid is $\Delta^{11:12}$-eicosenoic. **1951** A. W. JOHNSON et al. in E. H. Rodd *Chem. Carbon Compounds* IA. ix. 640, 9-Eicosenoic acid, gadoleic acid, $CH_3(CH_2)_9CH{:}CH(CH_2)_7COOH$ is a common component of fish and marine animal oils such as herring and shark liver oil. **1954** E. W. ECKEY *Vegetable Fats & Oils* xiv. 435 Investigations made after eicosenoic acid had been isolated from rapeseed oil and shown to exist in substantial proportion in hare's ear mustard oil confirmed the presence of this C_{20} monoethenoic acid in rapeseed oil and indicated that it occurs generally in oils of the Cruciferae. **1923** *Chem. Abstr.* XVII. 4447/2 (Index), Eicosoic acid (eicosanic acid), *n*-. **1951** I. L. FINAR *Org. Chem.* ix. 144 Some still higher acids are found in waxes: arachidic (eicosoic), $C_{20}H_{40}O_2$ (m.p. 77°), behenic (docosoic), $C_{22}H_{44}O_2$ (m.p. 82°), [etc.].

†**icosaeder.** *Obs.* [a. F. *icosaèdre* (1587), ad. late L. *īcosaedron*: see next.] = next.

1656 STANLEY *Hist. Philos.* v. (1701) 186/2 The Icosaeders [consist] of twenty [like sides].

icosahedron (ˌaɪkəʊsə'hiːdrən, -'hɛdrən). *Geom.* Also 6–8 **icosaedrum,** 6–9 **icosaedron,** 7 **eicosaedrum,** (8 **eicosihedron**). [a. Gr. εἰκοσάεδρον, neut. of εἰκοσάεδρος, f. εἴκοσι twenty + ἕδρα seat, base.] A solid contained by twenty plane faces; *spec.* the ***regular icosahedron,*** contained by twenty equal equilateral triangles.

1570 BILLINGSLEY *Euclid* XIII. xvi. 410 The opposite sides of an Icosahedron are parallels. **1571** DIGGES *Pantom.* IV. def. xvi. T ij b, Icosaedron.. *marg.* Icosaedrum. **1655–87** H. MORE *App. Antid.* (1712) 183 There are Five regular Bodies ..the Cube, the Tetraedrum, the Octaedrum, the Dodecaedrum, and the Eicosaedrum. **1785** REID *Int. Powers* VI. viii. 658 Five regular solid figures..the tetrahedron.. and the eicosihedron. **1881** ROUTLEDGE *Science* i. 25 To each element Plato assigns a geometrical solid: to earth, the cube; to fire, the pyramid; to air, the octahedron; to water, the icosahedron.

Hence **icosa'hedral** *a.*, of the form of an icosahedron; having twenty faces.

1828 in WEBSTER. **1855** MAYNE *Expos. Lex.*, Icosihedral.

‖**icosandria** (aɪkəʊ'sændrɪə). *Bot.* [mod.L. (Linnæus 1735), f. Gr. εἴκοσι twenty + ἀνήρ, ἀνδρ- man, male, taken as 'stamen'.] The twelfth class in the Linnæan Sexual System, containing plants with 20 or more stamens inserted on the calyx.

1753 CHAMBERS *Cycl. Supp.*, *Icosandria*... Of this class are the torch thistle, the myrtle, the storax, the almond, &c. **1794** MARTYN *Rousseau's Bot.* ix. 89 The situation of the stamens, which in the class icosandria, is either on the calyx or corolla.

Hence **ico'sander** [F. *icosandre*], a plant of the class *Icosandria*; **ico'sandrian, ico'sandrous** *adjs.*, belonging to the class *Icosandria*.

1828 WEBSTER, *Icosander*..*Icosandrian*. **1836** *Penny Cycl.* V. 253/1 *Icosandrous*. **1880** GRAY *Struct. Bot.* vi. §6. 249 *Icosandrous*..when a polyandrous flower has the stamens inserted on the calyx.

ˌicosiˌdodeca'hedron. *Geom.* [f. Gr. εἴκοσι twenty + δώδεκα twelve + ἕδρα seat, base.] A solid contained by twenty equilateral triangles and twelve regular pentagons, formed by replacing the twelve solid angles of the regular icosahedron by planes corresponding to the faces of a regular dodecahedron.

1570 BILLINGSLEY *Euclid* App. def. ii. 459. **1911** *Encycl. Brit.* XXII. 28/2 The icosidodecahedron..is a 32-faced solid, formed by truncating the vertices of an icosahedron so that the original faces become triangles. **1939** H. S. M. COXETER *Ball's Math. Recreations & Ess.* (ed. 11) v. 136 The compound of five cubes has the 30 facial planes of a triacontahedron. Reciprocally, the compound of five octahedra has the 30 vertices of an icosidodecahedron. **1972** *Science* 12 May 654 *(caption)* Icosidodecahedron, its first two stellations, and its final stellation.

ˌicosiˌtetra'hedron. *Geom.* and *Cryst.* [f. Gr. εἴκοσι twenty + τετρα- four + ἕδρα seat, base (cf. TETRAHEDRON).] A solid figure contained by twenty-four plane faces; *esp.* a form contained by twenty-four equal symmetrical trapeziums or deltoids, also called *deltohedron* or *trapezohedron*.

1831 BREWSTER *Optics* xxv. 214 The most common form of the analcime is the solid called the icositetrahedron, which is bounded by twenty-four equal and similar trapezia. **1879** RUTLEY *Stud. Rocks* x. 140 All the members of this group crystallise in the cubic system, the common forms being either the rhombic dodecahedron or the icositetrahedron.

So **icositetra'hedroid.**

1880 *Academy* 30 Oct. 314 Four-dimensional space may be built up with..ikosatetrahedroids.

i-coupled, -cupled, ME. pa. pple. of COUPLE *v.*

[**icre.** Error for *dicre* = DICKER *sb.*¹, the number ten, derived from a misinterpretation of quot. 1086 s.v. (xxxvi, dicras ferri), and reproduced in some mod. Dicts.

1610 HOLLAND *Camden's Brit.* I. 361 As we finde in the survey booke of England [*marg.* Doomesday-booke], the Kings demanded in maner no other tribute than certaine *Icres* of Iron [CAMDEN 1586 ferri Ieras; ed. 1607 ferri Icras], and Iron-barres.]

†**i-creoiced,** *ppl. a. Obs.* [f. ME. *cr(e)oice*, CROSS.] Crossed, signed with the cross.

a **1225** *Ancr. R.* 18 Cusceð ðe eorðe icreoiced mid te þume.

i-cried, ME. pa. pple. of CRY *v.*

icristned, ME. pa. pple. of CHRISTEN *v.*

i-croked, ME. pa. pple. of CROOK *v.*

i-crommet, ME. pa. pple. of CRAM *v.*

i-cruned, ME. pa. pple. of CROWN *v.*

-ics, suffix: see -IC 2.

ictal ('ɪktəl), *a. Med.* [f. ICT(US + -AL.] Of, pertaining to, or caused by an ictus (sense 2 c).

1950 PENFIELD & RASMUSSEN *Cerebral Cortex of Man* ix. 161 The ictal paralysis of normal function passes over into postictal paralysis. **1968** SCHMIDT & WILDER *Epilepsy* ii. 35 Ictal emotional experience is frequent among patients with temporal lobe epilepsy.

ictas, ictus, varr. IKTAS *sb. pl.*

icteric (ɪk'tɛrɪk), *a.* and *sb.* [ad. L. *ictericus*, a. Gr. ἰκτερικός jaundiced, f. ἴκτερος (see ICTERUS). Cf. F. *ictérique* (13th c. in Hatz.-Darm.).]

A. *adj.*

1. Belonging to, of the nature of, or affected with jaundice; jaundiced. (Sometimes referring to the yellow tint of the skin in that disease, or to the jaundiced eyes which see all things yellow.)

a **1600** J. MELVILL *Diary* (1842) 14 He died..anno 1575 in an icterik fevar. **1684** tr. *Bonet's Merc. Compit.* III. 96 That sort of Cœliack passion, which I think may be called an Icterick Loosness. **1799** M. UNDERWOOD *Treat. Dis. Childr.* (ed. 4) I. 29 *note*, An infant..whose finger nails were..of as deep a yellow as in any icteric adult. **1804** ANNA SEWARD *Lett.* (1811) VI. 141 Icteric vision. **1822–34** *Good's Study Med.* (ed. 4) I. 334 *note*, The icteric tint of the skin seems to be merely the result of an effusion of blood.

b. Used for the cure of jaundice.

1710 T. FULLER *Pharm. Extemp.* 14 Icteric Ale..cureth.. Icteric Persons.

2. ***icteric oriole***: a North American bird (*Icterus vulgaris*), having black and yellow plumage, with white spots on the wings; also called *troopial*.

1802 BINGLEY *Anim. Biog.* (1813) II. 114 The Icteric Oriole is, in size, somewhat smaller than a blackbird. **1816** KIRBY & SP. *Entomol.* (1843) I. 244 The icteric oriole is kept by the Americans in their houses for the sake of clearing them of insects.

B. *sb.* **1.** A person affected with jaundice.

1634 W. TIRWHYT tr. *Balzac's Lett.* (Vol. I.) 2 They resemble the Ictericks, who hauing the Iaundesse in their Eyes, see nothing which seemeth not vnto them to carry the same colour. **1684** tr. *Bonet's Merc. Compit.* IX. 314 When an Icterick was let bloud, it appeared all yellow.

2. A medicine for the cure of jaundice.

1727 SWIFT *Gulliver* III. vi, Administer to each of them lenitives..laxatives, cephalalgics, icterics.

ic'terical, *a.* [f. as prec. + -AL¹.] = prec. A. 1.

1649 JER. TAYLOR *Gt. Exemp.* II. Ad §12. 51 Our understandings if a crime be lodged in the will, being like ictericall eyes, transmitting the Species to the Soule with..colours of their own framing. **1697** EVELYN *Numism.* ix. 302 Icterical Persons. **1749** *Phil. Trans.* XLVI. 207 Ascitical and icterical Symptoms. **1822–34** *Good's Study Med.* (ed. 4) II. 30 A tedious icterical marasmus.

b. *transf.* Tinged with yellow.

1654 GAYTON *Pleas. Notes* III. vii. 110 His Diamond was of no spirituous and sparkling Water..the Don's was Ictericall, as if he had descended of the house of the Flavii, or that his Nurse had mix'd all his milke with Saffron.

Hence **ic'tericalness** (Bailey vol. II, 1727).

†**ic'tericie.** *Obs. rare.* [ad. med.L. *icteritia* (in Wr.-Wülcker), f. *icterus* = Gr. ἴκτερος jaundice. Cf. Sp. *ictericia*.] Jaundice.

1634 R. H. *Salernes Regim.* 205 It removeth a stopping matter the which causeth Ictericie.

icterine ('ɪktəraɪn), *a. Zool.* [f. ICTER-US + -INE.] **a.** Yellowish; esp. having yellow scales or plumage. **b.** Belonging to the family *Icteridæ* or sub-family *Icterinæ* of American passerine birds (typical genus *Icterus*: see ICTERIC A. 2).

1855 MAYNE *Expos. Lex.*, *Icterinus*,..yellow, or yellowish, as the *Cypræa icterina*: icterine. **1884** *Athenæum* 15 Nov. 628/2 An icterine warbler (*Hypolais icterina*) killed in Norfolk.

†**'icterism.** *Obs. rare.* [f. Gr. ἴκτερ-ος jaundice + -ISM.] Jaundice.

1660 STILLINGFL. *Iren.* II. v. §1 (1662) 201 Which prejudice being the Yellow-Jaundise of the soul, leaves such a tincture upon the eyes of the understanding, that till it be cured of that Icterism, it cannot discern things in their proper colours. **1662** —— *Orig. Sacr.* III. i. §14 Those who have an Icterism in their eyes.

icteritious (-'ɪʃəs), *a.* [f. med. (and mod.) L. *icteriti-a* jaundice + -OUS.] Jaundiced; also *fig.*

1609 BP. W. BARLOW *Answ. Nameless Cath.* 323 His gall ouer-flowes, and hee must voide it by his pen in his icteritious Pamphlet. **1684** tr. *Bonet's Merc. Compit.* IX. 316 The Ictericious dyscrasie of the bloud. **1822–34** *Good's Study Med.* (ed. 4) IV. 540 Absence of icteritious symptoms.

ictero- ('ɪktərəʊ), combining form of Gr. ἴκτερος jaundice, as in **ˌicteroge'netic** (*rare*), **ictero'genic** *adjs.*, causing jaundice.

1897 *Allbutt's Syst. Med.* IV. 38 This drug is the most notable of all icterogenetic poisons. **1903** DORLAND *Med. Dict.* (ed. 3) 331/1 Icterogenic. **1944** *Lancet* 16 Sept. 365/1 Icterogenic yellow fever vaccine. **1962** *Lancet* 19 May 1057/2 'The pill' should not be overlooked when the medicine-chest is scrutinised for potentially icterogenic drugs.

icterode ('ɪktərəʊd), *a.* [ad. Gr. ἰκτερώδης jaundiced.] = next, a.

1861 T. J. GRAHAM *Pract. Med.* 463 A continuance of the icterode appearance.

icteroid (ˈɪktərɔɪd), *a.* [f. Gr. ἴκτερ-ος jaundice + -OID.] **a.** Resembling or characteristic of jaundice. **b.** (See quot. 1897.)

1855 in MAYNE *Expos. Lex.* **1876** BARTHOLOW *Mat. Med.* (1879) 224 The skin assumes an icteroid hue. **1897** *Daily News* 12 June 3/1 Doctor Sanarelli..declared the cause of yellow fever to be a bacillus, named by him icteroid.

‖**icterus** (ˈɪktərəs). [L., a. Gr. ἴκτερος jaundice; also, a yellowish-green bird, by looking at which jaundiced persons were supposed to be cured.]

1. *Path.* The disease jaundice.

1706 PHILLIPS (ed. Kersey), *Icterus*, the Jaundice. **1802** *Med. Jrnl.* VIII. 240 Irritation..acting upon the hepatic system, is..the cause of icterus. **1886** *Lancet* 15 May 947/2 [He] pointed out that diabetes was not a disease, but a symptom like icterus.

b. *Bot.* A disease of plants in which the leaves turn yellow.

[**1807** *Edin. Rev.* XI. 85 To the natural decay of the leaves in Autumn, he has given the name of Icterus.] **1866** *Treas. Bot.*, *Icterus*, a name given to the yellow condition assumed by wheat and some other plants, under the influence of prolonged wet and cold... The golden hues of autumn belong clearly to another category.

2. *Zool.* **a.** A genus of American passerine birds, formerly nearly coextensive with the modern family *Icteridæ*, now restricted to the American orioles or hangbirds, a typical species being the troopial or icteric oriole, *I. vulgaris* (see ICTERIC A. 2).

1713 DERHAM *Phys.-Theol.* (1749) II. 25 *note*, The nest of the Guira tangeima, the Icterus minor, and the Jupujuba, or whatever other name the American Hang-nests may be called by.

ictic (ˈɪktɪk), *a. rare.* [irreg. f. L. *ictus* (*u-* stem: see ICTUS) + -IC.]

1. Of the nature of a blow or stroke; abrupt and sudden in its action.

1847 BUSHNELL *Chr. Nurt.* iv. (1861) 116 An abrupt, ictic grace. **1858** —— *Serm. New Life* 362 A naked, ictic force.

2. *Pros.* Pertaining to or due to the ictus or metrical stress.

1898 E. W. HOPKINS in *Amer. Jrnl. Philol.* XIX. 21 Dahlmann thinks it was an ictic conversion.

ictuate (ˈɪktjuːeɪt), *v. rare.* [f. L. *ictu-s* ICTUS + -ATE[3].] *trans.* To put the ictus on, to stress.

1822 J. TATE in *S. Parr's Wks.* (1828) VIII. 256 Closing a sentence of fury with the dimeter ictuated on the last syllable.

‖**ictus** (ˈɪktəs). [L., = blow, stroke, thrust, f. *icĕre* to strike, hit, smite.]

1. *Pros.* Stress on a particular syllable of a foot or verse; rhythmical or metrical stress. Used of Old English verse.

1752 NEWTON *Note Milton's P.R.* IV. 157, I think the ictus falls better in the common reading. **1784** J. B. SEALE *Anal. Grk. Metres* (1823) 3 In the Iambus and Trochee, the Arsis (or Ictus) is invariable, being upon the long syllable of each. **1823** J. BOSWORTH *Elem. Anglo-Saxon Gram.* 246 [quoting J. J. Conybeare] The ear is satisfied, not by the number of syllables, but by the recurrence of the accent, or ictus, if one may call it so. **1871** EARLE *Philol. Eng. Tongue* §621 It can hardly be a good line wherein this word [one], standing as an indefinite pronoun, receives the ictus of the metre. **1888** A. H. TOLMAN in *Publ. Mod. Lang. Assoc.* III. 21 March.. declares that 'the time from each ictus to the next is the same in any section'. **1953** F. P. MAGOUN in *Speculum* XXVIII. 458 The first down-beat or ictus in the off-verse does not here alliterate with the preceding on-verse.

2. *Med.* **a.** The beat of the pulse. **b.** *ictus solis* (Lat.): sunstroke.

1707 FLOYER *Physic. Pulse-Watch* 153 The Pulse is most properly consider'd in its Ictus, which shews the Vigor of spirits, and the Intervallum which shews the Heat of the Blood. **1811** HOOPER *Med. Dict.*, *Ictus*, a stroke, or blow. Hence *ictus solis* means a stroke of the sun.

c. A stroke, seizure, or fit. Also in some mod.L. phrases.

1890 GOULD *New Med. Dict.* 204/1 *Ictus*, a stroke or attack of disease coming without premonition. **1890** BILLINGS *Med. Dict.* I. 679/1 *Ictus sanguinis*, apoplexy. **1908** A. CHURCH *Dis. Nervous Syst.* 487 Especially severe attacks of tickling in the throat, arrest of respiration, unconsciousness, and epileptic attacks have been described as *ictus laryngeus*. **1931** I. S. WECHSLER *Textbk. Clin. Neurol.* (ed. 2) IV. 345 The clinical course [of apoplexy] may be conveniently divided into (1) the acute apoplectic stroke or ictus, and (2) the stage of paralysis. **1939** W. HAYMAKER tr. *Bing's Textbk. Nervous Dis.* xvii. 444 The most striking symptom of apoplectic stroke (*ictus apoplecticus*) is sudden loss of consciousness. **1961** *Lancet* 29 July 223/1 The conscious level chosen for stratification of patients in the trial was that at twenty-four hours after the ictus.

i-cud: see YKID, known, renowned.

i-cume(n, ME. pa. pple. of COME *v.*

†**i-cunde**, *sb. Obs.* Also i-kunde. [ME. *icunde* (*ü*), OE. *ȝecynd*, f. *cynd* nature, KIND *sb.*]

1. Nature; kind.

971 *Blickl. Hom.* 33 He wæs on anum hade tweȝra ȝecynda. *c* **1000** *Guthlac* 44 Wæstma ȝecyndu. *c* **1175** *Lamb. Hom.* 77 Nawiht efter flesces wille, ne efter likames ikunde. *Ibid.* 149 Þet brihte ikunde þet god haueð in ow ibroht of saule and of likame. *a* **1250** *Owl & Night.* 113 Seggeþ me hwo haveþ þis ido Ou nas never icunde þar to.

2. Inheritance; native land.

c **1205** LAY. 7909 Iulius Cesar..halt þer eower icunde. *Ibid.* 11199 He cleopede to Brutlonde þæt hit wes his icunde.

†**i-cunde**, *a. Obs.* [ME. (*ü*), OE. *ȝecynde*, f. *cynde* innate, natural, KIND *a.*] Natural; native.

Beowulf (Z.) 2697 Swa him ȝecynde wæs. *c* **1050** *Voc.* in Wr.-Wülcker 180/8 *Idioma, proprietas linguæ*, aȝen *uel* ȝecynde spræc. *c* **1205** LAY. 22165 Aȝif us ure icunde lond. *c* **1275** *O.E. Misc.* 56 Eueruych þer vnderstod his icunde speche.

Hence †**i-ˈcundeliche** *adv.*, naturally.

c **1175** *Lamb. Hom.* 99 An god is icundeliche on þreom Hadan. *a* **1250** *Owl & Night.* 1424 Heo stumpeþ and falþ icundeliche.

i-cunned, ME. pa. pple. of CUN, CON *v.*

†**i-cusse**, *v. Obs.* Pa. pple. i-cust. [ME. *icusse* (*ü*), OE. *ȝecyssan* (= OHG. *gikussen*), f. *cyssan* to kiss.] To kiss (mutually).

c **1205** LAY. 30042 Þas kinges wel ilomen mid luue heom icusten.

i-cweme, var. of I-QUEME *a.* and *v.*

i-cwethen, i-cweðen, ME. pa. pple. of QUETHE, I-QUETHE *v.*

icy (ˈaɪsɪ), *a.* Forms: [1 ísiȝ], 5 isy, 6 isie, 6–7 icie, ycie, 7 icey, 7– icy. [f. ICE *sb.* + -Y. Cf. Du. *ijzig*, Ger. *eisig*, Sw. *isig*. Used in OE., but formed anew in the 15th c.]

1. Abounding in, or characterized by the presence of, ice; covered or overlaid with ice.

[*Beowulf* (Z.) 33 Þær æt hyðe stod hringed-stefna isiȝ & utfus. *a* **1000** *Boeth. Metr.* xxiv. 45 Saturnus..is se cealda eall isiȝ tungel.] **1494** FABYAN *Chron.* VII. 431 Whan Saturne with his colde isy face The grounde with his frostys turnyth the grene to whyte. **1597** MIDDLETON *Wisd. Solomon* v. 6 Winter in her icy car. **1643** SIR T. BROWNE *Relig. Med.* I. §32 The ycie Ocean cracks, the frozen pole Thaws with the heat of the Celestial coale. **1796** H. HUNTER tr. *St.-Pierre's Stud. Nat.* (1799) II. 112 The flowers of the Icy Zones. **1848** DICKENS *Dombey* iv, Men, vying..who shall lie out first upon the yards to furl the icy sails.

2. Composed or consisting of ice. †*icy mountains* or *hills*, icebergs (*obs.*).

1600 HAKLUYT *Voy.* III. 79 Striuing against the streame, and beating amongst the Isie mountaines. **1659** D. PELL *Impr. Sea* 276 A sight of those huge Icy Mountains..which make such a dashing and crashing one against another. **1694** *Acc. Sev. Late Voy.* II. (1711) 29 In the Clifts of the Icy-hills on shoar. **1819** HEBER *Hymn*, From Greenland's icy mountains, From India's coral strand. **1820** SCORESBY *Acc. Arctic Reg.* I. 105 The icy cliff, from whence masses..were continually breaking. **1856** KANE *Arct. Expl.* I. xxv. 335 Huge icy stalactites seventy and a hundred feet long.

3. a. Resembling ice; having the nature or properties of ice; extremely cold, frosty; slippery.

1590 BARROUGH *Meth. Physick* v. xvi. 306 Sprinkle the pauements..dayly with water that is altogether ycie, and cold. **1598** FLORIO, *Sdrúsciolo*, slipperie,..gliding, isie. **1640** C. HARVEY *Journey* 26 We scramble to get up the banks Of icy honour. **1706** PHILLIPS (ed. Kersey), *Butter of Antimony*,..which some call Icy Oil of Antimony is a great Caustick, being us'd to eat proud Flesh. **1732** BERKELEY *Alciphr.* II. §26 What creates a love for icy liquors? **1784** COWPER *Task* VI. 137 Th' icy touch Of unprolific winter. **1886** *Law Times* LXXX. 195/1 An icy current was blowing about their feet.

b. *fig.* Of demeanour, character, speech, etc.

1594 SHAKS. *Rich. III*, III. i. 177 If he be leaden, ycie, cold, vnwilling, Be thou so too. **1638** DRUMM. OF HAWTH. *Irene* Wks. (1711) 168 An icy grandeur, erected by your selves. **1713** C'TESS WINCHELSEA *Misc. Poems* 351 The sixty Winters, that have..turn'd swift eager Love to icy Reasons. **1882** MISS BRADDON *Mt. Royal* III. i. 23 'He came—and he is dead', answered Christabel, in icy tones.

4. *Comb.*, as *icy-blue*, *-clear*, *-cold*; *icy-pearled* (having pearls or sparkling drops of ice), *icy-wheeled*.

c **1625** MILTON *Death of Fair Infant* iii, Mounting up in icy-pearled car. **1652–7** HEYLIN *Cosmogr.* 342 That Island which in times of old The Greeks did call Hibernia, ycie-cold. **1812** W. TENNANT *Anster F.* I. 12 John Frost Drove thro' mid air his chariot, icy-wheel'd. **1839** BAILEY *Festus* (1848) 238 Clear, cold, and icy-blue like a sea-eagle's eye. **1922** W. DE LA MARE *Down-adown-Derry* 93 Fleet-foot deer Lap of its waters icy-clear. **1925** BLUNDEN *Masks of Time* 41 Icy-clear The air of a mortal day shocks sense.

id[1] (ɪd). *Biol.* [Formed in German (1891) by Weismann: see first quot.] In Weismann's theory of heredity: A unit of germ-plasm or idioplasm.

1893 tr. *Weismann's Germ-Plasm* I. i. 62 We are led to the assumption of groups..composed of determinants, which in their turn are made up of biophors. These are the units which I formulated..long ago, and to which the name of *ancestral germ-plasms* was then given. I shall now speak of them as 'ids', a term which recalls the 'idioplasm' of Nägeli. **1893** M. HARTOG in *Contemp. Rev.* July 57 Each of the reproductive cells of an organism is supposed to contain in its nucleus a number of 'ids', and each id represents the personality of an ancestral member of the species or of an antecedent species. **1895** VINES *Text-bk. Bot.* 782 When..in hybridisation all the parental ids exert their full influence the offspring is precisely intermediate in character.

id[2] (ɪd). *Psycho-analysis.* [A use of L. *id* it, as a rendering of G. *es* it, which was adopted by Freud (*Das Ich und das Es* (1923)) following its use in a similar sense by G. Groddeck (*Das Buch vom Es* (1923)).] The inherited instinctive impulses of the individual, forming part of the unconscious and, in Freudian theory, interacting in the psyche with the ego and the super-ego. Also *attrib.*

[**1917** FREUD *Briefe* 5 June (1960) 316 [*To Georg Groddeck*] Ich muß Anspruch auf Sie erheben, muß behaupten, daß Sie ein prächtiger Analytiker sind, der das Wesen der Sache unverlierbar erfaßt hat. Wer erkennt, daß Übertragung und Widerstand die Drehpunkte der Behandlung sind, der gehört nun einmal rettungslos zum wilden Heer. Ob er das 'Ubw' [*sc.* Unbewußte, 'unconscious'] auch 'Es' nennt, das macht keinen Unterschied.] **1924** J. RIVIERE et al. tr. *Freud's Coll. Papers* II. xxi. 250 The essay..describes the various allegiances the ego owes, its mediate position between the outer world and the id, and its struggles to serve all its masters at one and the same time. [*Translators' note.*] To translate the German '*es*', which means 'it' and thus implies the impersonality of the mind apart from its ego, the Latin '*id*' has been selected. *Ibid.* 254 Keep in mind this dissection of the mental apparatus that I have proposed, namely, into ego, super-ego and id. **1927** J. RIVIERE tr. *Freud's Ego & Id* ii. 27 We need feel no hesitation in finding a place for Groddeck's discovery in the fabric of science. I propose to take it into account..by following Groddeck in giving to the other part of the mind, into which this entity [*sc.* the ego] extends and which behaves as though it were Ucs [*sc.* unconscious], the name of Id (Es). [*Note*] Groddeck himself no doubt followed the example of Nietzsche, who habitually used this grammatical term for whatever in our nature is impersonal and, so to speak, subject to natural law. **1942** *Essays & Stud.* XXVII. 12 Dreams..that fulfil the much darker wishes of the Id. **1943** H. READ *Educ. through Art* vi. 176 The super-ego is the direct representative of the unconscious, of the id, and hence the possibility, indeed, the inevitability, of a conflict with the ego. **1952** SHAFFER & LAZARUS *Fund. Concepts Clin. Psychol.* vi. 188 The forces which keep the id impulses in check as an adaptation to the pressures of the outside world comprise the ego. **1957** J. BRAINE *Room at Top* xxvi. 208 Roy, a quiet type normally, seemed to become, as Charles said, all Id when he'd had one over the eight. **1961** R. W. LUNDIN *Personality* i. 21 The id is entirely unconscious, having no contact with reality except through the ego. One may liken the id to the primitive or animal nature of man. **1962** R. FINE *Freud* xi. 156 The id is the source of all drives, the reservoir of instincts. **1965** C. M. & S. GROSSMAN *Wild Analyst* xii. 109 It became clear, when the two books [*sc.* Groddeck's *Das Buch vom Es* and Freud's *Das Ich und das Es*] were translated, that it had been wise to distinguish between the 'Id' and the 'It', because Freud's concept of the Id, broadened as it was, was still not as broad as Groddeck's concept of the It. *Ibid.* 110 He [*sc.* Groddeck] gave Freud the Id as a gift—he, too, had borrowed it, from Nietzsche. **1967** R. R. GREENSON *Technique & Pract. Psychoanal.* I. i. 20 The combing of her hair stirred up repressed id impulses which brought her into conflict with her ego and super-ego. .. There were indications that her ego already was relatively depleted and her id lacked adequate discharge possibilities. .. As a consequence the fantasies mobilized by the hair combing increased the id tensions to a point where they flooded the infantile defenses of the ego and involuntary discharges took place, eventuating in acute symptom formation.

-id, *suffix*[1], repr. F. *-ide*, L. *-id-us*, used to form adjectives, chiefly from verbs with *e*-stems, as *acidus* acid, f. *acē-re* to be sour, *āridus* arid, *fervidus* fervid, *frīgidus* frigid, *liquidus* liquid, *placidus* placid, *splendidus* splendid, *stupidus* stupid, etc., etc.; but also from a few verbs with *i*- or consonant stems, as *fluidus* fluid, f. *fluĕre* to flow, *vīvidus* vivid, f. *vīvĕre* to live; and occas. from substantives, as *fūmidus* fumid, f. *fūmus* smoke, *morbidus* morbid, f. *morbus* disease, *solidus* solid, f. *solum* ground, etc. The earlier Eng. words in *-id* came through Fr.; on the analogy of these, others have been taken from Latin direct; the suffix is not a living formative in Eng.

-id, *suffix*[2], corresp. to F. *-ide*, in sbs. derived from Latin sbs. in *-is*, *-id-em*, adopted from Greek sbs. in -ις, -ιδ-α. Such are *carotid* (ad. Gr. pl. καρωτίδ-ες), *chrysalid*, *hydatid*, *parotid*, *pyramid* (cf. F. *pyramide*). This formative occurs in certain botanical terms, as *amaryllid*, *epacrid*, *orchid*: etymologically these should denote the plants *amaryllis*, *epacris*, and *orchis* respectively, but they are actually used to denote a member of the order of which these are the typical genera (*Amaryllid-eæ*, *Epacrid-aceæ*, *Orchid-aceæ*).

b. *Astr.* Added to the name of a constellation to form the name of a meteor in a shower having its radiant point in that constellation, as *Andromedid*, *Leonid*, *Lyraid*, *Perseid*; also more widely used (cf. BIELID).

c. Used as a terminal element in the names of epic poems, as ÆNEID, HERACLEID, THEBAÏD.

-id, *suffix*[3], in zoological appellatives, sb. and adj.: (*a*) formed from Latin names of Families in *-id-æ*, pl. of *-idēs*, repr. Gr. -ίδης, patronymic suffix = 'son of': as *Araneid*, a member of the Family *Araneidæ*. (*b*) formed from Latin names of Classes, etc., in *-id-a*, taken as neut. pl. of *-idēs* = Gr. -ίδης: as *Arachnid*, a member of the Class *Arachnida*. Some of the terms have come through Fr. forms in *-ide*. See -IDAN.

-id, *suffix*^{4}, an early spelling of the chemical suffix -IDE, still retained by some, esp. in U.S.

-id, *suffix*^{5}, in the nomenclature of mammalian teeth, used to indicate a structure forming part of a tooth in the lower jaw. Cf. HYPOCONID, HYPOCONULID.

1897 H. F. OSBORN in *Amer. Naturalist* XXXI. 1006 The suffix *-id* is employed arbitrarily to distinguish the elements of the lower molars from those of the upper. **1949** A. S. ROMER *Vertebr. Body* x. 304 The names of specific cones are formed by adding..prefixes..and, where necessary, by suffixes: -ul(e) indicates a minor cusp, and -id a lower jaw element.

idæa, obs. (erron.) form of IDEA.

Idæan (aɪˈdiːən), *a.* Also **Idaian**. [f. L. *Īdæus*, Gr. Ἰδαῖος (f. *Īdā*, *Īdē*, Ἴδη) + -AN.] Of, belonging to, or dwelling on Mount Ida, either (*a*) a mountain in Asia Minor near the ancient Troy; or (*b*) the chief mountain in Crete, the birthplace of Zeus.

1590 SPENSER *F.Q.* II. vii. 55 Here eke that famous golden Apple grew,..For which th'Idæan Ladies disagreed. *Ibid.* II. viii. 6 Like as Cupido on Idæan hill. *a* **1649** DRUMMOND OF HAWTHORNDEN *Works* (1711) 7/1 Trembling Roofs of Trees..Which make Idæan Woods in every Crook. **1810** SCOTT *Lady of Lake* I. xxvi. 32 Where Ellen's hand had taught to twine The ivy and Idæan vine. **1820** SHELLEY *Prometh. Unb.* III. i. 97 Pour forth heaven's wine, Idæan Ganymede, And let it fill the Dædal cups like fire. **1876** GLADSTONE *Homeric Synchr.* 123 Teucer, son of Scamander and of an Idaian Nymph. **1921** *Public Opinion* 17 June 568/3 The sad dwellers on the Idaean plain. **1970** *Oxf. Classical Dict.* (ed. 2) 540/1 *Idaean dactyls*, literally the Fingers of Ida, but whether the Phrygian or the Cretan Ida and whether their name refers to craftsmanship, dwarfish size, or something else, the ancients were in doubt.

i-dæled, i-deled, ME. pa. pple. of DEAL *v.*

id al-fitr: see ID-UL-FITR.

Idalian (aɪˈdeɪlɪən), *a.* [f. L. *Idalius*: see -AN.] Of or belonging to the ancient town of Idalium in Cyprus, where Aphrodite was worshipped.

1599 NASHE *Lenten Stuffe* 34 Those debonaire Idalian nimphs and their spangled trappings. **1697** DRYDEN tr. *Virgil's Æneis* I. 955, I mean to plunge the Boy in pleasing Sleep, and, ravish'd, in Idalian Bow'rs to keep. **1799** T. CAMPBELL *Pleasures of Hope* II. 55 Some cottage-home.. With peace embosom'd in Idalian bow'rs! **1832** TENNYSON *Œnone* in *Poems* 60 Idalian Aphroditè oceanborn. **1928** J. H. MOZLEY tr. *Statius* I. 187 Golden Venus..on her way from the height of Eryx to the Idalian groves.

i-dampned, ME. pa. pple. of DAMN *v.*

-idan, in zoological appellatives, sb. and adj., formed on -ID^{3} with suffix -AN, meaning 'of or pertaining to', or 'a member of' the group designated by the suffix *-ida* or *-idæ*; as *arachnidan* (f. *Arachnida*) = *arachnid*; *ichneumonidan* (f. *Ichneumonidæ*) = *ichneumonid*.

idant (ˈaɪdənt). *Biol.* [Arbitrarily f. ID^{1}.] One of the chromatin bodies in the nucleus of a reproductive or other cell, regarded as consisting of 'ids' (see ID^{1}).

1893 tr. *Weismann's Germ-Plasm* I. i. 67 Those rod-like, loop-like, or granular masses of chromatin in the nucleus.. considered equivalent..to series or aggregations of ids, I have..proposed to call..*idants*. *Ibid.* III. Introd. 233 The germ-plasm in both nuclei..becomes contracted, so as to give rise to nuclear rods or idants..the number of these idants is the same in both of the conjugating cells. **1895** MIVART in *Harper's Mag.* Mar. 634.

iddingsite (ˈɪdɪŋzaɪt). *Min.* [f. the name of Joseph P. *Iddings* (1857–1920), American geologist + -ITE^{1}.] A red-brown to orange-brown silicate of calcium, magnesium, and trivalent iron having an indefinite composition and formed as an alteration product of olivine.

1893 A. C. LAWSON in *Bull. Dept. Geol. Univ. Calif.* I. 30 The common characteristic of all facies of these eruptive rocks is the presence, as a phenocryst of a mineral which.. has received but little attention... The most extended and satisfactory note that has yet appeared regarding it is by Prof. J. P. Iddings... For this reason and also in recognition of Professor Iddings' eminent services to the science of petrography, it is proposed to name the mineral iddingsite. **1900** H. E. GREGORY in *Bull. U.S. Geol. Survey* No. 165. 181 This alteration product appears somewhat like the iddingsite found in the Californian teschenite. **1961** *Amer. Mineralogist* XLVI. 96 The optical homogeneity of many 'iddingsites' suggests that, even if the material is not to be regarded as a definite compound with relatively fixed chemical constitution, there is some structural control over the alteration process. **1966** W. A. DEER et al. *Introd. Rock-Forming Min.* 5 The composition of both iddingsite and bowlingite show considerable variation.

iddyr, obs. form of UDDER.

iddy-umpty (ɪdɪˈʌmptɪ). Also **iddy-iddy-umpty**. Conventional verbal representation of the dots and dashes of the Morse code.

1906 *Punch* 24 Jan. 60/3 An 'Iddy Umpty' Idyll. **1914** *Daily Express* 15 Dec. 4/5 To see men practising the 'iddy-umpty', as they call it, with the back of a sheath-knife on the top of an empty tobacco-tin in lieu of a regulation 'dummy-key'. **1924** *Glasgow Herald* 23 June 10 For my sins of commission and of omission—as far as the worship of that fetish 'Iddy-Umpty' was concerned—I became for a time an inmate of the great signalling camp at Swanage. **1925** FRASER & GIBBONS *Soldier & Sailor Words* 126 *Iddy* (or *Itty*) *Umpty*, an expression first used in India in teaching the dot-and-dash Morse system to native troops. An 'Iddy Umpty' in that way came to be used as a term for a signaller.

ide^{1} (aɪd). [ad. mod.L. *idus*, ad. Sw. *id* (also *idmört*).] A cyprinoid fish (*Leuciscus idus* or *Idus melanotus*), inhabiting the fresh waters of northern Europe.

1839 YARRELL *Brit. Fishes* (1841) I. 396 A fine large specimen of the Ide..in the Gota Elf. **1839** *Penny Cycl.* XIII. 451 The Ide (*Leuciscus idus*, Cuvier), a species which is found in Norway, Sweden, Denmark, Russia. **1844–6** OWEN *Lect. Comp. Anat. Vertebr.* viii. 192 The long olfactory nerve in the Eel, the Ide or the Roach. **1884** *Century Mag.* Apr. 904/1 The gold-orfe or golden-ide [is] a fish bred for both ornament and the table.

ide^{2}: see IDES.

-ide, *Chem.*, a suffix used to form names of simple compounds of an element with another element or a radical. It is added to the stem or an abbreviated form of the name, and was first used in *ox-ide* (F. *oxyde*, Lavoisier) from *oxygen*, whence it was extended to other elements, sometimes displacing other derivatives in *-et*, *-uret*, previously used. Thus *chloride of nitrogen* or (more tersely) *nitrogen chloride*; *hydrogen arsenide* (*arseniuret*). The use of this suffix has been greatly extended in organic chemistry, notably in the generic names of various kinds of naturally occurring compounds, as GLYCOSIDE, PEPTIDE, SACCHARIDE (qq.v.); it is used *spec.* to form the names of glycosides from those of the corresponding sugars (as *galactoside* from *galactose*, *furanoside* from *furanose*).

In systematic terminology, a compound of oxygen with any other element is called an *oxide*; in other binary compounds *-ide* is combined with the (contracted) name of the more electro-negative of the two elements: thus *fluorine*, *chlorine*, *bromine*, *iodine* form with each other in order, and with any other element or radical except oxygen, *fluorides*, *chlorides*, *bromides*, *iodides*; sulphur, selenium, tellurium form with elements other than these, *sulphides*, *selenides*, *tellurides*; and so on. Examples are bromine chloride, sulphur bromide, carbon sulphide; hydrogen selenide, telluride, phosphide, arsenide, cyanide; boron carbide, boron hydride, silicon hydride, ethyl hydride; copper arsenide, carbide, nitride, hydrides of metals and organic radicals. The suffix is also used in AMIDE, ANHYDRIDE, CYANIDE *sb.*, ANILIDE, and other derivatives from names of compound radicals. *Mono-*, *di-*, *tri-*, *tetra-*, *penta-*, etc. are prefixed, to indicate the number of combining equivalents, as in sulphur *monochloride* S_2Cl_2 (= SCl), sulphur *dichloride* SCl_2, and so on.

1804 ROSCOE & SCHORLEMMER *Chem.* I. 121.

2. Used to form LANTHANIDE and later (by analogy) ACTINIDE, signifying a similarity in properties to lanthanum and actinium, respectively.

idea (aɪˈdiːə), *sb.* Also 6–7 *erron.* **idæa**. Pl. **ideas**; formerly sometimes **ideæ**. See also the earlier IDEE. [a. late L. *idea* (in Platonic sense), a. Gr. ἰδέα look, semblance, form, configuration, species, kind, class, sort, nature, (in Platonic philosophy) a general or ideal form, type, model, f. root ἰδ-, ἰδεῖν, to see: the word being thus analogous in derivation and original sense to L. *species* from *spec-ĕre* to see, behold. So It., Sp., Pg. *idea*; F. *idée*.

The original development of the word took place in Greek; and it was in the developed Platonic sense that the word was first adopted in the modern langs. (see branch I). Other applications of the word, however, became common by the end of the 16th c.: see the senses under II and III.]

I. General or ideal form as distinguished from its realization in individuals; archetype, pattern, plan, standard.

1. In Platonic philosophy: A supposed eternally existing pattern or archetype of any class of things, of which the individual things in that class are imperfect copies, and from which they derive their existence.

1430–1589 [see IDEE]. **1563** T. GALE *Institutes of Chirurg.* 11 As one myght thynke hymselfe ryght happye, though he neuer dyd attayne to Aristoteles *summum bonum*, or Plato his *Idæa*. **1603** HOLLAND *Plutarch's Mor.* 813 Idea is a bodilesse substance, which of it selfe hath no subsistence, but giveth figure and forme unto shapelesse matters, and becommeth the very cause that bringeth them into shew and evidence. Socrates and Plato suppose, that these Ideæ bee substances separate and distinct from Matter, howbeit, subsisting in the thoughts and imaginations of God—that is to say, of Minde and Understanding. **1652** GAULE *Magastrom.* *j b, Chymericall figments, Platonicall Ideaes, Cabbalisticall fancies. **1656** STANLEY *Hist. Philos.* v. (1701) 184/2 They define Idea an Eternal Exemplar of things which are according to Nature. For Idea's are the Eternal Notions of God, perfect in themselves. **1856** FERRIER *Inst. Metaph.* VI. xviii. 176 Plato..had merely succeeded in carrying our cognitions up into certain subordinate unities, certain inferior universals, called by him *ideas*. **1885** W. L. DAVIDSON *Logic of Definition* vi. 145 With Plato, the Idea is ontological or metaphysical... It is both an objective intelligible existence ('uncreated and imperishable') and a pattern, model, archetype or παράδειγμα.

2. a. The conception of anything in its highest perfection or supreme development; a standard of perfection; an ideal. (Cf. 1.) *Obs.* or *arch.*

1586 T. B. tr. *La Primaud. Fr. Acad.* Ep. Ded. A iij, Rather an Idæa of good life, than such a platforme as may be drawen from contemplation into action. **1606** BRYSKETT *Civ. Life* 61 Xenophon in his Ciropædia..hauing..vnder the person of Cirus, framed an idæa or perfect patterne of an excellent Prince. **1647** COWLEY *Mistr.*, *Not Fair* i, I thought you once as fair, As women in th' Idæa are. **1682** SIR T. BROWNE *Chr. Mor.* I. §28 How widely we are fallen from the pure Exemplar and Idea of our Nature. **1844** MRS. BROWNING *Drama of Exile* Poems 1850 I. 3 Thou [Lucifer] shalt be an Idea to all souls..whence to mark despair, And measure out the distances from good.

†**b.** A person or thing regarded as perfect in its kind; the ideal realized in an individual. *Obs.*

1591 *Troub. Raigne K. John* II. (1611) 100 Was euer any so infortunate, The right Idea of a cursed man? **1602** CAMPION *Bk. Airs* Wks. (Bullen) 27 It is th' Idea of her sex Envy of whom doth world perplex. **1627** JACKSON *Creed* XII. x. §2 Christ..was the idæa of legal Nazarites. **1651** *Life Father Sarpi* (1676) 65 The most excellent Senate (the very Idea of politick Christian prudence).

3. The conception of a standard or principle to be realized or aimed at; a conception of what is desirable or ought to be; a governing conception or principle; the plan or design according to which something is created or constructed.

1581 SIDNEY *Apol. Poetrie* (Arb.) 26 The skil of the Artificer standeth in that Idea or fore-conceite of the work. **1602** WARNER *Alb. Eng.* IX. lii, Scriptures Idea crouched in our Love to God and men. **1667** MILTON *P.L.* VII. 557 To behold this new created World..how good, how faire, Answering his great Idea. **1700** DRYDEN *Fables* Ded. 11 If Chaucer by the best idea wrought. **1840** MILL *Diss. & Disc.*, *Coleridge* (1859) I. 438 His mode..is to investigate what he terms the *Idea* of it, or what in common parlance would be called the principle involved in it. **1841** MYERS *Cath. Th.* IV. i. 182 The ground-plan of the Universe—the idea according to which it is. **1858** HAWTHORNE *Fr. & It. Jrnls.* II. 7 The statue has been restored, and..because the idea is perfect and indestructible, all these injuries do not..impair the effect.

4. In weakened sense: A conception or notion of something to be done or carried out; an intention, plan of action. ***big idea***: the purpose, intent. Freq. in ironic phr. ***what's*** (or ***what is***) ***the big idea?*** (orig. *U.S.*)

1617 MORYSON *Itin.* II. 245 You had alwaies in your owne judgement the certaine Idea thereof, as a thing that you resolved to doe. **1644** MILTON *Educ.* Wks. (1847) 98/2 That voluntary Idea, which hath long in silence presented itself to me, of a better education..than hath been yet in practice. **1770** BURKE *Corr.* (1844) I. 231 The idea of short parliaments is..plausible enough; so is the idea of an election by ballot. **1798** ROOT *Amer. Rep.* I. 44 If this performance meets with approbation..the author has it in idea to publish a second volume. **1861** HOLLAND *Less. Life* i. 12 We hear of women who are suddenly seized by an idea, as if it were a colic. **1908** G. H. LORIMER *Jack Spurlock* vii. 151 That's not the Big Idea, I know; it's the idiotic one, but the market for idiocy is unlimited. **1917** R. W. LARDNER *Gullible's Travels* (1926) iii. 83 Then we done a little spoonin' and then I ast her what was the big idear. **1927** A. P. HERBERT *Plain Jane* 52 But now I'm not wanted no more Unless it's for scrubbing a floor, And if that's what a person is for—Well, what's the Big Idea? **1933** M. LOWRY *Ultramarine* v. 220 What's the big idea not telling me before? **1937** A. CHRISTIE *Death on Nile* I. i. 35 You're crazy! What's the big idea? **1951** M. MCLUHAN *Mech. Bride* 43/1 Latch onto our big idea index for deep consolation? **1962** P. GREGORY *Like Tigress at Bay* vii. 76 Jill entered, her face pale. 'What was the big idea?'

†**5.** A pattern, type; the original of which something else is a copy; a preliminary sketch or draft; something in an undeveloped state. *Obs.*

1669 GALE *Crt. Gentiles* I. Introd. 1 Some rude Idea or first lines thereof were drawn many years past in mine Academic Studies. **1677** *Ibid.* III. 127 Those Pagan, Jewish, and Gnostic Antichrists..as forerunners and ideas of the great Roman Antichrist. **1670–98** LASSELS *Voy. Italy* 123 This was the first Cupola in Europe, and therefore the more admirable for having no Idea after which it was framed. **1692** RAY *Dissol. World* iv. (1732) 57 Those Ideas or Embryos may be..marred or deformed in the womb.

6. *Mus.* A musical theme, phrase, or figure, as conceived or sketched before being worked up in a composition.

1880 GROVE *Dict. Mus.* I. 165 [Beethoven's] sketch-books of that time are crammed with ideas.

II. Figure, form, image.

†**7. a.** A figure, representation, likeness, image, symbol, 'picture' (*of* something). *Obs.*

1531 ELYOT *Gov.* I. xxii, I haue..noted daunsinge to be of an excellent utilitie, comprehendinge in it wonderfull figures, or, as the grekes do calle them, *Ideae*, of vertues and noble qualities. **1594** SHAKS. *Rich. III*, III. vii. 13, I did inferre your Lineaments, Being the right Idea of your Father, Both in your forme, and Noblenesse of Minde. **1598** B. JONSON *Ev. Man in Hum.* II. iii, Hold up your head, do; and let the *Idea* of what you are, bee portray'd i' your face. **1634** SIR T. HERBERT *Trav.* 190 Where a top or high Mount is conspicuously set the Idæa of a horrible Caco-demon. **1641** FRENCH *Distill.* Pref. (1651) *iij, The Idea of a plant [may be made] to appear in a glasse, as if the very plant it selfe were there. **1707** *Curios. in Husb. & Gard.* 325 When a Body is..reduc'd into Ashes, we find again in the Salts, extracted from its Ashes, the Idea, the Image, and the Phantom of the same Body. **1714** SWIFT *Pres. St. Affairs* Wks. 1755 II. I. 211 A ship's crew quarreling in a storm.. is but a faint idea of this fatal infatuation.

†**b.** Form, figure (as a quality or attribute); configuration, shape; aspect; nature or character.

1594 Blundevil *Exerc.* III. I. ii. (1636) 279 The chiefe Idea or shape of Gods mind, which hath neither beginning nor ending, and therefore is compared to a Circle. **1653** H. More *Antid. Ath.* II. v. (1712) 54 Other solid Figures, which though they be not Regular, properly so called, yet have a settled Idea and Nature, as a Cone, Sphear, or Cylinder. **1677** Gale *Crt. Gentiles* III. 26 To demonstrate the vanitie of Philosophie from its own essential Idea or Nature. **1737** [S. Berington] *G. di Lucca's Mem.* 198 To return to the Idea of their Government, each Father of a Family governs all his Descendants.

†**c.** A 'figure' of speech or rhetoric; a form or way of speaking. *Obs.*

1642 Milton *Apol. Smect.* i, Whether a vehement vein throwing out indignation or scorn upon an object that merits it, were among the aptest ideas of speech to be allowed.

III. Mental image, conception, notion.

8. An image existing or formed in the mind.

†**a.** The mental image or picture of something previously seen or known, and recalled by the memory. *Obs.*

1589 Greene *Menaphon* (Arb.) 41 Me thinkes the Idea of her person represents it selfe an obiect to my fantasie. **1594** Spenser *Amoretti* xlv, Within my hart..The fayre Idea of your celestiall hew..remaines immortally. **1599** Shaks. *Much Ado* IV. i. 226 Th' Idea of her life shal sweetly creepe Into his study of imagination. **1662** J. Davies tr. *Olearius' Voy. Ambass.* 220 After he had earnestly view'd the Boy, and by that means Imprinted an Idea of him in his imagination. **1749** Fielding *Tom Jones* XIII. xi, Though I despaired of possessing you..I doted still on your charming idea. **1764** Foote *Mayor of G.* I. 19 Oh, Madam, I can never be alone; your sweet idea [*printed* idera] will be my constant companion.

b. More generally: A picture or notion of anything conceived by the mind; a conception.

1612 Brinsley *Lud. Lit.* vii. (1627) 84 To have an *Idæa* or generall notion of all in their heads. **1616** Bullokar, *Idea*, the forme or figure of any thing conceiued in the minde. **1651** Hobbes *Leviath.* II. xxxi. 190 To say we conceive, and imagine, or have an *Idea* of him [etc.]. **1659** Stanley *Hist. Philos.* XI. (1701) 448/2 Idæa's are notions of the Mind, and subsist in our Mind..as Similitudes and Images of Beings. **1662** J. Davies tr. *Mandelslo's Trav.* 284 Of this place I had heard so much..that I had framed to my self a certain Idæa of its greatnesse. **1712–14** Pope *Rape Lock* I. 83 Then gay Ideas crowd the vacant brain, While Peers, and Dukes, and all their sweeping train..appear. **1729** Switzer *Hydrost. & Hydraul.* 176 We acquire..an Idea of Solidity by the Touch. **1759** Johnson *Rasselas* xlvii, What space does the idea of a pyramid occupy more than the idea of a grain of corn? **1857** Maurice *Ep. St. John* xv. 242 This is the completest idea of love, the only complete idea we can have.

c. A conception to which no reality corresponds; something merely imagined or fancied.

1588 Shaks. *L.L.L.* IV. ii. 69 A foolish extrauagant spirit, full of formes, figures, shapes, objects, Ideas, apprehensions. **1622** Wither *Mistr. Philar.* Wks. (1633) 651 Is it possible that I Who scarce heard of Poesie Should a meare Idea raise To as true a pitch of praise As the learned Poets could? **1630** Prynne *Anti-Armin.* 156 Which make.. Predestination a meere Idæa. **1720** Waterland *Eight Serm.* 199 Not so destitute of..understanding, as to take the Substance of Father, or Son, to be an abstract Idea. **1871** R. W. Dale *Commandm.* i. 32 To the Jews, Jehovah was not a mere idea or a system of attributes.

d. *in idea* (= F. *en idée*), in conception or imagination; in mind, in thought: opposed to *in reality*.

1622 Mabbe tr. *Aleman's Guzman d'Alf.* II. I. i. 2 Albeit.. I were such an arrant Asse and Coxecombe, as you forsooth in your Idea would forme mee to be. **1632** B. Jonson *Magn. Lady* Induct., The author..hath phant'sied to himselfe, in Idæa, this Magneticke Mistris. **1701** Norris *Ideal World* I. ii. 16 Men talk..of things in idea..a line in idea, a circle in idea. **1807** Byron *Child. Recoll.* 45 Bright in idea gleams thy lofty spire. **1830** B'ness Bunsen in Hare *Life* (1879) I. ix. 347 How many vignettes did I make in my idea for my intended letter?

9. a. More widely: Any product of mental apprehension or activity, existing in the mind as an object of knowledge or thought; an item of knowledge or belief; a thought, conception, notion; a way of thinking.

c **1645** Howell *Lett.* (1655) III. xxvi. 38 One shall hardly find two in ten thousand that have exactly..the same tone of voice..or idæas of mind. **1690** Boyle *Chr. Virtuoso* I. 104 Either Congenite, or very easily and very early Acquir'd Notions and Idæas. **1713** Swift *Cadenus & Vanessa* 555 Ideas came into her mind So fast, his lessons lagg'd behind. **1728–46** Thomson *Spring* 1152 Delightful task! to rear the tender thought, To teach the young idea how to shoot. **1785** Reid *Intell. Powers* I. i. (1803) 36 In popular language idea signifies the same thing as conception, apprehension, notion. **1822** Hazlitt *Table-t.* II. iv. 60 People who have no ideas of their own are glad to hear what any one else has to say. **1888** J. Inglis *Tent Life Tigerland* 245 The marvellous way in which Western ideas are making progress in the minds of the natives.

b. A notion or thought more or less imperfect, indefinite, or fanciful; a vague belief, opinion, or estimate; a supposition, impression, fancy. *to have no idea*: (*a*) not to anticipate or expect (a situation or occurrence); (*b*) to be unable to comprehend; usu. in phr. *you have no idea.*

1712 W. Rogers *Voy.* 338 To give them an ill Idea of all those they..call Hereticks. **1737** [S. Berington] *G. di Lucca's Mem.* 58 The vast Ideas they had of their own Nation, valuing themselves above all other People. **1790** Burke *Fr. Rev.* 44 The very idea of the fabrication of a new government is enough to fill us with disgust and horror. **1852** E. Ruskin *Let.* 17 Apr. in M. Lutyens *Effie in Venice* (1965) II. 298 In two days he got it done and they are grateful you have no idea. **1852** Mrs. Stowe *Uncle Tom's C.* xxvi, 'You believe, don't you, that Topsy could become an angel ..if she were a Christian?' 'Topsy! what a ridiculous idea!' **1861** Dickens *Gt. Expect.* xi, So like Matthew! The idea! **1866** G. Macdonald *Ann. Q. Neighb.* xxx. (1878) 523, I had no idea you would be flooded. **1916** 'Taffrail' *Pincher Martin* vii. 114 He's that conceited, you've no idea.

c. Colloq. phr. *to get* (or *have*) *ideas* (*into one's head*): to conceive notions of a particular kind, usu. undesirable or harmful; *spec.* to entertain a notion or intention of being rebellious, violent, etc.

c **1848** F. A. Kemble *Let.* in *Rec. Later Life* (1882) III. 322 A young boy..brought up in a girl's convent, and taken out for a week, during which he..sups and gets tipsy at the mess, and, in short, 'gets ideas' of all sorts. **1932** H. C. Wyld *Universal Dict. Eng. Lang., To get ideas into one's head*, to cherish illusions. **1935** J. C. Squire *Reflections & Memories* 10 Babus would get ideas into their heads, but the Mutiny had taught its lesson and the redcoat had the situation well in hand. **1941** I. Baird *He rides Sky* 146 That's the second happy couple I've seen busted up in a month and it's cured me if I ever had ideas. I'd no more marry with a war on than jump over the moon. **1955** W. C. Gault *Ring around Rosa* vii. 82 Don't get any ideas, Brock Callahan. There are times when I simply—I mean, there's a definite therapeutical need for some form of release in a society as hectic as ——. *Ibid.* xiii. 156 Don't get any ideas, Callahan. This is an easy trigger.

d. Used after a possessive to denote a person's conception of an ideal, typical, or adequate example of the person or thing specified.

1903 G. B. Shaw *Man & Superman* III. 111 Is that your idea of a woman's mind? I call it cynical and disgusting materialism. **1907** —— *John Bull's Other Island* I. 7 Now thats my poor English idea of a whisky and soda. **1919** E. O'Neill *In Zone* in *Moon of Caribbees* (1923) 22 If this is your idea of a joke I'll have to confess it's a bit too thick for me to enjoy. **1933** —— *Ah, Wilderness!* (1934) I. 21 Gosh, he's always reading now. It's not my idea of having a good time in vacation. **1969** *Listener* 10 July 39/3 He would not be everyone's idea of a military dictator.

e. An idea worthy of consideration or capable of realization; a possibility; usu. in phr. *it's* (or *that's*) *an idea. colloq.*

1914 G. B. Shaw *Misalliance* 27 Thats an idea. Thats a new idea. I believe I ought to have made Johnny an author. **1919** —— *Inca of Perusalem* in *Heartbreak House* 197 Thats an idea. I will. **1942** A. Christie *Body in Library* i. 19 It *might* be. It's an idea, Jane. **1973** K. Giles *File on Death* i. 16 'I suppose I can take my Sergeant.'..'It might be an idea. .. Your Sergeant might wheedle his way where Chief Inspectors fear to tread.'

IV. Modern philosophical developments.

10. [from 8 and 9.] With Descartes and Locke: Whatever is in the mind and directly present to cognitive consciousness; that which one thinks, feels, or fancies; the immediate object of thought or mental perception.

With Hume and his followers: An impression of sensation, either as original or as reproduced and elaborated by association. With Reid, Dugald Stewart, and the Scottish school: The immediate and direct mental product of knowing, as distinguished from the object of knowledge, and from the action or process of knowing.

1666 *Phil. Trans.* I. 325 The Arguments devised against Atheists by Des Cartes, and drawn from the Idea's of our Mind. **1690** Locke *Hum. Und.* I. i, I must here in the Entrance beg Pardon..for the frequent use of the Word *Idea*... It being that Term, which, I think, serves best to stand for whatsoever is the Object of the Understanding when a Man thinks, I have used it to express..whatever it is, which the Mind can be employ'd about in thinking. *Ibid.* II. viii. §8 Whatsoever the Mind perceives in itself, or is the immediate Object of Perception, Thought, or Understanding, that I call *Idea*. **1709** Berkeley *Th. Vision* §45 When I speak of tangible ideas, I take the word idea for any the immediate object of sense, or understanding. **1710** —— *Princ. Hum. Knowl.* I. §2 The existence of an idea consists in being perceived. **1725** Watts *Logic* I. iii. §1 There has been a great controversy about the origin of ideas, viz. Whether any of our ideas are innate or no, that is, born with us, and naturally belonging to our minds. Mr. Locke utterly denies it; others as positively affirm it. *Ibid.* §2 A simple Idea is one uniform Idea which cannot be divided or distinguished by the Mind of Man into two or more Ideas; such are a Multitude of our Sensations, as the Idea of *Sweet, Bitter, Cold, Heat, White, Red, Blue, Hard, Soft.* **1739** Hume *Hum. Nat.* I. i. (1874) I. 311 By ideas I mean the faint images of these [impressions] in thinking and reasoning. **1762** Kames *Elem. Crit.* (1833) 478 This indistinct secondary perception of an object, is termed an idea. **1837–9** Hallam *Hist. Lit.* IV. iii. §107 The leading doctrine of Locke, as is well known, is the derivation of all our ideas from sensation and from reflection. **1843** Mill *Logic* IV. ii. §i, The metaphysical inquiry into the nature and composition of what have been called Abstract Ideas. **1860** Mansel *Proleg. Log.* i. 33 *Idea* has been indifferently employed by modern philosophers to denote the object of thought, of imagination, and even (under the representative hypothesis) of perception.

11. [from 1.] **a.** In the Kantian and transcendental schools: A conception of reason that transcends all experience; one of the *noumena* or ultimate principles apprehended by reason, as opposed to the conceptions of the understanding, which are confined to experience. **b.** In Hegelianism: The absolute truth of which all phenomenal existence is the expression; *the Idea*, the Absolute.

1838 *Penny Cycl.* XII. 99/1 Hegel distinguishes three species of thought..1. The *thought*...2. The *notion*...3. The *idea* , or thought in its totality and fully determined. *a* **1871** Grote *Eth. Fragm.* v. (1876) 138 This conception is what Kant would call an *Idea*—nothing precisely conformable to it, in its full extent, can ever exist in reality. **1874** W. Wallace *Logic of Hegel* Proleg. xxii. 174 This organism of thought, as the living reality or gist of the external world and the world within us, is termed the Idea. The Idea is the 'reality' and the ' ideality' of the world or totality, considered as a process beyond time. *Ibid.* xxiii. 181 *Idee* (idea) is the thorough adequacy of thought to itself, the solution of the contradictions which attach to thought, and hence, in the last resort, the coincidence or equilibrium of subjective notion and objectivity, which are the ultimate expression of that fundamental antithesis in thought. *Ibid.* §213. 304 The Idea is truth in itself and for itself,—the absolute unity of the notion and objectivity.

V. 12. *attrib.* and *Comb. idea-monger*; **idea(s) man**, a creative, inventive, or ingenious man.

1796 Coleridge in J. Cottle *Early Recoll.* (1837) I. 171 No poor fellow's idea-pot ever bubbled up so vehemently with fears, doubts, and difficulties. **1840** H. Reeve tr. *A. de Tocqueville's Democracy in Amer.* III. I. xiv. 123 For some few great authors..you may reckon thousands of idea-mongers. **1891** *Pall Mall G.* 10 Oct. 2/3 In most art matters we are quite eighteen years behind our idea-intoxicated neighbours. **1896** *Daily News* 26 Apr. 6/1 Mr. H...detests 'idea' politics and Republican 'sentiments' of every kind. **1909** *Englishwoman* Apr. 305 Ibsen.. was not merely an ideamonger, but a dramatist. **1923** *Glasgow Herald* 25 Jan. 4/2 Mr. Wells is a prolific idea-monger. **1938** 'E. Queen' *Four of Hearts* (1939) i. 10 You're an idea man, and that's what they pay off on in Hollywood. **1940** *Ann. Reg. 1939* 363 Bryan Wallace was appointed Ideas Man to the Government. **1954** Koestler *Invis. Writing* xxxi. 333 He looked like the nonchalant impresario and idea-man of the great Comintern variety show. **1958** [see *copywriter*]. **1960** *Guardian* 16 Nov. 7/3 David Bean, the ideas man, has specialized in exposing traps laid for consumers. **1967** *Ibid.* 17 Feb. 8/5 Dilettante ideas-men like Teilhard de Chardin.

idea (aɪˈdiːə), *v. rare.* [f. prec. sb.] †**a.** *trans.* To give a particular form or character to (cf. prec. 7 b). **b.** *intr.* To form ideas or notions.

1649 J. Ecclíston tr. *Behmen's Ep.* 84 Hee doth Idea, forme, and shape, in the same Being the wonders of the expressed Word. *Ibid.*, The humane Science..doth Idea, and shape it selfe both in good and evill, and maketh it selfe Essentiall therein. **1844** *Fraser's Mag.* XXIX. 133 According to him [Cousin], man should not be defined a reasoning, but an ideaing creature.

idea'd, ideaed (aɪˈdiːəd), *a.* [f. idea *sb.* + -ed².] Having an idea or ideas, *esp.* (in comb.) of a specified kind; expressing an idea, significant (quot. 1826).

1753 [see unidea'd]. **1826** *Blackw. Mag.* XIX. 106 Such a flood of idea'd words, that you..have been unable to slip in one of your long-treasured truisms. **1852** Reade *Peg Woff.* (1856) 204 Everybody could hear what anyone said; an excellent arrangement where ideaed guests only are admitted. **1868** Helps *Realmah* xiv. (1876) 387 Women are so persevering, and so one idea'd.

ideagenous (aɪdiːˈædʒɪnəs), *a.* [irreg. f. idea + -genous. (The etymological form would be *ideogenous.*)] Producing or giving rise to an idea.

1881 Huxley *Sc. & Cult.* ix. 235 Each sensory impression leaves behind a record in the structure of the brain—an 'ideagenous' molecule, so to speak.

ideagraph, etc., erron. ff. ideograph, etc.

ideal (aɪˈdiːəl), *a.* and *sb.* [a. F. *idéal* (16–17th c. in Hatz.-Darm.), ad. late L. *ideālis*, f. *idea* idea. Cf. It. *ideale*, Sp., Pg. *ideal.*]

A. *adj.* **1. a.** Existing as an idea or archetype; relating to or consisting of ideas (in the Platonic sense): see idea *sb.* 1.

1647 H. More *Song of Soul* I. II. x, His Ideall, And Centrall presence is in every Atom-ball. **1691–8** Norris *Pract. Disc.* (1711) III. 153 The Natural existence of things is founded upon their Ideal existence; if things had not first existed in Idea, they could never have existed in Nature. **1701** —— *Ideal World* I. i. 8 By the Ideal state of things I mean that state of them which is necessary, permanent and immutable, not only antecedent and præexisting to this, but also exemplary and representative of it..according to which it was made. **1896** Dk. Argyll *Philos. Belief* 88 Moulded on a mental plan..so clear, that every bone..and even in some cases the absence of a bone, can be referred with certainty to one ideal plan.

b. *Sociol.* **ideal type** [ad. G. *idealtypus* (M. Weber 1922, in *Grundriss d. Sozialökonomik* I. i. 3), f. ideal *a.* + *typus* type *sb.*¹], a hypothetical construct made up of the salient features or elements of a social phenomenon, or generalized concept, in order to facilitate comparison and classification of what is found in operation. Also (with hyphen) *attrib.* Hence **ideal-typical** *a.*, of or pertaining to an ideal type; **ideal typology**, the concept of ideal types.

1928 P. A. Sorokin *Contemp. Sociol. Theories* xii. 677 The outlined 'spirit of modern capitalism' is an example of one of the 'ideal types' of Max Weber. **1936** Wirth & Shils tr. *Mannheim's Ideology & Utopia* iv. 189 The pure types..of the utopian mind are constructions only in so far as they are conceived of as *ideal-types*. *Ibid.* 204 Max Weber always insisted that his general typology was created in order to characterize ideal-typical tendencies, and not immediately perceivable unique constellations. **1947** Henderson & Parsons tr. *Weber's Theory Social & Econ. Organiz.* I. i. 84 As a type ('ideal type') which has the merit of clear understandability and lack of ambiguity. **1949** R. K. Merton *Social Theory* xiv. 329 The Puritan ethic, as an ideal-typical expression of the value-attitudes basic to ascetic Protestantism generally, so canalized the interests of seventeenth-century Englishmen. **1962** T. B. Bottomore

Sociol. ii. 33 Weber's exposition of his 'ideal type' method. **1964** GOULD & KOLB *Dict. Social Sci.* 311/2 *Ideal-type analysis* denotes a method of sociological analysis associated with the name of M. Weber. **1964** I. L. HOROWITZ *New Sociol.* 42 Accounts of history that..were at best 'ideal-typologies' with strong subjective biases. *Ibid.* 456 The idealized or ideal-typical individual entrepreneur as against the political collectivity.

2. a. Conceived or regarded as perfect or supremely excellent in its kind; answering to one's highest conception. Cf. IDEA *sb.* 2, 3.

1613 R. CAWDREY *Table Alph.* (ed. 3), *Ideall*, proper. **1626** JACKSON *Creed* VIII. iii. §2 The Almighty Lord..the very law or Idæal rule of all righteousnesse. **1736** BOLINGBROKE *Patriot.* (1749) 177 The practice of morality..will never arrive at ideal perfection. **1843** RUSKIN *Arrows of Chace* (1880) I. 10 Ideal beauty is the generalization of consummate knowledge, the concentration of perfect truth. **1861** B'NESS BUNSEN in Hare *Life* II. v. 298 The sea-coast in the winter is to me an ideal enjoyment, by which I mean, completely the thing I like. **1874** GREEN *Short Hist.* iii. §1. 115 Sir Galahad, the type of ideal knighthood.

b. ***ideal language*** (Philos.): a supposed language which would mirror the world perfectly (cf. *logically perfect language*).

1922 B. RUSSELL in tr. *Wittgenstein's Tractatus* Introd. 8 The whole function of language is to have meaning, and it only fulfils this function in proportion as it approaches to the ideal language which we postulate. **1944** M. BLACK in P. A. Schilpp *Philos. B. Russell* 251 The 'ideal language' is, by definition, the symbolism which would be entirely free from the philosophical defects which Russell claims to find in ordinary language. **1953** G. E. M. ANSCOMBE tr. *Wittgenstein's Philos. Investigations* I. §81 It may look as if what we were talking about were an *ideal* language. **1963** R. CARNAP in P. A. Schilpp *Philos. R. Carnap* 29 When we found in Wittgenstein's book statements about 'the language', we interpreted them as referring to an ideal language; and this meant for us a formalized symbolic language. **1964** M. BLACK *Compan. to Wittgenstein's Tractatus* xx. 133 In this section W. seems to be subscribing to the ideal of an 'ideal language'. But cf. 5.5563*a* (ordinary language is perfectly in order). **1967** *Encycl. Philos.* VII. 361 The frequently recurring project of an ideal language is to be found for the first time in the very first extant treatise on language. **1973** A. KENNY *Wittgenstein* iv. 70 In an ideal language,..to each element of the propositional sign would correspond a single object in the world.

3. a. Of, pertaining or relating to, or of the nature of an idea, mental image, or conception.

1611 COTGR., *Ideal*, ideall; imaginarie, conceiued in th' imagination; onely in fancie. **1661** BOYLE *Style of Script.* 232 All things Related to her..Refreshing him with an Ideal, in the Absence of an Immediate Presence of her. **1759** JOHNSON *Rasselas* xlvii, An ideal form is no less real than material bulk: yet an ideal form has no extension. *a* **1862** BUCKLE *Civiliz.* (1873) III. v. 303 Starting from the so called nature of things, his first steps were ideal and from them he sought to advance to the actual.

b. Representing or embodying an idea or conception.

1846 RUSKIN *Mod. Paint.* (1851) II. III. I. xiii. §2 Any work of art which represents, not a material object, but the mental conception of a material object, is, in the primary sense of the word, ideal. **1874** MICKLETHWAITE *Mod. Par. Churches* 112 The crucifix..is an ideal, not a realistic representation.

4. a. Existing only in idea; confined to thought or imagination; imaginary: opp. to *real* or *actual*. Hence sometimes, Not real or practical; based on an idea or fancy; fancied, visionary.

1611 [see 3]. *a* **1637** STIRLING *Jonathan* XXV, Fed their fancies with Ideall shewes. **1757** HOME *Douglas* I, A river here, there an ideal line, By fancy drawn, divides the sister kingdoms. **1776** GIBBON *Decl. & F.* I. x. 272 They despised the ideal terrors of a foreign superstition. **1787** WINTER *Syst. Husb.* 168 These assertions are not ideal, but are founded on facts and experiments. **1803** W. TAYLOR in *Monthly Mag.* XIV. 492 Colour, time, space, may be said to have only an ideal reality. **1862** H. SPENCER *First Princ.* II. ii. §43 (1875) 144 Ideal sights and sounds are in the insane ..classed with real sights and sounds. **1877** E. R. CONDER *Bas. Faith* iii. 109 The facts are physical; their harmony is ideal. *Ibid.* 111 It is ideal, capable of existence only in thought; at all events inconceivable by us in any other way.

b. ***ideal construction*** (Philos.): a mental conception formed by abstracting properties found in experience and recombining or developing them; the process of forming such a conception.

1874 G. H. LEWES *Foundation of Creed* I. 288 Hume did not clearly understand that Science is essentially an ideal construction very far removed from a real transcript of facts. **1877** —— *Physical Basis of Mind* I. i. 8 This unity is only recognised in an *ideal construction* which lets drop all concrete differences. *Ibid.* III. i. 314 Science..is the systematisation of Experience under the forms of ideal constructions. **1883** F. H. BRADLEY *Princ. Logic* I. ii. 75 Ideal constructions connected, by an inference through identity of quality, with the real that appears in present perception. **1890** W. JAMES *Princ. Psychol.* I. xiii. 533 We have a *conception* of absolute sameness,..but this..is an ideal construction got by following a certain direction of serial increase to its maximum supposable extreme. **1901** G. F. STOUT *Man. Psychol.* (ed. 2) IV. vi. §7. 531 The external world as an ideal construction is a social product. **1917** J. GIBSON *Locke's Theory of Knowledge* iv. 78 The nature of ideal construction as the discovery of possible alternatives admitted by the nature of some universal. **1946** *Mind* LV. 153 Suppose, however, that Euclidean points are ideal constructions.

5. *Philos.* Regarding or treating ideas as the only real entities; of the nature of or pertaining to idealism; idealistic.

1764 REID *Inquiry* i. §7. 103 Des Cartes' system of the human understanding, which I shall beg leave to call the *ideal system.* **1792–1814** D. STEWART *Philos. Hum. Mind* (1843) 317 As Clarke..regarded the principles of the ideal theory as incontrovertible, it was perfectly impossible for him, with all his acuteness, to detect the flaw to which Berkeley's paradox owed its plausibility. **1836** EMERSON *Nature, Idealism* Wks. (Bohn) II. 160 The frivolous make themselves merry with the Ideal theory..as if it affected the stability of nature.

6. a. *Math.* Applied to a number or quantity which has no actual existence, but is assumed for some purpose in a system of complex numbers.

1860 H. J. S. SMITH in *Rep. Brit. Assoc.* 132 (Theory of Numbers) The assertion that a given complex number contains an ideal factor, is only a convenient mode of expressing a certain set of congruential conditions which are satisfied by the coefficients of the complex number. *Ibid.* 133 Every ideal number is a divisor of an actual number. **1875** B. PEIRCE in *Amer. Jrnl. Math.* (1881) IV. 216 The A, B, and C..may represent not merely the actual, but also the ideal, the impossible as well as the possible.

b. *Geom.* [ad. F. *idéal*, introduced in this sense by J. V. Poncelet (*Traité des Propriétés proj. des Figures* (1822) I. ii. §§50 ff.).] Having no proper existence in real Euclidean geometry as the thing so designated, but introduced into projective or complex geometry in order to do away with what would otherwise be exceptions to generalizations; chiefly in ***ideal point***, the single point (at infinity) at which two parallel lines are regarded as intersecting; similarly ***ideal line, plane***, the single line (or plane) at infinity that is regarded as containing all the ideal points (or lines) of a plane (or of space).

1879 *Encycl. Brit.* X. 389/1 We may say that all points at infinity in a line *appear* to us as one, and may be replaced by a single 'ideal' point. **1885** C. LEUDESDORF tr. *Cremona's Elem. Projective Geom.* xxi. 226 The segment *HH'* has been called an ideal chord of the conic... Accepting this definition we may say that a diameter contains the middle points of all chords, real and ideal, which are parallel to the conjugate diameter. **1937** B. C. PATTERSON *Projective Geom.* i. 4 Such considerations lead us to assume the existence, in each plane, of one and only one ideal line. It is the locus of all the ideal points of the plane, and it is also the line of intersection of the plane with all parallel planes. *Ibid.* 5 We assume..the existence of an ideal plane of space, the locus of all ideal points and ideal lines of space. **1962** W. T. FISHBACK *Projective & Euclidean Geom.* iv. 32 We created the projective plane by adding ideal points and an ideal line to the Euclidean plane.

7. *Comb.* as **ideal case**, one perfect or supremely excellent of its kind; **ideal copy** *Bibliogr.*, the most complete and perfect copy possible of an issue of a printed book, as properly described in a descriptive bibliography from the examination and analysis of multiple particular copies; **ideal fluid**, a hypothetical fluid that has no viscosity (no internal friction) and is incompressible; **ideal gas**, a hypothetical gas (which actual gases approach more or less closely in their behaviour) for which the product of the pressure and the volume (of a given mass) is proportional to its absolute temperature; **ideal home**, used, esp. in titles as *Ideal Home Exhibition, Ideal Home Magazine*, in the sense 'a well-designed functional house (and its contents)'; **ideal observer** *Philos.* (see quot. 1957); **ideal-real** *a.*, combining the ideal and the real; **ideal-realism**, a form of philosophy which combines the principles of idealism and realism; **ideal state**, an imaginary perfectly constituted political community, harmonious and stable; **ideal utilitarianism**, in ethics, any form of utilitarianism which takes other intrinsic goods besides pleasure as ultimate ends, together constituting an ideal end; so **ideal utilitarian**, an adherent of ideal utilitarianism; also as *attrib. phr.*, of or pertaining to such a theory.

1847 W. WHEWELL *Philos. Inductive Sci.* (ed. 2) XI. v. 49 A body left to itself will move on with unaltered velocity; ..(taking this as our Ideal Case) we find that all actual cases are intelligible. **1961** E. NAGEL *Struct. of Sci.* xiii. 463 A.. device commonly employed in the natural sciences is to formulate a law for a so-called 'ideal case'... For example, Galileo's law for freely falling bodies is formulated for bodies moving in a vacuum. **1949** F. BOWERS *Princ. Bibliogr. Descr.* ii. 113 An *ideal copy* is a book which is complete in all its leaves as it ultimately left the printer's shop in perfect condition and in the complete state that he considered to represent the final and most perfect state of the book... [*Footnote*] Nothing is invented in the description of an ideal copy. Instead, all the evidence to be gained from the examination of numbers of copies is analyzed..in order to discover what was the actual most perfect form of the book achieved by the printer within an issue. **1952** J. CARTER *ABC for Bk.-Collectors* 102 Though it is possible for an individual example of the book in question to conform to it, the 'ideal copy' is a sort of Platonic archetype, exhibiting the final intention of the author, publisher and printer at the completion of printing, in so far as this is capable of being established. **1969** E. W. PADWICK *Bibliogr. Method* iii. 29 Partly because each library is mainly concerned with its own collection, and partly because of the extreme rarity of many incunabula, bibliographical descriptions of these works are based more often than not on the examination of works in a single collection and not on the characteristics of an ideal copy. **1972** P. GASKELL *New Introd. Bibliogr.* 321 A bibliography based on analytical techniques is not the same thing as a catalogue of particular books... Indeed it does not describe particular books but ideal copies of its subjects, following the examination of as many actual copies as possible of each one. **1857** THOMSON & JOULE in *Proc. R. Soc.* VIII. 556 If a solid..be carried uniformly through a perfect liquid. [*Note*] That is, as we shall call it for brevity, an ideal fluid, perfectly incompressible and perfectly free from mutual friction among its parts. **1948** V. L. STREETER *Fluid Dynamics* i. 6 Many conclusions concerning the motion of a solid through an ideal fluid are applicable with slight modification to the motion of an airship through the air or to the motion of a submarine through the ocean. **1891** G. KAMENSKY tr. *Mendeléeff's Princ. Chem.* I. ii. 139 For a so-called perfect (ideal) gas, or for considerable variations of density, the elementary expression $pv = Ra(t + at)$, or $pv = R(273 + t)$ should be accepted. **1948** GLASSTONE *Textbk. Physical Chem.* (ed. 2) iii. 192 For a given mass of an ideal gas at constant pressure, therefore,..the volume is proportional to the absolute temperature. This relationship ..is the basis of an ideal gas scale of temperature. *Ibid.*, Instead of defining an ideal gas as one obeying the laws of Boyle and Gay-Lussac, it may be described as one to which Boyle's law is applicable, and whose internal energy is independent of its volume at all temperatures; it can be shown..that these two postulates include Gay-Lussac's law. **1913** R. FRY *Lett.* (1972) II. 371 You left a letter here from the Ideal Home Exhibition people asking Lewis to do decorations. *Ibid.* 373 I've not heard a word about the Ideal Home. Has it been a success..? **1925** A. HUXLEY *Those Barren Leaves* I. iv. 41 Agreeing..was a labour-saving device..a necessity in this Ideal Home. **1935** *Burlington Mag.* Jan. 3/2 The plans rather suggest an Ideal Home Exibition. **1967** K. GILES *Death in Diamonds* vi. 105 A big room furnished with a modernity which might be next year's Ideal Home. **1967** 'M. HUNTER' *Cambridgeshire Disaster* vi. 40 A baby grand piano..which gave a slightly Mayfairish touch of sophistication to the otherwise Ideal Homes format. **1969** *New Yorker* 29 Nov. 56/3 What d'you bet he considers it the Ideal Home? **1972** R. PERRY *Fall Guy* v. 86 The furniture wasn't out of Ideal Home..affording me no aesthetic pleasure whatsoever. **1952** R. FIRTH in *Philos. & Phenomenol. Research* XII. 317 (*title*) Ethical absolutism and the ideal observer. **1957** P. EDWARDS in Edwards & Pap *Mod. Introd. Philos.* 390 The..'ideal observer' theory of Adam Smith and others..maintains that 'X is good' can be translated into some such statement as 'If there were an omniscient, disinterested and dispassionate observer he would approve of X'. **1959** R. B. BRANDT *Ethical Theory* vii. 174 We must explain further the properties of the 'ideal observer'. **1971** T. D. CAMPBELL *Adam Smith's Sci. of Morals* vi. 128, I shall argue..that to present Smith's theory as a form of Ideal Observer theory is a mistake. **1972** J. RAWLS *Theory of Justice* §30. 185 Suppose that the ideal observer is thought of as a perfectly sympathetic being. **1886** *New Princeton Rev.* Jan. 22 (Cent.) The half-and-half systems, the ideal-real as they are called, held by so many in the present day in Germany, are in the position of a professedly neutral person between two hostile armies, exposed to the fire of both. **1874** W. WALLACE tr. *Hegel's Logic* Prolegomena xix. p. cxlvi, The measure dominates the conception of Plato's ideal state. **1892** B. JOWETT tr. *Plato's Dialogues* (ed. 3) V. Index 442 Ideal state, the, difficulty of. **1901** R. L. NETTLESHIP *Lect. Republic of Plato* (ed. 2) vi. 131 An outline is given of the institutions of the ideal state. **1931** L. R. PALMER tr. *Zeller's Outl. Hist. Greek Philos.* II. iii. 126 The Syracusan Hermocrates was to describe the degeneration from the original ideal state to the present. **1946** A. GRAY *Socialist Tradition* iii. 63 The actual description of life in the ideal state—the social gadgets—may appear trivial and puerile. **1952** K. R. POPPER *Open Soc.* (ed. 2) I. iii. 21 In believing in such an ideal state which does not change, Plato deviates radically from the tenets of historicism. **1967** *Encycl. Philos.* VI. 330/2 In the *Republic*, ..Plato delineates his famous Ideal State, or 'Callipolis'. **1970** J. PASSMORE *Perfectibility of Man* xii. 258 Kant looked forward..to an ideal State, or, in his later writings, to an 'ethical Commonwealth'. **1907** H. RASHDALL *Theory of Good & Evil* I. vii. 184 This view of ethics, which combines the utilitarian principle that Ethics must be teleological with a non-hedonistic view of the ethical end, I propose to call Ideal Utilitarianism. According to this view actions are right or wrong according as they tend to produce for all mankind an ideal end or good, which includes, but is not limited to, pleasure. **1930** W. D. ROSS *Right & Good* ii. 19 The theory of 'ideal utilitarianism', if I may for brevity refer so to the theory of Professor Moore. *Ibid.* 23 The 'ideal utilitarian' theory can only fall back on an opinion..that one of the goods is the greater. **1959** R. B. BRANDT *Ethical Theory* xiv. 355 Universal personal pluralism (often called 'ideal utilitarianism'). *Ibid.* xv. 385 Some ideal utilitarians (for example, Hastings Rashdall) think that qualities of character like veracity, sexual purity, and temperance have great intrinsic value. **1970** J. N. FINDLAY *Axiological Ethics* iii. 46 There is no reason why an ideal utilitarianism may not sometimes place so high a value on certain actions..as to let them outweigh all consequences.

B. *sb.*

1. a. A conception of something, or a thing conceived, in its highest perfection, or as an object to be realized or aimed at; a perfect type; a standard of perfection or excellence.

[**1623** COCKERAM, *Ideall*, a proper man.] **1796** F. A. NITSCH *Gen. View Kant's Princ. concerning Man* 52 Materialism, Idealism, Spiritualism, and Scepticism, are merely Ideals, which can only be approached, but never reached. **1798** W. TAYLOR in *Monthly Rev.* XXVI. 481 The ..dissertation..on the Ideals of the Greek artists. **1809–10** COLERIDGE *Friend* (1865) 125 The ideal to which..we should endeavour to approximate. **1845** M. PATTISON *Ess.* (1889) I. 1 Whether or no there be any perfect ideal of historical composition, the one best form of writing history for all ages and countries. **1859** MILL *Liberty* iii. (1865) 42/2 Advancing towards the Chinese ideal of making all people alike. *a* **1866** J. GROTE *Exam. Utilit. Philos.* xvii. (1870) 269 The notion of an *ideal*, of something which for whatever reason, *ought to be*, as distinguished from *what is*.

b. An actual thing or person regarded as realizing such a conception, and so as being perfect in its kind; a standard proposed for imitation.

a **1849** H. COLERIDGE *Ess.* (1851) II. 10 He seems to have made Donne his ideal. **1861** MAX MÜLLER *Chips* (1880) I. xiii. 310 His grandson speaks of him [Confucius] as the ideal of a sage. **1877** E. R. CONDER *Bas. Faith* i. 6 According to another authority God is the perfect ideal of which Nature is the imperfect realisation.

2. Something existing only as a mental conception; an imaginary thing.

1884 A. DANIELL *Princ. Physics* ix. 199 A rigid solid is one which, when a stress is applied to it, experiences no deformation.. This is an ideal; no substance is absolutely rigid.

3. *Math.* [a. G. *ideal* sb., introduced in this sense by R. Dedekind (in P. G. L. Dirichlet *Vorles. über Zahlentheorie* (ed. 2, 1871) Suppl. x. 452) after the adjectival use in *ideale zahl* ideal number (E. E. Kummer 1846, in *Ber. über die zur Bekanntmachung geeigneten Verh. d. K. Preuss. Akad. d. Wiss. zu Berlin* 87).] A subring that contains all products of the form *rx* and *xr*, where *r* and *x* are elements of the ring and of the subring, respectively; also called a *two-sided ideal*; *left* (or *right*) *ideal*, a subring that contains all products of the form *rx* (or *xr*).

1898 *Bull. Amer. Math. Soc.* IV. 228 The relation between Dedekind's ideals and Kronecker's forms is discussed. **1911** *Encycl. Brit.* XIX. 856/1 It is a fundamental theorem that every ideal can be resolved into the product of a finite number of prime ideals, and that this resolution is unique. **1937** A. A. ALBERT *Mod. Higher Algebra* (1938) xi. 253 Right ideals (right invariant subrings) are defined analogously, and we call 𝔐 an ideal (invariant subring) if it is both a right and a left ideal. When 𝔘 is commutative every right ideal is a left ideal so that every right or left ideal is an ideal. **1952** E. T. BELL *Math.* v. 80 The particular subvarieties of a ring called ideals have proved of great significance in the general theory of rings, particularly with regard to the structure or morphology of rings. Ideals entered modern algebra through the theory of algebraic numbers.. in the 1870s, but it was only in the 1920s and 1930s that their deeper relevance for much of algebra and algebraic geometry was recognized. **1969** F. M. HALL *Introd. Abstr. Algebra* II. vii. 181 An important example of an ideal is the subring of multiples of *n* in the ring of integers. *Ibid.*, Even when *R* is commutative not all subrings are ideals.

¶ See also BEAU-IDEAL.

idealess (aɪ'diːəlɪs), *a.* [f. IDEA *sb.* + -LESS.] Destitute of ideas; conveying no idea, meaningless.

1818 *Monthly Mag.* XLVI. 409 A few passages of good writing.. interlarded with idealess nonsense. **1856** MISS YONGE *Daisy Chain* II. v. (1879) 383 That stupid, idealess brother. **1875** *Contemp. Rev.* XXV. 800 The style of architecture.. is beyond words monotonous, idealess, soulless.

idealism (aɪ'diːəlɪz(ə)m). [ad. F. *idéalisme* (1752 in Hatz.-Darm.) or Ger. *idealismus*, f. IDEAL.]

1. *Philos.* Any system of thought or philosophy in which the object of external perception is held to consist, either in itself, or as perceived, of ideas (in various senses of the word: see IDEA *sb.*).

Subjective Idealism is the opinion that the object of external perception consists, whether in itself or as known to us, in ideas of the perceiving mind; ***Critical*** or ***Transcendental Idealism***, the opinion (of Kant) that it, together with the whole contents of our experience, consists, as known to us, but not necessarily in itself, of such ideas; ***Objective Idealism***, the opinion (of Schelling) that while, as known to us, it consists of such ideas, it consists also, as it is in itself, of ideas identical with these; ***Absolute Idealism***, (*a*) the opinion (of Hegel) that it consists, not only as known to us, but in itself, of ideas, not however ours, but those of the universal mind; (*b*) also applied more generally to other forms of idealism which do not suppose an independent reality underlying our ideas of external objects.

1796 W. TAYLOR in *Monthly Rev.* XX. 576 He [Parmenides] thus prepared arguments for scepticism, and made the first approaches towards idealism. **1803** —— in *Monthly Mag.* XIV. 487 The system of Berkeley.. is espoused under the name Idealism by writers of reputation in Germany. **1839** SIR W. HAMILTON *Discuss.* (1852) 196 A doctrine of Absolute Idealism was, without communication, contemporaneously promulgated by Berkeley and Collier. **1855** MEIKLEJOHN tr. *Kant's Critique of Pure Reason* 166 *note*, Formal or critical idealism—the theory of Kant—which denies us a knowledge of things in themselves and maintains that we can know only phenomena. **1856** DOVE *Logic Chr. Faith* v. i. §2. 270 Absolute Idealism means.. that thought is the all. **1865** LECKY *Ration.* (1878) I. 176 Shaftesbury retains a certain place as one of the few disciples of idealism who resisted the influence of Locke. **1872** MAHAFFY tr. *Kant's Prolegomena* 61 My having given this my theory the name of transcendental idealism, can authorise no one to confound it with the empirical idealism of Descartes. *Ibid.* 62, I now retract it [the word 'transcendental'] and desire this idealism of mine to be called critical. **1877** J. H. STIRLING *Annot. Schwegler's Handbk. Hist. Philos.* 420 The idealism of Fichte.. that reduced all to.. the ego.. was.. the subjective idealism. Then Schelling, who gave to the object an equal basis beside the subject, but still under an idealistic point of view, is said to have given rise to the objective idealism; while Hegel,.. because he subordinated all to thought alone, is styled the founder of the absolute idealism. **1886** CLIFFORD *Lect. & Ess., Nature of Things-in-Themselves* 276 It may very well be that I myself am the only existence, but it is simply ridiculous to suppose that anybody else is. The position of absolute idealism may, therefore, be left out of count. **1887** FLEMING & CALDERWOOD *Vocab. Philos.* 196 Subjective Idealism is the term applicable to the theories of Berkeley and Fichte. **1889** COURTNEY *Mill* 137 Idealism.. resolves all our notions of the external world into the subjective affections of the thinking self.

2. The practice of idealizing or tendency to idealize; the habit of representing things in an ideal form, or as they might be; imaginative treatment of a subject in art or literature; ideal style or character: opp. to *realism*. Also, aspiration after or pursuit of an ideal.

1829 I. TAYLOR *Enthus.* viii. 190 A transmutation of the objects of the devout affections into objects of imaginative delectation.. had tinged, more or less, with idealism, the religious sentiment of all but a few. **1841** W. SPALDING *Italy & It. Isl.* II. 350 The perfected idealism which reigns in his [Titian's] greatest works. **1871** FRASER *Life Berkeley* iii. 87 The project of social idealism which.. filled and determined his life in its middle period. **1890** HALL CAINE in *Contemp. Rev.* Apr. 479, I take realism to mean the doctrine of the importance of the real facts of life, and idealism the doctrine of the superiority of ideal existence over the facts of life.

b. (with *pl.*) An instance of this practice; an act or product of idealizing; an ideal representation.

a **1822** SHELLEY *Def. Poetry* i. in *Ess. & Lett.* (1840) I. 20 The highest idealisms of passion and power. **1861** THORNBURY *Turner* I. 316 [The Polyphemus] the most wonderful.. of Turner's idealisms. **1862** RUSKIN *Unto this Last* iv. 136 Three-fourths of the demands existing in the world are romantic; founded on visions, idealisms, hopes, and affections.

idealist (aɪ'diːəlɪst). [f. IDEAL + -IST; cf. F. *idéaliste* (18th c. in Hatz.-Darm.).]

1. *Philos.* One who holds a doctrine of idealism: see prec. 1. In first quot. One who holds the Platonic doctrine of ideas.

1701 NORRIS *Ideal World* I. iii. 182, I look upon St. Austin to be as great an Idealist as any in the world, and considering his authority, the greatest patron of the Ideal philosophy. **1737** W. LAW *On the Sacrament* 42 The Letter of Scripture.. that makes speculative Christians, Idealists, Critics, and Grammarians fall into Infidelity. **1803** W. TAYLOR in *Monthly Mag.* XV. 321 Nothing would remain tenable.. but the system of the idealists. *a* **1810** D. STEWART *Philos. Ess.* II. i. 56 Whereas Berkeley was sincerely and bona fide an idealist, Hume's leading object, in his metaphysical writings, plainly was to inculcate a universal scepticism. **1842** EMERSON *Addr., Transcendent.* Wks. (Bohn) II. 279 As thinkers, mankind have ever divided into two sects, Materialists and Idealists; the first class founding on experience, the second on consciousness. **1855** H. SPENCER *Princ. Psychol.* (1872) II. VII. xix. 500 Berkeley was not an Idealist: he never succeeded in expelling the consciousness of an external reality.

2. One who idealizes; an artist or writer who treats a subject imaginatively. Opposed to *realist*.

1805 MACKINTOSH in *Life* (1836) I. v. 232, I called Milton an idealist. **1861** TULLOCH *Eng. Purit.* ii. 284 Owen was the great dogmatist of the Puritan theological movement, Howe was its contemplative idealist. **1896** *Times* 27 Jan. 9 Once or twice this idealist, this formalist as his critics called him [Ld. Leighton], produced a portrait.. which showed that he could turn at pleasure to realism.

3. One who conceives, or follows after ideals. Sometimes *depreciatively*, One who cherishes visionary or unpractical notions.

1829 LYTTON *Disowned* (ed. 2) II. iii. 37 Findlater, you are a sceptic and an idealist. **1851** DIXON *W. Penn* vi. (1872) 54 The politics of Fox had.. their attraction for this idealist. **1884** CHURCH *Bacon* iii. 59 He was no mere idealist or recluse to undervalue or despise the real grandeur of the world.

4. *attrib.* or as *adj.* = next.

1875 JOWETT *Plato* (ed. 2) I. 421 Philosophers of the idealist school. **1884** in *Littell's Living Age* 16 Feb. 427 In a tender idealist exaltation. **1885** *Athenæum* 9 May 593/3 The various stages which the idealist problem has taken in modern philosophy.

idealistic (aɪdiːə'lɪstɪk), *a.* [f. prec. + -IC.]

1. Pertaining to or characteristic of an idealist; belonging to or having the character of idealism (in various senses: see these words).

1829 CARLYLE *Misc. Ess., Novalis* (1872) II. 207 As a Poet, Novalis is no less Idealistic than as a Philosopher. **1877** E. CAIRD *Philos. Kant* iv. 71 The idealistic individualism of Leibnitz. **1884** *Fortn. Rev.* Jan. 31 The best of all practical work is that produced in an idealistic spirit.

2. *Sociol.* In the theory of P. A. Sorokin, a type of culture which is a synthesis of spiritual and material values. Cf. IDEATIONAL *a.* 2 and SENSATE *a.*

1937 [see IDEATIONAL *a.* 2]. **1952** A. L. KROEBER *Nature of Culture* I. xviii. 165/2 These 'sensate', 'ideational', and 'idealistic' supersystems are not segments of cultures at all... They are essentially polar *qualities*. **1965** C. P. & Z. K. LOOMIS *Mod. Social Theories* vii. 466 European culture is classified as idealistic during the 12th to 14th centuries. **1967** T. PARSONS *Sociol. Theory & Mod. Soc.* IV. xii. 388 The idealistic pattern is conceived as intermediate between the two, not in the sense of a simple 'compromise', but rather of a synthesis which can achieve a harmonious balance between the two principal components.

Hence **idea'listical** *a. rare* = prec.; **idea'listically** *adv.*, in an idealistic manner.

1884 'VERN. LEE' *Euphorion* II. 9 The old idealistical decorations. **1886** W. J. TUCKER *E. Europe* 56 Independence, idealistically considered, is elysian, but when the sublime theory is brought into practice amongst a rude people.. with nothing but agricultural labour to fall back upon, their position undergoes a devastating change.

ideality (aɪdiː'ælɪtɪ). [f. IDEAL + -ITY; cf. F. *idéalité* (Littré).]

†**1.** The faculty of forming 'ideas' or archetypes: see IDEA *sb.* 1, IDEAL *a.* 1. *Obs.*

1701 NORRIS *Ideal World* I. Pref. 11 The Divine Ideality or that intelligible reason in the wisdom of God whereby things were made. **1704** *Ibid.* II. 282 When they [creatures].. had no existence but in the bosom of his own ideality.

2. The faculty or capacity of conceiving ideals; the imaginative faculty. (Introduced as a term of *Phrenology*.)

1828 G. COMBE *Constit. Man.* ii. §4 Ideality delights in perfection from the pure pleasure of contemplating it. **1838** SID. SMITH *Princ. Phrenol.* vii. 167 Gall denominated this the Poetical faculty; and Spurzheim changed it to its present name Ideality. *a* **1866** J. GROTE *Exam. Utilit. Philos.* xiii. (1870) 199 Moral imperativeness as based upon ideality or belief in higher fact. **1871** TYNDALL *Fragm. Sc.* (1879) II. xiv. 359 Poetry or ideality, and untruth are.. very different things.

3. The quality of being ideal.

a. The quality of expressing some idea.

1817 G. S. FABER *Eight Dissert.* (1845) II. 218 That crux of painful antiquaries, the origin and ideality of the far-famed Round Towers.

b. Ideal or imaginative character, esp. of a work of art: see IDEAL *a.* 2, 3 b.

1835 I. TAYLOR *Spir. Despot.* iii. 86 The ideality and the poetry of their religion. **1863** MRS. C. CLARKE *Shaks. Char.* xii. 315 No invention of the most ludicrously-florid fancy can surpass in incongruous ideality the real, and substantial, and solidly-stupid old watchman.

c. Ideal or non-real nature; existence in idea only (opp. to *reality*): see IDEAL *a.* 4.

1877 E. CAIRD *Philos. Kant* v. 88 The ideality of time and space.

4. with *pl.* Something ideal or imaginary; an idealized conception.

1844 R. P. WARD *Chatsworth* I. 39 [They] commenced their married life with amiable idealities about 'love in a cottage'. **1858** J. H. NEWMAN *Hist. Sk.* (1873) III. II. i. 221 Cicero.. is not a mere ideality, he is a man and a brother. **1875** LIGHTFOOT *Comm. Col.* (1886) 108 Those vague idealities which as.. æons, took their place in later speculations.

b. = IDEAL B. 1.

1860 T. L. PEACOCK *Wks.* (1875) III. 430 The intellectual qualities which constituted his ideality of the partner of his life.

idealization (aɪdiːəlaɪ'zeɪʃən). [f. IDEALIZE + -ATION; cf. F. *idéalisation* (Littré).] The action of idealizing or fact of being idealized.

1796 W. TAYLOR in *Monthly Mag.* II. 466 Is this irony?.. Or poetical idealization? **1853** DE QUINCEY *Autobiog. Sk.* Wks. I. 54 The devotion gave grandeur and idealisation to the sorrow. **1875** EMERSON *Lett. & Soc. Aims* i. 58 Our overpraise and idealization of famous masters. **1883** FAIRBAIRN *City of God* III. i. (1886) 233 They were not finely susceptible sons of genius and culture, imaginative men, capable of acts of splendid idealization.

b. A particular or concrete instance of this; an idealized representation.

1855 *Fraser's Mag.* LI. 702 This bust.. is a frank idealization. **1870** H. MACMILLAN *Bible Teach.* Pref. 13 Poets and artists teach us by their beautiful idealizations that the objects around us are not mere objects of sense.

idealize (aɪ'diːəlaɪz), *v.* [f. IDEAL + -IZE; cf. F. *idéaliser* (1794 in Hatz-Darm.).] *trans.* To make or render ideal; to represent in an ideal form or character; to exalt to an ideal perfection or excellence.

1795 W. TAYLOR in *Monthly Rev.* XVIII. 535 Italy is here idealized into a terrestrial paradise. *a* **1834** COLERIDGE *Shaks. Notes* (1849) 9 The tragic poet idealizes his characters. **1870** H. MACMILLAN *Bible Teach.* viii. 152 Creation is reflected and idealized in the mirror of the soul. **1884** *Pall Mall G.* 10 Sept. 1/1 Men who have been idealized after death.

b. *absol.* or *intr.* To represent something in an ideal form: to conceive or form an ideal or ideals.

1786 MATY *Meiner's Hist. Relig.* i. in *New Rev.* Feb. 62 Their [men's] natural propensity to idealize. *a* **1849** H. COLERIDGE *Ess.* (1851) II. 205 A portrait painter, idealise as he will, can only paint the sort of people that exist in his time.

Hence **i'dealized** *ppl. a.*; **i'dealizing** *vbl. sb.* and *ppl. a.*; also **i'dealizer**, one who or that which idealizes.

1817 COLERIDGE *Biog. Lit.* II. xxiii. 263 The idealized figures of the Apollo Belvidere, and the Farnese Hercules. **1821** —— in *Blackw. Mag.* X. 257 Dared I mention the name of my Idealizer. **1858** GLADSTONE *Homer* II. 216 The Hellenic mind.. [with] its active and idealizing fancy. **1869** LECKY *Europ. Mor.* I. xi. 293 The idealised suffering of the stage was unimpressive. **1876** LOWELL *Among my Bks.* Ser. II. *Dante* 67 There is no idealizer like unavailing regret. **1878** SEELEY *Stein* II. 490 It sometimes excites a suspicion of a little idealising.

idealless (aɪ'diːəllɪs), *a.* [f. IDEAL *sb.* + -LESS.] Without any ideal.

1880 'VERN. LEE' *Stud. Italy* iii. 149 While he was but a poor little feelingless, idealless scholar.

ideally (aɪ'diːəlɪ), *adv.* [f. IDEAL *a.* + -LY[2].] In an ideal manner.

†**1.** In 'idea' (sense 1) or archetype; in relation to a pattern or type. *Obs.*

1646 SIR T. BROWNE *Pseud. Ep.* III. ix. 124 A transmission is made materially from some parts, and Ideally from every one. **1678** CUDWORTH *Intell. Syst.* I. iv. §36. 582 The third

..doth actively display and produce into being what was.. contained..ideally or exemplarily in the second. **1701** NORRIS *Ideal World* I. ii. 36 As these figures..must first be conceived that they might be made, so they must be that they might be conceived, and consequently must exist ideally in order to their existing naturally.

2. In idea, mental conception, or imagination; imaginarily.

1598 FLORIO, *Ideale*, ideally, figuratiuely, formely, imaginatiuely [**1611** ideally or figuratiuely, by imagination]. **1816** COLERIDGE *Lay Serm.* 339 Reason and religion differ only as a twofold application of the same power. But if we are obliged to distinguish, we must ideally separate. **1860** TYNDALL *Glac.* II. xxvi. 374 The branches..have..been ideally prolonged across the moraines. **1872** GEO. ELIOT *Middlem.* lviii, It seemed now that her marriage was visibly as well as ideally floating her above the Middlemarch level. **1874** CARPENTER *Ment. Phys.* I. ix. §3 (1879) 410 The unexpected conclusion..that more than three dimensions in space are ideally possible.

3. In conformity with the ideal; in the highest conceivable perfection; in the way of supreme excellence.

1840 B'NESS BUNSEN in Hare *Life* (1879) II. iv. 243 Our ideally delightful journey. **1875** HAMERTON *Intell. Life* II. iii. 66 An ideally perfect history would tell the pure truth. **1885** *Manchester Exam.* 4 May 5/2 This fluid is..by no means an ideally pure water.

4. *Biol.* In relation to a general plan or archetype (of a class).

1859 DARWIN *Orig. Spec.* vi. 191 The swim-bladder is homologous, or 'ideally similar', in position and structure with the lungs of the higher..animals. **1896** DK. ARGYLL *Philos. Belief* 108 To designate this theoretically, or ideally, fundamental form.

i'dealness. [f. as prec. + -NESS.] Ideal quality or state, ideality.

1832 CARLYLE *Misc. Ess., Boswell* (1872) IV. 81 Ennoble the Actual into Idealness.

idealogical, etc., erron. ff. IDEOLOGICAL, etc.

†**i'dealty.** *Obs. rare.* [f. IDEAL *a.* + -TY; cf. *royalty*, etc.] A standard of excellence, an ideal.

1635 J. HAYWARD tr. *Biondi's Banish'd Virg.* III. 168 The world had now no more neede of any other exquisite patterne for the well-governing of Common-wealths, and Idealty of Princes.

ideate (aɪ'di:eɪt), *v.* [f. IDEA *sb.*: see -ATE[3]. Cf. It. *ideare*, Sp., Pg. *idear.*]

1. *trans.* To form the idea of; to frame, devise, or construct in idea or imagination; to imagine, conceive. (In early use with reference to Platonic 'ideas': see IDEA *sb.* 1.)

1610 DONNE *Pseudo-Mart.* 4 A State which Plato Ideated. *Ibid.* 248 As some Men have imagined..divers Idæas and so sought what a King, a General [etc.] should be, so these Men have Idæated what a Pope would be. **1656** SANDERSON *Serm.* (1689) 257 To quarrel at Gods gifts, if they be not such as we ..have ideated unto ourselves. **1682** SIR T. BROWNE *Chr. Mor.* I. §28 Could we..apprehend the Ideated Man..we might..comprehend our present Degeneration. **1864** WEBSTER, *Ideate*..To apprehend in thought so as to retain and recall; to fix and hold in the mind. (*Rare.*) **1893** *Nation* (N.Y.) 2 Feb. 81/3 Whether the index we had ideated is possible or not.

2. *absol.* or *intr.* **a.** To form ideas, to think. **b.** To devise or invent something imaginary.

1862 LEWES in *Blackw. Mag.* (1884) Feb. 177/1 The reality is implied in the very fact of impressions and ideas: there is something which is impressed, something which feels, which ideates. **1888** J. B. SMITH *Ideation* (title-p.), Experimental Proof that..Insects ideate and intercommunicate by these radiant Ideas or Physical Images.

i'deate, *a.* and *sb.* [ad. mod.L. *ideāt-us*, pa. pple. of **ideāre*: see prec.]

A. *adj.* **1.** Produced by or deriving its existence from a (Platonic) 'idea': see IDEA *sb.* 1.

2. Concerned with ideas as opp. to reality (cf. IDEA *sb.* 8).

1966 *New Statesman* 23 Sept. 434/3 A bad best-seller, its characters mere contrivances and its talk vacuously ideate. **1968** *Listener* 1 Aug. 149/1 It is not the absence of ideas but the absence of things..which most diminishes Williams's poems. He preached upon 'things' till it argued him ideate.

B. *sb.* The external object of which an idea or conception is formed.

1677 GALE *Crt. Gentiles* IV. 319 In us the Ideate or thing understood is before the Idea..but in God, his Idea is the original exemplar, and the Ideate in the Create but a.. reflexe image or similitude of the Divine Idea. [**1830** SIR W. HAMILTON *Discuss.* (1852) 76 Consciousness is converted with Perception,—Perception with Idea,—Idea with Ideatum.] **1854** FROUDE *Short Stud., Spinoza* (1867) II. 34 Body with all its properties is the object or ideate of mind. [**1885** J. MARTINEAU *Types Eth. The.* (1886) I. I. ii. 307 He objects to say outright that it is the ideatum which gives the idea.]

ideation (aɪdi:'eɪʃən). [f. IDEATE *v.*: see -ATION.] The formation of ideas or mental images of things not present to the senses.

1829 JAS. MILL *Hum. Mind* I. 42 As we say Sensation, we might also say Ideation; it would be a very useful word... Sensation is the general name for one part of our constitution.. Ideation for another. **1862** *Macm. Mag.* Apr. 507 In sensation the object of sense is present; in ideation it is absent, but remembered. **1879** HUXLEY *Hume* iv. 90 Of the mechanism of this generation of images of impressions or ideas (in Hume's sense), which may be termed *Ideation*, we know nothing.

ide'ational, *a.* [f. prec. + -AL[1].] **1.** Of or pertaining to ideation or the formation of ideas.

1853 CARPENTER *Hum. Phys.* (ed. 4) xiv. §788. 779 That state of consciousness which may be termed Ideational. *Ibid. Note*, If the use of the substantive Ideation be admitted, there can be no reasonable objection to the adjective ideational. **1879** HUXLEY *Hume* iv. 90 The rapidity and the intensity of this ideational process are..dependent upon physiological conditions. **1894** CREIGHTON & TITCHENER tr. *Wundt's Lect. Hum. & Animal Psychol.* xiii. 204 In both cases we are only dealing with a particular consequence of the principle of *ideational unity*. **1916** *Proc. Nat. Acad. Sci.* II. 631 Despite widespread interest in the evolution of reasoning, the comparative study of ideational behaviour has been neglected. **1958** *Times Lit. Suppl.* 12 Sept. 515/1 These regulators..are apprehended by, for instance, consciousness as 'archaic images' or 'ideational instincts'. **1970** *Jrnl. Gen. Psychol.* Oct. 144 The technique might differentiate more clearly for response style than for ideational content. **1971** J. Z. YOUNG *Introd. Study Man* xxxv. 489 It has also been called the 'area of ideational speech' or indeed 'word store'.

2. *Sociol.* A term used orig. by P. A. Sorokin (see quot. 1937) to describe a type of culture based on spiritual values and ideals, whose material needs are the minimum necessary to forward those ideals. (See also IDEALISTIC *a.* 2 and SENSATE *a.*)

1937 P. A. SOROKIN *Social & Cultural Dynamics* I. I. ii. 67 Of these two systems one may be termed *Ideational* culture, the other *Sensate*. *Ibid.* 68 Some [cultures] have contained a balanced synthesis of both pure types. This last I term the *Idealistic* type of culture. (It should not be confused with the Ideational.) **1944** H. P. FAIRCHILD *Dict. Sociol.* 148 *Ideational*,..a type of culture which exalts the spiritual above the material values. **1964** *Economist* 8 Aug. 563/1 Conservatism is not, like socialism, liberalism or democracy, an 'ideational' ideology but 'situational'. **1966** P. A. SOROKIN *Sociol. Theories Today* xi. 381 The phase of growth or 'spring' of Danilevsky-Spengler-Toynbee's civilizations is similar in several traits with Sorokin's ideational. **1970** G. A. & A. G. THEODORSON *Mod. Dict. Sociol.* 194 Rather than stressing the manipulation of the empirical world to improve the quality of life..the ideational culture emphasizes adjustment to the existing world.

ideationally (aɪdi:'eɪʃənəlɪ), *adv.* [f. IDEATIONAL *a.* + -LY[2].] By means of ideation.

1890 W. JAMES *Princ. Psychol.* II. xix. 127 Under ordinary circumstances, the entire brain probably plays a part in draining any centre which may be ideationally active. **1910** R. R. RUSK in *Brit. Jrnl. Psychol.* III. 379 The dissociation of the perceptually excited elements of consciousness from the ideationally excited factors. **1952** *Mind* LXI. 350 The interpretation..relates it [*sc.* the sensation] ideationally to other items.

ideative (aɪ'di:ətɪv), *a. rare.* = IDEATIONAL *a.* 1.

1887 *Alien & Neurol.* VIII. 215 (Cent.) The acoustic images, by awaking in the ideative field the correlated ideas, render the words spoken by another intelligible.

ideatum (aɪdi:'eɪtəm). *Philos.* [mod.L., neut. of *ideātus*: see IDEATE *a.* and *sb.*] = IDEATE *sb.*

1708 BERKELEY *Works* (1948) I. 100 The distinction between Idea and Ideatum I cannot otherwise conceive than by making one the effect or consequence of Dream, rêverie, Imagination, the other of sense & the Constant laws of Nature. **1889** 'SCOTUS NOVANTICUS' *Metaphysica Nova et Vetusta* (ed. 2) 81 We are entitled to start with..perfect equivalence between the idea and the ideatum. **1920** S. ALEXANDER *Space, Time & Deity* II. 84 The object..of which we are conscious as an idea or ideatum. **1933** *Mind* XLII. 303 Here the relation between a mode-factor in one attribute and its correlate in the other attribute is the absolutely unique relation of an idea to its ideatum.

idee (aɪ'di:). *Obs.* exc. in vulgar use. [a. F. *idée*, ad. late L. *idea*, Gr. ἰδέα: see IDEA *sb.*] = IDEA (in various senses).

1430–40 LYDG. *Bochas* IV. ix. (MS. Bodl.) lf. 222b/2 In the too scooles of prudent Socrates And of Plato which that bar the keie Of secre mysteries & of dyvyn Ideie. **1542** UDALL *Erasm. Apoph.* I. 123b, The Idees, that Plato deuised, & muche treacteth of, euen Aristotle laughed to skorne. **1573** G. HARVEY *Letter-bk.* (Camden) 102 Queint Idees bemone your imperfections, Or give me a type of such perfections. **1589** PUTTENHAM *Eng. Poesie* I. i. (Arb.) 19 God ..made all the world of nought, nor also by any paterne or mould as the Platonicks with their Idees do phantastically suppose. **1596** SPENSER *Hymn Heav. Love* 284 Thy bright radiant eyes shall plainely see Th' Idee of his pure glorie present still Before thy Face. **1647** H. MORE *Song of Soul* III. II. xxiv, Flush light she sendeth forth, and live Idees. **1848** LOWELL *Biglow P.* Ser. I. III. v, With good old idees o' wut's right an' wut aint.

‖**idée** (ide). The French word for 'idea' used in certain French phrases, as:

idée fixe (ide fiks): a fixed idea (see FIXED *ppl. a.* 2), an obsession.

1836 H. GREVILLE *Diary* 20 Feb. (1883) 88 The King.. has some *idée fixe* about marrying the Duke of Orleans. **1877** L. W. M. LOCKHART *Mine is Thine* (1878) I. vii, At all events, the attraction of the heart would require to be something out of the common run if it were to subdue this *idée fixe*. **1922** JOYCE *Ulysses* 245, I am sure he has an *idée fixe*, Haines said. **1941** AUDEN *New Year Let.* II. 29 Prefer our idées fixes to be True of a fixed Reality. **1953** C. DAY LEWIS *Italian Visit* ii. 28 Then fast, faster Drawn by the magnet of his *idée fixe*, Head down, tail up, he's charging the horizon. **1965** D. LODGE *Brit. Mus. is falling Down* viii. 133 'What's wrong?' Adam complained. 'Isn't everyone entitled to his *idée fixe*?' **1973** 'M. INNES' *Appleby's Answer* vi. 60 Not an *idée fixe* of mine... Jack of all trades, you might say. **1974** *Times Lit. Suppl.* 15 Feb. 162/1 Impatience in the search makes it fatally easy to freeze a hypothesis into a rigid system of *idées fixes*.

idée maîtresse (ide mɛtrɛs): a leading idea (cf. *master-idea* s.v. MASTER *sb.*[1] 26 b).

1939 *Times Lit. Suppl.* 16 Dec. 729/1 Mystified by M. Romains's apparent reluctance to confide his *idée maîtresse*, one could not always avoid an injured and carping note of appreciation. **1958** *Listener* 7 Aug. 193/2 The *idée maitresse* of his outlook. **1966** *Ibid.* 6 Oct. 500/2 The leading idea, the *idée maîtresse*, of the Enlightenment.

idée mère (ide mɛr): = *mother idea* (s.v. MOTHER *sb.*[1] 17 a).

1841 MILL *Let.* Aug. in *Works* (1963) XIII. 483, I think you should dwell much more..on the *idée mêre* of..the article. **1863** —— *Utilitarianism* v. 69 The *idée mère*, the primitive element, in the formation of the notion of justice, was conformity to law. **1908** H. JAMES *Awkward Age* Preface p. viii, They especially emphasise that truth of the vanity of the *a priori* test of what an *idée-mère* may have to give. **1916** G. SAINTSBURY *Peace of Augustans* i. 5 Dryden..had too much of the divine freedom and variety of poetry in him to follow up the *idées mères* of this couplet. **1931** R. FRY *Lett.* (1972) II. 653 It's a remarkable book even if it's hypothetical and he may have got an *idée mère*.

idée reçue (ide rəsy): a generally accepted notion or opinion (cf. RECEIVED *ppl. a.* 1).

1937 E. BOWEN in *New Statesman* 13 Mar. 418/1 He, too, lines up *idées reçues*. **1957** E. WILSON *Piece of my Mind* vii. 105 The foolish old *idée reçue* that Greek literature is the real thing and Latin a second-rate imitation. **1964** *Listener* 9 Jan. 92/2, I sympathized with his dismay that he should be considered right wing, because he did not accept left wing *idées reçues*. **1970** *Times* 23 Feb. 12/1 Your sort of pianist is always..unwilling to accept *idées reçues*, even when they come with most authoritative credentials. **1974** *Times Lit. Suppl.* 22 Mar. 303/2 It sweeps the *idées reçues* of sociologists, town planners and other rationalists into the dustbin.

†**i'deist.** *Obs.* [f. IDEA *sb.* + -IST.] = IDEALIST 1.

1697 J. SERGEANT (*title*) Solid Philosophy asserted against the Fancies of the Ideists. *a* **1704** LOCKE (L.), If that be so, I must..conclude, that the notionists and the ideists have their apprehensive faculties very differently turned.

idel, ideliche, -ly, obs. ff. IDLE, IDOL, IDLY.

i-deled, ME. pa. pple. of DEAL *v.*

‖**idem** ('aɪdɛm, 'ɪdɛm). [L. *īdem* masc., *ĭdem* neut. 'the same'.] The same word, name, title, author, etc., as mentioned before: used to avoid repetition. Abbreviated *id.*

14.. *Nom.* in Wr.-Wülcker 732/23 *Hec tectura*, thak. *Hoc tegimen, idem.* **1598** FLORIO, *Nolatore*, hyrer, a hackney man. *Noleggiante*, idem. *Nolesino*, idem. **1677** W. HUGHES *Man of Sin* II. iv. 83 *margin*, Id. ibid. c. 12.

†**i-deme**, *v. Obs.* [OE. *ᵹedéman* (= OHG. *getuomen*, Goth. *gadómjan*), f. *déman* to DEEM.] *trans.* To deem, judge.

a **900** CYNEWULF *Crist* 525 [He] wile..ᵹedeman dæda ᵹehwylce. *c* **1205** LAY. 4054 þus heo hit idemden. *Ibid.* 10441 Al weoren þa dæden al se heo idemden.

i-dem(e)d, ME. pa. pple. of DEEM *v.*

idemfaciend (aɪdɛm'feɪʃ(ɪ)ɛnd) *a.*, **idemfacient** (-'feɪʃ(ɪ)ənt) *a.*, **idemfactor** (-'fæktə(r)) [f. L. *idem* same + *faciend-us* to be made, *facient-em* making, *factor* maker, FACTOR *sb.*]: words used in multiple algebra: see quot.

1870 B. PEIRCE in *Amer. Jrnl. Math.* (1881) IV. 104 When an expression used as a factor in certain combinations overpowers the other factors and is itself the product, it may be called an idemfactor. When in the production of such a result it is the multiplier, it is idemfacient, but when it is the multiplicand it is idemfaciend.

idempotent (aɪ'dɛmpəʊtənt, ˌaɪdəm'pəʊtənt), *a.* and *sb.* [f. L. *idem* same + *potent-em* powerful, POTENT] **A.** *adj.* Of a quantity or element *a*: having the property that $a \times a = a$, where $\times$ represents multiplication or some other (specified) binary operation. Also applied to an operator or set for which this is true for any element *a* and to statements expressing this fact.

1870 B. PEIRCE in *Amer. Jrnl. Math.* (1881) IV. 104 When an expression..raised to a square or higher power..gives itself as the result, it may be called idempotent. **1937** A. A. ALBERT *Mod. Higher Algebra* (1938) iii. 88 A matrix E is called idempotent if $E^2 = E$. **1937** *Duke Math. Jrnl.* III. 629 We recall that $A \supset B$ if and only if $A = (A, B)$ and $B = [A, B]$, and that union and crosscut are associative, commutative, and idempotent operations. **1940** W. V. QUINE *Math. Logic* 56 A binary mode of statement composition..is said to be..idempotent if '$\phi \equiv .\phi\kappa\phi$' is true for all statements ϕ. **1941** BIRKHOFF & MACLANE *Surv. Mod. Algebra* xi. 313 All of these except for the idempotent laws and the second distributive law correspond to familiar laws of arithmetic. **1941** *Mind* L. 274 The element is only idempotent with respect to the combining relation defined as the combining relation of the group. **1950** W. V. QUINE *Methods of Logic* (1952) §1. 3 '*pp*' reduces to '*p*'. Conjunction is idempotent, to persist in the jargon. **1959** E. M. MCCORMICK *Digital Computer Primer* 181 It is further apparent..that $A + A = A$ and..that $A \times A = A$. These are sometimes referred to as the idempotent laws. **1967** A. GEDDES tr. *Dubreil & Dubreil-Jacotin's Lect. Mod. Algebra* i. 22 If every element of E is idempotent, the composition law is called idempotent and E is called an idempotent set.

B. *sb.* An idempotent element; also in more restricted use (see quot. 1958).

1941 BIRKHOFF & MACLANE *Surv. Mod. Algebra* i. 6 Prove that the following rules hold in any integral domain:..(h) the only 'idempotents' (that is, elements x satisfying $xx = x$) are 0 and 1. **1958** S. KRAVETZ tr. *Zassenhaus's Theory of Groups* (ed. 2) 182 The element e is called an idempotent if

$ee = e$ and if e is not a zero element. **1960** C. E. RICKART *Gen. Theory Banach Algebras* i. 35 Let 𝔄 be a Banach algebra and let e be a proper idempotent in 𝔄 (that is, $e \neq 0$, 1 and $e^2 = e$).

Hence **idempotence** (stress variable), **idem'potency**, the property of being idempotent.

1940 *Mind* XLIX. 461 The truth is that Eddington, in spite of all that he says about getting all the mathematics he wants out of the idempotency of the *J* symbols, employs them in accordance with the laws of ordinary algebra whenever he thinks fit. **1940** W. V. QUINE *Math. Logic* 60 In the case of conjunction and alternation, repetition of components has..been seen to be immaterial (idempotence). **1957** P. SUPPES *Introd. Logic* ix. 205 Equations (9) and (10) express what is usually called the idempotency of union and intersection. **1959** K. R. POPPER *Logic Sci. Discovery* 351 $p(aa, b) = p(a, b)$... This is the law of idempotence, sometimes also called the 'law of tautology'. **1960** P. SUPPES *Axiomatic Set Theory* ii. 27 The next three theorems assert the commutativity, associativity, and idempotence of union. **1968** *New Scientist* 16 May 339/1 Idempotency..occurs if an operation produces no change in the number or set on which it operates.

idemptitie, obs. form of IDENTITY.

idem sonans ('aɪdɛm 'səʊnænz). *Law.* [L., lit. = sounding the same.] Identity of sound in pronunciation; the occurrence in a document of a material word or name misspelt but having the sound of the word or name intended. Also *adj.*, homophonous *with*.

1848 WHARTON *Law Lexicon* 304/2 The courts will not interfere in setting aside proceedings on account of the misspelling of names, provided..there is an *idem sonans* between the pronunciation of the right name and that which is inserted in the proceedings; as Lawrance, instead of Lawrence, Reynell for Reynolds, Beniditto for Benedetto. **1856** *Newsp. & Gen. Reader's Compan.* II. §1749 The verb was unluckily *idem sonans* with another word. **1919** H. L. MENCKEN *Amer. Lang.* viii. 273 In America, with a language of peculiar vowel sounds and even consonant-sounds struggling against a foreign invasion unmatched for strength or variety..the legal rule of *idem sonans* is of much wider utility than anywhere else in the world.

-idene, *suffix.* *Chem.* [Prob. taken from ETHYLIDENE (ad. F. *éthylydène* (A. Lieben 1858, in *Compt. Rend.* XLVI. 663), f. *éthylène* with insertion of the *-yd-* of *aldehyde*).] Forming the names of bivalent organic radicals in which both valencies derive from the same atom. Cf. -YLIDENE.

1927 *Chem. Abstr.* XXI. 4576/1 *-idene* added to any radical usually means a double bond at point of attachment. **1966** *Nomencl. Org. Chem.* (I.U.P.A.C.) (ed. 2) A. 16 Bivalent and trivalent radicals derived from univalent acyclic hydrocarbon radicals whose authorized names end in '-yl' by removal of one or two hydrogen atoms from the carbon atom with the free valences are named by adding '-idene' or '-idyne', respectively, to the name of the corresponding univalent radical.

'ident, *a.* *Sc.* Also 6 **yden, ydan, ydant**. [Later form of ITHAND *a.*: cf. EIDENT.] Diligent, persistent. Hence **'identiy** *adv.*, diligently, attentively; persistently, continuously: cf. ITHANDLY.

1567 *Gude & Godlie B.* (S.T.S.) 16 Our Baptisme is not done all on ane day, Bot all our lyfe it lestis Identlie. **1573** *Satir. Poems Reform.* xl. 229 Quha preissis vprichtlie To serue the Lord mon..thame prepair for troublis Identlie. **1591** R. BRUCE *Serm.* vi. O iij, Mair ydant in this exercise. **1596** DALRYMPLE tr. *Leslie's Hist. Scot.* I. 111 Ydenly wt al diligence. *Ibid.* IV. 233 Thair ydan, still, and continual preichengs. *Ibid.* VII. 36 To wayt ydanlie vpon the kingis body. *Mod. Sc.* She is an ident lassie.

ident. Colloq. abbrev. of IDENTIFICATION (or *identification bracelet*), IDENTIFY *v.* orig. *U.S.*

1952 *Jewelers' Circular-Keystone* Sept. 65 (Advt.), Popular 'Idents' that build profitable sales. **1955** R. J. SCHWARTZ *Compl. Dict. Abbrev.* 90 *Ident*, identification (US Army). **1965** 'D. SHANNON' *Death-Bringers* (1966) i. 12 The group being showed thousands of mug shots at Records, hoping for a possible ident. **1966** M. & G. GORDON *Undercover Cat prowls Again* (1967) xiv. 95 It was so dark he couldn't make a positive ident until the girl was halfway along. **1967** R. J. SERLING *President's Plane is Missing* iii. 55 'Washington Center, Air Force One. Squawk ident.' 'Roger, identing.' **1970** P. LAURIE *Scotland Yard* ix. 196 A searcher..ploughs through the four thousand or so forms.. in the slim hope that one will match, giving him an 'ident'.

identic (aɪ'dɛntɪk), *a.* [ad. scholastic L. *identicus* (see IDENTITY): cf. F. *identique* (in Furetière 1690), It., Sp., Pg. *identico*.]

1. = IDENTICAL 1.

1664 BUTLER *Hud.* II. i. 149 The Beard's th' Identick Beard you knew. **1789** H. WALPOLE *Let.* in *Miss Berry's Corr.* (1865) I. 177, I concluded it must be a son..but asking my sister..she assured me it was..the identic being. *c* **1811** FUSELI in *Lect. Paint.* v. (1848) 465 The identic owner of those crutches. **1866** *Cornh. Mag.* Nov. 629 The new democratic axiom that aristocracy is a single and identic species of social vermin.

2. = IDENTICAL 2.

1649 G. DANIEL *Trinarch., Hen. IV*, ciii, Death, though it Estrange Perhaps, the Notion of Identike vse, Quickens a better Ray of Light in vs. **1751** HARRIS *Hermes* III. iv. (1786) 399 Whence..do these common Identic Ideas come? **1838** *Blackw. Mag.* XLIII. 768 Literature and pedagogism are in Germany identic in spirit. **1876** SKENE *Celtic Scotl.* I. 193 The Irish language still spoken there, which is identic with the Gaelic of the Scotch Highlands.

3. In diplomacy, applied to action or language in which two or more governments or powers agree to use precisely the same form, in their relations with some other power, so as to impress the latter by a simultaneous expression of unanimous opinion; esp. in *identic note*.

1863 KINGLAKE *Crimea* (1877) II. App. 391 The form of a simple identic declaration. **1879** in Dk. Argyll *East. Quest.* I. iv. 141 All appearance of identic action seemed to be undesirable. **1880** EARL GRANVILLE in *Times* 10 Aug. 6/1 Europe was unanimous in presenting an identic Note to the Porte.

identical (aɪ'dɛntɪkəl), *a.* and *sb.* [f. med.L. *identic-us* (see prec.) + -AL[1].]

A. *adj.* **1.** The same; the very same: said of one thing (or set of things) viewed at different times or in different relations. (Often emphasized by *same, very*.)

a **1633** AUSTIN *Medit.* (1635) 36 The Spirit..leades not every man in the same identicall path. **1774** C. J. PHIPPS *Voy. N. Pole* 13 To lend me the identical pendulum with which Mr. Graham had made his experiments. **1785** REID *Intell. Powers* III. i. 305, I cannot remember a thing that happened a year ago, without a conviction..that I, the same identical person who now remember that event, did then exist. **1809** MALKIN *Gil Blas* IV. ix. ¶4 This is the very identical man. **1832** HT. MARTINEAU *Demerara* ii. 23 The case is wholly changed by the second and third parties being identical. **1890** A. R. WALLACE *Darwinism* 2 Descended from one pair of ancestral crows of the same identical species.

2. a. Agreeing entirely in material, constitution, properties, qualities, or meaning: said of two or more things which are equal parts of one uniform whole, individual examples of one species, or copies of one type, so that any one of them may, for all purposes, or for the purposes contemplated, be substituted for any other.

1677 HALE *Prim. Orig. Man.* I. iv. 105 When we have to do with any thing whose very essence..consists in being greatest, there *majus* and *minus* do alter the very essence of the thing, and is identical with *magis* and *minus*. **1831** LAMB *Elia* Ser. II. *Ellistoniana*, 'I like Wrench'..'because he is the same natural, easy creature, on the stage that he is off.' 'My case exactly', retorted Elliston..'I am the same person off the stage that I am on'. The inference, at first sight, seems identical; but examine it a little, and it confesses only, that the one performer was never, and the other always, acting. **1860** WESTCOTT *Introd. Study Gosp.* iii. (ed. 5) 191 The incidents..are often identical and always similar. **1868** PEARD *Water-farm.* xiii. 129 A law..based on, and nearly identical with our present Fishery Act. **1896** DK. ARGYLL *Philos. Belief* 79 Crystals have no structure in the organic sense. They are cases of..cohesion of identical particles.

†**b.** *Geom.* Of figures: Equal and similar. *Obs.*

1806 HUTTON *Course Math.* I. 274 Identical figures, are such as have all the sides and all the angles of the one, respectively equal to all the sides and all the angles of the other, each to each; so that if the one figure were applied to, or laid upon the other, all the sides of the one would exactly fall upon and cover all the sides of the other.

c. *identical points* = *corresponding points* (CORRESPONDING *ppl. a.* 1 b).

1841 W. MACKENZIE *Physiol. Vision* xvi. 253 (*heading*) Corresponding or identical points of the retina. **1880** L. OWEN tr. *Giraud-Teulon's Elem. Treat. Function of Vision* I. ii. 16 The same object being depicted upon the two retinae, at homologous points, must give rise to a single sensation... This..has been called the doctrine of identical points. **1932** S. DUKE-ELDER *Text-bk. Ophthalm.* I. xxvii. 1028 Points on the two retinæ from which images are projected to the same place in the common visual field are called corresponding (or identical) points.

d. *identical twin*, one of a pair of twins who, as a result of being monozygotic, are of the same sex and very similar to one another in appearance; usu. *pl.* Opp. *fraternal twin*. Similarly *identical triplet*.

1889 S. SCHÖNLAND tr. *Weismann's Ess. Heredity* vi. 381 Under conditions of nutriment which are as identical as possible, *two* egg-cells develope into unlike twins, *one* into identical twins; although we cannot yet affirm that the latter result invariably follows. **1938**, **1941** [see FRATERNAL *a.* c]. **1964** M. ARGYLE *Psychol. & Social Probl.* vi. 77 The best method of studying the extent of genetic factors is by means of identical and fraternal twins. **1972** A. CHRISTIE *Elephants can Remember* xiv. 190 There was a project on hand..to follow up the general lives of selected pairs of identical twins. **1973** *Oxford Times* 6 Apr. 8 On Monday the first LP by the only identical triplet sisters act in British show business was released.

3. *Logic.* Said of a proposition, the terms of which denote the same thing; expressing an identity; as the propositions *A horse is a horse*; *man is a human being*.

1620 GRANGER *Div. Logike* II. 230 *Man is man*, viz. Subject to errours. *Note.* Identicall Axiomes. **1644** DIGBY *Two Treat.* II. ii. 18 The greatest assurance and the most eminent knowledge we can have of any thing is, of such Propositions as in the Schooles are called Identicall; as if one should say, Iohn is Iohn, or a man is a man. **1696** LORIMER *Goodwin's Disc.* vii. 40 The Major Proposition is self-evidently false, when stript of its Identical dress. **1810** BENTHAM *Packing* (1821) 247 Propositions, of the cast termed by logicians identical..which..leave every thing exactly as they find it: propositions declaring that what is right ought to be done, and what is wrong ought not to be done, and so forth. **1884** tr. *Lotze's Logic* 63.

4. *Alg.* **a.** Expressing identity, as *identical equation*, an equation which is true for all values of the literal quantities; as $(x + a)^2 = X^2 + 2ax + a^2$. **b.** Effecting identity, as *identical operation*, an operation which leaves the operand unchanged.

1875 TODHUNTER *Algebra* ix. §149 An *identical equation* is one in which the two sides are equal whatever numbers the letters stand for; for example, $(x + b)(x - b) = x^2 - b^2$ is an identical equation.

†**5.** Marking identity, identifying. *Obs.*

1704 HEARNE *Duct. Hist.* (1714) I. 22 An Eclipse either of the Sun or Moon is such a characteristical and identical Mark of a Year, that it is easy to distinguish it among an infinite Number of others.

B. *sb.* **1.** *pl.* Identical things.

1696 J. SERGEANT *Method to Sci.* 264 We can as easily define their Abstract Notions as we can the other, (or rather much more easily) and consequently Reduce them to their Identicals. **1903** J. GOTT *Lett.* (1918) 195 Most of the books ..worry me with endless and subtle refinements and hair-splitting distinctions between identicals. **1943** W. V. QUINE in *Jrnl. Philos.* 4 Mar. 113 One of the fundamental principles governing identity is that of *substitutivity*—or, as it might well be called, that of *indiscernibility of identicals*.

2. An identical twin.

[**1932** A. HUXLEY *Brave New World* i. 8 'Can you tell us the record for a single ovary..?'..' Sixteen thousand and twelve; in one hundred and eighty-nine batches of identicals.'] **1938** [see FRATERNAL *a.* c]. **1964** M. ARGYLE *Psychol. & Social Probl.* vi. 77 If it is found that identicals are more alike in some respect than fraternals, this suggests that the condition [*sc.* a mental disorder] is to some extent inherited.

Hence **i'denticalism** (*nonce-wd.*), the employment of an identical proposition.

1816 BENTHAM *Chrestom.* 294 'Let them not be too numerous':—this is plain identicalism..add—'without necessity', the identicalism is now topped by self-contradiction.

identically (aɪ'dɛntɪkəlɪ), *adv.* [f. prec. + -LY[2].] In an identical manner; in exactly the same way. (Often used intensively with *same*.)

1646 BP. MAXWELL *Burd. Issach.* in *Phenix* (1708) II. 293 A Bishop was no more in Scripture, but the same identically with Presbyter. **1796** MORSE *Amer. Geog.* I. 106 The language of the Sandwich Isles is almost identically the same with that of Otaheite. **1803** *Med. Jrnl.* IX. 469 Galvinism, which I certainly consider as the same fluid identically with electricity. **1842–3** GROVE *Corr. Phys. Forces* (1874) 174 The impossibility of any event identically recurring. **1884** tr. *Lotze's Logic* 328 If this force is of such a kind as to allow the object exposed to its influence to remain identically the same, the same effect would take place afresh in the object every fresh time we let the same cause operate on it.

b. *Alg.* In the manner of an identical equation (see IDENTICAL 4); for all values of the literal quantities.

1881 MAXWELL *Electr. & Magn.* I. 111 The first sum of terms vanishes identically.

i'denticalness. [f. prec. + -NESS.] The quality of being identical; sameness; identity.

1727 in BAILEY vol. II. **1748** RICHARDSON *Clarissa* (1811) IV. 201 She has a high opinion of her sex, to think they can charm so long a man so well acquainted with their identicalness. **1863** HAWTHORNE *Our Old Home, Civic Banquets* (1879) 354 There is a pervading commonplace and identicalness in the composition of extensive dinners.

identifiability (aɪ,dɛntɪfaɪə'bɪlɪtɪ). [f. IDENTIFIABLE *a.* + -ITY.] The property of being identifiable.

1898 W. JAMES in R. B. Perry *Tht. & Char. W. James* (1935) II. 369 The identifiability of these objects in different fields. **1959** P. F. STRAWSON *Individuals* i. 17 The possibility that the identifiability of particulars of some sorts may be in some *general* way dependent on the identifiability of particulars of other sorts.

identifiable (aɪ'dɛntɪfaɪəb(ə)l), *a.* [f. IDENTIFY + -ABLE.] Able to be identified; capable of identification.

1804 *Edin. Rev.* III. 306 They are easily identifiable. **1830** LYELL *Princ. Geol.* I. 94 Species identifiable with those now living in the Mediterranean. **1859** TENNENT *Ceylon* I. 574 Their names are scarcely identifiable with any now known. **1881** C. A. YOUNG *Sun* (Internat. Sci. Ser.) 82 A given substance is identifiable by its spectrum.

†**iden'tific**, *a.* *Obs. rare.* [ad. L. type **identificus*: see IDENTIFY.] Doing the same; concurring in action.

1678 GALE *Crt. Gentiles* III. 140 Ludovicus à Dola.. bends..his second part against the Jesuites to demonstrate, that a next, immediate, and identific concurse of God to al acts, both good and bad, cannot be defended by the artifice of their middle science. *Ibid.*, He establisheth..the hypothesis of Durandus, that the general concurse of God to acts of a natural order, specially such as are wicked, is not proxime, immediate and identific, but remote, mediate, and really distinct from the act of the creature.

So †**identifi'cality**, identity in action. †**iden'tifically** *adv.*, as to practical identity.

1668 H. MORE *Div. Dial.* I. xxvii. (1713) 57 That Extension which remains to you whether you will or no, is really and identifically coincident with the Amplitude of the Essence of God. **1716** M. DAVIES *Athen. Brit.* II. 423 Christ ..was distinguish'd from him [the Father] only by a.. Personally distinct By-Subsistent Identificality.

identification (aɪdɛntɪfɪ'keɪʃən). [n. of action f. IDENTIFY: see -FICATION.] The action of identifying or fact of being identified.

1. a. The making, regarding, or treating of a thing as identical *with* (†*to*) another, or of two or more things as identical with one another.

1644 DIGBY *Two Treat.* II. ii. 19 In them [identical propositions]..evidence ariseth out of the plaine Identification of the extreames that are affirmed of one another. **1656** BLOUNT *Glossogr.*, *Identification*, the making two things to be the same. **1749** P. SKELTON *Deism revealed* VI. (1751) II. 82 *Shep.* He may then be able..to join the soul or spirit of man to himself. *Dech.* Not so as to make but one person of both; such an identification I take to be impossible. **1805** R. WATSON *Charge* in *Misc. Tracts* (1815) I. 7, I am not ready to admit the Identification of the Romish Faith with Gospel Faith. **1856** STANLEY *Sinai & Pal.* i. (1858) 39 If there are insuperable objections to the identification of Serbâl with Sinai. **1884** GLADSTONE *Sp. Ho. Comm.* 28 Feb., The identification of the franchise in boroughs and counties.

b. The becoming or making oneself one with another, in feeling, interest, or action. Esp. in *Psychol.*, the (freq. unconscious) adaptation of one's ideas and behaviour to fit in with those of a person or group seen as a model.

1857 WILLMOTT *Pleas. Lit.* xi. 41 In Livy it will be the manner of telling a story, in Sallust, personal identification with the character. **1858** HOLLAND *Titcomb's Lett.* vii. 229 The thorough identification of husband and wife in feeling, pride of character and family. **1880** STEPHEN *Pope* iii. 62 He ..kept himself free from identification with either party. **1913** A. A. BRILL tr. *Freud's Interpr. of Dreams* iv. 126 Identification is a highly important factor in the mechanism of hysterical symptoms; by this means patients are enabled in their symptoms to represent not merely their own experiences, but the experiences of a great number of other persons. **1930** W. HEALY et al. *Struct. & Meaning Psychoanal.* v. 240 Identification is the unconscious molding of a person's own Ego after the fashion of one that has been taken as a model. **1950** *Brit. Jrnl. Psychol.* XLI. 176 It was ..clear from her stories and her behaviour at school that J. W. succeeded in making a 'good identification'. **1964** *Listener* 21 May 825/2 The participatory emotions...are mediated by processes variously known as empathy, *rapport*, projection, and identification. **1972** *Sci. Amer.* Jan. 36/3 Girls often are socialized in early childhood to satisfy their achievement needs passively by identification with the accomplishments of their father or their brothers.

2. The determination of identity; the action or process of determining what a thing is; the recognition of a thing as being what it is.

1859 LANG *Wand. India* 168 The identification of a child, who may be an heir to property, is not so light a matter as the purchase of a kitten. **1860** DICKENS *Uncomm. Trav.* v, I had taken, for purposes of identification, a photograph-likeness of a thief, in the portrait-room at our head police office. **1881** A. HERSCHEL in *Nature* No. 622. 507 The identification of their spectroscopic presence in certain meteor-streaks. **1887** *Times* 28 Sept. 3/6 The identification of habitual offenders in spite of their numerous disguises.

†**3.** Exact portraiture; realistic description; also, an instance of this. *Obs.*

1812 *Examiner* 25 May 327/2 The several Portrait Pieces are strong identifications of nature. **1842** MISS MITFORD in L'Estrange *Life* (1870) III. ix. 158 The power of identification, which is the salt of all literature from Horace to Scott.

4. A document such as a passport, driving licence, health card, or a disc or mark that serves to identify a person, or indicates his nationality, military unit, etc. Also *collect.*

1947 *Amer. College Dict.* 599/1 *Identification*, something that identifies one: *have you any identification?* **1958** P. KEMP *No Colours or Crest* vi. 100 We got good identifications—all from the 1st Alpine Division. **1964** MRS. L. B. JOHNSON *White House Diary* 10 June (1970) 164 What we should have done was to ask them all to wear some identification. **1965** M. BRADBURY *Stepping Westward* v. 272 Got any identification? **1970** *Globe & Mail* (Toronto) 28 Sept. 7/1 Once inside I was forced to produce my driver's licence, draft card, student I.D., and all other identification I had on me.

5. *attrib.* and *Comb.* [cf. IDENTITY 10], as ***identification badge, bracelet, card, mark, papers***; **identification beacon** *Aeronaut.* (see quot.); **identification disc**, a disc carried or worn by a person (usu. one in the armed forces), giving his name, etc., as a means of identification; **identification lamp, light**, a light (e.g. on an aircraft) that provides a means of identification; **identification panel**, a sign used to indicate the position of ground troops to friendly aircraft; **identification parade**, a parade of persons from among whom a suspect is to be identified; **identification patch** (see quot.); **identification plate**, the registered number plate of a motor vehicle; **identification signal** (see quot. 1918); **identification tag** *N. Amer.* = *identification disc*; also *transf.*

1945 Identification badge [see *film badge* (FILM *sb.* 7b)]. **1951** *Gloss. Aeronaut. Terms (B.S.I.)* III. 24 *Identification beacon*, a beacon displaying a coded light and identifying a geographical point. **1969** *New Yorker* 30 Aug. 57/2 (Advt.), The 17-jewel movement attaches to a rich gold.. identification bracelet. **1970** *Ibid.* 24 Oct. 48/2 He gave her his identification bracelet, from which he had had eight links removed. **1908** *Westm. Gaz.* 13 Feb. 5/2 An identification-card with his photograph on it. **1969** *New Yorker* 10 May 29/1 Residents will show identification cards to gain admittance. **1915** R. BROOKE *Let.* Mar. (1968) 665 Round my neck with my identification-disk. **1915** *Sphere* 11 Dec. p. iv/3 Copies of the soldiers' identification discs in gold. **1930** T. B. BRUCE *Missing* 13, I burnt all letters and papers.. keeping only my identification disc. **1935** H. G. WELLS *Things to Come* 15 An identification disk—his introduction card so to speak—will be carried. **1932** *Gloss. Aeronaut. Terms (B.S.I.)* (proofs) IX. 7 *Identification lamp*, a lamp mounted on an aircraft for purposes of recognition. **1933** *Gloss. Aeronaut. Terms (B.S.I.)* XIII. 78 *Identification light*, a light on or near a beacon having a character differing from, but serving to identify, it. **1946** R. A. MCFARLAND *Human Factors Air Transport Design* xii. 608 Accidents may arise from misinterpretation of identification lights on other aircraft. **1897** E. L. VOYNICH *Gadfly* III. i. 253 For you to go there just now, with all your identification marks; would be to walk into a trap with your eyes open. **1901** *Westm. Gaz.* 24 Apr. 3/2 He found fifteen other bodies, searched them for their identification marks. **1904** *Ibid.* 30 Aug. 4/3 The identification marks of the cartridges of all the known armies of the world. **1942** B. A. SHIELDS *Princ. Flight* vii. 231 When an aircraft is licensed, it is assigned an identification mark. *Ibid.*, The identification mark signifies the type of flying in which the airplane is permitted to engage. **1944** *Ann. Reg. 1943* 251 The Germans also resented the wearing..of.. colours of the R.A.F. aircraft identification marks. **1918** E. S. FARROW *Dict. Mil. Terms* 305 *Identification panels*, in aëroplane balloon signalling, panels which are displayed at the sound signal of the aircraft or upon the initiative of the command post. **1957** P. KEMP *Mine were of Trouble* viii. 139 We had white identification panels spread on the crest in front of us, to indicate our forward positions. **1903** *Westm. Gaz.* 28 Dec. 7/2, 300 men who had no workmen's identification papers. **1918** Identification papers [see GOOD *a.* C. 8]. **1927** W. E. COLLINSON *Contemp. Eng.* 78 The shortcomings of the identification parades at the police-station. **1965** W. SOYINKA *Road* 54 Perhaps..if you promised not to look in his face..so that you could not recognise him at an identification parade. **1966** A. SACHS *Jail Diary* xi. 109 Perhaps they are taking me to another cell, or they are going to put me on an identification parade. **1972** *Police Rev.* 10 Nov. 1472/3 You think it is necessary to hold identification parades in this case. **1918** E. S. FARROW *Dict. Mil. Terms* 305 *Identification patch*, tags placed upon the backs of the men's coats when advancing behind a barrage. **1901** *Motor-Car World* II. 74/1 Identification-plate. **1906** *Westm. Gaz.* 26 Aug. 8/2 The Commission recommends that identification plates should 'be rigidly fixed in an upright position'. **1909** *Ibid.* 24 June 4/1 Five marks for identification plates. **1918** E. S. FARROW *Dict. Mil. Terms* 305 *Identification signals*..which will identify the authority sending the communication..are assigned from division headquarters and each consists of one letter and one numeral. **1946** *Happy Landings* July 9/1 The identification signal could still be heard. **1918** Identification tag [see *dog tag* (DOG *sb.*[1] 21 a)]. **1918** E. S. FARROW *Dict. Mil. Terms* 305 An identification tag by which he can be identified if killed or wounded. **1960** J. J. ROWLANDS *Spindrift* 146 A small boy with an identification tag tied to his lapel walked silently beside the stewardess. **1964** GOULD & KOLB *Dict. Social Sci.* 244/2 Some students suggest that there is a great concern among those desirous of upward mobility to discard their ethnic identification tags.

identificational (aɪdɛntɪfɪˈkeɪʃənəl), *a.* *Linguistics.* [f. IDENTIFICATION + -AL.] Relating to being identified or not; involving identification.

1933 L. BLOOMFIELD *Lang.* xii. 203 The class-meaning is, roughly, 'identificational character of specimens'. **1964** E. A. NIDA *Toward Sci. Transl.* iii. 44 A communication..can be called identificational, for the source..exhibits a high degree of identification with the receptor.

identificatory (aɪdɛntɪfɪˈkeɪtərɪ), *a.* [f. IDENTIFICAT(ION + -ORY[2].] Serving to bring about identification (in various senses).

1943 *Internat. Jrnl. Psycho-Anal.* XXIV. 97/1 Thus identificatory thinking is employed for the purpose of avoiding what is unpleasurable and obtaining what is pleasurable. **1949** KOESTLER *Insight & Outlook* xii. 175 This identificatory rite survives with great vigour to our day in the ceremony of the eucharistic meal. **1959** P. F. STRAWSON *Individuals* ii. 82 Kant was very careful to empty this 'I' of referential, identificatory force. **1965** *Philos.* XL. 336 The relevant rules of difference are of course those of space-time and its trustworthiness as an identificatory medium. **1972** *Computers & Humanities* VII. 121 Each line includes identificatory information such as page number, abbreviated poem title, line number, and whether the line is a variant or not.

i'dentifier. [f. IDENTIFY + -ER[1].] **1. a.** One who identifies.

1889 *Evening Disp.* (Columbus, Ohio) 11 May, It was finally determined that the prisoner, attorneys and identifiers should step into a side room. **1959** E. FENWICK *Long Way Down* ii. 15 Where the hell's your identifier?

b. One who identifies himself with a cause, group, etc.

1966 *New Statesman* 8 July 56/3 He [*sc.* Mark Twain] lacked the moral or imaginative resources of other identifiers, like Dickens or Balzac.

2. a. That which identifies.

1894 'MARK TWAIN' in *Century Mag.* June 237/2 There was never a twin..that did not carry from birth to death a sure identifier. **1907** *Yesterday's Shopping* (1969) 633/2 Gamekeepers' identifiers...will burn for a period of 3 to 4 minutes. **1973** A. QUINTON *Nature of Things* iii. 61 The view that the identity of things through time is due to the presence in them of an identifying component or substance, an identifier, as I shall call it.

b. *Linguistics.* A linguistic element that has the function of identifying.

1946 [see DESCRIPTOR]. **1965** *Language* XLI. 73 The noun phrase..may be regarded as a string consisting of identifier tagmeme, manifested here by *a.*; [etc.].

c. *Computers.* A sequence of characters arbitrarily devised to identify or refer to a set of data, a location in a store, or a point in a program.

1958 *Communications Assoc. Computing Machinery* Dec. 11 Strings of letters and figures enclosed by delimiters represent new entities. However, only two types of such strings are admissible: 1. Strings consisting of figures ζ only represent the (positive) integers G (including 0) with the conventional meaning. 2. Strings beginning with a letter λ followed by arbitrary letters λ and/or figures ζ are called identifiers. They have no inherent meaning, but serve for identifying purposes only. **1960** *Computer Jrnl.* III. 67/2 An identifier may be used in an ALGOL 60 program as a simple variable. This means that the program, when ultimately translated and run on a computer, will associate a particular storage location with that identifier. The number held in this store at any stage in the calculation is called the current value of the variable. **1962** R. V. OAKFORD *Introd. Electronic Data Processing Equipment* vii. 245 An INPUT declaration defines one or more input-data sets, each of which is given a name in the form of an identifier. **1967** COX & GROSE *Organiz. Bibliogr. Rec. by Computer* II. 19 Such a file sequence carried an 8-character identifier and a sequence-number. **1968** CORLETT & TINSLEY *Pract. Programming* ii. 14 Reference is made to the memory of a computer by giving names or identifiers to variables... Identifiers are also used to denote labels which mark particular points in a program. **1973** *Computers & Humanities* VII. 144 The first ten columns contain identifiers for manuscript, book, question, and line number.

identify (aɪˈdɛntɪfaɪ), *v.* [ad. late L. *identificāre*: see IDENTITY and -FY. Cf. F. *identifier.*]

1. a. *trans.* To make identical (*with*, †*to* something) in thought or in reality; to consider, regard, or treat as the same.

1644 DIGBY *Two Treat.* II. vi. (1645) 63 A body..cannot be either like, or identified to nothing. **1669** BARROW *Expos. Creed* (1697) 89 All the divine perfections (being intrinsecal unto and identified with the divine nature or essence). **1781** GIBBON *Decl. & F.* xxviii. III. 82 *note*, Osiris, whom he identifies with Serapis. **1790** BURKE *Fr. Rev.* Wks. V. 191 They have incorporated and identified the estate of the church with the mass of private property. **1839–40** W. IRVING *Wolfert's R.* (1855) 35 So as to identify the surrounding scenes with those of which I had just been reading. **1856** FROUDE *Hist. Eng.* viii. (1858) II. 243 To identify their interests with those of the native chiefs. **1865** PUSEY *Truth Eng. Ch.* 8 That he identified the glory of God with the gaining fresh converts to the Roman Church.

b. (*a*) To make one in interest, feeling, principle, action, etc. *with*; to associate inseparably. Chiefly *refl.* and *passive.* (*b*) *to* ***identify oneself with***: *spec.* to model oneself on, esp. unconsciously; to feel oneself to be associated with or part of; freq. *absol.* with ellipsis of the refl. pron. Also occas. *intr.*, to perform or undergo such a process with regard to something unspecified.

1780 BURKE *Econ. Reform* Wks. III. 348 Let us identify, let us incorporate ourselves with the people. **1831** SCOTT *Abbot* Introd., They became identified with the literature of their country. **1849** LEWIS *Infl. Author. Matters Opin.* ix. §10 The abstinence of the State from identifying itself with one of the rival churches. **1859** MILL *Liberty* ii. 31 A legislature or an executive, not identified in interest with the people. **1866** LD. STRANGFORD *Select.* (1869) I. 102 A Crimean peace..is identified with the name of Stratford Canning.

1913 A. A. BRILL tr. *Freud's Interpr. of Dreams* iv. 126 If she has put herself in the place of her friend, or, as we may say, has identified herself with her friend. *Ibid.* 127 An hysterical woman identifies herself most readily..with persons with whom she has had sexual relations. **1940** 'G. ORWELL' *Inside Whale* 51 Sam Weller, Mark Tapley, Clara Peggotty..identify with their master's family. **1955** *Publ. Amer. Dial. Soc.* XXIV. 5 The teen-agers who almost compulsively identify with this semicriminal subculture. **1958** *Observer* 2 Feb. 14/3 Readers can immediately identify with her nice puzzled hero. **1958** M. ARGYLE *Relig. Behaviour* v. 40 Other investigators have studied the beliefs of children who..'identify' themselves with their parents —i.e. wish to be liked by them, wish to resemble them. **1959** *Listener* 31 Dec. 1174/2 An engaging series of attempts and failures to 'identify', as cricket-master at a prep school, or as a journalist on a go-getting daily. **1967** G. STEINER *Lang. & Silence* 81 Because we are trained to give psychological and moral credence to the imaginary..we may find it more difficult to identify with the real world. **1968** *Blues Unlimited* Sept. 8 Finally Tina came on and tore the joint up. She signified, the women identified and the men just drooled. **1969** *Times* 17 Oct. 18/5 Everyone identified madly and Biba's knew no failure. **1972** *Where* Jan. 18/2 Thus the parents, in conversation at home, are able to identify themselves with the place and people under discussion.

†**c.** *intr.* To be made, become, or prove to be the same; to become one *with*. *Obs.*

1683 E. HOOKER *Pref. Ep. Pordage's Mystic Div.* 103 Only as..conjoined with our affections, which commix, coincide, and as it were identifi with that grandest and Divinest Mysterie of Love, sciz. God made Flesh. **1790** BURKE *Fr. Rev.* Wks. V. 271 An enlightened self-interest, which..they tell us, will identify with an interest more enlarged and publick. *a* **1834** LAMB *Let. to Coleridge* in *Final Mem.* (1848) I. 83 Your taste and mine do not always exactly identify.

2. a. To determine (something) to be the same with something conceived, known, asserted, etc.; to determine or establish the identity of; to ascertain or establish what a given thing or who a given person is; in *Nat. Hist.* to refer a specimen to its proper species.

1769 BLACKSTONE *Comm.* IV. xxiii. (1830) 306 All indictments must set forth the christian name, sirname [etc.] ..of the offender: and all this to identify his person. **1797** BEWICK *Brit. Birds* (1847) I. 167 The above figure..it is hoped is sufficiently accurate to enable the ornithologist to identify this very small bird. **1828** WEBSTER s.v., The owner of the goods found them in the possession of the thief, and identified them. **1855** BAIN *Senses & Int.* III. i. §10 (1864) 473 A sailor identifies a speck in the horizon as a ship of a particular build. **1889** *Athenæum* 28 Sept. 421/1 Mr. Round ..has also identified as belonging to the reign of Stephen an elaborate hidated survey.

b. To serve as a means of identification for.

1886 J. WARD in *Encycl. Brit.* XX. 62/2 The voice perceived identifies Jacob, at the same time the hands identify Esau.

3. To discover, perceive; to localize. *colloq.*

1922 D. H. LAWRENCE *England, my England* 45 After a lapse and a new effort, he identified a pain in his head.

Hence **i'dentifying** *ppl. a.*, that identifies.

1828 in WEBSTER. **1872** *Daily News* 27 Apr. 3/4 The identifying warder is now one of the most important of the minor figures in our courts of justice. **1891** *Pall Mall G.* 14 May 6/1 The ornamental identifying medallions furnished to the members for wear during the tour.

identikit (aɪ'dɛntɪkɪt). Also **identi-kit.** [Blend of IDENTI(TY + KIT *sb.*[1]] A composite picture of a person whom the police wish to interview assembled from features described by witnesses. Also *transf.*

1961 *Observer* 12 Mar. 5/7 About forty police forces in this country are now testing an American device called an 'Identi-Kit', which is used to translate witnesses' descriptions of a person into visual terms. **1961** *Spectator* 1 Sept. 277 The identi-kit must depend..on the memory of the witness being questioned. **1962** *Times* 19 Apr. 13/2 The identi-kit method of political detection is not really very plausible here. **1963** *Listener* 19 Sept. 416/2 At their worst the genres of contemporary fiction provide no more than a kind of 'identikit' novel, prefabricated from ready-made elements. **1967** *Spectator* 29 Sept. 359/1 One at least managed to build up an identikit description of the soul: 'A most wonderful, delicate, small thing'. **1969** G. GREENE *Trav. with my Aunt* II. iii. 245, I don't resemble whatever identikit portrait you have of me. **1969** *Times* 13 Mar. 13/1 If one were looking at that time for an Identikit of an England side to defend the World Cup in Mexico in 1970 one would scarcely have recognized the person we were looking for. **1971** 'J. ASHFORD' *Bent Copper* vi. 43 He'd called in the D.C. from H.Q. who specialised in Identikit and..the D.C. had built up several faces. **1973** *Times Lit. Suppl.* 9 Mar. 255/1 The identikit of this regime [in Greece] is predictably unpleasant.

identism (aɪ'dɛntɪz(ə)m). [f. *ident(i)-* (see IDENTITY) + -ISM.] The system or doctrine of identity; spec. Schelling's metaphysical theory of absolute identity. (See IDENTITY 1.)

1857 W. FLEMING *Voc. Philos.*, *Identism* or identity.., or the doctrine of absolute identity, teaches that the two elements of thought, objective and subjective, are absolutely one.

‖**Identitätsphilosophie** (idɛnti'tɛːtsfilosofiː). Also i-. [G., identity-philosophy.] The term used for a system, propounded by, among others, F. W. Schelling (1775–1854), that assumes the fundamental identity of spirit and nature.

1866 H. SIDGWICK in A. & E. M. Sidgwick *Henry Sidgwick* iii. 151, I am coming more and more to the opinion that the whole 'Identitäts-philosophie' (Fichte, Schelling, and Hegel) is a monstrous mistake. **1905** W. JAMES *Meaning of Truth* (1909) v. 128 Humanism, here, is only a more comminuted *identitätsphilosophie*. **1905** —— *Ess. Radical Empiricism* (1912) iv. 134 This the post-Kantian idealists.. acknowledged by calling their doctrine an *Identitätsphilosophie*. **1938** *Mind* XLVII. 281 Spinoza's doctrine is not an Identitätsphilosophie; that is to say, the one and only substance has no underlying identical nature, which is only manifested in different ways in the attributes.

†**iden'titial,** *a. Obs. rare.* [irreg. f. next + -AL[1].] = IDENTICAL 1 or 2.

1635 *Grammar Warre* D vj b, That the Relatiue of substance identitiall, should agree in Gender, Number, and Person, with his Antecedent.

identity (aɪ'dɛntɪtɪ). Also 6 **idemptitie.** [ad. F. *identité* (Oresme, 14th c.), ad. late L. *identitās* (Martianus Capella, *c* 425), peculiarly formed from *ident(i)-*, for L. *idem* 'same' + *-tās, -tātem*: see -TY.

Various suggestions have been offered as to the formation. Need was evidently felt of a noun of condition or quality from *idem* to express the notion of 'sameness', side by side with those of 'likeness' and 'oneness' expressed by *similitās* and *ūnitās*: hence the form of the suffix. But *idem* had no combining stem. Some have thought that *ident(i)-* was taken from the L. adv. *identidem* 'over and over again, repeatedly', connexion with which appears to be suggested by Du Cange's explanation of *identitās* as 'quævis actio repetita'. Meyer-Lübke suggests that in the formation there was present some association between *idem* and *id ens* 'that being', whence *identitās* like *entitās*. But assimilation to *entitās* may have been merely to avoid the solecism of **idemitās* or **idemtās*. However originated, *ident(i)-* became the combining stem of *idem*, and the series *ūnitās, ūnicus, ūnificus, ūnificāre*, was paralleled by *identitās, identicus, identificus, identificāre*: see *identic, identific, identify* above.]

1. a. The quality or condition of being the same in substance, composition, nature, properties, or in particular qualities under consideration; absolute or essential sameness; oneness.

absolute identity, that asserted in the metaphysical doctrine of Schelling that mind and matter are phenomenal modifications of the same substance.

1570 BILLINGSLEY *Euclid* v. def. iv. 129 This likenes, idemptitie, or equallitie of proportion is called proportionallitie. **1603** HOLLAND *Plutarch's Mor.* 65 That the soule of this universall world, is not simple, uniforme and uncompounded, but mixed..of a certaine power of Identitie and of Diversity. **1654** Z. COKE *Logick* (1657) 88 Causall Identity is of them which agree in the causes. *Ibid.*, Accidentall Identity is of them that agree in Accidents. **1669** GALE *Crt. Gentiles* I. I. iii. 21 That the Phenicians were originally Canaanites, is manifest from the Identitie of their Languages. **1751** HARRIS *Hermes* Wks. (1841) 233 Is it not marvellous, there should be so exact an identity of our ideas? **1839** MURCHISON *Silur. Syst.* I. xxxv. 474 The organic remains are of great interest in establishing the geological identity between the coal measures of the Dudley district and those of distant parts of Great Britain. **1855** H. SPENCER *Princ. Psychol.* (1872) II. VI. vi. 59 Resemblance when it exists in the highest degree of all..is often called identity. **1863** FAWCETT *Pol. Econ.* II. ix. 265 There is no identity of interests between the employers and employed. **1876** TAIT *Rec. Adv. Phys. Sc.* viii. (ed. 2) 203 The identity of radiant light and heat. **1879** FROUDE *Cæsar* xviii. 298 United..by identity of conviction.

b. with *an* and *pl.* An instance of this quality.

1664 H. MORE *Myst. Iniq.* 264 How fully assured must we needs be of these Identities, the Agreements of these two Parallelisms. **1775** HARRIS *Philos. Arrangem.* Wks. (1841) 309 It is by a contrary power of composition that we recognise their identities. **1861** WRIGHT *Ess. Archæol.* I. vi. 91 The taking of resemblances of words for identities is one of the great stumbling-blocks of the philologist.

†**c.** Recurrence of the same; repetition. *Obs.*

1611 BIBLE *Transl. Pref.* 11 Wee haue not tyed our selues to an vniformitie of phrasing, or to an identitie of words. *a* **1619** FOTHERBY *Atheom.* II. xi. §6 (1622) 325 The soule is delighted with variety. It is dulled with identity.

2. a. The sameness of a person or thing at all times or in all circumstances; the condition or fact that a person or thing is itself and not something else; individuality, personality.

personal identity (in *Psychology*), the condition or fact of remaining the same person throughout the various phases of existence; continuity of the personality.

1638 RAWLEY tr. *Bacon's Life & Death* §5 The Duration of Bodies is Twofold; One in Identity, or the selfe-same Substance; the other by a Renovation or Reparation. **1690** LOCKE *Hum. Und.* II. xxvii. §6 The Identity of the same Man consists..in nothing but a participation of the same continued Life, by constantly fleeting Particles of Matter, in succession vitally united to the same organized Body. *Ibid.* §9 Consciousness always accompanies thinking,..in this alone consists personal Identity, i.e. the Sameness of a rational Being. **1739** HUME *Hum. Nat.* I. v. (1874) I. 323 Of all relations the most universal is that of identity, being common to every being whose existence has any duration. **1820** W. IRVING *Sketch Bk.* I. 85 He doubted his own identity, and whether he was himself or another man. **1832** G. DOWNES *Lett. Cont. Countries* I. 469 The fair city almost forfeits its identity, when disguised in a misty and murky atmosphere. **1885** 'E. GARRETT' *At Any Cost* v. 89 Tom.. had such a curious feeling of having lost his identity, that he wanted to reassure himself by the sight of his little belongings.

b. Personal or individual existence. *rare.* ? *Obs.*

1683 DRYDEN *Life Plutarch* 31 [Plutarch] doubtless beleiv'd the identity of one supream intellectual being which we call God. **1824** BYRON *Juan* XVI. cxx, How odd, a single hobgoblin's non-entity Should cause more fear than a whole host's identity.

†**3.** 'The self-same thing.' *Obs. rare.*

1616 BULLOKAR, *Identitie*, the selfe same thing. *a* **1619** FOTHERBY *Atheom.* II. iii. §2 (1622) 216 Life is not the cause of its owne liuing, but the very same identity with its liuing.

4. *Alg.* **a.** The equality of two expressions for all values of the literal quantities: distinctively denoted by the sign ≡. **b.** An equation expressing identity, an identical equation (IDENTICAL 4 a).

1859 BARN. SMITH *Arith. & Algebra* (ed. 6) 338 Such an expression as $(x + 1)^2 = x^2 + 2x + 1$, where one of the quantities, between which the sign of equality is placed, results from performing the operations indicated in the other, is called an Identity.

5. The condition of being identified in feeling, interest, etc. *rare.*

1868 GLADSTONE *Juv. Mundi* i. (1870) 5 He is in truth in visible identity with the age.

6. *Logic.* ***Law*** or ***Principle of Identity***, the principle expressed in the identical proposition *A is A.* Also *attrib.*, as ***identity formula, relation, sentence.***

1846 SIR W. HAMILTON *Reid's Wks.* 767 The four logical laws of Identity, Contradiction, Excluded Middle, and Reason and Consequent. **1851** MANSEL *Proleg. Log.* (1860) 196 This law of thought is expressed by the Principle of Identity 'Every A is A'. **1860** ABP. THOMSON *Laws Th.* (ed. 5) §114. 212 Criteria of Truth. 2nd Criterium. The Principle of Identity. **1889** FOWLER *Induct. Logic* Pref. (ed. 5) 19 *note*, Amongst the assumptions or pre-suppositions of reasoning, I have not included the so-called Law of Identity; as to say that all A is A, or a thing is the same as itself, appears to me to be an utterly unmeaning proposition. **1940** W. V. QUINE *Math. Logic* 232 *I* is..the identity relation $\hat{x}\hat{y}$ $(x = y)$. **1965** B. MATES *Elem. Logic* ix. 146 It will be useful to introduce a couple of obvious conventions for writing identity-formulas. *Ibid.* 149 The identity relation among the elements of one domain will be different from that among the elements of another. *Ibid.*, Thus every identity-sentence would be either trivial or absurd. **1967** *Encycl. Philos.* IV. 123/1 When we utter an identity sentence such as 'Venus is the morning star', what we wish to express..is that the terms 'Venus' and 'the morning star' both mean the same thing. **1970** J. D. CARNEY *Introd. Symbolic Logic* vii. 160 The identity relation has some rather special properties.

7. (*old*) ***identity***: a person long resident or well known in a place. *N.Z.* and *Austral.*

1862 *Otago, Its Goldfields & Resources* 9 The exclusive spirit of the 'old identity'. **1874** A. BATHGATE *Colonial Experiences* iii. 26 The term 'old identities' took its origin from an expression in a speech made by one of the members of the Provincial Council, Mr E. B. Cargill, who, in speaking of the new arrivals, said that the early settlers should endeavour to preserve their old identity... A comic singer [R. Thatcher] helped to perpetuate the name by writing a song. **1879** W. J. BARRY *Up & Down* xx. 197 The 'old identities' were beginning to be alive to the situation. **1889** *Bulletin* (Sydney) 28 Sept. 8/1 Many of the old identities of '52 and '53 will remember the license-hunting and shanty-raiding days. **1893** *Auckland Weekly News* 9 Dec. 7 Both these old identities are in possession of all their faculties to a wonderful degree. *Ibid.* 28 Another old identity passed away on Dec. 1 in the person of Mr. Thomas Hunt. **1929** 'M. BARNARD ELDERSHAW' *House Is Built* (1945) v. 111 He was the sort of man who becomes an old identity almost at once, so that the residents of the Parramatta Road..soon thought they had been seeing him drive past in his indescribably sailorly fashion all their lives. **1942** 'M. INNES' *Daffodil Affair* II. ii. 46 Ron's dad was a well-known identity Cobdogla-way. **1944** *Mod. Jun. Dict.* (Whitcombe & Tombs) 205 In Australia and New Zealand a very old resident in a place is called an 'old identity'. **1962** J. R. BERNARD in *Southerly* XXII. II. 97 We [Australians] add to ..identity that of outstanding local citizen. **1970** *N.Z. Woman's Weekly* 9 Nov. 19/1 Havelock North identity Mrs C. E. Turner-Williams..at 98 stitches happily on.

8. *Math.* **a.** An element of a set which, if combined with any element by a (specified) binary operation, leaves the latter element unchanged.

1894 *Bull. Amer. Math. Soc.* I. 61 Given an (abstract) group G_n..with elements s_1 = identity, s_2, s_n. **1937** R. D. CARMICHAEL *Introd. Theory Groups of Finite Order* xiii. 395 For every *a* we have $ai = a = ia$. Then we call *i* an identity with respect to the rule of combination of the group. *Ibid.* i. 17 Since the identity plays the role of unity in multiplication, it is often denoted by the symbol 1. **1941** BIRKHOFF & MACLANE *Surv. Mod. Algebra* i. 2 The number zero has the characteristic property that it leaves unaltered any number to which it is added; hence we say that zero is an 'identity element' for addition. By formal analogy, the 'unity' 1 is an identity for multiplication. **1966** MEYER & HANLON *Fun with New Math* i. 12 The number one is the multiplicative identity, for the product of it and any other number leaves the second number unchanged. **1971** E. C. DADE in Powell & Higman *Finite Simple Groups* viii. 254 The associativity in *G* easily implies that of multiplication in *FG*, and the identity 1_G of *G* is also the identity for *FG*.

b. A transformation that gives rise to the same elements as those to which it is applied.

1910 VEBLEN & YOUNG *Projective Geom.* I. iii. 65 The correspondence which makes every element of the system correspond to itself is called the identical correspondence or simply the identity, and is denoted by the symbol 1. **1959** E. M. PATTERSON *Topology* (ed. 2) ii. 20 If $A \subset B$, the transformation $i: A \to B$ defined by $i(^a) = a$ is a one-one transformation called an inclusion; in particular, if $A = B$, the inclusion $i: A \to A$ is called the identity. **1961** H. S. M. COXETER *Introd. Geom.* ii. 29 If the product of two transformations is the identity, each is called the inverse of the other, and their product in the reverse order is again the identity.

9. *S. Afr.* (See quot. 1924.)

1924 E. H. BROOKES *Hist. Native Policy S. Afr.* iii. 62 Most modern thinkers on the Native question argue as if there were no *via media* between the principle which refuses to acknowledge any real difference between Europeans and Natives, the policy of identity as we may call it,..and the principle which insists on the subordinate position of the Native in the body politic, the policy of subordination. **1961** *Listener* 30 Nov. 898/2 These influences..led in South Africa to the policy sometimes known as 'identity', of regarding all men as much the same. *Ibid.*, The earlier British policy of identity broke down.

10. a. *attrib.* and *Comb.* with the meaning 'that serves to identify the holder or wearer', as ***identity bracelet, card, certificate, disc, papers, patch***; also **identity element** *Math.* = IDENTITY 8 a; **identity matrix** *Math.*, a matrix in which all the elements of the principal diagonal are one and the remainder zero, so that its product with another matrix gives that matrix; **identity parade** = *identification parade.*

1968 J. IRONSIDE *Fashion Alphabet* 167 *Identity bracelet*, a gold or silver chain with a flat space for the owner's name. **1973** G. SIMS *Hunters Point* xiii. 124 On his wrists a gold watch and a gold identity bracelet. **1900** *Westm. Gaz.* 2 Jan. 3/1 When troops are going on service each man has issued to him what is known as a field dressing and an identity card. **1931** *Times Lit. Suppl.* 1 Jan. 2/2 He..forged an identity card, and procured a pistol. **1940** *Ann. Reg. 1939* 101 Some 65,000 enumerators, who..issued identity cards for all the persons mentioned in the forms. **1953** C. DAY LEWIS *Italian Visit* i. 14 The identity cards that inform us Not who we are or might be, but how we are interchangeable. **1961** *Daily Mail* 20 July 9/3 Millions of people may soon have to carry special medical identity cards... A card..would contain information about their illnesses..any special drugs they were taking. **1972** *Daily Tel.* 23 Nov. 6 The BBC is to tighten up security at its London studios and offices by issuing identity cards to staff. **1918** *Act 8 Geo. V* c. 6 §11 Every person who receives, detains or has in his possession any identity certificate, life certificate, or other certificate. **1909** *Daily Chron.* 15 June 5/5 Rations for three days, ammunition, field bandages, and identity discs were issued to the men. **1911** *Punch* 15 Mar. 181/1 By the March Army Orders the identity discs issued to officers and men in war time are in future to be issued to the former in peace time. **1915** 'I. HAY' *First Hundred Thousand* vi, Its called an Identity Disc. Every soldier on active service wears one. **1919** J. B. MORTON *Barber of Putney* i, In due course came vaccination and inoculation, and identity discs. **1956** R. ST. B. BAKER *Dance of Trees* vi. 79 When the top soil of Tel Fara was excavated we found modern spurs, identity discs, even a copy of the *Tatler*..reminders of the days of Allenby. **1902** *Trans. Amer. Math. Soc.* III. 486 There exists a left-hand identity element, that is, an element i_l such that, for every element *a*, $i_l a = a$. **1966** MAY & MOSS *New Math for Adults Only* vi. 33/2 Zero is the identity element in addition and one is the identity element in multiplication. **1941** BIRKHOFF & MACLANE *Surv. Mod. Algebra* viii. 197 Corresponding to the identity transformation $y_i = x_i$ *is the* $n \times n$ identity matrix *I*, which has entries 1 along the principal diagonal (upper left to lower right) and zeros elsewhere. **1908** *Daily*

Chron. 21 Feb. 4/6 The 'identity papers', which every man and woman in Prussia must carry about with them. **1955** 'A. GILBERT' *Is she Dead Too?* viii. 141 Put a gorilla in a set of ginger reach-me-downs and you could put up the pair of 'em in an identity parade and no one could tell the difference. **1973** E. LEMARCHAND *Let or Hindrance* vii. 69 We may ask you to come along to an identity parade. **1959** M. LEVIN *Eva* 37 The Ukrainians didn't have to wear identity patches, since the Germans considered them allies.

b. *Philos. attrib.* and *Comb.* as ***identity doctrine, sign, thesis***; **identity theory**, the materialist theory that physiological and mental perceptions are identical; hence ***identity theorist***, a person professing belief in the identity theory.

1920 S. ALEXANDER *Space, Time & Deity* II. 9 The statement..is a species of the identity doctrine of mind and body, maintaining that there are not two processes, one neural, the other mental, but one. **1950** W. V. QUINE *Methods of Logic* (1952) 211 It is the use of the identity sign between variables, rather than between singular terms, that is fundamental. **1965** HUGHES & LONDEY *Elem. Formal Logic* xxxvii. 258 We need one further symbol, which is written '=' and is known as the identity sign. **1951** G. HUMPHREY *Thinking* viii. 245 Inspired by the behaviourists one group of advocates of what may be called the 'identity theory' has stressed the importance of the so-called implicit speech movements which occur during thinking. **1966** *Amer. Philos. Q.* III. 227/2 Some philosophers..infer that the Identity Theory is an empirical theory. *Ibid.* 233/2 Some Identity Theorists are anxious to eliminate mental properties. **1967** *Encycl. Philos.* V. 339/1 The identity theorist uses the familiar philosophical distinction between significance and reference..to make the claim that mentalistic and physicalistic expressions..will turn out as a matter of empirical fact to refer to or denote one and the same thing, namely physical phenomena. **1954** H. FEIGL in P. A. Schilpp *Philos. R. Carnap* (1963) 259 The prima facie implausibility of the identity thesis arises..mainly from the psychological incompatibility of images such as of nervous tissue..with the qualities of some data of consciousness. **1967** *Philos. Rev.* LXXVI. 201 In recent years, a number of philosophers have argued in favor of materialism in the form of an identity thesis—that is, a thesis to the effect that mental events are identical with certain physiological events.

c. Belonging or relating to identity (sense 2), as in **identity crisis**, a phase of varying severity undergone by an individual in his need to establish his identity in relation to his associates and society as part of the process of maturing. Also *transf.*

1954 *Jrnl. Amer. Psychoanal. Assoc.* II. Apr. 327 George Bernard Shaw arranged for himself a psycho-social moratorium at the age of twenty when his identity crisis led him to leave..his family, friends and familiar work. **1959** *Listener* 29 Oct. 746/2 The prolonged identity crisis of this great young man. **1965** *Times Lit. Suppl.* 25 Nov. 1078/4 A sympathetic study of 'identity crisis' might appear peculiarly relevant to many Americans. **1968** *Internat. Encycl. Social Sci.* VII. 63/2 An era's identity crisis is least severe in that segment of youth which is able to invest its fidelity in an expanding technology. **1971** R. A. CARTER *Manhattan Primitive* (1972) xv. 137 Girl is on the verge of a breakdown, in deep identity crisis. **1971** M. MCCARTHY *Birds of America* 110 His college tutor, a stupid Freudian, had advised his mother that Peter had an 'identity problem'. **1974** *Times Lit. Suppl.* 19 Apr. 409/1 A middle-aged cuckold with piles and an identity crisis.

identlie, -ly: see IDENT.

ideo- ('aɪdi:əʊ, 'ɪdi:əʊ), combining form of Gr. *ἰδέα* IDEA, as in ˌ**ideoge'netic** *a.*, producing ideas or images; '**ideoglyph** = IDEOGRAPH; ˌ**ideoki'netic** *a. Path.*, denoting that form of apraxia in which the sufferer retains the motor ability to perform an action or movement and understands a request to perform it, but cannot perform it on request; **ideolatry** (-'ɒlətrɪ) [-LATRY], the worship of ideas; **ideo-motor** (-'məʊtə(r)) *a.* [MOTOR], applied by W. B. Carpenter to automatic muscular movements arising from complete occupation of the mind by an idea, and to the cerebral centres controlling such movements; so **ideo-'motion**, ideo-motor movement; '**ideophone** (-fəʊn) [Gr. *φωνή* voice, sound], (*a*) term used by A. J. Ellis (in contradistinction to *ideograph*) for a sound or group of sounds denoting an idea, i.e. a spoken word; (*b*) a term used principally in Bantu linguistics to refer to particular classes of onomatopœic and sound-symbolic words found in these languages; so **ideopho'netics**, the subject of 'ideophones'; hence **ideo'phonic** *a.*; **ideophonous** (-'ɒfənəs) *a.*, relating to spoken words as sounds denoting ideas; **ideopraxist** (-'præksɪst) *nonce-wd.* [Gr. *πρᾶξις* doing: see -IST], one whose practice is actuated by an idea, one who embodies an idea in action; **ideo-sen'sational** *a.*, compounded of ideas and sensations.

1904 *Jrnl. Philos.* 21 July 412 In the *ideogenetic thinking of artists, the word-symbols are not used. **1847** HINCKS *On Lett. Hieroglyph. Alph.* in *Irish Acad. Trans.* XXI. II. 3 We may give to these characters, and also to those which.. represent ideas without the intervention of words, the common name of *Ideoglyphs. **1908** *Jrnl. Nervous & Mental Dis.* XXXV. 636 There is a great variety of abnormal manipulations..of objects, which are described under the head of apraxia. These may be divided into (1) manifestations of ideomotor apraxia (*ideokinetic, of Liepmann, formerly motor apraxia). **1914** H. LIEPMANN in *17th Internat. Congr. Med.* XI. II. 100 Both limb-kinetic, and particularly ideokinetic apraxia, generally have ideational defective reactions admixed with them. **1933** W. R. BRAIN *Dis. Nervous Syst.* i. 95 Apraxia has been analysed by Liepmann into limb-kinetic apraxia.., ideo-kinetic apraxia, due to a dissociation between ideational and kinaesthetic processes, and ideational apraxia. **1947** F. B. WALSH *Clin. Neuro-Ophthalm*, i. 75/1 In ideokinetic apraxia there is a transferring of movement to other parts of the body, omission of movements, and the production of amorphous movements. **1869** BARING-GOULD *Orig. Relig. Belief* I. ix. 172 Idolatry exists in three forms: 1. Fetishism; 2. Symbolism; 3. *Ideolatry. **1886** *Syd. Soc. Lex.*, **Ideo-motion*, same as *Ideo-motor movements*. **1874** CARPENTER *Ment. Phys.* II. xiv. (1879) 557 His actions being directly prompted by the ideas with which he is possessed, and thus ..*ideo-motor..as distinguished from volitional. **1886** *Syd. Soc. Lex.*, *Ideomotor centre*, that part of the grey matter of the brain which excites muscular contraction under the influence of ideation. **1881** A. J. ELLIS *Synops. Lect. Lond. Dialectical Soc.* 2 Nov., Mimetics, ideographics, and *ideophonetics. Fixed ideograph, variable *ideophone, and their connection. **1909** *Cent. Dict.* Suppl., *Ideophone.* In *phonetics*, the auditory symbol of a word or phrase that is perceived as a whole and thus constitutes a single idea. Ideophones are distinguished as *sensory* or *motor*, according as the sound or group of sounds corresponding to the word or phrase is heard or spoken. **1935** C. M. DOKE *Bantu Ling. Terminol.* 118 *Ideophone*, a vivid representation of an idea in sound. A word, often onomatopoeic which describes a predicate, qualificative or adverb in respect to manner, colour, sound, smell, action, state or intensity. The ideophone is in Bantu a special part of speech, resembling to a certain extent in function the adverb. **1953** W. J. ENTWISTLE *Aspects of Lang.* xi. 360 The use of ideophones by Zulus and other Bantus shows that the quality of an action is of more interest to them than its specific nature. **1954** G. V. SMITHERS in *Archivum Linguisticum* VI. 73 Some English Ideophones. *Ibid.* 82 The term *ideophone* may as fittingly be applied to the English words of both groups [onomatopœic and imitative] as to those in other languages. **1955** L. W. LANHAM *Study of Gitonga of Inhambane* ix. 220 Certain irregular usages of the tenses given above are observable when ideophones are incorporated as predicative stems. **1964** *Afr. Lang. Stud.* V. 87 Examination.. brought to light, both in Swahili and in kindred languages of the Coastal area, a number of what have been..called ideophones. **1954** *Archivum Linguisticum* VI. 83 It seems that certain types, at least, of *ideophonic root can be struck out in various languages at various periods. **1962** G. FORTUNE *Ideophones in Shona* 37 Ideophonic forms, ideophonic constructions as well as ideophonic phonemes.. are peculiar to 'free expression' as contrasted with 'formal speech'. **1964** *N. & Q.* Oct. 372/2 An infallible sign that the word is an ideophonic formation. **1847** S. W. WILLIAMS *Mid. Kingd.* I. x. 464 The number of such *ideophonous compounds. **1831** CARLYLE *Sart. Res.* II. viii, He himself.. was among the completest Ideologists, at least *Ideopraxists: in the Idea (*in der Idee*) he lived, moved, and fought. **1886** GURNEY *Phantasms of Living* I. 464 **Ideo-sensational* would avoid this difficulty.

ideogram ('ɪdi:əʊgræm, aɪ-). [f. Gr. *ἰδέα* IDEA + -GRAM. Cf. mod.F. *idéogramme.*] = IDEOGRAPH. Also used in *transf.* senses, esp. of figurative diction.

1838 HINCKS in *Blackw. Mag.* July 106/2 Nor was Dr. Young less successful with the hieroglyphic ideograms (or symbolic characters direct and indirect), many of which he determined. **1882-3** F. BROWN in Schaff *Encycl. Relig. Knowl.* I. 583 A Shemitic pronunciation was given to characters used as ideograms. **1883** DELITZSCH in *Athenæum* 26 May 669/1 The Sumerian symbols or ideograms.. usually express the characteristics of the respective animals or objects which they represent. **1893** S. LAING *Hum. Orig.* 68 The idea of beauty being conveyed by an ideogram meaning 'a large sheep'. **1940** E. POUND *Let.* 16 Jan. (1971) 333 Early characters were pictures, squared for aesthetic reasons. But I think in a well-brushed ideogram the sun is seen to be rising. **1951** H. KENNER *Poetry E. Pound* 89 The Anglo-Saxon scholar's term for just such a vivid figure is 'kenning': the particulars by which the person or object in question is known. 'Whale-road', 'soul-bearer', are both ideogram and metaphor. **1959** N. G. L. HAMMOND *Hist. Greece* i. 34 The ideograms (signs which portray objects) and the symbols for numbers narrow the field of its interpretation somewhat, but much is left open to doubt. **1962** W. NOWOTTNY *Lang. Poets Use* iv. 78 The particulars which inhabit these schemes, though extraordinarily difficult to summate, permit themselves to be assimilated to a common ideogram of decline (of the year, of the day, of a fire). **1964** E. PALMER tr. *Martinet's Elem. Gen. Ling.* v. 152 The members of an American board of examiners showed that they agreed neither on the position of the accent in *ideogram* nor on the quality of the first two vowels of the word. **1972** *Times* 29 June 16/3 Traditional graphic symbols and ideograms..were used extensively by the Manding.

ideogrammic (ɪdi:əʊ'græmɪk), *a.* [f. IDEOGRAM + -IC.] Of the nature of an ideogram; expressed by means of symbols. Also **ideogra'mmatic** *a.*

1929 W. J. LOCKE *Ancestor Jorico* i. 15 The swift ideogrammic air-speed which Toby and Jones have invented between themselves is a mystery. **1951** H. KENNER *Poetry E. Pound* 84 Joyce's catalogue of Bloom's books in *Ulysses* is the simplest possible application of the ideogrammic method. **1962** Y. MALKIEL in Householder & Saporta *Probl. Lexicogr.* 22 Special features worthy of mention include: the use of abbreviations or peculiar ideogrammatic classifiers to mark for a given word its grammatical or semantic category. **1962** M. MCLUHAN *Gutenberg Galaxy* 22 No pictographic or ideogrammic or hieroglyphic mode of writing has the detribalizing power of the phonetic alphabet. **1967** *Punch* 18 Jan. 80 To others, the 'No Entry' sign (a highly ideogrammatic white bar on a red disc) variously indicated a pedestrian crossing, a level crossing, a Belisha beacon, the end of a speed limit, a first aid post, and a major road ahead.

ideograph ('ɪdi:əʊgrɑ:f, -æ-, aɪ-). Also erron. **ideagraph.** [f. as IDEOGRAM + -GRAPH.] A character or figure symbolizing the idea of a thing, without expressing the name of it, as the Chinese characters and most Egyptian hieroglyphics.

1835-40 HINCKS *On Hieroglyphics* (MS. B.M., Egypt. Antiq., 19 *e*), Hieroglyphic characters are either ideographs, that is, representations of ideas, or phonographs, that is, representations of sounds. **1838** *Blackw. Mag.* XLIII. 652 The old Egyptians in their hieroglyphics did..signify a wise ..man by the symbolic representation or ideagraph of a nose. **1883** SAYCE *Fresh Light fr. Anc. Mon.* 16 The frequent employment of ideographs, which denoted ideas and not sounds. *Ibid.* 19 Thus in English, the ideograph + may be pronounced 'plus', 'added to', or 'more', according to the pleasure of the reader. **1911** *Encycl. Brit.* XV. 172 The usual charge for advertisement is from 7d. to one shilling per line of 22 ideographs (about nine words). **1951** H. KENNER *Poetry E. Pound* 89 The Chinese ideograph, like the metaphor, deals in exceedingly condensed juxtapositions. **1972** *Computers & Humanities* VI. 259 There is a basic corpus of 2,444 morphemes, each corresponding to a single Chinese logograph (ideograph).

ideographic (ˌɪdi:əʊ'græfɪk, aɪ-), *a.* (*sb.*). (erron. idea-.) [f. as prec. + -IC. Cf. mod.F. *idéographique.*] **A.** *adj.* Of the nature of an ideograph; symbolizing an idea directly, as distinguished from the word or words by which it is expressed; relating to or composed of ideographs. Of ideographs: representing ideas pictorially or figuratively.

1822 *Q. Rev.* XXVIII. 189 Two Memoirs to prove, that neither the hieratic..nor the demotic..writing is alphabetic ..but ideographic. **1849** *Fraser's Mag.* XL. 419 The principle..whether phonetic or ideagraphic. **1862** H. SPENCER *First Princ.* II. xv. §123 (1875) 349 The picture-writing of the Mexicans was found to have given birth to a like family of ideographic forms. **1869** FARRAR *Fam. Speech* iv. (1873) 121 Chinese has only some 450 sounds, and yet has upwards of 40,000 ideographic signs. **1948** D. DIRINGER *Alphabet* 174 An outside initiative has suggested the replacing of the Japanese ideographic-syllabic script by the Latin alphabet. **1955** P. HERON *Changing Forms of Art* 109 This long picture..was new: it represented, as far as Picasso is concerned, the defeat of the plastic by the ideographic. **1964** M. A. K. HALLIDAY et al. *Linguistic Sciences* 49 The Chinese script is not ideographic: the symbols do not represent ideas, they represent formal items of the language. **1972** *Computers & Humanities* VI. 260 Because of an ideographic writing system extending back for 3,500+ years and still shared by all the Chinese languages, cognates can be visually identified.

B. *sb.* An ideographic character; *pl.* a method of writing in ideographic characters.

1846 WORCESTER cites *For. Q. Rev.* **1848** COTTRELL tr. *Bunsen's Egypt's Place* I. 496 The Ideographics comprise all non-phonetic signs. **1881** [see *ideophonetics* in IDEO-].

So **ideo'graphical** *a.* = prec.; hence **ideo'graphically** *adv.*, by means of ideographs.

1836 DU PONCEAU *Chinese Syst. Writ.* (1838) 48 Represent to yourself our hymn books..to be written ideographically, and to be sung *ad libitum*. **1842** BRANDE *Dict. Sci.* etc. 584/2 Ideographical writing is opposed to phonetic. **1880** SAYCE in *Nature* 19 Feb. 379 There was a limit to the number of ideas which could be represented ideographically.

ideography (ɪdi:-, aɪdi:'ɒgrəfɪ). Also erron. **ideagraphy.** [f. Gr. *ἰδέα* IDEA + -GRAPHY. Cf. F. *idéographie.*] The direct representation of ideas by graphic signs, as distinguished from phonetic symbols; writing consisting of ideographs.

1836 T. HOW (*title*) Ideagraphy. **1846** WORCESTER, *Ideography*, a system or treatise of short-hand writing. **1861** *Sat. Rev.* 14 Sept. 278 An erudite introduction upon North American 'Ideography'. **1869** FARRAR *Fam. Speech* iv. (1873) 120 They invented writing, but it stopped at hieroglyphics and ideography.

ideologic (aɪdi:əʊ'lɒdʒɪk), *a.* [f. IDEOLOG-Y + -IC. Cf. F. *idéologique* (1801).] = next, 1.

1857 T. E. WEBB *Intellect. Locke* v. 75 A complete solution of the great Ideologic problem.

ideo'logical, *a.* Also erron. **idealogical.** [f. as prec. + -AL[1].]

1. Belonging or relating to ideology (sense 1), or to the study of ideas.

1797 *Monthly Mag.* III. 286 Tracy..exhibits..a summary table of such ideological truths, as he conceives to be evident. **1843** MILL *Logic* IV. i. §4 Abstinence..from ideological discussions. **1886** *Proc. Philol. Soc.* 4 June p. xliii, He had compiled lists of ideological indices for over two hundred languages.

2. a. Relating to, or occupied with, an idea or ideas, esp. of a visionary kind; dealing with ideas as opposed to facts; ideal, speculative, idealistic. (Cf. IDEOLOGY 2.)

1837 *Blackw. Mag.* XLII. 407 Hence arises what Napoleon has called the ideological race of men. **1862** HEURTLEY in *Repl. 'Ess. & Rev.'* 167 It is an insult to his understanding to ask him to allow a so-called ideological application to supplant the natural and obvious meaning. **1869** *Pall Mall G.* 14 Oct. 10 If these tendencies are to be classified at all, they can only be classed in two divisions—the ideological (I intentionally avoid the word idealistic) and the materialistic.

b. Of or relating to an ideology (sense 4).

1914 *Atlantic Monthly* June 775/1 If Mr. Mencken's earnest seekers after truth wish to evolve ideological schemes of municipal taxation..then, indeed, the newspaper discussions of these questions would be

bewildering to these visionary workers in the realms of pure reason. **1925** M. EASTMAN *Since Lenin Died* iv. 32 Without realising this, you cannot penetrate beneath the ideological surface of the dispute which followed. **1937** *Times* 2 Nov. 17/2 Japan will be an absentee at Brussels... So will Germany... The inconvenience, to say no more, of ideological attitudes has been very swiftly illustrated. **1939** *Times* 2 Nov. 8/2 The attacks on Great Britain and France for waging ideological warfare (is not Communist warfare ideological?) and at the same time being actuated by imperialistic motives are an obvious contradiction in terms. **1940** E. POUND *Cantos* lv. 56 But his brat was run by his missus And they had an ideological war. **1952** *Ann. Reg.* *1951* 4 The rulers of Russia inherited imperialism and added to it an ideological imperialism. **1963** *Daily Tel.* 14 Oct. 12/2 Though it has been left this year to Albania to sponsor Communist China's membership, it will still be supported by her newly declared ideological foe, the Soviet Union, and by the victim of her aggression, India. **1969** *Guardian* 11 Sept. 7/2 Nor was he ever 'ideological', in the sense required by New Left dogmatists.

Hence **ideo'logically** *adv.*, in an ideological manner; in a non-literal sense.

1861 BP. S. WILBERFORCE *Ess.* (1874) I. 150 They ideologically suggest that, when it is asserted that our Lord miraculously fed the multitudes..no more is meant than that..he fed the souls of thousands with edifying moral discourses. **1862** HEURTLEY in *Repl. 'Ess. & Rev.'* 175 To be understood, not as literally and historically true, but only ideologically, or in a 'spiritualized sense'. **1957** P. WORSLEY *Trumpet shall Sound* iii. 67 It..represents a conscious step towards the establishment of forms of organization, which ..were independent both organizationally and ideologically. **1970** *Daily Tel.* 10 Jan. 12 As China's strength and numbers grow she becomes less prepared..to play second fiddle to Russia ideologically. **1971** *Ibid.* 3 Apr. 10/5 The Soviet system remains ideologically and politically committed to the destruction of our way of life.

ideologist (aɪdiːˈɒlədʒɪst). (erron. idea-.) [ad. F. *idéologiste*, f. *idéologie* IDEOLOGY: see -IST.]

1. One versed in ideology (sense 1); one who treats of the origin and nature of ideas.

1798 W. TAYLOR in *Monthly Rev.* XXV. 584 The ideologists of Paris. [**1862** *Mem. Lady Morgan* II. 40 Both she and Sir Charles were intimate with..the Comte de Tracy the *idéologiste*.] **1862** MAURICE *Mor. & Met. Philos.* IV. viii. §58. 500 The modern ideologists have claimed him as their progenitor.

2. A person occupied with an idea or ideas, esp. with such as are regarded as unpractical; a speculator; an idealist, a visionary, a mere theorist.

1831 CARLYLE *Sart. Res.* II. viii, We find our poor Professor..at last indignantly dismissed, almost thrown out of doors, as an 'Ideologist'. **1835** *Blackw. Mag.* XXXVIII. 323 Correspondence with the French propagandists, ideologists, and revolutionaires. **1847** EMERSON *Repr. Men, Napoleon* Wks. (Bohn) I. 368 The advocates of liberty, and of progress, are 'ideologists';—a word of contempt often in his [Bonaparte's] mouth. **1875** MERIVALE *Gen. Hist. Rome* li. (1877) 403 He derided the ideologists who were not content ..with taking the material world as he found it, and putting it to its practical uses.

3. A proponent or adherent of an ideology (sense 4).

1888 MARX & ENGELS *Manifesto of Communist Party* 14 Just as..the nobility went over to the bourgeoisie, so now a portion of the bourgeoisie goes over to the proletariat, and in particular a portion of the bourgeois ideologists, who have raised themselves to the level of comprehending..the historical movement. **1937** *Daily Herald* 20 Jan. 1/7 We are not content to see Europe arming feverishly under the contending standards of rival ideologists.

ide'ologize, *v.* [f. IDEOLOG(Y: see -IZE.] *trans.* To treat (a statement) ideologically.

1860 BP. S. WILBERFORCE *Ess.* (1874) I. 120 Could he.. call on any other speculator to stay the ideologizing process?

ideologue (aɪˈdiːəʊlɒg). Also erron. **idealogue**. [ad. F. *idéologue*, f. Gr. ἰδέα IDEA + -LOGUE.] = IDEOLOGIST 2.

1815 HEL. M. WILLIAMS *Pres. St. France* vii. 109 Leaving the ideologues of his council to arrange what he [Bonaparte] calls their revolutionary rubbish, such as sovereign people, equal rights, &c. **1882** *Spectator* 30 Dec. 1676 Unless by ill-fortune the Throne were filled by an idealogue. **1887** *Ibid.* 10 Sept. 1202 English workmen, we imagine, are not becoming ideologues, but some of their delegates are. **1955** *Times* 6 June 7/7 From outside it is so easy to think of the Russians as a nation of ideologues. **1961** *Spectator* 9 June 826 When the plotters and ideologues come up for trial. **1972** *Sat. Rev.* (U.S.) 20 May 34/2 Women's Liberation ideologues and strategists have advanced some fine, socially refined arguments. **1972** *Observer* 10 Dec. 36/2 One of the stated principles of this outfit's chief ideologues is to steer clear of the politicos.

ideology (aɪdiːˈɒlədʒɪ). [ad. F. *idéologie*: see IDEO- and -LOGY.]

1. a. The science of ideas; that department of philosophy or psychology which deals with the origin and nature of ideas. **b.** *spec.* Applied to the system of the French philosopher Condillac, according to which all ideas are derived from sensations.

1796 W. TAYLOR in *Monthly Rev.* XX. 569 Tracy read a paper [at the National Institute of France]..and proposed to call the philosophy of mind, ideology. **1797** *Monthly Mag.* III. 285 Tracy..proposes, that the science which results from this analysis, be named ideology, or the science of ideas, in order to distinguish it from the ancient metaphysics. **1832** SIR W. HAMILTON *Discuss.* (1852) 69 Ideologie (more correctly Idealogie)..has in France become the name peculiarly distinctive of that philosophy of mind which exclusively derives our knowledge from the senses. **1852** H. ROGERS *Ess.* I. vii. 377 The word 'ideas'..enters appropriately corrupted in the term ideology, as a name for a system of purely sensational philosophy. **1882** T. DAVIDSON tr. *Rosmini's Philos. Syst.* §10. 22 Ideology undertakes to investigate the nature of human knowledge.

c. The study of the way in which ideas are expressed in language.

1886 *Proc. Philol. Soc.* 4 June p. xliii, Valuable evidence.. could be derived from comparative ideology, a branch of the science of language that hitherto had been much neglected.

2. Ideal or abstract speculation; in a depreciatory sense, unpractical or visionary theorizing or speculation.

1813 J. ADAMS *Wks.* (1856) X. 52 Napoleon has lately invented a word, which perfectly expressed my opinion.. He calls the project ideology. **1827** SCOTT *Napoleon* VI. 251 Ideology, by which nickname the French ruler [Bonaparte] used to distinguish every species of theory, which, resting in no respect upon the basis of self-interest, could, he thought, prevail with none save hot-brained boys and crazed enthusiasts. **1839** CARLYLE *Chartism* vi. 148 Does the British reader..call all this unpleasant doctrine of ours ideology? **1881** SEELEY *Bonaparte* in *Macm. Mag.* XLIV. 164/2 He..put aside the whole system of false and confused thinking which had reigned since 1792, and which he called ideology.

3. = IDEALISM 1.

1835 J. B. ROBERTSON tr. *Schlegel's Philos. Hist.* (1846) 64 Infidel science, astonished at her own discoveries, which disconcert alike ideology and materialism.

4. A systematic scheme of ideas, usu. relating to politics or society, or to the conduct of a class or group, and regarded as justifying actions, esp. one that is held implicitly or adopted as a whole and maintained regardless of the course of events. Also *Comb.*

1909 *Westm. Gaz.* 4 May 10/2 It may be worth while giving some account of the ideology behind the German proposal, and of the details as worked out in the Conservative programme, bearing in mind that it is the scheme of a reactionary Agrarian party. **1936** WIRTH & SHILS tr. K. Mannheim (*title*) Ideology and Utopia. **1939** AUDEN in *I Believe* (1940) 22 It is despair at finding a solution to this problem which is responsible for much of the success of Fascist blood-and-soil ideology. **1955** E. SHILS in *Encounter* V. 52 (*title*) The end of ideology? **1966** D. JENKINS *Educated Society* iv. 177 The processes of ideology-formation can go on even in the most high-minded of circles. **1970** D. D. RAPHAEL *Probl. Pol. Philos.* i. 17 Ideology..is usually taken to mean, a prescriptive doctrine that is not supported by rational argument.

ideom(e, ideot, etc., obs. ff. IDIOM, etc.

ideomotion, -praxist, etc.: see IDEO-.

i-deoped, ME. pa. pple. of DEEP *v.*

ideoplasm (ˈɪdɪəʊplæz(ə)m). *Spiritualism.* [f. IDEO- + *-plasm* after ECTOPLASM.] = ECTOPLASM. So ˌ**ideo'plasmic** *a.*; ˈ**ideoplasmy** (see quot. 1961).

1926 A. CONAN DOYLE *Hist. Spiritualism* I. i. 7 Ectoplasm ..has also been called 'ideoplasm', because it takes on in an instant any shape with which it is impressed by the spirit. **1961** W. H. SALTER *Zoar* vi. 63 The hypothesis of 'ideoplasmy', that is to say, the view that materialisations are produced from the medium's energy and a substance ('ectoplasm') supplied by him with the assistance perhaps of the sitters, and that they take form in accordance with the thoughts of those present. *Ibid.* vi. 69 A clumsy attempt, whether ideoplasmic or fraudulent, to imitate the established conception of a spirit?

ideoplastic (ɪdɪəʊˈplæstɪk), *a.* [ad. F. *idéoplastie* (J. P. Philips *Cours théorique et pratique de Braidisme* (1860) ii. 44), adj. *idéoplastique*, f. IDEO- + PLASTIC *a.* 5.] Denoting those physiological or artistic processes which are supposed to be moulded or modified by mental impressions or suggestions; also, pertaining to the suggestive function of the imagination; so **ideo'plastically** *adv.*, in a manner influenced by mental or imaginative impressions; **ideo'plasty, ideo'plasy**, imagination in its suggestive capacity, esp. as modifying certain physiological functions or processes.

Somewhat specialized uses in spiritualistic writings are not clearly distinguishable from the above. Durand de Gros (see quot. 1901) and J. P. Philips (see etym.) are names of the same person.

1901 BALDWIN *Dict. Philos. & Psychol.* I. 507/2 *Ideoplastic*, applied to the physiological functions considered as liable to modification from suggested ideas (used originally by Durand de Gros). *Ibid.*, *Ideoplasy*, suggestions operative in the production of physiological changes. **1919** A. CONAN DOYLE *Vital Message* App. 209 We accept Dr. Geley's statement that they are 'ideoplastic'. **1929** *Encycl. Brit.* I. 51/1 For half a century no perceptible progress was made on the idea thrown out by Durand (1855, 1860) that a clear distinction should be effected between the 'ideoplastic' and hypotaxic phenomena. **1935** *Burlington Mag.* Mar. 110/1 As regards the ideoplastic character of pre-Greek art..it is called ideoplastic because the artist renders what he *knows* about the object rather than what he sees. *Ibid.* 121/2 He built up his works ideoplastically. **1943** H. READ *Educ. through Art* v. 136 Later writers..relate this two-fold distinction to Verworn's classification of primitive art as physioplastic and ideoplastic. **1960** *Times Lit. Suppl.* 12 Aug. 576/2 The 'ideoplasty' presumed to cause the body of a medium to extrude and model ectoplasm into the image, telepathically received, of old Aunt Kate. **1961** R. CROOKALL *Supreme Adventure* II. i. 60 The substance composing their environment resembles ectoplasm in being ideo-plastic and responding automatically to their thoughts, feelings, expectations, hopes and fears.

i-derued, ME. pa. pple. of DERVE *v.*

ides (aɪdz), *sb. pl.* Rarely in sing. ide. [a. F. *Ides* (12th c. in Hatz.-Darm.), ad. L. *Īdūs*, sb. pl.] In the ancient Roman calendar, the eighth day after the nones, i.e. the 15th of March, May, July, October, and the 13th of the other months.

The days after the nones were reckoned forward to the ides; hence such expressions as 'the sixth of the ides' (or 'the sixth ides', or 'the sixth ide') 'of June', loosely rendering L. *ante diem sextum Idus Junias* = June 8. See note s.v. CALENDS 1.

c **1330** R. BRUNNE *Chron.* (1810) 341 Idus þat is of May left I to write þis ryme, B letter & Friday bi ix þat ȝere ȝede prime. **1483** CAXTON *Gold. Leg.* 215 b/2 It was the iii ydees of Juyll. **1502** ARNOLDE *Chron.* 65 b/2 Somer..beginnithe the vij. Ide of may and lastith vnto the vij. Ide of august. **1576** FLEMING *Panopl. Epist.* 40 Dated the .7. of the Ides of June. **1601** SHAKS. *Jul. C.* I. ii. 17 Cæsar..Beware the Ides of March. **1641** HOWELL *Vote* in *New Vol. Lett.* (1650) I ij, The soft gliding Nones and every Ide. **1776** ABIGAIL ADAMS in *J. Adams' Fam. Lett.* (1876) 160 The 19th of April, ever memorable for America as the Ides of March to Rome and to Cæsar. **1834** LYTTON *Pompeii* I. iii, 'It stands fixed for the ninth ide of August', answered Pansa. **1847** EMERSON *Woodnotes* I. 45 Foreteller of the vernal ides, Wise harbinger of spheres and tides.

‖**id est**, two Latin words, meaning 'that is', used in works written in Latin to introduce an explanation of a word or phrase = 'that is to say'; retained in English in the same use, now usually in the abbreviated form *i.e.* (formerly often *i.*): see *Abbreviations*, under I the letter.

1598 FLORIO, *Gallina bagnata*, a wet hen, id est, a milke-sop. **1663** BUTLER *Hud.* I. i. 850 *Mira de lente*, as 'tis i'th Adage, *Id est*, to make a Leek a Cabbage. **1821** BYRON *Juan* IV. xciii, 'Arcades ambo', *id est*—blackguards both.

idiasm (ˈɪdɪæz(ə)m). [ad. Gr. ἰδιασμός peculiarity, f. ἰδιάζ-ειν to be peculiar, f. ἴδιος peculiar.] A peculiarity, mannerism.

1868 C. M. INGLEBY in *Athenæum* 12 Dec. 800/3 Among the causes which debase and enervate a language are..the use of idiasms generating euphemisms. **1877** —— *Shakespeare* I. vii. 118 The idioms, idiotisms, and, above all, the idiasms of Shakespeare [etc.]. **1893** *Nat. Observer* 21 Jan. 240/2 The owner's personal or peculiar whimsy or 'idiasm' is not only permissible, but is distinctly demanded.

idic (ˈɪdɪk), *a. Biol.* [f. ID¹ + -IC.] Pertaining to an id or ids.

1893 tr. *Weismann's Germ-Plasm* I. i. 63 Every id of the germ-plasm contains the whole of the elements which are necessary for the development of all subsequent idic stages.

i-diched, ME. pa. pple. of DITCH *v.*

idiely, idili, idillich, obs. ff. IDLY.

i-dight, i-diȝt, i-diht: see YDIGHT and DIGHT *v.*

-idin, *suffix. Chem.* [f. -ID(E + -IN¹.] Used to form the names of the anthocyanidins, as in *cyanidin, delphinidin, pelargonidin, peonidin.*

-idine, *suffix. Chem.* [f. -ID(E + -INE⁵.] Used to form the names of many organic compounds containing nitrogen which, with few exceptions (as *guanidine*), contain one or more rings; exp.: **a.** Certain amino derivatives (*a*) of simple monocyclic aromatic hydrocarbons, as *cumidine, cymidine, mesidine, toluidine, xylidine*, or of derivatives of such hydrocarbons, as *cresidine*; (*b*) of symmetrical bicyclic aromatic hydrocarbons, as *benzidine, naphthidine, tolidine.* **b.** Certain aminophenol ethers, as *anisidine, phenetidine.* **c.** Certain heterocyclic compounds with nitrogen in the ring (the use of the suffix in some cases implying that the ring is saturated), as *piperidine, pteridine, pyridine, pyrrolidine.* (Hence, in mod. systematic nomenclature, forming the suffixes *-iridine, -etidine* and *-olidine*, as in *aziridine.*) **d.** Pyrimidine nucleosides, as *cytidine, thymidine, uridine.* **e.** Certain alkaloids, as *anhalidine, pilocarpidine, quinidine.*

idio- (ˈɪdɪəʊ), repr. Gr. ἰδιο-, combining form of ἴδιος own, personal, private, peculiar, separate, distinct. Of compounds occurring in Greek, IDIOPATHY and IDIOSYNCRASY are Eng. representatives; but a number of recent scientific terms have been formed on Greek types, or even with a Latin second element, as *idio-muscular, -repulsive.* **idio'chromosome** *Cytology* = *sex chromosome.* **idi'ocracy** *nonce-wd.* [see -CRACY], personal rule or government. ˌ**idiocy'clophanous** *a.* [see CYCLO- and *idiophanous*], exhibiting axial interference figures without the use of polarizing apparatus. **idio'dinic** *a. Zool.* [Gr. δῖν-ος, δίν-η eddy, vortex, taken in sense 'pore'], having a special opening for the extrusion of genital products. †**idio-e'lectric** *a.* [see ELECTRIC], capable of being

electrified by friction. **idio'glossia** [Gr. *ἰδιόγλωσσος* of distinct tongue], a form of dyslalia in which the person affected consistently makes substitutions in his speech sounds to such an extent that he seems to speak a language of his own. **idio'glottic** *a.* [see GLOTTIC, and cf. Gr. *ἰδιόγλωσσος*], using words of one's own invention. **idio'gonaduct**, the gonaduct of an idiodinic animal. **'idiograph** [Gr. *ἰδιόγραφον*], one's private mark or signature; hence **idio'graphic** *a.*, (*a*) of or pertaining to an idiograph; (*b*) concerned with the individual, pertaining to or descriptive of single and unique facts and processes (opp. NOMOTHETIC *a.*). **idiolalia** (-'leɪlɪə) [-LALIA] = *idioglossia* above. **idi'olatry** *nonce-wd.* [Gr. *λατρεία* worship], self-worship. **idi'ometer** [-METER], an instrument for measuring the 'personal equation' of an observer, by observation of the transit of an artificial star whose actual motion is exactly known. **idio'muscular** *a. Path.* [see MUSCULAR], in ***idiomuscular contraction***, Schiff's term for the local contraction, under physical stimulus, of a muscle which is fatigued or dying, the movement not being transmitted to the whole length of muscular fibre. **idio'neural** *a. Path.* [see NEURAL] (see quot.). †**idi'onomy** [Gr. *-νομία* arrangement], individual constitution. **idi'ophanism**, idiophanous nature or property. **idi'ophanous** *a.* [Gr. *-φανής* appearing] = *idiocyclophanous*. **idiophone**, a percussion instrument that consists simply of elastic material (as metal, wood, etc.) capable of producing sound (as opp. to a MEMBRANOPHONE in which stretched skin is used as the agent of sound). **idio'phoneme** *Linguistics*, a phoneme in individual speech; hence **idiopho'nemic** *a.* **idio'phrenic** *a. Path.* [Gr. *φρήν* mind], 'Tuke's term for the form of insanity which is caused by disease of the brain itself' (*Syd. Soc. Lex.* 1886). **'idioplasm** *Biol.*, Nägeli's term for the special portion of protoplasm in a germ or cell which is supposed to determine the character of the resulting organism; hence **idioplas'matic** *a.* **idiopsy'chology**, the psychology of one's own mind; hence **idiopsycho'logical** *a.* **idiore'pulsive** *a.*, self-repelling. **idio'retinal** *a.*, applied to what is seen when the eyes are shut and there is no external stimulation of the retina. **idio'(r)rhythmic** *a.* [Gr. *ἰδιόρρυθμος* living in one's own way], of monastic institutions: allowing freedom to the individual (opposed to CŒNOBITIC); also as *sb.* **idio'static** *a.* [see STATIC], not employing any auxiliary electrification in the measurement of electricity: opposed to HETEROSTATIC. **idio'thalamous** *a. Bot.* [THALAMUS], 'having a different colour or texture from the thallus; a term used among lichens' (*Treas. Bot.* 1866). **'idiotype** *Chem.* [TYPE] (see quot.); hence **idio'typic** *a.* **ˌidioven'tricular** *a. Med.*, proper to the ventricle alone; used of the rhythm of contraction set up within the ventricle when the normal auricular stimulus to ventricular contraction is blocked.

1905 *Science* 20 Oct. 500/2 In type *B* all of the spermatozoa contain the same number of chromosomes.., but they are..of two classes, one of which contains a large and one a small '*idiochromosome'. **1920** L. DONCASTER *Introd. Study Cytol.* xi. 159 Most frequently the idio-chromosomes lag behind the autosomes in the spermatocyte anaphases, and the presence of such a lagging pair has sometimes been the first observed indication of the existence of a pair of idio-chromosomes. **1878** T. SINCLAIR *Mount* 103 No Jew of them all would..set up a theocracy, or *idiocracy, for this is the exact word, more eagerly and remorselessly. **1890** *Athenæum* 29 Mar. 408/3 'On Bertrand's *Idiocyclophanous Prism', by Prof. S. P. Thompson. **1883** E. R. LANKESTER in *Encycl. Brit.* XVI. 682/1 *note*, The Porodinic group is divisible into Nephrodinic and *Idiodinic, in the former the nephridium serving as a pore, in the latter a special (ἴδιος) pore being developed. **1828** WEBSTER, **Idioelectric*, electric *per se*, or containing electricity in its natural state. *Gregory*. **1830** R. KNOX *Béclard's Anat.* 160 They [hairs] are idio-electric. **1891** WHITE & BIRD in *Proc. R. Med. Chirurg. Soc. Lond.* III. 92 The two children..express themselves in..sounds..unlike those of any known language, but the same sound is always used by the same child to express the same word. Each child has thus a language of its own, and the authors have named the defect to which this peculiarity is due '*Idioglossia'. **1940** *Nature* 6 July 33/1 A child may develop idioglossia, that is, a language of its own; this is not a gibberish but is found on study to be subject to certain laws of sound-changes. **1961** W. R. BRAIN *Speech Disorders* xii. 137 For a number of years the child may not speak at all. Sooner or later, however, most patients acquire a vocabulary of their own which is comprehensible only to those who have been closely associated with them. This defective form of speech is called 'idioglossia' and 'lalling', and constitutes one form of dyslalia. **1888** H. HALE in *Science* 28 Sept. 146/1 The boy soon gave up his *idioglottic endeavors. **1883** E. R. LANKESTER in *Encycl. Brit.* XVI. 682/1 *note*, The genital ducts of Idiodinic forms may be called *Idiogonaducts, as distinguished from the Nephrogonaducts of nephrodinic forms. **1623** COCKERAM, **Idiograph*, priuate writings. **1656** BLOUNT *Glossogr.*, *Idiograph*, a private writing, or of one's own hand writing. **1897** *Westm. Gaz.* 27 Nov. 8/2 He had asked Sir William how he wrote his name phonetically, and he had given him an idiograph. [**1894** W. WINDELBAND *Geschichte & Naturwissenschaft* (1904) 12 Das wissenschaftliche Denken ist—wenn man neue Kunstausdrücke bilden darf—in dem einen Falle nomothetisch, in dem andern idiographisch.] **1909** *Cent. Dict.* Suppl., *Idiographic. **1931** A. WOLF in W. Rose *Outl. Mod. Knowl.* 570 History..is idiographic, that is to say, it is concerned with individuals and individual events in all their particularity. *a* **1943** R. G. COLLINGWOOD (1946) *Idea of Hist.* 166 Idiographic science, which is history. **1971** *Jrnl. Gen. Psychol.* Apr. 320 The findings imply that it is possible to study both normative and idiographic data about the emotional response to sound. **1931** ROBBINS & STINCHFIELD *Dict. Terms Disorders Speech* (Amer. Speech & Healing Assoc.) 15 **Idiolalia*, a form of dyslalia characterized by so extreme vowel and consonant substitution that a child's speech may be made unintelligible and appear to be another language to one who has not the key to the literal changes; but the same word is always used to express the same idea. **1933** S. M. STINCHFIELD *Speech Disorders* iii. 51 Idiolalia. This is a form of dyslalia characterized by the substitution of unusual and inaccurate sounds for vowels and consonants..; the same sound..is always used to express the same idea, however. Many refer to it as idioglossia. *a* **1626** BP. ANDREWES *Serm.* (1841–4) II. 393 (Cent.) Idolatry..differs but a letter from *idiolatry. **1881** *Daily News* 19 Sept. 6/2 The *idiometer invented by Colonel Walker was adopted by the Indian Survey Department. **1878** FOSTER *Phys.* I. ii. §2. 72 The wheal in many respects resembles a very slow or almost fixed contraction-wave, and has been called an '*idio-muscular' contraction. **1896** ALLBUTT *Syst. Med.* I. 109 The belief in the idiomuscular or, more truly, *idioneural action of the heart-muscle. **1651** BIGGS *New Disp.* ¶234 We have assigned the precedency and priority to purges from regular *Idionomy and propriety of natures with their appellatives. [**1913** C. SACHS *Real-Lexikon der Musikinstrumente* 195/1 Wir schlagen deshalb vor, dieser Klasse die Bezeichnung 'Idiophone', also 'ihrer Natur nach klingende' Instrumente zu geben.] **1940** C. SACHS *Hist. Mus. Instrum.* (1942) 455 The first of the five main classes is called **idiophones*. **1954** [see AUTOPHONE 2]. **1970** W. APEL *Harvard Dict. Mus.* (ed. 2) 414/1 Idiophones. Struck: triangle, gong, bell [etc.]. Shaken: rattle, sistrum, crescent. Plucked: Jew's harp, music box. Rubbed: glass harmonica, nail violin. **1971** *Sci. Amer.* Dec. 92/1 The instrument used to send messages in the Upper Congo is made solely of wood, and the entire instrument vibrates when it is struck. It is thus an idiophone, like metal gongs and the wood and metal bars of the xylophone and the glockenspiel. **1955** A. A. HILL in *Q. Jrnl. Speech* XLI. 255 The old concept of the phoneme turned on individual speech, the idiolect. Individual phonemic structures are therefore structures of *idiophonemes. **1958** —— *Introd. Ling. Struct.* iv. 58 Phonemes in individual speech can be called 'idiophonemes'. *Ibid.* iv. 60 Irregularities can characterize the over-all pattern as well as the *idiophonemic patterns. **1959** *Amer. Speech* XXXIV. 265 The diaphonemic inventory is a composite of all the idiophonemic inventories. **1889** MIVART in *Dublin Rev.* Oct. 293 Thus the *idio-plasm was changed more and more in the course of generations. **1890** WEISMANN in *Nature* 6 Feb. 320 The *idioplasmatic nature of the nuclear substance. **1886** F. L. PATTON in *New Princeton Rev.* Mar. 181 '*Idiopsychological' and 'heteropsychological' are the epithets employed to denote these two methods. *c* **1833** W. H. BROOKFIELD in *Life Tennyson* (1897) I. 126 At autopsychography I am not good, if I had any *idiopsychology to autopsychographize. **1828** WEBSTER, **Idio-repulsive*, repulsive by itself; as, the idio-repulsive power of heat. **1843** GROVE *Corr. Phys. Forces* (1846) 23 The early theories regard its phenomena as produced either by a single fluid idio-repulsive, but attractive of all matter, or else as produced by two fluids, each idio-repulsive but attractive of the other. **1890** BILLINGS *Med. Dict.* 679/2 *Idioretinal light. **1929** C. MURCHISON *Found. Exper. Psychol.* iv. 183 If the intensity of the stimulus is zero over the entire area of the retina, the accompanying experience is not typically a black, but is, instead, a dark gray, which is sometimes known as the 'idioretinal light' and is attributed to retinal self-excitation. **1938** R. S. WOODWORTH *Exper. Psychol.* xxii. 540 The readiest way of experiencing expanse color is to close the eyes and observe the gray field of idioretinal light. **1862** *Lond. Rev.* 17 May, They live..in regular monasteries, either of the stricter cœnobitic form..or under the laxer *idiorrythmic constitution. **1934** *Downside Rev.* LII. 483 But Mount Athos in 1928 still had nearly 5,000 monks, including the 'idiorrhythmics' with their very special kind of life. **1957** *Oxf. Dict. Chr. Ch.* 676/2 *Idiorrhythmic*, a term applied to certain monasteries on Mount Athos. **1960** D. ATHILL tr. *Valentin's Monks of Mt. Athos* 45 But the idiorhythmics keep their property? Indeed they do, and they have to look after it as well as possible because on their death everything they own goes to the monastery. **1880** J. E. H. GORDON *Electr. & Magn.* I. ix. 56 The accessory electrometer, or gauge, is called an *idiostatic electrometer. **1865–72** WATTS *Dict. Chem.* III. 242 **Idiotype*, a term applied by Guthrie..to bodies derived by replacement from the same substance, including the typical substance itself; ammonia..is *idiotypic with ethylamine, phenylamine, and all the organic bases derived from it by substitution, and these are idiotypic one with the other. **1909** *Heart* I. 70 The continuous ventricular rhythm, at about 30 per minute, met with in complete heart-block (*idioventricular rhythm). **1961** *Lancet* 9 Sept. 575/2 During this interval electrocardiographic monitoring should clarify the diagnosis of..idioventricular rhythm with inadequate cardiac output.

idioblast ('ɪdɪəʊblɑːst, -æ-). [f. IDIO- + -BLAST.]

1. *Bot.* An individual plant-cell of different nature or content from the surrounding tissue (Sachs).

1882 VINES *Sachs' Bot.* 84 It is not unusual for individual cells in a tissue otherwise homogeneous to become developed in a manner strikingly different from their neighbours; to such cells I have applied the term *Idioblast*.

2. *Cytology.* [a. G. *idioblast* (O. Hertwig *Zelle und Gewebe* (1893) I. ix. 272).] A hypothetical structural unit of living protoplasm. *Obs.* exc. *Hist.*

1893 *Nature* 2 Feb. 315 He [*sc.* O. Hertwig]..suggests the employment of the term 'Idioblasts' for the minute elementary particles, which Darwin called 'gemmules' in his hypothesis of pangenesis. **1925** E. B. WILSON *Cell* (ed. 3) 1134 *Idiosome*, the same as *idioblast, plasome, pangen* etc.

3. *Petrol.* [a. G. *idioblast* (F. Becke 1904, in *Compt. Rend. IX Sess. Congr. Géol. Internat.* II. 564)], a mineral crystal within a metamorphic rock which has developed its own characteristic crystal faces.

1920 A. HOLMES *Nomencl. Petrol.* 122 *Idioblast*, Becke, 1903, a term applied to pseudoidiomorphic crystals, such as garnet, occurring in metamorphic rocks. **1962** T. F. W. BARTH *Theoret. Petrol.* (ed. 2) 288 The majority of the minerals in metamorphic rocks are irregular in outline, xenoblasts; but some minerals are frequently bounded by their own crystal faces, idioblasts.

So **idio'blastic** *a. Petrol.*, (of a mineral crystal within a metamorphic rock) having its own characteristic crystal faces; (of a crystal face) having its own characteristic form; ***idioblastic order, series***, a ranking of minerals expressing their relative ability to develop idioblastic crystals when competing with each other.

1908 *Q. Jrnl. Geol. Soc.* LXIV. 482 Most of the hornblende existing in the amphibolite..is clearly secondary, and from its idiomorphic forms would be called 'recrystallized'... For such cases Prof. F. Becke has proposed the term idioblastic. **1954** H. WILLIAMS et al. *Petrogr.* ix. 166 It is possible to list metamorphic minerals in a generalized sequence—the crystalloblastic series (idioblastic order)—such that each tends to develop idioblastic surfaces against any other mineral placed lower in the series.

†**idi'ocrasy.** *Obs.* [ad. Gr. *ἰδιοκρᾱσία*, f. *ἰδιο-* IDIO- + *-κρᾱσία, κρᾶσις* mixing, tempering (CRASIS).] Peculiarity of physical or mental constitution; = IDIOSYNCRASY.

1681 tr. *Willis' Rem. Med. Wks.* Vocab., *Idiocrasie*, the proper disposition or temperament of a thing or body. **1684** tr. *Bonet's Merc. Compit.* Pref. 2 Several Mens Idiocrasie is various. **1755** JOHNSON, *Idiocrasy*, peculiarity of constitution.

Hence **idio'cratic, -al** *adjs.* = IDIOSYNCRATIC.

1727 BAILEY vol. II, *Idiocratical*, according to Idiocracy. [Hence in Johnson and mod. Dicts.] **1828** WEBSTER, *Idiocratic*. **1879** *Tinsley's Mag.* XXIV. 143 A few idiocratic remarks were gleaned.

idiocy ('ɪdɪəsɪ). Also 6 idiosy, 7 ideocy. [Possibly ad. Gr. *ἰδιωτεία* uncouthness, want of education, f. *ἰδιώτης* IDIOT; but perh. formed analogically on IDIOT, without reference to the Greek, after other sbs. in -CY from words in *-t*, as *prophet, prophecy*, etc. See also IDIOTCY. F. *idiotie* is recent.] The state or condition of being an idiot; natural absence or marked deficiency of ordinary understanding; extreme mental imbecility.

a **1529** SKELTON *Replyc.* 250 Your madde ipocrisy, And your idiosy, And your vayne glory Haue made you eate the flye. **1607** COWELL *Interpr.*, *Idiota inquirenda*..is a writ that is directed to the Excheator..to call before him the party suspected of Idiocie, and examin him. **1613** SIR H. FINCH *Law* (1636) 95 The king shall haue to his owne vse..all the possessions of a foole naturall, not of any other Ideot during his ideocy. **1765** BLACKSTONE *Comm.* I. viii. (1809) 306 When a man on an inquest of idiocy hath been returned an unthrift and not an idiot, no farther proceedings have been had. **1814** SCOTT *Wav.* ix, It was apparently neither idiocy nor insanity which gave that wild, unsettled, irregular expression to a face which naturally was rather handsome. **1874** MAUDSLEY *Respons. in Ment. Dis.* iii. 66 Idiocy is a defect of mind which is either congenital, or due to causes operating during the first few years of life.

b. Used *humorously* as a title.

1826 SCOTT *Woodst.* xxxiii, So please your idiocy, thou art an ass.

†**c.** *app.* Ignorance. *Obs.*

1598 SYLVESTER *Du Bartas* II. i. II. *Imposture* 323 The suspected vertue of This Tree Shall soon disperse the cloud of Idiocy, Which dims your eyes.

idiocyclophanous, etc.: see IDIO-.

idiogram ('ɪdɪəʊgræm). *Cytology* and *Med.* [ad. Russ. *idiogramma* (S. Navashin: in *Zhurn. Russk. Bot. Obshch.* (1921) VI. 171 he is reported as having used the term in his lectures for many years): see IDIO- and -GRAM.] = KARYOTYPE *sb.* 1 b: usually, a diagrammatic or systematized representation of a chromosome complement (of one cell or of many) indicating the number of chromosomes, their relative lengths, the position of the centromeres, etc.

1927 *Genetics* XII. 64 The relative size of the chromosomes, peculiar shape, and especially the presence of satellites (S. Nawaschin, 1912) and constrictions (Sakamura 1915, 1920) furnish criteria for distinguishing the members of a given complement, or using the terminology of S. Nawaschin, they characterize the idiogram or the specific arrangement of the diploid nuclear plates. **1934** L. W. SHARP *Introd. Cytol.* (ed. 3) ix. 128 The diagrammatic representation of a karyotype, as in Fig. 70, is called an idiogram (S. Nawaschin, 1921). **1957** C. P. SWANSON *Cytol. & Cytogenetics* (1958) v. 118 The shape and size of

chromosomes are his guideposts, and their constancy has enabled him to determine for purposes of comparison the karyotypes or idiograms (haploid complements) of many plants and animals. *Ibid.* xiii. 448 When represented in diagrammatic fashion.. the karyotype is usually referred to as an idiogram. **1966** D. M. KRAMSCH tr. *Grundmann's Gen. Cytol.* ii. 108 All the chromosomes of one set form the karyotype specific for each species and with such a chromosomal idiogram it is possible in certain cases to demonstrate relationships between the species. **1969** R. R. EGGEN in Davidsohn & Henry *Todd-Sanford Clin. Diagn.* (ed. 14) xxxii. 1224 (*caption*) Idiogram of a normal human cell... The male karyotype differs from the female in that male cells normally have a single X chromosome and therefore have only 15 group C chromosomes. **1971** *Nature* 11 June 887/1 The average forms of all chromosomes of a complement are defined by an idiogram, based on a large number of karyotypes. **1973** *Lancet* 24 Feb. 420/1 Strictly speaking the actual pictures [of chromosomes] are karyotypes, and an idiogram is a diagram of the chromosome state of an individual.

idiolect ('ɪdɪəʊlɛkt). *Linguistics.* [f. IDIO- after DIALECT.] The linguistic system of one person, differing in some details from that of all other speakers of the same dialect or language.

1948 B. BLOCH in *Language* XXIV. 7 The totality of the possible utterances of one speaker at one time in using a language to interact with one other speaker is an *idiolect*. **1948** R. A. HALL Jr. in *Studies in Linguistics* VI. ii. 31 Language exists in individuals, as a set of habits which each individual possesses (an *idiolect*). **1953** C. E. BAZELL *Ling. Form* 96 It must not be supposed that such [linguistic] systems are necessarily less determinate than for instance that of a single idiolect as recorded over a short space of time. **1953** J. B. CARROLL *Study of Lang.* ii. 10 Indeed each member of a speech community may be said to possess his own *idiolect*, his own personal variety of the language system. **1953** *Internat. Jrnl. Amer. Ling.* XIX. ii. Suppl. 40 Hockett defined 'idiolect' as the individual's total repertory of speech habits over a short period of time. **1958** A. A. HILL *Introd. Ling. Struct.* ii. 13 The English which is described in the personal dialect of a single speaker or, to use the technical term, a single idiolect. **1964** M. A. K. HALLIDAY et al. in J. A. Fishman *Readings Sociol. of Lang.* (1968) 158 A person's idiolect may be identified, through the lens of the various registers, by its grammatical and lexical characteristics. **1964** R. H. ROBINS *Gen. Ling.* ii. 51 The lower limit of dialect division comes down to the individual speaker, and for this limiting case of dialect the term *idiolect* (the speech habits of a single person) has been coined. **1970** W. LABOV in *Rep. 20th Round Table Meeting on Ling. & Lang. Stud.* 89 So we are dealing not with the idiolect of the investigator, but the idiolect of one isolated boy whose position in the community is quite uncertain.

Hence **idio'lectal** *a.*, of or pertaining to an idiolect; **idio'lectally** *adv.*

1953 *Internat. Jrnl. Amer. Ling.* XIX. ii. Suppl. 37 Utterances are swiftly and with assurance identified despite idiolectal differences. **1958** *Archivum Linguisticum* X. II. 146 Who..pronounces *cow* and *bough* with different diphthongs, unless idiolectally and idiosyncratically? **1965** *Language* XLI. 502 Idiolectal diversity is an inevitable result of the..productivity inherent in every single individual's linguistic habits. **1972** *Ibid.* XLVIII. 314 We believe these variations to be idiolectal rather than dialectal.

idiom ('ɪdɪəm). Forms: 6 ydiome, ideome, 6–7 idiome, 7 ideom, 7– idiom. [a. F. *idiome* (16th c. in Hatz.-Darm.), or ad. L. *idiōma*, Gr. ἰδίωμα peculiarity, property, peculiar phraseology (f. ἰδιό-εσθαι to make one's own, appropriate), f. ἴδιο-ς own, private, peculiar. Cf. It., Sp., Pg. *idioma*. The L. form was also used for some time.]

1. a. The form of speech peculiar or proper to a people or country; own language or tongue.

[**1575** GASCOIGNE *Cert. Notes Instr. Eng. Verse* §11 So woulde I wish you to frame all sentences in their mother phrase, and proper *Idioma*.] **1588** J. H[ARVEY] *Disc. Probleme* 41 A hawty Latin stile and antique Ideome. **1589** PUTTENHAM *Eng. Poesie* II. xii[i]. (Arb.) 127 To allow euery word polisillable one long time..which should be where his sharpe accent falls in our owne ydiome most aptly and naturally. **1674** R. GODFREY *Inj. & Ab. Physic* 48 The writings of Glauber, which were translated into the English Idiom. **1711** ADDISON *Spect.* No. 165 ¶3 The Histories of all our former Wars are transmitted to us in our Vernacular Idiom. **1860** FARRAR *Orig. Lang.* i. 20 The divine spark which glows in all idioms.

b. In narrower sense: That variety of a language which is peculiar to a limited district or class of people; dialect.

1598 FLORIO *Ital. Dict.* A iv a, So manie, and so much differing Dialects, and Idiomes, as be vsed and spoken in Italie. **1601** HOLLAND *Pliny* Pref. A iij b, That Dialect or Idiome which was familiar to the basest clowne. **1662** J. DAVIES *Mandelslo's Trav.* 226 The Chineses..when they speak, cannot understand one the other, by reason of the diversity of the Idioms and Dialects that is among the Inhabitants of several Provinces. *a* **1794** GIBBON *Misc. Wks.* (1814) I. 188 On the spot I read..the classics of the Tuscan idiom. **1874** REYNOLDS *John Bapt.* v. §3. 338 There were 'voices'..which expressed in some vernacular idiom of Hebrew or Greek the thoughts of the Almighty.

2. The specific character, property, or genius of any language; the manner of expression which is natural or peculiar to it: = IDIOTISM 2.

1598 E. GILPIN *Skial.* (1878) 39 Oh how the varges from his blacke pen wrung, Would sauce the Idiome of the English tongue. **1666** DRYDEN *Pref. Ann. Mirab.* Wks. (Globe) 39 The terms of arts in every tongue bearing more of the idiom of it than any other words. **1683** *Brit. Spec.* 39 The Idiom of it, as to the main, appears to be Teutonick. **1754** SHERLOCK *Disc.* (1759) I. vi. 189 To bring anything to light..is..in the Idiom of the English Tongue, to discover or reveal a thing. **1862** GOULBURN *Pers. Relig.* viii. III. (1873) 218 In their attempt to maintain idiom.

3. a. A form of expression, grammatical construction, phrase, etc., peculiar to a language; a peculiarity of phraseology approved by the usage of a language, and often having a signification other than its grammatical or logical one.

1628 DONNE *80 Serm.* vi. (1640) 52 There are certaine idioms, certaine formes of speech..which the holy Ghost repeats severall times. **1642** HOWELL *For. Trav.* (Arb.) 20 Every speech hath certaine Idiomes, and customary Phrases of its own. **1732** BERKELEY *Alciphr.* VI. §7 The Hebrew tongue, which, as every other language, had its idioms. **1871** *Pub. School Lat. Gram.* §122 The Adverbial use of the Attribute and Apposite is an important idiom.

b. A characteristic mode of expression in music, art, or writing; an instance of this.

1921 J. B. MCEWEN *First Steps Mus. Comp.* 5 To put it in somewhat colloquial terms, the composer of ancient music wrote melody, the composer of modern music writes tunes. It is no part of my purpose to make comparisons between these two idioms. *Ibid.*, An intentional reversion to the contrapuntal idiom. **1923** H. CRANE *Let.* 9 Feb. (1965) 121 Tate has a whole lot to offer when he finds his way out of the Eliot idiom. **1927** *Grove's Dict. Mus.* (ed. 3) II. 537/2 The folk-songs of all nations have been cultivated..for the sake, mainly, of their undoubted freshness and spontaneity of idiom as compared with pseudo-classical models. *Ibid.* 538/1 The study of this melodic music has suggested many harmonic idioms of notable freshness and beauty. **1939** *Burlington Mag.* Aug. 90/1 Buildings and industrial products which are now the accepted 'idiom' of design throughout the modern world. **1955** *Times* 9 May 3/1 We in this country have had experience of Anglo-American cooperation in film-making, and, whatever may be said in its favour from the practical, economic point of view, it certainly tends to blur and weaken the natural idiom and character of the countries involved. **1957** S. DANCE in S. Traill *Concerning Jazz* 43 The three great names in the presentation of jazz in the pure New Orleans idiom..were King Oliver, Jelly Roll Morton and Louis Armstrong. **1958** B. JAMES in P. Gammond *Duke Ellington* II. 145 Ellington's music had its origins in the New Orleans style, as has so much else worthwhile in the jazz idiom.

4. Specific form or property; peculiar nature; peculiarity. *Obs.* exc. as *fig.* of 1 or 2.

[**1596** FITZ-GEFFRAY *Sir F. Drake* (1881) 34 Vnpartiall Iudge of all, save present state, Truth's *Idioma* of the things are past.] **1644** DIGBY *Two Treat.* II. (1645) 143 Who can looke upon..those wondrous processions and idiomes [of the Godhead] reserved for Angels eyes? **1654** JER. TAYLOR *Real Pres.* 191 So we may say, this is Christs body, by the communication of the Idioms or proprieties to the bread with which it is united. **1658** R. FRANCK *North. Mem.* (1694) 177 It represents the idiom or form of a horn. **1828** MACAULAY *Ess. History* in *Misc. Writ.* (1889) 152 Connection..not so close as to destroy the idioms of national opinion and feeling. **1866** GEO. ELIOT *Let.* 15 Aug. (1955) IV. 301, I took unspeakable pains in preparing to write Romola—neglecting nothing I could find that would help me to what I may call the 'Idiom' of Florence, in the largest sense one could stretch the word to. **1870** G. M. HOPKINS *Jrnls. & Papers* (1959) 195, I noticed it [*sc.* snow]..sketched in intersecting edges bearing 'idiom'..I have no other word yet for that which takes the eye or mind in a bold hand..not being beauty nor true inscape yet gives interest. **1936** R. CAMPBELL *Mithraic Emblems* 46 To form the idiom of her flesh I faceted in clearest thought An arctic crystal in whose mesh Of frosty rays the sun is caught.

5. *Comb.* **Idiom Neutral**, an international language based on Volapük, devised chiefly by W. Rosenberger, and first published in English in 1903.

1903 W. ROSENBERGER (*title*) Idiom neutral. **1907** W. J. CLARK *Internat. Lang.* II. v. 99 The famous linguistic club of Nuremberg is remarkable for having gone through the evolution from Volapük to Idiom Neutral *viâ* Esperanto. **1922** A. L. GUÉRARD *Short Hist. Internat. Lang. Movement* II. vi. 137 Idiom Neutral is entirely based on the principle of greatest internationality, at least so far as root-words are concerned. **1949** M. PEI *Story of Lang.* (1952) VI. iii. 443 In 1902 an academy of Volapük experts devised a radical simplification of their tongue, which they rechristened Idiom Neutral.

idi'omacy. *rare*$^{-1}$. [f. L. *idiōmat-*, stem of *idiōma* IDIOM: see -CY.] Idiomatic quality.

1813 *Examiner* 15 Mar. 170/2 Its pert *slang* and ungrammatical idiomacy.

idiomatic (ɪdɪəʊ'mætɪk), *a.* [ad. Gr. ἰδιωματικ-ός peculiar, characteristic, f. ἰδίωμα (ἰδιώματ-) IDIOM. Cf. F. *idiomatique* (Littré).]

1. Peculiar to or characteristic of a particular language; pertaining to or exhibiting the expressions, constructions, or phraseology approved by the peculiar usage of a language, esp. as differing from a strictly grammatical or logical use of words; vernacular; colloquial.

1712 ADDISON *Spect.* No. 285 ¶4 Since..Phrases..used in ordinary Conversation contract a kind of Meanness by passing through the Mouths of the Vulgar, a Poet should take particular Care to guard himself against Idiomatick Ways of Speaking. **1784** tr. *De Lolme's Const. Eng.* Life 2, Pure idiomatic and attractive English. **1839** H. ROGERS *Ess.* II. iii. 136 The language of familiar dialogue and colloquial pleasantry..is always in a high degree idiomatic, both in the terms and phrases employed, and in the construction. **1875** JOWETT *Plato* (ed. 2) IV. 419 Hegel..thought..he gave his philosophy a truly German character by the use of idiomatic German words.

†**b.** Peculiar to one person, individual. *Obs.*

1765 HURD *Mor. & Polit. Dial.* Pref. 42 The *idiomatic* differences of expression, which flow not from the manners, but from some degree of study and affectation.

2. Given to or marked by the use of idioms peculiar to, or approved by, the usage of the language.

1839 HALLAM *Hist. Lit.* IV. vii. §32 IV. 529 They were more strictly idiomatic and English than their predecessors. **1870** LOWELL *Among my Bks.* Ser. I. 74 *note*, Like most idiomatic, as distinguished from correct writers, he [Dryden] knew very little about the language historically or critically.

So **idio'matical** *a.* = prec. Hence **idio'matically** *adv.*, in an idiomatic manner. **idio'maticalness**, the condition of being idiomatic.

1727 BAILEY vol. II, *Idiomatical..Idiomatically.* **1762** STERNE *Tr. Shandy* VI. xxxvii, To say a man is fallen in love ..carries an idiomatical kind of implication that love is a thing below a man. **1773** MONBODDO *Language* (1774) I. I. viii. 99 Qualities that are accidental, or idiomatical, that is, peculiar to the individual. **1779–81** JOHNSON *L.P., Addison* Wks. III. 110 If his language had been less idiomatical, it might have lost somewhat of its genuine Anglicism. **1840** DE QUINCEY *Rhetoric* Wks. XI. 70 Men wrote..idiomatically, because they wrote naturally and without affectation. **1898** F. HALL in *Nation* (N.Y.) LXVI. 341/3 Its character.. makes nothing either for or against the idiomaticalness of *in our midst*.

idio'maticism. *rare*$^{-1}$. [f. prec. + -ISM.] An idiomatic expression.

1862 *Parthenon* 26 July 397 'Occasional idiomaticisms', in such passages as it has been thought necessary to render literally will, we hope, be readily excused.

idiomaticity (ˌɪdɪəʊmə'tɪsɪtɪ). [f. IDIOMATIC *a.*: see -ICITY.] The quality or state of being idiomatic.

1965 *Language* XLI. 504 Mrs Palmer's translation is.. accurate, without sacrificing freedom or idiomaticity. **1971** T. F. MITCHELL in *Archivum Linguisticum* II. 57 Although such correspondences [as *make up to = flatter, make it up to = compensate*, etc.] are usually suggestive, they are apparently not a necessary condition of idiomaticity.

†**idi'omatism.** *Obs. rare*$^{-1}$. [f. Gr. ἰδιώματ- IDIOM + -ISM.] An idiomatic expression.

1771 *Acc. of Bks.* in *Ann. Reg.* 246/2 His style is..sometimes ungrammatical, and abounding with North-British terms and idiomatisms.

†**idiˌoma'tology.** *Obs. rare*$^{-1}$. [f. as prec. + -LOGY.] A collection of idioms.

1690 W. WALKER *Idiomat. Anglo-Lat.* Pref. 6 To translate some Englishes made in way of dialogue..whose latines.. may all be found in their respective heads of this Idiomatology.

idiomorphic (ɪdɪəʊ'mɔːfɪk), *a. Min.* [f. IDIO- + Gr. μορφή form + -IC.] Having its own characteristic form; *spec.* having its characteristic crystallographic faces: said of one of the constituent minerals of a rock. Hence **idio'morphically** *adv.*

1887 *Geol. Mag.* Mar. 123 The normal plutonic rocks are characterized by a structure in which idiomorphic constituents occur only in small proportion. **1888** W. S. BAYLEY in *Amer. Naturalist* Mar. 208 An idiomorphic mineral is one whose form is determined by the crystallizing forces acting within itself. An idiomorphic mineral is bounded by crystal planes. *Ibid.* 209 When..all of the constituents are idiomorphically developed, the rock is panidiomorphic.

idiomorphism (ɪdɪəʊ'mɔːfɪz(ə)m). *Min.* [f. IDIOMORPH(IC *a.* + -ISM.] The condition of being idiomorphic.

1908 *Q. Jrnl. Geol. Soc.* LXIV. 482 Professor F. Becke.. points out that, in the formation of the crystalline schists, the relative idiomorphism is not to be considered as denoting the order in which they have formed. **1951** TURNER & VERHOOGEN *Ing. & Metamorphic Petrol.* iii. 56 Idiomorphism seems..a doubtful criterion of early crystallization in the case of certain consistently idiomorphic accessories, such as apatite.

ˌidiopa'thetic, *a. rare.* [f. IDIOPATHY, after *pathetic*.] = IDIOPATHIC.

1661 LOVELL *Hist. Anim. & Min.* 337 The epilepsy..if idiopathetick, it is cured as before, by phlebotomy [etc.]. **1712** tr. *Pomet's Hist. Drugs* I. 164 It prevails against..Pains of the Head, whether Idiopathetick, or by Consent of Parts. **1846** WORCESTER cites *Month. Rev.*

So **idiopa'thetical** *a.* (Bailey vol. II. 1727).

idiopathic (ɪdɪəʊ'pæθɪk), *a.* [f. IDIOPATHY + -IC. Cf. F. *idiopathique* (1732 in Hatz.-Darm.).]

1. *Path.* Of a disease: Arising by itself in a particular part of the body; of the nature of a primary morbid state; not consequent upon or symptomatic of another disease.

1669 W. SIMPSON *Hydrol. Chym.* 88 If the diseases..be idiopathick. **1684** tr. *Bonet's Merc. Compit.* III. 69 The idiopathick Headach..requires Purging. **1796** *Nat. Hist.* in *Ann. Reg.* 405 It is a real and idiopathic disease. **1874** MAUDSLEY *Respons. in Ment. Dis.* iii. 80 Cases in which the insanity is owing to idiopathic disease of the brain. **1876** tr. *Wagner's Gen. Pathol.* 2 In many cases it is..important to recognize an affection as idiopathic or symptomatic.

2. Of the nature of a particular affection or susceptibility.

1846 SIR W. HAMILTON *Dissert.* in *Reid's Wks.* 854 The idiopathic affections of our several organs of sense, as Colour, Sound. **1857** BERKELEY *Cryptog. Bot.* §403. 368 The common mushroom has proved fatal in Italy... This does

not appear to depend upon any idiopathic phenomena, but upon the intrinsic character of the individual specimens.

So **idio'pathical** *a.* = prec.; hence **idio'pathically** *adv.*, in the manner of an idiopathic disease.

1828 WEBSTER, *Idiopathically*. **1835–6** TODD *Cycl. Anat.* I. 227/1 Disease..as it commences idiopathically within the vessel itself. **1846** WORCESTER cites *For. Q. Rev.* for *Idiopathical*. **1861** T. J. GRAHAM *Pract. Med.* 678 We must carefully watch for the symptoms of the complications, and treat them..much as when they occur idiopathically.

idiopathy (ɪdɪ'ɒpəθɪ). [ad. mod.L. *idiopathīa*, a. Gr. ἰδιοπάθεια (Galen): see IDIO- and -PATHY. Cf. F. *idiopathie*.]

†**1.** A feeling or sensation peculiar to an individual or class; an individual or personal state of feeling.

1647 H. MORE *Song of Soul* II. To Rdr., All men are so full of their own phansies and idiopathyes, that they scarce have the civility to interchange any words with a stranger. *Ibid.* (Interpret. unusual words), *Idiopathie*,..is ones proper peculiar πάθος, mine or thine, being affected thus or so upon this or that occasion. *a* **1688** CUDWORTH *Immut. Morality* (1731) 54 It is Impossible to demonstrate..that any two Men have the very same Phantasms or Ideas of Red or Green, these being Idiopathies.

2. *Path.* †**a.** A morbid condition originating in the part affected, and not occasioned by disease elsewhere. *Obs.* **b.** A disease not preceded or occasioned by any other; a primary disease.

a **1640** JACKSON *Creed* X. xxxiii. §9 The idiopathy as physicians speak is in the soul, the sympathy only in the spirit or conscience. **1671** *Phil. Trans.* VI. 2292 The Parts, which are primarily and by idiopathy affected in a Consumption. **1696** PHILLIPS (ed. 5), *Idiopathie*, in Physick, a primary Disease. **1833** *New Monthly Mag.* XXXIX. 129 This moral idiopathy, which neither proceeds from nor depends on any other disease,..this itch for seeing memorable places..is peculiarly English.

idiophanous, etc.: see IDIO-.

'idiopt. *rare.* [f. Gr. ἴδι-ος peculiar + stem ὀπτ- as in ὀπτήρ one who looks, ὀπτός seen.] One who has some peculiarity of vision.

1833 WHEWELL in Todhunter *Acc. W.'s Wks.* (1876) II. 153 The idiopt perceived scarcely any, if any, steady distinction between the two images.

idiorepulsive, -static, etc.: see IDIO-.

idiosome ('ɪdɪəʊsəʊm). [f. IDIO- + -SOME[4].]

†**1.** *Biol.* A supposed ultimate unit of living matter. *Obs.*

1894 C. O. WHITMAN in *Biol. Lectures 1893* (Wood's Hole, Mass., Marine Biol. Lab.) 123 It will find the secret of organization, growth, development, not in cell-formation, but in those ultimate elements of living matter, for which *idiosomes* seems to me an appropriate name. **1899** [see PANGENE].

2. *Cytology.* [Proposed (as F. *idiosome*) by C. Regaud (*Arch. d'Anat. microsc.* (1910) XI. 343) as a better word than *idiozome*.] = IDIOZOME.

1918 *Amer. Jrnl. Anat.* XXIV. 37 (*heading*) The development of the idiosome in the germ-cells of the male guinea-pig. **1934** L. W. SHARP *Introd. Cytol.* (ed. 3) xiv. 216 In another series of forms (mollusks, amphibia, other vertebrates) the Golgi bodies are closely aggregated about the centrioles where their lightly staining substance flows together to form the idiosome. **1953** O. E. NELSEN *Compar. Embryol. Vertebr.* iii. 126 The idiosome (idiozome) is a rounded body of cytoplasm which, in many animal species, takes the cytoplasmic stain more intensely than the surrounding cytoplasm.

idiosy, obs. form of IDIOCY.

†**idiosyn'crasical**, *a.* *Obs.* *rare*[−1]. [f. IDIOSYNCRAS-Y + -IC + -AL[1].]

= IDIOSYNCRATIC.

1633 HART *Diet of Diseased* Introd. 20 What shall I say of the Idiosyncrasicall..propriety of divers patients?

†**idio'syncrasis.** *Obs.* *rare.* [a. Gr. ἰδιοσύγκρᾱσις.] = next.

1654 WHITLOCK *Zootomia* Pref. a iij, Out of an Idiosyncrasis (or particular Temper) of my Fancy. **1797** *Monthly Mag.* III. 348 Lest the acrid humour..should be mistaken for the effect produced by an idiosyncrasis of the vessels.

idiosyncrasy (ɪdɪəʊ'sɪŋkrəsɪ). Also 7 **idiosygcrasye**, 7–8 **-syncrasie**, 7–9 (*erron.*) **-cracy**. [ad. Gr. ἰδιοσυγκρᾱσία, also -σύγκρᾱσις, f. ἰδιο- IDIO- + σύγκρᾱσις commixture, tempering (σύν together + κρᾶσις mixing, tempering, CRASIS).] A peculiarity of constitution or temperament.

1. The physical constitution peculiar to an individual (†or class). Now only *Med. spec.* An individual's hypersensitivity *to* a drug or other substance which is ingested or inhaled or which otherwise comes into contact with the body.

1604 F. HERING *Modest Def.* 29 The idiosygcrasye or particular Natures (as Galen calleth them) are vnknown. **1650** SIR T. BROWNE *Pseud. Ep.* III. xxviii. (ed. 2) 152 Whether Quailes from any idiosyncracy or peculiarity of constitution, doe innocuously feed upon Hellebore. **1744** BERKELEY *Siris* §87 Something in the idiosyncrasy of the patient that puzzles the physician. **1828** *Edin. Rev.* XLVII. 39 The special and apparently capricious varieties of digestive power, which the learned call Idiosyncrasy. **1875** H. C. WOOD *Therap.* (1879) 22 *Temperaments* are peculiarities of organization characterizing classes of individuals; *idiosyncrasies*, peculiarities belonging to single individuals. **1887** *Brit. Med. Jrnl.* 20 Aug. 431/1 Dr Daniel Bernouilli, of Basle, reports an instance of idiosyncrasy with respect to antipyrin. **1893** *Edin. Med. Jrnl.* XXXVIII. 627 No very tenable theory has been put forward to explain the reason of idiosyncrasy to drugs. **1912** *Jrnl. Amer. Med. Assoc.* 13 Apr. 1088 The view that the peculiar idiosyncrasies, so-called, with respect to certain articles of diet—strawberries, cheese..cow's milk, etc.—are forms of anaphylactic reactions is steadily growing. **1922** *Jrnl. Immunol.* VII. 128 Peculiar drug reactions, known as idiosyncrasies, were well recognized, but they were not identified as allergies until 1916. **1932** *Jrnl. Soc. Chem. Industry* 13 May 440/2 Mention was made..of the frequent lack of adequate proof of the supposed irritant action of certain dyes and of the difficulties due to idiosyncrasy. **1971** *Lancet* 25 Sept. 698/2 Idiosyncrasy to CS has not been reported, and the old and young do not seem to be at exceptional risk.

2. The mental constitution peculiar to a person or class of persons; individual bent of mind or inclination; a view or feeling, a liking or aversion, peculiar to a single person, race, or nation.

1665 GLANVILL *Scepsis Sci.* xiv. 90 The Understanding also hath its Idiosyncrasies, as well as other faculties. **1771** WESLEY *Wks.* (1872) VI. 128 There may be an idiosyncrasy—a peculiarity in your constitution of Soul. **1874** STUBBS *Const. Hist.* I. iv. 58 The pertinacious idiosyncrasy of the Gallic genius.

3. A mode of expression peculiar to an author.

1837–9 HALLAM *Hist. Lit.* III. vii. §34 III. 659 The style of Bacon has an idiosyncrasy which we might expect from his genius. *Ibid.* III. vi. §73 III. 329 The elaborate delineations of Jonson, or the marked idiosyncracies of Shakspeare. **1874** SAYCE *Compar. Philol.* i. 11 We must not..believe that we know a language because we can successfully imitate the idiosyncracies of a few of its literary men.

idiosyncratic (ˌɪdɪəʊsɪn'krætɪk), *a.* [f. prec., after Gr. συγκρᾱτικός: see -IC.] Pertaining to, or of the nature of, idiosyncrasy; due to individual disposition or susceptibility.

a **1779** WARBURTON *Div. Legat.* II. App. (1846) I. 315 His Lordship's idiosyncratic terrors, the terrors of a future State. **1870** LOWELL *Among my Bks.* Ser. I. (1873) 172 An idiosyncratic use of words. **1886** SYMONDS *Renaiss. Italy, Cath. React.* (1898) VII. xiii. 227 Our true critic renounces idiosyncratic whims and partialities. **1893** *Brit. Med. Jrnl.* 2 Sept. 555 The action—idiosyncratic or otherwise—of the above-named drug.

So **idiosyn'cratical** *a.* = prec.; hence **idiosyn'cratically** *adv.*, by inherent peculiarity of constitution.

1650 CHARLETON *Paradoxes* Prol. 16 The confederate vertue of the Unguent..idiosyncratically opposed to the essentiall hostility of that Acid. **1670** MAYNWARING *Vita Sana* vi. 70 The various natures..and idosyncratical [*sic*] properties of several bodies. **1863** LYTTON *Caxtoniana* I. 72 The man inveterately, idiosyncratically shy. **1893** PATMORE *Religio Poetæ* (1898) 40 Those of idiosyncratical enthusiasm.

idiot ('ɪdɪət), *sb.* Forms: 4 **ydyote**, 4–5 **ydiotte**, 4–6 **-ot(e**, **yd-**, **idyot**, 5 **idyote**, **-othe**, **ydeote**, 6 **ydeot(te**, **ideot(t)e**, **idiotte**, 4–7 **idiote**, 4–9 **ideot**, 4– **idiot**. [a. F. *idiot* (13th c. in Hatz.-Darm.) = It., Sp., Pg. *idiota*, ad. L. *idiōta* uneducated, ignorant person, ad. Gr. ἰδιώτης private person, common man, plebeian, one without professional knowledge, 'layman'; and so, ignorant, ill-informed person, f. ἴδιος private, own, peculiar.

In the 16th c., instances of the word are found with initial *n*, transferred from *an* (*a nidiot*:—*an idiot*); *nidiot* was further popularly corrupted to NIDGET (q.v.). With the latter cf. the modern vulgar pronunciation, sometimes graphically represented as *idget*.]

†**1. a.** A person without learning; an ignorant, uneducated man; a simple man; a clown. *Obs.*

This use is app. partly due to passages in the Vulgate or Greek N.T., esp. *Acts* iv. 13, *1 Cor.* xiv. 16.

1377 LANGL. *P. Pl.* B. XVI. 170, I..ȝede forth as an ydiote in contre to aspye After Pieres þe plowman. *c* **1440** CAPGRAVE *Life St. Kath.* I. 288 Ryght as be twelue ydiotes, sent Austyn seyth, hee meneth the apostellis, for thei not lerned were. **1483** CAXTON *Gold. Leg.* 287/1 The bisshop repreuyd hym sore as unconnyng and an ydeote. **1577** tr. *Bullinger's Decades* (1592) 23 A most common kinde of speech, wherewithall euen the verie idiots were acquainted. **1647** H. MORE *Poems* Pref., It would be safer to ask the judgment of young lads or Countrey idiots..then those lubricous wits and overworn Philosophers. **1657** (*title*) The Deuine Louer, or the Sainctly Ideots Deuotions. **1698** FRYER *Acc. E. India & P.* 374, I..confess my self an Ideot, understanding no other Language than Turkish. **1722** J. COVEL *Acc. Grk. Ch.* 353 There is also this very remarkable passage in the Cardinal; Idiotæ qui vident Picturas, Ideots who see these Pictures [etc.].

†**b.** *spec.* A layman. *Obs.*

c **1380** WYCLIF *Wks.* (1880) 46 We dwelten to-gidre in chirchis, & weren idiotis, & vnderloute to ale men. **1611** *Panegyr. Verses* in *Coryat's Crudities*, For he would not Take orders but remaine an Idiote. **1638** FEATLY *Strict. Lyndom.* I. 158 That hee that supplieth the place of the idiot or laye-man in answering for the people shall understand. **1660** JER. TAYLOR *Duct. Dubit.* I. ii. rule ii. §5 The holy and innocent ideot, or plain easy people of the Laity.

†**c.** One not professionally learned or skilled; also, a private (as opposed to a public) man. *Obs.*

1638 F. JUNIUS *Paint. Ancients* 75 If any one should bid an idiot take the instruments and mend what he blameth in the Artificers, he should never be able to doe it. **1651** JER. TAYLOR *Clerus Dom.* 54 In the form of Ideots and private persons. **1663** BOYLE *Exp. & Nat. Philos.* I. 17 Idiots admire in things the Beauty of their Materials, but Artists that of the Workmanship.

2. a. A person so deficient in mental or intellectual faculty as to be incapable of ordinary acts of reasoning or rational conduct. Applied to one permanently so afflicted, as distinguished from one who is temporarily insane, or 'out of his wits', and who either has lucid intervals, or may be expected to recover his reason.

By the older legal authorities an idiot is defined as one congenitally deficient in reasoning powers, a 'natural fool' (cf. quot. 1590), and this is still the common implication of the term. In quot. 1440 = *half-wit*.

a **1300** *Cursor M.* 10456 (Cott.) Þou sais to me als til a sott, Haldes þou me for ani idiot [*Gött.* a fole]? *c* **1386** CHAUCER *Wife's Prol.* 311 Wenestow make an ydyot of oure dame? *c* **1425** *Found. St. Bartholomew's* (E.E.T.S.) 13 He made and feyned hym-self vnwyse..and owtward pretendid the cheyr of an ydiotte. *c* **1440** *Promp. Parv.* 258/2 Idyote, neither fowle ne ryghte wyce (*H.* idyote, halfe innocent..), *idiota*. **1590** SWINBURNE *Testaments* II. 39 An Idiote, or a naturall foole is he, who notwithstanding he bee of lawfull age, yet he is so witlesse, that hee can not number to twentie, nor can tell what age he is of, nor knoweth who is his father, or mother, nor is able to answer to any such easie question. **1648** MILTON *Tenure Kings* (1650) 52 By the civil laws a foole or Idiot born shall lose the lands whereto he is born because he is not able to use them aright. **1690** LOCKE *Hum. Und.* II. xi. (1695) 77 Idiots make very few or no Propositions, and reason scarce at all. **1793** HOLCROFT tr. *Lavater's Physiog.* III. lii. 247 Who can explain wherein consists the difference of organization between an ideot and another man? **1845** STEPHEN *Comm. Laws Eng.* (1874) II. 62 Persons insane (in which class are..to be included idiots who have had no understanding from their birth, as well as lunatics who..have lost the use of their reason).

b. A term of reprobation for one who speaks or acts in what the speaker considers an irrational way, or with extreme stupidity or folly; a blockhead, an utter fool.

c **1375** *Sc. Leg. Saints, Theodera* 148 Wenand I ware sic a ydiot, þat þu suld wit my priuete. *a* **1568** COVERDALE *Bk. Death* III. iii. (1579) 258 O thou great ydiote, thou lamentest, that thy name and honour perisheth in this transitorie worlde. **1620** GRANGER *Div. Logike* 381 Many obdurate Popish Idiotes say, that all things are so deare..because there is so much preaching. **1713** ADDISON *Ct. Tariff*, He called them ideots and blockheads. **1796** BP. WATSON *Apol. Bible* 283 He would have been an ideot, had he put it in the power of his enemies to prove [etc.]. **1840** DICKENS *Barn. Rudge* li, You idiot, do you know what peril you stand in? [**1880** MRS. WHITNEY *Odd or Even?* xv. 136, 'I think people are "idgets"!' said Frances.]

†**c.** A man of weak intellect maintained to afford amusement to others; a household or court fool; a professional fool or jester. ***idiot's hood***, a fool's cap. *Obs.*

1526 *Will of T. Goldisburgh* (Somerset Ho.), To Richard Carlton my Idyot. **1586** G. WHITNEY *Emblems* I. 81 The ideot likes, with bables for to plaie. **1612** WOODALL *Surg. Mate* Wks. (1653) 297 He that's wise in his own conceit, puts on the Idiots hood. **1711** ADDISON *Spect.* No. 47 ¶2 Idiots are still in Request in most of the Courts of Germany, where there is not a Prince of any great Magnificence, who has not two or three dressed, distinguished, undisputed Fools in his Retinue.

3. *attrib.* or quasi-*adj.* **a.** Appositive, as ***idiot boy, fool, man, mother***. **b.** Of, pertaining to, or characteristic of an idiot or idiocy, idiotic; as ***idiot face, laugh, look***, etc.

1377 LANGL. *P. Pl.* B. XI. 308 *Ignorancia Non excusat episcopos nec* idiotes prestes. **1562** BULLEYN *Bk. Sicke Men* 69 b, Chaunged into ideotte fooles. **1647** H. MORE *Song of Soul* I. II. lv, A private idiot man. **1700** DRYDEN *Cymon & Iph.* 112 Long mute he stood, and..His wonder witness'd with an idiot laugh. **1711** SHAFTESB. *Charact.* (1737) I. 137 Why does an idiot-look and manner destroy the effect of all those outward charms? **1798** WORDSW. (*title*) The Idiot Boy. **1809** BYRON *Eng. Bards* 248 The tale of Betty Foy, The idiot mother of 'an idiot boy'. **1827** HOOD *Mids. Fairies* xciv, To hope my solemn countenance to wring To idiot smiles! **1871** R. ELLIS *Catullus* xxxvii. 6 Or if in idiot impotence arow you sit. **1885** STEVENSON *Dynamiter* xiii. 196 When I look upon your idiot face..the tears spring up.

4. *Comb.*, as ***idiot-born, -dull, -like*** adjs.; ***idiot-worshipper***. **idiot asylum**, a term formerly used for a hospital for the mentally ill; **idiot board** *colloq.*, a prompting board held before a television speaker but not projected on the film; **idiot box** *colloq.*, a television set; also *transf.*; **idiot card** *colloq.*, = *idiot board*; **idiot fringe**, (*a*) a fringe of hair in a style once worn (see quots.); (*b*) (*occas.*) = *lunatic fringe*; **idiot light** *colloq.*, a warning light, usu. red, that goes on when a fault occurs in a mechanical or electrical device; **idiot-proof** *a. colloq.* = FOOL-PROOF *a.*, esp. of equipment; **idiot sheet** *colloq.*, = *idiot board*; **idiot stick** *U.S. slang*, a shovel; **idiot stitch**, tricot-stitch, the easiest stitch in crochet work.

1866 J. MACGREGOR *Thousand Miles in Rob Roy Canoe* (ed. 2) vi. 104 Close to the inn was the idiot asylum, an old castle with poor demented women in it. **1880** 'MARK TWAIN' *Tramp Abroad* I. xxv. 250 They meant an asylum—an *idiot* asylum. **1952** *Newsweek* 4 Aug. 51/2 The Republicans and the Democrats got their 'idiot boards' free. **1961** G. MILLERSON *Technique Television Production* x. 194 (*caption*) Held-up cue card, idiot board, goof sheet. **1971** *Radio Times* 4 Nov. 6/4, I can never work with an auto-cue or idiot board. I learn my lines before the show. **1793** HOLCROFT tr. *Lavater's Physiog.* III. xxxvi. 186 The idiot-born cannot without a miracle become a philosopher. **1959** P. BULL *I know Face* xi. 193 The rationing period, when my very existence depended on the magic idiot-box. **1965**

Lancet 2 Jan. 46/2 Often they may be found, in semi-hypnotic state, watching the 'idiot box' with its endless stream of images and fullness of sound, all signifying nothing. **1972** P. FLOWER *Cobweb* ii. 72, I thought you spent all your time with the idiot box. **1973** *Ann. N.Y. Acad. Sci.* CCXI. 282 We assume that the modern general purpose computer is an idiot-box capable of performing only the simplest of routines. **1959** *Globe & Mail* (Toronto) 18 Sept. 1/7 No one held up an 'idiot card'—a prompter's card for actors who have forgotten their lines. **1960** B. KEATON *Wonderful World of Slapstick* (1967) 238 They had worked out an interesting technique for these foreign-language remakes. They used 'idiot cards'. On these the foreign words are spelled out in phonetic English and held up beyond camera range. **1969** *New Yorker* 27 Sept. 86/3 We had all the written questions put on idiot cards, and then the people read them before the camera. **1845** MRS. NORTON *Child of Islands* (1846) 152 Blind! and adder-deaf, and idiot-dull. **1886** H. BAUMANN *Londinismen* 81/1 *Idiot-fringe*, fransenartig auf die Stirn herabgekämmtes Haar der Fabrikmädchen, Hökerweiber u.s.w. **1923** J. MANCHON *Le Slang* 130 *Fringe*, le devant des cheveux dans la coiffure à la chien (habituelle chez les femmes de la basse classe). On dit aussi idiot-fringe. **1965** *Spectator* 5 Mar. 286/1 An article on a small and dying idiot-fringe sect of nationalists in North Germany. **1968** E. MCGIRR *Lead-Lined Coffin* iii. 173 He watched the idiot lights in the dashboard..for the warning red which would betoken he had lost the oil. **1971** M. TAK *Truck Talk* 88 *Idiot light*, a small light sometimes found on the front end of a tractor, the light turns on when the ignition is started. *a* **1603** T. CARTWRIGHT *Confut. Rhem. N.T.* (1618) 662 A childish and idiotelike pole. **1612** ROWLANDS *Knave of Hearts* B b, My Stockings Ideot-like, red, greene, and yealow. **1818** COBBETT *Pol. Reg.* XXXIII. 288 They, ideot-like, stand staring and sucking their fingers. **1977** *Economist* 8 Oct. 90/2 Viewdata's image could be bungled if the equipment proves not to be idiot-proof. **1985** *McGraw-Hill's Biotechnol. Newswatch* V. 21/2, I hate to use the term 'idiot-proof',..but our end-users for this assay are not technically trained. **1961** A. BERKMAN *Singers' Gloss. Show Business* 29 *Idiot sheet*, a large placard or paper roll, on which is [*sic*] printed the actual lines to be spoken by an announcer or performer. The printed characters are large enough to be seen from quite a distance from the camera. **1962** R. BRETZ *Techniques Television Production* 487 When cue cards first came into use for full script purposes, they were known derisively as 'idiot sheets'. **1942** BERREY & VAN DEN BARK *Amer. Thes. Slang* §75/32 *Shovel*, idiot stick. **1968** R. F. ADAMS *Western Words* (rev. ed.) 158/1 *Idiot stick*, what the miner calls his shovel; sometimes shortened to *idiot*. **1882** CAULFEILD & SAWARD *Dict. Needlework*, *Idiot stitch*, one of the names given to Tricot Stitch. **1606** SHAKS. *Tr. & Cr.* v. i. 7 Thou picture of what thou seem'st, and idoll of ideot-worshippers.

idiot, *v. nonce-wd.* [f. prec. sb.] *trans.* To call (any one) 'idiot'.

1864 TENNYSON *Aylmer's F.* 590 Much befooled and idioted.

‖**idi'ota.** *Obs. rare*⁻¹. [L. or It.: see IDIOT *sb.*] = IDIOT: in quot. in transf. sense.

1624 BP. MOUNTAGU *Gagg* To Rdr. 7 Many idle pamphlets in this very kinde have I seen in my dayes, but a verrier idiota saw I never any.

†**idi'otacy.** *Obs. rare*⁻¹. [irreg. f. IDIOT or L. *idiōta* + -ACY.] = IDIOCY.

1583 STUBBES *Anat. Abus.* I. (1879) 41 Vnder braue attyre sometime is couered great ydiotacy and folly.

idiotcy ('ɪdɪətsɪ). [irreg. f. IDIOT + -CY, q.v.] = IDIOCY, IDIOTISM.

1818 in TODD. **1839** F. BARHAM *Adamus Exul.* 34 It is but idiotcy to anatomise The fine degrees of guilt. **1851** H. MAYO *Pop. Superst.* (ed. 2) 76 Congenital idiotcy and imbecility. **1855** H. SPENCER *Princ. Psychol.* (1887) I. vii. §268. 470 A doctrine which makes idiotcy unaccountable. **1865** NICHOLS *Britton* II. 20 As long as they continue in their idiotcy [*en lour sotie*].

idiotic (ɪdɪ'ɒtɪk), *a.* [f. after Gr. ἰδιωτικ-ός (see next), or L. *idiōtic-us*; but in sense following IDIOT. Cf. F. *idiotique*.] Characteristic of or having the nature of an idiot or idiots; devoid of intellect; utterly stupid, senseless, or foolish.

1713 BENTLEY *Rem. Disc. Free-think.* xlix. II. 51 Maintaining that the Sun, Moon, and Stars were no bigger than they appear to the Eye, and other such Idiotic Stuff. **1809–10** COLERIDGE *Friend* (1837) III. 343 He may have an idiotic understanding, and what is far more common..an idiotic heart. **1877** BLACK *Green Past.* i, More..than he was likely to learn in any half-dozen years of his idiotic existence. **1887** *Spectator* 9 Apr. 491/2 Much that is idiotic and insufferable in modern strivings after fun.

idi'otical, *a.* Also 8 ideotical. [f. late L. *idiōtic-us* uneducated, ignorant, unskilful (a. Gr. ἰδιωτικός, f. ἰδιώτης: see IDIOT) + -AL¹.]

†**1.** Uneducated, unlearned, plain, ignorant. *Obs.*

idiotical psalms, ψαλμοὶ ἰδιωτικοί, psalms composed by uneducated persons or laymen, the use of which was forbidden by the Council of Laodicea.

1646 J. GREGORY *Notes & Obs.* To Rdr. (1650) ¶iv b, You may take it perhaps as forbidden by the Laodicean Canon among the Idioticall Psalmes. *a* **1652** J. SMITH *Sel. Disc.* (1821) 184 It [truth] speaks with the most idiotical sort of men in the most idiotical way. **1679** J. GOODMAN *Penit. Pardoned* III. ii. (1713) 283 It is not being..learned or idiotical, which makes so great a difference betwixt them. **1725** BLACKWALL *Sacr. Classics* I. 271 (T.) The language of the sublimest authors of Greece is, upon occasion, idiotical and vulgar.

†**2.** Private, personal, individual. *Obs. rare.*

1656 BLOUNT *Glossogr.*, *Idiotical*, private or belonging to private men. **1660** R. COKE *Justice Vind.* 7 He..absurdly prefers the obedience of the Commander..before the idiotical good of the Subject.

3. = IDIOTIC.

1656 BLOUNT *Glossogr.*, *Idiotical*,..belonging to an Idiot. **1751** SMOLLETT *Per. Pic.* (1779) IV. xci. 92 The ideotical hag. **1795** GIFFORD *Mæviad* (1811) 60, I recollect but two exceptions. Merry's idiotical Opera, and Mrs. Robinson's more idiotical Farce. **1834** H. MILLER *Scenes & Leg.* xxix. (1857) 443 Persons of an idiotical cast of mind.

Hence **idi'otically** *adv.*, in an idiotical manner; **idi'oticalness**, utter stupidity or irrationality.

1668 H. MORE *Div. Dial.* II. xi. (1713) 122 It is the Idioticalness of your phancy that makes you thus puzzled. **1668** WILKINS *Real Char.* 195 *Idioticalness*, being as a natural Fool. **1834** M. SCOTT *Cruise Midge* (1859) 279 That Idiotically serious kind of look that a man puts on who is conscious of having drank a little more than he should have done. **1860** GEN. P. THOMPSON *Audi Alt.* III. cxvi. 51 War idiotically begun, and carried on with contempt of the ordinary rules for escaping defeat.

‖**idioticon** (ɪdɪ'əʊtɪkən). [a. Gr. ἰδιωτικόν, neut. sing. of ἰδιωτικός (see IDIOTIC).] (See quot.)

1842 BRANDE *Dict. Sci.* etc., *Idioticon*, a word of frequent use in Germany, signifying a dictionary confined to a particular dialect, or containing words and phrases peculiar to one part of a country. **1883** *American* VI. 187 We wish somebody would compile a Philadelphia 'idioticon'. We have many local oddities: 'Gi'me', for 'give me'.

†**idiotish**, *a. Obs.* [f. IDIOT, or L. *idiōta* + -ISH.] = IDIOTIC.

1550 BALE *Image Both Ch.* I. (East) 118 Starke foolishenesse, all and moste ydiotishe dottage. **1614** T. ADAMS *Devil's Banquet* 327 Empirickes endanger not more bodies, than ideotish Priests soules. **1785** PALEY *Mor. Philos.* (1818) I. 354 As if he were mad or idiotish.

idiotism ('ɪdɪətɪz(ə)m). Also 7 **ideotism**. [In branch I. = F. *idiotisme* (16th c. in Hatz.-Darm.), ad. late L. *idiōtismus* common or vulgar manner of speaking, a. Gr. ἰδιωτισμός way or fashion of a common person, homely or vulgar phrase, f. ἰδιωτίζειν (see IDIOTIZE). In branch II. f. IDIOT + -ISM; cf. F. *idiotisme* (Cotgr.).]

I. †**1.** The speech, language, or dialect peculiar to a country, age, etc.: = IDIOM 1. *Obs.*

1588 J. H[ARVEY] *Disc. Probleme* 65 Some patcheries bungled up in an uplandish Ideotisme. *a* **1631** DONNE *Serm.* (1839) IV. xcv. 220 It is the language and Idiotism of the Church of God that the Resurrection is to be believed as an Article of Faith. *c* **1689** in Somers *Tracts* (1748) II. 433 By this Rule, Clemency and Tyrany should signify the same Thing; which, according to the Idiotism of our Days, are quite contrary.

†**2.** The peculiar character or genius of a language; idiomatic character: = IDIOM 2. *Obs.*

1605 J. DOVE *Confut. Atheism* 46 The same idiotisme and proprietye of speach in both Testaments vsed..doe shewe that they were written by one and the selfe-same spirit. **1683** DRYDEN *Life Plutarch* 96 We may have lost somewhat of the idiotism of that language in which it [a jest] was spoken. **1731** J. GILL *Trinity* ii. (1752) 23 In perfect agreement with the idiotism of the Hebrew language.

3. A peculiarity of phrase; a current deviation or departure from the strict syntactical rules or usages of a language; = IDIOM 3.

a **1615** DONNE *Ess. Divinity* (1651) 52 It satisfies me, for the phrase..that it is a meer Idiotism. **1683** CAVE *Ecclesiastici, Hilary* 212 Infecting their style with the peculiar Idiotisms of their own Country. *a* **1734** NORTH *Lives* II. 373 He once composed a Turkish dictionary, and showed the ordinary idiotisms and analogies of that language. **1882** *Century Mag.* XXIV. 637 An attempt..to conform to the 'idiotisms' of the English language.

†**b.** A technical term of science or art. *Obs.*

1655 BRAMHALL *Def. true Liberty* xix. 157 Must the Mathematician, the Metaphysician, and the Divine, relinquish all their tearmes of Art, and proper idiotismes?

c. A personal peculiarity of expression; an individualism (of language). *rare.*

1867 H. N. DAY *Art Discourse* §287 (1870) 260 Idiotism, or the use which is confined to an individual.

†**d.** *transf.* A peculiarity of action, manner, or habit. *Obs.*

1610 DONNE *Pseudo-Mart.* 90 Having made it habituall to them, and an Idiotisme of that Religion. **1639** FULLER *Holy War* IV. xvi. 196 The very language of their hands made them suspected..because they could not counterfeit the French idiotismes in managing their bucklers.

II. 4. Ignorance; lack of knowledge or culture.

1635 J. HAYWARD tr. *Biondi's Banish'd Virg.* A ij b, In discov'ring with his owne vile breath His Idiotisme, he'd be jeer'd to death. *a* **1652** BROME *City Wit* IV. i. Wks. 1873 I. 334 May Peasantry and Idiotism trample Upon the heads of Art and Knowledge.

5. The condition of being void of intellect or reason; = IDIOCY. Now *rare.*

1611 COTGR., *Idiotisme*, ideotisme, naturall follie [etc.]. **1632** BROME *North. Lasse* III. ii. Wks. 1873 III. 51 Direct Lunacie and Ideotism. **1710** LUTTRELL *Brief Rel.* (1857) VI. 594 Secretary to the commissions of lunacy and idiotism. **1822–34** *Good's Study Med.* (ed. 4) III. 62 Wit, madness and idiotism are as distinctly an heir-loom of some families as scrofula, consumption, and cancer of others.

b. Extreme folly, senselessness, or stupidity, exhibited in thought or conduct (cf. IDIOT 2 b).

1592 NASHE *P. Penilesse* (Shaks. Soc.) 40 New herrings, new! we must cry..or else we shall be christend with a hundred newe tytles of idiotisme. **1620** E. BLOUNT *Horæ Subs.* 363 [To] bee so farre carried away with this Ideotisme, which is both against Reason and Religion. **1745** ELIZA HAYWOOD *Female Spect.* (1748) II. 231 The folly or madness of such notions would..like other idiotisms, find pity [etc.]. **1764** WILKES *Corr.* (1805) II. 63 What idiotism it would be in me to trust myself to a ministry capable of such baseness. **1864** *Scotsman* 8 Apr., People get sympathy when they have damaged themselves by the perpetration of an idiotism.

†**'idiotist.** *Obs. rare.* [f. IDIOT (or its L. or Gr. original) + -IST.] = IDIOT 1.

1715 M. DAVIES *Athen. Brit.* I. 235 This sort of Meditation is still..in..practice amongst the Romish Idiotists and Vulgar People.

Hence †**idio'tistical** *a.*, used by the unlearned.

1715 M. DAVIES *Athen. Brit.* I. 77 The Idiotistical, or Vulgar Catholick Instrument, call'd the Rosary or Beads.

idiotize ('ɪdɪətaɪz), *v.* [f. as prec. + -IZE; cf. Gr. ἰδιωτίζ-ειν to put into common language.]

†**1.** *intr.* To act in a way peculiar to themselves (cf. IDIOTISM 3 d). *Obs.*

1716 M. DAVIES *Athen. Brit.* III. *Crit. Hist.* 11 Foreign Calvinists..disown and condemn our Dissenters for Idiotizing as well as Schismatizing.

2. *intr.* To become idiotic or stupid.

? *a* **1800** tr. *Montesquieu's Pers. Lett.* cix. (T.), It looks as if the heads of the greatest men idiotized, when they meet together.

3. *trans.* To make idiotic, to convert into an idiot; to make a fool of, befool.

1831 *Fraser's Mag.* IV. 580 They bethought them..how they might further idiotise the public. **1841** R. OASTLER *Fleet Papers* I. xlviii. 382 The invention..idiotizes all our former sages. **1886** T. HARDY *Mayor of Casterbr.* xxix, Henchard stood as if idiotised.

†**'idiotly**, *a. Obs. rare*⁻¹. [-LY¹.] = IDIOTIC.

1662 J. BARGRAVE *Pope Alex. VII* (1867) 95 This silly, iddiotly, coxcombly Cardinal Maidalchino.

'idiotry. [f. IDIOT + -RY.] **a.** *Sc. Law.* = IDIOCY. **b.** Idiotic or infatuated conduct, madness.

1597 *Lawes Sc. Parl.* (ed. Skene) Act Jas. III, c. 66 (heading) Anent the brieve of Idiotrie and furiositie. **1752** J. LOUTHIAN *Form of Process* (ed. 2) 286 Services of Idiotry and Furiosity to pay [fees] as general Services. **1757** WARBURTON *Note Pope's Prol. Sat.* 163, I still keep up my correspondence with him, notwithstanding his Idiotry. **1826** J. WILSON *Noct. Ambr.* Wks. 1855 I. 100 To emancipate the Catholics in order to destroy their religion..is pure idiotry. **1868** *Act 31 & 32 Vict.* c. 100 §101 The brieves of furiosity and idiotry hitherto in use are hereby abolished.

idiotype, etc.: see IDIO-.

idiozome ('ɪdɪəʊzəʊm). *Cytology.* Also **idiosome** (q.v. above). [ad. G. *idiozom* (F. Meves 1896, in *Anat. Hefte* (Abt. 2) VI. 315), f. IDIO- + Gr. ζῶμ-α loin-cloth, band, girdle.] A rounded structure present in the cytoplasm of developing germ cells in members of most animal groups, in certain of which it forms part of (or is associated with) the Golgi apparatus in spermatids and spermatocytes and develops into the acrosome of the spermatozoon.

1899 *Zool. Jahrbücher (Abt. für Anat.)* XII. 14 At the pointed end of the cell lies a spherical or oval body, homogeneous in appearance, which is stained more deeply by the action of Hermann's fixative than the enveloping cytoplasm... Meves..proposes for it the name 'Idiozom', which I shall adopt in the present paper... In the idiozome of the resting spermatogonium I have been unable to detect any granules which could be regarded as centrosomes. **1920** L. DONCASTER *Introd. Study Cytol.* vii. 102 The acrosome is described in some forms as arising from a mass of denser protoplasm known as the idiozome. **1928** C. W. METZ in E. V. Cowdry *Special Cytol.* II. xxxvi. 1282 The Golgi bodies ..usually appear first in the form of small granules or rods, which during the growth stages typically collect about the idiozome. **1952** G. H. BOURNE *Cytol. & Cell Physiol.* (ed. 2) vi. 254 The Golgi apparatus in developing male germ and other cells is frequently associated with a differentiated area of cytoplasm near the nucleus, called the idiozome.

idle ('aɪd(ə)l), *a.* (*sb.*). Forms: 1–6 **idel, ydel, idil,** 4–5 **ydul,** 4–6 **idyl,** *Sc.* **ydill, idell, -ul, ydil,** 5 **idylle, ydyll,** 5–6 **ydyl,** 5–7 **ydle,** 6 **ydell, idoll,** 6– **idle.** [OE. *ídel* = OFris. *idel*, OS. *îdal* empty, worthless (MDu. *idel*, *ydel*, Du. *ijdel*, *ijl*), OHG. *îtal* empty, useless, vain (MHG. *îtel*, G. *eitel* bare, mere, pure, worthless, vain; Sw. and Da. *idel* mere, pure, are from LG.). The orig. sense, was app. 'empty', but the ulterior etymology is obscure. The sense-development in Eng., which has produced senses 4–6, has been very different from that in Ger. and Du.]

A. *adj.* †**1.** Empty, vacant; void (*of*). *Obs.*

Beowulf (Z.) 2888 Lond-rihtes mot..monna æghwylc idel hweorfan. *c* **825** *Vesp. Psalter* cvi[i]. 9 Forðon ȝereorde sawle idle [L. *satiavit animam inanem*]. *c* **1000** ÆLFRIC *Hom.* II. 582 To hwan mæg ðis eorðlice hus ȝif hit ydel stent? *c* **1200** *Vices & Virtues* 23 Wuten we fare to ðessere idele saule and amti. *a* **1225** *Ancr. R.* 212 To hwamso is idel of god. **1340** *Ayenb.* 131 He is uol of zennes, and ydel of alle guode. **1388** WYCLIF *Gen.* i. 2 The erthe was idel [1382 veyn with ynne] and voide [L. *inanis et vacua*]. *c* **1450** tr. *De Imitatione* III. xxvii. 97, I am idel erþe & voide, til þou illumyne me.

2. a. Of actions, feelings, thoughts, words, etc.: Void of any real worth, usefulness, or significance; leading to no solid result; hence, ineffective, worthless, of no value, vain, frivolous, trifling. Also said of persons in respect of their actions, etc.

In OE., and early ME., frequent in *idle yelp*, boasting, vain-glory: see YELP.

c **825** *Vesp. Psalter* xiii[i]. 11 Dryhten wat ȝeðohtas monna forðon idle sind. *c* **950** *Lindisf. Gosp.* Matt. xii. 36 Eȝhuelc word idil [L. *otiosum*] þæt sprecende biðon menn [etc.]. *c* **1000** ÆLFRIC *Lev.* xxvi. 20 Eall eower ȝeswinc bið idel. *c* **1200** *Trin. Coll. Hom.* 129 On unnitte speche, and on iuele dede, and on idel þonc. *a* **1300** *Cursor M.* 28338 Idel gammes, chess and tablis. *c* **1374** CHAUCER *Boeth.* II. pr. vii. 46 (Camb. MS.) Yif yt be for the audience of poeple and for idil rumours. *c* **1440** *Promp. Parv.* 258/1 Idyl spekare, *vanidicus*. **1570–6** LAMBARDE *Peramb. Kent* (1826) 233 Beda speaketh there of the Northeast mouth of the flood Genlade: which speech of his were idle, if that water had none other mouthe but that one. **1576** FLEMING *Panopl. Epist.* 245 He is no idle talker. **1607** SHAKS. *Timon* IV. iii. 27 No Gods, I am no idle Votarist. **1617** MORYSON *Itin.* II. 47 The Schoolemens idle and absurd distinctions. **1709** SWIFT *Advancem. Relig.* Wks. 1755 II. I. 98 It is idle to propose remedies, before we are assured of the disease. **1802** MAR. EDGEWORTH *Moral T.* (1816) I. 217 He did not..waste his time in idle conjectures. **1857** BUCKLE *Civiliz.* I. xiii. 745 To argue against these opinions would be idle indeed.

†**b.** Void of meaning or sense; foolish, silly, incoherent; also (of persons) light-headed, out of one's mind, delirious (cf. IDLE-HEADED). *Obs.*

1548 HALL *Chron., Rich. III* 55 b, He..beganne a lytle to waxe ydle and weake in his wit and remembraunce. *Ibid., Hen. VIII* 219 b, She semed to bee in Traunses, and spake and uttered many foolishe and Idle woordes. *a* **1658** FORD, etc. *Witch Edmonton* IV. ii, *Kath.* Why do you talk so? Would you were fast asleep. *Frank.* No, no; I am not idle. **1658** A. FOX *Wurtz' Surg.* III. ii. 223 A patient that sleepeth much, and is idle withal in his sleep.

c. Without foundation: baseless, groundless.

1590 SPENSER *F.Q.* I. xii. 9 When they came where that dead Dragon lay..The sight with ydle feare did them dismay. **1617** MORYSON *Itin.* II. 235 The bruite that they should have come for Ireland was idle. **1849** MACAULAY *Hist. Eng.* vi. II. 153 He declared that Barillon must have been imposed upon by idle or malicious reports. **1878** BROWNING *La Saisiaz* 433 Idle hopes that lure man onward, forced back by as idle fears.

3. a. Of things: Serving no useful purpose, useless.

c **897** K. ÆLFRED *Gregory's Past.* xviii. 129 Ðær ðæt heafod bið unhal, eall ða limu bioð idelu, ðeah hie hal sien. *a* **1000** *Cædmon's Gen.* 106 Ðes wida grund stod..idel and unnyt. *c* **1566** J. ALDAY tr. *Boaystuau's Theat. World* R iv, As touching the eares, they are not idell, they are placed..hie and eminent for to receyve the sounde that naturally is borne hie. **1590** SHAKS. *Com. Err.* II. ii. 180 Vsurping Iuie, Brier, or idle Mosse. **1597** GERARDE *Herbal* I. lix. §1. 81 Out of the hole commeth a small idle or barren chaffie eare like unto that of Darnell. **1692** RAY *Dissol. World* (1732) 124 Which are no idle or useless Part. **1730–46** THOMSON *Autumn* 371 Caught in the meshy snare, in vain they beat Their idle wings, entangled more and more. **1834** DISRAELI *Rev. Epick* II. xxii, The idle shells On silent shores that none regard.

b. (See quot. 1956.)

1956 J. MASTERS *Bugles & Tiger* ii. 46 The word 'idle' meant anything the staff considered unsoldierly. We *were* idle; we had idle haircuts, idle rifles, idle bicycles; we *did* idle salutes, idle jumps. **1959** *News Chron.* 4 Aug. 1/4 'Idle' is a Brigade [of Guards] adjective that describes everything that is not perfection in execution. A bootlace undone is an idle bootlace. **1963** D. WALDER *Bags of Swank* vi. 65 Ransome looked at the lecturer's hip pocket now revealed as undone. 'Idle and naked,' he said loudly to Lilburne.

4. a. Of persons: Not engaged in work, doing nothing, unemployed. Freq. in phr. ***the idle rich***.

c **950** *Lindisf. Gosp.* Matt. xx. 6 Hwæt her stondes ȝe allen dæȝe idlo? [*c* **975** *Rushw. Gosp.* unnytte. *c* **1000** *Ags. Gosp.* idele]. *a* **1225** *Ancr. R.* 44 Lokeð also ich bid ou þet ȝe ne beon neuer idel. **1340** *Ayenb.* 206 Huo þet is ydel he him may naȝt longe hyalde þet he ne ualle in-to zenne. *c* **1450** *Mirour Saluacioun* 759 To devocionne evre and Contemplacionne Was sho gyven and nevre ydel. **1530–1** *Act 22 Hen. VIII*, c. 12 To arest the sayde vacaboundes and ydell persones. **1548** HALL *Chron., Hen. VIII* 119 b, They were never idle but doyng some thyng in one part or other. **1601** R. JOHNSON *Kingd. & Commw.* (1603) 179 The greater part of his men and horses were idle. **1764** BURN *Poor Laws* 143 They are idle for want of such work as they are able to do. **1865** MILL *Auguste Comte* 160 He allows of no idle rich. **1894** J. T. FOWLER *Adamnan* Introd. 74 He could not bear to be idle even for an hour. **1900** B. MATTHEWS *Confident To-Morrow* 178 Mr. Dircks wishes to shift the burdens of the worthy poor upon the shoulders of the idle rich. **1926** *Encycl. Brit.* I. 527/1 We must remember as a rule the 'idle rich' do not represent idle riches. **1938** *Times Lit. Suppl.* 11 June 403/3 The crew, Reds of various shades, mutiny and drive ashore the idle-rich passengers. **1960** C. DAY LEWIS *Buried Day* viii. 171 The idle rich, the boss class, fleeing.. from the wrath to come. **1964** M. ARGYLE *Psychol. & Social Probl.* xv. 185 There has been a decline of the old 'idle rich' upper middle class, living partly on unearned income and passing on wealth and advantages to its children. **1971** *Daily Tel.* 20 Oct. 10/4 More than 25,000 Coventry workers were idle yesterday as a result of the dispute.

†**b.** ***idle from***, not engaged in, free from. *Obs.*

c **1380** WYCLIF *Sel. Wks.* III. 359 For þei..ben y-dil fro many goode dedes. *c* **1440** *Jacob's Well* (E.E.T.S.) 238 þei were hyȝe in pride, & ydel fro gostly occupacyoun.

c. Of things, esp. time: Unoccupied; characterized by inaction or want of occupation. ***idle bread*** = bread of idleness (IDLENESS 4).

1297 R. GLOUC. (Rolls) 4020 þat ydel lif þat þine men abbeþ ylad. **1382** WYCLIF *Prov.* xxxi. 27 Idil bred she eet not [L. *panem otiosa non comedit*]. **1526** *Pilgr. Perf.* (W. de W. 1531) 235 All my ydell yeres & dayes. **1581** SIDNEY *Apol. Poetrie* (Arb.) 20 In these my..idelest times. **1601** SHAKS. *Jul. C.* II. i. 117 Breake off betimes; And euery man hence, to his idle bed. **1617** MORYSON *Itin.* II. 1 In which place.. whilest I passed an idle yeere [etc.] **1700** T. BROWN tr. *Fresny's Amusem. Ser. & Com.* 48 Persons..that have a great deal of Idle Time lying upon their Hands. **1783** COWPER *Epit. Hare* 31 Dozing out all his idle noons. **1850** CARLYLE *Latter-d. Pamph.* I. 47 Locking you up in temporary Idle Workhouses. **1870** E. PEACOCK *Ralf Skirl.* III. 234 Plough-Monday was an idle day.

d. ***idle worms***, worms humorously said to breed in the fingers of the idle.

[Cf. **1592** SHAKS. *Rom. & Jul.* I. iv. 65 (Qo. 1597) A little worme, Pickt [*later edd.* prickt] from the lasie finger of a maide [*Quartos 2–5 & Folio 1*, man, *Folios 2, 3, 4*, woman].] **1607** BEAUM. & FL. *Woman-Hater* III. i, Keep thy hands in thy muff, and warm the idle Worms in thy fingers' ends.

5. a. Of things: Inactive, unoccupied, not moving or in operation.

1522 MORE *De quat. Noviss.* Wks. 75/2 Mans mind is neuer ydle, but occupyed commonly either with good or euil. **1576** FLEMING *Panopl. Epist.* 350 All the Elementes and other celestiall bodies..are never ydle, but still occupied. **1655** MOUFET & BENNET *Health's Improv.* (1746) 87 As a standing Water corrupteth in a little Space, so an idle Air, rolled about with no Winds, soon putrefieth. **1720** WATTS '*How doth the little busy bee*' iii, Satan finds some mischief still For idle hands to do. **1822–34** *Good's Study Med.* (ed. 4) I. 365 Peruvian bark..is not an idle medicine; for if it do not assist it will be sure to injure. **1849** MACAULAY *Hist. Eng.* vi. II. 85 The power which the courts of law had thus recognised was not suffered to lie idle. **1877** RAYMOND *Statist. Mines & Mining* 302 The mine..was idle for the first six months of the year. **1898** *Daily News* 18 June 3/1 We don't keep the pits idle for the fun of the thing.

b. Of machinery. ***to run idle***, to run loose, without doing work or transmitting power.

idle wheel, idle-wheel, †(*a*) a safety-wheel to come into operation in case of the ordinary wheel breaking down; (*b*) an intermediate wheel used for connecting two geared wheels when they cannot be brought sufficiently near to gear directly, or when it is necessary that the 'follower' should revolve in the same direction as the 'leader', which would not be the case if they geared directly. *idle pulley*, the loose pulley of the 'fast-and-loose pulley' arrangement.

1805 *Specif. W. Milton's Patent* No. 2890 As near..to each active wheel as a workman may think proper, low, strong idle wheels..are to be placed..ready in case of an active wheel coming off, or breaking, or an axle-tree failing, to catch the falling vehicle. **1842** R. WILLIS *Princ. Mechanism* 205 If a wheel A be placed between two other wheels C and B it will not affect the velocity ratio of those wheels..but it does affect the directional relation; for..in consequence of the introduction of the intermediate axis of A, B and C will revolve in the same direction. Such an intermediate wheel is termed an idle wheel. **1873** C. P. B. SHELLEY *Workshop Appliances* (1885) 187 The wheel which is always in gear with the pinion is brought also into gear with the backshaft wheel, the second wheel running idle. *Ibid.* 239 The central pulley is 'idle', that is to say it runs loose upon the shaft. **1875** KNIGHT *Dict. Mech.* 1171/2 Another description of idle-wheel..is [a wheel] caused to rest upon a belt to tighten it, to perfect its adhesion to the band-wheels over which it runs. **1884** F. J. BRITTEN *Watch & Clockm.* 124 An idle wheel introduced causes the follower to rotate in the same direction as the driver.

c. *Electr.* Of a wire on an armature: having no electromotive force induced in it. Of a component of an alternating current: 90° out of phase with respect to the voltage; wattless, reactive.

1884 S. P. THOMPSON *Dynamo-Electr. Machinery* iii. 33 Where the coils are working in series, it has been considered advantageous to arrange the commutator to cut out the coil that is in the position of least action, as the circuit is thereby relieved of the resistance of an idle coil. *Ibid.* vii. 126 The advantage originally claimed for this construction, namely, that it allows less of the total length of wire to remain 'idle' on the inner side of the ring, is rather imaginary than real. **1904** R. M. WALMSLEY *Electr. in Service of Man* II. vi. 1069 This current..contributes nothing to the power, and is therefore often referred to as the idle current. **1908** SLINGO & BROOKER *Electr. Engin.* (new ed.) ix. 354 The portions connecting the horizontal limbs are always idle, inasmuch as they do not cut, but only slide through, the lines of force.

d. Of money: out of circulation.

1931 *Times Lit. Suppl.* 19 Feb. 124/2 It may be thought that saving cannot exceed investment because idle money automatically becomes the basis of bank credit. **1965** SELDON & PENNANCE *Everyman's Dict. Econ.* s.v. Dishoarding. A distinction is made between 'active' money in circulation and financing current transactions and 'inactive' money held in idle balances.

6. Addicted to doing no work; lazy, indolent. †***idle bellies***, indolent sluggards or gluttons (cf. *Titus* i. 12).

a **1300** *Cursor M.* 27238 Yong man idel, and ald man dill. **1398** TREVISA *Barth. De P.R.* VI. xvi. (1495) 200 He is slowe and ydle and lesyth in ydlenes the tyme that is graunted to traueylle in. **1530** *Compend. Treat.* (1863) 48 The ydle bellyes wolde have had leyser Inough to put forth a nother well translatyd. **1634** CANNE *Necess. Separ.* (1849) 246 The dumb dogs, caterpillars, and idle bellies, never had a better proctor than this. **1726** SHELVOCKE *Voy. round World* (1757) 28 They were very idle, and there was no driving them on faster. **1828** SCOTT *F.M. Perth* xiv, The Prince is unhappily a dissipated and idle youth.

†**7.** In quasi-*adv.* use = IDLY. *Obs.*

c **1300** *Cursor M.* 28991 (Cott. Galba) If þat ȝerning idell be, for idell prayand tald er we. **13..** *Guy Warw.* (A.) 7102 'Sir erl', quaþ Gij, 'þer-of speke nouȝt, Al idel þou hast me þer-of bisouȝt'. **1663** PEPYS *Diary* 29 Oct., The Queene mends apace, they say; but yet talks idle still.

8. a. Parasynthetic combs., as ***idle-bellied***, ***-brained***, ***-handed***, ***-minded*** (so ***-mindedness***), ***-pated***, ***-thoughted***, ***-witted*** adjs. Also ***idle-looking*** adj.; IDLE-HEADED.

1340 *Ayenb.* 218 þou ne sselt naȝt sseawy þe beuore me, ydel-honded. **1532** FRITH *Mirror to know Thyself* (1829) 272 Idle-bellied monks, canons, & priests. **1564** *Brief Exam.* *****iiij, To beleue euery fonde meanyng, as suche ydle brayned Durandes do bryng. *a* **1613** OVERBURY *Charac., Sexton* Wks. (1756) 206 Let him be found never so idle pated, he is still a grave drunkard. **1615** CHAPMAN *Odyss.* XVIII. 285 Is the man idle-brain'd for want of rest? **1652** GAULE *Magastrom.* 177 Idle-witted and fantastical men. **1849** HARE *Par. Serm.* II. 187 None of you can be so idle-thoughted as to fancy you can escape. **1870** FREEMAN in Stephens *Life & Lett.* (1895) II. 10 Idle-looking, watering-place sort of folk. **1899** *Westm. Gaz.* 21 Aug. 2/3 The empty-headed and idle-minded exist in both sexes. **1899** *Leisure Hour* Dec. 153 Hence the dull lives of many children of the poor, their occasional trend towards mischief from sheer idle-mindedness. **1917** KIPLING *Years Between* (1919) 47 But the idle-minded overlings who quibbled while they died. **1927** T. WILDER *Bridge San Luis Rey* 100 Even the busiest mother stands for a moment idle-handed. **1928** *Oxford Poetry* 39 Because this place is full of moneyed young men And indolent phallophil idleminded girls.

b. Special combs.: **idle-back**, an indolent person; †**idle-being**, being idle, idleness; **idle Dick, Jack** *S. Afr.*, formerly used as a local name for the grass-bird, *Sphenœacus afer*; **idle-fellow**, formerly, a fellow of a college who had no formal duties; so **idle fellowship**; †**idle-pack**, an idler; **idle-peg** (see quot.); **idle-tongs**, = LAZY-TONGS.

1828 *Craven Dial.*, **Idle-back*, a lazy person. **1562** in Strype *Ann. Ref.* (1709) I. xxxi. 317 Giving themselves to gaming, drinking, or *idlebeing at Home. **1901** A. C. STARK *Birds S. Afr.* II. 168 *Sphenœacus natalensis.* Natal Grass-Bird... '*Idle Dick' and 'Lazy Dick' of English Colonists. **1919** R. FROST *Let.* 8 Aug. (1964) 132, I am going..to Ann Arbor to become an *idle-fellow of the University of Michigan for one year. **1884** in J. R. Ware *Passing Eng.* (1909) 157/1 Much has been said against what are called *idle Fellowships. **1909** J. R. WARE *Ibid.* 156/2 *Idle fellowships* (*Oxford and Cambridge*), the old as distinct from the new fellowships. Parliamentary action swept away towards the end of the 19th century most of these fatal sinecures. **1884** R. B. SHARPE *Layard's Birds S. Afr.* (rev. ed.) 281 It..will suffer itself to be taken with the hand rather than rise again; for this reason it has acquired the name of **Idle Jack* or *Lazy Dick*. **1893** A. NEWTON *Dict. Birds* 458 Idle Jack, a local name in the Cape Colony for *Sphenœacus africanus* (Grass-bird). **1624** BP. MOUNTAGU *Gagg* 326 You have playd the *Idle-pack, Addlehead, Ignavo or Negligent in the course of your book. **1747** HOOSON *Miner's Dict.*, **Idlepeg*, a peg of wood, driven into a hole in the Stoblade, to stop the Sweep from turning and save the winder the trouble of holding it. **1864** MARY EYRE *Lady's Walks in S. France* xiii. (1865) 163 Zigzag roads..which at a distance look like a huge pair of *idle-tongs.

B. *sb.* (absol. use of the *adj.*)

†**1. a.** That which is useless, vain, or frivolous. *Obs. rare.*

c **1000** *Canons of Edgar* c. 26 in Thorpe *Laws* II. 250 Ne idele spræce ne idele dæde..ne æfre æniȝ idel. *c* **1000** *Sax. Leechd.* III. 214 ȝif þu ȝesihst maneȝa get [= goats] ydel ȝetacnað. *c* **1175** *Lamb. Hom.* 153 Opene to behalden idel and unnet.

†**b.** ***in*** (earlier ***on, an***) ***idle***: In vain; without result; without cause (cf. IDLENESS 1). *Obs.*

c **1000** ÆLFRIC *Lev.* xxvi. 16 On idel ȝe swincaþ. *c* **1000** —— *Deut.* v. 11 Ne nemne ȝe drihtnes naman on idel. *c* **1200** ORMIN 12514 Onn idell & wiþþutenn ned & alls he wollde leȝȝkenn. **1297** R. GLOUC. (Rolls) 3071 It nis an ydel noȝt þat ich telle þis tydinge. **1382** WYCLIF *Prov.* xxiv. 28 Be thou not a witnesse in idil [1388 with out resonable cause] aȝen thi neȝhebore. *c* **1386** CHAUCER *Pars. T.* ¶ 522 Euery man that taketh goddes name in ydel, or falsly swereth with his mouth. *a* **1500** *Ragman Roll* 80 in Hazl. *E.P.P.* I. 73 Al in ydel here is thy labour.

†**2. a.** Idleness. *Obs.*

a **1000** in Kemble *Sal. & Sat.* (1848) 258 þe slep & þæt ydel fet unþeawas & unhælo þæs lichoman. *a* **1225** *Ancr. R.* 404 Idel acoaldeð & acwencheð þis fur. **1465** *Paston Lett.* No. 501 II. 183 A day lost in idyll can never be recoveryd. **1606** SYLVESTER *Du Bartas* II. iv. II. 1319 His brains' rich Talent buries not in Idle.

b. pl. ***the idles***: idleness as an affection or distemper. *colloq.*

1616 *Withals' Dict.* 558 *Hodie nullam lineam duxi*, I have beene sicke of the idles to day. **1681** W. ROBERTSON *Phraseol. Gen.* (1693) 753 Sick of the Idles.

c. [f. IDLE *v.*] The act of idling.

1883 FENN *Middy & Ensign* xxiv. 142 A good idle ashore would be very pleasant.

†**3.** An idle person, idler. *Obs.*

1633 EARL MANCH. *Al Mondo* (1636) 146 Industry in any calling makes a man capable of better imployment, whereas Idles are fit for nothing but temptations. **1709** *Rambling Fuddle-Caps* 13 Had I thought you'd have prov'd such an Idle.

4. [f. the vb.] Idling (of an engine); idling speed.

1939 C. H. FISHER *Carburation & Carburettors* iv. 96 If the throttle is closed completely the adjustment of the idling mixture is rendered too sensitive, hence it is usual to give a very small opening of the throttle when adjusting the idle. **1943** A. P. FRAAS *Aircraft Power Plants* vii. 134 As the throttle is opened farther..the idle needle is withdrawn very rapidly and so has no effect on fuel flow at powers above an idle. **1966** *McGraw-Hill Encycl. Sci. & Technol.* II. 478/2 Because of increased piston and other friction with a cold engine, greater throttle opening as well as more fuel is required for idle at that time. **1972** *Practical Motorist* Oct. 160/3 Start the engine and set the tick-over to 650 rpm, using the air screw. Now turn the jet adjusting screw one way or the other until the smoothest idle is achieved.

5. *attrib.* (in sense B. 4: cf. IDLING *vbl. sb.* 2), as ***idle jet***, ***needle***, ***nozzle***, ***power***, ***range***, ***stroke***.

1943 A. P. FRAAS *Aircraft Power Plants* vii. 119 A high metering head..is used to induce a flow of fuel through an idle jet. **1943** Idle needle [see sense B. 4]. **1968** C. F. TAYLOR *Internal-Combustion Engine* II. vi. 200 Further opening of the throttle gradually exposes the idle nozzle to the full manifold depression, which may be as much as 10 psi.. below atmospheric pressure in a normal idling engine. **1946**

R. H. THORNER *Aircraft Carburetion* ii. 65 The richest mixture is required at the carburetor during the lowest idle power. **1939** C. H. FISHER *Carburation & Carburettors* iv. 95 Since most engines idle with a manifold depression of about 16" of mercury,..any good carburettor can be made to deliver a wide band of mixture strengths covering the idle range. **1896** W. NORRIS *'Otto' Cycle Gas Engine* ii. 6 The idle strokes of the 'Otto' cycle are far from theoretically correct.

idle ('aɪd(ə)l), *v.* [f. prec. adj. (OE. had *ídlian* to come to nothing, become vain or useless.)]

1. *intr.* To move or saunter idly. *rare.*

1592 SHAKS. *Rom. & Jul.* II. vi. 19 The Gossamours, That ydles in the wanton Summer ayre. **1882** W. D. HOWELLS in *Longm. Mag.* I. 41 A clear brown brook..idles through the pastures. **1890** G. GISSING *Emancipated* II. I. xiv. 127 Cecily let her fingers idle upon the keys. **1938** M. K. RAWLINGS *Yearling* ix. 75 The woodbox was low and Jody idled outside to fill it.

2. a. To be idle; to spend the time in idleness.

1668 PEPYS *Diary* 20 July, Thence idling all the afternoon. **1698** FRYER *Acc. E. India & P.* 95 All the heat of the Day they idle it under some shady Tree. **1748** RICHARDSON *Clarissa* (1811) III. xxxi. 187 What do I keep fellows idling in the country for? **1853** KANE *Grinnell Exp.* xix. (1856) 149 Whether you ate or slept, or idled or toiled.

b. quasi-*trans.* *to idle* (time) ***away***, to pass in idleness.

1652 J. AUDLEY *England's Commw.* 8 Some idle away their time. *a* **1773** CHESTERF. (T.), Will you improve that hour instead of idling it away? **1813** E. S. BARRETT *Heroine* (1815) I. 29 Thus idling her precious time over the common occupations of life.

3. *trans.* To cause to be idle.

1788 E. SHERIDAN *Jrnl.* (1960) 138 And to compleat all, they beg'd him to see another person who idled him two hours more. **1826** MOORE *Mem.* (1854) V. 55 [I] have been a good deal idled these few days past. **1834** SIR W. R. HAMILTON in R. P. Graves *Life* II. 97 My little boy, now about two months old, has not idled me much as yet. **1892** STOPF. BROOKE *Short Serm.* 174 Some pursuit which idles you too much. **1968** *Globe & Mail* (Toronto) 5 Feb. 21/7 Gilchrist was..idled with a leg injury. **1972** *Nat. Geographic* Sept. 322 (*caption*) *Idled by war*, workers await the call to return to the Karnaphuli Rayon and Chemicals plant in Chandraghona.

4. a. *intr.* Of an engine: to run while disconnected from a load or out of gear, so that it performs no external or useful work; also, to run very slowly.

1916 [implied in IDLING *vbl. sb.* 1]. **1920** V. W. PAGÉ *Useful Hints Motorists* iii. 78 Turn petrol adjustment to the right.. until motor idles smoothly. **1925** A. W. JUDGE *Carburettors & Carburation* iii. 37 The ideal carburettor should:.. (4) Enable the engine to run very slowly when 'idling', without undue waste of fuel. **1932** CHATFIELD & TAYLOR *Airplane & its Engine* (ed. 2) viii. 169 Airplane engines must be able to idle, that is run very slowly, in order to keep the landing speed as low as possible. **1934** *Boys' Mag.* XLVII. 23/2 One after another the four engines were started, 'revved' with a deafening roar singly and all together, and then left quietly 'idling'. **1953** G. E. M. ANSCOMBE tr. *Wittgenstein's Philos. Investigations* I. §132 The confusions which occupy us arise when language is like an engine idling, not when it is doing work. **1965** P. H. SMITH *High-Speed Two-Stroke Petrol Engine* x. 212 The engine is..idling at tick-over speed. **1970** *Commercial Motor* 25 Sept. 64/2 Neither vehicle had much mileage on the clock which was probably the reason why the engines idled badly.

b. *trans.* To cause (an engine) to idle; ***to idle down***, to slow down and idle (an engine).

1925 E. W. KNOTT *Carburettor Handbk.* i. 41 It is surprising what a small degree of throttle opening is necessary to pass the requisite amount of mixture to 'idle' an engine. **1938** J. STEINBECK *Long Valley* 17 She heard him drive to the gate and idle down his motor. **1938** *Amer. Speech* XIII. 131/2 In case of some delay, the engineer may idle down or slow down the tractor. **1972** 'H. BUCKMASTER' *Walking Trip* 163 David slowed the car and idled it by the side of the road.

¶ Meaning obscure.

c **1460** *Towneley Myst.* xxx. 326 With youre bendys and youre bridyls of sathan, the whilke sir sathanas Idyls you for tha ilke.

Hence **idling** *ppl. a.*

1828 D'ISRAELI *Chas. I*, II. v. 119 Not to be idle in idling times. **1936** E. S. GARDNER *Case of Stuttering Bishop* (1937) iii. 41 The ever-present throbbing undertone of sound.. from idling motors. **1968** [see *idle nozzle* s.v. IDLE *sb.* 5].

idle, obs. form of ISLE.

† **'idleby, 'idlesby.** *Obs.* Also 6–8 -bie, -bee. [f. IDLE *a.* + -BY 2: cf. *rudesby*. (Sometimes associated with *bee*.)] An idle fellow; a loafer.

α. **1589** NASHE *Anat. Absurd.* A j b, Might Ouids exile admonish such Idlebies to betake them to a new trade. **1635** PAGITT *Christianogr.* II. 39 Purgatory made many idle-bees swim in delicacy and voluptuousnesse. **1708** MOTTEUX *Rabelais* (1737) V. 217 Idle Lusks, slothful Idlebies.

β. **1611** COTGR., *Claquedent*, a lazie rogue, idle luske, slouthfull idlesbie. **1617** tr. *De Dominis on Rom.* xiii. 12. 43 Such a swarme of idlesbies. *a* **1639** W. WHATELEY *Prototypes* I. iv. (1640) 31 It is easie for Satan to entangle with his temptations the Idlesbee. **1681** W. ROBERTSON *Phraseol. Gen.* (1693) 753, I have played the idlesby to day.

† **'idleful**, *a.* *Obs.* [f. IDLE *a.* + -FUL.] Full of idleness, idle.

1483 CAXTON *Cato* B iij b, Ydelful and veyne talkyng. *a* **1652** BROME *Queen & Conc.* v. vi. Wks. 1873 II. 116 Though our Queen..be mercifully idleful.

† **'idle-headed**, *a.* *Obs.* [Parasynthetic f. *idle head*; cf. IDLE *a.* 8 a.]

1. Of little understanding or intellect; silly, foolish; crazy.

1598 SHAKS. *Merry W.* IV. iv. 36 The superstitious idle-headed-Eld Receiu'd, and did deliuer to our age This tale of Herne the Hunter, for a truth. **1614** R. TAILOR *Hog hath lost pearl* I. B iij, Our audience commonly are very simple idle-headed people. **1631** *Celestina* I. 12 Shee is idle-headed, and almost out of her little wits.

2. Off one's head, out of one's wits; distracted, delirious.

1599 HAKLUYT *Voy.* II. II. 108 Crazed in minde and halfe out of his wits..for whether he were put in fright of vs..or of sudden ioy..hee became idle-headed, and for eight dayes space neither night nor day tooke any naturall rest, and so at length died for lacke of sleepe. **1621** BURTON *Anat. Mel.* III. iv. I. ii. (1651) 656 Hilarion..for want of sleep became idle-headed. **1694** R. L'ESTRANGE *Fables* 132 The house was rifled and her trinkets went away with the rest. Upon this loss she fell idle-headed.

† **idlehed, -head.** *Obs.* [-HEAD.] Idleness.

c **1250** *Gen. & Ex.* 28 Ðoȝ hic folȝen idel-hed. **1594** CAREW *Tasso* (1881) 117 When night out issewd bore Silence, and sweuens [*printed* sweums] roaming idlehed.

'idlehood. *arch.* [-HOOD.] Idleness.

c **1540** *Pilgr. T.* 356 in *Thynne's Animadv.* (1875) App. i. 87 Now be they takyn..& we expellyd for our ydelhod. **1820** SCOTT *Monast.* xii, Thy craven fear my truth accused, Thine idlehood my trus abused.

† **'idlelaik, -leȝc.** *Obs.* [f. as prec. + -LAIK, = ON. *-leikr* action, f. *leikr* play.] Idleness.

c **1200** ORMIN 4738 Idellleȝȝc iss hæfedd plihht & wiþþreþþ wiþþ þin sawle. *Ibid.* 7845 Þatt he Ne lisste nohht wiþþ ære Till naness kinness idellleȝȝc.

idlely, obs. form of IDLY.

'idleman. *rare.* One who has no occupation; †formerly, in Ireland, a 'gentleman', as opposed to a working-man.

1331 in Rymer *Fœdera* (1821) II. II. 812/2 Item quod nullus..ducat Kernes, nec gentes vocatas Idelmen. **1428** *Waterford Arch.* in *10th Rep. Hist. MSS. Comm.* App. v. 295 Whatt ever man..arreste ony ydelman for ony trespasse done upon forayne grounde..shal pay to the commynes xx^{ti}. *li.* **1683** TRYON *Way to Health* 511 There are another sort of things called Idle-men or Gentle-men (but nothing gentle do we find from them). **1832** CARLYLE *Misc.*, *Corn-Law Rhymes* (1857) III. 164 A man, Workman or Idleman.

† **'idlement.** *Obs.* [f. IDLE *v.* + -MENT.] Idle or profitless occupation, idling.

1622 MABBE tr. *Aleman's Guzman d'Alf.* I. 118 These good things were not conferred vpon them..to waste and consume these good blessings of God in vnnecessary Idlements. **1631** *Celestina* I. 12 Let us not spend the time thus in idlements.

idleness ('aɪd(ə)lnɪs). Forms: see IDLE *a.* [OE. *ídelnes*, f. *ídel* IDLE + *-nes* -NESS.]

† **1.** Vanity: ***in*** (or ***on***) ***idleness***, in vain (cf. IDLE *sb.* 1 b). *Obs.*

c **825** *Vesp. Psalter* iv. 3 To hwon lufiað ȝe idelnisse, and soecað leasunge. *Ibid.* cxxvi[i]. 1 Nemðe dryhten timbrie hus, in idelnisse winnað ða timbriað ða. **1303** R. BRUNNE *Handl. Synne* 756 Swere nat hys name yn ydulnesse. **1340** *Ayenb.* 164 Salomon..zayde his dom ine zuiche manere, 'ydelnesse, ydelnesse, ydelnesse, and al þet ich izi is ydelnesse'. **1398** TREVISA *Barth. De P.R.* XIX. cxvi. (1495) 919 It is not sayd in ydelnesse (thou hast made all in nombre weyghte and mesure). *c* **1400** *Rom. Rose* 3323 Ye may wele ..Youre wordis waste in idilnesse.

2. Groundlessness, worthlessness; triviality; ineptitude, futility.

1645 BOATE *Irel. Nat. Hist.* (1652) 56 Who seeth not the idleness of that fiction concerning a certain Fountain [etc.]? **1758** H. WALPOLE *Catal. Roy. Authors* (1759) II. 17 Who.. could accommodate their minds to the utmost idlenesses of litterature. **1885** SIR J. W. CHITTY in *Law Rep.* 31 *Ch. Div.* 361 The idleness of the proceedings will be afterwards discovered.

† **3.** Light-headedness, imbecility; delirium; also folly, foolishness, silliness. *Obs. rare.*

a **1536** TINDALE *Answ. More* etc. (1850) 282 Interpreted.. as spoken of idleness of the head, by the reason of sickness. **1541** R. COPLAND *Guydon's Quest. Chirurg.*, The sayde cauteres applyed to the sayd places auayleth to ydlenes, fallynge euyll, paynes of the heade. **1612–15** BP. HALL *Contempl.*, *O.T.* XVIII. iv, What an idleness it is for foolish hypocrites to hope they can dance in a net, unseen of heaven! **1645** BOATE *Irel. Nat. Hist.* (1652) 181 This Fever.. accompanied with..idleness or raving, and restlessness.

4. The state or condition of being idle or unoccupied; want of occupation; habitual avoidance of work, inactivity, indolence; an instance of this. (Now the ordinary sense.)

bread of idleness, bread not earned by labour; cf. *idle bread* (IDLE *a.* 4 c).

c **1000** *Eccl. Inst.* §3 in Thorpe *Laws* II. 404 Seo ydelnes is þære sawle feond. *c* **1205** LAY. 24913 Idelnesse makeð mon his monscipe leose. *c* **1375** *Sc. Leg. Saints*, *Ninian* 233 Suerdome & Idilnes forto fle. *c* **1450** tr. *De Imitatione* III. lix. 137 Nature loueþ idelnes & bodely reste. **1576** FLEMING *Panopl. Epist.* 355 Apelles..was such an enimie to ydlenesse, that his pencill was never drie, but still drawinge a line. **1606** SHAKS. *Ant. & Cl.* I. iv. 76 'Tis time we twaine Did shew our selues i' th' Field..Pompey Thriues in our Idlenesse. **1611** BIBLE *Prov.* xxxi. 27 She looketh well to the wayes of her housholde, and eateth not the bread of idlenesse [COVERD. her bred with ydilnes]. **1711** STEELE *Spect.* No. 96 ¶3 Playing at Dice with other Servants, and the like Idlenesses. **1751** JOHNSON *Rambler* No. 153 ¶3 Unable to support any of his children, except his heir, in the hereditary dignity of idleness. **1856** FROUDE *Hist. Eng.* (1858) I. i. 51 The state..insisted as its natural right that children should not be allowed to grow up in idleness.

idler ('aɪdlə(r)). [f. IDLE *v.* + -ER^1.]

1. One who idles or is idle; one who spends his time in idleness; an indolent person.

(It has been used as the title of a periodical.)

1534 T. DORSET in *Suppress. Monasteries* (Camden) 36, I havyng nothyng to doo, as an idler went to Lambhethe to the byshopis place, to see what newis. **1687** CONGREVE *Old Bach.* I. i, Come, come, leave business to idlers, and wisdom to fools: they have need of 'em. **1758** JOHNSON (*title*) The Idler. **1781** COWPER *Retirem.* 681 An idler is a watch that wants both hands, As useless if it goes as when it stands. **1836** HOR. SMITH *Tin Trump.* (1876) 202 All rich idlers may be termed the representatives of former industry and talent. **1862** TYNDALL *Mountaineer.* i. 5 Had I not been a worker previous to my release from London, I could not now have been so glad an idler. **1874** GREEN *Short Hist.* ix. §3. 616 To all outer seeming Charles was the most consummate of idlers.

2. *Naut.* 'A general designation for all those on board a ship-of-war, who, from being liable to constant day duty, are not subjected to keep the night-watch' (Smyth *Sailor's Word-bk.*); on board a whaler, one who is not required to assist in the capture of whales (*Cent. Dict.*).

1794 NELSON 30 July in Nicolas *Disp.* (1845) I. 464 The Agamemnon cannot get under weigh: she has only her boats' crews and Maltese, besides idlers. **1819** J. H. VAUX *Mem.* I. xx. 229 It was but fair that I should sleep every night, as all persons under the denomination of 'Idlers' invariably do in king's ships. **1840** R. H. DANA *Bef. Mast* ii. 3 Having called up the 'idlers', namely, carpenter, cook, steward, etc. **1882** NARES *Seamanship* (ed. 6) 98 Marines, Idlers or Daymen.

3. a. *Machinery.* An idle wheel: see IDLE *a.* 5 b.

1875 in KNIGHT *Dict. Mech.*

b. A wheel or roller that when in contact with a moving belt, tape, or the like transmits no power but serves to support it, guide it, or make it taut. Freq. *attrib.*

1899 G. D. HISCOX *Mech. Movements* II. 37 A single belt, with two idlers, for tightening and directing the half twist of the belt. **1908** [see *belt conveyor* (BELT *sb.*^{1} 6)]. **1951** *Wire Ropes in Mines* (Inst. Mining & Metall.) 290 Supporting idlers are necessary to prevent severe whipping and vibration, if the distance is great between the drum and head sheave. However, if it is at all possible, the installation of idler sheaves should be avoided. **1962** A. NISBETT *Technique Sound Studio* 256 On a tape deck, the idler presses the tape against the capstan when the drive is switched on. **1969** *Times* 2 May (Suppl.) p. viii/7 This means that idler rolls made to this design will operate on conveyors at speeds up to and in excess of 1,000 ft. a minute. **1970** *Jrnl. Soc. Dyers & Colourists* LXXXVI. 87/1 The web follows an up-and-down zigzag path over idler rollers. **1972** *Reader's Digest Repair Manual* 551/4 Incorrect speed is generally due to a worn idler wheel.

4. *Railways.* (See quots.)

1909 *Cent. Dict.* Suppl., *Idler*, in *railroading*, an empty car; an empty. **1962** *Amer. Speech* XXXVII. 133 *Idler*, an empty car which is coupled to another car having a load of logs longer than the car, thus permitting the load to be coupled into a train.

idlesby: see IDLEBY.

'idleset. *Sc.* [f. IDLE *a.* + (app.) SET *sb.*, in sense of 'setting, putting'.] The condition of being reduced to idleness; want of employment.

1591 R. BRUCE *Serm. Kirk Edin.* Y viij a Ane verie slight object or short idleset will enkindle them. **1596** DALRYMPLE tr. *Leslie's Hist. Scot.* VI. 329 That na true vertue war able to hurt the body sa mekle as ydleset or ryches. **1830** GALT *Lawrie T.* VII. ii. (1849) 308 Idleset was to me a poor trade. **1856** MRS. OLIPHANT *Katie Stewart* 36 Lady Anne hersel is never held in such idleset.

idleship ('aɪd(ə)lʃɪp). Forms: see IDLE *a.* [f. IDLE *a.* + -SHIP.]

† **1.** Vanity (= IDLENESS 1); ***in idleship***, in vain.

a **1250** *Prov. Ælfred* 286 in *O.E. Misc.* 120 Idilschipe and ouer-prute þat lereþ yong wif vuele þewes. *c* **1315** SHOREHAM 93 Take nauȝt hys name in ydelschepe. **1357** *Lay Folks Catech.* 183 The secund commandement biddes us noght take In ydelship, ne in vayne the name of our god.

† **2.** Inactivity, want of occupation, indolence.

1357 *Lay Folks Catech.* 534 Ydelship..makes men lathe to begyn any gode dedis. **1390** GOWER *Conf.* II. 59 If I mighte spede With any maner besinesse, There shulde me none idelship Departen from her ladyship. **1496** *Dives & Paup.* (W. de W.) VI. xiv. 255 The wyse man sayth That ydelshyppe hath taught moche malyce.

3. As a mock title, after *lordship*, etc.

1860 *Luck Ladysmede* (1862) I. 80 Here I find your young idleship..holding a fool's court of japers and talemongers as usual. **1865** K. H. DIGBY *Short Poems* (1866) 24 But to write verses I have taken, In hopes your idleship to waken.

idlesse ('aɪdlɪs). *arch.* Also idless. [A pseudo-antique formation from IDLE *a.*; see -ESS^2.

App. fashioned after *humblesse*; the 19th c. romantic use dates from Scott.]

Idleness, viewed in a poetic or romantic light; *dolce far niente*.

1596 SPENSER *F.Q.* VI. ii. 31 My daies I haue not lewdly spent, Nor spilt the blossome of my tender yeares In ydlesse. **1748** THOMSON *Cast. Indol.* I. v, As Idless fancied in her dreaming mood. **1805** SCOTT *Last Minstr.* I. ii, The tables were drawn, it was idlesse all. **1812** BYRON *Ch. Har.* II. xciv, Who thus..Hath soothed thine idlesse with inglorious lays. **1848** LYTTON *Harold* XI. iv, The game..which amused the idlesse of that age. **1871** R. ELLIS *Catullus* lxiv. 38 Necks soften of oxen in idlesse. **1873** BROWNING *Red Cott. Nt.-cap* 160 Till Norman idlesse stock our England too.

'idleteth, 'idlety. *Sc.* and *north.* [f. IDLE *a.* The suffix is app. the Romanic -TY, which has a Sc. variant *-teth*; cf. DAINTETH.] = IDLENESS 4.

1585 JAS. I *Ess. Poesie* (Arb.) 74 Sen that tyme is sic a precious thing.. Flee ydilteth, which is the greatest lat. **1591** R. BRUCE *Serm. Kirk Edin.* Aa vij b, The ministerie is a worke and no idleteth. **1808–80** JAMIESON, *Idlety*, idleness. *Idleties*, idle frolics. *Aberd.* **1865** B. BRIERLEY *Irkdale* II. 13 He're a bit gan to idlety.

‖**idli** ('ɪdlɪ). [Tamil.] A steamed cake of rice and black gram, popular in southern India.

1958 R. K. NARAYAN *Guide* i. 16 Give me coffee and *idli*, please, first thing in the day. **1961** K. NAGARAIAN *Chron. Kedaram* iii. 64 There was no lack of mirth or old-fashioned cheer; plenty of *pongal* and *idlis* were consumed. **1971** *Hindustan Times Weekly* (New Delhi) (Suppl.) 4 Apr. p. iv/3, I learnt Tamil.. even got initiated into the mysteries of *idlis*. **1971** *Illustr. Weekly India* 25 Apr. 49/1 Dev closes the generation gap between Hema and him by the handsome device of welcoming this *idli*-white 'It Girl' with open arms. **1972** *New Yorker* 26 Aug. 28/1 Sell this poor child two *idlies*. Give him freshly made ones, not yesterday's. *Ibid.*, The *idlies*—so soft and pungent, with green chutney spread on top.

'idling, *vbl. sb.* [f. IDLE *v.* + -ING[1].] **1. a.** The action of the verb.

1843 BETHUNE *Sc. Fireside Stor.* 132 This course of idling .... was now drawing to a close.

b. *spec.* with reference to engines (see IDLE *v.* 4).

1916 R. T. NICHOLSON *Bk. of Ford* 151 You will run very economically, but you will find starting and 'idling' very difficult. **1925** A. W. JUDGE *Carburettors & Carburation* iv. 57 For slow running, or 'idling', two adjustments are provided. **1949** I. KATZ *Princ. Aircraft Propulsion Machinery* xx. 216 Idling is desirable from the standpoint of warm-up prior to flight. **1966** *McGraw-Hill Encycl. Sci. & Technol.* II. 478/1 Slight intake or exhaust valve leaks can make smooth idling impossible.

2. *attrib.*, as ***idling-place***; *spec.* designating parts of an engine concerned with idling, as ***idling adjustment, condition, jet, mixture, passage, screw, speed.***

1924 B. G. ELLIOTT *Automobile Repairing* x. 133 Carburettors which have *idling adjustments may be adjusted to overcome loading. **1940** *Chambers's Techn. Dict.* 437/1 *Idling adjustment*, a setting of the slow-running jet and throttle position of a carburettor, so as to give regular idling. **1943** A. P. FRAAS *Aircraft Power Plants* vii. 131 The model *H* idle system depends on a small hole in the tip of the metering pin to restrict the fuel flow under *idling conditions. **1929** *Motor World* 11 Jan. 23/2 In the new Zenith a special *idling jet, fed by its own independent compensating jet, is employed. **1942** B. A. SHIELDS *Air Pilot Training* xiii. 216 The engine is supplied with fuel for starting and idling by a special arrangement called an idling jet. **1959** *Motor Manual* (ed. 36) iii. 55 Here the *idling mixture is adjusted manually. **1925** A. W. JUDGE *Carburettors & Carburation* iv. 100 There is a slow running, or *idling passage, of the usual pilot jet type. **1879** GEO. ELIOT *Theo. Such* xviii. 315 An *idling-place of dilettanteism. **1972** *Drive* New Year 99/2 The throttle-stop, or *idling screw, will be found where the accelerator cable meets the carburettor; the mixture screw is at the base of the carburettor. **1932** CHATFIELD & TAYLOR *Airplane & its Engine* (ed. 2) viii. 139 The *idling speed is generally about 200 r.p.m. when the airplane is at rest on the ground. **1973** M. WOODHOUSE *Blue Bone* xii. 128, I.. opened the hood, screwing up the throttle control rod a couple of turns to raise the idling speed.

idlish ('aɪdlɪʃ), *a. rare.* Somewhat idle.

1865 CARLYLE *Fredk. Gt.* XX. vi. IX. 109 Not pleasant.. to an idlish man in weak health.

idly ('aɪdlɪ), *adv.* Forms: 1 **idellice,** 4 **ideliche, idillich, idili, ydilly,** 6 **idlelie, ydlelye, id-, ydelly, idiely, idlie,** 6–7 **idely,** 6–8 **idlely,** 6– **idly** [f. IDLE *a.* + -LY[2].]

1. Vainly, in vain; uselessly; frivolously, carelessly, ineffectively (cf. IDLE *a.*, senses 2–3).

c **825** *Vesp. Psalter* lxxxviii. 48 [lxxxix. 47] Nales soðlice idellice [L. *vane*] ðu ȝesettes bearn monna. *c* **1380** WYCLIF *Serm.* Sel. Wks. II. 341 þanne Crist hadde died for nouȝt and ideliche, wiþouten cause. **1382** —— *Deut.* v. 11 Thow shalt not mystaak the name of the Lord thi God idillich. **1565** JEWEL *Def. Apol.* (1611) 262 If ye list to cauill.. and.. idlely to play with the words and phrases of the ancient Fathers. **1625** HART *Anat. Ur.* II. xi. 122 [It] is not a thing so slightly to be passed ouer, as many may idlely imagine. **1700** ASTRY tr. *Saavedra-Faxardo* II. 89 When a Prince idlely squanders away his subjects fortunes. **1764** GOLDSM. *Trav.* 256 Thus idly busy rolls their world away. **1807** G. CHALMERS *Caledonia* I. I. iv. 121 Stukeley idly placed Colania, at Colechester, or Peebles. **1842** MRS. BROWNING *Grk. Chr. Poets* (1863) 70 Our heart is stirred, and not 'idly'. **1871** R. ELLIS *Catullus* v. 11 Then once heedfully counted all the thousands, We'll uncount them as idly.

†**b.** Incoherently (from affection of the brain), deliriously. *Obs.*

1565–73 COOPER *Thesaurus, Aliena loqui*,.. to speake idiely in sickenesse. *a* **1601** ? MARSTON *Pasquil & Kath.* III. 93 My brother will not liue long, he talkes idlely alreadie. **1632** tr. *Bruel's Praxis Med.* 399 They which talk idlely with amazednes.. for the most part die.

2. In an idle or lazy way; without working; inactively, indolently (cf. IDLE *a.*, senses 4–6).

1375 BARBOUR *Bruce* IV. 411 Othir syndry ȝeid thame by, As thai war masteris, ydilly. **1528** TINDALE *Obed. Chr. Man* Wks. (1573) 154/2 To get thee into a den, and lyue idlely, profitable to no man. **1547** *Act 1 Edw. VI*, c. 3 §10 Going loitering idlely about. **1613** PURCHAS *Pilgrimage* (1614) 309 They.. live idly upon almes. **1651** ISAACKSON in *Fuller's Abel Rediv., Andrewes* (1867) II. 160 He lived not idlely. **1736** FRANKLIN *Ess.* Wks. 1840 II. 81 He that idly loses five shillings' worth of time, loses five shillings. **1808** SCOTT *Marm.* VI. xx, And why stands Scotland idly now? **1874** GREEN *Short Hist.* iii. §5. 139 Sheriffs had stood idly by while the violence was done.

Ido ('i:dəʊ). [In this language, = offspring.] An artificial language, based on ESPERANTO, selected by the 'Delegation for the Adoption of an Auxiliary International Language' (founded at Paris in 1901), and made public in 1907. Hence **'Idist, 'Idoist,** a student or speaker of Ido; also ***attrib.***

The official name is 'Linguo Internaciona di la Delegitaro (Sistema Ido)'.

1908 *Daily Chron.* 7 Sept. 7/2 The new language has been named 'Ido', and its inventor [M. de Beaufront, of Geneva] claims that it is easier to learn and is more methodical than Esperanto, its parent. **1916** H. G. WELLS *Mr. Britling* I. v. §§10 ' There would be no English, no Germans, no Russians. Just Esperantists'..'Or Idoists,' said Herr Heinrich. **1922** O. JESPERSEN *Lang.* xviii. 347 Anyone who has written much in Ido [etc.]. **1926** *Encycl. Brit.* III. 906/1 In 1907 two Frenchmen, Messrs. Couturat and de Beaufront, produced a modification of Esperanto which they named simplified Esperanto. Owing to Esperantist protests, the 'linguo internaciona' was renamed Ido... The Idists claim that Ido is Esperanto rendered more scientific and natural. *Ibid.*, The chief Idist grammarian, Dr. Max Talmey, advocates what he calls 'Improved Ido' or 'Ilo' or 'Arulo'. **1928** O. JESPERSEN *Internat. Lang.* I. 24 The practical experiences of Volapükists, Esperantists and Idists .. have shown that the fears of sceptics are groundless with regard to pronunciation. **1946** H. JACOB *On Choice of Common Lang.* 79 The British section of the Ido-union. **1947** —— *Planned Auxiliary Lang.* 57 Idists practising the language for many years.

†**i-do,** *v. Obs.* [OE. *ȝedón* to put, do, make, = OS. *gidôn*, OHG. *gituon*, f. *dón* to DO.] *trans.* and *intr.* To do.

971 *Blickl. Hom.* 37 Eallum þæm godum þe ænig mon ȝedeþ his þæm nehstan. *a* **1000** *Andreas* 342 Hwæt þu us to duȝuðum ȝedon wille. *c* **1000** *Ags. Gosp.* Luke xxiii. 37 Ȝif þu si iudea cining, ȝedo þe halne. *c* **1175** *Lamb. Hom.* 29 He nule nefre mare eft ȝedon þeo sunnen. *c* **1205** LAY. 3612 Al heo iduden efter hire lare.

i-do, ME. pa. pple. of DO *v.*

idocrase ('aɪdəʊkreɪs). *Min.* [a. F. *idocrase* (Haüy 1796), f. Gr. εἶδος form, figure + κρᾶσις mixing, mixture (see CRASIS).] = VESUVIANITE.

1804 W. NICHOLSON tr. *Fourcroy's Chem.* II. 415 The idocrase is met with among the substances ejected from volcanos. **1811** PINKERTON *Petral.* II. 516 Several remarkable parasitic stones; such as I. The *Vesuvian* of Werner, and *idocrase* of Hauy. **1844** ALGER *Min.* 30 Idocrase occurs crystallized, either solitary or in groups. **1879** RUTLEY *Study Rocks* x. 142 Idocrase or Vesuvian is in its chemical composition closely allied to the lime-alumina garnets.

i-dodded, ME. pa. pple. of DOD *v.*

i-doȝt: see YDOUGHT.

idol ('aɪd(ə)l), *sb.* Forms: *α.* 3 **ydele, idele,** 4 **idel.** *ββ.* 4–6 **ydol(e,** 5–6 **ydoll,** 5–7 **idoll,** 6 **idole,** 4– **idol.** [ME. a. OF. *id(e)le*, and *idole*, ad. late L. *īdōl-um* (also *īdŏl-um* in Prudentius *c* 400, Sedulius *c* 470), image, form, spectre, apparition, in eccl. use 'idol', a. Gr. εἴδωλον image, phantom, idea, fancy, likeness, in LXX 'idol', f. εἶδος form, shape. The early OF. *idele, idle* (11th c.), represent the Latin '*īdŏlum*, the accentuation following that of the Greek. The current Fr. *idole* was adapted in 13th c. from L. *īdōlum*.]

The order of appearance of the senses in English does not correspond to their original development in Greek, where the sequence was apparently: 'appearance, phantom, unsubstantial form, image in water or a mirror, mental image, fancy, material image or statue', and finally, in Jewish and Christian use, 'image of a false god'. In English this last was, under religious influence, the earliest, and in ME. the only sense; hence (as also in Fr.) came sense 2. These are the only popular uses of the word. The other uses are 16th c. adoptions of earlier Greek senses, often however coloured by association with sense 1.

I. From Jewish and Christian use.

1. An image or similitude of a deity or divinity, used as an object of worship: applied to those worshipped by pagans, whence, in scriptural language, = false god, a fictitious divinity which "is nothing in the world' (1 Cor. viii. 4).

c **1250** *Gen. & Ex.* 1871 Godes ðat rachel hadde stolen.. And oðre ydeles broȝt fro sichem. *a* **1300** *Cursor M.* 11759 Al þair idels in a stund Grouelings fel vnto þe grund. **1340–70** *Alex. & Dind.* 754 For ȝour ydil idolus don ȝou ille wirche. **1382** WYCLIF *1 Cor.* viii. 4 We witen for an ydol is no thing in the world, and that ther is no God but oon. **1388** —— *Wisd.* xiv. 8 But the idol [1382 maumet] which is maad bi hond is cursid, bothe it, and he that made it. **1484** CAXTON *Fables of Æsop* vi, A man whiche had in his hows an ydolle the whiche oftyme he adoured as his god. **1553** EDEN *Treat. Newe Ind.* (Arb.) 17 Y^e priestes which serue ye Idols are had in chiefe reuerence. **1600** J. PORY tr. *Leo's Africa* I. 6 Some are Gentiles which worship Idols; others of the sect of Mahumet. **1651** HOBBES *Leviath.* IV. xiv. (1839) 650 But the name of idol is extended yet further in Scripture, to signify also the sun, or a star, or any other creature, visible or invisible, when they are worshipped for gods. **1727** DE FOE *Syst. Magic* I. i. (1840) 27 Their dumb idols, whom they called by the name of the holy gods. **1840** CARLYLE *Heroes* IV. (1858) 275 Idol is *Eidolon*, a thing seen, a symbol. It is not God, but a Symbol of God; and perhaps one many question whether any the most benighted mortal ever took it for more than a Symbol. **1860** PUSEY *Min. Proph.* 51 To say that it was made, was to deny that it was God. Hence the prophets so often urge this special proof of the vanity of idols.

b. Applied polemically to images or figures of divine beings and saints, and, more generally, to any material object of worship in a Christian church.

1545 BRINKLOW *Compl.* 52 [He] set vp in the same place another idol of S. Iohan Baptyst. **1554** T. SAMPSON in Strype *Eccl. Mem.* (1721) III. App. xviii. 47 Out of this mischievous idol the mass. **1566** in Peacock *Eng. Ch. Furniture* (1866) 44 One Rood with Marie and John and the rest of such Idolles was brent. *Ibid.* 45 Item an Idoll of all halowes—cut in peces by Mr. william ffearnes a year past. **1598** J. DICKENSON *Greene in Conc.* (1878) 122 Like to Idols, lay-mens bookes. **1608–11** BP. HALL *Epist.* I. vi. Wks. (1627) 284 The famous Kentish idoll moued her eyes and hands by those secret gimmers which now euery puppet-play can imitate. **1630** (*title*) The Great Idol of the Mass overthrown; a Sermon.. By a Protestant. **1839** KEIGHTLEY *Hist. Eng.* II. iv. 46 These various impostures were exposed at St. Paul's whither also were brought other idols from all parts of the country.

†**c.** A representation of a deity under some monstrous and non-natural form. *Obs.*

c **1400** MAUNDEV. xv. (1839) 164 Summe worschipen symulacres and summe ydoles. But betwene Symulacres and ydoles is a gret difference. For symulacres ben ymages made after lyknesse of men or of wommen, or of the sonne, or of the mone, or of ony best, or of ony kyndely thing. And ydoles is an ymage made of lewed wille of man, þat man may not fynden among kyndely thinges. As an ymage þat hath iiij hedes, on of a man, another of an hors, or of an ox, or of sum oþer best þat no man hath seyn.

2. *fig.* Any thing or person that is the object of excessive or supreme devotion, or that usurps the place of God in human affection. **a.** A thing.

[**1557** N. T. (Genev.) *1 John* v. 21 Babes kepe your selues from idoles.] **1562** A. SCOTT *Poems* (S.T.S.) i. 119 In sum hartis is gravit new agane Ane image, callit cuvatyce of geir; Now, to expell þat idoll.. God gif þe grace. **1639** T. BRUGIS tr. *Camus' Mor. Relat.* 351 It is only to save their purses that mettle, whereof they make their Idoll. **1706** PHILLIPS (ed. Kersey), *Idol*,.. any Object of one's Fondness. **1737** [S. BERINGTON] *G. di Lucca's Mem.* 4 Money, the Idol of other People, was the least of his Care. **1771** MACKENZIE *Man Feel.* xviii. (1803) 40 His darling idol, was the honour of a soldier. **1831** BREWSTER *Newton* (1855) II. xxii. 286 He tells him that space is now the idol of Englishmen.

b. A person so adored.

1591 SHAKS. *Two Gent.* II. iv. 144 *Pro.* Was this the Idoll, that you worship so? *Val.* Euen she. **1639** T. BRUGIS tr. *Camus' Mor. Relat.* 270 Whom shee openly cals her servant, and makes of him her Idoll. **1797** BURKE *Corr.* IV. 433 They who make a man an idol, when he is off his pedestal will treat him with all the contempt with which blind and angry worshippers treat an idol that is fallen. **1820** W. IRVING *Sketch Bk.* I. 44 How can she bear neglect? she has been the idol of society. **1839** THIRLWALL *Greece* VI. lii. 266 A hero who was the idol of his army.

II. From classical Greek (and Latin) use.

†**3.** An image, effigy, or figure of a person or thing; esp. a statue. *Obs.*

1548 HALL *Chron., Hen. VI* 115 The citezens of Orleaunce, had buylded in the honor of her, an Image or an Idole. **1583** STANYHURST *Æneis* II. (Arb.) 51 He rash charged with launce thee mystical idol. **1591** SPENSER *Ruins Rome* v, Her brave writings.. In spight of time.. Doo make her Idole through the world appeare. **1605** VERSTEGAN *Dec. Intell.* iii. (1628) 72 His Idoll was after his death honored prayed and sacrificed vnto.

†**b.** A counterpart, likeness, imitation; = IMAGE *sb.* 4, 4 c. *Obs.*

1590 SPENSER *F.Q.* II. ii. 41 Men.. Doe her adore.. As th' Idole of her makers great magnificence. **1641** *Chapman's Bussy D'Ambois* Plays 1873 II. 61 So women.. Are the most perfect Idols [1607 images] of the Moone. **1667** MILTON *P.L.* VI. 101 Th' Apostat in his Sun-bright Chariot sate, Idol of Majestie Divine.

†**c.** Aspect, appearance, likeness; = IMAGE *sb.* 3.

1584 R. SCOT *Discov. Witchcr.* XV. ii. (1886) 325 Orobas cometh foorth like a horsse, but when he putteth on him a mans idol, he talketh of divine vertue.

†**4.** An inert inactive person (who has the form, without the proper activity or energy, of a man). = F. *idole*, but in Eng. naturally associated with *idle* = IDLER. *Obs.*

1579 TOMSON *Calvin's Serm. Tim.* 238/1 It is not an honour of idlenesse, to bee called to this state, and therfore that he must not play the idoll, but.. must giue himselfe to it.. and take paines about it.

5. A visible but unsubstantial appearance, an image caused by reflexion as in a mirror, an incorporeal phantom.

1563 W. FULKE *Meteors* (1640) 41 b, Men have seen.. two Sunnes.. They are nothing else but Idols or Images of the Sunne, represented in an equall.. watry cloud. *c* **1611** CHAPMAN *Iliad* XXIII. 94, I see we have a soul In th' underdwellings, and a kind of man-resembling idol. **1676** HOBBES *Iliad* (1677) 344 In hell there souls are, though they have no hearts, But idols only are, and forms of men. **1678** CUDWORTH *Intell. Syst.* I. v. 784 By the Idol of the Soul Plotinus seems to mean, an Airy or Spirituous Body. **1822** SHELLEY *Faust* II. 386 It is an enchanted phantom, A lifeless idol. **1886** STEVENSON *Dr. Jekyll* x. 114, I looked upon that ugly idol [his image] in the glass.

6. A mental fiction; a phantasy or fancy.

1577 VAUTROUILLIER *Luther on Ep. Gal.* 123 In their heart they stablish, not the righteousnes of the lawe.. but a mere fantasie and an Idoll of the lawe. **1684** tr. *Agrippa's Van. Arts* 335 They frame to themselves.. so many Idols and Phantomes of their own Imaginations about divine things. **1899** FINDLAY in *Expositor* Feb. 94 They hold and grasp the

very God in Christ, and are no longer mocked with vain idols and phantoms of blessedness.

b. *Logic.* A false mental image or conception; a false or misleading notion; a fallacy; = IDOLUM 2.

[**1620** BACON: see *Idolum*.] **1678** CUDWORTH *Intell. Syst.* I. v. § 5. 884 But this is a mere *idolum specus*, an idol of the cave or den. *Ibid.* 886 This is but another idol of the Atheists den. **1733** SHAW tr. *Bacon's Nov. Org.* I. Aph. xxxix, There are four Kinds of Idols that possess the Mind of Man... We will ..call the first Kind, *Idols of the Tribe*; the second, *Idols of the Den*; the third, *Idols of the Market*; and the fourth, *Idols of the Theatre.* **1785** REID *Intell. Powers* VI. viii. 652 To every bias of the understanding, by which a man may be misled in judging, or drawn into error, Lord Bacon gives the name of idol. **1877** CONDER *Bas. Faith* ii. 81 Impenetrability, so confidently assumed as a self-evident primary property of matter..is seen to be an idol of our imagination.

†**7.** A fictitious personation; a counterfeit, sham; a pretender. (By Spenser used of a magic counterfeit.) *Obs.*

1590 SPENSER *F.Q.* III. viii. 11 To walke the woodes with that his Idole faire. **1611** SPEED *Hist. Gt. Brit.* IX. xx. §17 She well knew that this Lambert was but an Idoll, hammered out of the hot braine of that Boutefew Richard Simon, yet shee embraceth the occasion, countenanceth the Imposture. **1612** DAVIES *Why Ireland* etc. (1787) 47 Those two idols or counterfeits which were set up against him in the beginning of his reign. **1622** BACON *Hen. VII*, 29 He knew the pretended Plantagenet to be but an Idoll. **1660** FULLER *Mixt Contempl.* (1841) 252 King Henry the Seventh was much troubled with idols..pitiful persons who pretended themselves princes.

†**8.** The phrase *idol shepherd* used in Zech. xi. 17 in Geneva Bible and 1611 (where the Vulg. has *O pastor* et *idolum*, LXX *οἱ ποιμαίνοντες τὰ μάταια*, and the Revised Version of 1885 'worthless shepherd'), was frequently used in 17th c. polemics, sometimes with allusion to idolatry, sometimes with *idol* taken as = 'counterfeit' or 'sham' (sense 7), sometimes associated with *idle* (see sense 4), and so 'neglectful of duty'. *Obs.*

[**1535** COVERDALE *Zech.* xi. 17 O Idols shepherde, that leaueth the flocke.] **1560** BIBLE (Genev.) *ibid.*, O idole shepherd that leaueth the flocke. **1575–85** ABP. SANDYS *Serm.* (Parker Soc.) 71 Wo therefore to the idle and idol pastor. **1590** H. BARROW in *Confer.* iii. 55 We are ledd vnto Idoles when we are ledd vnto such Ministers as you, which ..are Idole Shepherds and Ministers. **1611** BIBLE *Zech.* xi. 17 Woe to the idoll shepheard that leaueth the flocke. **1612** T. TAYLOR *Comm. Titus* ii. 1 All idle, and idoll, Ministers that thrust themselues in for Pastors, and can onely feed themselues. **1634** CANNE *Necess. Separ.* (1849) 121 Reading of homilies in the church..is said to be..but the instrument of foolish and idol shepherds.

9. *attrib.* (without hyphen).

Often not distinguishable from the combinations in 10. *c* **1585** R. BROWNE *Answ. Cartwright* 33 He will haue..an Idol christ to be the life of the church. *Ibid.* 34 What remaineth but an Idol or counterfet christ? **1623** B. JONSON *Underwoods, Celebr. Charis* viii, Nay, I will not let you sit 'Fore your idol glass a whit! **1648** GAGE *West Ind.* xviii. 124 Placing there their Idoll Saints and Images. **1697** DRYDEN *Virg. Georg.* IV. 307 Besides, not Egypt, India..more With servile Awe their Idol King adore. **1827** KEBLE *Chr. Y.* 17th Sund. Trin. v, What idol shapes are on the wall pourtray'd. **1854** *Proc. Soc. Antiq.* III. 51 William Sells..exhibited.. three sketches of an Idol Figure of Mexican appearance.

10. *Comb.* **a.** simple attrib. Of an idol, of idols, as ***idol-altar***, ***-chapel***, ***-chariot***, ***-clergy***, ***-dwelling***, ***-figure***, ***-form***, ***-graith***, ***-house***, ***-priest***, ***-procession***, ***-prophet***, ***-room***, ***-sanctuary***, ***-service***, ***-shrine***, ***-throne***. **b.** Pertaining to or connected with idols or idol-worship, idolatrous, as ***idol-devotion***, ***-enjoyment***, ***-feast***, ***-fire***, ***-folly***, ***-hope***, ***-hymn***, ***-ocean***, ***-offering***, ***-pressure***, ***-sacrifice***, ***-sin***. **c.** appositive, as ***idol-block***, ***-devil***, ***-gold***, ***-notion***, ***-self***, ***-snake***.

1611 BIBLE *1 Macc.* i. 54 They..builded *idole altars throughout the cities of Iuda. **1860** PUSEY *Min. Proph.* 572 The dust of the idol-altars was cast into the brook Kedron. **1613** PURCHAS *Pilgrimage* (1614) 93 To worship..not that Virgin, on Earth holie, in Heaven glorious; but these idol-conceits, and *idol-blockes of her. **1860** PUSEY *Min. Proph.* 41 Each *idol-chapel..which they had multiplied to their idols. **1613** PURCHAS *Pilgrimage* (1864) 142 They haue those *Idol-chariots, like vnto Towers, to the drawing whereof, many thousands of deuout persons put their helping-hand. **1608** SYLVESTER *Du Bartas* II. iv. IV. *Decay* 226 Ba'l's *Idol-Clergy hee [Jehu] doth bring to nought. **1600** HOLLAND *Livy* 1355 In old time they called this *Idoll-devill, Vejovis, because he was deprived of all power to helpe and doe good. **1613** PURCHAS *Pilgrimage* (1864) 136 Which [sacrifices] in *Idoll-deuotion were all bestowed after on the poore. **1816** BYRON *Ch. Har.* III. xci, *Idol-dwellings, Goth or Greek. **1860** PUSEY *Min. Proph.* 554 God would wring his idol-sacrifices and *idol-enjoyments from him. **1641** HINDE *J. Bruen* xxx. 95 Such Wakes, and *Idol-Feasts. **1832** TENNYSON '*Love thou thy Land*' 69 A wind to puff your *idol-fires, And heap their ashes on the head. **1827** KEBLE *Chr. Y.* 5th Sund. Easter vii, An *idol form of earthly gold. **1638** SIR T. HERBERT *Trav.* (ed. 2) 297 Whither the lustfull Spaniard brought it, with his *Idol-gold from ravisht Indya. **1860** PUSEY *Min. Proph.* 193 Bethel, the centre of their *idol-hopes. **1577** tr. *Bullinger's Decades* (1592) 1022 To sacrifice at the altars of their gods in *idoll-houses, that is to say, in their idol temples. **1882** *Archæol. Cantiana* XIV. 103 A temple or idol-house where King Ethelbert according to the rites of his tribe was wont to pray. **1827** KEBLE *Chr. Y.* 3rd Sund. Lent viii, What seem'd an *idol hymn, now breathes of thee. **1663** J. SPENCER *Prodigies* (1665) 98 Common Experience (the surest Corrector of all *Idol Notions and hasty Reasonings). **1711** SHAFTESB. *Charac.* (1737) I. 60 Having..consecrated in our-selves certain idol-notions, which we will never suffer to be unveil'd. **1608** SYLVESTER *Du Bartas* II. iv. III. *Schisme* 371 A hundred Prophets.. Resist their rage, and from sad drowning keep The wracked planks on th' *Idol-Ocean deep. **1613** PURCHAS *Pilgrimage* (1614) 65 Their Priests collusions to make gaines of the *Idol-offerings. **1634** SIR T. HERBERT *Trav.* 187 Truly these *Idoll Priests are in such great esteeme among them. **1677** GILPIN *Demonol.* (1867) 439 He became an idol-priest in Thessalonica. **1613** PURCHAS *Pilgrimage* (1864) 140 Sir Iohn Mandeuile reporteth the same Historie of their *Idoll-Procession, and the ashes of those voluntary Martyrs. **1662** STILLINGFL. *Orig. Sacr.* II. v. §2 He that prophesied in the name of an Idol..this was the *Idol-Prophet. **1605** SYLVESTER *Du Bartas* II. iii. IV. *Captaines* 637 Contemns the Fountains of God's sacred Law, From *Idoll-Puddles poysoning drink to draw. **1613** PURCHAS *Pilgrimage* (1614) 444 In the entries of their houses they have an *Idol-roome, where they Incense these Deities morning and evening. **1860** PUSEY *Min. Proph.* 28 Partaking of their *idol-sacrifices and idolatrous rites. *Ibid.* 150 That God would desolate the *idol-sanctuaries of Israel. *a* **1711** KEN *Urania* Poet. Wks. 1721 IV. 485 For *Idol-self great God dethrones. **1568** CHENY in Strype *Ann. Ref.* (1709) I. lii. 525 Whether..a godly man may be at *idol-service with his body, his heart being with God. **1649** G. DANIEL *Trinarch., Rich. II*, cclxxvii, This *Idol-shrine..can boast of greater things Then many Temples famed. **1608** SYLVESTER *Du Bartas* II. iv. IV. *Decay* 184 Thou brought'st Samaria to Thine *Idol-Sin. **1610** G. FLETCHER *Christ's Vict.* I. xxi, Dens where *idol-snakes delight Again to cover Satan from their sight.

d. objective and objective genitive, as ***idol-breaker***, ***-maker***, ***-monger***; ***idol-breaking***, ***-framing***, ***-mongering***, ***-serving***. **e.** instrumental and locative, as ***idol-anchored***, ***-hated***, ***-prone***, ***-wedded***, adjs.

1852 *Meanderings of Mem.* I. 211 A heathen lamp supplies With meagre beam his *Idol-anchored eyes. **1579** FULKE *Confut. Sanders* 593 The idolaters haue had two generall councels of their side, the *idoll breakers none. **1840** CARLYLE *Heroes* IV. (1858) 285 We are to consider Luther as a Prophet Idol-breaker. **1897** *Daily News* 12 Oct. 6/3 The bigoted Sikander, whose *idol-breaking zeal procured him the title of But-Shikan, or 'Iconoclast'. **1677** GALE *Crt. Gentiles* III. 33 It drew their *Idol-framing hearts to set.. their adoration on these creatures, the Sun, Moon and Stars. **1603** H. CHETTLE *Sheph. Spring Song* viii. in *Eng. Mourn. Garm.* F iv b, The godly Constantine..Purgde this Iles aire from *Idoll-hated sinne. *a* **1619** FOTHERBY *Atheom.* I. xi. §5 (1622) 121 In making himselfe an Idol-God, hee becommeth both an *Idol-maker, and an Idol it selfe. **1612–15** BP. HALL *Contempl.*, *O.T.* XVIII. i, Abandon those *idol-mongers, restore devotion to her purity. **1889** C. EDWARDES *Sardinia* 184 *Idol-mongering was a profitable line of life. **1605** SYLVESTER *Du Bartas* II. iii. III. *Law* 1121 (*Idol-prone) example leading them. **1606** *Ibid.* II. iv. II. *Magnificence* 645 *Idol-serving Nile. **1605** *Ibid.* II. iii. IV. *Captaines* 217 This *Idol-wedded Town.

f. Special comb.: **idol's day**, a day on which an idol is honoured; **idol-shell**, a tropical mollusc of the family *Ampullariidæ*.

1671 MILTON *Samson* 1297 This Idol's day hath been to thee no day of rest. **1861** P. P. CARPENTER *Mollusca* (Cent.), The true ampullarias, which are peculiar to tropical America, and are called idol-shells by the Indians.

†**'idol**, *v.* *Obs. rare.* [f. prec. sb.] *trans.* To make an idol of; to idolize. (See also quot. 1644.)

1598 SYLVESTER *Du Bartas* II. ii. II. *Babylon* 20 Good princes..Who idol not their pearly scepter's glory. **1607** *Lingua* II. ii. D iij, And when they haue thus Idold her [a lady-love] like Pigmalion, they fall downe and worship her. **1644** ABP. MAXWELL *Sacrosancta Reg. Maj.* xi. 115 They Idoled the Covenant so much, that they would renounce God, if he would not be..the God of the Covenant. *Ibid.* xv. 147 He resolveth to Idoll or serve corruptly the humour and state of the people where he liveth.

idola: see IDOLUM.

†**'idolant.** [f. IDOL *v.* + -ANT[1].] = IDOLATER.

1592 SYLVESTER *Tri. Faith* iii, A countlesse hoast of craking Idolants By Esay's faith is here confounded all.

†**ido'laster**, *sb.* and *a.* *Obs.* Forms: 4–5 ydolastre, -aster, 6 idolastre, (-estour), 7 idolaster. [a. OF. *idolastre* (now *idolâtre*), var. (by confusion with suffix *-astre*, *-âtre*) of *idol-*, *ydolatre*: see IDOLATER.]

A. *sb.* An early equivalent of IDOLATER 1.

c **1386** CHAUCER *Pars. T.* ¶675 What difference is bitwixe an ydolastre [*v.r.* ydolaster] and an Auaricious man. *c* **1430** LYDG. *Min. Poems* (Percy Soc.) 139 Or Austin cam, we slombryd in dirknesse, Lyk ydolastres. **1503** HAWES *Examp. Virt.* vii. st. 54 In whiche tyme they were ydolestours. **1555** W. WATREMAN *Fardle Facions* II. xi. 237 His [Mahomet's] father was an idolastre after the maner of the heathen. **1616** BULLOKAR, *Idolaster*, an Idolater.

B. *adj.* Idolatrous. (OF. *idolastre*, F. *idolâtre*, primarily adj.)

1584 HUDSON *Judith* iv. 358 Her yv'ry neck and brest of alabastre Made Heathen men of her more idolastre.

idolater (aɪ'dɒlətə(r)). Forms: α. 4 ydolatrour, 4–6 ydolatrer, 4–7 idolatrer, (6 ydol-, idolatrar). β. 6 ydolatre, -ater, -atour, idoloter, 7– idolator, 6– idolater. [Gr. *εἰδωλο-λάτρης* (N.T.), idol-worshipper, gave eccl. L. (Tertullian) *īdōlolatrēs*, later *-latra* (see IDOLOLATER), shortened in Romanic to *idola'tra* (Sp., Pg. *idola'tra*, It. *idola'tro*), OF. *idolatre*, *ydolatre*, whence (by confusion with the suffix *-astre*, *-âtre*) *idolastre*, *idolâtre* (see IDOLASTER). Our α form *idolatrer*, *-rour*, was either f. OF. *idolatre* + agent-suffix *-er*, *-our*, or was a native formation from *idolatr-y* (cf. *astronom-y*, *-er*, etc.) with same suffix; the β form *idolater*, *-our*, was either a phonetic simplification of *idolatrer*, *-our*, or ad. F. *idolatre*, *idolâtre*.]

1. A worshipper of idols or images; one who pays divine honours to an image or representation of a god, or to any natural object as a deity.

α. *c* **1380** WYCLIF *Wks.* (1880) 88 þes wickid ydolatrours. **1382** —— *1 Cor.* x. 7 Neithir be ȝe maad ydolatreris (that is, worschiperis of false mawmetis). *c* **1449** PECOCK *Repr.* II. iii. 153 Vsers of ymagis ben ydolatrers. **1474** CAXTON *Chesse* 63 They forgid ydolles and were ydolatreres. **1526** *Pilgr. Perf.* (W. de W. 1531) 194 Brought vp in Egipt amonge ydolatrars. **1557** N. T. (Genev.) *Eph.* v. 5 No..couetous person, which is an idolatrer. **1574** N. DANIEL in Grosart *Spenser's Wks.* I. 422 We lose the love of Idolatrars. **1624** DONNE *Devotions* Expostul. xx. (ed. 2) 492 The present execution of manifest Idolatrers.

β. **1526** *Pilgr. Perf.* (W. de W. 1531) 3 But takyng & gyuynge it to stockes and stones, as ydolatres, worshyppynge them for goddes. **1529** MORE *Suppl. Soulys* Wks. 315/1 Idolaters, Turkes, Saracens, and Painims. *c* **1540** *Pilgr. T.* 336 in *Thynne's Animadv.* (1875) App. i. 86 We be called fornicators when tyme we be ydolotors, & take antychrist for our hed. **1562** WINȜET *Cert. Tractates* i. Wks. 1888 I. 9 Ignorantis off God and ydolatouris. **1658** SIR T. BROWNE *Hydriot.* i. 3 The Chaldeans, the great Idolaters of fire. **1687** A. LOVELL tr. *Thevenot's Trav.* III. 38 If these Indian Women be Idolators, they go bare-faced; and if Mahometans, they are Vailed. **1710** NORRIS *Chr. Prud.* iii. 123 We call them idolaters..who pay that Religious Worship which is due only to God, to something else that is not God. **1841** KITTO *Bible Hist. Palestine* 222 Many superstitions..of the ancient idolaters. **1852** ROBERTSON *Lect. Ep. Cor.* xlvii. (1859) 430 The idolater is not merely he who worships images, but he who gives his heart to something which is less than God.

2. An adorer, idolizer, devoted admirer *of* (some person or thing).

c **1566** J. ALDAY tr. *Boaystuau's Theat. World* O ij b, Old covetous men, ydolaters of their treasures. **1652** COTTERELL *Cassandra* VI. (1676) 343 He was a Lover, or rather an Idolater of that sex. **1660** WILLSFORD *Scales Comm.* Pref. A v, The Parasites of the Rich, or the Idolaters of Fortune. **1781** COWPER *Retirem.* 220 The lover too..Tender idolater of absent charms. **1884** SWINBURNE in *19th Cent.* Oct. 554 Had not the idolators of either [author] insisted..on the superior claims of their respective favorite.

idolathite, -yte, erron. forms of IDOLOTHYTE.

idolatrer: see IDOLATER.

idolatress (aɪ'dɒlətrɪs). [f. IDOLATER + -ESS.] A female idolater. Also *fig.*

1613 PURCHAS *Pilgrimage* (1614) 243 Having to wife an Egyptian Idolatresse. **1667** MILTON *P. L.* I. 445 That uxorious King, whose heart..Beguil'd by fair Idolatresses, fell To Idols foul. **1796** SEWARD *Anecd.* (ed. 3) III. 26 Jeanne was burnt..as a sorceress, an idolatress, a blasphemer of God. **1860** PUSEY *Min. Proph.* 608 The marriage with idolatresses brought..the profanation by their idolatries.

idolatric (aɪdəʊ'lætrɪk), *a.* *rare.* [ad. mod.L. *īdōlatric-us* (15–16th c. in Du Cange), f. *īdōlatrīa*, for *īdōlolatrīa* idolatry: see -IC. Cf. F. *idolâtrique* (Littré).] = next.

1669 GALE *Crt. Gentiles* I. II. viii. 103 This Idolatric Deifying of the Sun. **1677** *Ibid.* III. 106 Enticed to Idolatric Adoration. **1716** M. DAVIES *Athen. Brit.* II. 422 Christ.. would look upon such an Honour..to be Idolatrick. [**1887** E. JOHNSON in *Antiqua Mater* 145 The quarter whence the anti-idolatric movement came.]

†**idolatrical** (aɪdəʊ'lætrɪkəl), *a.* *Obs.* [f. as prec. + -AL[1].] Of or pertaining to idolatry; idolatrous.

1550 ? HOOPER *Exam. Apparel* ***iv, We haue in our Church no publique worshyppyng of Idolles, no Heathenishe or idolatrical sacrifice. **1562** WINȜET *Cert. Tractates* iii. Wks. 1888 I. 28 He callis the saidis solenniteis idolatrical, superstitius. **1662** THORNDIKE *Just Weights & Meas.* xix, This is demonstration that the soul has nothing in it that is idolatrical. **1796** PEGGE *Anonym.* (1809) 177 If Christ be not God, their worship of him is idolatrical.

Hence †**ido'latrically** *adv.*, in an idolatrous way.

1669 GALE *Crt. Gentiles* I. II. viii. 103 An heart Idolatrically inclined.

†**ido'latrious**, *a.* *Obs.* *rare*$^{-1}$. [f. med.L. *idolatrī-a* IDOLATRY + -OUS: cf. *industri-ous*, etc.] = IDOLATROUS.

1563 *Homilies* II. *Idolatry* III. (1859) 224 The idolatrious [**1582** idolatrous] opinions of our image maintainers.

idolatrize (aɪ'dɒlətraɪz), *v.* [f. IDOLATR-Y + -IZE; cf. *botanize*, *rhapsodize*, *scrutinize*.]

†**1.** *intr.* To worship an idol or idols; to commit or practise idolatry. Also, *to idolatrize it*. *Obs.*

1592 DANIEL *Compl. Rosamond* xxii, All that honour thee Idolatrize. **1596** FITZ-GEFFRAY *Sir F. Drake* (1881) 26 Cease (fondlings) henceforth to idolatrize With Venus, your Carpathean-sea borne Queene. **1613–16** W. BROWNE *Brit. Past.* I. i, The Persians did idolatrise Unto the Sunne. **1628** WITHER *Brit. Rememb.* VII. 1321 With worldly Honor, some idolatrize. **1640** FULLER *Joseph's Coat* iv. (1867) 142 Hast thou not idolatrized to thy friend? **1664** H. MORE *Myst. Iniq.* 283 A Christian City or Polity Idolatrizing and debauching others with Idolatry. **1706** PHILLIPS (ed. Kersey), *To Idolatrize*, to commit Idolatry.

†**b.** ? To exercise an incitement to idolatry.
1601 CHESTER *Love's Mart.* 143 Ore my heart your eyes do idolatrize.

2. *trans.* To make an idol of, to worship idolatrously. Chiefly in *fig.* use: To adore, to admire excessively; to idolize.
1615 DANIEL *Hymen's Tri.* II. i, Idolatrize not so that Sex. **1631** BRATHWAIT *Whimzies, Traveller* 93 It hath brought him to idolatrize himselfe. **1637** GILLESPIE *Eng. Pop. Cerem.* III. ii. 16 The consecrated hoste which Papists Idolatrize. **1740** CHEYNE *Regimen* 9–10 Idolatrising the Creatures, the moral Powers..being erased [etc.]. **1830** *Blackw. Mag.* XXVIII. 244 An age which..idolatrizes the tangible and the material. **1894** GROSART in *Green Pastures* Introd. 10 We are so used to idolatrize Shakespeare because of his simply incomparable genius.

†**3.** To render idolatrous. *Obs. rare.*
1678 CUDWORTH *Intell. Syst.* I. iv. §36. 628 Christianity.. was thereby itself paganized and idolatrized.

Hence **i'dolatrizing** *vbl. sb.* and *ppl. a.*; **i'dolatrizer**, one who idolatrizes: an idolizer or idolater.
1614 T. ADAMS *Devil's Banquet* 2 Erring, adulterating, idolatrising Solomon. *a* **1619** FOTHERBY *Atheom.* I. vi. §2 (1622) 41 For, how should..idolatrizing, be sinne; if there were not a God? **1642** A. PROWSE *Let. to Friend in Lond.* 3 That minor part so much cryed up, and doted on by the Idolatrizers thereof. **1817** G. S. FABER *Eight Dissert.* IV. iii. (1845) I. 301 Balaam..a seer of the idolatrising Gentiles.

idolatrous (aɪ'dɒlətrəs), *a.* [f. IDOLATER, F. *idolâtre* + -OUS.]
1. Of, pertaining to, or of the nature of idolatry.
1550 BALE *Apol.* 55 Your papa..whyche appoynted them to hys ydolatrouse dayes of ydelnesse. **1592** GREENE *Groat's W. Wit* (1617) 37 Were it not an idolatrous oath, I would sweare by sweet S. George. **1662** STILLINGFL. *Orig. Sacr.* II. vii. §10 The Idolatrous customs of those Nations. **1765** T. HUTCHINSON *Hist. Mass.* I. iv. 428 The exception to the word Sunday was founded upon its superstitious idolotrous origin. **1841** ELPHINSTONE *Hist. Ind.* I. 443 Their religion, however, though idolatrous, has no resemblance whatever to that of the Hindús. **1863** W. PHILLIPS *Speeches* iii. 46 Idolatrous veneration for the state.

2. Used in or devoted to idol-worship. ? *Obs.*
1613 PURCHAS *Pilgrimage* (1614) 98 Because of the judgements for the idolatrous high places in it. **1647** FULLER *Good Th. in Worse T.* (1841) 103 He saw an idolatrous altar at Damascus. **1796** MORSE *Amer. Geog.* II. 555 The idolatrous temple of Jaganaut. **1800** *Asiat. Ann. Reg., Misc. Tr.* 232/1 The road extends through innumerable towns, with idolatrous temples.

3. Of a person: Worshipping images or idols; given to the worship of idols or false gods.
1600 E. BLOUNT tr. *Conestaggio* 9 So as whole Realmes which were Idolatrous, are now obedient to the Apostolique Sea. **1611** BIBLE *2 Kings* xxiii. 5 Hee put downe the idolatrous priests whome the kings of Iudah had ordeined to burne incense. **1671** MILTON *Samson* 1364 The Philistines Idolatrous, uncircumcised, unclean. **1790** GIBBON *Misc. Wks.* (1814) V. 189 Zangwebar, the coast of the Zenghis, was still savage and idolatrous. **1822** SHELLEY *Chas. I*, I. 85 To that idolatrous and adulterous torturer.

†**b.** Constr. *of*. *Obs. rare.*
1639 T. BRUGIS tr. *Camus' Mor. Relat.* 295 [He] Makes her a Countesse, and withall becomes so idolatrous of her, that [etc.].

Hence **i'dolatrousness**, the quality or condition of being idolatrous.
1583 GOLDING *Calvin on Deut.* xxxii. 189 The parties.. that turne away from this lawe through their idolatrousnesse. **1633** AMES *Agst. Cerem.* II. 487 The formalities of that Altar, conteyning all the idolatrousnesse that was in it. **1764** HARMER *Observ.* XXI. vi. 276 How came this notion of the idolatrousness of Nebuchadnezzar's command to be so universal?

idolatrously (aɪ'dɒlətrəslɪ), *adv.* [f. prec. + -LY².] In an idolatrous manner.
1583 STUBBES *Anat. Abus.* II. (1882) 112 Any thing that hath been idolatrously abused by the papists. **1637** GILLESPIE *Eng. Pop. Cerem.* III. ii. 23 That the Idolatrously minded might not find their pathes. *a* **1791** WESLEY *Serm.* lxxxiii. I. 18 Wks. 1811 IX. 433 They are..[not] permitted to love one another idolatrously. **1882–3** SCHAFF *Encycl. Relig. Knowl.* I. 88 The Assyrians..used very extensively drawings and figures of animals, but probably not idolatrously.

idolatry (aɪ'dɒlətrɪ). Forms: 3–6 **ydolatrie, -y, -ee,** 4–6 **idolatrye,** 4–7 **-ie,** 6 **-i,** 5– **idolatry.** [a. OF. *idol-, ydolatrie* (12th c. in Littré), mod.F. *idolâtrie* = It., Sp. *idolatria*, Pr. *ydolatria*, repr. late L. (and Common Romanic) *īdōlatrīa* (Vulgate, Acts xvii. 16), shortened form of eccl. L. *īdōlolatrīa* (Tertullian), a. Gr. (N.T.) *εἰδωλολατρεία*, f. *εἴδωλον* IDOL + *λατρεία* service, worship, LATRIA.]
1. The worship of idols or images 'made with hands'; more generally, the paying or offering of divine honours to any created object.
c **1250** *Gen. & Ex.* 4143 Ydolatrie, ðat was hem lef, ofte vt-wroȝte hem sorȝes dref. **1382** WYCLIF *Acts* xvii. 16 Seynge the citee ȝouun to ydolatrie. **1494** FABYAN *Chron.* V. xcvii. 71 He had forsaken his Idolatry, and was becomyn Seruaunt of the oonly God. **1526** TINDALE *1 Pet.* iv. 3 We have spent the tyme..in eatynge, drynkynge and in abhominable ydolatrie [**1611** idolatries]. **1699** BURNET *39 Art.* xxviii. (1700) 340 This we believe is plain Idolatry, when an Insensible piece of Matter, such as Bread and Wine, has Divine Honors paid it. **1781** COWPER *Hope* 499 The gross idolatry blind heathens teach. **1833** L. RITCHIE *Wand. by Loire* i. 9 [The cathedrals] those huge temples of Catholic idolatry. **1864** J. H. NEWMAN *Apol.* 413 In the midst of the abominable idolatries and impurities of that fearful time, they could not do otherwise.
attrib. **1621** BP. MOUNTAGU *Diatribæ* III. 547 In their Idolatry seruice.

†**b.** *pl.* Idolatrous things or objects. *Obs.*
1671 MILTON *P.R.* III. 418 To worship calves, the deities Of Egypt..And all the idolatries of heathen round.

2. Immoderate attachment to or veneration for any person or thing; admiration savouring of adoration.
c **1386** CHAUCER *Pars. T.* ¶674 Therfore seith seint Paul ad Ephesios 5° that an Auaricious man is the thraldom of ydolatrie [*v.r.* is thral to ydolatrie]. **1526** *Pilgr. Perf.* (W. de W. 1531) 6 They make all that loueth them inordynately to commytte ydolatry. **1557** N. T. (Genev.) *Col.* iii. 5 Couetousnes which is idolatrie. **1568** GRAFTON *Chron.* II. 92 [They] caused that place [where a popular man was executed] to be watched, that such Idolatrie should there no more be used. **1639** T. BRUGIS tr. *Camus' Mor. Relat.* 335 Those tearmes of Idolatrie which grow in the mouthes of lovers. **1780** COWPER *Progr. Err.* 461 Thou god of our idolatry, the Press. **1837** LYTTON *E. Maltrav.* II. i, He usually falls at last into the popular idolatry.

idole, obs. form of IDOL.

†**'idolet.** *Obs.* [f. IDOL *sb.* + -ET¹. Cf. It. *idoletto.*] A little idol.
1674 BLOUNT *Glossogr.* (ed. 4), *Idolet*, a little Idol. **1770** J. BARETTI *Journ. Lond. to Genoa* I. vi. 36 Descanting upon every rusty medal they have, upon every broken idolet.

'idol-,god. A deity that is an idol; a false god, an idol. Also *transf.*
1607 TOPSELL *Four-f. Beasts* (1658) 183 A monster, having a Mans face, and a Goats legs, they call it Silvanus, and place it in the rank of idoll Gods. **1608** SYLVESTER *Du Bartas* II. iv. IV *Decay* 481 Th' High-places down hee pashes ..burns th' Idol-gods to ashes. **1781** COWPER *Expostulation* 216 They set up self, that idol-god, within. *a* **1849** J. C. MANGAN *Poems* (1859) 81 Gold is lord and idolgod of all.

i'dolify, *v.* [f. IDOL *sb.* + -(I)FY.] *trans.* To make an idol of.
1838 SOUTHEY *Doctor* cxliv. V. 99 If it had been the fate of Nobs thus to be idolified.

†**ido'lillo.** *Obs.* [f. IDOL *sb.* + Sp. dim. suffix *-illo.*] A diminutive idol.
1646 J. GREGORY *Note & Obs.* (1650) 54 If the confluence could haue beene perswaded..that these enshrined Idolillos of Diana..were no Gods because they were made with hands.

†**'idolish,** *a. Obs.* [f. IDOL *sb.* + -ISH.] Of or pertaining to idols or their worship; heathenish; also, idolatrous.
1577–87 HOLINSHED *Chron.* I. 120/2 Part of his commons louing this life..began to repaire their idolish churches, and fell to the worshipping of idols. **1605** BROUGHTON *Corrupt. Handl. Relig.* 95 The Mother of Beniamin, because she was somwhat idolish in her Fathers Theraphin, dyed as soone as twelue starres arose to Iacob. **1641** MILTON *Ch. Govt.* II. Concl. (1851) 175 When they have stufft their Idolish temples with the wastefull pillage of your estates.

idolism ('aɪdəlɪz(ə)m). [f. IDOL *sb.* + -ISM.]
1. The practice of idolatry.
1608 SYLVESTER *Du Bartas* II. iv. v. *Decay* 502 Much less permits he..one signe to stand Of idolism, or idle superstition. *Ibid.* 518 A people wholly drown'd In idolism, and all rebellious sins. **1816** COLERIDGE *Statesm. Man.* 365 Till they have cast out the common idol..and with it the whole service and ceremonial of idolism.

2. The action of idolizing, or making an idol (*of* anything); an idolization.
1825 COLERIDGE *Aids Refl.* (1848) I. 328 The vaunted Mechanico-corpuscular philosophy, with both its twins, Materialism on the one hand, and Idealism, rightlier named subjective Idolism, on the other. *Ibid.* (1858) I. App. 477 The idolism of the unspiritualized understanding. **1834** *Blackw. Mag.* XXXV. 35 Justice, Modesty..and other poetic idolisms of his new Pantheon.

3. A false mental image or notion, a fallacy: cf. EIDOLON, IDOLUM 2.
1671 MILTON *P. R.* IV. 234 How wilt thou reason with them, how refute Their Idolisms, Traditions, Paradoxes? **1897** W. P. KER *Epic & Rom.* 208 Quite unaffected by the common medieval fallacies and 'idolisms'.

idolist ('aɪdəlɪst). [f. as prec. + -IST.] A believer in or worshipper of idols; an idolater. Also *attrib.*
1614 SYLVESTER *Bethulia's Rescue* II. 498 You shall..make ruddy Mocmur's Floud, With Idolist Assyrian Armies bloud. **1624** F. WHITE *Repl. Fisher* 230 This Idolist heapeth conclusion vpon conclusion. **1671** MILTON *Samson* 453, I.. to God have brought Dishonour, obloquy, and op't the mouths Of Idolists, and Atheists. **1818** J. BROWN *Psyche* VII. 217 Idolists fall prostrate, scar'd At the rude gods, themselves prepar'd.

Hence **ido'listic** *a.*, recognizing idols, idolatrous.
1846 SARA COLERIDGE in *Mem. & Lett.* II. 92 The fault is not in the poet but in the gross idolistic system to which he adhered.

idolization (,aɪdəlaɪ'zeɪʃən). [f. next + -ATION.] The action of idolizing.
1853 JERDAN *Autobiog.* III. xii. 169 It but weakly expressed the idolisation which the constant watch over the expansion of that..most natural Intelligence inspired. **1885** *Spectator* 30 May 705/2 An idolisation of childhood.

idolize ('aɪdəlaɪz), *v.* [f. IDOL *sb.* + -IZE.]
1. a. *trans.* To make an idol of, to render to (a person or thing) such adoration or worship as is commonly given to an idol; hence, to venerate, adore, or love to excess. (Cf. IDOLATRIZE *v.* 2.) Also *absol.*
1598 SYLVESTER *Du Bartas* II. ii. IV. *Columnes* 763 Whose soule, seduced by his erring eyes, Doth some proud Dame devoutly Idolize. **1644** CROMWELL *Sp.* 9 Dec. in *Carlyle*, They [my soldiers] do not idolise me, but look upon the Cause they fight for. **1790** BURKE *Fr. Rev.* Wks. V. 249 The affectation, which..has prevailed in Paris..for idolizing the memory of your Henry the Fourth. **1834** LYTTON *Pompeii* III. iii, From my childhood upward I have idolised the dreams of Virtue. **1882** MISS BRADDON *Mt. Royal* I. iii. 97 He idolizes you, and he lets all the world see it. **1919** M. K. BRADBY *Psycho-Anal.* 65 For instance, one person may be prone to jealousy, another to idolise.

b. In literal sense: To make into an idol, to worship as an idol or idolatrously. ? *Obs.*
1669 GALE *Crt. Gentiles* I. II. ii. 15 The Moon is the same ..with Diana, which the Gauls greatly idolized. **1722** J. COVEL *Acc. Grk. Ch.* 354 The Brasen Serpent..when it was abused and Idolized. **1824** T. FENBY *Paraphr. Isa.* ix. 7 He ..Carveth a log of soundest wood To idolize.

2. *intr.* To practise idolatry (cf. IDOLATRIZE *v.* 1).
1631 H. SHIRLEY *Mart. Souldier* II. iii. in Bullen *O. Pl.* I. 200 Twas I that taught thee first to Idolize. **1652** GAULE *Magastrom.* Ep. Ded. A ij b, Then the Jewish Apostates Idolized with it and by it. *a* **1864** FAIRBAIRN (WEBSTER 1864), To idolize after the manner of Egypt.

Hence **'idolizing** *vbl. sb.* and *ppl. a.*
1637 GILLESPIE *Eng. Pop. Cerem.* III. iv. 50 The Idolizing of the Ceremonies. **1677** GILPIN *Demonol.* (1867) 365 A sinful idolizing of the creature. **1870** RUSKIN *Aratra Pent.* II. §33 The second great condition for the advance of the art of sculpture is that the race should possess, in addition to the mimetic instinct, the realistic or idolizing instinct.

idolized ('aɪdəlaɪzd), *ppl. a.* [f. prec. + -ED¹.]
a. Made into an idol; considered or treated as an idol. **b.** Revered or loved to excess.
1646 BP. MAXWELL *Burd. Issach.* 28 That too too much Idolized Reformation. **1649** MILTON *Eikon.* i. Wks. (1851) 346 To throw contempt and disgrace..upon this his Idoliz'd Book. **1705** STANHOPE *Paraphr.* II. 242. **1852** MISS YONGE *Cameos* (1877) IV. i. 13 She had cared little for her husband in comparison with her idolized brother.

idolizer ('aɪdəlaɪzə(r)). [f. as prec. + -ER¹.] One who idolizes.
1660 H. MORE *Myst. Godl.* VII. i. 281 Over-doting Idolizers of the Faculty of Free will. **1757** FOOTE *Author* I. Wks. 1799 I. 134, I thought these midwives to the muses were the idolizers of you, their favourite sons. **1840** ALFORD in *Life* (1873) 25 What wonder then if we became idolizers of Byron? **1889** H. F. WOOD *Englishman Rue Caïn* i, He was a dreaming idolizer, and idolizers are foredoomed.

idolo-, combining form of Gr. *εἴδωλον* IDOL, as in ‖**idolodou'lia** [Gr. *δουλεία* DULIA], veneration of an inferior kind given to idols or images. **idolo'graphical** *a.*, descriptive of idols. **i'dolomancy** [Gr. *μαντεία* divination by idols]. **idolo'mania,** †**ido'lomany** [MANIA], an infatuated devotion to idols; zealous idolatry.
1579 FULKE *Confut. Sanders* 608 It vexeth you that Maister Iewell calleth your worshippinge of Images *Idolodoulia, because you will not haue it Idololatria. **1826** SOUTHEY *Lett.* (1856) III. 539 Recorded in their extraordinary *idolographical work. **1652** GAULE *Magastrom.* 165 *Idolomancy, [divining by] Idolls, Images, Figures. **1624** GEE *Foot out of Snare* iii. 19 The practice of the people among them..is no lesse than *Idolomania. **1660** TRAPP *Comm. Isa.* xl. 19 So do the Turkes at this day [forbid images], to the shame of Papists' Idolomania. **1624** BP. MOUNTAGU *Gagg* xlv. 310 Then your *Idolomanie in Images, with stocks and stones, were clean dashed. **1654** TRAPP *Comm. Ps.* cxv. 4 The like Idolomany is at this day found among Papists.

idoloclast (aɪ'dɒləklæst). [f. IDOLO- + Gr. *-κλάστης* breaker, after *iconoclast.*] A breaker or demolisher of idols, an iconoclast.
1843 HARE in *Arnold's Hist. Rome* III. Pref., In an idolatrous age, one of the men we most need is an idoloclast ..Such an idoloclast we had in Dr. Arnold. **1846** DE QUINCEY *Sophocles' Antigone* Wks. XIV. 204 Many idoloclasts, who will expose the signs of disease, which zealots had interpreted as power.

Hence **idolo'clastic** *a.* = ICONOCLASTIC.
1851 *Beddoes' Poems* Mem. 21 To the transient popularities of the day..a mind so idoloclastic would show but little homage. **1852** *Tait's Mag.* XIX. 19 Applying to poetry the great idoloclastic test of resolution into prose.

†**ido'lolater.** *Obs.* [ad. eccl. L. *īdōlolatrēs*, later *-latra*, a. Gr. *εἰδωλολάτρης* (in N.T.), f. *εἴδωλο-ν* IDOL + *-λατρης* worshipper.] = IDOLATER.
a **1641** BP. MOUNTAGU *Acts & Mon.* (1642) 66 Idololaters they were..and Founders of Idololatry, in his opinion. *Ibid.* 46, 63.

†**idolo'latric,** *a. Obs.* [f. med.L. type **īdōlolatric-us*, f. *īdōlolatrīa* IDOLOLATRY; cf. IDOLATRIC.] Idolatrous.
a **1711** KEN *Hymnotheo* Poet. Wks. 1721 III. 351 Think how Mankind by Hell was captive led, In Rites Idololatrick born and bred.

†**idolo'latrical,** *a. Obs.* [see -ICAL.] = prec.
1550 HOOPER *Serm. Jonas* Ep. *iij, He had remoued all grosse and sensible Idololatry: and with the swerde had taken away all the Idololatricall priests. **1654** JER. TAYLOR

Real Pres. 336 As they have ordered the businesse, they have made it superstitious and Idololatrical. **1679** T. BARLOW *Invoc. Saints & Ador. Cross* 13 Stupidly irrational and.. highly Idololatrical.

†**idolo'latrify**, *v. Obs.* [f. L. *īdōlolatrī-a* IDOLOLATRY + -FY: cf. *glorify*] *trans.* To make the object of idolatry.

a **1641** BP. MOUNTAGU *Acts & Mon.* (1642) 45 False, Idololatrified Pagan gods.

†**ido'lolatrous**, *a. Obs.* [f. IDOLOLATER (or its source) + -OUS.] = IDOLATROUS.

a **1641** BP. MOUNTAGU *Acts & Mon.* (1642) 88 The maine multitude of rebellious and Idololatrous Israelites. *Ibid.* 232 Those.. Idololatrous Priests.

†**ido'lolatry**. *Obs.* [ad. L. *īdōlolatrīa* or Gr. εἰδωλολατρεία, f. εἴδωλο-ν IDOL + λατρεία service; (the etymological form from which *īdōlatria* IDOLATRY was contracted).] = IDOLATRY.

1550 HOOPER *Serm. Jonas* vi. 146 b, The vtward behauour and gesture of the receauer [of the sacrament], should want al kind of suspicion, shew, or inclinacion of Idololatrye. *a* **1641** BP. MOUNTAGU *Acts & Mon.* (1642) 219 Inducements, incitements to Idololatry, and all manner of impiety.

idoloter, obs. form of IDOLATER.

†**i'dolothism**. *Obs. rare.* [irreg. from next + -ISM.] The practice of offering to idols.

1607 *Schol. Disc. agst. Antichr.* I. i. 11 We haue viewed the signe of the Crosse in his Idolothisme considered in generall. *Ibid.* 20 The Apostle.. in steed of saying Fly from Idolothisme, saith, flye from Idolatrie. *a* **1640** J. BALL *Answ. Canne* ii. (1642) 24 Flie from idolothisme.

†**ido'lothyous**, *a. Obs.* Also erron. -thious. [f. Gr. εἴδωλο-ν IDOL + θύ-ειν to sacrifice + -OUS; after *idolothyte*.] Offered or sacrificed to an idol.

1607 *Schol. Disc. agst. Antichr.* I. i. 23 The thing being knowen to be Idolothious, a protestation that we honor not the Idol, serueth not the turne. **1637** GILLESPIE *Eng. Pop. Cerem.* II. ix. 39 What needed Paul to write so much against the scandall of meates, and against the scandall of Idolothious meats? *Ibid.* III. iv. 47 The Idolothyous Ceremonies.. are become Idols to those who have retained them.

idolothyte (aɪ'dɒləθaɪt), *a.* and *sb.* ? *Obs.* In 6 -atheit, 7 -othite, -yt, 7–8 -athite, 8 -yte. [ad. eccl. L. *īdōlothyt-us* (Tertullian), a. Gr. εἰδωλόθυτος offered to idols, f. εἴδωλο-ν IDOL + θυτός sacrificed.]

A. *adj.* Offered to an idol.

1562 A. SCOTT *Poems* (S.T.S.) i. 153 Paull biddis nocht deill wᵗ thingis idolatheit. **1637** GILLESPIE *Eng. Pop. Cerem.* II. ix. 38 The eating of Idolothyte Meats.

B. *sb.* A thing offered to an idol. Chiefly *pl.* (= Gr. neut. pl. εἰδωλόθυτα Acts xv. 29, 1 Cor. viii. 1).

1579 FULKE *Heskins' Parl.* 372 They did eate Idolothytes of the sacrifice. **1607** *Schol. Disc. agst. Antichr.* I. i. 9 The Canon Law doth reackon a Pagan poeme to bee an Idolothite not to be vsed. **1703** *Moderation a Virtue* 9 The Apostles Decree about Idolothytes, Blood, Things strangled, and Fornication.

Hence **idolo'thytic** *a.*, of or characterized by the eating of meats sacrificed to idols.

1889 HUXLEY *Ess. Controverted Quest.* (1892) 431 Those who assert the lawfulness of eating meat offered to idols.. I have called 'idolothytic' Christians.

†**idolous**, *a. Obs.* [f. IDOL *sb.* (or L. *īdōl-um*) + -OUS.] **a.** Of the nature of an idol. **b.** Addicted to idols, idolatrous.

1546 BALE *Eng. Votaries* I. (1550) 70 b, Was not thys.. good wholsom counsell of thys Idolous Byshop? **1550** —— *Image Both Ch.* II. K viij b, When such an Image or Idoluse prince is thus vp set or constituted by authoryty. **1550** —— *Apol.* 22 Now wyll I cause that ydolous stynkynge monstre.. to shew himself abroad in hys owne proper persone. **1617** COLLINS *Def. Bp. Ely* II. ix. 389 An idolous peice of work.

†'**idolry**. *Obs.* [f. IDOL *sb.* + -RY.] = IDOLATRY.

1535 STEWART *Cron. Scot.* II. 46 The faith of Crist and halie kirk to knaw.. And idolrie for to abhor alhaill. *Ibid.* 303 The faith of Christ he hes forȝet full quyte, And turnit hes to ydolrie full tyte.

'**idol-'temple**. The temple of an idol.

1577 [see *idol-house* s.v. IDOL 10]. **1631** WEEVER *Anc. Fun. Mon.* 450 An Idoll Temple, dedicated to Apollo. **1776** MICKLE tr. *Camoens' Lusiad* 3 Levell'd to the dust The idol-temples and the shrines of lust. **1860** PUSEY *Min. Proph.* 387 The one end of all was to form one great idol-temple, of which the centre and end was man, a rival worship to God.

i-doluen, ME. pa. pple. of DELVE *v.*

‖**idolum**, **-on** (aɪ'dəʊləm, -ɒn). Pl. idola (also 7 -aes, -ums). [L. *īdōlum*, a. Gr. εἴδωλον IDOL. Cf. also EIDOLON, and see IDOL 6, 7.]

1. An image or unsubstantial appearance; a spectre or phantom; a mental image, an idea.

1619 PURCHAS *Microcosmus* lviii. 568 The Constitution of the Soule, which is conflate of the Mind, Spirit, and Animall Soule, or Idolum. **1647** H. MORE *Song of Soul* III. II. xxxi, If like be known by like, then must the mind Innate idolums in it self contain; To judge the forms she doth imprinted find Upon occasions. **1857** T. E. WEBB *Intellectualism Locke* iv. 68 If by the inadvertent utterance of the wrong spell the magician has evoked a host of idola, he has himself furnished the counter-spell by which they are to be exorcised.

2. A false mental image or conception; a fallacy.

[**1620** BACON *Nov. Org.* I. xxxix, Quatuor sunt genera *Idolorum* quæ mentes humanas obsedent. Iis (docendi gratiâ) nomina imposuimus; vt primum genus, *Idola Tribûs*; secundum, *Idola specûs*; tertium, *Idola Fori*; quartum, *Idola Theatri* vocentur.]

1640 G. WATTS tr. *Bacon's Adv. Learn.* v. iv. §3 As for the Elenchs of Images or Idolaes; certainly Idolaes are the profoundest Fallacies of the mind of man. **1654** WHITLOCK *Zootomia* 255 To come to the second Bench of Censurers, fitted with peevish exclusive Notions, or Idola made by Education, Tradition, etc. **1678** CUDWORTH *Intell. Syst.* I. v. §1. 679 This opinion.. can be accounted no other than an *idolum specus* (as some affect to phrase it: *note*—Lord Bacon in his *Novum Organon*) or a prejudice of men's minds. **1865** LECKY *Ration.* (1878) I. 403 Bacon.. was pre-eminently noted for his classification of the *idola* or distorting influences that act on the mind. **1874** SAYCE *Compar. Philol.* ii. 63 What were intended to be mental landmarks become what Bacon expressively termed Idola, empty assumptions and misconceptions.

'**idol-,worship**. The worship of idols.

1667 MILTON *P.L.* XII. 115 Bred up in Idol-worship. **1712** S. CLARKE *Doctr. Trin.* I. i. §3. 61 Beware of Idol-worship. **1875** HELPS *Ess.*, *Self-Discipline* 19 It is idol-worship to substitute the form for the spirit.

Hence '**idol-,worshipper**.

a **1619** FOTHERBY *Atheom.* I. xi. §5 (1622) 121 In making himselfe an Idol-God, hee becommeth.. an Idol-worshipper.

Idomenian, **-enean** (aɪdəʊ'miːnɪən, aɪdəʊmɛ'niːən), *a.* and *sb.* [f. *Idomeneus*, f. Gr. Ἰδομενεύς, a king of Crete + -AN.] **A.** *adj.* Of or belonging to a race imagined by Thomas Reid, an 18th-c. metaphysician, to have no sense but sight, and to believe that space has only two dimensions. **B.** *sb.* A member of this race.

1764 T. REID *Inquiry Human Mind* vi. 252 'The Idomenians,' saith he, 'are many of them very ingenious, and much given to contemplation.' *Ibid.* 255 The geometry of the Idomenians agrees in every thing with the geometry of visibles. *Ibid.* 257 A person of great genius, who is looked upon as having had something in him above Idomenian nature. *Ibid.*, The Idomenian faculties were certainly intended for contemplation. *Ibid.* 258 Every Idomenian firmly believes, that two or more bodies may exist in the same place. **1871** A. C. FRASER *Life Berkeley* x. 400 The invisibility of that sort of distance can thus be proved even to the Idomenian. **1890** W. JAMES *Princ. Psychol.* II. xx. 214 One of Reid's Idomenians would frame precisely the same conception of the external world that we do, if he had our intellectual powers.

i-don, ME. pa. pple, of DO *v.*, I-DO *v.*

idoneal (aɪ'dəʊniːəl), *a. rare.* [f. L. *idone-us* + -AL¹.] = IDONEOUS.

1760 *N. & Q.* 7th Ser. (1888) VI. 403 Tho' they have Parts, with Fortune at their Will; Fine paper too, idoneal Types for Jargon.

idoneity (aɪdəʊ'niːɪtɪ). [ad. late L. *idoneitās*, *-tātem*, f. *idoneus* (see next). Cf. F. *idonéité*, It. *idoneità*.] Fitness, suitableness or aptitude.

1617 COLLINS *Def. Bp. Ely* II. x. 488 We are not to meane it of morall idoneity, or morall sufficiencie, but of Ecclesiasticall. **1668** HOWE *Bless. Righteous* (1825) 139 They want the.. meetness, the aptitude or idoneity for the inheritance of the Saints in light. **1822** C. BUTLER *Remin.* (1823) I. 32 To inquire and report upon the learning.. and general idoneity of the purchaser.

idoneous (aɪ'dəʊniːəs), *a.* Now *rare.* [f. L. *idone-us* fit, suitable + -OUS.] Apt, fit, or suitable.

a **1615** *Brieue Cron. Erlis Ross* (1850) 5 Quhilk Mark abbot enterit in the monasterie.. and fande the said place destitute of idonius personis, ornamentes, etc. **1626** *Waterf. Arch.* in *10th Rep. Hist. MSS. Comm.* App. v. 337 Two idoneows and decent persons shall be.. elected wardens of the said yeelde. **1680** BOYLE *Produc. Chem. Princ.* II. 71 Salt-peter is slowly generated in the earth by gradual.. Alterations of some Idoneous Matter. **1726** AYLIFFE *Parergon* 39 An Ecclesiastical Benefice.. ought to be conferr'd on an Idoneous Person. **1822** SYD. SMITH *Ess.* Wks. (1869) 418 A bitter, bustling, theological Bishop,.. the idoneous vehicle of abuse against the Establishment.

Hence **i'doneousness**, fitness, idoneity.

1727 BAILEY vol. II, *Idoneousness*, fitness, meetness. **1848** *Blackw. Mag.* Nov. 527 The scattered rays of idiosyncrasy and idoneousness.

idorgan ('ɪdɔːgən). *Biol.* [Arbitrarily f. ID-EAL + ORGAN.] An ideal or potential organism.

1883 P. GEDDES in *Encycl. Brit.* XVI. 842/2 The colonies of Protozoa are mere idorgans.

i-dorue(n, ME. pa. pple. of DERVE *v.*

i-doublet, ME. pa. pple. of DOUBLE *v.*

idous, obs. f. HIDEOUS.

i-douted, ME. pa. pple. of DOUBT *v.*

i-douwed, ME. pa. pple. of DOW *v.*², to endow.

idra, **idre**, obs. ff. HYDRA.

i-drad, ME. pa. pple. of DREAD *v.*

i-drahen, **i-drawe(n**, ME. pa. pple. of DRAW *v.*

i-drede, ME. pa. pple. of DREAD *v.*

†**i-dree**, *v. Obs.* [OE. *ȝedréoȝan*, f. *dréoȝan* to DREE.] *trans.* To do, perform, endure, suffer.

Beowulf (Z.) 2726 þæt he dæȝ-hwila ȝe-droȝen hæfde. *c* **950** *Lindisf. Gosp.* Matt. ix. 20 Wif ðiu blodes flouing.. ȝeðolade *vel* ȝedroȝ. *c* **1175** *Lamb. Hom.* 29 We moten idreȝan ure wil þe hwile þe we beoð ȝunge. *c* **1205** LAY. 6708 He ne mihte idriȝen [*c* **1275** þolie] to ihæren þene muche drem. *a* **1225** *Juliana* 27 Hwil þat eauer six men mahten idrehen beaten hire beare bodi.

i-dreufe, ME. pa. pple. of DRIVE *v.*

idrialin ('ɪdrɪəlɪn). [f. as next + -IN.]

1. *Min.* The name originally given by Dumas (in 1832) to IDRIALITE.

1844 DANA *Min.* (ed. 2) 517 Idrialin.

2. *Chem.* The essential constituent of idrialite, $C_{42}H_{28}O$, forming colourless scales which melt at a very high temperature.

1838 T. THOMSON *Chem. Org. Bodies* 748 When *branderz* is distilled, idrialin comes over in brilliant plates, light and micaceous,.. burning with the exhalation of a balsamic odour. **1838** *Penny Cycl.* XII. 397/1 Idrialin was obtained by M. Dumas from a mineral found in the quicksilver mines of Idria. **1865–72** WATTS *Dict. Chem.* III. 242 Idrialin heated with strong sulphuric acid forms a solution of a fine blue colour, like that of sulphindigotic acid.

idrialite ('ɪdrɪəlaɪt). *Min.* [Named from *Idria* in Austria where the mineral is found in the quicksilver mines: see -LITE.] A mineral hydrocarbon, called also inflammable cinnabar; 'it is massive and opaque, with greasy lustre, and greyish or brownish-black colour' (Watts). (It was made known to chemists by Payssé in 1814, and was at first named by Dumas, 1832, *idrialin*.)

1849 J. NICOL *Min.* 523 Idrialite.. burns with a thick smoky flame. **1868** DANA *Min.* (ed. 5) 738 Dumas separated the idrialite by treatment with oil of turpentine.

idrious, **idromancer**, **idropise**, **idrosis**, obs. ff. HYDRIOUS, HYDROMANCER, HYDROPSY, HIDROSIS.

i-driuen, **i-dronken**, **i-drowe**, ME. pa. pples. of DRIVE, DRINK, DREE *vbs.*

idryl ('ɪdrɪl, -aɪl). *Chem. Obs.* exc. *Hist.* [a. G. *idryl* (C. Bödeker 1844, in *Ann. d. Chem. u. Pharm.* LII. 102), f. IDR(IALIN 2 + -YL.] **a.** A mixture of fluoranthene and other hydrocarbons (see quot. 1952) orig. obtained from the mercury ores of Idrija, in north-west Yugoslavia, and thought to be a single compound. **b.** = FLUORANTHENE.

1845 C. BÖDEKER in *Chem. Gaz.* 15 Feb. 73 One of the products obtained in the working of the bituminous mercurial ores in Idria is the so-called *Stupp*, a soft black mass mixed with globules of mercury. It was supposed to contain idrialine, but in its stead another hydrocarbon was found, idryle C^3H, and a more accurate examination has proved that idrialine.. is an oxide of idryle. **1866** H. WATTS tr. *Gmelin's Hand-bk. Chem.* XVII. 477 Idryl. $C^{42}H^{14}$... The crystals are nearly colourless, with a tinge of yellowish-green... Idryl assumes a golden-yellow colour in cold oil of vitriol. **1877** *Chem. News* 16 Nov. 222/2 G. Goldschmidt, 'Idryl'. This body, found by Bödeker in Idria, is ascertained to consist of several hydrocarbons... Besides chrysen, pyren, anthracen, phenanthren, a new hydrocarbon, $C_{15}H_{10}$, was isolated, and receives the name originally applied to the mixture. **1892** ROSCOE & SCHORLEMMER *Treat. Chem.* (new ed.) III. vi. 523 Fluoranthene, $C_{15}H_{10}$, is found in coal-tar, and is also identical with idryl, one of the constituents of 'stuppfett'. **1926** H. G. RULE tr. *Schmidt's Text-bk. Org. Chem.* II. xvii. 513 Fluoranthene or Idryl, m.p. 110°, b.p. 250° (at 60 mm.). **1952** *Chem. Rev.* L. 483 In 1844 Boedeker.. distilled these ores, with production of a similar hydrocarbon which he named idryl. Much later Goldschmiedt.. showed.. that idryl consisted of anthracene, phenanthrene, chrysene, pyrene, and a hitherto unknown hydrocarbon, $C_{15}H_{10}$, to which he gave the name idryl. Simultaneously with Goldschmiedt's discovery, Fittig and Gebhard.. isolated.. a hydrocarbon which was named fluoranthene and was claimed to be identical with Goldschmiedt's idryl.

i-dubbed, **i-dubled**, **i-durked**, **i-dust**, **i-dut**, ME. pa. pples. of DUB, DOUBLE, DARK, DUST, DIT *vbs.*

†**i-duȝe**, *a. Obs.* [Cf. OE. *duȝan* to be of use, avail (see DOW *v.*¹).]. Profitable, advantageous.

a **1250** *Owl & Night.* 1582 þat gode wif.. fondeþ hu heo muȝe Do þing þat him beo iduȝe.

‖**id-ul-fitr** ('iːdʊlfɪtr). Also (a better form) id al-fitr. [Arab. *'īd al-fiṭr*.] The Feast of breaking the Ramadan Fast, or Lesser Bairam, celebrated on the 1st of the month of Shawwāl: one of the two major festivals in Islam.

1734 G. SALE tr. *Koran* Prelim. Disc. vii. 150 The first of them is called, in Arabic, *Id al fetr*, i.e. The Feast of breaking the fast, and begins the first of Shawâl, immediately succeeding the fast of Ramadân. **1832** G. A. HERKLOTS tr. *Shurreef's Qanoon-e-Islam* xxiv. 261 The *Eed-ool-fitr* (or feast of alms), called also the feast of *Rumzan*, is observed on the first day of the month *Shuwal*. **1836** E. W. LANE *Acct. Manners & Customs Mod. Egyptians* II. 238 It is also called '*Eed el-Fitr* (or the Festival of the Breaking of the fast). **1896** E. SELL *Faith of Islám* (ed. 2) vi. 319 A very usual form of the Khuṭbah of the 'Idu'l-Fiṭr which is preached in Arabic is as follows... We praise and thank him for the 'Idu'l-Fiṭr, that

great blessing, and we testify that beside him there is no God. **1909** *Daily Chron.* 18 Oct. 6/4 Undisturbed by the hum of the traffic in Holborn, the Imam lifted up his voice, and..droned out the Idul-Fitr prayer. **1970** *Cambr. Hist. Islam* II. 907 'Īd al-Fiṭr, 'the Feast of the Breaking of the Fast' or *al-'Īd al-Ṣaghīr* (the Small Feast), held after the end of Ramaḍān, the month of fasting. **1972** *Mainichi* (Japan) *Daily News* 6 Nov. 11/4 (Advt.), Kobe Muslim Mosque. Idul-Fitr prayers will be held at 9.00 a.m. on Tuesday, November 7th.

Idumæan (aɪdjuːˈmiːən, ɪd-), *sb.* and *a.* Also -ean. [f. L. *Idūmæa*, a. Gr. Ἰδουμαία, f. Heb. *Edōm* Edom + -AN.] **A.** *sb.* A member of the race inhabiting Idumæa. **B.** *adj.* Of or belonging to Idumæa or Edom, an ancient kingdom situated between Egypt and Palestine.

c **897** ÆLFRED tr. *Gregory's Pastoral Care* (1871) 387 Ezechiel... cwæð ðæt hie wolden weorðan forlorene & oferwunnene mid orsorgnesse, swa swa Idumeas wæron. **1382** WYCLIF *3 Kings* xi. 1 Forsothe kyng Salomon to brennyngly louede many hethen wymmen, the douȝter forsothe of Pharao, and Moabitis, and Amonytis, and Ydumees, and Cidonees, and Ethees. **1537** tr. *Original & Sprynge of Sectes* 55 Idumeans. **1602** LODGE tr. *Josephus' Workes* 679 Simon the sonne of Cathla,..spake vnto the Idumæans from a tower, and commanded them to cast down their armes. **1737** W. WHISTON tr. *Josephus' Works* 381 He fell upon the Idumeans, the posterity of Esau, at Acrabattene. **1838** *Penny Cycl.* XII. 437/1 The Idumæans marched to the assistance of Jerusalem when it was besieged by Titus. **1863** *Chambers's Encycl.* V. 343/1 The family was of Idumean descent. *Ibid.* 499/2 The Idumæan, Antipater. **1880** *Encycl. Brit.* XI. 754/1 Herod was the name of a family of Idumæan origin. **1936** C. ROTH *Short Hist. Jewish People* viii. 78 The age-long enmity between the Jews and Idumaeans (Edomites), which had found its expression in the raids of Judah the Maccabee, culminated in the final subjection of the country. **1968** P. NEEDHAM tr. *Gelzer's Caesar* v. 251 The Idumaean Antipater, the minister of the Jewish High Priest Hyrcanus.

idyll, idyl (ˈaɪdɪl, ɪd-). Also 7 eidyl(l. See also IDYLLIUM. [ad. L. *idyllium* (*ēdyllium*), a. Gr. εἰδύλλιον a short descriptive poem, dim. of εἶδος form, picture. Cf. F. *idylle*. Now commonly with pronunc. (ɪd-). (See Fowler *Mod. Eng. Usage* (1926) 253, R. Bridges in *S.P.E. Tract* (1929) XXXII. 403, and A. C. Gimson *Everyman's Eng. Pronouncing Dict.* (1969) 241.)]

1. A short poem, descriptive of some picturesque scene or incident, chiefly in rustic life. ***prose idyll***, a prose composition treating subjects of the same kind in a poetic style. (and derivs.).

1601 HOLLAND *Pliny* II. 296 Those amatorious eidyls and eclogues of Theocritus among Greek Poets, of Catullus and Virgil among vs. **1658** PHILLIPS, *Idyl*, a kinde of Eclogue, or Pastoral Poem, such as was written by Theocritus, Moschus, and others. **1799** W. TAYLOR in Robberds *Mem.* (1843) I. 243 The descriptive parts of this idyll..are unsurpassable. **1859** J. H. STIRLING *Crit. Ess.*, *Tennyson* (1868) 61 The Idyll or Idyl..is, on the whole, Tennyson's favourite form of rhythmical composition. **1873** SYMONDS *Grk. Poets* x. 306 The name of the Idyll sufficiently explains its nature. It is a little picture. Rustic or town life, legends of the gods, and passages of personal experience supply the idyllist with subjects. Generally there is a narrator, and in so far the Idyll is epic; its verse too is the hexameter. **1879** *World* 16 Apr., An Idyl is..not necessarily concerning pastoral matters, though from the prevalence of such topics in the idyls of Theocritus, the general notion is that idyllic and pastoral are almost convertible terms. **1888** BARRIE (*title*) Auld Licht Idylls. [Prose.]

2. *transf.* An episode or a series of events or circumstances of pastoral or rural simplicity, and suitable for an idyll.

1841-4 EMERSON *Ess.*, *Poet* Wks. (Bohn) I. 164 The pairing of the birds is an idyll, not tedious as our idylls are. **1869** LECKY *Europ. Mor.* II. v. 296 Nausicaa, whose figure shines like a perfect idyll among the tragedies of the Odyssey.

3. *Mus.* 'A composition, usually instrumental, of a pastoral or sentimental character' (*Cent. Dict.*).

4. *Comb.* **idyll-pastoral** *a.*, pastoral in subject and idyllic in form.

1849 E. C. OTTÉ tr. *Humboldt's Cosmos* II. 434 The artificial form of idyl-pastoral romances, and didactic poems.

idyller (ˈaɪdɪlə(r)). [f. prec. + -ER[1].] The author of an idyll.

1895 *Brit. Weekly* 7 Feb. 258 That life which lies just behind to-day..and would soon be quite forgotten if it were not for the 'idyller', who has saved some of the best for us.

idyllian (aɪˈdɪlɪən), *a. rare.* Also 8 **idilian**. [f. L. *idylli-um* IDYLL + -AN.] = IDYLLIC.

1716 M. DAVIES *Athen. Brit.* II. 150 Of all the Poetick Salts, the Epick is most Pure..the Eclogist and Idilian the most Country-wise and Native. **1844** THIRLWALL *Greece* VIII. lxvi. 416 A pleasing idyllian episode in a life divided between the senate and the camp. **1863** MARY HOWITT *F. Bremer's Greece* I. i. 15 The country is of idyllian beauty.

idyllic (aɪˈdɪlɪk), *a.* [mod. f. Gr. εἰδύλλι-ον IDYLL + -IC. Cf. F. *idyllique*.]

a. Of, belonging to, or of the nature of an idyll. **b.** Forming a suitable theme for an idyll; full of natural simple charm or picturesqueness.

1856 MRS. STOWE *Dred* II. 68 How perfectly cool and inviting you look! Really, quite idyllic! **1861** *Sat. Rev.* 7 Sept. 248 The *Amante and Madonna* of Ciullo d'Alcamo..to us appears to display a genuine and wonderful idyllic power. **1862** LOWELL *Biglow P.* Ser. II. ii, Much might be..said on the topick of Idyllick and Pastoral Poetry. **1874** FARRAR *Christ* xlii, At Nazareth, with all its idyllic memories of His boyhood, and His mother's home. **1897** DOWDEN *Fr. Lit.* IV. iv. 326 An Utopian visionary, an idyllic dreamer.

Hence **iˈdyllical** *a. rare*; **iˈdyllically** *adv.*; **iˈdyllicism**.

1874 SYMONDS *Sk. Italy & Greece* (1898) I. viii. 164 The female heads are singularly noble and idyllically graceful. **1876** SAINTSBURY in *Academy* 30 Dec. 622 They spend the winter idyllically. **1885** STEVENSON *Dynamiter* 117 A process..of idyllical simplicity. **1941** L. MACNEICE *Poetry of Yeats* v. 86 This snob idyllicism. **1964** *Economist* 25 Jan. 294/1 There is little idyllicism left.

ˈidyllism. [See -ISM.] The peculiar character or nature of an idyllic poem or scene.

1873 S. WARD in *Longfellow's Life* (1891) III. 219 The omission of those dramatic contrasts..makes your masterpiece soothing and tender, almost to idyllism.

idyllist (ˈaɪdɪlɪst). Also **idylist**. [f. IDYLL + -IST.] A writer of idylls; an idyllic poet.

1799 W. TAYLOR in Robberds *Mem.* (1843) I. 243, I should not think the English idyllist wise, who made himself a character in such a scene. **1873** [see IDYLL 1]. **1886** *Athenæum* 6 Feb. 207/2 Ready to measure himself with the idylist of another age.

‖**iˈdyllium, -on.** *Obs.* Also 6 idilion. Pl. idyllia (-ums, -ons). [a. L. *idyllium*, a. Gr. εἰδύλλιον: see IDYLL.] = IDYLL.

1579 E. K. *Gloss. Spenser's Sheph. Cal.* Aug., Such pretie descriptions..vseth Theocritus, to bring in his Idyllia. *Ibid.* Oct., This Æglogue is made in imitation of Theocritus his xvi. Idilion. **1647** H. MORE *Poems* Pref., Every Poem is an Idyllium. **1717** LADY M. W. MONTAGU *Let. to Pope* 1 Apr., Theocritus..I do not doubt, had he been born a Briton, but his Idylliums had been filled with descriptions of thrashing and churning. **1727-41** CHAMBERS *Cycl.* s.v., Theocritus is the oldest author who has written idyllions. **1809** W. IRVING *Knickerb.* (1861) 51 To sing, in soft Bucolic or negligent Idyllium, the rural beauties of the scene.

idyllize (ˈaɪdɪlaɪz), *v.* [f. IDYLL + -IZE.] *trans.* To make into an idyll; to render idyllic.

1886 SYMONDS *Renaiss. It.*, *Cath. React.* (1898) VII. viii. 12 The force of the poem [Tasso's *Jerusalem Delivered*] is..idyllised in the episode of Erminia among the shepherds.

idyot(e, idyothe, obs. forms of IDIOT.

idyous, obs. form of HIDEOUS.

Idzo, var. IJO *sb.* and *a.*

ie-, former spelling of JE-, as in *Iealousie, Iesus*: see I, the letter.

-ie, earlier form of -Y suffix, primarily in words from OF. *-ie* or *-e*, as *astronomie, fancie, citie, duetie*; but often extended also to words from OE. *iȝ*, as *icie, stonie*, and from other sources; in mod. use known chiefly as the Sc. spelling, now also often adopted in England, of the diminutive *-y* in *birdie, dearie, doggie, Jeanie, Willie*, etc.

1727 W. MATHER *Yng. Man's Comp.* 9 English Words that end with the sound of *i*, may be indifferently writ with a *y*, or *ie*; Safety or Safetie, Bounty or Bountie, but you must never end them with an *i* only, as Bounti, Safeti, for we have no English words so terminated. **1887** J. S. WINTER *A Siege-Baby* II. 7 Now, my chickie, let me go.

iebet, ieobet, obs. ff. GIBBET.

i-egged, ME. pa. pple. of EGG *v.*[1]

ieie (ˈiːeɪ,iːeɪ). Also **ie**. [Hawaiian.] A climbing screw-pine of the genus *Freycinetia*, esp. *F. arborea*, whose prop-roots yield a fibre. Cf. KIE-KIE.

1883 C. F. G. CUMMING *Fire Fountains* I. vii. 128 Vines without number, the most notable being one called the *ié*. **1903** R. C. L. PERKINS in *Fauna Hawaiiensis* I. 400 All those [birds] that were utilised could readily be caught by a bait of flowers, excepting perhaps the Ou, and this bird probably not less easily on account of its fondness for the ripe Ieie. **1915** W. A. BRYAN *Nat. Hist. Hawaii* xvi. 211 Another plant peculiar to the lower woods..is the ieie, a climbing shrub. **1970** S. CARLQUIST *Hawaii* xvii. 337 (*caption*) The flowers of the ieie are surrounded by short leaves bright orange in color.

iekyll, obs. f. ICKLE *sb.*, icicle.

ield, obs. f. YIELD.

i-eled, ME. pa. pple. of ELE *v.*[1] *Obs.*, to anoint.

ielefloure, ielopher, obs. ff. GILLYFLOWER.

i-ended, ME. pa. pple. of END *v.*[1]

ieniuer, obs. f. JUNIPER.

i-eode, pa. t. of I-GO *v. Obs.*

-ier, a suffix forming nouns designating position, employment, or profession, derived from sbs., rarely agent-nouns from vbs., (1) in words of ME. age, in which the suffix is unstressed, and varies (or has varied) with *-yer*, as *collier, bowyer*, (2) in words of later date (since 16th c.), in which the suffix is stressed, and varies with -EER[1], as *bombardier, cashier, cannoneer* (*-ier*), *financier*.

1. In words of ME. age, the suffix is of obscure and app. of diverse origin. Among the earliest examples are *cottier* (*cotier*), *tilier*, and *bowyer*: the first is a. OF. *cotier* = med.L. *cotārius*, and its retention of *-ier* is remarkable, because OF. *-ier* normally became *-er* in AFr. and Eng., as in *butler, draper, farmer* (see -ER[2] 2); *tiliere* (1250–1400), 'tiller, cultivator', appears to be an analogical formation on OE. *tilia*, early ME. *tilie*, on the analogy of such pairs as OE. *hunta*, ME. *huntere*, since the etymological formation would have been *tilere*; for *bowyer* (1297 *bowiare*, *a* 1450 *bowȝere, bowyere*), the suggestion has been made that the *i, y*, represents the *ȝ* of ME. *boȝe*, BOW; but this is doubtful. Other examples are *collier* (15th c. *koliere, cholier, colyer*, etc.), *lawyer* 1362 (but also, *a* 1400, *lawer*), *lockyer* (1407 *lokier*), *brazier* (1400–50 *brasier, brasyere*), *hellier, hillyer* (15th c. *helier, helyer, hillyer*), *spurrier a* 1450, *halyer* 1479 (*haulyer* 1577), *grazier c* 1500. Of *glazier* (*a* 1400), *clothier, hosier, sawyer* (*a* 1500), *farrier, pavier, -iour* (16th c.), there exist as early (in some cases earlier) forms in *-er*; *courier, cozier, furrier*, are 16th c. forms altered from ME. or OF. agent-nouns in *-our*; *drovier, glosier, kiddier*, are 16th c. variants of *drover, gloser, kidder*; *lovier* a late vulgarism for *lover*. In other words, as *carrier, courtier, currier, soldier*, the suffix is really *-er* (or earlier *-our*), the *i* belonging to the Eng. or F. vb. stem. (See also -IOUR.)

2. In words of later introduction, the suffix is the F. *-ier* (:—L. *-ārius*: see -ARY). The earlier of these, as *bombardier, cannonier* (*-eer*), *cashier, cavalier, chevalier, halberdier, harquebusier*, date from 16th c.; others, as *brigadier, carabinier* (*-eer*), *cuirassier, financier, fusilier, gondolier, grenadier*, from 17th or 18th c. Some, as *cordelier*, have taken the place of an earlier form in *-er*, which goes back to ME. Many of these also occur with the spelling *-eer*, expressing the English pronunciation; in some this spelling has been established, and from them -EER[1] has become a living English suffix, as in *auctioneer, charioteer, pamphleteer*.

ierapigre: see HIERA PICRA.

ierarch, ierarchie, obs. ff. HIERARCH, -Y.

i-erded, -et, ME. pa. pple. of ERDE *v. Obs.*, to dwell.

‖**ier-oe** (ˌiːərˈoː). *Sc.* Also **heir-oye**. [Gael. *iar-ogha*, f. *iar* after + *ogha* grandchild.] A great-grandchild.

1701 BRAND *Descr. Orkney* 71 (Jam.) There was also one Laurentius in the parish of Waes, whose heir-oyes do yet live there, who arrived at a great age. **1786** BURNS *Ded. to G. Hamilton* xiv, May health and peace, with mutual rays, Shine on the evening o' his days; Till his wee curlie John's ier-oe..The last sad mournful rites bestow!

i-escad, ME. pa. pple. of ASK *v.*

iesserand, obs. f. JAZERANT.

iest(e, obs. ff. GEST, JEST.

iesyne, var. GESINE *Obs.*, childbed.

i-eten, ME. pa. pple. of EAT *v.*

iethe, ieþe, var. of EATH *Obs.*, easy.

iette, iettour, obs. ff. JET, JETTER.

iewise, var. of JUISE *Obs.*

iey, obs. f. EYE.

if (ɪf), *conj.* (*sb.*). Forms: 1 **ȝif, ȝyf** (**ȝef, ȝife, ȝib**), 2–5 **ȝif, ȝef,** 3 **ȝief, ȝeif, ȝuf,** (*Ormin*) **ȝiff,** 3–5 **ȝyf, yef,** (also 4 **ȝiue, yif(f, yhef,** 4–5 **ȝeue, yeue,** 5 **ȝife, ȝyfe, yiffe, yeffe, ȝeff**); ? 3, 4– **if,** (4 **ef,** 4–6 **yf,** 5 **yff,** 5–6 **iffe,** 5–7 **iff**). See also GIF. [OE. *ȝif* (early WS. rare *ȝief*), late WS. *ȝyf* (Northumbr. rare *ȝef*), corresp. (more or less) to OFris. *ief, gef, ef* (*jof, of*), OS. *ef* (*of*) (MLG. *jof*, MDu. *jof, of*, Du. *of*) 'if', OHG. *ibu* (*oba, ubi*), MHG. *obe, ob*, Ger. *ob* 'whether, if', ON. *ef* 'if', Goth. *ibai* 'whether, lest', *jabai* 'if, even if, although'. The phonetic relations of the various forms. and their OTeut. type or types, have not been satisfactorily determined. By many considered to represent one or more cases of the sb. represented by OHG. *iba* str. f., 'condition, stipulation, doubt', ON. *if, ef* neut., *ifi, efi* wk. masc., 'doubt, hesitation' (whence *ifa, efa* vb. 'to doubt', Sw. *jäf* 'exception, challenge', *jäfva* 'to make an

exception against, to challenge'), the conj. thus meaning originally 'on condition', 'on the stipulation (that)'; but it has not been certainly determined whether the conj. is thus derived from the sb., or the sb. founded on the conj. A notable point in ME. is the development of the northern form GIF, q.v.]

A. I. Introducing a clause of condition or supposition (the protasis of a conditional sentence).

On condition that; given or granted that; in (the) case that; supposing that; on the supposition that.

1. *With the conditional clause or protasis in the indicative.* The indicative after *if* implies that the speaker expresses no adverse opinion as to the truth of the statement in the clause; it is consistent with his acceptance of it.

(In modern use the indicative is preferred to the subjunctive in cases which lie near the border-line of 1 and 2.)

a. Conditional clause in *present* (or *pres. perf.*) *indicative*; α. with principal clause in present (or pres. perf.) indicative.

Beowulf (Z.) 447 Ac he me habban wile d[r]eore fahne ȝif mec deað nimeð. **971** *Blickl. Hom.* 27 Þas ealle ic þe sylle, ȝif þu feallest to me. *c* **1000** *Ags. Gosp.* Matt. xviii. 15 ȝyf he þe ȝehyrð, þu ȝestaþelast þinne broðor. *c* **1200** *Vices & Virtues* 33 ȝif ðu ðus dost, ðanne berest þu þin rode. **1382** WYCLIF *John* i. 25 What therfore baptysist thou, if thou art not Crist, nethir Elye, nether prophete? *a* **1450** *Knt. de la Tour* (1868) 5 For yef ye do, the dede praiethe for you. **1611** BIBLE *Gen.* iv. 7 If thou doe [**16..** doest] well, shalt thou not be accepted? and if thou doest [COVERD. do] not well, sinne lieth at the doore. —— *Jas.* ii. 17 Euen so faith, if it hath not works, is dead, being alone. **1777** SHERIDAN *Sch. Scand.* II. ii, She's six and fifty if she's a day. **1861** JULIA KAVANAGH *French Wom. of Lett.* I. viii. 214 If I have not married, it is because I have not loved. **1864** BOWEN *Logic* vi. §3. 165 If A is true, O is false, E false, and I true... If A is false, O is true. If E is false, I is true. **1878** MORLEY *Crit. Misc.* Ser. I. *Carlyle* 200 If he does see it, he rides roughshod over it.

β. with principal clause in future indic. (or its equivalent).

c **1000** *Ags. Gosp.* John viii. 52 ȝif haw mine spræce ȝehealt ne bið he næfre dead. *c* **1200** ORMIN 673 ȝiff he seþ þatt mann iss ohht Forrfæredd off hiss sihhþe, He wile himm færenn. *a* **1250** *Owl & Night.* 904 ȝet i þe wulle an oder segge ȝif þu hit const a riht bilegge. **1297** R. GLOUC. (Rolls) 10997 ȝuf we doþ ou wrong wo ssal ou do riȝt? *c* **1300** *Harrow. Hell* 119 ȝef thou revest me of myne, Y shal reve the of thyne. *c* **1340** *Cursor M.* 14754 (Trin.) ȝif ȝe þis temple felle to grounde I shal hit rise in litil stounde. *c* **1440** *Partonope* 6263 Gyff I scape fro thens on lyve Agayn to prysoun I shall come as blyfe. **1596** SHAKS. *Merch. V.* III. i. 70 If we are like you in the rest, we will resemble you in that. **1633** *Costlie Whore* I. i. in Bullen *O. Pl.* IV, Ile tell another tale, if they have done. **1776** *Trial of Nundocomar* 73/2 If you do not give a plain answer to a plain question, you will be committed. **1816** J. WILSON *City of Plague* I. ii. 36 I'll give thee half of it If thou speak'st truly. *Mod.* If he does it, he will be punished.

γ. with principal clause in imperative.

a **900** *Martyrol.* in *O.E. Texts* 178 And ȝif monn minne noman nemneð in æniȝre frecennisse.. ðonne ȝefylȝe se ðinre mildheortnesse. *c* **1000** *Ags. Gosp.* Matt. xviii. 15 Soþlice ȝyf þin broþor synȝað [*Lind.* synnȝiȝa; *Rushw.* firniȝe *vel* synȝiȝe] wið þe, ga and styr him. *Ibid.* 16 ȝyf he þe ne ȝehyrð [*L.* ȝeheres; *R.* ȝe-hereþ], nim þonne ȝyt ænne oððe tweȝen to þe. *c* **1200** *Trin. Coll. Hom.* 31 ȝef þe is lef þin hele, heald þin cunde. **1340** *Ayenb.* 187 Yef þou hest ynoȝ of guode, yef largeliche, and yef þou hest lite, of þo litle yef gledliche. **1388** WYCLIF *Matt.* xviii. 16, 17 If he herith thee not, take with thee oon or tweyne.. And if he herith [*v.r.* here] not hem, seie thou to the chirche. **1535** COVERDALE *Gen.* xlvii. 6 Yf thou knowest that there be men of actiuyte amonge them, make them rulers of my catell. **1611** BIBLE *Job* xxxviii. 18 Declare if thou knowest it all. —— *Philem.* 18 If hee hath wronged thee or oweth thee ought, put that on mine account. **1680** DRYDEN *Ovid's Met.* I. [= *Lat. l.* 761] (1717) 35 If I am Heav'n-begot, assert your Son By some sure Sign. *Mod.* If they are not good, throw them away.

δ. with principal clause of other forms.

1611 BIBLE *2 Cor.* xi. 4 If he that commeth preacheth another Iesus.. ye might well beare with him. **1821** BYRON *Cain* I. i. 91 If I shrink not from these.. Why should I quail from him who now approaches? *Mod.* If records are to be trusted, there was no famine this year.

b. Conditional clause in *past* (or *pluperf.*) *indic.*, with principal clause in indic. or imper.

c **825** *Vesp. Psalter* vii. 4, 5 ȝif ic dyde ðis, ȝif is unreht-wisnis in hondum minum, ȝif ic aȝald ðæm ȝeldendum me yfel, ic ȝefallu [etc.]. *a* **1000** *Cædmon's Gen.* 661 ȝif þu him heodæȝ wuht hearmes ȝespræce he forȝifð hit þeah. *c* **1000** *Ags. Gosp.* John xiii. 14 ȝif ic þwoh eowre fet.. ȝe sceolon þwean eower ælc oðres fet. **1297** R. GLOUC. (Rolls) 8835 ȝif enie of is men misdude þe pouere.. vengance he nom stronge. *c* **1330** R. BRUNNE *Chron.* (1810) 40 If he had pes at euen, he had non at morow. *c* **1386** CHAUCER *Knt.'s T.* 257 If that Palamon was wounded sore Arcite is hurt as moche as he or moore. **1600** SHAKS. *A.Y.L.* III. ii. 41 If thou neuer was't at Court, thou neuer saw'st good manners: if thou neuer saw'st good maners, then thy manners must be wicked .. Thou art in a parlous state. **1832** TENNYSON *Lotos-eaters* 33 If his fellow spake, His voice was thin. **1835** THIRLWALL *Greece* I. vii. 267 If Amyclae was the Achaean capital, we can the better understand how it might be able to hold out. **1855** LEWES *Goethe* ii. (1875) 11 But if the town was heedless, not so were the stars. *Mod.* If he had loved her before, he now adored her.

c. Conditional clause in *future indicative* (or its equivalent), with principal clause in indic. or imper. Now *arch.* (supplied by a).

(*Béo* is here considered as future.)

c **825** *Vesp. Psalter* xii. 5 [xiii. 4] Ða swencað me ȝefiað, ȝif onstyred ic beam. **835** in *O.E. Texts* 448 Ann ic his freoðomunde, ȝif he ðonne lifes bið. *c* **1000** *Ags. Gosp.* Matt. v. 37 Soðlice ȝyf þær mare byð, þæt bið of yfele. *c* **1205** LAY. 482 ȝif þou þis nult iþolien þe scal beon þa wrse. **1297** R. GLOUC. (Rolls) 716 ȝif þou wole ȝut.. more.. wite of me, Al .. þe ground icholle segge þe. *c* **1375** *Cursor M.* 9439 (Laud) Yf þou wolle my forebode hold Thow shalt be lord as I þee told. **1382** WYCLIF *Matt.* xviii. 15 ȝif thi brother shal synne [**1388** synneth, **1611** shall trespasse] in thee, go thou and reproue hym.. ȝif he shal heere [**1388** herith] thee, thou hast wonnen thi brother. **1582** N.T. (Rhem.) *ibid.*, If thy brother shal offend against thee, goe and rebuke him. If he shall heare thee, thou shalt gaine [**1611** hast gained] thy brother. **1611** BIBLE *Matt.* xviii. 19 If two of you shall agree.. as touching any thing that they shall aske, it shall bee done for them.

2. *With the conditional clause or protasis in the subjunctive, and the principal clause or apodosis in the indicative or imperative.* The subjunctive after *if* implies that the speaker guards himself from endorsing the truth or realization of the statement; it is consistent with his doubt of it.

a. Conditional clause in *present subjunctive*; α. with principal clause in imperative.

Beowulf (Z.) 452 Onsend hiȝelace ȝif mec hild nime. **805** in *O.E. Texts* 442 ȝif hio.. bearn næbbe.. þonne foe he to ðæm londe. *a* **900** *Ibid.* 176 ȝif men ferlice wyrde unsofte, oððe sprecan ne maeȝe, halȝa him ðis wæter. *c* **950** *Lindisf. Gosp.* Mark xii. 19 Moses us awrat þæt ȝef huælc.. broðer dead sie.. and forletes þæt wif.. onfoe broðer his hlaf ðæs ilce. *c* **1000** *Ags. Gosp.* Matt. iv. 3 ȝyf þu godes sunu sy [Vulg. *es*; *Lind.* ðu arð, *Rushw.* siæ, *Hatt.* syo] cweð þæt þas stanas to hlafe ȝewurðon. *Ibid.* 6 ȝyf þu godes sunu eart [V. *es*; *L.* arð; *R.* sie; *H.* ert]. *c* **1325** *Metr. Hom.* 52 Ilk dai mak we a iorne Till heuin, ef we god men be. **1382** WYCLIF *Matt.* iv. 3 ȝif thou be [**1388** art, TINDALE *and all vv. to* **1611** be, *R.V.* art] Goddis sone, say that these stoons be maad looues. *c* **1430** *Two Cookery-bks.* 9 ȝif it be lente or fyssday take brothe of þe freysshe fysshe. **1534** TINDALE *Luke* xiii. 9 If it beare not then, after that, cut it downe [*later vv.* thou shalt cut it downe]. **1611** BIBLE *John* xx. 15 Sir, if thou haue borne [Vulg. *sustulisti*; WYCLIF, *Genev.*, *Rhem.*, *R.V.* hast; TINDALE, CRANMER have borne] him hence, tell me where thou hast layd him. —— *Phil.* ii. 1 If there bee therefore any consolation in Christ.. Fulfill ye my ioy. **1759** JOHNSON *Idler* No. 78 ¶5 If there be any man faultless, bring him forth into publick view. *Mod.* If he come to-morrow, send for me.

β. with principal clause in future indic. (or its equivalent).

13.. *Cursor M.* 6675 (Gött.) If he to min auter fly Men sal him þein draw to die. *c* **1386** CHAUCER *Prol.* 500 If gold ruste, what shal Iren doo? *c* **1400** MAUNDEV. (1839) iii. 25 ȝif thou kysse me, thou schalt have alle this Tresoure. *Ibid.* (Roxb.) v. 14 If þou ga noght, þou schall hafe grete harme. *c* **1450** MYRC 67 ȝef thow do þus thow schalt be dere To alle men that sen and here. **1526** TINDALE *Luke* x. 6 And yf the sonne of peace be thare, youre peace shall rest apon hym. **1533** MORE *Debell. Salem* Wks. 956/1 He that dyeth in deadly sinne, shall goe to the deuill, if goddes word be true. **1611** BIBLE *Judg.* xvi. 17 If I bee shauen.. I shall become weake, and bee like any other man. **1818** CRUISE *Digest* (ed. 2) II. 142 If part of the money.. be paid off, and a farther sum is borrowed.. no redemption will be granted unless both sums are paid.

γ. with principal clause in pres. indic.

c **1400** MAUNDEV. (Roxb.) Prol. 2 If we be riȝt childer of Criste, we awe for to chalange þe heritage þat oure fader left to vs. *Ibid.* i. 4 If a man come fro þe west partys of þe werld .. he may.. wende thurgh Almayne. **1450** MYRC 22 Luytel ys worthy þy prechynge, ȝef thow be of euyle lyuynge. **1526** TINDALE *John* i. 25 Why baptisest thou then yf thou be nott Christ, nor Helias? **1596** SHAKS. *Merch. V.* III. i. 71 If a Iew wrong a Christian, what is his humility? **1611** BIBLE *John* xv. 18 If the world hate you, ye know that it hated me before it hated you. **1648** JENKYN *Blind Guide* i. 7 If I be so young, I am in part excused for my illiteratenesse. **1654** Z. COKE *Logick* (1657) 118 [Ps. cxxvii. 1] If the Lord keep not the citie, the keepers watch in vain. **1839** *Times* 11 Apr., If we be not all Durhamised within another month, it is not from any sensible relaxation in the work of projected mischief. **1851** E. A. LITTON *Ch. of Christ* iv. (1898) 163 If it [the Church] be in its essence as visible a body as the republic of Venice, we have no need of faith to realise its existence.

δ. with principal clause of other form.

1662 STILLINGFL. *Orig. Sacr.* I. vi. §4 If we believe Joseph Scaliger, there could not be an Eclipse of the Sun at the time affirmed by Tarrutius. **1697** DRYDEN *Virg. Georg.* IV. 736 For sev'n continu'd Months, if Fame say true, The wretched Swain his Sorrows did renew.

b. Conditional clause in *past subjunctive* (in past sense), with principal clause in indic. or imper.

a **1400** *Octouian* 841 Yef he were er y-bete sore, Thanne was he bete moche more. **1593** SHAKS. *Rich. II*, I. iii. 201 If euer I were Traitor, My name be blotted from the booke of Life. **1601** —— *Jul. C.* III. ii. 84 If it were so, it was a greeuous Fault, And greeuously hath Cæsar answer'd it. **1850** TENNYSON *In Mem.* cxxii, If thou wert with me, and the grave Divide us not, be with me now.

c. Conditional clause in subjunctive with *should* in present or future sense ('if it should rain to-day or to-morrow') with principal clause in imperative, or in future, present, or pres. perf. indicative ('do not come', 'I shall not come', 'I am prepared for it', 'I have planned something else').

1821–3 ROGERS *Italy* xviii. 1 If ever you should come to Modena.. Stop at a Palace near the Reggio-gate. **1838** DICKENS *Nich. Nick.* vii, If you should go near Barnard Castle, there is good ale at the King's Head. **1850** TENNYSON *In Mem.* xliv, If such a dreamy touch should fall, O turn thee round, resolve the doubt. *Mod.* If you should come across him, tell him that I am looking for him.

3. *With both protasis and apodosis in the subjunctive.* Expressing a mere hypothesis which is admittedly not true or realized, and stating what would be the logical or natural consequence of its truth or realization.

a. Conditional clause in *past subjunctive*, with present or future sense ('if you came', 'should come', 'were to come' now or to-morrow). *spec.* ***if I were you.***

898 *O.E. Chron.* an. 894 Swa þæt he mehte æȝþerne ȝeræcan ȝif hie æniȝne feld secan wolden. *c* **1000** *Ags. Gosp.* John viii. 42 ȝif god wære eowre fæder, witodlice ȝe lufedon me [*Lind.* ȝif god faeder iuer uoere ȝie ualde lufiȝa.. mec]. *c* **1250** *Kent. Serm.* in *O.E. Misc.* 27 He hit wolde slon, yef he hit michte finde. *c* **1300** *Havelok* 1974 Yif he ne were, ich were nou ded. *a* **1307** *Thrush & Night.* in *Rel. Ant.* I. 241 This world were nout ȝif wimen nere. *c* **1380** WYCLIF *Serm.* Sel. Wks. I. 217 If Peter were now alyve.. he wolde seie þei weren not prestis of Crist. **1382** —— *John* xviii. 30 If this were not a mysdoer, we hadden not bitakun hym to thee [**1582** *Rhem.*, If he vvere not a malefactour, vve vvould not haue deliuered him vp to thee]. **1529** MORE *Dyaloge* II. Wks. 200/1 Yet wer it a dampnable errour to worship anye if we shoulde worship none at all. *c* **1615** FLETCHER *Mad Lover* I. i, If I were given to that vanity.. What a most precious subject had I purchased. **1766** GOLDSM. *Vic. W.* xvi, And if I were a king, it should be otherwise. **1814** JANE AUSTEN *Mansf. Park* I. vi. 109 If I were you, I should not think of the expense. *Ibid.* 112 'Mr Rushworth,' said Lady Bertram, 'if I were you, I would have a very pretty shrubbery. One likes to get out into a shrubbery in fine weather.' **1849** MACAULAY *Hist. Eng.* i. I. 3, I should very imperfectly execute the task.. if I were merely to treat of battles and sieges. **1869** TROLLOPE *Phineas Finn* II. xli. 30 'Of course you'll go,' said Phineas. 'I should, if I were you.' *a* **1899** *Mod.* If he were to come, what should we do? If he came, I should take to flight. If I were you, I would not do it. If they should meet you, it would be awkward. **1974** D. GRAY *Dead Give Away* vi. 65 I'd lay off stirring up trouble for a bit if I were you.

b. Conditional clause in *pluperf. subj.*, with past sense ('if he had come', 'would have come').

1382 WYCLIF *John* xi. 21 Lord, if thou haddist be here, my brother hadde not be deed [**1539** CRANMER, Lord, yf thou haddest bene here, my brother had not dyed]. **1482** *Monk of Evesham* (Arb.) 50 He hadde browghte plesaunte worde and tytyngys of my dampnacyon to hys father the deuyl, yeffe the mercye and goodnes of my lorde sente Nycholas had not wythstonde hym. **1614** BP. HALL *Recoll. Treat.* 610 If they had beene as hot for God, as they were for themselves, it had beene happy. **1665** SIR T. HERBERT *Trav.* (1677) 120 Shame it were, if.. we had gathered nothing. **1818** CRUISE *Digest* (ed. 2) III. 419 If he had altered it.. it would descend to the sister of the whole blood. **1819** SHELLEY *Cenci* II. i, If he Had killed me, he had done a kinder deed. **1849** MACAULAY *Hist. Eng.* vii. II. 256 All his difficulties would have been greatly augmented if Anne had declared herself favourable to the Indulgence. *Mod.* If he would have consented, all would have been right.

4. In pregnant senses:

a. Even if, even though; though; granted that.

c **1340** *Cursor M.* 579 (Fairf.) Þe saule wiþ-outen wene to ilk a man hit ys vn-seyne, if [*Cott.* þof; *Gött.* þou; *Trin.* þouȝe] hit of alle haue a siȝt. [**1340** HAMPOLE *Psalter* lxxi. 14 (15th c. MS.) Honorable.. is þe name of pore before him, gife it be dissipised before men.] **1572** R. H. tr. *Lauaterus' Ghostes* (1596) 197 If Spirites of their owne accorde woulde gladly tell vs many thinges: yet wee must not giue eare vnto them. **1848** [see TWITCH *v.*[1] 8 a]. *a* **1899** *Mod.* If he did say so, you needn't believe him. If they are poor, they are at any rate happy. **1965** *New Statesman* 16 Apr. 598/3 If Mr Stewart is top of the Tory pops, other ministers are also high up in the charts. **1967** *Listener* 17 Aug. 205/1 If my father's people were mill-workers.., my mother's people were agricultural workers. **1969** *Ibid.* 24 Apr. 585/1 If Mozart was a life-long admirer of J. C. Bach, his views on Clementi were disparaging, to put it mildly.

†**b.** = If it is certain or true that; as sure as. *Obs. rare.*

1605 SHAKS. *Macb.* III. iv. 74 If I stand heere, I saw him.

5. *if that* (north. *if at*) was formerly in use for the simple 'if'. Now *arch.*

c **1200** ORMIN Ded. 249 He shall o Domess daȝȝ Uss gifenn heffness blisse, ȝiff þatt we shulenn wurrþi ben. *a* **1300** *Dame Siriz* in Wright *Anecd.* 3 If that thou me tellest skil I shal don after thi wil. **1307** *Elegy Edw. I*, iv, Aȝein the hethene forte fyhte.. Myself ycholde ȝef that y myhte. *c* **1340** *Cursor M.* 5869 (Fairf.) Þai salle for-soþ if atte I may Wirk ij dayes werk a-pon a day. *c* **1386** CHAUCER *Prol.* 144 She wolde wepe, if that she saugh a Mous Kaught in a trappe, if it were deed or bledde. *c* **1450** *Guy Warw.* (C.) 1809 Yf þat y may, Wyth my handys y schall assay. **1509** BARCLAY *Shyp of Folys* (1874) I. 165 In the meane space, if that death vntretable Arrest the. **1605** SHAKS. *Lear* v. iii. 262 If that her breath will mist or staine the stone, Why, then she liues. **1821** BYRON *Sardan.* IV. i. 482 If that you conquer, I live to joy in your great triumph.

6. The conditional clause is often elliptical, and may dwindle down to *if* and a word or phrase sufficient to suggest the complete sense; so ***if not*** (= if a thing is, be, or were not), formerly sometimes = 'unless, except'; ***if any*** (see ANY *a.* 2); ***if anything***, if in any degree, perhaps even; ***if not, why not*** (see WHY *adv.* 4 b).

c **1320** *Sir Tristr.* 725 Knowe it ȝiue ȝe can. **1560** BIBLE (Genev.) *Dan.* iii. 18 Our God.. wil deliuer vs.. But if not, be it knowen to thee, o King, yt we wil not serue thy gods. **1642** *Perkins' Prof. Bk.* ii. §139. 61 He hath not authoritie to deliver it, if not by commandement. **1665** SIR T. HERBERT *Trav.* (1677) 173 Frogs are of great vertue, if physically used. **1711** If any [see ANY *a.* 2]. **1766** GOLDSM. *Vic. W.* v, We are not to judge of the feelings of others by what we might feel if in their place. **1836** G. C. LEWIS *Let.* 15 July (1870) 54 The writer says that the wages are nearly equal; if anything, the King's wages are rather the lowest. **1845** M. PATTISON *Ess.* (1889) I. 13 The style of Bede, if not elegant

Latin, is yet correct, sufficiently classical. **1851** H. Spencer *Social Statics* xxviii. 392 If anything, we were comparatively deficient in these respects. **1873** Lytton *Kenelm Chillingly* II. iv. vi. 257 Shall I ever be in love? and if not, why not? **1882** *Knowledge* II. 70 So that she might be cured, if possible. **1884** *Illustr. Lond. News* 5 July 18/1 He measured six feet two, if an inch; he weighed eighteen stone, if a pound. **1895** R. H. Sherard in *Bookman* Oct. 16/2 [He] labours hard over his proofs of the book, though little, if at all, over the newspaper proofs. **1909** P. A. Vaile *Mod. Golf* v. 92 If anything, touch the grass first. **1921** *Wireless World* IX. 187/1 L. M. T... asks..(3) If a diagram he sends is correct and, if not, why not. **1931** Belloc *Hist. Eng.* IV. ii. i. 260 If anything the ritual of King-worship was even more exaggerated in her case than in the case of Henry or of Edward. **1944** K. A. Esdaile *St. Martin in the Fields* ii. 50 If anything, the destruction was greater than in 1547. **1967** *Listener* 23 Feb. 261/1 At the start of every month I have to send him an account..of my earnings, if any.

7. The conditional clause alone (by aposiopesis of the principal clause) is sometimes used as an exclamation to express (*a*) a wish or determination, e.g. *If I had only known!* (sc. I would have done so and so); (*b*) surprise or indignation, e.g. *If ever I heard the like of that! The wretch! if he has not smashed the window!*

c **1000** *Ags. Gosp.* Luke xix. 42 ȝif þu wistest and witodlice on þysum þinum dæȝe þe ðe to sybbe synt. **1382** Wyclif *ibid.*, If thou haddist knowe, and thou, and sotheli in this thi day. **1637** Rutherford *Lett.* (1862) I. 393 If this kingdom would glorify the Lord in my behalf! **1702** Vanbrugh *False Friend* iii. ii, If he is not equipped for a housebreaker! **1846** *Swell's Night Guide* 49 And, so help me never! if his nibs didn't go and dossed with her the same night. **1914** *Sat. Even. Post* 4 Apr. 10/1 'If it ain't Frisco Red!' exclaimed one prone figure. **1925** T. Dreiser *Amer. Trag.* I. xvii. 145 'Oh, Gee, well, ain't that the limit?'..'If you aren't the grouch.' *Ibid.* II. iii. 184 Well, by jing, if it ain't Tom.

¶ *If* of the conditional clause is often omitted (esp. with the subjunctive), its effect being usually given by inverting the order of subject and verb.

Formerly sometimes without inversion, esp. after *than*, and after *glad* (where *if* was perhaps confused with *that*).

c **1275** Lay. 9295 Ac þare nadde he hi-come, nere hit [*c* 1205 ȝif hit nere] for swikedome. **1297** R. Glouc. (Rolls) 2473 Abbe þou poer ynou þou miȝt be glad & bliþe. **1377** Langl. *P. Pl.* B. Prol. 165 Were þere a belle on here beiȝ.. Men myȝte wite where þei went. *c* **1386** Chaucer *Man of Law's T.* 34, I were right now of tales desolaat, Nere that a Marchant..Me taughte a tale. *c* **1460** *Towneley Myst.* ii. 339 Be I taken I be bot dede. **1601** Shaks. *Jul. C.* iii. ii. 232 Were I Brutus, and Brutus Antony, there were an Antony, Would ruffle vp your Spirits. **1613** —— *Hen. VIII*, iii. ii. 456 Had I but seru'd my God, with halfe the Zeale..he would not in mine Age Haue left me. **1649** Lovelace *To Lucasta, on going to the Wars*, I could not love thee (Deare) so much, Lov'd I not Honour more. **1707** Watts *Hymn*, '*When I survey*' v, Were the whole realm of nature mine, That were a present far too small. **1747** Morell *Joshua* Air, O had I Jubal's lyre..To strains like his would I aspire. **1813** Byron *Corsair* i. xvii, In three days (serve the breeze) the sun shall shine On our return. **1838** Lytton *Richelieu* ii. i, Were Richelieu dead—his power were mine. *Mod.* I will come to-morrow, please God. Should you desire an interview, I shall not refuse to meet you. Should you find them, kindly let me know. You would see for yourself, were you here. Had they been careful this need not have happened.

1523 Ld. Berners *Froiss.* (1812) I. cccl. 794 The lordes.. spared no more money than it had fallen fro the clowdes. **1654** Dorothy Osborne *Lett.* (1888) 279 What would I give I could avoid it when people speak of you? **1761** Murphy *All in Wrong* iv. iv, Whatever he produces..I shall be glad you will, at any time, send to me. **1782** Miss Burney *Cecilia* viii. viii, I shall be glad you will inform me of it. **1802** tr. *Ducray-Duminil's Victor* IV. 227, I would give something he was here. **1806** Southey in *Life* (1850) III. 26, I should be glad this compromise were made.

8. Phrases. (See also even *if*, what *if*.)

†**a. all if, if all**: even if, even though, although. (See all C. 10 a, b.) *Obs.*

a **1300** *Cursor M.* 4246 (Cott.) Alle if [*Gött.* Al þou] þaire trauþe al sundre ware. *c* **1300** *Ibid.* 27674 (Cott. Galba) If all him-self neuer vnderstode. *c* **1340** *Ibid.* 1991 (Fairf.) Al if na rayne on erþ felle. **1340–1557** [see all C. 10 b].

b. an if, and if (see an *conj.* 2, and C. 1 b) = If. (Also occas. *if an.*) *arch.*

1297 R. Glouc. (Rolls) 282 An doȝter..Ich ȝivis þe to þi wif & ȝif þou wolt bileue here. **1394–1857** An if, and if [see and C. 1 b]. **1588, 1817** An if [see an *conj.* 2]. **1749** If an [see an *conj.* 2].

c. as if, followed by a clause containing a past subjunctive (sometimes ellipt.: cf. 6), or an infinitive expressing purpose or destination: As the case would be if; as though. (See as *conj.* 9 b.)

Also followed by a clause containing the present tense. Further examples in Fowler *King's Eng.* (ed. 3) pp. 165–6.

[*a* **1000** *Kent. Glosses* 219 in Kluge *Angelsächs. Lesebuch* 59 *Vel ut si avis festinet*, oððe swa ȝif efst fugel.] *c* **1290** *Michael* 411 in *S. Eng. Leg.* I. 311 Ase ȝif þov heolde ane clere candele bi-side an Appel riȝt. *c* **1410** Love *Bonavent. Mirr.* xxxiv. (Gibbs MS.) lf. 64 As ȝeue he herd oure lord bydde hym ryse. **1535** Coverdale *Prov.* vii. 23 Like as yf a byrde haisted to the snare. **1615** G. Sandys *Trav.* 136 Buying pewter, brasse, and such like implements, as if to set up house-keeping. **1693** Dryden tr. *Persius' Satires* I. 61 As if 'tis nothing worth that lies conceal'd. **1751** H. Fielding *Amelia* II. v. iii. 110 They seem indeed to be overburthened with Limbs, which they know not how to use, as if when Nature hath finished her Work, the Dancing-Master still is necessary to put it in Motion. **1766** Goldsm. *Vic. W.* iii, He defended his opinions with as much obstinacy as if he had been my patron. **1821** Shelley *Adonais* xi, One..Washed his light limbs as if embalming them. **1845** M. Pattison *Ess.* (1889) I. 8 Treating history as if it were a series of *tableaux vivants* intended to please the eye. **1862** Thackeray *Philip* II. viii. 173 As if a coarse woman..has a right to lead a guileless nature into wrong! **1963** D. Storey *Radcliffe* xxxvi. 367 As if everything that appears to live..is simply imitating some distant and incoherent ideal.

†**d. but if**: unless, except. *Obs.*

c **1200–1596** [see but *conj.* 10 b].

†**e. if case be (that)**: if it befall or happen (that). Also *if case that.* (See case *sb.*[1] 11.)

1525 Ld. Berners *Froiss.* II. cxi. [cvii.] 318 If case that my doughter haue sonne or doughter by hym. **1535–1630** [see case *sb.*[1] 11].

f. if so be (that), if it happen that, supposing that: a somewhat rhetorical equivalent of simple 'if'. *arch.* and *dial.* (Also occas. *if so were that*; ellipt. † *if so.*)

[**1390** Gower *Conf.* III. 5 And if so is that thou so be, Tell me thy shrift, in privete. **1414** *Rolls Parlt.* IV. 22 ȝif hit be so that they axke you by spekyng, or by writyng.] **1495–6** *Plumpton Corr.* (Camden) 114 Thynking that to be our next way, if so were that we wold not advise you to com not up by the pryvie seale. *a* **1547** Surrey *Æneid* iv. 820 If so that yonder wicked head must needes Recover port. **1559** Morwyng *Evonym.* 175 If so be it the mesure of the bloud excied three sextares. **1611** Bible *Josh.* xiv. 12 If so be the Lord will be with me, then I shall bee able to driue them out. **1665** Sir T. Herbert *Trav.* (1677) 173 If so be we left the Road,..they would wind about our horses legs. **1749** Chesterf. *Lett.* (1792) II. cciii. 269 If so be that I can get that affair done by the next post, I will not fail for to give your Lordship an account of it. **1861** *Cornh. Mag.* Aug. 183 'It's my opinion that any man can be a duke if so be it's born to him.'

g. if and when, in reference to a future time but with a strong element of doubt.

1926 Fowler *Mod. Eng. Usage* 254/1 *If & when.* Any writer who uses this formula lays himself open to entirely reasonable suspicions on the part of his readers... There is the suspicion that he is a timid swordsman who thinks he will be safer with a second sword in his left hand. **1940** G. B. Shaw *Matter with Ireland* (1962) 283 If and when the situation becomes grave enough to convince America that I have no alternative, I will reoccupy your ports. **1963** *Amer. Speech* XXXVIII. 255 If and when a study of local words in Missouri appears, we will be able to trace the same patterns in that state too.

II. 9. Introducing a noun-clause depending on the verb *see*, *ask*, *learn*, *doubt*, *know*, or the like: Whether. †Also, formerly, *if that.*

Beowulf (Z.) 273 Þu wast ȝif hit is swa we soþlice secgan hyrdon. *Ibid.* 1319 Frægn ȝif him wære æfter neod-laðu niht ȝe-tæse. *a* **1175** *Cott. Hom.* 219 Aȝen chire to chiesen ȝief [h]y wolden hare sceappinde lufie. *c* **1200** *Trin. Coll. Hom.* 81 Sum fortocne..warbi we mihten cnowen ȝif it soð were þat þu seist. *a* **1400** *Isumbras* 241 Aske we thiese folkes of þaire mete, And luke ȝife we maye any gete. **1481** Caxton *Reynard* (Arb.) 38 He loked..a boute yf ony body had seen hym. **1594** *First Pt. Contention* (1843) 37 We should not question if that he should live. **1611** Bible *Gen.* viii. 8 Hee sent foorth a doue from him, to see if the waters were abated. **1697** Dryden *Virg. Georg.* iii. 163 Observe, if he disdains to yield the Prize. **1717** Prior *Alma* iii. 71 She doubts if two and two make four. **1895** *Law Times Rep.* LXXIII. 623/1 He asked if his wife was there.

10. *Comb.* **if-clause**, a clause of condition or supposition introduced by the word *if*; **if-shot, if-stroke** *Cricket*, 'a stroke considered to be unsound and likely to cause the batsman's dismissal if the ball is hit' (Lewis).

1893 Turner & Hallidie *Primary Eng. Gram.* 113 The *if*-clause tells us *when*, or *under what circumstances* the desert would be a paradise. **1904** C. T. Onions *Adv. Eng. Syntax* 57 A Complex Sentence consisting of an Adverb Clause of Condition (if If-Clause, sometimes called the Protasis) and a Principal Clause (sometimes called the Apodosis) is called a Conditional Sentence. **1926** Fowler *Mod. Eng. Usage* 576/2 It [*sc.* the word *were*] is entirely out of place in an *if*-clause concerned with past actualities & not answered by a *were* or *would be* in the apodosis. **1964** *English Studies* XLV. 85 The meaningful weight of the complete sentence may move from the *if*-clause to the headclause. **1966** G. N. Leech *Eng. in Advertising* vi. 61 Favourite openings are..*if* clauses. **1897** K. S. Ranjitsinhji *Jubilee Bk. Cricket* iv. 165 In its worst form this [slipping the ball] is commonly known nowadays as the 'if-stroke'. Originally it was called the 'but-stroke', after its great exponent, the Sussex wicket-keeper [Butt]; but some wag suggested that it should be called in preference the 'if-stroke', because if you hit the ball you are nearly sure to be out. **1920** D. J. Knight in P. F. Warner *Cricket* 36 It is essentially an 'if' shot, and must, to a certain extent, be unsound. **1922** *Cricketer Ann. 1922–23* 62 We will not indulge in 'cowshots' or 'ifshots'.

B. *sb.* The conditional conjunction (see A.) used as a name for itself; hence, a condition, a supposition. (Cf. but.) Often in the tautological collocation *ifs and ands* (*ans*): see and C. = if.

1513 More *Rich. III* (1883) 47 What, quod the protectour, thou seruest me, I wene, with iffes and with andes. **1532** —— *Confut. Tindale* Wks. 537/1 Though he put in for shame repentaunce thereunto, with Iffes. *c* **1585** R. Browne *Answ. Cartwright* 24 By his iffs and supposings. **1613** *Answ. Uncasing of Machivils Instr.* G, With ifs and ands he begins to say. **1670** Dryden *1st Pt. Conq. Granada* ii. i, *Abdal.* If I am king, and if my brother die—*Lyndar.* Two ifs scarce make one possibility. *a* **1711** Ken *Sion* Poet. Wks. 1721 IV. 409 Ah if, sad if! Love should decay! **1849** Hare *Par. Serm.* II. 455 We are always raking up some if or other, to disturb our faith. **1868** Geo. Eliot *Sp. Gipsy* ii. 214 'Tis but a mirror, shows one image forth, And leaves the future dark with endless 'ifs'.

Hence **if** *v.*, to say or use 'if': only in ***iffing***.

1687 R. L'Estrange *Answ. Diss.* 21 The Letter is iffing of it now again too; with a 'What if the Mercenary Ministers [etc.]'. **1887** *Pierre* (Dakota) *Collegian* II. No. 3. 2 But iffing will not endow a college.

i-fa, early ME. form of foe.

†**i'fads**, *int. Obs.* In 7 y'fads, i'vads. [A parallel form to *y'facks*, *i'fags*, *i'fegs*.] In faith.

1672 Wycherley *Love in Wood* iii. ii, Would you sell us? 'Tis like you, y'fads!

i-failed, i-failled, ME. pa. pples. of fail *v.*

i-faired, ME. pa. pple. of fair *v.*, to make fair, beautify.

i'faith, in faith: see faith *sb.* 12 b.

†**i-falle**, *v. Obs.* [OE. *ȝefeallan* (= OHG. *gefallan*), f. *feallan* fall *v.*] *intr.* To fall, befall.

Beowulf (Z.) 2835 He eorðan ȝefeoll. *c* **1000** *Ags. Ps.* (Th.) lxviii. 9 Me eac fela þinra edwita on ȝefeollon. *c* **1250** *Kent. Serm.* in *O.E. Misc.* 29 So iuel auenture þet wyn failede.

i-falle(n, ME. pa. pple. of fall *v.*

†**i-fang, i-fo**, *v. Obs.* Forms: see fang *v.*[1] [OE. *ȝefón* (= OHG. *gifâhan*, MHG. *gevâhen*, Goth. *gafahan*), f. *fón* (see fang *v.*[1]).] *trans.* To lay hold of, take, grasp, seize.

c **888** K. Ælfred *Boeth.* xxxix. §1 Ær he ȝefehþ þæt. *c* **1000** Ælfric *Colloq.* in Wr.-Wülcker 93/12 Swa hwæt swa ic ȝefo. *c* **1175** *Lamb. Hom.* 131 Ðe mon þe wel deð he wel ifehð. *c* **1205** Lay. 7254 Þæt is a muchel æit-lond..þet Bruttes ærest ifeng. *Ibid.* 8231 Ȝif ich hine mai eower ifon [*c* 1275 ohwa fon]. *Ibid.* 22583 He on uaste iueng fæiere his iweden. *a* **1250** *Owl & Night.* 612 Ȝif ich hit mai ifo. *Ibid.* 1645 Þu seist þat gromes þe ifoþ. *a* **1300** *Floriz & Bl.* 694 He him nolde aȝen ifo.

†**i-fare**, *v. Obs.* Forms: see fare *v.*[1] [OE. *ȝefaran* (= OHG. *gifaran*, *givaran*), f. *faran* to fare.] *intr.* To go, proceed, fare.

c **950** *Lindisf. Gosp.* John i. 43 Ðæs on merne walde ȝefara in galileam. *c* **1000** *Cædmon's Gen.* 1355 Eall..under hrof ȝefor. *c* **1205** Lay. 6090 Þus i-uor [*c* 1275 ferde forþ] al Belin king. *Ibid.* 26595 Þus heo iuerden fiftene milen.

i-fare(n, ME. pa. pple. of fare *v.*, to journey, go.

†**i-fast**, *v. Obs.* [OE. *ȝefæstan* (= OHG. *gifestan*, MHG. *gevesten*), f. *fæstan* fast *v.*[1]] *trans.* To make fast, confirm, settle.

c **950** *Lindisf. Gosp.* Mark xii. 1 Wingeard ȝesette monn ..& ȝefæste [*Ags. Gosp.* ȝesette] ða ðæm lond-bigencgum. *c* **1205** Lay. 22551 Þis forward he iuaste, and ȝisles he funde. *a* **1300** *Fall & P.* 95 in *E.E.P.* 15 Al in helle were i-fast.

i-fast, -e, ME. pa. pple. of fast *v.*[1] and [2].

i-fat, ME. pa. pple. of fet *v.*

ifé ('ɪfeɪ). Also **ife**. [Native name.] A tropical African plant, *Sansevieria cylindrica*, of the family Liliaceæ, which yields a fibre formerly used as a substitute for hemp.

1859 *Curtis's Bot. Mag.* LXXXV. 5093 About three years since there were received at the Foreign Office, and transferred to the Admiralty, samples of a peculiar fibre and cordage under the name of Ifé, said to be derived from a new plant at the Portuguese settlement, Angola. **1866** Lindley & Moore *Treas. Bot.* II. 617/2 Ife. An Indian name for *Sanseviera* [sic] *cylindrica*. **1892** P. L. Simmonds *Commercial Dict. Trade Products* (rev. ed.) 462/1 Ife, a name in India for the *Sansievera* [sic] *cylindrica*, a plant useful for its fibre.

Ife ('iːfeɪ). The name of a town in Western Nigeria, the religious centre of the Yoruba people, used *attrib.* to designate the art of the Yoruba people, *spec.* the bronzes and terra-cottas of which the first examples were found there in 1912.

[**1913** R. Blind tr. *Frobenius' Voice Afr.* I. xiv. 293 Various comparatively coarse stone monuments are raised above the earth in Ifé. Below it we found old sculptured stonework..bronze work far exceeding that of Benin in its perfection and representative skill, and at last some terra-cottas amazing to those who inspect them.] **1939** *Burlington Mag.* LXXV. 152/2 The Ife terra-cottas and bronzes show the most diverse racial characteristics, from the Semitic.. running through all the ranges to the Negroid. **1949** Fagg & Underwood in *Man* XLIX. 2 (*caption*) The exhibition of Ife bronzes at the British Museum, July–September 1948. **1959** *Chambers's Encycl.* II. 609/2 All the Ife heads are technically and artistically on the highest level. The portrait-like treatment, with absolutely correct proportions, is extremely realistic and the modelling is of a beautiful sensitiveness and vitality. As works of art they rank even higher than the more impersonal and conventional Benin heads. **1960** *Times* 5 Oct. 18/7 The features of the Ife heads suddenly appear again.

i-fed, ME. pa. pple. of feed *v.*

†**i''fegs**, *int. Obs.* exc. *dial.* Forms: (with or without apostrophe) 7 **i'fac(k, i'feck, i'fex**, 7–8 **i'-, y'facks, i'-, y'-, efackins**, 8 **i-, efags, efacks, i-, efecks, efeclings, ifackins**, 9 **i'fakins.** [Perversions of *i' faith, in faith*: see fegs and i'fads.] Used, esp. by 17th and 18th c. dramatists, as a trivial oath amounting to a simple asseveration: In faith, by my faith.

1610 B. Jonson *Alch.* i. ii, *Dap.* I-fac, I doe not. You are mistaken. *Fac.* How! sweare by your fac?.. *Dap.* I'fac's no

oath. *a* **1625** FLETCHER *Nice Valour* IV. Wks. (Rtldg.) II. 467/1 I'fex have they. **1673** WYCHERLEY *Gentlem. Dancing-Master* II. ii, *Mrs. Caut.* Y'facks, but you shan't. I'll ask him. .. *Don.* Y'fackins, but you shan't ask him! **1709** STEELE *Tatler* No. 137 ¶2 He.. will tell you, That I'fackins, such a Thing is true. **1742** FIELDING *J. Andrews* I. xiv, Ifags! the gentleman has caught a traitor. *Ibid.* II. xiv, Ifacks, a good story. **1775** SHERIDAN *Duenna* III. vi, Efecks, Father, I should have guessed as much. **1785** HUTTON *Bran New Wark* 16 Good friends, these er sad duings, efeclings. **1825** BROCKETT, *I'fakins*, in faith—a frequent asseveration.

b. In earnest.

1687 CONGREVE *Old Bach.* IV. iv, Nay, dear Cocky, don't cry, I was but in jest, I was not ifeck.

i-feined, ME. pa. pple. of FEIGN *v.*

ifel, obs. form of EVIL *a.*

i-fel(l, pa. t. of I-FALL.

i-fele: see YFELE *v.*, to feel.

i-felle: see YFELL *v.*, to fell.

i-felled, i-feld, ME. pa. pple. of FELL *v.*

i-feng, pa. t. of FANG, I-FANG *v.*, to seize.

†**i-feond, -de.** *Obs.* [OE. *ȝefíend, -fýnd* pl.: see FIEND.] Enemies.

c **1000** *Ags. Gosp.* Luke xxiii. 12 Hiȝ wæron ær ȝefynd him betwynan. *c* **1205** LAY. 9876 þa ær weoren ifeonde, makede heom to fr[e]onde. *Ibid.* 16077 þu hauest..þine ifan þe biuoren, & þine ifeond bæften.

i-fere: see YFERE *sb.* and *adv.*

i-fered, ME. pa. pple. of FEAR *v.*, to terrify.

-iferous, combining form of the suffix -FEROUS.

i-fesid, ME. pa. pple. of *fese*, FEEZE *v.*[1], to drive.

i-fet, ME. pa. pple. of FET *v.*, to fetch.

i-fetered, i-fetred, ME. pa. pple. of FETTER *v.*[1]

i-fethered, i-feþered, ME. pa. pple. of FEATHER *v.*

iff. A written form of abbreviation of the phrase 'if and only if', always read as 'if and only if', used in *Math.* and *Logic* to introduce a condition that is necessary as well as sufficient, or a statement that is implied by and implies the preceding one.

1955 J. L. KELLEY *Gen. Topology* vii. 232 *F* is equicontinuous at *x* iff there is a neighborhood of *x* whose image under every member of *F* is small. **1961** R. R. STOLL *Sets, Logic, & Axiomatic Theories* i. 5 Two sets are equal iff (if and only if) they have the same members. **1964** T. O. MOORE *Elem. Gen. Topol.* i. 2 We use 'iff' as an abbreviation for 'if and only if'. **1965** B. MATES *Elem. Logic* viii. 137 $\phi \in \Delta$ iff ϕ is derivable from Δ. **1971** G. HUNTER *Metalogic* 16 Hereafter we abbreviate 'if and only if' to 'iff'. **1972** *R. Inst. Philos. Lect.* V. 34 An integer *n* is prime iff the only integers which divide it without remainder are itself and one.

iffy ('ɪfɪ), *a. orig. U.S.* [f. IF *conj.* + *-f-* + -Y[1].] Of a question, proposal, prospect, etc.: full of 'ifs', contingent, doubtful.

1937 *World this Week* 9 May, Very 'iffy', Mr. Roosevelt might characterize such talk. **1941** *Chicago Daily News* 17 Jan., The President had been asked the status of some proposal, or of some event.. whether this event was likely to happen... The president replied that the whole thing was 'iffy'. **1941** BAKER *Dict. Austral. Slang* 37 *Iffey*, uncertain, unsound, 'chancey'. **1941** *Time* 14 July 15/3 His chances of pulling out a plum were rather iffy. **1963** *Weekly News* (Auckland) 5 June 39/1 This gamble..is far too 'iffy' to be classed as a prudent business procedure. **1963** *Times* 12 June 12/7, I have no comment to make on it. As Mr. Roosevelt said, this would be giving hypothetical answers to 'if-y' questions. **1971** E. FENWICK *Impeccable People* xiii. 72 We knew this was rather an iffy tenant, morally speaking, before we rented. *Ibid.* 73 Now..she looks a little iffier. **1973** *Listener* 20 Sept. 364/2 If the Police do their job, if the new law is effectively enforced, these are very 'iffy' points indeed.

-ific, comb. form of the suffix -FIC, q.v.

-ification, comb. form of suffix -FICATION, q.v.

The *-i-* is always present, either as the L. stem-vowel or its representative, as in *glori-(a)-fication, molli-fication, fruct-i-fication*, or as connecting vowel, as in *oss-i-fication*.

i-fiht, early ME. form of FIGHT *sb.*

i-find: see YFIND *v.*, to find.

i-flemed, i-flemd, ME. pa. pples. of FLEME *v.*, to chase.

i-floured, i-flured, ME. pa. pple. of FLOWER *v.*

i-flown, -en, i-floȝen, ME. pa. pple. of FLEE *v.*

i-fo, i-foman: see FOE, FOEMAN.

i-fo, i-fon: see I-FANG *v.*, to seize.

i-foghte(n, i-foȝten, i-fohten, ME. pa. pple. of FIGHT *v.*

i-folde(n, ME. pa. pple. of FOLD *v.*

i-fonded, ME. pa. pple. of FAND *v.*, to try.

i-fongen, ME. pa. pple. of FANG, I-FANG *v.*

i-forth-: see YFORTH *v.*, AFFORD *v.*

i-fostered, ME. pa. pple. of FOSTER *v.*

i-founded, ME. pa. pple. of FOUND *v.*

i-frede: see FREDE, YFREDE *v.*, to feel.

i-free, i-freoȝen: see YFREE *v.*, to set free.

†**i-freond, -de**, *sb. pl. Obs.* [OE. *ȝefríend, -frýnd*, f. *fréond*, FRIEND.] Friends.

c **1000** *Ags. Gosp.* Luke xxiii. 12 On ðam dæȝe wurdun herodes and pilatus ȝefrynd. *c* **1205** LAY. 7715 Feond-scipe aleggen, makien feolle ifreond. *Ibid.* 11591 Her king wende þat heo weoren ifreonde.

i-fret, i-fretten, ME. pa. pples. of FRET *v.*

i-friȝed, ME. pa. pple. of FRY *v.*

i-frore(n, ME. pa. pple. of FREEZE *v.*

ifso'ever, *adv. nonce-wd.* [After *when-, wheresoever.*] If in any circumstances; if ever.

1847–57 DE QUINCEY *Secr. Societies* Suppl. note, Wks. VII. 300 Some bold fictions that should for ever stop the mouth of the Christian, whensoever or ifsoever any opening dawned for uttering a gleam of truth.

Ifugao ('iːfuːgaʊ), *sb.* and *a.* [Native name.] **A.** *sb.* The name of a people of northern Luzon in the Republic of the Philippines, of a member of this people, and of their Malayo-Polynesian dialect. **B.** *a.* Of or pertaining to the Ifugao people. Also '**Ifugaon.**

1859 J. BOWRING *Visit to Philippine Islands* viii. 171 This race [*sc.* Itaneg] has a mixture of Chinese blood, the Ifugaos of that of the Japanese. **1875** F. JAGOR *Trav. Philippines* v. 55 [Dialects of] Nueva Vizcáya: Gaddan, Ifugao, Ibilao, Ilongote. **1900** F. H. SAWYER *Inhabitants Philippines* I. xxviii. 271 The Ifugaos, who bear a strong resemblance to the Japanese, inhabit a territory in central Nueva Vizcaya. *Ibid.* 272 The Spaniards built and garrisoned a chain of forts in the Ifugao territory to keep them in order. **1901** A. G. ROBINSON *Philippines* x. 166 Following these tongues [*sc.* Visayan, Ilocano]..are the Pampangan..Ibanag, Ifugao, Ibilao [etc.]... Most of them are dialects, though sufficiently different to be practically unintelligible to those of other groups. **1914** D. C. WORCESTER *Philippines Past & Present* xx. 535, I assured him that we were friends who had come to get acquainted with the Ifugaos. *Ibid.* 536 An Ifugao climbed down from above. *Ibid.* 537 My mission to the Ifugao country was to establish kindly relations with the people. **1944** W. E. HARNEY *Taboo* (ed. 3) 21 The Melville Island native shield..may have come from the shields of the 'Ifugao' of the Philippine Islands. **1964** E. A. NIDA *Toward Sci. Transl.* iii. 50 In Ifugao in the Philippines and in Moré, a language of the Haute Volta, 'hair' and 'feathers' are included under the same term. **1968** R. NELSON *Philippines* 131 (*caption*) The Ifugaos are talented and artistic woodcarvers. *Ibid.* 133 (*caption*) An Ifugaon peasant.. leaving his tobacco field.

i-fuled, ME. pa. pple. of FOUL *v.*

i-fulled, i-fullet, ME. pa. pple. of FILL *v.*

i-furn: see FERN *adv.* and *a.*, former, -ly.

i-furred, ME. pa. pple. of FUR *v.*

†**i-fuse**, *v. Obs.* [ME. *ifusen* (ü), *ivusen*:—OE. *ȝefýsan*, f. *fýsan* to hasten, FUSE *v.*[1]]

1. *trans.* To cause to make haste, hasten, hurry.

Beowulf (Z.) 217 Winde ȝefysed flota. *a* **1000** *Cædmon's Exod.* 54 Werod wæs ȝefysed. *c* **1205** LAY. 22123 He wolde hine ifusen to ane bare walme.

2. *intr.* To make haste, to hasten.

c **1205** LAY. 503 An horsen & an foten forð heo ifusten. *Ibid.* 28946 Forð heo iuusden.

-ify, combining form of the verbal suffix -FY, q.v.

i-fynd: see YFIND *v.*, to find.

i-ga, i-gan, ME. forms of I-GO *v.*

i-gabbet, ME. pa. pple. of GAB *v.*[1]

†**igad, i'gad** (ɪ'gæd), *int. Obs.* Variant of EGAD; see GOD, and cf. ICOD.

1671 VILLIERS (Dk. Buckhm.) *Rehearsal* I. (Arb.) 37, I gad, I'll e'en kneel down, and he shall cut my head off. *Ibid.* V. 111 I'l justifie it to be as grand to the eye, every whit, I gad, as that great scene in Harry the Eight, and grander too, I gad. **1700** CONGREVE *Way of World* V. xiv, I'gad, I understand nothing of the matter. **1728** VANBR. & CIB. *Prov. Husb.* IV. i, I'gad, if I don't keep a tight Hand on my Tit, here, she'll [etc.].

i-gaderen: see GATHER *v.*

†**i-gain**, *adv.* and *prep. north. dial. Obs.* [a. ON. *í gegn* again, in turn, against; corresp. to OE. *ongeȝn, onȝéan*: see AGAIN.]

A. *adv.* In reply, in turn; again.

c **1325** *Metr. Hom.* 47 And he igain to thaim gan sai, Crist ..am I noht. *Ibid.* 149 This ermet..bad him com igain.

B. *prep.* Against; to meet.

c **1325** *Metr. Hom.* 4 And stithe stand igain the fend. *Ibid.* 149 The monkes com al him igaine.

Hence (with genitival *-es*) **i'gaines, egaynes**, in same sense.

a **1300** *Cursor M.* 469 (Gött.) Saint mychal..Ras egaynes him forto fight. *c* **1325** *Metr. Hom.* 54 Quat thou hauis done In licheri igaines me.

i-gan, pa. t. of I-GIN *v. Obs.*

igarape (igara'pe). Also **-apé, -ipe.** [Pg.] In South America, a tributary or other water-channel wide enough for a canoe.

1853 A. R. WALLACE *Trav. Amazon* ii. 41 Sometimes we would start down the igaripé in the montaria, not returning till late in the afternoon. *Ibid.* vii. 168 The word *igaripé*, applied to all small streams, means 'path of the canoe'. **1860** MAYNE REID *Odd People* 38 Travelling can only be done by water, either upon the great rivers, or by the narrow creeks (igaripes) or lagoons. **1866** L. AGASSIZ IN *Atlantic Monthly* July 58/1 We turned..into a narrow stream, which has the character of an Igarapé in its lower course. **1933** *Discovery* Jan. 24/2 It is intersected by innumerable water-ways, the igarapés, along which the tide ebbs and flows. **1944** S. PUTNAM tr. *E. da Cunha's Rebellion in Backlands* ii. §1. 59 The filling of the river [*sc.* Amazon] brings a stoppage of life. Caught in the meshes of the *igarapés*, man displays a rare stoicism.

i-gast, *a. Obs.*: see AGEST.

†**i-gastliche**, *adv. Obs.* [Cf. AGHAST.] Fearfully, terribly.

c **1205** LAY. 17869 Of him comen leomen igastliche scinen.

igasuric (ɪgə'sjʊərɪk), *a. Chem.* [ad. F. *igasurique*, f. *igasur*, the Malay name for St. Ignatius' Bean: see -IC.] In ***igasuric acid***, an acid contained in small quantities in the St. Ignatius' bean, *nux vomica*, and the root of *Strychnos colubrina.*

1830 LINDLEY *Nat. Syst. Bot.* 215 Igasuric acid occurs in combination with Strychnia in nux vomica and the St. Ignatius bean. **1865–72** WATTS *Dict. Chem.* III. 242 Igasuric acid precipitates acetate of lead.

So **iga'surate**, a salt of igasuric acid. **iga'surine**, a poisonous alkaloid found in *nux vomica*, discovered by Desnoix in 1853.

1855 MAYNE *Expos. Lex.*, *Igasurate.* **1865–72** WATTS *Dict. Chem.* III. 243 The igasurates are for the most part soluble in water and in alcohol. *Ibid.*, Igasurine crystallises in colourless prisms, having a silky lustre. **1879** H. C. WOOD *Therap.* 308 The igasurates of strychnia and of brucia.

Igbirra ('ɪgbɪrə). Also **Igbira.** [Name of an area in Kabba province, Northern Nigeria.] The name of a tribe in Northern Nigeria; a member of this tribe; also, their language.

1863 J. THOMAS *Jrnl.* 24 July in *Jrnls. & Notices Native Missionaries River Niger* (1864) 88 He went to our school-room and offered a prayer in Igbira. **1880** MRS. G. STURGE tr. *Burdo's Niger & Benueh* xv. 265 (*heading*) Attack by the Igbiras. **1883** R. N. CUST *Sk. Mod. Lang. Afr.* I. xi. 226 Williams, a Negro Catechist..has lately made Translations into Igbira, some of which are used in Divine Service. **1925** C. K. MEEK *Northern Tribes Nigeria* II. vii. 114 The Igbira mummify the body by pouring in gin or beer. **1958** J. S. COLEMAN *Nigeria* i. 24 Some of these [pagan tribes] were organized into unconsolidated village groups..others (for example, Igbirra, Bede, Bachama, and Igala) had achieved a certain measure of tribal unity. **1967** *Encycl. Brit.* XIII. 233/1 The native authority for Igbirra division, inhabited mainly by a tribe of the same name, consists of an elected council representative of the five Igbirra clans.

Igbo: see IBO *a.* and *sb.*

Igdrasil: see YGGDRASIL.

i-gederen, -unge: see GATHER *v.*, GATHERING.

i-geng, obs. form of GANG *sb.*

i-gerd, pierced, ME. pa. pple. of GIRD *v.*[2]

c **1380** *Sir Ferumb.* 2729 Duk Basyn..þorȝ þe heued i-gerd þer was, & ful doun ded.

i-gered, ME. pa. pple. of GEAR *v.*

i-gessyd, ME. pa. pple. of GUESS *v.*

iggerant: see IGNORANT *a.* 5.

‖**iggri, iggry** ('ɪgrɪ), *int.* Also **iggoree** *adv.* [Representing Egyptian colloq. Arab. pronunc. of *ijri*, imper. of *jarā* to run.] Hurry up! Also as *sb.* in phr. ***to get an iggri on.***

1919 W. H. DOWNING *Digger Dial.* 29 *Iggoree*, quickly. **1925** FRASER & GIBBONS *Soldier & Sailor Words* 127 *Iggry* (*iggri*),..a phrase in use in the Egyptian Expeditionary Force. 'Iggry Corner' at Bullecourt was so named by Australian troops who had been stationed in Egypt, as being an exceptionally dangerous locality from shell fire, where it was necessary to move rapidly. **1946** *Penguin New Writing* XXVIII. 173 'Come on, Chalky,' he pleaded, 'get an iggri on!'

i-ȝarwed, ME. pa. pple. of YARE *v.*

i-ȝete, ME. pa. pple. of EAT *v.*

i-ȝilde, i-ȝolde(n, i-ȝoulde, i-ȝulde, ME. pa. pple. of YIELD *v.*

i-ȝirnd, ME. pa. pple. of YEARN *v.*

i-ȝote(n, i-ȝotten, ME. pa. pple. of YETE *v.*, to pour, melt.

ight, var. *eighte*, AUGHT *sb.*^{1} *Obs.*, possession.
1390 GOWER *Conf.* II. 378 This Priamus had in his ight [*MS. Fairfax* 3 yhte] A wife and Hecuba she hight.

iʒt, obs. var. OUGHT *v.*

i-gilt, ME. f. GILT *ppl. a.*

†**i-gin**, *v. Obs.* [A parallel form to OE. *onginnan*, AGIN *v.*] To begin; in pa. t. = *gan.*
c **1205** LAY. 18127 In are brade strete he igon [*c* **1275** i-gan] mete þreo cnihtes.

†**i-ginet**, *pa. pple. Obs.* [Cf. GIN *v.*^{2}] Contrived, devised.
a **1225** *Leg. Kath.* 1981 þis pinfule gin wes o swuch wise iginet.

i-gistned, i-gladed, i-glewed, ME. pa. pples. of GESTEN, GLAD, GLUE *vbs.*

‖**igloo** (ˈɪgluː). [Eskimo, = house.]

1. An Eskimo dome-shaped hut; esp. one built of blocks of compact snow.
[**1662** J. DAVIES tr. *Olearius' Voy. Ambass.* 71 The Groenlanders speak fast,.. Iglun, a House.] **1856** KANE *Arct. Expl.* I. xxix. 380 The hut or igloë [of Smith Sound Eskimos].. was a single rude elliptical apartment, built not unskillfully of stone, the outside lined with sods. **1864** C. F. HALL *Life with Esquimaux* xi. (1865) 170 [They] commenced sawing out snow-blocks, while I carried them to a suitable spot for erecting the igloo. **1878** NARES *Polar Sea* I. iii. 53 The settlement of Etah.. consisted of three stone igloos, and one hut roofed over with canvas.

2. The cavity in the snow above a seal's breathing hole (Ogilvie, 1882).

3. *transf.* A small dome-shaped building or construction (see quots.).
1956 W. A. HEFLIN *U.S. Air Force Dict.* 262/2 *Igloo*.., a dome-shaped or rounded structure, usually made of reinforced concrete and earth, normally used for storage of explosives. **1969** *Jane's Freight Containers 1968–69* 438 (*caption*) A moulded fibreglass igloo unit as used by Delta Airlines. **1970** *Observer* 19 Apr. 6/8 The nerve gas is to be stored in 100 concrete igloos. **1970** *New Scientist* 21 May 382/2 The main advantage is that the igloos, unlike most other emergency shelters, can be made on the site; hence there are no major transport problems. **1972** *Evening Telegram* (St. John's, Newfoundland) 28 June 12/7 Igloos are spun-glass shells shaped to fit the bellies of jet-liners or the fuselages of all-cargo DC-8s. The use of the system is one of the main reasons for the rapid growth in air cargo operations.

i-gloset, ME. pa. pple. of GLOZE *v.*^{1}

i-gloupet, ME. pa. pple. of GULP *v.*

i-glyden, ME. pa. pple. of GLIDE *v.*

i-gnahen, i-gnawe, ME. pa. pple. of GNAW *v.*

igname, early f. YAM.

†**igˈnaro.** *Obs.* [a. It. *ignaro* adj.:—L. *ignārus* 'ignorant'; the use in English may have been derived from Spenser. In F., *ignare* sb. occurs in the 14th c.] An ignorant person, ignoramus.
[**1590** SPENSER *F.Q.* I. viii. 31 His name Ignaro did his nature right aread.] **1620** SANDERSON *Serm.* II. 158 Your mere ignaro's, what they err, they err for company; they judge not at all. **1634** HEYWOOD & BROME *Lancash. Witches* I. H.'s Wks. 1874 IV. 175 A meere Ignaro, and not worth acknowledgement. **1644** BP. MAXWELL *Prerog. Chr. Kings* Ded. 9 Ignaroes who are better versed in the Statutes and Acts of Parliament, than in the Acts of Christ. **1686** GOAD *Celest. Bodies* I. xvii. 110 We poor Ignaro's.

Ignatian (ɪgˈneɪʃ(ɪ)ən), *a.* and *sb.* Also 7 **Ignasian, Ignation.** [f. personal name *Ignati-us* (see def.) + -AN.] **A.** *adj.*

1. Pertaining to Ignatius Loyola (1491–1556), or to the Order of Jesus founded by him.
1605 WILLET *Hexapla in Gen.* 184 Thus farre this Ignatian sectarie. *c* **1610** SYLVESTER *Hen. Gt.* Ded. Sonn., O! just revenge, rout out th' Ignatian Pack. **1626** L. OWEN *Spec. Jesuit.* (1629) 68 The same Ignatian societie. **1679** *Let. Vind. Ref. Ch.* 8 These Ignatian Loyolists do very much derogate from Gods Great Attributes of Justice and Sanctity.

2. Of or belonging to St. Ignatius, bishop of Antioch, martyred at Rome early in the 2nd century; esp. in ***Ignatian Epistles***, letters attributed to him, the authenticity of which, in the various forms in which they have been handed down, has been the subject of much controversy.
[**1647** USSHER (*title*) Appendix Ignatiana, continens genuinas ejus epistolas.] **1832** MURDOCK tr. *Mosheim's Eccl. Hist.* (1841) I. 89 Indeed the whole subject of the Ignatian epistles is involved in much obscurity and perplexity. **1846** W. CURETON *Vindic. Ignat.* Appx., Opinions of various learned men respecting the Ignatian Epistles from the year 1650 down to the discovery of the Syriac Version.

B. *sb.* A follower of Ignatius Loyola; a JESUIT.
1613 PURCHAS *Pilgrimage* (1614) 393 This also was the Ignatians device. **1626** L. OWEN *Spec. Jesuit.* (1629) 15 Take notice, what foule mouth companions these Ignatians are. *a* **1683** OLDHAM *Wks.* (1685) 2 A sear'd Ignatian's Conscience, Harden'd, as his own Face, with Impudence.

Hence **Igˈnatianist** = IGNATIAN B.
1716 M. DAVIES *Athen. Brit.* III. *Crit. Hist.* 4 Made by the said Ignatianists for the Popish Schools.

Ignatius' Bean. = Bean of St. Ignatius (see BEAN *sb.* 4), the poisonous seed of *Strychnos Ignatii.* Also, in South America, applied to the medicinal seed of *Fevillea trilobata* and some other cucurbitaceous plants.
1751 SIR J. HILL *Mat. Med., Fruits* xiii. 506 (*heading*) Faba Sancti Ignatii, St. Ignatius's Bean. **1753** CHAMBERS *Cycl. Supp., Ignatius's-Bean*,.. it is a dry and hard fruit, or kernel of a fruit, of the size of a large hazel-nut. **1822–34** *Good's Study Med.* (ed. 4) I. 627 The nux vomica and Ignatius's bean.. combine, with an intense bitter, a most active narcotic virtue. **1880** BENTLEY & TRIMEN *Medic. Plants* III. *Sub Tab.* 179 The.. name of St. Ignatius' Beans.. is also used in South America to designate the seeds of several medicinal Cucurbitaceous plants.

†**igˈnave**, *a. Obs. rare*$^{-0}$. [ad. L. *ignāvus*: see next.] Slow, sluggish. Hence †**igˈnavely** *adv.*
1657 *Physical Dict.*, *Ignave*, cowardly, sluggish. **1657** TOMLINSON *Renou's Disp.* 501 They do it so ignavely.

†**ˈignavy.** *Obs.* [ad. L. *ignāvi-a*, n. of quality f. *ignāvus* idle, sluggish, f. I-^{2} = *in-* not + *gnāvus* busy, diligent.] Sluggishness, slowness, sloth.
1543 JOYE *Confut. Winchester's Art.* a iv b, Our own sluggishnes negligence and ignauye is the cause therof. **1545** —— *Exp. Dan.* xii. 234 What ignauy and sleugth is ther to any godly reformacion? **1657** TOMLINSON *Renou's Disp.* 97 The violence.. may be obtunded, or its ignavy excited. [**1850** CARLYLE *Latter-d. Pamph.* iv. (1872) 122 Nations, sunk in blind ignavia, demand a universal-suffrage Parliament to heal their wretchedness.]

†**ˈigneal**, *a. Obs. rare*$^{-1}$. [f. L. *igne-us* IGNEOUS + -AL^1. Cf. F. (medical) *ignéal.*] Fiery.
1669 WORLIDGE *Syst. Agric.* (1681) 7 Igneal Flames, and Claps of Thunder.

†**ˈignean**, *a. Obs.* [f. as prec. + -AN.] Fiery.
1635 PERSON *Varieties* I. 12 The Comets.. and falling Stars, etc. whereof many are neighbours with this Ignean-sphere, we visibly see. *Ibid.* II. iv. 61 Comets being of the number of ignean and fiery meteors.

†**igneduct.** *Obs. rare*$^{-1}$. [irreg. f. L. *igni-s* fire, after *aqueduct.*] A vent or passage for fire.
1676 HODGSON in *Phil. Trans.* XI. 763 The mouth of these Igneducts.

igneo-ˈaqueous, *a.* [f. *igneo-*, as comb. form of L. *igneus* igneous + AQUEOUS.] Due to the agency of both fire and water.
1882 *Sidereal Messenger* I. 215 We may look upon the state of igneoaqueous solution.. as one in which the water-substance is in a gaseous state.

igneous (ˈɪgnɪːəs), *a.* [f. L. *igne-us* of fire, fiery (f. *igni-s* fire) + -OUS. (F. has *igné*, It. *igneo.*)]

1. Of, pertaining to, or of the nature of fire; fiery.
1664 H. MORE *Myst. Iniq.* Apol. 496 There are many instances how Igneous and Lucid they [the bodies of angels] are. **1777** PRIESTLEY *Matt. & Spir.* (1782) I. xx. 267 The soul.. was first conceived to be an aerial, or an igneous substance. **1830** LYELL *Princ. Geol.* I. 327 Earthquakes and igneous exhalations. **1876** PAGE *Adv. Text-bk. Geol.* ii. 39 Volcanoes, earthquakes, and other igneous phenomena.

2. Resulting from, or produced by, the action of fire; *esp.* in *Geol.* Produced by volcanic agency (opposed to AQUEOUS 3).
1665 GLANVILL *Scepsis Sci.* xx. 127 Ignorant of the immediate way of Igneous solutions. **1796** KIRWAN *Elem. Min.* (ed. 2) I. 455 The igneous origin of basalts. **1812** SIR H. DAVY *Chem. Philos.* 48 The analysis of mineral bodies.. in experiments.. on their igneous fusion. **1830** LYELL *Princ. Geol.* I. iv. 58 Basalt and other igneous rocks. **1858** GEIKIE *Hist. Boulder* viii. 146 The cleft.. has been once filled by a wall of igneous rock called a trap-dyke.

ignescent (ɪgˈnɛsənt), *a.* and *sb. rare.* [ad. L. *ignēscent-em*, pres. pple. of *ignēscere* to take fire, become inflamed, inchoative of **ignēre*, f. *igni-s* fire.]

A. *adj.* Kindling, bursting into flame; firing up. *lit.* and *fig.*
1828 WEBSTER, *Ignescent*, emitting sparks of fire, when struck with steel; scintillating, as ignescent stones. *Fourcroy.* **1882** HALL CAINE *Recoll. Rossetti* 132 The outbursts of her ignescent hate.

B. *sb.* An ignescent body or substance.
a **1828** tr. *Fourcroy* in Webster (1828), Many other stones beside this class of ignescents, produce a real scintillation when struck against steel.

†**ignible**, *a. Obs. rare*$^{-1}$. [ad. L. type **ignī-bilis*, f. *ignī-re* to IGNITE: see -BLE.] Capable of ignition; ignitable.
1678 R. R[USSELL] *Geber* II. I. III. xii. 80 A metallick Body.. ignible (or sustaining Ignition).

†**ˈignic**, *a. Obs. rare*$^{-1}$. [f. L. *ignis* fire + -IC.] Of or pertaining to fire.
1612 STURTEVANT *Metallica* II. v. 59 Terrica is an Ignick Inuention, for the cheaper making of all kinds of Burnt-earths. **1855** MAYNE *Expos. Lex.*, *Ignicus*,.. ignic.

ignicolist (ɪgˈnɪkəlɪst). [f. L. *igni-s* fire + *-cola*, f. *col-ĕre* to worship + -IST. Cf. F. *ignicole* (1752).] A fire-worshipper.
1816 T. MAURICE *Ruins Babylon* II. 43 In whatever region of the earth this infatuated race of ignicolists took up their abode, the sacred fire immediately began to burn. **1859** R. F. BURTON *Centr. Afr.* in *Jrnl. Geog. Soc.* XXIX. 340 The ancient Persians were ignicolists, adoring etherial fire.

igniferous (ɪgˈnɪfərəs), *a.* [f. L. *ignifer*, f. *igni-s* fire: see -FEROUS.] Fire-bearing; producing fire. Also *fig.* Hence **igˈniferousness.**
1618 DEKKER *Owl's Almanack* 11 The manner how to dash it [fire] out of the igniferous flint. **1727** BAILEY vol. II, *Igniferousness*, fire-bearing or producing Quality. **1756** C. LUCAS *Ess. Waters* III. 114 This same igniferous matter was but.. a piece of lime. **1889** *Fabian Ess.* 209 The igniferous orators of the Socialist party.

igˈnific, *a.* [f. L. type **ignific-us*, f. *igni-s* fire: see -FIC.] Producing fire.
1753 B. MARTIN *Philos. Brit.* II. 280 If the ignific Particles of Light are sufficiently condensed.. by a.. Burning-Glass, they become ardent and burn.

†**igˈnifluous**, *a. Obs. rare.* [f. late L. *igniflu-us* (f. *igni-s* fire + *flu-us* flowing) + -OUS.] Flowing with fire.
1623 COCKERAM, *Ignifluous*, full of fire. **1659** D. PELL *Impr. Sea* 277 The Sea, which is sometimes of such an ignifluous lustre, as if it were full of Starrs. **1721** in BAILEY; hence in some mod. Dicts.

igniform (ˈɪgnɪfɔːm), *a. rare.* [f. L. *igni-s* fire + -FORM.] Of the form of fire.
1744 BERKELEY *Siris* §322 Democritus held the soul of the world to be an igniform deity. **1844** WOOD tr. *Bacon's Nov. Org.* II. §7. 129 We must examine.. whether that spirit is.. aeriform or igniform.

ignify (ˈɪgnɪfaɪ), *v. rare.* [f. L. type **ignificāre*, f. *igni-s* fire: see -FY. (Cf. late L. *ignefacĕre.*)] *trans.* To set on fire, to cause to burn.
a **1586** SIDNEY *Arcadia* (1598) 575 O *tace, tace*, or all the fat wil be ignified. **1656** BLOUNT *Glossogr.*, *Ignify*, to burn. **1690** LEYBOURN *Curs. Math.* 445 It is also probable, that the Solid parts of the Sun.. are thoroughly ignified in the same manner as the Bricks in the Roof and Sides of a Furnace are. **1706** E. WARD *Hud. Rediv.* I. v. 18 Let the Memorial.. Be doom'd to ignify our Pipes. **1848** LOWELL *Fable for Critics* 813 There is Bryant, as quiet, as cool, and as dignified, As a smooth, silent iceberg, that never is ignified.

Hence **ignified** *ppl. a.*; **ignifying** *vbl. sb.*
1659 STANLEY *Hist. Philos.* XIII. (1701) 599/2 Falling-Stars.. may be made either by pieces broken off from the true Stars.. or from a company of ignifying Atoms, meeting and joining together to effect it. **1763** W. STUKELEY *Palæogr. Sacra* 72 The sun formed, out of the ignifyed part of matter.

ignigenous (ɪgˈnɪdʒɪnəs), *a. rare.* [f. L. *ignigena* fire-born (epithet of Dionysus), f. *igni-s* fire + *-genus*, from *gen-* stem of *gignĕre* to produce + -OUS.] Produced by fire, or by the action of fire.
1727 BAILEY vol. II, *Ignigenous*, ingendred in or by Fire. **1818** *Blackw. Mag.* II. 379 How difficult it is to distinguish between ignigenous and Neptunian formations. *a* **1852** MACGILLIVRAY *Nat. Hist. Dee Side* (1855) 5 The obdurate primary and ignigenous rocks.

ignimbrite (ˈɪgnɪmbraɪt). *Geol.* [f. L. *ign-is* fire + *imbr-is*, *imber* shower of rain, stormcloud + -ITE^1.] Any pyroclastic rock, typically a welded tuff, deposited from or formed by the settling of a NUÉE ARDENTE.
1932 P. MARSHALL in *N.Z. Jrnl. Sci. & Technol.* XIII. 200 The type of rocks formed in this way varies greatly, but it is suggested that they should all be included in a separate group, for which the name 'Ignimbrite' seems satisfactory. **1959** A. MCLINTOCK *Descr. Atlas N.Z.* 11 Early in the Pleistocene Period, huge eruptions there formed a plateau of rhyolitic rock known as 'ignimbrite', some 10,000 square miles in extent. **1962** E. A. VINCENT tr. *Rittmann's Volcanoes* ii. 80 Ignimbrites, or welded tuffs, are formed in enormous quantities from overflowing glowing clouds in fissure eruptions of very acid magmas. The incandescent ash particles are intimately fused to one another and attain a largely pseudoliquid state, especially in the deeper portions of the deposit, so that the massive rock which results often shows columnar jointing and is easily confused with a rhyolitic lava. **1969** C. OLLIER *Volcanoes* vii. 73 Ignimbrite will be used here in the sense of Cook (1966). This is a rock unit term, and should not be used as a petrological term: several petrological types can give rise to ignimbrites though rhyolite and andesite predominate. Neither does the term imply any post-depositional alteration such as welding, though this may be present. **1970** *Nature* 12 Sept. 1125/1 This.. is matched in volume only by the large welded tuff sheets of the central North Island of New Zealand, the type locality for ignimbrite.

†**igˈniparous**, *a. Obs. rare*$^{-1}$. [f. L. *igni-s* fire + *-par-us* bringing forth + -OUS.] (See quot.)
1684 tr. *Bonet's Merc. Compit.* XIX. 770 Nothing is more igniparous or productive of fire [than Nitre].

ignipotent (ɪgˈnɪpətənt), *a.* [f. L. *ignipotent-em* having power over fire, an epithet of Vulcan, f. *potens* powerful.] Ruling or having power over fire.
1656 BLOUNT *Glossogr.*, *Ignipotent*, mighty by fire. **1715–20** POPE *Iliad* XXI. 398 Th' pow'r ignipotent her word obeys. **1813** H. & J. SMITH *Rej. Addr.*, *Fire & Ale* xii, But, spite of her shrieks, the ignipotent knight.. To the skies in a sky-rocket bore her.

Hence †**igˈnipotence.** *Obs. rare*$^{-0}$.
1727 BAILEY vol. II, *Ignipotence*, efficacy, prevalency against or power over Fire.

ignipuncture (ɪgnɪˈpʌŋktjʊə(r)). *Surg.* [f. L. *igni-* fire + PUNCTURE.] Puncture with a white-hot styliform cautery.
1886 *Syd. Soc. Lex.*, *Ignipuncture*, Ricket's mode of treating disease.. by the introduction of platinum needles at

a white heat. **1888** *Medical News* LIII. 216 (Cent. Dict.) Each gland should be treated by ignipuncture.

‖**ignis fatuus** ('ɪgnɪs 'fætjuːəs). [med. or mod.L., = foolish fire.] A phosphorescent light seen hovering or flitting over marshy ground, and supposed to be due to the spontaneous combustion of an inflammable gas (phosphuretted hydrogen) derived from decaying organic matter; popularly called *Will-o'-the-wisp*, *Jack-a-lantern*, etc.

It seems to have been formerly a common phenomenon; but is now exceedingly rare.

When approached, the *ignis fatuus* appeared to recede, and finally to vanish, sometimes reappearing in another direction. This led to the notion that it was the work of a mischievous sprite, intentionally leading benighted travellers astray. Hence the term is commonly used allusively or fig. for any delusive guiding principle, hope, aim, etc.

1563 W. Fulke *Meteors* (1640) 11 b, This impression seene on the land, is called in Latine, *Ignis fatuus*, foolish fire, that hurteth not, but only feareth fooles. **1658** Phillips, *Ignis fatuus*, a kind of slight exhalation set on fire in the night time, which ofttimes causeth men to wander out of their way. **1663** Butler *Hud.* I. i. 509 An *Ignis Fatuus* that bewitches And leads Men into Pools and Ditches. **1688** J. Clayton in *Phil. Trans.* XVII. 789 *Ignes fatui*, tho there be many boggy Swamps and Marshes, are seldom, if any are seen there. **1774** Goldsm. *Nat. Hist.* (1862) I. xxi. 134 Floating bodies of fire..the *ignis fatuus*, or wandering fire. **1813** Sir H. Davy *Agric. Chem.* i. (1814) 26 To avoid being led astray by the *ignis fatuus* the most secure method is to carry a lamp.

fig. **1599** *Broughton's Lett.* xii. 40 To fetch light from their Heathenish *Ignis fatuus*. **1631** *Star Chamb. Cases* (Camden) 31 For Sr Arthur Savage, he is the *primum mobile*, the *ignis fatuus* that misleades all the rest. **1777** J. Adams in *Fam. Lett.* (1876) 264 What an ignis fatuus this ambition is? **1824** Byron *Juan* xv. liv, Following the 'ignes fatui' of mankind. **1896** Dk. Argyll *Philos. Belief* Pref. 7 That ignis fatuus of the time—uniformity of worship throughout the three kingdoms.

attrib. **1808** Byron *To youthful friend* xvii, An ignis-fatuus gleam of love.

ignitable, -ible (ɪg'naɪtəb(ə)l, -ɪb(ə)l), *a.* [f. ignite *v.* + -able, -ible.] Capable of being ignited.

1646 Sir T. Browne *Pseud. Ep.* II. i. 52 Such bodies only strike fire as have a sulphur or ignitible parts within them. **1823** J. Badcock *Dom. Amusem.* 64 The explosion of an ignitible substance. **1851** *Fraser's Mag.* XLIV. 497 Some dense street of ignitable warehouses. **1860** J. Whiteside *Italy* xi. 106 Two piles of wood, mixed with ignitable materials. **1880** Kinglake *Crimea* VI. viii. 174 To find ignitible substances.

Hence **ignitability, -ibility**.

1809 *Europ. Mag.* LV. 20 Accident..from the ignitability of the materials. **1925** Coward & Wheeler *Ignition of Firedamp* 20 The ignitibility of any mixture by an electric spark is inversely proportional to the rate of movement of flame in that mixture. *Ibid.* 21 The relative ignitibilities of a wide range of inflammable methane-air mixtures. **1953** Kirk & Othmer *Encycl. Chem. Technol.* XI. 326 Ignition temperature, ignitibility, stability, and hygroscopicity are important in determining the certainty of functioning [of pyrotechnic compositions]. **1966** *Lancet* 24 Dec. 1404/1 Comparing circumstances in pure oxygen at 1 atmosphere with those in air at the same pressure one finds that there is a thousandfold increase in the ignitability of most substances.

†**ignite**, *a. Obs.* [ad. L. *ignīt-us*, pa. pple. of *ignī-re* (see next).] Intensely heated, in a state of white or red heat; glowing with heat, fiery. Also *fig.* hot, ardent.

1560 Rolland *Crt. Venus* III. 814 That we micht knaw his cheritie Ignite, Ardent, and hait. **1635** Person *Varieties* II. 55 These vaporous exhalations, whereof all the ignite and fiery Meteors..are composed. *a* **1650** *Venim. Qual. Tobacco* in Arb. *Jas. I, Counterbl.* (1869) App. 86 Tobacco is an ignite Plant. **1671** R. Bohun *Wind* 173 The ignite and suffocating Air, which infests the Burning Zone. *Ibid.* 175 The Ignite Damps..that finding no Vent, cause Earthquakes..if they escape through the Pores of the Earth. **1673** Ray *Journ. Low C.* 83 A Purse made of Alumen plumosum..put into a Pan of burning Charcoal till it was thoroughly ignite. **1704** J. Pitts *Acc. Mahometans* 72 Without..any other prolifick Heat, but that of the Sun, and such ignite Particles as the Earth may afford.

ignite (ɪg'naɪt), *v.* [f. prec., or L. *ignīt-* ppl. stem of *ignīre* to set on fire, f. *igni-s* fire.]

1. *trans.* To subject to the action of fire, to make intensely hot, to cause to glow with heat; in chemical use, *spec.* to heat to the point of combustion or chemical change.

1666 Evelyn *Diary* 3 Sept., Ye heate with a long set of faire and warme weather had even ignited the aire and prepar'd the materials to conceive the fire. **1795** Pearson in *Phil. Trans.* LXXXV. 327 A piece of the substance was ignited to whiteness, and then quenched in a large bulk of cold water. **1838** C. Tomlinson *Stud. Man. Nat. Philos.* I. i. 44 By incandescence we mean a glowing heat; and this is altogether different from ignition, since in the latter process the body is chemically changed; and generally speaking, a body can be ignited but once, whereas a body may be brought to a state of incandescence many times. **1853** W. Gregory *Inorg. Chem.* 187 The liquid is now evaporated to dryness, and the dry residue ignited and melted in a covered platinum vessel. **1889** *Nature* 31 Jan. 325/2 On evaporating a quantity and igniting in a platinum dish.

2. a. In popular use: To set fire to, to kindle.

[**1755** Johnson, *Ignite*, to kindle, to set on fire. A chymical term.] **1823** J. Badcock *Dom. Amusem.* 64 His preparation would not ignite any substance whatever, even gun-powder. **1860** Tyndall *Glac.* I. xxv. 189 Half a box of matches was consumed in the effort to ignite it [a lamp]. **1874** Holland *Mistr. Manse* iv. 125 We shrink and shrivel in the flames That low desire ignites and feeds.

b. *fig.* To light up, as if on fire.

1871 Tyndall *Hours of Exercise* ix. 94 Over the rugged face of the Breithorn itself the light fell as if in splashes, igniting its glaciers.

3. *intr.* To take fire; to begin to burn.

1818 Todd, *Ignite*, to become red-hot. A term of chymistry. **1828** Webster, *Ignite*, to take fire; to become red with heat. **1846** Greener *Sc. Gunnery* 90 A serious accident occurred..from the fuse of a shell igniting. **1885** *Manch. Exam.* 10 July 5/1 The gas ignited, and the explosion followed.

4. *trans.* and *intr.* To strike (an arc).

1917 *Proc. IRE* V. 298 It is assumed that the arc ignites every third time on the edges. **1919** E. W. Stone *Elem. Radiotelegr.* (1920) viii. 152 The arc is now 'struck' or ignited by this potential. **1933** [see ignitron].

Hence **ig'niting** *vbl. sb.* and *ppl. a.*

1813 T. Busby *Lucretius* v. 1382 From friction..might spring The igniting cause.

ignited (ɪg'naɪtɪd), *ppl. a.* [f. ignite *v.* + -ed¹.] **a.** Made glowing or incandescent. **b.** Set on fire, kindled. †**c.** *fig.* Hot, ardent.

a **1691** Boyle *Hist. Air* (1692) 61 Masses of ignited matter thrown up a great way into the air. **1744** Berkeley *Siris* §212 Plato..enumerating the ignited juices, names wine in the first place, and tar in the second. **1807** T. Thomson *Chem.* (ed. 3) II. 277 When this acid is placed on ignited coals, it emits a dense aromatic fume. **1871** Tyndall *Fragm. Sc.* (1879) I. v. 132 In a cylindrical beam..I placed an ignited spirit-lamp. **1875** *Ure's Dict. Arts* III. 384 Pinching..ignited rods of iron between indented rollers.

igniter (ɪg'naɪtə(r)). [f. as prec. + -er¹.]

1. a. One who ignites. **b.** A device to set fire to an explosive or combustible.

1883 *Q. Rev.* Apr. 514 The slow-burning fuse would give its igniter a minute or so of grace to walk quietly away. **1884** *Health Exhib. Catal.* 129/2 Patent Igniters and Instantaneous Fuses. **1886** D. Clerk *Gas Engine* viii. 205 The first few explosions cause a condensation of water upon the points and the spark then fails... The igniters then require to be uncoupled. **1887** *Sci. Amer.* 17 Sept. 187/2 An infernal machine..provided with a time exploder or igniter. **1902** *Min. Proc. Inst. Civil Eng.* CXLIX. 453 The hydrocarbon vapour sucked in from the carburettor..causes the igniter to glow brightly. **1905** H. J. Spooner *Motors & Motoring* 46 The principal features of the sparking plug or igniter. **1907** *Westm. Gaz.* 18 Nov. 10/2 The low-tension plugs and igniters are neatly placed in the sides of the cylinder heads. **1950** J. V. Casamassa *Jet Aircraft Power Syst.* xiv. 206 When the engine reaches a predetermined speed, the starter, ignition coils, and the flame igniters are automatically cut out. **1950** *Sci. News* XV. 78 One class [of propellants], called hypergols, react as soon as they come together, a property which eliminates the need for an igniter of some sort. **1954** J. W. T. Walsh *Textbk. Illuminating Engin.* (ed. 2) xii. 172 A special form of distance controller..switches on the igniter just before the gas is admitted to the burner. **1962** F. I. Ordway et al. *Basic Astronautics* x. 417 The solid rocket motor is composed of a cylindrical combustion chamber, a nozzle, a solid propellant grain, and an igniter.

2. *Electronics.* Also **ignitor**. A small rod of some refractory material that dips into the pool of mercury in an ignitron and serves as an auxiliary anode for restriking the arc in each cycle.

1933 *Electronics* VI. 166/1 At the present stage of development [of the ignitron] the instantaneous current required by the igniter to start the arc reliably is from 5 to 30 amperes. **1937** A. V. Eastman *Fund. Vacuum Tubes* iv. 107 One of the major problems in the design of Ignitrons is to make certain that the anode will pick up the discharge as soon as the igniter strikes. **1952** Young & Bueche *Fund. Electronics & Control* vi. 253 Because the ignitor can be controlled to cause initiation of the arc at any point in the positive half cycle, the average anode current flow can be controlled as in the case of thyratrons. **1962** C. Susskind *Encycl. Electronics* 361/1 In pulse-type circuits where capacitors are discharged, the ignitor can be made to start the discharge in less than 1 μsec.

ignitible, -tibility: see ignitable.

ignition (ɪg'nɪʃən). [f. med. or mod.L. *ignītiōn-em*, n. of action f. *ignī-re* to ignite. Cf. F. *ignition* (16th c. in Hatz.-Darm.).]

1. The action of subjecting to the full action of fire; *esp.* Heating to the point of combustion, or of chemical change with evolution of light and heat; the condition of being so heated or on fire.

1612 Woodall *Surg. Mate* Wks. (1653) 271 Ignition is calcination, the fire reducing violent bodies into Calx. **1666** Boyle *Orig. Formes & Qual.* 297 Silver will indure Ignition for a good while before it be brought to Fusion. **1685** —— *Effects of Mot.* ii. 10 The parts may be not onely intensely heated, but brought to an actual ignition. **1794** G. Adams *Nat. & Exp. Philos.* I. ix. 354 Bodies in certain degrees of heat appear luminous. A body which is thus rendered luminous is said to be ignited, and the effect itself is called ignition. **1807** T. Thomson *Chem.* (ed. 3) III. 163 It loses no weight in any degree of heat below ignition. **1811** A. T. Thomson *Lond. Disp.* (1818) 557 The crucible must be heated above 700° of Fahrenheit, which is the point of ignition of zinc. At this temperature the metal inflames, burning with a dazzling white and green flame. **1827** Faraday *Exp. Res.* xxxviii. 218 A portion of the gas..caused dull ignition of the platina. **1838** [see ignite *v.* 1].

2. a. The action of setting fire to anything; the process or fact of taking or catching fire, or beginning actually to burn; also, *loosely*, burning.

1816 T. L. Peacock *Headlong Hall* viii, The progress of the ignition, which having reached its extremity, the explosion took place. **1839** Bailey *Festus* (1854) 169 Like burning banners o'er a fiend-host there Arrested in ignition. **1840** *Statem. Steam Navig.* 44 Fire, from spontaneous ignition of coal in the bunkers. **1846** C. G. Addison *Contracts* II. iv. §3 (1883) 734 As the insurers take upon themselves only the risk of fire, they will not be responsible unless there has been actual ignition of the property insured. **1863** Tyndall *Heat* i. 9 By friction a lucifer-match is raised to the temperature of ignition.

b. A means of igniting or setting on fire. *spec.* A means of producing the spark in an internal-combustion engine; an ignition system, or the device that activates it.

1881 Greener *Gun* 101 This arm [Demondion's breech-loading percussion gun] is one of the first in which cartridges containing their own ignition were used. **1906** *Daily Chron.* 12 May 3/5 All good cars nowadays have the two independent ignitions, the accumulator and coil, and the magneto driven by a cog-wheel on the engine shaft. **1961** W. Hartley *Motorist's Home Repair Bk.* v. 70 There is no need to do more than insert the starting handle and have the engine turned over slowly (with the ignition switched off, of course!) while a petrol-moistened piece of silk is held against the commutator. **1972** J. Gores *Dead Skip* (1973) xiv. 97 A..Mustang with the driver's window open and the key in the ignition.

3. *Electronics.* The striking or initiation of an arc.

1919 E. W. Stone *Elem. Radiotelegr.* (1920) viii. 152 The potential existing across the arc at this instant is termed the extinction voltage as distinguished from that at ignition. It is less than the ignition voltage. **1927** J. G. Tarboux *Electr. Power Equipm.* iv. 128 The ignition anode is now drawn up by the spring..and at the point of rupture with the mercury an arc is started. **1945** *'Electr. Engineer' Ref. Bk.* x. 3 The action of the mercury-arc rectifier requires the cathode spot to be produced first by some auxiliary device before the arc can be established. This is generally effected by drawing an arc between the cathode and a small auxiliary anode, a process termed ignition. **1962** *Newnes Conc. Encycl. Electr. Engin.* 380/1 The ignitron differs from the other mercury-arc rectifiers..in the method used for ignition of the arc.

4. *attrib.* and *Comb.* (esp. in terms relating to internal-combustion engines and motor vehicles), as †*ignition box*, †*chamber*, *circuit*, *system*; **ignition advance**, the extent to which the moment when the spark occurs precedes the moment of greatest compression of the mixture in a cylinder of an internal-combustion engine, usu. expressed in terms of the angle between the two corresponding positions of the crank-shaft; **ignition coil**, an induction coil in an internal-combustion engine for converting a low-voltage current into one whose voltage is sufficient to produce the spark; **ignition key**, a key for operating an ignition switch in the form of a lock; **ignition lag**, the delay following the occurrence of the spark (in a spark-ignition engine) or the injection of the fuel (in a compression-ignition engine) before the pressure first begins to rise as a result of combustion; **ignition plug** = *sparking plug*; **ignition point** = *ignition temperature*; **ignition rating** (see quot. 1940); **ignition switch**, the switch by means of which the ignition circuit of a motor vehicle may be closed or opened (thereby allowing the engine to be started, or stopping it); **ignition temperature**, the lowest temperature at which a combustible substance in air will ignite and continue to burn; **ignition tube**, (*a*) *Chem.*, a small cylindrical vessel of heat-resistant glass in which a substance may be heated for purposes of analysis; †(*b*) a *hot tube* (hot *a.* 12 c) in some early internal-combustion engines.

1908 H. E. Wimperis *Internal Combustion Engine* viii. 282 It is permissible to set the ignition to take place..slightly before the dead centre... This reduces the arc of ignition advance throughout which the magneto is called upon to generate an effective spark. **1946** A. W. Judge *Mod. Petrol Engines* ii. 32 For weaker mixtures the flame rates are lower so that a greater ignition advance is necessary than for correct or slightly rich mixtures. **1900** G. D. Hiscox *Horseless Vehicles* xi. 184 The ignition of the charge is effected by heating the nickel tubes projecting about 2½ inches from the rear ends of the cylinders into the ignition box. **1894** B. Donkin *Text-bk. Gas, Oil, & Air Engines* I. xi. 140 At a given moment, a zig-zag passage in the slide valve is brought opposite the ignition chamber, and opens communication between it and the admission port into the cylinder. **1907** R. B. Whitman *Motor-Car Princ.* vi. 74 While wire is sometimes used on ignition circuits for the return as well as the lead, the most usual method is to utilise the metal of the engine to return the current to its source. **1900** G. D. Hiscox *Horseless Vehicles* vii. 127 (*heading*) Electric ignition coils. **1953** I. Frazee et al. *Automotive Fuel & Ignition Syst.* vii. 247 The ignition coil must produce sufficient voltage and current to ignite the fuel mixture at the various engine speeds encountered. **1933** D. L. Sayers *Murder must Advertise* ix. 155, I have the ignition keys of both cars. **1934** *Punch* 3 Oct. 388/3 Stepping into Humbottle's car am surprised to hear burst of gruff laughter... This probably explained by absence of ignition-key. **1962** J. Braine *Life at Top* xix. 190 She turned the ignition key; the car jerked forward convulsively, then stopped. 'Put it in neutral first,' I said. **1972** *Police Rev.* 1 Dec. 1577/3 They removed the ignition keys and sent a

message by radio for an officer to attend with the breath test equipment. **1932** *Fuel* XI. 187/1 At a definite temperature the ignition lag becomes infinitely great and ignition no longer takes place. **1900** G. D. Hiscox *Horseless Vehicles* vii. 130 (*heading*) Electric ignition plug. **1902** A. C. Harmsworth et al. *Motors* viii. 161 The ignition plugs may be examined to see that they are not coated with oil. **1933** I-B. O. Sneeden *Introd. Internal Combustion Engineering* ix. 164 The number of ignition plugs per cylinder is not limited to one. Two are often used. **1887** *Proc. Amer. Acad. Arts & Sci.* XXII. 483 In..trials, which I made with sound pine wood, I soon found that the ignition point was greatly affected by the way in which the sample was heated. *Ibid.* 486 The ignition point of the pine wood varied from 330°.. to 218°. **1922** Glazebrook *Dict. Appl. Physics* I. 338/2 The ignition points of oils are frequently required in connection with internal combustion engine problems. **1922** *Wireless World* IX. 727/1 Extensive use was made of portable accumulators..on motor cycles. The intermittent discharge through a trembler contact gave an apparent duration of double the hours at..a certain current. This led to the ignition rating of portable cells which is..misleading..for wireless work. **1940** *Chambers's Techn. Dict.* 437/2 *Ignition rating*, a special rating (in ampere-hours, q.v.) employed for accumulators used for supplying ignition systems; it is generally twice the continuous rating at a low discharge rate. **1952** *Ellery Queen's Mystery Mag.* XIX. 31/2 There was a car parked in front of the entrance, a Ford coupe, 1937... The key was in the ignition switch. **1902** A. C. Harmsworth et al. *Motors* viii. 159 The magneto ignition system..consists of a magneto-electric rotary machine, combined with a series of mechanical contact-breakers. **1943** A. P. Fraas *Aircraft Power Plants* viii. 140 The so-called battery ignition system has been used almost universally in automobiles... All the larger and many of the smaller aircraft engines make use of magneto ignition systems. **1956** H. E. Milburn *Motor-Cars To-Day* vi. 115 A normal ignition system consists of an induction coil, a condenser, a contact breaker, a distributor, a sparking plug for each cylinder of the engine, a switch, and the necessary connecting wires. **1881** *Jrnl. Iron & Steel Inst.* II. 679 (*heading*) Ignition temperature of mixed gases. **1897** F. Grover *Pract. Treat. Mod. Gas & Oil Engines* xix. 196 (*heading*) Ignition temperatures of explosive gaseous mixtures. **1968** *Fuel* XLVII. 119 According to D. W. van Krevelin the ignition temperature of coal depends on experimental conditions such as furnace design, way of heating, particle size, oxygen concentration and coal rank. **1874** F. Clowes *Elem. Treat. Pract. Chem.* II. 30 (*heading*) Small ignition tubes. **1890** W. Robinson *Gas & Petroleum Engines* vii. 229 The average life of ignition tubes in the Differential was 180 hours, and in the Cycle engine 120 hours. **1962** A. Atkinson *Compl. Pract. Chem.* xii. 272 Heat a little of the substance in an ignition tube or in a small dry test-tube until no further change occurs.

†**ig'nitious**, *a. Obs. rare*$^{-1}$. [f. IGNITION: see -IOUS.] Susceptible of ignition.

1753 B. Martin *Philos. Brit.* II. 278 Bodies are hotter or colder, as they contain a greater and lesser Quantity of ignitious particles.

ignitive ('ɪgnɪtɪv), *a. rare.* [f. L. stem *ignīt-* (see IGNITE *v.*) + -IVE: cf. *unitive.*] Having the property of igniting or taking fire.

1823 J. D. Hunter *Captiv. N. Amer.* 174 The Indians.. are acquainted with its combustible or ignitive properties.

ignitor, var. IGNITER 2.

ignitron (ɪg'naɪtrɒn). *Electronics.* [f. IGNIT(E *v.*, IGNIT(ION + -T)RON.] A kind of mercury-arc rectifier capable of handling large currents and having a pool cathode, a single anode, and an igniter to initiate the arc afresh in each cycle (the timing of this being used to control the output).

1933 D. D. Knowles in *Electronics* VI. 164/1 The Ignitron* is the latest arrival in the rapidly growing family of industrial electronic tubes. It is a tube in which conductivity is established by igniting the arc. [**Note*] Pronounced like the word 'ignite'. **1951** *Engineering* 14 Sept. 323/3 The ignitrons, which are water-cooled,..act as an electronic contactor which controls the current in the primary of the welding transformer. **1962** *Newnes Conc. Encycl. Electr. Engin.* 380/2 The larger ratings of ignitron are constructed with a double-walled stainless steel envelope, water being circulated in the jacket so formed for cooling. **1967** H. Cotton *Adv. Electr. Technol.* xv. 726 Typical applications of the ignitron are (*a*) small-power spot welding, (*b*) large-power control of variable-speed d.c. motors, such as certain types of colliery winder.

ignivomous (ɪg'nɪvəməs), *a.* [f. late L. *ignivom-us* (Lactantius), f. *igni-s* fire + *vom-ĕre* to vomit: see -OUS.] Vomiting fire. Also *fig.*

1603 Harsnet *Pop. Impost.* 70 What a Monstrous Coyle would Six or Seaven Ignivomous priests keepe in hell. **1639** Fuller *Holy War* III. xxii. (1647) 150 This ignivomous curre..did bark at and deeply bite the poore Albigenses. **1659** Stanley *Hist. Philos.* XIII. (1701) 580/1 Ignivomous Eruptions, as that of Ætna. **1674** *Phil. Trans.* IX. 239 There are other ignivomous Mountains besides Hecla; yet all are cover'd with Snow. **1711** Derham *Ibid.* XXVII. 275 The Mouth of the ignivomous Cavern. **1869** Phillips *Vesuv.* iv. 97 Throughout the whole of 1812 this small opening was ignivomous.

Hence **ig'nivomousness**.

1727 Bailey vol. II, *Ignivomousness*, Fire vomiting Quality, such as that of Vulcano's or burning Mountains.

ignobility (ɪgnəʊ'bɪlɪtɪ). [ad. L. *ignōbilitās*, n. of quality f. *ignōbilis* IGNOBLE, after *nobility*: see -ITY.] The quality of being ignoble.

1. Lowliness, humbleness, meanness (of birth or station).

1483 Caxton *Gold. Leg.* (1493) 267b, His ignobylite or vnworthines was torned in to sublymite and heyth. *a* **1520** Barclay *Jugurth* 10a, He dysdayned þe ignobylite of Jugurth for asmoche as he was vnlyke vnto them of byrth. **1624** Heywood *Gunaik.* II. 99 Modestie..illustrates the ignobility of birth. **1793** T. Taylor *Sallust* ix. 50 That nobility or ignobility of parents may be predicted from the stars.

b. *the ignobility*, the whole body of persons not of the nobility; the commons. *rare.*

1546 Langley *Pol. Verg. de Invent.* I. x. 20b, Very many of the ignobilitee wer promoted into the degree of Senatours. **1610** *Histrio-m.* IV. 11 Urgent need makes Princes bend their knee As servile as the ignobilitie. **1835** *Fraser's Mag.* XI. 315 The nobility, like the ignobility, was divided into the two ranks of landed and landless proprietors.

2. Want of nobility (of nature or disposition); meanness or baseness of character.

1549 Bale in Leland *Itin.* Cijb, A more sygne of ignobylytye can not be sene, then to hyde such noble monumentes. *c* **1610** *Women Saints* 4 Much ignobilitie were it, for a potent and riche Prince..to cast his affection on a begger woman. **1737** Whiston *Josephus, Antiq.* IV. viii. §15 Nor let servants be admitted to give testimony, on account of the ignobility of their soul. **1842** J. Martineau *Chr. Life* (1867) 297 Selfishness secretly conscious of its ignobility.

ignoble (ɪg'nəʊb(ə)l), *a.* (*sb.*) Also 5 innoble. [a. F. *ignoble* (14–15th c. in Hatz.-Darm.) = It. *ignobile*, Sp. *innoble*, ad. L. *ignōbilis*, f. I-^{2} = *in*- not + *gnōbilis*, *nōbilis* NOBLE.]

1. Not noble in respect of birth, position, or reputation; of low birth or humble station.

a. Of persons, their birth, family, condition, etc.

1494 Fabyan *Chron.* VII. 335 All must pay hym [death] dette, Noble and innoble. **1548** Hall *Chron., Edw. IV* 192 Of all men, as well noble as ignoble, as well of riche as of poore. **1593** Shaks. *3 Hen. VI*, IV. i. 70 You must all confesse, That I was not ignoble of Descent. **1617** Moryson *Itin.* III. 133 The Gentlemen doe not meddle with trafficke ..they thinke such trafficke ignoble and base. **1683** *Brit. Spec.* 191 To be ranked among the Peasantry and the Ignoble. **1738** Wesley *Ps.* XLV. xiv, Daughter of Heaven, tho born on Earth..Forget the first ignoble Birth. **1869** Freeman *Norm. Conq.* (1876) III. xi. 59 A West-Saxon house which, two generations back, had been undistinguished, perhaps ignoble. **1875** Jowett *Plato* (ed. 2) V. 313 No man..will be allowed to exercise any ignoble occupation.

b. Of animals, compared with each other or with man.

In *Ornith.* applied to those birds of prey, such as the kites and buzzards, which are not used in falconry. In *Falconry* applied to the short-winged hawks, such as the goshawk and sparrow-hawk, which chase or rake after the quarry, in contradistinction to the noble or long-winged falcons, which stoop to the quarry at a single swoop.

1661 Lovell *Hist. Anim. & Min.* 234 Peacock-fish..Is an insipid and ignoble fish. **1664** Power *Exp. Philos.* I. 38 This more ignoble creature [the great Black Snail] hath also a circulation of its nutritive humour. **1774** Goldsm. *Nat. Hist.* (1776) V. 129 The more ignoble race of birds make up by cunning and assiduity what these claim by force and celerity. **1829** Lytton *Devereux* I. ii, As the human eye is supposed to awe into impotence the malignant intentions of the ignobler animals. **1833** R. Mudie *Brit. Birds* (1841) I. 79 The old division of noble and ignoble hawks,..so well understood, when falconry was a general field sport.

c. Of things, places, etc. (Often passing into 2.)

1611 Coryat *Crudities* (1776) I. 23 This Clermont is a meane and ignoble place, having no memorable thing therein, worthy the obseruation. **1635–56** Cowley *Davideis* IV. 351 Like some fair Pine o'relooking all th' ignobler Wood. **1666** Boyle *Orig. Formes & Qual.* (1667) 41 Some.. maintain it to be possible to transmute the ignobler Metals into Gold. **1713** Young *Last Day* III. 234 My strength exhausted, fainting I descend, And chuse a less, but no ignoble, theme.

2. Not noble in disposition, nature, or quality; mean, base, sordid; dishonourable. Of persons, their actions, aims, desires, etc.

1592 Nashe *P. Penilesse* (ed. 2) 19a, His beggerly parsimony and ignoble illiberaltie. **1594** Shaks. *Rich. III*, III. v. 22 Here is the Head of that ignoble Traytor, The dangerous and vnsuspected Hastings. **1660** Milton *Free Commw.* Wks. (1847) 449/1 The worst and ignoblest sort of men. **1667** — *P.L.* II. 227 Thus Belial..Counsel'd ignoble ease, and peaceful sloath. **1695** Addison *Poems, King*, His Toils for no Ignoble ends designed. **1703** Pope *Thebais* 233 With scandal arm'd, th' ignoble mind's delight. **1851** Ruskin *Mod. Paint.* I. Pref. to ed. 2. 32 Every kind of knowledge may be sought from ignoble motives, and for ignoble ends. **1871** Dixon *Tower* IV. x. 96 The most ignoble year in an ignoble reign.

B. as *sb.* chiefly in pl. *ignobles*, persons not of noble rank; commoners. (In quot. 1808, used as = persons of ignoble character.)

c **1610** Sylvester *Honour's Fare-well* 42 A holy Mirrour, Reducing Nobles, from Ignobles' Errour. *a* **1761** Law tr. *Behmen's Myst. Magnum* xxii. (1772) 98 Be it either by Nobles or Ignobles, none excepted. **1808** E. S. Barrett *Miss-led General* 19 *note*, The Reader may..think that ignobles would be a more proper term [than *nobles*].

ignoble (ɪg'nəʊb(ə)l), *v. rare.* [f. prec. adj., as the opposite of ENNOBLE.] *trans.* To make ignoble or infamous; *fig.* to make of bad repute.

1590–2 Bacon *Disc. Praise Q. Eliz.* in Spedding *Lett. & Life* (1861) I. 142 The Invincible Navy..ignobling many shores and points of land by shipwreck. *a* **1614** Donne *Βιαθανατος* (1644) 80 By confiscation, and by condemning the memory of the delinquent, and ignobling his race. **1628** Gaule *Pract. The.* (1629) 105 The Person dignifies the Place, the Place ignobles not the Person. **1870** E. Peacock *Ralf Skirl.* III. 188 Early sorrow had prevented or ignobled much that was good in him.

ignobleness (ɪg'nəʊb(ə)lnɪs). [f. IGNOBLE + -NESS.] The quality of being ignoble (in either sense of the adj.); ignobility.

1625 K. Long tr. *Barclay's Argenis* I. xiv. 39 Wilt thou staine by the ignoblenesse of the skirmish, eyther thy death or victory? *a* **1661** Holyday *Juvenal* 71. **1741** Middleton *Cicero* II. ix. 329 [Antony] Reproached him with the ignobleness of his birth. **1879** Farrar *St. Paul* xxxi. II. 62 It was not with the world's..rank, but its ignobleness.. divine forces were allied.

†**ig'noblesse.** *Obs. nonce-wd.* [f. IGNOBLE, after *noblesse.*] = prec.

c **1611** Chapman *Sonn., to Earl Montgomrie*, Though Ignoblesse, all such workes defaces As tend to Learning, and the soules delight.

ignobly (ɪg'nəʊblɪ), *adv.* [f. IGNOBLE + -LY^{2}.] In an ignoble manner; lowly, meanly, basely, dishonourably.

1591 Shaks. *1 Hen. VI*, II. v. 35, I, Noble Vnckle, thus ignobly vs'd, Your Nephew..comes. **1607** — *Timon* II. ii. 183 No villanous bounty yet hath past my heart; Vnwisely, not ignobly haue I giuen. **1718** Rowe *Lucan* IX. 453 Yet now, ignobly, you with-hold your Hands, When nearer Liberty your Aid demands. **1746–7** Hervey *Medit.* (1818) 57 Let others..ignobly fawn, or anxiously sue for preferments. **1878** Lecky *Eng. in 18th C.* I. iii. 398 No sooner had the hour for action arrived than he shrank ignobly from the helm. **1878** W. S. Gilbert *H.M.S. Pinafore* I, She says I am ignobly born.

ignominious (ɪgnəʊ'mɪnɪəs), *a.* [a. F. *ignominieux* (14–15th c. in adv. *ignominieusement*, Hatz.-Darm.) = It., Sp. *ignominioso*, or ad. L. *ignōminiōsus*, f. *ignōminia* IGNOMINY.]

1. Full of ignominy; involving shame, disgrace, or obloquy; shameful, disgraceful, discreditable.

In recent use sometimes in weaker sense, 'lowering to one's dignity or self-respect'.

1526 *Pilgr. Perf.* (W. de W. 1531) 205b, The ignomynyous and shamefull deth of the crosse. **1607** Dekker & Webster *Sir T. Wyat* D.'s Wks. 1873 III. 111 You free your Countrie..From Ignominious slauerie. **1781** Gibbon *Decl. & F.* (1869) I. xviii. 499 The ignominious terms of peace were rejected with disdain. **1833** Ht. Martineau *Charmed Sea* i. 7 Taddeus..prepared to go into ignominious exile. **1869** Rawlinson *Anc. Hist.* 82 Carthage consented to conclude an ignominious peace.

2. Of persons: Covered with ignominy; deserving ignominy; infamous.

1577 Vautrouillier *Luther on Ep. Gal.* iv. 27 (1615) 220b, Such as before were strong, full, rich, glorious..shall become feeble, hungrie, poore, ignominious. **1599** Sandys *Europæ Spec.* (1632) 63 The most Reprobate Ignoble Ignominious and wicked race, that ever the world was yet pestered with. **1667** Milton *P.L.* VI. 395 Then first with fear surpris'd and sense of paine, Fled ignominious. **1712** Blackmore *Creation* VII. 80 Where wilt thou hide thy ignominious head? **1724** Swift *Drapier's Lett.* iii. Wks. 1778 III. 388 To be sacrificed to one single, rapacious, obscure, ignominious projector.

Hence **igno'miniously** *adv.*, in an ignominious manner; with ignominy or dishonour; shamefully. **igno'miniousness**, the quality of being ignominious.

1615 G. Sandys *Trav.* 89 Men ignorant in letters, studious for their bellies, and ignominiously lazie. **1727** Bailey vol. II, *Ignominiousness*. **1781** Gibbon *Decl. & F.* xxx. III. 167 The death of the royal captive, who was ignominiously beheaded, disgraced the triumph of Rome and of Christianity. **1844** Ld. Brougham *Brit. Const.* xv. (1862) 223 He was sentenced..to ride ignominiously on a horse with his face towards the tail.

ignominy ('ɪgnəmɪnɪ). [a. F. *ignominie* (15th c. in Hatz.-Darm.), ad. L. *ignōminia* disgrace, dishonour, f. I-^{2} = *in*- not + **gnōmen*, *nōmen* name, reputation.]

1. Dishonour, disgrace, shame; infamy; the condition of being in disgrace, etc.

1540 Morysine *Vives' Introd. Wysd.* Ciijb, They ingender ignominye and shame. **1548** Hall *Chron., Hen. VIII* 171 This ignominie shalbe ever newe and not dye, till you have obteigned the double honor, against all your enemies. **1617** Moryson *Itin.* II. 217 Degrading, and other notes of ignominy, which in military discipline are used. **1727** Swift *Gulliver* II. ii, The ignominy of being carried about for a monster. **1839** Thirlwall *Greece* II. xv. 312 Even his successes had been purchased with ignominy. **1860** Motley *Netherl.* I. i. 10 He had been..obliged to leave the country, covered with ignominy.

2. Ignominious or base quality or conduct; that which entails dishonour or disgrace.

1564 Becon *Wks.* Gen. Pref. Cij, The ignominie of all Priests is, to looke for their owne gayne and profite. **1643** Sir T. Browne *Relig. Med.* I. §40, I am not so much afraid of death, as ashamed thereof: 'tis the very disgrace and ignominy of our natures. **1828** Macaulay *Ess., Hallam* (1887) 94 He [Churchill] then repays by ingratitude the benefits which he has purchased by ignominy.

†**ig'nomious**, *a. Obs.* Shortened form of IGNOMINIOUS. (Cf. next.)

1574 Rich *Mercury & Sold.* Lvijb, Leaving..their renowne defaced and their life..ignomious. **1581** Marbeck *Bk. of Notes* 98 If thou doe gather, it is ignomious vnto thee: for infamie will thereby come. *a* **1598** Peele *Sir Clyomon*

Prol., Worthy writers' works, Wherein, as well as famous facts, ignomious placed are.

†**'ignomy.** *Obs.* Shortened form of IGNOMINY.
1534 WHITINTON *Tullyes Offices* I. (1540) 32 They seme to drede..their repulsion from dignyte as an ignomye and infamye. **1549** COVERDALE, etc. *Erasm. Par. Titus* ii. 30 Vexed with many afflictions and ignomies. **1650** J. HALL *Paradoxes* 36 Fame..when once it declines brings double ignomy. **1704** HEARNE *Duct. Hist.* (1714) I. 100 The good Effect of virtuous Actions..and the contrary Evil and Ignomy attending vicious Ones. **1805** tr. *Desforges' Eugene & Eugenia* II. 93 The shame, the reproach, the ignomy, cast upon..their name.

ig'norable, *a.* [ad. L. *ignōrābilis* unknown, f. *ignōrāre* to IGNORE: see -ABLE. Cf. F. *ignorable.*] Capable of being ignored; of which one may be ignorant.
1856 FERRIER *Inst. Metaph.* 433 The only possible object of ignorance—the only ignorable—if so barbarous a word be permissible. **1866** —— *Grk. Philos.* I. 483 The knowable alone is the ignorable.

†**igno'ramo.** *Obs.* An Italianized or Hispanicized form of IGNORAMUS 2.
1623 LISLE *Ælfric on O. & N. Test.* To Rdr. 26, I bewaile these Ignoramoes.

ignoramus (ɪgnɒˈreɪməs). Pl. **-uses** (-əsɪz), also †**-us.** [L., = 'we do not know', (in legal use) 'we take no notice of [it]'.]

†**1.** The endorsement formerly made by a Grand Jury upon a bill or indictment presented to them, when they considered the evidence for the prosecution insufficient to warrant the case going to a petty jury. Hence quasi-*sb.* or *ellipt.*, esp. in the phrases ***to find, return, bring in (an) ignoramus***; more rarely in passive, ***to be found, returned ignoramus.*** Also *transf.* an answer which admits ignorance of the point in question; *fig.* a state of ignorance.
(The words now used in the finding of the Grand Jury are 'not a true bill', or 'not found' or 'no bill'.)
a **1577** SIR T. SMITH *Commw. Eng.* II. xxii, If they doe not find it true, they write on the back-side, *Ignoramus*, and so deliver it to the Justices. **1598** FLORIO *Ital. Dict.* Ep. Ded. a iv a, I haue seene the best, yea naturall Italians..giue it ouer, or giue their verdict, with An *ignoramus.* **1607** COWELL *Interpr., Ignoramus*, is a word properly used by the grand Enquest..and written upon the Bill..when as they mislike their evidence, as defective, or too weak to make good the presentment. **1626** BERNARD *Isle of Man* (1627) 102 On the backe of this Inditement..they [the grand jury] write either *Ignoramus*, or *Billa vera.* **1631** *Star Chamb. Cases* (Camden) 2 At the precedent Assizes the Grand Jury found an ignoramus. **1658** J. JONES *Ovid's Ibis* 88 As for Medusa's brother I return ignoramus. **1682** *Enq. Elect. Sheriffs* 14 An *Ignoramus* brought in upon an Indictment against the Earl of Shaftsbury. *a* **1734** NORTH *Exam.* I. ii. §119 (1740) 95 Bills preferred to Grand Juries for High Treason duly proved were returned Ignoramus which was the Form for rejecting the Bill. **1742** FIELDING *J. Andrews* II. xi, If you can prove your innocence..you will be found ignoramus, and no harm will be done. **1769** BLACKSTONE *Comm.* IV. xxiii. (1809) 305 The grand jury..used formerly to endorse on the back of the bill, '*ignoramus*', or, we know nothing of it. **1827** HALLAM *Const. Hist.* (1876) II. xii. 450 The grand jury of London, in their celebrated ignoramus on the indictment preferred against Shaftesbury.
fig. **1613** BEAUM. & FL. *Honest Man's Fort.* v. iii, Wouldst thou come To point of marriage with an ignoramus? **1661** GLANVILL *Van. Dogm.* ix. 78 It hath changed its site..yet whether that were caused by its translation from us, or ours from it, sense leaves us in an Ignoramus.

b. *attrib.* as in ***ignoramus jury, crew, Whig*** (alluding to the Grand Jury which rejected the bill against the Earl of Shaftesbury, 1681).
c **1680** *Roxb. Ball.* (1883) IV. 562 With nose cock't up, and visage like a Fury, Or Foreman of an Ignoramus Jury. **1681** *Ibid.* IV. 351 All her Pride was re-assumed By the Ignoramus Whigs. **1683** *Ibid.* (1885) V. 325 With all your Ignoramus Crew, That Justice hate, and Treason brew. **1682** DRYDEN *Dk. Guise* Prol. 43 Let ignoramus juries find no traitors, And ignoramus poets scribble satires. **1828** MACAULAY *Ess., Hallam* (1889) 87 Where were..the members of ignoramus juries?

2. An ignorant person.
[In reference to the origin of this, cf. Ruggle's *Ignoramus* (acted 1615) 'written to expose the ignorance and arrogance of the common lawyers', in which 'Ignoramus' is the name of a lawyer. The word occurs also in the following title, evidently in legal connexion: 'The Case and Arguments against Sir Ignoramus, of Cambridge, in his Readings at Staple's Inn', by R. Callis, Serjeant at Law (1648). See also quot. 1634 below.]
a **1616** BEAUMONT *Vertue of Sack* in *Poems* (1653) Nj, Give blockheads beere, And silly *Ignoramus*, such as think There's powder-treason in all Spanish drink. **1634** *Grammar Warre* D vij, All students of Ignorance, with these bussards of Barbary, Ignoramus and Dulman his Clearke, were..exiled for euer out of all Grammar; and all false Latine was euer after confiscated to their vse. **1641** *Vox Borealis* in *Harl. Misc.* (Malh.) IV. 434 So many of their commanders are ignoramusses in the very vocables of art. **1675** COCKER *Morals* 8 By verbal sounds, who makes his small parts famous, But proves himself the greater Ignoramus. **1683** KENNETT tr. *Erasm. on Folly* 48 Who is so silly as to be Ignoramus to a Proverb? **1790** COWPER *Lett.* 10 May, So ignorant am I and by such ignoramuses surrounded. **1853** C. BRONTE *Villette* vi, I am quite an ignoramus, I know nothing—nothing in the world.

Hence †**igno'ramus'd** *ppl. a.*, freed from prosecution by the *ignoramus* of the Grand Jury.
a **1734** NORTH *Exam.* Chronol., 1681. July 8th. College ignoramus'd in Middlesex. Oct. 19th. Rouse ignoramus'd.

ignorance (ˈɪgnərəns). Also 4-6 **ig-, ygnoraunce,** (5 **ignorence,** 6 **yngnorance**). [a. F. *ignorance* (12th c. in Littré) = It. *ignoranzia*, Sp. *ignorancia*, ad. L. *ignōrāntia*, f. *ignōrānt-em* IGNORANT.]

1. a. The fact or condition of being ignorant; want of knowledge (general or special).
a **1225** *Ancr. R.* 278 Sunne & ignorance, þet is, unwisdom & unwitenesse. *a* **1340** HAMPOLE *Psalter* cxlv. 6 þe blynd in ignoraunce he makis seand in wisdome. *c* **1380** WYCLIF *Serm.* Sel. Wks. II. 32 He..þat synneþ of ignoraunce. **1490** CAXTON *Eneydos* xxviii. 110 Proserpyne..maketh theyr memorye to wexe feble and conuerteth it in to ygnoraunce. **1573** J. SANFORD *Hours Recreat.* (1576) 104 Marvell is the daughter of ignoraunce. **1601** SHAKS. *Twel. N.* IV. ii. 49-50 This house is as darke as Ignorance, thogh Ignorance were as darke as hell. *a* **1635** NAUNTON *Fragm. Reg.* (Arb.) 15 It was the maxime that over-ruled the foregoing times, that ignorance was the mother of devotion. **1742** GRAY *Ode Prospect Eton Coll.* 99 Where ignorance is bliss, 'Tis folly to be wise. **1768** BEATTIE *Minstr.* II. xxx, Be ignorance thy choice, where knowledge leads to wo. **1862** SIR B. BRODIE *Psychol. Inq.* II. v. 147 Much of the evil which exists in the world may be traced to mere ignorance.

b. Constr. of (†*in*, or dependent clause).
1390 GOWER *Conf.* III. 79 Thou..of thy self hast ignorance. **1566** *Acts & Constit. Scotl.* To Rdr. *iij, Thair is..na excusatioun to the man pretendand Ignorance of the Law. **1613** PURCHAS *Pilgrimage* (1614) 595 Oversights of Writers, through negligence or ignorance in forren names. **1847** L. HUNT *Men, Women & B.* I. i. 1 The supposition is founded on an ignorance of the nature of the human mind. **1872** RUSKIN *Eagle's N.* §16 National ignorance of decent art is always criminal.

c. With *an* and *pl.*: An instance or example of ignorance. *rare.*
1749 C. WESLEY in Bp. Lavington *Enthus. Methodists* (1754) I. ii. 76 That very weak Sermon..which is an *Ignoratio Elenchi* (an Ignorance of the Point in Question). **1758** BLACKSTONE *Study of Law* in *Comm.* I. (1809) 7 An ignorance in these must always be of dangerous consequence. **1817** J. SCOTT *Paris Revisit.* (ed. 4) 62 Difficulties which the ignorances and violence of the people have frequently thrown in the way of their princes. **1881** *Modern Rev.* Jan. 136 All falsities and ignorances are eliminated.

†**2.** With *an* and *pl.* An act due to want of knowledge; an offence or sin caused by ignorance.
c **1425** *Prymer* (E.E.T.S.) 62 [Ps. xxv. 7] Lord, remembre þou not þe trespassis of my ȝougþe, and myn ignoranncis. **1549** *Bk. Com. Prayer, Litany*, That it may please thee..to forgeue us all our synnes, negligences, and ignoraunces. **1598** YONG *Diana* 6 He neuer committed any ignorance, that might turne to the hurt or hinderance of his faith. **1611** BIBLE *1 Esdras* viii. 75 Our sinnes are multiplied aboue our heads, and our ignorances haue reached vp vnto heauen. [**1841** TRENCH *Parables* xxii. (1877) 377 Sin is oftentimes an ignorance.]

3. (In full ***the time*** or ***days of ignorance***; tr. Arab. *jāhilīyah* state of ignorance, f. *jāhil* ignorant.) The period of Arabian history previous to the teaching of Muhammad.
1788 GIBBON *Decl. & F.* V. l. 185 Of the time of ignorance which preceded Mahomet, seventeen hundred battles are recorded by tradition. **1895** A. MENZIES *Hist. Relig.* 213 The Arabs called the period before Islam the 'time of ignorance'; in that period they considered their race had no history. **1904** W. P. KER *Dark Ages* 14 The student of heroic poetry may admire the temper of the Arabian Dark Ages—'the Ignorance'. **1937** P. H. HITTI *Hist. Arabs* vii. 87 The term *jāhilīyah*, usually rendered 'time of ignorance' or 'barbarism', in reality means the period in which Arabia had no dispensation, no inspired prophet, no revealed book.

†**'ignorancy.** *Obs.* Also 6 **yngnorancye.** [ad. L. *ignōrāntia*: see prec. and -ANCY.] The quality of being ignorant; = IGNORANCE 1.
1526 TINDALE *Eph.* iv. 18 Thorowe the ignorancy that is in them. **1545** ASCHAM *Toxoph.* To Gentlem. Eng. (Arb.) 19 They can neyther folowe it, bycause of theyr ignorauncie. **1588** GREENE *Pandosto* (1843) 4 Rather frowne at my impudencie, then laugh at my ignorancie.

ignorant (ˈɪgnərənt), *a.* (*sb.*). Also 6 **yngnorant.** [a. F. *ignorant* (14th c. in Littré) = It., Sp. *ignorante*, ad. L. *ignōrans, ignōrānt-em*, pres. pple. of *ignōrāre* not to know: see IGNORE.]

A. *adj.* **1. a.** Destitute of knowledge, either in general or with respect to a particular fact or subject; unknowing, uninformed, unlearned. †*Ignorant Friars*: see IGNORANTINE.
c **1374** CHAUCER *Boeth.* v. met. iii. 124 (Camb. MS.) What wyht þat is al vnkunnynge and ignoraunt. **1483** CAXTON *Cato* 2 b, To therudicion and lernynge of them that ben ygnoraunt. **1500-20** DUNBAR *Poems* lxx. 17 We ar so beistlie, dull, and ignorant, Our rudnes may nocht lichtlie be correctit. **1661** *Grand Debate* 59 The same words are to be read by the ablest and ignorantest man. **1693** tr. *Emilianne's Hist. Monast. Ord.* xiv. 144 The Order of the Brothers of Charity, called otherwise..Ignorant Fryars. **1709** LADY M. W. MONTAGU *Let. to Miss A. Wortley* 21 Aug., I shall return to London the same ignorant soul I went from it. **1797** BEWICK *Brit. Birds* (1847) I. 73 To mislead the ignorant and credulous. **1855** MOTLEY *Dutch Rep.* v. iii. (1866) 704 There were..none so ignorant as not to know his deeds.

b. *fig.* or *transf.* of things.
1611 SHAKS. *Cymb.* III. i. 27 His Shipping (Poore ignorant Baubles!) on our terrible Seas..crack'd..'gainst our Rockes. **1718** J. CHAMBERLAYNE *Relig. Philos.* (1730) I. viii. §1 That the Origin thereof can be ascribed to nothing less than an Accidental and Ignorant Cause. **1875** 'MARK TWAIN' in *Atlantic Monthly* Jan. 71/1 This fellow had..an ignorant silver watch and a showy brass watch chain. **1892** —— *Amer. Claimant* Pref., It ought to be the ablest weather that can be had, not ignorant, poor-quality, amateur weather.

2. *Const.* **a.** With *in*: Uninformed or unskilled in, not acquainted with (a subject). *rare.*
1526 *Pilgr. Perf.* (W. de W. 1531) G b, For that we sholde not be ignoraunt feble & weyke in these thynges. **1563** W. FULKE *Meteors* (1640) 56 The ignorant in Philosophy must be admonished, that all things are full, nothing is empty. **1662** J. DAVIES tr. *Olearius' Voy. Ambass.* 180 Finding the Muscovian Pilot..absolutely ignorant in the business of Navigation. **1833** I. TAYLOR *Fanat.* i. 2 Ignorant in the chief article of the case.

b. with *of*: Having no knowledge of; hence †unconscious of, innocent of, having no share in (also ***ignorant to***). (In quot. 1755, taking no notice of, ignoring.)
1483 CAXTON *G. de la Tour* Ij b, Ignoraunt of this faytte. **1530** in W. H. Turner *Select. Rec. Oxford* 85 He is yngnorant to the acte. **1548** HALL *Chron., Edw. IV* 195 b, Of thys the erle of Warwycke was nothyng ignorant. **1615** G. SANDYS *Trav.* 64 Of cards and dice they are happily ignorant. *a* **1716** SOUTH *Serm.* III. 278 In some things, it is much more difficult for a Man..to be Ignorant of his Duty than to Learn it. **1755** *Man* No. 38 ¶5 To be ignorant of calumny more effectually stops its progress than vindication. **1862** BRODIE *Psychol. Inq.* II. v. 144 They are ignorant of many things with which we are well acquainted.

c. with dependent clause.
c **1532** *Remedie of Love* xxxiv, As a wanton lambe full ignorante How he is pulled and drawen to be bounde. **1551** ROBINSON tr. *More's Utop.* Ep. P. Giles (Arb.) 24, I am..ignorant in what sea that ylande standeth. **1586** A. DAY *Eng. Secretary* To Rdr. (1625) A iv, Being..nothing ignorant what great perfection is to be required in such a one. **1698** FRYER *Acc. E. India & P.* 114 They being ignorant how the Veins lye. **1791** MRS. RADCLIFFE *Rom. Forest* ix, I am ignorant that till now I ever made you this offer. **1866** GEO. ELIOT *F. Holt* i. (1868) 22 She was ignorant what sort of man Harold had become now.

3. *transf.* **a.** Showing absence of knowledge; resulting from ignorance.
1509 HAWES *Past. Pleas.* XIV. (Percy Soc.) 56 Besyde my draughtes rude and ignoraunt. **1604** SHAKS. *Oth.* IV. ii. 70 Alas, what ignorant sin haue I committed. *Mod.* This is a mere ignorant statement.

†**b.** That keeps one in ignorance. *nonce-use.*
1611 SHAKS. *Wint. T.* I. ii. 397 If you know ought which do's behoue my knowledge..imprison't not In ignorant concealement.

†**4.** Of things: Unknown. *Obs.*
(Cf. L. *ignārus* in sense of *ignōtus.*)
1547 HOOPER *Answ. Bp. Winchester* Ded. A ij b, It is not ignorant unto youe what may be done by the vertue of a fere and well orderyd oracion. **1548** UDALL *Erasm. Par. Luke* xviii. 139 b, It was not ignoraunt to him what thyng the blynde man wished to haue. **1612** CHAPMAN *Widowes T.* v. i, Whence he is, tis ignorant to vs. **1634** SIR T. HERBERT *Trav.* 219 It seemes ignorant that, long before, our Countrimen had embraced Christ by the preaching of Joseph of Arimathea.

5. *dial.* and *colloq.* Ill-mannered, uncouth.
¶Sometimes written as *iggerant* in imitation of vulgar speech.
1886 R. E. G. COLE *Gloss. Words S.W. Lincs.* 71 *Ignorant*, ill-mannered. **1886** F. T. ELWORTH *West Somerset Word-Bk.* 363 *Ignorant*, wanting in manners. The usual description of a rough, uncouth lout. **1946** K. TENNANT *Lost Haven* (1947) xvii. 273 He used the word 'ignorant' in the country sense of knowing nothing of good manners. **1965** *Listener* 22 July 137/3 He writes what he *thinks* 'a Puerto Rican' is thinking (very elemental, Latin, iggerant, dumb, baffled, passionate). **1966** 'L. LANE' *ABZ of Scouse* 49, I jes' can't stan' that feller, 'e's plain bloody 'iggerant. **1968** *New Society* 22 Aug. 266/1 Ignorant, meaning 'bad-mannered', is non-U.

B. *sb.* **a.** An ignorant person. Now *rare.*
c **1480** HENRYSON *Mor. Fab.* 7 Who is enemie to science and cunning, Bot ignorants who vnderstandeth not? **1563** FOXE *A. & M.* 716 We must nedes judge you an ignoraunt herin. **1627** H. BURTON *Baiting Pope's Bull* 2 Ignorants write their marke, in stead of their names. **1700** CONGREVE *Way of World* III. xiii, Ah! to marry an ignorant that can hardly read or write! **1863** MRS. C. CLARKE *Shaks. Char.* xvi. 394 The pretty ignorants had lost their fascination for him. **1874** MICKLETHWAITE *Mod. Par. Churches* 239 Church authorities..too often entrust their buildings to ignorants.

†**b.** *pl.* An order of friars: see IGNORANTINE.
1693 tr. *Emilianne's Hist. Monast. Ord.* xix. 220 Besides these Orders, there is mention made..of the Ignorants.

Ignorantine (ɪgnəˈræntɪn), *a.* and *sb. Eccl. Hist.* [ad. F. *ignorantin*, f. *ignorant* IGNORANT, after *bénédictin, capucin*, etc.: see -INE.] ***Ignorantine friars, Ignorantines***: a name applied to themselves in humility by the members of a religious order, the Brethren of Saint-Jean-de-Dieu, founded in 1495 to minister to the sick poor; they were introduced into France by Mary de Medici, and subsequently devoted themselves to the instruction of the poor (cf. IGNORANT *a.* 1 quot. 1693 and *sb.* b). Hence, 'by confusion, and sometimes in mockery' (Littré), the name is given in France to the 'Brethren of the Christian Schools', or 'Christian Brothers', a community founded *c* 1680, for the spread of education among the poor.
1861 M. ARNOLD *Pop. Educ. France* 37 Both the 'Ignorantine Friars' and the old village pedagogues are greatly regretted in the country. **1882-3** SCHAFF *Encycl. Relig. Knowl.* II. 1061 Ignorantines..the name of the members of an institution founded in the beginning of the 18th century in France, by the abbot Baptiste de la Salle.

ignorantism ('ɪgnərəntɪz(ə)m). *rare.* [f. IGNORANT + ISM. Cf. F. *ignorantisme.*] A system which exalts or favours ignorance; = OBSCURANTISM.

1856 *Sat. Rev.* II. 214/2 The aim of these censors is, obviously, to institute a sort of Protestant Ignorantism—a new religious hierarchy, in which readiness to pronounce one or two commonplace Shibboleths shall send a man to the top of the scale.

'ignorantist. = OBSCURANTIST.

1882 OGILVIE (Annandale) Suppl.

ignorantly ('ɪgnərəntlɪ), *adv.* [f. IGNORANT *a.* + -LY^{2}.] In an ignorant manner; without knowledge.

1495 *Act 11 Hen. VII*, c. 63 *Preamble*, In the which Acte ..the seid Francis Lovell was ignorauntly lefte oute and omitted. **1526** TINDALE *Acts* xvii. 23 Whom ye then ignorantly worship, hym shewe I vnto you. **1600** J. PORY tr. *Leo's Africa* II. 38 Extreme paine of the stomacke, which ignorantly they call, the paine of the hart. **1644** MILTON *Educ.* Wks. (1847) 99/1 An ambitious and mercenary or ignorantly zealous divinity. **1784** COWPER *Tiroc.* 108 Taught of God they may indeed be wise, Nor ignorantly wand'ring miss the skies.

'ignorantness. *rare*$^{-1}$. [f. as prec. + -NESS.] = IGNORANCE.

1632 LITHGOW *Trav.* VIII. 373 My Dragoman, doubting of his passage,..which arose from his ignorantnesse thereof. **1727** in BAILEY vol. II.

‖**ignoratio elenchi**: see next, 3.

ignoration (ɪgnɒ'reɪʃən). [ad. L. *ignōrātiōn-em*, n. of action f. *ignōrāre* to IGNORE.]

†**1.** The fact or condition of being ignorant; mistaking or misunderstanding through want of knowledge. *Obs.*

1612 H. AINSWORTH *Annot. Ps.* vii. *heading*, The word properly signifieth Aberration, or Ignoration.

2. The action of ignoring or treating as unknown; disregarding; the fact of being ignored.

1865 *Standard* 12 June 6/6 After long years of ignoration, let us coin the word, it is wanted in our language, Cherubini is about to be recognized. **1872** HARDWICK *Tradit. Lanc.* 63 The faith in the tradition produced a more tragic result than the most superstitious could have dreaded from its ignoration. **1881** *Q. Rev.* 212 The reply to that is that it is an entire ignoration of human nature.

3. *Ignoration of the Elench*, a rare anglicized repr. of the more usual Scholastic Latin **ignoratio elenchi** (ɪgnɒ'reɪʃɪəʊ ɪ'lɛŋkaɪ), a logical fallacy which consists in apparently refuting an opponent, while actually disproving some statement different from that advanced by him; also extended to any argument which is really irrelevant to its professed purpose.

1588 WHITAKER *Disp. Script.* (1849) 287 (Stanf.) This fallacy is that called *ignoratio elenchi*. **1638** CHILLINGW. *Wks.* II. 102 (Stanf.) Here was no *petitio principii* in Dr. Potter, but rather *ignoratio elenchi* in you. **1843** MILL *Logic* V. vii. §3 The fallacy of *Ignoratio Elenchi*,..also called by Archbishop Whately the Fallacy of Irrelevant Conclusion. **1866** FOWLER *Deduct. Logic* VIII. §4 The fallacy of Irrelevancy (or, as it is sometimes called, shifting ground) is technically termed *Ignoratio Elenchi*, i.e. ignorance of the syllogism required for the refutation of an adversary..this has now received a wider meaning. Whenever an argument is irrelevant to the object which a speaker or writer professes to have in view, it is called an ignoratio elenchi.

ignore (ɪg'nɔə(r)), *v.* [ad. F. *ignorer*, or L. *ignōrāre* not to know, to be ignorant of, mistake, misunderstand, disregard, ignore, f. I-^{2}, *in-* not + **gnōr-āre*, f. stem *gnō-* to know (cf. *gnārus* knowing).

In sense 1 the word occurs frequently in the works of Robert Boyle, with whom it has been erroneously supposed to have originated (cf. Aubrey's *Lett.* (1813) II. 159, and Bentley *Phalaris* Pref. 86). Todd, who points out that Johnson was wrong in holding this view, adds 'but it is a word not worthy to be used'. This sense appears to have become obs. by 1700, though occasionally used later (cf. quot. 1860). Sense 3 appears in the 19th c., and was *c* 1850 still used with apology.]

†**1.** *trans.* Not to know, to be ignorant of. *Obs.* or *rare.*

1611 COTGR., *Ignorer*, to ignore, or be ignorant of, to want skill, not to know. *c* **1612** SYLVESTER *Tropheis Henrie Gt.* Wks. (1621) 1088 Who durst not speak, his mildnes did ignore. **1620** SHELTON *Quix.* IV. ii. II. 21 Ignoring what competent Thanks she might return him..she cast herself down at his Feet. **1665** BOYLE *Occas. Refl.* IV. xv. (1848) 262 There are others..desirous to be taught by me, the little that I know, and they ignore. **1674** R. GODFREY *Inj. & Ab. Physic* 173 Good in an Apothecaries Hand, who ignores their Dose or Composition. [**1755–89** JOHNSON, *Ignore*,.. this word Boyle endeavoured to introduce, but it has not been received. **1776** G. CAMPBELL *Philos. Rhet.* (1801) I. 352 They appear as spots in his work. Such is the appearance which the terms opine, ignore, adroitness..have at present in the writings of some ingenious men.] **1860** R. F. BURTON *Centr. Afr.* II. 206 The 'principal men' at the southern extremity ignored the extent northward.

2. Said of a Grand Jury: To return (a bill) with the endorsement 'not a true bill', 'not found', or 'no bill': see IGNORAMUS 1; to reject as unfounded or having insufficient evidence; to refuse acceptance of.

1830 DE QUINCEY *Bentley* Wks. VII. 176 The word ignore, which he threw in the teeth of Mr. Boyle..is, in fact, Hibernian, which Bentley did not know; and in England is obsolete, except in the use of grand juries. (*Note* in *Wks.* 1857) It was written in the summer of 1830, at which time no vestige of a suspicion had arisen that very soon the word would be called back; or rather would be raised from a lifeless toleration in law-books to a popular and universal currency. It was a word much wanted..Yet there are pedants who..would even now (1857) ignore this indispensable word. **1838** *Penny Cycl.* XII. 460/1 When the bill is found not to be true, or, as it is frequently called, 'ignored', the accused is discharged..Sometimes, when the bill is ignored on account of some slip or error, the judge will direct the accused to be kept in custody. **1893** *Law Times* XCV. 28/1 The Lord Chief Justice suggested to the Grand Jury to ignore the bills, but they returned true bills.

3. To refuse to take notice of; not to recognize; to disregard intentionally, leave out of account or consideration, shut 'one's eyes to'.

1801 W. TAYLOR in Robberds *Mem.* I. 381 It is the worst symptom about your rise, that you ignore your former friends. **1832** B'NESS BUNSEN in Hare *Life* (1879) I. ix. 395 It was resolved to ignore this invitation. **1837** CARLYLE *Fr. Rev.* III. I. i, Happily human brains have such a talent of taking up simply what they can carry, and ignoring all the rest. **1851** LD. SHAFTESBURY in Hodder *Life* (1886) II. 358 They began by reviling me, they now *ignore* me, as the phrase goes. **1854** EARL OF CARLISLE *Diary Turk. & Grk. Waters* 189 Mr. Finlay says that the modern Greeks wholly ignore (I beg pardon for the use of the word) the whole period from Alexander the Great to Lord Palmerston. **1856** FROUDE *Hist. Eng.* (1858) I. ii. 161 He could not ignore an important feature of necessary evidence.

Hence **ig'noring** *vbl. sb.* and *ppl. a.*; also **ig'norer**, one who ignores.

1615 SYLVESTER *St. Lewis* 274 Th' hopefull Arrogance Sprung from ignoring of our Ignorance. **1841–4** EMERSON *Ess.*, *Manners* Wks. (Bohn) I. 213 Society loves..an ignoring eye, which does not see the annoyances, shifts, and inconveniences, that cloud the brow..of the sensitive. **1883** *Athenæum* 11 Aug. 167/1 The ignoring of this distinction. **1895** *Columbus* (Ohio) *Chron.* 12 Jan. 1/1 A sweet ignorer of the laws Of etiquette and rules of dress.

†**ig'noscency.** *Obs. rare.* [ad. late L. *ignōscentia*, abstr. sb. f. *ignōscĕre* to pardon, forgive, f. *in-* not + *(g)nōscĕre* to take notice of.] Forgiveness; forgiving spirit.

1647 TRAPP *Comm. Matt.* xviii. 3 And become as little children..in simplicity, humility, innocency, ignoscency. *Ibid.*, *1 Cor.* xiv. 20 In innocency and ignoscency.

†**ig'noscible,** *a. Obs. rare*$^{-0}$. [ad. L. *ignōscibilis* (rare), f. *ignōscĕre* to pardon: see -BLE.]

1656 BLOUNT *Glossogr.*, *Ignoscible*, tollerable, to be pardoned. Hence in PHILLIPS, BAILEY, etc.

†**ignote,** *a.* and *sb. Obs.* [ad. L. *ignōtus*, f. I-^{2}, *in-* not + *gnōtus*, *nōtus* known. Cf. It., Sp. *ignoto.*]

A. *adj.* Unknown.

1623 COCKERAM, *Ignote*, vnknowne. **1633** COWLEY *Poet. Bloss.*, *A Vote*, Th' ignote are better than ill known. **1639** G. DANIEL *Ecclus.* xlii. 60 Things secret, and Ignote. **1663** *Flagellum, or O. Cromwell* (1672) 137 Persons..of such mean and ignote extractions. *a* **1697** AUBREY *Lives, Hobbes* (1898) I. 366 They were both ignote to foreigners.

B. *sb.* A person unknown.

1639 G. DANIEL *Ecclus.* ix. 33 Leave not a proved freind; for an Ignote Comes but at hazard. *a* **1670** HACKET *Abp. Williams* I. (1692) 162 In a letter that an ignote wrote. *Ibid.* II. 144 Such Ignotes were not courted, but pass'd over.

†**ig'notion.** *Obs. nonce-wd.* [Noun of action f. L. *ignōscĕre*; intended as a negative of *notion*.] An ignorant notion; a notion falsely so called.

1647 WARD *Simp. Cobler* (1843) 19 These wits..cry up and downe in corners such bold ignotions of a new Gospell.

†**'ignotism.** *Obs.* [irreg. f. L. *ignōt-us* unknown + -ISM.] A mistake due to ignorance.

1737 *Gentl. Mag.* VII. 336/1 It has 92 Errors or *Ignotisms* in it.

‖**ignotum per ignotius** (ɪg'nəʊtəm pər ɪg'nəʊʃɪəs or ɪg'nəʊtɪəs). [late L., lit. the unknown by means of the more unknown.] An attempt to explain what is obscure by something which is more obscure, leading to 'confusion worse confounded'.

c **1386** CHAUCER *Canon's Yeoman's Tale* 1457 And Plato answerde vnto hym anoon, 'Take the stoon that Titanos men name.' 'Which is that?' quod he. 'Magnasia is the same,' Seyde Plato. 'Ye, sire, and is it thus? This [is] *ignotum per ignocius* [v.r. *ignotius*]. What is Magnasia, good sire, I yow preye?' *c* **1450** LYDGATE *Secrees* (1894) 588 With goldeyn Resouns in taast moost lykerous, Thyng per ignotum prevyd per ignocius. **1584** R. SCOT *Discov. Witchcr.* III. xvii. 67 Confuteth that opinion by a notable reason, called *Petitio principij*, or rather, *Ignotum per ignotius*. *a* **1734** R. NORTH *Examen* (1740) II. i. 28 When he drops his own Authority, and brings Fact to confirm all, the vouching that Fact by his own pure Parole, is a Cheat termed *Ignotum per ignotius*. **1888** *Athenæum* 22 Dec. 843/2 When Arabic names are twisted and mis-copied..the identification of sites resolves itself into a case of 'ignotum per ignotius'. **1931** *Times Lit. Suppl.* 30 July 590/3 [He] even goes so far on one occasion as to explain an Egyptian *chiaoush* as being analogous to an Indian *chobdav*, which to some readers may be a case of *ignotum per ignotius*. **1935** *Ibid.* 2 May 289/1 A distinct failure to escape the imputation of *ignotum per ignotius*.

†**i-go,** *v. Obs. Pa. t.* i-eode. [OE. *ȝegán* (= OHG. *gigân*; cf. OE. *ȝegangan*, OS., OHG. *gigangan*), f. *gán* to GO.]

1. *intr.* To go, pass.

c **900** tr. *Bæda's Hist.* II. xvi. (1890) 144 Heo meahte ȝegan ..ofer eall þis ealond. *c* **1205** LAY. 25773 Bi-halues þe iga and bihald ȝeorne, ȝif þu miht afinden oht of þan feonden. *a* **1225** *Ancr. R.* 208 Longe beon unbishoped & falsliche igon to schrifte.

2. *trans.* To go into, invade.

c **1205** LAY. 4253 Seoððen Bruttes hit [Bruttaine] ieode [*c* **1275** hadde]. *Ibid.* 26376 While þine aldren France ieoden [*c* **1275** bi-ȝeode].

i-go, i-gon, ME. pa. pple. of GO *v.*

i-goded, ME. pa. pple. of *gode*, GOOD *v.*

i-gon, pa. t. of I-GIN *v.*, to begin.

Igorot ('i:gərəʊt). Also Igolot(e), Igorrot(e), Ygorrote. [ad. Sp. *Ygolote* (A. de Morga, 1609), f. the native name.] Name of a people inhabiting northern Luzon in the Republic of the Philippines. Also as *collect. sing.* and *attrib.*

1821 W. WALTON tr. *T. de Comyn's State of Philippine Islands* p. xli, An expedition was also sent against the Igorrots, inhabiting the mountains of the interior, where gold is obtained. *Ibid.* ii. 32 The Igorrot Indians, who occasionally come down from the mountains to barter with the Christians, use certain coarse jars or vessels of copper. **1840** *Penny Cycl.* XVIII. 88/2 The Ygorrotes, who inhabit the mountains east of the Gulf of Lingayen, are distinguished by a peculiar physiognomy and a lighter colour. **1875** F. JAGOR *Trav. Philippines* 131 The Ygorrotes are not Christians. **1885** *Encycl. Brit.* XVIII. 753/1 The Igorrotes or Igolotes proper (for the name is by many writers very loosely applied to all the pagan mountain tribes of Luzon) inhabit the districts of Bangued, Lepanto, Tiagan, Bontoc. **1898** D. C. WORCESTER *Philippine Islands* 438 One of the Igorrote peoples is believed to be descended from the followers of the Chinese invader Limahong. **1903** BARROWS in *Philippine Jrnl. Sci.* Oct. 796 The powerful and numerous Igorot of northern Luzon. **1914** D. C. WORCESTER *Philippines Past & Present* I. 343 This once prosperous little Igorot hamlet had been burned by the Spaniards. **1925** K. MAYO *Isles of Fear* 256 The Igorots proper, however, number only about 70,000. **1957** *Encycl. Brit.* XII. 75/1 There are..two broad groupings of the Igorot as a whole. **1967** WERNSTEDT & SPENCER *Philippine Island World* III. ix. 349 The peoples and cultures of the North Luzon Highlands... Popular reference adopted the term 'Igorot' for the whole population,..although the term properly is only the Tagalog word for 'mountain-dwelling' or 'mountaineer'.

i-goven, ME. pa. pple. of GIVE *v.*

i-grad, ME. pa. pple. of GREDE *v.*, to cry.

i-graithed, i-greithed, ME. pa. pple. of GRAITH *v.*

i-gramed, i-gremed, ME. pa. pple. of GREME *v.*

i-gra(u)nted, ME. pa. pple. of GRANT *v.*

i-graven, ME. pa. pple. of GRAVE *v.*

†**i-'grede.** *Obs.* [f. I- *pref.*^{1} + GREDE cry.] Crying, clamour.

a **1250** *Owl & Night.* 1641 Mid ȝulinge and mid igrede.

†**i-grete,** *v. Obs.* [OE. *ȝegrétan*, f. *grétan* to GREET.] *trans.* To greet.

c **1000** ÆLFRIC *Hom.* II. 526 þæt we maȝon ure frynd ȝeseon and ure siblingas ȝegretan. *a* **1175** *Cott. Hom.* 227 Se ængel..ȝegrette hi. *c* **1275** *Death* 99 in *O.E. Misc.* 174 Alle ..þat..feire þe igretten. *c* **1315** SHOREHAM 119 þo was þat mayde was y-gret.

Hence †**i-gretinge** *vbl. sb.*, greeting.

1258 *Eng. Proclam. Hen. III*, Henr' þurȝ godes fultume king on Engleneloande..Send igretinge to alle hise holde ilærde and ileawede.

†**i-gripe,** *v. Obs.* [OE. *ȝegrípan* (= OHG. *gagrîfan*, MHG. *gegrîfen*), f. *grípan* to GRIPE.] *trans.* To gripe, grip, lay hold of.

c **1205** LAY. 25680 þa men þa he igripeð. *a* **1225** *Juliana* 73 Igripe ha me eanes. *a* **1225** *St. Marher.* 12 þis milde meiden margarete igrap him.

i-gripen, ME. pa. pple. of GRIPE *v.* and IGRIPE *v.*

i-grithed, i-griðed, ME. pa. pple. of GRITH *v.*, to pacify, etc.

i-groten, ME. pa. pple. of GREET *v.*, to weep.

i-grounde(n, ME. pa. pple. of GRIND *v.*

i-growe(n, ME. pa. pple. of GROW *v.*

†**i-grure** (*ü*). *Obs.* = GRURE, horror, terror.

c **1205** LAY. 812 Heo heom aweihten mid heora wæles igrure.

iguana (ɪ'gwɑ:nə). Forms: 6 iuanna, iwana, 6, 9 iguano, 7 yguana, guana, wana, gwane, gwayn, 7– iguana. [a. Sp. *iguana*, repr. the Carib name

iwana (variously given by early writers as *hiuana, igoana, iuanna, yuana*).]

1. A large arboreal lizard of the West Indies and South America, *Iguana tuberculata*, which attains to a length of five feet or more; also, in Zoology, the name of the genus, which includes the ***horned iguana*** of San Domingo, and other species; and loosely applied to other lizards of allied genera.

1555 EDEN *Decades* 126 Foure footed beastes..named Iuannas, muche lyke vnto Crocodiles, of eyght foote length, of moste pleasaunte taste. **1600** HAKLUYT *Voy.* III. 675 Store of fish, foule, deere, and Iwanas. *Ibid.* 815 *Iguanos* which are a kinde of Serpents, with foure feete, and a long sharpe tayle. **1604** E. G[RIMSTONE] tr. *D'Acosta's Hist. W. Ind.* IV. xxxviii. 313 The flesh of the Yguanas is a better meate. **1607** G. PERCY in Purchas *Pilgrimes* (1625) IV. 1686 We also killed Guanas, in fashion of a Serpent, & speckled like a Toade vnder the belly. **1617** RALEIGH *Apol.* 37 [South America] hath plenty of..Tortoyses, Armadiles, Wanaes. **1630** CAPT. SMITH *Trav. & Adv.* 54 Gwanes they have, which is a little harmlesse beast, like a Crokadell or Aligator, very fat and good meat. **1648** GAGE *West Ind.* xix. 143 Another kind of meat they feed much on which is called *Iguana.* **1796** STEDMAN *Surinam* I. 147 That species which is here called the iguana, and by the Indians the wayamaca, is seldom above 3 feet long. **1841** ELPHINSTONE *Hist. Ind.* I. 15 Iguanas, and other lizards, are found in all places. **1859** TENNENT *Ceylon* II. VII. ii. 122 The hideous but harmless iguano..moves slowly across the high-road. **1880** A. R. WALLACE *Isl. Life* ii. 27 The peculiarly American family of the iguanas is represented by two genera in Madagascar.

2. A name used in Africa for a large monitor lizard of the genus *Varanus*, esp. *V. niloticus*, the aquatic Nile monitor.

1753 N. OWEN *Jrnl. Slave-Dealer* (1930) 32 They [*sc.* the Bulums] eat alegators, guanas and long worms. **1801** J. BARROW *Acct. Trav. S. Afr.* I. v. 346 None of the people with me could testify to have seen any other species of that genus [*sc.* crocodile] frequenting the water, except Iguanas, from six to ten feet in length. **1803** T. WINTERBOTTOM *Acct. Native Africans Sierra Leone* I. iv. 69 Although they have several species of lizards, they use only one as an article of diet, the *guana*, lacerta iguana, which they esteem delicate food. **1834** T. PRINGLE *Afr. Sk.* II. vi. 210 One of the deep lagoons formed by the river, and which the [Moravian] brethren have named the Leguan's Tank, from its being frequented by numbers of the large amphibious lizard called the leguan or guana. **1875** J. J. BISSET *Sport & War* xx. 179 Hence [*sc.* from under water] the 'Iguana', a small kind of crocodile, proceed on shore at night and take chickens from the hen-roosts. **1900** H. A. BRYDEN *Animals Afr.* xv. 174 In South Africa this reptile [*sc.* the Nile Monitor] is often miscalled an 'iguana'. **1947** J. STEVENSON-HAMILTON *Wild Life S. Afr.* xxxv. 315 There are two large monitor lizards or leguaans of the genus *Varanus* found in South Africa. These are sometimes called 'iguanas', though the true iguanas are almost all confined to the New World, and the popular term may be merely a corruption of this name. **1964** J. P. CLARK *Three Plays* 30 They struggled like Two iguanas till outspent, they stopped.

Hence **i'guanian** *a.*, resembling an iguana, belonging to the iguana family, *Iguanidæ*; *sb.*, one of this family; also **i'guanid**. **i'guaniform** *a.*, having the form or structure of an iguana. **i'guanoid** *a.* and *sb.* = *iguanian.*

1838 *Penny Cycl.* XII. 441/1 Only one Iguanian belongs to Europe, the common Stellio. **1854** OWEN *Skel. & Teeth* in *Circ. Sc., Organ. Nat.* I. 200 In the iguanians..this synchondrosis is obliterated. **1855** MAYNE *Expos. Lex.*, *Iguanoides*,..iguanoid. **1864** OWEN *Power of God* 46 The Iguanian lizards [are] peculiar to the Western or American hemisphere. **1878** *19th Cent.* Dec. 1048 Madagascar possesses iguanoid lizards (*Hoplurus* and *Chalarodon*).

iguanodon (ɪ'gwɑːnədɒn, -æ-). *Palæont.* [f. IGUANA + Gr. ὀδούς, ὀδοντ- tooth, after *mastodon*, etc.

Mantell, in *Petrif. & their Teachings* (1851) 231–2, states that the name was suggested to him by the Rev. W. D. Conybeare.]

A large herbivorous lizard found fossil in the Wealden formation; it was from twenty-five to thirty feet long, and from its teeth and bones is considered to have resembled in many respects the iguana; whence the name.

1830 LYELL *Princ. Geol.* I. 123 The huge iguanodon might reappear in the woods, and the ichthyosaur in the sea. **1854** F. C. BAKEWELL *Geol.* 56 The length of the Iguanodon must have been nearly 70 feet.

i'guanodont (-dɒnt), *a.* and *sb.* [See prec.] **a.** *adj.* Having teeth like those of the iguana. **b.** *sb.* A saurian so characterized; a member of the family *Iguanodontidæ* of extinct dinosaurs, typified by the iguanodon.

i-gurd, i-gurt, ME. pa. pple. of GIRD *v.*

i-hacked, ME. pa. pple. of HACK *v.*

i-had, ME. pa. pple. of HAVE *v.*

i-haded, ME. pa. pple. of HADE *v.*[1], to ordain.

i-hal, var. of YHOLE.

†**i-hald, i-hold**, *v. Obs.* [OE. *ȝehealdan* (= OS. *gihaldan*, OHG. *gihaltan*), f. *healdan*:—**haldan* to HOLD.] *trans.* To hold, maintain, observe, keep, preserve.

Beowulf (Z.) 2620 He frætwe ȝeheold fela missera. *c* **1000** *Ags. Ps.* (Th.) cxviii[i]. 101 þæt ic þine word mihte wel ȝehealdan. *c* **1000** *Ags. Gosp.* Luke xi. 21 Se stranga ȝewæpnud his cafertun ȝehealt. *c* **1175** *Lamb. Hom.* 65 Hwenne ic i-halde þa ibode. *a* **1200** *Moral Ode* 56 in *Lamb. Hom.*, Giue hies [= he it] for godes luue, þenne deþ hes wel ihalden [*Jesus Coll. MS.* iholde]. *c* **1205** LAY. 5505 [He] wolde aȝen king Belin feht ihalden.

i-halden, ME. pa. pple. of HOLD *v.*

i-halewed, i-halwed, i-halȝed, ME. pa. pple. of HALLOW *v.*[1]

i-halowed, ME. pa. pple. of HALLOW *v.*[2]

†**i-handle**, *v. Obs.* [OE. **ȝehandlian* (= MHG. *gehandeln*), f. *handlian* to HANDLE.] *trans.* To handle.

c **1205** LAY. 14390 Ne preost ne na biscop ne nauere ihandled godes boc.

i-handled, i-hondled, ME. pa. pple. of HANDLE *v.*

i-haneked, (?) ME. pa. pple. of HANK *v.*

i-haspet, ME. pa. pple. of HASP *v.*

i-hat(te, i-heat, ME. pa. pple. of HEAT *v.*

i-hate(n, ME. pa. pple. of HIGHT *v.*[1]

i-hated, ME. pa. pple. of HATE *v.*

i-heawen, i-hewe, ME. pa. pple. of HEW *v.*

i-hed, of HIDE *v.*: see YHID.

†**i-hede**, *v. Obs.* [OE. *ȝehýdan, ȝehédan*, f. *hýdan*, HIDE *v.*[1]] *trans.* To hide, conceal.

c **888** K. ÆLFRED *Boeth.* xxxix. §8 He hit..ȝehyt and ȝehelt. *c* **1320** *Seuyn Sag.* (W.) 1314 He ne wiste..Whar he mighte hit best i-hede.

i-heied, i-hei(ȝ)et, ME. pa. pple. of HIGH *v.*

i-heled, ME. pa. pple. of HELE *v.*[2], to hide.

†**i-helmed**, *pa. pple. Obs.* [OE. *ȝehelmod* (= OHG. *gehelmôt*), pa. pple. of *(ȝe)helmian*, f. *helm* HELM *sb.*[1]] Helmed.

c **1000** ÆLFRIC *Gram.* xliii. (Z.) 256 *Galeatus*, ȝehelmod. *c* **1205** LAY. 26277 Gerin & Beof..and Walwain..iburned and ihelmed.

i-hende, var. of YHENDE, at hand.

i-hent, ME. pa. pple. of HENT *v.*

†**i-hente**, *v. Obs.* [OE. *ȝehentan*, f. *hentan* to HENT.] *trans.* To grasp; to hold, uphold.

905 *O.E. Chron.*, Eall þæt hie ȝehentan mehton. *c* **1230** *Hali Meid.* 21 For þi was wedlac ilahet in hali chirche..to ihente þe unstronge.

i-heorted, ME. form of HEARTED *ppl. a.*

i-heouwed: see HUED.

i-hercned, ME. pa. pple. of HEARKEN *v.*

i-herd, ME. pa. pple. of HEAR, YHERE, HERY *vbs.*

i-here, var. of YHERE *v.*

i-hered, -et, -i(e)d, ME. pa. pple. of HERY *v.*

i-hert, ME. pa. pple. of HURT *v.*

i-het, ME. pa. pple. of HEAT *v.*

i-heveȝed, i-hevied, weighed down, ME. pa. pple. of HEAVY *v.*

a **1225** *Ancr. R.* 332 þe neoðere [grindstone]..is iheueȝed [*MS. T.* iheueȝet] her mid herde uorte beon cwite of herdre. *c* **1374** CHAUCER *Boeth.* v. met. v. 133 (Camb. MS.) So þat thy thoght ne be nat I-heuyed ne put lowe.

i-hewed, ME. pa. pple. of HEW *v.*, HUE *v.*

i-hid, ME. pa. pple. of HIDE *v.*: see YHID.

†**i-hire**, *v. Obs.* [OE. *ȝehýran*, f. *hýran, hýrian* to HIRE.] *trans.* To hire.

c **1000** ÆLFRIC *Hom.* II. 74 Đæs hiredes ealdor ȝehyrde wyrhtan into his winȝearde. *c* **1250** *Kent. Serm.* in *O.E. Misc.* 34 Godalmichti i-hierde werkmen in-to his winyarde.

†**i-hitte**, *v. Obs.* [f. I- *pref.*[1] + *hitte*, HIT *v.*] *trans.* To hit.

c **1205** LAY. 314 He wende to sceoten þat hea der, & ihitte [*c* **1275** hitte] his aȝene fader.

ihleite ('iːliːaɪt). *Min.* [Named 1876 after Ihle, superintendent of mines at Mugrau, Bohemia: see -ITE.] A hydrous iron sulphate, found as a yellow efflorescence on graphite.

1876 *Amer. Jrnl. Sci.* Ser. III. XII. 151 Prof. Schrauf has announced a new mineral under the name Ihleite.

i-hoded, ME. pa. pple. of HADE, HODE, to ordain.

i-hoked, ME. form of HOOKED *a.*

i-hol: see YHOLE, whole.

†**i-hold.** *Obs.* [OE. *ȝeheald* 'keeping, guarding'.] Place of shelter or abode; hold.

a **1250** *Owl & Night.* 621 þar inne ic habbe god ihold A wintre warm a sumere cold.

i-hold, var. I-HALD, to hold.

i-holden, ME. pa. pple. of HOLD *v.*

i-hole(n, of HELE *v.*[1], to hide.

i-hon, i-honge: see YHONG *v.*, to hang.

i-hondsald, ME. pa. pple. of HANDSEL *v.*

a **1225** *Juliana* 7 Ha wes him sone ihondsald þah hit hire unwil were.

†**i-horned**, *a. Obs.* [Cf. OE. *ȝehyrned* (= MHG. *gehürnet*), f. I- *pref.*[1] + *horned.*] Horned.

[*c* **1000** *Sax. Leechd.* III. 266 ȝyf seo sunne..hine [the moon] onælð riht þwyres þonne byð he emlice ȝehyrned.] *a* **1225** *St. Marher.* 9 In his ihurnd heauet. **1387** TREVISA *Higden* III. 397 In liknesse of Iubiter i-horned. *a* **1415** LYDG. *Temp. Glass* 8 Derk Diane, ihorned, noþing clere.

i-horyed, ME. pa. pple. of HORY *v.*, to pollute.

c **1425** *Eng. Conq. Irel.* 138 The lond shal be I-horyed & I-steyned wyth grete slaght of men.

i-hosed, early ME. form of HOSED *a.*

c **1275** in *O.E. Misc.* 91 þayh we her hoppen ihosed and ischode. **1387** TREVISA *Higden* (Rolls) I. 29 þat boþe i-hosed and i-schod Goddes peple may passe þerby.

i-hote, ME. pa. pple. of HIGHT *v.*[1]

‖**ihram** (ɪ'rɑːm, iːx'rɑːm). Also 8 hir(r)awem. [Arab. *iḥrām* (f. *ḥarama* to forbid: cf. HAREM), a kind of dress used by the Arabs in Spain and Africa; 'sacred state' (Freytag).]

1. The dress worn by Mohammedan pilgrims, consisting of two pieces of white cotton, the one girded round the waist, and the other thrown over the left shoulder.

1704 J. PITTS *Acc. Mohometans* vii. 80 They take off all their cloaths, covering themselves with two Hirrawems, or large white Cotton Wrappers. **1811** tr. *Niebuhr's Trav. Arabia* xii. in Pinkerton *Voy.* X. 20 Pilgrims, in their first journey to Mecca, are obliged to assume the Ihhram immediately after passing Cape Wardan. **1819** T. HOPE *Anastasius* (1820) II. iv. 68 An ihram in rags, an old mat torn to pieces. **1862** *Lond. Rev.* 30 Aug. 187 The time had..arrived for changing our usual habiliments for the 'ihrâm' or pilgrim-costume of two towels, and for taking the various interdictory vows involved in its assumption.

2. The state in which a pilgrim is held to be while he wears this distinctive garb, during which time many acts of ordinary life are held unlawful.

1704 J. PITTS *Acc. Mahometans* 79 On this side Mecca, where all the Hagges..do enter into Hirawem, or Ihram. *Ibid.* 95 The eighth Day after the said two months, they all enter into Hirrawem again.

IHS, in ME., med.L., etc., also written IHS, Ih̄s, IHC, Ih̄c, representing Greek *IHΣ* or *IHC*, a MS. abbreviation of the word *IH(ΣOY)Σ* or *IH(COY)C*, Jesus; also used as a symbolical or ornamental monogram of the sacred name. Mediæval Latin texts have commonly *ih̄c* or *ih̄s, ih̄m, ih̄u* (with or without a stroke over or across the *h* (ħ), or other mark of abbreviation) for *Iesus, Iesum, Iesu.* In ME., the usual form was *ih̄u* = *Jesu*; less frequently *ih̄s, ih̄c*, or *ih̄us.* These abbreviations were in later times often erroneously expanded as *Ihesus, Ihesum, Ihesu.*

The Romanized form of the abbreviation would be IES, but from the entire or partial retention of the Greek form in Latin MSS. as IHC or IHS, and subsequent forgetfulness of its origin, it has often been looked upon as a Latin abbreviation or contraction, and explained by some as standing for I*esus* H*ominum* S*alvator*, Jesus Saviour of men, by others as I*n* H*oc* S*igno* (*vinces*), in this sign (thou shalt conquer), or I*n* H*ac* S*alus*, in this (cross) is salvation.

[*a* **600** *Codex Bezæ* Luke vi. 5 (Greek text) ΕΙΠΕ ΔΕ Ο ΙΗC ΠΡΟC ΑΥΤΟΥC. (Latin text) DIXIT AUTEM IH̄S AD EOS. *c* **950** *Lindisf. Gosp.* (Latin text) Matt. iii. 13 Tunc uenit ih̄s a galilaea in iordanen.] *a* **1240** *Wohunge* in *Cott. Hom.* 269 Ihu, swete. *c* **1250** *Kent. Serm.* (Laud MS. 471, lf. 128b), Cvm natus esset ihc in betleem iude. **1377** LANGL. *P. Pl.* B. III. 154 Bi ih̄us with here ieweles ȝowre iustices she shendeth. *Ibid.* XVI. 144 Iudas iangeled þere-aȝein ac Ih̄us hym tolde. **1540** *Churchw. Acc. St. Giles, Reading* (ed. Nash) 59 Paid to the Wardens of Ihc Masse towardes the prestes wages xiij^s iij^d. **1678** *Trial of Coleman* 27 L. *Chief Just.* What Inscription was upon the Seal? *Mr. Oates. I.H.Σ.* with a Cross, in English it had the Characters of *I.H.S.* **1721** STRYPE *Eccl. Mem.* III. App. xlviii. 145 JHS is God with us [quoting a title of 1559, which had 'Jesus is God with us'.] **1897** *Daily News* 30 Nov. 7/7 The monograms IHS and XPC, which are so often to be seen in our churches, sorely puzzle a portion of the congregation.

i-hud(de, ME. pa. pple. of HIDE *v.*: see YHID.

†**i-hudeket**, *ppl. a. Obs.* [ME., f. *hudeken* vb., app. repr. an OE. **hydecian*, deriv. of *hýdan* to hide.] Hooded.

a **1225** *Ancr. R.* 424 (Cott. MS.) Vte, gan i-mantlet; þe heaued i-hudeket.

i-hurnd: see I-HORNED.

i-hurt, ME. pa. pple. of HURT *v.*

i-huseled, ME. pa. pple. of HOUSEL *v.*

†**i-hwat**, *pron.* *Obs.* [OE. *ʒehwæt*, neut. of *ʒehwá* every one: = OLG. *gihvat*, neut. of *gihvê*.] Everything.

a **900** CYNEWULF *Crist* 1002 Ac þæt fyr nimeð þurh foldan ʒehwæt. *a* **1250** *Owl & Night.* 1056 Lym and grune & wel ihwat [*Cott. MS.* eiwat] Sette and leyde þe for to lacche.

i-hwer: see YWHERE.

i-hwilc, -illc, early ME. forms of OE. *ʒehwylc* EACH, q.v.

†**i-hwulen**, *v.* *Obs.* [ME., f. *hwule* (*ü*), in Ancren Riwle = *hwil* WHILE, time.] *intr.* To have time, be at leisure.

a **1225** *Ancr. R.* 44 Hwon so ȝe euer muwen ihwulen. *Ibid.* 422 Ne mei heo nout i-hwulen uorto hercnen mine lore.

i-imped, ME. pa. pple. of IMP *v.*

I-iron: see I the letter.

iiwi (iː'iːwɪ). [Hawaiian.] A Hawaiian bird, the honeycreeper *Vestiaria coccinea*, whose red feathers were formerly used to make the cloaks of native chiefs.

1779 J. KING *Jrnl.* Mar. in Cook *Voy. Pacific Ocean* (1784) III. vi. 119 The birds of these islands are as beautiful as any we have seen... Another is of an exceeding bright scarlet colour;..its native name is *eeeeve*. **1890** WILSON & EVANS *Aves Hawaiienses* I. 1 Vestiaria Coccinea. Olokele or Iiwi. *Ibid.* 3 The call-note of the 'Iiwi' is peculiar. **1899** A. H. EVANS in *Cambr. Nat. Hist.* IX. vii. 564 The splendid feather-cloaks of the Hawaiian kings..were of old chiefly composed of the plumage of the 'Mamo' (*Drepanis pacifica*) and the 'Iiwi' (*Vestiaria coccinea*). **1915** W. A. BRYAN *Nat. Hist. Hawaii* xxxi. 430 The beautiful red iiwi..is infested with three genera [of bird-lice]. **1944** G. C. MUNRO *Birds Hawaii* 93 With bright scarlet body, black wings and tail, and rose colored, inch long, curved bill, the iiwi is one of the most beautiful of the Hawaiian native birds. **1970** S. CARLQUIST *Hawaii* xi. 198 Iiwis are still relatively common in a number of forest areas of the Islands.

Ijo ('iːdʒəʊ), *sb.* and *a.* Also **Ejo, Idzo, Ijaw.**

A. *sb.* The name of a tribe inhabiting the Niger delta, on the coast of Nigeria; a member of this tribe; the language of this tribe. **B.** *adj.* Of or pertaining to the Ijo tribe.

1856 W. B. BAIKIE *Narr. Voy. Niger* iii. 40 The people are of the same tribe as those who inhabit the tract of country up to the Rio Formoso, where however they are called Ejo or Ojo, by which name also they are known at Abó, at Brass, and even at Bonny. By English palm-oil traders they are often termed Jo-men. **1883** R. N. CUST *Sk. Mod. Lang. Afr.* I. 220 Within the Idzo Language-Field many of the Ibo-speaking Races reside. **1906** A. G. LEONARD *Lower Niger* II. i. 52 So extremely touchy and sensitive are these people—the Ijo particularly so,—so easily piqued and disturbed, even by the mildest of chaff, that they have no hesitation in taking their own lives or the lives of others, on the spur of the moment. *Ibid.* I. iv. 42 An examination of the six or more dialects of Ijo and the five of Bini..shows that they are dissimilar not only to each other, but to the other neighbouring tongues. **1926** P. A. TALBOT *Peoples S. Nigeria* IV. iii. 82 Ijaw is a very primitive negro tongue, perhaps the most ancient in West Africa, and..has not the smallest affinity with any other. **1958** J. S. COLEMAN *Nigeria* xviii. 390 Demands for a separate state were made by minority groups in the Middle Belt in the Northern Region, by the Ijaw peoples of the Delta area, and elsewhere. **1966** M. CROWDER *Story Nigeria* v. 80 The Ijo exported dried fish and salt, which they panned in the salt water creeks, to the peoples of the hinterland in exchange for vegetables and tools. **1971** P. YOUNG in J. Spencer *Eng. Lang. W. Afr.* 180 The Nigerian poet and novelist, Gabriel Okara. His novel *The Voice* exhibits a highly idiosyncratic syntax obtained, according to Okara, by a direct substitution of the syntax of his native Ijaw for normal English syntax.

ijolite ('iːjəʊlaɪt). *Petrogr.* [ad. G. *ijolith* (Ramsay & Berghell 1891, in *Geol. Fören. i Stockholm Förh.* XIII. 304), f. *Ijo*, Sw. rendering of Finnish *Ii*, the name of a village and district on the Finnish coast near Oulu and also the initial element in the names of local geographic features, as *Iijärvi*, *Iijoki*, *Iivaara*: see -LITE.] A plutonic igneous rock consisting essentially of nepheline and pyroxene and containing no felspar.

1897 A. HARKER *Petrol.* (ed. 2) 52 The 'ijolite' of Ramsay and Berghell from Finland, a nepheline-pyroxene-rock free from felspar but sometimes rich in garnet. **1962** W. T. HUANG *Petrol.* iv. 139 Much of the ijolite on Alnö Island, Sweden, and Magnet Cove, Arkansas, contains abundant melanite garnet.

Hence **ijo'litic** *a.*, resembling or of the nature of ijolite.

1938 *Mineral. Abstr.* VII. 36 Masses of limestone and ijolitic intrusives. **1954** H. WILLIAMS et al. *Petrogr.* iv. 72 Most of these ijolitic rocks..owe their characteristics largely to contamination of magma by assimilation of limestone. **1966** R. L. JOHNSON in Tuttle & Gittins *Carbonatites* I. 221 Here there are a number of carbonatite complexes, which include granites, syenites, nepheline syenites and small amounts of ijolitic rocks within their limits.

ijs, obs. spelling of ICE.

ik, ME. form of I *pron.*

i-kakeled, ME. pa. pple. of CACKLE *v.*

†'**ikary, 'icary.** *Obs.* In 6 ickary. [ad. Russ. *ikra* caviare.] = CAVIARE.

1591 G. FLETCHER *Russe Commw.* (1857) 12 Of ickary or cavery, a great quantitie is made upon the river of Volgha, out of the fish called bellougina, the sturgeon. **1662** J. DAVIES tr. *Olearius' Voy. Ambass.* 87 The spawn of Fish, especially that of Sturgeon, they order thus... The Muscovites call it Ikary, and the Italians Cavaiar. [**1887** *Pall Mall G.* 15 Feb. 11/1 Can you use the roe of any other fish but sturgeon and sterlet as caviar, or ikra, as you call it?]

‖**ikat** ('ikat). [Mal., lit. 'to tie, fasten'.] A technique of fabric decoration common in Indonesia and Malaysia, in which warp or weft threads, or both, are tied at intervals and dyed before weaving; also, a fabric of this kind.

1931 C. F. IKLÉ (*title*) Ikat technique and Dutch East Indian ikats. **1942** *Ciba Rev.* Aug. 1586 The ikat process can be applied to the warp, the weft, or to both systems of the threads of a fabric. **1953** C. A. GIBSON-HILL *Malay Arts & Crafts*, §Hand-woven cloths. A variant form (of cloth) is sometimes introduced by a tie-and-dye technique (*ikat chuai*), in which short lengths of the woof are tied round with dye-proof strips of banana leaf and the skein then immersed in the dye. **1959** *Chambers's Encycl.* IV. 703/1 A.. technique known as *ikat* is practically limited to Indonesia. In this method the warp threads of a cloth are set out before weaving and tied at intervals before dyeing. **1968** *Encycl. Brit.* XII. 180/1 In the textiles in *batik* (wax-resist) and *ikat* (pre-dyed thread)..Indonesian art has shown a continuing vigour.

i-kauȝt, i-kaut, ME. pa. pple. of CATCH *v.*

‖**ikbal** ('ikbal). [Turkish.] A member of the harem of an Ottoman Sultan.

1910 *Encycl. Brit.* XII. 950/2 The so-called Odalisks..are subdivided according to the degree of favour.., into *Ikbals* ('Favourites') and *Geuzdés* (literally the 'Eyed' ones), those whom the sultan has favourably noticed. **1937** *Times Lit. Suppl.* 16 Jan. 36/3 The Sultan selected his favourites, or *ikbals*. **1956** A. D. ALDERSON *Struct. Ottoman Dynasty* ix. 80 If the relationship showed any signs of permanence, she was promoted to the rank of 'Ikbal' (Fortunate). **1962** J. FLEMING *When I grow Rich* iii. 40 She had ceased to be an *ikbal* (the name given to those members of the harem who actually slept with the Shadow of God upon Earth).

ike (aɪk), colloq. abbrev. of ICONOSCOPE 2.

1937 *Amer. Speech* XII. 101 As the microphone is a *mike* so the television iconoscope is an *ike*. **1947** L. A. SPOSA *Television Primer* 224 *Iconoscope* (*Ike*), a cathode-ray camera pickup tube developed by RCA.

ike: see IKEY *sb.* and *a.*

‖**ikebana** (ɪkiː'bɑːnə). [Jap., f. *ikeru* to keep alive, arrange + *hana* flower.] The art of Japanese flower arrangement in which flowers are formally displayed according to strict rules, sometimes with other natural objects.

1901 F. BRINKLEY *Oriental Series: Japan* III. i. 9 Another remarkable outcome of the Military epoch was the art of flower arrangement. The name applied to it, *ike-bana*, or 'living flower', explains at once the fundamental principle.. that the flowers must be so arranged as to suggest the idea of actual life. **1934** A. KOEHN *Art Jap. Flower Arrangement* 2 The word 'ikebana' is used for all forms of Japanese Flower Arrangement. **1960** KOESTLER *Lotus & Robot* II. vii. 191 It has its charm; and so has ikebana, the Art of Flower Arrangement. **1965** W. SWAAN *Jap. Lantern* xix. 227 Chrysanthemums are particularly popular for *ikebana*. **1966** *New Statesman* 3 June 809/1 On a pole in the street..I saw a signboard that advertised a local *ikebana* school. **1967** 'G. BLACK' *Wind of Death* x. 197 There was no *ikebana* flower arrangement.

i-keled, ME. pa. pple. of KELE *v.* to cool.

†**i-ken, i-kenne**, *v.* *Obs.* [OE. *ʒecennan* to make known, confess, f. *cennan* to declare, attest, KEN.] *trans.* To make known, mention; to know, recognize.

c **1000** *Hymns* x. 4 (Gr.) Ic ðe ecne God ænne ʒecenne. *c* **1205** LAY. 4844 þis weoren þeos kinges strætte þe ich i-kenned [*c* **1275** i-nemnid] habbe. *Ibid.* 28559 Mon i þan fihte non þer ne mihte ikenne [*c* **1275** icnowe] nenne kempe.

i-kenned, -kend, -kent, ME. pa. pple. of KEN.

†**i-kepe**, *v.* *Obs.* [f. ME. *kepe*, KEEP.] *trans.* To keep, receive, observe. (In quots. the sense is that of KEEP *v.* 5, 6c, to watch for, wait for, intercept, ward off.) Hence **i-kepynge, -unge** *vbl. sb.*, taking 'keep', heeding, regarding.

a **1225** *Ancr. R.* 156 God hit is ine silence ikepen Godes grace. *c* **1230** *Hali Meid.* 23 Driue adun swireforð wiðuten ikepunge. *a* **1250** *Owl & Night.* 1225 And grete duntes beoþ þe lasse ȝef me ikepth mid iwarnesse.

i-kept, ME. pa. pple. of KEEP *v.*

i-kest, ME. pa. pple. of CAST *v.*

i-ket, ME. pa. pple. of CUT *v.*

ikey ('aɪkɪ), *sb.* and *a.* *slang* and *dial.* Also **ike, iky, I-.** Familiar abbreviated form of the Jewish name *Isaac* (also **ikeymo**, f. *Isaac* and *Moses*), used typically for: a Jew or someone taken to be or resembling a Jew; also, a (Jewish) receiver, moneylender, etc.; *transf.*, a loafer; a tip, information; (*Austral.*) a bookmaker. As *adj.*, (*a*) artful, crafty, knowing, 'fly'; (*b*) having a good opinion of oneself, 'stuck-up'.

Derogatory and offensive in all uses as applied to persons.

1835 DICKENS *Sk. Boz* (1836) 1st Ser. II. ii. 44 'Let me alone,' replied Ikey, 'and I'll ha' vound up..in five seconds.' **1864** HOTTEN *Slang Dict.*, *Ikey*, a Jew 'fence'. **1870** LEYBOURNE in Farmer & Henley *Slang* (1896) IV. 2 My name it is ikey Bill, A Whitechapel Covey am I. **1881** *Punch* 10 Sept. 110/1 'Arf ikey of course, put-up bizness. **1887** PARISH & SHAW *Dict. Kentish Dial.* 83 *Ikey*, proud. **1889** BARRÈRE & LELAND *Dict. Slang*, *Ikey* (popular), a Jew;.. Also said of any one who thinks himself knowing, smart, and has a great opinion of himself. **1892** CHEVALIER in Farmer & Henley *Slang* (1896) IV. 2 Artful little ikey little ways. **1897** I. SCOTT *How I stole 10,000 Sheep in Austral. & N.Z.* 33 Jim now hit on a rather 'Iky' way to do the ride to Wellington. **1906** RUSSELL & RIGBY *Making of Criminal* i. 7 His clothes are so very poor that he does not like..'to show himself up' by appearing in them, especially if they are of a kind only affected by the professional loafer or 'ikey'. **1913** D. H. LAWRENCE *Sons & Lovers* ix. 241, I want people to think we're awful swells. So look ikey. **1922** JOYCE *Ulysses* 458 Three cheers for Ikey Mo! **1927** T. PRENTIS *Music-Hall Memories* 16 Sez as I'm as ikey as the Dook of Boocle-oo. **1934** *Bulletin* (Sydney) 18 Apr. 11/1 She laid the odds, as smartly and acutely, I'll bet, as any trousered Ikey Mo. **1936** J. G. BRANDON *Dragnet* xiii. 132 'E passed the ike, that there was somethink on there. **1941** *Penguin New Writing* III. 69 Go indoors an' 'elp yer sister with the washing-up, you lazy young ike. **1942** P. ABRAHAMS *Dark Testament* I. xiii. 72 Any guy his pal. Chink, ike. **1954** J. SYMONS *Narrowing Circle* xxx. 135 I'm a Hackney Jew, Dave. At school they called us Ikeymoes and Jewboys. **1966** F. SHAW et al. *Lern Yerself Scouse* 36 *Yer very ikey*, you are very dandified. **1969** *Private Eye* 6 June 14 (*caption*) Pull your head in, ikey mo! **1972** R. PLAYER *Oh! Where are Bloody Mary's Earrings* vi. 168 The Ikeys will win—you can stake your life on that.

Hence **ike, 'iky** *v.* (see quot. 1932); **'ikeyness**, the quality of, or an act of, being ikey.

1911 D. H. LAWRENCE *White Peacock* vii. 484, I haven't been to see them lately—can't stand Meg's ikeyness. **1932** *Amer. Speech* VII. 401 *Iky*, to jew down the price; to cheat. 'He ikied me out of my turn.' **1960** WENTWORTH & FLEXNER *Dict. Amer. Slang*, *Ike v.*, to cheat; to lower the price by haggling; to 'Jew down'.

i-kid, known, renowned: see YKID and KYTHE *v.*

i-knawe(n, i-knowe, ME. pa. pples. of KNOW *v.*

i-knede, ME. pa. pple. of KNEAD *v.*

†**i-knit, i-cnutte**, *v.* *Obs.* [OE. *ʒecnyttan*, f. *cnyttan* to KNIT.] *trans.* To tie, fasten, attach.

c **1000** *Ags. Gosp.* Matt. xviii. 6 þæt an cwyrn-stan si to hys swyran ʒecnytt. *c* **1050** *Ags. Gloss.* in Wr.-Wülcker 342/29 Gecnyttan. *c* **1205** LAY. 29272 He..lette..to þan sparewen uoten uaste heom icnutten.

i-knit, -yt, ME. pa. pple. of KNIT *v.*

ikon, variant of ICON.

i-koruen, ME. pa. pple. of CARVE *v.*

iktas ('ɪktəs), *sb. pl.* *N. Amer. colloq.* Also **ectas, ictas, ictus, iktics, iktus.** [Chinook.] Goods; belongings; things.

1856 *Democratic State Jrnl.* (Sacramento, Calif.) 4 Oct. 3/1 They are getting short of blankets and other *ictas*. *a* **1861** T. WINTHROP *Canoe & Saddle* (1863) iv. 53 My motley retinue followed me humbly, bearing 'ikta', my traps, and their own plunder. **1892** in *Brit. Columbia Hist. Q.* (1941) Oct. 302 They chiefly took their pay in blankets and provisions and other ectas—the balance in coin. **1951** R. P. HOBSON *Grass beyond Mountains* 101 We got eighteen horses, a summer's grub and all the ictus we need for the time being. **1965** S. G. LAWRENCE *Forty Yrs. on Yukon Telegraph* vi. 34, I must get some iktics together and hide.

i-kume(n, ME. pa. pple. of COME *v.*

i-kunde, var. of ICUNDE, nature.

ikunolite (ɪ'k(j)uːnəʊlaɪt). *Min.* [Named after the *Ikuno* mine in Hyōgo prefecture, Japan, where it was first found: see -LITE.] A bismuth sulphide, Bi_4S_3, that contains some selenium in place of sulphur and occurs as grey foliated masses.

1959 A. KATO in *Mineral. Jrnl.* II. 398 The chemical properties and X-ray studies clarified this mineral to be a new species of the composition $Bi_4(S, Se)_3$ with rhombohedral symmetry. The writer has called this mineral ikunolite after the locality name. **1961** *Mineral. Abstr.* XV. 43/2 Ikunolite resembles joseïte-A (Bi_4TeS_2) in structure, crystallography, and optical properties. **1962** *Amer. Mineralogist* XLVII. 1431 The bismuth sulfide mineral ikunolite (Bi_4S_3) was first described by Kato (1959)... A second occurrence of this mineral has recently been found in specimens from the bismuth-molybdenite pipes at Kingsgate in the New England district of New South Wales.

i-kupled, ME. pa. pple. of COUPLE *v.*

ikyl, obs. f. ICKLE *sb.*, icicle.

†**il, ile.** *Obs.* [OE. *igil*, *il* = OHG. *igil* (MHG., Ger. *igel*), MLG., MDu., Du. *egel*, ON. *igull*, going back, with Lith. *ežýs*, Gr. ἐχῖνος, to a pre-Teut. **eghĭ-nos*, *-los*, a deriv. of *eghi-*, Gr. ἔχι-ς adder.] A hedgehog. (In OE. also a porcupine.)

c **897** K. ÆLFRED *Gregory's Past.* xxxv. 241 Se iil..ʒewint he to anum cliewene and tihð his fet sua he inmest mæʒ and ʒehyt his heafod. *Ibid.*, Đonne bið ðæs iles heafud ʒesewen. *c* **1000** ÆLFRIC *Gloss.* in Wr.-Wülcker 123/21 *Istrix*, se mara igil. *c* **1050** *Martyrol.* in Cockayne *Shrine* 55 He [St.

Sebastian] wæs ðara [stræla] swa full swa igl..biþ byrsta. *a* **1200** *Fragm. Ælfric's Gram.*, etc. (Phillipps 1838) 8 Prikiende so piles on ile.

Hence †**iles pil, ilespil, ilspile** [OE. *píl* pointed stick, dart, prickle], prop. a spine of a hedgehog, but used as the name of the hedgehog itself.

a **1225** *Ancr. R.* 418 Ne bere ȝe non iren, ne here, ne irspiles [*v.rr.* yleslipes, ylespilles] felles. *c* **1305** *St. Edmund* 47 in *E.E.P.* (1862) 88 As ful as an illespyl is of pikes al aboute. **1387** TREVISA *Higden* (Rolls) I. 339 þere lakkeþ also ..ilspi[les], [*v.r.* ilspiles; *Caxton* ylespiles], wontes and oþere venemous bestes.

il, obs. form of ILL.

il-[1], assimilated form in L. of the prefix IN-[2] before initial *l*, which is written in the same way in Eng., as in *il-lation, il-luminate.* Usually only one *l* is heard; but both (or a prolonged *l*) may be pronounced when distinctive emphasis is laid on the prefix, as in *il-lision, il-lude*, distinguished from *e-lision, e-lide.* For the varieties of meaning, 'in, on, into, upon', see IN-[2].

il-[2], assimilated form in L. of the negative prefix IN-[3] before initial *l*, which remains in the same form in Eng., as in *il-legal, il-legitimate, il-literate.* Also used in forming negatives in English on the analogy of L., as in ILLOGICAL, ILLOYAL, and in such nonce-words as *il-level, il-locomotive*, etc. When the main stress immediately follows, an effort is often made to give the separate effect of the prefix by pronouncing both *l*'s, or combining them in one prolonged *l*; this is especially the case when rhetorical stress is laid on the prefix, as in 'You call this a Liberal measure; I consider it thoroughly *il*-liberal'.

-il, -ile, *suffixes*, the Eng. representatiaves of L. *-ilis* and *-īlis*, forming adjectives, sometimes also substantives, as in *fossilis* fossil, *civīlis* civil; *agilis* agile, *juvenīlis* juvenile. These suffixes are in origin the same, viz. *-lis* with connective *-i-*, which with *-i-* stems as *civi-s, hosti-s*, and in some other words, gave *-īlis.* In OF., the latter came down as *-il*, e.g. *Aprīl-em, Avril*, April; the former regularly lost the post-tonic *ĭ*, and became *-le* (for *-l'*), as in *humil-em* humble, *habil-em* able, *fragil-em, fraisle, fraile, frêle* frail, *gracil-em, graisle, gresle, grêle.* L. words *adapted* in OF. at an early date took the ending *-il* masc., *-ile* fem., e.g. *civil, civile*; later words have the ending *-ile* only, as *agile, facile, fossile.* Very few of these words in Eng. have the suffix in *-il*, e.g. *civil, fossil, utensil*; in the 17th c. we find occasionally *-il* for L. *-ilis*, e.g. *difficil, docil, fertil, steril*; but modern usage in Eng. as in French has levelled *-ilis* and *-īlis* under the common form *-ile.* In Walker's Pronouncing Dictionary *-ile* from *-īlis* is pronounced (-aɪl), and *-ile* from *-ilis* as (-il); but the more recent tendency is to extend (aɪl), with some exceptions, to all the words.

2. Following cl.L. and med.L. ordinal numerals of the type *quartīlis, quintīlis, sextīlis* (Eng. QUARTILE, etc.), *-ile* (-aɪl) is used in *Statistics* to form substantives denoting (*a*) those values of a variate that divide a population into the indicated number of groups, equal in size, and (*b*) the groups themselves; so *octile* and *quartile* (1879), *decile* (1882), *percentile* (1885).

Ila (ˈiːlə), *sb.* and *a.* Also **Ba-ila.** [Native name.] **A.** *sb.* **1.** An African of a Bantu people in Zambia (formerly Northern Rhodesia); also used as collect. sing. = this people. **2.** The Bantu language of this people. **B.** *adj.* Of or pertaining to this people or their language.

1907 E. W. SMITH *Handbk. Ila Lang.* i. 1 The Ila language is spoken by the Baila,..a people living in North-West Rhodesia. *Ibid.* i. 3 In Ila, as in all Bantu languages, alliteration..is not an accident of style, it is the very essence of the language. **1911** *Encycl. Brit.* III. 359/2 Next is a group which might be styled the Subiya-Tonga-Ila, though some authorities think that Tonga and Ila deserve to be ranked as an independent group. **1920** SMITH & DALE (*title*) Ila-speaking peoples of Northern Rhodesia. *Ibid.* p. xxvii, They are very mixed, but now the language of them all is Ila. **1956** W. V. BRELSFORD *Tribes N. Rhodesia* viii. 55 The Ila have a great and deserved reputation as fighting men, but their comparative paucity in numbers and the possession of great herds of cattle made them a constant prey to the bigger tribes of Barotseland. **1959** *Chambers's Encycl.* I. (*caption*, facing p. 140) A chief of the Ila peoples, photographed wearing ivory bracelets and *impande*, the insignia of office. *Ibid.* II. 109/2 The Ba-ila live in independent communities. **1960** R. C. BELL *Board & Table Games* I. 121 *Chisolo.* This is played by the Ba-ila speaking peoples of Northern Rhodesia. **1970** P. OLIVER *Savannah Syncopators* 26 The Ila and Tonga people are neither of them West African,.. being of the Middle Zambesi 2,300 miles away.

i-laced, ME. pa. pple. of LACE *v.*

i-lad, ME. pa. pple. of LEAD *v.*

i-lade, ME. pa. pple. of LOAD *v.*

i-laft, ME. pa. pple. of LEAVE, YLEAVE *vbs.*

‖**Ilag** (ˈiːlag). [Ger. abbrev. form of *Internierungslager.*] A prison-camp for civilian internees in Nazi Germany.

1941 WODEHOUSE *Berlin Broadcasts* in *Performing Flea* (1961) i. 261 An Oflag is where captured officers go. Stalags are reserved for N.C.O.s and privates. The civil internee gets the Ilag.

†**i-lahe(n**, *v. Obs.* [OE. *ȝelaȝian*, f. *laȝa* LAW, *laȝian* to make a law, ordain.] *trans.* To ordain or appoint by law.

1014 WULFSTAN *Sermo ad Anglos* (Napier 1883) 157 On hæþenum þeodum..þe ȝelaȝod is to ȝedwol-goda weorðunge. *c* **1230** *Hali Meid.* 21 For þi was wedlac ilahet in hali chirche. *Ibid.* 23 Godd haueð ilahed hit.

i-lahet, ME. pa. pple. of LOW *v.*, to abase.

i-laht, ME. pa. pple. of LATCH *v.* and I-LECCHE *v.*, to seize.

i-laid, ME. pa. pple. of LAY *v.*

ilala (ɪˈlɑːlə). *S. Afr.* Also **lala.** [Zulu.] A fan palm, *Hyphæne natalensis*, native to the coastal region of Natal.

1868 J. CHAPMAN *Trav. S. Afr.* II. 464 *Ilala*, Hyphæne. **1884** E. P. MATHERS *Trip to Moodie's* 29 There is a natural drink..which..goes by the name of kaffir beer..it is the exudation of a native palm tree (*ilala*). **1911** *Encycl. Brit.* XIX. 253/2 Of palms there are two varieties [in Natal], the ilala (*Hyphaene crinita*), found only by the sea shore and a mile or two inland, and the isundu (*Phoenix reclinata*). **1954** T. V. BULPIN *Ivory Trail* iv. 44 He..passed the hot hours in plaiting a hat from lala palm leaves. *Ibid.* xi. 114 The elephants..also had a liking for this potent lala palm wine. **1966** D. VARADAY *Gara-Yaka's Domain* viii. 89 He ruled the troop like a despot from his rocky keep above a growth of ilala palms.

Ilamba, var. LAMBA *sb.* and *a.*

iland, obs. (and etymological) spelling of ISLAND.

i-lapped, ME. pa. pple. of LAP *v.*

i-last(e: see YLAST(E, to suffer, continue, last.

†**ilastical**, *a. Obs.* [erron. for **hilastical*, f. Gr. type *ἱλαστικός, f. stem of ἱλάσκεσθαι to propitiate.] Propitiatory, expiatory.

1649 BP. REYNOLDS *Serm. Hosea* iii. 1 The sacrifices.. were Ilasticall propitiatory, or expiatory. **1671** FLAVEL *Fount. Life* ii. 30 Ilastical or expiatory for Satisfaction.

†**i-latet**, *a. Obs.* [f. ME. *lat* LATE *sb.*, ON. *lát* manner, mien.] Mannered.

a **1225** *Juliana* 33 As þu biwistest daniel bimong þe wode liuns ilatet se luðere. *c* **1230** *Hali Meid.* 33 ȝif þu art unwurðlich & wraðeliche ilatet.

i-laðed, -et, ME. pa. pple. of LATHE *v.*

ilb (ɪlb). Also **ailb, elb.** [Arab.] A spiny tree of the genus *Zizyphus*, esp. *Z. spina-Christi*, found in North Africa and the Middle East.

1894 *Kew Bull.* 330 *Zizyphus Lotus* Linn. A tree 20–30 feet high. Very common in Hadramaut. Native name, 'Ailb'. Extends through North Africa and South Europe. **1914–16** E. BLATTER *Flora of Aden* 158 *Zizyphus spina Christi*... Arabic name: Elb. **1940** F. STARK *Winter in Arabia* 118 It is only because of the English peace that he can count on the safe and quiet possession of his own waterless strip of 'ilb trees and plough. **1963** *Times* 12 Mar. 12/6 One looks out over fields of millet and barley, waving date palms and sturdy *ilb* trees.

ilche: see EACH, ILK.

Ilchester (ˈɪltʃɪstə(r)). The name of a town in Somerset, used *attrib.* or *ellipt.* as *sb.* to designate a cheese mixed with beer, chives, and spices.

1963 *Guardian* 11 Jan. 7/7 Mr Ken Seaton, landlord of the Ilchester hotel, Ilchester, has developed a new cheese, made with beer and chives and spices. He calls it Ilchester. **1965** T. FITZGIBBON *Art Brit. Cooking* 132 Ilchester cheese is a recent commercially blended cheese made in Ilchester, Somerset, from Cheddar cheese, Worthington beer, spices and chives. **1965** *Harrods Food News* May, Ilchester is Cheddar with Beer and Spices. **1967** T. A. LAYTON *Wine & Food Soc. Guide Cheese & Cheese Cookery* ii. 68 Ilchester cheese is the creation of a Yorkshireman, Ken Seaton, who hit upon the recipe almost by accident only six years ago. **1971** *Selfridge Christmas Food Catal.* 10/2 Ilchester cheese with Beer and Chives. 4 oz. pot, each 17½ p.

ild, obs. f. YIELD (in phr. *God ild*).

ild, obs. f. *illed*, pa. pple. of ILL *v.*

-ild: see GRUCCHILD.

ilde, obs. by-form of ISLE, AISLE.

ildell, contracted form of *ilk del*, every part: see ILK *a.*[2]

ildre, obs. f. ELDER *a.* and *sb.*[3]

†**ile**[1]. *Obs.* [ad. L. *īle* or *īle-um* (see ILEUM and ILIUM). Cf. F. (pl.) *iles* (13th c.).] = ILEUM.

1601 HOLLAND *Pliny* I. 342 The small guts..through which the meat passeth: in others it is named Ile. **1656** [see ILIACAL]. **1706** PHILLIPS (ed. Kersey), *Ile*, the Cavity or Hollowness from the Chest to the Thigh-Bones, the Flank that contains the small Guts.

ile[2], var. of AIL *sb.*[2], awn of barley, etc.

1706 PHILLIPS (ed. Kersey), *Iles*, or *Oils* (Country-Word), the Spires or Beards of Corn.

ile, obs. f. ILL, ISLE, AISLE; a former spelling of *I'll* = I will; a vulgar or dial. pronunciation (now esp. in U.S.) of OIL.

-ile, *suffix*: see -IL.

ˈ**ileac**, *a.* A refashioning of ILIAC *a.* after L. *īleus*, Gr. ἰλεός, or ILEUM.

1822–34 *Good's Study Med.* (ed. 4) I. 162 The treatment of ileac passion. **1855** MAYNE *Expos. Lex.*, *Ileac Passion.*

i-leaded, ME. f. LEADED *a.*

i-leafe, i-leave, *v.*: see YLEVE to leave, YLEVE to believe.

ileal (ˈɪlɪəl), *a.* [f. ILE(UM + -AL.] Of, within, or supplying the ileum.

1893 in *Funk's Stand. Dict.* **1895** R. T. MORRIS *Lect. Appendicitis* v. 100 (*heading*) The experimental production of ileal intussusception with carbonate of sodium. **1902** D. J. CUNNINGHAM *Text-bk. Anat.* 802 The ileal branch [of the superior mesenteric artery]..turns upwards and to the left in the lowest part of the mesentery. **1934** LAKE & MARSHALL *Surg. Anat. & Physiol.* xxxiii. 521 An appreciable degree of obstruction of the small gut ('ileal stasis'). **1971** *Brit. Med. Bull.* XXVII. 26/2 Epidemics of ileal obstruction were first recognized in 1964.

i-leanet, ME. pa. pple. of LENE, to lend.

i-learet, ME. pa. pple. of LERE, YLERE, to teach.

†**i-lecche**, *v. Obs.* [OE. *ȝelæccan*, f. *læccan* to seize: see LATCH *v.*] *trans.* To lay hold of, catch.

c **1000** *Ags. Gosp.* John vi. 15 Hiȝ woldon..hine ȝelæccean and to cynge don. *a* **1100** *O.E. Chron.* an. 1087 þa Englisce men..ȝelæhton of þam mannon..ma. *c* **1205** LAY. 29260 Swið monie he ilahte. *a* **1225** *Juliana* 73 Ilecche ha me eft, ne finde ich na leche. **1399** LANGL. *Rich. Redeles* III. 336 He was lyghtliche y-lauȝte and y-lugged of many.

i-lefde, pa. t. of YLEVE *v.*, to believe.

i-leid, ME. pa. pple. of LAY *v.*

ileitis (ɪlɪːˈaɪtɪs). *Path.* [f. ILE-UM + -ITIS.] Inflammation of the ileum.

1855 in MAYNE *Expos. Lex.*

i-lend, ME. pa. pple. of LENE, LEND *vbs.*

i-lengd, -ed, ME. pa. pple. of LENG *v.*, to prolong.

†**i-lenge**, *v. Obs.* [OE. *ȝelengan* to prolong, f. *lengan*, f. *lang* LONG.] *intr.* To continue one's journey; to attain *to*, get as far as.

c **1205** LAY. 17834 Leteð me ilenge [*c* **1275** bringeþ me] riht to Stanhenge.

i-lengthed, pa. pple. of LENGTH *v.*, to lengthen.

ileo- (ˌɪlɪːəʊ, ˌaɪ-), used as combining form of ILEUM, in terms of anatomy, pathology, etc.: as **ileo-cæcal** (-ˈsiːkəl) *a.*, related to or connected with the ileum and the cæcum; as in ***ileo-cæcal valve***, a valve consisting of two semilunar folds at the opening of the ileum into the cæcum; the name is sometimes restricted to the lower of these. **ileo-colic** (-ˈkɒlɪk) *a.*, relating to or connected with the ileum and the colon; as in ***ileo-colic artery***, a branch of the superior mesenteric artery; *ileo-colic valve* = *ileo-cæcal valve* (sometimes restricted to the upper fold of this). **ileo-colitis** (-kəʊˈlaɪtɪs), inflammation of the ileum and colon. ˌ**ileocoˈlostomy** *Surg.* [-STOMY], the operation of joining, and creating a passage between, a part of the ileum and a part of the colon so that the intervening part of the intestines is bypassed; the connection so formed. ˌ**ileo-ileˈostomy** *Surg.* [-STOMY], the operation of joining, and creating a passage between, two parts of the ileum so that the intervening part is bypassed; the connection so formed. **ileo-parietal** (-pəˈraɪɪtəl) *a.*, connecting the ileum and the bodywall, as the ***ileo-parietal band*** in Brachiopods. ˌ**ileo-ˈsigmoid** *a.*, between or connecting the ileum and the sigmoid flexure of the colon. ˌ**ileosigmoiˈdostomy** *Surg.* [-STOMY], the operation of joining, and creating a passage between, the sigmoid flexure of the colon and a part of the ileum so that the intervening part of the intestines is bypassed; the connection so formed. **ileostomy** (ɪlɪːˈɒstəmɪ) [Gr. στόμα mouth], the operation of attaching the ileum to

the abdominal wall and constructing an artificial anus so that the intestinal contents are evacuated directly from the ileum; also, the opening or artificial anus thus made.

1847 CRAIG, *Ilio-cæcal valve..Ilio-colic artery..Ilio-lumbar artery.* **1876** tr. *Wagner's Gen. Pathol.* 33 In the ileo-cæcal region. **1897** ALLBUTT *Syst. Med.* III. 823 In ilio-colic invaginations. **1886** *Syd. Soc. Lex., Ileo-colitis.* **1887** *Trans. Internat. Med. Congr. 9th Session* I. 485 An ileo-colostomy or ileo-rectostomy..should be done in all cases of irreducible ileo-cæcal invagination. *Ibid.* 475 Intestinal anastomosis, by making an ileo-colostomy by lateral apposition of the ileum to colon below the invagination. **1967** J. H. GARLOCK *Surg. Alimentary Tract* ix. 427 In the same category, one may include the bypassing operation of ileocolostomy. **1887** *Trans. Internat. Med. Congr. 9th Session* I. 479 Two adjacent coils of the ileum were united by making an ileo-ileostomy. **1889** *Lancet* 16 Mar. 531/1 Jejuno-ileostomy and ileo-ileostomy were performed in identically the same way. **1901** N. SENN *Pract. Surg.* xxiii. 833 Jejuno-ileostomy and ileo-ileostomy by apposition with decalcified bone-plates..is an operation almost devoid of danger. **1878** BELL tr. *Gegenbaur's Comp. Anat.* 311 The ileoparietal band..attached to the hind gut. **1903** Ileo-sigmoid [see *colo-colic* adj.]. **1968** J. C. GOLIGHER et al. *Ulcerative Colitis* xiii. 237 The first such operation involving an ileo-sigmoid anastomosis was recorded by Lilienthal as early as 1901. **1892** *Lancet* 16 Apr. 864/2 (*heading*) Ileo-sigmoidostomy (Senn's method) for intestinal obstruction due to malignant disease of the hepatic flexure of the colon. **1964** H. E. BACON *Cancer Colon, Rectum & Anal Canal* xv. 806/1 Ileosigmoidostomy..shortcuts the entire colon and renders it more or less functionless. **1890** BILLINGS *Med. Dict.* I. 682/1 Ileostomy. **1891** T. BRYANT in *Lancet* 3 Jan. 1/1 The operation I am about to describe may well be called 'ileostomy'. **1926** *Brit. Jrnl. Surg.* XIII. 711 Against ileostomy, however, we urge the loss of an important sphincter and portion of the digestive tract. **1968** J. C. GOLIGHER et al. *Ulcerative Colitis* xiii. 236 The creation of a terminal ileostomy. **1968** COLCOCK & BRAASCH *Surg. Small Intestine in Adult* xiii. 179 The great majority of patients with ulcerative colitis who need surgery will require a complete removal of the colon and rectum and an ileostomy. *Ibid.* 181 A temporary ileostomy appliance is cemented to the skin over the ileostomy. **1971** M. SPARSBERG (*title*) Ileostomy care.

† **'ileon.** *Obs.* [med.L. (in Gr. form) = ILEUM. Cf. F. *iléon.*] = ILEUM.

1495 *Trevisa's Barth. De P.R.* v. xlii. 158 The seconde grete gutte highte Yleon. **1594** [see next]. *a* **1661** HOLYDAY *Juvenal* 80 The ileon, one of the guts..is six times longer than our whole body. **1707** FLOYER *Physic. Pulse-Watch* 111 Inflammation of the Ileon. **1767** GOOCH *Treat. Wounds* I. 401 In the Jejunum..and in the Ileon.

† **'ileos.** *Obs.* [cf. prec., and ILEUS.] = ILEUM.

1594 T. B. *La Primaud. Fr. Acad.* II. 350 Then followeth the third small intraile, called Ileos by the Græcians [*margin*, The Ileon or folded Gut]. **1706** [see ILEUS 1].

† **'ileous,** *a. Obs. rare.* [f. L. ILE-UM + -OUS.] Belonging to the ileum; = ILIAC *a.* 1.

1657 TOMLINSON *Renou's Disp.* 628 It cures..cholical and ileous dolours.

† **i-ler,** *a. Obs.* Also 3 ilær. [OE. *ȝelǽr* (Sweet), f. *lǽr* empty, LERE.] Empty.

c **1205** LAY. 15961 þa þa water wes al ilædden & þe put wes ilær. **1297** R. GLOUC. (Rolls) 11221 þe clerkes adde þe stretes sone iler.

ilesite ('aɪlzaɪt). *Min.* [Named, 1881, after M. W. Iles, who described it.] Hydrous sulphate of manganese, zinc, and iron, resulting from the decomposition of pyrite and sphalerite.

1881 *Amer. Jrnl. Sc.* Ser. III. XXII. 490 *Ilesite*, a white friable mineral with a bitter, astringent taste.

ilespil(e, a hedghog: see IL *sb.*

† **i-lete.** *Obs.* [f. LETE *sb.*] Manner, bearing.

a **1250** *Owl & Night.* 403 He is wis þat hardeliche Wiþ his fo berþ grete ilete. *Ibid.* 1446 Hwanne ich iseo þe tohte ilete þe luve bringþ on þe ȝunglinge.

i-lete(n, ME. pa. pple. of LET *v.*

i-lethered, ME. form of LEATHERED *ppl. a.*

ilet-hole, obs. f. EYELET-HOLE.

i-leue, i-leve: see YLEVE *v.*

i-leued, ME. form of LEAVED *a.*

‖ **ileum** ('ɪliːəm, 'aɪ-). *Anat.* [late or med.L. *īleum*, for which classical L. had only *īlia* (pl. of *īle* or *īlium*, with a dat. sing. *īliō*), in the sense (1) flanks, loins, (2) small guts, entrails. The form *īleum* (*īleon, -os*) seems to have arisen from a confusion of this with *īleus*, Gr. εἰλεός (see ILEUS, ILIAC), whence also its restricted sense.] The third portion of the small intestine, succeeding the jejunum and opening into the cæcum.

1682 T. GIBSON *Anat.* (1697) 47 This Membrane in the small Guts, especially the Ileum, is full of wrinkles. **1706** PHILLIPS (ed. Kersey), *Ileum*, or *Ileon*, the third of the small Guts, so call'd by reason of its great turnings, and being about 21 Hands-breadth in Length. **1843** J. G. WILKINSON *Swedenborg's Anim. Kingd.* I. v. 179 The ileum, folded in wreathing gyres.

‖ **ileus** ('ɪliːəs, 'aɪ-). [L. *īleus*, *īleos*, a. Gr. ἰλεός or εἰλεός colic, 'iliac passion', app. f. εἴλειν to roll.]

1. *Path.* A painful affection (frequently fatal), due to intestinal obstruction, esp. in the ileum: also called *iliac passion.*

1706 PHILLIPS (ed. Kersey), *Ileus*, or *Ileos*, the small or thin Gut; also the twisting of the small Guts, when their Coats are doubled inward, and there is such a Stoppage that nothing can pass downward. **1732** ARBUTHNOT *Rules of Diet* 351 An Ileus..is commonly called the Twisting of the Guts, but is really either a Circumvolution or Insertion of one part of the Gut within the other. **1785** *Med. Commun.* 266 (heading), History of a Case of Ileus, where great benefit was derived from the application of a blister.

2. *Anat.* = ILEUM.

1706 [see 1].

i-lewed, early ME. form of LEWD *a.*

ilex ('aɪlɛks). Also 6–8 **ilix.** [a. L. *īlex, īlic-em* holm-oak.]

1. The holm-oak or evergreen oak (*Quercus Ilex*).

1398 TREVISA *Barth. De P.R.* XVII. lxxxiii. (1495) 654 Ilex is a manere oke, a tree that beeryth maste. **1506** GULYFORDE *Pilgr.* (Camden) 53 The tre called Ilex, that then stode byfore Abrahams dore is now wasted. **1601** HOLLAND *Pliny* I. 458 Of the Ilex or mast-Holme tree, there be two sorts. **1768** BOSWELL *Corsica* i. (ed. 2) 45 The Ilex, or ever-green oak, is very common here. **1787** P. BECKFORD *Lett. fr. Italy* (1805) I. 416 (Stanf.) A beautiful wood, enlivened in winter by the ilix and the cork tree, both ever-greens. **1789** G. WHITE *Selborne* lxi. (1875) 302 The ilexes were much injured. **1867** LADY HERBERT *Cradle L.* viii. 216 Tabor, with ..its base skirted with dwarf oak, ilexes, and arbutus.

b. *attrib.* and *Comb.*

1829 SOUTHEY *Sir T. More* Ded. 6 Spain's mountain passes, and her ilex woods. **1860** W. G. CLARK in *Vac. Tour.* 61 A steep ilex-clothed hill. **1887** RUSKIN *Præterita* II. iii. 92, I went..for a walk through its ilex groves.

‖ **2.** In modern Botany, the name of a genus of *Aquifoliaceæ*, comprising numerous trees and shrubs, of which the most familiar is the common holly (*I. Aquifolium*).

1565–73 COOPER *Thesaurus, Aquifolia*, a wilde tree with pricking leaves..a kinde of Ilix. **1838** *Penny Cycl.* XII. 443/1 Besides the common Holly.., the genus Ilex comprehends a large number of species.

i-leye(n, ME. pa. pple. of LIE *v.*

ilia, pl. of ILIUM.

iliac ('ɪlɪæk), *a.*[1] (*sb.*) Forms: 6 **yliac, -ake, ilyacke,** ? **ylike,** 7 **iliack(e, -ak, -aque, illiack(e, yliacke,** 8–9 **illiac,** 7– **iliac.** [a. F. *iliaque* or ad. late L. *īliac-us* (in Cælius, *passio īliaca*, also *īliacī* sufferers from colic); the L. is in form a deriv. of *īlia* (see ILIUM), but the suffix is Greek (*-ακός*), and the sense goes with L. *īleus*, Gr. εἰλεός, ἰλεός, colic, iliac passion; hence it would appear that *īleus* from Gr. εἰλεός was associated with *īlia*, and that *passio īliaca* was interpreted as 'pain of the ilia', and the adj. extended in late or med.L. to mean 'of or pertaining to the ilium'.]

1. Properly, Of the nature of the disease called ILEUS; but commonly understood as = Pertaining to or affecting the ILEUM. ***iliac passion*** [late L. *passio iliaca*] = ILEUS 1: cf. *colic passion* = colic.

[**1398** TREVISA *Barth. De P.R.* VII. xlix. (1495) 263 This passyon callyd Colica hath a cosyn that hyghte *Iliaca passio*, and hath that name of a gutte that hyghte Ilion.] **1519** HORMAN *Vulg.* 42b, Etyng esith the ylike passion and greueth the colik. **1601** HOLLAND *Pliny* II. 39 Them that are troubled with the Iliack passion, to wit, the paine and ringing of the small guts. **1707** FLOYER *Physic. Pulse-Watch* 111 In an Iliac Passion there is great Pain and Inflammation of the Ileon. **1746** R. JAMES *Moufet's Health Improvem.* Introd. 49 Inflammatory iliac Pains. **1856** MRS. CARLYLE *Lett.* II. 297 Some derangement of the bowels,..always expected to terminate fatally in iliac passion.

2. Pertaining to the flank, or to the ilium or flank-bone.

iliac artery, each of the two arteries, right and left, into which the abdominal aorta divides; each of these again divides into two, the *external* or *anterior*, and the *internal* or *posterior iliac arteries*. ***iliac bone***, the ilium. ***iliac fossa***, the depression on the inner side of the ilium, in which the iliac muscle lies. ***iliac muscle***, a muscle lying close to the ilium, and inserted, together with the psoas magnus, into the small trochanter of the femur; it serves for flexure of the hip-joint. ***iliac vein***, each of the two veins, right and left, formed by the union of the *external* and *internal iliac veins*, and uniting to form the inferior vena cava.

1541 COPLAND *Guydon's Quest. Chirurg.* H ij a, The parties called yliac are ouer the haunches. **1615** CROOKE *Body of Man* 838 From the vtter branch of the byfurcation of the Illiack trunke..do issue three veynes. **1741** A. MONRO *Anat.* (ed. 3) 205 The internal Iliac Muscle. **1840** E. WILSON *Anat. Vade-M.* v. 284 The internal iliac artery. **1854** OWEN *Skel. & Teeth* in *Circ. Sc., Organ. Nat.* I. 221 The iliac bones [of the swan]..are remarkable for their length, and for the number of the vertebræ..to which they are anchylosed. **1855** HOLDEN *Hum. Osteol.* (1878) 173 The inner surface of the ilium is slightly excavated, so as to form the 'iliac fossa'.

† **B.** *sb.* **1.** Short for *iliac passion. Obs.*

1542 BOORDE *Dyetary* x. (1870) 257 For them the whiche haue the Ilyacke or the colycke. [*c* **1550** LLOYD *Treas. Health* (1585) A viij, The paynes of the small guttes, called yliaca.]

2. Short for *iliac artery*, etc.

1782 A. MONRO *Compar. Anat.* (ed. 3) 35 The umbilical arteries rise..from the internal iliacs. **1822–34** *Good's Study Med.* (ed. 4) IV. 17 [The umbilical cord] consisting of an artery from each of the fœtal iliacs, and a vein running to the fœtal liver.

Iliac ('ɪlɪæk), *a.*[2] [ad. L. *Iliacus*, a. Gr. Ἰλιακός: see ILIAD.] Pertaining or relating to ancient Ilium; Ilian.

1878 GLADSTONE *Homer* 37 The other epics of the Iliac Cycle differ in their narrative from the Iliad.

† **i'liacal,** *a. Obs.* [f. as ILIAC + -AL[1].] = ILIAC *a.*[1]

1646 SIR T. BROWNE *Pseud. Ep.* v. v. 239 Two Arteries.. arising from the Iliacall branches. **1654** JER. TAYLOR *Real Pres.* 42 A man does not eate bullets or quicksilver against the Iliacal passion, but swallowes them. **1656** BLOUNT *Glossogr., Iliacal*,..of or belonging to the Iles or small guts.

iliacus (ɪ'laɪəkəs). *Anat.* [late L.: see ILIAC *a.* (*sb.*).] = *iliac muscle* (s.v. ILIAC *a.* 2). Also † ***iliacus internus, iliacus muscle.***

1615 H. CROOKE *Descr. Body Man* x. vi. 744 The thighes are each of them bent by two [muscles] called Psoas and Iliacus. *Ibid.* xxxviii. 811 The second Bender is called Iliacus internus the inward haunch-Muscle. **1726** W. CHESELDEN *Anat. Humane Body* (ed. 3) II. ii. 123 Iliacus internus, arises from the concave part of the ilium, and from its lower edge, and passing over the ilium near the os pubis, joins the former muscle [*sc.* psoas magnus], and is inserted with it, to be employed in the same action. **1733** G. DOUGLAS tr. *Winslow's Anat. Expos. Struct. Human Body* I. III. x. 53 The Iliacus and Psoas thus united pass under the Ligamentum Falloppii. **1875** *Encycl. Brit.* I. 840/2 The thigh can be bent on the abdomen by the action of the psoas, iliacus, and pectineus, which lie in front of the joint. **1967** G. M. WYBURN et al. *Conc. Anat.* vi. 158 The iliacus and psoas muscles pass behind the inguinal ligament and the iliacus joins the tendon of the psoas.

Iliad ('ɪlɪæd). [ad. L. *Īlias, Īliad-*, a. Gr. Ἰλιάς (1) sc. γῆ, the Troad, Troy, (2) sc. γυνή, a Trojan woman, (3) sc. ποίησις, the Iliad; f. Ἴλιος, Ἴλιον Ilion, Ilium, Troy, the scene of the Trojan war. Cf. F. *Iliade* (16th c. in Littré).]

1. One of the two great epic poems of ancient Greece (the other being the *Odyssey*) traditionally attributed to Homer, describing the ten years' siege of Ilium or Troy by the Greeks.

Sometimes used, with ordinal numeral, for one book of the Iliad: hence formerly in pl. for the whole poem.

1579 GOSSON *Sch. Abuse* (Arb.) 16 Homers Iliades in a nutte shell; a Kings picture in a pennie. **1715–20** POPE *Iliad* Pref., The descriptions of his battles, which take up no less than half the Iliad. **1828** WHATELY *Rhet.* in *Encycl. Metrop.* 250/1 No one would believe it possible for such a work as the Iliad, e.g. to be produced by a fortuitous shaking together of the letters of the alphabet. **1876** GLADSTONE *Homeric Synchr.* 163 In the Sixth Iliad.

attrib. **1791** COWPER *Let.* 10 Mar., I have two French prints..both on Iliad subjects.

2. *transf.* and *fig.* **a.** An epic poem like that of Homer, or a poem describing martial exploits.

1619 BRENT tr. *Sarpi's Counc. Trent* i. (1676) 2 The Iliad of our age. **1674** W. J. (*title*) English Iliads; or, a Sea-Fight reviewed in a Poem. **1831** CARLYLE *Sart. Res.* III. iii, Certain Iliads, and the like, have, in three-thousand years, attained quite new significance.

b. A long series of disasters or the like (Gr. ἰλιὰς κακῶν, Demosthenes); a long story or account.

1609 BP. W. BARLOW *Answ. Nameless Cath.* 359 Her stay brought forth..an Iliad of miseries. **1611** SPEED *Hist. Gt. Brit.* IX. xxiv. (1632) 1212 [They] heaped an Iliade of curses vpon the heads of the Executioners. **1698** FRYER *Acc. E. India & P.* 307 Fevers, Gout, Falling-sickness, and an Iliad of Distempers. **1796** BURKE *Regic. Peace* II. Wks. VIII. 233 It opens another Iliad of woes to Europe. **1865** *Times* 29 Apr., An opportunity of learning a whole Iliad of finance in a comparative nutshell.

Hence **Ili'adic** *a.*, of or pertaining to the Iliad; **'Iliadist,** (*a*) a singer of the Iliad, a rhapsodist; (*b*) a writer of 'Iliads' (see 2 a); **'Iliadize** *v.*, to relate in the manner of the Iliad.

1599 NASHE *Lenten Stuffe* 31 M. Vlisses..of whome it is Illiadizd that your very nose dropt sugar candie. *a* **1711** KEN *Hymnotheo* Poet. Wks. 1721 III. 289 The Iliadists in Scarlet Robes are drest..To picture what they sing of..Wars, and Blood of Greeks and Trojans slain. **1858** CARLYLE *Fredk. Gt.* I. i. (1872) I. 16 All real Poets, to this hour, are Psalmists and Iliadists after their sort. **1892** AGNES M. CLERKE *Fam. Stud. Homer* i. 29 The experience of the Iliadic bard. **1897** S. BUTLER *Authoress of Odyssey* Pref. 6 The leading Iliadic and Odyssean scholars.

iliahi (iːlɪ'ɑːhɪ). [Hawaiian.] One of several trees of the genus *Santalum*, esp. *S. freycinetianum*, which grow in Hawaii and yield an aromatic wood.

1825 W. ELLIS *Jrnl. Tour Hawaii* 247 *Iliahi*, sandalwood. **1888** W. HILLEBRAND *Flora Hawaiian Islands* 389 *Santalum*. ..The following species are weakly defined, and all furnish an equally fragrant wood..while the name of the tree is 'Iliahi'. **1915** W. A. BRYAN *Nat. Hist. Hawaii* xv. 219 The iliahi furnished the first article of export which attracted commerce to the islands. **1970** S. CARLQUIST *Hawaii* xiv. 269 Typical of this low stature is the coastal iliahi, or sandalwood (*Santalum ellipticum* var. *littorale*), which is a low, rounded shrub with succulent leaves, gray-green in color. Inland sandalwoods are all trees.

Ilian ('ɪlɪən, 'aɪlɪən), *a.* (*sb.*). [f. *Ili*(*um* + -AN.] Of or pertaining to any of the successive towns

of Ilium in the Trojan Plain; also as *sb.*, an inhabitant of Ilium.

1582 R. STANYHURST tr. *Virgil's Æneis* I. (Arb.) 26 Whilst stood the great Ilian empyre. **1626** G. SANDYS tr. *Ovid's Met.* XIII. 222 To th'Ilian Court I went. **1847** J. LEITCH tr. *Müller's Anc. Art* 483 Coins of the Ilians. **1869** TOZER *Highl. Turkey* I. 44 The site of the ancient Village of the Ilians. **1876** GLADSTONE *Homeric Synchronism* 34 He appears as the representation of the Dardanian Branch, with a sidelong jealous eye towards the predominating Ilian House of Priam. **1881** *Jrnl. Hellenic Stud.* II. 18 After the victory, he [*sc.* Alexander] gave substantial proof of gratitude to the Ilian gods and heroes. **1888** *Encycl. Brit.* XXIII. 579/2 The temple of the Ilian Athene. *Ibid.*, It was politic to recall the legend of Roman descent from Æneas. Lucius Scipio and the Ilians were alike eager to do so. **1927** W. W. TARN *Hellenistic Civilisation* ii. 70 Antigonus I..created three sectional Leagues: the Ionian..the Ilian..and the Islanders. **1941** M. ROSTOVTZEFF *Social & Econ. Hist. Hellenic World* I. iii. 154 Some of the leagues that had existed before, such as the Ionian, Aeolian, Ilian (?), Lycian, and Carian leagues in Asia Minor. **1957** *Encycl. Brit.* XXII. 505/1 In their temple of Athena the Ilians showed him arms which had served in the Trojan war.

Iliat ('ɪlɪɑːt). Also **Eylat, Ilat, Iliaut, Iliyat, Illyat.** [Turkish *īlāt*, pl. of *īl* country, wandering pastoral tribe (cf. *rūm-eyli* 'country of the Romans', Rumelia).] One of several tribes of nomads scattered throughout Persia.

1840 *Penny Cycl.* XVII. 472/1 The wandering tribes of Persia are comprehended under the general term of *Iliyats* or *Ilat*, and are found in every part of Persia. **1865** *Chambers's Encycl.* VII. 420/2 The nomad or pastoral tribes, or eylats (*eyl*, a clan), often spelt *illyats*, are of four distinct races—Turkomans, Kurds, Lûurs, and Arabs. **1888** *Encycl. Brit.* XXIII. 661/1 They are known by the name of Ilāt or Iliyāt. **1902** D. G. HOGARTH *Nearer East* 160 The nomad 'Iliats' who wander here and there.

ilich, -e, obs. forms of ALIKE: see YLIKE.

ilicic (aɪ'lɪsɪk), *a. Chem.* [f. L. *īlex, īlic-em* (see ILEX 2) + -IC.] Of or pertaining to the holly; in *ilicic acid*, an acid contained in the leaves of the holly. So **'ilicate**, a salt of ilicic acid; **'ilicin**, the non-nitrogenous bitter principle of the holly.

1861 MISS PRATT *Flower. Pl.* III. 394 Dr. Rousseau of Paris..found therein the existence of a hitherto unknown principle, called *Ilicine.* **1865–72** WATTS *Dict. Chem.* III. 244 Ilicic acid. *Ibid.*, Colourless ilicate of calcium is obtained. *Ibid.*, The ilicin extracted from the residue by alcohol..is a bitter, amorphous, brown, very hygroscopic mass.

i-lided, ME. form of LIDDED.

i-lift(e, ME. pa. pple. of LIFT *v.*

iligant ('ɪlɪgənt), *a.* Also **illigant.** ¶ Used, chiefly as an Irishism, for ELEGANT *a.* (sense ¶8).

1819 M. WILMOT *Let.* 3 Sept. (1935) 16 An *illigant* black silk dress. **1822** M. EDGEWORTH *Let.* 4 Mar. (1971) 361 We have an excellent job landau..and quite *iligant* coachman horses and *all*—for one pound per day. **1833** DICKENS *Lett.* (1965) I. 20, I..will not give you the trouble of deciphering any more of my iligant writing. **1846** *Punch* XI. 79 A large assortment of most iligant blunderbuss's. **1888** *Cornhill Mag.* Sep. 277 An' it looked an iligant counthry an' all in a glimmerin' green. **1898** J. D. BRAYSHAW *Slum Silhouettes* 21 It was agreed on all hands that he was 'an illigant corpse, and as foine a bhoy as ever was stretched'. **1939** JOYCE *Finnegans Wake* I. 14 She found hersell sackvulle of..small illigant brogues, so rich in sweat.

i-light, -liȝt, -liht, of LIGHT *v.*

i-like, obs. f. ALIKE: see YLIKE.

†**i-likeness.** *Obs.* [OE. *ȝelícnes* (= OS. *gelicnessi*, OHG. *gilîhnessi*, Ger. *gleichnis*), f. *ȝelíc* (see ALIKE, LIKE) + -NESS.] Likeness, image, similitude.

c **1000** ÆLFRIC *Gen.* i. 26 Uton wircean man to andlicnisse and to ure ȝelicnisse. *c* **1175** *Lamb. Hom.* 127 He wes imacad to monne ilicnesse. *a* **1225** *Juliana* 21 He..biheold hire lufsume leor lilies ilicnesse. *a* **1225** *Ancr. R.* 360 ȝif we beoð i-imped to þe iliknesse of Godes deaðe.

i-likned, ME. pa. pple. of LIKEN.

ilima (ɪ'liːmə). [Hawaiian.] A shrub of the genus *Sida*, esp. *S. fallax*, bearing yellow or orange flowers.

1888 W. HILLEBRAND *Flora Hawaiian Islands* 43 *Sida*... A large genus, distributed over the warmer regions of the entire globe.—Nat[ive] name of all species: 'Ilima'. **1915** W. A. BRYAN *Nat. Hist. Hawaii* xv. 209 Two species of ilima occur in the lower zone throughout the group. Their bright yellow flowers, so much used in leis, are well known. **1920** *Glasgow Herald* 16 Apr. 8 Three magnificent wreaths of ilima, the Hawaiian royal flowers. **1970** S. CARLQUIST *Hawaii* xiv. 269 *Sida fallax*, the ilima, is a mat with yellow-orange flowers and finely hairy white leaves, common near the shores of all the islands.

i-limed, of LIME *v.*; ME. form of LIMBED *a.*

†**i-limp,** *v. Obs.* [OE. *ȝelimpan*, f. *limpan* LIMP *v.*[1]] *intr.* To happen, befall.

975 *O.E. Chron.* an. 973 Ða þa ðis ȝelamp. *a* **1000** *Boeth. Metr.* xxvi. 34 Ða sio tid ȝelomp þæt hi þæt rice ȝereaht hæfdon. *a* **1175** *Cott. Hom.* 231 Hit ȝelamp þat an rice king wes. *c* **1175** *Lamb. Hom.* 93 þa com his wif saphira and nuste hwet hire were ilumpen wes. *a* **1225** *Ancr. R.* 54 More wunder ilomp [*v.r.* ilimpes].

†**'iling.** *Obs. rare.* [quasi *aisling*, f. *ile*, AISLE.] = AISLE.

1456–7 *Durham Acc. Rolls* (Surtees) I. 151 Pro operacione ..super lez Ilynges in aula predicta.

ilio- (,ɪlɪəʊ), used as combining form of ILIUM 3 in anatomical terms, as

ilio-aponeu'rotic *a.*, connected with the ilium, and of the character of an aponeurosis. **ilio-'dorsal** *a.*, 'relating to the dorsum of the ilium' (*Syd. Soc. Lex.*). **iliopecti'neal** *a.* [L. *pecten* comb], relating to the crest or comb of the ilium which forms part of the brim of the pelvis, or to the ilium and the pectineus muscle. ‖**ilio'psoas**, the iliac and psoas muscles regarded as forming one muscle. Esp. in comb. with adjs. relating to other parts of the body with the sense 'relating to or connecting the ilium and...', as **ilio-'caudal, -coccy'geal, -'costal, -'femoral, -hypo'gastric, -'inguinal, -'ischiac, -ischi'atic, -'lumbar, -pero'neal** [Gr. περόνη fibula] (applied to muscles connecting the ilium and the fibula; also as *sb.*); **ilio-pso'atic, -'pubic, -'sacral, -sci'atic** = *ilio-ischiatic*, **ilio-'scrotal, -'tibial, -trochan'teric,** *adjs.* (*Syd. Soc. Lex.*).

1831 R. KNOX *Cloquet's Anat.* 193 *Ilio-lumbar Ligament*.. by which the fifth lumbar vertebra and the os innominatum are connected. **1840** G. V. ELLIS *Anat.* 126 The last dorsal and ilio-inguinal nerves. **1840** E. WILSON *Anat. Vade M.* (1851) 259 The ilio-femoral articulation. **1845** TODD & BOWMAN *Phys. Anat.* I. 141 The strong ilio-sacral ligaments, which tie the bones together behind. **1866** HUXLEY *Preh. Rem. Caithn.* 92 The depth of the true pelvis, from the iliopectineal eminence to the tuberosity of the ischium. **1870** ROLLESTON *Anim. Life* 21 The iliopectineal spine..is absent. **1871** HUXLEY *Anat. Vert.* vi. 294 In.. birds..The iliosciatic interval is..converted into a foramen. **1879** HOLDEN *Anat.* (ed. 4) 400 The two muscles..may be considered as one, and are sometimes called the ilio-psoas. **1883** MARTIN & MOALE *Vertebr. Dissect.* 163 The sciatic nerve..issues from the pelvis by the ilio-sciatic foramen.

ilio-cæcal, -colic: see ILEO-.

ilion, obs. var. ILIUM.

ilis, obs. pl. of ISLE.

†**i-lited, -et,** *ppl. a. Obs.* [f. ON. *litr* hue, countenance (= OE. *wlite*).] Hued, coloured.

a **1225** *Leg. Kath.* 1433 Se rudie and se reade ilitet eauereuch leor.

i-lithe, -liðe, ME. form of LITHE *a.*

i-lithe(n, ME. pa. pple. of LITHE *v.*, to go, travel.

i-lithered, of LITHER *v.*, to hurl with a sling.

-ility, compound suffix (F. *-ilité*, L. *-ilitās*), consisting of -ITY added to adjs. in *-il* (*civility*), *-ile* (*servility*), or *-le* (*ability*).

1865 MRS. GASKELL *Wives & Dau.* xxxi, He heard of his successor's affability, and sociability, and amiability, and a variety of other agreeable 'ilities'.

ilium ('ɪlɪəm). *Anat.* Pl. **ilia.** Also 4–7 **ilion,** 6 pl. **ilions.** [L. *īlium* that part of the abdomen which extends from the lowest ribs to the pubes, groin, or flank; in classical L. only in pl. *īlia* (from *īle* or *īlium*) flanks, sides, also entrails.

In mediæval medical Latin a Græcized form *īlion*, deduced from pl. *īlia*, was in use, whence the early forms in the quots. (Cf. F. *ilion* (16th c. in Paré), now also *ilium*.) See also ILEUM, now used in one of the senses of *ilium*.]

†**1.** The third portion of the small intestine; the ILEUM. *Obs.*

1388 WYCLIF *Lev.* iii. 15 The calle which is..bisidis ilion [*v.r.* the ilion: 1382 biside the reyne guttes]. **1398** TREVISA *Barth. De P.R.* VIII. xlix. (1495) 263 The gutte that hyghte Ilion is a smalle gutte and longe biclypping other guttes aboute. **1541** COPLAND *Guydon's Quest. Chirurg.* H iv a, Ye sklendre gut that hyght Ylion..it hath many reuolucyons. **1681** tr. *Willis' Rem. Med. Wks.* Vocab., *Ilion*,..the thin gut or small gut. **1827** ABERNETHY *Surg. Wks.* I. 121 The villous coat of the ilium.

†**2.** *pl.* The parts of the body beneath the ribs on each side; the flanks (L. *īlia*). *Obs.*

1590 BARROUGH *Meth. Physick* III. xlii. 171 Cupping glasses fastened to the ilions, and the loines. **1706** PHILLIPS (ed. Kersey), *Ilia*, the Flanks, the side-parts of the lower Belly between the last Rib and the Privities.

3. The anterior or superior bone of the pelvis, the hip-bone; it occurs in most vertebrates above fishes, and has various forms and relative positions; usually (as in man) it articulates with the sacrum, and anchyloses with the ischium and pubis, forming together with these latter the *os innominatum.*

1706 PHILLIPS (ed. Kersey) s.v. *Coxæ Os*, In Infants it consists of three Bones, viz. Ilium, Ischium, and Os Pubis. **1727–41** CHAMBERS *Cycl.* s.v. *Innominatum*, Three bones; viz. the ilium, the pubis and ischium. **1831** R. KNOX *Cloquet's Anat.* 115 The Anterior and Inferior spinous process of the ilium. **1872** MIVART *Elem. Anat.* 178 A widely expanded upper part joins the sacrum and extends down to the socket for the thigh. This is the ilium.

i-live: see YLEVE *v.*, to believe.

ilixanthin (aɪlɪk'sænθɪn). *Chem.* [f. ILEX holly + Gr. ξανθός yellow + -IN.] A yellow colouring matter ($C_{17}H_{22}O_{11}$) obtained from the holly.

1865–72 WATTS *Dict. Chem.* III. 244 The leaves gathered in January contain scarcely any ilixanthin, while those gathered in August contain a large quantity. *Ibid.*, The ilixanthin crystallises out in straw-yellow microscopic needles. *Ibid.* 245 Neutral or basic acetate of lead produces in the aqueous solution of ilixanthin a splendid yellow precipitate.

ilk (ɪlk), *a.*[1] (*pron.*) Now *Sc.* Forms: α. 1 **ylca, illca,** 1–3 **ilca, (ilica),** 2 **ilc,** 3–6 **ilke,** 4–5 **ylk,** 4–6 **ylke, (6 elke),** 3–6, 9 **ilk.** β. 2–4 **ilche.** γ. 4 **ich,** 4–5 **iche.** [OE. *ilca* m., *ilce* f. and n., inflected as weak adj., app. f. the pronominal stem *i-*, *ī-* (cf. Goth. *i-s* he, Lat. *i-s*, *i-dem*) + *-líc* = Goth. *-leiks* (see LIKE); cf. OE. *hwelc, swelc* WHICH, SUCH = Goth. *hwileiks, swaleiks*. As in *such, which*, etc., the *k* was in southern and midland ME. palatalized to *ch*; but the word survives only in the north.]

†**1.** Same, identical; ***the (this, that) ilk***, the same, the identical, the very same (person, thing, etc. already mentioned, or specified in a clause following). Freq. in statements of time, ***that ilk day, night, year***, etc. Sometimes with addition of *same, self*. (See also THILK.) *Obs.*

α. **805–31** *Charter* in *O.E. Texts* 444 Of ðaem ilcan londe. *a* **1000** *Andreas* 752 (Gr.) þis is se ilca ealwalda god. **1154** *O.E. Chron.* an. 1135 þat ilc ȝær warth þe king ded. *a* **1250** *Owl & Night.* 99 þat ilke best þat fuleþ his owe nest. *a* **1300** *Cursor M.* 1284 (Gött.) Seth went..To paradis þat ilke day [*Trin.* þe same day]. *Ibid.* 1918 Bi þat ilk same day. *c* **1330** R. BRUNNE *Chron.* (1810) 61 þat ilk self ȝere. *c* **1400** *Rom. Rose* 1333 Ryght in that ilke same place. **1483** CAXTON *Gold. Leg.* 388/1 That the ylke god shold be blessyd. **1556** LAUDER *Tractate* 49 At this ilke compt quhat salbe said To thame? β. *c* **1200** *Vices & Virtues* 23 Ðe ilche gode wille. **1258** *Proclam. Hen. III*, Al on þo ilche worden. **1340–70** *Alisaunder* 448 þis cumlich Kyng þat ilche kith wynnes. γ. **13..** *Guy Warw.* (A.) 4303 þat ich while his lyoun ȝede out of þe pauiloun. *c* **1330** *Amis & Amil.* 850 Y seighe it meself this ich day. *c* **1480** *Kyng & Hermit* 91 in Hazl. *E.P.P.* I. 17 Send me grace this iche nyght.

†**2.** absol. ***the, that ilk***: **a.** The same person or persons. Also with *same, self*. *Obs.*

a **1000** *Boeth. Metr.* ix. 24 Se ilca het ealle acwellan. *a* **1100** *O.E. Chron.* an. 1058 Se ylca sænde..pallium hider to lande. *c* **1200** *Trin. Coll. Hom.* 55 Wo þo ilche þat ben mihti to drinken. *a* **1225** *Leg. Kath.* 1097 þe ilke self is Godes sune. *c* **1340** *Cursor M.* 18141 þis blisful kyng hit is þat iche [*Laud MS.* eche; *Cott. MS.* ilk]. *a* **1366** CHAUCER *Rom. Rose* 416 That ilk is she that pryvely Ne spareth never a wikked dede. **1390** GOWER *Conf.* I. 323, I am, quod he, that ilke same, Which men Diogenes calle.

†**b.** The same thing. ***with that ilke, in that ilke***, at that very moment. *Obs.*

c **755** *O.E. Chron.* an. 755 Hie cuædon þæt tæt ilce hiera ȝeferum ȝeboden wære. *a* **1300** *Cursor M.* 13451, I dar noght sai quere þis was þat ilk or nai. *a* **1375** *Joseph Arim.* 565 A whit kniht..Rydes to tholomer, rad wiþ þat ilke, Baar him doun of his hors. *c* **1375** *Sc. Leg. Saints, Mathou* 181 þat Ilk suld þai haf done til ȝow. *c* **1420** *Anturs of Arth.* ii, Hir sadille semyde of þat ilke. **1500–20** DUNBAR *Poems* lxxxii. 27 Sen as the world sayis þat ilk. *a* **1650** *Robin Hood's Death* 56 in Furniv. *Percy Folio* I. 54 Downe she came in that ilke.

3. ***of that ilk***, of the same place, territorial designation, or name: chiefly in names of landed families, as *Guthrie of that ilk, Wemyss of that ilk* = Guthrie of Guthrie, Wemyss of Wemyss. *Sc.*

1473 in *Acc. Ld. High Treasurer Scot.* I. 68 Gevin to the Justice Schire Dauid Guthere of that Ilk, knycht. **1536** BELLENDEN *Cron. Scot.* XVII. vii. (1821) II. 509 Alexander Elphinstoun of that ilk. **1542** LYNDESAY *Heraldic Notes* Wks. (E.E.T.S.) V. 609 Scot of Balwery.—Wemyss of that ilk.—Lwndy of that ilk. **1596** DALRYMPLE tr. *Leslie's Hist. Scot.* I. 126 King James, the fyfte of that ilke. **1816** SCOTT *Antiq.* xxiv, Then they were Knockwinnocks of that Ilk. **1860** GEN. P. THOMPSON *Audi Alt.* III. civ. 12 A canon and two choristers sent from St. George's to the hospital of that ilk.

¶ Erroneously, ***that ilk***: That family, class, set, or 'lot'. Also, by further extension, = kind, sort.

1790 J. FISHER *Poems* 155 Ilk ane a cap an' cloak o' silk Has got, as if she was a lady, An' that indeed, o' nae sma' ilk. **1845** MIALL in *Nonconf.* V. 212 Mr. Hume, or Mr. Roebuck, or any member of that ilk. **1881** *Annihilation* 8 It has been left for our friend Dr. —— and that ilk, to discover the long mistake. **1881** J. A. MORGAN *Shakes. Myth.* i. 36 Milton was the enemy of all the ilk. **1897** *Evesham Jrnl.* 23 June (E.D.D.), The horses most famous for marvellous exploits must have blood as well as bone, but only certain districts of the Green Isle can produce this ilk. **1899** *Westm. Gaz.* 29 June 3/2 Two very new hats of quite another 'ilk'. *Ibid.* 6 July 3/2 A coat of this 'ilk' is quite another matter from the coat of the tailor costume. **1969** *Times* 8 May 8/6 This habit is confined to Tory backbenchers like..Rear-Admiral Morgan Giles and others of that ilk. **1973** E. MCGIRR *Bardel's Murder* ii. 42 One doesn't like or dislike a fellow of that ilk... He was a kind of barrow boy in a shop.

ilk, *a.*[2] (*pron.*) Now *Sc.* Also 4–5 **ylke,** 4–6 **ilke.** [The northern and north-midland form of *ilch*, *iche* = southern *ælch, æche*, EACH: which see for the derivation and earlier history. After 1500 only in Sc., and now less usual than ILKA.]

1. Followed immediately by a substantive: = EACH 1 a; every.

c **825–1430** [see EACH A β]. *c* **1330** R. BRUNNE *Chron. Wace* (Rolls) 413 Now schul we seye of ylke parti. *c* **1400** MAUNDEV. (Roxb.) Pref. 2 Thurgh whilk ilk man es saued.

*c*1440 *Promp. Parv.* 258/1 Iche, or ylke, *quilibet.* *c*1460 *Towneley Myst.* xiv. 214 In ilk cuntre. 1508 Kennedie *Flyting w. Dunbar* 315 Thy elderis banis ilk nycht ryssis and rattillis. *a*1670 Spalding *Troub. Chas. I* (1829) 76 To raise 13*s.* 4*d.* out of ilk chalder of victual. 1767–95 Macneill *Will & Jean* iv, Tracing Will in ilk direction, Far frae Britain's fostering isle. 1837 R. Nicoll *Poems* (1842) 77 Ilk rugged mountain's curl.

b. Phrases: ***ilk deal*** (contracted ***il del, ildell***), every whit, completely. ***ilk-day's***, every-day's, ordinary, usual (cf. ILKA b). ***on ilk half***, on every side, all round. (Cf. EACH 1 d.)

*c*1300 *Havelok* 818 Þe siluer he brouthe hom il del. *c*1330 R. Brunne *Chron.* (1810) 29 [He] wan þe lond ilk dele. *c*1350 *Med. MS.* in *Archæol.* XXX. 351 Gadir of ye gres ildell. *a*1400–50 *Alexander* 731 Vnbehalde þe wele on ilk halfe. *c*1470 Henry *Wallace* III. 80 Our ilk dayis ger. 1513 Douglas *Æneis* IV. ix. 63 Sche has hir command done ilk deill. 1720 T. Boston *Hum. Nat. Fourf. St.* (1797) 317 He must take up his ilk-day's Cross.

2. *absol.*; esp. in ***ilk other***, each other (see EACH 5).

*c*1330 R. Brunne *Chron. Wace* (Rolls) 1823–4 Ilk oþer pulled, ilk oþer schok, Wiþ fet in fourche ilk oþer tok. 1596 Dalrymple tr. *Leslie's Hist. Scot.* I. 77 Ilk knew vthir well. *Ibid.* IV. 233 The vther sevin, ilk according to his power.

ilka (ˈɪlkə), *a.* Now *Sc.* Also (before vowels) **ylkan, ilkan(e.** [Orig. two words *ilk a* (*an*), i.e. ILK *a.*^{2} + A (the indefinite article); but from 15th c. usually written as one: cf. *each a* in EACH 1 b.] Each, every.

*c*1200 Ormin 5726 Illc an unnclene lusst. *a*1300 *E.E. Psalter* lxxxviii[i]. 13 In ilka land. *c*1330 R. Brunne *Chron.* (1810) 26 Þorgh þe gode Northeren slayn wer ilka man. —— *Chron. Wace* (Rolls) 1060 So wel was loked ylkan entre. 1340 Hampole *Pr. Consc.* 53 Ilk a thyng þat God has wroght. *Ibid.* 5970 Of ilkan Idel word and thoght. And of ilkan ydel dede. *c*1375 *Sc. Leg. Saints, Paulus* 68 Prechinge ilkaday agane þe Iowis. *c*1400 Maundev. (Roxb.) Pref. 2 Ilke a gude Cristen man þat may. 1483 *Cath. Angl.* 194/2 Ilkaday, *cotidie, cotidianus.* 1500–20 Dunbar *Poems* xxxiii. 82 A stanchell hang in ilka lug. 1686 G. Stuart *Joco-ser. Disc.* 39 Latin he speaks at ilka sentence. 1724 Ramsay *Tea-t. Misc.* Ded., To ilka lovely British lass. 1816 Scott *Antiq.* xv, That will be just five-and-threepence to ilka ane o' us. 1869 C. Gibbon *R. Gray* xvii, Ilka day makes ye the mair precious to me.

b. Phrases: ***ilka deal***, every whit (cf. ILK *a.*^{2} 1 b, EACH 1 d). ***ilka day***, week-day; *attrib.* (also ***ilka day's***) every-day (cf. ILK *a.*^{2} 1 b).

*a*1300 *Cursor M.* 26671, I haue mi hert soght ilk a delle. *c*1330 R. Brunne *Chron.* (1810) 69 Þat he wild hold his oth, & 3eld him þe coroun of Inglond ilkadele. *c*1450 *St. Cuthbert* (Surtees) 6023 He did his bysynes ilk a dele. 1768 Ross *Helenore* II. 85 Well neiper, I hae heard your tale, An' even fairly at it ilka dale. 1806 *Falls of Clyde* II. ii, Twa hours ..On ilka days, on Sundays sax or seven. 1818 Scott *Hrt. Midl.* xvi, What did ye do wi' your ilka-day's claise yesterday? 1822 Galt *Sir A. Wylie* I. xxx. 282 In ilka-day meals, I am obligated to hae a regard for frugality.

ilkane, ilkone, *pron.* Now *Sc.* [Orig., and still often, two words, i.e. ILK *a.*^{2} + *ane* ONE.

In mod. Sc., stressed *ilk 'ane* (*eane, yen*), and *'ilk-ane* (*ilkin*); also often *'ilka 'ane* (*yen*).]

Each one, each (absolutely); see EACH 1 c.

α. *c*1200 Ormin 503 Þat illc an shollde witenn well. *a*1300 *Havelok* 2357 Ilkan hauede ful god stede. *c*1375 *Sc. Leg. Saints, Johannes* 151 Skantly had Ilkane of þa a singill clath. *a*1400–50 *Alexander* 3602 Foure hundreth Olyfants.. With ilkane, bunden on his bake, a borden castell. *c*1470 Henry *Wallace* x. 1005 Thai brynt thaim thar ilkan. 1508 Dunbar *Tua Mariit Wemen* 404, I banyst..his brethir ilkane. 1597 Montgomerie *Cherrie & Slae* 882 Ilk ane vse thair awin. *Mod. Sc.* Gang hame ilk ane (yen) o' ye! Thay had ilk-ane (ilkin) a rung in his hand.

β. *c*1330 R. Brunne *Chron. Wace* (Rolls) 931 Men & wymen & children ylkone. *c*1400 *Chaucer's Doctor's T.* 113 (Harl. MS.) Þurgh þe lond þay praysed hir ilkoone [*six texts* echone]. 1420 *E.E. Wills* (1882) 52, I will þat ilkon off þ^e other thre ordirs..haue x marc. 14.. *Sir Beues* (MS. C.) 4313+10 Þat þey schulde arme þem ylkoon.

'ilkin, *a.* (*pron.*) [In sense 1 perh. f. ILK *a.*^{2} + KIN; in sense 2 a phonetic weakening of ILKANE.]

†**1.** *adj.* Each kind of, each, every. *Obs.*

*a*1300 *Cursor M.* 10831 Haf redi ilkin thing. *c*1470 Henry *Wallace* v. 602 Off ilkyn wicht scho kepyt her fra blame. 1674–91 Ray *N.C. Words, Gloss. Northumb.* 143 Ilkin, *quilibet.*

2. In mod. Sc. a frequent pronunciation of *ilkane.*

Mod. Sc. Take ilkin a dog wi' ye.

ill (ɪl), *a.* and *sb.* Also 2–6 **ille,** (4 **ile, hil(l, hyl),** 4–6 **yll(e, yl,** 4–7 **il,** (5 **el,** 6 **yle).** [Early ME. *ill*, a. ON. *illr* ill, bad, wicked, difficult, injurious, etc. Ulterior etymology unknown; not related to OE. *yfel*, EVIL.

As an adjective, *ill* is now much less used in general English than as an adverb, and survives chiefly in certain connexions, as *ill health, ill humour, ill temper, ill success*; as an adverb (the opposite of *well*), it is, in certain constructions, regularly hyphened to the word which it qualifies, e.g. *ill-advised, ill-bred, ill-conditioned, ill-spelt*, etc.: in imitation of these, apparently, and from the feeling that it is not a general adjective, but one that goes only with particular substantives, the adjective is also often hyphened to its sb., as in *ill-humour, ill-will*, etc.; but this is quite unnecessary; *ill humour* stands to *ill-humoured* just as *grey hair* to *grey-haired.*

Although *ill* is not etymologically related to *evil*, the two words have from the 12th c. been synonymous, and *ill* has been often viewed as a mere variant or reduced form of *evil*. This esp. in Sc., where *v* between two vowels early disappeared, and *devil, even, Levenax, preve, shovel, Steven*, became *deil, ein, Lennox, pree, shool, Steen*, so that *evil* might have become *eil*; hence, in 15–16th c. Sc., *euil, euyl* is found often written where *ill* was the word pronounced: e.g.

1500–20 Dunbar *Poems* xli. 10 (Bannatyne MS.) Be 3e ane tratlar, that I hald als ewill [*rimes* thrill, will, still]. 1560 Rolland *Crt. Venus* IV. 117 And take the best, and set on syde all euill [*rimes* till, will, fulfill]. 1662 *Epitaph* (on Bailie Sword) *at St. Andrews*, The svord doeth often kill..This svord doeth no svch eivell.]

A. *adj.*

1. Morally evil; wicked, iniquitous, depraved, vicious, immoral, blameworthy, reprehensible.

a. Of persons. *Obs.* exc. *dial.* Common in *Sc.*

*a*1200 *Moral Ode* 74 in *Cott. Hom.* 165 Lutel lac is gode lof þet kumeð of gode wille And ec-lete muchel 3eue of þan þe herte is ille. *a*1300 *Cursor M.* 886 (Gött.) Qui did þu þus, þu ille womman? 1340 Hampole *Pr. Consc.* 6141 Þe gude sal be sette on his right hand, And þe ille on his lefte syde sal stand. 1422 tr. *Secreta Secret., Priv. Priv.* 169 More deppyr in the turmentis of helle shall bene the ille Prynces, than the ill subiectes. 1566 T. Stapleton *Ret. Untr. Jewel* IV. 31 A very ill man, being justly excommunicat. *c*1680 Beveridge *Serm.* (1729) I. 513 They hurry him from one ill company to another. 1737 Whiston *Josephus, Hist.* I. iii. §2 The calumnies which ill men..contrived. 1813 Hogg *Witch of Fife* i Quhair haif ye been, ye ill womyne, These three lang nightis fra hame? 1861 Gen. P. Thompson *Audi Alt.* III. clvii. 165 Let us hope that while there are ill ministers, there shall be no lack of unpalatable truth. 1865 G. Macdonald *A. Forbes* xiii. 49 Takin' up wi' ill loons like Sandy Forbes. 1871 M. S. De Vere *Americanisms* 493 In Texas, the word *ill* has the..signification of 'immoral'; and 'an ill fellow' means 'a man of bad habits'.

b. Of conduct or actions. Now somewhat *arch.*

*c*1200 Ormin 6647 Þatt mann iss fox..And full off ille wiless. *a*1300 *Cursor M.* 42 Alle oure dedis, Both gode and ille. 1513 More in Grafton *Chron.* (1568) II. 808 To amende and chaunge hys yll lyfe. 1701 *Stanley's Hist. Philos.* Biogr. 3 Creating..a Horrour for what is Base and Ill. 1736 Butler *Anal.* I. iii. Wks. 1874 I. 54 Ill or mischievous actions should be punished. 1829 Landor *Imag. Conv.* Ser. II. *Barrow & Newton* II. 50 Correct your own ill habits. 1870 Morris *Earthly Par.* I. I. 307 Many tales..Of the ill deeds our fathers used to do.

c. Of estimation, repute, opinion, or name: Such as imputes or implies evil in the person or thing referred to.

1483 *Cath. Angl.* 195/1 An ille fame, *infamia.* 1546 J. Heywood *Prov.* (1867) 63 He that hath an yll name, is halfe hangd. 1640–4 Ld. Finch in Rushw. *Hist. Coll.* III. (1692) I. 124 That ill opinion which may perhaps be conceived of me. 1741 Watts *Improv. Mind* I. iii. §4 Prone to put an ill sense upon the actions of their neighbours. 1760–72 H. Brooke *Fool of Qual.* (1808) I. vii. 123 At a house of ill report, where she formerly had kept a milliner's shop. 1870 Spurgeon *Treas. Dav.* Ps. xxxvii. 6 The darkness of his sorrow and his ill-repute shall both flee away.

2. a. Marked by evil intent, or by want of good feeling; malevolent, hostile, unfriendly, adverse, unkind, harsh, cruel. (See also ILL BLOOD, ILL TREATMENT, ILL WILL.)

*c*1330 R. Brunne *Chron. Wace* (Rolls) 3960 Wyþ schrewes he digde hem many yl pul. *c*1360 *Ipotis* 285 in Horstm. *Altengl. Leg.* (1881) 344 Adam onswerde wordes ille. 1548 Hall *Chron., Edw. IV* 232 b, Revilyng hym with suche yll wordes, and so shamful termes. 1640–4 Ld. Finch in Rushw. *Hist. Coll.* III. (1692) I. 124 Ill office I never did to any of the House. 1680 Allen *Peace & Unity* 27 To forbear all hard speeches, and ill reflexions on them that differ from them. 1808 Jamieson, s.v. 'He's very ill to his wife.' 1819 Shelley *Cenci* v. iv. 150 Ill tongues shall wound me. 1849 Macaulay *Hist. Eng.* xiv. II. 458 In spite of the ill offices of the Jesuits. 1868 J. H. Blunt *Ref. Ch. Eng.* I. 395 The ill-feeling against the foreign residents.

b. Of an animal: Of evil disposition; fierce, savage, vicious. Now *dial.*

1480 Caxton *Chron. Eng.* clxxxvi. 162 The forsayd dragon shold be ladde by an ylle grehounde. 1574 Hyll *Ord. Bees* ix, The fierce bees are very ill. 1860 Bartlett *Dict. Amer., Ill*, vicious,..common in Texas; as, 'Is your dog ill?' meaning, is he vicious? 1888 *Jrnl. Amer. Folk-lore* I. No. 2 The negro..says a horse that is cross, or threatens harm, is ill, though in excellent health.

3. a. Doing or tending to do harm; hurtful, injurious, pernicious, noxious, mischievous, prejudicial; dangerous. Prov. ***ill weeds grow apace.***

1340–70 *Alex. & Dind.* 157 Addrus and ypotamus, and oþure ille wormus. *c*1375 *Sc. Leg. Saints, Ninian* 203 Þare he saw sawyne il seide. 1523 Fitzherb. *Husb.* §20 The thistyll is an yll wede. 1546 J. Heywood *Prov.* I. x. (1867) 22 Ill weede growth fast. 1597 Shaks. *2 Hen. IV*, II. i. 106 Prawnes..I told thee they were ill for a greene wound. 1611 —— *Wint. T.* II. i. 106 There's some ill Planet raignes. 1669 Evelyn *Diary* 10 July, It will be of ill consequence. 1850 Tennyson *In Mem.* lxxxvi, Doubt and Death, Ill brethren. 1860 Hawthorne *Marb. Faun* (1879) II. v. 54 The good or ill result.

†**b.** Unwholesome, injurious to health. *Obs.*

*c*1470 Henry *Wallace* II. 155 Ill meyt and drynk thai gert on till hym giff. 1640 Quarles *Enchirid.* iv. 55 Ill diet may hasten them unto their journey's end. 1726 Swift *Gulliver* I. i, Dead by immoderate labour and ill food.

4. Causing pain, discomfort, or inconvenience: offensive, painful, disagreeable, objectionable.

*c*1220 *Bestiary* 526 Wiles ðar [? ðat] weder is so ille. *a*1300 *Cursor M.* 16774 (Gött.) [Þ]at bitter drinc..he tasted it, bot ..it was selcuth ill. *c*1400 Maundev. (Roxb.) xvii. 79 Ill dremes and fantasies. 1548 Hall *Chron., Hen. VIII* 103 Great raine and yll wether. 1609 Bible (Douay) *Ps.* xxxiii. 22 The death of sinners is verie il. 1655 *W. Fulke's Meteors* Observ. 174 Copper..giveth no ill taste or smell to meat boyled in it. 1715 De Foe *Fam. Instruct.* I. i. (1841) I. 32 If it be but a little ill weather. 1852 Miss Yonge *Cameos* II. ix. 113 A knight riding up to him, told him he would die an ill death. 1876 Gladstone *Homeric Synchr.* 185 They fell into ill weather which destroyed their vessel.

5. Of conditions, fortune, etc.: Miserable, wretched, unfortunate, unlucky; disastrous, unfavourable, untoward, unpropitious. Prov. ***it's an ill wind that blows nobody good.***

*c*1250 *Gen. & Ex.* 4038 Quo-so wile cursing maken, Ille cursing sal him taken. 1450–70 *Golagros & Gaw.* 1243 Ane gude chance or ane ill. 1562 J. Heywood *Prov. & Epigr.* (1867) 140 It is an yll wynde that blowth no man to good. 1580 Sidney *Arcadia* III. (1622) 349, I go blindfold whether the course of my ill-happe carries me. 1611 Bible *Isa.* iii. 11 Woe vnto the wicked, it shall be ill with him. 1634 Sir T. Herbert *Trav.* 98 It was his ill fate, to be a sleepe, as old Abbas was going a hunting. 1725 Pope *Odyss.* xxiv. 176 Ill fortune led Ulysses to our isle. 1771 *Antiq. Sarisb.* Salisb. Ballad 21 *note*, The Church..was founded in an Ill-hour.. for the Steeple was burnt down by lightening, the day after 'twas finished. 1879 Froude *Cæsar* vii. 61 Choosing an ill moment for a revolution.

6. Difficult, troublesome, hard. (Usually with *dative inf.*, as 'ill to please'.)

*c*1330 R. Brunne *Chron.* (1810) 181 Þat castelle was fulle strong, & ille for to wynne. 1517 Torkington *Pilgr.* (1884) 2, I passyd an ill mountayne all a lone. 1551 Turner *Herbal* I. Pvb, Epimedum..is strange and yll to fynde. 1580 Sidney *Arcadia* (1622) 4 A defeate, where the conquered kept both field and spoile: a shipwrack without storme or ill footing. 1644 Evelyn *Diary* 12 Apr., The country dos not much molest the traveller with dirt and ill way. 1647 Sprigge *Anglia Rediv.* I. iv. (1854) 25 By reason of the moat, the access was ill to it. 1711 *C.M. Lett. to Curat* 57 He was not ill to please. 1838 Tupper *Proverb. Philos., Beauty* (ed. 9) 308 Beauty is intangible, vague, ill to be defined.

7. a. In privative sense: Not good; of deficient or inferior quality or condition; of little or no worth; defective, poor, imperfect, unsatisfactory, not up to the standard; faulty, erroneous; (of an agent or his work) unskilful, inexpert (*at*), inefficient.

*a*1300 *Cursor M.* 21805 Þis tale, queþer it be il or gode, I fand it written o þe rode. *c*1400 Maundev. (Roxb.) xiv. 64 A full ill land and sandy and lytill fruyt berand. 1470–85 Malory *Arthur* VI. xvi, I am an ylle clymber and the tree is passynge hyghe. 1500–20 Dunbar *Poems* xxxiv. 56 Ane browstar swoir the malt wes ill. 1592 Shaks. *Rom. & Jul.* IV. ii. 6 'Tis an ill Cooke that cannot licke his owne fingers. 1602 —— *Ham.* II. ii. 120, I am ill at these Numbers: I haue not Art to reckon my grones. 1653 Walton *Angler* Ep. Ded. 1, I have made so ill use of your former favors. 1727 Swift *Gulliver* III. iv, So ill an ear for music. 1782 Mann in *Lett. Lit. Men* (Camden) 423 He has the ill-taste to prefer London to Paris. 1800 Addison *Amer. Law Rep.* 62 The declaration was ill, in not alledging [etc.]. 1833 Lamb *Elia* Ser. II. *Wedding*, I am ill at describing female apparel. 1870 Ruskin *Lect. Art* i. (1875) 3 The first shoots of it enfeebled by ill gardening.

b. Of manners or behaviour: Not up to the standard of propriety; improper.

1586 A. Day *Eng. Secretary* I. (1625) 22 We rebuke the ill demeanors of our children. 1601 Shaks. *Twel. N.* I. v. 162 *Ol.* What manner of man? *Mal.* Of verie ill manner: hee'l speake with you, will you, or no. 1655 Fuller *Hist. Camb.* iii. 54 Ill Manners occasion Good laws, as the Handsome Children of Ugly Parents. 1773 Goldsm. *Stoops to Conq.* II. iii, My host seems to think it ill manners to leave me alone. 1875 Jowett *Plato* (ed. 2) I. 15, I shall have to praise myself, which would be ill manners.

8. a. Of health or bodily condition: Unsound, disordered. Hence, of persons (formerly, also, of parts of the body): Out of health, sick, indisposed, not well; almost always used predicatively.

(The prevailing mod. sense.)

*c*1460 *Towneley Myst.* xiii. 231 Bot a sekenes I feyll that haldys me full haytt..Therfor full sore am I and yll. *c*1575 G. Harvey *Letter-bk.* (Camden) 168, I..am yet as il almost as ever I was..But as soone as I shal recoover mi helth [etc.]. 1598 Sylvester *Du Bartas* II. i. III. *Furies* 582 Th' Il-habitude [turned] into the Dropsie chill. 1599 Shaks. *Much Ado* III. iv. 54 By my troth I am exceeding ill, hey ho. 1628 Winthrop *Let.* 7 Apr. in *Hist. New Eng.* (1853) I. 420 My hand is so ill as I know not when I shall be able to travel. 1637 Brian *Pisse-Proph.* (1679) 115 Whereas he..before.. was sick but a little in jest, he feels himself iller already with this message. 1660 Pepys *Diary* (1875) I. 127 My eye was very red and ill, in the morning. 1687 A. Lovell tr. *Thevenot's Trav.* I. 227 There was one little Child ill of the Small-pox. 1698 [see ILL HEALTH, ILL-HEALTH. 1712 W. Rogers *Voy.* 160 Another lying dangerously ill. 1806 *Med. Jrnl.* XV. 380, I..could get no other account from her, than that 'she was ill all over'. 1843 Sir C. Scudamore *Med. Visit Gräfenberg* 50 One month after this attack, he was taken ill in a similar way. 1849 James *Woodman* xii, Children are well and ill in a day. 1871 Napheys *Prev. & Cure Dis.* 33 Prolonged ill-health. 1897 Mamie Dickens *My Father* 66 A solemn clergyman..summoned to administer consolation to a very ill man.

b. = SICK *a.* 2.

1928 C. F. S. Gamble *Story N. Sea Air Station* 244 Before they could be attended they were given too much food and were violently ill as a result. 1929 A. Conan Doyle *Maracot Deep* 153 The sight was so horrifying that we were all ill.

9. In special collocations (often unnecessarily hyphened): **ill desert**, the fact of deserving ill, demerit, blameworthiness (so ***ill deserving***); **ill ease**, discomfort, uneasiness; † **ill eye** = *evil eye* (see EVIL *a.* 6); **ill fame** (see 1 c.); esp. in ***house of ill fame*** (see HOUSE *sb.* 11); **ill grace** (see GRACE *sb.*); † **ill hail** (see HAIL *sb.*^{2} 2); **ill house**, a house of ill fame; **ill part** (see PART *sb.*); † **ill rule**, disorderly conduct, misrule (also *attrib.*); **ill**

success, imperfect success (sense 6); often = want of success, failure (cf. 5); **ill temper** (see TEMPER *sb.*); **ill thief** (*Sc.*), the devil: see THIEF; † **ill year**, misfortune, disaster [app. suggested by GOODYEAR]. See also ILL BREEDING, ILL HUMOUR, etc.

1736 Butler *Anal.* I. vi. 113 Vitious and of *Ill-desert. **1861** G. Moberly *Serm. Beatit.* 14 None knows, as he knows, his own weakness and personal ill-desert. *a* **1850** Rossetti *Dante & Circ.* II. (1874) 280 My life seems made for other lives' *ill-ease. **1615** G. Sandys *Trav.* 138 To defend them from mischances, and the poison of *ill eies. **1697** Dryden *Virg. Past.* III. 159 What Magick has bewitched the Woolly Dams, And what ill Eyes beheld the tender Lambs? **1749** Fielding *Tom Jones* XIV. iii, If he had the least suspicion of me keeping an *ill house. **1556** *Nottingham Rec.* IV. 111 For kepyng of *ylle reulle howrs in hyr howsse. **1580** Hollyband *Treas. Fr. Tong*, *Berlans*,.. houses of ill rule or gaming. **1615** G. Sandys *Trav.* 145 *Ill successe of the Christian armies. **1665** Pepys *Diary* 20 Aug., My Lord is unblameable in all this ill-successe. **1796** Morse *Amer. Geog.* I. 291 The ill success of these expeditions. **1876** Bancroft *Hist. U.S.* II. xxii. 25 Disheartened by former ill-success. **1598** Barret *Theor. Warres* 120, I wish the *ill yeare to his Eggars and setters-on.

10. In *Comb.*: see ILL- below.

B. *sb.* [absolute use of the adj.]

1. Evil, in the widest sense (= EVIL *sb.* 1 a); the opposite of good. (Now chiefly in antithesis with *good*.)

a **1300** *Cursor M.* 939 Bath þe god and il knauand. **1340** Hampole *Pr. Consc.* 1615 Wa till yhow þat says with will þat ille es gud and gud es ill. *a* **1400–50** *Alexander* 4216 Þat we cuthe any-gates gesse betwyx gud and ill. *c* **1605** Rowley *Birth Merl.* II. ii, Great good must have great ill as opposite. **1734** Pope *Ess. Man* IV. 111 What makes all physical or moral ill? **1850** Tennyson *In Mem.* liv, Oh yet we trust that somehow good Will be the final goal of ill.

2. a. Moral evil, depravity, wickedness, iniquity, sin, wrong-doing. *arch.*

a **1300** *Cursor M.* 501 Þai mai neuermar held til il. *c* **1375** *Sc. Leg. Saints, Paulus* 800 In yll þe tyrand had sic Ioy. **1426** Audelay *Poems* 8 Mon.. has fre choys.. Weder he wyl do good or ylle. **1580** Sidney *Ps.* v. ii, Thou hatest all whose workes in ill are plac'd. **1608–33** Bp. Hall *Medit. & Vows* (1851) 58 Those men, which will ever be either doing nothing, or ill. **1697** Ken *Hymn, 'Glory to Thee'* ii, Forgive me, Lord, for Thy dear Son, The ill that I this day have done. **1711** Steele *Spect.* No. 79 ¶9 Many People call themselves Virtuous, from no other Pretence to it but an Absence of Ill. **1818** Shelley *Rev. Islam* x. vi, Strange natures made a brotherhood of ill. *Ibid.*, Each one the other thus from ill to ill did lure.

† **b.** A wicked or sinful act, a misdeed. *Obs.*

13.. *E.E. Allit. P.* B. 577 Alle illez he hates as helle þat stynkkez; But non nuyez hym.. As harlottrye vnhonest. *a* **1340** Hampole *Psalter* vii. 3 Pride.. is rote of all illes. *a* **1533** Ld. Berners *Gold. Bk. M. Aurel.* (1546) Gg iv b, To chastyse vs for our ylles. **1604** Eliz. Grymeston *Miserere* xix. in *Misc.*, If thou sinne offrings hadst desired.. How gladly those for all my illes I would haue yeelded thee! **1675** Otway *Alcib.* IV. i, And set her Ills off with a winning Dress. **1741** Mrs. Montagu *Lett.* I. 271 Who does an ill receives a punishment.

3. † **a.** Hostile, malevolent, or unfriendly feeling, ill will: in phr. ***in ill***, etc.; ***to take*** (a thing) ***in*** (***at, to***) ***ill*** = to take it ill, take offence at it. *Obs.*

1303 R. Brunne *Handl. Synne* 5660 Ȝyt ȝaue he hyt with no gode wylle, But kast hyt aftyr hym with ylle. *c* **1330** —— *Chron.* (1810) 25 Whan Alfrid & Gunter had werred long in ille. *c* **1340** *Cursor M.* 21898 (Fairf.) Againe him we were in il. *a* **1400** *Octavian* 1152 Syr, take hyt not yn ylle. *c* **1430** *Syr Gener.* 7447, I besech you take it not at yl. *a* **1440** *Sir Degrev.* 442 Y pray yow take hit not to ille. **1500–20** Dunbar *Poems* xxx. 20 Tak it nocht in ill.

b. In reference to opinion or the expression of it: Something blameful, unfavourable, unfriendly, or injurious. (Perh. orig. the *adverb*: cf. next 2 b.)

1414 Brampton *Penit. Ps.* 18 Ne with here tungys blemysch my name, And speke me ille. **1569** J. Rogers *Gl. Godly Loue* 184 Not once one to hear yl of another. **1656** B. Harris *Parival's Iron Age* (1659) 264 Many began now to speak ill of him. **1778** Mad. D'Arblay *Diary* Aug., I will allow no man to speak ill of [him].. that he does not deserve. **1891** E. Peacock *N. Brendon* I. 177 Plumer knew no ill of him. *Mod.* I can think no ill of him.

4. Evil as caused or inflicted; harm, injury, mischief.

c **1375** *Sc. Leg. Saints, Paulus* 582 Þat man has done gret il ay To þame, þat ar to þe lele men. **1470–85** Malory *Arthur* XIV. v, What dost thow here? He ansuerd I doo neyther good nor grete ylle. *a* **1533** Ld. Berners *Huon* cxlvi. 552 Al the ylles and damages that he hath done to you. **1611** Bible *Rom.* xiii. 10 Loue worketh no ill to his neighbour. **1689–90** Temple *Health & Long Life* Wks. 1731 I. 284 The only Ill of it lies in the too much or too frequent Use. **1760** 'Portia' *Polite Lady* xxvii. 123 Lest I should do myself more ill than good. **1816** Scott *Old Mort.* xiv, Wad there be ony ill in getting out o' thae chields' hands an' ane could compass it?

5. a. Evil as suffered or endured; misfortune, calamity, disaster, trouble, distress. † ***to give oneself ill***, to distress or trouble oneself, to grieve.

a **1300** *Cursor M.* 3037 'Abraham', [the angel] said, 'giue þe not ill'. *a* **1340** Hampole *Psalter* xxii. 5, I sall dred nan ill. *a* **1400** *Isumbras* 93 Thay wepede sare and gaffe thame ille. *a* **1450** *Le Morte Arth.* 821 He.. Sighed sore, and gaff hym ylle. **1502** Atkinson tr. *De Imitatione* III. xix. 212 As gladly shall I take by thy grace yll as good, bitter thynges as swete. **1598** Yong *Diana* 33 One day I do conforme me to my fortune, And to my griefe.. Next day mine yll doth vex me, and importune My soule with thoughts of griefe. **1660** F. Brooke tr. *Le Blanc's Trav.* 141 They have their nativity cast to know if good or ill shall befall them. **1771** Mackenzie *Man Feel.* xl. (1803) 76 We frequently observe the tidings of ill communicated as eagerly as the annunciation of good. **1842** Tennyson *Two Voices* 107 Still heaping on the fear of ill The fear of men, a coward still.

b. (with *pl.*) A misfortune, a calamity, a disaster; an adversity.

a **1340** Hampole *Psalter* cxxxix. 7 Many yllys are agayns me. **1546** Heywood *Prov.* (1867) 10 Of two yls, choose the least. **1548** Hall *Chron., Edw. IV* 209 (According to the olde proverbe) one yll commeth never alone. **1665** Dryden *Ind. Emperor* II. ii, The Ills of Love, not those of Fate, I fear. **1742** Gray *Ode Prospect Eton Coll.* 61 No sense have they of ills to come. **1796** H. Hunter tr. *St.-Pierre's Stud. Nat.* (1799) I. 95 We communicate to each other only the ills of life. **1888** Bryce *Amer. Commw.* II. xlv. 182 To enact some measure meant to cure a pressing ill.

6. Bodily disorder, disease, sickness. (Chiefly *Sc.* or *north.*) Frequent in popular names of diseases or distempers. ***comitial ill***, epilepsy: see COMITIAL 1 b. See also *child-ill* s.v. CHILD *sb.* 22.

c **1375** *Sc. Leg. Saints, Jacobus minor* 577 Full besyly can he spere Of his seknes þe manere, And of þe cause als of þe Ile. **1450** Myrc 365 That maketh a body to cache el. **1513** Douglas *Æneis* VIII. Prol. 139 Sum langis for the liffyr ill to lik of ane quart. **1588** Greene *Perimedes* 8 Mightie men cannot brooke the touch of their ill. **1652** Falling-ill [see FALLING *ppl. a.* 5]. **1819** Shelley *Peter Bell* I. iii, Peter now grew old, and had An ill no doctor could unravel. **1893** *Northumbld. Gloss.*, *Ill*, a disease. The 'milk ill' and the 'quarter ill' are diseases common among sheep.

† **7.** ***the ill***: That which is faulty or erroneous; the wrong side in an argument. *Obs.*

c **1330** R. Brunne *Chron.* (1810) 100 Þe bisshop schewed him skille þat he mayntend þe ille.

8. In *Comb.*: see ILL- II below.

ill (ɪl), *adv.* Forms: (? 2) 3–5 **ille**, 3–5 **ylle**, 3–6 **yll**, 3– **ill**, (4 **il**). [Early ME. *ille*, f. ILL *a.*; cf. ON. *illa* adv., Sw. *illa*, Da. *ilde*.] In an ill manner, badly.

(Like other advs., *ill* is, for syntactical reasons, hyphened to a following adj., when the latter is used attributively, as 'an *ill-built* house', but not when used predicatively, as in 'the house is *ill built*'. But examples of the unnecessary use of the hyphen in the latter construction are very frequent.)

1. Wickedly, sinfully, blameworthily. (In modern use, with weakened force and associated with other senses, esp. 6 b.)

c **1205** Lay. 5426 Þe king wes stille: & þa swiken speken ille. *c* **1250** *Gen. & Ex.* 1706 Sichem.. hire ille bi-nam. *a* **1300** *Cursor M.* 6531 Son he herd tiþand tell þat his folk had ful il don. *c* **1330** R. Brunne *Chron.* (1810) 49 He betraied my lord, & my sonne fulle ille. *Ibid.* 163 Þe dede þat I did ille. **1601** in Farr *S.P. Eliz.* (1845) II. 433 My youth ill-spent, and worne by women's guile. **1726** Shelvocke *Voy. round World* (1757) 8 Plausible pretences for behaving as ill as they pleased. **1793** Gouv. Morris in Sparks *Life & Writ.* (1832) III. 46 He, being a little more drunk than usual, behaved extremely ill.

2. With malevolent action, in an unfriendly manner, unkindly, harshly, wrongfully.

c **1300** *Havelok* 1952 Hwo haues þe þus ille maked, þus toriuen, and al mad naked? **1582** N. Lichefield tr. *Castanheda's Conq. E. Ind.* lxxix. 162 b, The enimies.. handeled our men very ill. **1773** Mrs. Chapone *Improv. Mind* (1774) II. 16 Those who treat you ill without provocation. **1830** Macaulay *Let. to Napier* 16 Sept. in Trevelyan *Life* (1876) I. 200 If you had used me ill, I might complain.

b. With unfavourable estimation, blamefully: chiefly in phr. ***to speak, think***, etc. ***ill*** (of); so † ***to hear ill***, to be ill spoken of (see HEAR 12).

1548 Hall *Chron., Hen. VIII*, 189 Thei grudged, and spake ill of the hole Parliament. **1615** G. Sandys *Trav.* 66 He [is] ill reputed of that forbeareth so to do. **1631** Sanderson *Serm.* II. 8 All our speeches and actions are ill-interpreted. **1644** Milton *Areop.* (Arb.) 51 Nationall corruption, for which England hears ill abroad. **1712** Addison *Spect.* No. 439 ¶4 A Man.. Inquisitive after every thing which is spoken ill of him. **1849** Macaulay *Hist. Eng.* ii. I. 169 Ill as he thought of his species, he never became a misanthrope.

c. With hostility, aversion, displeasure, or offence: chiefly in phrases ***to like ill*** = † (*a*) to displease (*obs.*), (*b*) to dislike, be displeased with (*arch.*); ***to take ill*** = to take offence at, take amiss.

c **1200** Ormin 18279 He.. ræfeþþ þe þin allderrdom And tet [= thee it] maȝȝ ille likenn. *a* **1310** in Wright *Lyric P.* xx. 61 Alle we shule deye, thah us like ylle. **14..** *Tundale's Vis.* 1033 Of that syght lykyd hym full yll. **1596** Harington *Metam. Ajax* Pref. (1814) 2 Some will take it ill.. because they doe ill understand it. **1664** Evelyn *Sylva* xvii. §2. 36 The Aspen.. takes it ill to have his head cut off. **1701** Rowe *Amb. Step-moth.* Ded., The Town has not receiv'd this Play ill. **1849** Macaulay *Hist. Eng.* x. II. 627 This suggestion was so ill received that he made haste to explain it away. **1854** H. Miller *Sch. & Schm.* (1858) 480 Mr. Stewart.. liked the move of his neighbour.. exceedingly ill.

3. Sorely, painfully, grievously, unpleasantly. *Obs.* exc. *dial.*

a **1275** *Prov. Ælfred* 652 in *O.E. Misc.* 137 Þe bicche bitit ille. *c* **1400** *Destr. Troy* 10976 He gird hir to ground, and greuit hir yll. *c* **1489** Caxton *Sonnes of Aymon* xvi. 367, I praye you gete me some mete, for I am yll a hungred. *a* **1550** *Christis Kirke Gr.* xv, Sum fled and ill mischievit. *Mod.* (*Yorkshire dial.*) He was ill clemmed.

† **4.** Banefully, hurtfully, injuriously. *Obs.*

1483 *Cath. Angl.* 195/1 Ille, *male, perniciose.* **1600** E. Blount tr. *Conestaggio* 34 They chose rather to counsell him ill and please him, then to advise him well and contradict him. **1642** Milton *Apol. Smect.* Introd., Wks. (1847) 80/2 As with him whose outward garment hath been injured and ill bedighted.

5. Unfavourably, unpropitiously; unfortunately, unhappily.

c **1325** *Metr. Hom.* 149 Ic haf sped ful ille. *c* **1460** *Towneley Myst.* xxvii. 6 Yll was thou ded, so wo is me that I it ken. **1593** Shaks. *3 Hen. VI*, II. v. 55 Ill blowes the winde that profits no body. **1600** E. Blount tr. *Conestaggio* 35 If it succeeded ill, the losse would be generall. **1657** R. Ligon *Barbadoes* (1673) 25 A Town ill scituate; for if they had considered health.. they would never have set it there. **1741** Richardson *Pamela* (1824) I. xxii. 273 Let them be young or old, well-married or ill-married. **1770** Goldsm. *Des. Vill.* 51 Ill fares the land.. Where wealth accumulates, and men decay. **1864** Doran *Their Majesties Serv.* I. 21 But for the sympathy of the Earl of Leicester, it would have gone ill with these players.

6. Of manner or quality of performance: **a.** Not well; defectively, imperfectly, poorly; hardly, scarcely. Sometimes (with mixture of sense 3), With trouble, difficulty, or inconvenience.

a **1300** *Cursor M.* 23851 (Gött.) Ill worth [*Fairf.* worþi] it es to tell þe feild, þat noght again þe sede will ȝeild. *a* **1400** *Isumbras* 558 Poure mene þat myghte ille goo. *c* **1460** *Towneley Myst.* xiii. 1 Lord, what these weders ar cold! and I am yll happyd. **1586** A. Day *Eng. Secretary* I. (1625) 31 Things.. ill beseeming or unworthy their reputation. **1654** Z. Coke *Logick* (1657) 35 A man cutteth ill if he have a blunt knife. **1667** Milton *P.L.* XI. 163 Ill worthie I such title should belong To me transgressour. **1725** Pope *Odyss.* VI. 79 Blushes ill-restrained betray Her thoughts. **1832** Ht. Martineau *Life in Wilds* iii. 34 We can ill spare him. **1839** Murchison *Silur. Syst.* I. xxiv. 301 The upper Ludlow rock is ill developed. **1849** Macaulay *Hist. Eng.* iv. I. 484 With an intemperance which.. ill becomes the judicial character.

b. Badly, faultily, improperly; unskilfully.

1540 Hyrde tr. *Vives' Instr. Chr. Wom.* (1592) I ij, If thou answere not quickly, thou shalt be called proude, or ill brought up. **1579** Spenser *Sheph. Cal.* June 72, I play to please myselfe, all be it ill. **1632** J. Hayward tr. *Biondi's Eromena* 138 Not many words, and those few ill exprest. **1670** Sir S. Crow in *12th Rep. Hist. MSS. Comm.* App. v. 15 The silke.. beeing ill woven will shrink. **1697** Dampier *Voy.* I. 139 The Houses are but low and ill built. **1728** Pope *Dunc.* I. 66 Figures ill pair'd, and Similes unlike. **1774** Chesterf. *Lett.* (1792) I. lett. 42 (tr.) 134 Shop-keepers, common people, footmen and maid-servants, all speak ill. **1873** M. Arnold *Lit. & Dogma* (1876) 85 The admitted duties themselves come to be ill-discharged. **1895** *Westm. Gaz.* 2 Apr. 2/2 The entertainer.. recited, by no means ill, the celebrated 'All the world's a stage' speech.

7. Phrases. **a.** ***ill at ease***: see EASE *sb.* 7 b; hence ***ill-at-easeness*** (nonce-wd.), the state of being ill at ease. **b.** ***ill-to-do***: in poor circumstances, poor needy (the opposite of *well-to-do*). ***ill-off***: in an unprosperous condition, badly off (the opposite of *well-off*): see OFF.

a. 1565 Sir T. Gresham in Burgon *Life* (1839) II. 443, I am right sorry that my Lady.. is yll at ease. **1734** Pope *Ess. Man* IV. 119 The virtuous son is ill at ease When his lewd father gave the dire disease. **1870** Morris *Earthly Par.* I. I. 349 Ill was the King at ease. **1882** Spurgeon *Treas. Dav.* Ps. cxx. 9 As ill-at-ease among lying neighbours as if he had lived among savages. **1890** Miss Broughton *Alas!* I. xxiii, Elizabeth's evident ill-at-easeness.

b. 1853 Lynch *Self-Improv.* v. 115 A most honourable ill-to-do class.. fighting a good fight with poverty. **1887** Pater *Imag. Portraits* 2 He is not ill-to-do, and has lately built himself a new stone house. **1889** *Charity Organis. Rev.* May 221 There is room for doubt whether the well-to-do man's conviction of the ill-to-do man's discomfort really leads to useful action.

8. In *Comb.*: see ILL- III. below.

ill (ɪl), *v.* *Obs.* exc. *dial.* [f. ILL *a.*]

† **1.** *trans.* To contrive maliciously. *Obs.*

a **1340** Hampole *Psalter* lxxxii. 3 On þi folke þai illid counsaile [L. *malignaverunt consilium*].

† **2.** To cause ill or evil to; to harm, hurt, injure, wrong. *Obs.*

c **1220** [see ILLING]. **1503** Hawes *Examp. Virt.* v. xxvi, That wyll payre and yll thy name. **1583** T. Watson *Centurie of Loue* c. (Arb.) 137 To pacyfie my minde, By illing him, through whome I liu'd a slaue. **1586** Warner *Alb. Eng.* III. xviii. 52 My wretched Cause of your repaire, by wicked Romaines ild. **1614** Sylvester *Panaretus* 454 Appeerd an Old-man (as one deeplie illd).

3. To speak ill of, abuse, malign, disparage.

c **1530** H. Rhodes *Bk. Nurture* in *Babees Bk.* 100 To ill thy foe, doth get to thee hatred and double blame. **1674–91** Ray *N.C. Words* 39 *To ill*, to reproach, to speak ill of another. **1683** Meriton *Yorksh. Dialogue* 15 You Ill my Farm, for you have said to some, You'r quite undone and beggar'd sine you come. **1878** *Cumberld. Gloss.*, Do n't ill a body if you can't say weel o' yan.

ill (in 3 **illen**), scribal var. of HILL *v.*[1] to cover.

a **1300** *Body & Soul* 69 (MS. Digby 86, lf. 196 b), Þe þridde dai flod shal flouen þat al þis world shal illen [*MS. Harl.* 2253 lf. 57 a, hylen: *rimes* swyle, myle, while].

ill-, in combination.

A. General uses. **I.** From ILL *adj.*

1. a. In attributive relation: see ILL *a.* 9; also ILL BLOOD, ILL BREEDING, ILLFARE, ILL HUMOUR, ILL LUCK, ILL NATURE, ILL-USAGE, ILL WILL.

b. Parasynthetic compounds: see 8.

II. From ILL *sb.*

2. Objective and obj. genitive, as † ***ill-abearing*** (enduring evil), † ***-aboding*** (= ILL-BODING), ***-breeding***, ***-designing***, ***-dispersing***, ***-divining***, ***-doing***, ***-halsening***, ***-intending***, ***-persuading***,

-presaging, -uttering, adjs.; ***ill-deemer, -doer, -doing, -dreader, -foreboder, -thinker***, sbs.; ILL-WILLER, -WILLING, -WISH, -WISHER.

1615 Chapman *Odyss.* XIII. 455 Bound to this *ill-abearing destiny. **1626** Jackson *Creed* VIII. xxvi. §4 This unseasonable *ill-aboding desire..‘ Give us a king to judge us’. *a* **1711** Ken *Psyche* Poet. Wks. 1721 IV. 269 Ill-aboding Birds who hate the Day. **1710–11** Swift *Examiner* (J.), The craft of *ill designing men. **1791** Burke *App. Whigs* Wks. VI. 83 To encourage ill-designing men. **1594** Shaks. *Rich. III*, IV. i. 53 O *ill dispersing Winde of Miserie. **1592** —— *Rom. & Jul.* III. v. 54, I haue an *ill Diuining soule. **1738** Swift *Pol. Conversat.* 89 *Ill Doers are ill Deemers. **1815** Scott *Guy M.* liii, It is the ill-doers are ill-dreaders. **1868** Helps *Realmah* i. (1876) 2 The ill-doings of all the ill-doers who [etc.]. **1611** Shaks. *Wint. T.* I. ii. 70 We knew not The Doctrine of *ill-doing. **1715** Leoni *Palladio's Archit.* (1742) II. 95 Temples erected to ill-doing Gods. **1782** Burns *Poem*, Oh why the deuce should I repine, And be an *ill foreboder? **1602** Carew *Cornwall* 1 b, This *ill-halsening hornie name hath..opened a gap to the scoffes of many. **1703** Congreve *Tears Amaryllis* 89 Skreams of *ill-presaging Birds. **1787** Burns *Death Sir J. Blair* 1 The lamp of day, with ill-presaging glare, Dim, cloudy, sunk beneath the western wave. *c* **1515** *Cocke Lorell's B.* 11 Surmowsers, *yll thynkers, and make brasers. **1606** Shaks. *Ant. & Cl.* II. v. 35 The Gold I giue thee, will I melt and powr Downe thy *ill vttering throate.

3. Instrumental and dative, as ***ill-deceived*** (deceived by evil), ***ill-inclining*** (inclining to evil).

1627–77 Feltham *Resolves* I. xxvi. 46 The ill-inclining soul. **1647** H. More *Poems, Insomn. Philos.* xxiii, Their ill-deceived soul.

III. From ILL *adv.*

In 6 and 7 the hyphen is only syntactic, being required when the qualified adj. is used attrib., but unnecessary when it is predicative: cf. ILL *adv.* Introd. note.

Both elements have usually a main stress, but one or other may predominate according to the construction; in particular, combinations like *ill-built, ill-fated, ill-fitting*, standing before a sb., have usually the stronger stress on *ill*. Cf. *an 'ill-built house, the chimney is 'ill 'built; an 'ill-fated prince, an 'ill-fitting dress, a child by no means ill-'favoured.*

4. With verbs, as ***ill-husband, ill-judge, ill-requite***; ILL-TREAT, ILL-USE. **ill-favour** *v. trans.*, to treat badly, to be inimical to or hostile towards. (Two stresses.)

1639 T. Brugis tr. *Camus' Mor. Relat.* 271 Whether..he illhusbanded the mind of Parmene. **1657–8** *Burton's Diary* II. 362, I hope they will never ill-requite it. **1673** *Lady's Call.* 54 To what can we more reasonably impute [it]..then to our ill-husbanding the means of grace? **1815** *Sporting Mag.* XLVI. 21 Shelton again ill-judged his distance. **1899** F. J. Crowest *Beethoven* 128 His environment generally throughout his early life ill-favoured the contemplative mood. **1908** *Westm. Gaz.* 21 Aug. 2/1 Fortune ill-favoured them in many skirmishes.

5. With adjectives derived from verbs, as †***ill-agreeable, ill-effaceable, ill-manageable, ill-observant***.

1614 Raleigh *Hist. World* III. (1634) 8 Ill-agreeable to the holy Scriptures. **1813** C. Lofft in E. H. Barker *Parriana* (1829) II. 79 *note*, A very ill-manageable portion of time. **1842** Sir A. de Vere *Song of Faith* 83 Ill-observant eyes. **1860** Pusey *Min. Proph.* 523 The ill-effaceable spot of ungodliness.

6. With pres. pples., or adjectives of ppl. form, forming adjs., as ***ill-according, -agreeing, -beseeming, -calculating, -consisting, -contenting, -fitting, -going, -greeting, -guiding, -neighbouring, -perfuming, -resounding, -smelling, -sounding, -succeeding, -suiting, -yoking***, etc.; ILL-FARING, -JUDGING, -LOOKING. (Stress: see under III. above.)

1611 Bible *Wisd.* xviii. 10 There sounded an *ill-according crie of the enemies. **1623** in Rushw. *Hist. Coll.* (1659) I. 94 The disposition of that People being..so malignant and *ill-agreeing with us. **1886** W. J. Tucker *E. Europe* 198 With an *ill-befitting air of haughtiness. **1592** Shaks. *Rom. & Jul.* I. v. 76 Put off these frownes, An *ill beseeming semblance for a Feast. **1893** A. S. Eccles *Sciatica* 39 *Ill-fitting joints in the woodwork. **1665** Boyle *Occas. Refl.* II. viii. (1848) 123 Telling the Strokes of an *ill-going Clock. **1634** Milton *Comus* 406 Lest some *ill-greeting touch attempt the person Of our unowned sister. **1592** Shaks. *Ven. & Ad.* 919 His *ill-resounding noise. **1897** Allbutt *Syst. Med.* III. 889 Ill-looking and often *ill-smelling mucus. **1693** Dryden *Juvenal* Introd. (1697) 88 He was forc'd to crowd his Verse with *ill-sounding Monosyllables. **1590** Spenser *F.Q.* I. ii. 2 Their bootelesse paines, and *ill succeeding night. **1643** Milton *Divorce* I. xiii, The forcible continuing of an improper and *ill-yoking couple.

7. With past pples., or adjectives of the same form, forming adjs.: **a.** in senses 1–4 of the adv., as ***ill-achieved, -acquired, -begotten, -behaved, -celebrated, -composed, -erected, -gendered, -invented, -meant, -occupied, -requited, -spent, -won***; ILL-AFFECTED, -DISPOSED, -GOT, -GOTTEN; **b.** in sense 5, as ***ill-adventured, -annexed, -bested, -constructed, -foreseen, -joined, -knotted, -met, -pleased, -wedded***; **c.** in sense 6, as ***ill-accoutred, -acted, -adapted, -adjusted, -armed, -arranged, -assorted, -balanced, -brought-up, -built, -cemented, -chosen, -clad, -coined, -coloured, -concealed, -conceived, -concerted, -conducted, -considered, -contrived, -cured, -defined, -digested, -directed, -dissembled, -done, -drawn, -dressed, -equipped, -fed, -fitted, -founded, -furnished, -governed, -grounded, -guided, -informed, -joined, -lighted, -lit, -made, -managed, -matched, -mated, -nurtured, -paid, -performed, -qualified, -regulated, -roasted, -ruled, -spun*** (*c* 1460), ***-strung, -supported, -taught, -tuned, -understood, -ventilated, -worded, -written, -wrought, -yoked***, etc.; ILL-ADVISED, -BRED, -SORTED, q.v. (Stress: see under III. above.)

These quasi-combinations can be formed with almost any pa. pple., or adj. in *-ed*, and their number (esp. in group c.) is practically unlimited. Only a few are here illustrated.

1777 Robertson *Hist. Amer.* (1778) II. VI. 169 A very slender and *ill-accoutred train of followers. **1848** Mill *Pol. Econ.* II. v. §1. 293 The same reckless prodigality with which they squandered any other part of their *ill-acquired possessions. **1640** Habington *Castara* III. (Arb.) 127 Like some dull *ill-acted part. **1878** W. James *Coll. Ess. & Rev.* (1920) 53 If his powers correspond to the wants of this social environment, he may survive, even though he be *ill-adapted to the natural or ‘outer’ environment. *Ibid.*, Individuals who, by their special powers, satisfy these desires are protected by their fellows and enabled to survive, though their mental constitution should in other respects be lamentably *ill-‘adjusted’ to the outward world. **1903** *Daily Chron.* 25 June 4/1 In this ill-adjusted world men have to take what they can get. *a* **1649** Drumm. of Hawth. *Poems* Wks. (1711) 42 The ship-wreck of my *ill-adventured youth. **1593** Shaks. *Lucr.* 874 *Ill-annexed Opportunity. **1807** J. Barlow *Columb.* vi. 225 Ridgefield and Compo saw his valorous might, With *ill armed swains put veteran troops to flight. **1942** W. S. Churchill *End of Beginning* (1943) 32 China, ill-armed or half-armed, has..withstood the main fury of Japan. **1814** *Ill-assorted [see ASSORTED *ppl. a.*]. **1849** Macaulay *Hist. Eng.* iv. I. 430 The misery of an ill assorted marriage. **1938** W. S. Churchill *Into Battle* (1941) 29 Three..Ministers of the Crown have been..prejudiced by being given..ill-assorted tasks. **1864** G. M. Hopkins *Poems* (1948) 119 The clouds come like *ill-balanced crags. **1956** K. Clark *Nude* vii. 284 Could fill an ill-balanced nature with destructive envy. **1611** Cotgr., *Mal-avenant*,..*ill behaued. *a* **1592** H. Smith *Wks.* (1867) II. 477 O *ill-bestid. Poor in store, in wealth a wretch. **1579–80** North *Plutarch* (1676) 800 This *ill-brought-up Tyrant. **1704** *Addr. Tiverton* 16 Oct. in *Lond. Gaz.* No. 4066/8 To enable Your Majesty to break the *ill-celebrated Ballance of Power. **1580** Sidney *Arcadia* (1622) 166 The ungratefull treason of her *ill-chosen husband. **1784** Cowper *Task* IV. 379 *Ill-clad and fed but sparely. **1779–81** Johnson *L.P.*, *Shenstone* Wks. IV. 219 His words *ill-coined, or ill-chosen. **1605** Shaks. *Macb.* IV. iii. 77 In my most *ill-compos'd Affection. **1895** B. M. Croker *Village Tales* 38 As time wore on, there actually arose an *ill-concealed jealousy of their old corps. **1960** *Farmer & Stockbreeder* 8 Mar. 63/3 The report of the Cook Committee was awaited with ‘ill-concealed impatience’. **1839** Mill in *Westm. Rev.* Apr. 497 There is a notion abroad that they are the *ill-conditioned and ill-conducted portion. **1835** —— in *London Rev.* II. III. 116 In the English aristocracy there has surely been..crude and *ill-considered legislation enough. **1956** E. E. Evans-Pritchard *Nuer Relig.* iii. 96 It was because this was not appreciated by British administrators that the role..of the prophets was very largely misunderstood and their treatment of them ill-considered. **1847** Mill *Let.* 19 June in *Works* (1963) XIII. 721 The long paper..is full of unfinished & *ill constructed..sentences. **1944** R. Chandler *Let.* 26 Jan. in *R. Chandler Speaking* (1966) 42 A column and a half of respectful attention will be given to any fourth-rate, ill-constructed, mock-serious account of the life of a bunch of cotton pickers in the deep south. **1655** Fuller *Ch. Hist.* IX. vi. §67 Homes..small and *ill-contrived. **1866** Tate *Brit. Mollusks* iv. 110 Its conical shell with a shallow *ill-defined umbilicus. *a* **1849** Poe *Works* (1865) I. 418 Some feeble and *ill-directed efforts resulted in complete failure on their part, and, of course, in total triumph on mine. **1947** *Mind* LVI. 132 They have thus been led to offer facile, but ill-directed, rebutments of the refutation. **1879** Geo. Eliot *Theo. Such* xvi. 291 *Ill-done work. **1956** *Nature* 10 Mar. 446/2 At present we are *ill-equipped to do so. **1962** W. Nowottny *Lang. Poets Use* i. 5 The exhausted and ill-equipped army. **1649** G. Daniel *Trinarch.* To Rdr. 100 Little spoone-Meats cull From Stowe's *ill-fardled dry fatt. **1671** Milton *Samson* 1504 Thy hopes are not *ill founded. **1685** tr. *Arnauld & Nicole's Logic* I. iii. 68 Such a Presumption and Rashness is a sign of an *ill-govern'd and ill-qualified mind. **1860** Ruskin *Unto this Last* in *Cornh. Mag.* Sept. 281 In the inactive or ill-governed nation, the gradations of decay and the victories of treason work out also their own rugged system of subjection and success. **1642** Fuller *Holy & Prof. St.* III. xx. 207 Overhot *illgrounded Zeal. **1824** *Ill informed [see INFORMED *ppl. a.* 2 b]. **1961** New Eng. Bible *Rom.* x. 2 To their zeal for God I can testify, but it is an ill-informed zeal. **1679** Burnet *Hist. Ref.* (1820) I. II. 505 Sanders's charge on her, was an *ill-invented calumny. **1905** W. Holman Hunt *Pre-Raphaelitism* I. iii. 46 With small and *ill-lit studios, and without means to pay models, he [*sc.* Haydon] could never do justice to his intellectual conceptions. **1719** De Foe *Crusoe* II. iv, Such refractory, *ill-matched fellows. **1667** Milton *P.L.* XI. 684 The product Of those *ill-mated Marriages. **1538** Starkey *England* II. i. 155 For the takyng away of thes *yl-occupyd personys. **1700** Dryden tr. *1st bk. Homer's Ilias* 255 My *ill-paid pains to mourn. **1890** W. James *Princ. Psychol.* I. x. 369 The only service that transcendental egoism has done to psychology has been by protests against Hume's ‘bundle’-theory of mind. But this service has been *ill-performed. **1946** A. L. Bacharach *Brit. Mus.* i. 12 The Churches, who never seemed to realise the paralysing effect their badly written, ill-performed music was having on their congregations. **1861** Trollope *Orley F.* (1862) I. xxi. 161 An angry *ill-pleased wife is no pleasant companion for a gentleman on a long evening. **1685** *Ill-qualified [see *ill-governed*]. **1790** Burke *Fr. Rev.* Wks. V. 233 The best of the unqualified or ill-qualified monarchies. **1803** Chalmers *Let.* in *Life* (1851) I. 483 The *ill-regulated mind of Rousseau was the victim of a thousand infirmities. **1600** Shaks. *A.Y.L.* III. ii. 38 Like an *ill roasted Egge, all on one side. *a* **1553** Udall *Royster D.* III. ii. (Arb.) 39 A sight Of him that made vs all so *yll shent. *c* **1460** *Towneley Myst.* ii. 435 *Ill spon weft ay comes foule out. **1640** Habington *Castara* III. (Arb.) 117 How can I turne to jollitie My *ill-strung Harpe. **1733** A. Baxter *Inquiry Human Soul* II. xxvi. 81 The Atheist's *ill-supported, tottering world. **1611** Shaks. *Wint. T.* I. ii. 460 His *ill-ta'ne suspition. **1644** Milton *Educ.* Wks. (1847) 100/1 All their childish and *illtaught qualities. **1595** Shaks. *John* II. i. 197 These *ill-tuned repetitions. **1580** Sidney *Arcadia* (1622) 407 That *ill-vnderstood intercession. **1596** Shaks. *1 Hen. IV*, v. iv. 88 *Ill-weau'd Ambition, how much art thou shrunke? **1643** Milton *Divorce* II. ix, The distresses and extremities of an *ill-wedded man. **1500–20** Dunbar *Poems* xvii. 19 *Ill-won geir riches not the kin. **1826** J. W. Croker in *C. Papers* (1884) I. xi. 325 An *ill-written, ill-spelled, ill-folded, ill-sealed letter. **1599** Marston *Sco. Villanie* I. i, Like Aphrogenias *ill-yoked marriage.

IV. 8. Parasynthetic combs., in which *ill-* is sometimes of adverbial, sometimes of adjectival origin. (Thus *ill-intentioned* is opposed to *well-intentioned*, but *ill-humoured* to *good-humoured*.) ***ill-complexioned, -countenanced, -eyed, -featured, -figured, -flavoured, -headed, -mouthed*** (*c* 1375), ***-neighboured, -noised, -nosed, -odoured, -principled, -savoured, -savoury, -scented, -spirited, -tasted, -visaged***, adjs. See also ILL-CONDITIONED, -DEEDY, -FAVOURED, -HUMOURED, -LOOKED, -MANNERED, -NATURED, -STARRED, -TEMPERED, -TONGUED, -WILLED, -WILLY. (Stress: see under III. above.)

a **1726** Collier (J.), Envy..meagre and *ill complexioned. **1638** F. Junius *Paint. Ancients* 41 Hard-favoured, *ill-countenanced damsels. **1670** *Moral State Eng.* 90 Lame, thin-faced, *il-eyed. **1513** More *Rich. III* (1883) 5 *Ill fetured of limmes. **1860** Froude *Hist. Eng.* xxviii. V. 367 She was short and *ill-figured. **1748** *Anson's Voy.* II. iv. 164 The..tobacco..was not *ill flavoured. **1596** Spenser *F.Q.* IV. i. 3 Whilest every man, Surcharg'd with wine, were heedlesse and *ill-hedded. **1599** Shaks. *Much Ado* III. i. 64 A launce ill headed. *c* **1375** *Sc. Leg. Saints, Bertholomeus* 235 With gret noyse and *ilmowtht late. **1580** Sidney *Arcadia* (1622) 203 A Gitterne, il-played on, accompanied with a hoarse voice..made them looke the way of the *ill-noysed song. **1646** J. Gregory *Notes & Obs.* (1650) 169 The bald *ill-nos'd Galilæan. **1741** Richardson *Pamela* I. 160 She is so *ill-principled a woman. **1583** Stubbes *Anat. Abus.* II. (1882) 65 A slouenly, *ill sauoured, and vncleane fellowe. **1598** Sylvester *Du Bartas* II. i. I. *Eden* 102 Sweet as Roses smelt th' *ill-savory Rew. **1596** Shaks. *1 Hen. IV*, v. v. 2 *Ill-spirited Worcester, did we not send Grace, Pardon, and tearmes of Loue to all of you? **1651–3** Jer. Taylor *Serm. for Year* (1678) 298 Bitter and *ill-tasted drugs. **1865** G. M. Hopkins *Poems* (1948) 142 And John shall lie, where winds are dead, And hate the *ill-visaged cursing tars. **1894** Ill visaged [see VISAGED *a.*].

B. Special Combs.: **'ill-a'ccustomed** *a.*, (*a*) little accustomed or habituated to something; (*b*) having little custom, little frequented by customers; **ill assurance**, want of assurance; †**ill-boned** *a.*, having diseased or injured bones; **ill-born** *a.*, of evil birth or origin; **ill-content, ill-contented** *adjs.*, discontented, †displeased; **ill-convenient** *a.*, inconvenient, ill-suiting (now *vulgar*); so **ill-convenience**, †**ill-conveniency**; **ill-customed** *a.*, (*a*) having little custom; (*b*) characterized by a bad custom or fashion; **ill-deserving** *a.*, deserving of ill; so **ill-deserver**; **ill-faced** *a.*, having an unpleasing face or aspect, ugly; **ill-famed** *a.*, of bad fame or repute; †**ill-fancied** *a.*, inelegant in design; **ill-fashioned** *a.*, of an ill fashion, or badly fashioned; †**ill-favourably** *adv.*, (*a*) = ILL-FAVOUREDLY; (*b*) with disfavour, unfavourably; **ill-formed** *a.*, badly formed, or having a bad form; so **ill-formedness**; **ill-friended** *a.*, ill provided with friends; †**ill-habited** *a.*, having an ill habit of body, unhealthy, disordered; **ill-hearted** *a.*, having an evil heart, ill-disposed, malicious; †**ill-language** *v. trans.*, to use ill language about, speak ill of; †**ill-lettered** *a.*, ill taught, illiterate; †**ill-liking** *a.* [see LIKING *a.*], in bad condition; **ill-lived** (-laɪvd) *a.*, leading a bad or immoral life; **ill-meaning** *a.*, meaning evil, malicious in intent; †**ill-minded** *a.*, having an evil mind or disposition, unfriendly, hostile, malicious; hence †**ill-mindedness**; †**ill-monied** *a.*, ill supplied with money, poor; †**ill-part** *a.*, playing an evil part; **ill-scraped** *a. Sc.*, not scraped clean, foul; **ill-seeming** *a.*, of evil appearance or aspect; **ill-shaped, -shapen** *adjs.*, badly shaped, or of a bad shape; ill-contrived, awkward; †**ill-speak** *v. trans.*, to speak evil of, slander, traduce; †**ill-stated** *a.*, in an evil state or condition; †**ill-thewed** *a.*, ill-mannered; **ill-thriven** *a.*, that has thriven badly; badly grown, sickly, stunted; peevish, ill-disposed; †**ill-wresting** *a.*, wresting any one's words or actions to his disadvantage.

1669 Woodhead *St. Teresa* I. 314 Some Souls so infirm and *ill-accustomed..though of a noble Nature. **1828** Miss Mitford *Village Ser.* III. (1863) 65 But one ill-accustomed shop. **1905** *Macm. Mag.* Dec. 151 As they grew out of the restive sensitiveness of youthful *ill-assurance,..they turned with gratitude towards their parent. *c* **1909** D. H. Lawrence *Collier's Friday Night* (1934) ii. 51 Ernest (flushing up at the sound of her ill-assurance). **1645**

RUTHERFORD *Tryal & Tri. Faith* xvii. (1845) 184 There is a Saviour's hand..to wheel in an *ill-boned soul. **1640–4** in Rushw. *Hist. Coll.* III. (1692) I. 215 To have strangled their *ill-born Resolutions in the Cradle. **1701** DE FOE *True-born Eng.* I. 132 From this amphibious ill-born mob began That vain, ill-natured thing, an Englishman. *c* **1489** CAXTON *Sonnes of Aymon* xxiii. 496 Whan the frenshe men sawe the grete cruelnes of Charlemagn..they were *yll contente. **1864** TENNYSON *En. Ard.* 558 So the three..Dwelt with eternal summer, ill-content. **1582** N. LICHEFIELD tr. *Castanheda's Conq. E. Ind.* lxxix. 163 With this spoyle the king..remained so *ill contented. **1643** MILTON *Divorce* I. ii, When the household estate..is so illcontented. **1694** SALMON *Bates' Disp.* (1713) 658/1 Leaving out the Opium it may be given..twice a day, without any *ill Conveniency. **1719** *Mem. Lewis XIV*, v. 53 Liable to a thousand Illconveniencies. **1740** GARRICK *Lying Valet* II, It will be *ill-convenient to pay me to-morrow. **1864** *Cornh. Mag.* IX. 207 They're always a-coming at illconvenient times. **1611** RICH *Honest. Age* (1614) 26 But an *ill customed shoppe, that taketh not fiue shillings a day. **1870** RUSKIN *Lect. Art* ii. 39 Forbid them to make what is ill-customed, and unrestrained..and without order. **1675** tr. *Camden's Hist. Eliz.* III. (1688) 364, I have bestowed Benefits upon *Ill-deservers. **1625** K. LONG tr. *Barclay's Argenis* I. xii. 31 The *ill-deserving King. **1734** WATTS *Reliq. Juv.* (1789) 154 So profane and ill-deserving a rout of men. **1590** SHAKS. *Com. Err.* IV. ii. 20 He is deformed..*Ill-fac'd, worse bodied, shapelesse. **1645** QUARLES *Sol. Recant.* II. 14 Let such as always are at wars With their own fortunes, curse their ill-fac'd stars. **1483** *Cath. Angl.* 195/1 *Ille famed, *infamatus.* **1897** F. WHYTE *Engl. Stage* 103 A street where ill-fed and ill-famed Frenchmen were..beginning to congregate. **1716** LADY M. W. MONTAGU *Let. to Lady X——* 1 Oct., I never ..saw so many fine clothes *ill-fancied. **1600** E. BLOUNT tr. *Conestaggio* 211 Fortified..with *ill fashioned trenches. **1821** SCOTT *Kenilw.* xxii, His ill-fashioned gaberdine. **1576** NEWTON *Lemnie's Complex.* (1633) 15 They..make the body to breake out *ilfavourably..with scabs. **1643** *True Informer* 27 It hath made the Venetian..to looke but ilfavourably of us. *a* **1672** A. BRADSTREET *Several Poems* (1678) 236 Thou *ill-form'd offspring of my feeble brain. **1690** LOCKE *Hum. Und.* IV. iv. §16 They..make bold..to destroy ill-formed and mis-shaped Productions. **1972** *Language* XLVIII. i. 82 These have to do with (1) dialect variations and (2) degree of *ill-formedness. **1972** A. MAKKAI *Idiom Struct. Eng.* 84 Let us now examine a few cases of lexemic illformedness. **1637** RUTHERFORD *Lett.* (1862) I. 246 She is not that *ill-friended. **1642** ROGERS *Naaman* 845 It becomes as meat to an *ill habited stomach. *a* **1617** HIERON *Wks.* (1619–20) II. 489 Many an hollow and *ill hearted counterfait. **1786** BURNS *Twa Dogs* 180 Fient haet o' them 's ill-hearted fellows. **1678** CUDWORTH *Intell. Syst.* I. iv. §36. 551 Neither was this Trinity of Divine Subsistences only thus *ill-languag'd by the Pagans generally. **1604** F. HERING *Modest Defence* 32 In illiberal and *illettered Natures. **1648** SANDERSON *Serm.* II. 241 They [trees] become *ill-liking and unfruitful. **1633** BP. HALL *Occas. Medit.* §56 A scandalous and *ill-lived Teacher. **1633** G. HERBERT *Temple, Glance* ii, The malicious and *ill-meaning harm. **1681** *Lond. Gaz.* No. 1619/4 Designing and ill-meaning Men. **1611** COTGR., *Malenthalenté*, maliciously affected, *ill-minded. **1726** AMHERST *Terræ Fil.* II. 8 Ill-minded priests. **1681** CROWNE *Hen. VI*, II. 14, I see..Too much *ill-mindedness in all this fury. **1608** TOURNEUR *Rev. Trag.* IV. ii. Wks. 1878 II. 110, I thinke thou art *ill-monied. **1601** MUNDAY & CHETTLE *Death Robt. Earl Huntington* D ij b, Let king Iohn, that *ill part personage..Of chaste Matilda let him make an end. **1858** M. PORTEOUS *Souter Johnny* 32 Mare than ae *ill scrapit tongue Misca'd ye sair. **1884** PAE *Eustace* 67 To put up with your ill-scraped tongue. **1596** SHAKS. *Tam. Shr.* V. ii. 143 Like a fountaine troubled, Muddie, *ill seeming. **1592** —— *Rom. & Jul.* V. i. 44 Skins Of *ill shap'd fishes. **1589** PUTTENHAM *Eng. Poesie* III. xxii. (Arb.) 263 Such manner of vncouth speech did the Tanner of Tamworth vse..I hope I shall be hanged to morrow; for I feare me I shall be hanged, whereat the king laughed..to heare his *ill shapen terme. **1582** N. T. (Rhem.) *Acts* xix. 9 *Il-speaking the way of the Lord before the multitude. **1605** SYLVESTER *Du Bartas* II. iii. IV. *Captaines* 1010 An *ill-stated body. **1647** H. MORE *Song of Soul* II. i. I. xx, Certes they be *ill thew'd and baser born. **1806** FORSYTH *Beauties Scotl.* IV. 58 Short *ill-thriven furze. **1843** LEVER *J. Hinton* xviii. (1878) 130 A little cross-grained, ill-thriven old fellow. *c* **1600** SHAKS. *Sonn.* cxl, Now this *ill wresting world is growne so bad, Madde slanderers by madde eares beleeued be.

†**i'llabile**, *a.* *Obs. rare.* [f. IL-^{2} + LABILE.] Not liable to slip, fall, or err; infallible. Hence †**illa'bility**, quality of being 'illabile'.

1740 CHEYNE *Regimen* iv. 140 It would seem..that all Creatures..must..be labile, fallible, and peccable, and that even infinite wisdom and power could not make a creature.. illabile, infallible, and impeccable. *Ibid.*, That secondary nature of eternal infallibility, illability, and impeccability. *Ibid.* 276.

†**i'llaborate**, *a.* *Obs. rare.* [ad. late L. *illabōrāt-us*: see IL-^{2} and cf. ELABORATE.] Unlaboured; not highly finished- unfinished.

1631 BRATHWAIT *Whimzies, Traveller* 95 So indigested are his collections, and so illaborate his style as the Stationer shunnes them. **1639** T. DE GREY *Compl. Horsem.* To Rdr., In this illaborat work of mine. **1656** BLOUNT *Glossogr.*, *Illaborate*, done or made without labor, plain, unlaboured. **1751** EARL ORRERY *Remarks Swift* (1752) 12 The style of it must be illaborate, and void of all freedom and vivacity.

Hence †**i'llaborateness**, 'the Quality of being effected without Labor and Pains' (Bailey 1727).

†**illa'borious**, *a.* *Obs.* *rare*$^{-1}$. [f. IL-^{2} + LABORIOUS.] Not laborious; lazy.

a **1631** DONNE *Serm.* lxxii. 728 This in-industrious and Illaborious man that takes no paines.

ill-accustomed: see ILL- B.

†**i'llacerable**, *a.* *Obs.* *rare*$^{-0}$. [ad. late L. *illacerābilis*: see IL-^{2} and LACERABLE. Cf. F. *illacérable.*] Not liable to be torn or rent. Hence †**i'llacerableness**.

1623 in COCKERAM. **1656** in BLOUNT *Glossogr.* **1727** BAILEY vol. II, *Illacerableness.*

†**i'llachrymable**, *a.* *Obs.* *rare*$^{-0}$. [ad. L. *illacrimābilis* unwept; unmoved by tears, pitiless, f. *il-* (IL-^{2}) + *lacrimābilis*: see LACHRYMOSE.] (See quots.) Hence †**i'llachrymableness**.

1623 COCKERAM, *Illachrymable*, pittilesse, vnmercifull. **1658** PHILLIPS, *Illachrymable*, pittilesse, also unpittied [*ed.* 1678 uncapable of weeping]. **1731** BAILEY (Vol. II), *Illacrymableness*, uncapableness of weeping. **1755** JOHNSON, *Illachrymable*, incapable of weeping.

illachry'mation. *rare.* [noun of action f. L. *illacrimāre* to weep over.] (See quots.)

1656 BLOUNT *Glossogr.*, *Illachrymation*, a weeping or bewailing. **1855** MAYNE *Expos. Lex.*, *Illacrymatio*, term for excessive weeping: illacrymation.

ill-advised ('ɪləd'vaɪzd), *a.* [ILL- 7 c.] Done without wise consideration or deliberation, injudicious, imprudent; sometimes, ill-counselled, following, or resulting from, bad advice. (Of persons, their actions, etc.)

c **1592** MARLOWE *Massacre Paris* I. iii, Your grace was ill-advis'd to take them. *a* **1600** HOOKER *Eccl. Pol.* VI. iv. §4 They which with ill-advised modesty seek to hide their sin like Adam. **1677** *Govt. Venice* 321 Vittor Amedeus was very ill-advised to deliver Pignerol to the French. **1728** YOUNG *Love Fame* iii. 52 To make that hopeless, ill-advis'd attack. **1818** SCOTT *Rob Roy* vi, The unfortunate and ill-advised James II. **1880** MᶜCARTHY *Own Times* III. xlv. 355 The ill-advised undertaking had to be given up.

Hence **ill-ad'visedly** (-ɪdlɪ) *adv.*, in an ill-advised manner, injudiciously, imprudently.

1879 FROUDE *Cæsar* xxi. 353 So ill-advisedly, so against all my counsels, the whole business has been conducted. **1884** *Pall Mall G.* 29 Dec. 2/1 The Board, ill advisedly..refused to forward this appeal.

†**i'llæs(e**, *ppl. a.* *Obs. rare.* [ad. L. *illæs-us* unhurt, f. *il-* (IL-^{2}) + *læsus* pa. pple. of *lædĕre* to injure. Cf. ILLESED.] Unhurt, uninjured.

1597 A. M. tr. *Guillemeau's Fr. Chirurg.* 10/2 The seconde table..illæse or vnhurte. *Ibid.* 37 b/1 The middle of the Legge [is] as yet illæs.

†**i'llæsive**, *a.* *Obs.* *rare*$^{-1}$. [f. IL-^{2} + L. *læs-*, ppl. stem of *lædĕre* to injure + -IVE.] Harmless.

1627–47 FELTHAM *Resolves* I. lxxxiv. 259 These they might sweeten with illæsive games.

†**i'llætible**, *a.* *Obs.* *rare*$^{-0}$. [For **illætable*, ad. L. *illætābilis*, f. *il-* (IL-^{2}) + *lætābilis* joyful.] 'Sorrowfull' (Cockeram 1623).

ill-affected ('ɪlə'fɛktɪd), *a.* [ILL- 7 a.]

†**1.** Affected with illness or indisposition; diseased. *Obs.*

1604 F. HERING *Modest Defense* A ij, As if a bleare-eyed man should not seeke remedy for his ill-affected eyes. **1615** [see AFFECTED II. 3]. **1665** NEEDHAM *Medela Medic.* 379 In Scorbutick and other ill-affected bodies. **1727** BRADLEY *Fam. Dict.* s.v. *Dimness*, The ill-affected Colour of the Eye.

2. Not well disposed towards some person or thing; unfriendly, disaffected.

1596 SPENSER *State Irel.* Wks. (Globe) 647/2 When all his parishioners are soe..ill-affected unto him, as they usually be to all the English. **1654** G. GODDARD in *Burton's Diary* (1828) I. Introd. 192 To prevent the election of delinquents and ill-affected persons. **1884** *Manch. Exam.* 16 Oct. 5/2 Somewhat better affected, or perhaps a trifle less ill-affected.

†**3.** Not viewed with favour; disliked. *Obs.*

1627 E. F. *Hist. Edw. II* in *Select. fr. Harl. Misc.* (1793) 33 This makes the ill-affected return of this our favourite, more infamous and hated.

Hence **ill-a'ffectedness**, ill-affected condition.

1648 HERRICK *Hesper.*, *Prognostick* (1869) 262 Nought but a kingdoms ill-affectednesse.

Illano (iː'ljɑːnəʊ). Also I(l)lanon, I(l)lanum. [Native name.] A member of a Moro people of Mindanao in the Republic of the Philippines; also, the language of this people. (Cf. MORO^2.) Hence **Illa'noan** *a.*

1779 T. FORREST *Voy. New Guinea* xii. 302 They possess an island in the very heart of the Philippines, called Burias, where has been a colony of Illanos, for many years. **1821** W. WALTON tr. *T. de Comyn's State of Philippine Islands* viii. 231 Long have the inhabitants of the Philippines deplored.. the ravages committed on their coasts and settlements by.. the Malanos, Ilanos and Tirones Moors and others. **1840** *Penny Cycl.* XVIII. 87/1 He was informed that the Illanos from that island [*sc.* Magindanao] had formed a settlement on Burias. **1848** F. S. MARRYAT *Borneo* 21 Pirate's Bay, so called from its being a favourite resort of the Illanoan pirates. **1898** F. T. BULLEN in *National Rev.* Aug. 857 There is yet another small section of the inhabitants of this Archipelago, who were once the terror of the surrounding seas... These have long been known as 'Illanons'. **1900** F. H. SAWYER *Inhabitants Philippines* 364 The Moros Illanos.. inhabit the country between the Bay of Iligan and Illana Bay, also round Lake Lanao, the Rio Grande and Lake Liguan. **1957** *Encycl. Americana* XIX. 472a/1 Some of the best-known Moro groups are the..Lanao Filipinos (divided into the Maranaos and Ilanums or Iranums). *Ibid.* XXI. 751/1 The principal languages and dialects with the number of persons speaking each were divided into the following groups:..Ilanon-Lanao-Lanao..109. Ilanon-Lanao-Maranoy..170,195.

†**i'llapsable**, *a.*^{1} *Obs.* *rare*$^{-1}$. [f. IL-^{2} + LAPSABLE.] Not liable to fall.

1662 GLANVILL *Lux Or.* viii. 86 They may be morally immutable and illapsable: but this is grace, not nature.

i'llapsable, *a.*^{2} *rare*$^{-0}$. [f. ILLAPSE *v.* + -ABLE.] Capable of illapsing, or liable to illapse.

In recent Dicts.

illapse (ɪ'læps, ɪll-), *sb.* Now *rare.* [ad. L. *illapsus* a gliding, falling, or slipping in, f. *illābī* to slip, etc. in: see IL-^{1} and LAPSE.]

1. The act of gliding, slipping, or falling in, of gently sinking into or permeating something.

a. *Theol.* Said of spiritual influences, esp. in ***the illapse of the Holy Spirit*** and equivalent expressions. (Freq. in 17th c.)

1614 JACKSON *Creed* III. xxi. §20 Testimonies..for the plentiful manner of effusion [of the Holy Ghost] and placid illapse into the souls of every sort. **1640** BP. REYNOLDS *Passions* iv. 27 By immediate illapse of Truth into the Vnderstanding. **1663** J. SPENCER *Prodigies* (1665) 80. **1796** J. OWEN *Trav. Europe* I. 55 The illapses of the spirit were sometimes made subservient to the impulses of the flesh. **1881** F. E. WARREN *Liturgy Celtic Ch.* ii. §10. 106 Praying for the illapse of the Holy Ghost.

b. Of the vital principle, heat, passion, etc.

1677 HALE *Prim. Orig. Man.* III. vi. 277 When the Matter is fitly prepared, there is an illapse of this Vital, Formative, Spiritual Principle into it. **1727–46** THOMSON *Summer* 1262 Thus life..is oft preserved By the bold swimmer in the swift illapse Of accident disastrous. **1768** MURPHY *Zenobia* IV. i. 10 Beware, my friend, and steel thy heart Against the sweet illapse of gentler passions.

†**c.** Of a tributary stream. *Obs.* *rare*$^{-1}$.

1753 MURPHY *Gray's-Inn Jrnl.* No. 30 ¶1 A River which admits..the tributary Illapse of several lesser Streams.

2. A gentle gliding movement. *rare*$^{-1}$.

1835 J. HARRIS *Gt. Teacher* (1837) 155, I will do this by illapses so gentle, by a process so natural.

illapse (ɪ'læps, ɪll-), *v.* Now *rare.* [f. L. *illaps-us*, pa. pple. of *illābī*: cf. LAPSE *v.*] *intr.* To fall, glide, or slip in. Hence **i'llapsing** *vbl. sb.*

1666 G. HARVEY *Morb. Angl.* xvi. 189 Their cure, when at any time illapsed into that Disease, is easier performed. **1677** HALE *Prim. Orig. Man.* IV. iv. 320 The illapsing of Souls into prepared Matter. *a* **1711** KEN *Hymns Festiv.* Poet. Wks. 1721 I. 193 Israel's sweet Singer sang Ideas bright, Illaps'd from Heav'n with true poetick Height. **1835** T. AIRD in *Blackw. Mag.* XXXVII. 180 A nymph..Near walking on the checkered floors of woods, Or far illapsing through their green retreat.

i'llapsing, *ppl. a.* *rare*$^{-1}$. [f. IL-^{2} + LAPSING.] That does not fall or slip.

1740 CHEYNE *Regimen* i. 28 The only mean, by which fallible, free lapsed Creatures..could be brought to an illapsing state of Stability.

i'llapsive, *a.* *rare*$^{-1}$. [f. as ILLAPSE *sb.* + -IVE.] Characterized by an illapse (of the divine Spirit).

1819 KNOX & JEBB *Corr.* II. 367, I know little..of illapsive communication.

†**i'llaqueable**, *a.* *Obs.* *rare*$^{-1}$. [f. L. *illaqueāre*: see ILLAQUEATE *v.* and -BLE.] Capable of being ensnared.

1678 CUDWORTH *Intell. Syst.* I. iv. §15. 268 Whether or no a Philosopher be temptable by it, or illaqueable into it.

†**i'llaqueate**, *ppl. a.* *Obs.* *rare*$^{-1}$. [ad. L. *illaqueāt-us*, pa. pple.: see next.] Ensnared.

1548 HALL *Chron.*, *Hen. VI* 165 b, The..labirynth, in the which he and hys people were enclosed and illaqueate.

illaqueate (ɪ'lækwɪeɪt), *v.* Now *rare* or *Obs.* [f. L. *illaqueāt-*, ppl. stem of *illaqueāre*, f. *il-* (IL-^{1}) + *laqueāre* to snare, f. *laqueus* noose, snare.] *trans.* To catch as in a noose; to ensnare, entrap, entangle.

1548 HALL *Chron.*, *Edw. IV* 239 b, The devel is wont with such wytchcraftes, to wrappe and illaqueat the myndes of men. **1650** tr. *Caussin's Ang. Peace* 38 Errour illaqueates some men. **1717** BULLOCK *Woman a Riddle* I. i. 8, I have inadvertently..illaqueated my self in an irrecoverable confusion. *a* **1834** COLERIDGE *Lit. Rem.* (1836–9) III. 298 Let not..his scholastic retiary versatility of logic illaqueate your good sense.

Hence **i'llaqueated** *ppl. a.*, **i'llaqueating** *vbl. sb.*

1664 H. MORE *Myst. Iniq.* 65 The illaqueating of mens consciences. *Ibid.* 465 Vexatious colluctations betwixt the injured body and the illaqueated Conscience.

†**illaque'ation**. *Obs.* [n. of action f. L. *illaqueāre* to ILLAQUEATE.]

1. The action of catching or entangling in a noose or snare; entrapping or entangling in argument; the condition of being entangled or ensnared.

1605 BACON *Adv. Learn.* II. xiv. §5. 54 The more subtile fourmes of Sophismes, and Illaqueations. **1646** SIR T. BROWNE *Pseud. Ep.* VII. xi. 361 The word ἀπήγξατο..doth not onely signifie suspension, or pendelous illaqueation.. but also suffocation, strangulation or interception of breath. **1699** EVELYN *Let. Archd. Nicholson* 10 Nov., Mem. (1857)

III. 378 They wholly gave themselves up to learn to wrangle, and the arts of illaqueation.

2. 'A snare, anything to catch another; a noose' (J.).

†**i'llate**, *v. Obs. rare.* [f. L. *illāt-*, ppl. stem of *inferre* to bring in, INFER.]

1. *trans.* To bring upon, occasion, cause.

1533 *St. Papers, Hen. VIII*, VII. 438 Restitution of dammagis to them illatid bi them specialli, whome the Pope sent thither agein the Turk.

2. *intr.* ? To be related, to relate.

1653 R. SANDERS *Physiogn., Moles* lxii. 19 This is of the nature of Jupiter and Saturn, and illateth to the right shoulder of Cepheus.

†**i'llatebrate**, *v. Obs. rare*$^{-0}$. [f. L. *illatebrāt-*, ppl. stem of *illatebrāre* (rare) to lie hid, f. *latebra* hiding-place.] *intr.* 'To hide in corners' (Cockeram 1623). Hence †**illate'bration**, 'a hiding, or seeking of corners' (Blount *Glossogr.* 1656).

illatinate (ɪ'lætɪnət), *a.* (*sb.*). *rare.* [f. IL-[2] + LATIN *a.* and *sb.* + -ATE[2], after ILLITERATE *a.*] Having no knowledge of Latin; ignorant of Latin. Also as *sb.*

1922 S. LESLIE *Oppidan* xxv. 345 They appeal even to the illatinate. **1941** E. MARSH tr. *Horace's Odes* Preface p. vii, Unless the version can give the illatinate reader some notion of Horace's quality as a poet, it is a superfluity.

illation (ɪ'leɪʃən). [ad. late L. *illātiōn-em*, n. of action from *inferre*, *illāt-um* to bring in, INFER. Cf. F. *illation* (1521 in Godefroy).]

1. The action of inferring or drawing a conclusion from premisses; hence, that which is inferred, an inference, deduction, or conclusion.

1533 MORE *Debell. Salem* Wks. 956/1 Hys illacion that he maketh vpon the same woordes of mine. **1565** HARDING in Jewel *Repl. Harding* (1611) 342 In framing his reason by way of illation. **1637** GILLESPIE *Eng. Pop. Cerem.* I. viii. 26 What ground of consequence can warrant such an illation from these premisses? **1781** WESLEY *Wks.* (1872) XIII. 463 By illation, I suppose he [Locke] means the inferring one thing from another. **1832** AUSTIN *Jurispr.* (1879) II. 1053 In the process of syllogising there is not really an illation or inference. **1886** *N. & Q.* 7th Ser. I. 251/1 It is permissible to smile at such an illation from such a major and minor.

2. *Eccl.* The Eucharistic Preface to the *Tersanctus*, as occurring in the primitive and some later liturgies, corresponding to the Preface in the Roman and Anglican liturgies.

1863 NEALE *Ess. Liturg.* 75 We now come to.. Illations; or, as they have been variously called, Prefaces, Contestations, or Prayers of the Triumphal Hymn. *Ibid.* 77 The Gallican has a different Illation for every principal festival.

illative (ɪ'leɪtɪv), *a.* and *sb.* [ad. late L. *illātīvus*, f. *illāt-*, ppl. stem of *inferre* (see prec.): cf. F. *illatif* (1617 in Godefroy).]

A. *adj.* **1.** Of words: Introducing or stating an inference; esp. in ***illative particle***.

1611 W. SCLATER *Key* iii. 20. 328 First reason..collected from the illatiue particle *therefore*. **1647** FARINGDON *Serm.* ii. 23 Which word is not causal, but illative. *a* **1703** BURKITT *On N.T., Heb.* ii. Pref., Our apostle draws an inference..as appears by the illative particle 'therefore' at the head of the first verse. **1864** BOWEN *Logic* vii. 220 Connected by an illative particle, *because, then, therefore*, &c.

2. Of the nature of, or arising from, an inference or illation; inferential.

1637 GILLESPIE *Eng. Pop. Cerem.* IV. viii. 40 The promissorie part is illative upon and relative unto the matter of the assertorie part. *a* **1716** SOUTH *Serm.* (1744) VIII. 89 There is a great deal of difference between a mere illative necessity, which consists only in the logical consequence of one thing upon another, and between a causal necessity [etc.]. **1864** BOWEN *Logic* vi. 156 Logic takes notice only of what is called illative Conversion, in which the Convertend and the Converse must either both be true, or both be false, together. Thus the Conversion of *No A is B*, into *No B is A*, is illative.. But the Conversion of *Some A are not B*, into *Some B are not A*, is not illative.

3. Of or pertaining to illation or inference; characterized by illation.

1870 J. H. NEWMAN *Gram. Assent* ix. §3. 354 The faculty or talent, which I call the Ratiocinative or Illative Sense, being parallel to *phronesis* in conduct, and to taste in the Fine Arts. **1876** L. CAMPBELL in *Contemp. Rev.* June 101 The English idiom is neither adversative nor illative in the same degree with the Greek.

4. *Gram.* Denoting the case expressing motion into.

1890 A. S. GATSCHET *Klamath Indians* 483 The suffix marks as well (1) a motion or direction toward an object or into a place or country, as (2) a stay or rest at or in a place, region, country. It is more frequently used in the former sense, and hence I have called the case the illative case. **1958** A. S. C. ROSS *Etym.* 167 *Illative case*, the case of 'motion towards', as in Finnish *Helsinkiin* 'to Helsinki'. **1959** [see ELATIVE *a.*]. **1968** C. J. FILLMORE in Bach & Harms *Universals in Linguistic Theory* 9 Redden..finds five case indices in Walapai..and identifies each of these with terms taken from the tradition of case studies:..*-l* is illative/inessive, [etc.].

B. *sb.* **1.** An illative particle.

1591 PERCIVALL *Sp. Dict.* E, A Coniunction..some are.. Illatiues, as, *assi*, so. **1659** O. WALKER *Instruct. Oratory* 102 Such illatives omitted..cause much ambiguity. *a* **1868** C. BYINGTON *Gram. Choctaw Lang.* (1870) viii. 54 Conjunctions are divided into the following classes:.. Illatives; therefore, wherefore, on account of, yomohmi hokvt, yomahmi hokah. **1870** F. A. MARCH *Compar. Gram. Anglo-Saxon Lang.* §481 Causals and illatives are very often omitted.

†**2.** An illative clause. *Obs.*

1604 TOOKER *Fabr. Church* 39 My Illative therfore is, the Bishop..did call other Ministers into a part of the Charge. **1651** JER. TAYLOR *Clerus Dom.* 13 This discourse was occasioned by our Saviours illative: All power is given me, goe yee therefore and teach.

Hence **i'llatively** *adv.*, in the way of inference.

1655 BP. RICHARDSON *On O. Test.* 434 Most commonly taken illatively. **1827** WHATELY *Logic* II. ii. §4 (1836) 78 Every proposition may be illatively converted.

†**i'llatrate**, *v. Obs. rare*$^{-0}$. [f. L. *illatrāt-*, ppl. stem of *illatrāre* (rare), f. *il-* (IL-[1]) + *latrāre* to bark.] 'To scoffe or barke at a thing' (Cockeram 1623). Hence †**illa'tration**, 'a barking against one' (Blount *Glossogr.* 1656).

illaudable (ɪ'lɔːdəb(ə)l), *a.* [ad. late L. *illaudābilis*: see IL-[2] and LAUDABLE.] Not laudable; unworthy of praise or commendation.

1589 PUTTENHAM *Eng. Poesie* I. xvi. (Arb.) 50 The bad and illawdable parts of all estates and degrees were taxed by the Poets in one sort or an other. **1670** MILTON *Hist. Eng.* v. Wks. (1851) 230 His actions are diversly reported, by Huntingdon not thought illaudable. **1754** RICHARDSON *Grandison* (1781) II. xxviii. 259 Young Ladies are too apt to make secrets of a passion that is not in itself illaudable. **1828** CARLYLE *Werner* in *Misc. Ess.* (1872) I. 102 Grounded on no wicked or even illaudable motive.

Hence **i'llaudably** *adv.*, in a way not to be praised. *rare.*

17.. BROOME (J.), It is natural for people to form, not illaudably, too favourable a judgment of their own country. **1888** *Scott. Leader* 14 July 4 The *miles gloriosus* whom he has illaudably encountered.

illau'dation. *rare.* [f. IL-[2] + LAUDATION: cf. F. *illaudation* (in Godefroy).] The opposite of laudation; censure.

1848 *Blackw. Mag.* LXIV. 503 The temper of direct praise is always wholly genial; that of lauding by illaudation has in it perforce an ungenial element.

i'llaudatory, *a. rare.* [f. IL-[2] + LAUDATORY.] Not laudatory; not characterized by praising.

1845 *Blackw. Mag.* LVII. 787 Unqualified praise from the illaudatory pen of Ritson.

‖**i'llaun.** *Irish.* [ad. Ir. *eileán*, *oileán* (prob. ad. ON. *eyland*, *øyland*).] An islet.

1882 *Cornh. Mag.* Mar. 321 Tiny illauns and carrigeens, which barely afford a foothold to the passing gull. **1895** *19th Cent.* Mar. 422 Their curraghs were cast ashore and dashed to pieces against the illaun.

Illawarra (ɪlə'wɒrə). The name of a district in New South Wales, used *attrib.* to designate certain trees native to the region.

1884 A. NILSON *Timber Trees N.S.W.* 39 *C*[*argillia*] *australis*.—Black Plum; Illawarra Plum. *Ibid.* 82 *F*[*renela*] *rhomboidea*.—Illawarra Mountain Pine. **1889** J. H. MAIDEN *Useful Native Plants Austral.* 422 *Elæocarpus reticulata* var. *Kirtoni*, is known as 'Illawarra Ash', or 'Mountain Ash'. **1904** —— *Forest Flora N.S.W.* I. 9 *Ficus rubiginosa*... Vernacular Names.—'Port Jackson Fig', 'Illawarra Fig', from the best known localities. **1907** *Ibid.* II. 53 This tree [sc. *Callitris Muelleri*] is usually known as Cypress Pine. The names 'Port Jackson Pine' and 'Illawarra Mountain Pine' should be received with caution, as *C. cupressiformis* may be included. **1965** *Austral. Encycl.* IV. 58/2 The Port Jackson, Illawarra, or rusty fig (*F. rubiginosa*) is confined in its native state to New South Wales, but is extensively planted as a shade and ornamental tree throughout Australia.

b. In full ***Illawarra*** (***dairy, milking***) ***shorthorn***: see quot. 1911.

1911 *N.Z. Jrnl. Agric.* May 274 The breed..known as the Illawara Milking Shorthorn, a dairy type of Shorthorn evolved on the south coast districts of the State from a Shorthorn-Ayrshire foundation, but now bred for about thirty years to a Shorthorn dairy type. *Ibid.*, One very good point of the Illawara is that while it is a heavy producer, the milk is generally of a very satisfactory butterfat standard. **1912** M. A. O'CALLAGHAN *Dairying in Australasia* vii. 111 The Scotch type of Ayrshire is nearly as different from the Australian type, as is the English shorthorn dairy cow from what we know as the Illawarra dairy Shorthorn. **1934** *Bulletin* (Sydney) 25 July 41/1 Southern India is to try Australia's own dairy cattle—the Illawarra shorthorn from the N.S.W. South Coast. **1965** *Austral. Encycl.* V. 64/1 During the nineteenth century a special breed of dairy cattle, the Australian Illawarra Shorthorn, was developed.

'ill-being. *nonce-wd.* [f. ILL *adv.* + BEING *vbl. sb.*] 'Ill' or unprosperous condition; employed as the antithesis of *well-being*.

1840 CARLYLE *Heroes* v. (1872) 178 The test of vital well-being or illbeing to a generation. **1884** H. SPENCER *Man v. State* 113 Philanthropists..insuring the future ill-being of men while eagerly pursuing their present well-being.

'ill-be'loved (see ILL- III), *a.* [f. ILL *adv.* + BELOVED.] Not well-beloved; not beloved; disliked.

1546 BALE *Sel. Wks.* (1849) 182 They are not so ill-beloved of their country merchants. **1622** MABBE tr. *Aleman's Guzman d'Alf.* II. 147 There is not a man..that hath so bad a name, or is so ill belou'd, as he is. **1785** J. TRUSLER *Mod. Times* II. 169 There is seldom a person dies that is so ill-beloved, but [etc.]. **1876** GEO. ELIOT *Dan. Der.* xlv, His ill-beloved nephew.

ill blood, 'ill-'blood. [See ILL *a.* 2, BLOOD *sb.* 5; cf. *bad blood*, BAD 6.] Unfriendly or angry feeling, animosity; strife.

1624 CAPT. SMITH *Virginia* 178 Finding this..might breed ill bloud. *c* **1645** HOWELL *Lett.* (1655) I. iii. 121 It was fear'd this..would have bred ill blood. **1703** BURCHETT *Naval Trans.* III. xvii. (1720) 365 This Action..bred ill Blood between him and Raleigh. **1809** WELLINGTON *Let. to J. Villiers* 19 May in Gurw. *Desp.* IV. 346 The embarrassment and ill-blood which it occasions. **1844** DICKENS *Mart. Chuz.* ii, Don't let there be any ill-blood between us, pray.

'ill-'boding, *a.* [ILL- 2.] That bodes or portends evil; of evil omen.

1591 SHAKS. *1 Hen. VI*, IV. v. 6 Malignant and ill-boading Starres. **1641** MILTON *Reform.* II. (1851) 45 There cannot be a more ill-boding signe to a Nation. **1720** WELTON *Suffer. Son of God* II. xxviii. 740 Unhappy Time! Ill-boding hours! **1855** SINGLETON *Virgil* I. 101 Dogs ill-omened, and ill-boding birds, Afforded presages.

ill-boned, -born: see ILL- B.

'ill-'bred, *a.* [f. ILL *adv.* + BRED *ppl. a.*[1]] Badly brought up; characterized by ill breeding, unmannerly, rude. (Of persons, their actions, etc.)

1622 MABBE tr. *Aleman's Guzman d'Alf.* I. v. 130, I was not so ill bred, but that I knew..when it was lawfull for me to speake. **1634** SIR T. HERBERT *Trav.* 15 Some Dutch-ill-bred Sayler. **1673** [R. LEIGH] *Transp. Reh.* 39 These Arminians are the rudest ill bred'st persons. *c* **1704** PRIOR *Henry & Emma* 462 The ill-bred question, and the lew'd reply. **1834** LYTTON *Pompeii* I. i, An ostentatious, bustling, ill-bred fellow. **1892** E. REEVES *Homeward Bound* 311 [In Spain] It is not considered ill-bred to stare at ladies.

ill breeding, 'ill-'breeding. [ILL *a.* + BREEDING *vbl. sb.*] Bad or inferior breeding or bringing up; hence, Bad manners, rudeness.

1800 MRS. HERVEY *Mourtray Fam.* II. 136 Declamations against the ill-breeding of modern young men. **1819** BYRON *Juan* I. clxxiv, To say the best, it was extreme ill-breeding.

ill-coloured, -ored ('ɪl'kʌləd), *a.* [f. ILL *a.* + COLOUR *sb.* + -ED[2]; or f. ILL *adv.* + *coloured*, pa. pple. of COLOUR *v.*]

1. Having a bad, unpleasant, or inferior colour.

1435 MISYN *Fire of Love* 78 Noyd & disesyd, wonedyd & ill-colorde. **1721** *Wodrow Corr.* (1843) II. 581 He..is turned blue and ill-coloured. **1748** *Anson's Voy.* II. viii. 219 If the bottom be muddy, the pearl is dark and ill-coloured. *a* **1776** R. JAMES *Dissert. Fevers* (1778) 24 Ill-coloured spots all over him.

2. *fig.* Having an evil appearance; that does not 'look well'.

1631 SANDERSON *Serm.* II. 12 Some things..if they be not evil, yet are ill-coloured..and carry in their faces some resemblance or appearance of evil.

3. Badly coloured or painted.

1749 BERKELEY *Let. to Prior* 2 Feb. in Fraser *Life* viii. (1871) 319 The third is a copy, and ill-coloured.

illcome ('ɪlkəm), *a. rare.* [f. ILL *adv.* + COME *pa. pple.*] Unfortunately come or arrived: not welcome.

1579 J. STUBBES *Gaping Gulf* C iij, A most illcome guest therefore. *a* **1592** GREENE *George a Greene* Wks. (Rtldg.) 264 *K. James.* My Lord of Kendal, you are welcome to the court. *K. Edw.* Nay, but ill-come as it falls out now. **1875** *Athenæum* 21 Aug. 237/3 Always welcome, and as often illcome.

ill-conditioned ('ɪlkən'dɪʃənd), *a.* [f. *ill condition* + -ED[2].] Having bad 'conditions' or qualities; of an evil disposition; in a bad condition or state. In Geometry, applied to a triangle which has very unequal angles, such as that by which a star's parallax is determined.

1614 RALEIGH *Hist. World* III. (1634) 5 His owne sonne.. being an ill conditioned Boy. **1694** SALMON *Bates' Disp.* (1713) 678/1 Gun-shot Wounds, and other malign and ill condition'd Ulcers. **1771** SMOLLETT *Humph. Cl.* 6 May Let. i, That a woman..should place her affection upon such an ugly, ill-conditioned cur. **1796** C. MARSHALL *Garden.* viii. (1813) 107 When roots reach a weak, ill-conditioned soil the trees must fail. **1850** MRS. JAMESON *Leg. Monast. Ord.* (1863) 386 This woman also proved ill-conditioned and thankless. **1897** ALLBUTT *Syst. Med.* III. 911 Peritonitis.. of an ill-conditioned kind.

Hence **ill-con'ditionedness**, the state or quality of being ill-conditioned.

1866 MISS MULOCK *Noble Life* v. 76 Ill-health, ill-humour and ill-conditionedness of every sort. **1875** TAIT in *Gd. Words* No. 1. 21 The ill-conditionedness of the triangle.

ill-content, -convenient, -customed, etc.: see ILL- B.

illd, obs. f. *illed*, from ILL *v.*

ˌ**ill-'deedy**, *a.* Now *Sc.* Also 6 evil-deedy (see note under ILL *a.*). [f. *ill deed* + -Y[1]: cf. DEEDY *a.*] Given to evil deeds, mischievous.

c **1460** *Towneley Myst.* XXX. 574 Riche and ille-dedy, Gederand and gredy. **1535** LYNDESAY *Satyre* 4028 Luke quhat it is to be evil-deidie. **1536** BELLENDEN *Cron. Scot.* (1821) I. 58 He favourit evill dedy men. **1728** RAMSAY *Anacreontic on Love*, Cupid, that ill-deedy geat. **1824** SCOTT *Redgauntlet* ch. vii, Where that ill-deedy hempy is.

ill-deserver, -deserving: see ILL- B.

ill-disposed (ˈɪldɪˈspəʊzd), *a.* [f. ILL *adv.* + DISPOSED.]

1. Having a bad disposition; disposed to evil or harm; immoral, wicked; malignant, malevolent; unpropitious.

1432-50 tr. *Higden* (Rolls) II. 367 The ylle disposede woman. *c* **1460** FORTESCUE *Abs. & Lim. Mon.* xvi. (1885) 149 Yll dyspôsed emperours..had slayn grete parte off þe senatours. **1622** BP. ANDREWES *Sermons*, If rugged or uneven the way, if the weather ill-disposed. **1800** *Asiat. Ann. Reg.*, *Misc. Tr.* 181/1 The country towards Bhopaulputtun was so ill-disposed towards us. **1863** BARING-GOULD *Iceland* 249 A hard-hearted ill-disposed fellow.

†**2.** In a bad state of health; unwell, indisposed.

1600 HAKLUYT *Voy.* III. 660 We lost not any one, nor had one ill disposed to my knowledge. *c* **1645** HOWELL *Lett.* I. v. xxxv, My Lord of Sunderland is still ill dispos'd.

3. Badly disposed or arranged.

1726 LEONI *Designs* Pref. 1/2 Ill-disposed and mis-matched Scraps. **1777** ROBERTSON *Hist. Amer.* (1783) III. 214 The apartments..were ill-disposed, and afforded little accommodation.

4. Not disposed (*to do* something); disinclined.

1771 GOLDSM. *Hist. Eng.* xlvii. IV. 307 The people..were never so ill disposed to receive him, as at the very time he pitched upon to make a descent.

Hence **ill-diˈsposedness** (-ɪdnɪs), state or quality of being ill-disposed.

1628 BP. HALL *Old Relig.* (1686) Ded., The ignorance and ill-disposedness of some cavillers that taxed this course.

ill-doer, -doing: see ILL- 2.

ill-ease: see ILL *a.* 9.

†**illeceˈbration.** *Obs. rare.* [n. of action f. late L. *illecebrāre* to entice, allure, f. *illecebra*: see ILLECEBROUS.] The action of alluring; enticement, allurement.

1624 HEYWOOD *Gunaik.* VII. 364 The Syrens..insinuating into the eares of man by their severall illecebrations or enticements. *a* **1704** T. BROWN *Wks.* (1760) IV. 292 Modesty..restrains..the great familiarity of pleasant illecebrations.

illeceˈbrose, *a.* [See next.] 'Full of allurements, very inticing' (Bailey vol. II, 1727).

†**iˈllecebrous,** *a. Obs.* [ad. L. (ante- and post-classical) *illecebrōsus*, f. *illecebra* charm, lure, enticement, f. *illicĕre* to entice (see ILLECT).] Alluring, enticing, attractive.

1531 ELYOT *Gov.* I. vii, The illecebrous dilectations of Venus. **1586** W. WEBBE *Eng. Poetrie* (Arb.) 45 Such illicibrous workes and inuentions, as among them..myght obtaine passage. **1599** R. LINCHE *Anc. Fiction* K ij, Rockt asleep with the illecebrous blandishments thereof. **1656** BLOUNT *Glossogr.*, *Illecebrous*, that enticeth or allureth.

ˈilleck, *sb.* ? *Obs.* A name in Cornwall of a fish, the gemmous dragonet, *Callionymus lyra.*

1602 CAREW *Cornwall* 32 a, Of flat [fish there are] Brets, Turbets, Dories, Illeck, Tub [etc.]. **1880** *West Cornw. Gloss.*, *Illick*, *ellick*, the red gurnard.

†**iˈllect,** *v. Obs. rare.* [f. L. *illect-*, ppl. stem of *illicĕre* to allure, entice, f. *il-* (IL-[1]) + **lacĕre* to entice: cf. ALLECT.] *trans.* To allure, entice.

1529 S. FISH *Supplic. Beggers* 6 Had not theyre superfluous rychesse illected theym to vnclene lust and ydelnesse. **1531** ELYOT *Gov.* I. vii, It were therefore better that no musike were taughte to a noble man, than..he shuld ..by that be illected to wantonnesse. **1534** MORE *On the Passion* Wks. 1315/1 Into the fleshly body can the deuyll enter..to illecte styrre and drawe vs to his purpose.

Hence †**illecˈtation** [late L. *illectātio*], allurement, enticement; †**iˈllective** *a.*, attractive, enticing; *sb.* an enticing agent.

1652 GAULE *Magastrom.* 269 Carpocrates..practised..all other machinations, malignations, inductions, illectations. **1706** PHILLIPS, *Illective*, Allurement, Inticement.

ill effect, ill-effect. [ILL *a.* 5, EFFECT *sb.* I.] (Usually in *pl.*) A harmful or deleterious effect, an unpleasant consequence.

1675 in McHutchin & Quirk *Isle of Man Charities* (1831) 6 The mean provision of the Clergy in that Isle, and the ill effects which necessarily attend upon the same. **1704** *Hist. Man* xlvii. 195 Envy, and the ill Effects of it. **1767** A. YOUNG *Farmer's Lett. People* 193 It has a very ill effect upon our tillage. **1845** *Douglas Jerrold's Shilling Mag.* I. 174 Equal ill effect, either from his liking the Princess too much, or too little. **1884** W. PYE *Surg. Handicraft* 531 One year after the accident he..could go to a ball and dance every dance without any ill effects. **1923** R. LYND *Blue Lion* xxi. 162 It would be mere perversity to quarrel with these [dishes] because there are no ill-effects from eating them. **1971** J. Z. YOUNG *Introd. Study Man* xxii. 294 Any genes that confer reproductive advantage early in life will be selected, even if they are pleiotropic and have ill-effects later.

illegal (ɪˈliːgəl), *a.* and *sb.* [a. F. *illégal* (14th c.) or ad. med.L. *illegālis*, f. *il-* (IL-[2]) + *legālis* LEGAL.] **A.** *adj.* **1. a.** Not legal or lawful; contrary to, or forbidden by, law.

1626 [implied in ILLEGALNESS]. **1639** FULLER *Holy War* II. viii. (1647) 54 Gibellinus..concluded the election of Ebremarus to be illegall and void. *a* **1654** SELDEN *Table-t.* (Arb.) 75 In all times the Princes in England have done something illegal, to get money. **1769** *Junius Lett.* xxxv. 166 They have set aside a return as illegal. **1817** W. SELWYN *Law Nisi Prius* (ed. 4) II. 925 Intended for carrying on an illegal commerce. **1855** MACAULAY *Hist. Eng.* xxi. IV. 605 To print such a tract without the approbation of the licenser was illegal.

†**b.** Lawless, irregular. *Obs. rare.*

1728 R. MORRIS *Ess. Anc. Archit.* 20 How preferable the Beauties of ancient Architecture are to the illegal Practices of our modern Builders.

2. Special Comb.: **illegal immigrant**, orig. a Jew who entered or attempted to enter Palestine without official permission during the later years of the British mandate; now used more generally; so ***illegal immigration***; **illegal operation**, an abortion procured illegally.

1939 *Times* 31 May 11/1 These illegal immigrants come practically penniless, and have no documents to indicate their origin. **1946** *Times* 23 Sept. 4/3 The British 'clamp down' on illegal immigrants. **1949** KOESTLER *Promise & Fulfilment* vi. 59 The hunting down of 'illegal immigrants' became gradually an obsession with the Palestine authorities. **1963** J. JOESTEN *They call it Intelligence* II. viii. 73 Once in this country, Abel headed straight for New York, a good place for an illegal immigrant. **1970** [see B. *sb.* 1]. **1970** *Times* 2 July 1/4 Police..took away 40 men who had come from the Punjab... All the men had been established as illegal immigrants. **1939** *Times* 31 May 11/1 Illegal immigration into Palestine probably dates back to Turkish times, but it is now assuming alarming proportions. **1969** *New Yorker* 29 Nov. 151/1 Moshe Pearlman..an organiser of illegal immigration to Palestine..for all his wit and sophistication, still takes his Zionism very seriously. **1910** CHESTERTON *G. B. Shaw* 145 Mr. Granville Barker's play of *Waste*, in which the woman dies from an illegal operation. **1927** *Rev. Eng. Stud.* Oct. 433 There is a very interesting misuse of words..due..to a yet older human failing: taboo. As instances may serve *lavatory*, *illegal operation*, *social evil*, *a certain disease*. **1938** 'M. BENNEY' *Scapegoat Dances* iv. 46 He had given his knowledge, time, and money to relieving the distresses of the street-walkers..when necessary, performing illegal operations on them. **1943** G. GREENE *Ministry of Fear* I. ii. 24 A man who deals in something disreputable—pornographic books or illegal operations. **1958** *New Statesman* 7 June 722/1 Estimates suggest that something like 200,000 illegal operations are performed every year in this country.

B. *sb.* **1.** = *illegal immigrant.*

1939 *Times* 31 May 11/1 Placing the illegals in concentration camps is no solution. **1946** KOESTLER *Thieves in Night* 328 The old tramper was lost—but there were two others on their way with eight hundred illegals this time. **1960** H. AGAR *Saving Remnant* viii. 208 The British announced that all future 'illegals' would be taken to Cyprus. **1970** *Sunday Times* (Colour Suppl.) 1 Feb. 29/4 In the year 1968 alone 142,000 illegal immigrants were caught. .. There is no onus upon an employer not to take on illegals.

2. A Soviet secret agent working in a foreign country.

1968 W. GARNER *Deep, Deep Freeze* xii. 133 An Illegal's first job was to pass vital information with the minimum of delay. **1969** —— *Us or Them War* xxxiii. 251 What if he'd come over as an 'illegal', with a long-term programme? **1969** H. MACINNES *Salzburg Connection* xx. 281 We'd like to catch that colonel and the rest of his illegals.

illegality (ɪliːˈgælɪtɪ). [ad. F. *illégalité* (14th c.): see prec. and -ITY.]

1. The quality or condition of being illegal.

1639 FULLER *Holy War* II. xx. (1647) 70 The illegality of his election was rectified. **1647** CLARENDON *Hist. Reb.* II. §72 Mr. Hambden the most Popular man in the House, and the same who had defended the Suit against the King in his own Name, upon the Illegality of Ship-money. **1691** T. H[ALE] *Acc. New Invent.* p. lxxii, The illegality of granting Forfeitures before Conviction is now out of fashion. **1771** BURKE *Sp. on Middlesex Elect.* Wks. 1877 VI. 131 How long the people are bound to tolerate the illegality of our judgments. **1840** THIRLWALL *Greece* VII. lvi. 136 The charge of illegality was well grounded.

b. An instance of this, an illegal act or practice.

1898 *Daily News* 22 June 7/1 Bishops must..deal with ritualistic illegalities within their diocese.

†**2.** = ILLEGITIMACY. *Obs. rare.*

1749 FIELDING *Tom Jones* I. iii, She took the child in her arms, without any apparent disgust at the illegality of its birth.

illegalize (ɪˈliːgəlaɪz), *v.* [f. ILLEGAL *a.* + -IZE.] *trans.* To render illegal.

1818 in TODD. **1866** *Cosmopolitan* 28 Apr. 472/2 The official presence of representatives from the bogus State of Western Virginia illegalises its functions.

illegally (ɪˈliːgəlɪ), *adv.* [f. ILLEGAL *a.* + -LY[2].] In an illegal manner.

1628 BP. HALL *Old Relig.* iv. 23 The reformed..being by that Church illegally condemned for those points, are not heretickes. **1765** BLACKSTONE *Comm.* I. xvi. (1809) 459 The bastard shall..be settled in the parish, from whence she [the mother] was illegally removed. **1884** *Law Times Rep.* LI. 335/2 A police constable procured a warrant to be illegally issued without a written information on oath.

iˈllegalness. *rare.* [f. as prec. + -NESS.] = ILLEGALITY.

1626 *Impeachm. Dk. Buckhm.* (Camden) 69 The Article.. touching the illegalness of embarguing. **1727** in BAILEY vol. II: whence in later Dicts.

illegibility (ɪlɛdʒɪˈbɪlɪtɪ). [f. ILLEGIBLE *a.*: see -ITY.] The quality of being illegible.

1818 TODD, *Illegibility*, incapability of being read. **1853** MRS. CARLYLE *Lett.* II. 219 My hand shakes so, you must excuse illegibility.

illegible (ɪˈlɛdʒɪb(ə)l), *a.* [f. IL-[2] + LEGIBLE.] Not legible, that cannot be read; esp. of written characters: Undecipherable.

[**1615** P. GORDON *Barbour's Bruce* Pref., It was an old tome, almost inlegeable in manie places.] **1640** HOWELL *Dodona's Gr.* (1645) 55 The secretary poured the ink-box all over the writings and so defaced them that they were made altogether illegible. **1791** MRS. RADCLIFFE *Rom. Forest* ix, Here several pages of the manuscript were..totally illegible. **1851** RUSKIN *Mod. Paint.* I. Pref. to 2nd ed. 33 It is no excuse for illegible writing, that there are persons who could not have read it had it been plain. **1866** G. MACDONALD *Ann. Q. Neighb.* v. (1878) 58 Mrs. Oldcastle's face..was illegible.

†**b.** Unreadable, because of language or matter.

1756 *Gentl. Mag.* XXVI. 37/2 Let plodding Sloan his taste for authors boast, The most illegible esteem the most. **1822** JEFFREY *Let.* in Ld. Cockburn *Life* II. Let. xc, Clarissa Harlowe and Sir C. Grandison owe all their attraction to their length;..an abstract of either would be illegible. **1828** *Edin. Rev.* XLVII. 203 Sir Michael Scott, again—being all magic, witchcraft, and mystery—is absolutely illegible.

Hence **iˈllegibly** *adv.*, in an illegible manner.

1818 in TODD. **1860** MOTLEY *Netherl.* (1868) I. i. 2 The diligent old man..could write so illegibly.

illegit, illegit. (ɪlɪˈdʒɪt), colloq. abbrev. of ILLEGITIMATE *a.* (*sb.*).

1913 A. LUNN *Harrovians* viii. 152 'Was he a blooming illegit?' asked Kendal. **1952** 'C. BRAND' *London Particular* xiii. 166 She was supposed to be having this illegit. **1955** J. CANNAN *Long Shadows* v. 86 Perhaps Mousie's illegit was a boy. **1958** 'C. CARNAC' *Long Shadows* xv. 200 Somerset House..registers the illegits..as carefully as the rest. **1962** C. WATSON *Hopjoy was Here* iii. 33 The mother is *Miss* Cork. Miriam's illegit. **1967** E. COXHEAD *Thankless Muse* iii. 61 She's a year younger than me and it's only a matter of minutes before she'll bring home the illegit. **1973** *Nation Rev.* (Melbourne) III. 31 Aug. 1463/1 If it was an illegit, why no mention in the womens lib chapter?

illegitimacy (ɪlɪˈdʒɪtɪməsɪ). [f. ILLEGITIMATE: see -ACY.] The quality, state, or condition of being illegitimate; *spec.* bastardy.

1680 WOOD *Life* (O.H.S.) II. 493 The King's declaration concerning the illegitimacie of the duke of Monmouth. **1751** EARL ORRERY *Remarks Swift* (1752) 5 The other suggestion concerning the illegitimacy of his birth, is equally false. **1864** DORAN *Majesties' Serv.* I. 80 His mother had addressed him..by an epithet referring to his illegitimacy. **1882-3** SCHAFF *Encycl. Relig. Knowl.* 2412/1 He..was fully aware of its illegitimacy..as doctrinal evidence. **1898** F. HALL in *Nation* (N.Y.) LXVI. 341/1 The [alleged] illegitimacy of [the expression] *in our midst.*

illegitimate (ɪlɪˈdʒɪtɪmət), *a.* (*sb.*) [f. L. *illēgitim-us* (see ILLEGITIME), after LEGITIMATE *a.*]

A. *adj.* **1.** Not legitimate, not in accordance with or authorized by law; unauthorized, unwarranted; spurious; irregular, improper.

1645 MILTON *Tetrach.* (1851) 194 Who shall judge of public honesty? the Law of God..or the illegitimat Law of Monks and Canonists? **1790** BURKE *Fr. Rev.* Wks. V. 117 A thing not only vicious in itself, but..rendering our whole government absolutely illegitimate, and not at all better than a downright usurpation. **1874** H. R. REYNOLDS *John Bapt.* III. i. 132 Illegitimate aspirants to the prophetic and priestly offices. **1876** TREVELYAN *Macaulay* I. v. 281 A living embodiment..of illegitimate curiosity.

2. *spec.* **a.** Not born in lawful wedlock; not recognized by law as lawful offspring; spurious, bastard. (The earliest sense in Eng.)

1536 *Act 28 Hen. VIII*, c. 7 §3 Elysabeth the kynges doughter illegyttimate borne vnder the same mariage. **1555** W. WATREMAN *Fardle Facions* I. v. 72 Ther is no child emong them, though it be borne of a bought woman slaue, that is compted illegitimate. **1606** SHAKS. *Tr. & Cr.* v. vii. 18, I am a Bastard begot, Bastard instructed, Bastard in minde, Bastard in valour, in euery thing illegitimate. **1827** JARMAN *Powell's Devises* (ed. 3) II. 343 The testator having four children, three legitimate and one illegitimate, (the latter being the child of himself and his wife born before their marriage). **1879** FROUDE *Cæsar* xii. 152 There is no record of any illegitimate children.

b. Not in accordance with rule or reason; not correctly deduced or inferred.

1599 SHAKS. *Much Ado* III. iv. 50 O illegitimate construction! I scorne that with my heeles. **1664** H. MORE *Myst. Iniq.*, *Apol.* 513, I propound all these waies of division as false and illegitimate. **1773** REID *Aristotle's Log.* iv. §4. 82 As to the illegitimate modes, Aristotle has taken the labour to try and condemn them. **1864** BOWEN *Logic* vii. 184 Throwing out at once all [the Syllogistic forms] that are illegitimate.

c. Naturally or physiologically abnormal. By Darwin applied to the irregular or abnormal fertilization of plants.

1615 CROOKE *Body of Man* 334, I call that a lawfull or legitimate birth which commeth in due time, & that illigitimate which happeneth before or after the due time. **1661** LOVELL *Hist. Anim. & Min.* 411 The scirrhus thereof ..if it be illegitimate and degenerat into a cancer; it's cured, by universal evacuation. **1868** DARWIN *Anim. & Pl.* xviii. II. 166 The illegitimate unions of reciprocally dimorphic or trimorphic plants. **1875** *Ibid.* (ed. 2) xix. II. 166 These illegitimate plants, as they may be called, are not fully fertile.

d. *Racing.* Formerly applied to steeplechasing and hurdle racing as distinguished from flat-racing.

So called from the fact that before the formation of the Grand National Hunt Committee these forms of racing were not under any rules and were not recognized by any racing tribunal.

1888 *Daily Chron.* 31 Oct. (Farmer), A much smarter performer at the illegitimate game than she was on the flat. **1889** Barrère & Leland *Dict. Slang* I. 481/2 *Illegitimate* season, also called the dead season. **1898** A. E. T. Watson *Turf* viii. 171 The Jockey Club gave no countenance to 'illegitimate' sport.

e. Of drama: more concerned with spectacle than with literary quality. Cf. LEGITIMATE *a.* 2 b.

1812 *Dramatic Censor 1811* 158 We are grieved to behold that hunger for spectacle, and the illegitimate Drama, which so glaringly prevails with the more numerous and coarser part of an English Public. **1842** *Times* 28 Jan., A magnificent Barbary lion, trained for performing in the illegitimate drama, 105 guineas. **1949** *Archit. Rev.* CV. 122/1 The popular tradition, which cared little about lines of demarcation between the 'legitimate' and 'illegitimate' stage.

B. *sb.* **a.** A bastard. **b.** One whose position is viewed as in some way illegitimate; *spec.* a free settler in Australia (*Obs.* exc. *Hist.*).

1673 [R. Leigh] *Transp. Reh.* 47 Some of your papers may ..dye the common death of illegitimates. **1827** P. Cunningham *N.S. Wales* II. 116 The legitimates, such as have legal reasons for visiting this colony; and the illegitimates, or such as are free from that stigma. **1836** (*title*) The Bar Sinister, or Memoirs of an Illegitimate. **1856** J. Glyde *Suffolk* 87, In 1842, the illegitimates were, in Suffolk, 8·1 per cent. **1941** Baker *Dict. Austral. Slang* 37 *Illegitimates*, free settlers (obs.). **1945** —— *Austral. Lang.* ii. 42 These were the type of people who styled themselves the *aristocracy*, *sterling*..and, since they had no 'legal' reasons for coming to Australia..also bore the title *illegitimates*. **1966** G. W. Turner *Eng. Lang. Austral. & N.Z.* i. 9 Historians..may draw on *illegitimates* or *pure merinos* as the Australian equivalent of a donnish joke, but they are not current in general Australian speech.

illegitimate (ɪlɪ'dʒɪtɪmeɪt), *v.* [f. prec.: cf. LEGITIMATE *v.*] *trans.* To declare or pronounce illegitimate; to bastardize.

1611 Cotgr., *Morte-main*,..the succession of, or estate left by, illegitimated bastards. **1624** T. Scott *Vox Cœli* 7 To illigitimate Don Anthony,..who was the first and neerest heire vnto that Crowne. *a* **1715** Burnet *Own Time* (1766) II. 84 They were by Acts of Parliament illegitimated. **1828** D. le Marchant *Rep. Claims Barony Gardner* p. xi, Evidence which the English law deems sufficient, for illegitimating children, born during the matrimony of their maternal parent.

illegitimately (ɪlɪ'dʒɪtɪmətlɪ), *adv.* [f. ILLEGITIMATE *a.* + -LY^2.] In an illegitimate manner; unlawfully; without authority; spuriously.

a **1633** Austin *Medit.* (1635) 12 Lest he should have beene justly cast out by those Infidels, as one Illegitimatly borne. **1835** *Fraser's Mag.* XI. 689 This is illegitimately deduced from his own premises. **1868** Darwin *Anim. & Pl.* xviii. II. 166 Seedlings of *Lythrum Salicaria*..raised from plants illegitimately fertilised by their own form pollen.

ille'gitimateness. *rare.* [f. as prec. + -NESS.] = ILLEGITIMACY.

1643-60 Hexham *Dutch Dict.*, *Onechtschap*, Bastardize, or Illegitimatenesse. **1661** Morgan *Sph. Gentry* II. i. 5 A distinction of illegitimatenesse of Birth.

illegitimation (ɪlɪdʒɪtɪ'meɪʃən). [f. ILLEGITIMATE *a.*, after *legitimation*: cf. obs. F. *illégitimation* in sense 2 (16th c. in Godefroy).]

1. The action of declaring illegitimate; a declaration of illegitimacy.

1553 *Act 1 Mary* Sess. 2. c. 1 §2 In which said two Acts was contained the illegitimations of your most noble person. **1588** Allen *Admon.* 52 The sentence declaratory of Pius Quintus..against the said [Queen] Elizabeth..concerning her illegitimation and vsurpation and inhabillite to the Crowne of England. **1622** Bacon *Hen. VII*, 28 Richard the third had a Resolution..to disable their Issues vpon false and incompetent Pretexts; the one, of Attaindor; the other, of Illegitimation. **1818** W. Taylor in *Monthly Rev.* LXXXVII. 534 To found his title to the crown on the illegitimation, or bastardization of the children of Edward IV.

†**2.** Illegitimate condition: = ILLEGITIMACY.

1594 Parsons *Confer. Success.* II. vi. 134 They proue the illegitimation of these children of the Earle of Hartford, for that it could neuer be lawfully proued that the said earle and the lady Catherin were married. **1665** Sir T. Herbert *Trav.* (1677) 243 To his illegitimation he added incest. **1707** J. Chamberlayne *State Gt. Brit.* II. vi. 101 A Baston, or a Bordure Gobonne, or some Mark of Illegitimation.

illegitimatize (ɪlɪ'dʒɪtɪmətaɪz), *v.* [f. ILLEGITIMATE *a.* + -IZE.] *trans.* = ILLEGITIMATE *v.*

1811 *Chron.* in *Ann. Reg.* 136 Thereby illegitimatizing the children. **1860** Froude *Hist. Eng.* VI. xxx. 100 Until her [Mary's] accession had been sanctioned by Parliament, and the act repealed by which she was illegitimatized.

†**illegitime**, *a.* *Obs. rare.* [a. F. *illégitime* (15th c.), ad. L. *illēgitimus*, f. *il-* (IL-^{2}) + *lēgitimus* LEGITIMATE.] = ILLEGITIMATE *a.*

1502 *Ord. Crysten Men* IV. xxi. (1506) 234 If he were.. bygame, illegittime, or concubinarie. **1669** Gale *Jansenism* 72 This Ordinance is neglected by all as illegitime.

ille'gitimize, *v.* [f. L. *illēgitimus* (see prec.) + -IZE; cf. *legitimize*.] *trans.* = ILLEGITIMATE *v.*

1856 Froude *Hist. Eng.* II. xi. 491 When both his sisters were illegitimized.

illeism ('ɪlɪɪz(ə)m). *nonce-wd.* [f. L. *ille* that man, he: after *egoism*.] Excessive use of the pronoun *he* (either in reference to another person or to oneself in the third person).

1809-10 Coleridge *Friend* (1818) I. 36 For one piece of egotism..there are fifty that steal out in the mask of tuisms and ille-isms. **1817** —— *Biog. Lit.* 4 An *index expurgatorius* of certain well known and ever returning phrases, both introductory and transitional, including the large assortment of modest egotisms and flattering illeisms.

So **'illeist**, one who makes much use of the pronoun *he*, or writes of himself as *he*.

1832 *Blackw. Mag.* XXXII. 241 Your intense egotist cunningly avoids the use of the first personal pronoun. He is, in fact, an Ille-ist.

†**i'llepid**, *a.* *Obs. rare*$^{-0}$. [ad. L. *illepidus* rude, unpleasant, f. *il-* (IL-^{2}) + *lepidus* pleasant, graceful. Cf. OF. *illepide* (Godef.).] (See quots.)

1656 Blount *Glossogr.*, *Illepid*, without delectation or Grace, unpleasant. **1658** Phillips, *Illepid*, dull and unpleasant in conversation.

†**i'llesed**, *ppl. a.* *Obs. rare*$^{-1}$. [f. L. *illæs-us* (see ILLÆSE) + -ED^1.] Uninjured, unimpaired.

1551 W. Copinger in Foxe *A. & M.* (1563) 831/1, In thys my appeale reserued on my behalfe illesed.

illess, *a.*: see ILL-LESS.

i'llevel, *a.* *nonce-wd.* [IL-^{2}.] Not level.

1856 H. Mayhew *Rhine* 107 The little illevel street.

†**i'lleviable**, *a.* *Obs. rare.* [f. IL-^{2} + LEVIABLE.] That cannot be levied or collected.

1650 in Hale *Sheriffs Accompts* (1683) 96 So much of the said Firmes as..are become illeviable. *a* **1676** Hale *Ibid.* vii. 67 Obsolete, illeviable Firmes. **1706** Phillips, *Illeviable*, that cannot be levy'd, rais'd, or recover'd, as *An illeviable Debt*.

ill-faced, -famed, etc.: see ILL- B.

illfare ('ɪlfɛə(r)). [f. ILL *a.* + FARE *sb.*^{1} 7.] The condition of faring or 'getting on' badly; infelicity; adversity; the opposite of *welfare*. (In recent use only as *nonce-wd.*) Used more or less *joc.* in phr. ***the Illfare State*** (opp. *Welfare State*).

c **1300** *Cursor M.* 27680 (Cott. Galba) He has ioy of oþer mens ill fare. **1474** Caxton *Recuyell of Troye* (1892) 169 This was to their vnhapp and ylfare. **1640** Quarles *Enchirid.* I. 25 It much conduces to the dishonor of a King, and the illfare of his Kingdome, to multiply Nobilitie. **1871** Ht. Martineau in *Athenæum* (1879) 31 May 695 Thoughts on the operation of natural religion on human welfare or illfare. **1952** C. Palmer (*title*) The British Socialist Ill-fare State; an examination of the Welfare State. **1962** *Punch* 28 Feb. 352/1 What is the Illfare State?

'ill-'faring, *a.* [f. ILL *adv.* + FARING *ppl. a.*] Faring badly, in bad condition; ill-conditioned. Hence †**,ill-'faringly** *adv.*, in an ill-conditioned manner.

a **1400** *Sir Perc.* 848 Siche ille farande fare. **1580** Sidney *Arcadia* III. Wks. 1725 II. 627 The ill-faring word of farewel. **1589** Puttenham *Eng. Poesie* III. ix. (Arb.) 169 When I consider..how ill faring the Greeke terme would sound in the English eare. *Ibid.* III. xxiii. 281 Another.. spake as ill-faringly in this verse.

ill-fated ('ɪl'feɪtɪd: see ILL- III), *a.*

1. Having or destined to an evil fate.

1710 Pope *Windsor For.* 311 Let softer strains ill-fated Henry mourn. **1805** Wordsw. *Fidelity* viii, The day When this ill-fated Traveller died. **1875** Jowett *Plato* (ed. 2) I. 278 Are not the miserable ill-fated? **1882** J. Taylor *Sc. Covenanters* 29 That ill-fated effort to retrieve the Royal cause.

2. Fraught with or bringing bad fortune.

1715-20 Pope *Iliad* I. 9 Declare, O Muse! in what ill-fated hour Sprung the fierce strife. **1729** T. Cooke *Tales, Proposals*, etc. 26 In an illfated Day Philander led The virgin Charmer to the Vi'let Bed.

ill-faur'd, *a.* *Sc.* = ILL-FAVOURED, q.v.

†**ill-favorited**, *a.* *Obs. rare*$^{-1}$. = ILL-FAVOURED.

1579 G. Harvey *Letter-bk.* 83 The ilfavoritid sprites and divells that nowe so truble and infecte the world.

ill-favoured, -ored ('ɪl'feɪvəd), *a.* Also (*Sc.*) ill-faur't, -faur(e)d, -fawrd, -fa'ard, -fard. [f. ILL *a.* + FAVOUR *sb.* 9 + -ED^2.] Having a bad or unpleasing appearance, aspect, or features; ill-looking, uncomely. (Chiefly of persons.)

1530 Palsgr. 316/1 Ill favoured, *layt.* **1576** Fleming *Panopl. Epist.* 237 A deformed and ylfavoured bodie. **1611** Bible *Gen.* xli. 27 The seuen thin and ill fauoured kine. **1708** Swift *Abol. Christianity* Wks. 1755 II. I. 89 An ill-favoured nose. **1809** in Skinner *Misc. Poetry* 109 (Jam.) Sae proud's I am..O' my attempts to be a bard, And think my muse nae that ill-fawrd. *a* **1810** Tannahill *Poems* (1846) 80 He had an ill-faur't tawtie face. **1840** Dickens *Barn. Rudge* vi, Who is this ill-favoured man?

b. *transf.* Offensive (to some other sense than sight, or to the mind); objectionable.

1552 Latimer *Serm. Lincolnsh.* (1562) 140, I my self.. haue felt such an ylfauored vnwholesom sauor. **1578** Lyte *Dodoens* VI. lxvi. 742 The whole plant is of a strong il-fauoured stinking sauour. **1788** V. Knox *Winter Even.* I. III. iv. 258 These are vulgar, ill-favoured virtues. **1818** Scott *Rob Roy* xviii, Blackguard loons o' excisemen and gaugers.. the ill-fa'ard thieves. **1865** *Pall Mall G.* 4 May 1 Democracy is an ill-favoured word to English ears.

ill-favouredly (ˌɪl'feɪvədlɪ), *adv.* [f. prec. + -LY^2.] In an ill-favoured manner; in a bad or unpleasing way or style.

1545 Ascham *Toxoph.* II. (Arb.) 140 He that shot ilfauouredlye shulde be mocked. **1644** Milton *Areop.* (Arb.) 41 The rare morsell..so ilfavourdly imitated by our inquisiturient Bishops. **1678** Cudworth *Intell. Syst.* I. iv. §18. 310 Men commonly pronouncing Exotick words ill-favouredly. **1724** Ramsay *Tea-t. Misc.* (1733) I. 86 Illfardly wad she crook her mou'.

ill-favouredness (ˌɪl'feɪvədnɪs). [f. as prec. + -NESS.] The quality of being ill-favoured; ugliness, uncomeliness, objectionableness.

1565-73 Cooper *Thesaurus*, *Deformitas*..vncomelinesse, ill fauourednesse. **1571** Golding *Calvin on Ps.* xlv. 17 Although the illfavourednes of the cross darken the glorie of the Church before the world. **1656** Earl Monm. *Advt. fr. Parnass.* 220 Like those glass eyes which squint eyed people wear to honest the ill-favouredness of their faces. **1721** Bailey, *Deformity*, Ugliness, Ill-favouredness.

ill-formed, -friended, etc.: see ILL- B.

†**'illful**, *a.* *Obs. rare.* [f. ILL *sb.* + -FUL.] Full of evil; harmful, pernicious.

1615 T. Adams *White Devill* 38 In many arts, the more skilful the more il-full.

ill-given ('ɪl'gɪv(ə)n), *a.* Now only *Sc.* Also ill-gi'en. Addicted to evil courses or conduct; 'ill-disposed, ill-inclined, malevolent' (Jam.).

a **1568** Ascham *Scholem.* II. (Arb.) 155 Salust was..ill geuen by nature, and made worse by bringing vp. **1819** R. Anderson *Cumberld. Ball.* 159 I's pestert wid an ill-gien weyfe. **1866** Carlyle *Remin.* (1881) I. 256 An ill-given, unserviceable kind of entity.

ill-got ('ɪl'gɒt: see ILL- III), *a.* [f. ILL *adv.* + *got*, pa. pple. of GET *v.*] = next.

1593 Shaks. *3 Hen. VI*, III. ii. 46 Things ill got had ever bad success. **1693** J. Dryden, jun. in *Dryden's Juvenal* xiv. (1697) 352 The Fabled Dragon never guarded more The Golden Fleece, than he his ill-got Store. **1725** Pope *Odyss.* XIV. 107 Of their ill-got spoils possess'd. **1753** A. Murphy *Gray's-Inn Jrnl.* No. 43 ¶4 According to the old Proverb, Ill got, Ill gone. **1848** J. A. Carlyle tr. *Dante's Inferno* XIX, Keep well the ill-got money.

ill-gotten ('ɪl'gɒt(ə)n), *a.* [f. ILL *adv.* + *gotten*, pa. pple. of GET *v.*] Gained by evil means.

1552 Latimer *5th Serm. Lord's Pr.* in *Serm.* (1562) 40 b, Yll gotten goodes. **1668** R. Steele *Husbandman's Calling* v. (1672) 125 The third heir seldom enjoys ill-gotten goods. *a* **1859** Macaulay *Hist. Eng.* xxiii. V. 45 Is compelled to disgorge his ill-gotten gains.

ill-habited, -hearted, etc.: see ILL- B.

ill health, ill-health. [ILL *a.* 7, HEALTH *sb.* 2 a.] An unsound, disordered condition of health; that state of health which is characterized by the presence of some disease or by the imperfect functioning of the physical processes.

1698 J. Locke *Let.* 6 Apr. in H. R. F. Bourne *Life J. Locke* (1876) II. 464 As for writing, my ill-health gives me little heart or opportunity for it. **1717** [see PHILOSOPHICAL *a.* 3]. **1732** Pope *Hor. Sat.* II. ii. 87 Ill health some just indulgence may engage. **1782** Miss Burney *Cecilia* iii. 32 The ill health of her uncle had hitherto prevented her. **1783** Johnson *Let.* 22 Sept. (1892) II. 336 That I have not written sooner, you may impute to absence, to ill-health, to any thing rather than want of regard. **1814** Jane Austen *Mansf. Park* I. ii. 38 Lady Bertram, in consequence of a little ill-health, and a great deal of indolence, gave up the house in town. **1855** Macaulay *Hist. Eng.* III. xi. 63 Danby..under the plea of ill health..withdrew from court. **1911** A. C. Benson *Diary* 31 Aug. (1926) 220 The pictures of her [*sc.* Mrs. Carlyle] in 1854..are hauntingly terrible—the mixture of ill-health and unhappiness very conspicuous. **1931** J. S. Huxley *What dare I Think?* ii. 61 They have..rescued many people from ill-health.

ill humour, 'ill-'humour. [Properly two words: ILL *a.* + HUMOUR *sb.*]

†**1.** A disordered or morbid bodily 'humour' (see HUMOUR *sb.* 2). *Obs.*

a **1568** Ascham *Scholem.* II. (Arb.) 115 Surelie mens bodies be not more full of ill humors, than commonlie mens myndes..be full of fansies. **1665** Boyle *Occas. Refl.* IV. xix. (1848) 281 It would..breed ill Humours and Diseases.

†**2.** An evil or malignant inclination (HUMOUR *sb.* 6 b). *Obs.*

1636 E. Dacres tr. *Machiavel's Disc. Livy* II. xiii. 325 The Romanes having had some sent of this ill humour, that had possessed the Latins.

3. A disagreeable, irascible, or sullen mood or frame of mind (HUMOUR *sb.* 5); crossness, moroseness, sullenness, bad temper. (In this sense often hyphened.)

1748 G. White *Serm.* (MS.), To bear with the ill Humours and Vices of those from whom they have worldly Expectations. **1776** Bentham *Fragm. Govt.* Wks. 1838 I. 230 It is with men that they are in ill-humour, not with laws. *a* **1872** Maurice *Friendship Bks.* i. (1874) 21 Dean Swift.. the best and most perfect specimen of ill-humour.

ill-humoured ('ɪl'hju:məd), *a.* [f. prec. + -ED^2.] Having or showing ill humour (see prec. 3); bad-tempered, morose.

1687 Congreve *Old Bach.* III. x, Love, they say..will.. make illhumoured people good. **1876** Bancroft *Hist. U.S.* VI. xlix. 360 Joseph II overcame his ill-humored demurs.

Hence **,ill-'humouredly** *adv.*, in an ill-humour.

1795 SEWARD *Anecd.* (ed. 2) I. 171 Marguerite ill-humouredly retorted [etc.]. **1859** GEN. P. THOMPSON *Audi Alt.* II. xcix. 89 What is the use of parading this ill-humouredly?

ill-husband *v.*: see ILL- 4.

†**i'lliable,** *a. Obs. rare.* [f. IL-^{2} + LIABLE.] Not liable.

1649 G. DANIEL *Trinarch., Rich. II,* cclxxviii, That the King might Act secure, and be Illyable to other men's Account. *Ibid., Hen. IV,* cxxiii, Whose Station They knew Illyable, to any frame Of Processe.

illiberal (ɪ'lɪbərəl, ɪll-), *a.* (*sb.*) [a. F. *illibéral* (14th c.), ad. L. *illiberālis* mean, sordid, f. *il-* (IL-^{2}) + *liberālis* LIBERAL.]

1. Not befitting or of the nature of a free man; not pertaining to or acquainted with the liberal arts (see LIBERAL), without liberal culture, unscholarly; ill-bred, ungentlemanly, unrefined; base, mean, vulgar, rude, sordid.

1535 STEWART *Cron. Scot.* II. 42 Ane Planctius, quhilk wes ane rycht soft man, Without ingyne or jeopardie in weir .. Illiberall, and richt seindell wes trew. *c* **1590** MARLOWE *Faust.* i. 35 This study fits a mercenary drudge .. Too servile and illiberal for me. **1599** HAKLUYT *Voy.* II. II. 92 Mechanicall & illiberall crafts. *a* **1619** FOTHERBY *Atheom.* II. i. §1 (1622) 172 No Art, neither liberall, nor illiberall. **1641** HINDE *J. Bruen* xxxviii. 120 To celebrate their Festivals with such illiberall plays and sports. **1641** WILKINS *Math. Magick* I. ii. (1707) 5 In Propriety of Speech those Employments alone may be styled Illiberal, which require only some bodily Exercise, as Manufactures, Trades. **1748** CHESTERF. *Lett.* 27 Sept., Every word or phrase you .. cannot find in Caesar, Cicero, Livy, Horace, Virgil, and Ovid, is bad, illiberal Latin. **1751** *Ibid.* 18 Mar., Your hand-writing is one, which is indeed shamefully bad, and illiberal. **1837–9** HALLAM *Hist. Lit.* I. I. v. §32. 352 Most of the youth .. betook themselves to mechanical or other illiberal employments. **1853** RUSKIN *Stones Ven.* II. vi, There should not .. be a trenchant distinction of employment, as between .. men of liberal and illiberal professions. **1875** JOWETT *Plato* (ed. 2) V. 79 No man will be allowed to exercise any illiberal occupation.

transf. **1607** TOPSELL *Serpents* (1658) 604 Serpents have many Epithets given unto them, as illiberal, perfidious, treacherous .. and such like.

2. Not generous in respect to the opinions, rights, or liberty of others; narrow-minded, bigoted; opposed to liberal principles in ecclesiastical, political, or commercial relations.

a **1649** CHAS. I (J.), The charity of most men is grown so cold, and their religion so illiberal. **1713** STEELE *Guardian* No. 1 ¶3 The affinity between all works which are beneficial to mankind is much nearer, than the illiberal arrogance of Scholars will .. allow. **1759** ROBERTSON *Hist. Scot.* II. I. 120 Popery .. of the most bigotted and illiberal kind. **1866** FELTON *Anc. & Mod. Gr.* II. x. 459 The unwise and illiberal policy of the great powers [towards Greece]. **1885** *Law Times* 10 Jan. 181/2 We cannot .. think that any court would put so illiberal a construction upon sect. 7.

3. Not free or generous in giving; stingy.

1623 COCKERAM, *Illiberall,* couetous, base. **1695** WOODWARD *Nat. Hist. Earth* (1702) 257 Earth did not deal out their Nourishment with an over-sparing or illiberal Hand. **1752** MASON *Elfrida* 8 More apt .. to err, In giving mercy's tide too free a course, Than with a thrifty and illiberal hand To circumscribe its channel.

4. *Comb.,* as *illiberal-minded.*

1805 *Simple Narrative* I. 21 His imperious illiberal-minded wife.

B. *sb.* (*nonce-use* from 2.) One who is not liberal in opinions, etc.; one who is opposed to Liberalism in politics.

1818 LADY MORGAN *Autobiogr.* (1859) 1 They all turn *moi, pauvre chétive,* into political capital in the fund of Illiberals. **1827** *Hist. Europe* in *Ann. Reg.* 112/1, I may be a Tory, and an illiberal. **1871** RUSKIN *Fors Clav.* I. i. 6, I am a violent Illiberal; but it does not follow that I must be a Conservative.

Hence **i'lliberalism, i'lliberalness,** illiberality, illiberal principles.

1727 BAILEY vol. II, *Illiberalness,* Niggardliness, Unbountifulness, Meanness of Spirit. **1839** in *Spirit Metropol. Conserv. Press* (1840) II. 370 No real corruption, no real illiberalism, will be tolerated in any administration whatever. **1851** *Blackw. Mag.* Feb. 197 The now fulfilled prophesies of Illiberalism. **1865** *Sat. Rev.* 11 Mar. 276/1 This slough of intolerance, and illiberalism, and servility.

illiberality (ɪlɪbə'rælɪtɪ). [a. F. *illiberalité* (14th c.), ad. L. *illiberālitāt-em*: see prec. and -ITY.] The quality of being illiberal (in the various senses of the adj.); meanness; uncharitableness; niggardliness, stinginess.

1581 MULCASTER *Positions* xxxix. (1887) 206 To be recovered from illiberalitie in trade. **1589** PUTTENHAM *Eng. Poesie* I. xx. (Arb.) 57 Parsimonie and illiberalitie are greater vices in a Prince then in a priuate person. **1607–12** BACON *Ess., Parents & Childr.* (Arb.) 274 The illiberalitye of Parentes in allowance towardes theire Children is an harmefull errour. **1775** SHERIDAN *Rivals* Pref., There will always be found a petulance and illiberality in their remarks. **1831** BREWSTER *Newton* (1855) I. iv. 100 The illiberality of England to her scientific institutions.

illiberalize (ɪ'lɪbərəlaɪz), *v.* [f. ILLIBERAL *a.* + -IZE.] *trans.* To render illiberal.

1807 W. TAYLOR in *Ann. Rev.* V. 568 It illiberalizes science. **1840** MILL *Diss. & Disc., Coleridge* (1859) I. 464 One who is to be dreaded by Liberals lest he should illiberalize the minds of the rising generation.

illiberally (ɪ'lɪbərəlɪ), *adv.* [f. ILLIBERAL *a.* + -LY^2.] In an illiberal manner: see the adj.

c **1611** CHAPMAN *Iliad* III. 378 There is no God given more illiberally To those that serve thee than thyself. **1667** *Decay Chr. Piety* xiv. ¶2 One that had been bountiful only upon surprize and incogitancy, illiberally retracts and contradicts his original design. **1753** CHESTERF. *Lett.* (1792) IV. ccxcix. 19 Nineteen, an age at which most of your countrymen are illiberally getting drunk in Port at the University. **1818** HALLAM *Mid. Ages* (1872) I. 498 The spirit of their administration was not illiberally exclusive.

†**illi'centiate,** *a. Obs. rare*$^{-1}$. [f. IL-^{2} + LICENTIATE.] Unlicensed.

a **1659** *Lady Alimony* I. iii. A iv b, *Tim.* Surly Sir, your design! *Hax.* To ruine your Design, illicentiate Play-wright.

†**illi'centious,** *a. Obs. rare*$^{-1}$. Done without license, unlawful, illegal.

1622 MALYNES *Anc. Law-Merch.* 461 Derogating many illicentious customes which grew by peruersnesse and corruptnesse of nature.

illicit (ɪ'lɪsɪt, ɪll-), *a.* Also 7 -ite. [a. F. *illicite* (14th c.), ad. L. *illicitus,* f. *il-* (IL-^{2}) + *licitus* pa. pple. of *licēre* to be allowed.] Not authorized or allowed; improper, irregular; *esp.* not sanctioned by law, rule, or custom; unlawful, forbidden.

a **1652** J. SMITH *Sel. Disc.* viii. 390 To purge and reform our hearts and all the illicit actions and motions thereof. **1664** H. MORE *Myst. Iniq.* 274 Corrupting Christianity with the illicite Doctrines and practices of Idolatry. **1748** *Anson's Voy.* I. ix. 85 The illicit commerce carried on to the river of Plate. **1806** SURR *Winter in Lond.* (ed. 3) II. 248, I am the offspring of illicit love. **1815** *European Mag.* LXXIII. 154 Between the 6th and 7th bars .. are formed two illicit fifths. **1845** M^{c}CULLOCH *Taxation* II. x. (1852) 365 Illicit distillation is but little prevalent. **1866** GEO. ELIOT *F. Holt* i. (1868) 25 Interested in stories of illicit passion.

b. Of an agent: That does something illegal.

1884 S. DOWELL *Taxes in Eng.* IV. I. i. 5 [This] enabled the illicit manufacturer to compete successfully with the fair trader.

c. *Logic. illicit process*: that form of syllogistic fallacy in which a term not distributed in the premisses is distributed in the conclusion.

1827 WHATELY *Logic* 88 To infer a universal conclusion [from a particular minor premise] would be an illicit process of the minor. **1866** FOWLER *Induct. Logic* (1869) 91 This fallacy is called *illicit process* of the major or minor, according as the term illegitimately distributed in the conclusion is the major or minor term.

Hence **i'llicitly** *adv.,* in an illicit manner. **i'llicitness,** unlawfulness (Todd, 1818).

1812 J. HENRY *Camp. agst. Quebec* 221 Captain Smith skulked thither illicitly. **1856** DOVE *Logic Chr. Faith* IV. ii. §3. 200 They introduce illicitly and unconsciously the idea of *mind.* **1872** YEATS *Growth Comm.* 225 A more profitable trade was illicitly carried on with the Spanish settlements.

†**i'llicitous,** *a. Obs. rare* [f. as ILLICIT + -OUS.] = ILLICIT. Hence †**i'llicitously** *adv.,* unlawfully.

1611 COTGR., *Illicite,* illicitous, vnlawfull. *Illicitement,* illicitously, vnlawfully. *a* **1693** URQUHART *Rabelais* III. xi. 88 That sort of Lottery is .. illicitous.

illigant, var. ILIGANT *a.*

†'**illigate,** *v. Obs. rare.* [f. L. *illigāt-,* ppl. stem of *illigāre* to fetter: see next.] *trans.* To bind or fetter; to bind with a spell.

1658 BROMHALL *Treat. Specters* I. 127 There were two thus illigated for three years space, and then reconciled, and had a very fine child.

†**illi'gation.** *Obs. rare.* [ad. L. *illigātiōn-em,* n. of action from *illigāre* to fetter, entangle, f. *il-* (IL-^{1}) + *ligāre* to bind.] Entanglement.

1727–77 FELTHAM *Resolves* II. xxi. 205 Not apprehending the hardship of others, by reason of the Beckonings and Illigations of pleasure. **1656** BLOUNT *Glossogr., Illigation,* an inwrapping, or intangling.

†**i'llighten,** *v. Obs.* [app. an alteration of ALIGHTEN *v.*^{3}, after *illuminate,* etc.; cf. ENLIGHTEN.] *trans.* To illuminate, enlighten. *lit.* and *fig.* (Freq. in 17th c.)

1555 J. PHILPOT in Coverdale *Lett. Mart.* (1564) 241 The knowledge of God which hath illightned your mynde with the true religion of Christ. **1592** *Greene's Groat's W. Wit* Addr., Wit may .. be termed the worlds goggle-eyde Lampe, which illightning all darkens its owne. **1641** HINDE *J. Bruen* xv. 50 This was the worke of grace, being illightened himselfe to illighten others. **1647** TRAPP *Comm. Col.* iv. 13 A Minister must be like the Sun, that .. illighteneth all round about it. **1693** G. FIRMIN *Rev. Mr Davis's Vind.* ii. 15 The understanding being illightned to see this Christ.

Hence †**i'llightened** *ppl. a.,* †**i'llightening** *vbl. sb.*; also †**i'llightener,** an enlightener.

1597 DANIEL *Civ. Wars* IV. lxxxv, When as th' illightned soule discovers cleere Th' abusing shewes of Sense. **1629** SIR W. MURE *True Crucifixe* 238 Illightened eyes did view the tree of life. **1638** FEATLY *Transub.* 65 The illightner .. of antiquities. **1656** JEANES *Fuln. Christ* 299 For the illightning of any mind, though never so darke.

illimitability (ɪˌlɪmɪtə'bɪlɪtɪ). [f. next + -ITY.] The quality or condition of being illimitable; illimitableness; boundlessness.

1841 *Blackw. Mag.* L. 62 The first and strongest [impression] the stranger wandering through London feels, is the idea of illimitability. **1880** VEITCH *Descartes' Method* Introd. 137 To know one's own limit is to know one's own illimitability.

illimitable (ɪ'lɪmɪtəb(ə)l, ɪll-), *a.* (*sb.*) [f. IL-^{2} + LIMITABLE: cf. F. *illimitable.*] That cannot be limited or bounded; having no determinable limits; limitless, boundless.

1596 SPENSER *Hymn Heav. Love* 57 The heauens illimitable hight. **1634** W. TIRWHYT tr. *Balzac's Lett.* (vol. I.) 198, I might seeme to .. prescribe lawes to what is illimitable. **1725** POPE *Odyss.* xx. 75 Tost thro' the void illimitable space. **1805** FOSTER *Ess.* IV. ii. 137 The attempt to comprehend the illimitable soul. **1840** CARLYLE *Heroes* I. (1841) 13 This huge illimitable whirlwind of Force, which envelops us here. **1871** L. STEPHEN *Playgr. Europe* (1894) 75 An illimitable appetite.

B. *sb.* That which is illimitable; an illimitable thing.

1884 BROWNING *Ferishtah, Plot-culture* 35 Clean-cut from out and off the illimitable. **1895** *Pop. Sci. Monthly* Mar. 677, I see only unbounded space and indefinite time, and within those illimitables a finite world.

i'llimitableness. [f. prec. + -NESS.] The quality of being illimitable; boundlessness.

1845 *Chr. Remembr., Laud* in Mozley *Ess.* (1878) I. 155 Restless illimitableness distresses the age. **1866** *Spectator* 17 Nov. 1282/2 When we apply the epithet infinite to space or time, this notion of perfection changes into that of illimitableness.

illimitably (ɪ'lɪmɪtəblɪ), *adv.* [f. as prec. + -LY^2.] In an illimitable manner; without limitation or possibility of limit.

1755 JOHNSON, *Illimitably.* **1798** *Hist.* in *Ann. Reg.* 88 These [projects] were illimitably extensive. **1866** *Spectator* 17 Nov. 1282/2 Degrees of infinity, i.e. of magnitudes, each of which is illimitably large or small. **1879** L. STEPHEN *Johnson* iv. 96 He talked and drank tea illimitably.

†**i'llimitate,** *a. Obs.* [ad. late L. *illīmitāt-us,* f. *il-* (IL-^{2}) + *līmitāre* to limit, f. *limit-em* LIMIT.] Unlimited, unbounded.

1602 FULBECKE *Pandectes* 11 Alexander the great .. did claime a generall and absolute power indefinite & illimitate ouer all men. **1604** T. WRIGHT *Passions* v. §4. 197 An illimitate and boundlesse sea. **1640** R. BAILLIE *Canterb. Self-convict.* 120 They tell us .. that the power of all true kings is .. absolute and illimitate.

illimitation (ɪlɪmɪ'teɪʃən). *rare.* [f. IL-^{2} + LIMITATION; cf. F. *illimitation.*] The condition or fact of being unlimited; freedom from limitation.

1610 BP. HALL *Apol. Brownists* §23 Their Popes supremacy, infallibility, illimitation. **1836–7** SIR W. HAMILTON *Metaph.* (1877) II. xxxviii. 374 Of these two repugnant opposites, the one is that of Unconditional or Absolute Limitation; the other that of Unconditional or Infinite Illimitation.

illimited (ɪ'lɪmɪtɪd, ɪll-), *a.* [f. IL-^{2} + LIMITED.] Not limited; unlimited; unbounded, unrestrained.

1602 FULBECKE *Pandectes* 61 The vnsatiable couetousnes and illimited encroachment. **1645** E. CALAMY *Indictm. agst. Eng.* 13 Some plead for an illimited toleration of all Religions. **1738** W. WILSON *Def. Reform. Princ. Ch. Scotl.* v. (1769) 318 The King was obliged to take a most illimited oath. **1827** AIKMAN *Hist. Scot.* III. IV. 467 The illimited power of the bishops. **1855** LYNCH *Lett. to Scattered* vi. 81 Human wrath may be blind, illimited, or selfish.

Hence **i'llimitedly** *adv.,* unlimitedly, unboundedly. **i'llimitedness,** the quality of being illimited, unlimited quality or degree.

a **1614** DONNE *Βιαθανατος* (1644) 46 This naturall Law, of Selfe-preservation .. doth not so rigorously, and urgently, and illimitedly binde, but that [etc.]. **1647** CLARENDON *Hist. Reb.* VIII. §86 The absoluteness and illimitedness of his Commission. **1722** WOLLASTON *Relig. Nat.* v. 70 He must exist in the best manner illimitedly and infinitely. **1843** GALLENGA *Italy, Past & Pr.* (1848) I. 111 New faith .. in the illimitedness of our human faculties.

illination, erron. form of ILLINITION.

†**illine,** *v. Obs. rare.* [f. L. *illinĕ-re,* f. *il-* (IL-^{1}) + *linĕ-re* to smear. Cf. obs. F. *illiner* (Cotgr.).] *trans.* To smear, besmear.

1615 CROOKE *Body of Man* 209 A yellow oily humor wherewith the passage .. is illined or smeared.

†**i'llineal,** *a. Obs. rare* [f. IL-^{2} + LINEAL.] Not lineal; 'out of line'.

1647 WARD *Simp. Cobler* 34 Kingdomes .. unsound in their foundations, illineall in their superstructures.

†'**illing,** *vbl. sb. Obs. rare.* [f. ILL *v.* + -ING^1.] **a.** Evil-doing, injuring, harming; speaking ill. **b.** Being or becoming ill; illness.

c **1220** *Bestiary* 419 [The fox] gelt hem here billing raðe wið illing, tetogeð and tetireð hem. *c* **1575** BALFOUR *Practicks* (1754) 600 Of thame that have spokin with Inglishmen in illing of Scotland .. in tressounabill manner. **1719** D'URFEY *Pills* IV. 91 To prevent her own Heart's illing.

illinition (ɪlɪ'nɪʃən). Also erron. **-ation.** [n. of action from L. *illinīre* (Columella, Pliny), late variant of *illinĕre* to smear (see ILLINE).]

1. The smearing or rubbing in or on, of ointment, liniment, or the like. **b.** *concr.* That which is smeared or rubbed in.

1684 tr. *Bonet's Merc. Compit.* XIV. 472 Upon the application or illinition of any fat things, presently Pustules arise. **1822–34** *Good's Study Med.* (ed. 4) IV. 257 A flannel shirt dipped in the oil..continues to be worn, after fresh illinations, till a cure is obtained.

2. *transf.* †**a.** A calcining process, in which metals were 'anointed' with certain solutions (see quot. 1678). *Obs.* **b.** *concr.* A thin crust of extraneous matter formed on the surface of metals; hence, a coating of foreign matter on other substances.

1678 SALMON *Lond. Disp.* VI. viii. 834 Potential Calcination, which is done by Corrosion, is either by Immersion, Amalgamation, Cementation, Fumigation, or Illinition. *Ibid.*, By Illinition, or Anointing, which is done by anointing plates of Metal with the Solution of Sal Niter, Sal Armoniack, Sal Gem, or Common Salt. **1683** PETTUS *Fleta Min.* II. 21 There are other ways of Calcinations..of Metals; viz. by..Illinations. **1796** KIRWAN *Elem. Min.* (ed. 2) I. 165 [Asbestinite] is sometimes disguised by a thin crust or illinition of black manganese. **1811** PINKERTON *Petral.* I. 306 Leaving on broad cloth a farinaceous illinition.

illinium (ɪ'lɪnɪəm). *Chem.* [Named after the University of *Illinois*, where the work reported in quot. 1926 was carried out: see -IUM.] A disused name for the element now called PROMETHIUM.

1926 J. A. HARRIS et al. in *Nature* 5 June 792/2 X-ray analysis confirmed the theory and showed the presence of element number 61 in those fractions... The name assigned to the element is Illinium (Il). **1939** [see FLORENTIUM]. **1947** *Nature* 4 Jan. 8/2 The names 'masurium' and 'illinium' are so firmly rooted in text-books and tables that recent work on artificial isotopes of the elements 43 and 61 is sometimes referred to as the production of species of masurium and illinium. **1951** J. R. PARTINGTON *Gen. & Inorg. Chem.* (ed. 2) xvi. 436 Promethium, an artificial element, fills the place of atomic number 61 missing in the natural rare-earth series, the supposed natural 'illinium' not having been confirmed. **1962** [see FLORENTIUM].

Illinoian (ɪlɪ'nɔɪən), *sb.* and *a.* [f. ILLINOI(S + -AN.] **A.** *sb.* A native or inhabitant of the state of Illinois.

The more usual form is ILLINOISAN.

1835 C. F. HOFFMAN *Winter in West* II. 246 The Yankees ..call us old Illinoians 'Suckers'. **1867** A. D. RICHARDSON *Beyond Mississippi* xi. 132 Most readers have heard Ohioans spoken of as 'Buckeyes',..Illinoians as 'Suckers'.

B. *adj. Geol.* Of, pertaining to, or designating the third Pleistocene glaciation in North America, now generally identified with the Riss glaciation in the Alps. Also *absol.*, the Illinoian glaciation or the deposits it produced.

1896 T. C. CHAMBERLIN in *Jrnl. Geol.* IV. 875 While returning from my last visit to the field in which the Kansan, Illinoian, Iowan, and Wisconsin formations were seen in close succession, I made a memorandum of impressions respecting their relative ages. **1899** *Bull. Geol. Soc. Amer.* X. 116 The color of the Illinoian till, where fresh and unweathered, is quite like that of the Iowan, and the boulders are somewhat similar... Judging by the changes that had been wrought in the surface of the Illinoian before the loess was laid down on it, this sheet of till is at least 5 or 6 times as old as the Iowan. **1934** R. A. DALY *Changing World of Ice Age* i. 29 In the Middle West of North America, five Glacial stages have been proved, and named, from oldest to youngest, the Nebraskan, Kansan, Illinoian, Iowan, and Wisconsin stages... However, the Iowan glaciation may have been merely a phase of the Wisconsin. **1957** J. K. CHARLESWORTH *Quaternary Era* I. xxiii. 466 Lakes were impounded by Illinoian ice in Pennsylvania and Illinois on the older drift and for a short time in Iowa..on the Illinoian drift by the displacement of the Mississippi. *Ibid.* II. l. 1528 F. Leverett..estimates post Early Wisconsin time as 70,000 years and obtains *c.* 200,000 years since the Illinoian, more than 500,000 years since the Kansan, and probably one million years since the Nebraskan. **1970** B. MEARS *Changing Earth* xv. 384/1 A eustatic fall of 500 feet, more or less, seems likely for the Illinoian stage.

Illinois (ɪlɪ'nɔɪ). Also 8 **Il(l)inese.** Pl. **Illinois.** [Amer. Indian.] **1.** *pl.* The members of a confederation of Algonquian Indian tribes formerly inhabiting an area in and around the state of Illinois.

[**1670** *Relations des Jésuites* (1858) 86 Les Ilinois peuples tirans au Sud, ont cinq grands Bourgs.] **1703** tr. *Lahontan's New Voy. N.-Amer.* I. 231 Some Ilinese at Chegakou. **1722** D. COXE *Descr. Carolana* 16 The River of the *Alinouecks*, corruptly by the French call'd *Illinois*. **1766** R. ROGERS *Ponteach* II. ii, This same Chekitan a Captive led The fair Donanta from the Illinois. **1834** J. M. PECK *Gazetteer Illinois* 102 The Illinois, a numerous nation of Indians who were destitute of the cruelty of savages. **1907** F. W. HODGE *Handbk. Amer. Indians* I. 598/2 Seemingly belonging to the Illinois. **1949** *Chicago Tribune* 20 Feb. (Grafic Mag.) 14/4 These Indians called themselves *Illini* (the native word for men) but the French called them *Illinois*.

2. The language of this people.

1703 tr. *Lahontan's New Voy. N. Amer.* I. xvi. 130 About two a clock in the Morning two Men approach'd to our little Camp, and call'd in *Illinese*, that they wanted an Interview. **1933** L. BLOOMFIELD *Lang.* iv. 72 The languages..of the Great Lakes region (..Illinois, Miami, and so on).

3. *attrib.* or quasi-*adj.* Of or pertaining to the Illinois Indians or to the state of Illinois.

1703 tr. *Lahontan's New Voy. N. Amer.* I. 231 Upon the Ilinese Lake, and the adjacent Country. **1764** J. GRANT *Let.* Dec. in *Amer. Hist. Rev.* (1915) XX. 827, I find Your Lordships' have included the Illinois Indians in the Northern District. **1785** T. JEFFERSON *Notes Virginia* (1787) 37 Paccan, or Illinois nut..grows on the Illinois. **1785** H. MARSHALL *Arbustrum Amer.* 69 *Juglans pecan.* The Pecan or Illinois Hickery. This tree is said to grow plenty in the neighborhood of the Illinois river. **1818** M. BIRKBECK *Lett. from Illinois* 104, I am an Illinois farmer. **1857** [see COMBINE *sb.* c]. **1861** *Daily Dispatch* (Richmond, Va.) 1 Aug. 2/3 The consternation in Washington, upon the arrival there of the Illinois Xerxes [*sc.* Abraham Lincoln], was indescribable. **1865** *Trans. Illinois Agric. Soc.* V. 865 The Chick-pea has again been heralded as a valuable acquisition upon the prairies under the name of Illinois coffee. **1948** *Chicago Tribune* 26 June I. 7/8 Starved Rock obtained its name from a legend which says that a band of Illinois Indians perished there in 1769.

Illinoisan (ɪlɪ'nɔɪən, -'ɔɪzən). Also **Illinoisian.** [f. ILLINOIS + -AN.] A native or inhabitant of the state of Illinois. Cf. ILLINOIAN *sb.*

1836 *Public Ledger* (Philadelphia) 14 Oct. (Th. 447), The Illinoisans are called Suckers. *c* **1848** W. WHITMAN in *Amer. Speech* (1961) XXXVI. 297 Illinoisians [are called] *Suckers*. **1855** *N.Y. Tribune* 31 Dec. 6/1, I had told him I was an Illinoisian, and an editor. **1890** W. WHITMAN *Compl. Prose Works* (1892) 504 Abraham Lincoln, familiar, our own, an Illinoisian. **1947** *Illinois: Descriptive & Hist. Guide* 3 He who would describe a typical Illinoisan may well find..that his only valid generalization is that an Illinoisan is one who resides in Illinois. **1948** *Aurora* (Illinois) *Beacon-News* 7 Nov. 3/1 The Illinoisan..boarded the Truman victory special at Union station here to welcome the President home. **1972** *Jrnl. Illinois State Hist. Soc.* LXV. 245 Nor should Illinoisans be surprised that politics is ever present.

illipe(e, var. ILLUPI.

illipsis, erron. for ELLIPSIS.

1749 *Power Pros. Numbers* 63 An Illipsis will often help the Rhythmus, by contracting two Syllables into one, as '*tis*, *don't*: for *it is*, *do not*.

† **'illiquated,** *ppl. a. Obs. rare*⁻⁰. [f. L. *illiquāt-us*, pa. pple. of *illiquāre* to flow into, f. *il-* (IL-[1]) + *liquāre* to melt, *liquārī* to be liquid, to flow.] 'Melted down' (Bailey vol. II, 1727).

† **illi'quation.** *Chem. Obs.* [ad. L. type **illiquātiōn-em*, f. *il-* (IL-[1]) + *liquātio* melting, LIQUATION.] The melting or infusing of one substance into another.

1612 WOODALL *Surg. Mate* Wks. (1653) 271 *Illiquation*, is the commission of terrene bodies with Metalline (as of Lapis cadmia with cuprum) but so as each retains his own substance. **1678** PHILLIPS (ed. 4) *List Barbarous Words, Illiquation*, an Infusing dry things into liquid.

† **i'lliquefact,** *v. Obs.* [f. L. *illiquefact-us* melted, liquefied, f. *il-* (IL-[1]) + *liquefactus* liquified.] *trans.* To liquefy; to melt.

1599 A. M. tr. *Gabelhouer's Bk. Physicke* 257/1 Take Terebinthine..and illiquifactede Hoggesgreace..liquefye them together. **1609** J. DAVIES *Holy Roode* (1876) 15 (D.) See how the sweat fals from His bloodlesse browes, Which doth illiquefact the clotted gore.

illiquid (ɪ'lɪkwɪd, ɪll-), *a. Law.* [f. IL-[2] + LIQUID. Cf. obs. F. *illiquide.*] **a.** Of a right, debt, or claim: Not clear or manifest; not ascertained and constituted either by a written obligation or by a decree of a court.

1694 LD. FOUNTAINHALL in M. P. Brown *Suppl. Decis. Crt. Sess.* (1826) IV. 207 That in such illiquid rights, where they had not obtained possession, it was hard to put an estimate and value thereon. **1880** MUIRHEAD *Gaius* IV. §51 A sort of anticipatory limitation, commonly called taxation, following on an illiquid claim. **1884** *Law Times Rep.* LI. 581/2 To ascertain whether the claim was liquid or illiquid.

b. Of an asset, investment, etc.: not easily or readily realizable. Hence **illi'quidity,** the character of being illiquid.

1913 *Globe* 24 Oct. 6/4 Is cottage property a safe investment for the Reserve Fund? It is an illiquid asset, and a sudden drain on a fund thus locked up might be very inconvenient. **1927** *Glasgow Herald* 18 Apr. 9 The illiquidity of credit in Japan. **1930** *Times* 26 Mar. 26/7 Slow and illiquid loans and investments. **1948** G. CROWTHER *Outl. Money* (rev. ed.) ii. 80 There is some difference between having a variety of small loans in different degrees illiquid, and being closely associated..with one or two large concerns that are known to be doing badly. **1971** *Nature* 5 Feb. 363/2 Some of the officers of the British Association seem to be hoping that they can solve their chronic problem of what is called illiquidity by merging either with the Royal Society of Arts or with the Royal Institution. **1972** *Real Estate Rev.* Winter 27/2 Illiquidity is generally valued at about 1·5 percent to 2·0 percent in most analyses of the capitalization rate, so the equity trust shareholder holds his own quite nicely in the return contest upon closer inspection. **1973** M. WOODHOUSE *Blue Bone* xv. 167 One is liquid or illiquid at awkward times, just as with any other business.

'illish, *a. rare.* [f. ILL *a.* + -ISH.] Somewhat ill or unwell; indisposed.

1637 BRIAN *Pisse-Proph.* (1679) 77 They are not sick..but are illlish or not well. **1679** *Trial of White & Other Jesuits* 21, I saw you in the afternoon when you were a little illish.

illision (ɪ'lɪʒən, ɪll-). Now *rare.* [ad. L. *illīsiōn-em*, n. of action f. *illīdĕre* to strike or dash against.] The action of striking against something.

1603 HOLLAND *Plutarch's Mor.* 1059 Clearches..having set this downe, that the vigour and firmitude of things, is the illision and smiting of fire. **1658** SIR T. BROWNE *Pseud. Ep.* (ed. 4) III. xxvii. 221 Aristotle..affirmeth this sound [humming of bees] to be made by the illision of an inward spirit upon a pellicle or little membrane about the precinct or pectoral division of their body. **1855** MAYNE *Expos. Lex.*, *Illisio*,..an illision.

† **i'llite,** *v. Obs. rare*⁻¹. [f. L. *illit-*, ppl. stem of *illinĕre* (ILLINE).] *trans.* To smear, anoint.

1657 TOMLINSON *Renou's Disp.* 294 Deleates black skars if illited with Oxegall. **1657** *Phys. Dict.*, *Illited*, anointed.

illite ('ɪlaɪt). *Min.* [Named after the state of ILL(INOIS: see -ITE[1].] Any of a group of clay minerals that belong to the mica group and are characterized by a lattice that does not expand through the absorption of water; *esp.* a mineral structurally and chemically similar to muscovite but differing in having more water and silicon and less potassium. Also used as a generic term for these minerals.

1937 R. E. GRIM et al. in *Amer. Mineralogist* XXII. 816 There remains only the alternative of giving a new name to the mica occurring in argillaceous sediments, and the term *illite*, taken from the State of Illinois, is here proposed. It is not proposed as a specific mineral name, but as a general term for the clay mineral constituent of argillaceous sediments belonging to the mica group. **1944** *Mineral. Mag.* XXVII. 60 Illite is not a stable mineral under humid temperate conditions. *Ibid.* 61 According to Fleischer, bravaisite may be the specific mineral species in illites. **1953** R. E. GRIM *Clay Mineral.* iii. 36 Grim, Bray, and Bradley gave the general formula for illites as $(OH)_4K_y(Si_{8-y}{\cdot}Al_y)(Al_4{\cdot}Fe_4{\cdot}Mg_4{\cdot}Mg_6)O_{20}$. In muscovite y is equal to 2, whereas in illite y is less than 2 and frequently equal to 1 to 1·5. According to the formula, illites would include both trioctahedral and dioctahedral types, and no attempt was made to differentiate between biotite and muscovite types of crystallization. At the present time the name illite is generally used, and will be used herein, for clay-mineral micas of both dioctahedral and trioctahedral types and of muscovite and biotite crystallizations. **1957** R. C. MACKENZIE *Differential Thermal Investigation of Clays* x. 260 Studies by Jackson et al. (1952) and Barshad (1954) suggest that illite itself should be considered as an interstratified mineral with mica and montmorillonite layers. **1959** C. S. HURLBUT *Dana's Man. Min.* (ed. 17) v. 463 Illite is the chief constituent in many shales. **1962** W. A. DEER et al. *Rock-Forming Min.* III. 213 The structure of illite is essentially that of a mica in that it contains layers with a plane of octahedrally coordinated cations sandwiched between two inward pointing sheets of linked $(Si, Al)O_4$ tetrahedra. *Ibid.* 214 A less common illite in which sodium is the inter-layer cation is called brammallite (Bannister, 1943). **1972** *Nature* 28 Jan. 220/1 The essential point about the quickclays is that they contain non-swelling clay minerals such as illite, chlorite and vermiculite, but not montmorillonite.

Hence **i'llitic** *a.*, containing, composed of, or characteristic of illite.

1949 KIRK & OTHMER *Encycl. Chem. Technol.* IV. 31 The illite group of minerals occurs abundantly in marine shales and in many soils, particularly in soils derived from illitic shales. **1963** D. W. & E. E. HUMPHRIES tr. *Termier's Erosion & Sedimentation* vi. 153 On the recent volcanic rocks of the northwest coast of Sumatra, H. Erhart (1954) has observed illitic soils between sea level and a height of 4,000 feet. **1972** *Nature* 28 Jan. 220/1 There are also, however, quickclays containing more than 80% particles finer than 2 μm, mainly of illitic nature.

illiteracy (ɪ'lɪtərəsɪ). [f. ILLITERATE: see -ACY.] **a.** The quality or condition of being illiterate; ignorance of letters; unlearnedness, absence of education; *esp.* inability to read and write. Also used more generally in sense: ignorance, lack of understanding (of any pursuit, activity, etc.). Cf. ILLITERATE *a.* (*sb.*)

1660 S. FISHER *Rusticks Alarm* Wks. (1679) 222 They have..nourish'd up Illiteracy itself. **1774** WARTON *Hist. Eng. Poetry* (1775) II. 280 To reform the illiteracy of the clergy. **1782** W. F. MARTYN *Geog. Mag.* I. 24 The illiteracy of Mahomet made it necessary for him to find some more learned associate. **1880** S. C. BUXTON *Hand-bk. Pol. Quest.* 43 That literate voters are induced to plead illiteracy so that the briber may know which way they vote. **1888** *Pall Mall G.* 3 Sept. 7/2 Comparative illiteracy, as tested by marks instead of names in the registers of marriage. **1965** W. LAMB *Posture & Gesture* x. 128 Our 'illiteracy' in physical behaviour communications is related to our puppet-like proclivities. **1970** *Nature* 11 Apr. 96/1 The responsibility for carrying out the act was left to local authorities, many of which are apparently more alarmed at being thought to provide 'sex on the rates' than by the widespread sexual illiteracy in the British population. **1973** *Times Lit. Suppl.* 15 June 660/5 Combating what was not yet called physical illiteracy and teaching girls and women ease and freedom of carriage and movement.

b. An error due to want of learning.

1725 POPE *Shaks.* Pref. (Jod.), The many blunders and illiteracies of the first publishers of his works.

illiteral (ɪ'lɪtərəl, ɪll-), *a. rare.* [f. IL-[2] + LITERAL.] Not literal.

1765 B. DAWSON *Texts on Logos* 251 (L.) A translation most of all unexact and illiteral.

illiterate (ɪ'lɪtərət), *a.* (*sb.*) Also 6 **illitturate,** 6–7 **illeterate,** 7 **illitterate.** [ad. L. *illitterāt-us* (less correctly *illīt-*) unlettered, unwritten, f. *il-* (IL-[2])

+ *litterātus* (*līt-*) furnished with letters, learned, liberally educated (see LITERATE).]

A. *adj.* **1. a.** Of persons: Ignorant of letters or literature; without book-learning or education; unlettered, unlearned; *spec.* (in reference to census returns, voting by ballot papers, etc.) unable to read, i.e. totally illiterate. Also, more generally, characterized by ignorance or lack of learning or subtlety (in any sphere of activity). Cf. ILLITERACY.

1556 LAUDER *Tractate* 453 No more can Iudgis Illitturate Discus ane mater. *a* **1635** NAUNTON *Fragm. Reg.* (Arb.) 50 Neither [was he] illiterate; for he was, as he would often professe, a friend to Sir Philip Sidney, and there are of his now extant, some fragments of his Poem. **1670** W. CLARKE *Nitre* 29 Every illiterate person talks of Brimstone in Lightning. **1748** CHESTERF. *Lett.* (1792) II. clii. 38 The word *illiterate*, in its common acceptation, means a man who is ignorant of those two languages [Greek and Latin]. **1826** E. IRVING *Babylon* II. VIII. 291 The illiterate fishermen of Galilee overcame the wit and learning of Greece and Rome. **1881** *Echo* 13 Jan. 1/5 The illiterate voter appeared rather prominently in the proceedings. **1953** *Ann. Reg. 1952* 397 The pre-war type of speculative builder's house, which by its illiterate design.. had been largely responsible for the poor reputation of English suburban architecture. **1956** C. S. LEWIS *Let.* (1966) 268 One must first distinguish the effect which music has on.. people like me who are musically illiterate and get only the emotional effect. **1962** *Sunday Times* (Colour Suppl.) 10 June 4 The 'traditionalists', who are in the main musically illiterate.

b. Of things: Characterized by or showing ignorance of letters, or absence of learning or education; unlearned, unpolished.

1597 A. M. tr. *Guillemeau's Fr. Chirurg.* * 6 b, The harshnes of my illeterate and rude stile. **1621** BURTON *Anat. Mel.* I. ii. III. xv. (1651) 134 The Civil Law with us.. an illiterate and barbarous Study. **1781** GIBBON *Decl. & F.* II. 75 The disadvantage of an illiterate education. **1870** MAX MÜLLER *Sc. Relig.* (1873) 102 The.. crowd of bookless or illiterate religions.

2. In sense of L. *illĭtterātus*: Unfurnished with letters, not written upon; not expressed in words; unwritten; inarticulate. *rare.*

1645 MILTON *Tetrach.* (1851) 198 Confidently to those who have read good books, and to those whose reason is not an illiterate booke to themselves I appeale. **1715** tr. *C'tess D'Aunoy's Wks.* 428 All good Council we refuse, And our Illiterate Sorrows only bear. **1888** E. PEACOCK in *Cath. Househ.* 18 Aug. 11/1 Some few old bells.. are without any inscription, but these 'illiterate' bells are very rare.

B. *sb.* An illiterate, unlearned, or uneducated person; *spec.* (in reference to census or polling returns, etc.), a person unable to read.

1628 WITHER *Brit. Rememb.* v. 1737 Not as a weakling, or illiterate. **1710** STEELE *Tatler* No. 200 ¶3 There is no manner of Competition between a Man of Liberal Education and an Illiterate. **1865** *Pall Mall G.* 13 Sept. 4/1 We have been told that the intellectual tests we have introduced into our army will exclude from it the dashing illiterates whose stout hearts and strong thews and sinews made it what it was under the Duke. **1883** *Athenæum* 3 Feb. 152/2 Regarding the number of 'cannot reads'.. Iowa is the 'banner State', having out of its total population but 2·4 per cent. of illiterates. **1893** *Times* 3 Aug. 7/3 [He] stated that in Ireland the illiterates were 21 per cent. of the electors.

† **i'lliterated**, *a. Obs.* [f. as prec. + -ED¹.] = prec. 1.

1589 NASHE *Pref. Greene's Menaphon* A iij b, Our vnexperienced and illiterated Punies. **1621** VENNER *Tobacco* in *Baths of Bathe* (1650) 405 Apothecaries and other base illiterated Empericks.

i'lliterately, *adv.* [f. ILLITERATE + -LY².] In an illiterate, unlettered, or unlearned manner.

1684 N. S. *Crit. Enq. Edit. Bible* iv. 23 Those things.. with which the Jews, half asleep, are illiterately contented. *a* **1743** SAVAGE *To John Powell* 47 To unread 'squires illiterately gay; Among the learn'd, as learned full as they.

i'lliterateness. [f. as prec. + -NESS.] The quality or condition of being illiterate; want of learning or education; illiteracy.

1631 R. BYFIELD *Doctr. Sabb.* *, The illiteratenesse and vanitie of the Title. **1748** RICHARDSON *Clarissa* (1811) IV. xxix. 161 The extreme illiterateness and indocility of this maid are surprising. **1865** RUSKIN *Sesame* 103 Childish illiterateness, and want of education in the most ordinary habits of thought.

‖ **illiterati** (ɪlɪtəˈrɑːtɪ, -ˈeɪtaɪ), *sb. pl.* [ad. L. *illitterātī*, pl. of *illitterātus*.] Illiterate, unlearned, or uneducated people. Cf. ILLITERATE *sb.*

1788 H. WALPOLE *Let.* 4 July (1905) XIV. 51 A lower species, indeed, is that of the scribes.. who every night compose a journal for the satisfaction of such *illiterati*. **1822** *Blackw. Mag.* XI. 608 Ye're the most tinkler-tongued pack of illiterati. **1962** *Listener* 22 Nov. 877/1 Weekly periodicals for the younger *illiterati*.

illiterature (ɪˈlɪtərətjʊə(r)). [f. ILLITERATE, after *literature*. Cf. F. *illittérature* (Littré).] Want of learning; illiterateness, illiteracy.

1592 R. D. *Hypnerotomachia* 18 b, The cause.. doth proceed from ignorance, and hath his beginning from illiterature. **1602** WARNER *Alb. Eng.* Epit. (1612) 399 The Obstinacie and Illiterature of the shallow people. **1726** AYLIFFE *Parergon* 208 The more usual Causes of this Deprivation are.. Illiterature, or Inability for the Discharge of that Sacred Function, Irreligion [etc.]. **1844** S. R. MAITLAND *Dark Ages* 11 Such regal curiosities of literature, or illiterature, would have been highly interesting. **1866** *Pall Mall G.* 31 May 4 It cannot efface his antecedents as a representative of illiterature.

† **i'llitered**, *a. Obs. rare*⁻¹. [f. *illiterate*, with Eng. suffix *-ed*, as in *lettered*.] Illiterate, unlettered.

1612 T. TAYLOR *Comm. Titus* i. 9 Rude and illitered men.

† **i'llition.** *Obs.* [ad. L. type **illitiōn-em*, n. of action f. *illinĕre* (see ILLINE).] Smearing, anointing.

1657 TOMLINSON *Renou's Disp.* 318 In drink or illition it confers against the bitings of Scorpions. **1855** MAYNE, *Illitio*,.. old term for the process of anointing; illition.

ill-judge *v.*: see ILL- 4.

ill-judged (ˈɪlˈdʒʌdʒd: see ILL- III), *a.* Done without judgement, injudicious, unwise.

1717 GARTH *Ovid's Met.* Pref. (1732) **** ij b, Nor do I remember he has err'd above once by ill-judg'd Superfluity. **1769** *Junius Lett.* xxxv. 155 To pay a very ill-judged compliment. **1820** W. IRVING *Sketch Bk.* (1859) 40 Recrimination on our part would be equally ill-judged. **1828** TYTLER *Hist. Scot.* (1864) I. 53 An ill-judged economy.

'ill-'judging, *a.* [f. ILL *adv.* + *judging*, pres. pple. of JUDGE *v.*]

1. Judging adversely or malevolently.

a **1715** WYCHERLEY *Consol. Cuckolds* Wks. (1728) II. 166 Injurious, spightful, and ill-judging Town. **1725** POPE *Odyss.* XVIII. 422 Thy ill-judging thoughts the brave disgrace.

2. Judging faultily or mistakenly; uncritical; injudicious.

a **1684** ROSCOMMON *Prospect of Death* iv, To their ill Judging Pallate sweet. **1717** PRIOR *Alma* I. 64 Our ill-judging wives and daughters Mistake small beer for citron waters. **1838–42** ARNOLD *Hist. Rome* II. xxxv. 415 This noble people rejected with indignation the proposal of some ill-judging orators.

ill-languaged, -lettered: see ILL- B.

ill-less, illess (ˈɪllɪs), *a. Sc.* [f. ILL *sb.* + -LESS.] Free from ill; having no evil designs; harmless, innocent.

a **1670** SPALDING *Troub. Chas. I* (1829) I. 334 His majestie, as a most gracious illess prince, haveing no mind of such plotts. **1823** GALT *Entail.* I. viii. 62 The illess laddie. **1823** G. BEATTIE *Jamie West* in *Life* (1863) 296 Poor ill-less creature!

ill-liking, -lived: see ILL- B.

† **ill-looked** (ˈɪlˈlʊkt), *a. Obs.* Also 7 **ill-lookt.** [f. ILL *a.* + LOOK *sb.* + -ED².] Having an evil aspect or evil looks; ill-looking, ugly. (Chiefly of persons.)

1636 MASSINGER *Bashf. Lover* III. iii, Ill-looked devil, Tie up thy bloody tongue! **1722** DE FOE *Col. Jack* (1840) 7 A surly ill-looked.. boy. **1821** SCOTT *Kenilw.* xxix, A huge, ill-made and ill-looked fellow.

ill-looking (ˈɪlˈlʊkɪŋ), *a.* [f. ILL *a.* or *adv.* + *looking*, pres. pple. of LOOK *v.*] Of evil or repulsive appearance, ugly; the opposite of *good-looking*. (Chiefly of persons.)

1633 FORD *Broken H.* II. i, Son of a cat, ill-looking hounds-head. **1725** DE FOE *Voy. round World* (1840) 101 Strange, ugly, ill-looking fellows. **1840** DICKENS *Barn. Rudge* vii, She was not absolutely ill-looking.

Hence ˌ**ill-'lookingness.**

1796 COLERIDGE *Lett.* (1895) 209 Laugh in the faces of gloom and ill-lookingness.

ill luck, 'ill-'luck. [ILL *a.* 5 + LUCK *sb.*] Bad or unfavourable luck; bad fortune, misfortune.

1548 HALL *Chron.*, *Edw. IV* 203 This good chaunce happed to kynge Edward, by the yll lucke of kynge Henry. **1598** SHAKS. *Merry W.* v. v. 120 Sir Iohn, we haue had ill lucke; wee could neuer meete. **1781** MAD. D'ARBLAY *Dairy* 14 Sept., He.. had a run of ill-luck. **1791** 'G. GAMBADO' *Ann. Horsem.* ix. (1809) 106 As ill luck would have it, the curb broke. **1844** DISRAELI *Coningsby* III. iv, Who always lamented his ill-luck.

attrib. **1634** MILTON *Comus* 845 Helping all urchin-blasts, and ill-luck signs.

ill-mannered (ˈɪlˈmænəd), *a.* [f. ILL *a.* + MANNER *sb.* + -ED².] Having or showing bad manners; unmannerly, rude. (Of persons, their actions, etc.)

1422 tr. *Secreta Secret.*, *Priv. Priv.* (E.E.T.S.) 226 Tho that haue the flesshe of the brestis lytill and dry bene ille-ymanerite and bene lykenyd to apys. **1573** J. SANFORD *Hours Recreat.* (1576) 175 A faire yong man, but yll mannered. **1623** MASSINGER *Bondman* v. iii, *C.* You are foul-mouthed. *A.* Ill-mannered too. **1681** DRYDEN *Span. Friar* v. ii, Curb your ill-mannered zeal. **1897** *Daily News* 20 May 7/1 Our Royal family are getting a little tired of the well-meant, but at the same time ill-mannered, homage of well-dressed crowds.

Hence ˌ**ill-'manneredly** *adv.*, in an unmannerly way, rudely. Also ˌ**ill-'mannerly** *a.*, unmannerly.

1663 PEPYS *Diary* 21 Mar., The worst that I ever said was that that was insolently or ill-mannerdly spoken. **1840** J. H. NEWMAN *Lett.* (1891) I. 426 Then I bethought myself, 'How ill-mannerly!'

ill-meaning, -minded, etc.: see ILL- B.

ill nature, 'ill-'nature. [ILL *a.* + NATURE.] Malevolent disposition or character; unkindly feeling; churlishness, spitefulness.

1691 WOOD *Life* 25 June (O.H.S.) III. 365 He was told.. that a great deal of ill nature was expressed in my book. **1704** SWIFT *T. Tub* Apol., If good and ill nature equally operated on mankind. **1861** DUTTON COOK *P. Foster's D.* i, Why need we barter ill-nature with each other?

ill-natured (ˈɪlˈneɪtjʊəd), *a.* [f. prec. + -ED².]

† **1.** Of evil or bad nature or character; malignant. *Obs.*

1645 FULLER *Good Th. in Bad T.* (1841) 32 Must the earth.. be sad, because some ill-natured star is sullen? **1665** NEEDHAM *Medela Medic.* 261 A good humor.. drawn out of the Bodie by common, ill-natur'd Purgers. **1775** NOURSE in *Phil. Trans.* LXVI. 433 The wound.. was more inflamed; and the edges of it looked thick and ill-natured. *a* **1788** POTT *Chirurg. Wks.* II. 449 An ill-natured fungus.

2. Of evil disposition; having, or showing, malevolent character or feeling; unkindly, churlish, spiteful. (Of persons, their actions, etc.)

1635–56 COWLEY *Davideis* I. 562 Ah cruel Father, whose ill-natur'd Rage Neither thy Worth, nor Marriage can asswage! **1668** WILKINS *Real Char.* Ep. b ij b, Some Ignorant and ill-natured men.. would have exposed them to contempt and ruine. *a* **1704** T. BROWN *Eng. Satire* Wks. 1730 I. 29 My lord Rochester was always witty, and always very illnatur'd. **1865** MISS MULOCK *Christian's Mistake* v. 111 The world is filled, not.. with only bad and good, but with an intermediate race which is merely ill-natured. **1869** TROLLOPE *He Knew* etc. xvi. 126 People say such ill-natured things.

b. Irritable in temper; peevish, cross. *Sc.*

1825–80 JAMIESON s.v., He has a very kind heart; but O! it's hard to live wi' him, he's sae ill-natured. **1843** BETHUNE *Sc. Fireside Stor.* 80 I'm aye ill-natured when I think that you had some hand in driving my best.. friend, from the house in which she was born and bred.

Hence ˌ**ill-'naturedly** *adv.*, in an ill-natured manner; ˌ**ill-'naturedness** (*rare*), churlishness.

1654 WHITLOCK *Zootomia* 486 That Soule hath.. some jarring ill-naturednesse. **1683** VILLIERS (Dk. Buckhm.) *Rehearsal* I. (ed. 4) 7 Phoo, Pox, That's ill natur'dly done of 'em. **1865** *Cornh. Mag.* Oct. 404 After all they may not mean them ill-naturedly.

illness (ˈɪlnɪs). [f. ILL *a.* + -NESS.] The quality or condition of being ill (in various senses).

† **1.** Bad moral quality, condition, or character; wickedness, depravity; evil conduct; badness. *Obs.*

c **1500** *Melusine* 261 That we were consentyng to the ylnesse & dysobedyence of Claude ayenst our souerayne lord naturel, your fader. **1553** LATIMER *Serm. Lincoln* ix. 148 When we doe ill, we shall receiue our rewarde for our ilnes. **1605** SHAKS. *Macb.* I. v. 21 Thou.. Art not without Ambition, but without The illnesse should attend it. **1690** NORRIS *Beatitudes* (1694) I. 81 Besides its own proper Illness, 'tis farther to be detested upon the Scandal of its Parentage. **1718** PRIDEAUX *Connect. O. & N. Test.* II. II. 75 The endangering of the whole Jewish State by the illness of his Conduct.

† **2.** Unpleasantness, disagreeableness; troublesomeness; hurtfulness, noxiousness; badness. *Obs.*

1595 MAYNARDE *Drake's Voy.* (Hakluyt Soc.) 16 Wearied with the ilnes of the waye. **1606** THOMAS *Dict.* s.v. *Inconsonantia*, By reason of their vnaptnes and illnesse of sound, when two vowels or letters can not be pronounced. **1690** LOCKE *Hum. Und.* II. xxi. (1695) 142 By the darkness of the Night, or illness of the Weather. **1718** BERKELEY *Jrnl. Tour Italy* 12 Apr., Wks. 1871 IV. 593 Land flat, marshy, hardly inhabited for the illness of the air.

3. Bad or unhealthy condition of the body (or, formerly, of some part of it); the condition of being ill (ILL *a.* 8); disease, ailment, sickness, malady. Also with *an* and *pl.* (The only current modern sense, *badness* being now used in the other senses.)

1689–90 TEMPLE *Ess.*, *Health & Long Life* Wks. 1731 I. 184 Rue is of excellent Use for all Illness of the Stomach. **1692** — *Mem.* 1672–79 (R.), While his illness lasted and the event was doubtful, all was in suspence. **1703** ROWE *Fair Penit.* I. i. 323 They told me you had felt some sudden Illness; Where are you sick? **1776** GIBBON *Decl. & F.* I. xiii. 392 From the inclemency of the weather, and the fatigue of the journey, he soon contracted a slow illness. **1838** LOCKHART *Scott* lxxx, In the family circle Sir Walter seldom spoke of his illness at all. **1875** JOWETT *Plato* (ed. 2) III. 280 Athletes.. are liable to most dangerous illnesses if they depart.. from their customary regimen.

† **i'llocable**, *a. Obs. rare*⁻⁰. [ad. L. *illocābil-is* that cannot be disposed of in marriage, f. *il-* (IL-²) + *locāre* to give in marriage, to let, hire: see -BLE.] 'That cannot be hired or placed out' (Bailey 1721).

illocal (ɪˈləʊkəl, ɪll-), *a.* [ad. late L. *illocāl-is*, f. *il-* (IL-²) + *locālis* LOCAL.]

1. Not local, having no place or location in space.

1601 DEACON & WALKER *Spirits & Divels* 93 They are not most simple, most infinite, illocal, nor omnipotent powers. **1678** CUDWORTH *Intell. Syst.* I. v. 783 To suppose these finite and particular Beings to be thus illocal and immoveable. **1893** FAIRBAIRN *Christ in Mod. Theol.* II. II. iii. 355 His miraculous power is illocal and universal.

† **2.** Out of place, misplaced. *Obs. nonce-use.*

1804 Anna Seward *Lett.* (1811) VI. 180 Not to be considered as impertinent, or (if I may be allowed to coin a word, which is lawfully compounded) illocal.

Hence **i'llocally** *adv.*, in an illocal manner; without reference to place or location.

1678 Cudworth *Intell. Syst.* I. v. 776 It is indivisibly, and unmultipliedly, and illocally, there..present with that which is naturally divisible, and multipliable, and in a place.

illocality (ɪləʊ'kælɪtɪ). [f. ILLOCAL + -ITY.] The quality or condition of being illocal.

1678 Cudworth *Intell. Syst.* I. v. 783 The Fourth and Last Objection, against Incorporeal and Vnextended Substance, is from that Illocality, and Immobility, (which will follow thereupon), of Humane Souls. **1768–74** Tucker *Lt. Nat.* (1852) I. 310 The notion of illocality is at least as old as Aristotle. **1857–8** Sears *Athan.* II. viii. (1859) 178 The early Lutheran divines..describe the Lord's post-resurrection body as endowed with the qualities of 'impalpability, invisibility, and illocality'.

i'llocomotive, *a. nonce-wd.* [See IL-².] Not locomotive, not moving readily.

1835 *New Monthly Mag.* XLIV. 464 To cast the slough of this expensive and il-locomotive humanity, and find yourself afloat with all the necessary apparatus of life.

illocution (ɪləʊ'kjuːʃən). *Philos.* [f. IL-¹ + LOCUTION.] An act such as ordering, warning, undertaking, performed in saying something. Hence **illo'cutionary** *a.*

1955 J. L. Austin *How to do Things with Words* (1962) viii. 99, I shall refer to the doctrine of the different types of function of language..as the doctrine of 'illocutionary forces'. *Ibid.* 101 Act (B) or Illocution: He urged (or advised, ordered, &c.) me to shoot her. *Ibid.* ix. 109 It is the distinction between illocutions and perlocutions which seems likeliest to give trouble. *Ibid.* 113 We must avoid the idea..that the illocutionary act is a *consequence* of the locutionary act. **1955** [see EO IPSO *advb. phr.*]. **1963** M. Furberg (*title*) Locutionary and illocutionary acts. **1964** *Philos. Rev.* LXXIII. 58 Describing and evaluating..are only two among hundreds of kinds of illocutionary force. **1972** J. Rawls *Theory of Justice* §62. 406 Nor do I oppose the view that a certain illocutionary force is central to 'good'. **1973** *Times Lit. Suppl.* 5 Oct. 1161/5 The illocutionary act was the act performed by a speaker *in* saying something, such as the act of asking or answering a question.

illogic (ɪ'lɒdʒɪk, ɪll-). [f. IL-² + LOGIC, after next.] The opposite or reverse of logic; want of logic, illogicalness.

1856 J. Skelton in *Edin. Ess.* 88 An article pervaded by the fervid illogic of Mr. Kingsley's mind. **1887** *Pall Mall G.* 1 Apr. 4 There is..one delicious bit of logic—or rather illogic—in this morning's chorus. **1889** *Sat. Rev.* 7 Dec., The illogic of the official position is clear. **1955** *Bull. Atomic Sci.* Apr. 131/1 So there was no illogic or softheadedness in the Commission's concern about the dangers inherent in the investigative process or in clearance determinations. **1965** *Sunday Times* (Colour Suppl.) 23 May 21/1 There's no room for illogic in an Ellery Queen mystery. **1972** *Nature* 1 Sept. 54/2 With the same illogic with which the Englishman will eat cow but not dog, will hang game but not chicken.

illogical (ɪ'lɒdʒɪkəl, ɪll-), *a.* [f. IL-² + LOGICAL.] Not logical; devoid of or contrary to logic; ignorant or negligent of the principles of sound reasoning.

1588 Fraunce *Lawiers Log.* I. xii. 56b, Illogicall lawyers who thinke it a fruiteles poynt of superfluous curiositie to understand the woords of a mans owne profession. **1663** Cowley *Verses & Ess., Shortness of Life* (1669) 137 What is there among the actions of Beasts so illogical and repugnant to Reason? **1788** *Warburton's Div. Legat.* III. iv. Wks. II. 95 Though their principles were often unnatural, their conclusions were rarely illogical. **1850** Kingsley *Alt. Locke* i. (1876) 14 A foolish and illogical antipathy.

illogicality (ɪlɒdʒɪ'kælɪtɪ). [f. prec. + -ITY.] Illogical quality or character; want of logic or sound reasoning, illogicalness; unreasonableness. Also with *pl.* an instance of this.

1830 *Blackw. Mag.* XXVIII. 874 The utter illogicality of any argument drawn from their misery. **1873** H. Spencer *Study Sociol.* xvi. (1877) 396 The illogicalities and absurdities to be found..in current opinions. **1882** *Athenæum* 15 July 72/1 Another instance of unpoetic illogicality.

illogically (ɪ'lɒdʒɪkəlɪ), *adv.* [f. prec. + -LY².] In an illogical manner; without reference or recourse to logical reasoning.

1660 R. Coke *Justice Vind.* 54 They..most illogically confound the relations of agencie and patiencie in the same subject. **1752** Warburton *Serm.* xiii. Wks. IX. (R.), He would infer, and not illogically on such a..Principle, that [etc.]. **1869** *Spectator* 24 July 861 The affair..was settled English fashion, illogically and stupidly, but finally.

i'llogicalness. [f. as prec. + -NESS.] Illogical quality or character; illogicality.

1639 Hammond *Serm., Pastors Motto* Wks. 1683 IV. 546 The illogicalness of the inference. **1683** O. U. *Parish Churches no Conventicles* 7 We may plainly see the Illogicalness of his Arguing. **1890** *Daily News* 10 Mar. 5/3 That curious illogicalness which the rural magisterial mind is sometimes 'very cunning in'.

illo'gician. *nonce-wd.* [f. IL-² + LOGICIAN.] The reverse of a logician; an illogical reasoner.

1884 A. Birrell *Obiter Dicta* Ser. I. 182 The baffled illogician, persecuted in one position, flees into another.

illogicity (ɪləʊ'dʒɪsɪtɪ). *rare.* [f. IL-² + LOGIC + -ITY. Cf. F. *illogicité.*] Illogicalness, illogicality.

1886 *Daily Tel.* 9 Apr. 5/1 The measure..is pervaded by one obvious illogicity.

ill-omened ('ɪl'əʊmɛnd), *a.* [parasynth. f. *ill omen* + -ED².] Having or attended by bad omens; ill-starred; inauspicious.

1685 Dryden *Thren. August.* 48 Soon as the ill-omened rumour reached his ear. **1738** Glover *Leonidas* II. 285 Which you exact from these ill-omen'd lips. **1832** Lytton *Eugene A.* I. iv, Without the porch..stood the ill-omened traveller. **1884** Mrs. C. Praed *Zero* xi, My blessing might be ill-omened.

illoricated (ɪ'lɒrɪkeɪtɪd, ɪll-), *a. Zool.* [f. IL-² + LORICATED.] Without a lorica or hard shell-like covering. So **i'lloricate** *a.*

1861 J. Hogg *Microsc.* II. ii. (ed. 5) 294 These are designated illoricated, which means shell-less.

illote (ɪ'ləʊt, ɪll-), *a.* [ad. L. *illōt-us.*] Unwashed.

1845 Ford *Handbk. Spain* I. 62 The cutaneous stucco by which his own illote carcass is Roman cemented.

illow, obs. var. of HILLO.

1688 R. Holme *Armoury* II. ix. 186/2 We say..Illow, Illow, there, there to the Grey-hound..when we encourage them to follow their chase.

illoyal (ɪ'lɔɪəl, ɪll-), *a.* [f. IL-² + LOYAL.] Not loyal; unloyal, disloyal.

1626 in Rushw. *Hist. Coll.* (1659) I. 397 The voice had nothing undutiful, or illoyal in it. *c* **1630** *App.* ibid. I. 34 Routs, Riots, illoyal assemblies. *c* **1694** D'Urfey *Pills* (1719) III. 77 Which made some call him Jacobite, Or otherwise Illoyal.

So **i'lloyalty**, disloyalty.

1882 in *Standard* 25 Sept. 3/1 (transl. Let. of Bismarck) A piece of cowardice and illoyalty.

ill-placed ('ɪl'pleɪst: see ILL- III), *a.* **a.** Badly placed or situated. **b.** Misplaced, that is 'out of place', inopportune.

1655 H. Vaughan *Silex Scint.* I. *Mount of Olives* i, Such ill-plac'd wit. **1662** Gerbier *Princ.* 14 A Pallace, like Cardinal Wolseyes ill-placed one..on a low ground by the River side. *a* **1797** H. Walpole *Mem. Geo. II* (1847) I. v. 115 Awkward and ill-placed panegyrics. **1832** Lytton *Eugene A.* I. x, An ill-placed and ill-requited attachment.

ill-scraped, -seeming: see ILL- B.

'ill-'seasoned, *a.* **a.** Badly seasoned or flavoured. **b.** Unseasonable.

1612 Drayton *Poly-olb.* xviii. 300 Some, his ill-seasond mouth that wisely vnderstood. **1640** Habington *Castara* III. (Arb.) 138 Oreflowed by an ill season'd raine. **1843** Judge Coleridge in *Arnold's Life* (1844) I. i. 20 So acute a perception of what was ill-seasoned, or irrelevant.

'ill-'set, *a.* [f. ILL *adv.* + SET *ppl. a.*]

1. Badly set or placed; in quot. 1622, in reference to type-setting; in quot. 1660 *fig.*

1622 Middleton *Changeling* II. i. (1653) C iv b, Like an ill set book, Whose faults might prove as big as half the volume. **1660** R. Coke *Power & Subj.* 130 Ignorance, and an ill-set Conscience, excuseth no more from doing what he ought.

2. 'Evil-disposed, ill-conditioned, having evil propensities' (Jam.). *Sc.*

1776 C. Keith *Farmer's Ha'* xxxviii. (Jam.), Auld luckie cries: 'Ye're o'er ill set; As ye'd hae measure, ye sud met'.

ill-shaped, -shapen: see ILL- B.

ill-sorted ('ɪl'sɔːtɪd: see ILL- III), *a.* [f. ILL *adv.* + *sorted*, pa. pple. of SORT *v.*]

1. Badly assorted or arranged; ill-matched.

1691 Norris *Pract. Disc.* 217 Without this, the Harmony of the Universe would be very defective, and its parts disproportionate and ill-sorted. **1725** Watts *Logic* IV. ii. §3 Ideas ill-joined, ill-sorted, or ill-disposed. **1755** Smollett *Quix.* (1803) II. 131 His ill-sorted armour. **1819** Byron *Juan* I. li, He and his wife were an ill-sorted pair.

2. Badly suited; put 'out of sorts'; displeased, 'upset'. *Sc.*

1815 Scott *Guy M.* xlv, Ye'll be ill-sorted to hear that he's like to be in the prison at Portanferry.

ill-speak *v.*: see ILL- B.

ill-starred ('ɪl'stɑːd), *a.* [f. ILL *a.* + STAR *sb.* + -ED².] Born under, or having one's fortunes governed by, an evil star (according to astrological belief); unfortunate, unlucky, ill-fated.

1604 Shaks. *Oth.* v. ii. 272 How dost thou looke now? Oh ill-Starr'd wench, Pale as thy Smocke. *a* **1763** Shenstone *Elegies* vi. 31 Ill-starr'd birds, that, listening, not admir'd. **1867** Howells *Ital. Journ.* 268 That ill-starred prince.

b. *transf.* Of actions, etc.: Disastrous.

c **1704** Prior *Henry & Emma* 593 A useless sorrow, and an ill-starr'd love. **1835** Miss Sedgwick *Linwoods* (1873) I. 143 The worst ill luck in life..is an ill-starred marriage.

ill-tempered ('ɪl'tɛmpəd), *a.* [partly f. ILL *adv.* + *tempered*, pa. pple. of TEMPER *v.*; partly parasynth. f. *ill temper* + -ED².]

†**1.** Having the 'humours' or elements badly 'tempered' or mixed; having a disordered 'temper' or constitution; in an unhealthy condition, distempered; in quot. 1661, unwholesome. *Obs.*

1601 Shaks. *Jul. C.* IV. iii. 115 When greefe and blood ill temper'd, vexeth him. **1661** Lovell *Hist. Anim. & Min.* 67 The liver [of a hart] is very bad, and ill tempered. **1664** Pepys *Diary* 28 June, This day put on a half-shirt..it being very hot; and yet so ill-tempered am I grown, that I am afeared I shall catch cold. **1685** tr. *Gracian's Courtiers Orac.* 135 The Paradox is a proof of an ill-tempered mind.

2. Having a bad temper; ill-conditioned; morose, cross, peevish. (In first quot. scarcely distinguishable from 1.)

1601 Shaks. *Jul. C.* IV. iii. 116 When I spoke that, I was ill temper'd too. **1825** J. Neal *Bro. Jonathan* II. 64 You cross-grained, ill-tempered, good for nothing whelp. **1849** James *Woodman* ii, I could trust her well enough, cross and ill-tempered as she is.

Hence **ˌill-'temperedly** *adv.*, in an ill-tempered manner; **ˌill-'temperedness**, the quality or condition of being ill-tempered (in quot. used *arch.*; cf. sense 1 above).

1860 Ruskin *Mod. Paint.* V. VI. viii. §11 The ruggedness and ill-temperedness [of a branch]. **1894** E. F. Benson *Dodo* 302 Remonstrate hastily and ill-temperedly.

illth (ɪlθ). [f. ILL *a.* + -TH¹.] Used by and after Ruskin as the reverse of *wealth* in the sense of 'well-being': Ill-being.

1860 Ruskin *Unto this Last* iv. 126 As mere accidental stays and impediments acting not as wealth, but (for we ought to have a correspondent term) as 'illth'. **1886** O. Lodge *Inaug. Addr.* in *L'pool Univ. Coll. Mag.* Mar. 136 A hundred sovereigns may be no wealth, but the direst illth, to the drowning wretch in whose pockets they serve only as a load to drag him to destruction. **1889** G. B. Shaw *Fabian Ess.* I. 22 (Sub-heading) 'Illth'.

ill-thrived, -thriven: see ILL- B.

'ill-'timed, *a.* [f. ILL *adv.* + *timed*, pa. pple. of TIME *v.*] Badly timed; occurring or done at an inappropriate time; unseasonable.

1692 *Vindication* Pref. A ij b, How can Zeal for so good a thing..be ever Ill-timed? **1725** Pope *Odyss.* xv. 78 The ill-tim'd efforts of officious love. **1791** Cowper *Iliad* VI. 399 Thy sullen humours, Paris, are ill-timed. **1838** Thirlwall *Greece* V. 93 Agesilaus..saw that such severity would be now very ill-timed.

ill-tongued ('ɪl'tʌŋd), *a.* [f. ILL *a.* + TONGUE *sb.* + -ED².] Having an evil or malicious tongue; speaking evil; slanderous; using bad language.

a **1300** *E.E. Psalter* cxxxix. 12 [cxl. 11] Man il-tunged, ai spekand. *a* **1536** *Calisto & Melib.* B ij a, A yll tongyd wrech, wyll ye not see? **1693** Congreve in *Dryden's Juvenal* xi. Note vii, Thersites. An Impudent, Deformed, Ill-Tongu'd Fellow. **1859** Cornwallis *New World* I. 215 The most ill-tongued ruffians that ever escaped from a penal settlement.

ill-treat (ˌɪl'triːt), *v.* [f. ILL *adv.* + TREAT *v.*; after the phrases *ill treated, ill treatment*; cf. ILL-USE.] *trans.* To treat badly; to deal harshly, unkindly, or cruelly with; to ill-use, maltreat.

[*a* **1704** Locke (J.), Where men find themselves ill treated.] **1794** Bloomfield *Amer. Law Rep.* 18 The Negro should not be ill-treated. **1818** Cobbett *Pol. Reg.* XXXIII. 398 When we see a man ill-treating any dumb creature. **1878** J. P. Hopps *Jesus* xii. 43 They began to mock him and to ill-treat him.

Hence **ˌill-'treater**, one who ill-treats.

1895 W. Platt *Women* 94 The illtreaters of women.

ill treatment, ill-treatment. [ILL *a.* 2, TREATMENT 1. Cf. ILL-TREAT *v.*] Bad or unfavourable treatment; rough handling; harsh or unsympathetic dealings.

1667 T. Sprat *Hist. R. Soc.* 401 A just occasion of lamenting the ill Treatment which has bin most commonly given to Inventors. **1676** Locke *Jrnl.* 23 Aug. in *Ess. Law Nature* (1954) 275 Making yourself an enemy to all by ill-treatment. **1677** —— tr. *Nicole's Ess.* (1828) 112 Ill treatment and persecutions would certainly fall to their lot. **1713** Steele *Guard.* No. 47 ¶9 The ill treatment which the protestants have met with. **1811** A. Graydon *Mem.* 292 In revenge for some real or supposed ill-treatment. **1818** *Public Ledger* 8 Apr. 3/2 Alledged ill-treatment during a short confinement in that prison. **1864** E. B. Pusey *Daniel* i. 21 Who revenge on man their illtreatment at the hand of man. **1879** G. Meredith *Egoist* II. v. 94 He contemplated her with an air of stiff-backed ill-treatment. **1905** Chesterton *Heretics* 79 A permanent possibility of selfishness arises from the mere fact of having a self, and not from any accidents of education or ill-treatment.

†**'ill-'turned** (see ILL- III), *a. Obs.* [f. ILL *adv.* + *turned*, pa. pple. of TURN *v.*] **a.** Badly turned, shapen, or expressed. **b.** Having an evil turn of mind, ill-disposed.

a **1637** B. Jonson tr. *Horace's Art of Poetry* Wks. (Rtldg.) 737/2 He'd bid blot all, and to the anvil bring Those ill-torn'd verses to new hammering [*delere jubebat, Et male tornatos incudi reddere versus*]. *a* **1704** Locke (J.), A mixture of rudeness and ill turned confidence. *a* **1715** Burnet *Own Time* (1753) V. 197 The capital gentry of England..appeared to be ill turned and not to apprehend the dangers. **1768–74** Tucker *Lt. Nat.* (1852) II. 676 Horace directs to send back the ill-turned line to the anvil.

illucidate (ɪ'l(j)uːsɪdeɪt), *v. rare.* [Formed, after L. *ēlūcidāre* to ELUCIDATE, with prefix IL-¹, either by phonetic confusion of the two prefixes, or to impart the force of 'on, upon', as in L. *illūcēre*,

illūmināre to shine on.] *trans.* To shed light upon; to make clear, clear up, elucidate.

a **1545** BOORDE *Pronost.* Prol. in *Introd. Knowl.* (1870) Forewords 25 Astronomy doth illucydat all the other lyberal sciences. **1656** BLOUNT *Glossogr.*, *Illucidate*, to enlighten or give light, to cleer, or explicate cleerly. **1833** SIR W. HAMILTON *Discuss.* (1852) 173 The instance adduced to illucidate the one method.

Hence **illuci'dation**, the action of throwing light upon something; **i'llucidative** *a.*, tending to throw light upon something.

1658 PHILLIPS, *Illucidation*, a giving light, also an explaining or making clear. **1848** TALFOURD *Lamb's Final Mem.* vii. 256 The following may..be added to these, as illucidative of his too brief raptures.

illude (ɪ'l(j)u:d), *v.* Now *rare.* Also 6 illud. [ad. L. *illūdĕre* to make sport of, jest or mock at, ridicule, occas. to trick, impose upon, f. *il-* (IL-[1]) + *lūdĕre* to play. Cf. obs. F. *illuder* (Godef.).]

†**1.** *trans.* To mock, make sport of, deride. *Obs.*

1516 *Lyfe St. Birgette* in *Myrr. our Ladye* (1873) Introd. 56 Where he was Illudyd, Crucyfyed and buryed. *a* **1572** KNOX *Hist. Ref.* Wks. 1846 I. 196 Nether wold I that ye should begyn to illud the trewth with sophistrie. **1669** GALE *Crt. Gentiles* I. II. ii. 22 It illudes, or mocks the worshippers of these Idols. *a* **1704** T. BROWN *Sat. Antients* Wks. 1730 I. 23 To refute or illude that which is opposed to him.

2. To trick, impose upon, deceive with false hopes.

1447 BOKENHAM *Seyntys* (Roxb.) 112 Illudyd by thi goddesse clepyd dyan. **1548** UDALL, etc. *Erasm. Par. John* xx. 120 Supposyng them to be deceyued and illuded by some vision. **1670** G. H. *Hist. Cardinals* III. III. 293 Full of hypocrisie and dissimulation, to lull and illude one another. **1872** M. COLLINS *Two Plunges for Pearl* I. iii. 64 They had allowed their imaginations to illude them.

absol. **1836** F. MAHONEY *Rel. Father Prout, Songs France* iv. (1860) 294 None among us seeks to illude By empty boast of brotherhood.

†**b.** To cheat out *of* (something). *Obs.*

1541 *Act 33 Hen. VIII*, c. 16 §1 Illuded and deceyved thereof.

†**3.** To evade, elude. (In quot. 1820, *absol.*) *Obs.*

In some instances there is prob. confusion with *elude*.

1553 BRENDE *Q. Curtins* 21 (R.) [He] cutt with his sworde the cordes a sunder: therby either illuding, or else fulfiling theffect of the prophesie. **1599** *Broughton's Let.* xiii. 44 One place in Plato excepted, which the Reuerend Father hath notably illuded. **1820** MOIR in *Blackw. Mag.* VII. 627 The magic rainbow..Receding, and illuding ever.

Hence **i'lluded** *ppl. a.*; **i'lluding** *vbl. sb.* and *ppl. a.*

a **1547** *Proclam. Hen. VIII* in Burnet *Hist. Ref.* (1715) III. II. 76 To the great Deceyte, illudyng and seducyng of our Subjects. **1577** FENTON *Gold. Epist.* 192 Giuing no other credite to it than as a vision or illuding suggestion. **1610** HEALEY *St. Aug. Citie of God* 62 To passe the time in vaine commendations of the labours of illuded antiquitie. **1696** LORIMER *Goodwin's Disc.* vii. 136 An illuding and mocking of them. **1745** WARTON *Pleas. Melanch.* 185 The woodman's stroke, or distant tinkling team..alarms The illuded sense. **1887** *Athenæum* 3 Dec. 745/1 They [women] come across unfavourable specimens of the illuding sex.

†**i'lludent**, *a. Obs. rare*$^{-1}$. [ad. L. *illūdens, -entem*, pres. pple. of *illūdĕre* to ILLUDE.] Deceiving, deceptive; mocking.

?*a* **1550** *Phylogamus* in *Skelton's Wks.* (1843) I. Introd. 116 O poete so impudent..To thee the goddes prudente Minerua is illudente!

i'lluder. *rare.* [f. ILLUDE + -ER[1].] One who illudes; a mocker, deceiver.

1550 BALE *Apol.* 53 O Illuders of ryghteousnesse! **1598** SYLVESTER *Du Bartas* II. ii. III. *Colonies* 121 False Berosus and such fond Deluders, (Their zealous Readers insolent Illuders).

illuk ('ɪlʊk). [Sinhala.] The name used in Sri Lanka (Ceylon) for a coarse grass, *Imperata cylindrica*; = LALANG.

1864 G. H. K. THWAITES *Enumeratio Plantarum Zeylaniæ* v. 369 *I*[*mperata*] *arundinacea*... Common in the hotter parts of the island. Nom. vulg. 'Illook'. The leaves make an excellent thatch. **1931** E. K. COOKE *Geogr. Ceylon* II. x. 164 The grass of Talawa is usually long and coarse, very different from the average patana grass; it usually reaches about three or four feet in height. The best known species are mahna and illuk. **1950** [see CHENA]. **1956** R. W. SZECHOWYCZ in S. Haden-Guest et al. *World Geogr. Forest Resources* xxii. 485 There is a total absence of undergrowth [in the savanna forest zone of Ceylon], and the herb layer consists of grasses, of which *Imperata cylindrica* (illuk) is the most prominent.

illume (ɪ'l(j)u:m), *v.* [A poetical shortening of ILLUMINE: cf. *relume*, also used by Shaks. Perhaps influenced by F. *allumer*, *rallumer* (Of. *alumer, ralumer*), also OF. *enlumer*, of which the stem *-lumer* came through *-*lumner*, from L. *-lūmināre*.] = ILLUMINE: almost exclusively *poetic*.

1. *trans.* To light up; to make shining or bright, to brighten.

1602 SHAKS. *Ham.* I. i. 37 When yond same Starre..Had made his course t' illume that part of Heauen Where now it burnes. **1788** WOLCOTT (P. Pindar) *Peter's Pension* Wks. 1812 II. 17 Train-oil instead of Wax was bid t'illume The goodly company and Dancing-room. **1791** COWPER *Odyss.* XIX. 42 Pallas from a golden lamp illumed The dusky way before them. **1821** SHELLEY *Hellas* 69 A second sun array'd in flame, To burn, to kindle, to illume. **1875** BEDFORD *Sailor's Pocket Bk.* v. (ed. 2) 131 It illumes to a greater extent the atmosphere.

2. *transf.* and *fig.* To 'light up' (the face), as a smile; to enlighten or illuminate (the mind or understanding).

a **1764** LLOYD tr. *Voltaire's Henriade* Poet. Wks. 1774 II. 222 Descend, and with thy strong and purest light My verse illume! **1795** SOUTHEY *Vis. Maid Orleans* III. 146 Loftier thoughts illume The enlighten'd glance. **1804** J. GRAHAME *Sabbath* 311 A smile illumes The face of some. **1862** NEALE *Hymns East. Ch.* (1866) 57 Till through fast-closed doors Thou camest Thy Disciples to illume.

†**3.** To set alight, kindle. Also, *fig. Obs. rare.*

1728 POPE *Dunc.* III. 260 Yon suns, he rears at pleasure higher, Illumes their light, and sets their flames on fire. **1744** AKENSIDE *Pleas. Imag.* I. 363 She by this Illumes the headstrong impulse of desire.

Hence **illumed** (ɪ'l(j)u:md), *ppl. a.* Also **i'llumer**, one who or that which illumes.

1836 I. TAYLOR *Phys. The. Another Life* (1857) 179 A wide illumed landscape. **1854** KEIGHTLEY *Mythol. Anc. Greece* (ed. 3) 384 Castor being the Illumer.

i'llume, *sb. poet. rare.* [f. prec. vb.] Illumination.

1838 J. STRUTHERS *Poetic Tales* 37 The lightnings flashed their dread illume. *c* **1882** E. DICKINSON *Poems* (1955) III. 1069 Better an ignis fatuus Than no illume at all.

illuminable (ɪ'l(j)u:mɪnəb(ə)l), *a.* [ad. L. *illūmināabil-is*, f. *illūmināre*: see ILLUMINE *v.* + -ABLE.] Capable of being illumined or illuminated.

1730–6 BAILEY (folio), *Illuminable*, capable of being enlightened. **1891** H. JONES *Browning* 250 A drench of utter dark not illuminable by white.

illumi'nado, obs. variant of *illuminato*, with Sp. ending -ADO: see ILLUMINATI.

1672 H. MORE *Brief Reply* 17 For there are some high-flown Illuminado's, that hold that lying with another mans wife is not Adultery in them though it be so in others.

illuminance (ɪ'l(j)u:mɪnəns). *Optics.* [f. L. *illūmin-āntem* (see ILLUMINANT *a.* and *sb.*) + -ANCE.] The amount of luminous flux per unit area; = ILLUMINATION 1 b.

1943 D. H. JACOBS *Fund. Optical Engin.* iv. 66 We have derived equations that give the illumination (or illuminance) only at points on the axis of the system. **1949** H. MARGENAU et al. *Physics Princ. & Applications* xliv. 621 Illuminance is expressed in lumens/ft^2 (foot candles) or lumens/m^2 (luxes). **1955** R. C. BROWN *Textbk. Physics* IV. l. 902 The illumination (sometimes called 'intensity of illumination' and also illuminance) of a surface is defined as the luminous flux incident per unit area on the surface. **1961** F. W. WEYMOUTH in Hirsch & Wick *Vision Aging Patient* iv. 41 Since the extent of dark adaptation is..curtailed with age, the performance at low levels of illuminance begins to decline even before the age of 40 years. **1970** *Nature* 24 Jan. 347/2 Each pattern..was projected.. at an average screen illuminance of 3 millilamberts.

illuminant (ɪ'l(j)u:mɪnənt), *a.* and *sb.* [ad. L. *illumināant-em*, pres. pple. of *illūmināre* to ILLUMINATE.] **A.** *adj.* Lighting up, enlightening.

1677 GALE *Crt. Gentiles* IV. 493 Chrysostom stiles it [divine illumination] the illuminant Intellect. **1886** E. WORSDELL *Gosp. Divine Help* viii. (1888) 153 'Types' and sacrifices were 'a shadow of the good things to come', and therefore not illuminant of them.

B. *sb.* That which illumines or illuminates; an illuminating or lighting body, substance, or agent; a source of illumination.

In Webster 1864 noted as *Obs.* but subsequently in common use as a general term for artificial agents of light.

1644 DIGBY *Two Treat.* I. xiii. (1645) 139 The refraction is made towards the perpendicular drawn from the illuminant to the superficies. **1686** BOYLE *Enq. Notion Nat.* iv. 117 The Bodies that are endow'd with it [light]..as the Planets by participation from an External Illuminant. **1875** BEDFORD *Sailor's Pocket Bk.* v. (ed. 2) 133 The illuminants or combustibles have consisted of animal or vegetable oils. **1882** *Pall Mall G.* 20 Mar. 2/1 The incandescent lamp as a domestic illuminant. **1895** CROCKETT *Sweetheart Trav.* 232 He carried no illuminant with him except a few lucifer matches.

i'lluminary, *a.* and *sb. rare.* [f. ILLUMINE *v.*, after *luminary*.]

A. *adj.* Tending to illumine; illuminative.

1730–6 BAILEY (folio), *Illuminary*, of or pertaining to Illuminating.

†**B.** *sb.* = ILLUMINATION. *Obs.*

1692 LUTTRELL *Brief Rel.* (1857) II. 608 The kings birth day..ringing of bells, illuminaries and bonefires.

illuminate (ɪ'l(j)u:mɪnət), *ppl. a.* and *sb.* Also 6–7 -at. [ad. L. *illūmināt-us*, pa. pple. of *illūmināre* (see next).

In use as pa. pple. and ppl. adj. before the introduction of ILLUMINATE *v.*, of which it subsequently served as pa. pple., but was gradually displaced by *illuminated*.]

A. *pa. pple.* and *adj.*

1. Lighted up; made bright by light. *arch.*

1432–50 tr. *Higden* (Rolls) I. 307 Callede Delon..in that hit was illuminate of the son a fore other londes. **1555** EDEN *Decades* 265 Shorter nyghtes..illuminate of the moone. **1603** HOLLAND *Plutarch's Mor.* 1218 He could see the earth no more, but the Isles all bright and illuminate with a mild and delicate fire. **1753** SHORT in *Phil. Trans.* XLVIII. 362 The illuminate limb of the Moon. **1845** LONGF. *To a Child* 106 This rustic seat..With its o'er-hanging golden canopy Of leaves illuminate with autumnal hues.

2. Enlightened spiritually; divinely taught or inspired; in technical use, converted, baptized. Sometimes *contemptuous* = professing to have the inner light.

1563 WINȜET *Four Scoir Thre Quest.* Wks. 1888 I. 90 The haly penitent man Serapion, quha..wes illuminat be the spirit of prophetie. **1579** J. FIELD tr. *Calvin's 13 Serm.* Ded. Bjb, Ioyning and conixing so neere with Anabaptists, the spirituall illuminate, Pelagians, and other merite mongers. **1594** NASHE *Unfort. Trav.* 27 You may bee counted illuminate botchers for a while, but your end will bee Good people pray for vs. **1613** PURCHAS *Pilgrimage* (1614) 489 The illuminate Elders of the Familists. **1617** MORYSON *Itin.* I. I. v. 72 Cloysters..of repenting or illuminate women, so they call whores entring Cloysters. **1672** CAVE *Prim. Chr.* I. viii. (1673) 211 Speaking to the illuminate or Baptized. *a* **1677** BARROW *Serm.* (1686) III. xxiii. 258 The most illuminate Seraphims. **1909** *Westm. Gaz.* 19 May 4/2, I once knew a follower of the Rosy Cross, an illuminate member.

3. Enlightened intellectually; well-informed, learned. *arch.*

1579 FULKE *Heskins' Parl.* 121 The illuminate doctor cryeth out agaynste his obcecate and blind enemies. **1605** BACON *Adv. Learn.* I. vii. §3 If they be illuminate by learning. **1649** J. ECCLISTON tr. *Behmen's Ep.* (1886) 84 As the illuminate mind shall well see.

4. = ILLUMINATED 5.

1851 R. H. STODDARD *Hymn to Flora*, Illuminate missals open on the meads, Bending with rosaries of dewy beads.

B. *sb.* A spiritually or intellectually enlightened person, or one claiming to be so; one initiated into 'the mysteries'. *arch.* Also *spec. pl.* = ILLUMINATI b.

1600 W. WATSON *Decacordon* (1602) 100 That bold attempt against such illuminates, and men sitting neare vnder God Almighties knee. **1612** T. JAMES *Jesuits' Downf.* 14 Every Iesuit takes vpon him to be an illuminate, an inculpate guider of soules. **1683** TRYON *Way to Health* 262 This great Philosopher and Illuminate of his Age. **1860** LOWELL in *Atlantic Monthly* Aug. 248 The illuminate too often looks upon the stems and flowers of language..as mere handles by which to pull up the grimy tubers. **1889** F. HALL in *Nation* (N.Y.) XLIX. 334/3 Not one of these illuminates has given proof of..even a moderate acquaintance with [etc.]. **1906** *Edin. Rev.* July 49 The influence of the German 'illuminates' on the French lodges. **1946** G. G. SCHOLEM *Major Trends Jewish Mysticism* (rev. ed.) iv. 121 The outspoken illuminates and ecstatics.

illuminate (ɪ'l(j)u:mɪneɪt), *v.* Also 6 illum-, yllumynate, *pa. t.* (*Sc.*) illumnat. [f. L. *illūmināt-*, ppl. stem of *illūmināre* to throw light on, light up, brighten, set in a clear light, make illustrious; in med.L. to baptize, to kindle, to paint or limn in colours; f. IL-[1] + *lūmen* light.]

1. a. *trans.* To light up, give light to.

1535 STEWART *Cron. Scot.* II. 604 Ane feild of birneist gold so bricht, That all the land illumnat with greit licht. *a* **1545** BOORDE *Pronost.* Prol. in *Introd. Knowl.* (1870) Forewords 25 Lyke to the son..illumynatynge as well the inferyal planetes as the superyal planetes. **1667** MILTON *P.L.* VII. 350 God made two great lights..And set them in the Firmament of Heav'n To illuminate the Earth. **1718** LADY M. W. MONTAGU *Let. to C'tess Bristol* 10 Apr., The mosque [is] illuminated with a vast number of lamps. **1736** J. MCURE in *Z. Boyd's Zion's Flowers* (1855) App. 32/2 It is illuminated with 41 windows. **1872** YEATS *Techn. Hist. Comm.* 139 Most dwellings were illuminated by brands or torches of pinewood.

b. To give light to, or remove blindness from (the eyes), esp. *fig.* in religious sense.

1582 BENTLEY *Mon. Matrones* II. 209 Illuminate mine eies ..O good Lord, that I sleepe not in darkenes. **1596** SPENSER *Hymne Beautie* 20 Doe thou vouchsafe with thy love-kindling light T' illuminate my dim and dulled eyne. **1638** SIR T. HERBERT *Trav.* (ed. 2) 74 He commands his sonnes eyes..to be forfetted, but the poyson is more mercifull, leaving one eye a little illuminated. **1671** FLAVEL *Fount. of Life* x. 30 To sin with eyes clearly illuminated with the purest Light.

c. To direct a beam of any kind of radiation at (an object or region): used esp. of radio waves and microwaves in connection with radar and telecommunication.

1942 [implied in ILLUMINATED *ppl. a.* 1 b]. **1947** CROWTHER & WHIDDINGTON *Science at War* I. 6 The power radiated proved ample to detect aircraft, flying at a height.. sufficient to bring them within the space 'illuminated', at the range of 75 miles. **1948** POLLARD & STURTEVANT *Microwaves & Radar Electronics* iv. 126 The..antenna pattern from a 30-inch-diameter dish illuminated at 3·2 centimeters..is shown. **1957** R. WATSON-WATT *Three Steps to Victory* 470 Of the secondary radiations, excited by 'illuminating' the craft by ground installations emitting light, heat, sound or radio-waves, the first two are excluded by atmospheric absorption. **1973** *Physics Bull.* Mar. 149/1 A cold cathode discharge source..provided a beam of electrons which could illuminate an object such as an aperture or a wire grid.

2. To shed spiritual light upon; to enlighten spiritually; in quot. 1698, to bring the Gospel to. (In mod. use consciously figurative from 1.)

1538 STARKEY *England* II. i. 143 That hyt may plese Hym ..to yllumynate and lyght our hartys and myndys. **1548–9** (Mar.) *Bk. Com. Prayer* Litany, That it maye please thee to illuminate all Bishops, pastours, and ministers..with true knowledge and vnderstandyng of thy word. **1611** BIBLE *Heb.* x. 32 The former dayes, in which after yee were illuminated, ye indured a great fight of afflictions. *a* **1656** HALES *Sin agst. H. Ghost* Tracts (1677) 13 Anciently, to be illuminated signified to be Baptized. **1698** FRYER *Acc. E. India & P.* 271 St. Basil illuminated the lower Armenia. **1719** DE FOE *Crusoe* II. vi, That He..would further illuminate them with a beam of his heavenly grace. **1875** MANNING *Mission H. Ghost* iv. 99 Faith therefore

illuminates us to know that God is the end for which we were made.

3. To enlighten intellectually; to give knowledge or understanding to.

c **1566** J. Alday tr. *Boaystuau's Theat. World* I iij b, Excellent Doctors in this Universitie.. by whose good condition and doctrine all Europe is at this daye illuminated. **1635** J. Hayward tr. *Biondi's Banish'd Virg.* 91 Disciplines illuminate the intellect. **1776** Boswell *Let. to Johnson* 20 Feb., You have illuminated my mind, and relieved me from imaginary shackles of conscientious obligation. *Mod. Testimonial*, I cannot imagine a teacher more gifted to lead, encourage, and illuminate a body of young students.

4. To throw light upon (a subject); to make luminous or clear; to elucidate. Also *absol.*

1586 Ferne *Blaz. Gentrie* To Gentlem. Inner Temple, Other autentique probacions did illuminate and give information. **1604** R. Cawdrey *Table Alph., Illuminate*, to inlighten, or make plaine. *a* **1624** Swinburne *Spousals* (1686) 17 Which Reason might be illuminated with sundry Examples. *a* **1748** Watts (J.), My health is insufficient to amplify these remarks, and to illuminate the several pages with variety of examples. **1791** Boswell *Johnson* Feb. an. 1744, The various incidents [in Johnson's 'Life of Savage'] are.. illuminated throughout with so much philosophy. **1851** D. Wilson *Preh. Ann.* (1863) II. iv. iv. 267 All combine to illuminate the oscure period of.. history.

5. To make resplendent or illustrious; to shed a lustre upon.

1601 Shaks. *Jul. C.* i. iii. 110 What trash is Rome?.. When it serues For the base matter, to illuminate So vile a thing as Cæsar. **1632** Lithgow *Trav.* x. 497 The chiefest Gentry... All which in each degree.. illuminat the soyle with grandure. **1830** D'Israeli *Chas. I* III. iv. 43 Hampden was to have illuminated with his genius this new order of government. **1850** Robertson *Serm.* Ser. iii. vii. 103 Self-sacrifice illuminated by love.

6. To decorate profusely with lights, as a sign of festivity or in honour of some person or some event.

1702 *Lond. Gaz.* No. 3842/1 The whole City being in an extraordinary manner illuminated. **1717** tr. *Frezier's Voy.* 204 The Steeples of the Church were adorn'd with Ensigns .. and illuminated with Lanthorns. **1863** *Illustr. Lond. News* 28 Mar. 358/2 The hotels.. and places of business were illuminated with.. transparencies and variegated lamps.

7. a. To set alight, light, kindle. *rare.*

1658 Willsford *Secrets Nat.* 66 [It] will extinguish a torch that is lighted, and being immediately put in again, it will illuminate it. **1849** Thackeray *Pendennis* xxxviii, The butler.. illuminated the antique Gothic chandelier.

b. *intr.* To take fire, to light up; of a town, etc.: to be decorated with lights as a sign of festivity or celebration. Also, to become excited (see also quot. 1926).

1706 Defoe *Review* 2 Mar. 108 The other Gentleman and his Man coming, and holding a real Candle up to Decide it, Affirm'd the Doctors Candle was Lighted; the Grave Gentleman went on, with an *Ay, I think it does begin to Illuminate.* **1801** *Med. Jrnl.* V. 583 The wood.. when it begins to illuminate, is mostly deprived of its resinous particles. **1843** *Punch* IV. 256 If Stockport and Paisley do not.. illuminate when they shall hear the glad tidings, then is the spirit of manufacture dead to gratitude. **1871** 'Mark Twain' *Sk. New & Old* (1875) 176 For eight-and-forty hours no soul in all the barony but did dance and sing, carouse and illuminate, to celebrate the great event. **1926** Wood & Goddard *Dict. Amer. Slang* 24 *Illuminated*, lit, drunk. **1927** E. H. C. Moberly Bell *Life & Lett. C. F. Moberly Bell* 96 The people illuminate, and go mad with frenzy for Gordon, and curse the Mahdi. **1972** *Jrnl. Social Psychol.* LXXXVII. 90 Subjects were asked to estimate the probability that an alleged peer.. would shock them when a light illuminated.

8. To decorate (an initial letter, word, or text, in a manuscript) with gold, silver, and brilliant colours, or with elaborate tracery and miniature designs, executed in colours; to adorn (a manuscript, inscription, text, etc.) with such decorative letters and miniatures. †Formerly, also, to colour a map.

(In this sense it has taken the place of ENLUMINE.)

1706 Phillips, *To illuminate*,.. to draw in Gold and Colours the beginning Letters and other Ornaments, as it is done in many old Manuscript Books; to lay Colours upon Maps and Prints. **1710** Hearne *Collect.* (O.H.S.) III. 47 Some of the Letters are illuminated. **1774** Warton *Hist. Eng. Poetry* Dissert. ii. (1775) I. 42 He was so fond of letters, that he did not disdain to bind and illuminate books. **1864** *Linnet's Trial* II. iii. viii. 88 That shall be the text which I choose, to illuminate and hang up in my bedroom.

Hence **i'lluminating** *ppl. a.*; **i'lluminatingly** *adv.*, in an illuminating way.

1632 Lithgow *Trav.* i. 31 The splendor of the illuminating Image. **1643** Milton *Divorce* ii. iii, The illuminating guidance of Gods Law. **1780** Cowper *Table Talk* 712 To shed illuminating rays On every scene and subject it surveys. **1854** Tomlinson *Arago's Astron.* 127 Each point of the illuminating surface will project.. a light which will diminish in the inverse proportion of the squares of the distances. **1891** G. Meredith *One of our Conq.* III. xii. 249 It was the more illuminatingly damnatory for being recognized as the sentiment which no father should feel. **1965** *Language* XLI. 216 The adjective structures illuminatingly discussed by Lees. **1972** *Nature* 28 Jan. 204/2 Another examination scheme has also proved illuminatingly effective.

illuminated (ɪ'l(j)uːmɪneɪtɪd), *ppl. a.* [f. ILLUMINATE *v.* + -ED[1]: cf. ILLUMINATE *a.*]

1. a. Lighted up; made light, luminous, or resplendent.

1664 Power *Exp. Philos.* ii. 91 Such like illuminated ayr as this we breathe in. **1715** tr. *Pancirollus' Rerum Mem.* I. i. vi. 17 The Bononian Stone.. if exposed a while to the illuminated Air, will imbibe the Light. **1831** Brewster *Optics* Introd. 2 Light is emitted from every point of a luminous or of an illuminated body. **1884** F. J. Britten *Watch & Clockm.* 85 Illuminated dials for turret clocks are as a rule made of opalescent glass.

b. Made, or being, the target of (non-visible) radiation of some kind.

1942 J. C. Slater *Microwave Transmission* vi. 275 The illuminated region can be considerably greater than the distance between poles. **1950** J. D. Kraus *Antennas* xii. 345 An antenna with a uniformly illuminated circular aperture 10 wavelengths in diameter has a gain of 600 or nearly 28 db with respect to a $\frac{1}{2}$-wavelength dipole antenna. **1966** Tolstoy & Clay *Ocean Acoustics* vi. 198 The dimensions of the illuminated area are much larger than the acoustic wavelength.

2. Having or claiming spiritual enlightenment.

1606 G. W[oodcocke] tr. *Ivstine* Ll iv b, Anabaptists.. trusting vnto illuminated reuelations. **1768** H. Walpole *Hist. Doubts* Pref. 3 All very ancient history except that of the illuminated Jews is a perfect fable. **1863** Geo. Eliot *Romola* i. i, Every revelation.. has many meanings, which it is given to the illuminated only to unfold.

3. Enlightened intellectually.

1661 Boyle *Style of Script.* (1675) 123 They believe them to have been endowed with very illuminated intellectuals. **1791** Paine *Rights of Man* (ed. 4) 10 That august, illuminated and illuminating body of men. **1831** Carlyle *Sart. Res.* iii. viii, 'But is it not the deepest Law of Nature that she be constant?' cries an illuminated class.

4. Of or belonging to various societies or orders called *illuminati*. Also *absol.* = ILLUMINATI.

1634 Canne *Necess. Separ.* (1849) 271 One of the illuminated fathers of the Familists. **1686** tr. *Bouhours' St. Ignatius* ii. 77 In Spain certain Visionaries, who were call'd the Illuminated, or Men of new Lights. **1802** *Edin. Rev.* I. 17 The object of the Illuminated Orders was probably.. unattainable.

5. a. Of letters, writing, manuscripts, etc.: Adorned with brilliant colours, metallic pigments, etc. (see ILLUMINATE *v.* 8). Also as *sb. rare.*

1712 Hearne *Collect.* (O.H.S.) III. 372 Not only the Black, but all the Red (commonly call'd Illuminated Letters) are printed. **1765** Blackstone *Comm.* (1774) I. 255 A copy of this act, elegantly engrossed and illuminated. **1856** Emerson *Eng. Traits, Truth* Wks. (Bohn) II. 51 Illuminated missals. **1923** E. Pound *Let.* 12 May (1971) 187 Price 25 dollars per copy, and 50 and 100 bones for Vellum and illuminateds.

b. *College slang.* Of a text: Having an interlinear translation.

1851 B. H. Hall *College Words* 261 *Illuminated* books are preferred.. to ponies or hobbies, as the text and translation in them are bought nearer to one another.

‖**illuminati** (ɪl(j)uːmɪ'neɪtaɪ, ɪluːmɪ'nɑːtiː), *sb. pl.* Also *sing.* **illuminato** (-'ɑːtəʊ); †plur. **-oes.** [Plural of L. *illūminātus*, It. *-ato* 'enlightened', used in fig. sense.] A name assumed by or applied to various societies or sects because of their claim to special enlightenment in religious, or (later) intellectual, matters.

a. Applied to a sect of Spanish heretics which existed in the 16th c. under the name *Alumbrados* or 'enlightened'; subsequently, to a similar but obscure sect of Familists which arose in France in Louis XIII's reign.

1599 Sandys *Europæ Spec.* (1632) 166 An other pestilent Sect there was not long since of the Illuminati in Aragon. **1652** R. Boreman *Countr. Catech.* ii. 5 The Illuminatoes of the times, the Anabaptists. **1686** tr. *Bouhours' St. Ignatius* ii. 77 The Inquisitors.. were induced to believe, that.. the Person.. might either be an Illuminato or a Lutheran. **1749** Bp. Lavington *Enthus. Methodists & Papists* (1754) I. ii. 114 The Alumbrado's or Illuminati of Spain.

b. Used to render Ger. *Illuminaten*, the name of a celebrated secret society, founded at Ingolstadt in Bavaria, in 1776, by Professor Adam Weishaupt, holding deistic and republican principles, and having an organization akin to freemasonry; hence applied to other thinkers regarded as atheistic or free-thinking, e.g. the French Encyclopædists.

1797 J. Robison (*title*) Proofs of a Conspiracy against all the Religions and Governments of Europe, carried on in the secret meetings of Freemasons, Illuminati, and Reading Societies. **1798** Washington *Lett.* Writ. 1893 XIV. 119 The doctrines of the Illuminati and principles of Jacobinism. **1802** Kett *Elem. Gen. Knowl.* 71 (Jod.) The Freethinkers of England, the Philosophists of France, and the Illuminati of Germany.

c. *gen.* Persons affecting or claiming to possess special knowledge or enlightenment on any subject: often used satirically.

1816 T. L. Peacock *Headlong Hall* i, The conversation among these illuminati soon became animated. **1846** H. Rogers *Ess.* I. iv. 157 What was dark to himself was happily quite clear to these illuminati [the alchemists]. **1850** Marg. Fuller *Life without & Life within* (1860) 41 Wilhelm is deemed worthy of admission to the society of the Illuminati, that is, those who have pierced the secret of life, and know what it is to be and to do. *a* **1878** Sir G. Scott *Recollect.* iii. (1879) 111 All thanks and honour.. to the older Pugin, however much our illuminati may sneer. **1887** *Contemp. Rev.* Apr. 592 An illuminato like Katkoff may write as if Russia was invincible; practical men know better.

i'lluminating, *vbl. sb.* [f. ILLUMINATE *v.* + -ING[1].] The action of the verb ILLUMINATE. Also *attrib.*, as **illuminating engineering**, the branch of engineering and applied science concerned with the design, installation, and modification of artificial lighting; so **illuminating engineer**.

c **1561** Veron *Free-will* 4 b, Without the illuminating and inspiration of the holye ghost. **1860** Reade *Cloister & H.* I. 12 He had made several trials at illuminating. **1906** (*title*) Transactions of the Illuminating Engineering Society. **1907** *Installation News* Nov. 3 That latest addition to the ever-growing family of specialists—the Illuminating Engineer —is providing the electrical industry and press with a good deal to think about. **1930** *Engineering* 31 Jan. 143/2 The development of the science of illuminating engineering has been continuous during the past few decades.

illumination (ɪl(j)uːmɪ'neɪʃən). [a. F. *illumination* (14th c., Oresme), ad. L. *illūminātiōn-em*, n. of action f. *illūmināre* to ILLUMINE, ILLUMINATE.]

1. a. The action of illuminating; the fact or condition of being illuminated; a lighting up, a supplying of light. Also *techn.* in sense 1 c. of ILLUMINATE *v.*

circle of illumination: see CIRCLE *sb.* 2 a.

1563 W. Fulke *Meteors* (1640) 11 Fyre scattered in the ayre, or illuminations, are generated in the lowest region of the ayre. **1603** Holland *Plutarch's Mor.* 1292 Mercurie.. plaied at dice with the Moone, and won from her the seventieth part of every one of her illuminations. **1766** tr. *Beccaria's Ess. Crimes* xi. (1793) 44 The illumination of the streets during the night at the public expense. **1784** Cowper *Task* iv. 274 The glowing hearth may satisfy awhile With faint illumination. **1816** Playfair *Nat. Phil.* II. 83 The circle separating Day from Night, or the light from the dark hemisphere of the earth, is called the Circle of Illumination. **1869** Tyndall in *Fortn. Rev.* 1 Feb. 226 The source of illumination chosen was the electric light... The dirt and filth.. were strikingly revealed by this method of illumination. **1942** J. C. Slater *Microwave Transmission* vi. 275 Vertically the illumination falls off gradually in intensity as the poles are approached. **1948** Pollard & Sturtevant *Microwaves & Radar Electronics* iv. 127 A horn feed illumination is the most widely favored. **1966** Tolstoy & Clay *Ocean Acoustics* vi. 199 It is convenient to measure the scattered signal relative to the signal reflected by a mirror-like surface when the illumination factor, source position, receiver position, etc., are the same.

b. *Optics.* Degree of lighting up; the intensity of the light falling upon a surface, as measurable by the amount incident on each unit of the surface.

1863 Atkinson tr. *Ganot's Physics* §410 The illumination of a surface placed in a beam of parallel luminous rays is the same at all distances. **1875** *Ure's Dict. Arts* II. 881 Experiments for determining the relative illumination of the different lights. **1943, 1955** [see ILLUMINANCE].

c. Directly *fig.* or in fig. context.

1646 Sir T. Browne *Pseud. Ep.* i. v. 18 Our understandings being eclipsed.. we must betake our selves to wayes of reparation, and depend upon the illumination of our endeavours. **1662** Stillingfl. *Orig. Sacr.* ii. v. §5 Nature is sensible of.. the imperfection of its own light, and therefore seems rather to require further illumination. **1825** Lamb *Elia* Ser. ii. *Superannuated Man*, The prospect.. threw something of an illumination upon the darker side of my captivity.

2. a. Spiritual enlightenment; divine inspiration; †*spec.* baptism (*obs.*). (The earliest sense in Eng.)

1398 Trevisa *Barth. De P.R.* ii. viii. (MS. Harl. 614) 10 b/2 He clepeþ & bringeþ þe neþer ordris, to be parteners of þe illumynacioun of þe schynynge of god. *c* **1450** tr. *De Imitatione* iii. Contents xxvii, A praier for illuminacion of mynde. **1570** Dee *Math. Pref.* 15 Speciall priuiledge of Illumination, or Reuelation from heauen. **1640** Habington *Castara* iii. (Arb.) 112 Confounding with supernaturall illumination, the opinionated judgement of the wise. **1725** tr. *Dupin's Eccl. Hist. 17th C.* I. v. 57 Besides the Name of Baptism.. they gave it also the Name of Illumination, of Light, of Circumcision. **1845** H. J. Rose *Theology* in *Encycl. Metrop.* II. 872/1 Ecclesiastical History gives us several instances of similar claims to prophecy and divine illumination. **1857** Keble *Eucharist. Adorat.* 15 In baptism we are illuminated, in illumination adopted.

b. *pl.* An instance of this; an inspiration; a revelation.

c **1340** Hampole *Prose Tr.* 17 Þe deuelle entirs þan by fals illumynacyons, and fals sownnes and swetnes, and dyssaues a mans saule. **1634** Sir T. Herbert *Trav.* 220 Madoc ingeniously perusing the older illuminations and seeing in some things the prophecie of this authentique Bardh. **1764** Harmer *Observ.* ix. vi. 250 Worship God.. to Whom in justice you ought to ascribe these illuminations. **1878** C. Stanford *Symb. Christ* i. 12 Whose soul was.. visited with preternatural illuminations.

3. Intellectual enlightenment; information, learning; †occas. in *pl.*, intellectual gifts. Also, the 'enlightenment' or doctrines of the *Illuminati*.

1634 Sir T. Herbert *Trav.* 12 They [Columbus and Americus] had an Antecessor from whose writings and Plats they had their illuminations. **1658** Evelyn *Diary* 27 Jan., These and the like illuminations, far exceeded his age. **1692** Ray *Dissol. World* iii. ix. (1732) 401 After further Illumination they were better informed. **1862** Lewes *Stud. Anim. Life* i. 41 From the illumination of many minds on many points, Truth must finally emerge. **1881** J. C. Shairp *Aspects Poetry* iv. 105 To turn the tide against the Illumination, of which Voltaire, Diderot, and the host of Encyclopædists were the high priests. **1886** Dowden *Shelley* I. 534 The materialistic philosophers of the French Illumination. **1893** Sir R. Ball *Story of Sun* 75 The illumination which mathematics alone can afford.

4. a. The lighting up of a building, town, etc. (now usually in a decorative way, with coloured lights arranged in artistic designs, etc.), in token

of festivity or rejoicing. **b.** with *an* and *pl.* An instance of this; also *pl.* the lights, or figures composed of lights, used in such decoration.
1691 LUTTRELL *Brief Rel.* (1857) II. 293 With many bonefires and illuminations at night. **1698** FRYER *Acc. E. India & P.* 94 A Time of Solemnity sometimes kept for several Weeks together with Illuminations on their Houses. **1767** FRANKLIN *Lett.* Wks. 1887 IV. 39 At the Church of Notre Dame, where we went to see a magnificent illumination, with figures, etc. **1823** BYRON *Juan* VII. xliv, When London had a grand illumination.. So that the streets of colour'd lamps are full. **1864** *Daily Tel.* 20 Sept., The illuminations were really magnificent.
attrib. **1797** MRS. RADCLIFFE *Italian* xiii, It was an illumination night.
†**5.** Elucidation. *Obs. rare*⁻¹.
1656 B. HARRIS *Parival's Iron Age* I. xvi. 32 For the restauration of learning, and for the illumination and illustration of Sciences. **1658** PHILLIPS, *Illumination*, the same [as *Illucidation*, an explaining or making clear].
6. a. The embellishment or decoration of a letter or writing with bright or luminous colours, the use of gold and silver, the addition of elaborate tracery or miniature illustrations, etc.: see ILLUMINATE *v.* 8. **b.** with *pl.* The designs, miniatures, and the like, employed in such decoration. †**c.** Formerly, also, the colouring of maps or prints.
1678 PHILLIPS (ed. 4), *Illumination*,.. a laying colours upon Maps or Printed Pictures; so as to give the greater light, as it were, and beauty to them. **1856** RUSKIN *Mod. Paint.* III. IV. viii. §9 The distinctive difference between illumination and painting proper, being, that illumination admits no shadows, but only gradations of pure colour. **1858** HAWTHORNE *Fr. & It. Jrnls.* II. 112 Beautiful illuminations, the vermilion and gold of which looked as brilliant now as they did five centuries ago. **1870** RUSKIN *Lect. Art* v. 138 Perfect illumination is only writing made lovely; the moment it passes into picture making it has lost its dignity and function.

illuminatism (ɪˈl(j)uːmɪnətɪz(ə)m). [f. ILLUMINAT-I or Ger. *Illuminat-en* + -ISM.] = ILLUMINISM.
1798 HAN. MORE *Fem. Educ.* (1799) I. 42 Poetry as well as prose, romance as well as history, writings on philosophical as well as on political subjects, have thus been employed to instil the principles of Illuminatism. **1842** *Blackw. Mag.* LI. 52 There would be ample materials.. in the mesmerism of France, and the illuminatism of Germany.

illuminatist[1] (ɪˈl(j)uːmɪnətɪst). [f. as prec. + -IST.] = ILLUMINIST.
1851 S. JUDD *Margaret* II. vii. (1871) 274 A third sect, who are less despised, and yet are more contemptible—the Illuminatists. **1880** T. FROST *Forty Years' Recoll.* 13 The day dreams of the Illuminatists, St. Simon and Fourier.

iˈlluminatist[2]. *rare.* [f. ILLUMINATE *v.* + -IST.] An illuminator of manuscripts.
1845 J. SAUNDERS *Cabinet Pict. Eng. Life, Chaucer* 101 It is the monks leaving work.. but the caligrapher and the illuminatist stir not.. they go on busier than ever.

illuminative (ɪˈl(j)uːmɪneɪtɪv, -ətɪv), *a.* (*sb.*) [f. L. *illūmināt-*, ppl. stem of *illūmināre* to ILLUMINATE: see -ATIVE. Cf. F. *illuminatif* (15th c., Gerson).]
1. Having the property of illuminating, lighting up, or affording light.
1644 DIGBY *Two Treat.* I. iv. (1645) 38 The illuminative action of fire. **1706** PHILLIPS, *Illuminative Month*,.. that space of Time, during which the Moon gives Light, or is to be seen betwixt one Conjunction and another. **1870** J. SCOFFERN *Stray Leaves Science* 106 Carbon.. united with hydrogen.. becomes ordinary illuminative gas.
fig. **1855** CARLYLE in Wemyss Reid *Life Ld. Houghton* (1891) I. xi. 526 The sight of your face will be illuminative to everybody in these premises.
2. Having the quality or claim of illuminating spiritually or intellectually; *spec.* applied to the second stage of spiritual advancement: see quots.
1649 JER. TAYLOR *Gt. Exemp.* I. v. iii. 90 After.. the punitive part of repentance is resolved on, and begun, and put forward.. we then enter into the illuminative way of religion; and set upon the acquist of virtues and the purchase of spiritual graces. **1654** GAYTON *Pleas. Notes* IV. xxv. 287 Illuminative and inspired physick he detested. **1669** WOODHEAD *St. Teresa* I. xxii. (1671) 144 After many yeares first passed through the Purgative way, and some advance made in the Illuminative. **1830** SOUTHEY in *For. Rev. & Cont. Misc.* V. 318 The purgative, illuminative, and unitive stages of devotion. **1858** CARLYLE *Fredk. Gt.* VI. vii. II. 108 A glimpse into the interior of the Berlin Schloss.. which will be illuminative to the reader. **1872** LIDDON *Elem. Relig.* iv. 129 Revelation must be not merely illuminative, but remedial.
b. Const. *of. rare.*
1701 NORRIS *Ideal World* I. iii. 157 Upon the contrary supposition, that of God's knowing the creatures in themselves, the consequence will be, that the creatures are freely illuminative of their Creator.
3. Pertaining to the illumination of writing.
1870 T. NICHOLS *Handy Bk. Brit. Mus.* iv. 393 The finest and richest specimen of Anglo-Saxon illuminative art.
B. *sb.* An illuminating agent. *rare.*
a **1711** KEN *Hymnotheo* Poet. Wks. 1721 III. 246 The Book inspir'd.. There all Inflammatives of Love Divine; There all sublime Illuminatives shine.

iˈlluminatively, *adv. rare.* [f. ILLUMINATIVE *a.* + -LY².] In an illuminative way.
1925 T. DREISER *Amer. Trag.* (1926) II. III. xxviii. 349 These hard, white-painted walls brightly lighted.. by incandescent lamps in the hall without at night—yet all so different from Bridgeburg,—so much more bright or harsh illuminatively.

illuminato, sing. of ILLUMINATI.

illuminator (ɪˈl(j)uːmɪneɪtə(r)). [ad. L. *illūminātor*, agent-n. f. *illūmināre* to ILLUMINATE. Cf. F. *illuminateur* (17th c.).]
1. He who or that which illuminates or gives light; an illuminating agent.
1598 FLORIO, *Illuminatore*, an illuminator or light-giuer. **1755** JOHNSON, *Illuminator*, one who gives light. **1834** *New Monthly Mag.* XLII. 260 Steam and gas.. are the grand facilitators and illuminators of the intercourse of the most distant provinces. **1883** *Century Mag.* XXVI. 339 To produce a cheap illuminator from water.
b. *techn.* Applied to various instruments or devices.
(*a*) In a microscope or other optical instrument: A lens or mirror for concentrating the light. (*b*) In Surgery: An instrument for directing a strong light into any cavity of the body, or for illuminating an internal part. (*c*) A glazed opening in a floor, the deck of a ship, etc., to admit light to the part beneath.
1837 GORING & PRITCHARD *Microgr.* 9, Fig. 4 is an illuminator for opaque objects.
2. One who illuminates or enlightens spiritually.
(The earliest sense in Eng.)
1485 CAXTON *Chas. Gt.* (1881) 15 The holy ghoost, confirmatour and Illumynatour of al good werkes. *a* **1711** KEN *Hymns Evang.* Poet. Wks. 1721 I. 180 For heav'nly Truth dispos'd, Then their Illuminatour they adore. **1866** J. G. MURPHY *Comm. Exod.* xxviii. 30 The Lord above is the great Illuminator of the darkened soul.
3. One who enlightens intellectually, who imparts instruction or knowledge; applied contemptuously to the 18th century Illuminati.
1777 PENNANT *Zool.* IV. Advt. 4 That wonderful man (after Ray) the greatest illuminator of the study of Nature. **1790** *Hist. Europe* in *Ann. Reg.* 11/1 The new illuminators, who despised all experience, and disdained all wisdom but their own. **1809–10** COLERIDGE *Friend* (1865) 214 The light of philosophy, when it is confined to a small minority, points out the possessors as the victims, rather than the illuminators, of the multitude. **1862** F. HALL *Hindu Philos. Syst.* 215 *note*, It is one's self that apprehends, and.. the illuminator desiderated by the Vedāntins is superfluous.
†**4.** One who makes resplendent or illustrious.
1605 VERSTEGAN *Dec. Intell.* vii. (1634) 203 The poet Geffery Chaucer, who.. is of some called the first illuminator of the English tongue.
5. One who embellishes letters with gold and colours, or manuscripts with ornamental writing so embellished: see ILLUMINATE *v.* 8.
[**1655** FULLER *Hist. Camb.* 24 *Illuminatores*, such as gave light and lustre to Manuscripts.] **1699** WANLEY in *Lett. Lit. Men* (Camden) 286 It seems to me to have been the name.. of the Illuminator. **1708** HEARNE *Collect.* 8 Oct. (O.H.S.) II. 138 They are.. of a.. large size for yᵉ use of yᵉ Illuminators. **1762–71** H. WALPOLE *Vertue's Anecd. Paint.* (1786) I. 69 The most valuable artists of that age were the illuminators of manuscripts. **1841** W. SPALDING *Italy & It. Isl.* II. 244 Fra Angelico, educated as an illuminator of manuscripts.

iˈlluminatory, *a. rare.* [f. L. *illūmināt-* (see ILLUMINATE *v.*) + -ORY.] Illuminative; explanatory. (In quot. 1762, applied to the colouring of a map.)
1762 tr. *Busching's Syst. Geog.* VI. 512 In the leaf containing the whole dutchy of Silesia, the division of the county is erroneously marked,.. the principality of Jauer belonging to the prefecturate of Breslau.. whereas the illuminatory strokes include it within that of Brieg. **1822** WHEWELL *Let. to Hare* 17 July in Todhunter *Acc. W.'s Wks.* (1876) II. 47 You have time plenty to look forwards to the commencement of your illuminatory course in October.

illumine (ɪˈl(j)uːmɪn), *v.* Also 4–6 illumyne, yll-. [a. F. *illuminer* (12–13th c. in Hatz.-Darm.), ad. L. *illūmināre*.] = ILLUMINATE *v.*
1. *trans.* To light up, shed light upon; to shine upon or into; to light up in token of rejoicing or honour.
1375 BARBOUR *Bruce* VIII. 228 Thair speris, thair pennownys, & thar scheldis Of licht Illumynit all the feldis. **1447** BOKENHAM *Seyntys* (Roxb.) 22 A ful greth lyht Illumyned sodeynly that derk presoun. **1500–20** DUNBAR *Thistle & Rose* 41 Illumynit our with orient skyis brycht. **1667** MILTON *P.L.* I. 666 The sudden blaze Far round illumin'd hell. **1794** SULLIVAN *View Nat.* I. 375 Clouds.. illumined by the sun. **1852** TENNYSON *Ode Wellington* viii, When the long-illumined cities flame Their ever-loyal iron leader's fame. **1860** TYNDALL *Glac.* I. xxvii. 202 The Aiguille and Dôme were most singularly illumined.
fig. ? *a* **1550** in *Dunbar's Poems* (1890) 322 Jesus the sterne of most bewte In the is rissin.. Fro dirknes to illumyne the. **1856** *Sat. Rev.* II. 465/2 Casual expressions.. illumine hidden depths in the man's heart and character.
b. To give light or sight to (the eyes).
1548 HALL *Chron., Hen. VIII* 188 b, When god had illumined the eies of the kyng. **1567** *Triall Treas.* (1850) 30 Who ilumineth myne eyes to see my saluation.
c. *intr.* To become light or bright; to be illuminated.
1500–20 DUNBAR *Thistle & Rose* 21 All the houss illumynit of hir lemys. *Ibid.* 157 All the land illumynit of the licht. **1773** J. ROSS *Fratricide* IV. 598 (MS.) The clouds uprise, and Heav'n's dark hemisphere Illumines as they pass.
1801 ANNA SEWARD *Lett.* (1811) V. 395 Our city illumines tomorrow.
2. To enlighten spiritually; to convert; to inspire. (The earliest sense in Eng.)
c **1340** HAMPOLE *Prose Tr.* 14 When the resone.. es illuminede with grace for to be-halde Godde and gastely thynges. **1382** WYCLIF *Heb.* vi. 4 Hem that oonys ben illumyned [L. *illuminati*]. *c* **1489** CAXTON *Sonnes of Aymon* xiv. 336 Good lord, ye created and made our fader Adam.. and yllumyned him with the grace of the holi gost. **1554** in Strype *Eccl. Mem.* (1721) III. App. xvii. 43 Which faith is.. wrought by the H. Ghost.. Where through.. the mind is illumined. **18..** I. WILLIAMS *Hymn, 'Disposer Supreme'*, The lights thou hast kindled In darkness around, O may they illumine Our spirits within.
3. To enlighten mentally or intellectually. *rare.*
a **1529** SKELTON *Bowge of Courte* 20 Ignoraunce full soone dyde me dyscure, And shewed that in this arte I was not sure; For to illumyne, she sayde, I was to dulle. *c* **1532** *Remedie of Love* xxx, O ye muses nine Whilom ye were wont to be mine aide & light, My penne to direct, my braine to illumine. **1667** MILTON *P.L.* I. 23 What in me is dark Illumine. **1784** *De Lolme's Eng. Const.* Life, Whose labours delighted and illumined mankind. **1847** LYTTON *Lucretia* II. vi, This benighted mind, only illumined by a kind of miserable astuteness.
4. To brighten as with light, to make radiant.
1508 DUNBAR *Goldyn Targe* 258 Thy fresch anamalit termes celicall This mater coud illumynit haue full brycht. **1592** SHAKS. *Ven. & Ad.* 486 And as the bright sun glorifies the sky, So is her face illumined with her eye. **1851** LONGF. *Gold. Leg.* I. *Castle Vautsberg*, Like a happy lover Who illumines life with dreaming! **1871** R. ELLIS *Catullus* lxiv. 34 Delight their faces illumines.
5. To illuminate (manuscripts, etc.); also *fig.*
1717 POPE *Let. to Lady M. W. Montagu* Oct., She.. had his sonnets curiously copied out, and illumined with letters of gold. **1738** —— *Epil. Sat.* II. 121 To Cato Virgil pay'd one honest line; O let my Country's Friends illumine mine!
Hence **iˈllumined** *ppl. a.* **iˈllumining** *vbl. sb.* and *ppl. a.* (*lit.* and *fig.*)
1382 WYCLIF *2 Cor.* iv. 6 To the illumynynge of the Science of the Cleernesse of God. **1526** *Pilgr. Perf.* (W. de W. 1531) 1 b, The sentences of illumyned doctours concernynge perfeccyon. **1641** MILTON *Reform.* II. (1851) 68 The third Subsistence of Divine Infinitude, illumining Spirit. **1727–41** CHAMBERS *Cycl.* s.v., The sect of illumined was revived in France in the year 1634.. but they were so hotly pursued by Louis XIII, that they were soon destroyed. The brothers of the rosy cross, are sometimes also called illumined. **1777** G. FORSTER *Voy. round World* I. 55 We procured a bucket full of the illumined sea-water. **1860** PUSEY *Min. Proph.* 426 Another illumining of the Holy Spirit came for the benefit of those who received the prophecy.

‖**Illuminé** (ilymine). Also **Illuminee** and with lower-case initial. [a. F. *illuminé*, pa. pple. of *illuminer* to ILLUMINE, used subst.: see -EE.] One of the Illuminati.
1794 A. PAGET *Let.* in *Paget Papers* (1896) I. 20 It would be highly interesting to Your Lordship to get some information relative to the people called *Illuminés*. **1799** *Lett. Lit. Men* (Camden) 450 Having its Ministry, Councils, and Army filled with *Illuminés* who are by profession enemies to Monarchy. **1800** W. TAYLOR in *Monthly Mag.* VIII. 600 The order of Illuminees went to work only with the weapons of oral and written instruction. **1816** SCOTT *Antiq.* I. xiii. 289 A simple youth whispered me that he was an *Illuminé*, and carried on an intercourse with the invisible world. **1927** R. FRY *Let.* 19 Aug. (1972) II. 605 Simon Bussy.. said.. that I was an *illuminé* who imagined such things and then got excited about them.

illuminer (ɪˈl(j)uːmɪnə(r)). Also 5 **illumynour**, **-are**, 7, 9 **-or**. [f. ILLUMINE *v.* + -ER¹. In 15th c. found also with AF. ending *-our* (:—OF. *-eor*, *-eur*: *-ātōrem*), whence also later *-or*. For 16th c. Sc. form in *-are*, see -AR³.]
1. An illuminator; an enlightener. *lit.* and *fig.*
c **1450** tr. *De Imitatione* III. ii. 65 Lorde god, inspirour & illumynour of prophetes. **1483** CAXTON *Gold. Leg.* 1/2 (R. Suppl.) We haue grete nede of a doctour.. of a condyter, of a lighter or illuminer. **1526** *Pilgr. Perf.* (W. de W. 1531) 180 b, An illumyner or a gyuer of lyght. **1655** FULLER *Ch. Hist.* IV. i. §48 A great Refiner, and Illuminer of our English tongue.
†**2.** A source of light; a luminary. *Obs.*
c **1500** *Lancelot* 3 The brycht and fresch illumynare Uprisith arly in his fyre chare. **1686** GOAD *Celest. Bodies* I. xiii. 75 The Pyramid of Illumination.. enlarges her basis so much the more as the Illuminor is remote.
†**3.** An illuminator of manuscripts, etc. *Obs.*
a **1661** FULLER *Worthies, Cambridgesh.* I. (1662) 161 The best Illuminer or Limner of our age. **1824** J. JOHNSON *Typogr.* I. 605 The whole body of monks, scribes, illuminors, and readers.

illuminism (ɪˈl(j)uːmɪnɪz(ə)m). [ad. F. *illuminisme* (in Dict. Acad. 1835), f. *illuminer* to ILLUMINE: see -ISM.] The doctrine or principles of the ILLUMINATI, or of any sect so called; *gen.* a theory, doctrine, or practice which involves belief in or claim to extraordinary spiritual or intellectual enlightenment, or an aim or purpose to bring about such enlightenment in society.
1798 W. TAYLOR in *Monthly Rev.* XXVII. 509 The history of illuminism will form a most interesting chapter in modern ecclesiastical annals. **1811** SHELLEY *Let. to Godwin* 2 Mar., The very great influence which some years since was gained by Illuminism. **1840** *Fraser's Mag.* XXI. 548 In Spain, Illuminism associated itself with freemasonry. **1856** R. S. VAUGHAN *Mystics* (1860) II. VIII. ix. 99 In that age of professed Illuminism, in the times of Voltaire and Diderot,

when universal *Aufklärung* was to banish every mediæval phantasm. **1861** H. Browne in *Aids to Faith* vii. 295 The very principle of illuminism was, that there is, in man's inmost consciousness, an intuitional knowledge of truth. **1879** Farrar *St. Paul* xxxix. II. 266 Conceited illuminism is as deep an offence against charity as saintly self-satisfaction.

illuminist[1] (ɪ'l(j)uːmɪnɪst). [f. as prec.: see -IST.] One who holds the doctrine of illuminism; one who claims to have or aims at a high spiritual, intellectual, or moral enlightenment; one of the *Illuminati*. Also *attrib.*

1840 *Fraser's Mag.* XXI. 549 Malte-Brun.. was likewise an Illuminist refugee. **1866** *Contemp. Rev.* I. 380 The illuminists of last century—Voltaire and his school. **1871** Morley *Crit. Misc.* I. 117 The mystical, or, as he [de Maistre] said, the illuminist side of his mind. **1887** Dowden *Shelley* I. iii. 112 How Sparticus Weishaupt founded the Society of Illuminists.

Hence **illumi'nistic** *a.*, pertaining to illuminism, or the illuminists.

1860 in Worcester citing *Eclectic Rev.*

i'lluminist[2]. [f. ILLUMINE *v.* + -IST.] A professional illuminator of manuscripts, etc.

1816 Singer *Hist. Cards* 104 Rude outlines.. intended to pass through the hands of the Illuminist.

illuminize (ɪ'l(j)uːmɪnaɪz), *v.* [f. as prec. + -IZE.]

1. *intr.* To be an illuminist; to play the illuminist.

1800 Coleridge *Let. to Southey* 25 Jan. Lett. 1895 I. 323 If to act on the belief that all things are the process, and that inapplicable truths are moral falsehoods, be to illuminize, why then I illuminize!

2. *trans.* 'To initiate into the doctrine or principles of the Illuminati' (Webster 1828 citing *Amer. Review*).

illuminized (ɪ'l(j)uːmɪnaɪzd), *ppl. a. rare.* [f. ILLUMINIZE *v.* + -ED[1].] Initiated (see ILLUMINIZE *v.* 2).

1920 *19th Cent.* July 104 A great Masonic meeting which was held in 1786 at Frankfurt—whither the headquarters of illuminised Freemasonry were removed after the famous Congress.

illuminometer (ɪl(j)uːmɪ'nɒmɪtə(r)). [f. ILLUMIN(ATION + -O + -METER.] A photometer, *esp.* one for measuring the illumination of surfaces (rather than the intensity of light sources).

1895 Houston & Kennelly in *Operator & Electr. World* 9 Mar. 309/2 The question at issue is.. the degree of illumination actually produced, and this question cannot be decided by the photometer, but requires the use of an illumination measurer or illuminometer. *Ibid.* 310/2 We call our instrument an illuminometer and have filed applications for a patent on the same. **1908** *Illuminating Engineer* (London) I. 714/2 It was proposed to use it [*sc.* Houston and Kennelly's photometer] for candlepower photometry as well as for the measurement of illumination. The unfortunate name 'illuminometer' was given to the instrument, and.. this mongrel word is sometimes used at the present day. **1953** Kirk & Othmer *Encycl. Chem. Technol.* XI. 326 The luminous intensity of the flame.. can be measured by an illuminometer consisting of a barrier-layer photocell connected to a micro-ammeter. **1971** *Jrnl. Gen. Psychol.* LXXXIV. 125 Exposure times of 40, 150, and 3500 msec and luminances of three and 30 fc, as read with a Macbeth Illuminometer, were employed.

illuminor: see ILLUMINER.

†**i'lluminous**, *a.*[1] *Obs.* [f. IL-[1] + LUMINOUS: after *illumine*, etc.] Bright, illuminatory.

c **1485** *Digby Myst.* (1882) III. 623 þe bemys of grace xal byn Illumynows. **1560** Rolland *Crt. Venus* III. 180 And sa the richt salbe Illuminous. **1745** Eliza Heywood *Fem. Spect.* (1748) II. 208 It is not from below we are to expect any illuminous emanations.

illuminous (ɪ'l(j)uːmɪnəs, ɪll-), *a.*[2] *rare.* [f. IL-[2] + LUMINOUS.] Non-luminous, opaque, dark.

1656 Blount *Glossogr.*, *Illuminous* (*illuminosus*), without light. **1842** Sir H. Taylor *Edwin the Fair* II. ii, This life.. to him Is but a tissue of illuminous dreams.

‖**illupi** ('ɪluːpɪ). *East-Ind.* Also illupie, illipe(e, illoopoo, ilpa, illupa. [Tamil *iluppai* or *iruppai*, Malayālam *iruppa*.] An evergreen tree, *Bassia longifolia* (N.O. *Sapotaceæ*), a native of Southern India. ***illupi oil***, a fixed solid oil obtained from the seeds of this tree. ***illipe butter***, any of various vegetable fats.

1832 H. Piddington *Eng. Index Plants India* 148 Illipee. **1842** W. B. O'Shaughnessy *Bengal Dispensatory*, Illupei, Illupi. **1858** Simmonds *Dict. Trade*, *Illipe Oil*, *Illoopoo Oil*, a solid oil expressed from the seeds of *Bassia longifolia*. *c* **1865** Letheby in *Circ. Sc.* I. 95/1 *Ilpa oil*, or *Eloopei unnay*, .. is expressed from the seeds of the Illupie tree.. that is.. abundant in the Madras Presidency. **1875** *Ure's Dict. Arts*, *Illoopa oil*.. used in India for illuminating purposes, and for the manufacture of soap. **1904** J. Lewkowitsch *Oils, Fats, & Waxes* (ed. 3) II. xiv. 702 The commercial fat is a mixture of Mowrah seed oil with Mahua butter or illipe butter, the fat from *Bassia latifolia*. **1911** *Encycl. Brit.* XX. 47 Mahua butter, Illipé butter. **1951** A. E. Bailey *Industr. Oil & Fat Products* (ed. 2) vi. 141 Mowrah fat, or illipé butter, which is obtained from the Indian plant *Bassia longifolia*, resembles shea butter in being relatively unsaturated, and correspondingly soft.

†**i'llure, i'llurement.** Alterations of ALLURE, ALLUREMENT, under the influence of words having prefix *il-*.

1582 N. T. (Rhem.) *2 Cor.* xi. 3 *note*, The sweet mouthes and illurements of Heretickes. **1638** Sir T. Herbert *Trav.* (ed. 2) 218 [He] illured from Babylon six hundred thousand soules. **1651** *Burton's Anat. Mel.* III. ii. III. iv. 494 If these illurements [*earlier edd.* allurements] do not take place for Simierus. *a* **1661** Fuller (Webster), The devil insnareth the souls of many men, by illuring them with the muck and dung of this world, to undo them eternally.

ill usage, 'ill-'usage. [Properly two words like *harsh usage*, *worse usage*, but commonly hyphened under the influence of *ill-used*.] The action of using or treating ill; bad or unkind treatment.

[**1569** in J. Hooker *Life Sir P. Carew* (1857) 234 The cruel and ill usages of my L. Deputy and Sr Peter Carew.] **1621** Burton *Anat. Mel.* I. ii. IV. ii, Too much severity and ill usage. **1818** Cobbett *Pol. Reg.* XXXIII. 298 They seldom fail to shew their just resentment of ill-usage. **1867** Trollope *Chron. Barset* I. i. 5 A manifest struggle to do his duty in spite of the world's ill-usage.

ill-use (ˌɪl'juːz), *v.* [Properly two words, *ill* adv. + *use* vb., which under the influence of *ill-used* (aided, perhaps, by *abuse*, *misuse*) have come to be hyphened.] *trans.* To 'use' or treat badly; to deal cruelly, unkindly, or inconsiderately with.

1841 Browning *Pippa* Introd. 30 If thou ill-usest Me, who am only Pippa. **1858** Ld. St. Leonards *Handy-Bk. Prop. Law* xiii. 80 The object of the Act was to protect mothers from the tyranny of husbands who ill-use them. **1876** T. Hardy *Ethelberta* (1890) 79, I would.. never desert you, ill-use me how you might!

ill-used ('ɪl'juːzd), *pa. pple.* and *ppl. a.* [Orig. two words, *ill* adv. and *used* pa. pple., hyphened when used attrib.; now treated as pa. pple. of prec. vb.] Badly 'used' or treated; ill-treated.

1594 Shaks. *Rich. III*, IV. iv. 396 (1623) Sweare not by time to come, for that thou hast Misvs'd ere vs'd, by times ill-vs'd [o]repast [*Qos.* misused.. o'erpast]. *c* **1600** —— *Sonn.* xcv, The hardest knife ill-used doth lose his edge. *a* **1656** Bp. Hall *Rem. Wks.* (1660) 109 Those.. guests who finde themselves ill used. **1765** Smollett *Trav.* xli. (1766) II. 255 If I am ill-used at the post-house in England, I can be accommodated elsewhere. **1832** Tennyson *Lotos-Eaters* 165 An ill-used race of men.

Hence ˌ**ill-'usedness**, condition of being ill-used.

1869 Mrs. Whitney *We Girls* vi. (1873) 95 A tone of quiet ill usedness.

i'llusible, *a. rare.* [f. L. *illūs-*, ppl. stem of *illūdĕ-re* to ILLUDE: see -IBLE.] Capable of being illuded or deceived.

a **1631** Donne in *Select.* (1840) 98 God is not an illusible God, to be carried with promises, or purposes only.

illusion (ɪ'l(j)uːʒən). Also 4–5 **illusyon(e**, 4–6 **-sioun**, 6 **-tion**. [a. F. *illusion* (12th c. in *Oxf. Psal.* lxxviii. 4), ad. L. *illūsiōn-em* mocking, jeering, (in Vulg.) deceit, illusion, n. of action f. *illūdĕre* to ILLUDE.] The action of illuding, the condition of being illuded; that whereby one is illuded.

†**1.** The action of deriding or mocking; derision, mockery. Also (with *pl.*) an instance of this. *Obs.*

(App. only as transl. of, or in reference to, L. *illūsio*.)

1382 Wyclif *Isa.* lxvi. 4, I shal chesen the illusiouns [1388 scornyngis] of hem. *c* **1450** *Mirour Saluacioun* 4601 Remyttyng the to pilat after this illusionne. **1526** *Pilgr. Perf.* (W. de W. 1531) 249 b, On his betrayenge and illusyons, how he was mocked & scorned before Anna and Cayphas. **1567** *Ps. lxxix.* in *Gude & Godlie B.* (S.T.S.) 118 Our nichtbouris.. leuch at vs with greit Illusioun. **1656** Blount *Glossogr.*, *Illusion*, a mocking or scorning.

2. †**a.** The action, or an act, of deceiving the bodily eye by false or unreal appearances, or the mental eye by false prospects, statements, etc.; deception, delusion, befooling. *Obs.*

c **1340** Hampole *Prose Tr.* 17 Wha-so þan will here aungells sange, and noghte be dyssayuede by feynynge.. ne by illusyone of þe enemy. *c* **1386** Chaucer *Can. Yeom. Prol. & T.* 120 To muchel folk we doon illusion. *c* **1470** Henry *Wallace* VII. 5 With suttelte and wykkit illusione, The worthi Scottis to put to confusione. **1529** More *Dyaloge* I. Wks. 130/2 Done by the deuil.. for the illusyon of them that with ydolatry had deserued to be deluded. **1613** Shaks. *Hen. VIII*, I. ii. 178, I told my Lord the Duke, by th'Diuels illusions The Monke might be deceiu'd. **1695** Woodward *Nat. Hist. Earth* VI. (1702) 249 This had been little better than a downright Illusion and abusing of him.

b. The fact or condition of being deceived or deluded by appearances, or an instance of this; a mental state involving the attribution of reality to what is unreal; a false conception or idea; a deception, delusion, fancy.

1571 *Satir. Poems Reform.* xxviii. 17 Can I nocht tell gif be Illutioun, Or gif be feir sic fantaseis we tak. **1613** Purchas *Pilgrimage* (1614) 158 The illusions of their bewitched mindes. **1665** Stillingfl. *Protest. Relig.* 600 [They] have fallen into many illusions and deceitful fancies. **1719** Young *Revenge* V. ii, Let us talk of Love, Plunge ourselves deep into the sweet illusion. **1772** Priestley *Inst. Relig.* (1782) I. 314 They could not be under an illusion themselves. **1862** H. Spencer *First Princ.* II. iii §46 (1875) 158 A sense of universal illusion ordinarily follows the reading of metaphysics. **1875** Emerson *Lett. & Soc. Aims*, *Immortality* Wks. (Bohn) III. 286 The youth puts off the illusions of the child.

3. Something that deceives or deludes by producing a false impression; a deceptive or illusive appearance, statement, belief, etc.; in early use often *spec.* An unreal visual appearance, an apparition, phantom.

c **1374** Chaucer *Troylus* V. 368 Prestes of þe temple tellen þis That dremes ben þe reuelacions Of goddes, and.. That þey ben Infernals illusions. *c* **1384** —— *H. Fame* I. 493 O Criste.. Fro Fantome and Illusion Me save. **1494** Fabyan *Chron.* V. c. 75 Whiche is nat comely to any Cristen Relygyon to gyue to any suche fantastycall illusions any mynde or credence. **1602** Shaks. *Ham.* I. i. 127 Stay Illusion: If thou hast any sound, or vse of Voyce, Speake to me. **1659** B. Harris *Parival's Iron Age* 161 Their pretexts were but illusions, to amuse, and baffle the good intentions of the Germans. **1715–20** Pope *Iliad* II. 19 Jove.. bids an empty phantom rise to sight.. Swift as the word the vain Illusion fled. **1749** Smollett *Regic.* III. i. (1777) 52 Come, smiling hope—divine illusion! come. **1849** Robertson *Serm.* Ser. IV. ix. (1876) 78 These were all an illusion and a phantasma, a thing that appeared, but did not really exist.

4. a. Sensuous perception of an external object, involving a false belief or conception: strictly distinguished from *hallucination*, but in general use often made to include it, and hence = the apparent perception of an external object when no such object is present, or of attributes of an object which do not exist. Also (with *pl.*) an instance of this.

1774 Goldsm. *Nat. Hist.* (1776) II. 147 Hitherto.. they only seem to fortify the organ for seeing distinctly; but they have still many illusions to correct. **1794** Sullivan *View Nat.* II. xlviii. 381 In lifting our eyes to the firmament, we see all the stars, as it were, attached to the same dome. But, this is merely an optical illusion. **1850** Robertson *Serm.* Ser. III. vi. 84 You may paint a picture in which rocks, trees, and sky are never mistaken for what they seem, yet produce all the emotion which real rocks, trees and sky would produce. This is illusion. **1858** Hawthorne *Fr. & It. Jrnls.* I. 193 Frescos brought to such perspective illusion, that the edges seem to project into air. **1859** Hulme tr. *De Boismont's Hallucinations* i. 21 We define.. an illusion as the false appreciation of real sensations. **1881** J. Sully in *Nature* XXIV. 185 As distinguished from hallucinations, illusions 'must always have a starting-point in some actual impression, whereas a hallucination has no such basis'. **1886** Gurney, etc. *Phantasms of Living* II. 184 Illusion consists either in perceiving a totally wrong object in place of the right one.. or in investing the right object with the wrong attributes.

b. ***the argument from illusion*** (Philos.): the argument that the objects of sense-experience, usually called ideas, appearances, or sense-data, cannot be objects in a physical world independent of the perceiver, since they vary according to his condition and environment.

1932 H. H. Price *Perception* ii. 27 It is commonly held that the *Argument from Illusion* (as it is called) is sufficient to refute Naïve Realism. **1936** A. J. Ayer *Lang., Truth & Logic* viii. 228 The so-called argument from illusion. **1940** —— *Found. Empirical Knowl.* i. 3 The answer is provided by what is known as the argument from illusion. **1959** J. L. Austin *Sense & Sensibilia* (1962) iii. 20 The primary purpose of the argument from illusion is to induce people to accept 'sense-data'. **1971** A. Flew *Introd. Western Philos.* 353 We can characterize the Argument from Illusion as the attempt to show that.. what we actually see is never things but only the appearances of things.

5. A name given to a thin and very transparent kind of tulle.

1857 *Lawrence* (Kansas) *Republican* 28 May 3 Lace, Gimp, Straw, Silk, Blend, Hair and Illusion Bonnets. **1865** F. B. Palliser *Hist. Lace* xxxv. 423 M. Doguin, who afterwards used the fine silks, and invented that popular material first called 'zephyr', since 'illusion'. **1869** L. M. Alcott *Little Women* II. xiv. 207 She put on Flo's old white silk ball dress, and covered it with a cloud of fresh illusion. **1873** *Young Englishwoman* Jan. 50/1 White muslin, trimmed with white lace, illusion veil. **1887** B. Farjeon *While Golden Sleep* 8 Pale blue silk, looped up with illusion and forget-me-nots. **1902** *Daily Chron.* 13 Dec. 8/4 It was trimmed with ruches of black tulle illusion. **1967** *Boston Sunday Herald* 30 Apr. v. 2/3 The headpiece was a lace mantilla with an illusion veil.

6. *attrib.* and *Comb.*, as ***illusion effect***; ***illusion-disturbing***, ***-proof*** adjs.

1909 W. M. Urban *Valuation* ix. 275 The elimination of illusion-disturbing moments is a conscious process. **1971** *Jrnl. Gen. Psychol.* LXXXV. 77 Differences in the magnitude of the illusion-effect were introduced. **1924** G. B. Shaw *Saint Joan* p. xvi, Napoleon or any other illusionproof genius.

Hence **i'llusionless** *a.*, not characterized by illusions.

1897 G. B. Shaw in *Academy* 16 Jan. 67/2 Illusionless conversation.. when the old people in Ibsen.. tell each other the frozen truth. **1964** S. Bellow *Herzog* 229 His face was illusionless, without need of hypocrisy.

i'llusionable, *a. rare.* [f. prec. + -ABLE.] Liable to illusions.

1879 E. J. Payne in *Academy* 6 Sept. 167/1 One who had been in the maturity of his powers and reputation when those illusionable youths were in their cradles.

illusional (ɪ'l(j)uːʒənəl), *a.* [f. ILLUSION + -AL.] Pertaining to, characterized by, or subject to illusions.

1900 Dorland *Med. Dict.* 317/1. **1923** *Daily Mail* 1 Mar. 4 On reception into prison he was suspicious, illusional, and confused. **1942** *Art Digest* 15 Jan. 30 She also goes in for illusional effects, such as an interwoven lost-and-found

sensation in *Malaga Cathedral* and the vaporous beach scene *Le Bar*.

i'llusionary, *a.* [f. as ILLUSIONABLE *a.* + -ARY.] Characterized by illusions; of the nature of an illusion; illusory.

1886 *Cornh. Mag.* Nov. 513 A romantic and an illusionary temperament. **1890** *Blackw. Mag.* CXLVIII. 534/2 An illusionary, dream-like light which had had no touch of earthly reality about it.

illusioned (ɪ'l(j)uːʒənd), *ppl. a.* [f. as ILLUSIONAL *a.* + -ED².] Full of illusions.

1920 *Glasgow Herald* 6 July 6 A fervent but illusioned admirer. **1921** GALSWORTHY *To Let* III. vi. 267 Even his love felt tainted, less illusioned, more of the earth. **1971** *Guardian* 11 Oct. 10 We remain totally illusioned..about the general good intentions of those who practise the art of government.

illusionism (ɪ'l(j)uːʒənɪz(ə)m). [f. ILLUSION + -ISM.] **1.** Theory or doctrine pertaining to or dealing with illusions; the theory that the material world is an illusion.

1843 *For. Q. Rev.* II. 351 From illusionism (the theory of Bishop Berkeley) to mysticism. **1882** *Athenæum* 14 Jan. 51/3 It contains what profess to be adequate analyses of..the 'akosmism of Brahmanism' and the 'absolute illusionism of Buddhism'.

2. The use of illusionary effects in art or sculpture.

1951 M. L. WOLF *Dict. Arts* 345/2 *Illusionism*, the effort in painting or sculpture to create as nearly as possible an illusion of visual reality. **1960** [see FANTASIST]. **1961** M. LEVY *Studio Dict. Art Terms* 62 *Illusionism*, the practice of Trompe L'Oeil painting. **1962** *Times* 6 Apr. 17/3 It [*sc.* the attitude and style of pop-art] is a gaudy glamorization of its subject which deliberately crashes its visual gears from abstract pattern right through to *trompe-l'oeil* illusionism.

illusionist (ɪ'l(j)uːʒənɪst). [f. as prec. + -IST.] **1.** One who holds the theory of illusionism; one who disbelieves in objective existence.

1843 *For Q. Rev.* II. 343 While the pantheist and the illusionist are discussing systems, the masses enact that there is no God. **1862** F. HALL *Hindu Philos. Syst.* 166 *note*, It tells with equal relevancy in confutation of the illusionists (*máyávádin*) and crypto-Bauddhas (*prachhannabauddha*).

2. One who produces illusions; *spec.* a conjuror or sleight-of-hand performer.

1850 *Punch* XIX. 215/2 The novel trick of shifting the lectern, will be introduced by that celebrated illusionist, the Rev. Mr. Cozens. **1864** *Daily Tel.* 6 Sept., In compliance with a request from the illusionist, four gentlemen advanced from the body of the hall to co-operate in a portion of the evening's entertainments. **1894** *Times* 7 Aug. 6/2 The illusionist..succeeded in mystifying his audience by producing a living tree on a piece of glass.

3. (See quots.)

1864 WEBSTER, *Illusionist*, one given to illusion. **1883** *Harper's Mag.* Apr. 699/1 He [the impressionist] is a good antidote against the 'illusionist', who sees too much, and then adds to it a lot that he does *not* see.

Hence **illusio'nistic** *a.*, pertaining to illusionism or the illusionists.

1911 *Encycl. Brit.* XXIII. 482/1 The lighting is carefully calculated with a view to illusionistic effect under the local conditions. **1938** *Mod. Lang. Rev.* Oct. 549 The tendency..to employ an illusionistic realism for the purpose of sensationalism..is what lies behind Wölfflin's conception of 'baroque'. **1944** *Burlington Mag.* Aug. 199/1 Compared with this the Byzantine solution may still be called illusionistic. **1958** *Times* 24 Sept. 3/1 They [*sc.* Dali's pictures] are irritatingly artificial concoctions with passages ..quite amazingly inept for a specialist in illusionistic devices. **1968** *Times* 21 Dec. 19/1 There was an upsurge of decorative architecture in Bavaria, Franconia and Swabia. It was illusionistic and what the writer calls 'a-tactonic'.

illusive (ɪ'l(j)uːsɪv), *a.* [f. L. *illūs-*, ppl. stem of *illūdĕre* to ILLUDE + -IVE.] That tends to illude or deceive by unreal appearances; productive of illusion or false impression; deceptive; illusory.

1679 JENISON *Popish Plot* 38 As if all were but an apparition or an illusive thing. **1755** J. G. COOPER *Tomb Shaks.* (R.), In yonder mead behold that vapour Whose vivid beams illusive play, Far off it seems a friendly taper To guide the traveller on his way. **1813** SCOTT *Trierm.* Concl. i, A vain illusive show, That melts whene'er the sun-beams glow. **1856** FROUDE *Hist. Eng.* ix. (1858) II. 399 The efforts at a combination had hitherto been illusive and ineffectual. **1893** W. H. HUDSON *Patagonia* 208 The mysterious illusive city, peopled by whites..is to moderns a myth.

Hence **i'llusively** *adv.*, in an illusive manner, by an illusion; **i'llusiveness**, illusive or deceptive quality.

1727 BAILEY vol. II, *Illusiveness*. **1818** TODD, *Illusively*. **1824** *Examiner* 246/2 Water was never more illusively lucid. **1829** I. TAYLOR *Enthus.* ix. 248 A vein of illusiveness runs through every page. **1839** *Fraser's Mag.* XIX. 327 The illusion loses its illusiveness.

illusor (ɪ'l(j)uːsə(r)). *rare.* [ad. late L. *illūsor*, *-ōrem*, agent-n. from *illūdĕre*, *illūs-* to ILLUDE.] A deceiver, deluder.

1382 WYCLIF *2 Pet.* iii. 3 In the laste dayes illusours [*Gloss* or scorners, or deceyuours] shulen come in deceyt. **1483** CAXTON *Gold. Leg.* 9/1 (R. Suppl.) They be sayd illuseurs and deceyuours, by cause they deceyued herodes. **1886** STUBBS *Med. & Mod. Hist.* viii. 197 Though he proffered peace he only wanted money; he was an illusor, and they would have nothing to do with him.

illusory (ɪ'l(j)uːsərɪ), *a.* [ad. late L. *illūsōri-us* of a mocking character, ironical, f. *illūsor*: see prec. and -ORY. Cf. F. *illusoire*.] Having the quality of illuding or tending to deceive by unreal prospects; of the nature of an illusion; illusive.

In first quot. as *sb.* = an illusory or illusive thing; an illusion.

1599 Q. ELIZ. *Let.* (N.), To trust him uppon pledges is a meare illusorye. *a* **1631** DONNE in *Select.* (1840) 79 A false, an illusory, and a sinful comfort. *a* **1691** BOYLE *Refl. Theol. Distinction* §2 It is not an arbitrary or illusory distinction. **1794** SULLIVAN *View Nat.* I. 25 The illusory offspring of the imagination. **1866** J. MARTINEAU *Ess.* I. 256 The promise is for the present illusory. **1866** ROGERS *Agric. & Prices* I. xxv. 621 The price given..is illusory. **1883** FROUDE *Short Stud.* IV. III. 256 Much illusory physiology was based on this hypothesis.

Hence **i'llusorily** *adv.*, in an illusory manner, by an illusion; **i'llusoriness**, deceptiveness of appearance.

a **1631** DONNE *Six Serm.* i. (1634) 32 That that Pilate did illusorily..wash his hands from the bloud of any of those men. **1727** BAILEY vol. II, *Illusoriness*. **1869** FARRAR *Fam. Speech* iii. (1873) 88 The utter illusoriness of the accidental resemblances in the unborrowed words. **1880** J. CAIRD *Philos. Relig.* v. 136 This very feeling of the instability and illusoriness of the world. **1898** *Westm. Gaz.* 1 Sept. 2/1 The way in front was illusorily barred by swiftly flowing water.

†**i'llustrable**, *a. Obs.* [f. L. type **illustrābil-is*, f. *illustrā-re* to ILLUSTRATE: see -BLE.] = next.

1658 SIR T. BROWNE *Gard. Cyrus* ii. 43 Solution and consolidation, union and division, illustrable from Aristotle in the old *Nucifragium* or nutcracker. **1668** G. C. in *H. More's Div. Dial.* To Rdr. a ij, How illustrable that passage is from the last Section of the 7. Chapter of Des Cartes his Meteors.

illustratable (ɪlə'streɪtəb(ə)l, -'lʌstrətəb(ə)l), *a.* [f. ILLUSTRATE *v.* + -ABLE.] Capable of being illustrated.

1850 D. G. ROSSETTI *Let.* in W. B. Scott *Autobiog.* (1892) I. xxi. 283 An illustratable paper. **1887** *Scot. Leader* 17 Dec. 4 The gradual reduction of animal organs was illustratable by innumerable examples.

†**i'llustrate**, *ppl. a. Obs.* [ad. L. *illustrāt-us*, pa. pple. of *illustrāre* to ILLUSTRATE.]

A. as *pa. pple.* Illustrated, illuminated, lighted up, enlightened: see ILLUSTRATE *v.*

1526 *Pilgr. Perf.* (W. de W. 1531) 285 O wolde god I.. were illustrate or lyghtned with the lyght and felynge therof. **1548** UDALL, etc. *Erasm. Par. Acts* ix. Fivb, Thin-warde eyes of his soule, wer in the meane space clearely illustrat. **1619** J. BAINBRIDGE *Descr. Late Comet* 10 The Comet..at first was illustrate with a bright resplendence. **1671** *True Non-conf.* 334 These things need not to be illustrat.

B. as *adj.* Illuminated, resplendent, clear; lustrous, illustrious.

1562 A. SCOTT *Poems* (S.T.S.) i. 1 Welcum, illustrat Ladye, and oure quene. **1583** SHAKS. *L.L.L.* v. i. 128 This most gallant, illustrate and learned Gentleman. **1601** CHETTLE & MUNDAY *Death Robt. Earl Huntington* v. ii. in Hazl. *Dodsley* VIII. 315 Bright sun, retire; gild not this vault of death With thy illustrate rays. **1669** *Addr. Yng. Gentry Eng.* 110 The Philosophy, we grope after..here, will..by the first approaches of the light of our never setting day, be plain and illustrate to us. **1704** HEARNE *Duct. Hist.* (1714) I. 136 That admirable work, the Lives of the most illustrate Men, Greeks and Romans.

Hence †**i'llustrately** *adv.*

1634 *Simple Reasons* in *Harl. Misc.* (Malh.) IV. 181 Our faith in God, and loyalty to the King, are most translucently light..refulgently light, illustrately light.

illustrate ('ɪləstreɪt, ɪ'lʌstreɪt), *v.* [f. L. *illustrāt-*, ppl. stem of *illustrāre* to light up, illuminate, clear up, elucidate, embellish, set off, render famous or illustrious; cf. *illustr-is* ILLUSTRE. For the stress see CONTEMPLATE *v.*]

†**1. a.** *trans.* To shed light upon, light up, illumine. *Obs.*

1625 N. CARPENTER *Geog. Del.* I. ii. (1635) 35 The beames of the Sun illustrate and lighten the Moone. **1681** COTTON *Wond. Peak* (ed. 4) 82 The Windows..Illustrating the noble Room. *a* **1717** PARNELL *Hymn for Morning* (Seager), The light, serenely fair, Illustrates all the tracts of air.

†**b.** Directly *fig.* esp. To illuminate (the mind). *Obs.* or *arch.* (The earlier use.)

1526 *Pilgr. Perf.* (W. de W. 1531) 125 It dyd so illustrate or lyghten theyr vnderstandynge, that [etc.]. **1665** BOYLE *Occas. Refl.* (1848) 55 The Mind of Man. Illustrated by the Beams of Heavenly Light, and Joy. **1728** EARBERY tr. *Burnet's St. Dead* II. 62 Virtue and Truth in their Fulness of Light, illustrating the whole World. **1872** BROWNING *Fifine* xxix, Quick sense perceives the same Self-vindicating flash illustrate every man And woman of our mass.

†**2.** To make lustrous, luminous, or bright; to set off with bright colours; *gen.* to beautify, adorn. *Obs.*

1592 NASHE *P. Penilesse* (ed. 2) 17b, There is no study, but it [Poetry] doth illustrate and beautify. **1634** SIR T. HERBERT *Trav.* 59 The wals..have beene illustrated with Gold, which in some places is visible. **1650** BULWER *Anthropomet.* 165 They illustrate their Arms and Hands, their Legs and Feet, with painted flowers and birds. **1748** RICHARDSON *Clarissa* (1811) III. iii. 29 Her head-dress was a Brussels-lace mob..A sky blue ribband illustrated that.

3. To set in a good light; to display to advantage; to show up.

1603 H. CROSSE *Vertues Commw.* (1878) 51 The deformitie of the one doth much illustrate and beautifie the other. **1628** PRYNNE *Love-lockes* 55 The onely meanes therefore for men to enhance, illustrate, and set out their Beautie, is to neglect it. **1686** W. DE BRITAINE *Hum. Prud.* xi. 53 Honour and Greatness add nothing to me, but to illustrate my Humility. **1757** H. WALPOLE *Mem. Geo. II*, III. 75 Pitt though..apt enough to take any step to illustrate his own measures. **1843** DICKENS *Mart. Chuz.* (1844) ii. 10 Charity..did so well set off and illustrate her sister! **1917** *Mod. Lang. Rev.* XII. 205, I do not desire to illustrate my version of 'the Fause Knight', but merely to claim that it throws new light on the subject matter of the original ballad.

4. To shed lustre upon; to render illustrious, renowned, or famous; to confer honour or distinction upon. Now *rare*.

1530 PALSGR. 589/2, I illustrate, I bring to lyght or make noble or worthy. **1624** HEYWOOD *Gunaik.* To Rdr., Women, such as have..beene illustrated for their Vertues, and noble actions. *a* **1794** GIBBON *Mem.* in *Misc. Wks.* (1814) I. 235 Mr. Wedderburne..who now illustrates the title of Lord Loughborough. **1834** SIR W. HAMILTON *Discuss.* (1852) 377 Under this system, no men of distinguished merit have illustrated our Universities. **1858** J. H. NEWMAN *Mission of Benedictine Order* in *Sel. Ess.* (1902) 191 The famous Congregation of Cluni, illustrated by St. Majolus, St. Odilo, Peter the Venerable. **1931** [see DITHER *sb.* b]. **1952** G. SARTON *Hist. Sci.* I. xi. 277 We now come to the greatest mathematician of the century, the first man to illustrate the name of Hippocrates.

5. To throw the light of intelligence upon; to make clear, elucidate, clear up, explain.

1538 COVERDALE *New Test.* Prol., Thou shalt see that one translation declareth, openeth, and illustrateth another. **1620** GRANGER *Div. Logike* 116 Argument that is brought to confirme, and illustrate must be more manifest..then that which is to be confirmed, and illustrated. **1691** NORRIS *Pract. Disc.* 77 When Revelation had illustrated the obscure Text of Reason. **1793** BEDDOES *Let. Darwin* 29 Many experiments upon animals, tending to illustrate this important subject. **1874** KINGSLEY *Lett.* (1878) II. 452 You have..illustrated it by quotations and metaphors which are sound and to the point.

6. To make clear or evident by means of examples, to elucidate; to give an example, instance, or illustration of; to exemplify. Also *absol.*

1612 BRINSLEY *Lud. Lit.* xiii. (1627) 183 Illustrated by a few more examples. **1732** BERKELEY *Alciphr.* II. §4, I can illustrate this doctrine of Lysicles by examples. **1786** W. THOMSON *Watson's Philip III* (1793) II. VI. 224 To illustrate the advantages of vigilance and foresight. **1849** MACAULAY *Hist. Eng.* I. ii. 162 Perhaps no single circumstance more strongly illustrates the temper of the precisians than their conduct respecting Christmas day. **1863** O. M. MITCHELL *Astron. Bible* 168 The subject is difficult. Permit me to illustrate. **1874** GREEN *Short Hist.* iii. §4. 129 No city better illustrates the transformation of the land in the hands of its Norman masters. **1895** F. HALL in *Nation* (N.Y.) LXI. 363/2 Very likely the usage which has been illustrated is a good deal older.

7. To elucidate (a description, etc.) by means of drawings or pictures; to ornament (a book, etc.) in this way with elucidatory designs. Said also of the pictures themselves.

1638 F. JUNIUS *Paint. of Ancients* 128 That the cleerest grounds an Artist is able to propound, are yet illustrated and cleered by Picture. **1676** RAY *Corr.* (1848) 123 [Few readers are] willing to take the pains to read..such [anatomical] descriptions, unless illustrated by figures. **1773** COOK *1st Voy.* Introd. (R.), The engravings which illustrate and adorn the account of this voyage. **1800** *Med. Jrnl.* III. 20, I shall subjoin two curious cases..together with a drawing to illustrate one of them. **1827** HONE *Table Bk.* I. 171 A gentleman engaged to assist in illustrating this work. **1873** TRISTRAM *Moab* i. 3 His camera illustrated the results of the expedition with about 80 excellent photographs. **1891** *Daily News* 9 Apr. 3/5 Journals which did not formerly illustrate now do so, and book and magazine literature are more than ever illustrated to meet the popular taste.

†**8.** To clear (the head or brain). *Obs.*

1684 tr. *Bonet's Merc. Compit.* XIX. 680 Some Cephalicks ..though they be less grateful to the Palate or Stomach..yet illustrate the Brain.

Hence **illustrating** *vbl. sb.* and *ppl. a.*

1598 HAKLUYT *Voy.* I. 352 To the illustrating of the Queenes most excellent Maiestie, the honour and commoditie of this her highnesse Realme. **1620** GRANGER *Div. Logike* 157 It hath speciall use in illustrating, and amplifying. **1681** FLAVEL *Meth. Grace* ix. 197 An illustrating work of the Spirit upon the minds of sinners. **1790** BURKE *Fr. Rev.* Wks. V. 80 Our liberty has a pedigree and illustrating ancestors. **1840** M. EDGEWORTH *Let.* 30 Dec. (1971) 574 The *illustrating* speech of the Irishman to the waiter of 'I'd wish to have the ham and the butter separate'.

illustrated ('ɪləstreɪtɪd, ɪ'lʌstreɪtɪd), *ppl. a.* (*sb.*) [f. ILLUSTRATE *v.* + ED¹.]

1. †**a.** Illuminated, made lustrous or bright (*obs.*). **b.** Having pictorial illustrations.

1831 (Dec. 31) *Olio or Museum Entertainm.* IX. No. 1 (*First Article*) Illustrated article: Two nights in Beauchamp tower. **1832** *Fraser's Mag.* VI. 393 The child in his illustrated look had the air as of a mighty triumphant victor. **1842** (*title*) The Illustrated London News. **1891** *Daily News* 9 Apr. 3/5 A paper..on Photography and Illustrated Journalism.

2. as *sb.* An illustrated newspaper or magazine. (In quot. 1879 = Illustrated London News.)

1879 *Echo* 10 Feb. 4/1 Looking at Illustrateds or Punches. **1892** STEVENSON & L. OSBOURNE *Wrecker* (ed. 2) 45 It may fit me for a position on one of the illustrateds.

illustration (ɪlə'streɪʃən). [a. F. *illustration* (13th c. in Godef.), ad. L. *illustrātiōn-em* (Quintilian), n. of action f. *illustrāre* to ILLUSTRATE.] The action or fact of illustrating.

The sense-history is parallel to that of ILLUMINATION, the meaning 'spiritual enlightenment' being the first to appear.

†**1.** Lighting up, illumination, enlightenment. *Obs.*

a. spiritual (the earliest sense) or intellectual.

c **1375** *Sc. Leg. Saints, Egipciane* 40 He had sic infusione of godis illustracione. **1526** *Pilgr. Perf.* (W. de W. 1531) 126 b, The persone that receyueth suche illustracyon or lyght, is all quvet & restfull bothe in soule & body. **1604** T. WRIGHT *Passions* VI. 322 The manifold inspirations of God, the illustrations of his holy Angels. **1612** DRAYTON *Poly-olb.* To Rdr. A vj b, Then hast thou the Illustration of this learned Gentleman, my friend, to explaine euery hard matter of history. **1653** LD. VAUX *Godeau's St. Paul* 344 A divine illustration cleared his understanding.

b. physical.

a **1631** DONNE 80 *Serm.* viii. (1640) 81 Such an illustration, such an irradiation, such a coruscation.. that by that light.. he could have read in the night. **1681** WHARTON *Disc. Soul World* Wks. (1683) 647 We see no Adustion in Comets but only some Illustration. **1764** *Phil. Trans.* LIV. 326 This unusual and very remarkable illustration of the atmosphere continued the whole evening.

2. The action of making or fact of being made illustrious, brilliant, or distinguished; distinction. Also, An example, means or cause of distinction.

1616 BULLOKAR, *Illustration*, a making famous or noble. **1649** JER. TAYLOR *Gt. Exemp.* I iv. 41 He [Christ] came not in pompous and secular illustrations. **1760–72** H. BROOKE *Fool of Qual.* (1809) III. 46 They have invested this their head [the king] with all possible illustration: he concentrates the rays of many nations. **1776** ADAM SMITH *W.N.* v. i. III. (1869) II. 360 In Rome it [law].. gave a considerable degree of illustration to those citizens who had the reputation of understanding it. **1850** MERIVALE *Rom. Emp.* (1865) I. ii. 61 The illustration of his family dated only from his father. **1855** THACKERAY *Newcomes* I. vii. 71 My maxim is, that genius is an illustration, and merit is better than any pedigree.

3. The action or fact of making clear or evident to the mind; setting forth clearly or pictorially; elucidation; explanation; exemplification.

1581 MARBECK *Bk. of Notes* 491 It is a figure called Illustration, by the which the forme of things is so set foorth in words, that it seemeth rather to be seene with the eies, then heard with the eares. **1588** FRAUNCE *Lawiers Log.* I. i. 3 By explication and illustration, or proofe and conclusion. **1657** J. SMITH *Myst. Rhet.* 172 Antithesis, is also the illustration of a thing by its opposite. *a* **1704** T. BROWN *Declam. Adverbs* Wks. 1730 I. 40 What need I bring more topicks for illustration? **1853** RUSKIN *Stones Ven.* II. vi, I have confined the illustration of it to architecture.

b. With *an* and *pl.* That which serves to illustrate or make clear, evident, etc.; an elucidation, explanation; an example, instance.

1585 T. WASHINGTON tr. *Nicholay's Voy.* II. iii. 33 John de Maire of Belges in his illustrations of Gaule. **1646** SIR T. BROWNE *Pseud. Ep.* VI. viii. 312 Some, from whom wee receive the greatest illustrations of Antiquity, have made no mention hereof. **1649** BLITHE *Eng. Improv. Impr.* To Rdr., Some illustrations upon some of the former passages. **1832** (*title*) Views in New York.. Picturesque Drawings.. with Historical, Topographical and Critical Illustrations by Th. G. Fay. **1860** TYNDALL *Glac.* I. xxii. 154 An illustration of the principle which runs throughout nature. **1896** DK. ARGYLL *Philos. Belief* 62 A passing image or illustration of some one.. aspect of life.

4. The pictorial elucidation of any subject; the elucidation or embellishment of a literary or scientific article, book, etc., by pictorial representations.

1813 BRITTON *Redcliffe Church* Pref. 9, I was also tempted to enter more fully into the illustration of the building. **Mod.** The artists engaged in the illustration of this sumptuous work. Process plates used in the illustration of cheap periodicals.

b. An illustrative picture; a drawing, plate, engraving, cut, or the like, illustrating or embellishing a literary article, a book, etc.

[**1816** (*title*) A Cabinet Illustration of Great Britain; in a series of near 300 Elegant Views.] **1817** *Advt.* in *Q. Rev.* Feb., Westall's Illustrations to the Works of Walter Scott, Esq. In 8vo, beautifully engraved from the Paintings of R. Westall, R.A. **1822** W. J. HOOKER (*title*) Botanical Illustrations: being a Series of Figures designed to illustrate the Terms employed in.. Lectures on Botany. **1828** *Lit. Gaz.* 9 Feb. 84/3 The Illustrations of the book are worthy of George Cruikshank. **1839** T. MOORE (*title*) The Epicurean: a Tale with Vignette Illustrations by J. M. W. Turner, R.A. **1842** (May 14) *Illustr. Lond. News* No. 1, Selections from the illustrations of the numerous works which the press is daily pouring forth. **1851** RUSKIN (*title*) The Stones of Venice.. with Illustrations drawn by the Author. **1888** *Nature* 23 Aug. 385 The book is one which is especially noteworthy for the beauty of its illustrations. **1898** *Navy & Army Illustr.* 23 July 412 Our next illustration shows a boat.. engaged in sounding.

illu'strational, *a.* [f. prec. + -AL[1].] Of or pertaining to illustration; illustrative. Also as *sb.*

1885 BOWEN in *Law Times Rep.* LIII. 610/2 Putting, in an emphatic and illustrational way.. that the advowson is a right of presentation that concerns and affects lands. **1926** R. FRY *Transformations* 147 Rodin's concern is with the expression of character and situation, it is essentially dramatic and illustrational. **1955** P. HERON *Changing Forms of Art* III. xi. 168, I believe Sutherland's phantasy is essentially illustrational, poetic, non-plastic. **1959** *Listener* 6 Aug. 206/1 Everything in fiction as in life had to satisfy his [H. James's] 'appetite for the illustrational'.

illustrative (ɪ'lʌstrətɪv), *a.* [f. L. *illustrāt-*, ppl. stem of *illustrāre* to ILLUSTRATE + -IVE.]

1. Serving or tending to illustrate, make clear or elucidate; explanatory, elucidatory; affording an illustration or example; exemplificatory. Const. *of.*

1643 SIR T. BROWNE *Relig. Med.* I. §45 Unspeakable mysteries in the Scriptures are often delivered in a vulgar and illustrative way. **1792** MARY WOLLSTONECR. *Rights Wom.* vi. 260 Till some fortuitous circumstance makes the information dart into the mind with illustrative force. **1828** COLE *Scarborough Collector* 1 The following paragraphs, illustrative of the accompanying etching. **1867** SMILES *Huguenots Eng.* ii. (1880) 22 The life of Palissy.. is eminently illustrative of his epoch. **1868** BROWNING *Ring & Bk.* IX. 805 Lest ye miss a point illustrative. **1869** TYNDALL *Notes Lect. Light* §110 Taking, as an illustrative case, the passage from air into water.

†**2.** Shining, illuminative. *Obs. rare.*

1686 GOAD *Celest. Bodies* II. xii. 320 Bright and Illustrative, as Pliny said but now.

i'llustratively, *adv.* [f. prec. + -LY[2].] In an illustrative manner; by way of, or by means of, illustration; so as to illustrate.

1646 SIR T. BROWNE *Pseud. Ep.* IV. xii. 214 Delivered Hieroglyphically, metaphorically, illustratively. **1822–56** DE QUINCEY *Confess.* (1862) 204 Treating the question illustratively rather than argumentatively.

illustrator ('ɪləstreɪtə(r)). [Agent-n. in L. form f. ILLUSTRATE *v.* Cf. late L. *illustrātor* (Lactantius); F. *illustrateur* (15th c. in Godef.).] One who or that which illustrates, in the various senses of the vb.; one who gives or draws illustrations; the artist who illustrates a book or periodical.

1598 FLORIO, *Illustratore*, an illustrator, a glorifier, a giuer of honors. *c* **1611** CHAPMAN *Homer's Iliads* Sonn. Gg v b, The right graciovs Illustrator of vertue.. the Earle of Montgomrie. **1632** BURTON *Anat. Mel.* (ed. 4) III. ii. v. v. 585 Leonitius his illustrator Garceus. **1689–90** in *Wood's Life* 30 Jan. (O.H.S.) III. 323 'An illustrator', or 'picturer of great letters in books'. **1812** W. TAYLOR in *Monthly Rev.* LXVIII. 499 From Herodotus and his illustrators. **1834** E. BRAYLEY (*title*) Graphic and Historical Illustrator of the Popular Superstitions and Customs of Wales. **1870** DICKENS *Lett.* (1880) II. 439 You please me with what you say of my new illustrator. **1879** J. C. BROWN *Ethics Geo. Eliot* 114 She stands out as the deepest, broadest, and most catholic illustrator of the true ethics of Christianity.

i'llustratory, *a.* [f. L. *illustrāt-* (see ILLUSTRATIVE) + -ORY.] Illustrative.

a **1734** NORTH *Exam.* (1740) 660 Introductory, illustratory, preparatory abuses of Truth [etc.]. **1806** SCOTT *Fam. Lett.* 5 July (1894) I. ii. 36 Dryden's works.. with notes critical and illustratory by the Editor.

illustratress ('ɪləstreɪtrɪs). [f. ILLUSTRATOR + -ESS.] A female illustrator.

1866 F. J. FURNIVALL in *Reader* 10 Mar. 248/3 The illustratress of the present book. **1888** *Sat. Rev.* 29 Dec. 785/2.

†**illustre**, *a. Obs.* Also 6 illuster, -are, ir. [a. F. *illustre* (15th c. in Hatz.-Darm.) illustrious, ad. L. *illustris* clear, bright, lustrous, plain, evident, distinguished, famous.] Illustrious.

1500–20 DUNBAR *Poems* vii. 1 Illuster Lodovick, of France most Christin king. *c* **1532** DU WES *Introd. Fr.* in *Palsgr.* 1036 Right illustre & prosperous lady. **1550** VERON *Godly Sayings* (1846) 20 The faythful subjectes of this victoriouse and illustre realme. **1585** JAS. I. *Ess. Poesie* To Rdr. (Arb.) 20 The deuine and Illuster Poëte, Salust du Bartas. **1612** MONNIEPENNIE *Abridgem. Scot. Chron.* I. 4 Some of the valiant illustre noble acts of your Highness. *a* **1653** G. DANIEL *Idyll* v. 66 Illustre Bassa.

†**illustre**, *v. Obs.* [a. F. *illustre-r* to light up, illumine (*obs.*), render illustrious, illustrate, ad. L. *illustrā-re* (see ILLUSTRATE *v.*).]

1. *trans.* To light up, illumine; to brighten.

1490 CAXTON *Eneydos* xxvii. 96 To go sprede abrode his newe lyght to illustre and illumyne the landes. **1591** SYLVESTER *Du Bartas* I. i. 534 And, all illustred with Light's radiant shine. **1606** *Ibid.* II. iv. II. *Magnif.* 107 With Vertue's luster Thou ought'st (at least) thy Greatnesse to illuster.

2. To render illustrious or distinguished; to confer distinction upon.

1530 PALSGR. 589/2 This noble acte illustreth your fame above al your ancesters. **1548** HALL *Chron., Hen. VIII,* 71 For to decore and illustre the same assembly.. thei shall.. do some faire feate of armes. **1657** REEVE *God's Plea* 46 As ye valew your places, illustre them.

Hence **i'llustred** *ppl. a.*, made illustrious.

In quot. 1649 used punningly with reference to a possible formation from IL-[2], meaning 'having no lustre'.

1512 *Helyas* in Thomas *E.E. Prose Rom.* (1858) III. 142 The illustred and noble quene. *a* **1649** DRUMM. OF HAWTH. *Poems* Wks. (1711) 22 Thy muse not-able, full, il-lustred rimes, Make thee the poetaster of our times.

†**i'llustrement**. *Obs. rare.* [f. ILLUSTRE *v.* + -MENT.] Illumination.

1599 R. LINCHE *Anc. Fiction* F, [The Sun] absenting his irradiance from the world's illustrement.

†**illu'stricity**. *Obs.* [Erroneously f. L. *illustris* + -ITY: see -ICITY.] Illustriousness. In quot. 1637, illustrious personage.

1637 BASTWICK *Answ. Inform. Sir J. Banks* 9 That their illustricityes might.. see his innocency. **1761** MISS TALBOT *Let. to Mrs. Carter* 1 Aug., See the short date of human illustricity. **1794** *Hist.* in *Ann. Reg.* 84 A name of great illustricity in the annals of France.

illustrious (ɪ'lʌstrɪəs), *a.* (Also 7 illustrous, *Sc.* -uows.) [f. L. *illustri-s* + -OUS.]

†**1.** Lighted up, having lustre or brilliancy; luminous, shining, bright, lustrous. *Obs.*

c **1605** ROWLEY *Birth Merl.* IV. v, From the igniferous body Seven splendent or illustrious rays are spread. **1668** CULPEPPER & COLE *Barthol. Anat.* II. vi. 100 Light, the companion of the Spirits, by which the blood receives a more Illustrious color. **1713** DERHAM *Phys.-Theol.* v. ix. 350 A Diamond.. he observed to be more illustrious at some times than others. **1886** DOWDEN *Shelley* I. xi. 476 He and Peacock.. made the darkness illustrious with fireworks.

†**2.** Clearly manifest, evident, or obvious. *Obs.*

1654 FULLER *Two Serm.* 21 The Foundations [of Religion] may be destroyed as to all outward visible illustrious apparition. **1762** KAMES *Elem. Crit.* (1788) II. 495 The final cause of uniformity is illustrious. **1792** T. TAYLOR *Proclus* I. Dissert. 62 They demand our assent.. from the illustrious certainty they possess.

3. Possessing lustre by reason of high birth or rank, noble or lofty action or qualities; distinguished, eminent; renowned, famous. **a.** Of persons.

(Sometimes used as a title of courtesy in addressing or speaking of persons of high rank. Cf. ILLUSTRISSIMO.)

1588 SHAKS. *L.L.L.* I. i. 178 Armado is a most illustrious wight, A man of fire, new words, fashions owne Knight. **1605** —— *Lear* v. iii. 135 Conspirant 'gainst this high illustrious Prince. *c* **1614** SIR W. MURE *Dido & Æneas* I. 733 And O! I wish ȝour brave, illustruows prince.. Were heir. **1692** DRYDEN *St. Euremont's Ess.* 204 There are Illustrious Debauchees, but there never was an Illustrious Miser. **1759** ROBERTSON *Hist. Scot.* VII. II. 150 She was an agreeable woman, rather than an illustrious Queen. **1809** *Med. Jrnl.* XXI. 90 The only tribute we can pay to the illustrious dead. **1855** PRESCOTT *Philip II*, I. II. iii. 176 Several of these victims were not only illustrious for their rank, but yet more so for their talents and virtues.

b. Of things.

c **1566** J. ALDAY tr. *Boaystuau's Theat. World* Q iij b, Acknowledging in him his proper figure and illustrious marke. **1632** J. HAYWARD tr. *Biondi's Eromena* 13 His Illustrious deeds, his renowne acquir'd. **1701** *Stanley's Hist. Philos.* Biog. 7 Mr. Des Cartes has given us an illustrious Instance of the Use of this Method in his Meditations and Method. **1820** LAMB *Elia* Ser. I. *Two Races Men*, One leaf of the illustrious folio.

c. ***most illustrious***: the special epithet of the Order of St. Patrick.

[**1783** *London Gaz.* 4–8 Feb. 1/1 The King has been pleased to order Letters Patent to be passed under the Great Seal of the Kingdom of Ireland, for creating a Society, or Brotherhood, to be called Knights of the Illustrious Order of St. Patrick.] **1858** B. BURKE *Bk. Orders Knighth.* 102 (*heading*) The Most Illustrious Order of Saint Patrick. **1971** *Whitaker's Almanack* 259 The Most Illustrious Order of Saint Patrick... *Ribbon*, Sky Blue. *Motto*, Quis separabit?.. (No conferments since 1934).

¶ In the following passage in the Shakspere folios, in the sense 'not lustrous, dull' (IL-[2]) whence editors have substituted *illustrous, inlustrous, unlustrous.*

1611 SHAKS. *Cymb.* I. vi. 109 (1623) An eye Base and illustrious as the smoakie light That's fed with stinking Tallow.

i'llustriously, *adv.* [f. prec. + -LY[2].] In an illustrious manner; †luminously, brightly, resplendently; clearly, conspicuously; brilliantly.

1638 CHILLINGW. *Relig. Prot.* I. v. §18. 259 A Church thus illustriously and conspicuously visible. **1715–20** POPE *Odyss.* XI. 358 In beauty's cause illustriously he fails. **1748** RICHARDSON *Clarissa* (1811) III. iii. 28, I never.. beheld a skin so illustriously fair. **1869** GOULBURN *Purs. Holiness* vii. 62 In the Cross of His Son God is most illustriously seen.

i'llustriousness. [f. as prec. + -NESS.]

1. Illustrious quality or condition; †brilliance, resplendency; distinction; illustrious rank or position.

1650–66 WHARTON *Poems* Wks. (1683) 383 Farewel to all our New Nobility: Good-night Illustriousness. **1660** JER. TAYLOR *Duct. Dubit.* I. iv. 126 The illustriousness of the birth. **1682** MRS. BEHN *False Count* IV. ii, An't please your Illustriousness. **1889** *Harper's Mag.* Mar. 501/1 Academies which can vie with ours in the illustriousness of their members.

2. [tr. G. *durchlaucht.*] With possessive adjective as a title of dignity or honour given to German princes.

1929 'S. N. D.' *Sir W. Howard Visct. Stafford* iv. 48 His Electoral Illustriousness, the Prince Palatine of the Rhine.

‖**illustrissimo** (ɪlə'strɪsɪməʊ, It. illu'strisimo), *a.* and *sb.* (Anglicized illustrissim.) [It., ad. L. *illustrissimus*, superl. of *illustris* (ILLUSTRE *a.*).]

a. *adj.* Most illustrious; used as a title of courtesy in addressing or speaking of Italian nobles, whence sometimes applied to others. **b.** *sb.* A man of noble rank, one of the Italian nobility.

1623 WEBSTER *Devil's Law Case* II. i, Your switching up at the horse-race, with the illustrissimi. **1681** *Disc. Tanger* 21 The Illustrissimo's of Tetuan. **1768–74** TUCKER *Lt. Nat.* (1852) I. 475 Mynheer, dear Doctor, celeberrimous Doctor, insignite illustrissim Doctor. **1829** SCOTT *Anne of G.* xix, Nor will we sauce your mess with poison like the wily Italian, and call you all the time *Illustrissimo* and *Magnifico*.

illustrous: see under ILLUSTRIOUS.

†**i'llutible**, *a. Obs. rare*$^{-0}$. [ad. late L. *illutibilis* (Nonius), f. *il-* (IL-[2]) + *luĕre, lut-* to wash: see -IBLE.] (See quot.)

1623 COCKERAM, *Illutible*, that cannot be washed away. **1656** in BLOUNT *Glossogr.*

illuvial (ɪ'l(j)uːvɪəl), *a.* *Soil Sci.* [f. IL-¹ + *-luvial*, as in ALLUVIAL, ELUVIAL *adjs.*] = ILLUVIATED *ppl. a.*; also, resulting from illuviation.

1924 *Geol. Mag.* LXI. 451 Three main horizons are generally recognized,..the A or eluvial horizon, the B or illuvial horizon, and the C horizon, which consists of the parent material. **1932** G. W. ROBINSON *Soils* iv. 92 We may also distinguish a type of clay which has been enriched by illuvial accumulation. **1952, 1963** [see ELUVIAL *a.* 2].

illuviation (ɪl(j)uːvɪ'eɪʃən). *Soil Sci.* [f. prec. + -ATION.] The deposition of salts or colloids in a soil horizon from percolating water which has removed them from another, generally superior, horizon. So **i'lluviated** *ppl. a.*, having received material by illuviation.

1928 *Bull. Amer. Soil Survey Assoc.* IX. 31 Illuviation. *Ibid.* 37 The illuviated horizons of the solum. **1932** *Forestry* VI. 28 The different horizons are designated by capital letters... 'B' the horizon of illuviation or deposition. **1949** W. W. WEIR *Soil Sci.* (ed. 2) vi. 116 Horizons, commonly topsoil layers, that have lost materials through eluviation are described as eluvial or eluviated; and horizons, commonly subsoil layers, that have received the materials, illuvial or illuviated. **1955** F. E. BEAR *Chem. of Soil* i. 37 In pedology, the term eluviation has been applied to the loss of material from the surface horizon, and the term illuviation, to the gain of material by the subsoil horizon.

†**illu'xurious**, *a.* *Obs. rare*⁻¹. [f. IL-² + LUXURIOUS.] Not luxurious; void of luxury.

1751 EARL ORRERY *Remarks Swift* ix. (1752) 72 The widow Vanhomrigh and her two daughters quitted the illuxurious soil of their native country for the more elegant pleasure of the English court.

ill will, ill-will ('ɪl'wɪl), *sb.* [In early use northern, corresp. to ON. *illvili*, f. *ill-r* adj. + *vili* sb. 'will'. In ME. usually written as two words: cf. *evil will*, OE. (*his*) *yfela willa*.

Cf. also L. *malevolentia*, of which, and the adjs. *malevolens*, *malevolus*, this and the following words are often the English renderings.]

1. Evil or hostile feeling or intention towards another; malevolence, malice, enmity, dislike.

a **1300** *Cursor M.* 7834 (Cott.) Qua lais hand in feloni.. Or of hill wil him mai not quitte. *c* **1340** *Ibid.* 25947 (Fairf.) Þat first was þoȝt wiþ iuel il wille. *c* **1375** *Sc. Leg. Saints, Mathias* 390 Þe Iowis, þat tuk tent here til, For Inwy and gret ill wyll. *a* **1533** LD. BERNERS *Huon* lxx. 240 Ye do me greate wronge to owe me youre yll wyll. **1596** DALRYMPLE tr. *Leslie's Hist. Scot.* x. 474 Jnuie, ilwil, adulatione or flatrie. **1600** SHAKS. *A.Y.L.* III. v. 71 Why looke you so vpon me? *Phe.* For no ill will I beare you. **1755** YOUNG *Centaur* i. Wks. 1757 IV. 108 It is both folly, and vice, to bear any man ill-will. **1828** SCOTT *F.M. Perth* xxvii, How comes it, then, that thy steps are haunted by general ill-will?

attrib. *a* **1832** BENTHAM *Deontology* Wks. 1834 II. 263 Correspondent to that same good-will fund there is an ill-will fund.

†**2.** ***with an ill will***, unwillingly. *Obs.*

1601 R. JOHNSON *Kingd. & Commw.* (1603) 61 They are drawne from their houses with an ill will.

Hence †**ill-will** *v. trans.*, to regard with ill will, wish evil to.

1568 NORTH tr. *Gueuara's Diall Pr.* (1582) 423 The beloued of the Princes is commonly ill willed of the common weale.

ill-willed ('ɪl'wɪld), *a.* *Obs.* exc. *dial.* [f. prec. *sb.* + -ED². Cf. ON. *illviljaðr*, L. *malevolus*.]

1. Feeling or cherishing ill will, malevolent.

a **1340** HAMPOLE *Psalter* ix. 39 Altobreke þe arme of þe synful and of þe ill willd. *Ibid.* civ. 14 In my prophetis willis noght be illwillid. **1477** EARL RIVERS (Caxton) *Dictes* 15 Ignoraunt folkis..froward and il-willed. **1483** *Cath. Angl.* 195/1 Ille wylled,..*malivolus*. **1825** BROCKETT, *Ill-willed*, malevolent, illnatured.

†**2.** Unwilling, reluctant. *Obs.*

1549 COVERDALE, etc. *Erasm. Par. Rom.* 41 Not to teache you, as ignoraunte, neither to commaunde you, as people ylwylled.

ill-willer ('ɪl'wɪlə(r)). [Late ME., f. ILL *adv.* (or *sb.*) + *willer*: cf. the earlier *il-willand* sb. (see next) in same sense; also the parallel *evil-willer*, *well-willer*, and the expressions *to will* one *ill*, *evil*, or *well*.] One who wishes evil to another; one who cherishes ill will or hostile feeling.

c **1500** *Melusine* 211, I haue be yl wyller bothe to you & to your lady [cf. 158 ayenst alle your euyl willers]. **1557** PAYNEL *Barclay's Jugurth* 87 Al the purposes of mine yllwyllers and aduersaries. **1678** MARVELL *Def. Howe* Wks. 1875 IV. 230 He seems to be no ill-willer to transubstantiation. **1690** *Andros Tracts* II. 28 Some of those Male-contents and Ill-wilers of their Neighbours. **1780** JOHNSON *Lett. to Mrs. Thrale* 21 June, His illwillers are very unwilling to think he can ever more sit in parliament. [*Not in J.'s Dict.*] **1828** SCOTT *F.M. Perth* xix, I have ill-willers enough. **1876** BANCROFT *Hist. U.S.* I. ix. 285 Ill-willers to New England were already railing against its people.

'ill-'willing, *a.* *rare.* [f. ILL *adv.* or ? *sb.* + WILLING *ppl. a.* Cf. OE. *yfel-willende*, L. *malevolens*.]

1. Wishing evil to another; cherishing ill will; malevolent. In first two quots. as *sb.* = ILL-WILLER.

a **1300** *Cursor M.* 6829 If þou find oþin ilwilland [*v.r.* ill-willand]..his beist ligand. *a* **1300** *E.E. Psalter* xliii. 6 In þe sal blaw with horn our il wiland. **1741** RICHARDSON *Pamela* (1824) I. v. 240 This same ill-willing world might think it was.

†**2.** Unwilling; in quot. 1579–80 as *adv.* Unwillingly. *Obs.*

c **1520** BARCLAY tr. *Sallust* 82 b, And compelled them that were frowarde and ylwillyng to labour. **1579–80** NORTH *Plutarch* (1676) 281 The People went very ill willing, and they had much ado to keep them together.

Hence **ill-'willingness** = ILL WILL 1.

a **1340** HAMPOLE *Psalter* xxxiv. 20 Restore my saule fra ill willandnes of þaim. **1580** HOLLYBAND *Treas. Fr. Tong*, *Malveuillance*, ill willingnesse.

ill-willy ('ɪl'wɪlɪ), *a.* Chiefly *Sc.* [f. ILL WILL *sb.* + -Y. Cf. EVIL-WILLY.] Cherishing ill will; malevolent, malignant, ill-disposed.

[**1500–20** DUNBAR *Poems* lxxv. 32 Be warme hairtit and nocht ewill willie, *Bannatyne MS.* illwillie]. **15..** *Almanak of Year* 1386, 5 Saturne es colde and drie, and ilwilly. *a* **1568** *Wife of Auchterm.* viii, Than thair cumis ane illwilly cow, And brodit his buttock. **1611** COTGR., *Maling*,..ill-willie. **1721** KELLY *Sc. Prov.* 11 (Jam.) An ill-willy cow should have short horns. **1819** W. TENNANT *Papistry Storm'd* (1827) 124 Syn baith the Bears now shine ill-willie.

'ill-'wish, *v.* [f. ILL *adv.* (or *sb.*) + WISH *v.*] *trans.* To wish evil to; to bring misfortune upon, or bewitch, by wishing evil, according to a popular belief in some rural districts (cf. *evil eye*). Also *absol.* Hence **ill-wish** *sb.*, the evil or misfortune wished.

1853 T. Q. COUCH in J. Brand *Observations Pop. Antiq.* (1870) III. 101 The witch's malice, or, as it is termed, 'the ill-wish'. **1865** R. HUNT *Pop. Rom. W. Eng.* Ser. II. 80, I believe I was illwished once. **1879** 'E. GARRETT' *House by Works* I. 162, I fear they almost ill-wished her when her husband hired lodgings for her at the seaside. **1899** S. BARING-GOULD *Bk. of West* II. 16 A bard, and after him a saint, might not ill-wish unless he had been refused a just request. *Ibid.*, If he ill-wished unjustly, then it was held that the ill-wish returned on the head of him who had launched it.

ill-wisher ('ɪl'wɪʃə(r)). [f. ILL *adv.* (or *sb.*) + WISHER: cf. *well-wisher*.] One who wishes evil to another; an ill-willer.

1607 HIERON *Wks.* I. 445 These ill-wishers to the Iewes. **1716** ADDISON *Freeholder* No. 55 Propagated by the ill-wishers to our constitution. **1827** HALLAM *Const. Hist.* (1876) II. ix. 123 His ill-wishers knew how to irritate the characteristic sensibility of the English on this topic.

illy ('ɪllɪ), *adv.* Now chiefly *U.S.* [f. ILL *a.* + -LY².] In an ill manner; badly; ill.

1549 DK. SOMERSET *Let. Sir T. Hoby* 24 Aug. in Strype *Eccl. Mem.* II. App. EE. 106 In Norfolk, gentlemen, and al serving men for their sakes, are as illy handled as maybe. **1594** CAREW *Huarte's Exam. Wits* v. (1596) 62 In the morning we learne best..and at the euening illy. **1681** R. KNOX *Hist. Ceylon* IV. iv. 133 They might see, how illy they were served. **1785** JEFFERSON *Writ.* (1894) IV. 100 Beauty is jealous, and illy bears the presence of a rival. **1795** SOUTHEY *Joan of Arc* VIII. 634 Thou dost deem That I have illy spared so large a band. **1848** LOWELL *Fable for Critics* 59 He don't sketch their bundles of muscles and thews illy. **1849** W. IRVING *Goldsmith* (Tauchn.) 56 Never were two beings more illy assorted than he and Goldsmith. **1898** T. HARDY *Wessex Poems* 170 Even the rank poplars bear Illy a rival's air. **1903** *Atlantic Monthly* July 116 Which is far better than if it had rushed into illy considered legislation. **1904** CLAIBORNE *Old Virginia* 268 (Th.), I dropped one of my gauntlets,..which I could illy afford to lose. **1925** T. DREISER *Amer. Trag.* (1926) II. xlvi. 57 By contrast with Sondra, how illy-dressed in the blue traveling suit..she had equipped herself for this occasion. **1927** C. A. & M. R. BEARD *Rise Amer. Civilization* II. 213 To meet a crisis of this kind labor was illy prepared. **1965** *Sat. Rev.* (U.S.) 5 June 28/1 *The Blue Hen's Chick* is no graceful memoir of a life well or illy spent.

Illyrian (ɪ'lɪrɪən), *a.* and *sb.* [f. L. *Illyrius*, a. Gr. Ἰλλυριός.]

A. *adj.* **1.** Of or pertaining to the Illyrians or to ancient Illyria (or Illyricum), a country lying east of the Adriatic and at an early period extending northwards to the Danube.

1553 N. GRIMALDE tr. *Cicero's Bookes of Dueties* (1558) II. f. 88ᵛ Bargulus, the Illirian robber, of whom mention is made in Theopompus. **1593** SHAKES. *2 Hen. VI*, IV. i. 108 Bargulus the strong Illyrian Pyrate. **1678** J. DAVIES tr. Appian (*title*) The History of Appian, of Alexandria. In Two Parts. The First, consisting of the Punick, Syrian, Parthian, Mithridatick, Illyrian, Spanish, and Hannibalick, Wars. **1776** GIBBON *Decl. & F.* I. i. 27 The provinces of the Danube soon acquired the general appellation of Illyricum, or the Illyrian frontier. **1797** *Encycl. Brit.* II. 714/2 The Heneti, an Illyrian people. **1880** *Ibid.* XII. 709/1 The Danube..was the limit of the Illyrian tribes towards the north. **1935** HUXLEY & HADDON *We Europeans* vi. 179 The Dinaric (Illyrian) type [of people] is found on both sides of the northern Adriatic, the Illyrian mountain system with extensions to the north and south. **1953** [see BANDKERAMIK].

b. Of or belonging to Illyria, a former division of Austria-Hungary, since 30 October 1918 forming part of Yugoslavia.

Illyrian Provinces, a division, made by Napoleon Bonaparte in 1809, of various Austrian territories lying north and east of the Adriatic, and abolished in 1814–15, after which it was made a nominal kingdom of the Austrian Empire.

1820 C. KELLY *Hist. French Revolution* I. xiii. 614 The treaty of Vienna has given to France a great extent of territory on the Adriatic sea: this territory is formed into the Illyrian republic. **1838** *Penny Cycl.* XII. 445/2 Napoleon,.. in 1809, gave to several tracts of territory ceded by Austria .. the name of the Illyrian Provinces. **1845** *Encycl. Metrop.* XIII. 1084/2 Meanwhile the war in the Illyrian provinces.. received a fresh complication from the secession of Bavaria from the French alliance. *Ibid.* XX. 559/1 The Emperor of Austria rules the Illyrian Kingdom with uncontrolled authority. **1921** *19th Cent.* May 856 The Illyrian provinces ..provided a strong bulwark against Austria. **1965** *New Cambr. Mod. Hist.* IX. xi. 331 The Illyrian provinces taken from Austria in 1809 remained directly under the control of Napoleon through a governor-general.

c. In literary use, pertaining to the regions lying along the east coast of the Adriatic.

This corresponds to the literary use of *Illyria*, which was retained even when the name had no political significance.

1852 M. ARNOLD *Empedocles on Etna* I. ii. 41 The Adriatic breaks in a warm bay Among the green Illyrian hills... There those two live, far in the Illyrian brakes. **1853** TENNYSON *To E.L.* in *Poems* 352 Illyrian woodlands, echoing falls Of water. **1950** J. C. FENNESSY *Way to Sea* xvii. 131 Lapis lazuli blue as the Illyrian sea.

d. Used in the names of breeds of dog that originated in this part of Yugoslavia, as ***Illyrian hound***, ***Illyrian sheepdog***.

1935 *Discovery* Oct. 310/2 The fierce dogs of the Yugoslav South..are now officially called Illyrian Sheepdogs. **1948** A. LOKAR in B. Vesey-Fitzgerald *Bk. Dog* II. 519 The Illyrian Sheepdog is..the best-known Yugoslav sheep-herding dog and is in big demand in the hills in summer, and in the valleys when the sheep and goats come down for winter feeding. **1964** E. F. DAGLISH tr. *Schneider-Leyer's Dogs of World* 198 The Illyrian Hound is not directly descended from the oft-mentioned Celtic Hound. **1971** F. HAMILTON *World Encycl. Dogs* 376 Illyrian Hound. This medium-sized hound is named for Illyria, that ill-defined region of present-day Yugoslavia which borders the Adriatic.

2. Pertaining to the group of ancient dialects represented by the modern Albanian; also, to a division of the eastern branch of the Slavonic languages.

1607 TOPSELL *Four-f. Beasts* 10 Cynocephales, are a kinde of Apes... In the French, Germain, and Illyrian tongues, they. are called of some Babian. **1824** J. JOHNSON *Typographia* II. 444 The names to the above letters are in the Illyrian and Servian tongues. **1833** *Penny Cycl.* I. 256/2 The hypothesis of the Albanians being descended from the Illyrians, cannot receive confirmation from comparing it with the old Illyrian tongue. **1928** C. DAWSON *Age of Gods* xvi. 375 Our knowledge of the Illyrian languages is so slight.

B. *sb.* **1.** One of an Indo-European people who inhabited ancient Illyria, and who were conquered by the Romans in the third and second centuries B.C.

1584 B. RICH tr. *Herodotus' Famous Hystory* f. 62ᵛ, The people Eneti comming of the Illyrians. **1788** LEMPRIÈRE *Classical Dict.* s.v. *Pausanias*, He accompanied the prince in an expedition against the Illyrians. **1880** *Encycl. Brit.* XII. 709/1 It would not be easy to draw any line of demarcation at this early time between the Illyrians and their neighbours on the west, south, and east. **1928** C. DAWSON *Age of Gods* xiv. 325 The Bronze Age in Eastern Europe. The Thracians and the Illyrians. **1935** HUXLEY & HADDON *We Europeans* vii. 213 The Albanians are in part the descendants of the old Illyrians and are noteworthy for the preservation of many archaic customs and of a primitive form of Aryan language. **1949** *Oxf. Classical Dict.* 966/1 Zeus..is found as 'Father', which attribute is very common in Greek too, among the Romans, Indians, and Illyrians.

2. An inhabitant of the former Austrian kingdom of Illyria.

1836 N. WISEMAN *Lect. Doctr. Cath. Ch.* I. vii. 256 M. Boraga, an Illyrian, obtained permission of the Bishop to open a new mission among the Indians on the Grand River.

3. A member of the Slavonic race now living in the territory of ancient Illyria; also applied loosely to any people inhabiting this region, without reference to the various political meanings of the name.

1845 *Encycl. Metrop.* XIII. 533/2 Fortunately at this crisis he [*sc.* Leopold II] obtained the support of the Illyrians.

4. The language of Illyria, or the group of ancient dialects represented by the modern Albanian; also, a division of the eastern branch of the Slavonic languages, spoken in the same or adjacent districts.

1888 J. WRIGHT tr. *Brugmann's Elem. Compar. Gram. Indo-Gmc. Lang.* I. 12 Russian..Bulgarian and Illyrian. **1904** [see ETEOCRETAN *a.* and *sb.*]. **1912** W. W. SKEAT *Sci. Etym.* 127 There is, however, sufficient evidence to show that the Old Illyrian was an independent descendant from the original Indo-germanic stock. **1958** P. KEMP *No Colours or Crest* v. 76 Indeed Albanian, which is supposed to be derived from ancient Illyrian, must be one of the most difficult of European languages to learn.

So **I'llyric** *a.* [ad. L. *Illyricus*, Gr. Ἰλλυρικός], **I'llyrican** *sb.* = ILLYRIAN *sb.* 4. Hence **'Illyrism**, (*a*) advocacy of Slovene, Croatian, and Serb nationalism; (*b*) see quot. 1957; so **'Illyrist** *a.* and *sb.*

1753 R. CLAYTON *Jrnl. from Cairo to Sinai* 34 We had in our company persons who were acquainted with Arabic, Greek,..Illyrican, German [etc.]. **1838** *Penny Cycl.* XII. 447/2 Antient Illyria..was inhabited by a people called by the general name of the Illyric nations. **1854** E. O. S. *Hungary & its Revolutions* 236 Louis Gay, a young man of literary attainments,..took the lead in a movement which obtained the name of Illyrism. **1877** *Encycl. Brit.* VI. 783/2 The so-called Morlacks, or Dalmatians proper, who..speak a Slavonic dialect usually distinguished as the Illyric. **1910** *Ibid.* VII. 475/2 A nationalist or 'Illyrist' party was formed ..to combat Hungarian influences. *Ibid.*, Conflicts between Illyrists and Magyarists. *Ibid.*, The Hungarians had obtained a royal manifesto hostile to Illyrism. **1957** *Ibid.* XX. 789/2 Between the Slovenes and the Croats there are transition dialects, and about 1840 there was an attempt (Illyrism) to establish a common literary language.

ilmenite (ˈɪlmənaɪt). *Min.* [Named, 1827, from the Ilmen Mountains (in southern Urals), where found.] Oxide of iron and titanium found in brilliant black crystals and in many varieties.

1827 *Edin. New Philos. Jrnl.* III. 187. **1894** BOWKER in *Harper's Mag.* Jan. 410/1 Ilmenite, or titanic iron (Fe Ti)$_2$ O$_3$.. an ore in which one of the iron molecules of hematite is replaced by the metal titanium.

ilmenorutile (ˌɪlmənəʊˈruːtaɪl, -ɪl). *Min.* [ad. G. *ilmenorutil* (N. von Kokscharow *Materialen zur Mineralogie Russlands* (1854–7) II. 352): see ILMENITE and RUTILE.] A black variety of rutile containing iron, niobium, and tantalum.

1861 H. W. BRISTOW *Gloss. Mineral.* 189/2 *Ilmenorutile*, Von Kokscharow. A variety of Rutile occurring in the form of the fundamental pyramid, without any prismatic planes. **1929** *Encycl. Brit.* XIX. 774/1 The colour [of rutile] is usually reddish-brown, though.. black in the ferruginous varieties ('nigrine' and 'ilmenorutile'). **1962** W. A. DEER et al. *Rock-Forming Min.* V. 35 Apart from the ferroan and ferrian varieties of rutile, there is also the niobian variety, or ilmenorutile, with up to 60 per cent. of Fe(Nb,Ta)$_2$O$_6$ with Nb > Ta. **1968** *Daily Tel.* 12 Nov. 14/4 The ilmenite mines are in the Jeseniky mountain range near the Polish border, and in Pisek, south of Pilsen, where the mines contain ilmeno-rutile, a more complex mineral suitable for the production of thorium as a trigger for H-bombs, as well as titanium.

Ilocano (iːləʊˈkɑːnəʊ). [Philippine Sp., f. *Ilocos*, the name of two provinces, lit. 'river men', f. Tagalog *ilog* river.] **a.** A member of a people inhabiting the north-western part of Luzon in the Republic of the Philippines. **b.** The language of this people. Also *attrib.* So **I'locan** *a.* and *sb.*; **I'loko, Y'loco.**

1840 *Penny Cycl.* XVIII. 88/2 The other tribes that are numerous, the Pampanga, Zambales, Pangasinan, Ylocos, and Cagayan, inhabit the other plains and lower country. **1885** *Encycl. Brit.* XVIII. 753/1 Other tribes of the Philippines—the Ilocanes, Pampangos, Pangasinanes,.. Vicols, &c. **1898** D. C. WORCESTER *Philippine Islands* 438 Of these [tribes] the Tagalogs and Ilocanos are the most important. **1900** F. H. SAWYER *Inhabitants Philippines* 250 Many converted Tinguianes and Igorrotes who speak the Ilocan dialect. **1901** *Rep. Philippine Comm.* III. 400 The first booklets in Ilocano are in Tagalog characters. **1905** F. W. ATKINSON *Philippine Isl.* 238 The Ilocanos, who inhabit the northern province of Ilocos Norte, Ilocos Sur, and Unión, in Luzón. **1914** D. C. WORCESTER *Philippines Past & Present* I. 21 The Ilocanos are one of the eight civilized peoples who collectively make up the Filipinos. **1925** K. MAYO *Isles of Fear* 50 Families..of the energetic Ilocano tribe. **1958** G. MIKES *East is East* 88 The twenty million inhabitants of the islands [*sc.* Philippines] have about seventy native tongues... Sugbuanon, Iloko, Bikol and Samarnon are not among the major forces of civilisation, nor is even Tagalog, the most widespread and most cultivated of the native tongues. **1962** H. C. CONKLIN in Householder & Saporta *Probl. Lexicogr.* 135 In passing, it may be noted that pronoun systems in Tagalog, Ilocano..and some other Philippine languages exhibit very similar..semantic relationships. **1964** E. A. NIDA *Toward Sci. Transl.* ix. 195 On the other hand some languages, e.g. Quechua, Aymara, Ilocano and Eskimo, include much more in the verb than is included in the Greek verb.

i-loȝen, ME. pa. pple. of LIE *v.*², to tell lies.

i-loke(n, ME. pa. pple. of LOCK *v.*

i-loked, ME. pa. pple. of LOOK *v.*

i-lome: see YLOME *adv.*, frequently.

i-lomp, pa. t. of I-LIMP *v.*

i-long *adv.*: see ALONG¹ and YLONG.

i-lope(n, ME. pa. pple. of LEAP *v.*

i-lore(n, ME. pa. pple. of LOSE *v.*: see also LORN.

i-losed, ME. pa. pple. of LOOSE *v.*

ilot, var. of ISLOT, islet.

ilote, obs. f. HELOT.

i-loten, ME. pa. pple. of LOT *v.*

i-loued, ME. pa. pple. of LOVE *v.*

i-lowe(n, ME. pa. pple. of LIE *v.*²

ilpa: see ILLUPI.

†**ilsample**, a perversion of ENSAMPLE, to suggest *ill sample, ill example.*

1588 *Marprel. Epist.* (Arb.) 5 But euerie Lord B[ishop] in England, as for ilsample, Iohn of Cant. **1589** *Marprel. Epit.* (1843) 52 That is the ilsample of Archbishop Titus.

ilsemannite (ˈɪlsəmənaɪt). *Min.* [ad. G. *ilsemannit* (H. Höfer 1871, in *Neues Jahrb. f. Mineral., Geol. u. Palaeont.* 567), f. the name of J. C. *Ilsemann* (1727–1822), German chemist: see -ITE¹.] A black or dark blue secondary molybdenum mineral, perhaps a hydrated oxide of molybdenum, $Mo_3O_8.nH_2O$, which occurs as earthy masses or crusts and as a blue stain and dissolves in water to give a blue solution.

1871 *Jrnl. Chem. Soc.* XXIV. 1173 Ilsemannite... The author gives this name to native molybdic molybdate, $MoO_2.4MoO_3$, occurring at Bleiberg in Carinthia, as a bluish-black to black, mostly earthy or cryptocrystalline deposit, between groups of crystals of barium sulphate. **1923** *Bull. U.S. Geol. Survey* No. 750. 16 Ilsemannite, like wulfenite, is probably formed from some unknown mineral, perhaps a sulphide. **1951** *Amer. Mineralogist* XXXVI. 611 In general, most mineralogists seem to have applied the name 'ilsemannite' to any molybdenum compound or mixture which is water soluble and turns the solution a typical molybdenum-blue color. **1959** *Econ. Geol.* LIV. 257 Ilsemannite is forming rapidly on the walls of the older mine workings.

ilspile, a hedgehog: see IL *sb.*

i-luve, var. of YLEVE, to believe.

i-luved, ME. pa. pple. of LOVE *v.*

ilvaite (ˈɪlvəaɪt). *Min.* [Named, 1811, from Ilva, Elba, where it is found.] A black crystalline silicate of iron and calcium, called also lievrite.

1816 R. JAMESON *Syst. Min.* II. 75. **1868** DANA *Min.* (ed. 5) 297.

i-lyche, i-lyke: see ALIKE, YLIKE.

im-¹, assimilated form of the suffix IN-², before *b, m, p*. This assimilation took place in Latin during the later classical period, and remains in French and English (although *in-* (*en-*) was not infrequent before *p* in OF. and ME.). In words that survived in living use, L. *in-, im-* became in OF. *en-, em-*. These words were taken into ME. in their current Fr. form; but from the 14th c. onward, there was a marked tendency to alter the French back into the Latin form of the prefix. Hence, many words are found with both *em-* and *im-*, in some cases one, in some the other, being ultimately prevalent, while in others, as *empanel, impanel*, the variation still continues: see EM-, and IN-². In this Dictionary, words thus varying in the prefix are treated under the prevalent spelling, or under that which analogy favours, whether EM- or IM-, a cross-reference being given under the other spelling. In words more recently derived from Latin (or from Italian) *im-* is the regular form.

Words in *im-* are chiefly verbs and their derivatives, and may be thus classed:

a. Words in *im-* taken from L. (or Romanic), directly or through later French, as *imbibe, imbue, imburse, immerge, immure, impact, impede, impend, implore, imprecate.* **b.** Words in which OF. *em-* has been altered back to *im-* in AF. or Eng., as *impair, impeach, implead, impoverish.* **c.** Words formed in Eng. on the analogy of the preceding, from sbs., adjs., or verbs, not only of Romanic, but also of native Eng. or other origin. The earlier of these began with *em-* (being the form of EN- before a labial), which was afterwards altered to *im-* (as in b); after this, later formations arose with *im-* from the first. Such are, from sbs., *imbarge, imbrute, immantle, immould, impalace, imperil, impocket; imbark, imbarn, imbook, imbud, immind, immire, immud*; from adjs., *impeevish* (cf. *imbrutish*), *impoor*; from verbs, *imbake, imbreathe, imbrighten, impave, impight, implunge, impleach.* In some of the last, *im-* may have been felt as a variant of IN-¹. For the sense expressed by the prefix, see IN-².

In words in *imm-*, usually only one *m* is pronounced; but when a rhetorical stress is laid on the prefix, or it is necessary to make plain its force in a nonce-word or an unusual word, as *immind, immire, immud*, both *ms*, or a prolonged *m*, may be pronounced.

im-², assimilated form in L. of the negative prefix IN-³ before *b, m, p*, which retains the same form in English, as *imbonity, immemorial, impossible.* In *imm-*, only one *m* is ordinarily pronounced (the prefix being thus reduced to *i-*), but *im-* may be kept separate where emphasis or distinctness requires, as in *im-malleable, im-mixed.*

im, obs. form of HIM.

I'm (aɪm), colloq. contraction of *I am.*

i-maad, i-mad, ME. pa. pple. of MAKE *v.*

i-mæht: see MIGHT *sb.*

image (ˈɪmɪdʒ), *sb.* Forms: 3–6 **ymage**, (4 **ymag**, 6 **ymadge**), 4– **image**. [a. F. *image* (13th c. in Littré), in 11th and 12th c. *imagene* = Pr. *image, emage*, It. *im(m)agine*, Sp. *imagen*, Pg. *imagem*, ad. L. *imāgo, imāgin-em* imitation, copy, likeness, statue, picture, phantom; conception, thought, idea; similitude, semblance, appearance, shadow; app. containing the same root as *im-itārī* to IMITATE.]

1. An artificial imitation or representation of the external form of any object, esp. of a person, or of the bust of a person. **a.** Such an imitation in the solid form; a statue, effigy, sculptured figure. (Often applied to figures of saints or divinities as objects of religious veneration.)

a **1225** *Leg. Kath.* 1476 Ichulle lete makie þe of gold an ymage. *a* **1300** *Cursor M.* 2298 For freind ded þat þam was dere did make ymage o metal sere. *c* **1375** *Sc. Leg. Saints, Agnes* 387 þan vent he to þe ymag in hy, & mad hire prayere deuotely. **1388** WYCLIF *Exod.* xx. 4 Thou schalt not make to thee a grauun ymage..thou schalt not herie tho, nether thou schalt worschipe. *c* **1400** MAUNDEV. (1839) xv. 164 An ymage, þat haþ .iiij. hedes. *c* **1450** *Mirour Saluacioun* 1316 With the ymage of godde Hamone yᵗin wroght craftily. **1526** TINDALE *Acts* xv. 20 Abstayne them selves from filthines of ymages [WYCLIF symulacris; 1611 Idoles]. **1563** *Homilies* II. *Agst. Idolatry* I. (1859) 178 We should not have images in the temple for fear and occasion of worshipping them. **1615** G. SANDYS *Trav.* 8 The Inchantresse having made two Images of her beloved, the one of clay, the other of waxe. **1782** PRIESTLEY *Corrupt. Chr.* I. IV. 384 Gregory the second [was] strenuous for the worship of images. **1860** PUSEY *Min. Proph.* 379 Graven and molten images, the idols which men adore..shall be their destruction.

b. (Less usually) Such an imitation delineated, painted, executed in relief, etc. upon a surface; a likeness, portrait, picture, carving, or the like. (Now *rare* or *Obs.* exc. in allusions to Matt. xxii. 20.)

c **1305** *Pilate* 142 in *E.E.P.* (1862) 115 Anon þo he þe ymage [on Veronica's kerchief] iseȝ he was [h]ol anon. **1362** LANGL. *P. Pl.* A. I. 48 God..asked..whom þe ymage was lyk þat þer-Inne [on the penny] stod. **1382** WYCLIF *Matt.* xxii. 20 Whos is this ymage, and the wrytyng aboue? **1548** HALL *Chron., Hen. VIII* 207 b, The one clothe was embraudered with the image of an old man. **1601** R. JOHNSON *Kingd. & Commw.* (1603) 97 Hee gave them a red banner with the image of the crucifixe painted therein. **1713** STEELE *Guard.* No. i. ¶ 1 Mr. Airs..has taken care to affix his own image opposite to the title-page. **1839** YEOWELL *Anc. Brit. Ch.* ii. (1847) 22 Their coinage of gold and silver with Cæsar's image.

†**c.** Applied to the constellations, as figures or delineations of persons, etc. *Obs.*

1481 CAXTON *Myrr.* III. xx. 178 The sterres whyche be named ben all fygures on the heuene and compassed by ymages. **1594** BLUNDEVIL *Exerc.* VII. xxxviii. (1636) 714 The 48 Images of the fixed stars..otherwise called Constellations. **1674** MOXON *Tutor Astron.* I. §10 The Images called Constellations, drawn upon the Celestial Globe.

d. *fig.* Applied to a person: (*a*) as simulating the appearance of some one, or considered as unreal; (*b*) as compared in some respect to a statue or idol.

1548 HALL *Chron., Hen. VII* 37 b, Hearyng that this feyned duke was come, and had heard that he [Perkin Warbeck] was but a peinted ymage. **1559** W. CUNNINGHAM *Cosmogr. Glasse* 1 Those most miserable men (yea, rather Images, and pictures of men, then very men in dede). [**1599** SHAKS. *Much Ado* II. i. 9 The one is too like an image and saies nothing.] **1741** RICHARDSON *Pamela* (1824) I. xxiii. 35 Can the pretty image speak, Mrs. Jervis? I vow she has speaking eyes! **1852** MRS. STOWE *Uncle Tom's C.* xx. 204 'How old are you, Topsy?' 'Dun no, missis', said the image, with a grin that showed all her teeth.

(*c*) In pregnant use, a person attracting amused or contemptuous glances, a 'sight'. *colloq.*

1851 H. MAYHEW *London Labour* I. 193/1 One boy, whose young woman made faces at it, got quite vexed and said, 'Wot a image you're a-making on yourself!' **1880** *Punch* 25 Dec. 298/2 Uncle Bowpot, the florist, lives here. Sech a rummy old image he is. **1898** CONRAD *Tales of Unrest* 138 How goes it, you old image? **1937** PARTRIDGE *Dict. Slang* 420/2 *You little image*, a term of affectionate reproach.

2. a. An optical appearance or counterpart of an object, such as is produced by rays of light either reflected as from a mirror, refracted as through a lens, or falling on a surface after passing through a small aperture.

Such an appearance may also be a mere subjective impression on the sense of sight, as an AFTER-IMAGE (q.v.), and the ***negative*** or ***accidental image*** seen after looking intently at a bright-coloured object, and having a colour complementary to that of the object.

An image produced by reflexion or refraction is called in Optics a ***real image*** when the rays from each point of the object actually meet at a point, a ***virtual image*** when they diverge as if from a point beyond the reflecting or refracting body.

c **1315** SHOREHAM 27 In a myrour thou myȝt fol wel thiselve se, Bote nauȝt the ymage schefte. **1548** HALL *Chron., Rich. III* 34 b, As perfectely as I sawe my awne Image in a glasse. **1563** W. FULKE *Meteors* (1640) 41 b, Appearing as though there were manny Sunnes, whereas indeed there is but one, and all the rest are images. **1651** HOBBES *Leviath.* I. ii. 6 From gazing upon the Sun, the impression leaves an image of the Sun before our eyes a long time after. **1674** BOYLE *Excell. Mech. Hypoth.* 7 When we see the Image of a Man cast into the Air by a Concave Spherical Looking-glass. **179.** COWPER *Poplar Field* 4 Nor Ouse on his bosom their image receives. **1833** N. ARNOTT *Physics* II. II. 211 The size of an image formed behind a lens is always proportioned to the distance of the image from the lens.

b. *transf.* (*a*) A collection of heat-rays concentrated at a particular point or portion of space, analogous to an image formed by light-rays. (*b*) *Electr.* (See quot. from Maxwell.)

1873 TYNDALL *Lect. Light* v. 181 The substantial identity of light and heat..[is proved by] the formation of invisible heat-images. **1873** MAXWELL *Electr. & Magn.* I. xi. 191 An imaginary electrified point, which has no physical existence ..but which may be called an electrical image, because the action of the surface on external points is the same as that which would be produced by the imaginary electrified point if the spherical surface were removed. **1885** WATSON & BURBURY *Math. Th. Electr. & Magn.* I. 115 Every electrified system within the sphere has its image outside of the sphere. .. No closed surface except a sphere or infinite plane generally gives rise to an image.

3. a. *abstractly.* Aspect, appearance, form; semblance, likeness. (Now only in allusions to,

or uses derived from, biblical language, esp. Gen. i. 26, 27.)

c **1300** *Cursor M.* 12371 Ye þat he has wroght to men.. efter his aun ymage. **1382** WYCLIF *1 Cor.* xv. 49 Therfore as we han born the ymage of the ertheli man, bere we and the ymage of the heuenly. **1548** HALL *Chron., Hen. VI* 92 b, Whiche child was judged..to have the very ymage..and lovely countenaunce of his noble parent. **1602** SHAKS. *Ham.* v. ii. 77 By the image of my Cause, I see The Portraiture of his. **1611** BIBLE *Gen.* i. 27 God created man in his owne Image, in the Image of God created hee him. *a* **1700** DRYDEN (J.), The face of things a frightful image bears. **1781** GIBBON *Decl. & F.* xxvii. III. 43 The affability of his manners displayed the image of his mind. **1857–8** SEARS *Athan.* xi. 99 We grow into the image of what we love.

†**b.** *concr.* A visible appearance; a figure; an apparition. *Obs.* or *arch.*

1530 TINDALE *Prol. Deut.* Wks. (1573) 22/1 Ye saw no image when God spake vnto you, but heard a voyce onely. **1548** HALL *Chron., Hen. III* 53 b, Y^t semed to hym beynge a slepe y^t he sawe diverse ymages lyke terrible develles. **1602** SHAKS. *Ham.* I. i. 81 Our last King, Whose Image euen but now appear'd to vs. **1697** DRYDEN *Virg. Georg.* IV. 588 The slipp'ry God will..various Forms assume, to cheat thy sight; And with vain Images of Beasts affright. **1832** TENNYSON *Mariana in South* vi, An image seem'd to pass the door, To look at her with slight.

4. a. A thing in which the aspect, form, or character of another is reproduced; a counterpart, copy. **living image**, a person with a striking resemblance to another; similarly **spit and image**: see SPIT *sb.*² 3 b and *spitting image*.

a **1300** *Cursor M.* 1116 (Gött.) He [God] wil þat he by þe vtrage, þat murtherrt sua his aun ymage. **1393** LANGL. *P. Pl.* C. XXI. 328 As þow by-gyledest godes ymage. *a* **1540** BARNES *Wks.* (1573) 346/1 It were better for you to burne those Idolles and to warme this true image of God there by. **1594** SHAKS. *Rich. III*, II. ii. 50, I haue bewept a worthy Husbands death, And liu'd with looking on his Images. **1620** GRANGER *Div. Logike* 147 Sleepe is the image of death. **1697** DRYDEN *Virg. Georg.* IV. 70 Hollow Rocks that.. double Images of Voice rebound. **1821** BYRON *Sardan.* I. ii. 400, I have loved, and lived, and multiplied my image. **1829** G. GRIFFIN *Collegians* (ed. 2) I. ix. 187 Sure I'd know that face all over the world,—your own livin' image, ma'am. **1884** in *N. & Q.* (1963) Mar. 106/1 (*title*) Her living image. **1889** KIPLING *Life's Handicap* (1891) 28 At the end..stood the livin' spit an' image o' mysilf worked on the linin'. **1895** Spit and image [see SPIT *sb.*² 3 b]. **1896** DK. ARGYLL *Philos. Belief* 184 In ourselves the external and the internal worlds meet, and we are the image and embodiment of both. *a* **1899** *Mod.* He is the very image of his father. **1931** R. CAMPBELL *Georgiad* i. 15 Here's the first number—see, upon the cover, The living image of a country lover. **1961** L. WOOLF *Growing* iv. 232 When I saw the priest—I have seen his spit and image in many cathedrals,..—I had no doubt that he was God's financial adviser.

b. A thing that represents or is taken to represent something else; a symbol, emblem, representation.

(In mod. use scarcely distinguishable from prec.)

c **1566** J. ALDAY tr. *Boaystuau's Theat. World* E ij, Bloud.. whiche is..the image and figure of sinne. **1602** SHAKS. *Ham.* III. ii. 248 This Play is the Image of a murder done in Vienna. **1613** PURCHAS *Pilgrimage* (1614) 13 The silent Moone..constant image of the worlds inconstancie. **1620** GRANGER *Div. Logike* 164 The name is a note, signe, image, or symboll noting, and representing the nature of the thing. **1804** W. TENNANT *Ind. Recreat.* (ed. 2) II. 248 This noisome dungeon..affords..an image of the gate of Tartarus, rather than the porch of Paradise.

c. A thing in which some quality is vividly exhibited, so as to make it a natural representative of such quality; a type, typical example, embodiment. (Now always *of* the quality; formerly also *of* a person: see quots. Cf. 'the *picture* of health'.)

1548 HALL *Chron., Hen. VI* 174 b, [He] sawe that Andrewe..of his frend was sodainly transformed, into the image of his extreme enemy. **1593** SHAKS. *2 Hen. VI*, I. iii. 179 Image of Pride, why should I hold my peace? **1605** —— *Lear* II. iv. 91 They are sicke, they are weary, They haue trauail'd all the night? meere fetches, The images of reuolt and flying off. **1691** tr. *Emilianne's Obs. Journ. Naples* 127 Never in my life did I see such an Image of Devotion. **1821** SHELLEY *Prometh. Unb.* I. 296 An awful image of calm power. **1879** MISS BRADDON *Clov. Foot* x, Mr. Sampson dropped his cigar, and sat transfixed, an image of half amused astonishment.

5. a. A mental representation of something (esp. a visible object), not by direct perception, but by memory or imagination; a mental picture or impression; an idea, conception. Also, with qualifying adj.: a mental representation due to any of the senses (not only sight) and to organic sensations.

c **1374** CHAUCER *Boeth.* v. met. iv. 129 (Camb. MS.) Stoyciens..wenden þat ymagis and sensibilitees, þat is to seyn sensible ymaginacions..weeren empreynted in to sowles, fro bodies with-owte forth. **1390** GOWER *Conf.* III. 255 So as him thought on his corage Where he portreieth her ymage. **1597** HOOKER *Eccl. Pol.* v. xix. §3 Conceipts are images representing that which is spoken of. **1601** SHAKS. *Twel. N.* II. iv. 19 Such..all true Louers are, Vnstaid and skittish..Saue in the constant image of the creature That is belou'd. **1704** ADDISON *Italy* Pref. (1733) 12, I have only cited such Verses as have given us some Image of the Place. **1797** MRS. RADCLIFFE *Italian* i. (1826) 6 She endeavoured to dismiss his image from her mind. **1874** SULLY *Sensat. & Intuit.* 87 The current of images that daily sweep through consciousness. **1890** W. JAMES *Princ. Psychol.* I. ix. 266 A deaf and dumb man can weave his tactile and visual images into a system of thought quite as effective and rational as that of a word-user. *Ibid.* xiv. 592 We then saw no need of optical and auditory images to interpret optical and auditory sensations by. **1897** tr. *Ribot's Psychol. of Emotions* xi. 145 In the two following cases the 'olfactory image' only exists in a single instance. **1899** *Amer. Jrnl. Psychol.* Oct. 25 Haptical images, beside being vague and ill defined, offer peculiar difficulties. **1904** E. B. TITCHENER in *Jrnl. Philos., Psychol. & Sci. Methods* 21 Jan. 38, I have no doubt, in my own case, of the existence of visual and auditory images... I have no doubt, from the reports of others, of the existence of free kinaesthetic images, verbal or other. **1923** H. G. BAYNES tr. *Jung's Psychol. Types* xi. 554 When I speak of image in this book, I do not mean the psychic reflection of the external object, but a concept essentially derived from a poetic figure of speech; namely, the *phantasy-image*, a presentation which is only indirectly related to the perception of the external object... Although, as a rule, no reality-value belongs to the image, its significance for the psychic life is often thereby enhanced, *i.e.* a greater *psychological* value clings to it.

b. A concept or impression, created in the minds of the public, of a particular person, institution, product, etc.; *spec.* a favourable impression; esp. in phr. ***public image***. Cf. *brand-image*. Also *attrib.* and *Comb.*, as ***image-builder***, ***-building***. Cf. IMAGE-MAKER.

Quots. 1908 are isolated uses. This sense developed from advertising parlance in the late 1950s.

1908 CHESTERTON *All Things Considered* 179 When courtiers sang the praises of a King they attributed to him things that were entirely improbable... Between the King and his public image there was really no relation. **1908** G. WALLAS *Human Nature in Politics* ii. 84 The origin of any particular party may be due to a deliberate intellectual process... But when a party has once come into existence its fortunes depend upon facts of human nature of which deliberate thought is only one. It is primarily a name, which, like other names, calls up when it is heard or seen an 'image' that shades imperceptibly into the voluntary realisation of its meaning... Emotional reactions can be set up by the name and its automatic mental associations.

1958 J. K. GALBRAITH *Affluent Soc.* xiii. 152 The first task of the public relations man, on taking over a business client, is to 're-engineer' his image to include something besides the production of goods. **1959** I. ROSS *Image Merchants* (1960) i. 17 The whole breed may be called the Image Merchants—the men who endlessly 'create', 'delineate', 'adumbrate' and 'project' the most flattering 'images' of their clients. 'Image' is perhaps the favorite noun in public relations..whether the image be that of a corporation, an industry, a product. **1960** *Punch* 16 Mar. 379/2 What..is the *image* of chemical warfare which you are projecting to the public at the moment? **1961** *Listener* 2 Nov. 732/2 He [*sc.* John Reith] created what in modern jargon would be called a public image of the B.B.C. Programmes moved with smooth efficiency..behind a screen of anonymity. **1962** *Ibid.* 27 Sept. 460/2 Mr Gaitskell has improved his image by his determination at Scarborough and after. **1964** *Economist* 3 Oct. 49/1 Mr Goldwater's professional image-builders. **1965** *New Society* 22 Apr. 7/1 An image is a surface presentation intended to elicit favourable responses, whether..justified by the actual reality or not; a reputation was related to the actual and enduring characteristics. **1966** G. N. LEECH *Eng. in Advertising* xx. 182 The relation between metaphor and image-building can be seen in extracts from a campaign for Kellogg's Corn Flakes. **1966** 'C. E. MAINE' *B.E.A.S.T.* v. 61 'Are you warning me off or telling me to join the queue?' 'Neither, I'm just image building.' **1967** M. ARGYLE *Psychol. Interpersonal Behaviour* vii. 125 Butlers, Lord Mayors, and film stars, as well as teachers, psychotherapists, and salesmen, all need to project a certain image of professional competence. **1967** *Economist* 28 Jan. 347/2 In these soft, image-conscious days (in Britain anyway) not many of the big ones would care to abuse this position. **1967** *Daily Tel.* 21 Feb. 16/4 This master-stroke of image-building, the climax of a long campaign, can mean one of two things. **1969** *New Yorker* 27 Sept. 86/3 About the only piece of image advertising I did at Bates was for the Chase Manhattan Bank. **1971** *Physics Bull.* Jan. 12/3 The ivory tower image dies hard even though few academic physicists can succeed these days in research without establishing wide contacts outside their own departments. **1973** *Listener* 15 Nov. 662/3 [*Princess*] *Anne*:..The trouble with horses—this is why one has such a terrible image, horsey image—is that if you have anything to do with them they do take up an awful lot of time.

6. A representation of something to the mind by speech or writing; a vivid or graphic description.

1522 MORE *De quat. Noviss.* Wks. 84/2, I shal put the a more ernest ymage of our condicion. **1578** J. DERRICKE (*title*) The Image of Irelande. **1717** LADY M. W. MONTAGU *Let. to Pope* 1 Apr., Theocritus..has only given a plain image of the way of life amongst the peasants. **1817** COLERIDGE *Sibyl. Leaves* (1862) 129 In a casual illustration [he] introduces the image of woman, child, or bird.

7. *Rhet.* A simile, metaphor, or figure of speech.

1676 [see ICON 3]. **1750** JOHNSON *Rambler* No. 4 ¶7 Incongruous combinations of images. **1846** TRENCH *Mirac.* vi. (1862) 188 To speak of death as a sleep, is an image common to all languages. **1896** DK. ARGYLL *Philos. Belief* 260 The image of the Creator walking in the garden..the angels with flaming swords to prevent return—all these are splendid..images, but they are images none the less.

8. *Math.* The element or set into which a given element or set is mapped by a particular function or transformation; const. *of* the element *by* or *under* the function. ***inverse image***, the set of all elements that are mapped into a given element or set by the function or transformation.

1889 *Cent. Dict.*, s.v. *Image.* When imaginary quantities are represented by points on a plane, a point representing any given function of a quantity represented by another point, the former point is said to be the image of the latter. **1905** J. PIERPONT *Lect. Theory Functions Real Variables* I. iv. 146 Let $u_1 = f_1(x_1 \ldots x_n) \ldots u_m = f_m(x_1 \ldots x_n)$ be defined over a domain X... When x ranges over X, u..runs over the domain U. It is convenient for brevity to call U the image of X. **1959** E. M. PATTERSON *Topology* (ed. 2) ii. 19 Any correspondence which associates with each element of a set A a unique element of a set B is called a function or transformation from A to B, and is denoted by $f{:}A \to B$... If $a \in A$, the element of B corresponding to a is called the image of a by or under f, and is denoted by $f(a)$. If $C \subset A$, the elements of B related to elements of C by f form a set $f(C)$ called the image of C by f. If $b \in f(A)$, the set of all elements $a \in A$ such that $b = f(a)$ is called the inverse image of b by f. **1965** J. J. ROTMAN *Theory of Groups* ii. 17 Let $f{:}G \to H$ be a homomorphism. Prove that the image of $f = \{h \in H{:}h = f(x)$ for some $x \in G\}$ is a sub-group of H. **1972** E. HILLE *Methods Classical & Functional Analysis* ii. 56 A mapping T from $\mathfrak{X}$ into $\mathfrak{Y}$ is a collection of ordered pairs (x, y), $x \in \mathfrak{X}$, $y \in \mathfrak{Y}$, such that every x of $\mathfrak{X}$ belongs to one and only one pair (x, y). Here $y = T(x)$ is called the image of x induced by T. .. Note that y may be the image of several points x and it is not excluded that all of $\mathfrak{X}$ may be mapped on a single point y.

9. *Radio.* An undesired signal whose frequency is as much above that of the local oscillator of a superheterodyne receiver as the signal sought is below it, so that if allowed to reach the frequency converter it too will give rise to the intermediate frequency (and consequently be heard as interference). Freq. *attrib.*, as ***image frequency***, ***interference***.

1932 F. E. TERMAN *Radio Engin.* xiii. 467 One of the chief functions of the tuned radio-frequency input amplifier is to prevent simultaneous reception of two stations in this way. By tuning this amplifier to the desired signal, the undesired or 'image' frequency is discriminated against. **1940** *Amat. Radio Handbk.* (ed. 2) 24/2 Interference is still likely to result from an incoming signal of such a frequency as to produce the correct intermediate frequency. This is known as 'image' or 'second channel interference'. **1950** K. HENNEY *Radio Engin. Handbk.* (ed. 4) xvii. 802 Since the function of the converter is to produce the difference between applied frequencies, it cannot distinguish between the signal and the image and produces i-f output from each. **1962** *B.B.C. Handbk.* 130 The selectivity of the receiver is improved and this reduces 'second channel', alternatively called 'image', interference. This is generally characterized by an irritating whistle of constantly changing pitch, sometimes accompanied by unwanted morse signals and programme modulation. Much of the interference experienced in the short-wave broadcast bands is due to such image effects. **1967** R. L. SHRADER *Electronic Communication* (ed. 2) xviii. 392/1 A second RF amplifier will reject the image very well. However, at frequencies in the 30-MHz range, for example, even the two RF amplifiers may not reject images satisfactorily.

10. *Comb.*, as ***image-apprehension***, ***-association***, ***-bearer***, ***-brilliance***, ***-complex***, ***-field***, ***-formation***, ***-graver***, ***-monger***, ***-motif***, ***-pattern***, ***-sound***, ***-substitute***, ***-type***, ***-war***, ***-work***, ***-world***; ***image-bearing***, ***-crowded***, ***-laden***, ***-like***, ***-ridden***, ***-seeing*** adjs.; **image cluster** (see CLUSTER *sb.* 3 b); **image converter**, an image tube, *esp.* one for converting an invisible image formed by infra-red or other invisible radiation into a visible one; **image dissector**, a kind of television camera tube in which a photo-emissive surface receives the image and the corresponding pattern of emitted electrons is deflected in a scanning pattern to and fro across a point anode, producing the video signal; †**image-doter**, one who dotes on or is superstitiously devoted to images or idols; so †**image-doting** *a.*; †**image-douly** [Gr. δουλεία: see DULIA]; **image frequency**: see sense 9 above; **image iconoscope**, a kind of television camera tube combining the iconoscope and the image dissector, the target plate receiving not the optical image (as in the former) but a pattern of emitted electrons produced by the image at a photo-emissive surface (as in the latter); **image intensifier**, an image tube or other device in which an image is formed by light or other radiation on a photo-emissive or photo-conductive surface and the resulting flow of electrons utilized to produce a corresponding visible image of increased brightness; **image interference**: see sense 9 above; **image-man**, a man who makes or sells images; **image-mug**, a mug or pitcher in the form of an image or bust; **image orthicon**, a kind of television camera tube in which a flow of electrons, produced as in an image tube, strikes a thin glass sheet and forms on it a pattern of positive charges corresponding to the picture, the video signal being derived from the variation this produces in a scanning electron beam that strikes the other side of the sheet (neutralizing the charge at that point) and returns to the electron gun and associated electron multipliers with an intensity reduced in accordance with the magnitude of the neutralized charge; **image toy**, a small decorative figure in earthenware, esp. one made in the 18th century by John Astbury (see ASTBURY) or Thomas Whieldon; **image tube**, an electron tube in which an image, formed by light or other electromagnetic radiation on a photo-emissive surface, causes it to emit a corresponding flow of electrons which may be

used to reproduce the image in a different form (as in an image converter or an image intensifier). Also IMAGE-BREAKER, -MAKER, -WORSHIP, etc.

1962 I. M. Crombie *Exam. Plato's Doctrines* I. iii. 120 The criteria employed in calling things ducks do not constitute more than an *image-apprehension of duckdom. *a* **1930** D. H. Lawrence *Apocalypse* (1932) 97 The curious *image-association. The oriental loved that. **1950** *Essays & Stud.* III. 39 The striking image-associations of this passage were noted by W. Clemen in *Shakespeares Bilder*. **1884** A. Murray *Like Christ* xxxi. 238 *Image-bearers of God..live a Godlike, live a Christlike life. **1889** *Anthony's Photogr. Bull.* II. 137 In removing the skin with the accompanying *image-bearing film from the waxed plate, be sure that the whole is uniformly dry. **1946** *Nature* 19 Oct. 533/2 Under the title 'geometrical properties of visual instruments' are discussed such questions as field-size..and *image-brilliance in different parts of the field. **1946** E. A. Armstrong *Shakespeare's Imagination* 184 As no two poets employ the same *image clusters, therefore works of doubtful provenance can be assigned to a poet with certainty if it contains clusters..characteristic of writings known to be authentic. **1961** *N. & Q.* Apr. 156/2 Particular stress is put on imagery and image-clusters in the cases of *Edward III* and *The Two Noble Kinsmen*. **1963** *Ibid.* Sept. 332/1 One's faith in image-clusters as evidence for authorship tends..to be diminished by such a coincidence. **1966** *English Studies* XLVII. 302 A Bible-inspired *image-complex in Vaughan's poems. **1946** *Electronic Engin.* XVIII. 157/1 The principle of the infra-red *image convertor is fairly well known. **1950** P. Parker *Electronics* xvii. 843 An image converter is a device which converts an image formed by light-rays on a photo-cathode into one formed by electron beams... The name image converter is generally kept, however, for tubes in which the electron image is formed on a fluorescent screen. **1952** *Electronic Engin.* XXIV. 307/1 The case of an image convertor of the ME1200 type will enable infra-red photographs to be taken using normal high-speed emulsions. **1959** *Proc. IRE* XLVII. 905/1 A group of American astronomers have undertaken the development of an image-converter tube which permits the electron image to emerge through a thin membrane or foil to expose an external photographic plate. **1968** L. Levi *Appl. Optics* vi. 266 Image converters greatly enhance night vision..and have in this capacity served in both military and zoological applications. **1911** W. B. Yeats *Plays for an Irish Theatre* p. ix, We feel our minds expand convulsively or spread out slowly like some moon-brightened *image-crowded sea. **1934** P. T. Farnsworth in *Jrnl. Franklin Inst.* CCXVIII. 411 Means for producing these saw-tooth currents and means for synchronizing them between the '*Image Dissector', or transmitting tube, and the..receiving tube, are discussed. **1968** *Brit. Med. Bull.* XXIV. 261/2 A non-storage camera tube of the type known as an 'image dissector' also possesses some very favourable properties, particularly in so far as resolution is concerned. **1629** Sir W. Mure *True Crucif.* 1139 *Image-doatars God's decreit Striue to make Irrite. **1649** Milton *Eikon.* xxviii, An inconstant, irrational and *Image-doting rabble. **1579** Fulke *Confut. Sanders* 623 Confesse that your *Image-Douly is no better then Idolatrie. **1968** *Brit. Med. Bull.* XXIV. 261/1 The only instruments of real interest at the moment seem to be those capable of automatic measurement of optical density at many different points of an *image field. **1923** J. S. Huxley *Ess. Biologist* ii. 81 Even in the most 'intelligent' of birds or mammals, the power of *image-formation is very probably absent, and the power of concept-formation..certainly so. **1972** *Jrnl. Social Psychol.* LXXXVII. 37 Mental imagery and image formation have recently become a topic of concern again. **1579–80** North *Plutarch* 629 (R.) Cephisodotus the *image-graver. **1939** *Proc. IRE* XXVII. 547/1 These *image iconoscopes are practical working tools, advanced well beyond the laboratory stage. **1957** Amos & Birkinshaw *Television Engin.* (rev.) I. iv. 75 Image iconoscopes, in common with all high-velocity tubes, have tended to be superseded by image orthicons in nearly all television services. **1939** L. M. Myers *Electron. Optics* viii. 449 We might term the device an *image intensifier. *Ibid.* 450 An image intensifier was indeed the unrealised and unrealisable dream of the mechanical optical television engineer. **1954** *Radiology* LXIII. 870 An ideal image intensifier would receive only information-bearing X-ray signals from the subject and construct therefrom an image of arbitrary size and brightness. **1959** *Proc. IRE* XLVII. 909/1 An entirely different principle of image amplification is used in the solid-state image intensifier... In the simplest form of this device, a phosphor layer is placed between two conducting plates to which an electric field of about 100 v is applied. If an ultraviolet image is focused on the screen thus formed, a marked increase in light emission is produced. **1967** *New Scientist* 25 May 485/2 At Herstmonceux experiments are in progress on a number of different types of image intensifier to find the most suitable system to be used in conjunction with the 100-in. Newton telescope. **1904** *Westm. Gaz.* 27 Aug. 6/2 This heavily-scented, *image-laden atmosphere. **1943** D. Gascoyne *Poems 1937–1942* 33 Blows back With long-held burning breath through eyeholes bored By image-laden rays. **1561** T. Norton *Calvin's Inst.* III. 266 They do proue their righteousnes with obedience and good workes, not with a bare & *image-like visor of fayth. **1827** Hone *Every-day Bk.* II. 313 The board of the '*image-man'. **1553** Becon *Reliques of Rome* (1563) 92 S. Athanasius proueth euidentlye agaynste all *Image-mongers [etc.]. **1937** U. Ellis-Fermor *Some Recent Res. Shakes. Imagery* 25 This [*sc.* Kolbe's *Shakespeare's Way*]..has some illuminating suggestions about the underlying *image-motifs in the plays. **1945** *Birmingham* (Alabama) *News* 29 Oct. 9/1 The product of RCA engineers..the device is known as an '*image orthicon'. **1946** *Proc. IRE* XXXIV. 428/2 The image orthicon derives its increased sensitivity over the iconoscope and orthicon from (1) the higher photosensitivity of a conducting photocathode relative to that of an insulating mosaic; (2) the multiplication by secondary emission of the electron image at the target; and (3) the use of an electron multiplier for the signal current. **1953** Amos & Birkinshaw *Television Engin.* I. v. 101 The image orthicon tube may be regarded as a combination of an orthicon tube with an image stage similar to that used in the image iconoscope. **1971** H. E. Ennes *Television Broadcasting* i. 20 There are three basic types of pickup tubes used in television cameras: the image orthicon, the vidicon, and the lead oxide. The image orthicon is used primarily in monochrome studio and field cameras for live pickups. **1947** C. Day Lewis *Poetic Image* 84 Its *image-pattern is so skilfully composed from certain theme-images. **1949** A. M. Farrer *Rebirth of Images* i. 22 The evidence for the unity of the Johannine writings..lies in the identity of image-pattern in the Gospel and the Apocalypse. **1935** Auden & Isherwood *Dog beneath Skin* I. 33 Our impulses are unseasonal and *image-ridden. **1929** A. Huxley *Holy Face* 21 *Image-seeing and poetical. **1929** D. H. Lawrence *Pornogr. & So On* (1936) 73 It is, for him, complete for he is void of image-seeing imagination. **1925** I. A. Richards *Princ. Lit. Crit.* 119 But the degree of correspondence between the *image-sounds, and the actual sounds that the reader would produce, varies enormously. *Ibid.* 120 *Something* takes the place of vivid images in these people and..provided the *image-substitute is efficacious, their lack of mimetic imagery is of no consequence. **1957** Mankowitz & Haggar *Conc. Encycl. Eng. Pottery & Porcelain* 115/1 **Image toys*, earthenware, stoneware or porcelain figures. **1960** H. Hayward *Antique Coll.* 147/1 *Image toys*, contemporary designation of mid-18th cent. Staffordshire pottery figures. **1971** *Country Life* 2 Dec. 1505/1 Pioneer maker of image toys in Staffordshire was John Astbury (1688–1742), his colours restricted to the browns and whites of his burnt clay. **1936** *Jrnl. Optical Soc. Amer.* XXVI. 187/2 The construction of the photosensitive cathode to be used in any given *image tube will, of course, depend upon the spectral region in which maximum sensitivity is desired. **1940** Zworykin & Morton *Television* iv. 91 The image tube is of importance because it can be combined with the Iconoscope to make a television pick-up tube which is many times more sensitive than the normal Iconoscope. **1969** *New Scientist* 10 July (Optics Suppl.) 21/1 Objects illuminated with non-visible radiation..can be seen with the aid of these devices. The image tube can also intensify very faint images..so that they become visible. **1971** *Nature* 3 Sept. 37/1 The difficulties associated with studying very faint [celestial] objects are very great, because of the increasing difficulty in detecting photons against the natural and man-made noise, even with the use of image-tube techniques. **1925** I. A. Richards *Princ. Lit. Crit.* 123 If this were not the case the absence of glaring differences between people of different *image-types would be astonishing. **1751–73** Jortin *Eccl. Hist.* (1846) II. 179 The history of the *image-war is written by Maimburg. **1904** *Daily Chron.* 8/2 Immersed in this innocent, harmless, *image-world. **1953** R. Manheim tr. *Cassirer's Philos. Symbolic Forms* I. 78 All live in particular image-worlds, which do not reflect the empirically given, but which rather produce it in accordance with an independent principle.

image (ˈɪmɪdʒ), *v.* [f. IMAGE *sb.*: in the 15th c. instances (in sense 4) app. a. F. *imager* (13–14th c.).]

1. *trans.* To make an image of; to represent or set forth by an image (in sculpture, painting, etc.); to figure, portray, delineate. Also *fig.*

a **1790** Warton *Ecl.* iv. (R.), Shrines of imag'd saints. **1821** Shelley *Prometh. Unb.* III. iv. 173 Those imaged to the pride of kings and priests. **1844** Mrs. Browning *Drama Exile* Poems 1850 I. 84 He images his Master's wounds! **1856** Froude *Hist. Eng.* x. II. 408 Traces of the fair beauty of the monastic spirit we may yet see imaged in the sculptured figures..upon the floors of our cathedrals. **1957** A. C. Clarke *Deep Range* xv. 129 The familiar rocky terrain was imaged on TV and sonar screen. **1970** *Physics Bull.* Nov. 490/2 Figure 1*a* shows the simplest possible optical system which includes both a parallel beam in which the working space can be placed (*B*) and a lens which can image it on to a receptor.

2. To form an optical image of, esp. by reflexion; to reflect, mirror.

1792 S. Rogers *Pleas. Mem.* II. 159 Hail, noblest structures imaged in the wave. **1860** Tyndall *Glac.* I. iv. 35 The houses on the margin of the lake were also imaged to a certain height.

3. a. To form an image or counterpart of; to copy, imitate, *rare.*

c **1611** Chapman *Iliad* Ep. Ded. 83 They his clear virtues emulate, In truth and justice imaging his state.

b. To be an image or counterpart of; to resemble. *rare.*

1701 Norris *Ideal World* I. v. 231 The Divine Ideas..are not imaging or imitative, but archetypal representatives. **1725** Pope *Odyss.* XIX. 445 None imag'd e'er like thee my master lost.

4. To form a mental image of; to conceive.

†**a.** something to be executed: To devise, plan. (The earliest sense: now *Obs.* or merged in next.)

c **1440** *Jacob's Well* 1 He ymagyth and castyth beforn in his herte, how he wyll makyn it. **1460** Capgrave *Chron.* (Rolls) 200 Thei..told him who Mortimer had ymaged his deth. [**1855** Browning *Grammar. Fun.* 69 Image the whole, then execute the parts.]

b. an object of perception or thought: To imagine, picture in the mind, represent *to oneself*.

a **1708** J. Philips (J.), Image to thy mind How our forefathers to the Stygian shades Went quick. **1781** J. Moore *View Soc. It.* (1790) I. xli. 447 We image to ourselves the Tarpeian Rock as a tremendous precipice. **1847** J. Wilson *Chr. North* (1857) I. 245 Image to yourselves the scenery of rivers and lakes. **1860** J. McCosh *Intuitions* I. i. 11 The mind of man has the power of imaging or representing in old forms by the memory, and in new forms by the imagination, whatever it has at any time known or experienced. **1924** T. H. Y. Trotter *Music & Mind* v. 56 Whether or not it is necessary for the listener to image in his mind the scene to be represented is a moot point. **1972** *Science* 16 June 1208/1 Some recall past events by imaging the scene.

5. To represent or set forth in speech or writing; to describe (esp. vividly or graphically).

a **1628** F. Grevil *Hum. Learning* cv, Hence striue the Schooles, by first and second kinds Of substances, by essence, and existence, That Trine and yet Vnitednesse diuine To comprehend, and image to the sense. **1712** Addison *Spect.* No. 315 ¶5 Satan's Approach to the Confines of the Creation, is finely imaged in the beginning of the Speech. **1796** W. Taylor in *Monthly Rev.* XX. 513 Who can describe her charms, who can image forth her beauty? *a* **1853** Robertson *Lect.* ii. (1858) 64 If only his Redeemer had been differently imaged to him.

6. To represent by an emblem or metaphor; to symbolize, typify.

1816 Shelley *Alastor* 505 O stream!..Thou imagest my life. **1860** Pusey *Min. Proph.* 37 He..shews forth His resistless power, imaged by His creatures in whom the quality of power is most seen, 'I will be as a lion'. **1871** Smiles *Charact.* i. (1876) 26 The heathen deities at least imaged human virtues.

Hence ˈ**imaging** *vbl. sb.* and *ppl. a.*

1666 Dryden *Ann. Mirab.* Pref., Wks. (Globe) 40 The delightful imaging of persons, actions, passions, or things. **1701** [see 3 b. above]. **1880** G. Meredith *Tragic Com.* (1881) 290 The sun-tracing would not deceive, as her own tricks of imageing might do. **1920** S. Alexander *Space, Time & Deity* I. 25 In imaging the act of mind is provoked from within. **1920** J. Laird *Study in Realism* iv. 67 Imaging has a different bodily margin from perceiving. **1943** *Mind* LII. 333 'Imagination' sometimes means the forming and contemplating of mental images, visual, auditory or other; this is more appropriately called 'imaging'. **1953** H. H. Price *Thinking & Experience* viii. 236 All these people, whose thoughts are concerned with the spatial relations of things..would be completely at a loss if the power of visual imaging suddenly deserted them. **1971** *Sci. Amer.* Aug. 83/1 'Imaging' is a control process in which verbal information is remembered through visual images; for example, Cicero suggested learning long lists (or speeches) by placing each member of the list in a visual representation of successive rooms of a well-known building.

imageable (ˈɪmɪdʒəb(ə)l), *a.* Also 7 **imagible.** [f. IMAGE *v.* + -ABLE.] Capable of being imaged, esp. in the mind.

1691 E. Taylor *Behmen's Theos. Philos.* 42 Whatever hath Limits of number and measure is imagible. **1809–10** Coleridge *Friend* (1818) III. 90 Whatever is admitted to be conceivable must be imageable. **1864** *Reader* 21 May 657 The concepts of the mind are divided into imageable and unimageable.

ˈ**image-ˌbreaker.** One who breaks or destroys images (as being idolatrous); an iconoclast.

1596 Dalrymple tr. *Leslie's Hist. Scot.* v. 269 A counsel..haldne at Nice against the secte of Jmagebrekeris. **1614** Earl Stirling *Dooms-day* ix. (R.), Image-breakers, foes to Papall power. **1859** Gullick & Timbs *Paint.* 62 The Iconoclasts (or image-breakers) of the Eastern church.

So ˈ**image-ˌbreaking** *sb.*, iconoclasm; *adj.*, iconoclastic.

1654 Whitlock *Zootomia* 208 That Learned Iconoclastes, that Image-breaking Enemie to Intellectual Idolatry [Bacon]. **1840** Carlyle *Heroes* vi. 319 It is tragical for us all to be concerned in image-breaking and down-pulling.

imaged (ˈɪmɪdʒd), *a.* [f. IMAGE + -ED.]

1. [f. the vb.] Represented by an image (physical or mental); sculptured, portrayed; reflected; imitated; imagined.

c **1718** Prior *Solomon* III. 368 His ear oft frighted with the imag'd voice Of heav'n, when first it thunder'd. *a* **1790** [see IMAGE *v.* 1]. **1868** Browning *Ring & Bk.* x. 124 The saints in imaged row. **1872** Geo. Eliot in J. W. Cross *Life* (1885) III. 169 You are often among my imaged companions both in dreaming and waking hours. **1889** W. B. Yeats *Wanderings of Oisin* II. 23 Between the lids of one The imaged meteors had shone and run. **1935** W. Empson *Poems* 13 Drink deep the imaged solid of the bone.

2. [f. the sb.] Adorned with an image or images. Of porcelain: Decorated with human figures.

1797 Southey *Lett. Journ. Spain* xxiii. (1799) 301 An imaged crucifix.

imageless (ˈɪmɪdʒlɪs), *a.* [f. IMAGE *sb.* + -LESS.]

a. Without an image or images.

1821 Shelley *Prometh. Unb.* II. iv. 116 The deep truth is imageless. **1883** Sir M. Monier-Williams *Relig. Th. India* viii. 227 Becaraji has numerous imageless shrines. **1885** Miss Harrison *Stud. Grk. Art* iii. 85 The worship of an imageless Jehovah. *a* **1930** D. H. Lawrence *Last Poems* (1932) 214 The gods are nameless and imageless.

b. Special Comb.: ***imageless thought*** (see quot. 1934); so ***imageless thinking***.

1896 G. F. Stout *Analytic Psychol.* I. I. iv. 85 An imageless thought is no absurdity, however opposed such a conception may be to..those who..regard consciousness as a kind of picture gallery. **1909** E. B. Titchener *Lect. Exper. Psychol. Thought-Processes* iii. 113 Binet..gives illustrations of imageless thought that must undoubtedly be classed with the conscious attitudes. **1920** S. Alexander *Space, Time & Deity* I. 213 Observation..has convinced us of the existence of 'imageless thinking', which seemed so inconceivable to some earlier psychologists. **1921** B. Russell *Analysis of Mind* xi. 226 Similar remarks apply to the general idea of 'imageless thinking', concerning which there has been much controversy. **1934** H. C. Warren *Dict. Psychol.* 131/2 *Imageless thought*, an idea, thought, or train of thinking which is wholly lacking in sensory contents. **1948** R. S. Woodworth *Contemp. Schools Psychol.* (ed. 2) iv. 74 Watson pointed an accusing finger at the 'imageless thought' controversy. **1953** J. B. Carroll *Study of Lang.* iii. 74 One outcome of Wundt's work..was the discovery, around 1900, of 'imageless thought'—a kind of subjective behaviour, noted in the process of thinking, which could not be described as..sensation and perception. **1972** *Science* 12 May 630/2 This casual attitude toward definition means that he need never ask whether..there are 'imageless' concepts or thoughts.

†**'imagely**, *a. Obs. rare.* [f. as prec. + -LY¹.] Characterized by images; idolatrous.

1561 DAUS tr. *Bullinger on Apoc.* (1573) 244 Old Rome is lost, and that mighty Monarchie decayed.. new Rome shall perish also with her Imagely Empire.

'image-,maker. a. A maker of images (usually in sense 1 a); a sculptor, carver, statuary.

1500 *Nottingham Rec.* III. 82 Thomas Hyll, image-maker. 1579-80 NORTH *Plutarch* (1676) 145 Phideas the Image-maker.. has undertaken to make the Image of Pallas. 1621 BP. MOUNTAGU *Diatribæ* III. 530 A very vehement inuectiue against Image-makers. 1875 JOWETT *Plato* (ed. 2) III. 130 If you are not.. an imitator or an image-maker.

b. *fig.* (in sense 5 b of image).

1960 *Guardian* 7 Oct. 17/4 [Owing] to the failure of the image-makers.. neither candidate seems to have put across a strong or provocative personality. 1969 *Times* 1 Aug. 6/7 The image-makers said that he was the family's best politician. 1971 *Daily Tel.* 23 Mar. 13/1 The population at large are as inwardly proud of their political rough-houses as they are of such image-makers as Ned Kelly, the waterless outback and Aussie-rules football.

So **'image-,making** *sb.* and *a.*

a 1930 D. H. LAWRENCE *Last Poems* (1932) 83 The gibe of image-making love. 1953 S. SPENDER *Creative Element* 50 For Yeats, spiritualism put him in touch, as he thought, with the image-making collective unconscious of all civilizations. 1967 *Listener* 3 Aug. 140/3 Darwin and Einstein.. must have been endowed with an extraordinary capacity of image-making to be able to see the world in a startlingly new shape. 1972 E. LUCIE-SMITH *Eroticism in Western Art* xv. 262 Since erotic art obeys the necessity to be specific, photography.. offered powerful competition to more traditional kinds of image-making in this field.

imager ('ɪmɪdʒə(r)). Forms: 4-5 **ymageour(e**, 5-6 **-er**, 7- **imager**, (7 **-eur**). [ME. *ym-*, *imageour*, a. OF. *ym-*, *imageur* (14th c. in Godef.), f. *image*; the surviving *imager* may repr. OF. *ymagier*, *imager* (12th c. in Hatz.-Darm.), or exemplify the frequent Eng. change of *-eur*, *-our*, to *-er* (-ER² 3).]

†**1. a.** A maker of images; a sculptor, carver. *Obs.*

13.. *K. Alis.* 7689 [7677] (Laud MS.), Þis ymage is made after Þee, I dude it an ymageoure Casten after Þi vigoure. 1413 *Pilgr. Sowle* (Caxton 1483) IV. xxxvii. 84 More helply is a Carpenter or a potter than an Organer, a peynter or an ymager. 1532 HERVET *Xenophon's Househ.* (1768), Good ioyners, good peynters, good ymagers. 1603 HOLLAND *Plutarch's Mor.* 1296 Lysippus also the Imager did very well to reproove Apelles the painter.

†**b.** Applied to a painter. *Obs. rare.*

1591 SYLVESTER *Du Bartas* I. vi. 750 This more peer-less learned Imager, Life to his lovely Picture to confer, Did not extract out of the Elements A certain secret Chymick Quint-essence.

2. One who images or graphically describes. Also, one who forms a mental image or images; something that reproduces an image (e.g. in radar).

1894 STOPF. BROOKE *Tennyson* xiv. 427 The poet as the emotional imager of life. 1960 A. HUXLEY *Let.* 17 July (1969) 893 Your work with imagers sounds very interesting. Have you any idea why some people visualize and others don't? 1963 *Listener* 28 Mar. 547/2 One regular hypnagogic imager has amusing images that would form excellent subject matter for a Walt Disney cartoon. 1967 C. L. WRENN *Word & Symbol* 10 Poets have always regarded themselves as.. the bearers of truth and imagers of reality. 1971 *Daily Tel.* (Colour Suppl.) 10 Dec. 34/1 The Army regards radar as an integral part of the night-vision family; just as important as image intensifiers or thermal imagers.

imagerial (ɪmɪ'dʒɪərɪəl), *a. rare.* [f. IMAGERY + -AL¹.] Relating to or of the nature of imagery; figurative, symbolic.

1849 *Fraser's Mag.* XL. 368 The imagerial descriptions of Holy Writ. 1852 *Househ. Words* IV. 230 Herat is called, after the imagerial way of the Easterns, the key of India.

Hence **ima'gerially** *adv.*, in the way of imagery; figuratively, symbolically.

1879 G. MEREDITH *Egoist* II. ii. 40 Imagerially, [they are] the frozen North on the young brown buds bursting into green.

imagery ('ɪmɪdʒrɪ, 'ɪmɪdʒərɪ). Forms: 4-6 **ymagerie**, **-y(e**, 4-7 **imagerie**, **-ye**, (5 **emagery**, **ymagry**, 6 **emygerie**, **imagrye**), 6- **imagery**. [a. OF. *imagerie* (13th c. in Hatz.-Darm.), f. *imagier* IMAGER: see -ERY.]

1. Images collectively; carved figures or decorations; image-work, statuary, carving. More rarely referring to pictures. Also in *pl.*

a 1325 *Prose Psalter* xcvi[i]. 7 Ben hij alle confounded Þat anouren ymagerie. *c* 1384 CHAUCER *H. Fame* III. 100 Many subtile compassinges, Rabewyures, and pynacles, Ymageries and tabernacles. *c* 1400 *Destr. Troy* 1562 Ymagry ouer all amyt Þere was. 1591 SPENSER *Ruines of Time* 96 Wrought with faire pillours and fine imageries. —— *Virg. Gnat* 103 His cup embost with Imagery. 1695 W. HALIFAX in *Phil. Trans.* XIX. 92 A Statue, which the Turks, zealous enemies of all Imagery, have thrown down. 1712 E. COOKE *Voy. S. Sea* 246 The Imagery they made, their Drawings and Paintings of all lively Colours. 1870 MORRIS *Earthly Par.* I. II. 588 He had wrought most godlike works in imagery. 1878 GEO. ELIOT *Coll. Breakf. P.* 429 Chambers of imagery in the soul [see Ezek. viii. 12].

†**b.** Figured work on a textile fabric, as in tapestry; embroidery. *Obs.*

1390 GOWER *Conf.* II. 320 She wafe a cloth of silke all white With letters and ymagery. 1480 *Wardr. Acc. Edw. IV* (1830) 117 A counterpoynt of arras silk with ymagery. 1553 *Lanc. Wills* (Chetham Soc.) I. 91, ij pillowes and a coveryng of imagerie. 1613-14 in Willis & Clark *Cambridge* (1886) I. 452 [Item] ij peeces of ffyne tapestrie of silke Imagrie. 1777 WARTON *Odes* v. v, Each room, array'd in glistering imagery.

c. *transf.* The pictorial elements of a natural scene or landscape; scenery; nature's 'image-work'.

1647 H. MORE *Poems* 195 As doth a looking-glasse [reflect] such imag'rie As it to the beholder doth detect. 1774 WARTON *Hist. Eng. Poetry* xxxvii. (1840) III. 35 Descriptive poetry and the representations of rural imagery. 1799 WORDSW. '*There was a Boy*' 23 The visible scene.. With all its solemn imagery, its rocks, Its woods. 1827 POLLOK *Course T.* v, Scotia's northern battlement of hills.. The standard still of rural imagery.

†**2.** The use of images in worship; idolatry. *Obs.*

c 1440 *Boctus* (Laud MS. 559) lf. 7b, He trowed all in Idolatrye And in fals ymagerye. 1561 J. PARKHURST *Injunct.*, The.. frames or Tabernacles deuised to aduance Imagerie, holy water stones also to be.. clean taken away. 1624 F. WHITE *Repl. Fisher* 208 This Aduocate of Imagerie should first of all haue declared, what hee vnderstandeth by Worship of Images.

†**3.** The making of images; the art of statuary or carving; *rarely*, the art of painting. *Obs.*

1531 ELYOT *Gov.* III. xxvi, Alexander.. came to the shoppe of Apelles, the excellent paynter, and.. raisoned with hym of lines, adumbrations, proportions, or other like thinges pertainyng to imagery. 1576 NEWTON *Lemnie's Complex.* (1633) 53 He in his art of Imagery so artificially handled his worke.. that all other Carvers and Statuaries.. set him before them as an absolute Patterne for imitation. 1611 COTGR., *Stuc*,.. a compounded morter or clay.. verie fit for Imagerie.

†**4.** The way in which a thing is imaged or fashioned; workmanship, make, figure, form, fashion. *Obs.*

c 1590 GREENE *Fr. Bacon* i. 64 She is beauties ouermatch, If thou suruaist her curious imagerie. 1661 FELTHAM *Resolves* liii. 295 They are our Brethren, and pieces of the same Imagery with our selves. *a* 1667 JER. TAYLOR *Whole Duty Clergy* I. Wks. 1831 IV. 175 Dress your people unto the imagery of Christ.

†**5.** An imaging, portrayal, or visible presentation of anything. *Obs. rare.*

c 1718 PRIOR *Solomon* II. 385 What can thy imagery of sorrow mean?

†**6.** A material representation or embodiment of something; = IMAGE *sb.* 4, 4 c. *Obs.*

1596 FITZ-GEFFRAY *Sir F. Drake* (1881) 76 Heavens counterfaite, Fames Pyramis, honours imagerye. *a* 1649 DRUMM. OF HAWTH. *Poems* Wks. (1711) 47 Aithen, thy tears pour on this silent grave.. And Niobe's imagery become.

7. †**a.** The formation of mental images; imagination, fancy, groundless belief. *Obs.* **b.** The result of this; mental images collectively or generally.

1611 SPEED *Hist. Gt. Brit.* IX. xxi. (1632) 1047 Nor is she to be condemned vpon the imagerie of his suspicious head. 1651 HOBBES *Leviath.* II. xxvii. 156 Leaveth the Law of Nature.. and followeth the imagery of his own.. brain. *a* 1667 JER. TAYLOR (J.), Things of the world fill the imaginative part with beauties and fantastick imagery. 1712 ADDISON *Spect.* No. 417 ¶1 Any single Circumstance of what we have formerly seen often raises up a whole Scene of Imagery. 1819 SHELLEY *Masque of Anarchy* lii, Like a dream's dim imagery.

8. The use of rhetorical images, or such images collectively; descriptive representation of ideas; figurative illustration, esp. of an ornate character.

1589 PUTTENHAM *Eng. Poesie* III. xix. (Arb.) 248 Resemblance by Pourtrait or Imagery. *Ibid.* 250 When we liken an humane person to another in countenaunce, stature, speach or other qualitie, it is.. called.. resemblaunce by imagerie or pourtrait. *a* 1700 DRYDEN (J.), I wish there may be in this poem any instance of good imagery. 1791 BOSWELL *Johnson* (1831) I. 78 The whole of it [*Irene*] is rich in thought and imagery. 1858 J. H. NEWMAN *Hist. Sk.* (1873) III. IV. vi. 385 The glowing imagery of prophets.

9. *attrib.*, as †**imagery work** = sense 1 (and 1 b).

1500 in *Ann. Reg.* (1768) 134 A counterpane of Imagery work. 1560-1 in Willis & Clark *Cambridge* (1886) I. 442 For wypinge owte the Imagery worke vppon the walles.

'image-,worship. The worship of images; idolatry.

1628 BP. HALL *Old Relig.* x. §1. 91 There was an act made for Image-worship. 1732 BERKELEY *Alciphr.* VI. §24 Moses.. not approving the image-worship of the Egyptians. 1877 *Outl. Hist. Relig.* 64 The image-worship which prevailed among them at the time of Mohammed.

So **'image-,worshipper**, one who worships images, an idolater; **'image-,worshipping** *sb.*, image-worship; *adj.*, that worships images.

1563 *Homilies* II. *Agst. Idolatry* I. (1859) 178 Such image worshippers shall never come into the inheritance of the kingdom of heaven. 1565 CALFHILL *Answ. Treat. Crosse* (1846) 138 Called.. of Image-worshippers an Image-enemy. *Ibid.* 156 By applying that to image-worshipping which made nothing at all to purpose.

imagic ('ɪmɪdʒɪk), *a.* [f. IMAGE *sb.* + -IC.] Image-like.

1937 'C. CAUDWELL' *Illusion & Reality* 237 The manifest content is imagic phantasy. 1953 *Essays in Crit.* III. 431 'Soundlessly' shares with 'Spawning' the imagic honours. 1957 N. FRYE *Sound & Poetry* 136 The 'New Criticism', chiefly concerned with the imagic and referential meaning (semantic) levels.

†**imagilet.** *Obs. rare.* [? for *imagelet* (f. IMAGE + -LET *dim. suffix*).] A small image; a statuette.

a 1661 FULLER *Worthies, Staffordsh.* III. (1662) 38 Italy affords finer Alabaster (whereof those Imagilets wrought at Leghorn are made).

imagina'bility. [f. next + -ITY.] The quality of being imaginable.

1830 COLERIDGE *Ch. & St.* (ed. 2) 233 In order to the imaginability of a circular line. 1953 G. E. M. ANSCOMBE tr. *Wittgenstein's Philos. Investigations* I. 120 There is a lack of clarity about the role of *imaginability* in our investigation.

imaginable (ɪ'mædʒɪnəb(ə)l), *a.* Also 4 **ym-**. [ad. late L. *imāginābilis* (Boethius), f. *imāgināre* to IMAGINE: see -BLE.]

Capable of being imagined; conceivable.

a. In ordinary adjectival (chiefly predicative) use.

c 1374 CHAUCER *Boeth.* v. pr. iv. 128 (Camb. MS.) Reson.. comprehendeth the thinges ymaginable & sensible. 1532 MORE *Confut. Tindale* Wks. 547/1 Hys worde, whych he by a meane to vs not imagynable continually speaketh vnto them. 1638 SIR T. HERBERT *Trav.* (ed. 2) 265 Such a dreadfull noyse, as is scarce imaginable. 1651 HOBBES *Govt. & Soc.* x. §2. 150 Nor is it imaginable which way publick treasures can be a grievance to private subjects. 1750 tr. *Leonardus' Mirr. Stones* 51 The human understanding extends itself to things intelligible and the imagination to things imaginable. 1852 H. ROGERS *Ecl. Faith* (1853) 76 Miracles are, at least, imaginable.

b. Frequently used to emphasize the absolute or universal nature of a statement, being placed after a sb. preceded by *all the* or a superlative, esp. *the greatest*, or between *all*, *every*, or *no*, and the sb.

1647 CLARENDON *Hist. Reb.* I. §23 Urged with all the artifice and address imaginable. 1656-9 B. HARRIS *Parival's Iron Age* (ed. 2) 98 The People.. held him still, for the Authour of all imaginable mischief to the Kingdom. 1692 WASHINGTON tr. *Milton's Def. Pop.* v. M.'s Wks. (1847) 376/1 Guilty of the greatest crimes imaginable. 1709 STEELE *Tatler* No. 41 ¶9 The Elector of Cologne is making all imaginable Hast to remove from hence to Rheims. 1711 ADDISON *Spect.* No. 123 ¶4 He had all the Duty and Affection imaginable for his supposed Parent. 1798 MALTHUS *Popul.* (1817) II. 379 Under the best form of government imaginable. 1880 L. STEPHEN *Pope* iii. 73 'Ass' is the vilest word imaginable in English or Latin. 1884 *Law Rep.* 25 Ch. Div. 491 There is no imaginable reason why the Court should not have power to sanction them.

Hence **i'maginableness** (Bailey vol. II, 1727).

i'maginably, *adv.* [f. prec. + -LY².] In an imaginable manner, conceivably.

1648 *Scot. Mist Dispel'd* 40 What can imaginably then be the meaning? 1685 BOYLE *Effects of Mot.* v. 61 A scarce imaginably little force may suffice to impel them. 1894 HOWELLS in *Cosmopolitan* Mar., A waste and ruined field.. which had imaginably once been the grounds about a pleasant home.

i'maginal, *a.*¹ [app. f. IMAGINE *v.* + -AL¹.] **a.** Of or pertaining to the imagination. Also, of or pertaining to a mental image. †**b.** Imaginable. *Obs. rare.*

Quot. *a* 1901 is perh. a transferred use of IMAGINAL *a.*²

1647 H. MORE *Song of Soul* I. I. xvi, No might imaginall May reach that vast profunditie. *Ibid.* II. i. II. xxx, That inward life's th' impresse imaginall Of Natures Art. *Ibid.* pt. IV. xxi, They would be alike wise, Know one anothers thoughts imaginall. 1658 J. WEBB tr. *Calprenède's Cleopatra* VIII. ii. 181 With all imaginall pomp. *a* 1901 F. W. H. MYERS *Human Personality* (1903) I. Gloss. p. xviii, *Imaginal*,.. metaphorically applied to transcendental faculties shown in rudiment in ordinary life. 1925 [see ATTITUDE 5]. 1925 J. E. TURNER *Theory Direct Realism* iv. 42 The imaginal and ideal elements, although of course they are undoubtedly present in the percipient's mind, never reveal themselves to him in their proper nature. 1935 *Brit. Jrnl. Psychol.* Apr. 445 The imaginal retention of a previously perceived common element. 1951 G. HUMPHREY *Thinking* ii. 32 Pure intellection as contrasted with thinking on imaginal terms. *Ibid.* iv. 129 Sensory aspects of experience which we may call imaginal, affective and cognitive.

Hence **i'maginally** *adv.*

1925 I. A. RICHARDS *Princ. Lit. Crit.* xviii. 157 As the eye wanders imaginally from point to point the relations between the parts of the picture-space change.

imaginal (ɪ'mædʒɪnəl), *a.*² *Entom.* [f. L. *imāgin-*, stem of IMAGO + -AL¹.] Of or pertaining to an insect imago. *imaginal disk*: see quot.

1877 HUXLEY *Anat. Inv. Anim.* vii. 449 The apodal maggot, when it leaves the egg, carries in the interior of its body certain regularly arranged discoidal masses of indifferent tissue, which are termed *imaginal disks.* These imaginal disks undergo little or no change until the larva encloses itself in its hardened last-shed cuticle, and becomes a pupa. 1885 *Athenæum* 25 Apr. 539/1 Reserving the two others to rear to the imaginal condition. 1891 F. W. MYERS in *19th Cent.* Apr. 642 What are called 'imaginal characters'—points of structure which indicate that the larva has descended from an imago.

†**i'maginant**, *ppl. a.* and *sb. Obs.* [ad. L. *imāginānt-em*, pres. pple. of *imāgināre* to imagine.]

A. *ppl. a.* That imagines.

1626 BACON *Sylva* §901 Introd., The Force of Imagination.. either vpon the Body Imaginant, or vpon another Body.

B. *sb.* One who imagines; an imaginer.

1605 BACON *Adv. Learn.* II. xi. §3. 46 The bodie of the Imaginant. **1626** —— *Sylva* §902 There is no doubt, but that Imagination and Vehement Affection worke greatly vpon the Body of the Imaginant. **1663** J. SPENCER *Prodigies* (1665) 223 The single testimony of some superstitious and melancholy Imaginant.

†**imagi'narian.** *nonce-wd.* [See -ARIAN.] One who occupies himself with imaginary things.

1830–3 MONTGOMERY *Lect. Poetry* 216 The greatest realists, and the greatest imaginarians,—if I may coin a barbarous word for a special occasion.

imaginarily (ɪ'mædʒɪnərɪlɪ), *adv.* [f. next + -LY².] In an imaginary way; in imagination.

1593 NASHE *Christ's T.* (1613) 69 My heart shall receiue an iniunction imaginarily to disinherite him. **1631** R. H. *Arraignm. Whole Creature* xvi. 285 Perplexed with what he eyther really or imaginarily wanteth. **1779** G. KEATE *Sketches fr. Nat.* (ed. 2) I. 53 On he would go, tho' imaginarily ill. **1874** MOTLEY *Barneveld* II. xi. 36 The places which they are now imaginarily to leave.

imaginary (ɪ'mædʒɪnərɪ), *a.* (*sb.*) Also 4 **ymag-**, 6 **imaginarie.** [ad. L. *imāgināri-us*, f. *imāgo, imāgin-* IMAGE: see -ARY¹.]

A. *adj.* **1. a.** Existing only in imagination or fancy; having no real existence. (Opposed to *real, actual.*) ***imaginary museum*** = *musée imaginaire* (see MUSÉE 2).

1382 WYCLIF *Rev.* Prol., Sum visioun is bodili..sum is spiritual, or ymaginarie, as whanne we seen slepinge, or ellis wakinge we biholden the ymagis of thingis, bi whiche sum other thing is signefied. *c* **1510** MORE *Picus* Wks. 17/1 How shorte, howe vncertain, how shadowe like, false, imaginary it is. **1651** HOBBES *Leviath.* III. xxxiv. 210 The word *Ghosts*, which signifieth..the Imaginary inhabitants of mans brain. **1709** LADY M. W. MONTAGU *Let. to Anne Wortley* 21 Aug., After giving me imaginary wit and beauty, you give me imaginary passions, and you tell me I'm in love. **1727** SWIFT *Gulliver* IV. vi, Besides real diseases, we are subject to many that are only imaginary, for which the physicians have invented imaginary cures. **1792** COWPER *Let.* 29 July Wks. 1835–7 III. 60 You may think there is much of the imaginary in it. **1883** FROUDE *Short Stud.* IV. III. 265 Rich men could not easily abandon substantial enjoyments in pursuit of so imaginary an object. **1963** *Times Lit. Suppl.* 23 Aug. 642/5 Mr. Skelton's readers are given hardly any notion of the imaginary museums in which poets roam and of which they too must be habitués if they are to appreciate poems more than superficially. **1967** *Listener* 25 May 679/2 Marino's *Galeria*, the 'imaginary museum' where one assembles one's favourite works of art from a number of different locations.

b. Said of lines, etc., assumed to be drawn through or between certain points.

1601 HOLLAND *Pliny* II. 397 If a woman make three imaginary circles round about them [etc.]. **1601** R. JOHNSON *Kingd. & Commw.* (1603) 229 An imaginarie line to be drawn from Suaquen to..Meroe. **1703** MOXON *Mech. Exerc.* 220 Each two Centers..shall have an imaginary Axis pass between them. **1837** WHEWELL *Hist. Induct. Sc.* (1857) I. 111 Imaginary lines drawn upon it.

c. *Math.* Applied to quantities or loci having no real existence, but assumed to exist for the purpose of generalization, or of extending a formula to all cases; such are the square root of a negative quantity, or any expression involving such a root, or any point, curve, etc. denoted algebraically by such an expression. (Imaginary quantities are sometimes called *impossible quantities.*) Also *transf.* Relating to imaginary quantities or loci, as ***imaginary geometry, projection***, etc. (Opp. to *real.*)

[**1637** DESCARTES *Géométrie* 380 Les..racines..ne sont pas tousiours reeles; mais quelquefois seulement imaginaires.] **1706** W. JONES *Syn. Palmar. Matheseos* 127 The Original Components or Roots of all Equations, may be either Affirmative, Negative, Mix'd, or Imaginary. **1816** tr. *Lacroix's Diff. & Int. Calculus* 98 The coefficient $\frac{dy}{dx}$ assumes an imaginary value. **1841** J. R. YOUNG *Math. Dissert.* i. 30 Expressions which in their common algebraic character denote imaginary or impossible quantities. **1859** BARN. SMITH *Arith. & Algebra* (ed. 6) 201 The square root or any even root of a negative quantity is called an Imaginary quantity. **1882** MINCHIN *Unipl. Kinemat.* 215 The remaining portion of this equipotential locus is..the (imaginary) circle which cuts the circle of poles orthogonally.

†**2.** Relating to the imagination; imaginative.

1595 SHAKS. *John* IV. ii. 265 My rage was blinde, And foule immaginarie eyes of blood Presented thee more hideous then thou art. *c* **1600** —— *Sonn.* xxvii, My soul's imaginary sight Presents thy shadow to my sightless view. **1677** GILPIN *Demonol.* (1867) 143 Satan had a power..to fix upon their imaginary faculty the species, images, or characters of what was to be suggested.

†**3.** Of the nature of an image or representation. *Obs.*

1593 SHAKS. *Lucr.* 1422 Much imaginarie worke was there ..A hand, a foote, a face, a leg, a head Stood for the whole to be imagined. **1669** WOODHEAD *St. Teresa* I. xxviii. 192 This Vision, though it be Imaginary (or representing itself by way of Image to me), was never seen by me with the eyes of my Body.

†**4.** Supposed; putative. *Obs.*

a **1631** DONNE *Serm.* xxv. 250 His Imaginary father Joseph.

†**5.** Imaginable; that can be imagined. *Obs.*

1653 ASHWELL *Fides Apost.* 12 Clearing my way as I go, of al Imaginary rubs and obstacles. **1687** A. LOVELL tr. *Thevenot's Trav.* III. 20 All imaginary enquiry was made after them, but..there was no news to be had.

B. *sb.* †**1.** An imagination; a fancy. *Obs.*

1709 MRS. MANLEY *Secret Mem.* (1736) III. 208 False glittering imaginaries. **1748** RICHARDSON *Clarissa* (1811) I. 224 And Cowley thus addresses beauty as a mere imaginary. *Ibid.* II. xiii. 81 The lovers imaginaries (her own notable word) are by that time gone off.

2. *Math.* An imaginary quantity or expression: see 1 c above.

1864 in WEBSTER. **1883** CAYLEY *Presid. Addr. Brit. Assoc.* 19 Sept., The circular functions..are connected through the theory of imaginaries.

Hence **i'maginariness** (Bailey vol. II, 1727).

†**i'maginate,** *ppl. a.* Chiefly *Sc. Obs.* [ad. L. *imāgināt-us*, pa. pple. of *imāgināre* to IMAGINE. (Sometimes const. as pple.)] Imagined; imaginary.

1533 BELLENDEN *Livy* II. (1822) 112 The faderis war sa commovit for this tressoun, recentlie imaginate, that..thay retretit thair sentence. **1563** WINȜET *Four Scoir Thre Quest.* Wks. 1888 I. 119 Gif ȝe appreue na Kirk..except an imaginat inuisible Kirk. **1588** A. KING tr. *Canisius' Catech.* 210 Na thing can be imaginat mair intolerable nor mair vnhappie. **1601** HOLLAND *Pliny* VII. xii. 161 The imaginate facultie of other living creatures is unmoveable.

†**i'maginate,** *v. Obs.* [f. L. *imāgināt-*, ppl. stem: see prec. and -ATE³.] *trans.* To imagine.

1563 WINȜET *Four Scoir Thre Quest.* Wks. 1888 I. 120 Or quhiddir imaginat ȝe ȝour Kirk to be inuisible? —— *Wks.* (1890) II. 22 Bot peraduentuir..we imaginat thir thingis. **1570** LEVINS *Manip.* 41/44 Imaginate, *imaginari.*

imagination (ɪmædʒɪ'neɪʃən). Also 4–6 with *y* for *i* and -cio(u)n, etc.; 6–7 **immagination.** [a. F. *imagination* (12th c.), ad. L. *imāginātiōn-em*, noun of action from *imāgināri, -āre* to IMAGINE.]

1. The action of imagining, or forming a mental concept of what is not actually present to the senses (cf. sense 3); the result of this process, a mental image or idea (often with implication that the conception does not correspond to the reality of things, hence freq. *vain* (*false*, etc.) ***imagination***).

a **1340** HAMPOLE *Psalter* xxxvii. 7 Þe fende þat..trauails my saule in vayn ymaginaciouns. **1377** LANGL. *P. Pl.* B. xx. 33 Wenynge is no wysdome ne wyse ymaginacioun. **1450–1530** *Myrr. our Ladye* 41 Anon ymaginacions of the same thynges come to his mynde. *c* **1460** FORTESCUE *Abs. & Lim. Mon.* ix. (1885) 128 We nede in this case to vse coniecture and ymaginacion. **1576** FLEMING *Panopl. Epist.* 193 They..accounted his undoubted divinations, madde immaginations. **1690** LOCKE *Hum. Und.* III. v. §12 When we speak of Justice, or Gratitude, we frame to our selves no Imagination of any thing existing. **1761** HUME *Hist. Eng.* III. xlv. 8 *note*, Could such an imagination ever have been entertained by him? **1829** JAS. MILL *Hum. Mind* (1869) I. vii. 239, I am said to have an imagination when I have a train of ideas. **1896** DK. ARGYLL *Philos. Belief* 223 The truths which they proclaimed were facts and not imaginations.

†**2.** The mental consideration of actions or events not yet in existence. **a.** Scheming or devising; a device, contrivance, plan, scheme, plot; a fanciful project. *Obs.* exc. as a biblical archaism.

c **1385** CHAUCER *L.G.W.* 1523 *Hypsip.*, With-outen any othir affeccioun Of loue or euyl ymagynacyoun. *c* **1400** MAUNDEV. (1839) xxiii. 251 Alle here lust and alle here Ymaginacioun is for to putten alle Londes undre hire subieccioun. **1535** COVERDALE *Lam.* iii. 60 Thou hast herde their despytefull wordes (O Lorde) yee and all their ymaginacions agaynst me. **1548** HALL *Chron., Rich. III* 47 b, That mischevous ymaginacion whiche he nowe newely beganne and attempted. **1660** *Trial Regic.* 9 In no Case else Imagination, or Compassing, without an actual effect of it, was punishable by our Law. **1709** SWIFT *Advancem. Relig.* Wks. 1755 II. I. 117 These airy imaginations of introducing new laws for the amendment of mankind. **1760–72** H. BROOKE *Fool of Quality* (1809) III. 47 Any imagination.. tending to change the nature or form of any one of the three estates.

†**b.** Impression as to what is likely; expectation, anticipation. *Obs.*

1623 BINGHAM *Xenophon* 29 As soone as it was day, all set forward..imagining that by sun-set they should reach to Villages of the Babylonian Territorie. Neither were they deceiued in their imagination. **1628** HOBBES *Thucyd.* (1822) 106 The sickness—the only thing that exceeded the imagination of all men. **1654** MARVELL *Corr.* Wks. 1872–5 II. 11 To tell you truly mine own imagination, I thought he would not open it while I was there.

3. That faculty of the mind by which are formed images or concepts of external objects not present to the senses, and of their relations (to each other or to the subject); hence frequently including memory. (Sometimes called the 'reproductive imagination'; cf. sense 4.)

1340 *Ayenb.* 158 Oþerhuil hit is ase to þe poȝte, oþer ase to þe ymaginacion. **1398** TREVISA *Barth. De P.R.* III. vi. (Tollem, MS.), The þridde hat ymaginacion: þerby þe soule biholdeþ þe liknesse of bodily þingis þat beþ absente. **1485** CAXTON *Chas. Gt.* 1 The comune understondyng is better content to the ymagnacion local. **1541** COPLAND *Guydon's Quest. Chirurg.* E j b, In the fyrste parte of the ventricle before is put yᵉ common blode. In the seconde yᵉ vertue of ymagynacyon. **1601** SHAKS. *All's Well* I. i. 93, I haue forgott him. My imagination Carries no fauour in't but Bertrams. **1639** T. BRUGIS tr. *Camus' Mor. Relat.* 320 The very features of the faces..remained so ingraven in his imagination. **1751** HARRIS *Hermes* Wks. (1841) 219 We have ..a faculty called imagination or fancy..which retains the fleeting forms of things, when things themselves are gone, and all sensation at an end. **1797** MRS. RADCLIFFE *Italian* i. (1826) 5 The beauty of her countenance haunting his imagination. **1840** MILL *Diss. & Disc., Bentham* (1859) I. 353 The Imagination..to which the name is generally appropriated by the best writers of the present day [is] that which enables us, by a voluntary effort, to conceive the absent as if it were present.

4. The power which the mind has of forming con cepts beyond those derived from external objects (the 'productive imagination').

a. The operation of fantastic thought; fancy.

c **1386** CHAUCER *Miller's T.* 426 Men may dyen of ymaginacion So depe may impression be take. **1390** GOWER *Conf.* III. 98 (MS. Fairfax 3) Full of ymaginacion, Of dredes and of wrathfull þoghtes. **1601** SHAKS. *Twel. N.* II. v. 48 Looke how imagination blowes him. **1645** BOATE *Irel. Nat. Hist.* (1652) 75 As if in very deed he had..seen and suffered all those things, which his weak imagination..did figure unto him. **1834** MEDWIN *Angler in Wales* I. 275 And I fancied, though it might be imagination, that her's trembled too.

b. The creative faculty of the mind in its highest aspect; the power of framing new and striking intellectual conceptions; poetic genius.

1509 HAWES *Past. Pleas.* XIV. (Percy Soc.) 53 Upon hys ymaginacyon He made also the tales of Caunterbury. **1590** SHAKS. *Mids. N.* V. i. 14 And as imagination bodies forth The forms of things vnknowne; the Poet's pen Turnes them to shapes, and giues to aire nothing, A locall habitation, and a name. **1657** R. LIGON *Barbadoes* (1673) 19 Nor can imagination frame so great a beauty. **1762** KAMES *Elem. Crit.* (1833) 480 This singular power of fabricating images without any foundation in reality, is distinguished by the name of *imagination.* **1871** DARWIN *Desc. Man* I. ii. 45 The Imagination is one of the highest prerogatives of man. By this faculty he unites, independently of the will, former images and ideas, and thus creates brilliant and novel results.

5. The mind, or a department of the mind, when engaged in imagining; hence, the operation of the mind generally; thinking; thought, opinion. Now *rare* or *Obs.*

c **1384** CHAUCER *H. Fame* II. 220, I wille Tellen the a propre skille, And worthe a demonstracion In myn ymagynacion. **1390** GOWER *Conf.* III. 303 Now is she red, now is she pale, Right after the condition Of her ymagination. *c* **1500** *Three Kings Sons* 138 The kynge..in his ymaginacion thought to make a grete assaute vpone the Turkes loggyng. **1548** HALL *Chron., Edw. IV* 239 b, Conjectures, which as often deceyve the imaginacions of fantastical folke. **1632** J. HAYWARD tr. *Biondi's Eromena* 12 That neither she..nor others..came thereby to lose or gaine in the imagination of others. **1662** J. DAVIES tr. *Olearius' Voy. Ambass.* 181 Upon the first sight thereof, it run into our imagination, that they were the Cosaques.

6. *attrib.* and *Comb.*, as ***imagination-consciousness, -game, -image, -mill, -monger, -process, -world***; ***imagination-liberating, -manufactured, -stirring, -stunning*** adjs.

1901 E. B. TITCHENER *Exper. Psychol.* I. I. 1 An *imagination-consciousness, our mind as it is when we are imagining something. **1926** E. BOWEN *Ann Lee's, & Other Stories* 53 But the *imagination-game palled upon him. **1890** W. JAMES *Princ. Psychol.* II. xviii. 50 *Imagination-images..feel subject to our spontaneity [etc.]. **1933** R. TUVE *Seasons & Months* i. 28 It was not the *imagination-liberating concept of Nature. **1902** *North Amer. Rev.* Dec. 768 The [Christian] Science..secures to him life-long immunity from *imagination-manufactured disease. **1899** *Harper's Mag.* Dec. 40/1 His *imagination-mill was hard at work in a minute. **1889** *Pall Mall G.* 28 June 3/2 To the exclusion of other industrious *imagination-mongers. **1890** W. JAMES *Princ. Psychol.* II. xviii. 72 The *imagination-process *can* then pass over into the sensation-process. In other words, genuine sensations *can* be centrally originated. **1892** 'MARK TWAIN' *Amer. Claimant* x. 88 The *imagination-stunning material development of this century. **1904** *Daily Chron.* 19 Oct. 8/1 This glimpse into the *imagination-world of London.

imaginational (ɪmædʒɪ'neɪʃənəl), *a.* [f. prec. + -AL¹.] Of or pertaining to the imagination.

1856 R. A. VAUGHAN *Mystics* (1860) I. 128 Within the depths of thine own soul thou wilt find a threefold heaven —the imaginational, the rational, and the intellectual. **1865** J. GROTE *Treat. Moral Ideas* iv. (1876) 48 We should have an imaginational knowledge or a quasi-sensation.

imaginative (ɪ'mædʒɪneɪtɪv, -ətɪv), *a.* (*sb.*) Forms: 4–5 **ymagyn-, ymagin-, -atyf, -yff, -if, -iff,** (6 **-ife, -yfe, -yue**), 6– **imaginative.** [a. OF. *imaginatif* (14th c.), ad. late L. *imāginātīvus*: see IMAGINE *v.* and -ATIVE.]

1. Of persons: Given to imagining; endowed with or specially characterized by imagination. †**a.** Full of thoughts, plans, designs, or devices (so OF. *imaginatif, -ive*). *Obs.* **b.** Full of idle fancies; fanciful. **c.** Having exceptional powers of fancy or inventive genius.

c **1386** CHAUCER *Frankl. T.* 366 No thyng list hym to been ymaginatyf. **1485** CAXTON *Paris & V.* 47 For allewaye he was pensyf and ymagynatyf. **1509** HAWES *Past. Pleas.* VIII. (Percy Soc.) 29 It was the guyse..Of famous poets ryght ymaginatife. **1525** LD. BERNERS *Froiss.* II. clxxxi. T T ij b, The kynge enclyned well therto, but the duke of Burgoyne who was sage and ymagynatyue wolde nat agree therto. **1592** WYRLEY *Armorie, Chandos* 38 This courteous knight, sage, imagenative, Found to his foes much warlike busines. **1626** BACON *Sylva* §903 The Witches themselues are Imaginative, and beleeue oft-times, they doe that, which they doe not. **1841** D'ISRAELI *Amen. Lit.* (1867) 617 Philosophers were often in peril of being as imaginative as poets. **1853** KANE *Grinnell Exp.* xxxi. (1856) 267 Men became moping, testy, and imaginative.

2. Of, pertaining to, or concerned in the exercise of imagination as a mental faculty.
c **1374** CHAUCER *Boeth.* v. pr. iv. 129 (Camb. MS.) Ymaginacion..enuyrowneth & comprehendeth alle thinges sensible, nat by reson sensible of deemynge, but bi reson Imaginatyf. **1581** SIDNEY *Apol. Poetrie* (Arb.) 33 The imaginative and iudging powre. **1647** H. MORE *Poems* Notes 349 Every sensitive and imaginative act. **1783** BLAIR *Rhet.* xxxviii. II. 322 Poetry..included then, the whole burst of the human mind; the whole exertion of its imaginative faculties. **1817** COLERIDGE *Biog. Lit.* I. iv. 88 Milton had a highly imaginative, Cowley a very fanciful mind.

†**3.** Imaginable. *Obs. rare*$^{-1}$.
1387-8 T. USK *Test. Love* III. i. (Skeat) I. 20 In that heuen shul they dwel..without any ymaginatife yuel in any halue.

†**4.** Existing only in the imagination; unreal, fancied, imaginary. *Obs.*
1561 T. NORTON *Calvin's Inst.* IV. xvii. 124 a, Onely an imaginatiue forme and not rather a naturall truth of bred. *a* **1603** T. CARTWRIGHT *Confut. Rhem. N.T.* (1618) 454 His righteousnesse imputed unto us, is not an imaginative, but a true righteousnesse. **1646** H. LAWRENCE *Comm. Angells* 8 An imaginative sight being onely within, in the imagination, consequently appeares to him onely, which so sees it.

5. Characterized by, or resulting from, the productive imagination; bearing evidence of high poetic or creative fancy.
1829 SCOTT *Guy M.* Introd., The imaginative tale of Sintram and his Companions, by Mons. Le Baron de la Motte Fouqué. **1873** BLACK *Pr. Thule* vi, He had sketched out an imaginative picture of the scene. **1874** GREEN *Short Hist.* vii. §7. 415 No great imaginative poem had broken the silence of English literature for nearly two hundred years.

†**B.** *sb.* Imaginative faculty; imagination. *Obs.*
[**1377** LANGL. *P. Pl.* B. XII. 1, I am ymagynatyf, quod he, Idel was I neuere, þouȝe I sitte bi my-self in sikenesse ne in helthe.] **1412-20** LYDG. *Chron. Troy* I. vi, Fordulled is myne imagynatyfe. *c* **1430** —— *Min. Poems* (Percy Soc.) 95 Seothe and considrithe in yowr imagynatif. **1641** MILTON *Animadv.* xiii. Wks. (1847) 71/2 Your Doctor's scarlet, which through your eyes infecting your pregnant imaginative with a red Suffusion, begets a continual thought of blushing.

imaginatively (ɪˈmædʒɪneɪtɪvlɪ), *adv.* [f. prec. + -LY[2].] In an imaginative fashion; in imagination.
1564 J. RASTELL *Confut. Jewell's Serm.* 140 The body of Christ is, onelye..imaginatiuelie in the Sacrament. **1662** PETTY *Taxes* 83 Others are but potentially or imaginatively rich. **1833** LAMB *Elia* Ser. II. *Barrenness Imag. Faculty Mod. Art*, Hogarth excepted, can we produce any one painter within the last fifty years..that has treated a story imaginatively? **1871** FARRAR *Witn. Hist.* ii. 59 The Christologies..are morally noble, and imaginatively beautiful.

imaginativeness (ɪˈmædʒɪneɪtɪvnɪs). [f. as prec. + -NESS.] Imaginative nature or quality.
1664 H. MORE *Myst. Iniq.* II. I. xiii. 294 'Ως therefore referrs to the Imaginativeness of the Representation. **1846** RUSKIN *Mod. Paint.* I. II. VI. i. §15 The exquisite imaginativeness of the lines. **1884** CHURCH *Bacon* ix. 220 Some bright touch of his incorrigible imaginativeness, ever ready to force itself in.

imaginator (ɪˈmædʒɪneɪtə(r)). *rare.* [ad. L. type **imāginātor*, agent-n. f. *imāginārī* to IMAGINE.] One who imagines.
a **1641** BP. MOUNTAGU *Acts & Mon.* (1642) 491 The Docitae [*read* Docetae] or Imaginators..held nothing reall, what hee [Christ] was, what hee did, what hee suffered, but all onely seeming so and in appearance. **1835** *Fraser's Mag.* XI. 612 Would not the imaginator of such a thing have been treated as a maniac? **1882** *Athenæum* No. 2867. 471 These masterly delineators and imaginators of fairyland.

†**iˈmaginatory,** *a. Obs. rare.* [ad. L. type **imāginātōri-us*; cf. prec.] **a.** Imaginary. **b.** Imaginative.
a **1618** RALEIGH *Apol.* 27 To satisfy his Majesty, that my designe was not Imaginatory but true. **1660** S. FISHER *Rusticks Alarm* Wks. (1679) 305 The dark and dismal Dreamings..which have entered and centered themselves in thy Imaginatory Mind.

imagine (ɪˈmædʒɪn), *v.* Forms: 4-6 ymagyn(e, -gene, 5-6 ymagine, imagyne, -gene, 6 ymagin, -en, imagyn, -en, ymmagen, immagin(e, -gyne, 6-7 imagin, 5- imagine. [a. F. *imaginer* (1297 in Hatz.-Darm.), ad. L. *imāgināre* to form an image of, represent, fashion, in middle voice *imāginārī* to picture to oneself, fancy, imagine, f. *imāgin-em* IMAGE.]

I. *trans.* **1. a.** To form a mental image of, to represent to oneself in imagination, to picture to oneself (something not present to the senses).
1340 HAMPOLE *Pr. Consc.* 6847 Alle þe men of cristianté Couthe noght, thurgh witt, ymagyn right, Ne descryve swa hydus a sight. *c* **1400** MAUNDEV. (Roxb.) xxv. 114 Þai er so curiously made þat na man may ymagyn mare curious. *c* **1566** J. ALDAY tr. *Boaystuau's Theat. World* M, A thing.. that it is not possible for man to ymagine the like without seeing. **1601** R. JOHNSON *Kingd. & Commw.* (1603) 188 By the multitudes of people (before spoken of) you may imagine the state of his forces. **1638** F. JUNIUS *Paint. of Ancients* 19 Phidias..had a singular abilitie to imagine things invisible after a most majesticall manner. **1739** HUME *Hum. Nat.* II. ii. (1874) I. 339 'Tis an establish'd maxim in metaphysics.. That nothing we imagine is absolutely impossible. **1780** A. YOUNG *Tour Irel.* 288 Surrounded by the most tremendous mountains that can be imagined. **1862** H. SPENCER *First Princ.* I. ii. §11 (1875) 34 The non-existence of space cannot, however, by any mental effort be imagined. **1874** GREEN *Short Hist.* viii. §5. 511 Milton's imagination is not strong enough to identify him with the world which he imagines.

b. with *obj. clause.*
1586 A. DAY *Eng. Secretary* I. (1625) 101, I cannot easily imagine how you may be served better. **1656-9** B. HARRIS *Parival's Iron Age* (ed. 2) 108 They could not imagine, that the said Dam..would be able to hinder their passage. **1697** DAMPIER *Voy.* I. 175, I cannot imagin wherefore they are called so.

2. To create as a mental conception, to conceive; to assume, suppose (as a mathematical line or figure). Also with *obj. clause* or *obj.* and *inf.*
c **1380** WYCLIF *Serm.* Sel. Wks. I. 168 Þei seien, þere is noon siche, but siche oon þei ymagynen. *c* **1391** CHAUCER *Astrol.* I. §14 This forseide grete Pyn in maner of an extre is ymagyn[e]d to be the Pol Artyk. *Ibid.* II. §39 The longitude of a clymat ys a lyne ymagined fro Est to west. **1522** MORE *De Quat. Noviss.* Wks. 75/1 Imagine your self in the same case, & I think ye wil think yea. **1549** *Compl. Scot.* vi. 48 ȝe sal ymagyn ane lyne that passis throucht the spere..; at the endis of the said lyne ȝe sal ymagyne tua sternis. **1568** GRAFTON *Chron.* II. 1298 Imagine you see before your eyes your wyves, and daughters in daunger. **1617** MORYSON *Itin.* III. 215 This law is thus practised..imagining there be three brothers, Thomas, John, and Andrew, and it happening, that Thomas first dies leaving [etc.]. **1659** D. PELL *Impr. Sea* 85 That hee would strongly imagine Cato..to bee in presence.

3. To conceive in the mind as a thing to be performed; to devise, plot, plan, compass. Also with *inf.* Now a biblical or legal archaism.
[**1351** *Act 25 Edw. III*, Stat. v. c. 2 Q^a^nt homme fait compasser ou ymaginer la mort nostre Seign^r^ le Roi.] *c* **1380** *Sir Ferumb.* 3244 Ymagened y haue anoþer þyng to conquery þe tour at ones. *c* **1426** *Paston Lett.* No. 4 I. 12 Purposyng and imaginyng to putte William Paston in drede. **1491** *Act 7 Hen. VII*, c. 23 Preamb., Richard White.. traitrously ymagened and compassed the dethe and destruccion of oure seid Souvereigne Lord. **1535** COVERDALE *Ps.* ii. 1 Why do..the people ymagyn [*R.V. marg.* meditate] vayne thinges? *Ibid.* lxi[i]. 3 How longe wil ye ymagin myschefe agaynst euery man? **1548** HALL *Chron., Hen. VIII* 112 Now that the Frenchemen..daily imagened to destroye the Englishe pale. **1632** J. HAYWARD tr. *Biondi's Eromena* 34 The Count could imagine no possible meanes to overtake the Admirall. **1707** J. CHAMBERLAYNE *St. Gt. Brit.* II. vi. 100 To imagine the Death of the Prince..is made High Treason. **1747** *Gentl. Mag.* XVII. 151/1 Lord Lovat ..did..traitorously compass and imagine the death of his majesty. **1769** BLACKSTONE *Comm.* IV. vi. (1830) 78-9 What is a compassing or imagining the death of the King, &c. These are synonymous terms; the word *compass* signifying the purpose or design of the mind or will..But, as this compassing or imagining is an act of the mind, it cannot possibly fall under any judicial cognizance, unless it be demonstrated by some open, or overt, act. **1839** KEIGHTLEY *Hist. Eng.* II. 29 Fisher..also was arraigned for imagining to deprive the king of his title and dignity.

†**4.** To consider, ponder, meditate, bethink oneself. (With *obj. clause.*) *Obs.*
c **1386** CHAUCER *Clerk's T.* 542 Now gooth he ful faste ymaginyng, If by his wyues cheere he myght se..that she Were chaunged. *c* **1430** LYDG. *Min. Poems* (Percy Soc.) 242 Lyggyng allone I gan to ymagyne, How with foure tymes departyd is the yeer. *a* **1533** LD. BERNERS *Gold. Bk. M. Aurel.* (1546) O v, Euer he imagined, howe to do plesure to the peple. **1582** N. LICHEFIELD tr. *Castanheda's Conq. E. Ind.* lxxii. 149 [He] did imagine againe what course he might best take to reuenge himselfe.

5. To conjecture, guess, suspect, suppose.
a. with *simple obj.*, *obj. clause*, or *obj.* and *inf.*
c **1385** CHAUCER *L.G.W.* 1410 *Hypsip.*, This Pelleus hadde gret enuye, Imagynynge that Iason myghte be Enhaunsede so..That from his regne he myghte ben put a doun. **1477** EARL RIVERS (Caxton) *Dictes* 67 Ymagyne no thing to be in him, but that, that is nedfulle goode and couenable. **1548** HALL *Chron., Rich. III* 46 b, No suche fraude suspectynge, nor yet any treason ymagenynge. **1648** GAGE *West Ind.* vi. 18 They presently imagined the truth that hee could not come thither but with some Spaniard. **1700** S. L. tr. *Fryke's Voy. E. Ind.* 36 In vain did I imagine many things, to be the natural causes of it.

b. with *obj.* and *complement.*
1526 *Pilgr. Perf.* (W. de W. 1531) 197 b, Whiche in no wyse..ought to be ymagyned in ye deite. **1559** W. CUNNINGHAM *Cosmogr. Glasse* Pref. A iv b, The situation of Paradice..some imagen it ether in heaven or in the harts of the quiet and faithfull. **1634** SIR T. HERBERT *Trav.* 2 Wee bore up to speake with them, imagining them Enemies and men of warr, but they proved Flemings and our Friends. **1774** C. J. PHIPPS *Voy. N. Pole* 48 We imagined ourselves in rather more than eighty degrees and a half. **1792** W. ROBERTS *Looker-on* No. 33 ¶10 Except you opened his mouth, you might imagine him in the full prime and mettle of his years.

6. a. To form an idea or notion with regard to something not known with certainty; to think, suppose, fancy, 'take into one's head' (*that*); often implying a vague notion not founded on exact observation or reasoning.
1548 HALL *Chron., Hen. VIII* 153 b, The greate Turke.. imagened that hys time was come, to do some greate act in Christendom. **1576** FLEMING *Panopl. Epist.* 156 It is not to be surmised, nor imagined, that the mention of these matters is unseasonable. **1641** J. JACKSON *True Evang. T.* III. 199 A plot..invented, one would imagine, not by men, but by Cacodæmons. **1687** A. LOVELL tr. *Thevenot's Trav.* II. 83 You must not imagine to find such lovely Grass-plats and borders of Flowers as are in Europe. **1726** SHELVOCKE *Voy. round World* (1757) 75 In short one would imagine it impossible that any thing living could subsist in so rigid a climate. **1759** JOHNSON *Rasselas* ix, I doubt not of the facts which you relate, but imagine that you impute them to mistaken motives. **1802** MAR. EDGEWORTH *Moral T.* (1816) I. i. 7 He did not imagine that he could reform every abuse. **1863** GEO. ELIOT *Romola* II. iv, Tito felt that Romola was a more unforgiving woman than he had imagined.

b. *colloq.* To believe or suppose. Also used with aposiopesis in phr. ***can you imagine?***
1947 N. MARSH *Final Curtain* x. 150 We all opened our letters yesterday morning, at breakfast. Can you imagine? I got down first and really—such a shock! **1952** E. GRIERSON *Reputation for Song* iii. 20 'Is your mother coming down?' 'I imagine so.' **1961** *Guardian* 25 May 10/4 Naïvely imagining that MI 5 was only blood-hounding those with suspected Cliveden or Mosley ideas. **1968** D. DEVINE *Sleeping Tiger* i. 12 Peter borrowed the Jag to bring her here and he scraped it on the gate! Can you *imagine?* **1971** C. BONINGTON *Annapurna South Face* iii. 28 At times, though, in these hectic weeks of organization, as I imagine happens with any expedition, it seemed we should never make our deadline for packing all our gear ready to go to India. **1973** *Listener* 20 Dec. 841/2 This prospect must bring a lot of cheer to the Speaker... I imagine that after Mr Ford's swearing-in he slept the sleep of the just.

II. *intr.* †**7.** To think, meditate; to form designs. *Obs.* (*intr.* to 3 and 4.)
1377 LANGL. *P. Pl.* B. XIII. 289 With Inwit and with outwitt ymagenen and studye As best for his body be. *c* **1460** ROSS *La Belle Dame sans Mercy* 14 Þer-vpon a while I stood musyng, and in my self gretly ymagynyng. **1462** *Pol. Poems* (Rolls) II. 270 The fals traytours agayne hym ymagynynge. **1589** COGAN *Haven Health* ccxvii. (1636) 241 Divines that imagine and study upon high and subtile matters.

8. To form mental images or ideas; to exercise the imagination. (*intr.* to 1 and 2.)
1631 WIDDOWES *Nat. Philos.* 52 Pleasant dreames are when the spirits of the braine, which the soule useth to imagine with, are most pure and thin. **1700** T. BROWN tr. *Fresny's Amusem. Ser. & Com.* 5 He who Imagines Briskly, Thinks Justly, and Writes Correctly, is an Original [Author]. **1809** SYD. SMITH *Wks.* (1859) I. 183/2 If it can be shown that women may be trained to reason and imagine as well as men [etc.].

9. *to imagine of*: = sense 1. (Cf. *conceive of, think of, know of.*)
1586 A. DAY *Eng. Secretary* I. (1625) 61 A minde..that could never so much as thinke or imagine of things contemptible. **1587** TURBERV. *Trag. T.* (1837) 153 Imagine of their joyes, Whom filthie sinne did linke. **1825** SCOTT *Talism.* iv, In his wildest rapture the knight imagined of no attempt to follow or to trace the object of such romantic attachment.

Hence **iˈmagining** *ppl. a.*, that imagines.
1660 S. FISHER *Rusticks Alarm* Wks. (1679) 348 Alas poor imagining Man!

†**imagine,** *sb. Obs. rare*$^{-1}$. [f. prec. vb.] ? Device, contrivance: cf. IMAGINEMENT.
1594 PEELE *Battle Alcazar* II. Introd., By this imagine was this barbarous Moor Chas'd from his dignity and diadem.

imagined (ɪˈmædʒɪnd), *ppl. a.* [f. IMAGINE *v.* + -ED[1].]
1. Invented, planned, designed. In later use only with *advs.*, as *ill-*, ***well-imagined.***
1509 HAWES *Past. Pleas.* xxxiv. (Percy Soc.) 110 Fantasy ..hath the hole aspecte, The ymagyned matter to bring to finysshement. **1658** CLEVELAND *Rustick. Ramp.* Wks. (1687) 491 By false, subtile, and imagined Language. **1809** KENDALL *Trav.* II. xxxvi. 19 A bridge will shortly be completed, of..well-imagined construction. **1822** SCOTT *Pirate* xii, Large and ill-imagined additions, hastily adapted to the original building.

2. Conceived (in the mind), supposed, fancied.
1549 *Compl. Scot.* vi. 49 The pole antartic is bot ane ymaginet point. **1609** BIBLE (Douay) II. *Hist. Table* 1082 Everie towne and village had their peculiar imagined goddes. **1667** MILTON *P.L.* v. 263 As when by night the Glass Of Galileo..observes Imagind Lands and Regions in the Moon. **1883** FROUDE in *19th Cent.* Aug. 233 Byron was a world's wonder for imagined wickedness.

†**iˈmaginement.** *Obs. rare*$^{-1}$. In 5 ym-. [f. IMAGINE *v.* + -MENT. Cf. OF. *ymaginement* image.] Contrivance, subtlety.
c **1470** HARDING *Chron.* CXX. v, Some in his sherte put oft tyme venemyng..Some in his hose, by great ymagenement.

imaginer (ɪˈmædʒɪnə(r)). [f. as prec. + -ER[1]. Cf. OF. *imagineur.*] One who imagines.
1483 *Cath. Angl.* 195/1 An Imaginer, *molitor, excogitator.* **1525** LD. BERNERS *Froiss.* II. clxvii. [clxiii.] 462 Men of warre inclosed in fortresses are sore imagyners, and whan their imaginacion inclyneth to any yuell dede, they wyll craftely colour it. **1678** CUDWORTH *Intell. Syst.* I. v. 700 As if the strength of imagination were such that it could not only create phancies but also real sensible objects, and that at a distance too from the imaginers. **1880** SIR E. REED *Japan* II. 238 He must be but a poor traveller and a weak imaginer.

imagines, pl. of IMAGO.

imagining (ɪˈmædʒɪnɪŋ), *vbl. sb.* [f. IMAGINE *v.* + -ING[1].] The action of the verb IMAGINE, in various senses; imagination.
c **1340** HAMPOLE *Prose Tr.* 40 In ymagynynge of þe manhede of oure Lorde. *c* **1385** CHAUCER *L.G.W.* Prol. 331 (MS. Gg. 4. 27) For hate or for Ielous ymagynyng. *c* **1430** LYDG. *Min. Poems* (Percy Soc.) 211 What may avaylle al your ymagynynges? **1548** HALL *Chron. Hen. VIII* 32 While these thynges were thus in commonynge and immagenyng. **1605** SHAKS. *Macb.* I. iii. 138 Present Feares Are lesse than horrible Imaginings. **1685** SOUTH *Serm.* (1697) I. 441 Our own Common Law looks upon a Man's raising Arms against ..his Prince, as an Imagining, or Compassing of his Death. **1812** BYRON *Ch. Har.* To Ianthe ii, Guileless beyond Hope's imagining! **1871** PALGRAVE *Lyr. Poems* 72 In hopeless chase of vain imaginings.

i'maginist. *nonce-wd.* [f. IMAGINE *v.* + -IST.] An imaginative person.

1815 JANE AUSTEN *Emma* xxxix. III. 43 How much more must an imaginist, like herself, be on fire with speculation and foresight!

†**i'maginous,** *a. Obs. rare.* [? f. L. *imāgo, imāgin-em* image + -OUS (cf. doubtful L. *imāginōsus*) or ? f. IMAGINE *v.* (cf. *ravenous*).] Imaginative; full of fancies.

1608 CHAPMAN *Byron's Conspir.* III. i, Till..man hath cast the beames, Of his imaginouse fancie through it. **16..** GATAKER *Joy of Just* in *Serm.* (1637) 235 Others that be awaked out of this imaginous sleepe.

Imagism ('ɪmɪdʒɪz(ə)m). Also **imagism.** [f. IMAGE *sb.* + -ISM.] **1.** Name given to a movement in poetry, originating in 1912 and represented by Ezra Pound, Amy Lowell, and others, aiming at clarity of expression through the use of precise visual images.

In the early period often written in the Fr. form *Imagisme.*

1912 E. POUND *Let.* 1 Aug. (1971) 38 I should like the name 'Imagisme' to retain some sort of a meaning. It stands, or I should like it to stand for hard light, clear edges. *Ibid.* 12 Aug. (1971) 39 If you want to drag in the word Imagisme you can use a subtitle 'an anthology devoted to Imagisme, vers libre and modern movements in verse' or something of that sort. **1913** *Poetry* (Chicago) Mar. 198 (*title*) Imagisme. Some curiosity has been aroused concerning *Imagisme*... Editor's Note—In response to many requests for information regarding *Imagism* and the *Imagistes*, we publish this note by Mr. Flint... *Imagism* is not necessarily associated with Hellenic subjects, or with *vers libre* as a prescribed form. **1915** E. POUND *Let.* Jan. (1971) 48 If I had acceded to A. L.'s [*sc.* Amy Lowell's] proposal to turn 'Imagism' into a democratic beer-garden, I should have undone what little good I had managed to do by setting up a critical standard. **1917** *North Amer. Rev.* CCV. 106 The third characteristic of The New Poetry, and particularly of Imagism, is what might be metaphorically described as faithfulness to the architectural line. **1924** T. MAYNARD *Our Best Poets* 198 Imagism brings together, with an indulgent catholicism, those who use metre with a brilliant exactness, and those who use only cadence. **1929** A. NOYES *Return of Scare-Crow* iv. 52 The sharp-edged imagism with which our younger writers are experimenting today. **1931** G. HUGHES (*title*) Imagism and the Imagists. **1967** *Listener* 2 Mar. 297/2 Pound may have believed that his imagism..was an alternative to symbolism, but there is no reason now for us to agree with him.

2. *Philos.* (See quot. 1953.)

1952 R. I. AARON *Theory of Universals* ii. 20 It might be argued that what Hobbes was attacking..was imagism rather than conceptualism, the notion [*i.e.* imagism] that there must be an image before us whenever we universalize. **1953** H. H. PRICE *Thinking & Experience* viii. 234 The theory that thinking consists in operating with mental images..has no generally accepted name. I am going to call it 'Imagism'.

Imagist ('ɪmɪdʒɪst), *sb.* (and *a.*) Also **imagist** and in Fr. form **Imagiste.** [f. as prec. + -IST.] **1.** An adherent of Imagism (sense 1). Also *attrib.* or as *adj.*

1912 E. POUND *Let.* Aug. (1971) 10 I send you all that I have on my desk—an over-elaborate post-Browning 'Imagiste' affair and a note on the Whistler exhibit. *Ibid.* Oct. (1971) 11 I've had luck again, and am sending you some *modern* stuff by an American, I say modern, for it is in the laconic speech of the Imagistes, even if the subject is classic. **1913** [see IMAGISM 1]. **1914** R. ALDINGTON in *Egoist* 1 June 201/1 (*title*) Modern poetry and the Imagists. *Ibid.* 202/1 Why do we call ourselves 'Imagists'?.. I think it is a very good and descriptive title... Let me say from memory what I, as an Imagist, consider the fundamental doctrines of the group... We do not say 'O how I admire that exquisite, that beautiful..woman'..but we present that woman, we make an 'Image' of her, we make the scene convey the emotion. **1915** *Egoist* 1 May 70/2 One of the first 'Imagist' poems by T. E. Hulme. **1919** *Hist. Amer. Lit.* II. 266 *Isle of la Belle Rivière*..was written in what is now called imagist verse, at the age of thirty. **1922** *Edin. Rev.* July 101 In much of the work of the imagists..we find a more or less conscious, and more or less effective yielding to that influence. **1931** [see GROUND *sb.* 11 b]. **1931** [see IMAGISM 1]. **1960** AUDEN *Homage to Clio* 42 No 'imagist' poem can be more than a few words long. **1970** *English Studies* LI. 269 This period also saw the birth and death of other more obviously revolutionary groups such as the Vorticists, Imagists, [etc.].

transf. **1962** *Times* 3 May 18/4 Two of the most rip-roaring imagists of European action-painting. **1962** *Listener* 27 Sept. 484/2 The Pirandellists, the Symbolists, the Kafkarians, the Imagists.

2. *Philos.* An adherent of imagism (sense 2). Also *attrib.* or as *adj.*

1948 *Mind* LVII. 481 He [*sc.* Ewing] backs it up with his criticisms of Behaviourist accounts of Belief and Verbalist and Imagist accounts of Thinking. **1953** H. H. PRICE *Thinking & Experience* viii. 239 The Imagist does not deny that words have meaning, but he holds that they have it only indirectly, as substitutes for images. *Ibid.* 241 The starting point of the Imagist theory..is private thinking, and private thinking of the 'free' symbol-using kind. **1972** *Science* 12 May 630/2 Thus he can adopt an imagist theory of meaning after carefully listing several objections to it which are never answered.

Hence **ima'gistic** *a.*, of or pertaining to Imagism (both senses); **ima'gistically** *adv.*

1916 E. POUND *Let.* 17 Apr. (1971) 76 Some of the things [*sc.* poems] seem to me 'just imagistic', neither better nor worse than a lot of other imagistic stuff that gets into print. **1921** H. CRANE *Let.* 22 July (1965) 63 In an imagistic way [this] singularly seems to agree with the substance of your opinion. **1940** *Kenyon Rev.* 277 The words 'fog' and 'bloody'..must be taken not only..imagistically but symbolically. **1944** *Mind* LIII. 216 Imagistic, literary, associative, or other kinds of meaning. **1963** *Listener* 14 Feb. 300/3 This imagistic language is carried to its logical conclusion in the controversial ending to the film. **1969** *Jrnl. Eng. & Gmc. Philol.* LXVIII. 219 The reason is imagistically indicated in the immediately preceding lines. **1973** *Times Lit. Suppl.* 2 Nov. 1348/3 He works for the most part imagistically, spacing small, autonomous chunks of perception around a page, resolutely subduing 'theme' to the eye-stopping images which compose it.

imago (ɪ'meɪgəʊ). Pl. **imagines** (-'eɪdʒɪniːz) and **imagos.** [A modern application of L. *imāgo* IMAGE, representation, natural shape, etc. (First used by Linnæus, *Syst. Nat.* ed. 12 (1767) I. II. 535.)] **1. a.** *Entom.* The final and perfect stage or form of an insect after it has undergone all its metamorphoses; the 'perfect insect'.

1797 *Encycl. Brit.*, *Imago*, in Natural History, is a name given by Linnæus to the third state of insects, when they appear in their proper shape and colours. **1816** KIRBY & SP. *Entomol.* I. iii. 67 The states through which insects pass are four: the egg, the larva, the pupa, and the imago. *Ibid.* 71 This Linné termed the imago state..because..it is now become a true representative or image of its species. **1847** SELBY in *Proc. Berw. Nat. Club* II. No. 5. 208 Species, whose imagos only appear..at uncertain..intervals. **1881** ANDERSON in *Science Gossip* No. 202. 223 In the year following, the larvæ of *Vanessa polychloros* swarmed on the elms..[but] neither caterpillars nor imagines have since been noticed.

b. *transf.* The perfect stage of other animals that undergo a metamorphosis.

1854 OWEN *Skel. & Teeth* in *Circ. Sc., Organ. Nat.* I. 189 The conversion of the cartilaginous skull of the larva to the ossified one of the imago, or perfect frog.

c. *fig.*

1921 *19th Cent.* Feb. 214 Since 1914 every constituent element that has been supposed to go to the making of great men—spacious times, tension, supreme effort, turmoil, battle, revolution—has abounded, but the imago has not emerged.

2. *Psychoanalysis.* A subjective image of someone (esp. a parent) which a person has subconsciously formed and which continues to influence his attitudes and behaviour. So ***father-imago, mother-imago.***

1916 B. M. HINKLE tr. *Jung's Psychol. of Unconscious* (1918) 492 Here I purposely give preference to the term 'Imago' rather than to the expression 'Complex', in order.. to invest this psychological condition, which I include under 'Imago', with living independence in the psychical hierarchy... 'Imago' has a significance similar on the one hand to the psychologically conceived creation in Spitteler's novel..and on the other hand to the ancient religious conception of 'imagines et lares'. **1919** M. K. BRADBY *Psycho-Anal.* 59 That web of ideas and emotions which is woven in the course of the child's life round the image of the parent or 'parent imago'. **1924** J. RIVIERE et al tr. *Freud's Coll. Papers* II. xxviii. 313 If the physician should be specially connected in this way with the father-imago (as Jung has happily named it) it is quite in accordance with his actual relationship to the patient. **1927** W. E. COLLINSON *Contemp. Eng.* 107 Most educated people will by now have heard of the Oedipus complex and will have a nodding acquaintance with libido and imago and may have, with distressing results, tried on themselves the method of free-association. **1948** M. KLEIN in S. Lorand *Psycho-Analysis Today* 65 The super-ego of the child does not coincide with the picture presented by its real parents, but is created out of imaginary pictures or *imagos* of them which it has taken up into itself. **1956** R. F. C. HULL tr. *Jung's Coll. Wks.* V. iv. 57 In most of the existing religions it seems that the formative factor..is the father-imago, while in the older religions it was the mother-imago. **1967** BRUSSEL & CANTZLAAR *Chambers's Dict. Psychiatry* 121 *Imago*, in Jung's *analytical psychology*, a conception of another person that one acquires in infancy or childhood and carries through to adulthood in the unconscious.

imagy ('ɪmɪdʒɪ), *a.* [f. IMAGE *sb.*: see -Y[1].] Of the nature of an image.

1937 *Aristotelian Soc. Suppl. Vol.* XVI. 213 We could suggest that an event has two sorts of constituents, *sensible* ones and *imagy* ones. **1953** H. H. PRICE *Thinking & Experience* vii. 201 The type-word 'cat' has *imagy* tokens as well as overtly perceptible ones.

i-maked, -et, ME. pa. pple. of MAKE *v.*

‖**imam, imaum** (ɪ'mɑːm). Forms: 7 **eemawm, imman,** 8 **emaum,** 9 **imawm, imám,** 7– **imam,** 8– **imaum;** also 7– **iman.** [a. Arab. *imām* leader, president, etc., f. *amma* to go before, precede. The form *iman* is that used in F. and Sp.]

1. The officiating priest of a Mohammedan mosque.

1613 PURCHAS *Pilgrimage* (1614) 301 Then ariseth another Priest of another order called Imam, and readeth a Psalme aloude. **1625–6** —— *Pilgrims* II. 1609 Immediately after euery one is cleansed and come into the Moschea, the Eemawm which is the Parish Priest beginnes to pray. **1687** A. LOVELL tr. *Thevenot's Trav.* II. 102 The director of the Prayers, who says the Prayers, and makes the rest say them; ..in Turkey he is called the Imam. **1717** LADY M. W. MONTAGU *Let. to Abbé Conti* 17 May, The outside of the mosque is adorned with four towers, vastly high, gilt on the top, from whence the imaums call the people to prayers. **1775** R. CHANDLER *Trav. Greece* (1825) II. 59 The Turks.. had erected a pulpit..for their iman or reader. **1815** ELPHINSTONE *Acc. Caubul* (1842) II. 278 The Imaums of towns have fees on marriages, burials, and some other ceremonies, and are maintained by them and the gifts of their congregation. **1884** F. BOYLE *Borderland* 257 The chief imam condemned such an interpretation of the law.

2. A title given to various Mohammedan leaders and chiefs.

Applied to **a.** the Caliph, as sovereign of the community, and (now or formerly) to other independent princes, e.g. the chief of Oman; **b.** the twelve chiefs of Islam recognized by the Ithnashari Shiites, of whom Ali, Hasan, and Husain were the earliest; **c.** the founders of the four orthodox sects of Mohammedans; **d.** the author of the leading treatise on any subject.

1662 J. DAVIES tr. *Olearius' Voy. Ambass.* 373 On these twelve Saints they bestow the quality of Imam, or Prelate. **1698** FRYER *Acc. E. India & P.* 220 The Prince of this Country [Muscat] is called *Imaum*, who is Guardian of Mahomet's Tomb, and on whom is devolved the Right of Caliphship. **1728** MORGAN *Algiers* I. vi. 171 The Khalifa of Bagdad..the legitimate Successor of Mahomet, and Sovereign Imaum or Pontiff of all the Mussulmans. **1753** HANWAY *Trav.* (1762) II. x. iv. 241 The Mascats are a tribe of Arabians..they are subject to an Iman, who has an absolute authority over them. **1804** W. TENNANT *Ind. Recreat.* (ed. 2) I. 220 Hossein.—This holy Imawm is believed not only to have been a saint, but a martyr. **1883** C. J. WILLS *Mod. Persia* 108 Where are buried the imams, or saints, of the Sheahs, Hussein and Hassan, one of the greatest shrines of Persian pilgrims. **1899** *Daily Chron.* 7 Mar. 7/3 By the treaty of 1862 France and Great Britain entered into a mutual engagement to respect the independence of the Imam of Muscat.

Hence **i'mamate** [cf. F. *imamat*], **i'mamship,** the dignity of imam.

1727–41 CHAMBERS *Cycl.* s.v. *Imam*, The Mahometans do not agree among themselves about this imamate, or dignity of the imam. **1860** J. GARDNER *Faiths World* II. 120/2 A number of the Schiites..denied the right of Moussa to the Imámate. **1895** *Pall Mall G.* 2 Dec. 2/2 The man who has given the trouble is the claimant to the Imamship of Sanaa—the titular ruler of the country before the Turks occupied it in 1872.

imambara (ɪ'mɑːmbərə, ɪmɑːm'bɑːrə). Also **imambarah, -barra, -bra, imaum-.** [Hind., f. Arab. IMAM + Hind. *bāṛā* enclosure.] In India, a building in which Shiite Muslims assemble at the time of Muharram; the gardens, courtyards, etc., surrounding such a building; also, any large tomb.

1837 E. EDEN *Jrnl.* 28 Dec. in *Up Country* (1866) I. ix. 87 In the afternoon we went to see the Emaumberra and Rooma Durwanee, two of the most magnificent native buildings I have seen yet. **1867** J. FERGUSSON *Hist. Archit.* II. v. viii. 702 In Lucknow there..is..one building especially, the Imambara, which..is not unfit to be spoken of in the same chapter as the earlier buildings. **1883** *Encycl. Brit.* XV. 49/2 The immense Imámbára, or mausoleum of Asaf-ud-daulá [at Lucknow]. **1886** YULE & BURNELL *Hobson-Jobson*, Imaumbarra. **1907** *Westm. Gaz.* 4 Apr. 10/2 The imambra connected with the Mohammedan morgue at Lucknow. **1955** J. TERRY *Charm Indo-Islamic Archit.* 40 (*heading*) Imambara, Lucknow, 18th century. A large hall built by a king of Oudh for famine-relief work. **1964** A. A. A. FYZEE *Outl. Muhammadan Law* (ed. 3) 319 An imāmbāra is a private apartment set apart by a member of the Ithnā 'Asharī Shiite faith for the performance of certain ceremonies at Muḥarram and other times; it is not a public place of worship like a mosque.

Imam Bayildi (ɪ'mɑːm 'bɑːjɪldɪ). Also **Imam Baildi.** [Turk., lit. = the priest fainted (supposedly from pleasure at, or because of the cost of, the dish).] A dish consisting of aubergines stuffed with an onion-and-tomato mixture and cooked in oil.

1935 M. MORPHY *Recipes of all Nations* 767 This vegetable [*sc.* the aubergine] is extremely popular in Turkey, and one of the commonest ways of preparing it is called *Imam Baïldi*..'the Swooning Imam'—the Imam having fainted with delight when he first partook of this wondrous dish. **1952** HOWE & ESPIR *Sultan's Pleasure & other Turkish Recipes* 75 *The fainting imam* (Pathcan Imam Bayildi). There is an amusing story connected with this traditional dish. **1958** I. ORGA *Turkish Cooking* 114 *Aubergine Imam Bayildi*... Take the onion mixture and fill the aubergines with this then lay them side by side in a wide-bottomed saucepan. **1969** R. STOUT *Death of Dude* (1970) xii. 176 Eggplant stuffed with a purée which the Turks call *Imam Baïldi*—'Swooning Imam'. Onions browned in oil, tomatoes, garlic, salt and pepper. **1972** J. RATHBONE *Trip Trap* x. 111 'Some more Imam Bayildi?' He motioned to the aubergine stew. **1973** *Guardian* 26 Jan. 11/1 A dish of aubergine..named Imam Bayildi or The Imam Fainted.

i-maned, obs. form of MANED *a.*

i-mang: see YMONG.

‖**imaret** (ɪ'mɑːrɛt, 'ɪmərɛt). [a. Turk., a. Arab. *imārat* 'rendering habitable', hence 'hospice'.] A hospice for the accommodation of pilgrims and travellers in Turkey.

1613 PURCHAS *Pilgrimage* (1614) 299 Their Hospitals they call Imarets... They found them for the reliefe of the poore, and of Trauellers. **1638** SIR T. HERBERT *Trav.* (ed. 2) 124 We found a neat Carravansraw or Inne, the Turks call them *Imareths*, the Indians *Sarrays*. **1817** MOORE *Lalla R., Veiled Prophet* III. 315 Many a dome and fair roofed imaret.

Imari (ɪ'mɑːrɪ). The name of a town in the north-west of the Japanese island of Kyushu, used *attrib.* and *ellipt.* to denote a type of Hizen porcelain.

1875–80 AUDSLEY & BOWES *Keramic Art Japan* I. 5 The productions of these numerous factories are usually exported from the seaport of Imari, and are therefore commonly known as Imari ware. **1878** J. J. YOUNG *Ceramic Art* vi. 175 The chief kinds of [Japanese] porcelain are the Hizen (also called Imari and Arita), [etc.]. **1890** B. H. CHAMBERLAIN *Things Japanese* 284 The second variety of Kutani ware may often be mistaken for 'old Japan' (i.e., Imari porcelain). **1902** *Encycl. Brit.* XXIX. 725/1 In the

term 'Hizen porcelains' are included not merely the richly decorated Imari ware—the 'Old Japan' of Western collectors [etc.]. **1954** H. GARNER *Oriental Blue & White* 63 The so-called 'Old Imari' wares. **1954** G. SAVAGE *Porcelain* 43 The *Imari* style is also Japanese, and was based on native textiles and brocades. **1969** *Guardian* 16 July 18/2 Japanese Kakiemon and Imari patterns were copied at Canton for shipment to Europe. **1970** *Ashmolean Mus. Rep. Visitors 1969* 47 Oil jug, Japanese export Imari porcelain, overglazed in red and gold. **1971** *Times* 5 Apr. 14/5 Delicate [chamber] pots in Imari porcelain and Wedgwood.

i-mariet, ME. pa. pple. of MARRY *v.*

i-martred, ME. pa. pple. of MARTYR *v.*

imbace: see EMBASE.

†**im'bake**, *v.* *Obs. rare.* [f. IM-[1] + BAKE *v.*] *trans.* To encrust, cake.

1632 HEYWOOD *1st Pt. Iron Age* IV. Wks. 1874 III. 329 Troilus..lyeth imbak'd In his cold blood.

imbalance (ɪm'bæləns). [f. IM-[2] + BALANCE *sb.*] An unbalanced condition; a lack of proper proportion or relation between corresponding things.

Orig. a technical term in Ophthalmology but now used generally in many subjects and contexts.

1898 *Ophthalmic Rec.* VII. 87 Some advocates of operative interference for ocular imbalance in the functional neuroses fail to recognize the fact that heterophoria, or even squint, may be only a symptom. **1930** G. HAMILTON *Med. Social Terminol.* 25 *Intellectual imbalance*, the state of an individual with special abilities or disabilities, markedly competent in some respects and deficient in others, but not well integrated or compensated. **1934** *Scrutiny* III. III. 230 It is a matter of common observation that a high degree of artistic discrimination can go along with an extreme paucity or imbalance of general emotional life. **1937** *Nature* 16 Jan. 90/2 The operating mechanism [of the human constitution] is the autonomic nervous system, which, especially in sensitive subjects is liable to..pass into imbalance or dysfunction, and eventually permanent disease. **1949** S. DUKE-ELDER *Text-bk. Ophthalm.* IV. xlvi. 3964 Operative treatment is the alternative measure to correct a heterophoria, and is particularly applicable in essential imbalance when the cause is anatomical. **1949** JANIS & FADNER in H. D. Lasswell et al. *Lang. Pol.* II. viii, This Coefficient of Imbalance is intended to be applicable to all types of communications..except those in which the communication is arbitrarily restricted to specified symbols. **1952** *N.Y. Times* 6 May 28/2 The trade imbalance and the drain of gold and hard currency reserves have lessened. **1953** *Manch. Guardian Weekly* 7 May 3/3 Which will prevent their own budgets from remaining in disastrous imbalance. **1954** *New Biol.* XVI. 80 While the maintenance of an adult organism is achieved by the exact balance of synthetic and degradative processes, growth is realized by a degree of imbalance in which synthetic processes predominate. **1957** *Economist* 7 Sept. 780/1 Increasing the existing imbalance between male and female employment. **1957** *English Studies* XXXVIII. 97 A remarkable corrective to this imbalance appeared in the writings of Henry Sweet. **1957** *Listener* 26 Dec. 1080/3 Shows clearly the imbalance created by an exodus of young persons (predominantly females) from the rural areas. **1961** *Lancet* 22 July 211/1 Imbalance in the mental diet results in greed. **1962** *Ibid.* 2 June 1167/2 Though the mammalian body has striking powers of recovery from the effects of long-maintained hormonal imbalance, there must be limits to the stresses which can safely be imposed. **1967** *Boston Sunday Globe* 21 May H 3/1 The imbalance problem [proportion of black and of white people] could be solved in such a setup... The 20 or so schools in a park would be able to share many facilities and personnel. **1969** *Times* 5 Aug. 9/5 The imbalance in the world's financial system has become grotesque. **1970** *New Society* 5 Feb. 222/1 Imbalances between homes and people emerge. **1973** *Sci. Amer.* Sept. 133/3 The marked increase in the average salary reflects both the imbalance of supply and demand for health workers and, more important, the highly desirable increased value placed on such workers.

imbalm, -ment, etc.: see EMBALM, etc.

†**imbalsa'mation.** *Obs. rare*[−1]. [f. IM-[1] + BALSAMATION.] Embalming; in quot. *fig.*

1803 W. TAYLOR in *Ann. Rev.* I. 355 [To] provide for his memory that clerical inbalsamation which perfumed and hallowed for ages the reliques of Constantine.

im'ban, *v.* *rare*[−1]. [ad. med.L. *imbannīre* to interdict: see IM-[1] and BAN *v.*] *trans.* To interdict, proscribe, excommunicate.

1808 J. BARLOW *Columb.* VIII. 223 Enslave my tribes! what, half mankind imban? **1828** WEBSTER, *Imban*, to excommunicate, in a civil sense; to cut off from the rights of man.

im'band, *v.* *rare*[−1]. [f. IM-[1] + BAND *sb.*[3]] *trans.* To form or enrol into a band.

a **1812** J. BARLOW (Webster, 1864), Beneath full sails imbanded nations rise.

imbank, -ment: see EMBANK, etc.

†**imban'kation.** *Obs. rare.* [n. of action from *imbank*, EMBANK.] Embankment.

1776 G. SEMPLE *Building in Water* 118 Till a substantial Imbankation may be erected. *Ibid.* 119 A substantial Road, or Imbankation.

imbannered, var. of EMBANNERED.

imbap'tize, *v.* *rare.* [f. IM-[1] + BAPTIZE *v.*] *trans.* To baptize by immersion; in quot. *fig.*

1855 BAILEY *Mystic* 34 He at their hest..his soul In the moon's argent streams did imbaptize, And purified his spirit in the sun.

imbar, etc., var. of EMBAR *v.*, etc.

†**im'barge**, *v.* *Obs.* Also inbardge. [f. IM-[1] + BARGE *sb.*[1]] *trans.* To embark.

1596 DRAYTON *Leg. Rob. of Norm.* (D.), As when the soueraigne we embarg'd doe see. **1604** CAWDREY *Table Alph.*, *Imbarge, Imbarke*, see *embarke*. **1627** DRAYTON *Agincourt*, etc. 78 Whither his friends she causd him to inbardge.

imbarge, imbargo, var. EMBARGE, EMBARGO.

imbark (ɪm'bɑːk), *v.* Also 7 em-. [f. IM-[1] + BARK *sb.*[1]] *trans.* To enclose in or clothe with bark. Also *fig.*

1647 H. MORE *Poems* 256 Embarked as in a tree..A fading life we lead. **1649** LOVELACE *Poems* 159 Imbark thee in the Lawrell tree. **1815** MRS. TRENCH *Rem.* 328, I..am not always imbarked and rooted in my geraniums and myrtles. *a* **1822** SHELLEY *Pr. Wks.* (1880) III. 69 It is leaning forward upon a knotty staff imbarked and circled by a viper.

imbark, -ation, etc.: see EMBARK, etc.

†**im'barn**, *v.* *Obs.* Also 8 em-. [f. IM-[1] + BARN *sb.*] *trans.* To gather into a barn or barns; to garner. Also *fig.*

1610 *Acta Capit. Christ Church, Canterbury* 17 July (MS.), To ymbarn in the Barnes..all or the more part of the tythe corne. **1610** *Chester's Tri., Rumor's Sp.* 28 To imbarne them in hell's restlesse rest. **1686** PLOT *Staffordsh.* 354 If they have not room to imbarn their Corn, they..set it up in ricks. **1796** *Ann. Agric., Thanet* XXVII. 521 (E.D.S.) They em-barn as much as they can of their corn.

imbarque, -barrass, -barren, -base: see EMBARK, etc.

imbases, obs. pl. of EMBASSY.

imbassador, -ator, -etor, -itor, etc., obs. ff. AMBASSADOR.

imbassage: see EMBASSAGE.

†**im'bastardize**, *v.* *Obs. rare*[−1]. [f. IM-[1] + BASTARDIZE. Cf. It. *imbastardire*, obs. F. *embastardir*; also *bastardize, abastardize.*] *trans.* To render bastard or degenerate.

1649 MILTON *Eikon.* Pref., Imbastardiz'd from the ancient Nobleness of thir Ancestors.

imbasure, var. EMBASURE.

imbathe, -battle, -bay: see EMBATHE, etc.

imbauba (ɪm'bɔːbə, ɪmbə'uːbə). [a. Pg. *imbaúba, umbaúba*, f. Tupi *ambauba, umbauba.*] A Brazilian tree of the genus *Cecropia*, esp. *C. peltata*, which has a hollow stem and yields a softwood timber; also called *trumpet-tree, trumpet-wood.* Cf. CECROPIA I.

1849 R. SPRUCE *Notes of Botanist on Amazon & Andes* (1908) I. i. 39 Many leaves are grey or hoary beneath, as in the Cecropias (or Imba-úbas, as they are called by the Indians). **1924** RECORD & MELL *Timbers Trop. Amer.* 145 There are various species of *Cecropia* in Brazil, at least twelve in the Amazon region, and they are generally known by the name of 'imbaúba' or 'embaúba'. **1927** R. R. GATES *Botanist in Amazon Valley* iv. 83 Another characteristic tree fringing the bank..in front of the main forest, is imbauba. **1931** B. MIALL tr. *Guenther's Naturalist in Brazil* xvii. 319 Another kind of Aztec ant inhabits the interior of the trunk of the Imbauba-tree.

imbeam (ɪm'biːm), *v.* *nonce-wd.* [f. IM-[1] + BEAM *sb.* Cf. EMBEAM.] *trans.* To cast as a beam.

1839 BAILEY *Festus* xxiv. (1848) 303 Oh! let not a planet-like eye Imbeam its tale on thine.

†**imbear**, *v.* *Obs.* [app. for *imbare* or *unbare.*] *trans.* To make or lay bare.

1657 W. MORICE *Coena quasi Κοινή* Def. xv. 206 To have their lips by the weight of jewels pendent in them drawn down over their chins to the imbearing of their teeth.

imbeasell, -beazell, -becile, obs. ff. EMBEZZLE.

imbecile ('ɪmbɪsɪl, -iːl, ɪmbɪ'siːl), *a.* (*sb.*) Forms: 6 -ill(e, 7–8 -il, 7– -ile. [a. F. *imbécille* (15–16th c. in Godef.), now *imbécile* (admitted by the Acad. 1835), ad. L. *imbēcill-us, -is*, weak, feeble in body or mind (a word of unknown composition).

From an erroneous impression that the L. word was *imbecilis* (so stated in Bailey's Folio, repeated by Johnson, and made the basis of argument by Walker), the spelling *imbecile*, found in 17th c., was established in 18th c. The pronunciation (ɪm'bɛsɪl), connected with the confusion of this word and EMBEZZLE (see IMBECILE *v.*) was usual down to the beginning of 19th c., and was preferred by Walker 1791, though (ɪmbɪ'siːl), after Fr. *imbécile*, is said to have been 'the more fashionable'.]

1. In general sense: Weak, feeble; esp. feeble of body, physically weak or impotent.

1549 *Compl. Scot.* vi. 37 The..laubirs that i tuke..gart al my body be cum imbecille ande verye. **1597** A. M. tr. *Guillemeau's Fr. Chirurg.* *vj, Their importunate assaultes on the imbecille walles of my answers. **1599** —— tr. *Gabelhouer's Bk. Physicke* 17/2 He may..drinck verye smalle, and imbecille wynes, and take heede of all manner of strong wynes what soever. **1659** D. PELL *Impr. Sea* To Rdr. d vij b, My prayer..that God would prosper this open and imbecil Peece to every one of their Souls. **1730** BAILEY, *Imbécile*, Weak, Feeble. **1797** GODWIN *Enquirer* II. xii. 428 An old man who..has..something imbecil in his motions. **1813** SHELLEY *Q. Mab* viii. 152 His stunted stature and imbecile frame. **1855** MACAULAY *Hist. Eng.* xiv. III. 424 The administration had..been constantly becoming more and more imbecile. **1856** EMERSON *Eng. Traits, Wealth* Wks. (Bohn) II. 74 The robust rural Saxon degenerates in the mills..to the imbecile Manchester spinner.

2. Mentally weak; of weak character or will through want of mental power; hence, Fatuous, stupid, idiotic. (The chief current use.)

[**1755** JOHNSON, *Imbécile*, weak; feeble; wanting strength of either mind or body. (No quot.) **1799–1805** WORDSW. *Prelude* IX. 585 His days he wasted,—an imbecile mind.] **1804** MATILDA BETHAM *Biog. Dict. Celebr. Wom., Pulcheria*, She alone had sustained the imperial dignity, under the reign of her weak and imbecile brother. **1846** DE QUINCEY *Glance Wks. Mackintosh* Wks. XIII. 63 But he had the misfortune to be 'imbecile'..in fact, he was partially an idiot. **1866** GEO. ELIOT *F. Holt* i. I. 42 The news came..that Durfey, the imbecile son, was dead.

b. Of actions: Marked by mental feebleness or fatuity; hence, Inane, stupid, absurd, idiotic.

1861 MRS. BROWNING *Mother & Poet* xv, 'Twere imbecile, hewing out roads to a wall. **1897** MARY KINGSLEY *W. Africa* 581 Bees..getting beneath the waterproof sheets over the bed, and pretending they can't get out and forthwith losing their tempers, which is imbecile, because the whole four sides of the affair are broad open.

c. *Comb.*, as ***imbecile-minded.***

1825 R. H. FROUDE *Rem.* (1838) I. 191 Imbecile-minded people.

†**3.** Made away with, squandered, or dissipated: cf. IMBECILE *v.* 2, EMBEZZLE. *Obs. rare.*

a **1677** BARROW *Serm. on Creed* xxii. Wks. 1686 II. 324 We in a manner were got out of God's possession: were, in respect to him become imbecil and lost: we were like sheep gone astray.

B. *sb.* One who is imbecile; a person of weak intellect.

1802 NUGENT *Let.* 19 Nov. in Dk. Buckhm. *Court Geo. III* (1855) III. 236 Le Clerc was an imbecile; but he is no more. **1838** LYTTON *Alice* 100 These haughty imbeciles shall fall into the trap they have dug for us. **1873** HAMERTON *Intell. Life* XI. iv. (1875) 419 We are not all of us exactly imbeciles in money matters.

Hence **imbecilely** *adv.*, in an imbecile manner; stupidly, idiotically.

1847 R. W. HAMILTON *Disq. Sabbath* v. (1848) 177 [The pulpit] may be imbecilely filled. **1870** *Daily News* 20 Sept., The Mobiles are peasants..when I speak to them they nudge each other, and grin imbecilely.

†**im'becile**, *v.* *Obs.* Also 6–7 -ill. [The history of this word can scarcely be disentangled from that of EMBEZZLE *v.* The latter (in 15–16th c. *embesil(l, imbesill*) was evidently thought to be derived from L. *imbēcill-us, -is*, or F. *imbécille*, weak; thence arose a series of spellings and senses connecting it with this supposed derivation, the ultimate result of both being *imbecil(l* in the sense to impair, weaken: see EMBEZZLE *v.*]

1. *trans.* To make imbecile, weak, or impotent; to impair, weaken, enfeeble, debilitate. See EMBEZZLE *v.* 2.

The modern instance is a nonce-use from the adj., having no historical relation to the 16–17th c. word.

1539–40 ABP. PARKER *Corr.* (Parker Soc.) 12, I would be loth now that any man should enter to imbecile the thing. **1546** LANGLEY *Pol. Verg. De Invent.* I. i. 1 b, These.. imbecilled their health, procured diseases. **1566** DRANT *Horace, Sat.* I. v, [They] so imbecill all theyr strengthe, that they are naught to me. **1574** NEWTON *Health Mag.* 26 To imbecile and hinder health. **1651** JER. TAYLOR *Holy Dying* iii. §7 It is a sad calamity, that the fear of death shall so imbecil man's courage and understanding. [**1851** W. ANDERSON *Exposure Popery* (1878) 239 What an imbecile you are—with your judgment imbeciled by some lust.]

2. (In senses of EMBEZZLE *v.*) To do away with the force of, annul, abrogate, make away with, take away dishonestly.

c **1546** in Brand *Hist. Newcastle* (1789) I. 258 The dede of the foundacion was lost or imbecilled away long syns. [**1548** GEST *Pr. Masse* in H. G. Dugdale *Life* (1840) App. i. 76 Thee pryvee masse..embecilleth and taketh out of our hartes Christ. *Ibid.* 131 To disanul and embecyl Christ his sonnes death.] **1563–87** FOXE *A. & M.* (1684) I. 301 By whom..the Authorities of old Grants, Statutes, Laws and Priviledges, and imbecilled and abrogate. **1580** HOLLYBAND *Treas. Fr. Tong, Appetisser*, to diminish, to lessen, to imbesill. **1637** GATAKER *Marriage Duties* Serm. 194 (L.) The provident and faithfull keeping and preserving of provisions..that they be not imbecilled or made away. **1650** JER. TAYLOR *Holy Living* iii. §2 Guardians of pupils and widows, not suffering their persons to be oppressed, or their states imbezill'd.

Hence †**imbeciled** *ppl. a.*; †**imbeciling** *vbl. sb.*

1549 ALLEN *Jude's Par. Rev.* xvi. 25 This is imbeselynge and diminyshe of their power and dominion. **1578** BANISTER *Hist. Man* I. 28 Vlna is the further downward, the more imbecilled, and weakened. **1599** A. M. tr. *Gabelhouer's Bk. Physicke* 117/2 It exsiccateth and also calefyeth the imbicilled stomacke.

imbecilic (ɪmbɪ'sɪlɪk), *a.* [f. IMBECILE *sb.* + -IC.] Characteristic of an imbecile; idiotic.

1918 D. FLATAU *Yellow English* xxxv, Looking round with an imbecilic grin. **1927** *Daily Express* 3 Dec. 4 Courteline.. collected..the most hideous and imbecilic portraits he could find. **1960** 'A. BURGESS' *Right to Answer* ii. 18 There was a kind of imbecilic helper in the public bar. **1968** *Punch* 7 Feb. 194/1 Extrovert delegates prance about singing, blowing horns and shouting imbecilic slogans.

Hence **imbe'cilically** *adv.*, in an imbecile manner.

1946 B. MARSHALL *George Brown's Schooldays* 28 Pretended not to pray or looked imbecilically heathen.

imbecilitate (ɪmbɪ'sɪlɪteɪt), *v.* [f. IMBECILITY, after *debilitate, facilitate*, etc.: see -ATE^3 7. In 17th c. *imbecill-*: see note to IMBECILE *a.*] *trans.* To render imbecile, weak, or feeble; to enfeeble.

1653 A. WILSON *Jas. I*, 58 The man being skilful in natural Magick, did use all the Artifice his subtilty could devise, really to imbecillitate the Earl. **1689** G. HARVEY *Curing Dis. by Expect.* iv. 18 A Man or Woman..being never so little imbecillitated in their Lungs. **1809** *Edin. Rev.* XV. 96 The same cause..imbecilitates..the superintendance of their official superiors. **1821** *Blackw. Mag.* VIII. 364 A great effect in imbecilitating the understanding.

imbecility (ɪmbɪ'sɪlɪtɪ). Forms: 6–7 **imbecillitie**, **-ilitie**, 6–8 **-illity**, 7– **-ility**; (6 **-yllyte**, **-ite**, **-illyte**, **-bicillitye**, 7 **-besilitie**). [a. F. *imbécillité* (14th c. in Littré), ad. L. *imbēcillitātem*, n. of quality f. *imbēcillus*, *-is*, IMBECILE. For the single *l*, see note to the adj.] The condition or quality of being imbecile.

1. Weakness, feebleness, debility, impotence.

a **1533** FRITH *Disput. Purgat.* Wks. 31 (R.) Sith we are not of power and habilitie to performe the law of God.. lamentyng our imbecillitie that we can do him no further pleasure. **1538** STARKEY *England* II. i. 176 The imbecyllyte of mannys nature. **1596** BARROUGH *Meth. Physick* (ed. 3) 458 It is a singular help against the imbecillity of the kidneis. **1624** WOTTON *Archit.* in *Reliq.* (1672) 32 Such [Arches].. for the natural imbecillity of the sharp Angle itself..ought to be exiled from judicious eyes. **1774** GOLDSM. *Nat. Hist.* I. 272 If anything can give us a picture of complete imbecility, it is a man when just come into the world. **1783** JOHNSON *Let. to Taylor* 22 Nov., Another evidence of its own imbecillity. **1822–34** *Good's Study Med.* (ed. 4) I. 139 The imbecility of the liver is..obvious in most cases [of dyspepsia]. **1838** SIR W. HAMILTON *Logic* xxx. (1866) II. 113 The imbecility of the human intellect in general. **1855** MACAULEY *Hist. Eng.* xv. III. 585 The misery of the Irish people and the imbecility of the Irish administration.

b. Incompetency or incapacity (*to do* something).

1767 BLACKSTONE *Comm.* II. 265 A tenant for life, for years, at will, or a copyholder, cannot prescribe, by reason of the imbecillity of their estates. **1812** J. J. HENRY *Camp. agst. Quebec* 146 Its imbecility to restrain us was apparent. **1822** LAMB *Elia* Ser. II. *Confess. Drunkard*, Languid enjoyment of evil with utter imbecility to good.

c. with *an* and *pl.* An instance of weakness, infirmity, or debility.

1541 R. COPLAND *Galyen's Terap.* 2 Ej, Dyspathies, Metasyncrises, Imbecyllitees, fyrmytudes and sondry other such names. **1619** T. MILLES tr. *Mexia's, etc. Treas. Anc. & Mod. T.* II. 380/2 Catarrhes, rheumes, and other imbecillities. **1727** SWIFT *Gulliver* IV. x, Such imbecillities of nature. **1862** H. SPENCER *First Princ.* I. v. §27 (1875) 98 Those imbecilities of the understanding.

2. Mental or intellectual weakness, esp. as characterizing action; hence, silliness, absurdity, folly; a specimen or example of this.

Medically and pathologically, *imbecility* is generally used to denote a defect of mental power of less degree than idiocy and not congenital.

1624 CAPT. SMITH *Virginia* VI. 222 Giue mee leaue to excuse my selfe of so much imbecillitie, as to say, that in these eighteene yeeres..I haue not learned, there is a great difference betwixt the directions and iudgements of experimentall knowledge, and the superficiall coniecture of variable relation. **1803** *Med. Jrnl.* IX. 339 Can a stronger proof of the fallacy and imbecility of the Brunonian System be required? **1862** FORBES WINSLOW in *Times* 2 Jan., I class the case..as a case of imbecility. In medical language it would be termed a case of *amentia* as distinguished from *dementia*. **1874** MAUDSLEY *Respons. in Ment. Dis.* iii. 66 Imbecility is..weakness of mind owing to defective mental development. **1888** J. INGLIS *Tent Life Tigerland* 4 The sneers and stupid imbecilities of the untravelled..sceptic.

imbed, imbellish: see EMBED *v.*, EMBELLISH.

imbed, *v.*, **imbedded**, *ppl. a.*, varr. EMBED *v.*, EMBEDDED *ppl. a.*

†**imbellic**, *a. Obs.* [f. IM-^{2} + L. *bellic-us* warlike, f. *bellum* war: cf. L. *imbellis*.] Unwarlike.

?**1620** FELTHAM *Resolves* I. [II.] v. 18 The Imbellicke peasant, when hee comes first to the field, shakes at the report of a Musket. **1623** COCKERAM, *Imbellicke*, cowardly, not for warre.

†**imbellious**, *a. Obs.* [f. L. *imbelli-s* unwarlike (f. *im-* (IM-^{2}) + *bellum* war) + -OUS, after *rebellious*.] Unwarlike, cowardly.

1602 WARNER *Alb. Eng.* Epit. (1612) 357 The voluntarie subiection of this their imbellious Countrie. **1627** H. BURTON *Baiting Pope's Bull* 5 [They] cannot possesse generous Princes with an imbellious feare of such *bruta fulmina*. **1628** —— *Israel's Fast* 2 Ignoble and imbellious Spirits.

†**imbe'nignity**. *Obs. rare.* [f. IM-^{2} + BENIGNITY.] Unkindness.

1675 R. BURTHOGGE *Causa Dei* 84 By reason of their Imbenignity, Inexorableness, and Inclemency.

imber, obs. and var. f. EMBER; obs. f. IMBAR *v.*

imberb (ɪm'bɜːb), *a. rare.* [ad. F. *imberbe*, f. L. *imberbis* (see IMBERBIC *a.*).] Beardless.

1923 A. HUXLEY *Antic Hay* iii. 42 A face of such childish contour and so imberb that he looked like a little boy playing at grown-ups.

†**im'berbic**, *a. Obs. rare*$^{-0}$. [f. L. *imberbis* (f. *im-* (IM-^{2}) + *barba* beard) + -IC.] Beardless.

1623 COCKERAM, *Imberbicke*, without a beard.

imbesel(l, **-il(l**, **-bezel(l**, **-il(l**, etc., obs. ff. EMBEZZLE.

imbetter, var. of EMBETTER *v.*

imbi'bation, erron. f. IMBIBITION.

1826 *Blackw. Mag.* XIX. 659 Preferable for forenoon imbibation. **1883** H. DRUMMOND *Nat. Law in Spir. W.* 325 It lived, henceforth, by simple imbibation, upon the elaborated juices of its host.

†**im'bibbed**, *a. Obs. rare.* Wearing a bib.

1611 COTGR., *Embaveté*, imbibbed; that, as a child, hath a bib, or mocket put before his breast, to keepe him from drivelling thereon.

imbibe (ɪm'baɪb), *v.* Also 4 **enbibe**, 5 **embybe**, 6 **enbybe**, **embibe**. [Partly a. F. *imbiber* to soak or penetrate with moisture, *refl.* to be soaked or penetrated with moisture, to soak *into*, later (esp. in pa. pple.) to imbue, in 18th c. to drink in, imbibe; partly ad. L. *imbibĕre* in cl. L., to conceive or imbibe (opinions, etc.), later in lit. sense, to drink in, inhale, f. *im-* (IM-^{1}) + *bibĕre* to drink.

The F. *imbiber* was app. formed from L. as an active verb to correspond to the pa. pple. *imbu* (prob. ad. L. *imbūtus*), and as such took to itself the meanings of L. *imbuĕre*, which the Eng. verb adopted together with those of L. *imbibĕre*. The early forms in Eng. suggest a French origin, though *imbiber* is not recorded before 16th c.]

I. †**1.** *trans.* To cause to absorb moisture or liquid; to soak, imbue, or saturate with moisture; to steep. *Obs.*

c **1386** CHAUCER *Can. Yeom. Prol. & T.* 261 And oure matires enbibyng [*Corpus* enbykynge, *Petw.* enbykinge] And eek of oure matires encorporyng And of oure siluer citrinacion. **1489** CAXTON *Faytes of A.* II. iv. 96 Towe of flaxe that wel embybed were with oyle. *a* **1529** SKELTON *Agst. the Scottes* 79 Unto your Grace for grace now I call To gyde my pen, and my pen to enbybe. **1558** WARDE tr. *Alexis' Secr.* I. I. (1580) 2 b, When it is almoste waxen drie, embibe or water it again. **1686** W. HARRIS tr. *Lemery's Chym.* (ed. 3) 31 That portion of the water wherewith the earth was imbibed. **1799** G. SMITH *Laboratory* I. 426 Imbibe that powder with strong white vinegar. **1804** *Captive of Valence* I. 144 Could a minister..have the wickedness to imbibe with slow poison that bread which, at his voice, was to become the body of his Divine master?

†**b.** *fig.* To IMBUE. Cf. F. *imbiber* (see etymol.).

1622 MALYNES *Anc. Law-Merch.* 163 This question is friuolous..and breedeth but contention to imbibe Merchants braines with them. **1707** *Curios. in Husb. & Gard.* 263 In regard to Fruits..we may imbibe them..with a Medicinal, Purgative Power.

†**c.** With inverted construction: To instil *into*.

1746 W. HORSLEY *Fool* xxvii. ¶4 Until such villainous Principles are thoroughly imbibed into us by the Enemies of our Peace. **1812** J. J. HENRY *Camp. agst. Quebec* 6 He wished to imbibe into the minds of his children a taste for mechanics.

II. 2. *trans.* To 'drink in', absorb, or assimilate (knowledge, ideas, etc.); to take into one's mind or moral system.

1555 EDEN *Decades* To Rdr. (Arb.) 57 They may also herewith imbibe trewe religion. **1652** EVELYN *State France* (R.), After the facile and more smooth languages are once thoroughly imbibed. **1690** LOCKE *Hum. Und.* II. xiii. (1695) 90 Those confused Notions are Prejudices it [the Mind] has imbibed from Custom, Inadvertency, and Common Conversation. **1746** HERVEY *Medit.* (1818) 65 Imbibe the precious truths. **1858** HOLLAND *Titcomb's Lett.* vi. 139 Young women are apt to imbibe another bad habit, namely, the use of slang. **1874** GREEN *Short Hist.* viii. §5. 507 Charles ..had imbibed his father's hatred of the Presbyterian system.

3. Of a person or animal: To drink in, drink (liquid); to inhale (the air, tobacco smoke).

1621 VENNER *Tobacco* in *Baths of Bathe* (1650) 402 They that..for every light occasion imbibe or take down this fume. *a* **1791** BLACKLOCK *Ps.* i. (R.), The wild horse.. Imbibes the silver surge, with heat opprest, To cool the fever of his glowing breast. **1828** SCOTT *F.M. Perth* xvi, Oliver..raised it to his head with a trembling hand, imbibed the contents with lips which quivered with emotion. **1859** LANG *Wand. India* 397 The mess-room, where more cheroots were smoked, and more weak brandy-and-water imbibed. **1874** HELPS *Soc. Press.* ii. 16 The population imbibe fresh air.

4. Of a thing: To suck up, drink in, absorb (moisture). Also *absol.*

1641 FRENCH *Distill.* i. (1651) 33 Let this Salt imbibe as much of the Oil..as it can. **1667** BOYLE *Orig. Formes & Qual.* (ed. 2) 339 A Plant that grows by some petrifying Spring by Imbibing that water is at length turn'd into a Stone. **1781** COWPER *Friendship* 184 So barren sands imbibe the shower. **1813** SIR H. DAVY *Agric. Chem.* (1814) 239 The roots imbibe fluids from the soil by capillary attraction. **1860** TYNDALL *Glac.* II. xxxi. 412 Water..will be partly imbibed by the adjacent porous ice.

5. To take up, absorb, or assimilate (a gas, rays of heat or light, etc.); to take (solid substances) into solution or suspension.

1626 BACON *Sylva* §290 The Aire doth willingly imbibe the Sound as gratefull, but cannot maintaine it. **1631** JORDEN *Nat. Bathes* ii. 8 Earth may be confused with water, but not imbibed, and will sink to the bottom again. **1725** POPE *Odyss.* VI. 111 While the robes imbibe the solar ray. **1744** BERKELEY *Siris* §122 Such salts are readily imbibed by water. **1807** T. THOMSON *Chem.* (ed. 3) II. 434 When volatile oils are exposed to the open air..they imbibe oxygen with rapidity. **1823** J. BADCOCK *Dom. Amusem.* 142 Having incorporated the mixture well, add of Frankfort black as much as it will imbibe. **1834** MRS. SOMERVILLE *Connex. Phys. Sc.* xv. (1849) 132 The heat of the sun's rays which the earth imbibes.

†**6.** *transf.* and *fig.* To absorb, swallow up. *Obs.*

1664 H. MORE *Myst. Iniq.* 261 So as it may appear that the one does wholly imbibe the other. **1678** CUDWORTH *Intell. Syst.* I. v. 771 No One Magnitude, can be Imbibed or Swallowed up into another. **1712** SWIFT *Poems, Midas* 77 The torrent merciless imbibes Commissions, perquisites, and bribes.

Hence **im'bibed** *ppl. a.*, †absorbed; **im'bibing** *vbl. sb.*, †steeping, saturation. †**im'bibement** *Obs. rare*, imbibing, imbibition. **im'biber**, one who or that which imbibes or drinks; †an absorber.

1584 R. SCOT *Discov. Witchcr.* XIV. i. (1886) 294 Termes of art; as (for a tast) their subliming, amalgaming, engluting, imbibing, incorporating. **1592** LYLY *Galathea* II. iii, Our [alchemists'] instruments..decensores, Violes, manuall and murall, for enbibing and conbibing. **1669** WORLIDGE *Syst. Agric.* (1681) 60 The imbibing or steeping of Corn, or any other Seeds in rich Wines. **1684** BOYLE *Porousn. Anim. & Solid Bod.* vi. 96 Evaporation of the imbibed Particles of water. **1696** PHILLIPS (ed. 5) s.v., The Imbibement of Principles, the sucking or drinking in of Principles in our Infancy. *a* **1735** ARBUTHNOT (J.), Salts are strong imbibers of sulphureous streams. **1870** *Even. Standard* 17 Sept., The imbiber of absinthe.

imbibition (ɪmbɪ'bɪʃən). [a. F. *imbibition* (14th c. in Godef. *Compl.*), ad. L. **imbibitiōn-em*, n. of action f. *imbibĕre* to IMBIBE.] The action of imbibing (in the various senses of the vb.).

†**1.** Soaking or saturation with liquid, steeping or solution in liquid; combination of solid and liquid by this process; an instance of this; *concr.* a solution. ***to lie in imbibition***, to lie a-soak or a-steep. *Obs.*

1471 RIPLEY *Comp. Alch.* VI. xxviii. in Ashm. (1652) 168 Mo Imbybycyons many must we have yett. **1594** PLAT *Jewell-ho.* I. 36 Water wherein good store of Cow dung hath lyen in imbibition. **1626** BACON *Sylva* §298 The Congruity of Bodies..if it be more, maketh a perfecter Imbibition, and Incorporation. **1662** J. DAVIES tr. *Olearius' Voy. Ambass.* 64 They steep the seed..in..an imbibition of fair water and Sheep's dung. **1678** R. R[USSELL] *Geber* III. II. II. vi. 185 Mixed with them by frequent Imbibitions, etc. continually grinding, imbibing, calcining and reducing.

2. Drinking in, sucking in, absorption; assimilation by absorption: usually of moisture or matter in solution, but sometimes of aeriform bodies or of solid particles by a liquid.

1601 HOLLAND *Pliny* II. 139 After this imbibition, when that the Frumenty hath thus drunk vp all the water. **1672** BOYLE in *Phil. Trans.* VII. 5159 A kind of Imbibition..of certain Particles of an Aereal Nature by the Water. **1770** WATSON *Ibid.* LX. 329 An imbibition of the particles of the several salts into the pores of the water. **1826** KIRBY & SP. *Entomol.* IV. 89 That their nutrition is by imbibition or immediate absorption. **1875** BENNETT & DYER *Sachs' Bot.* 710 Imbibition is the term given..to the capacity of organised structures to absorb water between their molecules with such force that they are thus driven apart. *Ibid.* 711 When wood distends on imbibition or contracts on desiccation.

b. Drinking. (Affected use.)

1844 J. T. HEWLETT *Parsons & W.* xxxix, The imbibition of a little..strong beer. **1896** ALLBUTT *Syst. Med.* I. 485 The free imbibition of port.

3. The imbibing, 'drinking in', or absorption of knowledge, opinions, etc.

1603 HOLLAND *Plutarch's Mor.* 50 The imbibition of good nourture in childhood. **1859** HOLLAND *Gold F.* xxv. 296 Every imbibition of truth. **1883** H. DRUMMOND *Nat. Law in Spir. W.* 352 If all one's truth is derived by imbibition from the Church.

imbibitional (ɪmbɪ'bɪʃənəl), *a.* [f. IMBIBITION + -AL.] Of, pertaining to, or resulting from imbibition.

1916 *Science* 6 Oct. 502/2 (*heading*) Imbibitional swelling of plants and colloidal mixtures. **1924** *Jrnl. Agric. Sci.* XIV. 204 (*heading*) Remarks and observations on imbibitional soil moisture. **1931** E. C. MILLER *Plant Physiol.* iv. 166 Very strong imbibitional forces may be developed within the plant even when the cell walls and protoplasm contain considerable water. **1959** *Chambers's Encycl.* VI. 331/2 In the early stages of water absorption by the barley grain,.. the imbibitional pressure may reach 900 atm.

imbind, imbitter, imblaze: see EMBIND, etc.

imblemish, var. of EMBLEMISH *Obs.* Hence †**im'blemishment**, defacement, injury.

1529 *Art. against Wolsey* i. in Ld. Herbert *Hen. VIII* (1649) 266 To the great imblemishment and hurt of your said Royall Jurisdiction.

imblossom, obs. var. of EMBLOSSOM.

†**imboard**, *v. Obs. rare*$^{-0}$. [IM-^{1}.] *trans.* = IMPLANK, q.v.

imboase, -boce, imbocer, etc., obs. forms of EMBOSS, etc.
1552 HULOET, Imbocer or chaser of plate.

imboasted: see IMBOSTED.

imbody, imbog, imboil, imbolden: see EMBODY, etc.

†**im'bolish**, *v. Obs.* [app. a perversion of ABOLISH by confusion of *a-* prefix with *em-*, *im-*.] *trans.* To do away with; to make away with.
1592 GREENE *Disput.* 7 Yeelding to the Mace, to imbollish Paules libertie. —— *Theeves falling out* (1615) C ij, The harme you do, is to imbollish mens goods, and bring them to pouerty.

imbolster, imbolt: see EMBOLSTER, INBOLT.

imbonga, imbongo, varr. MBONGO.

†**im'bonity.** *Obs. rare*⁻¹. [ad. late L. *imbonitās* (Tertullian), f. *im-* (IM-²) + *bonitās* goodness.] The reverse of goodness; unkindness.
The quot. is an echo of Tertullian's 'omnis duritia et imbonitas et insuavitas' (*Orat. ad Martyr.* 3 ad init.).
1621 BURTON *Anat. Mel.* I. iv. I. (1624) 186 All feares, griefes, suspitions, discontents, imbonities, insuavities.

†**im'book**, *v. Sc. Obs.* Also imbuik, -buke. [f. IM-¹ + BOOK *sb.*] *trans.* To enter in a book; to book, enrol, register.
1587 *MS. R. Long* (Brit. Mus.), To regester, imbooke, or incronicle all such worthye persons..as by there valyant actes have deserved perpetuall remembraunce. **1618** in Row *Hist. Kirk* (1842) 319 Selected..wise brethren, should, with the clerk, forme the acts, see them imbooked. **1620** W. SCOT *Apol. Narr.* (1846) 76 He said he wold not suffer them to be imbooked.

imborder, var. of EMBORDER.

†**im'bordure**, *v. Obs.* Also 5–6 en-, 6 em-. [f. IM-¹ + BORDURE.] *trans.* To encompass with a border; *spec. Her.* to furnish with a bordure of the same tincture (distinguished from BORDURING, used when the bordure was of a different tincture from the field). Always in pa. pple. or vbl. sb.
1486 *Bk. St. Albans, Her.* B iij a, Ther be vi. Differences in armys..Labell and Enbordunyng for lordis. **1562** LEIGH *Armorie* (1597) 110 b, This sometime is termed emborduring, because it is of the same that the field is off. **1572** BOSSEWELL *Armorie* II. 36 b, Of Armes enbordured, or with borders. **1610** GUILLIM *Heraldry* I. v. (1611) 17 You shall say that he beareth such metale colour or furre imbordured. **1658** PHILLIPS, *Imborduring*, a term in Heraldry, when the field and circumference of the field are both of one mettal, colour, or fur. **1730–6** in BAILEY (folio). **1775** in ASH.

imborsation (ɪmbɔːˈseɪʃən). *rare.* [ad. It. *imborsazione*, n. of action f. *imborsare*, f. *im-* (IM-¹) + *borsa* purse. Cf. IMBURSE *v.*] An Italian mode of election to magistracies, in accordance with which the names of the candidates were put into a bag or purse to be drawn by lot.
1787 J. ADAMS *Wks.* (1851) V. 180 The imborsations are made, and eight hundred names are put in the purses.

‖**imboscata** (imboˈskata). *Obs.* also em-. [It.] = AMBUSH, q.v.
1595 SAVIOLO *Practice* I. i, To drawe the enemy either into some imboscata or place of aduantage. **1820** SCOTT *Monast.* xxi, To set upon me here as in an *emboscata*.

imbose, obs. form of EMBOSS.

†**imbosk**, *v. Obs.* Also 6 -bosque. [ad. It. *imboscare* 'to enter or goe into a wood, to take couert or shelter as a Deere doeth... Also to lay in ambush' (Florio), f. *im-* (IM-¹) + *bosco* wood. Cf. EMBOSS *v.*²] *refl.* To hide or conceal oneself.
1562 J. SHUTE *Cambine's Turk. Wars* ii. 11 Scanderbeg went as secretly as possyble, to imbosque him selfe neare to that place. **1612–20** SHELTON *Quix.* III. viii. (1675) 46 Sancho..requesting him to depart..and imbosk himself in the mountain. **1657** S. W. *Schism Dispach't* 221 He cares not ..what contradictions he maintains, so he can but imbosk himself handsomely in them.
b. *intr.* for *refl.*
1641 MILTON *Reform.* I. Wks. (1847) 10/1 They seek the dark, the bushy, the tangled forest, they would imbosk.

imbosom, imboss(e: see EMBOSOM, EMBOSS.

imbost, obs. var. of EMBOSSED *ppl. a.*², foaming at the mouth from exhaustion.

†**im'bost**, *sb. Obs.* [cf. prec. and next.] Foam (from the mouth of a beast).
1677 N. COX *Gentl. Recreat.* I. 78 Yet will that [Stream] with the help of the Wind, lodge part of the Steam and Imbost [*printed* Imbosh], that comes from him, on the Banks. **1727** R. BRADLEY *Fam. Dict.* s.v. *Hart*, The Steam and Imbost.

†**im'bost**, *v. Obs. rare.* [f. *imbost*, pa. pple. of *imboss*, EMBOSS *v.*² (sense 3).
App. the pa. pple. or pa. t. was taken as the vb. stem; whence a new pa. pple. *imbosted*: cf. *graff, graft, grafted*.]

1. *trans.* To drive (a hunted beast) to extremity; to cause to foam at the mouth: = EMBOSS *v.*² 2.
1590 COKAINE *Treat. Hunting* D j, He will close vp his mouth as though he had not been imbosted or hunted that day.
2. *intr.* To foam, as a result of hard running: = EMBOSS *v.*² 3.
1590 COKAINE *Treat. Hunting* C iv, Who so hunteth unbreathed hounds..in hot weather, causeth them to imbost and surbate greatly.
Hence †**im'bosted, -boasted** *ppl. a.*, foaming at the mouth (like a madman).
1628 FELTHAM *Resolves* II. lxxxvi. 249 Sure, they borrow it..from the imboasted [*ed.* 1709 raging] Savage, and from tormenting spirits.

imbosture, imbound, imbow, imbowel, imbower, imbox, imbrace, etc.: see EMB-.

imbraid, var. of EMBRAID *v.*¹ *Obs.*, to upbraid.

imbraist, obs. f. *embraced*: see EMBRACE.

imbrake, var. EMBRAKE *v. Obs.*, to entangle.

†**im'branch**, *v. Obs.* Also en-, in-. [f. IM-¹ + BRANCH *sb.*] To graft on the stock: see quot.
1577 B. GOOGE *Heresbach's Husb.* (1586) 72 Three kindes of Grafting, betwixte the barke and the woode, in the stocke, and emplastring or inoculation. The first sort they call grafting, the seconde imbranching, the thirde inoculation or imbudding. **1598** FLORIO, *Incalmare*, to engraffe, to imbranch [**1611** inbranch]. *Incalmatura*, an enbranching.

†**im'brand**, *v. Obs. rare.* [f. IM-¹ + BRAND *sb.*] *trans.* To arm with brands or swords.
1610 G. FLETCHER *Christ's Vict.* I. xl, The heav'nly hierarchies, Burning in zeal, thickly imbranded were.

imbrangle, imbrase: see EMB-.

imbrasier, obs. var. *imbraserie*, EMBRACERY.
1589 *Sir T. Smith's Commw. Eng.* II. xiii. 72 The Matters in this Court are..Conspiracies, Champarties, Imbrasier [*so in edd.* 1594, 1609, 1633].

†**im'brate**, *v. Obs. rare.* [ad. It. *imbrattare* (Florio, 1598).] *trans.* To defile, sully, pollute.
1542 *St. Papers, Hen. VIII*, IX. 155 The thinges of this State semith to be fowle imbratid by corruptid factions.

imbrauthery, imbrayder, obs. forms of EMBROIDERY, EMBROIDER.

imbreast (ɪmˈbrɛst), *v. rare*⁻¹. [f. IM-¹ (= EM-) + BREAST *sb.*] *trans.* To hold in one's breast or bosom; to EMBOSOM.
1867 BAILEY *Univ. Hymn* 12 Who in Himself imbreasts both thee and heaven.

imbreathe (ɪmˈbriːð), *v.* Also 6 imbrethe, 7 imbreath. [f. IM-¹ + BREATHE *v.*; partly a variant of EMBREATHE, partly of INBREATHE.]
1. *trans.* To breathe in, inhale. Also *fig.*
1574 J. JONES *Nat. Beginning Grow. Things* 14 The hart cooled by the dayly imbrething of yᵉ aire. **1871** FARRAR *Witn. Hist.* iv. 131 The curse of a Paganism..must have been imbreathed with the first lessons of consciousness even by innocent childhood.
2. a. To inspire, instil. **b.** To inspire *with*.
1601 BP. W. BARLOW *Eagle & Body* (1609) F ij a, The Soules..returning vnto God, who first imbreathed them. **1641** H. AINSWORTH *Orth. Found. Relig.* 19 His soule was imbreathed of God. **1647** TRAPP *Comm. Rev.* xxii. 6 Those holy men spake no otherwise then as they were acted or imbreathed by the holy Ghost. **1657** —— *Comm. Ps.* xl. 3, I cannot breath out a desire after him, except he first imbreath me therewith. **1811** W. TAYLOR in *Monthly Mag.* XXXI. 345 A sceptical philosophy..pervades the treatise, which imbreathes contentment and philanthropy. **1825** COLERIDGE *Aids Refl.* 4 God transfused into man a higher gift and imbreathed a self-subsisting soul.
Hence **im'breathed** *ppl. a.*, inhaled, imbibed; **im'breathing** *vbl. sb.*, inhaling, inspiration.
1574 [see 1]. **1691** E. TAYLOR *Behmen's Theos. Philos.* 237 The Imbreathing whence Man became a Living Soul. **1841** CLOUGH *Early P.* x. 8 Imbreathed draughts of wine.

imbrech, var. EMBREACH.

imbred, imbreed, var. INBRED, INBREED.

†**imbreke.** *Obs.* A plant: house-leek.
1597 GERARDE *Herbal* App., Imbreke is Housleeke.

†**im'breve**, *v. Sc. Obs.* Also imbrew. [ad. med.L. *imbreviāre* 'in Breves redigere, describere' (Du Cange): see BRIEF *sb.* Cf. OF. *embrever*, EMBREVE.] *trans.* To put into the form of a brief.
1583 *Leg. Bp. St. Androis* 1104, I sall leave blankis for to imbreue thame [*printed* imbrew; *rime* believe thame]. **16..** *Balfour's Practicks* (1754) 53 Sic complaintis as pertenis to the King and his crown..sould be imbrevit and keipit untill the cuming of the Justice in the burrow court.

imbreviate (ɪmˈbriːvɪeɪt), *v.* Also 7 (*Sc.*) imbreviat. [f. med.L. *imbreviāt-*, ppl. stem of *imbreviāre* (see prec.).] *trans.* To put into the form of a brief; to enrol, register.
1609 SKENE *Reg. Maj.* 58 The Schiref sall cause imbreviat, and put in writ the names of the twelue assisours. **1636** PRYNNE *Remonstr. agst. Shipmoney* 27 The King..caused all the ships..to be imbreviated by this Writ. **1865** NICHOLS *Britton* I. 14 Let the coroner cause their names and the names of the pledges to be imbreviated [tr. AF. *enbrever*].

imbrew, obs. f. IMBREVE, IMBRUE.

‖**imbrex** (ˈɪmbrɛks). Pl. imbrices (ˈɪbrɪsiːz). [L. *imbrex*, f. *imber* a rain-shower.]
1. *Archæol.* A curved roof-tile (see quot. 1857).
1857 BIRCH *Anc. Pottery* (1858) I. 165 The joints of the flat roof tiles were covered by the imbrex, or rain-tile, which was made semi-cylindrical, the sides generally upright with an arched top. *Ibid.* II. 229. **1888** *Jrnl. Anthrop. Inst.* Feb. 193 The absence of 'imbrices', which are a necessary adjunct in the formation of a Roman tiled roof.
2. One of the scales or overlapping pieces of an imbrication.
1890 in *Cent. Dict.*

imbricate (ˈɪmbrɪkət), *a.* (*sb.*) [ad. L. *imbricāt-us*, pa. pple. of *imbricāre* to form like a gutter-tile, to cover with rain-tiles, f. *imbrex, imbric-em.*]
†**1.** Formed like a gutter-tile or pantile. *Obs.*
1656 BLOUNT *Glossogr.*, *Imbricate*, square and bent like a roof or gutter-Tile, which the Latines call *Imbrex*; also covered with such a Tile. **1661** LOVELL *Hist. Anim. & Min.* Introd., The nailes are in all that have toes; but the ape's are imbricate [= Pliny, *H.N.* XI. xlv. 101 *ungues imbricati*].
2. Covered with or composed of scales or scalelike parts overlapping like roof-tiles; e.g. said of the scaly covering of reptiles and fishes, of leaf-buds, the involucre of *Compositæ*, etc.
1656 [see 1]. **1760** J. LEE *Introd. Bot.* (1788) 25. **1794** MARTYN *Rousseau's Bot.* vi. 68 One of the most common forms also of the calyx in this class [*Compound Flowers*], is the *imbricate* or that which is made up of several rows of folioles, lying over each other like tiles on a roof. **1826** KIRBY & SP. *Entomol.* IV. 320 [Antennae] *Imbricate*, when the summit of each joint is incumbent upon the base of that which precedes it. **1830** LINDLEY *Nat. Syst. Bot.* Introd. 24 In Penæaceæ both valvate and imbricate æstivation exists.
b. Of leaves, scales, etc.: Overlapping like tiles.
1796 P. RUSSELL *Acc. Ind. Serpents* 7 (T.) Two rows..of larger scales, ovate and imbricate. **1852** DANA *Crust.* I. 483 Branchiæ..composed each of imbricate plates in two series.
3. = IMBRICATED 4.
1890 *Cent. Dict.* s.v., An imbricate pattern.
B. as *sb.* A reptile, fish, or other animal covered with imbricated scales.
1862 DANA *Man. Geol.* vii. 277 The Devonian ganoids are of three kinds..Imbricates having the scales arranged like shingles.

imbricate (ˈɪmbrɪkeɪt), *v.* [f. L. *imbricāt-*, ppl. stem of *imbricāre*: see prec.]
1. *trans.* To place so as to overlap like roof-tiles. Also with *together* (in *fig.* sense).
1784 tr. *Beckford's Vathek* (1786) Notes 315 Trains of peacocks..whose quills were set in a long stem, so as to imbricate the plumes in the gradations of their natural growths. **1874** COUES *Birds N.W.* 435 Each feather is thus folded or imbricated over the next succeeding.
2. *trans.* and *absol.* To overlap like tiles.
1820 HOGG *Treat.* in *Beck's Florist* (1850) 272 The petals [of a carnation] should be regularly disposed alike on every side, imbricating each other. **1854** WOODWARD *Mollusca* II. 213 Flattened prisms..arranged..obliquely to the surfaces of the shell, the interior of which is imbricated by their outcrop. **1873** SIR C. W. THOMSON *Depths of Sea* iv. 164 In all essential family characters they agree. The plates imbricate in the same directions and on the same plan.

imbricated (ˈɪmbrɪkeɪtɪd), *ppl. a.* [f. prec.]
†**1.** (See quot.) *Obs.*
1704 J. HARRIS *Lex. Techn.*, *Imbricated* is used by Mr. Tournefort, and some other Botanists, to express the Figure of the Leaves of some Plants, which are hollowed in, like an Imbrex, or Gutter-Tile. **1727–41** CHAMBERS *Cycl.*
2. Composed of parts (leaves, scales, or the like) which overlap like tiles. Also, covered by overlapping leaves, scales, etc.
1753 CHAMBERS *Cycl. Supp.*, *Imbricated shell*,..any species of shell-fish, whose shells are elevated into transverse ridges, lying over one another at the base, in the manner of the tiles on a house-top. **1759** B. STILLINGFL. *Econ. Nat.* in *Misc. Tracts* (1762) 79 On this earth the imbricated liverworts find a bed to strike their roots in. **1858** GEIKIE *Hist. Boulder* iv. 46 Imbricated like the cone of the Scotch fir. **1882** *Garden* 1 Apr. 212/3 Another beautiful variety, having large and finely imbricated flowers.
3. Of leaves, scales, etc.: Arranged so as to overlap each other, after the manner of roof-tiles.
1753 CHAMBERS *Cycl. Supp.* s.v. *Leaf*, *Imbricated leaf*,.. leaves placed over one another in the manner of the tiles of a house, or like the scales of fishes. **1777** PENNANT *Zool.* IV. 101 (Jod.) Pecten with about thirty echinated imbricated rays. **1806** GALPINE *Brit. Bot.* 20 Glumes, imbricated on every side. **1861** HULME tr. *Moquin-Tandon* II. III. i. 70 The Common Wood-louse... The body is oval..composed of a number of imbricated rings.
4. Resembling in pattern a surface of overlapping tiles: = IMBRICATE *a.* 3.
1875 FORTNUM *Majolica* iii. 32 Sometimes ornamented.. with chequered, 'chevroné' or imbricated patterns.

imbricately (ˈɪmbrɪkətlɪ), *adv.* [f. IMBRICATE *a.* + -LY².] In an imbricated manner or order.
1846 DANA *Zooph.* (1848) 592 The pinnules, when unexpanded, imbricately crowded.

imbricating ('ɪmbrɪkeɪtɪŋ), *ppl. a.* [f. IMBRICATE *v.* + -ING².] Overlapping like tiles.

1830 LINDLEY *Nat. Syst. Bot.* 229 Flowers not.. surrounded by imbricating bracteæ. **1851-6** WOODWARD *Mollusca* 156 *Chiton Squamosus*..shell composed of 8 transverse imbricating plates.

imbrication (ɪmbrɪ'keɪʃən). [n. of action: see IMBRICATE *v.* and *adj.*]

†**1.** ? The dropping of water from roof-tiles. *Obs.*

1650 BULWER *Anthropomet.* 68 Robbing the Eyes of their natural Pent-house or Water-table, they expose them bare to imbrications.

†**2.** (See quots.) *Obs.*

1656 BLOUNT *Glossogr.*, *Imbrication*, a covering with Tile. **1658** PHILLIPS, *Imbrication*, a..bending like a gutter-tile, also a covering with tile.

3. An overlapping as of tiles; a decorative pattern imitative of this.

1713 DERHAM *Phys.-Theol.* VIII. iv. (1752) 370 A well-made tegument, beset with bristles, adorned with neat imbrications. **1831** R. KNOX *Cloquet's Anat.* 247 Their edges also overlap each other, presenting the appearance of imbrication, to use the language of botanists. **1854** WOODWARD *Mollusca* II. 327 Shell..armed in front with rasp-like imbrications. **1870** ROLLESTON *Anim. Life* 43 The imbrication of the spinous first dorsal fin.

imbricative ('ɪmbrɪˌkeɪtɪv), *a.* [f. IMBRICATE *v.*: see -ATIVE. Cf. F. *imbricatif, -ive.*] = IMBRICATE *a.* 2 a.

1855 MAYNE *Expos. Lex.* s.v. *Imbricativus*, Most botanists call estivation *imbricative*, that which Candolle terms *irregular*. **1880** GRAY *Struct. Bot.* IV. ii. 135 Imbricate or Imbricative is the general name for æstivation (or vernation) with overlapping.

imbri'cato-. Combining form from L. *imbricāt-us*, = imbricately-, imbricated and ——; as ***imbricato-granulous***, having imbricated granulations.

1852 DANA *Crust.* I. 212 Areolets partly granulous and imbricato-granulous.

†**'imbrid,** *a. Obs.*⁻⁰ [ad. L. *imbrid-us*, f. *imber* rain.] 'Wet, rainy' (Cockeram, 1623).

†**im'brier,** *v. Obs.* [f. IM-¹ + BRIER *sb.*] *trans.* To entangle as among briers.

1605 CHAPMAN *All Fooles* iv. Dram. Wks. 1873 I. 171 Ye shall see, if..I leave not both these gullers wits imbrier'd. **1622** MABBE tr. *Aleman's Guzman d' Alf.* I. 113 Amidst how many Brambles and Bushes..must he im-bryer..himselfe withall. **1690** J. PALMER in *Andros Tracts* I. 30 That they were imbryar'd in an Indian-war.

im'briferous, *a. rare.* [f. L. *imbrifer* (f. *imber* a shower): see -FEROUS.] Rain-bringing, showery.

1813 T. FORSTER *Atmosph. Phænom.* (1815) 80 The imbriferous quality of the atmosphere.

imbrighten, obs. var. of EMBRIGHTEN.

imbring, obs. var. of *embering*, EMBER².

imbring, var. of INBRING *v. Obs.*

†**im'bristled,** *a. Obs. rare.* [f. IM-¹ (= EM-) + BRISTLE *sb.* + -ED¹.] Covered as with bristles.

1599 NASHE *Lenten Stuffe* 9 All the fennie Lerna betwixt, that with reede is so imbristled.

†**imbro'cado**¹. *Obs.* [Alteration of It. *imbroccata*, as if from Sp.: see -ADO. Spelt also EMBROCADO.] = IMBROCCATA.

?*c* **1600** *Distracted Emp.* IV. ii. (Bullen *O.P.* III. 233) Favorytts are not without their steccados, imbrocados, and punt[to]-reversos. **1613** WITHERS *Abuses Stript* I. v, They are for nothing but the Imbrocado. **1657** R. LIGON *Barbadoes* (1673) 52 Some of these Portugal Negroes..play at Rapier and Dagger very skilfully, with their Stockadoes, their Imbrocados, and their Passes.

†**imbro'cado**². *Obs.*⁻⁰ [Alteration of It. *imbroccato* (Florio): cf. *brocado*, BROCADE *sb.*, and EMBROCADO *v.*] = BROCADE *sb.* 1.

1656 in BLOUNT *Glossogr.* **1658** PHILLIPS, *Imbrocado*, cloth of Gold or Silver.

imbrocate, obs. var. EMBROCATE.

†**imbro'ccata.** *Obs.* [a. It. *imbroccata* 'a thrust at fence, or a venie giuen ouer the dagger' (Florio), f. *imbroccare* 'to giue a thrust at fence ouer the dagger', f. *brocca* stud, nail (cf. BROACH *sb.*¹).] A pass or thrust in fencing (see above).

1595 SAVIOLO *Practice* 9 The maister shall..breake the same imbroccata or foyne outward from the lefte side. **1598** B. JONSON *Ev. Man in Hum.* IV. vii, I would teach these nineteene, the speciall rules, as..your Stoccata, your Imbroccata, your Passada.

fig. **1599** B. JONSON *Cynthia's Rev.* V. ii, You have your passages and imbrocatas in court-ship, as the bitter bob in wit.

imbroder, -ery, obs. ff. EMBROIDER, -ERY.

†**im'broglid,** *ppl. a. Obs. rare*⁻¹. [var. of *embroiled* (see EMBROIL *v.*²), influenced by It. *imbrogliare*.] Embroiled; involved in a quarrel.

1670 COVEL *Diary* (Hakl. Soc.) 247, I had liked to have been imbroglid for disputing it.

imbroglio (ɪm'brəʊljəʊ). Also **em-**. [a. It. *imbroglio* 'an entangling, an enwrapping, a garboile', etc. (Florio), f. *broglio* confusion: see BROIL *sb.*¹ and *v.*²]

1. A confused heap.

1750 GRAY *Long Story* 66 Into the drawers and china pry, Papers and books, a huge imbroglio. **1850** CARLYLE *Latter-d. Pamph.* viii. (1872) 283 It will lie there an imbroglio of torn boughs. **1864** BROWNING *A Likeness* 42, I keep my prints an imbroglio, Fifty in one portfolio.

2. A state of great confusion and entanglement; a complicated or difficult situation (esp. political or dramatic); a confused misunderstanding or disagreement, embroilment.

1818 LADY MORGAN *Flor. Macarthy* I. iv. 235 The object of this farcical embroglio was the fanciful and accomplished ideologist. **1833** J. W. CROKER in *C. Papers* 23 Apr. (1884), A financial imbroglio would be immediate anarchy and general ruin. **1836** MRS. CARLYLE *Lett.* I. 57 No household imbroglios. **1864** *Reader* 8 Oct. 458/2 The play is exceedingly clever in its intrigue and imbroglio. **1879** FARRAR *St. Paul* xlii. II. 351 Matters had fallen into a hopeless imbroglio. **1885** STEVENSON *Dynamiter* 60 The terms of the letter, and the explosion of the early morning, fitted together like parts in some obscure and mischievous imbroglio.

3. 'A passage, in which the vocal or instrumental parts are made to sing, or play, against each other, in such a manner as to produce the effect of apparent but really well-ordered confusion' (Grove *Dict. Mus.* 1880).

imbroider, -ery, imbroil: see EMB-.

†**imbroin,** *v. Obs.* Var. EMBROYN, to befoul.

1566 PAINTER *Pal. Pleas.* I. 74b, He was imbroined and arraied with the dunge..whereof the Iakes was full.

†**im'brotheled,** *a. Obs. rare*⁻¹. [f. IM-¹ + BROTHEL *sb.* + -ED.] Placed in a brothel.

1593 DONNE *Sat.* ii. 64 Worse than Imbrotheld strumpet's prostitute.

imbrother, -browder, obs. ff. EMBROIDER.

imbrown, obs. f. EMBROWN.

imbrue (ɪm'bru:), *v.* Forms: 5 **enbrewe, en-, imbrowe,** 6–7 **imbrewe,** 6–8 **em-, imbrew,** 6– **em-, imbrue.** [a. OF. *embreuver* 'to moisten, bedeaw, soake in, soften with liquor; also, to die, indue, imbue' (Cotgr.), metathetic form of *emb(e)uvrer, embev(e)rer*, f. *em-*:—L. *im-* + *-bevrer* (It. *-beverare*):—**biberāre*, f. L. *bibĕre* to drink.]

†**1.** *trans.* To stain, dirty, defile. *Obs.*

1430 [see IMBRUED]. *c* **1460** J. RUSSELL *Bk. Nurture* 331 Enbrewe not youre table..ne þer-vppon ye wipe youre knyffes. *c* **1475** *Babees Bk.* 157 Whanne ye shalle drynke, your mouthe clence..Youre handes eke that they in no manere Imbrowe the cuppe. **1555** EDEN *Decades* 100 When their fingers are imbrued with any ounctuous meates. **1579** TOMSON *Calvin's Serm. Tim.* 119/2 How can a man touche whot pitche..and be not embrued? **1593** NASHE *Christ's T.* 13 b, Stayning Berries, which embrued my hands.

2. To stain, dye (one's hand, sword, etc.) *in* or *with* (blood, slaughter, etc.).

1529 MORE *Dyaloge* IV. Wks. 259/1 From howre to howre embruinge theyr handes in bloode. **1577** HANMER *Anc. Eccl. Hist.* (1619) 337 Thy right hand is embrued with slaughter and bloodshed. **1649** CROMWELL *Let.* 17 Sept. in *Carlyle*, These barbarous wretches, who have imbrued their hands in so much innocent blood. **1658** R. WHITE tr. *Digby's Powd. Symp.* (1660) 138 A clout or rag of cloth embrued with the blood. *c* **1704** PRIOR *Henry & Emma* 273 These hands in murder are imbrued. **1813** SCOTT *Rokeby* IV. vi, Who has not heard how brave O'Neale In English blood embrued his steel? **1848** MRS. JAMIESON *Sacr. & Leg. Art* (1850) 335 They started back, unwilling to imbrue their hands in the blood of their host.

b. Said of blood or bleeding wounds. Now *rare.*

1597 DANIEL *Civ. Wars* Wks. (1717) 103 A Spring of Blood..embru'd the Face Of that accursed Caitiff. **1636** G. SANDYS *Paraphr. Ps.* CXXXVI. Ægyptians..Whose wounds the thirsty Earth imbrew. **1776** MICKLE tr. *Camoens' Lusiad* 459 His son's life-gore his wither'd hands imbrews. **1814** CARY *Dante, Inf.* XII. 124 Shallow more and more the blood became, So that at last it but imbrued the feet.

†**3.** In pregnant sense (*with blood* understood): **a.** said of a person; also *absol.*; **b.** of a weapon piercing a part; **c.** with the weapon as object: to thrust, plunge, flesh. *Obs.*

a. 1597 SHAKS. *2 Hen. IV*, II. iv. 210 What? shall wee haue Incision? Shall wee embrew? **1715-20** POPE *Iliad* XIV. 602 What chief, what hero, first embru'd the field?

b. *c* **1580** SIDNEY *Ps.* XXXVII. x, Their swordes shall their own hartes imbrew. **1590** SHAKS. *Mids. N.* V. i. 350 Come trusty sword: Come blade, my brest imbrue.

c. 1590 SPENSER *F.Q.* III. xii. 32 A murdrous knife..The which he thought..In her tormented bodie to embrew. **1703** POPE *Thebais* 722 In their hearts embrues her cruel claws. **1749** SMOLLETT *Regic.* V. vi, And in th' assassin's heart Imbru'd my faithful steel.

d. *Her.* To stain with blood: see IMBRUED.

†**4.** To soak, steep *in*, or saturate *with* any moisture. Also *absol. Obs.*

c **1555** HARPSFIELD *Divorce Hen. VIII* (Camden) 200 The stones were imbrued with the tears of her devout eyes. **1590** BARROUGH *Meth. Physick* VIII. (1639) 443 When all these [materials] be bruised, imbrue them in the juyce of Fumitory. **1634** SIR T. HERBERT *Trav.* 211 One out of curiositie I tasted of, which..malignantly bit..my mouth and lips, as if Vitrioll and Sulphur had beene imbrued.

†**5.** *fig.* To steep *in*; to imbue *with*; to infect.

1565 HARDING in Jewel *Def. Apol.* (1611) 344 Cornelius Agrippa..was imbrewed with Heresies that sprang vp in his time. **1610** ROWLANDS *Martin Mark-all* B iv b, Their mindes were imbrued with such follies. **1639** GENTILIS *Servita's Inquis.* (1676) 868 It is done for fear lest they should be embrewed with some false Doctrine. **1674** N. FAIRFAX *Bulk & Selv.* 43 'Whereness' is a word, which..is almost quite embrew'd in Body if not altogether.

¶**6.** 'To pour, to emit moisture' (J.).

1590 SPENSER *F.Q.* II. v. 33 Some bathed kisses, and did soft embrew The sugured licour through his melting lips.

Hence **im'bruing** *vbl. sb.*

c **1475** *Babees Bk.* 147 On the borde lenynge be yee nat sene, But from embrowyng the clothe yee kepe clene. **1552** HULOET, *Imbruynge*, Loke defilynge.

imbrued (ɪm'bru:d), *ppl. a.* [f. prec. + -ED¹.] Stained, dyed, etc., esp. with blood or slaughter: see prec.

c **1430** *Stans puer* 38 in *Babees Bk.* 29 With mouþ enbrowide þi cuppe þou not take. *a* **1600** HOOKER *Eccl. Pol.* VI. v. §8 He hath not the body of our Lord in his foul imbrued hands. *a* **1628** F. GREVIL *Mustapha* I. i. Wks. (1633) 82 Persia, our old imbrued enemy. **1647** W. BROWNE tr. *Gomberv. Polex.* II. IV. 119 The most imbrued and greatest murtherers amongst the Arabians.

b. *Her.* Stained with blood.

1610 GUILLIM *Heraldry* IV. xiv. (1679) 251 He beareth Sable a Cheveron between 3 Spears heads, Argent, their points embrued, proper, by the name of Morgan. **1787** PORNY *Elem. Herald. Gloss.*, *Imbrued*, is said of Spears heads spotted with blood. **1863** BOUTELL *Her. Hist. & Pop.* 244 A dexter hand..holding erect a dagger, imbrued, all ppr.

im'bruement. *rare.* [f. as prec. + -MENT.] Tincture, infusion, imbuing.

1859 J. S. BLACKIE *Let.* 20 Sept. (1909) 143 To the gratification of the old Adam, but with no imbrument [*sic*] to the new. **1864** in WEBSTER. **1890** TALMAGE *Fr. Manger to Throne* 150 Being of a receptive nature with strong imbruement of religious instinct.

imbrute (ɪm'bru:t), *v.* Also **em-**. [f. IM-¹ + BRUTE *sb.*¹]

1. *trans.* To degrade to the level of a brute; to make bestial, brutalize.

1640 BP. REYNOLDS *Passions* xvi. 165 Wee finde how farre naturall corruption..can imbrute the Manners of Men. **1667** MILTON *P.L.* IX. 166, I..am now constraind Into a Beast, and mixt with bestial slime, This essence to incarnate and imbrute. **1742** YOUNG *Nt. Th.* II. 347 Dismounted ev'ry great and glorious aim; Embruted ev'ry faculty divine. **1875** MANNING *Mission H. Ghost* x. 267 To indulge his love of pleasure so as to soften, to debase, to imbrute himself.

2. *intr.* To sink or lapse to the level of a brute; to become bestial or degraded.

1634 MILTON *Comus* 468 The soul grows clotted by contagion, Embodies, and embrutes. *a* **1760** I. H. BROWNE *Poems, On a fit of Gout*, So when the mind imbrutes in sloth supine, Sharp pangs awake her energy Divine.

Hence **im'bruting** *vbl. sb.* and *ppl. a.*

1809 KNOX & JEBB *Corr.* I. 497 That embodying and embruting of the soul, which is the true antipode to pure and undefiled religion. **1830** H. N. COLERIDGE *Grk. Poets* (1834) 307. **1866** FELTON *Anc. & Mod. Gr.* II. I. i. 253 The imbruting despotism of a barbarous conqueror.

imbruted (ɪm'bru:tɪd), *ppl. a.* Also **em-**. [f. IMBRUTE + -ED¹.] Degraded to the level of a brute; brutalized.

1765 BEATTIE *To Churchill* 121 Thy gross imbruted sense. **1809-10** COLERIDGE *Friend* (1837) III. 208 The fetisch of the imbruted African. **1835** LYTTON *Rienzi* II. vii, A degenerate and embruted people.

imbrutement (ɪm'bru:tmənt). [f. IMBRUTE + -MENT.] The action of IMBRUTE *v.*; brutalization.

a **1837** SIR S. E. BRYDGES cited in Worcester. **1869** BUSHNELL *Wom. Suffrage* i. 12 For poor women to justify their imbrutement in a specially disgusting livelihood.

†**im'brutish,** *v. Obs. rare.* [f. IM-¹ + BRUTISH *a.* Cf. EMBRUTISH.] = IMBRUTE *v.* 1.

1639 LAUD *Confer. w. Fisher* §16. 60 All that have not imbrutished themselves and sunke below their species.

†**im'bud,** *v. Obs. rare.* [f. IM-¹ + BUD *sb.*] To graft by inoculation.

1577 [see IMBRANCH].

imbud, var. of EMBUD *v.*

imbue (ɪm'bju:), *v.* Also 6–7 **imbew.** [Found *c* 1550; ad. L. *imbuĕre* to wet, moisten, tinge, stain, imbrue, imbue. In earlier examples only in the pa. pple. *imbued*, answering to the L. pa. pple. *imbūt-us*, but prob. influenced by the synonymous F. *imbu* (found from 16th c.), now treated as pa. pple. of a vb. *imboire* (refashioned from OF. *emboire*, pa. pple. *embeü*, *embehu*, *embu*), but, as shown by the early forms *imbut* (1507 in Hatz.-Darm.), *imbuit* (*c* 1530 in Godefroy *Compl.*), prob., in its origin, ad. L. *imbūtus*. There was also F. *imbuer*, pa. pple. *imbué*, in occas. use 1560–1600.

1755 JOHNSON, *Imbue*,..this word, which seems wanted in our language, has been proposed by several writers, but not yet adopted by the rest.]

1. *trans.* To saturate, wet thoroughly (*with* moisture); to dye, tinge, impregnate (*with* colour or some physical quality).

1594 CAREW *Tasso* (1881) 72 Ornes and Ceders with sweete sent imbewd. —— *Huarte's Exam. Wits* (1616) 198 They had their bones, their sinewes, and their flesh, so imbewed with Manna and his qualities, that..they longed after nothing else. **1663** BOYLE *Exper. Hist. Colours* III. xlviii. §6 Copper plentifully dissolved in aqua fortis, will imbue several bodies with the colour of the solution. **1725** BRADLEY *Fam. Dict.* s.v. *Sallet*, It is incredible how small a Quantity of Oil in this Quality will suffice to imbue a very plentiful Quantity of Sallet-Herbs. **1818** WORDSW. *On Even. extraord. Beauty* ii, Beamy radiance, that imbues Whate'er it strikes with gem-like hues. **1818** BYRON *Ch. Har.* IV. xxix, Parting day Dies like the dolphin, whom each pang imbues With a new colour as it gasps away. *c* **1878** *Oxford Bible-Helps* 255 Cere-cloth, imbued with unguents and spices.

b. To imbrue (with blood).

1850 MERIVALE *Rom. Emp.* (1852) II. 355 The refractory legions imbued with the blood of their officers. **1874** HOLLAND *Mistr. Manse* xx. 210 Hands in kindred blood imbued.

2. To impregnate, permeate, pervade, or inspire (*with* opinions, feelings, habits, etc.).

1555 EDEN *Decades* 168 The nations seeme apte..to be imbued with good maners. **1591** SPENSER *Ruines Rome* xxiv, What fell Erynnis with hot burning tongs, Did grype your hearts with noysome rage imbew'd? **1667** MILTON *P.L.* VIII. 216 Thy words with Grace Divine Imbu'd. **1736** BERKELEY *Disc. to Magistrates* Wks. III. 415 To imbue the multitude with such notions as may control their appetites. **1822** HAZLITT *Table-t.* Ser. II. v. (1869) 118 He is so thoroughly imbued with the spirit of his authors. **1865** M. ARNOLD *Ess. Crit.* x. (1875) 419 How deeply the prejudices of the multitude imbued the educated class also.

Hence **im'buement**, the action of imbuing, the fact of being imbued.

a **1693** URQUHART *Rabelais* III. xiii. 101 An Imbuement from its Divine Source. **1864** in WEBSTER.

†**imbu'ition.** *Obs. rare*—0. [irreg. from *imbue*: cf. IMBUTION.]

1658 PHILLIPS, *Imbuition*, a thorough moistning, also a seasoning, also a staining.

imbull, var. of EMBULL.

†**im'burden**, *v. Obs. rare*—1. [f. IM-[1] + BURDEN *sb.*] *trans.* To lay as a burden.

1557 *Sarum Primer* Ps. xxxii, For daie and night hath thyne hand been imburdeined upon me.

†**im'buried**, *pa. pple. Obs.*—0 [f. IM-[1] + BURIED.] Entombed; 'layd in bed' (Cockeram, 1623).

imburse (ɪm'bɜːs), *v.* Now *rare.* Also 6 ymburss, 7 emborse, emburse. [ad. late and med.L. *imbursāre* (It. *imborsare*, OF. *enborser*, F. *embourser*), f. *im-* (IM-[1]) + *bursa* purse: cf. *disburse, re-imburse.*]

1. *trans.* To put into one's (or a) purse; to stow away, store up.

c **1530** *Debate Somer & Wynter* in Hazl. *E.P.P.* III. 37 Thou sellyst in to exyle my goodes & monè ymburssed. **1678** *Pol. Ballads* (1860) I. 208 Then Titus..oft did on Pickering call, His charity to imburse. **1721** BAILEY, *To imburse*, to put into Stock of Money. **1755** JOHNSON, *To Imburse*, to stock with money. This should be *emburse* from *embourser*. **1871** MARIA F. ROSSETTI *Shadow of Dante* (1884) 56 Round holes, 'purses' in which these money-sinners are imbursed from sight.

†**b.** *transf.* To pour as into a purse. *nonce-use.*

1692 J. SALTER *Triumphs Jesus* 6 Fountains and Rivers with an eager Course Wou'd to the Ocean all their Floods imburse.

2. †**a.** To enrich. *Obs.* **b.** To pay, refund.

1641-6 EARL MONM. tr. *Biondi's Civil Warres* IV. v. 132 The spoiles, estimated at 1600000. Crownes..emborsed them that were the Authors or Permitters thereof. **1721** BAILEY, *Emburse*, to restore or refund Money owing. **1890** *Daily News* 25 Nov. 2/1 The Bank naturally desires to be imbursed for the double work.

im'bursement. *rare.* [f. prec. + -MENT.] The action of supplying with money; payment.

1665 MANLEY *Grotius' Low C. Warres* 94 Provision was made for Imbursement of all Charges, by giving to him.. whatever Towns the Enemy held beyond the Maze. **1762** tr. *Busching's Syst. Geog.* V. 537 He..was obliged..for the imbursement thereof to grant certain prefecturates, places and estates.

imbushment, obs. form of AMBUSHMENT.

imbusy, var. of EMBUSY *v. Obs.*

†**im'bute**, *v. Obs. rare.* [f. L. *imbūt-*, ppl. stem of *imbuĕre* to IMBUE.] *trans.* To steep, soak. Hence †**im'bution**, steeping, soaking.

1657 TOMLINSON *Renou's Disp.* 53 An Infusion or rather ..an Imbution. *Ibid.* 586 Fumatory, in whose succe their Powders must be..imbuted.

imbuya (ɪm'bwiːjə). Also **imbuia, embuia.** [ad. Pg. *imbuia*, f. the local name for the tree.] A Brazilian timber tree, *Phoebe porosa*, or the wood obtained from it.

1919 *Jrnl. Forestry* XVII. 156 Embuia is the timber de luxe of the four southern Brazil States. **1929** *Tropical Woods* XVIII. 17 Imbuia, or Embuia, one of the best known hardwood timbers of southern Brazil, is used in the United States to a limited extent as a substitute for Walnut, and is sometimes sold as Brazilian Walnut. *Ibid.* 19 The wood of Imbuia varies from yellowish or olive to chocolate-brown, either plain or beautifully variegated and figured. **1947** J. C. RICH *Materials & Methods Sculpture* x. 289 *Imbuya* is a brown wood imported from Central and South America. It is occasionally called Brazilian walnut because of the similarity of its color to walnut. It is softer than black walnut and is usually available in logs and thin planks. **1956** *Handbk. Hardwoods* (Forest Prod. Res. Lab.) 115 Imbuya is also known as 'Brazilian walnut' or embuia (Brazil). **1969** B. J. RENDLE *World Timbers* II. 100 Imbuya is variable in colour, from yellowish-brown to chocolate-brown, and may be plain or variegated. **1971** *Cape Times* 13 Feb. 14/6 (Advt.), Solid imbuia kist with brass trims: excellent condition.

i-medled, ME. pa. pple. of MEDDLE.

i-meind, i-meint, of MENG *v.*, to mingle.

†**i-mele**, *v. Obs.* [OE. *ȝemǽlan* (= OHG. *gimahalan*, MHG. *gemahelen*), f. *mǽlan* to speak: see MELE *v.*] *intr.* To speak, say.

a **1000** *Cædmon's Gen.* 787 (Gr.) Adam ȝemælde and to Euan spræc. *a* **1240** *Ureisun* 48 in *Cott. Hom.* 193 Ne mei.. no muð imelen..Hu muchel god ðu ȝeirkest wið-inne paradise.

†**i'melle**, *prep.* and *adv. Obs.* Also 4 **in melle**, 4 **ymel**, 5 **ymelle**. [Of Norse origin: cf. OSw. *i mælli*, Sw. *emellan*, Da. *imellem* = ON. *í milli, í millum*, f. ON. *meðal* MIDDLE; cf. AMELLE.]

A. *prep.* Amid, among.

13.. *E.E. Allit. P.* A. 1126 To loue þe lombe his meyny in melle. *c* **1386** CHAUCER *Reeve's T.* 251 (Ellesm. & Heng.) Lo whilk a cowplyng is ymel [*Other MSS.* a-mong, be twene, bitwixe, ytwix] hem alle. *c* **1400** *Rowland & O.* 84 Oure noble kynge..His doghety men I-melle. *c* **1440** *MS. Linc. Med.* lf. 287 (Halliw.) Whenne the leves are dryede ynowghe and bakene y-melle the stones.

B. *adv.* Together; = AMONG *adv.* 3.

c **1420** *Liber Cocorum* (1862) 24 Hew þyn henne and do þer to þenne þy henne and ȝolkes of eyren imelle.

i-melled, ME. pa. pple. of MELL *v.*, to mix.

i-melt, of MELT *v.*

i-membred, obs. f. MEMBERED *a.*

†**i-mene**, *adj.* and *adv. Obs.* [OE. *ȝemǽne* = OS. *gimēni*, OFris. *gemēne*, OHG. *gimeini* (Ger. *gemein*, Du. *gemeen*), Goth. *gamains* common:—OTeut. **gamaini-z*, cognate with L. *communis.*]

A. *adj.* Common (to a number), shared or owned in common.

c **1000** *Ags. Gosp.* Matt. viii. 29 Hwæt ys þe and us ȝemæne? *c* **1050** *Suppl. Ælfric's Voc.* in Wr.-Wülcker 177/10 *Compascuus ager*, ȝemæne læs. *c* **1175** *Lamb. Hom.* 101 Heo dudan heore þing heom ȝemene. *c* **1200** ORMIN 5506 Swa þatt ȝe muȝhenn alle imæn þatt rihhte weȝȝe follȝhenn. *c* **1230** *Hali Meid.* 23 þat is to alle iliche imeane. *a* **1250** *Owl & Night.* 628 Hit is fele other wiȝte imene.

B. *adv.* In common, together.

c **1200** *Trin. Coll. Hom.* 31 Ne haue þu naht þin oȝen wif, ac oðer mannes imene. *a* **1225** *Ancr. R.* 90 Cume we nu eft aȝan & speken of alle imene. *c* **1400** *R. Gloucester's Chron.* (Rolls) 1015 + 106 in *App.* 805 Mid ech god man ymene þus argal was out ydriue.

Hence †**i-'mennesse** [OE. *ȝemǽnnesse*], communion, fellowship, society.

c **1050** *Martyrol.* in Cockayne *Shrine* 127 Sealdon hi þær in þara fæmnena ȝemænnesse. *a* **1240** *Lofsong* in *Cott. Hom.* 217, I bileue..on holi chirche, imennesse of haluwen.

i-meng(e)d, ME. pa. pple. of MENG *v.*, mingle.

imergency, obs. f. EMERGENCY.

imerinite (ɪmə'riːnaɪt). *Min.* [a. F. *imerinite* (A. Lacroix *Minéral. de la France* (1910) IV. 787), f. *Imerina* (F. *Imérina*), name of a region in central Madagascar: see -ITE[1].] A colourless or pale blue hydrated silicate of sodium, magnesium, and iron, $Na_2(Mg,Fe^{II},Fe^{III})_6Si_8O_{22}(O,OH)_2$, related to richterite.

1913 *Mineral. Mag.* XVI. 363 Imerinite... A soda-amphibole containing only a small amount of sesquioxides and so allied to soda-richterite. **1963** W. A. DEER et al. *Rock-Forming Min.* II. 353 The names imerinite (Lacroix, 1921) and szechenyite (Krenner, 1900), used for members of the richterite series from Madagascar and Burma respectively, serve no useful purpose and should be abandoned.

i-merked, ME. pa. pple. of MARK *v.*

i-merred, of MAR *v.*

i-met, i-mett, of MEET *v.*

†**i-met.** *Obs.* [OE. *ȝemet* (= OS. *gimet*, OHG. *gamez, kimez*), f. OE. *metan*, Goth. *mitan* to measure] Measure: moderation.

c **975** *Rushw. Gosp.* Matt. vii. 2 In ðæm ȝemete þe ȝe metaþ. *c* **1000** *Endowm. Men* 25 in *Exeter Bk.*, þy læs he..of ȝemete hweorfe. *c* **1175** *Lamb. Hom.* 137 Biðon ilke imet ðe ȝe meteð. *a* **1225** *Ancr. R.* 286 Euerich þing me mei, þauh, ouerdon. Best is euer imete.

†**i-mete**, *a. Obs.* [OE. *ȝemǽte* (= OHG. *gemâze*, MHG. *gemêze*), f. *mǽte* MEET *a.*] Moderate; meet, fit, appropriate.

[*a* **1000** *Cædmon's Daniel* 492 (Gr.) Wearð him hyrra hyȝe ..þonne ȝemet wæ re.] *c* **1175** *Lamb. Hom.* 105 Temperantia þet is metnesse on englisc, þet mon beo imete on alle þing. *c* **1205** LAY. 6584 He wes of his speche ælche monne imete. *a* **1300** *Leg. Rood* (1871) 30 Hi ne miȝte it make Imete.

Hence †**i-metnesse**, moderation.

c **1175** *Lamb. Hom.* 101 Imetnesse is alre mihta moder.

i-mete *v.*: see YMETE, to meet.

i-mete(n, ME. pa. pple. of METE *v.*, to measure.

†**i-metlich**, *a. Obs.* [OE. *ȝemetlíc*, f. *ȝemet*, I-MET *sb.* + *-líc*, -LY[1].] Moderate; meet; of moderate size.

c **888** K. ÆLFRED *Boeth.* xiv. §2 Mara..ȝesceafta þonne he beþurfe oððe him ȝemetlic seo. *c* **1000** *Father's Instruct.* 87 in *Exeter Bk.*, Wisfæst and ȝemetlice. *c* **1205** LAY. 21783 An imetliche broc þe of þan mere ualleð.

imhofite ('ɪmhɒfaɪt). *Min.* [ad. G. *imhofit* (G. Burri et al.: see quot. 1965), f. the name of Josef *Imhof*, 20th-c. Swiss mineral collector: see -ITE[1].] A soft, white sulphide of thallium and arsenic occurring as tiny monoclinic plates.

1965 G. BURRI et al. in *Chimia* XIX. 409 [*English summary of an article in German.*] The description of a new thallium arsenosulfosalt, imhofite, found in the Lengenbach quarry, is given. **1969** *Mineral. Abstr.* XX. 15/2 The structures of the following complex sulphides are summarized:.. imhofite, proustite, [etc.]... The greater part of these minerals are from Lengenbach, Binn valley, Switzerland.

†**i'mid**, *adv.* and *prep. Obs.* [Northern var. of AMID. The *i-* (varying with *e-*) might be merely a phonetic weakening, or it might be from *in*: cf. *in middum* in Rushw. Gosp., *inmiddes* in Cursor M. (*imyddes* in Hampole), *in mydde* in Morte Arthur.] Amid, amidst; in the middle (of).

a **1300** *Cursor M.* 6612 (Gött.) þai fand bot wormis crouland imyd [*Cott.* emid, *Fairf.* amid]. **1340** HAMPOLE *Pr. Consc.* 5167 Imyd þe erthe withouten it falles.

So †**i'middes** *prep.* = AMIDST.

1340 HAMPOLE *Pr. Consc.* 5185 Ierusalem..þat standes imyddes þe world so wyde.

imidazole (ɪ'mɪdəzəʊl). *Chem.* [ad. G. *imidazol* (Hantzsch & Weber 1887, in *Ber. d. Deut. Chem. Ges.* XX. 3119), f. *imid* IMIDE + AZ(O- + *-ol* -OLE.] **a.** A colourless, crystalline, heterocyclic compound consisting of the five-membered ring NH–CH=N–CH=CH. Also called GLYOXALINE. **b.** Any of the derivatives of this compound.

1892 *Jrnl. Chem. Soc.* LXII. 313 Derivatives obtained by displacing a CH group in these by N are designated imidazole = $C_3H_3(NH)N$, oxazole = $C_3H_3(O)N$, and thiazole = $C_3H_3(S)N$ respectively. **1900** E. F. SMITH tr. *V. von Richter's Org. Chem.* (ed. 3) II. 480 The glyoxalines or imidazoles. **1936** L. J. DESHA *Org. Chem.* xxiv. 493 Pyrazole and imidazole, $C_3H_4N_2$, are isomers differing in the relative positions of the nitrogen atoms. **1946** [see GLYOXALINE]. **1951** A. GROLLMAN *Pharmacol. & Therapeutics* xi. 216 Certain imidazole derivatives also exert actions similar in some respects to the sympathetic amines. **1953** R. H. WILEY in H. Gilman *Org. Chem.* IV. viii. 787 The imidazole nucleus is found naturally in the amino acid histidine..; in the purines..; in biotin..; and in histamine. **1968** [see GLYOXALINE]. **1968** L. A. PAQUETTE *Princ. Mod. Heterocyclic Chem.* vi. 185 Imidazole and pyrazole..readily form salts with metal ions.

imide ('ɪmaɪd, ɪ'maɪd). *Chem.* [Purposely altered from AMIDE; first formed as F. *imide* (A. Laurent 1835, in *Ann. de Chim. et de Phys.* LIX. 400).] Any compound containing the group –NH– (or the substituted form –NR–) attached either to two atoms of a metal or to one or two carbon atoms (which strictly should form part of an acidic group or groups).

1850 DAUBENY *Atom. The.* viii. (ed. 2) 248 Imidogen, by which name Laurent intended to express ammonia shorn of 2 of its hydrogen atoms. **1857** W. A. MILLER *Elem. Chem.* III. 231 The imides are bodies formed from the amidated acids by depriving these compounds of two equivalents of water. **1865-72** WATTS *Dict. Chem.* III. 246 *Imides*, monamides, in which 2 at. hydrogen are replaced by a diatomic radicle. **1869** *Eng. Mech.* 2 July 339/1 *Imides*.. bodies intermediate between the amides and nitrites, supposed to contain a hypothetical radicle, imidogen. **1892** E. F. SMITH tr. *V. von Richter's Chem. Carbon Compounds* (ed. 2) 365 The imides result by substituting the divalent acid radicals for two of the hydrogen atoms of ammonia. **1950** N. V. SIDGWICK *Chem. Elements & their Compounds* I. 666 Imides proper $R{\cdot}C{\Large\langle}^{OH}_{NH}$ (cyclic imides like phthalimide are of course of a different type) are scarcely known except as possible tautomeric forms of amides; their alkyl derivatives, the imino-ethers $R{\cdot}C{\Large\langle}^{O\cdot R}_{N\cdot R}$, change easily and irreversibly into the disubstituted amides $R{\cdot}C{\Large\langle}^{O}_{NR_2}$. **1951** C. R. NOLLER *Textbk. Org. Chem.* xiii. 195 The monoacyl derivatives of ammonia, primary amines and secondary amines, having the general formula $RCONH_2$, $RCONHR$, or $RCONR_2$, are known as amides. Diacyl derivatives of ammonia, $(RCO)_2NH$, and of primary amines, $(RCO)_2NR$, also are known and are called imides. Except for the cyclic imides..their preparation usually is more difficult. **1962** P. J. & B. DURRANT *Introd. Adv. Inorg. Chem.* xix. 695 The imides, for example lithium imide Li_2NH, contain the group >NH. Lithium, calcium, germanium, tin, and lead form imides.

Hence **i'mido-**, combining form of prec., as in *imidocaprylic* acid, *imidocaprylimide*, *imidosulphonic* acid, *imidosulphonate*, etc.

1881 WATTS *Dict. Chem.* VIII. 381 The products are imidocaprylic acid and imidocaprylimide.

imidic (ɪ'mɪdɪk), *a. Chem.* [In first quot. ad. F. *imidique* (A. Haller 1895, in *Compt. Rend.* CXX. 1194), but in later use prob. independently formed: see IMIDE and -IC.] Of the nature of an imide; in mod. use applied to organic acids of the type R·C(NH)OH and their derivatives.

1895 *Jrnl. Chem. Soc.* LXVIII. I. 648 Compounds containing the group NHRR' might be called imidic acids. **1919** *Decennial Index Chem. Abstr. 1907–1916* 3325/1 Imidic acids. **1951** I. L. FINAR *Org. Chem.* ix. 161 Imidic esters, which are also known as imino-ethers, are best prepared by passing dry hydrogen chloride into a solution of an alkyl cyanide in anhydrous alcohol. **1965** C. R. NOLLER *Chem. Org. Compounds* (ed. 3) xiv. 272 The tautomeric form of an amide, $\mathrm{R\overset{\overset{NH}{\|}}{C}-OH}$, is a nitrogen analog of a carboxylic acid and is known as an imidic acid. Although the imidic acids cannot be isolated because of the greater stability of the amide form, their derivatives are easily prepared.

†**i-milce, -milse,** *v. Obs.* Also **imilze.** [OE. *ȝemiltsian*, f. *miltsian* f. *milts* mildness, mercy: see MILCE.] *trans.* To have mercy upon, pardon.

c **1000** *Ags. Gosp.* Matt. xx. 34 Ða ȝe-miltsode he him. *c* **1000** *Ags. Ps.* (Spelm.) lvi. 1 (Bosw.) ȝemiltsa me God ȝemiltsa min. *c* **1175** *Lamb. Hom.* 39 Bute we inwarliche imilcien and forȝeuen þan monne. *c* **1205** LAY. 16837 Imilze þu Octa & his iueren . . ȝif heo wulleð cristindom . . vnderfon.

iminazole (ɪ'mɪnəzəʊl). *Chem.* [f. IMIN(E + AZ(O- + -OLE.] = IMIDAZOLE.

1901 *Jrnl. Chem. Soc.* LXXX. I (*heading*) Preparation of substituted iminazoles. **1926** H. G. RULE tr. *Schmidt's Text-bk. Org. Chem.* III. iii. 578 The ring system of the iminazoles, like that of the pyrazoles, consists of three carbon and two nitrogen atoms... Iminazole, the parent compound of the series, is formed . . by the action of ammonia on glyoxal, and hence is also known as glyoxaline. **1968** [see GLYOXALINE].

imine ('ɪmiːn). *Chem.* [ad. G. *imin* (A. Ladenburg 1883, in *Ber. d. Deut. Chem. Ges.* XVI. 1150), formed by altering *amin* AMINE (cf. IMIDE, AMIDE).] Any compound containing the group =NH (or the substituted form =NR) attached to one carbon atom that forms part of a non-acidic organic group, or containing it in symmetrical compounds of the type R·NH·R; also applied (unsystematically) to other compounds in which it is attached to two carbon atoms (strictly, atoms forming part of non-acidic groups), esp. when they are part of a ring (as in ethylene imine, $(CH_2)_2NH$).

1883 *Jrnl. Chem. Soc.* XLIV. 910 (*heading*) Imines. **1889** G. M'GOWAN tr. *A. Bernthsen's Text-bk. Org. Chem.* 194 If two hydrogen atoms in a molecule of ammonia are replaced by a divalent alcohol radicle, 'Imines', e.g. ethylene imine, $(C_2H_4)NH''$, result. **1909** *Proc. Chem. Soc.* XXV. 309 Some confusion exists owing to the present system of nomenclature adopted for the imino-compounds. These substances, which possess the group C:NH, are obviously just as different from the secondary amines having the group $\mathrm{{C \atop C}\!>\!NH}$ as the ketones with the group C:O are different from the ethers with the group $\mathrm{{C \atop C}\!>\!O}$, yet the general name of imine is applied to both these classes. **1935** *Jrnl. Amer. Chem. Soc.* LVII. 2328/1 (*heading*) The preparation of ethylene imine from mono-ethanolamine. **1950** N. V. SIDGWICK *Chem. Elements* I. 666 Imines of the type $\mathrm{{C \atop C}\!>\!C=N\cdot H}$ rarely occur and are always unstable. **1967** I. L. Finar *Org. Chem.* (ed. 5) I. viii. 181 Aldehydes react with primary amines to form imines (Schiff bases)... $\mathrm{R\cdot CHO + R'NH_2 \rightarrow R\cdot CH{=}NR' + H_2O}$. **1970** AMBROSE & EASTY *Cell Biol.* viii. 267 The sugar molecules form imine linkages (=NH) with the partially dissociated protein complexes.

imino(-) (ɪ'miːnəʊ). *Chem.* Comb. form of IMINE; also used *attrib.* as quasi-*adj.* So ***imino-chloride, -compound; iminosulphonic acid;*** **imino-acid**, any organic acid that contains an imino-group; also (now *rare*), an imidic acid; **imino-ester** or **-ether**, any compound that contains –C(NH)OR and is consequently an ester of an imidic acid; more correctly called an *imido-ester*; **imino-group**, the group =NH as it occurs in imines (in quot. 1906 it denotes what is more correctly called an *imido-group*).

1903 *Jrnl. Chem. Soc.* LXXXIV. I. 692 The formation and properties of some iminoacid anhydrides of the type of the hypothetical iminoformic anhydride, NH:CH·O·CH:O. **1937** Imino-acid [see *imino-ether* below]. **1953** FRUTON & SIMMONDS *Gen. Biochem.* iii. 49 The hydrolysis of a protein leads to the formation of a variety of amino acids... The compounds having the general formula shown are termed α-amino acids, whereas proline and hydroxyproline are more correctly designated α-imino acids; for convenience, however, these two cyclic compounds are also called amino acids. **1961** *Jrnl. Clin. Invest.* XL. I. 843/1 Since nearly all of the hydroxyproline of the body is found in collagen, it has been suggested . . that the urinary excretion of the imino acid may be an important index of collagen metabolism. **1967** *New Scientist* 24 Aug. 375/1 The precise proportion of the imino-acid hydroxyproline in the important protein collagen. **1900** *Jrnl. Chem. Soc.* LXXVIII. I. 295 The authors think it probable that aliphatic substituted imino-chlorides of aromatic acids are readily decomposed into alkyl chlorides and aromatic nitriles or their polymerides. **1904** *Ibid.* LXXXV. 1726 (*heading*) The formation and reactions of imino-compounds. **1924** C. HOLLINS *Synthesis Nitrogen Ring Compounds* vii. 203 The yield of imino-compound . . was very small. **1908** *Jrnl. Chem. Soc.* XCIV. I. 419 The catalysis of imino-esters. **1935** H. J. LUCAS *Org. Chem.* xxi. 314 In the presence of anhydrous hydrogen chloride, nitriles add alcohols to form imino esters: $\mathrm{CH_3C{\equiv}N + HOC_2H_5 \rightarrow CH_3\underset{\underset{OC_2H_5}{|}}{C}{=}NH}$. **1951** C. R. NOLLER *Chem. Org. Compounds* xiii. 242 The corresponding *O*-alkyl derivatives, $\mathrm{R\overset{\overset{NH}{\|}}{C}-OR}$, are known and are called imido esters (less correctly imino esters or imido ethers). **1897** *Jrnl. Chem. Soc.* LXII. II. 804/2 (Index), Imino-ethers. **1937** TAYLOR & BAKER *Sidgwick's Org. Chem. Nitrogen* (rev. ed.) v. 154 The imino-ethers, which can also be regarded as esters of imino-acids and are sometimes called imino-esters have the general formula R·C(OR'): NH. **1906** *Jrnl. Chem. Soc.* LXXXIX. II. 1837 The members of the former class contain the grouping $\mathrm{CO\!<\!{NH\cdot CO\cdot \atop NH\cdot CO\cdot}}$, whereas in no member of the latter class is this grouping present... Each of the imino-groups contained in the above-mentioned grouping, being connected with two carbonyl groups, will be possessed of acidic properties. **1966** NOWAKOWSKI & CLARKE tr. *Kretovich's Princ. Plant Biochem.* i. 16 Proline, strictly speaking, is not an amino acid, as it contains an imino group (=NH). **1896** *Jrnl. Chem. Soc.* LXX. II. 911/1 (Index), Iminosulphonic acid.

Examples of the general use (without hyphen) as quasi-*adj.*

1901 *Proc. Chem. Soc.* XVII. 61 A liquid base of 'imino' odour. **1937** F. C. WHITMORE *Org. Chem.* I. 226 This product loses water to form the imino analog of formaldehyde, $H_2C{=}NH$.

imipramine (ɪ'mɪprəmiːn). *Pharm.* [Rearrangement of some elements of *dimethyl*-amino*propyl*-imino*dibenzyl*, a systematic name for this compound: see -INE⁵.] A tricyclic tertiary amine, $C_{19}H_{24}N_2$, given orally as the hydrochloride, a white crystalline compound, in the treatment of endogenous depression.

1958 *Amer. Jrnl. Psychiatry* CXV. 459 (*heading*) The treatment of depressive states with G 22355 (imipramine hydrochloride). **1960** *Brit. Med. Jrnl.* 30 Jan. 348/2 We have . . noted the development of jaundice and also hypomania in patients receiving therapeutic doses of imipramine. **1963** *Lancet* 23 Mar. 638/2 The administration to pregnant rabbits of imipramine ('Tofranil') led to the development of fœtal abnormalities. **1964** HAFLIGER & BURCKHARDT in M. Gordon *Psychopharmacol. Agents* I. iii. 77 Imipramine has no influence upon monoamine oxidase. *Ibid.* 89 The most frequent side effecs of imipramine . . include dryness of the mouth, sweating, disturbance of accommodation, constipation, insomnia, and giddiness. **1965** *Nursing Times* 5 Feb. 187/1 Either electro-convulsive therapy or one of the antidepressant drugs (such as imipramine—Tofranil) will probably be used. **1965** J. POLLIT *Depression & its Treatment* iv. 58 Imipramine is effective mainly in Type S classical (retarded) depressions, and in depressed patients of middle age and over. It is less valuable in atypical depression, and in sensitive or hysterical personalities the ordinary mild side effects may cause bitter complaint. **1972** *Brit. Med. Jrnl.* 1 Apr. 45/2 These fairly substantial figures do not support the view that imipramine is liable to cause fetal abnormalities if given to pregnant women.

i-mist, ME. pa. pple. of MISS *v.*

imit ('aɪmɪt). *nonce-wd.* [f. L. *īm-us* lowest, after *summit*; cf. med.L. *īmitās*.] Lowest point.

1885 TAIT *Properties Matter* iv. §85. 72 A watercourse is thus the stream-line drawn from a col so as to pass through an *Imit*, or lowest point of the surface.

imitability (ˌɪmɪtə'bɪlɪtɪ). [f. IMITABLE: see -ITY.] The quality of being imitable.

1678 NORRIS *Coll. Misc.* (1699) 159 The various modes of Imitability or Participation. **1701** —— *Ideal World* I. v. 254 This account . . so far as it states the ideality of God upon his imitability or participability, is truly Platonic. **1887** W. M. ROSSETTI in *Shelley Soc. Papers* 6 Outside the precincts of imitability.

imitable ('ɪmɪtəb(ə)l), *a.* [a. F. *imitable* (16th c.), ad. L. *imitābilis*, f. *imitārī* to imitate: see -ABLE.]

1. Capable of being imitated.

1598 FLORIO, *Imitabile*, imitable, that may be imitated. **1656** COWLEY *Pindar. Odes, Praise Pindar* i, Pindar is imitable by none. **1711** STEELE *Spect.* No. 133 ¶1 We secretly believe the Part of the dying Person imitable by ourselves. **1880** L. STEPHEN *Pope* viii. 198 All poets who have any marked style are more or less imitable.

†**2.** Deserving of imitation. *Obs.*

1550 NICOLLS *Thucyd.* 6 That whiche shalbe founden to be therein Imitable and good to followe. **1682** SIR T. BROWNE *Chr. Mor.* I. §12 The worst of times afford imitable examples of virtue. **1742** RICHARDSON *Pamela* IV. 82 Such advantageous Lights, as shall . . make the Vice that ought to be censured, imitable. **1781** R. TWINING in *Twining Fam. Papers* (1887) 16 Wishing that painters and sculptors would confine their labours to imitable subjects.

Hence '**imitableness**, imitable quality.

1633 AMES *Agst. Cerem.* II. 493 The reason of this imitablenesse is the same. **1774** A. GIB *Pres. Truth* I. 332 The perpetual obligation and imitableness of the precepts and examples.

†'**imitably,** *adv. Obs.* [f. prec. + -LY².] By way of imitation or counterfeiting.

1616 J. LANE *Cont. Sqr.'s T.* 174 And theareof imitablie deignes declaime, To force a truith out of neutralitie.

†**imi'tamen.** *Obs. rare*⁻¹. [a. L. *imitāmen*, f. *imitārī* to imitate.] An imitation; a counterfeit.

1677 GALE *Crt. Gentiles* III. 51 Al the Phenician Baalim and Grecian Demons were but Idolatric Imitamens or Apes of the true Messias.

'**imitancy.** *nonce-wd.* [f. L. *imitānt-em*: see next and -ANCY.] The quality or property of imitating; imitativeness.

1832 CARLYLE *Misc. Ess., Boswell's Johnson* (1872) IV. 88 The servile imitancy . . of Mankind might be illustrated under the different figure . . of a Flock of Sheep. **1850** —— *Latter-d. Pamph.* i. (1872) 37 Not 'humanity' or manhood . . apehood rather,—paltry imitancy, from the teeth outward.

'**imitant.** *rare.* [f. L. *imitānt-em* imitating, pres. pple. of *imitārī* to imitate: see -ANT.] That which imitates; a counterfeit article or product.

1888 *Sci. Amer.* 3 Mar. 135/2 To lower the quality and . . to foster the use of imitants and adulterants.

imitate ('ɪmɪteɪt), *v.* Also 7 imm-. [f. L. *imitāt-*, ppl. stem of *imitārī* to copy, etc.]

1. *trans.* To do or try to do after the manner of; to follow the example of; to copy in action.

1534 MORE *On the Passion* Wks. 1346/1 He that so receiueth the bloude of hys redemer, that he will not yet imitate and follow his passion. **1600** E. BLOUNT tr. *Conestaggio* 18 Beseeching the King to . . imitate the example of his auncestors. **1668** CULPEPPER & COLE *Barthol. Anat.* I. xviii. 50 Spigelius whom Laurenbergius of Rostoch does faithfully imitate, has assigned other uses to these Capsulæ. **1697** DAMPIER *Voy.* I. 7 The Children imitating their Parents. **1781** GIBBON *Decl. & F.* xxviii. III. 75 *note*, In the form and disposition of his ten books of epistles, he imitated the younger Pliny. **1876** MOZLEY *Univ. Serm.* vii. (1877) 158 We are to imitate others so far as they possess moral qualities which are of general and common service.

b. Sometimes with implication of incongruity or of specific purpose: To mimic, counterfeit.

1613 PURCHAS *Pilgrimage* (1614) 558 The Hyæna . . will imitate humane voyce, and . . having heard the name of some of the Shepheards will call him. **1660** F. BROOKE tr. *Le Blanc's Trav.* 381 Of Apes and Monkies there are . . that will imitate all they see. **1727** DE FOE *Syst. Magic* I. iii. (1840) 76 It remains a question here, by what power . . the magicians of Egypt . . in short mimicked or imitated the miracles of Moses and Aaron. **1738** SWIFT *Pol. Conversat.* 73 *Miss.* (imitating Lady Answerall's Tone) Very pretty!

†**c.** Said of undesigned similarity of action. *Obs.*

1601 R. JOHNSON *Kingd. & Commw.* (1603) 169 Herein it should seeme they immitate the opinion of the Stoikes. **1602** PATERICKE tr. *Gentillet* 77 The Paynims also imitated this of Moses his sacrifices, that they immolated the like beasts.

†**d.** With *inf.*: To endeavour, make an attempt *to do* something. *Obs.* exc. *dial.*

a **1626** BACON (J.), We imitate and practise to make swifter motions than any out of your muskets. *a* **1825** FORBY *Voc. E. Anglia, Imitate*, to attempt; to endeavour. Ex. A child, or a sick person 'imitated to walk'.

2. To make or produce a copy or representation of; to copy, reproduce.

1590 SPENCER *F.Q.* II. xii. 42 A place pickt out by choyce of best alyve, That natures worke by art can imitate. **1638** F. JUNIUS *Paint. of Ancients* 19 Some Artificers . . can imitate the workes of others most accurately. **1687** A. LOVELL tr. *Thevenot's Trav.* 73 They do what they can to imitate the Galleasses of Venice. **1860** TYNDALL *Glac.* II. vii. 260 By such means it is possible to imitate the phenomena of the firmament.

b. 'To pursue the course of (a composition) so as to use parallel images and examples' (J.).

1700 DRYDEN *Fables* Pref. (Globe) 496 The adventures of Ulysses in the Odysseis are imitated in the first six books of Virgil's Æneis. *a* **1732** GAY (J.), For shame! what, imitate an ode! *a* **1832** SCOTT *Frederick & Alice* note, This tale is imitated, rather than translated, from a fragment.

3. To be, become, or make oneself like; to assume the aspect or semblance of; to simulate: **a.** intentionally or consciously; **b.** unintentionally or unconsciously.

1588 SHAKS. *L.L.L.* IV. iii. 265 Red . . Paints it selfe blacke, to imitate her brow. **1601** —— *Twel. N.* III. iv. 418 For him I imitate. **1615** G. SANDYS *Trav.* 7 In habite they imitate the Italians. **1654** Z. COKE *Logick* (1657) 138 The conclusion must imitate the more unworthy and weaker part that is premised. **1749** FIELDING *Tom Jones* IV. xii, The diseases of the mind . . imitate those of the body. **1839** MURCHISON *Silur. Syst.* I. xiv. 179 Where they may be seen in countless profusion, imitating in their outline, horse-shoes, rings, almonds, etc. *Mod.* A lath painted to imitate iron.

Hence '**imitated** *ppl. a.*; '**imitating** *vbl. sb.* and *ppl. a.*

1591 PERCIVALL *Sp. Dict.*, *Remedamiento*, imitating. **1686** PLOT *Staffordsh.* 284 This imitating quality . . becomes involuntary. **1697** DRYDEN *Æneid* x. 905 This hand appear'd a shining sword to wield, And that sustain'd an imitated shield. **1745** ELIZA HEYWOOD *Fem. Spectator* (1748) IV. 24 In this imitating age there will be few fond enough of vice to be out of the fashion.

†'**imitate,** *sb. Obs. rare.* [ad. L. *imitāt-us* an imitation, f. *imitārī* to IMITATE.] An imitation.

1669 GALE *Crt. Gentiles* I. III. i. 15 The Greek Rapsodies and Rapsodists, were but Satanic Imitates of the Hebrew Psalmodists.

imitation (ɪmɪˈteɪʃən). Also 6 ymy-, imytacion. [ad. L. *imitātiōn-em*, n. of action from *imitārī* to IMITATE: perh. through F. *imitation*.]

1. a. The action or practice of imitating or copying. † ***arts of imitation*** = imitative arts.

1502 ATKYNSON tr. *De Imitatione (title)* A full deuoute & gosteley treatyse of yᵉ Imytacion & folowynge yᵉ blessyd lyfe of our most mercifull sauiour cryst. **1520** WHITINTON *Vulg.* (1527) 3 Many fresshe wyttes by that blynde imitacyon be deceyued. **1638** F. JUNIUS *Paint. of Ancients* 150 Concerning the manifold use of these Arts of imitation. **1727** DE FOE *Syst. Magic* I. i. (1840) 7 Adam's posterity learnt to speak more immediately from him and Eve their mother, by mere imitation of sounds. **1769** *Junius Lett.* v. 28 An example for imitation. **1820** COLTON *Lacon* ccxvii, Imitation is the sincerest of flattery. **1876** MOZLEY *Univ. Serm.* ii. 26 Imitation, as well as nature, is the source of particular virtues.

b. Phrase: ***in imitation of*** (cf. F. *à l'imitation de*). Also † ***after the, according to the, out of an imitation of***; † ***in his imitation*** (cf. F. *à son imitation*).

1579–80 NORTH *Plutarch* (1676) 3 They learned it not of the Arabians.. neither did they it after the imitation of the Missians. **1585** T. WASHINGTON tr. *Nicholay's Voy.* II. xxi. 58 According to the imitation of the auncient Græcians and Romaines. **1586** A. DAY *Eng. Secretary* I. (1625) 20 In imitation of the best and most learned judgements of our time. **1594** CAREW *Huarte's Exam. Wits* (1616) 133 That which this notable man vsed to doe.. I am now also resolued to doe in his imitation. **1651** HOBBES *Leviath.* II. xxix. 170 To see the late troubles in England, out of an imitation of the Low Countries. **1823** RUTTER *Fonthill* 25 Carved timber work, painted in imitation of old oak.

c. *Psychol.* The adoption, whether conscious or not, during a learning process, of the behaviour or attitudes of some specific person or model.

[**1807** WORDSWORTH *Poems* II. 153 The little Actor cons another part.. As if his whole vocation Were endless imitation.] **1895** J. M. BALDWIN *Mental Development* xii. 351 First.. biological or organic imitation... Second: we pass to psychological, conscious, or cortical imitations. *Ibid.* 352 *Plastic Imitation.* This phrase is used to cover all cases of reaction or attitude, toward the doings, customs, opinions of others, which once represented more or less conscious adaptations.. but which have become what is ordinarily called 'secondary automatic' and subconscious. **1899** H. C. WARREN tr. *Tarde's Social Laws* 42 Giving the word imitation the very wide meaning accorded to it.. by Mr. Baldwin.. one might regard imitation as the fundamental fact, not only of social and psychological life, but of organic life as well, where it would appear as the necessary condition of habit and heredity. **1903** E. C. PARSONS tr. *Tarde's Laws of Imitation* p. xiv, By imitation, I mean every impression of an inter-psychical photography.. willed or not willed, passive or active. **1924** F. H. ALLPORT *Social Psychol.* x. 239 Before the rise of a really critical science of behavior the term 'imitation' enjoyed wide repute in social theory... Our treatment of imitation must therefore be mainly negative. **1946** D. MCCARTHY in L. Carmichael *Manual of Child Psychol.* 497/1 An interesting controversy.. on the problem of the relationship between imitation and comprehension of language. **1968** *Internat. Encycl. Social Sci.* VII. 96/1 Learning by vicarious experience has historically been referred to as 'imitation'.

2. The result or product of imitating; a copy, an artificial likeness; a thing made to look like something else, which it is not; a counterfeit.

1601 SHAKS. *Jul. C.* IV. i. 37 One that feeds On Objects, Arts, and Imitations. **1638** F. JUNIUS *Paint. of Ancients* 349 So is the imitation of an imitation much more hard and difficult. **1768** JOHNSON *Pref. Shaks.*, Imitations produce pain or pleasure, not because they are mistaken for realities. **1875** JOWETT *Plato* (ed. 2) III. 66 They are not true philosophers, but only an imitation. **1876** HUMPHREYS *Coin-Coll. Man.* 405 Modern imitations of ancient coins.

3. *Literature.* 'A method of translating looser than paraphrase, in which modern examples and illustrations are used for ancient, or domestick for foreign' (J.); a composition of this nature.

1656 COWLEY *Pindar. Odes, Praise Pindar*, In imitation of Horace his second Ode, B. 4. *a* **1721** PRIOR (*title*) The Lady's Looking-Glass. In imitation of a Greek Idyllium. **1734** WATTS *Reliq. Juv., Hebr. Poet*, The Difficulty of a just Translation of the Psalms of David.. an Apology for the Imitation of them in Christian Language. **1870** CHRISTIE in *Dryden's Wks.* (Globe) 488 Dryden's imitations, or, as he himself calls them, translations of Chaucer and Boccacio, were made in 1698 and 1699.

4. *Mus.* The repetition of a phrase or melody, usually at a different pitch, in another part or voice, either with the same intervals, rhythm, motion, etc. (***exact imitation***), or with these more or less modified (***free imitation***: see also AUGMENTATION, DIMINUTION, INVERSION).

1727–41 CHAMBERS *Cycl.*, *Imitation*, in music, a kind of composition wherein one part is made to imitate another either throughout the whole piece, which is one of the kinds of canon, or only during some measures, which is a simple imitation. **1880** OUSELEY in Grove *Dict. Mus.* I. 765 If the imitation is absolutely exact as to intervals it becomes a Canon.. Imitation may take place at any interval or at any distance. *Ibid.* 569 A specimen of simple imitation at the octave..; from such a small germ as this.. the.. modern fugue has been gradually developed.

5. *attrib.* Made (of less costly material) in imitation of a real or genuine article or substance.

1840 H. REEVE tr. *A. de Tocqueville's Democracy in Amer.* III. I. xi. 100 Imitation-diamonds are now made which may be easily mistaken for real ones. **1858** GREENER *Gunnery* 241 The fitting-up of an imitation gun for the African market.. with an imitation musket for the same. **1871** *Post Office Directory Leather Trades* 66 (*heading*) Imitation leather makers... Kid leather dressers... Kid reviver makers. **1895** *Oracle Encycl.* II. 125/1 Imitation tortoise-shell combs. **1902** *Encycl. Brit.* XXVIII. 611/1 This is a very different thing from the imitation diamond so common in shop windows. Here the chemist has only succeeded in making a paste or glass.. wanting the hardness and 'fire' of the real stone. **1904** GOODCHILD & TWENEY *Technol. & Sci. Dict.* 303/1 *Imitation parchment*, ordinary paper passed through a bath of sulphuric acid, which has the peculiar effect of 'toughening' the fibres. **1904** *Westm. Gaz.* 6 Oct. 4/2 Contempt of imitation jewels, imitation furs, imitation lace. *Ibid.*, A lovely coat of.. imitation sealskin. **1916** E. POUND *Lustra* 53 The small child in the soiled-white imitation fur coat. **1929** D. H. LAWRENCE *Pansies* 124 Will the Proustian lot go next? And then our English imitation intelligentsia? **1937** E. J. LABARRE *Dict. Paper* 159/1 Imitation art paper is a highly finished printing [paper] prepared by the addition of a heavy percentage of china clay to the pulp and a water-finish. **1940** *Chambers's Techn. Dict.* 552/1 *Mock leno*, a fabric in which openwork effect is produced by a grouping of threads, which, however, do not cross, as they do in leno and gauze fabrics. Also called imitation gauze. **1954** *Paper Terminol.* (Spalding & Hodge) 32 *Imitation kraft*, a quality of wrapping paper made from unbleached sulphite, mechanical pulp and waste papers and coloured brown to give the appearance of Kraft. **1957** *Encycl. Brit.* IV. 775/2 Imitation gauze weaves.. are.. largely utilized in the production of.. embroidery cloths. *Ibid.* XIII. 850 A/2 The first feasible imitation leathers were based on patents issued in the United Kingdom in 1851. *Ibid.* XIX. 635/1 Imitation rum is produced by flavouring a neutral spirit.. with high-ester Jamaican rum or with artificial essences. **1963** R. R. A. HIGHAM *Handbk. Papermaking* 282 *Imitation art*, paper which is highly finished by the action of super-calendering and water finishing and which contains a high percentage of china clay in the furnish.

imitational (ɪmɪˈteɪʃənəl), *a.* [f. prec. + -AL¹.] Of, pertaining to, or characterized by imitation.

1833 *Q. Rev.* XLIX. 517 Weak and merely imitational as many of the pieces included in this volume are. **1874** SAYCE *Compar. Philol.* vi. 237 Roots are not emotional or imitational cries, although they may have grown out of them.

imitationist (ɪmɪˈteɪʃənɪst). [f. as prec. + -IST.] One who practises imitation, or gives imitations; 'a mere imitator, one who wants originality'.

In mod. Dicts.

imitative (ˈɪmɪteɪtɪv), *a.* (*sb.*) [ad. late L. *imitātīv-us*, f. *imitārī* (see -ATIVE); cf. F. *imitatif*.]

1. Characterized by or consisting in imitation. ***imitative arts***, the arts of painting and sculpture; ***imitative word***, a word which reproduces a natural sound.

1584 TWYNE *Æneid* Life A vij, There are three kinde of stiles in a Poeme, ether Actiue, ether Imitatiue which Graecians call *Dramaticum*. **1697** DRYDEN *Virg. Georg.* II. 282 Ploughing is an imitative Toil, Resembling Nature in an easie Soil. **1753** HOGARTH *Anal. Beauty* xi. 91 It is allowed by the most skilful in the imitative arts. **1853** RUSKIN *Stones Ven.* II. vi, This is the error.. of merely imitative painters of still life, flowers, &c. **1865** TYLOR *Early Hist. Man.* ii. 15 Words which are evidently imitative, like 'peewit'.

b. Const. *of*.

1700 DRYDEN *Palamon & A.* II. 527 This temple.. Was imitative of the first in Thrace. **1849** FREEMAN *Archit.* I. I. v. 93 Some of them are.. directly imitative of the timber construction. **1867** MISS BROUGHTON *Not wisely* II. ii. 36 Walking.. in a manner feebly imitative of the human gait.

2. Given to imitation; prone to imitate, copy, or mimic.

1752 HUME *Ess. & Treat.* (1777) I. 216 The human mind is of a very imitative nature. **1827** GIFFORD *Ford's Plays* Introd. 36 At present, we are become an imitative, not to say a mimic, race. **1837** SYD. SMITH *Wks.* (1867) II. 249 Human beings are very imitative.

3. That imitates the appearance of something else; simulative; fictitious; counterfeit.

1838 DICKENS *Nich. Nick.* xxv, Dazzling articles of imitative jewellery almost equal to real.

† **B.** as *sb.* (See quot.) *Obs.*

1678 PHILLIPS (ed. 4), *Imitatives*, in Grammar, those sort of Verbs which express any kind of Imitation; as *Patrissare*, to take after the Father, or imitate his actions, humor, or fashion.

Hence **ˈimitatively** *adv.*, in an imitative manner; **ˈimitativeness**, imitative quality.

a **1846** MARTINEAU cited in Worcester for *Imitativeness*. *a* **1849** POE *H. B. Hirst* Wks. 1864 III. 209 His chief sin is imitativeness. **1879** *Cassell's Techn. Educ.* v. 279 If plants are employed as ornaments they must not be treated imitatively. **1973** *Daily Tel.* (Colour Suppl.) 9 Feb. 7/2 The imitativeness in these films is even more striking than their lack of artistry.

imitator (ˈɪmɪteɪtə(r)). Also 6 imm-, 6–7 -our, -er. [ad. F. *imitateur* (14th c.), ad. L. *imitātōr-em*, agent-noun f. *imitārī* to IMITATE.] One who imitates, copies, or follows another; one who produces an imitation of anything. Also *transf.* of things.

1523 LD. BERNERS *Froiss.* Pref. (1812) I. D ij, In semblable wyse dyd his imytator, noble duke Theseus. **1541** COPLAND *Galyen's Terapeut.* 2 G ij b, Medycyne ought to be immytatour.. of nature. **1585** T. WASHINGTON tr. *Nicholay's Voy.* III. xvii. 102 b, This they doe to shew themselves true immitatours of their Prophet. **1695** BLACKMORE *Pr. Arth.* v. 565 Let your bright Virtues Imitators draw. *a* **1832** BENTHAM *Man. Pol. Econ.* Wks. 1843 III. 71 In new inventions, protection against imitators is not less necessary than in established manufactures protection against thieves. **1859** DARWIN *Orig. Spec.* xiv. (1873) 376 We never find an imitator living remote from the form which it imitates.

Hence **ˈimiˌtatorship**, the office of an imitator.

1599 MARSTON *Sco. Villanie* III. viii. 218 When to seruile imitatorship Some spruce Athenian pen is prentized, Tis worse then Apish.

imitatress (ˈɪmɪteɪtrɪs). [f. prec.: see -ESS¹.] = next.

a **1834** COLERIDGE in *Lit. Rem.* (1836) I. 220 We all know that art is the imitatress of nature. **1865** PUSEY *Eiren.* 26 Superstition, the false imitatress of true piety. **1889** *Standard* 30 Sept. 5/4 The imitatress of the Second Catherine.

imitatrix (ɪmɪˈteɪtrɪks). [a. L. *imitātrix*, fem. of *imitātor*.] A female imitator.

1606 *Sir G. Goosecappe* II. ii. in Bullen *O. Pl.* III. 53 The most witty Imitatrixes of them. **1611** SPEED *Hist. Gt. Brit.* IX. xx. (1632) 972 Our Dutchesse was but an imitatrix. **1745** A. BUTLER *Lives of Saints, Isidore* (1847) V. 194 He made her a faithful imitatrix of his virtues. **1893** *Cornh. Mag.* May 495 Nature is a subtler imitatrix.

† **ˈimitature.** *Obs. rare.* [f. L. *imitāt-*, ppl. stem (see IMITATE) + -URE.] Imitation.

1652 H. COGAN tr. *Scudery's Ibrahim* I. ii. 27 She gave me her picture, which she had drawn in imitature, by beholding her self in a glass.

imma, var. IMMY.

immaciated, obs. var. of EMACIATED.

1748 *Anson's Voy.* III. vii. 362 Their own immaciated ship-mates.

† **iˈmmaculable**, *a. Obs. rare.* [ad. late L. *immaculābilis*, f. *maculāre* to spot: see -BLE.] Incapable of stain.

1624 FISHER in F. White *Repl. Fisher* 449 The bodie of Christ is.. in things impure immaculable.

immaculacy (ɪˈmækjʊləsɪ). [f. IMMACULATE: see -ACY.] Immaculate condition or quality.

1799 E. DU BOIS *Piece Family Biog.* I. 19, I.. will not.. sully the immaculacy of my page with a reflection [etc.]. **1817** J. SCOTT *Paris Revis.* (ed. 4) 252 Perrone is called the *pucelle*, because it had never been violated by an enemy; but her immaculacy is now more than questionable. **1863** MRS. C. CLARKE *Shaks. Char.* ii. 55 He sees through Professor Jaques's pretended immaculacy. **1892** W. WATSON *Epigr.* Poems 116 Insulted by a flower's immaculacy, And mock'd at by the flawless stars he stands.

immaculate (ɪˈmækjʊlət), *a.* Also 5 in-. [ad. L. *immaculātus*, f. *im-* (IM-²) + *maculātus* spotted, MACULATE.]

1. Free from spot or stain; pure, spotless, unblemished, undefiled. In *fig.* senses.

c **1430** LYDG. *Min. Poems* 79 The kyng of hevene blis; That.. Into a virgyns wombe immaculate Descendid. *c* **1460** in *Pol. Rel. & L. Poems* 81 Heyle towre of Dauid & vyrgyn immaculat! **1491** CAXTON *Vitas Patr.* I. li. (W. de W. 1495) 107 b, To haue kepte my soule Inmaculate and undefoylled. **1548** HALL *Chron., Hen. VII* 56 Their counsayll infected and corrupted the kynges clene and immaculate conscience. **1653** H. MORE *Conject. Cabbal.* (1713) 235 This Life is pure and immaculate Love, and this Love is God. **1781** GIBBON *Decl. & F.* xxiii. (1869) I. 653 The exercise of their sacred functions requires an immaculate purity. **1850** MRS. JAMESON *Leg. Monast. Ord.* (1863) 180 Convinced of his wife's immaculate purity.

† **b.** Constr. *from*. *Obs.*

1579 FULKE *Heskin's Parl.* 373 As they were imaculate from faults of their bodies, so he.. was immaculate from sins. **1790** GIBBON *Misc. Wks.* (1814) III. 507 His chastity was immaculate from sin or scandal.

c. ***Immaculate Conception***, the conception of the Virgin Mary, as held to have been free from the taint of original sin: in 1854 declared to be an article of faith of the Roman Church.

1687 BURNET *Trav.* i. (1750) 31 The Dominicans.. were .. obliged to assert, that she was born in Original Sin.. By this the Dominicans began to lose Ground extremely in the Minds of the People, who were strongly prepossess'd in favour of the immaculate Conception. **1782** PRIESTLEY *Corrupt. Chr.* I. IV. 380 The university.. declared for the immaculate conception. **1861** STANLEY *East. Ch.* viii. (1869) 264. **1871** FREEMAN *Norm. Conq.* IV. xviii. 137 The feast of the Conception—not yet declared to be immaculate—of our Lady.

d. ***immaculate lamb***, applied to Christ, after L. *agnus immaculatus* (Gr. ἀμνὸς ἄμωμος), 1 Pet. i. 19.

c **1450** *Cov. Myst.* (Shaks. Soc.) 272 This immaculat lombe that I xal ȝow ȝeve Is.. bothe God and man. **1526** *Pilgr. Perf.* (W. de W. 1531) 10 The immaculate lambe Jesu Chryst, the sone of God. **1772** FLETCHER *Logica Genev.* 209 The personal righteousness of the immaculate Lamb of God. **1858** NEALE tr. *Bernard de M.* 388 He, Lamb Immaculate.

2. Free from fault of flaw. (Chiefly in negative or ironical use.)

1832 W. IRVING *Alhambra* II. 147 The words of the immaculate Fredegonda. **1856** DOVE *Logic Chr. Faith* I. i. §2. 48 The Sceptical philosophy is by no means so immaculate. **1863** BRIGHT *Sp. Amer.* 26 Mar., You are not immaculate and.. your wisdom.. is not absolutely perfect.

b. Of manuscripts or printed books: Absolutely free from textual errors.

1841 MYERS *Cath. Th.* III. xiii. 49 They [the Jews] believed.. that all the manuscripts of their Law were immaculate, and the same to a letter. **1862** BURTON *Bk. Hunter* (1863) 65 Editions which claim a sort of canonization as immaculate, as for instance the Virgil of Didot and the Horace of Foulis.

3. In literal senses: **a.** Spotlessly clean or neat.

1735 POPE *Donne Sat.* IV. 253 A white-glov'd Chaplain.. in immac'late trim, Neatness itself impertinent in him. **1853** J. BROWN *Horæ Subs.* Ser. I. (1882) 169 Then out to parade ..in proper trim, pipe-clay immaculate. **1856** MRS. STOWE *Dred* I. iv. 52 Every plait of her immaculate cap.

b. *Nat. Hist.* Without coloured spots or marks; unspotted.

1797 BEWICK *Brit. Birds* (1847) I. 54 He describes the male bird to be of an immaculate white. **1828** STARKE *Elem. Nat. Hist.* II. 198 Abdomen..with spots and angulated bands of brown and white; legs immaculate. **1847** HARDY in *Proc. Berw. Nat. Club* II. No. 5. 236 Thorax narrowed towards the base, immaculate.

Hence **i'mmaculately** *adv.*, spotlessly, stainlessly, faultlessly.

a **1711** KEN *Hymnarium* Poet. Wks. 1721 II. 4 Thou art God alone, Thy Nature is immaculately pure. **1870** DISRAELI *Lothair* lvii, Those cheeks usually so immaculately fair.

i'mmaculateness. [f. prec. + -NESS.] The quality of being immaculate.

1641 J. JACKSON *True Evang. T.* II. 103 The immaculatenesse of the Lambe. *a* **1843** in Southey *Comm.-pl. Bk.* Ser. II. (1849) 374 They set themselves against S. Thomas Aquinas, taking advantage of his unpopular doctrine respecting the immaculateness. **1869** *Athenæum* 1 May 597/2 Mr. Lee..struggles hard to prove the immaculateness of his client.

†**immacu'lation.** *Obs. rare.* [f. IMMACULATE *a.*: see -ATION, and cf. med.L. *immaculātio.*] Immaculate condition.

1609 W. M. *Man in Moone* (Percy Soc.) 47 Beautie sitteth enthronized on her browes..immaculation on her necke.

†**i'mmailed,** *a. Obs. rare.* [f. IM-[1] + MAIL *sb.* + -ED.] Clad in mail; mailed.

1613–16 W. BROWNE *Brit. Past.* II. iv, Instructed swarmes Of men immayl'd.

†**imma'licious,** *a. Obs. rare.* [f. IM-[2] + MALICIOUS.] Not malicious; having no evil intent.

1662 PETTY *Taxes* 63 When the executors of them [penal laws] keep them hid until a fault be done, and then shew them terrible to the poor immalicious offender.

immalleable (ɪ'mælɪ:əb(ə)l, ɪmm-), *a. rare.* [f. IM-[2] + MALLEABLE.] Not malleable; incapable of being hammered out; unyielding (*to* force).

1675 BOYLE *Mech. Orig. Corrosiveness* Exp. xi. 24 It [aqua-fortis] quickly frets the parts assunder, and reduces it [tin] to an immalleable substance. **1682** *Mem. Sir E. Godfrey* 79 (T.) How immalleable does it render their stony natures to the force of all humane impressions. **1876** JEVONS *Logic Prim.* 19 When it cannot be so hammered out, it might be called immalleable; but..we generally call such a piece of metal brittle.

immanacle (ɪ'mænək(ə)l, ɪmm-), *v. rare.* [f. IM-[1] + MANACLE.] *trans.* To put manacles on; to handcuff; to fetter.

1634 MILTON *Comus* 665 Thou canst not touch the freedom of my mind..although this corporal rind Thou hast immanacled. **1810** F. DUDLEY *Amoroso* I. 45 He found her on the floor..bleeding and immanacled.

imma'nation. *rare.* [f. IM-[1], after EMANATION.] A flowing or entering in.

a **1834** LAMB *Let. to Coleridge* (L.), A quick immanation of continuous fantasies.

immane (ɪ'meɪn), *a. arch.* [ad. L. *immānis* monstrous, huge, savage, f. *im-* (IM-[2]) + *mānus* hand.]

1. Monstrous in size or strength; huge, vast, enormous, tremendous.

1615 CHAPMAN *Odyss.* ix. 268 A man in shape immane, and monsterous. **1679** EVELYN *Sylva* xvi. (ed. 3) 71 What immane difference then is there between the twenty fourth of Feb. and commencement of March? *a* **1734** NORTH *Lives* I. 101 An immane conceit of himself and of his own worth. **1835** HOGG in *Fraser's Mag.* XI. 516 So wild, unearthly, and immane.

2. Monstrous in character; inhumanly cruel or savage.

1602 FULBECKE *2nd Pt. Parall.* 38 To cutte his bodie in peeces..is a thing verie immane. **1644** BULWER *Chiron.* 12 The immane cruelty of Hieron, the Tyrant of that City. *c* **1860** O. W. HOLMES in *Pages fr. Old Vol. Life* (1891) 44 That immane and nefandous Burke-and-Hare business.

Hence **i'mmanely** *adv.*, hugely, monstrously, inhumanly; **i'mmaneness** (Bailey vol. II, 1727).

1612 R. SHELDON *Serm. St. Martin's* 27 Christ.. mercilesly hoysed vp, immanely pitched down with the crosse. **1670** MILTON *Hist. Eng.* I. (1851) 23 A man.. Valiant, Liberal, and fair of Aspect, but immanely Cruell.

immanence ('ɪmənəns). [f. IMMANENT *a.*: see -ENCE.] The fact or condition of being immanent; indwelling. Also *attrib.*, as **immanence philosophy**, a theory evolved in Germany at the end of the nineteenth century that reality exists only through being immanent in conscious minds.

1816 COLERIDGE *Lay Serm.* 341 Its state of immanence.. is reason and religion. **1847** LEWES *Hist. Philos.* (1867) II. 106 Bruno anticipated Spinoza in his conception of the immanence of the Deity. **1883** EDERSHEIM *Life Jesus* (ed. 6) II. 521 Conscious immanence in Him [Christ], and of His Word in us are the indispensable conditions of our privileges. **1901** BALDWIN *Dict. Philos. & Psychol.* I. 520/2 The immanence-philosophy (philosophy of the immediately given or science of pure experience) is the doctrine of a group of recent German thinkers. **1931** W. R. B. GIBSON tr. *Husserl's Ideas* II. ii. 133 Apart from perception, we find a variety of intentional experiences which essentially exclude the real immanence of their intentional objects. **1953** D. H. FREEMAN tr. *Dooyeweerd's New Critique Theoret. Thought* I. I. i. 112 It appears, that also modern phenomenology and Humanistic existentialism move in the paths of immanence-philosophy. **1970** D. M. LEVIN *Reason & Evidence in Husserl's Phenomenology* i. 16 If we suppose that the absence of spatial profiles could be a sufficient condition for immanence, then it would seem that we should have to consider mathematical entities and axioms as immanent objects.

immanency ('ɪmənənsɪ). [f. as prec.: see -ENCY.] The quality of being immanent; indwellingness.

1659 PEARSON *Creed* 170 The immanency and inherency of this power in Jesus. **1866** *Reader* No. 170. 318/1 The immanency and perfect unity of the two. **1886** *Westm. Rev.* Oct. 469 Christ..never reflected on transcendency and immanency.

immanent ('ɪmənənt), *a.* [ad. late L. *immanēnt-em*, pres. pple. of *immanēre*, f. *im-* (IM-[1]) + *manēre* to dwell, remain. Cf. F. *immanent* (14th c.).]

1. Indwelling, inherent; actually present or abiding *in*; remaining within.

In recent philosophy applied to the Deity regarded as permanently pervading and sustaining the universe, as distinguished from the notion of an external *transcendent* creator or ruler.

immanent principle (with Kant), a principle limited to the realm of experience: opposed to ***transcendental principle***.

1535 LYNDESAY *Satyre* 3460 Quhen our foirfather fell, Drawing vs all, in his loynis immanent, Captive from gloir. **1610** T. HIGGONS *Serm. Pauls Crosse* (1611) 13 He hath an immanent loue dwelling in him. **1637** GILLESPIE *Eng. Pop. Cerem.* Ep. B ij, That we may forget to distinguish betwixt evills immanent and evills imminent. **1659** PEARSON *Creed* (1741) 86 The power of miracles cannot be conceived as immanent or inhering in him. **1836** *Blackw. Mag.* XXXIX. 454 The man Whose form enshrouding immanent Deity Mourned from the cradle to the cursed tree! **1858** J. MARTINEAU *Stud. Chr.* 310 They have not cared to recognize it [the external world] as the shrine of immanent Deity. **1898** J. R. ILLINGWORTH *Divine Immanence* iii. 71 It remains then that we..conceive of God as at once transcending and immanent in nature.

2. ***immanent act*** (***action***): an act which is performed entirely within the mind of the subject, and produces no external effect; opposed to a *transient* or *transitive* act. Now *rare*.

This distinction, formulated in Scholastic philosophy, is the connexion in which the word most freq. occurred during the 17th and 18th centuries.

1613 PURCHAS *Pilgrimage* (1614) 5 The workes of God, which are either inward and immanent, or outward and transient. **1677** HALE *Prim. Orig. Man.* I. i. 28 The internal and immanent Faculties and Acts of the reasonable Soul.. are Intellect and Will. **1785** REID *Intell. Powers* II. xiv. (1803) I. 306 Logicians distinguish two kinds of operations of the mind; the first kind produces no effect without the mind, the last does. The first they call immanent acts; the second transitive. **1836–7** SIR W. HAMILTON *Metaph.* (1870) II. xxv. 118 A cognition is an immanent act of mind. **1847** DE QUINCEY *Milton v. Southey & Landor* Wks. XII. 177 In metaphysical language, the moral of an epos or a drama should be immanent, not transient..it should be vitally distributed through the whole organisation of the tree, not gathered or secreted into a sort of red berry..pendent at the end of its boughs.

Hence '**immanently** *adv.*, in immanent manner.

a **1711** KEN *Hymnarium* Poet. Wks. 1721 II. 73 Immanently will'd Within thy glorious self the Fiat pass'd.

imma'nental, *a.* [f. prec. + -AL[1].] Of or pertaining to the immanence of the Deity. Also, of or pertaining to philosophical immanence.

1885 J. MARTINEAU *Types Eth. Th.* (1886) I. I. ii. 119 The mysteries of the Immanental Metaphysics. **1897** W. M. URBAN *Hist. Princ. Suff. Reason* i. 8 The postulate of an immanental logic..becomes a permanent element. **1909** —— *Valuation* i. 9 The immanental reference..is a present state, referring, not beyond the present state, but to something more deeply implicit. **1920** A. S. PRINGLE-PATTISON *Idea of God* (ed. 2) 219 This lower pantheism..is common in the popular cults of the East, where the immanental unity of the divine is little more than the idea of a teeming nature. **1930** C. J. WRIGHT *Miracle in Hist.* 214 Theism can only abide with the recognition of the immanental activity of God in His universe. **1955** *Scottish Jrnl. Theol.* VIII. 88 This process is illustrated in religions which tend towards cosmic pantheism, impersonal fatalism, Platonic idealism, immanental piety, rigorous legalism, and ego-centric eudaemonism.

immanentism ('ɪmənəntɪz(ə)m). [f. IMMANENT *a.* + -ISM.] Belief in immanence, esp. the immanence of the Deity. So '**immanentist** *a.*, holding or characterized by this belief; also as *sb.*, one who believes in the immanence of the Deity.

1907 *Hibbert Jrnl.* July 919 Immanentism..explains away rather than explains that irrational fact of experience which we call evil. **1916** C. C. MARTINDALE *Life Mgr. R. H. Benson* II. 392 To this Immanentist school would thus belong St. Teresa, Dame Juliana of Norwich,..and Francis de Sales. **1918** M. D. PETRE *Modernism* x. 207 He has been charged with immanentism. **1930** *Times Lit. Suppl.* 14 Aug. 648/2 Mr. Wright stands for a modern, liberalizing and immanentist theology. **1931** *Ibid.* 22 Oct. 812/2 The pure phenomenology which resolves Being into Becoming by a sheer immanentism. **1945** *Mind* LIV. 275 Immanence and transcendence are logical complementaries, and..few thinkers can long afford to remain mere immanentists or mere transcendentists. **1952** *Mind* LXI. 102 Aristotle criticised Platonic doctrine, attacking the theory of Ideas from the 'immanentist' standpoint. **1965** *Rev. Eng. Stud.* XVI. 94 Mr. Miller speaks of the feeling that God is near at hand as God's 'immanence'... The Victorian age was notoriously a period in which immanentist theologies were fashionable.

i'mmanifest, *a. rare.* [f. IM-[2] + MANIFEST. Cf. OF. *immanifeste.*] Not manifest or evident.

1646 SIR T. BROWNE *Pseud. Ep.* VI. vi. 294 A time not much unlike that which was before time, immanifest and unknowne. **1674** BOYLE *Nat. & Preternat. State Bodies* 3 If the Body were under any violence, 'twas exercis'd by usual, but often immanifest Agents. **1789** T. TAYLOR *Proclus* II. 115. **1840** J. H. NEWMAN *Lett.* (1891) II. 316 The suppressed premiss is not immanifest.

Hence **i'mmanifestness.**

1822 T. TAYLOR *Apuleius* 276 The immanifestness of the art by which they were made.

†**i'mmanity.** *Obs.* [ad. L. *immānitās*, f. *immānis* IMMANE. Cf. F. *immanité* (16th c.).] The quality of being immane.

1. Hugeness; monstrosity, enormity.

1604 CAWDREY *Table Alph.*, *Immanitie*, beastlie crueltie, or hugenesse and greatnes. **1663** COWLEY *Ess. Verse & Prose, Liberty* (1688) 81 If the immanity of so many Vices had not been covered and disguised. **1667** POOLE *Dial. betw. Protest. & Papist* (1735) 45 The Immanity of their Blasphemies against God.

2. Monstrous cruelty; atrocious savagery.

1557 NORTH tr. *Gueuara's Diall Pr.* 115a/1 To shewe more their immanitie..they dranke the bloude of him that was lately alyue. **1563–87** FOXE *A. & M.* (1684) III. 649 Not to be accounted inhumanity, but rather immanity and beastly cruelty. *a* **1619** FOTHERBY *Atheom.* II. ii. §6 (1622) 207 Those notable immanities, which Dolabella exercised, vpon the body of Trebonius. **1699** BENTLEY *Phal.* xvi. 512 Phalaris the Tyrant came to that degree of Cruelty and Immanity, that he devour'd sucking Children.

†**immansuete,** *a. Obs. rare*$^{-0}$. [ad. L. *immansuētus*: see IM-[2] and MANSUETE.] 'Ungentle, untractable, outragious, wilde' (Blount 1656).

imman'tation. [ad. med.L. *immantātiōn-em*, n. of action from *immantāre* to clothe with a mantle, f. *mantum* mantle.] The investiture of a newly-elected pope with the *mantum* or mantle.

1871 *Academy* 15 Dec. 562/2 Some other ceremonial rites ..associated by custom with the 'tractatio', namely, the change of name, the adoration, and the 'immantation'.

immantle (ɪ'mænt(ə)l, ɪmm-), *v.* Also 7 **em-**, 9 **en-**. [f. IM-[1] + MANTLE.]

1. *trans.* To cover or enwrap with, or as with, a mantle. Chiefly *fig.*

1601 HOLLAND *Pliny* I. 1 Vnder the pourprise and bending cope whereof [heauen], all things are emmanteled and couered. *c* **1620** T. ROBINSON *Mary Magd.* 425 From top to toe, she was immanteled With purest Lawne. **1626** AILESBURY *Passion Serm.* 27 The Sunne..is immantled with a miraculous eclipse. **1719** LONDON & WISE *Compl. Gard.* 37 The verdant Foliage..Immant'ling the laden Branches. **1850** TENNYSON *In Mem.* lxxxix, Immantled in ambrosial dark. **1881** W. WILKINS *Songs of Study* 40 The calm that enmantles thine head.

†**2.** To place round as a fortification. (Cf. *dismantle.*) *Obs. rare.*

1601 HOLLAND *Pliny* II. 345 The walls that he caused to be built and emmanteled about other towns.

i'mmanuable, *a. Obs.* [f. IM-[2] + MANUABLE.] Unmanageable, incapable of being controlled.

1608 TOPSELL *Serpents* (1658) 735 When a horned Serpent hath bitten a man or beast..he falleth mad, his eyes grow dim, and his nerves immanuable.

i'mmarble, *v. rare.* [f. IM-[1] + MARBLE *sb.* Cf. EMMARBLE.] *trans.* To convert into marble; to make cold, hard, or immovable, as marble. Hence **immarbled** *ppl. a.*

1642 VICARS *God in Mount* 17 Such was their..immarbled impudence. **1839** BAILEY *Festus* (1854) 170 The immarbled madness of this orb.

†**immar'cescence.** *Obs.*$^{-0}$ [f. L. *immarcēsc-ĕre* (see next) + -ENCE.] 'Unfadingness, incorruptibleness' (Phillips, 1658).

immarcescible (ɪmɑ:'sɛsɪb(ə)l), *a.* Now *rare*. Also erron. 6–9 **-cessible**, (7 **-able**). [ad. late L. *immarcēscibilis*, f. *im-* (IM-[2]) + *marcēscĕre*, *marcēre* to fade, wither.] Unfading; incorruptible, imperishable; esp. in ***immarcescible crown*** (***of glory***).

(*Immarcescibilis corona* 'unfading garland' occurs in Paulinus Nolanus (*a* 431 A.D.) *Carm.* 15. The Vulgate has *hereditas immarcescibilis*, *1 Pet.* i. 4; *corona incorrupta*, *1 Cor.* ix. 24.)

1542 BECON *Pathw. Prayer* xlviii. R vj, The immarcessible [*ed.* 1543 vncorruptible] crowne of glory. **1548–9** (Mar.) *Bk. Com. Prayer, Form consecr. Bishops*, Ye may receyue the immarcessible [1662 never-fading] croune of glory. **1640** HOWELL *Dodona's Gr.* (1645) 168 Palms of Victory and immarcessible ghirlands of glory and triumph to all eternity. **1654** VILVAIN *Theorem. Theol.* Suppl. 238 Man was made

immortal or immarcescible, and fel from it by sin. **1708** *Addr. fr. Jersey* in *Lond. Gaz.* No. 4453/1 May he reward your Piety..with an immarcessible Crown of Glory. **1858** E. CASWALL *Masque Mary* 54 Children of Mary's care, and like herself of bloom and fragrance immarcessible.

Hence **immar'cescibly** *adv.*, unfadingly; **immar'cescibleness**, imperishableness.

1652 BP. HALL *Invis. World* III. xii, A crown.. immarcessibly eternal, a crown of righteousness. **1727** BAILEY vol. II, *Immarcessibleness*, never fading Nature.

immarginate (ɪ'mɑːdʒɪnət, ɪmm-), *a. Entom.* and *Bot.* [f. IM-² + MARGINATE.] Having no distinct or separate margin.

1826 in KIRBY & SP. *Entomol* IV. 327. **1880** GRAY *Struct. Bot.* (ed. 6) 416/1 *Immarginate*, not margined or bordered. **1881** SPRUCE in *Jrnl. Bot.* X. No. 217. 15 Papillose, immarginate, sharp-pointed leaves.

†**i'mmartial,** *a. Obs. rare.* [f. IM-² + MARTIAL.] Not martial; unwarlike.

c **1611** CHAPMAN *Iliad* VII. 206 Assay not me like one Yong and immartiall. **1615** —— *Odyss.* ix. 638 To oppose their least Against a man immartial, and a guest.

†**i'mmask,** *v. Obs. rare.* [f. IM-¹ + MASK *sb.* or *v.* Also INMASK.] *trans.* To cover as with a mask; to disguise.

1596 SHAKS. *1 Hen. IV*, I. ii. 201, I haue Cases of Buckram for the nonce, to immaske our noted outward garments.

†**i'mmatchable,** *a. Obs.* [f. IM-² + MATCHABLE.] That cannot be matched; unmatchable.

1596 DRAYTON *Legends, T. Cromwell* IV. 346 Men in those times immatchable for wit. **1630** *R. Johnson's Kingd. & Commw.* 198 For the store of shipping they are also immatchable.

†**i'mmatchless,** *a. Obs. rare.* [f. IM-¹ + MATCHLESS, by confusion with prec.] Matchless.

1595 MARKHAM *Sir R. Grinvile, To the fayrest* ix, Thou great Soveraigne of the earth, Onelie immatchlesse Monarchesse of harts. **1609** ARMIN *Maids of More-Cl.* (1880) 118 Go and returne as Paris did from Greece, With that immatchles Helen.

immaterial (ɪmə'tɪərɪəl), *a.* (*sb.*) Also 5 -iell, 6–7 -iall, (6 in-). [ad. med.L. *immateriālis*, f. *im-* (IM-²) + *materiālis* MATERIAL *a.* In 1398, prob. a. F. *immatériel* (14th c.).]

1. Not material; not consisting of matter; incorporeal; spiritual.

1398 TREVISA *Barth. De P.R.* I. (1495) 3 The contemplacyon of the heuenly Ierarchyes immaterielles. **1527** ANDREW *Brunswyke's Distyll. Waters* A j, That the corruptyble shall be made incorruptible, and to make the materyall inmateryall. **1570** BILLINGSLEY *Euclid* I. def. i. 1 Number is more simple and pure then is magnitude, and also immateriall. **1641** WILKINS *Mercury* xix. (1707) 78 That strange immaterial Power of the Loadstone. **1748** HARTLEY *Observ. Man* II. i. 31 If God be not an immaterial Being, then Matter may be the Cause of all the Motions in the Material World. **1830** LYELL *Princ. Geol.* I. 76 Demons, ghosts, witches, and other immaterial and supernatural agents.

b. *pl.* as *sb.*: Things that are non-material.

1661 GLANVILL *Van. Dogm.* vii. §2. 67 Thus more perfect apprehenders misconceive Immaterials: Our imaginations paint Souls and Angels in as dissimilar a resemblance. **1682** SIR T. BROWNE *Chr. Mor.* III. §14 Lodge immaterials in thy head: ascend unto invisibles. **1730** W. HARTE *Ess. Satire* 32 As well might Nothing bind Immensity, Or passive Matter Immaterials see.

2. Having little substance; flimsy, slight. *rare.*

1606 SHAKS. *Tr. & Cr.* V. i. 35 Thou idle, immateriall skiene of Sleyd silke!

†**3.** Not pertinent to the matter in hand. *Obs.*

1598 J. DICKENSON *Greene in Conc.* (1878) 162 Had I intituled this discourse, A Looking Glasse, the Metaphor had not been wholly immateriall. **1632** LITHGOW *Trav.* x. 488 Your absurd pretence: Your immateriall proofes.

4. Of no essential consequence; unimportant.

Johnson says 'This sense has crept into the conversation and writings of barbarians; but ought to be utterly rejected': it is, however, the opposite of *material* in the sense of 'important' found from 1528 onwards.

1698 FRYER *Acc. E. India & P.* 77 After some immaterial Discourse they returned to their Tents. **1748** HARTLEY *Observ. Man* II ii. 155 Small immaterial Variations excepted. **1804** W. TENNANT *Ind. Recreat.* (ed. 2) II. 213 Only employed..for coarse purposes, where colour and appearances are totally immaterial. **1893** CHITTY in *Law Times Rep.* LXVIII. 431/2 The question of notice becomes immaterial after my finding that there was no agreement.

Hence **imma'terially** *adv.*; **imma'terialness**.

1646 SIR T. BROWNE *Pseud. Ep.* III. vii. 119 For the visible species of things strike not our senses immater[i]ally. **1727** BAILEY vol. II, *Immaterialness*, immateriality.

immaterialism (ɪmə'tɪərɪəlɪz(ə)m). [f. prec. + -ISM, after *materialism.*]

1. The doctrine that matter does not exist in itself as a substance or cause, but that all things have existence only as the ideas or perceptions of a mind.

1713 BERKELEY *Hylas & Phil.* III. Wks. 1871 I. 352 You tell me indeed of a repugnancy between the Mosaic history and Immaterialism. **1777** J. BERINGTON (*title*) Immaterialism Delineated, or a view of the First Principles of Things. **1862** F. HALL *Hindu Philos. Syst.* 237 Berkeley maintains, that objects of sense are only ideas, they having no existence in themselves and apart from perception. This is immaterialism.

2. *nonce-use.* = IMMATERIALITY 1 b.

1824 BYRON *Juan* XVI. cxiv, For immaterialism's a serious matter; So that even those whose faith is the most great In souls immortal, shun them tête-à-tête.

immaterialist (ɪmə'tɪərɪəlɪst). [f. as prec. + -IST.] One who holds the doctrine of immaterialism.

1724 SWIFT *Let. to Ld. Carteret* 3 Sept., Dr. George Berkeley..going to England very young..became the founder of a sect there called the Immaterialists. **1822–34** *Good's Study Med.* (ed. 4) III. 34 The metaphysical immaterialists of modern times freely admit that the Mind has No Place of existence. *a* **1829** J. YOUNG *Lect. Intell. Philos.* xxix. (1835) 290 Hartley himself was a decided immaterialist.

immateriality (ɪmətɪərɪ'ælɪtɪ). [f. IMMATERIAL + -ITY.]

1. The quality or character of being immaterial or not of the nature of matter:

a. said of forms of energy, or of the conceptions of pure mathematics.

1570 DEE *Math. Pref.* 19 The purity, simplicitie, and Immateriality, of our Principall Science of Magnitude. **1653** H. MORE *Conject. Cabbal.* (1662) 130 We may be assured, that Immateriality was the work of the First Day, a Monad or Unite being so express a signification of the nature thereof. **1814** SHELLEY *Deism* Pr. Wks. 1888 I. 321 Light, electricity, and magnetism..seem to possess equal claims with thought to the unmeaning distinction of immateriality. **1863** TYNDALL *Heat* ii. §22 (1870) 27 The experiment.. which really proved the immateriality of heat.

b. said of spiritual beings or essences.

a **1652** J. SMITH *Sel. Disc.* iv. 86 A demonstration of the soul's immateriality. **1678** CUDWORTH *Intell. Syst.* I. i. §22. 21 He [Pythagoras] asserted the Immortality of the Soul, and consequently its Immateriality. **1710** BERKELEY *Princ. Hum. Knowl.* Pref., Of the existence and immateriality of God. **1859** SMILES *Self-Help* iii. (1860) 66 Speculations as to the immateriality and immortality of the soul.

c. Slightness, flimsiness. *rare.*

1886 STEVENSON *Dr. Jekyll* 109 The trembling immateriality, the mist-like transience, of this seemingly so solid body in which we walk attired.

2. An immaterial thing, existence, or essence.

1847–8 H. MILLER *First Impr.* xiv. (1857) 229 After originating these buoyant immaterialities, projected them upon the broad current of time.

3. The quality of being unessential or unimportant.

Mod. The immaterialitiy of the consideration.

immaterialize (ɪmə'tɪərɪəlaɪz), *v.* [f. IMMATERIAL + -IZE.] *trans.* To render immaterial or incorporeal.

Hence **imma'terialized** *ppl. a.*

1661 GLANVILL *Van. Dogm.* xii. 109 Though possibly Assiduity in the most fixed cogitation be no trouble or pain to immaterializ'd spirits. *a* **1711** KEN *Hymns Festiv.* Poet. Wks. 1721 I. 401 Simon..His Body had subdu'd, That he his Flesh might immaterialize. **1856** *Tait's Mag.* XXIII. 656 Our theologians immaterialize Heaven too much.

†**imma'teriate,** *a. Obs.* [f. IM-² + MATERIATE.] = IMMATERIAL.

1626 BACON *Sylva* §114–5 (Observ.) After long Inquiry of Things, Immerse in Matter, to interpose some Subject which is Immateriate or lesse Materiate. **1653** H. MORE *Conject. Cabbal.* (1662) 75 Philo makes all Immateriate Beings to be created in this first day.

imma'triculate, *v. rare.* [f. IM-¹ + MATRICULATE *v.* Cf. F. *immatriculer.*] *trans.* To matriculate. In quot. 1814 *fig.*

1718 BYROM *Jrnl. & Lit. Rem.* (1854) I. i. 39 Mr. Piper was immatriculated here yesterday. **1764** *Mem. G. Psalmanazar* 222, I was not indeed immatriculated. **1814** *Sporting Mag.* XLIV. 66 It would be an acquisition..if this species [of deer] were immatriculated in our parks.

So **immatricu'lation,** 'matriculation, especially in a German university' (Funk, 1893).

1891 FLÜGEL *German-Eng. Dict.*, *Immatriculation*, (im)matriculation.

immature (ɪmə'tjʊə(r)), *a.* [ad. L. *immātūrus* untimely, unripe, f. *im-* (IM-²) + *mātūrus* MATURE.]

1. Occurring before its time; untimely, premature. (Almost always said of death.) *Obs.* or *arch.*

1548 HALL *Chron., Rich. III* 48b, Ye sodein and immature death of his wife. **1621** BURTON *Anat. Mel.* I. ii. IV. vii. (1651) 163 Prince Henries immature death. **1726** LEONI *Alberti's Archit.* I. 7/1 The whole Frame..falls into dangerous Distempers and immature old Age. **1858** HAWTHORNE *Fr. & It. Jrnls.* I. 215 The design being prevented by his immature death.

2. Not mature; not arrived at the perfect or complete state; unripe. **a.** Of fruits. Now *rare.*

1599 A. M. tr. *Gabelhouer's Bk. Physicke* 5/2 Water of immature wallenuttes. **1692** TRYON *Good House-w.* xiv. (ed. 2) 104 Many other Fruits are gathered and eaten whilst they are immature. **1727** BRADLEY *Fam. Dict.* s.v. *Cider*, Cider.. made of green immature Fruit.

b. Of other things, in respect of physical growth.

1641 G. SANDYS *Paraphr. Song Sol.* VIII. iii, We have a Sister immature. **1667** MILTON *P.L.* VII. 277 The Earth..in the Womb as yet Of Waters, Embryon immature involv'd. **1845** DARWIN *Voy. Nat.* ix. (1879) 201 The young cells.. contain quite immature polypi. **1880** GÜNTHER *Fishes* 176 Immature males do not differ externally from the old female.

c. Of things immaterial.

[**1635** J. HAYWARD tr. *Biondi's Banish'd Virg.* 76 This project..being..immature in the fertile soyle of his braine-plot.] **1665** BOYLE *Occas. Refl.* IV. iv. 71 The green and immature Essays of early Writers. **1701** ROWE *Amb. Step-Moth.* V. i, As yet the Secret Is immature. **1823** DE QUINCEY *Lett. Educ.* v. (1860) 111 Presented to the immaturest student. **1851** D. WILSON *Preh. Ann.* (1863) II. IV. viii. 451 In these immature centuries.

d. *Ophthalm.* Of a progressive cataract: characterized by a marked but incomplete opacity, with the lens usually swollen and its superficial layers still largely transparent.

1850 B. E. BRODHURST *Of Crystalline Lens & Cataract* 57 The terms mature, and immature,..are well adapted to express the stage of progress at which any particular cataract may have arrived. **1904** L. W. FOX *Dis. Eye* xii. 311 The special difficulties..in removing a cataract before maturity are that parts of the cortex, clear at the time of operation, will remain adherent to the capsule of the lens, and later undergo the process of opacification... Some operators, however, operate on immature cataracts, washing out the tenacious material with a syringe. **1970** A. H. KEENEY *Ocular Exam.* ix. 143/2 Early (incipient or immature) cataracts cause changes in refraction..marked by increasing myopia at an age when refraction should either be stable or show increasing hyperopia.

e. Of a soil: not having a fully developed profile. Of a soil profile or its parts: not fully developed.

1926 C. F. MARBUT in Tansley & Chipp *Study of Vegetation* vii. 139 In every region there are hillside soils as well as alluvial and colluvial deposits in which the texture profile will not be well developed because of the short time during which the material has been subjected to the forces of soil development. Such soils are immature or have imperfectly developed profiles. **1927** N. M. COMBER *Introd. Sci. Study Soil* xiii. 139 Glinka divides all soils in the first instance into two groups:—(1) Immature or endodynamomorphic soils, in which the processes of formation have not had full play..(2) Mature or ektodynamomorphic soils, in which the processes of formation have had full play. **1963** D. W. & E. E. HUMPHRIES tr. *Termier's Erosion & Sedimentation* vi. 138 When erosion is greater than the rate of formation, the soil is immature. **1968** R. W. FAIRBRIDGE *Encycl. Geomorphol.* 273 These soils (lithosols) are immature and without soil profiles.

immatured (ɪmə'tjʊəd), *ppl. a.* [f. IM-² + MATURED.] Not matured; left immature.

1803 LEYDEN *Scenes Infancy* IV. 358 The Seeds of genius immatur'd by haste. **1835** CHALMERS *Nat. Theol.* I. II. iii. 263 The immatured buddings of animal and vegetable formation.

immaturely (ɪmə'tjʊəlɪ), *adv.* [f. prec. + -LY².] In an immature way; in an unripe condition; prematurely.

1620 VENNER *Via Recta* (1650) 291 They immaturely die by some acute disease. **1736** LEDIARD *Life Marlborough* II. 31 This high Opinion..appear'd to be too rashly and immaturely formed. **1751** WATSON in *Phil. Trans.* XLVII. 177 This prevents the falling of the fruit immaturely. **1887** A. DE VERE *Ess.* I. 237 Though he died young, he did not die immaturely.

imma'tureness. [f. as prec. + -NESS.] The quality of being immature; immaturity.

1665 BOYLE *Occas. Refl.* Ded., The Immatureness of some of them would..make many think they come forth Unseasonably.

immaturity (ɪmə'tjʊərɪtɪ). [ad. L. *immātūritāt-em* untimely haste (Cicero), unripeness (Suetonius), f. *immātūrus* IMMATURE.] The quality or condition of being immature.

†**1.** Prematureness; untimeliness. *Obs.*

c **1540** tr. *Pol. Verg. Eng. Hist.* (Camden) I. 199 Hee was prevented..bie the immaturitie of his deathe, skarcelie having accomplished the yᵗ. yeare of his reigne. **1670** G. H. *Hist. Cardinals* I. II. 43 His words (though spoke with some kind of hast and immaturity).

2. Unripeness; imperfect or incomplete state.

1606 HOLLAND *Sueton.* 54 The immaturity of young espoused wives. **1651** GATAKER *Whitaker* in *Fuller's Abel Rediv.* (1867) II. 112 His immaturity of years. **1764** HARMER *Observ.* V. ii. 54 When the grapes shall not be gathered, as they were wont before to be, in a state of immaturity. **1845** STOCQUELER *Handbk. Brit. India* (1854) 102 The men and women who chiefly compose the society leave home in their immaturity. **1877** DOWDEN *Shaks. Prim.* vi. 82 The poem of later date..exhibits far less immaturity.

b. with *pl.* An immature plant, production, etc.

1651 BIGGS *New Disp.* ¶77 Their own cruelties, infamy, immaturities. **1850** H. MILLER *Footpr. Creat.* x. (1874) 181 That the rich vegetation of the Coal Measures had been.. composed of magnificent immaturities of the vegetable kingdom.

†**i'mmaze,** *v. Obs. rare.* [f. IM-¹ + MAZE.] *trans.* To involve as in a maze or labyrinth.

1631 BRATHWAIT *Eng. Gentlew.* (1641) 294 That love-sicke girle, who became so immazed in loves error. **1647** WARD *Simp. Cobler* 22 The..Planters..had immazed themselves in the most intolerable confusions and inextricable thraldomes.

immeability (ɪmiːə'bɪlɪtɪ). [f. IM-² + L. *meābilis* passable (f. *meāre* to pass): see -BILITY.] Inability to pass or flow (through a channel).

1731 ARBUTHNOT *Aliments* vi. §29 (R.) The viscidity and immeability of the matter impacted in them. **1752** WATSON in *Phil. Trans.* 350 That the immediate cause..is the immeability of the nervous fluid through the nerves.

immeasurability (ɪˌmɛʒ(j)ʊərəˈbɪlɪtɪ). [f. next + -ITY.] = IMMEASURABLENESS.

1824 DE QUINCEY *Analects fr. Richter* Wks. XIV. 139 In sight of this immeasurability of life. **1882** *Fraser's Mag.* XXV. 490 A sense of unfitness, bred perhaps of the immeasurability of the surroundings.

immeasurable (ɪˈmɛʒ(j)ʊərəb(ə)l, ɪmm-), *a.* Also 5 ynmes-, ymeas-, 6 immes-, 7 immes. [f. IM-² + MEASURABLE *a.* Cf. 16th c. F. *immésurable.*] Not measurable; that cannot be measured; immense.

1440 J. SHIRLEY *Dethe K. James* (1818) 25 His tirannye ynmesurable, without pite or mercy. *a* **1532** MORE *Confut. Tindale* Wks. 590/1 Tyl he..for theire immesurable outrage ..finallye reiecteth and refuseth them. **1667** MILTON *P.L.* VII. 211 The vast immeasurable Abyss. *c* **1790** COWPER *Notes Milton's P.L.* I. 50 The immeasurable distance to which these apostate spirits had fallen from God. **1838** DICKENS *Nich. Nick.* xiii, To the immeasurable delight and admiration of all the readers thereof. **1869** J. MARTINEAU *Ess.* II. 40 Geology makes me familiar with immeasurable times.

i'mmeasurableness. [f. prec. + -NESS.] The quality or condition of being immeasurable; incapability of being measured.

1561 T. NORTON *Calvin's Inst.* IV. 77 Nor doeth [he] with immeasurablenesse of correction breake the bonde of felowship. **1628** GAULE *Pract. The.* (1629) 130. **1876** GEO. ELIOT *Dan. Der.* v. xxxv, Novelty gives immeasurableness to fear.

i'mmeasurably, *adv.* [f. as prec. + -LY².] To an immeasurable extent or degree; beyond measure; immensely, vastly.

1631 GOUGE *God's Arrows* I. §43. 71 Anger is mis-ordered, when it is..immeasurably moved. **1760** H. WALPOLE in *Four C. Eng. Lett.* 267 The Anthem..being immeasurably tedious. **1878** HUXLEY *Physiogr.* 67 The process is immeasurably slower.

immeasured (ɪˈmɛʒ(j)ʊəd, ɪmm-), *a.* [f. IM-² + MEASURED. Cf. F. *immesuré.*] Not measured; unmeasured; immense, vast.

1590 SPENSER *F.Q.* II. x. 8 Such dreadful wights, As far exceeded men in their immeasurd mights. **1622** DRAYTON *Poly-olb.* xix. (1748) 334 Four such immeasur'd pools, philosophers agree, I' th' four parts of the world undoubtedly to be. *a* **1745** BROOME *Poems, Death* (R.), A stream, that..glides To meet eternity's immeasur'd tides! **1828** MOIR in *Blackw. Mag.* XXIII. 294 The forests and valleys..Within the immeasured circumference.

†**imme'ation.** *Obs. rare.* [n. of action f. L. *immeāre* to pass into, to enter, f. *im-* (IM-¹) + L. *meāre* to go, pass.] A passing in; entrance, ingoing.

1675 J. J[ONES] *Brit. Ch.* (1678) 574 These mutual immeations, or Christ in us, and we in Christ.

†**imme'chanical,** *a. Obs.* [f. IM-² + MECHANICAL *a.*]

1. Of phenomena, etc.: Not mechanical; not of physical or material nature, origin, etc.

1715 CHEYNE *Philos. Princ. Relig.* I. (1716) 43 The Cause of the Motion of this subtill Fluid, which is the Cause of Gravity, is in itself Immechanical. **1748** HARTLEY *Observ. Man* I. i. 33 Some suppose this Effect to be immechanical, and to arise from the immediate Agency of God. **1796** W. MARSHALL *W. England* I. 176 The crooks being cleared, by hand, in a somewhat immechanical manner.

2. Of persons: Without mechanical or practical knowledge or skill; untechnical.

1737 BRACKEN *Farriery Impr.* (1757) II. 87 A very illiterate Way of speaking, and exceeding immechanical. **1751** EARL ORRERY *Remarks Swift* (1752) 91 Fine strokes of just satyr on the wild and immechanical enquiries of the philosophers..of that age.

Hence **imme'chanically** *adv.* (Craig, 1847.)

†**i'mmechanism.** *Obs.* [f. IM-² + MECHANISM: cf. prec.] Non-mechanical property; inertia.

1740 CHEYNE *Regimen* 45 However their Acts may be suspended, sopited, or destroyed by gross Matter, and the Im-mechanism of Bodies.

immediacy (ɪˈmiːdɪəsɪ). [f. next: see -ACY.]

1. a. The quality or condition of being immediate; freedom from intermediate or intervening agency; direct relation or connexion; directness.

1605 SHAKS. *Lear* V. iii. 65 He..Bore the Commission of my place and person, The which immediacie may well stand vp, And call it selfe your Brother. **1658** GURNALL *Chr. in Arm.* verse 14. xiv. §1 (1669) 55/1 There is the immediacy of his providence. **1660** S. FISHER *Rusticks Alarm* Wks. 431 The immediacy..of those first Scriptures from God to us. **1875** H. JAMES *R. Hudson* i. 10 Questions..bearing with varying degrees of immediacy on the subject. **1885** STEVENSON in *Contemp. Rev.* Apr. 549 A strange freshness and immediacy of address to the public mind.

b. *Logic* and *Philos.* (See IMMEDIATE 2 b.)

a **1834** COLERIDGE *Lit. Rem.* (1838) III. 315 Spiritual verities, or truths of reason *respective ad realia*..are differenced from the conceptions of the understanding by the immediacy [*printed* immediatcy] of the knowledge. **1836-7** SIR W. HAMILTON *Metaph.* xxiii. (1859) II. 78 If Reid did not maintain this immediacy of perception..he would at once be forced to admit one or other of the unitarian conclusions of materialism or idealism. **1864** BOWEN *Logic* viii. 265 The reduction of a Hypothetical Judgment to a Categorical shows very clearly the Immediacy of the reasoning in what is called a Hypothetical Syllogism. **1874** W. WALLACE *Logic of Hegel* §12. 16 The *a priori* aspect or immediacy of thought, where there is a mediation, not made by anything external but by a reflection into itself, is another name for universality.

2. The condition of being the immediate lord or vassal: see IMMEDIATE 1 b.

1762 tr. *Busching's Syst. Geog.* IV. 446 Varel lost its immediacy, or independency, and stands at present under the superiority of Oldenburg. *Ibid.* V. 299 The Emperors Charles IV. and Wenceslaus engaged to maintain it in its immediacy on the Empire. **1818-48** HALLAM *Mid. Ages* (1872) I. 23 *note*, The immediacy of vassals in times so ancient is open to much controversy.

3. The condition of being immediate in time (see IMMEDIATE 4).

1856 W. A. BUTLER *Hist. Anc. Philos.* I. 453 The sage will ..ensure his certainty in the immediacy of enjoyment, carefully rejecting all intensive suggestions of past or future. **1898** *Chr. World* 17 Mar. 15/4 On a subordinate point like the immediacy of the Second Coming.

4. *pl.* Immediate needs.

1923 H. G. WELLS *Men Like Gods* III. iv. 288 The old things and the foul things, customs, delusions, habits,.. base immediacies, triumph over us!

immediate (ɪˈmiːdɪət), *a.* (*sb.*, *adv.*) Also 5 immeadiat, 5-7 ymmediat(e, 6 y-, imediat(e, immediat; 5-6 inmediate. [ad. med.L. *immediātus* (the adv. *immediātē* was frequent in the feudal sense: see IMMEDIATELY), f. *im-* (IM-²) + *mediātus* MEDIATE. Cf. F. *immédiat* (Cotgr.).]

A. *adj.* **1.** Said of a person or thing in its relation to another: That has no intermediary or intervening member, medium, or agent; that is in actual contact or direct personal relation.

a. Of a person.

1548 HALL *Chron., Hen. VIII* 48 b, The Dolphyn desyred ..[them] to be two of his immediat aides. **1686** in Keble *Life Bp. Wilson* i. (1863) 27 Nothing unbecoming an immediate servant and follower of Christ. **1781** GIBBON *Decl. & F.* xvii. II. 51 The emperor conferred the rank of Illustrious on seven of his more immediate servants. **1822** LAMB *Elia* Ser. II. *Confess. Drunkard*, My next more immediate companions.

b. *spec.* In *Feudal* language, said of the relation between two persons one of whom holds of the other directly, as in ***immediate lord, tenant, tenure***; also elliptically = Holding directly of the sovereign or lord paramount, *spec.* in Germany, of the Emperor.

1543-4 *Act 35 Hen. VIII*, c. 4 The chiefe lorde or lordes immediate, of whom suche..houses be holden. **1548** HALL *Chron., Rich. III* 51 Ready to serve..their natural and immediate lord Jasper erle of Pembrooke. **1614** SELDEN *Titles Hon.* 229 To be free from either a mediat, or immediat Tenure of him. **1660** *Trial Regic.* 10 The King is immediate from God. **1818-48** HALLAM *Mid. Ages* (1872) II. 92 The inferior nobility..having now become immediate, abused that independence. **1863** H. COX *Instit.* I. iii. 11 The King's immediate tenants were bound to attend his court.

c. Of a thing.

1563 W. FULKE *Meteors* (1640) 44 All men have taken them as immediate miracles, without any naturall means or cause. **1597** HOOKER *Eccl. Pol.* v. lvii. §6 The true immediate cause why baptisme..is necessary. *a* **1628** PRESTON *Effectual Faith* (1631) 51 He doth it by an immediate voice, by which he speaketh immediately to our spirits. *a* **1763** SHENSTONE *Ess.* 95 Objects..less calculated to strike the immediate eye. *a* **1862** BUCKLE *Misc. Wks.* (1872) I. 4 The immediate object of all art is either pleasure or utility.

2. a. Of a relation or action between two things: Acting or existing without any intervening medium or agency; involving actual contact or direct relation: opposed to *mediate* and *remote*.

1533 MORE *Apol.* Wks. 893/1 As longe as the Prelates pretend that their authoritye is so hygh and so immediate of God, that the people are bounde to obeye theim. **1625** in Rymer *Foedera* (1726) XVIII. 240/2 By Our owne ymmediate commaunde and for Our owne ymmediate Service. **1709** BERKELEY *Th. Vision* §59 Bodies operating on our organs by an immediate application. **1712** W. ROGERS *Voy.* 26 We are desirous of an immediate Traffick with them. **1864** BOWEN *Logic* i. 2 Each [Intuition] is *immediate*, —that is, it does not come through the intervention of any other state of mind. *Ibid.* ii. 34 They rest upon the immediate testimony of consciousness.

b. *spec.* ***immediate inference*** (*Logic*): an inference drawn from a single premiss and therefore arrived at without the intervention of a middle term; sometimes called 'interpretative inference', because it renders explicit what was implicit in the original proposition. ***immediate knowledge*** (*Philos.*): knowledge of self-evident truth; intuitive knowledge, as distinguished from that arrived at by means of demonstration or proof.

1624 DE LAUNE tr. *Du Moulin's Logick* 166 Of immediate propositions..some are immediate in regard of the subject, and others are immediate in regard of the cause. **1843** MILL *Logic* Introd. §5 Whatever knowledge has been acquired otherwise than by immediate inference. **1866** FOWLER *Deduct. Logic* ii. (1869) 73 Of Immediate Inferences the most important forms are Oppositions, Conversions, Permutations. **1874** WALLACE *Logic of Hegel* §24. 45 When we compare the different forms of knowledge with one another, the first of them, immediate or intuitive knowledge, may perhaps seem the finest, noblest and most appropriate. *Ibid.* §64. 108 The difference between philosophy and the asseverations of immediate knowledge rather centres in the exclusive position which immediate knowledge takes up and in its opposition to philosophy.

3. a. Having no person, thing, or space intervening, in place, order, or succession; standing or coming nearest or next; proximate, nearest, next; close, near. In reference to place often used loosely of a distance which is treated as of no account.

1602 SHAKS. *Ham.* I. ii. 109 You are the most immediate to our throne. **1611** HEYWOOD *Gold. Age* III. Wks. 1874 III. 49, I am Iupiter, King Saturnes sonne, immediate heire to Crete. **1800** KNOX & JEBB *Corr.* I. 3 Immediate neighbourhood I have none, save one family. **1866** ROGERS *Agric. & Prices* I. xxiii. 598 In immediate proximity to the mines. **1888** J. INGLIS *Tent Life Tigerland* 183 This took us both away from the immediate vicinity of the plot. *Mod.* I know no one of the name in the immediate neighbourhood. I have made it known to my immediate neighbours on each side.

b. ***immediate constituent*** (Linguistics): a grammatical subdivision of a sentence, phrase, or word, which can sometimes be analysed into further such constituents; in the case of a word, so as to reveal its morphological structure. (Opp. *ultimate constituent*.)

1933 L. BLOOMFIELD *Lang.* xiii. 210 The principle of immediate constituents will lead us..to class a form like *gentlemanly* not as a compound word, but as a derived secondary word, since the immediate constituents are the bound form *-ly* and the underlying word *gentleman*. **1943** *Language* XIX. 79 In separating immediate constituents, one attempts to disturb as little as possible the relationship between the meaning of the parts of the combination and the meaning of the combination as a whole. **1958** A. A. HILL *Introd. Ling. Struct.* viii. 127 Immediate constituent analysis is the process of segmenting a complex construction by successive single cuts. **1961** R. B. LONG *Sentence & its Parts* 491 Immediate Constituents. This term is often used of what are here called simply components. **1963** F. G. LOUNSBURY in J. A. Fishman *Readings Sociol. of Lang.* (1968) 45 Linguistic analysis proceeds by the method of 'immediate constituents', i.e., by division of a larger unit into two immediate constituents... In the end, a systematic pursuit of a different set of policies in immediate-constituent division would, in fact, produce a different grammar of the same language. **1963** J. LYONS *Structural Semantics* ii. 14 It has sometimes been assumed that all the sentences of a particular language can be analysed syntactically in terms of the immediate-constituent, or phrase-structure model. **1964** R. H. ROBINS *Gen. Ling.* vi. 240 The processes of immediate constituent analysis..by which the longest and most complex sentences can be reduced by analysis to successive expansions of one of a few simple basic sentence structures. **1967** F. P. DINNEEN *Introd. Gen. Ling.* ix. 263 In analyzing the sentence *Poor John ran away*, Bloomfield found that it contains five morphemes: *poor, John, ran, a-*, and *way*. They are also the ultimate constituents of the sentence, but the immediate constituents are *Poor John* and *ran away*. **1971** P. GAENG *Introd. Princ. Lang.* v. 91 The sentence *The rebellious students walked to the dean's office* consists of two main parts —two immediate constituents—namely, *the rebellious students* and *walked to the dean's office*. Each part, in turn, consists of two parts, and each of these consists of two parts, until by cutting the sentence into smaller and smaller groupings, we reach the level of single words or morphemes, the ultimate constituents.

4. a. Of time: Present or next adjacent; of things: Pertaining to the time current or instant.

1605 BACON *Adv. Learn.* I. ii. § 3 Those of the later or immediate times. *a* **1641** BP. MOUNTAGU *Acts & Mon.* (1642) 172 Equall with, or immediate unto the Apostolicall times. **1771** *Junius Lett.* xlix. 257 If the event had not disappointed the immediate schemes of the closet. **1845** M. PATTISON *Ess.* (1889) I. 2 Our own immediate age is confessedly rich in works of the historical class. **1879** FROUDE *Cæsar* xv. 252 The immediate future was thus assured.

b. Occurring, accomplished, or taking effect without delay or lapse of time; done at once; instant.

1568 GRAFTON *Chron.* II. 1362 There was immediat order geven to Edward Lorde Clynton..with all expedicion to prepare himselfe. **1586** A. DAY *Eng. Secretary* I. (1625) 89, I did..at the first use some delaies in imediate dispatch of the thing. **1603** SHAKS. *Meas. for M.* V. i. 378 Immediate sentence then, and sequent death, Is all the grace I beg. **1667** MILTON *P.L.* VII. 176 Immediate are the Acts of God, more swift Then time or motion. **1748** SMOLLETT *Rod. Rand.* viii, Some loose silver for our immediate expenses. **1774** C. J. PHIPPS *Voy. N. Pole* 64 The hopes we had..entertained of the immediate effect of an Easterly wind in clearing the bay. **1855** MACAULAY *Hist. Eng.* IV. 596 That he must either consent to an immediate surrender, or prepare for an immediate assault. *Mod.* An immediate reply will oblige.

c. ***immediate access store***: in a computer, a store whose access time is negligible compared with the time required for other operations.

1960 G. N. LANCE *Numerical Methods for High Speed Computers* i. 5 The memory..can usually be separated into distinct parts. Firstly, there is the high-speed or immediate access store. **1964** F. L. WESTWATER *Electronic Computers* iv. 79 Magnetic core stores are often referred to as immediate access stores (I.A.S.).

5. That directly touches or concerns a person or thing; having a direct bearing.

1725 DE FOE *Voy. round World* (1840) 324 They began to think of their more immediate work. **1791** BURKE *App. Whigs* Wks. 1842 I. 515 Their own more immediate and popular rights and privileges. **1816** BYRON *Ch. Har.* III. lxxvi, But this is not my theme; and I return To that which is immediate. **1833** BROWNING *Pauline* 340, I rudely shaped my life To my immediate wants. **1878** BOSW. SMITH *Carthage* 28 She allowed her colonies to trade only so far as suited her own immediate interests. **1896** DK. ARGYLL *Philos. Belief* 78 Any mere arrangement which is destitute of obvious or immediate utility.

†**6.** Uninterrupted in course; direct. *Obs. rare.*

1634 Sir T. Herbert *Trav.* 4 Teneriffa is thought to equall..in height..any other Land in the World, allowing its immediate ascent from the Ocean. *Ibid.* 59 The immediate ascent is twenty two foot high.

†**B.** *sb.* (*pl.*) Immediate acts or communications. *Obs.*

1645 Rutherford *Tryal & Tri. Faith* (1845) 382 Christ is speedy, and swift as a roe;..especially in his immediates.

†**C.** as *adv.* (In some cases perh. L. *immediātē*, as formerly in Fr. and It.) Immediately. *Obs.*

1532 More *Confut. Tindale* Wks. 692/1 Hys other fower chapters immediate before. **1601** R. Johnson *Kingd. & Commw.* (1603) 135 Lord of those which hold of him immediate. **1626** Bacon *Sylva* §366 Bodies enflamed, wholly, and Immediate.

immediately (ɪˈmiːdɪətlɪ), *adv.* Forms: see IMMEDIATE. [f. prec., or rather L. *immediāt-us* + -LY². it is actually found before the adj. as the Eng. equivalent of L. *immediātē*.] In an immediate way; the reverse of *mediately*.

1. Without intermediary, intervening agency, or medium; by direct agency; in direct or proximate connexion or relation; so as to concern, interest, or affect directly, or intimately; directly.

1412–20 Lydg. *Chron. Troy* v. xxxvi. (MS. Digby 230) If. 178/2 Fro Troye were sente lettres..To pallamides immediatly directe. **1530** Baynton in *Palsgr.* Introd. 12 The frenche men borowe theyr wordes immediatly of the latines. **1592** West *1st Pt. Symbol.* §35 An Obligation by contract is gotten either mediately or immediatlie. Immediatlie by a mans owne proper contract. **1598** Hakluyt *Voy.* I. 64 Canow..was immediatly vnder the dominion of the Tartars. **1662** Stillingfl. *Orig. Sacr.* II. vii. §8 All positive precepts comming immediately from God. **1690** Locke *Hum. Und.* II. xxiii. (1695) 160 We immediately by our Senses perceive in Fire its Heat and Colour. **1691** Ray *Creation* II. (1704) 428 Insects useful to Mankind, if not immediately, yet mediately. **1788** Priestley *Lect. Hist.* III. xv. 121 An article of information the most immediately necessary to a reader of history. **1843** Mill *Logic* I. iii. §4 Feelings..immediately occasioned by bodily states. **1864** Bowen *Logic* i. 2 Not..immediately, but only through the medium of what is called a Concept.

b. Of feudal tenure (and *transf.*): see IMMEDIATE 1 b.

1488–9 *Act 4 Hen. VII*, c. 17 The lord of whom suche..hereditamentes be holden ymmediatly. **1574** tr. *Littleton's Tenures* 31 a, The Abbot shal holde immediatlye the same tenementes by knightes service of the Lorde of his grauntour. **1647** N. Bacon *Disc. Govt. Eng.* I. xvi. (1739) 32 All the Lands in England became mediately or immediately holden of the Crown. *c* **1670** Hobbes *Dial. Com. Laws* (1681) 202 Homage done to the King immediately. **1863** H. Cox *Instit.* III. ii. 604 All subjects' lands were held mediately or immediately under grants from him [the king].

2. With no person, thing, or distance, intervening in time, space, order, or succession; next or just (preceding or following, before or after); closely; proximately; directly.

1466 *Mann. & Househ. Exp.* (Roxb.) 168, vj. dayes immedyatly folwyng. **1476** Sir J. Paston in *P. Lett.* No. 771 III. 153 Inmediately afftr the dycesse off the Duke. **1552** Abp. Hamilton *Catech.* (1884) 46 The wordis that ar writtin immediatly afore the text. **1668** Culpepper & Cole *Barthol. Anatomy* I. xvii. 45 The Liver, under which it [right kidney] rests immediately. **1672** Cave *Prim. Chr.* III. iv. (1673) 351 So immediately opposite to the whole tenor of the Gospel. **1774** C. J. Phipps *Voy. N. Pole* 61 The ice immediately about the ships. **1853** Jerdan *Autobiog.* IV. 63, I lost my immediately elder brother. **1860** Tyndall *Glac.* I. ix. 63 Another peal was heard immediately afterwards. *Mod.* Fire broke out in the premises immediately adjoining.

3. Without any delay or lapse of time; instantly, directly, straightway; at once.

1420 *Proclam.* in Rymer *Foedera* (1709) 917/1 Sho shall take and have in the Roialme of France, immediately from the tyme of oure Dethe, Dower, to the Somme of Twenty Mill Francs Yerly. ? *a* **1500** *Chester Pl.* xiii. 107 He bade me goe immeadiatlye. **1590** Shaks. *Mids. N.* II. ii. 156 Either death or you lle finde immediately. **1711** Addison *Spect.* No. 94 ⁋9 He had only dipped his Head into the Water, and immediately taken it out again. **1877** Watts *Fownes' Inorg. Chem.* (ed. 12) 213 A crystalline precipitate immediately forms.

b. as *conj.* (ellipt. for *immediately that*). The moment that; as soon as. Cf. DIRECTLY 6 b.

1839 Asa Gray *Lett.* I. 28 Immediately this was done I completed an arrangement with my publishers. **1856** *Q. Rev.* June 182 Immediately they came upon the ground, fourteen of them were netted. **1896** Welton *Manual of Logic* (ed. 2) II. iii. §90 The diagrams..should be self-interpreting immediately the principle on which they are constructed is understood.

immediateness (ɪˈmiːdɪətnɪs). [f. IMMEDIATE + -NESS.] The quality or condition of being immediate; immediacy; directness (of action, thought, relation, etc.); absolute (or in loose use, relative) proximity in time or place.

1633 Ames *Agst. Cerem.* II. 298 Let any man looke..and he shall finde, that (merit, necessitie, and immediatnesse set a part) significant Ceremonies are externall acts of religious worship. **1691–8** Norris *Pract. Disc.* (1711) III. 141 The immediateness, the inwardness of his Essential Presence and Union with the Soul. **1704** —— *Ideal World* II. v. 283 The immediateness of the perception. **1863** J. G. Murphy *Comm. Gen.* xli. 32 The certainty and immediateness of the event. **1882** Stevenson *New Arab. Nts.* (1884) 229 The immediateness of our peril.

†**immediˈation.** *Obs.* [f. IM-² + MEDIATION, after *immediate*.] Immediate or direct action, communication, etc. (The reverse of *mediation*.)

1569 J. Sanford tr. *Agrippa's Van. Artes* 22 b, Of Mediations, and Immediations. **1677** Gale *Crt. Gentiles* IV. 292 God workes al immediately, not only by the Immediation of his Virtue but also by the Immediation of his Essence.

immediatism (ɪˈmiːdɪətɪz(ə)m). [as next + -ISM.]

1. The principle or practice of immediate action; formerly, in *U.S. Hist.*, applied to the policy of the immediate abolition of slavery.

1835 H. G. Otis in *Liberator* V. 144 They [abolitionists] have enriched the nomenclature with a new word, *immediatism.* This..is the opposite of *gradualism*, another new coinage. **1880** O. Johnson *Garrison* 45 Mr. Garrison had learned the doctrine of immediatism from Dr. Beecher.

2. The quality of being immediate; immediateness, immediacy.

a **1825** D. Stewart cited by Worcester.

immediatist (ɪˈmiːdɪətɪst). [f. IMMEDIATE + -IST.] One who practises or advocates immediate action; spec. in *U.S. Hist.*, one who advocated the immediate abolition of slavery.

1835 H. G. Otis in *Life of W. L. Garrison* (1885) I. 500 [He (Otis)..denied that the Scriptures were anywhere opposed to slavery; repeated that Christ] 'was not an immediatist'. **1852** W. Goodell in *Slavery & Freedom* (1882) 424 Those who professed to be opposed to slavery, and..only deprecated the imprudent measures of the *immediatists.* **1888** F. H. Stoddard in *Andover Rev.* Oct., The gospel of the Immediatist,—work while the day lasts.

immediaˈtorial, *a.* [f. IM-² + MEDIATORIAL.] Not mediatorial.

1851 Robertson *Lect. Ep. Cor.* xxix. (1889) 272 We shall know Him, when the mediatorial has merged in the immediatorial.

immedicable (ɪˈmɛdɪkəb(ə)l), *a.* Also 6 ymed-. [ad. F. *immedicable* (Cotgr.) or L. *immedicābilis*, f. *im-* (IM-²) + *medicābilis* MEDICABLE.] Incapable of being healed, incurable, irremediable.

1596 R. L[inche] *Diella* i. (1877) 7 With fatall and ymedicable wound. **1660** Willsford *Scales Comm.* 100 Glutted with excesse, [they] become immedicable by those surfeits. **1744** Armstrong *Preserv. Health* II. 220 More immedicable ills. **1822–34** *Good's Study Med.* (ed. 4) IV. 107 A disease immedicable by the healing art.

b. *transf.* and *fig.*

1533 More *Answ. Poysoned Bk.* Wks. 1075/1 Through his immedicable malyce he fell of himselfe. **1645** Milton *Colast.* Wks. (1851) 359 For another perversnes, or immedicable disaffection. **1813** Coleridge *Lett.* (1895) 612 There remains an immedicable But. **1880** Swinburne *Study Shaks.* ii. 167 Immedicable scepticism of the spirit.

Hence **iˈmmedicableness**, incurableness; **iˈmmedicably** *adv.*, incurably.

1727 Bailey vol. II, *Immedicableness*, incurableness. **1867** P. Bayne in *Contemp. Rev.* Nov. 351 Madness, be its visions gay or gloomy, is immedicably sad.

immeˈdicinable, *a. rare.* [f. IM-² + MEDICINABLE.] Not medicinable; incurable.

1826 Mrs. Shelley *Last Man* II. 328 Fallen..from health to immedicinable disease.

Immelmann (ˈɪməlmæn). Also erron. Immelman. The name of F. *Immelmann* (1890–1916), a German fighter pilot, used alone or *attrib.* in ***Immelmann turn***, to designate an evasive manœuvre in the air. Also as *v. intr.*, to execute this manœuvre.

1917 B. K. Adams *Amer. Spirit* (1918) 27 Next I tried the so-called Immelman turn. **1918** J. M. Grider *War Birds* (1927) 206 As I half rolled on top of him, he half rolled too and when I did an Immelman, he turned to the right and forced me on the outside arc and gave his observer a good shot at me. **1919** *Conquest* Dec. 68/1 One of the most useful stunts employed during the war was the 'Immelman turn', its name being that of the aviator who introduced it. In this manœuvre the machine rears up suddenly, turns sideways over the vertical, and emerges in the opposite direction. **1923** W. T. Blake *Flying* 43 *Immelmann turn.* This manœuvre is more commonly termed a 'half-roll' in England. **1934** V. M. Yeates *Winged Victory* III. viii. 254 He could turn better than the Pfalz, and felt he was winning the duel. After its tail, round and round. It straightened and he fired but it immelmanned away. He went after it, but it dived away all out. **1942** *R.A.F. Jrnl.* 27 June 18 Three outside snap rolls, a flick at 110 m.p.h., a stall off an Immelman and a power inverted spin. **1952** J. Steinbeck *East of Eden* xiv. 131 It..made Immelmann turns..and flew over the field upside down. **1967** *Boston Sunday Herald* 14 May (Comic Section), Wow! A loop th' loop! How about a Immelmann turn?

immelodious (ɪmɪˈləʊdɪəs, ɪmm-), *a.* [f. IM-² + MELODIOUS.] Not melodious; unmelodious.

1601 Chester *Love's Mart.* xcix, My immelodious discord I vnfret. **1616** Drumm. of Hawth. *Sonn.*, *To his Lute*, When immelodious Winds but made thee move. **1652** Caryl *Exp. Job* xi. 3 Little birds..troublesome..with uncessant, immelodious chirpings. **1822–34** *Good's Study Med.* (ed. 4) I. 429 Immelodious Voice. **1892** *Illustr. Lond. News* 15 Oct. 474/2 Master who crown'st our immelodious days With flower of perfect speech.

iˈmmember, *v. rare.* [f. IM-¹ + MEMBER *sb.*] *trans.* To incorporate as a member.

1871 Tylor *Prim. Cult.* II. 188 Incorporated or immembered in things they cannot quit.

†**immeˈmor**, *a. Sc. Obs. rare.* Also **immemoir** (= -ōr). [ad. L. *immemor*, f. *im-* (IM-²) + *memor* mindful.] Unmindful, forgetful.

1535 Stewart *Cron. Scot.* II. 673 This king Malcolme..wes nocht immemor The greit kyndnes that gude Edward befoir Schew him. *Ibid.* 699 This king Edgair, of quhome I schew befoir, Of gratitude wald nocht be immemoir.

immemorable (ɪˈmɛmərəb(ə)l), *a.* [ad. L. *immemorābil-is*, f. *im-* (IM-²) + *memorābilis* MEMORABLE. Cf. 16th c. F. *immémorable*.]

1. Not memorable; not worthy of remembrance.

1552 Huloet, Immemorable, or vnworthy remembraunce, *immemorabilis.* **1616** Bullokar, *Immemorable*, not worthy to be remembered. **1768** *Woman of Honor* I. 222 Poor immemorable insignificants. *Ibid.* II. 109 Not one jot more immemorable. **1880** Disraeli *Endym.* I. xi. 87 An ancient, and in its time, even not immemorable home.

b. as *sb.*

1768 *Woman of Honor* I. 79 Contented with being one of those immemorables, or cyphers of high life.

†**2.** = IMMEMORIAL. *Obs.*

1665 J. Webb *Stone-Heng* (1725) 90 As to Age..they be of most immemorable Antiquity. **1796** Burney *Mem. Metastasio* III. 85 A right by immemorable prescription. *Ibid.* III. 161.

Hence **iˈmmemorableness**, 'unworthiness to be remembered' (Bailey vol. II, 1727).

†**iˈmmemorate**, *a. Obs.* In 5 ymmemorat. [ad. L. *immemorātus*, f. *im-* (IM-²) + *memorātus*, pa. pple. of *memorāre* to bring to mind, remind.] ?Unmindful. (Cf. IMMEMOR.)

c **1400** *Beryn* 2626 Soveren lord celestiall!..ymmemorat of lyes, Graunt me grace to morowe! so þat God be plesid, Make so myne answere.

immemorial (ɪmɪˈmɔərɪəl), *a.* [ad. med.L. *immemoriāl-is*, f. *im-* (IM-²) + *memoriālis* (Suetonius) MEMORIAL. Cf. F. *immémorial* (16th c. in Littré).] That is beyond memory or 'out of mind'; ancient beyond memory or record; extremely old.

1602 Fulbecke *Pandectes* iv. 19 In making title by prescription and continuance of time immemoriall. **1696** Whiston *Th. Earth* II. (1722) 124 Which..was the immemorial beginning of the Ancient Year long before the time of Moses. **1765** Blackstone *Comm.* I. Introd. 64 They receive their binding power, and the force of laws, by long and immemorial usage. **1847** Tennyson *Princ.* VII. 206 The moan of doves in immemorial elms. **1872** Wharton *Law-Lex.* (ed. 5), *Immemorial usage*, a practice which has existed time out of mind; custom; prescription.

Hence **immeˈmorialness** (Bailey vol. II, 1727).

immemorially (ɪmɪˈmɔərɪəlɪ), *adv.* [f. prec. + -LY².] In an immemorial manner; from time immemorial; 'time out of mind'; by immemorial prescription of usage.

1614 Selden *Titles Hon.* 38 Their own immemorially possest right. **1661** Boyle *Style of Script.* (1675) 99 The truth and authority of the Scriptures..hath been immemorially believed by the learned'st men in the world. **1769** Blackstone *Comm.* IV. xxxii. (1830) 404 This prerogative, being founded in mercy, and immemorially exercised by the crown. **1855** Milman *Lat. Chr.* IV. i. (1883) II. 164 Small, independent, and immemorially hostile tribes.

†**immeˈmorious**, *a. Obs. rare*⁻¹. [f. IM-² + MEMORIOUS.] Unmindful, forgetful.

1602 W. Bas *Sword & Buckler* C*, We..Of our owne birth haue immemorious beene.

immense (ɪˈmɛns), *a.* (*sb.*) Also 5 emense, (6 imminens), 7 imens. [a. F. *immense* (1360 in Godefroi) = It., Pg. *immenso*, Sp. *inmenso*, ad. L. *immensus* immeasurable, boundless, f. *im-* (IM-²) + *mensus*, pa. pple. of *metīrī* to measure.]

1. Unmeasured; so great that it has not been or cannot be measured; immeasurably large; of boundless extent; infinite. ? *Obs.*

1599 Daniel *Musoph.* (R.), That immense and boundless ocean Of nature's riches. **1640** Habington *Castara* III. (Arb.) 131 Great God! when I consider thee Omnipotent, Æternall, and imens. **1677** Gale *Crt. Gentiles* IV. 464 God [is] not circumscribed or defined to any space, but immense in his Being. **1736** Butler *Anal.* I. iii. 89 The material world appears to be in a manner boundless and immense. *a* **1770** Jortin *Serm.* (1771) VI. viii. 159 The Scripture represents the Goodness of God as immense.

2. Much beyond the ordinary measure or size; extremely great or large; vast, huge.

1490 Caxton *Eneydos* xxvi. 92 My teeres and emense wepynges. **1575** Laneham *Let.* (1871) 55 So imminens & profuse a charge of expens. **1660** F. Brooke tr. *Le Blanc's Trav.* 148 The immense Armies brought..by the Persian Kings against the Grecians. **1748** *Anson's Voy.* I. ix. 88 Those immense hills called the Andes. **1849** Macaulay *Hist. Eng.* vii. II. 252 The immense fine which the Court of King's Bench had imposed. **1895** Ld. Esher in *Law Times Rep.* LXXIII. 701/2 The statute..was minutely dissected at immense length.

b. of persons in relation to actions or qualities.

1631 Weever *Anc. Fun. Mon.* 798 He was..little of stature, but immense in wit and vnderstanding. *Mod.* He is an immense eater.

3. *slang.* Superlatively good, fine, splendid, etc.

1762 *Gentl. Mag.* 86/2 Here's cream—damn'd fine—immense—upon my word! **1869** Lowell *Lett.* II. 43 The poem turned out to be something immense, as the slang is nowadays. **1883** F. M. Crawford *Dr. Claudius* iii. (1892) 47 You look like a crown prince..Perfectly immense.

†**b.** as *adv.* Immensely. *Obs. slang.*

1754 Murphy *Gray's-Inn Jrnl.* No. 89 ¶25 An immense fine Woman. **1772** *Ann. Reg.* II. 191 A long while everything was *immense* great and *immense* little, *immense* handsome and *immense* ugly.

B. as *sb.* Immense, boundless, or vast extent; immensity.

1791 E. Darwin *Bot. Gard.* I. 258 Bade with cold streams the quick expansion stop, And sunk the immense of vapour to a drop. **1805** T. Lindley *Voy. Brasil* (1808) 40 The rear was brought up by..other troops, and an immense of rabble. **1829** Carlyle *Novalis* in *Misc.* (1869) II. 285 A kingdom of Devouring..a baleful Immense. **1872** Blackie *Lays Highl.* 37 Let others probe the immense of Possibles.

immensely (ɪˈmɛnslɪ), *adv.* [f. IMMENSE + -LY[2].] In an immense degree; immeasurably, infinitely; very greatly, vastly, hugely: in colloquial use often a hyperbolical intensive = exceedingly, to an extent which one does not presume to measure or limit.

1654 tr. *Martini's Conq. China* 108 They immensely augmented their Armies, by the access of the China's Souldiers. **1738** Swift *Pol. Conversat.* 82 She's immensely rich. *a* **1742** Bentley (J.), The void space of our system is immensely bigger than all its corporeal mass. **1746–7** Hervey *Medit.* (1818) 173 O ye Heavens, whose azure arches rise immensely high, and stretch immeasurably wide. **1860** Tyndall *Glac.* I. iii. 27 The chances of safety are immensely in his favour. **1886** Ruskin *Præterita* I. 241 Charles wrote that he was enjoying himself immensely.

immenseness (ɪˈmɛnsnɪs). [f. as prec. + -NESS.] The quality of being immense; immeasurableness, infinity; vastness, hugeness. Now usually expressed by IMMENSITY.

1610 Donne *Pseudo-Mart.* 185 The Immensnesse of this power averts me from beleeving it to bee just. **1633** T. Adams *Exp. 2 Peter* i. 17 The immenseness of the Deity. **1798** Pennant *Hindoostan* I. Introd. 2 To retain the immenseness of their knowledge.

†**iˈmmensible,** *a. Obs.* [a. F. *immensible* or ad. L. **immensibilis*, f. *im-* (IM-[2]) + *mens-*, ppl. stem of *metīrī* to measure: see -IBLE.] Immeasurable; immense.

1579 J. Jones *Preserv. Bodie & Soule* I. xlvi. 123 Almightie, Euerlasting, Immensible, and only wise God. **1630** *R. Johnson's Kingd. & Commw.* 19 Divided from either angle by so immensible a tract of Sea.

immensikoff (ɪˈmɛnsɪkɒf). ? *Obs.* [See quot. 1896.] Jocular name for a heavy overcoat.

1870 D. J. Kirwan *Palace & Hovel* xxxiv. 504 The chorus ..of a popular street and music-hall song, which every one is now humming in London..as follows: '..I fancy I'm a Toff; From top to toe I really think I looks—Immensekoff.' **1889** *Pall Mall Gaz.* 25 Sept. 6/1 Heavy swells clad in Immensikoffs, which is the slang term, I believe, for those very fine and large fur robes affected by men about town. **1896** Farmer & Henley *Slang* IV. 3/1 *Immensikoff*, a fur-lined overcoat. From the burden of a song, 'The Shoreditch Toff', sung (*c*1868) by the late Arthur Lloyd, who described himself as Immensikoff, and wore an upper garment heavily trimmed with fur. **1911** A. Bennett *Hilda Lessways* I. vii. 70 His white muffler and large overcoat (which Dayson called an 'immensikoff').

immensity (ɪˈmɛnsɪtɪ). In 5 -itee. [a. F. *immensité* (14th c. in Hatz.-Darm.) or ad. L. *immensitās*, n. of quality f. *immensus* IMMENSE.] The quality or condition of being immense.

1. Immeasurableness, boundlessness, infinity.

c **1450** *Mirour Saluacioun* 1384 He filled heven and erthe with his inmensitee. **1603** Holland *Plutarch's Mor.* 1033 Infinity and immensity of excesse and defect. **1630** Prynne *God no Impostor* 34 Whose vast immensities..doe farre transcend our..finite vnderstandings. **1662** Stillingfl. *Orig. Sacr.* III. ii. §10 It is repugnant to the immensity of God. **1690** Locke *Hum. Und.* II. xiii. §4 This Power of repeating, or doubling any Idea we have of any distance.. without being ever able to come to any stop or stint..is that which gives us the Idea of Immensity. **1803–6** Wordsw. *Intimations* viii, Thou, whose exterior semblance doth belie Thy Soul's immensity. **1874** Symonds *Sk. Italy & Gr.* (1898) I. i. 11 The universe..becomes important to them in its infinite immensity.

2. Vast magnitude; vastness, hugeness.

1652 A. Wilson in Benlowes *Theoph.* To Author, Her poor little Orb appears to be A very Point to their Immensitie. **1790** Castles in *Phil. Trans.* LXXX. 347 The immensity of their number. **1883** *Fortn. Rev.* May 613 The immensity of the disaster increased the intensity of the disgrace.

b. An immense quantity or deal.

1778 Mad. D'Arblay *Diary* 3 Aug., I have an immensity to write. **1834** Ht. Martineau *Farrers* vii. 116 They say that an immensity of money will be raised by this income tax. **1862** Carlyle *Fredk. Gt.* IX. viii. (1872) III. 135 Having drunk immensities of Hungary wine. **1888** Rye *Records* 99 *note*, A very slight expenditure of labour would save an immensity of searchers' time.

3. That which is immense. **a.** *absolutely*, Infinite being or existence; infinity; infinite space.

a **1631** Donne *Holy Sonn., Annunciat.* ii. (R.), Thou.. shutt'st in little room Immensity, cloister'd in thy dear womb. **1688** Prior *Ode Exod.* iii. 6 The mysterious gulf of vast immensity. **1695** Blackmore *Pr. Arth.* II. 598 Immensity is wrapt in Swadling Bands. **1753** Hanway *Trav.* (1762) I. IV. lvii. 262 Who fills immensity with his presence. **1843** Carlyle *Past & Pr.* IV. iii, This Worker.. has to..collect the monitions of Immensity. **1860** Tyndall *Glac.* II. i. 239 Immensity is filled with this music.

b. An (or the) immense extent *of* something; a thing of immense or unmeasured extent.

1794 Mathias *Purs. Lit.* (1798) 265 It's tendency is to the ocean, to which it pays it's last tribute, and is finally lost in that immensity. **1821** Byron *Cain* II. ii. 390 Did ye not tell me that..what I have seen, Yon blue immensity, is boundless? **1853** Kane *Grinnell Exp.* xlii. (1856) 382 This solid immensity of varied ice. **1879** F. Harrison *Choice Bks.* (1886) 3 A pathless immensity beyond our powers of vision or of reach.

c. *pl.* Beings or things that are immense or infinite.

1839 Bailey *Festus* xxii. (1848) 280 A spirit nobler..Than all these bright immensities. **1843** Carlyle *Past & Pr.* IV. iii, He who can and dare trust the heavenly Immensities, all earthly Localities are subject to him.

†**iˈmmensive,** *a. Obs.* [ad. obs. F. *immensif, -ive* (16th c. in Godef.), f. *immense* IMMENSE: see -IVE.] Immeasurable, immense.

1604 T. Wright *Passions* v. §4. 4. 195 Some drops of amabilitie..from the immensiue Ocean of thy bountie. **1622** Malynes *Anc. Law-Merch.* 266 When workes are clogged with immensiue charges in the beginning, it choketh the benefit euer after. **1635** Swan *Spec. M.* v. §2. (1643) 143 The Sunnes immensive heat. **1648** Herrick *Hesper.*, *To live merrily*, This immensive cup Of aromatike wine.

immensurable (ɪˈmɛnsjʊərəb(ə)l, -ʃər-), *a.* [a. F. *immensurable* (15th c. in Godef.), or ad. late L. *immensūrābilis* (5th c.), f. *im-* (IM-[2]) + *mensūrābilis* MENSURABLE.] Immeasurable.

1535 Stewart *Cron. Scot.* II. 426 In meit and drink, and sleip also wes he Immensurabill and out of temperance. **1612** W. Parkes *Curtaine-Dr.* (1876) 18 Exorbitant desire.. illimitlesse, and immensurable. **1714** Derham *Astro-Theol.* I. iii. (1715) 23 What an immensurable space is the Firmament. **1807** F. Buchanan *Journ. Mysore* III. 469 The rank of the different casts..the immensurable superiority of the Brahmans above the rest of mankind.

Hence **immensuraˈbility, iˈmmensurableness,** immensurable quality or condition.

1675 Sterry *Freedom Will* 41 We must attribute this immenseness, or immensurableness to Him. **1678** Phillips (ed. 4), *Immensurability*, a being uncapable to be measured.

†**iˈmmensurate,** *a. Obs.* [ad. late L. *immensūrāt-us* (5th c.), f. *im-* (IM-[2]) + *mensūrātus*, pa. pple. of *mensūrāre* to MEASURE.] Unmeasured, immense.

1654 W. Mountague *Devout Ess.* II. ix. §1. 168 An immensurate distance from it. **1720** Welton *Suffer. Son God* I. ii. 28 In Thy Immensurate and perfect Felicity. **1766** G. Canning *Anti-Lucretius* II. 117 Space immensurate.

†**immerˈcurial,** *a. Obs.* *rare*$^{-1}$. [f. IM-[2] + MERCURIAL.] Not mercurial, mobile or yielding.

1637 Pocklington *Altare Chr.* xxv. 148 Some of Gr[antham] and others of that Immercuriall wood, may be so knotty and sturdy, that if you come with your Herculean armes to twine and twist them..they will cracke in the bending like a gunne.

immerd (ɪˈmɜːd), *v. rare.* [ad. L. type **immerdāre*, f. *im-* (IM-[1]) + *merda* dung; cf. It. *immerdare*, F. *emmerder*.] *trans.* To bury in or cover with ordure.

1635 Quarles *Embl.* Ded., Let Dors delight to immerd themselves in dung. **1651** W. Ames *Saints Security* (1652) 33 Doe wee..see some eminent professor..immerd himselfe in the dung of worldly wickednesse. **1875** Browning *Aristoph. Apol.* 1660 Make a muckheap of a man, There.. he remains, Immortally immerded.

immerge (ɪˈmɜːdʒ, ɪmm-). *v.* Now *rare.* (Also erron. **emerge.**) [ad. L. *immergĕre* to dip, plunge, sink (into), immerse, f. *im-* (IM-[1]) + *mergĕre* to MERGE. Cf. F. *immerger*.]

1. *trans.* To dip, plunge, put under the surface of a liquid; to immerse.

1624 *Harington's Sch. Salerne* II. 37 The eyes are not only to be washed, but being open plainly, immerg'd. **1655** Fuller *Ch. Hist.* II. iv. §4 They pour not water upon the Heads of Infants, but immerge them in the Font. **1664** Power *Exp. Philos.* II. 107 The deeper you immerge the Tube, the higher still will the Quicksilver in the Tube rise. **1770** *Phil. Trans.* LX. 304 A second method of preserving birds is, by immerging them in spirits. **1828** Hutton *Course Math.* II. 271 Immerge it in boiling water.

†**b.** *fig.* To 'drown', 'submerge'. *Obs.*

1644 *Jus Populi* 34 The right of Fathers..is now emerged or made subordinate. **1765** *Meretriciad* 11 Nor let thy wit immerge thy reason too.

2. *transf.* and *fig.* To plunge into a state of action or thought, way of living, etc.; = IMMERSE *v.* 2.

1611 Speed *Hist. Gt. Brit.* IX. viii. (1632) 583 [They] immerge themselues and their abetters into bottomlesse seruitudes and distresses. **1750** Johnson *Rambler* No. 65 ¶7 We entangle ourselves in business, immerge ourselves in luxury. **1829** Landor *Imag. Conv.* Wks. 1846 II. 49/2 [He] would immerge his country for twenty years in the most calamitous war.

3. *intr.* (for *refl.*) To plunge or dip oneself in a liquid; to sink. Also *transf.* and *fig.*

1706 Baynard in Sir J. Floyer *Hot & Cold Bath* II. 226 They have recovered by immerging into Cold Water. **1747** Wesley *Prim. Physic* (1762) 76 Immerge up to the Breast in a warm Bath. **1779–81** Johnson *L.P.*, *Swift* Wks. III. 380 He was now immerging into political controversy. **1841** Emerson *Addr., Meth. Nature* Wks. (Bohn) II. 227 And then immerge again into the holy silence and eternity out of which as a man he arose.

†**b.** *spec.* of a celestial body: To enter the shadow of another in an eclipse, or to disappear behind another in an occultation; to sink below the horizon. *Obs.*

1704 J. Hodgson in *Phil. Trans.* XXV. 1638 At London she [the moon] immerg'd at 38 minutes past 5. **1775** R. Chandler *Trav. Asia Minor* (1825) I. 4 The lower half of the orb soon after immerged in the horizon. **1786–7** Bonnycastle *Astron.* x. 172 When the satellite immerges into, or emerges out of Jupiter's shadow.

†**c.** Of a title or estate: To become merged or absorbed in that of a superior, so as no longer to have separate existence; to MERGE. *Obs.*

1750 Carte *Hist. Eng.* II. 868 Most of the great nobility had been destroyed..the bulk of their estates immerging into the crown. **1752** *Ibid.* III. 552 Her son..to whom the title of Lennox upon its immerging in the crown, had been granted.

immergence (ɪˈmɜːdʒəns). [f. IMMERGE *v.* + -ENCE; cf. *emergence*.] The action of immerging, plunging, or sinking into anything.

1859 Todd *Cycl. Anat.* V. 99/1 The pancreatic duct..at the point of its immergence into the intestinal canal. **1878** F. Ferguson *Life Christ* II. x. 268 On our way to the immergence of the Jordan.

†**immergent,** *a.*[1] *Obs.* Erroneous spelling of EMERGENT, in sense 'Unexpectedly arising', 'urgent'.

1655 Fuller *Ch. Hist.* v. iii. §4 Used upon all extra-ordinary, and immergent cases. **1792** Washington *Lett.* Writ. 1891 XII. 248 On no occasion (unless very immergent ones).

iˈmmergent, *a.*[2] *rare.* [f. IM-[2] + MERGENT.] Not merging into something else.

1837 H. H. Wilson *Sánkhya Káriká* 46 A discrete principle is mergent; the undiscrete, immergent (indissoluble).

iˈmmerger. [f. IMMERGE *v.* + -ER[1].] One who or that which immerges or plunges into water, etc.; *spec.* a diving bird.

1890 in *Cent. Dict.*

†**iˈmmerit,** *sb. Obs.* [f. IM-[2] + MERIT: cf. L. *immeritus* undeserved.] Want of merit; demerit.

1628 Wither *Brit. Rememb.* I. 967 That Machivillian crew, who to endeare Their base immerits, fill the royal eare With tales. *a* **1641** Suckling (J.), My own immerit tell me it must not be for me. **1750** Warburton *Doctr. Grace* Wks. 1811 VIII. 406 The immerit of good Works.

†**iˈmmerit,** *v. Obs.* [Back-formation from next.] *trans.* Not to merit or deserve. Only in †**iˈmmeriting** *pres. pple.* and *ppl. a.*, undeserving.

1635 R. Carew in *Lismore Papers* (1888) Ser. II. III. 222 Those honorable fauours..vouthsafed vnto poore immeritinge me. **1659** *Lady Alimony* II. v. in Hazl. *Dodsley* XIV. 307 Perish'd by th' immeriting touch Of a misshapen boor! **1676** Baker in Rigaud *Corr. Sci. Men* (1841) II. 10 Immeriting so immense pains and favour from you.

†**iˈmmerited,** *ppl. a. Obs.* [f. IM-[2] + MERITED, after L. *immerit-us*, in sense 'undeserved'.] Unmerited, undeserved.

1600 W. Watson *Decacordon* (1602) 165 He is become so proud..since this immerited authority came vpon him. **1667** Waterhouse *Fire Lond.* 123 Upon view of his mercies immerited. *a* **1703** Burkitt *On N.T., Rom.* xi. 6 Put into this state by mere grace, and immerited favours.

†**immeriˈtorious,** *a. Obs.* [f. IM-[2] + MERITORIOUS] Not meritorious; undeserving.

1642 Vicars *God in Mount* 85 An unjust and immeritorious eulogie or elogie. **1753** *Ess. Celibacy* 81 It is therefore immeritorious..to place human perfection in a solemn and formal round of devotional exercises.

Hence **immeriˈtoriously** *adv.*, undeservingly.

1675 O. Walker, etc. *Paraph. St. Paul* 99 All easily, and immeritoriously, stand in..the truth.

†**iˈmmeritous,** *a. Obs.* *rare*$^{-1}$. [f. L. *immerit-us*, that has not deserved, undeserving + -OUS.] Undeserving, without merit.

1645 Milton *Colast.* Wks. (1851) 372 A frothy, immeritous and undeserving discours.

†**iˈmmersable,** *a. Obs.* *rare*$^{-0}$. [ad. L. *immersābilis* 'that cannot be sunk' (Horace), f. *im-* (IM-[2]) + **mersābilis*, f. *mersāre* to dip in, immerse. Cf. IMMERSIBLE[1].] Incapable of being drowned.

[**1623** Cockeram II, Not to bee Drowned, *immeasurable*.] **1676** Coles, *Immersable*, which cannot be drowned, uncapable of immersion. **1730–6** Bailey (folio), *Immersable*, that cannot be dipped, etc.

immersal (ɪˈmɜːsəl). *rare.* [f. IMMERSE *v.* + -AL.] = IMMERSION 2.

1901 Greenough & Kittredge *Words* 98 Theological and philosophical studies are also pursued with vigor, and this means an immersal in Latin.

immerse (ɪˈmɜːs), *v.* [f. L. *immers-*, ppl. stem of *immergĕre* to dip, plunge (see IMMERGE).]

1. *trans.* To dip or plunge into a liquid; to put overhead in water, etc.; *spec.* to baptize by immersion.

1613 CAWDREY *Table Alph.* (ed. 3), *Immersed*, dipped, or plunged. **1684–5** BOYLE *Min. Waters* 83 Before the Water we immers'd it in was near boyling hot. **1772** HUTTON *Bridges* 65 The thickness of the pier when dry; and..the thickness when the pier is immersed in water. **1805** *Med. Jrnl.* XIV. 573 The other index..lies in the tube of the spirit-thermometer immersed in the alcohol. **1879** *Cassell's Techn. Educ.* IV. 354/2 Effected by immersing the meat in a solution of salt or pickle.

b. *transf.* To plunge into, to bury, imbed, involve, or include in other things.

1695 WOODWARD *Nat. Hist. Earth* (1702) 10 Heterogeneous Bodies, which I found immersed and included in the Mass of this Sandstone. **1700** DRYDEN *Theodore & Hon.* 89 He stood, More than a mile immers'd within the wood. **1745** tr. *Columella's Husb.* IV. xxx, Cuttings, a foot and a half long, being immersed into the ground. **1809** MALKIN *Gil Blas* II. i. ¶3 We kenned the old cripple, immersed in an elbow chair. **1860** TYNDALL *Glac.* I. xviii. 133 A traveller immersed to the waist in the jaws of a fissure.

†**c.** *fig.* To cause to enter; to involve, enclose, include; to merge, to sink. *Obs.*

1605 BACON *Adv. Learn.* II. viii. §1 Other formes..are more immersed into matter. *Ibid.* xvii. §9. **1627–77** FELTHAM *Resolves* II. xlix. 256 We ought..to immerse our private in the public safety. **1734** WATTS *Reliq. Juv.* lxxiii, The bulk of mankind, whose souls are immersed in flesh and blood.

2. *transf.* and *fig.* To plunge or sink into a (particular) state of body or mind; to involve deeply, to steep, absorb, in some action or activity. Chiefly *pass.* or *refl.*

1664 H. MORE *Myst. Iniq.* Apol. 534 It would engage them not to immerse themselves so much into the world, but to live holily. **1712** W. ROGERS *Voy.* 54 The Portuguese immers'd themselves in Debt to the Company. **1790** COWPER *Lett.* 19 Apr., A youth immersed in Mathematics. **1856** DOVE *Logic Chr. Faith* v. ii. 314 We are immersed in difficulties which we cannot explain. **1861** BUCKLE *Civiliz.* (1873) II. viii. 469 He was immersed in the most grovelling superstition.

3. *intr.* for *refl.* To plunge oneself, sink, become absorbed. *lit.* and *fig.* Now *rare* or *Obs.*

1667 *Decay Chr. Piety* xix. ¶2 When they find any proneness to immerse in faction. **1739** tr. *Algarotti on 'Newton's Theory'* (1742) II. 191 Must it not decline towards this Medium and immerse into it?

†**iˈmmerse,** *ppl. a. Obs.* [ad. L. *immers-us*, pa. pple. of *immergĕre* to IMMERGE.] Immersed.

1626 BACON *Sylva* §114–5 (Observ.), I practise, as I doe aduise..after long Inquiry of Things, Immerse in Matter, to interpose some Subject, which is Immateriate, or lesse Materiate. **1647** H. MORE *Song of Soul* To Rdr. 6/1 While I was so immerse in the inward sense and representation of things.

immersed (ɪˈmɜːst), *ppl. a.* [f. IMMERSE *v.* + -ED[1].] Dipped, plunged, or sunk in, or as in, a liquid. Also *fig.*

1678 CUDWORTH *Intell. Syst.* I. iv. §36. 553 He does not seem to understand thereby, such a deeply Immersed Soul, as would make the World an Animal, and a God. **1812** PLAYFAIR *Nat. Phil.* (1819) I. 181 The centre of gravity of the immersed part.

b. Baptized by immersion.

1892 *Daily News* 1 Nov. 6/6 My question is whether [he] is an immersed believer?

c. Growing wholly under water.

1860 GRAY cited in Worcester.

d. *Biol.* Sunken or embedded in a surface.

1826 KIRBY & SP. *Entomol.* IV. 314 *Immersed*, when they [the eyes] are quite imbedded in the head. **1833** SIR W. HOOKER *Smith's Eng. Flora* V. I. 172 *Urceolaria cinerea*—apothecia immersed solitary. **1870** J. D. HOOKER *Stud. Flora* 159 *Sium angustifolium*..Fruit shorter than in *S. latifolium*, with more immersed vittæ.

†**e.** *Astron.* Plunged in darkness, eclipsed.

1667 BOYLE in *Phil. Trans.* II. 597 The Light of the immersed Body. **1854** MOSELEY *Astron.* xviii. (ed. 4) 85 The enlightened hemisphere now includes the south pole, and the north is immersed.

iˈmmersement. *rare.* [f. IMMERSE *v.* + -MENT.] A plunge, a plunging.

1827 LYTTON *Pelham* xlix, After..various immersements into back passages, and courts, and alleys. **1903** W. JAMES *Let.* 29 Dec. in R. B. Perry *Tht. & Char. W. James* (1935) II. 331 Your letter finds me in my nineteenth day of immersement, with grippe, still weak as a 'cat'.

†**immersible** (ɪˈmɜːsɪb(ə)l), *a.*[1] *Obs. rare.* [f. L. type *immersibil-is, f. *im-* (IM-[2]) + **mersibilis*, f. *merg-ĕre*, *mers-* to dip, immerse: see -IBLE. Cf. IMMERSABLE.] That cannot sink in water; 'that cannot be drowned' (Blount *Glossogr.* 1656).

1693 I. MATHER *Cases Consc.* (1862) 274 If Witches are immersible, how came they to die by drowning in Bohemia?

Hence †**immersiˈbility**, incapability of sinking.

1693 I. MATHER *Cases Consc.* (1862) 274 This pretended Gift of Immersibility attending Witches.

iˈmmersible, *a.*[2] *rare.* [f. IMMERSE *v.* + -IBLE.] Capable of being immersed.

1846 in WORCESTER; whence in later Dicts. (some of which erroneously cite Blount and Coles).

immersion (ɪˈmɜːʃən). (Also *erron.* emersion.) [ad. late L. *immersiōn-em* (Arnobius), n. of action from *immergĕre* (see IMMERGE). Cf. F. *immersion* (14th c. in Hatz.-Darm.).] The action of immerging or immersing.

1. a. Dipping or plunging into water or other liquid, and *transf.* into other things.

c **1450** *Mirour Saluacioun* 1407 Thas whilk in watire takes duwe immersionne. **1658** PHILLIPS, *Immersion*, a dipping, ducking, or plunging in. **1664** POWER *Exp. Philos.* II. 123 After immersion thereof into the vessel of Quicksilver. **1693** SOUTH *Twelve Serm.* (1698) III. 86 Holding the Soul of Man to be a Spiritual Immaterial substance [they accounted for its] failures and defects..from its Immersion into, and intimate conjunction with matter. **1710** ADDISON *Tatler* No. 221 ¶5 The Doctor..gives her Two or Three total Emersions in the Cold Bath. **1860** TYNDALL *Glac.* I. xvi. 116 Being checked at intervals by a bodily immersion in the softer and deeper snow. **1882** VINES *Sachs' Bot.* 876 Immersion in warm or cold water. **1885** *Century Mag.* XXIX. 744/1 The Monitor, with only twelve feet immersion, could take any position.

b. The administration of Christian baptism by the dipping or plunging of the whole person in water: distinguished from *affusion* or *aspersion*.

1629 DONNE *80 Serm.* xxxi. (1640) 309 In Baptisme we are sunk under water, and then raised above the water, which was the manner of baptizing in the Christian church, by immersion, and not by aspersion, till of late times. **1751–73** JORTIN *Eccl. Hist.* IX. (1846) I. 165 [It] requires of the bishops and presbyters that they should make use of a three-fold immersion in baptism under pain of being deposed. **1822** J. FLINT *Lett. Amer.* 114 The immersion of seven Baptists in a pool. **1852** HOOK *Ch. Dict.* s.v., Immersion is the mode of baptizing first prescribed in our office of public baptism.

c. *Alch.* Reduction of a metal in some solvent.

1683 PETTUS *Fleta Min.* II. 21 There are other ways of Calcination especially of Metals; viz. by..Immersion. **1696** PHILLIPS, *Immersion*,..the putting Metals or Minerals, into some Corrosive, that they may be reduced to a Calx.

d. *Ceramics.* The application of the glaze to pottery by dipping it into a vessel filled with the glaze-cream.

2. *transf.* and *fig.* **a.** Absorption in some condition, action, interest, etc.

1647 H. MORE *Song of Soul* To Rdr. 7/1 Others, whom sensuall immersion or the deadnesse of Melancholy have more deeply seiz'd upon. **1722** WOLLASTON *Relig. Nat.* ix. 213 Immersion in vice and ignorance. **1840** ALISON *Europe* (1849–50) VIII. lv. 564 Austria was about to take advantage of his immersion in the Peninsular War.

b. A method or system of teaching (or learning) a foreign language in an environment where all communication is conducted in the language, esp. at a school, etc., run for this purpose. Freq. *attrib.*, as ***immersion course, school.*** Chiefly *N. Amer.*

1965 *New Statesman* 19 Nov. 811/1 (Advt.), Berlitz 'total immersion' courses. Berlitz 'immersion' courses. The 4–6 week 'Blitz' courses for busy international executives. **1966** *Official Gaz.* (U.S. Patent Office) 25 Oct. TM190 The Berlitz Schools of Languages of America... Berlitz Total Immersion for educational service of classroom instruction in foreign languages. First use Aug. 10, 1964. **1972** *Time* 13 Nov. 35/2 I've been taking immersion courses in French, you know. Some of my friends say what I really need is an immersion course in English. **1976** *Globe & Mail* (Toronto) 25 Aug. 9/5 In cautioning against putting too much emphasis on early French immersion for the majority of children, the report says such programs may harm children with learning difficulties. **1976** *Maclean's Mag.* 1 Nov. 21/1 In Winnipeg,..Ecole Sacre-Coeur, the city's largest immersion school, recorded a jump in enrollment from 334 to 560 students between 1974 and 1975. **1982** *English World-Wide* III. I. 50 The term 'second language immersion' describes such programmes in circumstances where pupils with the *same* linguistic and cultural background experience a home-school language switch, which is the case of Hong Kong students in E[nglish]-m[edium] schools. **1986** *Toronto Star* 28 May D1/1 (Advt.), Lovely bungalow on super large lot. Walk to French immersion & all schools.

3. *Astron.* The disappearance of a celestial body behind another or in its shadow, as in an occultation or eclipse: opp. to *emersion*.

1690 LEYBOURN *Curs. Math.* 818 The greatest.. Immersion of the Moon into the Shadow does not then happen. **1706** PHILLIPS (ed. Kersey), The *Immersion of a Star* (in Astron.), is when it approaches so near the Sun, as to lie hid in its Beams. **1774** M. MACKENZIE *Maritime Surv.* v. 111 If it is the apparent Time of an Immersion, or Emersion, that is observed. **1808** PIKE *SourcesIssiss.* II. (1810) 131, I observed two immersions of Jupiter's satellites. **1971** *Nature* 17 Dec. 406/1 None of the light curves showed any signs of an atmosphere on Io: in all cases the curves were flat just before and after occultation with abrupt changes in intensity at immersion and emersion.

4. *Microscopy.* The introduction of a liquid, as water or oil, between the object-glass and the object.

1875, 1877 [see 5].

5. *attrib.*, as (sense 1) ***immersion bath***, (1 b) ***immersion robe***, (4) ***immersion fluid, lens, objective, paraboloid, system.*** (sense 1) **immersion foot**, a condition similar to trench foot caused by prolonged exposure of the feet to wet and usually cold conditions; **immersion heater**, a heater (usually electric) whose element may be immersed in the liquid to be heated; *esp.* one having a thermostatic control and designed to be fixed inside a domestic hot-water cylinder; **immersion suit**, a garment designed to give the wearer buoyancy when in the water and to provide insulation from the cold.

1897 ALLBUTT *Syst. Med.* III. 60 Where external treatment is carried out..by simple hot *immersion baths. **1877** *Athenæum* 3 Nov. 569/3 Dr. Edmonds gave a description of his new Immersion Paraboloid, and explained its use..salts of lead in glycerine being specially recommended as the *immersion fluid. **1941** *Lancet* 6 Dec. 690/1, I have never seen a case of *immersion-foot, and for its adequate description we must await the reports of those whose war experience has brought them greater opportunities of observing it. **1967** *New Scientist* 25 May 449/3 In the Pacific during the second World War a warm water variety of immersion foot was common. **1969** J. McM. MENNELL *Foot Pain* v. 104 Immersion foot is similar to trench foot, but the wet environment seems to be more important than the cold; it may occur with relatively warm immersion. **1914** M. LANCASTER *Electr. Cooking, Heating, Cleaning* 208 The water in cylinder A..is heated by the *immersion heater B. *Ibid.* 209 An additional immersion heater could be fitted, current for which would pass through the meter...to be switched on if at any time the demand for hot water were much beyond the ordinary requirements. This auxiliary immersion heater could be controlled automatically by a thermostat..switch. **1935** *Jrnl. R. Aeronaut. Soc.* XXXIX. 455 The lubricating oil being kept at a temperature by immersion heaters in the oil tanks. **1936** *Archit. Rev.* LXXX. p. lxii/3 In many parts of the country ..automatically controlled immersion heaters are being fitted as auxiliary heaters to fuel fired boilers. **1944** T. A. LONGMORE *Med. Photogr.* 140 The immersion heater is an electrically heated poker or element which is placed in the developer to raise its temperature and is withdrawn before the solution is put to its normal use. **1951** *Good Housek. Home Encycl.* (1956) 76/1 Portable immersion heaters and boiling rings. **1958** *House & Garden* Mar. 70/2 The Agamatic also provides hot water—in the summer an immersion heater takes over. **1963** *Times* 8 Jan. 5/5 Mrs. Henderson told him that she decided not to have a bath, left the immersion heater on, and went to bed. **1875** KNIGHT *Dict. Mech.*, **Immersion-lens*, an achromatic objective for the microscope, which is used with a drop of water between the front lens and the glass cover of the object examined, to prevent the extreme refraction of the luminous pencils if air is present. **1877** *Immersion paraboloid [see *immersion fluid* above]. **1894** H. GARDENER *Unoff. Patriot* 28 As he arose from the water his face was radiant, and when he had removed his *immersion robe, his eyes filled with happy tears. **1951** R. H. DAVIS *Deep Diving & Submarine Operations* (ed. 5) I. xiv. 275 *Immersion suits can be worn ..to protect the escaper from the cold, and..to keep him afloat. **1968** *New Scientist* 15 Feb. 348/1 The immersion suit consists essentially of a double-layer rubber suit which can be inflated... Not only does this provide flotation but also excellent insulation.

immersionism (ɪˈmɜːʃənɪz(ə)m). [f. IMMERSION + -ISM.] The doctrine or practice of immersion in baptism.

1845 J. A. JAMES in *Ess. Chr. Union* iv. 166 Independency, Immersionism or Methodism. **1884** *Ch. Times* 413/1 The Baptistic craze of immersionism.

So **iˈmmersionist**, one who advocates or practices baptismal immersion; in quot. 1880 used *playfully* = bather.

1846 WORCESTER (citing HINTON). **1880** LUBBOCK in *Jrnl. Linn. Soc.* XV. No. 83. 173 Leaving the doomed immersionist to her hard fate. **1897** *Chicago Advance* 20 May 668/3 Connected with immersionist churches.

†**iˈmmersive,** *a. Obs.* [f. L. *immers-*, ppl. stem of *immergĕre* (see IMMERGE) + -IVE.] Characterized by or involving immersion.

1635 SWAN *Spec. M.* 143 (L.) The sun's immersive heat doth so boil the water in the cloud,..it looketh red when it falleth. **1694** SALMON *Bates' Disp.* (1713) 448/2 You are to take pure Sol; it is made pure by an immersive Calcination.

immesh, var. of ENMESH *v.*

†**iˈmmethoded,** *a. Obs. rare*[−1]. [f. IM-[2] + METHOD *sb.* + -ED[2].] Having no method; unmethodical.

1653 WATERHOUSE *Apol. Learn.* 157 Their sudden thoughts, immethoded discourses, and slovenly sermocinations.

immethodic (ɪmɪˈθɒdɪk, ɪmm-), *a.* [f. IM-[2] + METHODIC.] = next.

1858 CARLYLE *Fredk. Gt.* I. i. (1872) I. 9 As if there were not in Nature, for darkness, dreariness, immethodic platitude, anything comparable to him.

immethodical (ɪmɪˈθɒdɪkəl, ɪmm-), *a.* [f. IM-[2] + METHODICAL.] Not methodical; having no method; unmethodical.

1605 G. POWEL *Refut. Epist. by Puritan Papist* 54, I will not follow the Libeller in his immethodicall and idle Digressions. **1684** tr. *Bonet's Merc. Compit.* VI. 171 Although this Remedy be accounted..Empirical, immethodical and incertain. **1708** HEARNE *Collect.* 7 May (O.H.S.) II. 107 A very flat immethodical, and poor leaden Discourse. **1821** LAMB *Elia* Ser. I. *Old & New Schoolm.*, My reading has been lamentably desultory and immethodical.

immeˈthodically, *adv.* [f. prec. + -LY[2].] In an immethodical manner; without method; unmethodically.

1624 BURTON *Anat. Mel.* Democr. to Rdr. (ed. 2) 9 He jumbles vp many things together immethodically. **1704** HEARNE *Duct. Hist.* (1714) I. 126 He may both be led astray, by consulting Authors of uncertain Credit, and..by immethodically disposing those good ones he does look into. **1779–81** JOHNSON *L.P., Garth* Wks. III. 26 His notions are half-formed, and his materials immethodically confused.

imme'thodicalness. [f. as prec. + -NESS.] Immethodical quality or condition; want or absence of method; unmethodicalness.

1661 BOYLE *Style of Script.* (1675) 60 Sometimes, too, the seeming immethodicalnesse of the New Testament.. is due to the inconvenient distinction of chapters and verses now in use. *a* **1690** HOPKINS *Serm.* xxi. (R.), Immethodicalness breeds confusion.

immethodize (ɪ'mɛθədaɪz), *v.* [f. IM-^{2} + METHOD + -IZE.] *trans.* To emancipate from method; to render unmethodical.

1811 LAMB *Ess. Trag. Shaks.*, A mighty irregular power of reasoning, immethodized from the ordinary purposes of life.

immetrical (ɪ'mɛtrɪkəl, ɪmm-), *a.* [f. IM-^{2} + METRICAL.] Not metrical; unmetrical.

1598 CHAPMAN *Iliad* To Rdr., French and Italian most immetrical, Their many syllables in harsh collision. **1884** SWINBURNE in *19th Cent.* May 779 Cowley's 'immetrical' irregularity. **1895** *Athenæum* 22 June 796/1 When the word following *the* begins with a vowel, the line is absolutely immetrical.

Hence **i'mmetrically** *adv.*, **i'mmetricalness.**

1862 F. HALL *Sánkhya-sára* Pref. 12 *note*, With respect to the immetricalness of the tenth *Káriká.* **1885** SWINBURNE in *19th Cent.* Jan. 73 The right-hand margin of the line thus immetrically printed.

†**immew** (ɪ'mju:), *v. Obs.* [f. IM-^{1} + MEW *v.*] *trans.* To mew or coop up; to keep in restraint or confinement.

16.. *Song* in Lloyd *Mem.* (1668) 96 (T.) My soul is free as ambient air, Although my baser part's immew'd.

immigrant ('ɪmɪgrənt), *a.* and *sb.* [ad. L. *immigrānt-em*, pres. pple. of *immigrāre* to IMMIGRATE, after *emigrant* (1754).]

A. *adj.* Immigrating.

1805 SOUTHEY *Let. to C. W. W. Wynn* 6 Apr. in *Life* (1850) II. 323 To let the immigrant monastics associate together here. **1885** E. A. SHÄFER in *Proc. Roy. Soc.* XXXVIII. 90 As to the origin of these immigrant cells, it may be regarded as certain that they have passed inwards from the epithelium. **1897** *Daily News* 31 Aug. 4/7 Both [races] are immigrant, and European, not indigenous to the soil.

B. *sb.* One who or that which immigrates; a person who migrates into a country as a settler.

1792 BELKNAP *Hist. New Hampsh.* III. Pref. 6 There is another deviation from the strict letter of the English dictionaries which is found extremely convenient in our discourses on population... The verb *immigrate* and the nouns *immigrant* and *immigration* are used without scruple in some parts of this volume. *Ibid.* III. 473. **1809** KENDALL *Trav.* II. lv. 252 *Immigrant* is perhaps the only new word, of which the circumstances of the United States has in any degree demanded the addition to the English language. *a* **1817** T. DWIGHT *Trav. New Eng.* etc. (1821) II. 232 Immigrants are crowding to it from New-Hampshire, Massachusetts, and Rhode Island. **1876** GLADSTONE *Homeric Synchr.* 216 The son of Perseus, a foreigner and immigrant into Greece.

attrib. **1864** D. A. WELLS *Our Burden & Strength* 24 The immigrant landing depot in New York City. **1969** *Times* 18 July 4/8 Wolverhampton's Grove School.. was described as the '90 per cent immigrant school'. *Ibid.*, There was some criticism.. at this high proportion of immigrant children. **1971** *Economist* 12 June 31/2 Those [*sc.* children] born in England to immigrant parents cease to be classified as immigrant school-children after their parents have been here 10 years, while those born overseas remain within the category no matter how long they have been in England. **1973** *Times* 9 Nov. 2/4 Allowance must be made for immigrant children to adjust to a new social and educational environment.

immigrate ('ɪmɪgreɪt), *v.* [f. L. *immigrāt-*, ppl. stem of *immigrāre* to remove or go into, f. *im-* (IM-^{1}) + *migrāre* to MIGRATE.]

1. *intr.* To come to settle in a country (which is not one's own); to pass into a new habitat or place of residence (*lit.* and *fig.*).

1623 COCKERAM, *Immigrate*, to goe dwell in some place. **1651** CHARLETON *Ephes. & Cimm. Matrons* II. (1668) 67 In exchanging words, they exchange spirits: and immigrate into the wishes they utter. **1792** [see IMMIGRANT *sb.*]. **1845** McCULLOCH *Taxation* I. iii. (1852) 94 If foreign labourers.. be permitted freely to immigrate into the country.

2. *trans.* To bring in or introduce as settlers. (Cf. EMIGRATE 2.)

1896 *Daily News* 13 Feb. 5/7 By carving out a new autonomous district, to which the Armenians would be immigrated. **1898** *Westm. Gaz.* 14 May 2/3 The expense of immigrating coolie labour from the East Indies.

Hence **'immigrated, 'immigrating** *ppl. adjs.*

1869 FARRAR *Fam. Speech* iii. (1873) 100 Professor Munk ..believes that the Phœnicians were an immigrating race. **1882** *Rep. to Ho. Repr. Prec. Met. U.S.* 541 In Venezuelan Guyana, where immigrated Corsicans are the principal miners. **1885** E. A. SCHÄFER in *Proc. Roy. Soc.* XXXVIII. 89 The carrying of fatty particles into the lacteals.. by the immigrating leucocytes.

immigration (ɪmɪ'greɪʃən). [n. of action from IMMIGRATE: see -ATION.] **1. a.** The action of immigrating; entrance into a country for the purpose of settling there. Also *attrib.*

1658 PHILLIPS, *Immigration*, a going to dwell, a passing into. **1774** WARTON *Hist. Eng. Poetry* Diss. i. (1840) I. 18 The Saracens.. at their immigration into Spain about the ninth century. **1792** J. FREEMAN in Belknap *Hist. New Hampsh.* III. 476 The product is 21553, the amount of immigrations into New-Hampshire in 23 years. **1804** C. B. BROWN tr. *Volney's View Soil U.S.* 262 *note*, There is a large party in the state who abhor and discourage immigration. **1858** GLADSTONE *Homer* I. 284 Successive immigrations of bodies of refugees. **1872** *Atlantic Monthly* Apr. 456/1 Natives of Europe.. not included in the immigration reports [etc.]. **1879** *Bradstreet's* 10 Dec. 2/3 It is our idea that immigration societies are doing us no good. **1880** D. M. GORDON *Mountain & Prairie* 298 Such companies, spurred into activity by the prospect of profitable land sales, will probably be more zealous than Government immigration agents. **1890** *Stock Grower & Farmer* 25 Jan. 7/2 Col. Edward Haren, of the immigration department of the Sante Fe, is in the city on his return from Albuquerque. *Ibid.* 22 Feb. 3/2 This territory has never had an immigration 'boom'. **1904** F. BRADSHAW *Alien Immigration* 121 When the alien has passed the Immigration Department his troubles are not yet over. **1905** *Act 5 Edw. VII* c. 13 §1 An immigrant shall not be landed in the United Kingdom from an immigrant ship except at a port at which there is an immigration officer appointed under this Act. **1906** *Daily Chron.* 21 May 1/7 Mr. Seddon, Premier of New Zealand, has challenged the right of the British Government to interfere with Australasian immigration legislation. **1907** *Westm. Gaz.* 30 Jan. 8/2 The Premier [of Australia] has.. liberalised the immigration regulations. **1922** *Encycl. Brit.* XXXII. 854/1 By the Immigration Act passed in 1921 the number of immigrants admitted from any one country in the year July 1 1921 to June 20 1922, was restricted to 3% of the persons of that nationality resident in the United States in 1910. **1926** *Ibid.* III. 21/1 Since the opening of immigration [into Palestine] with promulgation of the Immigration Ordinance (1920) [etc.]. **1949** KOESTLER *Promise & Fulfilment* iv. 40 It is conceivable that they could have achieved sufficient pressure at least to mitigate the immigration bar of 1939. *Ibid.* vi. 56 Except the small number of those who already held pre-war immigration certificates. *Ibid.* 60 The majority.. were Zionists.. who at the eve of the war had been waiting for their turn on the immigration quota. **1969** *Times* 19 July 8/3 The controversy over Britain's immigration policy. **1971** 'D. HALLIDAY' *Dolly & Doctor Bird* ii. 25 He carried a Turkish passport through Immigration Controls. **1973** P. GEDDES *Ottawa Allegation* v. 63 The immigration officer.. took his time over Fender's passport.

b. *absol.*, the immigration checks or authorities. *colloq.*

1966 F. HOYLE *Oct. First* i. 5 We got into London airport more or less on time. Quickly we were into the reception hall and through immigration. **1972** J. POTTER *Going West* 17 He produced his passport and transit card for immigration.

2. *collect.* The body of immigrants. *U.S.*

1852 H. STANSBURY *Exped. Valley Gt. Salt Lake* 126 In the autumn, another large immigration arrived under the president, Brigham Young, which materially added to the strength of the colony. **1857** *Trans. Illinois Agric. Soc.* II. 365 The immigration was generally a moral, correct people. **1948** *Sat. Rev.* (U.S.) 17 July 20/1 A far vaster immigration ..began pouring through the city portals.

immigrator ('ɪmɪgreɪtə(r)). *rare.* [agent-n. in L. form from IMMIGRATE.] One who immigrates; an immigrant.

1836 LYTTON *Athens* (1837) I. 98 If no Egyptian Hierophant accompanied the immigrators.

immigratory ('ɪmɪgreɪtərɪ, -ətərɪ), *a. rare.* [f. as prec., after *migratory.*] Of or pertaining to immigration.

1897 *Naturalist* Jan. 13 The season has been marked by two very pronounced movements [of birds]. The first of them, probably both immigratory and emigratory, during the first week in September.

†**i'mmind, in'mind,** *v. Obs.* [f. IM-^{1} + MIND *sb.*] *trans.* To put in mind, to remind.

1647 M. HUDSON *Div. Right Govt.* II. x. 146 To immind man of his owne infirmity. **1657** TRAPP *Comm. Ezra* vi. 19 To inmind them of that signal mercy. **1660** S. FISHER *Rusticks Alarm* Wks. (1679) 477 The Bible, which doth.. immind men, that forget them to mind the Light and Spirit.

imminence ('ɪmɪnəns). [ad. late L. *imminēntia*, f. *imminēnt-*: see IMMINENT and -ENCE.]

1. The fact or condition of being imminent or impending.

1655 FULLER *Ch. Hist.* III. i. §28 Rufus..on the imminence of any danger or distress..promised them the releasing of their taxes. **1782** *Hist. Europe* in *Ann. Reg.* (1783) 56/2 The imminence of the danger. **1850** MERIVALE *Rom. Emp.* (1852) II. 6 The apparent imminence of intestine war.

2. That which is imminent; impending evil or peril.

1606 SHAKS. *Tr. & Cr.* V. x. 13, I..dare all imminence that gods and men Addresse their dangers in. **1882** *Quain's Med. Dict.* 1151/2 The morbid imminences of this age are few.

imminency ('ɪmɪnənsɪ). [f. as prec.: see -ENCY.] The quality of being imminent; imminent character.

1665 R. B. *Comment 2 Tales* 36 In regard both of the apparency and imminency of that danger. **1806** *Ann. Reg.* 224 Until the precise extent and imminency of the danger should be ascertained. **1871** MACDUFF *Mem. Patmos* i. 15 This predicted imminency of the Advent.

imminent ('ɪmɪnənt), *a.* Also 6–8 *erron.* **iminent, eminent** (see EMINENT 6). [ad. L. *imminens, -ēnt-em*, pres. pple. of *imminēre* to project or lean over, overhang, impend, be near, f. *im-* (IM-^{1}) + *-minēre*, as in *ēminēre*: cf. EMINENT. Cf. F. *imminent* (14th c. in Hatz.-Darm.).]

1. Of an event, etc. (almost always of evil or danger): Impending threateningly, hanging over one's head; ready to befall or overtake one; close at hand in its incidence; coming on shortly.

1528 GARDINER in Pocock *Rec. Ref.* I. l. 115 Fear..being so imminent and lately felt. **1555** EDEN *Decades* 103 Preseruation from so many imminent perels. **1593** SHAKS. *2 Hen. VI*, V. iii. 19 You haue defended me from imminent death. **1604** —— *Oth.* I. iii. 136 Haire-breadth scapes i' th' imminent deadly breach. *a* **1661** FULLER *Worthies* (1840) III. 3 Presaging their intended and imminent destruction. **1769** ROBERTSON *Chas. V* (1813) III. VII. 26 To oppose, first of all, the nearest and most imminent danger. **1875** STUBBS *Const. Hist.* III. xviii. 27 Invasion was imminent. **1883** C. J. WILLS *Mod. Persia* 330 In an Austrian lottery..a drawing was imminent.

†**2.** Remaining fixed or intent (*upon* something). *Obs.* [L. *imminēre* in sense 'to be intent upon'.]

1641 MILTON *Reform.* II. 65 Their eyes ever imminent upon worldly matters.

3. In literal sense: Projecting or leaning forward; overhanging.

1727 W. MATHER *Yng. Man's Comp.* 27 *Eminent*, famous. *Iminent*, over head. **1858** HAWTHORNE *Fr. & It. Jrnls.* (1872) I. 38 Heights began to rise imminent above our way.

†**4.** Confused with IMMANENT. *Obs.*

1605 VERSTEGAN *Dec. Intell.* iv. (1628) 108 This.. requireth an imminent reason to be sought for. **1644** HUNTON *Vind. Treat. Monarchy* v. 40 Now Legislation is an imminent Act, consisting in a meer expression of an Authoritative Will. **1677** GILPIN *Demonol.* (1867) 24 Our present formed thoughts, the immediate and imminent acts of the mind. **1856** DOVE *Logic Chr. Faith* v. i. §2. 272 The moral law of the conscience is the most..imminent of all that can be called Knowledge.

†**5.** Confused with EMINENT *a. Obs.*

1642 J. VICARS *God in Mount* 15 Some imminent Scots.

imminently ('ɪmɪnəntlɪ), *adv.* (Also 6–7 *erron.* emi-: see EMINENTLY 5.) [f. prec. + -LY^{2}.] In an imminent manner; impendingly; threateningly.

1548 HALL *Chron., Edw. IV* 219 The evill fate and destenie of her husbande, whiche eminently [**1568** GRAFTON 706 iminentlye] before hir iyes, she sawe to approche. **1646–1670** [see EMINENTLY 5]. **1786** BURKE *W. Hastings* Wks. 1842 II. 154 [He] did..shake the whole foundation of British authority, and imminently endanger the existence of the British nation in India. **1898** *Daily News* 10 Sept. 5/3 The left attack..was, I think, never imminently dangerous.

immingle (ɪ'mɪŋg(ə)l, ɪmm-), *v.* [f. IM-^{1} + MINGLE *v.*] *trans.* To mix or blend intimately; to mingle, intermingle.

1606 HOLLAND *Sueton.* 199 (R.) Let earth with fire imingled be. **1649** EVELYN *Liberty & Serv.* v. Misc. Writ. (1805) 33 Crimes so easily immingle themselves. **1726–46** THOMSON *Summer* 551 Where purity and peace immingle charms. **1848** CLOUGH *Bothie* v. 28 Themselves..accepted into it, immingled, as truly Part of it as are the kine in the field.

b. *intr.* (for *refl.*).

1848 CLOUGH *Amours de Voy.* III. 9 Where, upon Apennine slope, with the chestnut the oak-trees immingle.

Hence **i'mmingling** *vbl. sb.*

1855 PUSEY *Doctr. Real Presence* Note I. 114 He is divided indivisibly in all, on account of the immingling (ἐμμιξιν).

†**i'mminish,** *v. Obs.* Also 5 **enmenuse, emenische.** [ME. *enmenuse*, a. OF. *enmenuisier*, *emmenuisser*, repr. L. type **inminūtiāre* (see AMENUSE), refashioned as *emenish*, and ultimately (after L. *imminuĕre*) as *imminish*. Cf. AMINISH, DIMINISH, MINISH.]

a. *trans.* To diminish; to belittle; **b.** *intr.* To become less, decrease.

14.. *Life Alexander* (*MS. Lincoln* A. i. 17 lf. 32) (Halliw.) And his gudnesse be nathynge enmenuste therby. *Ibid.* lf. 48 Macedoyne salle waxe ay lesse and lesse, and emenische day bi day. **1562** COOPER *Answ. Priv. Masse* (Parker Soc.) 163 So to imminish and debase the weight of Christ's Commandments. **1565–73** —— *Thesaurus*, *Leuare authoritatem*,..to imminish.

†**'imminute,** *a. Obs.* [ad. L. *imminūt-us*, pa. pple. of *imminuĕre* to lessen, f. *im-* (IM-^{1}) + *minuĕre* to lessen.] Diminished, lessened.

a **1681** WHARTON *Eclipses* Wks. (1683) 106 In those Eclipses..we suffer by reason of the Imminute Influence of the Sun toward us.

†**immi'nution.** *Obs.* [ad. L. *imminūtiōn-em*, n. of action f. *imminuĕre*: see prec.] Diminution, lessening, decrease.

1590 BARROUGH *Meth. Physick* v. iv. (1639) 269 This.. sodaine and often imminution of the tumour. **1657** J. COSIN *Canon Script.* ii. 14 Without any Addition, Imminution, or Alteration. **1788** *Warburton's Div. Legat.* v. ii. *Note* H., Wks. III. 205 Where is the absurdity of Dr. Spencer's gradual declension or imminution of the Theocracy?

immi'raculous, *a. nonce-wd.* [f. IM-^{2} + MIRACULOUS.] Non-miraculous.

1880 FAIRBAIRN *Stud. Life Christ* xii. (1881) 200 These.. records of so-called miraculous events—so finely natural and immiraculous in tone.

†**i'mmire,** *v. Obs.* Also 7 **en-.** [f. IM-^{1} + MIRE *sb.*] *trans.* To immerse in mire; also *fig.*

1611 FLORIO, *Imbuare*, to enmud, to enbog, to enmire. **1652** URQUHART *Jewel* Wks. (1834) 280 Most of them do immire their spirits into worldly projects.

immiscibility (ɪmɪsɪ'bɪlɪtɪ). [f. next + -ITY: cf. F. *immiscibilité* (Littré).] The quality of being immiscible; incapacity of mixing.

1807 *Edin. Rev.* X. 145 He has investigated..the causes of this immiscibility. **1881** *Athenæum* 6 Aug. 165/2 Equally

typical was his [Landor's] immiscibility. 'The worst of John Bull', once said a famous American, 'is that he won't mix'.

immiscible (ɪ'mɪsɪb(ə)l), *a.* [f. IM-[2] + MISCIBLE. Cf. F. *immiscible* (Littré, who cites a L. *immiscibilis* from Quicherat).] That cannot be mixed; incapable of mixture. Usu. *spec.* of a liquid: incapable of forming a true solution *with* or *in* another liquid.

1671 J. WEBSTER *Metallogr.* xxvi. 336 Wismuth..of a brittle immiscible earth. **1751** *Phil. Trans.* XLVII. 258 A blackish liquid..absolutely immiscible with water. **1833** CHALMERS *Const. Man* (1835) II. vii. 30 Like water and oil, they are immiscible. **1934** A. J. MEE *Physical Chem.* x. 436 (*heading*) Vapour pressure of a mixture of immiscible liquids. **1964** D. F. EGGERS et al. *Physical Chem.* viii. 276 Steam distillation is frequently used to carry over organic substances immiscible in water.

Hence **i'mmiscibly** *adv.*, without capability of mixture.

1884 H. D. TRAILL *New Lucian* 116, I would that the hosts of darkness were thus immiscibly divided from the army of light.

†**i'mmiserable**, *a.* *Obs.* *rare*$^{-0}$. [ad. L. *immiserābilis* unpitied, f. *im-* (IM-[2]) + *miserābilis* MISERABLE.] 'Whom none pittieth' (Cockeram, 1623).

immiserization (ɪˌmɪzəraɪ'zeɪʃən). Also (slightly earlier) **immiseration**. [f. IM-[1] + MISER(ABLE *a.* + -IZATION; tr. G. *verelendung*.] The act of making or becoming progressively more miserable; pauperization, impoverishment. So **iˌmmiserifi'cation**, in the same sense; **i'mmiserize** *v. trans.*, to impoverish.

1942 J. A. SCHUMPETER *Capitalism, Socialism & Democracy* (1943) iii. 22 The glowing indictment of 'exploitation' and 'immiserization'. **1948** R. STRAUSZ-HUPÉ in *Philos. of Sci.* X. 270 Fifty years ago the Revisionists pointed out the fallacies of Marx's theory of the immiseration of the proletariat. **1971** J. VAIZEY *Social Democracy* 37 The general trend of real wages, after 1850, was upwards, and the general immiserisation of the proletariat was not brought about. *Ibid.* 48 The international industrial system had been created; the proletariat was not immiserised; and the modern nation-state had been created. **1975** D. MCLELLAN *Marx* iii. 44 Marx was thinking in terms of trends and projected into the future tendencies that he saw in contemporary society. One of the most important of these trends was the immiserization of the proletariat. Marx was usually chary of claiming that the proletariat would become immiserized in any absolute sense.

†**i'mmiss**, *v.* *Obs.* Also 7 **immise**. [f. L. *immiss-*, ppl. stem of *immittĕre* to IMMIT. With *immise* cf. *premise*.] *trans.* = IMMIT.

1647 J. HALL *Poems* II. 100 Whether the Sun will er'e immise Light to mine eyes. **1669** GALE *Crt. Gentiles* I. III. iii. 46 A Splendour..immissed into that dark Mater.

immission (ɪ'mɪʃən, ɪmm-). Now *rare*. [ad. L. *immissiōn-em*, n. of action f. *immittĕre* to IMMIT. Cf. obs. F. *immission*] The action of immitting; insertion, injection, admission, introduction. The opposite of *emission*.

1578 BANISTER *Hist. Man* VIII. 102 The strife therof ['how the sight is made'] as yet is vnder iudgement, as touchyng emission, and immission. **1612** DRAYTON *Poly-olb.* x. Notes 165 The Northwinde (much accounted of among builders.. for immission of pure ayre). **1651** JER. TAYLOR *Serm. for Year* I. xxii. 281 God does not give immissions and miracles from heaven to no purpose. **1713** DERHAM *Phys.-Theol.* 5 *note*, After such frequent Compressures, and immission of fresh Air. **1856** MASSON *Ess., Wordsw.* 349 The..theory of ..alternate immission and withdrawal of power, as regulating the progress of the universe.

b. *spec.* in Eucharistic use: = COMMIXTION 6.

1846 MASKELL *Anc. Liturgy* 115 *note*, The mystical intention of the Immission into the Cup. **1877** J. D. CHAMBERS *Div. Worship* 378 The Solemn Immission into the Chalice of one Portion or of one Hostia. *Ibid.* 386.

c. That which is immitted.

1526 *Pilgr. Perf.* (W. de W. 1531) 146 Immyssyons of the ennemy, that be euyll suggestyons. **1649** JER. TAYLOR *Gt. Exemp.* Pref. ⁋32 Faith is presented to be an infused grace, an immission from God.

†**i'mmistion**. *Obs.* [n. of action from L. *immiscē-re* to mix intimately: see IMMISCIBLE and -ION[1].] Intimate mixture or mingling.

1658 tr. *Porta's Nat. Magic* x. xv. 272 By continual solution and immistion, so to distil them [etc.].

immit (ɪ'mɪt), *v.* Now *rare* or *Obs.* [ad. L. *immittĕre* to send in, introduce, etc., f. *im-* (IM-[1]) + *mittĕre* to send.] *trans.* To put in, insert, inject, infuse; to let in, admit, introduce (things material or immaterial): the opposite of *emit*.

1578 BANISTER *Hist. Man* I. 24 The..heades [of the ribs] are immitted into the bodyes of the Vertebres. **1652** GAULE *Magastrom.* 20 It was his dream (divinely immitted). **1669** BOYLE *Contn. New Exp.* II. (1682) 141 The Air being immitted. **1705** GREENHILL *Art of Embalming* 273 This Balsamic Liquor thus Clysterwise immitted into the Intestins. **1834** G. S. FABER *Prim. Doctr. Election* (1836) *Pref.* 18 It [new doctrine] has, as Tertullian speaks, been *immitted* or *let in* or *introduced* at a later period.

immitigable (ɪ'mɪtɪgəb(ə)l), *a.* [ad. L. *immītigābilis*, f. *im-* (IM-[2]) + *mītigābilis* MITIGABLE.] That cannot be mitigated, softened, or appeased; implacable; not to be toned down.

1576 FLEMING *Panopl. Epist.* 19 What cause was there.. that the malice of my minde should be immitigable? **17..** HARRIS (J.), Did she mitigate these immitigable, these iron-hearted men? **1814** SOUTHEY *Roderick* XVII, He..on his flesh ..inflicts Fierce vengeance with immitigable hand. **1831** TRELAWNEY *Adv. Younger Son* III. 138 For four or five days and nights the pain was immitigable. **1887** SWINBURNE *Stud. Prose & Poetry* (1894) 188 The principle or the impulse of universal and immitigable charity.

Hence **i'mmitigably** *adv.*, in an immitigable manner or degree.

1824 *Westm. Rev.* I. 437 The most unavoidably and immitigably painful incidents of life. **1832** HT. MARTINEAU *Each & All* vii. 104 Mr. Bland looked as immitigably solemn as ever. **1854** N. HAWTHORNE *Eng. Note-Bks.* II. 308 Much that is most valuable must be immitigably rejected.

immittance (ɪ'mɪtəns). *Electr.* [f. IM(PEDANCE + (AD)MITTANCE.] Admittance or its reciprocal, impedance: used when it is desired to refer to both quantities without making a distinction between them.

1957 D. WOODS in *Proc. Inst. Electr. Engin.* CIV. c. 507/2 Immittance is the basic parameter of any a.c. measuring system for electrical quantities. [*Note*] Immittance is used to convey the general idea of impedance or admittance. **1960** CLEMENT & JOHNSON *Electr. Engin. Sci.* xi. 341 Each element *R, L,* and *C* of a network has an immittance to sinusoidal current. **1969** P. M. CHIRLIAN *Basic Network Theory* viii. 496 We can eventually calculate the input current $I_1(s)$. This will be expressed as $V_2(s)$ times some function of the immittances of the ladder network.

immix (ɪ'mɪks), *v.* Now *rare*. [The pa. pple. *immixt* is found in 15th c.; also a vb. IMMIXT; both from L. *immixt-us*, pa. pple. of *immiscēre*. The present stem *immix* was of later appearance, and due to the analysis of *immix-t* as a pa. pple. of Eng. formation, implying a present of this form. Cf. COMMIX, ADMIX, which had a like origin.] *trans.* To mix in (*with* something else); to mix intimately, mix up, commingle.

1432-50 tr. *Higden* (Rolls) I. 295 The peple..kepe the maneres and consuetudes of Frenche men, to whom thei were immixte. **1528** GARDINER in Pocock *Rec. Ref.* I. l. 113 We immixed such things and reasons as might serve. **1563-87** FOXE *A. & M.* (1596) 58/1 The boie immixed the eucharist, and dropt it in softlie into the mouth of the old man. **1596** SPENSER *F.Q.* IV. iii. 47 Amongst her teares immixing prayers meeke. **1671** MILTON *Samson* 1657 Samson with these immixt, inevitably Pulled down the same destruction on himself. **1791** BURNS *Elegy Miss Burnet* iv, Ye heathy wastes immix'd with reedy fens. **1882** F. W. MYERS *Renewal of Youth* 205 How oft shall evening's slant and crimson fire Immix the earthly and divine desire!

b. *refl.* To involve, or 'mix oneself up' (*in* or *with* something).

1593 R. BARNES *Parthenophil* xxxiii. in Arb. *Garner* V. 357 Lest my better part To milder objects should itself immix. **1671** *True Nonconf.* 124 Immixing themselves by privilege in secular Courts and affaires. **1748** J. GEDDES *Compos. Antients* 244 Having..immixed himself with the real τὸ ὄν.

c. *intr.* (for *refl.*).

1681 *No Protestant-Plot* 9 Many others..immix with them, and cooperate to promote their designs.

Hence **i'mmixed** *ppl. a.*, mixed up, commingled.

1855 BAILEY *Mystic* 80 Millet and lentil, and a thousand grains, As many and as immixed as Psyche slipped Through her sad fingers. **1858** —— *The Age* 199 Nor host immixed that by Propontic wave Its ranks deployed.

†**i'mmixable**, *a.* *Obs.* [f. IM-[2] + MIXABLE.] Incapable of being mixed; immiscible.

1641 WILKINS *Math. Magick* II. iv. (1648) 175 Fill it with such liquors as may be clear of the same colour, immixable.

†**immixt, immixed** (ɪ'mɪkst), *a.* *Obs.* [orig. ad. L. *immixt-us*, f. *im-* (IM-[2]) + *mixtus* MIXED.] Not mixed, unmingled, pure, simple.

1622 S. WARD *Life of Faith in Death* (1627) 101 The soule is..elder and more excellent sister to the body immixt and separable. **1638** SIR T. HERBERT *Trav.* (ed. 2) 339 They [the Chinese] are the most ancient and immixt people in the Universe. *a* **1640** JACKSON *Creed* XI. i. §2 The divine nature or Godhead is simple, pure, and immixt. **1659** EVELYN *Let. to Boyle* 3 Sept. in *B.'s Wks.* (1772) VI. 291 To assure you ..how pure and immixed the design is from any other than the public interest.

Hence †**i'mmixtness, -edness**.

1646 H. LAWRENCE *Comm. Angells* 125 Sincerity is immixednesse, and rightnesse of ends.

†**i'mmixt**, *v.* *Obs.* *rare*. [f. L. *immixt-*, ppl. stem of *immiscēre*: see IMMIX. Cf. the parallel early vbs. *admixt, commixt*.] *trans.* = IMMIX.

1432-50 tr. *Higden* (Rolls) I. 13 Take some versus of that nowble..poete called Homerus and adde or immixte theym unto his werkes. **1523** *St. Papers Hen. VIII*, IV. 89 Immyxting..your certificates and communications with drede of raysing of the Kinges armye.

†**i'mmixtion**. *Obs.* *rare*. In 7 **immixion**. [f. L. *immixt-*, ppl. stem of *immiscēre*: see -ION[1].] The action of mixing in.

1653 R. G. tr. *Bacon's Hist. Winds* 181 Of winds which are made by immixion of vapours.

†**i'mmixture**[1]. *Obs.* *rare*. [f. IM-[2] + MIXTURE, after IMMIXT *a.*] The condition of being unmixed; freedom from mixture; purity, simplicity.

1648 W. MOUNTAGUE *Devout Ess.* I. xiv. §3. 190 That wherein our love is the most defective, which is simplicity and immixture.

immixture[2] (ɪ'mɪkstjʊə(r)). [f. L. *immixt-*, ppl. stem of *immiscēre* to IMMIX + -URE, as if ad. L. **immixtūra*: cf. *admixture, commixture*.] The action of immixing or mixing up; intimate mixture, commingling; the fact of being 'mixed up' or involved (*in* something).

1859 GULLICK & TIMBS *Paint.* 240 The immixture of oil with the colours. **1865** J. GROTE *Treat. Moral Ideas* ii. (1876) 28 The immixture of the pollen with the stigma. **1888** BRYCE *Amer. Commw.* xxiv. (1889) I. 256 To avoid an immixture in political strife. **1889** STEVENSON *Master of B.* vi. 166 Repenting the temerity of my immixture in affairs so private.

immobile (ɪ'məʊbaɪl, -ɪl), *a.* Also 4 **in-mobill**, 5 **immobyle**, 6 **-il**, **immoble**, **imoble**. [a. F. *immobile* (13th c. in Hatz.-Darm.), ad. L. *immōbilis*, f. *im-* (IM-[2]) + *mōbilis* MOBILE.] Incapable of moving or of being moved, immovable (*lit.* and *fig.*); fixed, stable. Also less strictly: That does not move; motionless, stationary. (In first quot. = IMMOVABLE A. 3.)

c **1340** HAMPOLE *Prose Tr.* 11 Thou sall noghte couatye þe hous or oþer thynge mobill or in-mobill of þi neghtbour with wrange. **1490** CAXTON *Eneydos* xix. 69 Eneas..holdyng hys syght alwayes Immobyle atte anothre syde than vpon dydo. **1545** JOYE *Exp. Dan.* v. (R.), It is not laufull to breke them [laws]: but they be ferme and immoble. **1549** *Compl. Scot.* vi. 48 Al the thyng that circuitis this..fyrst mobil, is immobil and mouis nocht. **1559** W. CUNNINGHAM *Cosmogr. Glasse* 17, I do imagine..A. D. to be the axe tree, and imoble. **1677** GALE *Crt. Gentiles* IV. 141 Frequent repeted custome in sin renders the conscience..obdurate..whereby sin becomes necessary and immobile. **1859** G. MEREDITH *R. Feverel* xxxviii, The fruits hung immobile on the boughs. **1864** *Mattie, a Stray* I. 200 His immobile features did not alarm the young suitor.

immobilism (ɪ'məʊbɪlɪz(ə)m). [ad. F. *immobilisme* (also used).] A policy or attitude of extreme conservatism or opposition to progress.

1949 *Time* 17 Oct. 34 Successful 'immobilism' (patient compromise, appeasement, moderation). **1955** *Times* 5 May 10/7 The Radicals..wished to remain a party of the left; social and political *immobilisme* (opposition to progress) was the best ally of Communism. *Ibid.* 24 Aug. 6/1 There could be no question of allowing themselves to be swayed by a question of superstition or of fetishism, which would be contrary to national dignity. But in any case, M. Faure added, it had been clearly agreed that they would not adopt a policy of immobilism. **1959** *Economist* 21 Feb. 662/2 This outright *immobilisme* [among farmers] condemns itself. **1961** *Encounter* XVII. II. 21 The notorious *immobilisme* of French society. **1967** *Economist* 8 Apr. 110/2 Mr Callaghan will have made a sad present to industrial immobilism if he throws any such opportunity for reducing surtax away.

†**immo'bilitate**, *v.* *Obs.* *rare*. [f. med.L. *immōbilitāt-*, ppl. stem of *immōbilitāre*, f. *immōbilis* IMMOBILE: cf. *mōbilitāre* to render movable.] *trans.* To render incapable of movement.

1654 VILVAIN *Theorem. Theol.* ii. 46 Adams supernatural Grace given to corroborat him, did not immobilitat his wil to evil.

immobility (ɪməʊ'bɪlɪtɪ). [a. F. *immobilité* (13-14th c. in Hatz.-Darm.) or ad. L. *immōbilitās, -tātem*, n. of quality f. *immōbilis* IMMOBILE.] The quality or condition of being immobile; incapacity of moving, or of being moved; fixedness, stability; motionlessness. (*lit.* and *fig.*).

1483 CAXTON *Gold. Leg.* 25 b/1 In dyvynyte, in eternite, in situacion of immobylyte. *a* **1617** BAYNE *On Eph.* (1658) 55 The immobility of Gods word. **1664** POWER *Exp. Philos.* III. 153 A Magnetical Demonstration of the Earth's Immobility. **1732** ARBUTHNOT *Rules of Diet* 367 A Palsy is an Immobility of a Muscle from Relaxation. **1818** CRUISE *Digest* (ed. 2) I. 263 Estates for years are considered in law as chattels real, being an interest in real property, of which they have one quality, immobility, which denominates them real. **1860** W. COLLINS *Wom. White* I. ix. 102 There was an unnatural immobility in her face.

b. *concr.* = IMMOVABLE B. (*nonce-use*).

1873 BROWNING *Red Cott. Nt.-cap* 132 Still is for sale.. that same château With all its immobilities.

immobilize (ɪ'məʊbɪlaɪz), *v.* [ad. F. *immobiliser* (1835 *Dict. Acad.*), f. *immobile*: cf. *mobilize*.]

1. *trans.* To render immobile; to fix immovably; to keep (a joint or limb) without motion for surgical purposes; to render (troops) incapable of being mobilized; to withdraw (specie) from circulation, holding it against bank-notes.

1871 *Daily News* 4 Jan., To oblige the enemy to immobilize around us considerable forces. **1872** *Contemp. Rev.* XX. 581 [It] puts an end to the idea of future progress by immobilizing the organization of the present. **1879** *St. George's Hosp. Rep.* IX. 769 The patient..had his limb placed upon a cushion without being immobilised. **1892** *Pall Mall G.* 12 Dec. 6/3 The Italian écus, being immobilized in the State and in the Latin Union treasuries. **1898** M. P. SHIEL *Yellow Danger* 131 The whole Allied navy ..had been almost immobilised for lack of steam-fuel.

2. *Soil Sci.* and *Bot.* To convert (a plant nutrient) from a form in which it can be utilized by a plant to one in which it cannot; to assimilate and thereby render unavailable to (other) plants. Also *absol.*

1951 *Proc. Soil Sci. Soc. Amer.* XV. 168/2 Fertilizer and nonfertilizer nitrogen must have been absorbed and immobilized in proportion to their relative available concentrations in the soil. **1952** L. M. Thompson *Soils & Soil Fertility* ix. 135 If there is a deficit of nitrogen in the added organic matter, the microbes will immobilize ammonia and nitrates from the soil. **1958** *U.S. Dept. Agric. Yearbk. 1957* 760/1 The addition of fresh straw or sawdust to the soil may greatly increase the number of bacteria. These remove available nitrogen and phosphorus from the soil and immobilize them within their cells. **1967** Fried & Broeshart *Soil—Plant Syst.* vii. 240 Soluble phosphates that are applied to the soil are generally immobilized. **1971** *Nature* 9 Apr. 403/1 *Becium homblei*.. grows on soils rich in copper, and it has been shown to accumulate heavy metals. Other plants also have this characteristic, and their ability to immobilize in insoluble form.. has been noted.

Hence **immobili'zation**, the action or process of immobilizing; *concr.* specie withdrawn from circulation.

1882 *Quain's Med. Dict.* 780/1 Immobilization [of a diseased joint] should not be continued longer than necessary. **1894** *Daily News* 28 July 7/4 The immobilisation of the Italian banks will be distributed as follows: To the Bank of Italy about 400 million francs [etc.]. **1951** *Proc. Soil Sci. Soc. Amer.* XV. 166/2 Immobilization is here used to denote the process of conversion of inorganic nitrogen to organic combinations either through plant uptake or through microbial absorption. **1952** L. M. Thompson *Soils & Soil Fertility* ix. 132 Either plants or microorganisms may convert NH_4^+ or NO_3^- to organic form (chiefly protein). The conversion of inorganic compounds to organic form is called immobilization. **1956** *Proc. Soil Sci. Soc. Amer.* XX. 217/2 The tie-up (immobilization) or release (mineralization) of soil nitrogen depends very much on the chemical composition of the material undergoing decomposition. **1970** *Analytical Biochem.* XXXIII. 341 The physical entrapment of enzymes in insoluble matrices seems to provide a general method of immobilization.

immobilized (ɪ'məʊbɪlaɪzd), *ppl. a.* [f. IMMOBILIZE *v.* + -ED^{1}.] Rendered immobile or stationary.

1923 *Edin. Rev.* Jan. 179 The left and centre of the enemy was held... It was now possible to attempt a decisive attack on an immobilised enemy.

immoble, obs. var. of IMMOBILE.

†**i'mmodelize**, *v.* *Obs. rare.* [f. IM-^{1} + MODELIZE.] *trans.* To model, mould, fashion.

1649 J. Ellistone tr. *Behmen's Ep.* vi. §37 The formed or immodellized Science. *Ibid.* vii. §9 The pride of the Devill .. hath so imprinted and immodellized it selfe on the Image of man.

†**i'mmoderacy.** *Obs. rare.* [f. IMMODERATE: see -ACY.] Immoderateness, want of moderation, excess.

1682 Sir T. Browne *Chr. Mor.* II. §1 The strength of delight is in its seldomness.. Mediocrity is its Life and immoderacy its Confusion. **1686** Goad *Celest. Bodies* II. iv. 195 All Verdure by the immoderacy of the Season is parch'd and burnt.

†**immoderancy.** *Obs. rare.* [ad. late L. *immoderāntia*, f. *im-* (IM-^{2}) + *moderānt-em*, pres. pple. of *moderārī* to MODERATE.] = prec.

1646 Sir T. Browne *Pseud. Ep.* I. ii. 7 He by a decollation of all hope annihilated his [God's] mercy, this by an immoderancy thereof destroyed his justice.

immoderate (ɪ'mɒdərət), *a.* Also 5 in-. [ad. L. *immoderāt-us* unbounded, unrestrained, excessive, f. *im-* (IM-^{2}) + *moderātus* MODERATE.]

1. Not moderate; exceeding usual or proper limits; excessive, extravagant, too great.

1398 Trevisa *Barth. De P.R.* XIII. xxvi. (1495) 460 Inmoderate heete greuyth fysshe. **1533** Elyot *Cast. Helthe* (1539) 48 a, Immoderate slepe maketh the body apt vnto palsies. **1601** F. Godwin *Bps. of Eng.* 471 By reason of these immoderate expenses he became so bare, that [etc.] **1712** Budgell *Spect.* No. 277 ¶14 Her Necklace was of an immoderate length. **1855** Macaulay *Hist. Eng.* xxi. IV. 576 His immoderate zeal against the unfortunate clan.

b. Of persons: Wanting in moderation; going beyond reasonable bounds in action or opinion; extreme.

c **1450** Lydg. *Secrees* 939 In his departyng whoo is inmoderat, This to seyn whoo is nat mesurable In his Rychesse but disordinat, Is Callyd prodigus. **1638** F. Junius *Paint. of Ancients* 279 Pindarus was immoderate in the ornaments of his poesie. **1791** Burke *Th. French Aff.* Wks. VII. 45 The.. government.. which the immoderate republicans began so very lately to introduce into Holland. **1890** *Daily News* 12 Dec. 3/3 Mr. Labouchere .. said .. He was not a moderate but an immoderate Liberal.

†2. Unrestrained in feeling, passions, or conduct; intemperate. *Obs.* (exc. as implied in 1).

1497 Bp. Alcock *Mons Perfect.* B iij, A man wrothe is so immoderat that he knowith not what he sayth. **1567** Maplet *Gr. Forest* Pref., I therefore desire a Reader not learned, but vnskilfull: yet rather learned than immoderate. *a* **1635** Naunton *Fragm. Reg.* (Arb.) 55 Those immoderate courses of his youth. **1659** D. Pell *Impr. Sea* 19 *note*, Alexander was continent, yet immoderate. **1696** Phillips (ed. 5), *Immoderate*, observing no measure, intemperate beyond excess.

†3. Without limits, boundless; very great. *rare.*

c **1480** *St. Ursula* (Roxb.) A vij, To be theyr guides he sent his aungels bryght Athwart them to hauven thrugh his immoderate myght. **1635–56** Cowley *Davideis* II. 745 An heav'nly Maid walks in .. Immod'rate Grace Spoke things far more than Human in her Face.

immoderately (ɪ'mɒdərətlɪ), *adv.* [f. prec. + -LY^{2}.] In an immoderate manner or degree; beyond just or reasonable limits; excessively, in excess, extravagantly, too much.

1482 *Monk of Evesham* i. (Arb.) 20 Why he sorowde and wepte so imoderately. **1529** More *Suppl. Soulys* Wks. 336/2 His goodes y^{t} he hath immoderatelye gathered and gredily kept together. **1617** Moryson *Itin.* I. 240 The men .. died .. by eating immoderately thereof. **1712** Steele *Spect.* No. 296 ¶7 The Ladies.. laugh immoderately all the Time. **1858** Doran *Crt. Fools* 286 His arms and legs were immoderately long.

immoderateness (ɪ'mɒdərətnɪs). [f. as prec. + -NESS.] The quality or condition of being immoderate; want of moderation; excess.

1579 Twyne *Phisicke agst. Fort.* II. xliii. 62 a, Vnmeasurablenesse and immoderatnesse is to be eschewed. **1681** H. More *Exp. Dan.* Pref. 81 Nor is there any thing of Immoderateness or Extravagancy in this my zeal. **1714** tr. *T. à Kempis' Chr. Exerc.* IV. xvi. 254 This may be either by immoderateness or indiscretion.

immoderation (ɪmɒdə'reɪʃən). [a. F. *immodération* (15th c.), or ad. L. *immoderātiōn-em*, f. *im-* (IM-^{2}) + *moderātio* MODERATION.] The opposite of moderation; immoderateness, excess.

1541 Copland *Galyen's Terap.* 2 E j b, In competent and commoderacyon of smal conduites lyeth and consisteth the helth. And .. in vncompetence and immoderacyon in them the dysease. **1640** Bp. Hall *Chr. Moder.* (ed. Ward) 6/1 Immoderation in drinking. **1650** Venning *New Command Renewed* Pref., Who would undertake to moderate the extreme immoderation of our days? **1727** Bradley *Fam. Dict.* s.v. *Balm of Paracelsus*, It .. cures .. the Immoderation of the Menses. **1875** Manning *Mission H. Ghost* viii. 221 Many who have begun by some small immoderation .. have ended .. in a bondage of habitual excess.

†b. *pl.* Excesses; immoderate or intemperate acts.

1614 Bp. Hall *Heaven vpon Earth* §18 All immoderations are enemies, as to health, so to peace. **1679** Puller *Moder. Ch. Eng.* (1843) 320 Those who are for parity in the Church have great disparities, and very disproportionate measures in their own immoderations.

immodest (ɪ'mɒdɪst), *a.* [ad. L. *immodest-us*, f. *im-* (IM-^{2}) + *modestus* MODEST. Cf. F. *immodeste* (1549 R. Estienne).] Not modest, void of modesty.

1. Void of modesty in self-assertion or pretension; arrogant, forward, impudent.

1570 Levins *Manip.* 92/43 Immodest, *immodestus.* **1591** Shaks. *1 Hen. VI*, IV. i. 126 With this immodest clamorous outrage. **1635–56** Cowley *Davideis* I. *Notes* ¶3, I hope this kind of Boast .. will not seem immodest. **1672** Wilkins *Nat. Relig.* I. vii. 88 This were to subvert the credit of all history; which is so immodest a thing as any sober man would be ashamed of. **1771** N. Nicholls in *Corr. w. Gray* (1843) 133 If you think this an immodest request, you may do as much or as little of it as you please.

2. Wanting a due sense of decorum or decency; improper, indelicate, indecent, lewd, unchaste.

1590 Spenser *F.Q.* II. vi. 37 A foe of folly and immodest toy. **1597** Shaks. *2 Hen. IV*, IV. iv. 70 To gaine the Language, 'Tis needfull, that the most immodest word Be look'd vpon, and learn'd. **1634** Sir T. Herbert *Trav.* 196 Tis so made to open, that as they goe along, the least aire gives all to all mens immodest viewes. **1722** De Foe *Relig. Courtsh.* I. ii. (1840) 63, I have heard his father make him speak lewd words and sing immodest songs. **1826** Scott *Woodst.* iii, Whate'er of such lawless idleness and immodest folly hath defiled the land.

immodestly (ɪ'mɒdɪstlɪ), *adv.* [f. prec. + -LY^{2}.] In an immodest manner.

1. With excessive self-assertion; arrogantly.

1600 E. Blount tr. *Conestaggio* Apol. A iij, To surmise that I have spoken of them, either with passion or immodestlie. **1617** Moryson *Itin.* II. 123, I will not speake injuriously of your deserts, nor immodestly of mine owne. **1870** Lowell *Among my Bks.* Ser. I. (1873) 138 Himself not immodestly claimed the civic wreath for having saved the lives of fellow-citizens.

2. Improperly, indelicately, indecently.

1576 Woolton *Chr. Manual* L iij b (T.), He would have us live soberly;—not wantonly, not immodestly, not incontinently. **1590** Spenser *F.Q.* II. xii. 16 Throwing forth lewd wordes immodestly. *a* **1638** Mede *Diatr.* 259 (T.) These Corinthian women .. discovered their faces immodestly in the congregation. **1881** Miss Braddon *Asph.* I. 217 She wears .. her petticoats immodestly scanty.

immodesty (ɪ'mɒdɪstɪ). [ad. L. *immodestia*, f. *im-* (IM-^{2}) + *modestia* MODESTY. Cf. F. *immodestie* (1564 J. Thierry).] Want of modesty.

1. Excess of self-assertion or pretension; arrogance, forwardness; impudence.

1605 *Play Stucley* in Simpson *Sch. Shaks.* (1878) I. 161 Count it not in me immodesty To love the man whom heaven appointed for me. **1651** Baxter *Inf. Bapt.* 214, I thought it would seem meer pride and immodesty in me to send Arguments to you. **1681–6** J. Scott *Chr. Life* (1747) III. 635 To expose the great Immodesty of Crellius, who .. will needs persuade the World, that by the Word in the Chaldee Paraphrase is no where meant a Person. **1869** Ruskin *Q. of Air* §137 It belongs to all immodesty to defy or deny law, and assert privilege and license. **1893** *Independent* (N.Y.) 19 Oct., I may without immodesty say [etc.].

†b. In wider sense: Want of moderation or restraint. *Obs. rare.*

1665 Manley *Grotius' Low. C. Warres* 69 By his cruelty towards Priests, and all other kinds of immodesty.

2. Want of the sense of decorum or decency; impropriety, indelicacy; unchastity.

1597 Daniel *Civ. Wars* VIII. (R.), She shames to think that ought within her face Should breed th' opinion of immodesty. **1638** Sir T. Herbert *Trav.* (ed. 2) 182 Never regarding they were naked; .. I wondred .. at their immodesty. **1685** Baxter *Paraphr. N.T.*, *1 Pet.* iv. 3 We did too long live .. in immodesties .. and in excess of wine. **1859** Tennyson *Enid* 960 It seem'd an easier thing At once .. to strike her dead, Than to cry 'Halt', and to her own bright face Accuse her of the least immodesty.

†**immodish** (ɪ'məʊdɪʃ, ɪmm-), *a.* *Obs. nonce-wd.* [f. IM-^{2} + MODISH.] Not according to the mode; unfashionable. Hence †**i'mmodishly** *adv.*, unfashionably.

1649 G. Daniel *Trinarch.* To Rdr. 72 A Band Im-modeish, or, I wot not what Small singularity of Beard, or None. **1690** *Moral Ess. & Disc.* Pref. 2 So immodishly qualified.

†**i'mmodulate,** *v.* *Obs.* *rare*$^{-0}$. [f. L. *immodulāt-us* inharmonious, f. *im-* (IM-^{2}) + *modulāt-us*: see MODULATE.] (See quot.)

1623 Cockeram, *Immodulate*, to doe a thing without due proportion.

i'mmodulated, *ppl. a.* *rare.* [f. IM-^{2} + *modulated*, pa. pple. of MODULATE *v.*: cf. prec.] Not modulated; without vocal modulation.

1765 *Patriotism* v. in *Sch. Satire* (1802) 318 While, lib'ral of th' immodulated note He screams thro' all his dissonance of throat. **1878** Symonds *Shelley* 11 His voice was .. harsh and immodulated.

†**i'mmoisture,** *v.* *Obs.* [f. IM-^{1} + MOISTURE.] *trans.* To imbue with moisture, to moisten.

1523 Skelton *Garl. Laurel* 698 Of Pliades .. Immoysturid with mislyng.

†**immolate,** *ppl. a.* *Obs.* or *arch.* [ad. L. *immolāt-us*, pa. pple. of *immolāre*: see next. (In early examples const. as *pa. pple.*: see next, and -ATE^{2}.)] Sacrificed, immolated.

1534 More *On the Passion* Wks. 1296/1 The nyght .. wher in was immolate and offered in sacryfyce the vnspotted lambe. **1551** Gardiner *Explic. Cath. Fayth* 148 (R.) Whether Christ be daily immolate or only ones. **1830** W. Phillips *Mt. Sinai* III. 32 Nor were unconsumed The reeking victims immolate.

immolate, ('ɪməʊleɪt), *v.* [f. L. *immolāt-*, ppl. stem of *immolāre*, orig. to sprinkle with sacrificial meal (*mola salsa*), f. *im-* (IM-^{1}) + *mola* meal. The pa. pple. seems to have been the part first used: cf. prec.]

1. *trans.* To sacrifice, offer in sacrifice; to kill as a victim. (Properly, and now only, of sacrifices in which life is taken.)

1548 Hall *Chron., Hen. VII* 6 b, As though he should be a dewe sacrifice or an host immolated for the .. homicide. **1619** H. Hutton *Follies Anat.* (Percy Soc.) 48 Pan did the first fruites of his fold present: .. Ceres did immolate .. Autumn's rich prime, and Terra's golden mines. **1660** F. Brooke tr. *Le Blanc's Trav.* 126 They will cut themselves to immolate the bloud to their Idol. **1794** Sullivan *View Nat.* V. 327 The horrible custom of immolating the captives of war at the tombs of those who had been slain in battle. **1851** D. Wilson *Preh. Ann.* (1863) I. v. 158 Human victims were immolated to the Thunderer.

†b. *absol.* or *intr.* To offer sacrifice, to sacrifice.

1628 J. Hume *Jewes Deliv.* i. 10 They were wont to immolate and sacrifice vnto their heathenish Gods. **1660** F. Brooke tr. *Le Blanc's Trav.* 15 In a certain place there, the Marabouts immolate at this time.

2. *trans.* and *fig.* To give up to destruction, or to severe suffering or loss, for the sake of something else; to 'sacrifice'.

1634 W. Tirwhyt tr. *Balzac's Lett.* (vol. I.) 91 Should I immolate my selfe to publique scorne. **1665** Boyle *Occas. Refl.* v. ix. (1848) 333 To immolate their own inclinations and desires .. to their Vanity. **1797** Burke *Regic. Peace* III. Wks. VIII. 278 They had offered to immolate at the same shrine the most valuable of the national acquisitions. **1874** H. R. Reynolds *John Bapt.* v. i. 306 The religion of Christ never immolates the Church at the Shrine of the priesthood.

Hence '**immolated,** '**immolating** *ppl. adjs.*

1548 [see 1 above]. **1715–20** Pope *Iliad* XXI. 145 In vain your immolated bulls are slain. **1858** J. Martineau *Stud. Chr.* 139 His [Jesus'] voluntary .. spirit .. becomes officiating priest, and strikes his own person with immolating blow.

immolation (ɪməʊ'leɪʃən). [ad. L. *immolātiōn-em*, n. of action f. *immolāre* to IMMOLATE. Cf. F. *immolation* (13th c.).]

1. The action of immolating or offering in sacrifice; sacrificial slaughter of a victim; sacrifice.

1534 More *On the Passion* Wks. 1296/1 Pascha in thebrew sygnyfyeth immolacion. **1552** Abp. Hamilton *Catech.* III. vii. (1884) 202 The immolatioun and sacrifice of the Paschal lambe. **1613** Purchas *Pilgrimage* (1614) 66 Immolations,

yea of their owne children. **1646** SIR T. BROWNE *Pseud. Ep.* v. viii. 246 In the Picture of the Immolation of Isaac, or Abraham sacrificing his son. **1844** LINGARD *Anglo-Sax. Ch.* (1858) I. i. 31 Immolation of victims to the gods of paganism.

b. Applied to the sacrifice of the mass.

1548 RIDLEY *Answ. Queries touching Mass* iii, The Representation and Commemoration of Christ's Death and Passion, said and done in the Mass, is called the Sacrifice, Oblation, or Immolation of Christ. **1624** GATAKER *Transubst.* 5 That immolation of Christ's flesh which is done with the Priest's hand. **1849** ROCK *Ch. of Fathers* I. i. 17 St. Beda..held that the immolation of this sacrifice was an injunction laid upon the priesthood of His Church by Christ Himself.

c. *concr.* That which is immolated; a sacrificial victim, a sacrifice, an oblation.

1589 WARNER *Alb. Eng.* II. Prose Addit. (1612) 339 An Immolation or burnt sacrifice, offered to the Infernall Deities. **1595** B. BARNES *Spir. Sonn.* in Farr *S.P. Eliz.* I. 51 Thou precious immolacion of mankinde! **1651** C. CARTWRIGHT *Cert. Relig.* I. 291 That which is offered and consecrated by the Priest, is called a sacrifice,..a holy immolation.

2. *fig.* Devotion to destruction or severe loss for the sake of something else; 'sacrifice'.

c **1690** *Let. to Tillotson* in Somers *Tracts* (1748) II. 243 Has not Mammon been made a God, and a Crown an Idol, to which the Prince of Orange and his Adherents have sacrific'd the Lives of many thousands of Men,..besides a vast Treasure, tho' it is not fit to be named after the other two Immolations? **1828** D'ISRAELI *Chas. I,* II. viii. 186 Richelieu, by many an immolation, saved his country from intestine wars. **1847** EMERSON *Repr. Men, Swedenborg* Wks. (Bohn) I. 334 This immolation of genius and fame at the shrine of conscience.

immolator (ˈɪməʊleɪtə(r)). [ad. L. *immolātor*, agent-n. f. *immolāre* to IMMOLATE.] One who immolates or offers in sacrifice.

1652 GAULE *Magastrom.* 303 When the hoste escaped from the Immolator (a direfull omen for the sacrifice to avoid the Altar). **1660** BURNEY *Κέρδ. δῶρον* (1661) 2 Manasses, an immolator to Devills. **1847** DISRAELI *Tancred* III. iv, The holy race supplied the victim and the immolators.

†**immole**, *v. Obs. rare.* [ad. L. *immolāre*: cf. F. *immoler* (15th c.).] *trans.* = IMMOLATE *v.*

1609 BIBLE (Douay) *Eccl.* ix. 2 To him that immoleth victimes.

†**iˈmmoment**, *a. Obs. rare*⁻¹. [Arbitrary f. IM-² + MOMENT *sb.*] Of no moment; trifling.

1606 SHAKS. *Ant. & Cl.* v. ii. 166 Some Lady trifles.. Immoment toyes.

†**iˈmmomentary**, *a. Obs. rare*⁻¹. [f. IM-² + MOMENTARY.] = next.

1662 S. FISHER *Answ. Bp. Gauden* Wks. (1679) 50 Outward Observations concerning Meats, Drinks, Dayes, Times, Postures..and other..Immomentary Formallities.

immomentous (ɪməʊˈmɛntəs), *a. rare.* [f. IM-² + MOMENTOUS.] Not momentous; of no moment; unimportant.

1726 *J Ker's Mem.* Pref. 1 Neither, are..his Remarks immomentous. **1805** ANNA SEWARD *Lett.* (1811) VI. 236 Our newspapers cease to assert the Austrian defeat immomentous. **1898** *Speaker* 5 Mar. 294 The Soul 'so immomentous' to Mrs. Watson.

†**iˈmmonarchize**, *v. Obs. nonce-wd.* [f. IM-¹ + MONARCHIZE.] *trans.* To confer monarchy upon; to make into a monarch.

1679 OATES *Myst. Iniq.* 29 They might..by that means absolutely Immonarchise themselves.

†**iˈmmonastered**, *ppl. a. Obs. nonce-wd.* [f. IM-¹ + *monaster*, early form of MONASTERY + -ED.] Shut up in a monastery.

1622 DRAYTON *Poly-olb.* xxiv. 103 Immonastred in Kent.

immoral (ɪˈmɒrəl), *a.* (*sb.*) [f. IM-² + MORAL. Cf. F. *immoral* (18th c., Raynal).] The opposite of *moral*; not moral.

1. Not consistent with, or not conforming to, moral law or requirement; opposed to or violating morality; morally evil or impure; unprincipled, vicious, dissolute. (Of persons, things, actions, etc.)

1660 R. COKE *Power & Subj.* 80 If a man be obliged to his will, then..every man is obliged to do any thing because he hath willed it, then which there is nothing can be more immoral and destructive to all society. *a* **1715** BURNET *Own Time* I. III. 533 A learned but a very immoral man. **1736** BUTLER *Anal.* II. Concl, The same dissolute immoral temper of mind. **1841** MACAULAY *Ess., Comic Dramatists* (1887) 596 Morality is deeply interested in this—that what is immoral shall not be presented to the imagination of the young and susceptible in constant connection with what is attractive. **1848** WHARTON *Law Lex., Immoral contracts*, all contracts founded upon considerations *contra bonos mores*, are void. **1860** PEARSON in *National Rev.* Oct. 370 The times were gross, and their literature is often impure, but it is not immoral; it does not debauch the soul.

†**2.** Not having a moral nature or character; non-moral. *Obs. rare.*

a **1761** SHERLOCK *Serm.* II. 130 (L.) Whatever reason they [brutes] have, it is..exercised only with regard to their own wants and desires, and this renders them immoral agents.

B. *sb.* (*nonce-uses*, in opposition to *moral* sb.: see quots.)

1863 W. C. DOWDING *Life Calixtus* xv. 131 To sketch the morals (or *immorals*) of the times he lived in. **1896** AINGER in *B'ham Inst. Mag.* Mar. 292 It is thought foolish now to point a moral. At the same time what may be called an immoral, is held..eminently artistic.

Hence **iˈmmoralness**, immorality.

1727 in BAILEY vol. II.

immoralism (ɪˈmɒrəlɪz(ə)m). [ad. G. *immoralismus* (Nietzsche), f. IMMORAL *a.* + -ISM.] The reverse or negation of moralism; a system of thought or practice which rejects moral law.

1907 *Athenæum* 23 Mar. 348/1 The system..of Nietzsche, with all its blasphemy and immoralism. **1918** *Hibbert Jrnl.* Apr. 378 The sickly social idealism..which treated the most healthy immorality so much more harshly than it treated the most unhealthy immoralism. **1929** B. H. STREETER *Primitive Church* v. 179 The theoretic basis of Gnostic immoralism was a distinction between the ultimate Good God and the more or less evil Creator of the material universe. **1973** E. R. DODDS *Anc. Concept of Progress* 105 Nietzsche himself recognized the affiliation of his immoralism to the sophistic movement.

immoralist (ɪˈmɒrəlɪst). [f. IMMORAL *a.* + -IST, after *moralist.*] An advocate of immorality, or opponent of morality.

1697 C. LESLIE *Snake in Grass* (ed. 2) 90 Those who would improve this Principle..to justifie Immoralists. **1857** MISS MULOCK *Th. ab. Wom.* vii, That arch *im*-moralist, that high-priest of intellectual self-worship, Goethe. **1880** *Contemp. Rev.* Mar. 482 The appeal so eagerly made by artistic immoralists to science.

immorality (ɪmɒˈrælɪtɪ). [f. as prec. + -ITY, after *morality*.]

1. Immoral quality, character, or conduct; violation of moral law; wickedness, viciousness. (Now often used specifically of sexual impurity.)

c **1566** J. ALDAY tr. *Boaystuau's Theat. World* N viij, From thence the immorralitie and lingring of proces do procede. **1664** H. MORE *Myst. Iniq.* Apol. 533 Simply to speak what is false has no immorality at all in it. Other-wise no Man might dispute or pronounce a false Axiome. **1697** COLLIER (*title*) A short View of the Immorality and Profaneness of the English Stage. **1879** FROUDE *Cæsar* ii. 11 The educated Greeks..had no horror of immorality as such. **1894** SIR E. SULLIVAN *Woman* 29 The distinction society draws between immorality in women and immorality in men is monstrous: ..to assume, as men often do, that immorality is a glory to them, whilst it is a disgrace to women, is absurd.

2. with *an* and *pl.* An instance or species of this; an immoral act or practice; a vice.

a **1631** DONNE in *Select.* (1840) 70 The immoralities..that thou dost towards men, in scandalizing them, by thy sins. **1751–73** JORTIN *Eccl. Hist.* (R.), The writing of books or epistles under borrowed names, and imposing them as genuine upon the public, is..an immorality. **1859** LANG *Wand. India* 276 Deceit and falsehood are not regarded as immoralities in the eyes of Asiatics. **1876** MOZLEY *Univ. Serm.* viii. 162 Injustice is of all immoralities not the one most easily condoned.

iˈmmoralize, *v. rare.* [f. IMMORAL + -IZE.] *trans.* To render immoral.

a **1754** FIELDING *Fathers* Prol., May it decrease in favour; And be its fame immoralized for ever! **1898** *Westm. Gaz.* 24 Sept. 4/2 Even doors, fences, and planks from the wooden houses were torn down..to serve as fuel to cook for the troops... Such immoralised people the Spaniards are when they are..in a fix.

immorally (ɪˈmɒrəlɪ), *adv.* [f. as prec. + -LY².] In an immoral manner.

1727 in BAILEY vol. II. **1798** COLEBROOKE tr. *Digest Hindu Law* (1801) I. 347 Not afraid of acting immorally. **1894** *Chicago Advance* 16 Aug., A perverted mind and a depraved will, irrationally and immorally swayed hither and thither by its environment.

†**immoˈration**. *Obs. rare.* [n. of action from L. *immorārī* to stay upon or at, f. *im-* (IM-¹) + *morārī* to tarry.] The action of resting or dwelling *upon* something.

1640 BP. REYNOLDS *Passions* xi. 102 Stay and immoration of the Mind upon the Object loved. **1666** SPURSTOWE *Spir. Chym.* Pref. (1668) 5 It is a work of..difficulty..to make any considerable immoration, upon those subjects.

†**immorigerous**, *a. Obs.* [f. IM-² + MORIGEROUS (in *Timon*, *c* 1600).] Unyielding, obstinate: disobedient, rebellious; uncivil.

1623 COCKERAM, *Immorigerous*, rude, vnciuill. **1624** D. CAWDREY *Humilitie Saints Liverie* 40 How immorigerous and obstinate to the commands of God! **1649** JER. TAYLOR *Gt. Exemp.* II. ix. 122 Ungentlenesse, and an immorigerous Spirit. **1678** CUDWORTH *Intell. Syst.* I. v. 699 Immorigerous, Stiff, and Inflexible. **1732** STACKHOUSE *Hist. Bible* I. 150 (T. Suppl.) Such creatures as are immorigerous, we have found out expedients to reclaim.

¶**b.** *catachr.* Not refined or elegant, 'rude'.

1647 R. BARON *Cyprian Acad.* 11 We were as well content in our immorigerous roomes, as others in the magnificent structures of our Royall Soveraigne.

Hence †**immoˈrigerousness**, uncomplying obstinacy.

1649 JER. TAYLOR *Gt. Exemp.* I ii. 64 All degrees of delay are degrees of immorigerousnesse, and unwillingnesse.

immortable (ɪˈmɔːtəb(ə)l), *a.* [f. IMMORT(AL *a.* + -ABLE.] Having the capacity to live after death. So **immortaˈbility**.

1922 J. Y. SIMPSON *Man & Attainment of Immortality* xiii. 275 The contention that eternal life..is morally conditioned, that man, in short, is immortable rather than immortal. **1930** S. D. MCCONNELL (*title*) Immortability. An Old Man's Conclusions. **1950** S. EDDY *You will survive after Death* 3 We may have at least..'immortability'—a fitness in the quality of human personality for survival.

immortal (ɪˈmɔːtəl), *a.* and *sb.* Also 4–5 **in-**. [ad. L. *immortāl-is* (in pl. = the gods), f. *im-* (IM-²) + *mortālis* MORTAL. Cf. F. *immortel* (13–14th c. in Hatz.-Darm.), It. *immortale*.]

A. *adj.* **1. a.** Not mortal; not liable or subject to death; deathless, undying; living for ever.

c **1374** CHAUCER *Troylus* I. 103 So aungelli was hyre natyf beaute þat lyke a þyng inmortal semede sche. *c* **1386** —— *Man of Law's T.* 541 Immortal god that sauedest Susanne Fro fals blame. **1494** FABYAN *Chron.* 6 All these were Mynystris of god immortall. **1526** TINDALE *1 Tim.* i. 17 So then vnto god kynge everlastynge immortall invisible and wyse only be honoure and prayse for ever and ever. **1529** MORE *Dyaloge* I. Wks. 155/1 What if ye woulde..wene that bestes had immortall soules as men haue? **1656–9** B. HARRIS *Parival's Iron Age* (ed. 2) 59 Departed out of this fraile life, to the immortall one. **1742** YOUNG *Nt. Th.* VII. 1398 Souls immortal, made for bliss. **1885** FINLAYSON *Biol. Relig., Etern. Life* 87 A human soul might be immortal—in the sense of living on for ever,—and yet might never have ..'eternal life'—the true spiritual life of fellowship with God.

b. *transf.* Pertaining to immortal beings or immortality; heavenly, divine.

1535 COVERDALE *2 Esdras* ii. 45 These be they, that haue put of the mortall clothinge and put on the immortall. **1606** SHAKS. *Ant. & Cl.* v. ii. 283, I haue Immortall longings in me. **1803–6** WORDSW. *Intimations* ix, Our Souls have sight of that immortal sea Which brought us hither.

2. a. In wider sense: Not liable to perish or decay; everlasting, imperishable, unfading, incorruptible.

1630 *R. Johnson's Kingd. & Commw.* 140 Of the Lawes in force, some are fundamentall..and immortall..others are Temporall. **1644** MILTON *Areop.* (Arb.) 45 The race, where that immortall garland is to be run for. **1752** HUME *Pol. Disc.* xii. 303 The world itself probably is not immortal. **1776** ADAM SMITH *W.N.* I. xi. III. (1869) I. 220 The precious metals..are not necessarily immortal any more than they [the coarse metals].

b. *spec.* Of fame, or of famous works or their authors: Lasting through an unlimited succession of ages; that will not fade from the memory of men; remembered or celebrated through all time.

1514 BARCLAY *Cyt. & Uplondyshm.* (Percy Soc.) 18 [They] have in batayle..Won fame immortall, and excellent honours. **1632** MILTON *L'Allegro* 137 Soft Lydian airs, Married to immortal verse. **1738** SWIFT *Pol. Conversat.* Introd. 4 King William the Third, of ever glorious and immortal Memory. **1756** C. LUCAS *Ess. Waters* II. 18 As our Immortal Boyle has demonstrated, they are compound bodies. **1840** ALISON *Europe* (1849–50) VIII. liv. 464 Saragossa..has now..become immortal in the rolls of fame. **1873** HAMERTON *Intell. Life* IX. vi. (1875) 331 It was during tedious years of imprisonment that Bunyan wrote his immortal allegory. **1928** E. C. WEBSTER *Pot Holes* 3, I am as fond of Burns as any, and have read a good deal of his poetry, ..but I am not one of those who believe that the Immortal Memory can only be preserved by a yearly pickling in alcohol. **1959** *Times* 17 Apr. 15/3 His record of devotion to the 'Immortal Memory'—a toast which he had proposed all over Scotland and England—was typical of this special cult which the wandering Scot has carried all over the globe. **1973** *Listener* 15 Mar. 344/2 The Johnson celebration..the toast to 'the immortal memory'.

†**c.** *immortal herb*: = IMMORTELLE. *Obs.*

1731–7 MILLER *Gard. Dict., Xeranthemum*,..is vulgarly call'd the Immortal Herb, because the Flower of it may be kept for many Years, for it has rigid Petals, which crackle as if they were Plates of Metal.

3. a. In hyperbolical use: Lasting, perpetual, constant, 'undying', 'eternal'.

1538 STEPHEN in Ellis *Orig. Lett.* Ser. III. III. 223 With immortal thanckes for youre inestymable goodnes towarde me. **1586** A. DAY *Eng. Secretary* I. (1625) 75 The.. immortall hate, that all good men beare to..such kind of crueltie. **1669** PEPYS *Diary* 29 Jan., I have made myself an immortal enemy by it. **1681** TEMPLE *Mem.* III. Wks. 1731 I. 356 An immortal Body of six thousand brave English, which were by Agreement to be continually recruited. **1696** PHILLIPS (ed. 5), *Immortal*,..abusively said of things that last longer than People would have them, such a Woman has an immortal Clack.

†**b.** *colloq.* Superhuman, inhuman, excessive. *Obs.*

c **1540** tr. *Pol. Verg. Eng. Hist.* (Camden No. 29) 208 Then he besowght ayd, wherby, throwgh his immortal benyfyt, he might returne safely unto his owne nobylytie. *a* **1627** HAYWARD *Four Y. Eliz.* (Camden) 95 A most immortall and mercilesse butcherie did arise.

B. *sb.* **1.** An immortal being; one not subject to death. In *pl.*, esp. as a title for the gods of classical mythology.

16.. WALLER (J.), The Paphian queen,..Like terror did among th' immortals breed, Taught by her wound that goddesses may bleed. **1684** BUNYAN *Pilgr.* II. 8 She thought she saw..her Husband in a place of Bliss among many Immortals. **1774** J. BRYANT *Mythol.* III. 87 (Jod.) There was a war carried on against the Titans of Babylonia, whom he styles the Immortals. **1791** COWPER *Iliad* XVI. 542 Under yon great city fight no few Sprung from Immortals. *a* **1854** H. REED *Lect. Eng. Lit.* vii. (1878) 236 Man..is an immortal, gifted with a soul.

2. *fig.* **a.** In *pl.* a title for the royal bodyguard of ancient Persia (see quot. 1838); also, for other troops.

1803 *Edin. Rev.* II. 62 The English expedition was opposed to their immortals, to troops covered with trophies and scars. **1823** CRABB *Technol. Dict., Immortals* (*Mil.*), a

term of derision applied to soldiers who never see war. **1838** THIRLWALL *Greece* II. xv. 253 A body of 10,000 Persian infantry, the flower of the whole army, who were called the Immortals, because their number was kept constantly full.

b. A person, esp. an author, of enduring fame: cf. A. 2 b. Usually in *pl.*

Applied familiarly to the forty members of the French Academy (F. *les quarante immortels*), with a side reference to the fact that their number is always filled up; hence sometimes to the Royal Academicians in England.

1882 FROUDE *Carlyle* I. 421 He might not have been the Carlyle, who has conquered for himself among the Immortals.

3. That which is immortal; immortality.

1841 JAMES *Brigand* i, As if the immortal within us were telling the mortal of anxieties and griefs, and dangers approaching. **1844** MRS. BROWNING *House of Clouds* xiii, Love secures some fairer things, Dowered with his immortal.

Hence **i'mmortalism**, a doctrine of or belief in immortality; **i'mmortalist**, one who believes in immortality; **i'mmortalness** = IMMORTALITY; **i'mmortalship** [f. the sb.], the personality of an immortal (used as a burlesque title).

1796 W. TAYLOR in *Monthly Rev.* XXI. 509 Doctrines of freedom of the will, immaterialism, *immortalism, and theism. *a* **1667** JER. TAYLOR *Funeral Serm.* 392 (L.) The inhabitants of Ister..were called *Immortalists, because.. they saw this clearly, that virtuous and good men do not die, but their souls do go into blessed regions. **1817** W TAYLOR in *Monthly Rev.* LXXXIII. 15 Deists and atheists, immortalists and mortalists. **1616** R. C. *Times' Whistle* etc. (1871) 151 Then shall our corruptible flesh put on *Immortalnesse and incorruption. **1816** G. COLMAN *Br. Grins, Fire* xliii, Up their *immortalships all bounced.

immortality (ɪmɔː'tælɪtɪ). [ME. a. F. *immortalité* (12–13th c. in Godef. *Compl.*), ad. L. *immortālitās*, f. *immortālis* IMMORTAL.]

1. The quality or condition of being immortal; exemption from death or annihilation; endless life or existence; eternity; perpetuity.

conditional immortality: see CONDITIONAL A. 1.

a **1340** HAMPOLE *Psalter* xxix. 10 þat i may get þe state of immortalite. **1432–50** tr. *Higden* (Rolls) I. 5 A story is..the memory of life..renewenge as thro immortalite thynges like to peresche. **1526** TINDALE *1 Cor.* xv. 53 This mortall must put on immortalite. **1529** MORE *Dyaloge* I. Wks. 156/1 When we..saye we shall dye..and tourne all to duste, we.. nothing entende thereby to denye immortalite of our soule. **1685** BAXTER *Paraphr. N.T., Matt.* xxii. 31–2 The Sadducees denied..the immortality of the Soul, and all our life after this. **1719** WATTS *Ps.* CXLVI. i, My days of praise shall ne'er be past While..immortality endures. **1885** FINLAYSON *Biol. Relig., Etern. Life* 86–7 The word 'Immortality' is often used..loosely. When we speak of 'the immortality of the soul', we sometimes simply emphasize the fact that the soul survives the death of the body; but, at other times, we mean that the soul is destined to exist..for ever.

attrib. **1654** WHITLOCK *Zootomia* 85 If you will believe them [quacks], you would take their Closets..to be Immortality Offices.

2. The condition of being celebrated through all time; enduring fame or remembrance.

1535 COVERDALE *Wisd.* viii. 13 By the meanes of her I shal optayne immortalite, and leaue behinde me an euer-lastinge memoriall. **1608** SHAKS. *Per.* III. ii. 30 Virtue and cunning were endowments greater Than nobleness and riches.. immortality attends the former, Making a man a god. **1800–24** CAMPBELL *Lines on Poland* 22 In Fate's defiance.. Poland has won her immortality. **1866** R. W. DALE *Disc. Spec. Occ.* viii. 252 Shakspeare's immortality is secure.

immortalizable (ɪ'mɔːtəlaɪzəb(ə)l), *a.* [f. IMMORTALIZE + -ABLE.] Capable of being immortalized, or of becoming immortal.

1895 in *Daily News* 1 Oct. 5/5 That man is not so much intrinsically immortal as immortalisable.

†**i'mmortalizate**, *v.* *Obs. rare.* [f. IMMORTAL + -IZE + -ATE.] *trans.* = IMMORTALIZE.

1566 PAINTER *Pal. Pleas.* I. 114 Which he placed over the gate of his castell to immortalizate the great chastitie of his ..wife.

immortalization (ɪˌmɔːtəlaɪ'zeɪʃən) [f. next + -ATION. Cf. F. *immortalisation* (16th c. in Littré).] The action of immortalizing, or fact of being immortalized.

1603 FLORIO *Montaigne* (1634) 630 His [Alexander's] concepts about his immortalization. **1830** *Blackw. Mag.* XXVIII. 846 'That amber immortalization', (the expression of a man of genius). **1897** *Westm. Gaz.* 25 Oct. 10/2 It is.. surprising that none of our newly-made millionaires should have sought the immortalisation which the endowment of a great observatory gives.

immortalize (ɪ'mɔːtəlaɪz), *v.* [f. IMMORTAL + -IZE. Cf. F. *immortaliser* (16th c. in Littré).]

1. *trans.* To render immortal.

a. To endow with endless life; to exempt from death.

1633 EARL MANCH. *Al Mondo* (1636) 28 The body glorified..shall..be purified, perfected, and immortalized. **1875** E. WHITE *Life in Christ* III. xx. (1878) 283 He..will complete the process by immortalising your mortal bodies also at the resurrection.

b. To make (a thing) everlasting, confer endless existence upon; to perpetuate.

c **1566** J. ALDAY tr. *Boaystuau's Theat. World* S ij, Printing ..is the treasurer that immortaliseth the monuments of our spirites. **1592** DAVIES *Immort. Soul* cxxviii, Mortal things desire their like to breed, That so they may their kind immortalize. **1688** SOUTH *Serm.* (1697) I. 520 What are most of the Histories of the World, but Lyes? Lyes immortalized. **1715** tr. *C'tess D'Aunoy's Wks.* 407 The King desir'd her not to immortalize her Grief. **1841** MYERS *Cath. Th.* III. §41. 157 Errours.. generated by immortalising, as it were, merely temporary forms of expression.

c. To cause to be remembered or celebrated through all time; to confer enduring fame upon. (The prevailing sense.) Also *absol.*

1589 GREENE *Menaphon* (Arb.) 69 Holde, take thy fauors ..and immortalize whom thou wilt with thy toyes. **1591** SHAKS. *1 Hen. VI*, I. ii. 148 Driue them from Orleance, and be immortaliz'd. *c* **1665** MRS. HUTCHINSON *Mem. Col. Hutchinson* (1838) 12/1 The gentile virtues, that so immortalize the names of Cicero, Plutarch [etc.]. **1790** COWPER *My Mother's Pict.* 8 Blest be the Art that can immortalize. **1821–30** LD. COCKBURN *Mem.* 211 A genius.. who has immortalized Edinburgh,—Walter Scott. **1856** GRINDON *Life* iii. (1875) 31 Those exquisite shapes which ancient Art immortalized in marble.

2. *intr.* To become immortal; to attain immortality or enduring fame. *rare.*

1737 POPE *Hor. Ep.* II. i. 54 Say at what age a Poet grows divine?.. End all dispute; and fix the year precise When British bards begin t'immortalize?

Hence **i'mmortalized** *ppl. a.*; **i'mmortalizing** *vbl. sb.* and *ppl. a.*

1611 COTGR., *Immortalization*, an immortalization, an immortalizing. **1669** GALE *Crt. Gentiles* I. III. iv. 59 These Divine immortalising drinks, Nectar and Ambrosia. **1694** F. BRAGGE *Disc. Parables* I. 4 The word of God..will spring up ..to the nourishing..nay the immortalizing of men. **1858** SEARS *Athan.* II. xii. 250 [Christ] the great Exemplar of immortalized human nature.

immortalizer (ɪ'mɔːtəlaɪzə(r)). [f. prec. + -ER[1].] One who or that which immortalizes.

1710 TOLAND *Refl. Sacheverell's Serm.* 9 That they might have an Immortalizer in each Province. **1831** *Blackw. Mag.* XXIX. 525 The insidious immortalizer of frail beauty. **1885** tr. *Hehn's Wand. Pl. & Anim.* 414 To comfort one's self with the hope of a life after death..as the Getae did whom Herodotus calls οἱ ἀθανατίζοντες, the immortalizers.

immortally (ɪ'mɔːtəlɪ), *adv.* [f. IMMORTAL + -LY[2].]

1. In the way of immortal life or existence; endlessly, eternally, for ever.

a **1529** SKELTON *Dethe Northumbld.* 147 His right noble estate Immortally whiche is immaculate. **1597** SHAKS. *2 Hen. IV*, IV. iv. 144 He that weares the Crowne immortally, Long guard it yours. **1756** LAW *Lett. import. Subj.* 132 The first divine..nature of Adam, which was to have been immortally holy in union with God, is lost. **1855** BROWNING *Any Wife to Any Husband* ix, Therefore she is immortally my bride; Chance cannot change my love, nor time impair.

b. Perpetually; without withering.

1858 HAWTHORNE *Fr. & It. Jrnls.* (1872) I. 2 Green fields —immortally green, whatever winter can do against them.

2. *colloq.* To a degree beyond that of mortals; infinitely. [Cf. Cicero's *gaudeo immortaliter*.]

c **1540** tr. *Pol. Verg. Eng. Hist.* (Camden No. 29) 153 But King Edward, rejoysing immortally for the victory [etc.]. **1621** BURTON *Anat. Mel.* I. ii. IV. vii. (1676) 100/2 As he [Matth. Paris] saith of Edward the first at the news of..his Sons birth, *immortaliter gavisus*, he was immortally glad. **1883** *Harper's Mag.* June 134/2 How immortally beautiful that girl was!

immortase, -ese, -ise, obs. ff. AMORTIZE.

1462 J. PASTON in *P. Lett.* No. 461 II. 113 Certeyn livelode to be immortesid therto. **1487** *Ibid.* No. 893 III. 331 That ought [out] of the seide maners schuld be perpetually immortaysed a serteyn londe. **1657** HOWELL *Londinop.* 67 For the immortising and propriation of the Priory.

‖**immortelle** (ɪmɔː'tɛl, Fr. ‖imɔrtɛl). [Fr. (short for *fleur immortelle*), fem. of *immortel* IMMORTAL.] A name for various composite flowers of papery texture (esp. *Helichrysum orientale*, and other species of *Helichrysum*, *Xeranthemum*, etc.) which retain their colour after being dried: = EVERLASTING B. 4. Also *attrib.* and *Comb.*, *transf.*, and *fig.*

1832 *Backwoods Canada* iv. (1836) 45 The white love-everlasting, the same that the chaplets are made of by the French and Swiss girls to adorn the tombs of their friends, and which they call immortelle; the Americans call it life-everlasting. **1838** MISS PARDOE *River & Desert* II. 17 A tall black cross, crowned with immortelles. **1867** LADY HERBERT *Cradle L.* ix. 139 Cliffs..covered..with a beautiful bright lavender-coloured immortelle. **1883** 'MARK TWAIN' *Life on Mississippi* xlii. 431 A milder form of sorrow finds its inexpensive and lasting remembrancer in the coarse and ugly but indestructible 'immortelle'—which is a wreath or cross or some such emblem, made of rosettes of black linen, with sometimes a yellow rosette at the conjunction of the cross's bars,—kind of sorrowful breastpin, so to say. **1890** A. MARTIN *Home Life Ostrich Farm* i. 21 Pink and white *immortelles*, gladioli, ixias, and irises of all kinds abound. **1929** D. H. LAWRENCE *Pansies* 6 Anyhow I offer a bunch of pansies, not a wreath of *immortelles*. I don't want everlasting flowers. **1936** *Times Lit. Suppl.* 21 Nov. 935/1 Poor little immortelles surviving from that old gorgeous efflorescence of linguistic misuse. **1960** R. G. HAGGAR *Conc. Encycl. Cont. Pott. & Porc.* 67/2 *Blaublümchenmuster*, (German) blue flower pattern: 'aster' or 'immortelle' pattern. *Ibid.* 239/2 Early [Klösterle] wares were decorated in blue with popular Meissen 'Immortelle' and 'bird on rock' designs. **1963** V. NABOKOV *Gift* iii. 153 Even if he had put on the light the immortelle-like yellowness of daytime electricity would have been no help at all. **1968** E. LOVELACE *Schoolmaster* i. 7 The immortelle holds its scarlet blossoms still. **1970** *New Yorker* 22 Aug. 38/3 The old man was himself like a trophy of immortelles. **1971** E. M. ROACH in J. Figueroa *Caribbean Voices* I. 22 The giant immortelles Splash fire on the hills.

†**i'mmortgage**, *v.* *Obs. rare.* [f. IM-[1] + MORTGAGE.] *trans.* = MORTGAGE *v.*

1575 *Galway Arch.* in *10th Rep. Hist. MSS. Comm.* App. v. 426 The said Clan Teige shuld not immortgadge or put to pledge anny..of ther landes.

immortification (ɪˌmɔːtɪfɪ'keɪʃən). [ad. eccl. L. *immortificātio* (cf. *immortificātus* in A Kempis *De Imitatione*), f. *im-* (IM-[2]) + *mortificātio* MORTIFICATION. Cf. F. *immortification* (Fr. de Sales).] Want of mortification; a condition of the soul in which the passions are not mortified.

1626 T. H[AWKINS] *Caussin's Holy Crt.* 330 Sometime it [sadness], proceedeth from a great immortification of passion. **1649** JER. TAYLOR *Gt. Exemp.* I. iv. §4. 121 Immortification of spirit is the cause of all our..spiritual indispositions. *Ibid.* v. §9. 151 A state of infirmity, but..also of sin and death, a state of immortification. **1854** FABER *Growth in Holiness* viii. (1872) 133 In a spiritual man impatience to die would be no trifling immortification.

So **i'mmortified** *a.* [repr. med.L. *immortificātus*], not mortified.

1854 FABER *Growth in Holiness* viii. (1872) 115 One of the common delusions of immortified effeminacy.

†**i'mmotable**, *a.* *Obs. rare.* [ad. late L. *immōtābilis*, f. *im-* (IM-[2]) + *mōtābilis* (Vulgate) moving, movable, f. *mōtāre*, freq. of *movēre*, *mōt-* to move.] = IMMOVABLE.

1577 tr. *Bullinger's Decades* (1592) 844 Opinions..firme and immotable.

†**i'mmote**, *ppl. a.* *Obs.* [ad. L. *immōt-us*, f. *im-* (IM-[2]) + *mōtus* moved, pa. pple. of *movēre* to MOVE.] Unmoved (*lit.* and *fig.*).

1601 WEEVER *Mirr. Mart.* B iij b, A needle plac'd in equall distance, Betwixt a Load-stone and an Adamant, By either drawne..stands immote. **1685** COTTON tr. *Montaigne* II. 180 With an immote and unyielding constancy.

†**i'mmote**, *v.* *Obs. rare*[−1]. [f. *immōt-*, ppl. stem of late L. *immovēre* to move into or upon, place upon, f. *im-* (IM-[1]) + *movēre* to move.] *trans.* To convey or put upon something.

c **1420** *Pallad. on Husb.* IV. 109 Oyldregges salt effunde vppon the roote; Ffor grettest treen..vj congeus or iiij of hit ymmote [*immoueas*].

immotile (ɪ'məʊtɪl, -aɪl), *a.* [f. IM-[2] + MOTILE: cf. IMMOTE *ppl. a.*] Not motile; incapable of movement.

1872 H. C. WOOD in *Smithsonian Cont. to Knowl.* (1874) XIX. 213 Propagation by means of three immotile organs, generally placed upon distinct plants. **1875** BENNETT & DYER *Sach's Bot.* 789 The lateral leaflets of *Desmodium gyrans* are..immotile when the temperature of the air is below 22° C.

†**i'mmotion**. *Obs. nonce-wd.* [f. IM-[1] + MOTION.] ? Impulse. (App. fantastically used.)

1706 VANBRUGH *Mistake* IV. Wks. (Rtldg.) 452/1 By certain immotions, which—um—cause, as one may suppose, a sort of convulsive—yes,—hurricanious, um [etc.].

immotioned (ɪ'məʊʃənd, ɪmm-), *a.* *rare.* [f. IM-[2] + MOTION *sb.* + -ED[2].] Without motion, motionless.

1821 MOIR in *Blackw. Mag.* X. 641 Still and immotioned are the leafless woods. **1834** —— *Bride Lochleven* xvii. 37 She lay..Immotioned as a statue overthrown.

immotive (ɪ'məʊtɪv, ɪmm-), *a.* [f. IM-[2] + MOTIVE *a.*] Unmoving, or incapable of movement.

1627–47 FELTHAM *Resolves* I. lxii. 190 Laid in the stillness of an immotive calme. **1860** *Encycl. Brit.* XXI. 973/1 Almost insensible and immotive.

†**i'mmould**, *v.* *Obs.* [f. IM-[1] + MOULD: cf. INMOULD.] *trans.* To enclose as in a mould.

1610 G. FLETCHER *Christ's Vict.* II. xlix, So fabled Homer old, That Circe, with her potion, charm'd in gold, Vs'd manly soules in beastly bodies to immould.

†**i'mmound**, *v.* *Obs.* [f. IM-[1] + MOUND *sb.*] *trans.* To surround or enclose with a mound or mounds.

1591 SYLVESTER *Du Bartas* I. iii. 218 These straight and narrow streamed Fennes, And In-land Seas, which many a Mount immounds. **1610** W. FOLKINGHAM *Art of Survey* II. ii. 49 Collaterage Actiue, as..haying, hedging or shawing, immounding, impayling, immuring.

immovability (ɪmuːvə'bɪlɪtɪ). Also 4 **inmoeu(e)ablete**. [f. as next: see -ITY.] The quality or condition of being immovable; immovableness.

c **1374** CHAUCER *Boeth.* V. pr. vi. 134 (Camb. MS.) So as it ne may nat countrefeten it..for the inmoeuablete þat is to seyn þat is in the eternite of god. **1742** tr. *Algarotti on 'Newton's Theory'* II. 183 Our Speculations..to prove the Immoveability of the Sun. **1854** *Blackw. Mag.* LXXV. 56 A Tribunal..whose members..enjoy..immovability from office. **1868** LOCKYER *Guillemin's Heavens* (ed. 3) 343 Modern astronomical observation..has..exploded the idea of the immovability of the stars.

immovable (ɪ'muːvəb(ə)l), *a.* (and *sb.*) Also 4 **inmoeueable**, 5 **inmeuable**, 5–6 **immoov(e)able**, 6–

immoveable. [f. IM-² + MOVABLE. Cf. obs. F. *immo(u)vable*.] That cannot be moved.

A. *adj.* **1.** *lit.* That cannot be moved physically; firmly fixed; incapable of movement. Often less strictly: Motionless, stationary, fixed.

1387-8 T. USK *Test. Love* III. iv. (Skeat) l. 207 No reason defendeth, that some thing ne maie be in time temporell mouing, that in eterne is immouable. *c* **1440** *Promp. Parv.* 262/1 Inmeuable, *immobilis*. **1555** EDEN *Decades* 325 Armies of men passe ouer the immouable ise. **1596** SPENSER *F.Q.* v. ii. 35 The earth was in the middle centre pight, In which it doth immoueable abide. **1662** J. DAVIES tr. *Mandelslo's Trav.* 214 They lie down all along upon the ground, immovable as Statues. **1774** C. J. PHIPPS *Voy. N. Pole* 157 By these means the point of suspension of the pendulum is rendered much more immovable. **1831** R. KNOX *Cloquet's Anat.* 168 The articulations are naturally divided into..the moveable and the immoveable. **1831** BREWSTER *Newton* (1855) I. xi. 255 In his eyes the sun stood immovable in the centre of the universe.

2. *fig.* Not subject to change; unalterable, fixed. ***immovable feast***: see FEAST *sb.* 1.

c **1374** CHAUCER *Boeth.* v. pr. vi. 173 (B.M. Addit. MS.) þis ilke infinite moeuyng of temporel þinges folwiþ þis presentarie estat of þe lijf inmoeueable. *a* **1533** LD. BERNERS *Gold. Bk. M. Aurel.* (1546) Pij b, The..realm of Egypt.. hadde a lawe immouable. **1663** J. SPENCER *Prodigies* (1665) 312 Kingdoms..increasing to a greatness in the eye of sense immovable, and at last concluding in soil and dirt. **1706** PHILLIPS s.v. *Moveable Feasts*, The Immoveable Feasts are those, which..constantly fall on the same Day of the Month. **1871** R. ELLIS *Catullus* lxiv. 209 Words which his heedful soul had kept immovable ever.

b. Incapable of being diverted from one's purpose: steadfast, unyielding.

1534 ELYOT *Doctr. Princes* 8 It becometh..to princes in matter of justice, to have the minde immoueable. **1600** E. BLOUNT tr. *Conestaggio* 16 Resting immooveable in his counsels, and most obstinate in his opinion. **1759** JOHNSON *Rasselas* xviii, Heroes immovable by pain or pleasure. **1849** DICKENS *Dav. Copp.* xxiii, Mr. Jorkins has his opinions on these subjects... Mr. Jorkins is immovable.

c. Incapable of being stirred or affected with feeling; emotionless, impassive.

1639 BRUGIS tr. *Camus' Mor. Relat.* 229 His silence and his immoveable countenance gave..an answer which was not favourable. **1837** DICKENS *Pickw.* ii, His features were immovable.

3. *Law.* Not liable to be removed; permanent: applied to lands, houses, etc., as opposed to *movable* goods.

c **1449** PECOCK *Repr.* III. i. 277 Immouable godis. **1590** SWINBURNE *Testaments* 65 Of immoueable thinges, as of houses, or of demeanes, or of glebe, and such like, ecclesiasticall persons can not dispose by their testaments. **1651** HOBBES *Leviath.* II. xxiv. 130 All commodities, Moveable, and Immoveable. **1726** AYLIFFE *Parergon* 84 When an Executor begins to meddle with the immoveable Estate, before he has seiz'd on the moveable Goods. **1871** MARKBY *Elem. Law* §117 Thus land is..both physically and legally immoveable.

B. *sb.* (*Law.*) A piece or article of property that is immovable (see A. 3); almost always in *pl.* Immovable property, as land and things adherent thereto, as trees, buildings, servitudes.

1588 J. MELLIS *Briefe Instr.* Bj, This..Inuentorie of all my goods, moueables, and immoueables. **1677** *Govt. Venice* 193 Contracts..relating to the buying of Houses, Lands, or Ships (Ships being accounted immovables in Venice by reason of its scituation). *a* **1832** BENTHAM *Princ. Penal Law* Wks. 1843 I. 513 If he has property, it consists either in immoveables, or in moveables. **1884** *Law Times Rep.* LI. 119/1 The property..is, as regards immovables, governed by the law of England.

immovableness (ɪˈmuːvəb(ə)lnɪs). [f. prec. + -NESS.] The quality or condition of being immovable (*lit.* and *fig.*).

1617 MINSHEU *Voc. Hispan.-Lat.*, *Immobilidad*, immoueablenesse. **1727** BRADLEY *Family Dict.* s.v. *Earth*, Their system of the Immoveableness of the Earth. **1748** RICHARDSON *Clarissa* (1811) I. xlv. 353 The immoveableness I have shown. **1851** HAWTHORNE *Snow Image, Main Street* (1879) 74 With sullen but self-complacent immovableness.

immovably (ɪˈmuːvəblɪ), *adv.* [f. as prec. + -LY².] In an immovable manner (*lit.* and *fig.*); fixedly, steadfastly, unalterably.

1435 MISYN *Fire of Love* 46 Hym-self in only desire of hys makar in-moueabily. **1628** LE GRYS tr. *Barclay's Argenis* 81 He immoueably persisted on his former shew of mildnesse. **1761** STERNE *Tr. Shandy* III. iv, She leaned upon her elbow immovably. **1843** J. G. WILKINSON *Swedenborg's Anim. Kingd.* I. ii. 60 The upper jaw is immoveably fixed to the bones of the cranium.

†**immoved** (ɪˈmuːvd, *poet.* ɪˈmuːvɪd, ɪmm-), *ppl. a. Obs.* [f. IM-² + *moved*, pa. pple. of MOVE *v.*] Unmoved, motionless; unaltered.

1600 HEYWOOD *1st Pt. Edw. IV*, v. Wks. 1874 I. 76 An immovèd, constant, fixèd Star. **1634** —— *Maidenh. well Lost* I. ibid. IV. 109 We are fixt and stand immou'd. **1659** SHIRLEY *Content. Ajax & Ulysses* i, Did he stand immoved As I, when I received upon my casque A mighty javelin?

immram (ˈɪmram). Also **imram**. Pl. **im(m)rama**. [ad. O.Ir. *imram* (mod.Ir. *iomramh*), f. *imm-rá* to row around.] Any of the stories of fabulous sea voyages written in Ireland in the seventh and eighth centuries. Also *attrib.*

1895 A. NUTT in K. Meyer *Voy. of Bran* iv. 161 The *imrama* literature has been investigated by Professor Zimmer with all his wonted acuteness. **1917** *Mod. Philology* XV. 450 The *imram* is a sea-voyage tale in which a hero, accompanied by a few companions, wanders about from island to island, meets Otherworld wonders everywhere, and finally returns to his native land. **1948** M. DILLON *Early Irish Lit.* vi. 124 Of the seven immrama mentioned in the two lists of sagas, only three have come down to us. **1951** G. TURVILLE-PETRE *Heroic Age of Scandinavia* ix. 94 It is by no means improbable that the *Immrama* contain distorted descriptions of scenes, which the hermits had witnessed on their travels. **1962** *Guardian* 14 Dec. 7/4 The suggested relation between 'Gulliver's Travels' and the Early Irish *immram*. **1964** G. JONES *Norse Atlantic Saga* i. 7 The best known of the Irish *Imrama*..records the travels of St. Brendan. **1967** DILLON & CHADWICK *Celtic Realms* viii. 200 The briefer account of Brendan's voyage is included in the *Vita*,..and we thus possess two apparently independent accounts of the saint's *immram*.

†**i'mmud**, *v. Obs.* Also **enmud**, **emmudde**. [f. IM-¹ + MUD.] *trans.* To enclose or bury in mud.

1611 FLORIO, *Inuolutare*, to enmud, to enmire. **1644** DIGBY *Nat. Bodies* xxxvi. 315 It is naturall for such cold creatures to emmudde [*ed.* 1645 immud] themselues.

immund (ɪˈmʌnd), *a. rare.* [ad. L. *immundus*, f. *im-* (IM-²) + *mundus* clean, pure. Cf. F. *immonde*.] Unclean, impure; filthy, foul.

1621 BURTON *Anat. Mel.* I. ii. II. v, Through their owne nastinesse and sluttishnesse, and immund sordid maner of life. **1861** MRS. NORTON *Lady La G.* Prol. 48 Where birds immund find shelter dank. **1875** H. S. CUNNINGHAM *Chron. Dustypore* (1877) 288 Great were the cleansings, the white-washings..in many an immund old town and ill-odoured village.

†**immun'dicity**. *Obs.* [ad. obs. F. *immondicité* (1480 in Godef.), irreg. f. *immondice* impurity, ad. L. *immunditia* IMMUNDITY. (The form was perh. influenced by *impudicité* IMPUDICITY.)] Uncleanness, impurity; filthiness. **b.** *concr.* in *pl.* Impurities.

1530 LYNDESAY *Test. Papyngo* 212 O fals warld, fy on thy felycitie, Thy Pryde, Auaryce, and Immundicitie! **1541** R. COPLAND *Guydon's Quest. Chirurg.* Qiij, He hath no receptacle where to holde the sayd immundycytees. **1660** tr. *Amyraldus' Treat. conc. Relig.* I. iii. 40 Exempt from the contagion of their immundicity.

†**i'mmundified**, *ppl. a. Obs. rare.* [f. IM-² + MUNDIFIED.] Not mundified, uncleansed.

1597 A. M. tr. *Guillemeau's Fr. Chirurg.* 46b/1 Then followeth the mundifyed and cleane compresse thervnder, in the steade of the immundifyed.

immundity (ɪˈmʌndɪtɪ). *rare.* [f. L. *immund-us* IMMUND + -ITY: cf. L. *immunditia*, but this gave F. *immondice*.] Uncleanness, filthiness, impurity.

1870 E. H. PEMBER *Trag. Lesbos* Pref. 11 The ascription to Sappho of the various extravangances and immundities of the common myth.

immune (ɪˈmjuːn), *a.* (*sb.*) [ad. L. *immūn-is* exempt from a public service, burden, or charge, free, exempt, f. *im-* (IM-²) + *mūnis* ready to be of service, *mūnus* service, duty; cf. obs. F. *immune* 'exempt, free, priviledged, discharged from' (Cotgr. 1611).

Found in the general sense from 15th to 17th c. Reintroduced *c* 1880 (perh. from Fr. or Ger. use) in connexion with the investigation of the nature of infectious diseases and their prevention by inoculation and the like.]

1. Free (*from* some liability); exempt. *Obs.* in general sense since 17th c.

c **1420** *Pallad. on Husb.* VI. 237 O Sone of God..of synys drope or fraude immuyn. **1653** E. CHISENHALE *Cath. Hist.* 263 These Provincials were free and immune without appealing to the See of Rome. **1658** J. ROBINSON *Eudoxa* ix. 48 The Cochlearia..will not abide the French Air, (which is immune from it).

2. a. *spec.* Having immunity from hurtful bodily influences, as the influence of poison, the contagion of infectious diseases, and the like, esp. when rendered so by inoculation, etc. (Cf. IMMUNIZE.) Also *transf.* and *fig.*, wholly protected *from* something injurious or distasteful; not susceptible or responsive *to* something.

1881 *Local Govt. Board, Rep. Medical Officer* 200 Pasteur further states that the animals inoculated with the mitigated virus remain immune against further attacks of anthrax. **1888** F. P. COBBE in *Fortn. Rev.* Feb. 226 But (to use the new medical barbarism) we are never 'immune' altogether from the contagion. **1888** E. R. LANKESTER in *Watts' Dict. Chem.* s.v. *Bacteria*, An animal which had survived an attack of the virulent *B. anthracis* was thereby rendered 'immune' to subsequent attacks, just as one attack of small-pox renders its survivor 'immune' in regard to that disease. **1891** WOODHEAD *Bacteria* 372 He was able by inoculation to render an animal immune to the action of the more virulent anthrax bacillus. **1894** *Sat. Rev.* 17 Nov. 529 The new serum has the power..of rendering those who surround the patient immune from the poison. **1898** *Times* 25 Aug. 5/1 They had not been able to render animals immune from the attacks of the parasites. **1898** MERCIER in *Brit. Med. Jrnl.* 3 Sept. 586/1 There is for every insane person a certain sphere of conduct for which he ought to be entirely immune from punishment. **1900** *Daily News* 5 July 3/2 A man whose achievements should render him immune from all mud throwing. **1922** D. H. LAWRENCE *England, my England* 235 Among the graves, she felt immune from the world. **1944** A. HOLMES *Princ. Physical Geol.* xvii. 367 No place can be regarded as permanently immune from shocks. **1947** *Jrnl. R. Aeronaut. Soc.* LI. 293 Ice guards..proved of considerable value during the war when used on aircraft which themselves were not completely immune from icing. **1955** *Sci. Amer.* June 96/3 The magnetic-core memory..is relatively immune to unwanted electrical disturbances. **1973** *Human World* Feb. 8 The vision of the future that is to carry them through is the high-rise block of flats, the motorway... And if the 'underprivileged' prove immune to sense and prosperity? Well, thinks Mr Maddox, they can't. **1973** *Sci. Amer.* Feb. 83/1 The system is extremely complicated and therefore would be rather expensive and not as reliable or immune to functional failure as one would like. **1973** *Daily Tel.* 7 Mar. 18 Orwell was a bad poet and immune to the arts (though a most likeable man). **1974** *Ibid.* 16 Feb. 9/1 The white pawns are immune from Black's bishop.

b. as *sb.* An immune individual.

1898 *Westm. Gaz.* 29 Apr. 7/1 Regiments (mainly composed of negroes from the Southern States and other yellow fever immunes). **1909** *Rep. Brit. Assoc. Adv. Sci.* 764 All extracted immunes [*sc.* wheat plants immune to yellow rust] should breed true to this feature. **1951** WHITBY & HYNES *Med. Bacteriol.* (ed. 5) viii. 105 After an epidemic the community remains free from that disease until the proportion of immunes declines and the density of susceptibles is once more raised to pre-epidemic level.

3. *Med.* **a.** (Only in *attrib.* use.) Relating to immunity or its development; serving to bring immunity about.

1907 MUIR & RITCHIE *Man. Bacteriol.* (ed. 4) xix. 484 Various substances..remove the opsonic property from a normal serum, while they have no effect on an immune-opsonin. **1928** L. E. H. WHITBY *Med. Bacteriol.* ii. 19 The immune substances produced by the animal are termed antibodies. **1946** K. LANDSTEINER *Specificity Serological Reactions* (rev. ed.) i. 4 The immune antibodies..react as a rule only with the antigens that were used for immunizing and with closely similar ones. **1953** S. RAFFEL *Immunity* iv. 40 (*heading*) Mechanisms of acquired immunity. Antibody as a specific immune mechanism. **1969** *Times* 24 Mar. 4/7 Antilymphocytic serum..combats the particular immune defence mechanism responsible for rejecting tissue grafts.

b. Specific collocations: ***immune body*** = ANTIBODY; ***immune globulin***, (*a*) a preparation containing antibodies obtained from normal individuals or from ones immunized against a specific disease, and suitable for use as an antiserum; (*b*) = IMMUNOGLOBULIN; ***immune response***, the reaction of the body to the introduction into it of an antigen; ***immune serum***, serum which contains antibodies, esp. one which can confer immunity to the corresponding antigen on a recipient; = ANTISERUM b; ***immune system***, the part of the body's make-up and functioning responsible for producing an immune response and maintaining immunity.

1899 MUIR & RITCHIE *Man. Bacteriol.* (ed. 2) xix. 485 Ehrlich has recently applied his theory of antitoxines to the lysogenic action of sera towards bacteria and red corpuscles. .. His observations show that the body specially developed in the blood of the animal treated—the '*immune-body', enters into firm combination with the red corpuscles. **1900** P. EHRLICH in *Proc. R. Soc.* LXVI. 443, I have sought..to make clear the mechanism concerned in the action of these two components—the stable, which may be designated 'immune body', and the unstable, which may be designated 'complement'—which, acting together, effect the solution of the red blood corpuscles. **1937** Immune body [see AMBOCEPTOR]. **1971** HERBERT & WILKINSON *Dict. Immunol.* 91 *Immune body*, obsolete synonym for antibody. **1935** *Jrnl. Amer. Med. Assoc.* 17 Aug. 493/1 The use of *Immune Globulin (Human) in the modification of measles has been known for a considerable period. **1948** H. J. PARISH *Bacterial & Virus Dis.* ix. 67 Placental extract or 'human immune globulin' is an extract of placental globulins and has approximately the same potency as adult serum. **1958** —— *Antisera, Toxoids, Vaccines & Tuberculins* (ed. 4) ix. 78 Large pools of adult plasma normally contain a variety of protective antibodies..located mainly in the gamma fraction of the globulin or, as it is sometimes called, the immune globulin. **1966** *Lancet* 24 Dec. 1403/2 A technique of immunodiffusion of serum through agar gave a sensitive and fairly accurate measure of the concentrations of the three main classes of immune globulins—γ G, γ M, and γ A. **1953** *Jrnl. Nat. Cancer Inst.* XIV. 755 The over-all pattern presented is one of interference with an *immune response of the host. **1963** GELL & COOMBS *Clin. Aspects Immunol.* i. 5 Before we can understand much about 'immune' responses and their results, protective or damaging, on the host, we need to know more about the separation of antibody responses from the 'cellular' responses which result in delayed (non-antibody dependent) sensitivity. **1964** *New Scientist* 1 Oct. 10/2 The 'immune response' is an important feature of a vertebrate animal's defence mechanism. **1902** R. T. HEWLETT *Man. Bacteriol.* (ed. 2) v. 140 For the lysis of a given quantity of bacteria a certain amount of *immune serum is necessary. **1946** K. LANDSTEINER *Specificity Serological Reactions* (rev. ed.) i. 7 Sera that contain antibodies as the result of the injection of antigens are called 'immune sera' (antisera). **1955** *Sci. Amer.* Mar. 65/2 In experimental work, antibody, or what is known as immune serum, is produced by injecting virus into an animal. **1970** GOLD & PEACOCK *Basic Immunol.* vii. 247 Chiefly noted in man in connexion with immune serum therapy, serum sickness has also been widely studied as an experimental disease in laboratory animals. **1955** *Internat. Arch. Allergy & Appl. Immunol.* VII. 5 With the protein *immune systems, the weight of antigen injected intravenously corresponded..to one-half the amount of antibody. **1965** *N.Y. Times* 24 Oct. IV. 8/3 Enlisting the body's own natural defense mechanisms—primarily the immune system—to fight cancer is one approach. **1970** *Ann. Rev. Microbiol.* XXIV. 534 Virus infections can profoundly affect the functional capacity of the immune system. **1984** J. F. LAMB et al. *Essent. Physiol.* (ed. 2) iv. 76 The immune system identifies invaders, switches itself on, generates defenders armed specifically to deal with whatever invaders are

around, kills them and switches itself off before the body is unduly harmed. **1986** *Daily Tel.* 16 Sept. 11/1 These young women have a 10 to 30 per cent chance of developing the disease [*sc.* Aids], which kills by destroying the immune system thus exposing sufferers to a variety of lethal infections.

i'mmune, *v. rare.* [f. the adj.] *trans.* To render immune.

1849 G. S. FABER *Let.* 16 May in R. Chapman *Father Faber* (1961) xi. 220, I think if a little experience does not immune me to the row.. I *must* go to the back. **1928** HARDY *Coll. Poems* 431 The vision That immuned me from the chillings of misprision.

immunist (ɪ'mjuːnɪst). [ad. F. *immuniste,* f. *immunité* IMMUNITY.] One who enjoys an immunity (see IMMUNITY 1).

1897 MAITLAND *Domesday & Beyond* ii. 277 It is conceded that the 'immunist' (it is convenient to borrow a term that French writers have coined) is entitled to many of the fines and forfeitures that arise from offences committed within his territory. *Ibid.* 288 The land-lord.. is an immunist, or is the king, who.. occupies the position of an immunist.

immunity (ɪ'mjuːnɪtɪ). Also 4 **ynmunite,** (6 **emenyte,** 7 **emunity**), **imunity.** [ad. L. *immūnitās* freedom from public services or charges, in med.L. privileged place, sanctuary, f. *immūnis* IMMUNE: see -ITY, and cf. F. *immunité* (1341 in Godef. *Compl.*).]

1. *Law.* Exemption from a service, obligation, or duty; freedom from liability to taxation, jurisdiction, etc.; privilege granted to an individual or a corporation conferring exemption from certain taxes, burdens, or duties. Also less strictly or in non-technical use: Non-liability, privilege. (Cf. FRANCHISE.)

1382 WYCLIF *1 Macc.* x. 34 Dais of ynmunite [*Gloss* or fraunchise], and of remissioun, to alle Jewis that ben in my rewme. **1549** LATIMER *6th Serm. bef. Edw. VI* (Arb.) 161 There is sum place in London, as they saye, *immunitie, impunitie.* What should I call it? a preueledged place for whoredome. **1579–80** NORTH *Plutarch* (1676) 970 The Senate.. in favour of his Profession, gave immunity to all others that from that time forth did practise Physick. **1613** PURCHAS *Pilgrimage* (1614) 327 Enriching.. the place with name of a Citie, with building and immunitie. **1623** CONWAY in Ellis *Orig. Lett.* Ser. I. III. 155 His Majesty fore-sawe an infinite liberty, a perpetuall emunity graunted to the Roman Catholiques. **1641** MILTON *Ch. Govt.* I. iii, A foul injury and derogation.. of that birth-right and immunity which Christ hath purchas'd for us with his blood. **1827** HALLAM *Const. Hist.* (1876) I. v. 243 The English subject continued to pride himself in his immunity from taxation without consent of parliament. **1897** MAITLAND *Domesday & Beyond* ii. 270 In an ordinary case the clause of immunity will first contain some general words declaring the land to be free of burdens in general, and then some exceptive words declaring that it is not to be free from certain specified burdens.

b. with *pl.*: A particular exemption or privilege.

1538 STARKEY *England* II. i. 151 Certayn pryuylegys and prerogatyf.. as.. he schold not be constraynyd to go forth to warre.. wyth such other lyke immunytes and pryuylegys. **1571** *Act 13 Eliz.* c. 29 §5 All manner of Liberties Fraunchises Immunyties.. geven or graunted to the said Chauncellor Maisters and Schollers of either of the said Universities. **1690** CHILD *Disc. Trade* (1694) 117 Merchandizing.. the purchasing of an Immunity or Monopoly to the prejudice of our country. **1759** ROBERTSON *Hist. Scot.* (1813) I. I. 15 Civil privileges and immunities were the consequence of their victories. **1828** SCOTT *F.M. Perth* vii, He is the Provost of Perth, and.. must see the freedoms and immunities of the burgh preserved. **1872** YEATS *Growth Comm.* 128.

2. *spec.* (*Eccl.*) Exemption of ecclesiastical persons and things from secular or civil liabilities, burdens, or duties; as the exemption of the clergy from lay jurisdiction, or of church property from secular taxation, and the freedom of sanctuary from invasion. Chiefly with *an* and *pl.*

1513 MORE in Grafton *Chron.* (1568) II. 768 God forbid that any man should.. breake the immunite and libertie of that sacred Sanctuarie. **1524** *Sc. Acts Jas. V* (1814) 286 That the fredomez and liberteis of halikirk, with all priuelegis & emenyteis thairof.. be obseruit. **1563–87** FOXE *A. & M.* (1596) 93/2 Men of the clergie.. he indued with speciall privileges and immunities. **1609** SKENE *Reg. Maj., Stat. Robt. II,* 49 How oft ane manslayer takes him self to the immunitie of the kirk. **1610** BP. CARLETON *Jurisd.* 161 These immunities which Emperours and Princes haue giuen to the Church, the Church ought to inioy without disturbance, and to withdraw such immunities, were high sacriledge and impiety. **1711** *Lond. Gaz.* No. 4831/2 The Congregation of Immunities have.. had under their Consideration the Affairs of Naples, where the Viceroy has caused several Criminals of State to be taken forcibly out of the Churches, whither they had fled for Sanctuary. **1883** FROUDE *Short Stud.* IV. I. iii. 34 The question of the immunities of the clergy had been publicly raised.

†**3.** Freedom from ordinary restraints; undue freedom, licence. *Obs.*

[**1549**: see 1.] **1583** STUBBES *Anat. Abus.* I. (1877) 143 The arguments of tragedies is anger, wrath, immunitie, crueltie, iniurie, incest, murther. **1639** MASSINGER *Unnat. Combat* IV. ii, To pay your debts, and take your lechery.. With all your other choice immunities. *a* **1680** BUTLER *Rem.* (1759) I. 126 And he.. Is sentenc'd and deliver'd up To Satan.. For vent'ring wickedly to put a Stop To his Immunities and free Affairs.

4. Freedom or exemption *from* any natural or usual liability, or from anything evil or injurious.

1592 tr. *Junius on Rev.* xxii. 1 Freedome and immunity from all evil. **1677** HALE *Contempl.* II. 162, I have no cause to hope for an Immunity from Trouble, so long as I have no Immunity from Sin. **1683** BOYLE in *Phil. Trans.* XVII. 634 Three thousand Grains of Water, (whose Immunity from common Salt we try'd apart). **1756** BURKE *Subl. & B.* I. xv, Nor is it, either in real or fictitious distresses, our immunity from them which produces our delight. **1854** C. BRONTE in Mrs. Gaskell *Life* 437 It is long since I have known such comparative immunity from headache. **1894** J. T. FOWLER *Adamnan* Introd. 32 Ireland has enjoyed an immunity from snakes.

5. The condition of being immune from or insusceptible to poison, the contagion of a specific disease, or the like; immunization: see IMMUNE *a.* 2. [So mod.F. *immunité* (Littré).]

1879 *St. George's Hosp. Rep.* IX. 715 In one of the five instances.. the apparent immunity must have lasted for at least two years, that being the interval between the two diphtheritic visitations. **1887** *Oxf. Biol. Mem.* tr. *E. du Bois Reymond* 408 The immunity of vipers from their own poison proved by Fontana. **1896** ALLBUTT *Syst. Med.* I. 564 The animal remains passive while the immunity-conferring substances are applied to its tissues.

6. *proposed use.* (See quot.)

1879 W. E. HEARN *Aryan Househ.* x. 232 Outside this association there.. was the Household, considered as a corporate body, without any relation to other Households. .. The independent position of the Household may be called Immunity, as opposed to Community.

immunization (ɪmjuːnaɪ'zeɪʃən). [f. next + -ATION.] The action or immunizing or fact of being immunized.

1893 VIRCHOW in *Westm. Gaz.* 17 Mar. 7/1 It is also a kind of immunisation which.. has also great drawbacks; for this hardening against unjust attacks leads very easily to a similar indifference towards just attacks, and.. it finally leads also to indifference to praise and recognition. **1894** *Lancet* 3 Nov. 1044 Artificial immunisation, even against diseases liable to recurrence, such as anthrax. **1896** ALLBUTT *Syst. Med.* I. 561 The process of immunisation is 'accumulative'.

immunize ('ɪmjuːnaɪz), *v.* [f. IMMUNE + -IZE.]

1. *trans.* To render immune from or insusceptible to poison, or infection.

1892 in *Brit. Med. Jrnl.* 20 Feb. 379–80 (transl. fr. German) Emmerick succeeded in protecting animals by inoculating them with the tissue juices of immunised animals. **1894** *Westm. Gaz.* 21 Aug. 2/3 Experience in the new methods of immunising. **1894** *Lancet* 3 Nov. 1065 The immunising power of the serum. **1894** *Sat. Rev.* 17 Nov. 529 In 1891.. Professor Hankin pointed out that the injection of the serum of animals.. immunized by repeated inoculations, had a preventive or curative effect by destroying or neutralizing in the blood the products of disease-producing microbes. **1895** *Pop. Sci. Monthly* Feb. 515 Prof. Carl Fraenkel first immunized guinea-pigs against diphtheria.

2. *intr.* Of an organism or substance, regarded as an antigen: to produce immunity in an individual into which it is introduced.

1942 *Jrnl. Bacteriol.* XLIII. 405 Strains we have classified as weakly antigenic (in so far as they fail to immunize significantly against homologous virus injected intra-cerebrally). **1951** WHITBY & HYNES *Med. Bacteriol.* (ed. 5) viii. 108 It is possible to kill bacteria without so altering their antigenic structure that they no longer immunize against living bacteria. **1973** *Nature* 30 Mar. 330/1 The ability of lactating mammary gland to immunize against D1 and D2 mammary tumour growth.

immunizer ('ɪmjuːnaɪzə(r)). [f. IMMUNIZE *v.* + -ER[1].] That which renders immune; *occas.*, one who uses or advocates immunization.

1927 *Daily Express* 18 June 9/2 'Immuniser' for Cancer... It may well be that chemical and medical research will discover this natural immuniser, which will strengthen resistance to cancer in all individuals. **1931** *Amer. Jrnl. Cancer* XV. 627 Formalin.. is a less potent immuniser than antiserum. *Ibid.*, No single mode of treatment is entirely satisfactory both as a 'destroyer' and as an 'immuniser'. **1950** G. B. SHAW *Farfetched Fables* 90 Lying advertisements of panaceas, prophylactics, elixirs, immunizers, vaccines, antitoxins, vitamins, and professedly hygienic foods. *Ibid.*, They are in fact exalting every laboratory vivisector and quack immunizer above Jesus and St. James.

immuno- (ɪ'mjuːnəʊ, 'ɪmjuːnəʊ), used as comb. form of IMMUNE *a.*, IMMUNITY, IMMUNOLOGY, and related words. (In the following words secondary stresses are in general left unmarked, since they vary in the manner indicated above.)

immuno-assay (ɪmjuːnəʊ'æseɪ), a bio-assay performed by means of immunological methods; **immunobi'ology** = IMMUNOLOGY (see quot. 1970); so **immunobio'logic, -bio'logical** *adjs.*; **immuno'chemistry,** chemistry as applied to immunology; the chemistry of immunological phenomena; so **immuno'chemical** *a.*, of or pertaining to immunochemistry; using the methods of immunochemistry; **immuno'chemically** *adv.*; **immuno'chemist,** a student of or expert in immunochemistry; **immunode'ficiency,** a reduction in the normal immune defences of the body or in some necessary component of the immune system; freq. *attrib.*; hence **immunode'ficient** *a.*; **immunodi'ffusion,** diffusion of immunologically active substances; a technique for investigating antigens and antibodies by observing any precipitates that may form when initially separate portions of them are allowed to intermingle by diffusion through a gelatinous or other medium; **immuno-eˌlectropho'resis,** a technique for characterizing the proteins in a mixture (such as serum) by first separating them by electrophoresis and then subjecting them to immunodiffusion (in the same or a different medium); so **immuno-eˌlectropho'retic** *a.*, **-pho'retically** *adv.*; **immunofluo'rescence,** a method of demonstrating antibodies (or antigens) in microscopic preparations by introducing corresponding antigens (or antibodies) labelled with a fluorescent dye; fluorescence emitted by such preparations; so **immunofluo'rescent** *a.*, of, pertaining to, or involving this method; **immunoge'netic** *a.*, of or pertaining to immunogenetics; so **immunoge'netically** *adv.*; **immunoge'netics,** the related study of immunology and genetics, either as a branch of genetics in which immunological methods and knowledge are employed, or as the study of the genetic aspects of immunological phenomena and substances; **immunohæma'tology** (*U.S.* **-hematology**), the immunology of the blood; so **immunohæmato'logic, -'logical** *adjs.*; **immunopa'thologist,** a student of or expert in immunopathology; **immunopa'thology,** the pathology of the immune response; the study of immunological phenomena and substances in relation to pathology; hence **immunopatho'logic, -'logical** *adjs.*; **immunoprophy'laxis,** the prevention of disease by immunization; so **immunoprophy'lactic** *a.*, of or pertaining to immunoprophylaxis; *sb.*, an agent that prevents (a) disease by producing immunity; **immunosu'ppressant,** an agent which has an immunosuppressive effect; also *attrib.*; **immunosu'ppressed** *a.*, (of an individual) rendered unable to react immunologically to an antigen; **immunosu'ppression,** the suppression of the immune response of an organism; **immunosu'ppressive** *a.*, suppressing the immune response of an organism; **immunosympa'thectomy** [-ECTOMY, used *loosely*], the destruction of many of the sympathetic ganglia of a new-born animal by injection of an antiserum for the appropriate nerve growth-factor; so **immuno-sympa'thectomized** *ppl. a.*, treated in this way; **immuno'therapy,** treatment of disease by the production of immunity (whether by the introduction into the individual of appropriate antibodies, etc., or by the stimulation in it of an immune response); **immunotrans'fusion,** the transfusion of blood which has been previously immunized against the recipient's infection.

1959 *Nature* 21 Nov. 1648/2 We have previously reported on the immuno-assay of beef insulin. **1969** R. HALL et al. *Fund. Clin. Endocrinol.* xiv. 258/1 The hormone that reacts with anti-insulin serum in the immunoassay technique for insulin accounts for only a small part of the total ILA in plasma. **1930** *Jrnl. Amer. Med. Assoc.* 12 Apr. 1188/2 [*tr. a Finnish title*] Immunobiologic conditions in tuberculosis. **1959** *Biol. Abstr.* XXXIII. 1822/1 A few statements on the reflex mechanism of immunobiological processes. **1966** E. D. DAY *Found. Immunochem.* vii. 87 One definition [of *hapten*] is immunobiological. **1957** (*title*) Journal of microbiology, epidemiology and immunobiology. **1970** ALEXANDER & GOOD *Immunobiol. for Surgeons* i. 1 In its older and classical meaning, it [*sc.* immunology] was the study of immunity, the processes by which oganisms defend themselves against infection... More recently, cellular immunity has been recognized as being important in processes which have to do with recognition phenomena, self-characterization, growth and development, heredity, aging, cancer, and transplantation. With this expansion, immunology has exceeded the limits of its original meaning, and immunobiology has become a preferable term for this expanding field. **1925** C. H. BROWNING *Immunochem. Stud.* 15 The immunochemical properties of serum. **1948** KABAT & MAYER *Exper. Immunochem.* i. 5 The application of immunochemical methods has extended far beyond the study of immunity to disease and has become a valuable tool in the characterization of proteins and polysaccharides. **1960** *Jrnl. Immunol.* LXXXV. 37 (*heading*) Immunochemical studies of human serum Rh agglutinins. **1961** WEBSTER, Immunochemically. **1966** *Lancet* 31 Dec. 1435/1 In certain human antiserums, dog insulin is immunochemically distinguishable from pork insulin although both have the same aminoacid sequence. **1948** M. HEIDELBERGER in Kabat & Mayer *Exper. Immunochem.* p. vi, The immunochemist is in possession of a store of marked molecules, antigens and antibodies, each as distinctively marked with respect to the other as if it contained a radioactive tracer element. **1970** *Nature* 18 July 229/2 Immunochemists from ten laboratories cross matched almost seventy antibodies to the proteins of the vertebrate eye lens when an international working party on crystallin

immunochemistry met in..Edinburgh University. **1971** NOSSAL & ADA *Antigens, Lymphoid Cells, & Immune Response* i. 2 The key discoveries about lymphocytes and antibody-producing cells..have been less fully digested by immunochemists. **1907** S. ARRHENIUS *Immunochem.* p. vii, I have given to these lectures the title 'Immuno-chemistry', and wish with this word to indicate that the chemical reactions of the substances that are produced by the injection of foreign substances into the blood of animals, *i.e.* by immunisation, are under discussion in these pages. **1956** *Nature* 3 Mar. 426/2 Virulent and protective avirulent strains have been studied comparatively by the methods of immunology, immunochemistry and biochemistry. **1970** Immunochemistry [see *immunochemist* above]. **1969** *Biol. Abstr.* L. 10692/2 The immunological distinction between cellular and humoral immunity furnishes, for the immuno-deficiency diseases, a convenient and logical classification based on immunological data, evolution and phylogenetics. **1983** *Oxf. Textbk. Med.* I. IV. 44/2 Selective IgA deficiency is the most common immunodeficiency. **1971** *Jrnl. Pediatrics* LXXIX. 642 (*heading*) Vaccine-related paralytic poliomyelitis in an immunodeficient child. **1976** *Nature* 27 May 313/1 Both the SV40-transformed mouse cell lines.. and the hybrid clones are tumorigenic in immunodeficient 'nude' mice. **1959** *Nature* 30 May 1512 (*heading*) Cellulose acetate as a medium for immunodiffusion. **1966** *Lancet* 24 Dec. 1403/2 A technique of immunodiffusion of serum through agar gave a sensitive and fairly accurate measure of the concentrations of the three main classes of immune globulins. **1971** *Nature* 8 Jan. 119/2 Antibody studies were made using immunodiffusion techniques set up with cerumen suspensions and with IgA and IgG antibody. The IgA or IgG antibody was then placed in the centre well; diffusion was allowed to take place..and precipitin lines were recorded. **1958** *Federation Proc.* XVII. 530/2 (*heading*) Starch gel immunoelectrophoresis. **1964** G. H. HAGGIS et al. *Introd. Molecular Biol.* ii. 25 (*caption*) The identification of protein fractions present in human plasma using immuno-electrophoresis. **1968** H. HARRIS *Nucleus & Cytoplasm* v. 104 The antigens..were isolated as antigen-antibody complexes by immuno-electrophoresis. **1955** WILLIAMS & GRABAR in *Jrnl. Immunol.* LXXIV. 158 (*heading*) Immunoelectrophoretic studies on serum proteins. **1970** J. T. BARRETT *Textbk. Immunol.* v. 114 A valuable modification of gel precipitation tests is the immunoelectrophoretic procedure of Grabar and Williams. **1961** A. J. CROWLE *Immunodiffusion* iv. 101 According to Ryback (1959), plasmin exists immunoelectrophoretically as two zones in the beta region. **1960** *Jrnl. Biophysical & Biochem. Cytol.* VII. 43 (*heading*) Observations of measles virus infection of cultured human cells. I. A study of development and spread of virus antigen by means of immunofluorescence. **1961** *Lancet* 16 Sept. 663/2 The nuclear immunofluorescence obtained with heated and unheated sera was compared. **1971** tr. *K. Federlin's Immunopath. Insulin* 32 In direct immunofluorescence, the tissue is first covered with a layer of labelled antibody or antigen, then freed from the uncombined agent by several washings, and finally mounted with a coverslip. **1959** *Proc. Soc. Exper. Biol. & Med.* CI. 289 (*heading*) Quantitative determination of infectious units of measles virus by counts of immunofluorescent foci. *Ibid.* 290/2 The cells were.. prepared for immunofluorescent microscopy. **1970** HARRIS & SINKOVICS *Immunol. Malignant Dis.* i. 37 Other immunofluorescent studies by Morton have demonstrated antibodies to osteosarcoma in the serum of patients with this tumor. **1936** IRWIN & COLE in *Jrnl. Exper. Zool.* LXXIII. 85 (*heading*) Immunogenetic studies of species and of species hybrids in doves. **1970** W. H. HILDEMANN *Immunogenetics* iii. 86 The newest area in which immunogenetic characterization of microorganisms has provided substantial insights involves the many viruses capable of inducing cancer. *Ibid.* vii. 224 (*heading*) Immunogenetic concepts of cancer and aging. **1971** *Nature* 12 Nov. 103/1 The paternal strains, A/J and A2G respectively, are immunogenetically identical at the major H-2 histocompatibility locus. **1947** M. R. IRWIN in *Adv. Genetics* I. 133 The term 'immunogenetics' was proposed by the author some years ago to designate studies in which the technics of both genetics and immunology were employed jointly... The term indicates the study of genetic characters as yet only detectable by immunological reactions. **1965** P. L. CARPENTER *Immunol. & Serol.* (ed. 2) ix. 265 The use of serologic techniques in genetics is expanding. Genes control the formation of antigenic substances, so detection of antigens provides an objective and useful tool for study of genes. The term immunogenetics is applied to this field of research. **1971** J. A. BELLANTI *Immunol.* iii. 60 Immunogenetics includes all those processes concerned in the immune response which may have a genetic basis. In the past, the term has been largely restricted to mean genetic markers on immunoglobulin polypeptide chains. **1954** *Amer. Jrnl. Clin. Path.* XXIV. 1333 It is just 50 years ago that the first immunohematologic test was introduced by Donath and Landsteiner. **1959** H. S. LAWRENCE *Cellular & Humoral Aspects Hypersensitive States* v. 133 (*heading*) Immunohematologic disease. **1967** *Biol. Abstr.* XLVIII. 172/2 (*heading*) Significance of immuno-hematological methods of investigation. **1950** *Brit. Med. Jrnl.* 16 Sept 673/1 (*heading*) Immuno-haematology. **1954** *Amer. Jrnl. Clin. Path.* XXIV. 1334 Serologic technics applied to the study of diseases of blood added up to what is called immunohematology, a separate and distinct subdivision of hematology... Immunohematology encompasses diseases of blood of which the causes, the pathogenesis, or the clinical manifestations have been shown to be determined by an antigen-antibody reaction. **1972** Immunohematology [see *isoagglutinogen* s.v. ISO-]. **1960** *Federation Proc.* XIX. 208/2 (*heading*) An immunopathologic study of avian nephrotoxic nephritis in the rabbit. **1959** GRABAR & MIESCHER *Immunopath.* 17 Attention has been focussed on the immunopathological consequences of leucocyte isoantigens. *Ibid.* 41 Much data of interest to immunopathologists. **1970** *Nature* 19 Sept. 1196/2 Studies on the amino-terminal sequences of a number of myeloma and pathological immunoglobulin chains also evoked much interest among the immunopathologists. **1959** GRABAR & MIESCHER *Immunopath.* 13 Immunopathology presumably covers all immune phenomena associated with general pathology—the majority of the reactions of course being physiogenic and beneficial to the host—others again being inconsequential or even harmful. **1971** K. FEDERLIN (*title*) Immunopathology of insulin. **1960** *Biol. Abstr.* XXXV. 168/2 (*heading*) Poliomyelitis: the present status of some epidemiological and immunoprophylactic problems. **1964** D. F. GRAY *Immunol.* x. 95 Immuno-prophylactic procedures include not only the long-term protection afforded by active immunization against a number of the epidemic and endemic diseases to which urban man is prone, but also short-term passive protection against immediately anticipated infection. **1972** *Lancet* 21 Oct. 876/1 Administration of B.C.G. to mice who no longer have palpable disease does not prolong their life... This is true whether or not B.C.G. had been given as an immunoprophylactic. **1964** *Canad. Jrnl. Public Health* LIII. 346 (*heading*) Advances in the immunoprophylaxis of smallpox. *Ibid.*, In the last twenty years progress in this field [*sc.* smallpox] has been less dramatic than in other fields of immunoprophylaxis of virus diseases, such as poliomyelitis or measles. **1972** *Lancet* 21 Oct. 875/2 (*heading*) Immunoprophylaxis and immunotherapy of leukæmia with B.C.G. **1965** *Jrnl. Immunol.* XCV. 1019/1 Immunosuppressant compounds such as chloramphenicol .., actinomycin D.., 6-mercaptopurine..and corticosteroids. **1970** M. C. VALE tr. *Nezlin's Biochem. Antibodies* v. 282 One of the most active immunosuppressants is cyclophosphamide. **1967** *Jrnl. Nat. Cancer Inst.* XXXVIII. 754/1 Pretreatment..with this alkylating agent resulted in..increased growth and earlier tumor deaths in the immunosuppressed animals. **1965** *Jrnl. Immunol.* XCV. 1019/1 The mechanism of acriflavine-induced immunosuppression remains unknown. **1968** *New Scientist* 13 June 557/1 Reports of increasing success in combating graft rejection, following improvements in tissue typing and immunosuppression. **1963** *New England Jrnl. Med.* CCLXVIII. 1315 (*heading*) Prolonged survival of human-kidney homografts by immunosuppressive drug therapy. **1968** *Observer* 5 May 3/3 To stem any rejection of the new heart, Mr West is now receiving immuno suppressive treatment with a drug. **1970** BALNER & BEVERIDGE *Infections & Immunosuppression Subhuman Primates* 194/2 Most of the immunosuppressive agents currently in use are entirely non-specific, that is to say they depress all aspects of immune reactivity and thereby the immunological defences against infectious microorganisms as well. **1961** LEVI-MONTALCINI & ANGELETTI in Kety & Elkes *Regional Neurochem.* VII. 369 The injected and untreated animals did not differ from each other. Immunosympathectomized mice became pregnant, nursed and took care of the litter as controls. **1964** *Nature* 26 Dec. 1315/1 'Immunosympathectomized' rats, in which extensive irreversible atrophy of the peripheral sympathetic system is produced by injecting, during the first few days of life, an antiserum to nerve growth factor.., appear healthy, grow, reproduce and have normal gastro-intestinal function. **1962** *Internat. Jrnl. Neuropharmacol.* I. 163 Immunosympathectomy performed in newborn mice, results in a striking depletion of NA in the heart of the same adult animals. **1972** J. B. MARTIN in Steiner & Schönbaum *Immunosympathectomy* xii. 196 The use of immunosympathectomy in analyzing the importance of adrenergic innervation of individual glands is limited to some degree by the incomplete effect produced by the antisera to nerve growth factor. Thus, immunosympathectomy should be valuable in investigations of the role of sympathetic innervation of those glands (pineal, pituitary, thyroid) in which denervation is nearly complete. It is of limited use in studies of the abdominal glands or genital tract. **1913** R. L. CROCKETT in *N.Y. State Jrnl. Med.* XIII. 213/2 For some time I have been trying to discover what place (if any) vaccine therapy or, as I prefer to call it—immuno-therapy—had in the branches to which I limit my practice. **1937** *Jrnl. Amer. Med. Assoc.* 19 June 2171 Further investigations on active immuno-therapy of whooping cough. **1969** *Daily Colonist* (Victoria, B.C.) 9 Oct. 40/4 He said immunotherapy—injection of materials into the body to stimulate development of tumor-resistant anti-bodies—had been successful with eight of his patients. **1971** J. A. BELLANTI *Immunol.* xix. 510 Immunotherapy is passive immunization through the use of serum or gamma globulin which confers temporary protection to one host by the introduction of antibodies actively produced in another. **1919** A. E. WRIGHT in *Lancet* 29 Mar. 500/2 The therapeutic method here employed is..a combined method of serum therapy and transfusion. We may perhaps call it 'immuno-transfusion'. **1941** KOLMER & TUFT *Clin. Immunol.* x. 256 To increase the amount of protective antibody in the donors's blood, the donor may be injected with vaccine prior to the withdrawal of his blood. This type of transfusion is referred to as immunotransfusion.

immunogen (ɪ'mjuːnəʊdʒən). *Biol.* and *Med.* [f. IMMUNO- + -GEN.] **1.** An antigenic substance, or a preparation of it, believed to reside in the ectoplasm of the bacterial cell and to be removed by washing.

Immunogen has been registered as a proprietary name in Great Britain and the U.S.A.

1923 *Trade Marks Jrnl.* 31 Jan. 181 Immunogen... Parke Davis & Company. **1923** *Official Gaz.* (U.S. Patent Office) 18 Dec. 550/1 Immunogen... Immunizing Agents Used for the Prophylaxis and Treatment of Diseases of Bacterial Origin. **1926** HORDER & FERRY in *Brit. Med. Jrnl.* 31 July 179/2 As it would appear from these results..that the antigenic or immunizing portion of the bacterial cell is more ectoplasmic than endoplasmic in origin, it is proposed to call this type of antigen an 'ectoantigen', and for products prepared in such a manner as to contain only this ectoantigen the designation 'immunogens' is suggested, to distinguish them from other antigenic products already in use. **1928** *Jrnl. Amer. Med. Assoc.* 15 Dec. 1914/2 There is no difference between vaccines and immunogens. Their sphere of action is the same. Generally speaking it would be best to prepare vaccines or immunogens from 'autogenous material', but when that is not practicable commercial preparations may be used. **1929** J. W. BIGGER *Handbk. Bacteriol.* (ed. 2) vi. 88 'Immunogens' (Horder & Ferry) are the washings of bacteria. They are stated to contain the immunizing substances of bacteria without the toxins. **1934** *Jrnl. Amer. Med. Assoc.* 22 Sept. 939/2 A little girl..was given..doses of catarrhal immunogen (Parke-Davis) on biweekly visits. *Ibid.*, Immunogen (Parke, Davis & Co.) may be a mixture of antigenic substances. It is not on the accepted list of New and Nonofficial Remedies.

2. Any substance that elicits an immune response or produces immunity in the recipient (see quots.).

1959 A. D. BUSSARD in *Ann. Rev. Microbiol.* XIII. 280 The following terms will be used..in the course of this review: immunogenicity: ability of a substance to direct the formation of a specific antibody; antigenicity: ability of a substance to react with an antibody under a given set of conditions. An immunogen is a substance exhibiting immunogenicity and an antigen, a substance exhibiting antigenicity. **1971** S. O. FREEDMAN et al. *Clin. Immunol.* i. 3 Although the terms immunogen and antigen are frequently used interchangeably, they are not necessarily synonymous. Immunogenicity may be defined as the capacity of a substance to initiate a humoral or cell-mediated immune response, whereas antigenicity may be defined as the capacity of a substance to bind specifically with the antibody molecules whose formation it has elicited... Employed correctly, the term immunogen specifies that a substance acts at the afferent limb of the immune response... Most conventional antigens possess both immunogenic and antigenic capacities. **1972** *Science* 2 June 1028/3 Pneumococcal polysaccharides are generally considered weak immunogens since they elicit poor primary antibody responses.

immunogenic (ɪmjuːnəʊ'dʒɛnɪk), *a.* *Biol.* and *Med.* [f. IMMUNO- + -GENIC.] Of, pertaining to, or possessing the ability to elicit an immune response.

1933 *Jrnl. Amer. Med. Assoc.* 24 June 2013/2 (*heading*) An immunogenic paradox. **1934** *Index Medicus* XV. 637/2 Appearance of impedin in production of specific opsonin by local application of immunogenic salves to skin. **1942** *Jrnl. Bacteriol.* XLIII. 397 There is ample evidence in the literature to suggest that fixed virus strains differ in their immunogenic properties. **1962** *Lancet* 5 May 965/1 This incidence had been reduced by early vaccines, but more recent batches had not been sufficiently immunogenic. **1971** *Nature* 4 June 286/3 Why cells become more immunogenic after neuraminidase treatment is not yet clear.

Hence **immunoge'nicity**, immunogenic property. Also **immuno'genesis**, the formation or production of antibodies; bodily processes, collectively, that constitute an immune response.

1944 *Science* 16 June 496 Minute amounts..exhibited marked antityphoid immunogenicity. **1948** BIESTER & SCHWARTE *Dis. Poultry* (ed. 2) 567 The criteria of immunogenesis and pathogenesis. **1950** *Jrnl. Bacteriol.* LIX. 263 Textbooks..commonly state that a high degree of encapsulation is responsible for the reportedly poor immunogenicity of this fungus. **1956** *Jrnl. Immunol.* LXXVI. 217/1 It is demonstrated that the immunogenicity of immune globulin is suppressed by the simultaneous injection of other serum components. **1960** A. HOFMAN et al. tr. A. N. Gordienko (*title*) Control of immunogenesis by the nervous system. **1968** D. OSOBA in B. Cinader *Regulation Antibody Response* xii. 232 (*heading*) The regulatory role of the thymus in immunogenesis. **1970** *New Scientist* 19 Mar. 543/1 Irradiation with gamma rays, which render it non-infective without..loss of mobility or immunogenicity.

immunoglobulin (ɪˌmjuːnəʊ-, ˌɪmjuːnəʊ 'glɒbjʊlɪn). *Biochem.* and *Med.* [f. IMMUNO- + GLOBULIN.] Any of the group of proteins present in the serum of vertebrates which are characterized by their structure, in being a mixture of larger ('heavy') and smaller ('light') polypeptide chains, linked usu. by disulphide bonds, and by their function in that all known antibodies are immunoglobulins.

1959 J. F. HEREMANS in *Clin. Chim. Acta* IV. 643 The data ..seem to point to the existence of a system of closely related, though not identical, proteins which are capable of acting as antibodies. These are: (a) γ-globulin (7S, low carbohydrate content, heterogeneous mobility)..; (b) β_{2A}-globulin (also 7S, high carbohydrate content, high mobility)..; and (c) β_{2M}-globulin (19S, high carbohydrate content, high mobility). The outlined similarities in nature and function clearly call for the adoption of a common name for all these substances. A word such as 'immunoglobulins' would seem to be suitable. **1965** *New Scientist* 11 Mar. 626/1 The body's 'immune' defence mechanism against bacteria, viruses and other foreign materials depends largely on the presence in the blood serum of a family of proteins known as immunoglobulins. **1970** GOLD & PEACOCK *Basic Immunol.* iii. 93 A new nomenclature was proposed in which the prefix γ or Ig stood for immunoglobulin and a suffix denoted the particular class of immunoglobulin. Thus the 7S, 160,000 M.W., gamma-globulins became IgG or γG, the macroglobulins became IgM or γM, and the third class of immunoglobulins, IgA or γA... Two other classes of human immunoglobulin, IgD..and IgE.., are now known. **1970** ROTHSCHILD & WALDMANN *Plasma Protein Metabolism* xvi. 259 The immunoglobulins are a group of structurally related proteins produced by plasma cells and lymphocytes. **1970** *Nature* 12 Dec. 1040/1 These studies have shown that immunoglobulins are composed of light chains (molecular weight 23,000) and heavy chains (55,000) which are linked through disulphide bonds. **1971** *Ann. N.Y. Acad. Sci.* CXC. 8 The lamprey has 6·6S and 14S immunoglobulins which have similar light and heavy chains.

immunology (ɪmjʊ'nɒlədʒɪ). [f. IMMUN(ITY + -OLOGY.] The science which treats of the phenomena and causes of immunity (sense 5).

1910 *Jrnl. Amer. Med. Assoc.* 5 Mar. 828/1 Relations between pharmacology, immunology and experimental therapy. **1911** *Ibid.* 25 Feb. 578/2 The science of immunity, or immunology, would explain the mechanism by which the animal body is enabled to resist disease. **1947** *Nature* 4 Jan. 15/2 The hope that they [*sc.* incipient cancers] may elaborate specific antigenic substances, and thus provide serological

tests, goes back to the first years of immunology. **1963** GELL & COOMBS *Clin. Aspects Immunol.* p. xvii, Immunology has two aspects, its use as a tool and its investigation as a biological phenomenon.

Hence **immuno'logic** (chiefly *U.S.*), **-'logical** *adjs.*, of or pertaining to immunity or immunology; **immuno'logically** *adv.*, from the point of view of immunology; as regards the phenomena, properties, etc., of immunity; **immu'nologist**, an expert in or student of immunology.

1912 *Jrnl. Exper. Med.* XVI. 635 Hemolysins, precipitins, or other bodies included in the province of the immunologist. **1914** BILLINGS & IRONS *Forchheimer's Therapeusis Internal Dis.* V. iii. 121 *(heading)* Immunological reactions in diagnosis. **1919** Immunologic [see ALLERGY a.]. **1929** R. T. HEWLETT in *Syst. Bacteriol.* (Med. Res. Council) III. 375 Dickson had previously observed that the Nevin cheese strain differed immunologically from other strains with which he was working. **1955** *Sci. News Let.* 12 Mar. 168/1 Because of his lack of gamma globulin, the Minnesota boy has what his doctors term almost complete 'immunologic paralysis', meaning the mechanism in his body that should help him develop immunity, or resistance, to disease has been paralyzed. **1960** *New Biol.* XXXI. 103 It seems..that any potentially antigenic material which comes into contact with the cells during the stage of immunological immaturity fails subsequently to cause antibody formation. **1963** *Times* 25 Jan. 7/7 In such a case the twins are immunologically tolerant of each other's tissues. **1967** W. O. WEIGLE *Natural & Acquired Immunologic Unresponsiveness* i. 1 The evidence available suggests that the acquisition of an immunologic unresponsive state to self is not genetically determined, but is acquired early in life before maturation of the immune mechanisms. **1968** *Sunday Tel.* 28 Jan. 4/4 Dr. M. C. Botha, the immunologist who conducted the tests. **1973** J. GOODFIELD *Courier to Peking* x. 120 You hear the voice of the true immunologist. *Ibid.* 126 The question was a highly technical one and understanding it demanded a thorough background in immunological theory.

†**i'mmural**, *v. Obs.* [f. IM-[1] + MURAL (f. L. *mūrus* wall).] *trans.* To wall in.

1662 J. BARGRAVE *Pope Alex. VII* (1867) 121 The corps were at their length immuralled in thecas or, as it were, in hollow shelves dug in to the wall.

†**i'mmurate**, *ppl. a. Obs.* [ad. L. *immūrātus*, pa. pple. of *immūrāre* to IMMURE.] Immured.

1593 R. BARNES *Parthenophil* Madr. vii. in Arb. *Garner* V. 364 O chaste desires, which held her heart immurate In walls of adamant unfoiled!

immuration (ɪmjʊə'reɪʃən). [f. IMMUR(E *v.* + -ATION.] = IMMUREMENT.

1895 POLLOCK & MAITLAND *Hist. Eng. Law* I. II. ii. 427 Stephen Langton seems to have condemned two of the laity to that close imprisonment which was known as immuration. **1959** J. L. M. TRIM in Quirk & Smith *Teaching of Eng.* iii. 77 [Speech training] may easily lead to..an increasing immuration of the individual instead of the liberation which education should bring. **1963** *Yale Rev.* Winter 291 The first, the cloistered family, guarded the purity of the flesh and preserved the ideal of chastity through the Dark Ages by immuration.

immure (ɪ'mjʊə(r)), *v.* Also 6 **emure**. [ad. med.L. *immūrāre*, f. *im-* (IM-[1]) + *mūrus* wall (cf. late L. *mūrāre* to wall). Cf. F. *emmurer*, which may be the immediate source.]

†**1.** *trans.* To wall in, to surround with a wall or walls; to fortify. (= late L. *murare.*) *Obs.*

1598 SYLVESTER *Du Bartas* II. i. IV. *Handie-crafts* 375 With stones..And clayie morter..he immures his fort. **1615** G. SANDYS *Trav.* 114 These [walls]..appeare to have immured but a part of the Citie. **1698** FRYER *Acc. E. India & P.* 75 An Altar..immured by a Square Wall. **1746** *Tour through Ireland* ix. 187 It is certain the Town was immured long before that Date.

absol. **1636** G. SANDYS *Paraphr. Div. Poems, Eccl.* iii. (1648) 4 A time to batter down, a time t'immure.

2. To shut up or enclose within walls; to imprison; to confine as in a prison or fortress.

1588 SHAKS. *L.L.L.* III. i. 126 Thou wert emured, restrained, captiuated, bound. **1594** —— *Rich. III*, IV. i. 100 Pitty, you ancient Stones, those tender Babes, Whom Enuie hath immur'd within your Walls. *c* **1645** HOWELL *Lett.* I. VI. I, 'Tis not so tedious to me, as to others to be thus immur'd (in the Fleet). **1791** MRS. RADCLIFFE *Rom. Forest* iii, Too long I had been immured in the walls of a cloister. **1847** DISRAELI *Tancred* I. ii, Resolved to break his son's spirit by keeping him immured in the country. **1879** DIXON *Windsor* I. ii. 17 As rebels..they were immured in jail.

†**b.** To shut off, exclude, seclude *from*. *Obs.*

1616 R. C. *Times Whistle* v. 2328 Whom carnall sence & appetite immures From God & goodnesse. **1652–62** HEYLIN *Cosmogr.* III. (1682) 130 They live immured from the sight of the World.

3. *transf.* and *fig.* To enclose, encompass, encircle, surround; to shut in, confine. Now *rare*.

1583 STUBBES *Anat. Abus.* I. (1877) 23 A pleasant..Iland, immured aboute with the Sea. **1588** SHAKS. *L.L.L.* IV. iii. 328 Loue first learned in a Ladies eyes, Liues not alone emured in the braine. **1634** SIR T. HERBERT *Trav.* 135 The lodge here is in a craggie place immured betwixt two Hils. **1725** POPE *Odyss.* XXIII. 44 Immur'd we sat, and catch'd each passing sound. **1820** SCORESBY *Acc. Arctic Reg.* I. 298 In situations far immured among the northern ice.

b. *refl.* To shut oneself up.

1586 WARNER *Alb. Eng.* II. vii. (1612) 30 They and their King, immure themselves at length. **1627** MAY *Lucan* II. (1631) 19 Himselfe immuring in Brundusium's hold. **1751** JOHNSON *Rambler* No. 180 ¶9 Men bred in shades and silence, taught to immure themselves at sunset. **1826** DISRAELI *Viv. Grey* III. i, To immure himself for three years in a German University.

4. To build into a wall; to build up or entomb in a wall. Also *transf.*

1675 E. WILSON *Spadacr. Dunelm.* 9 Hairs, Straws, Grains of Sand [etc.] are frequently found immured in Hailstones. **1808** [see IMMURED]. **1851** [see IMMURING]. **1863** SIR G. SCOTT *Glean. Westm. Abb.* (ed. 2) 64 The end of the tomb has been immured in the lower part of the chapel of King Henry V.

Hence **i'mmuring** *vbl. sb.*

1610 W. FOLKINGHAM *Art of Survey* II. ii. 49 Immounding, impayling, immuring, skirting, Girding. **1851** J. H. NEWMAN *Cath. in Eng.* 115 The torturings, the starvings, the immurings, the murderings proper to a monastic establishment.

†**i'mmure**, *sb. Obs. rare.* In 7 **emure**. [f. IMMURE *v.*] Something that immures; a wall.

1606 SHAKS. *Tr. & Cr.* Prol. 8 Their vow is made To ransacke Troy, within whose strong emures The rauish'd Helen..sleepes.

immured (ɪ'mjʊəd), *ppl. a.* [f. IMMURE *v.* + -ED[1].] Enclosed in walls or as in walls; imprisoned, confined; built up in a wall.

1596 *Edward III*, II. i. 17 The prisoner of immured dark constraint. **1651** *Life Father Sarpi* (1676) 6 Among those immured Hermites of Saint Hermagora. **1740** GRAY *Let.* in *Poems* (1775) 81 The doors..we saw opened to him, and all the other immured Cardinals came thither to receive him. **1808** SCOTT *Marmion* II. xxv. *note*, A female skeleton, which, from the shape of the niche, and the position of the figure, seemed to be that of an immured nun.

immurement (ɪ'mjʊəmənt). [f. IMMURE *v.* + -MENT.] The action of immuring or condition of being immured; imprisonment, confinement.

1736 BAILEY (folio) Pref., *Immurement*, an inclosing between two Walls, a Punishment used in Popish Countries. **1753** SMOLLETT *Ct. Fathom* (1784) 178/1 By the interposition of his wife, whose aim was not the death but immurement of his daughter. **1835** *Fraser's Mag.* XI. 275 Her melancholy immurement and tragic end.

immusical (ɪ'mjuːzɪkəl, ɪmm-), *a.* Now *rare.* [f. IM-[2] + MUSICAL.] Not musical or harmonious; unmusical.

1626 BACON *Sylva* §101 All Sounds are either Musicall Sounds..which Sounds are euer Equall; As Singing..Or Immusicall Sounds; which are euer Vnequall; Such as are the Voice in Speaking, all Whisperings,..all Percussions. **1679** *Refined Courtier* 13/1 We ought industriously to refrain from singing, especially if the voice be immusical. **1706** A. BEDFORD *Temple Mus.* ii. 34 What our..Writers fancy of their..Scales, is known to be utterly Immusical. **1890** *Standard* 26 Mar. 3/8 They were not an immusical nation.

Hence **i'mmusically** *adv.*, unmusically.

1694 S. S. *Loyal & Impart. Satirist* Ded. A iij, Ingenious Whimseys, which sound but immusically to a Judicious Ear.

immutability (ɪmjuːtə'bɪlɪtɪ). [f. IMMUTABLE + -ITY; after F. *immutabilité*, L. *immūtābilitās.*] The quality of being immutable; unchangeableness, invariableness, unalterableness.

1594 HOOKER *Eccl. Pol.* III. xi. §3 Did any part of that [God's] will require the immutability of laws concerning church polity? **1611** BIBLE *Heb.* vi. 17 The immutabilitie of his counsell. **1718** *Freethinker* No. 64 ¶8 No Nation ever insisted, so rigorously, upon this Immutability of Laws, as the Locrians. **1863** DARWIN in *Life & Lett.* (1887) III. 8 He has really entirely lost faith in the immutability of species.

immutable (ɪ'mjuːtəb(ə)l), *a.* Also 5 **in-**. [ad. L. *immūtābil-is*, f. *im-* (IM-[2]) + *mūtābilis* MUTABLE. (Also in 15–16th c. F.)]

1. Not mutable; not subject to or susceptible of change; unchangeable, unalterable, changeless.

1412–20 LYDG. *Chron. Troy* II. xvi, He was..Perseuerant and of will immutable. **14..** *Circumcision* in *Tundale's Vis.* (1843) 97 Sothfast kyng whos regne is inmutabull. **1526** TINDALE *Heb.* vi. 18 By two immutable thynges (in which it was vnpossible that god shulde lye). **1651** HOBBES *Leviath.* I. xv. 79 The Lawes of Nature are Immutable and Eternall. **1710** PRIDEAUX *Orig. Tithes* iv. 170 This grant shall remain firm, and immutable. **1821** J. Q. ADAMS in *C. Davies' Metr. Syst.* III. (1871) 131 To find..some immutable standard of linear measure. **1875** JOWETT *Plato* (ed. 2) IV. 42 We speak of eternal and immutable justice, but not of eternal and immutable pleasure.

b. *techn.* Not subject to variation in different cases; invariable: used e.g. of markings which are the same in all the individuals of a species.

1621 HEYLIN *Microcosmus* 2 The greater circles are either Immutable as the Æquator, [or] Mutable as the Meridian, Horizon. **1706** PHILLIPS, *Immutable Circlis*..are the same to all the Inhabitants of the Earth. **1796** H. HUNTER tr. *St.-Pierre's Stud. Nat.* (1799) II. 73 Nature bestows on every being that which is adapted to it..according to the Latitude for which it is destined... Some of these adaptations are..immutable, and others variable.

¶**2.** [IM-[1].] = mutable: cf. IMMUTE *v.* *Obs.*

1581 MARBECK *Bk. of Notes* 867 If salvation were by us to be gotten, then we are so immutable that we should every minute of an houre, cast away ourselves.

Hence **i'mmutableness**, the quality of being immutable, immutability.

1610 DONNE *Pseudo-Martyr* xi. 345 In power of binding, and all validities, except immutablenesse..equall to Diuine. *a* **1687** H. MORE *Conject. Cabbal., Def.* (1712) App. viii. 184 The steddiness and immutableness of the Matter.

immutably (ɪ'mjuːtəblɪ), *adv.* [f. prec. + -LY[2].] In an immutable manner; without possibility of or liability to change; unchangeably.

1601 DENT *Pathw. Heaven* 282 To be immutably good, is proper onely to God. *a* **1711** KEN *Hymnar.* Poet. Wks. 1721 II. 33 God ever is immutably the same. **1855** MOTLEY *Dutch Rep.* II. v. (1866) 229 Immutably determined to permit no change of religion within his dominions.

immutate ('ɪmjuːtət), *a. rare.* [ad. L. *immūtāt-us*, f. *im-* (IM-[2]) + *mūtātus*, pa. pple. of *mūtāre* to change.] Unchanged.

1788 J. LEE *Introd. Bot.* III. xi. (ed. 4) 213 Having two Cotyledons; and these are either, *Immutate*, unchanged; ..*Plicate*, folded;..*Duplicate*, doubled [etc.].

†**immu'tation.** *Obs.* [ad. L. *immūtātiōn-em*, n. of action f. *immūtāre*: see next. Cf. obs. F. *immutation.*] Mutation, change, alteration, transformation. (In quot. 1704 = HYPALLAGE.)

c **1540** tr. *Pol. Verg. Eng. Hist.* (Camden) I. 195 The younger abatid their pride, while they endevored novelties and immutation. **1589** PUTTENHAM *Eng. Poesie* III. xii. (Arb.) 175 Defect, or surplusage..or immutation in the same speaches..altering either the congruitie grammaticall, or the sence, or both. **1647** H. MORE *Song of Soul* I. I. xxiii, What delightfull immutations Of her soft flowing vest we contemplate! **1669** GALE *Crt. Gentiles* I. III. iii. §10 Which reason of the immutation of this Light, is given by Moses, Gen. i. 14. **1704** J. HARRIS *Lex. Techn.*, *Hypallage* or *Immutation*, a Grammatical Figure..As in this Instance, *Dare Classibus Austros*, instead of *Dare Classes Austris.*

†**i'mmute**, *v. Obs.* [ad. L. *immūt-āre*, f. *im-* (IM-[1]) + *mūtāre* to change.] *trans.* To produce a change in; to change, alter, transform.

1613 SALKELD *Treat. Angels* 106 (L.) God can immediately immute, change, corrupt, destroy, or annihilate whatsoever pleaseth His divine majesty. **1646** SIR T. BROWNE *Pseud. Ep.* II. v. 86 Although the substance of gold be not sensibly immuted or its gravity at all decreased. **1661** GLANVILL *Van. Dogm.* xxi. 206 That..would be more immuted by those greater alterations which are in cadaverous solutions.

†**i'mmute**, *a. Obs. rare.* [Irregular shortening of *immuted.* (Cf. *elated, elate.*)] Unchanged.

1639 G. DANIEL *Ecclus.* xxvi. 53 Soe fixt doth vertue stand, and soe Immute, With her whose thoughts are truly resolute.

immutilate (ɪ'mjuːtɪlət), *a. rare.* [ad. late L. *immutilāt-us*, f. *im-* (IM-[2]) + *mutilātus* (see MUTILATE).] Unmutilated; without mutilation.

1890 T. W. ALLIES *Peter's Rock* 333 A maintainer of the Catholic and Apostolic faith immutilate.

i'mmutual, *a. rare.* [f. IM-[2] + MUTUAL.] Not mutual.

1768 W. DONALDSON *Life & Adv. Sir B. Sapskull* II. 6 The symmetry of the figure will be disproportioned to the design, and the harmony of the whole immutual and unadjusted.

immy ('ɪmɪ). Also **imma**, **immie**. [perh. f. IMITATION.] **a.** (See quot. 1928.) **b.** A type of marble used by children.

1928 *Funk's Stand. Dict.*, *Immy*, a choice marble made in imitation, as of a cornelian or an agate. **1936** *Fortune* June 36/2 Like glass for stained-glass windows and water tumblers, marble glass has a soft lime base, which makes an immie so resilient. **1941** BAKER *Dict. Austral. Slang* 37 *Imma*, a type of marble. **1952** [see AGATE *sb.* 1 b]. **1972** *Sat. Rev.* (U.S.) 29 Jan. 8 Shooting marbles was played by four or five boys kneeling around a circle... In the center there were a lot of marbles—'immies', as they were known.

†**i-mone**. *Obs.* [f. I-[1] + *mone* MOAN.] Moan.

1297 R. GLOUC. (Rolls) 1195 He was sori & made gret imone [*most MSS.* mone].

i-mong: see YMONG.

i-mored, ME. pa. pple. of MORE *v.* *Obs.*, to root.

i-motet, ME. pa. pple. of MOOT *v.*

imp (ɪmp), *sb.* Forms: 1 **impa**, (? **impe**), 3–7 **impe**, 4–6 **ympe**, (5 **hympe**, 6 **himp**, **emp**, 6–7 **ymp**), 6– **imp**. [OE. *impa* (or ? *impe*), pl. *impan*, goes with *impian* to IMP: see next. Cf. also mod.G. *impf*, Da. *ympe*, Sw. *ymp*. Welsh *imp* graft, scion, is from ME. Fr. *ente* (whence MDu. *ente*, Du. *ent*) is ultimately from the same source.]

†**1.** A young shoot of a plant or tree; a sapling; a sucker, slip, scion. *Obs.*

c **897** K. ÆLFRED *Gregory's Past.* xlix. 381 Sio haliȝe ȝesomnung Godes folces, ðæt eardað on æppeltunum, ðonne hie wel begað hira plantan & hiera impan, oð hie fulweaxne beoð. *a* **1225** *Ancr. R.* 378 Ȝunge impen me bigurt mid þornes, leste bestes ureten ham þeo hwule þet heo beoð meruwe. *c* **1386** CHAUCER *Monk's Prol.* 68 Of fieble trees ther comen wrecched ympes. *c* **1425** *Seven Sag.* (P.) 1697 The lorde hadde an hympe gode, Tha[t] in a fayr herber stood. **1578** LYTE *Dodoens* IV. lxi. 524 The first springes or tender impes of the Artechok. **1601** HOLLAND *Pliny* XIII. viii, About the foot of the tree it bears many yong imps, which are such suckers of the sap, that they draw away all the goodnesse. **1669** WORLIDGE *Syst. Agric.* (1681) 104 When the young Imps or Seedlings are sprung up, you must be very careful in keeping them from weeds. **1672** MARVELL *Reh. Transp.* I. 133 [Ivy] is a sneaking insinuating Imp.

†**b.** In fig. context, applied to persons. *Obs.*

1377 *Pol. Poems* (Rolls) I. 218 Thus ben this lordes ileid ful lowe; The stok is of the same rote; An ympe biginnes for to growe. 1596 SPENSER *F.Q.* IV. xi. 26 [Oxford] that faire City, wherein make abode So many learned impes, that shoote abrode, And with their braunches spred all Britany.

†2. A shoot or slip used in grafting; a graft.

1377 LANGL. *P. Pl.* B. v. 137, I was..þe couentes Gardyner for to graffe ympes. 1483 *Cath. Angl.* 195/1 An Impe, *ubi* A grafte. 1513 BRADSHAW *St. Werburge* I. 2004 The lytell graffe or ympe transcendeth the tree. 1599 H. BUTTES *Dyets drie Dinner* D viij, An Almond-tree-Imp, inserted to a Mastick stick. 1669 W. SIMPSON *Hydrol. Chym.* 270 The scions, imps, and grafts of fruit trees. 1706 PHILLIPS, *Imp*,..a kind of Graft to be set in a Tree.

†b. In fig. context, applied to persons. *Obs.*

1583 GOLDING *Calvin on Deut.* xxi. 124 If this bee happened to the natural braunches what shall become of the impes (that are graffed into the Tree)? 1612-15 BP. HALL *Contempl., O.T.* IX. i, God never did more for the naturall olive, then for that wild Impe which hee hath graffed in. 1613-16 W. BROWNE *Brit. Past.* I. ii. (N.), Poor Doridon, the impe Whom nature seem'd to have selected forth To be ingraffed on some stocke of worth.

3. Scion (esp. of a noble house); offspring, child (usually male). *Obs.* since 17th c., exc. as a literary archaism, or as partly continued in 5.

c1412 HOCCLEVE *Ball. Pr. Henry* in *De Reg. Princ.* (Roxb.) 195 In the presence Of Kynges ympe and Princes worthynesse. 1548 HALL *Chron., Hen. VIII* 242 b, That his sonne prince Edward, that goodly ympe, maie long reigne over you. 1575 *Appius & Virg.* I. in Hazl. *Dodsley* IV. 112 By her I have a virgin pure, an imp of heavenly race. 1584 *Epit. Ld. Denbigh in Beauchamp Chapel, Warwick*, Heere resteth the body of the noble Impe Robert of Dvdley.. sonne of Robert Erle of Leycester. 1611 SPEED *Hist. Gt. Brit.* VII. xii. 264 His sad lamenting sonne Faustus, a vertuous Impe of those impious parents. 1808 SCOTT *Marm.* I. Introd. 37 My imps,..hardy, bold, and wild, As best befits the mountain child. a1845 JOANNA BAILLIE *Poems, To a Child* i, Whose imp art thou, with dimpled cheek,..thou urchin sly?

b. = 'child', *fig.* and *transf. Obs.* or *arch.*

c1380 WYCLIF *Wks.* (1880) 334 A frere þat is a confessour to kyng or to a duke is ympe or pere to a bishop. 1536 *Act 28 Hen. VIII*, c. 10 §1 Dyvers sedicious..persones, being impes of the said Bisshopp of Rome. 1555 W. WATREMAN *Fardle Facions* II. viii. 179 Enuie cannot dwell ther, ne none of her impes. 1621 QUARLES *Div. Poems, Esther* vii, Art thou ..that Impe of Glory? 1645 PAGITT *Heresiogr.* (1647) 126 This opinion is easily discovered to be an Impe of Pelagianisme. 1796 BURKE *Bill for shorten. Durat. Parl.* Wks. 1812 V. 386 My honourable friend has not brought down a spirited imp of chivalry to win the first atchievement. 1809 W. IRVING *Knickerb.* VII. iv. (1849) 400 That imp of fame and prowess, the headstrong Peter.

4. *spec.* A 'child' of the devil, or of hell.

a. with parentage expressed: Applied to wicked men, and to petty fiends or evil spirits.

1526 *Pilgr. Perf.* (W. de W. 1531) 63 Suche appereth as aungelles, but in very dede they be ymps of serpentes. 1538 BALE *Gods Promises* in Dodsley *O. Pl.* (1780) I. 13 An ympe though I be of helle, deathe and dampnacyon. 1563 *Homilies* II. *Rebellion* IV. (1859) 577 Those most wicked imps of the devil. 1583 STUBBES *Anat. Abus.* I. (1877) 111 An impe of Sathan. c1648 BILLINGSLEY *Infancy of World* (1658) 94 The Devil's Impe the Pope. 1706-7 FARQUHAR *Beaux Strat.* IV. ii, What Witchcraft now have these two Imps of the Devil been a hatching here? a1806 K. WHITE *Poems, Despair* 46 Hither, ye furious imps of Acheron. 1821 SCOTT *Kenilw.* xxiv, Either Flibbertigibbet..or else an imp of the devil in good earnest.

b. Hence, with omission of the qualification: A little devil or demon, an evil spirit; esp. in 17th c., one of those with which witches were supposed to be familiar; now chiefly in art and mythology.

1584 R. SCOT *Discov. Witchcr.* VII. xv. (1886) 122 They haue so fraied vs with bull beggers, spirits, witches,.. tritons, centaurs, dwarfes, giants, imps. 1681 GLANVILL *Sadducismus* I. (1682) 18 The Imps of Witches are sometimes wicked spirits..that have been Sorcerers..in this life. 1693 C. MATHER *Invis. World* (1862) 83 We have seen even some of their own Children, so dedicated unto the Devil, that..the *Imps* have sucked them, and rendred them Venemous to a Prodigy. 1706 PHILLIPS, *Imp*, a familiar Spirit, said to be attending upon Witches. 1829 CARLYLE *Misc., Voltaire* (1872) II. 134 A scoffing man..shows more of the imp than of the angel. a1845 BARHAM *Ingol. Leg., Truants* iii, Three more frolicsome Imps, I ween, Beelzebub's self hath seldom seen. 1882 FROUDE *Carlyle* II. 53 Enjoying his work [of destruction] with the pleasure of some mocking imp.

c. Applied to a human being. (Often humorous.)

1633 D. R[OGERS] *Treat. Sacram.* I. 123 Will not this teach all the rest (except Impes and degenerate) to be much more so? 1750 GRAY *Long Story* 44 Thereabouts there lurk'd A wicked Imp they call a Poet. 1857 LOCKER *Lond. Lyrics, To Printer's Devil* I Small imp of blackness, off at once.

5. A mischievous child (having a little of 'the devil' in him); a young urchin: often used playfully.

(App. partly a continuation of sense 3, but largely influenced by 4 b.)

1642 in Miss Hickson *Irel. 17th Cent.* (1884) I. xviii. 196 Six Irish children of that town, who suddenly fell upon him, ..so that he by these wicked young imps, who were none of them..above eight years of age, quickly after died. 1727 SWIFT *Gulliver* IV. viii, I once caught a young male [Yahoo] of three years old,..but the little imp fell a squalling, and scratching, and biting. 1826 SCOTT in *Lockhart* i. *note*, I was never a dunce..but an incorrigibly idle imp. 1859 W. COLLINS *Q. of Hearts* (1875) 24 With a wild imp of a Welsh boy following her as guide and groom.

†6. A young man, a youth; fellow, man, 'lad', 'boy'. (Cf. CHILD, sense 7.) *Obs.*

1579 LYLY *Euphues* (Arb.) 33-5 There dwelt in Athens a young gentleman of great patrimony... It happened this young Impe to arive at Naples. *Ibid.* 108 This is..to admonish all young Imps and nouises in loue. 1648 GAGE *West Ind.* ix. 26 The mendicant Franciscan Fryers voweth ..poverty..Yet those wretched Impes live in those parts as though they had never vowed. 1889 R. BUCHANAN *Heir of Linne* i, Room there, you imps and loons.

7. A piece added on, to eke out, lengthen out, or enlarge something. (Cf. IMP *v.* 5.) †a. An additional tag to a bell-rope so that more than one person may pull at once: = EKE *sb.*[1] 2 a. b. *dial.* An addition to a beehive consisting of a wreath or wreaths placed underneath to increase its height: = EKE *sb.*[1] 2 b. c. *dial.* A length of twisted hair in a fishing-line.

1595 *Vestry Bks.* (Surtees) 123 Paid for vj emps to ye bell ropes, xijd. 1605 *Ibid.* 142 More for bell imps, xiiij *d.* 1606 *Ibid.* 144 For the greet bell ympes of the length of six feddom. 1615 W. LAWSON *Orch. & Gard.* III. x. (1668) 78 An imp is, three or four wreaths wrought at the Hive, the same compass, to raise the Hive withall. 1788 W. MARSHALL *Yorksh.* II. Gloss. (E.D.S.), *Imp*, an eke placed under a bee-hive. 1846 BROCKETT *N.C. Gloss* (ed. 3) I. 234 An addition to a beehive is called an 'imp', so also is a length of hair twisted, as forming part of a fishing-line.

8. *attrib.* and *Comb.*, as †*imp-garden, -garth, -yard* (nursery-garden, garden of plants), †*-tree*; *imp-like* adj.

1337-8 *Durham Acc. Rolls* (Surtees) I. 34 In..semine canab. emp. pro le ympyard. c1345 *Orpheo* 68 They seten hem down all thre, Fayr under an ympe-tre. 1446-7 *Durham Acc. Rolls* (Surtees) I. 84 Pro custodia orti Cellerarii vocati ympgarth. 1577 B. GOOGE *Heresbach's Husb.* (1586) 76 The orderyng of an Impe Garden..wherein as in a parke the young plantes are nourished. 1675 EVELYN *Terra* (1729) 35 Where Imp-Gardens are poor, the tender Plant does seldom thrive. 1831 J. HUNTER *Hist. Deanery Doncaster* II. 6 An imp-yard is what is now known by the term nursery-garden, as may be seen in The Booke of Husbandry by Barnaby Googe. 1866 CARLYLE *Remin.* I. 146 What a childlike and yet half imp-like volume of laughter lay in Frank.

imp (ɪmp), *v.* Forms: see the sb. [OE. *impian* (rare) = OHG. *impfôn* (rare), MHG. and Ger. *impfen*, beside which OHG. had (more commonly) *impitôn*, MHG. *imp(e)ten*. Da. *ympe*, Sw. *ympa* are from a LG. **impen*; Welsh *impio* is from Eng. F. *enter* (whence MDu. *enten, inten*, Du. *enten*, MLG. *enten*) is supposed to be ultimately from the same source.

The history of this vb. and the prec. sb. is in some points obscure, from want of evidence. The corresponding F. *enter* to graft, *ente* (for **empte*) graft, are referred by Darmesteter, etc., to late L. **emputāre*, **emputa*, the latter neuter pl. of Gr. ἔμφυτος, -ον implanted, engrafted: cf. ἐμφύειν to implant, ἐμφυτεύειν to implant, engraft, ἐμφυτεία implanting, engrafting. (There is evidence in the Salic Law for a med.L. *impotus, inpotus*, scion, graft.) This was presumably the source also of OHG. *impitôn* (not *impfitôn*), MHG. *imp(e)ten*; though some would refer it to L. *putāre* to prune. OE. *impian*, OHG *impfôn*, was evidently, from the OHG. lautverschiebung, a word of earlier adoption, but was prob. derived in some way from the same Gr. source (? from ἐμφυ-ειν); of this the OE. sb. *impa* (hardly *impe*) must then have been a derivative, on the analogy of agent-nouns in *-a*; so mod.Ger. *impf* from *impfen*.]

†1. *trans.* To graft, engraft. *Obs.*

c1000 *Gerefa* in *Anglia* IX. 262 On længtene eregian and impian, beana sawan, wingeard settan. 1377 LANGL. *P. Pl.* B. IX. 147 Impe on an ellerne, and if þine apple be swete, Mochel merueile me þynketh. 1413 *Pilgr. Sowle* (Caxton 1483) IV. ii. 58 Vpon that braunche was ymped a graf that was taken fro a free appel tree. 1553 T. WILSON *Rhet.* 26 b, To ympe or graffe yong settes. 1681 BURNET *Hist. Ref.* (1865) II. 530 He gave himself to gardening and used to graft and imp with his own hand.

†2. To plant (young shoots). *Obs. rare.*

c1420 *Pallad. on Husb.* III. 142 Then kest adoun thi scions here and there, And ympe in oon in euery stikis place.

3. *transf.* and *fig.* from 1 and 2. To 'engraft', implant; to inlay, set or fix in; to 'engraft' (as by marriage) in a family. *arch.*

1340-70 *Alisaunder* 616 A brem brasen borde..Imped in iuory..With goode siluer & golde gailich atired. c1400 *Rom. Rose* 5137 But Love..was so imped in my thought. c1425 *Hampole's Psalter* Metr. Pref. 50 Copyed has þis Sauter ben of yuel men of lollardry, And afturward hit has bene sene ympyd in wiþ eresy. 1596 SPENSER *F.Q.* IV. ix. 4 That headlesse tyrants tronke he reard from ground, And, having ympt the head to it agayne..made it so to ride as it alive was found. 1612-15 BP. HALL *Contempl., O.T.* XX. ii. (*Jehu and Jehoram*), Nothing is more dangerous than to be imped in a wicked family; this relation too often draws in a share both of sinne and punishment. 1613-16 W. BROWNE *Brit. Past.* II. ii, And when thy temple's well deserving bayes Might impe a pride in thee to reach thy praise. 1647 TRAPP *Comm. Matt.* i. 8 It was because they were imped in the wicked family of Ahab. 17.. BROWN *On Rom.* vi. 5 (Jam.) Believers are so closely united to Christ, as that they have been imped with him, like an imp joined to an old stock. 1876 BLACKIE *Songs Relig. & Life* 140 The new doctrine, which the times had imped Into his budding soul.

4. *Falconry.* To engraft feathers in the wing of a bird, so as to make good losses or deficiencies, and thus restore or improve the powers of flight; hence, allusively, with reference to 'taking higher flights', enlarging one's powers, and the like. In various constructions:

†a. To imp feathers *into* or *in* a wing, etc. *Obs.*

1477 *Paston Lett.* III. No. 794. 185 Like as the fawcon Which is alofte, tellith scorne to loke a down On hym that wont was her feders to pyke and ympe. 1580 LYLY *Euphues* (Arb.) 249 Ymping a fether to make me flye, when thou oughtest rather to cut my wing for feare of soaring. 1589 NASHE *Pasquil & Marf.* 11 Such an Eccho, as multiplies euery word..and ympes so many feathers vnto euery tale, that it flyes with all speede into euery corner of the Realme. 1641 BROME *Joviall Crew* II. Wks. 1873 III. 374 To see a swallow..with a white feather imp'd in her tail. 1706 PHILLIPS, *To Imp a Feather in a Hawk's Wing* (among Falconers), to add a new piece from an old broken stump.

b. To imp a wing (or bird) *with* feathers. *to imp the wings of*: to strengthen or improve the flight of.

1596 SPENSER *Hymn Heav. Beautie* 135 Gathering plumes of perfect speculation, To impe the wings of thy high flying mynd. 1598 DRAYTON *Heroic. Ep.* v. 78 Their Buzzard-wings, imp'd with our Eagles Plumes. a1618 SYLVESTER *Posthumi* Sonn. iv, Imping his broken wings with better plumes. 1648 MILTON *Sonn. to Fairfax*, The false North displays Her broken league to imp their serpent-wings. 1792 WOLCOTT (P. Pindar) *Ep. Ld. Macartney* 40 And [Fortune] with an Eagle's pinion imps an Owl. 1816 SOUTHEY *Lay of Laureate* Proem ii, My spirit imp'd her wings for stronger flight. 1852 JERDAN *Autobiog.* II. xviii. 251 At the same time Barry Cornwall first imped his wing in my grateful pages. 1886 SWINBURNE *Misc.* 145 The highest flight that Wordsworth's muse could attain when her wings were imped with plumes of religious doctrine.

c. To imp wings *on* or *to* a person; to imp *with* wings.

1633 G. HERBERT *Temple, Easter Wings* 9 If I imp my wing on thine, Affliction shall advance the flight in me. 1635 HEYWOOD *Londoni Sinus Salutis* Wks. 1874 IV. 289 These are Impt with no Icarian wings, But Plumes Immortall. 1669 *Addr. hopeful yng. Gentry Eng.* 34 To see a Gallant flutter..with no other wings than his Taylor has imp'd on. 1697 DRYDEN *Virg. Georg.* IV. 439 Imp'd with Wings, The Grubs proceed to Bees with pointed Stings. 1732 POPE *Ep. Bathurst* 41 Blest paper-credit!..That lends Corruption lighter wings to fly! Gold imp'd by thee can compass hardest things. 1814 CARY *Dante, Paradise* XXXII. 70 Behoved That circumcision in the males should imp The flight of innocent wings.

¶ App. by a misunderstanding of the hawking term, taken in the sense of 'To clip'.

1657 BP. H. KING *Poems* I. ii. (1843) 9 God shall imp their pride, and let them see They are but fools in a sublime degree. 1683 KENNETT tr. *Erasm. on Folly* 39 But imp the wings of his towering ambition. *Ibid.* 147 Her soaring wings are imp'd and all her enlivening faculties clogged.

5. To extend, lengthen, enlarge, add to; to eke *out* (that which is short or deficient); to mend, repair; to add on a piece to. (Cf. IMP *sb.* 7.)

1592 LYLY *Midas* V. ii, A woman's tongue ympt with a barbar's will proove a razor or a raser. 1606 CHAPMAN *Mons. D'Olive* Plays 1873 I. 221 All my care is for Followers to Imp out my Traine. 1661 SOUTH *Serm.* (1698) III. 188 An ill, restless, cross humour, which is imped with Smart, and quickned with Opposition. 1671 CLARENDON *Dialogues* in *Tracts* (1727) 306 We ought to imp out these unavoidable defects with an extraordinary civility and condescension. 1828 *Craven Dial.*, *Imp*, to add, to enlarge... It is a very common expression when applied to bee-hives. 1834 SIR H. TAYLOR *Artevelde* I. ii. (1849) 7 You have imped me with a new device.

6. *nonce-use.* To mock like an imp or demon.

1839 BAILEY *Festus* (1848) 112, I am..with the mightiest folly mocked Which ever imped a soul to madness.

imp. Abbreviation of *imperative, imperator, imperatrix, imperfect, imperial, impersonal, important, imprimatur, imprint, improvement.*

†im'pacable, *a. Obs.* [f. IM-[2] + L. *pācāre* to pacify, appease + -ABLE.] That cannot be pacified or appeased; implacable.

1571 FORTESCUE *Forest* 72 Seedes of impacable discorde and dissention. 1591 SPENSER *Ruines of Time* 395 Freed from bands of impacable fate. 1602 WARNER *Alb. Eng.* Epit. (1612) 356 The impacable Incursions of those barbarous and vndanted Pictes.

Hence **†impaca'bility**, implacability (*obs.*).

1602 WARNER *Alb. Eng.* Epit. (1612) 355 The Impacabilitie of the Pictes and Scotes.

†impa'cific, *a. Obs. rare* [ad. late L. *impācific-us*, or f. IM-[2] + PACIFIC. Cf. obs. F. *impacifique*.] Not pacific or peaceful; restless.

a1653 G. DANIEL *Idyll* i. 3 The Impacificke Seas of our owne feares And Iealousies.

impack (ɪm'pæk), *v. rare.* Also 7 em-. [f. IM-[1] + PACK *v.*] *trans.* To pack in; to press closely together into a mass; to pack up.

Hence **im'packing** *vbl. sb.*; **im'packment**, the action of impacking or state of being impacked (Webster 1864).

1611 FLORIO, *Impaccare*, to pack vp, to empack. *Ibid.*, *Imballamenti*, impackings or packes. 1867 I. I. HAYES *Open Polar Sea* 85 The ice was as closely impacked behind us as before us.

impact ('ɪmpækt), *sb.* [ad. L. type **impact-us* sb., f. ppl. stem of *impingĕre* to IMPINGE. Cf. mod.F. *impact*.] 1. a. The act of impinging; the striking of one body against another; collision. Chiefly in *Dynamics*, in reference to momentum.

1781 BP. WATSON *Chem. Ess.* (1784) I. 165 *note*, The same rule, by which common velocity of hard or non-elastic bodies after their impact..is calculated. 1795 SOUTHEY *Joan of Arc* VIII. 228 The English chief, Pointing again his arbalist, let loose The string; the quarrel, by that impact driven, True to its aim, fled fatal. 1862 *Times* 7 Mar., No such satisfactory results in the way of resisting the tremendous impact of the shot have been obtained from any

other target. **1863** TYNDALL *Heat* ii. §56 The impact of atoms of oxygen against atoms of sulphur. **1866** HUXLEY *Phys.* ix. (1872) 221 The impact of the vibrations of the luminous ether on the retina.

attrib. **1878** STEWART & TAIT *Unseen Univ.* iv. 146 We are ..driven to the impact theory as the only tenable one.

b. ***fig.*** Now commonly the effective action of one thing or person upon another; the effect of such action; influence; impression. Esp. in phr. ***to make an impact*** (***on***).

1817 COLERIDGE *Biog. Lit.* 63 In any given perception there is a something which has been communicated to it [the mind] by an impact, or an impression ab extra. **1874** STUBBS *Const. Hist.* I. i. 7 The impact of barbarian conquest split up the unity of the Latin tongue. **1946** *Sat. Rev. Lit.* (U.S.) 28 Dec. 15/1 The impact of the images, their skilful juxtaposition, and the bold page lay-outs make words superfluous. **1952** B. RUSSELL (*title*) The impact of science upon society. **1958** *Church Times* 8 Aug. 7/1 The story..is presented by means of narrative and dramatic episodes in a manner familiar to all radio-listeners, but it is the lighting which makes the great impact. **1965** *Listener* 26 Aug. 297/1 However much you give them, you are not going to make a significant impact on growth, though you may make an impact in the charitable sense. **1966** *Economist* 10 Dec. 1144/3 What has had an impact on food distributors, apparently, is the opening of an investigation by the Federal Trade Commission into supermarket games and stamps. **1967** E. SHORT *Embroidery & Fabric Collage* i. 18 The most dynamic colour combination if used too often loses its impact. **1969** LD. MOUNTBATTEN in *Times* (India Suppl.) 13 Oct. p. i/1 He [*sc.* Gandhi] made such an impact on me that his memory will forever remain fresh in my mind. **1973** *Daily Tel.* 5 Mar. 6/2 The main impact of the campaign will be made by full-page newspaper advertisements.

2. Special Comb.: **impact crater**, a crater or a hollow in the ground believed to have been produced by the impact of a meteorite; **impact extrusion**, a process for producing tubular objects in which metal in a die is struck by a punch that fits into it and forces the metal between their two surfaces and out of the die; **impact head** = *impact pressure*; **impact load**, a load imposed suddenly and for a short time, as when one body strikes another; **impact loading**, (the application of) an impact load; **impact pressure**, the total pressure in a moving fluid in the direction of flow, being equal (in the case of a fluid of negligible viscosity) to the sum of the dynamic pressure and the static pressure; **impact printer**, a printer that depends on mechanical pressure to transfer ink from a ribbon to the paper; so **impact printing**; **impact resistance** = *impact strength*; **impact strength**, the ability of a solid to withstand an impact or shock; strength as measured by an impact test; **impact test**, any of various tests for measuring the resistance of a body to suddenly applied stress in which it is broken, usually by a blow, under standard conditions; **impact tube**, a thin tube (usu. rigid with a right-angled bend) which may be placed in a flow of fluid with an open end facing upstream, so that the impact pressure in the fluid may be found by measuring the pressure in the tube; cf. *Pitot tube*.

1895 G. K. GILBERT in *Bull. Philos. Soc. Washington* XII. 265 The inquiry has followed three lines. First, an investigation of the ellipticity of lunar craters; second, an experimental investigation of the relation between incidence angle and ellipticity of impact craters; third, a more refined investigation of the orbital relations affecting the incidence angles of moonlets. *Ibid.* 291 Does the earth exhibit impact craters? If not, then erosion and sedimentation have destroyed them. **1965** R. B. BALDWIN *Fund. Survey Moon* vii. 66 If it can be shown that the impact craters on earth are ..similar to lunar craters..we will be on firm ground in considering that the lunar craters..were formed by the impacts..of meteorites. **1967** *Listener* 20 Apr. 521/2 Another impact crater is that at Wolf Creek in Australia, where the diameter is half a mile. **1935** *Metal Industry* 11 Oct. 373/1 A new..heavy duty press..for the cold impact extrusion of aluminium tubes and shells in one operation. **1963** H. R. CLAUSER *Encycl. Engin. Materials* 340/1 Parts produced by impact extrusion are essentially longitudinally oriented, e.g., collapsible tubes, cans, etc. **1928** G. MARTIN *Treat. Chem. Engin.* xvi. 3 A connection between the density of a fluid W and the power required to move it through a pipe of area A when the impact head is l_1 in. of water and the dynamic head is l in. of water. **1924** E. E. MANN *Introd. Pract. Civil Engin.* x. 166 Wind pressure on roofs is of the nature of an impact load. **1928** C. F. S. GAMBLE *Story N. Sea Air Station* 10 Her two stream-lined gondolas..were designed to be capable of sustaining severe impact loads when alighting on water. **1963** D. A. FIRMAGE *Fund. Theory of Struct.* iii. 56 Impact load is only a minor portion of the total load on any bridge. **1948** COURANT & FRIEDRICHS *Supersonic Flow & Shock Waves* iii. 240 The basic problem of wave propagation in a bar of elastic-plastic material is concerned with the motion resulting from impact-loading, i.e., from a velocity being suddenly imparted to one end of the bar and then maintained there. **1973** *Sci. Amer.* Feb. 85/1 It has been equipped with a grille structure that distributes the impact loading more uniformly. **1919** A. B. EASON *Flow & Measurem. Air & Gases* xiv. 237 The increase in the value of the impact pressure in the case of wind blowing directly on an opening will be due to the fact that more of the momentum of the air is destroyed than when air blows on the small area of the Pitot tube mouthpiece. **1966** DAILY & HARLEMAN *Fluid Dynamics* vi. 128 For liquids of small viscosity, Eq. (6·71) can be used to compute the velocity from the stagnation or impact pressure measured on the blunt nose of a probe in a steady flow. **1966** *IEEE Trans. Electronic Computers* XV. 794/1 The output includes an electromechanical actuator which propels a small hammer against a single or multipart paper pack and ribbon which together strike a moving font of type at the precise moment the type character desired to be printed is in collision position. Thus, this type of printing uses an 'on-the-fly' principle; it is called impact printing. **1970** *Computer & Humanities* V. 21 The board of directors..has approved a character set to be used on computer-driven impact printers handling machine-readable bibliographic information. **1985** *Personal Computer World* Feb. 111/1 (Advt.), Being an impact printer, the M-loog will print on virtually any paper. **1934** B. STOUGHTON *Metall. Iron & Steel* (ed. 4) xiii. 404 Impact Resistance of Steel.—The resistance of steel to shock decreases very much with lowered temperature. **1958** C. L. MANTELL *Engin. Materials Handbk.* III. 12 The impact resistance of standard malleable iron, measured by the Charpy test using a notch, 0·394-in. square bar, and 0·079-in. depth of notch is about 16·5 ft-lb. **1904** *Proc. Inst. Mech. Engin.* IV. 1227 The more or less consistent relation that appeared to exist in Messrs. Sankey and Kent-Smith's tests between impact strength and reduction of area. **1939** *Proc. Amer. Soc. Testing Materials* XXXVIII. II. 39 There are..8,000,000 molded phenol plastic telephones in use... The extent to which..breakage occurs..is determined largely by the impact strength of the molding material. **1952** WOOD & VON LUDWIG *Investment Castings for Engineers* x. 209 Both beryllium copper and aluminum bronze will develop higher tensile strength and hardness when heat treated, but they will not have good impact strength, whereas manganese bronze is one of the toughest cast metals available. **1967** M. CHANDLER *Ceramics in Mod. World* iv. 118 The impact strength of all ceramic materials..is rather low. **1899** W. C. UNWIN *Testing Materials of Construction* (ed. 2) 239 (*heading*) Example of an impact test. **1915** [see CHARPY]. **1918** *Machinery* 31 Jan. 477/1 Tensile impact tests, in which a sudden tensile stress is applied to a specimen by means of a falling weight, have also been practised..in recent years. **1943** F. D. JONES *Engin. Encycl.* (ed. 2) II. 680 The torsion impact test breaks the specimen by twisting. **1971** B. SCHARF *Engin. & its Lang.* iv. 24 The most common impact test in this country [*sc.* Great Britain] is the Izod test, in which a notched test piece fixed at one end is broken by a blow from a pendulum hammer, the energy absorbed in fracturing the specimen being recorded... Another method widely used in other countries and increasingly also in this country is the Charpy impact test, in which a notched test piece supported at both ends is broken by a blow from a striker, on the face opposite to and immediately behind the notch, the energy absorbed in fracturing the specimen being recorded. **1916** *Trans. Amer. Soc. Mech. Engin.* XXXVII. 1410 For high pressures, the manometer attached to the impact tube can be replaced by a mercury column or steam gage attached to a receiver in the main where velocity is largely reduced. **1934** J. H. PERRY *Chem. Engineers' Handbk.* 689 The length and shape of the tip, so long as the opening faces upstream, usually have little effect upon the head indicated by an impact tube. **1966** DAILY & HARLEMAN *Fluid Dynamics* ix. 178 The actual readings from impact tubes will depend both on the viscous effect and on the size of the pressure-sensing hole in the probe tip.

†**im'pact**, *ppl. a. Obs.* [ad. L. *impact-us*, pa. pple. of *impingĕre* to IMPINGE.] = IMPACTED (of which, in later use, it was prob. taken as a shortened form). Const. as *pple.* or *adj.*

1563 T. GALE *Antidot.* I. iv. 3 When..there are humours impacte in anye part. **1587** M. GROVE *Pelops & Hippod.* (1878) 81 From hir whose picture still I fynde within my brest impact. **1647** H. MORE *Song of Soul* III. I. ix, All these forms..That sense or phansie ever had impact. **1652** FRENCH *Yorksh. Spa* iv. 43 A cold, crass slimy morbifick, or a hot impact matter.

impact (ɪm'pækt), *v.* [orig., and usually, in pa. pple. *impacted*, which was prob. directly f. L. *impact-us* + -ED[1] (see IMPACT *ppl. a.* and IMPACTED); the verb proper being a later back-formation from this. See -ED[1] 2, and cf. COMPACT *v.*[1]]

1. *trans.* To press closely into or in something; to fix firmly in; to pack in.

1601 HOLLAND *Pliny* XX. xxi. II. 73 The seed of this hearbe remooveth the tough humours bedded in the stomacke, how hard impacted soever they be. **1709** BLAIR in *Phil. Trans.* XXVII. 75 These Pyramids, which receive the Hairs, are impacted in the Cutis. *a* **1791** WESLEY *Serm.* lxxxii. I. 5 Wks. 1811 IX. 417 Impact fire into iron, by hammering it when red hot. **1897** ALLBUTT *Syst. Med.* III. 835 A stone-like mass..which had become impacted in the lower ilium.

2. To stamp or impress (*on* something). *rare.*

1677 GALE *Crt. Gentiles* IV. Proem 4 Ideas or notions impacted on the mind. *Ibid.* 442 Every..Creature has a law impacted or impressed on its Being.

3. *intr.* **a.** To come forcibly into contact with a (larger) body or surface. Const. various preps.

1916 [see IMPACTING *ppl. a.* below]. **1929** 'SEAMARK' *Down River* vi. 172 Something impacted with a soft thud against Lingard's temple. **1945** *Jrnl. Sci. Instrum.* XXII. 191 A jet of air issuing from a slot and impacting on a plane surface. **1962** F. I. ORDWAY et al. *Basic Astronautics* v. 201 The Soviet Lunnaya Raketa was launched early in the afternoon of September 12, 1959 and impacted onto the Moon's surface just after midnight on September 14, Moscow time.

b. *fig.* To have a (pronounced) effect *on*.

1935 W. G. HARDY *Father Abraham* 370 For there was about them an air of eagerness and of shuddering expectation which impacted on his consciousness and fascinated even while it repelled him. **1956** *Oxf. Mag.* 8 Nov. 81/1 The Magazine..is not the place for consideration of national and international events except in so far as they impact on Oxford.

4. *trans.* To cause to impinge or impact *on*, *against*, etc.

1945 *Jrnl. Sci. Instrum.* XXII. 187 Experimental results for the efficiency of jets in impacting particles are correlated. **1964** K. STEWART in White & Smith *High-Efficiency Air Filtration* ii. 57 All impactors make use of the inertia effect which particles exhibit when the gas stream in which they are suspended is constrained to turn abruptly. The particle under suitable conditions cannot follow the stream lines and is impacted against a collecting plate. **1972** J. O. LEDBETTER *Air Pollution* A. v. 187 An aerosol moving toward an obstacle may impact particles on the obstacle.

Hence **impacting** *ppl. a.*, impinging, colliding.

1916 'BOYD CABLE' *Action Front* 95 No ping and smack of impacting lead hailed about them. **1961** *Sci. Amer.* Nov. 58/2 The impacting bodies may have been asteroids or comets. **1972** *Daily Tel.* 17 Apr. 6/8 These particles..cannot be measured or analysed from the Earth's surface. On the Moon, however, the impacting particles leave trails in the detector. **1973** *Nature* 13 July 68/2 Craters of the size of St Magnus Bay and The Firth would be formed by impacting meteorites of masses about 1 million tons.

impacted (ɪm'pæktɪd), *ppl. a.* [See IMPACT *v.*]

1. a. Pressed closely in, firmly fixed.

1683 SALMON *Doron Med.* II. 463 To melt (as it were) any impacted humor, though never so tough. *c* **1720** W. GIBSON *Farrier's Dispens.* i. (1734) 25 To ripen and dissolve hard impacted Humours. **1856** KANE *Arct. Expl.* I. xxi. 267 The fine impacted snow-dust of winter.

b. Applied *spec.* to fæces lodged in the intestine (cf. IMPACTION 2); also *transf.*, applied to (a part of) the intestine when so blocked.

1844 *Boston Med. & Surg. Jrnl.* XXX. 309 (*heading*) History of a case of impacted colon. **1850** *Lancet* 19 Jan. 80/2 The bowel is found in a state of great distention from an impacted mass closely adhering to its walls. **1875** *Cincinnati Med. News* VIII. 353 (*heading*) Remarkable case of impacted colon, with suppression of urine. **1902** J. P. TUTTLE *Treat. Dis. Anus* (1903) xiv. 545 Distressing symptoms are relieved either by the loosening up of an impacted fæcal mass, or possibly by the undoing of a volvulus or intussusception. **1972** F. A. JONES in Jones & Godding *Managem. Constipation* iv. 128 In some patients, impaction may have already led to severe symptoms, with acute distress, and it is then necessary to organize the immediate removal of the impacted faeces.

c. Applied to a bone fracture in which the broken parts are driven together so as to become locked.

1850 J. A. ORR *Princ. Surg.* II. xi. 153 Impacted fracture is when one broken extremity of the bone is driven into and lodged in the other. **1921** BAETJER & WATERS *Injuries & Dis. Bones & Joints* v. 102 When the fracture is just behind the head [of the femur] or in the middle of the neck, impaction is relatively rare. Fracture at the base is generally impacted. **1967** E. L. RALSTON et al. *Handbk. Fractures* vii. 116 Impacted fractures [of the humeral neck] even with angulation of 25 to 30 degrees are best treated with the use of a sling and swathe and early active exercises.

d. Applied to a tooth which, owing to obstruction by another tooth or by bone, fails to erupt properly and remains partly or wholly within the jaw-bone.

1876 H. MOON in T. Bryant *Pract. Surg.* (ed. 2) I. xiii. 546 In all cases where the impaction of a lower wisdom tooth is a source of irritation, the impaction should be at once got rid of... The serious results which may attend purulent inflammation about an impacted wisdom tooth, will receive notice later. **1928** H. PRINZ *Dis. Soft Struct. Teeth* i. 29 Impacted teeth usually do not cause painful symptoms unless they meet on their path of retarded eruption an obstruction or they exert pressure upon nerve fibers. **1971** COSTICH & WHITE *Fund. Oral Surg.* viii. 93/2 The maxillary third molars frequently fail to erupt but may not necessarily be regarded as impacted teeth.

2. a. That has impinged upon or struck something.

1952 *A.M.A. Arch. Industr. Hygiene & Occup. Med.* V. 464 Although the size of impacted particles can be measured under a microscope, the impaction principle..is used more as a method of sampling than as a method of determining the particle-size distribution.

b. That has been struck by an impacting body; also *fig.* (*U.S.*) of an area: affected by a larger demand than usual on public services, esp. schools.

1924 in *Sci. Amer.* (1974) July 12/1 One need only study a large raindrop falling into a still pool of water. There is first a surging outward of the impacted water. **1963** *Economist* 25 May 777/2 The..scheme for aid to 'impacted' areas (where schools are over-loaded). **1967** *Compton Yearbk.* 232/1 Funds were also earmarked for..federally 'impacted' areas, that is, areas where the families of federal workers had swollen school enrollments. **1970** *Time* 6 Apr. 12 Nixon..proposed that $1.5 billion in federal funds be made available to 'racially impacted areas'..to help desegregating school districts meet their special needs. **1971** *Nature* 16 July 162/2 The shape of a newly formed impact crater is caused by the sudden release of the kinetic energy of the impacting mass within a small volume somewhat below the original impacted surface.

impacter, var. IMPACTOR.

impaction (ɪm'pækʃən). [ad. L. *impactiōn-em*, n. of action f. *impingĕre* to IMPINGE.]

I. 1. The action of becoming, or condition of being, impacted or firmly fixed in.

1739 J. HUXHAM *Fevers* (1750) 176 To prevent the further Impaction of the obstructing Lentor. **1853** KANE *Grinnell Exp.* xxiv. (1856) 197 In case of accident or impaction further north. **1873** T. H. GREEN *Introd. Pathol.* (ed. 2) 42 Sudden obstruction of the circulation by the impaction of an embolus in one of the larger arteries. **1876** [see IMPACTED *ppl. a.* 1 d]. **1921** [see IMPACTED *ppl. a.* 1 c]. **1957** J. G. BONNIN *Textbk. Fractures* i. 8 Impaction is important in aiding fixation and indicates, as a rule, that little displacement has occurred. **1972** D. E. WAITE *Textbk. Pract. Oral Surg.* xi. 141 They also vary widely in degree of

impaction; some are partially erupted, while others are completely encased in bone.

2. *spec.* in *Med.* **a.** The lodging of a mass of (usu. hardened) fæces in the intestine so that defecation is prevented or impeded; hence, the obstruction of (a part of) the intestine in this way.

1853 *Assoc. Med. Jrnl.* I. 606 (*heading*) Impaction of the rectum from unground wheat. **1866** *Clin. Lect. & Rep.* (London Hospital) III. 193 Three cases of obstruction of the bowels..produced by the impaction of hardened fæces in the rectum, and colon. **1902** J. P. TUTTLE *Treat. Dis. Anus* xiv. 543 In simple constipation and in impaction there is always a channel for the escape of gases from the bowels. **1943** NILES & MARTIN in E. J. Stieglitz *Geriatric Med.* xxxv. 599 Rectal impaction is much more common in the aged. *Ibid.* Colonic impaction (scybala) is seen occasionally in old people, especially among those who are bedridden. **1972** [see IMPACTED *ppl. a.* 1 b].

b. *concr.* A mass of (usu. hardened) fæces lodged in the intestine so as to impede defecation.

1902 J. P. TUTTLE *Treat. Dis. Anus* xiv. 542 The author has known a patient to suffer from a continuous diarrhœa for six weeks..apparently from no other cause than an impaction of fæces in the sigmoid flexure. **1931** M. C. PRUITT *Mod. Proctology* xviii. 350 It is important to determine..whether the impaction is hard or soft. **1958** A. F. R. ANDRESEN *Office Gastroenterol.* 442 Small impactions can usually be induced to pass by means of a cleansing enema.

II. 3. The process of causing something to impinge or impact on something else (cf. IMPACT *v.* 4); also, the action of so impinging (cf. IMPACT *v.* 3).

1945 [see IMPACTOR 2]. **1952** *A.M.A. Arch. Industr. Hygiene & Occup. Med.* V. 476 Larger and heavier particles are thrown onto a collecting surface in front of the jet, while smaller and lighter particles escape impaction. **1956** P. L. MAGILL et al. *Air Pollution Handbk.* xii. 32 The impaction of aerosol particles on cylinders has been given considerable attention since it provides an insight into the functioning of fibrous filters. **1972** J. O. LEDBETTER *Air Pollution* A. vi. 230 Impaction devices..that depend upon the wind to carry out the impaction.

impactite (ɪm'pæktaɪt). *Geol.* [f. IMPACT *sb.* + -ITE[1], after TEKTITE.] Any piece of glassy material formed in or around a meteorite crater by the heat of impact.

1940 V. E. BARNES *N. Amer. Tektites* in *Univ. Texas Publ.* no. 3945, p. 558 Spencer's meteorite splash origin..is valid for the formation of certain glasses. Glasses of this type will be distinguished in general from most of those now included under tektites. These meteorite splashes should be given a distinctive name such as 'impactites'. This name was suggested by Dr. H. B. Stenzel. **1960** I. VIDZIUNAS tr. *Krinov's Princ. Meteoritics* vii. 435 This presence of numerous fragments of impactites in the area of meteoritic craters served as a basis for considering these objects to be fragments of fused terrestrial quartz sand. **1964** *New Scientist* 16 Jan. 160/1 The expert can easily distinguish tektites from..impactites (silica glass found around some meteorite craters).

impactive ('ɪmpæktɪv, ɪm'pæktɪv), *a.* [f. IMPACT *sb.* + -IVE.] Of, pertaining to, or characterized by impact; having an impact.

1934 F. SCOTT FITZGERALD *Tender is Night* 5 Feeling the impactive scrutiny of strange faces, she took off her bath-robe and followed. **1942** W. FAULKNER *Go down, Moses* 197 They faced one another, not close yet at slightly less than foils' distance, erect, their voices not raised, not impactive, just succinct. **1955** *Financial Times* 17 Jan. (Packaging Suppl.) 6/4 Mechanical tests have been devised for studying vibration, impactive shocks and compression loads in stacking. **1969** *Esquire* Feb. 20 Even more impactive, maybe, is The Spot, where the waitresses wear what they please.

im'pactly, *adv. rare.* [f. IMPACT *ppl. a.* + -LY[2].] With firm infixion or close pressure.

1862 *Jrnl. Soc. Arts* X. 325/2 A cube of 2½ inches, impactly secured, was subjected to a force of 200 tons.

im'pactment. [f. IMPACT *v.* + -MENT.] = IMPACTION.

1853 KANE *Grinnell Exp.* xx. 158 He..counseled us to prepare for the chances of an impactment [in the ice].

impactor (ɪm'pæktə(r)). Also impacter. [f. IMPACT *v.*: see -OR, -ER[1].] **1.** A device or machine that delivers impacts or blows.

1916 *Chambers's Jrnl.* Dec. 830/2 The impactor golf-machine is a new invention. **1950** J. H. PERRY *Chem. Engineers' Handbk.* (ed. 3) 1129/2 The Impactor..is a reversible hammer crusher without a discharge grating or cage. **1966** *McGraw-Hill Encycl. Sci. & Technol.* V. 471/1 To increase the effectiveness of the forging blows, the impacter forging machine was developed.

2. An impinger, esp. one in which the particles are deposited on a dry surface rather than in a liquid.

The distinction between impactors and impingers explained in quot. 1945 is rarely made.

1945 K. R. MAY in *Jrnl. Sci. Instrum.* XXII. 187 (*heading*) The cascade impactor: an instrument for sampling coarse aerosols. *Ibid.* 188 The method which has been adopted for depositing the sample is direct impaction of the particles on to glass slides which may be coated with a suitable medium. .. The terms 'impactor' and 'impaction' were suggested by Prof. J. H. Gaddum to avoid confusion with 'impinger' instruments... In 'impingers' a fine jet of air is directed at very high speed on to a flat surface to obtain the maximum efficiency of deposition of small particles. In the case of 'impactors' jet speeds are lower and larger particles are dealt with. **1956** P. L. MAGILL et al. *Air Pollution Handbk.* x. 30 Most cascade impactors are now operated using high air velocities. *Ibid.* 29 A single-stage impactor..is often useful because of its simplicity of operation. **1964** [see IMPACT *v.* 4]. **1971** *Nature* 12 Feb. 501/1 Partition of single uredospores between the first and second stage of a cascade impactor indicated a terminal velocity of 0·6 cm s^{-1}.

impail, obs. form of IMPALE.

impained: see IMPANED.

impaint (ɪm'peɪnt), *v.* [f. IM-[1] + PAINT *v.*] *trans.* To paint upon something, depict.

1596 SHAKS. *1 Hen. IV*, v. i. 80 Neuer yet did Insurrection want Such water-colours, to impaint his cause. **1729** SAVAGE *Wanderer* III. 83 O'er altars thus, impainted, we behold Half circling glories shoot in rays of gold.

impair (ɪm'pɛə(r)), *sb.*[1] *Obs.* or *arch.* Also 7 em-. [f. IMPAIR *v.*] An act of impairing; the fact of being impaired; impairment.

1568 NORTH tr. *Gueuara's Diall Pr.* (1582) 371 Halfe a dishonour, and an impair of his credit. **1598** CHAPMAN *Achilles' Shield* in *Homer* (1875) 13 Nor is it more impair to an honest and absolute man's sufficiency to have few friends, than [etc.]. **1612** —— *Widowes T.* Plays 1873 III. 36 Pocket it:..it's no impaire to thee: the greatest doo't. **1615** G. SANDYS *Trav.* 102 Such and such like affoord they yearely without empaire to themselues. **1677** HALE *Prim. Orig. Man.* IV. iii. 318 An impair of that Sovereignty and Dominion over the Creatures. **1848** J. A. CARLYLE tr. *Dante's Inferno* 28 To keep its beauty from impair.

'impair, *a.* (and *sb.*[2]) [Cf. F. *impair* unequal (1484 in Godef. *Compl.*), and *pair.*]

†**1.** (?) 'Unsuitable' (T.), unfit; inferior. *Obs.* (But the reading is disputed.)

1606 SHAKS. *Tr. & Cr.* IV. v. 103 (Fol. 1) Yet giues he not till iudgement guide his bounty, Nor dignifies an impaire [*Qo.* 1 impare; *Globe*, etc. impure] thought with breath.

2. a. Not paired; not forming one of a pair; odd. **b.** *sb.* An unpaired individual thing; an odd one. In roulette (with pronunc. ɛ̃pɛr), an odd number, or a number marked 'impair'.

1839–47 TODD *Cycl. Anat.* III. 829/1 This impair bone.. is..the representative of the superior occipitals of Cuvier. **1850** *Bohn's Hand-bk. Games* 348 (Roulette) The impair wins, when the ball enters a hole numbered impair. **1880** J. ABERCROMBY in *Academy* 23 Oct. 294/1 Grouping the letters in two sets of pairs and an impair, which again pairs with the other impairs. **1891** 'L. HOFFMAN' *Cycl. Card & Table Games* 626 If he places his money on Impair, he bets that the ball will drop into an odd number. **1902** *Encycl. Brit.* XXXII. 304/1 Pair indicates even numbers, impair odd numbers. **1966** 'W. HAGGARD' *Power House* xii. 125 The croupier was paying out. Mortimer was on the *Impair* side. **1973** L. MEYNELL *Thirteen Trumpeters* iv. 66 His right hand was..stretching out to place his stake on the next throw (a green on *pair*)... '*Impair*' was called.

impair (ɪm'pɛə(r)), *v.* Forms: α. 4 ampayr-i, anpayr-i, apayr-i, etc. (see APPAIR). β. 4–6 **enpeire, -peyre, -paire, -payre, empeyre,** 4–7 **empare, empeire, -paire, -payre,** 5 **enpare,** 7 **empair.** γ. 5–7 **impaire, -payre,** 6 **impeire, impere, inpayre,** 6–7 **impare,** 7– **impair.** [The current form *impair* is a partially Latinized refashioning of the earlier *empaire, empeire,* a. OF. *empeirer, ampeirer* to make worse:—Lat. type **impēiōrāre* to make worse, f. *im-* (IM-[1]) + *pēior* worse. The earliest form was *ampayre*, whence *apeyre* APPAIR. *Empeyre*, closest to contemporary French, was commonest in 15–16th c. Late in 15th c. the prefix began to be spelt *im-* after Lat., giving the current *impair*, which has superseded *empair* since *c* 1660. Cf. APPAIR, PAIR, EMPYRE.]

1. *trans.* To make worse, less valuable, or weaker; to lessen injuriously; to damage, injure.

[α. **1297–1643**: see APPAIR 1.]

β. *c* **1374** CHAUCER *Boeth.* IV. pr. iii. 93 (Camb. MS.) Thanne is the Meede of goode folk swich þat no day shal enpeyren it. *c* **1375** *Cato Major* IV. xxxiv. in *Anglia* VII, Empeyre þou nouȝt hire fame. **1494** FABYAN *Chron.* VII. ccxxxiv. 270 Y^e^ cytie of Danas..he assauted and enpayred very sore. **1548** HALL *Chron., Hen. VIII* 253 b, The possession might seme to be enpaired. **1576** FLEMING *Panopl. Epist.* 315 In hope that I shoulde recover my health, which sicknesse had empayred. **1602** FULBECKE *2nd Pt. Parall.* 22 Whereby hee was empeired and became worse. **1655** FULLER *Ch. Hist.* II. ii. §77 It never wastes nor empairs an Estate. **1658–78** PHILLIPS, *Empair* [**1696** (ed. 5) *Impair*].

γ. **1488–9** *Act 4 Hen. VII*, c. 19 The defence of this land ..[is] impaired. **1533** MORE *Debell. Salem* Wks. 1029/2 [It] yet helpeth not hys matter, but impayreth it much. **1667** MILTON *P.L.* v. 665 Satan..could not beare Through pride that sight, and thought himself impaird. **1703** MOXON *Mech. Exerc.* 239 No time will impair or decay those Grey Kentish Bricks. **1742** YOUNG *Nt. Th.* VII. 986 This argument is old; but truth No years impair. **1862** SIR B. BRODIE *Psychol. Inq.* II. II. 50 The best memory may be impaired by neglect.

b. *refl.*

1481 CAXTON *Myrr.* I. iv. 14 They empayre them self so moche that they may not lerne no good. **1484** —— *Curial* 3 Wyse men..for none auauncement ne hauyng of good enpayre not them self.

†**c.** *pass.* To be destitute *of*, or badly off for.

1591 HORSEY *Trav.* (Hakluyt Soc.) 255 If I wear impared of mony, he would send me out of his own treasur.

2. *intr.* (for *refl.*) To grow or become worse, less valuable, weaker, or less; to suffer injury or loss; to deteriorate, fall off, or decay. ? *Obs.*

[α. **1340–1581**: see APPAIR 2.]

β. *c* **1380** *Sir Ferumb.* 4691 þe power of hem enpayrede faste. **1486** *Bk. St. Albans* C vj b, The Eyghen will swell and empeyre in her hede. **1523** LD. BERNERS *Froiss.* I. ccxix. 279 The kynge..lay sore sicke..and euery daye he enpayred worse and worse. **1590** SPENSER *F.Q.* I. vii. 41 Flesh may empaire,..but reason can repaire. **1600** F. WALKER *Sp. Mandeville* 71 a, The sicke Gentleman daily so empaired in health.

γ. **1523** LD. BERNERS *Froiss.* I. ccxlv. 364 The prince dayly impered of a sicknesse. **1579** TWYNE *Phisicke agst. Fort.* II. xxviii. 205 a, All thinges impaire, and goe backewarde. **1648** BOYLE *Seraph. Love* (1660) 152 Cœlestial Pleasures..not impairing by being used Long. **1729** SWIFT *Lett. to Pope* Wks. 1761 VIII. 93 When years increase, and perhaps your health impairs. **1827** SOUTHEY in *Life* (1850) V. 284 His own health and faculties sensibly impairing day by day.

im'pairable, *a. rare.* [f. IMPAIR *v.* + -ABLE.] Capable of being impaired.

a **1665** J. GOODWIN *Filled w. the Spirit* (1867) 26 Though his power of executing..be not impaired, nor indeed impairable..by any negligence, unfaithfulness, or unfruitfulness of men. **1678** CUDWORTH *Intell. Syst.* I. iv. §36. 565 Souls..Self-improvable and Self-impairable.

impaired (ɪm'pɛəd), *ppl. a.* [f. IMPAIR *v.* + -ED[1].] **1.** Rendered worse; injured in amount, quality, or value; deteriorated, weakened, damaged.

1611 SPEED *Hist. Gt. Brit.* IX. viii. (1632) 563 He repaired with large diet his impayred lims and sinewes. **1719** BOLINGBROKE in *Swift's Lett.* (1766) II. 4 Those fancy'd ills, so dreadful to the great, A lost election, or impair'd estate. **1845** STOCQUELER *Handbk. Brit. India* (1854) 170 Hamilton ..was necessitated by an impaired constitution to return to England.

2. Of a driver or his driving: adversely affected by the influence of alcohol or narcotics. *Canad.*

1951 *Act* (Canada) 15 *Geo. VI* c. 47 §14 Driving while ability to drive is impaired. **1957** (*title*) Report on impaired driving tests (Crime Detection Laboratories of the Royal Canadian Mounted Police). **1967** W. S. AVIS et al. *Dict. Canad. Eng., Senior Dict.* 573/2 *Impaired driver*, one whose driving ability has been impaired by alcohol or narcotics. **1970** *Toronto Daily Star* 24 Sept. 37/1 Ange Gardien..was charged with impaired driving. **1972** *Evening Telegram* (St. John's, Newfoundland) 24 June 1/1 A police spokesman said the car received only slight damage. The driver was arrested and charged with impaired driving. **1973** *Kingston* (Ontario) *Whig-Standard* 18 Apr. 15/2 Another motorist.. was fined $175 and prohibited from driving for four months on a charge of impaired driving. **1973** *Daily Colonist* (Victoria, B.C.) 26 Apr. 41/3 Georg Edward Haines..was fined $350 following his plea of guilty to a charge of being impaired early Wednesday in Victoria while in care or control of a vehicle. *Ibid.*, Edward Weiland..pleaded guilty to a two-count Victoria charge of impaired driving and refusing to take a breath-analysis test. **1974** *Kingston* (Ontario) *Whig-Standard* 16 Jan. 5/4 A snowmobile operator was one of five persons assessed penalties ranging from $175 to $200 each in county court Tuesday on impaired driving charges.

impairer (ɪm'pɛərə(r)). [f. as prec. + -ER[1].] One who or that which impairs.

a **1586** SIDNEY *Arcadia* (1622) 215 The quiet mind (whereof my selfe empairer is). **1610** W. FOLKINGHAM *Art of Survey* I. x. 31 Wheat, Barley, Woade..are great impairers and soakers of the soyle. *a* **1779** WARBURTON (Mason), Immoderate labour and immoderate study are equally the impairers of health.

impairing (ɪm'pɛərɪŋ), *vbl. sb.* [f. as prec. + -ING[1].] The action of the verb IMPAIR; making worse, deterioration, impairment.

c **1380** WYCLIF *Wks.* (1880) 389 It is enpeyringe not oonly of oone estate of þe chirche, but of alle þre. *c* **1450** *Doctr. Galienis* in *Jyll of Breyntford* (Ballad Soc.) 39 With-oute þenpeyring of þy persone. **1513** DOUGLAS *Æneis* Concl. 10 And heir my nayme remane, but enparing. **1618** LATHAM *2nd Bk. Falconry* (1633) 7 Other dangers that may grow to the great impairing of her health. **1711** SHAFTESB. *Charac.* (1737) II. 174 The impairing of any one part must..tend to the disorder and ruin of other parts.

impairing, *ppl. a.* [f. as prec. + -ING[2].] That impairs.

1666 BOYLE *Orig. Formes & Qual.* (1667) 176 That Impairing Alteration of Texture we call Rottennesse.

impairment (ɪm'pɛəmənt). Forms: see IMPAIR *v.*; also APPAIRMENT. [a. OF. *empeirement*, mod.F. *empirement* (12th c. in Littré), f. *empeirer, empirer* to IMPAIR: see -MENT.] The action of impairing, or fact of being impaired; deterioration; injurious lessening or weakening.

1340 *Ayenb.* 148 Yef he ne deþ wyþ-oute emparement. *c* **1400** *St. Alexius* (Laud MS.) 255 To londe þai gonnen aryuen alle, Wiþouten enpeirement. **1531–2** *Act 23 Hen. VIII*, c. 9 §2 To the great impeirement & diminucions of their good names and honesties. **1611** SPEED *Hist. Gt. Brit.* IX. viii. (1632) 582 A greater impayrement of his hopes. **1651** *Life Father Sarpi* (1676) 98 A manifest impairment of his health. **1861** WYNTER *Soc. Bees, Brain Diffic.* 471 The following extraordinary impairment of memory.

impala (ɪm'pɑːlə, -'pælə). Also **impalla, mpala.** = PALLAH.

1875 W. H. DRUMMOND *Large Game & Nat. Hist. S. & S.-E. Afr.* vii. 330 The roibok or impalla..is about the size of a small reed-buck doe, though more slenderly made. *Ibid.*, These impalla..could easily distance any dog I possessed. **1886** W. M. KERR *Far Interior* I. ii. 29 It was here [*sc.* Boatlanama] that I shot my first antelope—a fine impala (*Æpyceros Melampus*), with a good head. **1888** P. GILLMORE *Days & Nights by Desert* xvii. 136 (*caption*) The Mpala Antelope (*Æpyceros Melampus*). **1896** [see PALLAH]. **1907** P.

FITZPATRICK *Jock of Bushveld* 302 We sat like statues as the impala walked out from its stall between Teddy's knees. **1931** *Times Lit. Suppl.* 3 Dec. 983/4 Graceful photographs of impalla, eland, and other antelope. **1947** J. STEVENSON-HAMILTON *Wild Life S. Afr.* xiii. 87 The impala (*Æpyceros melampus*)—Discovered by..Lichtenstein more than a hundred years ago, and variously termed impala, pallah, and rooibok, this antelope may claim to be one of the most beautiful and graceful members of the existing African fauna. **1965** A. NICOL *Truly Married Woman* 44 It was, after all, only a red-buck, an impalla, that they were afraid of. **1971** L. H. MATTHEWS *Life of Mammals* II. xiv. 394 Impala in East Africa do not move far from their restricted home range.

impalace (ɪm'pælɪs), *v.* Also 7 em-. [f. IM-[1] + PALACE.] *trans.* To place or install in a palace. Hence **im'palaced** (-ɪst) *ppl. a.*, installed in a palace.

1611 FLORIO, *Impalazzare*, to empallace. **1795** W. TAYLOR in *Monthly Rev.* XVIII. 543 In impalacing the magistrate. **1839** BAILEY *Festus* v. (1852) 62 One or two, impalaced, mitred, throned, And banqueted, burlesque.. The holy penury of the Son of God. *Ibid.* xxv. 438 The impalaced prisoner of the breast.

†**im'palatable**, *a. Obs. rare.* [f. IM-[2] + PALATABLE.] Not palatable, unpalatable.

1787 W. MARSHALL *Norfolk* II. 88 And render it altogether impalatable to stock. **1792** A. YOUNG *Trav. France* 115 A thing..equally impalatable and unconstitutional. **1814** MRS. WEST *Alicia De Lacy* IV. 68 The grandeur and luxury..were impalatable, because insecure.

†**impa'lation**. *Obs. rare.* [f. IMPALE *v.* + -ATION.] = IMPALEMENT 4.

1744 J. PATERSON *Comm. Milton's P.L.* 357 Impalation is a most tormenting punishment of malefactors.

impale (ɪm'peɪl), *v.* Forms: α. (6 enpale), 6–9 empale, 7 empail(e, (empall, empal). β. 6–7 impayl, (impall), 7 impail, (impal), 6– impale. [a. F. *empale-r* (Froissart), ad. med.L. *impālāre* 'in palum impingere' (Du Cange), f. *im-* (IM-[1]) + *pāl-us* stake (cf. late L. *pālāre* to support with stakes, prop up).]

1. a. *trans.* To enclose with pales, stakes, or posts; to surround with a palisade; to fence in. Now *rare*.

α. **1601** HOLLAND *Pliny* II. 516 Minding to mound and empale his cottage round about with a fence of an hedge. **1610** —— *Camden's Brit.* II. 73 (Ireland) Their country goeth under the tearme of *The English Pale*, because the first Englishmen..did empale for themselves certaine limits in the East part of the Iland. **1634–5** BRERETON *Trav.* (Chetham Soc.) 44, I saw a pool empaled wherein were pell-starts.

β. **1530** PALSGR. 590/1 I impale, I close a grounde or a parke with pales, *je emparque*. **1614** RALEIGH *Hist. World* III. (1634) 61 The same wall which..had preserved their lives, by holding out the enemy did now impale them. **1766** PORNY *Heraldry* iv. (1777) 64 The Pale denotes Strength and Firmness, and has been bestowed to impaling Cities. **1845** HOOD *Fairy Tale* 21 So he might impale a strip of soil.

b. *transf.* and *fig.* To surround or enclose as with a palisade; to shut in, hedge about, confine, hem in. Now *rare*.

α. **1581** J. BELL *Haddon's Answ. Osor.* 33 Men..that are empaled within the boundes of the Church. **1612** DRAYTON *Poly-olb.* ii. 24 Where Portland..doth overpeere the maine, Her rugged front empal'd (on every part) with rocks. **1675** GREW *Anat. Trunks* I. ii. §25 Every single Milk-Vessel being empaled or hemmed in with an Arch of Roriferous [vessels].

β. **1579** TOMSON *Calvin's Serm. Tim.* 899/1 Wee must.. keepe ourselues stil within the parke wherein God impaled us with his word. **1638** SIR T. HERBERT *Trav.* (ed. 2) 100 Welcomed by the Quene, who..impales him in her armes, and cryes for joy. **1725** POPE *Odyss.* XIX. 520 Bristles high impale his horrid chine. **1860** MAURY *Phys. Geog. Sea* (Low) x. §465 It would have been impaled in a nook of the very drop of water in which it was brought forth.

†**c.** *Mil.* To enclose or surround (troops) for defence, as with other troops, or with wagons, etc. (Improperly, To set in array, draw up.) *Obs.*

α. **1553** BRENDE *Q. Curtius* III. 28 Nabarzanes empaled the battell on the right hand with a great power of horse-men, and XXX. thousand slingers and archers. **1569** STOCKER tr. *Diod. Sic.* III. ii. 105 He enpaled his Campe with hys carriages. **1578** HUNNIS *Hiveful Honey*, Gen. xxiv. 16 Against these five, the other fower Their Battailes did empale. **1641** BAKER *Chron.* (1679) 232/2 The Battel.. consisted of a thousand Bill-men empaled with two thousand Pikes.

β. **1579** DIGGES *Stratiot.* 102 To set his souldyours that the best armed impale the rest. **1635** BARRIFFE *Mil. Discip.* cx. (1643) 343 Impaling the reere, with the Wagons, Carts, and Baggage. **1670** MILTON *Hist. Eng.* II. (1851) 60 The Legionaries stood..impal'd with light armed.

2. To surround for adornment; to encircle, as with a crown or garland; to border, edge (with decoration). *Obs.* or *arch.*

α. **1553** BRENDE *Q. Curtius* Dd vj, Garmentes of linnen clothe embrodered with golde, and empaled with purple. **1630** BRATHWAIT *Eng. Gentlem.* (1641) 247 A crowne of glory shall empale you. **1686** GOAD *Celest. Bodies* II. vii. 252, I cannot..empale each Page of this Discourse with a Black mourning Lig.

β. **1555** EDEN *Decades* 163 Fethers and quilles impaled with golde. **1589** GREENE *Menaphon* L iv b, He impalled the head of his yong nephew..with the crowne and diademe of Arcadie. **1644** BULWER *Chiron.* 69 A Hand..impail'd about with rayes. **1860** LD. LYTTON *Lucile* II. iv. §1. 126 All the laurels that ever with praise Impaled human brows.

3. a. *Her.* To combine (two coats of arms, as those of a husband and wife) by placing them side by side on one shield, separated palewise, i.e. by a vertical line down the middle. (Also said of one coat of arms, with the other as obj.)

α. **1611** SPEED *Hist. Gt. Brit.* VII. v. 212 Their..marriages are made knowne by the sculpture of an hand in hand, and the Coat-armes of the parties empaled. **1725** *Lond. Gaz.* No. 6382/3 The Escocheon of the Arms of the Order empaling those of the Sovereign. **1872** O. SHIPLEY *Gloss. Eccl. Terms* s.v. *Arms*, A bishop empales his family coat-of-arms with the arms of his see.

β. **1605** [see IMPALING *vbl. sb.*]. **1610** GUILLIM *Heraldry* VI. ii. (1611) 256 Receiued as an augmentation of honour.. impaled with her paternall coat. **1787** PORNY *Heraldry* (ed. 4) Gloss. **1882** CUSSANS *Her.* xii. (ed. 3) 166 A man marrying an Heiress..During her father's lifetime..her 'husband only impales her Arms.

†**b.** *fig.* To place side by side (for comparison, or as being equal in dignity). *Obs.*

1647 N. BACON *Disc. Govt. Eng.* I. lxxi. (1739) 193, I have thus impaled these three, that the Reader may the better discern how they relate each to other. **1655** FULLER *Ch. Hist.* I. v. §19 The Admission of St. Patrick..to be match'd and impaled with the Blessed Virgin in the Honour thereof. **1659** H. L'ESTRANGE *Alliance Div. Offices* Pref. 4 You may view them in one scheame..as they stand impaled.

4. a. To thrust a pointed stake through the body of, as a form of torture or capital punishment; to fix upon a stake thrust up through the body.

α. **1678** R. L'ESTRANGE *Seneca's Mor.* (1702) 193 Wild Beasts to devour us; Stakes to Empale us. **1713** ADDISON *Cato* III. v, Let them..be..empal'd and left To writhe at leisure round the bloody stake.

β. **1613** PURCHAS *Pilgrimage* (1614) 389 He impaled this Caragoses in the way on a sharpe stake fastened in the ground. **1660** F. BROOKE tr. *Le Blanc's Trav.* 100 *note*, To be impaled is to have a stake thrust thorough the fundament and to come out of the mouth. **1668** *Lond. Gaz.* No. 286/3 The Visier..caused the Greek to be impalled. **1828** G. W. BRIDGES *Ann. Jamaica* II. xv. 205 In a general massacre of the whites some were impaled by the savage hands of their own domestic slaves. **1859** TENNYSON *Vivien* 567 The King impaled him for his piracy.

b. *transf.* To transfix upon, or pierce through with, anything pointed; *fig.* to torment or render helpless as if transfixed.

a **1678** MARVELL *Poems, Soul & Body*, This tyrannic soul, Which, stretched upright, impales me so. **1807** SIR R. WILSON *Jrnl.* 27 Aug. in *Life* (1862) II. 363 The falcon often impales himself on the long and sharp beak [of the heron]. **1878** SMILES *Robt. Dick* v. 45 Impaling it with a pin.

c. *fig.* To transfix (a person) with one's gaze.

1877 *My Mother-in-Law* vi. 60 Mrs. Pinkerton devoted herself to impaling me with her eyes once in a while. **1903** *Critic* XLIII. 349/2 There was an impaling fierceness in his eyes.

impaled (ɪm'peɪld), *ppl. a.* [f. prec. + -ED[1].]

1. Fenced in, enclosed with a paling or fence. Also *fig.*

1549 COVERDALE, etc. *Erasm. Par. Jas.* 34 The empaled compasse of the teethe and lippes. **1586** J. HOOKER *Girald. Irel.* in *Holinshed* II. 147/1 These arrogant and disloiall parts of these impaled malecontents. **1652** in *N. & Q.* 8th Ser. (1893) IV. 77 That impaled ground called Hide Park. **1845** *Blackw. Mag.* LVII. 133 That impaled territory.

2. *Her.* Placed side by side on a shield divided palewise: see prec. 3.

1864 BOUTELL *Her. Hist. & Pop.* xiv. (ed. 3) 137 Neither the Heir nor the Cadets of any House bear the impaled Arms of their Father and Mother. **1882** CUSSANS *Her.* xii. (ed. 3) 166 Impaled Arms are not hereditary.

3. Transfixed upon a stake, etc.: see IMPALE *v.* 4.

impalement (ɪm'peɪlmənt). Also 7–9 em-. [a. F. *empalement* (1600 in Hatz.-Darm.), f. *empal-er* to IMPALE; but in recent use perh. directly from the Eng. vb.: see -MENT.] The action of impaling, or that which impales.

1. a. The action of enclosing with pales or stakes; *concr.* an enclosing fence or palisade.

1611 SPEED *Hist. Gt. Brit.* IX. xvi. §17. 818 To fortifie their battels with a Palizado, or empalement of stakes. **1665** J. WEBB *Stone-Heng* (1725) 154 The Impalement about them exactly square. **1786** tr. *Beckford's Vathek* (1868) 7 The prison..was encompassed by seven empalements of iron bars. **1828** WEBSTER, *Empalement*, a fencing, fortifying, or inclosing with stakes.

b. *transf.* and *fig.* (see IMPALE *v.* 1 b, c).

1598 BARRET *Theor. Warres* IV. i. 96 The impalement may be made of more shot in a ranke. **1641** MILTON *Ch. Govt.* I. ii, The rules of Church-discipline are..hedg'd about with such a terrible impalement of commands. **1814** CARY *Dante* (Chandos) 147 With penitential tears, That through the dread impalement forc'd a way.

†**2.** *Bot.* Applied by early botanists to the calyx, and, in composite flowers, to the involucre. *Obs.*

1671 GREW *Anat. Plants* I. v. §2 The general Parts [of the Flower] are most commonly three; the Empalement, the Foliation, and the Attire. The Empalement..I call that which is the utmost Part of the Flower, encompassing the other two. **1729** MARTYN in *Phil. Trans.* XXXVI. 28 The Empalement of the Lactuca is squamous. **1735–6** H. BROOKE *Univ. Beauty* IV. (R.), The flower's forensic beauties now admire, The impalement, foliation, down, attire. **1799** KNIGHT in *Phil. Trans.* LXXXIX. 202 The male and female parts within the same empalement.

3. *Her.* The marshalling of two coats of arms side by side on one shield divided palewise; the arms so marshalled.

1774 WARTON *Hist. Eng. Poetry* xxvi. (1840) II. 351 Two coats of arms, containing empalements of Cannynge and of his friends. **1882** CUSSANS *Her.* xii. (ed. 3) 165 Marshalling by Impalement is effected by slightly compressing the two Coats of Arms, and placing them in their entirety side by side on one Escutcheon.

4. a. The torture or punishment of impaling (see IMPALE *v.* 4).

1630 *R. Johnson's Kingd. & Commw.* 13 Tortures..as exoculations..impalements on stakes. **1727–41** CHAMBERS *Cycl.*, *Empalement*, or *Impalement*, a cruel kind of punishment, wherein a sharp pale, or stake, is thrust up the fundament through the body. **1813** BYRON *Corsair* II. ix, To-morrow's evening sun Will sinking see impalement's pangs begun.

b. The act or fact of being impaled upon rocks, the spikes of a gate, or the like.

1874 *Belgravia* Aug. 175 There was..one tall church-steeple which by the celerity of its approach appeared.. anxious that I should be impaled on its apex... I declare that the grotesqueness of the position of impalement—all legs and wings, like a cockchafer—..visibly occurred to me. **1885** *Austral. Med. Jrnl.* New Ser. VII. 436 A case of laceration of the rectum and jejunum by accidental impalement. **1887** *Graphic* 19 Mar. 307/2 His ship was rescued after impalement on a rock. **1921** *Contemp. Rev.* Aug. 272 Do you remember climbing the gate and just avoiding impalement? **1971** *Brit. Med. Jrnl.* 26 June 748/1 Perforation of the bladder following rectal impalement is extremely rare.

impaler (ɪm'peɪlə(r)). In 7–8 em-. [f. IMPALE *v.* + -ER[1].] One who or that which impales; applied by Grew to each of the calyx-leaves or sepals of a simple flower, and the bracts or phyllaries of a composite (cf. IMPALEMENT 2).

1671 GREW *Anat. Plants* I. v. §2 Each Empaler..being as another little Leaf. *Ibid.*, The continuation of all the three aforesaid Parts into each Empaler, is discoverable, I think, no where better than in an Artichoke, which is a true Flower, and whose Empalers are of that amplitude, as fairly to shew them all. **1969** *New Yorker* 6 Sept. 106/2 Ceauçescu.. probably the most popular Rumanian national leader since Vlad IV, called the Impaler, who successfully fought the Turks in the mid-fifteenth century.

†**impaletocked**, *pa. pple. Obs. nonce-wd.* rendering F. *empaletoqué* 'muffled, or lapt vp about the chinne, as with a Cassocke or Gaberdine' (Cotgr.): see PALETOT (in Cotgr. *palletoc*).

1653 URQUHART *Rabelais* I. xxi, His orison-mutterer impaletocked, or lap't up about the chin, like a tufted whoop.

impaling (ɪm'peɪlɪŋ), *vbl. sb.* [f. IMPALE *v.* + -ING[1].] The action of the verb IMPALE; *concr.* that which impales or is impaled.

1. The action of enclosing with or as with pales; *concr.* a paling or palisade: = IMPALEMENT 1.

1598 BARRET *Theor. Warres* 76 The Muskets of impaling ..doe roundly bestow their vollie in the face of the enemie. *c* **1600** NORDEN *Spec. Brit.*, *Cornw.* (1728) 21 Their Parkes of fallowe Deare, whereof remayne only..the ruyned impaylings. **1613** PURCHAS *Pilgrimage* VIII. vii. 643 At either end of that double empaling or entrance.

2. *Her.* = IMPALEMENT 3.

1605 CAMDEN *Rem.* (1637) 348 The impaling of his Armes with the Armes of Saint Edward. **1823** SCOTT *Let. to D. Terry* 29 Oct. in *Lockhart*, The different bearings of different families of the clan Scott, which with their quarterings and impalings will make a pretty display.

3. The action of transfixing on a pointed stake, etc. (see IMPALE *v.* 4, 4 b): = IMPALEMENT 4.

1615 G. SANDYS *Trav.* 62 Formes of putting to death.. impaling upon stakes. **1711** ADDISON *Spect.* No. 21 ¶7 Impaling of Insects upon the point of a Needle for Microscopical Observations. **1870** DICKENS *E. Drood* i, Set up by the Sultan's orders for the impaling of a horde of Turkish robbers.

impaling, *ppl. a.* [f. as prec. + -ING[2].] That impales: see the verb.

1649 G. DANIEL *Trinarch.*, *Hen. IV.* ccxxiv, The One-Eyed Scott..Breakes through impaleing Swords. **1742** FRANCIS *Horace*, *Odes* 35 (R.) Before thee stalks inexorable Fate, And grasps empaling nails, and wedges dread. **1903** [see IMPALE v. 4 c].

impall (ɪm'pɔːl), *v. rare.* [f. IM-[1] + PALL *sb*: see also *empall* s.v. EM- 1 a.] *trans.* To enfold or wrap in, or as in, a pall.

1852 J. JARVIE *Disc. & Misc. Writ.* 101 The chamber of the dead is impalled in silence and blackness.

impall, obs. (erron.) form of IMPALE.

impalla, var. IMPALA.

†**impallid** (ɪm'pælɪd), *v. Obs. rare.* [f. IM-[1] + PALLID; cf. L. *impallescĕre* to grow pale.] *trans.* To render pallid or pale.

1661 FELTHAM *Resolves* II. lvi, [Envy] the green sickness of the soul..impallids all the body to an Hectique leanness.

impalm (ɪm'pɑːm), *v. rare.* Also 9 em-. [f. IM-[1] + PALM *sb.*: cf. F. *empaumer*, in 16th c. *empaulmer*, It. *impalmare*, in the same or allied

senses.] *trans.* To grasp or take in the palm of the hand; also *fig.*

1611 COTGR., *Empaulmer*, to impaulme; to gripe, seise, lay full hand on. **1808** J. BARLOW *Columb.* IX. 42 Nature herself (whose grasp of time and place Deals out duration and impalms all space).

†im'palmed, *a. Obs. rare.* [f. IM-[1] + *palmed*, repr. L. *palmātus*, as in *tunica palmata*.] Worked or embroidered with palm-branches: said of the tunica worn by Roman generals in their triumphal processions.

1661 FELTHAM *Resolves* II. liii. 293 Her Conquerors impalmed Purples, and their lawrel'd Temples in their Turricular Chariots.

impalpability (ɪmpælpə'bɪlɪtɪ). [f. next + -ITY. Cf. F. *impalpabilité*.] The quality of being impalpable or imperceptible to the touch.

1605 M. SUTCLIFFE *Briefe Exam.* (1606) 100 The inuisibility and impalpability of Christes body in the sacrament. **1751–73** JORTIN *Eccl. Hist.* (1846) II. xxxviii. 161 A curious dispute, whether the bodies of the righteous, after the resurrection, should be solid, or thinner than the air? Gregory was for the palpability, and Eutychius for the impalpability. **1807** W. IRVING *Salmag* (1824) 361 A young lady whose unparalleled impalpability of waist was the envy of the drawing-room. *a* **1849** POE *Mellouba Tauba* Wks. 1864 IV. 293 The futility, the impalpability of their axioms.

impalpable (ɪm'pælpəb(ə)l), *a.* Also 6 **in-**. [a. F. *impalpable* (1517 in Hatz.-Darm.) or med.L. *impalpābilis*: see IM-[2] and PALPABLE.]

1. Incapable of being felt by the organs of touch; imperceptible to the touch; intangible. Said of things immaterial; also, of very fine powder, in which no grit is perceptible when it is rubbed between the fingers.

1509 HAWES *Past. Pleas.* XXIII. (Percy Soc.) 106 Though that aungell be invysyble, Inpalpable, and also celestiall. **1594** PLAT *Jewell-ho.* III. 88 So subtiliated .. as that it becam almost an impalpable powder. **1662** MERRETT tr. *Neri's Art of Glass* lxxvi, Grind it to an impalpable powder. **1791** COWPER *Odyss.* IX. 609 A thing impalpable, A shadow. **1873** W. LEES *Acoustics* III. iv. 100 Watery vapour, existing as an impalpable transparent gas.

2. *fig.* Incapable of being (readily) grasped or apprehended by the mind; producing no definite mental impression; 'intangible'.

1774 WARTON *Hist. Eng. Poetry* xlvii. (1840) III. 174 His own religion from its simple and impalpable form was much less exposed to the ridicule of scenic exhibition. **1838** PRESCOTT *Ferd. & Is.* (1846) I. Introd. 89 The almost impalpable beauties of style and expression. **1873** M. ARNOLD *Lit. & Dogma* (1876) 298 The impalpable and incognisable character of the subjects treated.

impalpably (ɪm'pælpəblɪ), *adv.* [f. prec. + -LY[2].] In an impalpable manner or degree.

1796 PEARSON in *Phil. Trans.* LXXXVI. 413 A light impalpably fine powder. **1864** J. H. NEWMAN *Apol.* 187 As a spirit .. within us .. working itself, though not in secret, yet so subtly and impalpably, as hardly to admit of precaution.

impalsy (ɪm'pɔːlzɪ), *v.* [f. IM-[1] + PALSY *sb.*[1]] *trans.* To affect with or as with palsy, to paralyse.

c **1750** SHENSTONE *Ruin'd Abbey* 205 The loyal soldier .. impalsy'd at the news .. drops the lifted steel.

impaludism (ɪm'pæljuːdɪz(ə)m). *Path.* [f. IM-[1] + L. *palus, palūd-em* marsh + -ISM.] 'The general morbid state, with predisposition to intermittent fevers and enlargement of the spleen, which is found in the dwellers in marshes' (*Syd. Soc. Lex.*).

1881 *Nature* No. 627. 24 On the parasitic nature of disorders arising from impaludism. **1889** *Lancet* 2 Feb. 252/2 A memoir on the parasite of impaludism.

impanate (ɪm'peɪnət, 'ɪmpənət), *ppl. a.* [ad. med.L. *impānāt-us*, pa. pple. of *impānāre* (see IMPANE).] Contained or embodied in bread: see IMPANATION.

1550 CRANMER *Defence* 33 a, As we haue God verely incarnate for our redemption, so shoulde wee haue him Impanate. **1551** GARDINER *Explic. Cath. Fayth* 115 (R.) In this mystery of the sacrament, in the whiche by the rule of our faithe Christes body is not impanate. *a* **1555** RIDLEY *Wks.* (Parker Soc.) 34 Saying: 'We grant the nature of bread remaineth .. and yet the corporeal substance of the bread therefore is gone, lest two bodies should be confused together, and Christ should be thought impanate'. **1563–87** FOXE *A. & M.* (1684) III. 648 That impanate God, whom Bucers Carcass had chased from thence. **1855** PUSEY *Doctr. Real Presence* Note A. 3 Guitmundus .. says [*trans.*] 'That Christ should be impanate, .. no ground requireth, nor did Prophets foretel, nor Christ shew, nor Apostles preach, nor the world believe'.

impanate, *v. rare.* [f. ppl. stem. of med.L. *impānāre*: see prec.] *trans.* To embody in bread.

1847 in CRAIG.

Hence **impanated** *ppl. a.* = IMPANATE *ppl. a.*

1579 FULKE *Heskins' Parl.* 257 Neither impanated, nor inuinated, nor inaccidentated. **1624** GATAKER *Transubst.* 145 Impanated or enclosed in bread. *a* **1740** WATERLAND *Wks.* VIII. 249 (R.) If the elements really contain such immense treasures, .. what have we to do but to look down to those impanated riches?

impanation (ɪmpə'neɪʃən). [ad. med.L. *impānātiōn-em*, n. of action f. *impānāre*: see IMPANE.] In Eucharistic theory: A local presence or inclusion of the body of Christ in the bread after consecration: one of the modifications of the doctrine of the real presence.

1548 GEST *Pr. Masse* in H. G. Dugdale *Life* App. i. (1840) 86–7 Thimpanacion of Christes bodye .. is .. soch a presence of Christes body in the bread wherwyth they both shuld be unseverably personed and have al theyr condicions and properties. **1576** WOOLTON *Chr. Manual* (Parker Soc.) 26 Nothing .. hath so greatly incensed .. the Saracens and Turks against Christians as .. the impanation of God. **1725** tr. *Dupin's Eccl. Hist 17th C.* I. VI. iii. 247 [Peter Martyr] attack'd Transubstantiation, and supported the Opinion of Luther concerning the Impanation. **1818** J. MILNER *End Relig. Controv.* III. (1819) 42 *note*, Osiander .. taught Impanation, or an hypostatical and personal union of the bread with Christ's body.

impanator ('ɪmpəneɪtə(r)). [ad. med.L. *impānātor-em*, agent-n. f. *impānāre* (see next).] One who holds the doctrine of impanation.

1855 PUSEY *Doctr. Real Presence* Note A. 4 [*transl.* the author of the 'de Sacramentis'] 'These His impanators the Lord Jesus slays with the word of His mouth, when .. He says, 'This is My Body'. He does not say, 'in this My Body lieth hid'. **1866** F. HARPER *Peace thr. Truth* 158 Others he distinguishes as impanators.

†im'pane, *v. Obs.* Also **inp-**. [ad. med.L. *impānā-re*, f. *im-* (IM-[1]) + *pān-is* bread.] *trans.* To embody in bread: see IMPANATION.

1547 BALE *Lett. Exam. Anne Askewe* 24 But now we must beleue that he commeth downe agayn, at the wyll of the prestes, to be inpaned or inbreaded .. lyke as he afore came downe .. to be incarnated or infleshed for our vnyuersall sowles helth. **1548** GEST *Pr. Masse* in H. G. Dugdale *Life* App. i. (1840) 87 Properly termed yᵉ impaning or enbreding therof.

†im'paned, *a. Obs.* In 7 **impained**. [f. IM-[1] + PANE + -ED[2].] Of a window: Having panes; fitted *with* (something) in each pane.

1635 BRATHWAIT *Arcad. Pr.* 218 A window impained with flaming lights.

impanel (ɪm'pænəl), *v.*[1] [f. IM-[1] + PANEL.]

1. *trans.* To fit with or as with panels.

1577 HARRISON *England* II. xii. (1877) I. 234 The claie wherewith our houses are impanelled, is either white, red, or blue.

2. To insert as a panel.

1861 SMILES *Engineers* VIII. xiv. II. 474 The painting of Westminster Bridge, impanelled in the wall over the parlour mantel-piece.

im'panel, im'pannel, *v.*[2]: another form of EMPANEL *v.*

†impantoufled, *ppl. a. Obs.* Also **-ofled**. [Rendering F. *empantouflé*.] (See quots.)

1611 COTGR., *Empantouflé*, impantofled, or wearing pantofles. [*Livre empantouflé*, a Booke with a thicke couer.] **1653** URQUHART *Rabelais* I. xxi, A huge impantoufled or thick-covered breviary.

†impapase, *v. Obs.* [f. IM-[1] + L. *pāpa* pope: the suffix perh. after Gr. παππάζ-ειν to call (any one) papa.] *trans.* To raise to the papacy; to make Pope.

1563–87 FOXE *A. & M.* (1596) 4/2 Pope Stephan the 4ᵗʰ, and pope Paschalis the 1ˢᵗ .. were impapased thorough discord without election of the emperor.

†im'paquet, *v. Obs.* [ad. F. *empaquet-er*, f. *paquet* PACKET: see also EMPACKET.] *trans.* To enclose in a packet.

1699 EVELYN *Let. to Dean of Carlisle* 10 Nov., Mem. 1857 III. 381 Of whom I had several letters impaqueted with many others.

†'impar, *sb. Obs.* [L. *impar* unequal, f. *im-* (IM-[2]) + *par* equal.] A thing unequal to another; *pl.* unequals.

1697 tr. *Burgersdicius his Logic* I. xxi. 84 Imparity is a diversity in quantity. Those things are said to be *impars* of which one is greater or less than another: .. so silver and gold, gold and virtues, are esteemed to be impars in this verse, *Vilius argentum est auro, virtutibus aurum.*

†impar, impare, *a. Obs.* [ad. L. *impar*, f. *im-* (IM-[2]) + *par* equal, even; cf. F. *impair* (1484 in Godef. *Compl.*).]

1. Of a number: Uneven; odd.

c **1430** *Art Nombryng* (E.E.T.S.) 6 In the place of the Impare sette a-side, put half of the even.

2. Unequal; unequally matched.

1535 STEWART *Cron. Scot.* I. 572 Becaus thair power that tyme wes impar, This Coell than wes sone put to the war [= worse].

imparadise, emparadise (ɪm'pærədaɪs), *v.* Also 6–7 **-ize**. [Corresponds to It. *imparadisare* (Florio) and F. *emparadiser* (17th c. in Littré); see IM-[1] and PARADISE.]

1. *trans.* To place in, or as in, Paradise; to bring into a state of rapture or supreme happiness; to transport, ravish.

α. **1592** CONSTABLE *Sonn.* VIII. iii, Though Death mee and my loue imparadizeth. **1592** DANIEL *Delia* Wks. (1717) 400 She that can my Heart imparadise. **1667** MILTON *P.L.* IV. 506 Imparadis't in one anothers arms. **1751** SMOLLETT *Per. Pic.* (1779) III. lxxxi. 88 We were imparadised in the gratification of our mutual wishes. **1845** *Bachelor Albany* (1848) 204 When he .. imparadised himself at Richmond.

β. **1598** FLORIO, *Paradisare*, to emparadize. **1610** G. FLETCHER *Christ's Vict.* IV. xliv, As in his burning throne he [David] sits emparadis'd. **1644** QUARLES *Barnabas & B.* 113 Emparadise thy soul in fresh delights. **1822** MILMAN *Martyr of Antioch* 84 Emparadised in bliss. **1851** SIR F. PALGRAVE *Norm. & Eng.* I. 49 The Greek emparadised by luxury and intellect.

2. To make a paradise of (a place or state).

a **1658** CLEVELAND *For Sleep* 29 Darkness emparadiz'd. **1776** MICKLE tr. *Camoens' Lusiad* 394 Song and joy imparadise the bowers. **1848** *Tait's Mag.* XV. 427 Improvements which would have literally imparadised the spot. **1849** MOIR in *Blackw. Mag.* LXVI. 565 The round white moon Emparadises midmost June.

Hence **im'paradised** (-aɪst) *ppl. a.*

a **1586** SIDNEY *Arcadia* (J.), This imparadised neighbourhood. **1606** FORD *Honor Tri.* (1843) 11 The fruition of imparadised content. **1853** TALFOURD *Castilian* IV. iii, The imparadised spirits of our saints.

†im'parallel, *a.* and *sb. Obs.* [f. IM-[2] + PARALLEL *a.* and *sb.*: cf. next.] **A.** *adj.* Unparalleled. **B.** *sb.* A thing unparalleled.

1641 TRAPP *Theol. Theol.* 173 What a deale of imparallell Rhetoricke is to bee read in that twelfth of Ecclesiastes! **1661** *Elegy Cleveland* 51 in *C.'s Wks.* (1687) 279 Poize this Imparallel; and you will find A Mine of Treasures in a Matchless Mind.

†imparalleled (ɪm'pærəlɛld), *a. Obs.* [f. IM-[2] + *paralleled*.] Without parallel, matchless, unparaleled.

1604 DRAYTON *Moses* III. (R.), Pisga .. Surveyeth the imparalleled land. **1639** T. BRUGIS tr. *Camus' Moral Relat.* 349 Image of a faithfull friend, and of a lover imparalelled. **1680** BURNET *Rochester* (1692) 168 A thing of such imparalelled Folly.

†im'parasite. *Zool. Obs.* [f. IM-[2] + PARASITE.] An animal that is not a parasite; applied by Kirby and Spence to certain insects. So **impara'sitic** *a.* (See quots.)

1816 KIRBY & SP. *Entomol.* (1843) I. 221 Those which are insectivorous only in their larva state may be .. divided into parasites and imparasites, meaning by .. the latter those that prey upon insects already dead. *Ibid.* 222 The Imparasitic insect devourers chiefly belong to the Hymenoptera.

†im'pardonable, *a. Obs.* Also 6 **inp-**. [f. IM-[2] + PARDONABLE. Cf. F. *impardonnable* (15th c. in Hatz.-Darm.).]

1. Not to be pardoned, unpardonable.

1523 LD. BERNERS *Froiss.* I. ccclxvi. 598 They shulde soore trespasse .. so yᵗ it shulde be inpardonable. **1647** N. BACON *Disc. Govt. Eng.* II. x. (1739) 56 Both King and People declare it an impardonable crime, by the Common Law. **1797** MRS. M. ROBINSON *Walsingham* I. 40 An act of disobedience which she deemed impardonable.

2. That gives no pardon. *rare.*

a **1625** BOYS *Wks.* (1630) 840 Leo the 10 so pilled and polled the .. nations .. with impardonable pardons, and mercilesse indulgences.

Hence **†im'pardonably** *adv.*, unpardonably. (In quot. actively = unforgivingly, mercilessly.)

1646 SIR T. BROWNE *Pseud. Ep.* VII. xvii. 379 He .. must impardonably condemne the obstinacy of the Jews.

impare, obs. form of IMPAIR *v.*, IMPAR *a.*

†im'parel, *v. Obs.* (See also EMPAREL.) Altered form of APPAREL *v.*

1556 *Chron. Gr. Friars* (Camden) 81 The iij. of August [1553] came in the qwenes grace .. goodly imparelde with alle the resydew of hare ladys.

imparesse, obs. form of EMPRESS.

1447–8 Q. MARG. *Petit. Hen. VI* in Willis & Clark *Cambridge* (1886) I. Introd. 63 The Imparesse of alle sciences and facultees, theologie.

imparfit, -ite, obs. forms of IMPERFECT.

imparidigitate (ɪm,pærɪ'dɪdʒɪtət), *a. Zool.* [f. L. *impar* unequal, uneven + DIGITATE.] Having an odd number of digits (fingers or toes) on each limb; perissodactyl.

1864 WEBSTER cites LEIDY.

imparipinnate (-'pɪnət), *a. Bot.* Also **-pennate**. [ad. mod.L. *imparipinnātus* (Linnæus, 1751): cf. prec. and PINNATE.] Pinnate (as a leaf) with an odd terminal leaflet.

1847 in CRAIG. **1870** BENTLEY *Bot.* 162 When a pinnate leaf ends in a single leaflet, it is impari-pinnate or unequally pinnate. **1876** HARLEY *Mat. Med.* (ed. 6) 665 Leaves exstipulate, imparipinnate.

imparisyllabic (-sɪ'læbɪk), *a.* (*sb.*) *Gram.* (Also 8–9 *erron.* **impara-**.) [f. L. *impar* unequal + SYLLABIC: cf. PARISYLLABIC.] Applied to Greek and Latin nouns which have not the same number of syllables in all the cases: e.g. nom. ὀδούς, gen. ὀδόντος; nom. *lapis*, gen. *lapidis*.

1730–6 BAILEY (folio), *Imparasyllabick*. (So ASH, CRAIG, etc.) **1774** J. BRYANT *Mythol.* I. 175 We must have regard to the oblique cases, especially in nouns imparasyllabic. **1796** PEGGE *Anonym.* (1809) 287 The imparisyllabic genitives of the third declension. **1813** S. PARR *Wks.* (1828) VII. 623 Markland's hypothesis upon the formation of the imparasyllabic genitive. **1854** DE QUINCEY *Autobiog. Sk.* Wks. II. 265 *note*, Of the nouns *Eicon* and *Doron* .. the first belonged to an imparisyllabic declension, .. the second not so.

B. as *sb.* An imparisyllabic noun.

1893 *Athenæum* 5 Aug. 189/2 The distinction of parisyllabics and imparisyllabics is barely indicated.

So †**imparisy'llabical** *a. Obs. rare*$^{-0}$.

1678 Phillips (ed. 4), *Imparisyllabical*, not consisting of a like number of syllables in every Case. **1721** in Bailey.

imparity (ɪm'pærɪtɪ). Now *rare* or *Obs.* [ad. late L. *imparitās*, f. *impar* unequal, uneven: see IM-[2] and PARITY. Cf. F. *imparité* (13–14th c.).]

1. The quality or condition of being unequal; inequality (in magnitude, degree, or rank): = DISPARITY 1.

1563 in Strype *Ann. Ref.* (1709) I. xxxv. 349 About matrimony and the virgin state, he had said, that there was no imparity, but the vow and dignity of both was equal. **1603** Holland *Plutarch's Mor.* 463 That there might be no imparitie nor inequality at all among his citizens. **1694** Crowne *Regulus* v. 58 A commonwealth bears no imparity: A great man is a tumor, a disease. **1702** *Toleration* 15 An unparallel'd imparity between your light Afflictions and the grievous Oppressions of other men. **1840** De Quincey *Style* III. Wks. 1860 XI. 265 You cannot affirm any imparity where the ground is preoccupied by disparity.

†**2.** The quality of being unlike; difference in nature or character, dissimilarity: = DISPARITY 2.

1608 Topsell *Serpents* (1658) 673 These claws stand not as other Birds do, three together and one by it self, but in imparity or dissimilitude, three on the one side, and two on the other. **1687** Towerson *Baptism* 167 There is this great imparity between the cases.

†**3.** Of numbers: The quality of not being divisible into two equal (integral) parts; unevenness; an uneven or odd number. *Obs.*

1646 Sir T. Browne *Pseud. Ep.* IV. v. 193 By parity or imparity of letters in mens names. **1658** —— *Gard. Cyrus* 70 By two and three, the first parity and imparity. **1659** T. Pecke *Parnassi Puerp.* 76 Love you Imparity?.. God, When He created Stars; created Odd.

impark (ɪm'pɑːk), *v.* Also 5 **inpark**, 6–9 **empark**. [a. AF. *enparker* (1304 in Godef.), OF. *emparquer*, f. *em-* (IM-[1]), + *parc* PARK.]

1. *trans.* To enclose or shut up in a park, as beasts of the chase; hence *gen.* to confine, shut up.

α. [**1304** *Year-bk.* 32–33 *Edw. I* (Rolls) 65 Puse no bestes enparker.] **1568** Grafton *Chron.* II. 641 The Capitaines strongly emparked themselves with high bankes, and depe trenches. **1614** Bp. J. King *Vine Palat.* 32 The wild boar of the forest.. that will not be held nor emparked within any laws or limits.

β. *a* **1400–50** *Alexander* 5499 Arteneus ane athill kemp alsso he in-parkis, And ane ser Tarbyn. **1491** *Act 7 Hen. VII*, c. 20 §5 The distres so taken.. bere awey imparke and reteigne unto the tyme that.. the.. rent.. be fully.. payed. **1589** Puttenham *Eng. Poesie* II. xi[i]. (Arb.) 112 Holding imparked as it were, Her people like to heards of deere. **1665** *Sir T. Roe's Voy. E. Ind.* in G. Havers *Della Valle's Trav.* 359 Their Deer are no where imparked. *a* **1678** Marvell *Poems* Wks. III. 198 What need of all this marble crust T'impark the wanton mole of dust?

2. To enclose (land) for a park; to fence in.

1535 *Act 27 Hen. VIII*, c. 22 They haue licence obteined.. of the kinges said highnes.. to imparke the same. **1548** Forrest *Pleas. Poesye* 87 Tenparke or enclose for hys Commoditee. **1611** Speed *Theat. Gt. Brit.* xxx. (1614) 59/1 Woods there are plenty, and many of them imparked. **1695** Kennett *Par. Antiq.* ix. 462 License to impark his woods there.

Hence **imparked** (ɪm'pɑːkt) *ppl. a.* (in quot. 1872 = surrounded by or situated in a park); **im'parking** *vbl. sb.*, enclosure of land for a park (also *gen.*); also **impar'kation** = prec.

1547 Hooper *Declar. Christ* Ded., One realm and island, divided from all the world by imparking of the sea. **1570–6** Lambarde *Peramb. Kent* (1826) 473 The pleasures of the emparked groundes here. **1710** *Lond. Gaz.* No. 4702/2 To bring in a Bill.. to encourage the imparking of Land. **1872** J. C. Jeaffreson *Woman in Spite of Herself* I. I. viii. 126 Their garden-girt villas and emparked mansions. **1880** *Antiquary* Dec. 233 To inquire into buildings lately destroyed for imparkation of lands.

imparl (ɪm'pɑːl), *v. Obs.* exc. *Hist.* Also 5–9 **em-**, 5–7 **-parle**. [a. obs. F. *emparler* to speak, plead, f. *em-* (IM-[1]) + *parler* to speak.]

†**1.** *intr.* To speak *together*, or *with* another, upon a matter; to confer, consult, parley. *Obs.*

[**1292** Britton II. xxi. §6 Et tauntost voysent les jurours en une part par eus mesmes pur enparler.] **1579–80** North *Plutarch* (1676) 25 The two Generals imparled together. **1599** Hakluyt *Voy.* II. I. 127 The Lord Baglione imparld with these hostages. **1600** Holland *Livy* IV. x, The captaine of the Volscians.. called the Consull forth to emparle.

2. *Law.* 'To have license to settle a litigation amicably; to obtain delay for adjustment' (Wharton *Law Lex.*). *Obs.* in practice; see next, 2.

1461 *Paston Lett.* No. 387 II. 8 They prayed heryng of the testament of my maister your fader, and therof made a nother mater.. be cause they had emparled to us by fore. **1531** *Dial. on Laws Eng.* I. xxvi. (1638) 41 He shall take a day to emparle at the same terme. **1613** Sir H. Finch *Law* (1636) 435 In an appeale of Robberie.. if the defendant plead a plea whereby his life should come in ieopardie, the Plaintife shall not emparle vnto it, but must answer *Sedente curia*. **1767** Blackstone *Comm.* II. xxi. 358 The demandant desires leave of the court to imparl, or confer with the vouchee in private; which is (as usual) allowed him. **1844** Williams *Real Prop.* I. ii. (1877) 47.

†**3.** *trans.* To talk over; to discuss. *Obs. rare.*

1600 Dymmok *Ireland* (1843) 50 [The matter] was first emparled between themselves in pryvate. **1805** in *Spirit Pub. Jrnls.* (1806) IX. 281 My Lord, your leave I humbly crave t' imparle it!

Hence **im-**, **em'parling**, conference, parleying.

1450–80 tr. *Secreta Secret.* (E.E.T.S.) 13 Whan this emparlyng is doone, than risith on of the wisist lordis.

imparlance (ɪm'pɑːləns). *Obs.* exc. *Hist.* Also 6–7 **em-**, **-aunce**, 7 **-eance**. [a. AF. **emparlaunce*, f. *emparler*: see prec. and -ANCE.]

†**1.** The action of speaking together upon a matter, esp. before taking action; conference, debate, discussion, parleying. *Obs.*

1579–80 North *Plutarch* (1676) 503 After this imparlance [with Eumenes], Antigonus compassed this Fort.. round about with a Wall. **1596** Spenser *F.Q.* v. iv. 50 With his Lord she would emparlaunce make. **1627** F. E. *Hist. Edw. II* (1680) 124 She will have no Impareleance, no discoursing. **1828** *Examiner* 273/2 This by way of imparlance; and now to revert to the bourne whence no suitor ever returns—Chancery.

2. *Law.* An extension of time to put in a response in pleading a case, on the (real or fictitious) ground of a desire to negotiate for an amicable settlement; a continuance of the case to another day; a petition for, or leave granted for, such delay. (Abolished in 1853.) Also *fig.*

1601–2 Fulbecke *1st Pt. Parall.* 59 In a Writ brought by one as sonne and heire to I. S., after imparlance the tenant cannot pleade to the Writte that hee is bastarde, or that hee is not heire. **1613** Sir H. Finch *Law* (1636) 434 *Emparlance* is when the defendant demandeth day to see if he may end the matter without further suite, which he may do once, but not oftner. **1713** Swift *Cadenus & Vanessa* 122 But with rejoinders and replies.. Demur, imparlance, and essoign, The parties ne'er could issue join. **1768** Blackstone *Comm.* III. xx. 299 The defendant.. before he pleads.. is intitled to demand one imparlance, or *licentia loquendi*, and may have more granted by consent of the plaintiff; to see if he can end the matter amicably without farther suit, by talking with the plaintiff. **1840** *Fraser's Mag.* XXII. 286 An imparlance was duly prayed of the bar. **1853** *Rules of Court, Trin. Term* xxxi, No entry or continuances, by way of imparlance.. or otherwise, shall be made upon any record.. or in the pleadings.

†**im'parlee.** *Obs. rare.* Also **emparle.** [f. as prec. after *parlee* PARLEY.] = IMPARLANCE.

1565 Stow *Eng. Chron.* 243b, They caused theyr trumpettes to sounde the blaste of emparle [Holinshed imparlée] that composition of eyther part myght be made to auoyde the imminent slaughter.

†**im'parlement, em-.** *Obs. rare.* [f. IMPARL *v.* + -MENT. Cf. OF. *emparlementé* adj. (1528 in Godef.).] = IMPARLANCE, IMPARLING.

1450–80 tr. *Secreta Secret.* (E.E.T.S.) 24 Haue emparlement with them of the nedis of thi Rewme.

†**imparler.** *Obs. rare*$^{-0}$. [f. IMPARL *v.* + -ER[1]: cf. OF. *emparlier*, *-ler* advocate.] One who 'imparls'.

1611 Cotgr., *Parlier*, a Pleader, Imparler.

imparour, imparre, obs. ff. EMPEROR, EMPIRE.

imparsonee (ɪmpɑːsə'niː), *a. Eccl. Law.* Also 7 **impersonee**. [f. med.L. *impersōnāta*, f. *im-* (IM-[1]) + *persōna* PARSON: after words like *appellee* (ult. ad. L. *appellātus*): see -EE[1].] In phr. ***parson imparsonee***, a clergyman duly presented, instituted, and inducted into a parsonage or rectory.

1607 Cowell *Interpr.* s.v. *Parson*, *Parson impersonee* (*persona impersonata*) is he that is in possession of a church. *Ibid.*, A Deane and chapter be persons impersonees of a benefice appropriated vnto them. **1613** Sir H. Finch *Law* (1636) 197 His plea must be, That the Church is full of his presentment, which a person impersonee cannot say. **1765** Blackstone *Comm.* I. xi. 391 When a clerk is thus presented, instituted, and inducted into a rectory, he is then .. in full and complete possession, and is called in law *persona impersonata*, or parson imparsonee. **1845** Stephen *Comm. Laws Eng.* (1874) II. Notes 677.

impart (ɪm'pɑːt), *v.* Also 5–6 **in-**, 5–7 **imparte**, 6–7 **empart**, 7 **impert**. [a. OF. *em-*, *impartir* (14th c. in Godef.), ad. L. *impartīre* (usu. *impert-*) to share, communicate, bestow, f. *im-* (IM-[1]) + *partīre* to PART.]

1. *trans.* To give a part or share of; to make another a partaker of; to bestow, give, communicate. (Usually (now only) with immaterial object, e.g. a condition, quality, etc.)

c **1477** Caxton *Jason* 139 But if [= unless] the goddes imparte to us of their grace we ben in grete daunger of our lyues. **1583** Stanyhurst *Æneis* III. (Arb.) 89 Thee stars imparted no light. **1599** B. Jonson *Ev. Man out of Hum.* III. i, Please you.. sir, to impart some ten groats, or half a crown to our use. **1609** Bible (Douay) *Exod.* vii. Comm., God doth not indurate by imperting malice, but by not imperting mercie. **1630** Prynne *Anti-Armin.* 137 If there be such a freedome of will.. imparted vnto all men. **1756** C. Lucas *Ess. Waters* I. 111 To the different solvents, it imparts different colors. **1858** Holland *Titcomb's Lett.* viii. 77 You are worth to society the happiness you are capable of imparting. **1875** Jowett *Plato* (ed. 2) I. 194 In a short time they can impart their skill to any one.

b. *absol.*

1601 B. Jonson *Poetaster* III. *ad. fin*, Did not Minos impart? *Cris.* Yes, here are twenty drachms he did convey. **1611** Bible *Luke* iii. 11 He that hath two coats, let him impart to him that hath none. **1853** Robertson *Serm.* Ser. III. xxi. 271 Let the rich impart to those who are not rich.

†**c.** *intr.* (with *with*). To part with. *Obs. rare.*

1606 G. W[oodcocke] tr. *Hist. Justin* 136a, They impart with many thousands of their store into Italy.

2. To communicate as knowledge or information; to make known, tell, relate. Const. *to*, formerly sometimes *with* (a person). *arch.* (or merged in 1).

a **1547** Surrey *Prisoner in Windsor* in *Tottell's Misc.* (Arb.) 14 The secrete thoughtes imparted with such trust. **1571** Digges *Pantom.* I. xxi. Gij a, I minde to imparte with my countrey men some suche secretes. **1596** Shaks. *Merch. V.* III. ii. 256 When I did first impart my loue to you. **1656–9** B. Harris *Parival's Iron Age* (ed. 2) 264 The Embassadours .. imparted the news to their friends. **1711** Addison *Spect.* No. 58 ¶2, I.. shall from Time to Time impart my Notions of Comedy. **1831** Brewster *Newton* (1855) II. xiv. 14 It does not appear that Newton imparted any of these methods to his mathematical friends.

†**b.** *refl.* To make known one's mind; to hold communication. *Obs.*

1625 Bacon *Ess.*, *Counsel* (Arb.) 321 King Henry the Seuenth.. imparted himselfe to none, except it were to Morton and Fox. **1647** Clarendon *Hist. Reb.* VI. §245 Imparting himself equally to all Men. **1653** H. More *Antid. Ath.* III. xiv. (1712) 132 This holy man that so freely imparted himself to Bodinus.

†**3.** To give a share of (something) to each of a number of persons; to distribute, divide, deal out.

1545 Joye *Exp. Dan.* iv. (R.), It behoueth vs.. (as saith Paul) diuyde trwely & imparte the worde of God to other. **1582** N. Lichefield tr. *Castanheda's Conq. E. Ind.* xiii. 32b, He imparted to his kinred, and diuided amongest them all his Lordships. **1601** B. Jonson *Poetaster* III. iv, Thou shalt impart the Wine, old Boy.

†**4.** To have or get a share of; to share, partake.

1581 J. Bell *Haddon's Answ. Osor.* 399 Yet ought not this power be.. emparted also with other Ministers in such wise. *a* **1639** Webster *Appius & Virg.* v. iii, Grieves it thee To impart my sad disaster? **1655** Heywood & Rowley *Fortune by Land* III. H.'s Wks. 1874 VI. 398, I am likely to impart his losse.

†**b.** *intr.* To share, take part, or partake *in*.

1471 *Arriv. Edw. IV* (Camden) 8 Thos that wowlde uttarly inparte with hym at beste and worste in his qwarell. **1615** Heywood *Foure Prentises* I. Wks. 1874 IV. 194 You offer wrong to impart in this my loue.

¶ See quot.

1530 Palsgr. 591/2, I inparte (Lydgate), I myxte thynges, I take parte of one and parte of another, *je mesle ensemble, je prens part dung et part dualtre.* [The reference to Lydgate has not been verified.]

Hence **im'parted** *ppl. a.*, **im'parting** *vbl. sb.* and *ppl. a.*

1611 Cotgr., *Communication*.. also, a participation, imparting, or making common a thing with others. **1653** T. Horton *Wisdome's Judgm. Folly* 59 Those whom God hath furnished with Estates.. should be so much the more imparting of them. **1848** R. I. Wilberforce *Incarnat. our Lord* xiv. (1852) 385 That holiness which is perfect must be the imparted holiness of Christ. **1952** *Mind* LXI. 309 Lying .. is the deliberate imparting of false information in order to deceive.

impartable (ɪm'pɑːtəb(ə)l), *a. rare.* [f. prec. + -ABLE.] Capable of being imparted, communicable: = IMPARTIBLE[2].

1653 F. G. tr. *Scudery's Artamenes* (1655) IV. VIII. II. 82 His secret thoughts which he conceived not impartable unto any.

impartance (ɪm'pɑːtəns). *rare.* [f. IMPART *v.* + -ANCE. (Not on L. analogies.)] = next.

1811 Shelley *Let. to Eliz. Hitchener* 18 Oct. (MS.), The balance between two opposing impartances of morality. **1828** Webster, *Impartance*, communication of a share.

impartation (ɪmpɑː'teɪʃən). [f. IMPART *v.* + -ATION. (The L. formation was *impertītio.*)] The action of imparting; impartment, communication.

1828 Webster cites Chauncey. *a* **1834** Coleridge *Confess.* (1849) 221 The miracle consisting in the impartation of a power to discourse. **1859** I. Taylor *Logic in Theol.* 294 The Divine impartation of religious truth. **1885** J. Brown *Bunyan* 186 The impartation of the new nature of sonship in Christ.

†**im'partener.** *Obs.* [irreg. f. IMPART *v.*: cf. *partner.*] One who imparts information; used by Puttenham as an equivalent of the rhetorical figure ANACŒNOSIS.

1589 Puttenham *Eng. Poesie* III. xix. (Arb.) 235 Another .. we call impartener, because many times in pleading and perswading, we thinke it a very good pollicie to acquaint our iudge or hearer or very aduersarie with some part of our Counsell.. and to aske their opinion [*marg.* Anachinosis, or the Impartener].

imparter (ɪm'pɑːtə(r)). [f. IMPART *v.* + -ER[1].] One who or that which imparts; a communicator, bestower.

1599 B. Jonson *Ev. Man out of Hum.* Dram. Pers., *Shift*, a thread-bare shark;.. lives upon lendings.. making privy searches for Imparters. **1652** Benlowes *Theoph.* 20 The Imparter of the guift. **1663** Boyle *Usefuln. Exp. & Nat. Philos.* v. Wks. 1772 II. 61 They may often learn that in a few moments, which cost the imparters many a year's toil and study. **1875** H. C. Wood *Therap.* (1879) 126 Alcohol.. its chief therapeutic value in acute disease is as a stimulant, a temporary imparter of power.. to bridge over some period of weakness.

impartial (ɪmˈpɑːʃəl), *a.* [f. IM-² + PARTIAL. Cf. F. *impartial* (1732 Dict. de Trévoux).]

1. Not partial; not favouring one party or side more than another; unprejudiced, unbiased, fair, just, equitable. (Of persons, their conduct, etc.)

1593 SHAKS. *Rich. II*, I. i. 115 Impartiall are our eyes and eares. **1601** CORNWALLYES *Ess.* (1617) Ciij, The most innocent and impartiall witnesses. **1693** SOUTH *Serm.* (1698) III. 72 A clear and a right Judging Conscience must be always Impartial;..it must judge all by Evidence, and nothing by Inclination. **1769** *Junius Lett.* xxxv. 161 Their sovereign, if not favourable to their cause, at least was impartial. **1838** THIRLWALL *Greece* II. xvi. 384 His cause was never submitted to an impartial tribunal.

†**2.** Not partial or fragmentary; entire, complete. *Obs. rare.*

a **1716** BLACKALL *Wks.* (1723) I. 5 The Obedience which God requires is impartial and universal, the Obedience of the whole Man.

¶**3.** Misused for *partial. Obs.*

1597 SHAKS. *Rom. & Jul.* Qo. 1, l. 1856 Cruel, vniust, impartiall destinies, Why to this day haue you preseru'd my life? **1620** *Swetnam the Woman Hater* (N.), You are impartial, and we do appeal From you to judges more indifferent.

impartialist (ɪmˈpɑːʃəlɪst). *rare.* [f. prec. + -IST.] One who professes impartiality; one who has or claims the character of being impartial.

1661 BOYLE *Style of Script.* (1675) 76, I am professedly enough an impartialist, not to stick to confess..that I read the Bible and the learnedst expositors on it, with somewhat particular aims. **1767** T. UNDERWOOD (*title*) The Impartialist; a Poem. **1883** *B'ham Weekly Post* 29 Sept 4/5 A movement set on foot by Conservative impartialists.

impartiality (ɪmpɑːʃɪˈælɪtɪ). [f. IMPARTIAL + -ITY. Cf. F. *impartialité* (1725 in Hatz.-D.).]

1. The quality or character of being impartial; freedom from prejudice or bias; fairness.

1611 COTGR., *Justice*,..vprightnesse, indifferencie, impartialitie. **1612–15** BP. HALL *Contempl.*, *N.T.* IV. iv, There must meet in God's ministers, courage and impartiality. **1749** FIELDING *Tom Jones* XVI. vi, It is almost impossible for the best parent to observe an exact impartiality to his children. **1802–12** BENTHAM *Ration. Evid.* Wks. 1843 VI. 350 Where is the cause in which any the slightest departure from the rule of impartiality is.. anything less than criminal on the part of the judge? **1836** H. ROGERS *J. Howe* Pref. (1863) 6 To maintain a tone of historic impartiality.

†**2.** Completeness: cf. IMPARTIAL 2. *Obs. rare.*

a **1716** BLACKALL *Wks.* (1723) I. 536 Whatever Commands thou art..pleased to lay upon us..grant that we may perform them..with such speed and Impartiality, as the holy Angels in Heaven do.

impartially (ɪmˈpɑːʃəlɪ), *adv.* [f. as prec. + -LY².] In an impartial manner; without favouring one more than another; without prejudice or bias; fairly, equitably.

1611 COTGR., *Justement*, iustly..indifferently, impartially. **1615** CHAPMAN *Odyss.* XIX. 292 God,..Whose equall hand impartially doth temper Greatnesse and goodnesse. **1711** STEELE *Spect.* No. 157 ⁋1 It is..hard..for a Man to judge of his own Capacity impartially. **1783** HAILES *Antiq. Chr. Ch.* iv. 70 They never..weighed impartially the evidence. **1835** BROWNING *Paracelsus* IV. 103 Another loved To hear impartially before he judged.

imˈpartialness. *rare.* [f. as prec. + -NESS.] The quality of being impartial; impartiality.

1643 W. GREENHILL *Axe at Root* 25 You see the severity of God in his impartiallnesse towards every tree. **1675** TEMPLE *Let. to Chas. II* 29 Jan., Wks. 1720 II. 322 A Thing that would give him Assurance of Your Majesty's Impartialness.

impartibility¹ (ɪmpɑːtɪˈbɪlɪtɪ). [f. IMPARTIBLE¹: see -ITY.] The quality or condition of being impartible or not subject to partition.

1656 JEANES *Fuln. Christ* 129 The impartibility, or indivisibility of the Godhead. **1750** CARTE *Hist. Eng.* II. 225 The elder sister and her issue should be preferred..as well on account of her primogeniture, as the impartibility of the Kingdom. **1764–7** LYTTELTON *Hen. II*, III. 121 (Seager) The impartibility of them [military fiefs] is ascribed by some writers to a constitution made by the emperor Frederick Barbarossa. **1788** T. TAYLOR *Proclus* I. 117 Those forms which, on account of their simplicity and impartibility, hold a superior rank among principles.

impartibility². *rare*⁻⁰. [f. IMPARTIBLE²: see -ITY.] Capability of being imparted; communicability.

1828 WEBSTER, *Impartibility*... 2. The quality of being capable of being communicated. [Hence in later Dicts.]

impartible (ɪmˈpɑːtɪb(ə)l), *a.*¹ (*sb.*) [ad. late L. *impartībilis*, f. *im-* (IM-²) + *partībilis* PARTIBLE.] Incapable of being parted or divided; not subject to partition or division into parts; indivisible. Now chiefly in legal use, of an estate.

1586 BRIGHT *Melanch.* xii. 58 In a nature so simple and impartible. **1640** BP. REYNOLDS *Passions* xxxii. 394 The soule,..being a spirituall and impartible substance, can.. have nothing severed from it. **1767** BLACKSTONE *Comm.* II. xiv. 215 When the emperors began to create honorary feuds ..it was found necessary..to make them impartible, or ..*feuda individua*, and in consequence descendible to the eldest son alone. **1788** T. TAYLOR *Proclus* I. 119 All of them pre-exist in intellect, but in an impartible..manner. **1890** *Times* 8 Mar. 4/1 The question..whether the estate..was partible or impartible.

B. as *sb.* Something that is indivisible.

1788 T. TAYLOR *Proclus* I. 118. **1789** *Ibid.* II. 7 Impartibles..are pure from corporeal place, and external motions.

†**impartible**, *a.*² *Obs. rare.* [f. L. *impartī-rī* (more correctly *impertīrī*) to impart: see -IBLE.] Capable of being imparted.

1631 T. POWELL *Tom All Trades* 142, I..desired to know so much..thereof as might be impartible to a freind of so small growth. **1730–6** BAILEY (folio), *Impartible*, that may be imparted.

impartibly (ɪmˈpɑːtɪblɪ), *adv.* [f. IMPARTIBLE¹ + -LY².] So as to be incapable of partition; indivisibly.

a **1631** DONNE 6 *Serm.* ii. (1634) 28 The soul of man is, indivisibly, impartibly, one entire. **1677** GALE *Crt. Gentiles* IV. 255 The Deitie..is multiplied in things partible impartibly,..i.e...is multiplied as to operations..yet without the least multiplicitie in it self. **1789** T. TAYLOR *Proclus* II. 419 For the soul does not contain the things.. according to magnitude, and locally, but impartibly, and without distance.

imparticipable (ɪmpɑːˈtɪsɪpəb(ə)l), *a.* (*sb.*) [f. IM-² + PARTICIPABLE.] Incapable of being participated or shared.

1789 T. TAYLOR *Proclus* II. 335 All participated hypostases..are reduced to imparticipable essences. **1816** —— *Proclus' Elem. Theol.* clxix. II. 409 Every multitude of unities which is participated by every imparticipable soul, is supermundane. **1839** BAILEY *Festus* ix. (1852) 133 Each star reigns, In imparticipable royalty. **1868** CUSSANS *Her.* xvi. 191 The title being imparticipable, it must necessarily remain unattached.

B. as *sb.* Something that is incapable of being shared.

1789 T. TAYLOR *Proclus* II. 359 Every imparticipable produces twofold orders of things participated.

impartite (ɪmˈpɑːtaɪt), *a. rare.* [f. IM-² + L. *partītus* divided, PARTITE.] Not divided into parts, undivided.

1862 F. HALL *Hindu Philos. Syst.* 248 The impartite intellect alone is subject and object of ignorance.

impartment (ɪmˈpɑːtmənt). [f. IMPART *v.* + -MENT. Cf. It. *impartimento* (Florio).] The fact of imparting, or that which is imparted; bestowal, communication, esp. of knowledge or information (cf. IMPART *v.* 2); a communication.

1602 SHAKS. *Ham.* I. iv. 59 It beckons you to go away with it, As if it some impartment did desire To you alone. **1647** M. HUDSON *Div. Right Govt.* II. x. 156 God ordained parents and Kings to be his instruments in the impartment of these outward blessings. **1683** PETTUS *Fleta Min.* I. Ded., Not to publish it, lest the Common sort of People should make an ill use of its impartments. **1824** HEBER *Jrnl.* (1828) I. 221 To ensure the gradual impartment of the sad news. **1882** WESTCOTT *Comm. Gosp. John* 22 The impartment of the Holy Spirit.

†**imˈparture.** *Obs. rare.* [f. as prec. + -URE: cf. *departure*.] The action of imparting.

1610 W. FOLKINGHAM *Art of Survey* I. iii. 6 The imparture of the innate facultie. *Ibid.* x. 28 This giues good increase, not so much through the imparture of any fattening facultie, as by fastening the wilde loose sand.

impassability (ɪmpɑːsəˈbɪlɪtɪ, -pæs-). [f. next: see -ITY.] The quality or condition of being impassable; with *pl.*, an impassable place, etc.

1772 MRS. DELANY *Lett.* Ser. II. I. 399 The impassibility of the ways between this and Whitehall. **1863** *Life in South* II. 225 The 'cane brakes' are such a network of impassabilities. **1880** MISS BIRD *Japan* I. 358 Ignorant of the impassability of the road to Odaté.

impassable (ɪmˈpɑːsəb(ə)l, -pæs-), *a.* [f. IM-² + PASSABLE.] That cannot be passed.

1. That cannot be passed along, through, or across; impossible to traverse or travel through.

1568 NORTH tr. *Gueuara's Diall Pr.* (1582) 446 A buckler or shield impassable. **1697** DAMPIER *Voy.* I. 167 All the Country..is full of impassable Woods. **1705** STANHOPE *Paraphr.* III. 550 The impassable Gulf fixed between us and all Happiness. **1844** H. H. WILSON *Brit. India* I. 453 It were most impolitic..to fix for ever impassable bounds to the public revenues. **1860** TYNDALL *Glac.* I. xii. 89 The glacier, though badly cut, was not impassable.

†**2.** That cannot pass (away or through). *Obs.*

1780 M. MADAN *Thelyphthora* II. 219 But the priesthood of Christ himself..is ἀπαράβατος, impassable from Him to any. **1832** *Examiner* 481/1 Bloated to a size as impassable through Heaven's gates, as is a camel through the needle's eye.

3. That cannot be 'passed' or made to pass. *rare.*

1865–6 H. PHILLIPS *Amer. Paper Curr.* II. 28 To cut a hole in each bill..thereby to render them impassable. **1887** *Pall Mall G.* 28 June 4/1 When a half a million gilt sixpences in circulation make half-sovereigns practically impassable.

Hence **imˈpassableness**; **imˈpassably** *adv.*

1727 BAILEY vol. II, *Impassableness.* **1801** CRUTWELL *Tour Gt. Brit., Lincolnsh.* (T.), No carts used to come here by reason of the impassableness of the boggy soil. **1828** WEBSTER, *Impassably.* **1865** MRS. WHITNEY *Gayworthys* xxix. (1879) 295 God knows what impassableness between their two suffering hearts.

‖**impasse** (ɛ̃pas, ɪmˈpɑs, -ˈpæs). [F. (Voltaire), f. *im-* (IM-²) + stem of *passer* to PASS.] A road or way having no outlet; a blind alley, 'cul-de-sac'. Also *fig.*, a position from which there is no way of escape, a 'fix'.

1851 H. GREVILLE *Leaves fr. Diary* 381 He ought to have given battle before plunging the country into this *impasse*. **1874** MIVART in Manning *Ess. Relig. & Lit.* III. 221 It is grammar and not reason which reduces them to this *impasse*. **1880** *Fortn. Rev.* Apr. 520 They find themselves in an impasse, unable to advance or retreat. **1882** H. C. MERIVALE *Faucit of B.* II. I. xxiv. 108 Somewhere off Piccadilly, among the curious little impasses of the Mayfair maze.

impassibility (ɪmpæsɪˈbɪlɪtɪ). Also 4–5 inp-. [a. F. *impassibilité* (13th c. in Hatz.-Darm.), ad. L. *impassibilitās* (tr. Gr. ἀπάθεια, Jerome), f. *impassibilis* (see next).] The quality of being impassible.

1. Incapability of, or exemption from, suffering; insusceptibility to injury.

a **1340** HAMPOLE *Psalter* lxvii. 38 He sall gif vertu of inpassibilite. **1496** *Dives & Paup.* (W. de W.) III. xiii. 148/2 Men shall haue there inpassybylyte & helth of bodye without all maner sekenesse. **1579** FULKE *Heskins' Parl.* 510 Christe is..God because of his impassibilitie, man for his passion. **1678** CUDWORTH *Intell. Syst.* I. iv. §15. 280 Incorruptibility, Perfection, Impassibility. *a* **1792** HORNE *Wks.* IV. xvii. (R.), The perfect impassibility of heaven. **1893** FAIRBAIRN *Christ in Mod. Theol.* 483 Theology has no falser idea than that of the impassibility of God.

2. Incapability of feeling or emotion, insensibility.

1603 HOLLAND *Plutarch's Mor.* 74 They..do terme those joyes, those promptitudes of the will..by the name of Eupathies, i.e. good affections, and not of Apathies, that is to say, Impassibilities. **1815** SOUTHEY in *Q. Rev.* XIII. 451 This impassibility..this Satanic indifference to the means which he used..and the misery which he occasioned, Marshal Soult possessed. **1840** MILL *Diss. & Disc.*, *A. de Vigny* (1859) I. 309–10 Spartan and Stoical impassibility. **1876** GEO. ELIOT *Dan. Der.* v. xxxv, Well-cut impassibility of face.

impassible (ɪmˈpæsɪb(ə)l), *a.* Erron. 6 -abyll, 7–9 -able. [a. F. *impassible* (13–14th c. in Hatz.-Darm.), or ad. eccl. L. *impassibilis*, f. *im-* (IM-²) + *passibilis* PASSIBLE.]

1. Incapable of suffering or pain; not subject to suffering. (Chiefly *Theol.*)

a **1340** HAMPOLE *Psalter* lxxi. 5 He is in generations in passybles, that ar of generations passiblis. **1502** *Ord. Crysten Men* (W. de W.) I. vii. H iv (Stanf.), They shall be Immortall and Impassyble. **1534** MORE *Comf. agst. Trib.* III. xxvi. (1573) 207 Tel him, that his body shalbe impassible, & neuer feele harme. **1667** *Decay Chr. Piety* Pref. A vj, That impassible state, where all tears shall be wiped from our eyes. **1782** PRIESTLEY *Corrupt. Chr.* I. I. 26 Cerinthus.. taught..that the Christ was impassible. **1871** ALABASTER *Wheel of Law* 108 An impassible, insensible, immovable spirit.

2. Incapable of suffering injury or detriment.

1491 CAXTON *Vitas Patr.* II. (W. de W. 1495) 220 b/2 The hauen of saluacyon Impassyble; that is to saye to the blysse that euer shall last without ende. **1624** GATAKER *Transubst.* 27 Christs body if it were broken and divided, would bee spoiled..but that it is impossible, because it is impassible. **1678** CUDWORTH *Intell. Syst.* I. v. 813 The Angelical Body, is so devoid of gross Matter, that it can pass through any Solid thing..being..more Impassible, than the Sunbeams. **1760–72** H. BROOKE *Fool of Qual.* (1809) II. 32 Virtue that I deemed to be impassible, unassailable. **1839** BAILEY *Festus* v. (1852) 60 Impassible as air, one great And indestructible substance as the sea.

3. Incapable of feeling or emotion; impassive, insensible, unimpressible.

1592 BACON *Confer. Pleas.* (1870) 5 If a man could make himself impassible of pleasure, he should make himself at one labor impassible of pain. **1690** NORRIS *Beatitudes* (1694) I. 46 Some Men of Rocky Hearts, and impassible Tempers, that could stand by, and see the whole World in Flames without any Concern. **1852** THACKERAY *Esmond* II. ix, He was impassible before victory, before danger, before defeat. **1876** GEO. ELIOT *Dan. Der.* VII. liv, Gwendolen, keeping her impassible air, as they moved away from the strand.

†**4.** Not to be endured, insufferable. *Obs. rare.*

1508 FISHER *7 Penit. Ps.* xxxviii. Wks. (1876) 56 Put your fynger nygh the fyre and full soone ye fele impassyble hete. **1665** T. MALL *Offer F. Help* vii, When the greatest sufferings approach you, say not they are invincible, impassable.

imˈpassibleness. [f. prec. + -NESS.] = IMPASSIBILITY.

1644 BP. HALL *Rem. Wks.* (1660) 122 The Impassiblenesse of the Spirit of God. **1667** *Decay Chr. Piety* viii. ⁋37 To..reserve all the sensualities of this world, and yet cry out for the impassibleness of the next. **1874** T. HARDY *Far fr. Mad. Crowd* I. xviii. 204 There was a change in Boldwood's exterior from its former impassibleness.

impassibly (ɪmˈpæsɪblɪ), *adv.* [f. as prec. + -LY².] In an impassible manner.

1677 GALE *Crt. Gentiles* IV. 253 God is also the Son, who always, eternally, influxibly, impassibly is begotten of the Father. **1872** GEO. ELIOT *Middlem.* IV. 353 He walked to the window, and gazed out as impassibly as he had done at the beginning of the interview.

†**imˈpassing**, *vbl. sb. Obs.* [f. IM-¹ + PASSING *vbl. sb.*] Passing or passage into.

1545 *Sc. Acts Mary* (1814) 451/1 þe tressonable Impassing of þe said george wᵗⁱⁿ þe partis of Ingland.

impassion (ɪmˈpæʃən), *v.* Also 6–9 em-. [ad. It. *impassionare* (Florio), f. *im-* (IM-¹) + *passione* PASSION.] *trans.* To fill or inflame with passion;

to infuse passion into; to stir the passions or feelings of; to excite deeply or strongly. Also *absol.*

1591 SPENSER *Daphn.* v, My soule it deepely doth empassion. **1593** NASHE *Christ's T.* (1613) 25 Sore am I impassioned for the storme thy tranquillity is in child with. **1647** H. MORE *Song of Soul* I. III. xxxiii, Doth not that sad sight..empassion his good spright With deeper sorrow? —— *Poems* 3 Lovers..impassion'd With outward forms. **1804** W. TAYLOR in *Ann. Rev.* II. 247 The whole narrative ..agitates and impassions like a novel. **1817** COLERIDGE *Biog. Lit.* 212 Metastasio..almost always raises and impassions the style of the recitative immediately preceding. **1894** STOPF. BROOKE *Tennyson* xii. 186 Its subject impassioned its writer.

impassionable (ɪm'pæʃənəbl), *a.* [f. IMPASSION *v.* + -ABLE.] Easily roused to passion; excitable.

1864 in WEBSTER.

impassionate (ɪm'pæʃənət), *a.*[1] Now *rare.* Also 6 **em-**. [ad. It. *impassionato*, pa. pple. of *impassionare* (see IMPASSION *v.*).] = IMPASSIONED. (In Spenser const. as pa. pple. of *impassion.*)

1590 MARLOWE *2nd Pt. Tamburl.* (*title-p.*), Tamburlaine, with his impassionate fury. **1596** SPENSER *F.Q.* v. ix. 46 With the neare touch whereof in tender hart The Briton Prince was sore empassionate. **1812** COLERIDGE in *Southey's Omniana* I. 238 The vehement and impassionate partizan of Mr. Wilkes.

impassionate, *a.*[2] Now *rare.* [f. IM-[2] + PASSIONATE. Cf. med.L. *impassiōnātus.*] Free from, or not governed by, passion; calm, dispassionate.

1621 BURTON *Anat. Mel.* I. iii. I. iii. (1676) 117/2 It stirs up dull Symptoms, and a kind of stupidity, or impassionate hurt. **1644** BP. HALL *Rem. Wks.* (1660) 123 It being the doctrine of that [Stoick] sect, that a wise man should be impassionate. **1664** LEIGHTON *Def. Mod. Episc.* Wks. (1868) 637 Upon the exactest (if impartial and impassionate) inquiry. **1850** *Tait's Mag.* XVII. 106/1 Spirits..whose dwelling is with simple impassionate truth.

impassionate (ɪm'pæʃəneɪt), *v.* Also 7 **em-**. [f. IMPASSIONATE *a.*[1]: see -ATE[3].]

1. *trans.* = IMPASSION.

a **1641** BP. MOUNTAGU *Acts & Mon.* (1642) 264 Alexandra ..was above all empassionated for his death. **1668** H. MORE *Div. Dial.* II. iv. 185 A very empassionating strain of Poetry. **1669** *Addr. hopeful yng. Gentry Eng.* 61 The object possessing and impassionating you. **1685** H. MORE *Para. Prophet.* 11 With a moving and empassionating Rhetorick. **1857** WHIPPLE *Character* iv. (1866) 97 Genius.. impassionates soaring imagination into settled purpose.

†**2.** *intr.* To be or become impassioned. *Obs.*

1639 G. DANIEL *Vervic.* 234 This fired my Rage; let it enflame thy verse, T' empassionate for me. **1646** —— *Poems* Wks. 1878 I. 63 How shall wee speake of him? what Numbers bring T'empassionate, and worthy Orgies sing?

impassionated, *ppl. a.* [f. as IMPASSIONATE *a.*[1] + -ED.] = IMPASSIONED.

1596 R. L[INCHE] *Diella* (1877) 52 What rare impassionated fits be these. *a* **1641** BP. MOUNTAGU *Acts & Mon.* (1642) 530 The Question was a long time canvased up and downe..with impassionated virulency. **1887** F. W. ROBINSON *In Bad Hands* etc. III. 11 The young, impassionated, handsome suitor.

im'passionately, *adv.* [f. IMPASSIONATE *a.*[1] + -LY[2].] In an impassioned manner, passionately.

1805 tr. *A. La Fontaine's Hermann & E.* II. 270 He beheld the Prince impassionately throw himself at her feet. **1839** *Fraser's Mag.* XIX. 362 [He] begged for succour, impassionately, though silently. **1869** *Daily News* 31 Aug., Their brethren in France impassionately and even reproachfully inviting them to return.

impassioned (ɪm'pæʃənd), *ppl. a.* Also 7–9 **em-**. [f. IMPASSION *v.* + -ED[1]; corresp. to It. *impassionato.*] Filled or inflamed with passion; having the feelings deeply moved or excited; passionate, ardent. (Of persons, or of feeling, speech, action, etc.)

1603 B. JONSON *Sejanus* v. x. Wks. (Rtldg.) 172/2 Fortune ..varying her empassion'd moods. **1667** MILTON *P.L.* IX. 678 The Tempter all impassiond thus began. **1791** MRS. RADCLIFFE *Rom. Forest* xi, Soft music..sounded the most tender and impassioned airs. **1838** SOUTHEY *Doctor* cxlvii. V. 128 Personification, a common figure..in all empassioned..speech. **1838** DICKENS *Nich. Nick.* vi, The tears fell..as she closed her impassioned appeal. **1889** MRS. A. FRASER *Lady Claud* I. ii. 30 He is impassioned of her.

Hence **im'passionedly** *adv.*; also **im'passionedness**.

1844 LD. HOUGHTON *Mem. Many Scenes, Venice*, Impassionedly The old Venetian sung those verses. **1876** W. GRAHAM *Mem. J. Macfarlane* vi. 301 He preached with plainness, directness..impassionedness. **1892** *Sat. Rev.* 9 Jan. 34/2 The impassionedly 'modern' Archdeacon.

im'passionment. *rare.* [f. IMPASSION *v.* + -MENT.] The action of impassioning or the fact of being impassioned.

1837 C. LOFFT, Jun. *Self-formation* II. xiii 226 His spirit ..vivid, flashing, and foaming to the highest pitch of impassionment when once thoroughly excited.

impassive (ɪm'pæsɪv), *a.* [f. IM-[2] + PASSIVE.]

1. Having the quality of not feeling pain; not subject or liable to suffering: = IMPASSIBLE 1.

1667 MILTON *P.L.* VI. 455 Too unequal work we find Against unequal armes to fight in paine, Against unpaind, impassive. **1708** ROWE *Royal Convert* v. i, The free, impassive Soul mounts on the Wing, Beyond the reach of Racks, and tort'ring Flames. *a* **1791** WESLEY *Serm.* lxv, While he was innocent, he was impassive, incapable of suffering. **1821** SHELLEY *Hellas* 680 O Slavery!..the free heart, the impassive soul, Scorn thy control!

2. Naturally without sensation; inanimate; not susceptible of physical impression or injury, invulnerable.

a **1687** COTTON *On Sleep* (R.), The lover meets the willing fair, And fondly grasps impassive air. **1711** POPE *Temp. Fame* 56 On the impassive Ice the light'nings play. **1780** BURKE *Sp. Econ. Reform* Wks. 1842 I. 243 Death.. domineers over every thing, but the forms of the exchequer. .. They are impassive and immortal. **1876** BLACKIE *Songs Relig. & Life* 35 Thou, like the thin impassive air, Dost cheat the grasp of subtlest-thoughted sage.

b. Deprived of feeling or sensation; insensible, unconscious.

1848 DICKENS *Dombey* i, The two medical attendants seemed to look on the impassive form with so much compassion and so little hope. **1871** ALABASTER *Wheel of Law* 194 The impassive state is only transient.

3. Deficient in, or void of, mental feeling or emotion; not susceptible to mental impressions; unimpressionable, apathetic; also, in good sense, not liable to be disturbed by passion, serene.

1699 GARTH *Dispens.* I. 4 To find How body acts upon impassive mind. **1725** POPE *Odyss.* IV. 313 Impassive and serene, The man entranc'd would view the deathful scene. **1856** FROUDE *Hist. Eng.* (1858) I. v. 399 Clement..had maintained an attitude of impassive reserve. **1871** H. AINSWORTH *Tower Hill* I. i, He looked hard at Sir Anthony, but could read nothing in the knight's impassive countenance. **1874** GREEN *Short Hist.* x. §1. 727 Even the impassive Chesterfield cried in despair, 'We are no longer a nation'.

4. Unendurable, intolerable: = IMPASSIBLE 4. *rare.*

1828 W. IRVING *Columbus* (1848) I. 38 A torrid zone.. separating the hemispheres by a region of impassive heat.

impassively (ɪm'pæsɪvlɪ), *adv.* [f. prec. + -LY[2].] In an impassive manner.

1828 in WEBSTER. *a* **1845** HOOD *Romance Cologne* viii, In her fond arms impassively he lies, Clay-cold to her caressing. **1871** *Daily News* 16 Aug., The same croupiers.. will impassively rake up your money.

impassiveness (ɪm'pæsɪvnɪs). [f. as prec. + -NESS.] The quality or condition of being impassive; want of feeling or emotion, insensibility, apathy.

1648 W. MOUNTAGUE *Devout Ess.* I. vi. §1. 53 The power of remaining in a calme apathy and impassivenesse in all offencive emergencies. **1657** PIERCE *Div. Philanthr.* Ded. 3 He hath communicable Attributes, as well as Attributes incommunicable; not only Impassivenesse, but patience. **1817** GODWIN *Mandeville* III. 364 (Jod.) The impassiveness with which Hell sometimes dowers her votaries. **1866** GEO. ELIOT *F. Holt* I. ii. 66 A handsome impassiveness of face.

impassivity (ɪmpæ'sɪvɪtɪ). [f. as prec. + -ITY.] = prec.

1794 T. TAYLOR tr. *Pausanias* cited in Webster 1828. **1822** —— *Apuleius* 307 Those human souls that descend into the regions of mortality with impassivity and purity were called ..heroes. **1837** CARLYLE *Fr. Rev.* III. IV. vii, Cold aristocratic impassivity, faithful to itself even in Tartarus. **1874** T. HARDY *Far fr. Mad. Crowd* iii, Compressing her lips to a demure impassivity.

impastation (ɪmpæ'steɪʃən). [n. of action f. IMPASTE *v.*: cf. F. *impastation* (1690 in Furetière).] The formation of a paste; also *concr.* (see quot. 1727).

1727–41 CHAMBERS *Cycl.*, *Impastation*, the mixtion of divers materials of different colours and consistences, baked or bound together with some cement, and hardened either by the air, or fire. Impastation is sometimes a sort of masons-work, made of stucco, or stone ground small, and wrought up again in manner of a paste. **1855** MAYNE *Expos. Lex.*, *Impastatio*, old term for the making of dry powders into a paste by means of some fluid: impastation.

impaste (ɪm'peɪst), *v.* Also 7–8 **em-**. [ad. It. *impastare* 'to empaste, to raise paste, to put into paste..Also to beplaister' (Florio, 1611), f. *im-* (IM-[1]) + *pasta* PASTE. Cf. F. *empâter*, in Cotgr. *empaster.*]

1. *trans.* To enclose in or encrust with or as with a paste.

1548–67 THOMAS *Ital. Dict.*, *Impastato*, impasted or raied with dirte. *a* **1747** R. CUMBERLAND *Mem.* (1806) I. 63 The.. hide grows stiff and hard, Scorch'd and impasted with the feverish heat. **1835** URE *Philos. Manuf.* 90 Wool and silk.. may be viewed with most advantage impasted in Canada balsam slightly thinned with oil of turpentine.

2. To make or form into a paste or crust.

1576 BAKER *Jewell of Health* 92 b, Of these make a paste, letting it to stand impasted together for certaine dayes. **1602** SHAKS. *Ham.* II. ii. 481 With blood of Fathers, Mothers, Daughters, Sonnes, Bak'd and impasted with the parching streets. **1662** MERRETT tr. *Neri's Art of Glass* xxxviii, Mixed, tempered, and impasted with the whites of Eggs.

3. *Painting.* To paint by laying on colour thickly.

1727–41 CHAMBERS *Cycl.*, *Empasting*, or *Impasting*, a term used in painting, for the laying on of colours, thick, and bold, or applying several lays of colours, so as they may appear thick. **1855** J. EDWARDS *Art Landscape Paint.* (ed. 10) 36 In oil painting, the shadows, or dark portions of the picture, are painted thinly; while the lights are laid on, or 'impasted', with a full pencil and a stiff colour. **1865** LESLIE & TAYLOR *Sir J. Reynolds* II. vi. 146 Heavily impasted pictures.

b. *transf.* To spread thickly (*on* a surface).

1888 G. GISSING *Life's Morning* I. vii. 290 [She] helped herself abundantly to marmalade, which she impasted solidly on buttered toast.

Hence **im'pasting** *vbl. sb.*; *spec.* in *Painting* (see 3); hence *transf.* in *Engraving* (see quot. 1864). Also *attrib.*

1727–41 [see 3]. **1822** HAZLITT *Table-t.* I. i. 17 *note*, The rich impasting of Titian and Giorgione. **1841** THACKERAY *On Men & Pict.* 111 When you wish to represent a piece of old timber,..this impasting method is very successful. **1855** J. EDWARDS *Art Landscape Paint.* (ed. 10) 36 In the lights of the foreground..the 'impasting' should be bold and free. **1864** WEBSTER, *Impasting*..2. (*Engraving*) (*a.*) An intermixture of lines and points to represent thickness or depth of coloring. (*b.*) The kind of work thus produced.

‖**impasto** (ɪm'pɑːstəʊ, -'pæs-). [It., n. of action f. *impastare* to IMPASTE.] **1.** *Painting.* The laying on of colour thickly; impasting, as a characteristic of style: see prec. 3. Also *attrib.*

1784 J. BARRY in *Lect. Paint.* vi. (Bohn 1848) 223 All that impasto, or embodying of colour, which may be necessary for certain lucid parts. **1838–9** HALLAM *Hist. Lit.* III. III. vi. §93. 341 A certain redundancy, as some may account it, gives fulness, or what the painters call *impasto*, to his style. **1859** GULLICK & TIMBS *Paint.* 6 In the works of the northern tempera painters there are very marked differences observable in their impasto or body of colour. **1880** *Spectator* 5 June 719 It is impossible to clean impasto work.

2. *Ceramics.* (See quots.)

1903 M. L. SOLON *Hist. Old French Faïence* 188 *Impasto*, clay or enamel colours laid so thickly on to the ware as to stand up in relief from its surface. **1960** R. G. HAGGAR *Conc. Encycl. Cont. Pott. & Porc.* 233/1 '*Impasto blue*', inky blue pigment which is applied thickly and stands up in slight but palpable relief on early 'oak-leaf' pots made at Florence.

impastoed (ɪm'pɑːstəʊd, -'pæs-), *ppl. a.* Encrusted with paste.

1923 *Blackw. Mag.* May 641/2 [He] thrust the point of his palette-knife under an impasto'd mass of paper.

†**im'pasture**, *v. Obs.* [f. IM-[1] + PASTURE *sb.*]

1. *trans.* To place or confine in a pasture; 'to set to feed; to turn out to graze' (Davies).

1612–15 BP. HALL *Contempl., N.T.* IV. i, Sheep..not guarded, not impastured, but strayed and lost. **1614** T. ADAMS *Fatal Banket* ii. Wks. 1861 I. 184 Adultery..sets paleness on his cheek, and impastures grief in his heart.

2. To turn into pasture-land, enclose for pasture.

1649 BLITHE *Eng. Improv. Impr.* (1653) 73 He will cast how he may Improve his Lands by Impasturing, and Enclosing of it.

impaternate (ɪmpə'tɜːnət), *a. Biol.* [f. IM-[2] + PATERN(AL *a.* + -ATE[2].] Produced parthenogenetically by a female without fecundation by a male.

1934 in WEBSTER. **1936** *Nature* 11 July 78/1 If the queen bee is diploid and heterozygous for a recessive factor, she.. would be expected to produce impaternate haploid drones, equal numbers of which would show the dominant or the recessive character. **1965** [see *deuterotoky* s.v. DEUTERO-].

†**im'patible**, *a. Obs.* Also 6 erron. **-able**. [ad. L. *impatibil-is*, *-petibilis*, insufferable, impassible, f. *im-* (IM-[2]) + *patibilis*, f. *pati* to suffer.]

1. Incapable of suffering, or of sustaining injury: = IMPASSIBLE 1, 2.

1541 R. COPLAND *Guydon's Quest. Chirurg.* 2 E j, The impatable and inalterable thynges to be the fyrste elementes. **1588** A. KING tr. *Canisius' Catech.* 76 b, It [the flesh of Christ] is inuisible, impatible, immortall. **1655** FULLER *Ch. Hist.* II. v. §15 The Devil..is a Spirit, and so impatible of materiall Fire.

2. Intolerable: = IMPASSIBLE 4.

1623 COCKERAM, *Impatible*, intolerable. **1659** D. PELL *Impr. Sea* 22 The heavy, severe, and impatible wrath of God.

impatience (ɪm'peɪʃəns). Forms: 3–6 **impacience**, (4 **in-**, 5 **inpaciens**, **ympacience**, 6 **impacyence**), 6– **impatience**. [ME. a. OF. *impacience* (12th c.), *-patience*, ad. L. *impatientia*, f. *im-* (IM-[2]) + *patientia* the quality of suffering, PATIENCE, f. *patī* to suffer: see -ENCE.] The fact or quality of being impatient; want of patience.

The *quality* was formerly more exactly expressed by IMPATIENCY: see -ENCY.

1. Want of endurance; failure to bear suffering, discomfort, annoyance, etc. with equanimity; irritability, irascibility.

a **1225** *Ancr. R.* 198 Þe eihteoðe hweolp is Impacience. Þesne hweolp fet hwose nis nout þolemod aȝean alle wowes, & in alle vueles. **1340** *Ayenb.* 33 Þe oþer poynt is inpacience, ..he ne may þolye be paciense, zuo þet non ne dar to him speke of his guode. *c* **1374** CHAUCER *Boeth.* II. pr. i. 21 (Cambr. MS.) [Thou] makest fortune wroth and Aspere by thine in-pacience. *c* **1421** HOCCLEVE *Complaint* 177, I full ofte Cawse had of angre and ympacience. **1591** SHAKS. *1 Hen. VI*, IV. vii. 8 Rough deeds of Rage, and sterne Impatience. **1632** LITHGOW *Trav.* x. 479 Men are rather killed with the impatience they have in adversity, then adversity it selfe. **1667** MILTON *P.L.* x. 1044 Rancor and pride, impatience and despite. **1846** TRENCH *Mirac.* vi. (1862) 185 Sore as the trial must have been, we detect no signs of impatience on his part.

b. With *of*: Incapacity of enduring; intolerance *of*.

c **1566** J. ALDAY tr. *Boaystuau's Theat. World* M ij, Bread made of chaffe.. the which the poore were forced to eate, by impacience and rage of hunger. **1607** TOPSELL *Four-f. Beasts* (1658) 106 Impatience of cold and wet. **1741** MIDDLETON *Cicero* I. vi. 495 An impatience of discipline. **1830** D'ISRAELI *Chas. I*, III. v. 74 His impatience of contradiction unfitted him.. for the council-table. **1876** BLACK *Madcap V.* xvii, The girl had an impatience of pretence of all kinds.

†**c.** With *inf.* (*obs.* or *arch.*): cf. IMPATIENT 1 c.

1575 LANEHAM *Let.* (1871) 6 Hee burst out in a great pang of impatiens to see such vncooth trudging too and fro. **1632** J. HAYWARD tr. *Biondi's Eromena* 137 With impatience to be longer bridled. **1683** *Brit. Spec.* 119 A tedious Impatience to see the horrible Actions of Nero forced St. Paul also to quit Rome.

2. *esp.* Intolerance of delay; restlessness of desire or expectation; restless longing or eagerness.

1581 MULCASTER *Positions* 262 Impacience, which can abide no tarying. **1632** J. HAYWARD tr. *Biondi's Eromena* 148 Hee with Impatience long'd for the appearance of the new day. **1712** LADY M. W. MONTAGU *Lett. to W. Montagu* 9–11 Dec. (1887) I. 79, I wait with impatience for.. your return. **1768–74** TUCKER *Lt. Nat.* (1852) I. 237 We find the uneasiness arising upon a delay of desire vulgarly styled impatience. **1878** M. A. BROWN *Nadeschda* 44, I asked in my impatience Each passing hour a question.

†**b.** With *of*: Impatient desire *of*. *Obs.*

(The sense here is practically the opposite of that in 1 b.)

1664 G. M. in *Marvell's Corr.* Wks. 1872–5 II. 104 Tyred with an extream impatience all day of removing from those Wisbies. **1702** *Eng. Theophrast.* 111 Out of a foolish impatience of being seen at Court. **17..** HURD (J.), The longer I continued in this scene, the greater was my impatience of retiring from it.

c. With *inf.*: cf. IMPATIENT 2 b.

1880 L. WALLACE *Ben-Hur* VII. iii, A return of impatience to see Him who is ever in my thought.

†**impatiency** (ɪmˈpeɪʃənsɪ). *Obs.* (or *rare archaism.*) Also 6 -ciency, -cyency, 7 -tientie. [ad. L. *impatientia*: see prec. and -ENCY.] The quality of being impatient.

1. = prec. 1: esp. as a quality or disposition. Also, with *pl.*, an instance or exhibition of this quality.

1526 *Pilgr. Perf.* (W. de W. 1531) 93 b, Testinesse or impacyency, is a frayle & hasty disposycyon, or rather accustomed & vsed vyce of angre. **1552** LATIMER *Serm. Lord's Prayer* vii. (1562) 45 He [the devil] goeth about.. to.. sturre vs to impatiency and murmuryng against god. **1658** *Whole Duty Man* vi. §16. 57 A calmness and quietness of spirit, contrary to the rages and impatiencies of anger. **1748** RICHARDSON *Clarissa* I. v. 35 His extraordinary prosperity adding to his impatiency.

b. With *of*: cf. prec. 1 b.

1557 PHAER *Æneid* VI. Argt., Those that through impaciencie of loue, had shortned their owne dayes. **1607** TOPSELL *Four-f. Beasts* (1658) 165 Their impatiency of cold. **1681** H. MORE *Exp. Dan.* 273 Their impatiency of that dark inglorious condition.

2. = prec. 2: esp. as a quality or disposition; also, with *pl.*, an instance of this.

1560 BECON *New Catech.* Wks. 1844 II. 143 Nothing doth more displease and offend God, than through impatiency to prescribe unto him the time when he shall help us. **1654–66** EARL ORRERY *Parthenissa* (1676) 764 In impatiencies above description [I] waited for the arrival of the Princess. **1664** MARVELL *Corr.* Wks. 1872–5 II. 129 Which [explanation] I do expect with the most vehement impatiency. **1684** LADY R. RUSSELL *Lett.* (1819) I. xiv. 40, I hope to wait without impatiency. **1889** STEVENSON *Master of B.* 287 My lord waited with growing impatiency.

b. With *inf.*: cf. prec. 2 c.

1647 CLARENDON *Hist. Reb.* III. §250 His Majesty's impatiency to see both Armies disbanded. **1742** RICHARDSON *Pamela* IV. 10, I had such an Impatiency to see him, having expected him at Dinner.

impatient (ɪmˈpeɪʃənt), *a.* (*sb.*) Forms: 4–6 **impacient, -cyent, inpacient,** 5 **-cyent,** 6– **impatient.** [a. OF. *impacient, impatient*, ad. L. *impatient-em*, f. *im-* (IM-²) + *patient-em* suffering, pres. pple. of *pati* to suffer.]

1. Not patient; not bearing or enduring (pain, discomfort, opposition, etc.) with composure; wanting in endurance; irritable, irascible, easily provoked. Also *transf.* of action or speech: Indicating impatience or irritation.

1377 LANGL. *P. Pl.* B. XVII. 337 Þowgh þat men make moche deol in her angre, And ben inpacient in here penaunce. **1413** *Pilgr. Sowle* (Caxton 1483) III. viii. 55 They nought ne couthe suffren but were yreful and inpacyent to al men aboute them. **1494** FABYAN *Chron.* v. xcvii. 71 The Kynge was thanne more impacient, and blamed yᵉ Relygion of his wyfe in moost impacyent maner. **1590** SHAKS. *Mids. N.* III. ii. 287 Will you teare Impatient answers from my gentle tongue? **1666** PEPYS *Diary* 20 Aug., [He] is much impatient by these few days sickness. **1712** STEELE *Spect.* No. 438 ¶4 You are of an impatient Spirit, and an impatient Spirit is never without Woe. **1851** TRENCH *Poems fr. East. Sources* 194 And by faith allayed to meekness Every wish and thought impatient.

b. With *of*: Unable or unwilling to endure or put up with; intolerant of.

1513 MORE in Grafton *Chron.* (1568) II. 758 Ambicious of aucthoritie, and impacient of partners. **1597** GERARDE *Herbal* I. xxxviii. §1. 55 Ginger is most impatient of the coldnes of these.. regions. **1601** SHAKS. *Jul. C.* IV. iii. 152 Impatient of my absence.. she fell distract. **1713** STEELE *Englishm.* No. 19. 121 The most ignorant are.. most impatient of Advice. **1893** LYDEKKER *Horns & Hoofs* 26 [Yaks] are extremely impatient of heat.

c. With *inf.* (obs. or arch.) or *dependent clause*. (With *inf.*, practically the opposite of 2 b.)

1565 EARL BEDFORD in Ellis *Orig. Lett.* Ser. I. II. 209 He was so impatient to see those thyngs he sawe and were dayly broughte to his Eares. **1615** G. SANDYS *Trav.* 145 The Jewes impatient that forrieners should possesse their countrey, raised a new commotion. **1632** J. HAYWARD tr. *Biondi's Eromena* 182 Impatient to stay till they would speake. **1877** MRS. OLIPHANT *Makers Flor.* xii. 299 Impatient to be thus forced out of his high work.

d. *fig.* (Said of things.)

1490 CAXTON *Eneydos* xxvii. 96 The see wexed right sore inpacyent and indigned. **1597** GERARDE *Herbal* II. xviii. (1633) 260 Impatient Lady Smocke.. The nature of this plant [*noli me tangere*] is such, that if you touch but the cods when the seed is ripe, tho'.. neuer so gently, yet will the seed fly all abroad with violence as disdaining to be touched. **1882** *Garden* 11 Mar. 169/1 Cherry is the most impatient tree we have to deal with under glass.

2. That does not willingly endure delay; uneasy or restless in desire or expectation. Const. *for*.

1592 SHAKS. *Rom. & Jul.* III. ii. 30 Tedious.. As is the night before some Festiuall, To an impatient child that hath new robes And may not weare them. **1599** —— *Hen. V*, IV. ii. 52 Their executors, the knauish Crowes, Flye o're them all, impatient for their howre. **1697** DRYDEN *Virg. Georg.* IV. 702 Strong Desires th' impatient Youth invade. **1728** POPE *Dunc.* III. 30 Impatient for the day. **1878** MORLEY *Carlyle* 174 Headlong and impatient souls. **1899** *Q. Rev.* Jan. 193 He has no impatient desire for the hurry of modern improvements.

b. With *inf.* Restlessly desirous, eagerly longing. (In quot. 1680 with *dependent clause.*)

1588 SHAKS. *L.L.L.* II. i. 238 All impatient to speake and not see. *a* **1680** BUTLER *Rem.* (1759) I. 3 All stood ready to fall on, Impatient who should have the Honour To plant an Ensign first upon her. **1718** LADY M. W. MONTAGU *Lett. to Mrs. Thistlethwaite* 25 Sept. (1887) I. 266, I am impatient to see the curiosities of this famous city. **1874** SYMONDS *Sk. Italy & Greece* (1898) I. ix. 180 Impatient to recover the lost jewel.

c. *transf.* and *fig.* Characterized by, or attended with, impatience of delay.

1703 ROWE *Ulyss.* III. i. 1230 This one impatient Minute. **1791** COWPER *Iliad* VIII. 304 Teucer, wide-straining his impatient bow. **1822** LAMB *Elia* Ser. II. *Detached Th. Bks.*, The five or six impatient minutes, before the dinner is quite ready.

†**3.** ? Intolerable, 'not to be borne' (J.). *Obs. rare.*

1590 SPENSER *F.Q.* II. i. 44 Ay, me! deare Lady, which the ymage art Of rufull pitty and impatient smart. **1646** SIR T. BROWNE *Pseud. Ep.* IV. x. 204 What absurd conceits they will swallow in their literals, an impatient example wee have in our owne profession.

B. as *sb.* An impatient person. (Sometimes with play on PATIENT *sb.*)

1502 *Ord. Crysten Men* (W. de W. 1506) I. vii. 67 The poor synner ought not to dyspayre hym, how be it that the sensualyte complayneth hym an impacyent. **1580** LUPTON *Sivqila* 130 When the Surgeon came before the Judge, and saw his poore Impatient there. ?**16..** *Seasonable Serm.* 39 (T.) Some ignorant impatients, when they have found themselves to smart with God's scourge. **1893** *Westm. Gaz.* 9 June 2/2 What the Unionist 'impatients' wants to get on at once to Clause 9.

imˈpatient, *v. rare.* [f. prec.: cf. F. *impatienter*, refl. *s'impatienter* to lose patience.] **a.** †*trans.* To await with impatience. **b.** *refl.* To become impatient, to lose patience. Hence †**imˈpatiented** *ppl. a.*, awaited with impatience.

1654–66 EARL ORRERY *Parthenissa* (1676) 382 As soon as the impatiented hour came, I went. *Ibid.* 538 At length the so impatiented night and hour came. **1813** SIR R. WILSON *Priv. Diary* II. 54 Amiable hosts, who did not impatient themselves even at the weather.

impatiently (ɪmˈpeɪʃəntlɪ), *adv.* [f. as prec. + -LY².] In an impatient manner.

1. Without endurance of suffering or discomfort; irritably. (In quot. 1593, Ardently, passionately.)

1490 CAXTON *Eneydos* vi. 25 His.. wyf bare it moche inpacyentli and sorowfully. **1593** NASHE *Christ's T.* (1613) 9, I love thee impatiently. **1601** SHAKS. *Jul. C.* II. i. 244 You.. too impatiently stampt with your foote. **1712** STEELE *Spect.* No. 424 ¶6 Speaking impatiently to Servants. **1816** SHELLEY *Alastor* 173 As if her heart impatiently endured Its bursting burthen.

2. With restless expectation or longing; with eager desire.

1632 J. HAYWARD tr. *Biondi's Eromena* 130 Impatiently expecting the Count of Bona's returne. **1766** GOLDSM. *Vic. W.* xxx, His sister ran impatiently to meet him. **1830** D'ISRAELI *Chas. I*, III. vii. 130 The Queen.. impatiently babbled the secret to Lady Carlisle. **1833** HT. MARTINEAU *Charmed Sea* i. 3 'Make haste!' cried the Russian, shaking his lance impatiently.

†**imˈpatientness.** *Obs. rare.* [-NESS.] The quality of being impatient; impatience.

1550 COVERDALE *Spir. Perle* xv. H vj b, Whensoeuer any [affliction or adversity] happen vnto hym, he is sore vexed wyth impacientnes. *Ibid.* xx. K v b, They power out al maner of impacientnes, bytternes, and spytefull poison against the rightuousnes of god. **1727** in BAILEY vol. II.

†**impatriˈotic,** *a. Obs. rare.* [f. IM-² + PATRIOTIC.] Not patriotic; unpatriotic. So †**imˈpatriotism,** want of patriotism.

1805 W. TAYLOR in *Ann. Rev.* III. 281 Nothing of impiety, but only of impatriotism. *Ibid.* 317 Every thing.. which infringes on our cosmopolitical duty is really impatriotic.

†**imˈpatron,** *v. Obs. rare.* [a. obs. F. *im-, empatroner, -patronir* (Godefroy, Cotgr.), a. It. *impatronire, impadronire* to make master of, put in possession of, f. *im-* (IM-¹) + F. *patron*, It. *padrone*, L. *patrōnus* PATRON, protector, master. Cf. EMPATRON.] *trans.* = IMPATRONIZE 1; *refl.* to make oneself master, possess oneself (of). Const. *with.*

1642 *Remark. Occur. North. Parts* 10 (D.) He.. impatroned himselfe with three peeces of ordinance.

†**imˈpatronage,** *v. Obs. rare.* [f. prec. after PATRONAGE.] *trans.* To put under a person's patronage; to dedicate.

1652 *F. Grevil's Sidney* Ep. ded. 2 His Matchless Poem seem'd providentially by him impatronag'd unto his Peerless Sister.

†**imˈpatronize,** *v. Obs.* [a. F. *impatroniser*, in 16th c. *-izer*: see IMPATRON and -IZE.]

1. *trans.* To put in possession *of*; usually *refl.* to take possession, make oneself master (*of*, also *upon*).

1577 FENTON *Gold. Epist.* 204 To confirme to him [Abraham] his promise, and to impatronize him of that religion for and in the name of such as shoulde descende of him. **1579** —— *Guicciard.* 537 To impatronise himselfe upon Rome and the whole estate ecclesiastike. **1600** J. PORY tr. *Leo's Africa* II. 388 They.. cast out of Africk the Romaines.. and wholie impatronized themselves of Barbarie. **1681** DUGDALE *Short View Late Troub. Eng.* 611 To impatronize themselves of many Cities and Strong-holds.

b. *transf.* To take possession of.

1611 COTGR., *Impatronisé*, impatronized, maistered. *a* **1649** DRUMM. OF HAWTH. *Hist. Jas. V*, Wks. (1711) 108 To impatronize and lay hold on the church rents and ecclesiastical goods. **1799** *Monthly Mag.* in *Spirit Pub. Jrnls.* (1800) III. 313 We him receiving and impatronising in our Dijon Infantry.

2. To patronize, favour.

1629 MAXWELL tr. *Herodian* (1635) 99 To make him away.. and to substitute another that would impatronize their lawlesse and licentious misdemeanours.

Hence †**imˌpatroniˈzation** (see quots.). *Obs.*

1611 COTGR., *Impatronisation*, an impatronization; th' absolute Maisterie, Seigneurie, or possession of. **1706** PHILLIPS, *Impatronization*, a putting into full possession of a Benefice. **1848** in WHARTON *Law Lex.*

impatshe: see IMPEACH.

impave (ɪmˈpeɪv), *v. rare.* [f. IM-¹ + PAVE *v.*] *trans.* To pave in; to set in a pavement.

1833 WORDSW. *Sonn. revis. Dunolly Castle*, There saw, impaved with rude fidelity Of art Mosaic, in a roofless floor An Eagle with stretched wings.

impavid (ɪmˈpævɪd), *a. rare.* [ad. L. *impavidus*, f. *im-* (IM-²) + *pavidus* fearful.]

Fearless, undaunted.

1857 G. LAWRENCE *Guy Liv.* xviii, He put the message into his pocket.. and won the rubber before he rose.. Impavid as the Horatian model-man. **1862** S. LUCAS *Secularia* 181 A high spirit.. resting impavid on its consciousness of right. **1897** *Globe* 12 Jan. 1/3 The flames were quenched, and the impavid student fared forth on his way.

Hence **imˈpavidly** *adv.*, fearlessly.

1849 THACKERAY *Pendennis* lxvi, Calverley and Coldstream would have looked on impavidly.

impaˈvidity. *rare.* [ad. L. type **impaviditās*, f. *impavidus*: see prec. and -ITY.] Fearlessness; in quot. used for 'foolhardiness'.

1604 PARSONS *3rd Pt. Three Convers. Eng.* 154 Not only Christian Diuyns, but heathen Philosophers also do accompt impauidity, or lacke of iust feare, as also audacity, presumption,.. for vices.

impawn (ɪmˈpɔːn), *v.* Also 6 **impaune;** 7 **empawn, -paun.** [f. IM-¹ + PAWN *v.* or *sb.*]

1. *trans.* To put in pawn; to pledge as security; to pawn.

1596 SHAKS. *1 Hen. IV*, IV. iii. 108 Let there be impawn'd Some suretie for a safe returne againe. **1625–6** PURCHAS *Pilgrims* II. 1269 He said he had impawned his Beard for a great summe to certaine Creditors. **1681** COLVIL *Whigs Supplic.* (1751) 63 Some of them empawn'd thir cloaks. **1814** MRS. J. WEST *Alicia de Lacy* III. 42 She offered to impawn the family jewels.

fig. **1838** EMERSON *War* Wks. 1884 XI. 196 A wise man will never impawn his future being and action, and decide beforehand what he shall do in a given extreme event.

b. *fig.* To pledge, plight (faith, etc.).

a **1628** F. GREVIL *Sidney* (1652) 32 My faith impawned to the Prince of Orange. *a* **1677** MANTON *Serm. Ps.* cxix. verse 92 Wks. 1872 VII. 426 God.. impawneth his truth with us to do us good. **1881** SWINBURNE *Mary Stuart* I. ii. 51 We held impawned The faith of Barnes.

2. *fig.* To risk the safety of, to put in hazard.

1613 SHERLEY *Trav. Persia* 23 Hee.. wished me to haue regard (if not to my selfe) yet to so many, which he did imagine were impawned in that misfortune by my meanes.

†**impay**, *v. Obs.* [f. IM-[1] + PAY *v.*: app. after It. *impagare* 'to pay home throughly' (Florio).] *trans.* To 'pay home', pay to the full what has been expended, reimburse, recoup.

1594 CAREW *Huarte's Exam. Wits* xiii. (1596) 229 It is a thing..vsed..to say such a one hath well impaied his trauaile, when he is well paied.

‖**impayable** (ɪm'peɪəb(ə)l, Fr. ɛ̃pɛjabl), *a.* [a. F. *impayable*, f. *im-* (IM-[2]) + *payer* (in OF.) to appease, satisfy, (mod.F.) to pay. Used in ME.; in mod. use often treated as French.]

†**1.** Implacable, unappeasable. *Obs.*

a **1340** HAMPOLE *Psalter* lxxxvii. 7 Impayable semes þi wraith.

2. That cannot be paid or discharged.

1797 S. J. PRATT in *Monthly Rev.* XXIII. 60 Impayable obligations. **1843** LD. HOUGHTON *Let.* in Wemyss Reid *Life* I. 300, I have mooted..the subject of the payment of the Roman Catholic Church in Ireland (which D'Orsay says is 'impayable').

‖**3. a.** Beyond price, priceless, invaluable. **b.** *colloq.* Going beyond ordinary limits; 'beyond anything' ('extraordinaire, très-plaisant, très-bizarre' Littré).

1818 LADY MORGAN *Autobiog.* (1859) 29, I must send you some of her notes, for they are *impayable.* **1823** SCOTT *Quentin D.* Introd., The cheese, the fruits, the salad..and the delicious white wine, each in their way were *impayables.* **1906** G. MEREDITH *Let.* 23 Nov. (1970) III. 1579 His [*sc.* Whistler's] tales of his student life in Paris..were *impayable.* **1954** P. BOTTOME *Against Whom?* xxiii. 177 As a patient, she is unsatisfactory..as a girl she is *impayable!*

impayl, impayre, obs. ff. IMPALE, IMPAIR.

impeach (ɪm'piːtʃ), *v.* Forms: α. 4–6 en-, empeche, 5–7 empeach. β. 5 enpesshe, enpesche, empeshe, 5–6 empesshe, -pesche, -peasche. γ. 6 impeche, impeache, 6– impeach. δ. 6 impesche, impeshe, (ympes(c)he), 7 impeash. ε. 6 *Sc.* empash, impash(e, impatshe, 6–7 em-, impasche, impass. [ME. *em-*, *enpechen*, later *empesche*, a. OF. *empechier*, *empeechier*, *empescher*, mod.F. *empêcher* (13th c. *empecier*, 12th c. (pple.) *empedicad* = Pr. *empedegar*):—late L. *impedicā-re* to catch, entangle (Ammianus), f. *im-* (IM-[1]) + *pedica* fetter, f. *pēs*, *ped-em* foot. In senses 4 and 5 treated as the representative of L. *impetĕre*. Cf. IMPEACHMENT.

The forms *empash*, *impashe* may be due to F. *empacher* (cf. Pr. *empaichar*); *impatshe* reflects It. *impacciare*; for the origin of the radicals of these forms, see DISPATCH *v.* (*Impeach* in Eng. displaced APPEACH *v.*, q.v. Cf. PEACH *v.*)]

A. Illustration of Forms.

α. *c* **1380** WYCLIF *Sel. Wks.* III. 294 þat wickid men..þere schullen dwelle in seyntewarie, and no man empeche hem bi processe of lawe. **1387–8, 1432–50** Enpeche [see B. 4]. **1494** FABYAN *Chron.* VII. ccxxxiii. 267 Y^{t} warke was for y^{t} tyme empeached and let. **1550** J. COKE *Eng. & Fr. Heralds* (1877) §153 You enpeche the welth of marchaundise. **1562** J. SHUTE *Cambine's Turk. Wars* 9b, Waiting continually to empeche him. **1650** tr. *Bacon's Hist. Life & Death* 51 That they might be (the Intention not at all empeached) both Safe and Effectual.

β. *c* **1474** CAXTON *Chesse* lf. 5a, Bodyly sight enpessheth and letteth..the knowleche of subtyll thinges. *c* **1477** —— *Jason* 49 The first man that..shold empesshe him of the royame of Mirmidone. **1483** *Pilgr. Sowle* (Caxton) v. i. 92b, Ther is nothyng that may therof enpeschen hym. **1530** PALSGR. 531/2, I empesshe or let one of his purpose. **1549** Empesche [see B. 1].

γ. **1533–4** *Act 25 Hen. VIII*, c. 9 §6 Any person..whiche shall be impeched to haue offended contrarie to the forme and effecte of this estatute. **1536** *Act 27 Hen. VIII*, c. 42 Any suche ordynaunce..as myght by annye meane hynder thadvauncement..of the..Worde of God..or impeache the knowlege of suche other good letters. **1577–87** HOLINSHED *Chron.* III. 963/1 Minded to impeach their passage. **1600**, etc. [see B. 3].

δ. **1548–67** THOMAS *Ital. Dict.*, *Impedire*, to let or impeshe. **1549** *Compl. Scot.* xv. 130 Mony dificil impedimentis.. maye impesche hym. **1567** FENTON *Trag. Disc.* 14 He went about to ympeshe his expedition. **1624** in Sir. R. Gordon *Hist. Earls Sutherland* (1813) 381 We will forbear to impeash your ma^{tie} any further.

ε. **1538** Impatshe [see B. 1b]. **1566** PAINTER *Pal. Pleas.* 34b, They were not able..to impache his corps, in tombe fast closed and buried. **1597** MONTGOMERIE *Cherrie & Slae* 808 Thy foly..Empashed him to pow. **1597** LOWE *Chirurg.* (1634) 124 To anoint..with the milke of a bitch which impasseth it to grow white. **1604** *Crt. Bk. Barony of Uric* (1892) 7 The Lard being impaschit throw thair dalie complenttis.

B. Signification.

†**1.** *trans.* To impede, hinder, prevent. *Obs.*

c **1380** WYCLIF *Sel. Wks.* III. 317 He schal dwelle þere alle his lif, and no man enpeche hym. **1480** CAXTON *Chron. Eng.* ccliii, They drad..that he wold have enpesshed that delyveraunce. **1533** BELLENDEN *Livy* IV. (1822) 320 The consulis, seand the tribunis impesche every thing that thay desirit afore the senate. **1549** *Compl. Scot.* vi. 56 The..eird empeschis the soune to gyf lycht to the mune. **1577–87** HOLINSHED *Scot. Chron.* (1805) II. 256 To impeach the Englishmen from setting on land any vittles there. *a* **1649** DRUMM. OF HAWTH. *Hist. Jas. I* Wks. (1711) 11 It hath been your valour..which heretofore empeached our conquest and progress in France. **1690** LEYBOURN *Curs. Math.* 586 A Ditch, of sufficient..breadth, and depth, to impeach the Assaults of an Enemy.

†**b.** *refl.* (= OF. *s'empêcher*, It. *impacciarsi*). To embarrass or trouble oneself. *Obs.*

1484 CAXTON *Curiall* 1 By thexample of me that empesshe my selue for to serue in the Courte Ryall. **1538** in Strype *Eccl. Mem.* (1721) I. xl. 313 Pole said he should do well not to impatshe himself with reading of the story of Nicolo Machavello.

†**c.** To hinder access to; to blockade. *Obs.*

1586 LD. BURGHLEY in *Leycester Corr.* (Camden) 360 Flieboates..are fittest to impeche thos kind of havens.

†**2.** To hinder the action, progress, or well-being of; to affect detrimentally or prejudicially; to hurt, harm, injure, endamage, impair. *Obs.*

1563 BP. SANDYS in Ellis *Orig. Lett.* Ser. I. II. 195 To preserve my honestie from malice whiche mynded to impeache yt. **1568** GRAFTON *Chron.* II. 391 They did empeche the honor of the kinges person. **1604** T. WRIGHT *Passions* I. iii. 12 The coldnesse of the water, earth, and ayre much impeacheth the vertue of his heate. **1691** E. TAYLOR *Behmen's Theos. Philos.* xvii. 25 Anything that might tend to impeach his perfection.

3. To challenge, call in question, cast an imputation upon, attack; to discredit, disparage.

1590 SHAKS. *Mids. N.* II. i. 214 You doe impeach your modesty too much To leave the Citty, and commit your selfe Into the hands of one that loues you not. **1600** J. PORY tr. *Leo's Africa* II. 42 Neither am I ignorant, how much mine owne credit is impeached. **1612** T. TAYLOR *Comm. Titus* i. 6 Because their name and honour was impeached. **1743** FIELDING *Conversation* Wks. 1784 IX. 364 It would by no means impeach the general rule. **1767** BLACKSTONE *Comm.* II. xxx. 444 A contract for any valuable consideration, as for marriage, for money, for work done,..can never be impeached at law. **1888** MISS GREEN *Behind Closed Doors* iv, My daughter's happiness is threatened and her character impeached.

4. *gen.* To bring a charge or accusation against; to accuse *of*, charge *with*.

c **1380** [see A. α]. **1387–8** T. USK *Test. Love* I. vi. (Skeat) l. 86 Whiche thing..I am bolde to mayntaine, and namely in distroiyng of a wrong, al shulde I therthrough enpeche myne owne frere, if he wer gilty. **1428** *Surtees Misc.* (1888) 3 He was empeched of forgeyng of fals osmundes. **1432–50** tr. *Higden* (Rolls) VII. 530 Godwyn was enpeched [L. *inculpatus*] for he had gadered so grete an oost. **1590** *Eng. Romayne Life* in *Harl. Misc.* (Malh.) II. 167 Nothing..that might impeach me either with error or vntrueth. **1648** *Art. Peace* §18 in *Milton's Wks.*, That no Person..be troubled, impeached, sued, inquieted or molested, for..any offence.. comprised within the said Act. **1794** GODWIN *Cal. Williams* 216 Go to the next justice of the peace and impeach us. **1840** DICKENS *Old C. Shop* lviii, Fearing every moment to hear the marchioness impeached.

b. Sometimes in restricted sense (see quot. 1617): To give accusatory evidence against; to 'peach' upon. (In quot. 1820 *absol.* To 'peach'.)

1617 MINSHEU *Duct. Ling.*, *To Impeach*, or accuse one guiltie of the same crime whereof he which impeacheth is accused. **1676** WYCHERLEY *Pl. Dealer* v. i, Like a Thief, because you know your self most guilty, you impeach your Fellow Criminals first. **1701** LUTTRELL *Brief Rel.* (1857) V. 59 A person, lately accused for robbing on the highway and acquitted, has impeach't 13 of his gang. **1731** FIELDING *Letter writer* II. ix, Would it not be your wisest way to impeach your companions? **1820** G. WATSON TAYLOR *Profligate* IV. i, The whole plot is laid open. Mr. Allcourt has impeached.

c. To find fault with (a *thing*), to censure.

1813 SCOTT *Trierm.* III. xxxviii, And so fair the slumberer seems, That De Vaux impeach'd his dreams. **1872** BROWNING *Fifine* lxxxv, Do you approve, not foolishly impeach The falsehood! **1876** GEO. ELIOT *Dan. Der.* v. xxxvi, Grandcourt's appearance..was not impeached with foreignness.

5. *spec.* To accuse of treason or other high crime or misdemeanour (usually against the state) before a competent tribunal: see IMPEACHMENT 5.

1568 GRAFTON *Chron.* II. 353 Whether the Lordes and commons might without the kings will empeche the same officers and justices upon their offenses in the parliament or not. **1647** CLARENDON *Hist. Reb.* III. §10 Mr. Pym at the bar [of the house of peers], and in the name of all the commons of England, impeached Thomas earl of Strafford..of high treason, and several other heinous crimes and misdemeanours. **1769** BLACKSTONE *Comm.* IV. xix. 261 The representatives of the people, or House of Commons, cannot properly judge; because their constituents are the parties injured; and can therefore only impeach. **1863** H. COX *Instit.* I. x. 229 Latimer was impeached and accused by the voice of the Commons. **1868** *Trial Andrew Johnson* 3 On Monday, February the 24th, 1868, the House of Representatives of the Congress of the United States resolved to impeach Andrew Johson, President of the United States, of high crimes and misdemeanors. **1883** G. T. CURTIS *Buchanan* II. xii. 247 In regard to the President, it was their duty to make a specific charge, to investigate it openly, and to impeach him before the Senate, if the evidence afforded reasonable ground to believe that the charge could be substantiated.

b. Applied to analogous judicial processes, e.g. the prosecution of state officials by the tribunes of ancient Rome.

1734 tr. *Rollin's Anc. Hist.* (1827) I. 353 Mago on his arrival at Carthage was impeached. **1838** ARNOLD *Hist. Rome* (1846) I. xiii. 231 One of the tribunes impeached him before the assembly of the tribes. **1840** THIRLWALL *Greece* VIII. 329 At Athens after his departure he was formally impeached and condemned to death.

Hence **im'peached** *ppl. a.*, **im'peaching** *vbl. sb.*

c **1400** MAUNDEV. (Roxb.) ix. 34 He myght seurly dwell in þat citee withouten empeching of any man. **1632** LITHGOW *Trav.* v. 179 The chiefe obstacle, and impeaching of so great an Army from taking it. **1751** EARL ORRERY *Remarks Swift* (1752) 60 The four impeached lords. **1827** HALLAM *Const. Hist.* (1876) III. xvi. 234 A charge against the impeached lords.

impeach (ɪm'piːtʃ), *sb.* [f. prec. vb.]

†**1.** Hindrance, impediment, prevention. *Obs.*

1511 in Tytler *Hist. Scot.* (1864) III. 385 The old worn pelt..who presently reigneth alone, and governeth without empeasche. **1605** P. WOODHOUSE *Flea* (1877) 18 Without all interrupting or impeach. **1611** SPEED *Hist. Gt. Brit.* VII. iv. §3. 205 These..got the..command of military affayres without impeach.

†**2.** Injury, damage, detriment. *Obs.*

1575 GASCOIGNE *Hearbes* Wks. (1587) 149 So farre thou mayst set out thy selfe without empeach or crime. **1586** BRIGHT *Melanch.* x. 47 The soul receiueth..no impeach, or impayre of cunning. **1625** tr. *Boccaccio's Decam.* II. 156 Without any impeach or blemish to his honor.

3. Challenge, calling in question; accusation, charge, impeachment.

1590 SHAKS. *Com. Err.* v. i. 269 Why what an intricate impeach is this? **1591** *Troub. Raigne K. John* II. (1611) 85 What kindship, lenitie, or Christian raigne, Rules in the man to beare this foul impeach? **1593** SHAKS. *3 Hen. VI*, I. iv. 60 It is Warres prize, to take all Vantages, And tenne to one, is no impeach of Valour. **1885** *Sat. Rev.* 14 Feb. 205/1 The delightful intricacy of this impeach..is highly characteristic.

impeachability (ɪmpiːtʃə'bɪlɪtɪ). [f. next + -ITY.] The quality of being impeachable.

1867 *Pall Mall G.* 10 Jan. 8 The inquiry instituted concerning the impeachability of President Johnson.

impeachable (ɪm'piːtʃəb(ə)l), *a.* Also 6 **empechable**. [f. IMPEACH *v.* + -ABLE.] Capable of being impeached, called in question, or accused; liable to impeachment; chargeable.

1503–4 *Act 19 Hen. VII*, c. 27 §9 The seid Maire..[shall] be nott hurted vexed impleted empeched nor empechable. **1533–4** *Act 25 Hen. VIII*, c. 14 [He] standeth in danger, and is impechable of heresie. **1678** *Lively Orac.* iv. §27. 292 Would God none but the Romanist were impeachable of this detention of Scripture. **1796** MORSE *Amer. Geog.* I. 573 All officers are impeachable. **1885** *Law Rep.* 10 Prob. Div. 192 Assuming the deed not to be impeachable on those grounds.

impeacher (ɪm'piːtʃə(r)). [f. as prec. + -ER[1].] One who impeaches.

†**1.** One who prevents, hinders, or impedes. *Obs.*

1641 MILTON *Ch. Govt.* I. vi, Instead of finding Prelaty an impeacher of Schisme or faction.

2. One who accuses or brings charges (of treason, etc.). See IMPEACH *v.* 4, 5.

1552 HULOET, Accuser or empeacher, *accusator.* **1656** EARL MONM. *Advt. fr. Parnass.* 178 The Prince..appeared a friend to the impeachers. **1788** (*title*) Reflexions on Impeachers and Impeaching; addressed to Warren Hastings, Esq. **1877** SYMONDS *Renaiss. Italy, Reviv. Learn.* 232 A violent impeacher and impugner of the living.

impeachment (ɪm'piːtʃmənt). Also 5–7 em-; for Forms, see IMPEACH *v.* [a. OF. *empechement*, *empeschement*, mod.F. *empêchement* (whence med.L. *impechementum*, *impechiamentum*), f. *empêche-r* to IMPEACH: see -MENT. In senses 4, 5, the word was treated as the repr. of med.L. *impetītio*, from *impetĕre* to attack, accuse, with which however it had no etymological connexion.] The action of impeaching.

†**1.** Hindrance, prevention, obstruction; impediment, obstacle. *Obs.*

1432 *Paston Lett.* No. 18. I. 31 Eny thing that mighte yeve empeschement or let therto. **1491** CAXTON *Vitas Patr.* (1495) 94 The devyll..came to vysyte hym for to gyue to hym empesshement & lettynge in his contemplacyons. **1531** ELYOT *Gov.* I. xv, Nowe haue I..declared the chiefe impechementes of excellent lernynge. **1569** STOCKER tr. *Diod. Sic.* II. xx. 72/2 Thus without empechement or stoppe, passed Cassander through the countrey of Thessaly. **1601** R. JOHNSON *Kingd. & Commw.* (1603) 140 He invaded Livonia without impeachment. **1621** *Sc. Acts Jas. VI* (1814) 696/2 To breid confusioun and Empaschement to þe lordis in..decyding of materis. *a* **1674** MILTON *Hist. Mosc.* iv, Boris..without impeachment now ascended the throne.

†**2.** Detriment, impairment, injury, damage. *Obs.*

1548 GEST *Pr. Masse* in H. G. Dugdale *Life* App. i. (1840) 136 Thee..unsufferable empechemente bothe of Christes honoure and our solles salvation. **1587** HARRISON *England* II. xxiii. (1877) I. 349 No man hath yet susteined anie manner of impeachment through the coldness of the water. **1591** SHAKS. *Two Gent.* I. iii. 15 To let him spend his time no more at home; Which would be great impeachment to his age. **1648** EVELYN *Mem.* (1857) III. 14 If they can attain the north without great impeachment..the game may yet be balanced to the purpose.

3. A calling in question or discrediting; disparagement, depreciation.

1568 GRAFTON *Chron.* II. 1281 Certaine armes..borne time out of minde, without chalenge or empechment. **1658** SLINGSBY *Diary* (1836) 213 Without an impeachment to their honour. **1794** GODWIN *Cal. Williams* 13 The reputation of my courage is sufficiently established not to expose it to any impeachment. **1830** HERSCHEL *Stud. Nat. Phil.* 111 The extreme injustice of this impeachment of their character.

4. Accusation, charge. *Obs.* exc. in phr. ***the soft impeachment***.

1387 TREVISA *Higden* (Rolls) VII. 165 If sche passe unhurte bare foot..uppon nyne brennynge cultres or schares, let here eskape of his enpechement [*ab impetitione ista*]. **1413** *Pilgr. Sowle* (Caxton) I. xxii. 17b, Thenne with an hye voys herd I one speke to my ful grete empesshement. **1594** SHAKS. *Rich. III*, II. ii. 22 The King prouok'd to it by the Queene, Deuis'd impeachments to imprison him. **1612**

T. TAYLOR *Comm. Titus* ii. 12 Be it thou beest neuer so harmles, that thou fearest no mans impeachment. **1775** SHERIDAN *Rivals* v. iii, Sir Lucius O'Trigger—ungrateful as you are—I own the soft impeachment—pardon my blushes, I am Delia. **1865** BUSHNELL *Vicar. Sacr.* Introd. (1868) 33 A considerable impeachment of heresy. **1892** STEVENSON *Across the Plains* 161 The Cigarette..denied the soft impeachment.

b. *Law.* ***without impeachment of waste*** (= law L. *absque impetitione vasti*): 'a reservation frequently made to a tenant for life, that no man shall proceed against him for waste committed' (Wharton *Law Lex.*).

1415 *E.E. Wills* (1882) 25, I wolle that..my weyf [haue] it to terme of her lyue wyth-oute empeschement of wast. **1503–4** *Act 19 Hen. VII*, c. 33 §1 To holde all the seid Maners..without impechment of Wast. **1767** BLACKSTONE *Comm.* II. xviii. 283 Unless their leases be made..without impeachement of waste, *absque impetitione vasti*; that is, with a provision or protection that no man shall *impetere*, or sue him, for waste committed. **1858** LD. ST. LEONARDS *Handy-Bk. Prop. Law* xvii. 124 Under your marriage settlement you are tenant for life, without impeachment of waste.

5. The accusation and prosecution of a person for treason or other high crime or misdemeanour before a competent tribunal; in Great Britain, 'the judicial process by which any man, from the rank of a peer downwards, may be tried before the House of Lords at the instance of the House of Commons' (*Dict. Eng. Hist.*); in U.S., a similar process in which the accusers are the House of Representatives and the court is the Senate.

1640–4 in Rushw. *Hist. Coll.* III. (1692) I. 356 The Lords sat upon the Impeachment against the Judges and Bishop Wren. **1667** MARVELL *Corr.* Wks. 1872–5 II. 221 This morning severall members of our House did..move the House to proceed to an impeachment against the Earle of Clarinden. **1754–62** HUME *Hist. Eng.* III. 15 (Seager) The first impeachment by the house of commons seems to have been carried up against Lord Latimer in the latter end of Edward the Third's reign. **1789** *Constit. U.S.* ii. §4 The President, Vice-President, and all Civil officers of the United States, shall be removed from office on impeachment for, and conviction of, treason, bribery or other high crimes and misdemeanors. **1805** S. CHASE in *Life Rufus King* (1897) IV. 444 Congratulations on my acquittal by the Senate of the Impeachment by the House of Representatives. **1827** HALLAM *Const. Hist.* (1876) II. ix. 105 The articles of Strafford's impeachment. **1867** *Nation* (N.Y.) 14 Feb. 121 Discussion of the power of the Senate to suspend the President [Johnson] during his impeachment.

impearl (ɪmˈpɜːl), *v.* Also 6–9 em-, (7–8 in-). [ad. F. *emperle-r* (16th c. in Littré) or It. *imperlare* (Florio): see IM-[1] and PEARL.]

1. *trans.* To deck with pearls or pearl-like drops: said of dew, rain, tears.

1591 SYLVESTER *Du Bartas* I. iii. 1117 The flowry Meads, Impearl'd with tears, the sweet Aurora sheads. **1598** FLORIO, *Imperlare*, to empearle or decke with pearles, to set with pearle. **1706** WATTS *Horæ Lyr.*, *To Mitio* II. 34 Heavenly dews, Nightly descending, shall impearl the grass. **1729** SAVAGE *Wanderer* II. 173 Here Love inpearls each moment with a tear. **1824** T. FENBY *On a Young Girl* i, Tears will soon her cheek impearl. **1876** JAS. GRANT *One of the 600*, vii, Groves and meadows all empearled with dew. *fig.* **1818** KEATS *Endym.* III. 102 On gold sand impearl'd With lily shells.

2. To make pearly or pearl-like.

a **1639** T. CAREW *Obseq. Lady Anne Hay* 52 Another shall Impearle thy teeth. **1794** *Poetry* in *Ann. Reg.* 421 Gems dissolv'd impearl her luscious drink.

3. To form into pearl-like drops.

c **1586** C'TESS PEMBROKE *Ps.* CXXXIII. (R.), The teares the morne doth shedd, Which ly on ground Empearled round. **1667** MILTON *P.L.* v. 747 Dew-drops, which the Sun Impearls on every leaf and every flouer. **1757** DYER *Fleece* I. 361 The crystal dews impearl'd upon the grass. **1839** BAILEY *Festus* i. (1852) 11 The spheres themselves are but as shining noughts Upon the mantle of the night impearled.

Hence **imˈpearled** *ppl. a.*

1598 DRAYTON *Heroic. Ep.* xx. 126 A rich impearled Coronet. **1881** ROSSETTI *Ball. & Sonn.* 162 Let Time see Its flowering crest impearled and orient.

impeccability (ɪmpɛkəˈbɪlɪtɪ). [ad. med.L. *impeccābilitās*, f. *impeccābilis* (see next). Cf. F. *impeccabilité* (1609 in Hatz.-Darm.).] The quality or character of being impeccable; freedom from liability to sin, wrong-doing, or error.

1613 SALKELD *Treat. Angels* 234 (L.) It doth cause an everlasting impeccability. **1627** [see IMPECCANCY]. **1670** G. H. *Hist. Cardinals* I. I. 27 Great Volumes in defence of the infallibility and impeccability of the Pope. **1725** tr. *Dupin's Eccl. Hist. 17th C.* I. v. 165 The Qualities of the Soul of Jesus Christ..its Knowledge, its Wisdom..and its Impeccability. **1879** G. MEREDITH *Egoist* III. viii. 151, I have never pretended to impeccability.

impeccable (ɪmˈpɛkəb(ə)l), *a.* (*sb.*) [ad. late L. *impeccābil-is*, f. *im-* (IM-[2]) + *peccāre* to sin: see -BLE. Cf. F. *impeccable* (15th c. in Godef. *Compl.*).]

1. Of persons: Not capable of or liable to sin; exempt from the possibility of sinning or doing wrong.

1531 LATIMER *Serm. & Rem.* (Parker Soc.) 325 No..judges..so deeply confirmed in grace, or so impeccable. *a* **1555** *Ibid.* 226 Though she never sinned, yet she was not so impeccable, but she might have sinned. **1670** G. H. *Hist. Cardinals* I. I. 25 The Pope is not only infallible, but also impeccable. **1736** BOLINGBROKE *Patriot.* (1749) 156 He knows that neither he nor his ministers are infallible, nor impeccable. **1849** ROBERTSON *Serm.* Ser. I. v. 71 No soul is absolutely impeccable.

2. Of things: Faultless, unerring.

1620 BP. HALL *Hon. Mar. Clergy* §8. 43 If we honor the man, must wee hold his pen impeccable? **1864** BOWEN *Logic* vii. 184 We need some more succinct mode than that of severally applying to each Syllogism all these Rules, before we can be satisfied that it is impeccable.

3. *sb.* One who is impeccable.

1748 RICHARDSON *Clarissa* (1811) IV. 7 A brace of impeccables, an't please ye. **1887** MARG. W. LAURENCE in W. Gladden *Parish Probl.* 144 A row of these same impeccables.

Hence **imˈpeccably** *adv.*, in an impeccable manner; without liability to sin.

1874 R. TYRWHITT *Sketch. Club* 221 Painters cannot..follow it [the Christian faith] impeccably.

impeccableness (ɪmˈpɛkəb(ə)lnɪs). [f. IMPECCABLE *a.* + -NESS.] The character or condition of being impeccable.

1696 J. SERGEANT *Method to Sci.* I. vi. 64 Original Sin, Impeccableness in the Saints in Heaven, Obdurateness in Sin in the Divels. **1901** F. H. BURNETT *Making of Marchioness* II. xiv. 233 With her ruby and her coronets and her lodging-house street, she is of an impeccableness—she does not even know she could be doubted. **1952** *New Yorker* 15 Nov. 166/2 They are inclined to be seduced by pieces whose chief charm rests in a thin, careful impeccableness.

†**imˈpeccance.** *Obs.* [ad. eccl. L. *impeccāntia*: see IMPECCANT and -ANCE.] = next.

1677 GALE *Crt. Gentiles* III. 160 The Scholemen have been great Champions for this Philosophic Pelagian Impeccance or state of Perfection in this life.

impeccancy (ɪmˈpɛkənsɪ). [ad. eccl. L. *impeccāntia* (Tertullian): see next and -ANCY.] The quality of being impeccant; sinlessness; inerrancy.

1614 BP. HALL *No Peace w. Rome* §5 She..stubbornely challenges unto her Chayre a certaine Impeccancy of judgement (that wee may borrow a word from Tertullian). **1627** DONNE *Serm.* clvii. Wks. (Alford) VI. 268 A present Impeccancy and a future Impeccability. *a* **1711** KEN *Preparatives* Poet. Wks. 1721 IV. 136 Life ne'er is wholly free from Sins, Impeccancy at Death begins.

impeccant (ɪmˈpɛkənt), *a.* [f. IM-[2] + L. *peccāns*, *peccānt-em*, pres. pple. of *peccāre* to sin.] Not sinning; sinless; unerring.

a **1763** BYROM *Ep. to G. Lloyd* (R.), Poor dogs of some sort, and impeccant half-asses. **1883** *Q. Rev.* Jan. 118 The pledger is certainly not always impeccant. **1890** *Standard* 5 Apr. 6/1 The hero..is neither impeccable nor impeccant.

impectinate (ɪmˈpɛktɪnət), *a.* *Entom.* [f. IM-[2] + PECTINATE.] Not pectinate; not comb-toothed: said of the antennæ of insects, and other parts, which are in other cases *pectinate*.

In recent Dicts.

impectoral (ɪmˈpɛktərəl), *a.* [f. IM-[2] + L. *pectus*, *pector-* breast + -AL[1], after *pectoral*.] Without a breast. (In quot. *humorous*.)

1860 RUSSELL *Diary India* I. i. 8 The gentlemen who preside over favourite dishes, such as an impectoral turkey.

impecuniary (ɪmpɪˈkjuːnɪərɪ), *a.* [f. IM-[2] + PECUNIARY.]

1. = IMPECUNIOUS.

1814 BYRON *Wks.* (1832) III. 95 Mr. Claughton, of impecuniary memory. **1825** LAMB *Eliana*, *Illustr. Defunct* (1867) 413 Many an impecuniary epicure has gloated over his locked-up warrant for future wealth. **1825** *New Monthly Mag.* XIII. 212 The impecuniary classes.

2. Not pecuniary; not having to do with money.

1855 BAGEHOT *Lit. Stud.* (1879) I. 268 It is in vain that in this hemisphere we endeavour after impecuniary fancies.

impecuniosity (ɪmpɪkjuːnɪˈɒsɪtɪ). [f. IMPECUNIOUS + -ITY.] The quality or condition of being impecunious; lack of money.

1818 SCOTT *Let. to J. B. S. Morritt* 7 Dec. in *Lockhart*, A certain degree of impecuniosity, a necessity of saving cheese parings and candle ends. **1850** W. IRVING *Goldsmith* 222 Hiffernan..elevated the emptiness of his purse into the dignity of a disease, which he termed impecuniosity. **1874** L. STEPHEN *Hours in Library* (1892) II. v. 145 He [Massinger], like most of his brethren, suffered grievously from impecuniosity.

impecunious (ɪmpɪˈkjuːnɪəs), *a.* [f. IM-[2] + PECUNIOUS. Cf. rare F. *impécunieux* (Littré).] Having no money, penniless; in want of money.

1596 NASHE *Saffron Walden* O ij b, A poore impecunious creature. **1599** B. JONSON *Cynthia's Rev.* v. ii, Put him out, an impecunious creature. **1859** *Daily Tel.* 14 Feb. 4/6 To this paradise of credit the simple and impecunious addressed their letters. **1891** MRS. RIDDELL *Mad Tour* 69 A train of impecunious camp followers.

imped (ˈɪmpɛd), *sb.* [f. IM-[2] + L. *pēs*, *ped-* foot.] A footless creature: used by R. Owen to render Aristotle's ἄπους.

1861 OWEN in *Life* (1894) II. 119 Aristotle had divided the group into bipeds, quadrupeds and impeds.

imped (ɪmpt, ˈɪmpɪd), *ppl. a.* [f. IMP *v.* + -ED[1].] Grafted, engrafted, implanted, eked: see IMP *v.*

c **1440** *Promp. Parv.* 259/2 *Impyd* (*Pynson* or graffed), *insertus.* **1587** TURBERV. *Trag. T.* (1837) 10 With ympèd quilles so prowde a pitch to flie. **1593** DRAYTON *Past.* Ecl. vii. 98 Cupid..Whose imped wings with spekled plumes be dight. **1621** FLETCHER *Pilgrim* I. i, None of your impt bravadoes.

impedance (ɪmˈpiːdəns). [f. IMPEDE *v.* + -ANCE.] **1.** *Electr.* **a.** The overall opposition to an electric current, arising from the combined effect of resistance *R* and reactance *X* and measured by the ratio of the e.m.f. to the resulting current (peak or r.m.s. values); it may be represented as a scalar quantity whose value is $\sqrt{(R^2 + X^2)}$ or as a complex number $R + jX$.

1886 HEAVISIDE *Electr. Pap.* (1892) II. 64 Let us call the ratio of the impressed force to the current in a line when electrostatic induction is ignorable the Impedance of the line, from the verb impede. *Ibid.* 126 The impedance may be independent of the frequency, or a constant. **1888** LODGE in *Rep. Brit. Assoc.*, Impedance of conductors to Leyden-jar discharges and to Lightning. **1923** E. W. MARCHANT *Radio Telegr.* ii. 15 If the conductor is a long straight wire it offers comparatively little obstruction or 'impedance' to the passage of a current; while, if it is wound up into a coil it will offer a very high 'impedance' to the passage of the high-frequency current. **1926** A. T. DOVER *Theory & Pract. Alternating Currents* iii. 49 The sides *OC*, *CE*, *OE* of triangle *OCE* are proportional to the resistance, reactance, and impedance respectively. On account of this feature the triangle *OCE*, when drawn to an ohm scale, is called the impedance triangle of the circuit. Impedance is therefore a complex quantity, i.e. it is only completely specified when its magnitude and inclination, or alternatively its two perpendicular components with respect to the current, are given. **1930** M. G. MALTI *Electr. Circuit Analysis* vii. 87 A sine voltage $E_{12} = 70 - j50$ is impressed on a series circuit of impedance $Z_L = 15$ cis 30° ohms. What is the complex expression for the current? **1931** MOYER & WOSTREL *Radio Handbk.* II. 76 The term $\sqrt{(R^2 + X^2)}$, known as the impedance of the circuit, takes the place in alternating-current calculations of the resistance in direct-current work. **1948** A. L. ALBERT *Radio Fund.* v. 128 If the impressed voltage is divided by the input current of *any* line, a value of impedance is obtained, and for *any* line this is called the input impedance. *Ibid.* 129 The characteristic impedance, usually designated by Z_0, is the input impedance of a line infinite in length. **1961** H. JASIK *Antenna Engin. Handbk.* xxxi. 2 A variable load impedance connected to a source will receive the maximum possible power from the source when it is adjusted to equal the complex conjugate of the impedance of the source. **1962** C. SUSSKIND *Encycl. Electronics* 422/2 The impedance of dynamic, ribbon, carbon, and magnetic microphones is nearly always less than 40,000 ohms and is essentially resistive.

b. Something that has impedance and may be made part of a circuit.

1935 CAMPBELL & CHILDS *Measurement of Inductance, Capacitance, & Frequency* xiii. 260 The unknown impedance Z is put in series with the known resistance R, and across them is connected a potential divider with slider Q. **1966** *McGraw-Hill Encycl. Sci. & Technol.* VII. 39/1 Standard resistors, capacitors, and inductors are often used as comparisons for unknown impedances.

2. *Mech.* and *Acoustics.* Any of several analogous properties of oscillatory mechanical systems that represent the force, pressure, etc., necessary to produce a given speed, rate of flow, etc., esp. ***mechanical impedance***, the ratio of the force on an oscillating body or particle to the resulting velocity; ***specific acoustic impedance***, in a wave, the ratio of the (excess) pressure at any point to the resulting particle velocity (i.e. the mechanical impedance per unit area of the wave-front); ***acoustic*** (or ***acoustical***) ***impedance***, the ratio of the average (excess) pressure over an imaginary surface in a wave to the resulting rate of volume flow across it (i.e. the specific acoustic impedance, averaged over the surface, divided by the area of the surface).

The qualifying adjs. are often omitted in contexts where there is no danger of ambiguity.

1919 A. G. WEBSTER in *Proc. Nat. Acad. Sci.* V. 275 (*heading*) Acoustical impedance, and the theory of horns and of the phonograph. *Ibid.*, The term 'impedance'..has been productive of very great convenience in the theory of alternating currents of electricity. Unfortunately, engineers have not seemed to notice that the idea may be made as useful in mechanics and acoustics as in electricity. In fact, in such apparatus as the telephone one may combine the notions of electrical and mechanical impedance with great advantage. *Ibid.*, If we have any oscillating system into which a volume of air *X* periodically enters under an excess pressure p, I propose to define the impedance by the *complex* ratio $Z = p/\dot{X}$. **1927** I. B. CRANDALL *Theory Vibrating Syst.* ii. 71 In most parts of the text it is convenient to take the mechanical impedance as the ratio of maximum force to maximum velocity. Strictly, the velocity is analogous to current density rather than to total current... The *acoustic* impedance per unit area, *divided by the area*, is what corresponds most closely to the electrical impedance. **1934** N. W. MCLACHLAN *Loud Speakers* i. 4 The difference between acoustical and mechanical impedance must not be confused. In the one case waves travel in some form of conduit or channel which impedes their progress. The greater the area the smaller the impedance. In the mechanical form something is being driven, so the greater the area driving the medium the greater the impedance opposing motion. **1936** P. M. MORSE *Vibration & Sound* vi. 192 A consideration of the behavior of the specific acoustic impedance of a plane wave will enable us to work out the details of its interaction with various mechanical systems. **1953** *Sci. News* XXIX. 11 Whenever in the layers lying

below the bed of the sea there is a sudden change in the acoustic impedance (that is in the product of the density of the material and the velocity of sound waves in it), there is a reflecting boundary. **1955** HUETER & BOLT *Sonics* ii. 33 The concept of acoustic impedance is useful in the analysis of lumped systems, such as cavity resonators, sirens, jets, etc. **1960** R. B. LINDSAY *Mech. Radiation* ix. 218 The excess pressure in a sound wave is taken to correspond with the electromotive force, and the volume current (the product of the particle velocity ξ and the area of the wavefront S) is assumed to be analogous to the electric current. Hence it is natural to define the acoustic impedance of a wave as $Z = Pe/X$, where X = volume current = $S\xi$. With the use of the complex notation for wave quantities the impedance will usually be complex. We first examine.. the case of a plane harmonic wave of angular frequency w... The impedance of such a wave is then $Z = \rho_0 V/S$, a real quantity. The numerator is called the specific acoustic impedance of a plane wave and denoted by Z_s. It is the impedance for a unit area of wavefront. **1961** BICKLEY & TALBOT *Introd. Theory Vibrating Syst.* xi. 139 The example is that of torsional waves on a shaft... The [angular] velocity is proportional to the transmitted torque... Now in the electrical analogy the ratio of force to velocity is that of e.m.f. to current, a ratio which the electrical engineer calls impedance. It is therefore convenient to call the ratio of transmitted torque to angular velocity (and the analogous quantity in other cases) the transmission impedance. **1963** C. T. MORROW *Shock & Vibration Engin.* I. vi. 127 A high impedance indicates that even a large force results in little motion; it suggests massiveness and rigidity. A low impedance indicates that motion is easy to produce; it suggests lightness and flexibility. A resistive impedance indicates that the energy supplied at the point is absorbed, as in a dashpot... A reactive impedance indicates that energy supplied is stored, as in.. a compressed spring.

3. Special Comb.: **impedance bond**, a kind of rail bond used to connect electrified rails in adjoining signalling sections, having a low resistance (so that the direct traction current can pass unhindered) and a high inductance (so that the alternating signalling currents are confined to their respective sections); **impedance-matching**, the adjustment of impedances in such a way as to minimize the power reflected or the reduction in the power transferred that occurs when an oscillatory current or other wave meets a change in impedance; also *attrib.*

1926 HARDING & EWING *Electr. Railway Engineering* (ed. 3) xix. 258 The development of the two-rail signal system making use of impedance bonds.. marked the beginning of a new era in the development of the new railway signal systems. Practically all of the automatic block signals which are being installed on both alternating- and direct-current railways at present are of this general type. **1967** G. F. FIENNES *I tried to run Railway* v. 49 Installing impedance bonds in the track. **1929** E. MALLETT *Telegr. & Telephony* vii. 160 Impedance matching is necessary in order that the maximum available power may be absorbed where it is required. **1934** *Jrnl. Inst. Electr. Engin.* LXXV. 803/2 Impedance-matching transformers have to be used at both ends of the screened lead-in feeder. **1968** *Listener* 22 Feb. 235/3 The bony levers [of the middle ear] reduce the amplitude of vibration and so serve as what an engineer would call an 'impedance-matching transformer'. This gives efficient transfer of energy from the air to the denser fluid in the cochlea of the inner ear.

impede (ɪm'pi:d), *v.* Also 7 **impeide**. [ad. L. *impedī-re*, lit. to shackle the feet, f. *im-* (IM-[1]) + *pēs, ped-em* foot.] *trans.* To retard in progress or action by putting obstacles in the way; to obstruct; to hinder; to stand in the way of.

1605 SHAKS. *Macb.* I. v. 29 All that impeides thee from the Golden Round, Which Fate..doth seeme To haue thee crown'd withall. **1698** FRYER *Acc. E. India & P.* 80 They would raise Objections on purpose to impede the Negotiation. *c* **1760** SMOLLETT *Ode to Leven-Water* 8 No rocks impede thy dimpling course. **1807** T. THOMSON *Chem.* (ed. 3) II. 546 Carbonic acid, instead of promoting, impedes the decomposition. **1855** MACAULAY *Hist. Eng.* xx. IV. 514 Adverse winds had impeded his progess through the Straits of Gibraltar. **1860** TYNDALL *Glac.* I. xxii. 155 My load, light as it was, impeded me.

b. *Astrol.* = IMPEDITE *v.* 2.

1819 [see IMPEDIMENT 4].

Hence **im'peded** *ppl. a.*; also **im'peder**, a person or thing that impedes.

1686 GOAD *Celest. Bodies* I. xiv. 78 Frost.. an impeder of their winter-marches. **1796–7** *Instr. & Reg. Cavalry* (1813) 190 The positions I, K, L, M. show the passage of obstacles by the impeded parts filing or marching ranks by three's round them.

†**im'pede**, *sb. Obs. rare.* [f. prec. vb.] The act of impeding; hindrance, impediment.

1659 *Lady Alimony* v. vi. in Hazl. *Dodsley* XIV. 362 To prune those wild luxurious sprays, Which give impede unto this spreading vine.

†**im'pedible**, *a. Obs.* [f. IMPEDE *v.* + -IBLE; f. L. type **impedībilis*: cf. It. *impedibile* (Florio).] That can be impeded, obstructed, or hindered. Hence †**impedi'bility**, liability to be impeded.

1655 JER. TAYLOR *Unum Necess.* vi. v. §73 (R. Suppl.) But the will is not impedible; it cannot be restrained at all, if there be any acts of life. **1677** GALE *Crt. Gentiles* IV. 404 Not impedible and frustrable in any manner. *Ibid.* 515 Where-ever there is passive power there is impedibilitie.

impedient (ɪm'pi:dɪənt), *a.* (*sb.*) [ad. L. *impedient-em*, pres. pple. of *impedīre* to IMPEDE.]

That impedes or hinders; obstructive, hindering.

1596 DALRYMPLE tr. *Leslie's Hist. Scot.* II. 164 A strang rebellioune in Kent.. to the legat Petilie is impedient, that he can mell na mair w[t] the Scottis. **1677** GALE *Crt. Gentiles* IV. 479 Nothing fails of its due perfection but from some cause either agent or impedient. **1879** M. PATTISON *Milton* 152 To a mind so disposed externals become, first indifferent, then impedient.

B. *sb.* An impeding or hindering agent.

1661 LOVELL *Hist. Anim. & Min.* 418 Cured by temperants, and impedients.

impediment (ɪm'pɛdɪmənt), *sb.* Also 5–6 **impedy-**, (5 **in-**, **enpedy-**, **impede-**, 6 **ympediment**). [ad. L. *impedīmentum* hindrance, impediment, pl. *-menta* baggage, f. *impedī-re* to IMPEDE.]

1. The fact of impeding or condition of being impeded; hindrance, obstruction; *concr.* something that impedes, hinders, or obstructs; a hindrance, an obstruction.

1398 TREVISA *Barth. De P.R.* v. xl. (1495) 156 To clense the eye syghte and to putte of the impediment and lette of the spyryte of lyfe. *a* **1420** HOCCLEVE *De Reg. Princ.* 1807 To begge, shame is myne impediment. *a* **1450** *Fysshynge w. angle* (1883) 6 Ye must know.. how many Impedimen[ts] þer ben yn anglyng. **1526** *Pilgr. Perf.* (W. de W. 1531) 31 Temporall rychesse is rather an impedyment or let, than fortheraunce. **1549** *Bk. Com. Prayer, Matrimony*, If either of you doe knowe any impedimente.. Yf no impedimente bee alleged. **1594** SHAKS. *Rich. III*, v. ii. 4 Thus farre.. Haue we marcht on without impediment. **1645** BOATE *Irel. Nat. Hist.* (1652) 67 These impediments are chiefly three in number, Cataracts, Weres, and Foards. **1662** *Bk. Com. Prayer, Matrimony*, If any of you know cause, or just impediment, why these two persons should not be joined together in holy Matrimony, ye are to declare it. **1722** SEWEL *Hist. Quakers* (1795) I. p. viii, Notwithstanding all these impediments I continually resumed this work. **1873** HAMERTON *Intell. Life* I. iii. (1875) 14 Impediments to his best activity.

†**2.** Something that impedes the functions or health of the body; a (physical) defect; an affection or malady. *Obs.*

1542 BOORDE *Dyetary* xii. (1870) 264 They be not good.. for the colycke nor the Ilyacke nor other inflatyue impedymentes or syckenesses. **1579** LANGHAM *Gard. Health* (1633) 461 Skuruy, and spreading scabs, and such like impediments. *c* **1585** *Faire Em* II. 471 What? is she deaf? a great impediment! **1657** R. LIGON *Barbadoes* (1673) 19 It was no decay or impediment in my sight that made me lose it.

b. *esp.* An organic obstruction to ready or distinct speech; a stammer or stutter.

1494 FABYAN *Chron.* VI. clxxiv. 170 He had an enpedyment in his tunge. **1539** BIBLE (Great) *Mark* vii. 32 One that was deaffe and had an impedyment in hys spech. **1809** J. WATSON *Instr. Deaf & Dumb* (title-p.) Hints for the Correction of Impediments in Speech.

3. (Chiefly *pl.*) Baggage, esp. of an army; IMPEDIMENTA.

c **1540** tr. *Pol. Verg. Eng. Hist.* (Camden No. 29) 219 All impedimentes being gatheryd into the middest of tharmy. **1598** BARRET *Theor. Warres* III. ii. 81 Then may the center containe the impedimentes and baggage of the armie. **1678** *Life Black Prince* in *Select. fr. Harl. Misc.* (1793) 51 Placing his carriages there, and all his other impediments. **1890** BOLDREWOOD *Col. Reformer* (1891) 265 As the progress of.. his party would necessarily partake of the nature of caravan movements, [he] decided.. to go ahead of his impediment.

4. *Astrol.* The 'impedited' condition of a planet: see IMPEDITE *v.* 2.

1819 J. WILSON *Compl. Dict. Astrol.* s.v. *Impeded*, The ☽ is impeded when in ☌, □, or ☍ of ☉, ♄, or ♂. If in ☌ or ☍, the impediment lasts four days, viz. two before and two after.

†**im'pediment**, *v. Obs.* [f. prec. sb.] *trans.* To put an impediment or obstruction in the way of; to obstruct.

1610 *Househ. Ord.* (1790) 337 Noise, whereby either their owne devotions may be diverted or that of others impedimented. **1631** T. POWELL *Tom All Trades* 162 Who ..impediment our Trade abroad. **1652** J. TAYLOR (Water P.) *Journ. Wales* (1859) 17 A reasonable hauen.. now.. much impedimented with shelvs, sands, and other annoyances.

‖**impedimenta** (ɪmpɛdɪ'mɛntə), *sb. pl.* [L., plur. of *impedīmentum*: see prec. sb.] Things which impede or encumber progress; baggage; travelling equipment (of an army, etc.).

1600 HOLLAND *Livy* Index II. Eeeeee j a/2 Enclosing the *impedimenta* or baggage in the mids, for safetie and securitie. *a* **1644** CHILLINGW. 9 *Serm.* vii. (1742) 81 Being so clogged and burdened with these *impedimenta*. **1834** MEDWIN *Angler in Wales* I. 28 [He] brought with him baggage enough to load a camel.. I have advised him to send on to that place his *impedimenta*. **1885** *Manch. Exam.* 22 Jan. 5/2 Leaving the camels and all impedimenta in the place where the troops had encamped.

impedimental (ɪmpɛdɪ'mɛntəl), *a.* [f. IMPEDIMENT *sb.* + -AL[1].] Of the nature of or constituting an impediment; obstructive; impeditive.

1654 W. MOUNTAGUE *Devout Ess.* II. vii. §2. 132 The impedimental stain, which intercepts her fruitive love. **1657** J. GOODWIN *Triers Tried* To Rdr. 5 It is as impedimental or destructive to the keeping of Gods commandments. *a* **1734** NORTH *Lives* (1826) I. 141 No.. impedimental forms of law shall stand against that equity. **1843** CARLYLE *Past & Pr.* IV. i, A distressing impedimental adjunct.

So **impedi'mentary** *a.*, in same sense.

1888 *Daily News* 20 Dec. 7/1 High heels and pointed toes ..eschewed.. as impedimentary to swiftness in walking.

impeding (ɪm'pi:dɪŋ), *ppl. a.* [f. IMPEDE *v.* + -ING[2].] That impedes or obstructs; hindering. Hence **im'pedingly** *adv.*, so as to impede.

1717 S. CLARKE *5th Reply to Leibnitz* 345 The contrary or impeding Force, which arises from the Resistance of Fluids to Bodies moved any way. **1805** SOUTHEY *Madoc* II. xviii, He dropt the impeding buckler. **1886** M. K. MACMILLAN *Dagonet the Jester* 154 The first thawings of the hard-bound road clung impedingly to our shoes.

†'**impedite**, *ppl. a. Obs.* [ad. L. *impedīt-us*, pa. pple. of *impedīre* to IMPEDE.] Impeded, obstructed, hindered; having an impediment, defective. *Astrol.*: see IMPEDITE *v.* 2.

1544 PHAER *Pestilence* (1553) L j a, You must consider whether he be impedit or no, and if he be impedite, there shalbe many sickenesses. **1635** SWAN *Spec. M.* (1670) 191 If Saturn.. shall behold the Moon, when she is impedite, with a quadrate or opposite aspect, then he fore-sheweth that there will be an Earthquake. **1662** GURNALL *Chr. in Arm.* verse 19 iii. §5 (1669) 491/2 Their impedite speech, and hesitant delivery. **1671** *True Nonconf.* 256 We know, the expressive facultie, where the organes are not impedite, to be.. subservient enough to the mindes conceptions.

impedite ('ɪmpɪdaɪt), *v.* Now *rare* or *Obs.* [f. L. *impedīt-*, ppl. stem of *impedīre* to IMPEDE.]

1. = IMPEDE 1.

c **1535** *Suppress. Monast.* (Camden) 23 To let, stoppe, impedite, and sclaunder your gracis mariage. **1612** WOODALL *Surg. Mate* Wks. (1653) 88 If the substance of the brain be offended, the functions thereof are impedited. **1650** BULWER *Anthropomet.* 84 To defend the Eye.. yet so, as it no way impedites vision. **1663** J. WALLIS in *Boyle's Wks.* (1772) VI. 457 Digestion.. seemed not to be much impedited.

2. *Astrol.* In *pass.*, said of a planet when its influence is hindered by the position of another.

1647 LILLY *Chr. Astrol.* xiii. 8 If she [the Moon] be impedited of the ☉ in a Nativity. *a* **1681** WHARTON *Disc. Soul of World* Wks. (1683) 669 How the Power and Dominion of this Star, then so strong and Powerful, should be thus Impedited. **1831** LYTTON *Godolph.* xxvii, For Jupiter in Cancer.. not impedited of any other star, betokened me indeed some expertness in science.

†**impe'dition.** *Obs.* [ad. L. *impedītiōn-em*, n. of action f. *impedīre* to IMPEDE.] The action of impeding or fact of being impeded; hindering.

1623 COCKERAM, *Impedition*, a hindering. **1676** R. GROVE *Vind. Conform. Clergy* (1680) 20 The brave man that speaks ..without the least impedition or hesitation. **1684** BAXTER *Par. Congreg.* 3 Not statedly, but only by some present impedition.

impeditive (ɪm'pɛdɪtɪv), *a.* [f. L. *impedīt-*, ppl. stem of *impedīre* to IMPEDE + -IVE.] Tending to impede or obstruct; of the nature of an impediment; obstructive.

1651 BP. HALL *Susurrium* xxii, Six legs to that unweildy body had been cumbersome, and impeditive of motion. *a* **1693** URQUHART *Rabelais* III. xvi. 133 The impeditive Interposition of many.. Rivers. **1881** G. MACDONALD *Mary Marston* I. iv. 88 A lovely fault.. but.. greatly impeditive to progress.

†**im'peevish**, *v. Obs. rare.* [IM-[1].] *trans.* To render peevish. Hence **impeevished** *ppl. a.*

1664 H. MORE *Myst. Iniq.* Apol. 561 They may serve the turn of particular impeevished spirits.

Impeian (pheasant): see IMPEYAN.

impeire, obs. form of IMPAIR *v.*

impel (ɪm'pɛl), *v.* Also 7–8 **impell**. [ad. L. *impell-ĕre*, in same senses, f. *im-* (IM-[1]) + *pellĕre* to drive; cf. also obs. F. *impeller* (16th c. in Godef.).]

1. *trans.* To drive, force, or constrain (a person) *to* some action, or *to do* something, by acting upon his mind or feelings; to urge on, incite.

1490 CAXTON *Eneydos* xxii. 78 He was strongli impelled in his corage by y[e] persuasions and harde lamentacions. **1577** tr. *Bullinger's Decades* (1592) 588 Will chooseth, for in it doth lie both to will and to nill: which are againe impeld by other powers and faculties. **1659** PEARSON *Creed* (1839) 12 Not.. upon their own motion, but as moved, impelled, and acted by God. **1732** POPE *Ess. Man* II. 68 Active its task, it prompts, impels, inspires. **1828** SCOTT *F.M. Perth* xxxi, I cannot tell what impels me to speak thus boldly. **1875** JOWETT *Plato* (ed. 2) V. 141 Human nature will impel him to seek pleasure instead of virtue.

2. In literal sense: To drive or cause to move onward; to impart motion to; to propel.

1611 FLORIO, *Impellere*, to impell, to thrust violently,.. to driue forward. **1646** SIR T. BROWNE *Pseud. Ep.* II. iv. 80 This effluvium attenuateth and impelleth the neighbour ayre. **1697** DRYDEN *Virg. Georg.* III. 316 O'er th' Elean Plains, thy well breath'd Horse Impels the flying Carr. **1793** BEDDOES *Calculus* 175 The heart.. impels the blood through the arteries. **1822** IMISON *Sc. & Art* I. 11 A ship impelled by the wind and tide. **1851** HAWTHORNE *Ho. Sev. Gables* xix. (1883) 338 Uncle Venner.. impelling a wheelbarrow along the street. **1861** HUGHES *Tom Brown at Oxf.* I. xiii. 245–6 One or two skiffs were coming home, impelled by reading men, who took their constitutionals on the water.

b. To force (a thing) *upon. rare.*

1760–72 H. BROOKE *Fool of Qual.* (1809) IV. 108 He cried, You must accept them as a token of our loves; and so he constrained and impelled them upon me.

Hence **im'pelled**, **im'pelling** *ppl. adjs.*

1685 BOYLE *Enq. Notion Nat.* vi. 217 The generality of impelled bodies do move either upwards, downwards [etc.].

1767 GOOCH *Treat. Wounds* I. 71 The impelling force of the blood. **1858** BUSHNELL *Serm. New Life* 305 Force which is cumulative, growing stronger and more impelling as it goes. **1858** LARDNER *Hand-bk. Nat. Phil., Hydrost.*, etc. 142 The impelling force acting only on one side of the centre.

impellent (ɪmˈpɛlənt), *a.* and *sb.* [ad. L. *impellent-em*, pres. pple. of *impellĕre* to IMPEL.]

A. *adj.* That impels, or drives on; impelling.

1620 GRANGER *Div. Logike* 167 *note*, The effect of the impellent cause. **1716** *Lond. Gaz.* No. 5459/4 For raising Water by the impellant force of Fire. **1875** VEITCH *Lucretius* 68 Where is the impellent power or δύναμις?

B. *sb.* A thing which impels or urges; an impelling force, agent, body, etc.

1644 DIGBY *Two Treat.* I. v. (1645) 47 By reason of the violent motion of the impellent. **1691** RAY *Creation* I. (1692) 70 Here is no appearing Impellent but the external Air. **1793** J. WILLIAMS *Calm Exam.* Ded., They must have equally an impellant or governor, to enforce obedience. **1836** CHALMERS *Mor. Philos.* Wks. V. 291 Curiosity is a great impellent to mental labour.

impeller (ɪmˈpɛlə(r)). [f. IMPEL *v.* + -ER[1].]

a. One who or that which impels.

1685 BOYLE *Enq. Notion Nat.* vi. 215 By other portions of matter (which are also extrinsical impellers) acting on them. **1707** S. CLARKE *2nd Def. Immat. Soul* (1715) 24 Is it possible to be an Effect produced without a Cause? Is it impelled without any Impeller? **1799** SOUTHEY *Lett.* (1856) I. 77 The first Impeller of all motions. **1889** FARRAR *Lives Fathers* I. i. 32 Clement is a moderator, Ignatius an impeller.

b. Also occas. **impellor**. A part of a machine or apparatus designed to impart motion to a fluid by rotation, esp. in a restricted space (as in a centrifugal pump or compressor).

1890 P. R. BJÖRLING *Pumps* 190 The pump being charged with water, the impeller or fan is set in motion at a great speed, imparting centrifugal motion to the water contained in the impeller, and so driven into the casing or body of the pump. **1923** *Daily Mail* 13 July 12 Cooling is by the thermo-syphon system assisted by a water impellor. **1934** *Archit. Rev.* LXXV. 203 Fresh air..is drawn into the eyes of the fans—the largest of which has a capacity of 641,000 cu. ft. of air a minute and an impellor diameter of 28 ft. **1942** R. A. BEAUMONT *Aeronaut. Engin.* 100/1 The mixture, thrown outwards at high velocity by the rapidly revolving impellor, passes through diffuser vanes into a chamber, from which it is delivered to the induction pipes. **1947** A. W. JUDGE *Mod. Gas Turbines* viii. 206 The compressor has a double-sided impeller with twenty-nine vanes on each side which enables the maximum air intake area to be obtained for a given tip diameter. **1956** MCCABE & SMITH *Unit Operations Chem. Engin.* vi. 282 In these machines mixing is done by a mechanically driven impeller, which creates a flow pattern in the liquid. *Ibid.* 283 The three main types of mixing impellers are paddles, turbines, and propellers. **1966** *McGraw-Hill Encycl. Sci. & Technol.* V. 334/2 A fluid coupling consists of an impeller on the input or driving shaft and a runner on the output or driven shaft... Impeller and runner are bladed rotors, the impeller acting as a pump and the runner reacting as a turbine.

impellingness (ɪmˈpɛlɪŋnɪs). *rare.* [f. IMPELLING *ppl. a.* + -NESS.] The quality of being impelling.

1922 F. H. BURNETT *Robin* i. 1 A certain impellingness of mood suggested that exercise would be a good thing.

impellor, var. IMPELLER.

†**imˈpen**, *v.*[1] *Obs.* [f. IM-[1] + PEN *sb.*[1] or *v.*[1]] *trans.* To shut in a pen or fold. (See also IMPENT.)

1627 FELTHAM *Resolves* I. [II.] lxvii. [lix.] 218 Like a sheepe impenn'd in the fold. **1661** —— *Lusoria* xxvii, O you Celestial Powers! why did you lend Accursed Man a Soul, to be impenn'd In womens Breasts?

†**imˈpen**, *v.*[2] *Obs.* Also em-. [f. IM-[1] + PEN *sb.*[2]] *trans.* To provide with pens or feathers.

c **1614** SIR W. MURE *Dido & Æneas* I. 22 By the, to climb Parnassus I aspyre, And by thy feathers to impen my flame. **1628** —— *Spir. Hymne* 214 On winges, with faith and hope empen'd.

†**imˈpend**, *v.*[1] *Obs.* [ad. L. *impend-ĕre* to lay out, expend, devote, employ, f. *im-* (IM-[1]) + *pendĕre* to weigh, pay out.] *trans.* To pay *to* some one; to spend, expend; to apply (money); to bestow.

c **1486** *Plumpton Corr.* 67 Ye shall bynd me..to impend unto your sayd mastership our prayer and service, according unto our duety. **1494** FABYAN *Chron.* VII. 354 For theyr fydelytie, whiche they to dayly impende. **1612** STURTEVANT *Metallica* (1854) 60 Monie to be impended and disbursed in Charges. **1669** BOYLE *Contn. New Exp.* ii. (1682) Pref. 9, I am almost ashamed to tell how much was impended on these Trials. *a* **1690** *R. Law's Mem.* (1818) 142 May they not also forbidd all tennants and vassals to pay.. rents to them, because they know not how they will impend them?

impend (ɪmˈpɛnd), *v.*[2] [ad. L. *impend-ēre*, in same senses, f. *im-* (IM-[1]) + *pendēre* to hang.]

1. *intr.* To hang or be suspended (*over*); to overhang. (With *indirect pass.*)

1780 A. YOUNG *Tour Irel.* 290 Bulging rocks..which seem to impend in horrid forms over the lake. **1803** K. WHITE *Clifton Grove* 224 Mournful larches o'er the wave impend. **1863** MRS. OLIPHANT *Salem Ch.* i. 5 Old Mr. Tufton, spiritual but homely, had been wont to impend over the desk and exhort his beloved brethren. **1878** H. S. WILSON *Alp. Ascents* i. 9 Impended over by great rock boulders.

2. *transf.* and *fig.* Of evil or danger: To hang threateningly or hover (*over*) as about to fall.

1599 MASSINGER, etc. *Old Law* v. i, Your father's curses, which have brought Vengeance impending on you. **1706** PHILLIPS, *To Impend*, to hang over one's Head, as Dangers or Judgments do; to be likely to happen. **1725** POPE *Odyss.* II. 191 Destruction sure o'er all your heads impends. **1849** MACAULAY *Hist. Eng.* iv. I. 515 Great dangers impended over the ecclesiastical and civil constitution. **1853** J. H. NEWMAN *Hist. Sk.* (1873) II. I. i. 12 Barbarism is ever impending over the civilized world.

3. Hence, *generally*, To be about to happen; to be imminent or near at hand.

1674 tr. *Martiniere's Voy. N. Countries* 141 Giving them notice of any accident or distemper impending. **1712–14** POPE *Rape Lock* I. 109, I saw, alas! some dread event impend. **1744** AKENSIDE *Pleas. Imag.* II. 68 The same glad task Impends. **1840** THIRLWALL *Greece* VII. 163 A war which was believed to be impending.

4. *trans.* To overhang, hover over; to be imminently near to. *rare.*

1652 GAULE *Magastrom.* 354 Thine own Art..lets thee not foresee what impends thee on earth. **1670** PENN *Case Lib. Consc.* 6 The dreadful Judgments that now impend the Nation. **1810** SHELLEY *Zastrozzi* xiii. Pr. Wks. 1888 I. 86 The alarming danger which impended her.

impendence (ɪmˈpɛndəns). [f. IMPENDENT: see -ENCE.] The fact or condition of being impendent; menacing attitude; imminence.

1657 PIERCE *Div. Philanthr.* 67 The impendence of but a temporall destruction. **1677** HALE *Prim. Orig. Man.* I. ii. 47 The impendence of a greater sensible evil. **1860** RUSKIN *Mod. Paint.* V. IX. iv. §12 The angry Apennine, dark with rolling impendence of volcanic cloud.

impendency (ɪmˈpɛndənsɪ). [f. as prec.: see -ENCY.] The quality or state of being impendent; imminent or threatening character; an impending circumstance.

a **1632** T. TAYLOR *God's Judgem.* II. iv. (1642) 49 Sloath.. hath many virulent and bitter impendencies. *a* **1660** HAMMOND *Wks.* (1683) IV. 492 The present impendency of God's punishments. **1848** TALFOURD *Final Mem. Lamb* 305 The constant impendency of this giant sorrow saddened to 'the Lambs' even their holidays.

impendent (ɪmˈpɛndənt), *a.* Now *rare.* [ad. L. *impendēnt-em*, pres. pple. of *impendēre*, IMPEND *v.*[2] Cf. obs. F. *impendent* (Cotgr.).]

1. = IMPENDING 1.

1611 COTGR., *Impendent*, impendent, hanging ouer, or vnto. **1692** RAY *Dissol. World* III. v. (1732) 347 A Rock of one of the impendent Cliffs. *c* **1790** IMISON *Sch. Art* I. 134 That part of the atmosphere impendant over England. **1856** RUSKIN *Mod. Paint.* III. IV. xviii. §17 The sky..is writhed into folds of motion, closely impendent upon earth. *Ibid.* IV. V. xvi. §40 Cliffs..impendent above strong torrents.

2. = IMPENDING 2.

a **1592** GREENE *Jas. IV* Wks. (Rtldg.) 206 Were I baser born, my mean estate Could warrant me from this impendent harm. **1667** MILTON *P.L.* II. 177 If.. Impendent horrors, threatning hideous fall One day upon our heads. **1741** WARBURTON *Div. Legat.* V. iii. II. 413 This impendent Desolation brings them to a Sense of their Folly. **1884** *Fortn. Rev.* June 762 The greatest impendent national evil.

impending (ɪmˈpɛndɪŋ), *ppl. a.* [f. IMPEND *v.*[2] + -ING[2].]

1. In literal sense: Overhanging.

1705–30 S. GALE in *Bibl. Topogr. Brit.* III. 38 A bower.. pleasantly shaded by the impending bushes. **1784** COWPER *Task* III. 193 Terribly arch'd and aquiline his nose, And overbuilt with most impending brows. **1854** HAWTHORNE *Eng. Note-Bks.* (1883) I. 583, The old house built by Philip English, in Salem..many-gabled, and impending.

2. Of evil, danger, etc.: That impends or is about to fall or happen; 'hanging over one's head'; imminent; near at hand.

1682 in Somers *Tracts* (1748) I. 193 To prevent impending Mischiefs. **1715–20** POPE *Iliad* II. 18 Nodding Ilion waits th' impending fall. **1837** W. IRVING *Capt. Bonneville* I. 160 There were symptoms of an impending storm. **1891** E. PEACOCK *N. Brendon* I. 263 A shower seemed impending.

†**imˈpendious**, *a.* *Obs.* *rare*$^{-0}$. [ad. L. *impendiōs-us* (Plautus), f. *impendi-um* outlay, expense, f. *impend-ĕre* IMPEND *v.*[1]] Lavish, extravagant. Hence †**imˈpendiousness**.

1623 COCKERAM, *Impendious*, spending more than needes. **1656** in BLOUNT *Glossogr.* **1727** BAILEY vol. II, *Impendiousness*, liberality, extravagant spending.

impenetrability (ɪmˌpɛnɪtrəˈbɪlɪtɪ). [f. next: see -ITY. Cf. F. *impénétrabilité.*]

1. The quality or condition of being impenetrable; incapability of being penetrated, entered, or pierced; inscrutability; unfathomableness; 'unsusceptibility of intellectual impression' (J.).

1706 PHILLIPS, *Impenetrability*, a being impenetrable. **1794** SULLIVAN *View Nat.* I. 373 Their excessive impenetrability to the action of cold. **1796** KIRWAN *Elem. Min.* (ed. 2) I. 37 The firmness, hardness, and impenetrability of minerals. **1848** C. BRONTË *J. Eyre* xvi, I will put her to some test..such impenetrability..is past comprehension. **1866** GEO. ELIOT *F. Holt* xvii, Jermyn's calculated slowness and conceit in his own impenetrability.

2. *Nat. Philos.* That property of matter in virtue of which two bodies cannot occupy the same place at the same time.

1665 GLANVILL *Scepsis Sci.* 44 That Quantity is Divisibility is presumed; but extension is before it, in nature, and our conception, and is the received notion, though perhaps Impenetrability is the truest. **1678** CUDWORTH *Intell. Syst.* I. v. 770 Tangibility and Impenetrability were..made by him the very essence of body. **1794** G. ADAMS *Nat. & Exp. Philos.* III. xxv. 67 The idea of impenetrability only supposes that two extended substances cannot be in the same place at the same time. **1877** E. R. CONDER *Bas. Faith* v. 222 Extension and impenetrability, long regarded as essential properties of matter, are now perceived to be properties not of atoms, but of masses of coherent molecules.

impenetrable (ɪmˈpɛnɪtrəb(ə)l), *a.* Also 5 inp-, 6–7 **impenitrable**. [a. F. *impénétrable* (14th c., J. de Vignay), ad. L. *impenetrābilis*, f. *im-* (IM-[2]) + *penetrābilis* PENETRABLE.] Not penetrable.

1. That cannot be penetrated, pierced, or entered; impossible to get into or through. Const. *to*, *by*.

1460 CAPGRAVE *Chron.* (Rolls) 133 The basnet was strong and inpenetrabel. **1585** T. WASHINGTON tr. *Nicholay's Voy.* IV. iii. 115 b, They had on their heads bourgonets, strong and impenetrable. **1603** DRAYTON *Bar. Wars* IV. lxx, Words ..Able to wound the impenitrablest Eares. **1667** MILTON *P.L.* IX. 1086 Woods impenetrable To Starr or Sun-light. **1687** *Lond. Gaz.* No. 2251/4 His Hull..not being impenetrable to our great Shot. **1794** S. WILLIAMS *Vermont* 98 Impenetrable to the rain. **1814** WORDSW. *Excurs.* II. *ad fin.*, The hills Lay shrouded in impenetrable mist. **1836** MACGILLIVRAY tr. *Humboldt's Trav.* xxv. 383 A kind of clay impenetrable by the roots of herbaceous plants. **1880** HAUGHTON *Phys. Geog.* v. 229 One impenetrable forest.

2. *transf.* and *fig.* Whose nature, meaning, etc. cannot be penetrated or discerned; inscrutable; unfathomable. **a.** Of things.

1531 ELYOT *Gov.* I. xxiii, Were the thing neuer so difficile (or as who saythe) impenitrable. **1692** DRYDEN *St. Euremont's Ess.* 285 Nothing is more impenetrable than its [the soul's] Nature, its Original, and its Duration. *a* **1704** T. BROWN *Praise Poverty* Wks. 1730 I. 93 The legerdemain must be clean and the Conveyance impenetrable to the eye of the people. **1823** LINGARD *Hist. Eng.* VI. 257 That the intention of proceeding to judgment might be kept an impenetrable secret. **1866** R. W. DALE *Disc. Spec. Occ.* vi. 188 Every article of it ends in impenetrable mystery.

b. Of persons, their appearance, actions, etc.

1718 *Freethinker* No. 75 ¶5 A long impenetrable Dissimulation. **1800** MRS. HERVEY *Mourtray Fam.* II. 154 She watched his countenance whilst she spoke, but it was impenetrable. **1802** MAR. EDGEWORTH *Moral T.* (1816) I. xv. 127 He was..impenetrable on this subject. **1882** OUIDA *Maremma* I. 70 She being a close and resolute woman, was impenetrable to the curiosity of her neighbours.

absol. as *sb.* **1811** *Henry & Isabella* II. 73, I hope you bring me some consolation from the fair impenetrable.

3. Impervious to intellectual or moral influences, impressions, or ideas.

1596 SHAKS. *Merch. V.* III. iii. 18 It is the most impenetrable curre That euer kept with men. **1601** ? MARSTON *Pasquil & Kath.* IV. 285 Looke, on my knees I creepe, Be not impenetrable, beautious youth! **1784** COWPER *Task* VI. 505 'And dost thou dream', the impenetrable man Exclaimed, 'that me the lullabies of age.. Can cheat?' **1865** M. ARNOLD *Ess. Crit.* v. (1875) 205 Aristocracies are, as such, naturally impenetrable by ideas.

4. *Nat. Philos.* Possessing the quality of impenetrability (see prec. 2).

1666 BOYLE *Orig. Formes & Qual.* (1667) 2 Bodies, by which I mean a Substance extended, divisible and impenetrable. **1717** S. CLARKE *Leibnitz's 5th Paper* 207 Some have fancied, that Man..became Solid, Opake, and Impenetrable by his Fall. **1829** *Nat. Philos.* I. *Pneumatics* ii. §7. 2 (U.K.S.) Air is impenetrable.

imˈpenetrableness. [f. prec. + -NESS.] The quality of being impenetrable; impenetrability.

1685 BOYLE *Enq. Notion Nat.* vi. 214 Since motion does not essentially belong to matter, as divisibility and impenetrableness are believed to do. **1748** RICHARDSON *Clarissa* (1811) I. xl. 301 This impenetrableness..is to be put among the shades in his character. **1866** GEO. ELIOT *F. Holt* xxxv, The cold impenetrableness which he preserved under the ordinary annoyances of business.

impenetrably (ɪmˈpɛnɪtrəblɪ), *adv.* [f. as prec. + -LY[2].] In an impenetrable manner; inscrutably; unfathomably.

1647 HAMMOND *Power of Keys* 96 Some man impenetrably obstinate. **1667** MILTON *P.L.* VI. 400 Invulnerable, impenitrably arm'd. **1759** ROBERTSON *Hist. Scot.* (1813) II. VIII. 43 The whole transaction remained as impenetrably dark as ever. **1857** H. B. BREEN *Mod. Eng. Lit.* 251 A poet so impenetrably shrouded in mysticism.

impenetrate (ɪmˈpɛnɪtreɪt), *v.* [f. IM-[1] + PENETRATE.] *trans.* To penetrate intimately.

1859 MISS MULOCK *Romant. T.* 318 Love..draws its light from its own essence, and pours it out in a sunshine-flood, surrounding and impenetrating the beloved with radiance. **1871** SMILES *Charac.* ii. (1876) 58 Society was impenetrated with vice and profligacy. **1892** *Black & White* 19 Mar. 377/2 So deeply has it impenetrated the daily life of the people.

impeneˈtration. [IM-[1].] Intimate penetration, permeation.

1861 BP. R. WILBERFORCE *Ess.* (1874) I. 177 The in-dwelling of Prophecy in the Church..is..the impenetration of its whole being by a miraculous power.

†**imˈpenetrative**, *a.* *Obs. rare.* [f. IM-[2] + PENETRATIVE.] Not having a penetrating quality.

1684 H. MORE *Answer* 396 The minds of most being.. slight, and impenetrative.

impenitence (ɪmˈpɛnɪtəns). [ad. late L. *impænitēntia* (Jerome), f. *impæniténs*

IMPENITENT: see -ENCE. Cf. F. *impénitent* (1630 in Hatz.-Darm.).] The fact or condition of being impenitent; want of penitence or repentance; hardness of heart; obduracy.

1624 BEDELL *Lett.* vii. 112 Impenitence of any deadly crime. **1667** MILTON *P.L.* XI. 816 Denouncing wrauth to come On thir impenitence. *a***1694** TILLOTSON *Serm.* II. cxix. (R.), Nor is one man's impenitence more blameable than another's; Chorazin and Bethsaida can be in no more fault for continuing impenitent, than Tyre and Sidon were. **1884** E. H. PLUMPTRE *Spirits in Prison* viii. 255 (tr. Dorner) There is no predestination to damnation, only continued impenitence can be the cause of that.

impenitency (ɪm'pɛnɪtənsɪ). [f. as prec.: see -ENCY.] The quality or state of being impenitent.

1563 GRINDAL *Serv. for Plague* Wks. (Parker Soc.) 92 As we through our impenitency do now most worthily feel thy justice punishing us. **1614** RALEIGH *Hist. World* II. (1634) 527 That the Sins which are not forsaken before the age of 52 yeares, shall be punished with finall impenitencie. **1732** BERKELEY *Serm. S.P.G.* Wks. III. 245 A mind not hardened by impenitency. **1864** J. WALKER *Faithf. Ministry* 143 Day by day hardening the Soul in deeper impenitency.

impenitent (ɪm'pɛnɪtənt), *a.* and *sb.* Also 6 -pœn-. [ad. L. *impænitēnt-em* (Jerome), also erron. *impœn-*, f. *im-* (IM-²) + *pænitens* PENITENT. Cf. F. *impénitent* (1570 in Hatz.-Darm.).]

A. *adj.* Not penitent or repentant; having no contrition or sorrow for sin; unrepentant, obdurate.

1532 MORE *Confut. Tindale* Wks. 613/1 [They] will.. wepe and repent in hell this foolish fruitlesse fashion of their impenitent repentance. **1582** N. T. (Rhem.) *Rom.* ii. 5 After thy hardnesse, and impenitent heart. **1597** HOOKER *Eccl. Pol.* v. lxviii. §8 Impœnitent and notorious sinners. **1709** STEELE *Tatler* No. 135 ¶2 Impenitent Criminals and Malefactors. **1898** J. CAIRD *Univ. Serm.* vii. 142 With God, to forgive an impenitent man and to continue to punish a penitent are equally impossible.

B. *sb.* An impenitent or unrepentant person.

1532 MORE *Confut. Tindale* Wks. 525/1 In thys kynde are there penitentes and impenitentes bothe. **1631** *High Commission Cases* (Camden) 207 That the body of the impenitent went not presently to hell but was condemned to hell when he dyed. **1734** WATTS *Reliq. Juv.* xxiii. *Distant Thunder*, These dark clouds.. hang over the nations, and are just ready to be discharged on the head of impenitents.

Hence **im'penitentness**, impenitency.

1727 BAILEY vol. II, *Impenitentness*, impenitence, unrelentingness.

impenitently (ɪm'pɛnɪtəntlɪ), *adv.* [f. prec. + -LY².] In an impenitent manner; without penitence, repentance, or contrition.

1631 GOUGE *God's Arrows* I. §10. 13 Sinnes impudently and impenitently committed. **1709** POPE *Ess. Crit.* 604 What crowds of these, impenitently bold, In sounds and jingling syllables grown old, Still run on Poets, in a raging vein. **1859** DICKENS *T. Two Cities* ix, Like some enchanted marquis of the impenitently wicked sort, in story.

†**im'penitible**, *a.* *Obs.* [f. IM-² + stem of L. *pænitēre* to repent + -IBLE.] Incapable of repentance. Hence †**im'penitibleness**.

*a***1614** DONNE Βιαθανατος (1644) 27 That there is in this life an impenitiblenesse, and impossibilitie of returning to God. *a***1631** —— *Serm.* xxvi. 262 Death.. concludes him and makes him Impenitible for ever. *Ibid.* l. 508 A finall Impenitence in this life and an Infinite Impenitiblenesse in the next. **1637** JACKSON *Serm. Luke* xiii. 5 Wks. 1844 VI. 132 Utterly cast off by God, or left in a state impenitible.

impennate (ɪm'pɛnət), *a.* and *sb.* *Ornith.* [f. IM-² + PENNATE, after mod.L. *Impenn-es.*]

A. *adj.* Featherless, wingless; *spec.* applied to the *Impennes*, a name given by Illiger, 1811, to certain swimming birds which have small wings covered with scale-like feathers, as the penguins. **B.** *sb.* A bird of this kind.

1842 BRANDE *Dict. Sci.* etc., Impennates, *Impennes*.

†**im'pennous**, *a.* *Obs. rare.* [f. IM-² + L. *penna* feather, pl. wings + -OUS.] Wingless.

1646 SIR T. BROWNE *Pseud. Ep.* III. xxv. 175 An earewigge.. is reckoned amongst impennous insects by many. **1658** PHILLIPS, *Impennuous*, having no feathers.

†**im'pense**, *v.* *Obs. rare.* [f. L. *impens-*, ppl. stem of *impendĕre*, IMPEND *v.*²] *intr.* To weigh *on*.

1797–1803 FOSTER in *Life & Corr.* (1846) I. 186 Make religious sentiments impense so powerfully on the mind.

†**im'pensely**, *adv.* *Obs.* [repr. L. *impensē* expensively, exceedingly, greatly, from *impens-us* expensive, considerable, great, pa. pple. of *impendĕre* to expend, IMPEND *v.*¹] Exceedingly, greatly.

1657 TOMLINSON *Renou's Disp.* 10 That which impensly heats, cools, moystneth or dryeth.

†**im'pensible**, *a.* *Obs. rare*⁻⁰. [f. L. type **impensibilis*, f. *im-* (IM-²) + **pensibilis*, f. *pendĕre, pens-* to weigh, pay.] 'Without reward, gratis' (Cockeram 1623).

†**im'pensively**, *adv.* *Obs.* [f. L. *impens-*, ppl. stem of *impendĕre* (IMPEND *v.*¹) + -IVE + -LY²: cf. *expensively*. The L. adv. was *impensē* (see IMPENSELY).] Exceedingly, greatly, immensely.

1620 VENNER *Via Recta* Introd. 11 It is at no hand to be allowed, except to such as are impensiuely hot. *Ibid.* ii. 38 It is.. impensiuely hurtfull to cold constitutions.

†**im'pent**, *pa. pple.* *Obs.* [f. IM-¹ + PENT, pa. pple. of PEN *v.*¹; or pa. pple of IMPEN *v.*¹] Pent in; shut in a pen or fold; enclosed; confined.

1633 P. FLETCHER *Purple Isl.* III. xii, As they runne in narrow banks impent. **1638–48** G. DANIEL *Eclog.* v. 67 When winds impent, Make Pelion tremble to Astonishment. **1649** —— *Trinarch., Hen. IV*, xxxiv, Neighbour Kings (Impent Wᵗʰ Horror at the fact, in their owne Right,) Hee Courts by his Ambassadors.

impeople, var. of EMPEOPLE *v.*, to fill with people; to people.

†'**imper**. *Obs.* [f. IMP *v.* + -ER¹.] One who imps or grafts; a grafter.

*c***1440** *Promp. Parv.* 259/2 Impare, or graffere,.. *insertor, surculator.*

†'**imperance**. *Obs.* [f. L. pres. ppl. stem *imperant-* (see next): see -ANCE.] Commanding quality, commandingness.

1595 CHAPMAN *Ovid's Banq. Sence* (1639) 35 Since vertue wants due imperance. **1598** —— in *Marlowe's Hero & Leander* III. *ad fin.*, If her soul.. found such imperance In her love's beauties.

†'**imperant**, *a.* *Obs.* [ad. L. *imperānt-em*, pres. pple. of *imperāre* to command.] Commanding, ruling.

1617 COLLINS *Def. Bp. Ely* II. ix. 359 Imperant only, not elicient; dirigent, not exequent, as your School-men loue to speak. **1691** BAXTER *Nat. Ch.* x. 47 They might.. by Imperant, Judicial and Executive power Govern them.

†'**imperate**, *ppl. a.* *Obs.* [ad. L. *imperāt-us*, pa. pple. of *imperā-re* to command, rule.]

A. as *pa. pple.* Commanded, ruled.

*c***1470** HARDING *Chron.* LXIII. vii, [He] reigned had and imperate In Brytain. **1560** ROLLAND *Crt. Venus* III. 260 It salbe sa, as I haif Imperat. **1677** HALE *Prim. Orig. Man.* I. i. 30 They are not acts that are imperate by the Will.

B. as *adj.* 'Commanded' *sc.* by the will; opp. to ELICIT *a.*, q.v.

1624 F. WHITE *Repl. Fisher* 544 All the actions elicite or imperate, which a sinner must performe.. that God may be pacified. *a***1652** J. SMITH *Sel. Disc.* IV. ix. (1821) 124 All the imperate motions of our wills. **1677** HALE *Prim. Orig. Man.* I. i. 29 The Spirits shot through the Nerves are the first and immediate Instruments of the Soul in its imperate acts. **1710** NORRIS *Chr. Prud.* iii. 135 By the Will those Motions or Operations (Imperate Acts as they are call'd) which are performed by the mediation of the Body.

†'**imperate**, *v.* *Obs.* [f. L. *imperāt-*, ppl. stem of *imperā-re* (see prec.).] *trans.* To command, rule, govern.

1599 A. M. tr. *Gabelhouer's Bk. Physicke* 109/2 He hath ordaynede for the Patiente this pectoralle Conserve.. and imperated him without cessatione to vse the same both day and night. **1633** AMES *Agst. Cerem.* I. 54 There be duties.. imperated or governed by religion. **1660** R. COKE *Power & Subj.* 13 My will is that which imperates all my actions.

impe'ration. *rare.* [n. of action from L. *imperāre* (see above).] The action of commanding.

1786–9 BENTHAM *Princ. Internat. Law* ii. Wks. 1838–43 II. 540 What is dominion? It is either the power of contrectation, or else that of imperation.. Under the head of the power of imperation is comprised all the power which the sovereign is accustomed to exercise.

imperatival (ɪmpɛrə'taɪvəl), *a.* *Gram.* [f. next + -AL¹.] Pertaining to the imperative mood.

1873 F. HALL *Mod. Eng.* 318 *Substantival* and its congeners.. *adjectival, affixal, diminutival, imperatival, nominatival.* **1875** LIGHTFOOT *Comm. Col.* (1886) 222 It is not.. that the participle itself has any imperatival force.

imperative (ɪm'pɛrətɪv), *a.* and *sb.* [ad. late L. *imperātīv-us* of or proceeding from a command, commanded (Macrobius), 'modus imperativus' (Martianus Capella), f. *imperāre, imperāt-* to command: see -IVE. Cf. F. *impératif*.]

A. *adj.*

1. a. *Gram.* Expressing command: applied to the verbal mood (or any form belonging to it) which expresses a command, request, or exhortation.

1530 PALSGR. Introd. 31 Modes: every parfyte verbe hath vi, the indicatyve, imperatyve [etc.]. **1581** R. GOADE in *Confer.* II. (1584) M ij b, It is the Imperatiue mode, and therefore a commaundement. **1665** WITHER *Lord's Prayer* 125 It is usual with the Prophets to express in the Imperative Mood, and by way of Prayer, those Benedictions which God hath decreed and promised to the Righteous. **1824** L. MURRAY *Eng. Gram.* (ed. 5) I. 112 The Imperative Mood is used for commanding, exhorting, entreating, or permitting.

b. ***imperative logic*** (*Philos.*): the theory of logical reasoning based on the commands and obligations contained in the imperative mood.

[**1839** MILL *Let.* 4 Nov. in *Works* (1963) XIII. 412 Above all mine is a logic of the indicative mood alone—the logic of the imperative, in which the major premiss says not *is* but *ought*—I do not meddle with.] **1939** *Philos. of Sci.* VI. 453 (*heading*) A logic of the doubtful. On optative and imperative logic. **1952** R. M. HARE *Lang. Morals* I. ii. 27 It is important to realize that *modal* imperative logic is as distinct from the logic of simple imperatives as in the case of the indicative mood. **1958** *Analysis* XVIII. 50 A thoroughgoing reduction of deontic logic to imperative logic would require Procrustean amputations.

2. Having the quality or property of commanding; of the nature of, characterized by, or expressing a command; commanding; peremptory.

1598 FLORIO, *Imperatiuo*, imperatiue, or commanding. **1612–15** BP. HALL *Contempl., O.T.* XV. iv, The suits of kings are imperative. **1794** GOUV. MORRIS in Sparks *Life & Writ.* (1832) II. 394 Subject to the imperative, and too often the imperious, mandates of a Committee. **1852** MRS. STOWE *Uncle Tom's C.* xxxii. 293 A female voice said something in a quick imperative tone.

3. Demanding obedience, execution, action, etc.; that must be done or performed; urgent; of the nature of a duty; obligatory.

1823 BYRON *Juan* VI. cxiv, But such precipitation may end ill, Even at your own imperative expense. **1843** LYTTON *Last Bar.* I. v, Science was of more imperative necessity than even Hunger. **1856** KANE *Arct. Expl.* II. 191 The condition of our sick men made it imperative that I should return at once. **1891** *Spectator* 4 Apr., The work is quite imperative, and its result will be most beneficial.

B. *sb.* **1.** *Gram.* The imperative mood, or a verbal form belonging to it (see A. 1).

1530 PALSGR. Introd. 36 *Je puis* wanteth his present imparatyve and his present optatyve. **1624** N. DE LAUNE tr. *Du Moulin's Logic* 108 Imperatives, Optatives, and Subjunctives enter not into an Enuntiation. **1727–41** CHAMBERS *Cycl.* s.v. *Mood*, I love, is a simple affirmation; love, an imperative. **1755** JOHNSON *Eng. Gram.*, The Imperative prohibitory is seldom applied in the second person.. without the word *do*; as *Stop him, but do not hurt him.* **1871** ROBY *Lat. Gram.* §581 The imperative present appears to consist of shortened forms of the indicative present.

2. a. An imperative action, speech, condition, etc.; an action, etc. involving or expressing a command; a command.

1606 BIRNIE *Kirk-Buriall* xvi, The Lords lawes are either imperatiues of good or inhibitiues of ill. **1633** T. ADAMS *Exp. 2 Peter* iii. 16. 1452 There be.. such mysticall allusions, such majesticall imparatives. **1837** SIR W. HAMILTON *Metaph.* xlvi. (1870) II. 516 The unconditional imperative of the moral law. **1868** BAIN *Ment. & Mor. Sc.* (1875) 459 There is no act however trivial which cannot be raised to the position of a moral act, by the imperative of society.

b. ***categorical imperative***: see CATEGORICAL A. 1 c.

1796 F. A. NITSCH *Gen. View Kant's Princ. concerning Man* 195 An Imperative.. which is founded upon reason itself.. is a Categorical Imperative which represents an action as necessary in itself. **1817** COLERIDGE *Biog. Lit.* 70 The unconditional command, or (in the technical language of his school) the categorical imperative, of the conscience. **1888** *Pall Mall G.* 29 Oct. 2/2 The practical importance of the doctrine of the Divinity of Christ has always seemed to me to lie in the fact that it invests His teaching with the authority of the Categorical Imperative.

imperatively (ɪm'pɛrətɪvlɪ), *adv.* [f. prec. adj. + -LY².] In an imperative manner; commandingly; †*Gram.* in or with the imperative mood.

*a***1603** T. CARTWRIGHT *Confut. Rhem. N.T.* (1618) 647 Whether it be turned Imperatiuely or Indicatiuely, it hurteth not us. *a***1710** BP. BULL *Serm.* I. i. (R.), The words, though they are delivered imperatively, yet are a plain promise. **1833** J. H. NEWMAN *Arians* I. ii. (1876) 37 A remedy, which.. the circumstances of the times imperatively required. **1866** GEO. ELIOT *F. Holt* xxxiii, Felix said, imperatively, 'Leave him there'.

imperativeness (ɪm'pɛrətɪvnɪs). [f. as prec. + -NESS.] The quality of being imperative; commandingness, authoritativeness; obligatoriness.

1840 *Fraser's Mag.* XXII. 196 That dictatorial imperativeness.. often associated with long service and high command. **1879** H. SPENCER *Data of Ethics* xi. §68. 187 The acts by which each maintains his own life must.. precede in imperativeness all other acts of which he is capable.

imperativism (ɪm'pɛrətɪvɪz(ə)m). *Philos.* [f. IMPERATIV(E *a.* and *sb.* + -ISM 2.] Reasoning based on the concept of obligation contained in the imperative mood (see IMPERATIVE *a.* 1 a and 1 b). Hence **im'perativist**, one who bases his reasoning on a concept of obligation; as *adj.*, of or pertaining to reasoning based on such a concept.

1926 R. B. PERRY *Gen. Theory of Value* iii. 79 They have been driven to adopt a metaphysical 'voluntarism' or 'imperativism'. **1950** S. E. TOULMIN *Exam. Place of Reason in Ethics* IV. xiii. 189 The 'imperativist' is prepared to consider the present account because it represents for him a sophisticated imperative theory. **1952** *Mind* LXI. 96 The imperativist analysis of moral indicatives cannot be correct. **1960** *Philos. of Sci.* XXVII. 374 This exposure tells against the 'imperativist' interpretation of law-sentences. **1963** W. SELLARS in Castañeda & Nakhnikian *Morality & Lang. of Conduct* 163 A rough approximation to more sophisticated analyses of the imperativist type. **1965** *Philos. Rev.* LXXIV. 108 It is Zink, and not the regiment of imperativists, emotivists,.. and noncognitivists, who is faithful to the insights of Moore and Wittgenstein.

‖**imperator** (ɪmpə'reɪtə(r)). Also 6 emp-. [L., agent-n. from *imperā-re* to command.]

a. In Roman History, a word originally meaning 'commander', under the Republic,

conferred by salutation of the soldiers on a victorious general; afterwards, under the Empire, confined to the head of the state, in whose name all victories were won, and thus the equivalent of its English representative, EMPEROR, q.v.

From the ancient Roman Emperors, it was continued as the Latin title of the Emperors of the East and West, and so of all monarchs who claimed 'imperial' rank or position. In this sense it was commonly assumed (in Latin documents) by the Old English kings from Æthelstan onward (see Freeman *Norm. Conq.* I. iii, and App. C); the OE. equivalent was *cásere* (cf. CÆSAR, KASER, KAISER), the OF. repr. was *empereor*, whence EMPEROR.

1579–80 NORTH *Plutarch* (1595) 679 Pompeyes souldiers saluted him by the name of Imperator. **1646** SIR T. BROWNE *Pseud. Ep.* VII. xvi. 374 Julius Augustus and Tiberius with great humility or popularity refused the name of Imperator. **1853** *W. Smith's Smaller Dict. Gr. & Rom. Antiq.* (1868) 211/1 After a victory it was usual for the soldiers to salute their commander as imperator, but this salutation neither gave nor confirmed the title, since the title as a matter of course was given with the imperium. **1867** FREEMAN *Norm. Conq.* I. iii. 145 From the days of Æthelstan onwards, our kings..appear in their public acts as *Basileus*, *Cæsar*, *Imperator*, *Imperator Augustus*.

b. *gen.* Absolute ruler, emperor; commander, ruler. (Cf. EMPEROR 3 b.)

1588 SHAKS. *L.L.L.* III. i. 187 [Cupid] King of Codpeeces, Sole Emperator and great generall Of trotting Parrators. **1596** *Edw. III*, II. ii. 26 She is as imperator over me; And I to her Am as a kneeling vassal. **1613** *Haga at Constant.* in *Harl. Misc.* (Malh.) III. 223 Supreme lord of the noble house of the Ottomans, and the imperator of all other rulers and lords in the world.

Hence **impe'ratorship**, the office of imperator.

1848 *Fraser's Mag.* XXXVIII. 242 This new theoretical Imperatorship consolidates itself. **1882–3** SCHAFF *Encycl. Relig. Knowl.* I. 407 His [Vespasian's] elevation to the imperatorship.

imperatorial (ɪmpɛrə'tɔərɪəl), *a.* [f. L. *imperātōri-us*, f. *imperātor* (see prec.) + -AL[1].]

1. Of, pertaining to, characteristic of, or befitting an imperator, emperor, or commander; imperial.

imperatorial province, a province of the ancient Roman empire, of which the Cæsar was himself the proconsul, the administration being by a *legatus* with prætorian power.

1660 BURNEY Κερδ. Δῶρον (1661) 15 St. Peter attributes to his Majesty the Imperatorial Title of Supream. *a* **1806** MACARTNEY *Wks.* I. 153 (Jod.) It calls for an unusual term in our language, an imperatorial control. **1823** DE QUINCEY *Lett. Educ.* iv. Wks. 1860 XIV. 77 A speech of imperatorial grandeur. **1832–4** —— *Cæsars* ibid. X. 228 *note*, In the imperatorial provinces, where the governor bore the title of *Proprætor*. **1878** SEELEY *Stein* II. 470 He was an imperatorial, a kingly man.

†**2.** Of or pertaining to absolute command; imperative. *Obs.*

1690 NORRIS *Beatitudes* (1692) 241 Moses deliver'd his Law after an Imperatorial way, saying, Thou shalt not do this.

Hence **impera'torially** *adv.*, in an imperatorial way; as an emperor.

1839 DE QUINCEY *Casuistry* Wks. VIII. 277 *note*, He provided..ropes of purple and of gold intertwisted, that he might hang himself imperatorially.

†**impera'torian**, *a.* *Obs.* [f. as prec. + -AN.] = IMPERATORIAL.

1640 SOMNER *Antiq. Canterb.* 365 That age as much affecting the Imperatorian Brevity, as ours abhorres it. *a* **1670** HACKET *Abp. Williams* I. (1692) 167 He [James I] did so little bear up with an imperatorian resolution against the method of their ways.

imperatorin (ɪmpɛrə'tɔərɪn). *Chem.* Also imperatrin. [f. Bot. L. *Imperatoria* (see below) + -IN.] A neutral substance discovered in the root of masterwort, *Imperatoria Ostruthium*, and afterwards proved to be the same as peucedanin.

1838 T. THOMSON *Chem. Org. Bodies* 820 Wackenroder, who examined it particularly, distinguished it by the name of *imperatrin*. **1866–72** WATTS *Dict. Chem.* IV. 386 *Peucedanin, Imperatorin*, $C_{12}H_{12}O_3$.

†**impera'torious**, *a.* *Obs.* [f. L. *imperātōri-us* + -OUS.] = IMPERATORIAL.

1625 SIR T. COVENTRY in Hacket *Abp. Williams* II. (1692) 9 His Majesty's Speech, though short, yet Full and Princely, and rightly Imperatorious. **1674** MILTON *Declar. Elect. King Poland* Wks. (1851) 463 The only (under God) imperatorious Valour and Prudence of Sobietski.

Hence †**impera'toriously** *adv.*, as a commander or general.

1620 GRANGER *Div. Logike* 318 Hee did it Strategicos, that is, Imperatoriously, or Nestoriously.

†**im'peratory**, *a.* *Obs.* [ad. L. *imperātōri-us*, f. IMPERATOR.] Imperatorial, imperial.

1616 CHAPMAN *Homer's Hymns, Hermes* 807 The mightie Imperatorie Art. *Ibid.* 997 In awe of thy high Imperatory hand.

†**im'peratrice.** *Obs.* Also emp-. [a. F. *impératrice* (16th c. in Littré), ad. L. *imperātrix, -trīcem*, fem. of IMPERATOR.] Empress.

c **1460** J. RUSSELL *Bk. Nurture* 1196 As pope, emperoure, Emperatrice, and Cardynalle. **1500–20** DUNBAR *Poems* lxxv. 61 Empryce of pryss, imperatrice. **1542** HENRY VIII *Declar.* 201 Dauid Kyng of Scottis did homage to Matilde the Emperatrice.

So ‖**impe'ratrix.**

1623 COCKERAM, *Imperatrix*, shee that commandeth. **1813** T. BUSBY *Lucretius* IV. *Comment.* xxxiii, The soul is her own imperatrix.

imperceable, -iable, var. of IMPIERCEABLE *a.*

imperceivable (ɪmpə'siːvəb(ə)l), *a.* Now *rare.* [f. IM-[2] + PERCEIVABLE.] Imperceptible.

a **1617** BAYNE *On Eph.* (1658) 137 The working of this is sweet and imperceivable. **1719** DE FOE *Crusoe* II. vi, In a manner to us imperceivable. **1819** W. LAWRENCE *Lect. Man* x. (1844) 377 There is no circumstance..which does not pass by imperceivable gradations into the opposite character.

Hence **imper'ceivableness**, imperceptibility; **imper'ceivably** *adv.*, imperceptibly.

1617 COLLINS *Def. Bp. Ely* II. viii. 297 This came vp secretly, closely, imperceiueably. *a* **1714** SHARP *Serm.* III. v. (R.), This imperceiveableness of the impressions made upon our souls by the Holy Spirit, was that which our Saviour signified to Nicodemus.

†**imperceived**, *a.* *Obs. rare.* [f. IM-[2] + *perceived*, pa. pple. of PERCEIVE *v.*] Not perceived or discerned.

1624 BP. MOUNTAGU *Immed. Address* 26 In a moment of Time, in imperceiued time, it passeth with speed from East to West. *a* **1691** BOYLE *Gen. Hist. Air* vi. (1692) 23 Finding the Bladder to be pump'd up, we would have tied up the contained Air, but could not do it by reason of an imperceiv'd Hole.

†**imper'ceiverant**, *a.* *Obs.* In 7 **imperseuerant.** [f. IM-[2] + PERCEIVERANT perceiving (*c* 1509).] Not perceiving, void of perception, undiscerning.

1611 SHAKS. *Cymb.* IV. i. 15 The Lines of my body are as well drawne as his..yet this imperseuerant Thing loues him in my despight.

imperceptibility (ˌɪmpəsɛptɪ'bɪlɪtɪ). [f. next: see -ITY.]

1. The quality or condition of being imperceptible; incapability of being perceived.

1677 GILPIN *Demonol.* (1867) 330 The wiles, depths, secrets, and devices of Satan..in their own nature imply a studied or designed secrecy and imperceptibility. **1794** MRS. PIOZZI *Synon.* II. 65 While metaphysicians expand their subtleties into imperceptibility.

†**2.** Incapability of perceiving. *Obs. rare.*

1786 tr. *Swedenborg's Chr. Relig.* §439 A total ignorance and imperceptibility of the delight of heavenly love.

imperceptible (ɪmpə'sɛptɪb(ə)l), *a.* (*sb.*) Also 7 inp-. [a. F. *imperceptible* (1425 in Hatz.-Darm.), ad. med.L. *imperceptibil-is*, f. *im-* (IM-[2]) + *perceptibil-is* PERCEPTIBLE.] Not perceptible; incapable of being perceived.

a. That by its nature cannot be perceived or discerned; naturally incapable of affecting the perceptive faculties.

1526 *Pilgr. Perf.* (W. de W. 1531) 201 b, Sodeynly in tyme imperceptyble he fourmed that moost blessed body in her wombe. **1603** HOLLAND *Plutarch's Mor.* 1019 As for the soule it is invisibile, yea and inperceptible to all the naturall senses. **1768–74** TUCKER *Lt. Nat.* (1852) II. 44 Some diseases..proceeding from an imperceptible vermin within us. **1840** HOOD *Kilmansegg, Christening* x, He..Seem'd washing his hands with invisible soap In imperceptible water.

b. So slight, gradual, subtle, or indistinct as not to be perceptible.

1635–56 COWLEY *Davideis* IV. 383 Strange Play of Fate! when might'iest humane things Hang on such small, Imperceptible Strings! **1737** [S. BERINGTON] *G. di Lucca's Mem.* 78 An imperceptible Dew, which tho' not so thick as a Fog, moisten'd the Surface of the Ground. **1853** RUSKIN *Stones Ven.* II. vi, The three classes..pass into each other by imperceptible gradations. **1880** GEIKIE *Phys. Geog.* iv. 216 The solid earth is subject to movements either sudden and violent, or slow and imperceptible.

B. *sb.* An imperceptible thing or creature; with *the*: that which is imperceptible.

1709 ADDISON *Tatler* No. 119 ¶2, I should be wonderfully pleased to see a natural History of Imperceptibles, containing a true Account of such Vegetables and Animals as grow and live out of Sight. **1862** H. SPENCER *First Princ.* II. xii. §93 (1875) 278 An entire history of anything must include its appearance out of the imperceptible and its disappearance into the imperceptible.

Hence **imper'ceptibleness**, imperceptibility.

1677 HALE *Prim. Orig. Man.* I. i. 18 By reason of their..subtilty and imperceptibleness to us. **1882** J. PARKER *Apost. Life* I. 15 The gradient has evermore lifted itself up by imperceptibleness of degree.

imperceptibly (ɪmpə'sɛptɪblɪ), *adv.* [f. IMPERCEPTIBLE + -LY[2].] In an imperceptible manner or degree; so as not to be perceived.

1603 FLORIO *Montaigne* (1634) 117 So doth our minde cast her points diversly and imperceptibly. **1734** BERKELEY *Visitat. Charge* Wks. 1871 IV. 653 Discourse..that imperceptibly glides from one subject to another. **1824** L. MURRAY *Eng. Gram.* (ed. 5) I. 213 The proposed variations ..are introduced and established almost imperceptibly. **1875** JOWETT *Plato* (ed. 2) IV. 276 The powers of sense and of reflection..pass imperceptibly into one another.

imperception (ɪmpə'sɛpʃən). [f. IM-[2] + PERCEPTION.] Absence or want of perception.

1662 H. MORE *Philos. Writ.* Pref. Gen. 16 Lay hold on that imperceptive part of the Soul, or on the Soul it self in the state of Silence or Imperception. **1663** CHARLETON *Chor. Gigant.* 64 An imperception of the majesty of his person. **1889** H. J. BARKER *Orig. English* i. 14 It is in this naïve imperception of distortion..that the whole humour of school-boyishness lies. **1961** W. R. BRAIN *Speech Disorders* xiii. 143 Hughlings Jackson..first recognized both agnosia and apraxia. He called the former 'imperception'. **1968** P. MCKELLAR *Experience & Behaviour* x. 260 The selective imperception of the virtuous actions or motivation of people we dislike.

imperceptive (ɪmpə'sɛptɪv), *a.* [f. IM-[2] + PERCEPTIVE.]

1. Not perceptive or perceiving; lacking perception; impercipient.

1661 RUST *Origen & Opin.* in *Phenix* (1721) I. 51 That Congruity..is more deeply pitch'd in her imperceptive Powers. **1768–74** TUCKER *Lt. Nat.* (1852) I. 302 Not producible by any combination whatsoever of imperceptive and inactive ingredients. **1880** GRANT WHITE *Every-Day Eng.* 87 Thus is the ear..habitually dull and imperceptive in regard to the utterance of the lips.

2. In pass. sense: Imperceptible. *rare.* (Cf. *unexpressive* in Shaks. and Milton.)

1876 MOZLEY *Univ. Serm.* iv. (1877) 95 Like some fragrant scent in the air, which comes and goes..and rises and falls in imperceptive waves.

Hence **imper'ceptiveness, impercep'tivity**, imperceptive quality or condition.

1662 H. MORE *Philos. Writ.* Pref. Gen. 16 Whose Imperceptiveness is no more Obstacle to her natural and plastical Operations, then [etc.]. **1681** GLANVILL *Sadducismus* I. 165 The third objection touching the Imperceptivity of an extended Substance.

†**im'perch**, *v.* *Obs. rare.* [f. IM-[1] + PERCH *v.*] To place *on* (something) as on a perch.

1786 *Europ. Mag.* IX. 293 Imperch'd on a post.

impercipient (ɪmpə'sɪpɪənt). *a.* (*sb.*) [f. IM-[2] + PERCIPIENT.] Not perceiving; lacking perception.

1813 C. LOFFT in E. H. Barker *Parriana* (1828) II. 77 *note*, A quality of impercipient substance. **1871** SIR H. HOLLAND *Recoll. Past Life* (1872) 180 A man singularly impercipient of natural beauty or grandeur. **1882** F. W. H. MYERS *Renewal Youth* 96 And is the World's in very truth An impercipient Soul?

B. *sb.* One who lacks perception.

1898 T. HARDY *Wessex Poems* 181 (*title*) The Impercipient.

So **imper'cipience**, lack of perception.

1891 T. HARDY *Tess* v. xlix. in *Graphic* 5 Dec. 665/2 Tess's warm outpouring lay awaiting him in a drawer..its ardour pitifully wasting itself on the cold darkness and impercipience of that receptacle. **1905** *Westm. Gaz.* 30 Sept. 4/1 It is only our physical or mental impercipience that leaves the sluggish..mind an easy prey to the promptings of vulgarity. **1925** A. QUILLER-COUCH *Charles Dickens* 71 A lost child, mooning incuriously along the hedgerows with an impercipience rivalling that of a famous Master of Trinity. **1971** *Country Life* 1 Apr. 785/2 H. G. Wells making one of his terrifying comments (terrifying for impercipience).

†**imper'cussively**, *adv.* *Obs. rare.* [f. IM-[2] + PERCUSSIVE + -LY[2].] Without percussion or striking.

1708 MOTTEUX *Rabelais* v. xx. (1737) 90 This caus'd the Pontiffs..to sacrifice to the great Deity in Silence, impercussively, without any vociferous..Sound.

†**im'perdible**, *a.* *Obs. rare.* [f. IM-[2] + L. *perdĕre* to lose + -IBLE.] That cannot be lost or destroyed. Hence †**imperdi'bility**, the quality of being imperdible, indestructibility.

1661 FELTHAM *Disc. Eccl.* ii. 11 Wks. 377 As they [wisdom and knowledge] are harder in their acquisition, so are they more imperdible and steddy in their stay. **1713** DERHAM *Phys.-Theol.* v. ix. 350 Neither are those pretious Things of greater use to the making of..Utensils..by means of their Beauty, Imperdibility, and Ductility.

†**im'pere.** *Sc. Obs. rare.* [a. obs. legal F. *impere* (Godef.), ad. L. *imperium*: see IMPERIUM.] A command, order.

1548 G. WISHART tr. *Swiss Confess. Faith* in *Wodrow Soc. Misc.* (1844) 22 We shulde be subject in holynes to the majestrate..so longe as his commandements, statutes and imperes evidently repugneth not with God.

impere, obs. form of IMPAIR *v.*

imperence ('ɪmpərəns). Also **-ance, impurence.** A vulgar corruption of IMPUDENCE, perh. associated with IMPERTINENCE.

1766 COLMAN & GARRICK *Cland. Marriage* v. 78, I wonder at your impurence, Mr. Brush. **1821** EGAN *Life London* II. ii. 192 She is blowing up the nasty fellow for his imperance. **1837** DICKENS *Pickw.* xiv, 'Let me alone, imperence', said the young lady.

So **imperent** ('ɪmpərənt) *a.*, vulgar corruption of *impudent*.

1838 JAS. GRANT *Sk. Lond.* 57 He's werry imperent, to make any reflekshuns o' the kind.

imperes, obs. form of EMPRESS.

imperfect (ɪm'pɜːfɪkt), *a.* (*sb.*) Forms: *α.* 4–5 **imparfit(e, inperfit(e, inparfit(e, -yt,** 5 **inperfyght,** 5–7 **imperfit,** (5–6 **-yt(e,** 6 **-fite, -fett).** *β.* 6 **imperfecte,** 6– **imperfect.** [ME. a. F. *imparfait* (1372 in Hatz.-Darm.) = It. *imperfetto*, Sp. *imperfecto*, Pg. *imperfeito*:—L. *imperfectus*, f. *im-* (IM-[2]) + *perfectus* PERFECT. Subseq. influenced by, and, in 16th c., assimilated to, the Latin

form.] A. *adj.* Not perfect; the opposite of perfect.

I. Ordinary senses.

1. Wanting some part or adjunct usually present, or necessary to the full form or development; not fully formed, made, or done; unfinished, incomplete; of less than the full amount; deficient.

c **1391** CHAUCER *Astrol.* I. §18 Som of hem semen perfit cercles, & somme semen inperfit. *c* **1440** *Gesta Rom.* II. xxi. 339 (Add. MS.) The child is not apte to serve god, in that he is inparfite. **1490** CAXTON *Eneydos* xiv. 49 The werkes.. that were begonne.. be lefte wythout eny more werkyng, alle Imperfyt. **1570** BILLINGSLEY *Euclid* XI. Def. i. 312 A line is the imperfectest kinde of quantitie. **1697** DRYDEN *Virg. Georg.* III. 667 A Snake.. Leaving his Nest, and his imperfect Young. **1782** PRIESTLEY *Corrupt. Chr.* I. Pref. 19, I did not think it right to leave any of the pieces imperfect. **1856** FROUDE *Hist. Eng.* (1858) I. ii. 92 The history of the time is too imperfect to justify a positive conclusion. **1884** BOWER & SCOTT *De Bary's Phaner.* 367 Those bundles which become imperfect by disappearance of the Tracheæ.

2. Wanting some quality or attribute necessary to full efficiency, normal condition, or ideal character; not coming up to the standard; not all that it should be; defective, faulty.

c **1340** HAMPOLE *Prose Tr.* 45 Othir saules þat ere in þis lyfe inperfite.. ne had noghte þe fullhede of charite.. sall haue þe lawere mede. **1494** FABYAN *Chron.* VII. 305 To brynge men of more inperfyght lyfe, into yᵉ place of men more parfyght. **1502** ATKYNSON tr. *De Imitatione* III. vi. 200, I am imperfite of vertu & feble in loue. **1605** SHAKS. *Lear* IV. vi. 5 Your other Senses grow imperfect By your eyes anguish. **1660** F. BROOKE tr. *Le Blanc's Trav.* 176 He had written them in French.. and withall in an imperfect and bad character. **1729** BUTLER *Serm.* Wks. 1874 II. 184 So imperfect a creature as man. **1872** RUSKIN *Eagle's N.* §88 Ignorance.. will produce what is imperfect, but not offensive.

†3. Positively faulty, vicious, evil. *Obs.*

1377 LANGL. *P. Pl.* B. xv. 50 'Þanne artow inparfit', quod he, 'and one of prydes knyȝtes'. *Ibid.* 127 Prestes inparfit and prechoures after syluer. **1393** *Ibid.* C. IV. 389 Al reson reproueþ such imparfit puple. **1611** COTGR., *Vicieux*,.. erronious, imperfect, vnsound. **1630** *R. Johnson's Kingd. & Commw.* 266 Their imperfect customes of drinking.

4. Of persons in respect of imperfect or defective action or accomplishment: Not fully instructed or accomplished *in*.

1570 *Henry's Wallace* XI. 1432 Blaym nocht the buk, thocht I be imperfyte [*c* **1470** wnperfyt]. **1605** SHAKS. *Macb.* I. iii. 70 Stay you imperfect Speakers, tell me more. **1650** SIR T. BROWNE *Pseud. Ep.* II. v. (1658) 98 A main Reason why the Ancients were so imperfect in the Doctrine of Meteors, was their ignorance of Gunpowder and Fire-works. **1676** tr. *Guillatiere's Voy. Athens* 221 If any of the Boys were out or imperfect, he was corrected by the next.. till the whole number of words were read. **1863** KINGLAKE *Crimea* (1876) I. xvii. 373 Any statesmen who forgot him in their reckoning must have been imperfect in their notion of political dynamics.

II. Technical senses.

5. *Gram.* Applied to a tense which denotes action going on but not completed; usually to the *past* tense of incomplete or progressive action (more fully called ***past imperfect***, formerly sometimes ***preter-imperfect***), as Gr. ἔγραφον , L. *scribēbam*, F. *j'écrivais*, Eng. *I was writing*.

In the grammar of the Semitic languages, now generally applied to the 'tense' or verbal form with prefixed pronominal elements, sometimes called *future* and *present*.

In Slavonic Grammar, formerly sometimes used for IMPERFECTIVE.

1530 PALSGR. 84 The preter imperfit tens, as *je parloye*. **1678** PHILLIPS (ed. 4), *Imperfect*, or *Preter-Imperfect Tense*. **1832** PINNOCK *L. Murray's Eng. Gram.* viii. §6. 129 The Imperfect Tense represents the action or event, either as past and finished or as remaining unfinished at a certain time past. **1866** MASON *Eng. Gram.* (ed. 7) §206 Nine Primary Tenses. A. 1. The Past Imperfect, showing that at a certain past time an action was going on; as *I was writing*.. B. 1. The Present Imperfect,.. as, *I am writing*.. C. 1. The Future Imperfect,.. as, *I shall be writing*. **1871** ROBY *Lat. Gram.* §549 Three [tenses] denoting incomplete action; the Present, Future, and Imperfect (sometimes called respectively, present imperfect, future imperfect, past imperfect). **1892** DRIVER *Heb. Tenses* (ed. 3) i, It will be better to acquiesce in the names now generally employed.. and to call them by the terms *perfect* and *imperfect* respectively. *Ibid.* iii, The imperfect in Hebrew, as in the other Semitic languages, indicates action as *nascent*, as evolving itself actively from its subject, as developing.

†6. *Arith.* **a.** Applied to a number which is not equal to the sum of its aliquot parts: opp. to *perfect*. (Cf. DEFICIENT A. 1 c.) **b.** Applied to a power (square, cube, etc.) whose root is an incommensurable quantity: opposed to a *perfect square*, *cube*, etc. *Obs.*

1557 RECORDE *Whetst.* A iv b, Imperfecte nombers be suche, whose partes added together, doe make either more or lesse then the whole number it self.. As 12, whose partes are 1, 2, 3, 4 and 6, which make 16. **1674** JEAKE *Arith.* (1696) 5 Imperfect numbers.. are those whose even parts added together, will not return the Primary Number. **1706** W. JONES *Syn. Palmar. Matheseos* 114 The Roots of Imperfect Powers are Incommensurable Quantities.

7. *Mus.* †**a.** In mediæval music, applied to a note when reckoned as twice (instead of three times) the length of a note of the next lower denomination; and hence to those 'modes', etc. characterized by such relative value of the notes. **b.** Applied to Plain Chant melodies which do not extend through the entire compass of the mode in which they are written (Grove *Dict. Mus.* s.v.). **c.** Sometimes applied to a diminished (as distinguished from a perfect) fourth, fifth, or triad: see DIMINISHED 4 a.

imperfect cadence: a cadence ending on some chord other than the direct chord of the tonic, usually that of the dominant, and having the effect of a partial close or stop (like that of a comma or semicolon in a sentence); also called a *half-close*. ***imperfect concords*** or ***consonances***: a name given to the thirds and sixths, major and minor.

1597 MORLEY *Introd. Mus.* 18 The Moode Imperfect of the more prolation is, when all go by two, except the Minome which goeth by three. *Ibid.* 19 The Moode Imperfect of the lesse prolation is, when all go by two: as two Longes to the Large, two Breeues to the Longe, two Semibreeues to the Breefe, and two Minomes to the Semibriefe. **1667** C. SIMPSON *Compend.* 40 Concords are.. Perfect and Imperfect.. Perfects are these, 5th, 8th with all their Octaves. Imperfects are a 3rd, 6th, and their Octaves. **1875** OUSELEY *Harmony* xiii. 156 When it is wished to make a kind of rest or division in a piece of music.. it is usual to employ what is called the Imperfect cadence, or half-close. **1877** STAINER *Harmony* xii, The most common position of the imperfect triad is its first inversion. **1880** C. H. H. PARRY in Grove *Dict. Mus.* I. 766 Mediæval writers (accustomed to look upon the number Three—the Symbol of the Blessed Trinity—as the sign of Perfection) applied the term Imperfect to all rhythmic proportions subject to the binary division... Thus, the Minim—always equal to two Crotchets only—was essentially Imperfect, in common with all other notes shorter than the Semibreve. The Large was also Imperfect, whenever it was made equal to two Longs [etc.]. *Ibid.* 768 An example of an Imperfect Cadence which concludes on a chord other than the Dominant. **1889** E. PROUT *Harmony* (ed. 10) i. §29 The consonant intervals are.. subdivided into perfect and imperfect consonances.

8. *Bot.* **a.** Applied to flowers in which any normal part is wanting.

Formerly, esp. to flowers having no corolla or perianth; now to those in which either stamens, or pistils, or both, are absent.

1704 J. HARRIS *Lex. Techn.*, *Imperfect Flowers* of Plants are such as want the *Petala*: and therefore they are sometimes called *Apetalous*, and sometimes *Stamineous*. **1855** MAYNE *Expos. Lex.*, *Imperfectus*, applied to flowers which want the anther, or pistil, or both: imperfect. **1860** LINDLEY *Sch. Bot.* i. 13 An amentum or catkin is a spike consisting of imperfect flowers.

b. Of a stage in the life cycle of a fungus: not producing or not known to produce sexual organs. Of a fungus, having (apparently) no sexual stage: belonging to the group designated ***imperfect fungi*** (or formally, in mod.L., *Fungi Imperfecti*), in which are included all those fungi which, because a sexual stage is missing or unknown, cannot be assigned to other taxa.

1895 M. C. COOKE *Introd. Study Fungi* xxii. 259 The group now under consideration is analogous, in external features, to the *Pyrenomycetes*, but wholly deficient of asci. The perithecia, or pseudoperithecia, include only stylospores, and have been assumed to be imperfect representatives, or imperfect stages or conditions, of the *Pyrenomyceteae*, and hence called 'imperfect capsular fungi'. **1898** *Jrnl. R. Microsc. Soc.* 660 (*heading*) Rabenhorst's cryptogamic flora of Germany (Fungi Imperfecti). **1908** *Ibid.* 626 Similar cultures were successfully carried through with *Gnomoniella tubiformis* on alder leaves, of which the 'imperfect' form was proved to be *Leptothyrium alneum*. **1952** C. J. ALEXOPOULOS *Introd. Mycol.* xiii. 312 A great many fungi are known which have septate mycelium and which, so far as anyone has been able to discover, reproduce only by means of conidia. Since these fungi apparently lack a sexual stage (perfect stage), we call them, commonly, 'imperfect fungi', and technically, Fungi Imperfecti. **1971** P. H. B. TALBOT *Princ. Fungal Taxon.* v. 77 The phase associated with asexual spores or sterile mycelia is known as the imperfect state of the fungus, while that associated with production of zygotes or of spores resulting from any type of sexual process is the perfect state.

9. *Law.* (See quots.)

1832 AUSTIN *Jurispr.* (1879) I. i. 101 An imperfect law (with the sense wherein the term is used by the Roman jurists) is a law which wants a sanction and which therefore is not binding. **1848** WHARTON *Law Lex.* 240/1 *Executory trusts.* In the case of articles of agreement, made in contemplation of marriage, and which are consequently preparatory to a settlement.. the trusts declared by them are said to be executory or imperfect, because they require an ulterior act to raise and perfect them. [See EXECUTORY *a.*[3]] **1872** *Ibid.* (ed. 5) *Imperfect obligations*, moral duties, such as charity, gratitude, etc. which cannot be enforced by law.

10. ***imperfect induction*** (*Philos.*): a term signifying induction (see INDUCTION 7) from an incomplete set of instances, usu. used in contrast to the notion of perfect induction.

[**1843** MILL *Logic* I. III. ii. §1. 352 The induction is asserted not to be perfect, unless every single individual of the class A is included in the antecedent.] *a* **1856** W. HAMILTON *Lect. Metaphysics & Logic* (1860) III. 325 This Imperfect Induction they [*sc.* logicians] held in contingent matter to be contingent. **1870** W. S. JEVONS *Elem. Lessons Logic* XXV. 213 The assertion that all the planets move in one direction round the sun.. is derived from Imperfect Induction; for it is possible that there exist planets more distant than the most distant-known planet Neptune. **1914** C. READ *Logic* (ed. 4) XV. 197 Imperfect Induction.. is.. the method of showing the credibility of an universal real proposition by an examination of *some* of the instances it includes. **1957** J. PASSMORE *100 Yrs. Philos.* i. 22 Conventionally, two sorts of induction had been distinguished: perfect and imperfect... We are driven back upon 'imperfect' induction, as.. the only sort of inductive inference.

11. ***imperfect competition*** (*Econ.*): competition diluted by elements of monopoly so that individual producers or consumers are able to exercise some control over the market price.

1881 F. Y. EDGEWORTH *Math. Psychics* II. 48 This condition, though not spontaneously generated by imperfect as by perfect competition, should be introduced *ab extra.* **1933** J. ROBINSON (*title*) The economics of imperfect competition. **1937** *Q. Jrnl. Econ.* LII. 529 'Imperfect competition' is a more familiar expression in England, while the term 'monopolistic competition' is more familiar in the United States. **1948** E. H. CHAMBERLIN *Monopolistic Competition* (ed. 6) p. ix, Monopolistic Competition is a fusion of the.. theories of monopoly and competition, whereas Imperfect Competition contains no monopoly. **1961** *Rev. Econ. Stud.* XXVIII. 182 Writers on imperfect competition in the product and factor markets have paid little attention to this question. **1969** D. C. HAGUE *Managerial Econ.* iv. 87 Imperfect competition, that is to say.. markets where there is not either pure competition or monopoly.

B. as *sb.*

1. *Gram.* The imperfect (i.e. past imperfect) tense: see A. 5 above.

1871 *Public Sch. Lat. Gram.* §66 The Imperfect expresses: (1) Action going on in time past along with other action.. (2) Action repeated or habitual in time past. **1873** F. HALL *Mod. Eng.* 324 Who, in the next place, devised our modern imperfects passive?

†2. *Mus.* An imperfect concord: see 7 (quot. 1667). *Obs.*

3. *pl.* Goods of which the quality is not high enough for them to be sold to the public, except at a reduced price.

1952 *Amer. Speech* XXVII. 264 Textile products which.. do not come up to standard quality are referred to as *imperfects*, *seconds*, and *run-of-the-mill*. **1962** E. GODFREY *Retail Selling & Organization* II. x. 95 The retail buyers.. buy up manufacturers' and wholesalers'.. factory imperfects. **1962** S. STRAND *Marketing Dict.* 358 *Imperfect*, merchandise below standard... In many cases imperfects are useful products, but because of a manufacturer's flaw.. they are removed from prime merchandise. **1969** *Observer* 9 Nov. 1/8 (Advt.), 'Imperfects' offered at a much reduced price.

†**im'perfect**, *v.* *Obs.* [f. prec. adj.] *trans.* To render imperfect; to destroy the perfection of.

1555 J. BRADFORD *Let.* in Coverdale *Lett. Mart.* (1564) 265, I deny transubstantiation.. wherby the Masse is mainteyned, christes supper peruerted, his sacrifice & crosse imperfetted, hys priesthode destroyed. *a* **1614** DONNE *Βιαθανατος* (1644) 179 As though the body of Christ could be imperfited. **1682** SIR T. BROWNE *Chr. Mor.* I. §28 Time, which perfects some Things, imperfects also others.

b. *Mus.* (See prec. 7 a.) Also *absol.*

1597 MORLEY *Introd. Mus.* Annot., This pricke standing in this place doeth imperfect. **1609** DOULAND *Ornith. Microl.* 54 A perfect Breefe can be imperfected, not onely by a Semibreefe.. but also of two Minims. *Ibid.* 55 The imperfecting Note doth goe before the Note that is imperfected.

†**im'perfected**, *a.* *Obs.* [f. IM-[2] + *perfected*, pa. pple. of PERFECT *v.*] Not perfected; incomplete, imperfect.

1552 HULOET, Imperfected, *infectus, i. non factus aut non perfectus.* *a* **1631** DONNE in *Select.* (1840) 100 Imperfected confessions (who perfects his confession?) leaue ill-gotten goods sticking upon thine heir. **1809–10** COLERIDGE *Friend* (1818) I. 158 The distinction between perfected and imperfected Obligations. **1829** E. JESSE *Jrnl. Naturalist* 297 The younger and imperfected creatures mine their way.. in the solid timber.

†**im'perfectible**, *a.*[1] *Mus.* *Obs.* [f. IMPERFECT *v.* + -IBLE.] Capable of being made imperfect (see IMPERFECT *a.* 7 a).

1609 DOULAND *Ornith. Microl.* 58 As oft as two alterable Notes are placed between two imperfectible Notes without a Pricke of Division, the Second is always altered.

imperfectible (ɪmpə'fɛktɪb(ə)l), *a.*[2] [f. IM-[2] + PERFECTIBLE. Cf. F. *imperfectible* (Littré).]

Incapable of being made perfect.

1869 FARRAR *Fam. Speech* iv. (1873) 115 Many of them apparently as imperfectible as the Ainos of Jesso or the Veddahs of Ceylon.

Hence **imperfecti'bility**, incapability of being made perfect.

1836 *Westm. Rev.* Apr. 241 The 'imperfectibility' of men's nature is visible in their lives. **1971** *Nature* 31 Dec. 523/1 The same principle of imperfectibility applies to all sex chromosome mechanisms.

imperfection (ɪmpə'fɛkʃən). [a. F. *imperfection* (12th c., Oxf. Ps.), or ad. L. *imperfectiōn-em*, f. *imperfectus* IMPERFECT *a.*]

1. The condition or quality of being imperfect (usually in sense 2 of the adj.); incompleteness; defectiveness, faultiness.

c **1380** WYCLIF *Sel. Wks.* III. 436 Seculer lordship þat clerkis hanne nou smacchiþ imperfeccioun on many maner. *c* **1386** CHAUCER *Pars. T.* ¶933 Ihesu crist is entierly al good in hym nys noon inperfeccion. *c* **1450** tr. *De Imitatione* I. iii. 5 All maner perfeccioun in þis worlde haþ a maner of imperfeccion annexed þerto. **1545** RAYNOLD *Byrth Mankynde* (1564) 18 b, Imperfection is, when that any perticuler creature doth lacke any propertie, instrument, or qualitie which commonly by nature is in all other, or the more part, of that kynd. **1667** MILTON *P.L.* VIII. 423 Man by number is to manifest His single imperfection, and beget Like of his like. **1772** PRIESTLEY *Inst. Relig.* (1782) II. 65 [They] bear the marks of human imperfection. **1875** JOWETT *Plato* (ed. 2) IV. 44 The necessary imperfection of language

seems to require that we should view the truth under more than one aspect.

2. (with *pl.*) An instance of this quality or condition; a detail or particular in which a thing is imperfect or faulty; a defect, fault, blemish.

1398 TREVISA *Barth. De P.R.* x. x. (1495) 380 Asshes hath this defawte and inperfeccyon, that though he be euery daye moysted..yet he is alwaye barayn. **1526** *Pilgr. Perf.* (W. de W. 1531) 1 b, Wherin..I myght loke, as in a..lokyng glasse ..and perceyue myne owne imperfeccyons. **1602** SHAKS. *Ham.* I. v. 79 No reckoning made, but sent to my account With all my imperfections on my head. **1774** C. J. PHIPPS *Voy. N. Pole* 87 Error [to] be attributed to the imperfections in the manner of measuring the distance. **1875** JOWETT *Plato* (ed. 2) V. 8 He has left imperfections, which would have been removed if he had lived a few years longer.

†**3.** *Mus.* The making of a note 'imperfect', or the condition of its being 'imperfect': see IMPERFECT *a.* 7 a. *Obs.*

1597 MORLEY *Introd. Mus.* 24 Imperfection..is the taking away of the third part of a perfect notes value. **1614** T. RAVENSCROFT (*title*) A briefe Discovrse of..Charact'ring the Degrees by their Perfection, Imperfection and Diminution, in measurable Musicke, against the common Practise and Custome of the Times. **1880** C. H. H. PARRY in Grove *Dict. Mus.* I. 767 Other ways in which the Perfection of certain notes may be changed to Imperfection.

4. a. *Printing. pl.* Letters that are wanting in a fount; types cast to make up a deficiency in a fount.

1681-5 FELL *Let. to Marshall* 24 Oct. (MS.), The compositor upon Mr. Junius his lexicon wants several imperfections, that we cannot supply without his Matrices. **1683-4** J. MOXON *Mech. Exerc. Printing* (1962) 344 When the Founder has not Cast a proportionable number of each sort of Letter, the wanting Letters are called Imperfections, as making the rest of the Fount unperfect. **1771** P. LUCKOMBE *Hist. & Art of Printing* 243 Less occasion to cast imperfections, which often prove very hurtful to a new fount of letter; as they are seldom exact to the prior sorts..: so that, was it not for the eagerness of the Compositor,..many a sort, cast for perfecting, would be returned. **1808** C. STOWER *Printer's Gram.* 56 It should be an invariable rule with master printers to examine imperfections before they go into the hands of the compositor. **1888** C. T. JACOBI *Printers' Vocab.* 61 *Imperfections*, short sorts required to perfect a typefounder's bill for a fount of a certain weight. **1924** *Southward's Mod. Printing* (ed. 5) I. xx. 124 The fount should be carefully examined with a view of ascertaining whether there are any imperfections—the founder's storekeepers sometimes making mistakes in the apportionment of particular letters. **1962** DAVIS & CARTER in J. Moxon *Mech. Exerc. Printing* 344 (*footnote*) Typefounders charge for sorts at a higher rate than for founts; but sorts to supplement a fount, if ordered within three months of delivery of the fount, are called 'imperfections' and charged at fount-price.

b. *Bookbinding.* A surplus or missing sheet of a work.

1683-4 J. MOXON *Mech. Exerc. Printing* (1962) 315 He Doubles or Quires up all the other Heaps and..writes upon them Imperfections of (the Title of the Book), and Writes on it the Signature of the Sheet that is Wanting. **1790** A. SMITH *Let.* 25 May in *Sotheby Catal.* (19 July 1937) lot 74, The bookbinder informed me..that one of the copies is imperfect, wanting the sheet E. I will beg the favour of you to send down the imperfection by the first parcel you send to Scotland. **1835** J. HANNETT *Bibliopegia* I. 13 If any sheet is wanting or belongs to another volume, or is a duplicate, the further progress of the work must be suspended, till the imperfection is procured or exchanged. **1888** C. T. JACOBI *Printers' Vocab.* 61 *Imperfections*, sheets required by a binder to make good books imperfect through bad gathering, collating, or spoiled sheets. **1963** KENNEISON & SPILMAN *Dict. Printing* 95 *Imperfections*, sheets rejected by the binder and returned to the printer to be replaced.

†**imper'fectious**, *a. Obs. rare.* [f. prec., after *factious*, etc.] Full of imperfection, faulty.

1594 *Taming of Shrew* (1844) 24 Come hither thou Imperfecksious slaue! **1608** MIDDLETON *Fam. Love* II. iv, Their behaviour wit and discourse..is as imperfectious and silly as your scholars new come from the university.

imperfective (ɪmpə'fɛktɪv), *a.* (*sb.*) [f. IMPERFECT *a.* + -IVE: cf. PERFECTIVE.]

A. *adj.* †**1.** Characterized by imperfection; imperfect.

a **1677** MANTON *Serm. Hebr.* xi. verse 16, Wks. 1873 XIV. 343 If we be imperfective, the fault is in ourselves. **1684** N. S. *Crit. Enq. Edit. Bible* xvi. 156 Their Copies are often defective and imperfective.

2. *Slavonic Grammar.* Applied (after Miklosich) to a form or 'aspect' of the verb expressing action not completed (either continuous, or repeated): opp. to *perfective*. (Cf. IMPERFECT *a.* 5, and terms in *-ive*, referring to the vb., as *active*, *passive*, *indicative*, *inchoative*, *desiderative*, etc.) Also, by extension, of a similar form or aspect in some non-Slavonic languages.

1887 MORFILL *Serbian Gram.* 32 The imperfective verbs express an action that is not completed, but this may be conceived either (*a*) as merely continuing, or (*b*) repeated at various times. **1889** —— *Russian Gram.* 37 The imperfective aspect has all the moods and tenses. The perfective wants the present tense and present participle. **1890** *Athenæum* 11 Oct. 478/3 The student will..then naturally ask how he is to distinguish the perfective from the imperfective aspect. **1899** MORFILL *Gram. Bohem. Lang.* 30 The imperfective verbs express an action that is not completed. **1912** [see DURATIVE *a.*]. **1924** [see ASPECT *sb.* 9 b]. **1955** *Word* XI. 546 In general it shows the action as completed (perfective) or incomplete (imperfective) relative to the time of the action of the main verb. **1957** R. W. ZANDVOORT *Handbk. Eng. Gram.* I. ii. 33 The aspect expressed by the present participle ..is called *imperfective* or *durative*. **1958** H. G. LUNT *Fund. Russian* 59 The imperfective aspect does not say anything about the end of the action. **1972** *Language* XLVIII. 169 By accident, some presents with imperfective meaning contained an *e*, e.g. *bher-e-* 'carry'.

B. *sb.* †**1.** = IMPERFECTION 2. *Obs.*

1601 CORNWALLYES *Ess.* II. xxvi. (1631) 9 Of all our delicacies, or imperfectives of any kind there is no Author but Affection.

2. An imperfective verb, case, or aspect.

1939 *Language* XV. 230 In a space of ten lines..there are four present imperfectives. *Ibid.*, The imperfectives, whether present or past, definitely indicate a repeated or a continuing action. **1949** *Ibid.* XXV. 403 There is only one present tense, namely an imperfective. **1949** *Archivum Linguisticum* I. II. 176 Imperfectives, if not iterative, become perfective by prefixing a preposition. **1962** K. KATZNER *Russian Review Text* 183 The Imperfectives are called the *Determinati* and the *Indeterminati*. **1962** *Word* XVIII. 17 These 'secondary' imperfectives enter, in turn, into a derivational relation with the 'primary' imperfectives. **1965** *Canad. Jrnl. Linguistics* Spring 117 Agentives are apparently built upon future duratives, not upon imperfectives. **1966** *Jrnl. Linguistics* II. ii. 249 The distribution 52% perfectives, 48% imperfectives, confirms that the relative frequency..of the Russian marked and unmarked members differs sharply. **1972** HARTMANN & STORK *Dict. Lang. & Ling.* 20 Ancient Greek, for example, had perfective, imperfective, and aorist.

Hence **imperfectivi'zation** *Gram.*, the making of a verbal form or tense 'imperfective'; the condition of being 'imperfective'.

1943 *Language* XIX. 273 The statement of 'means of imperfectivization' is a list of suffixes. **1962** *Word* XVIII. 15 Its function is basically grammatical, i.e. that of imperfectivization. **1966** *Jrnl. Linguistics* II. ii. 249 A formal distinction, as regards morphological potentiality, secondary imperfectivization, is made.

imperfectly (ɪm'pɜːfɪktlɪ), *adv.* [f. IMPERFECT *a.* + -LY².]

1. In an imperfect manner or degree; incompletely, defectively.

1377 LANGL. *P. Pl.* B. x. 464 Souteres and shepherdes.. passen..In-to þe blisse of paradys, for her pure byleue, þat inparfitly here knewe and eke lyued. **1563** W. FULKE *Meteors* (1640) 1 b, Bodies perfectly and imperfectly mixed ..They are called imperfectly mixed, because they are very soone changed into another thing..as snow into water. **1701** NORRIS *Ideal World* I. v. 247 They imitate his [God's] perfection imperfectly. **1797** BEWICK *Brit. Birds* (1847) I. 214 Its minute history is imperfectly known. **1845** FORD *Handbk. Spain* I. 66 When the traveller speaks the language imperfectly.

†**2.** *Gram.* (See IMPERFECT *a.* 5.) *Obs. rare.*

1530 PALSGR. Introd. 32 Thre dyvers tymes, imparfytly past, indiffynitly past, and more than parfytly past.

imperfectness (ɪm'pɜːfɪktnɪs). [f. as prec. + -NESS.] The quality or state of being imperfect; imperfection.

1382 WYCLIF *Ecclus.* xxxviii. 31 And his waking shal enourne the inparfitnesse. *c* **1400** MAUNDEV. (Roxb.) xv. 70 Me thoȝt grete schame þat Sarzenes..schuld þus reproue vs of oure inperfiteness. **1590** GREENWOOD *Answ. Def. Read Prayers* 9 If therbe allwaies spottes and imperfectnes in the true Church vpon earth. **1747** J. LIND *Lett. Navy* i. (1757) 11 The integrity of the intention, will..attone..for the imperfectness of the performance. **1853** RUSKIN *Stones Ven.* II. vi, I have only dwelt upon the rudeness of Gothic, or any other kind of imperfectness, as admirable, where it was impossible to get design or thought without it.

imperforable (ɪm'pɜːfərəb(ə)l), *a.* [f. IM-² + PERFORABLE.] That cannot be perforated.

1658 PHILLIPS, *Imperforable*, not to be bored through. Whence in BAILEY, JOHNSON, etc. **1895** *Columbus* (Ohio) *Disp.* 19 July 7/7 Leather..is not absolutely imperforable.

imperforate (ɪm'pɜːfərət), *a.* [f. IM-² + PERFORATE.] Not perforated; having no perforation, foramen, or opening. Chiefly in scientific and technical use; in *Anat.* said of parts of the body normally having an opening, when congenitally closed by malformation or in special cases; also of persons or animals so affected.

1673 RAY *Journ. Low C.*, *Venice* 200 One of these Glass-bubbles was perforated with a little hole..the other..was imperforate. **1739** S. SHARP *Operat. Surg.* (R.), Sometimes children are born imperforate. **1851-6** WOODWARD *Mollusca* 100 The whorls are closely coiled, leaving only a pillar of shell, or columella, in the centre: such shells are said to be imperforate. **1857** BULLOCK *Cazeaux' Midwif.* 44 Sometimes the hymen forms a complete imperforate Membrane. **1877** LL. JEWITT *Half-hours among Eng. Antiq.* 180 The use of these large imperforate beads..remains a mystery. **1887** L. HEITZMANN tr. *C. Heitzmann's Anat.* IV. 80 The clitoris..has two Corpora cavernosa, a Glans which is imperforate.

b. Of a sheet of postage, revenue, or other stamps: Not having the individual stamps separated by rows of perforations; hence of a stamp having the margin entire and not denticulated, as in 'perforated' specimens.

1885 E. B. EVANS *Philatelic Handbk.* 118 [1*d.* stamp] Watermark a Small Crown; imperforate. **1893** *Daily News* 28 July 5/2 Fine copies of the Canadian sixpenny [postage-stamp] 'imperforate'.

imperforated (ɪm'pɜːfəreɪtɪd), *a.* [f. IM-² + PERFORATED.] = prec.

1650 SIR T. BROWNE *Pseud. Ep.* VII. xvi. (1658) 453 As it happeneth sometimes in imperforated persons. **1754-64** SMELLIE *Midwif.* III. 503 A case in which the Anus was imperforated. **1851-6** WOODWARD *Mollusca* 83 A.. suggestion with respect to the nautili; namely, that the umbilicated specimens are the males,—imperforated shells, females. **1895** *Times* 2 Feb. 12/4 Ceylon.—4*d.* [postage stamp], rose, imperforated and unused, £130.

imperforation (ɪmpɜːfə'reɪʃən). [f. IM-² + PERFORATION. Cf. F. *imperforation* (Cotgr.).] The condition of being imperforate; an instance or case of this.

1656 BLOUNT *Glossogr.*, *Imperforation*, a closing or shutting up for want of boring or piercing. **1799** M. UNDERWOOD *Treat. Dis. Childr.* (ed. 4) II. 239 Imperforations of the vagina, the anus and the urethra. **1822-34** *Good's Study Med.* (ed. 4) III. 197 Where the cause [of deafness] is an imperforation of either of the passages. *Ibid.* IV. 99 A temporary imperforation of the urethra.

imperformable (ɪmpə'fɔːməb(ə)l), *a. rare.* [f. IM-² + PERFORMABLE.] That cannot be performed.

1693 CHAUNCY *Enq. Gosp. New Law* 28 How..illogical.. to conclude, that God will save the non-elect upon an imperformable condition. **1884** *Law Times Rep.* L. 252/2 To give damages for the non-performance of an inperformable agreement.

imperial (ɪm'pɪərɪəl), *a.* and *sb.* Forms: α. 4- **imperial**; also 4-7 **-all**, 4 **ymperyall**, 5 **imperiale**, **-ryal**, **-real**, 5-6 **-ryall(e**, **-ialle**, 6 **ymperiall**. β. 4-7 **emperial**, **-all**, 5 **-ialle**, **-eryal**, **-irial**. [a. OF. *em-*, *imperial* (12th c. in Hatz-Darm.), ad. L. *imperiālis*, f. IMPERIUM: see below, and -AL¹.]

A. *adj.* Pertaining to an empire or emperor.

I. 1. Of or pertaining to an empire, or to the empire in question; *orig.* belonging to the ancient Roman *imperium* or Empire; hence, to the Holy Roman (or German) Empire, or to any so-called Empire of modern times.

1390 GOWER *Conf.* III. 61 A great cronique emperiall. *c* **1400** *Rom. Rose* 6421 There shalle no jugge imperial, Ne bisshop, ne official, Done jugement on me. **1469** *Sc. Acts Jas. III* 20 Nov. in *Acts Parl. Scotl.* (1814) II. 95 þe Imperiale notaris. **1525** LD. BERNERS *Froiss.* II. ccxiv. [ccx.] 658 He..shewed certayne letters patentes apostolykes and imperyalles. **1548** HALL *Chron.*, *Hen. VIII* 169 b, The Duchie [Milan] is Imperiall, and in your gifte as many other seigniories bee. **1617** MORYSON *Itin.* I. 285 The Coynes of other Princes and free Cities, are stamped with the Imperiall Eagle. **1727-41** CHAMBERS *Cycl.*, *Imperial Chamber*, is a sovereign court, established for the affairs of the immediate states of the empire. **1851** D. WILSON *Preh. Ann.* (1863) II. III. ii. 67 The Northern limits of Imperial sway. **1861** M. PATTISON *Ess.* (1889) I. 45 High above, the Imperial double eagle figured in all its ugliness.

2. Of or pertaining to a sovereign state, which in its independence and importance ranks with an empire. **a.** Said of England, from the 16th c., in assertion of its independence of and sovereign equality with the 'Holy Roman' Empire (see quot. from Blackstone).

1532-3 *Act 24 Hen. VIII*, c. 12 This realme of England is an Impire..gouerned by one supreme head and kynge, hauynge the dignitie and royall estate of thimperiall crowne of the same. **1536** WRIOTHESLEY *Chron.* (Camden) I. 52 This realme is..an emperiall sea of itself. ? **1556** PARKER (*title*) A Defence of priestes mariages, stablysshed by the imperiall lawes of the Realme of Englande. **1660** *Trial Regic.* 11 What is an Imperial Crown? It is that, which, as to the Coercive part, is subject to no man under God. **1705** J. ANDERSON (*title*) Historical Essay showing that the Crown and Kingdom of Scotland is imperial and independent. **1724** SWIFT *Drapier's Lett.* Wks. 1755 V. II. 73 Ireland is, on the contrary, called in some statutes an imperial crown, as held only from God. **1765** BLACKSTONE *Comm.* I. vii. 242 The meaning..of the legislature, when it uses these terms of *empire* and *imperial*, and applies them to the realm and crown of England, is only to assert that our king is equally sovereign and independent within these his dominions, as any emperor is in his empire; and owes no kind of subjection to any other potentate upon earth.

b. Said, in more recent times, of the parliament, legislation, government, taxation, etc., of Great Britain, as distinct from those formerly possessed by its constituent kingdoms, from those of local application, and from those of colonies and foreign dependencies.

1774 BURKE *Amer. Tax.* Wks. II. 436 The parliament of Great Britain sits at the head of her extensive empire in two capacities: one as the local legislature of this island..The other, and..nobler capacity, is what I call her imperial character; in which..she superintends all the several inferiour legislatures. **1802** WINDHAM *Speeches Parl.* 24 May (1812) I. 341 The subject..appeared more especially unworthy of being entertained by the imperial parliament. **1858** J. B. NORTON *Topics* 142 All those things..which are from their nature imperial, require some one central controlling authority. *a* **1859** MACAULAY *Hist. Eng.* xvii. V. 56 The only power which such men as Washington and Franklin denied to the Imperial legislature was the power of taxing. **1865** *Times* 29 Apr., The improvement..was traced by Mr. Gladstone through every branch of the Imperial income. **1888** *Daily News* 15 Sept. 5/3 The United Kingdom is an 'Imperial' State—a State exercising 'imperium', or dominion over the colonies and other dependencies.

c. Designating certain decorations or orders.

1878 *London Gaz.* (Suppl.) 4 Jan. 113/1 The Queen has been graciously pleased..to institute and create an Order of Distinction, to be styled and designated 'The Imperial Order of the Crown of India'. **1902** *Encycl. Brit.* XXXI. 340/1 The Imperial Service Order was..instituted on 26th June 1902, to commemorate King Edward's coronation. *Ibid.*, The Imperial Order of the Crown of India is conferred for like purposes as the order of the Indian Empire. **1971** *Whitaker's Almanack* 261 The Imperial Service Order..

consists of the Sovereign and Companions (not exclusively male) to a number not exceeding 1325 of whom 750 may belong to the Home Civil Services and 575 to Overseas Civil Services.

d. ***Imperial Defence***: defence of Great Britain and of its dependent territories.

1897 G. S. CLARKE (*title*) Imperial defence. **1902** *Encycl. Brit.* XXVI. 401/1 The appointment in 1879 of a royal commission to consider the question of Imperial defence, which presented its report in 1882, led to a considerable development and reorganization of the system of Imperial fortifications. **1910** *Ibid.* III. 254/1 His [*sc.* A. J. Balfour's] institution of the permanent Committee of Imperial Defence, and of the new Army Council (1904), were reforms of the highest importance. **1938** *Ann. Reg. 1937* 67 The national defence was being quite adequately organised by the Committee of Imperial Defence.

e. Designating a policy or an institution concerned with the development of commerce between the constituent parts of the British Commonwealth (formerly the British Empire); esp. in ***imperial preference***, a system of tariff concessions granted by members of the British Empire or Commonwealth to one another.

1902 *Encycl. Brit.* XXVI. 397/2 The foundation of the Imperial Federation League—in 1884. *Ibid.* XXXIII. 393/1 The British Empire League, and the Imperial Trade Defence League endeavour to promote inter-Imperial trade. *Ibid.* 681/2 On 4th July she laid the foundation stone of the Imperial Institute. **1912** J. S. HUXLEY *Individual in Animal Kingdom* ii. 54 All the wheat in Canada, with Imperial Preference to help, would not keep her [*sc.* the English nation] from starvation. **1922** *Encycl. Brit.* XXX. 1016/2 At the end of April [1917] Mr. Bonar Law announced..that the Imperial War Cabinet had accepted the principle of Imperial Preference. *Ibid.* 1025/2 The main feature of the budget [1919] was the establishment at last of imperial preference. **1927** *Daily Tel.* 5 Mar. 8/7 Appreciation of the work of the Imperial Economic Committee and the Empire Marketing Board for the development of the market for Dominion produce in Great Britain. **1931** G. C. TRYON (*title*) Short history of imperial preference. **1958** *Listener* 18 Sept. 407/2 Both [*sc.* Australia and New Zealand] have sought to give foreign suppliers a better competitive position in their own markets by reducing imperial preferences to oil the wheels of reciprocity. **1971** A. SHONFIELD in A. Bullock *20th Cent.* xiv. 331/2 The Imperial Preference system was successful in helping the British industrial recovery in the 1930s.

3. a. Of or pertaining to the (or an) emperor.

c **1384** CHAUCER *H. Fame* III. 271 But al on hye above a dees Sit in a see imperiall..Y saugh perpetually y-stalled A femynyne creature. **1413** *Pilgr. Sowle* (Caxton 1483) v. xi. 101 Vnto thyn estate Imperyall no preysynge is that maye be peregal. **1549–62** STERNHOLD & H. *Ps.* ciii. 19 And by his power imperiall, he gouernes all the world. **1664** H. MORE *Myst. Iniq.* 262 They both aspired to a Majesty and Power plainly Imperial. **1726** SWIFT *Gulliver* I. i, A person of high rank from his Imperial Majesty. **1764** CHURCHILL *Candidate* 670 Where is the glory of imperial sway, If subjects none but just commands obey? **1832** G. R. PORTER *Porcelain & Gl.* 104 The honour of supplying the imperial [Chinese] court with porcelain. **1867** FREEMAN *Norm. Conq.* I. iii. 162 The Imperial titles and Imperial pretensions of the English Kings in the tenth and eleventh centuries.

b. *esp.* of the ancient Roman Emperors or the later Western and Eastern Emperors; *spec.* belonging to the party of the (Romano-German) Emperor.

c **1470** HARDING *Chron.* LXXX. vii, Maximian Kyng of greate Brytain By whole decre, and will of the senate, Was emperour of Roome, and ruled Almaigne..Wherfore we clayme the throne empirial. **1480** CAXTON *Chron. Eng.* ccli. (1482) 322 Frederyk duk of Osteryke was crouned with imperyal dyademe of pope nycholas the iiij. **1494** FABYAN *Chron.* IV. lxvii. 45 Whan yᵉ forsayd .ii. Emperoures had.. resygned and gyuen ouer all Imperyall dygnytie, this sayde Constancius wᵗ..Galerius, were made Emperours. *a* **1533** LD. BERNERS *Huon* xcix. 322 Thyther came themperour rychely armed with yᵉ armes imperyall. **1548** HALL *Chron.*, *Hen. VIII* 178 The towne of Cappe..became imperiall and turned to the Emperors part. **1585** T. WASHINGTON tr. *Nicholay's Voy.* II. xxi. 59 A slave unto the Emperor [the Sultan]..durst very well advance himselfe to come too the estate imperiall. **1588** SHAKS. *Tit. A.* I. i. 6 The Imperiall Diadem of Rome. **1658** SIR T. BROWNE *Hydriot.* (1896) 21 The faces of many imperial persons,..Cæsar, Claudius [etc.]. **1708** SWIFT *Predict.*, The pope..will die..and..be succeeded by a cardinal of the imperial faction. **1836** *Scenes of Commerce* 230 Robes of Tyrian dye constituted, among the Romans, the imperial purple. **1851** D. WILSON *Preh. Ann.* (1863) II. III. ii. 62 A series of imperial coins from Augustus to Diocletian. **1868** *W. Smith's Smaller Dict. Gr. & Rom. Antiq.* s.v. *Provincia*, The senatorian provinces were distributed among consulares and those who had filled the office of praetor..The imperial provinces were governed by *legati Caesaris*, with praetorian power, the proconsular power being in the Caesar himself, and the legati being his deputies and representatives.

4. *fig.* and *transf.* Of the nature or rank of an emperor or supreme ruler; ruling, commanding, supreme in authority.

1390 GOWER *Conf.* III. 213 Thus the sonne is over all The Chefe planet imperiall. *c* **1460** in *Pol. Rel. & L. Poems* (1866) 81 O Quene of hevyn imperyalle. **1541–2** *Act 33 Hen. VIII* in Bolton *Stat. Irel.* (1621) 184 Honours..to the estate and majestie of a king imperiall appertayning or belonging. **1590** SHAKS. *Mids. N.* II. i. 163 And the imperiall Votresse passed on, In maiden meditation, fancy free. **1696** PRIOR *To the King* 47 Imperial Britain on the sea looks down. **1697** DRYDEN *Virg. Georg.* III. 377 Every Creature, and of every Kind,..Not only Man's Imperial Race.

5. a. Having a commanding quality, demeanour, or aspect; majestic, august, lofty, exalted.

c **1374** CHAUCER *Boeth.* I. pr. i. 3 (Camb. MS.), I ne myhte nat knowen what þat womman was of so Imperial auctorite. *c* **1430** LYDG. *Min. Poems* (Percy Soc.) 11 This tabernacle of most magnyfycence Whas of his byldyng verry imperialle. **1508** DUNBAR *Gold. Targe* 254 O reuerend Chaucere, rose of rethoris all, As in our tong ane flour imperiall. **1617** MORYSON *Itin.* I. 137 Built by Pope Sixtus the fifth, with Imperiall magnificence. **1650** BULWER *Anthropomet.* 83 They would suffer none to reign over them, but Princes that had such imperial Noses. **1781** COWPER *Lily & Rose* 14 The Lily's height bespoke command, A fair imperial flower. **1849** MACAULAY *Hist. Eng.* i. I. 20 In so splendid and imperial a manner did the English people, properly so called, first take place among the nations of the world.

b. Assuming or affecting a commanding character or manner; domineering, imperious.

1581 MULCASTER *Positions* xxxvi. (1887) 136 Scholers by reason of their conceit which learning inflameth..become to imperiall to rest upon a litle. **1760–72** H. BROOKE *Fool of Quality* (1808) IV. 134, I am under the positive interdiction of an imperial thing called a husband. **1830** GALT *Lawrie T.* IV. i. (1849) 143 The squire he is mighty imperial.

6. Befitting an emperor of supreme ruler; of special excellence; magnificent; exceedingly fine or grand. (See also 8, 10.)

In quot. 1848 with humorous allusion to the 'imperial purple'.

1731 POPE *Ep. Burlington* 204 These are Imperial Works, and worthy Kings [cf. DRYDEN *Æneid* VI. 1177 To tame the proud, the fetter'd slave to free, These are imperial arts, and worthy thee [Rome]]. **1848** DICKENS *Dombey* xx, His imperial complexion was mainly referred by the faculty to that circumstance. **1871** E. F. BURR *Ad Fidem* v. 79 The marrow, and fatness of this imperial diet.

II. In special connexions and phrases.

7. Applied to those weights and measures appointed by statute to be used throughout the United Kingdom, instead of those various ones formerly in local use.

1838 T. THOMSON *Chem. Org. Bodies* 726, 10 ounces avoirdupois, of acid, for every imperial gallon of tar employed. **1843** *Penny Cycl.* XXVII. 202/1 *Imperial Measure.*—This measure supersedes the old corn, wine, and beer measures. **1854** DICKENS *Hard T.* i, Ready to have imperial gallons of facts poured into them. **1892** *Gardener's Chron.* 27 Aug. 241/3 At a cost of about £10 per imperial acre.

8. a. In names of various products or commodities of special size or quality. See also 10.

1664 EVELYN *Kal. Hort.* 72 *Plums*, Imperial, Blew, White Dates. **1719** LONDON & WISE *Compl. Gard.* 219 Imperial Lettuces, which are of an extraordinary Size. **1747** *Gentl. Mag.* XVII. 194 At morning store of cream, and tea, Either imperial, or bohea. **1795** A. ANDERSON *Narr. Brit. Emb. China* 186 That shrub which bears what is called the Imperial and gunpowder teas. **1892** WALSH *Tea* (Philad.) 74 The true Imperial tea..known in China as..the 'perfection of tea'.

b. Formerly the name of a size of paper: of printing-paper originally 22 by 32 inches, of writing-paper 22 by 30; later designating a number of different dimensions, but standardized at 22 or $22\frac{1}{2}$ by 30 inches (see B. 5 b below).

1668–9 WOOD *Life* (O.H.S.) IV. 82 To Mr. Hall, printer, for two large bibles of imperial paper, 19*li.* 10*s.* **1692** *Lond. Gaz.* No. 2819/4 The Draught consisting of 4 Sheets of Imperial Paper. **1859** GULLICK & TIMBS *Paint.* 286 The paper most generally used is of what is called 'Imperial' size. **1864** LOWNDES *Bibl. Man.* 2941 Wilson, Alexander. American Ornithology..Philadelphia, 1808–14. Imperial 4to. 9 vols.

c. Name of a particular make of roofing-slate, of large size ($2\frac{1}{2} \times 2$ ft.): cf. B. 5 c.

1823 P. NICHOLSON *Pract. Build.* xi. 396 The Imperial Slating, for roofs, is particularly neat, and is known by having its lower edge sawn; whereas all the other slates, used for covering, are only chipped square on their edges.

9. *Sporting slang.* Said of a fall on one's head or 'crown'.

1861 WHYTE MELVILLE *Mkt. Harb.* 134 Four imperial crowners at one and the same instant. **1889** R. S. S. BADEN-POWELL *Pigsticking* 75 The fall that followed was 'imperial'.

10. Phrases. ***imperial beard*** = B. 8; ***imperial blue***, an aniline blue dye, also called *spirit-blue*; ***imperial city***, (*a*) a city that is the seat of empire, or that is itself a sovereign or independent state; (*b*) one of those cities of the old German Empire which owned allegiance to the Emperor alone; †***cloth imperial***, a textile fabric in use in the Middle Ages, with figures woven in gold; app. so called as being made at Constantinople: see also B. 3; †***imperial crown***, the flower now called CROWN IMPERIAL (*Fritillaria imperialis*); ***imperial dome*** or ***roof***, a dome of pointed form, the vertical section of which is an ogee or curve of contrary flexure; ***imperial drink*** (formerly †***i. water***), a drink made of cream of tartar flavoured with lemons and sweetened; ***imperial elephant***, ***mammoth*** [tr. of *Elephas imperator* (J. Leidy 1858, in *Proc. Acad. Nat. Sci. Philadelphia* 10), which was later included in the genus *Mammuthus*]: a fossil mammal, *Mammuthus imperator*, found in Pleistocene remains in south-western North America; ***imperial pigeon***, a large fruit-eating pigeon, esp. one of the genus *Ducula*, found in south-eastern Asia, including India, and the Pacific region; ***imperial roof***, see *imperial dome* above; ***imperial water***, see *imperial drink* above; ***imperial yellow***, name of a kind of porcelain made in China, having a uniform yellow glaze, said to be reserved for the use of the imperial court; hence applied to other kinds imitating this in colour.

1859 JEPHSON & REEVE *Brittany* 13 The other soldier, with a huge *imperial beard. **1563** *Homilies* II. *Idolatry* II. (1640) 31 The *Emperiall citty Constantinople. **1586** A. DAY *Eng. Secretary* I. (1625) 25 We hasted thence to a city, called Noremberghe, being imperiall, situate in the high parts of Germany. **1601** R. JOHNSON *Kingd. & Commw.* (1603) 85 Geneva is an imperiall citty in Savoy. **1615** G. SANDYS *Trav.* 45 Taken from them Constantinople the Imperiall Citie. **1617** MORYSON *Itin.* I. 203 City of Erfurt..is a free City, but not an imperiall City; and paies some tribute to the Bishop of Metz, and to the Saxon Duke of Wineberg. [**1178** in Twysden *Hist. Anglic. Scripta* I. 602 Pannos quos Constantinopolis civitas vocat Imperiales.] *a* **1500** *York Fabric Rolls* (Surtees) 310 Two blue copes of *clothe imperialle. **1706** J. GARDINER tr. *Rapin on Gardens* (1728) 19 Then her gay gilded front th' *Imperial Crown Erects aloft. **1746–7** HERVEY *Medit.* (1818) 137 See the imperial crown, splendid and beautifully grand! **1886** *Syd. Soc. Lex.*, **Imperial drink.* **1897** ALLBUTT *Syst. Med.* III. 21 Plain water, barley water, lemonade or imperial drink may be allowed at will. **1913** W. B. SCOTT *Hist. Land Mammals W. Hemisphere* xii. 485 The largest of American proboscideans was the *Imperial Elephant. **1910** H. F. OSBORN *Age of Mammals* vi. 442 The Columbian and *imperial mammoths were for a time at least contemporaneous with the mastodon. **1945** A. S. ROMER *Vertebr. Paleont.* (ed. 2) xxi. 416 *M[ammuthus] imperator*, the imperial mammoth of southern North America, was more advanced in size and dental development. **1966** Imperial mammoth [see BALUCHITHERIUM]. **1864** T. C. JERDON *Birds India* III. 455 *Carpophaga sylvatica*... *Imperial Pigeon of Europeans in the South of India. **1895** *Jrnl. Bombay Nat. Hist. Soc.* X. 360 The green Imperial Pigeon..may be frequently met with nearly all over North Cachar. **1913** E. C. S. BAKER *Indian Pigeons & Doves* 103 Hodgson's Imperial Pigeon is less quarrelsome than most of the family. **1934** 'G. ORWELL' *Burmese Days* xiv. 211 Flo [*sc.* a dog]..came running excitedly up..with the big imperial pigeon in her mouth. **1967** D. GOODWIN *Pigeons & Doves of World* 384 The large species of fruit pigeons are often termed the imperial pigeons because of their impressive and majestic-looking if somewhat ponderous appearance. **1615** MARKHAM *Eng. Housew.* II. iii. (1668) 104 To make the *Emperial water. **1769** MRS. RAFFALD *Eng. Housekpr.* (1778) 327 To make Imperial Water. **1881** *Porcelain Works, Worcester* 35 The Persian turquoise, *Imperial yellow, mauve, Celeste, and other enamels present an interesting series. **1884** *Chr. World* (Fam. Circle ed.) 4 Nov. 260/4 Amongst the favourite colours are imperial yellow, Nile blue.

B. *sb.*

1. a. A member of the Emperor's party; a soldier of the Imperial troops: = IMPERIALIST 1.

c **1524** BP. OF BATH in Ellis *Orig. Lett.* Ser. II. I. 320 The Imperialles shall shortly receyve large sommys off monye. **1563** GOLDING (*title*) The Historie of Leonard Aretine concerning the Warres betwene the Imperialls and the Gothes for the possession of Italy. **1630** *R. Johnson's Kingd. & Commw.* 101 The Emperour and Germans, or if you please the Imperials. **1693** *Mem. Cnt. Teckely* IV. 58 The Imperials encamped as near them as possibly they could. **1890** T. W. ALLIES *Peter's Rock* 329 It came to a fierce struggle between the Italians on the Pope's side and the imperials.

†b. A decree or statute of the Emperor. *Obs.*

1614 SELDEN *Titles Hon.* 21 That great Volum of Lawes.. comprehending a collection out of the Digests, Code, Nouells, and other Imperialls, was titled τὰ βασίλικα.

c. An imperial personage. (In 16–17th c. used as = *emperor*.)

1588 SHAKS. *Tit. A.* IV. iii. 93 A matter of brawle, betwixt my Vncle, and one of the Emperialls men. **1591** —— *Two Gent.* II. iii. 5, I..am going with Sir Protheus to the Imperialls Court. **1628** J. GAULE *Pract. The.* (1629) 260 To quell and curbe the Seditious and Rebellious, to exact the Imperials Due, and mannage his Force. **1841** MOTLEY *Corr.* (1889) I. iv. 89 At twelve the Imperials [Emperor and Empress of Russia] retired and dismissed us.

2. †a. A former Flemish coin of the value of $2\frac{1}{2}$ rixdollars. *Obs.*

1674 R. GODFREY *Inj. & Ab. Physic* 48 Glauber..had receiv'd six hundred Imperials before hand. **1727–41** CHAMBERS *Cycl.* s.v. *Coin*, Flemish Coins.—Those of gold are imperials [etc.]... Imperial, 11*s.* 3*d.*

b. A Russian gold coin, formerly valued at 10 silver roubles, subsequently (1899) at 15.

1839 *Penny Cycl.* XV. 324/1 *Imperial*, a Russian gold coin, of 10 rubles... The English mint value of the imperial coined before 1763 has been given at 2*l.* 1*s.* 6*d.*.. The present value is 33*s.* 4*d.* **1897** *Daily News* 16 Jan. 3/2 The ukase..orders that imperials and half-imperials shall be minted with the inscriptions '15 roubles' and '$7\frac{1}{2}$ roubles' respectively.

†3. Short for *cloth imperial*: see A. 10. *Obs.*

1476 *Plumpton Corr.* 37 As for your cope..I send you a peice of baudkin, and another of impereal, to se whether ye will hafe of. **1483** *Wardr. Acc.* in *Antiq. Rep.* (1807) I. 49 ij canopies, one made of imperial, and the other of baldekyn. **1876** ROCK *Text. Fabr.* v. 39 At the end of the twelfth century there was brought to England from Greece, a sort of precious silk, named *Imperial*.

4. A case or trunk for luggage, fitted on, or adapted for, the roof of a coach or carriage. Also the roof or top of a carriage itself (F. *impériale*).

1794 W. FELTON *Carriages* (1801) II. Gloss., *Imperial*, a leathered case, which is placed occasionally on the roof of the body [of the carriage] for the purpose of carrying cloaths, etc. safe. **1796** NELSON 22 June in Nicolas *Disp.* (1846) VII. p. lxxxvi, In a Vessel lately taken by my Squadron is an imperiale full of clothes belonging to a General Officer. **1825** T. H. LISTER *Granby* xiv. (1836) 97 The carriage with its ponderous trunks and towering imperials, was actually at

the door. **1857** HUGHES *Tom Brown* I. i, Couriers and ladies'-maids, imperials and travelling carriages, are an abomination to me. **1875** J. H. BENNET *Winter Medit.* II. xi. 392, I was on the imperial or top of the diligence for the view, sitting next to the conductor.

5. a. A trade name for various articles of special size or quality: cf. A. 8, 10.

1858 SIMMONDS, *Dict. Trade, Imperial*, relating to royalty; any thing large, as a large decanter.

b. A size of paper: see A. 8 b above.

1712 *Act 10 Anne* in *Lond. Gaz.* No. 5018/3 For all Paper called.. Imperial fine 16s... per Ream. **1790** WOLCOTT (P. Pindar) *Ep. to Sylv. Urban* Wks. 1812 II. 261 His nice-discerning knowledge none deny On Crown, Imperial, Foolscap, and Demy. **1878** *Print. Trades Jrnl.* No. 25. 16 The sheet is somewhat large—the length of imperial. **1952** E. J. LABARRE *Dict. Paper* (ed. 2) 130/1 *Imperial.* Now standardized for writings and printings at 30″ × 22″ and for wrappings at 29″ × 22½″, for boards at 30″ × 22½″ and their multiples. **1968** *Specification Sizes Papers & Boards (B.S.I.)* 14 (*heading*) Table 2. Writing and printing papers and offset cartridges... Imperial.. 22 × 30. *Ibid.* 15 Table 3. Ledger papers... Imperial.. 22 × 30. *Ibid.* 17 Table 7. Paste boards; and duplex, triplex and ivory boards... Paste imperial.. 22½ × 30. *Ibid.*, Table 8. Drawing cartridges... Imperial.. 22 × 30.

c. A kind of roofing-slate: see A. 8 c.

1823 P. NICHOLSON *Pract. Build.* xi. 395 The Welsh Slates .. Imperials, 2 ft. 6 in. by 2 ft. *Ibid.* 396 Patent slating.. at the present time.. is composed of the Imperials, which are lighter, and much neater in appearance.

d. Short for *imperial water* or *drink*: see A. 10.

1827 *Blackw. Mag.* XXI. 829 Imperial, ginger-pop, soda-water, or lemonade.

6. Short for *imperial dome* or *roof*: see A. 10.

1826 ELMES *Bibliogr. Dict. Fine Arts, Imperial*, .. a kind of roof or dome which, viewed in its profile, is pointed towards the top, and widens itself more and more in descending towards its base. **1842–76** GWILT *Archit.* Gloss.

7. A game at cards. ? *Obs.*

1798 *Sporting Mag.* XII. 31 A general description of the game of Imperial. **1847–78** HALLIWELL, *Imperial*, a game at cards, mentioned as having been played by Henry VIII.

8. A small part of the beard left growing beneath the lower lip.

[**1829** BALZAC *La Maison du Chat-qui-Pelote* in *Œuvres* (1938) I. 64 Sa figure.. était encore animée par de petites moustaches relevées en pointe et noires comme du jais, par une impériale bien fournie,.. et par une forêt de cheveux noirs assez en désordre.] **1835** S. HORSLEY *Let.* in R. B. Gotch *Mendelssohn & his Friends in Kensington* (1934) 192 What with his black hair longer than ever, a *beard* which he is now cultivating to a great length, mustachios and an imperial,.. made you suspect the fact of his having escaped across the country from some wandering menagerie. **1838** H. MOZLEY *Let.* 2 Nov. in D. Mozley *Newman Family Lett.* (1962) 77 Mr. Sidney Herbert.. is.. a silly looking coxcomb, with a most disfiguring imperial. **1839** *Blackw. Mag.* Oct. 507/2 An imperial—*i.e.* a dirt-coloured tuft of hair. **1856** MISS BIRD *Englishw. Amer.* 366 Eccentricities of appearance in the shape of beards and imperials. **1859** O. W. HOLMES *Prof. Breakf.-t.* i. (1891) 4 A person with black whiskers and imperial.

imperial(l, -yal, obs. ff. EMPYREAL.

imperialism (ɪmˈpɪərɪəlɪz(ə)m). [f. IMPERIAL + -ISM: after *imperialist*.]

1. An imperial system of government; the rule of an emperor, esp. when despotic or arbitrary.

1858 *Westm. Rev.* Oct. 344 To lower the intellectual vigour of the nation,.. to exhibit to the world how the waywardness of mind will yield beneath the compression of a stern resolution—these are the tasks set itself by Imperialism. **1861** PEARSON *Early & Mid. Ages Eng.* xxxiv. (L.), Roman imperialism had divided the world into master and slave. **1861** GOLDW. SMITH *Irish Hist.* 18 There appears to be in the Keltic race a strong tendency to what is called Imperialism. **1869** *Times* 15 Oct., Imperialism, or, indeed, any worse form of despotism. **1870** *Daily News* 8 Sept. 3 That this meeting begs to express its delight at the downfall of Imperialism in France, and the proclamation in lieu thereof of the Republic.

2. The principle or spirit of empire; advocacy of what are held to be imperial interests. In nineteenth-century British politics, the principle or policy (1) of seeking, or at least not refusing, an extension of the British Empire in directions where trading interests and investments require the protection of the flag; and (2) of so uniting the different parts of the Empire having separate governments, as to secure that for certain purposes, such as warlike defence, internal commerce, copyright, and postal communication, they shall be practically a single state.

In the United States, *imperialism* was similarly applied to the policy of extending the rule or influence of the American people over foreign countries, and of acquiring and holding distant dependencies, in the way in which colonies and dependencies are held by European states.

1878 J. CHAMBERLAIN *Let.* 15 Oct. in J. L. Garvin *Life J. Chamberlain* (1932) I. 267 This infernal Afghan business is the natural consequence of Jingoism, Imperialism, 'British interests', [etc.]. *a* **1881** W. R. GREG *Misc. Ess.* Ser. I. ii. 39 Under the pretext of Imperialism and farseeing statesmanship, the habitual and hitherto incurable fault of our Governments—especially of Tory Governments—has been to look too far ahead. **1895** *Westm. Gaz.* 15 Jan. 2/2 'The Expansion of England'—with its firm grasp on the great possibilities of the New Englands beyond the sea, and its vivid realisation of the British Empire as 'a world-wide Venice with the sea for streets'—gave.. a decisive impulse to what may be called, in the slang of the day, 'the new Imperialism'. **1898** *Daily News* 28 May 2/2 That odious system of bluster and swagger and might against right on which Lord Beaconsfield and his colleagues bestowed the tawdry nickname of Imperialism. **1899** H. H. BANCROFT *New Pacific* viii. 145 The word imperialism is used in this connection in a modern, American sense, as applicable to the empire of industry as well as to domain... It [implies].. the extension of political and commercial influence, particularly in the Pacific. **1899** CARNEGIE in *North Amer. Rev.* Jan. 5 Imperialism implies naval and military force behind; moral force, education, civilization are not the backbone of Imperialism. **1899** J. L. WALTON in *Contemp. Rev.* Mar. 306, I define Imperialism as a principle or formula of statesmanship for interpreting the duties of government in relation to empire. **1899** LD. ROSEBERY in *Daily News* 6 May 4/2, I mean the greater pride in Empire which is called Imperialism... Sane Imperialism, as distinguished from what I may call wild-cat Imperialism, is nothing but this—a larger patriotism. **1914** *Cycl. Amer. Govt.* II. 152/1 As used in American politics, imperialism is employed to designate the policy on which the United States has embarked of acquiring territory not a part of the United States proper, nor contiguous to it.

3. Used disparagingly. In Communist writings: the imperial system or policy of the Western powers. Used conversely in some Western writings: the imperial system or policy of the Communist powers.

1918 *Manch. Guardian* 13 Dec. 7/4 The Menshevik and the small bourgeois parties have published a declaration calling on workers all over the world to rally to the support of the Russian Revolution against the Imperialism attacking it. **1939** VARGA & MENDELSOHN (*title*) New data for V. I. Lenin's 'Imperialism, the highest stage of capitalism'. **1957** C. HUNT *Guide to Communist Jargon* xxiv. 82 The term imperialism has largely replaced Capitalism in the Communist vocabulary. *Ibid.* 83 The essential features of imperialism are the concentration of capital, the merging of industrial and banking capital into 'finance capital' and the division of the world between national and international monopolies. **1957** *Encycl. Brit.* VI. 135/2 They [*sc.* the Communists] regarded the cause of World War II to be not German aggression but British and French imperialism. **1964** GOULD & KOLB *Dict. Social Sci.* 319/2 It is sometimes said that Russian control of East European countries is 'Russian imperialism'.

imperialist (ɪmˈpɪərɪəlɪst). [f. IMPERIAL *a.* + -IST: cf. F. *impérialiste* (16th c. in Littré).]

1. An adherent of the (or an) emperor (usually, 1600–1800, of the German Emperor); one of the emperor's party.

1603 KNOLLES *Hist. Turks* (J.), The imperialists imputed the cause of so shameful a flight unto the Venetians. **1644** VICARS *God in Mount* 202 Our Romish adversaries the Imperialists, even the most bloody and idolatrous House of Austria. **1656–9** B. HARRIS *Parival's Iron Age* (ed. 2) 119 Favouring the factions of the Guelphs, against the Gibellins, or Imperialists. **1677** I. MATHER *Preval. Prayer* (1864) 249 The Emperour Marcus Aurelius going to war against the Quads, Vandals, Sarmats and Germans.. the Imperialists were so cooped up by their numerous Enemies. **1786** W. THOMSON *Watson's Philip III*, VI. (1839) 347 Count Thorn, having in vain endeavoured to bring the Imperialists to an action.. set out for Prague. **1835** ALISON *Europe* xxiii. (1854) IV. 42 Sporck.. succeeded in joining the main body of the Imperialists. **1900** *Westm. Gaz.* 14 Sept. 2/2 It is interesting to note a new use of the word Imperialist in to-day's *Daily News*: 'A troop of American cavalry surprised 300 Imperialists at Shaho...' This is from Pekin—clearly Imperialist is to be the way of distinguishing the Chinese Imperial troops from rebel Boxers.

2. An advocate of imperial rule, or of an imperial form of government.

Esp. in France, an adherent of the Bonaparte family, under which the First and Second Empires were set up.

1800 W. TAYLOR in *Monthly Mag.* VIII. 599 These imperious imperialists are so effectually served as to bespeak at the same time a law against their antagonists in courts not allied. **1817** J. SCOTT *Paris Revis.* (ed. 4) 315 People of all parties, royalists, imperialists, and republicans, affected.. a fine indignant surprise at the bare suggestion.

3. An advocate of 'imperialism' in British or American politics.

1899 G. WYNDHAM in *Daily News* 23 Jan. 7/5 An Imperialist.. is a man who does accept the fact that his country is a part, is, indeed, the head and heart of an Empire scattered the whole world over. **1899** *Westm. Gaz.* 26 Jan. 2/2 An Imperialist is one who.. does not hesitate to do what is necessary to provide for the defence and development of the Empire. **1899** J. L. WALTON in *Contemp. Rev.* Mar. 306 The Imperialist feels a profound pride in the magnificent heritage of empire won by the courage and energies of his ancestry, and bequeathed to him subject to the burden of many sacred trusts. **1899** *Nation* (N.Y.) 27 Apr. 303/2 English setters-on of American Imperialists are just now loud in their cries that America must not 'retreat'. They trust we have too much pride and resolution to turn tail in the Philippines. **1900** *Congress. Rec.* 11 Jan. 766/2 The trouble with these imperialists is that they confound the Government of the United States with their puny President.

4. An advocate of 'imperialism' (sense 3).

1963 [see CAPITULATIONISM]. **1969** *Times* 8 Aug. 1/2 'We all know,' Mr. Katushev said, 'how violently the imperialists are fighting on all fronts.. to give support to anti-socialist forces.'

5. *attrib.* or as *adj.* Adhering or pertaining to imperialism; imperialistic. Also *Comb.*

1868 FREEMAN *Norm. Conq.* II. vii. 79 The first of the series of German or other Imperialist prelates. **1879** GREEN *Read. Eng. Hist.* xx. 103 The imperialist theories of the lawyers of his father's court. **1898** *Speaker* 31 Dec. 770 The English people is neither Imperialist nor Jingo. **1899** J. PULITZER in *Daily News* 2 May 4/3 The new departure from our [U.S.] constitutional government which the present imperialist policy means. **1937** [see CAPITALIST]. **1957** C. HUNT *Guide to Communist Jargon* xxiv. 83 Lenin does not seem to have regarded the actual possession of an empire as essential to it [*sc.* imperialism], so that, according to his theory, the United States is an imperialist Power, as communist propaganda daily represents it. **1967** H. ARENDT *Origins Totalitarianism* (new ed.) v. 130 The imperialist-minded businessmen were followed by civil servants who wanted 'the African to be left an African'. *Ibid.* viii. 257 The imperialist-inspired 'parties above parties' had never known how to profit from popular hatred of the party system as such. **1969** *Times* 8 Aug. 1/2 President Ceausescu [of Rumania] argued that the socialist world was strong enough to safeguard itself against imperialist tactics. *Ibid.* 21 Aug. 7/3 The Soviet Union stood revealed for what it now is—an imperialist power. **1973** D. MILLER *Chinese Jade Affair* xviii. 174 The K.M.T. group.. would probably suggest that K. Lawson was engaged in a typical Western imperialist plot.

imperiaˈlistic, *a.* [f. prec. + -IC.] Of, pertaining to, or characteristic of imperialists or imperialism.

1879 BALDW. BROWN in *Daily News* 30 Sept. 2/2 That Imperialistic rather than Imperial policy, whose tinsel glitter her keen and thrifty eye would at once have detected and despised. **1893** *Times* 2 Jan. 9/2 He denounced the imperialistic leanings of the richer classes and of the clergy of the Established Church. **1894** *Dublin Rev.* July 110 When, in an imperialistic age brutalism was spreading downwards. **1933** N. WALN *House of Exile* III. iii. 223 His remarks were a stirring appeal to the citizens of China to unite against the 'Imperialistic Foreign Devil'. **1958** [see COLONIAL *a.* 1 a]. **1969** *Listener* 24 Apr. 568/3 They show the unwavering will of the people to make up for all the damage done by these imperialistic traitors in the shortest possible time.

Hence **imperiaˈlistically** *adv.*, in an imperialistic way, after the manner of an imperialist.

1881 *World* 11 May 11/2 The little chapel over which Monsignor Goddard has presided so imperialistically. **1895** *Johannesburg Standard* 3 Aug. 4 The Colonist.. [is] Imperialistically loyal as far as is consistent with Colonial Conceit.

imperiality (ɪmpɪərɪˈælɪtɪ). Also 6 **emperyalite**, 7 **imperialitie**. [f. IMPERIAL *a.* + -ITY.]

†**1.** Imperial rank, power, or authority. *Obs.*

1534 WHITINTON *Tullyes Offices* III. (1540) 163 Manlius added more dayes to occupy the roume of his dictature or emperyalite than was due by the law. **1611** FLORIO, *Imperialità*, Empiry, Imperiality. **1629** tr. *Herodian* (1635) 5 They.. were.. deposed from their Imperialitie.

2. As a humorous title for an emperor or imperial personage; also collectively = imperial personages (cf. *royalty*).

1870 DICKENS *Lett.* III. 298 That the wind will pass over his Imperiality on the sands of France I have not the slightest doubt. **1878** OUIDA *Friendsh.* II. x. 118 They should not educate Royalties and Imperialities: they are much nicer when they can only say How-do.

¶ *Erroneously.* An imperial right or privilege.

In Webster 1828, with misprinted quot. from Tooke, in which the correct word is IMPERIALTY, q.v. Hence copied into later Dicts.

imperialize (ɪmˈpɪərɪəlaɪz), *v.* Also 7 **em-**. [f. IMPERIAL *a.* + -IZE.]

†**1.** *intr.* To act imperially, act the part of an emperor or absolute ruler. *Obs.*

1634 SIR T. HERBERT *Trav.* 157 They delight in tyranny and account Emperializing a qualitie proper for great Personages.

†**2.** *trans.* To render imperial; to attach to the party of the Emperor (e.g. against the Papacy).

1639 FULLER *Holy War* III. xxiv. (1647) 160 The Romanists cast away the witnesse of all Imperialized authours then living.

3. To render imperial; to cause to be, or belong to, an empire, or an imperial policy.

1805 *Times* in *Spirit Pub. Jrnls.* (1806) IX. 53 Whether.. their favourite luxury would be imperialized by the coronation to double their usual price. **1849** *Fraser's Mag.* XXXIX. 362 Those trading classes who would respect almost any constituted authority, or imperialised gensdarme who would keep the peace. **1878** *Scribner's Mag.* XV. 113/1 Napoleon's scheme for imperializing Mexico. **1880** L. WALLACE *Ben-Hur* 210 The expression of the cold, sharp, eagle features, imperialized in his countrymen [the Romans] by sway of the world through so many generations. **1880** MCCARTHY *Own Times* IV. 444 It was all part of an imperialising policy.

Hence **imperialiˈzation**, the action of imperializing.

1878 *N. Amer. Rev.* CXXVII. 405 The Government have blundered fatally in their struggles after 'imperialization'.

imperially (ɪmˈpɪərɪəlɪ), *adv.* [f. IMPERIAL *a.* + -LY².]

1. In an imperial manner; as, or by, an emperor or supreme ruler; with commanding demeanour or style, majestically; autocratically; in relation to, or in the way of attachment to, the empire.

1550 *Nicolls Thucyd.* 70 The prynces oftentymes vsed that same custome imperially and by constraincte. **1570** T. NORTON tr. *Nowel's Catech.* (1853) 196 God.. alone may everywhere gloriously reign, imperially rule, and triumph. *a* **1661** FULLER *Worthies* I. (1662) 297 His Sur-name, [Siveyer] so contemptible in English, sounds Imperially and Episcopally when latinized [Severus]. *a* **1704** T. BROWN *Praise Drunkenness* Wks. 1730 I. 37 She reigns imperially in Germany and Denmark. **1844** MRS. BROWNING *Lady Geraldine* lvi, She smiles them down imperially. **1881** *Daily News* 19 May 5 The project.. having been Imperially approved, passed in the usual course the Council of State.

b. *Comb.*, as *imperially-minded*.

1890 *Spectator* 3 May, From the point of view of an imperially-minded Englishman.

2. *Heraldry.* ***imperially crowned***: said of charges represented with an imperial crown, as distinguished from a ducal or other coronet: cf. DUCALLY.

1823 CRABB *Technol. Dict.*, *Imperially crowned*, an epithet for any charge, arms, crest, or supporters that are crowned with a regal crown. **1864** BOUTELL *Her. Hist. & Pop.* xix. 303 A lion rampant guardant or, imperially crowned ppr.

im'perialness. *rare.* [f. as prec. + -NESS.] Imperial quality, dignity, or style; also (with possessive) as a humorous title.

1701 BEVERLEY *Apoc. Quest.* 33 Let us..Compute the Time, from Constantines Celebrated Victorious Christian Imperialness, An. 312 to 475. **1890** *Illustr. Lond. News* 26 July 106/3 It was pitiful..to see her imperialness strain and fret at the silken meshes of love.

imperialty (ɪm'pɪərɪəltɪ). *rare.* [f. IMPERIAL + -TY, after *royal-ty*.]

†**1.** Imperial state or government, empire. *Obs.*

1600 W. WATSON *Decacordon* (1602) 173 The particular common-wealths, and regall Maiesties of England, France, Ireland, Scotland..together with the Imperialty of Cæsar. *Ibid.* 331 Imperialtie, and absolute raigne, rule, and authoritie. **1616** R. SHELDON *Miracles Antichrist* 165 (T.) A short Roman imperialty or empire, which followed upon the destruction of the sixth.

2. An imperial right or privilege; a tax levied by an emperor or empress. (Cf. *royalty*.)

1799 W. TOOKE *View Russian Emp.* II. 531 The late empress having..relinquished her imperialties on the private mines. *Ibid.* 537 These deliveries ceased with the other imperialties which the empress relinquished.

†**im'perible,** *a. Obs. rare.* [f. IM-^{2} + **perible*, f. L. *perīre* to perish: see -IBLE.] = IMPERISHABLE.

1614 SYLVESTER *Litt. Bartas* 761 O is there not another life imperible, Sweet to the guiltlesse, to the guilty terrible?

imperice, impericke, obs. ff. EMPRESS, EMPIRIC.

imperie, var. of IMPERY *Obs.*

imperil (ɪm'pɛrɪl), *v.* Also 6–9 **em-**. [f. EM- 1, IM-^{1} + PERIL *sb.*] *trans.* To bring into or put in peril; to endanger, hazard, risk.

α. **1596** SPENSER *F.Q.* IV. iv. 10 Braggadochio..never thought..His person to emperill so in fight. **1650** B. *Discolliminium* 53 [It] will..emperil the..Common-Wealth. **1856** FROUDE *Hist. Eng.* (1858) I. ii. 95 By the scandal of their lives they emperilled the stability of their order. **1862** MERIVALE *Rom. Emp.* xli. (1865) V. 68 A professional emulation..emperilled the tranquillity of the city.

β. **1632** B. JONSON *Magn. Lady* II. Chorus, Will I.. imperill the innocence, and candor of the Author, by his calumnie? **1775** ASH, *Imperil* (..not used), to endanger. **1849** GROTE *Greece* II. xliii. V. 300 Sicily..was already sufficiently imperiled by its formidable enemies in Africa. **1856** FROUDE *Hist. Eng.* (1858) II. vii. 191 Life and property were imperilled by an insecure succession.

Hence **imperilled, -iled** *ppl. a.*; also **im'perilment**, the action of imperilling, or condition of being imperilled.

1843 CARLYLE *Past & Pr.* I. ii, Fearful imperilment of the victory. **1846** GROTE *Greece* I. xvi. I. 551 The Dioscuri as the protectors of the imperiled mariner. **1868** BROWNING *Ring & Bk.* v. 1185 Cruelty, Oppression and imperilment of life. **1870** *Illustr. Lond. News* 29 Oct. 438 The means of saving or helping to save 19,687 imperilled lives.

†**im'perillous,** *a. Obs. rare.* [f. IM-^{1} + PERILOUS; after prec.] ? Perilous, dangerous.

1645 J. BOND *Occasus Occid.* 68 Both were taken away, by a kind of imperillous disease.

†**imperi'osity.** *Obs. rare.* [f. L. *imperiōs-us* IMPERIOUS + -ITY.] Imperiousness, arrogance.

1654 H. L'ESTRANGE *Chas. I* (1655) 138 These exorbitances of those sons of Eli..created a very great disgust..and many well enough affected to their Empire, did exceedingly blame their imperiosity.

imperious (ɪm'pɪərɪəs), *a.* Also 6–7 **em-**. [ad. L. *imperiōs-us* possessed of command, commanding, imperious, f. *imperium* command: see -OUS. Cf. F. *impérieux* (15th c. in Hatz.-Darm.).]

†**1.** Having the rank of, or belonging to or befitting, an emperor or supreme ruler; IMPERIAL.

c **1586** C'TESS PEMBROKE *Ps.* LXXXIX. ix, The orders Which his imperious hand for laws shall signe. **1588** SHAKS. *Tit. A.* IV. iv. 81 King, be thy thoughts Imperious like thy name. *c* **1592** MARLOWE *Massacre Paris* II. v, 'Tis more than kingly or emperious. **1632** HEYWOOD *2nd Pt. Iron Age* II. i. Wks. 1874 III. 380 Thetis, The Emperious goddesse of the Sea. ? **1650** *Don Bellianis* 118 Most mighty Sophy of Syconia, and imperious Soldan of this great Persian Monarchy. **1703** POPE *Thebais* 257 Can this imperious lord forget to reign?

†**2.** Exercising a commanding influence; ruling, sovereign, dominant; having a commanding position, aspect, demeanour, etc.; majestic, stately. *Obs.* (or merged in 3 or 4).

1592 DANIEL *Compl. Rosamond* Wks. (1717) 39, I joy'd the happiest Warmth..That ever yet imperious Beauty tasted. **1596** DRAYTON *Legends* iii. 474 It is Emperious, both o'r Love and Hate. **1613** PURCHAS *Pilgrimage* (1614) 366 Three Artes, that exercise most imperious power over the mindes of men; Physicke,..Religion,..Mathematicall Sciences. **1638** SIR T. HERBERT *Trav.* (ed. 2) 127 A brave Castle.. mounted upon an imperious hill. *Ibid.* 182 The imperious Mountaine Taurus. **1649** JER. TAYLOR *Gt. Exemp.* II. viii. 59 Faith and Repentance, those two potent and imperious faculties. *a* **1680** BUTLER *Remains* (1759) I. 264 For to instruct is greater than to rule, And no Command's s'imperious as a School. **1812–19** CRABBE *Tales, Dumb Orat.* 54 To his experience and his native sense He join'd a bold imperious eloquence.

3. Overbearing, domineering, dictatorial. (The prevailing modern sense.)

1555 [implied in IMPERIOUSLY 2]. **1574** WHITGIFT *Def. Aunsw.* I. Wks. (Parker Soc.) I. 164 By this word..all kind of domination is not signified, but that which is joined with a certain imperious cruelty. **1579–80** NORTH *Plutarch* (1676) 802 The over-licentious and imperious tyranny of Dionysius. **1613** HEYWOOD *Braz. Age* IV. Wks. 1874 III. 242 Th' Emperious Queene Doth tyranize ore captiue Hercules. **1653** R. SANDERS *Physiogn.* 76 An imperious commanding woman, that wears the Breeches. **1710** STEELE *Tatler* No. 231 ¶2 [She] had from her Infancy discovered so imperious a Temper (usually called a High Spirit). **1859** TENNYSON *Geraint & Enid* 190 A youthful face, Imperious, and of haughtiest lineaments. **1879** FROUDE *Cæsar* vii. 62 A proud, imperious aristocrat, contemptuous..of popular rights.

4. Urgent, absolute, overmastering, imperative.

1541 [implied in IMPERIOUSLY 3]. **1623** BINGHAM *Xenophon* 30 The day before he sent an Imperious commandement to deliuer vp our armes, and now this day he imploied messengers about a truce. **1663** COWLEY *Verses & Ess., Ode Liberty* i, Now wild Ambition with imperious force Rides, rains, and spurs them like th' unruly Horse. **1789** BENTHAM *Princ. Legisl.* xiii. §4 The laws of honour.. make it an imperious duty to succour the weak. **1877** E. R. CONDER *Bas. Faith* ii. 47 The imperious necessity which urges us. **1894** H. DRUMMOND *Ascent Man* 278 Hunger was early seen..to be the first and most imperious appetite of all living things.

imperiously (ɪm'pɪərɪəslɪ), *adv.* [f. prec. + -LY^2.] In an imperious manner.

†**1.** In the way of supreme or absolute rule, imperially, sovereignly; with a commanding aspect, majestically. *Obs.*

1596 DRAYTON *Legends* iv. 487 Those which late imperiously controld me. **1603** KNOLLES *Hist. Turks* (1638) 107 The proud Mamalukes..imperiously commanded as great Lords ouer the rest of the people. **1634** SIR T. HERBERT *Trav.* 188 Imperiously inthronized upon a brazen Mount. [**1839** *Fraser's Mag.* XIX. 127 He lived..with the convention, conventionally..with the empire, imperiously.]

2. In a domineering manner; overbearingly, arrogantly.

1555 EDEN *Decades* 62 Imperiously and with cruel countenaunce commaundinge the kynge..to gyue them vytayles. **1617** MORYSON *Itin.* III. 149 That England is..the Purgatory of Servants..because they..use their Servants imperiously. **1659** *Gentl. Calling* (1696) 33 To..behave themselves disdainfully and imperiously. *a* **1797** H. WALPOLE *Mem. Geo. II* (1847) III. v. 108 His natural temper..was imperiously blunt, haughty and contemptuous. **1871** H. AINSWORTH *Tower Hill* I. xv, 'See to it, or dread my resentment', cried Henry, imperiously.

3. In the way of an absolute command or demand; by overmastering necessity; urgently.

1541 BARNES *Wks.* (1573) 319/2 Which thyng I doe geue for a counsell, and doe not commaunde it imperiously. **1602** *2nd Pt. Return fr. Parnass.* v. i. (Arb.) 64 At what dore must we imperiously beg. **1803** T. JEFFERSON *Writ.* (1830) III. 503 Where circumstances imperiously oblige us to a prompt decision. **1855** MOTLEY *Dutch Rep.* v. ii. (1866) 685 So soon as his presence should no longer be imperiously required. **1875** H. C. WOOD *Therap.* (1879) 664 Every known substance refuses more or less imperiously to allow the passage of electricity.

imperiousness (ɪm'pɪərɪəsnɪs). [f. as prec. + -NESS.] The quality of being imperious.

†**1.** Imperial character or dignity; absolute rule or sovereignty; empire. *Obs.*

1574 WHITGIFT *Def. Aunsw.* I. Wks. (Parker Soc.) I. 151 Neither is this word 'εὐεργέται' of any such imperiousness, that Christ should forbid his disciples the name. **1630** *R. Johnson's Kingd. & Commw.* 508 Hee..gave way to his sonne Bajacet to fill the chaire of imperiousnesse. **1670** NARBOROUGH *Jrnl.* in *Acc. Sev. Late Voy.* I. (1711) 103 This they do to shew their Greatness and Imperiousness.

2. Overbearing character, disposition, or manner; domineering, arrogance.

a **1613** OVERBURY *A Wife* Wks. (1638) 139 His other Beast Imperiousnes, is yet more proudly loaden. **1673** *Lady's Call.* II. ii. ¶14. 70 The imperiousness of a woman do's often raise those storms, wherein her self is shipwrack'd. **1779–81** JOHNSON *L.P., Swift* Wks. III. 409 He [Swift] apparently flattered his own arrogance by an assumed imperiousness, in which he was ironical only to the resentful. **1870** *Spectator* 19 Nov. 1376 The imperiousness of which, when identified with Germany, Germans were in a degree proud.

3. Overmastering or imperative quality, urgency.

1667 PEPYS *Diary* 22 Oct., Which Sir J. Duncomb answered with great imperiousness and earnestness. **1828** TYTLER *Hist. Scot.* (1864) I. 228 The imperiousness of his demands experienced an immediate relaxation. **1894** *Chicago Advance* 4 Jan., Yielding to a sweet imperiousness which they could not resist, the tired mother and her daughters descended from the wagon.

†**im'perish,** *v. Obs.* [Another form of EMPERISH (app. f. OF. *empeirer, empirer*, perh. associated with *perish*).] *trans.* To impair, injure, make worse.

1494 FABYAN *Chron.* VII. 386 By reason of great plente of rayne whiche in that season fyll..yᵉ bokes were greatly imperisshed. **1545** RAYNOLD *Byrth Mankynde* IV. vi. (1634) 197 Weedes..among the good hearbs, will deforme and imperish the good grace of them. **1586** J. HOOKER *Girald. Irel.* in *Holinshed* II. 44/1 His vertues verie much imperished and blemished. **1603** DEKKER, etc. *Grissil* III. ii. (1841) 41, I thought (by the synteresis of my soul) I had not been imperished.

imperishability (ɪm,pɛrɪʃə'bɪlɪtɪ). [f. next: see -ITY.] The quality of being imperishable; imperishableness.

1813 T. BUSBY *Lucretius* III. Comment. iii, He could not ..admit the imperishability of the invisible compound of the soul. *a* **1822** SHELLEY *Ess. & Lett., Fut. State* (Camelot) 81 In what manner can this concession be made an argument for its imperishability? **1855** MILMAN *Lat. Chr.* XIV. iii. (1864) IX. 134 [Aquinas] repudiates..the Eternity of matter, the imperishability of the universe.

imperishable (ɪm'pɛrɪʃəb(ə)l), *a.* (*sb.*) [f. IM-^{2} + PERISHABLE: cf. F. *impérissable* (Cotgr. 1611).] That cannot perish; not subject to decay; indestructible, immortal, everlasting, enduring. Also as *sb.*

1648 W. MOUNTAGUE *Devout Ess.* I. v. §1. 37 Immaculate and imperishable formes. **1757** BURKE *Abridgm. Eng. Hist.* Wks. 1842 II. 509 That their gods should be represented under a human form, they thought derogatory to beings uncreated and imperishable. **1842** WORDSW. *Grace Darling* 15 But, verily, good deeds Do no imperishable record find Save in the rolls of heaven. **1874** SYMONDS *Sk. Italy & Greece* (1898) I. xi. 212 This..they owe partly to the imperishable nature of baked clay. *a* **1910** 'MARK TWAIN' *Mysterious Stranger* (1916) iii. 27, I am of the aristocracy of the Imperishables. **1964** *New Statesman* 3 Apr. 514/2, I have seen *Oliver Twist*,..and a number of Jules Verne's imperishables.

imperishableness (ɪm'pɛrɪʃəb(ə)lnɪs). [f. prec. + -NESS.] The quality of being imperishable; indestructibility, immortality.

1809–10 COLERIDGE *Friend* (1837) III. 111 The imperishableness of a spiritual nature. **1847–8** DE QUINCEY *Protestant.* Wks. VIII. 125 The heavenly truths, by their own imperishableness, defeat the mortality of languages. **1881** H. H. GIBBS *Double Standard* 44 Scarceness alone is not a sufficient qualification, nor imperishableness, nor portableness.

imperishably (ɪm'pɛrɪʃəblɪ), *adv.* [f. as prec. + -LY^2.] In an imperishable manner; in such a way as not to perish; indestructibly.

1816 BYRON *Ch. Har.* III. lxvii, Like yonder Alpine snow, Imperishably pure beyond all things below. **1855** MILMAN *Lat. Chr.* XIV. ii. (1864) IX. 75 This was ere long to be embodied in Poetry and more imperishably in Art. **1878** BAYNE *Purit. Rev.* II. 39 Shakespeare..expressed it perfectly and imperishably.

†**'imperite,** *a.* (*sb.*) *Obs.* [ad. L. *imperīt-us* inexperienced, unskilled, f. *im-* (IM-^{2}) + *perīt-us* experienced (cf. *ex-perīrī* to make trial of).] Unskilled, ignorant; as *sb.* an unskilled or ignorant person. Hence †**'imperitely** *adv.*, ignorantly.

1622 CALLIS *Stat. Sewers* (1647) 130 King Hen. 8. incorporated the Physitians..and gave them power by Charter to examine the Imperites. **1657** TOMLINSON *Renou's Disp.* 503 Vulgar apothecaries call this Syrupe Diacodium, but imperitely. **1708** MOTTEUX *Rabelais* v. xx, Rarely the Concomitants of the imperite Vulgar.

‖**imperium** (ɪm'pɪərɪəm). [L., = command, supreme authority or power, sovereignty, dominion.] Command; absolute power; supreme or imperial power; EMPIRE.

1651 T. GOODWIN *Wks.* (1862) IV. 144 All the operations of all the powers in it are immediately and entirely at the arbitrary *imperium* and dominion of the soul. **1678** CUDWORTH *Intell. Syst.* I. iii. §17. 163 We have no voluntary *imperium* at all upon the systole and diastole of the heart. **1838–42** ARNOLD *Hist. Rome* III. xlvii. 431 The consul's *imperium*, his absolute power of life and death. **1870** E. MULFORD *Nation* x. 166 (Stanf.) The sovereignty of the nation involves the right which is described in its formal phrase, as the imperium or eminent domain.

b. Lat. phr. ***imperium in imperio***, an empire within an empire, an independent or supreme authority exercised or claimed within the jurisdiction of another authority.

1752 CHESTERF. *Lett. to Son* 6 Jan., If he will not..admit their *imperium in imperio*..it becomes meritorious..to depose him. **1790** J. ADAMS *Wks.* (1854) IX. 564 Our new government is an attempt to divide a sovereignty; a fresh essay at *imperium in imperio*. **1886** MRQ. LORNE in *Contemp. Rev.* July 133 No State or Federal Government would willingly constitute an *imperium in imperio* formed of one race unit.

†**im'periwigged,** *a. Obs.* Periwigged.

1611 COTGR., *Emperruqué*,..imperiwigged, that weares a Periwig.

impermanence (ɪm'pɜːmənəns). [f. IMPERMANENT: see -ENCE; or f. IM-^{2} + PERMANENCE.] The fact or condition of being impermanent; want of permanence or continued duration.

1796 ANNA SEWARD *Lett* (1811) IV. 264 Melancholy impermanence of human blessings! **1893** HUXLEY *Evolution*

& *Ethics* 4 The most obvious attribute of the Cosmos is its impermanence. **1894** CROCKETT *Lilac Sun-bonnet* 108 The lucid impermanence of earliest dawn.

impermanency (ɪmˈpɜːmənənsɪ). [f. as prec.: see -ENCY.] The quality or state of being impermanent.

1648 W. MOUNTAGUE *Devout Ess.* I. vi. §2. 58 Distilling out of the serious contemplation of the mutability of all worldly happines, a remedy against the evill of that ficklenes and impermanency. **1889** HOWELLS *Hazard New Fort.* 131 March had a feeling of impermanency from what had happened.

impermanent (ɪmˈpɜːmənənt), *a.* [f. IM-² + PERMANENT.] Not permanent or lasting; unenduring; transient.

1653 H. MORE *Conject. Cabbal.* iii. (1662) 98 That Adam is here condemned to a mortal, flitting and impermanent state, till he reach his Æthereal or pure fiery Vehicle. **1762** ANNA SEWARD *Let.* Oct., Wks. 1810 I. p. xliv, The impermanent pleasures of the eye. **1883** HOWELLS *Woman's Reason* I. 28 The sense of our impermanent relation to the parental roof comes to us very early in life.

impermeability (ɪmpɜːmiːəˈbɪlɪtɪ). [f. next + -ITY. Cf. F. *imperméabilité*.] The quality or state of being impermeable.

1755 FRANKLIN *Lett.* Wks. 1840 V. 356 It does not appear to me that Père Beccaria doubts of the absolute impermeability of glass in the sense I meant it. **1889** *Nature* 19 Sept., Conclusive evidence of the impermeability of the strata. **1897** *Daily News* 30 July 5/7 He considered that the impermeability of the balloon was unsatisfactory.

impermeable (ɪmˈpɜːmiːəb(ə)l), *a.* [a. F. *imperméable* (Rabelais), or ad. late L. *impermeābil-is*, f. *im-* (IM-²) + *permeābilis* PERMEABLE.] Not permeable.

1. That cannot be passed through or traversed; impassable.

1697 EVELYN *Numism.* iv. 160 Attempts to discover the Nor-West and other hitherto impermeable Passages. **1808** J. BARLOW *Columb.* IX. 466 Between them stretch'd the impermeable main. **1854** HAWTHORNE *Eng. Note-Bks.* (1879) II. 350 Charing Cross..became absolutely impermeable.

2. *Physics.* That does not permit the passage of water or other fluid, liquid or gaseous.

1752 WATSON in *Phil. Trans.* XLVII. 554 To demonstrate, that glass is not absolutely impermeable to the electric fluid. **1827** STEUART *Planter's G.* (1828) 205 A bed of hard and impermeable clay. **1878** HUXLEY *Physiogr.* 21 Those [rocks] which refuse to allow water to soak in are said to be impermeable.

Hence **imˈpermeableness**, the quality of being impermeable, impermeability; **imˈpermeably** *adv.*, in an impermeable manner.

1846 WORCESTER, *Impermeably. Dr. Allen.* **1847** CRAIG, *Impermeableness.*

impermeated (ɪmˈpɜːmiːeɪtɪd), *a.* [f. IM-² + *permeated*, pa. pple. of PERMEATE *v.*] Not permeated, traversed, or penetrated; unpermeated.

1808 J. BARLOW *Columb.* IX. 50 A formless dark impermeated mass. **1847–9** TODD *Cycl. Anat.* IV. 521/1 A thin plate of bone, impermeated by vessels.

impermeator (ɪmˈpɜːmiːeɪtə(r)). [f. IM-¹ + late L. *permeātor*, agent-n. f. *permeāre* to PERMEATE.] In a steam-engine, an appliance for forcing oil into the cylinder in order to lubricate uniformly the walls of the cylinder and the piston.

In recent Dicts.

impermissible (ɪmpəˈmɪsɪb(ə)l), *a.* [f. IM-² + PERMISSIBLE.] Not permissible; not to be permitted or allowed.

1858 *Sat. Rev.* 30 Oct. 421/2 Morality is not allowed to say that the artist is on impermissible ground, for he is on the ground of real life. **1889** LIGHTFOOT *Ess.* '*Supernat. Relig.*' 181 He should consider it impossible and impermissible to suppose him guilty of any laches here.

†**imperˈmixt**, *a. Obs.* Also in-. [ad. L. *impermixt-us*, f. *im-* (IM-²) + *permixtus*, f. *per* through, thoroughly + *mixtus* mixed.] Unmixed, unmingled. Hence **imperˈmixtly** *adv.*, unmixedly, without mixture.

1629 DONNE *Serm.* cx. IV. 535 Goodness impermixt, intemerate and indeterminate goodness. *a* **1631** *Ibid.* lxiv. 648 Zeal cleanses us, but it must be Zeale impermixt as the Sun not mingled with our smoaky sooty factious affections. **1636** FEATLY *Clavis Myst.* xix. 188 Where divers candles.. in a room concur to enlighten the place, the light of them remaineth impermixt. **1677** GALE *Crt. Gentiles* IV. 288 It belongs to the Deitie to diffuse it self through althings impermixtly, but nothing through it.

†**imperˈmutable**, *a. Obs.* [f. IM-² + PERMUTABLE.] Not permutable; unchangeable.

1528 ROY *Rede Me* (Arb.) 108 Whose verite is impermutable. **1555** EDEN *Decades* 146 Wee see this order to bee impermutable. **1678** R. R[USSELL] *Geber* III. ii. II. xiv. 203 In Bodies there is somewhat impermutable..which cannot be taken away.

imperour, -owr, -ur, obs. ff. EMPEROR.

imperˈscriptible, *a.* [f. IM-² + **perscriptible*, f. L. *perscrībĕre* to put anything to paper, to write out, write down, register.] For which no written authority can be adduced; unrecorded.

1832 LEWIS *Use & Ab. Pol. Terms* iii. 31 An imperscriptable right is a right which was prior to the social compact. *a* **1843** SOUTHEY *Doctor* ccxli. (1862) 660 He frequently found cause to exercise the imperscriptible and inalienable right of altering and improving his own work.

†**imperˈscrutable**, *a. Obs.* [ad. L. *imperscrūtābil-is*, f. *im-* (IM-²) + *perscrūtāre* to search through, examine into: see -BLE.] Not to be searched out; unsearchable, inscrutable.

1526 *Pilgr. Perf.* (1531) 64 b, The dispensacyon of god is imperscrutable & farre beyonde mannes reason. **1652** GAULE *Magastrom.* 51 Are there not many naturall things imperscrutable to humane curiosity? **1681** GLANVILL *Sadducismus* I. 137 The Notion of a Spirit is so difficult and imperscrutable.

Hence †**imperˈscrutableness**, unsearchableness, inscrutableness.

1664 H. MORE *Myst. Iniq.* 410 The Incomprehensibleness and Imperscrutableness of the Divinity of our Saviour.

†**imperˈseverant**, *a.*¹ *Obs.* [f. IM-² + PERSEVERANT.] Not persevering, wanting in perseverance.

1594 BP. ANDREWES *Serm. bef. Q. Eliz. Hampton Crt.* in init., The Sodomites are an example of impenitent wilful sinners; and Lot's wife of imperseverant and relapsing righteous persons.

imperseverant, *a.*²: see IMPERCEIVERANT *a.*

impersistent (ɪmpəˈsɪstənt), *a.* [f. IM-² + PERSISTENT.] Not persistent or enduring.

a **1866** J. GROTE *Exam. Utilitarian Philos.* (1870) xix. 324 We ought..to know whether some races are strong and persistent,..others weak and impersistent, so as to yield to others and die out. **1888** H. T. BROWN in *Jrnl. Geol. Soc.* (1889) XLV. I. 7 An eroded and impersistent bed of hard, fine-grained, Coal-measure sandstone. **1965** G. J. WILLIAMS *Econ. Geol. N.Z.* iii. 27/2 Various impersistent shoots were worked in the Pandora and South Keep-it-Dark mines.

impersonal (ɪmˈpɜːsənəl), *a.* and *sb.* Also 6 imparsonall. [ad. late L. *impersōnāl-is*, f. *im-* (IM-²) + *persōnālis* PERSONAL. Cf. F. *impersonnel*.]

A. *adj.* **1.** *Gram.* A term applied to verbs when used only in the third person singular, as *it rains*, *it freezes*, *me thinks*, ME. *me hungreth*, *lest it ofthinke him*.

In Gr. and L., an impersonal vb. had no pronoun subject, e.g. ὕει, *pluit*, it rains; hence some have denied the name in English to verbs that have the subject *it*. Others have applied the term *unipersonal* to all verbs used only in the third person singular, whether with or without a pronoun subject. Impersonal verbs do not form a sharply defined class, since many ordinary verbs have impersonal constructions; in English, also, many verbs were formerly used impersonally which are now used in all the persons.

1520 WHITINTON *Vulg.* (1527) 2 b, If it be a verbe impersonal. **1530** PALSGR. Introd. 36 Verbes imparsonalles have no more but the thyrde parsone syngular. **1553** UDALL *Flowres* 11 (R.) Wher note that verbes impersonalles be oftentimes turned into personalles. *a* **1637** B. JONSON *Eng. Gram.* xvi, A verb is divided two manner of ways. First, in respect of persons, it is called personal, or impersonal. **1824** L. MURRAY *Eng. Gram.* (ed. 5) I. 170 As the word impersonal implies a total absence of persons, it is improperly applied to those verbs which have a person. **1841** LATHAM *Eng. Lang.* xxi. 319 These three [*meseems, methinks, me lists*] are the only true Impersonal Verbs in the English language..because no Pronoun accompanies them. **1850** *Ibid.* IV. xxvii. 342 In the old language impersonal verbs, or rather the impersonal use of verbs, was commoner than at present.

†**b.** By extension, applied to other parts of speech which have no inflexions. *Obs.*

c **1620** A. HUME *Brit. Tongue* (1865) 32 A word impersonal is quhilk in al formes of speach keepes one face, and this is adverb or conjunction. **1658** PHILLIPS, *Impersonal*, a term used in Gramar, and signifieth that word whether pronoun or verb which hath but one termination for all the three persons, or at least which wanteth a termination for one of them. [**1880** LEWIS & SHORT *Lat. Dict.*, *Impersōnātīvus* (sc. *modus*), the impersonal mood, i.e. the infinitive.]

2. Not pertaining to or connected with any particular person or persons; having no personal reference or connexion: said of things.

1630 BRATHWAIT *Eng. Gentlem.* (1641) 22 This unbounded fury may seeme to have a two-fold relation; either as it is proper and personall or popular and impersonall. **1841** EMERSON *Addr.*, *Method of Nature* Wks. (Bohn) II. 231 What is Genius but finer love, a love impersonal, a love of the..perfection of things? **1864** *Sat. Rev.* XVIII. 455/1 The most purely impersonal considerations of public duty. **1880** *Daily Tel.* 9 July, The jewels and other appointments of the harem are quite impersonal, belonging to the establishment and not to any of their successive wearers.

3. Not possessing or endowed with personality; not existing or manifested as a person.

1842 MANNING *Serm.*, *Myst. Sin* (1848) I. 4 It is most necessary for us ever to bear in mind the personality of Satan; for we are often wont to speak of sin, as we do of sicknesses or plagues, as if it were an impersonal thing. **1863** E. V. NEALE *Anal. Th. & Nat.* 95 Heraclitus..seemed to have called up a rival impersonal Deity, who must swallow up the personal gods of the popular faith. **1875** POSTE *Gaius* I. (ed. 2) 64 Slaves being regarded as impersonal men.

B. *sb.* **1.** *Gram.* An impersonal verb.

1612 BRINSLEY *Pos. Parts* (1669) 40 How are Impersonals declined? They are..only formed in the third Person singular, through all Moods and Tenses. **1845** STODDART in *Encycl. Metrop.* (1847) I. 63/1 The impersonals are of two kinds, active and neuter.

2. An impersonal thing or creature; an impersonality. *rare.*

1796 BURKE *Regic. Peace* IV. Wks. IX. 11 All those blessings..on him who found out abstraction, personification, and impersonals. In certain cases they are the first of all soporifics.

impersonalism (ɪmˈpɜːsənəlɪz(ə)m). [f. IMPERSONAL *a.* + -ISM.] The character of being impersonal; the absence of personal contacts. So **imˈpersonalist**, one who is, or aims at being, impersonal; **impersonaˈlistic** *a.*

1899 *Speaker* 9 Dec. 263/1 The weak point in the armour of the impersonalist is the dedication. **1908** *Daily Chron.* 26 May 3/4 The workmen are getting the impersonalism of Socialism without its humanity. **1920** F. M. FORD *Let.* 30 June (1965) 109 There is the whole open question of Impersonalism to discuss. **1932** J. C. POWYS *Glastonbury Romance* xxvi. 907 It was the appearance of Dave Spear's figure now—for the impersonalist had decided to disobey Zookey—that drove the tipsy giant to his next move. **1968** *Austral. Jrnl. Philos.* XLVI. 257 The existence of such principles, principles which are perfectly consistent as 'impersonalistic' principles are actually used but which would be inconsistent if 'impersonalistic' principles were used in the way being supposed, does not, however, give impersonalism any sort of advantage over nonimpersonalism.

impersonality (ɪmpɜːsəˈnælɪtɪ). [f. IMPERSONAL + -ITY.] The quality or condition of being impersonal; absence of personality.

1769 SIR W. DRAPER in *Junius Lett.* iv. 24 Junius..is pleased to tell me, that he addresses himself to me *personally*: I shall be glad to see him. It is his *impersonality* that I complain of. **1871** *Daily News* 26 Sept., The strangest thing to note is the impersonality of the events—the uncontrollable character of the movement; the annihilation of individual influence in the general rush. **1882** *Fraser's Mag.* XXVI. 65 The stability..of artistic form as contrasted with the fluctuating, changing impersonality of scientific fact. **1888** *Pall Mall G.* 19 Sept. 2/2 Editorial impersonality must give place to distinct and familiar personality.

b. An impersonal being or creation.

1876 HUMPHREYS *Coin-Coll. Man.* xvii. 210 Idealised impersonalities of the deities of the Greek mythology. **1881** *Daily Tel.* 12 Feb., The monopoly of governing power in an impersonality called 'the State'. **1897** W. P. KER *Epic & Rom.* 288 Kingdoms, Church and Empire. Of those great impersonalities there was little known in Iceland.

impersonalize (ɪmˈpɜːsənəlaɪz), *v.* [f. as prec. + -IZE.] *trans.* To render impersonal. Hence **imˌpersonaliˈzation**, the action of rendering impersonal; an impersonalized condition or form.

1880 A. B. GROSART *Willobie* p. vi, When you try to get near either or both, you have the same mysterious and baffling impersonalization of them.

impersonally (ɪmˈpɜːsənəlɪ), *adv.* [f. IMPERSONAL + -LY².] In an impersonal manner.

1. *Gram.* As an impersonal verb.

1580 BARET *Alv.* To Rdr. A vij b, *Adiect.* noteth a word Adiectiuelie taken:..*Imper.* Impersonallie taken. **1730–6** BAILEY (folio) s.v., The Verb *Rain* is used impersonally. **1870** R. C. JEBB *Sophocles' Electra* (ed. 2) 152/2 Aegisthus used πάρεστι impersonally = *licetne*?

2. Without personal reference, connexion, or feeling; without reference to any particular person.

1854 A. G. HENDERSON tr. *Cousin's Philos. of Kant* vii. 178 There is a state..where the reason manifests itself almost entirely impersonally. **1881** H. JAMES *Portr. Lady* xxxiii, He wished to describe him impersonally, scientifically. **1882** H. SPENCER *Princ. Sociol.* §533 The..laws which originate from personal authority, have inequality as their common essential principle; while the laws which originate impersonally, in the consensus of individual interests, have equality as their essential principle.

impersonalness (ɪmˈpɜːsənəlnɪs). [f. IMPERSONAL *a.* + -NESS.] Impersonal quality; absence of personality.

1871 P. BROOKS *Let.* 11 Jan. in A. V. G. Allen *Phillips Brooks* (1908) 247 When I see a small audience I lose the impersonalness of the thing. I think of individuals and that always puts me out. **1955** P. HERON *Changing Forms of Art* 233 In his painting it never matters one jot when his beautiful girl has a distinctly anonymous air. Her impersonalness is part of her charm. **1956** A. TOYNBEE *Historian's Approach to Relig.* iv. 44 The impersonalness of an oecumenical empire as an institution makes itself felt in the remoteness of its metropolis from the daily life of the great majority of its subjects.

impersonate (ɪmˈpɜːsəneɪt), *v.* [f. L. type **impersonāre*, f. *im-* (IM-¹) + *persōna* person: cf. *incorporāre* to INCORPORATE.]

†**1.** *trans.* To invest with an actual personality; to embody. *Obs.*

1633 EARL MANCH. *Al Mondo* (1636) 181 This soule of mine impersonated anew, and so inanimating my body againe.

2. To invest with a supposed personality; to represent in a personal or bodily form; to personify.

1624 BEDELL *Lett.* iii. 51 The rich man being in hell torments (in whose wordes I doubt not but our Sauiour doth impersonate and represent the conceits of many men liuing

in this world). **1755** WARBURTON *View Bolingbroke's Philos.* iii. Wks. 1811 XII. 203 That the Jews and Christians, as well as the Heathens, impersonated Chance under the name of Fortune. **1883** *Contemp. Rev.* Dec. 871 The conscience of the community is impersonated in its Government.

b. To manifest or embody in one's own person; to typify.

1855 MILMAN *Lat. Chr.* III. vi. (1864) II. 81 His age acknowledged Benedict as the perfect type of the highest religion and Benedict impersonated his age. **1863** KINGLAKE *Crimea* II. 1 [St. Arnaud] impersonated with singular exactness the idea which our forefathers had in their minds when they spoke of what they called 'a Frenchman'. **1874** STUBBS *Const. Hist.* I. ii. 27 His position was dignified and important, as impersonating the unity of the race.

3. To assume the person or character of; to play the part of; to act (a character); to personate.

1715 M. DAVIES *Athen. Brit.* I. 185 The Master and Disciple of the Dialogues often think fit..to impersonate other more surprizing Actors. **1863** MRS. C. CLARKE *Shaks. Char.* x. 257 None but persons of imagination and quick feeling should presume to impersonate any of his characters.

Hence **im'personated** *ppl. a.* = next.

a **1790** T. WARTON (Mason), The impersonated vices and virtues. **1878** GLADSTONE *Prim. Homer* xiii. 153 Of the impersonated Unseen no poet has made such effective employment.

impersonate (ɪm'pɜːsənət), *ppl. a.* [Short for *impersonated*, on analogy of other ppl. adjs. in *-ate*, *-ated*: see -ATE².] Embodied in a person; invested with personality; impersonated.

1820 KEATS *Isabella* l, If Love impersonate was ever dead. **1834** LD. HOUGHTON *Mem. Many Scenes, Spartans at Thermopylæ* (1844) 51 Heroic Dignity, impersonate In awful phantoms. *a* **1867** J. HAMILTON *Moses* iv. (1870) 68 We expect to find..the Sacred Scribe his own volume impersonate and alive.

impersonation (ɪmpɜːsə'neɪʃən). [n. of action from IMPERSONATE *v.*]

1. The action of impersonating or fact of being impersonated; representation in personal or bodily form; personification.

1800 *Collins' Poems* 128 *note* (Jod.), We include the Impersonation of Passions, Affections, Virtues and Vices. **1851** RUSKIN *Stones Ven.* (1874) I. App. 387 In figurative representation there is always impersonation.

b. *concr.* An instance of this; a person or thing impersonating or representing a principle, idea, etc.

1831 CARLYLE *Sart. Res.* III. vi, Man..the visible Manifestation and Impersonation of the Divinity. **1840** DICKENS *Barn. Rudge* iv, The very impersonation of good-humour and blooming beauty. **1850** MERIVALE *Rom. Emp.* (1865) II. xvi. 236 He proclaimed himself..the supreme impersonation of the laws.

2. The dramatic representation of a character.

1825 *Gentl. Mag.* XCV. I. 332/2 Her [Mrs. Siddons'] sublime impersonation of that heroic woman. **1881** *Athenæum* No. 2811. 348/1 For Herr Reichmann's impersonation of the leading *rôle* no words of praise could be too high.

impersonative (ɪm'pɜːsəneɪtɪv), *a.* [f. IMPERSONATE *v.*: see -ATIVE.] Having the faculty of impersonating; of the nature of or relating to histrionic impersonation.

1886 *Pall Mall G.* 9 Sept. 4/2 When she has thoroughly assimilated her lessons..then her impersonative talent will have unhindered way. **1890** *Ibid.* 2 June 3/2 He cannot make the novelist's characters live again. His talent is allusive, not impersonative.

impersonator (ɪm'pɜːsəneɪtə(r)). [agent-n. in L. form f. IMPERSONATE *v.*] One who impersonates or plays a part; an actor of a dramatic character.

1853 J. D. H. DALE tr. *Baldeschi's Cerem. Rom. Rite* 180 He who represents Christ will have the impersonator of the Evangelist on his right, and that of the crowd on his left. **1864** *Reader* 18 June, With one exception, all the characters are sustained by their former impersonators.

impersonatress (ɪm'pɜːsəneɪtrɪs). [f. prec. + -ESS.] A female impersonator.

1881 NORRIS *Matrimony* III. i. 11 The impersonatress of Madame de Sancerre played her part here to such purpose.

imperso'natrix. [fem. in L. form of *impersonator*: see -TRIX.] = prec.

1847 DE QUINCEY *Protestantism* Wks. VIII. 137 *note*, The ..old vulgar witch of England and Scotland was but an impersonatrix of the very same superstition.

impersonee, variant of IMPARSONEE.

impersonification (ɪmpə,sɒnɪfɪ'keɪʃən). [f. IM-¹ + PERSONIFICATION, after *impersonation*.] Personification; impersonation.

1799 MRS. J. WEST *Tale of Times* III. 38 A striking impersonification of suffering meekness. **1849** *Tait's Mag.* XVI. 319/1 A myth..is the ideal impersonification of a mighty impulse bestowed on the human mind. **1865** EMMELINE LOTT *Harem Life Egypt* I. p. ix, The far-famed Odalisques of the nineteenth century, those mysterious impersonifications of Eastern loveliness.

impersonify (ɪmpə'sɒnɪfaɪ), *v.* [f. IM-¹ + PERSONIFY, after *impersonate*.] *trans.* To represent in personal form; to personify. Hence **imper'sonified, imper'sonifying** *ppl. adjs.*

1804 ANNA SEWARD *Mem. Darwin* 186 An impersonified individual. **1864** *Daily Tel.* 15 Aug., It was not the lot of Robson, as it was of Rachel and of Kean, to impersonify the loftier emotions. **1883** GOSSE *17th Cent. Stud.* 64 Webster.. was only saved by his strong impersonifying habit of mind from falling into the mere historic dullness of such plays as *Perkin Warbeck* or *Sejanus*.

impersonize (ɪm'pɜːsənaɪz), *v. rare.* [f. IM-¹ + PERSONIZE, after *impersonate*.] *trans.* To personify, impersonate. Also *absol.*

1804 ANNA SEWARD *Mem. Darwin* 188 She impersonizes too lavishly. *Ibid.* 203 The impersonized elements received her. **1820** *Blackw. Mag.* VIII. 131 The various modifications and contentions of good and evil in this life, typified and impersonized by fairies, demons, &c.

Hence **impersoni'zation**, the action of personifying; impersonation.

1796 ANNA SEWARD *Lett.* (1811) IV. 192 Those lines in the centre, which present..an impersonization of winter. **1797** *Ibid.* 306 Dr. Darwin's impersonization of that death-breathing gale, in the Botanic Garden.

†**im'perspicable**, *a. Obs. rare.* In 7 in-. [ad. late L. *imperspicābil-is* inscrutable, incomprehensible, f. *im-* (IM-²) + *perspicābilis* that may be clearly seen, PERSPICABLE.] That cannot be seen or discerned; invisible.

1665 SIR T. HERBERT *Trav.* (1677) 133 It was so thick powdered with Oriental Pearl and glittering Gems, as made the ground of it inperspicable.

imperspi'cuity. [f. IM-² + PERSPICUITY.] The reverse of perspicuity or clearness; obscurity.

1659 O. WALKER *Instruct. Oratory* 98 [He] must in some things hazard the imperspicuity of his stile.

imper'spicuous, *a. rare.* [f. L. *imperspicu-us* not clear, obscure + -OUS; cf. PERSPICUOUS.] Not perspicuous or clear; obscure.

1721 BAILEY, *Imperspicuous*, not clear, or evident.

imperspirable (ɪmpə'spaɪərəb(ə)l), *a.* Now *rare.* [f. IM-² + PERSPIRABLE.] Incapable of perspiration.

1684 tr. *Bonet's Merc. Compit.* XVIII. 663 The humors are condensed, the skin made imperspirable. **1744** tr. *Boerhaave's Inst.* III. 299 A Cicatrix or imperspirable Crust is formed, instead of the Cuticle. **1844–57** G. BIRD *Urin. Deposits* (ed. 5) 311 Pulse quick and sharp; skin dry and imperspirable.

Hence **imperspira'bility**.

1744 MITCHELL in *Phil. Trans.* XLIII. 144 The Thickness and Density of the Skins of black and tawny People, or Imperspirability of their Bodies.

impersuadable (ɪmpə'sweɪdəb(ə)l), *a.* [f. IM-² + PERSUADABLE.] Not persuadable; that cannot be persuaded. Hence **imper'suadableness**.

a **104** T. BROWN *Two Oxford Scholars* Wks. 1730 I. 3 You break my heart..by your impersuadableness. **1891** J. M. MCNULTY in *Pall Mall G.* 24 Nov. 2/3 There is a personal hinderer in the spiritual life of men. He is mighty, malignant, spiritual, invisible, impersuadable.

†**imper'suasible**, *a. Obs.* [ad. med.L. *impersuāsibil-is*, f. *im-* (IM-²) + *persuāsibilis*, PERSUASIBLE.] = prec.

1576 FLEMING *Panopl. Epist.* 243 In this point he shall finde me impersuasible, and not to be exhorted. **1627** DONNE *Serm.* lxvi. 667 The imperswasible Recusant does so. **1667** *Decay Chr. Piety* ii. ⁋17 If it be his fortune to have as imperswasible an auditory.

So †**impersuasi'bility**, †**imper'suasibleness**; †**imper'suasibly** *adv.*

1549 HOOPER *Ten Commandm.* Pref., Wks. (Parker Soc.) 261 An impersuasibility, diffidence, incredulity, contumacy, or inobedience. **1654** WARREN *Unbelievers* 100 It signifies imperswasibility. **1659** HAMMOND *On Ps.* cxix. 70 Obstinately and imperswasibly bent upon their course. **1675** J. SMITH *Chr. Relig. App.* III. 14 The..imperswasibleness of the Sceptick.

impert, obs. form of IMPART.

†**im'pertinacy**. *Obs.* [f. next: see -ACY.] Erroneous form for IMPERTINENCY.

1584 LODGE *Alarum* Addr. Inns Court A ij b, Not according to the impertinacie of the injurye, but as equitye might countenance mee. *a* **1665** J. GOODWIN *Filled w. the Spirit* (1867) 374 We have..detected the insufficiency and impertinacy of such other grounds and reasons for their practice.

†**im'pertinat**, *a. Obs.* Erroneous form for IMPERTINENT *a.*

c **1450** HOLLAND *Howlat* 924 So pomposs, impertinat [*v.r.* impertinax] and reprovable.

impertinence (ɪm'pɜːtɪnəns), *sb.* [a. F. *impertinence*, f. *impertinent* IMPERTINENT: see -ENCE.] The fact or quality of being impertinent; that which is impertinent.

1. The fact or character of not pertaining to the matter in hand; want of pertinence; irrelevance.

1626 MASSINGER *Rom. Actor* III. ii, To cut off All tedious impertinence [I] have contracted The tragedy into one continued scene. **1653** MILTON *Hirelings* Wks. (1851) 352 Of like impertinence is that Example of Jacob, Gen. 28 22., who of his free choice..vow'd the Tenth of all that God should give him. **1726** DE FOE *Hist. Devil* I. vii. (1840) 78 The impertinence of this account would hardly have given it a place here. **1848** WHARTON *Law Lex.*, *Impertinence*, introducing into a pleading or an interrogatory to a witness in Chancery, long recitals, or unnecessary digressions.

b. (with *pl.*) An irrelevant fact or matter; an irrelevance.

1612 [see IMPERTINENCY 1 b]. **1675** BAXTER *Cath. Theol.* II. I. 1 Let us spend no time on such Impertinences, but speak that to the Matter. **1705** DE FOE *Mrs. Veal* Wks. 1840 V. 342 By her going off from her discourse abruptly to some impertinence. **1876** LOWELL *Among my Bks.* Ser. II. 131 To get a pack of impertinences on its shoulders.

2. The fact or character of being unsuitable, out of place, improper, or irrational; action or conduct of this character; inappropriateness, incongruity; triviality, trifling, folly, absurdity.

1629 MASSINGER *Picture* IV. iii, Still tormented With thy impertinence! **1664–93** SOUTH *12 Serm.* (1697) II. 122 A Petition, fraught with Nonsense and Incoherence, Confusion and Impertinence. **1676** MARVELL *Mr. Smirke* 28 To have done otherwise would have been the greatest Impert[in]ence and Folly. **1706** PHILLIPS, *Impertinence*,.. Extravagance, Silliness, Foolery, Nonsense. **1727** SWIFT *To a very Young Lady*, The hurry and impertinence of receiving and paying visits on account of your marriage being now over. **1769** *Junius Lett.* xxxv. ⁋1 Unacquainted with the vain impertinence of forms. **1823** LAMB *Elia* Ser. II. Pref., The impressions of infancy had burnt into him, and he resented the impertinence of manhood.

b. (with *pl.*) Something unsuitable, out of place, trivial, or irrational; an incongruity; a trifle, absurdity, piece of folly.

1603 HOLLAND *Plutarch's Mor.* 54 Forced and foolish figures..and such like impertinences or defects. **1645** EVELYN *Mem.* 27 Feb., We were taken up next morning in seeing the impertinences of the Carnival, when all the world are as mad at Rome as at other places. **1734** MRS. DELANY in *Life & Corr.* 475, I was not able to find one moment to write..from seven in the morning till eleven at night, I met with impertinences. **1869** GOULBURN *Purs. Holiness* xvii. 158 Any secular pursuit becomes an impertinence as regards the great end of our being.

3. Interference with what lies beyond one's province; unmannerly and offensive intrusion or taking of liberty; presumptuous or forward rudeness of behaviour or speech, esp. to a superior; insolence. (The chief current sense in colloq. use.)

1712 STEELE *Spect.* No. 410 ⁋1 Subjected to all the Impertinence she must meet with in that publick Place. **1773** MRS. CHAPONE *Improv. Mind* (1774) II. 80 Masters and mistresses sometimes provoke impertinence from their servants. **1810** *Sporting Mag.* XXXVI. 3 Impertinence is manifested by wilfully leaping over the boundaries of good manners. **1883** C. J. WILLS *Mod. Persia* 217 Being no archæologist, it would be impertinence were I to attempt a description.

b. (with *pl.*) An instance of this; an impertinent act; a piece of impertinence or rudeness.

1822 HAZLITT *Table-t.* Ser. II. vi. (1869) 132 We resent wholesome counsel as an impertinence. **1877** SPARROW *Serm.* xxi. 274 Social impertinences, involving more or less of disrespect.

c. An impertinent person.

1754 J. SHEBBEARE *Matrimony* (1766) I. 112 That little self-sufficient Impertinence, her Father. **1825** JAMIESON, *Impertinence*..2. An insolent person. *Aberd.*

im'pertinence, *v. rare.* [f. prec. sb.] *trans.* To treat with impertinence.

1756 H. WALPOLE *Lett. to H. Mann* (1834) III. 155, I do not wonder that you are impertinenced by Richcourt.

impertinency (ɪm'pɜːtɪnənsɪ). Now *rare.* [f. as IMPERTINENCE, with -ENCY, q.v. Cotgr. 1611 has '*Impertinence*, impertinencie, vnfitness, vnpropernesse'.] The quality of being impertinent.

1. The quality of being irrelevant; irrelevancy; = IMPERTINENCE 1.

1605 SHAKS. *Lear* IV. vi. 178 O matter, and impertinency mixt, Reason in Madnesse. **1610** GUILLIM *Heraldry* I. vi. (1660) 35 Which I doe passe over..for impertinency thereof to this place. **1699** BENTLEY *Phal.* xv. 486 'Twould be endless..to shew all the silliness and impertinency in the Matter of the Epistles. **1884** *Law Times* LXXVIII. 115/2 Motion that..several parts..of the bill of costs..might be expunged for scandal and impertinency.

b. An instance of this; = IMPERTINENCE 1 b.

1607–12 BACON *Ess.*, *Marriage* (Arb.) 266/1 Some.. whose thoughtes doe end with themselves, and doe accompt future tymes impertinencyes [*edd.* 1612, 1625 impertinences]. **1704** ADDISON *Italy* (1733) 67 All Answers ..are looked upon as Impertinencies or Interruptions.

2. The quality of being inappropriate or absurd; = IMPERTINENCE 2.

a **1629** SIR R. DUDLEY (*title*) A Proposition..to bridle the Impertinency of Parliaments. **1691** HARTCLIFFE *Virtues* 30 The Impertinency of worldly business is not yet become a burden too heavy for the mind to bear. **1727–41** CHAMBERS *Cycl.* s.v. *Astrology*, You boast much of the event of a few predictions, which, considering the multitude of those your art has produced, plainly confess its impertinency.

b. An instance of this; = IMPERTINENCE 2 b.

1589 PUTTENHAM *Eng. Poesie* III. xix. (Arb.) 212 A very foolish impertinency of speech, and not a figure. *a* **1656** HALES *Gold. Rem.* (1688) 201 Laborious Vanities, and learned Impertinencies. **1710** PALMER *Proverbs* 301 To neglect infancy, and leave children too long under the impertinencies of the baby and hobby-horse. **1742** RICHARDSON *Pamela* IV. 320 What Nursery Impertinencies are these, to trouble a Man with! **1793** COWPER *Let.* 5 Oct., My good intentions towards you..are continually frustrated ..by mere impertinencies, such as calls of civility.

3. Insolence; = IMPERTINENCE 3.
1653 Holcroft Procopius, Goth. Wars III. 106 We are amazed at the impertinency of these Gepædes; who..come here to offer the foulest scorne that can be. a 1714 Sharp Serm. IV. xviii. (R.), Wit and profaneness are infinitely different things, as likewise is wit and impertinency.
b. An instance of this; = IMPERTINENCE 3 b.
1628 Digby Voy. Medit. (Camden) 58 For some impertinencies and arrogancies did putt my chiefe masters mate out of his place. 1710 Lady M. W. Montagu Lett. to Burnet 20 July (1887) II. 4 You have already forgiven me greater impertinencies. 1842 Dickens Amer. Notes (1850) 136/1 There they are not the custom, and..would be impertinencies.

impertinent (ɪmˈpɜːtɪnənt), a. (sb.) Also 4 impertenent, 5 inpertynent, 6 impertynent, impartinent, -ynente. [a. F. impertinent (14th c. in Hatz.-Darm.) or ad. L. impertinēns, -ēnt-em not belonging, in med.L. 'ineptus, insulsus' (Du Cange), f. im- (IM-²) + pertinēns PERTINENT.]
†1. Not appertaining or belonging (to); unconnected, unrelated; inconsonant. ? Obs.
c 1380 Wyclif Serm. Sel. Wks. II. 31 Many men in þis world ben impertinent to erþeli lordis, for neiþer þei ben servantis to hem, ne þes lordis þeir worldly lordis. 1526 Pilgr. Perf. (W. de W. 1531) 166 Thynges that be eche to other impertynent & dyuerse. 1666 Ormonde MSS. in 10th Rep. Hist. MSS. Comm. App. v. 23 His private affayres and business (impertinent to anything relating to the said Lord Archbishop). 1809–10 Coleridge Friend (1837) III. 118 The more distant, disjointed and impertinent to each other and to any common purpose, will they appear.
2. Not pertaining to the subject or matter in hand; not pertinent; not to the point; irrelevant. Now rare exc. in Law.
c 1386 Chaucer Clerk's Prol. 54 Trewely as to my Iuggement Me thynketh it a thyng impertinent Saue that he wole conuoyen his mateere. 1530 Palsgr. 7 As for w is no letter used in the frenche tong..therfore as impertinent I passe it over. a 1571 Jewel Serm. bef. Queen (1583) A iij b, Let no man thinke these things are impertinent or from the purpose. 1610 Shaks. Temp. I. ii. 138 I'le bring thee to the present businesse Which now's vpon's: without the which, this Story Were most impertinent. 1642 Jer. Taylor Episc. (1647) 84 The allegation of S. Timothy's being an Evangelist, is absolutely impertinent, though it had been true. 1768 Blackstone Comm. III. xxvii. 443 The master is to examine the propriety of the bill: and, if he reports it scandalous or impertinent, such matter must be struck out. 1812 Mar. Edgeworth Vivian x. (1832) 196 He did not..digress to fifty impertinent episodes, before he came to the point. 1872 Wharton Law Lex. (ed. 5) 467/1 The Court may..direct the costs occasioned by any impertinent matter in any proceeding, to be paid by the party introducing it.
3. Not suitable to the circumstances; incongruous, inappropriate, out of place; not consonant with reason; absurd, idle, trivial, silly.
1590 Barrough Meth. Physick I. xxxiii. (1639) 53 Many ignorant practitioners..have endeavoured to cure this infirmity with many impertinent medicines. 1631 Weever Anc. Fun. Mon. 16 These superfluous and impertinent costs of funerall expenses. 1662 J. Davies tr. Olearius' Voy. Ambass. 80 The opinion the Muscovites have of themselves and their abilities, is sottish, gross, and impertinent. 1677 Hale Prim. Orig. Man. I. i. 13 In comparison of this, all other Knowledge is vain, light and impertinent. 1706 Phillips, Impertinent,..absurd, silly, idle. 1706 Estcourt Fair Examp. IV. i. 42 For my part, I think a Woman's Heart is the most impertinent part of the whole Body. 1849 Ruskin Sev. Lamps iv. §21. 111 There never was a more flagrant nor impertinent folly than the smallest portion of ornament in anything concerned with railroads.
†b. Unsuitable, unfitted for. Obs.
1594 Carew Huarte's Exam. Wits (1616) 177 A power impertinent for curing. Ibid. 183 To make clockes, pictures, poppets, and other ribaldries..impertinent for mans seruice.
†c. Of persons: Absurd, silly. Obs.
1639 T. Brugis tr. Camus' Mor. Relat. 205 As soone as a man brags, he is taken to be impertinent. 1681 Chetham Angler's Vade-m. xxii. §1 (1689) 143, I suspect myself to be Impertinent in saying thus much of the Conger, and Lampery. 1711 Steele Spect. No. 148 ¶7 The Ladies whom you visit, think a wise Man the most Impertinent Creature living.
4. Const. to (unto): in senses 2 and 3.
1532 More Confut. Barnes VIII. Wks. 740/1 Beyng as it is impertinent to the principall purpose. 1564 Brief Exam. C iij, I thynke it not impartinent vnto this matter. 1656 Hobbes Lib., Necess. & Chance (1841) 5 All the places of Scripture that he allegeth..are impertinent to the question. 1733 Neal Hist. Purit. II. 304 It is no impertinent story to our present purpose. 1849 W. Fitzgerald tr. Whitaker's Disput. 185 All the common disquisitions upon this place..however true in themselves, are foreign to the subject and impertinent to the matter in hand.
5. Of persons, their actions, etc.: Meddling with what is beyond one's province; intrusive, presumptuous; behaving without proper respect or deference to superiors or strangers; insolent or saucy in speech or behaviour. (The chief current sense in colloq. use.)
[1618 Sir D. Carleton Let. 4 Dec. in Crt. & Times Jas. I (1848) II. 111 They [the Armenians at the Synod of Dort] are decried from their impertinent boldness and impudence by all men.] 1681 Nevile Plato Rediv. 32, I have been impertinent in interrupting you. 1716 Lady M. W. Montagu Let. to Mrs. Thistlethwaite 30 Aug., It is publicly whispered, as a piece of impertinent pride in me, that I have hitherto been saucily civil to everybody. 1725 De Foe Voy. round World (1840) 91 A very useful, skilful fellow, but withal so impertinent and inquisitive that we knew not what to say to him. 1798 Nelson Let. to French Commander at Malta Oct., I feel confident that you will not attribute it either to insolence or impertinent curiosity. 1847 James Convict iii, He thought the stranger's tone rather impertinent. 1888 Miss Braddon Fatal Three I. iv, Fay has been most impertinent to me.
b. transf. of things.
1848 Dickens Dombey iv, Fenced up behind the most impertinent cushions. 1860 Sala Lady Chesterf. v. 83 The Lowther Arcade is vulgar and impertinent. 1861 Thackeray Four Georges iv. (1862) 221 Her fair hair, her blue eyes, and her impertinent shoulders.
B. sb. †1. An impertinent or irrelevant matter.
1628 Feltham Resolves I. Ep. Ded. A iij b, To apparell any more [of my thoughts] in these Paper vestments, I should multiply impertinents.
2. An impertinent person: see the adj.; now esp. a meddlesome, presumptuous, or insolent person; one who does or says that which he has no business to do or say, and which is considered a piece of presumption or insolence.
1635 A. Stafford Fem. Glory (1869) 5 This curious Impertinent. 1678 R. L'Estrange Seneca's Mor. (1702) 398 This Day I have had entire to my Self..For all the Impertinents were either at the Theatre..or at the Horse-match. 1682 Mrs. Behn City Heiress 39 Nay dear Impertinent, no more Complements, be gone! 1710 Palmer Proverbs 355 An inquisitive impertinent..medling where he has nothing to do. 1825 Lamb Elia Ser. II. Stage Illusion, When the pleasant impertinent of comedy..worries the studious man with taking up his leisure, or making his house his home. 1846 W. P. Scargill Purit. Grave 52 Henry St. John..rebuked the young impertinents.
Hence †**imˈpertinentness**, impertinency.
1670 Penn Truth Rescued fr. Impost. 66 The Frivolousness and Impertinentness of this Ribaldry to the Controversie in hand.

impertinently (ɪmˈpɜːtɪnəntlɪ), adv. [f. IMPERTINENT + -LY².] In an impertinent manner.
1. Without reference or relation to the subject in hand; not to the point; away from the matter or purpose; irrelevantly. Now rare.
c 1449 Pecock Repr. IV. iv. 442 Forto so inpertynentli speke. 1563 Homilies II. Cert. places Script. II. (1859) 380 Yet is there nothing so impertinently uttered in all the whole book of the Bible, but may serve to spiritual purpose. 1626 Jackson Creed VIII. iv. §7 A maxime..most impertinently applied to the point now in question. 1736 Chandler Hist. Persec. 452 How impertinently are both these instances alledged! 1838–9 Hallam Hist. Lit. II. III. i. §7. 374 A profusion of learning is scattered all around, but not pedantically or impertinently.
†2. Inappropriately, unseasonably, incongruously; in a way contrary to reason, good sense, or propriety; improperly, unbecomingly. Obs.
1640 Howell Dodona's Gr. 83 The blessedst of mortall Wights..began to be so impertinently importund, that a great part of Divine Liturgy was addressd solely to her. 1665 Boyle Occas. Refl. II. viii. (1848) 124 If..a Man speak either Unseasonably, erroneously, or Impertinently, he may, though he say little, talk too much. 1748 Smollett Rod. Rand. lxv. (1804) 475, I cannot help being impertinently circumstantial. a 1797 H. Walpole Mem. Geo. II (1847) I. i. 19 The brutum fulmen was applied to those who urged him with the orders of the House impertinently.
†b. To no purpose; with no effect. Obs.
1614 B. Jonson Barth. Fair IV. iv, I do thinke how impertinently I labour. 1665 Boyle Occas. Refl. (1848) 75 Half this precious time we impertinently trifle, or squander away. 1816 Coleridge Lay Serm. 335 To be impertinently busy, doing that which conduceth to no good purpose. 1823 Lamb Elia, Art. Com. Last C., Like Don Quixote, we take part against the puppets, and quite as impertinently.
3. Intrusively, presumptuously, saucily; in a manner contrary to what is due towards superiors or strangers (see IMPERTINENT 5).
1647 Clarendon Hist. Reb. I. §110 He was impertinently sollicitous to know what her Majesty said of him in private. 1711 Steele Spect. No. 79 ¶9 She is impertinently Blunt to all her Acquaintance. 1795 Phantoms of Cloister I. 170 He very impertinently walked up to her, and attempted to take her by the hand. 1802 Mar. Edgeworth Moral T. (1816) I. vii. 46, I would not interfere impertinently for the world. Mod. The maid answered her mistress most impertinently.

†**imperˈtransible**, a. Obs. [f. IM-² + med.L. pertransibilis, f. pertransīre, f. per through + transīre to cross, pass over or through.] That cannot be passed through or crossed. Hence †**impertransiˈbility**.
1677 Gale Crt. Gentiles IV. 227 What is infinite is incomprehensible and impertransible; as also adverse to al order, for in infinites there is no first or last. Ibid. 432 The distance between the power and act is, as to efficience, infinite and impertransible by any finite power. 1677 Hale Prim. Orig. Man. I. iv. 110 The Impertransibility of Eternity.

imperturbability (ɪmpətɜːbəˈbɪlɪtɪ). [f. next: see -ITY.] The quality or condition of being imperturbable or incapable of being agitated.
1831 Carlyle Sart. Res. II. vii, An imperturbability which passed, falsely enough, for courage. 1873 H. Rogers Orig. Bible vi. (1875) 231 This more than judicial imperturbability. 1888 Lowell in Daily News 26 July 6/3 This conduces certainly to peace of mind and imperturbability of judgment.

imperturbable (ɪmpəˈtɜːbəb(ə)l), a. [ad. late L. imperturbābil-is (Augustine, a 430), f. im- (IM-²) + *perturbābilis PERTURBABLE. Cf. F. imperturbable (1486 in Godef. Compl.).] Not capable of being or liable to be mentally perturbed, agitated, or excited; unexcitable; serene, calm.
c 1450 tr. De Imitatione III. liii. 126 Whan shal þere be sad pes, pes imperturbable and sure? 1775 Ash, Imperturbable, impossible to be disturbed, incapable of being disturbed. Dict. of Arts. 1797 W. Tooke Life Catherine 201 (Jod.) The Prince de Ligne had given the Empress Catherine the name of imperturbable, or immoveable. 1820 Scott Monast. xiv, Solemn and imperturbable gravity. 1860 Motley Netherl. (1868) I. viii. 524 Great was the embarrassment..even of the imperturbable Burleigh.
Hence **imperˈturbableness**, imperturbability.
1860 Pusey Min. Proph. 479 How great..was their constancy and imperturbableness. 1861 Holland Less. Life xiii. 182 A certain degree of mental repose—or what may be called imperturbableness—is necessary to influence.

imperturbably (ɪmpəˈtɜːbəblɪ), adv. [f. prec. + -LY².] In an imperturbable manner; without mental perturbation, agitation, or excitement; serenely, calmly.
1840 Carlyle Heroes i. (1858) 208 Trusting imperturbably in the appointment and choice of the upper Powers. 1866 Mrs. Whitney L. Goldthwaite v. (1873) 71 Her imperturbably goodnatured way. 1884 Seeley in Contemp. Rev. Oct. 492 The train of thought is imperturbably pursued.

imperturbation (ɪmpətɜːˈbeɪʃən). [ad. L. imperturbātiōn-em (Jerome, a 420), f. im- (IM-²) + perturbātio PERTURBATION.] Freedom from mental perturbation or agitation; calmness.
1648 W. Montague Devout Ess. I. xix. §2 In our copying of this equality and imperturbation, we must profess with the Apostle, We have not received the Spirit of the World, but the Spirit which is of God. 1871 M. Legrand Camb. Freshman (1878) 16 Collectedness of faculties, and imperturbation of feature.

imperturbed (ɪmpəˈtɜːbd), a. [f. IM-² + perturbed, pa. pple. of PERTURB v.: cf. L. imperturbātus, in same sense.] Not perturbed or agitated; undisturbed, unmoved, unexcited.
1721 Bailey, Imperturbed, undisturbed, serene, clear, calm. 1816 Scott Old Mort. xxxviii, The imperturbed Cuddie who was one of those persons who do not easily take alarm at any thing. 1835 Greswell Parables II. 420 Imperturbed rest.

impeˈrusably, adv. rare. [f. *imperusable adj. (f. IM-² + PERUSABLE) + -LY².] Unreadably.
1801 W. Taylor in Robberds Mem. I. 365 Proving, that very smoothly polished and laboriously wrought Antijacobin poetry may be imperusably dull.

†**imperˈverse**, v. Obs. rare. [f. IM-¹ + PERVERSE a.] trans. To render perverse.
1603 Florio Montaigne III. ix. (1632) 532 Favours relent me, feare imperverseth me [F. me roidit].

imperˈvertible, a. [f. IM-² + PERVERTIBLE.] Incapable of being perverted.
1850 Q. Rev. June 7 The far-seeing impervertible adroitness of the venerated chief.

†**imperˈvestigable**, a. Obs. rare. [f. IM-² + *pervestigable adj., f. L. pervestigāre to search out thoroughly: see -BLE.] That cannot be thoroughly investigated or traced out.
1656 Blount Glossogr., Impervestigable, that cannot be sought or found out. 1657–83 Evelyn Hist. Relig. (1850) I. 123 His being..is impervestigable and past finding out. 1699 Phil. Trans. XXI. 272 How impervestigable is the depth of Wisdom.

imperviable (ɪmˈpɜːvɪəb(ə)l), a. [f. L. impervi-us IMPERVIOUS: perh. by confusion with impermeable.] Incapable of being penetrated or passed through; impervious; impermeable.
1816 Scott Antiq. xv, Strong thick paper, imperviable by the curious eyes of the gossips. 1826 Chron. in Ann. Reg. 137/2 It renders [it] imperviable to water. 1867 H. Conybeare in Fortn. Rev. Nov. 505 An imperviable coating of gold which every shower would restore.
Hence **imperviaˈbility**, **imˈperviableness**, imperviousness.
1828 Edin. Rev. XLVII. 205 For imperviability and unhealthiness of climate, we may instance the vast forests..of Ceylon. 1847 Craig, Imperviableness, imperviousness.

†**imˈpervial**, a. Obs. rare. [f. L. impervi-us (see next) + -AL¹.] = next, 1.
1618 Chapman Hesiod II. 463 But then the gusts so fall, That oft the sea becomes impervial.

impervious (ɪmˈpɜːvɪəs), a. [f. L. impervi-us, f. im- (IM-²) + pervius PERVIOUS.]
1. Through which there is no way; not affording passage (to); not to be passed through or penetrated; impenetrable, impermeable, impassable.
1650 Bulwer Anthropomet. 226 Any skin..which should make the Neck [of the womb] impervious. 1663 Cowley Verses sev. Occas., Ode Harvey ii, A wall impervious between Divides the very Parts within. 1773–83 Hoole Orl. Fur. XLI. (R.), He wants no mail of proof whose skin was made Impervious to the javelin, dart, or blade. 1774 Pennant Tour Scotl. in 1772, 271 The western channel into it is impervious, by reason of rocks. 1807 T. Thomson Chem. (ed. 3) II. 490 Bricks and tiles should be impervious to water. 1813 W. Taylor Eng. Synonyms (1856) 282 The river is impervious that cannot be forded, and impassable

which cannot be crossed. **1858** Buckle *Civiliz.* (1869) II. viii. 562 An impervious desert.

2. *fig.* That one cannot get through or penetrate; in mod. use chiefly of a person or his mind, Not affording passage or entrance *to* (argument, feeling, etc.); 'impenetrable'.

1650 R. Stapylton *Strada's Low C. Warres* v. 137 What Councel-chamber can be impervious or inaccessible to royal bountie? **1794** Sullivan *View Nat.* I. 30 To render..that evident and clear, which would have otherwise been impervious. **1849** Macaulay *Hist. Eng.* v. I. 554 To reasons such as guide the conduct of statesmen and generals the minds of these zealots were absolutely impervious. **1857** Buckle *Civiliz.* I. xiii. 745 He had to deal with men impervious to argument.

im'perviously, *adv.* [f. prec. + -ly².] So as to be impervious; impenetrably.

1794 Sullivan *View Nat.* II. 293 Materials for an elucidation of a period almost imperviously involved in darkness. **1866** Howells *Venet. Life* (1883) I. vii. 111 The heavy wooden blinds [shut] imperviously.

imperviousness. [f. as prec. + -ness.] The quality of being impervious; impenetrability.

1727 in Bailey vol. II. (Hence in Johnson, etc.) **1869** Tyndall *Notes Lect. Light* §137 To a similar cause is due the whiteness and imperviousness of common salt, and of transparent bodies generally when crushed to powder. **1896** Dk. Argyll *Philos. Belief* 77 A modification of the same substance supplies imperviousness to the passage of air.

†**'impery.** *Obs.* Also 4 imperi, 6 -ye, 6–7 -ie. Cf. empery. [var. of empery, a. OF. *emperie* (11th c.), assimilated to the original L. *imperium*, supreme power, imperium, empire.]

1. Imperial or supreme rule or authority; command, dominion, sovereignty.

a **1300** *Cursor M.* 22269 Alsua of þe Imperi [*v. rr.* impire, empire] of rome. **1535** *Goodly Primer, Creed* in *Three Primers* (1848) 41 The Devil with all his impery, subtlety, and malice. *Ibid., Gen. Confession* 46 Honour, worship, impery, and rule be to thee, O Father. **1547** Hooper *Declar. Christ & Office* vi. Wks. (Parker Soc.) 48 Him that had the imperie and dominion of death, to say, the devil. **1604** Tooker *Fabrique of Ch.* 118 As for the Bishops..they have superiority but no Impery. **1657** Reeve *God's Plea* 36 Hath God this impery over us?

2. An empire.

1538 Leland *Itin.* I. p. xxii, So shaul yowr Majestie have this yowr Worlde and Impery of Englande. *c* **1552** Philpot *Exam. & Writ.* (Parker Soc.) 395 Ruled as these earthly kingdoms and imperies be.

3. A command, behest. *rare.*

1561 Jasper Heywood tr. *Seneca's Hercules* 1, At ease he doth myne imperie fulfyl.

impesh, -e, obs. forms of impeach.

impest, *v.* var. of empest *v.*

†**im'pester,** *v.* *Obs.* Also 7 em-. [a. OF. *empestrer* (now *empêtrer*) 'to pester, intricate, intangle' (Cotgr.), f. late L. **impastoriāre* (It. *impastojare*), f. *im-* (im-¹) + late L. *pastorium, -a*, It. *pastoia, pastora* a shackle or hopple for a horse.] *trans.* To hobble (a horse); to entangle, embarrass, encumber. Hence †**im'pesterment**, an entanglement, embarrassment, encumbrance.

1601 Bp. W. Barlow *Defence* 200 To extricate our inclosure within any maze of empestered errors. **1611** Cotgr., *Empestré*, impestered, intangled. **1646** Sir J. Temple *Irish Rebell.* ii. 3 Finding the City to grow daily more and more impestred with strangers. **1652** Urquhart *Jewel* Wks. (1834) 206 It would but intangle the minde with more impestrements. **1653** —— *Rabelais* ii. xxv, The two cables..intangled and impestered the legs of the horses. **1807** W. Irving *Salmag.* (1824) 321 Such..transposition of the foot, as might incontinently impester the legs of the Hoppingtots.

†**'impet.** *Obs. rare.* In 5 ympet. [ad. L. *impetus* violent impulse.] = impetus.

c **1440** *Gesta Rom.* lx. 247 (Harl. MS.) He sawe oon [ship] drivinge withe a grete ympet.

impeteous, obs. var. impetuous.

impeticos, *v.* A burlesque word put into the mouth of a fool: app. as a perversion of *impocket*, and perh. intended to suggest *petticoat*.

1601 Shaks. *Twel. N.* ii. iii. 27, I sent thee sixe pence for thy Lemon [*mod. edd.* leman], hadst it? *Clo.* I did impeticos thy gratillity.

impetiginous (ɪmpɪ'tɪdʒɪnəs), *a.* [ad. L. *impetīginōs-us*, f. *impetīgo*: cf. mod.F. *impétigineux* (Littré).] Pertaining to or of the nature of impetigo; 'scurfy; covered with small scabs' (J.).

1620 Venner *Via Recta* (1650) 282 Itch, tetters, and the like impetiginous affects in the flesh and skin. **1757** Brooke in *Phil. Trans.* LI. 80 Impetiginous disorders very common both in Maryland and Virginia. **1897** Allbutt *Syst. Med.* II. 158 All young children are to a considerable extent liable to impetiginous eczema.

‖**impetigo** (ɪmpɪ'taɪgəʊ). Pl. **impetigines** (-'ɪdʒɪniːz). [L. *impetīgo*, f. *impetĕre* to assail, attack: cf. *vertigo*.]

A name given to various pustular diseases of the skin, and in *pl.* to such diseases in general. Most of the diseases now so called are non-febrile and non-contagious; but ***impetigo contagiosa*** is an acute contagious disease with febrile symptoms.

1398 Trevisa *Barth. De P.R.* vii. lxiii. (1495) 278 Impetigo is a drye scabbe that comyth of more rysynge and fyry matere than Serpigo. **1527** Andrew *Brunswyke's Distyll. Waters* A ij, The same water withdryveth impetigines. **1669** *Addr. hopeful yng. Gentry Eng.* 20 The scrofulæ and luxuriant impetigos of fowl humors. **1803** *Med. Jrnl.* IX. 565 The leprosy of the Romans before the time of Cicero was the impetigo. **1876** Duhring *Dis. Skin* 78 Vesico-pustules are seen in..contagious impetigo.

impetious, obs. var. impetuous.

†**impe'tition.** *Obs.* [n. of action from L. *impetĕre* (ppl. stem *impetīt-*) to assail, attack, f. *im-* (im-¹) + *petĕre* to seek. (Used, app. from similarity of form, as noun of action to impeach.)] = impeachment 4.

1530–1 *Act 22 Hen. VIII*, c. 15 Al accomptes and al actions suites and impeticions for the same. **1605–6** *Act 3 Jas. I*, c. 27 §9 All manner of Deceites and Offences..all Impeticions and Punishmentes for the same. **1624** Gee *Foot out of Snare* App. 99 The most of their impetition..is a general railing against my discoueries. [**1721** Strype *Eccl. Mem.* II. xix. 402 (an. 1552) To have the premises..with impetition of waste during the life of the said Arch-bishop.]

impetous, obs. var. impetuous.

†**'impetrable,** *a.* *Obs.* [ad. L. *impetrābilis*, f. *impetrāre*: see impetrate *v.* and -ble. Cf. F. *impétrable* (1406 in Hatz.-Darm.).]

1. That may be impetrated or obtained.

1616 Bullokar, *Impetrable*, which may be obtained. **1628** Hobbes *Thucyd.* (1822) 149 Hope of pardon either impetrable by words, or purchasable by money.

2. Capable of obtaining or effecting something, successful.

1599 Nashe *Lenten Stuffe* 21 How impetrable hee was in mollyfying the adamantinest tiranny of mankinde.

†**'impetrant,** *a.* *Obs.* [ad. L. *impetrānt-em*, pres. pple. of *impetrāre*: see impetrate *v.* and -ant. Cf. F. *impétrant* (1468 in Godef. *Compl.*).] That impetrates or obtains.

1624 F. White *Repl. Fisher* 512 In the state and order of causes impetrant, or dispositiue conditions. *Ibid.* 517 They may be vsed..as dispositions and causes impetrant, and not as causes properly or condignely meritorious.

†**'impetrate,** *ppl. a.* *Obs.* Also *Sc.* -at. [ad. L. *impetrāt-us*, pa. pple. of *impetrāre*: see next.] Obtained by request, *esp.* by application to an authority; impetrated. (Const. chiefly as *pa. pple.*)

1528 Gardiner in Pocock *Rec. Ref.* I. l. 103 The said Commission might be, by an inhibition impetrate on like fashion, frustrate and letted. **1609** Skene *Reg. Maj.* 89 Gif the breive is impetrat, and raised..the assise sall proceid. *c* **1674** *Acc. Scotland's Grievances under Lauderdale* 24 Personal protections to debtors were most abusively impetrate. **1721–2** Wodrow *Hist. Suffer. Ch. Scot.* (1828) I. i. ii. 241 This was not the deed of Scotland but impetrate at London.

impetrate ('ɪmpɪtreɪt), *v.* [f. L. *impetrāt-*, ppl. stem of *impetrāre* to obtain by request or exertion, to procure, effect; f. *im-* (im-¹) + *patrāre* to bring to pass, accomplish, achieve.]

1. *trans.* To obtain by request or entreaty; to procure. Now chiefly *Theol.* (also in *Rom. Law*).

1533–4 *Act 25 Hen. VIII*, c. 14 The clergy..did impetrate and obteine by auctorite of parliament..that it shulde be lefull [etc.]. **1550** J. Coke *Eng. & Fr. Heralds* §61 (1877) 76 To impetrate a saulfconducte for hym. **1651** C. Cartwright *Cert. Relig.* i. 214 Good workes, which hee calles Merits, because they doe impetrate or obtaine a reward. **1692** *Covt. Grace Conditional* 5 That the Price paid by Christ..did fully impetrate, merit and purchase at the Fathers hands, the perfect and compleat Redemption of his Elect. **1862** Goulburn *Pers. Relig.* v. ii. (1873) 85 Powerful ..to impetrate from Him the highest blessings. **1880** Muirhead *Gaius* Digest 493 A conveyance he had impetrated by fraudulent representations.

absol. *a* **1643** J. Shute *Judgem. & Mercy* (1645) 192 Chrysostome sticks not to say that good works have the place of prayer with God, and impetrate.

†**b.** To bring to pass, procure, effect. *Obs.*

1647 Ward *Simp. Cobler* (1843) 71 Me thinks it should impetrate a Royall Redintegration.

2. To entreat, request, beseech, ask for. Now *rare.*

c **1565** Lindesay (Pitscottie) *Chron. Scot.* (1728) 46 To come straight to thy Clemency to impetrate Pardon for my Offence. **1651** Biggs *New Disp.* ¶ 80 It is to be impetrated of God alone, that he would vouchsafe [etc.]. **1681–6** J. Scott *Chr. Life* (1747) III. 5 To act on the Part of the Subject, in impetrating the Superior's Favour and Protection. **1818** Scott *Rob Roy* ix, A slight testimonial, sir, which I thought fit to impetrate from that worthy nobleman..MacCallum More. **1891** R. W. Dixon *Hist. Ch. Eng.* IV. 369 Application was made..for a prolongation of his life: which the Earl of Derby impetrated on his knees to the Queen.

b. To entreat or beseech (a person, etc.).

1881 F. G. Lee *R. Barentyne* viii. 103 Then we impetrate Fate, and abide our lot.

impetration (ɪmpɪ'treɪʃən). [ad. L. *impetrātiōn-em* obtaining by request, achievement, n. of action from *impetrāre*: see prec. Perh. in early instances a. AF. *impetraciour* (1292 in Britton).] The action of impetrating.

1. The action of obtaining or procuring by request or entreaty. (Chiefly *Theol.*)

1518 *Burgh Rec. Edinburgh* 10 Dec. (Jam. Suppl.), For the impetracioun of quhatsumeuir priuilege or fredomes thocht to thame profitable. **1526** *Pilgr. Perf.* (W. de W. 1531) 162 Impetracyon is yᵉ optaynynge of yᵉ peticyon. **1681** Flavel *Meth. Grace* To Rdr. 18 The former part contains the method of grace in the impetration thereof by Jesus Christ. **1854** Faber *Growth in Holiness* xv. (1872) 287 No prayer has such a power of impetration as that which comes from a will conformed to the will of God.

b. *Law.* The obtaining (of a writ).

a **1648** Ld. Herbert *Hen. VIII* (1683) 292 The said Cardinal did not know the impetration of the said Bulls to have been to the Contempt and Prejudice of the King. **1798** in Root *Amer. Law Rep.* I. 54 That more than three years had elapsed from rendering the judgment complained of, and the date and impetration of the plaintiff's writ.

c. 'The pre-obtaining of church benefices in England from the court of Rome, which belonged to the gift and disposition of the king, and other lay-patrons of this realm' (Tomlins *Law Dict.*).

[**1363** *Act 38 Edw. III*, Stat. 11, Aussi des impetracions & provisions, faites en meisme la Courte de Rome, des benefices & offices desglise appertenantz a la donacion.. notre dit sʳ. le Roi.] **1484** *Sc. Acts Jas. III* (1814) 166 (Jam.) Anent impetraciouns made in the Court of Rome in contrare our souuerane lordis priuilege. **1494** *Sc. Acts Jas. IV* (1597) §53 The impetration and purchasing at the court of Rome benefices electiue. **1856** Froude *Hist. Eng.* II. 7 That.. penalties..should be attached to all impetration of benefices from Rome by purchase or otherwise.

2. Petition, entreaty, supplication, request.

[**1292** Britton i. xxxii. §23 Par diligentes impetraciouns ad il esté..demaundé; *transl.* for that by continual claims he has been..demanded.] **1618** Gainsford *Perkin Warbeck* in *Select. Harl. Misc.* (1793) 64 The king went thither [to Our Lady of Walsingham] for the impetration of prosperity in his affairs, and overthrow and dissipation of his enemies. **1650** Elderfield *Tythes* 212 He should..reap some fruit of his own successful impetration. **1798** W. Wilberforce *Let. to Han. More* in *Life* (1838) II. 301, I have before expressed ..my earnest *impetration* that you would bear in mind [etc.]. **1873** B. Gregory *Holy Cath. Ch.* xvii. 196 Christ's own impetration..'That they all may be one'..must yet be answered. **1897** Maitland in *Eng. Hist. Rev.* Oct. 634 In the letter of 'impetration' that he [a litigant in the ecclesiastical courts] sent to Rome he named the persons whose appointment he desired.

impetrative ('ɪmpɛtreɪtɪv), *a.* *rare.* [ad. L. *impetrātīv-us*, f. ppl. stem of L. *impetrāre*: see impetrate *v.* and -ive.] = impetratory.

1612–15 Bp. Hall *Contempl., N.T.* iv. vi, O Saviour.. Thy prayers, which were most perfect and impetrative. **1656** Bramhall *Replic.* ix. 372 An impetrative Sacrifice, or an impetration of the fruit and benefit of his Passion by way of reall Prayer. **1884** R. S. Storrs *Divine Orig. Chr.* iv. 110 (Funk) [The mass] is to them a eucharistic and an impetrative sacrifice.

impetrator ('ɪmpɪtreɪtə(r)). [ad. L. *impetrātōr*, agent-n. f. *impetrāre* to impetrate.] One who impetrates or entreats.

1605 A. Willet *Hexapla in Genesin* 338 A blessing may be asked of them [angels] as the impetrators and intercessors for the same.

impetratory ('ɪmpɪtreɪtərɪ), *a.* [f. L. *impetrāt-*, ppl. stem of *impetrāre* + -ory. Cf. It. *impetratorio.*] Having the quality of obtaining by or as by request. (Chiefly *Theol.*)

1612–15 Bp. Hall *Contempl., N.T.* iv. ii, The least motion of a thought was in him impetratory. **1651** Jer. Taylor *Holy Dying* ii. §3 Alms..are preparatory to, and impetratory of the Grace of Repentance. *a* **1659** Bp. Brownrig *Serm.* (1674) I. iii. 38 Not a meritorious..but an impetratory Motive. **1881** T. E. Bridgett *Hist. Holy Eucharist* II. 139 Both as an impetratory or supplicatory, and as a propitiatory or satisfactory sacrifice.

†**impetre,** *v.* *Obs.* Also 5 empetre, empeter. [ME., a. OF. *empetre-r* (13th c.), *impetre-r* (14th c.), ad. L. *impetrāre*: see impetrate *v.*]

1. *trans.* = impetrate *v.* 2.

c **1374** Chaucer *Boeth* v. pr. iii. 123 (Camb. MS.) þat nis nat aproched no rather or þat men be-sekyn it and impetrent [*ed.* 1532 impetren] it. *a* **1450** *Knt. de la Tour* (1868) 51 Thei impetrithe [**1483** Caxton D ij, empetre] grace for them that be alyue. **1483** Caxton *Gold. Leg.* 94/2 Seynt Nychass.. impetred..of our lorde that thys tribulacion..sholde be to the helthe of the soules of them. **1494** Fabyan *Chron.* vii. (1533) II. 15/2 [They] rode to the kynge..to empeter grace for the sayde bayllyues.

2. = impetrate *v.* 1, 1 b.

a **1450** *Knt. de la Tour* (1868) 14 Fastinge..humblithe the herte, and impetret[h] pardon and grace of God. **1483** Caxton *Cato* B ij, To haue and impetre of them somme good after theyr deth. *c* **1500** *Melusine* 14 As lytel myrthe.. that he hath Impetred to oure moder by hys falshed.

impetulant (ɪm'pɛtjʊlənt), *a.* *rare*⁻⁰. [f. im-² + petulant.] Not petulant or peevishly impatient; free from petulance.

Hence **im'petulantly** *adv.*, without petulance.

1821 in *T. G. Wainewright's Ess. & Crit.* (1880) 197 To receive patiently and impetulantly.

impetuosity (ɪmˌpɛtjuːˈɒsɪtɪ). [a. F. *impétuosité* (13th c. in Godefroy *Compl.*), ad. L. *impetuōsitās*, f. *impetuōs-us*: see next and -ITY.] The quality or character of being impetuous; sudden or violent energy of movement, action, etc.; vehemence: **a.** of physical things or actions.

1585 T. WASHINGTON tr. *Nicholay's Voy.* II. xi. 46 The wynde and the rayne tooke us agayne wyth suche a furour and impetuosite. **1660** F. BROOKE tr. *Le Blanc's Trav.* 106 The tide runs.. with such fury and impetuosity, as it were mountains rolled up in water. **1687** A. LOVELL tr. *Thevenot's Trav.* I. 289 We entred the Town with so great Fury and Impetuosity, that the besieged begged Quarter. **1790** BEATSON *Nav. & Mil. Mem.* I. 244 They came down from the heights with the greatest impetuosity, and began their attack on the royal artillery. **1811** PINKERTON *Petral.* II. 536 Flames.. issued forth with great impetuosity. **1839** THIRLWALL *Greece* xlix. VI. 183 Their left wing was almost immediately broken by the impetuosity of his charge.

b. of feelings, temper, disposition, etc.

1639 DU VERGER tr. *Camus' Admir. Events* 12 Being not able any longer to beare the impetuosity of his appetites. **1749** FIELDING *Tom Jones* VI. v, You know the impetuosity of my brother's temper. **1872** BLACK *Adv. Phaeton* viii, This amiable self-discipline struggling with her ordinary frank impetuosity.

c. with *pl.* An instance of this quality; an impetuous movement, action, or feeling.

1632 LITHGOW *Trav.* V. 178 Indangered by violent and extreame impetuosities of raine. **1744** HARRIS *Three Treat.* III. I. (1765) 171 The Impulses of Appetite, the Impetuosities of Resentment may tempt us. **1815** *Hist. Mr. J. Decastro* IV. 253 Genevieve, with all her impetuosities, has, we confess, always been a favourite with us.

impetuous (ɪmˈpɛtjuːəs), *a.* Forms: α. 4 **impetuious, 5 impetuouse, ympetuous, inpytuous, 6 impytuous, (-petous), 6- -petuous.** β. 5 **inpeteous, (6 impeteous, -piteous, -pyteous, (-pytous, -pietouse), 6-7 impetious, 7 -pittious.** [a. F. *impétueux, -euse* (13th c. in Littré), ad. L. *impetuōs-us*, f. *impetu-s* (see below and -OUS).

The β forms suggest association with *piteous*.]

1. Of physical things or actions: Having much impetus; moving with great force or violence, or charaterized by violent motion; very rapid, forcibly rushing, violent.

c **1489** CAXTON *Blanchardyn* xxvi. 100 A right grete & Impetuouse tempeste rose. **1541** R. COPLAND *Galyen's Terapeut.* 2 G ij b, Yf the fluxyon be impetuous. **1600** F. WALKER *Sp. Mandeville* 64 a, A whirl-wind so strangely impetuous, that it amazed those that beheld it. **1692** RAY *Dissol. World* XI. v. (1732) 218 That great and impetuous River. **1794** S. WILLIAMS *Vermont* 98 Strength to resist the most impetuous winds. **1832** LANDER *Adv. Niger* II. x. 92 The river.. is much swollen.. its current more impetuous.

β. *a* **1533** LD. BERNERS *Gold. Bk. M. Aurel.* (1546) U v b, Roring and impiteous sees. **1542** BOORDE *Dyetary* ix. (1870) 250 Great and impyteous [*v.r.* impytous] wyndes. **1547** —— *Introd. Knowl.* xxi. 176 Great impietouse wyndes. **1602** SHAKS. *Ham.* IV. v. 100 The Ocean.. Eates not the Flats with more impittious haste. **1615** CROOKE *Body of Man* 175 A kinde of nimble violence and impetious motion.

2. Of feelings, etc., or of personal action or disposition, and hence of persons: Acting with or marked by great, sudden, or rash energy; vehement, violent, passionate, ardent.

1398 TREVISA *Barth. De P.R.* IV. x. (Tollem. MS.), Colerike men beþ generally wraþful, hardy,.. unstable, impetuious [**1495** inpeteous, **1535** impeteous; Lat. *instabiles, impetuosi*]. *c* **1425** *Found. St. Bartholomew's* (E.E.T.S.) 17 Wardid and defendyd, aȝenst ympetuous hostylyte. *a* **1628** PRESTON *Breastpl. Love* (1631) 207 A man that hath a more impetuous spirit than another. **1660** F. BROOKE tr. *Le Blanc's Trav.* 207 This Lords daughter had so impetuous a Love-passion for him. **1751** JOHNSON *Rambler* No. 167 ¶ 11 The impetuous vivacity of youth. **1849** MACAULAY *Hist. Eng.* vii. II. 170 His affection was as impetuous as his wrath. **1875** JOWETT *Plato* (ed. 2) I. 165, I mean the impetuous, ready to go at that which others are afraid to approach.

imˈpetuously, *adv.* [f. prec. + -LY².] In an impetuous manner; with great impetus or force; violently, vehemently; with sudden or rash energy.

1485 CAXTON *Chas. Gt.* 104 The ryver.. renneth so Inpytuously as a quarel out of an arbalastre. **1490** —— *Eneydos* x. 39 A clowde.. decended impetuously vpon the flote. **1590** SPENSER *F.Q.* II. xi. 18 [They] round about him flocke impetuously. **1664** POWER *Exp. Philos.* I. 70 For Motion the Spirits move impetuously down the nervous filaments. **1834** J. H. NEWMAN *Par. Serm.* (1837) I ix. 141 They are impetuously led on to wrong acts. **1871** H. AINSWORTH *Tower Hill* I. i, Henry rushed impetuously into the room.

imˈpetuousness. [f. as prec. + -NESS.] The quality of being impetuous; impetuosity.

c **1425** *Found. St. Bartholomew's* (E.E.T.S.) 46 Hastyly he went whedyr the ympetuousnes of the malicious woodenes ympellid hym. *c* **1530** L. COX *Rhet.* (1899) 83 Helpyng the shyp agaynst the impetuousnes of the storme. **1636** SANDERSON *Serm.* (1681) II. 56 We shall soon run into all extremities of evil with the greatest impetuousness that can be. **1675** *Art Contentm.* IV. xv. 199 The impetuousness of our desires. **1711** W. KING tr. *Naude's Ref. Politics* iv. 130 Those great rivers which flow with such impetuousness. **1875** JOWETT *Plato* (ed. 2) III. 7 Polemarchus has the frankness and impetuousness of youth.

impetus (ˈɪmpɪtəs). [a. L. *impetus* assault, onset, violent impulse, violence, force, vehemence, f. *impet-ĕre* to rush upon, attack, assail, f. *im-* (IM-¹) + *petĕre* to seek.]

1. The force with which a body moves or maintains its velocity and overcomes resistance; energy of motion; impulse, impulsion.

1656 HOBBES *Six Less.* Wks. 1845 VII. 285 The quantity of the impetus may be equal to the quantity of a time. **1667** *Phil. Trans.* II. 440 The Ball, being by the *Impetus* it acquired in descending, carried downwards. **1717** J. KEILL *Anim. Œcon.* (1738) 62 The Blood.. successively receives new *impetus's* from the Ventricles contracting themselves. **1794** SULLIVAN *View Nat.* II. 389 What is impetus, or force in a moving body? **1878** HUXLEY *Physiogr.* 174 Whether the stream.. retains sufficient impetus to carry it to our shores.

b. *Gunnery.* The altitude due to the initial velocity of a projectile, i.e. the space through which it must fall to attain an equal velocity; the force of projection as measured by this.

1807 HUTTON *Course Math.* II. 154 Having given the Direction, and the Impetus, or Altitude due to the First Velocity of a Projectile; to determine the Greatest Height to which it will rise. **1828** J. M. SPEARMAN *Brit. Gunner* (ed. 2) 249 The space due to the initial velocity is called the impetus.

2. In reference to immaterial things, as feelings, actions, etc.: Moving force, impulse, stimulus.

1641 *Compl. conc. Corrupt. & Grievances* 2 After that first heate and *impetus* of reformation.. the businesse went on no further. **1649** J. H. *Motion to Parl. Adv. Learn.* 29 To prosecute the hints and *impetus* of their owne inclinations. **1699** N. MARSH in *Lett. Lit. Men* (Camden) 296 Such juvenile *impetuses* ought to be repress'd. *a* **1714** M. HENRY *Wks.* (1835) I. 120 Struggling with the violent impetus of a particular lust. *a* **1830** HAZLITT in *Half Hours with Best Authors* II. 273 What also gave an unusual impetus to the mind of men at this period was the discovery of the New World. **1872** YEATS *Growth Comm.* 238 Fugitive Huguenots gave a fresh impetus to weaving.

Impeyan (ˈɪmpɪən), *a.* (*sb.*) Also **Impeian.** [Named by Latham, 1787, after Sir Elijah and Lady Impey, who tried to bring living specimens of the bird to England.]

Impeyan pheasant: a kind of East Indian pheasant (*Lophophorus impeyanus*), with crested head; the male has plumage of brilliant metallic hues. The name is sometimes extended to other species of *Lophophorus*. **b.** Of or pertaining to this pheasant. **c.** as *sb.* = Impeyan pheasant.

1870 BLAINE *Encycl. Rur. Sports* (ed. 3) §77 The Impeyan pheasant.. called by the Indians the 'bird of gold'. **1889** *Pall Mall G.* 8 Jan. 3/2 A store of Impeian, Argus, and Japanese pheasants. **1896** *Westm. Gaz.* 16 Jan. 1/2 The large hat.. was trimmed with shimmering impeyan feathers.

‖**imphee** (ˈɪmfiː). Also **imfe, imphie.** [*imfe*, native name in Natal.] A species of sugar-cane, *Andropogon saccharatus* Roxb. (*Holcus* Linn., *Sorghum* Pers.), also called African or Chinese Sugar-cane, Broom Corn, Sorgho, and Planter's Friend.

1857 *Country Gentleman* 11 June 379/2 A plant bearing the name of *Imphee*, or *Imphey*, or *Imphye*.. which it is alleged is identical with the Chinese Sugar Cane, has been introduced by Mr. Leonard Wray, from Southern Africa. **1862** T. BAINES *Jrnl.* 5 Apr. in *Explor. S.-W. Afr.* (1864) xiv. 438, I.. spent the intervening time with a circle of old fellows, who gave me imphi (holcus saccharatus) stalks to chew. **1880** *Silver's Handbk. Australia* 273 The imphee, or Planter's Friend, is well adapted to the Queensland climate. **1893** WATT *Dict. Econ. Prod. Ind.* VI. III. 277 This.. is said to be extensively grown in Africa and America, the plant of the former country being the Imphee, and of the latter the Sorgho, which is mainly cultivated on account of sugar.

†**imˈphrygiate**, *v. Obs. rare.* [f. IM-¹ + med.L. *phrygiāre* to embroider, 'acu pingere, opere Phrygio ornare' (Du Cange), f. *Phrygi-us* Phrygian.] *trans.* To embroider, work in embroidery.

1592 R. D. *Hypnerotomachia* 49 b, Little flying Byrdes, excellently imphrygiated of Museacall paynting.

‖**ˈimpi.** [Zulu, = body or company of people, esp. of armed men.] A body of Bantu warriors; a force, detachment, army.

1862 G. H. MASON *Zululand* xv. 200 There is always an 'Impi', (or army,) preparing for an attack on some neighbouring district. **1879** *Daily Tel.* 16 May, A Zulu impi.. managed to cut off the chief's cattle and to kill some of his followers. **1885** *Harper's Mag.* Mar. 652/1 His sabre.. clove a way through the Undi Impi at Isandhlwana. **1888** RIDER HAGGARD *Maiwa's Revenge* v. 123 The men looking round caught sight of the spears of Wambe's impi coming rapidly along. **1970** *Cape Times* 28 Oct. 2/9 Lands rich in grass and game and savage impis. **1971** *Rand Daily Mail* 4 Dec. 3/4 Dressed in full tribal regalia of leopard skin and feathers he led the dancing and singing impis who paid homage to their king.

†**ˈimpiate**, *v. Obs. rare*⁻⁰. [f. L. *impiāt-*, ppl. stem of *impiāre* to render impious, defile with sin, f. *impius* IMPIOUS.] *trans.* To pollute, defile. Hence †**impiˈation**, defilement.

1623 COCKERAM, *Impiate*, to defile with dishonestie. **1658** PHILLIPS, *Impiation*, a defiling.

†**ˈimpicate**, *v. Obs. rare*⁻⁰. [f. L. *impicāt-*, ppl. stem of *impicāre*, f. *im-* (IM-¹) + *pix, pic-em* PITCH.] *trans.* 'To cover with pitch' (Cockeram 1623).

impicture (ɪmˈpɪktjʊə(r)), *v.* Also 6 **en-**, 9 **em-**. [f. IM-¹ + PICTURE.]

1. *trans.* To represent as in a picture; to portray.

1520-30 SKELTON *Garl. Laurel* 892 Zeuxes, that enpictured fare Elene. **1787** *Generous Attachment* IV. 73 She tears the roses from the cheek of beauty, and impictures horror and despair. **1796-7** COLERIDGE *Lines to a beautiful Spring* 28 Like passing clouds impictured on thy breast. **1850** BLACKIE *Æschylus* I. 123 Behold.. The wild beasts of the woods by thine own hand Empictured. **1892** *Chamb. Jrnl.* 16 July 456/2 The lake, on the smooth steely surface of which the church and church-tower were impictured as in a mirror.

†**2.** To impress as with a picture. *Obs.*

1596 SPENSER *Astroph.* 163 His pallid face, impictured with death.

Hence **imˈpictured** *ppl. a.*, portrayed, depicted.

1814 CARY *Dante, Paradise* III. 12 The shape returns.. of our impictured lineaments.

impier, obs. form of EMPIRE, UMPIRE.

imˈpierce, var. of EMPIERCE *v.*

†**imˈpierceable**, *a. Obs.* Also 4-6 **-perciable**, 6 **-per-**, 7 **-pear-**, **-peirceable.** [f. IM-² + PIERCEABLE. Perh. representing an OF. **imperceable*.] Not pierceable; that cannot be pierced.

1387-8 T. USK *Test. Love* I. iv. (Skeat) I. 45 Ye armen your seruauntes ayenst al debates, with imperciable harneis. **1590** SPENSER *F.Q.* I. xi. 17 Never felt his imperceable brest So wondrous force from hand of living wight. **1647** WARD *Simp. Cobler* 73 Your weapons and armour are.. impierceable. **1691** E. TAYLOR *Behmen's Theos. Philos.* 189 So impierceable are their Rocky Hearts.

impiety (ɪmˈpaɪɪtɪ). Also 4 **impite.** [a. F. *impieté* (12th c.) or ad. L. *impietāt-em*, n. of quality f. *impius*: see IMPIOUS and -ITY.] Want of piety; that which is the opposite of piety.

1. Want of reverence for God or religion; irreligion; ungodliness; unrighteousness, wickedness.

a **1340** HAMPOLE *Psalter* lxxii. 6 Hilde þai er in wickidnes, & in þaire impite.. All bewrapped in wickedness against ther neightbour, & in impietie against god. **1548** HALL *Chron., Edw. IV* 200 The mother of this pernicious commocion was uncharitie, or very impietie. **1600** J. PORY tr. *Leo's Africa* II. 389 The impietie of Arrius and other heretikes. **1776** GIBBON *Decl. & F.* xiii. I. 387 The titles of the Divinity were usurped by Diocletian and Maximian.. Such extravagant compliments, however, soon lose their impiety by losing their meaning. **1875** JOWETT *Plato* (ed. 2) V. 155 The impiety of those who deny the existence of the Gods.

b. With *an* and *pl.* An instance of this; an impious, irreligious, or ungodly action, practice, etc.

1529 S. FISH *Supplic. Beggers* (1871) 11 So long shall it seme to euery man to be a greate ympiete not to gyue theim. **1611** BIBLE *2 Esdras* iii. 29 When I came thither, and had seene impieties without number. **1743** J. MORRIS *Serm.* vii. 197 He.. did not immediately chastise for their impieties. **1897** P. WARUNG *Tales Old Regime* 240 Each swore by the most impious of impieties that.. he would be its enemy.

2. Absence of natural piety, as of child to parent; want of dutifulness; hence, want of reverence or respect in general.

1588 SHAKS. *Tit. A.* I. i. 355 *Tit.* Bury him where you can, he comes not heere. *Mar.* My Lord this is impiety in you, My Nephew Mutius deeds do plead for him. **1674** tr. *Scheffer's Lapland* 34 It were impiety to believe this of all, since experience shews us the contrary. **1732** LAW *Serious C.* xxi. (ed. 2) 432 Can you think it a less impiety to contemn and vilify a brother? **1895** *Daily News* 2 Nov. 6/1 All this trivial chatter about the mere externals of De Quincey's life.. leaves upon our mind a disagreeable impression. It is impiety.. in its antique meaning. *Mod.* A gross instance of filial impiety.

†**imˈpight**, *pa. pple. Obs.* Also **in-**: see also EMPIGHT. [pa. pple. of *impitch*, f. IM-¹ + PITCH *v.*] Pitched or planted in; implanted, inserted.

1398 TREVISA *Barth. De P.R.* v. lii. (1495) 169 The knees ben holowe and rounde, for the legges and whyrlbones sholde be the easelyar inpyghte therin. **1633** P. FLETCHER *Purple Isl.* XI. xxix, Yet in her side deep was the wound impight.

†**imˈpignorate**, *pa. pple. Obs.* [ad. med.L. *impignorāt-us*, pa. pple. of *impignorāre*, f. *im-* (IM-¹) + *pignus, pigner-, pignor-* pledge, pawn, mortgage: cf. L. *pignerāre* to pledge.] Pledged, pawned, mortgaged.

1548 HALL *Chron., Hen. VII* 27 b, [They] borowed.. money, and for the repayment of the same, had morgaged and impignorate their landes. **1683-4** H. ROSE *Family of Rose of Kilravock* (Spalding Cl.) 58 For payment.. he gave the lands of Kinstearie, impignorat to him for 300 merks.

impignorate (ɪmˈpɪgnəreɪt), *v.* Chiefly *Sc.* Also **-pigner-.** [f. med.L. ppl. stem *impignorāt-* (see prec.).] *trans.* To place in pawn; to pledge, pawn, mortgage.

a **1639** SPOTTISWOOD *Hist. Ch. Scot.* VII. (1677) 519 The Earl had impignorated his estate. **1656** BLOUNT *Glossogr.*, *Impignerate.* **1732** E. ERSKINE *Serm.* Wks. 1871 II. 10 In his

oath he impignorates his holiness. **1754** ERSKINE *Princ. Sc. Law* (1809) 417 A wadset..is a right, by which lands, or other heritable subjects, are impignorated by the proprietor to his creditor in security of his debt. **1880** *Literary World* 17 Sept. 177/2 When Orkney and Shetland were impignorated to the Crown of Scotland.

impignoration (ɪm,pɪgnə'reɪʃən). [ad. med.L. *impignorātiōn-em*, n. of action f. *impignorāre*: see prec.] The action or fact of impignorating; pledging, pawning, mortgage.

1598 HAKLUYT *Voy.* I. 151 All arrestments, reprisals, and impignorations of whatsoeuer goods and marchandises in England and Prussia..are from henceforth quiet, free, and released. **1626** *Charges agst. Dk. Buckhm.* in Rushw. *Hist. Coll.* (1659) I. 347 A legal Impignoration, whereby the Estates personal and real of the Accomptants are made liable to be sold for the discharge of their debts. **1826** SCOTT *Mal. Malagr.* ii, The impignoration of moveables.

†**im'pigrity.** *Obs. rare*⁻⁰. [ad. L. *impigritāt-em*, n. of quality f. *impiger*, *impigr-*, f. *im-* (IM-²) + *piger* slow, sluggish.]

1623 COCKERAM, *Impigritie*, quicknesse, diligence. **1656** in BLOUNT *Glossogr.* **1658** in PHILLIPS. **1721** in BAILEY.

†**'impigrous,** *a. Obs. rare*⁻⁰. [f. L. *impigr-* (see prec.) + -OUS.]

1656 BLOUNT *Glossogr.*, *Impigrous*, diligent, quick, ready, not slow.

†**im'pile,** *v. Obs. rare.* [f. IM-¹ + PILE *sb.*] *trans.* To surround or enclose with piles or stakes.

1633 P. FLETCHER *Purple Isl.* II. xx, These three [common fences] round impile This regiment, and all the other Isle.

†**im'pillor,** *v. Obs. rare.* [f. IM-¹ + PILLOR *v.* to pillory.] *trans.* To put in the pillory; to pillory.

1645 W. HOOKE *New-Englands Sence* 5 But these have been..Imprisoned, Impillored, Fined. **1685** LUTTRELL *Brief Rel.* (1857) I. 360, 3 to be transported and one to be impillored.

imping ('ɪmpɪŋ), *vbl. sb.* [f. IMP *v.* + -ING¹.] The action of the verb IMP; grafting, engrafting; the repairing of a hawk's wing with adscititious feathers. In quot. 1340 *concr.* a shoot, scion, 'imp'.

a **1340** HAMPOLE *Psalter* cxliii. 13 Whas sunnys as new ympyngis in þaire ȝouthede. *c* **1440** *Promp. Parv.* 260/1 Impynge (*Pynson* or graffinge), *insertura.* **1575** TURBERV. *Faulconrie* 277 The laste maner of ymping is, when a feather is not quyte broken off but broosed. **1616** SURFL. & MARKH. *Country Farme* 352 To the end that you may not faile of this worke of imping. **1852** R. R. BURTON *Falconry in Valley of Indus* vii. 75 When the tail or the pinions are accidentally broken, the falconer..performs the process of 'imping' by neatly sewing and binding to the shaft a substitute which exactly matches the lost part.

b. *attrib.*, as ***imping needle.***

1575 TURBERV. *Faulconrie* 277 With an ymping needle layde in Vyneger and Salte, so close them togither as they may be thought to be one feather. **1674** N. COX *Gentl. Recreat.* II. (1677) 230 If a Feather be broken or bruised, he ..must have his Imping-needles.

impinge (ɪm'pɪndʒ), *v.* [ad. L. *imping-ĕre* (only trans.) to push, strike, drive (at or into), thrust, strike, or dash (against), f. *im-* (IM-¹) + *pangĕre* to fix, drive in.]

1. *trans.* To force or thrust (a thing) *upon* any one; to fasten or fix on forcibly. *rare.*

1535 JOYE *Apol. Tindale* 1 This with other haynous crymes whiche he impingeth vnto me in his pistle. **1825** SYD. SMITH *Sp.* Wks. 1859 II. 198/1 If this method of appealing to the absurdities of a past age, and impinging them upon the present age is fair and just.

2. To strike, dash, hurl a thing *upon* something else; *refl.* = 4.

1660 G. FLEMING *Stemma sacrum* 5 Before they did impinge themselves, and the Vessel, upon some new and worse dangers. **1829** T. L. PEACOCK *Misfort. Elphin* xi, He impinged his foot with a force that overbalanced himself.

3. To strike; to come into forcible contact with, collide with. Now *rare.*

1777 *Gamblers* 17 On being impinged by another ball, it will spin for some little time on its own center. **1794** G. ADAMS *Nat. & Exp. Philos.* II. xv. 139 Myriads [particles of light] can move all manner of ways without impinging one another. **1816** T. L. PEACOCK *Headlong Hall* iv, The degree of force with which I have impinged the surface. **1910** *Practitioner* July 109 The striker's thumb..impinges the skull of his opponent.

4. a. *intr.* To strike or dash; to come into (violent or energetic) contact; to collide. Const. *on*, *upon*, also *against*, †*at*.

1605 G. POWEL *Refut. Ep. by Puritan Papist* 38 The rockes of offence, whereat some of the ancient Emperours impinged. **1621** BURTON *Anat. Mel.* I. iv. I. 1676 134/2 A ship that is void of a Pilot, must needs impinge upon the next rock or sands, and suffer shipwrack. **1717** J. KEILL *Anim. Œcon.* (1738) 61 The Ventricles, when they contract, impinge upon the Blood, and..expel it. *a* **1774** GOLDSM. *Surv. Exp. Philos.* (1776) I. 176 Provided we know the weights of the two bodies, and their swiftness before they impinged. **1796** ATWOOD in *Phil. Trans.* LXXXVI. 130 The inclination of the masts and sails..and the direction in which the wind impinges on them. **1881** YOUNG *Every Man his own Mechanic* §1510 A flame which by means of the blowpipe is caused to impinge upon the charcoal.

b. Said of waves of light, sound, and the like.

1672 NEWTON in *Phil. Trans.* VII. 5087 Those, when they impinge on any Refracting or Reflecting superficies, must.. excite Vibrations in the aether. **1872** HUXLEY *Phys.* viii. 209 The aërial waves which enter the meatus all impinge upon the membrane of the drum. **1878** FOSTER *Phys.* III. ii. 397 The laws according to which rays of light impinging on the retina give rise to sensory impulses.

c. *fig.*

1614 P. FORBES *Def. Lawfull Ministers* §19. 35 They still reason, *ab authoritate negative*, and so, doe impinge foully, in all the sortes above specified. **1852** GLADSTONE *Glean.* IV. xxiii. 158 Here we impinge upon a dilemma hard as adamant.

5. To encroach or infringe *on* or *upon*.

1758 WARBURTON *Div. Legat.* Pref, Wks. 1811 IV. 59 Nor did the heat of reformation carry him to impinge upon any other of the nocturnal Rites, then celebrated in Rome. *c* **1800** LD. ELDIN in Ramsay *Remin.* v. (1870) 127 Had..my clients been caught..impingin on the patent richts. **1814** SCOTT *Wav.* xiv, Heaven forbid that I should do aught that might..impinge upon the right of my kinsman. **1884** *Illustr. Lond. News* 6 Sept. 219/1 In doing so, I should be impinging on the province of the reviewers.

Hence **impinging** (ɪm'pɪndʒɪŋ) *vbl. sb.* and *ppl. a.*

1704 NEWTON *Opticks* (J.), The cause of reflexion is not the impinging of light on the solid or impervious parts of bodies. **1794** SULLIVAN *View Nat.* II. 390 There must be as many impinging particles in the one, as there are gravitating particles in the other. **1844** RUSKIN *Arrows of Chace* (1880) I. 289 The power of reflection in water varies with the angle of the impinging ray. **1955** *Sci. News Let.* 14 May 308/1 Mercury vapor inside the vacuum tube gives the glow as its atoms are excited by impinging electrons.

impingement (ɪm'pɪndʒmənt). [f. IMPINGE + -MENT.] The action of impinging: **a.** Impact, collision. *lit.* and *fig.* **b.** Encroachment.

1671 *True Nonconf.* Contents, Prelatick exactions high impingements upon Christian Liberty. **1837** *Fraser's Mag.* XV. 732 The powers of reason have no similar incentives or impingement, but are a more direct emanation from the Deity. **1859** TENNENT *Ceylon* II. VII. i. 118 This tide-wave itself is..modified in its turn by impingement against the African continent. **1879** H. GEORGE *Progr. & Pov.* x. ii. (1881) 450 The effect of the impingement of civilization upon barbarism.

impingent (ɪm'pɪndʒənt). *a. rare.* [ad. L. *impingent-em*, pres. pple. of *impingĕre* to IMPINGE.] Impinging.

1759 PRINGLE in *Phil. Trans.* LI. 262 The immense velocity of the impingent body. *a* **1846** *Sat. Mag.* cited in Worcester.

impinger (ɪm'pɪndʒə(r)). [f. IMPING(E *v.* + -ER¹.] Any of various instruments for collecting samples of the particles suspended in air (or another gas), this being either drawn into a liquid or directed in a jet against a flat surface so that some particles are deposited.

1922 *Rep. Investigations U.S. Bureau of Mines* No. 2392. 3 The analytical procedure necessary when using this new impinger-bubbler apparatus is almost identical with that employed with the Palmer apparatus. **1932** *Jrnl. Industr. Hygiene & Toxicol.* XIV. 301/1 The Greenburg-Smith impinger was introduced in 1922. **1936** DRINKER & HATCH *Industr. Dust* vii. 116 The impinger flasks, stoppers, etc., should be washed..in..the sampling fluid. **1945** [see IMPACTOR 2]. **1972** BLAKESLEE & RECKNER in R. D. ROSS *Air Pollution & Industry* v. 270 Dry impingers are capable of depositing particles in distinct size ranges on surfaces such as microscope slides. Several units are connected in series, each containing an orifice which is aimed at the surface.

†**im'pinguate,** *v. Obs.* [f. ppl. stem of late L. *impinguāre*, f. *im-* (IM-¹) + *pingu-is* fat.] *trans.* To make fat; to fatten.

1620 VENNER *Via Recta* v. 85 It impinguateth and causeth the body to waxe grosse. **1666** G. HARVEY *Morb. Angl.* xviii. 214 Rhenish Wines..do accidentally impinguate. **1693** EVELYN *De la Quint. Orange Trees* 10 That the Mare of Wine did Impinguate, and Inrich the Ground.

Hence **im'pinguating** *ppl. a.*; also †**impin'guation**, fattening.

1620 VENNER *Via Recta* vii. 117 They yeeld a grosse, clammy, and an impinguating nourishment. **1640** G. WATTS tr. *Bacon's Adv. Learn.* IV. ii. (R. Suppl.), We receive into the body of medicine, the knowledge of the parts of man's body, of functions..of impinguation [L. *impinguatione*] and the like. *a* **1682** SIR T. BROWNE *Misc. Tracts* (1684) 16 Physicians..acknowledge a very nutritive and impinguating faculty in Pulses.

†**im'pingue,** *v. Obs. rare*⁻⁰. [ad. late L. *impinguā-re*: see prec.] 'To make fat' (Cockeram, 1623).

impious ('ɪmpɪəs), *a.* [f. L. *impi-us* without reverence (f. *im-*, IM-² + *pius*) + -OUS: cf. OF. *impieux*, *-euse* (15–16th c. in Godef.); mod.F. has *impie* (in Cotgr. 1611), ad. L. *impi-us.*]

1. Not pious; without piety or reverence for God and his ordinances; presumptuously irreligious, wicked, or profane: **a.** of persons, or things personified.

1594 *1st Pt. Contention* (1843) 31 Impious Yorke, and Bewford..Have all lymde bushes to betraie thy wings. **1624** GATAKER *Transubst.* 27 And who is so impious..as to eate thus that which he thinketh to be God? *a* **1704** T. BROWN *Dk. Ormond's Recov.* Wks. 1730 I. 50 E'er impious plow to wound the earth began. **1865** M. ARNOLD *Ess. Crit.* vii. (1875) 266 The Sunis recognise Abu Bekr, Omar and Othman..and regard the Shiahs as impious heretics. **1875** JOWETT *Plato* (ed. 2) I. 319 The impious, whoever he may be, ought not to go unpunished.

b. of actions, sayings, and the like.

1575–85 ABP. SANDYS *Serm.* (Parker Soc.) 199 If magistrates should command that which is impious..we have our answer well warranted:..'It is better to obey God than men'. **1638** SIR. T. HERBERT *Trav.* (ed. 2) 338 To touch their mouths or meat with fingers is held absurd and impious. **1667** MILTON *P.L.* v. 813 Canst thou with impious obloquie condemne The just Decree of God? **1718** PRIOR *Pleasure* 902 At Dagon's shrine I kindle impious flame. **1845** MAURICE *Mor. Philos.* in *Encycl. Metrop.* II. 638/1 An impious disregard of all the processes of his education.

2. Wanting in natural reverence and dutifulness, esp. to parents. *rare.*

1613 PURCHAS *Pilgrimage* (1614) 351 The Caspii shut up their parents..and there in respect of pietie (what more could the impious doe?) starve them to death. **1783** MORELL *Ainsworth's Lat. Dict.* IV. s.v. *Tullia*, The impious daughter of Servius Tullius..drove her chariot over the body of her aged father.

impiously ('ɪmpɪəslɪ), *adv.* [f. IMPIOUS *a.* + -LY².] In an impious manner; with impiety; with presumptuous wickedness or profanity.

1597 DANIEL *Civ. Wars* v. (R.), Ungrateful times! that impiously neglect That worth, that never times again shall show. **1693** CONGREVE in *Dryden's Persius* (1697) 400 So Vnbelievers impiously despise The sacred Oracles, in Mysteries. **1769** E. BANCROFT *Guiana* 320 Too many at the altar..impiously enter into engagements, without intending to fulfil them. **1864** SKEAT *Uhland's Poems* 314 My sacred ivy thou hast dared profane, And impiously dost call thyself my priest!

'impiousness. [f. as prec. + -NESS.] The quality of being impious; impiety.

1599 SANDYS *Europæ Spec.* (1632) 127 Who indeed doe blot out much impiousnesse and filth. **1695** LD. PRESTON *Boeth.* III. 113 *note*, The Impiousness of which Fact he ordered Papinian to excuse.

impir(e, impyre, etc., obs. ff. EMPIRE *sb.* and *v.* The usual Sc. forms in 16–17th c.

1513 DOUGLAS *Æneis* VI. xv. 14 To rewle the pepill vndir thyne impyre. **1559–60** *Cott. Lib. Cal.* B. ix, Seeing ambition has sa impyrit ower their reason. **1596** DALRYMPLE tr. *Leslie's Hist. Scot.* I. 3 Vnder the Impire of Ingland.

impish ('ɪmpɪʃ), *a.* [f. IMP *sb.* + -ISH.] Having the characteristics of an imp; pertaining to or characteristic of a little devil or mischievous urchin.

1652 GAULE *Magastrom.* 334 The news of the victory was ..carried to Rome by Castor and Pollux..or as others say, by the Impish divels themselves. **1834** BECKFORD *Italy* II. 8 Stimulated by impish children. **1876** T. HARDY *Ethelberta* (1890) 219 Teasing and worrying with impish laughter half suppressed. **1884** LADY VERNEY IN *Contemp. Rev.* Oct. 550 Spiteful, impish tricks.

Hence **'impishly** *adv.*, **'impishness.**

1864 WEBSTER, *Impishly.* **1872** LYTTON *Parisians* IX. ii, 'I shall have the wreath yet', cried [she] impishly. **1876** T. HARDY *Ethelberta* (1890) 303 When scheming any plot of particular neatness, which had less emotion than impishness in it. **1897** W. C. HAZLITT *Four Generat. Lit. Fam.* I. III. iii. 274 A half-witted fellow..whom the boys..impishly tormented.

impiteous (ɪm'pɪtɪəs), *a.* [f. IM-² + PITEOUS.] Ruthless, pitiless.

1877 SYMONDS *Renaiss. Italy, Reviv. Learn.* viii. 472 *note*, Exiled from home and fatherland by fate impiteous. **1882** —— *Animi Figura* 140 Sole 'neath heaven's impiteous stars. **1890** *Univ. Rev.* 15 June 231 Impiteous And hateful are the gods, and void of ruth.

impiteous, -tious, -tous, impittious, obs. varr. IMPETUOUS.

im'pitiably, *adv.* [f. IM-² + PITIABLY.] Without pity, mercilessly.

1835 *Fraser's Mag.* XII. 36 The antique barriers which impitiably and irrevocably divided mankind into castes have been swept away.

implaca'bility. [ad. late L. *implācābilitās*: see next and -ITY.] The quality or condition of being implacable.

1531 ELYOT *Gov.* II. vi, The implacabilitie or wrath insaciable, of those two capitaines. **1673** *Lady's Call.* I. iii. ¶19. 25 So to regulate their passions, that they never come within distance of implacability. *a* **1797** H. WALPOLE *Mem. Geo. II* (1847) I. ix. 262 His resentments were not softened by the implacability of their hatred to him. **1855** MACAULAY *Hist. Eng.* xii. III. 167 To James unpopularity, obstinacy, and implacability were the greatest recommendations that a statesman could have.

implacable (ɪm'pleɪkəb(ə)l, -'plækəb(ə)l), *a.* [a. F. *implacable*, ad. L. *implācābilis*, f. *im-* (IM-² + *plācābilis* PLACABLE. (By Spenser and Longfellow stressed on first (or third) syllable.)]

1. That cannot be appeased; irreconcileable; inexorable: of persons, feelings, etc.

1522 MORE *De Quat. Noviss.* Wks. 83/1 Bering implacable anger where they perceue themself not accepted. **1611** BIBLE *Rom.* i. 31 Couenant breakers..implacable, vnmercifull. **1751** JOHNSON *Rambler* No. 165 ¶3 That we should be harassed by implacable persecution. **1769** ROBERTSON *Chas. V* (1813) V. III. 340 He was, besides, the implacable enemy of Bourbon. **1827** LYTTON *Pelham* ii, If I, or any of his friends, was injured or aggrieved, his anger was almost implacable. **1875** STUBBS *Const. Hist.* II. xvi. 325 The earl of Warwick remained implacable.

b. Const. *to.*

1678 BUNYAN *Pilgr.* I. (ed. 2) 84 They thereby shew themselves to be implacable to good. **1785** T. BALGUY *Disc.* 62 The greater part of these sectaries were implacable to those who differed from them.

†**2.** That cannot be assuaged or mitigated. *Obs.*

1590 Spenser *F.Q.* ii. vi. 44 O how I burne with implacable fire. *Ibid.* iii. vii. 35. **1667** Milton *P.L.* vi. 658 Thir armor help'd their harm..which wrought them pain Implacable. **1862** Longf. *Wayside Inn* Prel. xiii, The plunge of the implacable seas, The tumult of the winds at night.

3. as *sb.* One who is implacable.

1748 Richardson *Clarissa* (1811) III. 2 As I have ordered it, the flight will appear to the implacables to be altogether with her own consent.

im'placableness. [f. prec. + -ness.] The quality of being implacable; implacability.

1631 Gouge *Gods Arrows* iii. §82. 338 It is mens implacablenesse which maketh God implacable. **1677** Gilpin *Demonol.* (1867) 466 Appearances of wrath and incompassionate implacableness. **1748** Richardson *Clarissa* (1811) II. xxx. 193 The implacableness of my brother and sister..he sets forth in strong lights. **1824** Southey *Bk. of Ch.* (1841) 506 The implacableness of their political hatred.

implacably (ɪm'pleɪkəblɪ, ɪm'plæk-), *adv.* [f. as prec. + -ly².] In an implacable manner; with enmity or resentment that cannot be appeased.

1631 Gouge *God's Arrows* i. §66. 109 Men may thinke the Divine wrath to be implacably incensed. **1751–73** Jortin *Eccl. Hist.* (R.), It is no wonder that men of this temper should have worried one another so implacably for Nestorianism [etc.]. **1876** Bancroft *Hist. U.S.* IV. xvii. 441 Burke..pursued Chatham implacably, and refused to come to an understanding with him.

†**im'placacy.** *Obs. rare*⁻¹. [f. L. *implācāt-us* unappeased (cf. implacable): see -acy.] Unappeased state or condition; implacableness.

c **1660** Wood *Life* (O.H.S.) I. 292 The smart of their implacasy.

im'placement, var. emplacement, situation, position, platform for a gun.

implacental (ɪmplə'sɛntəl), *a.* and *sb. Zool.* [f. im-² + placental (f. placenta + -al¹); cf. mod.L. *Implacentālia* neut. pl., name of the group.]

A. *adj.* Having no placenta, a term applied to the group of mammals consisting of the marsupials and monotremes (*Implacentalia*).

1839–47 Todd *Cycl. Anat.* III. 257/1 The quadrupeds.. above defined, are..implacental. **1865** Draper *Intell. Devel. Europe* xxiii. 562 Mammals, both placental and implacental.

B. *sb.* A mammal that has no placenta; a marsupial or monotreme.

1864 in Webster.

impla'centate, *a. Zool.* [f. im-² + placentate (f. placenta + -ate² 2): cf. mod.L. *Implacentata* = *Implacentalia*.] Having no placenta.

In Mod. Dicts.

†**im'plain,** *v. Obs. rare*⁻¹. [f. im-¹ + ? plain *a.*, in sense 'plane, flat, level'.] *trans.* To make smooth with plaster; to plaster smooth.

c **1420** *Pallad. on Husb.* i. 479 Oyl dregges mixt with clay thou must implayne [*v.r.* me may ymplayn] Thi wowes [= walls] with.

implaister, var. emplaster *v. Obs.*

†**implane,** *v.* [ad. late L. (Vulgate) *implānāre* to lead astray.] 'To deceive' (Cockeram, 1623).

†**im'planitude.** [f. im-² + L. *plānitūdo* evenness.] Unevenness, unlevelness; in quot. *attrib.*

1597 A. M. tr. *Guillemeau's Fr. Chirurg.* 46b/2 The vneven and implanitude collocation inferreth payn and recurvation in the Ioyncte.

†**im'plank,** *v. Obs. rare*⁻⁰. [im-¹.] *trans.* To enclose with planks.

1611 Florio, *Inassare*, to imboord or implanke.

implant (ɪm'plɑːnt, -'plænt), *v.* Also 6 **emplant.** [a. F. *implanter* to insert, engraft, etc. (also †*emplanter* to plant), f. *im-* (im-¹) + *planter* to plant.]

1. a. *trans.* To plant in, insert, infix. Chiefly *pass.*, To be set, fixed, or embedded *in* something, *e.g.* as a crystal in a matrix of another kind. Also *refl.*

1545 Raynold *Byrth Mankynde* 17 Before they emplant them self in the hedde of the stoone. **1578** Banister *Hist. Man* i. 15 The Opticke Sinew..is implanted into the middle of the eye. *a* **1705** Ray (J.), Another cartilage, capable of motion, by the help of some muscles that were implanted in it. **1811** Pinkerton *Petral.* I. 169 Patrinite sometimes occurs in globular masses, implanted in other rocks. **1831** R. Knox *Cloquet's Anat.* 75 The Teeth..are small bones.. implanted in the alveoli of both jaws.

b. *Med.* Surgically to place or insert (tissue, or something inorganic) in the body: used esp. when what is inserted does not correspond with what is naturally found at the site that receives it.

1886 W. D. Younger *Implantation of Teeth* 8, I have since tried implanting teeth which have been extracted for weeks and months. **1887** *Lancet* 12 Feb. 334/2 In his early attempts he used fresh teeth, which he obtained from other dentists.. and endeavoured to keep alive by implanting them in cocks' combs. **1919** *Jrnl. Amer. Med. Assoc.* 26 July 301/1 On the other hand, the pathologic opaque [corneal] graft, implanted in sound tissue, grows normal and in time becomes transparent. **1927** *Lancet* 15 Jan. 120/2 Animals not infrequently recover from tumours implanted into them. **1941** *Jrnl. Amer. Med. Assoc.* 27 Sept. 1070/1 In January 1940 a 200 mg. tablet of testosterone was implanted. After another month, hair appeared on the upper lip..and the penis further increased in size. **1952** *Brit. Jrnl. Radiol.* XXV. 423/2 A method of implanting redioactive Ta^{182} wire for the treatment of patients with carcinoma of the bladder is described. **1963** *Lancet* 12 Jan. 78/1 The amnion was prepared and implanted by the method of Troensegaard-Hansen (1956). In 8 cases where symptoms were unilateral the implant was placed in the affected leg. **1964** *Ann. N.Y. Acad. Sci.* CXI. 1063 During the past 3 years the pacemaker has been implanted in 43 patients ranging in age from 39 to 85 years.

2. a. To fix or instil (a principle, desire, opinion, etc.) *in* one. Chiefly *pass.*: To be firmly fixed or inherent *in.* (The ordinary use.)

a **1541** Barnes *Wks.* (1573) 323/1 They are both inclinations of nature, implanted of God. **1605** Timme *Quersit.* i. ii. 6 The diuine vertue which God hath put and implanted in all creatures. **1794** Sullivan *View Nat.* II. 389 Gravity, attraction, repulsion..are not powers implanted in matter, or possible to be made inherent in it. **1820** Scott *Abbot* i, So deeply is the desire of offspring implanted in the female breast. **1887** Bowen *Virg. Æneid* iii. 249 Take these words of the prophet—implant them deep in your heart.

†**b.** To engraft (a bud). Also *fig.*: cf. implantation 3. *Obs. rare.*

1660 Sharrock *Vegetables* 71 Till such time as the buds then implanted may be fast cemented. **1675** Brooks *Gold. Key* Wks. 1867 V. 30 Requiring men to be better Christians before they come to Christ, than commonly they prove after they are implanted into Christ.

3. a. To set in the ground; to plant. Also *fig.*

1610 W. Folkingham *Art of Survey* i. iii. 6 It implies that either the ground is very fertile in generall, or that they are implanted in Plots Sympathizing with their Natures. **1633** P. Fletcher *Purple Isl.* xii. lxxx, Upon her cheek doth Beauties self implant The freshest garden of her choicest flowers. **1753** L. M. tr. *Du Boscq's Accompl. Woman* I. 180 Those [herbs] which the gardiner implanteth. **1845** Stephen *Comm. Laws Eng.* (1874) II. 215 Trees, while still implanted in the ground, are parcel of the freehold. **1868** Helps *Realmah* viii. (1876) 208 Had implanted the seeds of fatal disease.

b. With inverted construction: To plant (ground, etc.) *with* something; to furnish *with* by insertion or implantation. Also *fig.*

1612–15 Bp. Hall *Contempl., N.T.* iv. xxxiii, Break up the fallowes of my nature, implant me with grace, prune mee with meet corrections. **1670** Milton *Hist. Eng.* iii. Wks. (1847) 503/2 Minds well implanted with solid and elaborate breeding. **1812** H. & J. Smith *Horace in Lond.* 121 Your heir ..May fell your groves, implant the lawn. **1919** *Lancet* 29 Mar. 490/2 We are dealing with serum implanted with gas-gangrene bacilli. *Ibid.* 493/2 An agar surface implanted with a serophytic organism. **1956** *Brit. Jrnl. Radiol.* XXIX. 509/1 When the whole area..has been 'implanted' with the introducing needles, their stilettes are removed and tantalum wires..are passed down their lumina. **1968** *Canad. Jrnl. Physics* XLVI. 671/1 A silicon sample implanted at room temperature with As ions. **1971** *Nature* 18 June 454/2 Sprague-Dawley male albino rats were stereotaxically implanted..with stainless steel cannula systems for the injection of..various amines.

4. *intr. Embryol.* To be or become implanted; to undergo implantation (sense 6).

1954 *Contrib. Embryol.* XXXV. 219/1 It appears..that the human blastocyst in the same stage of development implants earlier than that of the macaque. **1963** C. G. Hartman *Mechanisms Conception* vii. 349 After transfer to pseudopregnant hosts, the blastocysts implanted..with about the same frequency of success as blastocysts transferred without cultivation. **1967** Strong & Corney *Placenta in Twin Pregnancy* ii. 16 They may implant at adjacent sites so that the placentae in growing would fuse to form a dichorionic, but single placenta. **1970** *Sci. Jrnl.* June 48/1 Fertilization takes place in the Fallopian tube and some days later the fertilized egg implants into the lining of the uterus.

Hence **im'planting** *vbl. sb.* = implantation.

1597 Middleton in Farr *S.P. Eliz.* (1845) II. 536 Wisedomes haruest is with follie nipt..Her fruite all scattered, her implanting ript. **1620** Granger *Div. Logike* 49 The nighest end of Baptisme, is our implanting into the body of Christ.

implant ('ɪmplɑːnt, -plænt), *sb.* [f. implant *v.*]

a. Anything implanted, esp. within the body.

1890 *Sat. Rev.* 15 Nov. 551/2 It seemed to tell of an ineradicable implant of commercial hypocrisy. **1911** *Chem. Abstr.* V. 2499 However, since after extirpation of these implants the hypersensitiveness persisted, it would seem that sessile receptors are not essential. **1919** *Jrnl. Amer. Med. Assoc.* 26 July 301/1 A disk is cut from the opaque cornea and another from the transparent periphery, and the disks are transposed. The transparent implant being impermeable, like all autografts, becomes invaded by the abnormal elements surrounding it. **1952** *Brit. Jrnl. Radiol.* XXV. 421/1 A radon-seed implant has proved to be a useful method of treatment for early carcinoma of the bladder. **1961** J. N. Anderson *Appl. Dental Materials* (ed. 2) viii. 79 They [*sc.* chrome-cobalt alloys] can..be used as an 'implant' beneath the gum to which a denture may be fastened. **1963** [see implant *v.* 1 b]. **1968** *New Scientist* 11 Jan. 80/1 In recent years surgeons have been fitting an increasing number of implants to fix and repair damaged bones. **1968** *Brit. Med. Bull.* XXIV. 242/1 Radium implants for radiation therapy. **1968** *Canad. Jrnl. Physics* XLVI. 667/1 Since the implanted atoms are confined to a surface region less than 0·1 μ thick, a well-defined 'impurity' peak is observed in the scattering spectra. [*Note*] In the case of phosphorus implants..the mass difference between P and Si is too small for the 'impurity' peak to be resolved.

b. An act or operation of implanting something; an implantation.

1941 *Jrnl. Amer. Med. Assoc.* 27 Sept. 1069/1 Our more recent multiple 50 mg. pellet implants were performed with a trocar. **1970** *Times* 28 Apr. 5/4 French doctors today made the world's first implant of an atomic powered heart simulator into a human being.

implantable (ɪm'plɑːntəb(ə)l, -'plænt-), *a.* [f. implant *v.* + -able.] Capable of being implanted (in the body).

1960 C. N. Smyth *Med. Electronics* 253 (*heading*) An implantable pacemaker for the heart. **1965** *Adv. Biol. & Med. Physics* X. 367 It is conservatively estimated that over 4000 implantable cardiac pacemakers have been used to date with gratifying results. **1972** *Physics Bull.* June 336/2 Since there is no sign of complex implantable functioning organs at the present stage of medical engineering technology, devices which replace heart, lung, kidney or liver remain outside the body.

†**im'plantate,** *a. Obs. rare.* [f. L. type **implantāt-us*, pa. pple. of **implantāre* to implant.] Implanted.

1650 Charleton *Paradoxes* 34 There is a Magnetisme.. every where implantate in, and proper to, naturall bodies. *Ibid.* 56 Both the implantate and influent spirit depart hand in hand together. **1651** Biggs *New Disp.* ¶ 164 Their original inhærent and implantate vigour.

implantated, *ppl. a. rare.* [f. as prec. + -ed¹.]

1855 Mayne *Expos. Lex.*, *Implantatus*, applied to those crystals which are attached by one of their ends to the walls of an excavation hollowed in a rock: implantated.

implantation (ɪmplɑː'nteɪʃən, -plæn't-). [a. F. *implantation*, noun of action f. *implanter* to implant.] The action or process of implanting; the fact or manner of being implanted.

1. *Anat.* The insertion of an organ, muscle, etc.; esp. as to its manner and place. Cf. implant *v.* 1.

1578 Banister *Hist. Man* i. 13 The implantation of the teeth is not in one, as an other sheweth. **1615** Crooke *Body of Man* 815 They [two muscles] haue but one tendon and one implantation. **1650** Bulwer *Anthropomet.* 62 Ending in that part wherein the anteriour implantation of Temporal Muscle ariseth. **1854** Owen *Skel. & Teeth* in *Circ. Sc.*, *Organ. Nat.* I. 270 The teeth of the sphyræna are examples of the ordinary implantation in sockets. **1890** H. Ellis *Criminal* iii. 67 An implantation of the ears farther back than is normal.

2. The action of planting or setting in the ground. Also *fig.* Cf. implant *v.* 3.

a **1600** Hooker *Eccl. Pol.* vii. viii. §7 To make such provision for the direct implantation of his church. **1650** *Brief Disc. Fut. Hist. Europe* 15 By saving of Noahs family to preserve a seed for the implantation of a new. **1727–41** Chambers *Cycl.*, *Implantation*, one of the six kinds of transplantation, used by some for the sympathetic cure of certain diseases. [Process described.] *a* **1817** T. Dwight *Theol.* (1830) I. v. 135 The vegetable world..from its first implantation in the soil to its full growth.

†**3. a.** Engrafting. *Obs. rare.*

1652 Warren *Unbelievers* (1654) 23 The Gardners knife ..cannot cut off a branch, nor be helpful to the implantation of it, without the hand of the Gardner. **1660** Sharrock *Vegetables* 66 Apricots and Peaches, being secured upon their own stocks, will admit implantation unto another also.

†**b.** *fig. Theol.* 'Engrafting' into Christ. *Obs.*

1640 Bp. Reynolds *Passions* xi. 99 Hence we reade so often..of a Spirituall Implantation unto him [Christ] by Faith. *a* **1655** Vines *Lord's Supp.* (1677) 213 Baptism is first for insition and implantation. **1702** C. Mather *Magn. Chr.* iii. i. App. (1852) 346 A sinner's preparation for, implantation in, and salvation by, the glorious Lord Jesus Christ.

c. *Path.* The engrafting of a morbid or malignant growth.

1897 *Allbutt's Syst. Med.* III. 538 The observations of Hauser have thrown some light on the implantation of cancer on the ulcer. *Ibid.* 725 These [growths] are to be regarded..as examples of successful implantation or grafting of particles of malignant growth.

4. The introduction and fixing of a principle, idea, etc. in the mind. Cf. implant *v.* 2.

1653 H. More *Antid. Ath.* (1662) 26 The implantation of the Idea of God in the Soul. **1669** Gale *Crt. Gentiles* i. iv. 25 This desire of Navigation found a kind of natural implantation in these Phenicians. *a* **1708** Beveridge *Thes. Theol.* (1710) I. 362 The implantation of Christ's righteousness in sanctification, taking away the implantation of Adam's sin in us. **1875** E. White *Life in Christ* v. xxviii. (1878) 475 The moral judgment which is oftentimes appealed to by Christ as a correct rule of decision, because of divine implantation.

5. a. The firm placing or planting of the foot.

1870 Rolleston *Anim. Life* 59 By the protrusion and implantation of which [the muscular foot] into the soft bottoms of the ponds and streams in which these creatures [fresh-water mussels] live.

b. *Surg.* The (or an) operation of implanting something in the body (see implant *v.* 1 b). Also *attrib.*

1885 M. Hay tr. *H. von Ziemssen's Handbk. Gen. Therapeutics* II. 399 The method described by Bruns, and characterised by him as dry injection or implantation... In this, the drugs are likewise applied in thin cylinders or plugs, for the introduction of which..a special form of implantation needle is used. **1886** *Syd. Soc. Lex.*, *Implantation*,..the planting of a new sound tooth into the cavity from which a decayed one has been removed. Also, the engrafting of pieces of epidermis on the surface of an ulcer to promote skin formation. *Ibid.*, *Implantation*,

medicamental, the introduction of solid substances into the structures of the body, either to destroy a morbid growth or to produce a general therapeutical effect. *Ibid.*, *Implantation needle*, an instrument invented by Bruns for the practice of hypodermatic implantation. **1886** W. D. YOUNGER (*title*) Implantation of teeth and pericemental life. **1887** *Lancet* 12 Feb. 334/1 Implantation is the ingrafting of a natural tooth into an artificial socket. **1929** *Jrnl. Amer. Med. Assoc.* 1 June 1900/2 In cases..in which it is not possible to remove the oviducts without removing the ovaries, Michel cuts off a piece of one of the resected ovaries..and sutures it to the uterus... He obtained good results in six out of seven cases in which he used his method of auto-plastic implantation of a portion of an ovary. **1938** *Lancet* 10 Sept. 606/2 A very prolonged effect of certain androgens and œstrogens could be obtained by a single implantation, under the skin, of pure dry hormone in the form of crystals or compressed tablets. **1963** *Ibid.* 12 Jan. 77/2 Troensegaard-Hansen (1956) described the treatment of intermittent claudication by implantation of human amnion into the thigh. **1969** H. A. SALHANICK et al. *Metabolic Effects Gonadal Hormones* 723 The most direct experimental approach to this problem is by the intracranial implantation of small amounts of crystalline steroids.

6. *Embryol.* The attachment of the fertilized ovum (blastocyst) to the wall of the uterus.

1902 A. KEITH *Human Embryol.* viii. 96 The implantation of the ovum in the decidua is in the posterior wall of the uterus in over 60% of cases. **1936** F. J. TAUSSIG *Abortion* iv. 70 In about ten days from fertilization, the ovum is ready for implantation. **1969** KLOPPER & DICZFALUSY *Foetus & Placenta* iii. 62 Implantation begins on the 20th day of the cycle, and probably takes several days to complete... The great majority of implantations in the case of the human take place in the fundus of the uterus and in the posterior wall.

7. *Physics.* The introduction of ions into a crystalline structure by bombardment with an ion beam.

1965 *Nuclear Instruments & Methods* XXXVIII. 169/2 Implantations reported in this paper were made in a 24 inch radius calutron. **1967** *Canad. Jrnl. Physics* XLV. 4053 Because of the nonequilibrium nature of the implantation process, the relative number of impurities on substitutional and interstitial sites may differ from that observed following conventional thermal diffusion. **1973** *Sci. Amer.* Apr. 65/3 The accelerated-ion technique offers fairly precise control of both the number of ions implanted and the depth of implantation.

im'planted, *ppl. a.* [f. IMPLANT *v.* + -ED^1.]

1. That has been introduced or implanted; infixed.

1595 SOUTHWELL *St. Peter's Compl.* 72 What change of place can change implanted paine? **1861** MILL *Utilit.* 44 Whether the feeling of duty is innate or implanted.

2. In sense corresponding to IMPLANT *v.* 3 b: having something implanted or inserted into it; *spec.* containing implanted ions.

1965 *Nuclear Instruments & Methods* XXXVIII. 172/1 Fig. 7 shows variation in the sheet resistance of an implanted area with temperature. **1970** *New Scientist* 15 Oct. Suppl. 17/2 The Japanese..have already announced an implanted microwave transistor. **1973** WILSON & BREWER *Ion Beams* iv. 300 The oxide serves..to protect against compensation of the implanted region during a subsequent diffusion.

implanter (ɪm'plɑːntə(r), -'plænt-). [f. IMPLANT *v.* + -ER^1.] One who or that which implants.

1653 H. MORE *Antid. Ath.* I. v. §2. 17 There is an active and actual knowledge in a man of which these outward objects are rather the re-minders than the first begetters or implanters. **1883** A. H. SAYCE in *Contemp. Rev.* Sept. 392 The implanter of love in the hearts of men.

implaster, obs. var. EMPLASTER *sb.* and *v.*

implastic (ɪm'plæstɪk), *a.* *rare*$^{-1}$. [f. IM-^{2} + PLASTIC.] Not plastic, rigid. Hence **impla'sticity**, implastic quality or condition.

1822–34 *Good's Study Med.* (ed. 4) IV. 143 Labour delayed or injured from implasticity..of the soft parts. *Ibid.* 145 Cases of an implastic rigidity.

implastration, var. EMPLASTRATION, *Obs.*

implate (ɪm'pleɪt), *v.* *rare*$^{-0}$. [f. IM-^{1} + PLATE *sb.*] *trans.* 'To put a plate upon as a covering; to sheathe; as, to implate a ship with iron' (Webster, 1864).

implausi'bility. [f. next + -ITY.] The quality or condition of being implausible; want of plausibility.

a **1639** WOTTON in *Reliq.* (1685) 671 No doubt he had obtain'd a very important Office in this State, but for the implausibility of his Person. **1776** G. CAMPBELL *Philos. Rhet.* (1801) I. I. v. 175 Implausibility may be surmounted. **1926** B. FREEMAN *Towards Answer* 7 Perhaps the thing is an impossibility or an implausibility. **1966** G. N. LEECH *Eng. in Advertising* ii. 17 The other two examples are also freakish.. because of their contextual implausibility.

implausible (ɪm'plɔːzɪb(ə)l), *a.* [f. IM-^{2} + PLAUSIBLE.]

†**1.** Not worthy of applause; personally unacceptable. *Obs.*

1602 WARNER *Alb. Eng.* Epit., After his death him seuerally succeeded..his two Sons, Harold and Hardy Knought: Either of them implausible and burdenous to the English.

2. Not having the appearance of truth, probability, or acceptability; not plausible.

a **1677** BARROW *Serm.* (1683) II. xxvi. 369 By so impotent, so implausible and improbable means. **1730** SWIFT *Vind. Ld. Carteret* Wks. 1761 III. 190 Nothing can better improve political schoolboys than the art of making plausible or implausible harangues against the very opinion for which they resolve to determine. **1788** G. CAMPBELL *Four Gosp.* (1807) II. 84 This, though not implausible, is mere conjecture. **1794** BURKE *Petit. Unitarians* Wks. 1842 II. 475 When they mingle a political system with their religious opinions, true or false, plausible or implausible. **1971** *Nature* 5 Feb. 408/1 It is implausible that such animals should have preceded in time the small and structurally different species *Hipparion nagriensis* Hussain. **1974** *Daily Tel.* 20 Feb. 13/2 The play was..a highly stagey and implausible piece.

Hence **im'plausibleness**, implausibility; **im'plausibly** *adv.*, not plausibly.

1818 TODD, *Implausibly.* **1846** WORCESTER, *Implausibleness. Dr. Allen.* **1894** *Yellow Bk.* I. 75 That which is already fair is complete, it may be urged—urged implausibly. **1928** *Music & Lett.* July 234 Men..able to..write categorically though implausibly. **1965** *Chicago Tribune* 10 Aug., The principal river..was variously named Konomick, Killamick, Calamick and sundry other versions which some claim, implausibly, meant 'white beaver'.

impleach (ɪm'pliːtʃ), *v.* *poet. rare.* Also 6 **em-**. [f. IM-^{1} + PLEACH.] *trans.* To entwine, interweave. Hence **im'pleached** *ppl. a.*

1597 SHAKS. *Lover's Compl.* 205 Behold these tallents of their heir [= hair] With twisted mettle amorously empleacht. **1829** TENNYSON *Timbuctoo* 224 The fragrance of its complicated glooms And cool impleached twilights. **1865** SWINBURNE *Poems & Ball., Two Dreams* 175 Where the green shadow thickliest impleached Soft fruit and writhen spray and blossom.

implead (ɪm'pliːd), *v.* Forms: α. 4 **en-**, 4–5 **emplede**, 5–6 **emplete**, 6–9 **emplead**. β. 5–6 **implede**, **-plete**, 6 **ymplead**, 7 **impleade**, 6– **implead**. [ad. AF. *en-*, *empleder* = OF. *empleidier*, *-pledier*, *-plaidier*, etc., f. *em-* (EM-, IM-^{1}) + *plaidier* (F. *plaider*) to PLEAD.]

1. a. *trans.* To sue (a person, etc.) in a court of justice, raise an action against.

α. [**1292** BRITTON I. xii. §6 Et voloms, qe touz prisouns soint a touz responables a ceux qi les enplederount taunt cum eux serount en prisoun.] **1387** TREVISA *Higden* (Rolls) VII. 481 Kyng Stephene was..i-swore..þat he wolde enplede no man for his owne wordes. **1389** in *Eng. Gilds* (1870) 84 No brother ne sister of yis gylde ne enplede oþer in no place, for no dette ne trespas. *a* **1400** *Ibid.* 361 ȝef a foreyne empledy þe teþynge. *c* **1500** in Arnolde *Chron.* (1811) 33 That none of ye fraunches of the forsayd cite be empleted at our eschequer [etc.]. **1559** in Strype *Ann. Ref.* I. App. viii. 21 The kings..tenants in chief shall not be empleadid in the ecclesiasticall court.

β. **1458** in Ld. Campbell *Chancellors* (1857) I. xxii. 322 Wherfore I charge Robt. my sone..that he never vexe, implede, ne greve the forsaid Sir John. **1464** J. PASTON in *P. Lett.* No. 492 II. 163 Persones abill to plede and to be impletid. **1523** FITZHERB. *Surv.* 13 These manner of tenauntes shall nat plede nor be impleded of their tenementes by the kynges writte. **1611** BIBLE *Acts* xix. 38 If Demetrius and the craftesmen..haue a matter against any man, the law is open, let them implead [*R. V.* accuse] one another. **1765** BLACKSTONE *Comm.* I. xviii. 475 After a corporation is so formed and named, it acquires many powers..As..To sue or be sued, implead or be impleaded. **1879** FARRAR *St. Paul* xxxii. II. 57 Brethren who..might be impleading one another at law before the tribunal of a heathen Prætor. **1957** *Listener* 19 Dec. 1020/1 Can one implead the State concerned? *Ibid.*, At present you cannot implead a State in United Kingdom Courts except under the Warsaw Convention. **1964** *Welsh Hist. Rev.* II. 47 It was further stipulated that a similar arrangement would be adopted if Owain or Llywelyn or their heirs wished to implead any of the King's subjects. **1973** *N.Y. Law Jrnl.* 1 Aug. 1/7 The plaintiff sued the appellant for damages for fraudulent acts under the contract. The appellant impleaded the plaintiff's president on his guarantee.

†**b.** To plead or prosecute (a suit). *Obs. rare.*

1554 *Act 1 & 2 Phil. & Mary* c. 8 §35 The Title of all Lands..is..in your Courts only to be impleaded, ordered, tried and judged.

†**2.** To arraign, accuse, impeach. Const. *of*. *Obs.*

a **1600** HOOKER *Eccl. Pol.* VI. iv. §10 To implead the truth of this history, Cardinal Baronius allegeth that Socrates, Sozomen and Eudæmon were all Novatianists. *a* **1658** CLEVELAND *Gen. Poems* (1677) 143, I implead your Highness,..as Accessary to my Guilt. **1681–6** J. SCOTT *Chr. Life* (1747) III. 72 They were accused and impleaded by subtil and insinuating Orators before the Tribunals of their Enemies. **1814** MRS. J. WEST *Alicia de Lacy* IV. 174 The life and fame of an innocent woman were impleaded. **1846** LANDOR *Imag. Conv.* Wks. II. 193, I can easily pardon a smile if thou empleadest me of curiosity.

3. In various nonce-uses belonging or related to PLEAD *v.* †**a.** To allege as a plea. †**b.** To entreat. **c.** To plead *with*. **d.** To plead for.

1658 T. WALL *God's Rev. agst. Enemies Ch.* 20 Saul had never impleaded the intent of sacrifice..had it not yeilded him some hope to wipe off the guilt of his disobedience. **1682** *New News from Bedlam* 13 Now he rakes Hell and the Devil..And them impleads for to inspire his Muse. **1839** BAILEY *Festus* v. (1852) 60 Let monarchs..remember they are set on thrones As representatives..to implead with God and man. *a* **1850** ROSSETTI *Dante & Circ.* I. (1874) 137 How mayst thou be counselled to implead With God thine own misdeed, And not another's!

Hence **im'pleaded** *ppl. a.*, **im'pleading** *vbl. sb.*

1742 FRANCIS *Horace, Odes* II. i, O Pollio, thou the great defence Of sad, impleaded innocence. **1861** PEARSON *Early & Mid. Ages Eng.* xxxiii, Twelve others..who were to declare upon oath with whom the impleaded property lay. **1875** STUBBS *Const. Hist.* III. xx. 497 Redress for the impleading of a member during the session.

†**impleadable** (ɪm'pliːdəb(ə)l), *a.*^{1} *Obs.* [f. IMPLEAD *v.* + -ABLE.]

1. That may be sued (as a person) or prosecuted (as a suit).

1570–6 LAMBARDE *Peramb. Kent* (1826) 113 They be impleadable in their owne townes also, and not elsewhere. **1681** *Trial S. Colledge* 5, I am a Free-man of London, and I am not impleadable..any where out of the Liberties of the City. **1724** R. WELTON *Subst. Chr. Faith* 234 The rebellious and disloyal..are impleadable at a twofold bar. **1818** CRUISE *Digest* (ed. 2) V. 117 They would by that means become frank fee, and not impleadable in his court.

2. Capable or being pleaded or made a plea.

1648 J. GEREE *Might overcoming Right* (1649) 33 Those actions..shall be as impleadable by men. **1701** LUTTRELL *Brief Rel.* (1857) V. 26 That no pardon be impleadable to any impeachment in parliament.

†**im'pleadable**, *a.*^{2} *Obs.* [f. IM-^{2} + PLEADABLE.] Not to be pleaded against, or met by any plea.

1607 DEKKER *Knt.'s Conjur.* (1842) 48 In what a lamentable condition therefore stands the vnhappie prisoner; his inditement is impleadable, his evidence irrefutable, the fact irpardonable, the iudge impenitrable. **1614** T. ADAMS *Fatal Banquet* ii. Wks. 1861–2 I. 196 An impenetrable judge, an impleadable indictment, an intolerable anguish shall seize upon them.

†**im'pleader**. *Obs.* [f. IMPLEAD *v.* + -ER^1.] One that impleads, sues, or prosecutes another; a prosecutor, accuser, or impeacher.

a **1577** SIR T. SMITH *Commonw. Eng.* (1633) 109 In all judgements being two parties, the first we call the impleader, suiter, demander or demandant or plaintife. **1698** S. CLARKE *Script. Just.* iii. 13 Who is my adversary? (my impleader, or he that enters an Action against me). **1770** *Hist. Duelling* 3 (T.) The Gombette law..allowed the expedient of duelling to those impleaders, whom the administered oath to offenders did not sufficiently satisfy.

†**im'pleasing**, *a.* *Obs. rare.* [f. IM-^{2} + PLEASING.] Unpleasing, unpleasant.

1602 CAREW *Cornwall* 68 a, Let me lead you from these impleasing matters. *a* **1613** OVERBURY *A Wife* (1638) 103 Impleasing to all, as all to him.

impleat(e, var. IMPLETE *a.*, filled.

impledge (ɪm'plɛdʒ), *v.* Also 6–7 **empledge**, (6 *Sc.* **implaidge**). [f. EM- or IM-^{1} + PLEDGE. An Anglo-L. *implegiātus* occurs in the Laws of Henry I, suggesting that an Anglo-Fr. *emplegier* may have been in use. Cf. OF. *plegier*, 12th c.] *trans.* To put in pledge; to pledge, pawn; to give as security; to engage. Also *refl.*

α. **1548** HALL *Chron., Edw. IV* 239 The countye..which kynge Charles..had before engaged, and empledged to duke Philip. **1630** BRATHWAIT *Eng. Gentlem.* (1641) 147 Whosoever he be that marrieth a wife, empledging his faith unto her by a ring.

β. **1597** MONTGOMERIE *Cherrie & Slae* 1453 Implaidging and waidging Baith twa thair lyves for myne. *a* **1656** USSHER *Power Princes* II. (1683) 185 They have not onely impledged themselves the one into the other upon Earth, but also to God in Heaven. **1814** SCOTT *Ld. of Isles* I. viii, This auspicious morn, That bids the daughter of high Lorn Impledge her spousal faith to wed The heir of mighty Somerled. **1881** SWINBURNE *Mary Stuart* I. ii. 49 The great life's gage of England; in whose name Lie all our own impledged.

†**implefy**, *v.* *Obs.* *rare*$^{-0}$. In 7 **implefie**. [f. L. *implē-re* (see IMPLETE) + -FY.] To fill (Cockeram, 1623).

implement ('ɪmplɪmənt), *sb.* Forms: 6 **yn-**, **ymple-**, (**imply-**, **empell-**, **hympyll-**), 6–8 **impliment**, (7 **impell-**, **emploi-**, **imploye-**), 5– **implement**. [app. ad. L. *implēmentum* a filling up (f. *implēre* to fill; see IMPLETE) taken in the sense of 'that which serves to fill up or stock (a house, etc.)'; in which sense *implementa* occurs in an Anglo-L. letter of 1541 (see sense 1 below) and may have been in considerably earlier use. Of OF. *emplement*, from *empler* to fill, fill up, Godefroy cites only one example, in sense 'filling up, fulfilling, completing'. The word was evidently sometimes referred to EMPLOY *v.*, and so confused with *employment*, as if = 'thing employed or used'.]

I. 1. *pl.* Things that serve as equipment or outfit, as household furniture or utensils, ecclesiastical vessels or vestments, wearing apparel or ornaments, etc. In *sing.* An article of furniture, dress, etc.

[Cf. Letter of 1541, Rymer, XIV. 723 Cum omnibus et omnimodis vasibus, jocalibus, ornamentis, bonis, catallis, et Implementis.]

1454 *E.E. Wills* (1882) 132 Reparacions and implementis dwe to the..Cathedral Chirche of seynt powle. **1496–7** *Act 12 Hen. VII*, C. 13 §12 All other goodes and implementis of Houshold to be used in their Houses. **1505** in *Eng. Gilds* (1870) 327 Here ffolwyth the ymplementes of the Tayllourys halle. **1532** HERVET *Xenophon's Househ.* (1768) 36, I considered, howe great aboundaunce of implimentes was in that smalle vessele. **1566** in Peacock *Eng. Ch. Furniture* (1866) 77 Item one pax one cruitt one vall with all other empellmentes of supersticion. **1610** F. GODWIN *Bps. of Eng.* 218 He left for an implement of his house at Ely a woonderfull sumptuous and costly table. **1641** *Margate Par. Register* in *Macm. Mag.* XLIII. 196 A note of such goods and imployements as are belonginge to the parishe church of

St. John's yᵉ Baptist, in the Isle of Thanett. *a* **1656** USSHER *Ann.* VI. (1658) 522 To defray this, they were forced to.. make their women club their attyring implements, to make up the sum. **1687** A. LOVELL tr. *Thevenot's Trav.* I. 110 All the Sea-men have Capots, and it seems to me to be so necessary an Implement, not only for Sea-men, but for all that travel by Sea. *a* **1779** WARBURTON *Div. Legat.* II. iv. Wks. 1788 I. 253 A golden bough, we see, was an important implement, and of very complicated intention in the shews of the Mysteries. **1848** MRS. JAMESON *Sacr. & Leg. Art* (1850) 36 They wear the stole and alba as deacons, and bear the implements of the mass. **1851** D. WILSON *Preh. Ann.* (1863) II. iv. ix. 465 The use of the consecrated bell as one of the most essential ecclesiastical implements.

fig. a **1621** J. KING in Spurgeon *Treas. Dav.* Ps. xxxix. 4 Dispose of your bodies and souls, and all the implements of them both.

†**b.** In more general sense: Requisites. *Obs.*

1601 R. JOHNSON *Kingd. & Commw.* (1603) 38 More implements then a spacious sea coast are incident to this busines: he must have plenty of timber and cordage; he must be furnished with a people practised in sea affaires [etc.]. **1752** FIELDING *Amelia* Wks. 1775 X. 132 Water, cordials, and all necessary implements being brought, Miss Bath was at length recovered and placed in her chair.

2. *pl.* The apparatus, or set of utensils, instruments, etc. employed in any trade or in executing any piece of work; now chiefly in ***agricultural implements*** or as a synonym of 'tools'; frequent as a generic term for the tools, weapons, etc. used by primitive peoples, as ***flint implements***. In *sing.* A tool, instrument.

1538 LELAND *Itin.* III. 114 King Henry the vij..erectid.. 3 great Bruing Houses with the Implementes to serve his Shippes. **1567** *Richmond. Wills* (Surtees) 202 In the same garner..vj gaddes of yron..Other implements in the sayme garner. **1612** CHAPMAN *Widdowes T.* Wks. 1873 III. 76 My stay hath been prolonged With hunting obscure nooks for these emploiments [a crowbar and a halter]. **1616** SURFL. & MARKH. *Country Farme* 533 Thus you see the diuersitie of plowes..now it is meet to know the implements belonging to their draught. **1641** *Termes de la Ley, Implements*,..it is used for things of necessary use in any trade or mystery, which are implyed in the practice of the said trade. **1724** SWIFT *Drapier's Lett.* Wks. 1755 VI. II. 49 Wood hath..his tools and implements prepared to coin six times as much more. **1767** A. YOUNG *Farm. Lett. to People* 310 He should make drawings of every machine and implement of husbandry that differs from those of his own country. **1875** JOWETT *Plato* (ed. 2) I. 204 An artisan, who had all the implements necessary for his work. **1879** LUBBOCK *Sci. Lect.* v. 152 It is a great mistake to suppose that implements of stone were abandoned directly metal was discovered.

fig. **1645** MILTON *Tetrach.* Wks. (1847) 187/1 Those Sciential rules, which are the implements of instruction. **1862** GOULBURN *Pers. Relig.* v. IV. (1873) 288 The implements with which Christianity works. **1867** MILL *Inaug. Addr.* 7 The necessary mental implements for the work they have to perform.

b. Applied to a person; cf. *instrument, tool.*

1628 FORD *Lover's Mel.* II. ii, I am Trollio, Your honest implement. **1719** DE FOE *Crusoe* II. xiii, This..man was a most useful implement to us everywhere. **1741** RICHARDSON *Pamela* I. 115 The Messenger..was an Implement in his Master's Hands. **1849** MACAULAY *Hist. Eng.* iv. I. 511 That meanness which marked them out as fit implements of tyranny.

II. †**3.** Something necessary to make a thing complete; an essential or important constituent part. *Obs. rare.*

1632 LITHGOW *Trav.* I. 14 The Clergy, which are the two parts of the inhabitants, (besides the Jewes and Curtezans, which are the greatest implements of the other third part). **1650** FULLER *Pisgah* IV. vi. 101 Because they have utterly lost the mystery of making the blew ribband..an essentiall implement of the fringes.

4. *Sc. Law.* Fulfilment, full performance (cf. IMPLEMENT *v.* 1).

1754 ERSKINE *Princ. Sc. Law* (1809) 334 Obligations may be dissolved by performance or implement. **1862** SHIRLEY *Nugæ Crit.* iv. 195 Such conditions are clearly inconsistent with the duties..and it may fairly be doubted..whether implement of them could be enforced. **1868** *Act 31 & 32 Vict.* c. 100 §54 Such note shall not have the effect..of excusing obedience to or implement of the interlocutor reclaimed against.

III. 5. *attrib.* and *Comb.* **implement-bearing** = IMPLEMENTIFEROUS.

1862 *Illustr. Lond. News* 5 July 22/1 The implement and cattle departments were laid out with a masterly hand. **1872** SIR J. EVANS *Anc. Stone Implements* xxii. 426 The deposition of the implement-bearing beds..extended over a very considerable space of time. **1891** DK. ARGYLL in *19th Cent.* Jan. 26 Vigorous attempts have been made to treat all implement-bearing gravels as fluviatile.

implement (ˈɪmplɪmənt), *v.* [f. IMPLEMENT *sb.*] **1. a.** *trans.* To complete, perform, carry into effect (a contract, agreement, etc.); to fulfil (an engagement or promise).

1806 *Petit. T. Gillies of Balmakewan* 23 (Jam.) This was an obligation incumbent upon him, which the petitioners were entitled to insist that he should implement. **1833** *Act 3 & 4 Will. IV*, c. 46 §90 The decree or order of court has not been duly implemented. **1865** ALEX. SMITH *Summ. Skye* II. 138 He had seen the boatmen, and fully implemented his promise. **1879** *Times* 22 Nov. (Mr. Gladstone in Scotland), On that day..Mr. Gladstone is expected to implement no fewer than three engagements. **1909** *Westm. Gaz.* 30 Aug. 4/3 [The] council has been prepared to implement that agreement. **1950** C. MORRIS *Social Case-Work Gt. Brit.* 7 With the post-war flood of social legislation, social workers are required..to help to implement the laws. **1964** *Ann. Reg. 1963* 102 Henceforward the bargaining..continued until late in the year, with some decisions being announced and implemented piecemeal. **1969** *Times* 3 Sept. 11/6 Three years later Armageddon found him [*sc.* Churchill] ready at the Admiralty with plans and authority to implement that policy. **1972** *Daily Tel.* 27 June 2/7 The provision of the Act of which they are most apprehensive..has yet to be implemented by the Government.

b. To carry out, execute (a piece of work).

1837 WHITTOCK, etc. *Bk. Trades, Optician* (1842) 354 Any similar invention which he may be employed to implement for the contrivers.

c. To fulfil, satisfy (a condition).

1857 NICHOL *Cycl. Phys. Sci.* 63/1 The chief mechanical requisites of the barometer are implemented in such an instrument as the following. **1870** R. M. FERGUSON *Electr.* 38 How are the conditions of thermo-electricity implemented by the materials of the earth?

2. To complete, fill up, supplement.

1843 BURTON *Benthamiana* 166 Projects for implementing wages by pauper relief. **1855** BAIN *Senses & Int.* III. iv. §15 (1864) 604 The hearer must implement the process, by the force of his own mind.

3. To provide or fit with implements.

1886 *Edin. Rev.* Oct. 362 Whether armed for defence, or implemented for industry.

implemental (ɪmplɪˈmɛntəl), *a.* [f. IMPLEMENT *sb.* + -AL[1].] Of the nature of an implement or implements: †**a.** Essentially constituent; **b.** Instrumental, practically effective.

1676 MARVELL *Gen. Councils* Wks. 1875 IV. 154 All the ill that could have come of it would have been, that such kinds of bishops should have proved less implemental. **1746** W. HORSLEY *Fool* (1748) I. 11 A Statesman proper to govern this Implemental Common-wealth. **1874** BUSHNELL *Forgiveness & Law* iv. 220 The threefold substance of doctrine here set forth is to be his [the Holy Spirit's] implemental power.

implementation (ˌɪmplɪmənˈteɪʃən). [f. IMPLEMENT *v.* + -ATION.] The action of implementing; fulfilment.

1926 *Spectator* 16 Oct. 627/1 The Irish delegation will seek the implementation of co-equality with the States of the British Commonwealth. **1944** *Mind* LIII. 184 Professor Collingwood's *Principles of Art* attempted an implementation and restatement on the epistemological side. **1951** R. FIRTH *Elem. Social Organiz.* ii. 45 In a democratic society consent of the individual is ultimately necessary for the implementation of programmes. **1955** *Bull. Atomic Sci.* June 223/3 As a possible mode of implementation, I suggest that a civilian-directed Scientists Corps (SC) be set up within the Defense Department for an emergency. **1965** *Listener* 27 May 775/2 Such plans..were fundamentally sound in the practical potential of implementation. **1973** *Daily Tel.* 16 Mar. 6/4 The successful implementation of this policy is vital. The cost of failure is incalculable.

implementiferous (ˌɪmplɪmənˈtɪfərəs), *a. Geol.* [f. as IMPLEMENTAL *a.* + -(I)FEROUS.] Containing (stone) implements used by early man.

1881 *Nature* XXIII. 604 The well-known and accepted implementiferous river-gravels. **1894** J. GEIKIE *Gt. Ice Age* (ed. 3) 640 *note*, The valleys containing the implementiferous deposits.

†**im'plese**, var. *emplese*, EMPLESS, to please. *Sc.*

c **1375** *Sc. Leg. Saints, Egipciane* 1477 To succure all þat one his modir dere wil cal, & implese hyre with hartly wil & lef þare syne & serwe hyre til.

†**im'plete**, *a. Obs.* [ad. L. *implēt-us*, pa. pple. of *implēre* to fill up, f. *im-* (IM-[1]) + **plē-re* to fill.] Filled, replete (*with* something).

1568 C. WATSON *Polyb.* 8b, A Citie, impleate with inestimable treasure. **1597** A. M. tr. *Guillemeau's Fr. Chirurg.* 25/2 A little kinde of spoone full and implete with poulder of corrosiue. **1694** J. T. in *Phil. Trans.* XVIII. 111, I found..its Vesicles impleat with a grumous Blood.

implete (ɪmˈpliːt), *v. U.S.* [f. L. *implēt-*, ppl. stem of *implēre* (see prec.).] *trans.* To fill.

1862 *N.Y. Independent* 31 July 4 It was the purpose of Mr. Calhoun..to implete the Government silently with Southern principles. **1886** BEECHER in *Homilet. Rev.* (U.S.) May 421 He [God] impletes all lands, all breadths, above, below, everywhere.

implete, obs. var. IMPLEAD.

impletion (ɪmˈpliːʃən). [ad. late L. *implētiōn-em*, noun of action from *implēre*: see IMPLETE *a.*] **1.** The action of filling; the condition of being filled; fullness.

1583 STUBBES *Anat. Abus.* I. (1877) 104 Dooth not the impletion and sacietie of meates and drinks prouoke lust? **1646** SIR T. BROWNE *Pseud. Ep.* III. xvi. 145 Upon a.. plentifull impletion there may perhaps succeed a disruption of the matrix. **1650** GREENHILL *Ezekiel* 72 Impletion—when the Spirit..fills the heart of any with Divine graces and influences. **1822–34** *Good's Study Med.* (ed. 4) I. 146 The stomach and bowels have been accustomed to the stimulus of food, and a certain degree of impletion. **1863** H. JAMES *Subst. & Shadow* xv. 256 The depletion of his [man's] natural pride and self-seeking in order to his subsequent spiritual impletion with all Divine gentleness peace and innocence.

†**2.** Fulfilment, accomplishment (of prophecy).

1615 T. ADAMS *Leaven* 100 The impletion of scriptures, wᶜʰ had so prescribed of him. **1681** H. MORE *Exp. Dan.* App. ii. 293 The impletion of that Prophecy is..already past. *a* **1716** SOUTH *Serm.* (1744) X. 197 The very literal impletion of the prophecy.

3. *Bot.* The filling up of the disk or cup of a flower with petals, by the conversion of stamens, nectaries, etc. into petals; the 'doubling' of a 'single' flower, whereby it becomes *flore pleno.*

1788 J. LEE *Introd. Bot.* I. xx. (ed. 4) 61 The Impletion of Simple Flowers, is by the Increase either of the Petals, or of the Nectarium.

Hence **im'pletionist**, one who advocates impletion or filling up: see quot.

1883 *Sat. Rev.* 14 Apr. 464 Two general views on that question [Scotch crofters]..may be summarized by the two words 'impletionist' and 'depletionist'. *Ibid.*, The impletionist recommends..lowering of rents, increase of pasturage privileges, 'rooting in the soil', and all the rest of it.

†**im'pletive**, *a. Obs. rare.* [f. *implēt-*, ppl. stem of *implēre* (see IMPLETE *a.*) + -IVE.] Having the quality of filling.

1647 LILLY *Chr. Astrol.* xliv. 270 Such [medicaments] as are calefactive, warme and impletive. **1677** GALE *Crt. Gentiles* IV. 14 The Divine Bonitie, saith Proclus..is.. impletive of althings and conversive of althings into itself.

†**im'pletory**, *a. Obs. rare*[−1]. [f. as prec. + -ORY.] Characterized by fulfilment.

1647 TRAPP *Comm. Hebr.* x. 18 An Impletory remission, as now in the new Testament, not a promissory, as under the old.

†**'implex**, *a. Obs. rare.* [ad. L. *implex-us*, pa. pple. of *implectĕre* to entwine, f. *im-* (IM-[1]) + *plectĕre* to twist, plait. (Cf. F. *implexe*, 17th c.)] Involved; having a complicated plot.

1710 ADDISON *Spect.* No. 297 ¶2 The Fable..is, according to Aristotle's Division, either Simple or Implex. It is called Simple when there is no change of Fortune in it: Implex, when the Fortune of the chief Actor changes from Bad to Good, or from Good to Bad. **1779–81** JOHNSON *L.P., Cowley* Wks. II. 60 The fable is plainly implex, formed rather from the Odyssey than the Iliad.

†**implex**, *v. Obs. rare.* [f. L. *implex-*, ppl. stem of *implectĕre* (see prec.)] *trans.* To entwine.

1635 A. STAFFORD *Fem. Glory* cvij, These forme thy Ghyrlond. Wherof Myrtle green..is so implexed, and laid in, between.

†**implexed**, *ppl. a. Obs.* [f. prec. or L. *implex-us* IMPLEX *a.* + -ED[1].] Entwined; also *fig.* Involved, complicated; = IMPLEX *a.*

a **1619** FOTHERBY *Atheom.* II. iii. §3 (1622) 219 The often iteration, and implexed application of the termes, of One, and Many, and Being. **1678** CUDWORTH *Intell. Syst.* Pref. 2 A concatenation or implexed series of causes.

†**im'plexion**. *Obs. rare.* [ad. late L. *implexiōn-em*, noun of action from *implectĕre*: see IMPLEX.] Complication, intertwining.

1678 CUDWORTH *Intell. Syst.* I. ii. §22. 97 The mutual occursions and rencounters of atoms,..their cohesions, implexions, and entanglements.

im'plexous, *a. Bot.* [f. L. *implex-us* (see IMPLEX *a.*) + -OUS.] 'Entangled, interlaced' (*Treas. Bot.* 1866).

†**im'plexure**. *Obs. rare.* [f. L. *implex-* (see IMPLEX *a.*) + -URE.] An infolding, a fold.

1578 BANISTER *Hist. Man* VIII. 100 Nature..hath engrauen these cornered implexures, that in them the thinne Membran..might insinuate it selfe.

impliable (ɪmˈplaɪəb(ə)l), *a.*[1] *rare.* [f. IM-[2] + PLIABLE; cf. F. *impliable.*] Not pliable; inflexible.

a **1734** NORTH *Exam.* I. ii. §2 (1740) 32 All Matters rugged and impliable to the Design must be suppressed or corrupted. **1831** *Fraser's Mag.* IV. 320 The impliable and disjointed stuff they are obliged to render into tolerable English.

im'pliable, *a.*[2] [f. IMPLY *v.* + -ABLE.] Capable of being implied.

a **1865** ISAAC TAYLOR (F. Hall). [In mod. Dicts.]

implial (ɪmˈplaɪəl). *rare.* [f. IMPLY *v.* + -AL[1] II. 5: after *denial.*] An act of implying; implication.

1846 G. S. FABER *Lett. Tractar. Secess. Popery* 116 Let us test the amount of this mere implial.

†**im'pliance**. *Obs. rare.* [f. IMPLY *v.* + -ANCE.] The action of implying; implication.

1677 R. CARY *Chronol.* II. ii. III. viii. 237 Their Magistrate in Chief, at least 8 Years before this Convention, which must be the Apostle's impliance.

†**im'plicament**. *Obs. rare.* [ad. late L. *implicāment-um* entanglement, f. *implicāre*: see IMPLICATE and -MENT.] Entanglement.

c **1450** tr. *De Imitatione* II. viii. 49 Be pure and fre wiþin-furþe wiþout implicament or incombraunce of eny creature.

†**'implicancy**. *Obs. rare.* [ad. L. type **implicāntia*, f. *implicāre*: see IMPLICATE *v.* and -ANCY. Cf. F. *implicance* (17th c.).] Entanglement, confusion; contradiction of terms.

1638 CHILLINGW. *Relig. Prot.* I. v. §60. 276 He gives such evident reason of them, (which can hardly be done to prove implicancy true) that whereas you say, he will never be able to salve them from contradiction [etc.]. *Ibid.* vi. §2. 325 That science and knowledge..are Synonimous termes, and that a knowledge of a thing absolutely unknown is a plain implicancy, I think are things so plain, that you will not require any proofe of them.

implicans (ɪmplɪ'kænz). *Logic.* The pl. form used is **implicants**. [L., pres. pple. of *implicāre* (see IMPLICATE *v.*).] In implication (see IMPLICATION 2 c), the active proposition; the proposition that implies. Cf. also IMPLICATE *sb.* 2.

1921 W. E. JOHNSON *Logic* I. ii. 30 In the implicative function 'If *p* then *q*', *p* is the implicans and *q* the implicate. **1922** *Ibid.* II. x. 211 We shall take..the implicants and disjuncts to stand for particular propositions. **1930** L. S. STEBBING *Mod. Introd. Logic* v. 70 It is clear that the order of the implicans and the implicate is not indifferent. **1937** D. J. B. HAWKINS *Causality & Implication* 61 This factor consists in the implicans being given in reality, as opposed to merely given in thought. **1953** I. M. COPI *Introd. Logic* viii. 229 The constituent statement between the 'if' and the 'then' is called the *antecedent* (or the implicans). **1963** J. LYONS *Structural Semantics* vii. 189 Sentences of the form Np [etc.]..with their transforms and implicants..are well integrated in the field.

implicate ('ɪmplɪkət), *ppl. a.* and *sb.* Also 6 implicat, -plycate. [ad. L. *implicāt-us*, pa. pple. of *implicāre*; see IMPLICATE *v.*]

A. *adj.* **1.** Intertwined, twisted together; also, wrapped up *with*, entangled or involved *in*. Now *rare.*

1536 BELLENDEN *Cron. Scot.* (1821) I. p. lxii, The history of Scotland is sa implicat with the history of Ingland, that [etc.]. **1555** EDEN *Decades* 157 As the lycertes are implycate in the tayles of the vipers. **1583** STUBBES *Anat. Abus.* I. (1877) 129 The poore man is so implicate and wrapped in on euerie side. **1672** *Phil. Trans.* VII. 5134 The Veins appear to be strangely intangled and implicate. **1846** DANA *Zooph.* (1848) 273 Folia aggregated, and crowdedly implicate.

†**2.** Involved, intricate. *Obs.*

1555 EDEN *Decades* 98 What this implicate Hiperbole, or aduancement meaneth. **1588** FRAUNCE *Lawiers Log.* II. ii. 87 If you resolve such implicate propositions thus [etc.]. **1637** R. HUMPHREY tr. *St. Ambrose* II. 6 Wee see so manifold, so implicate, so confused questions of philosophie.

B. *sb.* †**1.** Entanglement, confusion: cf. IMPLICANCY. *Obs.*

1638 SANDERSON *Serm.* (1854) I. 181 It seemeth then to be a mere implicat, a contradiccion *in adjecto*, to say that a thing is sold, and yet for nothing.

2. That which is implied or involved.

1881 A. B. BRUCE *Chief End Revel.* vi. 266 But even without consulting the Scriptures we can determine for ourselves the speculative implicates of revelation. **1883** MAUDSLEY *Body & Will* I. vi. 95 The implicate of the moral imperative is not liberty but constraint. **1884** FAIRBAIRN in *Contemp. Rev.* 360 The doctrine and its implicates must simply be stated. **1900** [see *extraconscious* (EXTRA- 1)]. **1921** W. E. JOHNSON *Logic* I. iii. 35 From an implicative, combined with the affirmation of its implications, we may infer the affirmation of its implicate. **1937** D. J. B. HAWKINS *Causality & Implication* 61 What factor..must be present in order that the implicate should be dependent in being on the implicans. **1946** C. MORRIS *Signs, Lang. & Behavior* i. 22 A sign which is more general than another sign,..is an analytic implicate of the other sign. **1971** *Jrnl. Gen. Psychol.* Apr. 222 A theorem deducible only from the conjunction of axioms as their only implicate is, therefore, most probative of the theory that contains them.

Hence †'**implicately** *adv.*, by implication.

c **1555** HARPSFIELD *Divorce Hen. VIII* 152 It is in no other translation expressedly, but..it is there implicately.

implicate ('ɪmplɪkeɪt), *v.* [f. L. *implicāt-*, ppl. stem of *implicāre* to entangle, involve, connect closely, etc., f. *im-* (IM-[1]) + *plicāre* to fold, twist.]

1. *trans.* To intertwine; to wreathe, twist, or knit together; to entwine, to entangle.

1610 HOLLAND *Camden's Brit.* I. 550 The boughes and armes of trees twisted one within another, so implicated the woods together that [etc.]. **1666** BOYLE *Orig. Formes & Qual.* 402 [They] implicate, and intangle themselves together so, as to make, as it were, little knots. **1802** PALEY *Nat. Theol.* ix. §3 (1819) 113 Owing to the muscles employed in the act of deglutition being so implicated with the muscles of the lower jaw. **1833** J. HOLLAND *Manuf. Metal* II. 353 The various descriptions of wirework in which the open spaces are of fanciful forms, require to be carefully implicated by the hand.

fig. **1885** R. L. STEVENSON in *Contemp. Rev.* Apr. 551 The artist..takes up..two or more views of the subject in hand; combines, implicates, and contrasts them.

†**b.** *fig.* To entangle mentally, to confuse. *Obs.*

1625 SHIRLEY *Love-tricks* III. v, Good men of the jury..I will not implicate you with ambages and circumstances.

c. To entwine (things non-material) *in* or *with* (other things).

1826 E. IRVING *Babylon* I. Introd. 35 The church is a polity..wherewith he is to implicate all his hopes, desires, and prayers. **1836** H. COLERIDGE *North. Worthies* Introd. (1852) 20 The interests of individuals are so implicated in those of the community, that [etc.]. **1873** H. ROGERS *Orig. Bible* ii. (1875) 81 Christianity was not designed to be.. implicated with the fortunes of any earthly polity.

2. To involve: **a.** To involve in its nature or meaning, or as a consequence or inference; to imply; to comprise.

1600 W. WATSON *Decachordon* VII. vii. (1602) 195 Otherwise it implicates a contradiction. **1797** MRS. A. M. BENNETT *Beggar Girl* II. 103 Old Frazer..had..filled the office of looker at Castle Gowrand—a phrase that implicates the combined duties of steward and bailiff. **1802** MRS. E. PARSONS *Myst. Visit* II. 223 So much reserve and mystery ..assuredly implicated something wrong. **1829** I. TAYLOR *Enthus.* v. (1867) 109 If these doubtful opinions implicate inquiries which the unlearned can never prosecute. **1858** HAWTHORNE *Fr. & It. Jrnls.* (1872) I. 59 There was never any idea of domestic comfort..implicated in such structures. **1896** HOWELLS *Impressions & Exp.* 284 That first lesson of civilisation which my words implicate.

b. To involve (a person) *in* a charge, crime, etc.; to bring into actual connexion *with*; to show to be concerned. (Also without construction.)

1797 MRS. RADCLIFFE *Italian* xvi, These ruffians, who have dared to implicate that innocent victim..in the charge. **1808** PIKE *Sources Mississ.* III. App. 78 Duplicity..in some degree always implicates the character of a military man. **1849** MACAULAY *Hist. Eng.* iv. I. 503 In no conspiracy against the government had a Quaker been implicated. **1855** MILMAN *Lat. Chr.* VI. iii. (1864) III. 442 Each party strove to implicate the other with the name of an odious heresy. **1870** FREEMAN *Norm. Conq.* (ed. 2) I. App. 721 The Encomiast..does not say a word implicating Eadric.

c. To involve or include in the operation of something; to affect or cause to be affected in the action of something.

1798 T. JEFFERSON *Writ.* (1859) IV. 242 Your feelings have no doubt been much implicated by it. **1859** MILL *Liberty* v. (1865) 60/2 This question presents no difficulty, so long as the will of all the persons implicated remains unaltered. **1880** M. MACKENZIE *Dis. Throat & Nose* I. 144 It is much more rare for the muscles of the larynx and trunk to be implicated [in diphtheria]. **1887** *Alien. & Neurol.* VIII. 633 The brain is pathologically implicated in insanity.

Hence '**implicated** *ppl. a.*, inwoven, involved, intertwisted, entwined, etc. *lit.* and *fig.*; '**implicating** *ppl. a.*, intertwining.

a **1693** URQUHART *Rabelais* III. xxxvii. 308 The implicating Involutions and Fetterings of Gins. **1752** FAWKES *Descr. May* (R.), The painted birds their cunning fabrics made, Or on the oak, or implicated thorn. **1821** SHELLEY *Prometh. Unb.* II. iv. 87 The implicated orbits woven Of the wide-wandering stars. **1832** AUSTIN *Jurispr.* (1879) I. vi. 324 Where the performance of either of the promises is made by either to depend on the performance of the other, the several conventions are cross or implicated.

†'**implicateness**. *Obs. rare.* [f. IMPLICATE *a.* + -NESS.] The quality of being implicate; intricacy.

1685 H. MORE *Paralip. Prophet.* 103 [Arguments] without any implicateness or operosity from Authentic Testimonies.

implication (ɪmplɪ'keɪʃən). [ad. L. *implicātiōn-em* entwining or entangling, noun of action f. *implicāre* to IMPLICATE. Cf. F. *implication* (16th c.) complicity, contradiction.]

1. The action of involving, entwining, or entangling; the condition of being involved, entangled, twisted together, intimately connected or combined. Also *fig.*

c **1430** *Pilgr. Lyf Manhode* IV. xii. (1869) 182 Seculere implicacioun and worldliche ocupacioun. **1578** BANISTER *Hist. Man* VIII. 111 Comparable to the implications of the sinewes of the arme. **1623** COCKERAM, *Implication*, a wrapping in, or intangling. *a* **1635** NAUNTON *Fragm. Reg.* (Arb.) 43 Sir Thomas Perrot..married a Lady of great honour, of the Kings familiarity, which are presumptions of some implication. **1659** STANLEY *Hist. Philos.* XIII. (1701) 600/1 By implication of some Atoms cohering mutually to one another. **1728** EARBERY tr. *Burnet's St. Dead* I. 27 Distinguished from the corporeal machines and the implications of matter. **1832** AUSTIN *Jurispr.* (1879) I. vi. 325 A convention bilateral is formed by the implication of several unilateral conventions. **1843** J. MARTINEAU *Chr. Life* (1867) 14 The mystic implication of his nature with ours.

2. a. The action of implying; the fact of being implied or involved, without being plainly expressed; that which is involved or implied in something else.

1581 W. CHARKE in *Confer.* IV. (1584) Bbiij, Inferred in the scripture by good proofes of consequence and implication. **1657** CROMWELL *Sp.* 21 Apr. in *Carlyle*, It is but an implication, it is not determined. **1701** NORRIS *Ideal World* I. ii. 35 Here..is a plain implication of an intelligible human nature. **1790** PALEY *Horæ Paul.* Wks. 1825 III. 129 He does not say this is different from ordinary usage—this is left to implication. **1836** J. GILBERT *Chr. Atonem.* iii. (1852) 63 Facts, of which the clear implications can by no party be denied. **1879** H. SPENCER *Data Ethics* ii. §7. 20 These implications of the Evolution-Hypothesis, we shall now see harmonize with the leading moral ideas men have otherwise reached.

b. *by implication*: by what is implied though not formally expressed, by natural inference.

c **1555** HARPSFIELD *Divorce Hen. VIII* (Camden) 33 Though not by express words, yet by implication and meaning. **1615** J. STEPHENS *Satyr. Ess.* 54 It followes by implication that amongst posterity, some one must have precedence. **1793** T. JEFFERSON *Writ.* (1859) IV. 36 It does not give it to France, either expressly or by implication. **1870** FREEMAN *Norm. Conq.* (ed. 2) I. App. 659 The Chronicles..seem to call him Ealdorman by implication.

c. *Logic.* A relationship between propositions such that the one implies the other; also, a proposition asserting such a relationship. Also *attrib.*

1906 B. RUSSELL in *Amer. Jrnl. Math.* XXVIII. 202 The subject which comes next in logical order is the theory of *formal* implication. **1922** W. E. JOHNSON *Logic* II. vi. 152 When a formula of implication is used as a premiss in the process of deduction, its implicans must first be formally certified in order that its implicate may be formally certified. **1932** LEWIS & LANGFORD *Symbolic Logic* v. 93 The dot preceding the implication-sign. **1947** H. REICHENBACH *Elem. Symbolic Logic* §6.24 The expression to the left of the implication sign is called implicans. **1952** P. F. STRAWSON *Introd. Logical Theory* iii. 85 The futility of identifying conditional statements with material implications is obvious. **1954** I. M. COPI *Symbolic Logic* ix. 286 The proposition..may have its implication sign deleted. **1957** A. N. PRIOR *Time & Modality* i. 1 Moh Shaw-Kwei has attempted to lay down the conditions which entitle an operator to be considered as an implication-operator. **1963** W. SELLARS in Castañeda & Nakhnikian *Morality & Lang. of Conduct* 178 In other words, shall-statements, unlike implication statements, are in the object-language. **1968** J. LYONS *Introd. Theoretical Ling.* x. 446 Implication, in the sense in which it has been defined here, is in principle objectively testable.

3. The process of involving or fact of being involved in some condition, etc.

1873 T. H. GREEN *Introd. Pathol.* (ed. 2) 173 This implication of the lymphatics is much more marked than in the sarcomata [etc.]. **1897** ALLBUTT *Syst. Med.* III. 17 The younger the sufferers [from acute rheumatism] the greater the liability to cardiac implications.

implicational (ɪmplɪ'keɪʃənəl), *a. Logic.* [f. IMPLICATION + -AL.] Of, concerned with, or using implication.

1881 H. MACCOLL in *Phil. Mag.* XI. 40 (*title*) Implicational and equational logic. **1881** J. VENN *Symbolic Logic* xviii. 377 In this case the implicational mode of expression certainly tells its tale more simply and obviously. **1906** B. RUSSELL in *Amer. Jrnl. Math.* XXVIII. 198 Thus both *p* and not-*p* may be replaced, in implicational formulae, by equivalences. *a* **1943** R. G. COLLINGWOOD *Idea of Hist.* (1946) 262 This implicational relation is a compulsive one. **1951** J. ŁUKASIEWICZ *Aristotle's Syllogistic* 22 It is always easy to deduce from an implicational thesis the corresponding rule of inference. **1955** A. N. PRIOR *Formal Logic* 49 Łukasiewicz has shown that a single axiom for the 'implicational calculus' must contain at least 13 letters. **1964** *Language* XL. 264 Most of his universals are 'implicational', of the type 'if a language has a category of gender, it always has a category of number'. **1970** *Ibid.* XLVI. 551 These studies reveal that socially significant linguistic features occur in an implicational series such that the presence of some feature A in the speech of a certain individual means that the speaker will also be found to use features B, C, and D. *Ibid.* 552 Since implicational analysis requires binary decisions..how can such..decisions be made? **1971** *Newslet. Amer. Dial. Soc.* Feb. 16 Implicational analysis ..'attempts not to describe a set of speech acts but to model the idealized competence of the persons involved in those speech acts'. **1972** *Computer Jrnl.* XV. 292/2 One can define the set of all strings which are proofs in implicational calculus.

Hence **impli'cationally** *adv.*, in an implicational manner.

1922 W. E. JOHNSON *Logic* II. v. 108 Such a trio of equations are taken to be implicationally independent of one another. **1964** *Current Res. & Devel. Sci. Documentation* XIII. 220 Extensive investigations are also being carried out on procedures of proof in implicationally ordered formal systems.

implicative ('ɪmplɪkeɪtɪv), *a.* and *sb.* [f. IMPLICATE *v.* + -IVE.]

A. *adj.* Having the quality of implying; tending to imply or implicate. Also, containing at least implications or implications only.

1602 FULBECKE *2nd Pt. Parall.* 17 The receit of such goodes into the Inne is an implicatiue promise, that the goodes shall be safe. **1818** COLEBROOKE *Treat. Oblig. Contracts* I. 15 Implied or implicative contracts are such as reason and justice dictate. **1847** LEWES *Hist. Philos.* (1867) I. 94 That existence and knowledge were identical and mutually implicative. **1872** F. W. ROBINSON *Bridge of Glass* I. I. ix. 124 The words..were more in pity for the man.. than implicative of any thought for himself. **1910** WHITEHEAD & RUSSELL *Principia* I. i. 7 The Implicative Function is a propositional function with two arguments *p* and *q*. **1930** L. S. STEBBING *Mod. Introd. Logic* v. 71 The implicative proposition cannot be simply converted. **1955** A. N. PRIOR *Formal Logic* 61 A purely implicative formula. **1967** *Listener* 5 Oct. 422/3 Substitution of implicative features for defining features—that is, the use of emotive language—is the trade-mark of propaganda. **1971** *Language* XLVII. 341 For reasons that will soon become apparent, I suggest the terms 'implicative' and 'non-implicative' verbs.

†**B.** *sb.* That which implies; a statement or writing implying something more than it expressly states. *Obs. rare.*

1589 PUTTENHAM *Eng. Poesie* III. v. (Arb.) 163 This Eglogue..was misliked..as an implicatiue, nothing decent nor proportionable to Pollio his fortunes and calling.

Hence '**implicatively** *adv.*, by implication; **im'plicativeness**, the quality of being implicative.

1579 J. STUBBES *Gaping Gulf* E iv b, Which, as a former fayth, is implicatively excepted in any truce with an infidel. **1602** FULBECKE *Pandectes* 82 Such thinges as are not verballie forbidden, are implicatiuelie permitted. *a* **1676** HALE *Hist. Placit. Cor.* xlix. §2 (Mason) Virtually and implicatively, and by necessary consequence, it takes away clergy..in all those cases. **1932** *Times Lit. Suppl.* 2 June 411/3 Professor Trout's chapters on the systolic and diastolic implicativeness of 'religious rapport' and 'religious dominance'. **1951** J. MILES *Primary Lang. Poetry* 493 Richards allies emotion..to order, and so supports its implicativeness in shape and form and connotation. **1953** PARTRIDGE *Shaggy Dog Story* iii. 84 Many years ago *Collier's Weekly* published, implicatively as reminiscence, a 'shaggy dog' that must..rank very high.

†'**implicatory**, *a. Obs. rare.* [f. as prec. + -ORY.] Of entangling nature or character.

1642 *View Print. Bk. int. Observat.* 3 A Laborinth of implicatory and inextricable Errours. **1706** J. SERGEANT *Acc. Chapter* (1853) 38 To suppose that the brief..does not contain a sense implicatory and destructive to itself.

implicit (ɪmˈplɪsɪt), *a.* Also 7 implicite. [a. F. *implicite* or ad. L. *implicit-us*, later form for *implicāt-us* IMPLICATE *ppl. a.*]

†**1. a.** Entangled, entwined, folded or twisted together; involved. *Obs.*

1608 TOPSELL *Serpents* (1658) 767 Epithets..given to snakes..as..green, infolded or implicit, horrible. **1667** MILTON *P.L.* VII. 323 The humble Shrub, And bush with frizl'd hair implicit. *a* **1803** BEATTIE *Hares* 92 No hand had wove the implicit maze.

fig. **1614** LODGE *Seneca, Epist.* 239 How pleasant and expedite the life of those men is that follow them; how bitter and implicite theirs is that have beleeved opinion more then truth. **1620** GRANGER *Div. Logike* 117 Manner of handling, which is double, viz...infolded, or unfolded; implicite, or explicite.

†**b.** Involved in each other; overlapping. *Obs.*

1662 STILLINGFL. *Orig. Sacr.* I. v. §8 The uncertainty of heathen chronology, when..implicite years are given out for solid. **1704** HEARNE *Duct. Hist.* (1714) I. 284 They took implicit years for solid, and placed those Kings in a succession which were contemporary with one another.

2. a. Implied though not plainly expressed; naturally or necessarily involved in, or capable of being inferred from, something else. ***implicit function*** (see quot. 1892). ***implicit definition*** = *contextual definition.*

1599 in Harington *Nugæ Ant.* 57 Yet, because it is but implicit, I send again to know more clearly. **1613** PURCHAS *Pilgrimage* (1614) 366 Magike..which is by explicite or implicite compact with Divels. **1665** MANLEY *Grotius' Low C. Warres* 133 And the King of France, had with his promises, and some implicite threats, commended his Brother herein. **1720** WATERLAND *Eight Serm.* 237 The Scripture-proofs of the Eternity of God the Son, are..either implicite and indirect, or explicite and direct. **1816** tr. *Lacroix' Diff. & Int. Calculus* 160 Treating the subordinate variables as implicit functions of the independent ones. **1876** GEO. ELIOT *Dan. Der.* I. ii, Might she not be going in to buy something which had struck her fancy? This implicit falsehood passed through her mind. **1892** J. EDWARDS *Diff. Calculus* i. §8 (ed. 2) 3 If the function be not expressed directly in terms of the independent variable..the function is said to be *implicit.* **1959** K. R. POPPER *Logic Sci. Discovery* iii. 72 Sometimes the axioms are described as '*implicit definitions*' of the ideas which they introduce. **1961** E. NAGEL *Struct. of Sci.* v. 95 The fundamental assumptions of the theory provide only implicit definitions for the theoretical notions employed in them. **1973** A. QUINTON *Nature of Things* ix. 279 We can thus define a logical term as one whose meaning is wholly specified by implicit definitions.

†**b.** Of persons having some implied quality: Virtual, though not professed or avowed. *Obs.*

1610 DONNE *Pseudo-Martyr* 155 One may bee an implicite martyre, though he know not why he died. **1633** EARL MANCH. *Al Mondo* (1636) 114 Deferring as well as presuming, makes many men implicite Atheists. **1660** BURNEY *Κέρδ. Δῶρον* (1661) 130 All the kings of the Earth joyn their mutual forces for the Crown, when they design Justice; they are implicite confederates.

c. Of ideas or feelings: Contained in the mind without being clearly formulated; vague, indefinite. Now *rare.*

1659 *Gentl. Calling* (1696) 107 Men take up general and implicite prejudices. **1664** BUTLER *Hud.* II. i. 547 'Tis no implicite, nice Aversion T' your Conversation, Meine, or Person. **1690** LOCKE *Hum. Und.* I. ii. (1695) 11 The Understanding hath an implicit Knowledge of these Principles, but not an explicit. **1738** HUME *Hum. Nat.* I. §15 Views and sentiments..so implicit and obscure that they often escape our strictest attention. **1863** GEO. ELIOT *Romola* II. iii, Tito's implicit desires were working themselves out now in very explicit thoughts.

d. Virtually or potentially contained *in.*

1657 *Burton's Diary* (1828) II. 371 All those things were implicit in my eye in the oath. **1848** KINGSLEY *Saint's Trag.* II. viii, To evolve the blessing implicit in all heaven's chastenings. **1874** SAYCE *Compar. Philol.* vi. 245 The undeveloped conceptions that lay implicit in it have been severally marked off one from the other.

3. a. ***implicit faith*** (= eccl. L. ***fides implicita***), faith in spiritual matters, not independently arrived at by the individual, but involved in or subordinate to the general belief of the Church; hence, resting on the authority of another without doubt or inquiry; unquestioning, unreserved, absolute. So ***implicit belief, confidence, obedience, submission,*** etc.

[**1601** BP. W. BARLOW *Def. Prot. Relig.* 70 *Fidem implicitam*, a faith involved and folded within the Church beleefe. **1605** A. WOTTON *Answ. Pop. Articles* 29 Their *fides implicita*, their *Colliers faith*, which teaches them to beleeve as the Church doth, but never instructs them..in al the severall matters of beleefe.] **1610** DONNE *Pseudo-Martyr* Pref. C iij a, The implicite faith and blinde assent which you were used to give heretofore to the spirituall supremacy. *Ibid.* 195 The implicite obedience imagin'd to bee vowed to the Church in baptisme. **1640** QUARLES *Enchirid.* IV. lxxxix, Hee that beleeves with an implicite Faith, is a meere Empricke in Religion. **1647** CLARENDON *Hist. Reb.* VI. §388 An implicit Reverence for the Court. **1786** T. JEFFERSON *Writ.* (1859) II. 30 An implicit respect paid to the laws of the land. **1820** W. IRVING *Sketch Bk.* I. 98, I would place implicit confidence in an Englishman's description of the regions beyond the cataracts of the Nile. **1845** M. PATTISON *Ess.* (1889) I. 16 The Frank..learned with implicit belief his faith from the mouth of the Roman priest. **1869** FREEMAN *Norm. Conq.* III. xii. 244 These glaring contradictions..are quite enough to hinder us from putting implicit faith in a single uncorroborated detail.

†**b.** Hence (erroneously): Absolute, unqualified, unmitigated, as in ***implicit ignorance.*** *Obs.*

1625 BACON *Ess., Unity Relig.* (Arb.) 429 When the Peace is grounded, but vpon an implicite ignorance. *c* **1645** HOWELL *Lett.* (1650) II. II. 23 Prince Maurice..hath a limited allowance; nor hath he any implicit command when he goes to the field. **1651** BIGGS *New Disp.* ¶268 An implicite ignorance of a true and adæquate remedy.

c. *transf.* Of persons; Characterized by implicit faith, credulity, or obedience. ? *Obs.*

1694 R. FRANCK *North. Mem.* (1812) 293 This curious Dish Implicit Walton calls the Swallow-Fish. **1699** BURNET 39 *Art.* vi. (1700) 78 Too implicite in adhering to our Education, or in Submitting to the Dictates of others. *a* **1734** NORTH *Exam.* III. vi. §92 (1740) 491 Many are implicite under what is called Authority. **1748** RICHARDSON *Clarissa* (1811) III. lxii. 362 Be implicit. Am I not your general? **1826** LAMB *Elia* Ser. II. *Popular Fallacies*, Men are not such implicit sheep as this comes to.

¶ ? Confused with, or a mistake for, *explicit.*

1727 *Philip Quarll* 29 Pray be implicite, what King have we now? **1752** FIELDING *Amelia* Wks. 1775 X. 49, I am very implicit you see; but we are all among friends.

implicitly (ɪmˈplɪsɪtlɪ), *adv.* [f. prec. + -LY².]

1. By implication; impliedly, inferentially.

1610 DONNE *Pseudo-martyr* vii. §33. 215 All circumstances..by which they labour to..infirme the zeale of our side..doe appeare in them directly or implicitely. **1651** HOBBES *Govt. & Soc.* xiv. §8. 217 Every civill Law hath a penalty annexed to it, either explicitly, or implicitly. **1692** BENTLEY *Boyle Lect.* i. 6 He that denies this, doth implicitly deny his Existence. **1775** JOHNSON *Tax. no Tyr.* 33 We virtually and implicitly allow the institutions. **1862** H. SPENCER *First Princ.* II. iv. §53 (1875) 174 A certain conclusion is implicitly contained in certain premises explicitly stated.

†**b.** Not professedly or intentionally. *Obs.*

1625 DONNE *Serm.* 3 Apr. 43 Hee that does good ignorantly, stupidly, inconsiderately, implicitely, does good, but hee does that good ill.

†**2.** In an involved or confused manner. *Obs.*

1635 MEDE *Ep. to Twisse* 15 July, Wks. (1672) IV. 828 We have not (or but very implicitly and obscurely) reduced that ancient Commemorative Sacrifice of Christians.

3. With implicit faith, confidence, submission, etc.; unquestioningly.

1650 HOBBES *De Corp. Pol.* 132 There may be more Obedience required in him that hath the Fundamental Points explicated unto him, than in him that hath received the same but implicitly. **1662** J. DAVIES *Mandelslo's Trav.* 96 The young Prince implicitely crediting what was told him by his Favourite. **1712** STEELE *Spect.* No. 497 ¶1 They would lay by their animosities implicitly, if he bid them be friends. **1788** REID *Active Powers* III. ii. (1803) 549 They believe implicitly whatever they are told. **1860** MAURY *Phys. Geog. Sea* (Low) ii. §113 The slightest impulse..is immediately felt and implicitly obeyed.

imˈplicitness. [f. as prec. + -NESS.] The quality of being implicit; implicit belief or obedience; unquestioning character.

1679 JENISON *Popish Plot* 39 Let us wholly resign our belief to blind implicitenes. **1696** BP. OF LONDON *Charge* 20 Lest..by too much Implicitness we suffer Error to grow upon us. **1731** *Charac. Sir R. Steele* in *Town Talk* (1790) 148 This implicitness of conduct is the great engine of Popery framed for the destruction of good nature. **1864** S. WILBERFORCE *Ess.* (1874) I. 387 The Church of England..bows to its every sentence with the implicitness of Faith.

†**imˈplicity.** *Obs. rare.* [? a. F. *implicité* (Cotgr.), irreg. f. *implicite*, L. *implicitus*: cf. *complicité*, COMPLICITY.] Entanglement, complication, involution.

1602 WARNER *Alb. Eng.* Epit. (1612) 390 Fortune, that had so long time fauoured this noble Familie, now wrought it into a long-lasting implicitie of mischiefs. **1611** COTGR., *Implicité*, an implicitie, intanglement.

implied (ɪmˈplaɪd), *ppl. a.* [f. IMPLY *v.* + -ED¹.] Contained or stated by implication; involved in what is expressed; necessarily intended though not expressed: see IMPLY *v.* Often in legal phrases as ***implied contract*** (see quot. 1767), ***trust, warranty,*** etc.: see these words.

1529 MORE *Comf. agst. Trib.* I. Wks. 1146/1 Vnder a certaine condicion, either expressed or implied. **1665** GLANVILL *Scepsis Sci.* 26 The implyed assertion that the Soul moves not the body. **1767** BLACKSTONE *Comm.* II. i. 8 Founded upon a tacit and implied assent. *Ibid.* xxx. 443 Implied [contracts] are such as reason and justice dictate, and which therefore the law presumes that every man undertakes to perform. **1818** JAS. MILL *Brit. India* II. v. viii. 663 Under the implied as well as declared expectation that he would supply what had been remiss. **1875** JOWETT *Plato* (ed. 2) I. 393 [He] has entered into an implied contract that he will do as we command him.

impliedly (ɪmˈplaɪɪdlɪ), *adv.* [f. as prec. + -LY².] By implication, implicitly.

c **1400** *Apol. Loll.* 17 Þis sentence is clere..and publischid expresly & ympliȝeþly. *c* **1449** PECOCK *Repr.* II. v. 164 It is ther yn impliedli bi Holi Scripture leeful. *a* **1603** T. CARTWRIGHT *Confut. Rhem. N.T.* (1618) 664 Although not expresly, yet impliedly to a sufficient understanding. **1769** BLACKSTONE *Comm.* IV. iv. 63 This statute does not prohibit, but rather impliedly allows, any innocent recreation or amusement. **1884** SIR C. S. C. BOWEN in *Law Times Rep.* L. 217/2 The Act itself..does not say so in words, but it says so impliedly. **1964** *Mod. Law Rev.* XXVII. III. 266 Furthermore, it must be noted that union officials could equally be drawn into a 'conspiracy to intimidate impliedly'. **1970** [see CORPS 2 b].

impling (ˈɪmplɪŋ). *rare.* [f. IMP *sb.* + -LING.] A little imp.

1780 E. B. GREENE tr. *Apollon. Rhod.* IV. 206 There hissing implings boast their noxious birth. **1835** BECKFORD *Recoll.* 179 Withered hags, and meagre implings.

†**imˈplod,** *v. Obs. rare.* [f. IM-¹ + (?) PLOD *v.*] *trans.* To cause to plod, to involve in toilsome labour.

1609 LADY BOYLE in *Lismore Papers* Ser. II. (1887) I. 83, I am not imploded in commonwelth bisness as you are. **1642** ROGERS *Naaman* 19 The meer implodding and sadding thy thoughts. *Ibid.* 124 An heart overmuch implodded in the earth.

implode (ɪmˈpləʊd), *v.* [f. IM-¹ + L. *plōdĕre, plaudĕre* to clap, after EXPLODE; cf. IMPLOSION.]

1. *intr.* To burst inwards (cf. IMPLOSION 1). Also *trans.* and *fig.*

1881 TAIT in *Nature* XXV. 92 This bulb implodes, then the pressure is applied to the interior of the protected bulb, which, in its turn, explodes. **1913** J. MURRAY *Ocean* v. 97 Only those parts of the structure would be burst inwards ('imploded') into which water could not enter rapidly enough to equalise the pressure on the two sides, say, of an iron plate. **1973** *Sci. Amer.* Mar. 46/2 Applied evenly around the surface, these forces would suddenly implode the pellet to a density 100 times higher than that of lead.

2. *trans.* To utter or pronounce by implosion. Hence **imˈplodent,** an implosive sound (Funk); **imˈploded, imˈploding** *ppl. adjs.*

1963 *Observer* 17 Mar. 3/3 The 'jet' could be in the outer part of the galaxy, and might represent part of the imploding star which has broken away. **1964** M. MCLUHAN *Understanding Media* I. iii. 35 In our present electric age the imploding or contracting energies of our world now clash with the old expansionist and traditional patterns of organization. *Ibid.* v. 51 Individualism is not possible in an electrically patterned and imploded society.

imˈplorable, *a. rare.* [f. IM-¹ + L. *plōrābilis* lamentable, or f. IMPLORE *v.* + -ABLE.]

†**1.** Lamentable; = DEPLORABLE. *Obs.*

1535 STEWART *Cron. Scot.* II. 444 The grit ouirthraw and thirling of his ring, To him all tyme wes so implorabill.

2. That can or may be implored.

imploration (ɪmplɒˈreɪʃən). [a. obs. F. *imploration* (16th c.), or ad. L. *implōrātiōn-em*, noun of action from *implōrāre* to IMPLORE.]

1. The action of imploring; tearful supplication, earnest beseeching.

1577 FENTON *Gold. Epist.* 109 Dauid vsed no other solicitor for the remouing of Gods wrathe, then the imploration of a penitent heart. **1613–18** DANIEL *Coll. Hist. Eng.* (1626) 6 Their implorations preuailed not. **1658** COKAINE *Poems, Let. to Ld. Mohun* (1669) 81 The fluent Singer..would In imploration for Aide grow old. **1841** CATLIN *N. Amer. Ind.* (1844) II. lviii. 243 Their earnest implorations for divine forgiveness and mercy. **1889** LYMAN ABBOTT in *Chr. Union* (N.Y.) 10 Jan. 48 With the outcry of despairing imploration.

†**2.** Deploring; lamentation. *Obs. rare.*

1607 TOPSELL *Four-f. Beasts* (1658) 163 In token of their innocency, and imploration of their own weakness.

†**imploˈrator.** *Obs. rare*⁻¹. [Agent-noun in Latin form, f. *implōrāre* to IMPLORE; cf. obs. F. *implorateur* (16th c.).] One who implores or supplicates.

1602 SHAKS. *Ham.* I. iii. 129 Meere implorators of vnholy Sutes, Breathing like sanctified and pious bonds, The better to beguile.

imploratory (ɪmˈplɒrətərɪ), *a. rare.* [f. as prec.; see -ORY.] Of imploring or beseeching nature.

1832 *Examiner* 241/1 The tone of Lord Grey's speech..is depressed and imploratory. **1837** CARLYLE *Misc. Ess., Diam. Neckl.* vii. (1872) V. 164 On the 21st of March goes off that long exculpatory imploratory letter.

implore (ɪmˈplɔə(r)), *v.* Also 6 *Sc.* imploir. [ad. L. *implōrāre* to invoke or entreat with tears, f. *im-* (IM-¹) + *plōrāre* to weep, lament. Cf. F. *implorer* (R. Estienne, 1549).]

1. *trans.* **a.** To beg or pray for (aid, favour, pardon, etc.) with tearful or touching entreaties; to ask for in supplication; to beseech. †Formerly sometimes with two objects.

c **1540** tr. *Pol. Verg. Eng. Hist.* (Camden) I. 67 He himselfe imploringe the assistaunce and faithe of Carthumandua. **1563** WINȜET *Four Scoir Thre Quest.* Wks. 1888 I. 131 Haif we nocht iust cause to imploir the grace of God? **1632** J. HAYWARD tr. *Biondi's Eromena* 152 Hee might plainely discerne her dolorous gesture in the act of imploring his succour. **1654–66** LD. ORRERY *Parthenissa* (1676) 640 Permit me to implore you the promise that I shall receive no worse usage from you. **1687** DRYDEN *Hind & P.* III. 107 My daily bread is literally implor'd. **1791** MRS. RADCLIFFE *Rom. Forest* viii, He threw himself at her feet to implore forgiveness. **1849** MACAULAY *Hist. Eng.* vii. II. 224 He was perpetually surrounded by suitors imploring his interest.

b. To beseech, entreat, petition (a person) with deep emotion (to do something).

1603 SHAKS. *Meas. for M.* I. ii. 185 Implore her..that she make friends To the strict deputie. **1707** LADY M. W. MONTAGU *Lett. to Anne Wortley* 2 May (1887) I. 37, I have already told you I love you, and implored you not to forget me. **1838** LYTTON *Alice* I. x, 'Talk not thus, I implore you, Evelyn.' **1867** SMILES *Huguenots Eng.* xii. (1880) 204 The ladies of the household..implored him, with tears in their eyes, not to leave them.

c. To utter as a supplication.

1850 F. E. Smedley *Frank Fairlegh* xv. 136 'Gentlemen, don't ring the bells, pray,' implored the old man. **1853** C. Brontë *Villette* xvi, 'Do not let me think of them too often, too much, or too fondly', I implored. **1887** M. Corelli *Thelma* III. III. ii. 251 'Let me go with thee!' he implored, in broken accents. **1891** Hardy *Group Noble Dames* 101 'Oh, take it away—please take it away!' she implored.

2. *intr.* To utter touching supplications; const. *for* (a thing), *of* (a person).

1500–20 Dunbar *Poems* lxxxv. 55 Implore, adore, thow indeflore, To mak our oddis evyne. **1632** Lithgow *Trav.* VIII. 351 Holding up my hand, and imploring for our lives. **1870** H. Smart *Race for Wife* x, She flopped down on her knees, and implored for mercy. **1904** L. T. Meade *Love Triumphant* ii. 15, I implored of Granny to let us leave the cottage.

Hence **im'plored** *ppl. a.*

1659 Milton *Civ. Power Eccl. Causes* Wks. (1847) 413/2, I distrust not, through God's implored assistance, to make [it] plain by these following arguments.

†**im'plore,** *sb. Obs. rare.* [f. prec. vb.] An act of imploring; imploration, entreaty.

1590 Spenser *F.Q.* II. v. 37 He..urged sore, With percing wordes and pittifull implore, Him hasty to arise. **1607** *Barley-Breake* (1877) 29 Whose sudden sight her Fathers life-strings crackt, And falling downe, he ended his implore.

†**im'plorement.** *Obs. rare.* [f. IMPLORE *v.* + -MENT.] = IMPLORATION.

1611 Cotgr., *Requeste*,..intreatie, prayer, beseeching, inuocation, implorement.

im'plorer. *rare.* [f. as prec. + -ER[1].] One who implores.

1611 Cotgr., *Implorateur*, an implorer, beseecher [etc.]. *c* **1611** Chapman *Iliad* Ep. Ded., The most humble and faithful implorer for all the graces to your highnesse eternised by your diuine Homer. **1690** Boyle *Chr. Virtuoso* II. Wks. 1772 VI. 717 Those assistances, that God gives the faithful implorers, to enable them to obey and please him.

im'ploring, *vbl. sb.* [f. as prec. + -ING[1].] Supplication, beseeching.

1611 Cotgr., *Imploration*, an imploring,..beseeching. **1654–66** Ld. Orrery *Parthenissa* (1676) 513, I made many pressing implorings to suspend a little longer my return. **1896** in *Daily News* 27 May 7/4 We knelt at the Throne of the King of Kings with humble and earnest imploring.

im'ploring, *ppl. a.* [f. as prec. + -ING[2].] That implores or supplicates.

1654–66 Ld. Orrery *Parthenissa* (1676) 197 The fair Sophonisba, not as a Tryumphant Mistris, but an imploring Prisoner. **1771** Goldsm. *Hist. Eng.* I. 307 He threw himself in the most imploring manner upon his knees before his uncle. **1829** Southey *All for Love* VI. xxix, His imploring eye Bespake compassion. **1866** G. Macdonald *Ann. Q. Neighb.* xxvi. (1878) 452 She gave him one imploring look.

Hence **im'ploringly** *adv.*, in an imploring or supplicating way; **im'ploringness,** imploring quality.

1810 Southey *Kehama* x. ix, She stretch'd her hands imploringly. **1863** Mrs. Whitney *Faith Gartney* xxxvi. 334 Threading her way with a silent imploringness among the throng. **1876** Geo. Eliot *Dan. Der.* lxv, His voice took an affectionate imploringness. **1881** H. James *Portr. Lady* xxxvii, 'What on earth has he done to her?' he asked again imploringly.

implosion (ɪm'pləʊʒən). [n. of action from IMPLODE; cf. EXPLOSION.]

1. The bursting inward of a vessel from external pressure.

1880 W. B. Carpenter in *19th Cent.* Apr. 615 A sealed glass tube containing air, having been lowered (within a copper case) to a depth of 2,000 fathoms, was reduced to a fine powder almost like snow, by what Sir Wyville Thomson ingeniously characterised as an implosion.

2. *Phonetics.* (See quot.)

1877 Sweet *Handbk. Phonetics* §224 The implosion consists in closing the glottis simultaneously with the stop position, and then compressing the air between the glottis stoppage and the mouth one.

3. *fig.* (as the opposite of *explosion*).

1960 J. G. Ballard in D. Knight *100 Yrs. Sci. Fiction* (1969) 350 The population of Sumatra, for example, has declined by over fifteen per cent in the last twenty years... Do you realize that only two or three decades ago the Neo-Malthusians were talking about a 'world population explosion'? In fact, it's an implosion. **1964** M. McLuhan *Understanding Media* I. vii. 71 The rush of students into our universities is not explosion but implosion. *Ibid.* II. x. 92 Our speed-up today is not a slow explosion outward from center to margins but an instant implosion and an interfusion of space and functions.

implosive (ɪm'pləʊsɪv), *a.* and *sb.* [f. as prec. after EXPLOSIVE.] **1.** *Phonetics.* **a.** *adj.* Formed by implosion. **b.** *sb.* A sound formed by implosion.

1877 Sweet *Handbk. Phonetics* §224 Implosive Stops. **1880** Sayce *Introd. Sc. Lang.* iv. 285 Of the same nature as the clicks are the implosives peculiar to Saxon German, where no distinction is made between *d* and *t*, or *b* and *p*. **1890** Sweet *Primer Phonetics* §90 Some sounds are produced without either out- or in-breathing, but solely with the air in the throat or mouth. The 'implosives' are formed in the former, the suction-stops or 'clicks' in the latter way.

2. *fig.* (Cf. IMPLOSION 3.)

1964 M. McLuhan *Understanding Media* II. xi. 111 The implosive (compressional) character of the electric technology. *Ibid.* xix. 185 The implosive speed of the airplane. **1967** *Listener* 8 June 744/1 Television has an implosive effect on a culture.

Hence **im'plosively** *adv.*; **im'plosiveness.**

1877 Sweet *Handbk. Phonetics* §224 In Saxon German there is no distinction between *t* and *d*, etc., both being half-voiced, with the stop formed implosively. **1953** C. E. Bazell *Ling. Form* 42 If all initial occlusives are explosive and all final occlusives are implosive, it is obvious that two distinct conventions (explosiveness of initials and implosiveness of finals) need not be postulated.

imploy, -er, -ing, obs. forms of EMPLOY, etc.

imploy, var. of IMPLY: see EMPLOY 5.

†**im'ployable,** *a. Obs. rare.* [a. obs. F. *imployable*, f. *im-* (IM-[2]) + *ployer, plier* to bend, PLY.] Inflexible.

1603 Florio *Montaigne* I. i. 2 The effect of a couragious and imployable minde. *Ibid.* 408 Perswasion..of the fatall and imployable prescription of their dayes doth..embolden them in dangers.

†**im'ployment.** *Obs. rare*$^{-1}$. [f. *imploy* IMPLY + -MENT.] Implication, entanglement.

1598 Florio, *Impiego*, an imployment [**1611** an infoulding, an imployment].

imployment, obs. form of EMPLOYMENT; also, by confusion, of IMPLEMENT.

†**implume,** *a. Obs. rare.* [ad. L. *implūmis*, f. *im-* (IM-[2]) + *plūma* feather, PLUME.] Unfeathered, unfledged.

1536 Bellenden *Cron. Scot.* (1821) I. p. cxi, Thocht thow pas furth, as bird implume, to licht. **1658** Phillips, *Implume*, bare, without feathers.

†**im'plume,** *v.*[1] *Obs. rare*$^{-0}$. [? f. prec., or its source; cf IMPLUMED.] (See quot.)

1604 Cawdrey *Table Alph.*, *Implume*, to pull off the feathers.

implume (ɪm'pl(j)u:m), *v.*[2] *rare.* = EMPLUME *v.* 2, to plume, to feather.

1612 W. Parkes *Curtaine-Dr.* (1876) 28 That like to Iris had of late implum'd His curled branches. **1888** Swinburne in *19th Cent.* XXIII. 318 Swan-soft feathers of snow with whose luminous burden the branches implumed Hung heavily.

im'plumed, *a. rare.* [f. IM-[2] + PLUMED; cf. IMPLUME *a.* and *v.*[1]] Unfeathered, unfledged; deprived of feathers.

1604 Drayton *Owl* (R.), The poor implumed birds..Can point and say, This feather once was mine. **1605** A. Willet *Hexapla in Genesin* Ded., I..haue brought forth my implumed and vnfeathered birds. **1784** R. Bage *Barham Downs* I. 346 The implumed biped, lord of the earth. **1819** H. Busk *Vestriad* I. 367 Plum'd or implum'd the biped you despoil.

†**im'plumous,** *a. Obs. rare*$^{-0}$. [f. IM-[2] + PLUMOUS, L. *plūmōsus*, f. *plūma*: cf. L. *implūmis* IMPLUME *a.*] = prec.

1755 Johnson, *Unfeathered*, implumous; naked of feathers. **1818** in Todd; hence in mod. Dicts.

implunge (ɪm'plʌndʒ), *v.* Also 6 **emplonge,** 7 **emplunge.** [f. IM-[1] + PLUNGE *v.*] *trans.* To plunge *in* or *into* (also †*to*). Now *rare.*

1590 Spenser *F.Q.* III. x. 17 Malbecco..Into huge waves of griefe and gealosye Full deepe emplonged was. **1601** Dent *Pathw. Heaven* 324 The most dangerous gulfe of ignorance, wherein multitudes are implunged. **1639** Fuller *Holy War* I. xv. 22 He..implunged himself in much just hatred for his unjust dealing and treachery. **1855** Bailey *Mystic* 130 As since, In mountain tarn volcanic, throne and crown,..The imperial pagan of the west implunged.

†**im'pluvious,** *a. rare*$^{-0}$. [f. IM-[1] + PLUVIOUS.] 'Wet with rain' (Blount *Glossogr.* 1656). Hence †**im'pluviousness** (Bailey vol. II. 1727).

‖**impluvium** (ɪm'pl(j)u:vɪəm). [L. *impluvium*, f. *impluĕre* to rain into.] In ancient Roman houses, the square basin situated in the middle of the atrium or hall, which received the rain-water from the COMPLUVIUM or open space in the roof. (But sometimes also used in the same sense as *compluvium.*) **b.** (See quot. 1811.)

1811 Hooper *Med. Dict.*, *Impluvium*, the shower-bath. An embrocation. **1823** Crabb *Technol. Dict.* s.v., The impulvium differs from the compluvium, according to Festus in this, that the rain falls down into the Impluvium, but collects from different parts of the roof into the Compluvium. **1832** Gell *Pompeiana* I. viii. 146 The atrium ..with its impluvium near the centre, under which was a cistern. **1834** Lytton *Pompeii* I. iii, A square, shallow reservoir for rain water, (classically termed *impluvium*). **1856** Blackmore *C. Nowell* vi. (1881) 21 Trouble overflowed the impluvium.

imply (ɪm'plaɪ), *v.* Forms: α. 4 **enpliȝe,** 6 **emplie, -plye.** β. 4 **inpliȝe,** 5 **ymplie,** 4–7 **implie, -plye,** 6– **imply.** γ. 6–7 **imploy,** 6 **employ**: see EMPLOY *v.* (sense 5). [a. OF. *emplie-r*:—L. *implicāre* to infold, involve, f. *im-* (IM-[1]) + *plicāre* to fold; with subseq. substitution of the L. form of the prefix. The OF. vb. was orig. inflected, according to position of the stress: inf. *empli'er*, pres. ind. *em'pleie, em'pleies, em'pleiet, empli'ons, empli'ez, em'pleient*, imperative *em'pleie, empli'ez*; whence, by levelling, arose the two variant forms (1) *emplier*, and (2) *empleier*, later *emploier, employer*. Of these, mod.F. retains only the latter, while Eng. has *imply* from OF., and EMPLOY from later 15th c. F. *Imply* retained the classical L. sense of *implicare*, from which sense 2 appears to be a strictly English development; but instances of exchange between *imply* and *employ* are not infrequent in 16–17th c. (See sense 4 below, and EMPLOY *v.* 5.)]

†**1.** *trans.* To enfold, enwrap, entangle, involve: in *lit.* and *fig.* senses. *Obs.*

c **1374** Chaucer *Boeth.* v. met. i. 117 (Camb. MS.) The wateres I-medlyd wrappith or implieth many fortunel happis. *c* **1380** Wyclif *Serm.* Sel. Wks. I. 270 ȝif a prelate implie him wiþ seculer nedis. *c* **1400** *Apol. Loll.* 3 Hatyng to be enpliȝed wiþ seculer bisines. *c* **1450** tr. *De Imitatione* III. xxviii. 97 Wherto wrappist þou & ympliest þiself? *Ibid.* xxix. 98 Implie þe not wiþ þinges þat are not committed to þe. **1590** Spenser *F.Q.* I. iv. 31 An hatefull Snake, the which his taile uptyes In many folds, and mortall sting implyes. *Ibid.* vi. 6 Phœbus..His blushing face in foggy cloud implyes. *c* **1611** Chapman *Iliad* VI. 315 Lovely Theano took the veil, and with it she implies The great Palladium. **1823** Lamb *Elia* Ser. II. Pref., If it be egotism to imply and twine with his own identity the griefs and affections of another [etc.].

2. To involve or comprise as a necessary logical consequence; to involve the truth or existence of (something not expressly asserted or maintained).

1529 More *Dyaloge* I. Wks. 127/2 Two such thinges as imply contradiction. *a* **1557** Mrs. Basset tr. *More On the Passion* ibid. 1363/1 Y^e^ thing as ye principal point y^t^ briefly emplyeth al the rest. **1581** Lambarde *Eiren.* II. iii. (1588) 135 This 'Assault' doth not alwayes necessarily emplie a hitting. **1620** Granger *Div. Logike* 344 That axiome, is false which is inconsistent..or agreeth not with it selfe, but implieth a contradiction in it. **1653** Walton *Angler* i. 13 In Job.. mention is made of fish-hooks, which must imply Anglers in those times. **1789** Burke *Corr.* (1844) III. 127 There are situations in which despair does not imply inactivity. **1862** Stanley *Jew. Ch.* I. xvi, Often where no commendation is expressly given, it is distinctly implied.

b. With substantive clause as object.

1681–6 J. Scott *Chr. Life* (1747) III. 498 The Resurrection of the same Body doth not necessarily imply that all the same Matter shall be raised. **1876** Gladstone *Homeric Synchr.* 162 The text of the Poems implies that Sidon was the great and leading city.

c. Of a word of name: To involve by signification or import; to signify, import, mean.

c **1630** Risdon *Surv. Devon* §88 (1810) 85 *Villa* implieth a court house, or chief place in the lord's manor. **1660** Willsford *Scales Comm.* 21 This trading..is called Barter, derived from *Barato*, implying an exchange of commodities. **1737** [S. Berington] *G. di Lucca's Mem.* 126 Like a true Father of his People, which the Name..implies.

†**d.** To signify as much as, to be equivalent to.

1634 Sir T. Herbert *Trav.* 151 The horses feed usually of barley and chopt-straw put into a bag, and fastned about their heads, which implyes their manger.

†**e.** ? To mean or intend *for. Obs.*

1663 Cowley *Verses sev. Occas.*, *Ode Harvey* iii, From all the Souls that living Buildings rear, Whether imply'd for Earth, or Sea, or Air,..A strict Account to him is hourly brought.

3. To express indirectly; to insinuate, hint at.

1581 J. Bell *Haddon's Answ. Osor.* 36 He that forebyddeth a thyng to be done in after tyme, doth hee not covertly emplye that the same was done before? **1593** Drayton *Eclogues* i. 27 Whose wondrous workes thy Essence doe imply. **1641** Milton *Ch. Govt.* Pref., The reasons thereof are not formally..set downe, because to him that heeds attentively..they easily imply themselves. **1774** Goldsm. *Nat. Hist.* (1862) II. II. v. 49 His figure implies the stupidity of his disposition. **1849** Lytton *Caxtons* iii, Dimly implying some sort of jest, which he kept all to himself. **1870** Freeman *Norm. Conq.* (ed. 2) I. App. 636 It is not directly asserted, but it seems to be implied. *Mod.* What do you mean to imply?

†**4.** = EMPLOY *v. Obs.*

a **1533** Ld. Berners *Gold. Bk. M. Aurel.* (1546) Ee vj b, To leaue theyr riches to theyr vicious chyldren yl implied. **1658–9** Eliz. Bodvile in *Hatton Corr.* (Camden) 17 A mach which your Mother has implied a frind..about for you.

¶**5.** †**a.** = APPLY *v.* 5. *Obs.*

a **1625** Boys *Wks.* (1629) 264 That tenant deserues to be thrust out of house and home..that implieth all the best roomes vnto the basest offices.

†**b.** To ascribe, attribute: = APPLY *v.* 11. *Obs.*

a **1655** Webster & Rowley *Cure for Cuckold* I. i, Whence might this distaste arise?..Is it..your perverse and peevish will, To which I most imply it?

im'plyment, obs. f. EMPLOYMENT.

1614 G. Trevelyan in *Trevelyan Papers* (Camden) III. 136 Who landed in this harbor..and dispatcht that implyment of Scotland according his owne desyre.

impne, obs. form of HYMN.

impocket (ɪm'pɒkɪt), *v.* Also **em-**. [IM-[1].] *trans.* To put into one's pocket; to pocket.

1728 [? De Foe] *Carleton's Mem.* 57 The vulgar Sort stood staring, and with their Hands impocketted. **1796** *Mod. Gulliver's Trav.* 68 As soon as I had impocketed the gifts, he waved me to sit by him. **1884** *Punch* 1 Nov. 210/2 I did empocket thy gratulation [cf. Shaks. *Twel. N.* II. iii. 27]. **1887** M. B. Edwards *Next of Kin* II. ii. 17 There he sat.. hands impocketed.

†**im'poignant,** *a. Obs. rare*$^{-1}$. [f. IM-[2] + POIGNANT.] Not sharp or piquant.

1733 Cheyne *Eng. Malady* II. v. §10 (1734) 168 Such unprovoking and impoignant Viands.

impoison, -ing, etc., obs. var. EMPOISON, etc.

†**im'poke**, *v. Obs.* In 7 impoake. [f. IM-¹ + POKE *sb.*: after F. *empocher*.] = IMPOUCH.
1611 COTGR., *Empoché*, impoaked, impouched. *Ibid.*, *Ensaché*, insachelled, impoaked.

†**im'polarily**, *adv. Obs. rare*⁻¹. [f. IM-² + POLARY + -LY².] Not according to polarity.
1646 SIR T. BROWNE *Pseud. Ep.* II. iii. 68 Being impolarily adjoyned unto a more vigorous Loadstone, it will in a short time exchange it poles.

im'polarizable, *a.* [f. IM-² + POLARIZABLE.] Not capable of being polarized.
1882 MAIER tr. *Hospitalier's Electr.* II. iv. 240 The same may be said of Cloris Baudet's so-called impolarizable battery.

impolder (ɪm'pəʊldə(r)), *v.* [ad. Du. *inpolderen*: see IM-¹ and POLDER¹.] *trans.* = EMPOLDER *v.* Hence **im'poldering** *vbl. sb.*
1898 D. S. MELDRUM *Holland & Hollanders* 209 Into the sea that it is proposed to impolder, there falls, at Kampen, the river Ysel. **1899** *Pall Mall Gaz.* 13 Apr. 4/2 This impoldering and pumping, the raising and keeping of dykes and dams. **1901** *Speaker* 9 Mar. 633/2 It was about this time that Haarlem Mere was impoldered. **1929** *Encycl. Brit.* XI. 648/1 A great part of the Netherlands has now been impoldered. *Ibid.* 648/2 The largest impoldering scheme on record has now been commenced.

impolicy (ɪm'pɒlɪsɪ). [f. IM-² + POLICY, after *impolitic*: cf. F. *impolice*.] The quality of being impolitic; bad policy; inexpediency.
1747 MALLET *Amyntor & Theod.* Pref. 11 Those who governed Scotland under him, with no less cruelty than impolicy, made the people of that country desperate. **1798** MRQ. WELLESLEY in Owen *Desp.* (1877) 45 An act of such flagrant impolicy and injustice. **1827** HALLAM *Const. Hist.* (1876) II. viii. 92 The war itself was produced by the King's impolicy. **1856** FROUDE *Hist. Eng.* (1858) II. ix. 370 [They] expressed themselves in no measured terms at the impolicy of this most foolish action.

†**im'polished**, *a. Obs.* [f. IM-² + POLISHED.] Unpolished; devoid of polish; rude, unrefined.
1583 STUBBES *Anat. Abus.* I. Ep. Ded. (1877) 6 So rude and impolished a worke. **1617** MORYSON *Itin.* III. 68 At Constantinople.. the houses are commonly of impolished stone and flint. **1628** EARLE *Microcosm.*, *Blunt Man* (Arb.) 55 A blunt Man is one whose wit is better pointed then his behauiour, and that course, and Impollisht. **1684** N. S. *Crit. Enq. Edit. Bible* XXV. 226 His impolish'd and erroneous translation.

impolite (ɪmpəʊ'laɪt), *a.* [ad. L. *impolīt-us*, f. *im-* (IM-²) + *polīt-us* polished, POLITE. Cf. F. *impoli* (16th c.), It. *impolito* (Florio).]
†**1.** Not polished; wanting polish or smoothness of surface. *Obs.*
1621 BURTON *Anat. Mel.* III. i. II. iii. (1651) 423 Withered old men.. very harsh and impolite to the eye. **1657** TOMLINSON *Renou's Disp.* 459 Outwardly scabre and impolite.
†**2.** Wanting polish or refinement; unpolished, rude, rough. *Obs.*
1612 DRAYTON *Poly-olb.* x. Notes 169 Lest some more impolite hand hath sow'd many patches of base cloth into that more rich web. **1669** BOYLE *Contn. New Exp.* II. Pref. (1682) 9 A Book so impolite as this is. **1699** EVELYN *Mem.* (1857) III. 378 All those windings and meanders which rendered the study deserted as dull and impolite.
3. Wanting polite or courteous manners; uncivil, discourteous, rude.
1739 G. OGLE *Gualtherus & Griselda* 43 Polite or Impolite, I weigh not what is thought, but what is Right. **1836** JEFFREY *Let.* in Ld. Cockburn *Life* II. cxxviii, I am afraid I must have appeared very impolite in not having previously answered your letter of the 11th. **1870** MISS BROUGHTON *Red as Rose* I. 62 About the impolitest remark she could make.

†**impo'lited**, *a. Obs.* [f. L. *impolīt-us* see prec.) + -ED¹.] = prec. 2.
1597 A. M. tr. *Guillemeau's Fr. Chirurg.* *6b, Defilede and poluted with my impolitede stile.

impolitely (ɪmpəʊ'laɪtlɪ), *adv.* [f. IMPOLITE *a.* + -LY².] In an impolite manner; uncivilly, discourteously, rudely.
1730-6 in BAILEY (folio). **1775** in ASH. **1855** MACAULAY *Hist. Eng.* xv. III. 568 The bill.. was impolitely described as being neither good English nor good sense. **1865** *Athenæum* 28 Jan 122/1 They have, however, one virtue,.. they rarely lose their temper or speak impolitely.

impoliteness (ɪmpəʊ'laɪtnɪs). [f. as prec. + -NESS.] The quality of being impolite; want of politeness; incivility, discourtesy, rudeness.
a **1773** CHESTERF. *Charac.*, *Walpole* (1777) 20 The impoliteness of his manners seemed to attest his sincerity. **1837** *Lett. fr. Madras* (1843) 114 One has to dismiss one's own visitors, as they generally think it an impoliteness to go away of their own accord. **1839** THACKERAY *Major Gahagan* iv, It would have been the height of impoliteness.

impolitic (ɪm'pɒlɪtɪk), *a.* [f. IM-² + POLITIC. Cf. F. *impolitique* (1750 in Hatz.-Darm.).] Not politic; not according to good policy; unsuitable for the end proposed or desired; inexpedient.
a **1600** HOOKER (J.), He that exhorteth to beware of an enemy's policy, doth not give counsel to be impolitick. **1679** PRANCE *Addit. Narr. Pop. Plot* 19 As a Salvo for that impolitique Murder. **1783** A. HAMILTON in Sparks *Corr. Amer. Rev.* (1853) IV. 13, I often feel a mortification, which it would be impolitic to express. **1797** BURKE *Regic. Peace* iii. Wks. VIII. 353 The most unjust and impolitick of all things, unequal taxation. **1884** *Manch. Exam.* 21 May 5/3 It is impolitic to adopt an attitude of hostility to what is inevitable.

†**im'politic**, *v. Obs.* In 7 -ique. [f. IM-¹ + POLITIC *a.*] *trans.* To incorporate or engraft into the body politic.
1613 CHAPMAN *Bussy D'Ambois* Plays 1873 II. 149 Wee may impolitique our selues (as t'were) Into the kingdomes body politique.

†**impo'litical**, *a. Obs.* [f. IM-² + POLITICAL.] = IMPOLITIC *a.*
1748 RICHARDSON *Clarissa* lvii. (1811) VIII. 261 Out upon me for an impolitical wretch! **1775** W. CRAIG *Serm.* (1808) II. 35 Instead of being a prudent or humane Contrivance the Sabbath would become a very impolitical and hurtful one. **1791-1823** D'ISRAELI *Cur. Lit.*, *Polit. Nicknames*, The impolitical prosecution of Sacheverell. **1843** J. H. NEWMAN *Lett.* (1891) II. 414 A very impolitical step.

impo'litically, *adv.* [f. prec. + -LY².] = IMPOLITICLY.
1768 *Woman of Honor* III. 232 The solid advantages.. have been so impolitically sacrificed. **1816** SCOTT *Old Mort.* vi, A mere mask for treason, very impolitically allowed to those who are too great cowards to wear their principles barefaced. **1881** *Athenæum* 27 Aug. 263/2 It was near here that Ragnar Lodbrok was so impolitically cast into a pit full of snakes.

impo'liticalness. [f. as prec. + -NESS.] = IMPOLITICNESS, IMPOLICY.
1695 J. SAGE *Article* Wks. 1844 I. 275 The impoliticalness, the uncatholicalness of most, if not all, of these propositions.

impoliticly (ɪm'pɒlɪtɪklɪ), *adv.* [f. IMPOLITIC *a.* + -LY².] In an impolitic manner; not in accordance with good policy; inexpediently.
1608 BACON *Rep. in Ho. Comm.* in *Resuscitatio* (1661) 30 In the pursuites of their own Remedies.. they do it so impolitiquely. **1652-62** HEYLIN *Cosmogr.* II. (1682) 66 Impoliticklу dismembred from the chief of the House. **1751** JOHNSON *Rambler* No. 97 ¶33 Even fine faces, often seen, are less regarded than new faces, the proper punishment of showy girls, for rendering themselves so impoliticklу cheap. **1854** H. ROGERS *Ess.* (1860) II. 83 Those.. who have most impoliticly styled themselves.. the advocates of 'moral necessity'.

im'politicness. [f. as prec. + -NESS.] The quality of being impolitic; impolicy.
1680 R. MANSELL *Narr. Popish Plot* Addr. cij, The same wretched Impolitickness have they used in their other Actings. **1745** *Lond. Mag.* Index s.v. *Hungary, Queen of*, The Impolitickness of joining with her in an offensive War.

†**impo'llute**, *a. Obs.* Also 4 **inpolute**. [ad. L. *impollūt-us*, f. *im-* (IM-²) + *pollūtus* POLLUTED. Cf. F. *impollu*, in 1508 *impolut* (Godef.).] = next.
1382 WYCLIF *Heb.* vii. 26 It bycaam that such a man were bischop to vs, hooly, innosent, inpolute [*gloss* or ful clene]. **1563-87** FOXE *A. & M.* (1596) 279/1 A true bishop.. innocent, impollute.

†**impo'lluted**, *a. Obs.* [f. prec. + -ED¹; or f. IM-² + POLLUTED.] Unpolluted, undefiled.
1548 UDALL, etc. *Erasm. Par. John* xvii. 103 Kepe thou these cleane and impolluted from all contagious infeccions of the worlde. **1585** T. WASHINGTON tr. *Nicholay's Voy.* III. x. 86b, Too be impolluted of body and observants of virginite. **1662** H. MORE *Philos. Writ.* Pref. Gen. 9 The natural cohesion of Truth with an impolluted Soul.
So †**impollution**. *Obs. rare*⁻⁰.
1611 FLORIO, *Impolutione*, impolution, vndefilednesse.

‖**imponderabilia** (ɪm,pɒndərə'bɪlɪə), *sb. pl.* [neut. pl. of mod.L. *imponderābilis*, things that cannot be weighed.] Imponderables, imponderable factors.
1925 W. J. LOCKE *Great Pandolfo* xxiv. 300 A man beaten not by Fortune, not by the hostility of material influences, but by spiritual imponderabilia almost on the borderland of sanity and unreason. **1933** *Times Lit. Suppl.* 27 Apr. 283/2 The *imponderabilia* that constitute 'Toryism'. **1938** E. POUND *Let.* 12 May (1971) 316, I think Eliot would prefer your emendation. At any rate we are on ground of imponderabilia. **1942** E. WAUGH *Put out More Flags* ii. 111 Every week we have chamber music. There are certain *imponderabilia* at the Old Mill which, to be crude, have their market value. **1957** *Times* 17 Dec. 9/7 Tactically, the chiefs are in a weak position: but nobody can say what psychological *imponderabilia* may not be raked up if the attack is carried further.

imponderability (ɪm,pɒndərə'bɪlɪtɪ). [f. next + -ITY.] The quality of being imponderable.
1794 G. ADAMS *Nat. & Exp. Philos.* I. xii. 511 The imponderability of this principle [phlogiston] may be considered as a kind of axiom. **1847** in CRAIG.

imponderable (ɪm'pɒndərəb(ə)l), *a.* and *sb.* [f. IM-² + PONDERABLE. (Cf. F. *impondérable* Dict. Acad. 1835.)] **A.** *adj.* Not ponderable.
a. (Freq. in *Physics.*) Having no weight; destitute of weight: applied formerly to light, heat, electricity, etc., regarded as material substances, and later to the luminiferous 'ether'. Also *fig.*, incalculable, unthinkable.
1794 G. ADAMS *Nat. & Exp. Philos.* I. xi. 449 Phlogiston, a substance as imponderable as fire. **1822** IMISON *Sc. & Art* II. 33 Light.. is reckoned among the imponderable bodies. **1851** H. MAYO *Pop. Superst.* (ed. 2) 70 Mind, like electricity, is an imponderable force. **1854** EMERSON *Lett. & Soc. Aims*, *Poetry & Imag.* Wks. (Bohn) III. 146 The invisible and imponderable is the sole fact.
fig. **1814** SOUTHEY *Roderick* XXI. 192 Creeds like colours being by accident are therefore in the scale imponderable. **1959** *Manch. Guardian* 29 Jan. 5/5 It is not so much the calculable cost but the possible, imponderable one if things go wrong.
b. Having no appreciable weight; of extremely small weight or amount.
1846 G. E. DAY tr. *Simon's Anim. Chem.* II. 23 The bile-pigment in healthy bile is imponderable. **1963** D. W. & E. E. HUMPHRIES tr. *Termier's Erosion & Sedimentation* x. 194 They [*sc.* stratification joints] seem to result from those 'imponderable' particles.. which remain in suspension.
B. *sb.* An imponderable substance or agent. Now chiefly *fig.*, in sense 'something that cannot be estimated'.
1842-3 GROVE *Corr. Phys. Forces* 110 If it be admitted that one of the so-called imponderables is a mode of motion. **1858** O. W. HOLMES *Aut. Breakf.-t.* vi. 53 It is the imponderables that move the world,—heat, electricity, love. **1866** DK. ARGYLL *Reign Law* iii. (ed. 4) 158 Nothing which our scales can measure is lost when the 'vital force' is gone. It is the Great Imponderable. **1927** *Sunday Express* 22 May 12/4 It is not always possible to show gratitude by a gift... If we wish to keep ourselves free from the dreadful disease of ingratitude we should strive to remember these imponderables of life. **1938** S. BECKETT *Murphy* 20 Murphy's respect for the imponderables of personality was profound. **1952** M. MCCARTHY *Groves of Academe* (1953) vi. 110 'Fitness to teach' was an imponderable which he had no intention of pretending to weigh. **1960** *Times* 24 Oct. (Financial Rev.) p. xvii/5 Here the largest imponderable is first whether sufficient wool can be produced to meet the demand and secondly the challenge of synthetics. **1963** D. W. & E. E. HUMPHRIES tr. *Termier's Erosion & Sedimentation* xviii. 355 He [*sc.* A. Lombard] distinguishes between the 'imponderables' which are the salts in process of precipitation,.. and the 'ponderables' which sink rather quickly. **1964** M. GOWING *Britain & Atomic Energy* ix. 267 The British contribution was largely made up of imponderables. **1969** *Times* 17 Oct. 10/4 (*heading*) Farm imponderables in calculating cost of entry to Europe.
Hence **im'ponderableness**; **im'ponderably** *adv.*, without any weight.
1847 CRAIG, *Imponderableness*, the state of being imponderable. **1890** *Lippincott's Mag.* May 675 He saw her in that filmy light, imponderably poised.

†**im'ponderate**, *v. Obs.* [f. IM-¹ + L. *ponderāre*, *ponderāt-* to weigh, f. *pondus*, *ponder-* weight.] *trans.* To place a weight upon; to weight, load.
1667 WATERHOUSE *Fire Lond.* 41 [It] imponderates the judgement with a weightier note of Gods displeasure.

imponderous (ɪm'pɒndərəs), *a. rare.* [f. IM-² + PONDEROUS.] Without weight; imponderable.
1646 SIR T. BROWNE *Pseud. Ep.* II. v. 86 They produce visible and reall effects by imponderous and invisible emissions. **1798** *Monthly Rev.* XXVI. 560. **1827** CARLYLE *Germ. Lit.* in *Misc. Ess.* (1872) I. 24 Motion in *vacuo* is well known to be speedier and surer than through a resisting medium, especially to imponderous bodies. **1891** *Leisure Hour* Feb. 235/2 Those moral sureties which belong to the category of imponderous but important things.
b. *loosely.* Having no appreciable weight; 'weightless'; extremely light.
1851 CARLYLE *Sterling* III. v. 206 Deluges of scoriae, ashes and imponderous pumice-stones. **1858** —— *Fredk. Gt.* II. xiv. (1872) I. 127 Like an imponderous rag of conspicuous colour.
Hence **im'ponderousness** (Craig, 1847).

†**im'pone**, *v. Obs.* [ad. L. *impōn-ĕre* to put, place, or lay on, f. *im-* (IM-¹) + *pōnĕre* to place.]
1. *trans.* To place or set upon something; to impose.
1529 *St. Papers Hen. VIII*, II. 150 The proffyttes of suche imposicions, that is to say, of bestes, or other thyng, that at an entre or exployte shalbe imponed or had. **1530** *Ibid.* I. 364, I beseche you so to impone your favour, as that the vygor and seueryte of the lawe be not executed vpon thys thyng. **1709-29** V. MANDEY *Syst. Math.*, *Arith.* 70 Impone points,.. from the right hand, always intermitting two places.
b. To 'lay', stake, wager. (Of doubtful standing. Cf. IMPAWN.)
16.. SHAKS. *Ham.* v. ii. 155 (1623) The King sir ha's wag'd with him six Barbary Horses, against the which he impon'd as I take it, sixe French Rapiers and Poniards [*Qos.* 2-5 (1604-11) impaund, *Qo.* 6 (1637) impawn'd]. *Ibid.* 171 Why is this impon'd as you call it? [*Not in Qos.*]
2. *intr.* To impose *upon*.
1640 SIR E. DERING *Proper Sacrif.* (1644) 32 You will.. impone upon the ignorant.

imponent (ɪm'pəʊnənt), *a.* and *sb.* [ad. L. *impōnent-em*, pres. pple. of *impōnĕre*: see prec.]
A. *adj.* That imposes.
a **1882** T. H. GREEN *Prol. to Ethics* §323 Were there no Church.. Moral duties would still be associated with the imagination of an imponent authority, whose injunctions they would be supposed to be.
B. *sb.* One who imposes.
1842 PUSEY *Crisis Eng. Ch.* 45 While the Bishop.. regards the framers of Edward the Sixth's Articles as the imponents of ours, he sanctions the Catholic interpretation as much as ourselves. **1850** C. WORDSWORTH *Occas. Serm.* Ser. I. 132 The Articles are the Articles of the Church. She is the imponent. **1863** J. G. MURPHY *Comm. Gen.* xvii. 9-11 The parent is the voluntary imponent, and the child merely the passive recipient of the sign of the covenant.

impoof (ɪm'pu:f). Also **empofo, impofo, impoofo, impophoo.** [Zulu *i-mpofu*, f. *mpofu* tawny.] The common African eland, *Taurotragus oryx.*

1785 G. FORSTER tr. *Sparrman's Voy. Cape Good Hope* II. xiv. 205 In one of the places above referred to, I have mentioned that it [*sc.* the eland] is called by the Caffres *empofos*; I have since found.. that it is likewise called by the same nation *poffo.* **1834** *Penny Cycl.* II. 89/1 The Canna,.. improperly called *eland* or elk by the Dutch colonists of South Africa, and *impoof* by the Caffres. **1839** W. C. HARRIS *Wild Sports S. Afr.* x. 83 During the day I killed another impoofo, which actually measured nineteen hands two inches at the shoulder. **1875** *Encycl. Brit.* II. 101/2 The eland or impophoo (*Boselaphus Oreas*) is one of the largest of the antelopes. **1884** *Cassell's Nat. Hist.* III. 21 Writing on the hunting of these creatures, known in South Africa as the *Impoofo*, the same author [*sc.* W. Cornwallis Harris] remarks that, 'notwithstanding the unwieldy shape of these animals, they had at first greatly exceeded the speed of our jaded horses'. **1900** SCLATER & THOMAS *Bk. Antelopes* IV. 198 *Eland* of the Dutch at the Cape... *Impofo* of the Amandabele, Zulu, and Kafirs... *Mpofu* (Swaheli). **1964** E. P. WALKER et al. *Mammals of World* II. 1419 (*heading*) Elands; Elande, Eland Antilope, Impofo, Pofu, Siruwa (native names).

impoon (ɪm'pu:n). [Zulu *i-mpunzi.*] The grey duiker, *Sylvicapra grimmia*, a common small antelope of southern Africa.

1839 W. C. HARRIS *Wild Sports S. Afr.* 386 The Duiker. Duikerbok of the Cape Colonists. Impoon of the Matabili. **1868** *Chambers's Encycl.* X. 570/1 *Impoon* (*Antilope* or *Cephalopus mergens*),.. a small species of antelope, very plentiful in South Africa, in wooded districts. **1895** SCLATER & THOMAS *Bk. Antelopes* I. 205 *Duiker* and *Duiker-bok* of Dutch and English colonists... *Impunzi* or *Impuzi* of Matabili (also of Zulus and Swazis).

†im'poor, *v. Obs.* [f. IM-¹ + POOR: cf. *enrich.*] *trans.* To make poor; to impoverish.

1613 W. BROWNE *Sheph. Pipe* iii. 72 Neither waues, nor theeues, nor fire, Nor haue rots impoor'd this Sire.

†im'popular, *a. Obs.* [f. IM-² + POPULAR. Cf. mod.F. *impopulaire* (1835 Dict. Acad.).] Unpopular. Hence **†im'popularly** *adv.*

1721 SWIFT *Lett. to Pope* S.'s Wks. 1761 VIII. 24 The cause being so very odious and impopular. **1736** BOLINGBROKE *Patriot.* (1749) 240 They dipped the house of Hanover in our party-quarrels unseasonably.. and impopularly.

†im'porcate, *v. Obs. rare*⁻⁰. [f. L. *imporcāt-*, ppl. stem of *imporcāre* to put into furrows, f. *in* prep. + *porca* furrow.] Hence **†impor'cation.**

1623 COCKERAM, *Imporcate*, to make a ridge. [**1644** Ridiculed in *Vindex Anglicus* 5.] **1656** BLOUNT *Glossogr.*, *Imporcation*, making a balk in earing of Land.

†impo'rose, *a. Obs. rare.* [f. IM-² + POROSE.] = IMPOROUS.

1740 CHEYNE *Regimen* 308 Particles infinitly hard, indivisible, and imporose. *Ibid.* 341 They were hard, imporose, triangular, equilateral Prisms.

†impo'rosity. *Obs. rare.* [f. prec. + -ITY: cf. *porosity.*] The quality of being imporous.

1626 BACON *Sylva* §846 The Porosity, or Imporosity betwixt the Tangible Parts.

imporous (ɪm'pɔərəs), *a.* ? *Obs.* [f. IM-² + POROUS.] Not porous; having no pores.

1646 SIR T. BROWNE *Pseud. Ep.* II. i. 55 Its body is left imporous. **1671** R. BOHUN *Wind* 192 The most solid and imporous wood. **1691** RAY *Creation* i. (1692) 16 These Atomes.. all perfectly solid and imporous.

import (ɪm'pɔət), *v.* Also 5 inp-, 6 emport(e, ymporte, 6–7 importe. [ad. L. *importā-re* to carry or bring in, f. *im-* (IM-¹) + *portāre* to carry. Also, in part. ad. F. *emporter*, OF. *en porter*, L. **inde portāre* to carry away.]

I. From literal senses of cl. L. *importare.*

1. *trans.* To bring in; to introduce from a foreign or external source, or from one use, connexion, or relation into another.

1508 SKELTON *P. Sparowe* 216 That.. To me it myght importe Some pleasure and comforte. **1623** COCKERAM, *Impresse*, to import the forme of a thing. **1646** CRASHAW *Steps to Temple* 82 Good fortunes without gain imported be. **1651–3** JER. TAYLOR *Serm. for Year* (1678) 184 He that carries and imports into the understanding of his Brother notices of faith, and incomes of spiritual propositions. **1774** WARTON *Hist. Eng. Poetry* I. Diss. i. 36 They imported with them into England the old Runic language and letters. **1858** GLADSTONE *Stud. Homer* II. i. 31 The human element was gradually more and more imported into the divine. **1872** LIDDON *Elem. Relig.* i. 30 You hate the lie, and your hatred imports force into your contradiction. **1872** MIVART *Elem. Anat.* xii. 461 The function of importing oxygen into the blood.

2. *spec.* To bring in or cause to be brought in (goods or merchandise) from a foreign country, in international commerce. Opposed to *export.*

1548 HALL *Chron., Hen. VI* 169b, That the said estraungers imported and transported, into and out of this realme, all suche marchandises. **1670** TEMPLE *Lett. Ld. Berkeley* Wks. 1731 II. 217 Ireland runs every Year an eighth Part in Debt by importing so much beyond its Exportation. **1797** BURKE *Corr.* IV. 413 We import things of great value, and, in return, export little or nothing. **1841** W. SPALDING *Italy & It. Isl.* I. 91 There were collected duties *ad valorem* on merchandise imported and exported. **1861** GOSCHEN *For. Exch.* 17 A country which has large sums of interest to pay annually abroad, must import so much less or export so much more.

3. To convey to another, communicate (information, etc.). *Obs.* exc. as merged in 1 or 5 c.

1565 Q. ELIZ. in Ellis *Orig. Lett.* Ser. II. II. 304 Your letters of the xxiiijth of January directed to our Secretary, and by him imported to us and our Counsaile. **1589** PUTTENHAM *Eng. Poesie* I. xxi. (Arb.) 59 The profitable sciences were.. meete to be imported to the greater number of ciuill men for instruction of the people. **1726** CAVALLIER *Mem.* IV. 303, I was not able to import the variety of Torment that were used; and if I were, I would save his Majesty the pain of hearing the rehearsal of them. [**1847** EMERSON *Poems* (1857) 77 Hearts to hearts their meaning show, Sum their long experience, And import intelligence.]

†4. To bring about, cause, occasion; to carry with it or involve as a consequence or result. *Obs.*

1550 CROWLEY *Waie to Wealth* B vij a, Certenlye the greatnes of your sinnes importeth as present distruccion to you as if ye were the same Niniuites. *c* **1555** HARPSFIELD *Divorce Hen. VIII* (Camden) 29 It must needs then be a matter of marvellous moment.. that should induce and import a divorce between two such excellent personages. **1581** J. BELL *Haddon's Answ. Osor.* 219b, If these dealynges emporte not a generall overthrow of all Civill, and politicke governementes, let the accuser hym selfe deny it. **1615** G. SANDYS *Trav.* 87 Searched for concealed Slaves, and goods contrabanded; which found, import no lesse than losse both of ship and liberty. **1705** STANHOPE *Paraphr.* I. 24 The Salvation will import that Bliss which the Faithful expect.

5. a. To carry with it, as involved in its nature; to involve; to imply, betoken, indicate.

1529 MORE *Suppl. Soulys* Wks. 326/1 It importeth also plaine and open blasphemy. **1548** GEST *Pr. Masse* H v b, Honoure and prayer importe the presence of his glorye and maiestye where they be exhibited to him. *c* **1600** SHAKS. *Sonn.* cxxii, To keepe an adiunckt to remember thee, Were to import forgetfulnesse in mee. **1643** *Declar. Commons, Rebell. Ireland* 59 Their Lordships giving Warrant to print any Paper comming from his Majestie.. did not import their approbation of the contents thereof. **1657** J. SMITH *Myst. Rhet.* 31 Admitted to sacrifice to Him, which was a dignity importing honour. **1884** *Law Rep.* 26 Ch. Div. 131 Release.. by deed under seal.. imports valuable consideration and creates an estoppel.

b. To convey in its meaning; to bear the meaning of; to imply, signify, denote, mean.

1533 MORE *Debell. Salem* Wks. 956/1 If, he sayth, importeth alwaye a doubte. **1574** WHITGIFT *Def. Aunsw.* I. Wks. (Parker Soc.) I. 162 The words of Christ rather import the contrary. **1577** tr. *Bullinger's Decades* Pref., Euery Decade containing (as the word importeth) ten. **1581** MULCASTER *Positions* xxxvii. (1887) 163 The publike acknowledging of him to be such a one, as his title emporteth. **1615** G. SANDYS *Trav.* 139 Sarrack imports as much as a theefe. **1703** MAUNDRELL *Journ. Jerus.* (1721) 135 Heliopolis, or City of the Sun; for that the word imports. *a* **1716** SOUTH *Serm.* (1717) VI. 427 Having thus seen, what is imported in a Man's trusting his Heart. **1849** MACAULAY *Hist. Eng.* iii. I. 366 The levee was exactly what the word imports.

c. To bear as its purport; to convey as information; to express, state, make known.

c **1430** LYDG. *Min. Poems* (1840) 117 At goode leyser dothe the matier see, Whiche inportithe grete intelligence. **1576** FLEMING *Panopl. Epist.* 332 Hee beginneth his letter with.. a kinde of speache importing his inwarde gladnesse. **1595** T. P. GOODWINE *Caxton's Blanchardyn* i, Amongst many antient Chronicles importing the haughtie exploites of sundry nations. **1647** SIR E. NICHOLAS in *N. Papers* (Camden) 81, I cannot gett ready so soon as your letter imports. **1777** HOWARD *Prisons Eng.* (1780) 93 Over the gate is an inscription importing 'that it was erected by Pope Pius V in the year 1569'. **1849** MACAULAY *Hist. Eng.* iv. I. 518 They.. passed a resolution importing that they relied with entire confidence on His Majesty's gracious promise.

d. To signify (something coming); to portend.

1591 SHAKS. *1 Hen. VI*, I. i. 2 Comets importing change of Times and States. **1722** DE FOE *Plague* (1840) 22 That those two comets passed directly over the city, and that.. it was plain they imported something peculiar to the city alone. **1727** —— *Syst. Magic* I. vi. (1840) 159 Comets.. import great changes and troubles among men.

II. From med.L., It. *importare*, F. *importer.*

6. *intr.* To involve a considerable or weighty result (actual or possible); to be of consequence or significance; to be important, 'signify', matter. (Only in 3rd person; with various constructions, as in 7.) *arch.*

1588 R. PARKE tr. *Mendoza's Hist. China* 213 They did certifie him, that it was a thing that did import verie much. **1617** MORYSON *Itin.* I. 242 Neither imported it where we lodged. **1625** BACON *Ess., Unity Relig.* (Arb.) 427 The true Placing of them, importeth exceedingly. **1675** EVELYN *Terra* (1729) 35 So little does it import to have it profound. **1765** H. WALPOLE *Otranto* i. (1798) 26 What imported it to me whether I was seized a moment sooner, or a minute later? **1846** TRENCH *Mirac.* xxviii. (1862) 387 For them it greatly imports that they should understand this.

7. *trans.* To be of consequence or importance to; to relate to, have to do with; to concern. (Only in third person.)

a. with simple subject: (*a*) with personal object (? orig. *dative*).

1588 SHAKS. *L.L.L.* IV. i. 57 This Letter is mistooke: it importeth none here: It is writ to *Iaquenetta.* **1591** UNTON *Corr.* (Roxb.) 464, I humbly acknowledge her Majesties.. favor in lycensinge my retourne, which dothe very much importe me. **1649** BP. HALL *Cases Consc.* IV. vi. (1654) 349 So great a work and so highly importing us as matrimony. **1700** BP. PATRICK *Comm. Deut.* xxxiii. 1 To admonish their posterity.. of such things, as they thought most imported them. **1860** MILL *Repr. Govt.* (1861) 305 There is nothing which more vitally imports the American people, than to guard [etc.]. **1865** *Q. Rev.* CXVII. 280 It is a question that imports us nearly.

(*b*) with impersonal object.

1586 A. DAY *Eng. Secretary* I. (1625) 9 [Letters] bearing in them a resolute purpose.. importing the present affaires. **1653** H. COGAN tr. *Pinto's Trav.* vi. 14 Affairs very much importing the surety of the Fortress. **1703** ROWE *Ulyss.* IV. i, It may Import the Safety of my Royal Parents. *a* **1718** PENN *Innocency* Wks. 1726 I. 266 Religion.. which doth more essentially import the immortal Happiness of Men. **1815** MACKINTOSH *Sp. Ho. Comm.* 27 Apr., Wks. 1846 III. 315 The King's Ministers, whose character it does most deeply import.

b. with infin. phrase as subject, usually placed after the object, the verb being introduced by *it*; also (*poet.*) with impersonal construction, *it* being omitted. Here the sense often amounts to 'behove, be incumbent on, be the duty of'.

1561 NORTON & SACKV. *Gorboduc* I. ii. 5 Nowe more importeth mee the erst to vse Your faith and wisdome. **1579–80** NORTH *Plutarch* (1656) 86 Showing how much it importeth a nobleman and magistrate, ruleing weightie causes, to have his ears open to hear. **1632** J. HAYWARD tr. *Biondi's Eromena* I (Though a child) he knew already what it imported him to be last borne, and what it was to bee a younger Brother. **1663** CHARLETON *Chor. Gigant.* 41 It more imports us to proceed. **1761–2** HUME *Hist. Eng.* lxvii. (1806) V. 72 It imports us to get all the aid and assistance we can. **1820** SCOTT *Ivanhoe* xxxi, Let me say.. what it imports thee to know. **1868** FARRAR *Silence & V.* ix. (1875) 157, I know nothing which it more solemnly imports us to realize.

c. with subordinate clause as subject, the verb introduced by *it* as in b.

1588 *Orders for Span. Fleet* in *Harl. Misc.* (Park) I. 117 It importeth that all the armies do go close together. **1669** DRYDEN *Tyran. Love* V. i. Wks. 1883 III. 449 It much imports me that this truth I know. **1786** tr. *Beckford's Vathek* (1868) 41 What imports it you how I am employed? **1819** SHELLEY *Cenci* IV. iv. 77 It much imports your house That all should be made clear.

III. From Fr. *emporter.*

†8. a. To carry, lead, or induce (a person *to do* something). **b.** To influence in feeling, 'carry away', 'transport'. *Obs. rare.*

1649 EVELYN tr. *Le Vayer's Lib. & Servit.* iv. Misc. Writ. (1805) 18 The small inclination which their princes had to the sciences imported them.. to despise and neglect men of a life purely contemplative. **1652** —— *State France* ibid. 47 Women and children, who are commonly more imported with wonder and romance, than that solid and real emolument which is.. to be conveyed to us.

†9. To obtain, gain, win (victory). **b.** *intr.* To gain the victory, to prevail. **c.** *trans.* To gain the victory over; to conquer, overcome. (Cf. CARRY *v.* 16.) *Obs.*

1598 BARRET *Theor. Warres* III. ii. 75 The most valiantest and skilfullest therein do commonly import the victorie. **1600** HOLLAND *Livy* XLII. lxii. 1152 In the end, Romane constancie imported and had the upper hand. *Ibid.* lix. Epit. 1243 But Scipio imported and prevailed in the end. **1624** *Brief Inform. Aff. Palatinate* 50 The enemies.. had enterprised to import and conquer all the low Palatinate.

import ('ɪmpɔ:t, *formerly* ɪm'pɔət), *sb.* [f. IMPORT *v.*]

I. 1. The fact of importing or signifying something; that which a thing (esp. a document, phrase, word, etc.) involves, implies, betokens, or indicates; purport, significance, meaning.

1601 SHAKS. *All's Well* II. iii. 294 There's letters from my mother: What th' import is, I know not yet. **1685** SOUTH *Serm.* (1697) I. 425 Of all the Spiritual tricks and leger-demain,.. there is none so common, and of so fatal an import as these Two. **1719** YOUNG *Busiris* II. i. (1757) 37 Husband and King Are names of no mean import. **1781** COWPER *Expostulation* 126 Stiff in the letter, lax in the design And import of their oracles divine. **1817** BYRON *Manfred* II. ii. 190 She replied In words of dubious import. **1857** GLADSTONE *Glean.* VI. xl. 72 Such a construction.. follows the natural import of the words.

2. The quality or condition of having great or weighty significance; consequence, importance.

1588 SHAKS. *L.L.L.* V. i. 106 Importunate and most serious designes, and of great import indeed too. **1647** MAY *Hist. Parl.* III. ii. 39 Bristoll, a place of great import. **1703** ROWE *Ulyss.* IV. i, I have some Matters Of great and high Import. **1860** TYNDALL *Glac.* II. xiv. 308, I never supposed that passages.. of such cardinal import, could have been overlooked. **1872** BLACK *Adv. Phaeton* xxvii, Something of mighty import had just occurred.

II. 3. a. That which is imported or brought in; a commodity imported from abroad. (Usually in *pl.*) Opposed to *export.*

1690 CHILD *Disc. Trade* (1698) 167 The Imports exceed the Exports. **1746** LOCKMAN *To 1st Promoter Cambrick & Tea Bills* 24 Whence no supplies their imports cou'd create. **1769** BURKE *Late St. Nat.* Wks. II. 73 Your import is your own food; as much your own, as that you raise.. out of your own soil. **1845** MᶜCULLOCH *Taxation* II. x. (1852) 351 Every increase of imports is sure to occasion, directly or indirectly, an equal increase of exports.

b. *attrib.*

1769 BURKE *Late St. Nat.* Wks. II. 73 A merely luxurious consumption.. is the idea too generally and loosely annexed to our import article. **1796** COLQUHOUN *Police Metrop.* (1797) 107 It can generally be uttered.. at its full import value. **1817** F. ROBINSON in *Parl. Deb.* 565 In France the import duty on coals was nearly equal to our export duty. **1897** MARY KINGSLEY *W. Africa* 633 They are mainly carriers of import goods. **1963** A. MAIZELS *Industr. Growth & World Trade* vi. 150 An analysis has been made of the magnitude of the import-substitution that has in fact taken place in the industrial and semi-industrial countries since 1913. **1969** *Times* 13 Jan. 11/2 What many people wanted to know was how much £100 m. of import substitution was

worth to the balance of payments. **1971** D. E. WESTLAKE *I gave at the Office* (1972) 121 The import duty you pay now. .. The export duty you pay on the way out.

4. a. The action of importing; importation.

1797-8 WELLINGTON in Owen *Mrq. Wellesley's Desp.* (1877) 785 The import of Bengal articles ought to be as free for private traders as for the Company. **1861** GOSCHEN *For. Exch.* 11 It is an error..to look on the balance of trade as a mere question of import and export.

b. import-export: *a.*, of a business: engaged in both importing and exporting goods.

1955 G. GREENE *Quiet American* I. iii. 49 'Really? What kind of business?'.. 'Import, export.' **1965** 'W. HAGGARD' *Hard Sell* ii. 11 He had an import-export business, mostly import.

importa'bility. [f. IMPORTABLE *a.*²: see -ITY.] Capability of being imported or introduced.

1865 *Morning Star* 20 Apr., As regards the importability of the nervous disease, our danger..is apparently nothing, or next to nothing.

†**importable,** *a.*¹ *Obs.* Also 5-6 inp-. [a. F. *importable* (1328 in Godef.) = It. *importabile* (Florio), ad. L. *importābil-is* unbearable, insupportable, f. *im-* (IM-²) + *portābilis* bearable, PORTABLE.] That cannot be carried or borne; rarely *lit.* too heavy to be carried; usually *fig.* too grievous or painful to be borne, unbearable, unendurable.

c **1386** CHAUCER *Monk's T.* 524 (612) His peynes were importable. *c* **1400** *Rom. Rose* 6902 They wolde binde on folk alwey..Burdens that ben importable. **1440** J. SHIRLEY *Dethe K. James* (1818) 26 With the ymportible payne of turment, he cried then pitously. **1475** *Nottingham Rec.* II. 388 Many grete and importable charges and expensis. *a* **1533** LD. BERNERS *Huon* cxlv. 544 In all my lyfe I haue had but sorow, and heuynes, and dolours inportables. **1587** FLEMING *Contn. Holinshed* III. 1412/2 Vnder the importable yoke of the detestable inquisition of Spaine. **1632** SANDERSON *Serm.* (1681) I. 291 We lay upon our own shoulders..heavy and importable burdens. *a* **1651** CALDERWOOD *Hist. Kirk* (Wodrow Soc.) III. 662 The poorer sort could not bear the importable scafferie intended.

Hence †**im'portableness,** the quality of being insupportable; unbearableness. †**im'portably** *adv.*, unbearably, intolerably.

a **1420** HOCCLEVE *De Reg. Princ.* 356 It shalle us greeve Importably. **1559** ABP. PARKER *Corr.* (Parker Soc.) 99 That we be not hereafter importably charged with the setting forth of men of war. **1677** HALE *Contempl.* II. 199 Though the Yoke be the same, yet it finds no such severity and importableness in it.

importable (ɪm'pɔətəb(ə)l), *a.*² [f. IMPORT *v.* + -ABLE.] **a.** Capable of being brought in or introduced. **b.** That may be imported from abroad.

1533 MORE *Debell. Salem* xv. A ij b, Than is not the losse and the damage vnto the spyrytualtye alone, but harme is importable vnto the whole realme. **1753** HANWAY *Trav.* (1762) I. VII. xcv. 441 It is importable only under oath of being for private use. **1812** J. SMYTH *Pract. of Customs* (1821) 229 Rum is only importable in Casks of not less than 60 gallons. **1814** COLERIDGE in Smiles *J. Murray* (1891) I. 297 An attempt to import whatever is importable of either or of both into our own language.

importance (ɪm'pɔːtəns). [a. F. *importance* (1539 in R. Estienne), or ad. med.L. *importantia* (1496 in Du Cange) = It. *importanza*, Sp. *importancia*, f. *importans, -tant-em* IMPORTANT: see -ANCE.]

I. 1. a. The fact or quality of being important; the fact of importing or signifying much (or, with qualifying word, of having some degree of import); moment, significance, gravity, weight, consequence.

1508 WOLSEY in J. Gairdner *Lett. Rich. III & Hen. VII*, (Rolls) I. 439 [I have l]ernyd n[o th]yng of importance to be [written] to your grace. **1513** MORE in Grafton *Chron.* (1568) II. 765 Hee shewed his servauntes that he had tidinges of so great importaunce, that [etc.]. **1531** ELYOT *Gov.* II. viii, Emploienge treasour..on persones unworthy, or on thynges inconuenient, and of small importaunce. **1586** *Leycester Corr.* (Camden) 251 A towne of greatest importance. **1651** HOBBES *Leviath.* II. xxviii. 161 There is a question to be answered, of much importance. **1773** *Observ. State Poor* 89 The preservation of health is of not more importance, than the preservation of morals. **1844** H. H. WILSON *Brit. India* II. 501 A consideration of secondary importance. **1880** C. R. MARKHAM *Peruv. Bark* xii. 109 There was no bark trade in Peru of any importance.

b. Personal consequence, consideration, or dignity. (In first quot. humorously as a title.)

1678 DRYDEN *Limberham* v. i, *Pleas.* Your hand, sweet moiety. *Wood.* And heart too my comfortable importance. **1712-14** POPE *Rape Lock* I. 35 Fairest of mortals..thy own importance know, Nor bound thy narrow views to things below. **1776** PAINE *Com. Sense* (1791) 23 Men who look upon themselves born to reign, and others to obey, soon grow insolent;..their minds are early poisoned by importance. **1874** GREEN *Short Hist.* v. §1. 213 His family, though not noble, seems to have been of some importance.

c. Dignity of style or manner; an air of consequence; pompousness.

1607 *Barley-Breake* (1877) 14 The sacred traine with Musicke take the way, Where, with importance euery rite is done.

2. †**a.** An important matter, an affair of consequence (in quot. 1611, with qualifying context, of *slight* consequence). *Obs.*

1570 LEVINS *Manip.* 21/35 Importance, *magna res.* **1611** SHAKS. *Cymb.* I. iv. 45 It had beene pitty you should haue beene put together, with so mortall a purpose..vpon importance of so slight and triuiall a nature. **1664** BUTLER *Hud.* II. iii. 110 To whom all people, far and near, On deep importances repair. *a* **1670** HACKET *Abp. Williams* I. (1692) 14 He searched into the notable particularities of all kingdoms, republics and their churches, with all the importances that hung upon them.

b. One who is important; an important person.

1896 A. MORRISON *Child of Jago* ii. 26 The Importances from the platform came to find the tea. **1907** 'MARK TWAIN' *Christian Sci.* II. v. 147 To place the Virgin first, the Saviour second, and Mrs. Eddy third, seems to..make it an ascending scale of Importances, with Mrs. Eddy ranking the other two and holding first place.

c. An important thing.

1938 R. GRAVES *Coll. Poems* 129 And old importances came swimming back—Wine, meat, log-fires, a roof over the head.

†**3.** Urgency; importunity; solicitude. *Obs.*

1563-87 FOXE *A. & M.* (1684) III. 296 The shortness of time, and this said bringers importance is only the let. **1595** SHAKS. *John* II. i. 7 At our importance hither is he come, To spread his colours boy, in thy behalfe. **1624** HEYWOOD *Gunaik.* 43 [Stratonica] solicited him, and that with great importance, to select some beautifull ladie whom he best fancied. **1779-81** JOHNSON *Lives, Drake* Wks. IV. 389 A pinnace had passed by with sails and oars, and all the appearance of expedition and importance.

II. †**4. a.** = IMPORT *sb.* 1; signification, meaning, purport. *Obs.*

1552 HULOET, Importaunce, or meanynge, or signification of wordes. **1563** FOXE *A. & M.* 706 b, Many more wordes of like importance. **1611** SHAKS. *Wint. T.* v. ii. 20 The wisest beholder..could not say if th' importance were Ioy, or Sorrow. **1626** JACKSON *Creed* VIII. xix. §1 The multiplicity or variety of importances or significations of some one single word. **1709** STANHOPE *Paraphr.* IV. 524 They might..change it in common Speech, for another [word], of like Importance but different Character.

†**b.** Bearing, consequence. *Obs.*

1691 T. H[ALE] *Acc. New Invent.* 19 This wast [= waste] of Iron-work by Rust, and the ill importance of it, in its consequences.

III. †**5.** ? 'Means of support' (Jam.). *Obs.*

1505 *Seal of Cause* in Pennecuik *Blue Blanket* (1756) 42 It is weill knawne..that we uphald an altar situate within the Colledge-Kirk of St. Giles..and has nae importance to uphauld the same, but our sober oukleye Penny and upsets.

†**im'portancy.** *Obs.* [f. med.L. *importāntia*: see prec. and -ANCY.]

1. The quality of being important; = prec. 1.

1540 *Act 32 Hen. VIII*, c. 48 If the importancy or urgency of the cause..so requier. **1604** SHAKS. *Oth.* I. iii. 20 When we consider Th' importancie of Cyprus to the Turke. **1693** BEVERLEY *True St. Gosp. Truth* 13 According to the great Importancy of the word *Knowing* in Scripture.

b. An important matter; = prec. 2.

1623 COCKERAM, *Importancie, Importance,* a matter of much value. **1625** JACKSON *Creed* v. vi. §3 The great dissention..in such importancies enforceth such as thinke they have attained to some certainty in this point to reele and stagger. **1803** SOUTHEY in *Life* (1850) II. x. 241 Materials for a volume that should contain more real importancies than all travellers have yet brought home.

2. Urgency, importunity; = prec. 3.

1598-9 E. FORDE *Parismus* II. (1661) 141 In the end his suit grew to that importancy, that he would not be denied. **1624** HEYWOOD *Gunaik.* 204 Their importancie so far prevailed..that the first decree was quite abrogated. **1673** O. WALKER *Educ.* (1677) 38 Pressing all things great and small with the same vigour and importancy.

important (ɪm'pɔːtənt), *a.* [a. F. *important* (16th c. Montaigne) = It., Sp. *importante*, ad. med.L. *importans, -tantem*, f. *importāre* in its med.L. sense 'to be of consequence, weight, or force': see IMPORT *v.* II.]

1. a. Having much import or significance; carrying with it great or serious consequences; weighty, momentous, grave, significant.

1586 A. DAY *Eng. Secretary* I. (1625) 55 How much available then and important is it to every man to be frequented with learning. **1651** HOBBES *Leviath.* III. xl. 249 Wee may observe three points of important consequence. **1665** BOYLE *Occas. Refl.* II. xi. (1848) 131 This last and importantest of humane Actions. **1713** ADDISON *Cato* I. i, The great, the important day, big with the fate Of Cato and of Rome. **1843** MACAULAY *Lays Anc. Rome* Pref. (1864) 26 Hume..has overlooked one very important circumstance. **1845** M. PATTISON *Ess.* (1889) I. 13 Events most important to the understanding of his narrative.

b. *spec.* Of antiques or the like: very valuable.

1904 H. JAMES *Golden Bowl* II. xlii. 368 She had passed her arm into his, and the other objects in the room, the other pictures, the sofas, the chairs, the tables, the cabinets, the 'important' pieces, supreme in their way, stood out, round them. **1969** *Times* 18 Mar. 18/1 (Advt.), A highly important jewelled binding. **1973** *Country Life* 15 Nov. 76 An important tortoise shell and ormolu English Bracket Clock ..by Robert Hodgkin, London, *c.* 1720.

2. Having an air of importance or consequence; consequential, pompous, grandiose, pretentious.

1713 SWIFT *Cadenus & Vanessa* 376 Discoursing, with important face, On ribbons, fans, and gloves and lace. *a* **1732** GAY *Fables* II. iii, Fowls of all ranks surround his hut, To worship his important strut. **1876** J. WEISS *Wit Hum. & Shaks.* iii. 75 Parodying the important phrases and impotent exploits of the suburban constable.

†**3.** Urgent, pressing, importunate. *Obs.*

1590 SHAKS. *Com. Err.* v. i. 138 Antipholis, my husband, Whom I made lord of me, and all I had, At your important letters. **1599** —— *Much Ado* II. i. 74 If the Prince bee too important, tell him there is measure in euery thing. **1630** LENNARD tr. *Charron's Wisd.* III. vii. §8 (1670) 410 Not to be important to his friends, as they that are alwayes complaining.

4. Preceded by *more* or *most*: used as a kind of sentence adjective. Cf. IMPORTANTLY *adv.* 1.

This construction is discussed in R. Quirk et al. *Gram. Contemp. Eng.* (1972) §5.26 (p. 255).

1964 N. SPINRAD in D. Knight *100 Yrs. Sci. Fiction* (1969) 270 What were these quasi-stellar objects and, perhaps even more important, how were they giving off so much energy? **1965** J. C. DAVIS *Adv. Physical Chem.* x. 449 The carbon atom in its ground state is not completely described by hydrogen-like orbitals. More important, a carbon atom in a molecular configuration hardly resembles a free carbon atom. **1968** R. H. W. BROWN *Gardening Complete* vii. 192 It is a mistake to follow this advice too rigidly. One must wait until the soil is damp enough and, more important, warm enough. **1972** *Physics Bull.* Oct. 577/1 The participants must be fed with a stream of information at the crucial times. .. Most important of all, the foreign guests must be assured that the hosts will ease all problems of entry into their country. **1972** *Sunday Times* 22 Oct. 15/6 But, most important of all, it is now clear that reproducing a document which has been leaked in an unauthorised manner means [etc.]. **1973** *Sci. Amer.* Jan. 7 (Advt.), But most important of all, we begin by giving you the training you need to [etc.]. *Ibid.* 13/3 It can be readily synthesized from coal, oil or natural gas. More important, it can be produced simply by splitting molecules of water. **1973** *Daily Tel.* 13 Jan. 25/8 But, more important, a linked policy can be encashed—surrendered—before maturity date and the saver gets a high proportion of his savings returned to him.

5. *Comb.*, as ***important-looking*** adj.

1925 F. SCOTT FITZGERALD *Great Gatsby* iii. 45 On a chance we tried an important-looking door. **1926** 'C. BARRY' *Detective's Holiday* 42 Another important-looking person.

importantly (ɪm'pɔːtəntlɪ), *adv.* [-LY².]

1. In an important manner or degree; weightily, momentously.

Now esp. common as a kind of sentence adverb preceded by *more* or *most*; in some contexts it is interchangeable with *important* and so has the function of a quasi-*adj.* Cf. IMPORTANT *a.* 4.

1611 SHAKS. *Cymb.* IV. iv. 19 When they..haue both their eyes And eares so cloyd importantly as now. **1647** N. BACON *Disc. Govt. Eng.* I. lxv. (1739) 138 The publick was so importantly concerned. **1796** A. HAMILTON in *Washington's Writ.* (1892) XIII. 221 *note*, To render this act importantly and lastingly useful. **1861** WILSON & GEIKIE *Mem. E. Forbes* xiv. 498 Noting not a little that bore importantly upon questions that were engaging..attention. **1878** J. C. COLLINS *Introd. Tourneur's Plays* 25 Fifteen popular ballads ..some of which..importantly illustrate Shakespeare. **1938** C. WILLIAMS *He came down from Heaven* ii. 22 The main point is..the first outrage against *pietas*, and (more importantly) the first imagined proclamation of *pietas* from the heavens. **1941** *Jrnl. R. Aeronaut. Soc.* XLV. 309 Just as importantly, the chart is of extreme value in forming any decisions as to the desirability of modifying..the track. **1962** H. R. WILLIAMSON *Day Shakespeare Died* viii. 88 More importantly, Shakespeare, though using Holinshed as his main source, occasionally used Hall as the direct source of various passages. **1965** M. SPARK *Mandelbaum Gate* vii. 287 It appeared that Ruth assumed Barbara to be someone importantly on her side. **1965** *Listener* 27 May 791/1 Edward Dahlberg's mother is a sizeable part of his literary capital. He dealt with her importantly in two novels. **1969** *Nature* 1 Nov. 477/1 Most importantly, when the particles of the pair are brought together, they annihilate. **1972** *Ibid.* 31 Mar. 200/2 And, most importantly with an internal lipid bilayer, a membrane. **1972** *Times* 12 Apr. 16/5 Perhaps more importantly, income not applied to exclusively charitable purposes is not exempt from taxation. **1972** *Daily Tel.* 31 Oct. 14/6 But, importantly in this case, there is a well-built girl attendant who is chased about the stage by someone bearing a striking resemblance to the wild-eyed non-speaking member of the Marx Brothers team. **1972** *Times Higher Educ. Suppl.* 17 Nov., It will of course be recognized as a great modern dictionary, as we shall see presently; but more importantly,..for all the indications it gives of having registered the full impact of our so-called permissive age, is the way it preserves certain antique myths.

2. With an air of importance; consequentially.

1827-30 SIR J. BARRINGTON *Pers. Sk. Own Times* (ed. 2) II. 147, I will proceed at once to the little narrative thus importantly prefaced.

importation (ɪmpɔː'teɪʃən). [n. of action f. IMPORT *v.* (Hence in F.)]

1. The action of importing or bringing in.

a. *Commerce.* The bringing in of goods or merchandise from a foreign country: opp. to *exportation*.

1601 R. JOHNSON *Kingd. & Commw.* (1603) 79 Greate rivers, by which they may have cheap..importation or exportation of wares. **1776** ADAM SMITH *W.N.* IV. i. (1869) II. 23 Restraints upon the importation of such foreign goods for home consumption as could be produced at home. **1833** HT. MARTINEAU *Loom & Lugger* I. i. 3 To authorize a restricted importation of foreign silks.

fig. **1644** MILTON *Areop.* (Arb.) 66 [Licensing] hinders and retards the importation of our richest Marchandize, Truth.

attrib. **1808** J. ADAMS *Wks.* (1854) IX. 604 If I could lay an embargo, or pass a new importation law against corruption and foreign influence.

b. *gen.* Bringing in, introduction.

1666 J. SMITH *Old Age* 239 The Instruments..which serve for importation, and reception of the bloud and spirits. **1807** *Med. Jrnl.* XVII. 112 For more than fifty years..no importation of the disease into this city was suspected. **1874** PARKER *Gothic Archit.* I. iv. 141 The usual test of the importation of a new style.

2. *concr.* That which is imported or introduced; †imports collectively (*obs.*); an imported article, an import.

1664–5 PEPYS *Diary* 27 Jan., If the exportations exceed the importations. **1727** POPE *Thoughts Var. Subj.* in *Swift's Wks.* (1755) II. I. 230 Solomon's importation, Gold and apes. **1893** *Westm. Gaz.* 27 Mar. 7/2 Their eleven is entirely representative, and possesses no Scotch or Welsh importations. *Mod.* She is a recent importation, I fancy.

3. *Logic.* The inference that if a proposition implies that a second proposition implies a third, then the first and second together imply the third; the converse of EXPORTATION 4.

1903 B. RUSSELL *Princ. Math.* ii. 16 If *p* implies that *q* implies *r*, then *pq* implies *r*. This is the principle of importation. **1918** C. I. LEWIS *Survey Symbolic Logic* iv. 231 This theorem contains Peano's.. Principle of Importation. **1957** P. SUPPES *Introd. Logic* ii. 34 Law of Importation $[P\to(Q\to R)]\to[P \,\&\, Q\to R]$. **1965** HUGHES & LONDEY *Elem. Formal Logic* xv. 113 T 20 is known as the Law of Importation.., since its effect is to 'import' the antecedent of the consequent into the antecedent of the whole wff.

Hence **impor'tational** *a.*, of or relating to importation.

1935 *Mind* XLIV. 154 Importational logograms (analogous to definitions) are introduced by fiat.

imported (ɪm'pɔətɪd), *ppl. a.* [f. IMPORT *v.* + -ED[1].] Brought in from a foreign country, as merchandise; *gen.* brought in, introduced.

1660 WILLSFORD *Scales Comm.* 208 Whether imported or exported Goods. **1856** OLMSTED *Slave States* 97 The original stock of slaves, the imported Africans,.. probably required to be governed with much greater severity.

importee (ɪmpɔː'tiː). [f. IMPORT *v.* + -EE[1].] A person imported from abroad.

1858 CARLYLE *Fredk. Gt.* I. IV. vi. 445 Painter Pesne, a French Immigrant, or Importee,.. was sent for. **1888** *Scottish Leader* 19 Sept. 5 It was amongst the 'importees' that the row took place. **1955** *Caribbean Q.* IV. I. 50 The most recent census, taken in 1946, counted.. 3,500 East Indians, descendants of indentured importees.

importer (ɪm'pɔətə(r)). [f. IMPORT *v.* + -ER[1].] One who or that which imports or introduces; *esp.* a merchant who brings in or receives goods from abroad.

1700 S. SEWALL *Diary* 19 June (1879) II. 16 There is a Motion.. to get a Law that all Importers of Negros shall pay 40*s.* per head. **1845** MCCULLOCH *Taxation* II. iv. (1852) 197 It would then, like the generality of customs duties, fall wholly on the importers, or on the consumers here. **1866** CRUMP *Banking* x. 233 The Bank of England has for years been the only importer of bullion into the Mint. **1888** E. PULSFORD in *19th Cent.* Sept. 397 Up to the present year New South Wales has been a large importer of wheat.

importing (ɪm'pɔətɪŋ), *vbl. sb.* [f. IMPORT *v.* + -ING[1].] The action of the verb IMPORT, *esp.* in senses 1, 2; importation. Also *attrib.*

1640–4 in Rushw. *Hist. Coll.* III. (1692) I. 53 The Patent for the sole Trade to Guinney, and the sole Importing of Red-wood. **1895** SIR H. H. HOWORTH in *Athenæum* 2 Mar. 284/1 Some of his [Caxton's] words.. were French exotics of his own importing.

im'porting, *ppl. a.* [f. as prec. + -ING[2].]

†1. That 'imports' or signifies (see IMPORT *v.* 6); of much import; important. *Obs.*

1579 FENTON *Guicciard.* (1618) 33 The Admirall, with certaine others appointed to the gouernment and guard of Prouinces most importing. **1604** E. GRIMSTONE *Hist. Siege Ostend* 109 To garde the strongest places and most importing. **1654** H. L'ESTRANGE *Chas. I* (1655) 184 An Assembly so importing to the kings and kingdomes welfare.

2. That imports or brings in merchandise; engaged in importation.

1812 J. SMYTH *Pract. of Customs* (1821) 415 Register of Importing Ships. **1861** GOSCHEN *For. Exch.* 40 To sell the bills at a time.. when a premium may be given for them by the importing branch of the community.

†**im'portless**, *a. Obs. rare.* [f. IMPORT *sb.* + -LESS.] Without import or significance; trivial, unimportant.

1606 SHAKS. *Tr. & Cr.* I. iii. 71 That matter needlesse of importlesse burthen Diuide thy lips.

†**im'portment.** *Obs.* [f. IMPORT *v.* + -MENT.]

a. Signification, meaning, purport: = IMPORT *sb.* 1. b. Importance, consequence: = IMPORT *sb.* 2.

a **1624** BP. M. SMITH *Serm.* (1632) 2 Certaine things vttered.. vpon one speciall occasion, haue yet a generall drift or importment. **1658** W. BURTON *Itin. Anton.* 115 A Latine word for a Post, who speedily conveys news of Importment.

importraiture (ɪm'pɔətrətjʊə(r)). *rare.* [f. IM-[1] + PORTRAITURE.] The action of portraying in or upon something; *concr.* that which is portrayed (*lit.* or in writing), a portrait or description.

1836 *Fraser's Mag.* XIV. 9 Importraitures of passages in the external world, and in human life. **1842** *Ibid.* XXVI. 455 Here.. is an admirable importraiture for you. **1882** PHIL. ROBINSON *Noah's Ark* 28 Alterations from the received importraitures of the beasts.

†**impor'tray**, *v. Obs.* [f. IM-[1] + PORTRAY *v.*] *trans.* To portray or depict in or upon something.

1580 LYLY *Euphues* (Arb.) 311 Whome Philautus is now with all colours importraying in yᵉ Table of his hart.

†**im'portunable**, *a. Obs.* Also 5 in-. [f. IMPORTUNE *a.* (or ? *v.*) + -ABLE.]

1. Burdensome, onerous, grievous, heavy.

1482 *Paston Lett.* No. 867 III. 297 [They] wold have.. taryd hym there and his councell to his gret inportunabill charges. **1512** *Act 4 Hen. VIII*, c. 18 *Preamble*, To theyr greate importunable losse troble hurte and dammayge. **1529** MORE *Dyaloge* I. 23 b/2 Forbyddyng them to binde and lay vppon other pore mennys bakkes importunable burdeyns. **1611** SPEED *Hist. Gt. Brit.* IX. xxi. §3 They felt the weight of their done wrongs too importunable for them any longer to beare.

2. Troublesome; = IMPORTUNATE *a.* 2 b.

1566 DRANT *Horace, Sat.* I. ix. *argt.*, In generall he controwleth people inquisitiue, and importunable tatlers.

†**im'portunably**, *adv. Obs.* [f. prec. + -LY[2].] Persistently, pertinaciously; importunately.

1502 ATKYNSON tr. *De Imitatione* I. xiii. 161 The deuyl.. with a thousande snaris and subtilties importunably assaylynge vs.

importunacy (ɪm'pɔːtjuːnəsɪ). [f. IMPORTUNATE *a.*: see -ACY.] Pertinacity; pressing solicitation; = IMPORTUNITY 4.

1548 UDALL, etc. *Erasm. Par. Mark* vi. (R.), He gate hym not out of the way, nor commaunded them to departe for theyr importunacy. **1606** J. CARPENTER *Solomon's Solace* xxix. 120 The golden Calfe, which himselfe [Aaron] had made at the importunacie of our Fathers in the wildernes. **1655** DIGGES *Compl. Ambass.* 228 Overcome with the importunacy of their reasons, we did yield to take some further consideration. **1710** PALMER *Proverbs* 187 He, who made least to do, has often succeeded, when a rash, busie, importunacy has made an enemy of a friend. **1893** J. PULSFORD *Loyalty to Christ* II. 243 She is lauded by Jesus: her importunacy is triumphant.

im'portunance. [f. IMPORTUNE *v.* + -ANCE.] (?) Grievousness, gravity, seriousness.

1546 *St. Papers Hen. VIII*, XI. 91 The Kinges Majestie shulde.. be disapoynted of his enterpryse, which I besought Her to consider, and the greate importunance therof.

importunate (ɪm'pɔːtjuːnət), *a.* (*sb.*) [f. L. *importūn-us* + -ATE[2]. The use of the suffix is peculiar; perh. after *obstinate*, *fortunate*, *temperate*, or other adjs. expressing personal qualities.]

†1. Inopportune, unseasonable, untimely; = IMPORTUNE *a.* 1. *Obs.*

1529 [implied in IMPORTUNATELY 1]. **1552** HULOET, Importunate, or out of season, *importunus.* **1656–9** B. HARRIS *Parival's Iron Age* (ed. 2) 101 The inexorable executor of this importunate and unseasonable Command, was first chased away with stone.

†2. Burdensome; grievous, grave. *Obs.*

c **1540** tr. *Pol. Verg. Eng. Hist.* (Camden) I. 102 An importunate number of the barbarus people beeganne to moleste the Romaine imperie. **1548** HALL *Chron., Hen. VI* 152 b, When money was scante and importunate charges were dayly imminent. *Ibid., Hen. VII* 3 b, Beyng not hable to suffre the importunate heate, they cast away the shetes and all the clothes. **1577** FRAMPTON *Joyful News* I. (1596) 13 This water is also good for.. other dangerous and importunat diseases. **1663** COWLEY *Verses & Ess., Solitude*, When they are in love with a Mistress, all other persons are importunate and burdensome to them. **1824** LAMB *Elia* Ser. II. *Blakesmoor in H—— shire*, The pride of ancestry may be had on cheaper terms than to be obliged to an importunate race of ancestors.

†b. Troublesome; persistently troublesome. *Obs.*

1613 PURCHAS *Pilgrimage* (1614) 722 This New World.. hath to these importunate chapmen sold her freedome. **1660** H. MORE *Myst. Godl.* III. ii. 60 [The Sun] cannot.. free his own face of those importunate spots that ever and anon lie upon it like filth. **1691** RAY *Creation* II. (1692) 100, Lice, Fleas, and other noisom and importunate Insects.

3. Pressing, urgent; busy. *Obs.* or *arch.*

1542–3 *Act 34 & 35 Hen. VIII*, c. 2 §2 If.. the sayde collectours.. can not be thervnto admitted, by reason of importunate busines. *a* **1674** CLARENDON *Hist. Reb.* XIV. §136 The Earl remain'd in London whilst the enquiry was warm and importunate. **1877** BRYANT *Main-Dream* i, This maze of dusty streets, Forever shaken by the importunate jar Of commerce.

4. Persistent or pressing in solicitation; pertinacious.

1477 [implied in IMPORTUNATELY 4]. **1529** *Supplic. to King* (E.E.T.S.) 30 They.. will.. make importunate sute, and laboure to be in seruice with youre Magestye. *a* **1533** LD. BERNERS *Gold. Bk. M. Aurel.* x. (1546) F vj b, I am importune on you, that ye be not importunate on me. I pray you, that you praie not me. **1566** PAINTER *Pal. Pleas.* I. 69 Declaring how importunate his mother was to know. **1660** *Trial Regic.* 44 The King.. was importunate to know what they intended to do with Him. **1746** *Col. Rec. Pennsylv.* V. 53 Some of the Persons who supplied me with them grow Importunate for their money. **1863** MISS BRADDON *Eleanor's Vict.* ii, For the avoidance of importunate creditors. **1876** GEO. ELIOT *Dan. Der.* I. ii, Now came an importunate knock at the door; breakfast was ready.

B. as *sb.* An importunate person.

1881 *Jrnl. Educ.* 1 Mar. 49/2 He would have granted the fair importunates the examination without restriction.

importunate (ɪm'pɔːtjuːneɪt), *v.* [f. F. *importuner*: see IMPORTUNE *v.* and -ATE[3] 7.]

a. *trans.* To solicit persistently; = IMPORTUNE *v.* 3.

a **1598** ROLLOCK *Sel. Wks.* (Wodrow Soc.) II. 603 The widow who importunated the unrighteous Judge. **1600** F. WALKER *Sp. Mandeville* 85 b, Telling him that she was Lucrecia.. and importunating him with weeping and pittifull wordes. **1653** *Cloria & Narcissus* I. 117 Orestes.. began freshly to importunate his brother to the accomplishment of her request.

b. To obtain by importunity.

1891 *Pall Mall G.* 1 July 2/3 The degree of departure which outside bodies had been able to importunate from a somewhat pliant Senate.

importunately (ɪm'pɔːtjuːnətlɪ), *adv.* [f. IMPORTUNATE *a.* + -LY[2].] In an importunate manner.

†1. Inopportunely, untimely, unseasonably. *Obs.*

1529 MORE *Suppl. Soulys* Wks. 288/2 We do.. not yet importunatelye bereue you of your rest with cryinge at youre eares at vnseasonable tyme. **1658–9** *Burton's Diary* (1828) III. 168, I shall not say the Petition and Advice was unduly, but unseasonably and importunately obtained.

†2. In a burdensome or grievous way; grievously; troublesomely. *Obs.*

1564 GOLDING *Justin* xlii. (1570) 169 [Hymerus] through his tyrannous crueltie, vexed importunatlie both Babilon and manye other cyties. **1577** FRAMPTON *Joyful News* II. (1596) 50 Deseased with the tertian agewes, so importunatlie. **1638** BAKER tr. *Balzac's Lett.* (vol. III.) 4 Least I should be importuneately complementall.

†b. Gravely, exceedingly. *Obs.*

1660 tr. *Amyraldus' Treat. conc. Relig.* Pref. 5 An Expedient so importunately beneficial to Mankind, that scarce any Elogiums could be excogitated equal to their praise. **1690** LOCKE *Hum. Und.* III. x. (1695) 286 Men will not be so importunately dull as not to understand what others say.

3. With pressing or persistent action or purpose; pressingly.

1568 GRAFTON *Chron.* II. 792 He woulde importunatly [1513 MORE 'importunely'] pursue his appetite and have her. **1614** BP. HALL *Recoll. Treat.* 531 What do we now thus importunately catching at shadows? **1876** GEO. ELIOT *Dan. Der.* IV. xxix, His possible judgment of her actions was telling on her as importunately as Klesmer's judgment of her powers.

4. With persistent or pressing solicitation; with importunity.

1477 EARL RIVERS (Caxton) *Dictes* 137 He that axid importunatly after he is ones denied & refused his asking. **1529** S. FISH *Supplic. Beggers* Ded. (E.E.T.S.) 2 [They] haue begged so importunatly that they haue gotten ynto theyre hondes more then the therd part of all youre Realme. **1692** BP. OF CHESTER *Charge 5 May* 20 We need not doubt of God's help, if we sincerely and importunately pray for it. **1719** DE FOE *Crusoe* II. iv, They insisted importunately upon their demand. **1874** MOTLEY *Barneveld* II. xiv. 117 He instructed his envoy.. importunately and dictatorially to plead the cause.

importunateness (ɪm'pɔːtjuːnətnɪs). [f. as prec. + -NESS.] The quality of being importunate; importunity.

c **1530** L. COX *Rhet.* (1899) 67 Our lybertie is ouercome.. by the importunatnes of our wyues. **1549** LATIMER *3rd Serm. bef. Edw. VI* (Arb.) 93 He wyl beare your importunatenes, he wyll not be angrye at your cryinge and calling. **1635** R. CAREW in *Lismore Papers* Ser. II. (1888) III. 217, I am herevnto induced by the importunateness of my Masters. **1812** DE QUINCEY in H. A. Page *Life* (1877) I. viii. 169 Her sweet importunateness of action and voice.

importunator (ɪm'pɔːtjuːneɪtə(r)). [agent-n. in L. form from IMPORTUNATE *v.*] One who importunes, or solicits importunately.

1604 SANDYS *Relat. St. Relig. West Pts.* I iv b, Tyrannous importunators, and exactors of their own men. **1825** *New Monthly Mag.* XIV. 418 A flowing and ebbing of petitioners, claimants, and importunators of every kind.

importune (ɪmpɔː'tjuːn, ɪm'pɔːtjuːn), *a.* (*sb.*) Also 5 **yn-**, **in-**, 6 **ym-**. [ME. a. F. *importun*, *-une* (15th c. in Hatz.-Darm.) = It., Sp. *importuno*, ad. L. *importūn-us* unfit, unsuitable, inconvenient, troublesome, grievous, f. *im-* (IM-[2]): cf. *Portūnus* the protecting god of harbours, f. *portu-s* harbour, PORT. The same stem is found in *opportūn-us* OPPORTUNE.]

†1. Inopportune, untimely; unseasonable, unfit.

c **1425** [implied in IMPORTUNELY 1]. **1529** MORE *Comf. agst. Trib.* I. Wks. 1169/1, I haue thys daye done you much trybulacion with my importune obieccions, of very litle substaunce. **1597** A. M. tr. *Guillemeau's Fr. Chirurg.* *iv, Such fruictes are never importune, nether at anye time out of season. **1634** RAINBOW *Labour* (1635) 17 Both Importunate, and Importune Labour;.. the first is labour too earnest, too sollicitous; the second is labour out of its due time, unseasonable. **1650** BULWER *Anthropomet.* 120 These actions are somewhat importune and unwelcome guests at Feasts. **1704** SWIFT *Batt. Bks.* in *Misc.* (1711) 264 A Wild Ass, with Brayings Importune, affronts his Ear.

†2. Troublesome, burdensome; vexatious; grievous, heavy, severe, exacting. *Obs.*

c **1400** *Rom. Rose* 5632 And for he nyl be importune Unto no wight, ne honerous. **1412–20** LYDG. *Chron. Troy* I. v, The streyght waye is so importune, So dredeful eke and so full of rage. **1494** FABYAN *Chron.* VII. 486 By theyr inportune charges, the comynaltie was greatly enpoueryssbed. **1540**

Act 32 Hen. VIII, c. 43 Which is to peinfull chargeable intollerable and importune, for any man to susteine and abyde. **1590** Spenser *F.Q.* I. xii. 16 They did..often blame the too importune fate That heapd on him so many wrathfull wreakes. **1604** N. D. *3rd Pt. Three Convers. Eng.* 263 A detestable, cruell, horrible and importune monster. **1683** D. A. *Art Converse* 19 They cannot be but importune to us by their long and languishing narratives. **1864** Carlyle *Fredk. Gt.* xv. vi. IV. 90 Treaties, vaporous Foreshadows of Events..are importune to human nature, longing for the Events themselves.

†**3.** Pressing, urgent; busy. *Obs.*
c **1450** tr. *De Imitatione* III. Contents xliv. 61 That man be not importune in worldly erendes. *c* **1475** *Plumpton Corr.* (Camden) 33 The labor is so importune, that I cannot attend it without I shold do nothing ells. **1526** *Pilgr. Perf.* (W. de W. 1531) 129 The good aungelles contende not, they be not importune or to busy, they crye not. **1576** Fleming *Panopl. Epist.* 76 Although my busines be so weightie and importune, that I can obteine but little leasure. **1647** Ward *Simp. Cobler* 63 The importune Affaires of your Kingdome [are] perplexedly suspended.

4. Persistent or pressing in solicitation; pertinacious; irksome through persistency of request.
1447 Bokenham *Seyntys* Introd. (Roxb.) 6 The importune and besy preyere Of oon whom I love. *c* **1460** Fortescue *Abs. & Lim. Mon.* xx. (1885) 156 Importune suters wil gape vpon such reuersiouns. **1535** Coverdale *Luke* xviii. 5 Yet seynge this weddowe is so importune vpon me I will delyuer her. **1641** J. Jackson *True Evang. T.* III. 229 Our Saviour..made as though hee would have gone farther, that they might grow the more importune with him to stay. *a* **1734** North *Exam.* II. v. §83 (1740) 367 He was so importune in the Matter, that one of the Chiefs was provoked to say he spoke with a Cadence, but Nothing to the Purpose. **1890** E. Johnson *Rise Christendom* 106 Vices are importune spirits sent forth from Tartarus' caves.

†**B.** *sb.* [= F. *importun.*] One who is importune or troublesome in soliciting. *Obs.*
1589 Puttenham *Eng. Poesie* III. xxiv. (Arb.) 302 In Spaine it is thought very vndecent for a Courtier to craue, supposing that it is the part of an importune. *a* **1734** North *Exam.* (1740) 644 (D.) If justice must stay till such importunes are satisfied, there's a *ne plus ultra* of all law.

importune (ɪmpɔːˈtjuːn, ɪmˈpɔːtjuːn), *v.* [a. F. *importune-r* (1512 in Godef. *Compl.*) = It. *importunāre* (Florio), Sp. *importunar* (Percivall), med.L. *importūnārī, -āre*, f. *importūnus*: see prec.]

†**1.** *trans.* To burden; to be troublesome or wearisome to; to trouble, worry, pester, annoy.
1578 T. N. tr. *Conq. W. India* 140 Did so importune him and assure him of his going, he commaunded his fardage to be laden. **1598** Yong *Diana* 17 It was my ill hap, that one of them sat next vnto me, to make me infortunate as long as her memorie did importune me. **1661** Evelyn *Mem.* (1857) III. 136, I shall, whenever..it may least importune his privacy, make the inventory of particulars. **1781** Fletcher *Lett.* Wks. 1795 VII. 232 If bodies could move as quick as thought they would be importuned frequently with my company. **1788** Gibbon *Decl. & F.* lxx. VI. 607 Of his two immediate successors..Nicholas the Fifth, [was] the last who was importuned by the presence of a Roman emperor.

†**2.** To press, urge, impel. Also *absol.* *Obs.*
1603 Shaks. *Meas. for M.* I. i. 57 We shall write to you As time, and our concernings shall importune. **1615** Chapman *Odyss.* VI. 270 O queen, deign pity then, since first to you My fate importunes my distress to vow.

3. To solicit pressingly and persistently; to ply or beset with requests or petitions.
1530 Palsgr. 590/1, I importune one, I werye hym by importunate sute making to him for a mater. *c* **1585** *Faire Em* III. 699 A man that you do not a little esteem, hath long importuned me of love. **1590** Shaks. *Com. Err.* I. i. 127 My yongest boy..importun'd me That his attendant..Might beare him company in the quest of him. **1644** Milton *Areop.* (Arb.) 41 Ye were importun'd the passing it. **1676** Hobbes *Iliad* (1677) 298 'My friends', said he, 'importune me no more To eat or drink before we go to fight'. **1719** Young *Revenge* V. ii, He..importunes the skies for swift perdition. **1734** tr. *Rollin's Rom. Hist.* (1827) III. 25 The Kings themselves importuned him to that purpose. **1817** Byron *Beppo* lxii, Meantime the goddess I'll no more importune. **1849** Macaulay *Hist. Eng.* iii. I. 300 Some officers..after vainly importuning the government during many years, had died for want of a morsel of bread.
fig. **1586** A. Day *Eng. Secretary* I. (1625) 27 Being importuned by the dispatch of some present affaires..to have some conference with her Majestie, he went. **1601** Weever *Mirr. Mart.* C vj, No day which would not me to wars importune. *a* **1704** T. Brown *Praise Poverty* Wks. 1730 I. 98 The man that is importun'd with the craving pains of a hunger. **1800–24** Campbell *Song of Colonists* ii, A land, where beauties importune The Briton to its bowers.

4. To ask for (a thing) urgently and persistently; to crave or beg for.
1588 Shaks. *L.L.L.* II. i. 32 The daughter of the King of France..Importunes personall conference with his grace. **1596** Spenser *F.Q.* V. ix. 44 Then gan the Peoples cry and Commons sute Importune care of their owne publicke cause. *a* **1674** Clarendon *Hist. Reb.* xv. §34 It was very strange that any Men should importune the putting such a Question. **1695** Kennett *Par. Antiq.* ix. 228 The nobles..greatly importun'd his stay. **1870** Bryant *Iliad* II. XVI. 113 A little girl that by her mother's side Runs, importuning to be taken up.

5. a. *intr.* To make urgent solicitation; to be importunate.
1548 Q. Katheryn in Ellis *Orig. Lett.* Ser. I. II. 151, I wold not wyssche yow importune for hys good wyll, yf y^t^ cum nott frankely at the fyrst. **1661** Feltham *Resolves* I. xvii. 33, I will neither importune too much upon unwilling minds. **1761** Gray *Sketch own Char.*, Too poor for a bribe, and too proud to importune; He had not the method of making a fortune. **1871** R. Ellis *Catullus* viii. 13 He will not ask for pity, will not importune.

b. To solicit for purposes of prostitution.
1847 *Act 10 & 11 Vict.* c. 89 §28 Every Person who..commits any of the following Offences..may be committed to Prison... Every common Prostitute or Nightwalker loitering and importuning Passengers for the Purpose of Prostitution. **1943** C. E. Vulliamy *Polderoy Papers* 79 Even the prostitutes no longer 'importune', but hand you politely their cards. **1958** *Times* 17 Dec. 11/4 A severe national law already punishes any man who persistently solicits or importunes for immoral purposes.

¶**6.** To import, portend. (A Spenserian misuse.)
1590 Spenser *F.Q.* III. i. 16 But the sage wisard telles, as he has redd, That it importunes death and dolefull dreryhedd. **1598** Marston *Pygmal.* xxv. 130 Thus hauing said, he riseth from the floore, As if his soule diuined him good fortune..For all his thoughts did all good luck importune.

Hence **importuned** *ppl. a.*, **importuning** *vbl. sb.* and *ppl. a.*
1611 Chapman *Iliad* xx. *argt.*, The rest, all shunning their importun'd fates, Achilles beats even to the Ilian gates. **1660** Milton *Free Commw.* Wks. (1851) 427 Our once importuning Prayers against the Tyranny which we then groan'd under. **1660** Gauden *Gods Great Demonstr.* 40 His many forewarnings, importunings, and beseechings of men to flye from the wrath to come. **1720** Gay *Dione* in *Poems* II. 434 No Cleanthes interrupt my woe With importuning love. **1890** *Athenæum* 23 Aug. 254/2 The result of three years' constant importuning. **1958** *Times* 17 Dec. 11/4 The bill ignores the graver offence of importuning. This is mainly an activity of men. **1969** *Daily Tel.* (Colour Suppl.) 10 Jan. 7 Advertisements from importuning homosexuals.

importunely, *adv.* Now *rare.* Also 6 in-. [f. Importune *a.* + -ly[2].]

†**1.** Inopportunely, unseasonably. *Obs.*
c **1425** *Found. St. Bartholomew's* (E.E.T.S.) 25 He mevid hym..with goode and honeste wordes, opportunely and importunely. **1609** Bible (Douay) *Isa.* lviii. *Comm.*, Gods preachers must crie, and not cease to crie..opportunely, importunely, with al patience. **1716** M. Davies *Athen. Brit.* II. 260 How often has that Frenzical Arian Astrologer been told, and admonish'd Opportunely and Importunely.

†**2.** Grievously, troublesomely. *Obs.*
a **1656** Ussher *Ann.* (1658) 758 He..shewed them how proudly and importunely Antonius had answered to all his mild and just demands.

†**3.** Pressingly, persistently, pertinaciously. *Obs.*
1502 Atkynson tr. *De Imitatione* I. ix. 159 It is a synne of pertynacite & pryde any persone inportunly to offre theyr counsell and specially where they can lytle profyte. **1513** More *Rich. III* Wks. 63/1 Without any fear of God..he would importunely [1568 Grafton importunatly] pursue hys appetite, and haue her. *a* **1665** J. Goodwin *Filled w. the Spirit* (1867) 293 It is to be importunely troublesome unto the world, to quarrel almost with every man that comes in our way.

4. With urgent and persistent solicitation; importunately.
1464 *Plumpton Corr.* (Camden) 13 Thomas Eyr clamoreth upon mee importunly for money, so that gif I had any of my own, I wold have stopped him. **1526** *Pilgr. Perf.* (W. de W. 1531) 248 b, It wyll craue importunely for sustenaunce, rest, & other recreacyon. **1590** Spenser *F.Q.* II. viii. 4 He heard a voyce that called lowd and cleare..The Palmer lent his eare unto the noyce, To weet who called so importunely. **1672** J. Worthington *Gen. Pref. Mede's Wks.* e, Flattery and Covetous Ambition do importunely sollicite men to make a false judgment. **1850** J. S. B. Monsell *Parish Musings* (1875) 32 The very things we most desire Most importunely crave.

†**importunement.** *Obs.* [f. Importune *v.* + -ment.] The action or fact of importuning; earnest solicitation; an instance of this.
1635 Swan *Spec. M.* (1670) 474 Satan knoweth..that there be more sundry pressing importunements to read it, than can be shewed for the reading of any book beside.

importuner (ɪmpɔːˈtjuːnə(r), ɪmˈpɔːtjuːnə(r)). [f. as prec. + -er[1].] One who importunes.
1653 Waterhouse *Apol. Learn.* 187 Præclude..your ears..against all rash, rude, irrational, innovating importuners. **1876** Bancroft *Hist. U.S.* V. xlii. 21 Washington..was annoyed by shoals of selfish importuners.

importunity (ɪmpɔːˈtjuːnɪtɪ). [a. F. *importunité* (14th c. in Littré), ad. L. *importūnitās*, f. *importūnus*: see Importune *a.* and -ity.] The quality or condition of being importune.

†**1.** The condition of being unseasonable or inopportune; unseasonableness; an unsuitable time. *Obs.*
1489 Caxton *Faytes of A.* IV. xv. 274 The Importunytee of myn ignoraunce in reformyng of dyuerse argumentes. **1535** Coverdale *Ecclus.* xxxii. 6 Poure not forth wyszdome out of tyme, at an importunyte. **1579** J. Stubbes *Gaping Gulf* E vj, To snatch the crowne from hir heade by oportunity or importunity, which so euer come first. **1589** Puttenham *Eng. Poesie* III. xxiii. (Arb.) 274 Euery thing hath his season which is called Oportunitie, and the vnfitnesse or vndecency of the time is called Importunitie.

†**2.** Burdensomeness, trouble. *Obs.*
1475 *Bk. Noblesse* (Roxb.) 81 Late it be set in money to the remedie and socoure of this gret importunyte and necessite. **1662** J. Davies tr. *Olearius' Voy. Ambass.* 10 The Wagoners..are forc'd to make use of fire against the importunity of those Insects [Gnats]. **1739** J. Huxham *Ess. Fevers* (1750) 213 Very often the Importunity and violence of the Cough was to be appeased by Elixir Asthmaticum.

†**3.** Pertinacity or constancy of action. *Obs.*
1663 J. Spencer *Prodigies* (1665) 215 Many of them..continue for so many hours (if the importunity of Historians in this matter be of any consideration).

4. Troublesome pertinacity in solicitation.
c **1460** Fortescue *Abs. & Lim. Mon.* xii. (1885) 136 Through ymportunite off thair suyttes. **1526** Tindale *Luke* xi. 8 Because of hys importunite he woll ryse and geve hym as many as he nedeth. **1568** Tilney *Disc. Mariage* C vj, Of marvellous vertue is, to bee sufferable in the ymportunities of hys wyfe, sometimes..and in trifling consenting unto her. **1615** G. Sandys *Trav.* 19 With much importunitie and promise of reward..I got them to set me ashore. **1751** Smollett *Per. Pic.* (1779) III. lxxxi. 179 Tormenting me with his nauseous importunities. **1784** Cowper *Task* IV. 414 Knaves..liberal of their aid To clam'rous importunity in rags. **1875** Jowett *Plato* (ed. 2) I. 462 Fearing that our importunity might be troublesome.

†**impor'tunous**, *a.* *Obs. rare.* [f. L. *importūn-us* + -ous.] Burdensome, pestering.
1598 Yong *Diana* 412 Being now free from the importunous trouble of thy iealous husband.

†**im'portuous**, *a.* *Obs.* *rare*[−0]. [ad. L. *importuōs-us*, f. *im-* (im-[2]) + *portu-s* harbour, port.] 'Without port or haven' (Blount *Glossogr.* 1656).

†**im'porturait, -ate**, *pa. pple.* *Sc. Obs.* [for *importrait, impourtrait*, pa. pple. of Importray.] Portrayed in or upon something.
1501 Douglas *Pal. Hon.* III. lxviii, Palace and towris..Importurait of birdis and sweit flouris. **1553** *Douglas' Æneis* VIII. x. 79 For Vulcanus..Thare batellis all..Had thare importurate [*MS.* porturat] propirly and graue.

importure: see Emporture.

impos., colloq. abbreviation of Impossible *a.*
1924 Galsworthy *White Monkey* I. ix, 'If you're tired we could cut that.' 'My dear! Impos.!'

imposable (ɪmˈpəʊzəb(ə)l), *a. rare.* [f. Impose *v.* + -able.]

1. That may be imposed or laid on.
a **1660** Hammond (J.), They were not simply imposeable on any particular man, farther than he was a member of some church.

2. Capable of being imposed upon or cheated; gullible, dupable.
a **1734** North *Exam.* II. iv. (1740) 306 Much more monstrous is it to imagine readers so imposable upon to credit it upon any one's bare Relation. —— *Lives* (1826) I. 397 If he had been..a weak imposable wretch they had liked him much better.

Hence **im'posableness**, 'the state or quality of being imposable'.
1847 in Craig.

†**im'posal.** *Obs. rare.* [f. Impose *v.* + -al[1] 5: cf. *disposal, proposal.*] The action of imposing; imposition.
1641 R. Brooke *Eng. Episc.* I. iv. 17 They have had Authority above their owne (though I conceive, none for such rigid imposall). **1651** P. Sterry *Eng. Deliverance* (1652) 14 Being severe in the imposall of superstitious rites.

†**imposant.** *Obs. rare.* [a. F. *imposant*, pres. pple. of *imposer* to impose, formerly to impute.] One who imputes or charges.
1502 *Ord. Crysten Men* (W. de W. 1506) IV. xxi. 271 In besechynge the herers that they be not euyll dysposed or euyll content of the imposaunt, for he ymageneth to haue power to proue cryme that he imposeth.

impose (ɪmˈpəʊz), *v.* Also 6 **empose**. [a. F. *impose-r* (1302 in Godef.), earlier *en-, emposer* (11th c. in Littré), f. *em-, im-* (im-[1]) + *poser*, taken as repr. of L. *impōnĕre*: see Compose, Pose. Introduced first in special senses, e.g. 3, 2 b; the general sense being expressed by native words.]

I. *trans.*

1. To lay on or set on; to place or set in a position; to put, place, or deposit. *arch.*
1597 A. M. tr. *Guillemeau's Fr. Chirurg.* 16/2 The Chirurgiane [shall] impose the foresayed guttes agayne into their places..imposing or layinge the hande one the wounde. **1599** —— tr. *Gabelhouer's Bk. Physicke* 37/2 Impose therin linnen cloutes. **1615** Chapman *Odyss.* XIII. 207 She impos'd a stone Close to the cauernes mouth. **1781** Gibbon *Decl. & F.* xvii. II. 7 It was here likewise..that Xerxes imposed a stupendous bridge of boats. **1867** J. B. Rose tr. *Virgil's Æneid* 318 The mourners..on the tepid ground imposed more earth.

b. *Eccl.* To lay on hands in blessing, or in ordination, confirmation, etc.
1582 N. T. (Rhem.) *Mark* x. 16 And imposing hands vpon them, he blessed them. **1597** Hooker *Eccl. Pol.* V. lxvi. §1 When Israel blessed..Joseph's sons, he imposed upon them his hands and prayed. **1642** Jer. Taylor *Episc.* xxxii. 175 Bishops had a power of imposing hands, for collating of Orders, which Presbyters have not. **1658** Bramhall *Consecr. Bps.* vii. 177 What Priests did impose hands upon me.

c. To place in command or office; to appoint or set up authoritatively. Now *rare* or *Obs.* exc. as associated with 4.
1617 Moryson *Itin.* II. 57 And would be ready, after putting off the person which now was imposed on him, with much contentment to be commaunded by his Lordship. **1632** Lithgow *Trav.* III. 78 They have a Generall..who deposeth, or imposeth Magistrates. **1682** *Enq. Elect. Sheriffs* 20 So ungrateful a thing hath it always been to the People of England, to have Sheriffs imposed upon, and set over them,

otherwise than according to the course and direction of the Law.

d. *Printing.* To lay pages of type or stereotype plates on the imposing-stone or the bed of a press, and secure them in a chase, in such order that the printed pages shall follow each other in proper order when the sheet is folded.

1652 URQUHART *Jewel* Wks. (1834) 182 His [the setter's] plenishing of the gally, and imposing of the form. **1652** [see IMPOSITOR]. **1688** R. HOLME *Armoury* III. 122/2 *Imposing*, is the placing of the Pages that belong to a Sheet, within the Chase..in order, that when the Sheet is wrought off..all the Pages may be foulded into an orderly succession. **1824** J. JOHNSON *Typogr.* II. xiv. 495 The compositor who imposes a sheet must correct the chargeable proof of that sheet. **1875** KNIGHT *Dict. Mech.* 1172/1, 18, 24, 32 and 48mo. may be imposed in a similar manner, or may be so imposed as to be cut before folding.

2. *fig.* **a.** In general sense: to put, place; to place authoritatively. **b.** To apply authoritatively or bestow (a name or title) *upon, on*, †*to*. (In quots. 1500, 1566 with inverted construction.) Now associated with 4. †**c.** To put authoritatively (an end, conclusion, etc.) to. *Obs.*

1681 R. KNOX *Hist. Ceylon* 50 In whose service he imposeth greater confidence. **1818** JAS. MILL *Brit. India* II. IV. iv. 154 Lally had now..imposed upon the English so much respect, as deterred them from the siege.

b. *c* **1500** *Melusine* xix. 102 He was soone baptised and imposed to name Edon. *c* **1566** J. ALDAY tr. *Boaystuau's Theat. World* A vij, If thou wilt impose this worke a rapsodie, collation or gathering..thou shalt doe it no wrong. **1596** SPENSER *F.Q.* V. viii. 49 To prove her surname true, that she imposed has. **1605** CAMDEN *Rem.* (1637) 122 Riuers also haue imposed names to some men. **1669** GALE *Crt. Gentiles* I. I. vii. 36 The names, which the Phenicians imposed on those places. **1774** J. BRYANT *Mythol.* II. 294 The name was imposed antecedent to his birth. **1862** STANLEY *Jew. Ch.* (1877) I. ix. 183 The native names were altered, and new titles imposed by the Israelites.

c. **1541** R. COPLAND *Galyen's Terapeut.* 2 Hj, We wyl shew ye reason & maner to heale..than we wyl impose the ende of this fourth boke. **1581** SAVILE *Agricola* (1622) 197 To fiftie yeeres trauailes let this day impose a glorious conclusion. *c* **1611** CHAPMAN *Iliad* XXIV. 708 Before they had imposed the crown To these solemnities.

†**3.** To lay (a crime, etc.) to the account of; to impute, charge. *Obs.* (The earliest recorded use.)

1484 CAXTON *Fables of Æsop* 2 b, How he excused hym of that was imposed to hym. **1502** [see IMPOSANT]. **1596** DRAYTON *Legends* ii. 447 On him, the King..Impos'd my Death. **1599** SHAKS. *Hen. V*, IV. i. 157 The imputation of his wickednesse..should be imposed vpon his Father that sent him. **1663** GERBIER *Counsel* a viij a, It were a matter to impose as a charge upon the Author of such a Treatise.

4. To lay on, as something to be borne, endured, or submitted to; to inflict (something) *on* or *upon*; to levy or enforce authoritatively or arbitrarily.

1581 *N. Riding Rec.* I. 250 And further that the said Emprygham at an Admyrall Court dyd sett and empose greate and grevouse Fynes. **1588** SHAKS. *L.L.L.* v. ii. 850 Impose some seruice on me for my loue. **1593** —— *3 Hen. VI*, IV. iii. 58 What Fates impose, that men must needs abide. **1601** R. JOHNSON *Kingd. & Commw.* (1603) 174 They ..impose uppon the people al kinde of injuries. **1688** BUNYAN *Jerusalem Sinner* (1886) 52 These bloody letters were not imposed upon me. I went to the high-priest and desired them of him. **1703** POPE *Thebais* 398 On impious realms..impose Thy plagues. **1741** WATTS *Improv. Mind* I. vii. §11 To impose on a child to get by heart 'a long scroll of unknown phrases or words'. **1849** MACAULAY *Hist. Eng.* vi. II. 159 Pretending to abhor tests, he had himself imposed a test. **1854** J. S. C. ABBOTT *Napoleon* (1885) lxi. 471/1 [Alexander said] We have no wish to impose the Bourbons on the French people. **1875** JOWETT *Plato* (ed. 2) V. 58 Minos..imposed upon the Athenians a cruel tribute.

b. with double object (orig. dative of person and accusative of the thing).

1613 HEYWOOD *Silver Age* III. i. Wks. 1874 III. 126 For your sake I will impose him dangers, Such and so great. **1619** BRENT tr. *Sarpi's Counc. Trent* (1676) 499 Cardinal Crescentius..was wont..to impose them silence. **1810** tr. *Mad. de Stael Holstein's Libertine Husb.* I. 52 Her admirer, Dorville, was imposed silence. **1873** BROWNING *Red Cott. Nt.-cap* 221 Before the servant be imposed a task.

c. To put or levy (a tax, price, etc.) *on* or *upon* (goods, etc.).

1600 E. BLOUNT tr. *Conestaggio* 18 They imposed a newe custome upon the salt. **1660** F. BROOKE tr. *Le Blanc's Trav.* 228 [He] petitioned him he would bestow upon him the captive Princesse, or vouchsafe to impose a ransom on her. **1670** R. COKE *Disc. Trade* 15 To impose what wages they please upon their labours. **1863** H. COX *Instit.* III. ii. 601 That the Crown had the right to impose duties on foreign merchandise.

d. To put or subject (a person, etc.) *to* a penalty, observance, etc.

1568 NORTH tr. *Gueuara's Diall Pr.* (1619) 610 It is as necessary for the Courtier..to impose his tongue to silence. **1592** CONSTABLE *Sonn.* VII. vi, Thus long impos'd to euerlasting plaining. **1599** SHAKS. *Much Ado* v. i. 282 Impose me to what penance your inuention Can lay vpon my sinne.

e. *University* or *school slang.* To punish (a person) by an imposition: see IMPOSITION 5 c.

1887 J. R. MAGRATH (in *Let.*), Very lately a man was imposed for having missed chapel.

5. To obtrude or 'put' (a thing) *upon* (a person) by false representations; to palm or pass off.

1650 EVELYN *Mem.* 14 Dec., An impostor..had like to have impos'd upon us a pretended secret of multiplying gold. **1681-6** J. SCOTT *Chr. Life* (1747) III. 618 The God of Truth would never have empowered them to impose such a Cheat upon the World. **1712** tr. *Pomet's Hist. Drugs* I. 2 Take care..that Southernwood-seed be not imposed upon you for this. **1736** BOLINGBROKE *Patriot.* (1749) 142 A silly fellow can never impose himself for a man of sense. **1738** BIRCH *Milton* I. App. 73 First inventing a Falshood, and then imposing it on the World. **1837** MACKINTOSH, etc. *Hist. Eng.* V. i. 1 Thus early was he familiar with the art of imposing decorum for morality.

II. *intr.* (Often with *indirect passive*).

6. To put oneself *upon*: in various senses. **a.** To impose itself forcibly, authoritatively, or strikingly; to exert an influence *on*; to be of imposing character or appearance. †**b.** To encroach *upon*, to 'put' *upon*. *Obs.* **c.** To intrude, presume *upon*; to take advantage of.

a. **1625** BACON *Ess., Truth* (Arb.) 499 When it [Truth] is found, it imposeth vpon mens Thoughts. **1669** PEPYS *Diary* 30 Mar., They do think that I know too much, and shall impose upon whomever shall come next, and therefore must be removed. **1751** CHESTERF. *Lett.* (1792) III. ccxlv. 126 If you engage his heart, you have a fair chance for imposing upon his understanding, and determining his will. **1881** LUBBOCK *Addr. Brit. Assoc.* in *Nature* No. 618. 411 Mechanism that imposes through its extreme simplicity. **1883** LIEUT.-COL. STEWART in *Pall Mall G.* 23 Nov. 1/1 The troops, if not very formidable in quality, still impose through their number.

b. **1667** PEPYS *Diary* 9 Jan., There is no danger, in the passing this Bill, of imposing on his [the King's] prerogative. **1694** WOOD *Let.* June in *Life* (O.H.S.) III. 458 *note*, Imposing upon a generous person and making him a ridicule to the company..because of his then growing infirmity. *a* **1718** PENN *Wks.* (1726) I. 448 No Man is so accountable to his fellow Creatures, as to be imposed upon, restrained, or persecuted for any Matter of Conscience whatever.

c. **1670** COTTON *Espernon* Ded., I should not otherwise.. have presum'd to impose upon your Protection. **1883** C. J. WILLS *Mod. Persia* 46 An idle 'vagrom' man, who lives by imposing on the good nature of others. **1888** MRS. H. WARD *R. Elsmere* I. 88 She wished her son to impose upon her when it came to his taking any serious step in life.

7. To put a tax, to levy an impost (*upon*). ? *Obs.*

a **1618** RALEIGH *Prerog. Parl.* (1628) 51 To Impose upon all things brought into the Kingdome is very ancient. **1642** *Ord. Parl. Tonnage & P.* 11 To restraine the Crowne from imposing upon the people without their consent. **1642** in Clarendon *Hist. Reb.* v. §21 Desire a bill, (the only old way of imposing on our subjects). **1871** BROWNING *Pr. Hohenst.* 1814 Who scores a septett true for strings and wind Mulcted must be—else how should I impose Properly?

8. To practise imposture; with *upon, on*, to cheat or deceive by false representations.

1662 STILLINGFL. *Orig. Sacr.* I. ii. §9 The great reason the world hath been so long time imposed upon with varieties of books going under the name of Hermes Trismegistus. **1712** STEELE *Spect.* No. 300 ¶2 There are some so weak as to be imposed upon by fine Things and false Addresses. **1791** PAINE *Rights Man*, It can be of no real service to a Nation, to impose upon itself, or to permit itself to be imposed upon. **1873** H. ROGERS *Orig. Bible* i. (1875) 4 The counterfeit must have some resemblance to the genuine, else it would impose on nobody.

Hence **im'posed** *ppl. a.*, in the various senses of the vb.; also ***imposed-upon***: see sense 8 above.

1630 *R. Johnson's Kingd. & Commw.* 134 The imposed buildings [on London bridge], being so many, and so beautifull. **1642** JER. TAYLOR *Episc.* (1647) 139 To transplant them [words] to an artificiall, and imposed sense. **1706** DE FOE *Jure Div.* Pref. 27 They obtain'd so much upon the subjected Minds of the Poor imposed-upon Multitude. **1827** G. HIGGINS *Celtic Druids* 217 It generally consists of four stones, three upright and one imposed. **1847** GROTE *Greece* II. xxxiii. (1862) III. 202 Of the nineteen silver-paying satrapies, the most heavily imposed was Babylonia.

†**im'pose**, *sb. Obs. rare.* [f. IMPOSE *v.*] The imposition or laying on of a charge, duty, or task.

1591 SHAKS. *Two Gent.* IV. iii. 8 According to your Ladiships impose, I am thus early come. **1605** *Tryall Chev.* II. ii. in Bullen *O. Pl.* III. 293 But this impose is nothing, honour'd King.

imposement (ɪm'pəʊzmənt). *rare.* [f. IMPOSE *v.* + -MENT.] The action of imposing; imposition.

1664 H. MORE *Myst. Iniq.* xiii. 45 This imposement upon my self was a great ease and pleasure to the charitableness of my nature. **1896** *Columbus* (Ohio) *Disp.* 18 July 5/5 The residents..who are opposed to the imposement are fighting it.

imposer (ɪm'pəʊzə(r)). [f. IMPOSE *v.* + -ER[1].]

a. One who imposes: in various senses of the vb.

1597 HOOKER *Eccl. Pol.* v. lxxviii. §2 According to the mind of the first imposer of that name. **1641** MILTON *Animadv.* i, Civil politie, say you..came from arbitrary imposers. **1659** PEARSON *Creed* (1741) 189 The coronary thorns did not only express the scorn of the imposers,..but did also pierce his tender and sacred temples. **1681** H. MORE in *Glanvill's Sadducismus* Postscr., Præstigiator an Imposer on the sight. **1702** DE FOE *Occas. Conform.* in *Misc.* 315 An Oath is to be taken in the Sense of the Imposer, and a Sacrament, which is a Recognition of the most Sacred of Oaths, must be also taken in the Sense of the Imposer. **1860** TRENCH *Serm. Westm. Abb.* ix. 96 They might have cursed the imposers of those tasks. **1875** JOWETT *Plato* (ed. 2) I. 36 What that is to which the imposer of names gives this name of temperance or wisdom.

b. *Printing.* One who imposes (see IMPOSE *v.* 1 d).

1921 *Dict. Occup. Terms* (1927) §522 *Stone hand*, imposer; imposes type, which has been set up in page form, in correct position in chase or iron frame, for printing in sheets.

imposing (ɪm'pəʊzɪŋ), *vbl. sb.* [f. IMPOSE *v.* + -ING[1].]

1. The action of putting, placing, or laying on; imposition. *spec.* †**a.** The imposition of taxes, taxing. *Obs.*

1610 BP. CARLETON *Jurisd.* 289 This imposing of the Popes Iurisdiction vpon other nations. *a* **1618** RALEIGH *Invent. Shipping* 41 Certainly the imposing upon Coales.. can be no hinderance..to the Newcastlemen. **1668** GLANVILL *Plus Ultra* (1688) 148 [This] prevents all imperious Dictates and Imposings.

b. *Printing.* The arrangement of pages of type in a 'forme'. *attrib.* **imposing-stone, -table**, a slab of stone or metal on which pages of type or stereotype plates are imposed.

1727-41 CHAMBERS *Cycl.* s.v. *Printing*, The compositor.. carries them to the imposing or correcting-stone, there to range them in order, in a chase. **1824** J. JOHNSON *Typogr.* II. vii. 146 Imposing in quires may be carried on to any extent, by observing the following rule. *Ibid.* xiii. 482 The moment a sheet is composed and made up, he should order it to be imposed, provided there be room on the imposing-stone. **1846** *Print. Apparatus for Amateurs* 43 The arranging the pages of type for this purpose is called imposing, and this term also includes the placing of the furniture between the pages so as to make the necessary margin. **1883** *Scotsman* 9 May 11/7 A number of Imposing Tables.

2. with *upon*: Deception; imposition.

1658-9 *Burton's Diary* (1828) IV. 180 This is an imposing upon you.

imposing (ɪm'pəʊzɪŋ), *ppl. a.* [f. IMPOSE *v.* + -ING[2].] That imposes, in various senses of the vb.

1. That peremptorily enjoins; exacting.

1651 BOYLE *Occas. Refl.* (1665) II. v. ix. 179 A piece of Vanity, which, as imposing as Custom is wont to be, it has not yet dar'd to enjoyn. **1679** PENN *Addr. Prot.* II. 144 An Imposing Church..will be both Party and Judge: it requires Assent without Evidence, and Faith without Proof. **1772** MAD. D'ARBLAY *Early Diary* (1889) I. 149 He felt the utter impossibility of arguing with a man so imposing and so very ignorant. **1853** J. H. NEWMAN *Hist. Sk.* (1873) II. I. iv. 203 The more barbarous is a nation, the more imposing and peremptory are its claims.

2. That impresses by appearance or manner.

1786 W. THOMSON *Watson's Philip III* (1794) II. v. 133 Touched with an imposing delicacy on the irregularity of Ossuna's disposition. **1800** MRS. HERVEY *Mourtray Fam.* II. 15 She had such a majestic imposing air, that..many were disposed to make way for her. **1858** O. W. HOLMES *Aut. Breakf.-t.* i. 4 Audacious self-esteem, with good ground for it, is always imposing. **1860** TYNDALL *Glac.* I. xvi. 110 Mountains..of imposing magnitude.

3. Using deception; practising imposture.

1754 FIELDING *Voy. Lisbon* Wks. 1882 VII. 85 The imposing disposition of the people; who asked so much more than the proper price of their labour. **1796** J. OWEN *Trav. Europe* I. 72 The Dutch are represented as very trickish and imposing.

Hence **im'posingly** *adv.*, in an imposing manner; impressively. **im'posingness**, the quality of being imposing or impressive.

1812 SIR R. WILSON *Priv. Diary* I. 377 The whole scene is imposingly magnificent. **1813** L. HUNT in *Examiner* 22 Mar. 184/1 There is a pretty general breaking up of French imposingness over the Continent. **1876** GEO. ELIOT *Dan. Der.* v. xxxv, The white silk..might have something to do with the new imposingness of her beauty. **1880** MISS BIRD *Japan* I. 15 The British Consulate, imposingly ugly.

imposition (ɪmpəʊ'zɪʃən). Forms: 4 **imposiscion, -sicoun**, 5–6 **-sicion**, (6 **inpossession**), 5– **imposition**. [ME. ad. L. *impositiōn-em*, n. of action from *impōnĕre* to place upon, IMPOSE, or a. OF. *imposition, -icion* (1317 in Godef.). First used in the special senses 1 b, 2, 5.]

1. The action of putting, placing, or laying on. Also *concr.* A layer over something. *rare.*

1597 A. M. tr. *Guillemeau's Fr. Chirurg.* 38/2 The imposition of the fingers one the mouthes of the Veynes. **1599** —— tr. *Gabelhouer's Bk. Physicke* 54/2 On the sayed Straweberryes you must agayne strewe saulte, and agayne theron an impositione of strawberryes,..continuing the impositione of one on the other till the basen be repleate. **1833** MEDWIN *Shelley* (1847) II. 48 The imposition of my hand on his forehead, instantly put a stop to his spasms. **1888** *Pall Mall G.* 6 Dec. 5/1 A Japanese lacquer box..in various stages of development, from the imposition of colour on the first stone to the last.

b. *spec.* The laying on of hands in blessing, ordination, confirmation, etc. [L. *impositio*, Vulgate, Acts viii. 18.]

1382 WYCLIF *Bible* Pref. Ep. Jerome iii, The grace, the which is ȝouun to hym bi imposicoun [1388 puttyng to] of the prestis hond. **1548** CRANMER *Catech.* 230 The ministration of Gods worde..was deryued from the Apostles vnto other after theim by imposition of handes, and gyuynge the holy ghost. **1597** HOOKER *Eccl. Pol.* v. lxvi. §1 With prayers of spiritual and personal benediction the manner hath been in all ages to use imposition of hands, as a ceremony betokening our restrained desires to the party, whom we present unto God by prayer. **1660** JER. TAYLOR *Worthy Commun.* I. iii. 59 Thus we find that the grace of God is given by the imposition of hands. **1796** MORSE *Amer. Geog.* II. 157 Ministers, or preaching presbyters..alone can ..assist at the imposition of hands upon other ministers. **1885** *Catholic Dict.* (ed. 3) s.v., In two instances (the imposition of hands in ordination and confirmation) it [the rite] has received a sacramental efficacy.

c. *Print.* The imposing or arranging of pages of type in the forme.

1824 J. JOHNSON *Typogr.* II. vii. 144 A general outline for the imposition of whatever odd matter there may be at the

conclusion of a work. *Ibid.* xiv. 495 Pages..laid down for imposition, without folios or head lines, must be rectified by the person who has been slovenly enough to adopt this plan.

2. The action of attaching, affixing, or ascribing; bestowal (of a name, etc.).

1387–8 T. USK *Test. Love* II. iv. (Skeat) l. 141 Wel, quod I, this inpossession I wol wel understande. **1430–40** LYDG. *Bochas* I. i. (1544) 1 b, Adam made an imposicion..to those beastes all Of very reason what men should them call. **1599** HAKLUYT *Voy.* II. II. 89 Termed Cantam, which is rather the common name of the prouince, then a word of their proper imposition. **1709** STEELE *Tatler* No. 49 ¶1 The Imposition of honest Names and Words upon improper Subjects. **1870** J. H. NEWMAN *Gram. Assent* I. §2. 7 By our apprehension of propositions I mean our imposition of a sense on the terms of which they are composed.

†**3.** Imputation, accusation, charge. *Obs.*

1611 SHAKS. *Wint. T.* I. ii. 74 The Imposition clear'd, Hereditarie ours.

4. The action of imposing or laying as a burden, duty, charge, or task; the action of inflicting, levying, enjoining, or enforcing.

1593 SHAKS. *Lucr.* 1697 At this request..Each present Lord began to promise aide, As bound in Knighthood to her imposition. **1594** HOOKER *Eccl. Pol.* I. ii. §6 The Imposition of this Law upon himself is his own free and voluntary Act. **1621** BURTON *Anat. Mel.* I. ii. I. ii. (1651) 51 The superstitious impositions of fasts. **1841** MYERS *Cath. Th.* III. §34. 123 Opinions..not derived from forcible external imposition. **1845** MCCULLOCH *Taxation* I. iv. 108 The effects that would result from the imposition of taxes.

†**b.** The levying of a tax; taxation. *Obs.*

c **1374** CHAUCER *Boeth.* I. pr. iv. 9 (Camb. MS.) Coempcion..þat weere estabelyssed vp on the poeple by swich a manere imposiscion as who so bowhte a bossel corn he moste yeue the kynge the fifte part. **1628** in Clarendon *Hist. Reb.* III. §217 Any power of Imposition upon any Merchandizes.

5. Anything imposed, levied, or enjoined:

a. An impost; tax, duty; *spec.* in *pl.* duties upon imports and exports imposed by the royal prerogative.

c **1460** FORTESCUE *Abs. & Lim. Mon.* x. (1885) 132 He takith certayn imposicions made by hym selff vppon euery oxe. **1483** *Act 1 Rich. III*, c. 2 A new Imposition called a Benevolence. *a* **1533** LD. BERNERS *Huon* lx. 210 He hath reissyd vp in all his londes new taylles & gables & inpossessyons. **1689** BURNET *Tracts* I. 44 Those who stay behind, can scarce live and pay those grievous Impositions that are laid upon them. **1839** KEIGHTLEY *Hist. Eng.* I. 83 The lands of the church were also subject to the ordinary impositions for the public service. **1863** H. COX *Instit.* III. ii. 601 Prerogative impositions at the ports were dormant from the reign of Edward III. to that of Mary.

†**b.** A command, charge, or ordinance imposed or laid upon one. *Obs.*

1596 SHAKS. *Merch. V.* III. iv. 33, I doe desire you Not to denie this imposition, The which my loue and some necessity Now layes vpon you. **1601** HOLLAND *Pliny* II. 513 In those capitulations of peace..I find this expresse article and imposition, that they should not vse yron, but only about tillage of the ground. **1637** R. HUMPHREY tr. *St. Ambrose* I. 141 His imposition, 'let those in Iudea flie to the mountaines'. **1664** H. MORE *Myst. Iniq.* iii. 7 The decrees and ceremonial impositions of men.

c. A literary exercise or task imposed as a punishment at school or college. (Colloquially abbreviated *impo* or *impot.*)

1746 WARTON *Progr. Discontent* 121 When impositions were supplyd To light my pipe, or sooth my pride. **1785** —— *Minor Poems Milton* 422 note (Webster), Literary tasks called impositions. **1806–7** J. BERESFORD *Miseries Hum. Life* (1826) XII. Concl. 322, I have never forgotten the passage, since I once translated it at Oxford as an imposition. **1844** J. T. HEWLETT *Parsons & W.* xv, The penalty for transgressing this..was a long imposition—task some would call it. **1899** *Punch* 22 Feb. 88/2, I..got an 'impot' for cribbing a Greek exercise.

6. The action of imposing upon or deceiving by palming off what is false or unreal; an instance of this, an imposture.

1632 LITHGOW *Trav.* III. 108 When the flat contrary of his abjured impositions, is infallibly knowne to be of undoubted trueth. **1708** SWIFT *Death Partridge*, The predictions you printed..were mere impositions on the people. **1749** FIELDING *Tom Jones* XVI. ix, He was afraid Miss Western would never agree to an imposition of this kind. **1875** JOWETT *Plato* (ed. 2) II. 83 He who would either impose on others or escape imposition must know the truth.

impositive (ɪmˈpɒzɪtɪv), *a. rare.* [f. IM-² + POSITIVE *a.*] Not positive.

c **1856** DE MORGAN *Budget Paradoxes* (1872) 275 He [the psychological speculator] requires it to be granted that his system is positive and that your's is impositive.

†**impositor** (ɪmˈpɒzɪtə(r)). *Obs. rare.* [a. L. *impositor*, agent-noun from *impōnĕre* to IMPOSE.] One who imposes; = IMPOSER. †**a.** One who imposes a name. **b.** *Printing.* One who imposes the pages of type in a forme. **c.** The inflicter of a task or imposition.

1493 *Festivall* (W. de W. 1515) 122 b, Yf the imposytoure and gyuer of the name hath perfyte scyence and knowledge. **1617** MINSHEU *Ductor Ling.*, *Impositor*, in schooles he that put the names into a Rolle. **1656** BLOUNT *Glossogr.*, *Impositor*, the Impositor or Monitor in a School; also he that imposes the pages into a Form for the Press.

impossibilifiˈcation. *nonce-wd.* [f. IMPOSSIBLE: see -FICATION.] A rendering impossible.

1818 COLERIDGE in *Rem.* (1836) I. 88 Sovereigns and their courtiers were flattered by the degradation of nature and the *impossibilification* of a pretended virtue.

impossibilism (ɪmˈpɒsɪbɪlɪz(ə)m). [f. IMPOSSIBLE *a.* + -ISM.] Belief in ideas, especially on social reform, which cannot reasonably be put into practice. So **impossibilist** (ɪmˈpɒsɪbɪlɪst, -pɒˈsɪb-) *a.*, of or pertaining to such views; also as *sb.*, one who holds such impracticable views.

1885 G. B. SHAW *Let.* 14 Dec. (1965) 146 We detect..the ..anarchical impossibilism to which your proposition of private property in ideas..must lead in practice. **1892** —— *Let.* 22 Aug. (1965) 362 They had better circulate it among the Impossibilists. **1900** *Speaker* 3 Mar. 592/1 Even amongst those who were but recently impossibilist politicians saner views are prevailing. **1906** *Westm. Gaz.* 8 Feb. 7/2 We are predicting no impossibilist policy. **1909** *Ibid.* 17 Apr. 16/3 Impossibilists in Labour Politics. **1910** *Daily News* 3 Feb. 4/2 There is no fixed hostility, and no impossibilism of attitude. **1917** CHESTERTON *Short Hist. Eng.* 76 An idealism akin to impossibilism. **1921** *Public Opinion* 29 July 107/1 In a world largely controlled by fanatics, dreamers, and impossibilists, the one thoroughly practical policy is that of the League of Nations Union. **1939** *New Statesman* 18 Nov. 712/2 An exposure of Nazi impossibilism.

impossiˈbilitate, *v. rare.* [f. IMPOSSIBILIT-Y + -ATE³; cf. Sp. *imposibilitar*, It. *impossibilitare.*] *trans.* To render impossible.

1633 T. ADAMS *Exp. 2 Peter* ii. 14 It [covetousness] impossibilitates the entrance into heaven. **1646** CHAS. I *Let.* in Carte *Ormonde* (1735) III. 452, I..would do nothing to impossibilitate ayde [*printed* adye] from thence. **1834** SOUTHEY *Doctor* II. 116 How many accidents might for ever have impossibilitated the existence of this incomparable work!

impossibility (ɪmpɒsɪˈbɪlɪtɪ). [a. F. *impossibilité* (14th c.) or ad. L. *impossibilitāt-em*, f. *impossibilis* IMPOSSIBLE: see -ITY.]

1. a. The quality of being impossible.

1387–8 T. USK *Test. Love* III. iii. (Skeat) l. 14 Shewe me the absence of that impossibilite. **1526** *Pilgr. Perf.* (W. de W. 1531) 215 No lesse impossibilite it is, but rather more. **1548** HALL *Chron.*, *Hen. VIII* 110 To declare the impossibilite of this demaunde. **1647** CLARENDON *Hist. Reb.* I. §55 The impossibility that his Intelligence could be true. **1707** *Curios. in Husb. & Gard.* 187 The Impossibility they lie under of restoring them to their first State. **1754** EDWARDS *Freed. Will* I. iii. 19 Impossibility is the same as negative Necessity, or a Necessity that a Thing should not be. **1876** MOZLEY *Univ. Serm.* xi. (1877) 221 Where is the impossibility of a glorious and endless existence?

b. With *an* and *pl.*: An instance of this; an impossible thing; that which cannot be.

c **1500** *Three Kings' Sons* 112, I am not bounde to noon ympossibilite. **1570** BILLINGSLEY *Euclid* I. i. 9 A demonstration leadyng to an impossibilitie is that argument whose conclusion is impossible. **1691–8** NORRIS *Pract. Disc.* (1711) III. 73 The Impossibilities are of two sorts, Impossible Truths, and Impossible Goods. **1772** PRIESTLEY *Inst. Relig.* (1782) I. 28 Even divine power cannot produce impossibilities. **1828** CARLYLE *Misc.*, *Burns* (1872) II. 14 Is not every genius an impossibility till he appear?

†**2.** Impotence, inability. (So med.L. *impossibilitās.*) *Obs.*

c **1450** tr. *De Imitatione* III. vi. 71 Loue..pleyniþ neuere of impossibilite, for it demeþ itself miȝty to all þinges. **1553** LATIMER *Serm. Lord's Pr.* iv. (1562) 22 b, He woulde haue vs to know our owne impossibilitye and vnablenesse to doe any thyng. *Ibid.* vii. 45 Whan..we say, Leade vs not into temptation, we learn to know our own impossibilitie and infirmitie. **1654–66** LD. ORRERY *Parthen.* 534 News of his impossibility of doing it. **1796** *Plain Sense* II. 167 The utter impossibility of her father to afford any effectual assistance.

3. *Math.* The quality of being 'impossible' or imaginary. *rare.*

1673 WALLIS in Rigaud *Corr. Sci. Men* (1841) II. 557 Notwithstanding the impossibility of..the square root of a negative quantity.

4. *Comb.* **impossibility theorem** (see quots.). (Earlier known as the *possibility theorem*: see POSSIBILITY 4.)

[**1950** K. J. ARROW in *Jrnl. Pol. Econ.* LVIII. 342 The Possibility Theorem shows that, if no prior assumptions are made about the nature of individual orderings, there is no method of voting which will remove the paradox of voting discussed in Part I, neither plurality voting nor any scheme of proportional representation, no matter how complicated.] **1957** LUCE & RAIFFA *Games & Decisions* xiv. 333 (*heading*) Conditions on the social welfare function and Arrow's impossibility theorem. **1960** *Q. Jrnl. Econ.* LXXIV. 509 (*heading*) Proof of the Arrow impossibility theorem. **1967** K. J. ARROW in Laslett & Runciman *Philos., Politics & Society* 3rd Ser. 228 The following general theorem may be stated: There can be no constitution simultaneously satisfying the conditions of Collective Rationality, the Pareto Principle, the Independence of Irrelevant Alternatives, and Non-Dictatorship. The proof falls into two parts. It is first shown that if an individual is decisive for some pair of alternatives, then he is a dictator, contrary to the condition of Non-Dictatorship. Hence, no individual is decisive for any pair of alternatives, and the Impossibility Theorem itself then follows easily with the aid of the Pareto Principle. **1969** D. BLACK in *Jrnl. Law & Econ.* XII. ii. 227 The Impossibility Theorem shows that in the general case and apart from restrictions on the members' preferences, no committee procedure will be able to satisfy certain conditions which, Arrow suggests, a procedure might reasonably be required to meet, and that whichever committee procedure we may choose will, for certain sets of schedules, infringe one or more of the apparently reasonable conditions he specifies. **1971** W. LEE *Decision Theory & Human Behavior* iv. 103 Unhappily..reasonable conditions for deriving a social preference ranking from individual rankings are inconsistent with one another, i.e., in general there may be no social ranking conforming to the desired conditions, a conclusion known as Arrow's impossibility theorem.

impossible (ɪmˈpɒsɪb(ə)l), *a.* and *sb.* Forms: 3 **inpossibile**, 4 **in-**, **ympossible**, **impossibel**, 4–6 **impossyble**, 5 **inpossybyll**, **impossybul**, *Sc.* **impossibyll**, 4– **impossible.** [a. F. *impossible* (14th c.) = It. *impossibile*, or ad. (post-cl.) L. *impossibilis*, f. *im-* (IM-²) + *possibilis* POSSIBLE.]

A. *adj.* **1. a.** Not possible; that cannot be done or effected; that cannot exist or come into being; that cannot be, in existing or specified circumstances. Const. *to* or *for.*

The exact sphere in which the thing is declared to be impossible is sometimes expressed by the advs. *logically*, *mathematically*, *morally*, *physically* (see these words).

a **1300** *Cursor M.* 14761 It es bot foli al þi talking, And als an inpossibile [*Gött.* impossible] thing. **1340** HAMPOLE *Pr. Consc.* 6281 Swa witty and myghty es he þat na-thyng til hym impossibel may be. *c* **1460** *Towneley Myst.* xii. 373 Nothyng is inpossybyll sothly that god wyll. **1484** CAXTON *Fables of Æsop* v. i, None ought not to entermete hym to doo that that Impossyble is to hym. **1529** MORE *Dyaloge* I. Wks. 126/1 They..laughed therat as at an impossible lye. **1697** DAMPIER *Voy.* I. 274 We see that sometimes designs have been given over as impossible, and at another time..have been accomplished. **1751** SIR J. HILL *Rev. Wks. Roy. Soc.* (1780) 66 It becomes a wise Man not to think any Thing impossible. **1860** TYNDALL *Glac.* I. xi. 74 We reached a place where further advance was impossible.

b. with infinitive complement (now usually *active*, sometimes passive).

c **1400** MAUNDEV. (1839) xxvi. 265 Summe of hem trowed, it were an Inpossible thing to be. **1476** J. PASTON in *P. Lett.* No. 777 III. 164 It is non inpossybyll to bryng a bowght. **1484** CAXTON *Fables of Æsop* I. xvii, None ought to entermete hym self for to doo a thynge, whiche as for hym impossyble is to be done. **1561** T. NORTON *Calvin's Inst.* I. 5 b, His power impossible to be auoided, hangeth ouer them. **1656** WALLER *To my Ld. Protector* x, What may be thought impossible to do By us. **1667** MILTON *P.L.* IV. 548 The rest was craggie cliff..impossible to climbe.

c. Often qualifying an infinitive phrase, or substantive clause: commonly introduced by *it.*

1340–70 *Alex. & Dind.* 1108 To oure painede peple inpossible hit semeþ, þat ȝe oure manerus mihte mekliche endure. **1377** LANGL. *P. Pl.* B. x. 336 Poule preueth it inpossible riche men haue [*some MSS.* to haue] heuene. **1382** WYCLIF *Heb.* xi. 6 It is inpossible ony man for to plese God withoute feith. **1390** GOWER *Conf.* II. 153 To ben a god is inpossible. *a* **1400–50** *Alexander* 2707 Inpossible it semes A heuy As to be houyn [*Dublin MS.* to heff] on hye to þe sternes. **1526** *Pilgr. Perf.* (W. de W. 1531) 17 It was impossyble for them to..wynne the sayd lande. **1596** SHAKS. *Tam. Shr.* II. i. 285 It were impossible I should speed amisse. *c* **1712** LADY M. W. MONTAGU *Lett.* (1887) II. 1, I believed it impossible you should forget me. **1852** H. ROGERS *Ecl. Faith* (1853) 275 It is impossible that we should ever see levers perfectly inflexible. **1864** *Daily Tel.* 20 Sept., To give anything like a correct amount of the loss..would be impossible. **1890** *Law Times Rep.* LXIII. 766/2 It was impossible..for a loading berth to be secured.

2. *Math.* Having no possible or real value, imaginary.

1673 KERSEY *Algebra* I. 269 Impossible Roots are such whose values cannot be conceived or comprehended either Arithmetically or Geometrically; as in this Equation, $a = 2 - \sqrt{-1}$,..for no Number can be imagined, which being multiplied by itself according to any Rule of Multiplication will produce -1. **1830** GEN. P. THOMPSON *Exerc.* (1842) I. 226 Coming, like impossible roots, by pairs. **1874** TODHUNTER *Trig.* xix. §271 (1882) 216 If *n* be even, the last term..is possible..and the last term but one is impossible.

3. In recent use, with ellipsis of some qualification suggested by the context; as, impossible to deal with, to carry into practice, to do anything with, to get on with, to tolerate, to recognize; utterly unsuitable or impracticable, 'out of the question'.

1858 CARLYLE *Fredk. Gt.* III. vi. I. 247 Never was a spirited young fellow placed in more impossible position. **1865** M. ARNOLD *Ess. Crit.* Pref. 19 Oxford..adorable dreamer..home of lost causes, and forsaken beliefs, and unpopular names, and impossible loyalties! **1876** BESANT & RICE *Gold. Butterfly* II. 173 To all the world except Jack and Agatha, she was an impossible girl; she said things that no other girl would have said. **1884** *Harper's Mag.* May 911/2 The..ghosts..made the place absolutely impossible. **1886** G. ALLEN & MARY COTES *Kalee's Shrine* i. 17 The dear old ugly lady..in the speckly dress and impossible bonnet.

B. *sb.* **1.** = IMPOSSIBILITY. *rare* in *sing.*

c **1374** CHAUCER *Troilus* III. 476 (525) That wyst he wel an inpossible were. **1387–8** T. USK *Test. Love* II. iv. (Skeat) l. 152 If I graunte contradiccion, I should graunt an impossible. *c* **1440** CAPGRAVE *St. Kath.* IV. 662 Your secte ..May not stande..Right for þe impossibles whiche þer-inne ȝe hepe. **1472** J. PASTON in *P. Lett.* No. 701 III. 53 Your desyer..was an impossoybyl to be browght abowght. **1678** CUDWORTH *Intell. Syst.* I. ii. §5. 63 A bundle of incomprehensibles, unconceivables, and impossibles. **1789** T. TAYLOR *Proclus* II. 6 The nature of an impossible becomes known from the seventh [theorem]. **1866** MISS MULOCK *Christian's Mistake* 130 Heaven sometimes converts our impossibles and inevitables into the very best blessings we have.

2. With def. article: that which is or seems impossible.

1839 BAILEY *Festus* 266 He only holds Perfections, which are but the impossible To other beings. **1895** C'TESS MARTINENGO-CESARESCO *Liberation of Italy* xix. 394 Garibaldi..had always demanded the impossible of his men. **1904** *Daily Chron.* 6 May 7/5 The history of Christianity..had been a triumph of the impossible. **1916** HUNEKER *Ivory, Apes & Peacocks* 34 All three were

consumptives..; all three suffered from the nostalgia of the impossible. *a* **1930** F. NANSEN in *Penguin Dict. Mod. Quots.* (1971) 166/2 The difficult is what takes a little time; the impossible is what takes a little longer. **1972** *Pacifist* Nov. 3/1 Remember the Festival motto:—be realistic—demand the impossible.

C. *Comb.*, as ***impossible-looking***.

1871 CARLYLE in *Mrs. Carlyle's Lett.* I. 13 Certainly the impossiblest-looking literary problem I ever had. **1898** *Westm. Gaz.* 31 Mar., This impossible-looking constituency.

im'possibleness. *rare.* [f. prec. + -NESS] = IMPOSSIBILITY.

1447 BOKENHAM *Seyntys* (Roxb.) 29 Whan this Austyn sey the gret mischef.. And the impossybylnesse it to relef. **1642** ROGERS *Naaman* 101 The needlesnesse, difficulty, yea, impossiblenesse of prevailing. **1727** in BAILEY vol. II.

im'possibly, *adv.* [f. as prec. + -LY^{2}.] Not possibly; in an impossible fashion. Now chiefly in ***not impossibly*** = (just) possibly, perhaps.

1579–80 NORTH *Plutarch* (1656) 116 Rome..which..had impossibly attained unto so high glory and power..without the singular favour of the Gods. **1603** DRAYTON *Odes* viii. 7 S' impossibly I love you. **1667** MILTON *P.L.* IX. 360 Reason not impossibly may meet Some specious object by the Foe subornd. **1715–20** POPE *Iliad* v. 353 *note* (Seager), His enemy took..a rising ground, by which means he might not impossibly stand higher. *c* **1825** BEDDOES *Second Brother* II. ii, Let us forget what else is possible, Yea, hope impossibly! **1885** *Manch. Exam.* 28 May 5/3 The ceremony..may not impossibly be marred.

impost ('ɪmpəʊst), *sb.*^{1} [a. OF. *impost* (1429 in Hatz.-Darm.), now *impôt* = Sp. *impuesto*, Pg. *imposto*, ad. med.L. *impostus* or *impostum* (1272 in Du Cange) from L. *impostus*, *impositus*, pa. pple. of *impōnĕre* to IMPOSE. The corresponding It. *imposta* represents the fem. of the same pple. (cf. *mille equi de imposta*, an. 1302 in Du Cange).]

1. A tax, duty, imposition, tribute; *spec.* a customs-duty levied on merchandise. Now chiefly *Hist.*

The distinction suggested by Cowell, that *impost* properly denotes a duty on imported goods, and *custom* one on goods exported, is repeated by later dicts.; but there is no evidence that it was ever in accepted use.

1568 GRAFTON *Chron.*, *Hen. II*, II. 81 He neuer put any tribute, impost, or taxe vpon his subiectes. **1570** *Act 13 Eliz.* c. 4 §1 Customs, Subsidies, Imposts or other Duties within any Port of the Realm. **1601** R. JOHNSON *Kingd. & Commw.* (1603) 124 Keeping garrison there to receive the impostes, and customes of the ariving vessels. *a* **1618** RALEIGH *Prerog. Parl.* (1628) 51 The great taxe vpon wine is still called Impost, because it was imposed after the ordinary rate of payment had lasted many years. **1726** CAVALLIER *Mem.* IV. 274 That the Inhabitants of the Cevennes, whose Houses have been burned in the Wars, shall pay no Imposts for the Term of seven Years. **1789** *Const. U.S.* i. §10 The net produce of all duties and imposts, laid by any State on imports or exports, shall be for the use of the treasury of the United States. **1861** GOSCHEN *For. Exch.* 20 Import duties, or transit dues, and the whole range of Government imposts. **1874** GREEN *Short Hist.* viii. §5. 513 A bench of Judges..declared the new impost [ship-money] to be legal. *fig.* **1702** *Eng. Theophrast.* 236 Confidence is not the favour but the impost of a prince.

b. *attrib.*, as ***impost-fine***, ***-law***; also **impost-taker** (see quot. *a* 1700).

1588 *Acc.-Bk. W. Wray* in *Antiquary* XXXII. 54 Payd.. vj*s*. viij*d*. for an Impost Finne to the quens maiestie of xv. akers lande. *a* **1700** B. E. *Dict. Cant. Crew*, *Impost-taker*, one that stands by and Lends Money to the Gamester at a very high Interest. **1804** J. GRAHAME *Sabbath* (1808) 25 Ye who sit..divising impost-laws.

2. *Racing slang.* The weight which a horse has to carry in a handicap race.

1883 *Daily News* 25 June 2/1 The horse..has such a lenient impost that it will be easy to make him first favourite. **1887** *Ibid.* 7 Feb. 2/6 His light impost might enable him to win.

impost ('ɪmpəʊst), *sb.*^{2} *Arch.* [a F. *imposte* (1545 in Hatz.-Darm.), ad. It. *imposta*, of same derivation as prec.]

1. The upper course of a pillar or abutment, frequently projecting in the form of an ornamental moulding or capital, on which the foot of an arch rests.

Where there is no projection, the impost is said to be *continuous*.

1664 EVELYN tr. *Freart's Archit.* 130 Imposts..are nothing but their Capitels or more protuberant heads, upon which rest the ends of the Arches. **1712** J. JAMES tr. *Le Blond's Gardening* 74 An Arch adorn'd with Imposts. **1845** PETRIE *Eccl. Archit. Irel.* 178 Round pilastres, or semi-columns with flat imposts or capitals. **1850** J. H. PARKER *Gloss. Terms Grecian, Roman, Italian, & Gothic Archit.* (ed. 5) I. 258 It is better..to designate the mouldings as impost mouldings. *c* **1863** *Dict. Archit.* (Archit. Publ. Soc.) III. 15/1 The decorative impost, or point at which the ornamental impost moldings are placed, is frequently below the springing... In some archways the impost point is ornamental with horizontal moldings. **1901** R. STURGIS *Dict. Archit.* II. 464 *Impost block*, a member which gives direct support to one side of an arch, or to the adjoining parts of two arches.

†**2.** The hanging stile of a door or gate; hence, the leaf of a door or gate. *Obs. rare.*

1730 A. GORDON *Maffei's Amphith.* 295 Of these three Gates, the first..has no Marks of ever having had Imposts, ..the other..has two round Holes in the Stone of the Threshold..in them the Hinges of two parts of the Gates.. turned round, causing the Imposts to play [*facendo giocar le imposte*]. By this we discover the manner of the ancient Imposts, called *Postes* by the Latins.

3. A horizontal block supported by upright stones, as at Stonehenge. Also *attrib.*

1768 G. WHITE *Selborne* xxi. (1875) 74 These birds [daws] deposit their nests in the interstices between the upright and the impost stones of that amazing work of antiquity. **1769** *De Foe's Tours Gt. Brit.* I. 296 The outer Circle of Stone-henge..in its Perfection, consisted of 60 Stones, 30 Uprights, and 30 Imposts. **1852** T. WRIGHT *Celt, Roman & Saxon* ii. 59 Thirty upright stones sustaining as many others placed horizontally, so as to form a continuous impost.

†**impost,** *v.*^{1} *Obs. rare.* [app. ad. It. *impostare* 'to set on the impost or case to a door or window'.]

1. *trans.* To set or base on imposts.

1730 A. GORDON *Maffei's Amphith.* 327 The..Wall..has no Thickness..sufficient to impost another Roof of the Wall a-new. *Ibid.* 407 There being no Marks of Vaults on..the Wall, in which they may have been inlaid or imposted.

2. *intr.* To begin to curve inward; to spring, as an arch.

1730 A. GORDON *Maffei's Amphith.* 285 The Roofs do impost, or draw in above the thickness of the Arches.

'impost, *v.*^{2} *U.S. Customs.* [f. IMPOST *sb.*^{1}] *trans.* To classify (imported goods, etc.) according to their tariff designations and the rate of duties paid on them. Hence **'imposter**; **'imposting** *ppl. a.*

1884 *Harper's Mag.* June 57/2 (*New York Custom Ho.*), The entry papers..are..sent to an official who imposts them, or, in other words, classifies the articles therein described in separate columns according to the rate of duty that each is liable to pay. *Ibid.*, From the imposter the entries pass to other hands. *Ibid.*, Again they pass into the hands of the imposting and statistical clerks.

imposteme, obs. form of IMPOSTUME.

imposter, obs. f. IMPOSTOR; see IMPOST *v.*^{2}

†**impo'sterious,** *a. Obs. rare*$^{-1}$. [f. IMPOSTERY + -OUS; cf. IMPOSTORIOUS, -URIOUS.] = next.

1633 HART *Diet Diseased* III. xxx. 373 As for the signe of life and death by the blood sweaty drops, I hold it either imposterious or impious and superstitious.

†**im'posterous,** *a. Obs.* [f. *imposter*, IMPOSTOR, or perh. (from the date) IMPOSTURE + -OUS; cf. IMPOSTOROUS, -TROUS, -TUROUS.]

1. Of the nature of an imposture; false.

1562 BULLEYN *Bk. Simples* 44 a, Nothing, but the imposterous subtiltie of wicked people. **1607** BEAUM. & FL. *Woman-Hater* III. ii, To hold thy strictness false and imposterous. **1665** J. SPENSER *Vulg. Prophecies* 4 So imposterous and litigious an Argument as this is.

2. Having the character of an impostor.

a **1626** MIDDLETON *Mayor Queenborough* II. iii. 235 When thou'rt known to be a whore imposterous. *a* **1640** DAY *Parl. Bees* ix. (1881) 56 This Satyre is the Character Of an imposterous Quacksalver. **1652** GAULE *Magastrom.* 370 Executed for an imposterous traytor.

Hence †**im'posterously** *adv.*

1657 W. MORICE *Coena quasi Κοινὴ* Def. xi. 123 They would not dare to argue so imposterously.

†**im'postery.** *Obs. rare*$^{-1}$. [cf. prec.] Imposture: = IMPOSTORY, -TRY, -TURY.

1656 *Burton's Diary* (1828) I. 72 His riding into Exeter was a horrid piece of pageantry and impostery, but how to call that blasphemy in him I know not.

imposthume, etc.: see IMPOSTUME.

impostor (ɪm'pɒstə(r)). Forms: α. 6–7 **imposture**, (6 **-ur**). β. 7–9 **imposter**. γ. 7 **impostour**, 7– **impostor**. [a. F. *imposteur* (16th c.) = Sp., Pg. *impostor*, It. *impostore*, ad. late L. *impostor*, agent-noun f. *impōnĕre* to IMPOSE (ppl. stem *imposit-*, *impost-*). At its first adoption into English, the word was app. confused with the older IMPOSTURE, the termination being subsequently altered to *-er* and *-or*, the latter of which, agreeing with the original L. form, has survived.]

One who imposes on others; a deceiver, swindler, cheat; now chiefly, one who assumes a false character, or passes himself off as some one other than he really is.

α. **1586** JAS. VI in Ellis *Orig. Lett.* Ser. I. III. 21 To takk ..thaime to be malicious imposturis, as suirlie they are. **1591** HORSEY *Trav.* (Hakluyt Soc.) 161 Ther mett him an impostur or magician, which they held to be their oracle. **1634** SIR. T. HERBERT *Trav.* 145 Mahomet the great Imposture.

β. **1607** TOPSELL *Four-f. Beasts* 301 This thing haue the imposters of the World vsed for a Phyltre. **1687** T. BROWN *Saints in Uproar* Wks. 1730 I. 81 They are seven as arrant imposters as ever deluded the credulous world. **1845** FORD *Handbk. Spain* 113 The fanatics and imposters of the early ages.

γ. **1624** CAPT. SMITH *Virginia* III. xii. 94 Being found a meere Impostor, he dyed most miserably. *a* **1682** SIR T. BROWNE *Tracts* (1684) 3 The Impostour Barchochebas. **1711** ADDISON *Spect.* No. 35 ¶4 There is an Impostor abroad, who takes upon him the Name of this young Gentleman. **1825** LYTTON *Zicci* I. i, It is very clear that this Zicci is some impostor.

fig. **1605** SHAKS. *Macb.* III. iv. 64 These flawes and starts (Impostors to true feare).

attrib. **1660** F. BROOKE tr. *Le Blanc's Trav.* 14 The Impostor-Prophet Mahomet. **1678** WANLEY *Wond. Lit. World* IV. li. §10. 453/2 He commanded all those Impostor Priests to be crucified. **1738** WARBURTON *Div. Legat.* I. Ded. 40 What says our Imposter Jew to this? **1837** HT. MARTINEAU *Soc. Amer.* III. 70 An unworthy bondage of mean fear to some impostor opinion.

†**impo'storious,** *a. Obs. rare.* [f. IMPOSTORY + -OUS; cf. IMPOSTERIOUS, -TURIOUS.] Having the character of an impostor or imposture.

1623 HART *Arraignm. Ur.* II. ii. 43 An impostorious empiricke. *Ibid.* 44 Nothing else but impostorious conjecture. **1670** EVELYN *Mem.* 5 Aug., I was formerly acquainted with the impostorious Nunns of Loudune in France.

†**im'postorism.** *Obs. rare*$^{-1}$. [f. IMPOSTOR + -ISM; cf. IMPOSTURISM.] = IMPOSTURE.

1652 *Mercurius Democritus* 18–28 Aug. 162 Hocus Pocus Juglings, forgeries, and damn'd Impostorisms.

impostorous (ɪm'pɒstərəs). *a.* [f. IMPOSTOR, or perh. (from the date) orig. f. IMPOSTURE + -OUS; cf. IMPOSTEROUS, -TROUS, -TUROUS.]

†**1.** Of the nature of an imposture. *Obs.*

1548 HOOPER *Ten Commandm.* vii, That noman after there deathe shuld deceaue the people..with false and impostorous doctrine. **1652** GAULE *Magastrom.* 224 Rites and ceremonies..impostorous, prophane and impious.

2. Having the character of an impostor; practising imposture.

1611 SPEED *Hist. Gt. Brit.* IX. xx. §13. 944 Richard Simon, an ambitious and impostorous wretch. **1628** FORD *Lover's Mel.* I. ii, Thou..art indeed an impostorous empiric. **1657** W. MORICE *Coena quasi Κοινὴ* Def. xxvii. 273 His impostorous Physician assured him, that he could not live one day without his Medicines. **1882** CREIGHTON *Hist. Papacy* II. 458 *marg.*, Impostorous Embassy from the East.

im'postorship. [f. IMPOSTOR + -SHIP.] The office or character of an impostor.

1620 SHELTON *Quix.* III. xi. 68 This Vale of Tears where there's scarce anything without Mixture of Mischief, Impostorship or Villany. **1641** MILTON *Prel. Episc.* 23 An examiner, and discoverer of this impostorship. **1823** BENTHAM *Not Paul* 185 Should he..find himself stigmatized as an impostor;—find himself encountered by a certificate of impostorship. **1836** *Fraser's Mag.* XIII. 334 In the annals of literary, as well as political impostorship.

†**im'postory.** *Obs. rare.* [f. as prec. + -Y; cf. IMPOSTERY, -URY.] = IMPOSTURE.

1653 A. WILSON *Jas. I* 107 It could not be imagined that any thing of Impostory could result from him. **1655** FULLER *Ch. Hist.* x. iv. §56 The Disease of the Mother being the best Foundation to build such Impostourie thereon.

†**im'postrate,** *ppl. a. Obs. rare*$^{-1}$. [f. IMPOSTOR or IMPOSTURE + -ATE^{2}.] = IMPOSTROUS.

1632 LITHGOW *Trav.* I. 4 The impostrat quagmires of this abortive age.

impostress (ɪm'pɒstrɪs). [f. *imposter*, IMPOSTOR + -ESS; perh. after OF. *imposteresse* (Godefroy), but cf. *actor*, *-tress*, *hunter*, *-tress*.] A female impostor. Now *rare*.

1614 BACON *Let. to Jas. I* 11 Feb., The impostress Elizabeth Barton. **1665** WITHER *Lord's Prayer* 132 Reason is cryed down as an Impostress. **1772** *Poetry* in *Ann. Reg.* 212 No wonder if th' impostress had deceiv'd. **1839** PYE SMITH *Script. & Geol.* 179 It was an impostress under the name of philosophy.

†**im'postrix.** *Obs. rare.* [a med.L. *impostrix*, fem. of *impostor*.] = prec.

1655 FULLER *Ch. Hist.* v. ii. §47, I am heartily sorry that the gravity of John Fisher..should be so light, and the sharp sight of Sʳ Thomas More so blinde, as to give credit to so notorious an Impostrix. **1700** HICKES in *Pepys' Diary* 19 June, Some suspected her for an impostrix.

impostrous (ɪm'pɒstrəs), *a.* Also 7 **impost'rous.** [Abbreviation of IMPOSTEROUS or -OROUS: cf. *monster*, *-trous*.]

1. Having the character of an impostor.

1612 DRAYTON *Poly-olb.* xviii. 286 He that took th' impost'rous Ciprian king. **1850** GROTE *Greece* II. lxvii. VIII. 484 Aristotle..gave to the word Sophist a definition substantially the same as that which it bears in the modern languages 'an impostrous pretender to knowledge', a man who employs what he knows to be fallacy, for the purpose of deceit and of getting money.

2. Of the nature of an imposture.

1635 HEYWOOD *Hierarch.* v. 289 Further to speak of his impostrous lies. **1668** H. MORE *Div. Dial.* v. v. (1713) 412 The Idolatrous and Impostrous Church of Rome. **1810** BENTHAM *Packing* (1821) 26 As of the true and original jury, so of this impostrous modern substitute, the origin lies buried in obscurity. **1818** JAS. MILL *Brit. India* II. v. ix. 699 The outcry was groundless and impostrous.

So **im'postry** = IMPOSTERY, -ORY, -URY.

1585 T. WASHINGTON tr. *Nicholay's Voy.* III. xviii. 105 They returne to their houses triumphing of their impostrie.

†**im'postumate,** *ppl. a. Obs.* Also 8 **-thumate.** [Altered form of *apostumate*, APOSTEMATE *ppl. a.*, after IMPOSTUME.] Affected with impostumes; of the nature of an impostume. Also *fig.*

1601 HOLLAND *Pliny* XXVII. iv. II. 273 The leaves are singular good to be laid upon impostumat swellings. **1651–3** JER. TAYLOR *Serm. for Year* (1678) 187 He let his finger alone, and told him that his liver was impostumate. **1725**

POPE *Odyss.* xx. 358 This lord Ulysses ey'd; And thus burst out th' imposthumate with pride. **1754–64** SMELLIE *Midwif.* I. 132 The ovaria are sometimes.. inflamed, impostumate [etc.].

†**im'postumate**, *v.* *Obs.* Also 7–8 -thumate. [Altered form of *apostumate*, APOSTEMATE *v.*, after IMPOSTUME; cf. prec.]

1. *trans.* To affect with an impostume; to cause an impostume in. Also *fig.*

1592 NASHE *4 Lett. Confut.* L ij b, To corrupt the aire and impostumate mens ears with their pan-pudding prose. **1646** BUCK *Rich. III*, 53 So much our vices impostumate our fames. **1758** J. S. *Le Dran's Observ. Surg.* (1771) 220 Some fresh Stone having.. impostumated the Kidney.

2. *intr.* To swell into an impostume, to form an ulcerous tumour; to fester, 'gather'. Also *fig.*

1607 MARKHAM *Caval.* I. (1617) 68 Grosse and impostumating humors. *Ibid.* VII. 71 When those kernels doe swel and impostumate outwardly. **1712** ARBUTHNOT *John Bull* I. viii, The bruise imposthumated, and afterwards turned to a stinking ulcer. **1762** R. GUY *Pract. Obs. Cancers* 162 The Lump soon afterwards impostumated.

†**im'postumated**, *ppl. a.* Also 7–8 -thumated. [f. as prec. ppl. adj. and vb. + -ED¹.] Affected with, swollen into, of the nature of, an impostume; ulcerated. Also *fig.*

1576 BAKER *Jewell of Health* 131 b, Agaynst the Palsie of the tongue or other members, if they are impostumated or cankered. **1647** CLARENDON *Contempl. Ps.* in *Tracts* (1727) 471 Like the pain the impostumated patient suffers in the lancing his sore. **1712** *Perquisite Monger* 20 Intoxicated with Power, and imposthumated with Ambition. **1771** SMOLLETT *Humph. Cl.* 8 May, Putrid gums, imposthumated lungs.

impostumation, **-thumation** (ɪmpɒstjuːˈmeɪʃən). Now *rare*. [Altered form of *apostumation*, APOSTEMATION, after IMPOSTUME.]

1. The formation of an impostume; festering, suppuration.

1552 HULOET, Imposthumacion or runnynge of a sore, *suppurantia, suppuratio* [etc.]. **1643** I. STEER tr. *Exp. Chyrurg.* v. 13 Hereby commeth inflammation, impostimation, and divers times Gangrene. **1674** JOSSELYN *Voy. New Eng.* 184 They are troubled with a disease in the mouth or throat.. Quinsies, and Impostumations of the Almonds. **1886** *Syd. Soc. Lex.*, *Imposthumation*, the formation of an imposthume.

2. = IMPOSTUME *sb.* 1, 2.

1524 *St. Papers Hen. VIII*, IV. 185, I haue beene.. sore vexed.. with an impostumacion risen within my mouthe. **1607–12** BACON *Ess.*, *Seditions* (Arb.) 408 Maligne vlcers and pernicious impostumacions. *a* **1788** POTT *Chirurg. Wks.* II. 448 An abscess, or imposthumation which may be relieved or cured by an opening. **1807** *Med. Jrnl.* 216 Two or three small imposthumations appeared forming on the legs.

impostume, **-thume** (ɪmˈpɒstjʊm), *sb.* Now *rare*. Forms: 5–6 em-, en-, im-, -postem(e, -tym(e, -tome, -tume, 6–8 impostem, 7 imposthim, 6– impostume, -thume. [a. OF. *empostume* (also in 16th c. Eng.), altered form of *apostume*, *aposteme*; see APOSTEM.

A word which has undergone unusual corruption both in prefix and radical part. Originally Gr. ἀπόστημα abscess, L. *apostēma*, F. *apostème*. In OF. the ending was corrupted to *-stume* (whence ME. APOSTUME); in late OF. the initial *a* of the prefix *apo-* was, like *a-* prefix, sometimes confused with *em-*, making *empostume*. The Latin form of *em-* being *im-*, the word was modified in Eng. as *impostume*. The earlier ME. *apostume* was meanwhile aphetized as POSTUME, and this app. associated with the derivatives of L. *postumus*; when these were erroneously spelt *posthume*, *posthumous*, the erroneous *h* passed also into *apostume*, *impostume*; the spelling *imposthume* is occasional from *c* 1550, and prevalent (though not universal) from *c* 1700.]

1. A purulent swelling or cyst in any part of the body; an abscess.

c **1400** *Lanfranc's Cirurg.* 4 Contents, Cap. iiij of emposteme undire þe rote of þe ere. *Ibid.* 38 As it schal be teld in þe chapitle of an enpostyme [*MS. B.* aposteme]. *Ibid.* 52 An enpostym. *Ibid.* 54 Enpostemes. *Ibid.* 214 *heading*, Of empostyms of þe heed. **1483** *Cath. Angl.* 195/1 An Imposteme, *apostema*. **1525** LD. BERNERS *Froiss.* II. cv. [ci.] 307 By gambaldyng of the horse the impostume brake in his body. **1548** HALL *Chron., Hen. VI* (1809) 209 As though he had died of a Palsey or Empostome. **1552** HULOET, Imposthume, or botche, or course of euil humours. **1578** LYTE *Dodoens* I. lxiii. 93 Empostems, wennes, or harde swellings about the eares and throte. **1642** ROGERS *Naaman* 440 When the disease was ripe, he lets out the impostume. **1659** SOUTH *Serm.* (1697) I. 103 An Error in the judgment, is like an impostem in the Head. **1685** BOYLE *Enq. Notion Nat.* 228 Producing sometimes inward Imposthumes. **1738** STUART in *Phil. Trans.* XL. 327 Morbid Impostems or Tumors. **1748** tr. *V. Renatus' Distemp. Horses* 238 A Suppuration, which they call an Impostume. **1841** BREWSTER *Mart. Sc.* III. iii. (1856) 205 An imposthume in his brain, occasioned by too much study.

2. *fig.* **a.** With reference to moral corruption in the individual, or insurrection in the state: A moral or political 'festering sore'; the 'swelling' of pride, etc.

1565 CALFHILL *Answ. Treat. Crosse* (1846) 93 It openeth the festered sores, the pestilent imposthumes of our ill desires. **1622** MALYNES *Anc. Law-Merch.* 234 The three Impostumes of the world, namely, Warres, Famine, and Pestilence. **1685** R. YOUNGS in Sprat *2nd Pt. Relat. late Wicked Contrivance* (1693) 97 Several Imposthims they likewise haue sent abroad, which I can prove. **1702** *Eng. Theophrast.* 177 To hinder the impostume of bad humour from breaking. **1839** JAMES *Louis XIV*, I. 276 This most absurd and abusive imposthume upon an absurd and abusive system was called the Paulette. **1876** BROWNING *Pacchiar.* xxii, The imposthume I prick to relieve thee of,—Vanity.

†**b.** Applied to a gathering cloud or its contents.

1603 DRAYTON *Bar. Wars* II. xvi, From the swolne fluxure of the Clouds, doth shake A ranke Impostume upon every Lake.

†**c.** Applied to a person swollen with pride or insolence. *Obs.*

1621 FLETCHER *Isl. Princ.* I. iii, Dost thou know me, bladder, Thou insolent impostume?

†**im'postume**, **-thume**, *v.* *Obs.* Forms: see prec. [f. prec. sb.; cf. *apostume*, APOSTEME *v.*]

1. *intr.* To gather into an impostume or abscess; = IMPOSTUMATE *v.* 2.

c **1400** *Lanfranc's Cirurg.* 64 Whanne þat þou art sikir fro þe enpostemynge [*MS. B.* empostomynge]. **1527** ANDREW *Brunswyke's Distyll. Waters* B iij b, Good for impostumyng and payne in the gummes. **1580** HOLLYBAND *Treas. Fr. Tong*, *Apostumer & meurir*, to empostume, to runne. **1607** TOPSELL *Four-f. Beasts* (1658) 326 The knots will encrease daily, and inflame, impostume, and break. **1628** FELTHAM *Resolves* I. xxxvi. 111 Whatsoeuer is taken in, that is distastfull, and continues there vn-voyded, does daily impostume, and gather till at last it kills.

2. *trans.* = IMPOSTUMATE *v.* 1.

1645 G. DANIEL *Poems* Wks. 1878 II. 92 They are free Of that ranke venome which imposthumes Mee.

†**im'postumed**, **-thumed**, *ppl. a.* *Obs.* [f. IMPOSTUME + -ED.] = IMPOSTUMATED. *lit.* and *fig.*

c **1400** *Lanfranc's Cirurg.* I. iii. §6 *heading*, Off woundes Impostemede. *Ibid.* 58 þenke nouȝt to heele þe wounde as longe as it is enpostemed [*MS. B.* apostomyde]. *a* **1586** SIDNEY *Arcadia* III. (1622) 384 How can an impostumed hart but yeld forth euill matter by his mouth? **1628** SIR W. MURE *Fancies Farew.* iii. 3 Impostumde soares the patient most torment. **1651** CLEVELAND *Poems* 10 Th' impostum'd bubble of a wave. **1663** *Aron-bimn.* 65 To launce our impostum'd Ulcers.

†**im'posturage**. *Obs. rare*. [f. IMPOSTURE + -AGE.] The action of an impostor; imposture.

1654 GAYTON *Pleas. Notes* IV. viii. 230 Pardon my imposturage. **1656** *Artif. Handsom.* 127 To impute to the devils invention, or to count them any hurtfull imposturage.

†**im'postural**, *a.* *Obs. rare*. [f. as prec. + -AL¹.] = IMPOSTOROUS.

1588 J. HARVEY *Disc. Probl.* 71 The vnruly and presumptuous insolencie of such imposturall prophets. **1612** T. JAMES *Jesuits' Downf.* 1 A most impostural corporation, that haue cleane forsaken and forfeited the spirit of the Catholicke Church.

imposture (ɪmˈpɒstjʊə(r)), *sb.* [a. F. *imposture* (earlier *emposture*), ad. late L. *impostūra*, abstract sb. f. *impost-*, ppl. stem of *impōnĕre* to IMPOSE.]

1. The action or practice of imposing upon others; wilful and fraudulent deception.

1537 tr. *Latimer's 2nd Serm. bef. Convoc.* C vij, Great imposture commeth, when they that the common people take for the lyght, go aboute to take the sonne and the lyght out of the worlde. **1626** BACON *Sylva* §241, I see no great vse of it, but for Imposture. **1750** JOHNSON *Rambler* No. 79 ¶13 He that suffers by imposture has too often his virtue more impaired than his fortune. **1819** BYRON *Juan* I. cxxviii, You'd best begin with truth, and when you've lost your Labour, there's a sure market for imposture. **1878** MORLEY *Crit. Misc.* Ser. I. *Carlyle* 198 Imposture must come to an end.

†**b.** The deception of unreal or feigned appearances; illusion. *Obs.*

1643 SIR T. BROWNE *Relig. Med.* II. §5 The counterfeit griefes of those knowne and professed impostures [at a Play]. **1678** CUDWORTH *Intell. Syst.* I. i. §38. 47 There is something in us superiour to Sense, which judges of it, detects its Phantastry, and condemns its Imposture. **1794** SULLIVAN *View Nat.* II. 231 Nothing can secure the mind from error and imposture, but the precision arising from a candid philosophical spirit.

2. An act of fraudulent deception; a cheat, a fraud.

1548 HALL *Chron., Hen. VI* 153 By this pratye cautele and slyghe imposture. **1603** FLORIO *Montaigne* I. xxx. (1632) 103 A punishable imposture. **1759** ROBERTSON *Hist. Scot.* (1813) I. II. 115 The vigilance of the reformers detected these impostures. **1838** LYTTON *Calderon* i, He had submitted to an imposture.

b. A thing (or person) which is pretended to be what it is not.

1699 BURNET *39 Art.* xxii. (1700) 245 Many of the Bones which were carried about by Monks, were none of their Bones but Impostures. **1781** J. MOORE *View Soc. It.* (1790) I. i. 18 We were a gang of impostures.

†**3.** An obs. form of IMPOSTOR, q.v.

Hence **im'postureship** = IMPOSTORSHIP.

1608 T. MORTON *Preamb. Encounter* 39 A sportfull or rather execrable Impostureship of P.R.

†**im'posture**, *v.* *Obs.* [f. prec. sb.] **a.** *intr.* To practise imposture. **b.** *trans.* To impose upon, deceive. **c.** To declare or prove to be an imposture.

1622 H. SYDENHAM *Serm. Sol. Occ.* (1637) 92 Labouring to nullifie his acts, blemish his descent, imposture all his miracles. **1624** T. SCOTT *Belg. Souldier* 32 Spaine assembles armies, the Iesuites coniure, the Priests imposture. *a* **1659** *Lady Alimony* IV. vii, The Devil's a Witch, and has impostur'd them.

Hence **im'posturing** *vbl. sb.* and *ppl. a.*

1618 GAINSFORD *P. Warbeck* in *Select. Harl. Misc.* (1793) 60 Where the imposturing of priests hath got the upper hand of all religion and piety. **1624** *Gag for Pope* 71 Her abominable life and imposturing deceit. *a* **1641** BP. MOUNTAGU *Acts & Mon.* (1642) 214 Imposturing lewd Libels, counterfaited under the names of the Apostles.

†**im'postured**, *ppl. a.* *Obs.* [f. IMPOSTURE *sb.* or *v.* + -ED.] Falsified, adulterated; impostrous.

1619 *Pasquil's Palm* (1877) 149 False impostur'd wines doe hurt the eyes. **1648–99** J. BEAUMONT *Psyche* II. cxxxvi. (1702) 23 That face which I Wantonly scorn'd, and cast my love away Upon impostur'd Lust's foul Mystery.

†**impo'sturious**, *a.* *Obs. rare*⁻¹. [f. IMPOSTURY + -OUS; cf. IMPOSTERIOUS, -ORIOUS.] = IMPOSTROUS.

? *a* **1600** *Historie of Hamblet* iv, There are some imposturious companions that impute so much devinitie to the devell.

†**im'posturism**. *Obs. rare*. [f. IMPOSTURE *sb.* + -ISM.] The practice of imposture.

a **1640** DAY *Peregr. Schol.* (1881) 48 For she knew.. her base imposturisme would be discoverde. **1656** EARL MONM. *Advt. fr. Parnass.* 179 The cunning and imposturism which the princes of the world have used.

†**im'posturize**, *v.*¹ *Obs.* [f. *imposture*, or *impostor* + -IZE.] *intr.* To practise imposture. Hence **im'posturizing** *ppl. a.*

1603 HARSNET *Pop. Impost.* Pref., Imposturising Renegadoes that come fresh from the Popes Tyring House. *Ibid.* xxi. 134 Imposturising Sooth-sayers. **1624** GEE *Foot out of Snare* 44 Diuers other obseruations haue our imposturizing Renegadoes.

†**im'posturize**, *v.*² *nonce-wd.* [f. IM-¹ + POSTURIZE.] *trans.* To mimic the postures of.

1772 W. HUDDESFORD in *J. Granger's Lett.* (1805) 149 Your attempt to imposturize Tony will be vain, futile, useless... no one can tell but I how he looked, how he walked, how he scowled.

imposturous (ɪmˈpɒstjʊərəs), *a.* [f. IMPOSTURE + -OUS; cf. IMPOSTEROUS, -TOROUS, -TROUS.]

1. Of the nature of imposture; deceptive, fraudulent. Now *rare*.

1608 T. MORTON *Preamb. Encounter* 35 So suspicious and imposturous a Title. **1687** S. HILL *Cath. Balance* Pref., Methods of prescribing Tradition against imposturous Doctrines. **1852** GROTE *Greece* II. lxii. VIII. 50 They [the five thousand] did not even exist as individual names on paper, but simply as an imposturous nominal aggregate.

†**2.** Given to practising imposture; having the character of an impostor. *Obs.*

1611 SPEED *Hist. Gt. Brit.* IX. xxiv. (1632) 1175/2 The shamefull vntruth of those imposturous liers. **1668** H. MORE *Div. Dial.* III. xix. (1713) 220 An imposturous and bloody Priesthood! **1697** COLLIER *Immor. Stage* iii. 78 The English Œdipus makes the Priest-hood an imposturous Profession.

†**im'postury**. *Obs. rare*. [f. IMPOSTURE + -Y; cf. IMPOSTERY, -TORY, -TRY.] Imposture.

1615 G. SANDYS *Trav.* 107 Not long after the impostury of Mahomet. *Ibid.* 173 That Impostury of fetching fire from the Sepulcher upon Easter eve.

imposure (ɪmˈpəʊʒ(j)ʊə(r)). *rare*. [f. IMPOSE *v.* + -URE; cf. COMPOSURE.] An imposing; a laying on.

1682–3 *Case Indiff. Things* 49 It must issue in things inexpedient to Christians, or an unlawfulness in the Imposure. **1875** BROWNING *Aristoph. Apol.* 5463 At next quick imposure of decree.

impot: a schoolboy's abbreviation of IMPOSITION.

impotable (ɪmˈpəʊtəb(ə)l), *a.* [f. IM-² + POTABLE.] Undrinkable.

1608 A. WILLET *Hexapla in Exod.* 224 Bitter waters.. impotable and vnpleasant. **1885** *Pop. Sci. Monthly* XXVI. 532 Distilled water is made impotable and unhealthy by any traces of that [hydrochloric] acid.

†**im'pote**, *v.* *Obs. rare*⁻¹. [f. IM-¹ + L. *pōtāre* to drink.] *intr.* To drink heavily.

1721 BERKELEY *Let. to R. Nelson* 6 Oct. in Fraser *Life* iv. (1871) 93, I have bin at many tables and civilly used in a sober way without impoting.

impotence (ˈɪmpətəns). Also 5 -in, ym-. [a. F. *impotence* (13th c.) = Sp. *impotencia*, It. *impotenzia*, ad. L. *impotentia* (see next).]

1. Want of strength or power to perform anything; utter inability or weakness; helplessness.

a **1420** HOCCLEVE *De Reg. Princ.* 4654 Hir [= their] impotence Strecchiþ naght so fer as his influence. **1614** BP. HALL *Recoll. Treat.* 1036 Ready to cast imputations of levity, or impotence upon God. **1656** HOBBES *Lib., Necess. & Chance* (1841) 368 A sick or lame man's liberty to go.. is an impotence, and not a power or a liberty. **1671** MILTON *Samson* 52 O impotence of mind, in body strong! **1788** GIBBON *Decl. & F.* xliii. (1869) II. 612 Every accident betrayed the impotence of the government. **1851** JERROLD *St. Giles* xiv. 143 The old man.. wrung his hands in the very impotence of sorrow. **1870** SWINBURNE *Ess. & Stud.* (1875) 267 Alike by his powers and his impotences, by his capacity and his defect, Coleridge was inapt for dramatic poetry.

2. Want of physical power; feebleness of body, as through illness or old age.

1406 HOCCLEVE *La male regle* 443 As I saide, reewe on myn impotence, þat likly am to sterue yit or eeue. *c* **1445** LYDG. *Test.* in *Min. Poems* (Percy Soc.) 246 He can no moor diffence, Than crokyd age in his moost impotence. **1483** CAXTON *Gold. Leg.* 99b/1 It happed that two of them..a brother and a suster cam to y[m]potence. **1602** SHAKS. *Ham.* II. ii. 66 Greeued, That so his Sicknesse, Age, and Impotence Was falsely borne in hand. *a* **1674** MILTON *Hist. Mosc.* i, Any rich man who through age or other impotence is unable to serve the Public. **1836** H. COLERIDGE *North. Worthies* (1852) I. 21 Which [chronic diseases] slowly but surely reduce the body politic to a condition of impotence and dotage.

b. *Path.* Complete absence of sexual power: usually said of the male.

1655 FULLER *Ch. Hist.* II. vi. §17 Whilest Papists crie up this his incredible Continency: others easily unwonder the same, by imputing it partly to his Impotence, afflicted with an Infirmitie. **1798** MALTHUS *Popul.* III. ii. (1806) II. 111 Is it some mysterious interference of Heaven which..strikes the men with impotence and the women with barrenness? **1833–58** COPLAND *Dict. Pract. Med.* II. 319/2 Impotence may exist in either sex, but most commonly in the male.

†**3.** Lack of self-restraint, violent passion. *Obs.*

1634 MASSINGER *Very Woman* II. i, The being your sister would anew inflame me With much more impotence to doat upon her. **1667** MILTON *P.L.* II. 156 Will he, so wise, let loose at once his ire, Be ike through impotence, or unaware? **1715–20** POPE *Iliad* XXIV. 53 The dire Achilles..A lion, not a man, who slaughters wide In strength of rage and impotence of pride.

impotency (ˈɪmpətənsɪ). [ad. L. *impotentia* want of power, want of self-restraint, abstract sb. f. *impotens* IMPOTENT. Cf. prec. and see -ENCY.]

1. = IMPOTENCE 1.

In the 17th c. freq. used to denote moral weakness, inability to follow virtuous courses or to resist temptation.

c **1460** FORTESCUE *Abs. & Lim. Mon.* xix. (1885) 155 Ffor all such thynges come off impotencie, as doyth power to be syke or wex olde. **1552** LATIMER *Serm. & Rem.* (Parker Soc.) 149 Stories, wherein is mentioned the impotency of the devil. **1649** JER. TAYLOR *Gt. Exemp.* II. viii. 70 An impotency or disability to do good. **1675** BROOKS *Gold. Key* Wks. 1867 V. 303 The covenant of works is the lasting monument of man's impotency and changeableness. **1727** DE FOE *Syst. Magic* I. iii. (1840) 68 The first [magicians] gradually deposed themselves by their mere impotency. **1817** CHALMERS *Astron. Disc.* i. (1852) 28 The mind feels its own impotency in attempting to grasp them. **1871** MORLEY *Crit. Misc.* 23 Intellectual poverty and impotency.

2. a. = IMPOTENCE 2.

1440 J. SHIRLEY *Dethe K. James* (1818) 5 The greet age of the Kyng..the ympotencye of his lymmes and membirs, the febilenese of his persone. **1594** T. B. *La Primaud. Fr. Acad.* II. 365 They are taken with palsies, lamenesse, and impotencie in all their members. **1662** PETTY *Taxes* 4 It is unjust to let any starve, when we..limit the wages of the poor, so as they can lay up nothing against the time of their impotency and want of work. **1707** FLOYER *Physic. Pulse-Watch* 380 Swelling in the Hands and Feet, impotency of Walking. **1822–34** *Good's Study Med.* (ed. 4) IV. 96 When the impotency results from a paresis or paralysis of the local nerves..the case is nearly hopeless.

b. = IMPOTENCE 2b.

1594 CAREW *Huarte's Exam. Wits* (1616) 283 If these two separat each from other, vpon pretence of impotencie, and so hee take another wife, and shee another husband. **1644** MILTON *Jdgm. Bucer* xliii, She who..hath made her self unfit by open misdemeanours, or through incurable impotencies cannot be able, is not..to be esteem'd a wife. **1794** S. WILLIAMS *Vermont* 157 An evidence of weakness, impotency, and want of manhood. **1972** *Oxford Times* 28 July 7/1 An Oxford doctor is holding special surgeries for male undergraduates suffering from impotency. *Ibid.* 7/2 Male impotency is very common.

†**3.** = IMPOTENCE 3. *Obs.*

1542 N. UDALL in *Lett. Lit. Men* (Camden) 5 When he had oons shaken of that ympotencie of voluptuous appetites. **1635** N. R. *Camden's Hist. Eliz.* II. an. 27. 269 Letters were secretly sent whereby her womanish impotency might be thrust on to her own destruction. **1729** BUTLER *Serm. Compassion* Wks. 1874 II. 64 Persons..the most free from the impotencies of envy and resentment.

impotent (ˈɪmpətənt), *a.* (*sb.*) Also 5 in-. [a. F. *impotent* (14th c.) = It., Sp. *impotente*, ad. L. *impotent-em* powerless; usually, lacking self-restraint, f. *im-* (IM-^{2}) + *potens*, *potent-* POTENT.]

1. Having no power or ability to accomplish anything; powerless, helpless; ineffective.

1444 *Pol. Poems* (Rolls) II. 219, I sauh a krevys, with his klawes longe, Pursewe a snayl, poore and impotent. **1535** COVERDALE *Neh.* iv. 2 Saneballat..saide..What do the impotent Iewes? **1568** in H. Campbell *Love-Lett. Mary Q. Scots* App. (1824) 11 When any of the persons of the said councell shall depart, or become impotent to serve. **1671** MILTON *P.R.* II. 433 Yet Wealth without these three is impotent To gain dominion or to keep it gain'd. **1788** GIBBON *Decl. & F.* xliii. (1869) II. 610 The works of man are impotent against the assaults of nature. **1860** MOTLEY *Netherl.* (1868) I. ii. 25 The impotent monarch who occupied the French throne. **1896** DK. ARGYLL *Philos. Belief* 39 The finest microscopes..are impotent to detect the molecular and atomic constitution of any form of matter.

2. Physically weak; without bodily strength; unable to use one's limbs; helpless, decrepit.

1390 GOWER *Conf.* III. 383 And also for my daies olde That I am feble and impotent. *c* **1450** LYDG. *Secrees* 482 He was feble and Oold, And inpotent. **1538** STARKEY *Engl.* I. i. 3 He ys by syknes or age impotent and not of powar to helpe hym selfe. **1601** R. JOHNSON *Kingd. & Commw.* (1603) 184 Those onely who are impotent in their limes. **1709** STEELE *Tatler* No. 27 ¶2 The Fellow with broken Limbs justly deserves your Alms for his impotent Condition. **1853** C. BRONTE *Villette* iv, A rheumatic cripple, impotent hand and foot.

fig. **1604** SHAKS. *Oth.* II. i. 162 Oh most lame and impotent conclusion. **1871** FREEMAN *Hist. Ess.* (1872) 20 But he stops short in a most lame and impotent way.

b. Wholly lacking in sexual power; incapable of reproduction.

1615 G. SANDYS *Trav.* 7 Here it is a common practise to bewitch them: made thereby impotent with their wives, untill the charme be burnt. **1634** SIR T. HERBERT *Trav.* 148 Eight or ten lustfull women, by the law subjected to one (and he perhaps an impotent man). **1676** DRYDEN *Aurengz.* Ded. a j b, The Impotent Lover in Petronius. **1859** DARWIN *Orig. Spec.* ix. (1873) 250 Whole groups of animals and plants are rendered impotent by the same unnatural conditions.

†**3.** Not master of oneself; unable to restrain oneself; unrestrained, headlong, passionate. Also with *of*. *Obs.* [So L. *impotens*.]

1596 SPENSER *F.Q.* V. xii. 1 O sacred hunger of ambitious mindes, And impotent desire of men to raine! **1639** MASSINGER *Unnat. Combat* III. ii, An impotent lover Of women for a flash, but, his fires quenched, Hating as deadly. **1670** DRYDEN *1st Pt. Conq. Granada* V. i, Rash Men, like you, and impotent of Will, Give Chance no time to turn, but urge her still. **1715–20** POPE *Iliad* IV. 33 But Juno, impotent of passion, broke Her sullen silence.

B. *sb.* An impotent person.

1513 BRADSHAW *St. Werburge* I. 2268 And brought to the shryne this wretched impotent. **1596** *Edw. III*, III. iii, Whom should they follow, aged impotent, But he that is their true-born sovereign? **1662** PETTY *Taxes* 4 The maintenance..of impotents of all sorts. **1685** —— *Last Will* p. xi, As for impotents by the hand of God, the publick ought to maintain them. **1833** COLERIDGE *Lett.* (1895) 768 A similar institution might exist for a higher class of will-maniacs or impotents.

†**impoˈtential**, *a.* *Obs. rare.* [f. IM-^{2} + POTENTIAL.] Impotent.

1649 G. DANIEL *Trinarch., Rich. II*, lxxxv, It will adore An Onion..And tremble to its impotentiall Power. *c* **1700** *Earl Oswald* in Evans *O.B.* (1784) III. li. 303 Want, or secret dread, Or impotential age.

imˈpotentizing, *ppl. a.* *rare*$^{-1}$. [f. IMPOTENT *a.*: see -IZE, -ING^{2}.] That renders one impotent.

1920 JOYCE *Let.* 24 Oct. (1957) I. 149 Moly could also be absinthe the cerebral impotentising (!!) drink of chastity.

impotently (ˈɪmpətəntlɪ), *adv.* [f. IMPOTENT *a.* + -LY^{2}.]

1. Powerlessly, helplessly, ineffectively.

1611 COTGR., *Impuissament*, impotently, vnpowerfully. *a* **1652** J. SMITH *Sel. Disc.* II. i. (1821) 33 To imagine him so impotently mutable, that his favour may be won again with their uncouth devotions. **1742** YOUNG *Nt. Th.* V. 553 Some weep in earnest; and yet weep in vain;..Passion, blind passion! impotently pours Tears, that deserve more tears. **1868** KINGLAKE *Crimea* (1877) III. i. 64 He impotently watched the progress of Antemarre's brigade.

†**2.** Without self-restraint; ungovernably, unrestrainedly. *Obs.*

1621 BURTON *Anat. Mel.* III. ii. VI. v. (1651) 575 He loves her most impotently, she loves not him, and so e contra. **1630** B. JONSON *New Inn* I. Wks. (Rtldg.) 412/1, I have loved this lady long, And impotently with desire enough. **1653** H. MORE *Conject. Cabbal.* 203 (T.) The danger is of being impotently passionate.

†**ˈimpotentness.** *Obs.* *rare*$^{-0}$. [f. as prec. + -NESS.] Impotence.

1530 PALSGR. 234/1 Impotentnesse for age, *decrepitement*. **1727** BAILEY vol. II, *Impotentness*, want of Power or Strength, Weakness.

†**imˈpotionate**, *ppl. a.* *Obs. rare.* [ad. med.L. *impōtiōnāt-us*, pa. pple. of *impōtiōnāre* to poison, f. *im-* (IM-^{1}) + *pōtiōn-em* draught, *spec.* poisoned draught.] Poisoned.

1583 STUBBES *Anat. Abus.* I. (1877) 31 Any people..that hath drunke so deep of this impotionate Cup. *Ibid.* 105 Curious cookries and impotionate slibber sawces.

†**imˈpotionate**, *v.* *Obs.* *rare*$^{-1}$. [f. ppl. stem of L. *impōtiōnāre*: see prec.] *trans.* To poison.

1563–87 FOXE *A. & M.* (1596) 364/1 Certaine Lepers conspiring with the Turks and Iewes went about to impotionate, and infect all Christendome, by invenoming their fountains, lakes [etc.].

†**imˈpouch**, *v.* *Obs.* *rare*$^{-0}$. [f. IM-^{1} + POUCH, after F. *empocher*.] *trans.* To put into a pouch, bag, or pocket.

1611 COTGR., *Empoché*, impoakt, impouched. *Ibid.*, *Empocher*, to impouch, to put into a pouch or budget.

impound (ɪmˈpaʊnd), *v.* Also 6–7 **empound**, **impownd**. [f. EM- or IM-^{1} + POUND *sb.*^{2}]

1. a. *trans.* To shut up in a pound or pinfold (cattle legally seized).

1554 [see IMPOUNDING below]. **1569** in W. H. Turner *Select. Rec. Oxford* (1880) 327 To impounde..every of their catell put in above their rate. **1641** *Termes de la Ley*, *Parco fracto* is a Writ that lies against him that breakes any pownd and takes out the beasts which are there lawfully impownded. **1688** *Lond. Gaz.* No. 2399/4 A Bay Mare..having strayed and been impounded near Hogsden. **1807** VANCOUVER *Agric. Devon* (1813) 346 To exempt them from all liability of having their sheep impounded or taken up as estrays. **1851** HT. MARTINEAU *Hist. Peace* IV. ix. (1877) III. 24 Some cattle..had been impounded for tithe-payment.

fig. **1584** FENNER *Def. Ministers* (1587) 16 The other questions because they are driuen in ouer the hedge..wee will nowe impounde them.

b. *gen.* To shut up (cattle) in an enclosure.

1877 J. A. ALLEN *Amer. Bison* 575 The Indians..in the habit of hunting the buffalo by impounding them, or by driving them into an artificial enclosure. **1878** A. AYLWARD *Transvaal* ii. 17 The sun being set, and the cattle and stock impounded in their kraals and places of safety.

2. a. To shut in, enclose, confine (a person or thing) as in a pound.

1562 PHAER *Æneid* IX. C civ, King Latyns wife gets here no gage, Nor she thy fathers walls this time empoundes in cage. **1566** DRANT *Horace, Sat.* vi. Hvb, A fountayne bryghte, with stones empounded rounde. **1622** BACON *Hen. VII* 169 How to impound the Rebels, that none of them might escape. **1832** G. DOWNES *Lett. Cont. Countries* I. 2 On landing, we were impounded for about ten minutes within an enclosure of ropes and chains, before we were admitted into the Custom-house.

fig. **1574** R. SCOT *Hop Gard.* To Rdr., The Flemmings..seeking to impownde vs in the ignoraunce of our commodities. *a* **1639** WOTTON in *Reliq.* (1685) 240 As for Cæsar..they gave him at first only Illyricum and the nearer Gallia..(as it were to impound his spirits). *a* **1848** R. W. HAMILTON *Rew. & Punishm.* vii. (1853) 291 What right have they to impound the truth?

b. *spec.* To confine and store (water) in a reservoir; to confine water so as to form (a reservoir).

1861 W. FAIRBAIRN *Rep. Brit. Assoc.* lxiv, By this means forty million gallons of water per day are conveyed..into the Mugdock basin, where the water is impounded for distribution. **1893** TURNER & BRIGHTMORE *Princ. Waterworks Engin.* iv. 183 The entire site should be closely contoured at every foot of elevation, in order to determine the extent of the works required to impound the desired quantity of water. **1937** *Discovery* June 186/2 It [*sc.* the dam] impounds 1,400,000,000 gallons of water. **1959** *Chambers's Encycl.* IV. 355/2 The lake impounded by the Grand Coulee is 150 mls long. **1966** G. M. FAIR et al. *Water & Wastewater Engin.* I. ii. 6 Necessary reservoirs are impounded by throwing dams across the stream valley.

3. To seize or secure by legal right; to take legal or formal possession of (a document or the like) to be held in custody of the law.

1651 N. BACON *Disc. Govt. Eng.* II. vii. (1739) 40 Because they found them impounded in the Staple, they set all at liberty to buy and sell the same as they pleased. **1768** BLACKSTONE *Comm.* III. i. 12 The things distreined must in the first place be carried to some pound, and there impounded by the taker. **1851** DIXON *W. Penn* ii. (1872) 10 Officers came down from Seville..impounded his goods, his plate, his jewels. **1885** *Law Times* LXXIX. 39/1 Her life interest can be impounded for the benefit of the disappointed parties.

fig. **1782** *Hist. Eur.* in *Ann. Reg.* 141/2 To impound ..£520,000 of the public money..for the sole and exclusive service of the navy.

Hence **imˈpounded** *ppl. a.*; **imˈpounding** *vbl. sb.* and *ppl. a.* (as ***impounding reservoir***, a reservoir whose function is to store sufficient water to ensure an uninterrupted supply in times of relative drought). Also **imˈpoundable** *a.*, liable to be impounded; **imˈpoundage**, **imˈpoundment**, the act of impounding; **imˈpounder**, one who impounds or puts cattle, etc. into pound.

1554 *Act 1 & 2 Phil. & M.* c. 12 *Preamb.*, Disorder in taking of Distresses and impoundyng of Cattayle. **1611** COTGR., *Parchage*, impoundage, or an impounding. **1664–5** *Act 16–17 Chas. II*, c. 11 §9 Present sale thereof to make after the fowerth day of Impoundment. **1676** MARVELL *Mr. Smirke* 49 Whensoever a Christian transgresses these bounds once, he is impoundable, or like a wafe and stray whom Christ knows not, he falls to the Lord of the Mannor. **1828** WEBSTER, *Impounder*. **1875** *Encycl. Brit.* II. 225/1 With but little artificial addition, Loch Katrine, Loch Venachar, and Loch Drunkie were converted into impounding reservoirs, the first for the supply of the city, and the two latter for compensation. **1888** J. INGLIS *Tent Life Tigerland* 152 The bleating of an impounded kid. **1889** *Pall Mall G.* 26 June 1/3 A warning note as to the safety of the impounding reservoirs in this country. **1892** *Daily News* 6 Apr. 2/6 He could subpœna the officer of the Court to produce the impounded documents at Bow-street. **1893** TURNER & BRIGHTMORE *Princ. Waterworks Engin.* iv. 172 The first-mentioned requirement is satisfied by the formation of 'impounding-reservoirs', the office of which is to gather the irregular natural yield of surface-water, in order that it may be supplied at a uniform rate; the second is met by the construction of 'service-reservoirs', tanks and cisterns, from which water is distributed as required by the hourly demands of consumers. **1954** FAIR & GEYER *Water Supply & Waste-Water Disposal* viii. 188 In the absence of adequate natural storage, engineers resort to the construction of impounding reservoirs, or, more rarely, to the excavation of storage basins. *Ibid.* 192 Allowances for evaporation from the water surface that is created by the impoundage. *Ibid.* 195 When more than one reservoir is developed on a stream, the overflow from each impoundage becomes available to the reservoir next below. **1957** *Encycl. Brit.* XXIII. 432/2 Virtually all public regulatory authorities require that the impoundment be sufficiently great to provide for the release of compensation waters for downstream users. **1973** *New Yorker* 28 Apr. 29/3 There is some room for impoundment, but not to the tune of twelve billion dollars.

†**imˈpover**, *v.* *Obs. rare.* [Later form of EMPOVER, with IM-^{1}.] *trans.* To impoverish.

1535 *Goodly Primer*, *Song of Hannah*, The Lord impovereth, & he maketh rich. **1567** *Sc. Acts Jas. VI* (1814) 29/1 The Realme is vtterlie impouerit be euill cunȝe. **1634** BRERETON *Trav.* 31 Ghuest-houses, one for impovered and impotent persons, another for fatherless children.

impoverish (ɪmˈpɒvərɪʃ), *v.* Forms: 5 en-, empoveris, -poverys(s)h, inpoveryssh, 6

impoverys(s)h, -yshe, -ishe, 6–9 empoverish, 7 ym-, 6– impoverish. [ad. OF. *empoveriss-*, lengthened stem of *empov(e)rir*, *-pauvrir* to make poor, f. *em-*:—L. *im-* (IM-^{1}) + *povre*, *pauvre* POOR.]

1. *trans.* To make poor; to reduce to poverty.

1440 J. SHIRLEY *Dethe K. James* (1818) 8 Also of the gredi covatise that he oppressid and enpoverisid his comonalte. **1494** FABYAN *Chron.* II. xxxix. 27 He enriched hym self and inpouerysshed his subiects. **1555** EDEN *Decades* (Arb.) 54 England is in fewe years decayed and impoueryssshed. **1642** FULLER *Holy & Prof. St.* I. iii. 9 He that impoverisheth his children to enrich his widow, destroyes a quick hedge to make a dead one. **1771** *Junius Lett.* lvii. 295 Corruption.. impoverishes and enslaves the country. **1866** ROGERS *Agric. & Prices* I. xxix. 692 The trader was impoverished by high poor-rates.

†**b.** To reduce or diminish (wealth or a stock of anything). *Obs.*

1611 SPEED *Hist. Gt. Brit.* VIII. vii. §25. 405 A former warre against the French had empouerished much of their wealth. **1661** BOYLE *Style of Script.* (1675) 207 The dayes consecrated to God's service rather improve than impoverish our stock of time.

†**c.** To make bare, to strip *of* (some form of wealth). *Obs.*

1611 SPEED *Theat. Gt. Brit.* v. (1614) 9/2 Iron and glasse ..impoverish the country of woods. **1726** G. ROBERTS *4 Years Voy.* 391 They impoverished the Island of its Cattle.

2. To make weak or poor in quality or productiveness; to exhaust the strength or native quality of.

a **1631** DONNE in *Select.* (1840) 108 But when.. God shall deject, and impouerish, and evacuate that spirit. **1767** A. YOUNG *Farmer's Lett. People* 290 The unprofitable practice of ploughing up pastures..tends perpetually to impoverish them. **1784** TWAMLEY *Dairying* 29 Many People may think Water will hurt the Milk or impoverish the Cheese; experience shews it will not. **1876** MOZLEY *Univ. Serm.* v. 99 Such theories..impoverish the minds which they absorb. **1897** ALLBUTT *Syst. Med.* III. 81 Other depressing forces may have come into play impoverishing the blood.

im'poverished (-ɪʃt), *ppl. a.* [f. prec. + -ED^{1}.] Reduced to poverty; made poor, weak, etc.

a **1631** DONNE in *Select.* (1840) 16 Records of.. impoverished and forgotten, and obliterate families. **1753** N. TORRIANO *Gangr. Sore Throat* p. xii, An impoverished, and consequently an acrimonious State of Blood. **1772** BURKE *Dormant Claims Ch.* Wks. 1842 II. 498 An impoverished and degraded clergy. **1882** J. H. BLUNT *Ref. Ch. Eng.* II. 486 He found an impoverished exchequer.

im'poverisher. [f. as prec. + -ER^{1}.] One who, or that which, impoverishes.

1628 FELTHAM *Resolves* I. lxxi. 193 They are..mighty louers of their Pallates; and this is knowne an impouerisher. **1647** WARD *Simp. Cobler* 26 The very troublers and impoverishers of mankind. **1777** *Nat. Hist.* in *Ann. Reg.* 99/1 Rape and hemp are..impoverishers of the soil. **1827** HONE *Every-day Bk.* II. 12 Drink is..the impoverisher of their property. **1831** E. E. CROWE *Hist. France* III. x. 306 The rigid impoverisher of his own subjects.

im'poverishing, *vbl. sb.* [f. as prec. + -ING^{1}.] The action of the vb. IMPOVERISH.

1450 *Rolls of Parlt.* V. 206/2 Grauntes..made to the distruccion and fynall empovrysshing of the seid Monasterie. **1694** FALLE *Jersey* Pref. B iij, The impoverishing, if not undoing of the French. **1881** HENTY *Cornet of Horse* xvii. (1888) 176 The impoverishing of the nobles.

im'poverishing, *ppl. a.* [f. as prec. + -ING^{2}.] That impoverishes.

1598 J. DICKENSON *Greene in Conc.* (1878) 120 Boulstring vp with your bags their impouerishing braueries. **1876** T. HARDY *Ethelberta* (1890) 21 Country bookselling is a miserable, impoverishing, exasperating thing in these days.

im'poverishly, *adv.* *rare*$^{-0}$. [irreg. f. IMPOVERISH + -LY^{2}.] 'So as to impoverish'.

1847 in CRAIG. Hence in mod. Dicts.

im'poverishment. [ad. AF. *empoverissement*, f. *empoverir* to IMPOVERISH: see IM-^{2}.]

1. The fact or process of impoverishing or making poor; the condition of being impoverished; loss of wealth or means; that which has this effect.

1560 BECON *New Catech.* Wks. 1564 I. 367 b, To the empouerishment and losse of his goods. **1615** G. SANDYS *Trav.* 57 To abstaine from almes for feare of impoverishment. **1727** SWIFT *View St. Irel.* Wks. 1761 III. 169 All appeals for justice..to another country, are so many impoverishments. **1850** GROTE *Greece* II. lxiii. VII. 230 The ruin and impoverishment..inflicted by the Persian invasion of Attica. **1897** W. C. HAZLITT *Four Generat.* II. 134 His fondness for little dinners and other sweet impoverishments.

2. The process of making or becoming poor in quality; deterioration.

1618 LATHAM *2nd Bk. Falconry* (1633) 23 And on this impouerishment attendeth many other infirmities. **1669** W. SIMPSON *Hydrol. Chym.* 163 A further impoverishment of spirits. **1860** ADLER *Fauriel's Prov. Poetry* vii. 136 The natural tendency of languages towards disintegration and impoverishment. **1875** H. C. WOOD *Therap.* (1879) 489 Impoverishment and excessive fluidity of the blood.

impower, obs. var. EMPOWER.

impracticability (ɪmˌpræktɪkə'bɪlɪtɪ). [f. IMPRACTICABLE: see -ITY.]

1. The quality or condition of being impracticable. **a.** Incapability of being done or carried out; practical impossibility.

1747 *Gentl. Mag.* XVII. 524 Because of the impracticability of a march over the precipices. **1831** BREWSTER *Nat. Magic* xi. (1833) 293 The impracticability of foreseeing all the possible combinations of the parts. **1843** PRESCOTT *Mexico* (1850) I. 222 The impracticability of the attempt.

b. Incapability of being put to its purposed use, or of being dealt with; unserviceableness, unmanageableness; also intractability, stubbornness.

1764–7 LYTTELTON *Hen. II* (1769) II. II. 356 These great regular armies could not pursue them..from the impracticability of the country. **1766** SMOLLETT *Trav.* xxxiv. II. 183 Exposed to a variety of disagreeable adventures from the impracticability of the road. **1864** *Realm* 30 Mar. 4 A track..which, for steepness and apparent impracticability, more resembled the bed of a mountain torrent.

2. with *an* and *pl.* Something impracticable; a practical impossibility.

a **1797** H. WALPOLE *Mem. Geo. II* (1847) III. ii. 40 Lord Hardwicke..had clogged it with impracticabilities, absurdities, and hardships. **1881** *Blackw. Mag.* May 559 He was equally an impracticability while armour was employed.

impracticable (ɪm'præktɪkəb(ə)l), *a.* (*sb.*) Also 7 inp-. [f. IM-^{2} + PRACTICABLE: cf. F. *impraticable* (16th c.).]

1. Not practicable; that cannot be carried out, effected, accomplished, or done; practically impossible.

a **1677** BARROW *Serm.* (1810) I. 252 To attempt things impossible or impracticable. **1696** *Lond. Gaz.* No. 3226/2 Finding that design inpracticable. **1765** BLACKSTONE *Comm.* I. 244 Such distrust would render the exercise of that power precarious and impracticable. **1860** TYNDALL *Glac.* I. xxv. 182 Balmat pronounced the passage impracticable.

2. That cannot be put to use or practically dealt with; unmanageable, intractable, unserviceable. **a.** Of things generally.

1717 S. CLARKE *Leibnitz' 5th Paper* 181 The Fiction of a material finite Universe, moving forward in an infinite empty Space, cannot be admitted. It is altogether unreasonable and impracticable. **1821** CRAIG *Lect. Drawing* ii. 113 The colours become stiff and impracticable soon after they are applied. **1838** W. IRVING in *Life & Lett.* (1866) III. 123 Millions of acres which might..have remained idle and impracticable wastes.

b. Of roads, districts, etc.: Incapable of being used for passage; impossible to pass along, over, through, or to; impassable or inaccessible.

1653 CROMWELL *Sp.* 4 July in *Carlyle*, The way they were going in would be impracticable. **1711** ADDISON *Spect.* No. 165 ¶5 They took Post behind a great Morass which they thought impracticable. **1847** GROTE *Greece* II. xl. (1862) III. 435 The pass appeared impracticable. **1871** L. STEPHEN *Playgr. Europe* iii. (1894) 78 Cliffs so steep as to be perfectly impracticable.

c. Of persons, or their dispositions, etc.: Incapable of being 'managed', influenced, or persuaded; impossible to deal with or get on with; intractable, stubborn.

1713 ROWE *Jane Shore* I. i, And yet, this tough impracticable Heart Is govern'd by a dainty-finger'd Girl. **1768** GOLDSM. *Good-n. Man* II. i, A poor impracticable creature! **1809** MALKIN *Gil Blas* x. xi. (Rtldg.) 377 Scipio.. is one of those impracticable beings, on whom good example, good advice, and a good horsewhip, are equally thrown away. **1856** FROUDE *Hist. Eng.* (1858) II. vii. 203 Fisher must have been a hopelessly impracticable person.

B. as *sb.* An impracticable person: see 2 c.

1829 *Bengalee* 13, I was looked upon as an utter impracticable. **1870** EMERSON *Soc. & Solit.* ix. 187 Then the heady men, the egotists..the steriles, and the impracticables.

impracticableness (ɪm'præktɪkəb(ə)lnɪs). [f. prec. + -NESS.] The quality or condition of being impracticable. **a.** = IMPRACTICABILITY 1 a.

1653 CROMWELL *Sp.* 4 July in *Carlyle*, Having this discourse concerning the impracticableness of the thing. **1752** CARTE *Hist. Eng.* III. 449 The impracticableness of keeping her alive in prison. **1853** GEN. P. THOMPSON *Audi Alt.* (1858) I. xv. 52 The impracticableness of passing this desert.

b. = IMPRACTICABILITY 1 b.

a **1715** BURNET *Own Time, Q. Anne* (T. Suppl.), The greatest difficulty in these sieges was from the impracticableness of the ground. **1876** GEO. ELIOT *Dan. Der.* I. iii, No clerical magistrate had..less of mischievous impracticableness in relation to worldly affairs.

impracticably (ɪm'præktɪkəblɪ), *adv.* [f. as prec. + -LY^{2}.] In an impracticable manner or degree; impossibly; unmanageably.

1779–81 JOHNSON *L.P., Addison* Wks. III. 110 His morality is neither dangerously lax, nor impracticably rigid. **1966** *McGraw-Hill Encycl. Sci. & Technol.* X. 234/2 The tube would have to be made impracticably long to avoid cooling of the plasma by the ends. **1974** *Daily Tel.* 11 Mar. 9/2 These [proposals] are now generally recognised as impracticably complicated.

impractical (ɪm'præktɪkəl), *a.* [f. IM-^{2} + PRACTICAL.] Not practical; unpractical. Also = IMPRACTICABLE *a.*

1865 J. S. MILL in *Morn. Star* 6 July, 'How injudicious!' said one; 'How impractical!' said another. **1875** MERIVALE *Hist. Rome* xl. (1877) 294 A rigid and impractical declaimer. **1887** G. GISSING *Thyrza* I. xi. 228 He is..I'm afraid, so very, very impractical. **1925** T. DREISER *Amer. Trag.* (1926) I. I. ii. 11 For Clyde's parents had proved impractical in the matter of the future of their children. **1929** *Amer. Speech* IV. 331 'Impractical'..is more commonly used than either 'unpractical', or 'impracticable', as it seems to squint and have both meanings. **1931** J. T. ADAMS *Epic of Amer.* iv. 112 So impractical was American cotton culture considered that ..England seized eight bales. **1947** E. W. F. FELLER *Instrument & Control Manual* p. vii, The number of units to be controlled in a single plant all tend to render hand control impractical if not impossible. **1962** E. GODFREY *Retail Selling & Organiz.* ii. 21 On a busy ground floor, carpeting would be impractical. **1964** R. H. ROBINS *Gen. Ling.* i. 2 As an impractical ideal he [*sc.* the general linguist] would know something about every language. **1970** *Daily Tel.* 4 May 2/7 The scheme was reckoned to be the next best to transferable pensions, which the Government believes to be impractical at the moment. **1973** *Sci. Amer.* Mar. 113/2 The second calculating method..is too complicated and impractical to explain here.

impracticality (ɪmpræktɪ'kælɪtɪ). [f. IMPRACTICAL *a.* + -ITY.] The character of being impractical; impracticableness.

1916 H. S. WALPOLE *Dark Forest* I. iv, The Russian character..with its lack of restraint, its idealism, its impracticality. **1926** J. BUCHAN *Dancing Floor* II. x. 187 The impracticality of an entrance..at that point.

So **im'practicalness.**

1905 *Macm. Mag.* Nov. 55 He was accused of vagueness, impracticalness, generality.

impractically (ɪm'præktɪkəlɪ), *adv.* [f. IMPRACTICAL *a.* + -LY^{2}.] In an impractical manner; to an impractical or impracticable degree; not practicably.

1947 *Math. Tables & Other Aids to Computation* II. 359 Long sequences of accurate computations which would be impractically lengthy by any other slower means. **1959** E. M. MCCORMICK *Digital Computer Primer* viii. 115 It is generally impractically expensive to obtain the very large storage. **1974** *Sci. Amer.* Jan. 93/1 The forces toward the left between these lines are impractically high; normal playing is confined to the area toward the right.

†**im'pravable**, *a.* *Obs.* In 6 inp-. [f. IM-^{2} + L. *prāv-us* crooked, wrong, bad + -ABLE.] Incorruptible.

1542 BECON *Potat. Lent* Wks. 1564 I. 44 b, He that fasteth must..set before hys eyes alway the eye of the euerlastyng iudge and the inprauable iudgyng place.

impray (ɪm'preɪ), *v.* *rare*$^{-1}$. [f. IM-^{1} + PRAY, ? after L. *imprecārī*.] *trans.* To pray to, invoke.

1855 BAILEY *Spir. Leg.* in *Mystic*, etc. 72 Or warlike Don; Or Po, by Goths imprayed with murderous rites.

imprease: see EMPRISE, IMPRESS *sb.*^{2}

imprecate ('ɪmprɪkeɪt), *v.* [f. L. *imprecāt-*, ppl. stem of *imprecārī*, in senses 1 and 2, f. *im-* (IM-^{1}) + *precārī* to pray.]

1. *trans.* To pray for, invoke (something, usually from a deity). **a.** To invoke or call down (evil or calamity) *upon* a person.

1613 PURCHAS *Pilgrimage* (1614) 216 The falling sicknesse ..they vse to imprecate it to each other in their anger, as they also doe the plague. **1672** CAVE *Prim. Chr.* III. i. (1673) 220 Imprecating upon himself that he might be burnt. **1681–6** J. SCOTT *Chr. Life* (1747) III. 215 How importunately soever our past Guilts may imprecate the divine Vengeance upon us. **1753** SMOLLETT *Ct. Fathom* (1784) 45/2 She..imprecated a thousand curses upon his head. **1852** HAWTHORNE *Grandf. Chair* III. ix, There is scarcely a tongue..that does not imprecate curses on his name.

b. To pray for; to beg for, entreat (something good). *rare.*

1636 PRYNNE *Unbish. Tim.* (1661) 63 Priests and Presbyters who give Baptism and imprecate the Lords Advent to the Eucharist. **1664** LD. CARLISLE in *Marvell's Wks.* (1872–5) II. 110, I wish and imprecate to your Imperial Majestie all Happiness. **1861** LOWELL *Biglow P.* Ser. II. Introd., He..would only imprecate patience till he shall again have 'got the hang' (as he calls it) of an accomplishment long disused.

2. To pray (a deity), invoke, supplicate. Now *rare* or *Obs.*

1643 PRYNNE *Sov. Power Parl.* II. 39 b, Which I shall dayly imprecate the God of Peace speedily to accomplish. **1843** CARLYLE *Past & Pr.* II. viii, Imprecating the Lord.

†**3.** *absol.* or *intr.* To pray; to invoke evil. *Obs.*

1647 W. BROWNE tr. *Gomberville's Polexander* IV. ii. 204 Polexander, not knowing whom to accuse but his destinie, imprecated against himselfe. **1669** GALE *Crt. Gentiles* I. II. ix. 140 After they had imprecated on the head of the sacrifice, they cut it off. **1673** *Lady's Call.* I. 23 Aristides.. was so far from acting, or imprecating against them, that [etc.].

4. *trans.* To invoke evil upon (a person); to curse. Now *rare* or *Obs.*

1616 BULLOKAR, *Imprecate*, to curse and wish euill. **1641** J. JACKSON *True Evang. T.* I. 66 The Jewes imprecated themselves with 'His blood bee on us, and on our children'. **1760** DERRICK *Lett.* (1767) I. 90 View this..baseness and ingratitude of the Stuarts, and imprecate the name, ye infatuated friends of that family. **1879** MINTO *Defoe* iii. 33

His co-religionists were imprecating him as the man who had brought this persecution upon them.

Hence **'imprecating** *ppl. a.*, that imprecates, invoking a curse; whence **'imprecatingly** *adv.*, in the way of a curse.

1652 GAULE *Magastrom.* 280 Picus Mirandula..was envyously and imprecatingly told..that [etc.]. **1686** BURNET *Trav.* i. (1750) 40 He swore to them in a most imprecating Style, that he would never discover the Secret.

imprecation (ɪmprɪ'keɪʃən). [ad. L. *imprecātiōn-em*, n. of action from *imprecārī* to IMPRECATE: cf. F. *imprécation*, OF. *-acion* (14th c. in Littré).] The action, or an act, of imprecating.

1. a. The action of invoking evil, calamity, or divine vengeance upon another, or upon oneself, in an oath or adjuration; cursing.

1589 PUTTENHAM *Eng. Poesie* III. xix. (Arb.) 221 By way of exclamation or crying out..imprecation or cursing, obtestation or taking God and the world to witnes. **1649** MILTON *Eikon.* xii, The bare denyall of one man, though with imprecation, cannot in any reason countervaile. **1774** PENNANT *Tour Scotl. in 1772*, 184 A cairn on your head, is a token of imprecation. **1855** MILMAN *Lat. Chr.* v. xiii. (1864) III. 335 Arnulf's oath of fidelity..couched in terms of more than usual severity of imprecation.

b. (with *pl.*) An invocation of evil, a curse.

1603 HOLLAND *Plutarch's Mor.* 489 When he had powred out grievous imprecations against those unthankfull Xanthiens. **1639** HABINGTON *Castara* II. (Arb.) 88 Why lives the gamester, who doth blacke the night With cheats and imprecations? **1737** [S. BERINGTON] *G. di Lucca's Mem.* 277 He cursed himself with the most dreadful imprecations, if he were not [etc.]. **1849** MACAULAY *Hist. Eng.* vi. II. 145 He drove them from him with imprecations. **1883** FROUDE *Short Stud.* IV. I. x. 114 At each fierce imprecation he quenched a light, and dashed down a candle.

†**2.** A prayer, invocation, petition, entreaty. *Obs.*

1585 T. WASHINGTON tr. *Nicholay's Voy.* IV. ii. 115 After some imprecations made, [he] annoynted their sacrifice with oyle, milk and hony. **1631** WEEVER *Anc. Fun. Mon.* 374 Brute..made his imprecation to the Goddesse to this effect.

imprecator ('ɪmprɪkeɪtə(r)). [Agent-noun in L. form from IMPRECATE: see -OR.] One who imprecates or invokes evil.

1845 FORD *Handbk. Spain* I. 36 Bad luck seldom deserts the house of the imprecator.

imprecatory ('ɪmprɪkeɪtərɪ, -kəˌtərɪ, ɪmprɪ'keɪtərɪ), *a.* [f. L. *imprecāt-*, ppl. stem of *imprecārī* + -ORY.]

1. Expressing or involving imprecation; invoking evil or divine vengeance; cursing, maledictory.

1587 FLEMING *Contn. Holinshed* III. 400/2 An epitaph imprecatorie..is here placed as a conclusion of this his memoriall, and appliable vnto all..that antichristian and diabolicall succession. **1628** SIR S. D'EWES *Jrnl.* (1783) 46 This hexastich..of a like imprecatorie nature as the former. *a* **1792** G. HORNE in Spurgeon *Treas. Dav.* Ps. xxviii. 4–5 In most of the imprecatory passages the imperative and the future are used promiscuously. **1881** W. ROBERTSON SMITH *Old Test. in Jew. Ch.* vii. 207 The interpretation of the imprecatory Psalms.

†**2.** Of the nature of prayer or invocation; invoking blessing; invocatory. *Obs. rare.*

a **1625** BOYS *Wks.* (1629) 665 Other imprecatorie, by way of a good wish or salutation, the Lord be with you.

Hence **'imprecatorily** *adv.*, in the way of an imprecation or curse.

1874 E. P. CROWELL *Notes to Andria of Terence* 158 *Abin*, an interrogative form used imprecatorily.

†**im'preciable,** *a. Obs.* [ad. late L. *impretiābilis* (*-prēc-*) inestimable, f. *im-* (IM-^{2}) + *pretiāre* to prize (Cassiodorus): see -BLE.] Invaluable; beyond price.

1502 *Ord. Crysten Men* (W. de W. 1506) IV. xxi. 228 A man selleth the thynge imprecyable, and the whiche proprely may not be solde. **1650** BLOUNT *Glossogr.*, *Impreciable*, unpriseable, unvaluable.

imprecise (ɪmprɪ'saɪs), *a.* [f. IM-^{2} + PRECISE *a.*] Not precise; wanting in precision. Hence **impre'ciseness.**

1805 W. TAYLOR in *Ann. Rev.* III. 651 To say that no less can be acknowledged than this divine origin of law, is imprecise. **1830** —— *Germ. Poetry* I. 288, I have not abstained from confounding observations on the characters of this epopæa, with those which, according to Sulzer's imprecise plan of analysis, ought merely to have respected the majesty of this action. **1907** *Athenæum* 9 Mar. 282/3 He [*sc.* Henry James] must..deck it with the most elaborated precisions of impreciseness. **1943** A. L. ROWSE *Spirit Eng. Hist.* i. 11 An impreciseness which characterises the English mind.

imprecision (ɪmprɪ'sɪʒən). [f. IM-^{2} + PRECISION.] Want of precision; inexactness.

1803 W. TAYLOR in *Monthly Mag.* XIV. 487 The imprecision of this language arises from Berkeley's not having investigated what ideas are. **1815** *Ibid.* XXXVIII. 502 The slightest imprecision of outline may annihilate beauty. **1822–34** *Good's Study Med.* (ed. 4) II. 637 Scorbutus..could not therefore, without imprecision be used in a generic signification. **1954** W. STEVENS *Coll. Poems* 353 The romance of the precise is not the elision Of the tired romance of imprecision. **1971** *Nature* 4 June 274/1 For one thing, it pointed to strictly legal imprecisions in the legislation which at present regulates the use of transplants in Britain.

impredicable (ɪm'prɛdɪkəb(ə)l), *a.* Also 7 **in-.** [f. IM-^{2} + PREDICABLE.] That cannot be predicated. (In quot. 1864 *loosely* = that cannot be predicted.) Hence **imˌpredica'bility**, the condition of being impredicable.

1623 COCKERAM *Eng. Dict.* II, Not to be Spoken, *Ineffable, Inpredicable.* **1864** LOWELL *Rebellion* Prose Wks. 1890 V. 126 Dependent on a multitude of new and impredicable circumstances. **1880** F. HALL in *Nation* (N.Y.) XXXI. 276/1 Nor can we doubt that 'formal grammar', as impredicable of English..will cease to be a topic [etc.]. *a* **1899** *Mod.* Spiritual qualities are impredicable of physical things. **1906** P. LOWELL *Mars & its Canals* viii. 95 Even on Mars nothing in the way of weather is absolutely predicable but impredicability. **1937** A. SMEATON tr. *Carnap's Logical Syntax of Lang.* III. §38. 138 Russell showed that this antinomy can also be so formulated as to apply not only to classes but to properties as well (the antinomy of 'impredicable'..). *Ibid.* IV. §60a. 212 Hence a definition of the form given for 'impredicable' is obviously impossible. **1965** F. SOMMERS in M. Black *Philos. in Amer.* 272 For example, the term *clean* is impredicable of the equator. *Ibid.* 273 It becomes unnecessary to introduce special 'type' restrictions to account for impredicability.

impredicative (ɪm'prɛdɪkətɪv), *a.* [f. IM-^{2} + PREDICATIVE *a.*] Of a proposition, thing, etc.: not definable except in terms of a totality of which it is itself a part. Hence **im'predicatively** *adv.*; **impredica'tivity**, the state or quality of being impredicative.

1937 A. SMEATON tr. *Carnap's Logical Syntax of Lang.* IV. §44. 162 A thing is usually called impredicative (in the material mode of speech) when it is defined (or can only be defined) with the help of a totality to which it itself belongs. **1944** K. GÖDEL in P. A. Schilpp *Philos. B. Russell* II. iii. 138 What an impredicative definition would require is to construct a notion by a combination of a set of notions to which the notion to be formed itself belongs. **1963** W. V. QUINE *Set Theory* §34. 242 He [*sc.* Poincaré] called the suspect procedure impredicative. **1965** C. D. PARSONS in M. Black *Philos. in Amer.* 196 Such extensions..allow impredicatively defined classes. *Ibid.* 197 This can only be because the mathematics itself involves impredicativity.

impreg ('ɪmprɛg). Also **Impreg.** [Abbrev. of IMPREG(NATED *ppl. a.* 2.] A type of wood impregnated with a synthetic resin to improve its dimensional stability and resistance to distortion or decay.

1942 *Fortune* Oct. 180/2 F[orest] P[roducts] L[aboratory] makes a special 'impreg' by treating wood with raw resin so that the resin actually penetrates the wood cells. **1953** HUNT & GARRATT *Wood Preservation* (ed. 2) xi. 365 The shrinkage and swelling of wood..can be reduced..by first impregnating the wood (in thin sheets) with a solution of unpolymerized phenol-formaldehyde resin, then drying the wood at moderate temperatures, and finally heating the dry wood at about 300°C to polymerize the resin in place; the product formed is called Impreg. **1953** STAMM & HARRIS *Chem. Processing of Wood* (1954) viii. 226 Impreg was manufactured during World War II only for military users. **1967** R. H. FARMER *Chem. in Utilization of Wood* viii. 119 Uncompressed resin-impregnated wood was first made in the United States, where it is called Impreg.

impregn (ɪm'pri:n), *v.* Also 7 **-prægn.** Now only in poetic use. [ad. late L. *impræ̆gnā-re* to make pregnant, f. *im-* (IM-^{1}) + *prægnāre* to be PREGNANT. Cf. mod.F. *imprégner* (1690 in Hatz.-Darm.).]

1. *trans.* = IMPREGNATE *v.* 1, 2.

c **1540** tr. *Pol. Verg. Eng. Hist.* (Camden) I. 221 This woman..beinge impregned bie her husbande. **1647** H. MORE *Song of Soul* I. I. lviii, This all-spread Semele doth Bacchus bear, Impregn'd of love or On. **1748** *Phil. Trans.* XLV. 235 The Male impregns the Row which the Female has before deposited.

fig. *a* **1618** SYLVESTER *Tropheis Henry Gt.* 2 Since first Apollo lent the World his light, And Earth impregned with his heatfull might. **1657** PIERCE *Div. Philanthr.* Ded. 6 Once he terribly miscarried with what he had long been imprægn'd. **1727–46** THOMSON *Summer* 140 Th' unfruitful rock itself, impregn'd by thee, In dark retirement forms the lucid stone. **1839** BAILEY *Festus* i. (1852) 3 All souls, impregned with spirit, God-begot.

2. = IMPREGNATE *v.* 3, 4.

1652 BENLOWES *Theoph.* (Fancie upon Theophila), Magnetick Virtue's in her Brest Impregn'd with Grace, the noblest Guest. **1667** MILTON *P.L.* IX. 737 His perswasive words impregn'd With Reason. *a* **1769** J. G. COOPER *Hymn to Health* (R.), No wholsome scents impregn the western gale. *a* **1834** LAMB *Sonn.* iii, Impregning with delights the charmed air. **188.** R. G. H[ILL] *Voices Solit.* 172 The substance I will impregn With my light.

Hence **im'pregned, im'pregning** *ppl. adjs.*

1641 HOWELL *Vote* in *Lett.* (1650) II. 129 The Ocean..Is not for sail, if an impregning wind Fill not the flagging canvas. **1647** H. MORE *Song of Soul* I. II. v, True Soveraign Of working phancie when it floats amain With full impregned billows and strong rage. **1753** *Scots Mag.* XV. 76/1 To breathe the balm-impregned gale.

impregnability (ɪmprɛgnə'bɪlɪtɪ). [f. next: see -ITY.] The quality or condition of being impregnable; incapacity of being taken or reduced by force. *lit.* and *fig.*

1847 W. SMITH tr. *Fichte's Characteristics Present Age* 30 The supposed impregnability of the mode of thought which we have now described arises precisely in this way. **1861** MAINE *Anc. Law* vi. (1874) 202 The new or Praetorian Testament derived the whole of its impregnability from the *Jus Honorarium* or Equity of Rome. **1865** *Macm. Mag.* Nov. 13 The castle profited by the road in accessibility, but its impregnability was so far lessened. **1879** MENDELL *Art of War* iii. 77 Believing in the impregnability of these [mountain] chains.

impregnable (ɪm'prɛgnəb(ə)l), *a.* (*sb.*) Forms: 5–7 **imprenable**, (5 **inprenable**, 6 **inprennable, enprenabill**), 6 **impreignable, inpreyngnable, impreniable**, 6– **impregnable.** [Corrupted from *impreignable, imprenable*, a. F. *imprenable*, f. *im-* (IM-^{2}) + *prenable* able to be taken, f. *pren-*, stem of *prendre* to take. The *g* was evidently in imitation of the *g* mute in *reign, deign*, and the like, though it appears to have sometimes led in 16th c. to the pronunciation (nj).]

1. Of a fortress or stronghold: That cannot be taken by arms; incapable of being reduced by force; capable of holding out against all attacks.

1430–40 LYDG. *Bochas* VII. ix. (MS. Bodl.) lf. 360 b, Dreeding non enmy, for it was Imprenable. **1477** EARL RIVERS *Dictes* 129 Dimycrates saide pacience is a castell imprenable. **1530** PALSGR. 756/2 The castell whiche men wente had ben inprennable is throwen downe nowe. **1531** ELYOT *Gov.* I. xxvii, A fewe englisshe archers haue..also wonne impreignable cities and stronge holdes. *a* **1533** LD. BERNERS *Huon* lix. 203 Stondyng on a rocke on the see syde, it was impreyngnable. **1548** HALL *Chron., Edw. IV*, 228 What a folye was this in duke Charles, to besege a towne impregnable. **1553** BRENDE *Q. Curtius* C v, They said they knewe it to be impreniable. **1556** J. HEYWOOD *Spider & F.* lvii. 134 Se thenprenabill fort: in euery border. **1593** SHAKS. *3 Hen. VI*, IV. i. 44 Let vs be back'd with God, and with the Seas, Which he hath giu'n for fence impregnable. **1642** FULLER *Holy & Prof. St.* II. xix. 120 Such a mans soul is an impregnable fort. **1776** GIBBON *Decl. & F.* xiii. I. 369 Rendering his camp impregnable to the sallies of the besieged multitude. **1885** RUSKIN *Pleasures Eng.* 100 The Normans set themselves to build impregnable military walls.

2. *fig.* That cannot be overcome or vanquished; invincible, unconquerable, proof against attack.

1582 N. LICHEFIELD tr. *Castanheda's Conq. E. Ind.* ii. 4 b, Valyauntnesse of minde (for atteining of things impregnable). **1602** MARSTON *Ant. & Mel.* III. Wks. 1856 I. 37, I find them wondrous chaste, Impregnable. *a* **1661** FULLER *Worthies* (1840) III. 309 He wrote an excellent book ..containing impregnable truth. **1710** STEELE *Tatler* No. 101 ¶1 This Iniquity is committed by a most impregnable Set of Mortals, Men who are Rogues within the Law. **1856** KANE *Arct. Expl.* I. xxxii. 448, I do not fear the cold: we are impregnable in our furs. **1862** CARLYLE *Fredk. Gt.* VIII. v. (1872) III. 29 A man politely impregnable to the intrusion of human curiosity.

B. as *sb.* That which is impregnable. *rare.*

1803 *Gentl. Mag.* in *Spirit Pub. Jrnls.* (1804) VII. 43 Disappointed in attacking our impregnables.

im'pregnableness. *rare.* [f. prec. + -NESS.] = IMPREGNABILITY.

1603 KNOLLES *Hist. Turks* (1621) 1170 Discouraged with the impregnablenes of the place. **1647** CLARENDON *Contempl. Ps.* in *Tracts* (1727) 419 The strength and impregnableness of his castles and forts.

impregnably (ɪm'prɛgnəblɪ), *adv.* [f. as prec. + -LY^{2}.] In an impregnable manner; so as to be impregnable; invincibly, unconquerably.

1602 MARSTON *Ant. & Mel.* Induct., Wks. 1856 I. 5 So impregnably fortrest with his own content. **1661** J. STEPHENS *Procurations* 26 They make that Custome.. impregnably strong. *a* **1711** KEN *Anodynes* Poet. Wks. 1721 III. 445 Patient, resign'd, and humble Wills, Impregnably resist all Ills. **1821** SHELLEY *Hellas* 1004 If Greece must be A wreck, yet shall its fragments re-assemble, And build themselves again impregnably In a diviner clime.

impregnant (ɪm'prɛgnənt), *a.*^{1} and *sb.* [In sense A 1, f. IM-^{1} + PREGNANT; in senses A 2 and B, ad. L. *impræ̆gnānt-em*, pres. pple. of *impræ̆gnāre*: see IMPREGN and -ANT.]

A. *adj.* †**1.** Impregnated, pregnant. **a.** Caused to conceive; *fig.* rendered fruitful or productive. **b.** Imbued, saturated *with*. *Obs.*

1641 FRENCH *Distill.* v. (1651) 163 Vapours of Nitre.. bodying, and impregnant with Spirits of Nitre. **1643** SIR T. BROWNE *Relig. Med.* I. §16 [In the chaos] there was no deformity, because no forme, nor was it yet impregnant by the voice of God. **1670** E. BORLASE *Lathom Spaw* 5 The Water dies it with a rusty iron colour, one Argument of what it is impregnant with. **1712** ADDISON *Spect.* No. 303 ¶4 The Division of Hell into Seas of Fire, and into firm Ground impregnant with the same furious Element.

2. Impregnating. Also as *sb.* That which impregnates (cf. quot. 1664 s.v. IMPREGNATE *v.* 4). Now *rare.*

1661 GLANVILL *Van. Dogm.* xiv. 133 It [interest] is the Pole, to which we turn, and our sympathizing Judgements seldom decline from the direction of this Impregnant. **1825** COLERIDGE *Lit. Rem.* (1836) II. 340 This chaos, the eternal will,..acting as the impregnant, distinctive, and ordonnant power,—enabled to become a world. **1868** GEO. ELIOT *Sp. Gipsy* IV. 313 As the impregnant sap Of years successive frames the full-branched tree.

B. *sb.* A substance used for the impregnation of something else. (Cf. sense A 2.)

1933 H. BENNETT *Chem. Formulary* I. 441/1 Leather Soles, Impregnant for. **1948** KIRK & OTHMER *Encycl. Chem. Technol.* II. 546 The bitumens employed as felt impregnants are usually soft, low-melting materials of high fluidity in the molten condition. **1955** SEYMOUR & STEINER *Plastics for Corrosion-Resistant Applications* xii. 191 The sealing effect of the impregnant..is dependent upon an increase in molecular size of the resin used. **1959** *New Scientist* 30 July 127/3 Inside present day automotive

storage battery cells..a waffle-shaped network of lead holds the impregnant that keeps the battery alive.

†**impregnant**, *a.*² *Obs. rare.* [f. IM-² + PREGNANT *a.*] Not pregnant; sterile.

a **1659** OSBORN *Misc.*, *Queries* (1673) 610 That all things were not Created for their Own sakes, but the meer Interest of Nature, which abhors to be Idle, or to leave any in Impregnant Condition.

impregnate (ɪmˈprɛgnət), *ppl. a.* [ad. late or med.L. *impræg̃nāt-us*, pa. pple. of *impræg̃nāre*: see IMPREGN, of which this was also used as the pa. pple.] = IMPREGNATED (as *pa. pple.* or *adj.*).

1. Caused to conceive; pregnant; rendered fruitful or prolific. Also *fig.*

1545 RAYNOLD *Byrth Mankynde* II. vii. (1643) 133 All such women which be impregnate or conceiued. **1651** SIR E. SHERBURN *Salmacis* 7 The tumid Earth (As if impregnate with a fruitfull Birth) Swels gently up into an easie Hill. **1663** *Flagellum, or O. Cromwell* (ed. 2) 2 Nor were there any presagious dreams or fearful divinations of his Mother when she was impregnate with him. **1664** EVELYN *Sylva* (1679) 4 Being more impregnate with the Sun, Dews and heavenly Influences. **1849** *Fraser's Mag.* XL. 539 The leading impregnate thoughts, the ideas, or laws laid down for a poetical composition. **1855** SINGLETON *Virgil* I. 161 And oft without embraces any, by the wind Impregnate.

2. Imbued, saturated, filled, permeated *with* (some active principle). †In quot. 1661, Magnetized: cf. IMPREGNATE *v.* 4, quot. 1664.

1646 SIR T. BROWNE *Pseud. Ep.* III. xxi. 161 If the ambient aire be impregnate with subtile inflamabilities. **1661** GLANVILL *Van. Dogm.* xxi. 203 Let one move his impregnate needle to any letter in the alphabet, and its affected fellow will precisely respect the same. **1688** BURNET *Lett. Pres. St. Italy* 144 The Meadow..is impregnate with Salt, Iron, Nitre and Sulphur. **1715–20** POPE *Iliad* v. 968 Impregnate with celestial dew. **1818** BYRON *Ch. Har.* IV. lv, Thy decay Is still impregnate with divinity, Which gilds it with revivifying ray. **1851** WHITTIER *Chapel of Hermits* vi, O light and air of Palestine, Impregnate with His life divine!

¶ Erroneously for IMPREGNABLE.

1632 LITHGOW *Trav.* x. 506 Impregnate Forts, devalling Floods, and more Earth-gazing heights. **1721** D'URFEY *2 Queens Brentford* II. i, Bring me the Caitiff here before my Face, Tho' made Impregnate, as Achilles was.

impregnate (ˈɪm-, ɪmˈprɛgneɪt), *v.* [f. prec. or its source: see -ATE³ 3–5.]

1. *trans.* To make (a female) pregnant; to cause to conceive; to get with young; in *Biol.*, also, to fecundate the female reproductive cell or ovum.

1646 SIR T. BROWNE *Pseud. Ep.* III. xii. 134 Hermophrodites although they include the parts of both sexes..cannot impregnate themselves. **1707** NORRIS *Treat. Humility* viii. 352 She was to be impregnated by the overshadowings of the Holy Ghost. **1774** GOLDSM. *Nat. Hist.* (1776) VII. 31 Mr. Adanson has seen vast numbers of sea snails, united together in a chain, impregnating each other. **1841–71** T. R. JONES *Anim. Kingd.* (ed. 4) 363 By these the ova are developed, impregnated, and oviposited; and thus provision is made for..continuing the existence of the species.

b. *Bot.* Of the pollen or male reproductive cell in plants: To fertilize. †In quot. 1671, To cause to grow or develop (in the embryo plant).

1671 GREW *Anat. Plants* i. §44 The Lobes did at first feed and impregnate the Radicle into a perfect Root. **1769** E. BANCROFT *Guiana* 28 Their pistils are covered..with farina fæcundans,..which when mature falls into and impregnates the subjacent matrix. **1776** WITHERING *Brit. Plants* (1796) II. 401 Produced by the Pollen of the P. secunda, impregnating the germen of the P. rotundifolia.

c. *intr.* for *pass.* To become pregnant, to conceive. *rare.*

1711 ADDISON *Spect.* No. 127 ¶2 Were they, like Spanish Jennets, to impregnate by the Wind, they could not have thought on a more proper Invention.

2. *fig.* (*trans.*) To render fruitful or productive; to fertilize. (Also *absol.*)

1667 *Decay Chr. Piety* i. 1 Christianity is..so apt to impregnate the hearts and lives of its proselytes, that it is hard to imagine that any branch should want a due fertility. **1720** WELTON *Suffer, Son of God* II. xviii. 490 He left His Holy Spirit there..to Impregnate the Divine Seed that He had sown. **1860** SYMONDS in *Life* (1895) I. 345 Joy impregnates: sorrows bring forth.

3. To fill (a substance or portion of matter) *with* some active principle, element, or ingredient, diffused through it or mixed intimately with it; to imbue, saturate. In earlier use sometimes simply (with more direct allusion to 1) = to fill. (Most commonly in *passive*.)

1605 TIMME *Quersit.* I. iv. 15 The elements returne to their parents full and impregnated with celestiall forms. **1671** J. WEBSTER *Metallogr.* iv. 74 Sulpher, with which *Argent vive* is impregnated. **1732** ARBUTHNOT *Rules of Diet* 299 Water impregnated with some penetrating Salt. **1789** MRS. PIOZZI *Journ. France* I. 40 Savoy is impregnated with many minerals. **1808** *Med. Jrnl.* XIX. 110, I determined to impregnate his system with mercury by external inunction. **1847** SMEATON *Builder's Man.* 62 Attempts..to prevent the destruction of wood, by impregnating it with some substance capable of restraining its ravages.

b. *fig.* To imbue or fill *with* (active thoughts, feelings, principles, influences, moral qualities, etc.).

1652 J. HALL *Height Eloq.* p. xiv, We ought to nurture our souls to greatnesse, and impregnate them..to thoughts high and extraordinary. **1784** JOHNSON in *Boswell* 15 May, She has a constant stream of conversation, and it is always impregnated; it has always meaning. **1835** LYTTON *Rienzi* I. iv, He had sought to impregnate his colleagues with the same loftiness of principle. **1878** H. IRVING *The Stage* 24 Producing plays, the whole structure of which is impregnated with moral unhealthiness.

4. Said of the active principle or influence: To be diffused through (something); to permeate, interpenetrate, fill, saturate.

1664 POWER *Exp. Philos.* III. 158 The Magnetical Effluviums..proceed ab extrinseco &c. therefore do impregnate the Stone again, upon their re-admission. **1744** BERKELEY *Siris* §45 Light impregnates air, air impregnates vapour. **1746–7** HERVEY *Medit.* (1818) 89 This magnificent luminary..beautifies and impregnates universal nature. **1816** J. SMITH *Panorama Sc. & Art* II. 822 He suspended the birds by the feet..for the salts to impregnate the body.

Hence **impregnating** *vbl. sb.* and *ppl. a.*

1705 STANHOPE *Paraphr.* II. 73 The impregnating warmth of the Sun. **1846** J. BAXTER *Libr. Pract. Agric.* (ed. 4) I. 119 Then insects..become, in their journeyings of pleasure from flower to flower, the porters who bear the impregnating principle.

impregnated (ˈɪm-, ɪmˈprɛgneɪtɪd) *ppl. a.* [f. IMPREGNATE *v.* + -ED¹. It took the place of the earlier ppl. adj. *impregnate.*]

1. Made pregnant; caused to conceive; fertilized.

1789 BAILLIE in *Phil. Trans.* LXXIX. 75 In the impregnated uterus. **1881** MIVART *Cat* 317 The impregnated ovum becomes an embryo. **1885** GOODALE *Phys. Bot.* (1892) 436 The fertilized or impregnated oösphere is termed an oöspore.

2. Imbued or saturated with something; having some active ingredient diffused through it. *spec.* ***impregnated wood***, (*a*) wood saturated with a preservative; (*b*) = IMPREG.

1605 [see IMPREGNATE *v.* 3]. **1729** *Evelyn's Kal. Hort.* 206 A vessel of impregnated Water. **1790** KEIR in *Phil. Trans.* LXXX. 372 Adding water to the impregnated acid. **1877** RAYMOND *Statist. Mines & Mining* 280 An impregnated stratum of quartzite. **1942** *Amer. Jrnl. Bot.* XXIX. 552/1 A brown mold has been observed..on small pieces of impregnated wood. [**1942** *Fortune* Oct. 180/2 It [*sc.* 'compreg'] consists of layers of resin-impregnated wood that have been compressed together.] **1944** *Amer. Speech* XIX. 92 Plywood manufacturers..developed a technique by which the glue..is forced through the entire texture of all the plies in a laminated sheet, and 'impregnated wood' is the specific name of the resultant product. **1951** MACTAGGART & CHAMBERS *Plastics & Building* x. 114 This phenomenon [*sc.* impregnation of wood with synthetic resin] has resulted in the development of two types of impregnated wood called generally Impreg and Compreg. **1963** A. D. WOOD *Plywoods of World* IV. 141 Improved and impregnated wood is more difficult to work than solid timber.

impregnation (ɪmprɛgˈneɪʃən). [n. of action from IMPREGNATE *v.* Cf. F. *impregnation* (14th c. in Godef., and in Cotgr. 1611), which may be the source.]

1. The action or process of making pregnant; fecundation, fertilization. **a.** in animals.

1605 TIMME *Quersit.* I. iv. 15 Which impregnation commeth from no other than from those astrall seedes. **1633** BP. HALL *Hard Texts* 373 Upon her impregnation, the burden of her wombe shall force her to rest. **1799** *Med. Jrnl.* I. 3 It has been an opinion..that when an animal of a perfect order is brought forth an hermaphrodite, that it must have been the consequence of a double impregnation. **1878** BELL tr. *Gegenbaur's Comp. Anat.* 19 The egg-cell undergoes changes, which ordinarily commence after impregnation. **1880** GÜNTHER *Fishes* 157 Circumstances which render artificial impregnation more practicable [in fishes] than in any other class of animals.

b. in plants.

1735 J. LOGAN in *Phil. Trans.* Abr. VIII. 57 (*heading*) Experiments concerning the Impregnation of the Seeds of Plants. **1776** WITHERING *Brit. Plants* (1796) II. 262 In no plant may the process of impregnation be so distinctly seen. **1875** BENNETT & DYER *Sachs' Bot.* 485 Of pollen-tubes..only one usually grows to an extent sufficient to effect impregnation.

2. The action of imbuing or fact of being imbued with something; diffusion of an active element through a substance; saturation, *spec.* the saturation of wood with a preservative. Also *fig.*

1641 FRENCH *Distill.* i. (1651) 11 *Impregnation*, is when any dry body hath drank in so much moisture that it will admit of no more. **1691** RAY *Creation* I. (1692) 65 The Impregnation of the Blood with Air. **1790** KEIR in *Phil. Trans.* LXXX. 373 *note*, Colour communicated to oil of vitriol by impregnation with nitrous gas or vapour. **1847** SMEATON *Builder's Man.* 66 The impregnation of timber with corrosive sublimate. **1856** KANE *Arct. Expl.* I. xxix. 390 The impregnation of fatty oil through the cellular tissue makes a well-fed bear nearly uneatable. **1872** *Jrnl. Chem. Soc.* XXV. 186 It may be stated that the impregnation of wood with sulphate of copper, or with creosote oils, or their vapours, is of service in rendering the wood three or four times as lasting as unprepared material of the same quality. **1924** E. G. BLAKE *Seasoning & Preservation of Timber* iii. 24 If the principle of impregnation was to be universally adopted, the danger of the exhaustion of the world's supply would be deferred. **1946** CARTWRIGHT & FINDLAY *Decay of Timber* xiii. 258 Impregnation treatments are necessary whenever the timber is liable to be exposed to persistently damp conditions. **1968** *Gloss. Terms Timber Preservation* (*B.S.I.*) 18 *Impregnation*, strictly the saturation of wood with a preservative. Generally used to describe treatments giving a high loading of preservative in the wood, e.g. pressure treatments.

3. *concr.* **a.** That with which something is impregnated; an impregnating element, influence, etc.

1713 DERHAM *Phys.-Theol.* (J.), What could implant in the body such peculiar impregnations, as should have such power? **1756** C. LUCAS *Ess. Waters* II. 52 These several saline impregnations seemed nearly equally colorless and bright. **1838** T. THOMSON *Chem. Org. Bodies* 397 The least period that this impregnation is allowed to remain.

b. *Geol.* A mineral deposit consisting of a rock impregnated with ore, not forming a true vein.

1881 RAYMOND *Mining Gloss.*, *Impregnation*, an ore-deposit consisting of the country-rock impregnated with ore, usually without definite boundaries.

Hence **impreg'national** *a.*, of or relating to impregnation.

1888 J. T. GULICK in *Linn. Soc. Jrnl.* XX. 238 Impregnational Segregation is due to the different relations in which the members of a species stand to each other in regard to the possibility of their producing fertile offspring when they consort together.

im'pregnative, *a. rare.* [f. IMPREGNATE *v.*, or its source + -IVE.] Having the quality of impregnating *with* something; tending to impregnate.

1686 GOAD *Celest. Bodies* III. i. 377 An Aspect that is not ..so impregnative with Moisture, nor so potent.

impregnator (ˈɪm-, ɪmˈprɛgneɪtə(r)). [agent-n. in L. form from IMPREGNATE *v.*] One who impregnates.

1722 POPE *Let. to Gay* 13 July, Lett. 1735 I. 321 An Impregnator of the Barren. **1883** SIR M. MONIER-WILLIAMS *Relig. Th. India* xiii. 355 Let Prajā-pati be the Impregnator; let the Creator give the Embryo.

impregnatory (ɪmˈprɛgnətərɪ), *a.* [f. L. *impræg̃nāt-*, ppl. stem + -ORY.] Having the function of impregnating.

1857 BERKELEY *Introd. Cryptog. Bot.* §178. 200 The spermatozoids..vary a little in shape... There can, however, be little doubt that they are truly impregnatory organs.

†**impre'hend**, *v. Obs. rare*⁻¹. [f. IM-¹ + L. *prehendĕre*: see next.] *trans.* To take in, comprise.

1590 C. S. *Right Relig.* 22 This that Christ saith.. imprehendeth no other thing of Peter, but that which.. Peter himselfe speaketh.

So †**impre'hension**, undertaking. *Obs. rare*⁻⁰.

1611 FLORIO, *Imprensione*, an imprehension.

†**impre'hensible**, *a. Obs. rare*⁻¹. [a. OF. *imprehensible* (Godefroy), ad. late L. *impre(he)nsibilis*, f. *im-* (IM-²) + *prehendĕre*, *prehens-* to take, seize: cf. COMPREHENSIBLE.] Not to be grasped or seized; not to be apprehended.

1622 *Babington's Comf. Notes Numb.* xxix. Wks. II. 134 The imprehensible [*edd.* 1615, 1637 incomprehensible] sweetnesse of our blessed Sauiour.

impreignable, obs. form of IMPREGNABLE.

†**impre'judicate**, *ppl. a. Obs.* [f. IM-² + PREJUDICATE *ppl. a.*] Unprejudiced.

1640 R. BAILLIE *Canterb. Self-Convict.* Pref. 7 To the ful satisfaction of the whole world of free and imprejudicat mindes. **1646** SIR T. BROWNE *Pseud. Ep.* I. vii. 26 The solid reason of one man..with imprejudicate apprehensions. *a* **1677** BARROW *Wks.* (1686) III. xli. 473 Well-meaning, imprejudicate and uncorrupted persons.

Hence †**impre'judicately** *adv.*, without prejudice. *Obs.*

1654 VILVAIN *Theorem. Theol.* vi. 172 The previous Comment..impartialy perused, and imprejudicatly pondered.

†**im'prejudice**. *Obs.* [f. IM-² + PREJUDICE.] Absence of prejudice; unprejudiced opinion.

1806 W. TAYLOR in *Monthly Mag.* XXI. 401 Its bearing favours the cause of toleration and imprejudice.

†**impre'meditate**, *ppl. a. Obs. rare.* [f. IM-² + PREMEDITATE *ppl. a.* Cf. F. *imprémedité* (Cotgr.), It. *impremeditato* (Florio).] Unpremeditated.

1647 SALTMARSH *Spark. Glory* 166 Speakings to God in this..impremeditate or extemporary way.

So †**impremedi'tation**, want of premeditation.

1611 FLORIO, *Impremeditanza*, impremeditation.

impren(i)able, -prennable, obs. ff. IMPREGNABLE.

imprent, obs. form of IMPRINT.

†**imprepa'ration**. *Obs.* [f. IM-² + PREPARATION.] Want of preparation; unpreparedness.

1597 HOOKER *Eccl. Pol.* v. ii. §2 Impreparation and vnreadinesse. *a* **1656** BP. HALL *Rem. Wks.* (1660) 24, I strongly pleaded my indisposition of body, and my inpreparation for any such work. **1779** ELIZ. CARTER *Lett.* 5 Dec. (1808) II. 359 The awful stroke that hurried poor Lord Lyttelton from such a dreadful state of impreparation.

†**impre'paring**, *vbl. sb. Obs. rare*⁻⁰. [f. IM-² + PREPARING *vbl. sb.*] = prec.

1530 PALSGR. 234/1 Impreparyng, *impreparation.*

im'presa. Forms: 6–7 impresa, -so, 7 impreza, -prezza. [a. It. *impresa* (imˈpreza), undertaking,

attempt, device, etc.:—late L. **imprensa*: see EMPRISE, and cf. EMPRESS *sb.*^{2}, IMPRESE, IMPRESS *sb.*^{3}, IMPRESSA^1.]

1. An emblem or device, usually accompanied by an appropriate motto (cf. quot. *a* 1649).

1589 GREENE *Menaphon* (Arb.) 45 There was banding of such lookes, as euerie one imported as much as an *impreso*. **1598** YONG *Diana* 392 Making verses, impresas, and Anagrammes of her loue and name. **1602** MARSTON *Ant. & Mel.* v. Wks. 1856 I. 55, I did send for you to drawe me a devise, an Imprezza, by Sinecdoche a Mott. **1637** HEYWOOD *Lond. Mirr.* Wks. 1874 IV. 315 Every one of them expressing their natures and conditons in the impresaes of their shields. *a* **1649** DRUMM. OF HAWTH. *Disc. Impresas* Wks. (1711) 228 Though emblems and impresa's sometimes seem like other, .. the words of the emblem are only placed to declare the figures of the emblem; whereas, in an impresa, the figures express and illustrate the one part of the author's intention, and the word the other. **1653** URGUHART *Rabelais* I. ix, The device or impresa of my Lord-Admiral. **1865** F. B. PALLISER *Hist. Lace* 435 Then follow three pages in terzette, and p. 3. dorso, the impresa of the printer, a lion rampant, holding a sword in his fore paws. **1971** *English Studies* LII. 122 The last *impresa* in the supplementary chapter is almost certainly a personal device of Daniel's dedicatee, Sir Edward Dymoke.

†**2.** The sentence accompanying an emblem; hence, a motto, maxim, proverb. *Obs.*

1622 MALYNES *Anc. Law-Merch.* 230 The Impresa, *Sceptra fouent Artes*, may better be attributed to common-weales or popular gouernments, than vnto Monarchies or Kingdomes. **1630** BRATHWAIT *Eng. Gentlem.* (1641) 78 The Comicke Impreza: If wise, seeme not to know that which thou knowest. **1641** R. BROOKE *Eng. Episc.* I. iii. 5 For a Motto, and impreso, the Poets words,—*Et quæ non fecimus ipsi* [etc.].

impresario (‖impre'zario, now usu. ˌɪmprɪ'sɑːrɪəʊ). Also erroneously **impressario.** [It. *impresario* the undertaker of any business, contractor, etc., f. *impresa*: see prec.] One who organizes public entertainments; *esp.* the manager of an operatic or concert company.

1746 H. WALPOLE *Lett. to Sir H. Mann* 5 Dec., We have operas .. the Prince and Lord Middlesex *Impresarii*. **1751** *Ibid.* 18 June, Impresario Holderness. **1821** BYRON *Juan* IV. lxxx, A troop going to act In Sicily—all singers .. sold by the impresario. **1878** MORLEY in *Fortn. Rev.* Apr. 596 The Editor, the *impresario* of men of letters. **1887** EDNA LYALL *Knight-Errant* xix. (1889) 172 A man can't be in himself impresario, singer, and business agent all at once.

impréscience (ɪm'priːʃ(ɪ)əns). [f. IM-^{2} + PRESCIENCE.] Want of prescience or foreknowledge.

a **1859** DE QUINCEY *Posth. Wks.* (1891) I. 235 *note*, Acquiescing in total ventrine improvidence, imprescience, and selfish ease.

imprescribable (ɪmprɪ'skraɪbəb(ə)l), *a.* [f. IM-^{2} + PRESCRIBABLE.] Imprescriptible.

1887 *Westm. Rev.* Sept. 688 The ownership of land was by the law of the islands [Orkney] reserved to the descendants of the original occupant, by an inalienable and imprescribable entail.

imprescripti'bility. *rare.* [f. next + -ITY. Cf. F. *imprescriptibilité* (1732 in Hatz.-Darm.).] The quality of being imprescriptible.

? **1797** tr *Vattel's Law of Nations* (Webster 1828). **1806** W. TAYLOR in *Ann. Rev.* IV. 263 The imprescriptibility of royal titles form[s] no part of the law of nations.

imprescriptible (ɪmprɪ'skrɪptɪb(ə)l), *a.* Also 6 **inpre-**, 7 **impræ-**. [a. F. *imprescriptible* (16th c.), f. *im-* (IM-^{2}) + *prescriptible* PRESCRIPTIBLE.] Not subject to prescription; that cannot in any circumstances be legally taken away or abandoned; esp. in ***imprescriptible right*(*s***.

1563–87 FOXE *A. & M.* (1596) 330/1 The said lawe is called inprescriptible; for that it is *Ius fisci*. **1671** F. PHILLIPS *Reg. Necess.* 305 Those things which were granted or given in signe of subjection are impræscriptible. **1791** PAINE *Rights of Man* (ed. 4) 117 The natural and imprescriptible rights of man .. are liberty, property, security, and resistance of oppression. **1884** W. J. COURTHOPE *Addison* i. 3 The author of any ideal creation .. has an imprescriptible property in the fame of his work.

Hence **impre'scriptibly** *adv.*

1807 COXE *Austria* (Jod.), Imprescriptibly vested in the church.

†**im'prese, 'imprese.** *Obs.* Also 6 **ympreze**, 6–7 **imprease**, 7 **impreze**. [a. obs. F. *imprese* (1562 in Godefroy), ad. It. *impresa* IMPRESA.]

1. A device, emblem: = IMPRESA 1.

1588 FRAUNCE *Lawiers Log.* ¶ij, Hieroglyphikes, and Italian Impreses. **1589** *Pasquil's Ret.* 10 Scutchions, Emblems, Impreases, strange trickes, and deuises. **1590** R. W. *Three Lords London* (N.), That for his ympreze gives queene Junoes bird. **1604** EDMONDS *Observ. Cæsar's Comm.* VII. vii. II. 60 An Imprese with a circle, and a hand with a sharpe stile pointing towards the center with this motto: *Hic labor, hoc opus*. **1667** MILTON *P.L.* IX. 35 Emblazon'd Shields, Impreses quaint.

2. A motto: = IMPRESA 2.

1614 R. WILKINSON *Paire Serm.* 78 *Ich dien*, the word or imprease of the English prince. **1635** BRATHWAIT *Arcad. Pr.* II. 44 But whence the cause? eye the impreze, and it will informe thee. *c* **1811** LAMB *Melanch. Tailors* Wks. 1818 II. 186 The beautiful motto which formed the modest imprese of the shield.

fig. *a* **1659** *Lady Alimony* II. iii, Your choice has crown'd me; Nor shall track of time Raze out that Impreze which your free assent Has here ingraven.

Hence †**im'presed** *ppl. a.*, furnished with an imprese.

1590 R. W. *Three Lords London* (N.), Their shields ymprez'd with gilt copertiments.

impreso, variant of IMPRESA.

impress ('ɪmprɛs), *sb.*^{1} Also 6–7 **impresse**, (6 **empresse**). [f. IMPRESS *v.*^{1} Formerly also stressed *im'press*: see quot. 1627 and Johnson.]

1. The act of impressing or stamping; the 'stamp' (*of* anything); *concr.* a mark or indentation made by pressure, esp. one produced by a seal or stamp.

1592 *Nobody & Someb.* in Simpson *Sch. Shaks.* (1878) I. 354 Abasing of thy Soveraignes Coyne, And traitrous impresse of our Kingly seale. **1627** MAY *Lucan* VI. (1631) 14 Stamp'd his coines impresse In gold. **1706** WATTS *Horæ Lyr.*, '*Father, how wide thy glory shines*', The Labour of thy Hands, Or Impress of thy Feet. **1834** MEDWIN *Angler in Wales* I. 62 Bluish marks .. as if made by the impress of the fingers. **1876** HUMPHREYS *Coin-Coll. Man.* iv. 37 The reverse is incused with the impress of an amphora.

†**b.** A cast, mould. *Obs. rare.*

1695 WOODWARD *Nat. Hist. Earth* IV. (1723) 204 Having taken the Impresses of the Insides of these Shells.

c. = IMPRINT; impression.

1877 W. BOYD *Descr. Model Newsp.* vi, 'Tis a sheet octavoed,—handy; Fit in paper; impress clear. **1886** SYMONDS *Renaiss. It., Cath. React.* (1898) VII. ix. 50 Seven of his most important works .. bore the impress of Paris and Venice.

2. *fig.* **a.** Characteristic or distinctive mark; special character or quality stamped upon anything.

1590 GREENE *Mourn. Garm.* (1616) 58, I counted expence the empresse of a Gentleman. **1599** KYD *Solyman & Perseda* I. in Hazl. *Dodsley* V. 261 The fiery Spaniard, bearing in his face The impress of a noble warrior. **1636** FEATLY *Clavis Myst.* xvii. 218 Holinesse to God is the impresse of the regenerate. **1691** RAY *Creation* II. (1692) 148 They therefore who through the contrary Vices do deface and blot out this natural Character and Impress. **1832** DOWNES *Lett. Cont. Countries* I. 134 Of all the Swiss towns I have yet seen, Lucerne bears most strongly the impress of the middle ages. **1875** LYELL *Princ. Geol.* I. I. xii. 235 The physical sciences .. always bear the impress of the places where they began to be cultivated.

b. An impression upon the mind or senses. Now *rare*.

1591 SHAKS. *Two Gent.* III. ii. 6 This weake impresse of Loue, is as a figure Trenched in ice. **1651** JER. TAYLOR *Serm. for Year* I. Ep. Ded., Hearing is so effective an instrument of conveying impresses and images. **1691** RAY *Creation* I. (1692) 119 Only passive to the Instincts and Impresses thereof upon them. **1856** KANE *Arct. Expl.* I. xvi. 191 Some painful impress of solitary danger .. kept them closing up continually.

†**c.** An expression *of*. *Obs.*

1641 HINDE *J. Bruen* xxiii. 71 He .. writ it with his owne hand, to set it forth as an impresse of his chief desire.

3. *Comb.*, as ***impress copy***, a copy of writing, taken by pressure; a press-copy.

1885 *Pall Mall G.* 5 May 6/1 We use .. the .. Remington Type-writer, by which several legible copies can be printed by the aid of carbon paper, and also water impress copies.

impress ('ɪmprɪs), *sb.*^{2} Now *rare*. [f. IMPRESS *v.*^{2} Formerly stressed *im'press*: so in Bailey, Johnson, Ash.] Impressment; enforced service in the army or navy.

1602 SHAKS. *Ham.* I. i. 75 Such impresse of Ship-wrights, whose sore Taske Do's not diuide the Sunday from the weeke. **1606** —— *Ant. & Cl.* III. vii. 37 Your Marriners are Militers [muleteers], Reapers, people Ingrost by swift Impresse. **1758** JOHNSON *Idler* No. 5 ¶9 Our regiments would soon be filled without the reproach or cruelty of an impress. **1803** *Naval Chron.* IX. 420 We are all much alarmed .. with a military impress. **1832** MARRYAT *N. Forster* xiii, He could not prevail upon himself to accept a berth which was not protected from the impress.

b. *attrib.*, as ***impress-officer***, ***-service***; **impress-gang** = PRESS-GANG (Craig 1847).

1780 *Gentl. Mag.* L. 442 An impress officer .. thought it a fine opportunity to pick up some useful hands to serve his Majesty. *Ibid.* 443 The trial .. [of] a captain and lieutenant of the impress-service, or an action for illegally impressing and imprisoning the plaintiff. **1830** H. CROW *Mem.* 92, I have always considered the impress service as a thousand times worse than any negro trade whatever.

impress ('ɪmprɛs), *sb.*^{3} *Obs.* exc. *Hist.* [var. of IMPRESE, through association with IMPRESS *sb.*^{1}; cf. IMPRESSA as erroneous var. of IMPRESA. In 16–17th c. also *im'press*.]

1. An emblem, device: = IMPRESA 1.

1623 *Shaks.'s Rich. II*, III. i. 25 From mine owne Windowes torne my Household Coat, Raz'd out my Impresse [*Qos.* imprese]. **1694** *Phil. Trans.* XVIII. 38 These assumed the Name of *Investigantes*, with an Hound for their Impress, and .. *Vestigia lustrat*, for their Motto. **1790** BURKE *Fr. Rev.* Wks. V. 398 Their shields broken, their impresses defaced. **1868** CUSSANS *Her.* ix. 133 The Impress belonged exclusively to the Knight's person.

†**2.** A motto, sentence: = IMPRESA 2. *Obs.*

1611 CORYAT *Crudities* 303 This impresse is written ouer the dore in great letters. **1688** R. HOLME *Armoury* III. v. 253/2 Sentences are .. of the Learned termed a Period, Text, Aphorism, Axiome, Impress, Motto.

†**impress**, *sb.*^{4} *Obs.* [Variant of IMPREST *sb.*^{1}]

1. Money advanced, pay in advance: = IMPREST *sb.*^{1}

1600 E. BLOUNT tr. *Conestaggio* 28 He gave them impresse, and they remained for his service. **1633** T. STAFFORD *Pac. Hib.* III. xii. (1810) 597 Hee had received eight hundred duckets impresse.

b. *attrib.*, as ***impress-money***, earnest-money.

1617 MORYSON *Itin.* II. 273 [They] had taken impresse money from the King of Spaine. **1726** SHELVOCKE *Voy. round World* (1757) 38 Endeavouring to force them from Gravesend, before they had received their river pay, and impress money.

2. A charge made upon the pay of a naval officer who has not satisfactorily accounted for public money advanced to him (cf. IMPRESS *v.*^{3} 2).

1803 NELSON 12 July in Nicolas *Disp.* (1845) V. 132 That the simple receipt from the Captain of the Ship .. may be a sufficient Voucher for the disbursement of such money, and a full discharge from any impress against me.

†**im'press**, *a. Obs. rare.* [ad. L. *impress-us*, pa. pple. of *imprimĕre* to IMPRESS.] Impressed. ***impress species*** (Schol.L. *impressa species*): cf. IMPRESSED *ppl. a.*^{1} quot. 1704.

1704 NORRIS *Ideal World* II. vii. 335 These species are gross and material by way of distinction from those *express* species which are spiritualized. These *impress* species of bodies must then be little bodies.

impress (ɪm'prɛs), *v.*^{1} Also 4–6 **in-**, 4–7 **impresse**, 5–6 **impreise**. [f. L. *impress-*, ppl. stem of *imprimĕre*, f. *im-* (IM-^{1}) + *premĕre* to press (whence also obs. F. *impresser*). Partly answering in sense to OF. *empresser* to press, press or crowd upon, crush, print: cf. EMPRESS *v.*]

I. *trans.* To impress a thing *on*, *upon*, *in*, *into* something else.

1. To apply with pressure; to press (a thing *upon* another) so as to leave a mark; to produce by pressure (a mark *on*, †*in* some substance); to imprint, stamp.

c **1374** CHAUCER *Boeth.* v. met. iv. 130 (Camb. MS.) The notes and the figures Inpressed in manere of matere. **14..** *Circumcision* in *Tundale's Vis.* (1843) 99 In oure forhede when we Jesus imprese. **1590** SPENSER *F.Q.* III. xii. 33 Albe the wound were nothing deepe imprest. **1607** SHAKS. *Cor.* v. vi. 108 This Curre .. Who weares my stripes imprest vpon him. **1667** MILTON *P.L.* IV. 150 Fairest fruit .. On which the Sun more glad impress'd his beams. **1700** DRYDEN *Meleager & Atalanta* 219 The conquering chief his foot imprest On the strong neck of that destructive beast. **1784** COWPER *Task* I. 280 Not all its pride secures The grand retreat from injuries impress'd By rural carvers, who with knives deface The pannels. **1816** SHELLEY *Alastor* 515 He did impress On the green moss his tremulous step. **1856** STANLEY *Sinai & Pal.* i. (1858) 54 The foot-mark on the rock .. pointed out .. as impressed by his dromedary or mule. **1898** *Times* 25 Aug. 2/6 A signature impressed with a rubber stamp.

fig. **1649** J. ELLISTONE tr. *Behmen's Epist.* I. §39 Faith .. receiveth Christ into it selfe; it doth impress him into its hunger, with his heavenly flesh and blood.

2. a. *fig.* With immaterial object: esp. (in modern use) To 'stamp' (a character or quality) *upon* anything. Also *refl.*

1413 *Pilgr. Sowle* (Caxton 1483) IV. xxiv. 70 The ymage that first is impressid in to the sowle is most likely to abiden. **1586** A. DAY *Eng. Secretary* I. (1625) 66 He is yet very greene .. pliable to whatsoever may be impressed in him. **1667** MILTON *P.L.* XI. 182 Nature first gave Signs, imprest On Bird, Beast, Aire. **1791** MRS. RADCLIFFE *Rom. Forest* i, The image of virtue, which Nature had impressed upon his heart. **1867** H. MACMILLAN *Bible Teach.* xiii. (1870) 254 A beautiful character impresses itself upon the very features of the body. **1868** M. PATTISON *Academ. Org.* v. 121 The superstition .. that a use and direction, once impressed upon property by a founder, must be obeyed for ever.

b. *transf.* To produce or communicate (motion), exert (force), etc. by pressure. Const. *on*, *upon*.

1717 J. KEILL *Anim. Œcon.* (1738) 75 That Motion, which .. was impressed on the Coats of the Arteries by the Systole of the Heart. **1765** A. DICKSON *Treat. Agric.* (ed. 2) 209 The force impressed upon a ship by the wind. **1875** LYELL *Princ. Geol.* I. II. xx. 492 Movements .. impressed on a wide expanse of ocean. **1879** THOMSON & TAIT *Nat. Phil.* I. I. §262 A horse towing a boat on a canal is dragged backwards by a force equal to that which he impresses on the towing-rope forwards.

c. *Electr.* To apply or establish (an e.m.f. or a potential difference) by some external means.

1881 [implied in IMPRESSED *ppl. a.*^{1} 2]. **1918** *Wireless World* VI. 145 A certain steady voltage is impressed on the grids. **1930** [see IMPEDANCE 1 a]. **1948** A. L. ALBERT *Radio Fund.* v. 128 If a voltage is impressed across the input terminals .. the voltage will force a current into the line.

3. *fig.* To imprint (an idea, etc.) *on* (†*in*, *to*) the mind; to cause to take firm mental hold; to enforce, urge (a rule of conduct, etc.) *on* another.

c **1374** CHAUCER *Troylus* II. 1322 (1371) Yn good herte it mot som rouþe impresse, To here and se þe giltless in distresse. *c* **1400** MAUNDEV. (1839) xxix. 295 Thou scholdest thenke and impresse it in thi mynde, that nothing is inmortalle. **1500–20** DUNBAR *Poems* xi. 39 Sadlye in thy hart inpres *Quod tu in cinerem reuerteris*. **1590** SPENSER *F.Q.* II. xi. 5 So fowle and ugly, that exceeding feare Their visages imprest, when they approached neare. *Ibid.* III. iv. 49 So deepe the deadly feare of that foule swaine Was earst impressed in her gentle spright. **1649** J. ELLISTONE tr. *Behmen's Epist.* i. §39 That a man impresseth (or imagineth in his minde) to himselfe, that Christ is deade for his sinnes. *a* **1711** KEN *Divine Love* Wks. (1838) 238 Impress on my heart so tender a sense of thy sufferings. **1776** GIBBON *Decl. & F.* xi. (1869) I. 225 A few such examples impressed a

salutary consternation. **1838** DICKENS *Nich. Nick.* x, I am sure you will impress upon your children the necessity of attaching themselves to it early in life. **1863** GEO. ELIOT *Romola* II. xxi, This man had a power..of impressing his beliefs on others.

†**4.** To print, make a typographical 'impression' of. *Obs.* (Complemental adjunct usually absent.)

1508 FISHER *7 Penit. Ps.* Prol., I haue put the sayd sermons in wrytynge for to be impressed. **1533** *St. Papers, Hen. VIII*, I. 413 That the same Acte may be impressed, transumed, and set up on every churche dore in Englonde. **1658** J. ELLIOT in *Gosp. in New Eng.* (1659) 4 Let him..work under the Colledg Printer, in impressing the Bible in the Indian language. **1779–81** JOHNSON *L.P.*, *Pope* Wks. IV. 22 Lintot impressed the same pages upon a small Folio.

II. *trans.* To impress a thing *with*, *by* some instrument, or as an instrument does.

5. a. To exert pressure upon; to press; to mark (a thing) by means of pressure, esp. with a stamp, seal, etc. Const. *with*.

With quot. 1667 cf. IMPRESSION *sb.* 5.

1588 SHAKS. *L.L.L.* II. i. 236 His hart like an Agot with your print impressed. **1605** —— *Macb.* V. viii. 10 As easie may'st thou the intrenchant Ayre With thy keene Sword impresse. **1667** MILTON *P.L.* IV. 558 As a shooting Starr In autumn thwarts the night, when vapors fir'd Impress the Air. **1725** BRADLEY *Fam. Dict.* s.v. *Shepherd*, In impressing the Back near the Hips, if the Sheep does not bend, he judges 'em to be Sound and Strong. **1791** MRS. RADCLIFFE *Rom. Forest* viii, The Marquis seizing her hand, impressed it with kisses. **1874** L. STEPHEN *Hours in Library* (1892) I. vi. 200 The ring..was impressed with the seal of the Prophet.

b. To stamp, imprint, invest *with* a character, quality, etc.

1814 CARY *Dante, Paradise* XVII. 75 That mortal, who was at his birth imprest So strongly from this star. **1838** LYTTON *Alice* I. ii, The words were impressed with a wild and melancholy depth of feeling. **1868** GLADSTONE *Juv. Mundi* ii. (1869) 33 The people of Attica..had long been impressed with a markedly Pelasgian character. **1884** *Law Times Rep.* L. 374/1 Real property..impressed..with an implied trust for sale.

†**c.** To subject to *peine forte et dure*: see PRESS *v. Obs.*

1651 W. G. tr. *Cowel's Inst.* 273 In cases of Felony, he shall be impressed, viz. he shall be committed to the Prison ..where..being stripped naked, he shall be laid upon the bare ground..and his Arms and Legs pulled out by four ropes..hee shall be stretched out upon his back: Then..hee shall have so great a weight of Iron or Stone laid upon his Breast as hee is able to beare.

6. a. To produce a deep effect or impression on the mind or feelings of; to affect or influence strongly. Usually said of the instrument.

1736 BUTLER *Anal.*, *Nat. Virtue* Wks. 1874 I. 328 Brute creatures are impressed and actuated by various instincts and propensions. **1772** MACKENZIE *Man World* I. i. (1823) 420 He had come to that period of life when men are most apt to be impressed with appearances. **1846** DICKENS *Let. to Wills* 4 Mar., The letter..does not impress me favourably. **1851** RUSKIN *Stones Ven.* I, I could not but be solemnly impressed by the appearance of a circular temple. **1886** GURNEY, etc. *Phantasms of Living* I. 568 A man is telepathically impressed to conjure up his father's image. *absol.* **1823** BYRON *Juan* XII. lxix, Novelties please less than they impress.

b. To affect (a person) strongly *with* an idea.

1786 BURKE *W. Hastings* Wks. 1842 II. 131 To impress all the neighbouring princes..with an ill opinion of the faith, honour, and decency of the British nation. **1804** NELSON 1 Feb. in Nicolas *Disp.* (1845) V. 400 Impressed with the importance of this service..I felt justified..in ordering the Frigates to proceed immediately. **1838** THIRLWALL *Greece* xliv. V. 349 Some pains had been taken to impress the Athenian ambassadors with the same belief. **1878** J. W. EBSWORTH *Introd. Braithwait's Strappado* 26 Men.. impressed with an indignant scorn against uncleanness. *Mod.* He tried to impress me with his importance.

†**III.** *intr.* **7.** To press in; to press or throng about. *Obs.*

c **1386** CHAUCER *Merch. T.* 334 Heigh fantasye and curious bisynesse Fro day to day gan in the soule impresse Of Ianuarie aboute his mariage. **1412–20** LYDG. *Chron. Troy* I. v, The people ne wolde cesse Aboute them to gather and impreise. *c* **1480** *Crt. of Love* cxx, More and more impressen gan the dent Of Loves dart, while I beheld her face.

Hence **im'pressing** *vbl. sb.*[1] and *ppl. a.* *impressing cylinder* in a printing-machine: see quot.

1530 PALSGR. 234/1 Impressyng or printyng of a boke, *impression.* **1748** E. ERSKINE *Serm.* Wks. 1871 III. 351 The eye is an impressing organ; what we see with our eyes leaves an impression upon our minds. **1822** *Specif. Patent* No. 4640 Applegath 2 Applying the ink to the form of types, plates, or blocks, partly on one side of the impressing or printing cylinder, and partly on the other side.

impress (ɪm'prɛs), *v.*[2] [f. IM-[1] + PRESS *v.*[2], in same sense.

The latter, before the end of the 16th c., was evidently felt as the same word as PRESS *v.*[1] to subject to pressure or force, which easily led to a use of *impress*, as if to 'press in', 'press into service'.]

trans. To levy or furnish (a force) for military or naval service, to enlist; *spec.* to compel (men) to serve in the army or navy (in recent use, only the latter); to force authoritatively into service.

1596 SHAKS. *1 Hen. IV*, I. i. 21 Vnder whose blessed Crosse We are impressed and ingag'd to fight. **1605** —— *Macb.* IV. i. 95 Who can impresse the Forrest, bid the Tree Vnfixe his earth-bound Root? **1652–62** HEYLIN *Cosmogr.* IV. (1682) 123 The Inhabitants being able to impress 280 Horse for present service. **1679–88** *Secr. Serv. Money Chas. & Jas.* (Camden) 31 To Capt John Tyrwhite, for money by him disbursed for impressing 118 seamen for his said Majesties service. **1706** PHILLIPS, *To Impress Soldiers or Seamen*, to compel them to enter into the Publick Service. **1803** *Naval Chron.* IX. 335 Yesterday sailed the Diamond.. to impress men. **1835** MARRYAT *Jac. Faithf.* xliv, The seamen are impressed by force, the soldiers are entrapped by other means even more discreditable.

b. To take or seize by authority for royal or public service.

1749 J. POTE *Windsor Castle* 33 Commissioned to provide Stone, Timber, Lead, Iron and all other necessaries for the work and to impress carriages for their conveyance to Windsor. **1755** WASHINGTON *Lett.* Writ. 1889 I. 194, I impressed his wagons, and compelled him by force to assist in this work. **1863** H. COX *Instit.* III. viii. 715 Commissions ..authorizing different officers to impress both men and ships for the Royal service. **1875** STUBBS *Const. Hist.* II. xv. 288 The chief captain was empowered to impress men, vessels, victuals, and arms, paying however reasonable prices.

c. In various *fig.* and *transf.* senses: To enlist, force, or take into some service, press (a thing) into service in argument, etc.

1657 W. MORICE *Coena quasi Κοινὴ* Diat. vi. 314 How few uncase and impresse their pens against the enemies of our common faith. *a* **1680** BUTLER *Rem.* (1759) II. 194 He assumes a Privilege to impress what Text of Scripture he pleases for his own Use. **1779** MACKENZIE *Mirror* No. 12 ¶ 13 The toyman's little family of plaything figures..whom he had impressed into the service. **1825** T. JEFFERSON *Autobiog.* Wks. 1859 I. 108, I then meant..to withdraw from political life, into which I had been impressed by the circumstances of the times. **1832** HT. MARTINEAU *Ireland* iii. 43 Dan proceeded..to impress into his temporary service a horse which grazed in the neighbourhood. **1860** DICKENS *Uncomm. Trav.* ix, They had impressed a small school..to assist in the performances. **1869** FARRAR *Fam. Speech* ii. 42 Hypotheses into the service of which Philology was impressed.

Hence **im'pressing** *vbl. sb.*[2]

1641 in Rushw. *Hist. Coll.* III. (1692) I. 458 A Bill for Impressing of Souldiers. **1705** *Royal Proclam.* in *Lond. Gaz.* No. 4186/3 Officers Imployed in Impressing. *attrib.* **1863** *Morn. Star* 17 Dec. 5/6 The impressing agent has gone around.

†**im'press**, *v.*[3] *Obs. rare.* [Erroneously for IMPREST *v.*[1]: cf. IMPRESS *sb.*[4]]

1. *trans.* To advance (money): = IMPREST *v.*[1] 1.

1665 EVELYN *Diary* 19 Mar., £5000 impressed for the service of the sick and wounded prisoners. **1819** REES *Cycl.* s.v. *Auditor*, All monies impressed to any man for the king's service.

2. To charge with a deduction (the pay of an officer) in respect to public moneys or stores not accounted for by him: see IMPRESS *sb.*[4] 2.

1803 NELSON 12 July in Nicolas *Disp.* (1845) V, I..beg that their Lordships will exonerate them from the charge, and direct the Victualling Board not to impress their Accounts.

†**im'pressa**[1]. Erroneous form of IMPRESA (cf. IMPRESS *sb.*[3]).

a **1586** SIDNEY *Arcadia* (1622) 57 The Impressa in the shield, was a heauen full of starres, with a speech. **1656** EARL MONM. *Advt. fr. Parnass.* 410 The Impressa which he bore in his chief Standard, which was a writing Pen.

†**im'pressa**[2]. Erroneous f. IMPRESS *sb.*[1] (2 a).

1628 FELTHAM *Resolves* II. xix. 60 Surely, the Soule hath the reliqu'd Impressa's of diuine Vertue still..left within her. **1647** *Case Kingd.* 6, I observe now an Impressa of divine glory and excellency in many of their Practises.

im'pressable, *a. rare.* [f. IMPRESS *v.*[2] + -ABLE.] Liable to be impressed into service.

1865–6 H. PHILLIPS *Amer. Paper Curr.* II. 83 Wagons ..[were] made impressable for the use of the army.

impressed (ɪm'prɛst), *ppl. a.*[1] [f. IMPRESS *v.*[1] + -ED[1].] **1.** That is pressed or forced in, stamped upon something; stamped, marked by pressure or with impressions; in *Zool.* and *Bot.*, having an appearance of being stamped in; sunk in, depressed.

a **1420** HOCCLEVE *De Reg. Princ.* 644, I hertles was ay thurghe myne impressede drede. **1704** NORRIS *Ideal World* II. vii. 349 Which species..because they are imprinted by the objects they come from upon the outward senses, are therefore in their first state called impressed species, images, or phantoms. **1826** KIRBY & SP. *Entomol.* IV. 284 *Inaurate* ..when striæ or other impressed parts have a metallic splendour. **1845** LINDLEY *Sch. Bot.* v. (1858) 58 Seeds angular, impressed, brown speckled. **1854** WOODWARD *Mollusca* II. 216 Shell smooth or plaited, dorsal valve frequently impressed. **1876** TAIT *Rec. Adv. Phys. Sc.* ii. (ed. 2) 28 Change of motion is proportional to the impressed force.

2. *Electr.* Of an e.m.f. or potential difference: applied by some external means.

1881 *Jrnl. Soc. Telegr. Engin.* X. 271 Let *M* be the induction through the coil when its plane is at right angles to the lines of force of the external field, *wt* the angle turned through from this plane at time *t*..; then *Mw* sin *wt* is the impressed E.M.F. in the coil. **1929** *Encycl. Brit.* XXII. 408/1 A small current flows into the excited winding sufficient to produce a counter voltage equal to the impressed voltage. **1948** [see IMPEDANCE 1 a]. **1973** *Sci. Amer.* Oct. 125/1 Leakage through the capacitor should not exceed 10^{-10} ampere at an impressed potential of 10 volts.

Hence **im'pressedly** (-ɪdlɪ) *adv.*, in an impressed manner.

1640 G. WATTS tr. *Bacon's Adv. Learn.* IV. ii. (R. Suppl. s.v. *Malacissation*), Penetrating and insinuating remedies.. convay more easily and impressedly the virtue thereof.

impressed (ɪm'prɛst), *ppl. a.*[2] [f. IMPRESS *v.*[2] + -ED[1].] Enlisted; compelled to serve.

1605 SHAKS. *Lear* V. iii. 51 To..turne our imprest Launces in our eies Which do command them. **1768–74** TUCKER *Lt. Nat.* (1852) I. 573 You subject the impressed man to the same severities as the volunteer. **1803** *Naval Chron.* IX. 417 Volunteers and impressed men from the fleet.

impressibility (ɪmprɛsɪ'bɪlɪtɪ). Also **-ability.** [f. next: see -ITY.]

The quality of being impressible.

1751 tr. *Pernetti's Philos. Lett. Physiog.* xxxiii. 229 They [blue eyes] are sure Signs of a tender Impressibility and sympathising Disposition. **1811** W. TAYLOR in *Monthly Rev.* LXV. 12 When the change of scene had restored the impressability (may we call it?) of his senses [etc.]. **1860** W. COLLINS *Wom. White* (1861) 135 She seems to have parted with all her tenderness and all her impressibility. **1875** JEVONS *Money* v. 40 *Impressibility*,..the capacity of a substance to receive such an impression..as shall establish its character as current money.

b. A specimen or example of the impressible.

1820 *Examiner* No. 642. 495/1 [They] are all that fairy land can do for us. They are for younger impressibilities.

impressible (ɪm'prɛsɪb(ə)l), *a.* [f. IMPRESS *v.*[1] (or L. *impress-* ppl. stem) + -IBLE.] Capable of being impressed: **a.** Sensitive to impressions; susceptible, impressionable; **b.** That can be impressed on something.

1626 BACON *Sylva* §846 The Differences of Impressible and Not Impressible, Figurable and Not Figurable,..are Plebeian Notions. **1681** GLANVILL *Sadducismus* I. (1726) 18 An heightened and obstinate Fancy hath a great Influence upon impressible Spirits. **1780** COWPER *Progr. Err.* 355 The mind impressible and soft with ease Imbibes and copies what she hears and sees. **1856** KANE *Arct. Expl.* II. App. xi. 405 The instruments became very impressible to artificial elevation of temperature. **1874** MOTLEY *Barneveld* II. xxii. 404 Impressible, emotional, and susceptive, he had been accused of infirmity of purpose.

Hence **im'pressibleness**, impressibility; **im'pressibly** *adv.*, in an impressible manner. (In recent Dicts.)

impressing: see under IMPRESS *vbs.*[1] and [2].

impression (ɪm'prɛʃən), *sb.* Also 4–5 en-, 5 in-. [a. F. *impression* (13th c.), ad. L. *impressiōn-em* (in classical L. common only in the sense of 'irruption, onset, attack', but used by Cicero for 'emphasis' and 'mental impression', and in later L. for 'action of impressing or stamping'), n. of action from *imprimĕre* (ppl. stem *impress-*): see IMPRESS *v.*[1]]

1. The action or process of impressing, in various senses: *esp.* **a.** The action involved in the pressure of one thing upon or into the surface of another; also, the effect of this.

1444 *Pol. Poems* (Rolls) II. 218 Stable in the eyr is noon inpressioun. **1483** CAXTON *Gold. Leg.* 34 a/2 We ought to bere the crosse of Jhesu cryst..in the mouth by confession ..and in the vysage by contynuel impression. **1590** SPENSER *F.Q.* III. vi. 8 The fruitfull seades Of all things liuing, through impression Of the sunbeames..Doe life conceiue. **1592** SHAKS. *Ven. & Ad.* 566 What wax so frozen but dissolves with tempering, And yields at last to every light impression? **1613** PURCHAS *Pilgrimage* (1614) 505 Signatures of Natures owne impression. **1793** BEDDOES *Calculus* 175 The heart does not contract itself immediately upon the first impression of the blood. **1817** COLERIDGE *Biog. Lit.* 63 In any given perception there is a something which has been communicated to it [the mind] by an impact, or an impression ab extra. **1875** JOWETT *Plato* (ed. 2) III. 596 The creation of the world is the impression of order on a previously existing chaos.

†**b.** A charge, onset, attack, assault. *Obs.*

1402 HOCCLEVE *Let. Cupid* 233 Suche is the force of myn impressyon That sodenly I felle can hir bost. **1577–87** HOLINSHED *Chron.* I. 25/1 They were not able to susteine the violent impression of the armed men, and so fled. **1613** PURCHAS *Pilgrimage* (1614) 630 The Duke of Avero, with his Portugals, made a great impression into the Mores host. **1750** JOHNSON *Rambler* No. 21 ¶ 5 Elephants..by the violence of their impression..often threw the enemy into disorder. **1799** LD. KEITH 9 July in Nicolas *Disp. Nelson* (1845) III. 414 *note*, The Enemy have no intention of attempting an impression on the Island of Sicily.

†**c.** Oppression (so OF. *impression*). *Obs. rare.*

c **1470** HARDING *Chron.* CXXVIII. iv, Euery lorde..spoyled other..By greate impression and cruell sore raunson.

d. The impact or shock of any atmospheric or physical force. ? *Obs.*

1694 *Acc. Sev. Late Voy.* Introd. (1711) 22 To line them with the skins of Beasts, thereby to keep out the sharp impressions of the air. **1722** WOLLASTON *Relig. Nat.* ix. 168 He is in danger from falls, and all impressions of violence. **1799** KIRWAN *Geol. Ess.* 69 The traces of a violent shock or impression from the south are as yet perceptible in many countries. **1820** SCORESBY *Acc. Arctic Reg.* I. 330 [When a cold wind rises] the most hardy cannot conceal their uneasiness under its first impressions.

†**e.** In elocution or metre: A stress, emphasis.

1643 MILTON *Divorce* II. viii, To you he wrote this precept ..which (to you) must be read with an impression. **1824** L. MURRAY *Eng. Gram.* (ed. 5) I. 383 The intermixture of Pyrrhics and Spondees; in which, two impressions in the one foot make up for the want of one in the other.

2. a. A mark produced upon any surface by pressure, esp. by the application of a stamp, seal, etc. Hence, any depression, indentation, etc. such as would result from pressure; also, the

figure produced by stamping or sealing; a cast, mould, copy.

1398 TREVISA *Barth. De P.R.* XVI. lxxiv. (Bodl. MS.), He findeþ mater more able and obedient to his worchinge þe more noble impression he prenteþ þerein. *c* **1430** LYDG. *Min. Poems* (Percy Soc.) 51 Of crosse nor pile there is no recluse, Prynte nor impressioun in all thy seynt-warye. **1592** DAVIES *Immort. Soul* XIII. ii, When a Seal in Wax Impression makes. **1607** TOPSELL *Four-f. Beasts* (1658) 95 The horns like a rams.. with beaten notches or impressions. **1699** DAMPIER *Voy.* II. II. 103 The Impression in the Sand, seemed much like the Track of a Cow. **1713** BERKELEY *Hylas & Phil.* III. Wks. 1871 I. 346 As.. a seal [is said] to make an impression upon wax. **1756** C. LUCAS *Ess. Waters* III. 236 Impressions of fishes, and sometimes of fern.. are often found. **1851-6** WOODWARD *Mollusca* 276 Shell.. with a long and prominent ligament, and two adductor impressions. **1883** C. J. WILLS *Mod. Persia* 184 [He] breathes on his seal, and presses it firmly against the paper.. A very clear impression is thus produced.

fig. **1576** FLEMING *Panopl. Epist.* 372 Ignoraunce.. maketh him unmeete metall for the impressions of vertue. *c* **1600** SHAKS. *Sonn.* cxii, Your loue and pittie doth th' impression fill, Which vulgar scandall stampt upon my brow. **1784** COWPER *Task* VI. 983 If it bear The stamp and clear impression of good sense. **1847** PRESCOTT *Peru* (1850) II. 357 In his young and tender age he was to take the impression of those into whose society he was thrown.

†**b.** (See quot. and cf. sense 1, quot. 1483.) *Obs.*

1613 PURCHAS *Pilgr.* (1614) 300 The impression or signe of peace, which is done with bringing both hands over the face.

†**c.** A mark, trace, indication. *Obs.*

1613 PURCHAS *Pilgrimage* (1614) 671 For the Ethiopian names or crosses.. slaves.. might leave such impressions. **1615** G. SANDYS *Trav.* 81 Time hath left now no impressions of his barbarous labour. **1658** SIR T. BROWNE *Hydriot.* i. (1736) 8 Bones.. with fresh Impressions of their Combustion.

†**d.** *fig.* Stamp; creation; hence, rank. *Obs.*

A French usage; with quot. 1639 cf. D'Aubigné *un marquis de la nouvelle impression* (Littré).

1639 DU VERGER tr. *Camus' Admir. Events* 50 A gentleman of the new impression. **1677** *Govt. Venice* 23 'Tis every day to be seen in Venice, Noblemen of the last impression do marry Ladies of the first.

e. *Dentistry.* A negative copy of the teeth or oral cavity (from which a positive cast or model may be made) formed by bringing them into intimate contact with some substance that will take their shape.

1839 C. A. HARRIS *Dental Art* xxi. 350 Models of this kind are obtained by taking a wax impression of both jaws at the same time. **1878** C. HUNTER *Mech. Dentistry* i. 7 When the composition has become sufficiently hard, the impression is withdrawn from the mouth, and cold water should be allowed to flow over it. **1940** J. OSBORNE *Dental Mech.* i. 1 The introduction.. to the subject is the technique necessary for the accurate construction of a model, or positive likeness of the patient's mouth, from an impression or negative likeness.

3. a. The process of printing. Now *rare.*

1509 HAWES *Past. Pleas.* XLV. (Percy Soc.) 220 Go, little boke! I praye God the save From misse metryng by wrong impression. **1577-87** HARRISON *England* I. x. in *Holinshed* 44 At such time as I first attempted to commit this booke to the impression. **1602** T. FITZHERBERT *Apol.* Pref. 1 b, This Apology being written.. and made ready for the print.. it seemed good.. to stay the impression of it, vntil [etc.]. *a* **1794** GIBBON *Mem.* Misc. Wks. 1814 I. 260 The impression of the fourth volume had consumed three months. **1837-9** HALLAM *Hist. Lit.* I. I. iii. §73. 193 The number of scholars was still not sufficient to repay the expenses of impression.

b. The result of printing; a print taken from type or from an engraving or the like; a printed copy.

1559 *Primer* in *Priv. Prayers* (1851) 114 Neither to sel nor bye of any other impressions than suche as shal be Printed by the sayde Richard. **1589** NASHE *Ded. Greene's Menaphon* (Arb.) 10 Euerie priuate Scholler.. beganne to vaunt their smattering of Latine, in English Impressions. **1613** PURCHAS *Pilgrimage* (1614) 438 They print.. the letters not being therein set backeward, that in the impression they may appeare forward. **1698** FRYER *Acc. E. India & P.* 20 Bundles of Characters tied together to Ape Printing. What they make their Impression on, I cannot inform you. **1821** CRAIG *Lect. Drawing* vii. 381 He rubs the plate over with printing ink, as if an impression were about to be taken. **1832** BABBAGE *Econ. Manuf.* xi. (ed. 3) 72 Coloured impressions of leaves upon paper may be made by a kind of surface printing. **1869** MRS. HEATON *A. Dürer* II. iii. (1881) 215 Very early impressions of Dürer's engravings are seldom now to be met with.

c. The printing of that number of copies (of a book, etc.) which forms one issue of it; 'one course of printing' (J.); hence, the aggregate of copies thus printed: see EDITION *sb.* 3 b.

Sometimes distinguished from 'edition', as an unaltered reprint from standing type or plates; but often used as a more general term including both 'edition' and 'reprint': cf. quot. 1891.

1570-87 FOXE *A. & M.* (1684) III. 594 The Copy of which Dispensation.. is exemplified in our first Impression. **1592** NASHE *P. Penilesse* (ed. 2) 2 You write to mee my booke is hasting to the second impression. **1652** COLLINGES *Caveat for Prof.* (1653) A iij b, 6000 of his books being sold, if 1500 be allowed to an Impression. **1774** WARTON *Hist. Eng. Poetry* xix. II. 19 Of this translation there were six impressions before the year 1601. **1891** *Bibliog. Cat. Macmillan's Publications* Pref. 5 After careful consideration the Publishers decided to describe as an Edition an impression from type set up afresh either with or without alteration and read for press by a proof-reader. An impression from standing type or from Stereotype or Electrotype plates is described as a Reprint.

d. *Bibliogr.* In bibliographical classification and description, a subdivision of an edition, denoting all the copies printed at one time; chiefly applicable to books of the nineteenth and twentieth centuries.

1927 R. B. MCKERROW *Introd. Bibliogr.* II. iii. 175 When dealing with early books, 'edition' and 'impression' as a rule are the same thing, for the early printer normally distributed his type immediately it had been printed from, though there were.. exceptions to this. **1949** F. BOWERS *Princ. Bibliogr. Descr.* xi. 379 In its purest sense an *edition* of a book consists of all copies printed at any time or times from one setting of type, or its equivalent in the form of plates or monotype rolls; i.e., it is the sum of all impressions from one setting... All the copies of any single edition are not necessarily printed at any one time but may accumulate from a series of separate *impressions* removed from each other in date... Copies of each impression compose a part of an edition. **1972** P. GASKELL *New Introd. Bibliogr.* 315 It was not unusual in the nineteenth century for stereos to be used for ten successive impressions, and for electros to be used for as many as thirty; while, if a set of plates was kept as a 'mother' from which further sets could be made, the number of successive impressions of an edition that could be printed from plates was virtually unlimited.

4. The effective action of one thing upon another; influence; the effect of such action; a change produced in some passive subject by the operation of an external cause.

1390 GOWER *Conf.* III. 94 After thilke interstition, In which they take impression. **1471** RIPLEY *Comp. Alch.* IX. xi. in Ashm. (1652) 176 The Body of the Spryte takyth impression. **1576** BAKER *Jewell of Health* 116 a, Such oyles are made.. onely by impression.. as when symple medycines boyled, stieped, in common oyle, doe leave theyr vertues in it. **1648** BOYLE *Seraph. Love* xvi. (1700) 98 The Load-stone.. doth never rightly touch the amorous Steel without leaving an Impression. **1686** W. HARRIS *Lemery's Chym.* (ed. 3) 524 It is better to use vessels of Earth or Glass than those of Metals, because there is less fear of an Impression from those than from these. **1707** *Curios. in Husb. & Gard.* 330 Its fix'd Salt.. cannot devest it self of the Impression it had received from Nature, continuing always essencify'd with the same Qualities.. as the Plant from which it is extracted. **1800** *Asiat. Ann. Reg., Chron.* 7/1 The Coorugs, being unable to make any impression on the pagoda. **1822** IMISON *Sc. & Art* II. 120 One of the hardest of the metals; a file can scarcely make any impression on it. **1888** MISS E. BROWN *In Pursuit of Shadow* v. 78 The late rains seemed to have made but little impression on the streets of Moscow.

†**5.** *spec.* An atmospheric influence, condition, or phenomenon. ***fiery impression***, a comet, meteor, or the like. *Obs.*

1426 LYDG. *De Guil. Pilgr.* 3439 Off ellementys I am maystresse, Lady also & pryncesse Off wyndys and inpressyouns. **1530** PALSGR. 412 These impressyons of the eyer, 'hote, colde, fayre, foule [etc.]. ' **1563** W. FULKE *Meteors* (1640) 2 Divided into moist and drie impressions, consisting either of Vapors, or exhalations. **1657** S. PURCHAS *Pol. Flying-Ins.* I. iv. 10 Some leaving the hot impressions in the aire, attribute it to the driness of the earth. **1684** T. BURNET *Th. Earth* II. 64 Hot fumes and sulphureous clouds, which will sometimes flow in streams and fiery impressions through the air.

6. The effect produced by external force or influence on the senses or mind. **a.** An effect produced on the senses; a sensation, or sense-perception, in its purely receptive aspect.

1632 J. HAYWARD tr. *Biondi's Eromena* 107 The eye.. is more inclined to receive the impression of the one [black] than of the other [white]. **1651** HOBBES *Leviath.* II. xxvii. 156 The impressions our Senses had formerly received. **1736** BUTLER *Anal.* I. v. Wks. 1874 I. 89 Passive impressions grow weaker by being repeated upon us. **1807** T. THOMSON *Chem.* (ed. 3) II. 202 It has sourish taste at first, then makes a bitterish cooling impression, and at last leaves an agreeable sweetness. **1855** BAIN *Senses & Int.* I. ii. §22 (1864) 62 An impression of sound, a musical note, for example, is carried to the brain. **1875** JOWETT *Plato* (ed. 2) IV. 278 It is hard to say how much our impressions of hearing may be affected by those of sight.

b. An effect, especially a strong effect, produced on the intellect, conscience, or feelings. Esp. in phr. ***first impression***(*s*).

c **1374** CHAUCER *Troylus* v. 372 Ek oþere seyn þat þorugh Impressions [*v.r.* enpressiounnys] As yf a wight hath faste a þing in mynde.. cometh swich auysions. *c* **1386** —— *Sqr.'s T.* 363 In hire sleepe right for impression, Of hire Mirour she hadde Avision. **1576** FLEMING *Panopl. Epist.* 267 Madnesse kindleth diseases in the mynde, bycause that it worketh in them.. phantasticall impressions. **1655** FULLER *Ch. Hist.* II. ii. §69 Being over-rigid and severe, his Sermons made no Impression on his English Auditory. **1700** CONGREVE *Way of World* IV. i. 52 How shall I receive him? In what figure shall I give his Heart the first Impression? There is a great deal in the first Impression. *c* **1755** in R. Jackson *Hist. Rev. Pennsylvania* (1759) 270 It must have been while he was under the first Impressions given him by the Governor to our Disadvantage. **1759** FRANKLIN *Ess.* Wks. 1840 III. 407 While he was under the first impressions given him by the governor to our disadvantage. **1771** *Junius Lett.* xlix. 256 If they had made no impression upon his heart. **1773** SMOLLETT *Ode to Indep.* 30 He.. deeply felt the impression of her charms. **1843** DICKENS *Mart. Chuz.* (1944) v. 57 First impressions, you know, often go a long way, and last a long time. **1847** HUGH MILLER (*title*) First Impressions of England and its people. **1870** FREEMAN *Norm. Conq.* (ed. 2) I. App. 560 A deep impression had been made on the minds of Englishmen. **1924** E. O'NEILL *Welded* I. 90 The first impression of her whole personality is one of charm, partly innate, partly imposed by years of self-discipline.

c. In the philosophy of Hume (see quots.).

1739 HUME *Hum. Nat.* I. i. Wks. 1874 I. 311 Those perceptions, which enter with most force and violence, we may name *impressions.* **1742** —— *Ess. Hum. Und., Orig. Ideas* (1817) II. 16 By the term *impression*, I mean all our more lively perceptions, when we hear, or see, or feel, or love, or hate, or desire, or will... Impressions are distinguished from ideas, which are the less lively perceptions, of which we are conscious, when we reflect on any of those sensations or movements above mentioned.

d. An imitation or impersonation of a person or thing, done by a comedian as a form of entertainment.

1953 J. LAURIE *Vaudeville* 99 Some [beginners] just stuck to the regular 'impressions' and went through show biz getting by. **1969** *Times* 7 Nov. 13/3 An American entertainer ..joked, sang, went on singing, and did impressions. **1971** D. NATHAN *Laughtermakers* ii. 46 Peter would come in and do a few impressions of Kenneth Horne and others. *Ibid.* xiii. 227 Later on I'm going to do one or two impressions —I've got some good bird impressions, I eat worms.

7. A notion, remembrance, or belief, impressed upon the mind; hence *esp.*, a somewhat vague or indistinct notion remaining in the mind as a survival from more distinct knowledge. In modern use, often implying that the belief or idea is mistaken, esp. in ***under the impression.***

1613 PURCHAS *Pilgrimage* (1614) 2 That there is a God;.. This is a common notion, and impression, sealed up in the minde of every man. **1679** BURNET *Hist. Ref.* I. I. 170 They seemed to have strip't themselves of those impressions of pity and compassion, which are natural to mankind. **1837** CALHOUN *Wks.* (1874) III. 130, I am of the impression it may be both safely and conveniently used. **1860** RUSKIN *Unto this Last* (1862) iv. 131, I believe that many of our merchants are seriously under the impression that it is possible for everybody, somehow, to make a profit in this manner. **1865** —— *Sesame* ii. §86 Generally, we are under an impression that a man's duties are public, and a woman's private. **1867** W. F. HOOK *Lives Abps.* V. xxi. 356 Under the impression that they had been specially assisted by the saint. **1869** E. A. PARKES *Pract. Hygiene* (ed. 3) 64 That most fallacious of all evidence, a general impression, without a careful collection of facts. *a* **1899** *Mod.* I have an impression that I have somewhere met with it before. But it is a mere impression, and I may easily be mistaken.

8. *Painting.* **a.** 'The ground-colour, or that which is first laid on to receive the other colours'. **b.** 'A stratum of a single colour laid upon a wall or surface for ornament, upon outside work, or upon metals to protect from humidity' (Webster 1864).

9. *Comb.* **impression compound**, any impression material manufactured from a number of different ingredients, esp. one that is a non-elastic thermoplastic solid; **impression cup** (*Dentistry*), a cup or holder for the material used in obtaining a cast of the mouth; **impression cylinder**, in a printing-machine (see quots.); **impression material**, any substance used for taking dental impressions; **impression tray** = *impression cup.*

1903 *Dental Rec.* XXIII. 415 Do not think a good impression of a full denture cannot be taken in *impression compound. **1904** J. H. PROTHERO *Prosthetic Dentistry* iii. 22 Other impression materials.. are furnished by the dental supply houses and are called impression compounds. The usual claim made is that they are composed of materials that can be dried after the impression is taken. **1934** F. W. FRAHM *Princ. & Technics Full Denture Construction* vii. 84 A new impression compound has been added to our list of materials and is listed under the trade name of 'Dentocoll'. It is a hydro-colloidal, possessing unusual plasticity, some elasticity and a slight compressibility. **1965** PHILLIPS & SKINNER *Elem. Dental Materials* v. 37 As the formulas of the modern impression compounds are 'trade secrets', any discussion of composition cannot by very specific. In general, compounds are a mixture of waxes, thermoplastic resins, a filler, and a coloring agent. **1867** C. A. HARRIS *Dict. Med. Terminol.* 354/1 The plaster [of Paris].. is poured into an *impression cup, with high walls fitting loosely over the alveolar border. **1830** *Specif. Patent* No. 5988 Applegath 2, A is the cast-iron frame; B, the *impression cylinder, upon which the piece of material receives the impression. **1884** *Western Daily Press* 16 Sept. 5/6 Around the large cylinder were grouped from two to ten small impression cylinders. **1890** W. J. GORDON *Foundry* 186 The platen was impossible. Why not try Nicholson's impression cylinder? **1878** C. HUNTER *Mech. Dentistry* i. 2 Wax as an *impression material is now seldom used, composition (Godiva, or Stent) or plaster of Paris being now almost invariably employed. **1965** PHILLIPS & SKINNER *Elem. Dental Materials* iv. 33 If a rigid impression material has been used (i.e., plaster, compound, etc.), the mix of dental stone is poured into the impression carefully, preferably under vibration.

im'pression, *v. rare.* [f. prec. sb. Cf. F. *impressionner*, to which the current use (sense 2) may be due.]

†**1.** To stamp; make an impression. *Obs. rare*$^{-1}$.

1612 STURTEVANT *Metallica* (1854) 94 Peculiar Metallical instruments, which worke.. by pressing, impressing, impressioning or moulding.

2. *trans.* To make an impression on, to affect with an impression. In *pass.* To be affected.

1865 *Reader* 9 Sept. 291/1 Its busy roar of life is such that it is to all appearance but little impressioned by that sudden swerving [etc.]. **1892** *Argosy* Nov. 404 Impressioned as she had been by the mysterious music.

impressiona'bility. [f. next: see -ITY. Cf. mod.F. *impressionnabilité*.] The quality of being impressionable; susceptibility to impressions.

1835 *Blackw. Mag.* XXXVIII. 23 The joyous carelessness and prompt impressionability of that beautiful and healthful period of expansion and of growth. **1862** LYTTON *Str. Story* II. 226 Extreme impressionability to changes in temperature.

impressionable (ɪm'prɛʃənəb(ə)l), *a.* [a. F. *impressionnable*, f. *impressionner*: see -ABLE.]

1. Of persons or their feelings: Liable to be easily impressed or influenced; susceptible of impressions.

[**1835** *New Monthly Mag.* XLIV. 426 A nature which must be what the French so happily term *impressionable*.] **1836** T. HOOK *G. Gurney* (L.), She had a pretty face and an impressionable disposition. **1848** LONGF. in *Life* (1891) II. 133 He has real merit and quick, impressionable feelings. **1873** BLACK *Pr. Thule* (1874) 49 Attentions..such as must have driven a more impressionable man out of his senses.

2. Of things: **a.** Capable of being impressed. **b.** Sensitive to physical or chemical influences.

1878 MAXWELL in *Life* xiv. (1882) 455 Tinfoil thin enough to be impressionable by the metal style. **1889** *Anthony's Photogr. Bull.* II. 150 Sensitive or impressionable substances..which receive and retain the actinic energy.

So **im'pressionableness**, impressionability.

1858 *Chamb. Jrnl.* IX. 161 A nervous organisation of great delicacy, impressionableness, and excitability. **1881** G. MACDONALD *Mary Marston* I. vi. 101 A certain dropsical impressionableness of surface which made him seem and believe himself sympathetic.

im'pressional, *a.* [f. IMPRESSION *sb.* + -AL[1].] Of or pertaining to impressions; of the nature of an impression: in quot. 1860 = IMPRESSIONABLE.

1860 EMERSON *Cond. Life, Culture* (1861) 78 He must be musical, Tremulous, impressional. *a* **1882** J. QUINCY *Figures of Past* (1883) 279 The resemblance..could scarcely be called physical, and I am loath to borrow the word 'impressional' from the vocabulary of spirit mediums. **1920** S. ALEXANDER *Space, Time & Deity* II. 138 Impressional intensity, as Mr. Stout calls what Hume described as vivacity. **1969** *R. & E. Coordinator* (Res. & Engin. Council Graphic Arts Industry) Apr. 10/2 Principal advantages of the Mailander flatbeds are stated to be..the excellent control of plate inking and dampening and impressional squeeze in order to obtain the highest quality image with little..stock waste.

Hence **im'pressionalist** = IMPRESSIONIST; **impressio'nality**, impressional quality.

1876 *Nation* (N.Y.) 14 Sept. 163/2 There is no end to the descriptive efforts of the impressionalists. **1884** tr. *Brachet's Aix-les-bains* I. 96 The doctor directs the thermal course according to the impressionality of the patient.

im'pressionary, *a.* [f. as prec. + -ARY.] = IMPRESSIONISTIC *a.* 1.

1889 A. MEYNELL *The Newlyn School* in *Art Jrnl.* No. 53. 140 The beautiful lucid surface..capable of reflections which are in themselves an intricate yet distinctively impressionary study. **1891** *Athenæum* 27 June 831/2 An impressionary drawing of 'A Reception at Archbishop's House'. **1895** *Pall Mall G.* 11 Oct. 4/2 The most impressionary and modern of narrative descriptions—even whole sentences without any verb, which is your real impressionary style, as generally understood.

impressionism (ɪm'prɛʃənɪz(ə)m). [f. IMPRESSION *sb.* + -ISM: see next.]

†**1.** Applied to the philosophy of Hume: cf. IMPRESSION *sb.* 6 c. *nonce-use.*

1839 J. ROGERS *Antipopopr.* VI. ii. 202 All hail to Berkeley who would have no matter, and to Hume who would have no mind; to the Idealism of the former, and to the Impressionism of the latter!

2. The theory or practice of the impressionist school in art; the method of painting (or describing) things so as to give their general tone and effect, or the broad impression which they produce at first sight, without elaboration of detail.

1882 *Athenæum* 10 June 737/2 M. Duez, one of the fathers of Impressionism, seems to have modified and refined his practice. **1884** *Contemp. Rev.* July 141 The influence of impressionism is on the whole decreasing. **1888** *Ch. Times* 29 June 575/4 Impressionism is an excellent thing in its proper place, which is the artist's own sketch-book, not the completed canvas. **1899** *Q. Rev.* Apr. 536 In the case of Velasquez, Mr. R. A. M. Stevenson claims this ultimate development as distinct 'Impressionism'.

3. The literary presentation of some scene or emotion in its salient features, done in a few strokes.

1883 VERNON LEE in *Academy* 29 Dec. 426 Complete negation of all the elements most common in modern writing—namely, realism..and, if I may use an artist's word, impressionism in execution. **1892** *Pall Mall G.* 24 Mar. 6/1 A delightful freshness and vividness—a touch of unconscious literary impressionism, if the phrase may stand.

4. *Mus.* A style of composition, originating in the late 1880s with Debussy, characterized by its harmonic system, esp. in the use by Debussy of the whole-tone scale, and departing from the strong and direct structure and themes of the Romantic composers. Also used for a type of jazz with similar 'atmospheric' characteristics.

1889 G. B. SHAW *London Music 1888–89* (1937) 128 There is a great deal in Mefistofele that is mere impressionism; and like impressionism in painting it is enchanting when it is successful. **1908** W. H. DALY *Debussy* 31 So far as one can classify Debussy's use of a 'programme' at all, it is necessary to return to the comparison with painting, and style it impressionism. **1922** *Musical Opinion* May 698/1 Let it be thoroughly understood that impressionism is no more a matter of technique, of using dots, blobs and squares..any more than musical impressionism means the use of the whole-tone scale with its implied harmonies. **1934** C. LAMBERT *Music Ho!* I. 25 Impressionism, as I have said, is a term easily misused, and one may doubt the logic of its use as a musical term at all; but its association with the work of Debussy and his followers is so widespread that one may conveniently use it as a generic label for that period of disruption in music of which Debussy was the dominating figure. **1947** A. EINSTEIN *Music Romantic Era* xi. 149 His first symphonic poem *Les Éolides* (1876), inspired by Leconte de Lisle's poem, is rather a precursor of Impressionism. **1952** B. ULANOV *Hist. Jazz in Amer.* (1958) xii. 133 It was another sixteen years before the impact of Impressionism was again so directly felt in jazz. **1956** M. STEARNS *Story of Jazz* (1957) xiii. 146 The Debussyesque impressionism of Smith's 'Morning Air'. **1970** *Times* 27 Feb. 13/1 Mr. Fon..was keenly aware that impressionism for Debussy was not just a vague wash.

impressionist (ɪm'prɛʃənɪst), *sb.* (*a.*) [ad. F. *impressioniste*: see IMPRESSION and -IST.]

1. a. A painter who endeavours to express the general impression produced by a scene or object, to the exclusion of minute details or elaborate finish; also, a writer who practises a similar method; hence an impressionist painting, and in similar *transf.* uses.

1876 H. JAMES *Parisian Sk.* (1958) 131 An exhibition for which I may at least claim that it can give rise..to no dangerous perversities of taste is that of the little group of the Irreconcilables—otherwise known as the 'Impressionists' in painting. **1881** *Even. Standard* 1 Feb. 4/5 To create this misty sentiment is the aim of the modern impressionist. **1883** *Times* 3 Mar. 8 This artist..is something of an impressionist; though he does condescend ..to put into one point of his picture..a vast amount of elaborate work. **1891** *Ibid.* 20 Jan. 4/5 Velasquez and Frans Hals, the Great Twin Brethren of the Impressionists' worship. **1958** L. DURRELL *Mountolive* xi. 208 They would take a slow turn up and down the picture-gallery, with its splendid collection of Impressionists.

b. *attrib.* or as *adj.*

1876 H. JAMES *Parisian Sk.* (1958) 132 The 'Impressionist' doctrines strike me as incompatible, in an artist's mind, with the existence of first-rate talent. **1884** *Littell's Living Age* CLXI. 74 The Impressionist school. **1887** *Athenæum* 23 July 123 The great increase of so-called Impressionist pictures. **1892** MRS. H. WARD *David Grieve* II. 337, I should make one of the poetical impressionist painters who sway the public taste. **1893** R. FRY *Let.* 20 Sept. (1972) I. 154, I don't quite make out whether Elsie Howard is Impressionist; I suppose so, but I thought she was Ruskinian. **1894** G. MEREDITH *Let.* 5 July (1970) III. 1163 Beware of a hurried habit of mind that comes of addiction to Impressionist effects. **1933** *Burlington Mag.* Dec. 276/2 The Impressionist movement in England will never count for much. **1969** *Listener* 28 Aug. 274/3 A letter from the aged Earl Attlee in his own impressionist typewriting, full of splendidly sinister words like 'Ghsmberlian' and 'recollʒftian'.

2. *Mus.* A composer of impressionistic music. Also *attrib.*

1908 W. H. DALY *Debussy* 10 It is convenient, even if it is an incomplete definition of his altogether novel attitude towards music, to describe Debussy as an impressionist. He is something more than an impressionist as the term is commonly understood, although in his work there is not a little which recalls the methods and the points of view of the masters of impressionist painting. **1927** [see BITONALITY]. **1947** C. GRAY *Contingencies & Other Ess.* iii. 91 The so-called impressionists were anticipated by him [*sc.* Liszt] in many of their most characteristic effects and procedures, sometimes by as much as half a century. **1948** *Penguin Music Mag.* Oct. 46 The half-Tristanesque, half-impressionist Nocturne. **1952** B. ULANOV *Hist. Jazz in Amer.* (1958) xii. 132 The French Impressionist composers and their American disciples and imitators made a great impression upon Bix's generation of jazz musicians. **1955** R. BLESH *Shining Trumpets* (ed. 3) xii. 281 His borrowed effects from jazz, the Impressionists, and the French Romantics. **1959** D. COOKE *Lang. Mus.* i. 2 Medieval music was largely architectural in conception: the romantics were much concerned with the literary; the impressionists with the pictorial; modern music has swung back again to the architectural.

3. *Theatr.* A comedian whose act consists of imitations or impersonations of well-known personalities, etc. Cf. IMPRESSION 6 d.

1964 *Sun* (Sydney) 19 Nov. 40/5 Beside the virtuosity of American entertainer Frank Gorshin..all other impressionists fade almost into insignificance. **1973** 'E. MORECAMBE' in Morecambe & Wise *Eric & Ernie* II. 90 Most comedians start out as impressionists, but if they don't develop past that stage they never become big names. **1981** *Times* 28 Feb. 16 Like most modern impressionists, he 'took off' stars of stage, screen and radio.

impressio'nistic, *a.* [f. prec. + -IC.] **1.** Of or pertaining to impressionism; in the style of the impressionists. Also, in a general sense: subjective, unsystematic (formed directly from IMPRESSION *sb.* 7 and only indirectly influenced by senses of *impressionism, -ist*).

1886 *Sat. Rev.* 11 Dec. 782 In what is called impressionistic painting you paint something to suggest the temporary mood in which you looked at a certain scene or effect. **1891** *Athenæum* 28 Feb. 282/3 A new volume of poems, consisting of short impressionistic lyrics. **1891** G. MEREDITH *Let.* 15 Apr. (1970) II. 1025 You have at times.. insisted on your impressions. That is, you have put on your cap, sharpened your pencil, and gone afield as the Impressionistic poet. **1894** *Brit. Jrnl. Photog.* XLI. Suppl. 4 The hideous plague of impressionistic smudges. **1900** *Atlantic Monthly* LXXXVI. 78 As for the impressionistic writer about literature—he is apt to concern himself very little with this historical origin of a work of art. **1908** W. H. DALY *Debussy* 32 Debussy's music..deals..in suggestions. .. There is something swift, vague, and elusive, but strangely vivid and satisfying... But the broad, impressionistic methods are not taken to avoid difficulties of definition. **1909** W. JAMES *Pluralistic Universe* ii. 52 Impressionistic philosophizing, like impressionistic watch-making or land-surveying, is intolerable to experts. **1915** J. HUNEKER *Ivory, Apes & Peacocks* 38 Laforgue..was an ardent advocate of the Impressionistic painters. **1921** *Times Lit. Suppl.* 24 Feb. 114/1 The impressionistic reporter who asked Mr. Edison what he considered the chief mark of a truly valuable invention. **1933** *PMLA* XLVIII. 598 Such rather impressionistic terminology has been found suggestive and helpful in teaching. **1934** S. R. NELSON *All about Jazz* v. 101 All these are impressionistic music of the programme type. **1947** A. EINSTEIN *Music Romantic Era* vii. 69 Berlioz..made the two middle movements nothing but picturesque scenes—most finely impressionistic, most genuinely akin to French *plein air* painting. **1955** R. BLESH *Shining Trumpets* (ed. 3) xii. 268 An impressionistic montage of solo moods. **1958** R. A. BONE *Negro Novel in Amer.* ii. 68 The style is appropriately impressionistic, full of hyphenated adjectives aimed at vivid impressions of Harlem life. **1962** *Listener* 25 Jan. 195/3 Delius's impressionistic elusiveness. *Ibid.* 196/1 Its impressionistic string, harp and horn texture. **1973** *College English* XXXIV. 1103 Prosodic studies have tended toward tentative, impressionistic assertions and *ad hoc* methodology.

2. *Phonetics.* Non-systematic, subjective, non-structured; determined by the recorder's impressions of speech sounds, not by the sound-system of the language, dialect, etc., being recorded.

1939 H. KURATH *Handbk. Ling. Geogr. New England* iv. 122 The field workers' phonetic notations..are not phonemic, but on the contrary intentionally phonic, that is *impressionistic*. **1940** *Amer. Speech* XV. 145 This paper makes no claim to presenting a detailed impressionistic analysis of PM [i.e. Piedmont, U.S.] phonetics; it attempts merely to indicate a relative phonemic distribution. **1948** R. A. HALL *Leave Your Lang. Alone!* II. vi. 41 Trying to describe sounds in auditory, impressionistic terms is likely to give about as accurate results as would, say, describing chemical elements in terms of their smells. The impressions we get through our senses of hearing and smell just can't be stated in clear and analyzable enough terms to be of any use in scientific work. **1960** D. JONES *Outl. Eng. Phonetics* (ed. 9) 349 Systematic transcriptions have to be distinguished from transcriptions made on a general phonetic basis without reference to the needs of any particular language. The latter may be described as 'non-systematic' or 'impressionistic'. **1962** H. ORTON *Survey Eng. Dial., Introd.* i. 18 The merits and demerits of the impressionistic method need not be re-stated here. **1963** *Amer. Speech* XXXVIII. 127 The recording of the speech sounds is phonic (impressionistic) in intent. All premature phonemicization is strictly avoided.

impressionistically (ɪmprɛʃə'nɪstɪkəlɪ), *adv.* [f. IMPRESSIONISTIC *a.*: see -ICALLY.] In an impressionistic manner (in various senses); from the point of view of an impressionist.

1909 W. JAMES *Pluralistic Universe* iii. 92, I make no claim to understanding it, I treat it merely impressionistically. **1924** GALSWORTHY *White Monkey* II. ii, When you smile, Miss Collins, I see you impressionistically. **1924** J. A. HAMMERTON *Countries of World* III. 1507/1 Their flowers.. painted (impressionistically but with unerring truth of impression) in their frescoes. **1926** W. J. LOCKE *Old Bridge* I. i, I try to express myself..impressionistically. **1960** H. ORTON in *Orbis* IX. 337 The fieldworkers transcribed the informants' responses phonetically, and impressionistically, in the phonetic alphabet of the International Phonetic Association. **1964** F. BOWERS *Bibliogr. & Textual Crit.* II. iii. 51 The hypothesis is factually, not impressionistically, based.

impressionize (ɪm'prɛʃənaɪz), *v. rare.* [f. IMPRESSION *sb.* + -IZE.] **a.** *trans.* To make an impression on; to introduce impressions into, to portray as an impression or set of impressions. **b.** *intr.* To gather impressions.

1894 F. M. ELLIOT *Roman Gossip* i. 15 He had..imagined this *mise en scène* to impressionise his fellow-citizens. **1894** H. JAMES *Notebks.* (1947) 160, I must picture it [*sc.* a story to be written], summarize it, impressionize it, in a word—compress and confine it by making it the picture of what I see. **1905** D. SLADEN *Playing Game* I. i. 16 Instead of thinking Japan a God-forsaken country..he was impressionizing in an indolent æsthetic way.

im'pressionless, *a. rare.* [f. IMPRESSION + -LESS.] Without impression; void of impressions; unimpressible.

1864 in WEBSTER. **1889** *Eng. Illustr. Mag.* Apr. 500/1 A face as impressionless and vacant as the white door-post against which he lounged.

impressive (ɪm'prɛsɪv), *a.* [f. IMPRESS *v.*[1] + -IVE.]

†**1.** Capable of being easily impressed; susceptible (*to*); impressible. *Obs.*

1593 NASHE *Christ's T.* (1613) 50 She hath steeled my soft impressiue heart. **1603** DRAYTON *Bar. Wars* III. 58 (1605) Those pleasing raptures from her graces rise Strongly inuading his impressiue breast. **1663** J. SPENCER *Prodigies* (1665) 52 The multitude..cannot but be greatly impressive to any great and religious Perswasions concerning Prodigies. **1665** —— *Vulg. Proph.* 70 Men..of strong fancies, impressive tempers, and weak intellectuals.

†**2.** Conveying an impression *of. Obs. rare*$^{-1}$.

1791 J. HAMPSON *Wesley* III. 167 A freshness of complexion impressive of the most perfect health.

3. Characterized by making a deep impression on the mind or senses; able to excite deep feeling. Said usually of language or scenes; rarely of persons.

1775 ASH, *Impressive*, suited to make impression, making impression. **1791** NEWTE *Tour Eng. & Scot.* 189 That animated and impressive eloquence which usually distinguishes inventors and projectors. **1825** LAMB *Elia* Ser. II. *Barbara S——*, When that impressive actress has been bending over her in some heart-rending colloquy. **1860** TYNDALL *Glac.* I. viii. 59 The scene was exceedingly impressive.

4. *Comb.*, as ***impressive-looking*** adj.

1904 *Daily Chron.* 21 July 4/5 Even in these impressive-looking statistical tables little bits of cheerfulness obstinately obtrude themselves. **1925** T. DREISER *Amer. Trag.* (1926) II. xl. 10 Arabella Stark..in a large and impressive-looking car, was waiting.

im'pressively, *adv.* [f. prec. + -LY^{2}.] In an impressive manner; in a way fitted to impress.

1818 in TODD. **1830** D'ISRAELI *Chas. I*, III. vi. 110 The King..impressively assured him that he considered him the happiest man in England. **1841** ORDERSON *Creol.* xvii. 209 The funeral service was impressively performed. **1860** TYNDALL *Glac.* I. xvi. 115 My guide..repeating the warning more impressively before I attended to it.

im'pressiveness. [f. as prec. + -NESS.]

†**1.** The quality of being impressible; susceptibility to impressions. *Obs.*

1663 J. SPENCER *Prodigies* (1665) 57 That impressiveness of spirit which times of action and change..are generally attended with.

2. The character or quality of being impressive, or of making a deep impression on the mind, etc.

a **1805** PALEY *Serm. Several Subj.* iv. (1827) 632/1 We think a great deal more frequently about it..and our thoughts of it have much more of vivacity and impressiveness. *a* **1831** A. KNOX in *Rem.* (1844) I. 37 [It] makes them have the impressiveness of present facts. **1882** B. D. W. RAMSAY *Recoll. Mil. Serv.* I. viii. 172 He spoke.. with great impressiveness and eloquence.

im'pressment^{1}. *rare.* [f. IMPRESS *v.*^{1} + -MENT. In sense 2 for F. *empressement.*]

1. The action of impressing; exertion of pressure.

1865 BUSHNELL *Vicar. Sacr.* iii, Carried by mighty impressment, such as if by some unseen hydrostatic pressure.

2. Earnestness, ardour.

1854 'MARION HARLAND' *Alone* ix, Several young men dashed to the side of the carriage, with as much impressment as at a ball. **1880** L. WALLACE *Ben-Hur* 384 Simonides.. gave his farewell and the peace of the Lord with the impressment of a father.

impressment^{2} (ɪm'prɛsmənt). [f. IMPRESS *v.*^{2} + -MENT.] The act or practice of impressing or forcibly taking for the public service.

1796 MORSE *Amer. Geog.* I. 689 The loss to the citizens directly by the..British army, and indirectly by American impressments. **1829** MARRYAT *F. Mildmay* xxi, America looked upon our system of impressment as the sheet-anchor of her navy. **1866** ROGERS *Agric. & Prices* I. iv. 67 The right of the impressment of beasts for carriage was part of the ancient prerogative.

fig. **1834** H. MILLER *Scenes & Leg.* xvi. (1857) 232 There is no irregular impressment of the young and vigorous in the way of accident. **1876** E. MELLOR *Priesth.* App. D. 412 On three conditions only can such impressment of witnesses be justified.

†**im'pressor**^{1}. *Obs. rare.* [Agent-noun in L. form from L. *imprimĕre* to IMPRESS (cf. L. *pressor*, *expressor*).] One who, or that which, makes impressions.

1631 BRATHWAIT *Whimzies, Wine-soaker* 101 And now.. he hath had his evening lecture, and trenching home supported by his friendly impressor, makes every foote an indenture. **1661** GLANVILL *Van. Dogm.* i. 8 Their action is overcome by the strokes of stronger impressors. **1663** J. BEALE in *Boyle's Wks.* (1772) VI. 333 Fancy is the receiver and impressor.

†**im'pressor**^{2}. *Obs. rare.* [f. IMPRESS *v.*^{2} + -OR, after prec.] One who impresses or takes by force for the public service.

1781 R. H. LEE in Sparks *Corr. Amer. Rev.* (1853) III. 409 Let his mill and wagons have protection from the destructive talons of impressors.

impressure^{1} (ɪm'prɛʃ(j)ʊə(r)). Now *rare.* [f. IMPRESS *v.*^{1} + -URE, after *pressure.*]

1. The action of impressing or exerting pressure upon.

1649 J. ELLISTONE tr. *Behmen's Epist.* i. §37 The magnetick impressure, hunger, and desire, of the soule. *Ibid.* vi. §10 Comprehensive impressure or formation of the expressed word. **1784** *New Spectator* No. 16. 2/1 At an age when the twig bends under every impressure. **1875** SWINBURNE *Ess. & Stud.* 247 The subject..lay ready shapen for the strong impressure of his hand.

2. A mark made by pressure; an impression; an indentation.

1600 SHAKS. *A.Y.L.* III. v. 23 Leane vpon a rush, The Cicatrice and capable impressure Thy palme some moment keepes. **1601** —— *Twel. N.* II. v. 103 The impressure her Lucrece, with which she vses to seale. **1631** BRATHWAIT *Whimzies* Ep. Ded. 7 What else are characters but stampes or impressures, noting such an especiall place, person or office. **1848** JOHNSTON in *Proc. Berw. Nat. Club* II. No. 6. 289 Behind it a short mesial line..and a deep impressure still further backwards.

3. A mental or sensuous impression.

1607 MIDDLETON *Michaelm. Term* II. i, I knew not what fair impressure I received at first, but I began to affect your society very speedily. **1609** B. JONSON *Case is altered* I. iv, The impressure of those ample favours I have derived.. Would bind my faith. **1870** SWINBURNE *Ess. & Stud.* (1875) 182 One little *Requiescat*..leaves long upon the ear an impressure of simple, of earnest, of weary melody.

†**im'pressure**^{2}. *Obs. rare*$^{-1}$. [f. IMPRESS *v.*^{2} + -URE, after prec.] = IMPRESSMENT^{2}.

1680 *Nation's Interest in Relation to Pretens. Dk. York* 31 Their Bulwark against High Payments, and Impressures, demanded by the King.

imprest ('ɪmprɛst), *a.* and *sb.*^{1} [Appears in the 16th c. for the earlier PREST *a.* and *sb.* The prefix *im-* occurs in It. (and med.L.) *imprestāre* to lend, *impresto*, *imprestito* advanced, lent (cf. OF. *emprest* a loan), *imprestanza* (OF. *imprestance*) a loan, advance, but in English may have been partly due to a misunderstanding of the common phrase *in prest* (*money*): see PREST *a.*]

†**A.** *adj.* Of money: Lent, or paid in advance, advanced, esp. to soldiers, sailors, and public officials. *Obs.*

1570 *Act 13 Eliz.* c. 4. §1 Receiver of any Sums of Money imprest, or otherwise, for the Use of the Queen's Majesty. **1634** SIR T. HERBERT *Trav.* Ded. A ij b, Such imprest money I doe not like, but protest against it and the paymaster. **1658** PHILLIPS, *Imprest Money*, is money paid to Souldiers before hand. **1690** *Lond. Gaz.* No. 2580/4 Some Seamen..having received Imprest Money or Wages..have Absconded. **1737** *List Govt. Officers* in *J. Chamberlayne's St. Gt. Brit.* II. 87 Accomptant for Imprest Money for paying of Incidents. **1755** MAGENS *Insurances* II. 257 To insure the.. imprest Money advanced to Seamen.

B. *sb.*

1. a. An advance (of money) made to one who is charged with some business by the state, to enable him to proceed with the discharge of the same. †Formerly, also, advance-pay of soldiers or sailors.

1568 NORTH tr. *Gueuara's Diall Pr.* (1619) 678/1, I did accept in way of imprest, and not of gift. **1588** *Copy Let. to Mendoza* 20 For the Nauy of England..bargaines are already made, and Imprest of money deliuered, and certaine sent into the Estlands, for great store of al maritime prouisions. **1600** DEKKER *Gentle Craft* Wks. 1873 I. 11 They [the soldiers] have their imprest, coates, and furniture. **1617** MORYSON *Itin.* II. 242 Upon every Contract we make, we give the Victualers an imprest beforehand. **1633** T. STAFFORD *Pac. Hib.* III. xvii. (1810) 654 He had lately received a great imprest of Spanish money. **1723** *Lond. Gaz.* No. 6141/2 Navy-Office, Feb. 20, 1722..All Persons who have any Imprest standing out against them..are advised to bring in their Bills. **1748** *Anson's Voy.* I. i. 9 The Government agreed to advance them 10,000[£] upon imprest. **1863** H. COX *Instit.* III. vii. 690 The moneys drawn from the Exchequer are applied partly to final payments, and partly to advances or 'imprests'.

b. In general sense: An advance, a loan. (In quots. said of the borrower.)

1686 W. DE BRITAINE *Hum. Prud.* §37. 122 There is nothing which doth more impoverish a Prince, than Imprests of Money at great Usance. **1704** FLAMSTEED *Diary* 8 Nov. in Hone *Every-day Bk.* I. 1096, I would not cumber my..estate with imprests or securitys. **1957** F. KING *Man on Rock* iii. 81 He drew up a log-book for the car, checked the postage imprest. **1958** E. A. ROBERTSON *Justice of Heart* iv. 48 Off you go, see the foreign editor, get an imprest—don't imagine you can squander money on this trip, though!

c. ***Auditor of the Imprest*** (see quot. 1670). ***bill of imprest***, an order authorizing a person to draw money in advance: cf. *imprest-bill*.

1665 PEPYS *Diary* (1879) III. 331, I did get a bill of imprest to Captain Cocke to pay myselfe in part. **1668** *Lond. Gaz.* No. 277/4 All such Accounts as pass by the Auditors of Imprests. **1670** BLOUNT *Law Dict.*, *Auditor of the Prests or Imprests*, Are..Officers in the Exchequer, who take and make up the great Accompts of Ireland, Berwick, the Mint, and of any Money imprested to any Man for His Majesties service. **1741** BETTERTON *Eng. Stage* ii. 7 After he had so profitable a Post, as Auditor of the Imprest. **1781** *Act 21 Geo. III*, c. 56 §10 The Receipt of the Vice-Chancellor shall be allowed by the Auditor and Auditors of the Imprest.

2. *attrib.* and *Comb.*, as ***imprest-account***, ***-accountant*** (see quot. 1865); †**imprest-bill** = *bill of imprest*; †**imprest-office**, formerly, a department of the Admiralty which attended to the advances made to paymasters and other officials.

1615 SIR R. BOYLE in *Lismore Papers* (1886) I. 60 For this debt I have his imprest bills. **1666** PEPYS *Diary* (1879) IV. 123 The clearing of all my imprest bills. **1865** *Times* 17 Aug., The person to whom the advance is made is called the 'imprest accountant'. **1893** *Daily News* 27 Aug. 7/1 The 'imprest' account..related to sums advanced to officers for the purpose of making inquiries.

†**imprest**, *sb.*^{2} *Obs.* Also 7 **emprest**. [f. IMPREST *v.*^{2}: cf. IMPRESS *sb.*^{2}] = IMPRESSMENT^{2}.

1610 DONNE *Pseudo-Martyr* xi. §7. 326 To disobey the Kings emprest when hee leuies an Armie. **1627** J. CARTER *Expos. Serm. on Mount* 47 To bee compelled, by imprest from authority, to go a mile, a league, or more, at the officers pleasure. **1651** N. BACON *Disc. Govt. Eng.* II. xxii. (1739) 103 None were then compelled to enter into Service by Imprest, or absolute Command.

†**im'prest**, *v.*^{1} *Obs.* [ad. It. (and med.L.) *imprestāre* to lend: see IMPREST *sb.*^{1}, and the earlier PREST *v.*]

1. *trans.* To advance, lend (money).

1565 Q. ELIZ. *Let. to Bedford* in Robertson *Hist. Scot.* (1759) II. App. 28 The other 2000*l.*..to imprest some part thereof to the new numbers of the 600 footmen and 100 horsemen. **1646** SIR J. TEMPLE *Irish Rebell.* II. 3 Both of them had money imprested; Sir Thomas Lucas to compleat his Troope.., Captaine Armstrong to raise a new Troop. **1780** BURKE *Corr.* (1844) II. 331 The sum that shall be imprested by the exchequer to the bank, to answer these drafts. **1810** *Ann. Reg.* 453 These half-yearly accounts do not exhibit the money imprested to the conductor, or the balance due from him.

b. With inverted construction: To furnish (a person) with an advance of money.

1612 DAVIES *Why Ireland*, etc. (1747) 58 He should have four thousand Markes for the first year, whereof he should be imprested 2,000 li before hand. **1613** SIR R. BOYLE in *Lismore Papers* (1886) I. 23 This day I imprested [= imprested] my mother in lawe..wth 50^{li} ster. to sett the worck in hande.

2. To draw (a bill or money by a bill).

1617 MORYSON *Itin.* II. 207 Billes imprested upon accounts here. **1661** PEPYS *Diary* 13 June, So to the Wardrobe and got my Lord to order Mr. Creed to imprest so much upon me to be paid by Alderman Buckwell.

Hence **im'presting** *vbl. sb.*, advancing (of money), loan.

1565 Q. ELIZ. *Let. to Bedford* in Robertson *Hist. Scot.* (1759) II. App. 28 The impresting to him of 1000*l.* might stand him in stead for the help to defend himself. **1591** UNTON *Corr.* (Roxb.) 2 Greate sommes of money..by waie of impréstinge yealded to the said Kinge since he came to the crowne.

†**im'prest**, *v.*^{2} *Obs.* [f. *imprest*, *-pressed*, pa. pple. of IMPRESS *v.*^{2}, perh. confused with IMPREST *v.*^{1}] *trans.* To impress for the army or navy.

1645 *Martin's Echo* in Prynne *Fresh Discov. Prodig. Wand. Blazing Stars* 44 You have your Husbands, your Sons and Servants, Imprested from you. **1651** N. BACON *Disc. Govt. Eng.* II. xi. (1739) 62 Englishmen were anciently used to be imprested for the Wars in France. *a* **1680** BUTLER *Rem.* (1759) II. 174 He will join as many Shields together..to fortify the Nobility of a new made Lord, that will pay for the impresting of them, and allow him Coat and Conduct Money. **1704** *Royal Proclam.* 14 Dec. in *Lond. Gaz.* No. 4081/2 Captains..Imployed in Impresting Men for Our Fleet. **1708** *Ibid.* No. 4415/3 No Men shall be Imprested from any Merchant Ships.

†**im'prest**, *v.*^{3} *Obs. rare.* Erroneous for IMPRESS *v.*^{1} (Due to the confusion of *impress* and *imprest* in the two preceding vbs.) Hence **im'presting** *vbl. sb.*

1652 GAULE *Magastrom.* 93 Either the stars doe inflow and imprest, yea, portend, and signify perpetually, or not. **1659** *Gentl. Calling* (1696) 111 It is..the duty of those who are possest of this advantage, to use it to the impresting not of Vice, but Vertue.

†**im'prestable**, *a. Obs. rare.* [f. IM-^{2} + PRESTABLE.] That cannot be performed or rendered.

1683 *Last Speech J. Wilson* in *Cloud Witnesses* (1810) 225 Counting the cost and Seeing the cost of themselves imprestable. **1721** WODROW *Hist. Suff. Ch. Scotl.* II. 60 (Jam.) Sending against us an armed host of barbarous savages..for inforcing of a most unnatural bond, wholly illegal in itself, and imprestable by us.

†**im'pretiable**, *a. Obs. rare*$^{-1}$. [f. IM-^{2} + PRETIABLE.] Invaluable, priceless.

1638 O. SEDGWICKE *Sermon* (1639) 69 They [divine Truthes] are impretiable.

†**im'prevalence.** *Obs. rare*$^{-0}$. [see next and -ENCE.] = next.

1828 in WEBSTER; whence in later Dicts., with erroneous attribution to Bp. Hall: cf. next.

†**im'prevalency.** *Obs. rare*$^{-1}$. [f. IM-^{2} + PREVALENCY.] Unprevailing character; want of prevailing power.

a **1656** BP. HALL *Rem. Wks.* (1660) 276 He..triumphes in the impotence, and imprevalency of them all.

†**impre'varicable**, *a. Obs. rare*$^{-1}$. [f. IM-^{2} + PREVARICABLE.] That cannot be deviated from; invariable.

1644 DIGBY *Two Treat.* II. viii. 412 If then it be an impreuaricable law with all bodies, that none whatsoeuer can moue, vnlesse it be moued by an other [etc.].

†**impreve, -prieve**, *v. Sc. Obs.* Also 6 **ympreif, impryve, imprive, impreive**. Pa. pple. **improven** (-in). [ad. L. *improbāre* to prove bad, to reject, blame, disprove; cf. F. *improuver* to disapprove, blame. The form of the radical follows that of PREVE, *preive*, repr. OF. *proeve*, *preuve*, tonic form of *prover*, now *prouver*. Cf. APPREVE.]

1. *trans.* To disallow; to disprove.

1488 *Acta Dom. Conc.* 90 (Jam.) Ane instrument.. appreuand and ratifiand James Bonare of Rossy hir assignay, and imprevand James Bonare hir secund sone. **1564** *Acts Sederunt* 15 June (Jam.), Quhair ony person.. taks on hand to imprieve the execution of the precept. *c* **1575** BALFOUR *Practicks* (1754) 381 Improbatioun of writis, instrumentis or evidentis beand offerit, he that offeris him to impreive the samin, sould find the samin day and time cautioun to the uther partie. **1583** *Leg. Bp. St. Androis* 219

Wha swair that he had never sene it, And tuike in hand for to impryve it [*rime* mischevit]. **1609** SKENE *Reg. Maj.* 122 The direct maner of improbation be the witnes insert in the wreit quhilk is taken to be improven. **1617** *Sc. Acts Jas. VI* (1814) 546 (Jam.) In all cases except where the writtis so registrated ar offered to be improvin.

2. To rebuke, reprove.

1552 ABP. HAMILTON *Catech.* (1884) 61 Ympreif, repreif, exhort, with all suffering and doctrine.

impre'ventable, *a. rare*⁻⁰. [f. IM-² + PREVENTABLE.] That cannot be prevented (Webster 1864). Hence **impreventa'bility**, the state or quality of being impreventable.

imprevisible (ɪmprɪ'vɪzɪb(ə)l), *a. rare.* [f. IM-² + PREVISIBLE *a.*] That cannot be foreseen. Hence **imprevisi'bility**.

1887 *Mind* XII. 622 The notion of 'imprevisibility' is to be asserted without qualification as part of its meaning [i.e. of Free Will]. **1888** T. WHITTAKER *ibid.* XIII. 119 The whole conception of which these strictly 'imprevisible' acts form part.

impre'vision. *rare.* [f. IM-² + PREVISION.] Want of foresight; improvidence.

1883 W. J. STILLMAN in *Cent. Mag.* Oct. 825/2 The whole realm of beggary and imprevision will make a hitch forward.

‖**imprévu** (ǣprevy). Also imprevu. [Fr., f. IM-² + *prévu*, pa. pple. of *prévoir* to foresee.] The unexpected, the unforeseen.

1854 *Punch* 9 Sept. 106/2 Had he well read the people.., their love of *l'imprévu*? **1858** GEO. ELIOT *Let.* 2 Mar. in J. W. Cross *George Eliot's Life* (1885) II. viii. 13 Perhaps we may go to Dresden, perhaps not: we leave room for the *imprévu*. **1925** G. B. SHAW *Let.* 15 Dec. in *To a Young Actress* (1960) 88, I am prudent and foresee everything. My life lacks the imprevu. **1969** R. HARPER *World of Thriller* II. 65 Stendhal ..understood that without the '*imprévu*' there is no charm in human existence.

†**im'pride,** *v. Obs rare.* In 5 ynp-. [f. IM-¹ + PRIDE *sb.* (Cf. *incourage, inheart*, ME. forms of *encourage, enheart*.)] *trans.* To imbue with pride, make proud.

c **1425** *Found. St. Bartholomew's* (E.E.T.S.) 2 In prosperite nat ynpridid. In aduersite paciente.

imprieve: see IMPREVE.

imprimatur (ɪmprɪ'meɪtə(r)). [Lat. *imprimātur*, 3rd sing. pres. subj. pass. of *imprimĕre* to impress, imprint, in mod.L., to print.]

1. The formula (= 'let it be printed'), signed by an official licenser of the press, authorizing the printing of a book; hence as *sb.* an official license to print.

Now (in Great Britain and U.S.) only in works officially sanctioned by the Roman Catholic Church.

1640 SIR E. DERING *Sp. on Relig.* 23 Nov. iii. (1642) 7 To this I parallell our late *Imprimatur's*, Licences for the Presse. **1641** MILTON *Animadv.* i, Your proud *Imprimaturs* not to be obtain'd without the shallow surview, but not shallow hand of some mercenary, narrow Soul'd, and illitterate Chaplain. **1660** *Trial Regic.* [on p. facing title p.], Imprimatur; *J. Berkenhead.* **1712** ADDISON *Spect.* No. 445 ¶1 A Sheet of blank Paper that must have this new Imprimatur clapt upon it. **1779–81** JOHNSON *L.P.*, *Young* Wks. IV. 229 The vice-chancellor's *imprimatur*, for it was first printed at Oxford, is dated May the 19th, 1713. **1855** MACAULAY *Hist. Eng.* xxi. IV. 607 But Etherege's *She Would if She Could*..obtained the Imprimatur without difficulty. **1870** BALDW. BROWN *Eccl. Truth* 242 These tales..were circulated..with the imprimatur of the church. **1883** *Catholic Dict.* p. iv, *Imprimatur.* Henricus Eduardus Card. Archiep. Westmonast. Die 18 Dec. 1883. **1884** *Ibid.* (ed. 2), It has not been thought necessary to secure a fresh 'Imprimatur' for the additional matter in this edition; but it is submitted to the authority of the Church.

2. *fig.* Commendatory license, sanction.

1672 MARVELL *Reh. Transp.* I. 46 As things of Buffoonery do commonly, they carry with them their own *Imprimatur*. **1742** YOUNG *Nt. Th.* VII. 1404 Thus shall my title pass a sacred seal, Receive an *imprimatur* from Above. **1893** PATMORE *Relig. Poetæ* 121 Lord Rosebery affirmed that the test of true literature and its only justifiable *Imprimatur* is 'the thumb-mark of the artisan'. **1955** *Bull. Atomic Sci.* June 209/2 His calculations and conclusions bear no imprimatur of the Atomic Energy Commission. **1973** *N.Y. Law Jrnl.* 31 Aug. 3/1 It is well-settled contract law that courts do not give their imprimatur to such arrangements.

¶ Used confusedly = IMPRINT *sb.* 3. (Quot. 1971 is *fig.*)

1970 *Daily Tel.* 7 May 13/2 The agent, not the candidate, is the one liable to fines..if he..issues one word of election literature without his own and the printer's imprimatur on it. **1971** *Nature* 7 May 40/2 The site near Kültepe has been identified as the Assyrian karum Kanis and most of the tablets can thus be considered to bear the implicit imprimatur 'found at Kanis'.

‖**imprimatura** (imprima'tura). Also **imprimitura**. [ad. It. *imprimitura*.] A thin priming or ground, frequently coloured, applied to an artist's canvas or panel.

1951 R. MAYER *Artist's Handbk.* 434 *Imprimatura*, a veil or thin glaze of colour applied to a ground as a preliminary coating. Term not in very wide use. **1958** M. L. WOLF *Dict. Painting* 137 *Imprimatura*, in painting, a type of glaze applied as a toner to the canvas or other ground..an underpainting, intended to relieve the monotony of a white or gray background. **1967** J. N. BARRON *Lang. of Painting* 99 *Imprimatura*, a thin glaze or veil of color brushed or rubbed over the white of a ground... It may also be used at the same time to reduce, if necessary, the absorbency of the ground.

†**im'primature.** *Obs.* [app. f. F. *imprimer* to print + -ATE³ 7 + -URE, after such forms as *abbreviature*, etc.; but prob. influenced by IMPRIMATUR.] Printing; print, impression.

1762 A. CATCOTT *Deluge* (1768) 407 Things..that had not an existence when the imprimatures of the antediluvian animal and vegetable bodies were formed in the solid rock. **1813** J. THOMSON *Lect. Inflam.* Introd. 32 The right of imprimature..was denied by the faculty to a small work of Ambrose Parey's.

¶ Also, erroneous form of IMPRIMATUR.

1813 J. THOMSON *Lect. Inflam.* Introd. 32 A decree prohibiting..the publication of any medical books which had not previously obtained their imprimature.

†**imprime,** *v. Obs.* Also 6–7 em-. [f. IM-¹ + PRIME *a.* or *sb.*, or L. *prīm-us* first. The history of the hunting sense is obscure, and it may be a word of different origin.]

1. *trans. Hunting.* (See quots.)

1575 TURBERVILE *Bk. Venerie* 242 When he is hunted and doth first leave the herde we say that he is syngled or empryrned. **1590** COKAINE *Treat. Hunting* C iv b, Put your hounds softly vpon, for he wil fall oft at the beginning; which although the Huntsman see, yet must he giue libertie to the yoong houndes to imprime him themselues. **1656** BLOUNT *Glossogr.*, *Emprimed*, a term used by Hunters when a Hart first forsakes the Herd. **1706** PHILLIPS, *To imprime* (in Hunting), to unharbour, rouze, or dislodge a Wild Beast; A Deer is also said to be imprimed when she is forc'd to forsake the Herd. **1775** in ASH.

2. To begin, commence, initiate, enter upon.

1637 WOTTON in *Reliq.* (1651) 441 To trouble you..about the yet imperfected, though wel imprimed, Business of New-Windsor.

Hence **im'priming** *vbl. sb.*, beginning, commencement; entering upon action.

c **1633** WOTTON in *Reliq.* (1651) 455 After their impriming in France I could wish them to mount the Pirenies into Spaine. *a* **1639** *Ibid.* 6 These were both their springings and Imprimings, as I may call them.

†**im'prime,** *sb. Hunting. Obs.* [f. prec. vb.] The act of 'impriming' a deer.

1590 COKAINE *Treat. Hunting* C iv b, And being sure it his owne Deere, he may giue one gibbet, at euery imprime, and no more. **1703** *Rules Civility* 116 If you be a hunting the Buck [with a noble person],..suffer him to come in first to the death or imprime. **1741** *Compl. Fam. Piece* II. i. 293 If he be sunk, and the Hounds thrust him up, 'tis call'd an *Imprime*, and the Company all sound a *Racheat*.

†**'impriment.** *Obs. rare.* [ad. L. *impriment-em*, pres. pple. of *imprimĕre* to IMPRESS.] Something that impresses or imprints.

1762 STERNE *Tr. Shandy* V. xl, It is inherent in the seeds of all animals, and may be preserved..by consubstantials, impriments, and occludents [cf. IMPRINTER, quot. 1638].

†**im'primery.** *Obs.* Also -ie. [a. F. *imprimerie* printing, printing-house, f. *imprimer* to print, *imprimeur* printer: see -ERY.]

1. A printing-office or printing-house.

1663 *Signet Office Docquet Bk.* Aug. (P.R.O.), A new erected office for the surveyeing of the Imprimery and printing presses and to grant the same to Roger Le Strange Esqr., together with the sole lycencing of all ballads [etc.]. **1679** in Gutch *Coll. Cur.* I. 271 Several persons..furnish..an Imprimery, with all the necessaries thereof. *a* **1685** LD. ARLINGTON *To Oxford Univ.* (T.), You have those conveniences for a great imprimerie, which other universities cannot boast of. **1696** PHILLIPS (ed. 5), *Imprimery*, a Printing House.

2. Printing.

1681 WOOD *Life* 15 Mar. (O.H.S.) II. 529 Afterward he surveyed the places of imprimerie.

3. A print or impression.

1674 in BLOUNT *Glossogr.* (ed. 4). **1706** PHILLIPS, *Imprimery*..an Impression, or Print.

‖**imprimis** (ɪm'praɪmɪs), *adv.* or *adv. phr.* Also 5–6 in primis, inprimis, 7 in-primis. [L. assimilated form of *in prīmis*, lit. 'among the first things', 'in the first place'.] In the first place; first. Orig. used to introduce the first of a number of items, as in an inventory or will; thence in more general use. Now unusual.

1465 MARG. PASTON in *P. Lett.* No. 503. II. 189 Inprimis, a peyr brygandyrs, a salet [etc.]. **1548** HALL *Chron.*, *Hen. VIII* 147 b, In primis, the Frenche kyng sware to kepe peace. **1616** BULLOKAR, *Imprimis*, first of all. **1699** FARQUHAR *Const. Coup.* I. ii. Wks. 1892 I. 141 In a month's space, have I gained—let me see, *imprimis*, Colonel Standard. **1700** CONGREVE *Way of World* IV. v. Wks. (Rtldg.) 278/1 *Imprimis* then, I covenant, that your acquaintance be general. *a* **1774** GOLDSM. *New Simile* 15 *Imprimis*, pray observe his hat, Wings upon either side—mark that. **1842** E. FITZGERALD *Lett.* (1889) I. 89 What made you write the verses if you were not moved by the picture imprimis? **1860** *All Year Round* No. 63. 304 Imprimis, then, who can make a will?

†**imprimitive** (ɪm'prɪmɪtɪv), *a. Obs. rare.* [f. IM-² + PRIMITIVE.] Not primitive; not following primitive usage or tradition.

a **1726** W. REEVES *Serm.* (1729) 259 That scandalous contempt and ridicule which some imprimitive Divines of late have put upon it.

†**imprin'cipiate,** *a. Obs. rare*⁻¹. [f. IM-² + L. *principi-um* beginning + -ATE².] Without a beginning or origin.

1683 CAVE *Ecclesiastici, Eusebius* 31 God..has a proper, unbegotten, imprincipiate Deity.

imprint ('ɪmprɪnt), *sb.* Forms: 5 em-, enpraynt(e, enprinte, enprynte, 6 imprynte, *Sc.* imprent, 7– imprint. [ME. type *empreynte*, *-printe*, a. F. *empreinte* 'a stampe, a violent assault' (Cotgr.), ppl. sb. from *empreind-re* (pa. pple. *empreint*); the prefix subseq. conformed to L.: see next. *Empreinte* was a formation of the same class as *armée, assise, conduite*, etc.]

I. 1. a. A figure impressed or imprinted upon something; a mark produced by pressure on a surface; an impression, stamp.

1483 CAXTON *Gold. Leg.* 109 b/2 Thy seal wherein is thenprynte of the crosse. **1526** *Pilgr. Perf.* (W. de W. 1531) 304 The Vernacle, whiche is the very similitude & imprynte of thy blessed & gloryous vysage. **1585** JAS. I *Ess. Poesie* (Arb.) 31 As into the wax the seals imprent Is lyke a seale. **1835** J. BATMAN in Cornwallis *New World* (1859) I. 411, I requested the chief..to give the imprint of his mark. **1851** LONGF. *Gold. Leg.* v. *Devil's Bridge*, I showed you..a bowlder Marked with the imprint of his shoulder.

b. *fig.* A character impressed upon something; an attribute communicated by, and constituting evidence of, some agency; 'stamp', 'impression'.

c **1600** SHAKS. *Sonn.* lxxvii, The vacant leaues thy mindes imprint will beare. **1854** J. S. C. ABBOTT *Napoleon* (1855) I. xxxii. 490 He has left upon the Continent an imprint of beneficence which time can not efface. **1874** SYMONDS *Sk. Italy & Greece* (1898) I. xi. 215 The form-giver has stamped his thought..and fire has made that imprint permanent.

c. A representation or type of something.

1857–8 SEARS *Athan.* xvii. 148 Has God hung down these pictures..as the most perfect imprints of the good and fair?

2. †**a.** The condition of being printed, printed form, 'print' (in phr. *in enprinte*). *Obs.* **b.** The printing of a book, etc. **c.** Something printed, an 'impression' *of* a writing.

1480 CAXTON *Descr. Brit.* 57, I haue sette them in enprinte according to the translacion of Treuisa. **1485** —— *Chas. Gt.* 2, I late had fynysshed in enprynte the book of the noble & vyctoryous kyng Arthur. **1882** *N. & Q.* 6th Ser. V. 300/1 An imprint of a part of Roger Dodsworth's Yorkshire collections. *Mod.* (Review) In Mr. Martineau's opinion Zurich is the most probable place of imprint.

3. a. The name of the publisher, place of publication, and date, printed in a book, usually at the foot of the title-page (formerly often at the end of the book); also, the name of printer and place of printing, printed at the end of the book, or on the back of the title-page: these are distinguished as the ***publisher's imprint*** and ***printer's imprint***.

1790 *Brit. Crit.* Feb. (T.), The imprint, as it is called in technical language, 'E Typographeo Clarendoniano', or 'At the Clarendon Press'. **1860** SALA *Lady Chesterf.* Pref. 3 Many professional critics confine their labours to reviewing the title and imprint of a book. **1893** E. G. DUFF *Early printed Bks.* 138 From the time of Caxton's death, in 1491, to the time when his own name first appears in an imprint, Wynkyn de Worde printed five books.

b. Extended use: see quots.

1876 C. A. CUTTER *Rules Dict. Catal.* §136 The imprint consists of place of publication, publisher's name, date, number of volumes, typographic form, number of pages, and number of maps, engravings, and the like. **1972** *Times Lit. Suppl.* 27 Oct. 1276/5 (Advt.), Kahn & Averill (imprint of Stanmore Press Ltd.). **1973** *Ibid.* 2 Feb. 121/4 (Advt.), Diana Burfield who, before her resignation last summer after seventeen years with the imprint, was editorial director of Tavistock [Publications].

4. (With capital initial.) An old-style type face, named after the periodical for which it was designed.

1913 *Imprint* Jan. p. vi, The newly designed type in which our pages are presented to the reader was cut by the Lanston Monotype Company at our instance... The type has been christened Imprint Old Face. **1934** A. F. JOHNSON *Type Designs* iv. 120 The first acceptable book type to be cut after the Old Style of 1860 was the 'Monotype' Imprint of 1913. **1966** P. M. HANDOVER in K. Day *Bk. Typogr. 1815–1965* 160 Imprint was a reformed Caslon, regularised on the principles that had inspired old style which now resulted in another more distinguished face.

†**II. 5.** An onset, assault, charge. Cf. IMPRESSION 1 b. *Obs.*

c **1489** CAXTON *Blanchardyn* xx. 62 So moche he made atte the first empraynte, that ar euere his spere was broken, he threwe doune ded syx of his enemyes. —— *Four Sonnes Aymon* xx. 453 Eche of theim overthrew vii knightes at that enpraynt.

imprint (ɪm'prɪnt), *v.* Forms: α. 4–6 em-, en-, -print, -prynt, -prent, 5 empreynt, emprende, enprend. β. 5 inprent, impraynt, imprend, 5 (6 *Sc.*) imprent, 6 imprynt, 5– imprint. [ME. *empreynte-n*, *-prent-*, *-print-*, partly a. OF. *empreinte-r*, *-priente-r*, a secondary vb. (through *empreinte* sb.) from *empreind-re* (pa. pple. *empreint*) 'to print, also to assaile or set on with violence' (Cotgr.):—*empriembre*:—late pop. L. *impremĕre*, for cl. L. *imprimĕre* to impress, imprint; partly (in form *emprende*) immediately from *empreind-re*; the eventual form being largely due to the F. pa. pple. *empreint*

'imprinted', and the prefix conformed to L. as in IMPRINT *sb.*: cf. PRINT *v.*]

1. a. *trans.* To mark by pressure; to impress, stamp (a figure, etc. *on* something); to delineate by pressure. In first quot., to take an impression of (a solid body).

α. *c* **1386** CHAUCER *Merch. T.* 873 This fresshe May..In warm wex hath emprented [*Harl.* emprynted] the clyket And Damyan..The cliket countrefeted pryuely. *c* **1420** LYDG. *Thebes* 901 The Carectys of his woundes olde Upon his fete emprented wonder depe. **1502** *Ord. Crysten Men* (W. de W. 1506) I. iii. 20 Unto whome we haue enprynted in the forhede the sygne of the crosse.

β. *c* **1440** *Promp. Parv.* 262/1 Inprentyn (*MSS. K. & S.* imprentyn), *inprimo.* **1600** E. BLOUNT tr. *Conestaggio* 26 Leaving with them a Seale which did imprint with inke this word REII. *a* **1631** DRAYTON *Quest Cynthia* vii, Then looking on the ground, The shape of her most dainty foot Imprinted there I found. **1670–98** LASSELS *Voy. Italy* II. 22 The Volto Santo or print of our Saviour's face, which he imprinted in the handkerchief of St. Veronica. **1870** DICKENS *E. Drood* iii, Each sometimes stops and slowly imprints a deeper footstep in the fallen leaves.

†**b.** To portray (by some printing process). *Obs.*

1592 *Nobody & Someb.* in Simpson *Sch. Shaks.* (1878) I. 309 Let him be straight imprinted to the life; His picture shall be set on every stall.

†**2.** To impress (letters or characters) on paper or the like by means of type; to PRINT (a book or writing). *Obs.*

α. **1474** CAXTON *Chesse* Pref., By cause thys sayd book is ful of holsom wysedom..I have purposed to enprynte it. **1477** —— in *Earl Rivers' Dictes* 145 Here endeth the book named the dictes or sayengis of the philosophres enprynted by me William Caxton at Westmestre the yere of our lord .M.CCCC.lxxvij. **1493** *Petronilla* (*ad fin.*), Empryntyd by Rychard Pynson. **1496** *Bk. St. Albans, Fishing* 41 Yf it were enpryntyd allone by itself & put in a lytyll plaunflet. **1538** BALE *Thre Lawes* 1971 Enprent their declaracyon.

β. *c* **1500** *Love & Compl. Mars & Venus* (Colophon), Thys in pryntide in westmoster in kyng strete. For me Julianus Notarii. **1509** BARCLAY *Shyp of Folys* (title-p.), Inprentyd in the Cyte of London in Fletestre at the signe of Saynt George By Rycharde Pynson. **1548** HALL *Chron., Hen. VIII* 186 Willyam Tyndale had newly translated and imprinted the Newe Testament in Englishe. **1556** LAUDER *Tractate* (1864) 21 Imprentit, In the yeir of God Ane M.U.C.LUI. **1576** FLEMING *Panopl. Epist.* 114 *note*, So are the woordes set down in three auncient copies: and not..as in some bookes it is imprinted. **1611** BIBLE (*title-p.*), Imprinted at London by Robert Barker, Printer to the Kings most Excellent Maiestie. **1651** HOBBES *Leviath.* II. xxx. 176 Clean paper, fit to receive whatsoever..shall be imprinted in them. **1709** SWIFT *Merlin's Proph.*, In an old edition of Merlin's prophecies, imprinted at London..in the year 1530.

3. *fig.* **a.** To impress *on* or fix *in* the mind, memory, etc.; formerly often, to impress on one's own mind, consider or remember carefully.

α. *c* **1374** CHAUCER *Boeth.* v. metr. iv. 129 (Camb. MS.) Ymagynacions of sensible thinges weeren enpreynted [*Add. MS.* (*a* 1420) inprentid] in to sowles fro bodies with-owte forth. *c* **1386** —— *Merch. T.* 934 Ye been so depe enprented in my thoght. **1412–20** LYDG. *Chron. Troy* I. v, What that she sawe both in minde & thought She all emprynteth. *c* **1440** CAPGRAVE *St. Kath.* III. 580 Soo enprended it is On-to hir herte. **1493** *Festivall* (W. de W. 1515) 125 These vysyons were soo enprynted in this chyldes mynde. **1553** DOUGLAS *Æneis* XII. x. 16 Than of ane greter bargane in his entent All suddanly the figure dyd emprent [*MS.* imprent].

β. *a* **1420** [see *a c* 1374]. **1461** *Paston Lett.* No. 423 II. 66 Sorowe is imprended in myn hert. **1490** CAXTON *Eneydos* xiii. 48 Desirynge the presence of Eneas by Imagynacyon impraynted wythin the fauntasme of her entendemente. **1529** MORE *Comf. agst. Trib.* II. Wks. 1196/1 Some..haue with long and often thinking theron, imprinted that feare so sore in theyr ymaginacion. **1576** FLEMING *Panopl. Epist.* 24 Imprint this in thy memorie. **1643** MILTON *Divorce* II. iv, Not otherwise then to the law of nature and of equity imprinted in us seems correspondent. **1712** ADDISON *Spect.* No. 415 ⁋6 Every thing that is Majestick imprints an Awfulness and Reverence on the Mind of the Beholder. **1796** MORSE *Amer. Geog.* I. 95 It is the business of the women to notice every thing that passes, to imprint it on their memories. **1877** E. R. CONDER *Bas. Faith* ii. 75 As we are incorrectly wont to say, imprint themselves on the memory; but to speak more justly, which memory firmly retains.

b. To impress (a quality, character, or distinguishing mark) *on* or *in* a person or thing; to communicate, impart. In *pass.* of a quality, etc.: To exist strongly marked *in* or *on* a person, etc.

1526 *Pilgr. Perf.* (W. de W. 1531) 273 b, Why than sholde we be aboute to imprynt suche swetenesse in to carnall affeccyons? **1561** T. NORTON *Calvin's Inst.* I. 53 Euen in the vices themselues there remain emprinted some leauinges thereof. **1615** G. SANDYS *Trav.* 60 Repugnant to sound reason, and that wisedome which the Divine hand hath imprinted in his workes. **1744** AKENSIDE *Pleas. Imag.* III. 523 God alone, when first his active hand Imprints the secret byass of the soul. **1853** J. H. NEWMAN *Hist. Sk.* (1873) II. I. iii. 118 The misery and degradation which are at present imprinted on the very face of the soil.

4. a. *transf.* To make an impression or impressed figure upon; to stamp or impress (something) *with* a figure, etc.

c **1400** MAUNDEV. (1839) xxii. 239 Money..Of lether emprented or of papyre. **1596** DALRYMPLE tr. *Leslie's Hist. Scot.* I. 1 The way..sa deip imprented with the futstepis of thair foirbears. **1717** PRIOR *Henry & Emma* 655 She..sees his num'rous herds imprint her sands. **1818** MRS. SHELLEY *Frankenst.* i. (1865) 10 A land never before imprinted by the foot of man. **1856** STANLEY *Sinai & Pal.* xiv. (1858) 452 The roche..pointed out..as imprinted with the footstep of our Saviour.

b. *fig.* (*transf.* from 3 a and b). To impress *with* some feeling, quality, etc.; also of the quality, To be impressed upon, manifest itself in.

a **1732** GAY *Arachne* 107 Dread omnipotence imprints his face. **1765** H. WALPOLE *Otranto* i, Manfred..had imprinted her mind with terror.

5. *Animal Behaviour.* To bring about in (a social animal, usu. a young one) a state of habitual recognition of or trust in another animal or an object, which may thus come to be regarded as a parent; const. *to* or *on* the object of recognition. Also, of an animal or thing: to become established as an object of recognition or trust in the behaviour pattern of (a young animal) (quot. 1967): see IMPRINTING *vbl. sb.* 2. Usu. as *pa. pple.* **imprinted**.

1951 *Ibis* XCIII. 259 Young Partridges which had been caught after the fields had been mowed but were still only a few hours old had nevertheless already become definitely imprinted to their normal parents. **1956** W. H. THORPE *Learning & Instinct in Animals* vi. 116 The parent Cichlid fish may become imprinted to the young as well as the young to the parent. **1963** *Ibid.* (ed. 2) xv. 414 If young birds are kept together in groups they are harder to imprint than if they are kept singly. **1966** R. & D. MORRIS *Men & Apes* iii. 57 Monkeys imprinted on human beings as babies will readily accept them as sexual partners on reaching maturity. **1967** M. ARGYLE *Psychol. Interpersonal Behaviour* i. 23 Dogs raised by humans, may be imprinted by them, and human babies who are reared by wolves may fail to be imprinted by humans. **1972** *Nature* 2 June 287/2 Many hand-reared birds become imprinted on their human handlers if isolated from their parents at an early age. **1972** *Sci. Amer.* Aug. 25/3 We also took wild ducklings from their natural mother 16 hours after hatching and tried to imprint them to humans.

imprinted (ɪm'prɪntɪd), *ppl. a.*^{1} [f. prec. vb. + -ED^{1}.] Impressed, stamped, printed: see the verb.

1561 T. NORTON *Calvin's Inst.* I. 3 b, This imprinted persuasion of God is of most greate force. **1746–7** HERVEY *Medit.* (1818) 140 As the wax is turned to the imprinted seal. **1836** J. H. NEWMAN in *Lyra Apost.*, *Shame* iii, Saviour! wash out the imprinted shame. **1888** *Century Mag.* XXXVI. 763/1 The bearer of the imprinted piece of paper.

'imprinted, *ppl. a.*^{2} [f. IMPRINT *sb.* + -ED^{2}.] Bearing a bookseller's own imprint (IMPRINT *sb.* 3).

1926 *Publishers' Weekly* 17 July 181/2 A month before publication 300,000 imprinted postcards had been asked for. **1927** *Ibid.* 25 June 2371 Imprinted brochures are now ready for distribution.

imprinter (ɪm'prɪntə(r)). [f. IMPRINT *v.* + -ER^{1}.] One who or that which imprints or impresses; †a printer (*obs.*). With quot. 1638 cf. IMPRIMENT.

1548–9 (Mar.) *Bk. Com. Prayer* Colophon, The Imprinter to sell this Booke in Queres. **1561** T. NORTON *Calvin's Inst.* Pref. Contents, I doe pray and request the Readers that if they doe finde any [mistakes], they shall advertise the Imprinter. **1638** RAWLEY tr. *Bacon's Life & Death* 421 Malacissation is wrought, by Consubstantials; by Imprinters; and by Closers up. [BACON *Hist. Vitæ & Mortis* Canon xxvi. 443 Malacissatio fit, per Consubstantialia, Imprimentia, & Occludentia.] *a* **1849** J. C. MANGAN *Poems* (1859) 333 Are forty winters such faint imprinters Of age on a thing of thy mould?

imprinting (ɪm'prɪntɪŋ), *vbl. sb.* [f. as prec. + -ING^{1}.] **1.** The action of the verb IMPRINT, q.v.; †*spec.* printing (of books) (*obs.*).

c **1440** *Promp. Parv.* 262/1 Inprentynge, *impressio.* **1480** CAXTON *Chron. Eng.* cclvii. (1482) 336 Aboute this tyme [1455] the craft of enpryntynge was first founde in Magunce in Almayne. **1568** GRAFTON *Chron.* II. 637 This yere one named Johannes Fauscius, a Germain, first found out the noble science of Imprintyng in the Citie of Mentz. **1581** J. BELL *Haddon's Answ. Osor.* 480 b, The singular and most excellent Art of Emprinting. **1628** in Rushw. *Hist. Coll.* (1659) I. 621 The imprinting of such as are written against them, and in defence of the Orthodox Church, are hindred.

2. *Animal Behaviour.* The establishment of a behaviour pattern of recognition and trust, usu. directed at its own species, during a critical period of susceptibility in a (young) social animal, esp. in birds.

1937 K. LORENZ in *Auk* LIV. 262 This process of acquiring the biologically 'right' object of social reactions by conditioning them, not to one individual fellow-member of the species, but to the species as such, is so very peculiar that I have thought it necessary to use a particular word to describe it. I have called it 'Prägung' in German, which I propose to translate into English by the term 'imprinting'. **1953** J. S. HUXLEY *Evolution in Action* iv. 102 Young geese which have been hatched in an incubator will attach themselves to birds of other species or even to human beings and follow them about as if they were their real parents. This so-called 'imprinting' has to take place during a critical period soon after hatching, only takes a minute or so, and is then irreversible. **1967** M. ARGYLE *Psychol. Interpersonal Behaviour* i. 17 There may be 'imprinting' during the first year of life: the infant becomes attached to the dominant moving object in its environment, and does its best to follow that object. **1970** *Primate Behavior* I. 130 Imprinting data suggest that in birds early experiences before or during a critical period can influence social attachment in a relatively permanent fashion.

im'printing, *ppl. a.* [-ING^{2}.] That imprints: see the verb. In quot., †That imprints or impresses something on the mind, impressive (*obs.*).

c **1592** BACON *Confer. Pleas.* (1870) 12 Him that would offer the most pleasing object to the most imprinting sence.

Hence †**im'printingly** *adv. Obs.*, impressively.

1594 NASHE *Terrors of Night* G iij, To the end their naturall..portions might be more imprintingly apprehended.

imprison (ɪm'prɪz(ə)n), *v.* Forms: α. 3–4 **enprisone**, 4 **enprisounne**, **-presone**, 5 **-prisoun**, **-prysone**, **emprisone**, **-oun**, **-presoun**, 6 **enprison**, **-pryson**, 6 **emprison**. β. 5– **imprison**, (5–6 **in-**, 6 **impryson**, **ympreson**). [ME., a. OF. *en-*, *emprisoner* (12th c. in Hatz.-Darm.), mod.F. *emprisonner*, f. *en-*, *in-* (IN-^{2}) + *prison* PRISON: cf. Pr. *empreisonar*, It. *imprigionare*.]

1. *trans.* To put into prison, to confine in a prison or other place of confinement; to detain in custody, to keep in close confinement; to incarcerate.

α. **1297** R. GLOUC. (Rolls) 9521 Muche robberie me dude aboute in euerich toun, And bounde men & enprisonede, vor te hii finede raunson. *c* **1380** *Sir Ferumb.* 1181 Enprisone hem her wiþ-inne þy tours, & so þer let hem lye. *c* **1400** MAUNDEV. (Roxb.) vi. 19 Guytoga..empresound him in þe castell. *Ibid.* x. 40 He was emprisouned in many placez. **1568** GRAFTON *Chron.* II. 376 He did emprison them in dyverse prisons, commaundyng the jaylours to kepe them streyt in Irons. **1574** tr. *Littleton's Tenures* 43 a, He maye enprison his villaine.

β. *c* **1450** *R. Gloucester's Chron.* (1724) 464 *note* (MS. Coll. Arms) The Kynge..toke this Geffray, and imprisoned him. **1513** BRADSHAW *St. Werburge* I. 1599 And how into Egypt yonge Ioseph was solde, There was inprysoned by a false coniectour. **1522** MORE *De Quat. Noviss.* Wks. 84/1 In worse case be we, than those yt be taken & imprisoned for theft. **1611** BIBLE *Acts* xxii. 19 Lord, they know that I imprisoned [TINDALE presoned]..them that beleeued on thee. **1771** *Junius Lett.* xliv. 236 They have no legal authority to imprison any man. **1845** S. AUSTIN *Ranke's Hist. Ref.* III. 621 They imprison men and women, and make inquisition into their faith.

b. In more general sense: To confine.

c **1586** C'TESS PEMBROKE *Ps.* LXXI. iv, Since imprison'd in my mother Thou me freed'st. **1610** SHAKS. *Temp.* I. ii. 278 She did confine thee..Into a clouen Pyne, within which rift Imprison'd, thou didst painefully remaine A dozen yeeres. **1651** HOBBES *Leviath.* II. xxi. 107 All living creatures, whilst they are imprisoned..with walls, or chayns. **1682** CREECH *Lucretius* (1683) IV. 110 As when the hindring door Imprisons up the longing Eye no more. **1725** WATTS *Logic* II. iv. §6 If a Man imprison himself in his Closet, and employ the most exquisite Powers of Reason to find out the Nature of Things. *a* **1821** KEATS *Ode Melancholy* 19 If thy mistress some rich anger shows, Imprison her soft hand, and let her rave. **1841** LANE *Arab. Nts.* I. 97 Therefore will I put thee to death imprisoned in this bottle.

2. *transf.* and *fig.* To confine, shut up: in various connexions, in which either the confining agent or cause, or the object confined, or the nature of the confinement, or both, are other than physical, or in which the object is inanimate.

a **1533** LD. BERNERS *Gold. Bk. M. Aurel.* (1546) Nn vj, Thou enprysonedst my harte at thy wyndowe. **1576** FLEMING *Panopl. Epist.* 78 Alas..that we..should be thus imprisoned in perplexities. **1613** PURCHAS *Pilgrimage* (1614) 429 They have much gold, but hold it an high offence to imprison it..in Chests or Treasuries. *Ibid.* 739 An extreame Fogge, as double gard to that Iland (uncertaine weather to fortifie it, or to imprison them). **1634** SIR T. HERBERT *Trav.* 55 At this time such raine, thunder and lightning fell upon us, that wee were imprisoned in our Tents. **1671** MILTON *Samson* 8, I, a prisoner chained, scarce freely draw The air imprisoned also. **1675** TRAHERNE *Chr. Ethics* 519 It is a great mistake..so far to imprison our love to our selves, as to make it inconsistent with charity towards others. **1691** TRYON *Wisd. Dictates* 2 Imprison thy Tongue lest it imprison thee. *a* **1700** DRYDEN (J.), Try to imprison the resistless wind. **1820** KEATS *St. Agnes* ii, The sculptured dead..Emprison'd in black, purgatorial rails.

Hence **im'prisoned** *ppl. a.*, **im'prisoning** *vbl. sb.* and *ppl. a.*; **im'prisoner**, one who imprisons.

1529 MORE *Suppl. Soulys* Wks. 317/2 These poore emprisoned soules whome Christ..by his precious bloude..delyuered out of the lake of fyre wherin they lay bounden for their sinnes. *c* **1542** UDALL in *Royster D.* (Shaks. Soc.) p. xix, None ympresonyng, noo tormentes. **1615** G. SANDYS *Trav.* 243 Which heates the imprisoning rockes, when hot it growes. **1656** PRYNNE *Rights Eng. Freemen* 30 Any Levier of them [taxes], or imprisoner of refusers of them. **1855** MACAULAY *Hist. Eng.* xvii. IV. 107 The imprisoned officer was liberated. **1879** GEO. ELIOT *Theo. Such* 14 A partial release from the imprisoning verdict, that a man's philosophy is the formula of his personality.

†**im'prison,** *sb. Obs. rare.* [f. prec. vb.] Imprisonment.

1509 HAWES *Past. Pleas.* XXXIII. (Percy Soc.) 159 But yet they hoped for to have releve Of theyr imprison which did them so greve.

imprisonable (ɪm'prɪz(ə)nəb(ə)l), *a.* [f. prec. vb. + -ABLE.] **1.** Capable of or liable to imprisonment.

1622 CALLIS *Stat. Sewers* (1647) 133, I am of opinion that a person is both Fineable and Imprisonable. **1659** RUSHW. *Hist. Coll.* I. 533 He said he would prove a free man imprisonable upon command or pleasure, without cause expressed, to be absolutely in worse case then a villain.

2. Of an offence, etc.: for which a person can be imprisoned.

1971 *Daily Tel.* 31 July 11/2 Before a court recommends deportation of a Commonwealth citizen who has been convicted of an imprisonable offence, the offender must be given at least seven days clear notice.

imprisonment (ɪmˈprɪz(ə)nmənt). Forms: see IMPRISON *v.* [ME. *en-*, *emprisonement*, a. AF. *enprisounement* (Britton), OF. *emprisonnement* (13th c.), f. *emprisonner* to IMPRISON + -MENT.] The action of imprisoning, or fact or condition of being imprisoned; detention in a prison or place of confinement; close or irksome confinement; 'forcible restraint within bounds'; incarceration.

α. [**1292** BRITTON I. ii. §11 Sur peyne de enprisounement et de greef raunsoun.] **13..** *E.E. Allit. P.* B. 46 On payne of enprysonment & puttyng in stokkez. **1389** in *Eng. Gilds* (1870) 5 He sha[l] haue xiiij *d.* duryng hys enpresonement, euery wyk. *c***1440** *Jacob's Well* (E.E.T.S.) 93 In fals enprisonement, or fals qwest, or false dome. **1590** H. BARROW in Greenwood *Collect. Sclaund. Art.* D ij b, I.. haue euer since bene kept in most streight emprisonment.

β. **1415** *Proclam.* in *York Myst.* Introd. 34 Of payne of forfaiture of yaire wapen and inprisonment of yaire bodys. **1467** in *Eng. Gilds* (1870) 388 Inprisonment of hur bodyes at the kyngez wylle. **1513** MORE *Rich. III*, Wks. 52/1 For they would remembre their imprisonment. **1651** HOBBES *Leviath.* II. xxviii. 164 *Imprisonment*, is when a man is by publique Authority deprived of liberty. **1780** BURKE *Sp. Bristol previous to Elect.* Wks. III. 389 It is but six or seven years since a clergyman of the name of Malony..was condemned to perpetual imprisonment for exercising the functions of his Religion. **1817** W. SELWYN *Law Nisi Prius* (ed. 4) II. 851 An action for false imprisonment was brought by a native and inhabitant of Minorca..against the governor of the island.

b. *transf.* and *fig.* See IMPRISON *v.* 2.

1576 FLEMING *Panopl. Epist.* 226 Into the slavishe imprisonment of vices most detestable: yea, into that bondage it bringeth them. *c***1614** SIR W. MURE *Dido & Æneas* I. 211 At such impresonement they oft, repining, Lowd bellowing all break out. **1670** CLARENDON *Contempl. Ps.* in *Tracts* (1727) 611 No imprisonment is so unworthy, as to be inclosed by our servants, by our own narrow and sordid affections. **1856** KANE *Arct. Expl.* II. xviii. 187 The manly fortitude with which they bore up during this painful imprisonment.

†imˈprivacy, *v.* *Obs. rare.* [f. IM-¹ + PRIVACY.] *trans.* To place in privacy; to secrete.

*a***1670** HACKET *Cent. Serm.* (1675) 600 To what purpose doth..Saul imprivacy himself in a cave?

imprive: see IMPREVE.

†imˈproachable, *a.* *Obs.* In 6 improcheable. [f. IM-² + PROCHE *v.* to approach + -ABLE.] Unapproachable.

1571 DIGGES *Pantom.* I. xi. D ij b, With the ayde of two places to search out improcheable heightes.

improbability (ɪmprɒbəˈbɪlɪtɪ). [f. IMPROBABLE: see -ITY. Cf. F. *improbabilité* (1776).] The quality of being improbable; unlikelihood.

1598 FLORIO, *Improb[ab]ilita*, improbabilitie. **1617** MORYSON *Itin.* II. 245 The improbabilitie of their comming. **1690** LOCKE *Hum. Und.* IV. xv. 332 But there [are] degrees ..from the very neighbourhood of Certainty and Evidence, quite down to Improbability and Unlikeliness, even to the Confines of Impossibility. **1749** F. SMITH *Voy. Disc.* II. 332 The sending a Person over Land, carries not the least Air of Improbability with it. **1862** HEURTLEY in *Repl. to Ess. & Rev.* 144 There is no longer any antecedent improbability to be overcome.

b. with *an* and *pl.* An instance of this; an improbable circumstance; something unlikely.

1611 CORYAT *Crudities* 97 It is a meere improbability, yea and an impossibility, that this should be the true Serpent. **1612-15** BP. HALL *Contempl., O.T.* v. i, It is the praise of omnipotencie to worke by improbabilities. **1699** BENTLEY *Phal.* 76 Which is to add another Improbability to all that have gone before. **1876** MOZLEY *Univ. Serm.* v. 111 A universal empire..is..a physical improbability.

imˈprobabilize, *v.* *rare.* [f. IMPROBABLE + -IZE.] *trans.* To render improbable.

1820-27 BENTHAM *Princ. Judic. Proced.* Pref. Wks. 1838-43 II. 5/2 The fear of seeing real improvement obstructed and even improbabilized by the creation of new offices, with enormous salaries attached to them.

improbable (ɪmˈprɒbəb(ə)l), *a.* [ad. L. *improbābil-is*, f. *im-* (IM-²) + *probābilis* probable, likely: cf. F. *improbable* (1611 in Cotgr.).]

1. a. Not probable; not likely to be true; not easy to believe; unlikely.

1598 FLORIO, *Improbabile*, that cannot be prooued, improbable. **1600** E. BLOUNT tr. *Conestaggio* 90 They pleaded against the most Christian Queene, that her pretention was improbable. **1601** SHAKS. *Twel. N.* III. iv. 141 If this were plaid vpon a stage now, I could condemne it as an improbable fiction. **1710** STEELE & ADDISON *Tatler* No. 254 ¶2 Were they not so well attested, [they] would appear altogether improbable. **1770** *Junius Lett.* xxxix. 193, I think it was highly improbable. **1860** TYNDALL *Glac.* II. xxx. 407, I agree..in regarding the explanation as improbable.

b. Qualifying a clause, usually introduced by *it*.

1617 MORYSON *Itin.* I. 30 Though it bee improbable that there should be any want of waters. **1674** tr. *Scheffer's Lapland* 24 It is very improbable that so many Christian Kings should take no care of propagating their Religion. **1790** PALEY *Horæ Paul.* Rom. i. 11 It is in the highest degree improbable that it should have been the effect of contrivance and design. **1836** MACAULAY *Ess.*, *Temple* (1887) 448 When two armies fight, it is not improbable that one of them will be very soundly beaten. *Mod.* That he will succeed is highly improbable.

c. With complement. *rare.*

1647 CLARENDON *Hist. Reb.* VIII. §179 Nor was the design improbable to succeed. **1654-66** LD. ORRERY *Parthenissa* (1676) 241 His Love could not be more improbable of success than Perolla's had been.

2. In pregnant sense: Unlikely to 'do', suit, etc. Also, that does not 'look the part'.

1659 HAMMOND *On Ps.* civ. 16-18 And that in the most improbable soile. **1958** *Times* 18 Apr. 11/7 An immense arched building of blue painted woods decorated with an improbable metal dove. *Ibid.* 14 May 15/1 As if it were miraculous that this gentle and improbable individual should exist at all.

Hence **imˈprobableness**, improbability.

1727 in BAILEY vol. II.

improbably (ɪmˈprɒbəblɪ), *adv.* [f. prec. + -LY².] In an improbable manner; without likelihood.

(Usually qualifying the statement as a whole, and denoting that it is not likely to be true; now chiefly in ***not improbably***, an expression for 'with more or less probability'.)

1646 SIR T. BROWNE *Pseud. Ep.* IV. xiii. 229 That he lived and writ in these parts, is not improbably collected from the Epistles that passed betwixt him and Artaxerxes. **1670** MILTON *Hist. Eng.* III. Wks. (1847) 504/2 Dioneth, an imaginary king of Britain, or duke of Cornwal, who improbably sided with them against his own country. *a***1691** BOYLE (J.), He speaks very improbably. *a***1808** HURD *Proph.* App. (R.), A few years more may, not improbably, leave him without one admirer. *Mod.* He is coming to Oxford soon, and may not improbably call on me.

†ˈimprobate, *a.* *Obs.* *rare*⁻¹. In 6 (*Sc.*) -at. [f. L. *improbāt-us* blamed, condemned, or L. *improbus* wicked: see -ATE².] Wicked.

1596 DALRYMPLE tr. *Leslie's Hist. Scot.* IV. 220 Throuch his awne exemple the improbat he teached.

†improbate, *v.* *Obs.* *rare*⁻⁰. [f. L. *improbāt-*, ppl. stem of *improbāre* to disapprove, blame, condemn, reject, make void, f. *im-* (IM-²) + *probāre* to make good, pronounce good, approve.] *trans.* To disapprove, disallow.

1656 BLOUNT *Glossogr.*, *Improbate*, to disallow, to dispraise, or dislike.

improbation (ɪmprəʊˈbeɪʃən). [ad. L. *improbātiōn-em*, n. of action from *improbāre*: see IMPROBATE *v.* Cf. F. *improbation* (1504 in Hatz.-Darm.).]

†1. Disapprobation, disapproval. *Obs.*

1656 STANLEY *Hist. Philos.* v. (1701) 225/2 He with-holds from answering, either in approbation, or improbation of something. *a***1677** MANTON *Serm. Ps.* cxix. verse 143 Wks. 1872 IX. 16 God discovered his approbation and improbation then more by temporal mercies and temporal judgments. **1789** BENTHAM *Princ. Legisl.* Wks. 1843 I. 51 These, if they call it honour, will prefix an epithet of improbation to it, and call it false honour.

†2. Disproof, confutation. *Obs. rare* (in *gen.* sense: cf. next).

1551 RECORDE *Cast. Knowl.* IV. (1556) 118 As the firste improbation doth reproue the flatnes of the earth betwene easte and weste,..so this second confutation improueth the opinion of plainesse betwene south and north. **1657** TOMLINSON *Renou's Disp.* 275 The conjecture is not worth the improbation. **1657** *Physical Dict.*, *Improbation*, disproving.

3. *Sc. Law.* Disproof of a writ; an action brought to prove a document to be false or forged.

*c***1575** BALFOUR *Practicks* (1754) 381 Anent improbatioun. **1609** SKENE *Reg. Maj.* 122 The first is called the direct maner of improbation, be the witnes insert in the wreit, quhilk is taken to be improven. **1637** RUTHERFORD *Lett.* (1862) I. 422 Summons of improbation to prove our charters of Christ to be counterfeits, are raised against poor souls. **1752** J. LOUTHIAN *Form of Process* (ed. 2) 15 Indicting the Prisoner in the Terms of the Decreet of Improbation. **1861** W. BELL *Dict. Law Scot.*, *Improbation* is the disproving and setting aside of writs *ex facie* probative on the grounds of falsehood or forgery. The form of process by which this is generally done is an action of reduction-improbation.

improbative (ɪmˈprɒbətɪv), *a.* [f. L. *improbāt-*, ppl. stem of *improbāre* IMPROBATE *v.* + -IVE.]

1. Liable to improbation or disproof; not proved to be true or genuine.

1754 ERSKINE *Princ. Sc. Law* (1809) 517 Where witnesses attest a deed without knowing the granter, and seeing him subscribe..the deed is not only improbative, but such witnesses are declared accessory to forgery. **1866** *Guide to Elgin Cathedral* iv. 226 Some respect ought to be paid to universal tradition however improbative.

2. = IMPROBATORY.

1876 LOWELL *Among my Bks.* Ser. II. 44 'The form or mode of treatment', he [Dante] says, 'is..definitive, divisive, probative, improbative, and positive of examples'.

improbatory (ɪmˈprɒbətərɪ), *a.* [f. as prec. + -ORY.] Having the function of disproving; in *Sc. Law*, made in improbation or disproof of a writ.

1828 in W. Bell *Dict. Law Scot.* (1861) 76 [When the writing has been abidden by, the record is made up] by ordering a condescendence of articles improbatory, and answers containing articles approbatory, which shall be revised and accompanied with notes of pleas in law. **1861** *Ibid.*, These articles improbatory and approbatory consist of articulate averments and answers..setting forth the facts and circumstances relied on by the one party, as instructing the alleged forgery or falsehood, and by the other, as showing the writing to be genuine and fairly come by.

†improbe. *Obs. rare.* [a. OF. *improbe* (15th c. in Hatz.-Darm.), ad. L. *improbus* bad, wicked, f. *im-* (IM-²) + *probus* good.] A wicked person.

1484 CAXTON *Fables of Æsop* (1889) 1 The malyce off the euylle people, and the argument off the Improbes.

improbity (ɪmˈprɒbɪtɪ, -ˈprəʊbɪtɪ). [ad. L. *improbitās*, f. *improbus* wicked, persistent: cf. OF. *improbité* (14th c. in Godef. *Compl.*).]

†1. Persistency, perseverance. *Obs.* or *nonce-use.*

*c***1380** WYCLIF *Serm.* Sel. Wks. II. 154 Þis lastinge knocking is purging of man þat haþ lyved synfully; þis improbite to þis purpos is just tariyng of God. **1883** *Athenæum* 19 May 627 The reader who has had the improbity (in the untranslatable Latin sense of *improbus*) to follow M. Renan carefully.

2. Wickedness, want of principle or integrity.

1594 HOOKER *Eccl. Pol.* III. i. §7 Persons excommunicable, yea and cast out for notorious improbitie. **1695** LD. PRESTON *Boeth.* IV. 198 That the exuberant Improbity of ill Men may be repell'd and abated. **1731** MEDLEY *Kolben's Cape G. Hope* I. 27 His countrymen, among whom..all Improbity is abhorred. **1848** MILL *Pol. Econ.* I. vii. §5 The waste of wealth occasioned to Society by human improbity.

†ˈimprobous, *a.* *Obs. rare.* [f. L. *improb-us* or F. *improbe* + -OUS] Wicked, unprincipled. Hence **†ˈimprobously** *adv.*, wickedly; violently.

1657 TOMLINSON *Renou's Disp.* 295 One [nettle] whose leaves are improbously mordacious. *Ibid.* 596 Alas! the improbous do so impose upon us.

†improbration. *Obs. rare.* [f. IM-¹ + L. *probr-um* reproach + -ATION: cf. L. *exprobrātio* reproach, med.L. *improbrōs-us* disgraceful, and OF. *improperer* to reproach as shameful, address reproaches to (whence perh. an OF. *improperation*).] Reproach, reviling.

1526 *Pilgr. Perf.* (W. de W. 1531) 301 They dyd leade the bounden..with all..improbracyons, sclaunders, false contumelyes.

†improˈcerous, *a.* *Obs.* *rare*⁻⁰. [f. L. *imprōcēr-us* not tall + -OUS.] So **†improˈcerity**.

1656 BLOUNT *Glossogr.*, *Improcerous*, low, not tall. **1658** PHILLIPS, *Improcerity*, a lownesse, want of tallnesse.

†imˈprocreable, *a.* *Obs.* *rare*⁻⁰. [ad. L. *imprōcreābilis* that cannot be procreated.] So **†improcreaˈbility**. (See quots.)

1623 COCKERAM, *Improcreable*, not begotten. **1658** PHILLIPS, *Improcreability*, a barrennesse, or unaptnesse to procreate.

improcuraˈbility. *rare.* [f. **improcurable* (f. IM-² + PROCURABLE): see -ITY.] The condition of being unprocurable.

1876 MRS. WHITNEY *Sights & Ins.* II. xxxiii. 619 Absolute novelty and improcurability elsewhere or forever.

†improˈduced, *ppl. a.* [f. IM-² + PRODUCED.] Not produced from anything else; unproduced.

1662 STILLINGFL. *Orig. Sacr.* III. ii. §10 There will bee three real improduced things. **1692** RAY *Dissol. World* (1713) 4 They make no mention of the Creation of this Chaos, but seem to look upon it as self-existent and improduced.

improˈducible, *a.* *rare.* [f. IM-² + PRODUCIBLE.] Incapable of being produced; unproducible; unfit to be produced, unpresentable.

1704 NORRIS *Ideal World* II. viii. 381 We cannot produce them, and that because they are absolutely improducible. **1820** COLTON *Lacon* I. 93 Dr. Johnson was pronounced to be an improducible man by a Courtier.

†improˈduction. *Obs. rare.* [f. IM-² + PRODUCTION.] The condition of not having been produced from anything else.

1662 STILLINGFL. *Orig. Sacr.* III. ii. §10 The eternity and improduction of matter as the passive principle of things. **1678** CUDWORTH *Intell. Syst.* I. iv. §6. 197 Hermogenes and other[s]..assert the self-existence and Improduction of the Matter.

†improˈficience. *Obs.* *rare*⁻¹. [f. IM-² + PROFICIENCE.] = next.

1605 BACON *Adv. Learn.* II. vii. §7 This misplacing hath caused a deficience, or at least a great improficience in the Sciences.

improˈficiency. Now *rare.* Also 7 in-. [f. IM-² + PROFICIENCY.] Lack of proficiency; unskilfulness, backwardness.

1647 BOYLE *Let.* 20 Feb. in *Wks.* (1772) I. Life 35 The excellency of the Ministry, since waited on by such an improficiency, increases my presaging fears. **1661** FELTHAM *Resolves* II. xlv. 271 The least neglect does steal us into improficiency and offence. **1675** O. WALKER, etc. *Paraphr. Heb.* 21 Gently taxing their negligence and inproficiency. **1897** *Outing* (U.S.) XXX. 354/1 Knowing my own improficiency, I almost feared to tempt the giant game.

†**impro'ficuous**, *a. Obs. rare*$^{-1}$. [f. IM-^{2} + PROFICUOUS.] Unprofitable.

1650 BULWER *Anthropomet.* 53 We need not doubt to take away and freely to coerce that improficuous matter of hair.

†**im'profitable**, *a. Obs.* Also 4–5 in-. [f. IM-^{2} + PROFITABLE.] Not profitable, unprofitable.

a **1325** *Prose Psalter* lii[i]. 4 Hij ben made inprofitable. **1434** MISYN *Mending Life* xi. 124 Qwateuer he do, inprofetabyll & intollerabyll it semys. **1558** KENNEDY *Compend. Tractive* in *Wodr. Soc. Misc.* (1844) 125 Improffitable for our purpose. **1660** SHARROCK *Vegetables* 87 Weeds, fern, heath, broom and other improfitable vegetables. **1725** BRADLEY *Fam. Dict.* s.v. *Milk*, The only Way to make a Cow dry and utterly improfitable for the Dairy.

Hence †**im'profitableness**, unprofitableness.

a **1643** J. SHUTE *Judgem. & Mercy* (1645) 176 Cause..to wish that they had never seene your faces, because of your improfitablenesse.

improgressive (ɪmprəʊ'grɛsɪv), *a.* [IM-^{2} + PROGRESSIVE.] Not progressive; unprogressive.

1809–10 COLERIDGE *Friend* (1818) III. 179 Improgressive arrangement is not method. **1817** —— *Biog. Lit.* (1870) 222 The immense empire of China improgressive for thirty centuries. **1827** DE QUINCEY *Wks.* (1890) IV. 399 Cathedral cities in England, imperial cities without manufactures in Germany, are all in an improgressive condition.

Hence **impro'gressively** *adv.*, without making progress or advance; **impro'gressiveness**, the quality of being unprogressive, stationary character.

1827–48 HARE *Guesses* Ser. II. (1859) 310 The stormbeaten Atlantic, over which men had for ages been sailing to and fro almost improgressively. *Ibid.* 312 The other great scandal of philosophy, its improgressiveness, may easily be accounted for. **1839** *Fraser's Mag.* XIX. 105 It is this alleged improgressiveness of China that startles the imagination.

†**impro'lific**, *a. Obs.* [f. IM-^{2} + PROLIFIC.] Not prolific; unprolific.

a **1661** FULLER *Worthies, Hartfordsh.* II. (1662) 22 Many Worthies, who are..either improlifick, or have Children *in genitorum vituperium.* **1686** PLOT *Staffordsh.* 234 Imperfect, improlific eggs, which will never produce Chicken.

†**impro'lifical**, *a. Obs.* [f. IM-^{2} + PROLIFICAL.] = prec.

1646 SIR T. BROWNE *Pseud. Ep.* II. i. 50 That..which is not watery and improlificall will not conglaciate. **1656** BLOUNT *Glossogr.*, *Improlifical*,..not apt to have issue.

†**impro'lificate**, *v. Obs.* [f. IM-^{1} + PROLIFICATE *v.*] *trans.* To render prolific, to fertilize.

1646 SIR T. BROWNE *Pseud. Ep.* VII. xvi. 371 The inordinate longitude of the organ..may be a meanes to improlificate the seed. **1650** *Ibid.* (ed. 2) 151 A greater difficulty..is, how the sperm of the Cock improlificates and makes the ovall conception fruitfull.

†**impro'miscuous**, *a. Obs. rare.* [f. L. *impromiscu-us* + -OUS.] Unmixed, unmingled.

1656 in BLOUNT *Glossogr.* **1792** T. TAYLOR *Proclus* I. *Dissert.* p. lxxviii, The first is simple and impromiscuous.

†**im'prompt**, *a. Obs.* [ad. L. *imprompt-us*, f. *im-* (IM-^{2}) + *promptus* ready, PROMPT.] Not ready or prepared; unready.

1759 STERNE *Tr. Shandy* II. ix, So imprompt! so ill-prepared to stand the shock of it as Dr. Slop was.

impromptitude (ɪm'prɒm(p)tɪtju:d). [f. IM-^{2} + PROMPTITUDE: cf. prec.] Want of promptitude or quickness in action; unreadiness.

1887 *Story of a Kiss* III. xv. 267 His uncle's reproach of his 'impromptitude' was a different thing.

impromptu (ɪm'prɒm(p)tju:), *adv.*, *sb.*, *a.* [ad. L. *in promptū* in readiness, at hand (*promptus* readiness), written as one word and with the *n* changed to *m* before *p*, as in F. *impromptu* (Molière, 1659), whence also the adj. and sb. uses.]

A. *adv.* Without preparation or premeditation; off-hand, on the spur of the moment; extempore.

1669 LADY CHAWORTH in *12th Rep. Hist. MSS. Comm.* App. v. 11 Mr. Elliot..desired Mr. Titus to make some verses..which he did thus, impromptu [etc.]. **1788** BURNS *Let. to Mrs. Dunlop* 16 Aug., She sometimes hits on a couplet or two *impromptu*. **1791** BOSWELL *Johnson* (1816) I. 31 *note*, This was made almost *impromptu*. **1882** FARRAR *Early Chr.* II. 375 *note*, This was afterwards improved into the story that he [John] wrote the whole Gospel impromptu.

B. *sb.* Something composed or uttered without preparation or premeditation; an extemporaneous composition or performance; an improvisation. Also, a musical composition having the character of an improvisation.

1683 D. A. *Art Converse* 44 We must deal plainly and seriously with such men, waving all *in promptu's* and subtilities. **1693** DRYDEN *Juvenal* Introd. (1697) 37 They were made *extempore*, and were, as the French call them, *Impromptus*. **1776** JOHNSON *Poem* (*title*), To Mrs. Thrale, on her completing her thirty-fifth year, an impromptu. **1847** DISRAELI *Tancred* II. ix, Lady Constance..had a variety of conclusions on all social topics, which she threw forth..with the well-arranged air of an *impromptu*. **1880** GROVE *Dict. Mus.* I. 768/2 The two sets of pieces by Schubert known as Impromptus..were..not so entitled by him.

C. *adj.* **1.** Composed or uttered without preparation or premeditation; improvised; invented, produced, etc. on the spur of the moment and without previous thought.

1789 MRS. PIOZZI *Journ. France* I. 240 Who would risque the making impromptu poems at Paris? **1830** D'ISRAELI *Chas. I*, III. Pref. 4, I am not fortunate in impromptu replies. **1849** THACKERAY *Lett.* Apr., I daresay I shall have to make an impromptu speech.

2. Made or done on the spur of the moment; hastily made for the occasion, or converted to use in an emergency; extemporized, makeshift.

1764 MRS. HARRIS in *Priv. Lett. Ld. Malmesbury* I. 118 Lord North took an *impromptu* dinner with us yesterday. **1800** MRS. HERVEY *Mourtray Fam.* I. 67 They had a little *impromptu* ball. **1856** MISS MULOCK *J. Halifax* xxii. (1865) 215 My daughter encouraged me to pay this impromptu visit. **1872** BAKER *Nile Tribut.* viii. 128 We prepared an impromptu raft.

Hence **im'promptu** *v.*, to compose off-hand; to improvise, extemporize. **im'promptuary** *a.* = C. 1. **im'promptuist**, one who composes off-hand, an improviser.

1802 H. SWINBURNE in *Courts Europe* (1841) II. 334 The soldiers sing in the evening an endless German song, and the sailors impromptu in Danish. **1802–12** BENTHAM *Ration. Judic. Evid.* (1827) II. 2 Answers impromptuary. **1834** MEDWIN *Angler in Wales* I. 48 In a pelting rain, impromptu'd the following epigram. **1848** *Athenæum* 5 Aug. 773 Ballast-waggons..impromptued and filled up with seats. **1882** *Chamb. Jrnl.* 742/2 Theodore Hook..was a most prolific impromptuist. **1897** F. HALL in *Nation* (N.Y.) LXIV. 435/1 His impromptuary deliverances.

†**im'proof.** *Obs. rare.* [f. IMPROVE *v.*^{1}, after *prove, proof.*]

1. Disproof, refutation.

1641 J. JACKSON *True Evang. T.* II. 145 Now secondly for the Elench, and use of improofe.

2. Reproof, rebuke, censure.

1590 GREENWOOD *Answ. Def. Read Prayers* 30 The whole Scripture is..inspired of God, & profitable vnto doctrine, vnto improof, vnto correction. **1594** SOUTHWELL *M. Magd. Fun. Tears* To Rdr., That the reader may learn to love without improof of purity.

improper (ɪm'prɒpə(r)), *a.* [f. IM-^{2} + PROPER; after F. *impropre* (1372 in Hatz.-Darm.), L. *improprius.*] Not proper; the opposite of proper.

1. Not truly or strictly belonging to the thing under consideration; not in accordance with truth, fact, reason, or rule; abnormal, irregular; incorrect, inaccurate, erroneous, wrong.

Formerly sometimes without implication of blame or censure, e.g. said of a meaning given to a word which is not the 'proper' or literal one, but metaphorical.

1531 [implied in IMPROPERLY]. **1552** HULOET, Improper, *improprius, abusiuus.* **1581** MARBECK *Bk. of Notes* 877 When the Scripture saith, that the Lord God is unchaungeable, it is a proper speach, because he is so of his owne nature.. When it sayth: Hee went down to see the Tower of Babel, then it is an improper speach. **1649** ROBERTS *Clavis Bibl.* Introd. iii. 42 To eate Christs flesh—to pluck out our right eye..We cannot read any of these literally and properly.. therefore we must seek for a spiritual and improper sense. **1651** HOBBES *Leviath.* III. xxxiii. 201 Which to have said in the time of Joshua had been improper. **1701** tr. *Le Clerc's Prim. Fathers* (1702) 87 Of which one can only speak in metaphorical and improper Language. **1780** BURKE *Sp. Bristol previous to Elect.* Wks. III. 362 It is not lest you should censure me improperly, but lest you should form improper opinions on matters of some moment to you, that I trouble you at all upon the subject. **1870** TYNDALL *Lect. Electr. R. Instit.* 14 The conductors were called *non-electrics*, because they could not be so electrified. The division is improper, because if a conductor be insulated it can readily be electrified.

b. Not properly so called; ***improper fraction***: a fraction whose numerator is greater than (or equal to) its denominator, and whose value is therefore greater than (or equal to) unity. (Formerly applied to analogous fractions in Algebra.) ***improper diphthong***: see quot. 1824.

1542 RECORDE *Gr. Artes* (1575) 340 An Improper Fraction ..that is to saye, a fraction in forme, which in dede is greater than an Unit. **1610** FLETCHER *Faithf. Shepherdess* To Rdr., They [shepherds and shepherdesses in a Pastoral] are not to be adorned with any art but such improper ones as nature is said to bestow, as singing and poetry. **1674** JEAKE *Arith.* (1696) 44 Improper Fractions have alwayes the Numerator greater than the Denominator. **1806** HUTTON *Course Math.* I. 187 To Reduce an Improper Fraction to a Whole or Mixed Quantity. **1824** L. MURRAY *Eng. Gram.* (ed. 5) I. 36 An improper diphthong has but one of the vowels sounded: as, *ea* in eagle, *oa* in boat.

2. Not in accordance with the nature of the case or the purpose in view; unsuitable, unfit, inappropriate, ill-adapted.

1570 DEE *Math. Pref.* 33 Rather, then, either to want a name, or to haue to base and impropre a name. **1601** R. JOHNSON *Kingd. & Commw.* (1603) 90 The Hungarish horse by nature are not improper for war, being couragious, strong. **1665** BOYLE *Occas. Refl.* IV. xiii. (1848) 248 A Plain being a very improper place for such a purpose. **1702** ADDISON *Dial. Medals* ii. Misc. Wks. 1726 III. 52 [The quotation] is not improper to the occasion. **1774** C. J. PHIPPS *Voy. N. Pole* 50 As improper to be approached as a rocky lee shore. **1800** tr. *Lagrange's Chem.* I. 56 Hydrogen gas is improper for respiration.

3. Not in accordance with good manners, modesty, or decorum; unbecoming, unseemly; indecorous, indecent. Also *transf.* of a person.

1739 CHESTERF. *Lett.* (1792) I. xxxi. 108 It would be very improper and indecent if you were to fly your kite or play at nine-pins while you are with Mr. Maittaire. **1776** *Trial of Nundocomar* 106/2 It would be highly improper that their books should be wantonly subjected to curious and impertinent eyes. **1791** [see IMPROPER *v.*^{2}]. **1849** JAMES *Woodman* ii, It never occurred to her that there was anything improper in having them there. **1852** MRS. CARLYLE *Lett.* II. 177, I see single women besides myself at Verey's —not improper—governesses, and the like.

†**4.** ? Not proper or peculiar to an individual; general, common. *Obs. rare.*

[Quot. 1610 in 1 b is taken in this sense in recent Dicts.]

†**improper**, *v.*^{1} *Obs.* Forms: 4–5 **enpropre**, **-per**, 6 **empropre**, **-per**, 6–7 **impropre**, 5–7 **improper**. See also IMPROPRY. [ME. *en-*, *empropre*, app. repr. an AFr. **enproprier*, a variant (with change of prefix) of OF. *aproprier*, ad. L. *appropriāre* to APPROPRIATE. (No OF. *emproprier* or *improprier* is recorded, and the med. or mod.L. *improprīare* is cited by Du Cange only from English documents, and is presumably a latinization of the AFr. or Eng. word, though, in form, immediately f. L. *in* (IN-^{2}) into + *propri-us* own, private.) In Eng. *apropre*, APPROPRE, was in earlier use, app. with the same sense. The variant IMPROPRY corresponds to *apropry*.]

1. *trans.* To assign as a proper or private possession, to appropriate; = IMPROPRIATE *v.* 1.

c **1380** WYCLIF *Wks.* (1880) 81 But boþe þes ben enproprid to god. **1486** *Bk. St. Albans, Her.* B ij, That is to hym improperid bi lawe of armys. **1494** FABYAN *Chron.* VII. 441 He also had enproperyd vnto hym dyuerse wardys belongynge to the Kynge. **1526** *Pilgr. Perf.* (W. de W. 1531) 152 Persones..whose lyfe is aboue other impropered to contemplacyon. **1557** NORTH *Gueuara's Diall Pr.* 82 a, He that empropereth to him selfe that, whiche oughte to be common to al, is to be blamed of god, and hated of men. **1565** JEWEL *Repl. Harding* (1611) 383 If he would in like maner improper, and inclose the Sun beames, to comfort the rich. **1642** [? BP. HALL] *Mod. Confut. Animadv.* iii. 6, I have alwayes resolved that neither person nor cause shall improper me, further than they are good. [Cf. MILTON *Apol. Sm.* iii.]

2. *Eccl. Law.* = IMPROPRIATE *v.* 2.

1528 *Lett. Suppress. Monast.* (Camden) 2 To unite, annex, and improper the same unto the church of Saint Peters in Ipiswiche. **1529** MORE *Suppl. Soulys* Wks. 333/1 Many an abbey..haue the great parte therof in benefices geuen in and empropred vnto them. **1545** BRINKLOW *Compl.* 27 b, Parsonages and vicarages, which were..impropryd vnto them. **1601** F. GODWIN *Bps. of Eng.* 304 He impropred vnto our church the parsonage of Buckland Abbatis.

†**improper**, *v.*^{2} *Obs. nonce-wd.* [f. IMPROPER *a.*] *intr.* To behave improperly.

1791 H. WALPOLE *Corr.* (1837) III. 438, I am too old to be improper and you are too modest to be impropered to.

†**im'properate**, *v.*^{1} *Obs. rare*$^{-0}$. [f. ppl. stem of late L. *improperāre* to taunt, upbraid (Vulgate and Petronius), It. *improperāre* 'to vpbraid, to twit' (Florio), OF. *improperer*; cf. late L. *improperium* opprobrium, reproach (Heb. xi. 26, in Vulg.).] *trans.* To reproach, upbraid.

1623 COCKERAM, *Improperate*, to reproch. **1656** in BLOUNT.

†**im'properate**, *v.*^{2} *Obs. rare*$^{-0}$. [f. ppl. stem of L. *improperāre.*] *intr.* To hasten in.

1656 BLOUNT *Glossogr.*, *Improperate*,..also to make haste to go in.

†**imprope'ration**^{1}. *Obs.* [n. of action (prob. in OF.) from late L. *improperāre*, OF. *improperer*: see IMPROPERATE *v.*^{1}] The action of upbraiding or reviling; a reproach, taunt.

1502 *Ord. Crysten Men* (W. de W. 1506) II. ix. 112 Two other membres that is debates & improperacyons. **1526** *Pilgr. Perf.* (W. de W. 1531) 304 b, False contumeles, blasphemes, & improperacyons. **1603** HOLLAND *Plutarch's Mor.* 1235 That improperation and slander that went of him. **1643** SIR T. BROWNE *Relig. Med.* I. §3 Omitting those Improperations, and Terms of Scurrility betwixt us.

†**imprope'ration**^{2}. *Obs.* Erroneous form for IMPROPRIATION, after IMPROPER *v.*^{1}

1536 in Strype *Eccl. Mem.* (1721) I. App. lxxix. 187 At the time of the improperation. **1550** LEVER *Serm. Paul's Cross* E vj, Nothynge is so papystycall as improperacions of benefices be. **1624** DONNE *Serm.* xlvi. 466 This is an Improperation without Sacrilege..to make God mine owne.

†**imprope'ration**^{3}. *Obs. rare*$^{-0}$. [n. of action from IMPROPERATE *v.*^{2}] A hastening in.

1658 PHILLIPS, *Improperation*, a making haste.

improperium (ɪmprə'pɪərɪəm). *R.C. Liturg.* Pl. **-ia**. [late L., = reproach.] *pl.* A series of antiphons with responses forming part of the liturgical service of Good Friday, expressing the reproach or sorrowful remonstrance of Christ with the Jewish people; *sing.* one of these antiphons with its response.

1880 GROVE *Dict. Mus.* II. 1/1 The *Improperia* are sung, very softly, and without any accompaniment whatever, by two Antiphonal Choirs. **1884** ADDIS & ARNOLD *Cath. Dict.* 405/1 During the adoration the 'Improperia' are sung, each improperium being followed by the Trisagion in Greek and

Latin. **1959** *Collins Mus. Encycl.* 331/2 *Improperia*, part of the Roman liturgy for Good Friday.

improperly (ɪmˈprɒpəlɪ), *adv.* [f. IMPROPER *a.* + -LY².

The instance from Gower stands alone in date; the word, like its adj. IMPROPER, coming into general use in the 16th c. But *properly* is common from *c* 1225. The corresp. F. adv. *improprement* occurs in Oresme (14th c.).]

In an improper manner; wrongly, incorrectly, unsuitably, unbecomingly.

1390 GOWER *Conf.* I. 21 The world as of his propre kynde Was euere vntrewe and as þe blynde Improprelich he demeþ fame. **1531** ELYOT *Gov.* I. xxv, Modestie: whiche worde nat beinge knowen in the englisshe tonge,..they improprely named this vertue descretion. **1577** tr. *Bullinger's Decades* (1592) 463 Justification is properly attributed to the reconciling righteousnesse through Christ Jesus, and is improperly ascribed to the obeying righteousnes, or righteousnes of obedience. **1661–98** SOUTH *Serm.* III. 6 Merit, which we may not improperly define 'A Right to receive some good upon the score of some good done'. **1776** *Trial of Nundocomar* 97/1 The seal of Bollakey Doss was improperly made use of. **1879** *Cassell's Techn. Educ.* VI. 339/2 The heroic Jeanne Darc (commonly but improperly written d'Arc). **1885** *Law Rep.* 29 Ch. Div. 454 The lease.. has been by mistake improperly drawn.

imˈproperness. *rare.* [f. as prec. + -NESS.] The quality of being improper; impropriety.

1612 BRINSLEY *Lud. Lit.* viii. (1627) 110 For the impropernesse of the phrase in our speech. **1648** JENKYN *Blind Guide* i. 13 Faine to..snarle at the seeming impropernesse of a word. **1695** S. LOBB *Let. Dr. Bates* 11 The Improperness of Calling God Creditor, and Sin Debts otherwise than Metaphorically.

†**imˈproperty.** *Obs. rare.* [f. IMPROPER *a.* + -TY: cf. *property*.] = IMPROPRIETY.

1555 SHERRY *Treat. Fig. Gram. & Rhet.* 6 b, *Impropertie*, when a worde is brought into the talke hauing nothyng at al his owne proper signification. **1663** GERBIER *Counsel* a vj a, Ordering each part thereof, proper to its particular use, shunning all improperties.

†**imˈpropery.** *Obs.* [ad. L. *improperium* reproach, opprobrium; cf. F. *impróperie*: see IMPROPERATE *v.*¹] Reproach, upbraiding.

1542 BECON *Pathw. Prayer* ii. B vij b, Sara..desyrynge to be delyuered from the impropery & imbraydyng..of a certayne default.

†**improˈpitious,** *a. Obs. rare.* [f. IM-² + PROPITIOUS. Cf. F. *impropice* (15th c. in Littré).] Not propitious; unfavourable, unpropitious.

1638 WOTTON in *Reliq.* (1672) 574, I am sorry to hear.. that your dreams were impropitious.

†**improˈportion.** *Obs.* Also 5 in-. [IM-².] Want of proportion, disproportion.

c **1450** LYDG. & BURGH *Secrees* 1675 Yif..Ony evil humours Of qualitees gendre by in-proporcyon In the hed. **1604** T. WRIGHT *Passions* III. iii. 91 If there be but one eye ..out of square..the first thing almost we marke, is the improportion or disquaring of that part. **1675** BURTHOGGE *Causa Dei* 12 The seeming improportion of Infinite and Eternal Punishments to Finite Transgressions.

†**improˈportionable,** *a. Obs.* [f. IM-².] Not proportionable; = IMPROPORTIONATE.

1599 B. JONSON *Cynthia's Rev.* I. iii, [If she] could have dar'd so improportionable and abrupt a digression. **1621** SANDERSON *Serm.* I. 210 Profits improportionable to the pains and dangers men must undergo in them. **1661** *Grand Debate* 117 Forcing the..Liturgy, and Ceremonies, and that by improportionable penalties.

†**improˈportional,** *a. Obs.* [f. IM-² + PROPORTIONAL *a.*] = next.

1625 T. CRAUFURD *Hist. Univ. Edinb.* (1808) 99 A number improportional to the number of students, which in many years exceeded 16 score. **1784–98** in *Lect. Paint.* v. (1848) 203 The apparent objects in pictures should appear neither improportional nor deformed, on account of the distances and heights of the objects painted.

†**improˈportionate,** *a. Obs.* [f. IM-² + PROPORTIONATE *a.*] Not proportionate, out of proportion, disproportionate.

1581 MULCASTER *Positions* xxxvii. (1887) 146 To distribute their multitude to the best and easiest proportion of their owne state: which otherwise improportionate would breade an aposteme. **1652** GAULE *Magastrom.* 172 Acting and effecting at an improportionate distance. **1666** J. SMITH *Old Age* (ed. 2) 59 The Cavity is improportionate to the head of the humerus.

†**improˈportioned,** *ppl. a. Obs.* [f. IM-² + PROPORTIONED *ppl. a.*] Disproportioned: = prec.

1656 JEANES *Mixt. Schol. Div.* 40 Cognoscitive powers.. that can never reach spiritual substances, for they are improportioned unto it.

impropriate (ɪmˈprəʊprɪeɪt), *v.* [f. ppl. stem of med. or mod.L *impropriāre*: see IMPROPER *v.*¹ and cf. APPROPRIATE *v.*]

†**1.** *trans.* To make proper or peculiar *to* some person or thing: to make one's (or some one's) own; to appropriate. *Obs.*

1567 DRANT *Horace, Ep.* To Rdr. *vj, To impropriate it to me it were neither honestye, nor wysedom. **1612** T. TAYLOR *Comm. Titus* i. 3 In that period of time, which the wisdome of God hath impropriated unto them. **1651** HOBBES *Leviath.* IV. xlvi. 378 They..that impropriate the Preaching of the Gospell to one certain Order of men. **1672** MARVELL *Reh. Transp.* I. 279 In this imprudent and nauseous discourse, you have all along appropriated or impropriated all the Loyalty from the Nobility, the Gentry and the Commonalty, and dedicated it to the Church. **1703** MRS. CENTLIVRE *Stolen Heiress* II, The venerable man to whom this goodly mansion is impropriated.

†**b.** With inverted construction: To instal (a person) as proprietor. Const. *into. Obs. rare.*

1627–77 FELTHAM *Resolves* II. iii. 164 To impropriate my self into that which is not mine.

2. *spec.* To annex (an ecclesiastical benefice) to a corporation or person, as their corporate or private property; esp. **b.** (in later use) to place tithes or ecclesiastical property in lay hands.

Impropriate was in early use applied to the annexation of the tithes of a benefice to a religious house; at the Reformation most of these impropriations passed into lay hands, so that the word came to be specially associated with the lay possession of tithes, the synonym *appropriate* being subsequently taken to designate the original sense (with a covert allusion to the adjs. *appropriate* and *improper*): see IMPROPRIATION I.

1538 LELAND *Itin.* I. 41 Robert Sun to Hilbert Lacy impropriate booth this Hospital and S. Clementes yn the Castelle..to the new Priorie. **1587** FLEMING *Contn. Holinshed* III. 1302/1 The patronage and lordship of Woodburie..he gave and impropriated unto the vicars chorall of his church.

b. 1613 PURCHAS *Pilgrimage* II. vii. 113 Of nine thousand two hundred eighty and foure parishes in England..three thousand eight hundred fortie five were (as it is properly termed) impropriated. **1697** C. LESLIE *Snake in Grass* (ed. 2) 265 To maintain the Sacrilegious Impropriations which the Pope had made of the Tythes of the Secular Clergy, to endow their Monasteries: which Hen. VIII. instead of Restoring, did yet more Sacrilegiously Impropriate to the Laity. **1827, 1860** [see IMPROPRIATED].

impropriate (ɪmˈprəʊprɪət), *ppl. a.* [ad. med. or mod.L. *impropriāt-us*, pa. pple. of *impropriāre*: see prec. vb.]

1. Appropriated to some particular person or persons. ? *Obs.*

a **1600** HOOKER *Serm. Jude* 17–21 §19 Look upon Israel,.. to whom..the promises of Christ were made impropriate. **1612** T. TAYLOR *Comm. Titus* i. 1 A grace impropriate to the elect. **1706** DE FOE *Jure Div.* v. 8 If we dislike his Law, We must from his impropriate Lands withdraw.

2. *spec.* Of a benefice or its revenues: = IMPROPRIATED 2. (See IMPROPRIATE *v.* 2.)

1538 LELAND *Itin.* IV. 71 The Personage of Aulcester is impropriate to Aulcester Priory. **1555** *Act 2 & 3 Phil. & Mary* c. 4 §7 Rectories Personages and Benefices impropryate. **1631** *Star Chamb. Cases* (Camden) 66 The plaintiff Sr Edward Leech holdeth the tythes of the parsonage impropriate of Chesterfield, which tythes the Vicar of Chesterfield claymed to hold by an auncient composition. **1707** J. CHAMBERLAYNE *St. Gt. Brit.* I. i. 3 Hereof 3845 [parishes] are Churches impropriate, i.e. in Lay-Hands, where Lay-men receive the Tythes; or Appropriate, i.e. annexed to Church-Dignities. **1850** HT. MARTINEAU *Hist. Peace* IV. ix. II. 114 There were different kinds of tithes—the vicarial, rectorial, and impropriate. **1889** *Land Agent's Rec.* 6 Apr. 317, I pay the impropriate tithes as well.

imˈpropriated, *ppl. a.* [f. prec. vb. + -ED¹.]

1. Appropriated to some person or thing. ? *Obs.*

1632 LITHGOW *Trav.* I. 21 Italy was called so of Italus, a King in Sicily... The more impropriated names were Hesperia, because it is situate under the evening starre Hesperus: Latium..and Ænotria in regard of [etc.].

2. Of a benefice or tithes: Annexed to a corporation or held by a lay impropriator: see IMPROPRIATE *v.* 2, IMPROPRIATION I.

1661 BRAMHALL *Just Vind.* iii. 37 Why did they not restore the appropriated, (or, as we call them truely, impropriated tythes) to the Incumbents and lawful owners? **1827** HALLAM *Const. Hist.* (1876) II. viii. 66 A project of restoring all impropriated hereditaments to the church. **1860** FROUDE *Hist. Eng.* V. 355 The estates of the bishopric of Winchester were transferred to the crown in exchange for a few impropriated rectories.

†**b.** Of a person: Provided with an impropriation. *Obs. rare.*

?**1535** BYGOD *Treat. Impropr. Benefyces* B xi, Nowe my maisters impropriated or improper maisters..haue nat you ..dystroyed these holy and godly prouysyons, made for the mayntenance of goddes holy word.

Hence **imˈpropriatedly** *adv.*, by appropriation.

1847 R. W. HAMILTON *Disq. Sabbath* iii. (1848) 64 Every thing that can enter into the category of Christianity is impropriatedly his.

impropriation (ɪmprəʊprɪˈeɪʃən). [n. of action from IMPROPRIATE *v.*: see -ATION.]

1. The action of impropriating; the annexation of a benefice or its revenues to a corporation, office, or individual, esp. (*b*) (in later use) to a lay corporation or a lay proprietor.

By 17–18th c. law writers distinguished from *appropriation*: see quot. 1708, and APPROPRIATION 2. Although the distinction has app. no etymological or historical basis (cf. etymology of IMPROPER *v.*¹), the assignment of a benefice to a monastic house, and to a layman, being alike call *impropriation* in the 16th c., the later usage has been to restrict *impropriation* to the lay proprietorship of tithes or other ecclesiastical revenues.

?**1535** BYGOD (*title*) A treatyse concernynge impropriations of benefyces. **1549** LATIMER *6th Serm. bef. Edw. VI* (Arb.) 168 Wyth impropriacions he [the Devil] hath turned preachynge in to priuate Masses. **1575–85** ABP. SANDYS *Serm.* (Parker Soc.) 45 Rome hath robbed Christ of his honour, and by impropriations given his patrimony to idle fat monks to feed upon. **1660** R. COKE *Power & Subj.* 215 If the Pope did give Abbots and Priors power, being Ecclesiastical persons, to make divers Impropriations to their benefit, the King will take a power to take them all away, and convert them into Lay-fees, and incorporate them ..into particular mens estates. **1697** [see IMPROPRIATE *v.* 2 b].

(*b*) **1621** BURTON *Anat. Mel.* Democr. to Rdr. (1651) 64 No impropriations, no lay patrons of church livings. **1708** *Termes de la Ley* 396 *Impropriation* is properly so called, when the Advowson is in the Hands of a Layman, and Appropriation, when in the Hands of a Bishop, College, &c. **1741** RICHARDSON *Pamela* (1824) I. xxxii. 318 A bill for restoring to it [the church] all that it had lost by impropriations and other secularizations. **1868** J. H. BLUNT *Ref. Ch. Eng.* I. 25 *note*, Impropriations are the alienation of tithes to laymen.

b. The proprietorship conveyed by this action.

1631 WEEVER *Anc. Fun. Mon.* 356 The Churches..were impropriated to the Deane..by diuers Bishops; the Impropriations whereof were theirs at that time. **1849** STOVEL *Introd. Canne's 'Necess.'* 110 An impression..that, by appealing to the benevolence of individuals, the impropriations of church livings might be purchased and put in trust for the use of such ministers as they might approve.

c. An impropriated benefice; a living, tithes, etc., held by a religious house, or (in later use) by a layman or lay corporation.

1578 in Neal *Hist. Purit.* (1732) I. 367 Besides the impropriations in our shire. **1589** COOPER *Admon.* 78 Those lawes..whereby Impropriations and Patronages stande as mens lawfull possession and heritage. **1605** T. RYVES *Vicar's Plea* (1620) 98 The parsonages were heretofore..granted to the Monkes *in proprios vsus* from whence they haue their name of Impropriations. *a* **1661** FULLER *Worthies* (1840) II. 292 An impropriation which the Lord Gray of Wilton.. restored to the Church. **1761–2** HUME *Hist. Eng.* (1806) IV. lii. 105 Certain zealots had erected themselves into a society for buying in of impropriations, and transfering them to the church. **1778** *Eng. Gazetteer* (ed. 2) s.v. *Northleech*, A free grammar-school, endowed with the impropriation of Chedworth, worth 80l. a-year. **1861** TULLOCH *Eng. Purit.* I. 32 It required..that impropriations annexed to bishoprics and colleges be converted into regular rectorial livings.

†**2.** *gen.* The action of making proper or peculiar to some person or thing; appropriation; in quot. 1614, 'exclusive possession' (Todd). *Obs.*

1611 LOE *Bliss of Br. Beauty* (1614) 29 (T.) The Gnosticks had, as they deemed, the impropriation of all divine knowledge. **1654** WHITLOCK *Zootomia* 266 Is the Impropriation of some rich Beauty thy Designe? **1728** SIR J. BROWNE *Ess. Trade* (1729) 48 When..either their own Extravagance, or the general Impropriation of Things reduc'd any to Want, they hired themselves out to Labour.

†**b.** Something appropriated to a private owner; a property. *Obs.*

1651 HOBBES *Govt. & Soc.* Ep. Ded., What Nature at first laid forth in common, men did afterwards distribute into severall Impropriations. **1651** CLEVELAND *Poems* 7, I will never be your Impropriation.

3. The action of taking in the 'proper' or literal sense. *nonce-use.*

1825 COLERIDGE *Aids Refl.* (1848) I. 257 The impropriation of this metaphor—(that is, the taking it literally).

impropriator (ɪmˈprəʊprɪeɪtə(r)). [agent-n. in L. form, from med. or mod.L. *impropriāre* or IMPROPRIATE *v.*]

1. One to whom a benefice is impropriated; esp. = ***lay impropriator***, a layman in possession of a living or its revenues.

1622 T. SCOTT *Belg. Pismire* 27 The irreligious Impropriators, who prey vpon Church and State. **1635** PAGITT *Christianogr.* 229 The example of the Kings, Colledges, Bishops, Dean and Chapters giveth impropriators no allowance at al. **1695** KENNETT *Par. Antiq.* ix. 80 Upon this practise depends the custom..of the Rector or Impropriator maintaining the Chancel. **1794** GODWIN *Cal. Williams* ix. 43 Mr. Tyrrel, by the tenure of his manor, was impropriator of the great tithes. **1868** MILMAN *St. Paul's* xi. 273 A large portion of the tithes..had been alienated to the Crown..or to lay impropriators.

†**2.** *gen.* One to whom anything is appropriated, a proprietor, owner; one who appropriates or arrogates something to himself. *Obs. rare.*

1631 BRATHWAIT *Eng. Gentlew.* (1641) 283 Art not thou.. a Robber, who has received goods as a steward or dispenser; and entitlest thy selfe the impropriator or owner? **1660** E. MARTIN *His Opinion* ii. (1662) 23, I should condemn any man..for a most unconscionable Incloser and Impropriator, that should take upon himself to give another leave to speak, or write this or the like, which is as common for every one as the Air which wee breathe.

impropriatrix (ɪmˌprəʊprɪˈeɪtrɪks). [fem. in L. form of prec.: see -TRIX.] A female impropriator; a woman who holds a benefice.

1774 *Garton Inclos. Act* 5 The said Jane Cooke, Impropriatrix of the said rectory. **1801** H. GWILLIM *Coll. resp. Tithes* 1620 Upon a second trial a verdict was found for the impropriatrix.

†**improˈprietary.** *Obs. rare.* [A modification of the earlier APPROPRIETARY, conformed in the prefix to IMPROPRIATE, -ATOR, etc.] = IMPROPRIATOR I.

1637 HUMPHREY tr. *St. Ambrose* Ep. ded., Your endevours..to induce some improprietaries..to an enlargement of my poore maintenance.

impropriety (ɪmprəʊˈpraɪətɪ). [ad. F. *impropriété* (Calvin, 1560), or its source L. *improprietās*, f. *impropri-us* IMPROPER *a.*: cf. PROPRIETY *sb.*]

1. The quality of being improper. **a.** Want of accordance with the nature of the thing, or with reason or rule; incorrectness, erroneousness, inaccuracy.

1611 FLORIO, *Improprieta*, improprietie. **1612** DRAYTON *Poly-olb.* ii, The plaine truth (as wordes may certifie your eyes, sauing all impropriety of obiect) is that in the Poole are seated three Isles. **1646** SIR T. BROWNE *Pseud. Ep.* III. iv. 114 Then which words there can be none plainer, nor more evidently discover the improprietie of this appellation. **1776** ADAM SMITH *W.N.* IV. ix. (1869) II. 259 The following observations may serve to show the impropriety of this representation. **1843** MILL *Logic* I. ii. §4 We may therefore say, without impropriety, that the quality forms part of its signification.

b. Want of accordance with the purpose in view; unsuitableness, unfitness, inappropriateness.

1697 LUTTRELL *Brief Rel.* (1857) IV. 316 There appeared near 20 of the colledge of physitians to shew the impropriety of the medicine. **1774** C. J. PHIPPS *Voy. N. Pole* 212 The impropriety of the common process of distillation. **1875** JOWETT *Plato* (ed. 2) I. 234 The impropriety of holding a public discussion with such men.

c. Want of accordance with good manners or decorum; unbecomingness, unseemliness, indecency; morally improper conduct.

1751 JOHNSON *Rambler* No. 174 ¶13, I was convinced . . of the impropriety of my conduct. **1828** SCOTT *F.M. Perth* ix, The license and impropriety of the Duke of Rothsay's conduct was the more reprehensible in the public view, that he was a married person. **1884** *Law Times Rep.* LI. 247/2 The defendants obtained the property by misconduct, fraud, and impropriety.

2. with *an* and *pl.* An instance of improper language, conduct, etc.; a breach of propriety.

a **1674** CLARENDON *Hist. Reb.* XIV. §66 They had made themselves merry with some improprieties in the French. **1685** STILLINGFL. *Orig. Brit.* v. 283 We are not bound to follow any modern Writers in their Improprieties. **1755** JOHNSON *Dict.* Pref. ¶6 Every language has likewise its improprieties and absurdities, which it is the duty of the lexicographer to correct or proscribe. **1831** CARLYLE in Froude *Life* (1882) II. 229 How often do we find a conduct defaced by many a moral impropriety! **1888** J. INGLIS *Tent Life Tigerland* 185 Guilty of some terrible impropriety.

[**impropriety**[2], in Strype, by a misreading of *impropriate*, app. after *propriety* = property.

1721 STRYPE *Eccl. Mem.* III. xxxiv. 268 Rectories, parsonages, benefices, improprieties, glebe-lands, tithes. (The original document has 'Beneficis impropryate': see IMPROPRIATE *ppl. a.* 2, quot. 1555.)]

†**imˈproprious**, *a. Obs. rare.* [f. L. *impropri-us* IMPROPER + -OUS.] ? Lacking a proper form of its own.

1688 R. HOLME *Armoury* I. 12 Till the receiving of such forms we must account them as rude and improprious things.

†**imˈpropry, -rie**, *v. Obs.* [Of the same origin as *impropre*, IMPROPER *v.*[1]: cf. the parallel *apropre, aproprye*, under APPROPRE *v.*] *trans.* To appropriate, impropriate.

1526 *Pilgr. Perf.* (1531) 33 The partes of mannes body hath not theyr offyce for them selfe onely improprryed, but for the common wele of the hole body. **1535** CRANMER *Let. Cromwell* 2 Nov. in *Wks.* (Parker Soc.) II. 313 That I, pretending title to . . certain lands in Denham lately belonging to the house of Davyngton, and my brother in like manner to the benefice sometime impropried to the same. *a* **1571** JEWEL *On 2 Thess.* (1611) 114 Hee hath impropried the whole kingdome of Purgatorie to himselfe, and hath made it more gainefull than heauen and earth.

†**improˈsperity**. *Obs.* Also 6–7 in-. [f. L. *improsper* (see next) + -ITY: cf. *prosperity*.]

Want of, or the opposite of, prosperity; bad fortune, ill success, adversity; unprosperousness.

1528 LYNDESAY *Dreme* 848 Than quharein lyis our inprosperitie? **1634-61** FELTHAM *Resolves* II. xxxv. 254 God hath pronounc't an inprosperity to wickedness. **1660** GAUDEN *Anal. Covenant* 7 What improsperities, disorders, . . wars, spoils, and bloodshed. **1722** WOLLASTON *Relig. Nat.* v. 107 The prosperity or improsperity of a man . . does not intirely depend upon his own prudence or imprudence.

†**imˈprosperous**, *a. Obs.* [f. L. *improsper* unfortunate (f. *im-* (IM-[2]) + *prosper* favourable, prosperous) + -OUS.]

1. Not prosperous or thriving; unfortunate, unlucky, unsuccessful. (Of persons, enterprises, etc.)

1602 WARNER *Alb. Eng.* XII. lxxiv, Ah, falsed Matches, finished in the wrong of Others, might, By still improsperous Presidents, deterre from wronging Right. **1634** W. TIRWHYT tr. *Balzac's Lett.* (vol. I.) 168 That he no longer imploy those improsperous persons. **1727** BRADLEY *Fam. Dict.* s.v. *Fences*, The improsperous Condition of Wood-land and Plantations. **1829** T. L. PEACOCK *Misfort. Elphin* viii. 109 The household of Elphin was sufficiently improsperous during the absence of its chief.

2. Of fortune, etc.: Adverse to prosperity, unpropitious.

1598 GRENEWEY *Tacitus, Ann.* (1603) 70 As fortune was favourable to Augustus in government of state, so in household matters unluckie and improsperous. **1603** SIR C. HEYDON *Jud. Astrol.* ii. 101 The action of the starres . . became vnluckie and improsperous. *a* **1656** HALES *Gold. Rem.* (1688) 62 Bring upon them some improsperous Disease.

Hence †**imˈprosperously** *adv.*; †**imˈprosperousness**.

1594 DRAYTON *Matilda* 598 Thus like a rose . . The with'ring leaves impros'prously doth cast. **1647** HAMMOND *Power of Keys* iii. 39 The improsperousnesse of the cause of late in this kingdome hath moved some of them. **1658** *Whole Duty Man* xii. §9. 95 The strange improsperousness of ill gotten estates. *a* **1691** BOYLE (J.), This experiment has been but very improsperously attempted.

improvability (ɪmpruːvəˈbɪlɪtɪ). Also **improveability**. [f. IMPROVABLE *a.*[2]: see -ITY.] = IMPROVABLENESS.

1791 NEWTE *Tour Eng. & Scot.* 180 Since Great Britain has not yet come near to the *ultimatum* of its improveability. **1813** T. JEFFERSON *Writ.* (1830) IV. 194 One of the questions . . was on the improvability of the human mind. **1874** CARPENTER *Ment. Phys.* I. v. (1879) 205 The extraordinary improvability of the Perceptive faculty.

†**imˈprovable**, *a.*[1] *Obs. rare.* Also **improveable**. [f. IMPROVE *v.*[1] + -ABLE.] Capable of being disproved or refuted; to be censured or condemned.

1604 N. D. *3rd Pt. Three Convers. Eng.* 411 They were ashamed to bring forth so improueable a testimony. **1713** WARDER *True Amazons* 17 His Brain . . hath brought forth these improvable Maggots into the World.

improvable (ɪmˈpruːvəb(ə)l), *a.*[2] Also **improveable**. [f. IMPROVE *v.*[2] + -ABLE.] Capable of being improved; susceptible of improvement.

1. Capable of being turned to profit or account; that may be taken advantage of, or used profitably; serviceable. Now *rare*.

1646 SIR T. BROWNE *Pseud. Ep.* VI. xii. 338 The assayes of weaker heads affords oftentimes improveable hints unto better. **1665** BOYLE *Occas. Refl.* V. v. (1848) 314, I think it a less improvable Prerogative, to be able to coyn any Metal into mony, or call it in at pleasure. **1692** W. SHERLOCK *Fut. Judgem.* 316 Every thing that is improveable to the service and glory of God, is a talent. *a* **1734** NORTH *Lives* (1826) II. 8 Finding this project of a penny-post turn out so well, and apparently improvable. **1799** SOUTHEY *Lett.* (1856) I. 74 When I go over the houses I shall see how improvable they are.

2. Of land (orig. a specific use of 1, passing into sense 3): Capable of being profitably cultivated; adapted for cultivation; capable of being made better or more productive by cultivation.

1659 *Gentl. Calling* (1696) 27 Though a rich, yet still such an improvable Soil, as will encourage and reward his Husbandry. **1677** W. HUBBARD *Narrative* (1865) II. 72 All the Land improvable for such Uses, being already taken up. **1701** *Lond. Gaz.* No. 3720/4 The Premisses (which are very Improvable by Limestone on the Place). **1712** ADDISON *Spect.* No. 549 ¶3, I have got a fine spread of improveable lands. **1799** J. ROBERTSON *Agric. Perth* 245 After all, improveable is an indefinite term; and the last generation thought many spots unworthy of culture, which we now see converted into good arable land. **1813** G. EDWARDS *Meas. True Pol.* 25 The improveable land of the whole Kingdom.

3. Capable of being made better; that may be brought into a higher or more desirable condition.

1677 HALE *Prim. Orig. Man.* I. ii. 68 With Moral principles inherent in his Nature, and improvable by the exercise of his Faculties. **1712** W. ROGERS *Voy.* App. 56 Maps and Sea-Draughts are always improvable. *a* **1716** SOUTH *Serm.* (1717) IV. 81 Here is indeed something improveable into a bright and a noble Perfection. **1870** BLACK *Kilmeny* (1877) 284, I should not offer you the advice if I did not think you were improvable.

Hence **imˈprovably** *a.*, in a manner that admits of improvement.

1755 in JOHNSON. **1818** in TODD, and in mod. Dicts.

improvableness (ɪmˈpruːvəb(ə)lnɪs). [f. prec. + -NESS.] The quality of being improvable; capacity or susceptibility of improvement.

1652 BLITHE (*title*) The English Improver Improved . . discovering the Improveableness of all Lands. *a* **1660** HAMMOND *Wks.* I. 479 (R.) The Romish doctrines of the improvableness of attrition into contrition, by the priest's aid. **1878** MORLEY *Diderot* i. 8 Active faith in the improvableness of institutions.

imˈprovatory, *a. nonce-wd.* [irreg. f. IMPROVE *v.*[2], after *confirmatory*, etc.] Of improving nature or tendency.

1835 *New Monthly Mag.* XLV. 298 Three or four hundred letters . . hortatory, dehortatory, expostulatory, improvatory, and exclamatory!

†**improve**, *v.*[1] *Obs.* Also (6 **emprove**), 6–7 **improove**. [a. OF. *improver*, F. *improuver* (Oresme, 14th c.), ad. L. *improbāre* to condemn, reject, disapprove, f. *improbus* bad: cf. *probāre* to make good, f. *probus* good.]

1. *trans.* To prove to be wrong; to disprove, refute, confute (a statement, etc., or a person).

c **1449** PECOCK *Repr.* I. xiii. 70 For to improue and reproue the seid firste opinioun. **1531** TINDALE *Exp. 1 John* (1537) 8 Ye se . . how we haue manifestly improued the ypocrites in an hundreth textes. **1554** BRADFORD *Serm.* etc. (Parker Soc.) 91 Things which I have here brought forth to improve transubstantiation. **1581** J. BELL *Haddon's Answ. Osor.* 87 Whose doctrine when hee could by no meanes emprove, he rushed upon him like a Jolye Sycophaunte, with slaunders and reproches. **1606-10** R. FIELD *Hist. Ch.* (1628) 359 This we deny, and will in due place improve their error therein. **1620** GRANGER *Div. Logike* 336 A false Axiome is improoved two wayes.

2. To disapprove as bad; to disallow; to reprove, rebuke; to blame, censure, condemn.

1526 TINDALE *2 Tim.* iii. 16 All scripture geven by inspiracion of god is proffitable to teache, to improve, to informe. **1546** BALE *Eng. Votaries* 8 They haue improued that doctryne and taught the contrarye. **1551** ROBINSON tr. *More's Utop.* I. (Arb.) 54 When they had improued and disallowed my sayinges. **1560** ABP. PARKER *Corr.* (Parker Soc.) 130 We trust your gracious zeal towards Christs religion will not improve our doings. **1615** BEDWELL *Moham. Imp.* II. §63 This the Astronomers do denie: yea all Philosophers do improue this opinion. **1642** *Coll. Rights & Priv. Parl.* 10 When subjects doe improove wicked decrees.

improve (ɪmˈpruːv), *v.*[2] Forms: 5–6 enprow(e, improwe, emprow, emprou; 6–7 emproue, improue, 6–8 emprove, 7 improove, (8–9 *pa. pple.* (erron.) improven), 6– improve. [In 16th c. *en-*, *emprowe*, a. AFr. *en-*, *emprower*, *enprouwer*, *emprover* (1292 in Britton), a parallel form (with prep. *en* instead of *a*) of *aprower*, in med.(Anglo-)L. *appruare*, *approare*; f. OF. *en* into + *pro*, *prou*, *preu*, oblique case of *pros* profit, advantage: see APPROVE *v.*[2]

The normal phonetic descendant of the OF. verb would be *emprow*, *improw* (cf. *allow*) as in 16th c.; but, as in APPROVE *v.*[2], through confusion of *u* and *v*, and the influence of other words in which *-proue* stood for *-prove*, *improwe*, *improue*, has passed into *improve*.]

†**1.** *refl.* ***to improve*** (***improwe***) ***oneself*** (***of***): to make one's profit (of), to avail oneself (of) by using to one's profit. *Obs.*

Especially used of the lord's inclosing and bringing into cultivation of waste land: cf. APPROVE *v.*[2], and for the constr., *Cath. Angl.*, 'To approwe, *Approare, sicut domini se faciunt de vastis*'; i.e. as lords approwe (or improwe) themselves of wastes.

1523 FITZHERB. *Surv.* 5 It is to be inquered . . what of those wodes the lorde maye improwe him selfe & of howe many acres. *Ibid.* 6 If the lorde graunt a man commen with his catell within certayne meyres . . & boundes, the lorde shall nat improue hym selfe within those meyres and boundes. **1655** FULLER *Hist. Camb.* 6 The Townsmen . . unconscionably improving themselves on the Scholars necessities, extorted unreasonable rents from them.

2. *trans.* To turn (a thing) to profit or good account, to employ to advantage; to make profitable use of, take advantage of, avail oneself of, utilize; to make use of, use, employ.

†**a.** To lay out, invest, or employ *money* to profit; to put out to interest. *Obs.*

[**1292** BRITTON III. iii. §4 Et tut le profit qe il prist pur le mariage soit restoré as amis et as parentz la femme pur emprouer al oes la femme [let all the profit be restored to the woman's friends to *emproue* to the profit of the woman].] **1646** *Bury Wills* (Camden) 192 Item I give vnto Frances Browne, my grandchilde, fifty pounds, to be payd into her father's hands . . and to be improued by him for her vse, and to be payd to her at her age of sixteene years. **1658** *Whole Duty Man* xvii. §7. 140 To put his money in some sure hand, where he may both improve, and be certain of it at his need. *a* **1680** BUTLER *Rem.* (1759) I. 225 As if his Talent had been wrapt up in't Unthriftily, and now he went about Henceforward to improve, and put it out. *c* **1850** *Arab. Nts.* (Rtldg.) 356, I will . . improve the money I have obtained, in some way of merchandise.

†**b.** To turn *land* to profit; to inclose and cultivate (waste land); hence to make land more valuable or better by such means, and so, in later use, merged in sense 5. (Cf. also sense 3.) ? *Obs.*

The ancient sense, or something akin to it, was retained in 17–early 20th c. in the American colonies.

[**1292** BRITTON III. ii. §12 Villenage est tenement de demeynes de chescun seignur, baillé a tenir a sa volunté par vileins services de enprouwer al oes le seignur [the holding of a lord's demesne lands . . to *enprouwe* to the profit of the lord].] **1632** *Mass. Col. Rec.* (1853) I. 94 If the . . said John Winthrop shall . . suffer the said ileland to lye wast, and not improue the same, then this present demise to be voide. **1642** *Mass. Colony Laws* etc. §7 (Pickering) Where lands lye in common unfenced, if one man shall improve his land by fencing in several, and another shall not, he who shall so improve shall secure his lands against other men's cattle. **1653** *Early Rec. Lancaster, Mass.* (1884) 27 The Plantation or Sellect men shall determine the time, how Longe every man shall hold and Improue the said Lands for the proffit thereof. **1684** *Attorney Gen.* in *State Trials* (1735) VII. 574/2 All this piece of ground, of twenty acres, is built upon and improved. *a* **1687** PETTY *Pol. Arith.* (1690) 96 Tangier and Bumbay have . . been improved from a Desart condition to abound with People. **1700** EVELYN *Diary* 13 July, The land was . . thus improved for pleasure and retirement by the vast charge and industry of this opulent citizen. **1740** W. DOUGLASS *Disc. Curr. Brit. Plant. Amer.* 21 A good Farmer improves his Lands not by working them out of Heart . . but by manuring them, that they may yield the better Crops. **1906** L. L. BELL *Carolina Lee* 293, I could refuse an offer to improve my land, denuded and mortgaged as it is.

†**c.** To make profitable or advantageous use of, employ to advantage; to avail oneself of, utilize, use, employ as an instrument or means (*a thing*; also in American use, *a person* as an agent). *Obs.* or *dial.*

a **1529** SKELTON *P. Sparowe* 790 His [Chaucer's] mater is delectable, . . His Englysh well alowed, So as it is enprowed, For as it is enployed, There is no Englysh voyd. **1639** FULLER *Holy War* IV. xiii. 191 The Egyptians standing on the firm ground, were thereby enabled to improue and inforce their darts to the utmost. **1650** CROMWELL *Lett. Governor Edin. Castle* 12 Sept. (Query i) in *Carlyle*,

Improving the Covenant against the Godly and Saints in England. **1677** W. HUBBARD *Narrative* (1865) II. 75 Near some River..whose Streams are principally improved for the driving of Saw-mills. *Ibid.* 201 Such of the Women as were gifted at knitting and sewing, were improved to make Stockings and Garments. **1694** in Willis & Clark *Cambridge* (1886) II. 461 Materials that may be vsefull for yᵉ College, to be improved for that vse or to be sold. **1704** in B. Church *Hist. Philip's War* (1867) II. 137 All the Forces..that shall be improved in the Service to the Eastward of Casco-Bay. *c* **1710** CELIA FIENNES *Diary* (1888) 300 Every Corner is improved for Cupboards and necessarys. **1724** in *Early Rec. Lancaster, Mass.* (1884) 216, I endeavour to Improve the men constantly to the most advantage. **1798** in Root *Amer. Law Rep.* I. 173 The witnesses improved in the former trial were admitted.

d. (In American use.) To make use of or occupy *a place*.

1677 W. HUBBARD *Narrative* (1865) II. 71 Other Places adjoining were soon after seized, and improved for Trading and Fishing. **1782** *Rhode Island Colonial Rec.* (1864) IX. 512 That Josiah Flagg..have the liberty of improving the cellars under the state house in Providence, as repositories for the public stores. **1803** M. CUTLER in *Life, Jrnls. & Corr.* (1888) II. 114 We found in the octagon hall, which seemed to be improved as a levee room, a large company. **1828** WEBSTER, *Improve*..6. To use; to occupy; to cultivate. 'The house or farm is now improved by an industrious tenant.' This application is perhaps peculiar to some parts of the United States. **1863** HAWTHORNE *Old Home* (1883) I. 96 It has come to base uses in these latter days,—being improved, in Yankee phrase, as a brewery and washhouse.

e. To make good use of, turn to good account (an action, occurrence, event, season, time; now usually with *occasion*, *opportunity*, or the like).

1539 POLLARD, etc. in *St. Pap. Hen. VIII*, I. 619 [We] made so diligent enquirye and serche, that, with vigilante labour, we muche improvide the same. **1617** MORYSON *Itin.* II. 213 So far did we..improve our time..that..within two daies we made this Fort guardable. **1677** W. HUBBARD *Narrative* (1865) I. 245 An Opportunity..was let slip, and not improved. *Ibid.* 256 Yet was their Labour well improved, and followed with good Success. **1720** WATTS *Divine Songs* xx, How doth the little busy bee Improve each shining hour! **1748** RICHARDSON *Clarissa* (1811) VIII. 267 Then for improving a hint, thou wert always a true Englishman. **1774** J. ADAMS in *Fam. Lett.* (1876) 17 The fine weather..I hope has been carefully improved to get in my hay. **1844** LINGARD *Anglo-Sax. Ch.* (1858) I. ii. 78 He improved the opportunity. **1869** FREEMAN *Norm. Conq.* III. xii. 159 His next thought was how to improve the occasion. **1878** BOSW. SMITH *Carthage* 97 The Roman army improved the victory of their fleet by at once marching to Egesta.

f. To turn to account for spiritual profit or edification; *esp.* to preach or speak on, with a view to edification; now chiefly in ***to improve the occasion*** (which is felt as a contextual use of e).

1624 SANDERSON *Twelve Serm.* (1637) 487, I should also have desired..to have improved it [my Text] a little farther by a fourth Inference. **1650** W. BROUGH *Sacr. Princ.* (1659) 67 Teach me to improve my poverty. **1676** I. MATHER *K. Philip's War* (1862) 64 The news of this Blood-shed came to us..in the midst of the Sermon, the Scripture then improved being that *Isai.* 42, 24. **1677** W. HUBBARD *Narrative* (1865) II. 249 Sad Events should rather be improved to our own Instruction, than the condemning of others. **1705** STANHOPE *Paraphr.* I. Pref. 12 The Expounding and improving the Portions of Scripture recommended to us. **1816** SCOTT *Old Mort.* xviii, To improve the providential success which they had obtained by a word in season. **1823** SCORESBY *Whale Fishery* 127, I thought it my duty to address them, with the particular view of improving the serious impression evidently made upon them, by the awful death. **1857** LAWRENCE *Guy L.* viii. 66, I had..little opportunity for 'improving the occasion', as the Nonconformists have it.

†**3.** To enhance in monetary value; to raise the price or amount of. *Obs.*

As said of lands and rents, app. connected with senses 1 and 2 b, land that was 'emprowed' or inclosed and cultivated being enhanced in value or in rent.

1548 *Lansdowne MS.* 238, lf. 317 Noble men and gentlemen that haue not enprowed nor enhaunsed ther rentes. *Ibid.* lf. 324 Noble and gentlemen whiche had not emprowed nor enhaunsed ther rentes. **1616** BULLOKAR, *Improoue*, to raise rents higher. **1617** MORYSON *Itin.* II. 265 They improve their commodities to a treble price. *Ibid.* III. 148 Yet this prodigall age hath so forced Gentlemen to improve their revenews, as many of these grounds are by them disparked, and converted to feede Cattell. **1626** in *Crt. & Times Chas. I* (1848) I. 142 It will overthrow trade by the altering of the exchange,..improve Spain's bullion, enhance the price of all things. **1750** *Highlands of Scotland in 1750* (1898) 40 They have screwed their Rents to an extravagant Height (which they vitiously term improving their Estates).

†**4. a.** To make greater in amount or degree; to increase, augment, magnify, enlarge, intensify; to advance. *Obs.* (Now merged in 5.)

1509 HAWES *Past. Pleas.* (Percy Soc.) 124 Suche a one as thou..For thou thy selfe doost so much enprou Above the h[e]avens by exaltacion. **1676** LISTER in *Ray's Corr.* (1848) 125, I have much improved my Catalogue of Snails, having added five species thereto. *a* **1687** WALLER *To a Person of Honour* 8 You have advanc'd to wonder their renown, And no less virtuously improv'd your own. **1690** CHILD *Disc. Trade* (1694) 8 Some more particulars might be added, and those aforesaid further improved. **1727** *Philip Quarll* (1816) 56 He found seven peas;..and thinking they might..be improved to a quantity large enough to serve for a meal, he laid them by. **1771** GOLDSM. *Hist. Eng.* I. 103 This sum..only served to improve their desire for fresh exactions.

†**b.** To increase or augment (what is evil), to aggravate, make worse. *Obs.*

1615 HIERON *Wks.* I. 615 His tyranny began to be improued, and the burdens..were heauier then before. **1628** tr. *Camden's Hist. Eliz.* (1629) II. 380 Defect of health and strength, which the indisposition of the aire.., being a filthy, windy, and rainy day, much improoued. **1647** COWLEY *Mistress, Incurable* vii, As wholesome Medicines the Disease improve, There where they work not well. **1718** PENN *Maxims* Wks. 1726 I. 851 Thus Men improve their own Miseries, for want of an Equal and just Estimate of what they enjoy or lose. **1800** BP. PORTEUS *Lect. Matt.* xiii. (1802) I. 331 We all..have..by our own personal and voluntary transgressions, not a little improved the wretched inheritance we received from our ancestors.

5. To advance or raise to a better quality or condition; to bring into a more profitable or desirable state; to increase the value or excellence of; to make better; to better, ameliorate. (The prevailing modern sense, in which 2 b is now merged.)

1617 MORYSON *Itin.* II. 219 To himselfe, whose endeavours in that Kingdome had much improved her opinion of him. **1698** FRYER *Acc. E. India & P.* 182 The Mango (which they have improved in all its kinds to the utmost Perfection). **1706** PHILLIPS, *To Improve*, to better..to promote or advance, to bring to greater Perfection. **1733** P. LINDSAY *Interest Scot.* 167 The Reeds, Harness, Shuttles, and Temples,..lately given to the Weavers..have improven the Cloth in its Goodness much more. **1766** FORDYCE *Serm. Yng. Wom.* (1767) II. viii. 34 [She] had from her youth improved herself by reading. **1805** FORSYTH *Beauties Scotl.* (1806) III. 134 A large natural cave, which had been partly improven by art. **1862** SIR B. BRODIE *Psychol. Inq.* II. ii. 50 The habit of attention may be improved by exercise. **1888** J. INGLIS *Tent Life Tigerland* 184 The tobacco smoke had not improved his appearance, and..he..looked bad enough.

6. With *into*: **a.** (in sense 2), To make *into* or represent as, for the sake of turning to account; †**b.** (in sense 4), To turn *into* or represent as something greater, to magnify *into* (*obs.*); **c.** (in sense 5), To convert *into* something better.

1647 CLARENDON *Hist. Reb.* IV. §38 Taking all opportunities, uncharitably, to improve Mistakes, into Crimes. **1687** T. BROWN *Saints in Uproar* Wks. 1730 I. 74 Improve this mole-hill into a mountain. **1700** —— tr. *Fresny's Amusem. Ser. & Com.* 76 Sometimes, that a Witty Vertuous Woman will improve a Dull Heavy Country Booby, into a Man of Sence. **1688** SOUTH *Serm.* (1727) V. ix. 391 Did God vouch-safe such transcendent Blessings..only to be improved into the Food and Fewel of Intemperance? **1746** WESLEY *Princ. Methodist* 66 This very Thing you improve into a fresh Objection. **1758** LELAND *Philip of Macedon* I. i, It might have been the interest of Amyntas, to improve this incident of the birth of his son into a pledge of future happiness. **1818** JAS. MILL *Brit. India* II. IV. iv. 155 Preparations..for improving the blockade into more expeditious methods of reduction. **1846** J. W. CROKER in *C. Papers* (1884) III. xxiv. 67 The [potato] failure..was..(as the Methodists say) improved into an ostensible excuse for the measure [Corn Law repeal]. [Cf. sense 1 f.]

7. With *away* or a phr. of similar meaning: To remove, get rid of, lose, spend, or cause to disappear, by making improvements.

1780 CRAIG *Mirror* No. 69 ⁋5 My crops never paid for the expense of raising them: and..I found that I had improved away every shilling of my fortune. **1887** JESSOPP *Arcady* viii. 229 All the pinders are gone—improved off the face of the earth. **1887** J. BALL *Nat. in S. Amer.* 213 It is a question whether, like most native races..they will ultimately be improved out of existence.

8. *absol.* To make improvements. ***to improve on*** or ***upon***: to make or produce something better or more perfect than; to advance beyond. See IMPROVEMENT 6 b.

1699 BENTLEY *Phal.* 277 By long use and experience..he might improve upon his own Invention. **1748** J. GEDDES *Compos. Antients* 362 Longinus here seems to have improven on the orator. **1771** *Junius Lett.* lxvii. 331 The son has regularly improved upon the vices of his father. **1862** MERIVALE *Rom. Emp.* (1865) VI. xlviii. 64 *note*, It was not beyond [his] means..to improve on this political masterpiece. **1867** H. MACMILLAN *Bible Teach.* xiii. (1870) 253 We cannot improve upon nature. *Mod.* A tenant who improves ought to have the value of his improvements secured to him.

†**9.** *intr.* To increase, augment, become greater, advance, develop. *Obs.* (exc. as merged in 10).

1650 GREENHILL *Ezek.* 77 Iniquity improves in the going. *a* **1681** ALLESTREE *Serm.* (1684) I. 270 (L.) That fool..e'er long emproves into a wit. **1697** COLLIER *Ess. Mor. Subj.* II. (1702) 52 Admiration improves into Love. **1748** *Anson's Voy.* II. viii. 221 The relish improving upon them by degrees. **1776** JOHNSON *Let. to Thrale* 3 June, The lameness..has improved to a very serious and troublesome fit of the gout. **1809** W. IRVING *Knickerb.* I. iii. (1849) 48 Intimacy improves with time.

10. *intr.* To increase in value or excellence; to advance or rise to a more excellent condition; to become better.

1727 SWIFT *To a Young Lady*, It is a shame for an english lady not to relish such discourses, not to improve by them. **1737** [S. BERINGTON] *G. di Lucca's Mem.* 173 A Wine..mellowing and improving as it is kept. **1748** *Anson's Voy.* II. i. 111 This diversified landskip..still improved upon us the farther we advanced. **1796** JANE AUSTEN *Pride & Prej.* xii. 235 But afterwards she seemed to improve on you. **1805** PIKE *Sources Mississ.* I. App. (1810) 6 Their situation improves by a communication with the whites. **1834** MEDWIN *Angler in Wales* I. 49 The scenery improves, and becomes wilder in its character. **1866** CARLYLE *Inaug. Addr.* 174 In..the best of all possible conditions to improve by that book. **1885** *Manch. Exam.* 14 May 5/3 Our trade in the south has..improved.

†**improve**, *v.*³ *Obs.* [A variant of *aprove*, APPROVE *v.*¹, with change of prefix: perh. influenced by the corresp. change in IMPROVE *v.*²]

1. *trans.* To prove, establish, demonstrate, show to be true or real.

(*Improued*, in Hearne's *R. Glouc.* p. 466, is an error for *iproued*: cf. Rolls ed., line 9552.)

1613 in *Crt. & Times Jas. I* (1849) I. 246, I..will hope to improve my industry and diligence such as you shall find no fault to complain that [etc.]. **1633** BP. HALL *Hard Texts, N.T.* 137 Doe thou shew and improve this love of thine to me in this one point. **1650** BULWER *Anthropomet.* 183 These Amazons discarding the tendernesse of their Sex, and desiring to improve themselves Virago's. **1670** E. BORLASE *Lathom Spaw* 8 More..I am persuaded that Mr. Hooke in his Book hath improved to Admiration.

b. *intr.* To prove or turn out to be. *rare.*

1612 DAVIES *Why Ireland* etc. 95 Meanes for some great action, which..if hee had liued, woulde rather haue improued [ed. 1664 proved] a iourny into Fraunce then into Ireland.

2. *trans.* To approve, sanction, countenance.

1702 C. MATHER *Magn. Chr.* VII. 31 They that shall have too suddenly improved those Men, will be Partakers of their Sins.

improved (ɪmˈpruːvd), *ppl. a.* [f. IMPROVE *v.*² + -ED¹.]

1. Under cultivation; cultivated, cultured.

1617 MIDDLETON & ROWLEY *Fair Quarrel* II. Diij, The most improude yong souldier of seuen kingdoms. **1644** in J. Merrill *Hist. Amesbury, Mass.* (1880) 29 The improved lands..upon ye west side of ye Powwaus river. **1736** BUTLER *Analogy* I. iii. 82 Two or three men of the best and most improved understanding. **1775** A. BURNABY *Trav. N. Amer.* 78 The climate, soil, natural produce, and improved state of it, are much the same as of Rhode Island. **1818** JAS. MILL *Brit. India* I. I. i. 3 At that time the most improved and commercial part of Europe.

2. Turned to good account.

1641 J. SHUTE *Sarah & Hagar* (1649) 205 What a fruitful gain is to be made of our well-improved-afflictions!

†**3.** Made greater, increased, enhanced; aggravated. *Obs.*

1690 LOCKE *Hum. Und.* III. xi. §1 The natural and improv'd Imperfections of Language.

4. Made better or more serviceable; brought to a higher or more desirable condition.

1713 STEELE *Guardian* No. 2 ⁋3 He left behind him an improved paternal estate of six thousand pounds a year. **1799** H. HUNTER tr. *St.-Pierre's Stud. Nat.* I. Pref. 7 This new and improved Translation. **1800** MRS. HERVEY *Mourtray Fam.* I. 222 In consequence of her improved circumstances. **1817** J. BRADBURY *Trav. Amer.* 263 Improved implements and methods. **1849** R. V. DIXON *Heat* I. ii. 147 An improved air-pump of his own construction.

5. ***improved wood***, thin sheets of wood attached to each other by films of synthetic resin, thus improving its resistance to distortion, shrinkage, etc.

1940 *Jrnl. R. Aeronaut. Soc.* XLIV. 673 It..could be expected that..composite wood plastics, like..'improved' wood, such as commonly used in the modern aeroplane manufacture, would be suitable for the construction of petrol containers. **1957** *N.Z. Timber Jrnl.* Aug. 59/2 Certain commercial treatments to prevent movement owing to moisture variation in wood, have resulted in what is termed 'improved wood'. **1963** A. D. WOOD *Plywoods of World* IV. 138 Improved wood is the product of a combination of veneers..interleaved with a synthetic resin glue film.

improvement (ɪmˈpruːvmənt). Forms: see IMPROVE *v.*² [a. AF. *emprowement*, *empruement*, f. *emprower* IMPROVE *v.*² + -MENT.]

†**1. a.** The turning of a thing to profit or good account; profitable management or use; making the most of a thing for one's own profit; realization of the profits of anything; *concr.* profit. *Obs.* in *lit.* sense.

In early use, Anglo-Fr. and Eng., applied to the profitable cultivation of land by the owner, and to the collection of the proceeds of customs or imposts by the king's officers, as distinguished from the letting of land or taxes to a farmer, who managed them for *his* profit.

[*c* **1320** ? LANGTOFT *MS. Oxf. Fairf.* 24 lf. 12 Car le pays est gaste si ne se asseure niant Au roy ne a sa meinie pur son empruement. *a* **1400** *Lib. Custum.* lf. 175 (Rolls) I. 220 Quil ieit une commune huche de la compaignie..en la quele les remembraunces et les enprowemenz de la compaignie soient mis en sauve garde. *Ibid.* 222 Soit le surpluis..mis en commune huche a lenprowement de la compaignie. **1402** *Act 4 Hen. IV*, c. 24 Come nadgairs..ordeignez estoit..qe launage des draps..ne seroit mys a ferme, a graunt damage de nostre sieur le Roy annuelment, ordeignez est..qe le dit aunage purra estre commys a ferme ou en emprowement [*Rolls of Parl.* III. 508/1 en aprowement], solonc ladvys de Tresorer Dengleterre purle temps esteant.] **1453** *Rolls of Parl.* V. 268/2 It is ordeigned be Statute made in the tyme of Harry the fourth that the aunage of Cloth withinne this Roialme may be committed to ferme or in emprowement, after the advis of the Tresorer of Englond for the tyme beyng. **1478** J. PASTON in *Paston Lett.* No. 811. III. 217 Mastyr Yotton had..desyred me..to se th' enprowment of syche profytes as ar growing of hys chapell in Caster that ye gave hym. **1523** FITZHERB. (*title*) The Boke of Surueyeng and Improumentes. *Ibid.* 9 Rynning waters..as they be stored with fysshe, so dothe yᵉ profyte ryse to the lordes, wheder they go by way of improuement or set to ferme: wherof the bayly shall make accompte. *Ibid.* 10 And of mylnes there shall more be spoken of in the chapiter of waters, among the improwmentes.

†**b.** The profitable employment or investment of money; also (in religious use) of a 'talent'. *Obs.*

1655 STANLEY *Hist. Philos.* III. (1701) 75/2 His Father.. left him four-score Minæ which being entrusted with a Friend for Improvement they miscarried. **1702** ECHARD *Eccl. Hist.* (1710) 255 One who had made such good emprovement of his small portion of grace.

2. a. *spec.* The turning of land to better account, the reclamation of waste or unoccupied land by inclosing and bringing it into cultivation (*obs.*); hence, in later use, cultivation and occupation of land; merged at length in sense 5. Now (as in N.Amer., N.Z.), the turning of farmland to better account by the erection of buildings, fences, etc.

[**1302** *Year-bks. 30–1 Edw. I* (Rolls) 19 Le leu ou les avers furent pris est une Wastin, e lenpruement dil Wast apend a nous.] **1549–50** *Act 3 & 4 Edw. VI*, c. 3 (*title*) An Acte concerninge the ymprovement of Comons and Waste Groundes. **1625** BACON *Ess.*, *Riches* (Arb.) 235 The Improuement of the Ground, is the most Naturall Obtaining of Riches;.. But it is slow. **1677** YARRANTON *Eng. Improv.* 115 In these delightful Countries, there is no waste Lands, but all under improvement. **1767** A. YOUNG *Farmer's Lett. People* 250 All improvement ceases to be such when more money is spent in it than the advantages will repay. **1769** *Quebec Gaz.* 16 Feb. 3/1 The Possessors of such Concessions shall be entitled to such Part of them as shall be proportioned to the Improvements they have made thereon. **1888** J. INGLIS *Tent Life Tigerland* 301 The 'grants' were held under certain conditions of improvement clearly laid down and defined in the Waste Land Regulations. **1891** R. WALLACE *Rural Econ. Australia & N.Z.* xv. 225 Many [N.Z.] settlers naturally prefer the lease, as a perpetual leasehold is practically as good as a freehold, while it leaves a settler free to invest his capital in improvements. **1958** *New Yorker* 6 Sept. 37, I remember it as it originally was, for my brother and I, aged eight and six, accompanied my father when he went out to make the first 'improvements'.

b. *concr.* †A piece of land improved or rendered more profitable by inclosure, cultivation, the erection of buildings, etc. (*obs.* exc. in *U.S. dial.*). Now (in N. Amer., N.Z.), the buildings, fences, etc., themelves. (Now associated with senses 5, 6.)

1640 in *New Haven Col. Rec.* 1638–49 (1857) 43 If they remove, to sell nothing butt improvements. **1666** *Plymouth Col. Rec.* (1855) IV. 119. **1773** GOLDSM. *Stoops to Conq.* I. i, My aunt's bell rings for our afternoon's walk round the improvements. **1776** TWISS *Tour Irel.* 66 The gardens (termed *improvements* in Ireland, and *policies* in Scotland) are not extensive. **1800** ADDISON *Amer. Law Rep.* 249 Bought for a trifle a small improvement, to wit some trees deadened. **1817** J. BRADBURY *Trav. Amer.* 291 To purchase from the Backwoodsman what he calls his improvement.. The improvement consists in a log house, a peach, and perhaps an apple orchard, together with from ten to thirty or forty acres of land, inclosed, and partially cleared. **1841** W. DEANS *Let.* 25 Mar. in J. Deans *Pioneers of Canterbury* (1937) 33 Mr. Molesworth let a town acre of his for £240.. for 14 years, buildings and improvements to remain at the end of the lease. **1856** 'J. PHOENIX' *Phoenixiana* (1859) xxxiii. 202 Three other small buildings, unoccupied, a fence, and a grave-yard, constitute all the 'improvements' that have been made at the 'Playa'. **1908** *Indian Laws & Treaties* (U.S.) III. 382 Any person who.. shall be an actual resident upon any one such lot and the owner of substantial and actual improvements thereon. **1927** *Amer. Speech* May 358 *Improvements and land* (noun phrase), a farm with its buildings and cleared land. **1930** L. G. D. ACLAND *Early Canterbury Runs* viii. 180 The Studholmes had the Terrace Station... When they sold it about 1862.. the only improvements on it were a shepherd's hut and a set of sheep yards. **1949** *Lubbock* (Texas) *Morning Avalanche* 23 Feb. II. 3 Good 8 inch irrigation well, large loan, good improvements, possession.

†**c.** *fig.* Bodily or mental cultivation or culture; also an item of such personal culture, an accomplishment. *Obs.* exc. as merged in 5, 6.

1711 STEELE *Spect.* No. 41 ⁋2, I am a mere Man of the Town, and have very little Improvement, but what I have got from Plays. *a* **1716** SOUTH (J.), I look upon your city as the best place of improvement: from the school we go to the university, but from the universities to London. **1734** tr. *Rollin's Anc. Hist.* xv. §15 (1827) VI. 231 The fifth is of soldiers whose only improvement is war. **1738** BIRCH *Milton* M.'s Wks. 1738 I. 3 As well in voluntary Improvements, as in the perfecting of his School-exercises.

3. a. The making good use or turning to account of any person or thing (now *obs.* or *U.S. dial.*), or of any event or season; profitable use or employment.

c **1611** CHAPMAN *Iliad* VI. 484 To lead in fight, and give no danger pass Without improvement. **1677** W. HUBBARD *Narrative* (1865) II. 89 What Benefit and Improvement was ever made thereof [Gorges's Patent for Maine] by his Agents or Successors. **1697** DAMPIER *Voy.* I. 227, I have not heard of any improvement made of this commodity by our Countrymen anywhere. *Mod.* His prompt improvement of the opportunity was admirable.

b. The turning of anything to good account for spiritual or moral edification; *spec.* the profitable spiritual application of a text or incident.

1655 J. CLERK *Faithfull Steward* 30 A sober use and faithfull improvement of these his mercies. **1677** I. MATHER *Preval. Prayer* (1864) 268 That is the special Improvement which should be made of what hath been discoursed. **1678** R. L'ESTRANGE *Seneca's Mor.* (1702) 519 A great part of the End of them is lost, without such an Emprovement. **1705** STANHOPE *Paraphr.* II. 4 The Improvement I design to make of this passage. **1818** JAS. MILL *Brit. India* II. v. iv. 447 Such is the doctrine; the practical improvement is obvious. **1842** R. M. M'CHEYNE in *Mem.* (1872) 269 Seek a right improvement of this bereavement.

†**c.** In more general sense: Use; practice. *Obs. rare.*

1686 SOUTH *Serm.* (1727) V. i. 12 The Corruption of Men's Manners by the habitual Improvement of this vicious Principle. **1754** EDWARDS *Freed. Will* II. xi. (1762) 115 The good or bad State of the moral World depends on the Improvement they make of their moral Agency.

†**d.** In American use: Employment, occupation. (Cf. IMPROVE *v.*[2] 2c, d). *Obs.*

1703 S. SEWALL *Letter-bk.* 22 Apr. I. 282 Very few gray hairs are to be found in the Colony, in civil or sacred improvement. **1705** *Ibid.* 6 June 312, I have a good right to a third part of the said meadow, and am in the actual improvement of it. **1736** in *New Eng. Hist. Reg.* (1850) IV. 112.

†**4.** The action or process of enhancing, making or becoming greater or more complete, or an instance of this: **a.** Enhancement (of rent). **b.** Increase, enlargement, growth, development, advancement. **c.** Intensification or aggravation of evil. (See IMPROVE *v.*[2] 3, 4, 4b.) *Obs.*

1548 *MS. Lansdowne* 238, lf. 317 These great fines for landes and emprowment of rentes shall abate. **1607** HIERON *Wks.* I. 436 Thus the enlargement of Gods mercy.. is the greatest improuement of our sinne. **1617** *Ibid.* II. 70 This was nothing but an addition to his vexation, and an improuement of his griefe. **1646** SIR T. BROWNE *Pseud. Ep.* III. xvii. 149 The multiplication of Hares, which is by superfetation.. or an improvement of a second fruit before the first be excluded. **1674** tr. *Scheffer's Lapland* 34 A further cause of the little improvement of Christianity, is the vastness of the Country. **1727** *Philip Quarll* (1816) 59 He went to see the improvement of his peas and beans, which he found increased to admiration. **1772** PRIESTLEY *Inst. Relig.* (1782) I. 19 The earth itself is in a state of improvement. **1788** V. KNOX *Winter Even.* I. II. xv. 212 Not entirely intelligible to children under twelve or fourteen, unless in rare cases of premature improvement and sagacity.

†**d.** quasi-*concr.* An advanced stage, developed form, development (*of* something). *Obs.*

1692 SOUTH *Serm.* (1697) II. 60 Friendship is the Noblest and most Refined Improvement of Love. *a* **1716** *Ibid.* (1744) IX. iv. 105 A sin against this is the highest pitch, the utmost improvement, and.. the *ne plus ultra* of provocation.

†**e.** *concr.* Increase, produce. *Obs.*

1705 STANHOPE *Paraphr.* III. 29 The greatest part of the Wealth and Improvement there consisted in Sheep. **1719** DE FOE *Crusoe* I. xix, The improvement, or annual production, being distributed to charitable uses.

5. The action or process of making or becoming better; advance or increase in value or excellence; betterment, amelioration.

(Only gradually separable from the earlier senses of beneficial cultivation (2), and advancement or development (4).)

1647 CLARENDON *Hist. Reb.* I. §15 For the improvement of his Education, and giving an ornament to his hopefull Person. **1662** J. DAVIES tr. *Mandelslo's Trav.* 284 The quiet of the City, the wellfare of its Inhabitants, and the improvement of Trade. **1736** BUTLER *Anal.* I. v. Wks. 1874 I. 98 This moral principle is capable of improvement, by proper discipline and exercise. **1783** BLAIR *Rhet.* I. ii. 19 Exercise is the chief source of improvement in all our faculties. **1859** MILL *Liberty* 128 We are eager for improvement in politics, education, even in morals. **1875** JOWETT *Plato* (ed. 2) V. 96 A good education tends to the improvement of body and mind.

6. With *an* and *pl.*: **a.** An act of making or becoming better; a process, change, or addition, by which the value or excellence of a thing is increased; that in which such addition consists or by which anything is made better.

(In early use chiefly in reference to land; cf. 2 and 2b.)

1697 DRYDEN *Virg. Georg.* I. 122 Long Practice has a sure Improvement found, With kindled Fires to burn the barren Ground. **1705** STANHOPE *Paraphr.* II. 168 Religion is the highest Improvement of Humanity and Good-nature. **1739** CHESTERF. *Lett.* (1792) I. l. 181 You cannot imagine what alterations and improvements I expect to find every day, now that you are more than *Octennis*. **1774** C. J. PHIPPS *Voy. N. Pole* 11 With the new chain-pumps.. according to Captain Bentinck's improvements. **1776** ADAM SMITH *W.N.* I. i. (1869) I. 11 Many improvements have been made by the ingenuity of the makers of the machines. **1796** MRS. GLASSE *Cookery* xxi. 330 It is a great improvement to add the juice of two Seville oranges. **1870** *Echo* 16 Feb., Mr. Gladstone caused a general laugh by asking, 'What is an improvement?'.. the definition he gave seemed to meet with general approval—that it shall add to the letting value of the land, and must be suitable to the holding. **1888** J. INGLIS *Tigerland* 264 If the tan is occasionally rubbed into the pores of the skin it will be an improvement.

b. With *on* or *upon*: The production of something better or more perfect than (something previous), an advance upon; hence, the result of this, a thing that is better than (the former thing).

1712 ADDISON *Spect.* No. 273 ⁋4 (ed. 2) The Parts of Sinon, Camilla, and some few others, which are fine Improvements on the Greek Poet. **1782** PRIESTLEY *Corrupt. Chr.* I. III. 301 An improvement was made upon this doctrine. **1878** SPURGEON *Treas. Dav.* Ps. cvi. 7 We fear the sons are no great improvement upon the sires. **1896** *Newsagents' Chron.* 3 Oct. 3/3 The.. Magazine for October is a decided improvement on its predecessors.

7. *attrib.* and *Comb.*; **improvement lease**, in the United States and Australia, a lease granted with conditions of improvement to be made by the lessee.

1840 W. SEWALL *Diary* 15 Aug. (1930) 218/1 Henry and myself repairing fence west side of improvement ditch. **1849** E. CHAMBERLAIN *Indiana Gazetteer* (ed. 3) 34 They rented land on improvement leases, by which they were to have the use of from ten to twenty acres from seven to ten years, and often at the end of that time they were able to buy land for themselves. **1895** *Act* (New South Wales) 58 *Vict.* no. 18 §26 (*heading*) Improvement leases. **1900** *Daily News* 16 May 5/3 The new improvement undertakings of the Council. **1909** *Commonwealth Law Rep., High Court Australia* VII. 1, Sec. 26 of the *Crown Lands Act* 1895.. authorizes the Governor to grant 'improvement' leases of Crown lands which by reason of inferior quality, heavy timber, or other cause are not suitable for settlement until improved. **1909** *Daily Chron.* 30 Apr. 6/4 The improvement values added by enterprise. *Ibid.* 7/7 Housing and improvement schemes. **1909** *Westm. Gaz.* 19 May 2/2 The sale of sites in improvement areas. *Ibid.* 4/1 The trifling amount of improvement-sites which their predecessors have acquired. **1964** *Ann. Reg.* 1963 128 Then.. the Court decided that the Council of Ministers could not transfer municipal powers to improvement boards. **1972** *Guardian* 15 June 14 Improvement grants.. are overwhelmingly taken up by better-off owner-occupiers and speculative property developers.

improven, obs. (erron.) Sc. pa. pple. of IMPROVE *v.*[2]

improven, -in, pa. pple. of IMPREVE *v.*

improver[1] (ɪmˈpruːvə(r)). [f. IMPROVE *v.*[2] + -ER[1].] One who or that which improves.

†**1.** One who turns something to good account, or makes profitable use of it: in quot. 1647, one who cultivates or practises. *Obs.*

1647 CLARENDON *Hist. Reb.* I. §132 The greatest.. improvers of that Breeding, and those Qualifications with which Courts used to be adorned. **1654** WHITLOCK *Zootomia* 434 The ablest Improver of his time and parts. **1662** STILLINGFL. *Orig. Sacr.* III. ii. §18 This great improver and discoverer of the Mechanicall power of matter.

2. a. One who makes better; a person that increases the value or excellence of a thing, or brings it into a more desirable state. In early use, One who advances, develops, or makes more perfect (a branch of knowledge, etc.).

a **1661** FULLER *Worthies* xii. (1662) 41 Eminent Improvers of any art may be allowed for the Co-inventers thereof. **1713** GAY *Guardian* No. 149 ⁋18, I would counsel all our improvers of fashion always to take the hint from France. **1807** G. CHALMERS *Caledonia* I. II. vi. 310 The monks were.. the improvers of themselves, and the instructers of others, in the most useful arts. **1842** MRS. BROWNING *Grk. Chr. Poets* (1863) 120 An improver of the language. **1882–3** in Schaff *Encycl. Relig. Knowl.* 2132 An improver of other men's verses.

b. *spec.* One who applies himself to making land more productive or profitable. (Cf. IMPROVABLE 2, IMPROVEMENT 2). Now merged in 2.

1649 BLITHE (*title*) English Improver, or a new Survey of Husbandry. **1765** A. DICKSON *Treat. Agric.* II. (ed. 2) 274 May I be allowed to say, without giving offence to Improvers [etc.]? **1846** MCCULLOCH *Acc. Brit. Empire* (1854) I. 585 In 1723, a Society of Improvers was established at Edinburgh. **1883** *Contemp. Rev.* Dec. 861 Many landlords are great improvers. Many spend annually a third or half of their rent in improvements.

c. A thing that improves or makes better. *spec.* Short for *dress-improver*: see DRESS *sb.* 4a.

1669 STILLINGFL. *Serm.* ix. (1673) 167 Cold and nakedness, stripes and imprisonments, racks and torments? Are these the improvers of an excellent constitution? **1669** WORLIDGE *Syst. Agric.* v. §2. 61 [Chalk] after it is burned into Lime, becomes a very excellent Improver of Lands. **1777** LIGHTFOOT *Flora Scot.* II. 658 Fern cut while green, and left to rot upon the ground, is a good improver of land. **1872** *Young Englishwoman* Oct. 554/1 The improver consists of a thick calico foundation stiffened with whalebone.. furnished with strings to tie round the waist. **1884** *Pall Mall G.* 6 Sept. 7/2 She was searched, and her 'improver' was found to be so arranged as to hold 6 lb. of smuggled tobacco. **1887** *Daily News* 22 June 5/2 The hideous 'improver', which is one of the blots upon the picturesqueness of modern costume.

d. Any substance or preparation added to a foodstuff by a manufacturer or processor in order to improve it in some respect (e.g. in texture or keeping quality).

1902 LEFFMANN & BEAM *Food Analysis* 364 Improvers and Preservatives.—Mixtures of potassium nitrate, sodium chlorid, and other mineral preservatives with a little coloring-matter.. are sold for improving the appearance of meat. **1925** MOJONNIER & TROY *Technical Control Dairy Products* (ed. 2) xiii. 300 Several commercial products commonly known by the general term 'ice cream improvers' are in common use. These consist of rennet or pepsin mixed with certain powders such as milk sugar. These products react upon the casein in the mix, causing an increase in the viscosity. **1927** *Manch. Guardian Weekly* 11 Mar. 183/2 Indiscreet and provocative references in the press to 'improvers' and bleaching agents used in the preparation of flour for bread-making. **1960** W. J. FRANCE *Breadmaking & Flour Confectionary* xi. 109 Barbadoes and Demarara.—These sugars because of their colour, are useful brown bread improvers, adding a characteristic flavour to brown breads. **1970** FOX & CAMERON *Food Sci.* viii. 165 This ageing period can be dispensed with if the flour is treated with a minute quantity of one of a number of oxidizing agents which are called flour improvers. *Ibid.*, The first four of the improvers listed increase the whiteness of the flour by bleaching the carotene and xanthophyll, which.. give the flour a slight yellow tinge.

3. A person who works at a trade under an employer for the purpose of improving his or her knowledge or skill, and accepts the opportunity of such improvement wholly or in part instead of wages.

1858 SIMMONDS *Dict. Trade*, *Improver*, a learner. **1883** *Daily Tel.* 9 Apr. 7/6 (*Advt. Milliners*) Juniors or improvers.

1884 *B'ham Daily Post* 24 Jan. 3/5 (*Advt.*) Telegraph Clerks.—Wanted, Young Lady, as Improver. **1895** *Westm. Gaz.* 18 Sept. 3/1 His favourite plan is to take a situation as 'improver' to a working jeweller in a small way of business.

†**4.** = APPROVER². *Obs. rare.*

1670 BLOUNT *Law. Dict.* s.v. *Approve*, You may see what kinde of Approvers or Improvers were formerly in the Marches of Wales, authorized by the Prince thereof.

Hence **im'proveress**, a female improver; **im'provership**, the position of an improver (sense 3).

1744 J. PATERSON *Comm. Milton's P.L.* 305 Ceres was an inventress or improveress of husbandry. **1884** *Daily News* 3 Sept. 8/5 (*Advt.*) To Printers.—Improvership Wanted.

†**im'prover²**. *Obs. rare*⁻⁰. [f. IMPROVE *v.*¹ + -ER¹.] One who disproves, a confuter.

1611 FLORIO, *Improuatore*, an improouer.

†**impro'vided**, *a. Obs.* [f. IM-² + PROVIDED.]

1. Unprovided; unprepared.

1548 HALL *Chron., Edw. IV*, 247 b, He was in jeopardye of hys lyfe, and all improvided, for dread of death, coacted .. to sayle vnto Fraunce. **1622** BACON *Hen. VII*, 109 He was not to hope for any aide from Maximilian, for that hee was altogether improuided.

2. Unforeseen; unlooked for.

1590 SPENSER *F.Q.* I. xii. 34 To worke new woe and improvided scath.

improvidence (ɪm'prɒvɪdəns). [ad. L. *imprōvidentia*, f. *im-* (IM-²) + *prōvidentia* PROVIDENCE, foresight; cf. also obs. F. *improvidence* (16th c. in Godef.), It. *improvidenza*.] The fact or quality of being improvident; want of providence or foresight; thriftlessness.

1598 FLORIO, *Improvidenza*, improuidence, rashness. **1602** MARSTON *Ant. & Mel.* I. Wks. 1856 I. 11 Shee'le lift thee to improvidence, And breake thy neck from steepe securitie. *a* **1631** DONNE in *Select.* (1840) 88 Malice in other men or improvidence in myself, had ruined my fortune. **1786** BURKE *W. Hastings* III. iii. §15 His total improvidence in not taking any one rational security whatsoever against the inevitable consequences of those acts. **1836** H. COLERIDGE *North. Worthies* (1852) I. 40 Improvidence or treachery had left our shores defenceless. *a* **1862** BUCKLE *Misc. Wks.* (1872) I. 542 The only peculiarity I have found common to all barbarous nations is improvidence—indifference to the future.

improvident (ɪm'prɒvɪdənt), *a.* [f. IM-² + PROVIDENT: cf. prec., and L. *imprōvidus* not foreseeing, improvident.]

1. Of persons, their actions, etc.: Unforeseeing; that does not foresee or forecast the future.

1514 BARCLAY *Cyt. & Uplondyshm.* (Percy Soc.) 5 We finde yonge people be moche improvydent. **1597** DANIEL *Civ. Wars* III. xxix, When men well have fed, th' blood being warme, Then are they most improvident of harme. **1657** R. LIGON *Barbadoes* (1673) 25 They could not have been so improvident, as not to foresee the main inconveniences that must ensue. **1795** LD. AUCKLAND *Corr.* (1862) III. 306 The improvident, undignified, and unwise conduct of the German powers.

2. Not circumspect; heedless; unwary.

1591 SHAKS. *1 Hen. VI*, II. i. 58 Improuident Souldiors, had your Watch been good, This sudden Mischiefe neuer could haue falne. **1625** J. GLANVILL *Voy. Cadiz* (Camden) 58 They cutt of some few of our improvident and stragling men. **1650** BULWER *Anthropomet.* 162 Behold .. what the improvident curiosity of men hath thought on. **1765** BLACKSTONE *Comm.* I. 50 There is imminent danger of his employing that strength to improvident or oppressive purposes. **1849** GROTE *Greece* II. lv. (1862) V. 10 Amphipolis had been once lost by the improvident watch of Thucydidês and Euklês: it was now again lost by the improvident concessions of Nikias.

3. That fails to provide for future needs; thriftless.

1624 CAPT. SMITH *Virginia* IV. 110 So improuident as not to put Corne in the ground for their bread, but trusted to the store. **1788** PRIESTLEY *Lect. Hist.* V. xxxviii. 279 Great numbers .. will be improvident, spending every thing they have in the most extravagant manner. **1809–10** COLERIDGE *Friend* (1837) II. 199 They who live from hand to mouth, will most frequently become improvident. **1873** H. SPENCER *Stud. Sociol.* xv. 366 The English people are complained of as improvident. Very few of them lay by in anticipation of times when work is slack.

Hence **im'providentness** (Bailey vol. II, 1727).

†**improvi'dential**, *a. Obs. rare.* [IM-².]

1. Not providential; ungoverned by Providence.

a **1684** LEIGHTON *Serm.* Wks. (1868) 358 Though trouble be the general lot of mankind, yet it doth not come on him by an improvidential fatality.

2. Improvident: see next.

†**improvi'dentially**, *adv. Obs.* [f. prec. 2 + -LY².] = next.

1797 HOLCROFT *Stolberg's Trav.* (ed. 2) III. lxxxiii. 330 Chesnuts, which the mother, not improvidentially, had put in her pocket. **1819** CRABBE *T. of Hall* 32 The younger .. had rather improvidentially but happily married.

im'providently, *adv.* [f. IMPROVIDENT *a.* + -LY².]

1. In an improvident manner; without forethought; without providing for the future.

1607 DONNE *Lett.* (1651) 209, I went unprofitably and improvidently, to the utmost end of Truth. **1688** BOYLE *Final Causes Nat. Things* iv. 203 It must be casually or improvidently framed or placed. **1780** BURKE *Sp. Econ. Reform* Wks. III. 333 To recommit all its business to the council from whence it was very improvidently taken. **1868** ROGERS *Pol. Econ.* viii. (1876) 70 Agricultural labourers marry early and improvidently.

2. In an unforeseen or unanticipated manner. *rare.*

1885 E. F. BYRRNE *Entangled* I. I. viii. 139 Nature may treacherously and improvidently back-water; and he dreaded to be landed incontinently in the stagnation of satiety.

†**improving**, *vbl. sb.*¹ *Obs.* [f. IMPROVE *v.*¹ + -ING¹.] The action of IMPROVE *v.*¹; disproving, refutation.

c **1449** PECOCK *Repr.* I. i. 5 It is miche nede forto first .. vnroote and ouerturne tho thre trowingis .. bifore the improuyng of othere. *c* **1530** L. COX *Rhet.* (1899) 49 Argumentes for the prouinge or improuynge of compounde themes. **1574** WHITGIFT *Def. Aunsw.* II. 100 You shoulde haue kept you to the improuing of this generall proposition. **1611** FLORIO, *Improuatione*, an improouing.

improving (ɪm'pruːvɪŋ), *vbl. sb.*² [f. IMPROVE *v.*² + -ING¹.] The action of IMPROVE *v.*², q.v.; improvement.

1602 FULBECKE *2nd Pt. Parall.* 54 The improouing of ground from worse to better, is clearely permitted by our law. **1785** J. PHILLIPS *Treat. Inland Navig.* 49 Were it for nothing else but the improving of land .. the expence would be amply repaid.

b. *improving lease* (Sc. Law): a lease granted to a tenant for a longer period than the usual one, with the object of encouraging him to make permanent improvements on the holding by ensuring to him a longer enjoyment of their benefits.

1861 W. BELL *Dict. Law Scot.* s.v., A lease of ordinary endurance is a lease for nineteen or twenty-one years; and an improving lease is usually for thirty-eight or forty-two years.

im'proving, *ppl. a.* [f. as prec. + -ING².] That improves.

1. That makes better; *spec.* that improves the mind, understanding, or character; that makes agricultural improvements.

1665 BOYLE *Occas. Refl.* Introd. (1848) 24 The Sun, by his piercing and improving Beams, can not only make Diamonds sparkle, and Rubies flame, but [etc.]. **1736** BUTLER *Anal.* II. vi. Wks. 1874 I. 240 Temptations render our state a more improving state of discipline, than it would be otherwise. **1792** MARIA RIDDELL *Voy. Madeira* Ded. 6 After it has once undergone a few corrections from your improving hand. **1881** *Daily News* 14 Sept. 3/1 Should an improving farmer wish to leave for a finer opening in agriculture. **1884** G. ALLEN *Philistia* II. 11 Read a few verses of some improving volume every night.

2. Becoming better; advancing or increasing in excellence.

1694 F. BRAGGE *Disc. Parables* viii. 298 A soul so filled with grace as the improving soul will be. **1791** WASHINGTON *Lett.* Writ. 1892 XII. 49 The country appears to be in a very improving state. **1891** *Anthony's Photogr. Bull.* IV. 88 Improving powers of criticism.

Hence **im'provingly** *adv.*, in an improving manner; in the way of improvement.

1842 *Fraser's Mag.* XXVI. 520 Were he to disturb, however improvingly, the earlier songs. **1852** *Blackw. Mag.* LXXI. 461 How are we to amuse them?—Respectably of course; improvingly by all means.

improvisate (ɪm'prɒvɪzeɪt), *v.* Also **improvvisate**. [f. F. *improviser* or It. *improv(v)isare*: see IMPROVISE and -ATE³.]

= IMPROVISE. **a.** *trans.*

1832 J. H. NEWMAN *Lett.* (1891) I. 284, I was obliged to improvisate a padlock. **1837** *Tait's Mag.* IV. 453 It was easy to improvisate a paroxysm of royal rapture. **1837** *Fraser's Mag.* XVI. 413 He had improvvisated the verses.

b. *intr.* To speak extempore.

1838 JAS. GRANT *Random Recoll. Lds. & Com.* Ser. II. II. vii. 89 Few men in the house can improvisate better [than Mr. Gladstone].

im'provisate, *ppl. a. rare.* [ad. It. *improv(v)isato*, pa. pple. of *improv(v)isare* to improvise.] = IMPROVISED; unpremeditated, impromptu.

1847 in CRAIG. Hence in mod. Dicts.

improvisation (ɪmprɒvɪ'zeɪʃən, ˌɪmprəvaɪ'zeɪʃən). [n. of action from IMPROVISE, IMPROVISATE: cf. mod.F. *improvisation*.]

1. a. The action of improvising or composing extempore; also *concr.* verse, music, etc. so improvised.

1786 COLMAN *Prose Sev. Occas.* (1787) III. 166 Poor Tuscan-like Improvisation. **1811** SCOTT *Don Roderick* Introd. ix. *note*, The flexibility of the Italian and Spanish languages .. renders these countries distinguished for the talent of improvisation. **1834** GREVILLE *Mem.* 13 Aug. (1875) III. xxiv. 119 After dinner he [Theodore Hook] displayed his extraordinary talent of improvisation. **1872** GEO. ELIOT *Middlem.* xx, This speech .. was not indeed entirely an improvisation, but had taken shape in inward colloquy. **1876** LOWELL *Among my Bks.* Ser. II. 214 We can not expect in a modern poet the thrush-like improvisation .. that charm[s] us in our Elizabethan drama.

b. *spec.* of Old English verse.

1928 W. W. LAWRENCE *Beowulf & Epic Trad.* 3 We must agree to judge *Beowulf*, .. not as the improvisation of an untutored minstrel, but as a well-considered work of art. **1960** *English Studies* XLI. 5 The use of traditional diction is one thing; improvisation is something else again. The two need not go together and in *Beowulf* they most emphatically do not.

2. The production or execution of anything off-hand; any work or structure produced on the spur of the moment.

1874 SYMONDS *Sk. Italy & Greece* (1898) I. xi. 214 The terra-cotta decorations .. have all the spontaneity of improvisation. **1884** S. E. DAWSON *Handbk. Canada* 231 The Crystal Palace Opera-House, an improvisation on Dominion Square [Montreal].

improvi'sational, *a.* [f. IMPROVISATION + -AL.] Of or relating to improvisation, impromptu.

1923 *Theatre Arts Mag.* Oct. 328 He is always true to the great school of acting of the Italian improvisational comedy. **1958** *Times* 15 Dec. 3/4 His playing of Schubert's great B flat major sonata .. was far too improvisational and dreamy. **1970** P. OLIVER *Savannah Syncopators* 19 Jazz, at least in its early phases, was primarily a group music, using brass and wind instruments with rhythm background, employing improvisational techniques both collectively and in solo. **1972** *Jazz & Blues* Nov. 6 Orchestral textures, improvisational complexity, harmonic innovation. **1973** *Black World* Mar. 26 A stock feature of chanted sermons: the highly rhythmic, imaginative and improvisational rendering of the Word of God.

Hence **improvi'sationally** *adv.*

1946 R. BLESH *Shining Trumpets* (1949) ii. 33 The leader chants, often improvisationally, in strong declamatory phrases. **1963** *Times* 30 Apr. 15/4 Prokofiev's Seventh Sonata was also somewhat improvisationally showy instead of stable and strong.

improvisatize (ɪm'prɒvɪzətaɪz), *v. rare.* [irreg. f. IMPROVISATE + -IZE.] = IMPROVISATE, IMPROVISE.

1847 in CRAIG. **1860** A. L. WINDSOR *Ethica* vii. 382 Unlike Chatham, Mirabeau did not improvisatize.

improvisator (ɪm'prɒvɪzeɪtə(r)). [agent-n. in L. form, from IMPROVISE, IMPROVISATE, after It. *improv(v)isatore*, F. *improvisateur*.] One who improvises or composes extempore: an improviser. *spec.* of Old English verse.

1795 W. TAYLOR in *Monthly Rev.* XVIII. 125 The Italian improvisator never attempts a ballad without striking his mandolino. **1829** CARLYLE *Misc. Ess., Novalis* (1872) II. 183 The old guild of literary Improvisators. **1870** EMERSON *Soc. & Solit., Eloq.* Wks. (Bohn) III. 28 The world knows pretty well the style of these improvisators [Eastern story-tellers]. **1915** W. W. LAWRENCE in *PMLA* XXX. 400 A direct quotation of the lay sung by the improvisator. **1928** —— *Beowulf & Epic Trad.* 261 Each individual poet .. adapting, with the adroitness of the improvisator, bygone legends to the demands of special occasions.

‖**improvisatore**, **-provvisatore** (improv-viza'tore). *Pl.* -ori (-ori), also -ores. [It. *improvvisatore*, formerly *improvisatore* 'an extempore-sayer' (Florio), agent-n. from *improv(v)isare* to IMPROVISE.

(The non-etymological doubling of the *v* is a matter of mod. Italian phonetic spelling not generally followed in Eng.)]

An improvisator (Italian or of the Italian type).

1765 SMOLLETT *Trav.* (1766) II. xxvii. 56 One of the greatest curiosities you meet with in Italy, is the improvisatore; such is the name given to certain individuals, who have the surprising talent of reciting verses extempore, on any subject you propose. **1785** *Europ. Mag.* VII. 300 Metastasio .. was at his outset an *improvisatore*, or extempore poet. **1817** BYRON *Beppo* xxxiii, He patronised the Improvisatori .. Wrote rhymes, sang songs, could also tell a story. **1824** —— *Juan* xv. xx, Just as I feel the 'Improvvisatore'. **1841** W. SPALDING *Italy & It. Isl.* I. 370 The Eumolpus of Petronius .. fills up the only link required to complete the analogy between the classical and the modern improvvisatori. **1888** J. INGLIS *Tent Life Tigerland* 234 The musicians .. improvisatores, reciters of ancient legends.

attrib. **1800** SOUTHEY *Poet. Wks.* (1853) 213/1, I do not wish the *improvisatorè* tune. **1851** J. H. NEWMAN *Cath. in Eng.* viii. 302 The extempore and improvisatore mode of fabricating and fabling against us.

improvisatorial (ɪmprɒvɪzə'tɔərɪəl), *a.* [f. as IMPROVISATORY + -AL¹.] Of, pertaining to, or of the nature of an improvisator; relating to or having the power of extempore composition or oratory.

1822 *New Monthly Mag.* IV. 467 Singing .. some old Castilian air, to which he often adapts some improvisatorial words. **1860** J. WOLFF *Trav. & Adv.* I. 81 His improvisatorial powers have been already mentioned. **1886** *Athenæum* 14 Aug. 197/3 Hence, in the deepest and truest sense, Scott, often called the most improvisatorial, is the least improvisatorial of writers.

Hence **improvisa'torially** *adv.*, after the manner of an improvisator.

1886 TUPPER *My Life as Author* 385 Those who speak off-hand in prose or verse, 'inspirationally' as they call it, but as the outer world prefer to believe, improvisatorially.

improvisatorize (ɪmprɒvɪ'zeɪtəraɪz), *v. rare.* [f. IMPROVISATOR + -IZE.] **a.** *intr.* To play or act the improvisator. **b.** *trans.* To improvise.

1828 *Harrovian* 43 M—— read novels, and F—— improvisatorized in heroics. **1835** *Fraser's Mag.* XII. 541

Might not the mirthful poet of 'Dean-Bourn'..have improvisatorised the following trifle? **1837** *Ibid.* XV. 286 Tragedy and comedy were originally improvisatorised.

improvisatory (ɪmprəʊ'vɪzətərɪ), *a.* [f. IMPROVISATOR (or IMPROVISATE *v.*): see -ORY.] = IMPROVISATORIAL.

1806 W. TAYLOR in Robberds *Mem.* II. 138 Write with or without rime, as happens to accommodate best your improvisatory method of composition. **1886** SYMONDS *Renaiss. It., Cath. React.* (1898) VII. xi. 158 Marino had the improvisatory exuberance..of his birthplace.

‖**improvisatrice, -provvisatrice** (improv-viza'tritʃe). Pl. -trici (-tritʃi). [It. *improvvisatrice* (formerly *improvis-*), fem. of *improv(v)isatore*: see -TRICE.] A woman who improvises.

1804 MATILDA BETHAM *Biog. Dict. Wom.* 290 An honorary name given to the poetess (improvisatrice) D. Maria Maddalena Morelli Fernandez. **1838** *Penny Cycl.* XII. 452/2 Several ladies have distinguished themselves in the same art: they are styled improvvisatrici. **1844** MARG. FULLER *Wom. 19th C.* (1862) 28 We will not speak of the enthusiasm excited by actresses, improvisatrici, female singers. **1886** W. J. TUCKER *E. Europe* 338 The improvisatrice, the bewitching, supple siren stepped forward into the midst of the vacant space.

improvise (ɪmprəʊ'vaɪz, now usu. 'ɪmprəʊvaɪz), *v.* [a. F. *improvise-r* (1642 in Hatz.-Darm.), ad. It. *improvisare* (now *improvv-*) 'to sing or say extempore' (Florio), f. *improv(v)iso* IMPROVISO.]

1. *trans.* **a.** To compose (verse, music, etc.) on the spur of the moment; to utter or perform extempore.

1826 DISRAELI *Viv. Grey* II. i, He possessed also the singular faculty of being able to improvise quotations. *Ibid.* IV. ii, You must not improvise parliamentary papers. **1858** DORAN *Crt. Fools* 251 His happy facility of improvising rhymes. **1874** SYMONDS *Sk. Italy & Greece* (1898) I. vi. 115 The..funeral chant, improvised by women at funerals over the bodies of the dead.

b. *spec.* of Old English verse.

1915 W. W. LAWRENCE in *PMLA* XXX. 400 A thane of the king, skilled in story..entertains the company, improvising a song in honor of Beowulf. **1948** P. F. BAUM in *Mod. Philology* XLVI. 76 The minstrel..begins by improvising in verse an account of Beowulf's adventures which he had just learned about and had had little opportunity to work up beforehand. This..presupposes something different from the *Beowulf*, which certainly does not give the impression of improvising.

2. To bring about or get up on the spur of the moment; to provide for the occasion.

a **1854** E. FORBES *Lit. Papers* viii. (1855) 206 If a number of both sexes happen to assemble at the same house a dance is improvised. **1859** DICKENS *Lett. to Miss D.* 13 June (1880) II. 95 A tent improvised this morning.

3. *intr.* **a.** To compose, utter, or perform verse or music impromptu; to speak extemporaneously; hence, to do anything on the spur of the moment.

1830 H. N. COLERIDGE *Grk. Poets* (1834) 42 A noted English wit of the present day can improvise in rhyme even in our language. **1845** E. HOLMES *Mozart* 22 He sang, played, and composed extempore, played and transposed at sight..improvised on a given bass. **1880** VERN. LEE *Italy* IV. i. 147 He had the honour of improvising before cardinals and princesses.

b. *spec.* of Old English verse.

1892 J. EARLE *Deeds of Beowulf* 136 The minstrel did not merely narrate, but improvised in alliterative verse. **1961** W. WHALLON in *PMLA* LXXVI. 310 The oral poet cannot pause; he must improvise continuously with no apparent effort.

Hence '**improvising** *vbl. sb.*; also *attrib.*

1832 W. IRVING *Alhambra, Journey* (1896) 10 This talent of singing and improvising is frequent in Spain, and is said to have been inherited from the Moors. **1853** JERDAN *Autobiog.* III. ii. 20 [He] was..in superb trim to answer the calls for various improvising interludes.

impro'vise, *sb. rare.* [f. prec. vb.] An improvised composition; an improvisation.

1820 MRS. SHELLEY in Dowden *Shelley* (1887) II. 360 Go to the theatre and hear the Improvise of Sgricci. **1821** SHELLEY *Hellas* Pref., The poem..is a mere improvise.

improvised (ɪmprəʊ'vaɪzd, now usu. 'ɪmprəʊvaɪzd), *ppl. a.* [f. prec. vb. + -ED^1.]

Composed or uttered off-hand; invented or produced on the spur of the moment or for the occasion.

1837 CARLYLE *Fr. Rev.* III. I. iv, What part might be premeditated, what was improvised and accidental, man will never know. **1863** GEO. ELIOT *Romola* II. xxvi, [He] let Gaddi have the credit of the improvised welcome. **1873** SMILES *Huguenots Fr.* I. x. (1881) 214 By crossing their hands over each other, they..carried him along on this improvised chair. **1876** GEO. ELIOT *Dan. Der.* VIII. lxi, His improvised words had inevitably some drollery.

improvisedly (ɪmprəʊ'vaɪzɪdlɪ), *adv.* [f. prec. + -LY^2. In sense 2, for L. *improviso*, It. *improvvisamente*.]

1. In an improvised or unpremeditated manner; impromptu, extempore.

1882 H. C. MERIVALE *Faucit of B.* I. I. vi. 97 He..could dress up Plato's Republic improvisedly, in sympathetic and attractive English of his own.

†**2.** (*Sc.* **improvisitlie**). Without forethought, imprudently, precipitately. *Obs.*

c **1568** in H. Campbell *Love-Lett. Mary Q. Scots* App. (1824) 20 Humblie requiring..that pretendit and unlauchfull marriage quhairin sho was improvisitlie enterit to be dissolvit.

impro'viser. [f. IMPROVISE *v.* + -ER^1.] One who improvises; an improvisator. Also *attrib.*

1829 *Blackw. Mag.* XXVIII. 134 Earth holds no improvizer like Theodore. **1851** CARLYLE *Sterling* II. vi. (1872) 137 Essentially an improviser genius; as his Father too was. **1880** *Sat. Rev.* 26 June 830/2 There was a certain Maria Maddalena Morelli..known as poet and improviser, and much in request for her powers of social entertainment. **1948** P. F. BAUM in *Mod. Philology* XLVI. 76 Its meter and the variations exhibit by turns both the ease and freedom of the improviser and the careful workmanship of the artist.

†**impro'vision.** *Obs.* [f. IM-^{2} + PROVISION.] Want of provision or forethought.

1646 SIR T. BROWNE *Pseud. Ep.* III. ii. 108 Wherein..there would be a maine defect, and her improvision justly accusable, if [etc.]. **1649** JER. TAYLOR *Gt. Exemp.* III. §14. 41 The disadvantages of ignorance or improvision.

†**improviso** (ɪmprəʊ'vaɪzəʊ), *a. Obs.* [It. *improviso*, now spelt *improvviso* 'vnprouided, extempore' (Florio), = L. *imprōvīsus* unforeseen, unexpected, f. *im-* (IM-^{2}) + *prōvīsus*, pa. pple. of *prōvidēre* to foresee. (The word may also be taken as an adjectival use of the L. adv. *imprōvīsō* (also *dē imprōvīsō*, *ex imprōvīsō*) 'on a sudden, unexpectedly'.)] Improvised, extempore.

1786 MRS. PIOZZI *Anecdotes Johnson* (title of poem) Improviso translation of the following distich on the Duke of Modena's running away from the comet in 1742 or 1743. **1789** —— *Journ. France* I. 374 Our postillion sung improviso verses on his sweetheart. [**1839** *Standard* 29 Mar. in *Spirit Metrop. Conserv. Press* (1840) I. 142 An impassioned and *ex-improviso* survey.]

Hence **impro'viso** *v. trans.* (*nonce-wd.*), to improvise.

1835 *Blackw. Mag.* XXXVII. 518 He had *improvisoed* a joyous song.

improvvisatore, -trice: see IMPROVIS-.

imprudence (ɪm'pruːdəns). [ad. L. *imprūdentia*, n. of quality f. *imprūdēns* IMPRUDENT: see -ENCE. Cf. F. *imprudence* (Oresme, 14th c.), which may have been the immediate source.] The quality or fact of being imprudent; want of prudence, circumspection, or discretion; indiscretion, rashness.

[In Chaucer's *Parson's Tale* ⁋317, 'imprudence' is the reading in MSS. Harl. 7334, Petw. 635, Selden; but this is evidently an error: all MSS. have 'impudent' in the correlative ⁋323: see quot. 1386 in IMPUDENCE I.]

1541 R. COPLAND *Galyen's Terapeut.* 2 Bijb, The fyrste speake ouer lyghtly and to imprudently, yf it be imprudence to afferme a thynge impossyble. *c* **1645** HOWELL *Lett.* (1650) I. VI. iii. 253 To this day the Spanish council is taxed of improvidence and imprudence, that there was no use made of the hanse towns in that expedition. **1731** C'TESS SUFFOLK in *Swift's Lett.* (1766) II. 143 There is an epitaph in St. Patrick's cathedral, that will be a lasting monument of your imprudence. **1831** SIR J. SINCLAIR *Corr.* II. 85 Not taking those precautions against the weather.., I soon suffered for my imprudence.

b. with *an* and *pl.* An instance of this, an imprudent act.

1646–9 JER. TAYLOR *Apol. Liturgy* §95 It were a strange imprudence, choosingly, to entertain those inconveniences. **1768–74** TUCKER *Lt. Nat.* (1852) II. 361 If Eve had been deceived before by the serpent into some imprudences not criminal, she might have been aware of his wiles. **1889** LUBBOCK *Pleas. Life* II. iv. 64 Love at first sight sounds like an imprudence, and yet is almost a revelation.

†**im'prudency.** *Obs.* [ad. L. *imprūdēntia*: see prec. and -ENCY.] = IMPRUDENCE.

1576 BAKER *Jewell of Health* 122 a, Through the hastinesse and imprudencie of the worker. **1620** VENNER *Via Recta* viii. 166 The fault is rather to be attributed to our imprudency, and intemperancie. **1698** NORRIS *Pract. Disc.* IV. Pref., Men have a Toleration for their Imprudencies. **1792** A. YOUNG *Trav. France* 118 Some imprudencies in the manner of forcing the King's system. **1800** LAMB *Let. to Wordsworth* 10 Oct., It tickles one with the image of an imprudency, without the penalty usually annexed.

imprudent (ɪm'pruːdənt), *a.* (*sb.*) [ad. L. *imprūdēns*, *imprūdēnt-em*, f. *im-* (IM-^{2}) + *prūdēns*, contracted from *prōvidēns*, pres. pple. of *prōvidēre* to see before one, provide: see PRUDENT. Cf. F. *imprudent* (15–16th c. in Hatz.-Darm.).] Not prudent, wanting in prudence or discretion; the reverse of prudent; rash, heedless, indiscreet, incautious. **a.** Of persons.

c **1386** CHAUCER *Man of Law's T.* 211 Imprudent Emperour of Rome allas Was ther no philosophre in al thy toun? **1541** R. COPLAND *Galyen's Terapeut.* 2 Dj, O foole and imprudent Thessalus. **1548** HALL *Chron., Hen. VII* 46 He and his imprudent counsayll were fully resolved on this poincte. **1710** NORRIS *Chr. Prud.* ii. 71 Imprudent men are call'd Fools. **1893** TANNER *Steps Princ. Agric.* (ed. 2) 61 We are not so imprudent..as to destroy the bees that work for us.

b. Of conduct, actions, etc.

1599 HAKLUYT *Voy.* II. 35 (R.) Thus by the imprudent and foolish hardines of the French earle, the Frenchmen were discomfited. **1660** R. COKE *Power & Subj.* 15 Loss for the folly of imprudent actions. **1745** *De Foe's Eng. Tradesman* (1841) I. vii. 53 Nothing can be more imprudent and impolitic, as it regards himself and his family. **1827** D. JOHNSON *Ind. Field Sports* 10 *note*, When the rivers are.. rising, it would be imprudent to venture into them.

c. rarely with *of.*

1750 AKENSIDE *Odes* II. iv, Not imprudent of my loss to come.

†**B.** *sb.* An imprudent person. *Obs.*

1753 L. M. tr. *Du Boscq's Accompl. Wom.* I. 29 [It] is ever in the mouth of these Imprudents. **1767** *Woman of Fashion* I. 244 The little Imprudent—How could I expect a Miracle!

Hence **im'prudentness**, imprudence (Bailey vol. II, 1727).

†**impru'dential,** *a. Obs. rare.* [f. IM-^{2} + PRUDENTIAL: cf. IMPRUDENCE.] Not prudential; not marked by prudence; imprudent, improvident.

1649 MILTON *Eikon.* xxviii, The most unwise and imprudential Act as to civil Government.

imprudently (ɪm'pruːdəntlɪ), *adv.* [f. IMPRUDENT *a.* + -LY^2.] In an imprudent manner; with imprudence; indiscreetly, unadvisedly.

1541 [see IMPRUDENCE]. **1548** HALL *Chron., Hen. VI* 187 b, He so imprudently demeaned hymselfe, that..he came into the handes of his mortall enemies. **1685** BAXTER *Paraphr. N.T.* Matt. vi. 28 Christ here neither blameth..meet labour, nor would have it done imprudently and carelesly. **1781** GIBBON *Decl. & F.* xxix. III. 111 The new magistrate imprudently departed from the maxims of the court, and of the times. **1855** MACAULAY *Hist. Eng.* xx. IV. 403 William, with the ardour of a very young commander, had most imprudently offered battle.

impryve: see IMPREVE.

'**impship.** *rare.* [f. IMP *sb.*] The condition or station of an imp: in quot. as a mock title.

1684 OTWAY *Atheist* III, I hope your little Impship will be civil to me.

impsonite ('ɪmpsənaɪt). *Min.* [f. *Impson*, the name of a valley in Pushmataha Co., Oklahoma + -ITE^1.] An asphaltic mineral similar to albertite.

1901 G. H. ELDRIDGE in *Ann. Rep. U.S. Geol. Survey* XXII. I. 265 This differs from albertite, however, sufficiently, it is thought, to warrant a distinctive name, and for this, impsonite is suggested, after the valley in which it is chiefly found. **1951** E. N. TIRATSOO *Petroleum Geol.* xi. 292 Impsonite..seems to be a kind of end-product in the process of bitumen formation, having a very high proportion of fixed carbon and being infusible. **1965** E. T. DEGENS *Geochem. Sediments* v. 263 One may distinguish between the asphaltic, e.g. wurtzilite, elaterite, albertite, and impsonite, and the nonasphaltic pyrobitumens.

imp-tree: see IMP *sb.* 8.

impuberal (ɪm'pjuːbərəl), *a. rare.* [f. L. *impūbes*, *impūber-em* (f. *im-* (IM-^{2}) + *pūbes*, *pūber-em* of ripe age, of the age of puberty) + -AL^1.] Not come to puberty or maturity; immature.

1836–7 SIR W. HAMILTON *Metaph.* (1870) I. App. 409 In impuberal animals the cerebellum is in proportion to the brain proper greatly less than in adults.

im'puberate, *a. rare.* [f. as prec. + -ATE^2.] = prec. Also *absol.* as *sb.*

1880 MUIRHEAD *Gaius* II. §179 To our impuberate descendants *in potestate* we may..make a substitution in the manner already described. —— *Ulpian* xvi. §1 The death of any of those impuberates..secures for them the right of taking in full.

impuberty (ɪm'pjuːbətɪ). [f. L. *impūber-em* (see IMPUBERAL) + -TY, after *puberty.*] The condition of not having reached the state or age of puberty.

1785 PALEY *Mor. Philos.* III. vii. (1830) 220 Sentences of the ecclesiastical courts, which release the parties *à vinculo matrimonii* by reason of impuberty [etc.]..are not dissolutions of the marriage-contract, but judicial declarations that there never was any marriage.

impubic (ɪm'pjuːbɪk), *a. rare.* [irreg. f. L. *impūb-es*, *-is* (see IMPUBERAL) + -IC: cf. PUBIC.] = IMPUBERAL.

1876 GROSS *Dis. Bladder* etc. 140 In only six were the subjects impubic, the average age being the 20th year.

†**im'public,** *v. Obs. rare.* [f. IM-^{1} + PUBLIC.] *trans.* To make public; to publish.

1628 FELTHAM *Resolves* II. xci. 265 It hath made them slighted, ever since his passions so impublik'd [*ed.* 1709 proclaimed] them.

impudence ('ɪmpjʊdəns). Also 4–5 in-. [ad. L. *impudēntia* shamelessness, n. of quality f. *impudēns* IMPUDENT: see -ENCE. *Impud-ence* has the form of suffix derived through OF., while *impudency* has that formed directly from L.; but F. *impudence* is recorded only from 1539 (Hatz.-Darm.).]

The quality or fact of being impudent.

†**1.** Shamelessness; immodesty, indelicacy. *Obs.*

c **1386** CHAUCER *Pars. T.* ⁋317 [Twigs of Pride] There is ..Arrogance. Inpudence [*v.r.* Impudence]..Insolence.. and many another twig. **1406** HOCCLEVE *La Male regle* 62 My lustes blynde han causid thee to varie Fro me thurgh my

folie and inpudence. 1601 SHAKS. *All's Well* II. i. 173 *King.* Vpon thy certainty and confidence, What dar'st thou venter? *Hell.* Taxe of impudence, A strumpets boldnesse, a divulged shame. 1682 *Hereford Dioces. Reg.* 9 Oct., This deponent, blushing to see soe much impudence betwixt the said persons, immediatly went out of the same Chamber. 1712 J. DIGBY tr. *Epicurus' Mor.* 37 'Tis very well known, that Crates and Diogenes have made profession of Beastly Impudence, even in public places.

2. Shameless effrontery; insolent disrespect, insolence; unabashed presumption.

1611 SHAKS. *Wint. T.* III. ii. 57, I ne're heard yet, That any of these bolder Vices wanted Lesse Impudence to gaine-say what they did, Then to performe it first. 1656–9 B. HARRIS *Parival's Iron Age* (ed. 2) 26 The impudence of a certain Monk called Tetzel, exceeded so farre, as to presume to sell the Indulgences. 1697 DRYDEN *Virg. Georg.* II. 721 Some with Impudence invade the Court. 1715 DE FOE *Fam. Instruct.* I. iv. (1841) I. 73 Who will have the impudence to hinder us? 1838 DICKENS *Nich. Nick.* xiii, 'Confound his impudence!' muttered Squeers. 1884 PAE *Eustace* 69 He gave me a deal of impudence..just now.

b. with *an* and *pl.* A piece of impudence.

1885 T. MOZLEY *Remin. Towns* etc. I. 413 Any kind of head-covering was a weakness, or an impudence.

c. Applied to an impudent person.

1671 DRYDEN *Even. Love* II. 20 Peace, impudence, and see my face no more.

3. In a good or neutral sense: Freedom from shamefastness; cool confidence.

1619 FLETCHER, etc. *False One* IV. iii, Off, my dejected looks, and welcome impudence! My daring shall be deity, to save me. 1688 SHADWELL *Sqr. Alsatia* II. i, Learned lawyer of little practice, for want of impudence. 1692 DRYDEN *St. Euremont's Ess.* 133, I..will tell you with the utmost impudence that I esteem much more his Person, than his Works. 1824 W. IRVING *T. Trav.* I. 259, I had not enterprise nor impudence enough to venture from my concealment.

impudency ('ɪmpjʊdənsɪ). Now *rare.* [ad. L. *impudentia*: see prec. and -ENCY.]

1. Shamelessness, immodesty; = IMPUDENCE 1.

1548 UDALL, etc. *Erasm. Par. Matt.* xxvi. 117 Insomuche that he ioyned impudencie and unshamefastenes. 1577 BULL *Luther's Comm. Ps. Grad.* 237 The impudencie of the monks..was so great that I am ashamed to speak it. 1594 T. B. *La Primaud. Fr. Acad.* II. 329 Although too much shamefastnesse, when it is causelesse, is woorthy of blame.. yet is it more praise-woorthy then impudency. 1648 *Eikon Bas.* xxi. (1824) 218 Nor did his [Noah's] open infirmity justifie Chams impudency. 1864 *Fraser's Mag.* Oct. 508 Were she as naked as Diana, there should be no impudency on the figure of Imogen. 1892 *Harper's Mag.* Sept. 494/2 In his earlier tales he seemed to seek pleasure with the impudency of a splendidly healthy young faun.

b. with *an* and *pl.*

1628 WITHER *Brit. Rememb.* IV. 255 For those impudencies, Those riots, and those other foule offences. 1845 *Blackw. Mag.* LVIII. 369 The whole dialogue..is polluted with similar impudencies.

2. Shameless effrontery; = IMPUDENCE 2.

1529 FRITH *Antithesis* lxxviii. in *Pistle Chr. Rdr.* 102 What impudencye is this? I thinke he wold saye also that an Asse were a man yf he thought to gette eny avantage thorow it. 1615 CROOKE *Body of Man* 258 Some haue growne to that impudencie, that they haue denied a woman to haue a soule as man hath. 1655 H. MORE *App. Antid.* (1662) 162 That will..argue..rash boldness and blind impudency in him that shall return so irrational an Answer. 1871 BROWNING *Balaust.* 1604 Alas and yet again! How full is age of impudency!

b. with *an* and *pl.*

1624 CAPT. SMITH *Virginia* v. 194 It had beene a high impudency and presumption to haue medled with them. 1644 HAMMOND *Loyal Convert* 10 How, for their encouragement, are Lyes and brasse-brow'd Impudencies invented.

†**3.** = IMPUDENCE 3. *Obs.*

*c*1610 *Women Saints* 167 All humane helpe being despayred of..in fine, of holie and notable impudencie, she imitated the woman, that..pressed to touch the hemme of Christs garment.

impudent ('ɪmpjʊdənt), *a.* (*sb.*) Also 4–5 in-. [ad. L. *impudēns, impudent-em* shameless, f. *im-* (IM-²) + *pudēns* ashamed, modest, orig. pres. pple. of *pudēre* to make or feel ashamed. Cf. F. *impudent* (16th c. in Hatz.-Darm. and Godef. *Compl.*: but the latter has the adv. *impudemment* of 1461).]

†**1.** Wanting in shame or modesty; shameless, unblushing, immodest; indelicate. (In quot. 1628, 'without the means of decency'.) *Obs.*

*c*1386 CHAUCER *Pars. T.* ⁋323 Inpudent is he that for his pride hath no shame of hise synnes. 1533 UDALL *Floures* 90 Canis (sayth Donate) is a worde that menie vse to obiect vnto suche as be impudent shameles felowes. 1579 G. HARVEY *Letter-bk.* (Camden) 61 Setting the best and impudentist face of it that I can borrowe. 1611 BIBLE *Ecclus.* xix. 2 He that cleaueth to harlots will become impudent. 1628 HOBBES *Thucyd.* (1822) 101 Many for want of things necessary.. were forced to become impudent in the funerals of their friends. 1632 LITHGOW *Trav.* I. 26 Their impudent Curtezans, the most lascivious harlots in the world. 1659 D. PELL *Impr. Sea* 76 With impudent fore-heads, and with brows rubbed on brass-pots. 1732 GAY *Achilles* III, Then her bosom too is so preposterously impudent!

2. Possessed of unblushing presumption, effrontery, or assurance; shamelessly forward, insolently disrespectful.

1563–87 FOXE *A. & M.* (1684) III. 493 Thou art as impudent a Fellow as I have communed withal. 1583 FULKE *Defence* xix. 544 You are the most impudent advoucher, I think, that ever became a writer. 1638 BAKER tr. *Balzac's Lett.* (vol. III.) 123 Sufficient defence against the audaciousnesse of the most impudent. 1709–10 HEARNE in *Reliq.* (1857) I. 181 Some persons were so impudent (to speak in the canting phrase) as to huzza him. 1710–11 SWIFT *Lett.* (1767) III. 125 Oh faith, you're an impudent saucy couple of sluttekins for presuming to write so soon. 1829 LYTTON *Devereux* II. iv, Thou art an impudent thing to jest at us. 1848 DICKENS *Dombey* viii, Wickam is a wicked, impudent, bold-faced hussy.

b. Of conduct, actions, etc.

1597 SHAKS. *2 Hen. IV,* II. i. 135 You call honorable Boldnes, impudent Sawcinesse. 1639 T. BRUGIS tr. *Camus' Mor. Relat.* 246 [She] disclosed..[his] impudent attempt against the reverence of his marriage. 1755 YOUNG *Centaur* ii. Wks. 1757 IV. 134 Our impudent folly puts nature out of countenance. 1862 MARSH *Eng. Lang.* i. 10 An impudent fabrication of the fourteenth century. 1873 HALE *In His Name* vi. 64 This was the impudent reply of the largest boy of the group.

B. *sb.* A person of unblushing effrontery or insolence.

1586 T. B. tr. *La Primaud. Fr. Acad.* (1589) 404 No beast (as they say) is so shamelesse as an impudent. *Ibid.* 253. 1589 PUTTENHAM *Eng. Poesie* I. xxvii. (Arb.) 69 Defrauded of the reward, that an impudent had gotten by abuse of his merit. 1632 LITHGOW *Trav.* x. 434 Many dissembling impudents intrude themselves in this high calling of God.

impudently ('ɪmpjʊdəntlɪ), *adv.* [f. prec. + -LY².] In an impudent manner; with effrontery; shamelessly, insolently.

1561 T. NORTON *Calvin's Inst.* I. 25 Whosoeuer deny yᵗ it hath thus been done in time past, yea within our owne remembrance, they impudently lie. 1664–5 PEPYS *Diary* 19 Mar., Castlemaine lay impudently upon her back in her coach asleep. 1770 *Junius Lett.* xl. 207 A boy, impudently thrust over their heads. 1855 MACAULAY *Hist. Eng.* xiv. (1871) II. 72 An impudently false accusation.

'impudentness. *rare.* [f. as prec. + -NESS.] The quality of being impudent; impudence.

1599 SANDYS *Europæ Spec.* (1632) 19 Governours and Subjectes..striving as it were with other in an impudentnesse therein. 1727 in BAILEY vol. II.

impudicity (ɪmpjuː'dɪsɪtɪ). [a. F. *impudicité*, f. L. type **impudīcitās*, for cl. L. *impudīcitia*, f. *impudīc-us* shameless.] Shamelessness, immodesty.

1528 LYNDESAY *Dreme* 279 With thare prouocatyue Impudicitie, Brocht mony ane man to Infelicitie. 1577 HELLOWES *Gueuara's Chron.* 416, I bred thee chaste, and thou arte imbrued with impudicitie. 1674 tr. *Du Moulin's Papal Tyranny* 38 The luxury..the impudicity, the gluttony..that reigned in the Papal Court. 1824 LANDOR *Imag. Conv.* Wks. 1846 I. 55/2 This impudicity..seems to have always been a characteristic of the Italian race. 1883 BEECHER in *Chr. World Pulpit* XXIII. 372/3 Knowledge with women in Grecian days was a token of impudicity.

b. with *an* and *pl.*

1582 N. T. (Rhem.) *Mark* vii. 22 Theftes, auarices, wickednesse, guile, impudicities.

†**impudicous,** *a. Obs. rare.* [f. L. *impudīcus* + -OUS.] Immodest, indelicate, indecent.

1657 W. MORICE *Coena quasi Κοινὴ* Def. xii. 157 It may be a wanton and impudicous act in another to kiss a woman.

impugn (ɪm'pjuːn), *v.* Forms: 4 in-, yn-, 4–6 en-, (5 em-), 5–6 ym-, 4–7 **impugne**, 4–5 in-, impungne, 6 impounge (?), *Sc.* impung, 6– **impugn.** [a. F. *impugner* (1363 in Godefroy) = Pr. *im-*, *enpugnar*, Sp. *impugnar*, It. *impugnare*, ad. L. *impugnāre* to attack, assail, f. *im-* (IM-¹) + *pugnāre* to fight.]

†**1.** *trans.* To fight against: to attack, assail, assault (a person, city, etc.). *Obs.*

1382 WYCLIF *1 Macc.* xi. 41 Thei inpungneden Yrael. 1388 —— *Judg.* ix. 44 He roos..and enpugnyde [1382 aȝenfiȝtynge] and bisegide the citee. *c*1450 tr. *De Imitatione* III. xl. 110 þou dwellist amonge enemyes, þou art impugned on þe riȝt honde & on þe lifte honde. 1553 BECON *Reliques of Rome* (1563) 264 We are set in a slipperye place, and are impugned of deuills. 1603 KNOLLES *Hist. Turks* (1621) 35 He..laid siege unto Damascus..which he so notably impugned, that [etc.].

fig. 1651 HOBBES *Leviath.* Ded., The Outworks of the Enemy, from whence they impugne the Civill Power.

†**b.** To fight in resistance against; to withstand, resist, oppose. *Obs.*

1577 HANMER *Anc. Eccl. Hist.* (1619) 43 Josephus..which himselfe also at the first impugned the Romaines. 1591 *Troub. Raigne K. John* II. (1611) 107 Only the heart impugnes with faint resist The fierce inuade of him that conquers Kings. 1611 SPEED *Hist. Gt. Brit.* IX. v. §25 God ..will not leaue vs succourlesse, whiles in a just cause, we impugne a most vnjust Intruder. 1660 F. BROOKE tr. *Le Blanc's Trav.* 223 To impugn with all his power the Moores, Jews, and Idolaters.

transf. 1646 SIR T. BROWNE *Pseud. Ep.* VI. v. 291 The defect of alternation would utterly impugne the generation of all things.

2. To assail (an opinion, statement, document, action, etc.) by word or argument; to call in question; to dispute the truth, validity, or correctness of; to oppose as false or erroneous.

1362 LANGL. *P. Pl.* A. VIII. 155 Al þis makeþ me..to þenken..On Pers þe plouhmon and whuch a pardoun he hedde, And hou þe preost inpugnede hit. *c*1380 WYCLIF *Sel. Wks.* III. 350 þes sectis inpugnen þe gospel, and also þe olde lawe. 1415 HOCCLEVE *To Sir J. Oldcastle* 172 No man wolde Impugne hir right. 1494 FABYAN *Chron.* II. xliii. 29 This sayinge contraryeth and enpugnyth myne Auctor Gaufride. 1549 *Compl. Scot.* To Rdr. 12 Detractione.. reddy to suppedit & tyl impung ane verteous verk. *a*1614 DONNE *Βιαθανατος* (1644) 124 No man hath as yet, to my knowledge, impugned this custome of ours. 1678 CUDWORTH *Intell. Syst.* I. v. 642 It cannot be accounted less than extreme sottishness and stupidity of mind..thus to impugn a Deity. 1777 WATSON *Philip II* (1793) I. v. 181 An opinion which in France had always been impugned and rejected. 1847 DISRAELI *Tancred* I. v, The saint was scarcely canonised, before his claims to beatitude were impugned.

b. To assail the actions, question the statements, etc. of (a person); to find fault with, accuse. Now *rare.*

1377 LANGL. *P. Pl.* B. XIII. 123 One Pieres þe ploughman hath inpugned vs alle, And sette alle sciences at a soppe, saue loue one. 1491 CAXTON *Vitas Patr.* (W. de W. 1495) III. iii. 318b/1 Many hated hym & specyally theretykes; for he cessed not to enpugne & repreef theym. 1530 LYNDESAY *Test. Papyngo* 13 Quho dar presume thir Poetis tyll Impung, Quhose sweit sentence throuch Albione bene sung? 1596 SHAKS. *Merch. V.* IV. i. 179 Yet in such rule, that the Venetian Law Cannot impugne you as you do proceed. 1879 FARRAR *St. Paul* xl. II. 323 *note,* The Law, for the supposed apostasy from which he was impugned.

Hence **im'pugned** *ppl. a.*; **im'pugning** *vbl. sb.* and *ppl. a.*

*c*1400 *Apol. Loll.* 73 Inpungning of þe law of God. *c*1440 *Jacob's Well* (E.E.T.S.) 276 It techyth þe..to defende þi feyth wyth resouns fro inpugnyng of heretykes. 1599 SANDYS *Europæ Spec.* (1632) 94 For defence of impugned truth. 1802–12 BENTHAM *Rat. Judic. Evid.* (1827) III. 204 It should be allowable..to call upon the impugning witness.. to declare [etc.]. 1860 *Sat. Rev.* IX. 145/2 The impugned department will send down..a cohort of witnesses.

impugnable (ɪm'pjuːnəb(ə)l), *a.*¹ *rare.* [f. prec. + -ABLE.] Liable to be impugned.

1823 *New Monthly Mag.* VIII. 262 If any chance to be impugnable on the score of principles. 1847 DISRAELI *Tancred* IV. viii, Her reason..though not easily impugnable was not as satisfactory to his understanding as to his ear.

impugnable (ɪm'pʌgnəb(ə)l), *a.*² ? *Obs.* [f. IM-² + L. *pugn-āre* to fight + -ABLE; cf. EXPUGNABLE.] That cannot be assailed or overcome.

1570 LEVINS *Manip.* 3/27 Impugnable, *impugnabilis.* 1611 SPEED *Hist. Gt. Brit.* VII. v. 217 To withstand so puissant and impugnable an enemy. *Ibid.* x. i. (1632) 1242 If the Tower were impugnable.

Hence **impugna'bility.** ? *Obs.*

1837 G. S. FABER *Prim. Doctr. Justif.* iv. 167 So long as the canon of Tertullian shall flourish in its absolute impugnability.

†**im'pugnance.** *Obs. rare*⁻¹. In 6 in-. [f. L. *impugnāre* to IMPUGN: see -ANCE.] = IMPUGNATION.

1600 W. WATSON *Decacordon* IX. v. (1602) 308 Therefore doe we call traitors rebels: when they rise by resistance or inpugnance of their Princes authority.

†**im'pugnant,** *ppl. a. Obs. rare*⁻¹. [ad. L. *impugnāns, impugnānt-em*, or corresponding It. *impugnante*, pres. pple. of *impugnāre* to oppose, IMPUGN.] Repugnant, opposed.

1579 FENTON *Guicciard.* II. (1599) 95 Whether you ought to be the personage so impugnant and contrary to your proper resolution.

impugnation (ɪmpʌg'neɪʃən). ? *Obs.* [ad. L. *impugnātiōn-em*, noun of action f. *impugnāre* to IMPUGN: cf. obs. F. *impugnation.*]

†**1.** The action of attacking or assaulting (a person); *esp.* spiritual assault, temptation. *Obs.*

1398 TREVISA *Barth. De P.R.* IX. xxx. (MS. Bodl.), Aȝens þeese so manye inpungnacions we beþ ywarded and isocoured with spyrytual armoure. *c*1450 *Mirour Saluacioun* 3179 Oure lord has ordeyned yᵗ a man shalle haf here impugnacionne. 1602 T. FITZHERBERT *Apol.* 9 a, He receiued such a violent impugnation and persecution of all the bad priests in the cittie [Rome], that he was forced to depart thence. 1645 BP. HALL *Remedy Discontents* 108 The fift is a perpetuall impugnation, and self-conflict.

2. The action of impugning (an opinion, etc.); calling in question, disputing; impugnment.

1502 *Ord. Crysten Men* (W. de W. 1506) II. vii. 103 Impugnacyon of trouth the whiche is whan the persone of certayne malice ayen sayth unto the trouth of the fayth. 1529 MORE *Suppl. Soulys* Wks. 313/2 The impugnacion of that vncharitable heresye. 1692 NORRIS *Curs. Refl.* 'Ess. Hum. Und.' 21 Having considered our Author's Impugnation of Innate Principles. 1873 WAGNER tr. *Teuffel's Hist. Rom. Lit.* II. 95 It begins with a lengthy impugnation of the mythical opinions caused by the poets.

†**impug'nator.** *Obs. rare*⁻¹. [ad. late L. *impugnātor*, agent-n. f. *impugnāre* to IMPUGN; cf. F. (obs.) *impugnateur.*] = next.

1678 GALE *Crt. Gentiles* III. 123 The Iesuites themselves, who are his most puissant Impugnators, give him a more candid and favorable treatment.

impugner (ɪm'pjuːnə(r)). [f. IMPUGN *v.* + -ER¹.] One who impugns or assails.

1539 TONSTALL *Serm. Palm Sund.* (1823) 51 Redye to defende the faith ageynst the impugners of it. *a*1688 CUDWORTH *Immut. Mor.* (1731) 223 Some of these Strenuous Impugners of Immaterial and Incorporeal Substances. 1712 BERKELEY *Passive Obed.* §38 A.. prejudice which influenceth the impugners of non-resistance. 1818 HAZLITT *Eng. Poets* iii. (1870) 80 The way to defend Milton against all impugners is to take down the book and read it. 1890 *Spectator* 6 Sept., The impugners of the story..have failed to support their scepticism with anything that can properly be called evidence.

impugnment (ɪm'pjuːnmənt). [f. as prec. + -MENT.] The action or fact of impugning.

1840 E. HOWARD *Jack ashore* xlvii. (Stratm.), It must not be an impugnment to his manhood that he cried like a child. **1862** BURTON *Bk. Hunter* (1863) 63 The theses on which aspirants after university honours held their disputations or impugnments.

impuissance (ɪm'pjuːɪsəns). [a. F. *impuissance* (1361 in Littré): see IM-² and PUISSANCE. (By the Brownings stressed *impu'issance*.)]

1. Impotence, powerlessness, weakness.

1483 CAXTON *Gold. Leg.* 1/1 (R. Suppl.) In tyme whan man was vaynquysshed of ignoraunce and impuissaunce. **1602** PATERICKE tr. *Gentillet* 26 An impuissance to conserve himself. **1645** *City Alarum* 9 We have always hoodwinkt our selves with conceits of the kings impuissance till it came to tryal. **1762** STERNE *Tr. Shandy* V. xvi, He lay under an impuissance..of advancing above a line and a half in the compass of a whole summer's day. **1855** BROWNING *Saul* xviii, Why is it I dare Think but lightly of such impuissance? **1856** MRS. BROWNING *Aur. Leigh* IX. 469, I felt myself So safe in impuissance and despair I could not hurt you. **1884** BROWNING *Ferishtah, Cherries*, Never too much of faith In impuissance, man's.

†**2.** Want of self-control; cf. IMPOTENCE 3. *Obs.*

1667 WATERHOUSE *Fire Lond.* 95 When the light of reason is under a Bushel of passion; and impuissance is regent in the soul.

So †**im'puissancy** [see -ANCY]. *Obs. rare*⁻¹.

1701 BEVERLEY *Apoc. Quest.* 39 An Image of Supremacy; and yet Impuissancy.

impuissant (ɪm'pjuːɪsənt), *a.* [a. F. *impuissant* (15th c.): see IM-² and PUISSANT.] Impotent, powerless, weak.

1629 MAXWELL tr. *Herodian* (1635) 127 How im-puissant and dejected they are. **1652–62** HEYLIN *Cosmogr.* IV. (1682) 58 The Country made a prey to impuissant Enemies. **1853** GROTE *Greece* II. lxxxiv. XI. 113 An impuissant embrace of philosophy on the part of so great a potentate. **1863** LD. LYTTON *Ring Amasis* I. 188 Vain, and impuissant are the pity and commiseration of a feeble fellow-creature.

im'pulsatile, *a. rare*⁻¹. [f. IM-² + PULSATILE *a.*] Not characterized by pulsation.

1859 TODD *Cycl. Anat.* V. 288/1 In these vessels..its [the blood's] movement is impulsatile or venous.

impulse ('ɪmpʌls), *sb.* [ad. L. *impuls-us* a push against, f. ppl. stem of *impellĕre* to IMPEL.]

1. a. An act of impelling; an application of sudden force causing motion; a thrust, a push.

1650 ASHMOLE *Chym. Collect.* (ed. 3) 227 The Second lurketh in the bowels of the Earth, by the Impulse and action, whereof the Subterraneous vapours are driven upwards through Pores and Pipes. **1690** LOCKE *Hum. Und.* IV. x. §19 We cannot conceive how any thing but impulse of body can move body. **1752** HUME *Ess. & Treat.* (1777) II. 68 The impulse of one billiard-ball is attended with motion in the second. **1758** JOHNSON *Idler* No. 2 ¶1 He will wish to advance rather by the impulse of the wind, than the strokes of the oar. **1860** TYNDALL *Glac.* II. i. 228 To produce the impression of violet light a still greater number of impulses is necessary. **1872** HUXLEY *Physiol.* viii. 210 The chief agents in transmitting the impulses of the aërial waves. **1875** DARWIN *Insectiv. Pl.* x. 240 When a gland is first excited the motor impulse is discharged within a few seconds.

fig. **1692** BENTLEY *Boyle Lect.* i. 12 Driven on by the blind impulses of Fatality and Fortune. **1818** JAS. MILL *Brit. India* II. v. ix. 698 The total exemption of the deliberations in parliament from the impulse of the royal will. **1877** MRS. OLIPHANT *Makers Flor.* vi. 160 The early impulse of the Renaissance [was] just then beginning to influence the world.

b. *Path.* 'The shock felt on the chest-wall when the heart beats, or over an aneurysm during the cardiac systole.. *Cardiac impulse*, the apex beat of the heart' (*Syd. Soc. Lex.* 1886).

1879 *St. George's Hosp. Rep.* IX. 182 Of the Heart: No sensible impulse; sounds hardly audible. *Ibid.*, Area ill-defined; impulse diffused; sounds muffled.

2. *Dynamics.* **a.** An indefinitely large force enduring for an inappreciably short time but producing a finite momentum; such as the blow of a hammer, the drive of a bat, the impact of colliding balls, etc. **b.** The product of the average value *of* any force multiplied by the time during which it acts. (This extended use was introduced by Clerk Maxwell *Matter & Motion* 43.)

1796 HUTTON *Math. Dict.*, *Impulse*, the single or momentary action or force by which a body is impelled. **1806** —— *Course Math.* II. 132 The Momentum, or Quantity of Motion, generated by a Single Impulse, or any Momentary Force, is as the Generating Force. **1859** LUNN *Of Motion* 87. **1868** ROUTH *Rigid Dynamics* (ed. 2) 262 We may regard an impulse as the limit of a large finite force acting for a very short time. **1875** MAXWELL *Theory of Heat* (ed. 4) 88 The impulse of a force is equal to the momentum produced by it. **1868** W. K. CLIFFORD *Lect.* (1879) I. 76 A shuttlecock, which has its entire state of motion suddenly changed by the impulse of the battledore.

c. Aeronaut. ***specific impulse***: the ratio of the thrust produced in a rocket engine to the rate of consumption of propellant (expressed as mass, or weight, per second).

Equivalent to the impulse (sense 2 b) obtained per unit mass, or weight, of propellant.

1947 *Jrnl. Brit. Interplanetary Soc.* Mar. 101 The most important requirement is a low consumption, or to use a term more commonly employed in rocketry, a high 'specific impulse'; the specific impulse being the thrust obtained from the consumption of one unit of propellant mixture per second. **1950** *Sci. News* XV. 76 The most useful measure of the efficiency of a rocket is called 'specific impulse'. **1962** F. I. ORDWAY et al. *Basic Astronautics* x. 422 In the liquid fuel reactor hydrogen is bubbled through liquid uranium compounds. With this method specific impulses on the order of 1500 lb-sec/lb may be attained. **1971** P. J. MCMAHON *Aircraft Propulsion* iii. 116 In the foot-pound-second system, specific impulse has the units lbf-sec/lb. For many years it was the practice to define the specific impulse as the thrust divided by the *weight* flow rate of propellants. Using this definition the units of specific impulse became 'seconds'. *Ibid.* x. 298 The specific impulse of a cordite type propellant will be of the order of 2 000 N-s/kg when operating with a chamber pressure of 6 000 kN/m² and exhausting to 100 kN/m².

3. a. Force or influence exerted upon the mind by some external stimulus; suggestion, incitement, instigation. †Formerly, *esp.*, A strong suggestion supposed to come from a good or evil spirit.

1660 R. COKE *Power & Subj.* 177 If he by chance offend by the impulse of the Devil, let him make amends therefore. **1674** OWEN *Holy Spirit* (1693) 184 An immediate Revelation or Divine Impulse and Impression. **1701** G. HAMMOND (*title*) Discourse of Angels..also something touching Devils, Apparitions, and Impulses. **1798** WORDSW. *Tables turned* vi, One impulse from a vernal wood May teach you more..Than all the sages can. **1833** CRUSE *Eusebius* II. i. 49 Thomas, under divine impulse, sent Thaddeus as herald and evangelist. **1847** PRESCOTT *Peru* (1850) II. 138 He was not a man..to yield timidly to the impulses of others.

b. Incitement or stimulus to action arising from some state of mind or feeling.

1647 CLARENDON *Hist. Reb.* I. §60 His purpose.. proceeded only from himself and the impulse of his own Conscience. **1769** ROBERTSON *Chas. V* (1813) III. XI. 281 No motive to direct him but the impulse of ungovernable passions. **1833** HT. MARTINEAU *Charmed Sea* i. 2 Some ran on, under an impulse of curiosity. **1853** J. H. NEWMAN *Hist. Sk.* (1876) II. I. iii. 107 The inward impulse of gigantic energy and brutal cupidity urged them forward.

c. Sudden or involuntary inclination or tendency to act, without premeditation or reflection.

1763 BURKE *Corr.* (1844) I. 50, I act almost always from my present impulse, and with little scheme or design. **1861** GEO. ELIOT *Silas M.* ii. 12 He seemed to weave, like the spider, from pure impulse, without reflection. **1869** FREEMAN *Norm. Conq.* III. xiii. 281 Men..are apt to be guided by impulse rather than by judgement. **1876** T. HARDY *Ethelberta* (1890) 271 It was mere impulse.

4. a. The effect produced by impulsion; motion caused by the sudden application of force; momentum, impetus.

1715 DESAGULIERS *Fires Impr.* 8 A Ray..goes on by a compound Motion made up of its Impulse..and its constant tendency upwards. *a* **1721** KEILL *Maupertuis' Diss.* (1734) 25 The motion of such a Vortex..ought to give them some horizontal Impulse, and hurry them along in its own direction. **1856** KANE *Arct. Expl.* I. xii. 133 My team.. leaping them..and the impulse of our sledge carrying it across. **1878** HUXLEY *Physiogr.* 188 The impulse may be transmitted through the earth to an enormous distance.

fig. **1872** YEATS *Growth Comm.* 97 Orseolo gave a new impulse to navigation. **1874** GREEN *Short Hist.* vii. §7. 418 Circumstances..were giving a poetic impulse to the newly-aroused intelligence of men.

b. *Path.* 'The wave of change which travels through nerve and muscle in passing from rest into action' (*Syd. Soc. Lex.* 1886).

c. *Dancing.* (See quot. 1949.)

1949 SHURR & YOCOM *Mod. Dance* 190 *Impulse*, the impetus or impelling force used to initiate a movement sequence, such as a hip contraction or a hip release. **1968** J. WINEARLS *Mod. Dance* (ed. 2) ii. 64 Thus with continued forward impulses the pelvis moves in a backwards—downwards—forwards—upwards—circle with an accent at the bottom of the circle.

5. *Electr.* A sudden, momentary change in voltage or current from an otherwise steady (or slowly varying) value. (More commonly *pulse*.)

1883 E. ATKINSON tr. *Ganot's Elem. Treat. Physics* (ed. 11) x. vi. 850 As they are all connected together we get, not so much a series of separate impulses, as a continuous series of currents. **1904** *Daily Chron.* 10 Dec. 7/2 It [*sc.* a tape] is inserted in the aperture of the transmitting instrument, and by the perforations the electrical impulses are created and recorded at the receiving station. **1943** A. L. ALBERT *Fund. Telephony* ix. 206 The vertical movement of the selector switch is controlled by the electric impulses received from the subscriber's dial. **1971** H. E. ENNES *Television Broadcasting* vii. 347 The circuit works by virtue of the fact that spurious noise impulses normally are much narrower than the desired sync pulses.

6. *attrib.* and *Comb.*, esp. in various technical terms relating to the driving mechanism of a clock, as ***impulse-teeth***, etc.

1825 J. NICHOLSON *Operat. Mechanic* 520 The impulse-teeth consist of very small tempered steel pins, inserted on the surface of the rim of the wheel on one side only. **1879** *Cassell's Techn. Educ.* IV. 369/2 The impulse-arc of the balance..is determined by the radii of lever and roller. **1884** F. J. BRITTEN *Watch & Clockm.* 55 The escape wheel.. overtakes the impulse pallet and drives it on. *Ibid.*, The impulse roller. *Ibid.* 97 The impulse teeth..the impulse finger. **1901** *Daily Chron.* 3 Sept. 3/7 A genuine chivalrous impulse-desire—that natural desire for companionship. **1929** D. H. LAWRENCE *Let.* 1 Oct. (1962) II. 1204 You are working all the time from wrong impulse-sources. **1949** M. MEAD *Male & Female* xvii. 355 Modern psychology and modern literature emphasize the importance of impulse gratification.

b. Special Comb.: **impulse clock, dial**, a secondary clock operated by electrical impulses transmitted at regular intervals by a master clock; **impulse coupling** = *impulse starter*; **impulse-reaction turbine**, a turbine comprising two (or more) stages, one working on the principle of the impulse turbine and the other on that of the reaction turbine; **impulse starter**, a mechanical device which may be fitted to the magneto of an ignition system to cause its rotor to turn in a series of jerks instead of continuously, resulting in an increased voltage that facilitates the production of a spark at low speeds or when starting; **impulse tube**, a tube serving to expel a torpedo; **impulse turbine**, a turbine in which the working fluid undergoes no drop in pressure in the rotor, this being driven solely by the change it causes in the direction of flow; **impulse-wheel**, a form of turbine water-wheel driven by the impact of a jet upon it (*Cent. Dict.*).

1923 LANGMAN & BALL *Electr. Horology* v. 82 Clocks coming under this section are generally..designated as dials, impulse clocks, secondary clocks, journeyman clocks, sympathetic clocks, or step by step movements. **1951** S. J. WISE *Electr. Clocks* (ed. 2) iv. 67 An impulse or repeater clock is a device which receives the timed electrical impulses transmitted by a master clock, and translates them, through its wheelwork, into seconds, minutes and hours. **1916** Impulse coupling [see *impulse starter* below]. **1943** A. P. FRAAS *Aircraft Power Plants* viii. 147 To ensure a good spark at cranking speeds the magnetos for many of the smaller engines are fitted with an impulse coupling. **1931** F. HOPE-JONES *Electr. Clocks* ii. 6 Circuits of electrical impulse dials, in which a master clock transmits impulses every minute or half-minute to propel the hands. **1940** —— *Electr. Timekeeping* i. 6 After many years of futile attempts to apply electricity to horology, inventors turned their attention to systems of electrical impulse dials, an obviously sane and effective method of indicating uniform time throughout a large building. **1929** T. M. NAYLOR *Steam Turbines* i. 4 Combination turbines or disc and drum turbines, as they are often called, are a combination of impulse and reaction types of turbine. The first part of the turbine is impulse, and the remainder of the turbine is reaction, so that this type of turbine might be called impulse-reaction. **1951** *Engineering* 5 Oct. 438/3 The high-pressure turbine is of the impulse-reaction type. **1916** V. W. PAGÉ *Automobile Starting* iii. 224 The device..is known as the Eisemann impulse starter coupling. This may be attached to any model of Eisemann magneto and is said to have no effect upon its regular operation except at slow speeds, when it causes the armature to rotate in a series of jumps instead of at a uniform speed. **1940** W. E. CROOK *Electr. in Aircraft* vii. 93 The impulse starter..enables the engine to start on its own magnetos. It is a purely mechanical piece of apparatus, consisting essentially of a spring-loaded pawl and ratchet gear. **1877** *Illustr. London News* 14 Apr. 339/3 It is fired by what is called an 'impulse-tube', which..discharges the torpedo into the water. **1878** *Cassell's Family Mag.* 312/2 Direction is given to the torpedo by means of an iron impulse-tube built into the vessel. **1885** *Marine Engineer* 1 Sept. 144/2 The fish torpedoes lie side by side. Immediately behind them..are a couple of 'impulse tubes'. **1881** *Encycl. Brit.* XII. 524/1 In some turbines the whole available energy of the water is converted into kinetic energy before the water acts on the moving part of the turbine. Such turbines are termed Impulse Turbines, and they are distinguished by this that the wheel passages are never entirely filled by the water. **1906** W. H. S. GARNETT *Turbines* iv. 42 Impulse turbines..are unsuited for the development of high speed motion from low falls... For running, on the other hand, at low speeds under a high fall, the impulse turbine cannot be surpassed. **1971** P. J. MCMAHON *Aircraft Propulsion* v. 163 The extreme case of a zero reaction stage wherein all the pressure drop occurs in the nozzle blades is known as an 'impulse turbine' in accordance with steam turbine practice. A pure impulse turbine would rarely be used for an aero-turbine engine.

c. Of or pertaining to a purchase or purchases made on impulse, usu. at the point of sale of displayed goods, as ***impulse buyer, buying***, etc.

1959 *Times Lit. Suppl.* 29 May (Children's Books) 5 [Children's books] snarl 'impulse buyers' in the supermarket. **1959** *Sunday Express* 26 July 10/4 The Opposition Leader's Lady and Judy O'Grady are '*impulse buyers*' under the skin. **1959** *News Chron.* 18 Nov. 4/2 What the traders call 'impulse buying' is increasingly popular. **1962** *Sunday Express* 8 July 15/2 Top dressers..plunge with the odd '*impulse buy*'. **1963** *Punch* 27 Nov. 772 New Prime Minister..impulse-buys sixty Phantom 11s. **1964** *Punch* 6 May 655/3 Trolleys full of impulse-bought bargains. **1965** *Mod. Law Rev.* XXVIII. v. 557 None of the reasons given for minimising the importance of 'impulse sales' apply with special force to the book trade. **1967** L. J. BRAUN *Cat who ate Danish Modern* x. 88 These are little boutique items for the impulse buyer. **1968** 'S. JAY' *Sleepers can Kill* vi. 66 He goes into a shop..and buys a boat... An impulse buy, if ever there was one. **1972** *New Statesman* 26 May 709/3, I impulse-bought some crumpets the other day, because they were on the counter at the dairy.

im'pulse, *v.* [f. the sb. or f. L. *impuls-*, ppl. stem of *impellĕre* to IMPEL; cf. obs. F. *impulser*.]

trans. To give an impulse to; to impel; to instigate. Also *intr.*

1611 FLORIO, *Impulsare*, to impulse, to perswade often. **1614** RALEIGH *Hist. World* I. (1634) 34 With that force so impulsed and prest they are carried under the deepe Ocean. **1658** BROMHALL *Treat. Specters* I. 102 The Man being impulsed by some invisible spirit. **1689** T. PLUNKET *Char. Gd. Commander* 45 The Earth's fill'd with fraud and violence, Impulsed by the Jesuits influence. *a* **1711** KEN *Hymns Festiv.* Poet. Wks. 1721 I. 307 Love to the Cross his Soul impuls'd. *a* **1718** PENN *Tracts* Wks. 1726 I. 548 His

Good Angel or Spirit.. very often impuls'd or moved him to preach to the People. **1757** ELIZ. GRIFFITH *Lett. Henry & Frances* (1767) II. 55 The Centrifugal [power]..is a force impulsed upon all the planets, at their creation, that directs them forward, in a right line. **1931** *Times* 27 June 11/5 The interference is due..to..sparks in stays of masts, and to loose metallic contacts, which impulse the receiver in the same way as heavy atmospherics would do. **1936** *Nature* 12 Sept. 445/2 The law and governmental forms..clearly lag behind even economic developments as impulsed by scientific discovery. **1943** *Gloss. Terms Telecomm. (B.S.I.)* 62 *Impulsing signal*, a signal carrying the selective information to steer the call in the desired direction. **1949** E. C. BERKELEY *Giant Brains* iii. 41 This type of relay has the property of staying..in either position until the opposite coil is impulsed. **1960** *Lang. & Speech* III. 140 (*title*) Recurrently impulsed resonators in speech and psycho-physical studies. **1972** J. QUARTERMAIN *Rock of Diamond* xiii. 72 Her small voice..impulsed through the network of cables.

Hence **im'pulsing** *vbl. sb.*

1885 L. OLIPHANT *Sympneumata* xiii. 207 They may trace ..the radiant current through the human story of the Divine impulsings.

impulsion (ɪmˈpʌlʃən). Also 5-6 **ym-**. [a. F. *impulsion* (*c* 1315 in Godefroy *Compl.*), ad. L. *impulsiōn-em* influence, instigation, f. *impuls-*, ppl. stem of *impellĕre* to IMPEL; cf. IMPULSE *sb.*]

1. The action of impelling or forcing onward; also of striking upon, thrusting, pushing, or pressing against without producing motion; the condition of being thrust or pushed.

1432-50 tr. *Higden* (Rolls) IV. 199 The body of Tholomeus borne vn to the londe by the impulsion of the see. **1483** CAXTON *Gold. Leg.* 245/2 The deken fyll wyth the chalyce by thympulsion and threstyng of the paynems. **1581** W. STAFFORD *Exam. Compl.* iii. (1876) 78 Thus one thyng hanges vpon another, and sets forwarde one another, but one first of all is the chiefe cause of all this circuler motion and impulsion. **1655** STANLEY *Hist. Philos.* II. (1701) 73/2 The Wind that comes next presseth the first, forcing..it by frequent impulsions. **1774** GOLDSM. *Nat. Hist.* (1776) I. 4 That of attraction, which draws them towards the sun; and ..impulsion, which drives them strait forward into the great void of space. **1794** SULLIVAN *View Nat.* I. 54 The centrifugal force, or force of impulsion, is still unknown. **1835-6** TODD *Cycl. Anat.* I. 621/2 The impulsion of the water takes place on the surface of the tentacula. **1863** TYNDALL *Heat* vii. (1870) 209 The needle of the galvanometer is instantly deflected, and the limit of the first impulsion is noted.

transf. or *fig.* **1610** R. NICCOLS *Wint. Nts. Vis.*, *R. Curthose* in *Mirr. Mag.* 652 To see How griefes impulsions in my brest did beate. *a* **1626** BACON *Max. & Uses Com. Law* i. 1 To judge the causes of causes, and their impulsions one of another. **1844** MRS. BROWNING *Lady Geraldine* lviii, A vibration and impulsion to an end beyond its own.

†**b.** An impelling cause or occasion. *Obs.*

1605 BACON *Adv. Learn.* II. x. §3. 41 Medicine.. considereth causes of Diseases, with the occasions or impulsions.

†**c.** Attack, assault. *Obs.*

1631 WEEVER *Anc. Fun. Mon.* 146 The citie of Ierusalem being recouered against the impulsions of the Infidels.

2. a. External influence exerted upon mind or conduct; instigation, incitement.

1560 DAUS tr. *Sleidane's Comm.* 13 If the Frenche kynge conquere..it maye be that the Byshoppe of Rome throughe his impulsion will vndo oure Election. **1628** HOBBES *Thucyd.* (1822) 6 Atreus and Thyestes..at the impulsion of their mother slew this Chrysippus. **1676** MARVELL *Gen. Councils* Wks. 1875 IV. 127 'Tis meant that it was free from all external impulsion. **1829** I. TAYLOR *Enthus.* vii. 168 The few who might have done the same without impulsion. **1859** HOLLAND *Gold F.* xv. 171, I do not believe any man ever became thoroughly industrious, save under the impulsion of motives outside of labor.

b. Determination to action resulting from natural tendency or temporary excitement; impulse.

c **1530** L. COX *Rhet.* (1899) 77 Natural impulsion is angre, hatred, couetyse, loue, or suche other affections. **1586** BRIGHT *Melanch.* xii. 60 The other not only derection but impulsion also from an inward vertue. **1672** EACHARD *Hobbs's State Nat.* (1705) 108 This he did by a certain impulsion of nature. **1793** *Object. to the War Examined* 44 It can only be upon the like impulsion from which a drowning man catches at a twig. **1875** LOWELL *Under old Elm* 4 With sure impulsion to keep honor clear.

3. Tendency to onward motion imparted by some force or influence; impetus.

1795 CRAUFURD in *Ld. Auckland's Corr.* (1862) III. 290 Whether the impulsion be given by the people to their representatives, or..by the representatives to the people [etc.]. **1836-7** SIR W. HAMILTON *Metaph.* xli. (1870) II. 417 The impulsion which Kant had given to philosophy. **1881** *Manch. Exam.* 3 Mar. 4 A great impulsion has of late years been given to steam navigation in the Levant.

impulsive (ɪmˈpʌlsɪv), *a.* (*sb.*) [ad. med.L. *impulsīv-us* or a. F. *impulsif, -ive* (14th c.), f. L. *impuls-*, ppl. stem of *impellĕre* to IMPEL: see -IVE.]

A. *adj.* **1. a.** Having the property of impelling or producing impulsion; characterized by impulsion or impetus.

1604 DRAYTON *Moses* II, The goodly horse..Lies where but late disdainfully he trod,..[and] Stirs not when prick'd with the impulsive goad. *c* **1611** CHAPMAN *Iliad* v. 232 The force Of the impulsive chariot. **1621** G. SANDYS *Ovid's Met.* VI. (1626) 113 A shaft, which from th'impulsiue bow-string flew. **1794** SULLIVAN *View Nat.* II. 387 The impulsive motion of the planets..gives rise to numberless phænomena.

b. *Dynamics.* (See quot. and IMPULSE *sb.* 2.)

1803 J. WOOD *Princ. Mech.* i. 15 When a force produces it's effect instantaneously, it is said to be impulsive. **1807** HUTTON *Course Math.* II. 137 If the forces be impulsive or momentary, the motions will be uniform. **1879** THOMSON & TAIT *Nat. Phil.* I. I. §298 The shot is fired into the block in a horizontal direction..The impulsive penetration is.. nearly instantaneous.

2. Impelling or determining to action. ***impulsive cause*** (freq. in 17th c., now rare), originating or primary cause.

c **1555** HARPSFIELD *Divorce Hen. VIII* (Camden) 214 The cause impulsive moving the prætor to promulge this edict was [etc.]. **1621** SANDERSON *Serm.* I. 180 There is a kind of cause..which the learned..call the impulsive cause: and it is such a cause as moveth and induceth the principal agent, to do that which it doth. **1686** HORNECK *Crucif. Jesus* xii. 234 The love of God was the impulsive cause, but our sins were the instrumental cause, these brought him to the Cross. **1788** REID *Active Powers* III. II. i. (1803) 159 Some cool principle of action, which has authority without any impulsive force. **1865** RUSKIN *Sesame* 6 That thirst [for applause]..is..on the whole, the strongest impulsive influence of average humanity. **1894** *Month* Mar. 392 The impulsive cause of the granting of a dispensation is that which..moves the superior.

3. Of persons, their character, actions, etc.: Actuated or characterized by impulse; apt to be moved by sudden impulse or swayed by emotion.

1847 L. HUNT *Jar Honey* v. (1848) 58 The Scotch have shown a more genial and impulsive spirit in their songs and dances than the English. **1850** W. IRVING *Goldsmith* xxviii. 276 Who was very impulsive, and prone to acts of inconsiderate generosity. **1854** H. MILLER *Sch. & Schm.* xix. (1860) 208 One of those impulsive acts of which men repent at their leisure. **1867** FREEMAN *Norm. Conq.* I. vi. 558 Such conduct would not be that of a sentimental and impulsive hero. **1897** ALLBUTT *Syst. Med.* II. 851 Impulsive drunkenness or dipsomania is the result of an hereditary taint.

4. *Electr.* Consisting of, or of the nature of, an impulse or impulses.

1920 *Whittaker's Electr. Engineer's Pocket-Bk.* (ed. 4) 136 The passage of the spark in such a case appears to involve an impulsive rush of electricity, and the setting up of electric pulses in the neighbourhood of the spark gap can be demonstrated. **1940** *Chambers's Techn. Dict.* 440/2 *Impulsive current*, a current which comprises one or more impulses in one direction round a circuit, as in dialling. **1947** D. G. FINK *Radar Engin.* xi. 127 The impulsive type of noise (ignition interference and static) so commonly encountered on lower frequencies is generally absent in radar. **1962** *Newnes Conc. Encycl. Electr. Engin.* 466/2 Although the secondary winding [of a magneto] may have 10,000 turns, its voltage is not sufficiently impulsive, however. The contact-breaker is therefore arranged to short-circuit the primary.

†**B.** *sb.* An impelling agent or cause. *Obs.*

a **1628** PRESTON *Breastpl. Love* (1631) 29 Where love is, it is such a strong impulsive in the heart, it carries one on to serve and please the Lord in all things. **1659** H. L'ESTRANGE *Alliance Div. Off.* xi. 326 This was the genuine and true impulsive to Calvin, to write that letter.

impulsively (ɪmˈpʌlsɪvlɪ), *adv.* [f. prec. + -LY².] In an impulsive fashion; with, or by means of, impulse; by sudden impulse.

1768 STERNE *Sent. Journ.*, *Act of Charity*, The two ladies seemed much affected; and impulsively at the same time they both put their hands into their pocket. **1825** *Blackw. Mag.* XVIII. 295 Causes, which..bear impulsively, or hinderingly, upon every action. **1865** MISS MULOCK *Christian's Mistake* 2 He looked like a man who was not in the habit of acting hastily or impulsively. **1879** THOMSON & TAIT *Nat. Phil.* I. I. §317 A stated velocity in a stated direction is communicated impulsively to each end of a flexible inextensible cord.

impulsiveness (ɪmˈpʌlsɪvnɪs). [f. as prec. + -NESS.] The quality of being impulsive in feeling or action.

1659 D. PELL *Impr. Sea* To Rdr., A strong, and an unwithstanding impulsiveness that lay..upon my heart and spirit, till I went about it. **1863** GEO. ELIOT *Romola* Proem, Crude passions acted out with childish impulsiveness. **1884** W. J. COURTHOPE *Addison* v. 97 That impulsiveness of feeling..made him [Steele] the most powerful and persuasive advocate of Virtue in fiction.

impulsivity (ɪmpʌlˈsɪvɪtɪ). [f. IMPULSIVE *a.* + -ITY.] The character of being impulsive or acting on impulse, without reflection or forethought; impulsiveness. Hence **im'pulsivist**, one who acts on impulse.

1891 C. LOMBROSO *Man of Genius* 348 The psychology peculiar to the epileptic—impulsivity, double personality, childishness. **1895** tr. *M. Nordau's Degeneration* 120 Moral insanity, however, is not present in Verlaine. He sins through irresistible impulse. He is an Impulsivist. **1925** *Public Opinion* 24 Apr. 391/2 A man of exceptional ability and yet of a febrile impulsivity. **1969** D. A. WINN in Caplan & Lebovici *Adolescence* 256 Impulsivity was prominently a part of the suicidal behavior of most of the 60 adolescents in this study. **1971** *Jrnl. Gen. Psychol.* Oct. 273 This relationship would seem to indicate an underlying impulsivity as being a modest contributor.

†**im'pulsor.** *Obs.* [a. L. *impulsor*, agent-n. from *impellĕre* to IMPEL; cf. F. (obs.) *impulseur*.] One who, or that which, impels.

1653 H. MORE *Antid. Ath.* (1662) 151 Nor [can] Motion be communicated but by Impulse, nor Impulse without Impenetrability in the Impulsor. **1658** SIR T. BROWNE *Gard. Cyrus* ii. 43 The innitency and stresse being made upon the hypomochlion or fulciment in the decussation, the greater compression is made by the union of two impulsors. **1678** GALE *Crt. Gentiles* III. 136 So that God be the motor and impulsor..of the action and worke. **1700** S. PARKER *Six Philos. Ess.* 106 Independent of any foreign Impulsor.

impulsory (ɪmˈpʌlsərɪ), *a. rare.* [f. L. *impuls-*, ppl. stem of *impellĕre*: see IMPULSE *v.* and -ORY.] That tends to impel or force onward.

1659 D. PELL *Impr. Sea* 498 Hee gives some or other amongst you secret, and impulsory hints and warnings. **1845** G. OLIVER *Coll. Biog. Soc. Jesus* 171 Whatever he said ..was dictated by the impulsory act of his conscience.

†**im'pulverable,** *a. Obs. rare*⁻¹. [f. IM-² + PULVERABLE.] Incapable of being pulverized.

a **1691** BOYLE *Hist. Air* (1692) 169 Some good fine dried jalap..he found by the heat of the air to be melted, and by consequence to be impulverable.

impunctate (ɪmˈpʌŋktət), *ppl. a.* [f. IM-² + PUNCTATE.] Not punctate; not marked with points or dots.

1819 G. SAMOUELLE *Entomol. Compend.* 157 *Hyphydrus ovatus*, Obscure, ferrugineous, impunctate. **1846** HARDY in *Proc. Berw. Nat. Club* II. No. 14. 196 Foveæ impunctate. **1854** WOODWARD *Mollusca* II. 214 The loop, or brachial processes, are always impunctate.

†**im'punction.** *Obs. rare*⁻¹. [ad. L. type **impunctiōn-em*, f. *im-* (IM-¹) + *pungĕre* to prick, pierce; cf. PUNCTION.] Pricking or piercing.

1712 SIR G. WHELER *Liturgy* 138 Cabasilas hath nothing of chopping the bread..but impunction, and cutting, as by a Lance.

impunctual (ɪmˈpʌŋktjuːəl), *a.* [f. IM-² + PUNCTUAL.] Not punctual, behind time (Webster, 1864). So **impunctu'ality**, want of punctuality.

1790 *Observer* No. 139 ¶2 Unable to account for his impunctuality, some of his intimates were dispatched in quest of him. *a* **1804** ALEX. HAMILTON cited in Worcester.

impunctured (ɪmˈpʌŋktjʊəd), *ppl. a.* [f. IM-² + PUNCTURED.] Unpunctured; impunctate.

†**impune** (ɪmˈpjuːn), *a. Obs.* [ad. L. *impūn-is* unpunished; f. *im-* (IM-²) + *pœna* penalty, punishment, *pūnīre* to punish.] Unpunished; enjoying impunity.

1614 T. ADAMS *Fatal Banquet* ii. Wks. 1861 I. 235 The breach of our national statutes can not go impune by the plea of ignorance. **1615** —— *White Devill* 34 [Not a thing that] can priviledg or keep impune the injuries [etc.].

†**im'punely,** *adv. Obs.* [f. prec. + -LY².] With impunity; without punishment.

1614 T. ADAMS *Fatal Banquet* i. Wks. 1861 I. 184 The blood of his enemies shall not be impunely shed. *a* **1711** KEN *Hymns Evang.* Poet. Wks. 1721 I. 118 Shall he impunely sacred Law defie? **1715** D. JONES *Hist. House Brunswick* 380 A certain Militia Captain..(and that impunedly) order'd the Musick on his March to play, '*The King shall enjoy his Own again*'.

impung, -punge, obs. forms of IMPUGN *v.*

impunible (ɪmˈpjuːnɪb(ə)l), *a. rare.* [f. IM-² + L. *pūnīre* to punish + -IBLE.] Not punishable; unpunishable.

1660 R. COKE *Justice Vind.* 47 But Mr. Hobbs outruns the Constable, and makes the King or Civitas..impunible for whatsoever he shall do.

Hence **im'punibly** *adv.*, without punishment, with impunity.

1743 J. ELLIS *Knowl. Div. Th.* ii. 65 Xenophon represents the Opinion of Socrates, that..no Man impunibly violates a Law established by the Gods. **1865** MRS. WHITNEY *Gayworthys* xxiii. (1879) 230 She never lied, or stole, or slew, impunibly.

impunitive (ɪmˈpjuːnɪtɪv), *a. Psychol.* [f. IM-² + PUNITIVE *a.*] Adopting an attitude of resignation towards frustration; characterized by blaming neither oneself nor others unreasonably. Contrasted with INTROPUNITIVE *a.* and EXTRAPUNITIVE *a.*

1938 S. ROSENZWEIG in H. A. Murray *Explorations in Personality* vi. 587 He may experience emotions of embarrassment and shame, making little of blame and emphasizing instead the conciliation of others and himself to the disagreeable situation. In this case he will be more interested in condoning than in condemning and will pass off the frustration as lightly as possible by making references, even at the price of self-deception, to unavoidable circumstances. This type of reaction may be termed 'impunitive'. **1954** G. W. ALLPORT *Nature of Prejudice* xxi. 349 Some frustrated people..are so detached and philosophical about life's frustrations that they blame no one; they are impunitive. **1958** M. ARGYLE *Relig. Behaviour* viii. 90 A related personality variable is that of punitiveness: people are said to be extrapunitive if they react to frustration by aggression directed outwards, intropunitive if the aggression is directed inwards, and impunitive if they do not react aggressively at all.

Hence **im'punitively** *adv.*, in a way characteristic of an impunitive individual.

1958 M. ARGYLE *Relig. Behaviour* viii. 91 The humanitarians on the other hand responded impunitively. **1969** M. D. VERNON *Human Motivation* ix. 148 Unacceptable motivational tendencies..may be treated impunitively and denied entry to consciousness.

impunity (ɪmˈpjuːnɪtɪ). [ad. L. *impūnitās*, f. *impūnis* (see IMPUNE and -TY), or ad. F. *impunité*

(14th c. in Littré).] Exemption from punishment or penalty.

1532 MORE *Confut. Tindale* Wks. 716/2 For the safegard of heretikes, and impunitie of all mischieuous people. **1598** BARCKLEY *Felic. Man* (1631) 648 Wicked acts and misdemeanours are allured by impunity, as it were by rewards. **1660** R. COKE *Power & Subj.* 45 This unlimited power of doing anything with impunity, will only beget a confidence in kings of doing what they list. **1736** BUTLER *Anal.* I. ii. Wks. 1874 I. 41 Delay of punishment is no sort nor degree of presumption of final impunity. **1872** BLACK *Adv. Phaeton* xxv, You can't commit murder in this country with impunity.

b. In weaker sense: Exemption from injury or loss as a consequence of any action; security.

1800 *Med. Jrnl.* III. 50 Men of strong constitutions began to stimulate in excess very early in life, and continued in the practice for several years with impunity. **1806** *Ibid.* XV. 442 Mr. Fewster..had the small-pox in his youth, and was exposed to the infection with impunity for forty years. **1834** PRINGLE *Afr. Sk.* viii. 285 The venom of the most deadly snakes may be swallowed with impunity. **1856** KANE *Arct. Expl.* II. xiv. 142 Its runners..seem to bear with impunity the fierce shocks of the ice.

†**impu'ration.** *Obs. rare.* [f. L. *impūrus* IMPURE + -ATION: cf. L. *pūrāre* to purify.] The action of making impure; pollution. *lit.* and *fig.*

1614 BP. HALL *Recoll. Treat.* 833 The impuration or corruption of the Roman Church. *a* **1656** —— *Serm. Christ & Cæsar* Wks. 1863 V. 336 For these happy regions..may it please you to forbid their impuration by the noysome fogges and mists of those mis-opinions.

impure (ɪm'pjʊə(r)), *a.* (*sb.*) [ad. L. *impūr-us*, f. *im-* (IM-[2]) + *pūrus* pure. Cf. F. *impur*, *-e* (13th c. in Hatz.-Darm.).]

A. *adj.* **I. 1. a.** Containing some defiling or offensive matter; dirty, unclean.

1597 A. M. tr. *Guillemeau's Fr. Chirurg.* 46b/1 We then sowe a cleane white Compresse on the impured compresse, and then we draw away the impure compresse from vnder the Fracture. **1647** COWLEY *Mistress, Bathing in River* v, Thou No priviledge dost know Above th' impurest streams that thither flow. **1774** GOLDSM. *Nat. Hist.* (1776) I. 170 The impurest fresh water that we know, is that of stagnating pools and lakes. **1807** *Med. Jrnl.* XVII. 103 Want of due discrimination between the effects of an impure atmosphere and of contagion.

b. Not pure ceremonially; unhallowed, unclean.

1612–15 BP. HALL *Contempl., O.T.* XVIII. vi, His [God's] only command sanctifies those creatures, which, by a general charge, were legally impure. **1662** J. DAVIES tr. *Olearius' Voy. Ambass.* 204 Their meat..if it happen that any one..should blow or breath upon it, they cast it away as impure. **1804** W. TENNANT *Ind. Recreat.* (ed. 2) I. 120 An honest man, by touching impure food,..will be degraded. **1840** THIRLWALL *Greece* liv. VII. 49 The invader, who had touched the hallowed soil with impure feet. **1841** LANE *Arab. Nts.* (Rtldg.) 51 Dogs, which, according to the tenets of the Mussulman religion, are impure animals.

2. Not pure morally; defiled by sin; unclean, unchaste; filthy. **a.** of persons.

a **1536** TINDALE *Expos. Matt.* v. 6. 18 Impure and vnclean herted then ar al they that study to breake God's commaundementes. **1591** SPENSER *Teares of Muses* 120 The wretchednes of world impure. **1620** GRANGER *Div. Logike* 140 It is then more intollerable to serve an impure fellow. **1784** COWPER *Task* II. 751 Jockeys, brothellers impure, Spend-thrifts, and booted sportsmen. **1818** SHELLEY *Rev. Islam* X. vi, Those slaves impure, Each one the other thus from ill to ill did lure.

b. of actions or things.

1613 PURCHAS *Pilgrimage* (1614) 66 Astrologie, which..he defiled with impure Magicke. **1667** MILTON *P.L.* IV. 746 Defaming as impure what God declares Pure. **1780** COWPER *Progr. Err.* 584 The temple of impure delight. **1864** J. WALKER *Faithf. Ministry* 103 We fill the hearts of others with impure desires.

II. 3. Mixed with or containing some extraneous or foreign matter, esp. of an inferior or baser kind; contaminated, adulterated. **a.** Of things physical.

1626 BACON *Sylva* §98 The Oyly, Crude, Pure, Impure, Fine, Grosse Parts of Bodies, and the like. **1799** G. SMITH *Laboratory* I. 334 In this manner are extracted from roses.. the three impure parts, phlegm, water, and earthy residuum. **1811** PINKERTON *Petral.* I. 317 Another cove.. which affords a greyish impure steatites, spotted with black. **1816** J. SMITH *Panorama Sc. & Art* II. 370 Impure mercury also soils white paper, and the presence of lead may be detected by agitating the metal with water. **1838** T. THOMSON *Chem. Org. Bodies* 114 The catechuic acid obtained in this way was still impure.

b. Of things immaterial.

1704 NORRIS *Ideal World* II. iii. 179 That [act of the will] may be said to be impure or mixt, partly voluntary, partly involuntary. *Ibid.* 180, I call that an impure thought, whose object is material or corporeal. **1844** D. R. HAY *Orig. Geom. Diaper Designs* 3 Many of the kinds of ornaments called styles being themselves impure, in so far as they are destitute of the first principles of beauty. **1894** *Daily News* 6 Mar. 7/4 The testator died..possessed of considerable personal property, the pure personalty amounting to 25,000*l.*, and the impure to 3,500*l.* **1895** HOLMAN HUNT *ibid.* 14 Aug. 6/2 The nation has adopted the impure entanglements of the Art of previous races.

c. Of a language, style, etc.: Containing foreign idioms or grammatical blemishes.

1613 PURCHAS *Pilgrimage* (1614) 47 By reason of their traffique, it [the language] proved impure there also. **1814** [implied in IMPURELY].

d. Of a colour: Containing an admixture of some other colour or colours; also said of a spectrum when the colours overlap.

1860 TYNDALL *Glac.* II. i. 227 The rainbow is an imperfect or impure spectrum. **1869** —— *Fragm. Sc.* (1879) I. 115 The sky-blue is gradually rendered impure by the growth of the particles. **1882** P. G. TAIT in *Encycl. Brit.* XIV. 593/1 The spectrum produced in this way is very impure, i.e., the spaces occupied by the various homogeneous rays overlap one another. **1892** *Nature* 22 Sept. 485/1 'Impure'..may be an objectionable term to apply to a colour when mixed with white, but..it can only be used in that sense.

B. *sb.* An unchaste or lewd person; a harlot.

1784 *New Spectator* No. 3. 4/2 Balloon hats now adorn the heads of..the parading impures. **1825** C. M. WESTMACOTT *Eng. Spy* II. 24 Four fashionable impures. **1830** H. INGELO *Reminisc.* II. 282 The destiny of those unfortunate impures.

Hence **im'purist**, one who is not a purist.

1937 V. WOOLF *Writer's Diary* 3 Apr. (1953) 280 The purists and the impurists. **1959** 'F. NEWTON' *Jazz Scene* vi. 113 The jazz public has always been divided, but before the modernist revolution normally only into 'purists' and 'impurists'.

†**im'pure**, *v. Obs.* [f. IMPURE *a.*]

1. *trans.* To render impure; to defile.

1597 [see IMPURE *a.* 1]. **1612–15** BP. HALL *Contempl., O.T.* XX. iv, One drop of that wicked blood was enough..to impure and spill all the rest. **1641** *Answ. Vind. Smectymnuus* 59 To take up gold mislaid in a channell, which could not impure it. **1673** CARYL *Nat. & Princ. Love* 46 Sin did impure his whole inner Man.

2. *intr.* To become impure.

a **1618** SYLVESTER *Mem. Mortal.* lxx, Pure in she [the soul] came, there living she impures And suffers there a thousand woes the while.

impurely (ɪm'pjʊəlɪ), *adv.* [f. IMPURE *a.* + -LY[2].] In an impure manner; with impurity; corruptly.

1612 T. TAYLOR *Comm. Titus* i. 15 In generall, men impurely vse them two wayes. **1647** WARD *Simp. Cobler* 43 A Church impurely Reformed. **1813** W. TAYLOR *Eng. Synonyms* (1856) 52 *Fashionable* is impurely formed, and ought to mean able to be fashioned. **1814** —— in *Monthly Mag.* XXXVII. 118 The translators of the Bible use the word counsellor impurely, instead of adviser.

impureness (ɪm'pjʊənɪs). [f. as prec. + -NESS.] The quality of being impure; impurity.

1547–64 BAULDWIN *Mor. Philos.* (Palfr.) III. ii, The people ..by the impurenesse thereof [a palace] are with sundry vices corrupted. **1623** MIDDLETON *More Dissemblers* I. i, As void of all impureness as an altar. **1803** *Med. Jrnl.* X. 554 No doubt..as to the badness or impureness of the plant, as it was gathered in the beginning of July. **1861** G. MOBERLY *Serm. Beatit.* vi. 107 He becomes familiarized in all his life with the realities of impureness.

im'purify, *v. rare.* [f. IMPURE *a.* after PURIFY.] *trans.* To render impure.

1693 W. FREKE *Sel. Ess.* xxix. 166 Let no Temptation impurify thy Will. **1904** *Daily Chron.* 19 July 3/7 Impure aeration that..takes place in dirty, fœtid cowsheds impurifies it [*sc.* milk]. **1928** D. H. LAWRENCE *Let.* 18 Feb. (1962) II. 1040, I am having to impurify and dilute it [sc. *Lady Chatterley's Lover*] for the market.

Im'puritan. [f. IMPURE *a.*, after PURITAN.] **a.** One who practises impurity. **b.** A hostile term for one not a Puritan or opposed to Puritanism.

1617 DABORNE *Serm. Waterford* (1618) 11 There are a third Sect, and those are *puri quasi minime puri*, the impuritans of our time. **1627** J. CARTER *Expos.* 19 Not.. Impuritanes in any degree, whether walkers in the counsell of the ungodly, or [etc.]. **1647** WARD *Simp. Cobler* 29 If those who are tearmed Rattle-heads and impuritans, would take up a Resolution to begin in moderation of haire, to the just reproach of those that are called Puritans and Roundheads, I would honour their manlinesse. **1818** BENTHAM *Ch. Eng.* Introd. 27 It may moreover..be not unacceptable, to behold the difference between Puritans and Impuritans.

Hence **Im'puritanism**, the principles of an Impuritan as opposed to those of a Puritan; also, impure life or principles generally.

1818 BENTHAM *Ch. Eng.* Introd. 23 The difference between Church-of-Scotlandism and Church-of-Englandism:—between Puritanism, since that must be the name, and Impuritanism: between Presbyterianism and Episcopacy. **1892** *Chicago Advance* 25 Feb., The protest of the Puritan against the impuritanism of his time.

impurity (ɪm'pjʊərɪtɪ). [a. OF. *impurité* (15th c. in Littré) = mod.F. *impureté*, ad. L. *impūritās*, f. *impūrus*: see IMPURE *a.* and -TY.]

1. The quality or condition of being impure or of containing something foul or unclean; *concr.* foul or offensive matter, dirt.

1597 A. M. tr. *Guillemeau's Fr. Chirurg.* 11b/1 The matter, and all impuritye might therout have free passage. **1660** F. BROOKE tr. *Le Blanc's Trav.* 14 By reason of the impurity of the ayr, there is scarce any more then these two townes in the whole country. **1797** BEWICK *Brit. Birds* (1847) I. 156 Its entrails are shaken out, leaving only the body thus cleansed from all its impurities. **1806** *Med. Jrnl.* XV. 547 Wipe out the little subjacent drop of pus, in order to guard against impurity. **1860** RUSKIN *Mod. Paint.* VIII. i. §7 (1897) V. 175 Exclusive of animal decay, we can hardly arrive at a more absolute type of impurity than the mud or slime of a damp, over-trodden path, in the outskirts of a manufacturing town.

2. a. The state or condition of being morally impure; uncleanness, unchastity; defilement by sin.

1548 UDALL, etc. *Erasm. Par. John* xiii. 74 Excepte..the affeccions of his mynde be often purged from all impuritie of this worlde. *a* **1610** HEALEY *Theophrastus* (1636) 44 Impurity or beastlinesse is not hard to be defined. *a* **1711** KEN *Div. Love* Wks. (1838) 292 Let thy love, who art purity itself, create in me a perfect abhorrence of all impurity. **1874** SAYCE *Compar. Philol.* viii. 305 Sin and moral impurity are words which he would not understand.

b. With *an* and *pl.* That which is or makes impure morally; moral uncleanness or corruption.

c **1450** tr. *De Imitatione* III. liii. 126 Come, heuenly swetnes, & make fle fro þi visage all maner impurite. **1593** SHAKS. *Lucr.* 854 But no perfection is so absolute, That some impuritie doth not pollute. **1639** DU VERGER tr. *Camus' Admir. Events* To Rdr. aiјb, Novels..full of impurities, impieties. **1790** BEATTIE *Moral Sc.* I. ii. §6. 347 Let no visible or audible impurity..enter the apartment of a child.

3. a. The quality of containing some extraneous or foreign admixture, esp. of an inferior or baser kind; *concr.* foreign matter which detracts from the purity of any substance.

1605 TIMME *Quersit.* I. ix. 37 Saltes haue their corporall impurities. **1704** NORRIS *Ideal World* II. iii. 182 The metaphysical..impurity of thought is the..materiality of its object. **1750** tr. *Leonardus' Mirr. Stones* 25 These virtues are varied..by reason of..the purity or impurity of the matter. **1799** G. SMITH *Laboratory* I. 142 Neal the copper..to prevent ashes or other impurities getting to it. **1842** PARNELL *Chem. Anal.* (1845) 19 The hydrochloric acid of commerce is always contaminated with impurities which render it quite unfit for general use as a reagent.

b. An impurity atom; *esp.* an atom of dopant present at a normal lattice site in an impurity semiconductor.

1931 A. H. WILSON in *Proc. R. Soc.* A. CXXXIV. 279 Electrons on a foreign atom [in a semiconductor] do not take part directly in conduction. They must first be transferred by the effect of the lattice vibrations to an atom of the pure substance. In this case the main function of the impurities is to provide electrons for the upper unoccupied energy bands of the crystal, while acting as scatterers is only a secondary function. **1950** W. SHOCKLEY *Electrons & Holes in Semiconductors* i. 12 The conductivity [of the silicon] arises from the presence of arsenic atoms which are termed 'impurities', even though added deliberately in the otherwise pure silicon. *Ibid.* 14 Impurities with a valence of five are called 'donor impurities' because they donate an excess electron to the crystal; those with a valence of three are called 'acceptor impurities', since they accept an electron from somewhere else in the crystal.., thus leaving a hole to conduct. **1952** J. S. KOEHLER in W. Shockley et al. *Imperfections in nearly Perfect Crystals* vii. 206 The maximum value..of this force occurs when the impurity is two or three atomic distances from the dislocation. **1959** R. A. SMITH *Semiconductors* iii. 45 We must distinguish two types of impurity, substitutional impurities, which replace atoms of the host crystal on their lattice sites, and interstitial impurities which occupy positions in between the lattice sites. **1972** F. J. BAILEY *Introd. Semiconductor Devices* i. 21 By the addition of donor impurities to the silicon, large numbers of free electrons become available as current carriers.

4. Special Comb.: **impurity atom**, an atom that differs from the bulk of those present in a substance in being of a different element; **impurity level**, an energy level in a semiconductor that is due to an impurity atom and generally lies either just above the highest filled (valence) energy band (in the case of an acceptor) or just below the lowest empty (conduction) band (in the case of a donor); **impurity scattering**, scattering of current carriers by impurity atoms in a crystalline solid; **impurity semiconductor**, a semiconductor in which most of the carriers of electric current are electrons and holes from impurity atoms.

1939 A. H. WILSON *Semi-Conductors & Metals* i. 3 The [electrical] resistance in a metal is caused by the scattering of the electrons by irregularities in the crystal; these irregularities may be due to the presence of impurity atoms and strains or to the temperature motion of the atoms. **1949** *Physical Rev.* LXXV. 866/1 A substitutional impurity atom from the fifth group has one more valence electron than is required to fill the four valence bonds with neighboring silicon atoms. **1970** W. BOLLMANN *Crystal Defects* iv. 37 The elementary point defects are vacancies and interstitial atoms, and also impurity atoms. **1972** F. J. BAILEY *Introd. Semiconductor Devices* i. 21 The doping level refers to the ratio of impurity atoms to silicon atoms. For a transistor this may typically be $1:10^8$, i.e. one impurity atom for every hundred million silicon atoms. **1973** *Sci. Amer.* Feb. 93/2 If other atoms, which can be referred to as impurity atoms if their concentration is relatively small, are introduced into a helium discharge, the random collisions in the discharge will mix the impurity atoms with the helium atoms. **1933** R. H. FOWLER in *Proc. R. Soc.* A. CXL. 507 Semi-conductors with impurity levels full of electrons at low temperatures owe their conductivity to the excitation of electrons to band 1 both from the impurity levels and from band 2, the former predominating at ordinary temperatures. **1964** J. M. ZIMAN *Princ. Theory Solids* vi. 169 In a semiconductor there may also be scattering from a neutral impurity—where, for example, an electron has settled in a donor impurity level, or a hole is resident on an acceptor level. **1946** *Physical Rev.* LXIX. 258/2 (*heading*) Theory of impurity scattering in semiconductors. **1965** LINDMAYER & WRIGLEY *Fund. Semiconductor Devices* vii. 259 In crystals used for devices, thermal scattering and impurity scattering dominate the collision processes. **1946** *Trans. Amer. Inst. Electr. Engin.* Nov. 713/3 At low temperatures the conductivity of different samples varies by large factors. In this region silicon is said to be an impurity semiconductor. **1950** W. SHOCKLEY *Electrons & Holes in Semiconductors* i. 12 (*heading*) Impurity semiconductors; donors and acceptors.

impurple, obs. form of EMPURPLE *v.*

†**impurpure**, *v. Sc. Obs.* Also 7 em-. [f. IM-¹ + PURPURE, earlier form of PURPLE.] *trans.* To make purple; to empurple.

1552 LYNDESAY *Monarche* Prol. 146 Quhose donke impurpurit vestiment nocturnall, With his imbroudit mantyll matutyne. **1628** SIR W. MURE *Spir. Hymne* 114 Empurp'ring thy vnstained face.

imput, var. of INPUT *v.*, to put in.

imputability (ɪmpjuːtəˈbɪlɪtɪ). [f. IMPUTABLE: see -TY. So mod.F. *imputabilité*.] The quality or condition of being imputable.

1771 R. WATSON *Chem. Ess.* (1787) V. 175 There ariseth a proportionable imputability of conduct. **1831** BLAKEY *Free-will* 32 The entire absence of restraint..confers upon all human actions the character of moral imputability. **1857** T. E. WEBB *Intellectualism Locke* vii. 141 That which declares and measures the Moral Imputability of Actions. **1875** POSTE *Gaius* III. (ed. 2) 452 They..imply imputability, or responsibility for dolus and culpa.

imputable (ɪmˈpjuːtəb(ə)l), *a.* [ad. med.L. *imputābilis*, f. *imputāre* to IMPUTE: see -BLE. Cf. F. *imputable* (Oresme, 14th c.).]

1. That may be imputed *to* or assigned to the account of; chargeable, attributable.

1626 JACKSON *Creed* VIII. xxvii. §5 The errour is imputable onely to the Transcriber or Interpreter, not to the author. **1665** BOYLE *Occas. Refl.* Introd. (1848) 29 Apologies..for the Imperfections imputable to this Treatise. **1780** T. JEFFERSON *Corr.* Wks. 1859 I. 271 Their being exposed..to a want of covering, would be imputable to themselves only. **1845** LD. CAMPBELL *Chancellors* cxii. (1857) V. 217 No blame is imputable to him. **1880** MUIRHEAD *Gaius* IV. §163 *note*, Damages, the amount of the pursuer's loss imputable to the defender.

†**2.** Liable to imputation; open to accusation or censure; blameworthy, reprehensible, culpable. Cf. IMPUTE *v.* 3. *Obs.*

1660 JER. TAYLOR *Duct. Dubit.* I. ii, There being nothing that can render an action culpable or imputable [etc.]. **1710** SHAFTESB. *Charact.* II. II. i. (1737) II. 120 Some justly blameable and imputable Act. **1726** AYLIFFE *Parergon* 58 The law deems her to be a dutiful wife..in no wise imputable. **1784** J. BARRY in *Lect. Paint.* iv. (1848) 162 This fault..is hardly imputable, as it was not committed through ignorance but by election.

Hence **im'putableness**, the quality of being imputable; **im'putably** *adv.*, in a way that is imputable or chargeable with fault.

1678 NORRIS *Coll. Misc.* (1699) 298 'Tis necessary to imputableness of an Action, that it be avoidable. **1710** —— *Chr. Prud.* vii. 327 A man may sin by following his conscience..and that too imputably, if it was mistaken for want of care to inform it better.

†**Impu'tarian.** *Obs. rare*⁻¹. [f. IMPUTE *v.* + *-arian*, as in *Unitarian*, *Trinitarian*, etc.] One who holds the theological doctrine of imputed righteousness.

1668 PENN *Sandy Foundation* 28 Some..of the same spirit with the Satisfactionists and Imputarians of our time.

imputation (ɪmpjuːˈteɪʃən). [ad. late L. *imputātiōn-em*, n. of action from *imputāre* to IMPUTE. Cf. F. *imputation* (15th c. in Godef. *Compl.*).]

1. The action of imputing or attributing something, usually a fault, crime, etc., to a person; the fact of being charged with a crime, fault, etc.; (with *pl.*) an instance of this; accusation, charge.

1581 SIDNEY *Apol. Poetrie* (Arb.) 51 Nowe then goe wee to the most important imputations laid to the poore Poets. **1597** SHAKS. *2 Hen. IV*, v. i. 81, I would humour his men, with the imputation of beeing neere their Mayster. **1611** BIBLE *Transl. Pref.* 10 The imputation of Sixtus..that our people had bene fed with gall of Dragons in stead of wine. **1693** DRYDEN tr. *Juvenal* Ded. 7 Heaven be prais'd, our common Libellers are as free from the imputation of Wit, as of Morality. **1786** BURKE *W. Hastings* Wks. 1842 II. 202 The imputation of a new violation of faith. **1802–12** BENTHAM *Ration. Evidence* Wks. 1843 VII. 16 Individuals, really innocent, have sunk under a load of imputation heaped upon them by fallacious circumstantial evidence. **1871** MARKBY *Elem. Law* §258 Rashness or heedlessness may be a ground of criminal imputation.

2. *Theol.* **a.** The attributing to believers of the righteousness of Christ, and to Christ of human sin, by vicarious substitution; also, the imputing of the guilt of Adam's sin to all his descendants.

1545 JOYE *Exp. Dan.* iii. 45 b, In the remission of synnes and in the imputacion of rightwysnes and lyfe eternall. **1597** HOOKER *Eccl. Pol.* v. lvi. §11 We participate Christ partly by imputation, as when those things which he did and suffered for us are imputed unto us for righteousnesse. **1656** COWLEY *Misc.* Pref., No body can be justified by the Imputation even of anothers Merit. **1758** S. HAYWARD *Serm.* ix. 270 Of this kind is the imputation of Christ's righteousness, the imputation of our sins to him, and the imputation of Adam's sin to us. **1852** HOOK *Ch. Dict.* (1871) 383 Imputation is the attributing of a character to a person which he does not really possess.

b. *concretely.*

1642 ROGERS *Naaman* 13 Christ was no such large imputation of all grace, as Adam was of sin.

†**3.** Attribution of merit (to oneself); the making a merit of a thing. (So L. *imputāre*). *Obs.*

1628 EARLE *Microcosm.*, *Meere Gull* (Arb.) 93 A man that will spend his sixe pence with a great deale of imputation, and no man makes more of a pinte of wine then he.

4. An economic theory of value (see quot. 1965); also (freq. *attrib.*) a form of taxation levied on company profits, usu. in phr. ***imputation system, tax.*** Cf. IMPUTE *v.* 6.

1893 C. A. MALLOCH tr. *F. von Wieser's Natural Value* III. ii. 77 So far as this method succeeds in founding, upon the imputation of the return, a valuation of goods and a plan of production..it is the height of practical wisdom. To show that imputation in this sense is both allowable and practicable take one single case. **1931** A. GRAY *Devel. Econ. Doctrine* xii. 354 The most characteristic part of Wieser's contribution to the school lies in his doctrine of *Zurechnung*, which has been acclimatized in this country as 'imputation' or 'attribution'... In a sense the higher goods have no value until a value is 'imputed'..to them. **1934** F. A. VON HAYEK in C. Menger *Coll. Works* I. p. xv, He answers the problem of imputation..by saying that such quantities of the different factors as can be substituted for each other..must have equal value. **1938** E. ROLL *Hist. Econ. Thought* viii. 388 In the theory of distribution Menger is responsible for posing what is known as the problem of imputation; that is the problem of the value of goods of a higher order. **1965** SELDON & PENNANCE *Everyman's Dict. Econ.* 210 *Imputation*, the process of attributing value to productive resources in accordance with their contribution to the value of their products... The theory of imputation argued that the value of factors ('higher-order' goods) was *in all cases* determined by (imputed from) the value of the final ('lower-order') goods to whose production they contributed. **1971** *Daily Tel.* 17 Nov. 19/2 The Government..preferred to replace it not with the French *imputation* or tax credit method but with a two-rate system... The *imputation* system..would mean that all company profits..would be taxed at the rate of 50 p.c. **1972** *Accountant* 23 Mar. 366/1 The Chancellor..would introduce a new tax based upon the imputation system. *Ibid.*, Under the imputation system, the company will pay tax on its total profits. **1972** S. MARCUS *Finance Act 1972* i. 2 Under the new 1973 method, known as the 'imputation system', all profits (except capital gains) will be taxed at the same rate, whether they are distributed or not. **1973** *Daily Tel.* 31 Mar. 19/5 Dividend covers..have been adjusted to take into account the new corporation 'imputation' tax system. *Ibid.* 2 Apr. 20 The 'imputation' method of taxing company profits..becomes the technical core of investment.

imputative (ɪmˈpjuːtətɪv), *a.* [ad. late L. *imputātīv-us* (*c* 200 Tertullian), f. ppl. stem of *imputāre* to IMPUTE: see -IVE.]

1. Characterized by being imputed; existing or arising by imputation: esp. in reference to the theological doctrine of imputed righteousness.

1579 FULKE *Refut. Rastel* 794 All the iustice and holinesse of good men is but an imputatiue iustice. **1600** E. BLOUNT *Hospit. Incur. Fooles* A ij, Poets still..traduce your Ladyshyp with the imputatiue slanders of Niggardise and instability. **1691** SHADWELL *Scourers* II, A man would think we need no imputative wickedness. **1713** NELSON *Life Bp. Bull* 223 The imputative Righteousness of Christ. **1882–3** SCHAFF *Encycl. Relig. Knowl.* II. 1608 He fought for supralapsarian predestination, imputative justification, etc.

2. Given to making imputations.

1824 *Examiner* 756/1 Never being smart, ironical, or what we will venture to call imputative.

Hence **im'putatively** *adv.*, in an imputative manner; by imputation. **im'putativeness**, imputative character or quality.

c **1621** S. WARD *Life of Faith* (1627) 61 A Iust man, not onely imputatiuely, but inherently in part. *a* **1708** BEVERIDGE *Priv. Thoughts* vii. (1816) 65 The righteousness of God, radically his but imputatively ours. **1837** G. S. FABER *Prim. Doctr. Justif.* iv. 161 *note*, Of the Church of old ..it is said, on the same principle of imputativeness [etc.]. **1879** tr. *Meyer's Ep. Corinth.* II. v. 296 The γινεσθαι δικαιοσυνην θεου took place for men imputatively.

impute (ɪmˈpjuːt), *v.* Also 4 input, 6 inpute. [a. F. *imputer* (Oresme, 14th c.), earlier OF. *emputer*, ad. L. *imputāre* to bring into the reckoning, enter into the account, charge, f. *im-* (IM-¹) + *putāre* to clear up, settle, reckon.]

1. a. *trans.* To bring (a fault or the like) into the reckoning against; to lay to the charge of; to attribute or assign as due or owing *to* (†*into*, *unto*).

c **1375** *Sc. Leg. Saints, Margaret* 701 Ihesu, for þi pitte þu input nocht þis ded to me! **1490** CAXTON *Eneydos* xx. 73 A lyar, that dredeth not..to Impute to theym [the goddes] that they ben cause of thyn vntrouth. **1535** JOYE *Apol. Tindale* (Arb.) 30 Here he imputeth vnto me certain crimes. **1674** N. COX *Gentl. Recreat.* II. (1677) 173, I rather impute that fault to the ignorance, or negligence and harshness of the Faulconer. **1746** JOHNSON *Plan Dict.* Wks. IX. 185 We usually ascribe good, but impute evil. **1814** D'ISRAELI *Quarrels Auth.* (1867) 263 He had frequently imputed to the poet meanings which he never thought. **1869** SIR J. T. COLERIDGE *Mem. Keble* 353 No one could impute that he took them up hastily. **1875** SCRIVENER *Lect. Text N. Test.* 7 Variations such as we must at once impute to the fault of the scribe.

b. Less usually in a good sense: To set to the credit of; to ascribe or reckon *to*.

1574 tr. *Marlorat's Apocalips* 16 Imputing all thinges to Gods grace. **1611** BIBLE *Rom.* iv. 22 It was imputed to him for righteousnesse. **1767** JOHNSON *Let. to W. Drummond* 21 Apr., I hope you do not flatter me by imputing to me more good than I have really done. **1856** EMERSON *Eng. Traits, Universities* Wks. (Bohn) II. 89, I imputed to these English an advantage in their secure and polished manners.

2. *Theol.* To attribute or ascribe (righteousness, guilt, etc.) *to* a person by vicarious substitution: see IMPUTATION 2.

[**1539** BIBLE (Great) *Rom.* iv. 6 Dauid descrybeth the blessedfulnes of that man, vnto whom God imputeth ryghtewesnes wythout dedes.] **1583** FULKE *Defence* i. 121 The justice of Christ which is imputed unto us by faith. **1667** MILTON *P.L.* III. 291 Thy merit Imputed shall absolve them who renounce Thir own both righteous and unrighteous deeds. **1771** WESLEY *Wks.* (1872) V. 237 To all believers the righteousness of Christ is imputed. **1876** J. P. NORRIS *Rudim. Theol.* I. iii. 48 Luther's theory of imputation:—man's sin was imputed to Christ, and Christ's righteousness was imputed to man.

3. a. To charge, arraign, or tax *with* fault; to accuse. ? *Obs.*

1596 MUNDAY tr. *Silvayn's Orator* 25 You will impute me for favoring more the Plebeian then Patrician faction. **1625** FLETCHER *Noble Gent.* I. i, If you fail, Do not impute me with it; I am clear. **1639** GENTILIS *Servita's Inquis.* (1676) 886 They ought not to proceed but against the persons imputed. **1859** TENNYSON *Vivien* 824 They..that most impute a crime Are pronest to it, and impute themselves.

†**b.** *loosely.* To condemn, sentence. *Obs. rare.*

c **1540** *Pilgr. Tale* 455 in Thynne's *Animadv.* (1865) App. i. 90 O wyched worme..by god inputed to crepe apon thy brest.

†**4.** To reckon or take into account; to reckon, regard, consider. *Obs.*

1532 TINDALE *Exposit.* (Parker Soc. 1849) 89 God promiseth to forgive us our sins, and to impute us for full righteous. **1548** UDALL, etc. *Erasm. Par. John* xviii. 111 They..yet impute themselues pure and fre from murder. **1555** EDEN *Decades* 48 Yowe may..impute this to occupie the place of the tenthe. **1611** SPEED *Theat. Gt. Brit.* vi. (1614) 11/1 [K. Henry VI] for his holy life was imputed a Saint. **1673** MARVELL *Reh. Transp.* II. 5 They impute it for a great obligation. **1727** SWIFT *Prayer for Mrs. Johnson* ii, Accept and impute all her good deeds. *a* **1794** GIBBON (Webster 1864), If we impute this last humiliation as the cause of his death.

†**5.** To impart. *Obs.*

1594 J. DICKENSON *Arisbas* (1878) 63 Trust me, employ me, impute to me thy desires. **1633** G. HERBERT *Temple, Faith* ix, Thou didst make the sunne, Impute a lustre, and allow them bright. **1675** TRAHERNE *Chr. Ethics* 57 The value of the objects imputes a lustre and higher value to the light wherein they are enjoyed.

6. *Econ.* To attribute or assign (value) to a product or process by inference from the value of the products or processes to which it contributes.

1893 C. A. MALLOCH tr. *F. von Wieser's Natural Value* III. viii. 96 To each single item or quantity is imputed the smallest contribution which..can be economically aimed at by the employment of this particular item or quantity. **1893** W. SMART in C. A. Malloch tr. *F. von Wieser's Natural Value* p. xv, This determination of imputation by equations of return tells us nothing more than that certain shares *are* imputed to certain elements. **1945** E. HEIMANN *Hist. Econ. Doctrines* VIII. ii. 197 A problem..had greatly concerned the Austrians from Menger on, namely how separate shares in the product can be imputed to the cost factors when they invariably co-operate in production. **1950** DINGWALL & HOSELITZ tr. *Menger's Princ. Econ.* III. ii. 139 We logically impute this importance to the goods on whose availability we are conscious of being dependent. **1965** SELDON & PENNANCE *Everyman's Dict. Econ.* 210 The value of factors ..was *in all cases* determined by (imputed from) the value of the final..goods to whose production they contributed. **1973** *N.Y. Law Jrnl.* 2 Aug. 4/4 If interest is not provided for, the Internal Revenue Service may impute interest to any deferred payments.

Hence **im'puting** *vbl. sb.*; also **im'puter**, one who imputes or charges.

1611 COTGR., *Imputeur*, an imputor; a putter of thing vpon ..others. **1630** *Penit. Conf.* xii. (1657) 316 For the not imputing, the remitting, and covering of sin appertain to the righteousness of faith. *a* **1641** BP. MOUNTAGU *Acts & Mon.* (1642) 169, I wonder it is not vouched by the Imputers, that he was counterfaited by the Apostles themselves.

†**im'pute**, *sb. Obs. rare*⁻¹. [f. IMPUTE *v.*: cf. *repute*.] Imputation, charge.

1649 G. DANIEL *Trinarch., Rich. II*, xxv, Hee might be worthy blame, (If Royalty may fall vnder Impute).

impute, var. of INPUT *v.*, to put in.

imputed (ɪmˈpjuːtɪd), *ppl. a.* [f. IMPUTE *v.* + -ED¹.]

1. Charged (as a fault); attributed or ascribed.

1552 HULOET, Imputed, *obiectus*. **1590** SPENSER *F.Q.* II. i. 20 He shortly shall againe be tryde, And fairely quit him of th' imputed blame. **1690** LOCKE *Hum. Und.* II. ix. §22 To distinguish the primary, and real Qualities of Bodies, which are always in them..from those secondary and imputed Qualities, which are but the Powers of several Combinations of those primary ones. **1794** SULLIVAN *View Nat.* II. 299 Their imputed names were titles. **1891** CHURCH *Oxford Movem.* x. 169 The party soon had the faults of a party, real and imputed.

2. Ascribed by vicarious substitution.

1620 GRANGER *Div. Logike* 60 Imputed justice by which we are justified before God, is inherent in Christ. **1729** SWIFT *Libel on Delany*, Steel, who own'd what others writ, And flourish'd by imputed wit. **1849** ROBERTSON *Serm.* I. ix. 141 By imputed guilt is meant, in theological language, that a person is treated as if he were guilty. **1871** MACDUFF *Mem. Patmos* xiii. 173 The pure white garment of Christ's imputed righteousness.

3. *Econ.* Estimated, valued in relation to something else. Spec. ***imputed price, value*** (see quots.).

1909 WEBSTER, *Imputed value*, Econ., the value that a thing has merely for its utility in the production of something else;—called also *derived value*. **1929** *Encycl. Brit.* XXII. 960/2 Imputed price..is an estimate of the amount of money for which a given article or a given quantum of goods could be sold or bought. **1973** *Daily Tel.*

27 Mar. 23 (Advt.), With imputed tax credits this is equivalent to a franked payment of 6·5625 p per share.

Hence **im'putedly** *adv.*, by imputation.

1646 P. BULKELEY *Gospel Covt.* II. 173 When he hath made us imputedly righteous, he will have us inherently righteous also.

imputrescence (ɪmpju:'trɛsəns). [f. IM-² + PUTRESCENCE.] Absence of putrescence or decomposition.

1658 PHILLIPS, *Imputrescence*, a keeping from putrefaction, or rotting, an uncorruptiblenesse. **1823** *New Monthly Mag.* VII. 144 The magistrates..found his body with all the usual characteristics of animation and imputrescence.

imputresci'bility. [f. next + -TY.] The quality of being imputrescible or incorruptible.

1727 in BAILEY vol. II. **1797** PEARSON in *Phil. Trans.* LXXXVIII. 28 Its peculiar..distinguishing properties are, imputrescibility, facility of crystallization [etc.]. **1972** C. LÉVI-STRAUSS in P. Maranda *Mythology* xiii. 275 They are operators, which make it possible..to express..a set of equivalences connecting life and death, vegetable foods and cannibalism, putrefaction and imputrescibility, [etc.].

imputrescible (ɪmpju:'trɛsɪb(ə)l), *a.* [f. IM-² + PUTRESCIBLE.] Not subject to putrefaction or decomposition; incorruptible.

1656 in BLOUNT *Glossogr.* **1805** HATCHETT in *Phil. Trans.* XCV. 211 Tannin..renders the skins of animals insoluble in water, and imputrescible. **1852** MORFIT *Tanning & Currying* (1853) 47 It..thus forms insoluble and imputrescible compounds.

†**im'putrible,** *a. Obs.* Also 5 in-. [ad. late L. *imputribil-is* (*c* 400 Augustine, Jerome), f. *im-* (IM-²) + *putribilis* corruptible, f. *putrēre* to be rotten: see -IBLE.] Imputrescible; not subject to decomposition; not liable to rot or decay.

1430–40 LYDG. *Bochas* IV. i. (MS. Bodl. 263) lf. 212/1 Mirtis braunchis, which been Inputrible Enduryng euere and corupte nouht. *c* **1450** *Mirour Saluacioun* 1237 The Testamentis arke of Sethim a tree inputrible was made. **1607** TOPSELL *Four-f. Beasts* (1658) 15 It was afterward supposed he was buried therein, and was lively to be seen imputrible.

†**imputrid** (ɪm'pju:trɪd), *a. Obs.* [f. IM-² + PUTRID.] Not putrid: applied to a fever.

1684 tr. *Bonet's Merc. Compit.* VI. 188 Whether drinking of cold Water be proper in an imputrid continent fever. **1822–34** *Good's Study Med.* (ed. 4) I. 676 The species has been distinguished by a variety of names..imputrid synochus, which is that of Galen; imputrid continued fever ..that of Boerhaave; imputrid continent..that of Lommius.

imputt, imputter: see INPUT, etc.

'impy, *a. rare.* [f. IMP *sb.* + -Y.] Impish.

1845 *Whitehall* xxxvi. 244 A swarm of impy changelings.

†**im'pyre,** *a.* Obs. var. of EMPYRE, empyrean.

1552 LYNDESAY *Monarche* 6034 Frome erth, vp to the Heuin Impyre, All beis renewit by that fyre. **1567** *Gude & Godlie B.* (S.T.S.) 29 That thay sall cum..To gloir and joy, and heuin Impyre. *a* **1605** MONTGOMERIE *Misc. Poems* xiii. 10 That fervent fyre Of burning love impyre.

impyre, obs. form of EMPIRE.

impyteous, -pytous, -pytuous, obs. var. IMPETUOUS.

imram, var. IMMRAM.

imshi ('ɪmʃɪ). *Services' slang.* Also **imshee, imshy.** [Local Arabic (Berggren).] Be off, go away. Also as *vb.*

1916 *Anzac Book* 135/2 And the King-of-all-the-Huns said, 'It is enough, Imshee!' *Note*, Imshee is the Arabic for 'go away'. The Australasian Corps, which had so far employed it only to street hawkers in Cairo, used this war-cry on April 25. *Ibid.* 136/1 So they imsheed. **1919** *Athenæum* 28 July 664/2 'Imshy', go away (generally corrupted into something like 'hampshire'). **1942** *Word Study* Dec. 6/2 '*Imshi*,' said the drongo; 'you're *shikkered*!' **1965** G. MCINNES *Road to Gundagai* iv. 70 Now, imshee-allah!

‖**imu** ('imu). [Hawaiian.] 'In the Hawaiian islands, a pit used for baking meat or vegetables by means of heated stones' (*Cent. Dict.* Suppl., 1909).

1928 J. C. ANDERSEN *Myths & Legends Polynesians* 296 When he reached Makila, on the confines of Lahaina, he saw a number of people heating an *imu*, or ground oven. **1954** *Ellery Queen's Mystery Mag.* Oct. 43/2 Next came the ritual of putting the pigs into the *imu*. *Ibid.* 47/1 *Imu* pork, white and succulent inside crackling brown skin.

imunction, variant of EMUNCTION, *Obs.*

1601 HOLLAND *Pliny* XX. v, The imunction of the eies, with the juice thereof [*sc.* green onions], is thought to clense their cicatrises or cloudinesse of the eies.

i-munde: see YMUNDE.

†**i-mune, i-myne,** *v. Obs.* [OE. *ȝemunan*, *ȝemynan*, f. *munan* to remember.] *trans.* To bear in mind, remember.

971 *Blickl. Hom.* 55 Mid inneweardre heortan ȝemunan and ȝeþencan. *c* **1000** *Ags. Gosp.* Luke i. 72 ȝemunan [*Lindisf.* ȝemyndȝa] his haleȝan cyþnesse. *c* **1000** *St. Juliana* 721 in *Exeter Bk.*, þæt he mec..bi noman minum ȝemyne. *c* **1205** LAY. 16309 Wel ȝe hit maȝen imunen þat ich wulle mæinen.

i-munt, pa. pple. of MINT *v.*, to intend.

†**i-munte,** *v. Obs.* [OE. *ȝemyntan*, f. *myntan* to think, intend.] *trans.* To intend, determine.

c **1000** ÆLFRIC *Hom.* II. 126 Gregorius..ȝemunde hwæt he..Angelcynne ȝemynte. *c* **1205** LAY. 8038 For æuere more he mai imunnen þæt he him her imunten [*v.r.* imunte].

i-murðred, ME. pa. pple. of MURDER *v.*

i-mutation: see I I. 2 b.

i-mylded, ME. pa. pple. of MILD *v.*

in (ɪn), *prep.* Forms: α. 1– in; also 3 *Orm.* inn, 5 yn(e, ynne. β. 2–6 i, i-, 3–4 y, 6– i'. [Common Teut. = OFris., OS., OHG., Goth. *in*, ON. *í* (Sw., Da. *i*), cognate with L. *in*, Gr. ἐν.

In OE., in all those texts in which the word occurs, the full form *in* is used, but in early ME. the apocopated *i* became common in certain dialects.

In the *Ormulum*, *inn* (= *in*) is employed before vowels and *h*, and *i* before all consonants except *h*. Early southern texts, such as the *Lamb.* and *Cott. Homilies*, *Juliana*, *St. Kath.*, *St. Marher.*, *Ancr. R.*, etc., show a similar tendency, but with more or less irregularity, the MSS. often differing in this respect; on the whole, *i* is preferred when the prep. precedes the definite article or the demonstrative pronouns, as *i þe*, *i þis*, *i þat*. In some of these texts (*Ancr. R.*, *Lamb. Hom.*) the relations of the two forms are further complicated by the use of INE, which also appears (e.g. in *Ayenb.*, *Owl & Night.*, *Shoreham*) where *i* is rare or altogether wanting. The prevalence of *i* in these southern texts suggests that Ormin's use of this form was not due to Scandinavian influence, especially as northern writers (including Scottish down to 1600) always employed *in*, though *i'* is common in the modern dialects. In standard English from the time of Chaucer *in* has been the normal form; but former colloquial usage is sometimes retained in verse in the combination *i' th'*, or as an archaism in *i' faith*.

c **1175** *Lamb. Hom.* 79 Þe uisces iþe wetere and fuȝeles iþe lufte. *c* **1200** ORMIN Ded. 5 Broþerr min i Godess hus. *Ibid.* 506 To serrvenn i þe temmple. *c* **1205** LAY. 1231 Biȝende France i þet west. *a* **1240** *Sawles Warde* in *Cott. Hom.* 245, I þis hus is þe huse lauerd. **1610** SHAKS. *Temp.* I. ii. 84 All hearts i' th state. *Ibid.* 130 Ith' dead of darkenesse. *Ibid.* II. i. 147 I' th' Commonwealth. *a* **1734** [see 29]. **1785** BURNS *Vision* I. ii, Whan the day had clos'd his e'e, Far i' the west. **1855** BROWNING *Bp. Blougram's Apol.* 2 Cool i'faith! We ought to have our Abbey back you see.]

General Sense:— The preposition expressing the relation of inclusion, situation, position, existence, or action, within limits of space, time, condition, circumstances, etc. In ancient times, expressing also (like L. *in*) motion or direction from a point outside to one within limits; the two senses being determined by the case of the word expressing the limits, the former taking the *dative* (originally locative), the latter the *accusative* or case of direction. These cases being subsequently levelled, this distinction ceased to be practicable, and the latter relation is now ordinarily expressed by the compound *in-to*, INTO; but there are various locutions in which (either because the accompanying verb conveys the sense of motion, or through the preservation of an ancient phrase without analysis) *in* still expresses motion from without to within.

In OE. (as in OS. and to some extent in OFris.) the prep. *in* was displaced by the prep. *on* (WGer. *an*, Goth. *ana*), so that in classical and late WSaxon, and to some extent in other OE. dialects, *on* was used for both *on* and *in*, an emphatic or distinctive sense of 'in' being however expressed by *innan*. (See full details in Dr. T. Miller, *OE. Version of Bede*, Introd. xxxiii–xliv.) In Anglian, esp. in the north and west, *in* remained (though, under WSax. influence, often displaced by *on* in documents); and in ME. the distinction of *in* and *on* was gradually restored, though many traces of their former blending still remain. (See sense 2.)

The formal coincidence of *in* with the L. prep. *in* (with which it is originally cognate) led to its being employed, in translating from L., in senses or uses which were idiomatic in L., but not originally English. These also have affected the current contextual use of the preposition.

I. Of position or location.

Primarily *in* (of position) is opposed to *out of*: anything which is *in* a given space is not *out of* it, and *vice versa*. The compound *with-in*, is mainly an equivalent of *in* emphasizing the relation to limits. The simple relation-words nearest in sense to *in* are *at* and *on*, with which *in* sometimes has common ground, e.g. '*in* or *at* Oxford', '*in* or *on* a street', '*in* or *on* behalf of a man'. *In* may also have common ground with *with*, as 'to travel *in* or *with* a caravan, a railway train, etc.'.

1. a. Of place or position in space or anything having material extension: Within the limits or bounds of, within (any place or thing).

May relate to a space of any size, however large or small: e.g. *in* the universe, *in* the world, *in* heaven, *in* hell, *in* the earth, *in* the sea (otherwise *on* the earth, *on* the sea, *at* sea), *in* a ship, vessel, *in* a field, wood, forest, desert, wilderness (but *on* a heath, moor, or common), *in* (U.S. *on*) a street, *in* a house, carriage, box, drawer, nut-shell, drop of water, etc.

Also (U.S.) *in* school, attending a school, receiving education at a school = (U.K.) *at school* (cf. SCHOOL *sb.*¹ 1 b). In former times *in school* was also used in Britain in the sense 'attending a school': see quot. *c* 1205 s.v. SCHOOL *sb.*¹ 1 b. Also *c* 900 *Bæda's Eccl. Hist.* (1890) 190/12 Sum leornungmon in scole Scotta cynnes; *a* 1350 *Harley Lyrics* (1948) 63 Whil y wer a clerc in scole.

a **700** *Epinal Gloss.* 549 *In curia*, in maethlae. *c* **825** *Vesp. Psalter* viii. 2 Hu wundurlic is noma ðin in alre eorðan. *c* **1175** *Lamb. Hom.* 7 Þa children pleȝeden in þere strete. *Ibid.* 23 Þa men þe beoð in þe castel. *c* **1205** LAY. 17490 In þan brade uelde. **1297** R. GLOUC. (Rolls) 2 Engelond Iset in þe on ende of þe worlde as al in þe west. *c* **1330** R. BRUNNE *Chron. Wace* (Rolls) 8253 Þey are now saylynge in þe se. **1362** LANGL. *P. Pl.* A. I. 114 Summe in þe Eir, and summe in þe Eorþe, and summe in helle deope. **1426** *E.E. Wills* (1882) 73 My bachous in Wodestrete. **1470–85** MALORY *Arthur* x. i, In euery place he asked..after sir Launcelot, but in no place he coude not here of hym. **1551** RECORDE *Pathw. Knowl.* I. xxvii, The circle is not named to be drawen in a triangle, because it doth not touche the sides of the triangle. **1608** TOPSELL *Serpents* (1658) 741 Dryed in a furnace. **1653–1756** In the open air [see AIR *sb.* 3 b]. **1660** WOOD *Life* 4 Dec. (O.H.S.) I. 350 His chamber in Merton Coll. *a* **1707** BP. PATRICK *Autobiog.* (1839) 105, I never saw greater devotion in any countenance. **1711** ADDISON *Spect.* No. 10 ¶4 Spectators, who live in the World without having anything to do in it. **1818** SHELLEY *Rev. Islam* x. xv, The fish were poisoned in the streams; the birds In the green woods perished. **1828** SCOTT *F.M. Perth* ii, Adjacent to Couvrefew Street in which they lived. **1848** J. F. COOPER *Jack Tier* I. iii. 80 *In* a vessel is as correct as *in* a coach, and *on* a vessel, as wrong as can be; but you can say *on board* a vessel, though not 'on the boards of a vessel'. **1849** MACAULAY *Hist. Eng.* I. i. 150 The restored wanderer reposed safe in the palace of his ancestors. **1852** DICKENS *Bleak Ho.* vi, The wind's in the East. **1855** KINGSLEY *Heroes, Perseus* I. 4 They are..in the open sea. **1873** TRISTRAM *Moab* viii. 157 An orderly in the doorway. **1898** FLO. MONTGOMERY *Tony* 9 In a somewhat crowded train. **1916** 'TAFFRAIL' *Pincher Martin* xiv. 248 'When I was in the old *Somerset*, in nineteen-nine,' somebody would start the ball rolling, 'we had a fellow who'——. **1942** *Short Guide Gt. Brit.* (U.S. War Dept.) 8 The tales of Scott and Robert Louis Stevenson which many of you read in school. **1972** R. QUIRK et al. *Gram. Contemp. Eng.* 310 He's {at school (BrE) / in school (AmE)} (= 'He attends/is attending school'). He's in school (= (in BrE) 'He's actually inside the building—not, *eg* on the playing fields').

b. After *in*, the article is often omitted, esp. when the function of the place is the prominent notion; as in *bed*, in *chancery*, in *chapel*, in *church*, in *court*, in *hall*, in *prison*, in *school*, in *town*: see the sbs.

in earth, *in sea*, follow *in heaven*, *in hell*, which are treated like geographical proper names: see c.

c **1175** *Lamb. Hom.* 59 In eorðe, in heuene is his mahte. *a* **1300** *Cursor M.* 11793 (Gött.) Alle þai drouned in see. **1389** in *Eng. Gilds* (1870) 5 Be he in toun oþer out of toun. **1398** TREVISA *Barth. De P.R.* VI. xii. (1495) 196, I suffre not a woman to teche in chyrche. **1593** SHAKS. *3 Hen. VI*, III. ii. 70, I had rather lye in Prison. **1675** tr. *Machiavelli's Prince* (Rtldg.) 297 Strasburg..has a million of florins..in bank. **1744** BERKELEY *Siris* §77 A large glass every hour..taken in bed. **1852** DICKENS *Bleak Ho.* ii, In Chancery. Between John Jondyce [etc.]. *Mod.* Hundreds lay languishing in prison.

c. *In* is used with the proper names of continents, seas, countries, regions, provinces, and other divisions, usually also of large cities, esp. the capital of a country, and of the city or town in which the speaker lives. Cf. AT *prep.* 2.

c **900** *O.E. Chron.* an. 894 Þa ȝegaderedon þa þe in Norþhymbrum buȝeað & on East Englum. **971** *Blickl. Hom.* 211 Wæs he..in Italia afeded, in Ticinan þære byriȝ. *c* **1205** LAY. 10712 Wes Allec þe king in are temple in Lundenne. *a* **1300** *Cursor M.* 24765 Willam basterd, þat warraid in jngland ful hard. **1526** TINDALE *Matt.* iv. 13 Jesus..went and dwelte in Capernaum. **1686** F. SPENCE tr. *Varilla's Ho. Medicis* 176 The worthiest man in Europe. **1841** THACKERAY *Gt. Hoggarty Diam.* ix, We wished her at—Bath; certainly not in London. **1849** MACAULAY *Hist. Eng.* ii. I. 158 The Presbyterian system was fully established nowhere but in Middlesex and Lancashire.

†**2. a.** = ON (of position). *Obs.*

Partly a reaction from the blending of *in* with *on* in OE.; but partly also transl. L. *in*, and partly due to a different notion in reference to the sb.

Beowulf (Z.) 1952 Hio syððan well in gum-stole gode mære..breac. *a* **1000** *Riddles* xli. 98 (Gr.) Ne hafu ic in heafde hwite loccas. *a* **1000** *Cædmon's Dan.* 723 (Gr.) Engel drihtnes..wrat þa in waȝe worda ȝerynu. *c* **1250** *Meid. Maregr.* xlvii, Ho..Sette ir fot in is necke. **1297** R. GLOUC. (Rolls) 6179 Me slou is folc aboute in eche syde. *a* **1300** *Cursor M.* 8136 An heremite þar þai fand at ham, In þat montan. *Ibid.* 11819 In his heued he has þe scall. *a* **1300** etc., In a chair [see CHAIR *sb.* 1]. *c* **1305** *St. Andrew* 42 in *E.E.P.* (1862) 99 In þe Rode as þi louerd deide: ic wole sette þe. *c* **1380** WYCLIF *Wks.* (1880) 457 Þe pope sittiþ in his troone. *c* **1430** *Pilgr. Lyf Manhode* II. xcviii. (1869) 111 Þat oon bar þat ooþer in hire nekke. *c* **1449** PECOCK *Repr.* II. ii. 138 Sette him up an hiȝe in the eend of a long pole. *Ibid.* v. 166 Write sum..carect with cole..in the wal. **1480** *Robt. Devyll* 28 He kneled downe in the floore. *a* **1550** *Christis Kirke Gr.* xviii, His wyfe hang in his waist. **1607** TOPSELL *Four-f. Beasts* (1658) 241 The Rider must lay the rains in his neck. **1664** MARVELL *Corr.* Wks. 1872–5 II. 157 *note*, Farr from making any favourable impressions in the Tzar. **1692** S. PATRICK *Answ. Touchstone* 89 Antichrist is long ago in the Throne of the Roman Church. **1701** *Stanley's Hist. Philos.* Biog. 10 He ..spent his Time in the Solitary Top of a Mountain. **1730** A. GORDON *Maffei's Amphith.* 42 Flattering Fame is.. generally in the magnifying Side.

†**b.** = AT. *Obs.*

1647 CLARENDON *Hist. Reb.* VI. §85 Then was the General ..in the head of his Regiment..shot in the thigh. **1653** HOLCROFT *Procopius* 20 The Barbarians came up close, with Gelimer in the head of them. **1671** MILTON *P.R.* I. 98 Ere in the head of nations he appear.

3. *In* is now regular with collectives thought of as singular (*in an army, a crowd*); *among* with plurals, or collectives thought of as plural (*among the people*); but through Latin influence *in* was formerly used also with plurals.

c**825** *Vesp. Psalter* lxvi. 3 Ðæt we oncnawen..in allum ðiodum hælu ðin. a**900** CYNEWULF *Crist* 195 in *Exeter Bk.*, ȝen strengre is þæt ic..scyle..lifȝan siþþan fracoð in folcum. c**950** *Lindisf. Gosp.* Luke i. 28 ȝebloedsad ðu in wifum. c**1380** WYCLIF *Sel. Wks.* III. 445 Freris wold not here þis publischt in þe pepul. **1388** —— *Ps.* lxvi. 3 [lxvii. 2] That we knowe thi weie on erthe, thin heelthe in alle folkis. **1535** COVERDALE *Judith* viii. 21 Seinge ye are the honorable and elders in the people of God.

4. With numerals, nouns of quantity, and the like, expressing ratio or rate. Esp. of a gradient.

1598 W. PHILLIPS *Linschoten* (1864) 171 Commonly worth fiue and twenty or thirty in the hundred profit. a **1613** OVERBURY *Char., Creditour* Wks. (1856) 161 He takes ten groats i' th' pound. **1703** MOXON *Mech. Exerc.* 239 Dearer ..by about six Shillings in a Thousand. **1726** LEONI tr. *Alberti's Archit.* I. 74/1 A very good Rise for a slope is half an inch in every three foot. **1732** NEAL *Hist. Purit.* I. Pref. 7 Not one beneficed clergyman in six was capable of composing a sermon. **1761** WESLEY *Jrnl.* 23 June (1827) III. 62 Ninety-nine in a hundred were attentive. **1830**, etc. [see ONE 5 b]. **1840** [see GRADE *sb.* 10]. **1861**, **1868** [see GRADIENT *sb.* 1]. **1869** *Bradshaw's Railway Manual* XXI. 318 The gradients and curves are generally favourable, the steepest gradient being 1 in 82 ½. **1892** *Law Times* XCII. 147/1 A debtor..offered 6*s.* 8*d.* in the pound. **1923** *Michelin Guide Gt. Brit.* (ed. 7) facing p. 277, Gradients on roads are shown thus:..1 in 20 to 1 in 14. 1 in 14 to 1 in 10. 1 in 10 and over. **1973** E. COURSE *Railways S. Eng.: Main Lines* i. 29 Over the nineteen and a half miles from Redhill to Tonbridge the maximum gradient was 1 in 250.

5. a. Defining the particular part of anything in which it is affected.

a **1225** *Ancr. R.* 112 A lutel ihurt i þen eie derueð more þen deð a muchel iðe hele. a **1300** *Cursor M.* 7224 Man aght to dred þe brand þat brint him forwit in his hand. *Ibid.* 12184 Leui was wrath..And gaf him in þe heued a dint. a **1533** LD. BERNERS *Huon* cxlviii. 558 Huon..kyst her in the mouth. a **1618** RALEIGH *Prerog. Parl.* (1628) 45 He was knock't in the head by Parliament. a **1626** MIDDLETON *More Dissemblers* v. i, There's many..Whom I have nipp'd i' th' ear. **1703** MOXON *Mech. Exerc.* 36 You must mend it in that place. **1795** *Hist.* in *Ann. Reg.* 70 A masked battery took them in flank. **1858** CARLYLE *Fredk. Gt.* IX. ix. II. 491 King of the Two Sicilies..whom Naples, in all ranks of it, willingly homages as such. **1898** *Tit-Bits* 17 Sept. 484/1 The horse..is blind in one eye.

b. In phrases implying incidental distribution, e.g. *in parts, in places.*

1905 [see CURATE 2 b]. **1922** D. H. LAWRENCE *England, my England* 132 And I sensed I was a prisoner, for the snow was everywhere deep, and drifted in places. **1924** A. D. SEDGWICK *Little French Girl* II. v, The long iron staircase down the face of the cliff was almost as steep as a fire escape in places. **1973** *Listener* 8 Feb. 167/2 The Appeal Court.. found the [Warhol] film dull, dreary, and offensive in parts.

6. Expressing relation to that which covers, clothes, or envelopes, its material, its colour, etc., = clothed in, wearing, enveloped in, bound in, etc.: as a lady *in a court dress, in a Gainsborough hat, in muslin, in mourning, in white, in curl-papers,* a man *in armour, in slippers, in a wig,* a parcel *in brown paper,* etc. (*in* ARMS, and other idiomatic uses: see the substantives.) Cf. also 13 b.

a **1000** *Cædmon's Exod.* 212 (Gr.) Sæton æfter beorȝum in blacum reafum. a **1240** *Wohunge* in *Cott. Hom.* 277 Poure þu wunden was irattes and i clutes. c **1300** *Havelok* 1767 Comes a ladde in a ioupe. **13..** *Coer de L.* 5616 Our Crystene men ben armyd weel Both in yren and in steel. c **1386** CHAUCER *Knt.'s T.* 1261 Som wol ben armed in an haubergeon And in bristplate and in a light gypon. c **1430** *Life St. Kath.* (1884) 17 Þe company of martirs clothed alle in purpul. **1581** J. BELL *Haddon's Answ. Osor.* 28 b, The same was gaynsayd by some men in armes. **1710** ADDISON *Tatler* No. 221 ¶1 A little Boy in a black Coat. **1843** *Blackw. Mag.* LIV. 195 A lovely girl in mourning is sitting. **1843** *Fraser's Mag.* XXVIII. 324 A lady in black velvet is seated. **1868** DICKENS *Uncomm. Trav.* xx, A compactly-made handsome man in black.

7. The physical sense of location often passes into one more immaterial; e.g. *in a book, in an author,* come to mean 'in the course of the narrative or subject' of the book, or the writings of the author; *in a company, college, association,* or *party, in the army, the navy,* and the like, become = 'belonging to, or in the membership of the company, party, the army', etc. *in* COMPANY, *in* LEAGUE, etc.: see the sbs.

c**890** *O.E. Chron.* an. 878 þara monna þe in þam here weorþuste wæron. c **1175** *Lamb. Hom.* 7 Þis witeȝede dauid ..in þe saltere. a **1225** *Ancr. R.* 400 Ase he seið þuruh Sein Johan iðe Apocalipse. **1297** R. GLOUC. (Rolls) 56 We ssulleþ her after in þise boc telle of al þis wo. c **1340** *Cursor M.* 15563 (Fairf.) We salle ga in company & suffre baþe a sare. c **1460** *Towneley Myst.* xvi. 202 Syrs, I pray you inquere in all wrytyng, In vyrgyll, in homere, And all other thyng Bot legende. **1548** LATIMER *Ploughers* (Arb.) 17 All things that are written in Goddes boke. **1657** BP. KING *Poems* III. ix. (1843) 90 Let it no more in History be told. **1662** STILLINGFL. *Orig. Sacr.* III. ii. §5 So true is that of Balbus in Tully when he comes to discourse of the Nature of God. **1709** ADDISON *Tatler* No. 131 ¶11 A Friend of mine in the Army. **1849** MACAULAY *Hist. Eng.* iii. I. 325 The place of the clergyman in society had been completely changed by the Reformation. **1887** ANNE GILCHRIST in *Century Guild Hobby Horse* 13 Eblis in the Koran, Cain in the Bible are scarce so black as this royal phantom in his Escurial. **1890** *Law Times Rep.* LXIII. 685/2 The plaintiff applied for shares in this company.

8. With non-physical realms, regions of thought, departments or faculties of the mind, spheres of action, etc., treated as having extension or content.

c**888** K. ÆLFRED *Boeth.* i, Se wæs in boccræftum & on woruldþeawum se rihtwisesta. a **1000** *Cædmon's Dan.* 732 (Gr.) Sohton þa swiðe in sefan ȝehydum. a **1225** *Leg. Kath.* 607 In hire mod inwið. c **1300** *Havelok* 122 Sho is mikel in mi þouht. c **1400** *Three Kings Cologne* xiv. 50 3if þe werkis of god myȝt be comprehendit in mannys wit or reson. c **1470** HENRY *Wallace* I. 2 Hald in mynde thar nobille worthi deid. **1601** CORNWALLYES *Ess.* II. xlv, In no course is it more behovefull then in the life of a Souldier. **1645** FULLER *Good Th. in Bad T.* (1841) 33, I discover an arrant laziness in my soul. **1670** SIR S. CROW in *12th Rep. Hist. MSS. Comm.* App. v. 16 In my opinion a better designe. a **1770** JORTIN *Serm.* (1771) IV. vi. 114 A faith which dwells in the memory hath no influence on the heart. **1826** J. WILSON *Noct. Ambr.* Wks. 1855 I. 240 How canst thou thus in fancy burn with fruitless fires? **1849** MACAULAY *Hist. Eng.* vi. II. 39 All the thirty were in politics vehemently opposed to the prisoner.

II. Of situation, condition, state, occupation, action, manner, form, material, and other circumstances and attributes.

9. a. Of situation, i.e. kind or nature of position: e.g. *in the dust, in the mud, in snow, in clover, in hot water.* Often idiomatic: see the sbs.

a **900** CYNEWULF *Crist* 561 in *Exeter Bk.*, In cwic-susle ȝehynde & ȝehæfte. c **1175** *Lamb. Hom.* 47 Ieremie þe prophete stod..in þe uenne up to his muðe. **12..** *Relig. Songs* in Wright *Owl & Night.* (Percy Soc.) 75 Ich schal bernen in fur and chiverin in ise. **1382** WYCLIF *Job* xlii. 6 Therfore I myself repreue me, and do penaunce in dead cole and askis. **1481** CAXTON *Godfrey* cci. 293 Habandouned in ordure and fylthe. **1592** SHAKS. *Ven. & Ad.* 94 She bathes in water. **1697** DRYDEN *Virg. Georg.* III. 548 A hilly Heap, seven Cubits deep in Snow. *Ibid.* IV. 545 The sacred Altars are involv'd in Smoak. **1765** MRS. HARRIS in *Priv. Lett. Ld. Malmesbury* (1870)) I. 125 We are kept, to use the modern phrase, in *hot water.* **1849** TENNYSON *In Mem.* Prol. iii, Thou wilt not leave us in the dust. **1886** *Law Times* LXXX. 166/2 Hall..found his working about eighteen inches deep in water.

b. Situation expressed by material instruments: e.g. *in bonds, chains, fetters, leading-strings, in a cord, a leash, a rope, a string,* etc.

a **1200** *Moral Ode* 289 In þo loþe biende. c **1200** ORMIN 19975 Inn hiss cwarrterrne i bandess. c **1300** *Beket* 15 Al in feteres and in other bende. **1382** WYCLIF *Isa.* xlv. 14 Bounde in manycles thei shul wende. **1590** SPENSER *F.Q.* I. i. 4 And by her, in a line, a milkewhite lambe she lad. **1611** BIBLE *Job* xxxvi. 8 If they bee bound in fetters, and be holden in cords of affliction. **1712** STEELE *Spect.* No. 504 ¶5, I am to be hang'd in chains. **1862** C. HUDSON in *Peaks, Passes & Glaciers* Ser. II. I. 209 During the descent.. Melchior, Tuckett, and I, who were in the same cord with them, were..obliged to stop until they got down some of the more difficult rocks.

c. Situation as to light, darkness, and atmospherical environment.

Beowulf (Z.) 87 Se ellengæst..seþe in þystrum bad. a **1225** *Juliana* 31 As ha þrinne wes i þeosternesse. a **1300** *Cursor M.* 17811 (Gött.) Þe folk in dedeli mirknes stad. **1382** WYCLIF *Isa.* ii. 5 Go wee in the liȝt of the Lord oure God. **1553** T. WILSON *Rhet.* (1580) 160 Gropyng in the dark. **1605** SHAKS. *Macb.* I. i. 2 When shall we three meet againe? In Thunder, Lightning, or in Raine? **1648** BP. HALL *Breath. Devout Soul* xxix. 46 An inheritance in light: In light incomprehensible, in light inaccessible. **1697** DRYDEN *Virg. Georg.* III. 135 His thick Mane..dances in the Wind. *Ibid.* 473 Where basking in the Sun-shine they may lye. **1855** MACAULAY *Hist. Eng.* xxi. IV. 593 Privateers and smugglers who put to sea in all weathers. **1887** *Spectator* 27 Aug. 1148 Planting his potatoes in the rain.

d. Situation within the range of sensuous observation or the sphere of action of another. *in the eyes of*: see EYE *sb.* 4 c, d.

1388 WYCLIF *Ezek.* ix. 5 He seide to hem in myn heryng. a **1425** in *Rel. Ant.* I. 230 He is God, that all thinge made, and all thinge hath in his power. c **1460** *Towneley Myst.* i. 15 All is in my sight. **1667** MILTON *P.L.* III. 655 Those seav'n Spirits that stand In sight of God's high Throne. **1780** COWPER *Table T.* 97 There..the group is full in view. **1860** TROLLOPE *Framley P.* I. i, The living of Framley was in the gift of the Lufton family.

10. a. Of condition or state, physical, mental, or moral: e.g. *in a blaze, in debt, in doubt, in comfort, in health, in hope, in life, in love, in pain, in sickness, in solitude, in sorrow.* Also *in-work* (nonce-wd.), one who has work.

c**825** *Vesp. Psalter* ii. 11 Ðeowiað dryhtne in eȝe [L. *in timore*]. c**1175** *Lamb. Hom.* 59 He makede mon i rihtwisnesse. **1297** R. GLOUC. (Rolls) 328 Him þoȝte, þe ymage in is slep tolde him is chance. **1340** *Ayenb.* 250 Þer he him resteþ, þer he is in pais. c **1350** *Will. Palerne* 841 He semes bi semblant in sekeness ful harde. c **1450** *Merlin* 71, I am in certeyn of oon thynge, that he farith well and is in hele. **1535** COVERDALE *2 Chron.* xxi. 19 He dyed in euell diseases. **1602** *2nd Pt. Return fr. Parnass.* III. iii. (Arb.) 43 [He] throwes the booke away in a rage. **1666** PEPYS *Diary* 6 June, All the Court was in a hubbub. **1711** ADDISON *Spect.* No. 15 ¶6 Her Husband..has been in Love with her ever since he knew her. *Ibid.* No. 98 ¶1, I am highly pleased with the Coiffure now in Fashion. **1732** LEDIARD *Sethos* II. IX. 273 You are absolutely forbidden speaking to him in private. **1791** MRS. RADCLIFFE *Rom. Forest* ii, Egad, Master, you're in the right. **1793** BEDDOES *Calculus* 214 Supposing that the carbon is in a very attenuated state in the blood. **1846** MRS. GORE *Eng. Char.* 13 No sooner in print, than out of print. The reviews revere him. **1849** MACAULAY *Hist. Eng.* xiv. III. 482 The sea was in a blaze for many miles. **1924** GALSWORTHY *White Monkey* I. xii, The out-of-works and the in-works.

b. The condition may be expressed by a concrete sb.: e.g. *in calf, in kid, in cash, in drink, in liquor, in wine, in tears,* etc.: see the sbs. Cf. also BUD *sb.*[1] 4, FLOWER *sb.* 10, FOAL *sb.* 1 b, IN-CALF *a.*, IN-FOAL *a.*, IN-PIG *a.*, LEAF *sb.*[1] 3.

c **1460** *Towneley Myst.* xii. 111 What, art thou in ayll? a **1562** G. CAVENDISH *Wolsey* (1893) 217 Havyng a great multitude of artyfycers and laborers..dayly in wages. **1593** NASHE *Christs T.* (1613) 25 Sore am I impassioned for the storme thy tranquillity is in child with. **1596** SHAKS. *1 Hen. IV*, II. iv. 458, I doe not speake to thee in Drinke. **1697** DRYDEN *Virg. Past.* x. 19 For him the lofty Laurel stands in Tears. **1703** *Lond. Gaz.* No. 3971/4 Calve-Skins in the Hair. **1704** *Ibid.* No. 4034/4 John Jackson..aged near 40.. in his own Hair. **1754–64** SMELLIE *Midwif.* I. 400 Women in the first child seldom have after-pains. **1799** J. ROBERTSON *Agric. Perth* 196 Where the land has not lain for some time in grass. **1813** M. EDGEWORTH *Let.* 6 Apr. (1971) 10 The coffee tree in *red berry*... The palm tree in *fruit and flower.* .. The banana in *fruit.* **1847** TENNYSON *Princ.* Prol. 142 Sweet girl-graduates in their golden hair. **1849** MACAULAY *Hist. Eng.* i. I. 123 Leaving their castles in ruins. **1866** ROGERS *Agric. & Prices* I. xxvi. 642 Goats in kid. **1881** SHELDON *Dairy Farming* 8/1 If the cow is in milk. **1882** [see POD *sb.*[2] 1]. **1972** *Hilliers' Man. Trees & Shrubs* 83 Corylus avellana 'Contorta'... A winter feature when in catkin.

11. a. Of occupation or engagement: chiefly with nouns of action and vbl. sbs.

c **1205** LAY. 27767 Þer he heom funde i fihte. a **1300** *Cursor M.* 49 In riot and in rigolage Of all þere liif spend þai þe stage. **1340** *Ayenb.* 7 Þe ilke þet dispendeþ þane zonday and þe festes ine zenne and ine hordom. **1502** *Privy Purse Exp. Eliz. of York* (1830) 52 A servaunt..that cam in message to the Quenes grace. **1628** HOBBES *Thucyd.* (1822) 19 The Lacedemonians..are already in labour of the war. **1701** *Stanley's Hist. Philos.* Biog. 10 He..spent his Time.. in seriously bemoaning the Follies and Vanity of the World. **1754** HUME *Hist. Eng.* (1812) I. iii. 163 The King, in pursuance of his engagements, had indeed married Editha. **1838** DICKENS *Mem. Grimaldi* iv, In search of plunder. **1884** *Gd. Words* June 400/1 They have..been 'in' almost every variety of crime, from petty larceny down to downright murder.

b. In the process of, in the act of; in case of: often equivalent in sense to a temporal clause introduced by *when, while, if, in the event of.*

c **1400** MAUNDEV. (1839) iii. 19 Wee synne dedly, in schauynge oure berdes. *Ibid.*, Wee synne dedly, in etynge of bestes. **1477** EARL RIVERS (Caxton) *Dictes* 67 Gladdenesse, whiche encresses daily in me in lernynghe wysdom. ? a **1550** *Life Fisher* in *F.'s Wks.* (E.E.T.S.) II. p. liii, I am not affraid in gevinge you this counsell to take vpon my owne soul all the damage. **1591** SHAKS. *1 Hen. VI*, v. iii. 41 And may ye both be sodainly surpriz'd By bloudy hands, in sleeping on your beds. **1596** —— *Merch. V.* III. ii. 320 In paying it, it is impossible I should liue. **1607** *Stat.* in *Hist. Wakefield Gram. Sch.* (1892) 58 Leaves word thereof att their howses in theire beinge abrode. **1846** MCCULLOCH *Acc. Brit. Empire* (1854) II. 217 In estimating the chances which any candidate has of succeeding..no one ever thinks of inquiring into the politics of the tenants. **1864** HOLME LEE *In Silver Age* (1866) 408 Kindness is not a quality that perishes in the using. *Mod.* He was drowned in crossing the river.

†**c.** After the verb *be*, and some other verbs, *in* was formerly used to express the relation of occupation before a verbal sb. where it varied with *a* (A *prep.* 13), and is now omitted, the vbl. sb. functioning as a present participle active. *Obs.*

1509 HAWES *Past. Pleas.* (Percy Soc.) 79 Of many floures ..A goodly chaplet she was in makynge. **1535** STEWART *Cron. Scot.* I. 528 Richt quyetlie in hunting he is gone. **1580** LYLY *Euphues* (Arb.) 367 Camilla, whome he founde in gathering of flowers. **1675** BROOKS *Gold. Key* Wks. 1867 V. 577 A griping usurer, who was always best when he was most in talking of the world. **1737** WHISTON *Josephus, Antiq.* v. ii. §2 They went on still in taking the cities. *Ibid.* IX. xii. §3 He went on in worshipping them. **1808** SOUTHEY in C. C. Southey *Life* (1850) III. 137 You saw me in London everlastingly at work in packing my books.

†**d.** *In* (varying with A *prep.* 12) was formerly used with a vbl. sb. expressing the action or process to which a thing or person was subjected. (The prep. is now usually omitted, and the vbl. sb. functions as a present pple., passive in meaning: e.g. *while the ark was* (*in* or *a*) *building* (= in the process of building, being built). *Obs.* or *arch.*

c **1400** MAUNDEV. (Roxb.) vi. 21 When þe toure of Babilon was in makyng. **1465** MARG. PASTON in *P. Lett.* No. 533 II. 250 Whille the logge at Heylesdon was in the betyng down. a **1535** FISHER *Serm. Passion* Wks. (1876) 427 So the grasse is euer in eatyng, and neuer full eaten. **1620** *Frier Rush* 36, I haue a new Church in building. **1699** in Picton *L'pool Munic. Rec.* (1883) I. 326 New streets are built and still in building. **1869** FREEMAN *Norm. Conq.* III. xi. 45 While the symbolic act was in doing.

12. a. Of manner (way, mode, style, fashion).

1297 R. GLOUC. (Rolls) 1473 In þis manere þe brutons þis lond wuste þo. c **1305** *Pilate* 56 in *E.E.P.* (1862) 112 Þer ne miȝte so neuere non beo in none wise. c **1489** CAXTON *Sonnes of Aymon* xvi. 380 In lyke wyse dyde Alarde. **1559** BP. SCOT *Sp. Parl.* in Strype *Ann. Ref.* (1824) I. App. vii. 408 Every man..sholde..at large speke his mind in conscience in the contents of all the bills. **1608** W. SCLATER *Comm. Malachy* (1650) 196 The things there spoken of cannot in any hand agree to Elias. **1654** CROMWELL *Let.* 20 Jan. in *Carlyle*, What can be made out in this kind? **1691** T. H[ALE] *Acc. New Invent.* 62 In the manner anciently used. **1706** tr. *Dupin's Eccl. Hist. 16th C.* II. III. iv. 81 Begging him to take this their Remonstrance in good part. **1737** WHISTON *Josephus, Antiq.* II. i. §1 He was, in way of jest, called Adom. **1833** HT. MARTINEAU *Berkeley the Banker* I. IV. 92 He told several people in confidence. **1849** MACAULAY *Hist. Eng.* v. I. 619

He begged in piteous terms that he might be admitted to the royal presence. **1859** JEPHSON *Brittany* v. 54 The baptistery has been restored in Renaissance.

b. Of form, shape, conformation, arrangement, order. [The OE. example has the *accusative*.]

a **900** CYNEWULF *Crist* 725 in *Exeter Bk.*, þa he.. wæs in cildes hiw claðum biwunden. *c* **1400** MAUNDEV. (Roxb.) iv. 12 In likness of a dragoun. **1572** BOSSEWELL *Armorie* III. 7 Fiue Plates in crosse. **1598** SYLVESTER *Du Bartas* II. II. iii. *Colonies* 391 That vast Extent, where now fell Tartars hant In wandring troops. **1602** SHAKS. *Ham.* III. iv. 210 When in one line two crafts directly meet. **1605** —— *Lear* III. vi. 31 The foul fiend haunts poor Tom in the voice of a nightingale. **1667** MILTON *P.L.* III. 641 Under a Coronet his flowing haire In curles on either cheek plaid. *Ibid.* VII. 459 Among the Trees in Pairs they rose. **1694** LUTTRELL *Brief Rel.* (1857) III. 292 The agent.. is gone aside, and hath carried with him 2000£ in money belonging to the troop. **1710** ADDISON *Tatler* No. 221 ¶2 Whether I had best sell my Beetles in a Lump or by Retail. **1776** MICKLE tr. *Camoens' Lusiad* 339 He gives the prelude in a dreary sound. **1807** SOUTHEY *Espriella's Lett.* II. 395 Did he, contrary to the ordinary process, begin in rogue, and end in enthusiast? *c* **1820** S. ROGERS *Italy*, *Advent*, A hawk Flew in a circle, screaming. **1843** *Fraser's Mag.* XXVIII. 695 A cloak falls in easy folds down his back. **1855** MACAULAY *Hist. Eng.* xvi. III. 684 Within a few hours and a few acres had been exhibited in miniature the devastation of the Palatinate. **1891** *Law Rep.* Weekly Notes 82/2 A land company, who afterwards sold the adjoining land in building plots. **1895** *Scot. Antiq.* X. 79 In singles or in pairs men began to put in an appearance.

c. Of manner of speech or writing.

c **900** tr. *Bæda's Hist.* IV. xxiv. [xxiii.] (1890) 332 Heo .. ȝewat to þære ceastre, þe in Englisc is ȝehaten kwelcaceaster. **1297** R. GLOUC. (Rolls) 2430 þe heye god þat in vre tonge woden icluped is. *c* **1315** SHOREHAM 122 Hy makede joye in hare manere And eke in hare langage. *c* **1400** MAUNDEV. (Roxb.) ii. 5 þe table.. on þe whilk þe tytle was writen in Hebrew, in Grew and in Latyne. **1542** UDALL *Erasm. Apoph.* 106a, An herbe called.. in latin, Beta. **1680** EVELYN *Diary* 2 Sept., The discourse is in High Dutch. **1776** *Trial of Nundocomar* 22/2 Sometimes he wrote the bonds.. in Nagree, sometimes in Bengal. **1833** HT. MARTINEAU *Vanderput & S.* i. 3 He.. spoke in a strong French accent. **1845** M. PATTISON *Ess.* (1889) I. 13 Bede is writing in a dead language, Gregory in a living.

d. Often dependent upon a superlative or a commendatory epithet: within the sphere of (a particular class or order of things). *colloq.*

1866 RUSKIN *Crown Wild Olive* ii. §53 The newest and sweetest thing in pinnacles. **1879** [see THING *sb.*[1] 7]. **1911** W. J. LOCKE *Glory of Clementina Wing* ii, I may not be the latest thing in dandyism. **1966** G. N. LEECH *Eng. in Advertising* ix. 92 ABC: the first name in entertainment. **1974** *Radio Times* 3 Jan. 58/1 The most dazzling cruises in holiday history.

13. Of means or instrumentality: now usually expressed by *with*.

†**a.** Illustration of earlier uses. (Often a literalism of translation.) *Obs.*

c **825** *Vesp. Psalter* ii. 9 Ðu reces hie in ȝerde iserre [L. *in virga ferrea*]. *a* **1300** *E.E. Psalter* ibid., In yherde irened salt þou stere þa. **1382** WYCLIF *1 Cor.* iv. 21 Shal I come to ȝou in a ȝerd: or in charite? *c* **1450** tr. *De Imitatione* III. xlviii. 119 þan shal Iherusalem be serched in lanternes. **1503** *Act 19 Hen. VII.* c. 4 §3 No persone.. shall occupie or shote in eny Crosebowe. **1580** LYLY *Euphues* (Arb.) 445 It more delighteth them to talke of Robin hood then to shoot in his bowe. **1693** J. DRYDEN, jun. in *Dryden's Juvenal* (1697) 367 Penelope knew which of her Suitors cou'd shoot best in her Husband's Bow. **1753** CHESTERF. *Lett.* (1792) IV. ccxcix. 19 Getting drunk in Port. **1804** *Naval Chron.* XIII. 147 A French Ship.. ballasted in mahogany.

b. Uses in which the senses of *in* (*on*) and *with* (*by*) are both present: e.g. to cover *in* or *with* any envelope.

c **900** tr. *Bæda's Hist.* IV. xxiv. [xxv.] (1890) 346 He eal þa he in ȝehyrnesse ȝeleornian meahte, mid hine ȝemyndȝade. *a* **1225** *Leg. Kath.* 1035 In þis an þing he schawde.. þet he wes soð godd. *a* **1340** HAMPOLE *Psalter* xvii. 48 In herynge of ere he boghed til me. *c* **1440** *Jacob's Well* (E.E.T.S.) 137 þou wylt wretthe god in brekyng þe halyday. **1609** BIBLE (Douay) *1 Sam.* xviii. 6 The wemen came.. singing and dancing.. in timbrels of joy, and in cornettes. **1621** BURTON *Anat. Mel.* III. ii. III. iv. (1651) 495 Whom Iuno for pitty covered in her Apron. **1697** DRYDEN *Virg. Georg.* IV. 19 Progne, with her Bosom stain'd in Blood. **1880** CHURCH *Spenser* v. 137 He drowns us in words.

c. Here may be added the use of *in* after *eat*, *drink*, *pledge*, etc. Also = (eat or drink) out of.

1593 SHAKS. *2 Hen. VI*, II. iii. 60, I drinke to you in a Cup of Sack. **1621** BURTON *Anat. Mel.* II. iii. III. (1651) 323 A poor man drinks in a wooden dish, and eats his meat in wooden spoons. **1711** ADDISON *Spect.* No. 15 ¶4 Whether they keep their coach and six, or eat in plate. **1742** FIELDING *J. Andrewes* IV. ii, He was drinking her ladyship's health below in a cup of her ale.

14. Of material, constituents, and the like.

1663 GERBIER *Counsel* 94 They paint them also in strong oyle colour thrice over. **1686** tr. *Chardin's Trav.* 75 Our Ships Lading consisted in Salt, Fish, Caveare, Oyle, Biscuite. **1710** ADDISON *Tatler* No. 243 ¶1 The Statue of an Horse in Brass. **1722** DE FOE *Col. Jack* (1840) 23 It was in gold, all but 14*s.* **1852** DICKENS *Bleak Ho.* vi, Half-length portraits, in crayons. **1891** *Truth* 10 Dec. 1240/2 The long coat was also in green velvet, with sleeves and revers in green cloth.

15. Of degree, extent, measure.

c **1380** WYCLIF *Sel. Wks.* III. 510 Cristene men.. shulde have discerved most þank of God in degre possible to hem. **1601** SHAKS. *Twel. N.* I. v. 61 Misprision in the highest degree. **1649** CROMWELL *Let. to W. Lenthall* 14 Nov. in *Carlyle*, Only, in the general, give me leave humbly to offer [etc.]. **1667** MILTON *P.L.* v. 490 Differing but in degree, of kind the same. **1696** *Dupin's Eccl. Hist. 16th C.* I. 54 In the main they agree with ours. **1737** L. CLARKE *Hist. Bible* (1740) I. IX. 585 Without being in the least discouraged. **1843** *Fraser's Mag.* XXVIII. 647 Tears fell in profusion. **1845** STEPHEN *Comm. Laws Eng.* (1874) I. 79 Any act repealing in whole or in part any former statute. **1875** F. HALL in *Lippincott's Mag.* XVI. 750/1 Drift-wood was lying about in large quantities.

16. Expressing object, aim, or purpose: with an abstr. sb., as *in affirmation, answer, denial, memory, honour, proof, quest, recompense, reply, return, reward, scorn, search, testimony, token, witness, worship*, etc. See farther under the sbs.

It is possible that the object here was orig. accusative, and that these expressions came under sense 31.

a **1225** *Ancr. R.* 30 In hore wurðshipe siggeð oþer les oþer mo. **1297** R. GLOUC. (Rolls) 466 Brut.. let vair tabernacle in honour of him rere. *c* **1315** SHOREHAM 131 In tokne that pays scholde be. *c* **1400** MAUNDEV. (1839) iv. 31 In the worschipe of hem there is a fair chirche. **1526** *Pilgr. Perf.* (W. de W.) 1 Diuyded in to thre bokes, in the honour of the Trinite. **1667** MILTON *P.L.* IX. 552 She thus in answer spake. **1713** ADDISON *Cato* I. ii, I claim in my reward his captive daughter. **1805** SCOTT *Last Minstr.* IV. xii, Loudly the Beattison laughed in scorn. **1821** J. F. COOPER *Spy* viii, He went in quest of his new applicant. *Mod.* A holiday in honour of the event. He has written to the newspaper in reply to his assailant.

17. Expressing reference or relation to something: In reference or regard to; in the case of, in the matter, affair, or province of.

Used especially with the sphere or department in relation or reference to which an attribute or quality is predicated: see 33 b, c, 34–36.

18. With a following sb. forming attrib. phrases: ***in-car***, within a car; ***in-career***, of training, etc., received while in employment; ***in-churn***, of a method of machine-milking direct into a churn; ***in-company***, of training, etc., received while in the employment of a company; ***in-depth*** (see DEPTH I. 3 c); ***in-person*** (cf. PERSON *sb.* 11); ***in-pile***, within a nuclear reactor; ***in-plant***, within a 'plant' or factory; ***in-process*** (cf. PROCESS *sb.* 1), of any activity, etc., that is in process; ***in-process gauging*** (see quot. 1968); ***in-sack***, within a sack; ***in-service*** (cf. SERVICE *sb.*[1] 1), of training, etc.: received by a person while engaged on some activity; of an object: relating to its reliability, maintenance, etc., while in use. Cf. IN-COLLEGE *a.* (Cf. analogous uses mentioned near end of IN- *pref.*[1])

1968 *N.Y. Times* 7 Apr. 1/4 The sound problem was eventually solved with in-car speakers. **1971** *Daily Tel.* (Colour Suppl.) 4 June 39/1 These damp cloths are part of something the manufacturers.. don't seem to have heard of; in-car luggage. They seem to think you can put everything in the boot. **1973** *Times* 13 Feb. 24/1 A Lucas spokesman said yesterday: 'I can confirm that we shall be entering the in-car entertainment market this year.' **1968** *New Scientist* 3 Oct. 31/2 Whether in-career re-education will be best inside or outside universities is a matter for debate. **1970** *Physics Bull.* June 242/2 The engineers' survey.. includes unemployment and in-career training as well as remuneration figures. **1970** *Nature* 28 Nov. 814/2 In-career retraining may become very important in the future. **1955** J. G. DAVIS *Dict. Dairying* (ed. 2) 745 Probably the most important development has been the introduction of the 'In-Churn System'. In-churn milking passes the milk direct from the cow to the churn. *Ibid.*, In-churn recording.. is carried out by means of weighing scales. *Ibid.*, In-churn cooling. **1960** *Farmer & Stockbreeder* 16 Feb. 39/3 This new .. unit.. provides you with modern in-churn milking. **1966** *Ann. Rep. Travelers Insurance Co. (Hartford, Conn.) 1966* 26/2 Our in-company training programs. **1969** *Timber Trades Jrnl.* 13 Dec. 35/2 There were twin pillars to training —in-company training and, for young people in particular, further education. **1970** *Times* 28 Apr. 26/7 Having already completed most of the in-company training for the introduction of decimalization. **1955** L. FEATHER *Encycl. Jazz* i. 21 Although the white jazzmen rarely found opportunities for expressing themselves freely on 'in-person' jobs, the work.. on.. recording sessions compensated. **1957** S. DANCE in S. Traill *Concerning Jazz* 37 No experience of jazz can be so exciting or so illuminating as the in-person performance. **1959** *Spectator* 9 Oct. 469/1 On any one TV appearance Macmillan and Gaitskell must have been seen by more people than the sum total audience of their in-person tours. **1972** *Jazz & Blues* Nov. 18/1 Her recordings and in-person work illustrate that she is an artist who is always willing to experiment. **1960** *Times Rev. Industry* Dec. 16/2 Zirconium.. is useful for 'in-pile' equipment, such as fuel element supports, tubes for control equipment, flexible hose and packing pieces. **1961** *Times* 10 May 2 The work includes:—out-of-pile and in-pile testing. **1963** B. FOZARD *Instrumentation Nucl. Reactors* iii. 33 The second type of measurement is made with in-pile detectors. **1943** *Atlantic Monthly* Sept. 55 Few of them participate in in-plant training and upgrading programs. **1958** *Technology* Feb. 414/2 The proportion of in-plant to total training is.. low. **1959** *Times* 5 Feb. 2/5 They involve an application of this industry in in-plant technical scale studies. **1967** *Jane's Surface Skimmer Systems 1967–68* 62/2 The power source can be an in-plant air supply system or [etc.]. **1971** *Timber Trades Jrnl.* 21 Aug. 26/3 In-plant treatment will now be extended to other '1800' components. **1925** *Nat. Assoc. Cost Accountants Yearbk.* 24 Divide the average 'in process' inventories into the amount of transfers to finished stores. **1967** *New Scientist* 20 Apr. 140/1 In-process gauging, on the machine tool itself, could halt.. appalling waste. **1968** *Gloss. Terms Air Gauging (B.S.I.)* 13 *In-process gauging*, gauging carried out during processing, e.g. measurement of a workpiece whilst it is being machined. **1971** *Computers & Humanities* VI. 41 In-process corrections, however, are very difficult to make since holes cannot be erased. **1971** *Gloss. Terms Quality Assurance (B.S.I.)* 6 *In-process inspection*, product inspection carried out at various discrete stages in manufacture. **1958** *Times* 24 Nov. 15/4 For drying grass seed.., the in-sack drier had many advantages. **1960** *Farmer & Stockbreeder* 23 Feb. 100/1 (Advt.), Heat for.. in-sack grain drying. **1928** *Rep. Comm. Educ., U.S. Dept. Interior* 30 June 6 The movement for improving preservice and inservice training of teachers for rural schools. **1960** *Guardian* 13 July 5/4 Development of in-service training.. for staff nurses. **1963** F. F. LAIDLER *Gloss. Home Econ. Educ.* 48 *In-service training*, the continuing education and training given to a person after he/she has begun to work in a particular occupation. **1964** M. A. K. HALLIDAY et al. *Ling. Sci.* 264 He [*sc.* the primary school teacher] needs an appropriate training in his new task, either during his initial period of training as a teacher or by means of in-service training. **1967** *Technology Week* 23 Jan. 43/2 (Advt.), Such data may well reveal overdesign or design deficiencies, thus providing opportunities for improvement of safety characteristics, in-service reliability. **1972** *Lebende Sprachen* XVII. 72/2 The in-service performance of the trio is likely to dictate the specification for production models which are due to appear before the end of 1971.

III. Of time.

19. a. Within the limits of a period or space of time.

With *in the day, in the night*: cf. *by day, by night*, BY *prep.* 19 b.

Beowulf (Z.) 2 We Gardena in ȝear-daȝum þeod-cyninga þrym ȝe-frunon. *a* **900** *O.E. Chron.* an. 709 In foreweardum Danieles daȝum. **1297** R. GLOUC. (Rolls) 9129 In þe sixe & þrittiþe ȝer of his kinedom. **13..** *K. Alis.* 85 By cler candel, in the nyght. **1388** WYCLIF *Gen.* i. 1 In the bigynnyng God made of nouȝt heuene and erthe. *c* **1400** MAUNDEV. (1839) Prol. 4, I.. passed the see, in the ȝeer of oure lord Jhesu crist MCCCXXII. *c* **1500** *Melusine* lxii. 369 He was neuer in his dayes so aferd. **1588** SHAKS. *L.L.L.* I. i. 39 One day in a weeke to touch no foode. **1591** —— *Two Gent.* III. i. 178 Except I be by Siluia in the night.. Vnlesse I looke on Siluia in the day. **1650** TRAPP *Comm. Lev.* xxvi. 26 Common in times of famine. **1655** STANLEY *Hist. Philos.* I. (1701) 36/1 Pittacus was.. born in the thirty second Olympiad. **1710** STEELE *Tatler* No. 222 ¶1 Between the Hours of Twelve and Four in the Morning. **1812** T. JEFFERSON *Writ.* (1830) IV. 176, I think our acquaintance commenced in 1764. **1849** MACAULAY *Hist. Eng.* iv. I. 490 In the days of the Commonwealth.

b. With other sbs. implying time.

871–889 *Charter* in *O.E. Texts* 452 In þissum life ondwardum. *a* **1000** *Seafarer* 40 (Gr.) In ȝeoȝuþe. *a* **1240** *Wohunge* in *Cott. Hom.* 277, I þi burð tid. *Ibid.*, I þi cildhad. **13..** *Coer de L.* 4049 A spie, That hadde be Crystene in hys youthe. *c* **1440** *Jacob's Well* (E.E.T.S.) 277 To styen vp to heuen in ȝoure ende. **1555** EDEN *Decades* 245 They are neyther bytten with coulde in wynter nor molested with heate in summer. **1732** BERKELEY *Alciphr.* I. §11, I never saw a first-rate picture in my life. **1825** T. H. LISTER *Granby* vii. (1836) 43 You must be an archeress in the summer, and a skater in the winter. **1839** THIRLWALL *Greece* VI. 89 The education of the prince in his childhood.

c. With processes occupying time.

1711 ADDISON *Spect.* No. 126 ¶8 In all our Journey from London to his House we did not so much as bait at a Whig Inn. **1721** *Lond. Gaz.* No. 5954/1 In the Passage we had bad Weather. **1802** H. MARTIN *Helen of Glenross* IV. 73 In our descent down life. **1859** J. WHITE *Hist. France* (1860) 90 All the gentlemen's houses you see in a railway excursion.

20. Of the length of time occupied; in the course of.

1297 R. GLOUC. (Rolls) 1818 þer were in a moneþ [*so most MSS.; A has* wiþinne one monþe] seuentene þousend & mo Ymartred. **1388** WYCLIF *Exod.* xxxi. 17 In sixe daies God made heuene and erthe. *c* **1400** MAUNDEV. (Roxb.) xxxiii. 148 Men may saile it in seuen days. **1526** TINDALE *1 Cor.* xv. 52 We shall all be chaunged.. in a moment and in the twincklynge of an eye. **1611** BIBLE *Transl. Pref.* 11 The worke hath not bene hudled vp in 72 dayes. **1702** *Eng. Theophrast.* 163 Presumption leads people to infidelity in a trice. **1885** *Manch. Exam.* 15 May 5/6 From the Gatling Gun.. a trail of 1,000 bullets can be discharged in a single minute. *Mod.* The voyage to America can now be done in less than 7 days. By working hard he could make one in a week.

21. Of a limit of time: before or at the expiration of; within the space of.

a **1300** *Treat. Science* (1841) 138 Ther nis non.. That evereft i-heled beo, ac deyeth in a stounde. **13..** *Seuyn Sag.* (W.) 115 In time of seuen yere He sal be wise withowten were. **1513** MORE *Rich. III* (1641) 210 He dyed in three moneths. **1706** tr. *Dupin's Eccl. Hist. 16th C.* II. VII. xviii. 261 In Process of Time they might be corrupted. **1782** JOHNSON *Let. to Dr. Taylor* 8 July, I came back from Oxford in ten days. **1843** *Blackw. Mag.* LIV. 305, I rallied in a day or two. **1884** *Law Times Rep.* L. 231/2 Anything put into the defendants' well was certain in time to affect the supply.

22. Formerly (and still sometimes) used, where *at*, *on*, *during*, *for* are now in use, or where the preposition is omitted.

At is now ordinarily used with a point of time, e.g. *at this time, at the moment, at day-break, at sunset*; *on* in stating the date of an event, e.g. *on the first of May, on Monday next, on a summer morning*; *during* for the course or continuance of a period, for which *for* is also used, esp. in negative statements, e.g. *he has stayed for a week, I have not seen him for a long time*. For all these *in* occurs in earlier or dialectal use.

a. = *At.*

c **1175** *Lamb. Hom.* 121 þas pine.. ure drihten þolede.. in þisse timan. *a* **1225** *St. Marher.* 2 Wes in þe ilke time liuiende.. þet eadi meiden. **13..** *K. Alis.* 403 In the dawenyng He made efte his charmyng. *c* **1440** *Gesta Rom.* xci. 417 (Addit. MS.) He made this Eyre to sitte with hym .. in mete tyme. **1525** LD. BERNERS *Froiss.* II. cxix. [cxv.] 340 They departed.. in the brekynge of the daye. **1604** SHAKS. *Oth.* I. ii. 94 The Duke in Counsell? In this time of the night? *a* **1715** BURNET *Own Time* (1823) I. 315 But he.. got his offices to be published.. in a time when [etc.]. **1807** CRABBE *Par. Reg.* II. 456 No Sunday shower Kept him at home in that important hour. **1873** HAMERTON *Intell. Life* VI. ii. 205 When an architect in the present day has to restore some venerable church.

b. = *on.* [The OE. example has the *accusative.*]

a **900** *O.E. Chron.* an. 626 Her Eanfled..wæs ȝefulwad in þone halȝan æfen Pentecosten. *c* **1175** *Lamb. Hom.* 81 Þet me sculde in þe ehtuþe dei þet knaue child embsniþen. **1297** R. GLOUC. (Rolls) 8668 In a þores-dai it was. *c* **1400** MAUNDEV. (1839) Prol. 4, I..passed the see..in the day of Seynt Michelle. **1426** in *Surtees Misc.* (1888) 7 In þe Vigil of þe Assumpcion of our Lady. **1597** SHAKS. *2 Hen. IV*, I. ii. 233 Looke you..that our Armies ioyn not in a hot day. **1806–7** J. BERESFORD *Miseries Hum. Life* (1826) x. l, In a chilling evening..after you have carefully stirred a very ticklish fire.

c. = *during.*

1713 SWIFT *Corr.* Wks. 1841 II. 492 In all the time I have been conversant in business, I never before observed [etc.]. **1748** *Anson's Voy.* II. vii. 209 Captain Mitchel, in the whole time of his cruise, had only taken two prizes. *Ibid.* viii. 220 The succeeding four months in which we continued at sea.

d. = *for.* (Formerly only in negative sentences.)

1470–85 MALORY *Arthur* x. xxxvi, He made them to swere to were none harneis in a twelue monethe and a day. **1525** LD. BERNERS *Froiss.* II. xliv. [lxix.] (1812) 422 If they dranke moche..they coulde not helpe themselfe in two dayes after. **1601** HOLLAND *Pliny* (1634) II. 379 Wash it not off in three daies. **1669** PEPYS *Diary* (1879) VI. 1 To Westminster Hall, where I have not been..in some months. **1765** BLACKSTONE *Comm.* I. v. 228 It had not been practiced in some hundreds of years. **1793** SMEATON *Edystone L.* §265 They did not come back in some days. **1889** E. SALTUS *Tristrem Varick* xiv. 152 He was hungry as he had not been in months. **1924** C. MACKENZIE *Heavenly Ladder* xvi. 223 Mark had never been near his house in a year. **1957** R. A. HEINLEIN *Door into Summer* (1960) ix. 143 The place smelled like a vault that has not been opened in years. **1971** *Daily Tel.* 1 June 4/8 The first bridge across the Bosphorus in 2,300 years..is now being built. **1972** 'E. MCBAIN' *Sadie when she Died* xiii. 42 Arlene said that she had not played tennis in three years. **1973** *Sci. Amer.* Jan. 53/1 When Mariner 9 reached Mars on November 13, 1971, the greatest dust storm in more than a century was raging.

e. Where no preposition is now expressed.

1382 WYCLIF *Luke* i. 75 In hoolynesse and riȝtfulnesse bifore him in alle oure dayes. **1523** LD. BERNERS *Froiss.* I. ccxxxv. 332 In the same euennyng the two marshals.. commaunded euery man to drawe to their logynge, and in the next mornyng to be redy at sownyng of the trumpettes. **1603** SHAKS. *Meas. for M.* IV. iv. 9 Why should wee proclaime it in an howre before his entring? **1726** SWIFT *Gulliver* I. i, This engine..set out in four hours after my landing.

IV. Pregnant uses: sometimes due to ellipsis.

23. With reflexive pronouns: *in himself, in itself,* etc.: in his or its own person, essence, or nature; apart from any connexion with or relation to others; absolutely.

c **1200** ORMIN 3041 Jesu Crist Iss..soþ Godd inn himm sellfenn. **1340** *Ayenb.* 237 Þe sacrement þet is ymad..be þe hand of þe kueade ministre ne is naȝt lesse worþ ine himzelue. **1531** TINDALE *Exp. 1 John* (1537) 7 The scripture abydeth pure in herselfe. **1656** *Artif. Handsom.* (1662) 178 Suppose Artificial beautifying of the face be not in it self absolutely unlawful. **1843** MILL *Logic* I. iii. §7 Of things absolutely or in themselves. **1849** RUSKIN *Sev. Lamps* vii. §5. 189 Neither originality, therefore, nor change..are ever to be sought in themselves. **1870** FREEMAN *Norm. Conq.* (ed. 2) I. App. 739 The story may be true in itself.

24. In spiritual or mystical union with.

c **1315** SHOREHAM 2 Ydemyd we bethe In Adam and ine Eve. **1382** WYCLIF *1 Cor.* xv. 22 As in Adam alle men dyen, so and in Crist alle men schulen be quykenyd. —— *Rev.* xiv. 13 Blessed the deede men, that dien in the Lord. **1548–9** (Mar.) *Bk. Comm. Prayer, Communion* (Coll. ad fin.), Al our woorkes begonne, continued, and ended in thee. **1745** A. BUTLER *Lives of Saints* (1836) I. 23 It was their desire that he might follow his vocation in God.

25. In the person or case of.

c **1380** WYCLIF *Sel. Wks.* III. 341 Þe fend..moved þe emperour of Rome to dowe þis Chirche in þis preest. **1470–85** MALORY *Arthur* IX. xxv, Fy for shame..that euer suche fals treason shold be wrought or vsed in a quene and a kynges syster. **1589** SPENSER *F.Q.* (Let. to Raleigh), Sir Guyon in whome I sette forth Temperaunce. **1603** SHAKS. *Meas. for M.* II. iii. That in the Captaine's but a chollericke word, Which in the Souldier is flat blasphemie. **1653** H. MORE *Antid. Ath.* III. viii. (1712) 111 Which also happen'd in a Maid of his. **1707** *Glossogr. Anglic. Nova, Asa foetida,*.. good against fits in women. **1712** ADDISON *Spect.* No. 333 ¶7 It was..a..bold Thought in our Author, to ascribe the first Use of Artillery to the Rebel Angels. **1821** CLARE *Vill. Minstr.* I. 20 Dread no thief in me! **1854** J. SCOFFERN in *Orr's Circ. Sc., Chem.* 102 This instrument was found in the thermomultiplier of Nobili. **1868** FREEMAN *Norm. Conq.* II. x. 470 How great a captain England possessed in her future King. **1878** MORLEY *Crit. Misc.* Ser. I. *Carlyle* 201 Those who..found in the rules and discipline and aims of their system an acceptable expression for their own disinterested social aspirations.

26. a. Belonging to, as an internal quality, attribute, faculty, or capacity, inherent in; hence, within the ability, capacity, thought, etc. of.

a **1225** *Ancr. R.* 166 Þer ȝe schulen beon ine þrunge, auh reste and peis is in me. **1377** LANGL. *P. Pl.* B. XIX. 78 Al þe witte of þe worlde was in þo þre kynges. **1388** WYCLIF *John* i. 4 In hym was lijf. *c* **1400** MAUNDEV. (Roxb.) xxxiv. 156 And I, in þat in me es, makez þam parceneres of þam. **1591** SHAKS. *Two Gent.* III. i. 179 There is no musicke in the Nightingale. *c* **1600** G. HARVEY in *Shaks. C. Praise* 30 Shakespeare's..Lucrece, and his tragedy of Hamlet..have it in them to please the wiser sort. **1605** SHAKS. *Lear* II. iv. 177 'Tis not in thee To grudge my pleasures. *a* **1611** BEAUM. & FL. *Maid's Trag.* III. i, It is in me to punish thee. **1678** WANLEY *Wond. Lit. World* v. ii. §16. 469/2 A covetous Pelagian, and one that had nothing of worth in him. **1737** BRACKEN *Farriery Impr.* (1757) II. 129 As to the Notion..I think there is not much in it. **1775** SHERIDAN *St. Patr. Day* I. ii, You did not mean any rudeness, did you, Humphrey? Oh No, in deed, miss; his worship knows it is not in me. **1810** *Q. Rev.* Feb. 193 If a man has it in him, he can do anything any where. **1841** LYTTON *Night & Morning* (ed. 2) I. I. v. 103, I will work for you day and night. I have it in me. **1846** G. E. JEWSBURY *Sel. Lett. to Mrs. Carlyle* (1892) 224, I did care for him once, long and well—better than I have it in me to care for any man now. **1875** JOWETT *Plato* (ed. 2) I. 174 To prefer evil to good is not in human nature. *Ibid.* 332 An enquiry which I shall never be weary of pursuing as far as in me lies. **1889** *Nature* 11 Apr. 500 Anyone who has it in him to do heroic deeds. **1892** I. ZANGWILL *Childr. Ghetto* III. 52 That girl's got it in her, I can tell you. She'll take the shine out of some of our West-Enders. **1895** H. JAMES *Notebks.* (1947) 408, I didn't know I had it in me. **1919** BEERBOHM *Seven Men* 119 He looked to me to 'do something big, one of these days', and that he was sure I had it 'in' me. **1924** *Isis* (Oxf.) 30 Jan. 16/2 He may become a fine actor —he has it in him. **1928** FOY & HARLOW *Clowning through Life* 297, I didn't believe he had it in him. **1938** R. FINLAYSON *Brown Man's Burden* 79 They didn't think Kay had it in him to do it. **1958** *Listener* 13 Nov. 786/2 As between draughts and chess this is outweighed by the fact that there is more 'in' chess. **1960** M. SPARK *Bachelors* i. 2 'You must have it in you,' said Ronald, 'going all the way to Piccadilly for herbs.' **1973** 'E. MCBAIN' *Hail to Chief* ii. 30 If you could find it in yourself to go over to the hospital and identify your brother.

b. ***nothing, not much, little,*** etc., ***in it***: little or no difference between competitors or any persons or things that are compared. orig. *Racing slang.*

1914 in *Concise Oxf. Dict.* **1927** *Observer* 18 Dec. 19/3 The first round there was nothing much in it. In the second round Angus..punched Mansfield round the ring. **1929** S. E. THOMAS *Elem. Econ.* (ed. 4) xxix. 523 While in the course of a year Britain imports considerable quantities of gold, she also exports almost equally large quantities, and on balance there is usually very little in it.

c. *in it*: an advantage (to be received from something). Usu. in phr. ***what was*** (or *is,* etc.) *in it for* (someone).

1963 T. PARKER *Unknown Citizen* v. 140 He seemed to have an inbred suspicion of any kind of offered help, he wanted to know why people were giving it, what was in it for them. **1968** *Guardian* 2 Apr. 11/1 The 'Washingtonologists' in Moscow must be getting their files out to see what is in it for the Soviet Union—and for the world. **1971** 'A. GILBERT' *Tenant for Tomb* ii. 39, I can't see what there was in it for Mrs Plum.

27. In the hands of; in the control or power of; legally vested in.

c **1460** *Towneley Myst.* xvi. 92 In me standys lyfe and dede. ? *a* **1500** *Cov. Myst.* (1841) 311 Alle the poer lyth now in the. *a* **1532** LD. BERNERS *Huon* lxxxi. 250 You knowe well it is in me to cause Huon to dye. **1607** *Stat.* in *Hist. Wakefield Gram. Sch.* (1892) 65 The election..shall be in the Maister and Fellowes of Emanuel Colledge. *a* **1626** BACON *Max. & Uses Com. Law* (1636) 23 Lands possessed without any such title, are in the crowne, and not in him that first entreth. **1708** *New View Lond.* II. 484/1 The Living is a Rectory, the Advowson in the Bp. of London. **1837** WHEWELL *Hist. Induct. Sc.* (1857) I. 30 The government of Greece is in the king. **1884** LD. COLERIDGE in *Law Times Rep.* L. 45/2 The minerals, therefore, are in the trustees.

28. Partaking, sharing, associated, or actually engaged in. ***to be in it,*** to be one of those actually engaged as partners, competitors, etc.; to be in the running, to be a serious competitor, to count for something.

1728 W. CLELAND *Let. on Dunciad* in *Pope's Wks.* (Globe) 359 None, it is plain, was so little in their friendships, or so much in that of those whom they had most abused. **1792** *Hist.* in *Ann. Reg.* 13 Neither the Count d'Artois..nor Mr. de Calonne were in the secret. **1812** J. H. VAUX *Flash Dict.* s.v., To let another partake of any benefit or acquisition you have acquired by robbery or otherwise, is called putting him in it: a family-man who is accidentally witness to a robbery, &c., effected by one or more others, will say to the latter, Mind I'm in it. **1888** *Lady* 25 Oct. 374/1, I thought I really was in it at last, and knew what she meant. **1888** *Longm. Mag.* July 256 To those 'in it' every sound conveys a meaning. **1889** *Spectator* 21 Sept., 'Flying Childers' and 'Eclipse' would not be 'in it' with our modern cracks. **1902** H. JAMES *Wings of Dove* VI. xx. 298 'You scarcely call him, I suppose, one of the dukes.' 'Mercy, no—far from it. He's not, compared with other possibilities, "in" it.' **1907** F. H. BURNETT *Shuttle* xxxviii. 381 'Hope you had a fine time, Mr. Selden?' 'Fine! I should smile. Fine wasn't in it.' **1912** A. BENNETT *Matador* 272 We were completely outshone. I tell you, we were not *in* it, not anywhere near being in it! **1913** F. L. BARCLAY *Broken Halo* vi. 69 In fact, the Egyptian dynasties weren't in it! She was positively antediluvian! **1915** A. HUXLEY *Let.* Oct. (1969) 82 At present I share Balliol with one..man..who rather repels me at meals by his..habit of shewing satisfaction with the food: Sir Toby Belch was not in it. **1960** L. COOPER *Accomplices* IV. ii. 224, I thought the Party knew all the technique there is about handling people, but they're not in it with the Church. **1964** H. E. F. DONOHUE *Conversations with Nelson Algren* ii. 74 All people are killers, potentially. Tigers aren't in it with people. **1966** 'J. HACKSTON' *Father clears Out* 140 A fight in the snow is a tame affair and not in it with a hot summer contest. **1968** *Globe & Mail* (Toronto) 15 Jan. 9/4 We just weren't in this one... Nobody was going to beat them today.

29. Of representative character or capacity, as *in* NAME *of, in* RIGHT *of*: see the sbs.

30. Elliptical for (*a*) in the name of; (*b*) in the character of.

a **1734** NORTH *Lives* (1826) III. 203 'Ay, i' God, is it', said the lord. **1831** FR. A. KEMBLE *Let.* in *Rec. Girlhood* II. viii. 229, I am to come out in Bianca, in Milman's 'Fazio'.

V. Of motion or direction. See also 16.

31. Expressing motion or direction from without to a point within, or transition from one thing to another: = INTO.

In OE. this was the proper sense of *in* with the accusative: see above. The sense of 'into' is still retained after some verbs, as *put, cast, split, part,* where the sense implies motion, and in some idiomatic phrases which are no longer analysed.

†**a.** Illustrations of earlier usage, now *obs.* or *dial.*

c **825** *Vesp. Psalter* v. 8 Ic inga, dryhten, in hus ðin. **971** *Blickl. Hom.* 121 Þa hie..in þone heofon locodan æfter him. *a* **1000** *Hymns* vi. 27 (Gr.) Ne læd þu us..in costunge. *c* **1175** *Lamb. Hom.* 3 Goð in þane castel þet is on-ȝein eou. *Ibid.* 45 Muneȝing of þam hali gast þe he sende in his apostles. *c* **1220** *Bestiary* 230 Do we ðe bodi in ðe bale. *a* **1300** *E.E. Psalter* xxix. 12 [xxx. 11] Þou torned mi weping..In blisse. *c* **1386** CHAUCER *Knt.'s T.* 11 And broghte hire hoom with hym in his contree. *c* **1470** HENRY *Wallace* I. 147 His fadyr Malcom in the Lennox fled. *c* **1500** *Melusine* 369 Soone after [she] tourned herself in the figure of a serpent and so vanysshed away. **1509** *Bury Wills* (Camden) 111 Yff ony off my childern happyn to cumme in pouerte. **1535** COVERDALE *2 Esdras* iii. 4 And hast brethed in him the breth of life. **1570** *Tragedie* 127 in *Satir. Poems Reform.* x, Turnit day in nycht and nycht in day. **1596** DALRYMPLE tr. *Leslie's Hist. Scot.* I. 8 Dorpes and wynes..now growne in fair townes. **1680** in *12th Rep. Hist. MSS. Comm.* App. VII. 394 My daughter was brought in bed of another boy. **1697** DRYDEN *Virg. Georg.* III. 645 [The snake] retires..And in some secret Cranny slowly glides. **1785** BURNS *Death & Dr. Horn-bk.* xiv, Deil mak his king's-hood in a spleuchan!

b. Illustrations of current usage after the verbs *cast, fall, lay, put, throw, thrust,* etc., *divide, split, break,* etc.

a **900** *O.E. Chron.* an. 709 Wæs todæled..in tua biscopscira West Seaxna lond. **971** *Blickl. Hom.* 191 His lic ..in þa stowe asetton þe Uaticanus hatte. **1154** *O.E. Chron.* an. 1137 ¶2, & dide ælle in prisun, til hi iafen up here castles. *c* **1200** *Trin. Coll. Hom.* 21 And was his holie lichame leid in burieles, in þe holie sepulcre. *c* **1330** R. BRUNNE *Chron. Wace* (Rolls) 3618 Iþe barel of gold þey leid ilkon. **1390** GOWER *Conf.* I. 106 Full ofte he heweth up so highe That chippes fallen in his eye. *c* **1400** MAUNDEV. (Roxb.) xxxiv. 153 Þe prestez..hewez þe body all in smale pecez. *c* **1460** *Towneley Myst.* xxvi. 413 My catyf hart wyll breke in thre. **1491** *Act 7 Hen. VII,* c. 22 Preamble, The seid John..caste the seid writing in the fire. **1590** SHAKS. *Mids. N.* II. i. 108 Hoared headed frosts Fall in the fresh lap of the crimson Rose. **1591** —— *1 Hen. VI.*, I. iv. 52 They suppos'd I could ..spurne in pieces Posts of Adamant. **1697** DRYDEN *Virg. Georg.* IV. 766 He..in the Billows plung'd his hoary Head. **1836** FONBLANQUE *Eng. under 7 Administ.* (1837) III. 336 Is he put on the shelf, or cast in the lumber-room? *a* **1868** M. J. HIGGINS *Ess.* (1875) 118 The most judicious mode of putting a kicker in harness. **1876** MOZLEY *Univ. Serm.* vi. (1877) 142 This dreadful schism..which splits them, as it were, in two beings.

c. See also *in the face of*: FACE *sb.* 4.

†**32.** The sense of motion or direction formerly gave rise to various modifications. [Cf. L. *in* with *accus.*] *Obs.*

†**a.** = *upon, on.*

a **1225** *Leg. Kath.* 102 Ha..spende al þet oðer in neodfulle & in nakede. *c* **1305** *St. Lucy* 7 in *E.E.P.* 101 In fisciciens heo hadde ispend moche del of hire gode. *c* **1430** *Hymns Virg.* 97 Þan schal neuere myscheef in þee falle. **1490** CAXTON *Eneydos* vi. 26 Yᵉ grete..cryme, perpetred and commysed in the persone of sychee. **1535** STEWART *Cron. Scot.* II. 528 To put handis in ane crownit king. **1557** NORTH *Gueuara's Diall Pr.* 127 b/2 To caste their eyes onelye in that that is presente.

†**b.** = *against, towards.*

a **1300** *E.E. Psalter* xliii. 6 [xliv. 5] In þi name for-how in us risand. *a* **1340** HAMPOLE *Psalter* vi. 1 Forgifynge til him þat synnes in vs. *c* **1380** WYCLIF *Wks.* (1880) 158 To oure dettouris þat is to men þat han synned in vs.

†**c.** = *over.*

c **1430** LYDG. *Min. Poems* (Percy Soc.) 16 That noon enmyes have in him powere.

†**d.** = *unto, to.*

1523 LD. BERNERS *Froiss.* I. xxxvi. 50 Sir Water of Manny ..dyd set fyre in the strete ioyninge to the castell. *Ibid.* cclxxix. 417 Parte of them that had set the fyre in the towne. **1535** COVERDALE *2 Esdras* iii. 7 Thou appoyntedest death in him, and in his generacions.

VI. Constructional uses.

33. Expressing the relation which the action of a verb has to some indirect object: forming with the latter an adverbial adjunct to the verb, and often entering with it into an indirect passive: e.g. *to be believed in, to be dealt in, to be engaged in.* (See the verbs individually.)

a. To *believe, trust, hope* in, and the like. In OE., *believe* took *in* with the accus., = *into, unto, towards* (cf. L. *credere in Deum*, etc.).

c **825** *Vesp. Psalter* ii. 13 Eadȝe alle ða ðe ȝetreowað in hine [L. *confidunt in eum*]. *a* **1000** *Juliana* 434 in *Exeter Bk.*, þu in ecne god..þinne ȝetreowdes. *c* **1200** *Trin. Coll. Hom.* 19 He þe bileueð in god. **13..** *K. Alis.* 7348 Alisaunder him gan affye In his owne chivalrie. *c* **1400** MAUNDEV. (1839) xv. 166 In theise thinges..ther ben many folk that beleeven. **1553** Q. MARY in Strype *Eccl. Mem.* (1721) III. App. i. 3 For the special trust and affiance we have in you. **1753** CHESTERF. *Lett.* (1774) IV. 6, I hope in God she will give you the will of exerting them.

b. To *partake, share, concur, engage, join, deal* in; to *consist* in; to *succeed, fail, increase* in; to *delight, exult, glory, joy, rejoice, triumph* in; etc.

a **1225** *Ancr. R.* 38 Ȝif me..delen in his pinen. *a* **1300** *E.E. Psalter* ix. 3, I sal fayne and glade in þe. **1375** BARBOUR *Bruce* IV. 718 Thai men, that will study In the craft of astrology. *c* **1585** R. BROWNE *Answ. Cartwright* 68, I partake in another mans offring. **1593** SHAKS. *Lucr.* 77 To those two Armies that would let him goe, Rather then triumph in so false a foe. **1697** DRYDEN *Virg. Georg.* I. 13 Join in my Work. **1776** *Trial of Nundocomar* 68/1, I used, a long time ago, to trade in salt. **1795** *Hist.* in *Ann. Reg.* 5 All classes..concurred in this determination. **1845** S. AUSTIN *Ranke's Hist. Ref.* I. 185 A

regular war with France was not to be engaged in without negotiations.

c. With trans. vb.: To *instruct* (a person) in; to *convict, condemn, mulct* in; to *baffle, disappoint, limit* in; to *spend* (money, time, etc.) in. To *hold* in (honour, etc.): see HOLD *v.* 12 f.

a **1300** *Cursor M.* 2610 In despit sco haldes me. **1382** WYCLIF *2 Chron.* xxxvi. 3 The king of Egipt.. condempnede the lond in an hundrith talentis of syluer. **1490** CAXTON *Eneydos* vii. 33 To haue some prynce.. for tenstructe hym in doctrynes and good maners. **1588** SHAKS. *L.L.L.* II. i. 19 Spending your wit in the praise of mine. *a* **1715** BURNET *Own Time* (1823) II. 207 The crown had been.. limited in the power of raising money. **1838** THIRLWALL *Greece* xi. II. 24 The Athenians, who had been repeatedly baffled in their attempts. **1893** W. P. COURTNEY in *Acad.* 13 May 413/1 The money expended in the improvement of the site.

34. Expressing the relation of an *adjective* (often ppl.) to some sphere or department to which its qualification is limited: *in* and its object forming an adverbial adjunct of the adjective; e.g. *accomplished, adroit, at home, complete, diligent, eager, eloquent, great, learned, skilled, strong, weak* in; *attacked, grieved, hurt, marked, wounded* in; etc.

c **900** tr. *Bæda's Hist.* IV. xxiii[i.]. (1890) 332 Wæs heo.. æðele in woruld ȝebyrdum. *Ibid.* 334 In regollices lifes lare swiðe ȝeornful. *a* **1225** *Leg. Kath.* 525 In alle wittes of worldliche wisdome wiseste o worlde. **1382** WYCLIF *Acts* vii. 22 Moyses.. was myȝty in his wordis and werkis. **1477** EARL RIVERS (Caxton) *Dictes* 76 Right connyng in fisike and a good fisicien. **1526** TINDALE *Matt.* v. 3 Blessed are the povre in sprete. **1557** NORTH *Gueuara's Diall Pr.* (1582) 174 a, Pirrus.. was stout and hardy, valiant in armes, liberall in benefices, pacient in aduersities. **1605** SHAKS. *Macb.* IV. ii. 66 Though in your state of Honor I am perfect. **1665** BOYLE *Occas. Refl.* (1848) 294 To admire and thank him that is infinite in Beauty, and in goodness. **1711** ADDISON *Spect.* No. 81 ¶2 If Rosalinda is unfortunate in her Mole, Nigranilla is as unhappy in a Pimple. **1833** I. TAYLOR *Fanat.* i. 2 Ignorant in the chief article of the case. **1845** M. PATTISON *Ess.* (1889) I. 2 Rich in works of the historical class. **1884** *Law Times* LXXVII. 27/2 A railway company was held liable in damages. **1895** *Bookman* Oct. 22/2 Louis [XIV] was.. wanting in all the elements of true greatness.

35. Expressing the relation of a *substantive* (esp. one that involves an attribute) to a certain sphere.

c **1200** ORM. 5483 Þe firrste ȝife iss witt & skill Inn heofennlike þingess. **1382** WYCLIF *Dan.* i. 17 God ȝaue to these children science and discipline in ech boke. **1513** DOUGLAS *Æneis* I. Prol. 56 Nane is, nor was.. ne ȝit sal haue sic crafte in poetrie. **1571** CAMPION *Hist. Irel.* ix. (1633) 27 The Barbarians highly honoured him for his cunning in all languages. **1699** BURNET *39 Art.* xxv. (1700) 266 In all this Diversity there is no real difference. **1749** FIELDING *Tom Jones* I. x, He was himself a very competent judge in most kinds of literature. *a* **1770** JORTIN *Serm.* (1771) I. iii. 46 Those who have skill in arts.. in war.. in politics. **1830** T. TAYLOR *Argts. Celsus* etc. 63 Alacrity in the performance of things. **1849** MACAULAY *Hist. Eng.* i. I. 111 The Houses.. would have made no formal change in the constitution. **1859** C. BARKER *Assoc. Princ.* ii. 56 Young beginners in business. **1884** W. C. SMITH *Kildrostan* 48 Let nothing shake your trust in her.

36. Expressing the relation of *number* or *quantity* to the dimension or amount in question: e.g. *length, breadth, depth*, or the like.

c **1275** LAY. 21995 Hit his imete in brede fif and twenti fote. **1382** WYCLIF *1 Kings* vi. 2 The hows.. hadde sexti cubitis in length and twenti in brede. **1512** *Act 4 Hen. VIII*, c. 1 §1 The said Countie is thre score and ten myle in lenght. **1548** UDALL, etc. *Erasm. Par. Mark* i. (1552) 120 Fewe in numbre. **1710** BERKELEY *Princ. Hum. Knowl.* Introd. §12 A black line of an inch in length. **1875** JOWETT *Plato* (ed. 2) III. 306 The virtues, which are also four in number. **1882** W. SHARP *D. G. Rossetti* ii. 86 A man six feet two inches in height.

37. With a substantive (or adj.), forming an *adverbial phrase*, e.g. *in charity, in duty, in honour*; *in right*; *in common, in general, in especial*; *in fact, in (all) probability, in truth, in faith*; *in conclusion, in fine*; *in haste*; *in any case, in every way*; *in (all) the world*. See the *sbs.*; also INDEED.

a **1300** *Cursor M.* 13402 Þai fild a cupp þan son in hast. *c* **1386** CHAUCER *Pard. Prol.* 126 But herkneth lordynges in conclusioun Youre likyng is that I schal telle a tale. **1513** MORE *Rich. III*, in Grafton *Chron.* I. 781 In faith man.. I was never so sory. **1647** N. BACON *Disc. Govt. Eng.* I. iii. 8 In Charity, therefore, the English Church in those daies must be of mean repute for outward pomp. **1667** PRIMATT *City & C. Build.* 2 Consider.. what casualties it may in probability be subject unto. **1721** *St. German's Doctor & Stud.* 309 If a man buy a horse.. of him that in right had no property to him. **1802** MAR. EDGEWORTH *Moral T.* (1816) I. xii. 100 Debts, which he could not, in honour, delay to discharge. **1871** SMILES *Charac.* i. (1876) 11 Every one is.. bound in duty, to aim at reaching the highest standard of character. **1881** MRS. WALFORD *Dick Netherby* xiv. 162 Not a shilling in the world.

38. In many *prepositional phrases*, as *in* CASE *of*, *in* FACE *of*, *in* FAVOUR *of*, *in* FRONT *of*, *in* HONOUR *of*, *in* LIEU *of*, *in* PRESENCE *of*, *in* RESPECT *of*, *in* SPITE *of*, INSTEAD *of*; *in* REGARD *of*, *to*, *in* RESPECT *of*, *to*; *in* ORDER *to*, *in* PROPORTION *to*, *in* RELATION *to*; *in* COMMON *with*, *in* COMPANY *with*, *in* COMPARISON *with*, etc. See these words.

VII. *Phrases.*

39. in so far: in such measure or degree (as); to such extent (that). Still conventionally written thus (*Hart's Rules for Compositors*, ed. 37, 1967, p. 75) but also freq. as a single word or with hyphens.

1596 DALRYMPLE tr. *Leslie's Hist. Scot.* v. 269 Britannie was.. in sevin Regimentis, deuydet be the Saxonis,.. Jnsafar, that a certane and sure ordour of kingis coulde not weil be collected. **1836** H. TAYLOR *Statesman* xxxi. 232 A man's manners have much real and intrinsic significancy, in so far forth as they are the result of his individual nature and taste. **1847** GROTE *Greece* II. xlvii. (1862) IV. 183 Insofar the latter had good reason to complain. **1896** *Act 59 & 60 Vict.* c. 39 §1 (3) In so far as they are temporary in their duration. **1940** *Economist* 6 July 13/2 Insofar as it ensures that trade between the two participating countries shall be reciprocal, it is an extension of compensation trade. **1948** J. STEINBECK *Russ. Jrnl.* (1949) 10 The C-47's are a little run down insofar as upholstery and carpeting go. **1959** B. WOOTTON *Social Sci. & Social Path.* viii. 267 Differentiation between the one and the other will be called for only insofar as it affects the kind of treatment that is likely to be helpful. **1969** *Times* 31 Oct. 29/5 Enforcement, insofar as salaries are concerned, is costing nothing. **1971** *Watsonia* VIII. 205 The results of it will be used here in-so-far as they affect the classification of the group.

40. in that: in the fact that; in its being the case that; in presence, view, or consequence of the fact that; seeing that; as, because.

c **1440** *Gesta Rom.* II. xxi. 399 (Add. MS.) The child is not apte to serve god, in that he is inparfite. **1523** LD. BERNERS *Froiss.* I. cliv. 186 The kyng of Nauerr.. excused hymselfe honorably, in that he departed out of the realme of France. **1535** COVERDALE *Josh.* xxii. 31 We knowe, that yᵉ Lorde is amonge vs, in that ye haue not trespaced agaynst the Lorde. **1593** SHAKS. *2 Hen. VI*, III. i. 257 Let him dye, in that he is a Fox. *c* **1680** BEVERIDGE *Serm.* (1729) II. 302 In that they think they get good by such hearing.. they are really the worse for it. **1883** DOBSON *Fielding* i. 18 This is the more likely, in that Arne the musician.. was Fielding's contemporary at Eton.

41. See also INASMUCH, INSOMUCH, etc.

in (ɪn), *adv.* Forms. 1– in; 1 inn. 3–5 inne, 4 ynne, ine, 4–5 yn. [Common Teut.; OE. *in(n* = OFris., OS., OHG. *in* (MHG. *in, în*, Ger. *ein*), Goth. *inn-* (in composition with vbs.), ON. *inn* (Sw. *in*, Da. *ind*). The distinction between *adv.* and *prep.* is clearly marked in mod.Ger. *ein* beside *in*, in Scandinavian *inn, in, ind* beside *í, i*, and in English dialects which use *in* for the adv., *i'* for the prep. OE. *inn* was employed only with verbs expressing motion, the corresponding form to denote rest within a place being *inne* (see INNE), but during the ME. period the loss of the final vowel made the two words identical in form; in some texts it is doubtful whether the *e* of *inne, ynne* is of etymological significance or not.]

I. Of motion or direction. [OE. *inn, in.*]

1. a. Expressing motion from a point without certain limits to a place within these; so as to penetrate or pass into a certain space; esp. into a house or other building (see also under COME, GO, PASS, PUT, etc.). Frequently followed by preps. indicating the direction, extent, etc. of the movement, as ***in at, by, †on, through, to, under***, etc.; also ***in-a-doors*** (see A-DOORS).

Beowulf (Z.) 3090 Þa me ȝerymed wæs.. sið.. inn under eorðweall. *c* **893** K. ÆLFRED *Oros.* I. i. §14 Ða beah þæt land þær eastryhte, oþþe seo sæ in on ðæt lond. *c* **1000** *Ags. Gosp.* Matt. vii. 13 Gangað inn [*v.r.* in] þurh þæt nearwe ȝeat. *a* **1225** *Ancr. R.* 74 Hwose euer wule mei gon in. **13..** *K. Alis.* 349 In he cam to hire bour. *c* **1400** *Rom. Rose* 7004 My paleis and myn hous make I There men may renne ynne openly. **1596** SPENSER *F.Q.* VI. iii. 42 The groome went streight way in, and to his Lord Declar'd the message. **1673** RAY *Journ. Low C.* 23 At our Entrance in [to Breda] we passed [etc.]. **1719** DE FOE *Crusoe* II. i, In comes my nephew. **1722** —— *Col. Jack* (1840) 311, I was called in again. **1814** MRS. WEST *Alicia de Lacy* III. 215 We shall be never the nearer.. unless we can climb in at the.. window. **1894** BARING-GOULD *Kitty Alone* II. 101 Put the cob in, said he to the ostler.

†b. In OE. (poetry and prose) and in ME. poetry, *in* often precedes the verb with which it is construed. *Obs.*

c **1000** ÆLFRIC *Hom.* II. 520 Be ðam hunde ðe his hand eft inn abær. —— *Exod.* xxi. 3 Ga he ut mid swilcum reafe swilce he in com. —— *Ags. Gosp.* Matt. xxvi. 41 Waciaþ.. þæt ȝe in ne gan on costunge. *c* **1200** *Trin. Coll. Hom.* 91 þenne þe procession ut goð of ierusalem and eft þenne it in cumeð. **13..** *K. Alis.* 544 A dragon com yn fleon. **13..** *Coer de L.* 3305 They leten hem in come. *Ibid.* 6316 A stout Sarezyn gan in sterte. ? **1370** *Robt. Cicyle* 52 Let hym in come swythe faste. *a* **1400** *Sir Perc.* 1538 The portere.. Lete the knyghtis in fare. *c* **1440** *Ipomydon* 1110 Þe rede knyght anone in rode.

c. Used after auxiliary verbs, as *may, must, shall*, etc., or absolutely with imperative force, with omission of 'go', 'enter', 'get', or the like (cf. IN *v.* 5). Now chiefly *poet.* or *rhet.*

971 *Blickl. Hom.* 127 Duru þæt mannes heafod, ȝe þa sculdro, magan in. *a* **1225** *Ancr. R.* 74 Ase buruh wiðuten wal, þer ase uerd mei in oueral. **13..** *Coer de L.* 3842 The Sarezynes myght neyther in ne oute. **1340** *Ayenb.* 232 þet hy ne moȝe naȝt in. **1590** SHAKS. *Com. Err.* V. i. 37 This is some Priorie, in, or we are spoyl'd. **1595** —— *John* I. i. 171 In at the window, or else ore the hatch. **1627** SANDERSON *Serm.* (1681) I. 284 Unless God kept him back, he must on, and he must in, and he must in deep. **1668** DAVENANT *Man's the Master* III. i, Sure, this is Isabella's chamber; the door is open! I'll in, and take my leave of her. **1821** BYRON *Sardan.* II. i. 601 Let's in. **1857** TROLLOPE *Barchester T.* I. v. 62, I see that there are three trains in and three out every Sabbath.

d. Imperatively = 'take in'. Also *in with*.

1708 MOTTEUX *Rabelais* IV. xviii. (1737) 76 He cry'd, in with your Top-sails. **1857** *Merc. Marine Mag.* (1858) V. 1 In jib and main course.

2. Phrase. ***day in, day out***: as each day comes in or begins, and goes out or closes; continually. So with *week, year*, etc.

1839 LONGF. *Village Blacksmith* iii, Week in, week out, from morn till night. **1884** MISS WILKINS in *Harper's Mag.* July 303/2 Sitting and sewing as she did day in and day out.

3. Expressing motion in the direction of some central point; hence, position attained by (or as by) coming, bending, or pressing in; in proximity, within reach of, or near to some point or limit specified or implied; into or in close quarters.

1702 *Lond. Gaz.* No. 3781/4 Goes a little in with his Ancles. **1709–10** *Tatler* (J.), They [fencers] are in with you, if you offer to fall back without keeping your guard. **1812** *Sporting Mag.* XXXIX. 24 Crib always was in and fighting with him. **1872** BLACK *Adv. Phæton* (1878) 532 The swans were sailing close in by the reeds. **1888** R. HAGGARD *Maiwa's Revenge* iv, About five yards in, it [the path] took a turn. **1898** *To-Day* 5 Nov. 4/2 When you have a man 'fighting in', there is no possible time to use anything but your hands.

4. Into the bargain; in addition (to the legal amount); over and above, besides; as in to *get, give, throw* in: see the verbs.

1634 MASSINGER *Very Woman* III. i, He will not yield above a peck of oysters: If I can get a quart of wine in too, you are gone, Sir. **1718** *Free-thinker* No. 28 ¶1 To these [exquisite Faces] he threw me in Three Songs. **1836–9** DICKENS *Sk. Boz* 116 (Hoppe) And so you have the fight in gratis. **1864** Throw in [see INBREAD *sb.*]. **1886** [see GIVE 59 f].

II. Of position.

5. a. Within a certain space; esp. inside a house or other enclosed place, inside the usual place of abode, shelter, or safety.

In early ME. use chiefly northern, the southern word being orig. INNE.

a **1300** *Cursor M.* 14737 Ne wald he neuer o þaim blin, Till all war vte þat þar was in. *c* **1475** *Rauf Coilȝear* 94 Vndo the dure beliue! Dame, art thow in? **1719** DE FOE *Crusoe* I. i, Our ship rid forecastle in. **1793** SMEATON *Edystone L.* §287 To come home with her cargo in. **1805** COLLINGWOOD 6 Oct. in Nicolas *Disp.* (1846) VII. 81 *note*, I think at 5, or at 4, the Boats will be better in. *Mod.* Is Mr. A. in? He is not in at present. Do you know when I shall find him in?

b. On the inside, within. ***from in***, from the inside.

a **1300** *Cursor M.* 5615 An esscen kyst sco did be wroght, Did pik it sua, wit-oute and in [*Gött.* widuten and inne; *Trin.* wiþoute & ynne]. **1606** SHAKS. *Tr. & Cr.* III. iii. 97 Man, how dearely euer parted, How much in hauing, or without, or in, Cannot make boast to haue that which he hath. *c* **1860** H. STUART *Seaman's Catech.* 22 Reeve it from in out through the quarter block. **1873** TRISTRAM *Moab* iii. 43 A sheepskin coat with the woolly side in.

6. In various special senses.

In some of these the adverbial use may have arisen from the prep. by ellipse of a substantive; in others the verb *to be* takes the place of one implying motion. Hence *in* may be used in almost any sense arising from verbal combinations, and only the more common ones are illustrated here.

a. In prison, in confinement.

1597 SHAKS. *2 Hen. IV*, V. v. 40 Thy Dol.. is in base Durance, and contagious prision.. Dol is in. **1877** *Five Years Penal Servit.* iii. 147 It is the etiquette among prisoners never to ask a man what he is in for. The badge upon his left arm gives his sentence.

b. Engaged, involved, entangled in (an action, esp. an unlawful one). Cf. COUNT *v.* 2 b.

1588 SHAKS. *L.L.L.* IV. iii. 20, I would not care a pin, if the other three were in. **1602** MARSTON *Ant. & Mel.* IV. Wks. 1856 I. 49, I shall nere ha done when I am in, Tis harder for me end, than to begin. **1607** TOURNEUR *Rev. Trag.* V. iii, And now, my Lord, since we are in for ever. **1623** MASSINGER *Dk. Milan* II. *ad. fin.*, All my plots Turn back upon myself: but I am in, And must go on. **1884** 'MARK TWAIN' *Huck. Finn* xxxi. 321 As long as I was in, and in for good, I might as well go the whole hog. **1893** —— in *Century Mag.* Jan. 342/1, I could n't venture it now; I was in too deep.

c. Of a statesman or political party: In office, in power.

1605 SHAKS. *Lear* V. iii. 15 Talke of Court newes.. Who looses, and who wins; who's in, who's out. **1678** EARL OF ARRAN in *Lauderdale Papers* (1885) III. 102 Some people.. because they are not In themselves,.. must fall upon me. **1728** YOUNG *Love Fame* I. 214 Against reason.. 'tis equal sin To boast of merely being out or in. **1801** H. SWINBURNE in *Crts. Europe Last Cent.* (1841) II. 303 We are in a strange situation, half a ministry in, and half another out. **1880** *Daily Tel.* 22 Sept., Incorrigible revolutionists, who must attack a Minister because he is 'in'.

d. Of a player or a side in a game: In possession of the field, etc.; having the turn or right to play. Cf. INNINGS. Also of a batsman given 'not out' by the umpire.

1744 *Laws* [of Cricket] in *New Dict. Arts & Sci.* (1755) IV. 3459/1 Laws for the strikers, or those that are in. **1770** J. LOVE *Cricket* 24 The two last Champions even now are in. **1844** *Blackburn Standard* 17 July, The bowler asked 'in or out?' **1871** 'THOMSONBY' *Cricketers in Council* 32 Men who run with their bats in the air are constantly run out in cases where they would have been safely 'in' if they had adopted the contrary practice. **1874** J. D. HEATH *Croquet-Player* 69 Instructions to the player who is 'in'. **1884** *Lillywhite's Cricket Ann.* 55 He scored 33 out of 35 made while he was in. **1898** K. S. RANJITSINHJI *With Stoddart's Team* (ed. 3) iv. 70 He was given 'in' by the umpire when appealed to.

e. In legal possession of (an estate).

1818 CRUISE *Digest* (ed. 2) III. 350 Where the heir takes any thing which might have vested in the ancestor, the heir should be in by descent.

f. Of a ship's sails: Taken in, furled.

1769 FALCONER *Dict. Marine* (1789), *In*, the state of any of a ship's sails, when they are furled or stowed.

g. Of fire or light: Burning, lighted. Chiefly with certain verbs, e.g. *to keep in*; *to blow in*, the reverse of *to blow out*.

1662 SIR S. TUKE *Adv. Five Hours* v. i. in Hazl. *Dodsley* XV. 287 (Pedro.. lets the candle fall.. Diego takes up the candle.) Here's a fair trial for your maiden breath! Flora, blow't in again.. (Flora blows the candle in). **1711** ADDISON *Spect.* No. 72 ¶7 They observe the law.. which orders the Fire to be always kept in. **1793** SMEATON *Edystone L.* § 247 This evening's tide we worked with links, and it began to blow so fresh that we had much ado to keep them in. **1883** *L'pool Daily Post* 28 Dec. 5/3 By 3 o'clock the electric lights were in, as though it were in the evening. **1889** *Pall Mall G.* 2 Dec. 3/1 One has to think seriously before blowing in a furnace whether the price will be maintained long enough to leave him a profit. **1893** *Argosy* Jan. 23 We.. sat round the .. fire, which we kept in more for the sake of cheerfulness than warmth.

h. Of a train, coach, steamer, mail, etc.: Come in, arrived.

1870 MISS BRIDGMAN *R. Lynne* I. xv. 249 The 7.30 train would be in.

i. In the market; in season; in fashion.

1687 [see IN AND OUT 1 b]. **1851** MAYHEW *Lond. Labour* I. 85 During July cherries are in as well as raspberries. **1891** *Daily News* 24 Oct. 5/4 Savoys are in. **1923** *Ladies' Home Jrnl.* Sept. 50 Her hostess, in black silk crêpe, rejoices that trains are once more 'in', knowing the value of long lines and loose draperies. **1954** L. MACNEICE *Autumn Sequel* 131 Accomplishments were in, enthusiasm out. **1959** *Encounter* Sept. 60/2 Beckett is a fashionable reputation which is still 'in'. **1965** M. MORSE *Unattached* i. 24 Perhaps 'being at a party' is a qualification for being 'in'?

j. Of a school: in session, in progress. *Sc.* and *N.Z.*

1812 P. FORBES *Poems, chiefly in Sc. Dial.* 95 On Saturday, nae school being in. **1895** W. C. FRASER *Whaups of Durley* iii. 27 We would be stopped by a shout, 'The schule's in'. **1949** F. SARGESON *I saw in my Dream* I. vi. 40 But I don't remember nothing about when school was in.

k. well in. (*a*) *Racing.* Applied to a horse which has been treated leniently by the handicapper. (*b*) In comfortable or easy circumstances. *colloq.* orig. *Austral.* Also, profitably engaged in speculation.

(*a*) **1854** J. MILLS *Life Race-Horse* xvii. 111 The handicapper.. considerately classed me among the middle ones, and awarded 6 st. 12 lb. as my burthen. 'He's vell in,' said my owner,.. 'very vell in.' **1894** G. MOORE *Esther Waters* xxx. 247 Are the 'orses he backs what you'd call well in? **1898** A. E. T. WATSON *Turf* i. 16 A horse which is well in in a little handicap.

(*b*) **1891** [see WELL-IN *adj. phr.*]. **1902** WEBSTER Suppl., *Well in*, engaged in a profitable speculation in stocks; said of a speculator whose purchases have risen considerably in value on his hands. Hence, in a general sense, prosperous; well off; well to do. (*Colloq., Australia.*) **1913** M. ROBERTS *Salt of Sea* 158 If you ain't lucky you're bound to be dishonest,.. if you means to be well in all the time.

l. Of fortune or luck: favourable. (Cf. OUT *adv.* 23.)

1901 A. E. W. MASON *Clementina* i, His luck for the moment was altogether in. **1912** 'SAKI' *Chron. Clovis* 187 Her fellow-gamblers were always ready to entertain her.. when their luck was in.

III. Contextual uses.

7. With verbs, besides the senses 1–5, above, *in* has many contextual and idiomatic uses; e.g. expressing irruption, as in *break*, *burst*, *strike in*; penetration, as in *burn*, *cut*, *force*, *rub in*; enclosing, surrounding, or covering, as in *build*, *cover*, *fence*, *hem*, *roof*, *wall in*; acceding, yielding, as in *come*, *fall*, *give in*. See the verbs.

IV. Phrases, etc.

8. in for. [Cf. 6 b.]

a. †(*a*) Involved or engaged *in* some business or occupation *for* a specified time. (*b*) Involved in some coming event, etc. from which no escape is possible; finally committed or destined to do or suffer something.

1599 *Broughton's Lett.* viii. 26 Herein.. you are in for all day.. it is your element. **1658–9** *Burton's Diary* (1828) IV. 37 We are in for a month at this rate of speaking. **1773** GOLDSM. *Stoops to Conq.* IV, I was in for a list of blunders. **1835** *Fraser's Mag.* XI. 21 We are in for a speech. **1889** *Repent. P. Wentworth* I. xiv. 285 We are in for a pretty severe storm.

b. esp. in phrase *in for it*: Committed to a course of action; also, certain to meet with punishment or something unpleasant.

1698 FARQUHAR *Love and a Bottle* III. i, I've thrown my cast, and am fairly in for't. But an't I an impudent dog? *c* **1730** BURT *Lett. N. Scotl.* (1818) I. 91 As I am in for't I must now proceed. **1741** RICHARDSON *Pamela* II. 99, I am in for it now, over Head and Ears, I doubt, and can't help loving him. **1855** KINGSLEY *Plays & Purit.* 145 Raleigh finds himself 'in for it', and takes the island out of hand in the most masterly fashion. **1864** SALA in *Daily Tel.* 26 Feb., When.. the representative receives a lady's card.. He knows that he is in for it.. he has to exhibit the lions of the Capitol.

c. In the competition or race for some prize or thing to be gained. Cf. *go in for*: GO *v.* 82 e.

1850 SCORESBY *Cheever's Whaleman's Adv.* xiii. (1859) 182 Though not myself.. in for any share of the profits. *Mod.* Several good men are in for the librarianship. He is in for Moderations at Oxford.

d. In for a penny, in for a pound: see PENNY.

9. in with.

a. In agreement with; on friendly terms with. *to keep in with*: see KEEP *v.*

a **1677** MANTON in Spurgeon *Treas. Dav.* Ps. cxix. 98 A godly-wise man is careful to keep in with God. **1682** BUNYAN *Holy War* (Cassell) 115 They knew that.. against him they had been in with Diabolus. **1692** BULSTRODE in *15th Rep. Hist. MSS. Comm.* App. II. 21 He was a haughty proud man, in with King Charles the Second. **1714** SWIFT *Pres. St. Aff.* Wks. 1778 VI. 101 Those who pretended wholly to be in with the principles upon which her Majesty and her new servants proceeded. *a* **1875** W. ARNOT *Anchor of Soul* (1876) 72 When I am no longer in with my destroyer, I have the Omnipotent on my side. **1925** 'R. CROMPTON' *Still—William* vi. 112 So far County had persistently resisted the attempts of Mrs. Bott to 'get in' with it. **1942** E. PAUL *Narrow St.* xxiv. 213 Naturally, the Prime Minister was in with Stavisky, too. **1964** P. M. HUBBARD *Picture of Millie* ii. 15 We.. go along to the Carrack for a drink.. occasionally, but we're not really in with the people staying there.

b. *Naut.* Close in to, near (the land).

1708 *Lond. Gaz.* No. 4422/7 It proving close and dirty Weather,.. we could not venture in with Land. **1748** *Anson's Voy.* II. xiii. 275 We kept plying on and off the whole night, intending to keep well in with the land. **1800** SIR M. HUNTER *Jrnl.* (1894) 159 We sailed close in with the island.

†**c.** At close quarters with; even with. *rare*$^{-1}$.

1742 RICHARDSON *Pamela* III. 335, I can't say, but you're in with me now... Ay, by my Soul, you have nabbed me cleverly.

d. *to come in with* (see COME 63 n); *to fall in with* (see FALL *v.* 91).

10. See IN AND IN, IN AND OUT.

V. Combinations.

11. Participles and vbl. sbs., nouns of action, and agent-nouns, from verbs qualified by *in*, are formed by prefixing *in-*, when used as adjs. or sbs. The number of these is practically unlimited. See IN- *pref.*[1].

a. With *pres. pple.*, as *in-abiding*, that abides in; so *in-curling*, *in-flying*, etc. Also INBURNING, INBURSTING, INCOMING, etc., etc.

1889 J. SMITH *Fellowship* i. (1891) 26 The inabiding and inworking Christ. **1894** G. EGERTON *Keynotes* 66 Like the wave-note of the in-curling sea in the Mediterranean. **1894** *Outing* (U.S.) XXIV. 46/1 We lay.. in the bottom of the boat and.. waited for the in-flying game.

b. With *pa. pple.*, as *in-burnt*, that is burnt in; so *in-built*, *in-moulded*, *in-set*, etc. Also INBLOWN, INBOWED, INGROWN, INPOURED, etc.

17.. *Christmas Ba'ing* in Skinner *Misc. Poet.* (1809) 127 (Jam.) In came the insett Dominie Just riftin frae his dinner. **1848** A. H. tr. *Richter's Levana* I. ii. §7 An Indian slave, who wanders about with the inburnt stamps of his various masters. **1856** R. A. VAUGHAN *Mystics* (1860) I. 271 A man of true self-abandonment must be un-built from the creature, in-built with Christ. **1896** *Westm. Gaz.* 23 Apr. 8/1 Coffins.. made of heavy plate-glass, the sides and top being strengthened by an in-moulded network of wire.

c. With *vbl. sb.*, as *in-abiding*, an abiding in; so *in-flashing*, etc. Also INBEAMING, INBRINGING, etc., etc.

1850 W. ANDERSON *Regener.* (1871) 205 That there be a continuance of that inflashing of the truth into the.. soul. **1889** J. SMITH *Fellowship* (1891) 126 You enjoy the in-abiding of the mind of God.

d. With noun of action, as INBURST, INCAST, INCOME, INPOUR, etc., q.v.

e. With agent-noun, as INBRINGER, INCOMER, etc., q.v.

12. With sbs. Usually opposed to *out-*. (Cf. IN *a.*, which differs from this only in being written detached.)

a. That is, lives, lies, or remains *in*, or *within* (some understood place); internal: usually opposed to a person or thing which is *out* or external, as **'in-brother**, a resident brother of a fraternity or guild; **'in-burgess**, a burgess resident in the burgh; **'in-case**, a case of an in-patient; **'in-company**, a company employed at home or at headquarters; **in-maintenance**, maintenance for a person living in a workhouse or the like; **'in-patient**, a patient who remains in a hospital while under medical treatment, as distinguished from an *out-patient* who comes daily, or from time to time, to be attended to; now freq. used *attrib.*; **'in-pensioner**, a pensioner resident in a charitable institution.

1644 *MS. Acc. St. John's Hosp, Canterb.*, Receiued.. when he was admitted an *inbrother. **1479** *Burgh Rec. Aberdeen* (Spalding Club) I. 37 Of all otheris, outeburges and *inburgessis and indwellaris havand chavmer or house, a penny. **1741** in Gross *Gild Merch.* (1890) II. 200 The Foreign Burgesses and the Inn-Burgesses.. Those admitted by the Council or by the Mayor are called Inn-Burgesses by Copy of Court Roll. **1892** *Daily News* 13 July 5/5 A 'faction fight' has contributed a further contingent of '*in-cases' to the local hospitals. **1793** SMEATON *Edystone L.* §101 The out-company not to return home till the *in-company is carried out to relieve them. **1860** in C. S. DAVIES *Hist. Macclesfield* (1961) v. 267 *In-Maintenance of paupers £1027 s.5 d.9. **1885** *Encycl. Brit.* XIX. 475/2 Relief given in a workhouse is termed 'in (or indoor) maintenance' relief. **1905** *Daily Chron.* 1 Sept. 2/5 For every £1 spent on out-relief in 1902–3 no less than £7 12s. 4d. was expended on in-maintenance. **1760** MORE in *Phil. Trans.* LI. 938 Thinking, that if he was admitted an *in-patient at the hospital, he should be more likely to obtain a cure. **1879** *St. George's Hosp. Rep.* IX. 693 Four of these were also inpatients of the hospital. **1959** *Times* 13 Jan. 3/2 Inpatient therapy. **1965** *Mod. Law Rev.* XXVIII. v. 580 Persons who.. are receiving in-patient treatment for mental disorder. **1894** *Daily News* 12 Sept. 5/3 It would be very unfair to take the Hospital away from the *in-pensioners.

b. That is in office or power, as **'in-party** (cf. quot. 1817 in IN *a.*); **in-side** *Cricket*, the side which is batting.

1837 D. WALKER *Games & Sports* 224 Batters, belonging to the In-side. *a* **1860** WHATELY *Comm.-pl. Bk.* (1864) 172 An out-party will generally have more zeal.. among its members, than an in-party. **1882** *Australians in Eng.* 16 Matters are going wrong with the in-side.

c. Inside a person; inside the body; internal; as **'in-evidence**, internal evidence; †**'in-muscle**, an internal muscle; **'in-parts**, internal parts of the body (cf. quot. 1599 in IN *a.*). Also INMEAT.

c **1611** CHAPMAN *Iliad* v. 76 The region About the bladder, underneath th' in-muscles and the bone. *a* **1629** T. GOFF *Three Trag.* (1656) 208 This hand shall rip her breast, And search her inparts, but I'll find it out. **1662** STILLINGFL. *Orig. Sacr.* II. viii. §4 The in-evidence which is so much spoken of as an ingredient of the nature of faith.

d. Situated within limits, or nearer to the centre, or point of reference, as IN-FIELD, INLAND, IN-PARISH, IN-SHORE. **e.** In various other compounds, which see in their places.

13. Parasynthetic derivatives from sbs. forming adjs., as *in-backed*, having the back bent inwards. So IN-KNEED, IN-TOED.

1833 *New Monthly Mag.* XXXVIII. 33 The in-back'd slave, Who, laid face upward, hews the black stone down.

14. With verbs: see IN- *prefix*[1].

15. With adverbs and prepositions; as IN-ABOUT, IN-BETWEEN. *in on* (cf. ON *adv.* 13): participating in; being (one of a group) in possession of knowledge concerning (something).

1923 A. CHRISTIE *Murder on Links* viii. 101 You don't mean—that you're in on *that*? **1928** E. WALLACE *Gunner* xxiii. 189 As you're in on this, Gunner, you'd better see what I've said. **1935** M. M. ATWATER *Murder in Midsummer* xxv. 235 He'll want to be in on this. **1946** [see GROUND FLOOR b]. **1953** W. BURROUGHS *Junkie* (1972) ix. 83 They are in on narcotics, and they are connected with Communism. *Ibid.* xii. 121 If any one makes a good score, she puts out a grapevine to find out who was in on the job. **1958** B. NICHOLS *Sweet & Twenties* 197, I was very much 'in' on the birth of this song. **1959** *Listener* 12 Feb. 283/1 It does not work for the American reader, who is not in on the secret. **1970** R. LOWELL *Notebk.* 221 Anyway you should be in on it. Only In imagination can we lose the battle. **1973** 'M. INNES' *Appleby's Answer* xv. 128 Don't imagine I have the slightest wish to be in on your muckraking.

in, *a.* [IN *adv.* used *attrib.*, or as positive of INNER, INMOST.] **1.** That is in; that lies, remains, lives, is situated, or is used in or within; internal. (In most cases it is more usual to hyphen *in* to the sb.: see IN *adv.* 12.)

1599 CHAPMAN *Hum. days Myrth* Plays 1873 I. 76 All their in parts then fit to serue pesants or make curdes for dawes. **1615** CHAPMAN *Odyss.* v. 305 Up he rose, put on His in and out weed. **1681** W. ROBERTSON *Phraseol. Gen.* (1693) 734 You made it out by in and home proofs. **1693** *Answ. 'Just Measures'* 5 What's this but to say we may have one sort of Power to Govern the out Part, and another to guide the in? **1817** COBBETT *Pol. Reg.* XXXII. 62 The out party proposed to pass a law [etc.]. The in party said that such a law was unnecessary. **1818** *Ibid.* XXXIII. 469 To suppose .. that the out part of 'the regiment' would be disposed to call the in part of 'the regiment' to account. **1836** SOUTHEY *Lett.* (1856) IV. 464 Twenty-nine little volumes.. with one duke's arms on the outside, and another.. on the in. **1876** MRS. WHITNEY *Sights & Ins.* xxiv. 238 The outside and the in of a thing.

2. a. Fashionable, sophisticated; esoteric. Cf. IN *adv.* 6 i, IN-GROUP, IN-JOKE, IN-REFERENCE.

1960 *Spectator* 14 Oct. 555 A personable young *strip-peuse* at Vegas (as we 'in' people call Las Vegas). **1961** *Harper's Bazaar* Apr. 138/2 The *dahlings* of the profession—beloved by 'in' audiences who adore a coterie joke. **1965** *Melody Maker* 13 Feb. 10 Record companies release more discs in the belief that folk is the new 'in thing'. **1969** C. F. BURKE *God is Beautiful, Man* (1970) 107 He's got all the in stuff on and a big stick pin. **1969** *Daily Tel.* 2 July 19/6 The audience —totally committed to the 'pop' ideal and fully conversant with its idiomatic 'in' vocabulary—reacted suitably. **1970** O. NORTON *Dead on Prediction* ii. 41 It *is* the in place. You'd be surprised who you meet there.

b. With hyphen and so passing into IN- *pref.*[1]

1961 *Guardian* 29 Apr. 12/7 You will quickly find in N.Y. that the in-thing to do is to pronounce.. Broad*way*. **1965** *Punch* 17 Nov. 721/1 Gnomes, it judged, are now in-people —possibly even top people. **1968** *Daily Tel.* 15 Nov. 16/7 The pace-setters here are upper-class girls who treat swearing as a snobbish in-thing to do. **1969** J. BRAIDWOOD *Ulster Dialect Lexicon* 17, I am informed that it has become the in-word in all Northern Ireland Ministry of Agriculture pamphlets. **1969** *New Scientist* 9 Oct. 74/1 The words 'computer' and 'education' must be two of the most overworked in-words of the decade. **1969** *Word* Feb. 38/1 Change is a contemporary theme; change is one of those in-words at the moment. **1969** *Time* 11 Apr. 55 The magazine's critics still point to its smug, In-crowd perspective. **1970** *Times* Suppl. 9 May 26/4 The in-crowd calls it [*sc.* Casablanca] 'Casa', and I offer the information here for anyone who can use it to advantage.

in, *sb.* [f. IN *adv.*]

1. *pl.* **a.** In politics: The party which is in office (see IN *adv.* 6 c), usu. in phrase (*the*) ***ins and outs***.

1764 Chesterf. *Lett.* (1792) IV. ccclxxix. 201, I believe that there will be something patched up between the *ins* and the *outs*. **1774** H. Swinburne in *Crts. Europe Last Cent.* (1841) I. 16 What an epoch for ministers, both ins and outs! **1823** Byron *Juan* xiii. xxiv, Juan stood well both with Ins and Outs. **1884** Spurgeon in *Pall Mall G.* 19 June 11/1 Everything the Ins do the Outs denounce, and then the moment this denunciation has done its work, the Outs take the place of the Ins, and are abused in their turn, not because they are wrong, but because they are in.

b. In games: The side whose turn it is to play (see IN *adv.* 6 d).

1862 J. F. Campbell *Pop. Tales W. Highlands* IV. 37 *note*, The circle within which the 'ins' stand at the game of rounders. **1891** *Daily News* 4 Aug. 4/8 In an ocean-going steamship..a ball in the rigging or in the air funnels is the fortune of the ins.

2. ins and outs. a. Windings or turnings in and out, devious or tortuous turns to and fro in a road, a course of action, etc.; sinuous ramifications.

a **1670** Hacket *Abp. Williams* i. (1692) 152 Follow their Whimsies and their In and Outs at the Consulto, when the Prince was among them. **1809** Malkin *Gil Blas* vii. vi, Laura..required from me a faithful and true narrative of all my pros and cons, my ins and outs, since that..separation of ours. *a* **1845** Hood *Laying down the Law* ii, A celebrated judge, too prone to tarry To hesitate on devious ins and outs. **1862** Sala *Seven Sons* III. v. 83 The labour of following the ins and outs of the close-clustered carriages. **1878** R. H. Hutton *Scott* ii. 27 Keen appreciation of the ins and outs of legal method. **1889** Boldrewood *Robbery under Arms* xxii, He knew the ins and outs of the road better than any of us.

b. Those who are constantly entering and leaving the workhouse. Cf. *in-and-out class*, etc. (s.v. IN AND OUT, IN-AND-OUT *adv.* 4).

1884 *Daily News* 10 Dec. (Ware), There are considerable numbers of paupers..who find the workhouse a convenient retreat on emergency... They are known familiarly as 'the ins-and-outs'. **1896** *Rep. Poor Law Schools Comm.* xi. 71 The fluctuating class of children whose parents frequently discharge themselves from the workhouse and in a few days seek readmission. These cases are known among Poor Law officials as 'ins and outs'. **1905** *Rep. Brit. Assoc. Adv. Sci.* 467 The 'ins and outs' of Great Britain have characteristics which may be described as nomadic.

3. a. An introduction to someone of power, fame, or authority; influence with such a person. *colloq.* (orig. *U.S.*).

1929 E. D. Sullivan *Look at Chicago* (1930) ii. 21 His strong 'in' with police, built largely at the outset, with their organization's money. **1930** *Amer. Mercury* Dec. 454/1 *An in*, an introduction; to place in a position to bribe. 'Get me an in with the skipper of that precinct.' **1940** R. Chandler *Farewell, my Lovely* xxxvi. 276 It stands to reason that he had an in with the city government, but that don't mean they knew everything he did or that every cop on the force knew he had an in. **1947** J. Steinbeck *Wayward Bus* iv. 44 If her cousin was Clark Gable, why, that was an 'in' you couldn't beat. **1950** 'J. Tey' *To love & be Wise* xix. 248 A girl has a more difficult time getting an 'in' in a racket. **1958** N. F. Leopold *Life plus 99 Yrs.* iii. 58 He had some sort of special 'in' with Warden Westbrook of the jail and was allowed more privileges than the other reporters. **1961** J. Heller *Catch-22* (1962) xxi. 210 The only colonel he trusted was Colonel Moodus, and even he had an in with his father-in-law. **1962** J. Wain *Strike Father Dead* v. 210 He had always been meaning to base himself in Paris for a while; all he had been waiting for was what he called 'an in'. Well, now he had got the ideal in. **1966** J. B. Priestley *Salt is Leaving* xiii. 177, I have an *in* with a couple of the directors. **1973** E. McGirr *Bardel's Murder* i. 18 He wondered if she had an 'in' with some manufacturer.

b. ***to be on the in***: to have inside information. *U.S. colloq.*

1936 J. Steinbeck *In Dubious Battle* vi. 78 'You a big guy?' 'I'm on the in,' said the boy. **1942** Berrey & Van den Bark *Amer. Thes. Slang* §480/4 *On the in*, smarted up, wise (to), wised (up).

in (ɪn), *v.* Also 5–9 **inn**, 6–7 **inne**. [The OE. *innian, ʒeinnian*, appear to attach themselves in part directly to the adv. *inn*, IN, partly to be more immediately associated with the derivative, INN *sb.* In mod. use we distinguish IN *v.* from INN *v.* in accordance with their sense, but the formal distinction fails in the inflected forms *inned*, *inning*, and, in ME., even in the present forms *inn-en*, *inn-est*, *inn-eth*, *inne*; in some uses, also, it is possible that both notions were present. Cf. OHG. *innôn*, from the adv. *inn*.]

1. *trans.* To give or put in (*obs.*); to take in, include, inclose; *esp.* to take in, inclose or reclaim (waste or unprofitable land). Now *dial.*

11.. *Codex Exon.* 1 He hæfð ʒeinnod þæt ær ʒeutod wæs. **1387** Trevisa *Higden* (Rolls) VI. 367 Aluredus inned Londoun first and Colwulfus deel to his owne kyngdom. **1529** More *Dyaloge* iv. Wks. 278/1 The landes Inned by dyuers owners in the Isle of tenate. **1543–4** *Act 35 Hen. VIII*, c. 9 Wappinge Marshe..beyng longe tyme surrounded and over flowen wᵗ water was recovered and ynned by the saide Cornelys [Wanderdelf]. **1592** Bacon *Observ. Libel* in *Resuscitatio* (1661) 113 Wast, and unprofitable Ground Inned, Reclaimed, and Improved. **1640** Somner *Antiq. Canterb.* 290 Appledore mershes were inned in his time. **1852** *Humber Conserv. Act* 2038 Any part of the shores..shall be inned, gained, or reclaimed from the water. **1875** Parish *Sussex Gloss.* s.v., I inned that piece of land from the common.

2. To gather (grain, hay, or other produce) into the barn, stackyard, etc.; to harvest or house.

c **1407** Hoccleve *Bal. & Chanceon to H. Somer* 29 Haasteth our heruest as soone as yee may..Were our seed Inned wel we mighten pleye. **1496** *Dives & Paup.* (W. de W.) x. viii. 383/1 Thou shalt tylle and other shall in that thou tyllest. **1525** Ld. Berners *Froiss.* II. xxii. 55 Then he taryed tyll they had inned all theyr corne and vyntage. **1601** Holland *Pliny* I. 562 They make greater hast to cut it [Barley] downe, and to inne it. *a* **1605** Montgomerie *Poems* xlviii. 240 Notwithstanding all wes ind and bair. **1676** T. Clark in Hubbard *Narrative* (1865) II. 139 *note*, To fight the Enemie out of our Borders, that our English Corn may be inned in. **1743** *Lond. & Country Brew.* iv. (ed. 2) 253 When Barley is inn'd wet, it will heat or burn in the Mow. **1821** *Blackw. Mag.* VIII. 428 October either rots, or inns the stuff. **1847** *Tait's Mag.* XIV. 842 The brownie had inned the corn and threshed it.

b. To harvest (a field). Now *local.*

1646 in Picton *L'pool Munic. Rec.* (1883) I. 234 From the tyme of seedeing till the towne feild be inned.

3. To get in, gather in, collect. (Partly *transf.* from 2.)

1615 E. S. *Britain's Buss* in Arb. *Garner* III. 647 The same [money] is clearly inned again, together with all other charges. **1655** Fuller *Ch. Hist.* x. iii. §13 The profits of two former years, which the knight inned at his own cost. *a* **1700** B. E. *Dict. Cant. Crew, Fat*, the last landed, inned or stowed of any sort of Merchandize.

†**4.** To take in mentally, comprehend. *rare*⁻¹.

1603 Florio *Montaigne* ii. iv. (1632) 201 He hath assuredly understood and inned the very imagination, and the true conceit of the Author.

†**5.** *intr.* To go in, to enter; in 17th c. to make a beginning, to begin. *Obs.*

(The OE. instance is a late variant reading; it has app. no historical connexion with the 17th c. use.)

K. Ælfred *Boeth.* xxxii. §1 (Bodley MS. *a* 1200), He [se læcecræft] bið swiðe biter on muðe..ac he werodað syððan he innað, & bið liðe on ðam innoðe [*Cotton MS. a* 1000, ac he weredað siððan he innan bið, & swiðe liðe on ðæm innoðe]. **1633** P. Fletcher *Purple Isl.* i. i, The warmer Sun the golden Bull outran And with the Twins made haste to inne and play. **1639** J. Clarke *Paræmiol.* 13 We inne diversely, but end alike.

‖**in** (ɪn). *Lat. prep.* **I.** The Latin preposition *in*, (with the ablative case) 'in', (with accusative) 'into', enters into a number of phrases, chiefly of legal, logical, philosophical, or ecclesiastical origin, now or formerly current in English, of which the chief are given below.

In early use, the *in* seems occasionally to have been taken as the English preposition, and is thus found printed in roman type, while the rest of the phrase is in italics.

1. in ab'sentia, in (his, her, or their) absence.

1886 *Edin. Univ. Cal. 1885/6* 141 Conferred *in absentia.* **1938** *Times Lit. Suppl.* 5 Feb. 88/3 The clergy in general are likewise condemned, though *in absentia.* **1955** *Times* 11 July 9/3 A Goa military court has sentenced *in absentia* Peter Alvarez, former president of the Goa National Congress. **1961** L. Mumford *City in History* xiii. 386 Residences of royal power *in absentia*, like Londonderry, Philippeville, and Christiansand. **1965** *Listener* 7 Oct. 544/2 The *Occult Diary*..goes on principally to describe his relationship, both actual and telepathically *in absentia*, with his third wife. **1972** D. Bloodworth *Any Number can Play* xi. 92 The renegade..has been condemned to death *in absentia.*

2. in 'actu, in practice (as opp. to theory or potentiality).

[*a* **1680** S. Charnock *Works* (1684) II. 171 Some say..we are active *in actu exercito*, but not *in actu signato.* **1749** Chesterfield *Let.* 5 Dec. (1932) IV. 1453, I can only allow him *in actu primo* (to talk logic) and seldom *in actu secundo.*] **1902** W. James *Varieties Relig. Experience* xviii. 451 Whatever we may be *in posse*, the very best of us *in actu* falls very short of being absolutely divine. **1905** —— *Ess. Radical Empiricism* ix. 239 Radical empiricism, unable to close its eyes to the transitions caught *in actu*, accounts for the self-transcendency or the pointing..as a process that occurs within experience. **1907** —— *Pragmatism* vi. 222 Health *in actu* means, among other things, good sleeping and digesting.

3. in 'antis. *Class. Arch.* [see ANTA], denoting a building in which the side walls are prolonged beyond the front and the pilasters terminating them are in line with the columns of the façade.

1848 W. Smith *Dict. Greek & Roman Antiquities* (ed. 2) 1105/2 There were never more than ten columns in the end portico of a temple; and when there were only two, they were always arranged in that peculiar form called *in antis.* **1875** *Encycl. Brit.* II. 388/2 Temples in Antis, with a portico of two or four columns in front. **1955** L. Woolley *Alalakh* ii. 71 It is tempting to restore this as a temple *in antis*, with two columns between the projecting walls (or between reveals from those walls) on the analogy of Niqme-pa's palace front. **1973** *Country Life* 20 Sept. 763/3 Its original first-floor portico, with Ionic columns *in antis*, survives.

4. in 'capite, in chief (see CHIEF *sb.* 12), holding directly from the crown.

[**1275** in *Rot. Hundred.* (1812) d ij b, Jurati dicunt quod civitas London...tenetur in capite de domino Rege.] *a* **1558** Staunford *Kinges Prerog.* i. (1567) 6 a, It extendes to any landes..whether they be holden of the king in capite or not. **1593** Shaks. *2 Hen. VI*, iv. vii. 129 Men shall hold of mee in Capite. **1767** Blackstone *Comm.* II. 60 All tenures being thus derived..from the king, those that held immediately under him..were called his tenants in capite, or in chief.

5. in contu'maciam, applied to sentences given against persons in contempt.

1892 in *Stanford Dict. Anglicised Words* 460/2. **1918** *Wireless World* VI. 156 It was only because they were for the moment beyond reach of the Italian Courts that they were condemned *in contumaciam.* **1923** *Westm. Gaz.* 28 Dec., Several of these verdicts were passed in contumaciam.

6. in 'corpore = *in vivo.*

1906 *Rep. Brit. Assoc. Adv. Sci. 1905* 552 The nature of the substance contained in the serum was discussed. *In vitro* it has little power. *In corpore*,..the amount..necessary..is of no consequence. **1969** *Nature* 12 July 189/1 This is the first reported case of *in corpore* fertilization and development in the sea urchin, *Arbacia punctulata.*

7. in 'distans, at a distance (see ACTIO IN DISTANS).

1890 W. James *Princ. Psychol.* I. ii. 47 This blindness was probably due to inhibitions exerted *in distans.* **1909** —— *Pluralistic Universe* viii. 311 Remote professorial minds operating *in distans* upon conceptual substitutes for him [*sc.* God] alone.

8. in ex'tenso, at full length.

1826 *Congress Debates* II. ii. 1767 It might not suit the views of the Government, to give, *in extenso*, the instructions given to our Ministers. **1855** Thackeray *Newcomes* II. xx. 196 The evening papers gave Rowland's address, *in extenso.* **1906** *Rep. Brit. Assoc. Adv. Sci. 1905* 257 Star Streaming. By Professor J. C. Kapteyn. (Ordered by the General Committee to be printed *in extenso.*) **1965** *Mod. Law Rev.* XXVIII. v. 618 Nearly every section is quoted *in extenso.*

9. in ex'tremis, in the last agonies, at the very point of death.

a **1530** R. Pace *Let. to Wolsey* in Ellis *Orig. Lett.* Ser. iii. I. 199 Mr. Dean off Paulis hath lyen continually synst Thursdaye *in extremis* and is not yitt dedde. **1646** Evelyn *Diary* (1850) I. 230 An Irish Friar..confessing him..and other ceremonies used *in extremis.* **1764** G. Williams in J. H. Jesse *G. Selwyn & Contemp.* (1843) I. 321 The Master of the Rolls..tumbled out of his chair last Sunday at church, and is, they say, *in extremis.* **1840** Barham *Ingol. Leg., Lady Rohesia*, His lady was *in extremis.*

10. in 'forma 'pauperis, in the form or guise of a poor person (exempted from liability to pay the costs of an action: see PAUPER *sb.*); hence, in a humble or abject manner.

1592 Greene *Quip Upst. Courtier* E j b, The poore man that..pleads in *forma pauperis.* **1605** Sylvester *Du Bartas* ii. *Law* Ded. to Ld. Chauncelor, He is compell'd, *in forma pauperis*, To Plead. **1641** *Spiritual Courts* in *Harl. Misc.* (Malh.) IV. 420 Many of them were *in formâ pauperis.* **1711** Steele in *Spect.* No. 78 ¶10 We have been oppressed so many Years, that we can appear no other way, but *in forma pauperis.* **1883** *Wharton's Law Dict.* (ed. 7) 409/1 A person admitted to sue *in formâ pauperis* is not entitled to costs from the opposite party, unless by order of the Court or a judge.

11. in infi'nitum, to infinity, without end (cf. AD INFINITUM).

1564 Grindal *Fun. Serm. Emp. Ferdinand* in *Rem.* (1843) 4 And so *in infinitum*, until all years and days be clean past and expired. **1674** Boyle *Excell. Theol.* ii. iii. 146 Each of these parts is divisible..into other corporeal parts, lesser and lesser, *in infinitum.* **1790** Reid *Let. to J. Gregory* Wks. (1846) 86/1 Diminish the time, *in infinitum*, and the effect of a centripetal force is diminished *in infinitum.*

12. in 'limine, on the threshold, at the very outset.

1804 *Edin. Rev.* July 297 One objection, *in limine*, we feel ourselves called upon to make. **189.** S. Leathes *Testim. Earlier Proph. Writ.* 7 The supposition of super-natural teaching, which is *in limine* rejected by the critics.

13. in 'loco, (*a*) in place of; esp. **in loco pa'rentis**, in the place or position of a parent.

1710 *New Hampshire Prov. Papers* (1869) III. 434 George Jaffrey was this day elected..a Representative *in loco* Mark Hunkin. [**1785** Ld. Thurlow in W. Brown *Chancery Cases* (1820) I. 426 A provision..made directly, or as a portion by a parent or person *loco parentis.*] **1828** *Congress Debates* IV. i. 1335, I now stand to them, *in loco parentis*, in the place of a father. **1854** Thackeray *Newcomes* I. xvi. 157, I stood towards him *in loco parentis*; because he was as a child to me.

(*b*) in a (*or* the) place; locally.

1671 Locke *Essay Draft B* (1931) §94 p. 200 If it be said that it [*sc.* the soul] cannot change place, because it has none, for spirits are not *in loco* but *ubi*, I desire that distinction may be put into English or any other language and made intelligible. **1908** *Practitioner* Jan. 22 Some toxin either generated in loco..or reaching the skin from some distant focus of disease.

14. in 'medias 'res, into the midst of affairs, into the middle of a narrative.

1786 Han. More *Bas Bleu* 33 But be as epic as I please, And plunge at once in medias res. **1819** Byron *Don Juan* i. vi. **1883** Black *Yolande* I. xiii. 253 For good or ill, she determined to plunge *in medias res.*

15. in me'moriam, to the memory of, in memory of. Common as the commencement of an epitaph or commemorative inscription. Hence, after the title of Tennyson's poem, used as *sb.* = A memorial poem or writing.

1850 Tennyson (*title*) In Memoriam A.H.H. Obiit MDCCCXXXIII. **1895** *Daily News* 19 Oct. 6/1 The in memoriam of a bereavement, a breviary of a sorrowing parent's love.

16. in 'nomine, in the name (of): applied to (*a*) a motet or antiphon in fugal style, probably so called because originally used of a composition set to a text in which these words occurred, e.g., the Introit 'In nomine Jesu', the Psalm 'Deus, in nomine tuo'; (*b*) a free fugue in which the answer does not exactly correspond with the subject.

1636 C. Butler *Princ. Musick* 91 The *In-nomine's* of Parsons, Taverner, D. Ty, etc. **1876** Stainer & Barrett *Dict. Mus. Terms* s.v., The *in nomines* which exist are chiefly the production of composers of the 16th century. **1970** W. Apel *Harvard Dict. Mus.* (ed. 2) 412/2 Purcell's two 'In

nomine' compositions represent a late attempt at revival of the form.

17. in 'nubibus, in the clouds; not yet settled or decided; also, incapable of being carried out.

1583 BABINGTON *Commandm.* To Gentl. Glamorgan, Both the fee and freehold of the Church is in suspence, and *in nubibus.* **1624–5** J. CHAMBERLAIN in *Crt. & Times Jas. I* (1848) II. 506 The French match is still *in nubibus*, and few or none know yet what to judge of it. **1717–18** EYRE in Gilbert *Cases in Law & Equity* (1760) 266 It would Occasion great Delay, should the Plaintiff be put to take out a new Writ, whilst the Business is thus *in Nubibus.* **1848** THACKERAY *Van. F.* lxvi, 'Bah', said the other, 'the concert is a concert *in nubibus*'.

18. in 'nuce, in a nutshell, in a condensed form.

1854 GEO. ELIOT tr. *Feuerbach's Essence Christianity* II. xxii. 214 The religious man is happy in his imagination; he has all things *in nuce*; his possessions are always portable. **1948** L. SPITZER *Linguistics & Lit. Hist.* iii. 100 A reduction *in nuce* of the general aesthetics of Racine. **1972** *Times Lit. Suppl.* 7 Apr. 382/1 A grand summation and cosmology *in nuce.* **1973** *Times Lit. Suppl.* 26 Oct. 1307/1 The idea of the modern family as social democracy *in nuce.*

19. in 'partibus (infi'delium), in the regions of infidels; in countries inhabited by unbelievers. In *R.C. Ch.* describing a titular bishop in an uncivilized or a heretical country: see BISHOP 1 b.

1687 in Ellis *Orig. Lett.* Ser. III. IV. 314 The King having ..recommended Father Phillip Ellis, Dr. Gifford, and Dr. Smith, to be Bishops *in partibus.* **1787** BECKFORD *Italy* (1834) II. xiv. 73 He is become Archbishop, *in partibus.* **1885** *Catholic Dict.* (ed. 3) 88/2 Bishops *in partibus* can attend general councils.

20. in 'pectore = *in petto* (see PETTO).

1858 N. WISEMAN *Recoll. Last Four Popes* vii. 333 The Pope made this speech..in this form: 'Moreover, *we create* a cardinal of the Holy Roman Church,..whom, however, we reserve *in pectore.*' **1876** *Encycl. Brit.* V. 98/1 The change which Paul III. introduced consisted in confining the secret of the unpublished nominations [of cardinals] to his own breast, keeping it '*in pectore*'. **1963** *Times* 29 May 10/2 One suggestion about the current affairs discussed with Cardinal Cicognani is that the Pope is preparing to reveal the identities of the three Cardinals whom he created *in pectore* in 1960—a device by which the Pope may keep to himself the names of certain new appointments if he feels that the moment is inopportune to publish them.

21. in per'petuum, in perpetuity, to all time, for ever.

1642 tr. *Perkins' Prof. Bk.* iii. §239 If Lands or Tenements bee devised by Will, unto a man and his Assignees, *In perpetuum.* **1807** *Edin. Rev.* July 362 We ought not to annex, *in perpetuum*, to the office of cabinet-minister, one or two hundred more of close boroughs.

22. a. in pontifi'calibus, in pontificals, in the proper vestments of a pope, cardinal, archbishop, etc.

1494 FABYAN *Chron.* VII. 607 The deane and the chanons of Paulys, with whom also *in pontificalibus* came the archebysshop of Caunterbury. **1577–87** HOLINSHED *Chron.* III. 892/2 The cardinall..sat in pontificalibus vnder his cloth of estate. **1679** LUTTRELL *Brief Rel.* (1857) I. 29 At night were several bonefires, and particularly a very great one at Temple gate, where was a pope burnt in pontificalibus. **1788** H. WALPOLE *Remin.* iv. in *Lett.* 1857 I. p. cxii, He offered to proclaim the Pretender at Charing Cross in pontificalibus.

b. Also *in his, their,* etc. *pontificalibus*: see PONTIFICALIBUS.

23. in 'propria per'sona, 'in proper person', in his (her, etc.) own person.

1654 GAYTON *Pleas. Notes* III. vii. 113 He Knight-Errant, if he steale *in propria persona*, is Uncalendred for ever. **1762** SMOLLETT *Sir L. Greaves* xvi. (1793) II. 85 Believing he was the devil *in propria persona.* **1817** BYRON *Let. to Moore* 28 Jan. in Moore *Lett.* etc. (1830) II. 72 Marianna S**, *in propriâ personâ*..without a single word seizes her said sister-in-law by the hair. **1828** LYTTON *Pelham* III. xvii. 280 As they have never beheld me before, it would very little matter if I went in *propriâ personâ.* **1851** GEO. ELIOT *Let.* 28 Jan. (1954) I. 344 When am I to have Mr. Bray's promised letter? or to see him in propria persona. **1958** *Times* 19 Aug. 11/2 *Cosi fan tutte* was performed in the great hall of the Residenz, where Leopold and Wolfgang Mozart themselves had often been *in propriis personis.* **1967** *Listener* 23 Mar. 408/3 In Figaro he [*sc.* Rossini] has created the ideal character from which he can speak *in propria persona.*

24. in re, (*a*) in reality; (*b*) *Logic*, = EXTRA DICTIONEM (opp. *in voce*); (*c*) *Metaph.*, (of universals) dependent for their existence on the existence of the particulars that instantiate them, as Aristotle held; having real or objective, not merely mental, existence, but not separately from particulars (cf. ANTE REM); also **in 'rebus**; (probably taken by modern writers from Duns Scotus (*c.* 1264–1308)); (*d*) in the matter of, referring to, = RE *sb.*[2]

(*a*) **1602** W. WATSON *Decacordon* 145 Wherein the Iesuits ..had any speciall commoditie or gaine *in re* or *in spe* thereby. *a* **1680** S. CHARNOCK *Works* (1684) II. 853 Their Sacraments and ours were the same *in re*, though diverse in signs.

(*b*) **1847** [see IN DICTIONE]. **1906** [see EXTRA DICTIONEM].

(*c*) **1879** W. JAMES *Coll. Ess. & Rev.* (1920) 112 If they begin with a clear nominalistic note, they are sure to end with a grating rattle which sounds very like *universalia in re*, if not *ante rem.* **1904** [see ANTE REM]. **1907** W. JAMES *Pragmatism* vi. 221 Like wealth, health also lives *in rebus.* **1927** [see ANTE REM]. **1952** R. I. AARON *Theory of Universals* ii. 26 Locke here denies the *In Re* theory... The white itself is not *in re* but 'in the mind'. **1953** H. H. PRICE *Thinking & Experience* i. 10 The traditional Aristotelian doctrine of *universalia in rebus. Ibid.* ii. 56 There *are* universals, existing and subsisting *in rebus.*

(*d*) **1877** *Times* 18 Jan. 11/4 Court of Bankruptcy... In re B. and L. Harris. This was an adjourned sitting for public examination. The bankrupts, Messrs. Benjamin and Lawrence Harris, were merchants. **1886** *Athenæum* 20 Nov. 671/2 The alleged 'misrepresentation' *in re* Squeers *v.* Bentley. **1896** E. TERRY *Let.* 7 Dec. in *Ellen Terry & Bernard Shaw* (1931) 136 What do you mean by saying (in re The Philanderer) it is dull and bestial? **1955** *Times* 29 June 3/7 *In re* Hillier ([1954] 1 W.L.R. 700), but it did not occur to counsel in that case. **1972** *Times* 22 Feb. 14/5 In *In re Scarisbrick* ([1951] Ch 622) the Court of Appeal held that the distinction between a public or charitable trust and a private trust depended on [etc.].

25. in se *Philos.*, in itself. So **inseity** (ɪn'siːɪtɪ), in-itselfness.

1868 W. JAMES *Let.* 5 Apr. in R. B. Perry *Tht. & Char. W. James* (1935) I. xv. 269 To the Greeks a thing was evil only transiently and accidentally... Bystanders could remain careless and untouched—no after-brooding, no disinterested hatred of it *in se*, and questioning of its right to darken the world. **1879** —— *Coll. Ess. & Rev.* (1920) 94 Substance *in se* cannot be directly imaged by feeling. **1909** —— *Meaning of Truth* vii. 167 Useful to test truth by, the matrix of circumstance, he thinks, cannot found the truth-relation *in se.* **1899** A. E. GARVIE *Ritschlian Theol.* ii. 48 The thing which we represent for ourselves is an existence in itself (inseity). **1940** *Mind* XLIX. 177 The *otherness* of 'self' and 'other' need in no wise conceal the inseity of the 'other' from the 'self'.

26. in 'situ, in its (original) place; in position. Also *attrib.*

1740 W. STUKELEY *Stonehenge* iv. 21 Eleven of them are standing *in situ.* **1817** *Edin. Rev.* Mar. 180 Granite and clay slate are those [rocks] alone which appear *in situ.* **1845** J. C. ATKINSON in *Proc. Berw. Nat. Club* II. No. 13. 134 We shall find it *in situ* close by. **1894** *Nation* (N.Y.) 31 May 405/1 What actually remains *in situ* is the walls of the foundations. **1912** *Proc. Amer. Philos. Soc.* LI. 490 *In situ* forests occur frequently in shale beds. **1940** *Archit. Rev.* LXXXVII. 102/2 The foundations to receive the superstructure are formed of concrete in-situ posts. **1968** *Daily Tel.* 4 Nov. 9/6 Constructed entirely in in-situ concrete..it resembles a fortified gateway to the main hospital buildings. **1971** *Nature* 24 Dec. 432/1 The Department of the Environment, which has responsibility for *in situ* historical monuments in England.

27. in 'statu na'scendi, in the process of creation, formation, or construction.

1890 W. JAMES *Princ. Psychol.* II. xvii. 11 Black can only be felt in contrast to white..and in like manner a smell, a taste, a touch, only, so to speak, *in statu nascendi*, whilst, when the stimulus continues, all sensation disappears. **1927** B. MALINOWSKI *Sex & Repression in Savage Society* IV. i. 180 And let us clearly and explicitly recognize that we can never observe it [*sc.* culture] *in statu nascendi.* **1948** *Sci. News* VII. 112 The ENIAC has been in use for some time, the other machines are still *in statu nascendi.*

28. in 'statu pupi'llari, as a pupil or ward; under scholastic discipline; at the universities, designating all who have not the degree of Master.

1855 *Newsp. & Gen. Reader's Compan.* §571 A young Englishman..while still in statu pupillari. **1860** *Once a Week* 21 July 95/2, I fully admit that in later years we are all of us apt to grow sentimental about the traditions of our respective schools—I merely deny that we do so whilst we remain *in statu pupillari.* **1862** THACKERAY *Philip* III. x. 214 Other young women who are kept by over-watchful mothers too much *in statu pupillari.* **1882** *Standard* 25 Dec. 5 (Stanford), Academic and urban magnates, fellows, and tutors have predominated over guests who are *in statu pupillari.* **1903** 'SIGMA' *Personalia* 172 One of those dusky potentates *in statu pupillari*, who were nearly always represented at the Master's dinners. **1930** *Sunday Times* 12 Oct. 26/2 The possession of a motor-car makes it easy for a person *in statu pupillari* to spend a large part of his existence elsewhere than in the University. **1965** *Rep. Comm. Disciplinary Powers Vice-Chancellor & Proctors* (Univ. Oxf.) 8 Difficulties might arise if graduates *in statu pupillari* who, very often, do the same sorts of things as undergraduates, such as running university clubs, are not bound by the same regulations as their undergraduate colleagues.

29. in 'statu 'quo (ante, prius, or **nunc)**, in the same state (as formerly or now).

1602 W. WATSON *Decacordon* 174 The seculars are but *in statu quo prius*, and cannot be in a worse then they are in at this present. *c* **1645** HOWELL *Lett.* (1650) II. xlvii. 60 In *statu quo nunc* I am grown useless and good for nothing. **1687** *New Eng. Hist. & Gen. Reg.* (1850) IV. 222 Matters will never be againe *in Statu quo* here. **1688** T. TRAMALL in *Hatton Corr.* (Camden) II. 98 Things were put in statu quo, only Mr. Charnock was left out. **1717** LADY M. W. MONTAGU *Let. to Lady* [*Rich*] 17 June, However, my face is still *in statu quo.* **1817** BYRON *Let. to Murray* 2 Apr. in Moore *Life* (1830) II. 94 Of course I had the box remitted *in statu quo.*

30. in te'rrorem, as a warning, in order to terrify or deter others.

1612 J. CHAMBERLAIN in *Crt. & Times Jas. I* (1848) I. 213 Most men believe..that only it was done *in terrorem.* **1771** SMOLLETT *Humph. Cl.* To Dr. Lewis, 2 June, This [the pillory] is so far from being accounted a punishment *in terrorem*, that it will probably make his fortune. **1845** M. PATTISON *Ess.* (1889) I. 18 Exhibited *in terrorem* to the assembly. **1960** *Times* 12 Apr. 13/7 They operate mainly *in terrorem*; the potential tax avoider will not incur the cost and complication of a transaction unless he can be reasonably sure of its result. **1970** *Internat. & Compar. Law Q.* XIX. II. 214 Perhaps no more would be necessary than a criminal sanction against rent usury operating *in terrorem*, as exists in German law. **1971** *Daily Tel.* 1 July 4/6 This idea that the Treaty of Rome, like diamonds, is forever, is held *in terrorem* over people.

attrib. **1799** WASHINGTON *Lett.* Writ. 1893 XIV. 153 If the augmented force was not intended as an *in terrorem* measure the delay in Recruiting it is unaccountable.

31. in 'toto, as a whole, absolutely, completely, without exception.

[*a* **1639** WOTTON *Surv. Educ.* in *Reliq.* (1654) 293 Always I except Prodigious Forms, and meer natural Impotencies, which are unmanageable *In toto Genere.*] **1798** WASHINGTON *Lett.* Writ. 1893 XIV. 135 It was impossible to comply with them, and difficult to discriminate, for which reasons it was deemed best to reject them *in toto.* **1811** G. CONSTABLE *Let.* 31 Dec. in J. Constable *Corr.* (1962) I. 73 If my opinion was requested it would not be to give up your female acquaintance in toto. **1858** GREENER *Gunnery* 357 Many writers condemn *in toto* the Minié principle and its cup. **1893** STEVENSON *Catriona* 32, I decline *in toto* to hear more of it. **1954** M. BERESFORD *Lost Villages* vi. 186 In fact we cannot be all that certain that it was all that much less *in toto.* **1955** *Times* 4 May 22/6 These amounts, *in toto*, fall short of our requirements if the business is to continue to expand as it is doing. **1965** *Mod. Law Rev.* XXVIII. 595 Lord Cameron's reasoning is applicable *in toto* to the situation in *The Acrux.*

32. in 'transitu, in passing, on the way.

1620 *Reliq. Wotton.* (1654) 334, I had, *in transitu*, conferred with him your Christian ends. **1665** SOUTH *Serm. at Court* 23 They only please and affect the mind *in Transitu.* **1787** GROSE in Durnford & East *Rep.* (1794) II. 76 The consignor may seize the goods *in transitu*, if the consignee become insolvent before the delivery of them. **1882** LD. SELBORNE in *Law Rep.* 7 App. Cas. 576 But for the indorsement..the right of stoppage in transitu would have been well exercised.

33. in 'utero, in the uterus or womb, unborn.

1713 W. CHESELDEN *Anat. Humane Body* IV. iii. 170 It seems highly necessary, that the Ducts thro' which the Body receives Nourishment after the Birth, shou'd be kept open by a Fluid passing that way whilst it is in *Utero.* **1728** CHAMBERS *Cycl.* s.v. *Generation*, For that Dr. Harvey could never discover any thing of it *in utero.* **1795** W. TURNBULL in *Mem. Med. Soc. London* IV. 364 (*title*) A case where small-pox was communicated from the mother to the child in utero. **1871** A. MEADOWS *Manual of Midwifery* (ed. 2) III. ii. 156 The placenta, which..still remains for awhile in utero. **1901** [see STOMATITIC *a.*]. **1964** M. CRITCHLEY *Developmental Dyslexia* xiii. 75 Any theory of minimal brain damage—whether or not sustained *in utero*—is also unconvincing. **1966** *Lancet* 24 Dec. 1403/2 Stiehm et al. conclude that raised levels of γM or γA globulins at birth are presumptive of in-utero infection.

34. in 'vacuo, in a vacuum or empty space.

1660 EVELYN *Diary* (1872) I. 364 Various experiments *in vacuo.* **1716** CHEYNE *Philos. Princ. Relig.* I. 114 Supposing a body moving *in vacuo.* **1812** SIR H. DAVY *Chem. Philos.* 138 A wire of platina may be preserved in a state of intense ignition *in vacuo.* **1937** [see ELECTRONIC *a.* 1]. **1942** *Tee Emm* (Air Ministry) II. 140 It is more correct to regard a running fix as a means of approximating the position 'in vacuo' so to speak, when more precise methods are unobtainable. **1955** *Times* 25 May 15/3 Whatever meaning people might ascribe to the word 'tramp' *in vacuo.*

35. in 'vino 'veritas, truth comes out under the influence of alcohol; a drunken person tells the truth.

1594 LYLY *Mother Bombie* in *Wks.* (1902) III. III. iii. 199, I perceiue sober men tel most lies, for *in vino veritas.* **1616** T. ADAMS *Divine Herball* 27 And though the Prouerbe be, *In vino veritas*; yet as drunke as he is, you shall neuer haue truth break out of his lips. **1831** DISRAELI *Young Duke* III. IV. vi. 50 There was Cogit, who, when he was drunk, swore that he had had a father; but this was deemed the only exception to *in vino veritas.* **1927** D. H. LAWRENCE *Mornings in Mexico* 174 They say: *in vino veritas.* Bah! They say so much! **1936** N. MARSH *Death in Ecstasy* xii. 145 We had a clear case of *in vino veritas.* *a* **1953** E. O'NEILL *Long Day's Journey* (1956) IV. 145 Got to tell you now. Something I ought to have told you long ago... Not drunken bull, but 'in vino veritas' stuff.

36. in vitro ('viːtrəʊ). *Biol.* [lit. 'in glass'.] In a test tube, culture dish, etc.; hence, outside a living body, under artificial conditions; also *attrib.*, performed, obtained, or occurring *in vitro.*

1894 GOULD *Dict. Med.* 623/2 *In vitro*, in the glass; applied to phenomena that are observed in experiments carried out in the laboratory with microörganisms, digestive ferments, and other agents, but that may not necessarily occur within the living body. **1901** *Jrnl. Exper. Med.* V. 355 Serum obtained by immunising with one race did not necessarily give more than a trace of reaction in vitro and none whatever in vivo when tested with another race. **1912** BROQUET & SCOTT tr. *Burnet's Microbes & Toxins* x. 193 The neutralisation in an ordinary test-tube of a toxin by an antitoxin was one of the first and most brilliant '*in vitro*' experiments in immunity. **1925** C. H. BROWNING *Immunochem. Stud.* 14 These alcoholic extracts possess the property of reacting with heterophile antibody *in vitro.* **1955** *Sci. Amer.* June 88/3 Streptomycin has little or no activity against fungi *in vitro* , but it..controls blue mold of tobacco ..and rot of sugar beets—all fungus diseases. **1962** *Lancet* 5 May 936/2 The in-vitro results show that fucidin is very active..in sterilising cultures of staphylococcus at higher concentrations. **1974** *Nature* 22 Nov. 302/1 Onset of rapid haemoglobin formation in the blood islands of the developing chick blastodisc, both *in ovo* and *in vitro*, commences at the stage of the 6- to 7-somite embryo.

37. in vivo ('viːvəʊ). *Biol.* Within the living organism; also *attrib.*, performed, obtained, or occurring *in vivo.*

1901 [see *in vitro*]. **1947** *Sci. News* V. 78 Some chemical interchange between the plant and the bacteria must take place *in vivo* and be largely responsible for nitrogen fixation. **1962** VAN HEYNINGEN & WALEY in A. Pirie *Lens Metabolism Rel. Cataract* 336 Proteolytic enzymes are often characterized by their action on substrates which are not known to be the natural substrates of the enzyme *in vivo.* **1973** *Nature* 16 Feb. 457/2 The *in vivo* experiments were also carried out using mice bearing a 14 day old tumour.

38. In many other phrases: e.g. ***in ab'stracto***, in the ABSTRACT (*a.* 5); ***in ar'ticulo mortis***, in the article of death (cf. ARTICLE 2 b); at the point, or in the instant of death; ***in 'banco***, on the bench (see BANCO); ***in 'camera***, in (a judge's) private room, not in open court (see CAMERA 1 b); ***in 'cathedra***, in the chair of office, in the seat of authority: see CATHEDRA 2; ***in co'mmendam***: see COMMENDAM 1; ***in con'creto***, in the CONCRETE (*a.* 5); ***in de'liciis***, in favour, in affection; ***in de'posito***, in deposit (see DEPOSIT *sb.* 2 and DEPOSITUM); ***in 'dubio***, in doubt, in uncertainty; ***in duo'decimo***, ***in 'embryo***, ***in equi'librio***, ***in 'esse***: see the sbs.; ***in ex'celsis***, in the highest (heavens), in the highest degree; ***in 'fieri***: see FIERI; ***in fla'grante de'licto***, in the very act of committing an offence (cf. DELICT b); also (colloq.) ***in flagrante***; ***in 'folio***: see FOLIO 5; ***in 'foro consci'entiæ***, in the court of conscience (cf. FORUM 2 b); ***in 'fumo***, in smoke (in *Alchemy*); ***in 'genere***, in the genus, in general; ***in 'medio***, in the middle, in an unsettled state; ***in 'pari ma'teria***, in a like case or position; ***in 'plano***, on a plane surface; ***in 'posse***, in potentiality, in the condition of being possible: see POSSE; ***in po'tentia***, in potentiality; ***in 'primis***: see IMPRIMIS; ***in prin'cipio***, in the beginning: the first words of Genesis and St. John's Gospel in the Vulgate; ***in 'puris natu'ralibus***, in 'pure naturals' (cf. NATURAL *sb.*); in a purely natural condition, hence 'stark naked'; ***in 'rerum na'tura***, in nature, in the physical world; ***in 'sæcula sæcu'lorum***, to the ages of ages, to all eternity, for ever and ever; ***in 'specie***, in specific form, in the precise or identical form: see SPECIE; ***in 'tenebris***, in darkness, in a state of ignorance or doubt; ***in 'terminis***, in express terms, expressly.

1602 W. WATSON *Decacordon* ix. 310 Which if he can bring to passe..then shall the French be so fleeced *in *abstracto*..to be distracted out of their wits. **1630** [see *in concreto* below]. **1884** W. JAMES *Ess. Radical Empiricism* (1912) xii. 269 Let us fall back from all concrete attempts and see what we can do with his notion of through-and-throughness, avowedly taken *in abstracto*. **1920** D. H. LAWRENCE *Lost Girl* vii. 127 She existed *in abstracto* as far as he was concerned. **1928** O. JESPERSEN *Internat. Lang.* I. 22 Those who have spoken in favour of the idea *in abstracto*. **1933** *Times Lit. Suppl.* 13 Apr. 256/2 Towards the religious life of India Dr. Söderblom is kinder than many critics, but he, of course, is dealing with it *in abstracto* and not in its cruder manifestations. **1951** PARSONS & SHILS *Toward Gen. Theory Action* i. 99 The actor *in abstracto* is simply a set of properties by which he can be classified; in action he is involved in a system of relationships. **1967** *Word* XXIII. 385 We remember that the verb expresses nothing but the verbal idea in abstracto without containing any actualizing elements such as tense, mode, or voice. **1596** *Estate Eng. Fugitives* 75 (Stanf.) Visitation of sicke men *in *articulo mortis*. **1617** J. CHAMBERLAIN in T. Birch *Cour & Times James I* (1848) II. 1 The late lord chancellor left this world, being visited *in articulo mortis*, or not full half an hour before. **1825** SCOTT *Talisman* in *Tales Crusaders* IV. xv. 344 Nor did I mention it, save *in articulo mortis*,..to yonder reverend hermit. **1929** *Encycl. Brit.* VI. 231/1 Those under discipline were allowed to receive the eucharist when *in articulo mortis*. **1868** J. T. BENJAMIN *Sales* (1884) 409 The only case decided *in banco, that has been found on this point. **1872** E. BROWNING *Exposition Laws Marriage & Divorce* 5 The Judge may, and usually does sit **in camerâ* to hear suits for nullity of marriage, where the matters to be disclosed are unfit for the public ear. **1882** *Standard* 26 Dec. 5/7 The case is one that in England would be heard *in camera*. **1955** *Times* 25 June 11/7 All documents filed in the Court be confidential and kept secret, and that every application for an adoption order should be heard and determined *in camera*. *Ibid.* 14 July 5/1 A naval court martial held *in camera* to-day in H.M.S. Victory at Portsmouth. **1966** P. MOLONEY *Plea for Mersey* 34 Fearing that the evidence might be a bit lurid the judge ordered 'Clear the court! The evidence will be heard in camera.' The accused immediately asked 'What the Hell's "in camera"..?' **1970** *Guardian* 8 Aug. 9/2 The expurgated version of the in-camera sessions. **1602** W. WATSON *Decacordon* ix. 310 Though by the law Salique the Lady Infanta may be..put from her..lawfull claime to the whole kingdome of France, *in *concreto*. **1630** T. ADAMS *Workes* 633 And the Popes haue so wrought it and brought it about now, that they will not onely *in abstracto* bee had in reuerence; but *in concreto* be feared with obseruation. **1798** A. F. M. WILLICH *Elem. Critical Philos.* 39 A bare idea of a possible science, which is no where given *in concreto*. **1885** W. JAMES in *Mind* X. 41, I may satisfy him that the words mean for me just what they mean for him, by showing him *in concreto* the very animals and their arrangements, of which the pages treat. **1902** —— *Varieties Relig. Experience* ii. 31 Not a deity *in concreto*, not a superhuman person, but the immanent divinity in things ..is the object of the transcendentalist cult. **1936** C. S. LEWIS *Allegory of Love* vi. 289 The symbol..fits all, and gives *in concreto* a characteristic of our life. **1621** BURTON *Anat. Mel.* II. ii. IV. (1676) 172/2 Their cats which they have **in deliciis*. **1615** J. CHAMBERLAIN in *Crt. & Times Jas. I* (1848) I. 362 The place of Lord Warden of the Cinque Ports hath..remained in the lord chamberlain's hands as **in deposito*. **1602** W. WATSON *Decacordon* i. 21 Though to vs vnknowne to be of the same church triumphant **in excelsis*. **1882** *Athenæum* 23 Dec. 854 It is an uncritical guide-book *in excelsis*. **1927** *Melody Maker* Sept. 923/3 By all means strive to become a Frankie Trumbauer, or a Jimmy Dorsey, for that is musicianship and style *in excelsis*. **1965** *New Statesman* 30 Apr. 690/1 Tchaikovsky is the Victorian Artist *in excelsis*, grand, noble, compassionate. **1612** T. SHELTON tr. *Cervantes's Hist. Don Quixote* III. viii. 190 All was done *in *Flagrante*, there was no leisure to giue me torment, the cause was concluded. **1772** 'JUNIUS' *Lett.* II. lxviii. 314 A person positively charged with feloniously stealing, and taken *in flagrante delicto*, with the stolen goods upon him, is not bailable. **1876** tr. *P.J. van Beneden's Animal Parasites* 2 The sharper passes for an honest man as long as he has not been taken *in flagrante delicto*. *a* **1930** D. H. LAWRENCE *Phoenix* (1936) 17 But at last she caught him *in flagrante*. **1942** E. PAUL *Narrow St.* ii. 16 He saw, not his cringing wife and the imaginary lover he had always sworn to catch *in flagrante delicto*, but his swarthy waiter and a strange girl. **1972** D. BLOODWORTH *Any Number can Play* i. 2 A shocked Font-le-Baume caught them *in flagrante*. **1749** FIELDING *Tom Jones* IV. xi, As his Intention was truly upright, he ought to be excused *in *Foro Conscientiæ*. **1605** B. JONSON *Volpone* II. i. Wks. (Rtldg.) 183/2 When these practitioners come to the last decoction, blow, blow, puff, puff, and all flies *in *fumo*. **1474** CAXTON *Chesse* IV. i. *heading*, Of the chesse borde *in genere how it is made. **1609** HOLLAND *Amm. Marcell.* Annot. XIV. a iv, I leave it **in medio*. **1884** *Law Times* LXXVIII. 131/1 To keep the property *in medio* until the rights of the parties were ascertained. **1867** WHARTON *Law Lexicon* (ed. 4) 485/2 **In pari materiâ*, dealing with the same subject-matter. **1932** *Times Lit. Suppl.* 16 June 436/3 The comparison..on page 106 is not quite *in pari materia*: the three and a half million Churchfolk are adults, the thirty-five the whole population. **1955** J. L. AUSTIN *How to do Things with Words* (1962) ix. 112 Even the minimum physical action..is, being a bodily movement, *in pari materia* with at least many of its immediate and natural consequences. **1662** EVELYN *Chalcogr.* (1769) 98 Solid bodies may seem swelling, and to be embossed **in plano* by art. **1610** B. JONSON *Alch.* II. iii, The egg..is a chicken *in *potentia*. *c* **1386** CHAUCER *Prol.* 254 So plesaunt was his **In principio*. *c* **1570** *Pride & Lowl.* (1841) 23 Sure thou were not in principio. **1602** W. WATSON *Decacordon* vii. 204 As inclined to seeke for good to eschewe euill, and wishing after *summum bonum*, if *in *puris naturalibus* they could haue obtained it. **1633** SANDERSON *Serm.* II. 34 Compare thy self and him..*in puris naturalibus*, and thou shalt find no difference. **1859** *Harper's Mag.* June 46/2 The natives.. may be found not only in their primitive state, but even *in puris naturalibus*. **1930** D. H. LAWRENCE *Nettles* 18, I thought it was a commonplace That a man or a woman in a state of grace In puris naturalibus, don't you see, Had normal pudenda, like you and me. **1584** R. SCOT *Disc. Witch.* XIII. v. 292 Such as except we had seene..we would not beleeve to be **In rerum natura*. **1686** J. DUNTON *Lett. fr. New-Eng.* (1867) 21 Stuff'd with Wonders of my own Invention, and such as never were in rerum natura. **1593** PEELE *Edw. I* Wks. (Rtldg.) 382/2 To follow my fortune *in *secula seculorum*. **1716** POPE *Let.* 9 July (1956) I. 347 We begin to wish you had the singing of our Poets..to yourselves, in *Sæcula Sæculorum*. **1841** THACKERAY *Misc. Ess.* (1885) 219 So Pride and Hatred continue *in sæcula sæculorum*. **1890** [see *atom-like*]. **1940** *Penguin New Writing* I. 10, I thought of the British Raj as an unbreakable tyranny, as something clamped down, in saecula saeculorum, upon the will of prostrate peoples. **1668** DRYDEN *Even. Love* IV. ii, But, how she lost it, and how it came upon your finger, I am yet **in tenebris*. **1646** HAMMOND *Wks.* (1674) I. 254 'Tis said of Christ in Scripture **in terminis* that he was the day-spring to give light to them which sit in darkness. **1808** SCOTT *Life Dryden* in *Dryden's Wks.* I. 98 A contradiction *in terminis*.

II. The Italian prep. = Latin *in*, as in the phrases *in fresco*, *in petto*, for which see the sbs.

in, obs. f. INN; var. HIN *pron. Obs.*, him.

in-, *pref.*[1], the prep. and adv. IN, in combination with verbs, verbal derivatives, and other words. In original compound verbs, unaccented *in-* passed in WS. into *on-* (cf. IN *prep.*, General Sense): e.g. Goth. *inliuhtjan*, OHG. *inliuhten*, OE. *onliehtan* to enlighten, illuminate; Goth. *intandjan*, OE. *ontęndan* to set on fire, Goth. *inwandjan*, OE. *onwęndan* to turn, change. In such of these verbs as survived in ME., *on-* was normally reduced to *a-*. But, in late OE., numerous new verbs in *in-* appeared as glosses or literal renderings of Latin verbs in *in-*, e.g. *inbláwan* = L. *inflāre*, *inspīrāre* to blow in, *inbringan* = L. *inferre* to bring in, *inlǽdan* = L. *intrōdūcĕre* to lead in. The formation of these in similar circumstances continued in ME. to the close of the 14th c., when numerous examples occur in Wyclif. Among the ME. examples are *inclepe*, L. *invocāre* to call in, *indelve*, L. *infodĕre* to dig in, *inȝette*, L. *infundĕre* to pour in, *inloȝe*, L. *inflammāre* to inflame, *inwlappen*, L. *involvĕre* to enwrap, *inwrite*, L. *inscrībĕre* to inscribe. Few or none of these verbs have survived into mod. English. In OE. the adv. *inn*, *in*, was also freely used in collocation with verbs of motion or change of state. The position of the adv. was, with the finite tenses, variable; in the infinitive it generally stood before the vb., and in derived verbal sbs. and adjs. always so. In this position the adv. came at length to be written in combination with the vb., e.g. *income-n*, *incoming*, *income* sb., *indwelle-n*, *indwelling*, *indweller*, etc. In the infinitive and other verbal forms *in-* remained movable, and is now regularly placed after the verb, as in *come in*, *go in*, *call in*, *lead in*, etc.; but the derived sbs. and adjs. in which the position of *in-* was invariable, have become regular compounds with stress on *in-*, thus *incoming*, *income*, *incomer* (beside *come in*), *indwelling*, *indweller* (beside *dwell in*), *inlet*, *insight*, *intake*, etc. See IN *adv.* 11. (Cf. the parallel case of German verbs with movable prefixes, as *eingehen*, *einzugehen*, *eingegangen*, *gehe ein*, *er geht ein*, *wenn er eingeht*, *eingang*, *eingehend*; *eingeben*, *eingeber*; etc.) There are also various other formations, OE., ME., or modern, in which this prefix occurs, usually with the sense 'in, within, internal', e.g. OE. *inȝehyȝd*, *inȝeþanc* internal thought, intent, *inland* demesne land, ME. *inwit* conscience; mod. *inborn*, *inside*, *inward*, etc. In a few instances prepositional phrases with *in-* have given rise to attributive combinations, as *in-college* residents, *in-door* occupations.

As to the blending of this prefix and IN- *pref.*[2] in later use, see at the end of the latter.

b. *Geom.* Representing INSCRIBED *ppl. a.* 3, as in *in-centre*, *in-circle*, *in-sphere*.

in-, *pref.*[2], repr. L. *in-* adv. and prep., used in combination with verbs or their derivatives, less commonly with other parts of speech, with the senses 'into, in, within; on, upon; towards, against', sometimes expressing onward motion or continuance, sometimes intensive, sometimes transitive, and in other cases with little appreciable force.

Form-history. In earlier L., *in-* was generally retained unchanged before all consonants; but in later times it was assimilated to the following consonant, becoming *il-* before *l*, *im-* before a labial, *ir-* before *r*. These changes are retained in Eng.: e.g. *il-late*, *im-bue*, *im-mit*, *im-pel*, *ir-radiate*: see IL-[1], IM-[1], IR-[1]. In OF., in inherited words, *in-*, *im-*, became *en-*, *em-*; but learned words derived or formed from L., esp. in later times, regularly retained *in-*, *im-*. The French words were adopted in Eng. in their current form; but from the 14th c. onward, there was a growing tendency in words in which the L. derivation was evident, to change *en-*, *em-* back to L. *in-*, *im-*, as in the words of learned origin. This was even extended to some words which were not obviously, or not at all of L. origin, including some of those in which *en-*, *em-* was, as a living formative, prefixed to radicals of OE. or other origin. (See EN-.) Conversely, some words directly from L. were formed with the French *en-*, *em-*. Hence, a large number of words occur in the 15th and 16th c. with both forms of the prefix, and some have retained both forms to the present day, either with no distinction of sense, as in *enclose*, *inclose*, *enquire*, *inquire*, or with differentiation of use, as *ensure*, *insure*. The general tendency (though with numerous exceptions) has been to establish *in-*, *im-*, in words evidently derived from L., reserving *en-*, *em-*, for words formed in French and not having a L. type, or in which the L. type is disguised by phonetic change, and for words formed in Eng. on the analogy of these. In this Dictionary, current words are placed under their usual form, whether *in-* (*im-*) or *en-* (*em-*), or, in unsettled cases, in that which, on grounds of etymology or analogy, appears to be the preferable form; obsolete words have been dealt with on the same principles, and cross-references have been given to the form under which each word is treated.

Since IN-[1] and IN-[2] are identical in form, and to a great extent in sense, they come in later use to be felt as one and the same prefix; and it is this resulting prefix which appears in many words of later formation, formed upon native substantives or adjectives, in which *in-*, *im-*, has affinities at once with the prefix *en-*, *em-*, from French, and with OE. *in-*.

in-, *pref.*[3], the Lat. *in-*, cognate with Gr. α-, αν-, Com. Teut. *un-*, prefixed to adjs. and their derivatives, rarely to other words, to express negation or privation; as *fēlix* happy, *infēlix* unhappy, *utilis* useful, *inutilis* useless, *nocēns* hurtful, *innocēns* unhurtful, innocent, *doctus* learned, *indoctus* unlearned. In earlier Latin, *in-* was used before all consonants, but in later times was subjected to the same assimilations as IN-[2], as in *il-litterātus* illiterate, *im-mensus* unmeasured, immense, *ir-regulāris* without rule, irregular, and was besides reduced to *i-* before *gn*, as in *i-gnārus* ignorant; *i-gnōscĕre* not to take cognizance of, to overlook, forgive. In a few OF. words, L. *in-* became *en-* as in IN-[2], e.g. *inimīcus*, OF. *enemi* enemy, L. *invidia*, OF. *envie* envy; but most French words containing this prefix are of learned formation, and retain L. *in-*

(*il-*, *im-*, *ir-*); as is the case also in Eng. with words derived either through French, or from L. direct. In Eng. *in-* (*il-*, *im-*, *ir-*) is a living negative suffix for words of Latin or Romanic origin, freely used, even when no corresponding formation appears in Latin; in this use it interchanges to some extent with the OE. negative *un-*, which is used in native or thoroughly naturalized words, e.g. *incautious*, *uncautious*, *in-*, *un-ceremonious*, *in-*, *un-certain*, *in-*, *un-communicative*, *in-*, *un-devout*, *in-*, *un-distinguishable*. In such cases the practice in the 16th and 17th c. was to prefer the form with *in-*, e.g. *inaidable*, *inarguable*, *inavailable*, but the modern tendency is to restrict *in-* to words obviously answering to Latin types, and to prefer *un-* in other cases, as in *unavailing*, *uncertain*, *undevout*.

in-, *pref.*[4], of Teut. origin, prefixed to OE. and ME. adjs., with intensive force. In origin akin to IN- *pref.*[1], with the sense 'inly', 'intimately', 'thoroughly', and hence 'exceedingly', 'very'. Examples: OE. *indryhten* most noble, *infród* very wise, *inhold* thoroughly loyal; ME. *inred* deep red. (On this prefix in the cognate langs., see Hœfer '*Das intensive* IN', in *Germania*, new ser. III. 61.)

-in, *suffix*[1]. *Chem.* A modification of the chemical suffix -INE[5], introduced into systematic nomenclature by Hofmann *a* 1860, used systematically in Watts' *Dict. Chem.* in 1866, and subsequently adopted by the Chemical Society, for the names of neutral substances, such as glycerides, glucosides, bitter principles, colouring matters, and proteids, which are thus distinguished from names of alkaloids and basic substances in -INE. Examples, *albumin*, *casein*, *fibrin*, *globulin*, *mucin*, *myosin*, *pepsin*; *cerebrin*, *chitin*, *chondrin*, *gelatin*, *lecithin*; *acetin*, *alizarin*, *aloïn*, *arbutin*, *cerotin*, *curcumin*, *dextrin*, *hæmatin*, *indigotin*, *inulin*, *isatin*, *palmitin*, *purpurin*, *salicin*, *ulmin*, *vanillin*. Some of these were formerly spelt with *-ine*, and in that spelling had passed into popular use before the rectification of the nomenclature, esp. *dextrine*, *gelatine*, *margarine*, which are still commonly so spelt in non-scientific use. Also used systematically to form the names of certain unsaturated six-membered heterocyclic monocyclic compounds having no nitrogen atom in the ring, as *dioxin*. Cf. -INE[5].

1881 *Chemical Society, Instructions to Abstractors* ¶16 Basic substances should invariably be indicated by names ending in *-ine*, as *aniline*, instead of *anilin*, the termination *-in* being restricted to certain neutral compounds, viz. glycerides, glucosides, bitter principles, and proteids, such as *palmitin*, *amygdalin*, *albumin*. **1928** [see -INE[5]]. **1940** in PATTERSON & CAPELL *Ring Index* 21. **1957** E. H. RODD *Chem. Carbon Compounds* IVA. 4 Six membered rings in their least hydrogenated forms have names ending in '-in' when non-nitrogenous and '-ine' when nitrogenous.

-in, *suffix*[2], an obs. variant of -INE[1] in adjs., as *feminin*, *genuin*, etc.; also an occasional variant of -INE[4]:—L. *-īna*, as in *ruin*.

-in, *suffix*[3]. The adverb IN used as a suffix originally designating a communal act of protest by Negroes in the United States against racial segregation (cf. SIT-IN); subsequently indicating any group protest or large gathering for some common purpose. Examples are very numerous: e.g. ***apply-in***, BE-IN, ***bury-in***, ***chain-in***, ***cook-in***, ***drive-in***, ***eat-in***, FISH-IN, ***hate-in***, ***join-in***, ***kiss-in***, ***kneel-in***, ***lie-in***, LOVE-IN, ***marry-in***, ***mill-in***, ***pedal-in***, ***play-in***, ***pray-in***, ***read-in***, ***scrub-in***, ***sew-in***, ***shout-in***, ***sit-in***, ***sleep-in***, ***solve-in***, ***stall-in***, ***stand-in***, ***study-in***, ***sweep-in***, ***swim-in***, ***teach-in***, ***wade-in***, ***walk-in***. Chiefly attached to verb stem, but also to adjectives, e.g. ***fat-in***, ***nude-in***, and to substantives designating a participant in the protest or gathering, e.g. ***kneeler-in***, ***sitter-in***, ***wader-in***.

1960 *Newsweek* 16 May 34/1 Into the already-roiled waters of the South, Negroes will wade this summer in a campaign to break down segregation at public beaches—a wade-in counterpart to the widespread lunch-counter sit-ins of recent weeks. **1960** in *Amer. Speech* (1961) XXXVI. 282 Negro college students have initiated a new 'kneel-in' campaign..by attending services at white protestant Atlanta churches. **1961** in *Ibid.*, He called for *walk-ins* in art galleries and museums, *drive-ins* at segregated motels and roadside ice cream stands, *sit-ins* in court rooms, *study-ins* at segregated schools, and *bury-ins* to integrate cemeteries. *Ibid.*, Negro teen-aged boys in an impromptu swim-in at an undesignated beach drew a crowd of 300 shoving, shouting Memorial Day bathers and boaters yesterday. *Ibid.* 284 A Chattanooga, Tenn., Negro stand-in demonstrator says his son's life has been threatened. **1961** *Guardian* 26 May 11/1 The United Presbyterian Church of America.. recommended a 'kneel-in' campaign as a manifestation of the belief in the right of all people to worship regardless of race. **1961** *N.Y. Times* 9 Nov. 37 Last night, twenty-four students gathered in the campus library for an all-night 'read-in' demonstration. **1963** *Time* 30 Aug. 12 Demonstrators..prostrate themselves before bull-dozers at construction-site 'lie-ins'. *Ibid.*, The 'pray-in' at churches. **1964** *Economist* 25 Apr. 376/1 The threatened 'stall-in' of thousands of motor cars [by Negroes]. **1965** *N.Y. Times* 28 Mar. 2E/8 There have been sit-ins, lie-ins, stand-ins, eat-ins, shop-ins, sleep-ins, swim-ins, and sing-ins. **1965** *Economist* 19 June 1401/2 This week Mr Johnson countered the university 'teach-ins', protesting against his foreign policy, with a cultural 'play-in' demonstrating his respect for the arts. **1966** *Daily Tel.* 12 Aug. 11/3 William Bryden-Smith, aged 10, who wrote to us, wants to take part in the cook-in. **1967** *Ibid.* 3 Mar. 23/7 A 'kiss-in' to protest against Michigan University's stern regulations on 'public displays of affection' was described by students last night as the most enjoyable form of demonstration yet devised. **1967** *New Statesman* 17 Mar. 356/3 Last week police arrested scores of teenagers at a rave-in, and left-wing Catholics staged a pray-in. **1967** *Times* 28 Mar. 4/7 It took the police three hours to clear a 'mill-in' at the intersection of Haight and Ashbury streets, celebrated as the chief resort of the bearded and sandalled 'hippies' who travel to San Francisco from all over the United States to signify their dissent from modern society. **1967** *Observer* 11 June 10 If everyone was fat there'd be no war. No one would pass the physical.—A speaker at the New York Central Park 'Fat-in'. **1967** *Listener* 10 Aug. 188/3 This is a very exciting inversion of psychedelic soulfulness, a hate-in. **1967** *World Study* Dec. 7/1 *Chain-in*, demonstrators locking themselves to a city hall pillar,..until the mayor listened to their grievances. *Ibid.* 7/2 *Stand-in*, demonstrators lining up at a theater ticket booth until given admission to the theater, not simply to a segregated section in the rear of the house but to any area where a white patron—or a member of any race—may sit. **1968** *Lebende Sprachen* XIII. 68/1 Their action fits into a wave of unofficial, unconnected *nude-ins* so far this year in Golden Gate Park, starting with freebeachers dancing nude at the great be-in. **1968** *Listener* 26 Dec. 849/1 Charge of the Light Brigade, 20th-century style: a lie-in at Porton Microbiological Research Establishment. **1969** *New Yorker* 3 May 31/1 Another rally was held at the Campus Center, followed by what was termed a 'mill-in' at the Army, Air Force, and Marine recruiting site. **1969** *Daily Tel.* 29 Jan. 1/6 About 20 of the militants..ended their vigil yesterday with a 3 a.m. 'swim-in' in the basement pool. *Ibid.* 2 July 18/3 Practical tests in revolutionary rhetoric ('shout-ins'), wall-defacement and anti-Establishment violence. **1970** *Ibid.* 2 Mar. 16 To teach-in..and sit-in..have now been added walk-in and work-in. The first means the occupation of premises outside undergraduates' recognised territory, the second a teach-in during vacation. **1971** *Guardian* 28 Sept. 15/3 A student sleep-in began last night. **1973** *Daily Tel.* 3 Dec. 13/8 College catering would be disrupted by students alternately boycotting canteens and then holding mass eat-ins.

-ina, *suffix*[1], a Latin feminine suffix found in *reg-ina* queen, extended in It. or Sp., and thence in Eng. use, to form feminine titles, as *czar-ina* (for Russ. *tsaritsa*), and female Christian names, as *Alexandr-ina*, *Angel-ina*, *Christ-ina*, *Clement-ina*, *Georg-ina*, *Thomas-ina*, *Wilhelm-ina*, etc. (Cf. -INE[4].) It occurs also as a formative of some other words, as in *concertina*, *seraphina*, etc., names of musical instruments.

-ina, *suffix*[2], in words which are the neuter pl. of L. adjs. in *-īnus*, and in mod.L. words formed after them, used (in agreement with *animālia* animals, understood) to form names of groups of animals related to some typical genus, as *Bombycina* (genus *Bombyx*), etc.

†**ina'bilitate**, *ppl. a. Obs. rare*[−1]. [f. med.L. *inhabilitātus*, pa. pple. of *inhabilitāre* to declare unfit, f. *inhabilis* unfit, unable, etc.] Declared unfit or unable, disqualified.

1577 HELLOWES *Gueuara's Chron.* 259 They..were inabilitate of all power to commaund or to gouerne.

†**inabilite**, *v. Obs. rare*[−1]. [ad. med.L. *inhabilitāre* (see prec.), or a. obs. F. *inhabilite-r* (Oresme, 14th c.): cf. INHABILITY.] *trans.* To declare ineligible (for an office); to disqualify.

1432–50 tr. *Higden* (Rolls) VIII. 448 Takynge their benefices, and inabilitynge þeim to eny benefice afterwarde.

inability (ɪnəˈbɪlɪtɪ). Also 6–7 inhab-. [f. IN-[3] + ABILITY: cf. It. *inabilità*, F. *inhabileté*.] The condition of being unable; want of ability, physical, mental, or moral; lack of power, capacity, or means.

14.. *Goodly Ballad* L'Envoye, I haue besought my ladies Sapience Of thy behalfe, to accept in game Thine inabilite. **1526** *Pilgr. Perf.* (W. de W. 1531) 130 Knowynge our owne fraylty & inabilite, we shall thynke our selfe vnworthy. **1651** tr. *Life Father Sarpi* (1676) 23 The temperament and complexion have a great part in the habilities or inhabilities of men. **1684** T. BURNET *Th. Earth* I. 214 The cause of that driness and decay, or other inhability in the solid parts. **1754** EDWARDS *Freed. Will* I. iv. 25 The word Inability..has Respect to some stated Defect. **1843** CARLYLE *Past & Pr.* I. i, Instead of noble thrift and plenty, there is idle luxury alternating with mean scarcity and inability.

†**b.** *spec.* Bodily infirmity. *Obs.*

1640 in Grant *Burgh Sch. Scotl.* II. xii. (1876) 368 In regairid of his old aige and inhabilitie of bodie. *a* **1834** LAMB *Let. to Southey* in Talfourd *Lett.* (1837) I. iv. 107 A good field for dwelling on sickness, and inabilities, and old age.

c. Const. *for* (†*to*) something; *to do*, *of doing* something.

1644 *Direct. Publ. Worship* 6 Their own inability to so great a Worke. **1660** R. COKE *Justice Vind.* 4 He tells you of childrens inability of judging. **1676** SOUTH *Serm.* (1697) I. 407 Their Inability for, and frequent contrariety to the bringing about such designs. **1697** *Ibid.* (1698) III. 41 That Infinitely Greater Inability..to present Him with any Thing, which they were not first Beholden to Him for. **1712** STEELE *Spect.* No. 437 ¶3 Good Nature is only an Inability of observing what is faulty. **1805** N. NICHOLLS *Let.* in *Corr. w. Gray* (1843) 49 A want of love for general society, indeed an inability to it. **1867** DICKENS *Let. to Miss Hogarth* 21 Jan. (1880) II. 272 My distressing inability to sleep at night.

†**inable, -ment**, obs. forms of ENABLE, -MENT.

1648 W. MOUNTAGUE *Devout Ess.* I. x. §6. 118 They owe much of these furtherances and inablements to the civill Discipline and Politique literature of Courts. *Ibid.* xv. §1. 267 That treasure which is dispensed to us for our inablements to this discharge.

in-a'bout, *adv. Sc.* [f. IN *adv.* + ABOUT *adv.*] In or into proximity; about or close to a place.

1813 W. BEATTIE *Tales* 4 (Jam.) Just as I entered in-about, My aunt by chance was looking out. *Mod.* Come in-about here. There was a lot o' fowk in-about yesterday.

†**in'abrogable**, *a. Obs. rare.* [IN-[3].] Not abrogable; that cannot be abrogated or revoked.

1617 COLLINS *Def. Bp. Ely* Ep. Ded. 5 Their authoritie is inabrogable.

in absentia: see IN *Lat. prep.*

in'abstinence. [IN-[3].] Want of abstinence; failure to abstain.

1667 MILTON *P.L.* XI. 476 What miserie th' inabstinence of Eve Shall bring on men. **1863** W. LANCASTER *Praeterita* 77 Man, Ape of all change, whose fierce inabstinence Gulps at illusion.

†**inab'stracted**, *ppl. a. Obs. rare.* [IN-[3].] Not abstracted.

16.. *Hooker's Eccl. Pol.* VIII. i. §5 Names betokening accidents unabstracted [*v.r.* inabstracted], do betoken not only those accidents, but also together with them the subjects whereunto they cleave.

†**ina'busively**, *adv. Obs. rare.* [IN-[3].] Not abusively, properly.

a **1677** LD. NORTH *Light in Way Paradise* (1682) 91 (T.) That infinite wisdom..which resideth in the Deity, and which makes power to consist inabusively only there, as in its proper sphere.

†**inac'centuated**, *a. rare.* [IN-[2].] Accentuated, emphasized.

1716 M. DAVIES *Athen. Brit.* II. 304 The Jacobit Mobs Skreeking and Bawling one on top of the other with inaccentuated Clamours and Barbarous Huees.

inaccentu'ation. [IN-[3].] Unaccented condition. Also *fig.*

1867 C. J. SMITH *Syn. & Antonyms* s.v. *Accent*, Smoothness. Inaccentuation... Equableness. **1882** E. C. BABER in *R. Geog. Soc. Suppl. Papers* I. I. 157 In every step and movement there was a decision and exactness widely different from the sluggish inaccentuation of the Chinese physique.

inac'ceptable, *a.* [IN-[3].] Not acceptable, unacceptable.

1878 LECKY *Eng. 18th C.* II. viii. 445 The French made propositions of peace, but they appeared utterly inacceptable. **1908** *Westm. Gaz.* 22 Oct. 7/1 The Turkish Foreign Minister replied that the proposal was inacceptable. **1934** A. S. C. ROSS in *Neuphilol. Mitt.* XXXV. 129 The perpetuation of a Victorian prudishness (inacceptable in philology beyond all other subjects). **1938** E. BEVAN *Symbolism & Belief* v. 108, I am in the company of others who find Professor Alexander's philosophy in this respect inacceptable. **1970** H. BRAUN *Parish Churches* xii. 160 Such dreariness being inacceptable to the parish churchman.. Gothic forms began..to represent the appropriate Anglican architecture.

Hence ˌ**inaccepta'bility**, the quality or condition of being inacceptable.

1922 *Glasgow Herald* 13 May 8 Whatever..France's attitude..might be, the inacceptability of the memorandum as a whole appears to render equally null in her eyes this detail. **1957** J. S. HUXLEY *Relig. without Revelation* (rev. ed.) iv. 75 The inacceptability, to my growing intellectual interest, of any Christian theology proffered to me.

†**inac'cesse**, *a. Obs. rare.* [ad. L. *inaccessus* unapproached, unapproachable, f. *in-* (IN-[3]) + *accessus*, pa. pple. of *accēdĕre* to approach.] Unapproachable, inaccessible.

1555 ABP. PARKER *Ps.* xciv. 266 My God was rocke: as inaccesse [*rime* stresse] My trust and confidence.

inaccessibility (ˌɪnæksɛsɪˈbɪlɪtɪ). [f. next + -ITY. Cf. F. *inaccessibilité* (17th c. in Hatz.-Darm.).] The quality or condition of being inaccessible; unapproachableness. Also *fig.*

1665 MANLEY *Grotius' Low C. Warres* 317 The inaccessibility of the Marishes frighted them from their Design. **1798** PENNANT *Hindoostan* II. 73 The partial inaccessibility bestowed on them by nature. **1833** *Penny Cycl.* I. 389/2 The Jungfrau..owes its name to its supposed inaccessibility. **1843** MILL *Logic* III. xxi. §4 Accounted for by..their inaccessibility to observation. **1864** *Spectator* 1403 Should we prove our reliance on his inaccessibility to error?

b. (with *pl.*) An inaccessible place.

1862 CARLYLE *Fredk. Gt.* IX. x. (1872) III. 154 Going from Stollhofen..up into the inaccessibilities.

inaccessible (ˌɪnækˈsɛsɪb(ə)l), *a.* (*sb.*) Also 6–7 *erron.* -able. [a. F. *inaccessible* (14th c. in Hatz.-Darm.), ad. late L. *inaccessibilis*, f. *in-* (IN-^{3}) + *accessibilis* ACCESSIBLE.]

1. That cannot be reached, entered, or got to; that cannot be scaled or penetrated.

1555 EDEN *Decades* 253 The south partes..inaccessable by reason of great heate. **1603** KNOLLES *Hist. Turks* (1638) 281 The desperat danger..in climbing the inaccessible mountain. **1610** SHAKS. *Temp.* II. i. 37 Vninhabitable, and almost inaccessible. **1718** LADY M. W. MONTAGU *Let. to Abbé Conti* 31 July, The harbour..[is] inaccessible almost six months in the year. **1846** GROTE *Greece* I. xvii. (1862) II. 433 Its inaccessible acropolis defied them.

2. *fig.* That one cannot come into personal or close relations with; not open to advances or influence, unapproachable.

1583 STUBBES *Anat. Abus.* I. (1879) 35 The Lord our God, a spiritual..substance, incomprehensible, immensurable, and inaccessible. *a* **1665** J. GOODWIN *Filled w. the Spirit* (1867) 431 Fortify the spirit..of a man, to make it inaccessible unto..cares and fears. **1781** GIBBON *Decl. & F.* xxxiv. (1869) II. 265 This savage hero was not inaccessible to pity. **1896** 'M. FIELD' *Attila* I. 19 Always inaccessible To any suitor.

†**3.** (tr. Gr. ἄαπτος.) 'Not to be touched, resistless, invincible.' *Obs.*

c **1611** CHAPMAN *Iliad* I. 550 Curb your tongue in time, lest all the Gods..Too few be and too weak to help thy punish'd insolence, When my inaccessible hands shall fall on thee.

B. *sb.* That which is inaccessible. *rare.*

1812 KEATINGE (*title*) Eidometrian Local, Victorial, and Military, for Inaccessibles.

inac'cessibleness. [f. prec. + -NESS.] The quality of being inaccessible; inaccessibility.

1612–15 BP. HALL *Contempl., O.T.* XII. viii, Them that trusted to the inaccessiblenesse of the place. **1627** H. BURTON *Baiting of Pope's Bull* Ep. Ded. 3 Whose case.. became the more desperate, through the inaccessiblenesse of intercessors. **1769** *Scots Mag.* Sept. 526/1 Haughtiness and inaccessibleness, are crimes in a servant of the public. **1844** EMERSON *Ess.* Ser. II. i. 33 The inaccessibleness of every thought but that we are in, is wonderful.

inac'cessibly, *adv.* [f. as prec. + -LY^2.] In an inaccessible manner or degree; unapproachably.

1708 *Brit. Apollo* No. 82. 2/1 God is Inaccessibly Glorious. *a* **1785** GLOVER *Athenaid* XXI. Poems (1810) 151/2 Friendship's unremitted care Still in Sandauce's chamber held the queen Sequester'd, inaccessibly immur'd. **1816** SHELLEY *Alastor* 503 O stream! Whose source is inaccessibly profound.

†**inac'cessional,** *a.* *Obs. rare.* [IN-^{3}.] Unapproachable.

1654–66 LD. ORRERY *Parthen.* 97 A Lady, who possest the several Beauties of shape, stature, complexion, and features in so inaccessional a degree. *Ibid.* 137 To raise your insolence to an inaccessional height.

†**inaccidentate,** *v. Obs.* [f. IN-^{2} + ACCIDENT *sb.* (sense 6) + -ATE^3.] *trans.* To unite with the 'accidents' (in reference to transubstantiation).

1579 FULKE *Heskins' Parl.* 257 He [Christ] is neither impanated, nor inuinated, nor inaccidentated.

†**ina'ccommodate,** *a. Obs. rare.* [f. IN-^{3} + ACCOMMODATE *ppl. a.*] Not suited, unsuited.

1657 TOMLINSON *Renou's Disp.* 697 Some things he disallowed of as inaccommodate.

ina'ccordance. [IN-^{3}.] = next.

1822–34 *Good's Study Med.* (ed. 4) I. 61 Another cause of irregularity..is an inaccordance of time, or manner.

ina'ccordancy. [IN-^{3}.] The quality of being inaccordant; want of agreement or harmony.

1822–34 *Good's Study Med.* (ed. 4) I. 295 The contractile power of the one follows instead of keeping pace with the contractile power of the other, or evinces some other mode of inaccordancy. *Ibid.* IV. 102 An incongruity, inaccordancy, or want of adaptation in the constituent principles.

ina'ccordant, *a.* [IN-^{3}.] Not accordant; not in agreement or harmony; inharmonious. Hence **ina'ccordantly** *adv.*

1822–34 *Good's Study Med.* (ed. 4) II. 403 [They] belong to the same genus in botany, however inaccordant they may appear to the eye of an ordinary spectator. *Ibid.* III. 327 Violent motions sometimes separately and sometimes synchronously, but inaccordantly as to the number of throbs in a given time. *Ibid.* IV. 373 An organ, whose common function is so inaccordant with such a production. **1851** *Beddoes' Poems* Mem. 19 This unhesitating sacrifice of partial but inaccordant beauty..is..among the surest tests of the true artistic mind.

ina'ccountable, *a. rare.* ? *Obs.* [IN-^{3}.] Not to be reasonably accounted for; unaccountable.

1684 T. BURNET *Th. Earth* I. 216 To imagine that his years are to be understood one way, and those of his fellow-patriarchs another, would be an inaccountable fiction.

inaccuracy (ɪnˈækjʊərəsɪ). [f. next: see -ACY, and cf. *accuracy*.] The quality or condition of being inaccurate; want of accuracy, exactness, or precision; with *an* and *pl.*, an instance of this, an inaccurate statement.

1757 SYMMER in Ellis *Orig. Lett.* Ser. II. IV. 400 An inaccuracy with regard to one of the great privileges of the House had..been suffered to slip. **1772** *Junius Lett.* lxviii. 343 An appearance of inaccuracy in the use of terms. **1824** L. MURRAY *Eng. Gram.* (ed. 5) I. 29 Some examples of inaccuracy, in the use of the verb without its nominative case. **1883** A. ROBERTS *O.T. Revis.* vi. 131 The historical inaccuracies which the book contains.

inaccurate (ɪnˈækjʊərət), *a.* [f. IN-^{3} + ACCURATE.] Not accurate; inexact, incorrect, erroneous.

1738 WARBURTON *Div. Legat.* II. vi. Wks. 1811 II. 301 Men going into Antiquity under the impression of modern ideas, must needs form very inaccurate judgements of what they find. **1775–8** TYRWHITT *Chaucer* App. to Pref. (1860) 5 *note*, Leland is also inaccurate..in representing the edition by Thynne as coming next after that by Caxton. **1875** JOWETT *Plato* III. 620 Inaccurate modes of expression.

Hence **in'accurateness,** inaccuracy.

1873 WAGNER tr. *Teuffel's Hist. Rom. Lit.* II. 564 There are numerous inaccuratenesses.

in'accurately, *adv.* [IN-^{3}.] In an inaccurate manner; not accurately; incorrectly.

1669 FLAMSTEED in Rigaud *Corr. Sci. Men* (1841) II. 78 These appearances, which I had not inaccurately calculated. **1794** SULLIVAN *View Nat.* II. 316 Phænomena, inaccurately observed very often, and not always very fairly recorded. **1875** JOWETT *Plato* (ed. 2) III. 42 Quoting or alluding to Homer inaccurately.

inacquaintance (ɪnəˈkweɪntəns). [IN-^{3}.] The being unacquainted; want of acquaintance.

1607 MARKHAM *Caval.* III. (1617) 57 The very inacquaintance therewith will make him tyer euen in his best strength. **1779–84** W. RUSSELL *Europe* IV. 290 (Jod.) An inacquaintance with the principle of gravitation. **1879** GEO. ELIOT *Theo. Such* 96 He..took his inacquaintance with doctrines for a creative dissidence.

inacqui'escent, *a.* [IN-^{3}.] Not acquiescent.

1818 SCOTT *Hrt. Midl.* xiii, In the same dry inacquiescent tone of voice and manner.

So †**inacqui'escency,** want of acquiescence.

1647 SPRIGGE *Anglia Rediv.* I. i. (1854) 6 From an inacquiescency and dissatisfaction with the success of the present.

inact (ɪnˈækt), *v.*^{1} [f. IN-^{2} + ACT *v.*]

†**1.** *trans.* To bring into activity; to actuate.

1647 H. MORE *Philosoph. Poems* 348 *note*, The Mundane spirit..inacted by Psyche. **1660** —— *Myst. Godl.* x. ix. 514 He is inacted by the envy of Satan against the Kingdome of Christ. **1662** GLANVILL *Lux Orient.* xiv. 145 The soul..was united with the most subtile and æthereal matter that it was capable of inacting.

2. *intr.* To act *in* or *within. rare.*

1830 *Fraser's Mag.* I. 513 The principle is the all in all, precedes all, inacts in all.

inact, *v.*^{2}, obs. form of ENACT.

inaction (ɪnˈækʃən). [f. IN-^{3} + ACTION *sb.*: cf. F. *inaction* (1690 in Hatz.-Darm.).] Absence of action or activity; inertness, supineness.

1707 *Curios. in Husb. & Gard.* 63 In Winter, the Trees are in a state of Inaction. **1796** BURKE *Let. to Ld. Rockingham* Wks. 1842 II. 393 That your lordship should meet your friends with some settled plan either of action or inaction. **1861** STANLEY *East. Ch.* i. (1869) 35 In regard to missions the inaction of the Eastern Churches is well known. **1868** [see INACTIVITY b]. **1874** GREEN *Short Hist.* iii. §2. 120 The revelation of a danger at home..shook him out of his contemptuous inaction.

Hence **in'actionist,** one who advocates inaction; a member of a party of inaction.

1892 *Temple Bar Mag.* May 50 It is..his schemes for the reconstruction of society that most raise the gall of the great inactionist, who..fumes at interference.

inactivate (ɪnˈæktɪveɪt), *v.* [f. INACTIV(E *a.* + -ATE^3.] *trans.* To render inactive. So **in'activated** *ppl. a.*

1906 *Jrnl. Physiol.* XXXIV. p. xxxvi, If only the decomposition of the substrate is considered, heat inactivates enzymes completely. *Ibid.*, The presence of inactivated enzyme has a marked influence on the reaction between active enzyme and substrate. **1927** HALDANE & HUXLEY *Animal Biol.* ix. 189 When unaccustomed proteins enter their system, they [*sc.* higher animals] can..destroy or inactivate them. **1949** *Jane's Fighting Ships 1949–50* 358 She has been 'inactivated', and is laid up in a state of preservation as a potential fighting ship. **1955** *Times* 11 June 6/4 It said that the vaccine is composed of three types of viruses, mixed together after they had been inactivated or killed, but in some cases live viruses were found in the final mixture after tests. **1962** *Lancet* 5 May 941/1 The pattern of serological response to inactivated poliovirus vaccines has been..well documented. **1971** J. PHILIPS *Escape a Killer* (1972) II. ii. 136 The moment we inactivate the fence, we sound an alarm.

Also **inacti'vation,** the process of inactivating.

1906 DORLAND *Med. Dict.* (ed. 4) 353/2 *Inactivation*, the destruction of the activity of a serum by the action of heat or other means. **1936** *Brit. Jrnl. Psychol.* XXVI. 394 We shall employ the term 'impulse' in describing our experiments as implying the conscious activation and inactivation of the motor apparatus. **1946** *Nature* 27 July 121/1 The primary factor in heat damage seems to be an inactivation of the cell. **1968** *Economist* 6 July 16/3 Does the splendid nonsense word coined by the Americans, the 'inactivation' of Khe Sanh, signal another step in de-escalation?

inactivator (ɪnˈæktɪveɪtə(r)). [f. prec. + -OR.] That which inactivates; also, an individual considered in respect of his or her speed of metabolizing and so inactivating a drug in the body.

1944 *Biol. Abstr.* XVIII. 2662/3 (Index), Inactivator of vit. B_1 in diets of foxes. **1946** *Nature* 10 Aug. 201/1 The inactivator or inactivators involved are susceptible to heat and do not pass through a Seitz filter. **1960** *Times* 11 Nov. 17/2 Individuals could be divided into two categories: rapid and slow inactivators of the drug. **1970** PASSMORE & ROBSON *Compan. Med. Stud.* II. ii. 14/1 Patients who are 'slow inactivators' of isoniazid are more likely to develop peripheral neuritis if given the usual dose.

inactive (ɪnˈæktɪv), *a.* [f. IN-^{3} + ACTIVE: cf. F. *inactif* (1771 in Hatz.-Darm.).] **1.** Not active; characterized by absence of action or activity; not disposed to act; inert, indolent, sluggish; passive, quiescent.

1725 POPE *Odyss.* View Epic. Poem §3 Led away by the seeming Charms of an idle and inactive life. **1789** W. BUCHAN *Dom. Med.* (1790) 85 The inactive are continually complaining of pains of the stomach. **1818** CRUISE *Digest* (ed. 2) III. 231 The title to a barony, which has descended upon, and is vested in coheirs, remains in them in an inactive and dormant state. **1837** WHEWELL *Hist. Induct. Sc.* (1857) I. 159 This Alexandrian period, so inactive and barren. **1838** THIRLWALL *Greece* xxii. III. 207 The Spartans..were not entirely inactive this summer. **1866** ODLING *Anim. Chem.* 155 A converter of inactive or free, into active or combined oxygen. **1883** *Manch. Exam.* 13 Dec. 4/1 The money market to-day was very inactive.

2. *Chem.* [tr. F. (*moléculairement*) *inactif* (J. B. Biot 1840, in *Ann. de Chim. et de Physique* LXXIV. 403).] Not rotating the plane of polarization of polarized light. Often qualified by *optically*.

Pasteur adopted the term from Biot (*Jrnl. de Pharm. et de Chim.* (1848) XIII. 449).

1853 L. PASTEUR in *Chem. Gaz.* 1 Sept. 323 The latter [body]..resists isomeric transformation, and remaining without alteration in the quinicine, gives this its feeble deviation to the right. The other group, which..is very active, becomes inactive when the quinine is heated so as to become converted into quinicine; so that quinicine is nothing but quinine in which one of the active constituent groups has become inactive. **1857** W. A. MILLER *Elem. Chem.* III. v. 334 It [*sc.* another modification of tartaric acid] has been termed by Pasteur, inactive tartaric acid, in allusion to its want of action upon polarized light. **1905** *Jrnl. Physiol.* XXXII. p. xxxix (*heading*) The formation of inactive arginine by enzymes from proteids which yield optically active arginine on hydrolysis with acids. **1961** L. F. & M. FIESER *Adv. Org. Chem.* iii. 83 Properties of the two active and two inactive forms of tartaric acid are given in Table 3.2. A noteworthy point is that the *dl-* form, racemic acid, melts at a higher temperature than the optically active components.

So **in'activeness,** inactivity.

1678 C. HATTON in *H. Corr.* (Camden) I. 164 Complaining to yᵉ King of yᵉ weeknesse of yᵉ King's bench, by reason of yᵉ inactivenesse of yᵉ Lᵈ Ch. Justice.

in'actively, *adv.* [f. prec. + -LY^2.] In an inactive manner; inertly, sluggishly.

1730–6 in BAILEY (folio). **1755** in JOHNSON. [J. quotes Locke (*Educ.* §125), 'whether he inactively loiters it away', but in all edd. examined the word is 'unactively'.] **1837** HALLAM *Hist. Lit.* III. ii. §6 This pope was not inactively occupied in the great cause of subduing the Protestant heresy. **1876** BANCROFT *Hist. U.S.* xliii. V. 22 The Continental Congress..waited inactively for his appeals.

inactivity (ɪnækˈtɪvɪtɪ). [IN-^{3}. Cf. F. *inactivité* (1790 in Hatz.-Darm.).] The quality or condition of being inactive; want of activity; inertness, sluggishness; passiveness, quiescence.

1646 SIR T. BROWNE *Pseud. Ep.* I. v. 18 By a temperamentall inactivity we are unready to put in execution the suggestions or dictates of reason. ? **1723** POPE *Let. to Gay* 21 July, Lett. 1735 I. 326 Poor Fenton..died at Easthamstead, of Indolence and Inactivity. **1738** SWIFT *To Dr. King* 1 Virtue conceal'd within our breast, Is inactivity at best. **1830** KATER & LARDNER *Mech.* iii. 33 The term inactivity implying the absence of all force.

b. Phrase. ***masterly inactivity.***

1791 MACKINTOSH *Vind. Gallicæ* i. (1837) 44 The Commons, faithful to their system, remained in a wise and masterly inactivity, which tacitly reproached the arrogant assumption of the Nobles. **1831** CALHOUN *Wks.* (1874) V. 143 If the Government should be taught that the highest wisdom of a state is a wise and masterly inactivity, an invaluable blessing will be conferred. **1848** —— *Sp. Oregon Quest.* ibid. IV. 286, I venture to say 'a wise and masterly inactivity', in despite of the attempt to cast ridicule upon the expression. **1867** J. WYLLIE in *Edin. Rev.* Jan. [**1868** G. DUFF *Pol. Surv.* 71 The much-sneered-at policy of masterly inaction.]

i'nactor, obs. form of ENACTOR.

1614 RALEIGH *Hist. World* IV. vii. §1 Chosen Gouernours of the State, and inactors of Solons lawes.

in actu: see IN *Lat. prep.*

inactuate (ɪnˈæktjuːeɪt), *v. arch.* [f. IN-^{2} + ACTUATE.] *trans.* To make active, put in action, stir into activity.

1651 H. MORE *Second Lash* in *Enthus. Tri.* (1656) 179 How magnificent a state is the Soul of man in, when the life of God, inactuating her, shoots her along with himself through Heaven and Earth. **1652** H. MORE in R. Ward *Life More* (1710) 292 Those [Souls]..do very highly and vigorously Inactuate the Matter which falls to their Share for their Vehicles. **1662** GLANVILL *Lux Orient.* xiv. 160 The plastick in them is too highly awakened, to inactuate only an aerial body. [**1881** SHORTHOUSE *J. Inglesant* (1882) I. xvii. 310.]

Hence **inactu'ation,** a bringing into activity, the condition of activity.

1662 GLANVILL *Lux Orient.* xiii. 138 That they should be inconsistent in the supremest exercise and inactuation, is to me as probable. *Ibid.* xiv. 145 They [the creatures] were

then constituted in the inactuation and exercise of their noblest and most perfect powers.

inadaptability (ɪnədæptə'bɪlɪtɪ). [IN-³.] Want of adaptability; incapacity for adaptation.
1840 *Tait's Mag.* VII. 662 The inadaptibility of the soil. **1881** *Macm. Mag.* XLIV. 117 An inadaptability to their social environments.

ina'daptable, *a. rare.* [IN-³.] That cannot be adapted; incapable of adaptation.
In mod. Dicts.

inadaptation (ɪnædəp'teɪʃən). [IN-³.] Want of adaptation; the condition of not being adapted.
1855 in HYDE CLARKE *Eng. Dict.*

ina'daptive, *a.* [IN-³.] Not adaptive.
1886 *Athenæum* 9 Oct. 471/1 Among extinct ungulates there are two types of foot-structure—one adaptive, such as is seen to-day, and one inadaptive.

ina'dept, *a. rare.* [IN-³.] Not adept.
1875 H. S. CUNNINGHAM *Chron. Dustypore* (1877) 167 Is this the race which proclaims itself inadept at amusements, and which..loves to take its very pleasures sadly?

inadequacy (ɪn'ædɪkwəsɪ). [f. next, after *adequacy*.] The condition or quality of being inadequate; insufficiency.
1787 BONNYCASTLE *Astron.* xv. 244 The inadequacy of his natural powers. **1818** SCOTT *Rob Roy* xvii, My own inadequacy to sustain the task of a dissembler. **1834** PRINGLE *Afr. Sk.* ix. 291 The inadequacy of the income for the support of a family. **1879** FROUDE *Cæsar* i. 2 Inadequacy to some unforeseen position.

inadequate (ɪn'ædɪkwət), *a.* (and *sb.*) [IN-³.]
A. *adj.* **a.** Not adequate; not equal to requirement; insufficient. Also as *sb.*
1675 BOYLE *Reconcileablen. Reason & Relig.* I. ii, We can have but inadequate conceptions of them. **1690** LOCKE *Hum. Und.* II. xxxi. (1695) 207 Inadequate Ideas are such, which are but a partial, or incomplete representation of those Archetypes to which they are referred. **1792** *Anecd. W. Pitt* II. xxiii. 49 There had been a bargain, but the terms were inadequate. **1824** SYD. SMITH *Wks.* (1867) II. 192 It is astonishing what unworthy and inadequate notions men are apt to form of the Christian faith. **1880** C. R. MARKHAM *Peruv. Bark* xix. 214 He would then..have received some, though probably very inadequate, remuneration.
b. Const. *to*, and with *infin.*
1751 JOHNSON *Rambler* No. 126 ¶6 We must conclude ourselves safe when we see no danger, or none inadequate to our powers of opposition. **1788** GIBBON *Decl. & F.* xl. (1869) II. 476 His revenues were found inadequate to his expences. **1874** GREEN *Short Hist.* vi. §5. 318 The ordinary resources of the Crown..were inadequate to meet the expenses of war.
B. As *sb.* An inadequate person; one whose personality is in some way insufficient to meet the expectations of society.
1962 *Guardian* 7 Nov. 8/4 How can prison help a social inadequate through his troubles? **1963** T. PARKER *Unknown Citizen* 166 The majority of them are in fact the inadequates of whom Charlie Smith is typical. **1966** *Listener* 18 Aug. 226/1 The people that we are accustomed to call inadequates or weak characters. **1971** *Guardian* 26 Mar. 14/1 So-called 'inadequates' are the victims of society which is inadequate.

in'adequately, *adv.* [f. prec. + -LY².] In an inadequate manner or degree; insufficiently.
a **1691** BOYLE (J.), These pores they may either exactly fill, or but inadequately. **1736** BUTLER *Anal.* II. vi. Wks. 1874 I. 244 Signs often can be no more than inadequately expressive of the things signified. **1843** PRESCOTT *Mexico* (1850) I. 215 He..was very inadequately provided with supplies.

in'adequateness. [f. as prec. + -NESS.] The quality of being inadequate; inadequacy.
1681 FLAVEL *Meth. Grace* xii. 252 This comes to pass from the inadequateness..of the creature to the nobler and more excellent soul of man. **1796** *Hist.* in *Ann. Reg.* 66 The inadequateness of the successes obtained. **1873** M. ARNOLD *Lit. & Dogma* (1876) 60 This inadequateness of our speech.

inadequation (ɪnædɪ'kweɪʃən). *arch.* [IN-³.] Want of equivalence or exact correspondence.
1630 I. CRAVEN *Serm.* (1631) 29 Man..cannot [know the secrets] of anothers heart; nor those of his owne..but with inadequation to the truth. **1676** MARVELL *Mr. Smirke* 35 The difference arising only from the Inadequation of Languages. **1830** DE QUINCEY *R. Bentley* Wks. VII. 105 The continual inadequation (to use a logical term) of Greek to modern terms.

in'adequative, *a.* [f. IN-³ + ADEQUATIVE.] Not having exact equivalence; not of equal extension or comprehension. Hence **in'adequatively** *adv.*
1862 F. HALL *Hindu Philos. Syst.* 120 A characterization of *ákáśa* will serve to show how inadequatively it is represented by 'ether'.

inadherent (ɪnəd'hɪərənt), *a.* [IN-³.] Not adherent; not attached.
1855 in Mayne *Expos. Lex.* **1886** in *Syd. Soc. Lex.*

inadhesion (ɪnəd'hiːʒən). [IN-³.] The fact of not adhering; non-adhesion.
1796 KIRWAN *Elem. Min.* (ed. 2) I. 198 Its colour, inadhesion to the tongue and fingers. *Ibid.* 199.

inadhesive (ɪnəd'hiːsɪv), *a.* [IN-³.] Not adhesive, without the property of sticking.
1811 PINKERTON *Petral.* II. 474 Composed only of lapillo, pumice, and other substances of an inadhesive quality. **1832** BABBAGE *Econ. Manuf.* xi. (ed. 3) 79 Two kinds of ink.. mutually inadhesive. **1879** J. J. YOUNG *Ceram. Art* 22 Giving by the help of water a certain consistency to the inadhesive sand.

inadmissi'bility. [f. next + -ITY: cf. F. *inadmissibilité* (1835 in Hatz.-Darm.).] The quality or fact of being inadmissible.
1802-12 BENTHAM *Ration. Judic. Evid.* (1827) IV. 417 Whether through inadmissibility or through insufficiency [of the evidence]. *c* **1811** FUSELI in *Lect. Paint.* iv. (1848) 440 The admissibility and inadmissibility of Allegory in poems of supposed reality. **1881** WESTCOTT & HORT *Grk. N.T.* II. 209 The proved inadmissibility of the third supposition.

inadmissible (ɪnəd'mɪsɪb(ə)l), *a.* [IN-³. Cf. F. *inadmissible* (1475 in Hatz.-Darm.).] Not admissible; not to be admitted, entertained, or allowed.
1776 BURNEY *Hist. Mus.* I. 116 Who..contemn whatever theory suggests as visionary, and inadmissible in practice. **1786** T. JEFFERSON *Writ.* (1859) I. 557 To leave her in possession of our posts, seems inadmissible. *a* **1859** MACAULAY *Hist. Eng.* xxiii. V. 116 The demand which was made upon himself was altogether inadmissible. **1896** ALLBUTT *Syst. Med.* I. 402 Tea, coffee, and alcohol are inadmissible.

in-a-door, *adv.* = INDOORS *adv.* (App. only in Blunden.)
1932 BLUNDEN *Face of England* 14 We keep in-a-door unless compelled forth. **1937** —— *Elegy* 28 Hasten here in-a-door. **1949** —— *After Bombing* 36 And dog and cat run in-a-door.

†**in'adulable,** *a. Obs. rare*⁻⁰. [ad. L. *inadūlābilis*, f. *in-* (IN-³) + *adūlābilis* ADULABLE.] Not to be flattered.
1623 in COCKERAM. **1656** in BLOUNT *Glossogr.*

†**ina'dulterate,** *a. Obs. rare*⁻¹. [f. IN-³ + ADULTERATE *ppl. a.*] Unadulterated.
1648 HERRICK *Hesper.*, *Proof to no purpose*, Induc't that inadultrate same Streame to the spring from whence it came.

†**inad'vantage.** *Obs. rare*⁻¹. [IN-³.] Disadvantage.
1689 *Def. Liberty agst. Tyrants* 55 They which dye in that War seem to have this inadvantage.

inadventurous (ɪnəd'vɛntjʊərəs), *a.* [IN-³.] Not adventurous; unenterprising. Hence **inad'venturousness.**
1853 C. BRONTE *Villette* viii, Inadventurous, unstirred by impulses of practical ambition. **1867** C. J. SMITH *Syn. & Antonyms* s.v. *Adventurous*, Unenterprising, Inadventurous. *Ibid.* s.v. *Audacity*, Diffidence, Inadventurousness.

inadvertence (ɪnəd'vɜːtəns). [ad. Schol.L. *inadvertentia*: see next and -ENCE. Cf. OF. *inavertance* (Oresme, 14th c.), *inadvertance*.]
The fact or habit of being inadvertent; want of advertence, failure to observe or pay attention; inattention; also = INADVERTENCY.
1568 in Row *Hist. Kirk* (Wodrow Soc.) 36 He who slayes any upon suddentie and inadvertence. **1669** CLARENDON *Ess.* in *Tracts* (1727) 100 Incogitance, inadvertence, not thinking at all, not considering anything, which is degrading ourselves..by renouncing the faculties of a reasonable soul. **1786** BURKE *W. Hastings* Wks. 1842 II. 184 The said letter ..was, through inadvertence, laid before the board. **1872** J. G. MURPHY *Comm. Lev.* v. 18 The offences..are invariably acts of inadvertence. **1875** POSTE *Gaius* I. Introd. (ed. 2) 14 Inadvertence to the consequences of commission may be called heedlessness.
b. with *an* and *pl.* An instance of this; an act or fault of inattention; an oversight.
1725 WATTS *Logic* II. iv. §3 Such an Inadvertence or Mistake will expose you to great Error in Judgment. **1876** MISS BRADDON *Dead Men's Shoes* I. i. 6 Marriage is one of those inadvertences which can hardly go for nothing even in the easiest life. **1876** MOZLEY *Univ. Serm.* xv. 257 The mind broods over some passing inadvertence or fancied neglect till it assumes gigantic dimensions.

inadvertency (ɪnəd'vɜːtənsɪ). [ad. Schol.L. *inadvertentia*, f. *in-* (IN-³) + *advertentia* ADVERTENCY.] The quality or character of being inadvertent; heedlessness; also = INADVERTENCE.
1592 Q. ELIZ. in Ld. Campbell *Chancellors* (1857) II. xlvi. 302 If any person speak ill of the Emperor through a foolish rashness or inadvertency, it is to be despised. **1647** CLARENDON *Contempl. Ps.* in *Tracts* (1727) 460 If through inadvertency or unskilfulness they know not how to ask. **1755** JOHNSON *Dict.* Pref. *ad fin.*, Sudden fits of inadvertency will surprize vigilance. **1838** THIRLWALL *Greece* xi. II. 46 Defects..which might creep in through error and inadvertency.
b. with *an* and *pl.* = prec. b.
1647 CLARENDON *Hist. Reb.* II. §4 It was a fatal inadvertency that..these Canons..were never seen by the Assembly. **1748** RICHARDSON *Clarissa* (1811) IV. xxxv. 220 Forgive my inadvertencies! **1866** J. G. MURPHY *Comm. Exod.* vii. 6 Grave inadvertencies into which they are betrayed.

inadvertent (ɪnəd'vɜːtənt), *a.* [f. IN-³ + ADVERTENT.]
1. Of persons, their dispositions, etc.: Not properly attentive or observant; inattentive, negligent; heedless. In quot. 1653, Not having the faculty of observation.
1653 H. MORE *Antid. Ath.* II. v. §3. 53 The effects of an inadvertent form (λόγος ἔνυλος) of materiated or incorporated art or seminal reason. **1681-6** J. SCOTT *Chr. Life* (1747) III. vii. 89 If we are not wilfully deaf and inadvertent to it. **1694** KETTLEWELL *Comp. Penitent* 124 Whose unconstant Temper..is supine and inadvertent. **1718** *Freethinker* No. 21 ¶5 A Volume is thrown away upon the Inadvertent. **1863** J. G. MURPHY *Comm. Gen.* i. 3 Inadvertent critics object to God being described as speaking, or performing any other act that is proper only to the human frame.
2. Of actions, etc.: Characterized by want of attention or taking notice; hence, unintentional.
1724 SWIFT *Advice Grand Jury* Wks. 1761 III. 81 If such a writer should in one or two places happen to let fall an inadvertent expression. **1784** COWPER *Task* VI. 564 An inadvertent step may crush the snail, That crawls at evening in the public path. **1870** LOWELL *Study Wind.* 2 Another secret charm of this book is inadvertent humor.
Hence **inad'vertentness** (Bailey vol. II, 1727).

inad'vertently, *adv.* [f. prec. + -LY².] In an inadvertent manner; without due attention or thought; inattentively, heedlessly, carelessly; hence, unintentionally.
1678 CUDWORTH *Intell. Syst.* I. v. 747 They.. inadvertently give their assent to those Words in a Wrong Sense. **1756** BURKE *Subl. & B.* IV. xvii, If, after descending a flight of stairs, we attempt inadvertently to take another step in the manner of the former ones, the shock is extremely rude and disagreeable. **1803** WELLINGTON *Let. to Col. Collins* in Gurw. *Desp.* (1837) II. 140, I cannot approve of the expression inadvertently used in Colonel Stevenson's letter. **1866** G. MACDONALD *Ann. Q. Neighb.* xi. (1878) 214, I have already inadvertently broken my promise.

†**inad'verting,** *a. Obs. rare.* [f. IN-³ + *adverting*, pres. pple. of ADVERT *v.*] Inadvertent. Hence †**inad'vertingly** *adv.*, inadvertently.
1678 *Lively Orac.* viii. §26. 315 The vertue God has put there..can never be drawn out by drousy inadverting readers. **1715** M. DAVIES *Athen. Brit.* I. Y y iij a, Dr. Mills inadvertingly gives some handle to the Arians.

†**inad'vertisement.** *Obs. rare.* [f. IN-³ + ADVERTISEMENT I.] Want of attention or observation; inadvertence.
1682 SIR T. BROWNE *Chr. Mor.* III. §10 Forget not how assuefaction unto any thing minorates the passion from it; how constant objects loose their hints, and steal an inadvertisement upon us.

†**inad'vertist.** *Obs. rare.* [f. IN-³ + *advertist* from ADVERTISE *v.* 1-3.] One who habitually fails to take notice; an inadvertent person.
1679 HARBY *Key Script.* ii. 20 The insedulity of sleepy Inadvertists that mind nothing.

inadvisable (ɪnəd'vaɪzəb(ə)l), *a.* [IN-³.] Not advisable; unadvisable.
1870 *Daily News* 11 Feb., That it was inadvisable at the present time to add to the taxation. **1896** *Allbutt's Syst. Med.* I. 402 Sugar is inadvisable. **1953** *Times Lit. Suppl.* 25 Sept. 613/2 The idea..is that it would be inadvisable for Germany to annex parts of Austria. **1953** *Times* 3 Oct. 3/4 Coventry isolation hospital is now receiving only cases which it would be inadvisable to send..to the isolation hospital at..Birmingham.
Hence **inadvisa'bility**, unadvisableness.
1864 R. A. ARNOLD *Cotton Fam.* 429 The inadvisability of raising the rate of relief any higher. **1882** T. A. GUTHRIE *Vice Versâ* viii. (ed. 19) 153 He saw the inadvisability of mingling with the crowd.

inadvisedly (ɪnəd'vaɪzɪdlɪ), *adv. rare.* [IN-³.] Unadvisedly. So **inad'visedness.**
1652 HOWELL *Giraffi's Rev. Naples* II. 193 The Duke of Guise..was much taxed of inadvisednesse to leave the City. **1681** KETTLEWELL *Chr. Obed.* (1715) 561 They, who scarce ever sin wilfully at all..are wont most frequently through indeliberation and inadvisedness to miscarry. **1894** *Athenæum* 17 Nov. 671/1 She has entered upon the task somewhat inadvisedly.

-inæ, *suffix*, in words which are the fem. pl. of L. adjs. in *-īnus*, and in mod.L. words formed on this pattern, used (in agreement with *bestiæ* beasts, understood) to form names of sub-families of animals, as *Caninæ* (L. *canīnus* canine), *Felinæ* (L. *felīnus* feline).

inæqu-: see INEQU-.

inæsthetic (ɪnɪs'θɛtɪk), *a.* [IN-³.] Not æsthetic; void of æsthetic perception or taste.
1846 FORD *Gather. fr. Spain* 18 The Oriental inæsthetic incuriousness for things. **1877** MAY LAFFAN *Hon. Miss Ferrard* III. iii. 101 We are all utterly ignorant and inaesthetic.

†**in'affable,** *a. Obs.* [IN-³.] Not affable. Hence †**inaffa'bility**, want of affability.
1611 FLORIO, *Inaffabilità*, discourtesie, inaffabilitie. **1656** BLOUNT *Glossogr.*, *Inaffable*,..not affable, discourteous. **1665** S. CLARKE *Descr. Germany* 17 He is misliked for his inaffability.

inaffec'tation. *rare*⁻⁰. [IN-³.] Freedom from affectation; unaffectedness.
1658 PHILLIPS, *Inaffectation*, carelesseness, freeness from vain-glory.

†**ina'ffected,** *ppl. a. Obs. rare*⁻⁰. [IN-³.] = UNAFFECTED. Hence †**ina'ffectedly** *adv.*;

†**ina'ffectedness**, the quality of being unaffected or not touched in the feelings.

1617 MINSHEU *Ductor*, *Inaffected*, vi. unaffected. **1623** COCKERAM, *Inaffectedly*,..done carelessly. **1648** *Petit. Eastern Ass.* 28 Our apprehension of your inaffectednes with these our publike miseries.

†**ina'ffection.** *Obs. rare*$^{-1}$. [f. IN-^{3} + AFFECTION 1.] ? Want of power to affect or move.

1739 CIBBER *Apol.* iv. 93 In the just Delivery of Poetical Numbers, particularly where the Sentiments are pathetick, it is scarce credible, upon how minute an Article of Sound depends their greatest Beauty or Inaffection.

†**ina'ffectionate,** *a. Obs. rare.* In 6 ineff-. [f. IN-^{3} + AFFECTIONATE *a.* 2.] Unbiased, unprejudiced.

1558 KENNEDY *Compend. Tractiue* 94, I appele the conscience of the ineffectionat & godly redare diligentlie to considder [etc.]. **1563** *Reasoning Crosraguell & Knox* 20 b (Jam.), As the..ineffectionat readr may cleirly perceaue.

inage, var. ENAGE *v. Obs.*, to make old.

ina'gglutinable, *a.* [f. IN-^{3} + AGGLUTINABLE *a.*]

Incapable of being agglutinated (*by*).

1919 *Lancet* 4 Oct. 607/2 This inagglutinable strain was isolated from a case a few weeks before..experiments commenced. **1934** *Jrnl. R. Anthrop. Inst.* LXIV. 34 Every individual whose corpuscles were inagglutinable by the A and B sera. **1951** WHITBY & HYNES *Med. Bacteriol.* (ed. 5) xii. 203 It [*sc.* the Vi antigen] is not affected when the organisms are killed with 75 per cent alcohol, although they may then become inagglutinable by a Vi antiserum.

Also ,**inagglutina'bility**, the property of being inagglutinable.

1925 C. H. BROWNING *Bacteriol.* viii. 169 Occasionally typhoid bacilli when they have been recently obtained from the living body are not susceptible to agglutination by antiserum, but such inagglutinability usually soon disappears. **1948** *Biol. Abstr.* XXII. 897 Inagglutinability of red cells occurs.

ina'ggressive, *a. rare.* [IN-^{3}.] Not aggressive; unaggressive.

1876 W. E. HEARN *Aryan Househ.* xiv. 325 The strong individuality and the inaggressive nature of the early cults.

†**ina'greeable,** *a. Obs. rare*$^{-1}$. [IN-^{3}.] Not agreeable or accordant *to*.

1657 TOMLINSON *Renou's Disp.* 49 That..is most averse from and inagreeable to our nature.

†**in'aidable,** *a. Obs. rare*$^{-1}$. [IN-^{3}.] That cannot be aided or assisted; helpless.

1601 SHAKS. *All's Well* II. i. 122 The congregated Colledge haue concluded, That labouring Art can neuer ransome nature From her inaydible estate.

i-nailed, ME. pa. pple. of NAIL *v.*

†**in'aired,** *ppl. a. Obs. rare*$^{-1}$. [? f. IN-^{1} (or ? IN-^{3}) + AIR *sb.* + -ED.] ? Suspended in the air (or ? deprived of vital air).

1602 WARNER *Alb. Eng.* x. lix. 261 Natures Mynion [Absalom], Eyes Admier, and now in-ayred Earth, (For, hanging, Ioabs ruthles speare had vented vitall breath).

inajá (ɪnə'dʒɑː). [Tupi.] In full ***inajá palm***. A palm tree, *Maximiliana martiana* (*regia*), native to the Amazon region.

1849 R. SPRUCE *Notes of Botanist on Amazon & Andes* (1908) I. i. 45 The pinnate fronds of the..Inajá (*Maximiliana regia*) reach sometimes 40 feet in length. **1853** A. R. WALLACE *Trav. Amazon* ii. 33 Here also grew the Inajá, a fine thick-stemmed species, with a very large dense head of foliage. **1860** MAYNE REID *Odd People* 82 These nuts [*sc.* palm-nuts] are the fruit of several kinds of palms, but the best are those afforded by two magnificent species,—the 'Inaja' (*Maximilliana* [sic] *regia*), and the 'Urucuri' (*Attalea excelsa*). **1866** LINDLEY & MOORE *Treas. Bot.* II. 726/1 *M*[*aximiliana*] *regia*, the Inajá Palm of the Amazon, has a trunk a hundred or more feet high. **1927** R. R. GATES *Botanist in Amazon Valley* viii. 174 The Inajá..is one of the common palms of the Amazon. It produces enormous masses of ovoid fruits the size of a lemon. **1966** E. J. H. CORNER *Nat. Hist. Palms* xii. 283 As a major feature of vegetation, they [*sc.* South American palms] call for botanical investigation in every respect. For example, the babaçu.., cohune.., piassava.., and inajá.

inaka, var. INANGA.

ina'lacrity. *rare.* [IN-^{3}.] Want of alacrity.

1813 W. TAYLOR *Eng. Synonyms* (1856) 206 Men are.. indolent from insensibility, lazy from inalacrity. **1855** *Chamb. Jrnl.* IV. 219 Owing to..my unhappy inalacrity in dismounting.

inal'buminate, *a. rare.* [IN-^{3}.] Not furnished with albumen; exalbuminous.

1886 *Syd. Soc. Lex.*, *Inalbuminate*, applied to a plant embryo that is deprived of albumen, as in the Faba.

in,aliena'bility. [f. next + -ITY: cf. F. *inaliénabilité* (1722 in Hatz.-Darm.).] The quality of being inalienable; incapability of alienation.

1775 DE LOLME *Eng. Const.* II. x. (1784) 195 This inalienability of the executive power. **1855** MILMAN *Lat. Chr.* XIV. i. (1864) IX. 10 This property, instead of standing secure in its theoretic inalienability, was in constant fluctuation. **1885** *Law Times* LXXIX. 191/1 The present generation has seen a momentous change in the theory of inalienability.

inalienable (ɪn'eɪlɪənəb(ə)l), *a.* [f. IN-^{3} + ALIENABLE. Cf. F. *inaliénable* (16th c. in Hatz.-Darm.).] Not alienable; that cannot be alienated or transferred from its present ownership or relation.

c **1645** HOWELL *Lett.* (1650) II. x. 18 Their youth shall last alwaies with their lust, and love shall be satiated with onely one, where it shall remain inalienable. **1777** ROBERTSON *Hist. Amer.* (1813) II. VI. 248 Inalienable prerogatives of royalty. **1809–10** COLERIDGE *Friend* (1865) 120 This right of the individual to retain his whole natural independence..is absolutely inalienable. **1884** *Law Rep.* 27 Ch. Div. 163 This petition has been opposed..on the ground of the inalienable character of alimony.

Hence **in'alienably** *adv.*; **in'alienableness.**

1727 BAILEY vol. II, *Inalienableness*, incapableness of being alienated, or transferred to another by Law. **1769** ROBERTSON *Chas. V*, I. 170 (Seager) Some of the highest offices in the empire have been annexed to them inalienably. **1868** STANLEY *Westm. Abb.* i. 48 The ceremony of the coronation has been inalienably attached to the Abbey. **1885** *Law Times Rep.* LIII. 78/1 A married woman takes an interest under a settlement, vested in her inalienably.

inali'mental, *a. rare.* [IN-^{3}.] Not alimental; not affording nourishment.

1626 BACON *Sylva* §649 The Making of Things Inalimentall, to become Alimentall, may be an Experiment of great Profit, for Making new Victuall. **1656** in BLOUNT *Glossogr.* **1755** in JOHNSON. **1886** *Syd. Soc. Lex.*, *Inalimental*, not capable of affording nourishment.

inalterable (ɪn'ɔːltərəb(ə)l), *a.* [IN-^{3}.] Not alterable; not subject to alteration or change; unchangeable, immutable; unalterable.

1541 R. COPLAND *Galyen's Terapeut.* 2 Ej, The impatable and inalterable thynges to be the fyrste elementes. **1555** BONNER *Necess. Doctr.* 69 For the Godhed is inalterable and unpassible. *a* **1653** GOUGE *Comm. Heb.* vi. 2 The sentence at the last judgement will be inalterable. **1876** LOWELL *Among my Bks.* Ser. II. *Wordsw.* 211 He was to make men better, by opening to them the sources of an inalterable well-being. **1879** G. MEREDITH *Egoist* I. xviii. 331.

Hence **inaltera'bility,** unchangeableness; **in'alterably** *adv.*, immutably.

1631 GOUGE *God's Arrows* III. §78. 329 God was inalterably resolved utterly to destroy Amalek. **1714** DERHAM *Astro-Theol.* (1715) 75 *note*, Contrary to the received Opinion then, of the Heavens inalterability. **1856** W. A. MILLER *Elem. Chem.* §564 From its lightness and inalterability in the air, aluminum has been applied to the preparation of small weights. **1878** W. E. HENLEY in *Academy* 12 Oct. 355/1 Hopelessly and inalterably poor.

inam, variant of ENAM (*E. Indies*).

inam'bitious, *a. rare.* [IN-^{3}.] Not ambitious.

1729 T. COOKE *Tales, Propos.* etc. 90 Contented he enjoys what Nature yields, And inambitious plows his native Fields.

†**in'ambulate,** *v. Obs. rare*$^{-0}$. [f. ppl. stem of L. *inambulāre*, f. *in-* (IN-^{2}) + *ambulāre* to walk.] (See quot.) Hence †**inambu'lation.**

1656 BLOUNT *Glossogr.*, *Inambulate*, to walk up and down in a place. **1658** PHILLIPS, *Inambulation*, a walking from place to place.

i-named, ME. pa. pple. of NAME *v.*

inamel(l, enamil, obs. forms of ENAMEL.

†**in'amiable,** *a. Obs. rare*$^{-0}$. [IN-^{3}.] Not amiable, unamiable. Hence †**in'amiableness.**

1623 COCKERAM, *Inamiable*, unpleasant, not to be beloved. **1727** BAILEY vol. II, *Inamiableness*. **1818** in TODD; whence in mod. Dicts.

†**in'amicable,** *a. Obs. rare*$^{-1}$. [IN-^{3}.] Not amicable; unfriendly, hostile.

1683 TRYON *Way to Health* 127 In this season, which is inamicable to the pure Spirits of all such food.

inamissible (ɪnə'mɪsɪb(ə)l), *a.* Now *rare.* [IN-^{3}. Cf. F. *inamissible* (1617 in Hatz.-Darm.).] Not liable to be lost.

1649 JER. TAYLOR *Gt. Exemp.* III. xv. 38 As this is irremediable and irrecoverable, so is the other inamissible. **1662** GLANVILL *Lux Orient.* viii. (1682) 68 Had we been so fixt in an inamissible happiness. *c* **1771** FLETCHER *4th Check* Wks. 1795 III. 87 How can you infer, that the life of faith is inamissible? **1829** I. TAYLOR *Enthus* vi. (1867) 140 The Scriptures..declare..that virtue will be inamissible in heaven. **1886** STUART & MACPHERSON tr. *Ebrard's Chr. Apol.* I. §123. 287 With man..it is a monad cognizant of itself in inamissible identity with itself.

Hence **inamissi'bility, ina'missibleness,** the quality of being inamissible.

1727 BAILEY vol. II, *Inamissibleness*, uncapableness of being lost. **1742** tr. *Bossuet's Variat. Prot. Ch.* (1829) I. 357 The dogma called inamissability of justice. *a* **1861** W. CUNNINGHAM *Hist. Theol.* (1864) II. xxi. 89 The perseverance of the Saints..Romish divines usually call the inamissibility of justice or righteousness.

inamitie, var. of INEMITIE *Obs.*, enmity.

inamor, obs. f. ENAMOUR: see also INAMOUR.

inamorata (ɪnæmɒ'rɑːtə). Also 9 en-. [a. It. *in(n)amorata* mistress, sweetheart, fem. pa. pple. of *in(n)amorare*: see INAMORATE *v.*] A female lover, mistress, sweetheart.

1651 SHERBURNE *Forsaken Lydia* iii, The faire Inamorata who from farre Had spy'd the Ship which her hearts treasure bare. **1771** SMOLLETT *Humph. Cl.* 18 Let. i, On finding herself abandoned by her new admirer, in favour of another inamorata. **1841** CATLIN *N. Amer. Ind.* (1844) II. lv. 198 One of his little fair enamoratas, or 'catch crumbs' such as live in the halo of all great men. **1844** DISRAELI *Coningsby* VIII. vii, Percy is often in love..and never likes us to be very intimate with his inamoratas.

in'amorate, *a.* and *sb.* See also ENAMORATE. [ad. It. *in(n)amorato*: see below.] **A.** *adj.* Enamoured, in love. †**B.** *sb.* One in love, a lover.

1602 MARSTON *Antonio's Rev.* I. i. Wks. 1856 I. 76 Looke I not now like an inamorate? **1605** CHAPMAN *Mons. D'Olive* IV. i. F iij, His blood was framde for euerie shade of vertue, To rauish into true inamourate fire. **1612** HEYWOOD *Apol. Actors* III. 55 Deriding foolish inamorates who spend.. themselves in the service and ridiculous imployments of their mistresses. **1886** *Belgravia Mag.* LX. 97, I became over head and ears inamorate of the all-accomplished Ida.

Hence †**in'amorately** *adv.*, lovingly, fondly.

1599 NASHE *Lenten Stuffe* 5 It is so inamorately protected and patronized.

†**in'amorate,** *v. Obs. rare.* See also ENAMORATE. [ad. It. *inamorare*, now *innamor-*, 'to enamour, to fall in loue' (Florio), f. *in-* (IN-^{2}) + *amore* love.] *trans.* To inspire with love, to enamour. Hence †**inamo'ration,** enamourment.

1624 HEYWOOD *Gunaik.* I. 30 A confection, which..Jason gave to Medea to inamourat her. **1652** BENLOWES *Theoph.* IV. 51 The Inamoration.

inamorato (ɪnæmɒ'rɑːtəʊ). Also 8–9 en-. [a. It. *inamorato*, now *innamorato* lover, masc. pa. pple. of *in(n)amorare*: see INAMORATA.] A lover.

1592 GREENE *Upst. Courtier* D iv, He..asketh..whether hee wil haue his peak cut short and sharpe, amiable like an Inamerato. **1621** BURTON *Anat. Mel.* II. ii. IV. (1651) 282 Such Inamoratoes as read nothing but play-books. **1712** HUGHES *Spect.* No. 525 ¶5 All our Pretenders to Rhyme are professed Inamorato's. **1756** *Connoisseur* cxxiv. 21, I have lately taken a survey of the numerous tribe of Enamoratos. *c* **1763** *Babler* (1767) I. 164 No. 39 Various were the tricks related of this unhappy enamorato. **1772–84** COOK *Voy.* (1790) IV. 1317 Thinking it would be a bad precedent, and an encouragement to other enamouratoes. **1812** R. H. in *Exam.* 25 May 327/2 The kissing of a girl by two enamoratoes. **1831** T. L. PEACOCK *Crotchet Castle* xvi. (1887) 168 A mingled expression of mistrust, of kindness, and of fixed resolution, which the far-gone *inamorato* found irresistible. **1941** E. R. EDDISON *Fish Dinner* (1968) xiii. 221 How would you like Shelley for your *inamorato*? **1973** 'M. INNES' *Appleby's Answer* iii. 29 You must invite him to luncheon here. And invite me as well. I'd love to meet the *inamorato*.

†**inamo'retta.** *Obs.* A corruption of INAMORATA, perh. confused with *amorette*, *amoretto*.

1709 MRS. MANLEY *Secr. Mem.* (1736) II. 66 There are others..that lavish vast Sums upon their Inamoretta's. **1767** *Woman of Fashion* I. 231 You remember an Inamoretta of mine—Peggy Williamson. *Ibid.* I. 122.

†**inamour, -ed,** obs. forms of ENAMOUR, -ED.

1591 SYLVESTER *Du Bartas* I. iv. 738 The Stars-king all inamoured on thee, Full of desire, shines down direct upon thee. **1652** BENLOWES *Theoph.* IV. xcvi, Through her eyes Did love inamoring Passions rise. **1665** BOYLE *Occas. Refl.* (1848) 374 As absurd were it for us, to..fancy Piety ours, because our Discourses can possibly inamour others of it. **1729** T. COOKE *Tales, Propos.* etc. 42 In the flowry Vale inamour'd stray.

ina'movable, *a. rare.* [IN-^{3}. Cf. F. *inamovible* (18th c. in Hatz.-Darm.).] Not liable to be removed. Hence **inamova'bility** [cf. F. *inamovibilité*], the quality of not being removable.

1849 MILL *Ess.* (1859) II. 370 Declaring..that the inamovability of judges was inconsistent with republican principles. **1851** SIR F. PALGRAVE *Norm. & Eng.* II. 173 They rendered him [Hugh-le-Grand]..the inamovable Protector of the monarchy.

inanage'nnesis, *erron.* **inana'genesis.** [mod. f. Gr. ἴς, ἰν- fibre + ἀναγέννησις ANAGENNESIS, regeneration.] (See quot.)

1855 MAYNE *Expos. Lex.*, *Inanagenesis*,..muscular regeneration, or the reproduction of muscular fibre. **1886** *Syd. Soc. Lex.*, *Inanagenesis*.

inanaphysis (ɪnə'næfɪsɪs). [mod. f. Gr. ἴς, ἰν- fibre + ἀνάφυσις growing again.] 'A term for the renewed growth or increase of muscular fibre'.

1855 in MAYNE *Expos. Lex.* **1886** in *Syd. Soc. Lex.*

in and in, in-and-in, *adv.* and *sb.* [IN *adv.*]

A. *adv.* **1. a.** Further and further in; continually inwards; *esp.* in phrase ***to breed in and in***, to breed always within a limited stock (see BREED *v.* III); so ***to marry in and in***, to marry with near relatives, in successive generations.

1633 B. JONSON *Tale Tub* IV. ii, A weaver he was..his shittle Went in and in still. We [joiners] do lay Things in and in, in our work. **1765** *Treat. Dom. Pigeons* 61 Should he (as the term is) breed them in and in..the breed would degenerate. **1794** *Sporting Mag.* IV. 115 This practice is well known, under the term of breeding in-and-in. **1828** MACAULAY *Misc. Writings* (1860) I. 266 Their minds, if we may so express ourselves, bred in and in. **1875** JOWETT *Plato* (ed. 2) III. 163 The marrying in and in of the same family tends constantly to weakness or idiotcy.

b. Entirely in, sharing fully.
1926 J. Black *You can't Win* x. 131 We know you are 'right'.. That's why you are declared 'in and in' with the works.

c. *attrib.* (in quasi-*adj.* use).
1831 T. P. Thompson in *Westm. Rev.* XIV. 444 They maintained a sort of in-and-in communication with each other. **1874** Lubbock *Orig. & Met. Ins.* iv. 75 Avoiding in-and-in breeding. **1881** Sheldon *Dairy Farming* 13/1 The practice of close in-and-in breeding has..produced extraordinary results. **1891** *Pall Mall G.* 8 July 1/2 Sometimes it leads to 'in-and-in' marrying, and the royal families deteriorate or die of exhaustion. **1892** *Daily News* 19 Jan. 2/6 The charter was, in fact, nothing more nor less than an in-and-in system between two colleges which would have the main control of the faculties and the studies and the examinations.

2. (See quot.)
1926 *Paper Terminol.* (Spalding & Hodge) 14 *In and in*, a method of packing reams too large conveniently to travel flat. The ream is divided in half, and the two portions clasped in and in to each other.

B. *sb.* †**1. a.** The name given to a throw made with four dice, when these fell all alike or as two doublets. *Obs.*
1633 Shirley *Gamester* iii. iv, A curse upon these reeling dice! That last in-and-in was out my way ten pieces. **1668** Dryden *Even. Love* iii. i. Wks. 1883 III. 310 The highest duplet wins, except you throw in and in, which is called raffle. **1668** Davenant *Man's the Master* v. i, The devil's in the dice if you throw twice in and in, without any light.

†**b.** A gambling game, played by three persons with four dice; the player who threw *in and in* (see above) took all the stake. *Obs.*
A full description of the game is given in Cotton's *Compleat Gamester* (1680) 117.
1630 B. Jonson *New Inn* iii. i, He is a merchant still, adventurer, At in-and-in. **1671** Shadwell *Humourist* iii, I saw you..inveigle a third man at Six-penny In and In. **1674** Cotton *Compl. Gamester* (1680) 13, I have seen three persons sit down at twelve penny In and In [etc.].

2. A space which opens up and ever discloses something further in.
1890 J. H. Stirling *Philos. & Theol.* iv. 69 A boundless in and in of subjective internalities.

3. *slang.* (See quot.)
1935 *Evening News* 29 June 3/2 The '*in-and-in*' is simply the point at which the swindler apparently risks his own money with that of the dupe.

in and out, in-and-out, *adv.* and *sb.* (Cf. also *ins and outs*, IN *sb.* 2.)

A. *adv.* **1.** Alternately in and out; now in, now out.

a. Of motion.
[*a* **1240** *Sawles Warde* in *Cott. Hom.* 247 þe warliche loki hwam ha leote in ant ut.] **1503** Hawes *Examp. Virt.* ix. xiii, I was in a mase goynge in and oute. *a* **1641** Suckling *Ballad on Wedding*, Her feet beneath her petticoat Like little mice stole in and out. **1703** Dampier *Voy.* III. 19 This Rope serveth to hale the Boat in and out. **1897** Hall Caine *Christian* xi, Little knowing curls that went in and out on her temples.

b. Of position, condition, season, etc.
a **1635** Naunton *Fragm. Reg.* (Arb.) 52 Their affections had been more permanent, and not so in and out as they were, like an Instrument ill tuned. **1687** R. L'Estrange *Answ. Diss.* 22 'Tis not with Sermons, as 'tis with Mackrel, to be In, and Out. **1711** Addison *Spect.* No. 72 ¶7 The Fire ..has seen the Glass-house Fires in and out above an Hundred times. **1855** Dickens *Dorrit* i. xxix, He was much in and out.

†**2.** Inside out. *Obs.*
a **1533** Ld. Berners *Huon* lv. 187 When he had well proued him [a horse] and turned hym in and out. **1542** Udall *Erasm. Apoph.* 234 b, Cesar permitted hym to turne the tale in and out, and laie the wyte or blame on hymselfe. **1548** Udall, etc. *Erasm. Par. Luke* 138 a, Soodainly turned in and out clene arsie versie. *Ibid.* 151 a, O the course of thinges meruailously turned in and out.

3. Both in and out; inside and outside.
1895 *How to get Married* 113 A widow knows him [a man] in and out.

4. *attrib.* (quasi-*adj.*) in various senses; spec. ***in-and-out bolts*** (see quot. 1850); ***in-and-out boy, man***, someone in and out of prison; a burglar; ***in-and-out class***, those paupers who are now in and now out of the workhouse; ***in-and-out cottage***, a cottage of irregular plan; ***in and out family***, formerly, a family constantly entering and leaving a workhouse; ***in-and-out running***, alternate winning and losing of races (so ***in-and-out football***); ***in and out work***, work which is not continuous; also, irregular or unlawful practice.
1640 Bp. Hall *Episc.* ii. xvii. 182 What Ordination to that their In-and-out Office; have these succeeding and Momentary Presidents? **1824** Miss Mitford *Village* Ser. i. (1863) 239 Ah! the in-and-out cottage! the dear, dear home. **1841** R. H. Dana *Seaman's Manual* 111 *In-and-out*, a term sometimes used for the scantline of the timbers, the moulding way, and particularly for those bolts that are driven into the hanging and lodging knees, through the sides, which are called *in-and-out bolts*. *c* **1850** *Rudim. Navig.* (Weale) 126 *In and out*,..applied to those bolts in the knees, riders, &c., which are driven through the ship's sides, or athwartships, and therefore called 'In and out bolts'. **1855** Geo. Eliot in *Fraser's Mag.* June 699/2 Heavy-looking in-and-out corridors, such as one found only in German inns. **1885** *Referee* 26 Apr. 1/2 Now and again in-and-out running on the part of a horse subjects his owner to considerable annoyance. **1888** *Times* 26 June 4/5 Have you heard of what is called in-and-out running? **1888** 'R. Boldrewood' *Robbery under Arms* III. xviii. 277, I began to hear that there was a deal of in-and-out sort of work about my getting my freedom. **1897** *Westm. Gaz.* 31 July 2/3 Children of habitual tramps and of the 'in and out' classes. **1903** *Westm. Gaz.* 29 Sept. 10/1 His engagements are only for particular plays—'in and out' work. **1904** *Daily Chron.* 14 June 9/1 One notable 'In and Out' family entered and discharged itself sixty-two times from a London workhouse in one year. **1906** E. Dyson *Fact'ry 'Ands* viii. 97 It was in 'n' out sorter work. **1910** E. M. Forster *Howards End* v. 38 Oh, heavens! I've knocked the In and Out card down. **1936** H. G. Wells *Anat. Frustration* xv. 178 That does not close the Jewish problem for you. It merely brings you back to the fundamental age-long problem of this nation among the nations, this in-and-out mentality, the essential parasitism of the Jewish mycelium upon the social and cultural organisms in which it lives. **1937** C. Prior *So I wrote It* xvi. 191 Among the boys I knew, very few had either the courage or skill to tackle 'live gaffs' by night. Most of them were in-and-out boys. They did their eighteen months in Wandsworth or Pentonville, had a run of a month or so and went back to do a twenty-one or even a lagging. **1939** H. Hodge *Cab, Sir?* 221 An 'in and out job' is a passenger who comes back to his starting point. **1959** *Times* 31 Dec. 11/3 The discovery was announced in 1925 and met with a very in-and-out reception. **1960** *Encounter* Mar. 77/1 The *In-and-Out* Game is played... 'Everyone' knows that Hemingway is not so *In* as Faulkner. **1961** Partridge *Dict. Slang* (ed. 5) II. 1143/2 *In-and-out man*, an opportunist thief. **1961** *Times* 14 Apr. 5/4 Two clubs who have had an in-and-out season meet at Old Deer Park. **1970** *Guardian* 12 Sept. 11/2 Israeli casualties were..high... The alternative ..would be a quick 'in and out' operation. **1972** *Times* 15 Dec. 14/3 'In and out' records through lapsing..are not uncommon.

B. *sb.* ***The 'In' and 'Out'***, the name of the Naval and Military Club in London.
1925 Fraser & Gibbons *Soldier & Sailor Words* 127 *The In and Out*, the Naval and Military Club, 94, Piccadilly. So called familiarly from the words 'In' and 'Out', painted on the pillars of the approach to the courtyard in front. **1967** *Guardian* 21 Feb. 3/6 Two London clubs, the 105-year-old Naval and Military, better known as the 'In and Out', and the 92-year-old Devonshire, may merge.

Hence **in-and-outishness, -outism, -outness** *nonce-wds.*, irregularity of form or outline; **in-and-outer**, one who is only moderately skilled or is erratic in performance; one who holds office intermittently.
1824 Miss Mitford *Village* Ser. i. (1863) 5 A cottage..all angles, and of a charming in-and-outness. **1833** T. Hook *Widow & Marquess* viii, The in-and-outishness of the Quebec. **1836** —— *G. Gurney* III. iii. 135 Her figure was.. full of those in-and-out-isms which constitute in my mind true symmetry. **1905** *Outing* (U.S.) Feb. 572/2 Whippets run in more consistent form than horses, and there are few 'in-and-outers'. **1934** E. B. Marks *They all Sang* 210 He was an in-and-outer..and this was one of his 'out' periods. **1952** *Assoc. Press* 8 Oct., Reynolds has 30 knockouts among his 52 victories but he has been an in-and-outer. **1960** *Farmer & Stockbreeder* 29 Mar. 53/3 There are a great many 'in-and-outers' who know mighty little of the art of breeding. **1967** *Economist* 5 Aug. 496/1 The British unfamiliarity with the American concept of 'ins and outers' —men who alternate between private careers and public service.

inane (ɪˈneɪn), *a.* and *sb.* [ad. L. *inān-is* empty, useless, vain.]

A. *adj.* **1.** Empty, void.
1662 Glanvill *Lux Orient.* ix. (1682) 72 To have confined his omnipotence to work only in one little spot of an infinite inane capacity. **1850** Kingsley *Alt. Locke* xxx, Dilating into vast inane infinities. **1850** Carlyle *Latter-d. Pamph.* iii. (1872) 79 To live..like inane phantasms, and to leave their life as a paltry contribution to the guano mountains.

2. Of persons, their actions, etc.: Void or destitute of sense; silly, senseless; empty-headed.
1819 Shelley *Cenci* iii. i. 277 Some inane and vacant smile. **1843** Carlyle *Past & Pr.* ii. vii, We listen..to the inanest hubbub. **1852** Mrs. Jameson *Leg. Madonna* (1857) 12 We have merely inane prettiness. **1885** *Manch. Exam.* 11 Nov. 3/1 To us the book seems a very inane, tiresome, and purposeless affair.

3. *Comb.*, as ***inane-visaged*** adj.
1876 C. M. Davies *Unorth. Lond.* (ed. 2) 54 An inane-visaged man.

B. *sb.* **1.** That which is inane, void, or empty; void or empty space; vacuity; the 'formless void' of infinite space.
1677 Hale *Prim. Orig. Man.* iii. ii. 257 An infinite number of small imperceptible Bodies, that floated up and down in a vast infinite Inane. **1690** Locke *Hum. Und.* ii. vii. §10 The capacious mind of man..that..makes excursions into the incomprehensible Inane. **1700** S. Parker *Six Philos. Ess.* 5 Atoms..dispers'd and dancing in the great Inane. **1837** Carlyle *Fr. Rev.* III. vii. i, So much is getting abolished; fleeting swiftly into the Inane. **1868** Tennyson *Lucretius* 40, I saw the flaring atom-streams And torrents of her myriad universe, Ruining along the illimitable inane.

2. An empty-headed, unintelligent person.
1710 Pope *Let. to Cromwell* 17 May, Being all alike Inanes, we saunter to one another's habitations, and daily assist each other in doing nothing at all.

Hence **i'nanely** *adv.*, emptily, senselessly.
1883 *Harper's Mag.* May 894/1 What sport..sounds more inanely foolish than confetti-throwing? **1895** *Pall Mall Mag.* VII. 516 'Can't you push on a bit?' I said, somewhat inanely.

†**in-ane, in an(e, inane,** *adv. Sc.* and *north. dial. Obs.* [Northern form of ANON, q.v.] In one accord; in one and the same state; without cessation or interruption, continuously; straightway.
c **1320** *Sir Tristr.* 272 And euer he dede as þe sleiȝe And held his hert in an, þat wise. *c* **1450** Holland *Howlat* 47 Nerar that noyss in nest I nechit in ane. *Ibid.* 861 And, considerand the causs, concludit in ane That thai wald Natur beseike. **1513** Douglas *Æneis* vii. x. 89 The detestable weris, evyr in ane, Agane the fatis all, thai cry and rane. *Ibid.* ix. xiii. 66 On sik wys is he quhelmyt and confundit, That euer inane hys bos helm rang and soundit.

inanga (ˈinaŋa). Also **inaka** (the South Island form). [Maori.] **1.** The New Zealand name for a small fish, *Galaxias attenuatus*, the young form of which is called whitebait.
1845 E. J. Wakefield *Adventure N.Z.* II. 100 This fish is called *hinanga*, and resembles Blackwall whitebait in size and flavour. **1896** *Australasian* 28 Aug. 407/3 About the same size as this fish is the 'inaka' much used for bait. *a* **1939** 'R. Hyde' *Houses by Sea* (1952) 64 Brown women drying out inanga. **1944** *Mod. Jun. Dict.* (Whitcombe & Tombs) 209 *Inanga, Inaka*, the Maori name of the small fish called 'whitebait' in New Zealand; inanga in the north, inaka in the south. **1959** Tindale & Lindsay *Rangatira* x. 93 Every year shoals of the tiny, delicious inanga fish came up the creeks from the sea. **1962** *Post-Primary School Bull.* (N.Z.) XV. i. 26 Whitebait belongs to the species *Galaxias attenuatus*... The adult fish, called Inanga, reach a length of about four inches.

2. An evergreen shrub or small tree, *Dracophyllum longifolium*, belonging to the family Epacridaceæ and native to New Zealand.
1889 T. Kirk *Forest Flora N.Z.* 215 Mr. Charles Traill informs me that it [sc. *Dracophyllum longifolium*] is termed 'inaka' by the Maoris on Stewart Island. **1910** L. Cockayne *N.Z. Plants* 76 In similar situations [*sc.* along the coastline] the inuka (*Dracophyllum longifolium*) and the smaller New Zealand flax (*Phormium Cookianum*) are common. **1929** W. Martin *N.Z. Nature Bk.* viii. 126 The Inanga ranges in size from a small shrub..to a tree 15 to 30 ft. high. **1961** H. H. Allan *Flora N.Z.* I. 532 *D. longifolium*... Inanga... The Forsterian specimens I have seen are scrappy. **1968** *N.Z. Listener* 15 Mar. 6/5 Lying in its sheltered cove..complete with its own rata tree, inaka bushes, and great cushy heaps of golden-green moss.

†**in'angular,** *a.*[1] *rare.* [IN-[3].] Not angular.
1646 Sir T. Browne *Pseud. Ep.* iv. i. 180 Inangular postures upon the back, the belly and the feet.

in'angular, *a.*[2] *rare.* [IN-[2].] Situated in an angle.
a **1855** Ranken *Canada & Crimea* xiv. (1862) 258 Every embrasure was distinctly marked by its inangular dark patch of shadow.

in'angulate, *a. rare.* [IN-[3].] (See quot.)
1855 Mayne *Expos. Lex.*, *Inangulatus*, having no angles: inangulate. **1886** in *Syd. Soc. Lex.*

in'angulated, *ppl. a. Ent.* [f. IN-[2] + ANGULATED *ppl. a.*] Angled inwardly.
1898 *Proc. Zool. Soc.* 441 The inner stripe more or less strongly inangulated below median vein, the outer stripe zigzag.

†**ina'niloquent,** *a. Obs. rare*$^{-0}$. [f. L. *inānis* INANE + *loquent-em*, pres. pple. of *loquī* to speak.] Full of empty or idle talk. So †**ina'niloquous** *a.*; also †**ina'niloquence,** †**inanilo'quution.**
1656 Blount *Glossogr.*, *Inaniloquent*, that speaketh vainly, a babbler. **1658** Phillips, *Inaniloquution*, an idle or vain speaking. **1721** Bailey, *Inaniloquous*, vain Talking or Babling. **1727** Bailey vol. II, *Inaniloquence*, vain Talk, foolish Babbling.

†**inanimad'version.** *Obs.* [IN-[3].] = next. (In quot., An instance of this.)
1676 Marvell *Mr. Smirke* 15 A whole Cargo of Consequences which..will, upon search, be all found the Animadverters proper goods and Trade, his own Inconsequences and Inanimadversions.

†**inanimad'vertence.** *Obs.* [IN-[3].] Inadvertence, inattention.
c **1656** Bramhall *Replic.* 13 Not by chance or inanimadvertence, but upon premeditation. *Ibid.* 37 Their inanimadvertence might make the separation lesse Justifiable.

†**inanimad'vertency.** *Obs.* [IN-[3].] Inadvertency, inattentiveness.
1650 H. Brooke *Conserv. Health* 158 Neglect or inanimadvertency. **1658** W. Burton *Itin. Anton.* 42 Therein he doth but discover his own inanimadvertency. **1679** Harby *Key Script.* ii. 30 The Inanimadvertency of Ages could not comprehend these things.

†**in'animal,** *a. Obs. rare*$^{-0}$. [IN-[3].] = next.
1623 Cockeram, *Inanimall*, hee which is dead.

inanimate (ɪnˈænɪmət), *a.* (*sb.*) [ad. late L. *inanimātus* lifeless, f. *in-* (IN-[3]) + *animātus* ANIMATE. Cf. F. *inanimé*.]

1. Not animated or alive; destitute of life, lifeless; *spec.* not endowed with animal life, as in ***inanimate nature***, that part of nature which is without sensation, i.e. all outside the animal world.
1563-87 Foxe *A. & M.* (1684) III. 286 Shall we see Sacrifice and God's service done to an inanimate Creature, and be mum? **1643** J. Steer tr. *Exp. Chyrurg.* xvi. 65 Inanimate creatures, as Trees, and the like. **1784** Cowper *Task* i. 197 Nature inanimate employs sweet sounds, But animated Nature sweeter still. **1828** Scott *F.M. Perth* ii,

The beauties of inanimate nature. **1866** LIDDON *Bampt. Lect.* iv. 152 At His bidding life returns to inanimate corpses. **1880** MUIRHEAD *Gaius*, Digest 632 He who.. did damage to any inanimate property.. was liable in its highest value.

2. Without the activity or motion of life (*lit.* and *fig.*); spiritless, inactive, dull.

1704 POPE *Windsor For.* 308 From her roofs when Verrio's colours fall, And leave inanimate the naked wall. **1862** HELPS *Ess., Organ. Daily Life* (1875) 162 Organization should not be an inanimate, but a living, growing thing. **1871** R. ELLIS *Catullus* xvii. 24 If from stupor inanimate peradventure he wake him. **1884** PAE *Eustace* 10 His arms grasped the girl's inanimate form. **1893** *Daily News* 19 June 4/7 The stock markets were quite inanimate.

B. *sb.* An inanimate thing; that which is inanimate.

1652 GAULE *Magastrom.* 167 The very inanimates, whom words can in no wise effect or move. **1741** T. FRANCKLIN tr. *Cicero's Nat. of Gods* I. 65 Even Inanimates have their proper Stations assigned. **1836** KINGSLEY *Lett.* (1878) I. 36 My enjoyment was drawn.. from the beautiful inanimate in all its forms.

†**in'animate**, *v.*^{1} *Obs.* [f. ppl. stem of late L. *inanimāre* to animate, encourage, f. *in-* (IN-^{2}) + *animāre* to ANIMATE. (Sc. pa. ppl. *inanimat*, after L. *inanimāt-us*.)]

1. *trans.* To animate, infuse life into. Also *fig.*

1610 DONNE *Pseudo-Mart.* vi. 172 God inanimates.. euery man with one soule. **1647** R. STAPYLTON *Juvenal* 65 Stealing fire from the suns coach-wheeles, wherewith he inanimated his man of clay. **1679** M. RUSDEN *Further Discov. Bees* 59 Which matter so inanimated.. is called by some Sandarack, by others Bee-bread.

2. To animate, encourage, quicken.

1600 *Sc. Acts Jas. VI* (1814) 248 (Jam.) To continew in prosequuting the said actioun, quhairby vtheris.. may be thair exampill be inannimat to the lyik interpryisis. **1604** T. WRIGHT *Passions* v. 157 To inanimate their souldiours to battell. *a* **1631** DONNE *Six Serm.* iv. (1634) 5 In the shadow of death, the Lord of life should quicken and inanimate their hearts. **1670** G. H. *Hist. Cardinals* III. I. 251 To excite, and inanimate their Subjects to an expedition.

Hence †**in'animated** *ppl. a.*, endowed with life.

1689 *Def. Liberty agst. Tyrants* 57 Magistrates.. are but an inanimated and speaking Law.

†**in'animate**, *v.*^{2} *Obs. rare.* [f. INANIMATE *a.*^{1}] *trans.* To deprive of life.

1647 tr. *Malvezzi's Pourtract* 3 It wounds not, it inanimats not.

†**in'animated**, *a. Obs.* [f. IN-^{3} + ANIMATED *ppl. a.*] Not endowed with or having life.

1. = INANIMATE *a.* 1.

1646 SIR T. BROWNE *Pseud. Ep.* III. xxi. 159 Principles, which are.. common also unto inanimated constitutions. **1651** HOBBES *Leviath.* IV. xliv. 339 God that raised inanimated dust and clay into a living Creature. **1777** ROBERTSON *Hist. Amer.* (1813) II. VII. 286 Every representation of inanimated nature, is extremely rude and awkward. **1826** *Blackw. Mag.* XX. 676 With our religious spirit [we] embue all the ongoings of animated and even inanimated life.

2. = INANIMATE *a.* 2.

1753 SMOLLETT *Ct. Fathom* (1784) 183/2 Her faded lips, her pale cheek, and her inanimated features. **1788** CLARA REEVE *Exiles* II. 47, I behaved.. like a poor, inanimated, lifeless creature.

in'animately, *adv.* [f. INANIMATE *a.* + -LY^2.] Lifelessly, without animation.

1876 T. HARDY *Ethelberta* II. xliii. 199 'It makes no difference', said Mountclere, inanimately. **1881** *Standard* 8 Nov. 2/4 Having been rendered inanimately faint from his wounds.

in'animateness. [f. as prec. + -NESS.] Lifelessness; want of animation, life, or vivacity.

1654 W. MOUNTAGUE *Devout Ess.* II. ii. §3 Might not the motion have been accounted less perfect, by reason of the deadness and inanimateness of the subject mov'd? **1847** HARE *Vict. Faith* 34 The inanimateness of a bare intellectual belief.

†**in'animating**, *ppl. a. Obs. rare.* [f. IN-^{3} + ANIMATING *ppl. a.*] Not animating; not quickening.

1755 *Man* No. 26. 4 Being only inanimating or dead knowledge.

†**inani'mation**^{1}. *Obs.* [Noun of action from INANIMATE *v.*^{1}] Infusion of life, spirit, or vitality.

a **1614** DONNE *Βιαθανατος* (1644) 175 He hath preserued.. from that ordinary corruption of evill.. (as he is said to have done our B. Lady from originall sinne in her inanimation,) some of those acts of ours. **1625** —— *Serm.* cl., Wks. 1839 VI. 67 God hath given our zeal.. a new inanimation by this fire of tribulation. **1647** BP. HALL *Christ Mystical* (R.), This habitual joy.. arising from the inanimation of Christ living and breathing within us.

inanimation^2 (ɪnænɪ'meɪʃən). [IN-^{3}.] Inanimate condition; absence of life or liveliness.

1784 *New Spectator* No. 9. 8/2 The lines of Mrs. Bannister's inanimation. **1816** BENTHAM *Chrestom.* i. Wks. 1843 VIII. 12 The growth of the mind is retarded to an inordinate degree, by the state of inanimation in which it is kept. **1817** SHELLEY in Dowden *Life* II. 168 Towards evening I sink into a state of lethargy and inanimation. **1858** *Times* 19 Nov. 7/6 After such a long duration of inanimation she became perfectly conscious.

†**inanite**, *v. Obs. rare.* [f. L. *inānīt-*, ppl. stem of *inānīre* to make empty or void, f. *inānis* INANE.] *trans.* To empty.

a **1598** ROLLOCK *Wks.* (Wodrow Soc.) II. 460 He was so inanited as never creature was. —— *On 2 Thess.* (1606) 33 (Jam.).

ina'nitiate, *v.* [A back-formation from *inanitiation*, ineptly formed in French by Chossat, from *inanition*: Littré points out that the proper French form would be *inanisation*. In English Dictionaries from Dunglison; but not in Eng. use.] *trans.* 'To affect with inanition; to exhaust for want of nourishment'. So **inaniti'ation** [see above], 'Chossat's term for the gradual passage of the animal body into a state the end of which is *Inanition*' (*Syd. Soc. Lex.* 1886).

1857 DUNGLISON *Med. Lex.* 492 *Inanitiation*,.. The act of being exhausted for want of nourishment. One so exhausted is said to be *inanitiated*. (Hence in OGILVIE and later Dicts.)

inanition (ɪnə'nɪʃən). [ad. L. *inānītiōn-em*, n. of action f. *inānīre*: see INANITE; cf. F. *inanition* (14th c. in Hatz.-Darm.).] The action or process of emptying; the condition of being empty; *spec.* the exhausted condition resulting from want or insufficiency of nourishment. Also *fig.*

c **1400** tr. *Lanfranc's Cirurg.* 100 Of þe whiche drawynge þat ben .ij. causis coniunct: þe toon is repleccioun of þe senewe oþere of þe corde, þe oþer is in-anisioun. **1543** TRAHERON *Vigo's Chirurg.* II. iii. 17 Of inanition and repletion. **1615** CROOKE *Body of Man* 169 In the Dogge-appetite there is no Inanition or emptinesse of the parts, but an exquisite sense of suction. **1732** ARBUTHNOT *Rules of Diet* 308 Fevers proceed from too great Fulness in the beginning and too great Inanition in the latter end of the Disease. **1856** FROUDE *Hist. Eng.* II. 252 Anarchy.. is usually shortlived, and perishes of inanition. **1866** A. FLINT *Princ. Med.* (1880) 516 Inanition is a pathological condition entering into all diseases which interfere with the ingestion or the assimilation of aliment. **1875** JOWETT *Plato* (ed. 2) III. 123 Hunger and thirst are inanitions of the body.

inanity (ɪ'nænɪtɪ). [ad. L. *inānitās* emptiness, n. of quality f. *inānis* INANE. Cf. F. *inanité* (14th c. in Hatz.-Darm.).]

1. The quality or condition of being inane, empty, or void; emptiness.

1607 *Schol. Disc. agst. Antichr.* I. iii. 128 How ill God is pleased with that which is vaine, through inanitie of commoditie and of proffit which ought to bee in it. **1631** R. H. *Arraignm. Whole Creature* xiii. §3. 208 What shall fill.. the Inanity and Vacuity of the heart of man? **1649** G. DANIEL *Trinarch., Hen. IV*, cccxxv, Where pruneing Lawes lye by; till the inanitye Of Branches call 'em out, lest the whole Dye. **1744** ARMSTRONG *Preserv. Health* (1807) 29 The elemental tubes Collaps'd and shrunk with long inanity.

2. *fig.* **a.** Want of substance or solidity; the quality of being void of interest; inability to satisfy desire; unsatisfactoriness; vanity; hollowness.

1603 FLORIO *Montaigne* (1634) 625 Their inanity.. will sufficiently be felt, and doth sufficiently produce it selfe. **1684** *Contempl. St. Man* II. i. (1699) 135 O the inanity and emptiness of temporal Goods! **1751** JOHNSON *Rambler* No. 133 ¶4 Such helpless destitution, such dismal inanity.. All is gloomy privation or impotent desire. **1826** KIRBY & SP. *Entomol.* III. xxix. 55 He has placed the inanity.. of such high-sounding terms in their true name. **1877** FARRAR *Days of Youth* xxviii. 279 The inanity of its own cherished hopes.

b. Mental vacuity; lack of ideas or sense; frivolity, senselessness, silliness.

1753 C. SMART *Hilliad* (R.), Inanity will ever be the same. **1756** J. WARTON *Ess. Pope* I. iii. 201 The Rambler calls his [Walsh's] works Pages of Inanity. **1803** *Ann. Rev.* I. 400/2 This same topic is treated with similar inanity for thirteen pages more. **1878** LECKY *Eng. in 18th C.* II. ix. 529 The pretentious and verbose inanity of his theological writings.

c. Vacuity of existence; want of active interest; idleness, inaction.

1782 W. F. MARTYN *Geog. Mag.* I. 737 They consider any further exertions unnecessary, and retire again to the enjoyment of their favourite inanity. **1797** GODWIN *Enquirer* II. i. 165 A.. state of inanity and torpor. **1818** SCOTT *Hrt. Midl.* i, A fine gentleman, bred up in the thorough idleness and inanity of pursuit, which.. is absolutely necessary to the character in perfection. **1837** MISS SEDGWICK *Live & let L.* (1876) 92 Do not let us consider any occupation so vulgar as indolence and inanity.

3. with *an* and *pl.* An instance of vacuity or frivolity; an inane remark or practice.

1661 GLANVILL *Van. Dogm.* xvi. 153 To make good its resemblance to that Commentitious Inanity. **1807–8** SYD. SMITH *Plymley's Lett.* Wks. 1859 II. 160/1 The embroidered inanities and the sixth-form effusions of Mr. Canning. **1838** DICKENS *Nich. Nick.* xxviii, If this young lord does.. whisper his drivelling inanities in your ears. **1863** HOLLAND *Lett. Joneses* viii. 122 The vanities and inanities of fashion.

inantherate (ɪn'ænθərət), *a. Bot.* [f. IN-^{3} + ANTHER + -ATE^2.] (See quot.)

1866 *Treas. Bot.* 620/2 *Inantherate*, bearing no anther; applied to sterile filaments or abortive stamens.

inanthe'riferous, *a. Bot.* [IN-^{3}.] = prec.

1855 MAYNE *Expos. Lex.*, *Inantheriferus*, applied to a filament of a stamen which bears no anther: inantheriferous. **1886** in *Syd. Soc. Lex.*

†**in'antidotal**, *a. Obs. rare*$^{-1}$. [IN-^{3}.] Not antidotal, of no value as an antidote.

1639 G. DANIEL *Ecclus.* xviii. 50 Take the Cordiall To prevent Sicknes; In-antidotall Protraction makes it.

in antis: see IN *Lat. prep.*

†**in'anulate**, *v. Obs. rare*$^{-1}$. [f. It. *inanellare* 'to frounse, or crisp, or curle haires' (Florio, 1598), refashioned after L. *ānulus* ring: see -ATE^3.] *intr.* To curl, form ringlets.

1592 R. D. *Hypnerotomachia* 23 Theyr tresses of haire.. crisping and inanulating by their eares.

in'apathy. *rare*$^{-1}$. [IN-^{3}.] The absence or opposite of apathy; feeling, sensibility.

a **1846** *Edin. Rev.* cited by Worcester. Hence in later Dicts.

ina'pertous, *a. Bot. rare.* [f. L. *inapert-us* unopen + -OUS.] (See quot.)

1866 *Treas. Bot.* 620/2 *Inapertous*, not opened, although its habit is to open.

†**inapes**, var. of A-NAPES. *Obs.*

1552–3 *Inv. Ch. Goods, Staffs.* in *Ann. Lichfield* (1863) IV. 52 One vestement of fustian inapes.

†**ina'postate**, *a. Obs. rare*$^{-1}$. [IN-^{3}.] Not apostate; not revolted; loyally disposed.

1648 HERRICK *Hesper., To his brother Nicholas*, The man that will but lay his eares, As inapostate, to the thing he heares, Shall by [*printed* be] his hearing quickly come to see The truth of travails lesse in bookes then thee.

†**inappa'ration.** *Obs. rare*$^{-0}$. [ad. L. *inapparātiōn-em*, f. *in-* (IN-^{3}) + *apparātio* APPARATION.] 'Want of provision' (Cockeram, 1623).

ina'pparent, *a.* [IN-^{3}.] Not apparent or manifest; invisible; latent.

1626 DONNE *Serm.* lxxx. 823 Fire, a body more disputable and inapparant. **1655** STANLEY *Hist. Philos.* I. (1701) 24/2. **1694** SALMON *Bates' Dispens.* (1713) 316/1 Then the inapparent Writing done with the first Liquor appears black. **1753** N. TORRIANO *Gangr. Sore Throat* 23 A latent or inapparent Flooding.. which does not appear outwardly. **1898** J. CAIRD *Univ. Sermons* 371 These are the invisible realities, inapparent, impenetrable to sense. **1960** *New Scientist* 16 June 1521/3 This vaccine is then fed to the individual and produces an inapparent or mild infection which leads to immunity. **1970** *Ibid.* 15 Jan. 101/1 One of the most difficult variables in biological research—namely, inapparent infections, which can cause differing and misleading responses to experimental treatments.

†**ina'ppealable**, *a. Obs. rare.* [IN-^{3}.] = INAPPELLABLE.

1651 HOWELL *Surv. Venice* 14 All.. flagitious crimes.. they have inappealable power to punish.

inappeasable (ɪnə'piːzəb(ə)l), *a.* [IN-^{3}.] Not appeasable; not to be appeased.

1840 J. F. COOPER *Pathfinder* ii, The appetite of the aboriginal American for venison being seemingly inappeasable. *a* **1848** R. W. HAMILTON *Rew. & Punishm.* iii. (1853) 110 Inappeasable longings of the soul. **1851** DIXON *W. Penn* xxxiv. (1872) 321 These disorders were a source of inappeasable grief to Penn.

inappellable (ɪnə'pɛləb(ə)l), *a.* [f. IN-^{3} + L. *appellāre* to APPEAL + -BLE.] That cannot be appealed against; from which there is no appeal.

1825 COLERIDGE *Aids Refl.* (1848) I. 180 A supreme and inappellable tribunal. **1855** LEWIS *Credib. Early Rom. Hist.* xii. §9 II. 28 The absolute, undivided, and inappellable power of the dictator. **1887** T. A. TROLLOPE *What I remember* I. 320 The inappellable law of fashion.

Hence **inappella'bility**.

a **1834** COLERIDGE *Lit. Rem.* III. 25 The inappellability of the Councils.

inappen'diculate, *a. Zool.* and *Bot.* [IN-^{3}.] Not appendiculate; having no appendicles or minute appendages, as the branchiæ of certain molluscs or the anthers of certain plants.

1855 MAYNE *Expos. Lex.*, *Inappendiculatus*,.. applied by H. Cassini to the bracteæ of the pericline of the Synantheræ,.. inappendiculate. **1880** GRAY *Struct. Bot.* (ed. 6) 416/1. **1886** in *Syd. Soc. Lex.*

ina'ppertinent, *a. rare.* [IN-^{3}.] Not appertinent; impertinent.

1814 COLERIDGE in J. Cottle *Early Recoll.* (1837) II. 204 What, in a great commercial city, will not be deemed trifling or inappertinent.

inappetence (ɪn'æpɪtəns). [f. IN-^{3} + APPETENCE: cf. F. *inappétence* (16th c. in Hatz.-Darm.).] Lack of appetence; want of appetite, desire, or longing.

a **1691** BOYLE *Agst. Custom. Swearing* 106 [He] takes a long walk to the physician's lodging, to beg some remedy for his inappetence. **1733** CHEYNE *Eng. Malady* II. vii. §3 (1734) 188 Inappetence and Weakness of Digestion. **1859** TODD *Cycl. Anat.* V. 670/1 Irresistible impulse, alternating with total inappetence. **1887** MISS LINSKILL *In Exchange for Soul* III. lxiv. 228 His inappetence for spending money on himself.

inappetency (ɪn'æpɪtənsɪ). [f. IN-^{3} + APPETENCY: see -ENCY.] = prec.

1611 COTGR., *Anorexie*, inapetencie. **1647** LILLY *Chr. Astrol.* xliv. 280 There's inappetency of the Ventricle. **1733**

CHEYNE *Eng. Malady* II. v. §3 Loathing and Inappetency.. always attends..all Disorders. **1884** T. HARDY in *Independent* 7 Feb., Her virtues lay in no resistant force of character, but in a natural inappetency for evil things.

inappetent (ɪn'æpɪtənt), *a.* [IN-³.] Not appetent; without appetite or desire.
1796 COLERIDGE *Lett.* (1895) 176 Totally inappetent of food. **1803** *Monthly Mag.* XVI. 123 Inappetent, restless, and uneasy for want..of exercise. **1886** MISS LINSKILL *Haven under the Hill* II. i. 7 She awakened very slowly, and with an inappetent listlessness.

inappetible (ɪn'æpɪtɪb(ə)l), *a.* [IN-³.] Not appetible; that awakens no appetite or desire.
1874 McCOSH *Scott. Philos.* xix. (1875) 148 The place which the idea of an object..as appetible or inappetible has in all feeling.

inapplicability (ɪn,æplɪkə'bɪlɪtɪ). [f. next: see -ITY: cf. *applicability*.] The quality of being inapplicable; incapability of being fitly applied. Also with *an* and *pl.*, an instance of this.
1673 H. MORE *App. Antid. Idol.* xxxvi. 43 The inapplicability is so easily discoverable. **1792** BURKE *Let. to Sir H. Langrishe* Wks. VI. 301 The inapplicability of your own old principles to the circumstances that are likely to influence your conduct against these principles. **1820** L. HUNT *Indicator* No. 18 These scripture names of men.. have given rise to some curious inapplicabilities, as Adam Smith and David Hume, two infidel philosophers. **1884** W. J. COURTHOPE *Addison* i. 21 Retaining the old ideas.. without being able to perceive their inapplicability to the existing nature of things.

inapplicable (ɪn'æplɪkəb(ə)l), *a.* [IN-³. Cf. F. *inapplicable* (18th c.).] Not applicable; incapable of being applied (*to* some case); unsuitable (*to* the purpose).
1656 *Burton's Diary* (1828) I. 273 The late king cited statutes, but you declared them inapplicable in the case of the commission of array. *a* **1794** SIR W. JONES *Two Hymns to Pracriti* Argt., Lest European critics should consider a few of the images as inapplicable to Indian manners. **1839** JAMES *Louis XIV*, IV. 262 To show that this reasoning is inapplicable. **1881** LUBBOCK *Addr. Brit. Assoc.* in *Nature* No. 618. 409 Döppler's method was practically inapplicable, because the amount of effect on the colour would be utterly insensible.

in'applicableness. *rare*⁻⁰. [-NESS.]
1. = INAPPLICABILITY.
1730–6 BAILEY (folio), *Inapplicableness*, uncapableness of being applied to.
†**2.** = INAPPLICATION. (Cf. APPLICABLE *a.* 1.)
1727 BAILEY vol. II, *Inapplicableness*, heedlesness [*pr.* heedfulness], want of Application.

in'applicably, *adv.* [f. as prec. + -LY².] In a way not capable of application; unsuitably.
1864 in WEBSTER. **1884** LD. BURY in *Cyclist* 13 Feb. 251/1 That sex, which has been..perhaps inapplicably, termed the weaker.

in'applicate, *a. Bot.* [ad. mod.L. *inapplicāt-us*, f. *in-* (IN-³) + *applicātus* APPLICATE.]
1855 MAYNE *Expos. Lex.*, *Inapplicatus*, used by H. Cassini, to the bracteoles of the Synanthereæ, when they are not applied against the clinanthium: inapplicate. **1886** in *Syd. Soc. Lex.*

inapplication (ɪnæplɪ'keɪʃən). [IN-³. Cf. F. *inapplication* (1718 in *Dict. Acad.*).]
1. Want of application; the fact or habit of not applying oneself to one's duties.
1721 BAILEY, *Inapplication*, heedlesness. **1755** JOHNSON, *Inapplication*, indolence, negligence. *a* **1797** H. WALPOLE *Mem. Geo. II* (1847) II. viii. 259 The Prince excused his own inapplication on the foot of idleness. **1800** W. TAYLOR in Robberds *Mem.* I. 330 Inapplication, versatility, are, I suppose, the dangers of a mind like Henry's.
2. The condition of not applying or having no application to the case; inapplicability.
1784 J. BARRY in *Lect. Paint.* iii. (1848) 146 These rules.. appear to me to be very inconclusive, and much out of their place, when thus applied to prescribed forms..Besides their utter inapplication, these multiplied little rules seem [etc.].

inapposite (ɪn'æpəzɪt), *a.* [IN-³.] Not apposite, not to the point, out of place; impertinent.
1661 K. W. *Conf. Charac.*, *Pune Pulpit-filler* (1860) 84 Another sort..fill up their sermon with..a heaped congeries of impertinent and inapposite Scriptures. **1670** W. SIMPSON *Hydrol. Ess.* 130 He supposed my Answer to be inapposite only to that point afore-noted. **1809** HAN. MORE *Cœlebs* I. 236 (Jod.), I..forbore telling her how totally inapposite her application was. **1838–9** HALLAM *Hist. Lit.* IV. vii. §29 IV. 313 A name..inapposite to our purpose. **1862** F. HALL *Hindu Philos. Syst.* 260 In one respect, that illustration is inapposite.
Hence **in'appositely** *adv.*, in an inapposite manner, unsuitably, impertinently.
1620–55 I. JONES *Stone-Heng* (1725) 6 It may not inappositely be observ'd. **1823** BENTHAM *Not Paul* 69 Under the name so inappositely represented at present by the English word deacon. **1884** *Law Times* LXXVII. 307/1 An Act of Parliament inappositely described..as the 'Settled Land Act 1882'.

inappositeness (ɪn'æpəzɪtnɪs). [f. INAPPOSITE *a.* + -NESS.] The character or quality of being inapposite.
1893 E. SALTUS *Madam Sapphira* iii. 50 With an inappositeness which afterward was to occur to Nevius as curious. **1894** W. J. LOCKE *At Gate of Samaria* (1895) xii. 134 The words estranged them still further. They were pathetic in their ludicrous inappositeness.

inappreciable (ɪnə'priːʃɪəb(ə)l). Also 9 -tiable. [f. IN-³ + APPRECIABLE. Cf. F. *inappréciable* (15th c. in Hatz.-Darm.).] Not appreciable.
†**1.** That cannot be sufficiently appreciated, valued, or esteemed; invaluable, priceless. *Obs.*
1787 T. JEFFERSON *Writ.* (1859) II. 153 His knowledge and integrity render his value inappreciable. **1827** SCOTT *Napoleon* I. iii. 86 A barrier of inappreciable value. **1868** MILMAN *St. Paul's* xvii. 446 Gratitude for his inappreciable services.
2. Too inconsiderable to be estimated or valued; imperceptible; of no consequence.
1802 SMITHSON in *Phil. Trans.* XCIII. 14 Excepting an inappretiable quantity of virtue of lime. **1862** F. HALL *Hindu Philos. Syst.* 69 An atom is..inappreciable by any of the senses. **1878** HUXLEY *Physiogr.* 116 The rise from the river to their summits would be almost inappreciable in a diagram.
3. Not capable of being appreciated; beyond the appreciation of some person, etc.
1855 MISS COBBE *Intuit. Mor.* 36 Their libraries of wisdom, their galleries of beauty, inappreciable to beast and bird.
Hence **ina'ppreciably** *adv.*, without, beyond, or beneath appreciation; imperceptibly.
1860 PATMORE *Faithful for Ever* in *Sat. Rev.* 10 Nov. 590 One athirst, who comes thereby And inappreciably sips The deep with disappointed lips. **1893** F. HALL in *Nation* (N.Y.) LVI. 274/1 Inappreciably as the fact imports my contention. *Mod.* The difference is inappreciably minute.

inappreciation (ɪnəpriːʃɪ'eɪʃən). [IN-³.] Want of appreciation; failure to appreciate or estimate duly.
1864 in WEBSTER. **1869** J. MARTINEAU *Ess.* II. 120 This strange inappreciation of the relative position. **1881** MRS. C. PRAED *Policy & P.* I. 263 Embittered by disappointment and inappreciation.

inappreciative (ɪnə'priːʃɪətɪv), *a.* [IN-³.] Not appreciative; wanting in appreciation. Hence **ina'ppreciatively** *adv.*; **ina'ppreciativeness.**
1868 HOLME LEE *B. Godfrey* xxxi. 166 Colonel Godfrey's inappreciativeness of his darling. **1881** *World* 27 July 8/1 The religious papers have expressed themselves, not inappreciatively, but with a certain subacidity of grief. **1897** *Educat. Rev.* XIII. 69 Which makes even the dullest and most inappreciative peasant remove his hat.

†**inappre'hending,** *ppl. a. Obs. rare.* [IN-³.] That does not apprehend; inapprehensive.
1652 GAULE *Magastrom.* 161 It is not for the inapprehending part to have an ordaining power over the apprehensive whole.

inapprehensible (ɪnæprɪ'hɛnsɪb(ə)l), *a.* [IN-³. Cf. late L. *inapprehensibilis*, perh. the direct source.] Not apprehensible; that cannot be apprehended or grasped by the senses or intellect.
a **1641** BP. MOUNTAGU *Acts & Mon.* (1642) 25. **1642** MILTON *Apol. Smect.* Introd., Wks. (1851) 273 Those celestiall songs to others inapprehensible. **1841** EMERSON *Addr., Meth. Nature* Wks. (Bohn) II. 231 Your end should be one inapprehensible to the senses. **1872** *Contemp. Rev.* XX. 674 Sublimated into inapprehensible nothingness.

inapprehension (ɪnæprɪ'hɛnʃən). [IN-³.]
1. Want of apprehension; failure to apprehend or grasp mentally.
1744 WARBURTON *Wks.* (1811) XI. 362 An intire inapprehension of the very drift and purpose of it. *a* **1808** HURD *Serm.* Wks. 1811 VI. xxi. 306 It is not envy, but inapprehension, which sets them on work. **1843** POE *Purloined Letter* Wks. 1864 I. 277 The moral inapprehension by which the intellect suffers to pass unnoticed those considerations which are too obtrusively and too palpably self-evident.
2. Absence of apprehension of danger. *rare.*
1865 *Pall Mall G.* 2 Oct. 5 He took advantage of their inapprehension and defenceless condition to gratify the worst passions.

inapprehensive (ɪnæprɪ'hɛnsɪv), *a.* [IN-³.] Not apprehensive; without apprehension: **a.** that does not grasp mentally, or perceive by sense; **b.** that does not apprehend danger.
1651–3 JER. TAYLOR *Serm. for Year* I. v. 63 [They] remain stupid and inapprehensive. **1666** STILLINGFL. *Serm.* (1683) i. 5 When were they ever more secure and inapprehensive of their danger than at this time? *a* **1732** ATTERBURY *Serm.* (1737) III. 138 In respect of divine truth they may be altogether inapprehensive and stupid. **1867** BUSHNELL *Mor. Uses Dark Th.* 99 The more inward parts of the body are comparatively inapprehensive.
Hence **inappre'hensiveness.**
1652 SPARKE *Prim. Devot.* (1660) 172 Not out of a Stoical Apathy, or inapprehensivenesse, but out of a Christian magnanimity. **1836** *New Monthly Mag.* XLVIII. 456 In pure inapprehensiveness of the *juste milieu.*

inapproachable (ɪnə'prəʊtʃəb(ə)l), *a.* [IN-³.] That cannot be approached; inaccessible, unapproachable.
1828 in WEBSTER. **1856** RUSKIN *Mod. Paint.* IV. v. App. i, Many subjects..may be dealt with by this kind of art which are inapproachable by any other. **1858** HOBHOUSE *Italy* (1859) II. 158 The Forum and the vast arcades of the Basilica of Constantine were..almost inapproachable from filth. **1860** PUSEY *Min. Proph.* 427 His inapproachable light is darkness to eyes which would gaze on it.

Hence **ina'pproachably** *adv.*; **inapproach-a'bility**, unapproachableness.
1864 WEBSTER, *Inapproachably.* **1871** tr. *Lange's Comm. Jeremiah* 196 Defiant in its inapproachability.

inappropriable (ɪnə'prəʊprɪəb(ə)l), *a. rare.* [IN-³.] Not capable of being appropriated.
1851 S. JUDD *Margaret* II. ii. (1871) 201 Unreachable, inappropriable, anagogical.
Hence **ina'ppropriableness.**
1836 R. F. WILSON in *Newman's Lett.* (1891) II. 206 The 'inappropriableness' of Church property..to Church purposes different from those which the letter of the Founder's intentions prescribed.

inappropriate (ɪnə'prəʊprɪət), *a.* [IN-³.] Not appropriate; unsuitable to the particular case; unfitting, improper.
1804 *Ann. Rev.* II. 19/2 A rambling inappropriate retrospect of Indian history. **1848** DICKENS *Dombey* ii, [He] invaded the grave silence..with the singularly inappropriate air of 'A Cobbler there was'. **1883** H. DRUMMOND *Nat. Law in Spir. W.* Pref. (ed. 2) 13 Inappropriate Hybridism is checked by the Law of Sterility.

ina'ppropriately, *adv.* [f. prec. + -LY².] In an inappropriate manner; unfittingly.
1847 in CRAIG. **1867** FREEMAN *Norm. Conq.* I. App. 599 Verses not inappropriately chosen for the epilogue of his work. **1870–4** COCHRAN *Let.* in Anderson *Missions Amer. Bd.* IV. xxxvii. 314 This innovation..was not inappropriately followed by the suspension of the Sabbath-school and preaching service.

ina'ppropriateness. [f. as prec. + -NESS.] Inappropriate quality; unfitness, unsuitableness.
1847 in CRAIG. **1856** OLMSTED *Slave States* 124 The very levity and inappropriateness with which it is applied, shows a want of a right appreciation of it. **1876** MOZLEY *Univ. Serm.* i. 8 The inappropriateness of the punishment constitutes its injustice.

inapt (ɪn'æpt), *a.* [f. IN-³ + APT. Cf. INEPT.]
1. Not adapted to the purpose or occasion; unsuitable, inappropriate, inapposite.
1744 HARRIS *Three Treat.* III. i. (1765) 142 Others are Inapt, Incongruous, and Disagreeable. **1818** COBBETT *Pol. Reg.* XXXIII. 436 The occasion rendered this inapt and far-fetched. **1885** *Law Times* LXXVIII. 242/1 The words.. being altogether inapt to express more than one devolution of title.
2. Not apt; wanting in aptitude or skill; unskilful, awkward.
1860 *Sat. Rev.* IX. 600/2 Uncouth and inapt to charm the female heart. **1867** D. G. MITCHELL *Rural Stud.* 246 However inapt a man may be at..horticultural pursuits. **1895** *Current Hist.* (Buffalo) V. 820 The well-meant but hopelessly inapt attempt of the powers.

inaptitude (ɪn'æptɪtjuːd). [IN-³.] Want of aptitude. **1.** Unfitness, unsuitableness, inappropriateness.
a **1688** CUDWORTH *Immut. Mor.* (1731) 149 Such as are Cause, Effect..Equality, Inequality, Aptitude, Inaptitude, Symmetry, Asymmetry. **1790** BURKE *Fr. Rev.* Wks. V. 98 A moral and almost physical inaptitude of the man to the function. **1865** M. ARNOLD *Ess. Crit.* v. (1875) 194 Our excessive neglect of the idea and our consequent inaptitude for it.
2. Unreadiness, unskilfulness, unhandiness.
1620 E. BLOUNT *Horæ Subsec.* 103 Inaptitude to the former [honourable expences] shewes a man to be of a poore and ignoble spirit. **1715–16** STEELE *Town-Talk* No. 8 This inaptitude is too notorious to have left a nation..the least room for reporting any advantageous circumstance of this remarkable person. **1834** *Edin. Rev.* LIX. 54 There was such inaptitude in the English people. **1884** *West. Morn. News* 5 Sept. 4/5 Rags of fish and tough meat lead people daily to believe that national cookery is another name for old inaptitude.

in'aptly, *adv.* [f. INAPT + -LY².] In an inapt manner; unfitly, inappropriately.
a **1834** COLERIDGE cited by Worcester. **1859** C. BARKER *Assoc. Princ.* ii. 34 These associations may not inaptly be compared to the then military organization of the country. **1885** *Law Times* LXXVIII. 211/2 An auction is not inaptly called *locus penitentiæ.*

in'aptness. [f. as prec. + -NESS.] The quality of being inapt; inaptitude.
1795–1814 WORDSW. *Excursion* II. 70 The poor man.. unable to subdue Impatience through inaptness to perceive General distress in his particular lot. **1841** MYERS *Cath. Th.* III. §49. 186 Some sentence..to which it may attach itself with not more obvious inaptness. **1844** W. H. MILL *Serm. Tempt. Christ* iii. 68 That luxury..which..produces of itself inaptness for spiritual objects.

†**in'aquate,** *ppl. a. Obs.* [ad. L. *inaquāt-us*, pa. pple. of *inaquāre* to turn into water, f. *in-* (IN-²) + *aqua* water.] Converted or transformed into water. Hence †**ina'quation**, conversion into water.
1550 CRANMER *Defence* 33b, Ther foloweth no Impanation thereof, no more than the holy ghost is Inaquate, that is to say, made water, being sacramentally ioyned to the water in baptisme. **1551** GARDNER *Explic., Transubst.* 126b, The solution to the seconde reason is allmost as soundely handled, alludynge from impanation to Inaquation, although it was neuer sayde in Scripture, this water is the holy ghoost.

inarable (ɪn'ærəb(ə)l), *a.* [IN-^{3}.] Not arable; incapable of being ploughed.

1656 BLOUNT *Glossogr.*, *Inarable*, not arable, that cannot be plowed. [Hence in BAILEY, JOHNSON, etc.] **1843** CARLYLE *Past & Pr.* III. viii, No soil, not even an inarable one. **1866** —— *Remin.* (1881) I. 166 A place lying all in dimples and wrinkles.. grassy but inarable.

†**inarate**, *v. Obs. rare*$^{-0}$. [f. ppl. stem of L. *inarāre* to plough in; also to till, cultivate.] 'To till ground' (Cockeram, 1623).

inarch (ɪn'ɑːtʃ), *v.*^{1} Also 8–9 **enarch.** [f. IN-^{2} + ARCH *v.*^{1}] *trans.* To graft by connecting a growing branch without separating it from its parent stock; to graft by approach: see APPROACH *sb.* 10.

1629, etc. [see INARCHING]. **1671** EVELYN *Kal. Hort.* 76 (July) Graff by Approach, Inarch, or Inoculate Jasmines, Oranges. **1762** HUDSON in *Phil. Trans.* LII. 499 It appears ..that a tree inarched between two other trees, though its root be cut off.. will continue to grow. **1845** *Florist's Jrnl.* 77 The remedy consists in grafting or inarching the Chinese varieties on some more durable and luxuriant growing kind.

Hence **in'arched** *ppl. a.*, grafted by approach.

1741 *Compl. Fam. Piece* II. iii. 390 Cut the inarched Orange Stocks from the bearing Trees. **1898** BAILEY *Pruning Bk.* 388 Inarched Elms.

in'arch, *v.*^{2} *rare.* [f. IN-^{1} + ARCH *v.*^{1}] *trans.* To arch in, encompass like an arch. Hence **in'arching** *ppl. a.*

1882 F. W. H. MYERS *Renewal of Youth* 203 When all the embracing earth, the inarching blue, Seemed the soul's cage no wings might battle through. **1893** W. W. PEYTON *Memorab. Jesus* ix. 281 The Divine Presence whom Christ calls His Father, who inarched the Spirit of Jesus and infolded Him.

inarching (ɪn'ɑːtʃɪŋ), *vbl. sb.* [f. INARCH *v.*^{1}]

1. The action or process of grafting by approach.

1629 PARKINSON *Paradisi, Ord. Orchard* iv. 543 Inarching is another manner of grafting in the stocke. **1727** BRADLEY *Fam. Dict.* s.v. *Grafting*, Grafting by.. Enarching. **1863** ALCOCK *Capit. Tycoon* I. 325 The Japanese understand, and sometimes practise, the inarching of plants. **1898** BAILEY *Pruning Bk.* 389 The union [of trees and branches] takes place more rapidly if the bark is removed from the conjoined surfaces and the exposed parts of the wounds covered with wax. This is a species of inarching.

2. *transf.* = ANAPLASTY. *rare.*

1646 SIR T. BROWNE *Pseud. Ep.* III. ix. 127 We might abate the Art of Taliacotius, and the new inarching of noses. **1650** BULWER *Anthropomet.* 78.

†**inarchitec'tonical**, *a. Obs. rare*$^{-1}$. [IN-^{3}.] Not architectonic.

1665 J. WEBB *Stone-Heng* (1725) 113 Absurdly inarchitectonical Expressions.

†**in'arcious**, *a. Obs. rare.* [? f. IN-^{3} + ART + -(I)OUS: cf. *ingracious*.] Not technically or professionally skilled. (See ART *sb.* 4.)

1547 BOORDE *Brev. Health* Pref. 2 This sayde archane science to the whiche none inarciouse persons can nor shal atteine to the knowledge. *Ibid.* 3, I aduertise al inarcyous phisitions to beware.

†**in'ardent**, *a. Obs. rare*$^{-1}$. [IN-^{3}.] Not ardent or burning.

1730 *Phil. Trans.* XXXVI. 289 The upper yellow Liquor is separated from the inardent sulphureous.

†**in'argentate**, *v. Obs. rare*$^{-0}$. [f. ppl. stem of L. *inargentāre* to overlay with silver, f. *in-* (IN-^{2}) + *argentum* silver.] 'To gild or cover with silver' (Cockeram, 1623). Hence †**inargen'tation**.

1658 in PHILLIPS. **1721** in BAILEY.

in'arguable, *a. rare.* [IN-^{3}.] Not arguable.

a **1875** HELPS in *Gd. Words* (1884) Mar. 206 Love.. incomprehensible, indefinable, inarguable-about.

†**in'ark**, *v. Obs. rare.* [f. IN-^{1} or ^{2} + ARK *sb.*] *trans.* To put or enclose in an ark.

1595 MARKHAM *Sir R. Grinvile* (Arb.) 59 Greater, and better then inarked he, Which in the worlds huge deluge did suruiue. **1646** W. BRIDGE *Serm.* (1647) 17 Get your soules in-arked in all these promises.

inarm (ɪn'ɑːm), *v.* Also 9 **enarm.** [f. IN-^{1} or ^{2} + ARM *sb.*^{1}: cf. F. *embracer*, *-brasser* to embrace.] *trans.* To clasp within or as with the arms; to embrace; to throw the arms round. Hence **in'armed, in'arming** *ppl. adjs.*

1612 SELDEN *Illustr. Drayton's Poly-olb.* xiii. 223 Warwickshire.. you might call Middle-Engle for equality of distance from the inarming Ocean. **1713** M. HENRY *Wks.* (1835) II. 271/2 He [Christ] inarmed them [children], he took them into his embraces. **1839** BAILEY *Festus* xix. (1852) 276 As the twin tidal wave inarms the world. **1871** R. ELLIS *Catullus* lxiv. 28 Thee could Thetis inarm, most beauteous Ocean-daughter. **1875** BROWNING *Aristoph. Apol.* 11 Fire should have flung a passion of embrace About thee.. resplendently inarmed. **1876** —— *A Forgiveness* 126 Gallant and lady.. Enarming each the other. **1881** F. W. H. MYERS *Wordsworth* 43 Norway's inarming melancholy sea.

inarm, obs. form of ENARM, to arm.

1552 LYNDESAY *Monarche* 2150 Ane man of weir, Inarmit weill with sword and speir.

inar'ticulable, *a. rare.* [f. IN-^{3} + *articulable*, f. L. *articulā-re* to ARTICULATE + -BLE.] That cannot be articulated or pronounced articulately.

1801 W. TAYLOR in *Monthly Mag.* XII. 99 To unite in one termination b, d, g, v, or z, with p, t, k, f, or s, is inarticulable.

inarticulacy (ɪnɑː'tɪkjʊləsɪ). [f. INARTICULA(TE *a.* + -CY.] Inarticulateness.

1921 *Observer* 11 Sept. 10/2 That it has not done so.. we must ascribe.. to the inarticulacy of the scientist himself. **1927** M. SADLEIR *Trollope: a Comm.* 41 He has virtually entreated her forgiveness for his inarticulacy. **1951** A. BARON *Rosie Hogarth* 81 Perhaps it was this, more than his inarticulacy,.. that had held him back. **1970** *Listener* 30 July 157/2 Prone to miscarriages, inarticulacy, and general indecision. **1971** *Daily Tel.* 9 Oct. 9/6 'Y'know' and 'I mean' and other apologies for inarticulacy.

inarticulate (ɪnɑː'tɪkjʊlət), *a.* [ad. L. *inarticulāt-us*, f. *in-* (IN-^{3}) + *articulātus* ARTICULATE. Cf. F. *inarticulé*.] Not articulate: the opposite of ARTICULATE.

1. Not jointed or hinged; esp. in *Zool.* and *Bot.* Not having articulation; not composed of segments united by joints.

1607 TOPSELL *Four-f. Beasts* (1658) 449 The whole body inarticulate, and not well compounded for the outward sight. **1610** GUILLIM *Heraldry* III. xiii. (1611) 124 Such beasts as haue their feet Solid or Vndiuided or.. inarticulat, that is to say without toes. **1650** BULWER *Anthropomet.* xxi. 230 The Feet of women, which being naturally short and round, and also inarticulate. **1776** DA COSTA *Conchol.* 242 A hinge is inarticulate when not set with any visible joints or teeth. **1846** DANA *Zooph.* (1848) 639 Gorgonidæ forming an inarticulate solid stony axis. **1851** RICHARDSON *Geol.* viii. 229 Body inarticulate, soft and pulpy.

b. Of or belonging to the division *Inarticulata* of Brachiopods, with non-articulate valves, now called *Ecardines*.

In mod. Dicts.

c. Disjoined, unconnected, dislocated.

1852 G. W. CURTIS *Howadji in Syria* (1872) 26 (Funk) Heliopolis is a mass of sand mounds now, and a few inarticulate stone relics.

2. Of sound or voice: Not of the nature of articulate speech; not consisting of distinct parts having each a definite meaning; not uttered or emitted with expressive or intelligible modulations; without distinction of syllables: as a long musical note, a groan, or the sounds produced by some animals. Also, not clearly articulated, indistinctly pronounced.

1603 HOLLAND *Plutarch's Mor.* 643 A kinde of voice, not altogether inarticulate and insignificant. **1610** G. FLETCHER *Christ's Vict.* To Rdr., The inarticulate sounds of musique. **1662** STILLINGFL. *Orig. Sacr.* I. iii. §1 Had they not learned the inarticulate voice of the goats. **1670** DRYDEN *Tyran. Love* Pref., Solemn Musick, which is inarticulate Poesie. **1790** BEATTIE *Moral Sc.* I. i. §4. 81 Inarticulate sounds may be divided into musical sound and noise. **1828** WORDSW. *Power of Sound* xiii, Ye banded instruments of wind and chords Unite.. Your inarticulate notes with the voice of words! **1856** SIR B. BRODIE *Psychol. Inq.* I. ii. 50 In the attempt to do so he produced sounds which were wholly inarticulate.

b. Unable to speak articulately or distinctly; not using articulate speech; dumb.

1754 H. WALPOLE *Lett. to Mann* 28 Mar., The poor Earl, who is inarticulate with the palsy. **1850** CARLYLE *Latter-d. Pamph.* ii. (1872) 41 The heavy miseries pressing.. on the great dumb inarticulate class. **1855** THACKERAY *Newcomes* v, [She] was found.. in the morning, inarticulate, but still alive. **1870** MORRIS *Earthly Par.* I. I. 289 Then inarticulate with rage and grief Phineus turned on him.

c. *transf.* Having no distinct meaning.

1855 BRIMLEY *Ess., Poetry & Crit.* 191 Inarticulate gibberish. **1899** *Westm. Gaz.* 7 Feb., The beautiful comprehensiveness of these inarticulate Articles.

†**inar'ticulate**, *v. Obs. rare.* [f. IN-^{2} + ARTICULATE *v.*] *trans.* To joint in, joint together.

1713 DERHAM *Phys.-Theol.* IV. iii. Note 19 (1727) 124 In Man, and Quadrupeds, they are four, curiously inarticulated with one another.

inar'ticulated, *ppl. a.* [IN-^{3}.] Not articulated.

1. *Zool.* and *Bot.* Unjointed: = INARTICULATE *a.* 1.

1830 LINDLEY *Nat. Syst. Bot.* 280 Arborescent stems with rigid.. inarticulated leaves, called fronds. **1861** HULME tr. *Moquin-Tandon* II. II. 60 Lamarck.. associated the Polype or Compound Animals with Inarticulated Animals. *Ibid.* II. VI. i. 292 A sucker inclosed in an inarticulated sheath. **1877** HUXLEY *Anat. Inv. Anim.* viii. 466 In the inarticulated Brachiopods, our knowledge of the nervous system is very imperfect.

2. Of sound or voice: Not uttered articulately; = INARTICULATE *a.* 2.

1824 GALT *Rothelan* II. IV. viii. 169 She.. listened to the inarticulated menaces of his inflamed spirit. **1886** *Pall Mall G.* 22 Apr. 13/2 Cries of 'Out with the Premier, and give us a railroad', alternated with the fierce, inarticulated yells.

inar'ticulately, *adv.* [f. INARTICULATE *a.* + -LY^{2}.] In an inarticulate manner; without words or syllables; without distinct articulation or expression; with indistinct utterance, indistinctly.

a **1660** HAMMOND *Serm. God of Bethel* Wks. 1683 IV. 497 The Divine admonitions and holy laws whisper'd inarticulately in our hearts. **1760–72** H. BROOKE *Fool of Qual.* (1809) IV. 66, I muttered something, as I suppose, inarticulately, toward an answer. **1800** MRS. HERVEY *Mourtray Fam.* I. 215 Emma inarticulately attempted to express her regret at this unfortunate circumstance. **1884** SEELEY in *Contemp. Rev.* Oct. 501 They have.. but inarticulately striven to communicate it to others.

inar'ticulateness. [f. as prec. + -NESS.] The quality or condition of being inarticulate or of not using articulate speech; lack of clear articulation, indistinctness of utterance.

1731 BAILEY, *Inarticulateness*, the being not articulate, indistinct, confused. **1891** *Spectator* 14 Mar. 376/1 Not in the least discouraged by the banter his inarticulateness excited.

†**inarticu'lation**^{1}. *Obs.* [f. IN-^{2} + ARTICULATION: cf. INARTICULATE *v.*] The jointing of one thing into another; = ENARTHROSIS.

1578 BANISTER *Hist. Man.* I. 24 Certaine cauities.. of the three neither most ribbes seruyng also to their inarticulation. **1616** SURFL. & MARKH. *Country Farme* 472 For the better perfecting of this inarticulation, there are two edges or brimmes, that so they may the better ioyne together. **1634** T. JOHNSON *Parey's Chirurg.* VI. xlii. (1678) 165 Enarthrosis or Inarticulation is a kind of Dearticulation, in which a deep cavity receives a thick and long head.

inarticu'lation^{2}. *rare.* [IN-^{3}: cf. INARTICULATE *a.*] Absence of distinct articulation; inarticulate utterance.

1765 FRANKLIN *Lett.* Wks. 1887 III. 397, I might have mentioned inarticulation among the defects in common speech that are assumed as beauties in modern singing. *a* **1773** CHESTERF. (T.), The oracles meaned to be obscure; but then it was by the ambiguity of the expression, and not by the inarticulation of the words.

inartificial (ɪnɑːtɪ'fɪʃəl), *a.* [ad. L. *inartificiālis* (Quintilian), f. *in-* (IN-^{3}) + *artificiālis* ARTIFICIAL (used to render Gr. ἄτεχνος). Cf. F. *inartificiel* (16th c.).] Not artificial.

1. Not resulting from art or artifice; not produced by constructive skill; natural. Now *rare*.

1656 STANLEY *Hist. Philos.* VII. (1701) 329/1 There are.. two kinds of Fire, one artificial, requisite to the use of life, which converteth nutriment into it self; the other inartificial (so Cicero renders ἀτεχνικὸν) by which all things grow, and are preserved. **1660** JER. TAYLOR *Worthy Commun.* Introd. 8 It is nothing but a shining cloud.. cast into a contingent and inartificial shape. **1672** GREW *Philos. Hist. Plants* §8 When needful to add the preparations of Art to that of Nature; how to Enlarge those of Art, and Rectifie those which are indeed Inartificial.

2. Not in accordance with the principles of art; constructed without art or skill, rude, clumsy; inartistic.

1613 CAWDREY *Table Alph.* (ed. 3), *Inartificiall*, without art or skill. **1660** JER. TAYLOR *Duct. Dubit.* I. iv. (R.), For these and many other concurrent causes, the proceeding is inartificial and casual, and fit to lead the ignorant, but not the learned. **1671** in E. D. Neill *Virg. Carol.* (1886) 332 We are at continual charge to repair unskilfull and inartificial buildings. **1748** *Anson's Voy.* III. x. 412 The Chinese.. adhere to the rude and inartificial method of representing words by arbitrary marks. **1818** JAS. MILL *Brit. India* I. II. viii. 257 Their warlike instruments are rude, noisy and inartificial. **1830** HERSCHEL *Stud. Nat. Phil.* §326 Nothing could be.. more inartificial and unnatural than its classification. **1882** FARRAR *Early Chr.* II. 153 In the style of Papias, so inartificial and inexact, it cannot be regarded as certain that this is his meaning.

†**3.** Of an argument: Not according to the art of Logic; not deduced by logical methods from accepted premisses, but derived from authority or testimony. *Obs.*

1588 FRAUNCE *Lawiers Log.* I. ii. 10 Ramus divideth an argument into artificiall and inartificiall. **1639** FULLER *Holy War* III. xxvi. (1647) 157 The Legate used an inartificiall argument drawn from the authority of his place. *a* **1665** J. GOODWIN *Filled w. the Spirit* (1867) 339 There being two kinds of arguments or reasons.. whereby positions or tenets are wont to be proved, artificial and inartificial: by artificial, the meaning is, those that are levied and wrought out by the light and strength of the understanding from general principles; by inartificial, the testimony or consent of judgment amongst men about a matter. **1678** CUDWORTH *Intell. Syst.* Pref. 38 The Scripture-Faith, is not a meer Believing of Historicall Things, and upon Inartificiall Arguments, or Testimonies onely. **1725** WATTS *Logic* III. ii. §8 An artificial Argument is taken from the Nature and Circumstances of the Things;.. An inartificial Argument is the Testimony of another.

4. Not assumed or put on; artless, unaffected, natural. (Of personal qualities, actions, etc.; hence of persons.)

1664–5 EVELYN *Let. to Ld. Cornebery* Feb., This excesse, which.. proceeds from the honest and inartificial gratitude of [etc.]. **1779** MAD. D'ARBLAY *Diary* Jan., A rather pretty, pale girl; very young and inartificial. **1780** BURKE *Econ. Reform* Wks. III. 249 Any inartificial expression of the people's wishes. **1871** S. C. HALL *Bk. Memories* 383 His [Hogg's] vanity was so inartificial as to be absolutely amusing.

5. Without complexity or artifice; not elaborately designed or worked out; plain, simple, straightforward.

1823 J. F. COOPER *Pioneers* xi. (1869) 46 The 'long room' was but an extremely plain and inartificial temple. **1838–9** HALLAM *Hist. Lit.* I. iv. §23. I. 271 What is told in narration, according to the ancient inartificial form of tragedy, is finely told. **1893** H. WALKER *3 Cent. Scot. Lit.* I. 173 The thought

is without complexity, inartificial and, to a large extent, common property.

Hence **inartifici'ality**, inartificial character.

1847 L. HUNT *Men, Women, & B.* II. vi. 81 The defects, in want of character and probability..and inartificiality of ordonnance.

inartificially (ɪnɑːtɪˈfɪʃəlɪ), *adv.* [f. prec. + -LY².] In an inartificial manner; without art or technical skill; clumsily, unskilfully, inartistically; untechnically.

1623 COCKERAM II, Ilfauour'dly done, *Inconcinnately, Inarteficially.* **1647** JER. TAYLOR *Lib. Proph.* ii. 44 He did it so inartificially..that Arius thought he did not distinguish the persons. **1774** WHITE in *Phil. Trans.* LXV. 273 Her rude nest, consisting of fine grasses and feathers,..very inartificially laid together. **1815** SIMOND *Tour Gt. Brit.* I. 3 Three small dishes dressed very inartificially. **1831** SCOTT *Monast.* Introd., The incidents were inartifically huddled together. **1884** *Law Times Rep.* L. 254/1 The word 'heirs' would have been used inartificially, because used in reference to a legacy of personal estate simply.

b. In an artless or unaffected manner; simply, artlessly.

1825 *New Monthly Mag.* XVI. 300 The air..was sweetly and inartificially sung.

inartistic (ɪnɑːˈtɪstɪk), *a.* [IN-³.] Not artistic; not in accordance with the principles of art.

1859 GEO. ELIOT *A. Bede* 55 Inartistic figures crowding the canvass of life without adequate effect. **1875** JOWETT *Plato* (ed. 2) III. 191 This book is a very dull and inartistic performance.

b. Having no appreciation for or love of art; unskilled in art.

1875 STEDMAN *Vict. Poets* iv. (1887) 134 An inartistic nature and a dull or commonplace mind.

inar'tistical, *a.* [IN-³.] Not artistical; = prec. Hence **inartisti'cality**.

a **1849** POE *M. & L. Davidson* Wks. 1864 III. 226 The rhythm lapses in the most inartistical manner. —— *Longfellow, Willis*, etc. ibid. 348 The prevalence of this folly [speaking aside] detracts as much from the acting merit of our drama generally, as any other inartisticality. **1869** *Eng. Mech.* 31 Dec. 390/1 Minute and..inartistical notches.

inar'tistically, *adv.* [f. prec. + -LY².] In an inartistic manner; without conformity to the rules of art; without technical skill.

1862 'SHIRLEY' *Nugæ Crit.* viii. 348 The rude inscriptions on the tombs of these early christians,..inartistically scraped upon the stone. **1875** JOWETT *Plato* (ed. 2) V. 5 The externals of the scene, which are briefly and inartistically described, soon disappear. **1884** *Law Times Rep.* LI. 832/2 This last paragraph is rather inartistically drawn.

inasmuch (ɪnəzˈmʌtʃ), *adv.* [orig. three words *in as much* (in northern ME. *in als mikel*), subsequently sometimes written as two words, *in asmuch*, and now (esp. since 17th c.) as one.]

I. In phrase *inasmuch as*.

1. In so far as, to such a degree as, in proportion as, according as.

a **1300** *Cursor M.* 19596 Sua aght all preistes mar and less, In als mikel als in þaim es. *c* **1380** WYCLIF *Serm.* Sel. Wks. II. 206 Þe popis lawes in þis mater ben litil worþ but inasmyche as þei ben groundid of Goddis lawe or of resoun. **1526** TINDALE *Matt.* xxv. 40 In as moche as [*Ags. Gosp.* swa lange swa; WYCLIF as long as] ye have done it vnto won of the leest of these my brethren; ye have done it to me. **1577** *Test. 12 Patriarchs* (1604) 124 In as much as his mind is bent unto righteousness, he putteth away naughtiness. **1711** *Fingall MSS.* in *10th Rep. Hist. MSS. Comm.* App. v. 112 We are bound, inasmuch as it lyes in our power, to make satisfaction. **1836-7** SIR W. HAMILTON *Metaph.* ii. (1859) 32 God is only God inasmuch as he is the Moral Governor of a Moral World.

2. In that; in view of the fact that; seeing that; considering that; on the ground or for the reason that; since, because.

c **1386** CHAUCER *Nun's Pr. T.* 601, I haue to yow, quod he, ydoon trespas In as muche [*v.r.* moche] as I maked yow aferd Whan I yow hente. *c* **1450** LONELICH *Grail* xliii. 461 For In as Moche as God he was, he Ros Aȝen thorwgh his Owne Gras. **1545** BRINKLOW *Complaynt* 3 b, Inasmoch as there is no powr but of God. **1557** *N.T.* (Genev.) Ep. *iij, Euery man might fynde him in him selfe: in asmuche as we are all susteined and conserued by his vertue that dwelleth in vs. **1607** HIERON *Wks.* I. 193 He hath no iust cause to pleade against God; in as much as the conscience of his owne deserts will stop his mouth. **1771** WESLEY *Serm.* I. I. §5 Inasmuch as 'he was delivered for our sins'. **1818** CRUISE *Digest* (ed. 2) IV. 476 The recitals in the indenture of assignment were false, inasmuch as there never was any indenture of mortgage. **1870** DICKENS *E. Drood* iii, I am unable to reply that I am much the better for seeing you, Pussy, inasmuch as I see nothing of you.

II. †**3.** Without *as*: In an equal or like degree, likewise. *Obs.*

1727 SWIFT *Circumcision E. Curll* Wks. 1778 VII. 236 The wisest man that ever was, and inasmuch the richest, beyond all peradventure was a Jew.

†**in'asperate**, *v. Obs. rare.* [f. IN-² + L. *asperāre* to make rough or fierce, after *exasperate*: cf. Ital. *inasperare* (Florio), F. *enasprir* (Cotgr.), which may have served as models.] To provoke to cruelty or bitterness; to exasperate, embitter.

1599 SANDYS *Europæ Spec.* (1632) 242 Their doubt of farther inasperating the Turke in his Cruelty. *a* **1639** WOTTON in *Reliq.* (1685) 708 To sweeten the humours of that Family, not a little inaspirated by the Death of Alfonso.

ina'ssimilable, *a. rare.* [IN-³: so in mod.F.] Not assimilable, not capable of assimilation.

1886 in *Syd. Soc. Lex.*

inassimi'lation. *rare.* [IN-³.] Non-assimilation; failure to assimilate (food).

1885 *Alien. & Neurol.* VI. 541 It is one of the frequent occurrences in inassimilation that the organism is not uniformly well nourished.

inassuageable (ɪnəˈsweɪdʒəb(ə)l), *a.* [f. IN-³ + *assuageable*, f. ASSUAGE.] That cannot be assuaged or allayed.

1654 GAYTON *Pleasant Notes* III. v. 96 Don Mariotto, Knight of the Inasswagable Panch. **1887** G. GISSING *Thyrza* II. viii. 155 To bear the torture of an inassuageable desire.

†**ina'ssurance.** *Obs. rare.* [IN-³.] Want of assurance, uncertainty.

1614 JACKSON *Creed* III. Pref. a v a, Their inassurance of life eternall. **1675** EARL OF ESSEX *Lett.* (1770) 21 Not from any..unkindness or inassurance I have of his friendship.

inate, obs. form of INNATE.

ina'ttackable, *a. rare.* [IN-³.] Not attackable; that cannot be attacked; unassailable.

1832 *Fraser's Mag.* III. 234 The most precious, the most inattackable part of the existing system.

inattention (ɪnəˈtɛnʃən). [IN-³: perh. a. F. *inattention* (1701 in Hatz.-Darm.).] Want of attention; failure to attend, take heed, or fix the mind attentively upon any matter; want of observant care or notice; heedlessness, negligence.

1710 *Tatler* No. 187 ¶6 The universal Indolence and Inattention among us to Things that concern the Publick. **1759** ROBERTSON *Hist. Scot.* (1813) I. I. 30 This was not owing to the inattention of our princes. **1793** BEDDOES *Calculus* etc. 272 He was totally misled by some inattention in conducting his processes. **1839-40** W. IRVING *Wolfert's R.* (1855) 61, I recollected her inattention to my discourse of the preceding morning.

b. Want of courteous personal attention.

c **1792** HAYLEY *Let. to Cowper* (in *Sotheby's Catal.* July 1887), Damped by a little blank gloomy inattention from our great Friend. **1794** S. WILLIAMS *Vermont* 183 From the beardless countenance, and inattention of the Indian to the female.

inattentive (ɪnəˈtɛntɪv), *a.* [IN-³: cf. F. *inattentif* (1762 in *Dict. Acad.*).] Not attentive; not fixing or applying the mind steadily; not heedful or observant; negligent.

1741 WATTS *Improv. Mind* I. xv. §6 If we indulge the frequent rise and roving of passions, we shall thereby procure an unsteady and inattentive habit of mind. **1777** SHERIDAN *Sch. Scand.* IV. iii, She will find I have not been inattentive to her interest while living. **1784** COWPER *Task* VI. 120 All in sight of inattentive man. **1838** LYTTON *Alice* I 3 Or else Evelyn was peculiarly inattentive.

b. Not rendering personal attentions; neglectful.

1795 BURKE *Corr.* IV. 320, I hope you will not think me inattentive to you.

inattentively (ɪnəˈtɛntɪvlɪ), *adv.* [f. prec. + -LY².] In an inattentive manner; without paying attention or giving due heed; negligently.

1748 BUTLER *Serm.* Wks. 1874 II. 308 A kind of prejudice, to which perhaps most of us..may inattentively be liable. **1779-81** JOHNSON *L.P., Pope* Wks. IV. 41 Behaviour, inattentively deficient in respect. **1839** HALLAM *Hist. Lit.* II. II. v. §12 *note*, Corniani, and all the rest, must have read her very inattentively.

inattentiveness (ɪnəˈtɛntɪvnɪs). [f. as prec. + -NESS.] The quality or condition of being inattentive; want of attentiveness.

1754 RICHARDSON *Grandison* (1781) VI. lvi. 369 That inattentiveness to his own figure and appearance, which demonstrate the truly fine gentleman. **1785** PALEY *Mor. Philos.* V. v. (1830) 286 [The second inconvenience of a liturgy is] that the perpetual repetition of the same form of words produces weariness and inattentiveness in the congregation. **1884** J. PARKER *Apost. Life* III. 12 It hears tones that have not uttered themselves to inattentiveness.

†**inau'dacity.** *Obs. rare.* [f. L. *inaudax* not daring, timorous; cf. *audacity*.] Lack of boldness or resolution, timidity.

1594 CONSTABLE *Diana* VII. x, Such punie thoughts.. whose inaudacitie dares but base conceite.

inaudibility (ɪnɔːdɪˈbɪlɪtɪ). [f. next + -ITY.] The quality or condition of being inaudible; incapability of being heard.

1821 LAMB *Elia* Ser. I. *Old & New Schoolm.*, A whisper teases you by its provoking inaudibility. **1867** TYNDALL *Sound* vii. (1875) 272 The steamer was immediately turned and urged back to our last position of inaudibility. **1870** *Daily News* 17 Feb., The female witnesses were, with one exception, indistinct almost to inaudibility.

inaudible (ɪnˈɔːdɪb(ə)l), *a.* [ad. L. *inaudībil-is*, f. *in-* (IN-³) + *audībilis* AUDIBLE: cf. It. *inaudibile* (Florio, 1598.).] Not audible; not capable of being heard; imperceptible to the ear.

1601 SHAKS. *All's Well* V. iii. 41 Th' inaudible, and noiselesse foot of time. **1626** BACON *Sylva* §122 As the Bullet moueth so swift, that it is Inuisible, to the same Swiftnesse of Motion maketh it Inaudible. *a* **1770** C. SMART *Ode St. Cecilia* i, Ye, that inform the tuneful spheres, Inaudible to mortal ears. **1875** JOWETT *Plato* (ed. 2) I. 129 An echo in the room which rendered his words inaudible.

inaudibly (ɪnˈɔːdɪblɪ), *adv.* [f. prec. + -LY².] In an inaudible manner, so as not to be heard.

1798 WORDSW. *P. Bell* III. li, He Sets down his hoofs inaudibly. *a* **1822** SHELLEY *Summer Even.* 24 Its awful hush is felt inaudibly.

†**inau'dite**, *a. Obs. rare*⁻¹. [a. F. *inaudite* (Rabelais) ad. L. *inaudīt-us* unheard, f. *in-* (IN-³).] Unheard of.

1708 MOTTEUX *Rabelais* (1737) V. 229 Your placid Life, here inaudite before, Repletes the Town of Lugdun.

inaugur (ɪˈnɔːgə(r)), *v.* Now *rare*. Also -ure. [a. F. *inaugure-r* (14th c. in Littré), or ad. L. *inaugurāre* to INAUGURATE.]

†**1.** *trans.* = INAUGURATE *v.* 1; also *fig. Obs.*

a **1555** LATIMER (Webster 1864), Inaugured and created king. **1566** PAINTER *Pal. Pleas.* I. 32 [He] is worthy to be inaugured with a laurel crown of follie. **1611** SPEED *Hist. Gt. Brit.* IX. xxiv. §41. 1142 Shan, then chosen, proclaimed, and inaugured O'Neale, by an old shoo cast ouer his head, seized vpon his Fathers inheritance. **1631** HEYWOOD *London's Jus Hon.* 273 To inaugure you, in your Praetorium seate. **1644** H. LESLIE *Serm. Bless. Judah* 25 Howsoever the King be sometimes chosen by them, and alwayes inaugured by them. **1706** HEARNE *Collect.* 2 Feb. (O.H.S.) I. 176 Then 3 shall beat 5, be inaugur'd in Spain.

2. = INAUGURATE *v.* 5.

1890 'ANNIE THOMAS' *On the Children* II. x. 166 The opportunity of inauguring the half-days of cessation from commercial cark and care was welcomed gladly.

inaugural (ɪˈnɔːgjʊərəl), *a.* (*sb.*) [a. F. *inaugural* (17th c. in Hatz.-Darm.), f. *inaugurer* to INAUGURATE, after L. *augurālis*.] **A.** *adj.* Of or pertaining to inauguration; forming part of the ceremony of inauguration or of the formal commencement of any course or career.

1689 in Somers *Tracts* II. 332 Instances of auspicious inaugural Medals. **1708** HEARNE *Collect.* 12 May (O.H.S.) II. 108 Mr. Thwaites Greek Professor made his Inaugural Speech. **1805** T. JEFFERSON *Writ.* (1830) IV. 34 The satisfaction you express with the last inaugural address. **1841** ARNOLD *Let.* in Stanley *Life* (1844) II. x. 300 My Inaugural Lecture was so kindly received that it gives me great hopes of being able to do something. **1897** [see INAUGURATION 4]. **1898** A. W. W. DALE *Life of R. W. Dale* xii. 269 The inaugural meeting was attended by men of all parties.

B. *sb.* An inaugural speech or address. Also, an inaugural lecture at a university. *U.S.*

1832 *Reg. Deb. Congress U.S.* 5 May 2778, I turn now to the other points in the inaugural. **1860** BARTLETT *Dict. Amer.* s.v., 'Have you read the President's inaugural?' **1871** S. N. RANDOLPH *Dom. Life T. Jefferson* 289 He went in to deliver his inaugural. **1884** *Century Mag.* XXVIII. 504 A few days before one of his inaugurals. **1958** *Listener* 18 Sept. 429/3 That well-known story about Seeley's inaugural. **1965** J. A. W. BENNETT in J. Gibb *Light on C. S. Lewis* 44 The mere quotability of his Cambridge Inaugural may lead us to forget his positive achievement. **1967** *Listener* 26 Jan. 139/2 Enright's famous inaugural at the University of Singapore.

†**i'naugurate**, *ppl. a. Obs.* Also 6 -at. [ad. L. *inaugurāt-us*, pa. pple. of *inaugurāre*: see next.] Inaugurated, ceremoniously or formally installed into office: see next, 1. (Const. as *pa. pple.*)

1600 HOLLAND *Livy* XXVII. xxxvi. 655 Dolabella was inaugurat or installed king of the sacrifices. **1644** HAMMOND *Serm. Christ's Resurr.* Wks. 1683 IV. 529 The new state, to which Christ was inaugurate at his resurrection. **1681** W. ROBERTSON *Phraseol. Gen.* (1693) 533 That the consuls might be made and inaugurate.

inaugurate (ɪˈnɔːgjʊəreɪt), *v.* [f. L. *inaugurāt-*, ppl. stem of *inaugurāre* to take omens from the flight of birds, to consecrate or install after taking such omens or auguries, f. *in-* (IN-²) + *augurāre* to take auguries: see AUGUR *sb.* and *v.*]

1. *trans.* To admit or induct (a person) to an office or dignity by a formal ceremony; to consecrate, install, invest. Also with complement.

1606 WARNER *Alb. Eng.* XIV. lxxxii. (1612) 344 More to their proper Elements inaugurated none, Than shee to hers by-passed, he to his possessed Throne. **1612** DRAYTON *Poly-olb.* xvii. 260 The seat on which her Kings inaugurated were. **1637-50** ROW *Hist. Kirk* (Wodrow Soc.) 261 They behoved to be doctorated ere they were inaugurated bishops. **1708** OCKLEY *Saracens* (1848) 387 Yezid..was inaugurated Caliph on the new moon of the month Rejeb. **1786** BURNS *Let. to J. Kennedy* Aug., I have..made my public appearance, and am solemnly inaugurated into the numerous class. **1825** MACAULAY *Ess., Milton* (1851) I. 22 When Cromwell was inaugurated in Westminster Hall.

†**2.** To invest (a thing) with a sacred or supposed sacred character, etc. *Obs.*

1638 F. JUNIUS *Paint. Ancients* 136 The inaugurated Statues..being set up by skilfull enchaunters in..the temple, or else secretly digged in the ground, were thought to appease..the Gods, and to protect the Country. *Ibid.* 137 The inaugurated statues, which now adays..are called Talisman.

3. To make auspicious or of good augury; to confer solemnity or sanctity upon; to sanctify, consecrate. *rare.*

a **1639** WOTTON *Life Dk. Buckhm.* in *Reliq.* (1651) 79 Those beginnings of years were very propitious unto him, as

if Kings did chuse remarkable dayes to inaugurate their favours, that they may appeare acts as well of the Times, as of the Will. **1847** R. W. HAMILTON *Disq. Sabbath* i. (1848) 7 And now succeeds the Sabbath which inaugurates all these accomplishments,.. as it perfects, illustrates, and glorifies the wondrous Hebdomade.

4. 'To begin with good omens' (J.); to begin (a course of action, period of time, etc., esp. of an important character) with some formal ceremony or notable act; to commence, enter upon; to introduce, usher in; to initiate. (Sometimes merely grandiose for 'begin'.)

1755 JOHNSON, *To Inaugurate*,.. to begin with good omens, to begin. **1851** GALLENGA *Italy* i. 22 The revolution was to be inaugurated without a single deed of violence to any Italian. *a* **1861** MRS. BROWNING *Sabbath Morn. at Sea* v, And sky and heaven made mighty room To inaugurate the vision. **1865** LIVINGSTONE *Zambesi* xxi. 428 He would certainly have inaugurated a new era on the East Coast of Africa. **1876** GRANT *Burgh Sch. Scotl.* II. v. 159 The daily work of the school was inaugurated and generally concluded .. with the ceremony of engaging publicly in prayer.

5. To initiate the public use of, introduce into public use by a formal opening ceremony (a statue, fountain, building, etc.).

[**1838** ARNOLD *Hist. Rome* I. xiii. 237 The augurs were to attend in order to inaugurate the ground where the soldiers were to meet.] **1852** LD. COCKBURN *Jrnl.* (1874) II. 282 On the 18th instant, Steell's equestrian Statue of the Duke of Wellington was inaugurated, as it is now the fashion to call such proceedings. **1861** *Sat. Rev.* 22 June 630 Then, why is everything 'inaugurated'? It is silly enough to talk about the 'inauguration' of a new statue; but we have quite got beyond that.

¶ Erroneously explained in early Dicts.

1604 R. CAWDREY *Table Alph.*, *Inaugurate*, to aske counsell of soothsayers. **1656** BLOUNT *Glossogr.*, *Inaugurate* .. to ask counsel of the Augures what shall follow, to dedicate to soothsaying.

inauguration (ɪnɔːgjʊəˈreɪʃən). [ad. L. *inaugurātiōn-em* consecration or instalment under good auspices or omens, n. of action from *inaugurāre*: cf. F. *inauguration* (*-acion*), (14th c. in Hatz.-Darm.).] The action of inaugurating; formal induction, institution, or ushering in, with auspicious ceremonies.

1. Formal or ceremonial induction to an office or dignity; consecration, investiture, installation.

1569 in H. Campbell *Love Lett. Mary Q. Scots* App. (1824) 59 Our Soverane Lordis coronatioun and inauguratioun in his kingdom was ratyfeit and found gude. **1575–85** ABP. SANDYS *Serm.* (Parker Soc.) 56 Eusebius .. was appointed to celebrate with a sermon the inauguration of Constantinus the emperor. **1627** in *Crt. & Times Chas. I* (1848) I. 214 Dr. Bargrave's sermon at the King's Anniversary Inauguration, March 27. **1752** J. GILL *Trinity* vii. 143 The Father's solemn inauguration of him into his kingly office. **1789** A. HAMILTON *Wks.* (1886) VII. 44 The day .. of the inauguration of the President, which completed the organization of the Constitution. **1822** J. FLINT *Lett. Amer.* 121 The inauguration of the professors of the university of Lexington occasioned much stir to-day. **1861** MILL *Autobiog.* iv. (1874) 123, I have always dated from these conversations my own real inauguration as an original and independent thinker.

2. The formal or definite commencement or introduction of a course of action, an important era or period of time, etc.

1856 FROUDE *Hist. Eng.* I. 292 To the one it was the advent of Antichrist, to the other the inauguration of the millennium. **1872** YEATS *Growth Comm.* 219 It was the inauguration of privateering.

3. The formal introduction of something into public use with appropriate ceremonies, as the opening of a building or park, the unveiling of a statue, fountain, etc.

1861 [see INAUGURATE *v.* 5]. **1865** *Pall Mall G.* 31 Aug. 10/1 Another ludicrous perversion of a word of Latin origin is the popular use of the word 'inauguration' as applied to the uncovering of a statue or a monument.

4. *attrib.* usually in sense 1: = INAUGURAL.

1686 WOOD *Life* 6 Feb. (O.H.S.) III. 179 King's inauguration day kept very solemnly at Oxford. **1741** MIDDLETON *Cicero* I. vi. 425 Cicero was invited to the inauguration feast. **1772** FOOTE *Nabob* III. Wks. 1799 II. 314 An inauguration-speech is required. **1893** K. D. WIGGIN *Polly Oliver's Problem* (1894) xvii. 185 As it chances to be a presidential year, we will celebrate Inauguration Day. **1897** *Daily News* 5 Mar. 8/3 The inauguration exercises took place to-day .. Mr. McKinley delivered his inaugural address in the open air in front of the Capitol. **1948** *Denison* (Texas) *Herald* 1 July 4/3 That was when Inauguration Day was changed from March 4 to January 20, for Roosevelt's second term.

¶ Erroneously explained: cf. INAUGURATE *v.*

1658 PHILLIPS, *Inauguration*, an asking counsel of Augures or Soothsayers.

inaugurative (ɪˈnɔːgjʊərətɪv), *a. rare.* [f. as INAUGURATE *v.* + -IVE.] Having the function of inaugurating; inaugural.

1853 MISS SHEPPARD *Ch. Auchester* I. 317 The mother-sickness that is the very treble-string of humility to many a hero in his inaugurative exile. **1885** *Illustr. Lond. News* 21 Mar. 292 She gave an inaugurative dinner.

inaugurator (ɪˈnɔːgjʊəreɪtə(r)). [agent-noun from L. *inaugurāre* to INAUGURATE.] One who inaugurates; an introducer, initiator.

a **1834** COLERIDGE cited by Worcester. **1851** J. MARTINEAU *Stud. Chr.* (1858) 289 They have assumed .. that its agents and inaugurators must have been fully cognizant of its whole scope and contents. **1861** HUGHES *Tom Brown at Oxf.* i. (1889) 4 The inaugurators of these changes had passed away. **1877** SYMONDS *Renaiss. Italy, Fine Arts* 70 The inaugurator of the humanistic impulse of the fifteenth century.

† **iˈnauguratory**, *sb. Obs.* [f. L. *inaugurāt-* (see INAUGURATE *v.*) + -ORY: cf. *laboratory*, *observatory*.] A place for the ceremony of inauguration.

1665 J. WEBB *Stone-Heng* (1725) 120 His whole Endeavour hath been .. to make our Antiquity designed for an Inauguratory of Princes. *Ibid.* 174 Homage was paid .. not in a stony Inauguratory, but on an Hill.

inauguratory (ɪˈnɔːgjʊərətərɪ), *a.* [f. as prec. + -ORY.] Pertaining to inauguration; = INAUGURAL.

1775 JOHNSON *Journ. West. Isl., St. Andrews*, An inauguratory speech by the present chancellor. **1779–81** —— *L.P., Dryden* Wks. III. 390 Inauguratory gratulations. **1865** GROTE *Plato* I. v. 178 A sort of .. inauguratory composition for the opening of his school.

† **iˈnaugurer**. *Obs. rare.* [f. INAUGUR + -ER[1].] One who inaugurates a person to an office.

1636 W. SCOT *Apol. Narr.* (1846) 40 Commission was given to try the Chapter and the Inaugurers. **1695** J. SAGE *The Article* Wks. 1844 I. 261 The ordainers and inaugurers of the said Archbishop.

† **iˈnaugurize**, *v. Obs. rare*$^{-0}$. [f. IN-[2] + AUGURIZE.] *trans.* To inaugurate.

1611 COTGR., *Inauguré*, inaugurized, consecrated, dedicated.

inaunter, var. ENAUNTER, in case (that). *Obs.*

1551 R. ROBINSON tr. *More's Utopia* I. (Arb.) 57 That therefore the Skottes muste be .. readie at all occasions, in aunters the Englishmen shoulde sturre neuer so lytle. **1589** PUTTENHAM *Eng. Poesie* III. xiii[i]. (Arb.) 134 For your foote *amphibrachus* .. ye haue these wordes and many like to these 'rĕsīstĕd, dĕlīghtfŭll, rĕprīsăll, ĭnaūntĕr, ĕnāmīll'.

inaurate (ɪnˈɔːrət), *a. rare.* [ad. L. *inaurāt-us* gilded, pa. pple. of *inaurāre*, f. *in-* (IN-[2]) + *aurāre* to gild.] **a.** Gilded, covered with gold. **b.** *Entom.* Applied to parts having a metallic lustre.

1826 KIRBY & SP. *Entomol.* IV. 284 *Inaurate* .. when striæ or other impressed parts have a metallic splendour. **1855** MAYNE *Expos. Lex.*, *Inauratus* .. applied to pills which it was formerly usual to gild in order to prevent their taste being perceived in swallowing: inaurate.

† **inˈaurate**, *v. Obs. rare.* [f. ppl. stem of L. *inaurāre* to gild: see prec.] *trans.* To gild.

1623 COCKERAM II, To Gild with golde, *inaurate*.

Hence † **inˈaurated** *ppl. a. Obs.* = INAURATE *a.*; † **inauˈration**, gilding.

1623 COCKERAM, *Inaurated*, gilted, or couered with gold. **1706** PHILLIPS, *Inauration* (among Apothecaries), a gilding or covering of Pills,..etc. with Leaf-Gold. **1727** ARBUTHNOT *Coins* (J.), The Romans had the art of gilding .. but some sort of their inauration, or gilding, must have been much dearer than ours.

inˈaureole, *v. nonce-wd.* [f. IN-[2] + AUREOLE *sb.*] *trans.* To surround with or as with an aureole.

1897 F. THOMPSON *New Poems* 5 [Light] Did inaureole All her lovely body round.

† **inˈauspicate**, *a. Obs.* [ad. L. *inauspicāt-us* at which no auspices were taken, f. *in-* (IN-[3]) + *auspicātus* consecrated by auguries, started with good auspices: see AUSPICATE.] Ill-omened, inauspicious.

1632 VICARS tr. *Virgil's Æneid* v. [*Lat. l.* 635] (N.) With me come burn these ships inauspicate; For I Cassandra's ghost in sleep saw late. **1646** BUCK *Rich. III* 43 Though it bore an inauspicate face, it proved of a friendly event. **1668** R. STEELE *Husbandm. Calling* vii. (1672) 170 The raven .. is an unclean creature .. an inauspicate creature.

So † **inˈauspicated** *ppl. a. Obs. rare*$^{-0}$.

1623 COCKERAM II, Vnluckily done, *inauspicated*.

inauspicious (ɪnɔːˈspɪʃəs), *a.* [f. IN-[3] + AUSPICIOUS.] Not auspicious, not of good omen; of unfavourable presage, foreboding evil; ill-omened, unlucky, unfortunate.

1592 SHAKS. *Rom. & Jul.* v. iii. 111 O here Will I .. shake the yoke of inauspicious starres From this world-wearied flesh. *a* **1635** NAUNTON *Fragm. Reg.* (Arb.) 19 It was an unthrifty and inauspitious war. **1638** COWLEY *Love's Riddle* v. i, On that Trees Top an inauspicious Crow Foretold some ill to happen. **1711** SHAFTESB. *Charac.* (1737) II. I. §1. 192, I begin this inauspicious Work, which my ill Stars and you have assign'd me. **1781** GIBBON *Decl. & F.* xxiv. (1869) I. 695 The appearances of the victims threatened the most inauspicious events. **1828** D'ISRAELI *Chas. I*, II. ii. 55 Many inauspicious rumours were bruited among the people. **1856** KANE *Arct. Expl.* II. App. ii. 310 A tardy and inauspicious season.

inauˈspiciously, *adv.* [f. prec. + -LY[2].] In an inauspicious manner; with presage of evil.

1684 tr. *Agrippa's Van. Arts* lxvii. 219 Unless he know how to Govern his own House and Family, [he] is very inauspiciously prefer'd. **1797** BURKE *Regic. Peace* iii. Wks. VIII. 263 What had been so inauspiciously begun and so feebly carried on. **1884** *Leeds Merc.* 24 Oct. 4/4 [The Session] has commenced not inauspiciously.

inauˈspiciousness. [f. as prec. + -NESS.] The quality of being inauspicious; unluckiness.

1652 GAULE *Magastrom.* 130 The propitiousness of the fortunate, and inauspiciousness of the unfortunate, stars. *a* **1693** URQUHART *Rabelais* III. xxxiii. 277 The dismal inauspiciousness of the Holy Days. **1727** in BAILEY vol. II. Hence in Todd and mod. Dicts.

inauthentic (ɪnɔːˈθɛntɪk), *a.* [IN-[3].] Not authentic.

1860 MRS. BROWNING *Lett.* May (1897) II. 384 The serious intention, hid in those mummy wrappings, is not inauthentic. **1972** *Times Lit. Suppl.* 24 Mar. 342/2 This does not prevent the two schools of Zen from attacking each other as being inauthentic.

Hence **inauˈthentically** *adv.* **inauthenˈticity**, inauthentic character.

1883 *Q. Rev.* July 165 Their precariousness and inauthenticity. **1883** H. M. KENNEDY tr. *Ten Brink's E.E. Lit.* 389 Evidence of the inauthenticity of Asser's *Life of Alfred*. **1964** S. BELLOW *Herzog* (1965) 81 The cant and rant of pipsqueaks about Inauthenticity and Forlornness. **1965** *Philos. Rev.* LXXIV. 215 The philosopher he is attacking .. have written inauthentically. **1970** G. GREER *Female Eunuch* 152 The altruism of women is merely the inauthenticity of the feminine person carried over into behaviour.

inauthoritative (ɪnɔːˈθɒrɪteɪtɪv), *a.* [IN-[3].] Not authoritative; having no authority. Hence **inauˈthoritativeness**.

1659 GAUDEN *Tears Ch.* 53 Ignorance and impudence, inability and inauthoritativeness contend which shall be greatest. *Ibid.* 281 As if all we had done .. had been irregular, confused, inauthoritative. **1774** T. JEFFERSON *Autobiog.* App., Wks. 1859 I. 132 An act of Parliament had been passed .. against which act the Americans had protested, as inauthoritative. **1839** *New Monthly Mag.* LVI. 275 The only attempt at a connected Life .. is .. anonymous, and inauthoritative. **1888** *Nature* 8 Mar. 442/2 Far-reaching interests will not excuse inauthoritativeness [in statements].

† **inaˈvailable**, *a. Obs.* [IN-[3].] Of no avail; unavailing.

1650 HUBBERT *Pill Formality* 204 All the means in the world are invaileable. **1681** FLAVEL *Meth. Grace* i. 8 Without this [personal application of Christ to us by the Spirit] all is inavailable and ineffectual to our salvation.

inaˈvertible, *a. rare.* [IN-[3].] Not avertible; that cannot be averted.

1885 GOSSE *Fr. Shaks. to Pope*, A javelin, ponderous, invertible, lethal.

† **inaˈvoidable**, *a. Obs.* [IN-[3].] That cannot be avoided; unavoidable, inevitable. Hence † **inaˈvoidableness**; † **inaˈvoidably** *adv.*

1640 BP. REYNOLDS *Passions* xxvii. 274 By reason of the Neerenesse and Inavoydablenesse of the Evill. **1670–98** LASSELS *Voy. Italy* II. 199 These waters afford innumerable and inavoidable wetting places. **1674** R. GODFREY *Inj. & Ab. Physic* 122 Had she not been strong enough for both the Disease and the Remedy, Death had inavoidably followed.

† **inawe, enawe** (ɪˈnɔː, ɛˈnɔː), *v. Obs. rare.* [f. IN-[2] (EN-) + AWE *sb.*] *trans.* To put in awe or fear; to awe, overawe.

1642 SIR W. BRERETON *Let. to Cromwell* in *13th Rep. Hist. MSS. Comm.* App. I. 45 It would seem they [the Commissioners of Array] intend to enawe or expel our best ministers. **1645** —— *Let. to Lenthall* ibid. 317 Unless it be so that Sir Francis Gamull and Sir Richard Grosvenor .. do enslave and inaw them hereunto. **1645–6** *Ibid.* 336 Many of the citizens [of Chester] remain still so enthralled and enawed as that they dare not oppose nor resist.

i-nayled, ME. pa. pple. of NAIL *v.*

† **inˈazure**, *v.* Obs. var. *enazure*: see EN- 2.

1611 FLORIO, *Inazzurrare*, to inazure, to inblew.

† **inbalme, -bau(l)me**, obs. ff. EMBALM *v.*

1611 FLORIO, *Imbalsamare*, to inbalme.

in banco: see BANCO *sb.*

inbardge, variant of IMBARGE *v.*

† **inbark**, obs. form of EMBARK *v.*

1612 SYLVESTER *Lacrymæ Lacr.* 176 Wee Humbled Mourners may be Heav'nly Markt, In Mercies Vessell to be All inbarkt.

inbarn, variant of IMBARN *v.*

ˈin-basket. [Cf. IN *adv.* 12 a.] In an office, etc.: a basket or tray for incoming correspondence and other documents. Cf. IN-TRAY.

Sometimes written as two separate words with *in* regarded adjectivally.

1940 *Amer. Speech* XV. 247 His *incoming* mail is put in an *in-basket*. **1948** 'N. SHUTE' *No Highway* v. 130, I sighed and pulled my IN basket towards me, full of the arrears of work. **1957** J. BRAINE *Room at Top* xxviii. 217 My in-basket was full. **1970** *New Yorker* 26 Sept. 40/3 She sat down beside him with pencil and paper and let him churn up the contents of his 'in' and 'out' baskets.

† **inbassat, -et, inbassitour**, obs. forms of EMBASSADE or EMBASSIATE, AMBASSADOR.

c **1450** *St. Cuthbert* (Surtees) 7913 þe kyng made hym an Inbassitour. **1462** *Paston Lett.* No. 458 II. 110 The Erles of Warrewyk, of Essex .. and other go in to Scotland of inbassat.

‖ **inbat**, var. EMBAT (Turkish), northerly wind.

1775 R. CHANDLER *Trav. Asia M.* (1825) I. 70 The apartments are in the upper story .. open to the sea and the refreshing inbat.

inbatail, -batell, -battel, obs. ff. EMBATTLE *v.*[1]

inbathe, obs. form of EMBATHE.

†**inbay,** obs. form of EMBAY *v.*[1]

a **1608** SIR F. VERE *Comm.* (1657) 36 The ordinary and ready way to the town lay on that side low and inbayd to the foot of the hilly downs.

inbe (ɪnˈbiː), *v. poet. nonce-wd.* [f. IN-*pref.*[1] + BE *v.* A. 1¶ (centre column p. 2). Cf. L. *inesse.*] To be within.

1921 HARDY *Late Lyrics* (1922) 70 Where such inbe, A dwelling's character Takes theirs.

inbealch: see INBELCH *v.*

ˈin-ˌbeaming, *vbl. sb.* [f. IN *adv.* 11 c + BEAMING *vbl. sb.*] A beaming or shining in; illumination, irradiation.

1662 J. CHANDLER *Van Helmont's Oriat.* 290 Indeed, that is proper to the soul, by a singular radiation or in-beaming. **1663–70** SOUTH *Serm.* (1717) IV. 293 Boastings of new Lights, Inbeamings, and Inspirations.

ˈinˌbearing, *ppl. a. Sc.* [f. IN *adv.* 11 a + *bearing*, pres. pple. of BEAR *v.* (branch III).] Intrusive, officious, meddlesome.

a **1800** *Sir P. Spens* xv. in Child *Ballads* III. lviii. (1885) 28/1 Then out it speaks an auld skipper, An inbearing dog was hee. **1808–80** JAMIESON, *Inbearing*, officious, prone to embrace every opportunity of ingratiating one's self, especially by intermeddling in the affairs of others.

†**inˈbeat,** *v. Obs.* [f. IN-[1] + BEAT *v.*] *trans.* To beat in, drive in by beating.

c **1420** *Pallad. on Husb.* VI. 183 Then with a barre inbete hit, batte hit ofte, And playne hit rough. **1610** HOLLAND *Camden's Brit.* I. 319 The sandes and beach which the sea doth inbeate into the haven.

in-being, inbeing (ˈɪnˌbiːɪŋ). [f. IN *adv.* 11 c + BEING *vbl. sb.*]

1. The fact of being in; existence in something else; inherence, indwelling, immanence.

1617 DAYRELL *On the Church* 81 Were it not extreme folly ..because of this manner of enterance, to deny the in-being of the aforesaid men in the house? **1654** WARREN *Unbelievers* 107 'Tis such an union and in-being in Christ. **1776** J. NEILL 23 *Serm.* 88 Believing..[consists] in such a reception of them as gives them a real subsistence and in-being in the Soul. **1834** J. BROWN *Lett. Sanctific.* v. 295 Must not that be pleasant which is, if I may use the expression, a mutual inbeing in God?

2. Inward or essential nature; that which a thing is in itself.

1661 W. ANNAND *Panem Quotid.* 9 God giving Lawes for the inbeing of the National Church which he was then instituting. **1869** RUSKIN *Q. of Air* §135 Men get to know not only their income, but their inbeing—to know themselves.. what is in them, and what may be got out of them.

†**3.** An indwelling being: applied to the 'persons' of the Trinity. *Obs.*

1587 GOLDING *De Mornay* v. (1617) 53 In the same most single essence are three Persons or In-beings. *a* **1643** SUCKLING *Acc. Relig.* 115 This cannot be done, but by one of the three Inbeings, which is the word they use to expresse the Trinity by.

†**inˈbelch,** *v. Obs. rare.* [f. IN-[1] + BELCH *v.*] *trans.* To 'belch' or vomit in; to cast in.

1610 HOLLAND *Camden's Brit.* I. 341 The Ocean..is now so farre excluded by reason of sandy residence inbealched with the tides.

ˈinˌbending, *vbl. sb.* [f. IN *adv.* 11 c + BENDING *vbl. sb.*] A bending or curving inwards.

1881 MIVART *Cat* 221 For the lining of the lungs is but, as it were, a very deep and complex inbending and infolding of the body's external surface.

ˈinˌbending, *ppl. a.* [f. IN *adv.* 11 a + BENDING *ppl. a.*] That bends or curves inwards.

1622 DRAYTON *Poly-olb.* xxv. 7 To diuide Low Holland from the High, which on their Easterne side Th' in bending Ocean holds from the Norfolcan lands.

ˈinˌbent, *ppl. a.* [f. IN *adv.* 11 b + BENT *ppl. a.*] Bent or curved inwards; turned or directed inwards.

a **1586** SIDNEY *Astr. & Stella* xciv, So darke..that inbent eyes Can scarce discerne the shape of mine owne paine. **1623** LISLE *Ælfric on O. & N. Test.* Ded., Hauing thus with inbent heau'n begunne, See how this bulked world vnto thee bowes. **1625** —— *Du Bartas, Noe* 151 It is concave and convex, which is as much as to say inbent and out-bent. **1889** *Geol. Jrnl.* XLV. I. 152, I can distinguish no regular markings on the inbent surfaces of the radials between the spines.

in-beˈtween. [subst. or attrib. use of phr. *in between* (IN *adv.* + BETWEEN *prep.* or *adv.*).]

a. quasi-*sb.* (*a*) An interval; (*b*) A person who intervenes. **b.** quasi-*adj.* Placed between. Hence **in-beˈtweener, inbeˈtweener,** a person who takes up an intermediate position (chiefly *fig.*).

1815 JANE AUSTEN *Emma* I. iii, Busy..talking and listening, and forming all these schemes in the in-betweens. **1815** *Zeluca* I. 393 He's fallen in love with Lady Naglefort, because she's an in-between. **1898** *Westm. Gaz.* 22 Sept. 3/2 White or pale-coloured silk, with an in-between layer of chiffon. **1924** *Contemp. Rev.* Apr. 459 The undeserving and the in-betweeners far outnumber the deserving. **1927** C. SHAW *Let.* 17 May in Knightley & Simpson *Secret Lives of Lawrence of Arabia* (1969) xvii. 256 In Ireland... We had The Gentry and The People: nothing else. You will say 'but the in-betweeners?' They belonged to the people. **1939** C. E. SMITH in Ramsey & Smith *Jazzmen* 247 The inbetweeners are still there but the musician has become an individual. **1942** O. NASH *Good Intentions* (1943) 162 He was a born in-betweener... He always thought that there was much to be said on both sides. **1970** *S.A. Panorama* Feb. 25/1 He joined the London Polytechnic Studios. He started as an 'in-betweener'—the name given to the most junior apprentice.

†**inˈbill,** *v. Obs.* [f. IN-[2] + BILL *sb.*[3]: cf. also BILL *v.*[3]] *trans.* To enter in a 'bill' or list.

1461 *Paston Lett.* No. 391 II. 13 John Jeney enformed me ..ye ar inbylled to be made knygth at this Coronacion.

inbind (ɪnˈbaɪnd), *v.* [f. IN-[1] + BIND *v.*] To bind within (usu. in *pass.* and *fig.*); to bind within a book or manuscript (cf. INBOUND *a.*[2]).

1888 RUSKIN *Praeterita* (1889) III. i. 32 The most stern practical precept of that doctrine still holding me,—it is curiously inbound with all the rest,—was the Sabbath keeping. **1913** D. H. LAWRENCE *Sons & Lovers* x. 316 He had never been very closely inbound into the family. **1932** *Ampleforth Jrnl.* Spring 133 A transcription of the fragment inbound in the Sarum Missal in the monastery library.

in-bland, *adv. phr. Obs.* See BLAND *sb.*[1]

inblement, obs. form of EMBLEMENT.

†**inˈblind,** var of EMBLIND *v. Obs. trans.*, to produce blindness in; to blind.

1515 BARCLAY *Egloges* iv. (1570) C iv b/2 Such rusty meates inblindeth so our brayne, That of our favour the muses have disdayne.

†**inˈblow,** *v. Obs.* [OE. *inbláwan*, f. IN-[1] + BLOW *v.*, tr. L. *inflāre, inspīrāre.* See also ENBLOW.] *trans.* To blow or breathe into: **a.** to inflate, puff up; **b.** to inspire (also in bad sense). Hence †**inblown** *ppl. a.*

c **975** *Rushw. Gosp.* John xx. 22 In-bleow on hine & cwæð him on-foað ðone halȝan gast. **1042** *Charter* in *Land-Charters* (Earle) 242 ðif æniȝ þonne sy uppahofen & in-blawen on þa oferhyda þære ȝeættredan deofles lare. **1382** WYCLIF *1 Cor.* iv. 6 Oon aȝens anothir be inblowyn with pride. *Ibid.* viii. 1 Soþely science [*gloss* or kunnynge] inblowiþ [*gloss* wiþ pride]: charite edifieth. **1678** CUDWORTH *Intell. Syst.* I. iii. §29. 134 Bewitched enthusiasts..acted by a dark, narrow, and captivated principle of life, and (to use their own language) 'in-blown' by it. **1678** H. MORE *Postscr. Glanvill's Sadducismus* (1681) 48 Whether the inspired Scripture, or these inblown Buffoons, puffed up with nothing but ignorance..are to be believed.

†**inˈblue,** *v. Obs. rare*$^{-0}$. [IN-[2].] *trans.* To colour blue.

1611 FLORIO, *Inazzurrare*, to inazure, to inblew.

inboard (ˈɪnbɔəd), *adv.*, *prep.*, and *a. Naut.* [Properly a phrase, IN *prep.* + BOARD *sb.* V: cf. *on board*, etc. For form and sense cf. *inland.*]

A. *adv.* Within the sides of a ship or vessel; also, towards the centre of the vessel. Also *transf.*

1830 J. F. COOPER *Water Witch* III. vii. 216 Assured of the position of his enemy, he returned in-board. **1851** H. MELVILLE *Moby Dick* III. xlix. 306 Two of them clutched the gunwale..and..hurled themselves bodily in-board. **1853** KANE *Grinnell Exp.* xi. (1856) 83 It passes inboard through a block. **1863** *Sat. Rev.* 437 At every successive collision the eager spectators on paddle-boxes and other elevated standing-points were in danger of being knocked off. Luckily, those who were upset managed to fall inboard. **1894** *Times* 27 Mar. 11 Each leaf [of the Tower bridge] over-hangs the water 100ft. The shaft or pivot on which the leaf hinges is placed 13ft. 3in. inboard, and beyond this the short arm of the leaf extends 49ft. 6in. **1897** KIPLING *Seven Seas, Anchor Song*, Up, well up the fluke of her, and inboard haul! **1912** BELLOC *This & That* xxxviii. 284 We picked up the little buoy..and we got it in-board. **1958** *Engineering* 28 Mar. 393/1 Movable projectors are housed in the two cylindrical frameworks of the dumb-bell assembly in-board of the star globes. **1962** S. CARPENTER in *Into Orbit* 161 You make sure the abort handle is *inboard and locked.* **1963** *Times* 12 Feb. 15/6 Inboard-mounted disc brakes. **1967** *Autocar* 5 Oct. 7/2 The Triumph 2000 port face is 'inboard' of the holding-down studs. **1971** *Times* 16 Feb. 8/6 The unsprung weight has been reduced by mounting the front and rear suspension units inboard.

B. *prep.* Inside, within (a vessel). Cf. ABOARD B, BOARD *sb.* 14 b.

1864 ATKINSON *Stanton Grange* 2 A jerked pebble fell inboard the fractious vessel.

C. *adj.* Situated within or towards the centre of the vessel; interior; in quot. 1898 said of a 'sea' that has washed inboard. Also, applied to parts of vehicles, aircraft, etc.

1847 WEBSTER, Inboard cargo. *c* **1850** *Rudim. Navig.* (Weale) 126 *Inboard*, within the ship, as the inboard works, &c. **1876** C. H. DAVIS *Polaris Exp.* I. 29 New bulkheads and inboard works. **1886** *Forest & Stream* 13 May 316/3 The Hampton flattie is best described as a beamy sharpie with an 'inboard jib'. **1893** *Funk's Stand. Dict.*, Inboard stroke of the piston. **1898** *Blackw. Mag.* Sept. 377 This inboard sea gurgled gently. **1909** *Cent. Dict.* Suppl., In *mech.*, toward the inside; toward the main center or center-line: as, an inboard stroke of the piston; an inboard bearing. *Ibid.* s.v. *Profile. Inboard profile*, in ship-building, a plan which shows the internal arrangements of a vessel by a longitudinal vertical section at the centerline. **1921** *Rudder* July 5 Even in large sailing boats the use of an inboard engine is sometimes not advisable. **1936** *Discovery* Dec. 380/1 We were five boats in all, some inboard launches, others with outboard motors, which passed the inspection of the river police. **1945** *Times* 30 June 4/5 A new type of drive couples the engines to contra-rotating airscrews, 16 ft. in diameter. Those driving the inboard engines can be reversed on landing to act as brakes. **1948** 'N. SHUTE' *No Highway* iii. 66 Stop the inboard engines [of the aircraft] and turn back. **1951** *Yachting Monthly* Oct. 202 Her modest inboard-cutter sail plan is easily handled by two. **1956** LOOMIS *Hotspur Story* 183 With her new inboard rig *Hotspur* is now a single-headsail cutter. **1957** M. SWAN *Brit. Guiana* 202 In the old days when the mining men, the pork-knockers, went up the river they would paddle against currents which an inboard engine can now only just fight. **1959** E. K. WENLOCK *Kitchin's Road Transport Law* (ed. 12) 19/2 Inboard brakes, that is to say brakes acting on the axle shafts. **1971** *Power Farming* Mar. 57/3 A unique feature is the individual shaft bottom drive to each cutting disc, relieving the strain on the inboard drive components compared with other designs where the cutters are powered in train. **1972** *National Observer* (U.S.) 27 May 9/3 The inboard portions of the belts are short to prevent the lap belt from slipping over the hip bone onto the stomach, where the belt might cause serious injury in an accident.

†**inˈbody,** obs. var. of EMBODY *v.*

1596 DRAYTON *Leg.* iii. 47 Whilst here my Soule inbodyed did abide. **1611** FLORIO, *Incorporare*, to incorporate, to inbodie.

†**inˈbold,** var. of EMBOLD *v. Obs.*, to embolden.

a **1520** BARCLAY *Jugurth* (Pynson, ed. 2) 78 Whan he had assembled and inbolded with his words these fresshe fotemen.

†**inˈbolt,** *v. Obs.* Also imbolt. [f. IN-[1] + BOLT *v.*] *trans.* To bolt in, fasten in with bolts.

1632 LITHGOW *Trav.* x. 461 To disburden me of my irons, which being very hard inbolted [**1682** imbolted] he could not Ram-verse the Wedges for a long time.

inbond (ˈɪnbɒnd), *a. Building.* [f. IN-[1] + BOND *sb.*[1] 13 a.] Said of a brick or stone laid with its length across a wall (also called a *header*); also of a wall built wholly or mainly of bricks or stones thus placed. Opp. to *outbond.*

1842–76 GWILT *Archit.* Gloss., *Inbond Jambstone*, a bond-stone laid in the joint of an aperture. **1864** WEBSTER, *Inbond-stone*, a stone lengthwise across a wall; a header.

†**ˈinborgh, inborrow.** *Obs.* Forms: 1 in-borh, 2 inborȝ, inboreȝ, 3 inbor(e)we, (7 inborow). [OE. *inborh, -borȝes*, f. IN-[1] + *borh* security, BORROW *sb.*]

1. a. (In OE.) Security, bail. **b.** One who gives or offers security for another, a surety.

c **1000** *Ord. Dunsetas* c. 8 in Schmid *Gesetze* 362 þonne sette mon in-borh. *a* **1100** *Laws Edw. Conf.* c. 6 §1 ibid. 114 ȝif hwa þifðe betoȝen sy..þonne niman þa þe hit to-ȝebyreð on his æhtan in-borh. *c* **1175** *Lamb. Hom.* 73 Heore godfaderes and heore godmoderes scullen onswerie for hem et þe chirche dure and beo in borȝes et þe fonstan þet heo sculen beon bi-lefulle men. *c* **1200** *Trin. Coll. Hom.* 17 Here godfaderes..ben here boreȝes toȝenes gode ate chireche dure, and inboreȝes ate fanstone.

2. In phr. ***inborrow and outborrow*** (in 13th c. *inborewe and utborewe*), 'surety in and out', applied in 13th c. to the Earl of Dunbar, who became surety to the kings of England and Scotland respectively for persons permitted to pass out of the one realm into the other.

1210–12 *Red Bk. Exch.* lf. 147 (Rolls) 562 Comes Patricius [de Dunbar, tenet] baroniam de Beneleghe, ut sit inborewe et utborewe inter Reges Angliæ et Scotiæ. **1278–9** *Assize Roll* (*Northumb.*), 7 *Edw. I* in *Cal. Docts. rel. Scotl.* (1884) II. 42 [The jury present that..Earl Patrick holds his serjeanty in Northumberland by being] in-borwe et ut-borewe ad merk et mere [between the kingdoms]. **1610** HOLLAND tr. *Camden's Brit.* 815 In King Henrie the Third his time the Baronie of Patricke Earle of Dunbar: who also as we read.. was Inborow and Outborow betweene England and Scotland, that is to say, if I mistake it not, he was to allow and observe in this part, the ingresse and egresse of those that travailed too and fro betweene both Realmes.

inborn (ˈɪnbɔːn), *ppl. a.* [f. IN *adv.* + BORN *ppl. a.*]

†**1.** Of a person: Born in a place or country; native, aboriginal. *Obs.*

c **1000** *Germania* (N.S.) XI. 390 *Indigena*, inborena. **1609** HOLLAND *Amm. Marcell.* 371 The hills..were passable for none but the inborne inhabitants that knew the wayes verie well. **1627** SPEED *England* vii. §10 [They] put to the sword (almost) euery mothers childe of the in-borne Inhabitants. **1670** MILTON *Hist. Eng.* I. Wks. (1847) 476/2 Those old and inborn names of successive Kings. **1875** DASENT *Vikings* III. 270, I would sooner have given her to an inborn man, said the Earl.

2. a. Of a quality, etc.: Born in a person, existing in him from birth; implanted by nature; innate.

1513 DOUGLAS *Æneis* I. Prol. 97 (Comment), *Innative* is alsmekil to say as *inborn*, or that quhilk cumis til ony person ..throw thar forbearis. **1599** T. M[OUFET] *Silkwormes* 42 Whose inborne skil our want of witte controules. *a* **1625** FLETCHER *Nice Valour* v. iii, Merit, manners, And in-born virtue does it. **1725** POPE *Odyss.* XIX. 383 He whose in-born worth his acts commend. **1871** PALGRAVE *Lyr. Poems* 11 With some inborn sense Of courtesy. **1874** CARPENTER *Ment. Phys.* I. vi. §1 (1879) 227 An intellectual instinct inborn in Man.

b. Of an attribute or condition: In or into which one was born; inherited, hereditary. *rare.*

1816 BYRON *Ch. Har.* III. lxxxi, Bow'd to the inborn tyranny of years.

c. *transf.* Of a person: That was born such, or is such by nature; = BORN B. 1 b. *rare.*

1818 BYRON *Ch. Har.* IV. xciv, Bequeathing their hereditary rage To the new race of inborn slaves. 1878 BOSW. SMITH *Carthage* 439 The Arab is, in a sense in which it can hardly be said of any European nation, an inborn gentle-man. 1895 *Westm. Gaz.* 24 May 3/2 Every in-born artist has a natural method, like the song-birds of the air.

d. ***inborn error of metabolism***: any disorder or abnormality that is due to a hereditary fault in the metabolic processes of the body, generally attributable to the lack or alteration of some enzyme.

1908 A. E. GARROD in *Lancet* 4 July 3/1 Quite unlike that of the above metabolic diseases is the course of the anomalies of which I propose to treat in these lectures and which may be classed together as inborn errors of metabolism. 1909 —— (*title*) Inborn errors of metabolism. 1935 HARROW & SHERWIN *Textbk. Biochem.* xxviii. 716 The disease [*sc.* cystinuria], frequently referred to as an 'inborn error of metabolism' is rare. 1968 PASSMORE & ROBSON *Compan. Med. Stud.* I. xi. 24/2 Hereditary lack of the necessary enzyme, phenylalanine hydroxylase, leads to an inborn error of metabolism, phenylketonuria, in which phenylalanine.. is transaminated extensively to phenylpyruvic acid... Presence of phenylpyruvic acid in the blood and central nervous system leads to mental retardation.

†**ˌin-'borrow**, *v. Sc. Obs.* [f. IN-¹ + BORROW *v.*] *trans.* To redeem from pawn.

1541 *Aberdeen Reg.* V. 17 To requir Cristene Malisoun to inborrow hir kirtill quhilk sche hes lyand in wed. *Ibid.*, And requyr him to inborrow & inquytt ane ring of gold quhilk he laid in wed.

inborrow, *sb.*: see INBORGH.

†**in'bosom**, obs. var. of EMBOSOM *v.*

1610 HOLLAND *Camden's Brit.* II. 52 A country much mangled with many inlets and armes of the Sea inbosoming itselfe with manifold commodities. 1611 SPEED *Theat. Gt. Brit.* (1614) 131/2 Scotland.. inbosoming many loughes and inlets upon the East and West.

'inbound, *a.*¹ [f. IN *adv.* + BOUND *ppl. a.*¹: cf. *outbound.*] Bound inward or homeward.

1894 *Outing* (U.S.) XXIV. 473/1 Inbound vessels told of passing these valiant American schooners. 1967 *Jane's Surface Skimmer Systems 1967–68* 63/1 Inbound freight is sorted on arrival at terminal. 1971 D. POTTER *Brit. Eliz. Stamps* xiii. 144 Clever collectors with new issues of stamps purchased at the all-night post office in London, would rush to stations within 50 miles or so of London to post their covers on inbound services. 1973 D. WESTHEIMER *Going Public* ix. 127 Drivers on the inbound lanes slowed to a crawl.

'inbound, *a.*² [f. INBIND *v.*; cf. BOUND *ppl. a.*²] Of a leaf, gathering, etc., in a manuscript or book: bound within.

1953 D. C. C. YOUNG in *Scriptorium* VIII. 15 There is an inbound quaternion of blanks.

†**in'bound**, *v. Obs.* [f. IN-¹ + BOUND *v.*] *trans.* To inclose as a boundary; to bound. (See also EMBOUND.)

1600 FAIRFAX *Tasso* XVIII. xx, On the greene banks which that faire streame inbound, Flowers and odours sweetely smilde and smeld. 1627 SPEED *England* v. §1 Vpon the East Kent doth imbound it [Surrey]. 1649 BLITHE *Eng. Improv. Impr.* (1653) 47 Your Marsh Lands.. lye under the Levell of the Sea, and were it not inbounded by the banks,.. would all return to the Sea again.

†**in'bow**, *v. Obs.* [f. IN-¹ + BOW *v.*¹ In Wyclif rendering L. *incurvāre, inclīnāre.*]

1. *trans.* To bend into a curved or arched form; to incurve, arch. Cf. BOW *v.* 9, EMBOW *v.*¹ 2.

1382 WYCLIF *Isa.* lix. 8 The pathis of them inbowid [L. *incurvatæ*, 1388 bowid] ben to them. 1465 *Mann. & Househ. Exp.* (Roxb.) 496 Paid.. fore inbowenge of dyverse werke. *c* 1520 *Mem. Ripon* (Surtees) III. 202 Radulpho Turret inbowyng tymber per iij dies. 1552–1625 [see INBOWED below].

2. To bow or bend (towards); to incline.

1382 WYCLIF *Ps.* xliv. 11 Here, doȝter, and see, and inbowe [L. *inclina*] thin Eere. *Ibid.* cxiv. 2 For he inbowide his ere to me; and in my daȝis I shal inwardly clepe.

Hence †**in'bowed** *ppl. a.* [cf. EMBOWED], bent into an arch, curved, arched. †**in'bowing** *vbl. sb.*, curvature, arching, arched work.

1452 in Willis & Clark *Cambridge* (1886) I. 282, ij of the Bemys shalbe.. inbowed with lozinggys. *Ibid.*, iij sengulere Principalls in werkyng in inbowyng and in Scantlyon accordyng to the Principalls. 1465 Inbowenge [see 1]. 1552 HULOET, Beame of a rouffe, not beynge inbowed or fretted. 1556 in Willis & Clark *Cambridge* (1886) II. 564 The holle rooffe of ooke inbowed. 1625 BACON *Ess., Building* (Arb.) 551 For Inbowed Windowes [*Latin text* prominentes sive arcuatas], I hold them of good Vse.

†**'inbowed, in-bowed**, *a. Obs.* [f. IN *adv.* + *bowed*, pa. pple. of BOW *v.*] Bowed or bent inwards or concavely.

a 1586 SIDNEY *Arcadia* (1622) 92 He met her full.. With inbow'd bosom well for her prepared. *c* 1586 C'TESS PEMBROKE *Ps.* CXXIX. iv, Filling neither reapers hand Nor the binders inbowd lapp. 1658 A. FOX *Wurts' Surg.* II. vii. 68 Neither must the in-bowed scull be opprest with Cataplasmes. *Ibid.* xxvii. 180 There is a very small difference between a Fracture and an in-bowed bone.

So †**'inbowing** *ppl. a.*, bending inwards or concavely.

1603 OWEN *Pembrokesh.* (1891) 2 Diuerse other Inboweinge places.. where the sea occupieth a great Inlett.

†**in'box**, obs. var. of EMBOX *v.*, to enclose in a box.

1596 *Foxe's A. & M.* 361/2 Thinking to finde refuge at the presence of the transubstantiated God of the aultar there caried and inboxed.

†**in'brawn**, *v. Obs.* [f. IN-² + BRAWN *sb.* or *v.* Cf. *incrust.*] *trans.* To cover or encase as with a hard skin: cf. BRAWN *sb.* 5.

1576 FLEMING *Panopl. Epist.* 178, I should shew my self inbrawnd with foolishnes, when I see others usurping.. yet I me selfe to be so precise, as to absteine.

in-bread ('ɪnbrɛd), *sb.* [f. IN *adv.* + BREAD.] Bread 'thrown in'; the extra loaf or loaves allowed by a baker in each dozen. Cf. *baker's dozen*, s.v. BAKER 6.

1639 *Bury Wills* (Camden) 177 Fowre and twenty loaves of the said bread, wᵗʰ the inbread allowed by the baker for those twoe dosens of bread. *a* 1665 J. GOODWIN *Filled w. the Spirit* (1867) 377 As that which we call the in-bread is given into the dozen, there is nothing properly paid or given for it, but only for the dozen. 1864 HOTTEN *Slang Dict., Baker's dozen*, this consists of thirteen or fourteen; the surplus number, called the inbread, being thrown in for fear of incurring the penalty for short weight.

†**inbread** (ɪn'brɛd), *v. Obs.* Also **en-**. [f. IN-¹ or IN-² + BREAD.] *trans.* To embody in bread: = IMPANE, q.v.

1547 BALE *Lett. Exam. Anne Askewe* 24 At the wyll of the prestes, to be inpaned or inbreaded. 1548 GESTE *Pr. Masse* in H. G. Dugdale *Life* App. i. (1840) 87 The impaning or enbreding thereof [i.e. of Christ's body].

inbreak ('ɪnbreɪk). *rare.* [f. IN *adv.* + BREAK *sb.*¹, after *outbreak.*] A breaking in, irruption, invasion, forcible incursion.

1837 CARLYLE *Fr. Rev.* I. VII. x, Deshuttes and Varigny, massacred at the first inbreak, have been beheaded in the Marble Court. 1853 KANE *Grinnell Exp.* xli. (1856) 378 The first inbreak upon our desolate circle of ice and water that we had experienced in ninety-nine days. 1879 A. B. DAVIDSON in Expositor 255 The inbreak of Phœnician idolatry.

So '**inˌbreaking** *vbl. sb.*, a breaking in; *ppl. a.*, that breaks in.

1652 J. PAWSON *Brief Vind. Free Grace* 6 The out-breakings of corruption, the in-breakings of Satan. 1882 H. SCOTT HOLLAND *Logic & Life* (1885) 307 Waiting.. for the inbreaking of God's tremendous Majesty. 1891 MOULE *Suppl. Cambr. Rev.* p. lxi/2 The solemn gloom of judgment without the inbreaking sunshine of pardon.

inbreath ('ɪnbrɛθ). [f. IN *adv.* + BREATH.] A drawing in of the breath.

1921 R. GRAVES *Pier-Glass* 26 The deep in-breath, The breath roaring out. 1936 J. G. BRANDON *Dragnet* iv. 37 It was accompanied by a hissing inbreath from Ferradi. 1956 J. LOTZ in L. T. White *Frontiers of Knowledge in Study of Man* xiv. 212 In Swedish.. the word *ja*, 'yes', is very often spoken on the in-breath.

inbreathe (ɪn'briːð), *v.* [f. IN-¹ + BREATHE *v.* after L. *inspīrāre*. Cf. EMBREATHE, IMBREATHE.]

1. *trans.* To breathe (something) in. *lit.* and *fig.*

1382 WYCLIF *Ecclus.* iv. 12 Wisdom to his sonus inbrethede [1388 enspirith] life. 1574 J. JONES *Nat. Beginning Grow. Things* 19 A nother cause is contagiousnes which the ambient of compassing aire powreth and inbreatheth vpon those whome it doth enuiron. 1654 GATAKER *Disc. Apol.* 72 They cannot inbreath into us such knowledg that shal quiet and allay our.. hearts. *a* 1763 BYROM *Fragment* (R.), That inward, holy thing, inbreathed then. 1873 SYMONDS *Grk. Poets* x. 337 So true and delicate a spirit is inbreathed into the old forms.

2. To inspire (a person).

1851 [see INBREATHED]. 1883 *Presbyt. Messenger* 221 A soul saved and inbreathed by Jesus Christ. 1895 A. MURRAY *Holiest of All* 49 All prove to us how they were inbreathed by that Spirit of Christ.

3. To draw in as breath; to inhale, inspire.

1889 ILLINGWORTH *Probl. Pain* in *Lux Mundi* (ed. 10) 122 He felt himself inbreathing power from on high.

inbreathed ('ɪnˌbriːðd), *ppl. a.* [f. IN *adv.* 11 + BREATHED.] Breathed in; inspired.

c 1630 MILTON *At a Solemn Music* 4 Wed your divine sounds, and mixed power employ, Dead things with in-breathed sense able to pierce. 1851 SIR F. PALGRAVE *Norm. & Eng.* I. 200 The advantages which the inbreathed spirit receives. 1873 SYMONDS *Grk. Poets* x. 321 Brilliant with the inbreathed fancy of the North.

inbreather ('ɪnˌbriːðə(r)). [f. as INBREATHE + -ER¹.] One who inbreathes; an inspirer.

1873 SYMONDS *Grk. Poets* iii. 84 *Εἰσπνήλης* and *ἀΐτης* or 'inbreather' and 'listener'. 1880 A. RALEIGH *Way to City* 280 The very image of the Maker, the Inbreather.

inbreathing ('ɪnˌbriːðɪŋ), *vbl. sb.* [f. as prec. + -ING¹.] The action of the vb. INBREATHE; breathing in; inspiration.

1382 WYCLIF *2 Sam.* xxii. 16 Fro the inbrethinge of the spiryt of his woodnes. 1657 H. PINNELL *Philos. Reformed* 60 Man hath an Intellectual and immortal Soul, or Spirit by the inbreathing of God. 1678 R. BARCLAY *Apol. Quakers* (1841) 163 'There is', saith he, 'some lovely and some desirable thing in man, which is called the in-breathing of God, *ἐμφύσημα Θεοῦ*'. 1882 H. SCOTT HOLLAND *Logic & Life* (1885) 128 Man.. has withdrawn from him.. that essential inbreathing of God.

inbred ('ɪnˌbrɛd), *ppl. a.* (*sb.*) Also 7–8 **imbred**. [f. IN *adv.* 11 + BRED.]

1. Bred, engendered, or produced within; innate, native, inherent by nature.

a 1592 H. SMITH *Wks.* (1867) II. 481 O sin-bred hurt! O inbred hell! Nor full, nor fasting, never well. 1612 WOODALL *Surg. Mate* Wks. (1653) 206 Not onely the Sea, but also all other creatures.. cannot.. subsist without a natural inbred salt in them. 1660 BOYLE *New Exp. Phys. Mech.* Proem 2 Your inbred Curiosity, and love of Experimental Learning. 1738 WESLEY *Ps.* XXXVI. viii, The Pray'r is seal'd: We now foresee The Downfal of our inbred Foes. 1849 GROTE *Greece* II. lix. (1862) V. 237 He exhorted them to show their inbred superiority as Dorians.

β. 1627 HAKEWILL *Apol.* III. iv. (R.), To be wise, that is, to search the truth is a disposition imbred in every man. 1671 J. WEBSTER *Metallogr.* iv. 67 This imbred heat is sufficient. *a* 1715 BURNET *Own Time* (1766) I. 125 Out of the imbred love that all men have for their native country.

†**2.** Bred in a place, native; in quot. 1625 as *sb.* A native. *Obs. rare.*

1625 LISLE *Du Bartas, Noe* 100 The old Britton, the naturall Inbred of the country, was constrained to forsake it. 1638 F. JUNIUS *Paint. of Ancients* Ded. A iij, This translation befitteth rather the native fluency of one in-bred.

3. (Properly *in-bred.*) Bred in-and-in.

1892 STEVENSON *Across the Plains* 185 Sore-eyed, short-lived, inbred fishermen.

inbreed (ɪn'briːd), *v.* Also **imbreed**. [f. IN-¹ + BREED *v.*]

1. *trans.* To breed, engender, or produce within.

1599 SANDYS *Europæ Spec.* (1632) 83 These Iesuites.. endeavour.. to imbreed that fiercenesse and obstinacie in their schollers. 1641 MILTON *Ch. Govt.* II. Introd., To in-breed and cherish in a great people the seeds of vertu, and publick civility. 1647 N. BACON *Disc. Govt. Eng.* I. lxii. (1739) 121 The first and last Heresy that ever troubled this Island, was imbred by Pelagius. 1847 CLOUGH *Life & Duty* 49 Perplexing these that sleep, and in their folly Imbreeding doubt and sceptic melancholy. 1879 M. D. CONWAY *Demonol.* II. IV. xxiv. 293 The Church.. not wishing to imbreed in the popular mind a sceptical habit.

†**2.** To breed, bring up, or train *in* a course of action. *Obs. rare.*

1610 HOLLAND *Camden's Brit.* II. 39 Inbread and nuzeled in warlick exercises or robberies rather.

in-breeding ('ɪnˌbriːdɪŋ), *vbl. sb.* [f. IN *adv.* + BREEDING *vbl. sb.*] Breeding from animals of the same parentage or closely related; breeding in-and-in.

c 1842 E. J. LANCE *Cottage Farmer*, An in-breeding soon breaks up the inattentive keeper of domestic animals. 1881 J. P. SHELDON *Dairy Farming* 4/2 *In-breeding*,.. that is, the breeding for a time amongst near relations—generally results mischievously on the systems and on the fertility of the stock. 1882 *Standard* 23 Aug. 2/1 Over-preserving and 'in-breeding' are deteriorating the herds.

†**in'bridle**, var. of EMBRIDLE *v. Obs.*

1611 FLORIO, *Inbrigliare*, to inbridle, to insnaffle.

†**in'brier**, var. of IMBRIER *v. Obs.*

1611 FLORIO, *Infrascare*,.. to intangle, to inbrier, to inbush.

†**in'bring, ˌin-'bring**, *v. Obs.* Chiefly *Sc.* Also 4–7 **imbring**. Pa. t. and pple. **inbrought**; for Forms see BRING. [OE. *inbringan*, f. IN-¹ + BRING; transl. L. *offerre*, etc. See also EMBRING.]

trans. To bring in (*lit.* and *fig.*); to introduce; to adduce; to induce, cause to come; in *Sc. Law*, to bring in by legal authority, to produce in court, to confiscate (the goods of a condemned criminal).

c 1000 *Ags. Gosp.* Mark ii. 4 Þa hi ne mihton hine in-bringan [*c* 1160 in bringen] for þære mænigu. *c* 1325 *Metr. Hom.* 116 Bitakens tim quen lau imbroht knawing of sin. 1375 BARBOUR *Bruce* III. 268 Thusgat thaim confortyt the king; And, to confort thaim, gan Inbryng Auld storys. *c* 1400 tr. *Secreta Secret., Gov. Lordsh.* (E.E.T.S.) 81 Somtyme þis Reubarb is venomous, and inbrynges deth to hem þat takys hit ouer manere. 1563 WINȜET *Wks.* (1890) II. 21 Quhoumekle calamitie is inbrocht be the inductioun of a new doctrine. 1574 *Inv. R. Wardrobe* (1815) 200 To serche seik and inbring all our soverane lordis jowellis to his hienes use. 1609 SKENE *Reg. Maj., Stat. Robt. III* 57 Ilk Justitiar or his depute, sould cause his Clerk bring in all the extracts of his Justice aire.. And gif.. the saidis extracts are not imbrocht: that sall be imputed to them. 1619 SIR J. SEMPILL *Sacrilege Handl.* App. 17 Paul.. proueth both to imbring and bind other persons after coming, to the performance of things by them then represented. 1752 J. LOUTHIAN *Form of Process* (ed. 2) 55 Ordain all his moveable Goods and Gear to be escheat, and in-brought to his Majesty's Use. *Ibid.* 127 Ye denounce them our Rebels, and put them to our Horn, escheat, and in-bring all their moveable Goods and Gear to our Use. 1816 SCOTT *Old Mort.* xxxvi, His moveable goods and gear escheat and in-brought to his Majesty's use.

inbringer ('ɪnˌbrɪŋə(r)). Now *rare* or *Obs.* [f. IN *adv.* + BRINGER.] One who brings in, an introducer.

1557–75 *Diurnal Occurr.* (Bannatyne Club) 176 The in-bringaris of thir said Inglismen, strangers of this realme, wer James erle of Mortoun, Iohne erle of Mar. 1623 T. SCOTT *Projector* To Rdr. 2, I feare not what they bring in so much, as I doe the In-bringers. *a* 1670 SPALDING *Troub. Chas. I* (1792) I. 267 An evil patriot and special inbringer of thir innovations within the church.

'inˌbringing, *vbl. sb.* Now *rare* or *Obs.* [f. INBRING + -ING¹, or f. IN *adv.* + BRINGING *vbl.*

sb.] The action of bringing in; importation, introduction; bringing in under legal warrant. **1387** TREVISA *Higden* (Rolls) I. 29 An in-bryngynge to gretter knowleche in oþer bookes þat foloweþ. **1470** *Sc. Acts Jas. III*, II. 97/2 Þe Inbringing of bullion in þe Realme. *a* **1670** SPALDING *Troub. Chas. I* (1792) I. 292 For inbringing of men to his regiment. **1693** *Lond. Gaz.* No. 2936/3 Another Proclamation..for the better In-bringing of Their Majesties Excise. **1829** SCOTT *Rob Roy* Introd., The Earl of Argyle's service..in the inbringing of MacGregor, with a great many of the leading men of the clan, worthily executed to death for their offences, is thankfully acknowledged.

†**in'brothel**, *v. Obs. rare.* [Cf. IMBROTHELED.] *trans.* To place in a brothel. **1611** FLORIO, *Inbordellare*, to inbrothell.

†**in'brother**, *v. Obs. rare.* [f. IN-¹ + BROTHER.] *trans.* To admit as a brother. **1611** FLORIO, *Infratellare*, to inbrother.

†**in'brotherer**, obs. form of EMBROIDERER. **1577** FLEETWOOD in Ellis *Orig. Lett.* Ser. II. III. 56 On[e] Hayward, an inbrotherer, a Servaunt of my Lo. Wentworthes. **1610** *Canterb. Marriage Licenses* 10 July (MS.), Willi'mus Graues Ciuitatis Cant. Inbrotherer.

†**in'browded**, var. of EMBROWDED, embroidered. *c* **1440** *Promp. Parv.* 261/1 Inbrowdyd (*v.r.* inbrowdred), *intextus*. Inbrowdyd clothe (*Pynson* inbrowdred), *frigia*.

inbuche, obs. form of AMBUSH.

in-build (ɪn'bɪld), *v.* Also **inbuild**. [f. IN-¹ + BUILD *v.*] *trans.* To build in (see BUILD *v.* 2 b). Chiefly as **'in-,built** *ppl. a.* = *built-in* (BUILT *ppl. a.* 1 b). **1920** C. C. MARTINDALE in C. Hess *God & Supernatural* x. 342 Christ speaks of His faithful as pillars in-builded into that Temple which is Himself. **1923** *Daily Mail* 12 June 5 (Advt.), The difference between good and bad waterproofs being inbuilt, therefore invisible. **1961** *Times* 27 Mar. 5/3 The triphenyl tin compounds possess an inbuilt safety factor. **1961** *John o' London's* 7 Dec. 636/3 An in-built sense of humour. **1961** B. R. WILSON *Sects & Society* 7 The sect often in-builds a hard core of suspicion. **1965** *Catholic Herald* 5 Mar. 5/4 Any nation has an inbuilt resistance to immigrants. **1969** *Jane's Freight Containers 1968–69* 582/1 Basically it is a bi-directional roller beam with an inbuilt hydraulic jacking arrangement. **1971** *Daily Tel.* 15 Mar. 17/5 They are ten times brighter than the present traffic lights but contain an in-built device to ensure that no dazzle occurs.

†**in'bull**, var. of EMBULL *v. Obs.* **1432–50** tr. *Higden* (Rolls) VIII. 432 Messangers were sende from kynge Edwarde unto the pope for this accorde to be inbullede.

inburning ('ɪn,bɜːnɪŋ), *ppl. a.* [f. IN *adv.* + BURNING *ppl. a.*] Burning within or internally. **1596** SPENSER *F.Q.* IV. viii. 17 Her inburning wrath she gan abate.

inburst ('ɪnbɜːst), *sb. rare.* [f. IN *adv.* + BURST *sb.*; cf. *outburst*.] A bursting in, irruption. **1837** CARLYLE *Fr. Rev.* I. VII. ix, Like the infinite inburst of water; or say rather, of inflammable, self-igniting fluid. **1858** MASSON *Milton* I. 424 If there was no inburst of the essential Scottish spirit into English literature. **1872** G. MACDONALD *Wilf. Cumb.* II. xx. 291, I could see nothing for some time for the mighty inburst of a lovely light.

in'burst, *v. rare.* [f. IN *adv.* + BURST *v.*] *intr.* To burst in; to come in with suddenness and violence. So **'inbursting** *vbl. sb.* and *ppl. a.* *c* **1540** *Pilgr. T.* 220 in *Thynne's Animadv.* (1865) App. i. 83 Ther workes lay in pryson fast, till the kyng of glory in-brast. *a* **1876** H. BUSHNELL in *Butler's Bible Work* (1883) II. 326 The inbursting of a cloudless day on all the righteous dead. **1882** *Macm. Mag.* XLVI. 125 Sorely pressed by the inbursting Goths in the province of Mœsia.

†**inbush**, obs. variant of AMBUSH *v.*; also to cover with bushes, involve, entangle. *a* **1533** LD. BERNERS *Huon* ix. 25 Yᵉ knyghtes that were inbushyd in the wode. **1611** FLORIO, *Infrascare*,..to intangle, to inbrier, to inbush.

in-by(e ('ɪn'baɪ), *adv. Sc.* and *north. dial.* [f. IN *adv.* + BY *adv.*] **a.** In an inward direction; closer or further in towards the centre or interior of a house, farm, mine, etc. **1768** ROSS *Helenore* 66 (Jam.) That gate she halds, and as she weer [= wore] inby She does a lass among the trees espy. **1825–80** JAMIESON, *To gae inby*, is to go from the door towards the fire. **1851** GREENWELL *Coal-trade Terms Northumb. & Durh.* 31 *Inbye*, in the workings, or away from the shaft. **1899** *Westm. Gaz.* 16 Aug. 6/3 The passage is rather low, and we had to ride 'inby' [in a coal-mine].

b. *attrib.* as *inbye fields* (on a farm), *inbye servant*, *worker*, etc. Also used *absol.* or as *sb.* **1824** J. HOGG *Private Mem. Justified Sinner* 227 Gie up your crooning, or I'll pit you to an in-by place. **1894** J. CUNNINGHAM *Broomieburn* vi. 88 The inbye hand, Jock, would emerge from his bed in the stable-loft. **1918** *Border Standard* 18 May 2 Louping-ill or trembling is proving very destructive amongst in-by or park lambs. **1940** *Geogr. Jrnl.* XCVI. 108 Parallel galleries also served as inbye and outbye roads. **1958** *Rep. R. Comm. Common Land 1955–58* (Cmnd. 462) 274 *In-by land.* The term is widely used in the North of England and derives from the Scandinavian word (*by*) for a farm. Hence it means the fenced-in land nearest the homestead. **1960** *Farmer & Stockbreeder* 26 Jan. 56/1 Glanilyn Farm,..which has some 140 acres of in-bye... It was wasteful to use in-bye land. **1961** *Guardian* 18 Dec. 6/4 A large part of the 84 acres will be able to support pasture and contribute to the in-bye in the valley. **1971** *Country Life* 20 May 1259/1 Ewes and lambs on in-bye land at Lartington in Yorkshire.

†**inc**, *pron. Obs.* Forms: 1–3 inc, 2 ȝunc, ȝinc, hinc, 3 ȝunc, (*Orm.* ȝunnc), unk, hunke. [OE. *inc* = OS. *ink*, Goth. *igqis*, ON. *ykkr*, dat. and acc. dual of the second pers. pron. THOU. The acc. had in early OE. the fuller form *incit*, which has no parallel in the other Teut. languages. In late OE. altered (app. after the nom. dual *ȝit*, and the plur. *ȝe, eow*) to *ȝinc*, *ȝunc*, corrupted subseq. to *unk, hunk*.]

a. You two, both of you. **b.** To you two. *c* **1000** *Ags. Gosp.* Matt. ix. 29 Sy inc æftyr incrun ȝeleafan. *Ibid.* Mark i. 17 Ic do inc [*Hatton* ȝunc] þæt ȝyt beoð sawla onfonde. *c* **1175** *Lamb. Hom.* 93 Hwi iwearð hinc swa þet ȝit dursten fondian godes. *c* **1200** ORMIN 4493 Wiþþ unnclænnesess fule lusst, To filenn swa ȝunnc baþe. *a* **1225** *St. Marher.* 21 þe hali gast, þat glit of inc baðen. *c* **1230** *Hali Meid.* 11 Ne brec þu nawt tat seil þat seiled inc to gederes. *a* **1250** *Owl & Night.* 1733 Unk [*v.r.* Hunke] schal itide harm and schonde. *c* **1250** *Gen. & Ex.* 2830 Ic sal red Gunc boðen bringen read and sped.

Inc. U.S. abbreviation of INCORPORATED *ppl. a.* **1906** *Country Life in Amer.* May 16/1 (Advt.), The Engleside Company, Inc., Owners. **1928** *Publishers' Weekly* 16 June 2451/1 The retail business will be known as 'Dutton's, Inc.' **1936** MENCKEN *Amer. Lang.* (ed. 4) 244 An Englishman writes *Ltd.* after the name of a limited liability (what we would call *incorporated*) bank or trading company, as we write *Inc.* **1973** R. T. ELSON (*title*) The world of Time Inc.: the intimate history of a publishing enterprise.

‖**Inca** ('ɪŋkə). Also 6–8 Inga, 7 Ingua, Ynca. [Peruvian *inca* 'lord, king, emperor', also, more widely, 'man of the blood royal', the king being distinguished as *Capa Inca*, i.e. 'sole lord' (Garcilasso de Vega, *Comment. reales* (1609) I. xxiv).

(The form *inga* was, according to Garcilasso (himself of the race of Incas), a Spanish corruption.)]

1. The title of the emperor or king of Peru before its conquest by the Spaniards; also, one of the royal race of Peru, descended from Manco Capac and Mama Ocollo. [**1526** OVIEDO *Hist. Gen. y Nat. de las Indias* XLVI. xvii. (1855), Solo al superior señor le llaman Inga.] **1594** BLUNDEVIL *Exerc.* v. (1597) 275 In the Prouince Peru..yet vnder the Gouernement of their naturall King, which then was called Ingas. **1604** E. GRIMSTONE tr. *D'Acosta's Hist. W. Ind.* IV. xli. 320 The Ingua king of Peru. *c* **1645** HOWELL *Lett.* (1650) II. Introd. Poem 2 Which made the Indian Inca think they were Spirits which in white sheets the aer did tear. **1668** H. MORE *Div. Dial.* III. xvi. (1713) 210 Those of Peru frequently sacrifice their Children for the success of the affairs of their Ingua. **1777** ROBERTSON *Hist. Amer.* (1783) III. 23 The empire of the Incas or Lords of Peru. **1840** *Penny Cycl.* XVIII. 10/1 In 1780 the Peruvians took up arms against the Spaniards, under Tupac Amaro, an Inca. **1847** PRESCOTT *Peru* (1850) II. 143 The brows of the young Inca were encircled with the imperial borla by the hands of his conqueror.

2. Special comb. **Inca Cockatoo**, an adaptation of a German name, *Inka Kakadu* (cf. Reichenow, *Vogelbilder aus fernen Zonen* 1878–83), of the Pink or Leadbetter's Cockatoo of Australia; **Inca dog**, a South American species or sub-species of dog, *Canis ingæ* of Tschudi; **Inca tern**, a species of tern (*Nænia inca*), called also Bearded Tern.

The tern was originally described in 1826 by Lesson (*Voyage de la Coquille, Zoologie* 731) as 'Sterne des Incas' *Sterna inca*; placed by Boci (*Isis* 1844, p. 189) in a new genus *Nænia*, overlooking which Jardine in 1850 proposed to name it *Inca mysticalis*.

1887 MAC FARLANE in *Ibis* 204 There were numbers of.. the beautiful slate-black Inca Tern (*Nænia Inca*) with its curling white moustaches and cherry-red bill and feet.

†**in'cabinate**, *v. Obs.* [f. IN-¹ or ² + CABIN *sb.* + -ATE³ 7: cf. F. *encabaner*.] *trans.* To enclose as in a cabin or cabinet; to confine, restrict. **1672** *Mil. & Marit. Discipl.*, *Mil. Observ. Exerc. Port* ii. 177 This power was incabinated within the breast of Emperours, Kings and Generals.

†**in'cag**, *v. Obs. rare*⁻⁰. [f. IN-¹ or ² + CAG *sb.*¹] *trans.* To put into a cag or small cask. **1611** COTGR., *Encacqué*, incagged, put into a cag.

†**in'cage**, etc., obs. var. of ENCAGE, etc. *a* **1586** SIDNEY *Arcadia* IV. Wks. 1726 II. 750 Fitly incaged for death. *c* **1586** C'TESS PEMBROKE *Ps.* LVII. iii, My soule incaged lyes with lions brood.

Incaic (ɪŋ'keɪɪk), *a.* = INCAN *a.* Also **Incaean** (ɪŋkə'iːən), **Incarian** (ɪŋ'kɛərɪən) *adjs.* **1880** G. W. CABLE *Grandissimes* iv. 23 Possibly between the two sides of the occipital profile there may have been an Incaean tendency to inequality. **1909** *Cent. Dict.* Suppl., Incaic, Incarian. **1926** *Glasgow Herald* 30 Jan. 8 The ruins of an ancient Incaic village. **1937** *Jrnl. R. Anthrop. Inst.* 321 The resemblance to possibly pre-Incaic pottery from the vicinity. **1963** *Times* 9 Feb. 9/7 An intact group of thousands of Incaic and pre-Incaic tombs, some dating from about 1200 B.C., was found only a few weeks ago.

incalculability (ɪn,kælkjʊlə'bɪlɪtɪ). [f. next: see -ITY.] The quality of being incalculable. **1873** B. STEWART *Conserv. Energy* vi. §218 Such machines are eminently characterized by their incalculability. **1892** *Standard* 21 June 5/4 Mr. Gladstone's incalculability is a danger.

incalculable (ɪn'kælkjʊləb(ə)l), *a.* [f. IN-³ + CALCULABLE. So in F. (1789 in Hatz.-Darm.).]

1. That cannot be calculated.

a. That cannot be reckoned up; of an amount or number greater than can be computed; beyond calculation. **1795** BURKE *Scarcity* Wks. VII. 398 They may even in one year of such false policy, do mischiefs incalculable. **1815** W. H. IRELAND *Scribbleomania* 253 The incalculable benefits derivable from education. **1842** LYTTON *Zanoni* 28 They say his wealth is incalculable.

b. That cannot be reckoned or determined beforehand; incapable of being estimated or forecast. **1796** BURKE *Regic. Peace* i. Wks. VIII. 83 Passing, with a rapid, eccentrick, incalculable course, from the wildest anarchy to the sternest despotism. **1846** HAWTHORNE *Mosses* I. v. 127 Thrusting himself into an incalculable position.

2. Of a person or his disposition: That cannot be reckoned upon; such that his action cannot be estimated or forecast. **1876** GEO. ELIOT *Dan. Der.* v. xxxvii, Anxiety about the beloved but incalculable son. **1879** —— *Theo. Such* vi. 123 An uncertain incalculable temper.

in'calculableness. [f. prec. + -NESS.] The quality of being incalculable. **1864** in WEBSTER. **1879** GEO. ELIOT *Theo. Such* vi. 126 Ground for bearing with his diurnal incalculableness. **1897** *Daily News* 19 Feb. 5/2 It entirely falsifies the predictions as to the 'incalculableness' of the female vote.

in'calculably, *adv.* [f. as prec. + -LY².] In an incalculable manner; to an incalculable extent; beyond calculation; more than can be computed. **1806** MAURICE *Fall of Mogul* I. i. (Jod.), The sum incalculably vast demanded. **1837** HT. MARTINEAU *Soc. Amer.* II. 162 The population is advancing incalculably faster in Illinois than in Missouri.

†**in'calendared**, *pa. pple. Obs.* In 7 -ered. [f. IN-² + CALENDAR *v.* or *sb.* + -ED¹.] Entered in the calendar of saints; canonized. **1622** DRAYTON *Poly-olb.* xxiv. 78 These foure haue been for Saints preferd, And with their leader still doe liue incalendered.

incalescence (ɪnkə'lɛsəns). Now *rare* or *Obs.* [f. L. *incalēsc-ĕre*: see INCALESCENT and -ENCE.] The action or process of becoming hot or warm; rise of temperature; heating. **1646** SIR T. BROWNE *Pseud. Ep.* v. xxi. 270 Making no more thereof, then Seneca commendeth..that is, a sober incalescence and regulated æstuation from wine. **1669** BOYLE *Contn. New Exp.* I. (1682) 154 The Incalescence of solid bodies struck or rubbed against one another. **1749** LAVINGTON *Enthus. Method. & Papists* (1754) I. ii. 58 No sooner do the Inebriation and Incalescence go off, but a Sinking of the Spirits, a Coldness and Dullness take Place. **1761** *Descr. S. Carolina* 16 The greatest Incalescences of the Air, which..I have known take place in Twenty-four or Thirty Hours, were, 19 Degrees in the Spring, 24 in the Summer.

†**inca'lescency.** *Obs.* [f. as prec.: see -ENCY.] = prec. **1658** J. ROBINSON *Eudoxa* viii. 46 Though it produce an incalescency in the Spirits. **1691** RAY *Creation* II. (1692) 58–9 This Inunction is useful, indeed necessary..For preserving the ends of the Bones from an Incalescency.

incalescent (ɪnkə'lɛsənt), *a.* Now *rare.* [ad. L. *incalēscent-em*, pres. pple. of *incalēscĕre* to become warm or hot, f. *in-* (IN-²) + *calēscĕre* to grow warm.] Becoming hot or warm; increasing in warmth. *lit.* and *fig.* **1680** BOYLE *Produc. Chem. Princ.* IV. 213 There are many learned Chymists that looke upon incalescent Mercuries.. as Chymical non-entia. **1706** PHILLIPS, *Incalescent Mercury*, a Name given by Mr. Boyle to Mercury or Quick-silver.. which being mingled with a due Proportion of Leaf-Gold, or small Filings, would amalgamate, or turn to a Paste, and grow hot with the Gold. **1876** G. MEREDITH *Beauch. Career* I. xiv. 212 [His] bubbling generalizations..would ascend as incalescent adjectives to the popular idea of the sublime.

in-calf (ɪn'kɑːf), *a.* Also 6 encalf. [attrib. use of phrase *in calf*: see IN *prep.* 10 b.] Of a cow: That is in calf; pregnant. So **in'calving** *a.*; **in'calver**, a cow in calf. **1556** *Richmond. Wills* (1853) 90 To everye of the sonnes of Evan Haddocke..one encalf qwye. **1613** SIR R. BOYLE *Diary* in *Lismore Papers* (1886) I. 29, I delivered him 30 incalf cows and vj oxen. **1856** *Farmer's Mag.* Nov. 372 It is their common practice to purchase incalving cows. **1886** *Leeds Merc.* 22 Feb. 6/4 Not so many milch cows and incalvers. **1890** *Stratford-on-Avon Herald* 19 Dec. 6/2 Keeping in-calf cows on the pastures in the bleak days and chilly nights of October and November.

†**in'call**, *v. Obs.* [f. IN-¹ + CALL *v.*, after L. *invocāre* to call in, INVOKE.]

1. *trans.* To call in; to call upon, invoke. *a* **1340** HAMPOLE *Psalter* xiii. 9 God þai incald noght. *Ibid.* xix. 10 Here vs in day þat we inkall þe. *c* **1400** *Apol. Loll.* 95

Enchauntors..in callun fendis to ken hem þingis, or to telle hem þingis be for. **1563** WINȜET *Four Scoir Thre Quest.* lxxvii. Wks. 1888 I. 124 Gif we may incall the sanctis to pray for ws. **1637–50** ROW *Hist. Kirk* (Wodrow Soc.) 329 After incalling of the Lord's name.

b. To pray for, invoke, 'call down' (*on* a person). *rare.*

1563 WINȜET *Four Scoir Thre Quest.* lxii. Wks. 1888 I. 115 The Prophet incallis the wrayth of God on thame.

2. *intr.* **a.** To call *on* or *upon*: = 1. **b.** To pray *for, that.*

*a***1572** KNOX *Hist. Ref.* Wks. 1846 I. 162 That Sanctis should not be honored nor incalled upone. **1588** A. KING tr. *Canisius' Catech.* 20 b, Promised to al thame quha vnfeignedlie sal incal on the. **1589** R. BRUCE *Serm.* (Wodrow Soc.) 69 He man bow down and earnestly incall for the Spirit. **1591** *Ibid.* 202 The prophet incalled that the Sun should be brought back. **1663** R. BLAIR *Autobiog.* vi. (1848) 85 After incalling upon the name of the Lord.

Hence †**in'caller**, one who invokes, a suppliant.

1589 R. BRUCE *Serm.* (Wodrow Soc.) 149 Ye man be diligent incallers for mercie.

incalling, *vbl. sb.* [See the senses.]

†**1.** [f. INCALL + -ING^{1}.] Invocation, supplication.

1554 KNOX *Prayer* Sel. Writ. (1845) 44 The incallings of such as pray without Jesus Christ are vain.

2. [f. IN *adv.* + CALLING *vbl. sb.*] The action of calling in; invitation.

1669 R. FLEMING *Fulfill. Script.* (1801) I. 280 This truth anent the incalling of the Gentiles.

†**in'calm**, obs. var. of *encalm* (see EN-^{1} 2), to becalm.

1582 N. LICHEFIELD tr. *Castanheda's Conq. E. Ind.* vii. 17 b, The Tuesdaye after..hee was incalmed. *Ibid.* xxiv. 61 b, Eight great ships..wer incalmed.

incalver, incalving: see IN-CALF.

†**incameration** (ɪnkæmə'reɪʃən). *Obs.* [a. F. *incamération* = It. *incamerazione*, n. of action from F. *incamérer*, It. *incamerare*, f. *in-* (IN-^{2}) + It. *camera* chamber, the papal treasury: see CAMERA 2.] Annexation to the papal domain.

1670 G. H. *Hist. Cardinals* II. II. 161 He oppos'd the validity of the Bull for the incameration of Castro. **1727–41** CHAMBERS *Cycl.*, *Incameration*, in the apostolical chancery, the union of some land, right, or revenue to the domain of the pope.

incamp, -ment: see ENCAMP, -MENT.

Incan ('ɪŋkən), *a.* [f. INCA + -AN.] Pertaining to the Incas of Peru.

1885 *Stand. Nat. Hist.* VI. 216 We have no accurate knowledge of the Incan history earlier than the century before the invasion of the Spaniards.

†**in'cancred**, *ppl. a. Obs.* [var. *encankered*: see ENCANKER under EN-^{1} 2.] Cankered, converted into an ulcer or gangrene.

1562 SHUTE *Cambini's Turk. Wars* 68 There appeared in the raines of hys backe an incancred appostume, which dyd ..eate hys fleshe.

incandent (ɪn'kændənt), *a. rare.* [f. IN-^{2} + L. *candēnt-em* CANDENT, after L. *incandēscĕre*.] Shining white.

1854 DOBELL *Balder* xxiii. 116 Some great acropolis, Above the wondering eyes of ancient men..Sent out her idols round the incandent hill.

incandesce (ɪnkæn'dɛs), *v.* [ad. L. *incandēsc-ĕre* to become warm, glow, inflame, f. *in-* (IN-^{2}) + *candēscĕre* to become white.]

1. *intr.* To be or become incandescent; to glow with heat. Chiefly in pres. pple. **incan'descing** = INCANDESCENT.

1874 *Pop. Sci. Monthly* Jan., The heat of the incandescing body. **1880** *Edison's U.S. Patent* No. 230255 My electric lamp consists, essentially..of an *incandescing* conductor of high resistance hermetically sealed in a glass vacuum chamber. **1882** *Nature* XXVI. 357 To heat the incandescing body to an extremely high temperature.

2. *trans.* To render incandescent, cause to glow.

1883 SIR W. THOMSON in *Nature* XXVII. 278 The activity of the sun's radiation is..sixty-seven times greater than that of a Swan lamp per equal area, when incandesced to 240 candles per horse-power.

incandescence (ɪnkæn'dɛsəns). [f. INCANDESCENT: see -ENCE; so in F. (1798 in *Dict. Acad.*).]

1. The fact or condition of glowing with heat; the emission of light by a body heated to a high temperature; the state of being incandescent.

1794 J. HUTTON *Philos. Light* etc. 24 A body..heated far below the intensity necessary for incandescence. **1837** BREWSTER *Magnet.* 52 Incandescence does not give to bodies the power of coercing the magnetic influence. **1860** TYNDALL *Glac.* I. iii. 31 Meteorites..brought to incandescence by friction against the earth's atmosphere. **1881** SPOTTISWOODE in *Nature* No. 623. 547 The Swan, the Maxim, the Lane-Fox, and the Edison lamps, in which the light is due to the incandescence of a fine thread of carbon.

b. *transf.* Glowing or intense heat. *rare.*

1849 E. B. EASTWICK *Dry Leaves* 195 It was delightful to me after the incandescence from which I had just come.

c. *transf.* Matter in a state of incandescence or glow.

1853 KANE *Grinnell Exp.* xxviii. (1856) 230 We had parhelia..a mass of incandescence 22° from the sun. **1862** M. HOPKINS *Hawaii* 23 The descending lava presented a head of incandescence 200 rods in width.

2. *fig.* The state of becoming or being 'inflamed' with anger or other strong feeling; ardency, fervour.

1656 BLOUNT *Glossogr.*, *Incandescence*, a being or waxing very angry, or greatly inflamed. **1882–3** W. M. TAYLOR in Schaff *Encycl. Relig. Knowl.* II. 1015 Not with the earnestness of rant or roaring, but with that of fervid incandescence. **1898** *Daily News* 17 Nov. 5/5 An ally prone to velocity..and to sudden states of incandescence.

So **incan'descency** (*rare*), the quality or state of being incandescent.

1882 *Dredge's Elect. Illum.* I. 153 A platinum wire 18 B.W.G. and 15 feet long was raised to vivid incandescency.

incandescent (ɪnkæn'dɛsənt), *a.* (and *sb.*) [ad. L. *incandēscent-em*, pres. pple. of *incandēsc-ĕre* to INCANDESCE: so in F. (1798 in *Dict. Acad.*).]

1. a. Emitting light on account of being at a high temperature; glowing with heat.

1794 J. HUTTON *Philos. Light* etc. 172 The incandescent heat..would soon be carried away from the mass of coals, however great. **1822** IMISON *Sc. & Art* II. 27 If the heated body is not luminous or incandescent, as hot water, for instance. **1869** TYNDALL *Notes Lect. Light* 43 The spectrum of incandescent sodium-vapour consists of a brilliant band on the confines of the orange and yellow. **1876** PAGE *Adv. Text-bk. Geol.* i. 35 The hypothesis of an originally incandescent globe.

b. *gen.* Glowing, brightly shining, brilliantly luminous.

1867 J. HOGG *Microsc.* I. ii. 124 If any incandescent object be placed in a suitable position. **1871** B. TAYLOR *Faust* (1875) I. xxi. 181 Here gush the sparkles incandescent Like scattered showers of golden sand. **1872** C. KING *Mountain. Sierra Nev.* xi. 228 Through forest vistas, the incandescent snow greeted us.

c. *transf.* Intensely hot. *rare.*

1859 SALA *Tw. round Clock* (1861) 8 These are the shops to make your incandescent coppers hiss.

d. *techn.* Applied to that form of electric light produced by the incandescence of a filament or strip of carbon: the *glow-lamp* as distinguished from the *arc light*: see ARC *sb.* 5. Hence extended to various forms of gas and other lamps in which an appliance of a similar nature is used to increase the brightness of the flame.

[**1848** *Times* 2 Nov. 3/6 The Electric light..is not a flame, but is an incandescent light.] **1881** SIR W. THOMSON in *Nature* No. 619. 434 A Faure cell..charged and employed to excite incandescent vacuum-lamps. **1894** *Daily News* 7 Nov. 7/3 The use of the 'incandescent' or Welsbach burners is rapidly increasing..The leading features of the system are ..the incandescence of a cone or 'mantle' of filament, by which a soft, white, steady, and smokeless light is given. **1899** Incandescent gas lamps were introduced two years ago to light the streets of Oxford.

e. Also *sb.* An incandescent lamp or burner.

1908 S. FORD *Side-Stepping with Shorty* 38 It was dark, and about half a million incandescents had been turned on. **1925** C. R. COOPER *Lions 'n' Tigers* v. 143 The great, empty building, where only a few incandescents gleamed dully. **1971** *General Electric Investor* II. II. 5 Lucalox is giving Washington double the light output of its former mercury lighting and six times the levels of its original incandescents.

2. *fig.* Becoming or being warm or intense in feeling, expression, etc.; ardent, fiery; 'flaming up'.

1859 I. TAYLOR *Logic in Theol.* 340 Holy Scripture become resplendent; or, as one might say, incandescent; through-out, and taking effect on all minds. **1882** FARRAR *Early Chr.* II. 23 As he dwells on the point his words seem to grow incandescent with the writer's vehemence. **1894** *Westm. Gaz.* 27 Dec. 2/3 The 'incandescent passions' of the Anti-Semites.

Hence **incan'descently** *adv.*; also *fig.* 'hotly'.

1803 *Edin. Rev.* II. 184 More incandescently wrong-headed than any body else.

†**inca'nescence**. *Obs. rare*$^{-0}$. [f. as next + -ENCE.] (See quot.)

1656 BLOUNT *Glossogr.*, *Incanescence*, a waxing hoary or white headed. **1658** in PHILLIPS.

incanescent (ɪnkə'nɛsənt), *a. rare.* [f. L. *incānēscent-em*, pres. pple. of *incānēscĕre* to become white, f. *in-* (IN-^{2}) + *cānēscĕre* to become white, *cānēre* to be white.] = CANESCENT.

1866 *Treas. Bot.*, *Incanescent*, having a hoary or grey aspect, because of the presence of hairs upon the surface.

†**inca'nonical**, *a. Obs. rare.* [IN-^{3}.] Not canonical; uncanonical.

1637 C. DOW *Answ. to H. Burton* 105 b, Illegall, incanonicall proceedings. **1648** HERRICK *Hesper.*, *To his brother Nicholas*, Their large narrations, incanonicall.

†**in'canopy**, *v. Obs.* In 7 **incanope**. [f. IN-^{2} + CANOPY *sb.*] *trans.* To inclose in or as in a canopy.

1607 WALKINGTON *Opt. Glass* i. (1664) 1 Incanoped and intrenched in this darksome misty Cloud of Ignorance.

incanous (ɪn'keɪnəs), *a. Bot.* [f. L. *incān-us* hoary + -OUS.] Hoary with white pubescence.

1864 WEBSTER cites A. Gray.

in'cant, *v. Obs.* [ad. L. *incantā-re* to chant, make incantation, charm, enchant, bewitch, f. *in-* (IN-^{2}) + *cantāre* to sing, chant.] †**a.** *intr.* To use incantation or enchantment (*obs.*). †**b.** *trans.* To enchant, charm (*obs.*). **c.** *trans.* To raise by incantation. **d.** To chant, intone. Hence **in'canting** *vbl. sb.* and *ppl. a.*

1546 BALE *Eng. Votaries* I. (1550) 35 All vayn and craftye scyences..exorcising, incanting, & conjuring. **1658** BROMHALL *Treat. Specters* I. 38 They..have lesse incanting amongst them then formerly. **1665** SIR T. HERBERT *Trav.* (1677) 306 With incanting voices,..poesy, mirth, and wine, raising the sport commonly to admiration. **1926** *Chambers's Jrnl.* June 359/1 A little sorceress, talking to some spirit which she had incanted. **1959** *Times* 23 Sept. 3/7 The umpire incanting the score. **1961** M. SPARK *Prime of Miss Jean Brodie* ii. 22 They sat in the twilight eating toffees and incanting witches' spells.

†**incantate**, *v. Obs. rare*$^{-0}$. [f. ppl. stem of L. *incantāre*: see prec.] = prec.

1623 COCKERAM II, To Charme, *Incantate*.

incantation (ɪnkæn'teɪʃən). [a. F. *incantation* (13th c. in Godef. *Compl.*), ad. L. *incantātiōn-em*, n. of action from *incantāre*: see INCANT.]

The use of a formula of words spoken or chanted to produce a magical effect; the utterance of a spell or charm; more widely, The use of magical ceremonies or arts; magic, sorcery, enchantment.

1390 GOWER *Conf.* III. 45 With nigromaunce he wolde assaile To make his incantacion. **1527** ANDREW *Brunswyke's Distyll. Waters* D j, It is good dronke for them that hath eaten or hath in his body any incantacyon. **1616** CHAPMAN *Homer's Hymne to Hermes* 75 Thy vertue..Gainst Great-yll-causing incantation, To serue as for a Lance, Or Amulet. **1757** BURKE *Abridgm. Eng. Hist.* I. ii. (R.), Medicine was always joined with magick; no remedy was administered without mysterious ceremony and incantation. **1862** BURTON *Bk. Hunter* (1863) 315 Like the demons of old summoned by incantation.

b. with *pl.* An instance of this; *concr.* a magical formula chanted or spoken, or (more widely) any act or ceremony performed, to produce a magical effect; a spell, charm.

1412–20 LYDG. *Chron. Troy* I. ii. (MS. Digby 230) lf. 31/1 Oethes þe Kyng wᵗ ful greet laboure Made kepe it by incantacïouns. *a***1535** MORE *Let. Frith.* K ij b, To stoppe euery good mannes eares from suche vngracyouse incantacyons as thys mannes reasons be. **1602** WARNER *Alb. Eng.* XI. lxvii. (1612) 286 Loues Incantations so did he with Malice such defie. **1672** SIR T. BROWNE *Lett. Friend* §6 Amulets, Spells, Sigils, and Incantations, practised in other Diseases. **1774** PENNANT *Tour Scotl. in 1772*, 15 The old women, when they undertake a cure, mumble certain rhythmical incantations. *a***1854** H. REED *Lect. Eng. Lit.* vi. (1878) 195 The magic of the dark incantations of Shakespeare's witchcraft.

incantator ('ɪnkæn,teɪtə(r)). *rare.* [a. L. *incantātor*, agent-noun from *incantāre*: see INCANT.] One who uses incantation; an enchanter.

1447 BOKENHAM *Seyntys* (Roxb.) 85 Julyan anoon to the incantatour Thy craft he seyde is not worth a flykke. **1656** BLOUNT *Glossogr.*, *Incantator*, a charmer or enchanter. **1885** A. STEWART *Ben Nevis & Glencoe* I. 8 We have to beg the incantator not to direct the rats to the Lochaber shore.

incantatory (ɪn'kæntətərɪ), *a. rare.* [f. as prec. + -ORY.] Using, or of the nature of, incantation.

1646 SIR T. BROWNE *Pseud. Ep.* I. iii. 12 Fortune tellers, Juglers, Geomancers, and the like incantatory impostors. *Ibid.* I. iv. 16 Amulets, charms, and all incantatory applications. **1888** *Harper's Mag.* Aug. 332/2 It is wild, barbaric, incantatory—it is a monstrous musical conjuration.

†**in'canter**. *Obs. rare.* [f. INCANT. *v.* + -ER^{1}.] = INCANTATOR.

1829 *Examiner* 500/1 The flapping of great wings from a gigantic demon hovering over the incanters.

incanton (ɪn'kæntən), *v.* [f. IN-^{2} + CANTON *sb.*] *trans.* To make into or admit as a canton.

1705 ADDISON *Italy*, *Switzerland* 517 When the Cantons of Bern and Zurich propos'd, at a general Diet, the Incorporating Geneva in the Number of the Cantons, the Roman Catholick Party..propos'd at the same time the Incantoning of Constance, as a Counterpoise.

incapability (ɪnkeɪpə'bɪlɪtɪ). [f. next + -ITY.] The quality or condition of being incapable; incapacity, inability, incompetence: see the adj.

1632 SHERWOOD, Incapabilitie, or incapablenesse. *a***1641** SUCKLING (J.), You have nothing to urge but a kind of incapability in yourself to the service. **1665** BOYLE *Occas. Refl.* (1848) 371 An absolute Incapability of Love. **1793** HOLCROFT tr. *Lavater's Physiogn.* xlv. 228 There are capabilities and incapabilities in the countenance. **1868** MILL *Eng. & Irel.* 41 The difficulty of governing Ireland lies entirely in our own minds; it is an incapability of understanding.

incapable (ɪn'keɪpəb(ə)l), *a.* (*sb.*) [ad. med.L. *incapābil-is*, f. *in-* (IN-^{3}) + *capābilis* CAPABLE. (F. *incapable* is known from 1517 (Hatz.-Darm.); *capable* in Eng. from *c* 1560.)]

I. Not capable; the opposite of capable.

†**1.** Unable to take in, receive, contain, hold, or keep. Const. *of*. *Obs.*

c **1600** SHAKS. *Sonn.* cxiii, Incapable of more, repleat with you, My most true minde thus maketh mine eye vntrue. **1628** HOBBES *Thucyd.* (1882) 2 Attica being incapable of them itself, they sent out colonies into Ionia. **1683** D. A. *Art Converse* 104 The Mobility of their Spirits, and the Volubility of their Tongues, make them incapable of a Secret. **1841** L. HUNT *Seer* (1864) 2 This dandy would be incapable of his own wealth.

†**b.** Unable to receive or take calmly, put up with, or endure; impatient or intolerant *of*. *Obs.*

1643 SIR T. BROWNE *Relig. Med.* Pref., Men of my condition may be as incapable of affronts as hopeless of their reparations. **1712** STEELE *Spect.* No. 438 ¶4 Your Temper is Wanton, and incapable of the least Pain.

2. Unable or unfit to receive so as to be affected or influenced by; not open to or susceptible of; unable to 'take in' so as to realize, insensible to. Const. *of*. *Obs.* or *arch.*

1601 R. JOHNSON *Kingd. & Commw.* (1603) 64 Plato deemed the Cyrenians incapable of discipline, by reason of their long prosperitie. **1602** SHAKS. *Ham.* IV. vii. 179 As one incapable of her owne distresse. **1644** QUARLES *Barnabas & B.* (1851) 11 Lord, wherein am I more incapable of thy indignation [than Babel's proud king]? **1683** SIR W. SOAMES tr. *Boileau's Art Poetry* (R.), Decrepit age;—Incapable of pleasures youth abuse, In others blames what age does him refuse. **1830** HERSCHEL *Stud. Nat. Phil.* 81 If he refuse this, he is incapable of science.

3. Of such a nature, or in such a condition, as not to allow or admit of; not admitting or susceptible of. Const. *of*; also formerly with *inf.*

Equivalent to 'that cannot' with an infinitive passive; e.g. *incapable of measurement*, or *incapable of being measured* = 'that cannot be measured'.

1712 BUDGELL *Spect.* No. 401 ¶3 His Person..might.. make him believe himself not incapable to be beloved. **1748** *Anson's Voy.* II. viii. 219 The pearl oyster..was incapable of being eaten. **1871** B. STEWART *Heat* (ed. 2) §289 Unavoidable loss of heat which is incapable of accurate measurement. **1872** YEATS *Techn. Hist. Comm.* 430 Permanent, and incapable of being lost.

4. Not having the capacity, power, or fitness for a specified function, action, etc.; unable. Const. *of*; also formerly with *inf.*

With verbal nouns, or infinitives, equivalent to 'that cannot' with an infinitive active; e.g. *incapable of aspiration*, or *incapable of aspiring* = 'that cannot aspire'.

1610 SHAKS. *Temp.* I. ii. 111 Of temporal royalties He thinks me now incapable. **1611** —— *Wint. T.* IV. iv. 408 Is not your Father growne incapeable Of reasonable affayres? **1674** tr. *Scheffer's Hist. Lapland* 34 Their understanding.. incapable of discerning between true and false. **1781** GIBBON *Decl. & F.* xxix. III. 124 A claim, which they were incapable of supporting, either by reason, or by arms. **1783** *Hist. Miss Baltimores* I. 179, I..was almost incapable to utter a syllable. **1839** HALLAM *Hist. Lit.* I. iii. §95 Incapable, in the infancy of criticism, to discern authentic from spurious writings. **1842** MRS. CARLYLE *Lett.* I. 149, I am still incapable of much exertion. **1895** *Bookman* Oct. 22/2 Louis [XIV.]..was also quite incapable of appreciating genius in others.

b. In a good sense: Not having the depravity, effrontery, or moral weakness for a specified act, etc.

1755 YOUNG *Centaur* ii. Wks. 1757 IV. 136 The world.. was incapable of so great a guilt. **1828** SCOTT *F.M. Perth* xxvii, My foes..have laid things to my charge whereof I am incapable, even in thought. **1870** BRYANT *Iliad* I. v. 147 The valiant Diomede replied, Incapable of fear.

5. *absol.* Destitute of, or deficient in, ordinary capacity or natural ability; incompetent; without natural qualification.

In phr. ***drunk and incapable*** (in police reports), i.e. so drunk as to be incapable of taking care of himself.

1594 SHAKS. *Rich. III*, II. ii. 18 Incapeable, and shallow Innocents, You cannot guesse who caus'd your Fathers death. **1623** COCKERAM, *Incapable*, which cannot conceiue, a foole. **1849** MACAULAY *Hist. Eng.* vi. II. 158 That the finances might not be ruined by incapable and inexperienced Papists. **1883** C. J. WILLS *Mod. Persia* 139 In a few days he was found..drunk and incapable in the street.

6. Not having some external, *esp.* legal, qualification; not legally qualified or entitled; disqualified. Const. *of*; also formerly with *inf.*

1651 HOBBES *Leviath.* II. xix. 100 They are incapable of Election of any new Monarch. **1712** ADDISON *Spect.* No. 495 ¶8 The Jews..are in most, if not all, Places incapable of either Lands or Offices. **1769** *Resol. Ho. Commons* 17 Feb., John Wilkes Esq.:..was and is incapable of being elected a Member to serve in this present Parliament. **1818** HALLAM *Mid. Ages* (1872) I. 199 Incapable of property, and destitute of redress. **1855** MACAULAY *Hist. Eng.* xv. III. 518 That every person who..should presume to take any such office ..should be for life incapable of holding any public employment whatever.

II. †**7.** In passive sense = med.L. *incapābilis* that cannot be taken in or comprehended: That cannot be received or apprehended. Const. *to*. *Obs. rare.*

1591 SYLVESTER *Du Bartas* I. i. 162 God, of himselfe, incapable to sense In's Works reueales him t'our intelligence. *a* **1625** BOYS in Spurgeon *Treas. Dav.* Ps. xix. Introd., God is incapable to sense, yet he makes himself.. visible in his works.

B. *sb.* A thoroughly incompetent person; one without capacity or ability.

1809 BENTHAM *Plan Parl. Reform* (1817) 25 Many opulent, and thence idle incapables..crowd the list. **1838** LYTTON *Alice* XI. iv, Saxingham and his friends were imbeciles—incapables. **1861** J. G. SHEPPARD *Fall Rome* vii. 360 The guidance of an Incapable like Radagasius.

in'capableness. [f. prec. + -NESS.] The quality of being incapable; incapability.

1632 SHERWOOD, Incapabilitie or incapableness. **1642** ROGERS *Naaman* 4 Our incapablenesse of holy things. **1659** R. GELL *Amendm. Bible* 403 Nor to be understood onely according to the dulness or incapableness of the hearer. **1860** EMERSON *Cond. Life, Culture* (1861) 95 An incapableness of being dazzled or frightened.

in'capably, *adv.* [f. as prec. + -LY[2].] **a.** In an incapable or incompetent manner. **b.** To such a degree as to be incapable (in phr. ***incapably drunk***: see INCAPABLE 5).

1846 WORCESTER cites *Westm. Rev.* **1896** *Daily News* 19 Sept. 2/6 She was found incapably drunk in Rosehill-road.

†**inca'pacify,** *v. Obs. rare.* [f. L. *incapāx, incapāci-* + -FY: cf. *capacify*.] = INCAPACITATE.

1683 E. HOOKER *Pref. Ep. Pordage's Mystic Div.* 10 Then are you utterly incapacified as to the Concerns of these Mysteries and Sublimities.

incapacious (ɪnkəˈpeɪʃəs), *a.* [f. L. *incapāx, incapāci-* + -OUS: cf. It. *incapace* and CAPACIOUS.] Not capacious; the opposite of capacious.

1. Not of sufficient size to take in or contain something; not having space or room. **b.** Not able to contain much; not spacious or roomy; narrow, limited. (*lit.* and *fig.*)

1635 PAGITT *Christianogr.* App. 11 These my Letters are incapacious for mee to set downe at large the reasons. **1668** HOWE *Bless. Righteous* (1825) 4 The momentary pleasure of narrow and incapacious sense. *a* **1715** BURNET (J.), Souls that are made little and incapacious cannot enlarge their thoughts to take in any great compass of times or things.

2. Unable to comprehend or apprehend; not having mental capacity for something. Const. *of*; also formerly with *inf.* **b.** *absol.* Deficient in mental capacity or ability.

1617 MIDDLETON & ROWLEY *Fair Quarrel* II. ii, Can art be so dim-sighted, learned sir? I did not think her so incapacious. **1625** BP. MOUNTAGU *App. Cæsar* ix. 80 Buzzing them into popular eares and capacities, incapacious of them. **1627–77** FELTHAM *Resolves* II. lxiii. 293 Nature has doom'd him among the incapacious and silly. **1652** W. HARTLEY *Infant-Baptism* 10 [He] was incapacious to comprehend a rule or law. **1836** LANDOR *Peric. & Asp.* Wks. 1846 II. 404 The minds of them all..however incapacious, are carried to the utmost pitch of enthusiasm.

Hence **inca'paciousness**, the quality of being incapacious, want of capacity.

1727 in BAILEY vol. II. Hence in JOHNSON, TODD, etc.

incapacitant (ɪnkəˈpæsɪtənt). [f. INCAPACIT(ATE *v.* + -ANT[1].] A substance that can be used to incapacitate a person for a time without wounding or killing him.

1961 *Today's Health* Mar. 76 If the Chemical Corps succeeds in standardizing effective incapacitants, it will represent a significant advance. **1963** *Listener* 7 Feb. 238/2 The nature of the military 'incapacitants'..includes such 'psychic poisons' as lysergic acid diethylamide, LSD-25, which produces extreme mental confusion. **1968** *New Scientist* 29 Feb. 465/1 BZ, one of the standard US incapacitants produces dizziness, heart palpitation, urinary retention and constipation. **1970** *Daily Tel.* (Colour Suppl.) 20 Feb. 19 Incapacitants are also intended for 'humane' use; their idea is to render an enemy temporarily helpless and to put him out of action for short periods.

incapacitate (ɪnkəˈpæsɪteɪt), *v.* [f. INCAPACITY + -ATE[3]: cf. *capacitate*.]

1. *trans.* To deprive of capacity; to render incapable; to disqualify, unfit. Const. *for*, †*of*, *from*, or *inf.*

1661 SOUTH *Serm.* III. 170 There is an Universal stain and depravation upon Mans Nature, that does incapacitate him for the Fruition of God. **1666** G. HARVEY *Morb. Angl.* xii. 137 They are..incapacitated of digesting the alimonious humours into flesh. **1727** SWIFT *What passed in London*, Which might..incapacitate her to give ready and apt answers. **1830** HERSCHEL *Stud. Nat. Phil.* 91 A state that incapacitates us from reasoning, and almost from observation! **1877** S. COX *Salv. Mundi* vii. (1878) 152 A reward which his evil qualities and defects incapacitated him to receive. **1882** MRS. PITMAN *Mission L. Greece & Pal.* 254 My lameness does not incapacitate me..for the work of the day school.

2. To deprive of legal capacity; to disqualify in law.

1657 CROMWELL *Sp.* 21 Apr. in *Carlyle*, You have incapacitated public Preachers from sitting in Parliament. **1687** in *Magd. Coll. & Jas. II* (O.H.S.) 222 The order for incapacitating the late Fellows..was read. **1765** BLACKSTONE *Comm.* I. 162 A minor was incapacitated.. from sitting in either house, by the law and custom of parliament. **1885** *Law Rep.* 29 Ch. Div. 548 The death of one of two trustees does not incapacitate the other trustee from giving a good receipt for trust funds paid to him.

Hence **inca'pacitated, inca'pacitating** *ppl. adjs.*

1783 JOHNSON *Let. to Reynolds* 12 Apr. in *Boswell*, If you could procure the revocation of this incapacitating Edict. **1805** EUGENIA DE ACTON *Nuns of Desert* II. 73 The incapacitated situation of his servant. **1811** *Henry & Isabella* II. 59 Many instances of daughters supporting incapacitated parents. **1879** GEO. ELIOT *Theo. Such* ii. 37 To look always from overhead at the crowd of one's fellow-men must be in many ways incapacitating.

incapacitation (ɪnkəpæsɪˈteɪʃən). [n. of action f. INCAPACITATE.] The action of incapacitating or fact of being incapacitated; the rendering or being rendered incapable; disqualification.

a. general: cf. prec. 1.

1790 G. WALKER *Serm.* II. xix. 82 An incapacitation for the happiness of heaven. **1871** R. ELLIS *Catullus* xxi. 8 A wily wit defeated Pays in scandalous incapacitation.

b. legal: cf. prec. 2.

1770 BURKE *Pres. Discont.* Wks. 1842 I. 143 If they suffer this power of arbitrary incapacitation to stand, they have utterly perverted every other power of the house of commons. **1771** *Junius Lett.* xx. 93 *note*, The house of Commons..exceeded their boasted precedent of the expulsion and subsequent incapacitation of Mr. Walpole. **1855** MILMAN *Lat. Chr.* IV. viii. (1864) II. 385 A public sign of their incapacitation for secular business.

attrib. **1806** W. TAYLOR in *Ann. Rev.* IV. 210 Mr. Belsham applauds the clergy-incapacitation act.

incapacity (ɪnkəˈpæsɪtɪ). [ad. F. *incapacité* (16th c. in Hatz.-Darm.) = It. *incapacità* (Florio, 1598): see IN-[3] and CAPACITY.]

1. Want of capacity; inability, powerlessness; incompetence, natural disqualification; incapability. Also with *an* and *pl.*, an instance of this.

1611 FLORIO, *Incapacita*, incapacity, vncapablenesse. **1646** SIR T. BROWNE *Pseud. Ep.* III. i. 107 Wee doe not conceive..any such intolerable incapacity in the organs of divers other Quadrupedes. **1647** CLARENDON *Hist. Reb.* I. §141 The Lord Conway..for age and incapacity, was at last removed from the Secretary's office. **1712** STEELE *Spect.* No. 456 ¶2 The Incapacity of an Infant or a Lunatick. **1781** GIBBON *Decl. & F.* xxi. (1869) I. 589 His incapacity and ignorance were equal to his presumption. **1819** SHELLEY *Cenci* II. ii, The eldest son of a rich nobleman Is heir to all his incapacities. **1873** HAMERTON *Intell. Life* x. v. (1875) 391 Cerebral fatigue leading to temporary incapacity.

b. Const. *of*, *for*, or *inf.*: cf. INCAPABLE.

a **1665** J. GOODWIN *Filled w. the Spirit* (1867) 27 An utter incapacity of receiving the Spirit. **1681** LUTTRELL *Brief Rel.* (1857) I. 131 The incapacity of the emperor to hinder it. **1736** BUTLER *Anal.* I. iii. 100 Through incapacity of knowing better, and doing better for themselves. **1823** LAMB *Elia* Ser. II. *Old Margate Hoy*, The incapacity of actual objects for satisfying our preconceptions of them. **1856** OLMSTEAD *Slave States* 130 Feeling their own incapacity to take care of themselves.

c. Inability to take, receive, or deal with in some way. Const. *of*, *for*.

a **1655** VINES *Lord's Supp.* (1677) 165 He brings..a church into an incapacity of sacraments. **1665** GLANVILL *Def. Vain Dogm.* p. v, I fell into a violent feavour, which long detain'd me in an incapacity for matter of such a nature. **1896** *Allbutt's Syst. Med.* I. 411 Digestive incapacity for starch and milky food.

2. Legal disqualification, disability: with *an* and *pl.*, an instance of this, a disqualification or disability.

1648 *Art. Peace* c. 8 That all Incapacities imposed upon the Natives of this Kingdom..be taken away by Act to be passed in the said Parliament. **168.** in Somers *Tracts* I. 272 Persons of great Consideration and Credit..lying at present under an Incapacity. **1767** BLACKSTONE *Comm.* II. 257 There is one more incapacity of taking by descent. **1850** MERIVALE *Rom. Emp.* (1865) I. iv. 189 The laws..inflicted upon him civil incapacity to the fullest extent.

Incaparina (ɪnkæpəˈriːnə). [f. the initials of *I*nstitute of *N*utrition of *C*entral *A*merica and *P*anama + Amer. Sp. *f)ariña* powdered manioc f. L. *farina* flour, meal.] A preparation of vegetable protein, used as a dietary supplement.

1960 N. S. SCRIMSHAW in *Proc. Conf. Cottonseed Protein for Animals & Man* 18/1 The name Incaparina has now been adopted as a generic name to refer to any vegetable mixture developed by INCAP suitable for feeding to young children and containing at least 25% protein of a quality comparable to that of milk and other products of animal origin. **1964** *Listener* 28 May 886/2 'Incaparina', a mixture of cottonseed meal, maize, and several other ingredients, has been used widely in Guatemala. **1965** S. M. CANTOR in J. M. Leitch *Food Sci. & Technol.* III. 460 One of the most successful protein mixtures, Incaparina, a food product of plant origin, was developed by the Institute of Nutrition of Central America and Panama... Incaparina is an uncooked, dry powder which may be heated, flavoured, and consumed alone as a liquid, or it may be added to other foods. **1970** M. PYKE *Food Sci & Technol.* (ed. 3) xi. 212 The nutritional value of this preparation, which is marketed under the name of 'Incaparina', is sufficiently high to allow its being fed to young children as a substitute for milk.

†**in'capital,** *a. Obs. rare.* [IN-[3].] Not capital; not punishable with death.

1643 (*title*) Remonstrance of..poore distressed Prisoners ..committed for debt and other incapitall offences.

†**incapon,** *v. Obs. rare.* [f. IN-[2] + CAPON *v.*] *trans.* To castrate.

1611 FLORIO, *Incaponito*, incaponed, guelded.

incapsulate, -ation, var. ENCAPSULATE, -ATION.

in'captivate, *v. rare.* Also en-. [f. ppl. stem of med.L. *incaptīvāre*, f. *in-* (IN-[2]) + late L. *captīvāre* to CAPTIVATE: cf. It. *incattivare* (Florio).] *trans.* To take captive, bring into captivity.

1611 FLORIO, *Incattiuare*, to encaptiuate. **1683** TRYON *Way to Health* 563 That man should so prodigiously degrade, dishonour and incaptivate himself. **1771** T. HULL *Hist. Sir W. Harrington* I. 223 The radiant beams of your encaptivating splendor. **1882** OGILVIE (Annandale), *Encaptivate.*

incaptive: see ENCAPTIVE.

in-car attrib.: see IN *prep.* 18.

†**in'carcer,** *v. Obs. rare.* [a. F. *incarcérer* (1508 in Hatz.-Darm.), earlier *encarcerer* (1392 in Du Cange), ad. med.L. *incarcerāre* to imprison, f. *in-* (IN-^{2}) + *carcer* prison, jail.] = INCARCERATE *v.*

c **1620** Z. BOYD *Zion's Flowers* (1855) 23, I.. Incarc'rd lye within this floating In.

incarcerate (ɪn'kɑːsərət), *ppl. a. arch.* [ad. med.L. *incarcerāt-us*, pa. pple. of *incarcerāre*: see prec.] Incarcerated, imprisoned; confined, shut in. (Formerly constr. also as pa. pple. of next.)

1528 ROY *Rede Me* (Arb.) 48 They lose their goodes with oute mercy, And their boddies to be incarcerate. **1583** *Leg. Bp. St. Androis* Pref. 31 Tane and incarcerat, kepit heir and there. **1647** H. MORE *Song of Soul* III. III. x, While in this muddy world incarcerate They lie. **1752** J. LOUTHIAN *Form of Process* (ed. 2) I. 61 The Committer.. shall order his Liberation, or discharge his Imprisonment, if not incarcerate. **1827** H. COLERIDGE *Poems* (1833) I. 85 Breathes the mephitic and incarcerate fog. **1863** SALA *Capt. Dangerous* I. x. 285 Many.. lay incarcerate years after they had satisfied the Demands of their Creditors.

incarcerate (ɪn'kɑːsəreɪt), *v.* [f. ppl. stem of med.L. *incarcerāre*: see INCARCER and -ATE^{3}.]

1. *trans.* To shut up in prison; to put in confinement; to imprison.

1560 ROLLAND *Crt. Venus* II. 342 Tratour, I sall thy corps Incarcerate. **1637–50** ROW *Hist. Kirk* (Wodrow Soc.) 238 Mr. Andro Melvill, by great moyen.. obtained leave that a servant should be incarcerated with him in the Tower. **1654** in W. ROSS *Aberdour & Inchcolme* xi. (1885) 329 The Session desires the Bailȝie to cause apprehend and incarcerate presently Margaret Currie. **1833** L. RITCHIE *Wand. by Loire* 57 We were incarcerated a whole day in the prison.

2. *fig.* To shut up as in prison; to confine.

1640–4 in Rushw. *Hist. Coll.* III. (1692) I. 216 What is it .. to incarcerate the Liberty of the Subject under the Iron and weighty Chains of an Arbitrary Government? **1665** G. HARVEY *Advice agst. Plague* 9 Those dense bodies.. easily incarcerate the infected air.

Hence **in'carcerated** *ppl. a.*, imprisoned; *spec.* in *Path.*, variously used of a strangulated, obstructed, or otherwise irreducible hernia and of a retained placenta; **in'carcerating** *ppl. a.*, that incarcerates, imprisoning.

1742 YOUNG *Nt. Th.* IV. 665 From nature's continent.. this little isle of life, This dark, incarcerating colony, Divides us. **1783** POTT *Chirurg. Wks.* II. 76 Every symptom which attends an incarcerated rupture. *Ibid.* 186 The operation for the incarcerated bubonocele. **1822–34** *Good's Study Med.* (ed. 4) IV. 65 A troublesome phimosis either of the strangulating or incarcerating kind. **1823** BENTHAM *Not Paul* 19 The sweeping and incarcerating commission he had been intrusted with by the rulers. **1883** *19th Cent.* May 878 The incarcerating creditor was compelled to allow him a daily aliment. **1886** *Syd. Soc. Lex.*, *Hernia, incarcerated*,.. variously explained by authors. It is used by some.. as strangulated; by others, to signify.. an obstructed hernia; and by others, to denote a hernia which has become irreducible in consequence of thickening of, or fatty deposit in, the enclosed omentum or mesentery.

incarceration (ɪnkɑːsə'reɪʃən). [a. F. *incarcération* (13–14th c. in Littré), ad. med.L. *incarcerātiōn-em* imprisonment, n. of action from L. *incarcerāre*: see prec.] The action of incarcerating or fact of being incarcerated; imprisonment.

1536 BELLENDEN *Cron. Scot.* (1821) I. 179 Be lang seiknes and malancoly, quhilk he tuke for his incarceration. *a* **1649** DRUMM. OF HAWTH. *Jas. I* Wks. (1711) 4 He thought by gentle incarcerations to have restrained their malice. **1803** SYD. SMITH *Wks.* (1869) 31 Since the benevolent Howard attacked our prisons, incarceration has become not only healthy but elegant. **1855** MISS COBBE *Intuit. Mor.* 117 The deprivation of Personal Freedom constitutes.. an incarceration of the Soul.

b. *Path.* Obstinate constriction or strangulation of a hernia (see INCARCERATED); retention of the placenta in parturition.

1826 COOPER *Surg.* 461 The.. simple obstruction of a hernia, is essentially different from incarceration, or strangulation.

incarcerator (ɪn'kɑːsəreɪtə(r)). [Agent-noun in L. form from med.L. *incarcerāre* to INCARCERATE.] One who incarcerates or imprisons.

1820 J. CLELAND *Rise Glasgow* 82 Fees Paid by the Incarcerator to the Jailor. **1869** *Pall Mall G.* 19 Aug. 10 The amnesty is not a greater relief to the incarcerated than to the incarcerator.

†**in'cardinate,** *a. Obs.* Used humourously as a blunder for *incarnate*.

1601 SHAKS. *Twel. N.* V. i. 185 We tooke him for a Coward, but hee's the verie diuell incardinate.

incardinate (ɪn'kɑːdɪneɪt), *v.* [f. ppl. stem of med.L. *incardināre* to institute into an ecclesiastical benefice, f. *in-* (IN-^{2}) + *cardo, cardin-em* hinge, *cardinālis* a chief presbyter, a CARDINAL.]

trans. **a.** To institute as principal priest, deacon, etc. at a particular church or place (see *Cardinalis* and *Incardinare* in Du Cange); in quot. 1609 explained etymologically. **b.** To institute to a cardinalship, raise to the rank of cardinal.

1609 BP. W. BARLOW *Answ. Nameless Cath.* 7 A dignitie [that of Cardinal] denominated.. as being Incardinated (it is Gregories word) that is Mortized or riueted to a Church, as a hinge to a dore. [**1725** tr. *Dupin's Eccl. Hist. 17th C.* I. II. iii. 42 He who had a right to succeed was called *Incardinatus*; whereas he who had a Church in present was said to be *Ordinatus*.] **1862** HOOK *Lives Abps.* II. xii. 663 When he had accepted the office of Cardinal, but before he was incardinated. **1882–3** SCHAFF *Encycl. Relig. Knowl.* I. 403 Pope Pius V finally confined the title [*cardinal*] formerly applied somewhat vaguely to all priests appointed at a cathedral church.. to such among the clergy of the city of Rome as had been 'incardinated' by the Pope himself.

So **incardi'nation,** institution or formal incorporation.

1897 *Dublin Rev.* Oct. 483 A tribal badge, symbol of incardination in the sept.

in-career *attrib.*: see IN *prep.* 18.

†**inca'ressing,** *ppl. a. Obs. rare.* [IN-^{3}.] The opposite of caressing; treating coldly or harshly.

1608 MACHIN *Dumb Knt.* III, From this reproch, this incarressing humour Hath taught my soule a new philosophie.

Incarial (ɪŋ'kɛərɪəl), *a.* [f. mod.L. type **incāri-us*, or **incāri-s*, f. INCA (like L. *aquārius, contrārius*, or *familiāris, stellāris*) + -AL^{1}.] Of or pertaining to the Incas of Peru.

1863 *Intell. Observer* III. 229 Ascending the Cordillera, Incarial ruins will be met with continually. **1877** E. G. SQUIER *Peru* (1878) 454 The procession of Corpus Christi, in which the Incarial family, in regal native costume, take part.

incarmined (ɪn'kɑːmɪnd), *ppl. a.* [f. IN-^{2} + CARMINE *sb.* + -ED^{1}.] Imbued with carmine; dyed carmine or deep crimson.

1863 D. G. MITCHELL *My Farm of Edgewood* 210 Rosy cheeks and incarmined arms do not belong to the heroines of her dreams.

incarn (ɪn'kɑːn), *v.* Also 6 **en-**. [a. F. *incarner* (1372 in Hatz.-Darm.), ad. L. *incarnāre* (5th c.) to make flesh, f. *in-* (IN-^{2}) + *caro, carn-* flesh.]

1. a. *trans.* To cover with flesh, cause flesh to grow upon or in, heal over (a wound or sore).

c **1400** *Lanfranc's Cirurg.* 122 Leie aboute þe wounde.. a defensif of bole armonyak.. aftirward incarne it, þat is to seie brynge ouer fleisch, & aftirward consowde. **1543** TRAHERON *Vigo's Chirurg.* II. ix. 23 Than ye must mundifye the place, and incarne it, and seale it up. **1612** WOODALL *Surg. Mate* Wks. (1653) 31 This unguent doth digest and incarn wounds and ulcers. **1750** *Phil. Trans.* XLVII. 94 The wound was thoroughly deterged, incarned, and.. cicatrized. **1822–34** *Good's Study Med.* (ed. 4) II. 519 Here however the hollows are not incarned or filled-up with a new material.

b. *absol.* To cause flesh to grow; to induce healing.

1541 R. COPLAND *Guydon's Form.* S iv b, Ley it on with towe, and a playster, for it dryeth, encarneth, and conforteth. **1694** WESTMACOTT *Script. Herb.* 10 Another oyntment that doth digest, mundify, and incarn. **1758** J. S. *Le Dran's Observ. Surg.* (1771) Dict., *Epulotica*, Medicines that incarn and cicatrize.

c. *intr.* To become covered with flesh, to heal.

1689 MOYLE *Sea Chyrurg.* II. x. 57 You will know how it incarns by a reddish speck, which you will see on the end of your Tent when you take it out. **1776** *Phil. Trans.* LXVI. 438 As the wound incarned, the.. discharge lessened daily. **1822–34** *Good's Study Med.* (ed. 4) II. 43 Incarning and cicatrizing easily.

2. To embody in flesh, to incarnate. *rare.*

1563 [see INCARNED]. **1882** L. WINGFIELD *Gehenna* II. vii. 211 Next time that you're re-incarned, you'll be a Byron. **1904** HARDY *Dynasts* I. I. iii. 17 Did I incarn in moulds of all mankind. **1907** *Westm. Gaz.* 7 Feb. 8/2 Incarned as 'Superman' by G.B.S.

Hence **in'carning** *vbl. sb.* and *ppl. a.*

1721 QUINCY tr. *Hodges' Plague Lond.* 200 Incarning is gradually to be effected and the Ulcer slowly healed over. **1813** J. THOMSON *Lect. Inflam.* 611 To use several medicaments more or less humecting, digesting, deterging, incarning or desiccative, to the sundry burnt parts.

incarnadine (ɪn'kɑːnədɪn, -aɪn), *a.* and *sb. arch.* Also 7 **-in.** [a. F. *incarnadin, -ine* (16th c.), ad. It. *incarnadino*, var. of *incarnatino* carnation, flesh-colour, deriv. of *incarnato* INCARNATE.]

A. *adj.* Properly, Flesh-coloured, carnation, pale red or pink; but **b.** also used for various shades of crimson or blood-red (cf. CARNATION^{2}); in mod. use sometimes = Blood-stained (from Shaks. *Macb.* II. ii. 62: see INCARNADINE *v.*).

1591 SYLVESTER *Du Bartas* I. v. 609 Her wings and train of feathers (mixed fine) Of orient Azure and incarnadine. **1649** LOVELACE *Poems, To my Lady H.* (1864) 124 Whose white satin upper coat of skin, Cut upon velvet rich incarnadin, Has yet a body (and of flesh) within. **1658** PHILLIPS, *Incarnadin colour*, a flesh colour, or the colour of a Damask Rose. *c* **1872** in A. E. Lee *Hist. Columbus, Ohio* (1892) I. 710 The color ranged from a deep crimson to a light or pale incarnadine. **b. 1820** BYRON *Mar. Fal.* III. ii. 509 You'll.. calmly wash those hands incarnadine. *a* **1845** BARHAM *Ingol. Leg.*, *Jerry Jarvis's Wig*, His very fore head was incarnadine. **1888** WATTS-DUNTON in *Athenæum* 18 Aug. 225/1 And Night's black wings are glowing incarnadine From Dover cliffs to Gravelines tower With sparks—with fiery flakes, a ruddy shower On breeze and brine!

B. *sb.* Flesh-colour, blush colour; also, a crimson or blood-red colour (see A).

1622 PEACHAM *Compl. Gent.* (1661) 155 Incarnadine, or flesh colour. **1735** SEWEL *Dutch Dict.* (ed. 3), *Hoog rood*, Carnation-colour, incarnadine. **1820** BYRON *Mar. Fal.* IV. ii. 147 No Barbaric blood can reconcile us now Unto that horrible incarnadine. **1865** TRENCH *Gust. Adolphus* i. 49 To take the rich incarnadine of blood.

in'carnadine, *v. arch.* Also erron. **incarnardine.** [f. prec.] *trans.* To dye or tinge with incarnadine (see prec.); to redden.

Properly, to make flesh-coloured or carnation; but from Shakspere onward associated with the colour of blood.

1605 SHAKS. *Macb.* II. ii. 62 This my Hand will rather The multitudinous Seas incarnardine, Making the Greene, one Red. *a* **1639** CAREW *Poems* Wks. (1824) 85 A fourth [shall] incarnadine Thy rosie cheeke. **1791** COWPER *Iliad* XI. 480 His blood the glebe Incarnadines. **1831** L. RITCHIE *Capt. Conspirator* in *Remembrance* 144 The yellow oil-flower, incarnardined with gorgeous poppies, fluttered in the waving wind. **1845** LONGF. *Evening Star*, The painted oriel of the West Whose panes.. the sunken sun incarnadines. **1866** CONINGTON *Æneid* VI. 176 War, dreadful war, and Tiber flood I see incarnadined with blood.

fig. **1879** FARRAR *St. Paul* ix. (1893) 98 Not the only blood of which the stains had incarnadined his conscience.

Hence **in'carnadined** *ppl. a.*

1821 *Tales of Landlord* New Ser. *Witch Glas Llyn* II. 170 The fierce reflection glowed on the incarnadined waters of the Clowdoc.

incarnalize, var. of ENCARNALIZE *v.*

incarnate (ɪn'kɑːnət), *a.* [ad. L. *incarnāt-us* made flesh (common in 4th c. in Christian writers), pa. pple. of *incarnāre*: see INCARN. In sense 3 corresp. to F. *incarnat, -ate*, It. *incarnato* incarnate, flesh-coloured.]

1. Clothed or invested with flesh; embodied in flesh; in a human (or animal) bodily form. **a.** Of a person, soul, or spirit. (Sometimes const. as *pa. pple.*, esp. when used of Christ.)

In phr. ***a devil incarnate***, applied hyperbolically to a person (cf. DEVIL *sb.* 4), the true meaning is often more or less lost sight of, and the adj. becomes nearly = 'out-and-out', 'arrant'.

1395 PURVEY *Remonstr.* (1851) 53 A sone of perdicioun, and a devil incarnat othir in flesh. *a* **1420** HOCCLEVE *De Reg. Princ.* 3333 Mercy Crist caused to ben incarnate. **1494** FABYAN *Chron.* III. liii. 34 In the season that he was Kynge our Sauyour Criste Ihesus was incarnat of that moste blessyd virgyne our Lady. **1534** MORE *On the Passion* Wks. 1315/1 By his goinge fro the father, was nothynge ment, but his beynge incarnate in the worlde. **1548–9** (Mar.) *Bk. Com. Prayer, Commun.* (Nicene Creed), And was incarnate by the holy Ghoste, of the Virgin Mary. **1597** HOOKER *Eccl. Pol.* v. li. §2 The nature of God.. in the onely person of the Sonne is incarnate. **1609** ROWLANDS *Knaue of Clubbes* 31 Incarnate deuils, such as do Assume a humane shape. **1612–15** BP. HALL *Contempl., N.T.* I. ii, That God should be incarnate of a virgin was an abasement of His maiestie, and an exaltation of the creature beyond all example. **1738** WESLEY *Ps.* II. ii, And slay th' incarnate Deity. **1820** SCOTT *Abbot* xvii, Whether there be a devil incarnate in you or no. **1831** CARLYLE *Sart. Res.* I. iv. (1872) 21 You look on him almost with a shudder, as on some incarnate Mephistopheles. **1896** GLADSTONE *Will* §2 Commending myself to the infinite mercies of God in the Incarnate Son as my only and sufficient hope.

b. Of a quality or other abstraction: Embodied in human form; impersonated.

(In quot. *a* 1652 in extended sense: Put into a form adapted to human nature or comprehension; expressed 'after the manner of men'.)

c **1532** DU WES *Introd. Fr.* in Palsgr. 1056 We juge her a thought or understandynge incarnate. *a* **1652** J. SMITH *Sel. Disc.* vi. 183 Divine truth becomes many times in Scripture incarnate, debasing itself to assume our rude conceptions. **1839** CARLYLE *Chartism* v. (1858) 27 The quack is a Falsehood Incarnate. **1874** GREEN *Short Hist.* ii. §2. 64 Liberty and independence itself seemed incarnate in his [the Confessor's] name. **1880** OUIDA *Moths* III. 269 In his eyes Vere was purity incarnate.

c. Vaguely used: Enshrined.

a **1533** LD. BERNERS *Gold. Bk. M. Aurel.* (1546) Nn iij, The hertes incarnate in loue are lyttel satisfied with syluer. **1871** TYLOR *Prim. Cult.* II. 98 To remain incarnate in the memory of friends is something.

¶ Erron. used, as if f. IN-^{3} (= not).

1748 RICHARDSON *Clarissa* (1811) V. 46 (D.), I fear nothing.. that devil carnate or incarnate can fairly do against a virtue so established.

†**2.** Consisting of flesh; fleshy. *Obs. rare.*

1597 A. M. tr. *Guillemeau's Fr. Chirurg.* 13 b/1 All incarnate or fleshye partes of the bodye.

3. Flesh-coloured; light pink or crimson. *Obs.* exc. in *Bot.* as a rendering of L. *incarnātus*.

a **1533** LD. BERNERS *Gold Bk. M. Aurel.* (1546) Nn iv b, Well colowred face, incarnate tethe, ruddye lyppes. **1552** in Strype *Eccl. Mem.* (1721) II. xiv. 359, 4 Yards of Turkey silk incarnate. **1567** MARY STUART *Let.* in *Lamartine's M. Stuart* App. (1859) 174 Send to me half elle of incarnat Satin. **1578** LYTE *Dodoens* I. xiii. 21 Butter burre.. putteth forth a hollow stalke of a span long, set full of small incarnate floures at the toppe. **1656** BLOUNT *Glossogr.* s.v. *Incarnation*, An Incarnate colour is a Carnation colour, a flesh color, or of the colour of our Damask Rose. **1791** W. BARTRAM *Carolina* 104 The flowers.. are of a pale incarnate colour. **1859** DARWIN

Orig. Spec. iv. (1861) 99 The common red and incarnate clovers (*Trifolium pratense* and *incarnatum*).

Hence **in'carnately** *adv.*, in a bodily form.

1856 MRS. BROWNING *Aur. Leigh* VI. 46 Freedom's self.. Fixed in a feudal form incarnately To suit our ways of thought and reverence.

incarnate (ɪn'kɑːneɪt), *v.* Also 6 en-. [f. prec., or f. ppl. stem of L. *incarnāre*: see INCARN.]

1. *trans.* To render incarnate; to embody in flesh. In *pass.* to be embodied; to assume, or exist in, a bodily (esp. a human) form.

1533 TINDALE *Supper of Lord* Wks. (Parker Soc.) III. 245 They believed in Christ to be incarnated, and to suffer death. *a* **1556** CRANMER *Wks.* (Parker Soc.) I. 74 We say, that they [fathers and prophets of the old testament] did eat his body and drink his blood, although he was not yet born nor incarnated. **1598** BARCKLEY *Felic. Man* III. (1603) 227 That old Serpent..can by God's sufferance..incarnate himselfe, or possesse infants. *Ibid.* IV. 317 An English man italianated is a devil incarnated. **1624** DONNE *Serm.* ii. 16, I must not ask why God took this way to incarnate his Son. **1715** DE FOE *Fam. Instruct.* I. i. (1841) I. 20 He incarnated, by a miraculous birth, the divine nature into the human. **1844** MARG. FULLER *Wom. 19th C.* (1862) 18 The All-Sustaining incarnated himself to guard..the destinies of this world.

2. *transf.* and *fig.* **a.** To put into, express or exhibit in, a concrete or definite form; to realize, actualize, embody (an idea or other abstraction).

1591 HARINGTON *Orl. Fur.* I. lviii, There shall no foolish plaints, nor fained ire Hinder me to encarnat my desire. **1856** KINGSLEY *Misc., Froude's Hist. Eng.* II. 74 Forces which we can no more stop, by shrieks at their absurdity, from incarnating themselves in actual blood, and misery, and horror than [etc.]. **1878** DOWDEN *Stud. Lit.* 9 A political doctrine..expecting to be incarnated in institutions. **1885** CLODD *Myths & Dr.* I. vii. 122 The ennobling qualities incarnated in some hero..meet with admiring response.

b. To exhibit (in oneself) in bodily or human form; to be the living embodiment or type of; to impersonate, embody (a quality, etc.).

1806 R. CUMBERLAND *Mem.* (T.), If quick conception, true discrimination, and the happy faculty of incarnating the idea of his poet, are properties essential in the..composition of a great..actor. **1849** *Fraser's Mag.* XXXIX. 395 The truest artist..must be he who incarnates best the age's artistic tendencies. **1886** SYMONDS *Renaiss. It., Cath. React.* (1898) VII. x. 85 This friar incarnated the Venetian spirit.

†**c.** To cause to exist, or represent as existing, in a particular mode of being, or as a part of something else. †**d.** To entertain as an indwelling presence; to enshrine. *Obs.*

1643 MILTON *Divorce* II. iii, Nay this is..to incarnat sin into the unpunishing and well pleas'd will of God. *a* **1711** KEN *Hymns Festiv.* Poet. Wks. 1721 I. 213 O may I thee incarnate in my Heart.

†**3.** To cause flesh to grow upon or in (a wound or sore); to heal over: = INCARN I. *Obs.*

1543 TRAHERON *Vigo's Chirurg.* II. ii. 16 After mundification ye must incarnate the place, after thys forme. **1577** FRAMPTON *Joyfull Newes* II. (1596) 38 The Tabaco.. doth make them [wounds] cleane, and incarnate them. **1616** SURFL. & MARKH. *Country Farme* 223 The other Ointment is better to incarnate and consolidate all sorts of wounds. **1725** BRADLEY *Fam. Dict.* s.v. *Lucatellus Balsam*, It is used externally to deterge and incarnate green Wounds and Ulcers.

†**b.** *absol.* = INCARN I b. *Obs.*

1563 T. GALE *Antidot.* II. 13 Thys Unguent..incarnateth verye well. **1686** W. HARRIS tr. *Lemery's Course Chym.* (ed. 3) 628 Its Tincture..is discutient, detersive, good against Gangrenes, and to incarnate.

†**c.** *intr.* for *refl.* = INCARN I c. *Obs.*

1674-7 J. MOLINS *Anat. Obs.* (1896) 17 As the adjacent parts mundified, soe it incarnated. **1759** STERNE *Tr. Shandy* II. v, My uncle Toby's wound was near well..the surgeon ..told him, 'twas just beginning to incarnate.

†**4.** To make fleshly or carnal; to degrade from spiritual nature, despiritualize. *Obs.*

1667 MILTON *P.L.* IX. 166 That I..am now constrained Into a Beast, and mixt with bestial slime, This essence to incarnate and imbrute. *a* **1683** WHICHCOTE *Aphorisms*, Bad men [study] to incarnate their souls.

†**5.** To enclose or insert in the flesh. *Obs. rare.*

1662 J. CHANDLER *Van Helmont's Oriat.* 282 They cut off part of the garment, that they may incarnate a thread or rag thereof, within the skin of the forehead of every one that is bitten by a mad dog.

6. To convert (vegetable matter) into flesh.

1882 PLAYFAIR in *Macm. Mag.* XLV. 335 As is said in the west, it is cheaper to 'incarnate' Indian corn [i.e. by feeding cattle with it] than to send that bulky grain by railways.

Hence **in'carnated** *ppl. a.*; **in'carnating** *vbl. sb.* and *ppl. a.* (in various senses of the verb).

1549-62 STERNHOLD & H. *Ps., Quicunque vult*, Of the incarnating of Christ, our Lord, believe aright. **1576** BAKER *Jewell of Health* 148 a, In every incarnating and closing togyther and healing. **1597** A. M. tr. *Guillemeau's Fr. Chirurg.* 12/1 That newe incarnated fleshe, which, after the trepaninge, groweth therin. *Ibid.* 49 b/1 Any incarnatinge medicamentes. **1671** FLAVEL *Fount. Life* v. 14 He hath laid the foundation thereof so deep, in the Incarnating of his own Son. **1872** OUIDA *Genl. Matchmaking* (Tauchn.) 72 Little Fay was delightful—for all the world like a bit of incarnated sunshine. **1878** BAYNE *Purit. Rev.* vi. 224 The love of romantic young men for their incarnated ideals.

incarnation (ɪnkɑː'neɪʃən). [a. F. *incarnation*, in 12th c. Norman F. *incarnaciun* (Phil. de Thaun), ad. late L. *incarnātiōn-em* (in Hilary, Jerome, Ambrose, etc.), n. of action from *incarnāre*: see INCARN.]

1. The action of incarnating or fact of being incarnated or 'made flesh'; a becoming incarnate; investiture or embodiment in flesh; assumption of, or existence in, a bodily (esp. human) form.

a. *spec.* of Christ, or of God in Christ. Often *absol.* ***the Incarnation.*** (The earliest and still the prevalent sense. In early use often in reference to the Christian era: the date of the incarnation or birth of Christ.)

1297 R. GLOUC. (Rolls) 197 þe vifþe [age] was fram dauid to þe transmigracion Of babiloyne and þe sixþe to þe incarnacion, þat was vorte god was ibore. **1382** WYCLIF *Isa.* Gen. Prol., The principal entent of the profetis is to declare the mysterie of Cristis incarnacioun, passioun, resurreccioun, ascensioun, and the comyng to the general doom. ? *a* **1400** *Arthur* 626 þe yheer after þe Incarnacione, Vyf hundred fourty & two. *c* **1400** MAUNDEV. (Roxb.) xxxii. 146 þai trowe wele þe incarnacioun of Criste. **1477** EARL RIVERS (Caxton) *Dictes* 123 He was borne after the Incarnacion of oure lord ij. c. yeres. **1526** *Pilgr. Perf.* (W. de W. 1531) 179 b, The preemynence of his moost gracyous incarnacyon. **1597** HOOKER *Eccl. Pol.* v. li. §3 Taking..our flesh, and by his incarnation making it his owne flesh. **1653** WALTON *Angler* i. 13 Angling is much more ancient then the incarnation of our Saviour. **1726** tr. *Gregory's Astron.* I. 251 We are to take notice, that Dionysius, called Exiguus, was the Author of this Æra five hundred Years after Christ, from which time they began to reckon from the Nativity or Incarnation of Christ. **1860** PUSEY *Min. Proph.* 128 It is said, *The Word was made flesh*, whence we speak of the *Incarnation* of our Blessed Lord, i.e. 'His taking on Him our Flesh'.

b. In general sense.

1646 SIR T. BROWNE *Pseud. Ep.* VI. i. 274 The woman being formed out of the rib, was once removed from earth, and framed from that element under incarnation. **1684** T. BURNET *Th. Earth* I. 301 The incarnation, as I may so say, of a spiritual substance, is to me a kind of standing miracle. **1841** EMERSON *Meth. Nat.* Wks. (Bohn) II. 227 The thoughts he delights to utter are the reason of his incarnation. **1858** SEARS *Athan.* III. iii. 272 The reader will here distinguish carefully between two things—between the *resurrection* and the *re-incarnation* of the dead.

c. *fig.* The putting into, or assumption of, a concrete or definite form; 'embodiment'. ? *Obs.*

1615 CROOKE *Body of Man* 274 Before the birth or incarnation as we may say of Philosophy. **1648** HERRICK *Hesper., Julia's Picture*, How am I ravish'd, when I do but see The painter's art in thy sciography? If so, how much more shall I dote thereon, When once he gives it incarnation.

2. *concr.* **a.** A body, person, or form in which a soul, spirit, or deity is incarnated; an incarnate or embodied form (*of*).

1742 YOUNG *Nt. Th.* IX. 1341 When shall my soul her incarnation quit, And..Obtain her Apotheosis in Thee? **1836** EMERSON *Nature, Spirit* Wks. (Bohn) II. 167 The world..is a remoter and inferior incarnation of God. **1841** ELPHINSTONE *Hist. Ind.* I. iv. 167 Vishnu and Siva..and their incarnations now attract almost all the religious veneration of the Hindús. **1843** *Penny Cycl.* XXVI. 387/1 The other Avatâras, descents or incarnations of Vishn'u. *Ibid.*, His first incarnation was that of a fish. **1899** SAYCE *Early Israel* v. 181 The line of the Pharaohs, the incarnations of the Sun-God.

b. A person in whom some quality, attribute, principle, etc. is exhibited in a bodily form; a living type or representative, embodiment, impersonation (*of* a quality, etc.).

1833 L. RITCHIE *Wand. by Loire* 126 Blue-Beard, that incarnation of juvenile romance. **1847** LEWES *Hist. Philos.* (1867) II. 551 Great men are the incarnations of the spirit of the age. **1865** DICKENS *Mut. Fr.* III. iv, You incarnation of sauciness. **1874** STUBBS *Const. Hist.* I. x. 302 William Rufus ..a foul incarnation of selfishness in its most abhorrent form.

c. Loosely or by extension: A thing in which some quality, etc. is typically represented or exhibited; an embodiment (*of*).

1821 SHELLEY *Adonais* xiii, Splendours, and Glooms, and glimmering Incarnations Of hopes and fears, and twilight Phantasies. **1866** G. MACDONALD *Ann. Q. Neighb.* xiii. (1878) 244 The grounds about the Hall seemed the incarnation of a summer which had taken years to ripen to perfection.

†**3.** Conception (in the womb). *Obs. rare.*

1548-67 THOMAS *Ital. Dict.*, *Incarnacione*, the incarnation or engenderyng tyme. **1683** TRYON *Way to Health* 3 That quality that doth predominate in the Spirit at the incarnation and Birth, that very same property doth carry the upper Dominion in the Body.

4. The formation or growth of new flesh upon or in a wound or sore; healing up; granulation. Also *concr.*, a growth of new flesh.

1544 PHAER *Regim. Lyfe* (1560) Pij, Procede with mundification and incarnation, even as in other kindes of apostumes. **1699** *Phil. Trans.* XXI. 403 The external containing parts of the Neck began now to unite by Incarnation. **1783** POTT *Chirurg. Wks.* II. These were soon covered with an incarnation. **1822-34** *Good's Study Med.* (ed. 4) II. 18 From this period the process of incarnation commences.

5. Flesh-colour, carnation; a pigment or dye of this colour. *Obs.* or *arch.*

c **1485** *E.E. Misc.* (Warton Club) 73 For an incarnacion, take sable and saffrone and rede lede, and medylle heme welle togedyre. **1573** *Art of Limning* 8 b, If you wil make incarnations for Visages, or a fleshly colour for Images. **1821** BYRON *Cain* III. i, His little cheeks, In their pure incarnation.

b. *attrib.* or as *adj.* Flesh-coloured, light pink: = INCARNATE *a.* 3. *Obs.* or *arch.*

1562 TURNER *Herbal* II. 116 b, Damaske roses, incarnation roses, muske roses. **1652** URQUHART *Jewel* Wks. (1834) 242 A pair of incarnation velvet slippers. **1672** *Phil. Trans.* VII. 5172 The Dying of Wool of an Incarnation colour, with a kind of Moss growing in Malta.

†**6.** The plant CARNATION. *Obs.*

1538 TURNER *Libellus* A iij a, Herba quam uernacula lingua uocamus a Gelofer, aut a Clowgelofer, aut an Incarnacyon.

Hence **incar'nationist**, a believer in an incarnation; also *attrib.* or as *adj.* So also **incar'nationalist**.

1834 MEDWIN *Angler in Wales* I. 223 The new Incarnationists of Johanna Southcote. **1903** *Q. Rev.* Apr. 519 Wherever the Incarnationist idea originated, it did not originate in Hellenism. **1939** A. TOYNBEE *Study of Hist.* IV. 625 The Christology which Dr. Conybeare calls 'Incarnationist' ought properly to be called 'Conceptionist'. **1962** *Listener* 11 Jan. 68/2 This 'incarnationalist' type of doctrine—to be culled from almost every page of so very orthodox a teacher as our own Henry Scott Holland, for example—urges that the divine for us must mean the vision of a new humanity.

incarnational (ɪnkɑː'neɪʃənəl), *a.* [f. INCARNATION + -AL.] Of or relating to the theological doctrine of incarnation.

1912 F. VON HÜGEL *Eternal Life* viii. 166 Even the most general incarnational doctrine..must, then, be Superstition or Fanaticism for him. **1942** D. JENKINS *Nature of Catholicity* i. 12 This..widely influential tendency, with its affinities with historical Romanticism and the so-called 'Incarnational' theology, is a development of the Anglican doctrine of catholicity in the direction of Liberalism. **1954** D. L. SAYERS *Introd. Papers on Dante* 122 This Way, though it is perhaps more typically Western and might appear to be more typically Catholic and Incarnational than the other, has, I believe, never been fully mapped by any mystical theologian—unless we count Dante. **1971** *Daily Tel.* 29 July 6/3 His Christian faith is essentially this-worldly, 'incarnational', to use one of his favourite words.

incarnative (ɪn'kɑːnətɪv), *a.* and *sb.* [a. obs. F. *incarnatif*, *-ive* (early 16th c.), 'flesh-bringing, flesh-breeding' (Cotgr.), ad. med.L. *incarnātīvus*, It. *incarnativo* (Florio), f. as INCARNATE *v.* + -IVE.]

A. *adj.*

1. Having the quality of incarning; promoting the growth of flesh in a wound or sore.

c **1400** *Lanfranc's Cirurg.* 153 Medicyns comfortatiuis & incarnatiuis [*MS. B.* Incarnatyfes]. *Ibid.* 342 Regeneratiue, & incarnatiue [medicines], & facientes carnem nasci, ben oon to seie. **1541** R. COPLAND *Guydon's Quest. Chirurg.* Lj b, There ben thre maners. One is incarnatyue and it competeth to newe woundes, and fractures. **1563** T. GALE *Antidot.* I. ix. 6 Medicines incarnatiue, which doe also ingender fleshe. **1614** T. ADAMS *Devil's Banquet* 329 Your exulcerated sores cannot bee healed with incarnative salues. **1694** SALMON *Bate's Disp.* I. (1713) 312/2 Mercury is the Balsam of Nature, in which is an incarnative and regenerative Vertue.

†**2.** Humorously or blunderingly used for *incarnate* (here = 'arrant': see INCARNATE *a.* 1, note).

1594 GREENE & LODGE *Looking Glasse* I. Wks. (Rtldg.) 119/2 Paltry!..why, you incarnative knave, what are you that you speak petty treason?

B. *sb.* An incarnative medicine or application: see A. 1.

1568 SKEYNE *The Pest* (1860) 43 Curatiuis and incarnatiues succedis. **1643** I. STEER tr. *Exp. Chyrurg.* viii. 36 To Vlcers already mundified, it is best to use Incarnatives. **1720** BECKET in *Phil. Trans.* XXXI. 53 He scraped it with an Instrument for several Days, and drest it with Incarnatives, designing to have ingendred Flesh on it.

†**in'carned**, *ppl. a. Obs.* [f. INCARN *v.*] = INCARNATE.

1563 *Mirr. Mag.*, *Rivers* lvi, The duke of Glocestre that incarned devyll. **1871** T. H. NOYES *Hymns Mod. Man, Relig. Love* xiii, Prating That Godhead incarned ever trod The bye-paths of our pitiful Planet.

incarnifi'cation. *rare*$^{-0}$. = INCARNATION I.

1864 in WEBSTER.

†**in'carry**, *v. Obs.* [f. IN-^{1} + CARRY *v.*] *trans.* To carry or convey in; to mingle, mix.

1486 *Bk. St. Albans, Her.* D v a, Theys armis ar calde watteri: for ij. colowris ar incariet oon in to an other by the maner of water trobulde wᵗ wynde. **1646-7** in Swayne *Sarum Churchw. Acc.* (1896) 324 Carying and incarying the Organ Pipes 1s.

†**in'carve**, *v. Obs. rare.* Also en-. [f. IN-^{2} = EN-^{1} 3 + CARVE *v.*] *trans.* To carve in or upon something; to engrave.

1596 FITZ-GEFFRAY *Sir F. Drake* (1881) 22 Encarving characters of memorie. **1605** DANIEL *Queen's Arcadia* v. ii, He had incarv'd a woful Elegy. **1615** —— *Hymen's Tri.* Wks. (1717) 131, I found incarv'd, and fair incarv'd, these Words: Thy Sylvia, Thirsis, lives; and is return'd.

incase, -ment, var. of ENCASE, -MENT.

†**in'cask**, *v. Obs.* [f. IN-^{1} or ^{2} + CASK *sb.*] *trans.* **a.** To put into, or as into, a cask. **b.** To cover with, or as with, a casque or helmet.

1611 COTGR., *Enfusté*, inpiped, or incasked. **1612** SHELTON *Quix.* I. III. xiii. 256 Then did hee incaske his pate in his hat, which was so broad, as it might serue him excellently for a Quitasoll.

incast ('ɪnkɑːst, -æ-), *sb. local.* [f. vbl. phrase *cast in.*] Something 'thrown in'; a quantity of some commodity given in addition to the exact measure.

1798 R. DOUGLAS *Agric. Surv. Roxb. & Selkirk* 357 It is still usual in several places to give a pound of *incast*, as it is here called, to every stone of wool, and a fleece to every pack sold. **1863** MORTON *Cycl. Agric.* (E.D.S.), *Incast* (Roxb. & Selkirksh.), a pound in a stone of wool, and a fleece in a pack, usually given above measure.

†**in'cast,** *v. Obs.* [f. IN-^{1} + CAST *v.*] *trans.* To cast or throw in; *fig.* to suggest. Hence †'**incasting** *vbl. sb.*, throwing in; suggestion.

1398 TREVISA *Barth. De P.R.* v. xxiv. (1495) 132 Somtyme hoorsnes of the throte fallith by incastynge of powdre. *c* **1440** HYLTON *Scala Perf.* (W. de W. 1494) I. xxi, Yf they fele ony stiryng wythin by thyncastyng of thenmye, or elles fro wythout of ony of the deuylles prophets whiche men callen sothsayers. **1469** *Sc. Acts Jas. III* (1597) §34 The said poynding for mailles and annualles, in-casting and out-casting of tennentes, be deferred. **1616** J. LANE *Cont. Sqr.'s T.* IX. 63 Th' assailantes entries, evrie wheare to hinder, incastinge stooles, ropes, froes, chaines, manors, beddes, and all trassh whatsoever.

†**in'castellate, en-,** *v. Obs.* [f. ppl. stem of med.L. *incastellāre*, It. *incastellare* to INCASTLE: see IN-^{2}, and -ATE^3.] *trans.* To make into a castle; to fortify; to enclose (a well or cistern) with masonry: see CASTELLATED.

1538 LELAND *Itin.* I. 73 Began first to encastellate it. **1598** STOW *Surv.* viii. (1603) 46 And also incastelated the same round about. *Ibid.* xxxiii. 295 Incastellated the same in sufficient cesterns. **1601** F. GODWIN *Bps. of Eng.* 522 The Auncient mannor place at Arkland he did encastellate.

†**in'castellated,** *ppl. a. Obs.* [ad. It. *incastellato* 'hoof-bound, that is when a horses hoofe is dride vp, so that it sounds hollow' (Florio), F. *encastelé* (1606), according to Hatz.-Darm., related to It. *incastare*, *incastrare* to enchase, mortice, insert firmly.] Hoof-bound (as a horse).

1611 COTGR., *Encastellé*, incastellated, or narrow-heeled (as a horse). *Ibid.*, *Encastelure*, a being incastellated, or growing narrow heeled; a vicious, or painfull narrownesse in a horses heele. **1656** BLOUNT *Glossogr.*, *Incastellated* (Fr. *Encastellé*), narrow-heeled (as a horse). **1658** in PHILLIPS. **1676–1724** in COLES.

†**in'castle,** *v. Obs.* In 6–7 encastle, 6–8 incastell. [ad. med.L. *incastellāre* = It. *incastellare* (Florio), OF. *enchasteler* to furnish with a castle or castles, f. *in-* (IN-^{2}) + L. *castellum* CASTLE; cf. INCASTELLATE.] *trans.* To provide with castles; to fortify.

1586 J. HOOKER *Girald. Irel.* in *Holinshed* II. 47/2 Meth was alredie meetlie well and indifferentlie fortified and incastelled. **1611** FLORIO, *Incastellare*, to encastle, to fortifie with castles, to reduce or bring to a castle.

†**in'castled, in'castelled,** *ppl. a. Obs.* [ad. F. *encastelé*: see INCASTELLATED.] Hoof-bound.

1706 PHILLIPS, *Incastelled*, narrow Heel'd, or Hoof-bound, as *An incastelled Horse.*

'**incatch,** *sb. nonce-wd.* [f. vbl. phr. *catch in.*] A catching or sudden drawing in (of the breath).

1895 *Chamb. Jrnl.* XII. 782/1 There followed a fierce incatch of his breath, a hollowing of his lean cheeks.

incatenate (ɪn'kætɪneɪt), *v.* [f. It. and med.L. *incatenare* to enchain, f. *in-* (IN-^{2}) + L. *catēnāre* to bind with chains, *catēna* chain. Cf. F. *enchaîner.*] *trans.* To put in chains; to enchain, to fetter.

1839 *Blackw. Mag.* XLV. 689 He looks as embarrassed and incatenated, as a galley slave escaped from the *bagne* of Toulon.

incatenation (ɪnkætɪ'neɪʃən). [ad. med.L. *incatēnātiōn-em*, n. of action f. med.L. *incatēnāre*: see prec.] Putting in or fastening with chains; harnessing; a linking or being linked together.

1762 GOLDSM. *Cit. W.* cviii, Still..more triflingly sedulous in the incatenation of fleas, or the sculpture of a cherry-stone. **1885** *Q. Rev.* Oct. 362 The blank verse..had no variety, no incatenation, no harmony.

†**in'cathedrate,** *v. Obs.* [f. med.L. *incathedrāre*, f. *in-* (IN-^{2}) + *cathedra* chair, bishop's seat.] *trans.* To place in a chair; to chair; esp. to place in the *cathedra* or bishop's chair; to enthrone as a bishop.

1635 PAGITT *Christianogr.* 77 He was there incathedrated, and with great reverence received and esteemed. **1641** SIR E. DERING *Sp. Relig.* 21 June (1642) 72 You are in your selves but fellow-members of the same house with us.. untill by our Election, and by common suffrage you are Incathedrated.

†**in'causable,** *a. Obs. rare.* [IN-^{3}.] Not capable of being caused; having no cause.

1653 R. G. tr. *Bacon's Hist. Winds* 357 This is a most abstruse and hidden Motion..and in some things it seemes as it were to be incausable.

†**in'causative,** *a. Obs. rare.* [IN-^{3}.] Not causing.

1829 COLERIDGE *Lit. Rem.* (1836) IV. 3 Merely an antecedent, or an incausative alien antecedent in time.

†**in'cautelous,** *a. Obs.* [f. IN-^{3} + CAUTELOUS: cf. L. *incautēla* incaution.] Incautious, unwary, heedless.

1610 G. FLETCHER *Christ's Tri.* I. xix, The bold Physitian too incautelous, By those he cures himselfe is murdered. **1681** FLAVEL *Meth. Grace* xxviii. 485 The wiles and stratagems it makes use of to ensnare the incautelous soul. *a* **1734** NORTH *Exam.* II. iv. §110 (1740) 288 All Advantage of Cavil at the Expressions of the Judges, if any had been incautelous, was lost.

Hence †**in'cautelously** *adv.*; also †**in'cautelousness.**

1640 BP. REYNOLDS *Passions* xv. 144 This by incautelousnesse and Credulity. *a* **1656** HALES *Rem.*, *Serm. Rom.* xiv. 1 (R.) We grow sick many times by incautelously conversing with the diseas'd. **1693** BAMPFIELD *Repl. Dr. Wallis* 32 If it were not written incautelously.

†**in'cautely,** *adv. Obs.* [f. L. *incaut-us* incautious, *incaute* incautiously + -LY^2. Cf. the obs. F. equivalent *incautement.*] Incautiously, heedlessly.

1510 *Sheph. Kal.* vii. G v b, Ofte tymes Incautely Not takynge hede what they swere. **1657** W. MORICE *Coena quasi Κοινὴ* Def. xi. 126 It was incautely said so of him alone.

incaution (ɪn'kɔːʃən). [f. IN-^{3} + CAUTION, after L. *incautus*, etc.] Want of caution; carelessness, heedlessness, unwariness.

1715–20 POPE *Iliad* XXIII. 415 Lest thro' incaution failing, thou may'st be A joy to others, a reproach to me. **1800** *Med. Jrnl.* IV. 439 That disease..quickly spreads, from incaution, to the houses of their more opulent neighbours. **1884** HORNER *Florence* (ed. 2) I. xxi. 312 The accusation arose from the incaution of one of the monks.

incautious (ɪn'kɔːʃəs), *a.* [f. IN-^{3} + CAUTIOUS, after L. *incautus*, etc.] Not cautious; wanting in caution; careless, heedless, unwary, rash.

a **1703** POMFRET *Poet. Wks.* (1833) 27 Some swains, I own, impose upon the fair, And lead the' incautious maid into a snare. **1800** *Asiat. Ann. Reg.*, *Proc. E. Ind. Ho.* 101/2 If in an incautious moment that honourable director had written an imprudent letter. **1832** LEWIS *Use & Ab. Pol. Terms* Introd. 2 An incautious employment..of language. **1867** H. MACMILLAN *Bible Teach.* ii. (1870) 33 A single incautious step may be attended with the most fatal consequences.

incautiously (ɪn'kɔːʃəslɪ), *adv.* [f. prec. + -LY^2.] In an incautious manner; without caution; heedlessly, unwarily, rashly.

1733 ARBUTHNOT *On Air* (J.), A species of palsy invades such as incautiously expose themselves to the morning air. **1741** tr. *D'Argens' Chinese Lett.* vi. 32 The Sentence of Death pronounc'd ever so incautiously and bluntly. **1898** W. M. RAMSAY *Was Christ born in Bethlehem?* v. 115 He incautiously adopted a series of errors.

incautiousness (ɪn'kɔːʃəsnɪs). [f. as prec. + -NESS.] The quality of being incautious; heedlessness, rashness.

1796 JANE AUSTEN *Sense & Sens.* I. xv, Your eyes have been reproaching them every day for incautiousness. **1865** *Daily Tel.* 7 Nov. 6/5 The obloquy..is due in a great measure to the incautiousness of its votaries.

incavate ('ɪnkəveɪt), *v. rare*$^{-0}$. [f. ppl. stem of L. *incavāre*: see INCAVE, and cf. EXCAVATE.] *trans.* = INCAVE *v.*^{1}

1727 BAILEY vol. II, *Incavated*, made hollow. **1839** SMART, *Incavated*, made hollow; bent round or in. **1884** *Cassell's Encycl. Dict.*, *Incavate*, to make hollowed or concave.

incavate ('ɪnkəvət), *a. rare*$^{-0}$. [ad. L. *incavāt-us*, pa. pple. of *incavāre*: see prec.] Hollowed, bent inwards.

In recent Dicts.

incavation (ɪnkə'veɪʃən). [n. of action from L. *incavāre*: see INCAVATE.] **a.** The action of making hollow or bending inwards. **b.** A hollow or depression on a surface; a hollowed place.

1799 KIRWAN *Geol. Ess.* 79 The protuberance..in South America, corresponding with the incavation on the African side from the river of Congo to Cape Palmas. **1852** SEIDEL *Organ* 78 This lip is..not a separate part of the pipe, but merely an incavation on the foot.

†**in'cave,** *v.*^{1} *Obs.* [ad. L. *incavāre* to hollow, f. *in-* (IN-^{2}) + *cavāre* to hollow.] *trans.* To make hollow or concave; to bend inwards. Hence **in'caved** *ppl. a.*

a **1586** SIDNEY *Arcadia* II. (1622) 141 But bow all knees, now of her knees My tongue doth tell what fancie sees.. Whose bought incau'd doth yeeld such sight, Like cunning Painter shadowing white.

incave, encave (ɪn'keɪv, ɛn-), *v.*^{2} [f. IN-^{2}, EN-^{1} + CAVE *sb.* Cf. F. *encaver* (1295 in Godef. *Compl.*).] *trans.* To enclose or shut up in, or as in, a cave.

1604 SHAKS. *Oth.* IV. i. 82 Stand you a while apart..Do but encaue your selfe. **1615** G. SANDYS *Trav.* 307 (D.) The bristled Bore and Beare Incaued rage. **1729** SAVAGE *Wanderer* I. 158 There..Incav'd secure th' exulting eagle dwells. **1821** MOIR in *Blackw. Mag.* X. 301 The stayless element found its way to nether domes encaved. **1856** KANE *Arct. Expl.* II. xxvi. 264 The rocks seemed to close above our heads..a protecting cliff between us and the gale. We were completely encaved.

incavern, encavern (ɪn'kævən, ɛn-), *v.* [f. IN-^{2}, EN-^{1} + CAVERN *sb.*^{1}: cf. It. *incavernare* (Florio).] *trans.* To shut up in a cavern: = prec.

1611 FLORIO, *Incauernare*, to encaue, to encauerne, to endenne. **1612** DRAYTON *Poly-olb.* i. 6 Then Lid creeps on along, and taking Thrushel throws Herself amongst the rocks; and so incavern'd goes. **1836** F. MAHONEY *Rel. Father Prout*, *Literature & Jesuits* (1859) 178 Soothing the toils of the encaverned slave.

†**in'cavity.** *Obs. rare.* [f. IN-^{2} + CAVITY: cf. L. *incavāre* to INCAVE.] The quality of being bent inwards, hollowed formation, concavity.

1730 A. GORDON *Maffei's Amphith.* 135 Their Size, Sharpness, Incavity, and Form.

incawse, var. of ENCAUSE *v.*, *Obs.*

inceasible, erron. form of INCESSABLE *a.*

incede (ɪn'siːd), *v. rare.* [ad. L. *incēdĕre* to go on, f. *in-* (IN-^{2}) + *cēdĕre* to go, depart: cf. *recede*, *proceed.*] *intr.* To move on, advance; to move or march with measured or stately pace. Hence **in'ceding** *ppl. a.*; **in'cedingly** *adv.* (often with allusion to Virgil, *Æn.* I. 46).

1669 FLAMSTEED in Rigaud *Corr. Sci. Men* (1841) II. 79 The stars will appear to incede nearly under the same angle and spots of the moon. **1686** GOAD *Celest. Bodies* II. i. 142 In his Retrocession, when direct he incedes above it. **1822** *Blackw. Mag.* XI. 459 The majestic inceding step of the English Muse, as exemplified by Shakespeare and Milton. **1853** C. BRONTE *Villette* xxiii. (1863) 248 Even in the uttermost frenzy of energy is each mænad movement royally, imperially, incedingly upborne.

†**in'celebrated,** *a. Obs.* [f. IN-^{3} + CELEBRATED, after the L. equiv. *incelebrātus.*] Not celebrated; having no celebrity.

1538 LELAND *Itin.* II. 79 Ther was a Chapelle of Thomas Bekket on the Grene in Shirburn, it stondith but incelebratid.

So **ince'lebrity**, want of celebrity.

1803 COLERIDGE *Lit. Rem.* (1836) I. 256 A mournful proof of the incelebrity of this great and amazing work [Barclay's *Argenis*] among both the public and the people. **1812** EUSTACE *Class. Tour* (1821) IV. 342.

†**incend** (ɪn'sɛnd), *v. Obs.* (exc. as *nonce-wd.*) [ad. L. *incend-ĕre* to set on fire, kindle, f. *in-* (IN-^{2}) + **candĕre* to cause to glow, cf. *candēre* to glow, shine: cf. It. *incendere* to kindle, inflame.]

1. *trans.* To kindle, set alight, set on fire. In quot. 1872, to burn as incense (*nonce-use*).

1597 A. M. tr. *Guillemeau's Fr. Chirurg.* 32 b/1 A little peece or inche of a candle, which they incende and light. **1598** YONG *Diana* 149 Nor thou that I in flames am thus incended. **1624** QUARLES *Div. Poems*, *Sion's Sonn.* xx. 19 Thy breath..incends quick flames. **1705** C. PURSHALL *Mech. Macrocosm* 34 Steel incended by the stroak of a Flint. **1872** J. G. MURPHY *Comm. Lev.* iv. 12 It signifies merely to destroy by fire; whereas the other means to incend, or consume as incense.

2. To engender (bodily heat); to heat, inflame (the body or its organs).

1533 ELYOT *Cast. Helthe* III. iii. (1541) 54 a, Naturall heate, by withdrawinge of moysture, is to moche incended. **1574** NEWTON *Health Mag.* 5 Nothyng doth so muche incende and enflame naturall heate, as laboure and mooving. **1621** BURTON *Anat. Mel.* I. iii. III. i, They incend it [the brain] without measure.

3. To inflame, excite (the mind, passions, etc.); to incite to action.

1502 ATKYNSON tr. *De Imitatione* III. vi. 200 Loue knoweth no mesure; but it incendeth the louer oute of measure. **1531** ELYOT *Gov.* I. xxiii, The perfecte paterne of Industrie..to be understande of the reders. And..incende them to approche to the true practising therof. **1599** MARSTON *Sco. Villanie* II. vi. 201 Oh theres a line incends his lustfull blood. **1684** T. HOCKIN *Gods Decrees* 71 Spanish flies..given in a potion incend lust.

Hence **in'cending** *vbl. sb.* and *ppl. a.*

1533 ELYOT *Cast. Helthe* I. (1539) 11 b, Moche incendynge or adustion of bloude. **1772** NUGENT tr. *Hist. Friar Gerund* II. 328 The Persians offered to the sun.. incending pyres.

incendiarism (ɪn'sɛndɪərɪz(ə)m). [f. INCENDIARY + -ISM.] The practice of an incendiary. **a.** *lit.* The practice or act of maliciously setting fire to buildings or other property; the practice or commission of arson.

1837 LOCKHART *Scott* lxxix. an 1830, Every newspaper teemed with details of riot and incendiarism. **1850** KINGSLEY *Alt. Locke* xvii, With robbery, assassinations, vitriol-bottles, and midnight incendiarism. **1897** *Times* 23 Jan. 13/1 The Fulahs have proved themselves masters in incendiarism.

b. *fig.* The inflaming or exciting of passion, strife, or violence; inflammatory agitation.

1674–1710 BURNET *Serm. Royal Martyr* 5 Among the much-abused words of the late time were Incendiary and Incendiarism. **1836** MARRYAT *Midsh. Easy* (1863) 202 Already we have had a good deal of incendiarism about the country, and some..have advised sedition and conspiracy. **1860** L. HARCOURT *Diaries G. Rose* I. 156 Lord John Russell will do well to abstain from raking up the..embers of Whig incendiarism.

So **in'cendiarize** *v. trans.* (*nonce-wd.*), to infect with incendiarism; to inflame, 'set on fire'.

1859 *Blackw. Mag.* Mar. 291/2 Suspecting that we had picked up traitorous designs..and meant to incendiarise Constantinople with the same.

incendiary (ɪnˈsɛndɪərɪ), *a.* and *sb.* Also 7 en-. [ad. L. *incendiāri-us* causing conflagration, setting on fire, f. *incendi-um* burning, conflagration, f. *incendĕre* to INCEND: see -ARY.]

A. *adj.*

1. a. Consisting in, relating or petaining to, the malicious setting on fire of buildings or other property.

1611 SPEED *Hist. Gt. Brit.* IX. ix. §105. 626 An incendiary outrage at Norwich, where the Citizens set on fire the Priorie Church. *a* **1845** HOOD (*title*) An Incendiary Song. **1856** MISS MULOCK *J. Halifax* vii. (ed. 17) 76 The glare of some incendiary fire.

b. *Mil.* Adapted or used for setting on fire an enemy's buildings, ships, etc. Used esp. of a type of aerial bomb that ignites on impact.

1871 *Daily News* 14 Jan., Should they still be obstinate, a shower of incendiary shells of great size will be poured upon them. **1885** E. S. FARROW *Mil. Encycl.* I. 666/1 (*heading*) Incendiary fire-works.—The incendiary preparations are.. incendiary-match, and hot-shot. *Ibid.* 666/2 Incendiary-match is made by boiling slow-match in a saturated solution of niter, drying it, cutting it into pieces, and plunging it into melted fire-stone. It is principally used in loaded shells. **1892** E. BAKER *Prelim. Tactics* ii. 31 The ammunition carried per gun..is: ring shell, 84;..case, 8; incendiary shell, 6. **1911** *Aero* May 37/1 The following are reckoned..to be the principal offensive uses of the war-aeroplane: (1.) Attacking supply stores and setting them on fire with incendiary bombs. **1915** *Lancet* 12 June 1249/2 The incendiary bomb may cause a serious outbreak of fire. **1917** H. WOODHOUSE *Textbk. Naval Aeronaut.* (1918) xix. 120/2 The Zeppelins also dropped incendiary bombs intended to set places on fire. **1918** E. S. FARROW *Dict. Mil. Terms* 307 *Incendiary grenade*, a form of grenade designed to scatter molten metal upon bursting. **1935** *Jrnl. R. Aeronaut. Soc.* XXXIX. 164 Reference is made to incendiary bombs with magnesium alloy case and thermit filling. **1940** *Illustr. London News* 5 Oct. 435/2 The oil bomb, which may be of various sizes, is filled in some cases with petrol, thus becoming a tremendously powerful incendiary bomb. **1941** *Ann. Reg. 1940* 69 Though large numbers of incendiary bombs were dropped the damage done by fire was kept within fairly narrow limits.

2. *fig.* Having the character of inflaming or exciting the passions, esp. in regard to political matters; tending to stir up strife, violence, or sedition; inflammatory.

1614 T. ADAMS *Devil's Banquet* 22 Zeale is 1 hote; no incendiary, no praeter-naturall, but a super-naturall heate. **1777** BURKE *Corr.* (1844) II. 145 All incendiary acts and incendiary practices. **1847** EMERSON *Repr. Men, Montaigne* Wks. (Bohn) I. 336 Ideas are disturbing, incendiary, follies of young men, repudiated by the solid portion of society. **1853** BRIMLEY *Ess., My Novel* 263 To counteract the effect of incendiary publications.

B. *sb.*

1. a. A person who maliciously sets fire to a building or other property; one who wilfully or criminally causes a conflagration; one who commits arson.

1606 HOLLAND *Sueton.* 238 Others called him with open mouth Incendiarie [*marg.* Or firebrand because he burnt the Capitoll]. **1672** R. WILD *Poet. Licent.* 26 We would make Bonfires (sir) but that we fear Name of Incendiaries we may hear. **1769** BLACKSTONE *Comm.* IV. xvi. 220 Fire too frequently involves in the common calamity persons unknown to the incendiary, and not intended to be hurt by him. **1834** LYTTON *Pompeii* III. i, These are the incendiaries that burnt Rome under Nero.

†**b.** *gen.* A person or thing that kindles or sets on fire. *Obs.*

1654 H. L'ESTRANGE *Chas. I* (1655) 17 Instructions were issued out for the firing of them, and Sir Samuel Argall was appointed to be the incendiary. **1684** T. BURNET *Th. Earth* II. 47 The sun, and the central fire. These two great incendiaries, they say, will be let loose upon us at the conflagration.

c. Short for *incendiary bomb.*

1940 *Flight* 19 Dec. 522/2 The pilot found his objective at once and his incendiaries started four large fires. **1942** *R.A.F. Jrnl.* 13 June 24 You may have tried to put out an incendiary bomb by heaping..sand on it... No amount of sand will smother an incendiary. **1958** *Times Lit. Suppl.* 28 Mar. 176/1 In 1941 Lambeth Palace Library was heavily bombed. Incendiaries fell in the middle of the seventeenth-century Great Hall which was its centre.

2. *fig.* **a.** A person who inflames or excites the passions of men, esp. in regard to political matters; one who stirs up civil strife or violence; a mover of dissension or sedition: an inflammatory agitator, a 'firebrand'.

1631 GOUGE *God's Arrows* III. §93. 356 Campion, and other Seminaries and Incendiaries were sent by the Pope. **1672** MARVELL *Reh. Transp.* I. 163 He is an hot-headed Incendiary. **1704** J. BLAIR in W. S. Perry *Hist. Coll. Amer. Col. Ch.* I. 101 Playing the Incendiary by endeavouring to make differences among friends. **1775** ADAIR *Amer. Ind.* 462 Transforming them..into dangerous political incendiaries. *a* **1797** H. WALPOLE *Mem. Geo. III* (1845) III. i. 8 The Jesuits had been the incendiaries of the late insurrection. **1844** H. H. WILSON *Brit. Ind.* I. ii. I. 139 Native officers.. had been active in aggravating the irritation caused... The dismissal of the incendiaries..restored tranquillity.

†**b.** A thing that inflames or excites passion, strife, etc.; an incentive to evil. *Obs.*

1628 BURTON *Anat. Mel.* III. iii. I. ii. (ed. 3) 548 Causes or incendiaries of this rage. **1630** WADSWORTH *Pilgr.* vi. 58 Their intemperate drinking..was the incendiary of some quarrels. **1726** SHELVOCKE *Voy. round World* 286 We took a booty..which might have been made valuable, if discretion and prudence might have had the management of it; for want of which it proved a troublesome incendiary.

Hence **in'cendiaryship** (*nonce-wd.*), the office or personality of an incendiary.

1640-1 LD. DIGBY *Parl. Sp.* 9 Feb. 13 Was there a man peaceably affected, studious of the Quiet and Tranquillity of his Countrey? Their Incendiariships hath plagued him.

†**in'cendiate,** *v. Obs. rare.* [f. L. *incendi-um* conflagration, burning + -ATE[3] 7: cf. mod.F. *incendier.*] *trans.* To set fire to, burn, make a fire of. (*Affected.*) So **in'cendiated** *ppl. a.*, set on fire (*rare*⁻¹); †**incendi'ation,** conflagration; †**in'cendiator,** one who kindles or excites.

1653 *Several Proc. Parl.* 9–16 Aug. No. 4. 42 (Stanf.) The chief Incendiators of the most of the Troubles and Wars in Europe. **1700** RYCAUT *Hist. Turks* III. 302, I believe that this Incendiation did proceed from an Irruption of Subterranean Fires. *a* **1701** SEDLEY *Grumbler* I. i, He has lacerated, incendiated all his books. **1922** JOYCE *Ulysses* 702 The carbonised remains of an incendiated edifice.

incendijel (ɪnˈsɛndɪdʒɛl). orig. *U.S.* Also (*corruptly*) **incenderjel, incinderjell.** [f. INCENDI(ARY *a.* + JEL(LY *sb.*] An inflammable jelly used in incendiary weapons, composed of polystyrene, petrol, and benzene.

1966 *Air Force/Space Digest* (U.S.) Mar. 45/2 Nearly 700 day and night sorties were flown by B-57, A-1E, F-100, and F-8 aircraft, which dropped more than 450,000 pounds of incendijel. **1966** *New Statesman* 8 Apr. 496/1 The new jelly—or what US pilots refer to as 'incendijel'—is replacing the old soap-jelled gasoline napalm as used in Korea. **1967** (*title*) Modification kit for the MXY 377/E 32 incendijel mixing and transfer unit (U.S. Air Force Armament Lab.) (AD 830 504). **1967** *N.Y. Rev. Bks.* 20 Apr. 5/1 The Americans do not dissemble what they are up to. They do not seem to feel the need, except through verbiage: e.g., napalm has become 'Incinder-jell'. **1968** *Listener* 22 Feb. 244/2 The issues and living horror of the war disappear in a deadened, bureaucratic language—'incinderjell', 'the other side', 'body counts'. **1968** V. W. SIDEL in S. Rose *Chem. & Biol. Warfare* iii. 44 The name napalm has been retained as a generic one for weapons of this type. Recently the term has also been applied to a gel consisting of petrol, benzene, and polystyrene which is also called 'incenderjell' or Napalm-B.

†**in'cendious,** *a. Obs.* [ad. L. *incendiōs-us*, f. *incendium*: see -OUS.] = INCENDIARY *a.* Hence †**incendiously** *adv.* (Webster, 1856).

1823 J. D. HUNTER *Captivity N. Amer.* 5 The massacre of my parents and connections,..and the incendious destruction of their dwellings.

‖**in'cendium.** *Obs.* Also in anglicized form **incendy.** [L. *incendium* burning fire, conflagration, burning, f. *incendĕre*: see INCEND. Cf. in same sense It. *incendio.*] A conflagration; a volcanic eruption.

1637 NABBES *Hanniball & Scipio* III. iii, To prevent an incendium it is best To quench a brand before it fire the rest. **1667** *Obs. Burn. Lond.* in *Select. Harl. Misc.* (1793) 445 An incendy, a conflagration, a ruin and devastation by fire. **1669** *Phil. Trans.* IV. 967 A Chronological Accompt of the several Incendium's or Fires of Mount Ætna. **1750** R. ROE *Let. to Abraham Johnson* 12 Quench'd the fatal flames as spedily as Gulliver did the fam'd Lilliputian Incendium.

incendivity (ɪnsɛnˈdɪvɪtɪ). [f. the stem of L. *incend-ere* (see INCEND *v.*) + -IVITY.] The ability to effect ignition or set on fire.

1919 *Jrnl. Chem. Soc.* CXV. 103 These results clearly establish the fact that the incendivity of a spark does not depend on the total energy of the spark. **1972** *Physics Bull.* Aug. 454/3 Later laboratory measurements..of the incendivity of spark discharges showed that if the uniform field strength in a tank roof space away from any protrusions was 500 kV m⁻¹, then brush discharges having sufficient energy to ignite an inflammable hydrocarbon-air mixture could occur at metal protrusions.

Hence (as a back-formation) **in'cendive** *a.*, of or pertaining to incendivity; capable of effecting ignition.

1959 *Rep. Investigations U.S. Bureau of Mines* No. 5463. 19 Chemical composition alone is not sufficient to define the incendive character of an explosive. **1972** *Physics Bull.* Aug. 456/1 Differences between the incendive properties of metal to metal sparks and liquid to metal sparks. **1973** *Ibid.* Mar. 145/3 It draws attention to the risks of incendive sparks at or near deck openings resulting from static electricity.

†**in'cendment.** *Obs. rare.* [f. INCEND *v.* + -MENT.] The action of kindling or inflaming.

1647 W. BROWNE tr. *Gomberville's Polexander* III. v. 144 This love, being so ardent, could produce nothing but flames and incendments.

incensation (ɪnsɛnˈseɪʃən). [n. of action f. med.L. *incensāre* to INCENSE.] The action of perfuming with incense; censing.

1853 J. D. H. DALE tr. *Baldeschi's Cerem. Rom. Rite* 8 During the incensation of the Celebrant, he stands near the Deacon. **1890** T. E. BRIDGETT *Blund. & Forg.* iv. 101 A priest with a thurible continues the incensation. **1893** *Dublin Rev.* Apr. 281 The ceremony concludes, in the Byzantine rite, with..the incensation of the gifts.

incense (ˈɪnsɛns), *sb.* Forms: 3 **ansens,** 4 **ensense, encenz,** 4–5 **encense, encence,** 4–6 **encens, ensence,** 4–8 **ensens,** 5 **yncense,** 5–6 **incence,** 6 **insence,** 5– **incense.** [ME. *ansens, encenz*, a. OF. *encens* (12th c.), *ancens*, ad. eccl. L. *incensum* incense, lit. 'that which is set on fire', neuter of *incensus*, pa. pple. of *incendĕre* to set on fire. Altered through *ensence, encence* to *incense*, after L. An aphetic ME. form was CENSE *sb.*[1]]

1. An aromatic gum or other vegetable product, or a mixture of fragrant gums and spices, used for producing a sweet smell when burned.

c **1290** *S. Eng. Leg.* I. 178/22 Gold and mirre and Ansens. *c* **1340** *Cursor M.* 9358 (Trin.) Wel swotir hir vestiment þan encense þat is brent. *c* **1380** *Sir Ferumb.* 2545 þan was þar at hure fete of encenz a fair dentee, And of balme þat smylleþ swete & spycery gret plentee. *c* **1386** CHAUCER *Knt.'s T.* 1573 And moore encens in to the fyr he caste. *c* **1400** MAUNDEV. (Roxb.) xix. 87 þai bring..incense and oþer thinges swete smelland. **1526** *Pilgr. Perf.* (W. de W. 1531) 179 b, Some aduysed her to brenne incence in her cell. **1578** LYTE *Dodoens* II. xcvii. 280 His roote sauoreth like the Encens, which is called in Greke Libanos. **1610** MARKHAM *Masterp.* I. xciv. 186 Take the powder of gumdragant, Ensens, and damaske roses. **1666** DRYDEN *Ann. Mirab.* ccxcvii, The East with incense, and the West with gold, Will stand like suppliants to receive her doom. **1709** *Lond. Gaz.* No. 4518/4 For Publick Sale,..a good quantity of..Oil of Turpentine, Ensens alias Frankincense. **1850** J. GARDNER *Faiths World* II. 127 On the great day of atonement..having received incense from one of the priests, he [the high-priest] offered it on the golden altar. **1897** WILLIS *Flower. Pl.* II. 363 It [Styrax] is used medicinally and for incense.

2. The smoke or perfume of incense, esp. when burned as an oblation or in religious ceremonial.

c **1380** WYCLIF *Serm.* Sel. Wks. I. 341 Bi þe encence þei myȝten putte awey þe stynke of þe stable. **1390** GOWER *Conf.* III. 243 With encense He sacreth and doth reverence. **1483** CAXTON *Cato* I iv b, To pease God wyth encence and by good werkes. **1611** BIBLE *Ezek.* viii. 11 A thicke cloud of incense went vp. **1661** SOUTH *Twelve Serm.* (1698) III. 177 Like Incense, while it ascends to Heaven it perfumes all about it. **1739** GRAY *Let.* in *Poems* (1775) 69 We listened to this, and breathed nothing but incense for two hours. **1860** C. SANGSTER *Hesperus* etc. 181, I too Did offer incense in that solemn place.

3. *transf.* **a.** (In biblical language.) The smoke or odour of any burnt sacrifice. **b.** Any pleasant perfume or fragrance, as of flowers.

a **1340** HAMPOLE *Psalter* lxv. 14 [lxvi. 15], I sall offire til þe wiþ encens of wethirs [so WYCLIF 1382; 1611 incense of rammes]. **1667** MILTON *P.L.* IX. 194 Sacred Light began to dawne In Eden on the humid Flours, that breathd Thir morning Incense. **1712** POPE *Messiah* 24 With all the incense of the breathing spring. **1821** SHELLEY *Ginevra* 126 The matin winds from the expanded flowers Scatter their hoarded incense.

4. *fig.* Applied to something figured as a religious sacrifice, or as offered in the way of homage, *e.g.* prayer, praise, flattery; esp. when represented as grateful to the recipient.

[*a* **1340** HAMPOLE *Psalter* cxl. 2 My prayere be rightid as ensens in þi sight.] **1382** WYCLIF *Rev.* viii. 4 The smoke of the encensis of the preyers of halewis. **1593** SHAKS. *Lucr.* 194 Offer pure incense to so pure a shrine. **1614** EARL STIRLING *Domes-day* II. (R.), The sorrow of his saints doth move God much: No sweeter incence then the sighs of such. **1738** POPE *Univ. Prayer* 52 To thee..One Chorus let all Being raise, All Nature's Incense rise! **1746-7** HERVEY *Medit.* (1818) 195 Continue to add the incense of a dutiful life, to all the oblations of a grateful tongue. *a* **1854** H. REED *Lect. Brit. Poets* (1857) II. x. 22 The incense of flattery which his satellites were forever burning beneath his nostrils. **1879** FARRAR *St. Paul* I. 313 The king, to whom no incense was so sweet as the voice of popular applause.

5. *Comb.*, as *incense-breath, -cloud, -mist, -pan, -pot, -smoke*; *incense-bearing, -burning, -loaded* adjs.; **incense-blossom,** a blossom yielding 'incense' or fragrance; **incense-boat,** a boat-shaped vessel used to hold incense for transfer to a censer; †**incense-brass,** a rendering of Gr. χαλκολίβανον in Rev. i. 15 (1611 'fine brass', R. V. 1881 'burnished brass', but also explained as 'yellow frankincense'); **incense-breathing** *a.*, exhaling 'incense' or fragrance; **incense-burner,** (*a*) one who burns incense; (*b*) a vessel or stand in or on which incense is burnt; **incense-cedar,** the genus *Libocedrus*, esp. the White Cedar (*L. decurrens*) of Western North America; **incense-cup,** a cup or small vessel for burning incense; also applied to certain small vessels found in prehistoric graves; †**incense-frank** = FRANKINCENSE (*obs.*); **incense-tree,** a name for various trees yielding incense, esp. of the genera *Boswellia* (chiefly East Indian) and *Icica* (chiefly South American); also applied to a species of *Pittosporum*, from its fragrant flowers; **incense-wood,** the wood of *Icica heptaphylla*, a South American tree; †**incense-wort,** 'a kind of herb' (Phillips, 1706).

1818 SHELLEY *Rev. Islam* XII. xix, Many a lawny mountain With *incense-bearing forests. **1817** —— *To Constantia Singing*, Western isles with *incense-blossoms bright. **1853** J. D. H. DALE tr. *Baldeschi's Cerem. Rom. Rite* 8 He.. presents the *navicula* (or *incense-boat) to the Master of Ceremonies. **1866** R. F. LITTLEDALE *Incense* 19 The priest.. takes the incense-boat, and burns incense in the thurible, censing the altar five times. **1561** DAUS tr. *Bullinger on Apoc.* (1573) 17 b, The feete of the Lord are of Copper, or like to *Incens-brasse burnyng in a fire. For *Incensbrasse* is a word compounded of Brasse and Incence. **1750** GRAY *Elegy* v, The breezy call of *incense-breathing morn. *a* **1843**

SOUTHEY *Comm.-pl. Bk.* IV. 3 An *incense-burner to the idols. **1884** MILLER *Plant-n., Libocedrus,* *Incense Cedar. *a* **1835** MRS. HEMANS *Poems, To Picture Madonna,* And hath the crested helmet bow'd Before thee, midst the *incense-cloud? **1633** *True Trojans* III. vi. in Hazl. *Dodsley* XII. 498 An altar we descry, Where *incense-frank and amber fumes did fly In little rolling curls. **1842** FABER *Styrian Lake* etc. 37 The *incense-loaded air. *a* **1835** MRS. HEMANS *Poems, Minster,* Revealing Through *incense-mists their sainted pageantry. **1611** FLORIO, *Incensorio,* a censor, or *incense-pan. *a* **1661** HOLYDAY *Juvenal* 248 There was no such matter as the bringing of their incense in papers to the altars; there being, for that purpose, an incense-pan. **1699** DAMPIER *Voy.* II. I. 43 A little Altar, with two *Incense-pots on it. **1587** FENNER in Farr *S.P. Eliz.* (1845) II. 341 Spiknard, saffron, sweet canes, Cinomon, with the rest Of *incense-trees. **1855** KINGSLEY *Westw. Ho* xxi. (1889) 391 Shrubberies of heaths and rhododendrons, and woolly incense-trees. **1884** *Leisure Hour* Dec. 753/2 The Pittosporum or incense tree, as it is here called from the perfume which its pretty white flowers give out. **1866** *Treas. Bot.,* *Incense wood, *Icica heptaphylla.*

incense ('ɪnsɛns), *v.*^{1} Forms: see INCENSE *sb.* [a. F. *encenser* (*Chanson Roland,* 11th c.), corresp. to med.L. and It. *incensāre,* f. *encens, incensum, incenso,* INCENSE *sb.*]

1. *trans.* To fumigate or perfume (a person or thing) with incense, esp. in connexion with a religious ceremony; to burn or offer incense before (an image), or to (a deity); to cense.

1303 R. BRUNNE *Handl. Synne* 11093 Þey ensensede þe body. *c* **1375** *Sc. Leg. Saints, Baptista* 47 Þis zachary . . wes in þe tempil gan, . . til incense þe altere. **1401** *Pol. Poems* (Rolls) II. 44 Chorees children, with new senceres ensencen the auters of synne. **1496** *Dives & Paup.* (W. de W.) I. xv. 47/1 Now clerkes encense ymages & other. **1558** HETHE in Strype *Ann. Ref.* (1824) I. App. vi. 402 Kinge Ozias did take the censer to incense the aulter. **1613** PURCHAS *Pilgrimage* (1614) 144 An Idol-roome, where they Incense these Deities morning and euening. **1709** J. JOHNSON *Clergym. Vade M.* II. 194 They that . . did not . . with their own hands incense Idols. **1805** SOUTHEY *Madoc* II. ii, And those infernal Priests who guard him then . . At morning and at evening incense him, And mock him with knee-reverence. **1837** CARLYLE *Fr. Rev.* II. I. x, Neither . . shall any man or woman, self-styled noble, be 'incensed,'—foolishly fumigated with incense, in Church.

fig. **1729** STACKHOUSE *Body Divin.* IV. i. §2 (1776) II. 428 The prayers of the saints incensed with the merits of his sacrifice.

2. *transf.* To perfume with any pleasant odour; to suffuse with fragrance; to scent. (In quot. 1503, to drive *out* by diffusing fragrance.)

1503 HAWES *Examp. Virt.* IV. iii, Fragrant floures full of delycasy That all yll heyres [= airs] dyde ensence oute. **1727** A. HAMILTON *New Acc. E. Ind.* I. vii. 68 Some Powder of Benjoin, Myrrh or Frankincense, which produce a thick Smoke, that incenses or perfumes the whole Room. **1852** HAWTHORNE *Blithedale Rom.* iv, A goodly quantity of peat, which was crumbling to white ashes, . . incensed the kitchen with its not ungrateful odor. **1861** L. L. NOBLE *Icebergs* 303 Wild roses incensed the fresh air. **1884** J. PAYNE *1001 Nights* VIII. 20 She incensed herself with aloes-wood and scented herself with musk and ambergris.

3. *fig.* To offer flattering homage or adulation to; to flatter. ? *Obs.*

1732 *Gentl. Instr.* (ed. 10) 212 (D.) He . . now must be bought off and incensed by his Sovereign, as the Devil is by the Indians, that he may do no more harm. **1736** LD. HERVEY *Mem. Geo. II,* I. 319 Flatterers that were perpetually incensing his altars. **1762–71** H. WALPOLE *Vertue's Anecd. Paint.* (1786) III. 206 This was not the only instance in which the poet incensed the painter.

4. To burn or offer as incense (*lit.* and *fig.*).

1605 BACON *Adv. Learn.* II. *Concl.,* The good, if any bee, is due . . to be incensed to the honour first of the Diuine Maiestie, and next of your Maiestie. **1613** PURCHAS *Pilgrimage* (1614) 417 A Censer with Incense, which he incenseth. **1872** J. G. MURPHY *Comm. Lev.* iv. 11–12 The whole carcass of the bullock is burned, not incensed or turned into a sweet smell on the altar, but consumed by fire in the place of ashes.

5. *intr.* To burn or offer incense.

c **1386** CHAUCER *Sec. Nun's T.* 395 They nolde encense ne sacrifise right nought. **1388** WYCLIF *Luke* i. 9 He . . entride in to the temple, to encense. *c* **1449** PECOCK *Repr.* II. vi. 169 To encense to God or to a Seint bifore an auter. **1638** *Penit. Conf.* viii. (1657) 250 Such who . . through frailty had incensed unto Idols. **1870** *Daily News* 7 Feb., His Holiness . . afterwards walked round the coffin, incensing and sprinking holy water.

incense (ɪn'sɛns), *v.*^{2} Forms: 5 **encense,** 5–6 **ensense,** 5–7 **incence,** 6–7 **insence,** 6– **incense.** [a. OF. *incenser* (? *encenser*) (15–16th c. in Godef.), f. L. *incens-,* ppl. stem of *incendĕre* to set on fire, INCEND.]

†**1.** *trans.* To set on fire, kindle; to consume with fire, burn. *Obs.*

1470–85 MALORY *Arthur* XXI. xi, Syr Launcelot with his viij felowes wente aboute the hors bere syngyng & redyng many an holy oryson, & frankensens vpon the corps encensed. **1477** NORTON *Ord. Alch.* v. in Ashm. (1652) 64 Incenced with Heate. **1509** HAWES *Past. Pleas.* I. xv, Envyroned about With tongues of fyre as bright as any starre, That fyry flambes ensensed alway out. **1593** G. FLETCHER *Licia* (1876) 53 For why my heart with sighs doth breath such flame, That ayre and water both incensed be. **1625** BACON *Ess., Adversitie* (Arb.) 505 Vertue is like pretious Odours, most fragrant, when they are incensed, or crushed. *c* **1700** ADDISON *Milton imit. out of 3rd Æneid* (R.), Now belches molten stones and ruddy flame Incenst, or tears up mountains by the roots.

†**b.** To heat, make hot. *Obs.*

1621 BURTON *Anat. Mel.* I. i. I. iv. 12 Madnesse . . hath the same causes as the other [Phrensie], as Choler adust, and Blood incensed, Braines inflamed.

†**2.** *fig.* To inflame, excite, 'kindle' (passion or ardent feeling). *Obs.*

1599 MARSTON *Sco. Villanie* I. iii. 184 Shall Curio . . with bare groping touch Incense his lust? **1631** GOUGE *God's Arrows* I. §4. 7 These by their sinnes much incense Gods wrath. **1667** MILTON *P.L.* IX. 692 Will God incense his ire For such a petty Trespass? **1809** W. IRVING *Knickerb.* VII. vi. (1849) 410 Perplexities which bewildered the brain and incensed the ire of honest Peter.

†**3.** To inflame, excite, 'fire' (a person *with* some ardent feeling or passion). *Obs.* exc. as in b.

1435 MISYN *Fire of Love* 102 My saule truly with holy lufe was ensensyd. **1531** ELYOT *Gov.* I. ii, Some . . be incensed with glorie, some with ambicion. **1610** G. FLETCHER *Christ's Vict.* I. lx, And all incensed with love, With wonder and amazement, did her beauty prove. **1664** *Flodden F.* I. 1 You muses all my mind incense.

b. *spec.* To inflame with wrath, excite or provoke to anger, make angry, enrage, exasperate. (The current sense.)

1494 FABYAN *Chron.* VI. ccvii. 220 For the whiche he ensensed the kynge of Fraunce agayne hym in all that he myght. *c* **1586** C'TESS PEMBROKE *Ps.* LXXVIII. xvi, How ofte this crooked kind Incenst him in the desert every where. **1596** SPENSER *F.Q.* v. iii. 36 Much was the knight incenst with his lewd word. **1653** H. COGAN tr. *Pinto's Trav.* xxx. 119 They incensed the Inhabitants against him. **1749** FIELDING *Tom Jones* XVI. ii, This so incensed her father, that . . he departed from her with many hard words and curses. **1858** BRIGHT *Sp. India* 24 June, A thing likely to incense and horrify the people of India.

c. *fig.* To stir up, make violent or furious.

In quot. 1604 with mixture of sense 1.

1604 DEKKER *Honest Wh.* Wks. 1873 II. 133 Winds wrastling with great fires, incense the flames. **1615** G. SANDYS *Trav.* 2 A sea tempestuous and vnfaithfull; at an instant incensed with sudden gusts. *Ibid.* 25 A trade-wind blowing . . which when contrary to the streame, doth exceedingly incense it.

†**4.** To incite to some action; to urge, instigate, stir up, 'set on'. Const. *to* or *to do* something.

In some instances perhaps associated with INSENSE, *q.v.*

1531 ELYOT *Gov.* I. xiv, If nature . . wyll dispose them to that maner studie, they shall be therto the more incensed, and come unto it the better prepared and furnisshed. **1549** COVERDALE, etc. *Erasm. Par. 1 Pet.* 7 The Profession . . whereunto they ought rather to be encensed and allured by your honest behauiour. **1600** HOLLAND *Livy* XXVII. xlix. 665 [Asdrubal] when his men were weery and drew back . . incensed [*accendit*] them againe, one while by faire words and intreatie, another while by sharpe checks and rebukes. **1639** FULLER *Holy War* IV. xxviii. (1647) 217 By which speech he incensed the English to go on with him.

incensed ('ɪnsɛnst), *ppl. a.*^{1} [f. INCENSE *v.*^{1} (or *sb.*) + -ED.] Perfumed or accompanied with incense; filled with the smoke of incense.

1611 HEYWOOD *Gold. Age* I. Wks. 1874 I. 13 The Delphian God, Spake from the Incenst Altar. **1812** S. ROGERS *Columbus* v. 21 The incensed rites, and choral harmonies. **1866** NEALE *Sequences & Hymns* 131 Again shall banner, cross, and cope gleam thro' the incensed aisle.

incensed (ɪn'sɛnst, *poet.* ɪn'sɛnsɪd), *ppl. a.*^{2} [f. INCENSE *v.*^{2} + -ED^1.]

†**1. a.** *lit.* Set on fire, kindled. **b.** *fig.* (of anger, etc.) Kindled, excited. *Obs.*

1612 ROWLANDS *More Knaues Yet?* 27 Whose heauy wrath and iust incensed Ire, Hath sentenc'd me to euerlasting fier. **1663** J. SPENCER *Prodigies* (1665) 213 The coruscation of some incensed Exhalations breaking forth by pauses and intervals form the Clouds. **1694** tr. *Milton's Lett. State, To Pr. Transilvania* May an. 1655, Beseeching him to remove his incens'd Anger from his Subjects.

2. Inflamed with wrath, made angry, enraged.

1594 SHAKS. *Rich III,* II. i. 52 Betweene these swelling wrong incensed Peeres. **1667** MILTON *P.L.* v. 847 Hast'n to appease Th' incensed Father, and th' incensed Son, While Pardon may be found in time besought. **1681–6** J. SCOTT *Chr. Life* (1747) III. 16 He will appear against us as an incensed Judge in the Quarrel of his Father's Authority. **1838** THIRLWALL *Greece* xviii. III. 51 To abandon the Samians to the vengeance of their incensed sovereign.

3. *Her.* Said of an animal depicted with fire issuing from the mouth and ears.

1577–87 HOLINSHED *Chron.* III. 1256/2 The field . . charged with so many lions of the first rampants incensed gules. **1882** CUSSANS *Her.* vi. (ed. 3) 90.

Hence **in'censedness** (Bailey vol. II, 1727).

incenseless ('ɪnsɛnslɪs), *a.* [f. INCENSE *sb.* + -LESS.] Without incense.

1856 G. WILSON *Gateways Knowl.* (1859) 80 An opportunity . . which our modern incenseless worship does not supply.

incensement (ɪn'sɛnsmənt). Now *rare.* [f. INCENSE *v.*^{2} + -MENT.] The fact of being incensed; anger, wrath, exasperation.

1599 PORTER *Angry Wom. Abingd.* in Hazl. *Dodsley* VII. 316 Not for that your incensement Makes me make offer of it, but your health. **1601** SHAKS. *Twel. N.* III. iv. 260 His incensement at this moment is so implacable, that satisfaction can be none, but by pangs of death and sepulcher! **1624** HEYWOOD *Captives* III. i. in Bullen *O. Pl.* IV, Rather give him upp a Sacrifice To my lord's just incensement. **1821** *Examiner* 814/2 Popular incensement . . seems more to be indicated. **1867** OUIDA *Idalia* x. 126 Such a freedom . . now lashed him into vehement pain and incensement.

†**in'censer**^{1}. *Obs.* Forms: α. 4 **encenser, ensenser;** β. 5–6 **encensour, -or,** 6 **incensur;** γ. 7 **incenser.** [Two types: ME. *en'censer,* a. AF. *encenser,* OF. *encensier:*—late L. *incensārium* (Du Cange), f. *incensum* INCENSE; and ME. *encensor,* ad. OF. *encensoir,* med.L. *incensōrium* INCENSORY. Cf. CENSER.] A vessel in which incense is burned; a censer.

α. *c* **1380** WYCLIF *Wks.* (1880) 323 Somme of þise newe ordris hauen costy encenseris to encense beddis of men & of wymmen & to spoyle hem. **1382** —— *Exod.* xxxvii. 16 Ensensers [1388 censeris] of moost clene gold. **1387** TREVISA *Higden* (Rolls) V. 225 He ordeyned þat no [wo]man schulde . . doo ensens in þe ensencer [*v.rr.* senser, censer].

β. *c* **1400** MAUNDEV. (Roxb.) xi. 43 Foure encensours of gold. **1480** CAXTON *Ovid's Met.* XIII. xiii, Eneas . . gaf to the Kynge of his jewels . . a moche ryche encensor. **1563** WINȜET *Four Scoir Thre Quest.* lxii. Wks. 1888 I. 115 Be exemple of the incensuris of Dathan and Abiron.

γ. **1624** DARCIE *Birth of Heresies* xvi. 66 They had a portable Incenser, wherewith to incense.

incenser^2 ('ɪnsɛnsə(r)). Also 6 **encensour,** 9 **incensor.** [a. F. *encenseur* (14th c. in Hatz.-Darm.) agent-n. from *encenser,* INCENSE *v.*^{1} Subseq. conformed to Eng. type of vb. and suffix: see -ER^1 2.]

1. One who burns or offers incense.

1555 W. WATREMAN *Fardle Facions* II. xii. 270 An encensour with the censoure in his hande. **1775** R. CHANDLER *Trav. Asia M.* (1825) I. 167 Some of the inferior ministers . . the sacred herald, the incenser, the player on the flute.

2. *fig.* A flatterer: see INCENSE *v.*^{1} 3.

1873 LD. HOUGHTON *Monogr.* 36 The servility . . which degraded the incensor of Frederic the Great—M. de Voltaire.

incenser^3: see INCENSOR.

†**in'censial,** *a. Obs. rare.* In 6 **encencyall.** [f. *encens* INCENSE *sb.*: prob. immed. a. OF. *encensiel:* see -AL^1.] Pertaining to or resembling incense.

1493 *Festivall* (W. de W. 1515) 84 There is noo encence savoureth soo swete and gyueth so encencyall an odour . . as dooth good prayers.

in'censible, *a. rare*$^{-1}$. [f. L. *incens-,* ppl. stem of L. *incendĕre* to INCEND + -IBLE.] Capable of being incensed or excited in feeling.

1614 T. ADAMS in Spurgeon *Treas. Dav.* Ps. xxxv. 17 Were God like man, subject to passions, or incensible by the suggestions of the common barrator.

incensing ('ɪnsɛnsɪŋ), *vbl. sb.*^{1} [f. INCENSE *v.*^{1} + -ING^1.] The action of INCENSE *v.*^{1}; a perfuming with, or offering of, incense; censing.

1388 WYCLIF *Luke* i. 10 Al the multitude of the puple . . preiede in the our of encensyng. **1496** *Dives & Paup.* (W. de W.) I. xv. 47/1 In euery lawe thuryfycacyon or encensynge hath ben an hygh dyuyne worshyp. **1559** BP. COX in Strype *Ann. Ref.* (1709) I. App. xxii. 51 Images in the Church of Christ have been foully abused . . with . . clothing, gilding, incensing, and other kinds of honour. **1679** PULLER *Moder. Ch. Eng.* (1843) 137 As formal . . as any Romanist can be in his crosses and incensings. **1877** J. D. CHAMBERS *Div. Worship* 264 The elaborate incensing of the altar and of persons and things.

incensing (ɪn'sɛnsɪŋ), *vbl. sb.*^{2} [f. INCENSE *v.*^{2} + -ING^1.] The action of INCENSE *v.*^{2}; inflaming; †stirring up (*obs.*); a making angry.

1494 FABYAN *Chron.* VII. 350 The commons of yᵉ cytie were so ferre out of rule by ensensynge of ryotous persones. **1650** B. *Discolliminium* 53 The world never saw . . such incensing of forraigne hatred upon a Nation.

in'censing, *ppl. a.* [f. as prec. + -ING^2.] That incenses, inflames, or excites.

1599 MARSTON *Sco. Villanie* III. viii. 212 To streake himselfe, and with incensing touch To faint his force.

†**in'cension.** *Obs.* Also 4–5 **insencyon.** [ad. L. *incensiōn-em,* n. of action from *incendĕre* to INCEND: cf. OF. *incension* (1488 in Godef.).]

1. Burning; setting on fire; conflagration.

1432–50 tr. *Higden* (Rolls) I. 29 The iiij. ages of the world, from the plasmacion of Adam vn to the incension of the temple of the Iewes. **1626** BACON *Sylva* §23 Subtill or Windy Spirits are taken off by Incension or Euaporation. **1656** BLOUNT *Glossogr., Incension,* . . a burning or inflaming.

2. Bodily heating or inflammation.

1597 A. M. tr. *Guillemeau's Fr. Chirurg.* 17/2 The woundes of the belly are not so subiecte vnto inflammation or incensions. **1745** MORTIMER in *Phil. Trans.* XLIII. 477 Was it not for the Superabundance of aqueous Humours in Animals . . fatal Incensions would frequently happen.

3. The inflaming or exciting of passion or ardent feeling; incensement.

1675 BAXTER *Cath. Theol.* II. I. 2 Wars and blood-shed . . hath followed partly by this incension.

†**in'censive,** *a.* and *sb. Obs. rare.* Also 7 **insensive.** [a. obs. F. *incensif, -ive,* ad. L. type **incensiv-us,* f. *incens-,* ppl. stem of *incendĕre:* see INCEND and -IVE.]

A. *adj.* **1.** Of inflamed disposition, full of rage or wrath.

1563–87 FOXE *A. & M.* (1684) I. 90/2 Unto Christian piety and Religion, he was most incensive, and in the East Churches exercised cruel persecution.

2. Tending to inflame or excite passion or angry feeling.

1633 T. ADAMS *Exp. 2 Peter* ii. 1 Quarelling, and multiplying incensive terms. *a* **1677** BARROW *Wks.* (1686) III. x. 118 To be extremely hated, and inhumanely persecuted without any fault committed, or just occasion offered, is greatly incensive of humane passion.

B. *sb.* = INCENTIVE *sb.* 1

a **1618** RALEIGH *War* D vj b, Hence we may observe, that the very propagation of our kind, hath with it a strong insensive even of those daily Wars, which afflict the earth.

†**in'censor, -er.** *Obs.* [a. L. *incensor*, agent-n. from *incendĕre*: see INCEND *v.* Cf. obs. F. *incenseur* (16th c.). The form *incenser* might be agent-n. from INCENSE *v.*[2]] One who kindles, inflames, stirs up, or incites; an instigator.

c **1555** HARPSFIELD *Divorce Hen. VIII* (Camden) 254 The chief incenser and solicitor of the first divorce. **1576** NEWTON *Lemnie's Complex.* (1633) 7 The humours and spirits (which be the incensors and stirrers forward of the minde). **1613** *North's Plutarch* Add. Lives 1215 Seneca vnderstanding..how these lewd incensers did accuse him.. besought him [Nero] to hear him. *a* **1627** HAYWARD *Edw. VI* (1630) 55 Many priests..were incensors of the rage.

incensory ('ɪnsɛnsərɪ). [ad. med.L. *incensōrium*, f. *incensum* INCENSE: see -ORY. Cf. INCENSER[1].]

†**1.** ? A burnt offering, or ? an altar of burnt offering. *Obs. rare.*

c **1611** CHAPMAN *Iliad* XI. 686 A cup of gold, crown'd with red wine, he held On th' holy incensory pour'd [ἐπ' αἰθομένοις ἱεροῖσι].

2. A vessel for burning incense; a censer.

1645 EVELYN *Mem.* 17 Feb., Other saints lie here, decorated with splendid ornaments, lamps, and incensories of great cost. **1656** BLOUNT *Glossogr.*, *Incensory*, a Church-vessel to burn Incense in; a censing or perfuming pan. **1826** C. BUTLER *Grotius* Introd. 21 Chalices, patines, incensories, images..were fabricated. **1844** LINGARD *Anglo-Sax. Ch.* (1858) I. vii. 269 In some churches an incensory, or metallic vessel, was suspended from the roof.

incensurable (ɪn'sɛnsjʊərəb(ə)l, -ʃ(j)ʊər-), *a. rare.* [IN-[3].] Not liable to censure; not censurable or blameable.

1846 WORCESTER cites DWIGHT.

Hence **incensurably** *adv. rare.*

1846 WORCESTER cites SHELLEY.

†**in'cention.** *Obs. rare*—[0]. In 7 -sion. [ad. L. *incentiōn-em*, n. of action f. *incinĕre* to sing to, blow on an instrument, f. *in-* (IN-[2]) + *canĕre* to sing.] (See quot.)

1656 BLOUNT *Glossogr.*, *Incension* (*ab incino*), melody of Instruments, or of men singing together.

incentive (ɪn'sɛntɪv), *a.* and *sb.* [ad. L. *incentīvus* setting the tune, inciting, f. *incinĕre*: see INCENTION. In sense 2, app. confounded with INCENSIVE, and other derivatives of L. *incendĕre* to kindle, set on fire.]

A. *adj.* **1.** Having the quality of inciting or arousing to feeling or action; provocative, exciting.

1603 HOLLAND *Plutarch's Mor.* 1143 Pythia the Priestresse of Apollo, being once come downe from her three footed fabricke, upon which she receiveth that incentive spirit of furie, remaineth quiet. **1660** tr. *Amyraldus' Treat. conc. Relig.* I. viii. 109 Embellish'd with many beauties incentive of our Love. **1677** W. HUBBARD *Narrative* Postscr. 10 Instances of this nature should be Incentive unto us, to bless the Father of Lights. *a* **1734** NORTH *Lives* (1826) I. 371 The Lord Shaftesbury..made an incentive speech in the House of Lords. **1864** *Reader* No. 92. 405/2 Pleasing and incentive..to.. our mental faculties. **1866** CANDLISH *1 Ep. John* ix. 104 It is a stimulus and incentive impulse.

†**2.** Having the property of kindling or setting on fire. *Obs.*

1667 MILTON *P.L.* VI. 519 Part incentive reed Provide, pernicious with one touch to fire. **1708** J. PHILIPS *Cyder* I. (Seager), The cavern'd ground, With grain incentive [gunpowder] stor'd, by sudden blaze Bursts fatal.

3. Of or pertaining to a system of payments, concessions, etc., to encourage harder work or a particular choice of work.

1943 *Reader's Digest* Aug. 11/1 Mr. Charles E. Wilson.. is urging war industries to adopt 'incentive pay'—that is, to pay workers more if they *produce* more. **1948** *Ann. Reg. 1947* 283 In an effort to increase foreign trading various incentives were offered to exporters..a proportion of the foreign exchange..for the purchase of raw materials,..and 'incentive' goods for their workers. **1951** *Engineering* 2 Mar. 245/2 The body of the book is concerned with a description of the ['Armstrong Merit Sharing'] scheme... A series of 'requirements' is laid down to which it is considered that any incentive scheme should conform. **1952** 'VIGILANS' *Chamber of Horrors* 72 *Incentive bonus*, a bonus *in advance* as an encouragement, for workers, to work. **1957** *Encycl. Brit.* XXIII. 272/1 For a substantial number of wage earners compensation is defined in terms not of time units but of output, under various types of incentive systems. *Ibid.* 272/2 The essential characteristic of an incentive wage rate structure is that payment depends on output rather than work time. **1967** G. F. FIENNES *I tried to run Railway* iv. 31 Work Study became synonymous with incentive payments. **1970** T. LUPTON *Managem. & Social Sci.* (ed. 2) ii. 53 These controls were turned mainly to the manipulation of the incentive payment system.

B. *sb.* **1.** [L. *incentīvum.*] Something that arouses feeling, or incites to action; an exciting cause or motive; an incitement, provocation, 'spur'.

1432-50 tr. *Higden* (Rolls) I. 5 The incentiue of manhode. **1612** SELDEN *Illustr. Drayton's Poly-olb.* vi. 97 A musicall incentiue to warre. **1638** ROUSE *Heav. Univ.* i. (1702) 3 Let the Precepts and Patterns of Vertues..serve for Spurs and Incentives to Grace. **1665** BOYLE *Occas. Refl.* (1848) 9 Incentives to inflame our hearts with Charity and Zeal. **1713** STEELE *Englishm.* No. 50. 329 This Paper is principally designed as an Incentive to the Love of our Country. **1849** MISS MULOCK *Ogilvies* viii, With men of Lynedon's character opposition is often the greatest incentive to love.

2. An incentive payment, scheme, etc.

1948 [see adj. sense 3 above]. **1956** HICKMAN & KUHN *Individuals, Groups & Econ. Behavior* ii. 50 Debate about this central question has hinged in large part on the issue of incentives. *Ibid.* 60 Gordon enumerates several nonfinancial incentives of some apparent importance, including power, prestige, and security. **1960** H. C. WALLICH *Cost of Freedom* iii. 81 This leaves us with incentives in the narrower sense as the third element in the triad of forces upon which we rely to call forth initiative and effort. *Ibid.* 89 Labor and management performance is not the only place where we must look for the effects of incentives.

Hence **in'centively** *adv.*, incitingly.

1856 in WEBSTER.

incentor (ɪn'sɛntə(r)). Now *rare.* Also 6 -our, 9 (erron.) -er. [a. L. *incentor* singer, setter of a tune, inciter, from *incinĕre*: see INCENTION.]

1. One who excites or stirs up (strife, etc.); one who incites *to* action.

1563-87 FOXE *A. & M.* (1596) 79/2 The cheefe Capteine and incentour of which persecution was first Dioclesian. **1609** BP. W. BARLOW *Answ. Nameless Cath.* 172 They tooke him to be Incentor, the Stirrer or Procurer of the same. **1656** BLOUNT *Glossogr.*, *Incentor*,..a make-bate, or *Boutefeu.* **1658** PHILLIPS, *Incentor*, the same as *Incendiary.* **1718** PRIDEAUX *O. & N. Test.* II. II. 138 The chief Incentors of this War. **1895** *N. Brit. Daily Mail* 30 Aug. 5 A placard, declaring that all incenters to riot would be executed.

†**2.** (See quot.) *Obs.*

1656 BLOUNT *Glossogr.*, *Incentor*, he that singeth the descant. In singing there are three degrees, the first *Succentor*, the second *Incentor*, the third *Accentor.* **1678** PHILLIPS (ed. 4), *Incentor*, he that sings the middle part.

incentre, encentre, (ɪn-, ɛn'sɛntə(r)), *v. rare.* [f. IN-[2], EN-[1] + CENTRE: cf. It. *incentrare.*] *trans.* To centre *in* something; to place or fix in the centre.

1611 FLORIO, *Incentrare*, to encentre, or goe to the midle or centre. **1623** WILLIAMS *Let. to Dk. Buckingham* 15 June in Hacket *Life* I. (1692) 135 Nor is your Love incentred to me only in your own Breast. **1843** E. JONES *Sens. & Ev.* 111 Encentred in this meadow, one revolved Inquiring gaze.

incentre, in-centre ('ɪnsɛntə(r)), *sb. Geom.* Also (*U.S.*) **-center.** [f. IN-[1] b + CENTRE, CENTER *sb.*] The centre of an inscribed circle.

1903 E. H. ASKWITH *Course Pure Geom.* i. 12 The pedal triangle has for its incentre the orthocentre of the original triangle. **1904** HALL & STEVENS *School Geom.* III. 204 Given the base and vertical angle of a triangle, find the locus of the in-centre. **1963** R. A. ROSENBAUM *Introd. Projective Geom. & Mod. Algebra* i. 3 Prove that the bisectors of the angles of a triangle are concurrent. (The point of concurrency is the center of the inscribed circle, abbreviated 'incenter'.)

incept (ɪn'sɛpt), *v.* [f. L. *incept-*, ppl. stem of *incipĕre* to begin (see INCIPIENT). Cf. rare OF. *incepter* to begin = L. freq. *inceptāre* to begin, undertake.]

†**1.** *trans.* To undertake; to begin, commence, enter upon. *Obs.*

1569 NEWTON *Cicero's Olde Age* 7 b, Those things..were unluckely and in ill time incepted. **1641** *More's Rich. III* 245 Was not his first enterprise..begun and incepted by the murther of divers noble..and vertuous personages? **1802**, **1895** [see INCEPTED, INCEPTING below].

2. *intr.* To enter formally upon the office of a Master or Doctor in a University, and to be recognized as such by the Faculty; to complete the taking of a degree; = COMMENCE *v.* 4. (A term retained at Cambridge: now obs. at Oxford.) Hence *gen.* to enter upon one's career or office.

1852 C. A. BRISTED *Eng. University* (ed. 2) 348 The M.A. *incepts* in about three years and two months from the time of taking his first degree. **1888** MULLINGER in *Encycl. Brit.* XXIII. 835/1 What is technically known as admission to that degree [*licentia docendi*] was really nothing more nor less than receiving the chancellor's permission to incept. **1895** RASHDALL *Univ. Europe in Mid. Ages* I. v. 288 The 'Licentiate' was not regarded as a full 'Master' or 'Doctor' till be had 'incepted'. **1896** *Daily News* 28 Oct. 3/4 Cambridge..Permission to incept in surgery has been granted by the Degree Committee of the Special Board of Medicine to H. H. C——, M.A., M.B., of Clare College.

3. *trans.* (*Biol.*) To take in, as an organism or cell.

1863 H. J. CARTER in *Ann. Nat. Hist.* Ser. III. 45 Each time after incepting a grain it went away to some distance. **1885** E. A. SCHÄFER in *Proc. R. Soc.* XXXVIII. 88 The intussusception of particles is one of the most characteristic phenomena exhibited by amœboid cells, which will carry such incepted matters along with them in their slow movements from place to place.

Hence **in'cepted, in'cepting** *ppl. adjs.*

1802 PALEY *Nat. Theol.* xxvii. (1819) 482 In plants..the incepted organization, though formed within and through and by a preceding organization, is not corrupted by its corruption, or destroyed by its dissolution. **1861** M. PATTISON *Serm.* (1885) 60 The love of truth..which is as unmistakable in the incepting scholar as in the consummate scientific intellect. **1884** F. HALL in *Nation* (N.Y.) XXXIX. 338/3 An introductory guide to Sanskrit..for incepting students whose mother-tongue is English. **1893** FOWLER *Hist. C.C.C.* (O.H.S.) 277 One of the incepting Doctors. **1895** RAVEN *Hist. Suffolk* 58 The joint action of the village community, rather than the mandate of an incepting thane.

inception (ɪn'sɛpʃən). [ad. L. *inceptiōn-em*, n. of action from *incipĕre* to begin. Cf. OF. *inception, -cion* (15-16th c.).]

1. The action of entering upon some undertaking, process, or stage of existence; origination, beginning, commencement.

a **1483** *Liber Niger* in *Househ. Ord.* (1792) 18 From his first inception, tyll the day of his dethe, his house stode aftyr one vnyformitie. **1626** BACON *Sylva* §316 The Inception of Putrefaction hath in it a Maturation. **1677** HALE *Prim. Orig. Man* I. ii. 69 The very repugnancy in Nature of successive Beings to be without an inception, or eternal. **1827** JARMAN *Powell's Devises* II. 299 Cases in which..the devise, according to the state of events at the time of its inception, never could have had an object. **1866** GROVE *Contrib. Sc.* in *Corr. Phys. Forces* (1874) 211 Minute organisms which appear so to speak, full-blown at their inception. **1878** LECKY *Eng. in 18th C.* I. ii. 213 Between the inception and the execution of the project Louis XIV died.

2. In University use: The action of incepting; see quots. 1888, 1895, and cf. COMMENCEMENT 2.

c **1680** WOOD *Annals* (ed. Gutch, 1792) I. 60 After he had feasted the Scholars at his Inception, they like clownes left him. *Ibid.* 66 There was no scholar, if of any account, but did show himself bountiful at his Inception. **1841** PEACOCK *Stat. Cambridge* 11 There yet remained to be performed [before creation] the exercises of inception or commencement. **1888** MULLINGER in *Encycl. Brit.* XXIII. 835/1 By inception was implied the master's formal entrance upon, and commencement of, the functions of a duly licensed teacher, and his recognition as such by his brothers in the profession. **1895** RASHDALL *Univ. Europe in Mid. Ages* I. iv. 232 In our English Universities, conservative as they are in many things, every trace of the ceremony of Inception has at length unhappily disappeared; only the preliminary ceremonial of the License survives. *Ibid.* v. 452 An interval of half a year commonly elapsed between License and Inception... He was then free to give his formal inaugural lecture or rather disputation in the presence of the Faculty, to receive the Magisterial *biretta* and the book,..to receive the kiss of fellowship, and to take his seat upon the magisterial Cathedra.

3. The action of taking in, as an organism.

a **1849** E. A. POE (O.), The result is the immersion of the mouth and nostrils, and the inception, during efforts to breathe while beneath the surface, of water into the lungs.

inceptive (ɪn'sɛptɪv), *a.* and *sb.* [a. obs. F. *inceptif, -ive* (16th c. in Godef.), ad. L. type **inceptīv-us*, f. *incept-*, ppl. stem of *incipĕre* to begin: see -IVE.] **A.** *adj.*

1. Beginnning, commencing, incipient; relating to or of the nature of a beginning, initial.

1662 J. SPARROW tr. *Behme's Rem. Wks., 2nd Apol. Tylcken* 10 Whether is it an inceptive or beginning Mystery, or an Eternall one? *a* **1763** BYROM *Art Eng. Poetry* (R.), You see, in speaking, or by sound, or ink, The grand inceptive caution is to think. **1873** EARLE *Philol. Eng. Tongue* (ed. 2) §247 The various accents of the Newfoundland dog..are manifestations wonderfully like inceptive speech.

2. *Gram.* and *Logic.* Expressing the beginning of action, as ***inceptive verb, inceptive tenses, inceptive proposition***: see quots.

1656 TRAPP *Comm. Rom.* vii. 7 The word *concupisco* is inceptive. **1706** PHILLIPS s.v., Verbs Inceptive, the same as Inchoatives. **1725** WATTS *Logic* III. ii. §4 Inceptive and desitive propositions..as the fogs vanish as the sun rises; but the fogs have not yet begun to vanish; therefore the sun is not yet risen. **1751** HARRIS *Hermes* I. vii. Wks. (1841) 152 The three first of these tenses we call the inceptive present, the inceptive past, and the inceptive future. **1824** L. MURRAY *Eng. Gram.* (ed. 5) I. 128, 'I am going to write'; 'I am about to write'. These have been called the Inceptive future, as they note the commencement of an action. **1885** *Athenæum* 23 May 660/1 Nor has any attempt been made to give the inceptive force of the participle מצאת [being brought forth] in Gen. xxxviii. 25.

b. Beginning a word; initial.

1859 R. F. BURTON *Centr. Afr.* in *Jrnl. Geog. Soc.* XXIX. 54 *note*, This [*mvinyo*] is..supplied with the truly S. African inceptive *m* before a consonant.

†**3.** *Geom.* Used of a locus deficient in some particular dimension, but generating by its motion another which has that dimension. *Obs.*

1706 PHILLIPS, *Inceptive Magnitude*, a Word us'd by Dr. Wallis to express the first Principles in Geometry, which, though of no Magnitude themselves, are yet capable of producing such; thus a Point has no Magnitude it self, but is inceptive of a Line. **1727-41** CHAMBERS *Cycl.* s.v., So a line, though it have no breadth, is yet inceptive of breadth; that is, capable, by its motion, of producing a surface which has breadth.

B. *sb.* **1. a.** *Gram.* An inceptive verb. **b.** *Logic.* An inceptive proposition.

1612 BRINSLEY *Pos. Parts* (1669) 126 What mean you by Inceptives ending in *sco*? **1669** MILTON *Accedence* Wks. (1847) 466/1 Verbs called Inceptives ending in *sco*, borrow their Preterperfect Tense from the Verb wherof they are deriv'd, as *tepesco tepui* from *tepeo.* **1725** WATTS *Logic* II. ii. §6 Inceptives and desitives, which relate to the beginning or ending of any thing; as, the Latin tongue is not yet forgotten. No man before Orpheus wrote Greek verse. **1751** HARRIS *Hermes* I. vii. Wks. (1841) 154 A species of verbs..called inchoatives or inceptives.

†**2.** (*pl.*) Initial circumstances; beginnings. *Obs.*

1728 North *Mem. Musick* (1846) 14 In these inceptives of musick. *a* **1734** —— *Exam.* I. iii. §63 (1740) 171 One may observe a different Scope in each, as the Persons, however close to the Inceptives of the Movement, were differently circumstanced.

Hence **in'ceptively** *adv.*, in an inceptive way.

1856 in Webster.

inceptor (ɪn'sɛptə(r), -ɔː(r)). [a. L. *inceptor*, agent-n. from *incipĕre* to begin: cf. obs. F. *incepteur* (16th c.).]

1. One who incepts or is about to incept in a University.

1479 W. Paston [at Oxford] in *Paston Lett.* No. 830 III. 246, I wold be Inceptor be fore Mydsomer. **1552** Huloet, Inceptours or regent masters in the vniuersities, *candidati*. **1574** in Peacock *Stat. Cambridge* (1841) App. A. p. xxi. **1650** in Quincy *Hist. Harvard Univ.* (1840) I. 518 In case any of the Sophisters, Questionists, or Inceptors, fail in the premises..they shall be deferred to the following year. **1669** Evelyn *Diary* 10 July, Next followed the Disputations of the Inceptor-Doctors in Medicine..Then disputed the Inceptors of Law..Lastly, Inceptors in Theology. **1706** Hearne *Collect.* 7 Mar. (O.H.S.) I. 201 Dr. Hudson, then an Inceptor in Arts, bore a Musquet. **1865** *Standard* 5 July, The proctors [at Oxford] have, this morning, issued..the list of 'inceptors' of the present year—by which we mean the list of those who, by proceeding to some superior degree, have made themselves members of convocation. **1895** Rashdall *Univ. Europe* I. v. 453 The evening concluded with a banquet given at the expense of the Inceptor or a party of Inceptors to the Masters and others.

2. *gen.* A beginner. *rare*$^{-0}$.

1706 Phillips, *Inceptor*, a Beginner, or Enterprizer.

Hence **in'ceptorship**.

1831 Sir W. Hamilton *Discuss., St. Eng. Univ.* (1852) 405 The forms of Inceptorship, and the Examinations of some of the Nations, still connected the Faculty of Arts with this venerable site.

† **'incerate**, *v. Obs. rare*$^{-0}$. [f. ppl. stem of L. *incērāre* to spread wax on, overlay with wax, f. *in-* (IN-^{2}) + *cērāre* to wax, f. *cēra* wax.]

1623 Cockeram, *Incerate* [printed *Incernate*], to couer with wax, to seere. **1727** Bailey vol. II, *Incerated.*

† **ince'ration**. *Obs.* [n. of action from prec.; so in mod.F. (Littré).] The action of covering with wax; the bringing of a substance to the consistency of moist wax.

1610 B. Jonson *Alch.* II. iii, He's ripe for inceration, he stands warm, In his ash-fire. **1612** Woodall *Surg. Mate* Wks. (1653) 272 *Inceration* is the mixture of humidity with that which is dry, by a gentle and not hasty combibition to the consistence of mollified wax.

† **in'cerative**, *a. Obs. rare*$^{-0}$. [f. ppl. stem of L. *incērāre* (INCERATE *v.*) + -IVE.] (See quot.)

1611 Cotgr., *Inceratif*, inceratiue, waxing; cleauing, or sticking vnto. **1818** in Todd.

† **incere'monious**, *a. Obs. rare.* [IN-^{3}.] Void of ceremony; unceremonious.

1651 Bp. Hall *Susurrium* xvii, Another approves better of a simple and inceremonious devotion. **1687** *Good Advice* 40 Who..would not be brought to so Inceremonious a way of Worship as that of the Calvinists.

† **in'cern**, *v. Obs. rare*$^{-0}$. [ad. L. *incern-ĕre*, f. *in-* (IN-^{2}) + *cernĕre* to sift.] To sift (a matter); to examine closely.

1656 Blount *Glossogr.*, *Incerning*, sifting, trying by sifting, looking narrowly into. *Scotch Papers.* **1658** Phillips, *Incern*, to sift, to examine strictly.

† **in'cernicle**. *Obs. rare.* [ad. L. *incerniculum* sieve, f. *incernĕre*: see prec.] A sieve.

1657 Tomlinson *Renou's Disp.* 484 Sieves made of Horses hairs..called..sometimes excussive incernicles. **1657** *Physical Dict.*, *Incernicle*, a sieve.

incert, obs. erron. form of INSERT.

† **in'certain**, *a.* and *sb. Obs.* [a. F. *incertain* (Oresme, 14th c.), f. *in-* (IN-^{3}) + *certain*, after L. *incert-us* uncertain.]

A. *adj.* Not certain; = UNCERTAIN (in various senses).

1491 Caxton *Vitas Patr.* (W. de W. 1495) II. 280 b/2 All is incertayne duryng this lyfe. **1549** Coverdale, etc. *Erasm. Par. Jas.* iv. G j, Thys is a thinge moste incertayn, how long they shall lyue, and a thing moste certain that they shall not lyue longe. **1611** Shaks. *Wint. T.* v. i. 29 What Dangers.. May drop vpon his Kingdome, and deuoure Incertaine lookers on. **1655** Sir E. Nicholas in *N. Papers* (Camden) II. 293 What he will be able to doe is incertain. **1716** M. Davies *Athen. Brit.* II. To Rdr. 26 Christian Hope will or ought to be my not incertain support. **1741** T. Robinson *Gavelkind* ii. 16 All the Possessions were incertain; and this Incertainty was the cause [etc.].

B. *sb.* **1.** Uncertainty.

1502 *Ord. Crysten Men* (W. de W. 1506) II. xviii. 136 The incertayne of the houre of a moment and of the estate.

2. Name of an obsolete game at cards.

1689 Shadwell *Bury F.* I. i, With ombre, crimp, comet or incertain.

† **in'certain**, *v. Obs. rare.* [f. IN-^{2} + CERTAIN *a.*; cf. ENCERTAIN.] To make certain, assure.

1628 Feltham *Resolves* II. xxviii. 89 The first hath more incertain'd honor; but lesse safety: The latter is humbly secure.

[**incertain**, a frequent scribal and editorial error for *in certain*, in truth, certainly (CERTAIN *sb.* 7): e.g. in Pauli's *Gower* I. 150, 245, etc.]

† **in'certainly**, *adv. Obs.* [f. INCERTAIN *a.* + -LY^{2}.] = UNCERTAINLY, in various senses.

1530 Palsgr. 66 Other sixe used of their auctours incertaynly, sometyme as masculynes, sometyme as femynines. **1572** Huloet, To aunswere incertainly and ambiguouslye. **1612** Brinsley *Lud. Lit.* 65 The learners shall still goe incertainly and fearefully. **1714** Scroggs *Courts-leet* (ed. 3) 171 If the Verdict find the Matter incertainly.

† **in'certainty**. *Obs.* [a. OF. *incertaineté* (1477 in Godef.; in Cotgr. 1611), f. *incertain*, after *certaineté* CERTAINTY.] = UNCERTAINTY, in various senses.

1484 Caxton *Curiall* 6 To ryse & mounte fro certaynte to Incertaynte. **1579** Fenton *Guicciard.* I. (1599) 28 Mens.. hopes full of suspicions and incertainties. *c* **1600** Shaks. *Sonn.* cvii, Incertenties now crowne them-selues assur'de. **1684** B. Hale *Pref. to Contempl. St. Man* (1699) p. iii, Here thou mayest see the incertainty of Mortal Life. **1792** T. Jefferson *Writ.* (1859) III. 330 There is great incertainty in the meaning of the term.

incertitude (ɪn'sɜːtɪtjuːd). [a. F. *incertitude* (14th c. in Hatz.-Darm.), ad. L. type **incertitūdo*, f. *in-* (IN-^{3}) + *certitūdo* CERTITUDE.]

1. Subjective uncertainty; the state or condition of not being certain or sure of something; absence of assurance or confidence; doubt, hesitation.

1601 Holland *Pliny* XVIII. xxv. 586 The cause of this incertitude and difficultie [as to the beginning of Spring], is partly the convexitie of the cope of heaven, and partly the diverse climates observed in the globe of the earth. *a* **1631** Donne in *Select.* (1840) 207 The fearful man..falls into labyrinths, of incertitudes, and impertinencies, and.. anxieties, and irresolutions. **1677** Gale *Crt. Gentiles* III. 158 For Scepticisme and incertitude is the punishment of such temeritie. **1756** Burke *Vind. Nat. Soc.* Wks. I. 63 Thus we were brought back to our old incertitude. **1833** Alison *Europe* v. §63 (1849) I. 621 The king was distracted by the most cruel incertitude.

2. Objective uncertainty; uncertain or insecure condition; insecurity.

1603 Holland *Plutarch's Mor.* 875 The incertitude and instabilitie of this life. **1692** Locke *Toleration* i. Wks. 1727 II. 241 Let us grant..that in this Incertitude of Things, the safest..Way..is to follow his Dictates. **1802** Corry *Mem. A. Berkeley* 152 The incertitude of his reconciliation with Miss Vernon.

3. Indistinctness of visible forms; obscurity.

1883 *Century Mag.* XXVI. 821 Visit it..towards the close of day, when the gray incertitude lies on the mighty city.

incessable (ɪn'sɛsəb(ə)l), *a.* Now *rare* or *Obs.* Also 6 -ceissabill, 7 -ceassable, *erron.* -ceasible. [ad. L. *incessābil-is*, f. *in-* (IN-^{3}) + **cessābilis*, f. *cessāre* to CEASE: cf. F. *incessable* (15th c. in Godef.). In 16–17th c. sometimes assimilated to *cease*.] Of unceasing character; ceaseless, incessant.

1545 Raynold *Byrth Mankynde* IV. vi. (1634) 198 Incessable sweating. **1560** Rolland *Crt. Venus* IV. 492, I sall vphald his seruice Inceissabill. **1624** Heywood *Gunaik.* IX. 443 His liver and heart is perpetually tyred on by a ravenous vulture, who still renewes his inceasible torments. **1627–77** Feltham *Resolves* II. v. 168 The life of man is the Incessable walk of time.

incessably (ɪn'sɛsəblɪ), *adv.* [f. prec. + -LY^{2}.] Without cessation; ceaselessly, incessantly.

1398 Trevisa *Barth. De P.R.* II. viii. (MS. Harl. 614) 9 b/1 Also he meueþ incessable [*ed.* **1495** -bly] for sich a loue faileþ neuer. **1502** *Ord. Crysten Men* (W. de W. 1506) v. iii. 383 The lamentacyons, and the complayntes that they make in sessybly. **1893** *Proceed. World's Congr. Deaf* (1894) 174 Our deaf mute mimics continued incessably to give assault to these prejudices.

incessancy (ɪn'sɛsənsɪ). [f. next: see -ANCY.] The quality of being incessant or unceasing; unbroken continuance.

1615 Chapman *Odyss.* I. 248 Whose white bones wasting lie..with th' incessancy Of showers pour'd down upon them. **1665** R. B. *Comm. 2 Tales* 59 By the incessancy of his Prayers, Heaven's wrath was appeased. **1853** Lynch *Chr. Practicalness* in *Lett. to Scattered* etc. 350 The incessancy and vastness of human labour. **1883** *Contemp. Rev.* Sept. 457 The incessancy and minuteness of their bureaucratic study.

incessant (ɪn'sɛsənt). *a.* [prob. a. F. *incessant* (implied in *incessamment*, 1358 in Hatz.-Darm.), ad. late L. *incessānt-em*, (implied in *incessānter*), f. *in-* (IN-^{3}) + *cessānt-em*, pres. pple. of *cessāre* to cease.]

1. That does not cease; unceasing, ceaseless, continual, either in duration or repetition.

1532 More *Confut. Tindale* Wks. 362/1 These menne.. with their incessaunt searche fynde out false causes. **1590** Shaks. *Com. Err.* I. i. 71 The incessant weepings of my wife. **1666** Dryden *Ann. Mirab.* cclxxviii, And now four days the sun had seen our woes; Four nights the moon beheld th' incessant fire. **1726** Swift *Gulliver* I. ii, An incessant noise like that of a water-mill. **1852** M. Arnold *Future* vii, Cities will crowd to its edge In a blacker incessanter line. **1885** F. Temple *Relat. Relig. & Sc.* v. 140 The pivots of all the prophetical teaching are the incessant inculcation of justice and mercy.

b. *transf.* Of persons and things in reference to their action.

1749 Smollett *Regicide* III. iv, The rude flint Yields to the incessant drop. **1820** Shelley *Witch Atl.* l, The incessant hail with stony clash Ploughed up the waters. **1863** Bright *Sp. Amer.* 16 June, A few persons..have been incessant in their condemnation of the North.

† **2.** Unending, endless, everlasting. *Obs.*

1557 F. Seager *Sch. Vertue* 845 in *Babees Bk.*, Eternall blisse where incessaunt ioie continually is. **1561** Daus tr. *Bullinger on Apoc.* (1573) 26 Which doctrine surely is incessant or perpetuall to the Church of Christ. **1564** Bulleyn *Dial. agst. Pest.* (1888) 135 To thee, oh heauenlie father, be incessaunte honour and glorie.

3. quasi-*adv.* Without intermission or pause; unceasingly.

1557 Phaer *Æneid* VII. (1558) S iv, A swarme of bees beset the bows, Incessant thick with noise. **1703** Rowe *Ulyss.* I. i. 314 Do they not..call Incessant on his tardy Vengeance? **1871** B. Taylor *Faust* (1875) I. vi. 103 The world's a ball Doth rise and fall And Roll incessant.

incessantly (ɪn'sɛsəntlɪ), *adv.* [f. prec. + -LY^{2}: cf. F. *incessamment*, L. *incessānter*, both found earlier than the adj. on the type of which they are formed.]

1. In an incessant manner; without cessation; unceasingly.

14.. *Lament. Mary Magd.* lxxxv, Myne hert is wounded with thy charite, It brenneth, it flameth incessantly. **1481** Caxton *Godefroy* ccix. 306 Thise turkes..pourchaced incessantly alle the harme & euyl that they myght. **1534** More *Comf. agst. Trib.* I. Wks. 1161/1 When Sainct Peter was in prieson..the whole churche without intermission prayed incessantely for him. *c* **1611** Chapman *Iliad* XIX. 349 The frosty north wind blowes a cold thicke sleete..flakes after flakes, incessantly descending. **1682** Norris *Hierocles* 3 They incessantly enjoy the divine felicity. **1712** Budgell *Spect.* No. 404 ¶6 Cælia's Tongue runs incessantly. **1776** Gibbon *Decl. & F.* xii. I. 330 He was incessantly tormented by factions which he could not asswage. **1880** Haughton *Phys. Geog.* iv. 190 During which time heavy rain pours incessantly.

† **2.** For ever; perpetually. *Obs.*

1481 Caxton *Myrr.* I. i. 5 Certainly god was to fore, and shal be incessantly after without ende & withoute begynnyng.

† **3.** Without pausing; instantly; immediately.

1472 *Plumpton Corr.* (Camden) p. lxxvii, The said Joan making like response incessantly to the said Sir William. **1649** Lovelace *Poems* (1864) 41 My oathes..then with thee incessantly grew cold. **1700** Congreve *Way of World* v. viii, If I see him I fear I shall turn to Stone, and petrifie incessantly. *a* **1807** A. Addison *Charge to Jury* (Cent.), I shall incessantly order him to be stripped of his gown.

in'cessantness. [f. INCESSANT *a.* + -NESS.] The quality or condition of being incessant.

1727 in Bailey vol. II. **1865** M. Arnold *Ess. Crit.* v. (1875) 193 Because of this incessantness of his barking [he] cannot get listened to. **1890** *Spectator* 22 Nov., The men and women..will detest its sobriety, the incessantness of its officers' admonitions.

† **in'cession.** *Obs. rare.* [a. obs. F. *incession* 'pace, gait, or going' (Cotgr.), ad. L. *incessiōn-em*, n. of action from *incēdĕre* to go on, walk.] Onward motion; progression, locomotion.

1651 Biggs *New Disp.* ¶197 The slow and necessary incession of mediocrity. **1658** Sir T. Browne *Gard. Cyrus* iii. 56 The incession or locall motion of animals. **1845** M. J. Higgins *Ess.* (1875) 215 Elegant young men unsurpassable in speed, endurance, and oiliness of incession [in dancing].

incession, var. INSESSION, *Obs.*, a hip-bath.

incest ('ɪnsɛst). [ad. L. *incestus* (*u* stem) or *incestum* (neuter of *incestus* adj. impure, unchaste), from *in-* (IN-^{3}) + *castus* chaste, pure. Cf. OF. *inceste* (14th c. in Hatz.-Darm.). In sense 2, ad. L. *incestus*, F. *inceste*, an incestuous person.]

1. a. The crime of sexual intercourse or cohabitation between persons related within the degrees within which marriage is prohibited; sexual commerce of near kindred.

a **1225** *Ancr. R.* 204 Incest..is bitwhwe sibbe, vleshliche oðer gostliche. *a* **1300** *Cursor M.* 27942 Incest, þat es for to lij bi þat þi sibman has line bi, or if þou has don þat sin wit ani of þin aun kin. *c* **1440** *Jacob's Well* (E.E.T.S.) 162 Neyther may be weddyd to oþeres kyn, in-to þe fyfte degre, ne medle wyth hem; for ȝif þei don, it is incest. **1548** Udall *Erasm. Par. Luke* iii. (R.), Thys holy man coulde not abide such incest and vnnaturalnesse of mariage in a king's house. **1603** Shaks. *Meas. for M.* III. i. 139 Is't not a kinde of Incest, to take life From thine owne sisters shame? **1840** Macaulay *Ess., Ranke* (1851) II. 137 Its annals are black with treason, murder, and incest. **1868** Farrar *Seekers* III. iii. (1875) 299 Hideous charges of cannibalism and incest.

b. ***spiritual incest*** (in *R. C. Ch.*): (*a*) Marriage or sexual connexion between persons related by spiritual affinity, or with a person under a vow of chastity, etc. (*b*) The holding by the same person of two benefices, one of which depends on the collation of the other.

a **1225** [see 1]. **1532** More *Confut. Tindale* Wks. 361/1 Mayster Martine Luther hymself..toke out of religion a spouse of Christ..liueth with her openly..in shamefull incest and abhominable bycherye. **1727–41** Chambers *Cycl.* s.v., Spiritual incest is understood of a..beneficiary who.. holds two benefices, the one whereof depends on the collation of the other. Such a spiritual incest renders both.. benefices void.

†**2.** A person guilty of incest. *Obs. rare.*

1484 CAXTON *Fables of Æsop* VI. iv, Thow arte an inceste & lechour, For thow knowest naturelly both thy moder and thy doughter.

3. *attrib.* and *Comb.*

1633 FORD *'Tis Pity* v. iv, When my young incest-monger comes. **1819** SHELLEY *Let.* 16 Nov. (1964) II. 531 The incest scene of Amon & Tamar is tremendous. **1921** D. H. LAWRENCE *Psychoanal. & Unconscious* i. 20 At the root of almost every neurosis lies some incest-craving. *Ibid.* ii. 31 And this brings us finally to incest, even incest-worship. **1933** LD. RAGLAN *Jocasta's Crime* i. 6 Having eliminated reason, instinct, and religion as bases of the incest taboo, what have we left? The answer is magic. *Ibid.* ii. 15 There are no stronger upholders of the incest taboo than those very Australian tribes who believe that the child has no physical connexion with the father. **1946** KOESTLER *Thieves in Night* 162 The intimacy of life in the smaller Communes acts as a gradually materialising incest-barrier. **1949** —— *Insight & Outlook* xxiii. 323 Examples of such archetypes or primordial experiences are..the incest-motif. **1949** M. MEAD *Male & Female* ix. 199 Usually the primary incest-taboos are extended in various ways. **1963** A. HERON *Towards Quaker View of Sex* 56 Incest thoughts appear in human dreams. *Ibid.* 59 The sexual nature of this relationship is reinforced and with it feelings of incest-guilt, especially in the child. This situation may cause the boy or girl later to shirk contact with the opposite sex for fear of violating the incest barrier.

incestancy. *rare*$^{-1}$. [irreg. formation.] ? = INCEST.

1602 MIDDLETON *Blurt, Master-Constable* III. i. 71 Incestancy dwell on his rivell'd brow That weds for dirt.

†**in'cestial,** *a. Obs. rare.* [irreg. f. INCEST + -AL[1]: cf. *bestial.*] = INCESTUOUS.

1581 NUCE *Seneca's Octavia* I. iv, And with incestiall love benummed quite His brother Germanicks daughter. *Ibid.*, To which unlucky incestiall brydall bed.

incestuous (ɪn'sɛstjuːəs), *a.* Also 6–7 **-teous, -tious.** [ad. L. *incestuōs-us*, f. *incestu-s* INCEST: see -OUS; cf. F. *incestueux, -euse* (13th c. in Godef.).]

1. a. Guilty of incest.

1552 ABP. HAMILTON *Catech.* (1884) 10 Incesteous personis. *a* **1592** H. SMITH *Wks.* (1867) II. 368 Caius Caligula, that wicked and incestuous emperor. **1651** C. CARTWRIGHT *Cert. Relig.* I. 99 The [Romish] Church reputed those, who married together after their vowes, not only for adulterers, but also for incestuous persons. **1746** COLLINS *Odes, Fear* 38 Wrapt in thy cloudy veil, th' incestuous Queen Sigh'd the sad call her son and husband heard. **1855** MILMAN *Lat. Chr.* IV. vi. (1864) II. 319 The sway of an incestuous female Martina.

fig. **1591** SYLVESTER *Du Bartas* I. iii. 520 You City-Vipers, that (incestious) joyn Use upon use, begetting Coyn of Coyn!

†**b.** Loosely or more vaguely: Adulterous. *Obs.*

1632 HEYWOOD *1st Pt. Iron Age* II. Wks. 1874 III. 291, I would not for the world, Priam should send Incestious Hellen backe on tearmes of peace. **1681** COLVIL *Whigs Supplic.* (1751) 30.

2. a. Of the nature of or involving incest.

1532 MORE *Confut. Tindale* Wks. 394/2 These shameles heretykes liue in open shamefull incestuous lechery, and call it matrimonie. *c* **1555** HARPSFIELD *Divorce Hen. VIII* (Camden) 238 Incestuous copulation should not once be accounted under the name of marriage. **1581** MARBECK *Bk. of Notes* 486 He openlie condemned the incestious Matrimonie of Herode with Herodias. **1625** K. LONG tr. *Barclay's Argenis* V xix. 399 The feare of the mention of such an incestuous marriage. **1766** WARBURTON *Ded. to Freethinkers* Postscr., Wks. 1811 I. 182 Virtuous love, not adulterous or incestuous. **1838** THIRLWALL *Greece* xiii. II. 177 He had even trampled on the laws of Persia by an incestuous union with his sisters. **1879** GREEN *Read. Eng. Hist.* vii. 33 As the new Queen was Eadwig's kinswoman, the religious opinion of the day regarded his marriage as incestuous.

†**b.** *fig.* Applied to other crimes committed between persons nearly akin. *Obs.*

1744 ARMSTRONG *Preserv. Health* III. 536 (Seager) Her legions in incestuous murder [i.e. civil war] mix'd.

c. *Fig.* use of sense 2 a.

1869 D. G. ROSSETTI *Let* 27 Aug. (1965) II. 727 'Solemn poetry' belongs to the class of phrases absolutely forbidden I think *in* poetry. It is intellectually incestuous,—poetry seeking to beget its emotional offspring on its own identity. **1971** *Listener* 2 Sept. 307/3 Systematising..the old-boy network..would almost undoubtedly exacerbate the incestuous intolerance of the present scene.

†**3.** Begotten of incest. *Obs.*

1588 ALLEN *Admon.* (1842) 11 An incestuous bastard, begotten and borne in sinne, of an infamous curtesan. **1621** G. SANDYS *Ovid's Met.* x. (1626) 206 Th' incesteous infant, now at perfect groth Within the tree; indeuors to get forth.

in'cestuously, *adv.* [f. prec. + -LY[2].] In an incestuous manner: in the way of incest.

1549 COVERDALE, etc. *Erasm. Par. 1 Cor.* vii. (R.), Theyr children, as borne incestuously and by vnlawfull meanes. **1655** FULLER *Ch. Hist.* II. v. §27 An English Count who lived incestuously with his own Kinswoman. *a* **1700** DRYDEN (J.), Macareus and Canace, son and daughter to Æolus..loved each other incestuously.

in'cestuousness. [f. as prec. + -NESS.] Incestuous quality or character.

1649 BP. HALL *Cases Consc.* Addit. iii. (R.), The knowledge of the horrible incestuousness of this match.

inch (ɪnʃ), *sb.*[1] Forms: 1 ynce, ince, 3 unche, 4–6 ench(e, ynche, 4–7 ynch, 5–6 inche. 6 unch, *Sc.* insch, 4– inch. [OE. *ynce*:—**unkja*, a. L. *uncia* twelfth part, inch (cf. OUNCE). A word of early adoption, not in the other Teutonic languages.]

1. a. A measure of length, the twelfth part of a foot. Hence, a measure of surface and of solidity (explicitly ***square*** or ***superficial***, ***cubic*** or ***solid inch***) equal to the content respectively of a square or cube the sides of which are of this length.

c **1000** *Laws of Æthelbert* c. 67 ʒife ofer ynce, scilling; æt twam yncum, tweȝen. *c* **1000** *Laws of Ælfred* c 45 Wund inces lang. *c* **1000** in *Sal. & Sat.* (Kemble) 180 He [Adam] wæs vi and cx ynca lang. *c* **1205** LAY. 23970 He wunde afeng feouwer unchene long. *c* **1300** *Havelok* 1034 An inch or more. *c* **1380** *Sir Ferumb.* 3302 þer ne wanteþ noȝt enches foure. **1398** TREVISA *Barth. De P.R.* XIX. cxxix. (1495) 937 An ynche is leste parti of mesures of feldes. *c* **1440** *Jacob's Well* (E.E.T.S.) 128 þis is .v. inche thycke. *c* **1500** *Melusine* xix. 104 Whiche at his birth brought in hys mouthe a grete & long toth, that apyered without an ench long & more. **1559** W. CUNNINGHAM *Cosmogr. Glasse* 56 In..measures, we do go from a barly corne, to a finger breadth: from a finger breadth, to an unch: from an unch, to an hand breadth. **1588** SHAKS. *L.L.L.* v. ii. 193 The Princesse bids you tell, How many inches doth fill vp one mile? **1760** *Phil. Trans.* LI. 784, 9 London inches are equal to 8·447 Paris inches and decimals. **1824** R. STUART *Hist. Steam Engine* 200 A column of water equal to ten pounds on the [square] inch. **1837** WHEWELL *Hist. Induct. Sc.* (1857) I. 163 Each inch being the thickness of six grains of barley. *Mod.* The gill contains 8·665 cubic inches. The pint contains 4 gills or 34·660 inches.

b. As the unit of measurement of rainfall: That quantity of water which would cover a surface to the depth of an inch; equivalent to 3630 cubic feet on an acre, or about 4⅗ gallons on every square yard.

1845 STOCQUELER *Handbk. Brit. India* (1854) 264 The rains set in fairly at the beginning of June..Two inches in the twenty-four hours often fall; sometimes three. **1896** G. J. SYMONS *Brit. Rainfall* 20 On the western slope of Sca Fell, between it and Wastwater..mean fall about 90 inches. **1896** *Whitaker's Almanack* 53 An 'Inch of Rain' means a gallon of water spread over a surface of nearly two square feet, or 3630 cubic feet = 100 tons upon an acre.

c. As the unit of measurement of atmospheric or other pressure: That amount of pressure which balances the weight of a column of mercury, an inch high, in the mercurial barometer.

[**1727–41** CHAMBERS *Cycl.* s.v. *Barometer*, On the top of Snowdon-hill..Dr. Halley found the mercury lower by three inches eight tenths than at the foot thereof. **1835** *Penny Cycl.* III. 37/1 The mean height of the barometer in London is stated at 29·88 inches.] **1873** RALFE *Phys. Chem.* 134 Oil, to which a few drops of bile have been added, passes readily through animal membranes under the slight pressure of 0·068 to 0·132 inches of mercury. **1896** *Whitaker's Almanack* 602 Atmospherical pressure was least, 28·6 inches, on the 14th [Nov. 1894]; greatest, 30·6, on the 30th.

d. As a unit of measurement of the flow of water (esp. in mining, whence specifically called ***miner's inch***): That amount of water that will pass in 24 hours through an opening of 1 square inch under a constant pressure of 6 inches.

1858 LARDNER *Hand-bk. Nat. Phil., Hydrost.*, etc. 238 The rate of discharge from the orifice is called the inch of water, and is the hydraulic unit by which the discharge from pumps is expressed. **1877** RAYMOND *Statist. Mines & Mining* 90 *note*, One 24-hour miners' inch is equivalent to 2,230 cubic feet of water. *Ibid.* 95 Water at that time cost 75 cents an inch. **1882** *Rep. to Ho. Repr. Prec. Met. U.S.* 646 The nearest even figure, is 17,000 gallons in twenty-four hours, and, in the absence of any legal determination, this may be regarded as the approximately correct equivalent of a miner's inch of water.

2. *transf.* and *fig.* **a.** A very small measure, distance, amount, or degree; the least amount or part (of space, time, material or immaterial things); a very little; a 'bit'. Esp. in phr. ***within an inch of one's life*** (or †***skin***): almost to the point of death; so as to be nearly killed; freq. hyperbolically and *fig.*

a **1350** *Birth of Jesus* 40 in Horstmann *Altengl. Leg.* (1875) 66 þe tyme hem þoȝte longe Inouȝ, ech vnche hem þouȝte a sponne. *c* **1400** *Rom. Rose* 5101 But thou art not an inch the nerre. **1582** BENTLEY *Mon. Matrones* III. 360 Neither will I suffer my selfe..to depart one ynch from thy holie commandments. **1594** KYD *Sp. Trag.* IV. in Hazl. *Dodsley* V. 114 There is not left in him one inch of man. **1700** S. L. tr. *Fryke's Voy. E. Ind.* 76 Tho' thousands of their Men dropt, they would not give ground an Inch. **1726** G. ROBERTS *4 Yrs. Voy.* 30, I will drub you, you Dog, within an Inch of your Life, and that Inch too. **1781** COWPER *Let.* 4 Oct., Wks. (1876) 85 That I may avail myself of every inch of time. **1839** DICKENS *Nich. Nick.* xiii, I'll flog you within an inch of your life, and spare you that. **1854** B. P. SHILLABER *Life & Sayings Mrs. Partington* 81 I'll be tempered to whip you within an inch of your skin. **1894** H. NISBET *Bush Girl's Rom.* 156 He could not see an inch before him. **1896** W. D. HOWELLS *Impressions & Experiences* 74 The defendent..had invited her to come down the street to a certain point, and be beaten within an inch of her life. **1909** L. M. MONTGOMERY *Anne of Avonlea* xii. 126 The grammar class were parsed and analysed within an inch of their lives. **1932** 'E. M. DELAFIELD' *Thank Heaven Fasting* III. i. 250 She's always bullied Cecily within an inch of her life. **1939** L. M. MONTGOMERY *Anne of Ingleside* i. 12 He said that..everybody else would be dressed within an inch of her life. *Ibid.* iv. 30 If I had talked to my parents like that..I would have been whipped within an inch of my life.

b. Applied to material things: †(*a*) A small piece or fragment; (*b*) A person of small stature.

1573 *Satir. Poems Reform.* xxxix. 94 Thocht the wallis wes wycht, ȝit dowbell battrie brak thame al in inschis. **1884** BLACK *Jud. Shaks.* iv, You imp, you inch, you elfin queen, you!

3. Phrases. †**a.** ***at an inch, at inches***: close at hand; (ready) at any instant; in immediate readiness. *Obs.*

1547–64 BAULDWIN *Mor. Philos.* (Palfr.) VI. ii, Vpon this wicked rabble..crafty concupiscence waiteth as a seruant at inches. **1583** RICH *Phylotus & Emelia* (1835) 18 Attendaunt vpon her, and readie at an ynche to prouide her of any thing. **1586** J. HOOKER *Girald Irel.* in *Holinshed* II. 144/1 In such a readinesse to be at inches with them. **1618** FLETCHER *Loyal Subj.* IV. ii, Ile wait ye at an inch.

b. ***by inches, inch by inch***: by small degrees, by little and little, very gradually, bit by bit.

1607 SHAKS. *Cor.* v. iv. 42 All swearing..They'l giue him death by inches. **1652** COLLINGES *Caveat for Prof.* i. (1653) Biij, They were forced to..reforme by inches. **1700** CONGREVE *Way of World* IV. xii, No, don't kill him at once ..starve him gradually, inch by inch. **1719** F. HARE *Ch. Authority Vind.* 27 To dispute the ground inch by inch. **1833** MARRYAT *P. Simple* xxix, Wasting away, and dying, as they say, by inches. **1869** B. WILBERFORCE *Sk. Lives Domin. Missionaries Japan* 195 All these four martyrs expired by inches, after a series of torments.

c. ***every inch***: every bit, every whit; altogether, entirely, in every respect.

c **1420** *S. Etheldred* 720 in Horstm. *Altengl. Leg.* (1881) 298 þat ston was well ygraue..eueryche a neynche. **1520** *Caxton's Chron. Eng.* III. 24 b/1 This man was cursed every ynche. **1605** SHAKS. *Lear* IV. vi. 109, I, euery inch a King. **1684** WINSTANLEY *Rich. III, Life Shakspere*, A man of Arms, every inch of him. **1749** FIELDING *Tom Jones* VII. vii, I tremble every inch of me. **1809–10** COLERIDGE *Friend* (1837) III. 289 Lord Nelson was an admiral, every inch of him. **1893** EARL DUNMORE *Pamirs* II. 336 His..companion ..looks a soldier, every inch of him.

d. ***inches*** = stature; ***of inches***, of (considerable) height, tall. ***of one's inches***: in respect of one's height or stature.

1606 SHAKS. *Ant. & Cl.* I. iii. 40, I would I had thy inches. **1687** T. BROWN *Saints in Uproar* Wks. 1730 I. 73 A notable fellow of his inches, and metal to the back. **1768–74** TUCKER *Lt. Nat.* (1852) II. 629 Beware of servants instilling the prodigious importance of master or miss beyond all others of their inches. **1809** MALKIN *Gil Blas* v. i. ¶ 18 Pedro was what we call a tall fellow of his inches. **1885** *Graphic* 28 Feb. 214/2 In order to make the most of her inches she had acquired the habit of holding her head thrown back.

e. ***by inch of candle***: see CANDLE *sb.* 5 d. ***give him an inch and he'll take an ell***: see ELL[1] 1 b; also in extended use.

1546 J. HEYWOOD *Prov.* (1867) 78 Whan I gaue you an ynche, ye tooke an ell. **1640** HOWELL *Dodona's Gr.* 8 For soveraignty where she gets an inch, stickes not some-times to stretch it to an ell. **1844** DICKENS *Mart. Chuz.* (Househ. ed.) 311/1 Give John an inch in that way, and he was sure to take several ells. **1973** *Times* 21 Feb. 3/1 If you turn your back for an instant or give them an inch they will park their cars on it.

4. a. *attrib.* and *Comb.*, as ***inch-allotment, -diet; inch-deep, -high, -long, -thick, -wide*** adjs.

1611 SHAKS. *Wint. T.* I. ii. 186 Gone already Ynch-thick, knee-deepe. **1655** MOUFET & BENNET *Health's Improv.* (1746) 72 An exquisite thin Diet (called of Jobertus..the Inch-diet, wherein we eat by Drams, and drink by Spoonfuls). **1682** CREECH tr. *Lucretius* (1683) IV. 115 Little Puddles..Tho scarce Inch-deep. **1742** YOUNG *Nt. Th.* II. 360 Life's little stage is a small eminence, Inch-high the grave above. **1873** *Young Englishwoman* Apr. 194/2 Inch-wide lace. **1876** LOWELL *Among my Bks.* Ser. II. *Spenser* 189 Futile gossip and inch-long politics. **1884** BROWNING *Ferishtah, A Bean-stripe* 218 Aphis that I am, How leave my inch-allotment? **1899** *Westm. Gaz.* 11 May 4/2 Strings..of inch-wide black velvet. **1950** W. DE LA MARE *Inward Compan.* 89 From inch-wide eyes I scan their..flames. **1964** C. DENT *Quantity Surveying by Computer* iii. 31 The new 1-inch-wide eight-channel paper tape now in use on some computers.

b. *attrib.* Containing an inch in any dimension; of the length, thickness, etc. of an inch; as ***inch-board*** (board an inch thick), ***inch-line***, etc.; of the focal length of one inch, as ***inch object-glass***.

1646 SIR T. BROWNE *Pseud. Ep.* VII. xviii. 383 A candle out of a Musket will pierce through an inch board. **1683** KENNETT tr. *Erasm. on Folly* 93 To see through an Inch-board. **1836** MARRYAT *Midsh. Easy* (1863) 165 He asked Captain Hogg to bring on shore some inch line. **1837** GORING & PRITCHARD *Microgr.* 179 Suppose we have an inch triple achromatic object-glass. **1858** SIMMONDS *Dict.*, *Inch-stuff*, deal plank sawn to the thickness of an inch.

c. *attrib.* with prefixed numeral (*two-inch, six-inch*, etc.): Of the length, diameter, etc. of (so many) inches.

1559 in Boys *Sandwich* (1792) 739, xl m. of iii ynche plancke for the said jutties. **1698** DAMPIER *Voy.* 282 Condemned..to have three blows from each man in the ship, with a two-inch and a half rope on his bare back. **1798** NELSON *Let. to Nepean* 7 Aug. in A. Duncan *Life* (1806) 91, I have..brought off the two thirteen-inch mortars. **1825** NICHOLSON *Operat. Mechanic* 576 Three or four thicknesses of one and a half inch-deal. **1879** *Daily News* 12 Aug. 5/3 Fourteen of the Bacchante guns are seven-inch weapons.

d. Special Combs.: **inch-bones** *sb. pl.*, fragments of bone used as manure (distinguished from *bone-dust*: cf. c); **inch-measure, -rule, -tape**, a measuring rule or tape divided into inches; **inch-pound** (*Dynamics*), the work done in raising a pound weight vertically through an inch (cf. FOOT-POUND); **inch-taped** *a.* (*nonce-wd.*), covered with inch-

tape; **inch-worm**, a name for a geometer caterpillar, also called *looper* or *measuring-worm*; also *fig.*

1846 J. BAXTER *Libr. Pract. Agric.* (ed. 4) II. 353 The smaller bone-dust is ground the more effective it is as a manure..on the other hand large or drilled or *inch-bones, as they are called, remain longer in the soil undecomposed, but produce less immediate effect. On these accounts bone-dust is the more valuable manure for turnips, and inch-bones for wheat. **1851** MAYHEW *Lond. Labour* I. 377 (Hoppe) They all sell thimbles, needles, *inch-measures, bodkins, etc. **1850** DICKENS *Dav. Copp.* lx. 595 Neither will you find him measuring all human interests..with his one poor little *inch-rule now. **1896** *Westm. Gaz.* 9 Nov. 3/2 [He] measures the force of the temptation with an inch-rule. **1884** 'EDNA LYALL' *We Two* xxx, [She] has gone to fetch an *inch tape. **1939** DYLAN THOMAS *Map of Love* 6 'His mother's womb had a tongue that lapped up mud,' Cried the topless, *inchtaped lips. *a* **1861** T. WINTHROP *Life in Open Air* (1863) 123 All the green *inch-worms vanish on the tenth of every June. **1881** *Harper's Mag.* Oct. 656/1 A wriggling inch-worm,..awaiting..an opportunity to measure the length of your nose. **1949** *Sat. Even. Post* 12 Mar. 33/1 One evening the Main Line local hunched its cars together like an inchworm and skidded to a halt. **1954** BORROR & DELONG *Introd. Study Insects* xxvi. 522 The larvae of geometers are the familiar caterpillars commonly called inchworms or measuring-worms. **1959** G. MATTINGLY *Defeat of Spanish Armada* xx. 218 There was only one offset to the exasperation of this inchworm progress. **1970** R. LOWELL *Notebk.* 235 Have you ever seen an inchworm crawl on a leaf,..Feeling for something to reach something?

inch (ɪnʃ), *sb.*^{2} Also 5 ynche, 6 *Sc.* insche. [a. Gael. *innis* (ɪnɪʃ), genit. *innse* (iːnʃe) island, land by a river.] A small island. (Frequent in the names of small islands belonging to Scotland.)

c **1425** WYNTOUN *Cron.* Prol., I wes..made priowre Of the ynche wyth-in Loch-lewyne. *c* **1470** HENRY *Wallace* IX. 1147 Bot in Lochlewyn thair lay a cumpane, Apon that inch. **1596** DALRYMPLE tr. *Leslie's Hist. Scot.* I. 24 In the Sey selfe ar mony Iles and Inches nocht few, as the Mai, the Basse, the ile of S. Colme. **1605** SHAKS. *Macb.* I. ii. 61 Till he disbursed, at St. Colmes ynch, Ten thousand Dollars to our generall vse. **1793** *Statist. Acc. Scotl.* VIII. 597 There are some beautiful islands which are called *Inches.* **1805** SCOTT *Last Minstr.* VI. xxiii, To inch and rock the sea-mews fly.

b. Applied locally to a meadow by a river (as the Inches of Perth); also, to a piece of rising ground in the midst of a plain.

1799 J. ROBERTSON *Agric. Perth* 476 Such parts of the Carse [of Gowrie], as are elevated above the common level of the country are called *Inches* (which word signifies islands). **1863** LYELL *Antiq. Man* iii. (ed. 3) 54 The Celtic name of Inch being attached to many hillocks, which rise above the general level of the alluvial plains.

inch (ɪnʃ), *v.* [f. INCH *sb.*^{1}]

1. *intr.* To move, advance, or retreat, by inches or small degrees.

1599 SANDYS *Europæ Spec.* (1632) 213 And if he itch and inch forward one way for an ell, hee looseth an other. **1697** DRYDEN *Æneid* IX. 1065 Now Turnus doubts, and..with slow paces measures back the field, And inches to the walls. **1812** W. TENNANT *Anster F.* III. xlv, Inching along in motion retrograde. **1881** *Amer. Grocer* 20 July, Boys who did not play fair..would keep reaching over the line in order to get nearer the marbles in the ring and have a better chance to knock them out. This was called 'inching', and 'fen inchings' was the warning against such unfair play. **1888** *Chicago Advance* 29 Nov., Meanwhile, the celebrated case, possibly, will be inching along toward some final decision.

2. *trans.* To drive by inches or small degrees.

1667 DRYDEN *Maiden Queen* III. i, And so inch him and shove him out of the world. **1692** —— *Cleomenes* II. ii. (R.), He gets too far into the souldier's grace; And inches out my master. **1868** BROWNING *Ring & Bk.* III. 617 Like so much cold steel inched through his breast-blade. **1895** *Outing* (U.S.) Oct. 10/2 The children..inched their chairs closer and insisted there was not room for her between them.

3. To measure or compute the number of inches in.

1673 SHADWELL *Epsom Wells* I, E'er a horse in your Stable, weigh him and inch him. **1690** H. C[OGGESHALL] *Art Pract. Measuring* (*title-p.*), Gauging and Inching of Tuns. **1718** STEELE *Fish-Pool* 171 The Fish-Pool sloop being inched according to common gauging.

4. ***inch out***: **a.** To eke out by inches or small amounts.

1620 I. V. tr. *P. du Moulin's Serm. Rom.* i. 16.2 He hath inched out the skin of the Lion with that of the Foxe, adding craft to crueltie. **1622** MABBE tr. *Aleman's Guzman d'Alf.* II. 263 When I could not inch it out any further..I found my selfe then in that strait, that [etc.]. **1652-62** HEYLIN *Cosmogr.* II. (1682) 206 The Women cutting off their Hair to inch out their Tackle. **1654** E. JOHNSON *Wond.-wrkg. Prov.* 173 Corn incht out with Chesnuts and bitter Acorns. **1679** MRS. BEHN *Feign'd Curtizan* III. i, Cou'd you not..throw in a little Love and Constancy, to inch out that want of Honesty of yours? **1878** BROWNING *Poets Croisic* 127 There stands Paul erect, Inched out his uttermost.

†**b.** To deal out inch by inch, hence, by small amounts or sparingly. *Obs.*

1636 HENSHAW *Horæ Succ.* 300 God..doth..not requite it with a little, or inch out His blessings. *a* **1656** BP. HALL *Rem. Wks.* (1660) 267 In the inching out of the possibilities of our assurance by nice distinctions.

5. To divide or graduate into inches; to mark with lines an inch apart.

inchafe, inchain, inchair: see EN-.

in'chamber, *v. rare*$^{-0}$. [f. IN-^{2} + CHAMBER.] *trans.* To lodge in or as in a chamber.

1611 FLORIO, *Incamerare*, to chamber, to inchamber. **1611** COTGR., *Enchambré*, inchambred; lodged as in a chamber.

†**in'change**, *v. Obs. rare.* [f. IN-^{1} or ^{2} + CHANGE *v.*, after L. *immūtāre.*] *trans.* To produce change in; to change, alter.

1382 WYCLIF *Job* xiv. 20 Thou shalt inchaungen his face, and thou shalt senden hym out. —— *1 Cor.* xv. 51 Alle we schulen ryse aȝen, but not alle we schulen be inchaungid.

†**in'changeable**, *a. Obs. rare.* [IN-^{3}.] Not changeable; unchangeable, immutable. So **inchangea'bility**, unchangeableness.

1583 GOLDING *Calvin on Deut.* clxix. 1047 The calling of God..is without repentaunce, and inchaungeable. **1654** tr. *Scudery's Curia Pol.* 116 As for the word of a King, it ought to be inchangeable. **1773** KENRICK *Rhet. Gram.* vi. (Jod.), Almost all our English writers,..possessed with this inchangeability of accent and quantity, tell us, that all accented syllables are long.

inchant, inchanter, etc.: see ENCHANT, etc.

incharge: see ENCHARGE.

†**in'charitable**, *a. Obs.* [IN-^{3}.] Not charitable; uncharitable. Hence †**in'charitableness**, uncharitableness, †**incharitably** *adv.*

1496 *Act 12 Hen. VII*, c. 6 Their incharitable and inordinate Covetise. **1610** SHAKS. *Temp.* I. i. 44 You bawling, blasphemous incharitable Dog. **1670** PENN *Truth Rescued fr. Impost.* 5 The second discovery..is not less Incharitable, then the first was Proud and Impudent. **1679** —— *Addr. Prot.* II. 63 The Debate..fill'd this Kingdom with Incharitableness and Division.

†**in'charity.** *Obs.* [f. IN-^{3} + CHARITY: cf. prec.] Want of charity; uncharitableness.

1589 WARNER *Alb. Eng.* II. Prose Addit. (1612) 340 Least mine incharitie proue lesse pardonable than his Iniurie. **1602** *Ibid.* IX. liii. 237 Avarice, Incharitie and Pride. **1670** PENN *Case Lib. Consc.* 36 It is high Incharity to proceed so severely upon meer Suppositions. **1679** —— *Addr. Prot.* II. 90 Great must their Incharity and Presumption be, who [etc.].

incharm, inchase: see ENCHARM, ENCHASE *v.*^{2}

†**inchaste**, *a. Obs. rare.* [f. IN-^{3} + CHASE *a.*: cf. L. *incastus.*] Unchaste.

1599 PEELE *David & Bethsabe* Wks. (Rtldg.) 476/2 His inchaste and lustful fire.

†**in'chastity.** *Obs.* exc. as *nonce-use.* [f. IN-^{3} + CHASTITY: cf. L. *incastitās.*] Want of chastity; unchastity.

1586 MARLOWE *1st Pt. Tamburl.* V. ii, All blot of foul inchastity. **1613** HEYWOOD *Brazen Age* IV. Wks. 1874 III. 230 What will Diana Say when shee heares of our inchastity? **1671** H. M. tr. *Erasm. Colloquies* A iij b, To keep them from the temptation of inchastity. **1972** *Times Lit. Suppl.* 25 Aug. 1000/4 It is difficult..to imagine how sanctions against inchastity could be re-imposed.

inchaunt, etc.: see ENCHANT, etc.

Inche ('ɪntʃə). Also **Enche, Enc(h)ik, Inchi.** [Mal. *enche'*, *enchek*, *enchik* master, mistress.] In Malaysia, a prefixed title signifying respect, used for persons with no other special distinction; equivalent to 'Mr.'

The current official spelling (since 1972) is *Encik.*

1834 P. J. BEGBIE *Malayan Peninsula* ii. 83 It now only remains to mention the fate of Inchi Oowan Saban. **1897** *Jrnl. Straits Branch R. Asiatic Soc.* July 85 The following account of the method of rice cultivation..was written..by Inche Muhammad Ja'far. **1913** RANEE OF SARAWAK *My Life in Sarawak* xviii. 160 Inchi Sawal was a great stickler for grammar. **1937** *Jrnl. Malayan Branch R. Asiatic Soc.* XV. I. 63 Inche Abdul Raffar, Collector and Deputy Registrar, Ulu Selangor. **1951** *Proc. Legis. Council Fedn. Malaya* B159 Enche Abdullah: Sir, I beg to second the motion. **1972** *Straits Times* 4 May 1/5 Inche Ghafar clarified today that he had not made any offer for the formation of a coalition government.

inchear, variant of ENCHEER, *v.*

inched (ɪnʃt), *a.* Also 7 incht. [f. INCH *sb.*^{1} or *v.* + -ED.]

1. In combination, with numeral, etc. prefixed: Containing (so many) inches in length or other dimension. (With quot. 1894 cf. INCH *sb.*^{1} 3 d.)

1605 SHAKS. *Lear* III. iv. 57 To ride on a Bay trotting Horse, ouer foure incht Bridges. **1651-7** T. BARKER *Art of Angling* (1820) 28 The two inched hook is better. **1894** DU MAURIER *Trilby* II. 175 Any young squire, well-inched and well-acred, and well-whiskered.

2. Divided into or graduated in inches.

incheer, variant of ENCHEER *v.*

incher (ɪnʃə(r)). [f. INCH *sb.*^{1} + -ER^1.] In combination, with numeral prefixed, applied to something of so many inches in length, diameter, etc.

1885 *Cycl. Tour. Club Gaz.* Sept. 289/1 A tricycle of abnormal growth..a 96-incher. **1898** KIPLING in *Westm. Gaz.* 9 Nov. 9/2 Firing..with six-inchers, twelve-pounders, and Maxims all turned loose together.

†**in'cheson, in'chessoun**, var. of ENCHEASON.

a **1400-50** *Alexander* 343 þe incheson of his charme.

inchest, variant of ENCHEST *v.*

†**in'chete, -er**, obs. var. of ENCHEAT, -ER.

1483 *Cath. Angl.* 195/2 To Inchete, *fiscare.* *Ibid.*, An Incheter, *fiscator, fiscarius.*

†**in'child**, *v. Obs. rare.* [f. IN-^{2} + CHILD.] *trans.* To introduce as a child, to affiliate.

1611 FLORIO, *Infigliuolare*, to inchilde.

inchmeal ('ɪnʃmiːl), *adv.* (*sb.*) [f. INCH *sb.*^{1} + -MEAL, ME. *-mele*, OE. *-mælum.*] By inches; inch by inch; by small portions, little by little.

1548 COOPER *Elyot's Dict.*, *Vuciatim*, ynche by ynche, ynche meale. **1579** J. JONES *Preserv. Bodie & Soule* I. xxxi. 63 Some dyed Inch-mele, some were Famished, some Starued. **1583** FOXE *A. & M.* 2066/1 Thou shalt bee racked inchmeale. *a* **1734** NORTH *Exam.* II. iv. §108 (1740) 286 As Towns are taken Inch-meal. **1792** HOLCROFT *Road to Ruin* IV. iii, I would indeed starve inchmeal, rather than he should marry her! **1813** MAR. EDGEWORTH *Patron.* (1833) II. xxviii. 187 People..will stand to be cut to pieces inchmeal, rather than submit to a conqueror.

b. Also with *by* (giving the force of the lost inflexion).

1530 PALSGR. 833/1 By ynche meale, *menuement*, or *par poulcées.* **1549** CHALONER tr. *Erasm. on Folly* L iij b, They take upon theim to measure the sonne..as it were by ynche-meale. **1610** SHAKS. *Temp.* II. ii. 3 All the infections that the Sunne suckes vp From Bogs, Fens, Flats, on Prosper fall, and make him By ynch-meale a disease. *a* **1691** FLAVEL *Sea-Deliv.* (1754) 167 To lengthen our miserable lives a few hours, to die, as it were, by inch-meal. **1893** *National Observer* 18 Feb. 329/1 The ground must be fought by inch-meal.

inchoacy ('ɪnkəʊəsɪ). *rare.* [f. INCHOATE *a.*: see -ACY.] The state of being inchoate; incipiency.

1871 R. H. HUTTON *Ess.*, *Clough* (1880) II. 247 A picture of inchoacy I admit.

inchoant ('ɪnkəʊənt), *a. rare.* [ad. L. *inchoānt-em*, pres. pple. of *inchoāre*: see next.] Beginning, incipient, in an initial stage.

a **1876** M. COLLINS *Th. in Garden* (1880) II. 275 The projector of an inchoant and rather incoherent periodical.

inchoate ('ɪnkəʊət), *a.* (*sb.*) [ad. L. *inchoāt-us* (more correctly *incohātus*), pa. pple. of *inchoāre* (more correctly *incohāre*) to begin.] Just begun, incipient; in an initial or early stage; hence elementary, imperfect, undeveloped, immature.

1534 WHITINTON *Tullyes Offices* III. (1540) 117 No paynter..shoulde fynysshe that parte of Venus which inchoat [and] begon, Apelles left of imperfyte. **1581** E. CAMPION in *Confer.* II. (1584) H iv, It was a Church inchoate, beginning, not perfect. *a* **1626** BP. ANDREWES *Serm.* (1856) I. 109 His heavenly grace, which is glory inchoate, He imparteth to His Saints. *a* **1711** KEN *Hymns Festiv.* Poet. Wks. 1721 I. 409 You are in happy State; Our Bliss is only Inchoate. **1765** BLACKSTONE *Comm.* I. xv. 436 If a boy under fourteen, or a girl under twelve years of age, marries, this marriage is only inchoate and imperfect. **1821** SYD. SMITH *Wks.* (1859) I. 326/1 Many inchoate acts are innocent, the consummation of which is a capital offence. **1874** H. R. REYNOLDS *John Bapt.* viii. 473 The position I have ventured to maintain..as to the inchoate, imperfect, and transitional work of John. **1888** BURGON *Lives 12 Gd. Men* I. II. 181 All was as yet in an inchoate state.

b. as *sb.* A beginning, rudiment. *rare.*

1845 R. W. HAMILTON *Pop. Educ.* vi. (1846) 135 The drudgery of teaching and learning the barest inchoates of knowledge.

inchoate ('ɪnkəʊeɪt), *v.* [f. ppl. stem of L. *inchoāre* (prop. *incohāre*) to begin: see prec.]

1. *trans.* To begin, commence, initiate, take the first steps in.

a **1612** DONNE *Βιαθανατος* (1644) 182 This growth (Inchoated, increased, grown great, and perfected). **1647** H. MORE *Song of Soul* Notes 150/2 The great soul of the World does at least inchoate, and rudely delineate the fabrick of our body at first. **1746-7** *Act 20 Geo. II*, c. 43 §28 That royal burgh..which shall lie nearest to the place where such poynding was inchoated. **1868** BROWNING *Ring & Bk.* I. 1155 How he..Conceives and inchoates the argument.

b. To cause to begin, originate, bring about.

1654 WARREN *Unbelievers* 236 Any moral..inchoating our Justification. **1802** PALEY *Nat. Theol.* xxiii. (1819) 390 To inchoate the formation of an eye. **1845** STOCQUELER *Handbk. Brit. India* (1854) 113 Nor will it inchoate their ruin to expend a few rupees more than an accurate calculation of comforts might allow.

2. *intr.* To commence, make a beginning.

1654 VILVAIN *Epit. Ess.* VII. 75 At the Worlds origin this Book inchoats. **1767** A. CAMPBELL *Lexiph.* (1774) 7, I shall inchoate with one of its most delicious morsels of eloquence.

inchoated ('ɪnkəʊeɪtɪd), *ppl. a.* [f. prec. + -ED^1.] Begun, commenced; just begun, incipient, inchoate.

a **1631** DONNE *Serm.* lxiii. 633 The torment is an inchoative hell, so is the Person, The Wicked here, an inchoated Devill. **1651** C. CARTWRIGHT *Cert. Relig.* I. 205 This righteousnesse of ours is but inchoated and imperfect. **1762** KAMES *Elem. Crit.* ii. §6 (1833) 80 An inchoated gratification of the prevailing passion. **1826** *Q. Rev.* XXXIII. 298 There is a fine gradation between the inchoated conception and the completed purpose.

inchoately (ˈɪnkəʊətlɪ), *adv.* [f. INCHOATE *a.* + -LY^2.] In an inchoate manner or degree; incipiently.

1626 SCLATER *Exp. 2 Thess.* (1629) 52 Such as..are purged, though but inchoately, from all filthinesse of flesh and Spirit. **1675** O. WALKER, etc. *Par. Hebrews* 18 Here inchoately..hereafter absolutely. **1837** J. H. NEWMAN *Lett.* (1891) II. 235 Confirmation seals in their fulness..those sanctifying gifts..which are given inchoately, in Baptism.

inchoateness (ˈɪnkəʊətnɪs). [f. as prec. + -NESS.] The state or quality of being inchoate.

1845 J. H. NEWMAN *Ess. Developm.* 100 Defect or inchoateness in its doctrines. **1893** FAIRBAIRN *Christ Mod. Theol.* I. I. i. 30 It was their very differences and inchoatenesses that made it necessary for her to speak.

inchoation (ɪnkəʊˈeɪʃən). Also 7 incohation. [ad. late L. *inchoātiōn-em* (prop. *incohātiōn-em*) (Augustine), n. of action from *inchoāre* (*incohāre*) to begin.] Beginning, commencement; origination; initial or early stage.

1530 PALSGR. 403 Whan the tenses of *je vas* is joyned to an infynityve, he dothe betoken inchoacion. **1597** HOOKER *Eccl. Pol.* v. lvii. §6 But the inchoation of those graces, the consummation whereof dependeth on mysteries ensuing. **1652** T. WHITFIELD *Doctr. Armin.* 88 The life of Grace is an inchoation of the life of glory. **1768–74** TUCKER *Lt. Nat.* (1852) I. 215 An inchoation of virtue, or, as we may call it, the embryo or seedling not yet arrived to perfection. **1885** SIR H. TAYLOR *Autobiog.* I. xiv. 226 The members were to be, at the inchoation of the bodies, named by the Crown.

†**b.** *pl.* First steps, beginnings. *Obs.*

*a***1619** FOTHERBY *Atheom.* II. viii. §3 (1622) 284 The præparatiues vnto it: or rather indeed the inchoations of it. **1660** H. MORE *Myst. Godl.* VIII. v. 378 Having..some more weak inchoations of the life of Righteousness.

†**c.** The initial element of a word; a prefix. *Obs.*

*a***1661** FULLER *Worthies, Cornwall* I. (1662) 197 By Tre, Pol, and Pen,—You shall know the Cornishmen:..Some adde to these a fourth inchoation, viz. Car (which I guess to signify a rock).

inchoative (ɪnˈkəʊətɪv, ˈɪnkəʊeɪtɪv), *a.* and *sb.* [ad. L. *inchoātīv-us* (prop. *incohātīv-us*), f. ppl. stem of *inchoāre*, *incohāre* to begin: see INCHOATE *v.* and -IVE.]

A. *adj.* **1.** That is in an initial or incipient stage; rudimentary, inchoate; belonging to or of the nature of a beginning or commencement, initial.

*a***1631** [see INCHOATED]. **1633** T. ADAMS *Exp. 2 Peter* iii 1 This pureness is either imputative..Or inchoative, inherent pureness. **1662** J. CHANDLER *Van Helmont's Oriat.* 32 That the stable Ferments of places, should be as it were, the chief universal, simple, and inchoative or beginning Beginnings of Seeds. *a***1703** BURKITT *On N.T.*, *Gal.* v. 24 We must not understand this of a total, plenery, and final crucifixion, but inchoative only. **1865** CARLYLE *Fredk. Gt.* XXI. v. (1872) X. 45 The solution of the Polish Business is still in its inchoative stages.

2. *Gram.* Of verbs: Denoting the beginning of an action; inceptive.

1668 WILKINS *Real Char.* 450 Those particular Terminations which signifie a Verb to be Inchoative, Frequentative, Diminutive, are not without many exceptions. **1751** HARRIS *Hermes* I. vii. (1765) 126 These Inchoative Verbs are so peculiarly appropriated to the Beginnings of Time, that they are defective as to all Tenses, which denote it in its Completion. **1871** ROBY *Lat. Gram.* §634 The inchoative form sometimes exists alone, sometimes is used besides the ordinary stem.

B. *sb.* (*Gram.*) An inchoative verb; see A. 2.

1530 PALSGR. 403 They knowe neyther frequentatyves, nor inchoatyves, nor no suche sortes of verbes. **1678** PHILLIPS (ed. 4), *Inchoatives*, in Grammar..as *Calesco*, to grow hot, or begin to be hot. **1751** HARRIS *Hermes* I. vii. (1765) 126 The Latins..have a Species of Verbs, derived from others..called Inchoatives or Inceptives. **1871** ROBY *Lat. Gram.* §638 Inchoatives formed directly from noun stems.

inˈchoatively, *adv.* [f. prec. + -LY^2.] In an inchoative manner; in relation to the beginning or early stage; incipiently, initially.

1649 J. ELLISTONE tr. *Behmen's Epist.* vi. §60 The humane Science (which inchoatively is arisen from the Spiration of the Word). *a***1703** BURKITT *On N.T.*, *Heb.* iv. 10 This is done two ways, initially, inchoatively, and imperfectly in this life; fully, finally, perfectly, and completely in the next.

†**ˈinchpin.** *Obs.* Also 6–7 -pinne, -pyn. [app. f. INCH *sb.* + PIN *sb.*; but perh. (in sense 1) a popular corruption of some other word.]

1. A name among huntsmen for the sweetbread of a deer. But by some explained as 'the lower gut', or otherwise: see quots.

1576 TURBERV. *Venerie* 134 Take the caule, the tong, the eares, the doulcets, the tenderlings..and the sweetegut, which some call the Inchpinne..altogether for the Prince or chiefe. **1583** STANYHURST *Æneis* I. (Arb.) 24 Thee stags vpbreaking they slit to the dulcet or inchepyn. **1611** COTGR. s.v. *Boyau*, *Gras boyau*, as *Boyau culier*; In beasts called, the Inche-pinne, or Inne-pinne. **1616** BULLOKAR, *Inchepinne*, the lower gut of a Deere. **1637** B. JONSON *Sad Sheph.* I. vi, *Mar.* I gave them All the sweet morsels, called Tongue, Eares, and Doucets! *Rob.* What? and the inch-pin? **1688** R. HOLME *Armoury* II. 188/1 Inchpin are the Sweet-breds or sweet Gut in the Deer.

2. ? A pin of the length of an inch.

1571 GOLDING *Calvin on Ps.* xxi. 12 He compareth them to a But wherin an inchpin is woont to be set up.

†**inchristiaˈnation.** *Obs. rare*$^{-1}$. [f. IN-^{2} + CHRISTIAN + -ATION, forming noun of action.] Admission into Christianity or the Christian Church.

1654 GAYTON *Pleas. Notes* IV. xv. 253 That this learned contrivance of Mr. Curates could worke in Zoraidas Inchristianation, with the solemnity and rights belonging to it.

†**inchristiˈanity.** *Obs. rare.* [IN-^{3}.] Unchristian or non-Christian condition.

1611 FLORIO, *Inchristianita*, paganisme, barbarisme, inchristianitie.

†**inˈchurch**, obs. var. of ENCHURCH *v.*

in-churn *attrib.*: see IN *prep.* 18.

†**inˈcicurable**, *a. Obs. rare.* [ad. mod.L. *incicurābilis*, f. *in-* (IN-^{3}) + *cicurāre* to tame; see CICURATE and -ABLE.] That cannot be tamed; hence, of plants, incapable of being introduced into cultivation or naturalized.

1657 TOMLINSON *Renou's Disp.* 284 Schœnanthum..growing in India, whence it is brought to us..being incicurable by all art. **1776** HUNTER in *Evelyn's Sylva* 359 Those [trees]..strangers till of late, and believed incicurable here.

incide (ɪnˈsaɪd), *v.*^{1} ? *Obs.* Also 6 (erron.) inscide, inscyde. [ad. L. *incīdĕre* to cut into, f. *in-* (IN-^{2}) + *cædĕre* to cut; cf. INCISE *v.*]

1. *Surg.* (*trans.* or *intr.*) To cut into, cut, make incision.

1597 A. M. tr. *Guillemeau's Fr. Chirurg.* 16 b/2 The Needle..inscideth with her edges. *Ibid.* 31 b/1 They first inscyded the skinne wherwith the varix is covered. **1743** tr. *Heister's Gen. Syst. Surg.* (1750) 425 Takes a Lancet and therewith cautiously incides through the Cornea. **1784** COOK *3rd Voy.* III. ix. (R.), Cutting or inciding the fore-skin. **1799** W. G. BROWNE *Trav. Africa* etc. xviii. 258 After having incided with an ordinary knife, they sear the wound with an hot iron.

†**2.** *Med.* Of the action of internal remedies: To sever, loosen, disperse, resolve (a viscid humour, phlegm in the chest, etc.); = CUT *v.* 10. *Obs.*

1612 *Enchir. Med.* 89 It doth incide and attenuate, and by his drinesse doth resolue. **1684** tr. *Bonet's Merc. Compit.* III. 92 Such Medicines are convenient, as incide the cold and viscous humours. **1727–41** CHAMBERS *Cycl.* s.v., Those medicines are said to incide which consist of pointed and sharp particles; as acids and most salts. **1797** J. DOWNING *Disord. Horned Cattle* 30 These medicines..infallibly incide and remove heavy slime, and putrid matter.

incide (ɪnˈsaɪd), *v.*^{2} *rare.* [ad. L. *incidĕre* to fall upon, f. *in-* (IN-^{2}) + *cadĕre* to fall; cf. INCIDENT *a.*^{1}] *intr.* To fall *upon*; to have incidence.

*a***1774** GOLDSM. *Surv. Exp. Philos.* (1776) II. 393 The ray C inciding still less obliquely..will be less refracted. **1855** M. BRIDGES *Pop. Mod. Hist.* 423 The cruel inequality with which the gabelle incided upon certain rural districts.

incidence (ˈɪnsɪdəns). [a. F. *incidence* (15th c.), f. *incident* INCIDENT *a.*^{1}: see -ENCE.]

†**1. a.** = INCIDENT *sb.*^{1} 1; incidental matter. *Obs.*

1423 JAS. I *Kingis Q.* vii, Procede I will agayn to my sentence Off my mater, and leue all Incidence. **1525** LD. BERNERS *Froiss.* II. i. 3 In the same season there fell in Lombardye a marueylous insydence, which was moche spoken of throughe out all the worlde. *Ibid.* clii. [cxlviii.] 419, I knowe nat by what insydence certayne men layde in wayte on hym, and in the feldes set on him or he was ware. **1605** BACON *Adv. Learn.* II. viii. §3 Many operations have been invented sometimes by a casual incidence and occurrence. **1651** JER. TAYLOR *Holy Living* iii. §4 (1870) 153 He that hath wounded his neighbour is tied to the expenses of the Surgeon and other incidences.

†**b.** A casual circumstance. *Obs.*

1670 G. H. *Hist. Cardinals* II. I. 111 Since by way of incidence [It. *incidenza*, digression], I have spoken of Alms.

†**c.** = INCIDENT *sb.*^{1} 4 b. *Obs.*

1574 tr. *Littleton's Tenures* 47 a, Al the rente and service in suche case bee incidences to the reversion.

†**2.** Liability; natural tendency *to*. *Obs.*

1652 GAULE *Magastrom.* 112 A conscious and confest incidence to error..even in the very rule or art it self.

3. The act or fact of falling upon, coming in contact with, or affecting in some way.

1656 STANLEY *Hist. Philos.* IV. (1701) 135/2 It is enough that a Man be affected and reduced by incidence of one single pleasure. **1853** KANE *Grinnell Exp.* xxiv. (1856) 196 The great expanse..had up to this moment resisted the enormous incidence of a heavy gale. **1868** ROGERS *Pol. Econ.* ix. (1876) 93 The incidence of the event will be very probably obviated by the large use of machinery in agricultural operations. **1885** J. MARTINEAU *Types Eth. Th.* (ed. 2) I. I. xi. §8. 212 A partial incidence of the Divine thinking.

4. *Physics.* The falling of a line, or anything moving in a line (as a projectile, a ray of light, heat, etc.) upon a surface; the manner of such falling, esp. in regard to the inclination of the line of incidence to the surface.

angle of incidence, (*a*) the angle which the incident line, ray, etc., makes with the perpendicular or normal to the surface at the point of incidence (†formerly, also, the angle between the line, etc., and the surface); (*b*) the angle which the chord of an aircraft wing makes with the direction of the undisturbed air current. ***axis of incidence***, the perpendicular or normal to the surface at the point of incidence. ***cathetus of incidence*** (see CATHETUS, quot. 1751). ***plane of incidence***, the plane through the line of incidence and the normal to the surface. ***point of incidence***, ***incidence-point***, the point at which the line of incidence meets the surface. †***ray of incidence***, an incident ray, a ray which falls upon a reflecting or refracting surface.

1626 BACON *Sylva* §245 In Mirrours, there is the like Angle of Incidence, from the Object to the Glasse, and from the Glasse to the Eye. **1656** tr. *Hobbes' Elem. Philos.* Wks. 1839 I. 274, I call an angle of incidence, that which is made between a strait line and another line, strait or crooked, upon which it falls, and which I call the line reflecting. **1658** SIR T. BROWNE *Gard. Cyrus* iv. 67 This is also the law of reflexion in moved bodies and sounds, which..observe the rule of equality between incidence and reflexion. **1664** POWER *Exp. Philos.* I. 81 Every Ray of incidence is seven times refracted in the Eye before it reach the Retina. **1704** NEWTON *Opticks* (J.), In equal incidences there is a considerable inequality of refractions. **1727–41** CHAMBERS *Cycl.* s.v. *Axis*, *Axis of Incidence*, in dioptrics, is a right line drawn through the point of incidence, perpendicularly to the refracting surface. **1803** J. WOOD *Princ. Mech.* vi. 130 The velocity of the body after reflection is equal to it's velocity before incidence. **1854** TOMLINSON *Arago's Astron.* 3 DO will be the direction of the reflected ray, and the point I, where it cuts the surface of the mirror, will be the point of incidence. **1871** TYNDALL *Fragm. Sc.* (1879) II. viii. 129 The searcher welcomes every gleam, and seeks to augment his light by indirect incidences. **1908**, etc. [see ANGLE *sb.*^{2} 1 ¶]. **1948** *Sci. News* VII. 28 The pilot is able to increase or decrease the lift by altering the angle of incidence. *Ibid.*, As the angle of incidence increases, the lift also increases and the aircraft is able to climb, but if the tilt is made too large the flow on the upper surface separates and eddies are formed.

5. *Astron.* = IMMERSION 3.

1727–41 CHAMBERS *Cycl.* s.v. *Eclipse*, Immersion, or incidence of an eclipse, is the moment when part of the sun or moon's disk first begins to be hid.

6. *Geom.* The situation of one locus with respect to another when they have a common point or points, but do not completely coincide; e.g. of a point to a line on which it lies, of a point or a line to a plane in which it lies, or of two intersecting lines to each other. [From the German of Schubert, *Kalkul der Abzähl. Geom.* (1879) 25.]

7. a. Manner of falling upon or affecting in any way; the range or scope of a thing, the extent of its influence or effects.

1846 FONBLANQUE in *Life & Labours* (1874) 210 It is clear that the Duke has not mistaken the post hoc for the propter hoc, incidence for causation. **1851** DE QUINCEY *Ld. Carlisle on Pope* Wks. XIII. 24 The question..always is, Whether the differential feature..ought not to disturb the incidence of the legal rule? **1866** ROGERS *Agric. & Prices* I. xv. 266 The incidence of the Plague was general. **1871** EARLE *Philol. Eng. Tongue* §37 *On*, the preposition, exists in Saxon, but its area of incidence is different.

b. *spec.* in *Pol. Econ.* Of taxation (see quot. 1878).

1825 McCULLOCH *Pol. Econ.* I. 8 The incidence and effect of taxes and regulations. **1848** MILL *Pol. Econ.* v. vi. §1 (1876) 521 The real incidence of indirect taxation is every day more generally understood. **1878** JEVONS *Prim. Pol. Econ.* 127 It is often impossible to say what is really the incidence of a tax, that is, the manner in which it falls upon different classes of the population.

8. Special Comb.: **incidence wire** *Aeronaut.*, on a biplane (see quot. 1916).

1916 H. BARBER *Aeroplane Speaks* 143 *Incidence wire*, a wire running from the top of an interplane strut to the bottom of the interplane strut in front of or behind it. It maintains the 'stagger' and assists in maintaining the angle of incidence. **1928** V. W. PAGÉ *Mod. Aircraft* v. 175 These wires are called 'incidence wires', as they keep the planes in the proper angular relation to each other.

†**ˈincidency.** *Obs.* [See prec. and -ENCY.]

1. An incidental occurrence or circumstance; an incident.

1611 SHAKS. *Wint. T.* I. ii. 403 Declare What incidencie thou do'st ghesse of harme Is creeping toward me. **1663** J. SPENCER *Prodigies* (1665) 171 We have no reason why we should..vouchsafe the honor of a solemn notice to any such little incidencies as these. **1701** NORRIS *Ideal World* I. ii. 42 But ordinarily, and out of these singular incidencies..his way of procedure..is to act according to the general and stated laws of motion.

2. a. The quality of being liable to fall *to*. **b.** (with *pl.*) A thing incident or liable to befall or fall *to*.

1615 T. ADAMS *White Devill* 55 First the difficulty, to beare the bagge and not be couetous—secondly the usual incidency of the bagge to the worst men. *a***1662** HEYLIN *Laud* I. (1671) 53 If any other considerations of Profit, Preferment or Compliance, did prevail upon him..they may with charity be looked on as the common incidencies of Humane frailty. *a***1683** WHICHCOTE *Disc.* (1703) III. 426 Particular errours and misapprehensions in some things is an incidency to uprightness of heart.

3. *Physics.* = INCIDENCE 4.

1646 J. GREGORY *Notes & Obs.* Ep. Ded. (1650) 4 Rayes of incidency contract no warmth upon the Earth, unlesse reflected back upon their originall Sun. **1704** NORRIS *Ideal World* II. 245 As a certain subtile matter in its direct incidency is light.

fig. *a***1711** NORRIS (J.), He..receives a more vigorous joy from the reflexion than from the direct incidency of his happiness.

4. The falling of one line upon another, the meeting of lines.

1789 MORSE *Amer. Geog.* 346 Four streets intersect each other at right angles..whose incidencies form a spacious parade.

incident (ˈɪnsɪdənt), *sb.*[1] Also 5 incedent, 5-6 incydent. [a. F. *incident* (13th c.), subst. use of *incident* adj.; see INCIDENT *a.*[1]]

1. a. Something that occurs casually in the course of, or in connexion with, something else, of which it constitutes no essential part; an event of accessory or subordinate character.

1412-20 LYDG. *Chron. Troy* V. xxxvii, In Troye boke no more of hym I fynde.. Fro henceforth I can no processe reade But incydentes that beare no substaunce. **1525** LD. BERNERS *Froiss.* II. xl. 126 Yf an incydent had not ben or this, he had ben farre in the countrey of Hungery. **1533** MORE *Apol.* xxvi. Wks. 891/2 The touching of this matter is no part of my principall entent, but happeneth as an incident to fall in my waye. **1556** J. HEYWOOD *Spider & F.* lxi. 63 This present argument, Is: to principall case, but an incident. **1711** SHAFTESB. *Charac.* (1737) III. IV. ii. 220 Habitations of Defence against the Seasons and other Incidents. **1725** BRADLEY *Fam. Dict.* s.v. *Preserve*, Corn, by the Moisture of the Weather, want of turning, and some other Incidents, will grow musty. **1879** *Athenæum* 6 Sept. 305/1 Failures are inevitable incidents.

b. An occurrence or event, sometimes comparatively trivial in itself, which precipitates or could precipitate political unrest, open warfare, etc. Also, a particular episode (air-raid, skirmish, etc.) in war; an unpleasant or violent argument, a fracas.

1913 *Ann. Reg. 1912* I. 441 He had invariably done everything France wanted him to do, and, especially at the time of the Agadir incident, had rejected German.. advances. **1920** W. S. BLUNT *My Diaries* II. v. 138 Bramley ..had reported the incident in a serious light, and Cromer had taken it up seriously, seeing in it..a danger to the British occupation. **1920** T. E. LAWRENCE *Let.* 8 Aug. (1938) 313 Our communications are very bad, our defence positions all have both flanks in the air, and there seem to have been two incidents lately. **1930** *Economist* 30 Aug. 392/1 When some special 'incident' has occurred, a Mandatory Power frequently furnishes the Commission with additional information. **1937** V. BARTLETT *This is my Life* xiv. 245 There were very few 'incidents'. I visited almost every district of Berlin,..and I saw no man beaten.. but I came back..overwhelmed with shame that people could be proud of so much bullying. **1937** L. BROMFIELD *Rains Came* I. iv. 32 One impotent little man from Clapham, who was insolent to the Maharani, received for his pains a dismissal from the Civil Service for having made an 'incident'. *Ibid.* lv. 242 It was threatening to become an 'incident' which might unsettle the peace of India. **1938** *Encycl. Brit. Bk. of Yr. 1938* 296/1 Such incidents are bound to form an integral part of large-scale warfare under modern conditions. **1943** HUNT & PRINGLE *Service Slang* 40 There are no occasions, occurrences, or events in an airman's life. Anything that happens to him is an 'incident'..why, nobody knows. **1945** *Ann. Reg. 1944* 113 They [*sc.* the Home Guard] had given valuable aid to the Civil Defence Services in dealing with air-raid incidents. **1955** *Ann. Reg. 1954* 15 The number of 'incidents' in the Canal Zone increased. **1959** R. COLLIER *City that wouldn't Die* xi. 211 A warden doesn't write off an incident until he has personally made certain there is no one else on the premises. **1960** PARTRIDGE *Charm of Words* i. 23 If a business man speaks of incidents when he means quarrels, he has been influenced by journalism. **1973** G. GREENE *Honorary Consul* I. i. 23 The Governor didn't want any incidents.

2. a. An occurrence or event viewed as a separate circumstance.

1462 J. PASTON in *P. Lett.* No. 439 II. 89 This and what incedentes ye knowe, I preie yow by wrytinge certefie me in all hast. **1563-87** FOXE *A. & M.* (1684) III. 861 But of these incidents and occurrents here-after more. **1725** DE FOE *Voy. round World* (1840) 254 Rarities in nature, and surprising incidents, which foreigners expect. **1751** JOHNSON *Rambler* No. 154 ⁋11 The fortuitous collision of happy incidents. **1802-12** BENTHAM *Ration. Evid.* Wks. 1843 VI. 262 To relate incidents as they have really happened, is the work of the memory. **1828** SCOTT *F.M. Perth* v, Even the high-swelled hopes with which the late incident had filled him began to quail. **1874** L. STEPHEN *Hours in Library* (1892) I. i. 34 This book..shows a skill in selecting telling incidents.

†**b.** A matter, an affair. *Obs. rare.*

1485 CAXTON *St. Wenefr.* 21 After many wordes and causes leyd and after Innumerable incidentes and reasons alledged atte last they were al acorded. **1709** STEELE *Tatler* No. 25 ⁋4 Upon such Incidents as we decide by Combat. **1761** HUME *Hist. Eng.* II. xlii. 443 *note*, This parliament.. passed some remarkable incidents.

3. In the arts: **a.** A distinct piece of action in a play or poem; †in early use, an event subordinate to the main design (so F. *incident*).

1695 DRYDEN tr. *Du Fresnoy's Art Paint.* (J.), No person, no incident in the play, but must be of use to carry on the main design. **1709** STEELE *Tatler* No. 19 ⁋3 The Plot and Incidents of the Play are laid with that Subtilty of Spirit. **1727-41** CHAMBERS *Cycl.*, *Incident*, in a poem, is an episode or particular action, tacked to the principal action, or depending on it. **1863** MRS. C. CLARKE *Shaks. Char.* xiv. 350 A set-off against the pathetic incidents of the play. **1873** SYMONDS *Grk. Poets* vii. 205 The plays of Euripides are more rich in stirring incidents than those of his predecessors.

b. A single feature in a picture; especially one that does not form part of the main design or scene. *rare.*

1705 ADDISON *Italy* 379 The Prospect from the Capucin's Garden, which for the Extent and Variety of pleasing Incidents is, I think, the most charming. **1846** RUSKIN *Mod. Paint.* (1848) I. II. I. vii. §13. 86 Behind the 'Sacrifice for the Friends' of Giotto at Pisa, there is a sweet piece of rock incident.

†**4. a.** Something liable to attach itself to or connect itself with another thing; an accessory circumstance. Const. *to*, *unto* (rarely *into*). *Obs.* exc. as in b.

1649 BP. HALL *Cases Consc.* I. iv. (R.), There are two incidents into this practice which may render it not unwarrantable. **1660** R. COKE *Power & Subj.* 95 Treason does ever produce fatal and final destruction to the offender, and never attaineth to the desired end (two incidents inseparable thereunto). **1755** B. MARTIN *Mag. Arts & Sc.* II. xi. 236 Virgil, from the various Incidents of this Season, gives many singular and notable Epithets thereto.

b. *Law.* A privilege, burden, custom, etc. commonly or invariably attaching to an office, estate, or the like.

1628 COKE *On Litt.* 151 b, *Incident*, a thing appertaining to or following another as a more worthy or principall.. And of incidents some be separable, and some inseparable. **1670** BLOUNT *Law Dict.* s.v. *Advowzen*, Advowzen Appendant.. depends upon a Mannor, as appurtenant to it, termed by Kitchin an Incident that may be separated from the Subject. **1755** CARTE *Hist. Eng.* IV. 301 Their dignities had ceased for some ages to be an incident of their tenures. **1817** LD. LOUGHBOROUGH in *Douglass' Rep.* II. 727 A fine to be paid on the change of a tenant is almost a constant incident of a copyhold estate. **1876** DIGBY *Real Prop.* i. 48 Some of the 'incidents' of tenure by knight-service had their counterpart in tenure in socage.

†**c.** An incidental charge or expense. *Obs.*

1737 J. CHAMBERLAYNE *St. Gt. Brit.* II. III. 87 (List Officers Excise) Accomptant for Imprest Money for paying of Incidents. **1776** ADAM SMITH *W.N.* v. ii. (1869) II. 495 If the salaries of officers and other incidents, therefore, amount to more than ten per cent. **1776** G. SEMPLE *Building in Water* 38 An Estimate of the Expence..amounted to twenty thousand Pounds, and..we allowed the five hundred for Incidents.

5. *attrib.* and *Comb.* (also *incidents*). **incident book**, a book in which all relevant information is kept at an incident room; **incident office, post, room**, names for a centre set up by the police close to the scene of a crime, accident, or disaster, from which all operations are controlled and monitored.

1967 BAKER & WILKIE *Police Promotion Handbk.* IV. xxiii. 302 It will be clear from the list of duties that the manning of an Incident Post at the scene of a major disaster will call for a sufficiency of staff. **1971** 'J. FRASER' *Death in Pheasant's Eye* xxiii. 132 Three night men on duty in the Incidents Room. *Ibid.*, The Incidents Book was on Inspector Coates' table... The Incidents Book was the Bible of any murder investigation; every action was telephoned to the man who looked after the book. **1972** L. LAMB *Picture Frame* xviii. 154 Mr. Glover's incident office is in a red corrugated-iron hut. **1973** *Times* 12 Mar. 1/5 The murder hunt is being led by Detective Superintendent Brian Weight, who set up an incident room at Aylesbury police station.

incident, *sb.*[2]: see INCIDENT *a.*[2]

incident (ˈɪnsɪdənt), *a.*[1] Also 6 incydent(e, insedent, insident. [a. F. *incident* or ad. L. *incident-em*, pres. pple. of *incidĕre* to fall into or to, fall upon, happen to, etc., f. *in-* (IN-[2]) + *cadĕre* to fall. The senses of the English word are derived from med.L. rather than from F.]

I. 1. Liable or apt to befall or occur *to*; likely to happen; hence, naturally appertaining or attaching. **a.** Const. *to* (†*in*, *into*), rarely *on*.

1488 *Will of Statworth* (Somerset Ho.), To socour his simple body as they think incident and conuenient to him. **1530** RASTELL *Bk. Purgat.* III. xii, Punyshment..is incydent to the repentaunce whiche taketh away yͤ synne. **1534** MORE *Comf. agst. Trib.* II. Wks. 1177/2 Yf we well consyder these twoo thinges, tentation and persecucion, wee maye fynde that eyther of theym is incydente into the tother. **1578** LYTE *Dodoens* vi. lxxxvii. 771 A kind of corruption or maladie insident to the pine-tree. **1584** LYLY *Campaspe* v. iv, Commonly we see it incident in artificers to be enamoured of their owne workes. **1657** AUSTEN *Fruit Trees* I. 46 Which is not incident in this way of grafting. **1685** H. MORE *Para. Prophet.* 414 That the Time of the New Jerusalem is comprized in, or, at least, incident into, the Philadelphian Succession. **1744** WARBURTON *Wks.* (1811) XI. 407 Deliberation and after-thought are not incident to God. **1773** REID *Aristotle's Log.* v. §3 (1806) 119 The fallacies incident to categorical syllogisms. **1859** LANG *Wand. India* 359 The noise..incident on the striking of the tents and the breaking up of the little camp. **1888** BRYCE *Amer. Commw.* II. xxxvii. 43 A State government is a natural growth, which *prima facie* possesses all the powers incident to any government whatever.

b. without construction.

1570 DEE *Math. Pref.* 5 Both the one and the other hath fractions incident. **1597** HOOKER *Eccl. Pol.* v. lviii. §4 Baptisme is farre more necessarie then any such incident Rite or Solemnitie ordained for the better administration thereof. **1649** MILTON *Eikon.* xxvi, Æmulations..are incident among military men. **1653** *Woodall's Wks.* Pref. 9 To instruct them in the uses and dangers incident by mistakes. *a* **1677** MANTON *Serm. Ps.* cxix. verse 107. Wks. 1872 VIII. 96 Those in the highest station have their incident cares and troubles. **1898** *Daily News* 23 July 5/3 The Puerto Rico expedition, and the incident aggressive steps taken in the campaign.

2. *Law.* Attaching itself, as a privilege, burden, or custom, *to* an office, position, etc.

1491 *Act 7 Hen. VII*, c. 22 §2 Fees and annuyties incident to every or the same Offices. **1523** FITZHERB. *Bk. Surv.* 21 b, It is called a rent seeke, bycause there is no distresse insedent nor belongyng to the same. **1574** tr. *Littleton's Tenures* 21 a, Fealtie is incydent to everye manner of Service. *a* **1626** BACON *Max. & Uses Com. Law* (1636) 35 To this tenure by Knights service in chief, was incident that the King should have a certain summe of money, called aid. **1767** BLACKSTONE *Comm.* II. xi. 176 Where rent is reserved, it is also incident..to the reversion. **1876** DIGBY *Real Prop.* iii. 162 Every freeholder holding lands within the manor had, as of right, common of pasturage on the wastes as incident to his lands.

†**3.** Relating or pertinent *to*. *Obs.*

1557 *Ord. Hospitalls* Fiij, The Books of this Howse, incident to the matter. **1583** STUBBES *Anat. Abus.* II. (1882) 2 Such necessary questions, as are incident to my purpose. **1614** RALEIGH *Hist. World* III. (1634) 89 It is not my purpose to pursue the historie of the Persians..otherwise than as they shall be incident to the affaires of Greece.

†**4.** Apt to fall into; liable *to*; subject *to*. *Obs.*

1603 DRAYTON *Bar. Wars* I. lx, Men are not ever incident to losse, When Fortune seemes them frowardly to crosse. **1624** HEYWOOD *Gunaik.* I. 18 A wicked and irreligious man is subject and incident to fall into many distresses and casualties. **1647** W. BROWNE tr. *Gomberville's Polexander* III. iii. 84 Ah! ingratefull Zabaim, King incident to all crimes! **1676** W. HUBBARD *Happiness of People* 55 Spiritual Pride is an evil, the very best of Gods Children are incident unto. **1760** H. BROOKE *Fool of Qual.* (1808) I. 166 This state of mortality is incident to perpetual change and revolution. **1767** MRS. S. PENNINGTON *Lett. Diff. Subj.* IV. 16 The little complaints they [children] are incident to.

5. a. Occurring or liable to occur by the way, or in the course of something else of which it forms no essential part; casual; = INCIDENTAL 1. Now *rare* or *Obs.*

1523 LD. BERNERS *Froiss.* I. cccxix. 493 The duke of Lancaster was nat in the fauoure of the comen people, wherby dyuers incydents parels fell after in England. **1581** *Confer.* I. (1584) Fiv b, By occasion incident there was talke of a text of Scripture. **1699** BENTLEY *Phal* 309 The incident Mistakes, which he has run into, have not fail'd to increase in Number. **1716** M. DAVIES *Athen. Brit.* III. *Crit. Hist.* 53 That Doctrine, which those chance-Propositions or incident Expressions seem to insinuate.

†**b.** Of expenses or charges; = INCIDENTAL 1 b.

1652 *Act Commw. Sale Est. Ld. Dunbar*, etc., The Commissioners shall and may allow all incident charges for the necessary carrying on of this service. *a* **1680** BUTLER *Rem.* (1759) I. 230 With all the Charges incident. **1756** WASHINGTON *Lett.* Writ. 1889 I. 313 By this means the country loses..the sums of money which each man costs, besides many incident charges, such as horse hire. **1768** *Woman of Honor* III. 178 He put into my hand a bank note, more than sufficient to defray any incident charges.

6. Subordinate, subsidiary, accessory.

a. *Anat.* (See quot.)

1855 MAYNE *Expos. Lex.*, *Incident Spinal Nerves*..those of the spinal system of nerves which convey any impressions on, or irritation of the integuments, or mucous membranes, to the true spinal marrow.

†**b.** ***incident proposition***, a proposition inserted in a principal one, and introduced by a relative pronoun, as 'bodies, *which are transparent*, have many pores' (Watts); a subordinate relative clause.

1725 WATTS *Logic* II. ii. §5 The whole proposition is called the primary or chief, and the additional proposition is called an incident proposition.

II. 7. Falling or striking upon or against; acting upon anything from without. *esp.* of light: Falling or striking upon a surface often in photographic contexts. Const. *upon*.

1667 BOYLE in *Phil. Trans.* II. 606 Looking-Glasses..are conspicuous only by the incident beams of the Sun. **1710** J. CLARKE *Rohault's Phil.* (1729) I. 91 If the incident Body A, and the Body CDEF upon which it strikes, are void of all Elasticity [etc.]. **1716** CHEYNE *Philos. Princ. Relig.* I. 78 The Obliquity of the Incident Ray is great. **1831** BREWSTER *Nat. Magic* iv. (1833) 59 Mirrors..adjusted not only to one another, but to the light incident upon each. **1842-3** GROVE *Corr. Phys. Forces* (1874) 116 Transparent matter upon which light is incident. **1855** J. EDWARDS *Art Landscape Paint. Water Col.* 37 Illuminated by light actually incident upon the picture. **1864** H. SPENCER *Princ. Biol.* §169 That there may be continuous changes of structure in organisms, there must be continuous changes in the incident forces. **1951** G. H. SEWELL *Amateur Film-Making* (ed. 2) ii. 21 The makers of other meters have adopted the Incident-light principle and have provided modifying attachments for their instruments. **1952** J. F. DUNN *Exposure Meters* i. 22 The term 'incident light' is used instead of 'illumination' when we wish to consider only the strength of the light being received *from* the source irrespective of the angle of inclination of the surface receiving it. **1956** *Nature* 4 Feb. 231/1 Blocks of soil were..directly examined with the aid of the incident-light equipment of a Leitz 'Ortholux' microscope. **1962** M. L. HASELGROVE *Photographer's Dict.* 130 Light falling on a surface is said to be incident on the surface. In most photographic writing this term used without qualification refers to the light incident on the subject to be photographed.

†**8.** Opposed *to*, running counter *to*. *Obs. rare*$^{-1}$. [Cf. L. *incidĕre* to fall upon, attack, strike or dash against.]

c **1555** HARPSFIELD *Divorce Hen. VIII* (Camden) 74 There is no marriage, but only between the parents and children, of itself and immediately incident and repugnant to natural reason.

†**incident** (ɪnˈsaɪdənt), *a.*[2] and *sb.*[2] *Obs.* [ad. L. *incīdent-em*, pres. pple. of *incīdĕre* to INCIDE.]

A. *adj.* That 'cuts' the phlegm, etc. **B.** *sb.* An inciding medicine.

1753 CHAMBERS *Cycl. Supp.*, *Incidents*, or *Attenuants*, in the materia medica... To this class belong the roots of arum, asarabacca, acorus [etc.]. **1855** MAYNE *Expos. Lex.*, *Incidens*, having power to cut; formerly applied to medicines ..supposed to cause the phlegm to be discharged, by cutting, as it were..: incident.

incidental (ɪnsɪˈdɛntəl), *a.* (*sb.*) [f. INCIDENT *sb.* + -AL[1]. Cf. mod.F. *incidentel.*]

A. *adj.* **1. a.** Occurring or liable to occur in fortuitous or subordinate conjunction with something else of which it forms no essential part; casual.

1644 MILTON *Educ.* Wks. (1847) 98/1 Those incidental discourses which we have wandered into. **1697** DAMPIER *Voy.* I. 161 With an incidental Account of the first Inducements that made the Privateers undertake the passage. **1736** BUTLER *Anal.* II. Concl. 405 In Scripture, whether in incidental passages or in the general scheme of it. **1790** PALEY *Horæ Paul.* Rom. ii. 19 A circumstance as incidental, and as unlike design, as any that can be imagined. **1875** JOWETT *Plato* (ed. 2) III. 17 The simple and apparently incidental manner in which the last remark is introduced. **1876** E. MELLOR *Priesth.* viii. 371 There is scarcely any practice which is so corrupt as not to produce some incidental good.

b. Of a charge or expense: Such as is incurred (in the execution of some plan or purpose) apart from the primary disbursements.

1739 CIBBER *Apol.* (1756) II. 86 In the first six days of acting it, we paid all our constant and incidental expence, and shar'd each of us a hundred pounds. **1772** *Ann. Reg.* 224 For defraying the expences of the civil establishment of his Majesty's colony of West Florida, and other incidental expences attending the same. **1804** W. TENNANT *Ind. Recreat.* (ed. 2) I. 63 The house rent, and the incidental charges of a family. **1868** PEARD *Water-Farm.* x. 104 These calls sufficed..for the nursery, and incidental expenses.

c. ***incidental images, colours***: such as are perceived by the eye as a consequence of visual impressions no longer present.

1876 BERNSTEIN *Five Senses* 117 These prolonged impressions of light are called *incidental* images. *Ibid.* 120 The incidental colours..which are formed in the eye, are most interesting.

2. ***incidental to***: liable to happen to; to which a thing is liable or exposed. ***incidental upon***: following upon as an incident.

1616 CORYAT in J. Taylor (Water P.) *Wks.* (1630) II. 83 If I should happen to be destitute; a matter very incidentall to a poore Footman Pilgrim. **1665** T. MALL *Offer F. Help* 96 Those temptations that are incidental to a suffering state. **1732** BERKELEY *Alciphr.* I. §10, I, who am no great genius, have a weakness incidental to little ones. **1828** SCOTT *F.M. Perth* vi, The hesitation incidental to the use of a foreign language. **1851** H. SPENCER *Social Statics* 70 Others..may contend that..with the rightly constituted or moral man, correct conduct to others is merely incidental upon the fulfilment of his own nature. **1888** J. INGLIS *Tent Life Tigerland* 148 The dangers incidental to pigsticking.

3. a. Casually met with or encountered. *rare.*

1856 J. CUMMING *Script. Read. Deuteron.* viii. 143 The green moss and incidental flowerets break out from the rifts and rents. **1871** BLACKIE *Four Phases* i. 122 The..braying of an incidental ass. **1876** GEO. ELIOT *Dan. Der.* v. xxxviii, A store of magical articulation with which he..promised himself to frighten any incidental Christian of his own years.

b. Given to relating casual incidents. *nonce-use.*

1843 CARLYLE *Past & Pr.* II. v, Says the incidental Jocelin.

†**4.** = INCIDENT *a.*[1] 7. *Obs. rare.*

1813 T. BUSBY *Lucretius* IV. Comment. xv, The angle contained by the incidental ray.

5. Special collocations: ***incidental advertisement*** (see quot.); ***incidental music***, music played as an accompaniment or 'background' to a play or film, or to a radio or other performance or entertainment; ***incidental number***, a piece of incidental music; also *transf.*

1931 *Times Lit. Suppl.* 20 Aug. 636/3 'Incidental' advertisements, advertisements..which are printed in a separate gathering from the body of the book and sewn in at either the end or the beginnning. **1864** in H. J. Byron *Orpheus & Eurydice* 2 (*heading*) The incidental music selected and arranged by Mr. Frank Musgrave. **1928** *Melody Maker* Feb. 214 (Advt.), Liber's incidental music. **1938** *Oxf. Compan. Music* 464/1 Incidental music to plays has always been an important side-line of the art and business of the composer. **1904** W. D. ADAMS *Dict. Drama* I. p. vi, Musical Composers, the latter ranging from the writers of operas and operettas to the providers of 'incidental numbers' for plays. **1912** E. WYLIE (*title*) Incidental numbers.

B. *sb.* An incidental circumstance, event, charge, expense, etc.

1707 *Modest Enquiry* in *Sewall's Diary* (1879) II. 73 The accidental occasions of hiring Transport Ships, together with the other Incidentals that must necessarily accrue. **1726** POPE *Let. to Bethel* 9 Aug., Almost every body and every thing is a cause or object for humanity, even prosperity itself, and health itself; so many weak pitiful incidentals attend on them. **1866** ROGERS *Agric. & Prices* I. xxviii. 673 We should find in others a large bill for incidentals.

incidentalist (ɪnsɪˈdɛntəlɪst). [f. INCIDENTAL *a.* + -IST.] One who describes or insists on what is merely incidental and not essential.

1904 *Daily Chron.* 19 Nov. 3/1 Mr. Palmer may be described as an 'incidentalist'. **1924** H. E. FOSDICK *Mod. Use Bible* 163 Folk who insist on that kind of literal inerrancy in ancient documents are not Fundamentalists at all; they are incidentalists.

incidentality (ˌɪnsɪdɛnˈtælɪtɪ). *rare.* [f. INCIDENTAL *a.* + -ITY.] The quality of being incidental.

1791 *Deb. Congress U.S.* (1834) II. 1942 Hence the incidentality of this authority to the mere existence of Government is inferred.

incidentally (ɪnsɪˈdɛntəlɪ), *adv.* [f. INCIDENTAL *a.* + -LY[2].] **1.** In an incidental manner; as an incident, or a subordinate and casual circumstance.

1665 BOYLE *Occas. Refl.* (1848) 56 A Theme, that fell but incidentally under my consideration. **1736** BUTLER *Anal.* II. vii. Wks. 1874 I. 254 He mentions these gifts incidentally, in the most easy manner. **1855** MACAULAY *Hist. Eng.* xiv. III. 407 In the course of the debate a grave constitutional question was incidentally raised. **1879** R. K. DOUGLAS *Confucianism* iv. 94 The supreme object of learning should be truth, and incidentally self-improvement.

2. In point of fact: used to accompany a not immediately pertinent statement.

1925 T. DREISER *Amer. Trag.* (1926) I. I. ii. 15 Incidentally by that time the sex lure or appeal had begun to manifest itself. **1926** FOWLER *Mod. Eng. Usage* 264/2 *Incidentally* is now very common as a writer's apology for an irrelevance. **1961** A. HUXLEY *Let.* 8 Jan. (1969) 902 Pure perceptual receptivity is the basis, incidentally, of many Tantrik exercises. **1972** R. QUIRK et al. *Gram. Contemp. Eng.* 667 *Incidentally* adds explicitly that what is being said is a digression, if only slight, and an afterthought: The airlines charge half-price for students. Incidentally, I have already bought my ticket to New York.

inciˈdentalness. [f. as prec. + -NESS.] The quality or state of being incidental.

1730-6 in BAILEY (folio). **1775** in ASH. Hence in WORCESTER, etc.

†**inciˈdentary,** *a. Obs. rare.* [f. INCIDENT *sb.*[1] + -ARY. Cf. *accidentary.*] Casual, incidental. Hence **inciˈdentarily** *adv.*, incidentally.

a **1670** HACKET *Abp. Williams* II. (1692) 208 He had been near fifty years from the county of Carnarvan and the town of Conway, unless by incidentary visits. —— *Cent. Serm.* (1675) 621 They came together upon appointment, or incidentary occasions. *Ibid., Incarn.* iv, These 14 generations are reckoned up, and but 4 women incidentarily put into the catalogue.

incidented (ˈɪnsɪdəntɪd), *a.* [f. INCIDENT *sb.*[1] + -ED[2].] Filled with incidents, eventful.

1898 W. J. LOCKE *Idols* 274 In the course of an incidented life..I have found that discretion is the better part of virtue.

ˈincidentless, *a. rare.* [f. INCIDENT *sb.*[1] + -LESS.] Without incident; uneventful.

1782 MAD. D'ARBLAY *Diary* 26 Oct., My journey was incidentless, but the moment I came into Brighthelmstone I was met by Mrs. Thrale.

†**ˈincidently,** *adv. Obs.* [f. INCIDENT *a.*[1] + -LY[2].] In an incident manner; by the way, casually; incidentally.

1529 MORE *Dyaloge* I. xxii. 28 Y[e] author therfore incydently sheweth what harm hath happed sumtyme to fall to dyuerse of those yong men. **1570** *Act 13 Eliz.* c. 4 §9 Suche Charges as are necessarily and incidentlye to be spent and provided in theyr Offyces. **1640** BP. HALL *Episc.* II. xx. 201 It is but incidently in our way. **1716** M. DAVIES *Athen. Brit.* III. *Crit. Hist.* 54 As for such an Author's incidently mentioning some things [etc.]. **1824** *Westm. Rev.* I. 375 In so doing we may incidently afford some specimens of the original.

†**ˈincidentness.** *Obs. rare*$^{-0}$. [-NESS.]

1727 BAILEY vol. II, *Incidentness*, liableness.

†**inˈcider.** *Obs.* [f. INCIDE *v.*[1] + -ER[1].] One who or that which cuts; an 'inciding' medicine.

1598 FLORIO, *Incisore*, an incider or maker of an incision. **1720** BLAIR in *Phil. Trans.* XXXI. 33 Attenuaters and Inciders, as Salvia, Horminum. **1749** T. SHORT *Chron. Hist. Air*, etc. I. 260 The Cure consisted in repeated Lenitives, cooling Inciders, and Pectorals.

inˈciding, *vbl. sb.* ?*Obs.* [f. as prec. + -ING[1].] The action of INCIDE *v.*[1]; a cutting, incision.

1694 SALMON *Bate's Dispens.* (1713) 43/1 This Mixture has the Power of inciding, and attenuating. **1746** R. JAMES *Introd. Mouffet's Health's Improv.* 2 The first Part of Manducation is, the inciding, or cutting the Aliment with the fore Teeth.

inˈciding, *ppl. a.* ?*Obs.* [-ING[2].] Cutting; †loosening and removing phlegm or the like.

1678 SALMON *Pharm. Lond.* VI. ii. 814 *Inciding*, such as cut, attenuate and make matter or humors thin. **1758** J. S. *Le Dran's Observ. Surg.* (1771) 86 The Stroke..was inciding with regard to the first Table of the Bone. **1788** HOWARD *Encycl.* s.v. *Albugo*, A little of this powder..gradually absterges and wears off the spot by it's inciding quality.

inciduous (ɪnˈsɪdjuːəs), *a. rare.* [f. L. *incidĕre* INCIDE *v.*[2]: cf. *deciduous.*] Of a pulse: Undulating.

1822 GOOD *Study Med.* II. 26 The dicrotic, coturnising, and inciduous [pulses] proposed by Solano, as mere sub-varieties of the rebounding or redoubling. [Cf. DUNGLISON (ed. 1851) *Pulsus incidens*,..undulating pulse.]

incinderjell, var. INCENDIJEL.

†**inˈcinderment.** *Obs.* [f. **incinder* vb. (ad. F. *encendrer*:—L. *incinerāre*) + -MENT.] Reduction to ashes; incineration.

1609 J. DAVIES *Holy Roode* (1876) 26 (D.) Hee, like the glorious rare Arabian bird, Will soon result from His incinderment.

incinerable (ɪnˈsɪnərəb(ə)l), *a. rare.* [f. med.L. *incinerāre* to INCINERATE + -ABLE.] Capable of being burnt to ashes.

1658 SIR T. BROWNE *Hydriot.* iii. 23 Other incinerable substances were found so fresh, that they could feel no sindge from fire.

†**inˈcinerate,** *ppl. a. Obs.* [ad. med.L. *incinerāt-us*, pa. pple. of *incinerāre*: see next.] = INCINERATED. (Const. as *pa. pple.* or *adj.*)

1471 RIPLEY *Comp. Alch.* I. xix. in Ashm. (1652) 133 Thy Elements shalbe incynerate sone. **1526** *Pilgr. Perf.* (W. de W. 1531) 182 b, Our fyrst mother Eue with her husbande was incinerate and turned to dust after theyr deth. **1626** BACON *Sylva* §683 Fire burneth Wood, making it first Luminous; Then Blacke and Brittle; And lastly, Broken and Incinerate.

incinerate (ɪnˈsɪnəreɪt), *v.* [f. ppl. stem of med.L. *incinerāre* to reduce to ashes, f. *in-* (IN-[2]) + *cinis, ciner-em* ashes (of a fire): see -ATE[3].]

1. *trans.* To reduce to ashes, burn to ashes, consume by fire.

1555 EDEN *Decades* 334 The fyer whose force dooth incinerate or brynge to asshes..all creatures. **1626** BACON *Sylva* §87 The Heat..doth Incinerate and Calcinate. **1661-80** BOYLE *Scept. Chem.* I. 80 It is the Fire only that Incinerates Bodies. **1805** C. HATCHET in *Phil. Trans.* XCV. 216 Animal coal is incinerated with much more difficulty than vegetable coal or charcoal. **1884** *Manch. Exam.* 10 Mar. 5/3 A Crematorium..has been established, in which..forty bodies had been incinerated after the manner of the Romans of old.

2. *intr.* To become reduced to ashes.

1800 tr. *Lagrange's Chem.* II. 190 A light spongy charcoal, which easily incinerates when burnt in the open air. **1826** KIRBY & SP. *Entomol.* III. xxxiv. 396 Feathers, wool, hair, etc., when exposed to the action of fire liquify, more or less, before they incinerate.

incinerated (ɪnˈsɪnəreɪtɪd), *ppl. a.* [f. prec. + -ED[1].] Burnt or reduced to ashes.

1658 SIR T. BROWNE *Hydriot.* ii. 15 Near the same plot of ground..were digged up coals and incinerated substances. **1869** E. A. PARKES *Pract. Hygiene* (ed. 3) 37 The difference between the weight of the simply dried and the incinerated solids.

b. Reduced to 'ashes', i.e. to the dust of death.

1647 FARINGDON *Serm.* 55 (L.) That power which is requisite to raise a body now putrified and incinerated.

incineration (ɪnsɪnəˈreɪʃən). [a. F. *incinération* (14th c. in Hatz.-Darm.), ad. med.L. *incinerātio*, n. of action from *incinerāre* to INCINERATE.] The action or process of incinerating or burning to ashes; reduction to ashes.

a **1529** SKELTON *P. Sparowe* 536 The phenyx..Of whose incyneracyon There ryseth a new creacyon. **1678** SALMON *Pharm. Lond.* VI. ix. 834 Incineration is the burning a matter to Ashes, either with live coals, or by the help of Niter. **1756** C. LUCAS *Ess. Waters* III. 322 Some land plants give some sea salt by incineration. **1842** PARNELL *Chem. Anal.* (1845) 84 Organic matters may be removed by incineration.

b. Applied *spec.* (esp. in U.S.) to the cremation of the dead.

1880 *Nature* XXI. 239 The time for the complete incineration of the bodies was..about two hours. **1885** *Pall Mall G.* 28 Oct. 3/1 In America cremation—or, as it is called, incineration—is making rapid strides.

incinerator (ɪnˈsɪnəreɪtə(r)). [agent-n. in L. form from INCINERATE *v.*] One who or that which incinerates; *spec.* an apparatus for burning substances to ashes; a cremator.

1883 BENGLOSS in *Princeton Rev.* 149 The door of the incinerator is opened to receive the body. **1889** *Engineer* 18 Jan. Advts. p. xxvii, 'The Incinerator' (Dr. Sargeant's Patent) for destroying the refuse of Hospitals [etc.].

incipher, obs. form of ENCIPHER *v.*

incipience (ɪnˈsɪpɪəns). [f. INCIPIENT: see -ENCE.] Beginning, commencement, origination; the fact or condition of being incipient or in an early stage; with *pl.*, a beginning, a first step or stage.

1864 WEBSTER, *Incipience, Incipiency*, beginning; commencement. **1865** CARLYLE *Fredk. Gt.* XVIII. x. (1872) VII. 270 The dim incipiences of dawn. **1898** *19th Cent.* XLIV. 995 The wealth of England does not explain the incipience of the college system.

incipience, obs. (erron.) f. INSIPIENCE.

incipiency (ɪnˈsɪpɪənsɪ). [f. as prec. + -ENCY.] The quality or state of being incipient; incipience.

1817 T. L. PEACOCK *Melincourt* xxiii, If that ugly monster ..had not knocked us both down in the incipiency of our progression. **1834** *Fraser's Mag.* IX. 583 In the incipiency of his business. **1847** LEWES *Hist. Philos.* (1857) 14 The infinite as being in a constant state of incipiency. **1858** CARLYLE *Fredk. Gt.* IV. i. (1872) I. 274 She oversaw his.. first attempts at walking..incipiencies of speech. **1876** BARTHOLOW *Mat. Med.* (1879) 155 Dose..of quinia and morphia..given at the incipiency of the attack.

incipient (ɪn'sɪpɪənt), *a.* and *sb.* [ad. L. *incipient-em*, pres. pple. of *incipĕre* to begin.]

A. *adj.* **1.** Beginning; commencing; coming into, or in an early stage of, existence; in an initial stage.

1669 W. SIMPSON *Hydrol. Chym.* 164 Incipient putrefaction. **1764** GRAINGER *Sugar-Cane* IV. *note* (R.), The juice of the leaves drop'd into the eye will remove incipient films. **1779–81** JOHNSON *L.P., Addison* Wks. III. 56 The flying vapours of incipient madness. **1803** BEDDOES *Hygeia* x. 20 It is affirmed that the evening and..night are the seasons of most violence with incipient lunatics. **1813** SIR H. DAVY *Agric. Chem.* (1814) 302 A slight incipient fermentation is undoubtedly of use in the dunghill. **1837–9** HALLAM *Hist. Lit.* I. I. iv. 293 *note*, It is evident that Greek was just now incipient at Cambridge. **1869** GOULBURN *Purs. Holiness* vii. 57 The same instinct is found in an incipient and crude state among animals.

2. *Comb.* **incipient species**, a group of plants or animals in the process of becoming sufficiently distinct to be described as a full species.

1859 DARWIN *Origin of Species* ii. 52 A well-marked variety may be called an incipient species... It need not be supposed that all varieties or incipient species necessarily attain the rank of species. **1942** E. MAYR *Systematics & Origin of Species* vii. 156 Some subspecies are incipient species, or subspecies are potentially incipient species. **1963** DAVIS & HEYWOOD *Princ. Angiosperm Taxon.* iii. 100 There is a tendency to regard subspecies as incipient species. **1971** *Nature* 2 Apr. 275/2 In *D[rosophila] paulistorum* there are a number of incipient species (usually called 'semispecies').

B. *sb.* †**1.** A beginner; = INCEPTOR. *Obs.*

1589 NASHE *Anat. Absurb.* 39 This I speake to shew what an obloquie, these impudent incipients in Arts, are vnto Art. **1598** FLORIO, *Incipiente*, an incipient, a beginner.

2. *Heb. Gram.* The verbal 'tense' or form with prefixed servile letters, variously called Future, Present, and Imperfect.

1866 J. G. MURPHY *Comm. Exod.* iii. 14 It [present tense] is..the only form fit to express the Hebrew incipient.

Hence **in'cipiently** *adv.*, in an incipient manner.

1856 in WEBSTER. **1893** J. PULSFORD *Loyalty to Christ* II. 231 Christ is incipiently becoming the inrooted Righteousness of every man who..deplores his inherent sinfulness.

incipient, obs. (erron.) form of INSIPIENT.

‖**incipit** ('ɪnsɪpɪt). The L. word *incipit* = [here] beginneth, used by mediæval scribes in indicating the beginning of a new treatise, poem, division, etc. in a Latin or (sometimes) English MS.; hence, as *sb.* The beginning or first words or lines of a treatise or poem in a MS. Cf. EXPLICIT.

[**1377** LANGL. *P. Pl.* B, Incipit liber de Petro Plowman.] **1897** *Dublin Rev.* Oct. 473 The contents of each volume are fully given, for the most part with incipits and explicits. **1963** [see EXPLICIT b]. **1973** *Times* 2 Nov. 6/1 The *incipits*, or titular opening phrases, of more than 200 literary works current in Sumer in the early second millennium B.C.

'**in-,circle.** *Geom.* [f. IN *adv.* + CIRCLE *sb.*] An inscribed circle.

1883 W. H. H. HUDSON in *Nature* XXVIII. 7, I beg leave to suggest the following names: *circumcircle, incircle, excircle*, and *midcircle*.

incircle, incircule, obs. ff. ENCIRCLE *v.*

†**in'circlet.** *Obs. nonce-wd.* [f. IN-¹ or IN-² + CIRCLET.] A little circular curl or spiral.

a **1586** SIDNEY *Arcadia* II. xvii. (1622) 139 No purer then the prettie eares.. In whose Incirclets if ye gaze, Your eyes may tread a Louers maze.

†**in'circuit**, *v. Obs.* [f. IN-² + CIRCUIT *sb.* Cf. phrase 'in circuit'.] *trans.* To encircle, surround.

c **1650** in Johnston *Nat. Hist. E. Bord.* (1853) I. 91 This Towne was strengthened, environed, and is incircuited with strong walls and flankeirs.

†**incircumcised**, *a. Obs.* [f. IN-³ + CIRCUMCISED, after L. *incircumcīsus* or F. *inciconcis*.] Not circumcised; uncircumcised.

1483 CAXTON *Gold. Leg.* 65 b/2 And dauid said what is this incircumcised that hath despysed the hoost of the god of Israhel? **1554** KNOX *Godly Let.* A vj b, Beholde, theyr eares be incircumcised, they can not advert.

So †**incircum'cision**, uncircumcision.

a **1641** BP. MOUNTAGU *Acts & Mon.* (1642) 499 Heare this you Jewes and Gentiles, attend it Circumcision and Incircumcision.

†**in'circumscript**, *a. Obs.* [ad. late L. *incircumscript-us* (Prudens, *c* 400): see IN-³ and CIRCUMSCRIPT; cf. obs. F. *inciconscrit*, *incircumscript* (Godefroy).] Not circumscribed or limited; unbounded, infinite.

1677 GALE *Crt. Gentiles* IV. 248 God is without cause, without end, sempiterne and eternal..incircumscripte.

†**incircum'scriptible**, *a. Obs.* [ad. med.L. *incircumscriptibilis*, obs. F. *incircumscriptible*, *inciconscritible*: see IN-³ and CIRCUMSCRIPTIBLE.] Incapable of being circumscribed or limited.

1550 CRANMER *Defence* 28 a, God..is inuisible, immortall, incircumscriptible, incomprehensible. **1635** PAGITT *Christianogr.* I. iii. (1636) 106 Who can make an Image of God? who is invisible, incorporall, and incircumscriptible. **1652** E. BENLOWES *Theoph.* VIII. xvii, So there Th' incircumscriptible would circumscribed appear.

Hence †**incircum'scriptibleness.**

1615 BYFIELD *Expos. Coloss.* i. 17 The immensity of Christ's divine nature hath..incircumscriptibleness in respect of place.

incircumscription (ɪnsɜːkəm'skrɪpʃən). Now *rare.* [IN-³.] The condition of not being circumscribed or limited; boundlessness, infinitude.

1651 JER. TAYLOR *Serm. for Year* I. xxvii. 351 His mercy ..returns to its own centre and incircumscription, and infinity, unlesse it issues forth upon us. **1652** CHARLETON *Darkness Atheism* 2 Consider how impossible it must be..to behold invisibility, derive independency, calculate eternity, circumscribe incircumscription. **1865** *Union Rev.* III. 440 The tenet..is..at variance with the incircumscription of the Divine Nature.

†**incircum'spect**, *a. Obs.* [IN-³.] Not circumspect; incautious, heedless, imprudent.

1531 in W. H. Turner *Select. Rec. Oxford* 102 The incircumspect occupying of their crafts. **1532** TINDALE *Exp. Matt.* v–vii, Vnstable, inconstant, and lyght manered, full of wittes, after witted (as we call it,) incircumspect, inconsiderate, heady, rash. **1608** TOPSELL *Serpents* (1658) 770 With their teeth they bite and wound at unawares, incircumspect Mowers, and harvest-folks. **1651** BIGGS *New Disp.* ¶ 170 Incircumspect credulity.

Hence †**incircum'spectly** *adv.*; also †**incircum'spectness.**

1542 *Lam. & Piteous Treat.* in *Harl. Misc.* (Malh.) I. 236 Two shyppes of the Turcke..whiche incircumspectly fell into oure handes. **1568** C. WATSON *Polyb.* 85 a, The incircumspectness of Hanno hindered not the Carthaginenses only at this time, but also [etc.]. **1563–87** FOXE *A. & M.* (1596) 269/1 The Christians..entring into the munition incircumspectlie, were pelted and pashed with stones.

†**incircum'spection.** *Obs.* [IN-³.] Want of circumspection; heedlessness, unwariness.

1646 SIR T. BROWNE *Pseud. Ep.* I. xi. 45 Whereby he more easily led away the incercumspection of their beliefe. **1683** CAVE *Ecclesiastici, Eusebius* 33 He did it..through heedlessness and incircumspection.

incisal (ɪn'saɪzəl), *a. Dentistry.* [f. *incis-* stem of INCISOR, etc. + -AL.] Of, pertaining to, or designating the cutting edge or surface of an incisor or a canine tooth.

1916 M. DEWEY *Dental Anat.* ii. 44 The incisal edge of the central incisor is formed by the junction of the lingual and labial surfaces of the tooth. **1924** J. F. HOVESTAD *Pract. Dental Porcelains* xiv. 121 Frequent accidents to anterior teeth..causing loss of incisal corners or edges, have given the dentist great trouble. **1956** J. N. ANDERSON *Appl. Dental Materials* xxii. 300 The incisal edge of an anterior tooth is mainly enamel. **1969** *Gloss. Terms Dentistry* (*B.S.I.*) 80 *Incisal guidance*, the influence on mandibular movements exerted by the contacting surfaces of the mandibular and maxillary anterior teeth.

incise (ɪn'saɪz), *v.* Also 6 incyse, 7 incize. [a. F. *incise-r* (15th c. in Godef.), for OF. *enciser* (12th c. in Littré), f. L. *incis-*, ppl. stem of *incīdĕre* to cut into: see INCIDE *v.*¹]

1. a. *trans.* To cut into, make a cut or incision in; to cut marks or figures upon, engrave *with* figures.

1567 [see INCISING below]. **1610** MARKHAM *Masterp.* I. v. 14 Flesh being cut or incised into many parts, yet is euery part still flesh. *a* **1639** CAREW *Poems* Wks. (1824) 32 Fond man, that canst beleeve..that thy weake steele can incize The crystall case wherin it lyes. **1834** J. FORBES *Laennec's Dis. Chest* (ed. 4) 615 The other parts of the lungs were.. imbued with a yellowish frothy serum, which escaped from them when incised. **1873** J. GEIKIE *Gt. Ice Age* xxiv. 316 Glacial deposits were swept out of the valleys, and the solid rocks themselves deeply incised. **1876** GEO. ELIOT *Dan. Der.* VIII. lx, The wood was beautifully incised with Arabic lettering.

b. *absol.* To make a cut or incision.

1541 R. COPLAND *Guydon's Quest. Chirurg.*, etc., By incysynge, cuttynge, or scaturysyng. **1612** WOODALL *Surg. Mate* Wks. (1653) 1 It behoveth the Surgeon to regard if he incise deep. **1617** FLETCHER *Mad Lover* III. ii, Ye can incise To a hair's breadth without defacing.

c. *trans. Geol.* Of a river: to cut (a channel or valley) in an underlying landform. Also *absol.* Usu. as **incised** *pa. pple.* (cf. INCISED *ppl. a.* 3).

1893 *Science* 17 Nov. 278/1 The process by which the present ravines are forming is not a direct continuation of the process by which the gentler slopes of the upland were formed. The former are incised in the latter. **1896** *Nat. Geogr. Mag.* VII. 190 With the uplift of the region the meandering river would proceed to incise its channel beneath the uplifted surface. **1926** *Jrnl. Geol.* XXXIV. 31 Green River has a highly meandering course which is deeply incised in the rocks of the plateau. **1954** W. D. THORNBURY *Princ. Geomorphol.* vi. 147 Heavily loaded streams are more likely to cut laterally as they incise their valleys than those with lesser loads. **1972** *Science* 27 Oct. 409/2 Meandering rivers that have incised in bedrock and yet have maintained a sinuous pattern may be of two basic types.

2. To produce, form, or trace by cutting; to carve, engrave (a statue, figure, inscription, etc.).

c **1631** CAREW *Elegy Donne* in *D.'s Poems* (1633) 388, I on thy Tombe this Epitaph incise. **1656** STANLEY *Hist. Philos.* v. (1701) 178/2 'Twas Mars's Steel that Venus did incize. **1851** D. WILSON *Preh. Ann.* (1863) II. IV. ii. 246 Stones decorated with crosses, incised or in relief. **1876** BIRCH *Rede Lect. Egypt* 35 A nation..incising virtues and not vices for public consideration.

Hence **in'cising** *vbl. sb.* = INCISION.

1567 *Ann. Barber-Surg.* (1890) 315 The desections or incysynges of the body.

†**incise** (ɪn'saɪs), *a. rare*⁻⁰. [ad. L. *incīsus*, pa. pple. of *incīdĕre* (see prec.). Cf. *concise*.] = INCISED. Hence **in'cisely** *adv.*

1828 WEBSTER, *Incisely*, in the manner of incisions or notches. *Eaton.*

incised (ɪn'saɪzd), *ppl. a.* [f. INCISE *v.* + -ED¹.]

1. a. Cut into, having an incision made in it; marked by cutting.

1597 A. M. tr. *Guillemeau's Fr. Chirurg.* 20 b/1 Thrust cleane through the incisede skinne. **1743** *Lond. & Country Brewer* (ed. 4) 292 The best Staple incised Isinglass, two Ounces. **1800** *Med. Jrnl.* IV. 80 No inflammation could be traced on the margin of the incised gums. **1853** G. TATE *Addr. Berwick. Naturalists' Club*, Sketches of incised rocks at Ford and Bewick.

b. *Bot.* and *Zool.* Having marginal notches, as if cut or slashed; as a leaf or an insect's wing. Also in comb. = INCISO-, as in ***incised-crenate***.

1826 KIRBY & SP. *Entomol.* IV. 295 *Incised*, cut into equal marginal segments. **1870** HOOKER *Stud. Flora* 292 *Lamium album*..leaves..rarely deeply incised. *Ibid.* 294 *Teucrium chamædrys*; leaves petioled ovate incised-crenate. **1880** GRAY *Struct. Bot.* iii. §4. 98 The blade [of a leaf] is said to be *Incised*, when cut by sharp and irregular incisions more or less deeply.

2. Produced by cutting or incision; engraved.

1807–26 S. COOPER *First Lines Surg.* (ed. 5) 119 An incised wound, made with a clean sharp instrument..can have no foreign bodies in it. **1851** RUSKIN *Stones Ven.* I. xxi. §23 The ornaments on the armour are simply drawn with incised lines. **1879** LUBBOCK *Addr. Pol. & Educ.* ix. 173 Two stones, with incised crosses.

3. *Geol.* Of the channel of a stream, esp. a meander: cut abnormally deeply into underlying deposits or bedrock. Also, of a landform: cut by channels.

1899 W. M. DAVIS *Physical Geogr.* ix. 254 Incised meanders and cut-off spurs occur on the Allegheny river above Pittsburg. **1906** *Bull. Geogr. Soc. Philadelphia* IV. IV. 1 (*heading*) Incised meandering valleys. *Ibid.* 9 The Potomac river..exhibits some well-defined incised meanders in a valley of monoclinal strata. **1944** A. HOLMES *Princ. Physical Geol.* xi. 198 In Utah, where recent uplift has made possible the development of many deeply incised meanders.., there are several examples of such arches. **1968** R. W. FAIRBRIDGE *Encycl. Geomorphol.* 332/2 (*caption*) Incised etchplain. *Ibid.* 548/2 A meandering river valley that has cut down its bed into the bedrock, because of uplift or lowered base level, is called incised, intrenched, entrenched, inclosed or ingrown.

incisiform (ɪn'saɪzɪfɔːm), *a. Zool.* [f. L. *incīs-us* as stem of INCISOR + -FORM.] Having the form of an incisor tooth, esp. of that of a rodent.

1885 *Amer. Jrnl. Sci.* Ser. III. Mar. 187 In the genus Dinoceras there are three incisor teeth, and a small incisiform canine on each side.

incision (ɪn'sɪʒən). Forms: 5 incisyon (inscicioun), 6 incysyon, (insicion, -yon, 6–7 inscision(e, 7 incession, inscition, incissision), 5– incision. [a. F. *incision* (13–14th c. in Hatz.-Darm.), ad. L. *incīsiōn-em*, n. of action from *incīdĕre* to cut in, INCIDE *v.*¹ The 16–17th c. spelling in *insc-* arose from erroneously referring the word to L. *scindĕre, scissum* to divide, tear, cut: cf. *abscision, abscission*, and *scissors* (orig. *cysours, cizars*, F. *ciseaux*).]

1. The action of cutting into something; esp. into some part of the body in surgery.

1474 CAXTON *Chesse* 100 Instrumentis of yron and of siluer for to make incisions. **1547** BOORDE *Brev. Health* Pref. 4 That they [Surgeons] be circumspecte in insicyons. **1614** W. B. *Philosopher's Banquet* (ed. 2) 2 That put the knife to inscition, or the sawe to abscition. **1697** DRYDEN *Virg. Georg.* II. 111 We make a deep Incision in the Tree. **1794** S. WILLIAMS *Vermont* 89 Nor can they be easily withdrawn without tearing the flesh, but by incision. **1846** G. E. DAY tr. *Simon's Anim. Chem.* II. 422 On making incisions into the warm flesh of an animal just killed, we obtain, by pressure, an acid fluid. **1875** H. WALTON *Dis. Eye* (ed. 3) 576 'Incision' is suited when the iris will retract.

2. a. The effect of cutting into something; a division produced by cutting; a cut, gash.

c **1400** *Lanfranc's Cirurg.* 302 þou schalt make þe inscicioun of þe veine þe more long. **1564–78** BULLEYN *Dial. agst. Pest.* (1888) 47 Make the insicion long. **1609** W. BIDDULPH in T. Lavender *Trav.* (1612) 10 Out of these incisions and cuts proceedeth the masticke by drops. **1795** A. ANDERSON *Brit. Emb. China* xi. 133 The incision made from the top of the mountain to the surface of the road. **1879** STAINER *Music of Bible* 83 An incision in the surface of the cane.

b. *Bot.* and *Zool.* A deep indentation or notch having the appearance of being produced by cutting, as in the margin of a leaf or of an insect's wing, etc.

1578 LYTE *Dodoens* III. lxiii. 404 The leaues be white, with great and deepe incisions and cuttes. **1875** W. HOUGHTON *Sh. Brit. Ins.* 84 The incisions between some of the segments are deep black. **1877** F. HEATH *Fern W.* 22 The incisions reach down to the rachis, or mid-rib, of the frond.

†**3.** *Med.* The loosening and removal of obstructive or viscid humours: cf. INCIDE *v.*¹ 2. *Obs.*

1626 BACON *Sylva* §42 Abstertion..is plainely a Scouring off, or Incision of the more viscous Humours..And Cutting betweene them and the Part.

4. *fig.* Incisiveness, keenness of action or apprehension.

1862 TROLLOPE *N. Amer.* I. 303 The mind of the Englishman has more imagination, but that of the American more incision. *a* **1882** J. S. BLACKIE (O.), The bards performed the function of public censors with sharp incision.

¶**5.** In 17th c. often erroneously used for INSITION, engrafting.

1601 R. JOHNSON *Kingd. & Commw.* 132 These acquisitions are as it were incisions or graffings. **1681** FLAVEL *Meth. Grace* ii. 27 Implanted, or ingraffed by way of incision.

6. *Geol.* The cutting down and deepening of its channel by a river; a channel so made.

1906 *Bull. N.Y. State Mus.* No. 92. 333 So relatively inconspicuous are the incisions in this upland, that..the sky line will appear a nearly level one. **1914** *Jrnl. Geol.* XXII. 473 Lack of flats along the stream indicates that incision is still in progress. **1970** R. J. SMALL *Study of Landforms* ii. 65 A change of climate, leading to..a condition of stream underloading, will be accompanied by incision of the rivers into these deposits.

7. *attrib.* and *Comb.*, as ***incision operation***; **incision-knife**, a knife for making surgical incisions.

1611 COTGR., *Incisif*, cutting, launcing, opening, incision-making. **1612** WOODALL *Surg. Mate* Wks. (1653) 2 It is very ..needfull for the Surgeon to have at the least two incision Knives. **1808** BENTHAM *Sc. Reform* 29 The preservation of abuse..against the attacks of the probe, or the incision-knife. **1897** *Allbutt's Syst. Med.* II. 1131 During the seven years..121 incision-operations have been performed on hydatids within the great cavities of the body.

Hence †**in'cisioner** *Obs. nonce-wd.*, one who makes incisions, a surgeon.

1602 W. CLOWES *Struma* 33 A famous Incisioner and Licentiate Chirurgian of London.

incisive (ɪn'saɪsɪv), *a.* (*sb.*) Also 6 (*erron.*) inscisive. [ad. med.L. *incīsīv-us*, f. *incīs-* (see INCISE *v.*) + -IVE: cf. F. *incisif, -ive* (13–14th c. in Hatz.-Darm.).]

1. Having the quality of incising or cutting into something; cutting, penetrating with a sharp edge.

1597 A. M. tr. *Guillemeau's Fr. Chirurg.* 14 b/2 Inscisive or cuttinge pinser or tonges, to cutt of any splinters of bone. **1767** GOOCH *Treat. Wounds* I. 155 Take off the points of the needles or pins with incisive pincers. **1883** *Harper's Mag.* Nov. 824/2 The wet sand..is fed into the opening, and.. produces an incisive friction.

2. *Anat.* Applied to the incisor teeth (F. *dents incisives*; see INCISOR); and hence to parts or structures connected with these, as the ***incisive bones*** = the premaxillary bones.

1804 *Med. Jrnl.* XII. 549 In the first..the canine and incisive teeth, and in the latter the incisives only, perform the most essential part of mastication. **1842** E. WILSON *Anat. Vade M.* 34 Beneath the nasal spine, and above the two superior incisor teeth, is a slight depression, the incisive or myrtiform fossa. **1847** ANSTED *Anc. World* xv. 355 The incisive teeth and the extremities of the jaws.

†**3.** Sharp or keen in physical qualities or effects; cutting, piercing; in old *Med.* and *Phys.*, having the quality of 'cutting' or loosening viscid humours (see INCIDE *v.*¹ 2). *Obs.*

1528 PAYNEL *Salerne's Regim.* P iv, Whey..is incisiue or subtile. **1603** HOLLAND *Plutarch's Mor.* 1187 Now this aire by..incisive qualitie thereof, piercing in to the brasse.. forceth out of it a deale of rust. **1694** SALMON *Bate's Dispens.* (1713) 118/1 The Acid being alone, becomes incisive, and pricks the *Nervi Gustantes* by their Points.

4. *fig.* Sharp or keen in mental qualities; producing a highly clear and impressive mental effect; penetrating, acute, trenchant.

a **1850** MARG. FULLER *At Home & Abr.* (1860) 239 Their talk is..picturesque and what the French call *incisive*. **1854** EMERSON *Lett. & Soc. Aims, Poet. & Imag.* Wks. (Bohn) III. 162 An idea steeped in verse becomes suddenly more incisive and more brilliant. **1856** MRS. BROWNING *Aur. Leigh* II. 709 Her incisive smile. **1866** G. MACDONALD *Ann. Q. Neighb.* iii. (1878) 30 She said this in an incisive tone. **1880** *Times* 27 Dec. 7/1 Lord Grey always writes in an incisive and pungent style.

B. *sb.*

†**1.** *Med.* An 'incisive' drug: see A. 3. *Obs.*

1726 LEONI *Alberti's Archit.* II. 107/2 Physicians, for the cure of..Fevers, order the use of the juice of squills and of incisives.

2. *Anat.* An incisor tooth.

1804 [see A. 2].

b. *Entom.* 'The incisive edge of the mandible of a beetle' (*Cent. Dict.*).

incisively (ɪn'saɪsɪvlɪ), *adv.* [f. prec. + -LY².] In an incisive manner or style (*lit.* and *fig.*).

1871 *Athenæum* 2 Dec. 714 Equally incisively are the good people of Middlemarch brought before us face to face. **1879** *Cassell's Techn. Educ.* IV. 72/2 Some of the turning tools for iron also act incisively. **1894** *Chicago Advance* 24 May, [He] holds his convictions clearly and expresses them incisively and boldly.

incisiveness (ɪn'saɪsɪvnɪs). [f. as prec. + -NESS.] The quality of being incisive: usually in sense 4 of the adj.

1865 *Daily Tel.* 23 Oct. 4/5 That incisiveness of expression, that clearness of mind, for which he was famous. **1896** *Law Times* C. 393/1 The Doctor's reply..was not wanting in incisiveness.

inciso- (ɪn'saɪsəʊ), combining adverbial form of L. *incīsus* INCISED, in botanical and zoological terms, used in the sense 'incisedly——', 'incised and ——', as ***inciso-dentate, -denticulate, -lobate, -pinnatifid, -serrate*** adjs.

1847 W. E. STEELE *Field Bot.* 94 Leaves pinnate, leaflets cordate-ovate, inciso-lobate. **1848** DANA *Zooph.* 180 Lamellæ stout, broad dentate and inciso-dentate. **1870** HOOKER *Stud. Flora* 285 Leaves ovate-cordate inciso-serrate. *Ibid.* 462 *Asplenium Adiantum-nigrum*..pinnules petioled inciso-pinnatifid and serrate.

incisor (ɪn'saɪsə(r), -ɔː(r), -'saɪz-). *Anat.* and *Zool.* [a. med. and mod.L. *incīsor* lit. 'cutter', agent-n. from L. *incīdĕre* to cut, INCIDE *v.*¹] A tooth adapted for cutting; any one of the front teeth in either jaw, having a sharp edge and a single fang, situated between the canine teeth on each side, as in man and other mammals; hence extended to teeth of any character having this situation.

1672 SIR T. BROWNE *Lett. Friend* §12 In the burnt fragments of urns which I have enquired into, altho I seem to find few Incisors or Shearers. **1713** DERHAM *Phys.-Theol.* IV. xi. *note* (R.), Suppose the order of the teeth..inverted, the grinders set in the room of the incisors. **1831** YOUATT *Horse* v. (1847) 107 The horse has six incisors or cutting teeth in the front of each jaw.

b. *attrib.* (*a*) Adapted for cutting, as ***incisor forceps***; ***incisor tooth*** (= prec. sense). (*b*) Connected with the incisor teeth, as ***incisor artery, canal, foramen, fossa, nerve***.

1837 M. DONOVAN *Dom. Econ.* II. 289 The human teeth are chiefly incisor or cutting teeth, and molar or grinding teeth. **1841–71** T. R. JONES *Anim. Kingd.* (ed. 4) 215 Like the incisor teeth of rodent quadrupeds, they are therefore continually growing, and are thus always preserved sharp and fit for use. **1879** *St. George's Hosp. Rep.* IX. 635 Aided by strong cutting and incisor forceps, a partially decayed upper canine tooth was forcibly extracted. **1886** *Syd. Soc. Lex.*, *Incisor artery*, a branch of the inferior dental artery. It supplies the canine and incisor teeth... *Incisor nerve*, a branch of the inferior dental nerve. It supplies the canine and incisor teeth.

incisorial (ɪnsaɪ'sɔərɪəl), *a.* [f. as next + -AL¹.] Of or pertaining to the incisors; of the character of an incisor.

(In recent Dicts.)

incisory (ɪn'saɪsərɪ), *a.* [ad. L. type **incīsōri-us*, in F. *incisoire*, f. as INCISOR: see -ORY.]

1. Having the property of cutting, incisive: applied to the incisor teeth.

1594 T. B. *La Primaud. Fr. Acad.* II. 105 Right afore there are foure aboue, and as many beneath..which are called incisorie teeth. **1661** LOVELL *Hist. Anim. & Min.* 302 Sixteen [teeth], of which foure are incisory, two canine, and ten molar.

†**2.** Having a form as if cut; incised. *Obs.*

a **1693** URQUHART *Rabelais* III. viii. 70 Fig-tree-leaves..by reason of their..incisory notches, were..proper.

incisure (ɪn'sɪʒ(j)ʊə(r)). [ad. L. *incīsūra* a cutting into, an incision, f. *incīs-*, ppl. stem of *incīdĕre* INCIDE *v.*¹: see -URE.] A deep indentation in an edge or surface, caused or appearing as if caused by cutting; a cut, notch, slit, cleft; = INCISION 2.

1597 GERARDE *Herbal* II. ci. 353 One whole and entire leafe without any incisure at all. **1658** ROWLAND tr. *Moufet's Theat. Ins.* 936 Ventricle or belly, distinguished with five or six clefts or incisures. **1669** *Phil. Trans.* IV. 987 In..the structure of this Insect [silk-worm] he takes notice..of its eleven Rings or Incisures. **1774** GOLDSM. *Nat. Hist.* (1776) VIII. 116 Crooked jaws..in each of which are seen incisures, that look like teeth. **1819** G. SAMOUELLE *Entomol. Compend.* 342 Toothed like a saw, the incisures turned towards the extremities.

incitable (ɪn'saɪtəb(ə)l), *a. rare.* [f. INCITE *v.* + -ABLE: cf. mod.F. *incitable* (Littré).] Capable of being incited or urged to action. Hence **incita'bility**, capability of being incited.

1800 *Med. Jrnl.* IV. 560 The phenomena of fever differ.. according to the incitability or activity of the organic parts. **1881** LINCOLN tr. *Trousseau & Pidoux's Therapeutics* (ed 9) III. 297 The more an organ is incited, the less it is incitable. **1886** *Syd. Soc. Lex.*, *Incitability*, same as *Irritability*.

†**in'citament.** *Obs. rare*⁻¹. [ad. L. *incitāmentum*, f. *incitāre* to INCITE.] = INCITEMENT.

1579 FULKE *Heskins' Parl.* 9 The little incitament vnto vertue, that you suppose to appeare in the ballattes of Salomon.

incitant ('ɪnsɪtənt, ɪn'saɪtənt), *a.* and *sb.* [ad. L. *incitānt-em*, pres. pple. of *incitāre* to INCITE; cf. F. *incitant.*]

A. *adj.* That incites, stimulating.

1886 *Syd. Soc. Lex.*, *Incitant*,..moving, provoking... *Incitant force*, in Brown's System, a term applied to everything capable of acting on the living body and exciting the exercise of the faculties.

B. *sb.* That which incites; an inciting agent.

a **1802** E. DARWIN cited in Webster 1828.

†'**incitate**, *ppl. a. Obs. rare*⁻¹. [ad. L. *incitāt-us*, pa. pple. of *incitāre* to INCITE.] Incited, instigated.

1568 C. WATSON *Polyb.* 9 a, But [they]..being moved and incitate by the example of the Mamertines..violated and falsified their oath.

†'**incitate**, *v. Obs.* [f. L. *incitāt-*, ppl. stem of *incitāre* to INCITE; cf. prec.] *trans.* To incite.

1597 M. BOWMAN in *Guillemeau's Fr. Chirurg.* *ij, The excellence of this booke hath incitatede me to dedicate [it] to your Mtye. **1607** TOPSELL *Four-f. Beasts* (1658) 371 The Lamb being fastned upon the top of the pillar, doth incitate the hunger-starven heart of the Lion by his bleating. **1623** COCKERAM II, *To Anger one*, Exagitate, Irretate, Exasperate, Stimulate, Incitate.

incitation (ɪnsɪ'teɪʃən). [a. F. *incitation* (14th c.), ad. L. *incitātiōn-em*, n. of action f. *incitāre* to INCITE.]

1. The action of inciting; stirring up, incitement, stimulation, instigation.

c **1477** CAXTON *Jason* 89 b, Medea cam and mette with him by the incitacion and admonishment of loue. **1579** FENTON *Guicciard.* (1618) 89 This accident hapned..by the incitation of certaine souldiers. **1607** *Schol. Disc. agst. Antichr.* II. viii. 103 Pharoes seruants, by whose meanes and incitation Abraham had his Wife taken from him. **1710** ADDISON *Tatler* No. 255 ¶2 Is there any Thing that tends to Incitation in Sweetmeats more than in ordinary Dishes? **1842** SIR H. TAYLOR *Edwin* III. iii, The seculars By secret incitation hearten'd up, Will give their voices. **1881** LINCOLN tr. *Trousseau & Pidoux's Therapeutics* (ed. 9) III. 297 Brown was sometimes right in the pathological order, if the incitation is repeated and remains the same.

†**2.** That which incites or stimulates to action; a stimulus, incentive, incitement. *Obs.*

1622 SPARROW *Bk. Com. Prayer* (1661) 70 These words, Let us pray,..are an Incitation to prayer. *a* **1653** GOUGE *Comm. Heb.* xiii. 3 As an incitation this clause..implieth a due consideration of our own condition. **1709** STEELE *Tatler* No. 23 ¶7 This passion..the strongest and noblest Incitation to honest Attempts.

†**3.** Power in inciting. *Obs.*

1656 TRAPP *Comm. Matt.* xiii. 34 But now that form ('as I have loved you')..is matchless, and more full of incitation to fire affection. **1684** tr. *Bonet's Merc. Compit.* XVI. 553 Where need is of Medicines endued with a certain incitation.

†**in'citative**, *a.* and *sb. Obs. rare.* [a. obs. F. *incitatif, -ive*, ad. L. **incitātīv-us* (see -ATIVE), f. *incitāre* to INCITE.]

A. *adj.* Having the quality of inciting or stirring up; stimulative.

1490 CAXTON *Eneydos* vi. 90 She sayd to theym, wepynge these incitatyf wordes.

B. *sb.* An inciting or stimulating agent, medicine, etc.

1620 SHELTON *Quix.* IV. xiii. 103 Wallets..well provided at least with Incitatives that provoked to drink two Miles off.

†**in'citatory**, *a. Obs. rare.* [f. L. *incitāt-* (see INCITATE) + -ORY.] Tending to incite; stirring, stimulative.

1610 DONNE *Pseudo-Martyr* 151 We will..onely repeat Baronius his Panegyrique and Incitatorie Encouragement.

incite (ɪn'saɪt), *v.* Also 5 encyte, 5–6 incyte. [a. F. *inciter* (14th c.; OF. also *enciter*) = Sp., Pg. *incitar*, It. *incitare*, ad. L. *incitāre*, f. *in-* (IN-²) + *citāre* to set in rapid motion, rouse, stimulate, etc., frequentative of *ciēre, cit-um* to put in motion, stir, rouse; see CITE.] *trans.* To urge or spur on; to stir up, animate, instigate, stimulate. Const. *to do* something; *to* or *unto* some action.

1483 CAXTON *Cato* A viij, For to doo thys right canon admonesteth and inciteth us. **1490** —— *Eneydos* Contents 7 How Eneas encyted the patrons & maystres of his shyppes for to departe. **1502** ATKYNSON tr. *De Imitatione* I. xi. 161 The firste mocions that incyteth vs to synne. **1597** HOOKER *Eccl. Pol.* V. xi. §1 He incited all men vnto bountifull contribution. **1606** G. W[OODCOCKE] tr. *Hist. Ivstine* 9 a, The rather to incite him vppe vnto their ayde, [he] shewed the exceeding valour of their women. **1661** BRAMHALL *Just Vind.* vii. 221 The Pope incited the King of Spain to make war against the Republick. **1715–20** POPE *Iliad* IV. 499 These Mars incites, and those Minerva fires. **1812** G. CHALMERS *Dom. Econ. Gt. Brit.* 423 Manufactures were incited, and pushed forward, by every sort of encouragement. **1875** JOWETT *Plato* (ed. 2) I. 462 Each of us was urging and inciting the other to put the question. **1880** E. WHITE *Cert. Relig.* 24 A certainty, and an overflowing gladness in the heart, which are capable of inciting to heroic deeds.

b. To urge or provoke (some action).

1627 *Lisander & Cal.* V. 90, I could not finde any thing which might incite my stay after this losse.

Hence **inciting** *vbl. sb.*

1611 FLORIO, *Infugatione*,..a prouocation, or inciting vnto.

incitement (ɪn'saɪtmənt). [f. INCITE *v.* + -MENT: cf. F. *incitement* (16th c. in Littré), L. *incitāmentum*, f. *incitāre*.]

1. The action of inciting or rousing to action; an urging, spurring, or setting on; instigation, stimulation. † Also, the condition of being incited.

1594 CAREW *Huarte's Exam. Wits* (1616) 296 By his continuall incitement. **1647–8** COTTERELL *Davila's Hist. Fr.* (1678) 20 Chiefly by the incitement of the Cardinal. **1670** MILTON *Hist. Eng.* II. Wks. (1851) 64 Incens'd against him

..by the incitement of Roscius Cælius Legat of a Legion. **1803** *Med. Jrnl.* X. 53 Does the incitement of the influence which in Mr. Galvani's experiments, occasions the muscles of animals to contract, either wholly or in part depend upon any peculiar property of living bodies? **1876** E. H. CHAPIN *Faith & Life* vi. 105 The method of Christianity is not excitement, but incitement.

2. That which incites or rouses to action; an inciting cause or motive; stimulus, incentive, 'spur'.

a **1600** G. C. in Hakluyt *Voy.* III. 670 And she [Nature] must neede incitementes to her good, Euen from that part she hurtes! **1641** MILTON *Ch. Govt.* I. vii, Let us not therefore make these things an incumbrance..which God sends us as an incitement to proceed with more honour and alacrity. **1709** STEELE *Tatler* No. 3 ¶1 A good Play..must raise very proper Incitements to good Behaviour. **1875** JOWETT *Plato* III. 653 Pleasure, the greatest incitement of evil.

inciter (ɪn'saɪtə(r)). Also 7 incitor. [f. INCITE *v.* + -ER^1.] One who or that which incites or rouses to action; an instigator.

1598 FLORIO, *Impulsore*, an inciter, a perswader. **1611** COTGR., *Instigateur*, an instigator; stirrer, incitor, vrger, egger on. *a* **1626** BACON *Maxims & Uses Com. Law* xii. 53 The law accounteth the incitor as principall, though he be absent. *a* **1720** SHEFFIELD (Dk. Buckhm.) *Wks.* (1753) II. 190 The Romans..politickly encouraged that humour in every body, as being a constant inciter to virtue. **1813** L. HUNT in *Examiner* 15 Feb. 97/2 Inciters to robbery. **1893** BOYD CARPENTER *Son of Man* ii. 43 He is an inciter of revolution.

Hence **in'citress**, a female inciter.

1611 COTGR., *Concitatrice*, a concitatrix, incitresse, prouokeresse. **1654** GAYTON *Pleasant Notes* IV. vi, Bright Sun-beame, repairer and incitresse of my decaying heat.

inciting (ɪn'saɪtɪŋ), *ppl. a.* [f. INCITE *v.* + -ING^2.] That incites; stimulating, provoking. Hence **in'citingly** *adv.*

1855 MAYNE *Expos. Lex.*, *Incitans*,..applied to medicines .. which provoke or excite; inciting. **1856** WEBSTER, *Incitingly.* **1879** G. MEREDITH *Egoist* I. vii. 118 'My letters?' he said incitingly. 'I read them.' **1884** *Daily News* 3 Sept. 4/7 Mr. Gladstone has been a restraining not an inciting influence upon most of his followers.

incitive (ɪn'saɪtɪv), *a.* and *sb. rare.* [f. INCITE *v.* + -IVE; cf. INCITATIVE.]

A. *adj.* Having the quality of inciting; stimulative.

1888 T. W. HUNT in *New Princeton Rev.* Nov. 363 The style is thus instructive and incitive.

B. *sb.* An incentive, incitement.

1736 LEDIARD *Marlborough* I. 57 A proper Incitive to a constant Vigilance. **1881** J. F. T. KEANE *Journey Medinah* 194 He..will never, except under a very strong incitive, expose himself to unnecessary danger.

incito-motor (ɪn,saɪtəʊ'məʊtə(r)), *a. rare.* [f. INCITE *v.* + MOTOR, after EXCITO-MOTOR, q.v. Cf. F. *incito-moteur* (Littré).] Inciting to motion or muscular action; applied to the action of the nervous centres which determine the contraction of the muscles through the intermediation of the motor nerves. Also erroneously identified with *excito-motor*. So **in,cito-'motory** *a.*

1884 *Cassell's Encycl. Dict.*, Incito-motory. **1886** *Syd. Soc. Lex.*, *Incito-motor*, same as *Excito-motor.* **1893** DUNGLISON *Med. Dict.* (ed. 21), *Incitomotor*, epithet applied to an action the reverse of excitomotor, as muscular motion, commencing in the nervous centres, and exciting the muscles to contraction.

incitory (ɪn'saɪtərɪ), *a. rare.* [f. *incit-* stem of INCITE *v.*, etc.: see -ORY^2.] Having the quality of inciting; stimulative, provoking.

1941 A. WARREN in N. Foerster et al. *Lit. Scholarship* iv. 147 The second [group] holds art to be incitory, an invitation to action. **1949** WELLEK & WARREN *Theory of Lit.* iii. 27 Is some literature incitory and some cathartic? **1950** *N.Y. Times* 20 Apr. 1/8 He had used his employes for espionage and to gather material for 'fictitious reports of incitory character' for the voice of America.

incivic (ɪn'sɪvɪk), *a. rare*$^{-1}$. [f. IN-^{3} + CIVIC.] Having no civic spirit or virtues.

1795 W. TAYLOR in *Monthly Rev.* XVII. 505 Ye rise above the base Incivic herd, like Cato and Brutus, superior to a senate of cowards and hirelings.

† **in'civil**, *a. Obs.* [a. F. *incivil* (14th c.), ad. late L. *incīvīlis*, f. *in-* (IN-^{3}) + *cīvīlis* CIVIL.]

1. Not of the rank of a free citizen.

1549 *Compl. Scot.* xvii. 147 He that hed neuyr dune ane vailȝeant act contrar his enemeis, vas reput for ane inciuile villaine. *Ibid.* 150 Thy father vas ane mecanyc tailȝour discendit of inciuile pure pepil.

2. Not according to civil law.

1613-18 DANIEL *Coll. Hist. Eng.* (1621) 214 The Contract was made in prison, and therefore incivill, and not to be held by the right of Nations.

3. Savage, barbarous.

1586 MARLOWE *1st Pt. Tamburl.* I. i, Tamburlaine, that sturdy Scythian thief That..Daily commits incivil outrages.

4. Unmannerly, rude, clownish; impolite or uncourteous to others; uncivil.

1611 SHAKS. *Cymb.* V. v. 292 *Cym.* He was a Prince. *Gui.* A most inciuill one. The wrongs he did mee Were nothing Prince-like. **1683** D. A. *Art Converse* 117 They are rather not civil than positively incivil. **1707** *Reflex. upon Ridicule* 189 He is Proud, Haughty, Incivil.

Hence, † **in'civilly** *adv.*, † **in'civilness** (Bailey vol. II, 1727).

1671 *Plymouth Col. Rec.* (1856) V. 53 Hee did highly misdemean himselfe..by..bringing in off a mare inciuilly into the parlour of James Cole.

incivility (ɪnsɪ'vɪlɪtɪ). [ad. F. *incivilité* (1426 in Hatz.-Darm.), ad. late L. *incīvīlitāt-em*, f. *incīvīlis*; see prec. and -ITY.] The quality or condition of being incivil or uncivil.

† **1.** Want of civilization; uncivilized condition; savageness, barbarism. *Obs.*

1584 R. SCOT *Discov. Witchcr.* XI. iii. (1886) 153 The incivilitie and cruell sacrifices of popish preests. **1612** BREREWOOD *Lang. & Relig.* xiii. 118 In their incivility and many barbarous properties, they [Americans] resemble the old and rude Tartars. **1663** BLAIR *Autobiog.* iii. (1848) 57 The northern Irishes remaining obdured in their idleness and incivility. **1774** WARTON *Hist. Eng. Poetry* xvi. I. 423 The licentiousness of Boccaccio's tales..was not so much the consequence of popular incivility, as it was owing to a particular event of the writer's age. **1811** *Henry & Isabella* I. Pref. 5 That barbarous relic of feudal incivility, duelling.

† **2.** Want of good manners or good breeding; ill-bred behaviour. *Obs.*

1590 SHAKS. *Com. Err.* IV. iv. 49 *Curt...* Is not your husband mad? *Adri.* His inciuility confirmes no lesse. **1603** HOLLAND *Plutarch's Mor.* 42 Cowardise, follie, and perverse incivilitie, be the defects of learning, and are meere ignorance. **1650** BULWER *Anthropomet.* 113 They account it the greatest incivility in the world to let any thing fall in eating. **1673** *Rules Civility* 118 'Tis gross incivility to begin any person of Honour's health, and to address it to himself.

3. Ill-bred, uncivil, or uncourteous behaviour towards others; want of civility or politeness; discourtesy, rudeness.

1612 T. TAYLOR *Comm. Titus* iii. 2 It would be thought too much inciuilitie to stay a man from shooting his venomed arrowes. **1684** *Contempl. St. Man* II. x. (1699) 236 The irreverence and great incivility towards God in a Mortal Sin. **1769** LD. ROCHFORD in Ellis *Orig. Lett.* Ser. II. IV. 521 The Russian Ambassador appears personally satisfied with the excuses made for personal incivility, but considers his Court is highly insulted. **1849** MACAULAY *Hist. Eng.* iv. I. 454 At Council he [Guildford] was treated by Jeffreys with marked incivility.

b. An act of rudeness or ill-breeding.

1652 H. COGAN tr. *Scudery's Ibrahim* II. iv. 76, I had done an hundred incivilities to satisfie her. *a* **1693** LUDLOW *Mem.* I. 88 (R.) No person offered me the least incivility.

incivilization (ɪn,sɪvɪlɪ'zeɪʃən, -aɪ'z-). [f. IN-^{3} + CIVILIZATION.] Uncivilized condition; want of civilization.

1823 *New Monthly Mag.* IX. 169/2 His excuse is at best incivilization and ignorance. **1843** CARLYLE *Past & Pr.* III. v, A terrible worker; irresistible against..incivilisation. **1861** GRESLEY *Sophron & N.* 145 We have spoken, in a former paper, of the incivilization of China.

† **in'civilize**, *v. Obs. rare*$^{-1}$. [f. IN-^{2} + CIVILIZE; cf. It. *incivilire* 'to grow ciuill or mannerly' (Florio).] *trans.* To make civilized, to refine.

1603 FLORIO *Montaigne* III. vi. (1632) 512 Such hands as would gently have polished, reformed and incivilized, what in them they deemed to be barbarous and rude.

† **in'civilized**, *a. Obs. rare.* [IN-^{3}]. Not civilized; uncivilized.

1647 W. BROWNE tr. *Gomberville's Polexander* IV. iii. 240 One incivilis'd, and unworthy either to breathe or to serve her.

incivism ('ɪnsɪvɪz(ə)m). Also 9 -isme. [ad. F. *incivisme* (1791 in Hatz.-Darm.), f. *in-* (IN-^{3}) + *civisme* CIVISM.] The opposite of CIVISM; want of good citizenship.

a. In reference to the French Revolution: want of loyalty to the principles of the Revolution: regarded as a crime against the Republic.

1794 J. GIFFORD *Louis XVI*, 563 As the body guard which had been allotted to the king by the constitution was particularly suspected of incivism, it was disbanded. **1794** HERON *Inform. Powers at War* 185 None dare absent themselves; for, such an act of incivism would be punished with the loss of liberty and property. **1887** M. ARNOLD in *19th Cent.* May 634, I should not like to be brought before him as President of a Committee of Safety, on a charge of incivism.

b. In reference to other states and times.

1820 COLERIDGE *Lett., Convers.*, etc. I. 91 Judge Abbot.. put the question on the ground of incivism, and not on the religious ground. **1865** GROTE *Plato* I. viii. 303 Socrates is to be..exculpated from the charge of incivism. **1879** M. PATTISON *Milton* xii. 153 Milton will exclude Romanists from toleration, not on the statesman's ground of incivism, but on the theologian's ground of idolatry.

incize, inckling, obs. ff. INCISE, INKLING.

† **incla'mation.** *Obs. rare.* [ad. late L. *inclāmātiōn-em*, n. of action f. *inclāmāre* to cry out to, call upon, f. *in-* (IN-^{2}) + *clāmāre* to call.] A calling upon; invocation. Also, a cry, a loud call.

1612-15 BP. HALL *Contempl., O.T.* XVIII. ii, Steps forth a prophet of God, and interrupts that glorious service, with a loud inclamation of judgement. *Ibid.* vii, These idolatrous prophets now rend their throats with inclamations. **1613** CHAPMAN *Bussy D'Ambois* Plays 1873 II. 140 Cassandra's prophecie..when shee fore-tolde Troyes ruine: which succeeding made her vse This sacred Inclamation.

† **in'clamitate**, *v. Obs.*$^{-0}$ [f. ppl. stem of *inclāmitāre* (Plautus), frequentative of *inclāmāre*: see prec.] 'To call often' (Cockeram, 1623). Hence † **inclami'tation**, 'an often calling upon' (Phillips, 1658).

inclasp, obs. form of ENCLASP *v.*

in'claudent, *a. Bot. rare.* [IN-^{3}.] Not closing.

1840 PAXTON *Bot. Dict.*, *Inclaudent*, not closing.

† **in'clavate**, *v. Obs. rare*$^{-1}$. [f. med.L. *inclāvāt-*, ppl. stem of *inclāvāre* (f. L. *in-*, IN-^{2} + *clāvāre* to nail, f. *clāvus* nail): see -ATE^3.] *trans.* To nail or bolt in, fix firmly.

1666 J. SMITH *Old Age* 81 These [teeth] are more firmly inclavated and infixed into the jawbones by treble or quadruple roots.

incla'vation. *rare.* [n. of action f. prec.] The condition of being firmly fixed in, as of a tooth in its socket.

1855 MAYNE *Expos. Lex.*, *Inclaveatio*, term for the condition of a tooth in its socket; inclaveation.

inclave, obs. form of ENCLAVE *a. Her.*

incle, variant of INKLE *sb.* and *v.*

inclear, variant of ENCLEAR *v. Obs.*

'in-,clearing. [IN *adv.* 11 c.] The cheques, bills of exchange, etc., collectively, payable by a bank, and received through the Clearing-house for settlement; also *attrib.* as in **in-clearing book** (short '*in-book*) the entry book of these claims. Hence '**in-clearer**, the representative of a bank in the Clearing-house who receives the in-clearing; also called **in-clerk**.

[**1827** GILBART *Treat. on Banking* (1849) II. 442 The drafts which are drawn upon the house, and which have come in from the clearing..are called the 'clearing in'.] **1872** E. SEYD *Lond. Banking* 48 The..Banker..receives..25 batches of Cheques, all drawn upon his Bank..he..must enter them to his debit, into his 'in' or 'paid' clearing book. **1878** JEVONS *Money & Mech. Exchange* (ed. 4) 278 Messengers..walking round the desks..receiving [the parcels] of 'in clearing' or as they are called in New York, the ..Debit Exchanges. **1882** *Gilbart's Hist., etc. of Banking* (ed. Michie) II. 325 The In-Clearing Book of each clerk ought to agree..with the portions relating to him of the Out-Clearing Books of the other twenty six Clerks. **1884** HOWARTH *Clearing System* iv. 53 The 'in-clerk' is also at his post..and finds awaiting him several charges, which he enters on, as a continuation of the morning work. *Ibid.* iv. 54 Between half-past three and four..the in-clearers with lightning-like rapidity run the items in their in-books and cast them up.

inclemency (ɪn'klɛmənsɪ). [ad. L. *inclēmentia*: see next and -ENCY. Cf. F. *inclémence.*] The quality or condition of being inclement.

1. The opposite of mildness or temperateness of climate; severity of weather.

1559 W. CUNNINGHAM *Cosmogr. Glasse* Pref. A vj, In travailing, thou shalt not be molested with the inclemencye of th' Aere, boysterous windes [etc.]. **1603** KNOLLES *Hist. Turks* (1621) 70, I cannot.. longer endure the inclemencie and intemperature of the aire in this extreme hot season. **1725** BRADLEY *Fam. Dict.* s.v. *Planting*, Strong enough to bear the Inclemency of the weather. **1775** ADAIR *Amer. Ind.* 3, I saw..a white man..who, by the inclemency of the sun, ..was tarnished with as deep an Indian hue, as any of the camp. **1844** H. H. WILSON *Brit. India* II. 381 His march was delayed by the inclemency of the weather.

transf. **1864** HOWELLS *Venet. Life* vii. (1866) 95 Providence, tempering the inclemency of the domestic situation, sent them Giovanna.

b. With *pl.*: A particular instance of this.

1699 GARTH *Dispens.* 9 Deep sunk in Down, they..Avoid th' Inclemencies of Morning Air. **1748** *Anson's Voy.* II. xiv. 288 Not fit to struggle with the inclemencies of a cold climate. **1749** SMOLLETT *Regicide* V. vii, Who rest secure From all the inclemencies of stormy life. **1865** LUBBOCK *Preh. Times* xvi. (1878) 606 This gave him clothing against the varying inclemencies of the season.

† **2.** Want of clemency or kindliness of disposition; pitilessness, unmercifulness. *Obs.*

1598 FLORIO, *Inclemenza*, rigorousnes..mercilesnesse, inclemencie. **1610** BP. CARLETON *Jurisd.* 221 After his death Clement vsed all inclemency against me, setting vp another King. **1614** BP. HALL *Recoll. Treat.*, *Imprese of God* II. 667 The inclemencie of the late Pope laboring to forestall him in his just throne. **1658** PHILLIPS, *Inclemency*, rigour, sharpness, a being without pitty or compassion.

inclement (ɪn'klɛmənt), *a.* [ad. L. *inclēment-em*, f. *in-* (IN-^{3}) + *clēment-* CLEMENT; cf. F. *inclément* (1564 in Hatz.-Darm.).] Not clement.

1. Of climate or weather: Not mild or temperate; extreme; severe. (Usually applied to cold or stormy weather; rarely of severe heat or drought.)

1667 MILTON *P.L.* X. 1063 To shun Th' inclement Seasons, Rain, Ice, Hail and Snow. **1701** J. PHILIPS *Splendid Shilling* 94 When..th' inclement air Persuades men to repel benumbing frosts. **1742** YOUNG *Nt. Th.* III. 80 In this inclement clime of human life. **1760** BEATTIE *Past.* vii. Poems 157 Inclement drought the hardening soil would drain. **1853** J. H. NEWMAN *Hist. Sk.* (1876) II. I. i. 8 The North does but hold out to them a climate more inclement than their own.

transf. **1867** *Good Cheer* 11 This is not because the country to which they have been driven is ugly or inclement—it may or may not be such.

†**2.** Not merciful or kindly; pitiless, harsh, severe, cruel. *Obs.*

1621 MOLLE *Camerar. Liv. Libr.* v. iii. 330 Pope Clement the fift, was inclement and cruell. **1725** POPE *Odyss.* XIX. 288 O thou, she cry'd, whom first inclement fate Made welcome to my hospitable gate!

transf. **1861** L. L. NOBLE *Icebergs* 149 We have been tossing nearly all day upon a rough, inclement ocean.

Hence **in'clemently** *adv.*, pitilessly; **in'clementness** (Bailey vol. II, 1727).

1789 JAS. WHITE *Earl Strongbow* II. 167 By adhering inclemently to her recent resolution.

†**incle'mental**, *a. Obs. rare*⁻¹. [f. prec. + -AL¹.]

= INCLEMENT 1.

1709 *Brit. Apollo* II. No. 18. 3/2 To be lodg'd safe from Inclemental Air.

†**in'clension**. *Obs. rare.* [repr. L. *inclīnātiōn-em* INCLINATION: cf. DECLENSION.] The action of inclining.

1751 tr. *Female Foundling* I. 67 Making, with some Confusion, an Inclension of the Head. *Ibid.* I. 68 By a small Inclension of her Head.

†**in'clepe**, *v. Obs.* [f. IN-¹ + CLEPE *v.*; after L. *invocāre*, which it is used to translate.] *trans.* To invoke, call upon.

1382 WYCLIF *Rom.* x. 13 Forsoth ech man who euere schal inclepe the name of the Lord, schal be saaf. How therfore schulen thei inclepyn hym, into whom thei han not bileued? — *2 Cor.* i. 23 Forsoth I inclepe God witnesse in to my soule. *c* **1400** *Prymer* in Maskell *Mon. Rit.* (1846–7) II. 106 [Ps. xx. 9] Lord.. heere thou us in the dai that we shulen inclepe thee.

in-clerk: see IN-CLEARING.

inclinable (ɪn'klaɪnəb(ə)l), *a.* Also 6–8 en-. [a. OF. *enclinable* (*Roman de Rose*), in 16th c. *inclinable*, f. encliner, in 14th c. *incliner*, ad. L. *inclīnāre*: see INCLINE and -ABLE.]

1. Having a (mental) inclination or leaning in some direction; inclined, disposed. †**a.** *to* something. *Obs.* (Common from early 16th to late 18th c.)

1494 FABYAN *Chron.* VII. 324 Whan Lewys harde of these tydynges.. he was more inclynable vnto peace. **1526** *Pilgr. Perf.* (W. de W. 1531) 227 b, So meke & enclynable to the instruccions and mocyons of the holy goost. **1561** T. NORTON *Calvin's Inst.* I. xi. 22 b, The Jewes were forbidden images, because they were enclinable [*ed.* **1634** inclinable] to superstition. **1627–77** FELTHAM *Resolves* II. xix. 200 This King, being of a Noble Nature, and inclinable to mercy. **1682** LUTTRELL *Brief Rel.* (1857) I. 162 The Algerines.. are very inclinable to a peace with us. **1706** tr. *Dupin's Eccl. Hist. 16th C.* II. v. 85 The opinions of the Calvinists, to which he had been inclinable in his younger years. **1779** J. MOORE *View Soc. Fr.* II. xciv. 414 Sensibility renders the heart averse to scepticism, and inclinable to devotion.

b. *to do* something.

c **1500** *Three Kings Sons* 107 [They] founde the kynge enclynable y-nough to entende to thise matiers. **1546** GARDINER *Declar. Art. Joye* 41 b, God myght haue chaunged it.. and not haue made man inclineable to fall. **1647** FULLER *Good Th. in Worse T.* (1841) 86 A multitude is not so inclinable to save as to destroy. **1704** *Lond. Gaz.* No. 4060/5 Such Persons as are enclinable to furnish Pork. **1795** LD. AUCKLAND *Corr.* (1862) III. 283 This country is very low-spirited as to continental politics, and very inclinable to leave the Continent to go to the devil in its own way. **1826** LAMB *Elia* Ser. II. *Popular Fallacies* v, His master was inclinable to keep him, but his mistress thought otherwise.

†**c.** with other constructions, or *absol. Obs.*

1583 GOLDING *Calvin on Deut.* xxxii. 189 It is not for that God is inclynable, or for that he resembleth vs or for that hee is mooued thereto. *a* **1600** HOOKER (J.), A probable opinion, that divine authority was the same way inclinable. **1654** tr. *Scudery's Curia Pol.* 110 Too inclinable for factions. **1702** J. LOGAN in *Pa. Hist. Soc. Mem.* IX. 95 [This] made me inclinable that he should hold his hand. **1737** *Col. Rec. Pennsylv.* IV. 219 The Government of Pennsylvania has not appeared to me.. so inclinable for a good understanding and Harmony.

2. Favourably disposed; willing to accede, assent, or submit *to*; propitious, favourable; amenable; inclined to favour or side with some person or party.

c **1449** PECOCK *Repr.* II. xviii. 262 O God make the Patroun .. be to us inclynable. *c* **1555** HARPSFIELD *Divorce Hen. VIII* (Camden) 189 In case they found not the Pope so propice and inclinable to their desires as they looked for. **1632** LE GRYS tr. *Velleius Paterc.* 25 The Rhodians.. did then seeme .. more enclinable to the Kings part. **1692** SIR T. P. BLOUNT *Ess.* 78 They may have our minds easie and inclinable. **1709** HEARNE *Collect.* (O.H.S.) II. 290 He was recommended by the Lᵈ Clarendon.. wᶜʰ made some inclinable to him. **1759** W. HASTINGS in Beveridge *Hist. India* (1862) I. III. xii. 664 An argument that the nabob is inclinable to the French. **1880** FREEMAN in Stephens *Life & Lett.* (1895) II. 196, I am myself rather inclinable to them [Hittites]—as far as one can be inclinable to any non-Aryan creatures.

3. Having an inclination or tendency to some physical quality, character, condition, or action.

1607 NORDEN *Surv. Dial.* 211 You see this country inclinable to wood and timber much. **1616** SURFL. & MARKH. *Country Farme* 573 The meale.. falleth out to be more inclinable and readie to corrupt. **1683** *Lond. Gaz.* No. 1867/8 His Hair inclinable to Red. **1684** tr. *Bonet's Merc. Compit.* VI. 220 He.. was already inclinable enough to a Fever. **1700** J. WELWOOD *Mem.* 83 When he was warm in discourse, he was inclinable to stammer. **1784** TWAMLEY *Dairying* 125 A strong loomy soil inclinable to clay. **1789** G. KEATE *Pelew Isl.* 264 Of a middling stature, rather inclinable to be corpulent. **1805** *Log 'Sirius'* 20 Oct. in Nicolas *Disp. Nelson* (1846) VII. 134 *note*, Light airs, inclinable to calm.

4. Capable of being inclined or sloped.

1766 *Phil. Trans.* LVI. 2 The telescope was.. inclinable on all sides, so that it was easy to place it according to the motion of the sun.

†**in'clinableness.** *Obs.* [f. prec. + -NESS.] The quality or character of being 'inclinable'; inclination, readiness, willingness.

a **1617** HIERON *Wks.* (1619–20) II. 436 An inclineablenesse of will to doe him any seruice. *a* **1656** HALES *Gold. Rem.* (1688) 72 A general Inclineableness to Merciful Proceedings. **1718** HICKES & NELSON *J. Kettlewell* II. §34. 141 One of the main Objections.. was their Inclinableness to Popery. **1725** COLLIER *Several Disc.* 201 An Inclinableness to this Passion argues Weakness in us.

†**in'clinably**, *adv. Obs. rare.* [f. as prec. + -LY².] With an inclination or disposition (in quot., to some particular opinion or belief).

a **1641** BP. MOUNTAGU *Acts & Mon.* (1642) 142 He is not resolved where.. but most inclinably, upon the taking in of Jerusalem by Cn. Pompeius.

†**incli'nabo.** *Obs.* [A humorous application of L. *inclīnābo* I shall bow or incline.] A bow.

1640 R. BAILLIE *Canterb. Self-convict.* 52 A number of low cringes towards these elements.. a low inclinabo before the bread, when they set it downe.

†**in'clinary**, *a. Obs. rare.* [f. INCLINE *v.* + -ARY.] Belonging to inclination or disposition.

1628 FELTHAM *Resolves* II. [I.] xxxvii. 114 For worth in many men, we are more beholding to the defects of Nature, then their owne inclinary Loue.

†**'inclinate**, *a. Obs. rare.* [ad. L. *inclīnāt-us* inclined, pa. pple. of *inclīnāre* to INCLINE.] Inclined, sloping, oblique.

1571 DIGGES *Pantom.* III. ii. Q j b, Whether the Pyramis be direct or inclinate.

†**'inclinated**, *ppl. a. Obs. rare.* [f. as prec. + -ED¹.] = prec.

1757 PULTNEY in *Phil. Trans.* L. 66 The style is filiform, of the length of the stamina, and inclinated.

inclination (ɪnklɪ'neɪʃən). Also 5 en-. [ad. F. *inclination* (Oresme, 14th c.), ad. L. *inclīnātiōn-em*, n. of action from *inclīnāre* to INCLINE.]

I. 1. The action, or an act, of inclining or bending towards something: *spec.* **a.** A bending forward of the body or head in token of reverence or courtesy; a bow. (In quot. 1659, a bending.)

prayer of inclination, name for various prayers in the liturgies of the Eastern Church; *esp.* that between the Lord's Prayer and the Communion, also called the ***prayer of humble access***.

1483 CAXTON *Gold. Leg.* 437 b/1 There he maketh a depe enclynacion. **1526** *Pilgr. Perf.* (W. de W. 1531) 237 b, With genufleccyons or knelynges, inclinacyons, prostracyons, or other reuerence. **1613** PURCHAS *Pilgrimage* (1614) 300 With eight inclinations and foure prayings. **1659** PEARSON *Creed* Art. vi (T.), To sit, doth not [here] signify any peculiar inclination or flexion, any determinate location or position, of the body. **1712** ADDISON *Spect.* No. 305 ¶14 To furnish them with Bows and Inclinations of all Sizes, Measures, and Proportions. *c* **1850** *Arab. Nts.* (Rtldg.) 412 Having made him a courteous inclination of the head, she proceeded on her route. **1865** DICKENS *Mut. Fr.* I. viii, With a languid inclination of the head.

†**b.** The sloping or tilting of a vessel in order to pour out the liquor from it without stirring up the sediment; decantation. *Obs.*

1641 FRENCH *Distill.* i. (1651) 9 *Decantation*, is the pouring off of any liquor which hath a setling, by inclination. **1694** SALMON *Bate's Dispens.* (1713) 157/1 Separate the clear from the Fæces by Inclination. **1758** REID tr. *Macquer's Chym.* I. 306 Pour off the liquor by inclination, and wash the precipitate with fair water.

†**2.** *fig.* = DECLINATION 5, DECLINE *sb.* 1. *rare.*

1565 HARDING in Jewel *Def. Apol.* (1611) 370 Any other stocke, that ye can name since the inclination of the Roman Empire.

3. The fact or condition of being inclined; deviation from the normal vertical or horizontal position or direction; leaning or slanting position; slope, slant.

1530 PALSGR. 234/1 Inclynation, *inclinement*. **1590** SPENSER *F.Q.* III. vi. 44 There was a pleasaunt Arber, not by art But of the trees owne inclination made. **1664** POWER *Exp. Philos.* III. 167 The Angles of Inclination and Elevation will remain the same. **1796** H. HUNTER tr. *St.-Pierre's Stud. Nat.* (1799) II. 124 This inclination undergoes some varieties in certain mountain-trees. **1799** KIRWAN *Geol. Ess.* 335 A connexion between the inclination of the slip, and the elevation or depression of the strata. **1862** SMILES *Engineers* III. 175 The inclination of the gradients being towards the sea.

b. The amount of slope or deviation from the horizontal position.

1799 J. ROBERTSON *Agric. Perth* 494 The drain has an inclination of one foot in 100 yards. **1851** GREENWELL *Coal-trade Terms Northumb. & Durh.* 31 An underground self-acting plane should not have a less inclination than 1¼ inch to the yard. **1878** HUXLEY *Physiogr.* 143 When a river approaches the sea, the inclination of its basin usually diminishes.

c. *Dialling.* The amount by which the plane of an inclining dial (see INCLINE *v.* 9 b) deviates from the vertical.

1593 FALE *Dialling* 4 If the angle which the plat maketh with the horizon be accute or sharp, then it doth incline. The quantity of inclination is thus known. **1727–41** CHAMBERS *Cycl.*, *Inclination of a Plane*, in dialing, is the arch of a vertical circle, perpendicular both to the plane and the horizon, and intercepted between them.

d. The dip of the magnetic needle: see DIP *sb.* 4. Hence *attrib.* in ***inclination-chart***, ***-compass*** (= dipping-compass), ***-equator***, ***-pole***.

1678 HOBBES *Decam.* viii. 101 The same Needle placed in a Plain perpendicular to the Horizon, hath another Motion called the Inclination. **1839** G. BIRD *Nat. Phil.* 151 The dip or inclination of the needle.

attrib. **1870** R. M. FERGUSON *Electr.* 44 The first inclination chart was published by Wilke. **1870** R. A. PROCTOR in *Eng. Mech.* 14 Jan. 424/2 As we leave either inclination-pole, the dipping needle leaves its vertical position, and gradually approaches the horizontal.. until, along a curve lying midway between the two poles, the needle becomes exactly horizontal. This curve is called the magnetic inclination-equator.

e. An inclined surface; an incline. *rare.*

1841 *Penny Cycl.* XIX. 250/2 s.v. *Railway*, If.. any inclination occur so steep that the ordinary power cannot ascend it by a reduction of speed. *Ibid.*, On inclinations of much greater steepness.

4. *gen.* (chiefly in *Geom.*) The direction of a line, surface, or body, with respect to another line, surface, or body which has a different direction; the difference of direction of two lines, etc. regarded as 'leaning' or tending towards each other; usually, the amount of such difference measured by the angle which they make with each other (or would make if produced), called the ***angle of inclination***. In *Astron.* sometimes *spec.* the position of the plane of a planet's orbit in relation to that of the ecliptic, measured by the angle between them.

1570 BILLINGSLEY *Euclid* XI. def. iii. 313 Inclination or leaning of a right line, to a plaine superficies, is an acute angle. **1656** tr. *Hobbes' Elem. Philos.* Wks. 1839 I. 198 An angle, which is made by two planes, is commonly called the inclination of those planes. **1704** NEWTON *Optics* (J.), The two rays, being equally refracted, have the same inclination to one another after refraction which they had before; that is, the inclination of half a degree answering to the sun's diameter. **1714** DERHAM *Astro-Theol.* IV. iv. (R.), The other lying in the broad path of the zodiack at an inclination of twenty-three and a half degrees. **1760–72** tr. *Juan & Ulloa's Voy.* (ed. 3) I. 368 A course of above 200 leagues in a direct line from E. to W. with some, though insensible, inclinations to the S. **1812–16** J. SMITH *Panorama Sc. & Art* I. 538 The inclination of Mercury's orbit, to the plane of the ecliptic, is about 7°. **1880** GEIKIE *Phys. Geog.* i. 15 The alteration of the Seasons depends.. upon the inclination of the earth's axis in its yearly orbit.

b. Loosely used for the deviation of a line from the perpendicular to a given plane.

1854 BREWSTER *More Worlds* iv. 66 The small inclination of Jupiter's axis to the plane of its orbit, which is only about three degrees. **1868** LOCKYER *Guillemin's Heavens* (ed. 3) 31 The Sun's axis of rotation is but slightly inclined.. to the ideal plane in which our Earth moves round the Sun. If this inclination were nil [etc.].

II. 5. The action of inclining, bending, or directing the mind to something. ? *Obs.*

1509 HAWES *Past. Pleas.* xxxiv. (Percy Soc.) 110 Whan the comyn wytte hath the thinge electe, It werketh by all due inclynacyon For to brynge the mater to the hole effecte. **1529** MORE *Dyaloge* I. xxix. 45 b/1 That he shuld lede theym by secrete insperacyon and inclynacyon of theyr hartes in to all trouth. **1603** BP. MATTHEWS in Ellis *Orig. Lett.* Ser. I. III. 74 Thus presuming your Grace will yield favourable inclination to this my dutiful and lowly petition.

6. The condition of being mentally inclined or disposed to something, or an instance of such condition; a tendency or bent of the mind, will, or desires towards a particular object; disposition, propensity, leaning. **a.** *absol.*

c **1430** LYDG. *Min. Poems* (1840) 91 He.. holly gaf his inclynaciouns, Duryng his lyf, to every vicyous thyng. **1490** CAXTON *How to Die* 16 That he resiste his euyll enclynacyon. *a* **1540** BARNES *Wks.* (1573) 323/1 They are both inclinations of nature, implanted of God. **1667** MILTON *P.L.* II. 524 Each his several way Pursues, as inclination or sad choice Leads him perplext. **1704–5** J. LOGAN in *Pa. Hist. Soc. Mem.* IX. 376 There seems to be growing on the inhabitants, in the main, much better inclinations. **1767** *Junius Lett.* iii. 19 It was taken from him, much against his inclination. **1849** MACAULAY *Hist. Eng.* vi. II. 139 Clarendon's inclinations were very different: but he was, from temper, interest, and principle, an obsequious courtier. **1897** GLADSTONE *E. Crisis* 2 Inclination does not suffice to justify silence.

b. Const. *to*, *for* (†*of*, *after*, *toward*) something: *to do* something.

1398 TREVISA *Barth. De P.R.* VIII. i. (1495) 295 The more inclynacyon and appetyte it hath to spyrytuall fourme and shappe. **1533** MORE *Debell. Salem* Wks. 982/1 From the inclinacion toward pyty. **1548** HALL *Chron.*, *Edw. IV* 226 A certayn naturall inclination to make warre in Fraunce. **1553** BRENDE *Q. Curtius* v. 86 b, Alexander.. had in him more enclinacion of heate then of pacience. **1691** HARTCLIFFE *Virtues* 5 Enough to draw off all our Inclinations after this World. **1712** STEELE *Spect.* No. 264 ¶3, I have an Inclination to print the following Letters. **1845** M. PATTISON *Ess.* (1889) I. 18 The Frank warriors.. showed an inclination of executing at once the sentence. **1859** MRS. CARLYLE *Lett.* III. 17, I havn't time nor inclination for much letter-writing.

c. Liking, affection.

1647 COWLEY *Mistr., My Diet* iii, If you an Inclination have for me. **1711** STEELE *Spect.* No. 33 ¶1 Daphne, despairing of any Inclination towards her Person, has depended only on her Merit. **1874** MOTLEY *Barneveld* I. ii. 112, I love you with affection and inclination. **1882** STEVENSON *New Arab. Nts.* (1884) 195, I conceived that any inclination between a man and a woman would rather delay ..the step.

†**d.** General or permanent mental tendency; natural disposition; nature, character. *Obs.*

c **1386** CHAUCER *Wife's Prol.* 615, I folwed ay myn Inclination By vertu of my constellacion. **1508** DUNBAR *Poems* vii. 34 He of naturall inclinacioune Dois favour the. **1577** tr. *Bullinger's Decades* (1592) 638 He hath giuen to all creatures a certaine inclination and nature, which he hath made their owne. **1606** SHAKS. *Ant. & Cl.* II. v. 113 Bid him Report the feature of Octauia: her yeares, Her inclination, let him not leaue out The colour of her haire. **1713** DERHAM *Phys. Theol.* v. i. (1754) 270 There is the same Reason for the Variety of Genii, or Inclinations of Men.

7. A tendency, disposition, or propensity to some physical condition or quality; formerly, the general character or nature (of a thing): now only as *fig.* from 6 (with const. as in b).

1593 SHAKS. *Rich. II*, III. ii. 195 Men iudge by the complexion of the Skie The state and inclination of the day. **1616** [see INCLINED 4]. **1653** HOLCROFT *Procopius, Goth. Wars* I. 22 The whole inclination of the War depending on him. **1704** ADDISON *Italy* (J.), Though most of the thick woods are grubbed up since the promontory has been cultivated, there are still many spots of it which shew the natural inclination of the soil leans that way. **1899** *Warehouseman & Draper* 3 June 789 When he held yarn (or cloth) in such a manner that it could not shrink, and then immersed it in caustic soda, subsequently washing the caustic soda out again, the yarn no longer had any inclination to shrink.

8. *transf.* **a.** An action or practice to which one is inclined. (Chiefly referring to an infinitive clause.)

1526 *Pilgr. Perf.* (W. de W. 1531) 2b, Her naturall inclynacyon is to be abrode in the open ayre. **1734** tr. *Rollin's Anc. Hist.* (1827) I. II. vii. 219 Traffic was the predominant inclination. **1760–72** tr. *Juan & Ulloa's Voy.* (ed. 3) II. 348 The usual inclination of the wind in these seas ..is to follow the sun from E. to S., S.S.W. and N. **1796** MORSE *Amer. Geog.* I. 104 Thieving is a very prevalent inclination among them. **1885** F. TEMPLE *Relat. Relig. & Sc.* iii. 77 We do what it is our custom, our inclination, our character to do.

†**b.** A person for whom one has a liking; a favourite. (Also in *pl.* in same sense.) *Obs.*

1691 TEMPLE *Mem.* 1672–9, iii, This was the Character of Monsieur Hoept, who was a great Inclination of mine. **1712** ARBUTHNOT *John Bull* III. ii, Of the three brothers..Jack had, of late, been her inclination.

III. 9. *Gr.* and *Lat. Gram.* The throwing of the accent of an enclitic upon the last syllable of the word to which it is attached: see INCLINE *v.* 5.

1842 JELF *Gr. Gram.* (1851) I. 61 The inclination of the accent is naturally subject to the general laws of accentuation.

incli'national, *a. rare.* [f. prec. + -AL[1].]

a. Relating to slope or inclination to the horizon. **b.** Of or pertaining to mental inclination or disposition.

1821 W. TAYLOR in *Monthly Mag.* LII. 395 As he persisted in writing for the stage, it was deemed wiser to patronize his inclinational than his professional exertions. **1879** THOMSON & TAIT *Nat. Phil.* I. I. 397 There are two freedoms, one azimuthal, the other inclinational; the first neutral, the other unstable, when fly-wheel not rotating.

‖**inclinatorium** (ɪnklaɪnəˈtɔərɪəm). [mod.L. (cf. med.L. *inclīnatōrium* a couch); see next.] The inclination-compass or dipping-needle.

1849 MISS OTTÉ, etc. tr. *Humboldt's Cosmos* I. 172 *note*, Hardly twenty years after Robert Norman had invented the inclinatorium.

inclinatory (ɪnˈklaɪnətərɪ), *a.* ?*Obs.* [f. L. *inclīnāt-* (ppl. stem of *inclīnāre* to INCLINE) + -ORY, as if ad. L. **inclīnātōrius*.] Relating to or characterized by inclination or 'dip' (see INCLINATION 3 d). ***inclinatory needle*** = DIPPING-NEEDLE.

1613 M. RIDLEY *Magn. Bodies* Pref. 2 To have the Inclinatory-needle truly placed in his ring. **1625** N. CARPENTER *Geog. Del.* I. iii. (1635) 46 The Magneticall Inclinatory needle in euery eleuation of the Pole is.. disposed to the Axell of the Earth. *a* **1691** BOYLE *Unsucceed. Exper.* Wks. 1772 I. 343 In some men's hands it will not at all succeed, some hidden property in him that uses the [divining] wand being able, as they say, to overpower and hinder its inclinatory virtue. **1770** *Phil. Trans.* LX. 366 He got an inclinatory needle constructed at Basle. **1842** *United Serv. Mag.* I. 292 The attractive and repulsive power of the magnet, and its directive and inclinatory faculties.

Hence **in'clinatorily** *adv.*

1646 SIR T. BROWNE *Pseud. Ep.* II. ii. 60 Whether they be refrigerated inclinatorily or somewhat Æquinoxially, that is toward the Easterne or Westerne points.. If an iron or steele ..be held perpendicularly or inclinatorily unto the needle, the lower end thereof will attract the *cuspis* or southerne point.

incline (ɪnˈklaɪn), *v.* Forms: α. 4–6 **enclyne**, 4–8 **encline**; β. 5–6 **inclyne**, (6 **incleine**), 6– **incline**. [Ultimately from L. *inclīnāre* to bend inwards or towards, f. *in-* (IN-[2]) + *clīnāre* to bend. The ME. form, a. OF. *encliner*, was *encline*, usual before 1500, and still found after 1600; *incline*, after later F. *incliner* (Oresme, 14th c.), is rare before 16th c., the early examples being chiefly Sc. or northern.] To bend in the direction of some object or point expressed or implied: hence generally construed with *to*, *toward*, and the like.

I. *Transitive senses.*

1. To bend or bow (the head, the body, oneself) towards a person or thing, and hence forward or downward.

α. *c* **1305** 11000 *Virgins* 159 in *E.E.P.* (1862) 70 þe bodie aros vp alone And enclynede hire to þe heȝe weued. *c* **1400** MAUNDEV. (Roxb.) xxv. 115 Ilk man enclynez his heued toward þe erthe. **1483** CAXTON *Cato* A iv, Thou oughtest to enclyne and bowe thy kne. **1631** WEEVER *Anc. Fun. Mon.* 147 Kneeling close to the Sepulchre, enclining his head vpon the same.

β. *c* **1450** *Alexander* 1603 (Dubl. MS.) þan all þe Iewes.. Inclines þaim [*Ashm. MS.* Enclynes þam] to þis conquerour & hym on knees gretes. **1567** *Gude & Godlie B.* (S.T.S.) 44 Than he his heid culd inclyne. **1590** SPENSER *F.Q.* II. ii. 3 Oft himselfe inclyning on his knee Downe to that well. **1667** MILTON *P.L.* IV. 615 The timely dew of sleep, Now falling with soft slumbrous weight, inclines Our eye-lids. **1671** —— *Samson* 1636 With head a while inclined, And eyes fast fixed he stood. **1875** JOWETT *Plato* (ed. 2) I. 482 Socrates inclined his head to the speaker and listened.

b. To bend or turn *one's ear*(*s* towards a speaker, to give ear, listen favourably, attend (*to*).

1447 BOKENHAM *Seyntys* (Roxb.) 6 That holy virgyne Wych to synful prayers lyst hyr ere enclyne. **1535** COVERDALE *Ps.* xvi[i]. 6 Enclyne thine eares to me, and herken vnto my wordes. —— *Jer.* vii. 24 They were not obedient, they inclyned not their eares there vnto. **1548–9** (Mar.) *Bk. Com. Prayer, Commun.*, We beseche thee mercifully to inclyne thyne eares to us. **1708** POPE *Ode St. Cecilia* 127 When the full organ joins the tuneful quire Th' immortal pow'rs incline their ear. **1860** MOTLEY *Netherl.* (1868) II. xii. 122 It was unwise that he should incline his ear ..to those who counselled severe measures.

†**2.** *fig.* To cause to bow, obey, or be subject *to* a person or thing; to bring down, subject. *Obs.*

c **1450** tr. *De Imitatione* III. lix. 137 Redy..to be mekely enclyned & bowed to euery creature of man [kynde]. **1450** Q. MARGARET in *Four C. Eng. Lett.* 8 Inclynyng you to his honest desire at this tyme. **1483** CAXTON *Gold. Leg.* 29 b/1 He enclyneth the hye thynges doun.

3. To bend (the mind, heart, will, etc.) towards some course or action; to give a mental leaning or tendency to (a person); to dispose. Const. *to* something, or *to do* something. (See also INCLINED 3.)

α. *c* **1430** *Pol., Rel. & L. Poems* (1866) 166 þou..To him þin herte wolt hooli enclyne. **1509** FISHER *Fun. Serm. C'tess Richmond* Wks. (1876) 299 Here vnto his ryght-wysnes also sholde enclyne hym. **1552** *Bk. Com. Prayer, Commun.*, Encline our heartes to kepe thys lawe. **1642** ROGERS *Naaman* 441 Not whether the heart would of itselfe encline, but whether God enclines it.

β. **1483** CAXTON *Cato* B iij b, Oftentymes they inclyne or bowen them to suche playes. **1526** *Pilgr. Perf.* (W. de W. 1531) 19 b, Goostly pite, inclyneth hym to the same by inspiracyon. **1591** SOUTHWELL in *Imp. Consid. Sec. Priests* (1675) 80 So far hath he inclined fury to clemency. **1653** MILTON *Hirelings* Wks. (1847) 424/2 Such advice as God shall incline him..to propound. **1756** BURKE *Vind. Nat. Soc.* Wks. I. 9 You were inclined to the party which you adopted rather by the feelings of your good nature. **1771** WESLEY *Serm.* I. III. §8 To hear them speak..might incline one to think they were not far from the kingdom of God. **1839** THIRLWALL *Greece* xlvii. VI. 105 The language of Æschines inclines us to believe, that they did not adopt the motion of Demosthenes.

4. To cause to lean from the vertical or horizontal (or other given) position or direction; to bend, direct, or turn downwards; to slope, tilt.

1590 SPENSER *F.Q.* II. xii. 54 An embracing vine, Whose bounches hanging downe..did them selves into their hands incline. **1694** SALMON *Bate's Dispens.* (1713) 242/1 Then inclining the Glass, decant the Tincture. **1732** POPE *Ep. Cobham* 150 Just as the Twig is bent, the Tree's inclin'd. **1769** *Junius Lett.* xviii. (1804) I. 113 It is not the Printer's fault, if the greater weight inclines the balance. **1839** G. BIRD *Nat. Phil.* 221 So inclining them that they may lean against each other. **1860** TYNDALL *Glac.* 223 Bradley.. found that, owing to the velocity with which the earth flies through space, the rays of the stars are slightly inclined.

b. To bend the course of (something) in the direction of, towards, or *to* (some person or thing).

1712–14 POPE *Rape Lock* III. 66 Now to the Baron fate inclines the field. **1725** —— *Odyss.* I. 538 To this his steps the thoughtful prince inclin'd.

†**c.** To direct (something immaterial) towards a particular object; to apply, bestow. *Obs.*

1535 COVERDALE *Ezra* ix. 9 Oure God..hath enclyned mercy vnto vs. **1596** J. NORDEN *Progr. Pietie* (1847) 170 Such..will have regard unto the same, and incline help thereunto. *a* **1626** BACON *Max. & Uses Com. Law* iii. (1636) 22 The issue..shall encline and apply all the proofes as tending to that conclusion.

5. *Gr.* and *Lat. Gram.* To cause (a dependent word) to lean its accent upon the preceding word: see ENCLITIC *a.*

1751 HARRIS *Hermes* I. v. (1806) 84 [Certain pronouns] not only took their place behind the Verb, but even gave it their accent, and (as it were) inclined themselves upon it. And hence they acquired the name of Ἐγκλιτικαί, that is, Leaning or Inclining Pronouns. **1764** PRIMATT *Accent. Rediv.* 249 After giving some instances where they [words] are inclined.

II. *Intransitive.*

6. To bend the head or body forward or downward; to bend, stoop, bow: esp. in token of respect or courtesy. ? *Obs.*

α. **13..** *E.E. Allit. P.* A. 236 Enclynande lowe in wommon lore. **13..** *Gaw. & Gr. Knt.* 340 To þe kyng he can enclyne. *c* **1386** CHAUCER *Monk's Prol.* 14 If that any neighebore of myne Wol nat in chirche to my wyf en clyne. *c* **1500** *Melusine* xxxiii. 233 Whan she cam byfore her vncle she enclyned & honourably made to hym her obeyssaunce.

β. *c* **1400** MAUNDEV. (Roxb.) xi. 41 He inclynes þerto reuerently. *c* **1470** HENRY *Wallace* XI. 51 Wallace inclynd, and thankit this wys lord. **1547** BOORDE *Introd. Knowl.* xxiv. (1870) 185 Whan they do heare masse, & se the sacrament, they do inclyne. *c* **1658** MILTON *Sonn. Deceased Wife*, As to embrace me she inclined, I waked, she fled, and day brought back my night. **1667** —— *P.L.* XI. 250 Adam bowd low, hee [Michael] Kingly from his State Inclin'd not. *c* **1820** S. ROGERS *Italy, Ginevra* 27 She sits, inclining forward as to speak.

†**b.** With indirect obj. [Cf. OF. *encliner* to bow to, salute.] *Obs.*

1375 BARBOUR *Bruce* IV. 509 (Edin. MS.) Than went thai till the king in hy, And hym inclynyt curtasly. *c* **1400** *Destr. Troy* 2305 He enclynet the Kyng & closit his mowthe.

7. *fig.* To 'bow', submit, yield *to*; to 'bow down', condescend; to accede (*to*).

α. *c* **1440** *York Myst.* x. 245 To goddis cummaundement I sall enclyne. **1513** MORE *Rich. III* Wks. 65/2 He could not fynde in his hearte..to enclyne to theyr desyre.

β. *c* **1470** HENRY *Wallace* x. 1001 Baith hycht and waill obeyed all till his will..The byschoprykis inclynyt till his croune. **1500–20** DUNBAR *Poems* x. 25 All clergy do to him inclyne, And bow vnto that barne benyng. **1611** BIBLE *Ps.* XL, 1, I waited patiently for the Lord, and he inclined vnto me. **1866** *Standard* 24 Nov. 4/6 A favorite..is generally of that pliant temperament which never gives offence because it ever inclines before it.

8. To turn in mind, feeling, or action, in a given direction; to apply oneself (*to*); to favour, take sides, or show practical sympathy, with a person, party, or cause. (Now mostly with mixture of sense 9.)

α. *a* **1300** *Cursor M.* 25516 þou giue vs lauerd!.. Wit hand and werck, hert and will..To þe wit hert encline. *c* **1375** *Sc. Leg. Saints, Blasius* 181 Til enclyne fals godis till. **1535** COVERDALE *Acts* v. 36 All they y[t] enclyned vnto him were scatred abrode. **1548** HALL *Chron., Hen. VIII* 150 To judge to whiche parte he should moste encline, and geve credence.

β. **1500–20** DUNBAR *Poems* lxxxiv. 17 Se ȝe hir full suddanelie incleine To tak a crippill, or a creatour Deformit. **1530** PALSGR. 590/2, I inclyne..I applye my mynde to do a thyng. *a* **1580** *Farrant's Anthem, 'Lord, for thy tender mercies' sake'*, Give us grace..to decline from sin and incline to virtue. **1626** C. POTTER tr. *Sarpi's Hist. Quarrels Pope Paul V*, 107 Only the Great Chancellor and the Marshall Prainer inclined for the Pope. **1665** MANLEY *Grotius' Low C. Warres* 339 The very Common People..would not.. hearken or incline to any Thoughts of Peace. **1770** *Junius Lett.* xxxvi. 175 Your best friends are in doubt which way they shall incline. **1879** M. ARNOLD *Ess., Irish Cathol. & Brit. Lib.* 99 For England to incline one way is a sufficient reason for Ireland to incline another.

9. To have a mental leaning, bias, or favourable inclination towards something; to be disposed or inclined (see INCLINED 3). Const. *to* (*toward*, *for*) something, *to do* something.

a **1340** [see INCLINING *ppl. a.* 2]. **1375** BARBOUR *Bruce* IV. 722 (Edin. MS.) The constellatioun That kyndlik maners gifs thaim till, For to inclyne to gud or ill. *c* **1450** tr. *De Imitatione* III. lix. 138 Nature enclineþ to creatures, to hir ovne flesshe. **1548** HALL *Chron., Hen. VIII* 149 Whiche caused hym to encline to mariage. **1611** BIBLE *Judg.* ix. 3 Their hearts inclined to follow Abimelech; for they said, He is our brother. *a* **1703** WALLIS *Pref.* in J. Greenwood *Eng. Gram* (1711) 6, I rather encline to the contrary Opinion. **1722** DE FOE *Plague* (1754) 13, I enclin'd to stay and take my Lot in that Station in which God had plac'd me. **1771** GOLDSM. *Hist. Eng.* IV. 93 It was not,..without private reasons that Marlborough inclined for war. **1839** G. BIRD *Nat. Phil.* 290 The second theory..toward which philosophers of the present day generally incline. **1847** GROTE *Greece* II. xlvii. IV. 168, I incline to believe [etc.].

b. *elliptically.* To be inclined or disposed (to go, do, have, etc.); to desire.

1746 ELIZA HEYWOOD *Fem. Spect.* (1748) IV. 235 What they incline, they have not the power to inforce. **1777** WATSON *Philip II* (1793) III. xx. 72 To carry them to whatever place they should incline. **1795** MACKNIGHT *Apost. Epist.* I. 267 The unregenerated do not the good they incline, but the evil which they do not incline. **1834** CAMPBELL in *Brown's Lett. Sanctif.* vi. 320, I had not that assurance of my state which I inclined.

10. To have or take a direction or position which leans in a given direction from the vertical or horizontal; to slope, slant, bend downwards. Const. *to*, *towards*.

1568 GRAFTON *Chron.* II. 131 The Beame should stande upright..enclinyng to neyther partie. **1673** RAY *Journ. Low C., Pisa* 262 The Campanile or Steeple..so very much enclining or seeming to encline or lean to one side, that one would think it could not long stand upright. **1756–7** tr. *Keysler's Trav.* (1760) II. 64 The head inclines on one side. **1854** RONALDS & RICHARDSON *Chem. Technol.* (ed. 2) I. 81 The sole of the furnace is raised in the centre and inclines towards the sides. **1867** W. W. SMYTH *Coal & Coal-mining* 23 They are found to incline..more or less regularly from the moderate angles of 6 or 8° to as much as 25 or 30°.

b. *Dialling.* Said of a dial, the plane of which leans forwards from the wall against which it is placed: opposed to *recline*.

1593 FALE *Dialling* 4 If the angle which the plat maketh with the horizon be accute or sharp, then it doth incline. **1703** MOXON *Mech. Exerc.* 321 It is not upright, but Inclines or Reclines.

11. *gen.* To have or take a course or position turning away in the direction of some point, region, etc.; hence, generally, to have an oblique position or direction, so as to make angles with something else.

1553 EDEN *Treat. Newe Ind.* (Arb.) 39 Melcha is situate more toward the West, and Calicut more enclininge towarde the south. **1613** PURCHAS *Pilgrimage* (1614) 410 A course directly East, or inclining to the South. **1823** H. J. BROOKE *Introd. Crystallogr.* 163 The unequal angles at which the primary planes incline to each other at the edges. **1838** GUEST *Eng. Rhythms* I. 5 If they incline from each other, they will bulge inwards, if towards each other, they will bulge outwards.

b. *Mil.* To move in a direction at angles with the front of the formation, so as to gain ground to the flank while advancing.

1796–7 *Instr. & Reg. Cavalry* (1813) 19 At the order to Incline! each man makes a half face on his horse's fore feet ..and the whole will look to the hand to which they are to incline. **1847** *Infantry Man.* (1854) 47 The march of every body, except in the case of inclining, is made on lines perpendicular to its front. **1853** STOCQUELER *Milit. Encycl.*, *Incline*, to gain ground to the flank, as well as to the front.

12. *fig.* **a.** To turn or go aside in a given direction; to have a tendency, tend (*to*); in quot. 1615, to have relation, refer (*to*).

1509 HAWES *Past. Pleas.* xxxiii. (Percy Soc.) 163 My name is Falshed, I shall cause enclyne My neyghbours goods for to make them myne. **1568** GRAFTON *Chron.* II. 102 We.. intend so to proceede in this matter neither enclynyng on the right hande, neyther yet on the left. **1611** BIBLE *Prov.* ii. 18 Her house inclineth vnto death, and her pathes vnto the dead. **1615** CHAPMAN *Odyss.* I. 45 Inducing matter that inclined To wise Ulysses. **1788** GIBBON *Decl. & F.* lii. (1869) III. 272 Victory inclined to the side of the allies. **1884** LD. COLERIDGE in *Law Rep.* 12 Q. Bench Div. 322 The weight of authority inclines upon the whole in favour of the objection.

b. To tend towards some quality or condition; to have some attribute in an incipient degree. Const. *to* with noun or adj., or *inf*.

1589 COGAN *Haven Health* ccxviii. (1636) 252 Beere or ale being made of wheate malt encline th more to heat, for wheate is hot. **1599** H. BUTTES *Dyets drie Dinner* P iij b, Tobacco..of a tawny colour, somwhat inclining to red. **1699** DAMPIER *Voy.* II. I. 32 The weather is more mixt and uncertain (tho inclining to the wet extreme). **1749** FIELDING *Tom Jones* IV. ii, Sophia..was a middle-sized woman, but rather inclining to tall. **1797** BEWICK *Brit. Birds* (1847) I. 28 The top of the head..dark brown, inclining to black. **1835** MARRYAT *Jac. Faithf.* vi, He was stout and well-built, inclining to corpulence.

†**c.** To fall off, decay, wane: = DECLINE *v.* 10.

1612 [see INCLINING *vbl. sb.* 1 b, *ppl. a.* 1].

incline (ɪnˈklaɪn, ˈɪnklaɪn), *sb.* [f. the vb.]

†**1.** Mental tendency, disposition: = INCLINATION 6. *Obs.*

1600 W. WATSON *Decacordon* (1602) 140 All alike neare to God by creation, by redemption, by natures incline in euery one. *Ibid.* 193 This so gracious..incline of her Maiestie and honorable Counsell to mitigate our generall..affliction. *Ibid.* 273 A..sweete incline to mercy.

2. An inclined plane or surface; a slope, declivity (esp. on a road or railway).

1846 *Penny Cycl.* Suppl. II. 663/2 To fear that the train would be unable to ascend an incline of 16 feet per mile. **1883** C. J. WILLS *Mod. Persia* 112 We rode..under an arch-way and up a steep incline. **1887** LOWELL *Democr.* etc. 16 A railway train running down an incline.

b. *Mining.* More fully **incline-shaft**: A shaft or opening into a mine having considerable inclination or slope; distinguished from a (vertical) *shaft* and from a *level*.

1877 RAYMOND *Statist. Mines & Mining* 85 The incline-shaft is down 800 feet... The 600 and 700 foot levels are connected by a winze, which is 175 feet south of the incline. **1898** *Daily News* 12 July 2/7 In changing over to the new central incline shaft from the old shaft.

inclined (ɪnˈklaɪnd), *ppl. a.* Also 4–6 en-. [f. INCLINE *v.* + -ED[1].]

1. Having a direction leaning or falling away from the vertical or horizontal; sloping, slanting.

inclined plane, a material plane surface inclined at an acute angle to the horizon, constituting one of the mechanical powers.

1541 R. COPLAND *Guydon's Quest. Chirurg.*, From the nether parte it [the heart] is enclyned a lytell towarde the left syde, to gyue place to the lyuer. **1710** J. CLARKE *Rohault's Nat. Phil.* (1729) I. 87 The Force and the Weight will then support one another upon an inclined Plain. **1812–16** J. SMITH *Panorama Sc. & Art* I. 316 The inclined plane is any flat surface which forms an angle less than a right angle, with the plane of the horizon. **1821** CRAIG *Lect. Drawing* vii. 401 Turning the plate slowly round..in a somewhat inclined direction. **1833** LYELL *Princ. Geol.* III. 174 Sets of inclined and horizontal layers of sand. **1878** MARG. STOKES *Early Chr. Archit. Irel.* 3 The ancient features of the horizontal lintel and inclined sides are preserved in the doorways.

b. *gen.* Having a direction making an angle with something else (const. *to*; cf. INCLINATION 4).

1813 BAKEWELL *Introd. Geol.* (1815) 58 The sides of mountains which are most inclined to the horizon. **1840** LARDNER *Geom.* iv. 39 The sides of the triangle will be inclined to MN at the same angles as those at which they are inclined to its parallel A.

2. Having a physical tendency (*to* something, or *to do* something): = DISPOSED 5.

c **1384** CHAUCER *H. Fame* II. 241 Every Ryver to the see Enclyned ys to goo by kynde. **1726** LEONI tr. *Alberti's Archit.* I. 65/1 The Winds are naturally enclined to follow the Sun.

3. Having a mental bent, tendency, or propensity towards a particular object; favourably disposed; in the mood or mind for something: = DISPOSED 4. **a.** Following its sb.: Const. *to* or *for* something, *to do* something; also with adverb or adverbial phrase, as ***dishonestly inclined, that way inclined***.

1390 GOWER *Conf.* III. 179 Enclined to vertue or to vice. **1413** *Pilgr. Sowle* (Caxton 1483) IV. xxx. 78 He is enclyned to counceylle. **1548** HALL *Chron., Hen. VIII* 58 The kyng ever enclyned to mercy, sent theim apparell. **1596** DRAYTON *Leg.* iv. 173 Being besides industriously inclinde. **1603** SHAKS. *Meas. for M.* III. ii. 130 He was not enclin'd that way. **1651** HOBBES *Leviath.* I. viii. 38 A mans spirit, enclined to Godlinesse. **1703** DE FOE in *15th Rep. Hist. MSS. Comm.* App. IV. 62 If you find him inclined to have compassion. **1754** MURPHY *Gray's-Inn Jrnl.* No. 91 ¶ 1 Gentlemen that are inclined for Marriage. **1873** BLACK *Pr. Thule* vii, Ingram was now well inclined to the project. **1875** JOWETT *Plato* (ed. 2) I. 162, I wish Protagoras either to ask or answer as he is inclined. *Mod.* I don't feel much inclined for work.

b. In attributive construction; usually with preceding adverb, as ***well-inclined***.

1561 T. NORTON *Calvin's Inst.* I. 21 His fatherly bountie and enclined will to do good. **1619** VISC. DONCASTER in *Eng. & Germ.* (Camden) 201 Inducements heerunto strong inough to sway inclined mindes. **1710** STEELE *Tatler* No. 207 ¶ 1 A well inclined young Man.

†**4.** Having a particular disposition, character, or nature. *Obs. rare.* (Cf. INCLINATION 6 d.)

1583 STUBBES *Anat. Abus.* II. (1882) 65 He that is borne vnder Cancer, shall be crabbed and angrie, bicause the crab fish is so inclined. **1616** SURFL. & MARKH. *Country Farme* 28 He shall know how euerie moneth in the yeare will be enclined, by obseruing the inclination of the day of the Natiuitie, and of the Festiuall dayes following.

incliner (ɪnˈklaɪnə(r)). [f. as prec. + -ER[1].] One who or that which inclines; an inclining dial.

1609 W. SCLATER *Threefold Preserv.* (1610) D iv b, Another kind of Apostasie, which we call partiall, a fearfull incliner to this irrecouerable condition. **1690** LEYBOURN *Curs. Math.* 701 If the Plain pass between the Horizon and the Pole, the North Pole; and on the Incliners opposite to them, the South Pole must be elevated. **1703** MOXON *Mech. Exerc.* 331 If your Plane be an East Incliner, or a West Recliner.

inclining (ɪnˈklaɪnɪŋ), *vbl. sb.* Also 4–6 en-. [f. as prec. + -ING[1].] The action of the verb INCLINE; inclination.

1. A bending forward or downward; a bowing of the head or body in salutation or worship; a slope, declivity.

c **1400** MAUNDEV. (1839) xxii. 234 Þei gon..before the Emperour, with outen speche of ony woord, saf only enclynynge to him. ? *a* **1550** in *Dunbar's Poems* (S.T.S.) 322 Hevin, erd, and hell makis inclynyng. **1596** DALRYMPLE tr. *Leslie's Hist. Scot.* I. 30 A plane field, haueng na inclyneng or bowing.

†**b.** *fig.* A falling off, decline. *Obs.*

1612 T. TAYLOR *Comm. Titus* i. 6 (1619) 105 In the inclining of Salomons prosperitie, the first exception the Lord tooke against him was, that he loued many outlandish women.

2. Tendency, propensity, bent (physical or mental).

c **1384** CHAUCER *H. Fame* II. 236 Vnto whiche place euery thynge Thorgh his kyndely enclynynge Moveth for to come to. **1500–20** DUNBAR *Poems* xlvi. 52 To luve eik natur gaif thame inclynnyng. **1577** B. GOOGE *Heresbach's Husb.* II. (1586) 80 b, There is required a more enclining to the one parte. **1748** RICHARDSON *Clarissa* (1811) III. iii. 35 I'll tell thee my inclinings as I proceed. **1895** *Daily News* 20 June 6/1 He had many tastes and many inclinings outside the.. world of politics.

b. Party, following (cf. INCLINE *v.* 8). *Obs.* or *arch.*

1604 SHAKS. *Oth.* I. ii. 82 Hold your hands Both you of my inclining and the rest. **1752** MURPHY *Gray's-Inn Jrnl.* No. 10 ¶ 7 Mr. Plastic is a compleat Shaftesburian Philosopher; like all the Gentlemen of that inclining, he has a polite Taste for the imitative Arts. **1893** MCCARTHY *Dictator* I. 14 The flower that had come to be the badge of those of his inclining.

in'clining, *ppl. a.* Also 4–6 en-. [f. as prec. + -ING[2]. Cf. ENCLINANT.] That inclines, in various senses.

1. Leaning or bending from the vertical or horizontal (or other given) direction or position; bending downward or forward; sloping, slanting.

inclining dial: see INCLINE *v.* 10 b.

1612 DRAYTON *Poly-olb.* ix. Notes 149 Such composed quiet, as inclining Age affects. *a* **1682** SIR T. BROWNE *Let. to Friend* in *Hydriot.* (1736) 59 A large Pot was found, which lay in an inclining Posture. **1703** MOXON *Mech. Exerc.* 311 Inclining Planes, which lean towards you. **1772** *Ann Reg.* 76 This mountain is situated in a gently inclining plain. **1825** J. NICHOLSON *Operat. Mechanic* 518 The pendulum.. withdraws the detent..from the tooth, which now pushes off the detent, by acting on the inclining face of it. **1881** *N. & Q.* 22 Jan., Passing through a romantic gorge, where the inclining ridges met.

2. Having a tendency, leaning, or disposition *to* some particular thing; inclined, disposed; †disposed to comply with or favour a particular person, party, or cause (*obs.*).

a **1340** HAMPOLE *Psalter* xxiv. 1 Whils he has any affeccioun enclynand til any creature. **1604** SHAKS. *Oth.* II. iii. 346 For 'tis most easy The inclining Desdemona to subdue In any honest suit. **1649** G. DANIEL *Trinarch., Hen. IV*, clxxxviii, These Suggestions Made the enclineing Commons, All his friends. **1682** MRS. BEHN *City Heiress* 37 What Wit, what Art Can save a poor inclining heart? **1771** GOLDSM. *Hist. Eng.* III. 373 They supposed that he was more inclining to popery.

b. Of things: Tending, approximating.

a **1774** GOLDSM. *Surv. Exp. Philos.* (1776) II. 367 The more inclining to violet..would be the colour of the body which they composed.

inclinometer (ɪnklɪˈnɒmɪtə(r)). [irreg. f. L. *inclīnāre* + -METER: cf. DECLINOMETER.]

1. An instrument for measuring the vertical intensity of the earth's magnetic force, as shown by the inclination or dip of the magnetic needle.

1842 *Proc. Amer. Phil. Soc.* II. 237 A new induction inclinometer by Professor Lloyd of Dublin. **1851–9** *Man. Sci. Enq.* 91 It consists of a dipping-needle and graduated circle differing little from the accustomed form of an Inclinometer.

2. An instrument for measuring the inclination or slope of anything.

1852 *Mechanics' Mag.* LVII. 416/2 An improved apparatus, instrument, or means for ascertaining or setting off the slope or level of drains, banks, inclines, or works of any description..which the patentee calls an 'inclinometer'. **1898** *Tit-Bits* 16 July 313/3 A patent inclinometer, designed to register the exact roll or list to port or starboard of a vessel at sea or in harbour. **1913** *Captain* Sept. 1069/2 An inclinometer, to show the angle of ascent or descent. **1919** H. SHAW *Textbk. Aeronaut.* xiii. 169 Inclinometers of the spirit-level type, or constructed on the principle of the pendulum,..are inaccurate when the machine is subjected to an acceleration as in turning. **1960** [see GRADIOMETER a].

inclip (ɪnˈklɪp), *v. arch.* [f. IN-[1] + CLIP *v.*[1]] *trans.* To clasp, enclose, embrace.

1608 SHAKS. *Ant. & Cl.* II. vii. 74 What ere the Ocean pales, or skie inclippes, Is thine, if thou wilt ha't. **1855** SINGLETON *Virgil* I. 277 The tiny frames of his two sons Each snake, inclipping them, infolds.

incloise, -cloiss, obs. var. of INCLOSE.

incloister, -cloyster, var. of ENCLOISTER *v.*

†**in-clos**, *pple. Obs.* = ENCLOSE, enclosed.

c **1330** R. BRUNNE *Chron. Wace* (Rolls) 5107 Þyse Bretons þat were in-clos & byseged wiþ her fos. *c* **1475** [see ENCLOSE].

inclose, *v.* Variant form of ENCLOSE, being the legal and statutory form, in reference to the inclosing of common and waste lands; formerly a frequent and still an occasional variant in other senses: see ENCLOSE.

inclosed, -er, -ing, var. ff. ENCLOSED, etc.

inclosure. Variant form of ENCLOSURE, being the statutory form in reference to the inclosing of waste lands, commons, etc. Formerly also in other senses: see ENCLOSURE.

†**in'closurer.** [f. INCLOSURE + -ER.] One who 'squats' on an inclosure from a common or waste.

1665 *Lex Scripta I. of Man* (1819) 157 And so..turning Cottlers or Inclosurers on some Highway Side, are commonly given to pilfering and stealing, and intertainers of Vagabonds.

†**in'closyer**, obs. form of INCLOSER.

a **1529** SKELTON *Vox Populi* 366 Our covetous lordes.. With comons and comon ingenders With inclosyers and extenders.

incloude, -owd, obs. forms of ENCLOUD.

includable, variant of INCLUDIBLE.

include (ɪnˈkluːd), *v.* Also 5–6 enclude, 6 includ, 6 *pa. pple.* include. [ad. L. *inclūd-ĕre* to shut in, f. *in-* (IN-[2]) + *claudĕre* to shut.] *trans.* To shut in, enclose, confine, embrace, comprise, contain: predicated either of the agent or of the confining or containing limits or space.

1. a. *trans.* To shut or close in; to enclose within material limits; †to shut up, confine (*obs.*). Now only in *passive*: cf. INCLUDED *ppl. a.*

c **1420** *Pallad. on Husb.* IV. 338 The flouryng tre, the trunke in leed Enclude. **1432–50** tr. *Higden* (Rolls) VI. 169 That he includede a wicked spirite in a potte boylynge. *Ibid.* I. 39 Marianus a Scotte and a monke, included at a cyte callede Mangotia. **1500–20** DUNBAR *Poems* lxxxv. 78 Hospitall riall, the lord of all Thy closet did include. **1564** HAWARD *Eutropius* I. 10 The Romaynes which were here [in the capitol] included. **1570** BILLINGSLEY *Euclid* I. 7 That two right lines include not a superficies. **1571** DIGGES *Pantom.* III. viii. R j b, The circles semidiameter that encludeth the greater Hexagonum. **1588** FRAUNCE *Lawiers Log.* I. xvii. 62 b, They hedge in and include the ground. *a* **1592** GREENE *Jas. IV*, II. ii, O, that I were included in my grave. **1678** EVELYN *Diary* 23 July, Went to see Mr. Elias Ashmole's library and curiosities..He shew'd me a toade included in amber. **1750** tr. *Leonardus' Mirr. Stones* 151 It holds air included in it, and swims by the lightness of the air. **1784** COWPER *Task* VI. 244 He..includes In grains as countless as the sea-side sands, The forms with which he sprinkles all the earth. **1799** DAVY in Beddoes *Contrib. Phys. & Med. Knowl.* 158 The globe was..inserted horizontally in a vessel, so as to be perfectly included from light. **1857–8**

SEARS *Athan.* viii. 68 A spirit allied with seraphim included in this animal frame.

b. *fig.* (The limits, object, or inclusion being non-material.)

?*a*1550 *Dunbar's Poems* (S.T.S.) 325 The Souerane Senȝour of all celsitude.. Quhilk all thing creat, and all thing dois includ. **1567** *Gude & Godlie B.* (S.T.S.) 185 Of thair fude his flock we haif begylit.. And in fals belief hes thame includit. **1606** SHAKS. *Tr. & Cr.* I. iii. 119 Then euery thing includes it selfe in Power, Power into Will, Will into Appetite. **1609** BIBLE (Douay) *Jer.* xix. 9 The distresse, wherein their enemies shal include them. **1781** COWPER *Charity* 598 The soul, thus kindled from above.. Includes creation in her close embrace.

c. To enclose (in an area).

1662 STILLINGFL. *Orig. Sacr.* I. ii. §4 It was after included in its circuit. **1856** STANLEY *Sinai & Pal.* xiv. (1858) 459 The question whether the wall of Herod really ran so as just to exclude or just to include the present site.

2. To contain, comprise, embrace. **a.** To contain as a member of an aggregate, or a constituent part of a whole; to embrace as a subdivision or section; to comprise; to comprehend.

*c*1430 LYDG. *Min. Poems* (1840) 118 The moralite.. includithe in many sundry wise, No man shuld.. For no prerogatif his neyghburghe to dispise. **1494** FABYAN *Chron.* 5 This boke Includyth Storyes fele. **1591** SHAKS. *1 Hen. VI*, I. ii. 137 With Henries death, the English Circle ends, Dispersed are the glories it included. **1659** PEARSON *Creed* (1839) 370 In the number of the fifty days was both the day of the wave-offering and of Pentecost included. **1673** TEMPLE *Observ. United Prov.* i. (R.), I can-not affirm whether it [Flanders] only bordered upon, or included the lower parts of the vast woods of Ardenne. **1797** BEWICK *Brit. Birds* (1847) I. 70 It includes.. the Pie, Jay, Nutcracker, Chough, Chatterer, &c. **1843** MILL *Logic* I. v. §3 The proposition, Man is mortal, asserts, according to this view of it, that the class man is included in the class mortal. **1874** GREEN *Short Hist.* iv. §2. 167 The Great Council.. was held to include all tenants who held directly of the Crown.

b. To contain as a subordinate element, corollary, or secondary feature; to comprise virtually or by inference; to involve, imply.

1526 *Pilgr. Perf.* (W. de W. 1531) 128 In the vertue of fayth is vnderstande sure hope & perfyte charite: For whan fayth is perfyte, it encludeth them bothe. *a*1540 BARNES *Wks.* 228 (R.) Our mayster Christ sheweth that in fulfilling ii. of these commaundementes, bee all workes included. **1588** FRAUNCE *Lawiers Log.* I. i. 2b, [A proposition] which is contrarie to all reason, and includeth in it selfe a manifest contradiction. **1594** SHAKS. *Rich. III*, I. iii. 8 The losse of such a Lord, includes all harmes. *a*1763 SHENSTONE *Ess.* (1765) 144 Every good poet includes a critic. **1818** CRUISE *Digest* (ed. 2) IV. 174 A power of appointment, which relates to the land, includes a right to appoint either absolutely or with a new power of revocation and appointment. **1876** J. PARKER *Paracl.* I. iii. 24 The term God includes all other terms. **1883** *Contemp. Rev.* XLIII. 47 There is a love that includes friendship, as religion includes morality.

3. a. To place in a class or category; to embrace in a general survey or description; to reckon in a calculation, mention in an enumeration, etc.

1560 ROLLAND *Crt. Venus* III. 796 Bot I suppone thir wemen ar Include.. For to fulfill the number suspensiue. **1625** USSHER in *Lett. Lit. Men* (Camden) 132, I was bold to include you in a Letter to my Lo. of Landaff. **1794** SULLIVAN *View Nat.* I. 18 Men of feeble parts.. are not to be included in this number. **1843** MILL *Logic* I. i. §3 The enumeration has omitted nothing which ought to have been included. **1848** —— *Pol. Econ.* I. i. §1 It is necessary to include in the idea [of Labour] all feelings of a disagreeable kind.. connected with the employment of one's thoughts, or muscles, or both, in a particular occupation.

b. Const. *out*: to exclude (oneself or someone). Hence, pleonastically, ***to include*** (someone) ***in***.

This colloquial expression, which freq. indicates strong feelings of cynicism or disillusion, is attributed to the American film producer Sam Goldwyn.

1937 A. JOHNSTON in *Sat. Even. Post* 8 May 6/1 An ordinary man, on deciding to quit the Hays organization, might have turned to his fellow producers and said, 'Gentlemen, I prefer to stand aloof,' or, 'Gentlemen, I have decided to go my own way.' Sam [Goldwyn] said, 'Gentlemen, include me out.' **1938** *Hansard Commons* 8 Nov. 18/1 It may be that the First Commissioner of Works.. will now label the 'Aye' Lobby the 'Sez you' Lobby, and the other the 'Include me out' Lobby. **1946** WODEHOUSE *Joy in Morning* xvi. 140 Include me out... Nothing doing. **1958** G. MITCHELL *Spotted Hemlock* x. 101, I shall suggest giving you lunch and include him in. **1958** *Times Lit. Suppl.* 1 Aug. 435/1 He sees that our young men are angry; they do not see visions or dream dreams; they want neither to go back nor move forward: they only ask to be included-out of the social and historical process. **1959** M. STEEN *Woman in Back Seat* I. vii. 128 Oh, darling, please include me out! I can't bear affairs of that kind. **1967** WODEHOUSE *Company for Henry* ii. 39 You surprise me. A free meal, and he made no attempt to include himself in? **1969** V. GIELGUD *Necessary End* III. xv. 120 I'd like nothing better—in the immortal words—than to include myself out. **1971** *Daily Tel.* 13 Oct. 11/5 Half the in-jokes included me out, but I revelled in the way the actors caricatured famous folk. **1972** G. BROMLEY *In Absence of Body* iii. 33 Looking for clues? If so, include me in.

†**4.** To bring to a close: = CONCLUDE 5. *Obs.*

1591 SHAKS. *Two Gent.* V. iv. 160 We will include all iarres, With Triumphes, Mirth, and rare solemnity.

†**5.** To infer: = CONCLUDE 8. *Obs.*

1529 MORE *Suppl. Soulys* Wks. 291/1 Wherof he would include that.. yᵉ king must nedes graunt a licence to such lewd felowes to rayle vpon them.

Hence **including** *vbl. sb.*, inclusion.

1598 FLORIO, *Inclusione*, an including.

included (ɪn'klu:dɪd), *ppl. a.* [f. prec. + -ED¹.]

a. Shut in, enclosed, contained, comprised.

1552 HULOET, Included, *inclusus*. **1561** T. NORTON *Calvin's Inst.* IV. xiv. (1634) 637 *marg.*, They [the Sacraments] work not by secret included force. **1667** MILTON *P.L.* IX. 416 The onely two of Mankinde, but in them The whole included Race. **1727–41** CHAMBERS *Cycl.* s.v. *Cupping*, After the included air has been well heated. **1806** HUTTON *Course Math.* I. 275 If two Triangles have Two Sides and the Included Angle in the one, equal to Two Sides and the Included Angle in the other, the Triangles will be Identical, or equal in all respects. **1874** LYELL *Elem. Geol.* xiii. 176 The quartzose sand and the included shells are most ..[of] ochreous colour. **1884** TENNYSON *Becket* I. i, The included Danaë has escaped again Her tower.

b. *Entom.* Said of a clypeus or nasus, situated between two projecting portions of the supraclypeus or postnasus.

1826 KIRBY & SP. *Entomol.* IV. 313 *Included*, when the nose is included between the two sides of the Postnasus which run towards the upper lip.

c. *Bot.* Said of parts (esp. the style or stamens) which do not protrude beyond the corolla.

1847 W. E. STEELE *Field Bot.* 120 *Pyrola minor.* Stamens inflexed, equalling the straight, included style. **1880** GRAY *Struct. Bot.* (ed. 6) 416/1.

d. *Linguistics.* (See quot. 1933.)

1933 L. BLOOMFIELD *Lang.* xi. 170 When a linguistic form occurs as part of a larger form, it is said to be in included position; otherwise it is said to be in absolute position and to constitute a sentence. **1949** E. A. NIDA *Morphol.* (ed. 2) 76 Some morphemes occur in included position, either partial or complete. **1952** C. C. FRIES *Struct. of Eng.* XI. 253 These are the signals of 'included' sentences... In some sentences there are devices that signal the inclusion of two or more separate sentences within the structural pattern of a single free sentence unit. **1954** PEI & GAYNOR *Dict. Ling.* 98 *Included position*, the position had by a word, phrase or other linguistic form when it is part of a larger form and does not constitute a sentence in itself. **1962** B. M. H. STRANG *Mod. Eng. Struct.* v. 82 Linguistic structures may always be either ..absolute or included.

e. *Bot.* ***included phloem***, ***sapwood*** (see quots.).

1933 *Tropical Woods* XXXVI. 2 Included Phloem.—Phloem strands or layers included in the secondary xylem or certain dicotyledonous woods. (To replace *Interxylary Phloem.*) **1937** *Ibid.* L. 11 Strands of included phloem usually isolated, but occasionally linked by parenchyma. **1969** K. ESAU *Phloem* 3 In some genera a third category of phloem is found, *included phloem*, which consists of strands or layers embedded in the secondary xylem. **1933** *Tropical Woods* XXXVI. 3 Included Sapwood.—Masses or concentric zones included in the heartwood, which retain appearance and technical properties of sapwood. **1956** F. W. JANE *Struct. Wood* x. 212 Sometimes, heartwood is formed irregularly and patches of pale coloured wood are enclosed within the heartwood, a feature referred to as included sapwood.

†**in'cludent.** *Obs.* [ad. L. *inclūdent-em*, pres. pple. of *inclūdĕre* to INCLUDE.] = INCLUDER b.

1670 *Conclave wherein Clement VIII was elected Pope* 16 Upon this new relation he did animate Sforza, and Sfondrato, assuring them that the Includents of Santa Severina were but 34.

†**in'cluder.** *Obs.* [f. INCLUDE *v.* + -ER¹.] One who or that which includes.

1610 GUILLIM *Heraldry* III. xii. (1611) 120 The outmost includer which is the skinne.

b. *spec.* One who votes for the admission of a candidate. Cf. EXCLUDER b.

1670 G. H. *Hist. Cardinals* III. II. 282 They observ'd no great zeal either in the Excluders, or Includers.

includible (ɪn'klu:dɪb(ə)l), *a.* Also **-able**. [f. INCLUDE *v.* + -IBLE, after L. type **inclūdibilis*.] Capable of being included.

1890 D. G. BRINTON *Ess. Americanist* 399 These are with much difficulty or not at all includable in a graphic method. **1894** in *Voice* (N.Y.) 12 July, The exciting causes of spavin ..will appear to be fairly includible under two general heads.

[The citation from Bentham in some recent dicts. is erroneous: the word there being *ineludible*.]

including (ɪn'klu:dɪŋ), *ppl. a.* [f. INCLUDE *v.* + -ING².]

1. That includes, shuts in, encloses, or comprises.

1670 G. H. *Hist. Cardinals* III. III. 329 If the Head of the including Faction, offers the Head of the Excluding Party, to assist him at any time, in the Election of one of the Excludents. **1842** MANNING *Serm.* (1848) I. xiv. 197 God has given him a moral sight to discern the right as the test, and as the including form of true expediency. **1899** *Edin. Rev.* Apr. 318 The including shafts were masked by 'pans' or depressions.

2. *Including* pres. pple. often governs a sb. particularizing a person or thing included in a group previously (or afterwards) mentioned; = Inclusive of.

Syntactically, it may sometimes be viewed as agreeing with the word for the group, e.g. 'I met a large party including your brothers'; but often it appears to agree with an indefinite pronoun *one*, *we*, *you*, e.g. 'including [= if we, one, you include] servants, the party will number fourteen'. In the latter construction we have a kind of active of the passive absolute clause 'servants being included', or 'if servants are included'.

1853 RUSKIN *Stones Ven.* II. vi, A large body of English landscapists come into this class, including most clever sketchers from nature. **1864** *Daily Tel.* 20 Sept., These premises.. were.. in the occupation of several other warehousemen, including Mr. T. Tapling.

Hence **in'cludingly** *adv.*, inclusively.

*c*1449 PECOCK *Repr.* I. xix. 111 He theryn and therbi biddith includingli and closingli al it to be doon.

in'cluse, *a.* and *sb. Obs.* exc. *Hist.* [ad. L. *inclūs-us*, pa. pple. of *inclūdĕre* to shut in. Cf. obs. F. *enclus* anchorite (14th c. in Godef.), whence the form ENCLUSE, q.v.]

A. *adj.* Shut up as an anchorite.

*c*1340 HAMPOLE *Prose Tr.* 42 þou sall be safe as ane ankir incluse. *c*1440 HYLTON *Scala Perf.* (W. de W. 1494) I. xliv. **1715** M.DAVIES *Athen. Brit.* I. Pref. 20 The Incluse Anchoret Peter, from the Confines of Spain.

B. *sb.* An anchorite.

1432–50 tr. *Higden* (Rolls) VII. 81 A religious man and pilgreme.. whiche hade lernede of an incluse [TREVISA, of a man recluse] that sowles of dedde men were punysched for theire synnes in a place of the see nye to Sicille. **1868** KINGSLEY *Hermits* 330 Through these apertures the 'incluse' or anker, watched the celebration of mass, and partook of the Holy Communion. **1871** H. MACMILLAN *True Vine* vi. 268 Those incluses, or 'holy men of the stone', during the middle age lived for years in a small cell built up around them, beside the wall of a cathedral. **1881** T. E. BRIDGETT *Hist. Holy Eucharist* II. 180 The Incluse or Recluse.. was confined within fixed and narrow limits.

†**in'cluse,** *v. Obs.* [f. L. *inclūs-* ppl. stem: see prec. At first only in pa. pple. *inclused*, f. as prec. + -ED.]

1. *trans.* To enclose, shut up.

1432–50 tr. *Higden* (Rolls) IV. 141 This Cithero did write so subtily alle the batelle of Troy that hit semede as inclusede withynne the schelle of a nutte. **1474** CAXTON *Chesse* IV. ii. Riij b, Yf he be taken or deed or ellys Inclusid and shette up.. al is finysshed and lost. **1496** *Dives & Paup.* (W. de W.) VI. xiii. 253/1 Of wymen ancres so inclused is seldon herde ony of these defautes. **1570** *Satir. Poems Reform.* xii. 129 Keip not Capua quhil ȝone knaifis incluse ȝow. **1571** *Ibid.* xxxvi. 84 þe Quene wes in the Louche Inclusit. **1578** *Archpriest. Controv.* (Camden) I. 91 The inclused monkes of that Diocese. **1597** MONTGOMERIE *Cherrie & Slae* 282 Within my cairfull corpis incluissit, In presoun of my breist.

2. To close, shut (a house, the eyes, etc.). In quot. *intr.* for *refl.*

1500–20 DUNBAR *Poems* lxxiv. 46 My ene for paine incluse and steik.

inclusion (ɪn'klu:ʒən). [ad. L. *inclūsiōn-em*, n. of action f. *inclūdĕre*: see INCLUDE.]

1. The action of including (in various senses of the vb.); the fact or condition of being included; an instance of this.

1600 ABP. ABBOT *Exp. Jonah* 33 St. Austen.. doth by a secret inclusion compare this mind of man, to one who is to passe over a ditch. *c*1611 CHAPMAN *Iliad* XVI. 291 These Greeks.. Obtain'd a little time to breathe, but found no present vents To their inclusions. **1612** SELDEN *Illustr. Drayton's Poly-olb.* ix. 145 In this Kingdome the name of Frenchman hath by inclusion comprehended all kind of Aliens. **1646** SIR T. BROWNE *Pseud. Ep.* VI. iii. 286 Their Heliacall obscuration, or their inclusion in the lustre of the Sunne. **1677** HALE *Prim. Orig. Man.* 49 The inclusion and expansion of any natural inanimate particles of elementary Fire. **1827** JARMAN *Powell's Devises* (ed. 3) II. 95 The inclusion of the produce of the fund in the general residuary clause, may be considered as a mere arrangement of language. **1851** MANSEL *Proleg. Logica* (1860) 55 To illustrate the position of the three terms in Barbara by a diagram.. tends to confuse the mental inclusion of one notion in the sphere of another with the local inclusion of a smaller portion of a space in a larger. **1884** *Manch. Guard.* 24 Jan. 5/3 The questions involved in the inclusion of Ireland in the Bill. **1891** WELTON *Man. Logic* II. ii §94 On the class view the relation between subject and predicate is that of inclusion in a class.

2. *concr.* That which is included; *spec.* in *Min.*, a gaseous or liquid substance, or a small body, contained in a crystal or a mineral mass. More generally in technical use (e.g. *Cytology*, *Metallurgy*): any discrete body or particle which is recognizably different or distinct from the groundmass or relatively solid and homogeneous substance in which it is embedded.

1839 BAILEY *Festus* ix. (1852) 121 All the starry inclusions of all signs, Shall rise, and rule, and pass. **1881** *Nature* No. 616.355 Other sections.. are those on mineral inclusions, on the hardness and etching of crystal faces. **1896** E. B. WILSON *Cell* i. 15 The lifeless inclusions in the protoplasm have been collectively designated as *metaplasm* (Hanstein) in contradistinction to the living *protoplasm*. **1897** *Jrnl. Morphol.* XII. Suppl. 14 (*heading*) Discontinuous elements or inclusions. **1904** *20th Rep. Bureau Animal Industry, U.S. Dept. Agric.* 149 Borrel considers that his researches show that the microbe of sheep pox is ultramicroscopic and that the cellular inclusions described as parasites of vaccinia.. cannot be the true cause of the disease. **1913** *Jrnl. Iron & Steel Inst.* LXXXVII. 655 The various kinds of slag inclusions occurring in steel.. may be classified as follows: 1. Those.. dispersed throughout the metal, but mostly near the surface. 2. Those.. dispersed throughout the whole mass of the metal. 3. Small inclusions.. occurring between the crystals of the metal. **1939** A. JOHANNSEN *Descr. Petrogr. Igneous Rocks* (ed. 2) I. iii. 39 Von Leonhard used the term *Porphyr-Struktur* for that texture in which crystals, crystal fragments, grains, or flakes lie in a dense, unbroken groundmass. The inclusions, he said, are usually different from the groundmass and do not touch each other. **1960** F. C. STEWARD *Plant Physiol.* IA. i. 11 The metabolically active inclusions are the mitochondria, the microsomes, and the chloroplasts. **1966** *Nature* 28 May 879/2 Ice specimens.. prepared with inclusions of fine air bubbles. **1967** A. H. COTTRELL *Introd. Metall.* xxi. 390 There may additionally be local groupings of dislocations created round large foreign inclusions by thermal shrinkage strains.

3. *Math.* Usu. ***inclusion map(ping)***, ***function***. A mapping of a set *A* into a set *B* containing *A* which maps each element of *A* on to itself.

1949 *Ann. Math.* L. 956 The symbolism $f:(X', A') \subset (X, A)$ is read: *f* is the inclusion map of (X', A') into (X, A). **1956** E. M. PATTERSON *Topology* ii. 20 If $A \subset B$, the transformation $i:A \to B$ defined by $i(a) = a$ is a one-one transformation called an inclusion. **1962** B. MENDELSON *Introd. Topology* (1963) i. 30 Let $A \subset X$. The function $i:A \to X$.. is called an inclusion mapping or function. *Ibid.* iii. 111 Let the topological space *Y* be a subspace of the topological space *X*. Then the inclusion mapping $i: Y \to X$ is continuous. **1964** SZE-TSEN HU *Elem. Gen. Topology* i. 8 Consider the case $X \subset Y$. Then, the function $i:X \to Y$ defined by $i(x) = x \in Y$ for every $x \in X$ is called the inclusion function of *X* into *Y*... We write $i:X \subset Y$.

in'clusionist, *sb.* [f. prec. + -IST.] One who supports a principle or measure of inclusion.

1893 *Daily News* 12 July 4/8 Hours are enough..to transform them from exclusionists to inclusionists, from Federal Home Rulers to Colonial Home Rulers.

inclusive (ɪn'kluːsɪv), *a.* (*sb.*) [ad. med.L. *inclūsīv-us*, f. *inclūs-*, ppl. stem of *inclūdĕre* to INCLUDE: see -IVE. Cf. F. *inclusif*, *-ive*.]

A. *adj.* **1. a.** Having the character or function of including, enclosing, or comprehending.

1594 SHAKS. *Rich. III*, IV. i. 59 The inclusiue Verge Of Golden Mettall, that must round my Brow. **1814** WORDSW. *Excursion* IV. 678 Altar and image, and the inclusive walls And roofs of temples built by human hands. **1858** HAWTHORNE *Fr. & It. Jrnls.* II. 23 Between the two inclusive extremes of Phidias and Clarke Mills.

b. Characterized by including a great deal, or everything that naturally comes within its scope; comprehensive; all-embracing.

inclusive terms, ***payment***, etc.: such as include all accessory payments.

1601 SHAKS. *All's Well* I. iii. 232 Notes, whose faculties inclusiue were, More then they were in note. **1817** COLERIDGE *Biog. Lit.* I. xii. 242 In Latin we must too often be contented with a more general and inclusive term. **1876** J. PARKER *Paracl.* I. xiv. 229 In His self-resurrection our Lord repeated all His miracles in one inclusive act. **1880** MRS. WHITNEY *Odd or Even?* xv. 135 Not so deep or inclusive as to anticipate query. **1910** *Bradshaw's Railway Guide* Apr. 1061 Bath Hotel..Inclusive Terms from 7/6 per day. *Ibid.* 1067 Specimen Menus and very moderate Inclusive Rates per return. **1970** *Times* 21 Nov. 22/2 The first British inclusive holidaymakers are going out to the new summer resorts. **1972** *Times* 30 Sept. 11/4 Inclusive holidays offered by various tour operators.

c. Characterized by including, comprising, or taking in, as opposed to excluding or leaving out.

1651 BAXTER *Inf. Bapt.* (1656) 105 The word, 'To such' is ..rather inclusive as to them, then exclusive. **1665** T. MALL *Offer F. Help* 57 There are divers sorts of marks; some are exclusive..others are inclusive. **1670** G. H. *Hist. Cardinals* III. III. 328 He had not enough of the inclusive power. **1818** CRUISE *Digest* (ed. 2) 394 It is the nature of all human science and knowledge, to proceed most safely by negative and exclusive, to what is affirmative and inclusive.

d. ***inclusive of***, including or embracing (some specified thing or matter which is hereby taken in).

1709 *Brit. Apollo* II. No. 19. 1/1 Those Words..wou'd be Inclusive of Perjury. **1872** J. G. MURPHY *Comm. Lev.* v. 21 Fraud..and oppression are inclusive of most wrong done to a neighbor.

†**2.** Characterized by being included or comprehended in something else. *Obs.*

1616 BULLOKAR, *Inclusiue*, which containeth, or is contained. **1642** MILTON *Argt. conc. Militia* 36 What they declare to be Law the King by an inclusive judgement declareth to be Law also. **1735** H. BROOKE *Univ. Beauty* II. 327 Each note inclusive melody reveals.

3. quasi-*adv.* The term or terms named being included: = INCLUSIVELY 2.

Formerly sometimes treated as med.L. *inclusivè* adv.

1515 in Pitcairn *Crim. Trials* I. *261 Fra þe xiiij day forsaid inclusiue, to xx day of þe samyn exclusiue. **15..** *Almanack for Year* 1386, 49 Lat hym wythdraw the 3 fourt partes until þe 24 day of February inclusive. **1602** FULBECKE *Pandectes* 6 If you accompt from the first hower to the seuenth *inclusivè*. **1713** SWIFT *Cadenus & Vanessa* 148 I'll search where ev'ry virtue dwells, From courts inclusive down to cells. **1838** DE MORGAN *Ess. Probab.* 77 In 200 tosses, what is the chance that the number of heads shall lie between 97 and 103, both inclusive? **1873** HAMERTON *Intell. Life* XI. v. (1875) 427 From Monday till Saturday inclusive.

B. *sb.* An inclusive proposition or particle. Cf. EXCLUSIVE B. 1.

1533 MORE *Debell. Salem* Wks. 943/1 This man is so cunning in his inclusiues & exclusiues, that he dyscerneth nothing betwene copulatiues and disiunctiues.

inclusively (ɪn'kluːsɪvlɪ), *adv.* [f. prec. + -LY².]

1. In a way that includes; so as to include or be included. **a.** By way of comprehension within material limits.

1636 HENSHAW *Horæ Succ.* 111 God is inclusively in no place, and yet he is in every place. **1675** BROOKS *Gold. Key* Wks. 1867 V. 458 Repletively [God] is..everywhere, though inclusively nowhere.

b. By way of comprehension of particulars in a group, or of a part in a whole.

1578 *Almanack, New Calend.* in *Liturg. Serv. Q. Eliz.* (Parker Soc.) 441 An Almanacke, inclusively comprehending, not onely howe to finde the Epact for.. XXXII. yeeres to come, but also the Golden number. **1589** *Hay any Work* 29 Our callings are not onely inclusiuely, but also expressely in the worde. **1658** OSBORN *K. Jas.* Wks. (1673) 475 [It was] maintained that his Majesties Pardon lay inclusively in the Commission he gave him upon his setting out to sea. **1790** BURKE *Fr. Rev.* 88 He [man] abdicates all right to be his own governor. He inclusively..abandons the right of self-defence. **1809–10** COLERIDGE *Friend* (1865) 44 The intention of the agent, wherever it can be independently or inclusively ascertained.

2. With inclusion of the term or limit mentioned; one or both extremes being included. Cf. INCLUSIVE *a.* 3.

1597 MORLEY *Introd. Mus.* 70 In reckoning your distances ..you vnderstood mee exclusiuely, and I meant inclusiuely. **1607** TOPSELL *Four-f. Beasts* (1658) 247 They were celebrated in Olympus every fifth year inclusively, that is, after the end of every fourth year. *a* **1661** FULLER *Worthies* I. (1662) 98 He built the Church of Newberry from the Pulpit westward to the Tower inclusively. **1701** S. SEWALL *Diary* 14 Jan. (1879) II. 31 Singing of the 90th Psalm, from the 8th to the 15th verse inclusively. **1762** H. WALPOLE *Vertue's Anecd. Paint.* (1786) V. 274 Four small plates of kings from William I. to George I. inclusively. **1805** *East's Reports* V. 246 The word *until*..is used indifferently either inclusively or exclusively.

inclusiveness (ɪn'kluːsɪvnɪs). [f. as prec. + -NESS.] The quality of being inclusive.

1731 in BAILEY vol. II. **1881** WESTCOTT & HORT *Grk. N.T.* II. App. 32/1 The instinctive hankering after inclusiveness of text. **1885** G. H. TAYLOR *Pelvic & Hernic Therapeut.* 295 The adequacy of the means is shown in its scope and inclusiveness.

inclusivity (ɪnkluː'sɪvɪtɪ). *rare.* [INCLUSIVE *a.* + -ITY.] The quality of being inclusive.

1939 E. POUND *Let.* 2 Sept. (1971) 326 Re yr. extension of contents: The *real* work of a time is never done by more than four or five people with a fringe of occasional compositions. I suspect inclusivity. **1955** H. READ *Icon & Idea* ii. 36 But 'actuality' does not imply inclusivity.

in'clusory, *a. rare.* [f. L. *inclūs-*, ppl. stem (see INCLUSIVE) + -ORY.] Having the property of including various elements; = INCLUSIVE.

1775 WRAXALL *Tour North. Europe* 360 Dedicating it to the..Trinity, the..Virgin, and St. Bernard. These inclusory dedications were common in most countries.

†**in'coached**, *ppl. a. Obs.* Also en-. [f. IN-² + COACH + -ED¹.] Conveyed in a coach or carriage.

1599 R. FITCH in Hakluyt *Voy.* II. I. 264 The king goeth inc[o]ached, as they do all. *a* **1618** J. DAVIES *Wks.* (1876) 22 (D.) Tamburlaine..encoacht in burnisht gold.

†**inco'act**, *a. Obs. rare*⁻⁰. [ad. L. *incoact-us*, f. *in-* (IN-³) + *coactus* COACT *ppl. a.*] = next.

1616 BULLOKAR, *Incoact*, vnconstrained.

†**inco'acted**, *a. Obs rare* [f. L. *incoact-us* (see prec.) + -ED¹ 2: cf. COACTED.] Uncompelled, unconstrained.

1677 HALE *Prim. Orig. Man.* 312 A light and clear Intellect, a free and incoacted Will.

incoagulable (ɪnkəʊ'ægjʊləb(ə)l), *a.* [f. IN-³ + COAGULABLE.] That cannot be coagulated; incapable of coagulation. Hence **ˌincoagula'bility**, the property or state of being incoagulable.

1667 *Phil. Trans.* II. 556 Certain Bodies..in themselves invisible and incoagulable. **1672** BOYLE *Ess. Gems* I. Wks. 1772 III. 527 The remaining and incoagulable part of it may have been imbibed by the ambient air. **1822–34** *Good's Study Med.* (ed. 4) II. 648 The fluids of the body are loose and incoagulable. **1915** *Jrnl. Med. Res.* XXXII. 452 The leech extract incoagulable blood in vivo differs markedly from blood made incoagulable by receiving it into leech extract in vitro. *Ibid.* 454 In anaphylactic blood and in leech extract blood the probable explanation of a part at least of the incoagulability of the blood consists in a definite effect of these conditions on the blood platelets. **1964** W. G. SMITH *Allergy & Tissue Metabolism* ii. 17 Other workers demonstrated a deficiency in fibrinogen, platelets, and prothrombin as a cause of the incoagulability.

incoa'lescence. *rare.* [f. IN-³ + COALESCENCE.] Want of coalescence; non-coalescence.

1846 in WORCESTER (citing Walker).

incoa'lescible, *a. rare*⁻¹. [f. IN-³ + COALESCE *v.* + -IBLE.] Not capable of coalescing.

1821 *Tales of Landlord* New Ser. *Fair Witch Glas Llyn* I. p. vii, The incoalescible learning of Coke upon Littleton.

†**in'coated**, **en'coated**, *ppl. a. Obs. rare.* [f. IN-², EN- + COAT *sb.* + -ED¹.] (See quots.)

1611 FLORIO, *Incottato*, incoated, hauing a coat on. *Ibid.*, *Ingiubbato*, encoted, hauing a cote on.

†**in'cocted**, *a. Obs.* [f. L. *incoct-us* uncooked, raw + -ED¹ 2.] Uncooked, raw, crude; hence, undigested or indigestible.

1645 BP. HALL *Remedy Discontents* xii. 61 Meales usually sawced with an healthfull hunger, wherein no incocted Crudities oppresse Nature. **1657** TOMLINSON *Renou's Disp.* 92 Things incocted and untractable are cocted and made more mild.

†**in'coctible**, *a. Obs.* [f. IN-³ + COCTIBLE.] Indigestible.

1684 tr. *Bonet's Merc. Compit.* IX. 323 The Flower remains crude, incoctible, and insuperable.

†**in'coctile**, *a. Obs. rare*⁻¹. [f. IN-³ + COCTILE.] Crude, raw.

1684 tr. *Bonet's Merc. Compit.* XVIII. 606 A great Putrefaction..of a thick and incoctil nature.

†**in'coction**¹. *Obs.* [f. IN-², after *concoction*; cf. late L. *incoctio* a boiling in.] App. = *concoction* or *third concoction*: see CONCOCTION 1 b.

1607 WALKINGTON *Opt. Glass* 64 The first [engendered] after our aliment is blood, phleume is the first after incoction.

†**in'coction**². *Obs.* [IN-³.] Indigestion.

1651 tr. *Bacon's Life & Death* 41 Touching the prolongation of Life, and Reparation by Aliments, and Retardation of the Incoction of Old Age. **1684** tr. *Bonet's Merc. Compit.* VI. 179 Troubles and disorders about the Stomach..Want of appetite, Incoction.

incoercible (ɪnkəʊ'ɜːsɪb(ə)l), *a.* [f. IN-³ + COERCIBLE: cf. F. *incoercible* (18th c. in Hatz.-Darm.).]

1. That cannot be coerced, restrained, or overpowered by force; irrepressible.

1756 C. LUCAS *Ess. Waters* III. 126 Heat..when confined, causes incoercible explosions. **1804** W. TAYLOR in *Ann. Rev.* II. 337 They [the American ministers] must abide by the incoercible result of popular suffrage. **1896** *Daily News* 23 June 6/1 She called upon me while suffering from an attack of incoercible sickness.

2. Incapable of being confined; volatile.

1710 T. FULLER *Pharm. Extemp.* 192 Flatus..an invisible, impalpable, and incoercible Spirit. **1756** C. LUCAS *Ess. Waters* II. 166 An acid of extreme subtility, almost incoercible. **1835** KIRBY *Hab. & Inst. Anim.* I. Introd. 41 Speaking of the imponderable incoercible fluids, and specifying heat, electricity, the magnetic fluid [etc.].

†**b.** Incapable of being liquefied by pressure: formerly said of some gases. *Obs.*

1861 B. SILLIMAN, Jr. *Physics* (ed. 2) §256 It [the atmosphere] is composed of two incoercible gases, nitrogen and oxygen.

incoexistence (ɪnkəʊɛg'zɪstəns). *rare. nonce-wd.* [f. IN-³ + COEXISTENCE.] Absence of coexistence; the fact of not existing together.

1690 LOCKE *Hum. Und.* IV. iii. §12 There is yet another and more incurable part of ignorance which sets us more remote from a certain Knowledge of the co-existence, or inco-existence (if I may so say) of different ideas in the same subject.

incoffin (ɪn'kɒfɪn), *v.* Also 6 -en. [f. IN-² + COFFIN: cf. F. *encoffiner* (early 16th c. in Godef.).]

1. *trans.* To enclose in, or as in, a coffin.

1570–6 LAMBARDE *Peramb. Kent* (1826) 128 This good father (thinking to have procured some gaine to his Church, by veneration of the dead bodies..) persuaded the King to incoffen them, and to commit them to honorable buriall in Christeschurch at Canterburie. **1574** HELLOWES *Gueuara's Fam. Ep.* (1577) 343 The Citties did burie their dead.. incoffined with a certein wood of Cithia incorruptible. **1670** PENN *Gt. Case Lib. Consc.* Wks. 1782 III. 15 They condemn the Papists for incoffining the scriptures and their worship in an unknown tongue.

2. To hold or enclose like a coffin.

1633 FORD *Love's Sacr.* V. i, That sepulchre that holds Your coffin, shall incoffin me alive.

incog (ɪn'kɒg), *a.*, *adv.*, *sb.* [Colloquial abbreviation of INCOGNITO, INCOGNITA.]

A. *adj.* = INCOGNITO, INCOGNITA *a.*

1705 *Double Welcome* xl, He's now a Priest incog..with Sword and Wig. **1712** OLDISWORTH tr. *Horace' Odes* I. 23/1 He had a mind to be Incog. **1835** W. IRVING *Crayon Misc.* (1849) 227, I am apt to treat him with respect from the idea that he may be a great prince incog.

B. *adv.* = INCOGNITO *adv.*

1709 STEELE *Tatler* No. 34 ¶5 Mr. Justice Overdo..met with more Enormities by walking *incog.* **1777** SHERIDAN *Sch. Scand.* IV. iii, What! turn inquisitor, and take evidence incog? **1807** SIR R. WILSON *Jrnl.* 15 July in *Life* (1862) II. viii. 320 We hear..that Buonaparte went on the water incog. at Königsberg. **1840** HOOD *Kilmansegg, Courtship* x, A Foreign Count—who came *incog.*

C. *sb.* = INCOGNITO, INCOGNITA *sb.*

a **1700** B. E. *Dict. Cant. Crew*, *Incog*, for Incognito, a Man of Character or Quality concealed or in disguise. **1813** BYRON *Br. of Abydos* II. ix. *note*, I have seen the Capitan Pacha..wearing it [a Turkish sailor's dress] as a kind of *incog.* **1895** *Westm. Gaz.* 2 Aug. 2/1 The 'incog.' was kept very strictly. No visits were received, the local press was silent as the grave concerning the august visitors.

†**in'cogent**, *a. Obs. rare*⁻¹. [f. IN-³ + COGENT.] Not cogent; without force.

1667 WATERHOUSE *Fire Lond.* 157 But I forbear what mine Oratory is incogent in.

incogita'bility. *rare*⁻¹. [f. next: see -ITY.] The quality of being unthinkable; incapability of being thought.

1852 SIR W. HAMILTON *Discuss.* 602 We then predicate incogitability.

incogitable (ɪn'kɒdʒɪtəb(ə)l), *a.* [ad. late L. *incōgitābil-is*: see IN-³ and COGITABLE.] Unthinkable, inconceivable.

1522 MORE *De Quat. Noviss.* Wks. 78/2 To mynyster by subtylle and incogytable meanes..vnlawefull longyng to lyue. **1678** HOBBES *Decam.* v. 55 As for the conversion of Air into Water by Condensation..it is a thing incogitable. **1865** GROTE *Plato* I. ii. 108 Let us grant that Ens or Entia exist;

they would nevertheless (argued Gorgias) be incogitable and unknowable.

†**in'cogitance.** *Obs. rare.* [f. as next: see -ANCE.] Want of thought; = next.

1637 JACKSON *2nd Serm. Jer.* xxvi. 19 §3 The second incogitance is more pertinent to this place, and in itself more dangerous. **1659** STANLEY *Hist. Philos.* XIII. (1701) 611/1 We oppose not Prudence to any affection so much as to Incogitance, Ignorance, Folly.

†**in'cogitancy.** *Obs.* [ad. L. *incōgitāntia* thoughtlessness, f. *incōgitānt-em*: see next.]

1. Want of thought or reflection; thoughtlessness, heedlessness, negligence; inadvertence.

1612 SCLATER *Chr. Strength* 3 Infirmities..are, vsually, sins of incogitancie. **1621** BP. MOUNTAGU *Diatribæ* I. 39 It was peraduenture a slip of the pen vpon incogitancy. **1693** TYRRELL *Law Nat.* 160 Through some Errour, Weakness, or Incogitancy..they may often deviate from this great end. **1759** B. MARTIN *Nat. Hist. Eng.* I. *Wilts.* 104 An Argument of vulgar Incogitancy.

2. Want of the faculty of thought.

1649 JER. TAYLOR *Gt. Exemp.* II. viii. 83 The tremblings of the heart, the incogitancy of the minde..represent a death-bed to be but an ill station for a penitent. *c* **1673** *Reasonable Def. Seasonable Disc.* 20 Were not our Author furnished with a convenient talent of incogitancy, he could not but know.

incogitant (ɪn'kɒdʒɪtənt), *a.* [ad. L. *incōgitānt-em* unthinking, f. *in-* (IN-³) + *cōgitāns*, pres. pple. of *cōgitāre* to think.] That does not think.

1. Thoughtless; unthinking; characterized by want of thought; inconsiderate.

1628 JACKSON *Creed* VI. x. §1 By the incogitant use of these and the like scripture phrases. **1679** J. GOODMAN *Penit. Pardoned* II. i. (1713) 138 A light incogitant young man. *a* **1683** WHICHCOTE *Disc.* (1703) III. 194, I might have been incogitant all my days of these things, which when offered I know to be true. **1732** STACKHOUSE *Hist. Bible* (1767) VI. VIII. v. 512 So blind and incogitant that his Empress Messalina married herself to another man. **1893** F. HALL in *Nation* (N.Y.) 16 Feb. 123/1 If the ruling of an incogitant autocrat is to be preferred to the warrant of good usage.

2. Not having the faculty of thinking.

1702 HOWE *Living Temple* I. iii. §12 Wks. 1724 I. 45 As mind is a cogitant substance, matter is incogitant.

in'cogitantly, *adv.* [f. prec. + -LY².] Unthinkingly, thoughtlessly, without consideration or reflection.

1645 T. HILL *Olive Branch of Peace* (1648) 34 If they finde they did it rashly and incogitantly. *a* **1677** BARROW *Serm.* (1687) I. xiii. 184 Men almost as often speak incogitantly, as they think silently.

†**in'cogitate,** *a. Obs. rare*⁻¹. [ad. L. *incōgitāt-us*, f. *in-* (IN-³) + *cōgitātus*, pa. pple. of *cōgitāre* to think.] Not thought of; unexpected; unpremeditated.

1652 GAULE *Magastrom.* 95 The nature and property of a meer contingent is to be..unknown, sudden, indeterminate, incogitate.

incogitative (ɪn'kɒdʒɪteɪtɪv), *a. rare.* [f. IN-³ + COGITATIVE.] Unthinking; destitute of the thinking faculty.

1690 LOCKE *Hum. Und.* IV. x. §9 There are but two sorts of beings in the world..which..we will hereafter call cogitative and incogitative beings. **1706** CLARKE *Nat. & Rev. Relig.* Pref. (R.), From my using the word mere Matter, he concludes that I imagine there is another form of Matter, which is not a mere, bare, pure, incogitative Matter. **1813** BUSBY *Lucretius* III. *Comment.* xiv, If the seeds of heat, air, and vapour are as positively incogitative as those of the body.

Hence **in,cogita'tivity** (*rare*⁻¹), the quality of being incogitative or without the faculty of thought.

1722 WOLLASTON *Relig. Nat.* ix. 191 Is the same in effect as to say, that God may superadd a faculty of thinking to incogitativity.

‖**incognita** (ɪn'kɒgnɪtə, -'niːtə), *a.* and *sb.*¹ [It. *incognita*, fem. of *incognito* unknown.]

A. *adj.* Of a female: Unknown or disguised; having one's identity concealed or unavowed.

1668 DRYDEN *Mock Astrol.* III. Wks. 1701 I. 303 Being thus *incognita*, I shall discover if he make love to any of you. **1716** LADY M. W. MONTAGU *Let. to C'tess Mar* 3 Aug., I walked almost all over the town yesterday, *incognita*, in my slippers. **1884** RITA *Vivienne* V. v, She would go to Naples *incognita*.

B. *sb.* **1.** An unknown or disguised woman or girl; one whose identity is not made known. In 18th c. used often of a sweetheart.

1718 MRS. CENTLIVRE *Wonder* V. i. (Jod.), That's the lady's name of the house, where my *incognita* is. **1748** SMOLLETT *Rod. Rand.* li. (1804) 349 The whole was subscribed 'Your incognita'. **1807** ANNA M. PORTER *Hungar. Bro.* iii. (1832) 40 It will be impossible for me to see your incognita without knowing her by instinct. **1828** MISS MITFORD *Village* Ser. III. (1863) 465 Nobody knew any thing certain of the incognita, or her story.

fig. **1833** *Westm. Rev.* Jan. 41 The charms of that fair incognita the 'legitimate' drama.

2. Unknown or unavowed character or position (of a woman).

1882 *World* No. 399. 10 The Queen will not assume her incognita until she reaches Cherbourg.

‖**in'cognita,** *sb.*² *pl.* [L. *incognita*, neut. pl. of *incognitus* unknown; cf. next.] Unknown things or places.

1846 GROTE *Greece* (1854) I. 477 They [myths]..explained many of the puzzling incognita of the present. **1853** KANE *Grinnell Exp.* xxxi. (1856) 272 At this rate, we will in a few days be within the Baffin's Bay *incognita.*

†**incognite** (ɪn'kɒgnɪt), *a. Obs.* [ad. L. *incognit-us* unknown, f. *in-* (IN-³) + *cognit-us*, pa. pple. of *cognōscĕre* to get to know.] Unknown.

1609 *Ev. Woman in Hum.* II. i. in Bullen *O. Pl.* IV, All which to me are..Obsurde inigmaes, and to my studies Incognite Language. **1677** GALE *Crt. Gentiles* IV. 458 It becomes us..to receive..al the workes of Providence, albeit they may seem to many injust, because incognite and incomprehensible. **1678** T. JORDAN *Triumphs Lond.* Ded., By their [merchants'] Cost, Adventures, Diligence, and Vigilance, incognite Countries have been discovered.

in'cognitive, *a. rare*⁻¹. [f. IN-³ + COGNITIVE.] Destitute of the faculty of cognition; unable to take cognizance.

1862 F. HALL *Hindu Philos. Syst.* 154 God made the soul cognitive; and who shall make it incognitive?

‖**incognito** (ɪn'kɒgnɪtəʊ, -'niːtəʊ), *a.*, *adv.*, *sb.* Pl. -ti (-tiː). [It. *incognito* adj., adv., unknown, disguised, ad. L. *incognitus*: see INCOGNITE.

1652 H. COGAN tr. *Scudery's Ibrahim* I. ii. 39 He went..in that manner, which the Grandees of Italie do often make use of, whenas they travell, and which they call *Incognito.*]

A. *adj.* Unknown; whose identity is concealed or unavowed, and therefore not taken as known; concealed under a disguised or assumed character.

1649 EVELYN *Lib. & Servit.* iv. Misc. Writ. (1805) 22 They make it..their chiefest care to make themselves hidden and incognito. **1676** ETHEREDGE *Man of Mode* IV. i, A Fool is very troublesome, when he Presumes he is Incognito. **1732** LEDIARD *Sethos* II. VII. 70 This prince was incognito in Arabia. **1864** *Linnet's Trial* I. i. iii. 72, I only came for a couple of days..and I intended to have remained incognito.

b. Of a thing: Done or conducted under disguise.

1819 T. HOPE *Anastasius* (1820) II. ii. 30 Asses for incognito expeditions.

B. *adv.* With one's real name, title, or character undisclosed or disguised: used esp. in reference to royal or dignified personages who wish to conceal their identity or not to be openly recognized.

1649 EVELYN *Mem.* 12 July, Mr. Arthur Slingsby, who left England *incognito.* **1691** T. ROGERS *Disc. Trouble Mind* 384 A Christian in this World is like a King that travels *Incognito* in a strange land. **1709** PRIOR *Ladle* 2 The Scepticks think 'twas long ago Since Gods came down *Incognito.* **1800** MRS. HERVEY *Mourtray Fam.* II. 10 As you wished to do good incognito, I did not disclose your name. **1862** HOOK *Lives Abps.* II. iii. 211 He had passed incognito through Canterbury.

C. *sb.* **1.** An unknown man; one who conceals his identity; an anonymous person.

1638 BAKER tr. *Balzac's Lett.* (vol. II.) 228, I send you all I have of that admirable *Incognito.* **1784** COWPER *Let.* 22 Feb., The same *incognito* to all except ourselves made us his almoners this year likewise. **1797** E. DU BOIS *Piece Fam. Biogr.* II. 81 This for the incogniti. **1802** MAR. EDGEWORTH *Moral T.* (1816) I. xix. 163 This young incognito.

2. The condition of being unknown, anonymity; fictitious character; disguise; orig. in phrase *in incognito* (taken as L. or It.), in concealment, in an anonymous character.

[**1663** COWLEY *Verses & Ess.*, *Obscurity*, I think..that the pleasantest condition of life is *in incognito.* *c* **1669** LADY CHAWORTH in *12th Rep. Hist. MSS. Comm.* App. v. 12 The Prince of Thuscany..being in incognito.] **1822** HAZLITT *Table-t.* Ser. II. ii. (1869) 35 Never venturing out of their imposing and mysterious incognito. **1874** L. STEPHEN *Hours in Library* (1892) I. i. 12 Few writers would have preserved their incognito so long. **1886** W. ALEXANDER *St. Augustine's Holiday* 9 Proving that chance is God's incognito.

in,cogniza'bility. *rare.* [f. next: see -ITY.] The quality of being incognizable.

c **1860** *Lond. Rev.* No. 32. 541 His doctrine of the incognisability of the Infinite.

incognizable, -isable (ɪn'kɒgnɪ-, -'kɒnɪzəb(ə)l), *a.* [f. IN-³ + COGNIZABLE; cf. F. *inconnaissable* (†*incognoissable*), 16th c. in Hatz.-Darm.] Not cognizable; incapable of being known, perceived, or apprehended by the senses or intellect; incapable of recognition.

1852 M. ARNOLD *Human Life* 8 On life's incognisable sea. **1869** J. MARTINEAU *Ess.* II. 288 Why then describe these truths as intrinsically incognizable? **1880** *Churchman* No. 5. 331 The old coinage of years gone by had become incognisable by stress of wear and mutilation.

incognizance (ɪn'kɒgnɪ-, -'kɒnɪzəns). [f. IN-³ + COGNIZANCE.] Want of knowledge or recognition.

a **1856** SIR W. HAMILTON *Lect.* (1877) I. xix. 367 Now this incognisance may be explained. **1865** MRS. WHITNEY *Gayworthys* vi. (1879) 68 They would scarcely drift away from each other into utter incognizance and separation.

incognizant (ɪn'kɒgnɪ-, -'kɒnɪzənt), *a.* [f. IN-³ + COGNIZANT.] Not cognizant; without cognizance, knowledge, or apprehension *of*; unaware, unconscious *of*.

1837 *Fraser's Mag.* XV. 760 Being utterly incognisant of their inquiries, [she] merely shook her head. **1856** FERRIER *Inst. Metaph.* I. 81 A man..is never altogether incognisant, is never totally oblivious, of himself. **1878** RUSKIN *Notes Turner's Drawings* 88 Not incognizant of this joyful industry.

incognoscent (ɪnkɒg'nɒsənt), *a. rare.* [f. IN-³ + COGNOSCENT.] Unknowing, ignorant.

1827 W. G. S. *Excurs. Village Curate* 133, I pardon you, my choleric incognoscent octogenarian.

incognoscibility (ɪnkɒgnɒsɪ'bɪlɪtɪ). [f. next: see -ITY.] The quality or condition of being incognoscible; unknowableness.

1824 BENTHAM *Bk. Fallacies* I. i. §1 The incognoscibility, the expensiveness, the dilatoriness, the vexatiousness of the system of judicial procedure. **1838** SOUTHEY *Doctor* Interch. xix. V. 386 If..the Imperial Philosopher should censure the still incognoscible Author for still continuing in incognoscibility..I should remind him of the Eleusinian Mysteries. **1848** MILL *Pol. Econ.* V. viii. §3 (1876) 533.

incognoscible (ɪnkɒg'nɒsɪb(ə)l), *a.* [f. IN-³ + COGNOSCIBLE.] Unknowable, beyond cognizance.

1691 E. TAYLOR *Behmen's Theos. Philos.* 199 To some this Question may seem..so occult as if incognoscible [*printed* incogniscible]. **1838** *New Monthly Mag.* LIII. 304 The magnificence of that mind which dwelt..in the regions of the incognoscible. *a* **1843** SOUTHEY *Doctor* (1847) VI. Archch. 205 Incognito I am and wish to be, and incognoscible it is in my power to remain.

incoherence (ɪnkəʊ'hɪərəns). [f. IN-³ + COHERENCE; cf. It. *incoherenza* (Florio, 1611), F. *incohérence* (18th c. in Hatz.-Darm.).] The fact, condition, or quality of being incoherent.

1. *lit.* Want of cohesion.

1672 BOYLE *Hist. Fluidity* §16 Wks. 1772 I. 388 The smallness and incoherence of the parts do..make them easy to be put into motion. **1849** MURCHISON *Siluria* vii. 126 The ..shale..from its incoherence has been denuded for the most part.

2. Want of connexion; incompatibility, incongruity of subjects or matters.

1665 BOYLE *Occas. Refl.* Introd. Pref. (1848) 11 The Incoherence of the Subjects..may make them look so little of kin to one another, as scarce to appear the Productions of the same Pen. *a* **1674** CLARENDON *Hist. Reb.* XI. §202 Impracticable Particulars, which troubled the Parliament the less, for their incoherence, and impossibility to be reduced into practice. **1824** L. MURRAY *Eng. Gram.* (ed. 5) I. 494 The same author..says, 'There is not a single view of human nature, which is not sufficient to extinguish the seeds of pride'. Observe the incoherence of the things here joined together; making a view extinguish, and extinguish seeds.

3. a. Want of coherence or connexion in thought or language; incongruity, inconsistency; want of logical or rational consistency or congruity.

1611 FLORIO, *Incoherenza*, incoherence. **1643** MILTON *Divorce* II. ii, The incoherence of such a doctrine cannot, must not be thus interpreted. **1664–94** SOUTH *Twelve Serm.* II. 141 A Petition fraught with Nonsense and Incoherence, Confusion and Impertinence. **1778** BP. LOWTH *Transl. Isaiah* Notes (ed. 12) 189 This obscure incoherence is given to it by the false rendering of a Hebrew particle. **1829** I. TAYLOR *Euthus.* iv. (1867) 84 The intrinsic incoherence of heresy. **1871** BLACKIE *Four Phases* I. 98 Never was a greater amount of incoherence crammed into a short sentence.

b. with *an* and *pl.*: An instance of this; an incoherent statement or proceeding.

1658 BRAMHALL *Consecr. Bps.* vii. 157 A Testimony which is clogged with so many improbabilities, and incongruities, and incoherences. **1710** ADDISON *Whig Exam.* No. 4 (Seager) The system of his politicks, when disembroiled and cleared of all those incoherences and independent matters that are woven into this motley piece. **1859** I. TAYLOR *Logic in Theol.* 285 This mythic theory is a mass of incoherences.

4. *Physics.* The property (of waves, or of phenomena involving them) of being incoherent (sense 5); lack of a definite or stable phase relationship between waves at different points (in space or in time).

1938 *Physica* V. 785 In the usual treatment of interference and diffraction phenomena, there is nothing intermediate between coherence and incoherence... The first term is understood to mean complete dependence of phases, the second complete independence. **1958** *Physical Rev.* CI. 7/2 This is a classical type of incoherence, such as would result if we had an assembly of classical oscillators with random initial phase. **1971** K. R. BARNES *Optical Transfer Function* ii. 7 Spatial incoherence implies that the phases of the monochromatic components of the light from all points of the object are changing at random.

incoherency (ɪnkəʊ'hɪərənsɪ). [f. as prec.: see -ENCY.] The quality of being incoherent; = INCOHERENCE 2, 3.

1684 BUNYAN *Pilgr.* II. 186 There is an Incoherencie in their Words now, as there was before. **1751** EARL ORRERY *Remarks Swift* (1752) 51 The incoherency of situation is perhaps one of the most excusable faults in the collection. **1822–34** *Good's Study Med.* (ed. 4) II. 227 The pulse has been a hundred and forty..in a minute, with incoherency or delirium from the first night. **1843** BETHUNE *Sc. Fireside Stor.* 71 To believe, that the whole of his illness, and the incoherency of his speech, had been feigned to elude suspicion.

b. with *an* and *pl.* An instance of this quality; something incoherent.

1708 *Lond. Gaz.* No. 4417/3 Besides the many Absurdities and Incoherencies in the historical Part thereof. **1837–9** HALLAM *Hist. Lit.* III. iii. §1 ¶20 This cannot give a sanction to the incoherencies of Madness. **1856** MRS. BROWNING *Aur. Leigh* I. 7 The incoherencies of change and death.

incoherent (ɪnkəʊˈhɪərənt), *a.* (*sb.*) Also 7 **-hærent.** [f. IN-³ + COHERENT: cf. F. *incohérent* (18th c. in Hatz.-Darm.).]

A. *adj.* Not coherent.

1. a. Without physical coherence or cohesion; consisting of parts which do not stick or cling together; unconnected, disjoined, loose.

1695 WOODWARD *Nat. Hist. Earth* II. (1723) 123 Matter which was..lax, incoherent, and in Form of Earth, or of Sand. **1756** C. LUCAS *Ess. Waters* I. 40 Various earths..void of humidity are but loose, light, and incoherent dust. **1811** PINKERTON *Petral.* I. 340 Entire mountains of serpentine and ollite, which were only heaps of incoherent blocks. **1849** MURCHISON *Siluria* iv. 72 A mass of..incoherent slaty schists.

b. *transf.* and *fig.*

1768 BURKE *Corr.* (1844) I. 161 He spoke of the ministry as a strange incoherent composition, that certainly would not stand. **1849** GROTE *Greece* II. lvii. (1862) V. 105 The incoherent mixture of races. **1884** H. SPENCER in *Pop. Sc. Monthly* XXIV. 730 A comparatively small body of officials, coherent,..and acting under central authority, has an immense advantage over an incoherent public which has no settled policy.

2. Of abstract things (as schemes, actions, etc.): Consisting of or forming a group or series of incongruous parts; not connected or unified by any general principle or characteristic; inconsistent, uncoordinated.

1626 DONNE *Serm.* xxi. 211 But hath lost his Soule so long agoe in rusty and incoherent Sins, (not sins that produced one another as in Davids case). **1732** BERKELEY *Alciphr.* III. §11 An incoherent fortuitous system, governed by chance. **1871** TYLOR *Prim. Cult.* I. 2 They affirm, with Aristotle, that nature is not full of incoherent episodes, like a bad tragedy.

3. a. Of thought and mental phenomena, language, literary compositions, etc.: Without logical connexion or natural sequence of ideas; inconsistent, rambling, disjointed.

1632 SANDERSON *Twelve Serm.* 467 Whose discourse should be incohærent and vnjoynted. **1709** STEELE *Tatler* No. 60 ¶7 This incoherent Stuff was answer'd by a tender Sigh. **1791** MRS. RADCLIFFE *Rom. Forest* i, Sometimes she muttered an incoherent sentence. **1839** KEIGHTLEY *Hist. Eng.* II. 25 She used to utter much incoherent rhapsody.

b. Characterized or marked by incoherency of thought or expression.

1803 JANE PORTER *Thaddeus* i. (1831) 5 His voice was hurried and incoherent. **1845** T. ARCHER *Mem. & Disc.* 287 Listen to that preacher, unrhetorical, incoherent, ungrammatical. **1874** MAUDSLEY *Respons. in Ment. Dis.* vii. 245 Sometimes..there was an attack of incoherent and furious mania.

4. Incapable of cohering or coalescing; naturally different; incompatible, incongruous.

1643 MILTON *Divorce* I. x, To force a mixture of minds that cannot unite, and to sowe the furrow of mans nativity with seed of two incoherent and uncombining dispositions. **1704** SWIFT *Batt. Bks.* Wks. 1778 I. 425 His armour was patched up of a thousand incoherent pieces. **1708** W. KING *Cookery* (1807) 71 Hence mack'rel seem delightful to the eyes, Though dress'd with incoherent gooseberries.

5. *Physics.* Producing, involving, or consisting of waves that have no definite or stable phase relationship with one another.

1929 A. SOMMERFELD *Lect. Wave Mech.* vi. 91 In addition to secondary radiations of the same frequency as the incident light, we have also radiations of altered frequency. .. These modified radiations bear obviously no phase relationship with the exciting radiation, and might therefore be described as 'incoherent radiations'. **1953** C. E. HALL *Introd. Electron Microsc.* vii. 155 If two incoherent sources are observed with a microscope, the intensity at the image plane is the sum of the intensities from each one taken separately. **1959** BORN & WOLF *Princ. Optics* vii. 255 In beams from different sources, the fluctuations are completely uncorrelated, and the beams are said to be mutually incoherent. *Ibid.* x. 506 The light vibrations arising from different elements of the source may be assumed to be statistically independent (mutually incoherent), and of zero mean value. **1966** *McGraw-Hill Encycl. Sci. & Technol.* XII. 57/2 It is also useful to distinguish between coherent and incoherent scattering; the distinction is made on the basis of the ability of the scattered wave to interfere with the incident one. Inelastic scattering is always incoherent.

B. *sb.* That which is incoherent. *rare.*

1823 T. G. WAINEWRIGHT *Ess. & Crit.* (1880) 319 Perceptions..of coherents in incoherents.

incoherently (ɪnkəʊˈhɪərəntlɪ), *adv.* [f. INCOHERENT + -LY².] In an incoherent manner.

1651 HOBBES *Leviath.* III. xxxvi. 224 One that speaketh incoherently, as men that are distracted. **1790–3** BEATTIE *Moral Sc.* IV. i. §3 (R.) It being the nature of violent passion to unsettle the mind and make men speak incoherently. **1859** C. BARKER *Assoc. Princ.* ii. 57, I have endeavoured to place before you, I fear very incoherently and imperfectly, some account of the Trade Guilds of the Middle Ages. **1938** *Physica* V. 795 For equal illuminating and observing apertures the result will be that two points just separable by the objectives are incoherently illuminated. **1961** *Encycl. Dict. Physics* I. 723/1 Incoherently radiating oscillators may very quickly become coherent through their interaction with their common radiation field.

incoˈherentness. *rare*⁻⁰. [f. as prec. + -NESS.] Want of coherence; incoherence.

1727 in BAILEY vol. II. Hence in ASH, and mod. Dicts.

incohering (ɪnkəʊˈhɪərɪŋ), *a.* Also 8 **-hær-.** [f. IN-³ + COHERING.] That does not cohere: = INCOHERENT I.

1659 O. WALKER *Instruct. Oratory* 13 All which variety of in-cohering matter is to be joynted and set together in the second review. **1713** DERHAM *Phys.-Theol.* III. ii. 66 That they should..consist of lax, incohæring Earth. **1867** PAGE *Adv. Text-bk. Geol.* (ed. 4) 18 Some hard and compact, others soft and incohering.

incohesion (ɪnkəʊˈhiːʒən). [f. IN-³ + COHESION.] Want of cohesion.

1882 H. SPENCER *Princ. Sociol.* II. v. ii. 278 Our own Indian Empire..held together by force in a state of artificial equilibrium, threatens some day to illustrate by its fall the incohesion arising from lack of congruity in components. **1922** *Public Opinion* 17 Mar. 244/2 The interminable vacillation, procrastination and incohesion of the Government at home. **1924** *These Eventful Years* I. 157 All these regimes are dependent on British support as against the incohesion of tribes and sects.

incohesive (ɪnkəʊˈhiːsɪv), *a.* [IN-³.] Not cohesive; without cohesion; that has not the quality of sticking together.

1846 LANDOR *Imag. Conv.* Wks. II. 67 Turned out of an Italian mould..in a state too fluid and incohesive to stand in English. **1881** *Knowledge* No. 5. 88 Experiments..proving that all gases are composed of matter which is not merely incohesive, but is energetically self-repulsive.

†**incohible,** *a. Obs.*⁻⁰ [ad. late L. *incohibil-is*, f. *in-* (IN-³) + *cohibilis*, f. *cohibēre* to restrain.]

1656 BLOUNT *Glossogr.*, *Incohible*, that cannot be restrained.

†**inˈcoible,** *a. Obs.*⁻⁰ [ad. late L. *incoibil-is*, f. *in-* (IN-³) + **coibil-is*, f. *coī-re* to go or come together.] 'Not to be mingled' (Cockeram, 1623). Hence **incoiˈbility**, incapability of going together or mixing.

1671 E. MAYNWARING *Pract. Phys.* 81 The rejection and incoibility of Some.

incoˈincidence. [IN-³.] Want of coincidence or agreement.

?**1798** COLERIDGE *Lett.* (1895) 246 It were wrong indeed if an incoincidence with one of our wishes altered our respect and affection to a man. **1828** in WEBSTER.

incoincident (ɪnkəʊˈɪnsɪdənt), *a.* [f. IN-³ + COINCIDENT.] Not coinciding; not necessarily existing together; not identical.

1636 FEATLY *Clavis Myst.* xiv. 188 The graces of the Spirit, and the vertues of the mind are incoincident. **1812** SHELLEY *Let. to Godwin* 10 Jan. in Dowden *Life* (1887) I. 222 My Father's notions of family honour are incoincident with my knowledge of public good.

†**ˈincolant, incolent.** *Obs. rare.* [ad. L. *incolent-em*, pres. pple. of *incolĕre* to inhabit, for which *incolāre* (pres. pple. *incolānt-em*) also occurs in late L.] An inhabitant.

1597 MIDDLETON *Wisdom Solomon* xvi. 4 The sinful incolants of his made earth. **1602** WARNER *Alb. Eng.* XII. lxxii, As how the naturall Incolants the Iselanders subdew. *Ibid.* Epit. ¶1 The first Incolents, and of this our Iland.

†**ˈincolary.** *Obs. rare*⁻¹. [f. stem of L. *incola* inhabitant, *incolĕre* to inhabit + -ARY.] An inhabitant.

1652 URQUHART *Jewel* Wks. (1834) 245 The very Scyths and Sarmats, even to the almost subarctick incolaries.

†**incoled,** *ppl. a. Obs. rare.* [repr. L. *incolāt-us* (incorrectly explained in Du Cange): cf. COLE *v.*²] Cut into scallops or zigzag indentations.

1543 TRAHERON tr. *Vigo's Chirurg.* III. vi. 93 You must sewe of cloutes incoled or cheuerned, and laye them vpon yᵉ wounde wᵗ the past aforewrytten [L. *suantur pecie incolate & posite cum supradicta pasta*].

†**ˈincoler.** *Obs. rare*⁻¹. [f. as INCOLARY or obs. F. *incole* inhabitant (1530 in Godef.) + -ER¹.] An inhabitant.

1494 FABYAN *Chron* VI. cxlvii. 133 Not as inhabytans or incolers of Spayne, but that they were issuyd out of Affryca.

†**ˈincolist.** *Obs. rare*⁻¹. [f. L. *incolĕre* to inhabit + -IST.] An inhabitant.

1657 TOMLINSON *Renou's Disp.* 360 Which maladyes much molest the Germanes, and Septentrionall Incolists.

ˈin-ˌcollege, *a.* [IN *prep.* 18.] Residing within the buildings of a college; of or pertaining to teaching or administration within the precincts of a college. Cf. OUT-COLLEGE *a.*

1845 J. PYCROFT *Collegian's Guide* vi. 131 There is a list of the eleven in-collegemen. **1899** *N.E.D.* s.v. IN- *pref.*¹ ad fin., In-college residents. **1945** G. B. GRUNDY *55 Yrs. at Oxf.* 108 An in-college Bursar. **1966** *Rep. Comm. Inquiry Univ. Oxf.* II. 122 In-college teaching. *Ibid.* 143 In-college teacher.

incoloˈration. *rare*⁻⁰. [f. IN-³ + COLORATION.] 'Defect of colour' (*Syd. Soc. Lex.* 1886).

1855 in MAYNE *Expos. Lex.*

†**incoˈlumity.** *Obs.* Also 6 **-ite.** [a. OF. *incolūmité*, ad. L. *incolumitās* safety, soundness, f. *incolumis* safe, sound: see -TY.] Safety, soundness, freedom from danger.

1533 CATH. PARR tr. *Erasm. Com. Crede* 75 Not for the incolumite and preseruation of one cyte or of one nation, but for the helthe and saluation of the hole worlde. **1650** HOWELL *Giraffi's Rev. Naples* ii. (1652) 142 Some things.. that tended to the publique Incolumity and Welfare of the City. **1672** BOYLE *Hydrost. Disc.* II. v. Wks. 1772 III. 617 The cause of the incolumity of the tadpole is, that the pressure..of the particles of the water against one another is hindered..by the *principium hylarchicum.*

incombent, obs. form of INCUMBENT *sb.*

incomber, -bre, -brance, etc., obs. var. ENCUMBER, ENCUMBRANCE, etc.

†**inˈcomber,** var. of ENCUMBER *sb.*, *Obs.*, an encumbrance (on an estate), a mortgage.

1612 DEKKER *If it be not good* Wks. 1873 III. 358 Euen yet Raues hee for Bonds and incombers.

†**incomˈbining,** *a. Obs. rare*⁻¹. [IN-³.] Not combining, incapable of uniting; incompatible.

1643 MILTON *Divorce* I. x, Minds that can not unite..two incoherent and incombining dispositions.

incombustible (ɪnkəmˈbʌstɪb(ə)l), *a.* and *sb.* Also 5 **-able.** [ad. med.L. *incombustibilis*, or a. F. *incombustible* (14th c. in Hatz.-Darm.): see IN-³ and COMBUSTIBLE.]

A. *adj.* Incapable of being burnt or consumed by fire.

1460–70 *Bk. Quintessence* 10 Manye philosophoris clepiþ þis quinta essencia an oile incombustible. **1471** RIPLEY *Comp. Alch.* III. iii, So out of our stone precious, if thou be witty, Oyle incombustible and Water thou shalt draw. **1605** TIMME *Quersit.* Ded. 2 The 4 elements..having in every of them 2 other elements, the one putrifying and combustible, the other eternal and incombustible. **1646** SIR T. BROWNE *Pseud. Ep.* III. xiv. 140 There are in the number of Mineralls, some bodies incombustible; more remarkably that which the Ancients named Asbeston. **1799** G. SMITH *Laboratory* I. 427 To make an incombustible wick. **1874** tr. *Lommel's Light* 6 An infusible and incombustible substance, as chalk or magnesia.

B. *sb.* An incombustible substance or matter.

1807 T. THOMSON *Chem* (ed. 3) II. 95 The combustibles unite with each other..also with incombustibles and with metals. The incombustibles..do not unite with each other, nor with the metals.

Hence **incomˈbustibleness**, the quality of being incombustible; also **incombustiˈbility**.

1653 H. MORE *Antid. Ath.* III. ix. (1712) 114 The prodigious Weight of his body..As also the Incombustibleness thereof. *a* **1691** SIR T. ROBINSON in Ray *Creation* I. (1692) 84 The Bononia Stone..is remarkable for its shining quality. The Amianthus for its Incombustibility. **1747** *Gentl. Mag.* 535 Demonstrates its incombustibleness. **1861** BERESF. HOPE *Eng. Cathedr. 19th C.* vi. 225 Stone..is the most perfect material for groining, if for no other reason, at least for its comparative incombustibility.

income (ˈɪnkəm), *sb.*¹ Also 4–7 **in-com, incom, in-come,** 6 **incomme,** (**incombe, incumb**). [f. IN *adv.* + COME *v.*: cf. INCOME *v.*, and *come in*, COME *v.* 63.]

1. a. Coming in, entrance, arrival, advent; beginning (of a period of time, or an action). Now *rare*.

a **1300** *Cursor M.* 11127 At þe income of þe firth monet [*v.r.* first moneth] Ioseph him went to nazareth. ? *a* **1400** *Morte Arth.* 2171 But Kayous at the income was kepyd unfayre With a cowarde knyghte of þe kythe ryche. **1566** DRANT *Horace, Sat.* I. vi. (R.), At mine income, I lowted lowe, and muttred full demure. **1593** SHAKS. *Lucr.* 334 Pain pays the income of each precious thing. *c* **1611** CHAPMAN *Iliad* XVII. 482, I would then make in indeed, and steep My income in their bloods, in aid of good Patroclus. *a* **1670** BP. RUST in Glanvill *Lux Orient.* (1682) 192 Incomes of light and shade. **1840** *New Monthly Mag.* LX. 267 An annual income of one child, always strong and thriving, sometimes twins. **1898** *Westm. Gaz.* 25 Feb. 5/3 Where the management..do not systematically check the income of provisions supplied.

b. *spec.* The coming in of divine influence into the soul; spiritual influx or communication. (Common in 17th c.: now *Obs.* or *rare.*)

1647 J. HEYDON *Discov. Preserv. Fairfax* 11 God hath.. given you large experience of the incomes of God through Jesus Christ. **1678** R. BARCLAY *Apol. Quakers* XI. x. 368 The pure Incomes of his holy Life..flow in upon them. *a* **1694** J. SCOTT *Wks.* (1718) II. 375 Among the Turkish and heathen saints, there are as notorious instances of these sweet incomes and manifestations, as among our own. *a* **1708** BEVERIDGE *Thes. Theol.* (1711) III. 412 Consider.. what incomes of His grace..God vouchsafed to you. [**1849** WHITTIER *Marg. Smith's Jrnl.* Prose Wks. 1889 I. 161 She said..that no eye could see..the sweet incomes and refreshings of the Lord's spirit.]

†**c.** The act of 'coming in' with something (*e.g.* a statement or argument); the fact of being 'brought in' or adduced. *Obs.*

1654 JER. TAYLOR *Real Pres.* 23 Therefore we have the income of so many Fathers as are cited by the Canon-Law ..to be partly a warrant.

†**2.** A place at which one comes in, an entry or entrance. *Obs.*

a **1300** *Cursor M.* 10546 Quen þou ert common to þe cite O ierusalem, atte gilden yate, þar es an in-com [*Trin.* an entre] þat sua hatt.

†**3.** A fee paid on coming in or entering; entry-money, entrance-fee. *Obs.*

1549 LATIMER *2nd Serm. bef. Edw. VI* (Arb.) 50 Thy Tennant.. whom, wyth newe Incomes, fynes..and such lyke vnreasonable exactions, thou pilles, polles, and miserablie oppresses. **1549** in W. H. Turner *Select. Rec. Oxford* (1880) 199 What Proffitts and Incumbs are due to the Bailiffs. **1579** *MS. Indenture, Mappleton, Yks.*, 400 marks paid for a fyne or incombe. **1646** BRIDGE *Serm. John* i. 16. 27 There are no In-com's, no Incom's to be paid at our coming in to Jesus Christ. **1662** J. STRYPE *Let.* in E. F. King *Life Newton* 23, I shall have to pay but 10*s.* a year [for my chamber] besides my income, which may be about 40*s.* or thereabouts. **1712** *Act 12 Anne* c. 4 §4 So as no Fine Income or other Consideration be taken for the same.

†**4.** A person who comes in or has come in; a new-comer, incomer, immigrant. *Obs.*

1555 W. WATREMAN *Fardle Facions* I. iii. 35 Fower sondrie peoples, of the whiche..twaine ware alienes and incommes. **1570** LEVINS *Manip.* 161/45 Income, *incola, aduena.* **1804** TARRAS *Poems* 14 (Jam.) Lat's try this income, how he stands, An' eik us sib by shakin' hands.

†**5.** A thing that comes in (in addition, or by the way); something added or incidental. *Obs.*

1583 GOLDING *Calvin on Deut.* xiii. 76 Where as God promised the land of Chanaan..this was no parte of that Countrie: he gaue them this as an income or overplus. **1587** —— *De Mornay* ii. 22 Euill is neither a nature nor a substance, but an income or accident which is falne into natures and substances. **1602** WARNER *Alb. Eng.* XIII. lxxxviii. (1612) 322 But not that yll, productiuely, from Nature firstly springs. But as an In-come, hapning in the substance.

6. a. *spec.* That which comes in as the periodical produce of one's work, business, lands, or investments (considered in reference to its amount, and commonly expressed in terms of money); annual or periodical receipts accruing to a person or corporation; revenue. Formerly also in *pl.* = Receipts, emoluments, profits; but the plural is now used only in reference to more than one person. (The prevailing sense.)

1601 R. JOHNSON *Kingd. & Commw.* (1603) 196 Paying the expence of one yere with the income of another. **1633** HERBERT *Temple, Ch. Porch* xxvii, Never exceed thy income. **1646** H. LAWRENCE *Comm. Angells* 152 Hee hath beene at a great deale of paines and cost; now what are his in-comes? **1652** C. B. STAPYLTON *Herodian* 16 He scraped still and never was content, But studied more his Incoms to augment. **1697** DRYDEN *Virg. Georg.* II. 285 No Fields afford So large an Income to the Village Lord. **1789** *Loiterer* No. 43. 10 Having lived, what is called up to his income, that is a good deal above it. **1802** *Med. Jrnl.* VIII. 229 Income, in its usual acceptation, is a loose and vague term; it applies equally to gross receipts and to net produce: But when the Legislature had limited it to be synonimous with profits and gains, it became as clear and precise as any other word. **1866** GEO. ELIOT *F. Holt* ii. I. 76 No, I shan't attack the Church—only the incomes of the bishops, perhaps, to make them eke out the incomes of the poor clergy.

(ii) ***national income***: the income of a nation as a whole, *spec.* the aggregate amount available for distribution among the agents of production.

1878 *Encycl. Brit.* VIII. 258/1 The income tax returns given in the preceding tables furnish important materials for ascertaining, if only approximately, the national income of England. **1925** S. E. THOMAS *Elem. Econ.* xvi. 214 The total of the national income represents not only the reward which flows to land, capital, labour and enterprise: it is also the total available in the hands of all members of the community for purchasing goods and services. **1931** *Times Lit. Suppl.* 19 Feb. 124/2 The national income may be divided into the income (wages, salaries and interest) of the producers of capital and consumable goods respectively. **1964** GOULD & KOLB *Dict. Social Sci.* 452/2 The term national income is used in a generic sense to refer to the net value of all economic goods and services produced by a nation during a particular time, usually a calendar year... In a more specific sense...it denotes the aggregate of all income payments accruing to the factors of production. **1971** A. SHONFIELD in A. Bullock *20th Cent.* 327/1 Many of the European nations were used to earning up to one-quarter of their national income through sales abroad.

b. *fig.* Profit, proceeds; result, 'harvest'. Also in *pl.* (*obs.*).

1635 RUTHERFORD *Let. to M. Macknaught* 8 July, Christ will not be in your common to have you giving out anything for Him and not give you all incomes with advantage. **1687** BP. CARTWRIGHT in *Magdalen Coll. & Jas. II* (O.H.S.) 116 They are..afraid of the income of their evil practices. *a* **1902** S. BUTLER *Notebks.* (1912) i. 12 All progress is based upon a universal innate desire on the part of every organism to live beyond its income. **1939** T. S. ELIOT *Family Reunion* II. ii. 105 It is as if I had been living all these years upon my capital, Instead of earning my spiritual income daily. **1953** A. HUXLEY *Let.* 16 Nov. (1969) 688 He was a retired business man, living beyond his intellectual income.

c. *transf.* That which is taken in, as food (with reference to amount).

1896 *Allbutt's Syst. Med.* I. 162 Physiologists have shewn that the minimum daily income required by a healthy man performing his average daily work and maintaining his usual body weight is five per cent. of that body weight.

7. *attrib.* and *Comb.* (in sense 6), as ***income account***, ***bracket***, ***level***; ***income-earning***, ***-producing*** adj.; **income bonds**, bonds of a corporation or company, the interest of which is not cumulative, secured by a lien upon the net income of each several year, after payment of interest upon prior mortgages; **income funds, investment, share, stock**, investments regarded primarily as a source of income; **income group**, a section of the population graded according to income; **incomes policy**, a policy introduced in the U.K. by the Labour Government of 1964–70 for the control of inflation by attempting to restrict increases in wages, salaries, dividends, etc.; any similar programme.

1869 *Bradshaw's Railway Manual* XXI. 419 Add balance to credit of income account. **1889** *Daily News* 29 Nov. 6/2 In America, Income bonds are something like preference stock in England, but carrying no voting rights. **1940** Income bracket [see BRACKET *sb.* 5 c]. **1947** *Partisan Rev.* XIV. 482 The hard core of the stratum that lives off ideas..are the graduates of the fashionable Eastern colleges whose social origin is in the upper income-bracket groups. **1969** *Times* 30 Sept. 11/8 Good citizenship is not decided by income brackets. **1972** *Listener* 6 Apr. 467/1 A poor cabbie loses his girl because her family don't like his income bracket. **1909** *Daily Chron.* 22 Feb. 1/4 No doubt many an 'old alibi' has won the pension for some young wage-earning or income-earning person. **1946** KOESTLER *Thieves in Night* 88 Of these, 6,624 Work Days were spent on income-earning labour. **1969** *Times* 15 Nov. 16/1 The neglected income funds are..coming back into favour. **1934** B. J. NEWMAN in *Encycl. Social Sci.* XIV. 93 s.v. *Slum*, The worst structural and sanitary conditions and the most degraded occupancy, usually by the lowest income groups, of any given period. **1936** *Discovery* Apr. 98/2 For the income-groups below the adequacy level an increased consumption of milk, butter, eggs, fruit, vegetables, and meat is desirable. **1957** J. BRAINE *Room at Top* vii. 62 She possessed the necessary face and figure and the right income group. **1970** *Listener* 21 May 687/1 The boom in Swiss industry after the war led to..a flood of foreign workers, mostly Italians and Spaniards of the lowest income-groups. **1900** *Westm. Gaz.* 22 Oct. 9/3 This would give a good prospect of dividend for the ordinary shares, and so make those shares not a bad 'income' investment. **1928** M. DOBB *Wages* vi. 113 The potential supply of lawyers or doctors..will be almost entirely confined..to children of parents above the income-level which makes possible a somewhat costly public school and university career. **1951** M. MCLUHAN *Mech. Bride* (1967) 117/2 What would you say was the income level of this family group? **1955** T. H. PEAR *Eng. Social Differences* 136 According to occupation or income-level. **1965** *New Statesman* 19 Mar. 434/1 When he first goes into battle over a wage claim or a price increase—when an incomes policy is first translated into action. **1966** *Listener* 17 Mar. 391/1 The kind of incomes policy they advocate requires unemployment and short-time working to make it effective. **1969** H. PERKIN *Key Profession* v. 181 In terms of an incomes policy a long-term change in relativities was desirable in the national interest in order to restore the universities to a position from which they could compete. **1972** *Listener* 24 Aug. 239/2 The publicly and privately expressed views of the Bank of England that a formal incomes policy of some kind was needed. **1894** SIR J. HUTTON in *Daily News* 25 July 7/3 The acquisition of income-producing undertakings, such as tramways, water supply, &c. **1900** *Westm. Gaz.* 22 Oct. 9/3 Looking upon their shares as 'income shares' only. **1958** *Spectator* 27 June 849/3 A number of so-called 'income' shares in the consumer goods trades. *Ibid.*, The yields on 'income' stocks.

†**income** (ˈɪnkʌm), *sb.*[2] *Sc.* and *north. dial.* [f. IN *adv.* + COME. Cf. the earlier AN-COME, ONCOME.] A morbid affection of any part of the body, a swelling, impostume, tumour, or the like.

1808 in JAMIESON. **1822** GALT *Sir A. Wylie* III. xxii. 191 She had got an income in the right arm, and couldna spin. **1825** BROCKETT *N.C. Gloss.*, *Income*, any swelling or other bodily infirmity, not apparently proceeding from any external cause..or which has formed unexpectedly. *Ancome*, in the same sense, is an old word. **1834** M. SCOTT *Cruise Midge* (1863) 195 An Income is a tumour, sir; and mine was a very bad one. **1859** J. BROWN *Rab & F.* (1862) 13 She's got a trouble in her breast—some kind o' an income we're thinkin'.

†**inˈcome**, *v. Obs.* [OE. *incuman* = OHG. *inqueman*, *inchomen* (MHG. *inkomen*, Ger. *einkommen*), MDu., MLG. *incomen*, Du. *inkomen*; Da. *indkomme*, Sw. *inkomma*. Not an original compound vb., but a collocation of IN *adv.* + COME *v.*: see IN- *pref.*[1] and IN *adv.* 1 b. Now replaced by *come in*: see COME *v.* 63.] *intr.* To come in, to enter.

c **1000** ÆLFRIC *Lev.* xxiii. 10 And þonne ȝe incumaþ on þæt land þe ic eow sille. **1297** R. GLOUC. (Rolls) 1112 To kepe þe emperours folc ar hii to ver in come. *a* **1300** *E.E. Psalter* xxiii[i]. 7 King of blisse in come sal he. **13..** *Coer de L.* 3305 So that ye lat us inne come..They leten hem in come anon. *Ibid.* 3991 Thoo the cunstable herd telle, That the Crystene wer incomen.

ˈ**incomed**, *a. rare.* [f. INCOME *sb.*[1] + -ED[2].] Provided with an income.

1790 COWPER *Lett.* 26 Jan., Johnson, I believe, is tolerably well incomed.

incomeless (ˈɪnkəmlɪs), *a.* [f. INCOME *sb.*[1] + -LESS.] Without an income (sense 6).

1829 ARCHD. WRANGHAM in L'Estrange *Friendships Miss Mitford* (1882) I. 194 Taking possession..of a new and almost incomeless archdeaconry. **1899** *Daily News* 6 Mar. 4/2 The entirely incomeless woman to whom the full pension of £18 was adjudged.

incomer (ˈɪnˌkʌmə(r)). [f. IN *adv.* + COMER.] One who comes in: in the general sense (opposed to *outgoer*) and with various specific applications; e.g. **a.** One who comes in or has come in from another place or country; a visitor, immigrant, or foreign resident. **b.** One who comes in where he is unwelcome or troublesome; an intruder; an invader. **c.** One who comes into a position or office relinquished by another; a successor. **d.** *Sport.* A bird that flies towards the sportsman.

1526 TINDALE *Gal.* ii. 4 Be cause of incommers beynge falce brethren, which cam in amonge wother. **1613–18** DANIEL *Coll. Hist. Eng.* (1626) 32 To foster a party against so dangerous an incommer, that was like to thrust them all out of doore. *a* **1641** BP. MOUNTAGU *Acts & Mon.* (1642) 469 The Samaritans..would not confesse themselves.. Incommers from those trans-Euphratean nations. **1663** GERBIER *Counsel* B viij a, Kept Officers at the gates of the City, to invite all incomers to take refreshment in his Pallace. **1721** *New Hampsh. Prov. Papers* (1869) III. 817 *note*, Voted, yt all Pedlers and Incomers yt shall trade in this Province of New Hampshire shall pay $2\frac{1}{2}$ per cent. for all their trade. **1816** J. SCOTT *Vis. Paris* (ed. 5) 25 A body of troops is stationed, to take cognizance of incomers and outgoers. **1861** *Jrnl. R. Agric. Soc.* XXII. II. 325 Mutual accommodation between incomer and outgoer. **1878** BOSW. SMITH *Carthage* 44 Differences of manners, language and race between the native African and the Phoenician incomer. **1888** *Law Times Rep.* LVIII. 114/1 The outgoer is liable for one part and the incomer for the other half.

ˈ**income-tax.** [INCOME *sb.*[1] 6.] A tax levied in some countries on incomes. Also *attrib.*

In Great Britain first introduced as a war-tax in 1799; reintroduced in 1842, and maintained since. Assessed at a rate annually fixed by Parliament of so many pence per pound (*e.g.* a sixpenny or eightpenny income-tax), with exemptions or deductions for incomes below certain defined amounts.

1799 H. BEEKE (*title*) Observations on the Produce of the Income Tax, and its proportion to the whole Income of Great Britain. **1803** PITT in *G. Rose's Diaries* (1860) II. 17 He puts the income tax at 4,500,000*l.* **1819** BYRON *Juan* I. clxxxiii, The only mischief was, it came too late; Of all experience 'tis the usual price, A sort of income-tax laid on by fate. **1844** A. W. KINGLAKE *Eothen* viii. 111 The fear that my party might be a company of Income-tax commissioners. **1844** *Punch* VII. 206 Infernal things. The Income-Tax papers. **1846** MCCULLOCH *Acc. Brit. Empire* (1854) II. 401 The existing income-tax..certainly is a tax that should not be retained a moment after it can be dispensed with. **1862** TROLLOPE *Small House at Allington* (1864) I. iv. 36 Mrs. Cradell..who had also succeeded in getting her son into the Income-tax Office, had placed him in charge of Mrs. Roper. **1873** H. SPENCER *Stud. Sociol.* i. (1875) 16 An increased income-tax obliges you to abridge your autumn holiday. **1878** [see INCOME *sb.*[1] 6 a]. **1879** GEO. ELIOT *Let.* 23 July (1956) VII. 185, I have filled up one income-taxpaper for this district. **1902** *Encycl. Brit.* XXXIII. 194/2 An Income Tax Code. **1909** *Westm. Gaz.* 24 Sept. 5/3 Returns may be demanded in every income-tax district in which a person may reside. **1916** *Act 6 & 7 Geo. V* c. 24 §37 Income tax relief on war insurance premiums. **1920** A. E. HOUSMAN *Let.* 3 Sept. (1971) 178 The additional trouble in filling up my Income Tax return. **1927** BOWLEY & STAMP *Nat. Income 1924* 17 'Income-Tax' income exceeds ordinary income under certain heads, since it includes *inter alia* various losses which do not come out in the assessment. **1941** *Time* 1 Dec. 84/2 Now appealing a three-year sentence for income-tax evasion. **1950** T. S. ELIOT *Cocktail Party* II. 105 I'd like to see *you* filling up an income-tax form. **1959** *Listener* 2 July 23/2 These customers are known in agriculture as 'income-tax farmers'. **1966** *Ibid.* 5 May 663/1 A composer worth his salt should be able to set ..an income-tax demand to viable music.

†**inˈcomfortable**, *a. Obs. rare.* [IN-[3].] = UNCOMFORTABLE.

1574 HELLOWES *Gueuara's Fam. Ep.* 180 Impatient men are incomfortable to serve and of conversation perrillous. **1655** E. TERRY *Voy. E.-Ind.* 242 Our family was not exempted from that most incomfortable visitation.

incoming (ˈɪnˌkʌmɪŋ), *vbl. sb.* [f. IN *adv.* + COMING *vbl. sb.*]

1. The action or fact of coming in; entrance; arrival. (Opposed to *outgoing*.)

1382 WYCLIF *Ecclus.* i. 7 The multepliyng of the incomyng of it who vnderstod? *c* **1400** *Three Kings Cologne* 51 þe which is a C dayes iorney bitwix in-comynge and goynge. **1463** *Bury Wills* (Camden) 22 Liberte of fre owth goyng and in comyng at the gate be the strete syde. **1573** MORTON *Let. to Killigrew* 5 Aug. in Tytler *Hist. Scot.* (1864) III. 423 At the incoming of the queen's majesty's forces. **1649** BLITHE *Eng. Improv. Impr.* (1653) 54–5 To regulate them..for close shutting, and suitable opening, to the incomming of the Tide, out-going of the Floods. **1726–31** TINDAL *Rapin's Hist. Eng.* XVII. (1743) II. 72 *note*, The incoming of others into the Cabinet. **1825** HONE *Every-day Bk.* I. 491 With the incoming of spring there is an outgoing from town. **1868** HOLME LEE *B. Godfrey* xix. 108 Wardlaw ..watched for her in-comings and out-goings.

†**2.** Place of entrance; entrance, entry: = INCOME *sb.*[1] 2. *Obs.*

1382 WYCLIF *Ecclus.* l. 5 The incomyng of the hous, and of the porche he made large [**1388** alargide the entryng of the house]. *c* **1440** *Boctus* (Laud MS. 559) lf. 3 b, Hit was right at y[e] incomyng Of garabys lond. *c* **1511** *1st Eng. Bk. Amer.* (Arb.) Introd. 35/2 In the incomynge of euery cyte stande iij crosses.

†**3.** An entrance-fee: = INCOME *sb.*[1] 3. *Obs.*

1554–9 WATERTOUNE in *Songs & Ball.* (1860) 10 Be incomings and fynes many tenantes decaye.

4. Money that comes in, revenue: = INCOME *sb.*[1] 6. (Usually in *pl.*)

1596 DALRYMPLE tr. *Leslie's Hist. Scot.* IV. 252 Garnard King of Peychtis..bigit a gret hous w[t] a kirk and gaue it Rentis, and incuming of the nerrest feildis. **1820** SCOTT *Monast.* ix, More followers than he can support by honest means, or by his own incomings. **1848** MILL *Pol. Econ.* Prel. Rem. (1876) 4 Money..a convenient shape in which to receive his incomings of all sorts. **1881** *Sat. Rev.* 5 Feb. 185/1 The nominal incomings are 900*l.*

'incoming, *ppl. a.* [f. IN *adv.* + COMING *ppl. a.*] That comes in or enters: in the general sense, and with various specific applications; e.g. **a.** Entering upon a position or office vacated by another, succeeding. **b.** Coming in from abroad, immigrant. **c.** Coming in as profit, accruing. **d.** Of a period of time: About to begin; ensuing (*Sc.*). **e.** Of game: approaching the sportsman.

1753 *Stewart's Trial* App. 52 As to the agreement betwixt him and the incoming tenants, when he undertook to be their bouman. **1795** BURKE *Th. Scarcity* Wks. 1842 II. 249 The farmer should have a full incoming profit on the product of his labour. **1808** JAMIESON, *The incomin ook*, the next week. **1862** ANSTED *Channel Isl.* I. iii. (ed. 2) 50 Tracing the in-coming or out-going tide. **1870** *Daily News* 22 Sept., Pilots, for incoming vessels. **1876** PREECE & SIVEWRIGHT *Telegraphy* 146 The incoming line wire at A is attached to terminal I, and the compensating wire to terminal 4. **1892** W. W. GREENER *Breech-Loader* 211 It often happens that incoming and motionless ground game is shot over. *Mod. Sc.* Plans for the incoming year.

†in'comity. *Obs. rare*⁻⁰. [f. L. *incōm-is* unpleasant, after COMITY.] 'Discourtesy' (Blount *Glossogr.* 1656).

†inco'mmend, *v. Obs.* [IN-².] *trans.* To commit, entrust (*to* a person); = COMMEND *v.* I.

1574 HELLOWES *Gueuara's Fam. Ep.* 53 Many times did the Consul Scipio request the Numantins to incommend themselves to the clemencie of Rome. *Ibid.* 103 Warres to be good must be incommended unto the Goddes. **1590** H. BARROW *Brief Discov.* 1 The Gospell..deliuered and incommended by his holy Apostles and Prophets vnto vs and all posterities. **1598** BARRET *Theor. Warres* II. i. 27 The Ensigne to be incommended to the Ensigne-bearer. **1621** AINSWORTH *Annot. Pentat., Lev.* vi. 1 Of incommending a thing, and requiring it.

†inco'mmendable, *a. Obs.* [IN-³: cf. obs. F. *incommendable* (Cotgr.).] Not commendable or praiseworthy; discommendable.

c **1510** BARCLAY *Mirr. Gd. Manners* (1570) F ij, That suche thing semed earst honest and laudable, Nowe semeth dishonest, vile and incommendable. **1657** TOMLINSON *Renou's Disp.* 564 Tryphræ, as he describes them..are incommendable in faculties.

in commendam: see COMMENDAM I.

incommensurability (ɪnkə,mɛnsjʊərə'bɪlɪtɪ, -ʃər-). [f. as next + -ITY.] The quality or character of being incommensurable.

1570 BILLINGSLEY *Euclid* x. xviii. 247 According to their commensurability or incommensurabilitie. **1653** H. MORE *Conject. Cabbal.* (1713) 11 Wherein also is involved the Incompossibility and Incommensurability of things. **1785** REID *Intell. Powers* VI. vii. (1803) II. 387 Aristotle mentions the incommensurability of the diagonal of a square to its side. **1834** MRS. SOMERVILLE *Connect. Phys. Sci.* xii. (1849) 95 The incommensurability that exists between the length of the day and the revolution of the sun. **1841** J. R. YOUNG *Math. Dissert.* Pref. 9 The first [Dissertation] contains an attempt to prove the incommensurability of the circle.

incommensurable (ɪnkə'mɛnsjʊərəb(ə)l, -ʃər-), *a.* (*sb.*) [ad. med.L. *incommensurābilis*, also in Fr. (Oresme, 14th c.) which may be the intermediate source: see IN-³ and COMMENSURABLE.]

1. *Math.* Not commensurable; having no common measure (integral or fractional). Said of two or more quantities or magnitudes, or of one quantity or magnitude in relation to another (const. *with*, †*to*); also sometimes *absol.* = incommensurable with ordinary or 'rational' quantities, as the natural numbers; the same as *irrational* or *surd* (but not usually said, like these, of *roots*).

1570 BILLINGSLEY *Euclid* x. def. ii. 229 Incommensurable magnitudes are such, which no one common measure doth measure. **1571** DIGGES *Pantom.* III. viii. R j b, These lines for that they are some of them incommensurable, can not exactly be expressed, saue only in surde numbers. *a* **1688** CUDWORTH *Immut. Mor.* (1731) 271 That the Diameter of every Square is Incommensurable with the Sides. **1710** J. CLARKE *Rohault's Nat. Phil.* (1729) I. 33 Suppose ABCD to be a Square, it may be geometrically demonstrated, that the Side AB, is incommensurable to the Diagonal AC. **1837–9** HALLAM *Hist. Lit.* I. I. iii. §136. 242 The rules as to surd roots are referable to incommensurable magnitudes. *Mod.* The ratio of the circumference of a circle to its diameter (denoted by π) is an incommensurable quantity.

b. (in *Arith.*): Having no (integral) common measure except unity; prime to one another.

1557 RECORDE *Whetst.* B j, If thei haue no suche common diuisor, then are thei called incommensurable, as 18 and 25. **1806** HUTTON *Course Math.* I. 53 If it happen that the common measure thus found is 1; then the numbers are said to be incommensurable, or not having any common measure.

2. *gen.* Having no common standard of measurement; not comparable in respect of magnitude or value.

1660 R. COKE *Justice Vind.* 12 Whether such things so apprehended by the Senses, be pleasant, profitable, just or unjust..commensurable, or incommensurable. **1664** H. MORE *Myst. Iniq.* Apol. 539 Will not this Position prove as incommensurable to humane affairs and be laden with as great inconveniences? **1796** BURKE *Let. Noble Ld.* Wks. 1842 II. 260 Between money and such services..there is no common principle of comparison: they are quantities incommensurable. **1845** DE QUINCEY *Nat. Temperance Movem.* Wks. XII. 167 The two states are incommensurable on any plan of direct comparison. **1881** WESTCOTT & HORT *Grk. N.T.* II. 46 The rival probabilities represented by relative number of attesting documents must be treated as incommensurable.

b. *spec.* Not worthy to be measured *with*; not coming up to the standard of measurement of (something); utterly disproportioned to.

1799–1805 S. TURNER *Anglo-Sax.* (1836) I. III. iv. 188 The forces of either were so incommensurable with the numbers and bravery of the people they attacked. **1856** DOVE *Logic Chr. Faith* VI. §2. 340 His past life is incommensurable with infinity. **1892** STEVENSON & L. OSBOURNE *Wrecker* x. 173 Solutions, which I still dismissed as incommensurable with the facts.

B. *sb.* An incommensurable quantity, etc.: usually in *pl.*

1741 WATTS *Improv. Mind* I. i. §3 Puzzling enquiries concerning..incommensurables. **1812** *Edin. Rev.* XX. 94 Omitting to introduce any thing concerning the nature of incommensurables. **1845** H. ROGERS *Ess.* I. iii. 125 Melancthon was 'cutting and contriving' to perform impossibilities, to find a common measure of incommensurables.

inco'mmensurableness. *rare.* [f. prec. + -NESS.] The quality of being incommensurable; incommensurability.

a **1691** BOYLE *Advices judging Things* Wks. 1772 IV. 468 But [Euclid] contents himself to demonstrate the incommensurableness of the side and diagonal of a square. **1833** J. H. NEWMAN *Arians* II. iii. (1876) 164 The impropriety of the inquiry arises from the incommensurableness, not the coincidence, of the respective feelings.

inco'mmensurably, *adv.* [f. as prec. + -LY².] In an incommensurable manner or degree; incomparably.

1652 W. HARTLEY *Infant-Baptism* 9 Unless we affirm that the Death of Christ be incommensurably reparative to our fall in Adam. **1871** BROWNING *Pr. Hohenst.* 1830 The incommensurably Beautiful.

incommensurate (ɪnkə'mɛnsjʊərət, -ʃər-), *a.* [IN-³.] Not commensurate.

1. Not of equal or corresponding measure or degree; out of proportion, disproportionate, inadequate. Const. *with, to.*

1684 BOYLE *Porousn. Solid Bod.* iv. Wks. 1772 IV. 780 So they be not incommensurate to its pores. **1751** JOHNSON *Rambler* No. 127 ¶10 His improvement grows continually more incommensurate to his life. **1847** GROTE *Greece* II. xxxi. IV. 172 The four ancient tribes..had become incommensurate with the existing condition of the Attic people. **1856** FROUDE *Hist. Eng.* II. 251 That power, unfortunately, was incommensurate with their good will.

†b. Having parts or elements out of proportion; disproportioned. *Obs. rare.*

1650 BULWER *Anthropomet.* 186 The natural proportion of the body is depraved, and the Body made incommensurate.

2. Not having a common standard of measurement; = INCOMMENSURABLE.

a **1687** H. MORE (J.), The diagonal line and side of a quadrate..to our apprehension, are incommensurate. **1694** HOLDER *Disc. Time* (J.), If the year comprehend days, it is but as any greater space of time may be said to comprehend a less, though the less space be incommensurate to the greater. **1864** J. H. NEWMAN *Apol.* 374 Difficulty and doubt are incommensurate.

Hence **inco'mmensurately** *adv.*; also **inco'mmensurateness.**

1727 BAILEY vol. II, *Incommensurateness*, incommensurable Quality. **1825** COLERIDGE *Aids Refl.* (1848) I. 285 The utter incommensurateness and the unsatisfying qualities of the things around us. **1828** WEBSTER cites Cheyne for *Incommensurately*. **1841** *Blackw. Mag.* XLIX. 152 The incommensurateness of Christianity, under its present developments, to embrace and to form a rest for the new mental developments of society.

†incommensu'ration. *Obs. rare.* [IN-³.] Incommensurateness; disproportionateness.

1650 BULWER *Anthropomet.* 250 In knowing and judging of Commensuration or Incommensuration of a Body.

incommiscible (ɪnkə'mɪsɪb(ə)l), *a. rare.* [ad. L. *incommiscibilis*: see IN-³ and COMMISCIBLE.]

Incapable of being mixed together.

1620 WOTTON in *Reliq.* (1672) 501 Whose habits make us incommiscible. **1813** BP. JEBB *Let.* xlii. in *Life*, etc. 476 To blend materials, if not altogether incommiscible, at least very uncongenial. **1825** SOUTHEY in *Q. Rev.* XXXIII. 146 Incommiscible with matter.

Hence **incommisci'bility**, incapacity of being mixed together (or *with* something).

1646 SIR T. BROWNE *Pseud. Ep.* II. v. 90 By some antipathie, or incummiscibility therewith.

†inco'mmixed, -'mixt, *a. Obs.* [IN-³.] Not mixed together, or with something; unmingled.

1658 SIR T. BROWNE *Hydriot.* 28 Which preserved their bones and ashes incommixed. **1660** STANLEY *Hist. Philos.* IX. (1701) 352/2 Those fair things which are first, and Divine, and Incommixt, and always the same.

†inco'mmixture. *Obs.* [IN-³.] Freedom from mixture; unmixed condition.

1657–83 EVELYN *Hist. Relig.* (1850) I. 100 This incommixture and simple purity of parts and principles. *a* **1682** SIR T. BROWNE *Tracts* (1684) 135 In what purity and incommixture the Language of that People stood which were casually discovered in the heart of Spain.

incommo'bility. *rare*⁻¹. [ad. late L. *incommōbilitās*, f. *in-* (IN-³) + *commōbilis* easily moved: see -ITY.] Incapability of being moved or stirred to feeling.

1822 T. TAYLOR *Apuleius, Philos. Plato* II. 346 The attendants on this are indignation, and incommobility, which is called in Greek ἀοργησία, or a disposition incapable of being excited to anger.

†in'commodate, *v. Obs.* [f. ppl. stem of L. *incommodāre* to inconvenience, f. *incommod-us* inconvenient: see INCOMMODE *a.*]

1. *trans.* = INCOMMODE *v.* I.

1611 SPEED *Hist. Gt. Brit.* IX. vi. §24. 490 As wee may easily thinke that the French would gladly incommodate the King of England. **1648** EARL WESTMORELAND *Otia Sacra* (1879) 140 When the Scorching Noon-dayes heat, Incommodates the Lowing Neat. **1693** SIR T. P. BLOUNT *Nat. Hist.* 106 Tea..consumes superfluous Humours, which incommodate the Brain.

2. = INCOMMODE *v.* 2.

c **1555** HARPSFIELD *Divorce Hen. VIII* (Camden) 86 This definition doth nothing incommodate and hurt our cause. **1634** W. TIRWHYT tr. *Balzac's Lett.* (vol. I.) 182 Your Maiesty may bestow it without incommodating your affaires. **1682** H. MORE *Annot. Glanvill's Lux O.* 115 Incommodated by any dull cloudy obscurations.

†in'commodate, *ppl. a. Obs.* [ad. L. *incommodāt-us*, pa. pple. of *incommodāre*: see prec.] Incommoded; inconvenienced.

1622 MABBE tr. *Aleman's Guzman d'Alf.* II. 117 This incommodate accommodating of thy selfe will cost thee money. **1658** BAILLIE in Z. Boyd *Zion's Flowers* (1855) App. 35/1, I..am exceedingly incommodate. **1669** MORTON *New Eng. Mem.* 22 Scurvy, and other Diseases, which this long Voyage and their incommodate condition had brought upon them.

incommodation (ɪnkɒmə'deɪʃən). Now *rare* or *Obs.* [n. of action from L. *incommodāre* to INCOMMODE.] The action of incommoding, or fact of being incommoded; inconvenience.

1664 H. MORE *Myst. Iniq.* xx. 75 But to let pass these incommodations of the Body; Christianity may be made very uneasie and uncomfortable by several rackings and distractings of the Mind. **1779** SHERIDAN *Critic* I. ii, The assurance of crowd and incommodation at public places. **1857** *Chamb. Jrnl.* VIII. 8 Enjoyments were purchased at a rather dear rate in the incommodations connected with that coach.

†inco'mmode, *a.* (*sb.*) *Obs.* [a. F. *incommode* (16th c. in Godef. *Compl.*), ad. L. *incommodus* inconvenient, f. *in-* (IN-³) + *commodus* convenient: see COMMODE *a.*]

1. Inconvenient, troublesome; = INCOMMODIOUS I.

1672 WYCHERLEY *Love in Wood* Ded., To be obliging to that excess as you are..is a dangerous quality, and may be very incommode to you. **1686** tr. *Agiatis* 75 Think of gaining the esteem of the World, and never shew your self incommode. **1762–71** H. WALPOLE *Vertue's Anecd. Paint.* (1786) V. 202 If those streams of hair were incommode in a battle, I know nothing they were adapted to. *Ibid.* 264 Vertue was incommode; he loved truth.

2. Unsuitable, unfitting; = INCOMMODIOUS 4.

1678 GALE *Crt. Gentiles* III. 31 It seems more incommode to say that God moves and predetermines to al other acts.

B. *sb.* An inconvenience, incommodity.

1518 WOLSEY *Let. to Ambass. France* in Strype *Eccl. Mem.* (1721) I. i. 22 Advoiding sundry incommodes and inconveniences that might follow thereof.

incommode (ɪnkə'məʊd), *v.* [a. F. *incommode-r* (15th c. in Littré), ad. L. *incommodāre* to inconvenience: see INCOMMODATE *v.*]

1. *trans.* To subject to inconvenience or discomfort; to trouble, annoy, molest, embarrass, inconvenience.

1598 FLORIO, *Incomodare*, to incommode, to trouble, to disease [etc.]. **1672–3** MARVELL *Reh. Transp.* I. 111 The King would find himself incommoded with all that furniture upon his back. **1692** BENTLEY *Boyle Lect.* iii. 87 Every breath of wind would incommode us. **1748** RICHARDSON *Clarissa* (1811) V. viii. 96 Not that..I would incommode the lady. **1835** W. IRVING *Tour Prairies* 334 We had been, for some weeks past, so accustomed to sleep entirely in the open air, that, at first, the confinement of a chamber incommoded us. **1883** J. HAWTHORNE *Dust* II. 96 The revelation could be so managed as not to incommode anyone.

2. To affect with inconvenience; to hinder, impede, obstruct (an action, etc.).

1702 W. J. *Bruyn's Voy. Levant* liv. 210 A wooden Shed, which very much incommodes their marching in Procession. **1775** JOHNSON *Lett. to Mrs. Thrale* 13 July, The hay harvest is here very much incommoded by daily showers. **1802** *Med. Jrnl.* VIII. 37 The breathing was much incommoded when she reclined on a sofa or bed.

†incommodement (-'məʊdmənt). *Obs. rare.* [ad. F. *incommodément* (1549 in R. Estienne), f. *incommoder*: see -MENT.] Condition of being incommoded or inconvenienced.

1733 CHEYNE *Eng. Malady* 315 (L.), I persisted in my ordinary course of living and business, though with severe incommodement.

†inco'mmoderation. *Obs.* [IN-³.] The opposite of 'commoderation'; mixture (of 'humours') in undue proportions.

1612 WOODALL *Surg. Mate* Wks. (1653) 141 An Apostume is a tumour composed of three kinds of diseases

..Intemperature, Incommoderation, and Solution of continuity.

†inco'mmodiate, *v. Obs.* [irreg. f. INCOMMODI-OUS (or its source) + -ATE^3. Cf. COMMODIATE.] = INCOMMODE *v.*

1650 EARL MONM. tr. *Senault's Man bec. Guilty* 171 We ought to incommodiate our selves, to serve our friends. **1654** —— tr. *Bentivoglio's Hist. Warrs Flanders* III. vii. 426 It is not to be said..how much the Artillery was incommodiated. *Ibid.* 359, 363, 384.

incommodious (ɪnkə'məʊdɪəs), *a.* [f. IN-^{3} + COMMODIOUS; cf. F. *incommode*, L. *incommodus*.] Not commodious, or the opposite of commodious.

1. Causing inconvenience or discomfort; troublesome, annoying, disagreeable, inconvenient.

1551 ROBINSON tr. *More's Utop.* I. (Arb.) 48 Beside their dayly labour, their life is nothing hard or incommodious. **1654** tr. *Scudery's Curia Pol.* 131 The Slaves know that the lightest chaines are alwaies the least incommodious. **1713** DERHAM *Phys.-Theol.* III. iv. 80 Hills and Vales though to a peevish weary Traveller, they may seem incommodious and troublesome, yet are a noble Work of the great Creator. **1822-34** *Good's Study Med.* (ed. 4) IV. 289 It may be given in any form, though its disgusting taste points out that of pills as the least incommodious.

†b. Of persons or their dispositions: Troublesome, difficult to get on with. *Obs.*

1563-87 FOXE *A. & M.* (1596) 46/2 In the time of this Commodus, although he was an incommodious prince [etc.]. **1783** JOHNSON *Lett. to Mrs. Thrale* 20 Nov., A temper very incommodious in sickness, and by no means amiable in the tenour of life.

†2. Disadvantageous, hurtful, injurious. *Obs.*

1579-80 NORTH *Plutarch* (1676) 77 They cast also a certain moisture and steam..that is very hurtfull and incommodious. **1655** MOUFET & BENNET *Health's Improv.* (1746) 350 Whereas Honey is hurtful to choleric Complexions, Sugar is incommodious or hurtful unto none.

†3. Unprofitable, unfit, unsuitable; unbefitting, unbecoming. Const. *for*, *to*, or *inf.* *Obs.*

1553 EDEN *Treat. Newe Ind.* (Arb.) 41 There are manye wildernesses..lacking water, and incommodious for the lyfe of man. **1628** JACKSON *Creed* VI. xx. §5, I am not ignorant what censures pass upon this author for his incommodious speeches in this argument. **1714** STEELE *Lover* No. 20 (1723) 119 It was incommodious to the Circumstances of his Family.

4. Of places or the like: Not convenient for shelter, travelling, etc.; not affording good or sufficient accommodation; inconveniently small, narrow, etc.; uncomfortable.

1615 tr. *De Monfart's Surv. E. Indies* 7 A great bridge of boates..som-what incommodious by reason of the largenes and height of the Riuer. **1687** A. LOVELL tr. *Thevenot's Trav.* I. 10 The Streets of this Town are incommodious, in that one is always going either up hill or down hill. **1725** POPE *Odyss.* XIX. 220 An incommodious port. **1777** HOWARD *Prisons Eng.* (1780) 212 In March 1775, when the number of prisoners was 175, there were with them in this incommodious prison wives and children 46. **1859** DICKENS *T. Two Cities* II. i, Tellson's Bank was small, dark, ugly, and very incommodious.

inco'mmodiously, *adv.* [f. prec. + -LY^2.] In an incommodious manner or degree; inconveniently, uncomfortably; troublesomely.

1551 R. ROBINSON tr. *More's Utop.* II. (Arb.) 93 To thintent the sycke..shuld not lye to thronge or strayte, and therfore vneasely, and incommodiously. **1583** FULKE *Defence* xiii. 439 Neither was this Cyprian's fault alone, that he wrote of repentance many things incommodiously [marg. *imprudenter*] and unwisely. **1652** COGAN tr. *Scudery's Ibrahim* II. i. 15 It is certain, that I am not incommodiously inconstant. **1713** DERHAM *Phys.-Theol.* V. ii. (R.), Without this erect posture his eyes would have been the most prone, and incommodiously situated of all animals. **1784** COWPER *Task* I. 69 Incommodiously pent in, And ill at ease behind.

inco'mmodiousness. [f. as prec. + -NESS.] The quality of being incommodious; inconvenience, incommodity. Also with *pl.*, An inconvenience.

1624 DONNE *Serm.* V. cxxx. 330 If Abraham had any such doubts..of an Incommodiousness in so troublesome a Seal, of a Needlessness in so impertinent a Seal. **1640** SANDERSON *Serm.* II. 175 God hath so tempered the things of this world, that every commodity hath some incommodiousness, and every conveniency some inconvenience attending the same. *a* **1713** ELLWOOD *Autobiog.* (1765) 151 The Incommodiousness of the Place wherein he was kept, may have occasioned his Death. **1854** *Chamb. Jrnl.* I. 257 Bearing..evils altogether beyond masculine philosophy—even, it may be, incommodiousnesses that threaten health, nay, life itself. **1859** DICKENS *T. Two Cities* II. i, The partners in the House were proud of its smallness..proud of its ugliness, and proud of its incommodiousness.

incommodity (ɪnkə'mɒdɪtɪ). [a. F. *incommodité* (1389 in Hatz.-Darm.), ad. L. *incommoditās*, f. *incommodus*: see INCOMMODE *a.* and -ITY.]

1. Incommodious quality, condition, or state of things; inconvenience, disadvantage, discomfort.

1432-50 tr. *Higden* (Rolls) VI. 31 The gardyn of delices, where noon intemperaunce is or affliccioun of incommodite, but the fruicion of alle maner delices. ? *a* **1500** *Chester Pl.* xi. 5 Moche teene and incommodité Foloweth age. **1540-1** ELYOT *Image Gov.* (1549) 102 Nor there is any other thyng priuatelie dooen to our incommoditee. **1596** SPENSER *State Irel.* Wks. (Globe) 618/1 Declare your opinion..about the lawes of that realme, what incomodity you have conceaved to be in them. **1633** T. STAFFORD *Pac. Hib.* II. xv. (1810) 385 To bee exposed to the like incommoditie of cold and raine. **1773** JOHNSON *Let. to Boswell* 27 Nov., I came home last night, without any incommodity, danger, or weariness.

2. With *pl.*: An incommodious thing or circumstance; an inconvenience, disadvantage; a discomfort, annoyance. †Formerly also in stronger sense: Something hurtful, an injury, damage (cf. 1).

1432-50 tr. *Higden* (Rolls) VIII. 241 In the ende of herveste were so moche wete and reyne..whereby mony incommodites folowede. *c* **1450** tr. *De Imitatione* II. xii. 58 To suffre many contrary þinges & diuerse incomodites in þis wrecchid lif. **1579** FENTON *Guicciard.* I. (1599) 16 Touching their expedition by land it was full of incommodities. **1625** BACON *Ess., Usury* (Arb.) 541 It is good to set before vs, the Incommodities, and Commodities of Vsury. **1711** *Lond. Gaz.* No. 4919/2 The Incommodities of the Season will soon oblige the Troops to decamp. **1852** HAWTHORNE *Blithedale Rom.* vii. I. 107 As soon as my incommodities allowed me to think of past occurrences.

†in'commodous, *a. Obs. rare.* [f. L. *incommod-us* inconvenient (see above) + -OUS.] = INCOMMODIOUS.

1677 GALE *Crt. Gentiles* IV. 180 The Communitie..do best understand what is most commodous or incommodous for the preservation and promotion of their Societies.

†in'common, var. of ENCOMMON *v. Obs.*, to make common.

1627-47 FELTHAM *Resolves* I. lxxvi. 235 The way to make Honour last, is to doe by it, as men doe by rich Jewels; not in-common them to the every day eyes.

incommunicability (ɪnkə,mju:nɪkə'bɪlɪtɪ). [f. next + -ITY.] = INCOMMUNICABLENESS.

a **1639** CAREW *Song* (*title*) Wks. (1651) 82 Incommunicability of Love. **1660** JER. TAYLOR *Duct. Dubit.* II. ii. rule vi. §24 An act of so great simplicity and incommunicability that it hath neither brother nor sister, mother nor daughter, kiff nor kin. **1855** DE QUINCEY *Let. to Daughters* 3 Mar. in H. A. Page *Life* (1877) II. xviii. 100 To account for the incommunicability and to show that the accident of last night in George Square was no accident.

incommunicable (ɪnkə'mju:nɪkəb(ə)l), *a.* [f. IN-^{3} + COMMUNICABLE: cf. F. *incommunicable* (16th c., Calvin *Inst.*), mod.L. *incommūnicābilis*.]

1. Not communicable; that cannot be communicated or made common; incapable of being imparted or shared.

1577 tr. *Bullinger's Decades* (1592) 675 Hee..who doth communicate the incommunicable properties of God to creatures. **1608** WILLET *Hexapla in Exod.* 40 This name Iehouah is also incommunicable. **1672** WILKINS *Nat. Relig.* 104 Those are called incommunicable attributes, which are proper to God alone, and not communicated to any creature. **1760** C. JOHNSTON *Chrysal* (1822) III. 139 To wrest from the sovereign an essential part of the incommunicable power of the crown. **1814** SOUTHEY *Roderick* XVIII. 65 None shared or knew His deep and incommunicable joy.

b. *absol.* or as *sb.*

a **1641** BP. MOUNTAGU *Acts & Mon.* (1642) 32 A Reception of Superabundant Transcendency, Christs peculiar Incommunicable, which..is *ultra consortes*.

2. That cannot be communicated to another by speech; incapable of being told or uttered; ineffable, unspeakable, unutterable.

1664 SOUTH *Twelve Serm.* (1697) II. 79 How freely did Christ unbosom himself to his Disciples?..[not] in the extra-ordinary discoveries of the Gospel only, but also of those incommunicable Revelations of the Divine Love, in reference to their own personal interest in it. **1827** POLLOK *Course T.* v, Heard unutterable things, And incommunicable visions saw. *a* **1864** FERRIER *Grk. Philos.* (1866) 252 Its true meaning is utterly incommunicable by one being to another.

3. Not communicative; incommunicative.

1568 NORTH *Gueuara's Diall Pr.* IV. x. 136 Terrible iudges, seuere, intractable, collerick, incommunicable. **1831** SOUTHEY *Lett.* (1856) IV. 247 About the Essays or Colloquies I can tell nothing, Murray being incommunicable.

4. Not in communication (with others or with each other); not having inter-communication; without communication or intercourse.

1646 SIR T. BROWNE *Pseud. Ep.* VI. vii. 307 For the North and Southerne pole, are the invariable termes of that Axis whereon the heavens doe move, and are therefore incommunicable and fixed points. **1804** WORDSW. *Affliction Margaret* viii, Perhaps..thou..hast been summoned to the deep, Thou, thou and all thy mates, to keep An incommunicable sleep. **1865** GROTE *Plato* II. xxv. 266 The two worlds, though naturally disjoined, were not incommunicable.

inco'mmunicableness. [f. prec. + -NESS.] The quality of being incommunicable:

a. Incapability of being communicated, imparted, or shared.

1609 BP. HALL *No Peace with Rome* §8 Wee neither can nor dare arrogate vnto our selues those things which, by an holy reseruation and incommunicablenesse, are proper onely vnto the Highest. **1701** BEVERLEY *Glory of Grace* 11 The Incommunicableness of the Perfection of all the Attributes of God. **1882** MATHESON in *Expositor* Aug. 140 The Jew emphasized..the self-containedness, the incommunicableness of God.

†b. Want of inter-communication or intercourse.

1643 HERLE in T. Goodwin, etc. *Apol. Narration* Introd., The vindication of the Protestant party in generall, from the aspersions of Incommunicablenesse within it selfe, and Incompatiblenesse with Magistracy.

c. Incommunicativeness, reticence, taciturnity.

1835 *Edin. Rev.* LX. 280 His incommunicableness with his children accounts for the paucity of those familiar anecdotes.

incommunicably (ɪnkə'mju:nɪkəblɪ), *adv.* [f. as prec. + -LY^2.] In an incommunicable manner; in a way that cannot be communicated, imparted, or shared.

1627 HAKEWILL *Apol.* (1630) I. iv. i. 46 [Annihilation is] as incommunicably the effect of a power divine and above nature, as is the worke of the Creation it selfe. **1707** NORRIS *Treat. Humility* vii. 300 To usurp that praise and honour which is peculiarly and incommunicably due to him. **1882** FARRAR *Early Chr.* II. 430 Abide in the Unction. It is a thing absolutely real, incommunicably dissevered from all that is false.

b. Without communication or intercourse.

1892 STEVENSON *Across the Plains* 197 Each, in his own little world of air, stood incommunicably separate.

incommunicado (,ɪnkəmju:nɪ'kɑ:dəʊ), *a.* (or *adv.*) Also ‖incomunicado. [Sp. *incomunicado*, pa. pple. of *incomunicar* to deprive of communication.] Having no means of communication with other persons; isolated; in solitary confinement.

1844 G. W. KENDALL *Narr. Santa Fé Exped.* II. 255 Now that I was incomunicado—now that all intercourse with my friends was cut off,..my situation became irksome in the extreme. **1911** R. H. DAVIS *Once upon a Time* 57, I asked the official concerning Judge Rojas. 'Oh, yes,' he said readily. 'He is still *incomunicado*.' **1934** J. M. CAIN *Postman always rings Twice* x. 109 They can hold you forty-eight hours incommunicado. **1941** 'R. WEST' *Black Lamb* II. 310 This was an island: parts of it were even now *incommunicado*. **1952** M. MCCARTHY *Groves of Academe* (1953) v. 96 The defendant or victim in such cases as mine ought to be held incommunicado till his well-wishers have concluded their efforts. **1955** *Times* 4 May 10/6 The Dutch prisoners were arrested at the beginning of 1954 and held *incomunicado* for a considerable time. **1956** 'A. BRIDGE' *Lighthearted Quest* 42 Liners' captains, in her experience, kept themselves *incommunicado* except when on the high seas. **1962** I. MURDOCH *Unofficial Rose* vi. 57 Randall had been practically incommunicado for ten days. **1970** *Observer* 13 Sept. 4/7 The prisoners will be..detained again under the Terrorism Act by the Special Branch, permitted..to hold any person *incommunicado* for any length of time.

†inco'mmunicate, *a. Obs. rare*$^{-1}$. [f. IN-^{3} + COMMUNICATE *ppl. a.*] = next.

1668 HOWE *Bless. Righteous* (1825) 11 It is not happy by an incommunicate happiness, nor glorious by an incommunicate glory.

Hence **†inco'mmunicately** *adv.*, without communication.

1664 H. MORE *Myst. Iniq., Synopsis Proph.* 524 A singular or individual substance completely existing by itself, but not incommunicably, though incommunicately.

†inco'mmunicated, *ppl. a. Obs. rare.* [IN-^{3}.] Not communicated; uncommunicated; that is without communication.

1646 SIR T. BROWNE *Pseud. Ep.* III. xxiv. 171 Although in that indistinguisht masse, all things seemed one, yet separated by the voyce of God, according to their species they came out in incommunicated varieties, and irrelative seminalities. **1664** H. MORE *Antid. Idol.* ii. 18 Excellencies so far as we know incommunicated to any Creature.

inco'mmunicating, *a.* [IN-^{3}.] Not communicating, without communication.

a **1676** HALE *Hist. Com. Law* xii. (1713) 256 That Confusion and Disparity that would unavoidably ensue, if the Administration was by several incommunicating Hands. *a* **1682** SIR T. BROWNE *Tracts* (1684) 130 Even in their Northern Nations and incommunicating Angles, their Languages are widely differing. **1876** J. MARTINEAU *Ess., Addr.* etc. (1891) IV. 225 Incommunicating distances.

†incommuni'cation. *Obs.* [IN-^{3}.] Absence or want of communication or imparting.

1611 SCLATER *Key* (1629) 133 The third branch is incommunication, *Inuidia Canina*..the dog in the manger. **1628** J. DOUGHTY *Church-Schismes* 17 They inflicted vpon them abstension, or (as I may say) incommunication with the Church. **1653** MANTON *Exp. James* iii. 14 Envy discovereth itself..By incommunication: men would have all things inclosed within their own line and pale.

incommunicative (ɪnkə'mju:nɪkətɪv), *a.* [IN-^{3}.] Not communicative; not disposed for intercourse or conversation; uncommunicative.

1670 COLLINS in Rigaud *Corr. Sci. Men* (1841) I. 149 We cannot expect it from one here (who is incommunicative). **1716** M. DAVIES *Athen. Brit.* II. To Rdr. 15, I shall not imitate their incommunicative Tenaciousness. **1816** BYRON *Fragm., 'Could I remount'*, Or do they in their silent cities dwell Each in his incommunicative cell? **1851** HAWTHORNE *Grandfather's Chair* III. xi. (1879) 210, I am naturally a silent and incommunicative sort of character.

Hence **inco'mmunicatively** *adv.*; also **inco'mmunicativeness**.

1816 J. SCOTT *Vis. Paris* (ed. 5) 45 The officer resisted conversation with more firmness than is usual in France..and shut himself up in almost total incommunicativeness. *a* **1862** THOREAU *Cape Cod* vi. (1865) 109 Silently, and for the most part incommunicatively, going about their business. **1872** J. L. SANFORD *Estim. Eng. Kings, Chas. I,*

335 The overt act of a lie seemed frequently the best method of incommunicativeness.

incommuta'bility. [f. next + -ITY. Cf. mod.F. *incommutabilité* (1718 in *Dict. Acad.*).] The quality or condition of being incommutable.

1674 tr. *Boethius* 187 (T.) This order, by its own incommutability, keeps all things mutable within their several ranks and conditions. **1882-3** SCHAFF *Encycl. Relig. Knowl.* I. 48 Maimonides maintained the incommutability of the law.

incommutable (ɪnkə'mjuːtəb(ə)l), *a.* [ad. L. *incommūtābilis*, f. *in-* (IN-³) + *commūtābilis* COMMUTABLE: cf. F. *incommutable* (1381 in Hatz.-Darm.). In sense 2f. IN-³ + COMMUTABLE.]

1. Not changeable; not liable to change or alteration; unchangeable, immutable.

*c***1450** tr. *De Imitatione* III. iii. 66 But allas! for good incommutable, for mede inestimable, for soueryn worship, for endeles glory, men wol not suffre þe lest werynes. **1483** CAXTON *Gold. Leg.* 26b/2 The Incomutable deyte of the blessyd trynyte is without ony chaungyng. **1677** GALE *Crt. Gentiles* IV. 184 One uniforme, sempiterne, and incommutable Rule of Justice in al Times and Nations. **1842** CHALMERS *Lect. Rom.* I. 54 The giver of a perfect and incommutable law.

2. Not commutable; that cannot be commuted or exchanged; unexchangeable.

1775 HARRIS *Philos. Arrangem.* Wks. (1841) 331 The powers, though invisible, are incommutable; nor can those of the shipwright enable him to forge an anchor, or those of the smith enable him to construct a ship. *a***1806** HORSLEY *Serm.* (1811) 424 Notwithstanding the reality of those differences, and the incommutable nature of the two things.

Hence **inco'mmutably** *adv.*, unexchangeably; **inco'mmutableness**.

1828 WEBSTER, *Incommutableness*, the quality of being incommutable. *Incommutably*, without reciprocal change. **1855** W. H. MILL *Applic. Panth. Princ.* (1861) 197 But the first element of this name Eliakim..differs in its initial radical letter and etymology from 'Ἠλί..as completely and incommutably as do their respective correlations in Arabic, Allah and Ali.

†**incommutative,** *a. Obs. rare*⁻⁰. [IN-³.]

1656 BLOUNT *Glossogr.*, *Incommutative*, not to be changed or altered.

incompact (ɪnkəm'pækt), *a.* [IN-³.] Not compact; loosely put together; of loose consistency.

1616 BULLOKAR, *Incompact*, slight, not close ioyned. **1684** T. BURNET *Th. Earth* II. 55 These ruines..being not onely unequal in their surface, but also hollow, loose, and incompact within, as ruines use to be. **1759** tr. *Duhamel's Husb.* I. viii. (1762) 22 The earth itself loose and incompact.

b. *transf.* and *fig.*

1829 LANDOR *Wks.* (1846) I. 399/2 The empire of the Czars being already incompact and vast. **1852** SEIDEL *Organ* 116 Their tone is too braying and incoherent (or incompact). **1869** HADDAN *Apost. Succ.* iii. 55 An organized Church is a more effective instrument for the transmission of truth than the incompact school of a philosophical sect.

Hence **incom'pactly** *adv.*, **incom'pactness**.

1727 BAILEY vol. II, *Incompactness.* **1846** LANDOR *Wks.* I. 71/2 My memory..is apt to stagger and swerve under verses piled incompactly. **1898** *Blackw. Mag.* Oct. 540/1 The geese ..have a strange air of incompactness, mainly attributable to the independent character of many of their wing-feathers.

incom'pacted, *a. rare.* [f. IN-³ + COMPACTED *ppl. a.*¹] Not compacted; incompact.

1680 BOYLE *Scept. Chem.* v. Wks. 1772 I. 546 The other four elements might indeed be variously and loosely blended together, but would remain incompacted.

in-company *attrib.*: see IN *prep.* 18.

incomparability (ɪn,kɒmpərə'bɪlɪtɪ). [f. next: see -ITY.] The quality of being incomparable; incomparableness.

1603 FLORIO *Montaigne* (1634) 568 Truth hath her lets, discommodities, and incomparabilities with us. **1884** tr. *Lotze's Metaph.* 436 Opposing those who adduce the incomparability of things psychical and material as an objection against the possibility of any interaction between them.

incomparable (ɪn'kɒmpərəb(ə)l), *a.* (*adv.*, *sb.*) [a. F. *incomparable* (12–13th c. in Hatz.-Darm.), ad. L. *incomparābilis*, f. *in-* (IN-³) + *comparābilis* COMPARABLE.]

1. With which there is no comparison; unequalled in manner, kind, or degree; matchless, peerless, transcendent.

1412-20 LYDG. *Chron. Troy* I. vi, And of beaute ȝe bene incomparable. *c***1450** *Cov. Myst.* (Shaks. Soc.) 391 Heyl! incomparabil quen Goddis holy tron! **1533** ELYOT *Cast. Helthe* (1541) 35a, Honye..is of incomparable efficacy. *a***1661** FULLER *Worthies* (1840) II. 451 She was afterwards his incomparable wife. **1740** WARBURTON *Div. Legat.* IV. v. Wks. 1811 IV. 215 A new hypothesis..which hath the incomparable Sir Isaac Newton for its Patron. **1871** L. STEPHEN *Playgr. Europe* ix. (1894) 202 The squalor of an Italian town surrounds monuments of incomparable beauty. **1897** GLADSTONE *Let.* 20 Apr., Incredible shame, incomparable bungling.

2. Not to be compared (*with* or *to*).

1614 JACKSON *Creed* III. xi. §18 *marg.*, Vniuersall absolute obedience vnto men is incomparable with true loyalty vnto Christ. **1634** SIR T. HERBERT *Trav.* 116 Neere mountayne Taurus is now a Citie both great and famous, yet incomparable to what shee was in Ecbatans time. **1897** *Allbutt's Syst. Med.* III. 640 As knowledge becomes more accurate, the tables constructed in successive periods become incomparable. **1899** *Westm. Gaz.* 15 May 9/2 The British patent system..is incomparable, from every point of view almost, with the patent systems of Germany and the United States.

†**B.** *adv.* = INCOMPARABLY. *Obs.*

1482 *Monk of Evesham* (Arb.) 101 Mekyl more gladder and that yncomparable for the certen bydyng that he boode to haue the sight of god. **1526** *Pilgr. Perf.* (W. de W. 1531) 40b, Thou shalte be in heuen ruler of incomparable more treasure. **1664** POWER *Exp. Philos.* I. 6 The Gray, or Horse-Fly. Her eye is an incomparable pleasant spectacle.

C. *sb.* **1.** An incomparable or matchless person or thing.

1704 PENN in *Pa. Hist. Soc. Mem.* IX. 355 That there ever should be such a succession of incomparables. **1807** tr. *Three Germans* III. 19 This incomparable would be an evil to be dreaded in the city.

2. A name for a North American bird, the Nonpareil or Painted Bunting (*Cyanospiza* or *Passerina ciris*), so called from its gorgeous colouring, blue, green, yellow, and scarlet.

1889 *Cent. Dict.*, *Cyanospiza*..contains the common indigo-bird of the United States.., the lazuli finch.., the nonpareil, incomparable, or pape [etc.].

incomparableness (ɪn'kɒmpərəb(ə)lnɪs). [f. prec. + -NESS.] The quality of being incomparable.

1633 T. ADAMS *Exp. 2 Peter* iii. 5 Whose.. incomparableness of number, may well fill our hearts with admiration. **1733** FIELDING *Don Quixote Eng.* II. v, I will make thee a dreadful example to all future knights who shall dare dispute the incomparableness of that divine lady. **1882-3** SCHAFF *Encycl. Relig. Knowl.* II. 1003/1 It is from this centre that the ideas of his..incomparableness and glory irradiate.

incomparably (ɪn'kɒmpərəblɪ), *adv.* [f. as prec. + -LY²; cf. F. *incomparablement* (12–13th c.), L. *incomparābiliter*.] In an incomparable manner or degree; in a way that does not admit of comparison; beyond comparison.

*c***1422** HOCCLEVE *Learn to Die* 257 Goostly lucres & wynnynges..Exceedynge in value all eerthly thynges Inconparablely. *c***1450** *Mirour Saluacioun* 1263 Hire bemes ouer alle the sternes ere incomparabli bright. **1531** ELYOT *Gov.* I. xxvii, Shootinge in the longe bowe..incomparably excelleth all other exercise. **1634** HEYWOOD *Maidenhead* III. Wks. 1874 IV. 131 Does not the new Gowne the Prince sent my Mistresse, become her most incomparably? **1666** BOYLE *Orig. Formes & Qual.* (1674) 14 The structure even of the rarest watch is incomparably inferiour to that of a humane body. **1712** ADDISON *Spect.* No. 419 ¶7 Shakespear has incomparably excelled all others. **1855** EMERSON in *Scot. Rev.* (1883) 283 Incomparable things said incomparably well. **1870** ROGERS *Hist. Gleanings* Ser. II. 115 Strafford.. was incomparably the abler of the two.

†**incom'pared,** *a. Obs. rare*⁻¹. [IN-³.] Unmatched, matchless, peerless, incomparable.

1590 SPENSER *To Sir F. Walsingham* 1 That Mantuane Poetes incompared spirit.

incompass, obs. var. of ENCOMPASS *v.*

†**incom'passible,** *a. Obs. rare*⁻¹. [a. obs. F. *incompassible* incompatible (14th c. in Godef.), f. *in-* (IN-³) + *compassible*, a parallel form to COMPATIBLE.] Incompatible.

1630-56 SIR R. GORDON *Hist. Earls Sutherland* 413 (Jam.) It seemed to be incompassible in the persone of any subject, derogative to the king's honor, and insupportablie grievous to the leidges.

†**incom'passion.** *Obs.* [f. IN-³ + COMPASSION: so It. *incompassione*.] Want or absence of compassion or pity.

1625 SANDERSON *12 Serm.* (1637) 231 There are many publike and nationall sinnes,..our incompassion to our brethren miserably wasted with Warre and Famine in other parts of the world. **1630** *Ibid.* II. 259 Whilst we avoid the one extreme, that of incompassion, we may not fall into the other, that of foolish pity. **1675** *Art Contentm.* x. §7. 232 [They] look on our enjoiments and their sufferings thro' the contracting optics of ingratitude and incompassion.

†**incom'passionate,** *a. Obs.* [IN-³.] Not compassionate; void of compassion or pity.

1611 COTGR., *Impiteux*, pitilesse, incompassionate. **1623** SANDERSON *12 Serm.* (1637) 126 He was to wrestle with the unjust and bitter upbraidings of unreasonable and incompassionate men. **1674** FLATMAN *Review* 8 When incompassionate Age shall plow The delicate Amira's brow. **1679** *Establ. Test* 21 They will..repay them with the..most incompassionate Cruelty.

Hence †**incom'passionately** *adv.*, without compassion or pity; †**incom'passionateness**, lack of compassion, pitilessness.

1621 T. GRANGER *On Eccl.* 94 (T. Suppl.) The incompassionateness of other great men, which were merciless, cruel, and hard-hearted. **1638** FORD *Lady's Trial* II. iii, Plead not..without sense of pity So incompassionately.

incompatibility (ɪnkəmpætɪ'bɪlɪtɪ). [a. F. *incompatibilité* (15th c.): see next and -ITY.]

1. a. The quality or condition of being incompatible; incongruity, absolute inconsistency, irreconcilableness.

1611 COTGR., *Incompatibilité*, incompatibilitie, iarring, disagreement. **1614** SELDEN *Titles Hon.* 310 The incompatibilitie of the then vsd superstitions in the Camp, and Christianitie. **1690** LOCKE *Hum. Und.* IV. iii. §15 Incompatibility, or repugnancy to co-existence. **1763** SCRAFTON *Indostan* ii. (1770) 45 Hadjee Hamet..gave the world an instance more of the incompatibility of wickedness with happiness. **1831** BREWSTER *Optics* vii. §66. 73 The hypothesis..which others had rejected from its incompatibility with the phenomena of the spectrum. **1875** JOWETT *Plato* (ed. 2) V. 128 Divorces are readily allowed for incompatibility of temper.

b. (with *pl.*) An incompatible thing or quality.

1671 E. PANTON *Spec. Juvent.* 105 You may tell me that I propose Incompatibilities. **1759** DILWORTH *Pope* 80 They made him an absurd Compound of incompatibilities. **1822** LAMB *Elia* Ser. I. *Artif. Comedy Last Cent.*, The comedy, I have said, is incongruous; a mixture of Congreve with sentimental incompatibilities. **1853** KANE *Grinnell Exp.* xlvii. (1856) 442 It became a grave question, how to reconcile the incompatibilities of dog and goat.

†**2.** = INCOMPETIBILITY. *Obs. rare.*

1659 *Parl. Let.* 9 May in *England's Conf.* 14 We..urged their incompatibility to judge of the Members.

3. *Pharm.* The condition (of drugs) of being incompatible (sense 5); an instance of this.

1825 R. BEST *Tables Chem. Equivalents* 29 This table refers only to chemical incompatibility. The physician must decide for himself, on the propriety of combining those substances which it designates as incompatible with each other. **1877** R. FARQUHARSON *Guide Therapeutics* 14 Incompatibility may be of different sorts, and is generally divided into chemical and physiological. **1948** GROSS & GREENBERG *Salicylates* ii. 16 Incompatibility of salicylic acid has been reported with compounds of bismuth. **1969** J. A. BEVAN *Essent. Pharmacol.* lxv. 628 The whole problem of drug incompatibility is changing as our knowledge of drug metabolism enlarges. *Ibid.* 629 In Table 65-2 some common therapeutic drug incompatibilities are listed. **1970** A. & E. F. GROLLMAN *Pharmacol. & Therapeutics* (ed. 7) i. 20 Incompatibilities between drugs may also occur when they are mixed, as a result of physical or chemical changes.

4. *Biol.* **a.** The incapacity of cells or tissue from one individual to tolerate those of some other individual when an organic union of some kind is formed between them, esp. in grafting and transplantation, in the transfusion of blood, and in parasitism.

1904 *Mass. Agric. Exper. Station Techn. Bull.* No. 2. 15 After a close study of a large number of these defective unions, the writer has reached the opinion that they are almost always due to the incompatibility of stock and cion. **1916** J. LOEB *Organism as a Whole* iii. 46 A lesser though still marked degree of incompatibility exists also in lower animals for grafts from a different species. **1916** *Mem. N.Y. Bot. Garden* VI. 429 Between bloods of members of any one class there is no incompatibility in the form of agglutination. **1927** *Jrnl. Agric. Res.* XXXIV. 675 Reciprocal grafts between the pigmented and the nonpigmented varieties showed no incompatibility whatever, as they produced well-established unions. **1935** N. P. SHERWOOD *Immunol.* xii. 270 In discussing the incompatibility of species not closely related, Loeb mentions the rigid specificity requirements for successful skin grafting or organ transplantation. **1957** MAHLSTEDE & HABER *Plant Propagation* xvi. 277 Many theories have been proposed relative to the causes of incompatibility in grafted plants. **1970** *Woman's Own* 3 Jan. 26/3 Expectant mothers will be immunized against the development of the Rhesus incompatibility which can affect their babies. **1971** *Canad. Jrnl. Bot.* XLIX. 304/2 Parasite/host combinations are referred to by the corresponding genotypes under study which specify compatibility or incompatibility of the relationship.

b. Inability to succeed in sexual reproduction under circumstances where fertile gametes are produced and brought together; *orig.* used mainly of failure of crossing between different species, but now usu. *spec.* such inability (occurring in many species of fungi and angiosperms) between individuals belonging to the same species, which is genetically controlled and which usually acts to promote outbreeding.

1905 *Biol. Bull.* VIII. 320 The incompatibility was less marked... In general..the eggs crossed much more readily than did the California form. **1913** W. BATESON *Probl. Genetics* xi. 240 Whether the incompatibility between species is to be associated with that of the self-steriles also cannot be positively asserted. **1916** A. B. STOUT in *Mem. N.Y. Bot. Garden* VI. 335 The term incompatibility has been, of course, used to characterize a wide range of causes of failure in reproduction, but it can well be limited in its application to those causes existing in the plants themselves which prevent fertilization in and between plants with normal reproductive organs and gametes. *Ibid.* 336 We may distinguish two quite distinct types of incompatibility: 1. Anatomical incompatibility... 2. Physiological incompatibility. **1954** *Adv. Genetics* VI. 236 The widespread distribution and high frequency of incompatibility in the higher plants and fungi indicate that it is one of the most important outbreeding mechanisms in plants. **1966** J. R. RAPER *Genetics of Sexuality in Higher Fungi* iv. 52 The terms 'incompatibility' and 'incompatibility factors' as applied to this and other systems of self-sterility in the fungi are of more recent origin. **1970** *Bot. Gaz.* CXXXI. 139 (*heading*) Self- and interspecific incompatibility in the Convolvulaceae.

incompatible (ɪnkəm'pætɪb(ə)l), *a.* (*sb.*) [ad. med.L. *incompatibilis* (said of benefices); cf. F. *incompatible* (15th c. in Hatz.-Darm.), and see IN-³ and COMPATIBLE.] **A.** *adj.* Not compatible.

1. Of benefices, etc.: Incapable of being held together. [med.L. *incompatibilis*.]

1563-87 FOXE *A. & M.* (1596) 3/2 For infinite dispensations, as to dispense with age, with order, with benefices incompatible. **1637-50** ROW *Hist. Kirk* (1842) 57 Inacted, aganis pluralitie of offices incompatible in one man's persone. **1726** AYLIFFE *Parergon* 115 By the Canon Law Incompatible Benefices are Dignities, Parsonages and

other Benefices, which do by some Statute or approv'd Custom require a Personal Residence. **1872** O. SHIPLEY *Gloss. Eccl. Terms, Benefice incompatible*, means one which cannot be held with another.

2. a. Mutually intolerant; incapable of existing together in the same subject; contrary or opposed in character; discordant, incongruous, inconsistent.

1592 DANIEL *Rosamond* I iij, As heere beholde th' incompatible blood Of age and youth. **1628** T. SPENCER *Logick* 75 When the subiect, and the thing dissenting, doth abhorre each other, and are.. incompatible, than there is a totall opposition betweene them. **1692** BENTLEY *Boyle Lect.* ii. 66 The ideas of Matter and Thought are absolutely incompatible. **1755** FOX in H. Walpole *Mem. Geo. II* (1847) II. ii. 37 Yet.. are we on incompatible lines? **1816** T. L. PEACOCK *Headlong Hall* vii, Luxury and liberty are incompatible. **1871** BLACKIE *Four Phases* i. 18 He felt that to be a politician and a preacher of righteousness was to combine two vocations practically incompatible.

b. Const. *with*.

a **1635** NAUNTON *Fragm. Reg.* (Arb.) 24 A prudence which was incompatible with her Sisters nature. **1781** GIBBON *Decl. & F.* xxvii. III. 68 The use of the shield is incompatible with that of the bow. **1832** tr. *Sismondi's Ital. Rep.* xv. 319 Law and order seemed incompatible with the government of priests.

†**c.** Const. *to*. (Sometimes confused with INCOMPETIBLE.) *Obs.*

1641 R. GREVILLE (Ld. Brooke) *Episc.* 113 A trade, which yet they thinke not altogether incompatible to Preaching. **1652** GAULE *Magastrom.* 75 Is not the prescience or prævision of future things.. incompatible to the nature of any creature in heaven or earth? **1668** HOWE *Bless. Righteous* (1825) 101 Balaam knew it was incompatible to Him to lie or repent. **1790** ANNA M. JOHNSON *Monmouth* III. 11 She knew the unconditional liberation.. was incompatible to his Lordship's professions.

†**d.** Const. *of*: Intolerant *of*. *Obs.*

1605 RALEIGH *Introd. Hist. Eng.* (1693) 34 The English Nobility, incompatible of these new Concurrents, found.. a darkning of their Dignities by the Interposition of so many. **1613–18** DANIEL *Coll. Hist. Eng.* (1621) 24 A Nobilitie, stubborne, haughty, and incompatible of each other's precedency. **1646** BUCK *Rich. III* 51 He was now incompatible of any others precedency and propinquity.

†**3.** Unable to agree or 'get on' together; disagreeing, at variance. *Obs.*

1567 THROGMORTON *Let. to Eliz.* in Robertson *Hist. Scot.* (1759) II. App., The earle of Argyll, the Hamiltons and he be incompatible.—I do find amongest the Hamiltons, Argyll and the company two strange and sundry humours. **1605** BACON *Adv. Learn.* II. xxii. §13 Is there not a caution.. to be giuen of the doctrines of Moralities themselues.. leaste they make men too precise, arrogant, incompatible? *a* **1659** OSBORN *Defect. Rowe* Wks. (1673) 396 By which they have rendered themselves incompatible with any other Tenets than their own. **1722** DE FOE *Plague* (1884) 298 The Quarel remain'd, the Church and the Presbyterians were incompatible.

†**4.** Irreconcilable. *Obs. rare.*

1623 COCKERAM, *Incompactible*, vnreconcilable. **1635** R. BOLTON *Comf. Affl. Consc.* xvii. 321 They set themselves against godly Christians with incompatible estrangement, and implacable spite.

5. *Pharm.* Of a drug: reacting or interfering *with* another (specified) substance in such a way that the two should not be mixed or prescribed together; unsuited to simultaneous administration to a patient.

1812 J. A. PARIS *Pharmacologia* p. vii, The incompatible substances, i.e. all those which are capable of destroying its properties, or rendering its flavour, or aspect, unpleasant, or disgusting. **1855** R. G. MAYNE *Expos. Lex. Med. Sci.* (1860) 519/1 *Incompatible*, applied to substances which act chemically on each other, and which therefore cannot with propriety be prescribed together. **1881** R. FARQUHARSON *Guide to Therapeutics* (ed. 2) 24 Infusions containing tannic acid are incompatible with metallic salts generally. **1898** E. W. LUCAS *Pract. Pharmacy* xliv. 299 Incompatible substances cannot exist together in solution without mutual decomposition. *Ibid.* 301 Sodium bicarbonate is incompatible with solution of strychnia. **1917** E. A. RUDDIMAN *Incompatibilities in Prescriptions* (ed. 4) p. iii, The second object of the writer is to furnish the student of pharmacy with a list of incompatible prescriptions in such form that he may find out for himself what the trouble is. **1970** GOODMAN & GILMAN *Pharmacol. Basis Therapeutics* (ed. 4) 1716/1 Cationic substances and anionic substances.. are often incompatible with each other.

6. *Biol.* **a.** Exhibiting or causing incompatibility (sense 4 a). Const. *with*.

1904 *Mass. Agric. Exper. Station Techn. Bull.* No. 2. 14 When the two members are unlike in nature and in some way physiologically incompatible (whatever that may mean), the wound does not heal readily, owing to some sort of irritation which continues to be felt at this point. **1918** *Jrnl. Immunol.* III. 99 A patient of group I, for example, requires a donor of group I, the blood of all other groups being incompatible. **1936** *Jrnl. Pomol.* XIV. 360 Later, the sour orange also proved to be incompatible as a stock with imported varieties of this species. **1962** J. D. SMYTH *Introd. Animal Parasitol.* xxxii. 371 Physiological resistance. This type of resistance is due to some aspect of the host physiology being incompatible with that of the invading parasite at some stage in its life history. **1966** WRIGHT & SYMMERS *Systemic Path.* I. iv. 151/2 For transfusions.. under no circumstances should the donor's red cells be incompatible with the recipient's plasma. **1971** *Canad. Jrnl. Bot.* XLIX. 303 (*heading*) Transfer of ^{35}S from wheat to the powdery mildew fungus with compatible and incompatible parasite/host genotypes.

b. Having or exhibiting incompatibility (sense 4 b); unable to cross.

1905 *Biol. Bull.* VIII. 323 No eggs segmented, but neither did the eggs in the check experiment in sea water, showing that the eggs or the sperm were poor, or else incompatible. **1913** W. BATESON *Probl. Genetics* xi. 239, I first tried Cinerarias, which are usually self-sterile, but I found no incompatible pairs of plants. **1916** *Mem. N.Y. Bot. Garden* VI. 419 The parent species were cross-incompatible. **1937** GWYNNE-VAUGHAN & BARNES *Struct. & Devel. Fungi* (ed. 2) 5 Often, in these self-incompatible fungi, the sexual apparatus has partially or wholly disappeared. **1967** BRIGGS & KNOWLES *Introd. Plant Breeding* xv. 187 In *Gasteria*, pollen germination and tube development were not affected in incompatible pollinations.

B. *sb.* An incompatible person or thing.

a **1711** KEN *Psyche* Poet. Wks. 1721 IV. 280, I am all Resignation, all Desire. How can these Incompatibles conspire? **1751** HARRIS *Hermes* Wks. (1841) 183 Such syntax is in fact a blending of incompatibles; that is to say, of a defined substantive with an undefined attributive. **1848** H. ROGERS *Ess.* I. vi. 305 This union of incompatibles. **1885** *Pall Mall G.* 9 June 1/2 He might shed his incapables and his incompatibles, and build up a new Cabinet.

incom'patibleness. [f. prec. + -NESS.] The quality of being incompatible, incompatibility.

1608 *Dispute Kneeling Sacram.* 124 The incompatiblenes and disproportion of kneeling with the acts and demonstrations of reioycing. **1752** CARTE *Hist. Eng.* III. 615 Nothing but the incompatibleness of their two lives could have determined her to sign the warrant. **1825** COLERIDGE *Aids Refl.* (1848) I. 241 The incompatibleness of thy will and nature with Heaven and holiness and an immediate God.

incom'patibly, *adv.* [f. as prec. + -LY^{2}.] In an incompatible manner, so as to be incompatible with something else.

a **1711** KEN *Hymnarium* Poet. Wks. 1721 II. 100 Your Country's Heav'n, your Business to rejoice, God's Love is incompatibly your choice. **1755** in JOHNSON; and in mod. Dicts.

incom'pendious, *a. rare.* [IN-^{3}.] Not compendious, not economical; uneconomical.

1833 *Fraser's Mag.* VII. 307 The same failing purposer.. the same incompendious actor—the same too-lavish and too-sparing merchant.

†**incom'pensable,** *a. Obs. rare*$^{-0}$. [IN-^{3}: so mod.F. *incompensable* (Littré).] Incapable of being compensated.

Hence †**incom'pensableness** (Bailey vol. II, 1731).

1658 PHILLIPS, *Incompensable*, uncapable of being recompenced. **1721** in BAILEY; and in mod. Dicts.

incompetence (ɪn'kɒmpɪtəns). [a. F. *incompétence* (1549 in R. Estienne), f. *in-* (IN-^{3}) + *compétence*: after INCOMPETENT.]

†**1.** Inadequacy, insufficiency. *Obs.*

1663 *Flagellum, or O. Cromwell* (1672) 160 The niggardliness and incompetence of his reward.

2. a. The fact or condition of being personally or practically incompetent; want of competence; lack of the requisite ability, power, or qualification; incapacity.

a **1716** SOUTH *Serm.* (1744) VII. xiv. 302 That Incompetence arises from this: That no Man can judge rightly of two Things, but by comparing them together. **1795–1814** WORDSW. *Excurs.* VIII. 13 Therefore no incompetence of mine Could do them wrong. **1812** W. GODWIN in C. K. Paul *W. Godwin* (1876) II. 213 The feeling I had in myself of an incompetence for the education of daughters. **1874** MICKLETHWAITE *Mod. Par. Churches* 201 The incompetence of the tradesman to whom the work is entrusted.

b. *Med.* Inability to function correctly; *esp.* inadequacy of a valve or sphincter properly to regulate the passage of liquid or solid matter.

1876 *Trans. Clin. Soc.* IX. 47, I found.. on examination, incompetence of the aortic and mitral valves. **1890** F. TAYLOR *Man. Pract. Med.* 458 Incompetence of the aortic valves gives rise to a murmur during the dilatation of the ventricle. **1900** DORLAND *Med. Dict.* s.v., *Pyloric i*[*ncompetence*], passage of food undigested into the intestine. **1939** DIBLE & DAVIE *Path.* xxxii. 535 If there has been much necrosis, contraction, or deformity of the valve curtain, a definite degree of incompetence will be left. **1950** *Amer. Jrnl. Obstetr. & Gynecol.* LIX. 69 The symptoms of the incompetence of the internal os are chiefly those of habitual abortion. **1970** *Med. Jrnl. Austral.* 25 July 179/1 The incidence of round ligament vein incompetence in women greatly exceeds that of short saphenous vein incompetence. **1971** *Gut* XII. 102 Of 19 patients.., 17 (89%) exhibited duodenogastric reflux of barium indicating pyloric incompetence. **1971** *Biol. Abstr.* LII. 8355/1 Gonadotropic hormones, the prostate and an experimental model of its incompetence.

3. Of a logical conclusion: Want of legitimacy or propriety; faultiness: = INCOMPETENCY 3.

1837–8 SIR W. HAMILTON *Logic* (1860) II. 465 It shows at a glance the competence or incompetence of any Conclusion.

incompetency (ɪn'kɒmpɪtənsɪ). [f. prec. or INCOMPETENT: see -ENCY.]

1. a. The quality of being incompetent; inadequate ability, incapacity for what is required: = INCOMPETENCE 2. Also, with *pl.*, an instance of this.

1611 COTGR., *Incompetence*, incompetencie. *a* **1691** BOYLE *Ess. Intestine Motions* iv. Wks. 1772 I. 447 The incompetency of our eyes to discern the motions of natural bodies. *a* **1732** ATTERBURY *Serm. Isa.* lx. 22. ii. (Seager), The meanness and incompetency of the instruments that wrought this effect. **1782** PRIESTLEY *Corrupt. Chr.* II. x. 260 [The] utter incompetency of the bishops. **1862** H. SPENCER *First Princ.* I. v. §31 (1875) 109 Is it not proved that this incompetency is the incompetency of the Conditioned to grasp the Unconditioned? **1871** BLACKIE *Four Phases* I. 66 Exposing the manifold superficialities and incompetencies of the persons with whom he conversed.

b. *Med.* = INCOMPETENCE 2 b.

1865 J. H. BENNETT *Clin. Lect. Princ. & Pract. Med.* (ed. 4) VI. 577 (*heading*) Incompetency of aortic valves. **1892** W. OSLER *Princ. & Pract. Med.* v. 611 An acute dilatation of the left ventricle with relative incompetency of the mitral segments. **1950** *Amer. Jrnl. Obstetr. & Gynecol.* LIX. 69 The degree of incompetency [of the internal os of the cervix] may vary.

2. Legal incapacity, disability, or disqualification.

1650 HOBBES *Answ. Davenant's Pref. Gondibert* Wks. 1840 IV. 456 Having thus.. avoided the first exception, against the incompetency of my judgment, I am but little moved with the second, which is of being bribed by the honour you have done me. **1660** *Trial Regic.* 157 Concerning the competency or incompetency of the witness; the incompetency against him is this, that [etc.]. **1833** MYLNE & KEEN *Rep.* II. 245 The affidavits.. positively denied.. the testator's alleged incompetency to enter into the agreement. **1895** *Law Times Rep.* LXXIII. 23/2 The original incompetency to deal with it continued down to.. when the husband died.

3. Logical impropriety or illegitimacy.

1837–8 SIR W. HAMILTON *Logic* xxi. (1866) I. 424 The arguments.. by which it was attempted to evince the incompetency of this figure.

incompetent (ɪn'kɒmpɪtənt), *a.* (*sb.*) [a. F. *incompétent*, ad. late L. *incompetent-em*, f. *in-* (IN-^{3}) + *competent-em* COMPETENT.] **A.** *adj.* Not competent.

†**1.** Insufficient, inadequate. *Obs.*

1611 COTGR. s.v. *Rose, Chapeau, ou chapel de roses*, a small, sleight, incompetent, or lesse-then-due portion giuen a maid to her mariage. **1692** BENTLEY *Boyle Lect.* vii. 256 An incompetent Cause for the Formation of a World. **1789** A. HAMILTON *Wks.* (1886) VII. 25 The situations.. were yet incompetent to the full display of those.. endowments with which nature.. decorates a favorite. **1823** LAMB *Elia* Ser. II. *Tombs in Abbey*, A purse incompetent to this demand.

2. a. Of inadequate ability or fitness; not having the requisite capacity or qualification; incapable. Const. *to*, *to do* something. Rarely of things.

a **1635** NAUNTON *Fragm. Reg.* (Arb.) 39 Sir Francis Knowls was somewhat of the Queens affinity, and had likewise no incompetent Issue. **1647** CLARENDON *Hist. Reb.* I. §3, I may not be thought altogether an incompetent person, having been present as a Member of Parliament in Councils. **1693** N. MATHER *Pref. Owen's Holy Spirit* 3 It is not for so incompetent a person to say as writes this. **1800** COLERIDGE in C. K. Paul *W. Godwin* (1876) II. 13, I would gladly write any verses; but to a prologue or epilogue I am utterly incompetent. **1818** JAS. MILL *Brit. India* II. v. viii. 678 The Nabob, who was totally incompetent to his own defence. **1842** TENNYSON *Two Voices* 375 Much more, if first I floated free, As naked essence, must I be Incompetent of memory. **1869** TYNDALL *Notes Lect. Light* 41 A body placed in a light which it is incompetent to transmit appears black. **1880** L. STEPHEN *Pope* v. 131 He was no philosopher, and therefore an incompetent assailant of the abuses of philosophy.

b. *Med.* Unable to function correctly: used esp. of a valve or sphincter. (Cf. INCOMPETENCE 2 b.)

1863 W. BRAITHWAITE in *Retrospect Med.* XLVII. 69 If.. the aortic valvular segments are rendered incompetent, we have the aortic regurgitant current. **1879** *St. George's Hosp. Rep.* IX. 84 The mitral valves were puckered and incompetent. **1939** DIBLE & DAVIE *Path.* xxxii. 537 The aortic valves are incompetent and allow a certain quantity of blood to flow back into the left ventricle during diastole. **1950** *Amer. Jrnl. Obstetr. & Gynecol.* LIX. 69 An abortion due to an incompetent internal os. **1971** *Amer. Jrnl. Digestive Dis.* XVI. 307 Eight patients had free gastroesophageal relux through a weak, incompetent sphincter. **1971** *Amer. Jrnl. Dis. Children* CXXI. 481/2 The immunologic system may be incompetent or contribute to the etiology of the disease.

3. Not legally competent or qualified.

1597 DANIEL *Civ. Wars* III. (R.), Subjects.. judges incompetent To judge their king. **1650** HOBBES *Answ. Davenant's Pref. Gondibert* Wks. 1840 IV. 443, I lie open to two exceptions, one of an incompetent, the other of a corrupted witness. **1736** BUTLER *Anal.* II. iii. Wks. 1874 I. 187 The objections of an incompetent judgment. **1880** MUIRHEAD *Gaius* IV. §107 Further action.. is *ipso iure* incompetent.

4. Logically inadmissible or illegitimate.

1835 SIR W. HAMILTON *Discuss., Deaf & Dumb* (1852) 135 Dr. Whately's definition, is therefore, not only incompetent, but delusive. **1837–8** —— *Logic* xvii. (1866) I. 320 This process is wholly incompetent to the logician.

5. *Geol.* Of rock or a stratum: apt to flow or to be crushed when laterally compressed; incapable of forming a simple fold and supporting any overlying strata without being distorted by plastic flow. Also applied to structures and processes dominated by such strata.

1891–92 B. WILLIS in *Ann. Rep. U.S. Geol. Survey* (1893) XIII. II. 250 If the thrust be not powerful enough to raise the load there will be no uplift; or if the layers be so plastic that they yield to the thrust by swelling, then the principal result of deformation is change of form other than by simple flexure, and it assumes some phase of flowing. This is incompetent structure. **1923** *Jrnl. Geol.* XXXI. 506 Several attempts were made to reproduce the overfolds.. of the Alps by applying rotational stresses to models in which competent layers were placed between incompetent layers. **1949** C. M. NEVIN *Princ. Struct. Geol.* (ed. 4) iii. 54 Folding has been divided into two groups: competent folding, where the dominantly horizontal pressures are transmitted by the

competent beds acting as a strut; and incompetent folding where the forces are mostly vertical and the incompetent beds react passively. *Ibid.* 55 Immediately beneath the arch formed by a folded relatively competent bed a formation as incompetent as shale may rise as a broad simple arch, even at a considerable depth. **1967** A. I. LEVORSEN *Geol. Petroleum* (ed. 2) viii. 358 In these cases the salt mass acts as an incompetent formation, rising as a result of the deformation of the enclosing rocks. *Ibid.* 378 Folds in the relatively incompetent salt.

B. *sb.* An incompetent person.

1866 ALGER *Solit. Nat. & Man* IV. 248 These jealous incompetents had..hurled him down into a muddy pit of error. **1882** STEVENSON *New Arab. Nts.* (1884) 324 A dauber, an incompetent, not fit to be a sign-painter.

Hence **in'competentness**, incompetence (Bailey vol. II, 1727).

incompetently (ɪn'kɒmpɪtəntlɪ), *adv.* [f. prec. + -LY².] In an incompetent manner or degree; inadequately, insufficiently; with incompetence.

1649 JER. TAYLOR *Gt. Exemp., Beatit.* §9 He that fights for temporals..loses his title, by striving incompetently for the reward. **1772** BURKE *Sp. Ch. Claims Bill* Wks. X. 146 Not that the Church of England is incompetently endowed.

†**incompeti'bility.** *Obs.* [f. next: see -ITY.] The quality or condition of being 'incompetible'; incompetency, incapacity. Sometimes confused with *incompatibility*: see the latter, sense 2.

1664 HAMMOND *19 Serm.* Wks. 1684 IV. 604 The competibility of knowledge, and incompetibility of true faith with carnall desires. **1677** HALE *Prim. Orig. Man.* 122 The stress..rests not upon the incompetibility of an excess of one Infinitude above another, either in Intension or Extension, but the incompetibility of any multitude to be infinite.

†**incom'petible,** *a.* *Obs.* [f. IN-³ + COMPETIBLE.] Not competible; not within one's competence or capacity; not properly applicable or suitable *to*; inappropriate. Sometimes confused with *incompatible*: see the latter, 2 c.

1621 BP. MOUNTAGU *Diatribæ* III. 415 Puffed vp with incomparable and incompetible Titles of Learning. **1641** MILTON *Prel. Episc.* 5 For now the Pope was come to that height, as to arrogate to himselfe by his Vicars incompetible honours. **1650** *Exercit. Usurped Powers* 9 Take him as a usurper, and my allegiance is incompetible to him. **1655-87** H. MORE *App. Antid.* (1712) 186 Indivisibility is incompetible to a Spirit. **1684** BURNET *The. Earth* II. 139 The characters of the New Jerusalem..are very hard to be understood: some of them being incompetible to a terrestrial state, and some of them to a celestial.

Hence †**incom'petibleness** = INCOMPETIBILITY. (Confused with *incompatibleness.*)

1727 BAILEY vol. II, *Incompetibleness*, the Condition of a Thing, that will not square or agree with another.

incompletability, (ɪnkəm'pliːtəbɪlɪtɪ). Also -ibility. [f. INCOMPLETE *a.* + -BILITY.]

1. Incapability of being completed; = INCOMPLETABLENESS.

1829 CARLYLE *Misc., Novalis* (1872) II. 213 (*tr.* Novalis) Men often wondered at the stubborn Incompletibility of these two Sciences. **1898** *Q. Rev.* Apr. 86 This idea of the mysterious incompletability of existence.

b. *Logic* and *Math.* The property, inherent in certain kinds of logical or mathematical system, of being incapable of providing a proof of every true proposition that can be formulated within the language of the system, no matter how many of these propositions be taken as extra axioms of the system. Cf. INCOMPLETE *a.* 2 b.

1940 W. V. QUINE *Math. Logic* Pref. p. vii, Gödel's theorem regarding the incompletability of logic and arithmetic is derived along novel lines. **1950** —— *Methods of Logic* (1952) §42. 248 Church's argument makes essential use of Gödel's theorem of the incompletability of number theory. **1962** [see GÖDEL].

incompletable (ɪnkəm'pliːtəb(ə)l), *a.* *rare*⁻⁰. [f. IN-³ + COMPLETABLE.] That cannot be completed. Hence **incom'pletableness,** incapability of being completed. See INCOMPLETABILITY *a.*

1898 *Q. Rev.* Jan. 80 It is the infinity or physical incompletableness of the Universe which baffles the scientific understanding.

incomplete (ɪnkəm'pliːt), *a.* [ad. L. *incomplēt-us*, f. *in-* (IN-³) + *complētus* COMPLETE: cf. F. *incomplet, -plète*, in OF. *-plette* (1372 in Hatz.-Darm.).] **1. a.** Not complete; not fully formed, made, or done; not whole, entire, or thorough; wanting some part; unfinished, imperfect, defective.

c **1380** WYCLIF *Sel. Wks.* III. 342 Þe chesyng maad of man is fals signe, and incomplet, for to make Cristis viker. *a* **1600** HOOKER (J.), It pleaseth him in mercy to account himself incomplete and maimed without us. **1646** SIR T. BROWNE *Pseud. Ep.* III. xviii. 152 That they be comparativly incomplete wee need not to denie. **1665** BOYLE *Occas. Refl.* Ded., What I had written was In-compleat. **1711** J. GREENWOOD *Eng. Gram.* 114 If we consider whether an action be compleat or incompleat. **1817** G. ROSE *Diaries* (1860) I. 39 The abolition [of slavery] was incomplete even in England. **1863** P. BARRY *Dockyard Econ.* 91 The Resistance was delivered incomplete ten months after the contractor's agreement. **1871** PALGRAVE *Lyr. Poems* 79 Thou would'st be child for ever, Completer whilst incomplete.

b. In technical uses:

incomplete flower, a flower wanting one or more of the normal parts (calyx, corolla, stamens, or pistils). ***incomplete metamorphosis*** (in insects, etc.) = IMPERFECT metamorphosis. ***incomplete areolet***: see quot. 1826.

1760 J. LEE *Introd. Bot.* (1788) 95 Such as are incomplete. *Note*, Calyx or Corolla wanting. **1794** MARTYN *Rousseau's Bot.* ix. 96 Incomplete flowers only are found..on separate trees or plants. **1826** KIRBY & SP. *Entomol.* IV. 342 *Incomplete* [*areolets*], open areolets that terminate short of the margin. **1880** GRAY *Struct. Bot.* (ed. 6) 190 Flowers are incomplete, in which any one or more of the four kinds of organs is wanting.

2. a. Philos. ***incomplete symbol*** (see quot. 1910).

1910 WHITEHEAD & RUSSELL *Principia Math.* I. iii. 69 By an 'incomplete' symbol we mean a symbol which is not supposed to have any meaning in isolation, but is only defined in certain contexts. **1919** B. RUSSELL *Introd. Math. Philos.* xvii. 182 Classes are in fact, like descriptions, logical fictions, or (as we say) 'incomplete symbols'. **1930** L. S. STEBBING *Mod. Introd. Logic* ix. 156 The notion of an incomplete symbol is required in order to define what is meant by a 'logical construction'. **1956** J. O. URMSON *Philos. Analysis* iii. 30 Russell is now writing as though to show that 'X' is an incomplete symbol is tantamount to showing that there are no X's. **1967** R. A. GEORGE tr. *Carnap's Logical Struct. World* II. §27. 48 These other signs we call, after Frege, incomplete symbols. *Ibid.* 49 An incomplete symbol designates..a quasi object.

b. *Logic* and *Math.* Of a formal logical or mathematical system: containing true propositions for which no proof of validity is possible using only the formal rules of the system. Cf. INCOMPLETABILITY b.

1932 LEWIS & LANGFORD *Symbolic Logic* xi. 365 It is to be observed that there is an important respect in which each of these sets is incomplete and therefore open to further determination. **1937** A. SMEATON tr. *Carnap's Logical Syntax of Lang.* III. 100 Now, however, Gödel has shown that not only all former systems, but all systems of this kind in general, are incomplete. **1958** NAGEL & NEWMAN *Gödel's Proof* vi. 58 Gödel showed that *Principia* [*Mathematica*], or any other system within which arithmetic can be developed, is essentially incomplete. **1970** J. VAN HEIJENOORT tr. *Gödel's Completeness & Consistency* in *Frege & Gödel* 107 If *S* contains *Z*, *S* is incomplete, that is, there are in *S* propositions..that are undecidable on the basis of the axioms of *S*, provided that *S* is *w*-consistent.

†**incom'plete,** *v.* *Obs. rare*⁻¹. [f. prec. after COMPLETE *v.*] *trans.* To render incomplete, to destroy the completeness of.

1656 JEANES *Fuln. Christ* 26 Will Christ then..suffer any thing to prevaile against his Church, which is his fulness? What were that but to mayme and incompleate him?

incom'pleted, *a.* [f. IN-³ + COMPLETED.] Not completed; unfinished, incomplete.

1836 LYTTON *Athens* (1837) I. 408 One of those rude but serviceable instruments by which a more practical and perfect action is often wrought out from the incompleted theories of greater statesmen. **1889** *Electrical Rev.* 12 Apr. 415/2 The details of an incompleted research.

incompletely (ɪnkəm'pliːtlɪ), *adv.* [f. INCOMPLETE *a.* + -LY².] In an incomplete manner or degree; partially, imperfectly.

1651 BAXTER *Inf. Bapt.* 15 Those that are *de jure*, or incompleatly Disciples. **1777** WATSON *Philip II* (1793) I. IX. 363 Undisciplined, incompletely armed and disheartened. **1862** LATHAM *Channel Isl.* III. xv. (ed. 2) 368 It is only partially and incompletely that his request is attended to.

incompleteness (ɪnkəm'pliːtnɪs). [f. as prec. + -NESS.] **a.** The quality or state of being incomplete; want of completeness.

1643 MILTON *Divorce* Introd., Error..willingly accepts what he wants, and supplies what her incompleatnesse went seeking. **1664-5** BOYLE *Cause Condens. Air* Wks. 1772 II. 499 The incompleteness of the theory of cold. **1845-6** TRENCH *Huls. Lect.* Ser. I. i. 8 A book..underlying the same ..incompletenesses as every other work of men's hands. **1860** TYNDALL *Glac.* 33, I had often occasion to feel the incompleteness of my knowledge.

b. *spec.* in *Logic* and *Math.* (see INCOMPLETE *a.* 2 b.) Also *attrib.* in **incompleteness theorem,** the mathematical proof of incompleteness (cf. GÖDEL).

1932 LEWIS & LANGFORD *Symbolic Logic* xi. 365 This point of incompleteness can be brought out by contrasting examples. **1937** A. SMEATON tr. *Carnap's Logical Syntax of Lang.* III. §34a. 100 In spite of this necessary incompleteness of the method of derivation.., the method retains its fundamental significance. **1955** K. R. POPPER in P. A. Schilpp *Philos. of R. Carnap* (1963) 200 Gödel, by his two famous incompleteness theorems, had proved that one unified language would not be sufficiently universal for even the purposes of elementary number theory. **1957** P. SUPPES *Introd. Logic* iv. 70 Gödel's theorem on the incompleteness of elementary number theory is probably the most important theorem in the literature of modern logic. **1962** B. MELTZER tr. *Gödel's On Formally Undecidable Propositions* 62 The true source of the incompleteness attaching to all formal systems of mathematics, is to be found..in the fact that the formation of ever higher types can be continued into the transfinite. **1971** G. HUNTER *Metalogic* 257 This is Gödel's second incompleteness theorem.

incompletion (ɪnkəm'pliːʃən). [f. IN-³ + COMPLETION.] Incomplete or unfinished condition, incompleteness.

1804 *Miniature* No. 5 ¶1 He..only effects one design, that he may regret the incompletion of others. **1815** W. TAYLOR in *Monthly Mag.* XXXVIII. 43 His literary history of them would appear useless from incompletion. **1873** BROWNING *Red Cott. Nt-cap* IV. 762 Artist-preference For work complete, inferiorly proposed, To incompletion, though it aim aright.

incompletive (ɪnkəm'pliːtɪv), *a.* (*sb.*) *Gram.* [f. INCOMPLET(E *a.* + -IVE.] An aspect of the verb indicating incompletion of an action or process; = IMPERFECTIVE *a.* (*sb.*) 2.

1944 E. A. NIDA *Morphol.* II. ix. 130 This imperfective aspect, which may also be called 'atelic' or 'incompletive', is often associated with the future time, with the negative or with the potential. **1964** —— *Toward Sci. Transl.* ix. 200 In the Old Testament, however, the differences between the Hebrew completive and incompletive forms are essentially contrasts between kinds of action. **1964** *Language* XL. 77 Two aspect classes of the active voice are also marked by simulfixation: the incompletive, marked by the structural absence of a simulfix, and the completive, marked by the simulfix for active voice. **1968** *Ibid.* XLIV. 293 There are four aspects in Huixtec: timeless, incompletive, completive, and perfective.

incomplex (ɪn'kɒmplɛks, *formerly* ɪnkəm'plɛks), *a.* [ad. late L. *incomplex-us*, f. *in-* (IN-³) + *complex-us* COMPLEX: so F. *incomplexe* (1732 in Dict. Trévoux).] Not complex; not complicated or involved; simple.

1658 BAXTER *Saving Faith* vi. 36 Complex Objects, which are appointed to be the means of knowing the incomplex. *a* **1677** BARROW *Serm.* iv. Wks. 1686 II. 55 It is unintelligible how any incomplex thing..can be the complete or immediate object of belief. **1713** DERHAM *Phys.-Theol.* VII. ii. 382 The Ear is in Birds the most simple and incomplex of any Animals Ear. **1789** T. TAYLOR *Proclus* II. 49 The incomplex [theorems] are such composites as cannot be divided into simple theorems, as the fourth proposition. **1827** WHATELY *Logic* 59 Incomplex apprehension is of one object, or of several without any relation being perceived between them.

†**incom'plexed,** *a.* *Obs. rare.* [f. late L. *incomplex-us* (see prec.) + -ED¹.] Not complex; incomplex.

1628 T. SPENCER *Logick* 12 Aristotle giues his incomplexed things no name: but, thereby he meanes arguments. *Ibid.* 151 *Arguments*..those single, or incomplexed termes whereof wee spake in the former part.

†**incom'plexionate,** *a.* *Obs. rare*⁻¹. [IN-³.] Not 'complexionate'; not influenced by the mental 'complexion' or humour.

1660 H. MORE *Myst. Godl.* VI. xiii. 254 To intoxicate them with the same heat and noise in their enravished Imagination, whereby that still and small voice of Incomplexionate Reason cannot be heard.

incom'plexity. *rare.* [IN-³.] Absence of complexity; simplicity.

1782 V. KNOX *Ess.* (1819) III. clxxvi. 278 Artlessness, and incomplexity of fable.

†**incom'plexly,** *adv.* *Obs.* [f. INCOMPLEX *a.* + -LY².] In an incomplex manner; simply.

1677 GALE *Crt. Gentiles* IV. 313 The Divine Intellect understandes things complexe incomplexely; but the human Intellect understandes things most simple and incomplexe, complexely.

†**incom'pliable,** *a.* *Obs.* [f. IN-³ + COMPLIABLE.] Not able or ready to comply or act in concord; disagreeing, unconformable.

1625 BP. MOUNTAGU *App. Cæsar* I. vii. 60 Men intractable, insociable, incompliable with those that will not *ædificare ad dissensiones*. **1629** PRYNNE *Ch. Eng.* 137 Which ..of these irreconcilable, incompliable Assertions are the ancient..Doctrines of our Church. **1664** H. MORE *Myst. Iniq.* 448 You see how distorted, forced, and incompliable his Exposition is to the text.

Hence †**incom'pliableness,** the quality of being 'incompliable'; unconformable tendency.

1642 ROGERS *Naaman* 11 Convinced of their owne incompliablenesse to the grace of God offred. *Ibid.* 130 That wofull and desperate flinging out of the soule, and incompliablenesse of the spirit.

incompliance (ɪnkəm'plaɪəns). Now *rare.* [IN-³.] The fact or quality of being incompliant.

†**1.** Want of conformity or accordance. *Obs.*

a **1655** VINES *Lord's Supp.* (1677) 200 A streight rule discovers a crooked line by the incompliance of it to the rule.

†**2.** Unaccommodating disposition; want of complaisance. *Obs.*

a **1694** TILLOTSON *Serm.* (1743) I. iii. 101 All peevishness and incompliance of humour in things lawful and indifferent. **1697** COLLIER *Ess. Mor. Subj.* I. (1703) 79 A martial man, except he has been sweetened and polished by a lettered education, is apt to have a tincture of sowerness and incomplyance in his behaviour. **1770** LANGHORNE *Plutarch* (1879) I. 291/2 A peevishness of temper or incompliance of manners,..produce the most incurable aversions in a married life. **1805** FOSTER *Ess.* II. v. 178 Invested with a manner of sternness, reserve, and incompliance.

3. Failure to comply with a claim, desire, or request; non-compliance.

1708 *Diss. Drunkenness* 29 Will he baulk his Interest, and punish himself for so small an Incompliance? **1781** JOHNSON *Let.* 4 Apr., Mr. Johnson knows that Sir Joshua..will excuse his incompliance with the Call. *a* **1797** H. WALPOLE *Mem. Geo. II* (1847) III. i. 21 Pitt..foresaw incompliance on the Duke's part. **1885** R. W. DIXON *Hist. Ch. Eng.* xvi. (1893) III. 147 They wrote to complain, 18 July, adding that her incompliance in religion gave countenance to the disturbances.

incom'pliancy. *rare.* [f. INCOMPLIANT: see -ANCY, and cf. *compliancy*.] Incompliant character.

1658 OSBORN *Jas. I*, Wks. (1673) 519 The Incompliancy of the Episcopal Clergy and their natural propensity to dilate their power. **1798** LANDOR *Gebir* Wks. 1846 II 499/1 Thou..leanest on thy claim Till overwhelmed through incompliancy.

incompliant (ɪnkəm'plaɪənt), *a.* Now *rare.* [f. IN-[3] + COMPLIANT.] Not compliant.

1. Not yielding or disposed to yield to the desires or requests of others; unaccommodating, unsubmissive, uncompliant.

1707 *Reflex. upon Ridicule* 302 There are a sort of incompliant People that are all of a piece. **1709** STRYPE *Ann. Ref.* (1824) I. vii. 154 If they themselves held together, and remained incompliant with the steps that were taking, the Queen must be forced to keep them in the church. **1721** —— *Eccl. Mem.* II. xxix. 238 We find three incompliant prelates more this year under confinement in the Tower. **1830** D'ISRAELI *Chas. I*, III. xiii. 285 That reaction which inflames the incompliant to obstinacy.

2. Of things: **a.** Not in harmony, incompatible, not lending itself to some purpose. **b.** Unpliant, unyielding.

1647 SPRIGGE *Anglia Rediv.* III. v. (1854) 159 The narrowness of the ways..was altogether incompliant with the army's march. **1663** T. JORDAN *Royal Arb. Poesie* 22 Men act, that are between Forty and fifty, Wenches of fifteen; With bone so large, and nerve so incomplyant, When you call Desdemona, enter Giant. **1846** LANDOR *Wks.* II. 216/1 No branch of intellectual pleasure so brittle and incompliant as never to be turned to profit.

Hence **incom'pliantly** *adv.*, in an unyielding or unaccommodating manner.

1847 in CRAIG.

†**in'complicate,** *a. Obs. rare.* [IN-[3].] Not complicated; uncomplicated; simple.

1686 GOAD *Celest. Bodies* II. iii. 178 This belongs to the Chapter of Complicate Aspects, and our Method engages us yet to show the Influence only of the Single and incomplicate. *Ibid.* III. iv. 508 We seek for the Nature of the Single and Incomplicate Aspect. **1804** ANNA SEWARD *Mem. Darwin* 392 This incomplicate and so easily practicable system.

†**incom'plying,** *a. Obs. rare.* [IN-[3].] Not complying; incompliant. Hence †**incom'plyingness,** uncomplying character.

1640 W. BRIDGES *True Souldiers Convoy* 10 Now, God is very incomplying in all his wayes. **1654** H. L'ESTRANGE *Chas. I* (1655) 101 Usually they [kings] derive their asperity ..from the protervity and incomplyingnesse of their people. *a* **1732** ATTERBURY *Serm.* XXII. (L.), That obstinate resolution of mind, that stubborn incomplying virtue, which is requisite to preserve a man undefiled and blameless.

†**incom'portable,** *a. Obs.* [IN-[3].] Not to be borne, intolerable, insupportable.

a **1734** NORTH *Exam.* I. ii. §18 (1740) 39 It was..no new Device to shove Men out of their Places by contriving incomportable Hardships to be put upon them. *Ibid.* §53. 57 Setting up what was called the Country Party, to an incomportable Height.

†**incomposed** (ɪnkəm'pəʊzd), *a. Obs.* [f. IN-[3] + COMPOSED: cf. F. *incomposé* (15th c. in Godef.), L. *incompositus*.]

1. Not composite or compound; simple, uncompounded.

1634 W. TIRWHYT tr. *Balzac's Lett.* (1638) 242 A simple and incomposed substance..farre from all composition and mixture. **1655** STANLEY *Hist. Philos.* II. (1701) 62/1 He used the Ionick Dialect, plain and incomposed. **1657–83** EVELYN *Hist. Relig.* (1850) I. 189 [The Soul], being an act, is incomposed, and, could she die, would be annihilated.

2. Wanting in composure or orderly arrangement; disordered, disarranged; disturbed, agitated, discomposed.

1608 CHAPMAN *Byrons Trag.* Plays 1873 II. 256 When th' incomposd incursions of floods Wasted and eat the earth. *a* **1619** FOTHERBY *Atheom.* II. xi. §4 (1622) 318 Such vntuneable and incomposed noyse. **1667** MILTON *P.L.* II. 989 Him thus the Anarch old With faultring speech and visage incompos'd Answer'd. **1727–46** THOMSON *Summer* 491 The strong laborious ox, of honest front Which incompos'd he shakes. **1740** SOMERVILLE *Hobbinol* III. 339 With hasty Step, and Visage incompos'd, Wildly she star'd.

3. Indisposed (*to*), not in the proper state for. Cf. COMPOSE *v.* 14.

1660 J. S. *Andromana* I. i. in Hazl. *Dodsley* XIV. 198 That sweetness which bewitch'd men's hearts is grown So rugged, so incompos'd to all commerce, Men fear he'll shortly quarrel with himself.

Hence †**incom'posedly** *adv.*, in a disorderly or disturbed way; without composure; †**incom'posedness,** want of composure, disorderliness.

1612–15 BP. HALL *Contempl., O.T.* XI. vi, If she had spoken too loud and incomposedly, he might have had some just colour for this conceit. **1653** H. MORE *Antid. Ath.* I. x. (1662) 32 Whose limbs by force of the convulsion are moved very incomposedly and ilfavour'dly. *Ibid.* III. xvi. 141 A jumbled feculency and incomposedness of the spirits. *a* **1711** KEN *Man. Prayers* Wks.(1838) 426 If you find in any duty..incomposedness, and weariness of spirit.

incomposite (ɪn'kɒmpəzɪt), *a.* (*sb.*) [ad. L. *incomposit-us*, f. *in-* (IN-[3]) + *compositus* COMPOSITE.]

1. Not composite; not composed of parts; simple, uncompounded. Also as *sb.* Something simple or uncompounded.

1677 GALE *Crt. Gentiles* IV. 253 Thus Damascene, Orthodox. Fid. I. I. c. 15... 'The Deitie is not a composite: but in three perfect (Persons) one perfect, indivisible and incomposite (Essence)'. **1788** T. TAYLOR *Proclus* I. 44 Substances destitute of parts, simple, incomposite and indivisible. *Ibid.* 133 All the rest..he denominates incomposites.

b. *Arith.* ***incomposite number***: a number not composed of factors, a prime number. ? *Obs.*

1706 PHILLIPS s.v. *Number, Prime, Simple,* or *Incomposit Number*..is a Number, which can only be measur'd or divided by it self, or by Unity, without leaving any Remainder. **1776** HUTTON in *Phil. Trans.* LXVI. 479 The.. incomposite number 239.

2. Not properly composed or put together.

1879 SWINBURNE *Study Shaks.* ii. (1880) 97 The whole structure of the play if judged by any strict rule of pure art is incomposite and incongruous, wanting in unity, consistency, and coherence of interest.

incompossibility (ɪnkəmpɒsɪ'bɪlɪtɪ). Now *rare.* [f. next: see -ITY.] The quality or condition of being incompossible; total incompatibility. Also, with *pl.*, an instance of this.

1629 JACKSON *Creed* VI. II. xxix. §2 Whether we respect the contrariety of their natural dispositions or the incompossibility of their projects and engagements. **1630** RANDOLPH *Aristippus* (1652) 3 What should this Scotus meane by his possibilities and incompossibilities? My Cooper, Rider, Thomas and Minsheu are as farre to seek as myself. **1742** C. OWEN *Nat. Hist. Serpents* 66 By reason of some great Disproportion or Incompossibility. **1864** BOWEN *Logic* vi. 170 The Incompossibility, or the fact that the two Judgments cannot both be true. **1877** E. CAIRD *Philos. Kant* v. 83 The incompossibility of different things (i.e. the impossibility of different things existing together).

incompossible (ɪnkəm'pɒsɪb(ə)l), *a.* Now *rare.* [ad. schol.L. *incompossibil-is*, f. *in-* (IN-[3]) + med.L. *compossibilis* COMPOSSIBLE: cf. F. *incompossible* (1732 in Dict. Trévoux).] Not possible together; that cannot exist or be true together; wholly incompatible or inconsistent.

1605 *Answ. Discov. Rom. Doctrine* 21 The gouernment of their Eldership, or Presbitery (incompossible with Princes Supremacy) is the cheefest article of their religion. *a* **1640** JACKSON *Creed* X. xl. §5 Conditions..whose performance.. was very incompatible, though not incompossible with haughty pride or tenacious avarice. **1662** STILLINGFL. *Orig. Sacr.* III. i. (1702) 248 Things..which in nature seem wholly incompossible (as the schools speak). **1701** BEVERLEY *Glory of Grace* 12, I..illustrate this grand Point by an In-Compossible Supposition. **1864** BOWEN *Logic* vi. 169 To adopt the Hamiltonian word, the two Judgments are incompossible. **1877** E. CAIRD *Philos. Kant* Introd. v. 84 If there be any positive existences which are incompossible —i.e. which cannot be combined without opposition and conflict.

†**incom'posure.** *Obs.* [IN-[3].] The state of being 'incomposed'; discomposure, disorder.

1644 BULWER *Chiron.* 133 The incomposure of the Hands is to be avoided. **1655–87** H. MORE *App. Antid.* (1662) 177 That Birds prune their feathers..to rid themselves of that more uncouth and harsh sense they feel in their skins by the incomposure of their ruffled plumes. **1706** PHILLIPS, *Incomposure*, Disorder, Confusion.

†**incom'pound,** *a. Obs. rare.* [IN-[3].] = next.

1735 H. BROOKE *Univ. Beauty* IV. 68 With vision of internal powers profound, A pure essential unit, incompound.

†**incom'pounded,** *a. Obs.* [IN-[3].] Not compounded; uncompounded.

1603 HOLLAND *Plutarch's Mor.* 1252 The Hemitone in the Mese will be incompounded. **1735** H. BROOKE *Univ. Beauty* I. 199 An incompounded radiant form they claim, Nor spirit all—nor yet corporeal frame.

†**incom'poundness.** *Obs.* [f. IN-[3] + COMPOUND *a.* + -NESS.] The quality or state of not being compound.

1600 ABP. ABBOT *Exp. Jonah* 195 The single incompoundnesse of that self-moving soule..in comparison of the flesh. **1649** BLITHE *Eng. Improv. Impr.* (1653) 137 The onely sign..is the incompoundness of it.

incompre'hended, *a. rare.* [IN-[3].] Not comprehended; beyond comprehension.

1652 H. C. *Looking-Gl. Ladies* 15 Speech, that vast incomprehended measure. *Ibid.* 19 The great incomprehended phrase [God in Man]. **1839** I. WILLIAMS *Hymns fr. Paris Brev.* 160 Thrice holy, thrice Almighty Three, Incomprehended Trinity.

incompre'hending, *ppl. a. rare.* [IN-[3].] Not comprehending; wanting in comprehension or understanding. Hence **incompre'hendingly** *adv.*

1881 MRS. C. PRAED *Policy & P.* I. 195 Good Mrs. Ferris, incomprehending soul, knew nothing of [etc.]. **1885** —— *Head Stat.* 7 The Kanaka shook his head incomprehendingly.

†**incompre'hense,** *a. Obs. rare.* In 7 -ence. [ad. L. *incomprehens-us*, f. *in-* (IN-[3]) + *comprehensus* comprehended.] Not comprehended or comprised within limits; boundless, unlimited.

1606 MARSTON *Sophonisba* v. ii, Could no scope of glory.. Fill thy great breast, but thou must prove immense Incomprehence in vertue?

incomprehensibility (ɪnkɒmprɪhɛnsɪ'bɪlɪtɪ). [f. next: see -ITY: cf. F. *incompréhensibilité* (Montaigne, 16th c.).] The quality or state of being incomprehensible; an instance of this.

1. Incapability of being comprised or circumscribed within limits; boundlessness, infinitude.

1650 HOBBES *Treat. Hum. Nat.* xi. Wks. 1840 IV. 60 This it is which all men conceive by the name of GOD, implying eternity, incomprehensibility, and omnipotency. **1701** NORRIS *Ideal World* I. v. 302 The Divine nature, and..the same real infinity and incomprehensibility that essentially belongs to it. **1724** WATERLAND *Athan. Creed* 139. **1866** LIDDON *Bampt. Lect.* i. (1875) 29 When we confess the omnipresence and incomprehensibility of God.

†**b.** That which is incapable of limitation. *Obs.*

1610 HEALEY *St. Aug. Citie of God* 459 His [i.e. God's] wisdome..can comprehend all incomprehensibility, by his incomprehensible comprehension.

2. Incapability of being grasped by the mind; inconceivableness, unintelligibility.

1598 FLORIO, *Incomprehensibilità*, incomprehensibilitie. **1694** SOUTH *Twelve Serm.* (1698) III. 267 [The] constant, universal sense of all Antiquity Unanimously confessing an Incomprehensibility in many of the Articles of the Christian Faith. **1734** BERKELEY *Analyst* §49 This obscurity and incomprehensibility of your metaphysics. **1836–7** SIR W. HAMILTON *Metaph.* xxvi. (1859) II. 136 The incomprehensibility of the fact of consciousness.

b. Something inconceivable or unintelligible.

1651 tr. *Life Father Sarpi* (1676) 39 This ariseth..from some incomprehensibility that is met with. **1825** COLERIDGE *Aids Refl.* (1848) I. 141 On the score of any incomprehensibilities and seeming contradictions that might be objected to it. **1850** DE QUINCEY in H. A. Page *Life* (1877) II. xvii. 69 Such a result..would have been an impossibility, and not only so but also an incomprehensibility.

incomprehensible (ɪnkɒmprɪ'hɛnsɪb(ə)l), *a.* (*sb.*) [ad. L. *incomprehensibil-is*, f. *in-* (IN-[3]) + *comprehensibilis* COMPREHENSIBLE. Cf. F. *incompréhensible* (13–14th c. in Littré).]

1. That cannot be contained or circumscribed within limits; illimitable, boundless, infinite; immense. (Chiefly *Theol.*) *arch.* (Now chiefly in allusions to the use in the Athanasian Creed.)

a **1340** HAMPOLE *Psalter* cxliv. 3 He is incomprehensibil, for na stede na thoght may vmlouke him, bot all he passis. **1382** WYCLIF *Jer.* xxxii. 19 Gret in counseil, and incomprehensible in thenking. **1538** STARKEY *England* II. i 143 We cal to Hym who, by Hys incomparabul gudnes and incomprehensybyl wisdome, made..and rulyth al thyngys. **1548–9** (Mar.) *Bk. Com. Prayer, Athan. Creed,* The father incomprehensible [L. *immensus*], the sonne incomprehensible: and the holy gost incomprehensible. **1596** SHAKS. *1 Hen. IV*, I. ii. 209 The vertue of this Iest will be, the incomprehensible lyes that this fat Rogue will tell vs, when we meete at Supper. **1596** NASHE *Saffron Walden* 42 He is asham'd of the incomprehensible corpulencie thereof [i.e. of his book]. **1667** MILTON *P.L.* VIII. 20 The Firmament..And all her numberd Starrs, that seem to rowle Spaces incomprehensible. **1772** PRIESTLEY *Inst. Relig.* (1782) II. 113 The incomprehensible greatness and perfection of the divine being. **1865** *Morn. Star* 23 May, The principal word in this well-abused creed..is 'immensus', translated 'incomprehensible'.

2. That cannot be grasped by the understanding; beyond the reach of intellect or research; unfathomable by the mind. *Obs.* or *arch.* exc. as in b.

a **1340** HAMPOLE *Psalter* cxxxviii. 5 Incomprehensibile it is made for my syn, swa that .i. may neuer wyn til contemplacioun of the thorgh my myght. **1382** WYCLIF *Rom.* xi. 33 How incomprehensyble ben his domes, and his weyis vnserchable. **1435** MISYN *Fire of Love* 14 He treuly knawes god parfitly þat hym felys incomprehensibyll & vnabyl to be knawen. **1526** TINDALE *Rom.* xi. 33 Howe incomprehensible are his iudgementes. **1651** HOBBES *Leviath.* I. viii. 39 Incident to none but those, that converse in questions of matters incomprehensible. **1738** WARBURTON *Div. Legat.* II. App. Wks. 1811 II. 211 A God whose essence indeed was incomprehensible, but his attributes..discoverable by human reason.

b. In weaker or more general sense: That cannot be understood; inconceivable, unintelligible.

1604 CAWDREY, *Incomprehensible*, that cannot be conceiued, or vnderstood. **1638** BAKER tr. *Balzac's Lett.* (vol. II) 217 The carriage at Cazal, is a thing incomprehensible. **1719** W. WOOD *Surv. Trade* 299 For so many to believe it redounds to the Good of this Kingdom.. is to me incomprehensible. **1861** DICKENS *Gt. Expect.* ix, She was perfectly incomprehensible to me. **1884** L. DAVIES in *Contemp. Rev.* Mar. 306 He must be looked at as a 'prophet', or be put aside as an incomprehensible fanatic.

†**3.** That cannot be grasped or taken hold of (physically); incapable of being caught (quot. 1607); impalpable. *Obs. rare.*

1607 TOPSELL *Four-f. Beasts* (1658) 115 Jupiter, to avoid confusion, turned both the incomprehensible beasts into stones. **1621** BURTON *Anat. Mel.* I. ii. I. ii, That the Diuell being a slender incomprehensible spirit, can easily insinuate and winde himselfe into humane bodies. **1745** tr. *Columella's Husb.* x. Pref., Of the incomprehensible smallness of sand a rope cannot be made.

B. *sb.* An incomprehensible thing or being (in sense 1 or 2).

[1548–9 (Mar.) *Bk. Com. Prayer, Athan. Creed*, There be not three incomprehensibles, nor three uncreated: but one uncreated, and one incomprehensible.] **1678** CUDWORTH *Intell. Syst.* I. ii. §v. 63 That notion..is nothing but a bundle of incomprehensibles, unconceivables, and impossibles. *a* **1711** KEN *Hymnarium* Poet. Wks. 1721 II. 18 In the Incomprehensible I rest, By humble Ignorance we know the Godhead best. **1856** DOVE *Logic Chr. Faith* Introd. §5. 12 The incomprehensibles are the absolute and the infinite (to which in a secondary sense may be added the primary and the ultimate).

incompre'hensibleness. [f. prec. + -NESS.] The quality of being incomprehensible: = INCOMPREHENSIBILITY (in senses 1 and 2).

1611 COTGR, *Incomprehensibilité*, Incomprehensibleness. **1622** DONNE *Serm.* i. 3 The Incomprehensibleness of Man's Sin. **1631** GOUGE *God's Arrows* III. §72. 317 It implieth Gods incomprehensiblenesse, immutability, and all sufficiency. **1685** BAXTER *Paraphr. N.T., 1 Cor.* viii. 2 If they knew God, or any of his Works, they would know their Incomprehensibleness. **1862** H. SPENCER *First Princ.* I. iii. §21 (1875) 67 He realizes..the utter incomprehensibleness of the simplest fact, considered in itself. **1879** GEO. ELIOT *Theo. Such* I. 19 [They] recite to me examples of feminine incomprehensibleness as typified in their wives.

incompre'hensibly, *adv.* [f. as prec. + -LY².] In an incomprehensible manner or degree; †infinitely (*obs.*); beyond mental comprehension, inconceivably, unintelligibly.

1531 ELYOT *Gov.* III. xxx, Their soules..shall be incomprehensibly rewarded of the gyuer of wisedome. **1664** H. POWER *Exp. Philos.* I. 17 How incomprehensibly subtil must the Animal Spirits be, that run to and fro in Nerves included in such prodigiously little spindle-shank'd leggs. **1807** H. MARTYN in Sargent *Life* (1881) 223 O thou most incomprehensibly glorious Saviour! **1863** MRS. WHITNEY *Faith Gartney* xxvi. 247 Do we not—and most strangely and incomprehensibly—live two lives?

incomprehension (ɪnkɒmprɪ'hɛnʃən). [f. IN-³ + COMPREHENSION; after the prec. words.] The fact of not comprehending or grasping with the mind; want of comprehension; failure to comprehend or understand.

1605 BACON *Adv. Learn.* II. x. §2 It is the remote standing or placing thereof that breedeth these mazes and incomprehensions. **1677** GALE *Crt. Gentiles* IV. 295 From our ignorance and incomprehension of the least things in Nature. **1835** MRS. CARLYLE *Lett.* I. 50 Her perfect incomprehension of everything like ceremony. **1877** BLACKMORE *Erema* vii, Sam..feigned pure incomprehension of that glance.

incomprehensive (ɪnkɒmprɪ'hɛnsɪv), *a.* [IN-³.]

I. Not comprehensive.

1. Not understanding; deficient in mental grasp.

1652 W. HARTLEY *Infant-Baptism* 10 To manifest charity where the object for reception of benefit is incomprehensive. **1777** SHERIDAN *Trip Scarb.* I. ii, Thou art an incomprehensive coxcomb. **1827** *Blackw. Mag.* XXI. 852 Like an unskilful and incomprehensive general, who, heedless of the main breast-work of the battle, pursues his wing of victory beyond limits.

2. Not inclusive; not comprising all that it should or might.

1774 WARTON *Hist. Eng. Poetry* lxii. (1840) III. 406 A most incomprehensive and inaccurate title. **1851** [implied in INCOMPREHENSIVENESS].

II. †**3.** Not to be comprehended or understood; incomprehensible. *Obs.*

1656 STANLEY *Hist. Philos.* IV. (1701) 134/2 The first are comprehensive, the second incomprehensive, the Soul being weak in the discernment thereof by reason of.. motions, mutations, and many other causes. **1735** H. BROOKE *Univ. Beauty* III. Poems, etc. 1789 I. 217 Within, while wisdom dwells replete, Incomprehensive through his sacred seat. **1791** W. TAYLOR *Lessing's Nathan* I. (1868) 14 Methinks it brings us Just so much the nearer the incomprehensive First cause of preservation.

Hence **incompre'hensively** *adv.*; **incompre'hensiveness** (in quots. in sense 2).

1846 WORCESTER cites Perry for *Incomprehensiveness*. **1851** I. TAYLOR *Wesley* (1852) 81 The incomprehensiveness of the aspect under which it took its view of human nature. *a* **1856** SIR W. HAMILTON (O.), These are received only upon trust, as incomprehensively revealed facts.

†**incomprenable,** *a. Obs.* [a. OF. *incomprenable* incomprehensible, f. *in-* (IN-³) + *comprenable* understandable, f. *comprendre* to comprehend, understand.]

= INCOMPREHENSIBLE.

1502 *Ord. Crysten Men* (W. de W. 1506) II. xviii. 132 Hyer and incomprenable mater [orig. F. *plus haulte et incomprenable matiere*] as these the whiche foloweth. *Ibid.* IV. xxix. 333 Than cometh..so grete and so incomprenable batayll of dyscease, of sorowe, and of fere.

incompressibility (ɪnkəmprɛsɪ'bɪlɪtɪ). [f. next: see -ITY: cf. F. *incompressibilité* (1755 in Hatz.-Darm.).] The quality of being incompressible.

1730–6 in BAILEY (folio). **1740** CHEYNE *Regimen* 5 Water has its Incompressibility. *c* **1790** IMISON *Sch. Art* I. 149 The incompressibility of water, proved by the Florentine experiment. **1818** *Leigh's New Pict. Lond.* 312 The longitudinal incompressibility of timber.

incompressible (ɪnkəm'prɛsɪb(ə)l), *a.* [f. IN-³ + COMPRESSIBLE: cf. F. *incompressible* (Furetière, 1690).] That cannot be compressed or squeezed into smaller compass; incapable of compression.

1730–6 in BAILEY (folio). *a* **1743** CHEYNE (J.), Hardness is the reason why water is incompressible, when the air lodged in it is exhausted. **1782** A. MONRO *Anat.* 125 The middle fluid part is incompressible. **1858** LARDNER *Hand-bk. Nat. Phil., Hydrost.* etc. iii. 46 Liquids in general are treated in hydrostatics as incompressible bodies. **1876** tr. *Wagner's Gen. Pathol.* 158 The brain is quite incompressible.

b. *fig.* (In quot. 1824 = irrepressible.)

1823 W. TAYLOR in *Monthly Mag.* LVI. 129 That higher class of writers whose popularity [is] incompressible within the scanty limits of one country. **1824** *Examiner* 370/1 His incompressible mental independence subjected him to the rancorous..calumny of those who knew him not.

Hence **incom'pressibleness** (Bailey, folio, 1730).

†**in'compt,** *a. Obs.* [ad. L. *incom(p)t-us* unadorned, rough, f. *in-* (IN-³) + *comptus* combed, dressed, neat, COMPT.] Void of neatness; inelegant. Hence †**in'comptness,** inelegance.

1631 SIR J. DODERIDGE *Eng. Lawyer* 52 What horrid and incompt words hath Logicke and Philosophy endured. **1658** BROMHALL *Treat. Specters* I. 2 His beard incompt and squalid, and his hair disorderly hanging down. **1659** O. WALKER *Instruct. Oratory* 51 Metaphors; without which the speech shews incompt and naked. **1669** BOYLE *Contn. New Exp.* II. Pref. (1682) 7 There is no need of any farther apology, to excuse the incomptness of the style.

incomputable (ɪnkəm'pjuːtəb(ə)l, ɪn'kɒmpjuːtəb(ə)l), *a.* [f. IN-³ + COMPUTABLE *a.*] That cannot be computed or reckoned; incalculable.

1606 EARL NORTHAMPTON in *True & Perfect Relat.* Hh ij a, These two Lordes are in one Regiment incomputible. **1630** J. LANE *Cont. Sqr.'s T.* (Chaucer Soc.) 199 *note*, Thincomputible summes of theire expense. **1655** *Ref. Commw. Bees* 19 An incomputable sum of money. **1802** PALEY *Nat. Theol.* xx. (1819) 314 The variety of the seed-vessels is incomputable. **1847** BUSHNELL *Chr. Nurt.* viii. (1861) 215 At some incomputable distance of time.

incomunicado, var. INCOMMUNICADO.

†**incon'cealable,** *a. Obs. rare*⁻¹. [IN-³.] That cannot be concealed.

1646 SIR T. BROWNE *Pseud. Ep.* VII. x. 359 The inconceableable imperfections of our selves..will hourely prompt us our corruptions, and lowdly tell us we are the sons of earth.

inconceivability (ɪnkənsiːvə'bɪlɪtɪ). [f. next: see -ITY.] The quality or condition of being inconceivable; inconceivableness.

1847–8 H. MILLER *First Impr.* xvii. (1857) 302 Exactly the same degree of inconceivability attaches to 'the years of the Eternal'. **1865** MILL *Exam. Hamilton* iv. (1872) 63 The inconceivability and consequent unknowability of the Unconditioned. **1882** *Macm. Mag.* XLV. 405 The inconceivability of a popular revolution [in Russia].

b. An instance of this; something that is inconceivable.

1843 MILL *Logic* III. v. §9 (1856) I. 389 The action of mind upon matter..has appeared to some thinkers to be itself the grand inconceivability. **1863** E. V. NEALE *Anal. Th. & Nat.* 219 The three points where Mr. Spencer's theory falls foul of inconceivabilities. **1865** MASSON *Rec. Brit. Philos.* 393 He has had to assume an inexplicability, an inconceivability, a paradox, as nevertheless a fact.

inconceivable (ɪnkən'siːvəb(ə)l), *a.* (*sb.*) Also 8 -ceiveable. [f. IN-³ + CONCEIVABLE. Cf. F. *inconcevable* (1617 in Hatz.-Darm.).]

1. That cannot be conceived or realized in the imagination; unthinkable, unimaginable, incredible. Often with exaggerative force for 'hardly credible', 'incalculable', 'extraordinary', of things which transcend common experience.

a **1631** DONNE in *Select.* (1840) 147 The inexpressible and inconceivable love of Christ. **1646** H. LAWRENCE *Comm. Angells* 34 With an inconceivable dexterity and quicknes. **1721** BELLAMY *Th. Trinity* Introd. 3 There can be but one God, and..his Perfections are both infinite and inconceivable. **1748** *Anson's Voy.* III. ii. 310 There were inconceivable quantities of coco-nuts. **1822** IMISON *Sc. & Art* I. 222 Light appears to move with a velocity that is truly inconceivable. **1853** J. H. NEWMAN *Hist. Sk.* (1876) II. I. iv. 229 One thing is inconceivable,—that the Turks should, as an existing nation, accept of modern civilization.

2. *spec.* As a philosophical term.

The following distinctions in meaning, though disputed by some, are generally recognized: (*a*) Opposed to the fundamental laws of thought, self-contradictory, involving a contradiction in terms. (*b*) Repugnant to recognized axioms or established laws of nature. (*c*) Involving the dissolution of ideas which have become inseparably linked in the human mind. (*d*) Involving a combination of facts, which renders a proposition incredible to the ordinary mind. (*e*) Incapable of being represented by a mental image.

1655 H. MORE *Antid. Ath.* I. iii. 10 What is inconceivable or contradictious, is nothing at all to us. **1754** SHERLOCK *Disc.* (1759) I. iii. 136 The Objection represents a Mystery as a Thing inconceivable..irreconcileable to..Reason. **1785** REID *Intell. Powers* II. xiv. (1803) I. 305 Power without substance is inconceivable. **1829** SIR W. HAMILTON *Discuss., Philos. Unconditioned* (1852) 12 The Unconditioned is incognisable and inconceivable. **1865** MILL *Exam. Hamilton* vi. (1872) 86 The first meaning of Inconceivable is, that of which the mind cannot form to itself any representation..the first and most proper meaning. *Ibid.* 90 This extends the term *inconceivable* to every combination of facts which..appears incredible. It was in this sense that the Antipodes were inconceivable. *Ibid.* 93 He [Hamilton] gives to the term a third sense. 'We conceive a thing only as we think it within or under something else'..The inconceivable in this third sense, is simply the inexplicable. **1872** H. SPENCER *Princ. Psychol.* (ed. 2) II. VII. xi. §427 Let me here define what I mean by inconceivable, as distinguished from incredible or unbelievable. An inconceivable proposition is one of which the terms cannot by any effort be brought before consciousness in that relation which the proposition asserts between them. **1875** JOWETT *Plato* (ed. 2) IV. 271 Even these inconceivable qualities of space..may be made the subject of reasoning.

B. as *sb.* A thing or quality that cannot be conceived.

1706 WATTS *Horæ Lyr.* I. 56 Nothing's found in thee But boundless inconceivables, And vast eternity! **1836–7** SIR W. HAMILTON *Metaph.* xxxviii. (1859) II. 373 They confound together these exclusive inconceivables into a single notion. **1865** MILL *Exam. Hamilton* 63 Inconceivables are incessantly becoming Conceivables as our experience becomes enlarged.

inconceivableness (ɪnkən'siːvəb(ə)lnɪs). [f. prec. + -NESS.] The quality of being inconceivable.

1661 GLANVILL *Van. Dogm.* vi. 57 Wee need go no further for an evidence of its inconceivableness. **1690** LOCKE *Hum. Und.* IV. iii. §6 Men..who because of the inconceivableness of something they find in one, throw themselves violently into the contrary hypothesis. *a* **1740** ABERNETHY in *Reid's Intell. Powers* IV. iii. (1803) II. 63 The measure of impossibility to us is inconceivableness, that of which we can have no idea, but that reflecting upon it, it appears to be nothing. **1872** H. SPENCER *Princ. Psychol.* (ed. 2) II. §426 The inconceivableness of its negation is that which shows a cognition to possess the highest rank.

inconceivably (ɪnkən'siːvəblɪ), *adv.* [f. as prec. + -LY².] In an inconceivable manner or degree. Often exaggerative for 'extraordinarily', 'extremely', 'very highly'.

1651 BAXTER *Inf. Bapt.* 55 The Church of Christ is not in a worse condition now..but inconceivably better. **1711** STEELE *Spect.* No. 167 ⁋3 The ill Consequence of these Reveries is inconceiveably great. **1748** JOHNSON *Vision Theodore* ⁋6 Amazed to find it without foundation, and placed inconceivably in emptiness and darkness. **1750** —— *Rambler* No. 41 ⁋13 Though its actual existence be inconceivably short. **1866** J. MARTINEAU *Ess.* I. 19 The book is inconceivably absurd.

†**incon'ceptible,** *a. Obs. rare.* [IN-³.] = INCONCEIVABLE.

1677 HALE *Prim. Orig. Man.* 86 It is inconceptible how any such man that hath stood the shock of an eternal duration..should after be corrupted or altered. *Ibid.* 289 As it is utterly impossible that mankind should be without a beginning, so it is utterly inconceptible that he should have any other original but this.

†**incon'ception.** *Obs. rare.* [IN-³.] Want of conception or understanding.

1761 BP. HILDESLEY in *Richardson's Corr.* (1804) V. 153 As to the ladies, they may be allowed to understand no harm in what they read: but our sex, I doubt, have no pretensions to such a plea of inconception.

†**incon'cerned,** *a. Obs. rare*⁻⁰. [IN-³.] Unconcerned. Hence †**incon'cernedly** *adv.*; †**incon'cernedness.**

1688 *Ess. Magistracy* in *Harl. Misc.* I. 7 The parting with it tamely would argue the greatest stupidity and inconcernedness. **1695** J. SAGE *Article* Wks. 1844 I. 239 They inconcernedly quitted their pretensions.

†**incon'cerning,** *a. Obs. rare.* [f. IN-³ + CONCERNING *ppl. a.*] That does not concern one, that does not matter; unimportant.

1642 FULLER *Holy & Prof. St.* II. ix. 86 He is carefull not to entitle violence in indifferent and inconcerning matters to be zeal. **1650** BAXTER *Saints' R.* I. viii. (1662) 136 This Conviction is not met by meer Argumentation, as a man is convinced of some inconcerning Consequence by dispute.

†**incon'cernment.** *Obs. rare*⁻¹. [f. IN-³ + CONCERNMENT.] The fact of not being concerned or affected.

1671 *True Nonconf.* Pref., To contradict his asserting of Religious inconcernment in these matters.

†**incon'ciliable,** *a. Obs. rare.* Also -cilable, -cileable. [f. IN-³ + CONCILIABLE *a.* Cf. F. *inconciliable* (1752 in *Dict. Trévoux*).] Incapable of being conciliated or reconciled; irreconcilable.

1643 MILTON *Divorce* I. xiv, To kindle one another, not with the fire of love, but with a hatred inconcileable. **1661** R. L'ESTRANGE *State Divinity* 38 Their Principles are Inconciliable, save by the stronger malice they bear to the Government then to each other. **1694** —— *Fables* xlv. (1714) 59 An Alliance among those that Nature her self has divided by an Inconcilable disagreement.

†**incon'cinn, -e,** *a. Obs. rare.* [f. IN-³ + CONCINNE. Cf. L. *inconcinnus* awkward, unpolished.] Not adjusted or adapted; incongruous.

1660 H. MORE *Myst. Godl.* V. xvi. 183 To omit what is very inconcinne. **1678** CUDWORTH *Intell. Syst.* I. i. §16. 16 Asclepiades..supposed all the corporeal world to be made ..of Dissimilar and inconcinn Moleculæ, i.e. Atoms of different Magnitude and Figures.

† **incon'cinnate**, *a. Obs. rare.* Also 6 *erron.* -ite. [f. IN-^{3} + CONCINNATE *ppl. a.*] **a.** Awkward, clumsy. **b.** Not adapted; unsuitable.

1533 CATH. PARR tr. *Erasm. Com. Crede* 79 b, The very inconcinnite and unhandsome ioyninge or hangynge togeder of the speche and oration. **1657** TOMLINSON *Renou's Disp.* 495 Latter Writers..have rejected some [medicaments] as inconcinnate.

Hence † **incon'cinnately** *adv.*, inelegantly.

1623 COCKERAM II, Ilfauour'dly done, *Inconcinnately, Inarteficially.*

incon'cinnity. *Obs.* or *arch.* [ad. L. *inconcinnitās* inelegance, impropriety, f. *inconcinn-us*: see INCONCINN and -ITY.] Want of concinnity, congruousness, or proportion; inelegance, awkwardness; impropriety, unsuitableness.

1616 BULLOKAR, *Inconcinnitie*, vnaptnes: ill agreeing, disproportion. **1630** PRYNNE *Anti-Armin.* 160 This Text in respect of the inconcinnity of this phrase, and its incongruity to the Elect..cannot be aptly accommodated to them. *a* **1655** VINES *Lord's Supp.* (1677) 396 He hath corrected all inconcinnity by the glass, and composed his dress. **1664** H. MORE *Myst. Iniq.* 357 So are there also several Inconcinnities in it, and even Historical Defects. **1857** TRENCH *Defic. Eng. Dict.* 18 As..other little-used words are introduced, there is at least an inconcinnity in omitting these. **1861** —— *Ep. Seven Ch.* (ed. 2) 15 There is a certain apparent inconcinnity in the abstract *βασιλείαν* joined with the concrete *ἱερεῖς*.

† **incon'cinnous**, *a. Obs.* [f. L. *inconcinn-us* inelegant, absurd + -OUS: cf. CONCINNOUS.]

1. Incongruous.

1662 *Life & Death Sir H. Vane* 50 How grossly inconcinnous must it now appear to the common reason of all mankind that such as take upon them to be magistrates.. should give the rule to all other's consciences.

2. *Mus.* Inharmonious, contrary to the principles of harmony.

inconcinnous discord (or ***interval***): a discord or dissonant interval which cannot be used in harmony.

1727–41 CHAMBERS *Cycl.* s.v. *Concinnous*, Discords are distinguished into *concinnous* and *inconcinnous* intervals. **1760** STILES in *Phil. Trans.* LI. 716 Without one or other of which circumstances, the composition was held inconcinnous. **1811** REES *Cycl.* s.v., Inconcinnous intervals ..are such as are a comma flatter or sharper than perfect.

† **incon'cludency.** *Obs. rare*$^{-1}$. [f. next: see -ENCY.] The quality of being inconclusive; an instance of this, an inconclusive argument.

1654 HAMMOND *Answ. Animadv. Ignat.* ii. §1. 31 That learned Grammarian did never more passionately *δουλεύειν ὑποθέσει*, then in this heap of inconcludencies.

† **incon'cludent**, *a. Obs.* [f. IN-^{3} + CONCLUDENT.] = next.

1671 *True Nonconf.* 20 Your insinuation is General and inconcludent. *a* **1677** BARROW *Pope's Suprem.* (1687) 235 The Instances alledged..are inconcludent and invalid. **1726** AYLIFFE *Parergon* 447 An inconcludent Proof is so far from being good Evidence, that it renders the Matter still more doubtful and uncertain.

† **incon'cluding**, *a. Obs.* [f. IN-^{3} + CONCLUDING *ppl. a.*] That furnishes no ground for a conclusion; inconclusive.

a **1644** CHILLINGWORTH *Serm. Ps.* xiv. 1 §3 Which inference of his were weak and inconcluding. **1659** PEARSON *Creed* (1839) 72 [They] made use of very frivolous and inconcluding arguments. *a* **1677** BARROW *Disc. Unity Church* in *Pope's Suprem.* (1687) 316 The reasons alledged.. are insufficient and inconcluding.

incon'clusible, *a. rare.* [f. IN-^{3} + CONCLUSIBLE.] Not capable of being concluded; endless.

1660 S. FISHER *Rusticks Alarm* Wks. (1679) 439 That inconclusible Controversie, and Endless Entercourse, which I see J. O. and others are there engaged in. **1930** T. S. ELIOT *Ash-Wednesday* II. 18 Conclusions of all that Is inconclusible.

inconclusion (ɪnkən'klu:ʒən). [f. IN-^{3} + CONCLUSION. Cf. It. *inconclusione* 'an vncertaintie' (Florio, 1598).] The condition of reaching no conclusion; an inconclusive result, an unwarranted conclusion.

1847 FR. A. KEMBLE *Rec. Later Life* (1882) III. 289, I float comfortably enough over infinite abysses of inconclusion. **1886** TUPPER *My Life as Author* 380 It seems to me quite an inconclusion to give to the spirits of the dead..the seemingly miraculous powers exhibited.

inconclusive (ɪnkən'klu:sɪv), *a.* [IN-^{3}.]

1. Not conclusive in argument or evidence; that does not bring to an end (a doubt, dispute, or inquiry); not decisive or convincing.

1690 [implied in INCONCLUSIVENESS]. **1707** A. COLLINS *Reply Clarke's Def.* R., The author of the objection to that argument still thinks it inconclusive, and proposes to show its inconclusiveness in the following papers. **1838** T. THOMSON *Chem. Org. Bodies* 969 The experiments of Duhamel and Tillet are equally inconclusive. **1855** MILMAN *Lat. Chr.* XI. vi. (1864) VI. 108 Long and inconclusive debates took place on the legality of a Papal abdication. **1879** FROUDE *Cæsar* xi. 120 When evidence is inconclusive, probability becomes argument.

b. Given to inconclusion; undecided.

1836 SIR H. TAYLOR *Statesman* xxi. 142 He whose mind is not seasonably inconclusive, and cannot bear with a reasonable term of suspense, will either get wrong, or get right more tardily by means of after-thought and correction.

2. Not conclusive in action; reaching no final result or producing no conclusive effect.

1841 ELPHINSTONE *Hist. Ind.* I. 563 Even his Indian operations..are so far from displaying any signs of system or combination, that their desultory and inconclusive nature would lead us to deny him a comprehensive intellect.

incon'clusively, *adv.* [f. prec. + -LY^{2}.] In an inconclusive manner.

1755 in JOHNSON. **1863** MRS. C. CLARKE *Shaks. Char.* iii. 68 He reasons clearly and consistently, it may be inconclusively.

incon'clusiveness. [f. as prec. + -NESS.] The quality of being inconclusive.

1690 LOCKE *Hum. Und.* IV. xvii. §4 The weakness and inconclusiveness of a long artificial and plausible discourse. **1754** EDWARDS *Freed. Will* Concl. (ed. 4) 401 The inconclusiveness of the arguments he offers. **1856** FROUDE *Hist. Eng.* I. 324 The beauty of the form was insufficient to disguise the inconclusiveness of the reasoning.

incon'clusivism. *nonce-wd.* [f. as prec. + -ISM.] A theory or doctrine that conclusive evidence on metaphysical or religious questions is unattainable.

a **1866** J. GROTE *Exam. Util. Philos.* Introd. (1870) 9, I have no wish to originate any school of my own, and yet have strongly denounced..the writing merely to profess inconclusivism and scepticism.

† **incon'coct**, *a. Obs.* [f. IN-^{3} + CONCOCT *a.*] = next.

1596 BARROUGH *Meth. Physick* VI. ix. (1639) 366 If the same unctuosity doth more abound in the yonger wood, it is more inconcoct and excrementous. **1626** BACON *Sylva* §838 While the Body to bee Conuerted and Altered, is too strong for the Efficient..it is (all that while) Crude and Inconcoct; And the Processe is to be called Crudity and Inconcoction.

† **incon'cocted**, *a. Obs.* [IN-^{3}.] Not concocted; not fully digested or matured; raw, crude; not softened by ripening; unconcocted.

1605 TIMME *Quersit.* I. xiii. 60 By reason of his soliditie and hardness inconcocted. **1620** VENNER *Via Recta* viii. 190 They remaining crude and inconcocted in the body..doe at length settle and produce morbificall affects. **1646** SIR T. BROWNE *Pseud. Ep.* VI. xii. 338 Divers plants containe..an austere and inconcocted roughnesse, as Sloes, Medlers and Quinces. **1677** HALE *Prim. Orig. Man.* I. i. 23 Better..than when I was a Child, and had my organical Parts less digested and inconcocted.

† **incon'coction.** *Obs.* [f. IN-^{3} + CONCOCTION.] The fact or condition of being unconcocted or undigested.

1626 H. MASON *Epicure's Fast* v. 42 Let Fasts be moderate; lest..they weaken the stomacke and requiring greater refection afterward, they break out into crudity and inconcoction. **1626** [see INCONCOCT]. **1656** STANLEY *Hist. Philos.* v. (1701) 255/1 The end of Concoction..is mutation of the Essence, as when food is converted into flesh and blood..Inconcoction is an Imperfection in the opposite passive qualities, proceeding from defect of heat.

incon'crete, *a.* Now *rare.* [ad. late L. *inconcrēt-us* (*c* 320), f. *in-* (IN-^{3}) + *concrēt-us* CONCRETE.] Not concrete; abstract; immaterial.

a **1626** BP. ANDREWES *Serm.* (1841) I. 88 There is not..a more pure, simple, inconcrete procreation than that whereby the mind conceiveth the word within it. **1659** STANLEY *Hist. Philos.* XIII. (1701) 558/2 The Divine Nature, which is inconcrete, and, by reason of its Tenuity, cannot be touched nor struck. **1876** RUSKIN *Fors Clav.* lxvi. 180 Tell me one or two of the inconcrete results of separate evolution.

† **incon'culcate**, *v. Obs. rare.* [f. IN-^{2} + CONCULCATE *v.*] *trans.* To inculcate persistently.

1610 DONNE *Pseudo-Martyr* Advt. to Rdr., An ordinary Instrument of his..had oppugned his Lordships Booke, and iterated and inconculcated those his oppositions.

† **incon'current**, *a. Obs. rare*$^{-1}$. [IN-^{3}.] Not concurrent; = next.

1651 HOBBES *Leviath.* II. xxv. 136 Retarded also by the inconcurrent judgements, and endeavours of them that drive it.

† **incon'curring**, *a. Obs. rare*$^{-1}$. [IN-^{3}.] Not concurring; not acting in combination towards some end.

1646 SIR T. BROWNE *Pseud. Ep.* I. iv. 16 Deriving effects not only from inconcurring causes, but things devoid of all efficiencie whatever.

† **incon'cuss**, *a. Obs.* [ad. L. *inconcussus* unshaken, f. *in-* (IN-^{3}) + *concussus*, pa. pple. of *concutĕre* to dash together, shake violently.] = next.

1542 BECON *Pathw. Prayer* in *Early Wks.* (Parker Soc.) 144 Prayer is..the inconcusse, unshaken, and puissant custody or watch of the faithful. **1646** BUCK *Rich. III*, 60 An inconcusse and great resolution.

† **incon'cussed**, *a. Obs.* [f. as prec. + -ED^{1}.] Unshaken, firm, stable.

1432–50 tr. *Higden* (Rolls) I. 71 Trewely the fame of Paradise hathe stonde as inconcussede by vj. ml. yeres and more. *c* **1450** tr. *De Imitatione* III. xxxviii. 108 For so he may abide oon & þe same inconcussyd. **1623** COCKERAM, *Inconcussed*, stable, not to be shaken.

† **incon'cussible**, *a. Obs.* Also -able. [a. obs. F. *inconcussible*, f. *in-* (IN-^{3}) + **concussible*, f. L. *concuss-*, ppl. stem of *concutĕre* to shake violently: see -IBLE.] That cannot be shaken; firmly fixed, stable.

1589 PUTTENHAM *Eng. Poesie* II. xi[i.]. (Arb.) 113 As the roundell or Spheare is appropriat to the heauens..the Triangle to the ayre, and the Lozange to the water: so is the square for his inconcussable steadinesse likened to the earth. **1609** BELL *Theoph. & Remig.* 46 A pillar that is sublime, straight, inconcussible. **1715** M. DAVIES *Athen. Brit.* I. Pref. 32 To this inconcussable Maxim in our Legal Israel, the Sophistical Jesuit..could say nothing at all.

incondensable (ɪnkən'dɛnsəb(ə)l), *a.* Also -ible. [f. IN-^{3} + CONDENSABLE *a.*, which see in reference to the prevalent erroneous spelling *-ible.*] That cannot be condensed; incapable of being made more dense or compact; *spec.* incapable of being reduced to the liquid or solid condition.

1736 *Elaboratory laid open* 108 The tin pipe, for carrying off the incondensible fumes. **1812** SIR H. DAVY *Chem. Philos.* 85 Steam at 500 degrees of Fahrenheit would be equally incondensible with air at a range of temperature such as we can command below our common temperatures. **1828** WEBSTER, *Incondensable.* **1864** H. SPENCER *Biol.* I. 5 Carbonic oxide..is an incondensible gas.

Hence **incondensa'bility** (*erron.* **-ibility**), the quality of being incondensable.

1828 WEBSTER, *Incondensability.*

† **incon'dign**, *a. Obs.* [f. IN-^{3} + CONDIGN.] Unworthy, undeserving, undeserved.

c **1450** LYDG. & BURGH *Secrees* 1532 This lady lyst nat to parte the tresourys Of hir substaunce to my Childhood incondigne.

incondite (ɪn'kɒndɪt), *a.* [ad. L. *incondit-us* disordered, uncouth, f. *in-* (IN-^{3}) + *conditus*, pa. pple. of *condĕre* to put together.]

1. Consisting of parts which are ill arranged; ill constructed, ill composed: said esp. of literary and artistic compositions.

1634 JACKSON *Creed* VII. x. §2 Such incondite figures, or confused fancies as are thereon painted. **1708** J. PHILIPS *Cyder* II. (1807) 92 Now sportive youth Carol incondite rhythms with suiting notes. **1794** GIFFORD *Baviad* (1811) 48 O deign, To cast a glance on this incondite strain. **1832** AUSTIN *Jurispr.* (1879) II. xxxv. 619 An incondite collection or heap of single and insulated rules. **1871** CARLYLE in *Mrs. C.'s Lett.* I. 75 Plenty of incondite stuff accordingly there was [in the lecture].

2. Unformed, crude; without delicacy of finish; rude, unpolished, unrefined.

1539 TAVERNER *Gard. Wysed.* II. (1545) 2 a, I muste desyre you..to pardon myne incondite and grosse phrase. **1657** TRAPP *Comm. Ps.* cxvi. 1 An inarticulate incondite voice. **1822–34** *Good's Study Med.* (ed. 4) I. 434 Something far more rude and incondite must have preceded and paved the way for it [the alphabet]. **1871** KINGSLEY *At Last* II. xv. 262 The Negresses..forgot themselves, kicked up their legs, shouted to the bystanders, and were altogether incondite.

3. Rendering L. *incondita* qualifying *vox* 'utterance', and applied to interjections representing mere natural utterances.

[**1549** LILLY *Brev. Inst. Grammaticae Cognosc.*, Interjectio est pars orationis quae sub incondita voce subito perrumpentem animi affectum demonstrat..An interiection is a parte of speche whyche betokeneth a sodayne passion of the mynde under an unperfect voyce.] **1845** STODDART in *Encycl. Metrop.* (1847) I. 186/1 These variations then depend not on the articulation, but on the intonation; that is..on the elevation or depression of voice in pronouncing it: but this is not peculiar to the interjection *oh!* or to the 'incondite' interjections generally; for the same may be observed of any nouns or verbs used interjectionally.

Hence **in'conditely** *adv.*, in a crude or undigested condition; in an ill-constructed form.

1822–34 *Good's Study Med.* (ed. 4) I. 141 Its [the stomach's] fluids are poured forth too sparingly or too inconditely. **1880** F. HALL *Doctor Indoctus* 35 The rule here inconditely laid down admits, as worded, of a tedious variety of interpretations.

† **incon'ditional**, *a. Obs. rare*$^{-1}$. [f. IN-^{3} + CONDITIONAL.] Without qualifying or limiting conditions; unconditional.

1646 SIR T. BROWNE *Pseud. Ep.* I. iv. 15 When from that which is but true in a qualified sense an inconditionall and absolute verity is inferred.

Hence † **inconditio'nality**, the quality of being unconditional.

1696 LORIMER *Goodwin's Disc.* vii. 133 To answer the aforesaid Sophism taken from the Inconditionality and Independency of God's Will.

inconditionate (ɪnkən'dɪʃənət), *a.* (*sb.*) [f. IN-^{3} + CONDITIONATE: cf. mod.F. *inconditionné.*] Not subject to or limited by conditions; unconditioned.

1654 J. P. *Tyrants & Protectors* 28 The power of Government..is fiduciary, and not inconditionate. **1698** NORRIS *Pract. Disc.* IV. 148 The First of these is wholely Absolute and Inconditionate (there being nothing required of us to make sin pardonable to us).

B. *sb. Philos.* An entity which is unconditioned; a form under which the Unconditioned is conceived.

1829 SIR W. HAMILTON *Discuss., Philos. Unconditioned* (1853) 15 The Conditioned is the mean between two extremes,—two inconditionates. **1882** VEITCH *Life Hamilton* 230 The Unconditioned and the species, or Inconditionates which it contains—viz., Absolute and Infinite.

Hence **incon'ditionateness**, the quality of being unconditioned.

1693 BEVERLEY *True St. Gosp. Truth* (title-p.), The Inconditionateness of the Gospel Salvation.

inconducive (ınkən'djuːsıv), *a. rare.* [IN-³.] Not conducive, not tending towards an end or result; unconducive.

1848 *Tait's Mag.* XV. 354 Habits are formed inconducive to good government. **1867** C. J. SMITH *Syn. & Antonyms* s.v. *Applicable*, Inconducive, Inapplicable.

Inconel ('ınkənɛl). A proprietary name of various alloys which contain nickel (70–80%), chromium (12–19%), and iron (usually between 5% and 8%), and are useful for their strength and their resistance to corrosion and oxidation at high temperatures.

1933 *Official Gaz.* (U.S. Patent Office) 12 Sept. 263/2 International Nickel Company, Inc... *Inconel.* For Nickel Alloys and Alloys of Nickel, Chromium, and Iron. Claims use since Nov. 25, 1932. **1935** *Chem. Abstr.* XXIX. 7257 (*heading*) Corrosion resistance of nickel, of copper-nickel alloys, of nickel silver and of Inconel. **1938** *Jrnl. R. Aeronaut. Soc.* XLII. 962 A further development is the alloy 'Inconel' containing about 80 per cent. Ni., 13 per cent. Cr., 7 per cent. Fe., which can be hardened by work, but not by heat-treatment... Its resistance to heat-oxidation at very high temperatures finds application in silencers and exhaust manifolds. **1966** *McGraw-Hill Encycl. Sci. & Technol.* VII. 265/2 The Inconels (Nimonics in England) are advantageous in cyclic heating and cooling service where large temperature gradients exist. **1967** D. FISHLOCK *New Materials* ii. 23 Inconel X-750 (75 per cent nickel) is today used extensively for the structure of the 4104 m.p.h. X-15 rocket aircraft..whose skin..is designed to withstand 650°C.

inconey: see INCONY.

in'confidence. *rare.* [IN-³.] Want of confidence, distrust.

1626 W. SCLATER *Exp. 2 Thess.* (1629) 165 There may be obserued in many..inconfidence of at least, Timely Reuocation. **1811** *Henry & Isabella* I. 215 She looked with inconfidence on every one.

†**in'confident**, *a. Obs. rare.* [IN-³.]

1. Not confident, not trusting, distrustful.

1667 WATERHOUSE *Fire Lond.* 132 Whose project it is to keep us jealous and inconfident each of other.

2. Unfaithful, untrue to a trust. (Cf. CONFIDENT 6.)

1603 H. CROSSE *Vertues Commw.* (1878) 95 He is inconfident to whom mony is deliuered vpon trust to paie to an other, and doth either keep it back all, or deliuer but halfe.

†**incon'finable**, *a. Obs. rare.* [IN-³.] That cannot be confined; unconfinable.

1606 DEKKER *News fr. Hell* C ij, The raptures of that fierie and inconfinable Italian spirit. *a* **1641** BP. MOUNTAGU *Acts & Mon.* (1642) 494 Christ..had..transcendent, inconfinable power and authority.

†**incon'firmed**, *a. Obs. rare.* [IN-³.] Not confirmed; not become firm or strong.

1646 SIR T. BROWNE *Pseud. Ep.* IV. xii. 216 In the first septenarie doe most die..the infirmities that attend it are so many, and the body that receives them so inconfirmed.

†**incon'form**, *a. Obs.* [f. IN-³ + CONFORM *a.*] Not conformed *to*.

1659 GAUDEN *Tears Ch. Eng.* III. xi. 291 A way most charitable..and no way inconform to the will of God in his Word. **1663** CHARLETON *Chor. Gigant.* 26 Inconform to the Rule of the Close order.

inconformable (ınkən'fɔːməb(ə)l), *a.* [IN-³.] Not conformable; unconformable.

1. Not according in form, pattern, position, or character (*to*).

1612 STURTEVANT *Metallica* (1854) 81 *R.* Define an inconformable inuention. *A.* An inuention.. whose Protoplast..cannot be conformed to any former inuention in use. **1665** J. WEBB *Stone-Heng* (1725) 169 In Position not much inconformable to that in our Antiquity. **1670** *Famous Conclave wherein Clement VIII was elected* 24 There was nothing more detestable in a man, nor inconformable to a Christian, than ingratitude. **1670** G. H. *Hist. Cardinals* I. II. 34 To evince the antiquity of their Rights, which are in many things inconformable with the Roman. **1864** BOWEN *Logic* xii. 413 So strong is our assurance of the universality of the principle..that, when an anomalous or inconformable instance actually arises, we seek at once for the means of eliminating it, or explaining it away.

2. Of persons: Not disposed or wont to conform; of incompliant disposition or practice: esp., in *Eng. Hist.*, Not conforming to the usages of the established Church.

1633 AMES *Agst. Cerem.* II. 192 This calumniation concerning some inconformable suffered for a time. *a* **1662** HEYLIN *Laud* (1668) 201 Two of the Lecturers in that Diocess..they found obstinately inconformable to the Kings Directions. **1861** W. S. PERRY *Hist. Ch. Eng.* I. xvi. 592 There are scarcely any inconformable or troublesome ministers noted in this report.

†**incon'formist.** *Obs.* [f. IN-³ + CONFORMIST.] One who does not conform in matters religious or ecclesiastical; = NONCONFORMIST.

1633 AMES *Agst. Cerem.* II. 196 The Inconformists are by him tossed (as it were) in a blancket. **1634** CANNE *Necess. Separ.* (1849) 198, I will here lay down some few syllogisms, entirely made up between the Inconformists and Conformists. **1658** MANTON *Exp. Jude* vers. 22–3 The late bishops' courts were chiefly bent against the godly; a drunkard and an adulterer found more favour than a goodly inconformist.

inconformity (ınkən'fɔːmıtı). [f. IN-³ + CONFORMITY.] Want of conformity.

1. Want of correspondence in form or manner; want of agreement in character; dissimilarity; want of conformity *to* (†*unto*) or *with* a pattern.

1625 BACON *Ess., Innovations* (Arb.) 527 New Things peece not so well; But though they helpe by their vtility, yet they trouble by their Inconformity. **1661** R. L'ESTRANGE *Interest Mistaken* 65 We find an Inconformity of Practise to Profession. **1665** J. WEBB *Stone-Heng* (1725) 205 The Dissimilitude or Inconformity betwixt Stone-Heng and the Monuments in..Denmark. **1711** STRYPE *Parker* an. 1573 (R.), Neither did he, I believe, ever endeavour for it, knowing his own inconformity. **1890** J. MARTINEAU *Seat Author. Relig.* v. i. 593 The chief difference..lies in the conformity or inconformity of the seeming fact with expectations.

2. Refusal or omission to conform *to* some rule, standard, or fashion; want of conformity *with* a guide or pattern.

1594 HOOKER *Eccl. Pol.* IV. iv. §1 [abridging Cartwright, who, however, has not the word] Utter inconformity therefore with the church of Rome in these things, is the best and surest policie which the Church can vse. **1597** —— *E.P.* v. lxxxi. §11 It being better that the Church should want altogether the benefit of such mens labours, than indure the mischiefe of their inconformitie to good Lawes. **1651** HOBBES *Leviath.* I. xv. 74 Conformity or Inconformity of Manners to Reason. **1681** MANTON *Serm. Ps.* cxix. 80 Wks. 1872 VII. 346 God..taketh notice of our conformity and inconformity to his will.

3. *spec.* Want of conformity in worship; refusal to conform to the religious worship or ecclesiastical polity established or publicly recognized; = NONCONFORMITY.

1633 LAUD *Wks.* (1853) V. 320 His lordship certifies that he hath suspended a lecturer for his inconformity. **1644** BP. ST. ASAPH *Let. to Laud* in *Hist. Nonconf. Wales* (1861) 10 They were not any where troubled with Inconformity. **1667** J. CORBET *Disc. Relig. Eng.* 23 As for the Ministers of this Perswasion, some have called them Fools for their Inconformity. **1824** SOUTHEY *Bk. of Ch.* (1841) 447 Inconformity had become well nigh general. **1861** W. S. PERRY *Hist. Ch. Eng.* I. xiv. 510 We might almost imagine that..there was scarce any disaffection, inconformity, or difference of opinion prevalent.

b. An instance of this; a practice not in conformity with the recognized form of religion.

a **1662** HEYLIN *Laud* I. (1668) 124 All Calvinians are not to be counted as Puritans also; whose practices many of them abhor, and whose inconformities they detest.

inconfused (ınkən'fjuːzd), *a.* [f. IN-³ + CONFUSED; after L. *inconfūs-us.*] Not confused; free from confusion or mixture of the elements or essential parts.

1626 BACON *Sylva* §192 All the curious Diuersitie of Articulate Sounds, of the Voice of Man, or Birds, will enter at a small Cranny, Inconfused. **1647** HERRICK *Noble Numb., To God* (1869) 413 God's undivided, One in Persons Three, And Three in Inconfused Unity. **1660** STANLEY *Hist. Philos.* IX. (1701) 385/2 The Diastematick..manifests the mutation which is in all its parts which is inconfused and divided and disjoined.

Hence **incon'fusedly** *adv.*

1852 BP. FORBES *Nicene Cr.* 203 The union of the two natures in Jesus Christ has taken place, neither by disorder ..nor by confusion..but by synthesis; or personally,.. immutably, inconfusedly, unalterably, inherently, inseparably, in two perfect natures in one person.

†**incon'fusible**, *a. Obs. rare.* [ad. L. *inconfūsibilis* (Vulgate), f. *in-* (IN-³) + *confūsibilis* CONFUSIBLE. So F. *inconfusible* (15th c. in Godef.).] Incapable of being confused.

1565 CALFHILL *Answ. Treat. Crosse* (Parker Soc.) 140 He hath confounded, by confusion most wicked, that uniting and knitting together of the two natures, which are inconfusible, and in themselves distinct. **1652** BENLOWES *Theoph.* Ded. 22 The Immaculate Earth of the Humanity, Inseparable, Inconfusible, Inconvertible.

†**incon'fusion.** *Obs. rare*⁻¹. [f. IN-³ + CONFUSION, after L. *inconfūs-us.*] Absence of confusion; the condition of being unconfused.

1626 BACON *Sylva* §224 The Cause of the Confusion in Sounds and the Inconfusion in Species Visible; is, For that the Sight worketh in Right Lines, and maketh seuerall Cones.

†**incon'futable**, *a. Obs. rare*⁻¹. [IN-³.] Not confutable; not to be confuted.

1679 PENN *Addr. Prot.* II. 84 To which Malice and Slander he returned this Inconfutable Answer.

Hence †**incon'futably** *adv.*, in a way not to be confuted.

1664 JER. TAYLOR *Dissuas. Popery* i. §1. (1686) 6 The writings of the fathers were..full of proper opinions and such variety of sayings, that both sides eternally and inconfutably shall bring sayings for themselves respectively.

incongealable (ınkən'dʒiːləb(ə)l), *a.* ? *Obs.* Also **incongelable.** [f. IN-³ + CONGEALABLE: cf. F. *incongelable* (Cotgr. 1611).] Incapable of being congealed.

1623 COCKERAM, *Incongealable*, not to be frozen. **1665** BOYLE *Exper. Hist. Cold* iii. Wks. 1772 II. 517 This train oil ..swimming upon the surface of the water, and being incongealable by the cold, protects the subjacent water from the freezing violence of the cold.

Hence **incon'gealableness.**

1727 in BAILEY vol. II; also in some mod. Dicts.

†**incon'generous**, *a. Obs.* [IN-³.] Not of the same kind; the opposite of CONGENEROUS 1.

1646 SIR T. BROWNE *Pseud. Ep.* II. iii. 69 Certaine it is.. that the Loadstone will not attract even steele it selfe that is candent, much lesse the incongenerous body of glasse being fired.

incongenial (ınkən'dʒiːnıəl), *a.* [IN-³.] Not congenial; uncongenial. Hence **incongeni'ality.**

1797 HAIGHTON in *Phil. Trans.* LXXXVII. 184 The impression which these experiments at first made on my mind, was..not altogether incongenial to my wish. **1847** A. BENNIE *Disc.* 42 A sphere of usefulness that was by no means incongenial to his tastes. **1864** WEBSTER, *Incongeniality.*

†**in'congrue**, *a. Obs.* Also 5–6 -gru. [a. F. *incongru*, -*grue* (14th c. in Hatz.-Darm.), ad. L. *incongru-us*: see INCONGRUOUS.] = INCONGRUOUS.

1398 TREVISA *Barth. De P.R.* II. ii. (1495) 27 Yf the nominatyf caas & the verbe discord in person and in nombre, thenne the reason is incongrue. **1490** CAXTON *How to Die* 18 It oughte not to seme to none incongrue ne meruellous. *c* **1560** *Phylogamus* in *Skelton's Wks.* (1862) I. p. cxxxii, Thou wrytest thynges dyffuse, Incongrue and confuse, Obfuscate and obtuse. **1581** *Act 23 Eliz.* c. 3 §2 No Fine..shall be reversed..by any Writ of Error, for false or incongrue Latin.

Hence †**in'congruly** *adv. Obs.*, incongruously.

1483 *Cath. Angl.* 74/2 [In]congruly; [Lat.] *incongrue.*

incongruence (ın'kɒŋgruːəns). [ad. L. *incongruentia* (Tertullian), f. *incongruent-em* INCONGRUENT: see -ENCE.] Want of congruence; disagreement, incongruity.

1610 HEALEY *St. Aug. Citie of God* 900 Wherefore there shalbe no cause of dislike through incongruence of parts. *a* **1691** BOYLE *Hist. Fluidity* xix. Wks. 1772 I. 391 The humidity of a body..depends chiefly upon the congruity or incongruence of the component particles of the liquor in reference to the pores of those particular bodies, that it touches. **1845** *Blackw. Mag.* LVII. 381 This, not with any incongruence or disharmony. **1885** R. BRIDGES *Nero* I. ii, Foreseeing how The incongruence of time and place, the audience Of drunken sots would turn my best to worst.

in'congruency. ? *Obs.* [f. as prec.: see -ENCY.] = prec.

1604 CAWDREY *Table Alph.*, *Incongruencie*, want of agreement. **1684** T. BURNET *Th. Earth* II. 166 This is the first argument against the reciprocal production of mountains and the sea, their incongruency or disproportion.

incongruent (ın'kɒŋgruːənt), *a.* [ad. L. *incongruent-em*, f. *in-* (IN-³) + *congruent-em* CONGRUENT.] Not congruent; disagreeing, unsuitable, incongruous.

1531 ELYOT *Gov.* I. xiii, It shall nat be incongruent to our mater to shewe what profite may be taken by the diligent reding of auncient poetes. **1603** DEKKER *Grissil* (Shaks. Soc.) 21, I bought them of a penurious cordwainer, and they are the most incongruent that e'er I ware. **1655** *Fulke's Meteors* Observ. 172 Lead is an incongruent and malignant Metal to all others. **1772** SIR J. REYNOLDS *Disc.* v. (1876) 365 A harsh jarring of incongruent principles. *a* **1864** HAWTHORNE *Amer. Note-Bks.* (1879) II. 168 Things most incongruent to his hereditary stomach. **1893** H. WALKER *3 Cent. Scot. Lit.* I. i. 8 There is the additional improbability of incongruent circumstances. **1940** *Mind* XLIX. 349 Evident empirical facts (*i.e.*, rotational motion and incongruent counterparts) which Newton and Kant designated as rendering the relational theory untenable. **1951** A. GARDINER *Theory of Speech & Lang.* (ed. 2) 232 Grammar is, in the main, concerned with linguistic form in congruent function, and treats of incongruent function only in so far as this is building up new forms in which such function will be congruent. **1966** *Amer. Philos. Q.* III. 179/1 Kant made use of incongruent counterparts to establish a theory of space. **1972** *Jrnl. Social Psychol.* LXXXVI. 121 When a man's life style is incongruent with the demands of a task he must perform he will experience stress.

in'congruently, *adv.* [f. prec. + -LY².] In an incongruent manner; incongruously.

1568 C. WATSON *Polyb.* 19 a, Oftentimes of this fashion erreth Philinus incongruently and without reson. **1632** MASSINGER & FIELD *Fatal Dowry* IV. i, What fouler object in the world, than to see a young, fair, handsome beauty unhandsomely dighted, and incongruently accoutred? **1933** *Amer. Jrnl. Sci.* XXV. 277 Fayalite melts incongruently with separation of iron. **1970** *Nature* 19 Dec. 1144/1 The ruby laser permits fairly fast deposition rates even of 'difficult' materials and, in particular, allows preparation of thin films of compounds that normally evaporate incongruently.

incongruity (ınkən'gruːıtı). [ad. med.L. *incongruitās*, f. *in-* (IN-³) + *congruitās* CONGRUITY: cf. F. *incongruité* (1529 in Hatz.-Darm.) perh. the immediate source.] The

quality, condition, or fact of being incongruous; an instance of this.

1. Disagreement in character or qualities; want of accordance or harmony; discrepancy, inconsistency. (Now often with some colour of sense 2.)

1612 LD. ROCHESTER in Ellis *Orig. Lett.* Ser. II. III. 229 That incongruity betwixt your Highnes age and hirs is one inconvenience which neither syde can help. **1664** POWER *Exp. Philos.* II. 149 We have tried Oyl and Water, and no Motion at all was perceived, for the same reason of incongruity. **1672** MARVELL *Reh. Transp.* I. 269 Never was there such Incongruity and Nonconformity in their furniture. **1704** F. FULLER *Med. Gymn.* (1711) 251, I have often..admir'd the Incongruity of the Circumstances of Humane Life. **1807** REES *Cycl.* s.v. *Congruity*, Incongruity denotes an unfitness of their surfaces for joining together. Thus quicksilver will unite with gold..but will roll off from wood. **1850** KINGSLEY *Alt. Locke* xxvii, The quaint incongruity of the priestly and the lay elements in his speech.

b. (with *pl.*) An instance or point of disagreement; a discrepancy, an inconsistency.

a **1610** HEALEY *Epictetus' Man.* Ep. Ded., In extenuation of so many incongruities. *a* **1720** SHEFFIELD (Dk. Buckhm.) *Wks.* (1753) II. 112 We ought to believe it well and wisely done, whatever incongruities may appear in it. **1830** HERSCHEL *Stud. Nat. Phil.* 43 There we find no contradictions, no incongruities, but all is harmony. **1868** BAIN *Ment. & Mor. Sc.* xiii. (ed. 2) 315 The most commonly assigned cause of the Ludicrous is Incongruity; but all incongruities are not ludicrous.

2. Want of accordance with what is reasonable or fitting; unsuitableness, inappropriateness, absurdity.

1597 HOOKER *Eccl. Pol.* v. xx. §9 As if they who abolish legends could not without incongruitie reteine..Homilies. **1660** H. MORE *Myst. Godl.* VI. ii. 218 To shew there is no incongruity nor inconvenience in it. **1696** PHILLIPS (ed. 5), *Incongruity*,..Figuratively said of Faults committed against Civility, against Decency, and the received Customs of the World. **1751** JOHNSON *Rambler* No. 92 ¶1 Without incongruity..we cannot speak of geometrical beauty. **1875** JOWETT *Plato* (ed. 2) IV. 130 He felt no incongruity in the veteran..correcting the youthful Socrates. **1877** BLACK *Green Past.* xxiv, She thought it arose from a sarcastic appreciation of the incongruity of his presence there.

b. (with *pl.*) An instance of such disagreement; an inappropriate matter; an absurdity.

a **1626** BP. ANDREWES *Serm.* (1856) I. 333 How great, gross, and foul an incongruity it is to pour out ourselves into sin..when we go forth to correct sin. **1663** GERBIER *Counsel* 1 The incongruities committed by many undertakers of Buildings. **1748** SMOLLETT *Rod. Rand.* xlv, The only Expedient I know..is to lay hold of some incongruity he has uttered. **1882** A. MACFARLANE *Consanguin.* 16 There was an incongruity in using the two phrases as equivalent.

3. Want of harmony of parts or elements; want of self-consistency; incoherence. Also (with *pl.*) something incoherent or not self-consistent.

a **1532** *Remedie of Love* 2 This werke who so shal see or rede Of any incongruitie doe me not impeche. *a* **1653** GOUGE *Comm. Heb.* ii. 10 In this there is no great incongruity. **1729** BUTLER *Serm. Self-deceit* Wks. 1874 II. 122 Hence arises that amazing incongruity, and seeming inconsistency of character. **1823** SCOTT *Peveril* xxxii, Had Julian been inclined for mirth,..he must have smiled at the incongruity of the clerk's apparel. **1876** MOZLEY *Univ. Serm.* viii. 179 The whole story is one grand incongruity; a splendid illusion.

†4. *Gram.* Violation of the rules of concord; grammatical incorrectness; solecism. *Obs.*

1573–80 BARET *Alv.* I 97 Incongruitie, *solœcismus.* **1589** PUTTENHAM *Eng. Poesie* III. xxi. (Arb.) 256 Some maner of speaches..are euer vndecent, namely barbarousnesse, incongruitie, ill disposition. *Ibid.* xxii. 258 Your next intollerable vice is *solecismus* or incongruitie..that is by misusing the Grammaticall rules to be obserued in cases, genders, tenses, and such like. **1612** BRINSLEY *Lud. Lit.* xv. (1627) 199, I have found my schollers to misse most in these. .. Incongruity in their concords.

incongruous (ɪnˈkɒŋgruːəs), *a.* [f. L. *incongru-us* (f. *in-*, IN-^{3} + *congru-us*: see CONGRUOUS) + -OUS.] Not congruous; the opposite of congruous.

1. Disagreeing in character or qualities; not corresponding; out of keeping; disaccordant, inconsistent, inharmonious, unsuited. Const. *with, to.*

(Often with mixture of sense 2, stress being laid upon the inappropriateness or absurdity resulting from the want of correspondence.)

1611 COTGR., *Incongrue*, incongruous, vnagreeing. **1645** MILTON *Tetrach.* Wks. (1847) 184/2 All the ecclesiastical glue the liturgy or laymen can compound, is not able to soder up two such incongruous natures into the one flesh of a true beseeming marriage. **1666** BOYLE *Orig. Formes & Qual.* (1667) 5 If its Shape were incongruous to that of the cavity of the Lock, it would be unfit to be used as a Key. **1695** HUMFREY *Mediocria* 53 This is a Scheme I look on as incongruous with free reason. **1717** BULLOCK *Wom. a Riddle* I. i. 8 O Stupidity unparalleled, incongruous to all sense and breeding! **1787** G. WHITE *Selborne* i. 3 The cart way of the village divides..two very incongruous soils. **1821** J. Q. ADAMS in C. Davies *Metr. Syst.* III. (1871) 191 Here are two new measures of capacity altogether incongruous to the new system. **1830** LINDLEY *Nat. Syst. Bot.* 203 The number of stamens is incongruous with the lobes of the corolla. **1863** GEO. ELIOT *Romola* xii, There entered a figure strangely incongruous with the current of their thoughts.

2. Disagreeing or inconsistent with the circumstances or requirements of the case, or with what is reasonable or becoming; unbecoming, unsuitable, inappropriate, absurd, out of place.

1623 COCKERAM, *Incongruous*, absurd, disagreeable. **1630** PRYNNE *Anti-Armin.* 173 This..is no such incongruous, ridiculous nouell distinction. **1664** H. MORE *Myst. Iniq.* xxii. 85 As if a man should be acquitted and yet punished for the same crime, at the same Court, then which nothing is more foolish or incongruous. **1719** DE FOE *Crusoe* II. i, I have since often observed, how incongruous and irrational the common Temper of Mankind is. **1792** BURKE *Let. to Sir H. Langrishe* Wks. 1842 I. 548 It would be incongruous and absurd, to have the head of the church of one faith, and the members of another. **1804** J. GRAHAME *Sabbath* 267 Most miserable, most incongruous wretch! Darest thou spurn thy life, the boon of God? **1876** C. M. DAVIES *Unorth. Lond.* 106 The effect was slightly incongruous.

3. Having parts or elements not agreeing with each other; involving inconsistency or disagreement; not self-consistent; incoherent.

1658 T. WALL *Charac. Enemies Ch.* 43 Their confused and incongruous intermixture of the different parts of prayer. **1788** H. WALPOLE in *Walpoliana, Fr. Philos.* 50 Surely of all human characters a fanatic philosopher is the most incongruous, and of course the most truly ludicrous. **1880** L. STEPHEN *Pope* v. 135 The consequent alterations make the hero of the poem a thoroughly incongruous figure.

†4. *Gram.* Violating the rules of concord; grammatically incorrect. *Obs.*

1616 BULLOKAR, *Incongruous*, against rule of Grammar. **1678** R. BARCLAY *Apol. Quakers* xv. v. (1701) 526 It is incongruous to say *vos amas, vos legis*, that is *you lovest, you readest*, speaking to One.

†5. *Geom.* Not coinciding when superposed.

1656 tr. *Hobbes' Elem. Philos.* (1839) 180 Of crooked magnitudes, some are congruous, that is, are coincident when they are applied to one other; others are incongruous.

6. *Theory of Numbers.* Of two numbers: Not congruent; giving different remainders when divided by the modulus: see CONGRUENT 5.

1864 WEBSTER, *Incongruous Numbers.*

in'congruously, *adv.* [f. prec. + -LY^{2}.] In an incongruous manner; inconsistently; inappropriately; incoherently.

1641 CLARENDON *Ess.*, Tracts (1727) 228 The excellency of those pious fathers have intitled that age, how incongruously soever, to be looked upon as the primitive time. **1744** BERKELEY *Siris* §278 Nature..may not improperly and incongruously be styled the life of the world. **1822–34** *Good's Study Med.* (ed. 4) I. 715 There was a low muttering delirium, in which the patient spoke incongruously. **1847** DISRAELI *Tancred* II. xiv, Never were men more incongruously grouped. **1884** *Law Times* LXXVIII. 77/2 It shows incongruously beside the more prosaic business of the law.

†b. *Gram.* With violation of concord, ungrammatically. *Obs.*

c **1645** HOWELL *Lett.* (1650) I. 382 They speak of some towns called the Lacones, which retain yet, and vulgarly speak the old Greek, but incongruously. *a* **1684** KNATCHBULL *Annot. Tr.* 56 (T.) Saying, that Luke..writ incongruously; when, in truth, he is acknowledged by all expositors too knowing in the Greek to commit such a solecism.

†c. *Geom.* So as not to coincide. *Obs.*

1656 tr. *Hobbes' Elem. Philos.* (1839) 183 If they be incongruously applied, they will, as all other crooked lines, touch one another..in one point only.

in'congruousness. [f. as prec. + -NESS.] The quality of being incongruous; incongruity.

1727 in BAILEY vol. II. **1847–9** TODD *Cycl. Anat.* IV. 688/1 There is [in dreams] a complete incongruousness in the thoughts and images which pass through our minds. **1869** SEELEY *Lect. & Ess.* i. 18 It was a revolution which struck with incongruousness..the very instinctive impulses of men.

inconie: see INCONY.

†incon'jectable, *a. Obs.* [f. IN-^{3} + L. *conjectā-re* to conjecture, guess (see CONJECT) + -ABLE.] Used to render Gr. *ἀνείκαστος* 'unattainable by conjecture, immense' (Liddell & Scott).

1609 HOLLAND *Amm. Marcell.* XVII. iv. 85 Apollo powerful, Lord and Patron inconiectable of the Diademes [*κύριος διαδήματος ἀνείκαστος*], unto whom the Lord of Ægypt hath set up statues in this kingdome.

inconjoinable (ɪnkənˈdʒɔɪnəb(ə)l), *a.* (*sb.*) *rare.* [f. IN^{3} + CONJOIN *v.* + -ABLE.] That cannot be conjoined: in quot. as *sb.*

1844 SIR W. HAMILTON *Logic* II. App. 328 The Principle of Inconjoinables (i.e. What cannot be thought as with and beside each other, cannot exist with and beside each other).

†in'conjugated, *a. Obs.* [IN-^{3}.] Not coupled or paired: cf. CONJUGATION 4.

1578 BANISTER *Hist. Man* VIII. 112 Galene rehearseth besides all these a Nerue inconiugated, or hauyng no fellow.

inconjunct (ɪnkənˈdʒʌŋkt), *a. Obs.* [IN-^{3}.] Not in conjunction: *spec.* in *Astrol.*, said of two planets or their positions when they are so placed that neither affects the operation of the other; 'when a planet, house, or sign has no aspect or familiarity with another' (Wilson *Dict. Astrol.*, 1819). (Cf. ASPECT *sb.* 4.)

1603 SIR C. HEYDON *Jud. Astrol.* xxi. 469 All the rest beeing inconiunct, and out of familiaritie, and therefore without operation. **1647** LILLY *Chr. Astrol.* xix. 109 These are called Signes inconjunct, or such as if a Planet be in one of them, he cannot have any aspect to another in the Signe underneath. **1819** J. WILSON *Compl. Dict. Astrol.* 101 The ancient opinion was, that a planet, being five signs distant from any moderator or significator, was inconjunct, and had no effect on it whatever... The semisextile was likewise considered as an inconjunct position. *Ibid.* 277 Houses also are inconjunct; as the 1st with the 2d, 6th, 8th, and 12th.

inco'nnected, *a. rare.* [IN-^{3}.] Not connected; unconnected; disconnected.

Hence **inco'nnectedness.**

1742 WARBURTON *Pope's Ess. Man* I. 43 The best system cannot but be such a one as hath no inconnected void; such a one in which there is a perfect coherence and gradual subordination in all its parts. **17..** HURD *Epist. Writ.* (R.), To treat a number of inconnected and quite different subjects in the same measure. **1880** *Victorian Rev.* Dec. 196 In spite of the proverbial inconnectedness of the subject matter [of a Dictionary].

†inco'nnexedly, *adv. Obs. rare*$^{-1}$. [f. IN-^{3} + CONNEXED *ppl. a.* + -LY^{2}: cf. L. *inconnexus* unconnected.] In an unconnected way; without connexion.

1646 SIR T. BROWNE *Pseud. Ep.* IV. ix. 201 Ascribing hereto as a cause what perhaps but casually or inconexedly succeeded.

inconnexion, -ection (ɪnkəˈnɛkʃən). ? *Obs.* [IN-^{3}: cf. L. *inconnex-us*: see prec.] Want of connexion; unconnectedness.

1620 BP. HALL *Hon. Mar. Clergy* I. §3 Neither need wee any better or other proofe of the inconnexion of this vow with holy orders. **1678** PHILLIPS (ed. 4), *Inconnexion*..In Rhetorick it is the same as the figure *Asyntheton.* **1697** COLLIER *Immor. Stage* iv. §3 (1730) 150 This strangeness of Persons, distinct Company, and Inconnexion of Affairs. **1755** JOHNSON *Hist. Eng. Lang.* ¶4 Their speech..must have been artless and unconnected, without any modes of transition or involution of clauses; which abruptness and inconnection may be observed even in their later writings. **1813** T. BUSBY *Lucretius* III. Comment. xl, The utter inconnection of the time which passed before our being with that in which we live.

b. (with *pl.*) An instance of this; something unconnected with what precedes or follows.

1697 COLLIER *Ess. Mor. Subj.* II. (1703) 94 As to single ideas, inconnexions, and slight touches, my observation holds good.

†inco'nnexive, *a. Obs.* [IN-^{3}.] Of unconnected nature or character; without connexion.

1659 STANLEY *Hist. Philos.* III. II. 144 The Monads in the Duad are inconnexive to those of the Triad.

inconnu (ˈɪŋkənjuː, ‖ɛ̃kɔny). [Fr., unknown.]

1. A game fish, *Stenodus leucichthys*, belonging to the family Salmonidæ and found in Alaska and north-west Canada.

[**1806** S. FRASER *Lett. & Jrnls.* (1960) 231 The Indians also state that there are plenty white fish unconu some trout carp Jub, &c. in the fall of the year.] **1833** G. BACK *Jrnl.* 14 Aug. in *Narr. Arctic Land Expedition* (1836) iii. 101 La Prise set a net, which..produced a few white fish, a trout, and, what surprised the Indians, an inconnu. **1844** J. H. LEFROY *In Search Magnetic North* (1955) 99, I tried the Inconnu there, but it is far inferior to the Trout. **1905** D. S. JORDAN *Guide to Study of Fishes* II. iv. 67 The Inconnu, or Mackenzie River salmon, known on the Yukon as 'charr'.. belongs to this genus [sc. *Stenodus*]. **1943** *Beaver* Mar. 28 Inconnu (*Stenodus Mackenzii*), generally called 'conny', is a fish peculiar to the Mackenzie River. **1965** A. J. MCCLANE *Standard Fishing Encycl.* 424/1 Inconnu have fair food value and are utilized to a large extent by the Eskimos.

2. (ɛ̃kɔny.) An unknown person; a stranger. Also fem. **-e.**

1807 *Salmagundi* 4 Apr. 142 When we toast a frenchman, we merely mean one of those *inconnus*, who swarmed to this country, from the kitchens and barber's shops of Nantz, Bourdeaux, and Marseilles. **1829** G. GRIFFIN *Collegians* (ed. 2) I. xiii. 266 The lovely inconnue..felt her heart beat somewhat quickly. **1865** 'OUIDA' *Strathmore* I. v. 76 The jewels that sparkled on the hands of the fair inconnue. **1920** F. S. FITZGERALD in *Smart Set* July 15/2 Edith murmured a conventional 'Thanks loads—cut in later,' to the *inconnu.*

in'conquerable, *a. rare.* [f. IN-^{3} + CONQUERABLE.] Unconquerable.

1660 N. INGELO *Bentivoglio & Urania* (1682) I. 93 Alledging, That sin is inconquerable in this mortal body. **1905** *Daily Chron.* 4 Oct. 5/1 An inconquerable penchant to conspiracy. **1921** *Edin. Rev.* July 134 That rather ticklish matter, the government and command of the British Empire Navy,..does not present inconquerable obstacles to be overcome. **1946** W. S. CHURCHILL *Secret Session Speeches* 29 The inconquerable, the inexhaustible adaptiveness and ingenuity of the British mind.

inconscient (ɪnˈkɒnʃɪənt), *a. rare.* [f. IN-^{3} + CONSCIENT. Also in mod.F. (Dict. Acad. 1878): cf. L. *inconscius.*] Unconscious.

1885 *Alien. & Neurol.* VI. 486 The old doctrines.. suspected not the immense efficacy of the inconscient, which is the foundation of mental life. **1894** LD. SALISBURY *Pres. Addr. Brit. Assoc.* 7 Aug., Whether you believe that Creation was the work of design or of inconscient law, it is equally difficult to imagine how this random collection of dissimilar materials [the chemical elements] came together.

So **inconscience** (ɪnˈkɒnʃəns), unconsciousness.

1891 A. LYNCH *Mod. Authors* 96 The genuineness and inconscience of these elemental *motifs.*

inconsciently (ɪnˈkɒnʃ(ɪ)əntlɪ), *adv.* [f. INCONSCIENT *a.* + -LY^{2}.] Unknowingly.

1913 *Glasgow Herald* 18 Oct. 11/1 They stood, inconsciently perhaps, for some of the priceless intangible

things without which the millennium would be a sterile and bitter anti-climax. **1929** R. BRIDGES *Testament of Beauty* iv. 126 Held by the inborn love of Beauty inconsciently Of preference to imitate the more beautiful things.

†**inconscionable**, *a. Obs.* [IN-³.] Not having, or not regarding, conscience; unconscionable.
1596 SPENSER *State Irel.* Wks. (Globe) 619/1 Soe inconscionable are these common people, and so litle feeling have they of God. **1672** WYCHERLEY *Love in Wood* IV. i, Inconscionable, false woman..You cheated, trepanned, robbed, me of the five-hundred pounds!
Hence †**in'conscionableness**; †**in'conscionably** *adv.*
1634 STRAFFORD *Let. to Coke* in *Lett. & Disp.* (1739) I. 238 Most inconscionably the Landlords..had laid it upon the poor and bare Tenants. **1800** ADDISON *Amer. Law Rep.* 57 There is intrinsic inconscionableness in the bargain.

inconscious (ɪn'kɒnʃəs), *a.* Now *rare.* [f. late L. *inconsci-us* + -OUS: cf. CONSCIOUS.]
†**1.** Not privy to some deed: cf. CONSCIOUS 1.
1670 MILTON *Hist. Eng.* IV. (1851) 182 Miserably slain by his people, some say deservedly, as not inconscious with them who train'd Osred to his ruin.
2. Not conscious; unconscious.
1678 CUDWORTH *Intell. Syst.* I. iii. §34. 144 Concluding that all Matter and Substance as such, hath Life and Perception or Understanding Natural and Inconscious, Essentially belonging to it. **1790** *Norman & Bertha* II. 84 Miss Westbrook..had long entertained a penchant for him, of which..he was not inconscious. **1868** BROWNING *Ring & Bk.* III. 466 Each in turn Patting the curly calm inconscious head.
Hence **in'consciously** *adv. rare*, unconsciously.
1840 BROWNING *Sordello* VI. 148 He had inconsciously contrived forget, I' the whole, to dwell o' the points. **1873** —— *Red Cott. Nt.-cap* III. 386 Chatting and chirping sunk inconsciously To silence.

inconsecutive (ɪnkən'sɛkjʊtɪv), *a.* [IN-³.] Not consecutive; characterized by want of sequence; inconsequent.
1837 G. S. FABER *Prim. Doct. Justif.* v. 233 *note*, His argument is altogether lame and inconsecutive. **1853** —— *Reviv. Fr. Emperorship* 64 Mr. Elliott is far too hasty and too inconsecutive to be a safe guide. **1894** *Times* 24 Nov. 11/2 They follow one another in an absolutely inconsecutive and irrelevant manner.
Hence **incon'secutively** *adv.*; **incon'secutiveness**.
1836 G. S. FABER *Prim. Doctr. Election* II. vi. 330 An inconsecutiveness of reasoning which cannot be tolerated. **1845** *Bachelor Albany* 7 He had read a good deal, inconsecutively and superficially. **1880** M. PATTISON *Milton* xi. 138 The inconsecutiveness, the want of arrangement, are exaggerated.

inconsederat, obs. form of INCONSIDERATE.

inconsequence (ɪn'kɒnsɪkwəns). [ad. L. *inconsequentia* (Quintil.), f. *inconsequent-em* INCONSEQUENT. So F. *inconséquence* (17th c. in Hatz.-Darm.).] The fact or quality of being inconsequent; an instance of this.
1. Want of logical sequence; the character of an inference that does not follow from the premisses, or of an argument involving such an inference; inconclusiveness, illogicalness.
1588 FRAUNCE *Lawiers Log.* I. ii. 7 b, Syllogismes are the true and onely rules of consequence and inconsequence. **1653** GATAKER *Vind. Annot. Jer.* 174 Mr. S. himself could not but see the inconsequence of his own argument. **1764** HURD *Let. to Dr. Leland* (R.), Strange! that you should not see the inconsequence of your own reasoning. **1862** *Sat. Rev.* 18 Mar. 298 With a ludicrous inconsequence it labours to establish a necessary connexion between the mere consolidation of grants and efficiency in fundamental instruction.
b. (with *pl.*) An instance of this; a conclusion that does not follow from the premisses; an illogical inference or piece of reasoning.
1605 BACON *Adv. Learn.* II. xviii. §2 Men are vndermined by Inconsequences. **1656** HOBBES *Quest. Lib., Necess. & Chance* Wks. 1841 V. 425 And from *will work* to *doth work upon absolute necessity*, is another gross inconsequence. **1828** W. SEWELL *Oxf. Prize Ess.* 42 We cannot, without a gross inconsequence, deny them a proportionate result.
2. Want of sequence or natural connexion of ideas, actions, or events; irrelevance; disconnexion, inconsecutiveness; an instance of this, an irrelevant action or circumstance.
1842 POE *Marie Roget* Wks. 1864 I. 232 The whole of this paragraph must now appear a tissue of inconsequence and incoherence. **1846** —— *N. P. Willis* Wks. 1864 III. 33 The plot was a tissue of absurdities, inconsequences and inconsistencies. **1865** MERIVALE *Rom. Emp.* lxiii. VIII. 16 The inconsequence of the proceeding might easily be overlooked.
3. As a quality of persons, their thought, or action: **a.** The practice or habit of drawing inconsequent inferences; illogicalness of reasoning. **b.** The practice or habit of speaking or acting disconnectedly or without sequence.
1817 COLERIDGE *Biog. Lit.* 104 That fortunate inconsequence of our nature which permits the heart to rectify the errors of the understanding. **1856** MRS. BROWNING *Aur. Leigh* VI. 13 For what is lightness but inconsequence, Vague fluctuation 'twixt effect and cause Compelled by neither? **1876** GEO. ELIOT *Dan. Der.* xxxviii, That mingling of inconsequence which belongs to us all, and not unhappily, since it saves us from many effects of mistake.
†**4.** The being of no consequence or importance.
1759 *Compl. Letter-writer* (ed. 6) 218 My extreme inconsequence, and the little I can say. **1812** J. J. HENRY *Camp. agst. Quebec* 80 Being without arms, and in an unknown country, my inconsequence, and futileness lay heavy on my spirits.

†**in'consequency.** *Obs.* [f. as prec.: see -ENCY.] = prec. (in quot., in sense 1 b).
a **1641** BP. MOUNTAGU *Acts & Mon.* (1642) 142 Full of inconsequencies and absurdities. **1655** H. MORE *Antid. Ath.* App. i. §1. 294 To search and discover..any weakness or inconsequency in any Argumentation throughtout the whole Treatise. **1706** in PHILLIPS.

inconsequent (ɪn'kɒnsɪkwənt), *a.* (*sb.*) [ad. L. *inconsequent-em* without due sequence or connexion, f. *in-* (IN-³) + *consequent-em* CONSEQUENT.]
1. Not following as an inference or logical conclusion; falsely or erroneously inferred; illogical.
1627 HAKEWILL *Apol.* (J.), The ground he assumes is unsound, and his illation from thence deduced inconsequent. **1644** DIGBY *Two Treat.* II. (1645) 109 Inconsequent to the whole body of reason. *a* **1688** CUDWORTH *Immut. Mor.* (1731) 65 Not only ridiculously absurd and contradictious in themselves, but also altogether inconsequent from the same.
b. Not following naturally in the order of events; having no rational connexion with preceding or accompanying circumstances; irrelevant.
1881 H. JAMES *Portr. Lady* xxxix, She was checked..on her progress to the door, by an inconsequent request from Isabel. **1893** W. H. HUDSON *Patagonia* 143 Who that has noticed monkeys in captivity—their profound inconsequent gravity and insane delight in their own unreasonableness.
c. *transf.* Of things: That do not follow on, or carry out the purpose or design of something else.
1866 HOWELLS *Venet. Life* ii. 24 The narrowest, crookedest, and most inconsequent little streets in the world. **1898** *Westm. Gaz.* 24 Nov. 3/2 Inconsequent trimmings, that have no *raison d'être*, are well known to be the crime of the third-rate dressmaker.
2. Wanting in logical sequence of thought or reasoning; involving erroneous inference.
1579 FULKE *Heskins' Parl.* 430 Who euer heard a more shamelesse lye, or a more inconsequent argument? **1663** J. SPENCER *Prodigies* (1665) 120 A most inconsequent and presumptuous reasoning. **1794** J. HUTTON *Philos. Light* etc. 2, I wish to show the erroneous, or inconsequent way of reasoning, which has prevailed in physical investigation. **1877** E. R. CONDER *Bas. Faith* i. 24 Confused thought and inconsequent reasoning.
b. Wanting in sequence or connexion of ideas or subjects; characterized by irrelevance; disconnected, inconsecutive.
1869 MISS MULOCK *Woman's Kingd.* II. 15 She..began talking in her smoothly flowing, inconsequent way. **1891** MISS DOWIE *Girl in Karp.* 204 The trumpeters..blew long notes of inconsequent music.
3. *transf.* Of a person: Characterized by inconsequence in thought, speech, or action.
1794 SULLIVAN *View Nat.* V. 381 This to me, is the most clear; that the private Atheist is an inconsequent man, and an enemy to himself. **1813** SHELLEY *Notes Q. Mab* Poet. Wks. (1891) 47/1 A Necessarian is inconsequent to his own principles if he indulges in hatred or contempt. **1863** TROLLOPE *Rachel Ray* I. 250 Mrs. Ray was herself so inconsequent in her mental workings, so *shandy-pated*, if I may say so, that it did not occur to her [etc.].
4. Of no consequence, unimportant, not worth notice. *rare.*
1768 STERNE *Sent. Journ.* (1778) I. 202 (*The Rose*), I blush'd at many a word the first month—which I found inconsequent and perfectly innocent the second.
†**B.** *sb.* A conclusion that does not follow from the premisses; an illogical inference; a *non sequitur. Obs.*
1643 PRYNNE *Sov. Power Parl.* III. 128, To which I answer that this is a meer inconsequent.

inconsequential (ɪnkɒnsɪ'kwɛnʃəl). *a.* [IN-³.] Characterized by inconsequence; the opposite of CONSEQUENTIAL (in senses 3–6).
1. Characterized by inconsequence of reasoning, thought, or speech; = INCONSEQUENT 1–3.
1621 W. SCLATER *Tythes* (1623) Aja, So vtterly inconsequentiall are all arguments pretended against the diuine right of Tything. **1650** CROMWELL *Let.* 12 Sept. in *Carlyle*, I cannot let such gross mistakes and inconsequential reasonings pass without some notice taken of them. **1710** NORRIS *Chr. Prud.* iii. 117 The loose and inconsequential Reasoner..in his wild ramble may happen to light upon Truth. **1779–81** JOHNSON *L.P., Somerville*, The fiction is unnatural, and the moral inconsequential. **1837** J. H. NEWMAN *Proph. Office Ch.* 132, I do not say that such reasoning is, necessarily, inconsequential or unfair.
2. Of no consequence; = INCONSEQUENT 4.
1782 MISS BURNEY *Cecilia* IX. iii, As my time is not wholly inconsequential, I should not be sorry to have an early opportunity of being heard. **1791–1823** D'ISRAELI *Cur. Lit., Lit. Anecdotes*, A circumstance, which may appear inconsequential to a reader, may bear some remote or latent connexion. **1892** STEVENSON *Across the Plains* 306 An affair too simple and inconsequential for gentlemen of our heroic mould.
Hence as *sb.*; also **inconse'quentialism** (*nonce wd.*), inconsequential or disconnected nature.
1893 *National Observer* 15 Apr. 544/2 A practice that from its inconsequentialism was always pleasing. **1936** L. C. DOUGLAS *White Banners* xiii. 277 Exchanging inconsequentials and blandly taking each other's measure. **1936** *Mind* XLV. 334 The three protagonists may actually hold a few inconsequentials in common. **1957** *Economist* 2 Nov. 436 (Advt.), News never buried under frothy inconsequentials.

inconsequentiality (ɪnkɒnsɪkwɛnʃɪ'ælɪtɪ.)[f. prec. + -ITY.] Inconsequential quality or character: the opposite of CONSEQUENTIALITY.
1. = INCONSEQUENCE 1, 1 b.
1832 L. HUNT *Sir R. Esher* (1850) 258 His inconsequentialities were usually of a pleasanter character. **1858** R. CHAMBERS *Dom. Ann. Scot.* (1859) I. 127 A sense of the inconsequentiality of such reasoning at length came over them.
2. The quality of not being consequential.
1850 L. HUNT *Autobiog.* xv. (1860) 241, I used to rally him [Shelley] on the apparent inconsequentiality of his manner upon those occasions.

inconse'quentially, *adv.* [f. as prec. + -LY².] In an inconsequential manner; without logical sequence.
1754 WARBURTON *View Bolingbroke's Philos.* iii. Wks. 1811 XII. 225 He infers inconsequentially in supposing that from the inconsistency of a certain relation concerning revelation, there never was any revelation at all. **1879** TROLLOPE *Thackeray* ix. 197 He must mass his sentences inconsequentially.

inconsequentialness. [f. INCONSEQUENTIAL *a.* + -NESS.] Inconsequentiality.
1931 *Daily Express* 22 Sept. 10/6 The fact is, the profligacy of war expenditure, the high pay, the inconsequentialness of it all, led every one into bad, extravagant habits. **1956** *Essays in Crit.* VI. 117 Her English ..having a quality of inconsequentialness.

in'consequentism. *nonce-wd.* [f. INCONSEQUENT *a.* + ISM.] = INCONSEQUENCE 3.
1829 CARLYLE *Misc., Novalis* (1872) II. 214 (*tr.* Novalis) They..hold their views as results of weakness, as Inconsequentism.

in'consequently, *adv.* [f. INCONSEQUENT + -LY².] In an inconsequent manner.
1. Without logical sequence; in the way of erroneous inference; inconclusively.
1626 JACKSON *Creed* VIII. xxvii. §6, I could not condemn Maldonat for speaking inconsequently either to the truth itself, or to the authority of the Romish Church, wherein he lived. **1681** GLANVILL *Sadducismus* 113 How crazily and inconsequently they collect that the human Soul is nowhere. **1836** SIR W. HAMILTON *Discuss., Stud. Math.* (1852) 286 It would argue a mind incorrigibly false, to reason inconsequently on principles so obtrusive.
2. Without sequence or connexion of ideas or circumstances; not as a consequence of anything; irrelevantly.
1864 *Linnet's Trial* IV. iii. II. 248 'Are you not longing to see Kirkham again?' asked Brandon rather inconsequently. **1881** H. JAMES *Portr. Lady* xlii, And Edward Rosier looked all round, inconsequently, with his single glass.

in'consequentness. *rare.* [f. as prec. + -NESS.] The quality of being inconsequent.
1727 in BAILEY vol. II. **1856** J. YOUNG *Demonol.* IV. vii. 447 Often may the inconsequentness of the reasoning be unperceived. **1882** *Pop. Sci. Monthly* XX. 816 There is always some inconsequentness or incoherency in madness.

†**incon'sider**, *v. Obs. rare.* [f. IN-³ + CONSIDER *v.*: cf. INCONSIDERATE.] *trans.* Not to consider; to leave out of consideration.
1697 R. PEIRCE *Bath Mem.* I. ii. 29 We were forc'd to.. apply our selves wholly to the Consumption..and inconsider the Sciatica.

inconsiderable (ɪnkən'sɪdərəb(ə)l), *a.* (*sb.*) [a. F. *inconsidérable* (16th c. in Godef.), f. *in-* (IN-³) + *considérable.*] Not considerable; not to be considered.
†**1.** Incapable of being considered or reckoned, incalculable. (Cf. CONSIDER 6.) *Obs. rare.*
1598 FLORIO, *Inconsiderabile*, that cannot be considered, or imagined, inconsiderable. *a* **1631** DONNE *Serm.* (Alford) IV. cvii. 466 All that inexpressible inconsiderable Number made not up one Minute of this Eternity.
2. Not to be considered; unworthy of consideration; beneath notice; of no consequence, unimportant; insignificant, trifling. The opposite of CONSIDERABLE (senses 3–5).
1637 LAUD in *Collect.* (O.H.S.) I. 318 Nor is it altogether inconsiderable, that [etc.]. **1658–9** *Burton's Diary* (1828) III. 80, I never heard of the fellow. He is inconsiderable. **1699** BENTLEY *Phal.* 133 This Discovery of mine, if it be true, is no inconsiderable one. **1712** STEELE *Spect.* No. 302 ¶1 A trifling inconsiderable Circumstance. **1754** SHERLOCK *Disc.* (1759) I. xi. 311 This Earth was made for the Habitation of Men, wicked and inconsiderable as they are. **1806** SURR *Winter in Lond.* (ed. 3) II. 39 My uncle, in whose correspondence..Mr. Montagu has made no inconsiderable figure.
b. Hence, Of very small value, amount, or size.
1648 D. JENKINS *Wks.* 2 The place is of so inconsiderable a benefit that it is worth but 80. *l.* per Annum. **1654** SIR E.

Nicholas in *N. Papers* (Camden) II. 61, I know nothing of all the money he hath received,..which I assure you have not been inconsiderable sums. **1766** Smollett *Hist. Eng.* (1804) V. 264 A small fortification..defended by an inconsiderable garrison. **1796** Morse *Amer. Geog.* I. 450 Paukatuck river, is an inconsiderable stream. **1812** Chalmers *Dom. Econ. Gt. Brit.* 373 The American tribes.. are found to be inconsiderable in numbers. **1875** Scrivener *Lect. Text N. Test.* 9 But a few inconsiderable fragments of the New Testament still extant are older than the fiery reign of Diocletian.

†**3.** Inconsiderate, thoughtless. *Obs. rare.*

1640 [implied in INCONSIDERABLENESS 2]. *a* **1646** [implied in INCONSIDERABLY 2]. **1692** Locke *Educ.* 138 Questions which to a supercilious and inconsiderable Japaner would seem very idle. **1726** Leoni tr. *Alberti's Archit.* II. 100/1 The Region wherein an inconsiderable Architect has placed his City, may perhaps have those defects.

†**B.** *sb.* A point or circumstance not worth considering, or of no importance. Chiefly in *pl. Obs.*

1670 W. Simpson *Hydrol. Ess.* p. xiv, Both not so repleat with inconsiderables.

incon'siderableness. [f. prec. + -NESS.] The quality of being inconsiderable.

1. Unworthiness of being considered; small importance or consequence; slightness of value or amount; trifling amount; insignificance.

1646 Jenkyn *Remora* 16 The smallnes and inconsiderablenes of the pretext. **1663** Pepys *Diary* 5 Sept., I did inform myself well in things relating to the East Indys; both of the country..and the inconsiderableness of the place of Bombaim, if we had had it. **1730** A. Gordon *Maffei's Amphith.* 24 The Inconsiderableness of that Edifice. **1812** Chalmers *Dom. Econ. Gt. Brit.* 66 The cargoes..could not, from their inconsiderableness, have filled a mighty void, for any length of years.

†**2.** Thoughtlessness, want of consideration. *Obs.*

1640 Bp. Reynolds *Passions* xl. 522 A Depraved Understanding,..Depraved by Neglect and Inconsiderablenesse; not darkned by Ignorance.

incon'siderably, *adv.* [f. as prec. + -LY².]

1. To an inconsiderable, insignificant, or trifling extent; slightly, very little.

1727 Bailey vol. II, *Inconsiderably*, meanly, etc. **1753** Costard in *Phil. Trans.* XLVIII. 483 His number..differs inconsiderably from what they, most probably, made it. **1794** Sullivan *View Nat.* II. 325 Those islands..being but inconsiderably elevated above the surface of the water.

†**2.** Thoughtlessly, carelessly, inconsiderately. *Obs. rare.*

a **1646** J. Gregory *Terrest. Globe* in *Posthuma* (1650) 266 [It] was thwartly in it self, and, in the proof, inconsiderably don.

†**incon'sideracy.** *Obs. rare.* [f. INCONSIDERATE: see -ACY.] Inconsiderateness.

1748 Chesterf. *Lett.* (1792) II. cxli. 2 This is the common effect of the inconsideracy of youth. **1847** tr. *Feuchtersleben's Princ. Med. Psychol.* (Syd. Soc.) 271 Hence their..habitual absence of mind, inconsideracy, forgetfulness.

†**incon'siderance.** *Obs. rare.* [ad. L. *inconsiderāntia*, f. *inconsiderānt-em* acting inconsiderately: see -ANCE.] Want of consideration; inconsiderateness.

1549 Chaloner *Erasm. on Folly* S ij a, Unlesse he had laide folie and inconsideraunce to bote. *a* **1644** Chillingw. *Serm.* ii. §9 The cause of this practical atheism..was ignorance or rather imprudence, inconsiderance.

So †**incon'siderancy.** *Obs. rare*⁻⁰. = prec.

1599 Minsheu *Sp. Dict.* II, Inconsiderancie, *inadvertencia, inconsideracion.* **1623** Cockeram, *Inconsiderancie*, folly. **1706** Phillips, *Inconsiderancy*, Inconsiderateness, Unadvisedness, Rashness.

inconsiderate (ɪnkən'sɪdərət), *a.* (*sb.*) Also 5 **inconsederat.** [ad. L. *inconsiderāt-us* unadvised, thoughtless, inconsiderate; f. *in-* (IN-³) + *considerātus* CONSIDERATE.]

1. Of things, actions, etc.: Not properly considered; done or made without deliberation; thoughtless, unadvised, precipitate, rash. (Now often regarded as *transf.* from 2.)

c **1460** [implied in INCONSIDERATELY]. **1549** Coverdale, etc. *Erasm. Par. 1 Pet.* 7 That you geve none occasion unto their inconsiderate ignoraunce. **1612** T. Taylor *Comm. Titus* iii. 1 Sauls inconsiderate and rash oath. **1661** J. Stephens *Procurations* 1 Unseasonable and inconsiderate speaking. **1751** Earl Orrery *Remarks Swift* (1752) 181 Our inclinations are so apt to hurry us into inconsiderate actions. **1798** Malthus *Popul.* (1817) III. 52 We often draw very inconsiderate conclusions against the industry and government of states from the appearance of uncultivated lands in them. **1835** I. Taylor *Spir. Despot.* v. 219 An inconsiderate application of genuine principles to particular instances.

2. Of persons, etc.: Not characterized by consideration; acting without deliberation; thoughtless, imprudent, indiscreet, careless.

1595 Shaks. *John* II. i. 67 Rash, inconsiderate, fiery voluntaries. *a* **1635** Naunton *Fragm. Reg.* (Arb.) 33 You will never leave it untill you are knockt on the head, as that inconsiderate fellow Sidney was. **1660** Milton *Free Commw.* Wks. (1847) 448/1 If there be a king, which the inconsiderate multitude are now so mad upon. **1710** Pope *Let. to Cromwell* 17 Dec., Inconsiderate authors wou'd rather be admir'd than understood. **1833** Alison *Europe* (1849) I. i. §62. 105 There is enough here to arrest the attention of the most inconsiderate. **1875** Jowett *Plato* (ed. 2) I. 343 They are younger and more inconsiderate.

†**b.** Not thinking *of*, careless *of*, regardless *of*.

1607 Topsell *Four-f. Beasts* (1658) 343 The silly beast inconsiderate of all fraud cometh out and is taken. **1667** *Decay Chr. Piety* viii. ¶12 So wholly taken up with the contemplation and enjoyment of his own felicity, that he is utterly inconsiderate of that of his creatures. **1670** G. H. *Hist. Cardinals* III. III. 27 The innocent Popes..walk on careless and inconsiderate of what they do.

3. Without consideration or regard for the circumstances, claims, feelings, etc. of others.

1842 *The Visitor* (R.T.S.) 60 (Aunt Priscilla), She was not of an inconsiderate temper. She did not allow herself to utter remarks or censure without considering how they were likely to operate on the tempers and feelings of others. **1858–85** [implied in INCONSIDERATENESS 2] *Mod.* It was most inconsiderate to mention the matter in her hearing.

†**4.** Not held in consideration, unconsidered; of no importance; inconsiderable, trifling. *Obs.*

1655 E. Terry *Voy. E. Ind.* 15 When they had sold any one of their bullocks to us, for a little inconsiderate peece of brasse. **1657** *North's Plutarch* Add. Lives (1676) 42 But an inconsiderate person, of a base extraction. **1703** Moxon *Mech. Exerc.* 276 The difference of the thicknesses being so inconsiderate, is not discerned.

B. *sb.* An inconsiderate or thoughtless person.

1588 Shaks. *L.L.L.* III. i 79 O pardon me my stars, doth the inconsiderate take *salue* for *lenuoy*, and the word *lenuoy* for a *salue*? **1621** S. Ward *Iethro's Iustice of Peace* (1627) 8 Ambitious Inconsiderates..climbe into the chaire of honor. **1748** Richardson *Clarissa* (1811) III. 168, I was as willing as the gay inconsiderate to call another cause, as he termed it.

incon'siderately, *adv.* [f. prec. + -LY².] In an inconsiderate manner; without consideration or deliberation; thoughtlessly, unadvisedly, indiscreetly, rashly.

c **1460** Fortescue *Abs. & Lim. Mon.* xi. (1885) 136 Yff suche gyftis, and namely tho wich haue be made inconsideratle, or aboff the merytes off hem that haue thaim, were refourmed. *Ibid.* xiv. 143 Giftes..made off the kynges livelod inconsiderately, as not deseruet. **1591** Percivall *Sp. Dict.*, *Desatinadamente*, rashly, inconsiderately. **1594** T. B. *La Primaud. Fr. Acad.* II. 307 Such passions did neuer vse any consultation, but performed all things inconsideratly and at aduenture. **1603** Holland *Plutarch's Mor.* 205 He answereth not..inconsiderately, but with good advice and seriously. **1682** Norris *Hierocles* 13 Now the best way to doe this is not to use Oaths frequently, nor inconsiderately. **1742** Richardson *Pamela* IV. 422 Miss L., is of a remarkably soft Temper, tho' not so inconsiderately soft as Miss Cope. **1880** Muirhead *Gaius* II. §33 Our statement.. is not made inconsiderately.

incon'siderateness. [f. as prec. + -NESS.]

1. The quality of being inconsiderate; thoughtlessness, want of consideration; imprudence, rashness; an instance of this.

1591 Percivall *Sp. Dict.*, *Desatino*,..rashnesse, inconsiderateness, folly. **1594** T. B. *La Primaud. Fr. Acad.* II. 275 Our inconsideratenesse, our blockishnesse and ingratitude is the cause, why wee cannot learne this lesson. **1626** Bernard *Isle of Man* (1627) 67 Where Inconsideratenesse sits, there Audacitie and Foolehardinesse will waite. **1741** Middleton *Cicero* I. vi. 531 It shall be my care to check his inconsiderateness in this one article. **1855** Ld. Houghton in *Life* (1891) I. xi. 527 It is one of those inconsideratenesses with which I am continually reproaching myself.

2. Want of consideration for the claims or feelings of others.

1858 Holland *Titcomb's Lett.* iii. 190 Injustice and inconsiderateness will not go down especially when administered by a man's companion. **1885** *Manch. Exam.* 6 July 4/7 Servants..were often..treated with painful inconsiderateness.

inconsideration (ɪnkənsɪdə'reɪʃən). [a. F. *inconsidération* (16th c.), or ad. late L. *inconsiderātiōn-em* (Salvianus *c* 440), f. *in-* (IN-³) + *considerātiōn-em*, after *inconsiderāt-us* inconsiderate.]

1. Want of consideration; failure or refusal to consider; thoughtlessness of action; indiscretion.

1526 *Pilgr. Perf.* (W. de W. 1531) 90 b, Lechery, blyndnes of mynde, inconsideracyon or neglygence. **1570–6** Lambarde *Peramb. Kent* (1826) 91 Tymor standing by blamed him [the king] of great inconsideration. **1656** *Artif. Handsom.* 146 They are at first, through inconsideration or unwontednesse, scandalised at them. **1748** Richardson *Clarissa* (1811) I. 281, I had reason to impute full as much to my own inconsideration, as to his power over me. **1815** Jane Austen *Emma* III. xv, Faults of inconsideration and thoughtlessness. **1847** A. Bennie *Disc.* 52 This tranquillity is the result of inconsideration.

†**b.** (with *pl.*) An instance of this; an inconsiderate act; a failure to consider. *Obs.*

1579 Fenton *Guicciard.* (1618) 288 All men being much amazed at so great an inconsideration. **1649** Jer. Taylor *Gt. Exemp.* III. §15 (R.) The greatnesse of John's love, when he had mastered the first inconsiderations of his fear, made him to return.

2. Absence of consideration for others; inconsiderateness.

1872 W. R. Greg *Enigmas* (1873) iv. 178 Her [Nature's] merciless inconsideration for the individual where the interests of the Race are in question. **1885** *Pall Mall G.* 22 Sept. 4/2 A protraction of time which is frequently caused by the inconsideration of principals, who will drive off 'writing their letters' to the last moment. **1891** *Scenes Life Nurse* 63 In spite of the inconsideration shown by the lady, I felt very sorry for her.

†**incon'siderative,** *a. Obs. rare*⁻¹. [f. IN-³ + CONSIDERATIVE.] = INCONSIDERATE 1.

1684 *Def. Resol. Case Consc. conc. Symbol. Ch. Rome* 36 You never uttered a more inconsiderative saying.

inconsidered (ɪnkən'sɪdəd), *a. rare.* [IN-³: after L. *inconsiderāt-us*, F. *inconsidéré.*] Not considered, unconsidered; = INCONSIDERATE 1.

1630 Donne *Serm.* (Alford) I. xi. 220 God will scarce hearken to sudden inconsidered irreverent Prayers. **1894** *Pop. Sci. Monthly* XLIV. 460 Gradually by inconsidered increments the mightiest economic changes are made. **1895** *Westm. Gaz.* 30 Sept. 3/3 Greater harm is done to society by emotional and inconsidered charity, than by the refusal to help some cases of perhaps doubtful genuineness.

†**incon'sidering,** *a. Obs. rare.* [IN-³.] Unconsidering; = INCONSIDERATE 2.

1685 Cotton tr. *Montaigne* I. 586 One effect of its virtue, even in the most inconsidering sort of men.

inconsistence (ɪnkən'sɪstəns). Now *rare* or *Obs.* [f. INCONSISTENT (after *consistence*): see -ENCE. Cf. F. *inconsistance* (1755 in Hatz.-Darm.).]

1. Want of agreement or harmony (*with* something, or *between* things); = INCONSISTENCY 1.

1651 Hobbes *Leviath.* Concl. 390 There is..no such Inconsistence of Humane Nature, with Civill Duties, as some think. **1661** Marvell *Let. to Mayor of Hull* Wks. 1776 I. 27, I did not at all see what inconsistence there could be between Colonell Gilby's interest and mine. **1712** Berkeley *Passive Obed.* §51 The inconsistence of such a state with that manner of life which human nature requires. **1764** Harmer *Observ.* x. ii. 65 Some seeming inconsistence betwixt this and the preceding observation.

2. Want of agreement between the parts of a thing; = INCONSISTENCY 2.

1643 Milton *Divorce* II. viii, What may we do then to salve this seeming inconsistence? **1736** Butler *Anal.* II. vii. 361 Any inconsistence in its several parts. *a* **1797** H. Walpole *Mem. Geo. II* (1847) I. x. 319 [There was] no deviation, no inconsistence in his narrative.

3. Inconsistent action or conduct; = INCONSISTENCY 4.

1713 Bentley *Free-think.* i. (ed. 2) 9 These very Men.. are honour'd in other parts of his Book, and recommended as Free-thinkers. What inconsistence is this, what Contradiction? **1741** Richardson *Pamela* I. 91 Well, you may be gone from my Presence, thou strange Medley of Inconsistence! **1769** *Junius Lett.* xviii. (1804) I. 114 Mr. Grenville was, of all men, the person who should not have complained of inconsistence with regard to Mr. Wilkes. **1897** *Westm. Gaz.* 16 Feb. 3/2 Let them ignore the consistence or the inconsistence of the occupants of the two front benches.

4. With *an* and *pl.* An instance of inconsistence; an inconsistency.

1655 Fuller *Ch. Hist.* III. vii. §18 Else these inconsistences will not be reconciled. **1754** Edwards *Freed. Will* II. iv. 51 Nor will it help in the least its Absurdities and Inconsistences. **1802–12** Bentham *Ration. Judic. Evid.* (1827) V. 62 English jurisprudence will be found variegated by inconsistences.

inconsistency (ɪnkən'sɪstənsɪ). [f. as prec. (after *consistency*): see -ENCY.] The quality, condition, or fact of being inconsistent.

1. Want of consistency or congruity; lack of accordance or harmony (*with* something, or *between* things); incompatibility, contrariety, or opposition.

1699 Bentley *Phal.* 481 What an inconsistency is there between the LI and LXIX Epistles? *a* **1719** Addison *Chr. Relig.* II. iv, An eminent instance of the inconsistency of our Religion with Magic. **1818** Jas. Mill *Brit. India* II. IV. vii. 260 That disappointment and distress which their inconsistency with the matters of fact rendered a necessary consequence. **1853** Bright *Sp. India* 3 June, There is.. great inconsistency between the speech of the right hon. Gentleman and that which he proposes should be done.

2. Want of agreement or harmony between two things or different parts of the same thing.

1651 Baxter *Inf. Bapt.* 296 The inconsistency of sealing these two at once. **1721** Bellamy *Th. Trin.* 28 Which two [Persons], though different, are inseparably united; which nevertheless implies not the least Inconsistency. **1849** Macaulay *Hist. Eng.* x. II. 630 The one beauty of the resolution is its inconsistency. **1875** Jowett *Plato* (ed. 2) I. 110 Nor is there an inconsistency in wise and good fathers having foolish and worthless sons.

3. With *an* and *pl.* Something that is inconsistent; a discrepancy, incongruity.

1647 H. More *Song of Soul* II. App. xxix, If those single lights hither aspire, This strange prodigious inconsistency Groweth still stranger. **1668** Wilkins *Real Char.* b j, Affected phrases; which being Philosophically unfolded.. will appear to be inconsistencies and contradictions. **1713** Berkeley *Hylas & Phil.* III. Wks. 1871 I. 329, I know that nothing inconsistent can exist, and that the existance of Matter implies an inconsistency. **1833** I. Taylor *Fanat.* i. 6 A world of wonderous inconsistencies.

4. Of persons: Want of consistency in thought or action; *esp.* discrepancy between principles and practice, or between one action and another.

1665 Glanvill *Def. Vain Dogm.* 54 If he sayes otherwise elsewhere, 'tis only an argument of the inconsistency of Aristotle. **1745** Wesley *Answ. Ch.* 7, I am continually charged with Inconsistency herein. **1790** Han. More *Relig. Fash. World* (1791) 220, I dare not say this is hypocrisy, but surely it is inconsistency. **1836** Hor. Smith *Tin Trump.* (1876) 204 Inconsistency—the only thing in which men are consistent. **1874** Motley *Barneveld* I. viii. 349 James had given a new exhibition of his astounding inconsistency.

b. An instance of this; an inconsistent act.

1750 JOHNSON *Rambler* No. 14 ¶1 The many inconsistencies which folly produces, or infirmity suffers in the human mind. **1834** MACAULAY *Ess., Pitt* (1851) 298 The inconsistencies of which Pitt had been guilty. **1862** *Fraser's Mag.* July 19 Such people talk edifyingly enough of the sins of Church-goers—their 'inconsistencies'..their worldly gossip.

5. *Logic.* (See quot.)

1864 BOWEN *Logic* vi. 169 This new sort of Opposition or Incompossibility, as it exists between two Judgments which are alike in Quality, either both Affirmatives or both Negatives,..is called *Inconsistency*.

inconsistent (ɪnkən'sɪstənt), *a.* (*sb.*) Also 7-8 -ant. [f. IN-^{3} + CONSISTENT *a.*; cf. mod.F. *inconsistant*.] Not consistent.

I. 1. Of a substance: Without consistence or firmness, of incoherent nature. *rare. arch.*

1677 GREW *Exp. Solut. Salts* ii. §10 If the Particles of Water were themselves Fluid or Inconsistent and Alterable. **1718** J. CHAMBERLAYNE *Relig. Philos.* (1730) I. xi. §10 The whole Matter is so soft and inconsistent that it can hardly bear touching with the Hands. **1860** RUSKIN *Mod. Paint.* V. VIII. i. 159 The parts of a crystal are consistent, but of dust, inconsistent.

II. 2. Not consisting; not agreeing in substance, spirit, or form; not in keeping; not consonant or in accordance; at variance, discordant, incompatible, incongruous. **a.** Said of one thing in relation to another; const. *with*, †rarely *to*.

1646 SIR T. BROWNE *Pseud. Ep.* I. viii. 30 It containeth impossibilities and things inconsistent with truth. **1664** *Rhode Island Col. Rec.* (1857) II. 64 Whether ther be any lawes that are inconsistent to the present government. **1729** BUTLER *Serm. Forgiveness* Wks. 1874 II. 109 Resentment is not inconsistent with good-will. **1836** J. GILBERT *Chr. Atonem.* viii. (1852) 258 The benevolence of God..is not inconsistent with his determination to punish. **1870** JEVONS *Elem. Logic* ix. 76 The proposition, A, then, is inconsistent with both E and O. **1880** HAUGHTON *Phys. Geog.* iii. 163 *note*, Three combinations..give results inconsistent with the others.

b. Said of two or more things, in relation to each other.

c **1656** BRAMHALL *Replic.* v. 227 Thus he confoundeth Papall and Patriarchall Power, making things inconsistent to be one and the same thing. **1657** CROMWELL *Sp.* 21 Apr. in *Carlyle*, And it is a pitiful fancy..to think they are inconsistent. Certainly they may consist. *a* **1704** LOCKE *Posth. Wks.* (1706) 179 Can the same unextended indivisible Substance have different, nay inconsistent and opposite Modifications at the same time? **1857** MAURICE *Ep. St. John* xv. 247 Are these two passages inconsistent? **1875** ABP. THOMSON *Laws Th.* §124. 256 Two or more inconsistent views..may be formed at the same time.

†c. Applied to a benefice incapable of being held together with a fellowship. *Obs.*

1690 LUTTRELL *Brief Rel.* (1857) II. 85 Dr. Hern..having a liveing at St. Anns in Westminster, the bishop declared it inconsistent with his fellowship. **1691** *Case Exeter Coll.* 51 The Statutes of Exeter-College..would very imprudently have made that distinction betwixt Benefices consistent and inconsistent.

3. Wanting in harmony between its different parts or elements; self-contradictory; involving inconsistency. Said of a single thing, or of action including two or more courses.

1651 BAXTER *Inf. Bapt.* 277 For his humanity to reign actually, and to suffer at the same time, is inconsistent. **1658** BRAMHALL *Consecr. Bps.* v. 134 It had deserved more credit, then this silly, improbable, inconsistent Relation. **1774** J. BRYANT *Mythol.* I. 306 All which in time..gave rise to a most inconsistent system of Polytheism. **1856** FROUDE *Hist. Eng.* (1858) II. ix. 340 The language of the Roman see had been inconsistent, but the actions of it had been always uniform. **1860** ABP. THOMSON *Laws Th.* §84. 150 Inconsistent opposition lies between any two affirmative judgments which cannot be correct together, but may be false together.

4. Of a person: Not consistent in thought or action. **a.** Const. *with*, †rarely *to* (oneself, one's principles, etc.). **b.** *absol.* Acting in a way at variance with one's professed principles, or with one's conduct at another time.

a. 1709 STRYPE *Ann. Ref.* (1824) I. I. viii. 166 Many of these accused them to the Queen..as men that were inconsistent to themselves. **1709** STEELE *Tatler* No. 7 ¶1 Man is a Creature very inconsistent with himself. **1771** *Junius Lett.* xlviii. 252 You..are inconsistent with your own principles. **1887** FOWLER *Deductive Logic* (ed. 9) Examples 174 You are inconsistent with yourself.

b. 1742 YOUNG *Nt. Th.* II. 113 Ah! how unjust to nature, and himself, Is thoughtless, thankless, inconsistent man! *a* **1863** WHATELY *Comm.-pl. Bk.* (1864) 99 A man is..properly called inconsistent whose opinions or practices are at any one time at variance with each other; in short, who holds at once a proposition and its contradictory. **1875** JOWETT *Plato* (ed. 2) IV. 11 Nor..in speaking of God both in the masculine and neuter gender, did he [Plato] seem to himself inconsistent.

B. *sb.* (*pl.*) Things, statements, etc. which are inconsistent with each other or with something else.

1652 GAULE *Magastrom.* 147 Necessity and contingency have alwayes been held as contraries and inconsistents. **1655** FULLER *Ch. Hist.* I. ii. §4 As for other inconsistents with truth..they prove not that this whole Story should be refused, but refined. **1864** BOWEN *Logic* vi. 169 Two Inconsistents..cannot both be true.

inconsistently (ɪnkən'sɪstəntlɪ), *adv.* [f. prec. + -LY^{2}.] In an inconsistent manner.

1665 J. SPENCER *Vulg. Proph.* 109 (T.) A melancholy kind of madness..made him speak distractedly and inconsistently. **1681** H. MORE *Exp. Dan.* 86 Who will be sure never to interpret it inconsistently to his own corrupt Interest. **1720** WATERLAND *Eight Serm.* 262 The Text of St. John..is very inconsistently put together with this other Construction. **1831** LAMB *Elia* Ser. II. *Ellistoniana*, Adventitious trappings, which, nevertheless, sit not at all inconsistently upon him. **1881** W. B. POPE *Higher Catech. Theol.* 382 This plausible argument is inconsistently urged by the annihilationist.

†incon'sistentness. *Obs. rare*$^{-1}$. [f. as prec. + -NESS.] = INCONSISTENCY.

1647 H. MORE *Song of Soul* II. App. xlix, And what might come to passe Implies no contradictious inconsistentnesse. **1727** in BAILEY vol. II.

†incon'sistible, *a. Obs.* [f. IN-^{3} + CONSISTIBLE.] That cannot consist; inconsistent.

1660 R. COKE *Justice Vind.* Pref. 5, I was amazed to see such inconsistible and impossible things to come from Men, otherwise so learned. *a* **1734** NORTH *Exam.* III. viii. §59. 629 It hath a ridiculous Phiz, like the Fable of the old Man, his Ass, and a Boy, before the inconsistible Vulgar.

Hence **†incon,sisti'bility**, inconsistency.

1650 R. HOLLINGWORTH *Exerc. Usurped Powers* 30 An inconsistibility..of the things one with another.

†incon'sisting, *ppl. a. Obs.* [f. IN-^{3} + CONSISTING.] = INCONSISTENT.

1658 W. SANDERSON *Graphice* Pref. A secret inconsisting with common capacities. **1679** PENN *Addr. Prot.* II. 216 Obstinately..maintaining inconsisting Things with the Faith, Peace and Prosperity of the Church. **1705** S. WHATELY in W. S. Perry *Hist. Coll. Amer. Col. Ch.* I. 167 As Clandestine, as Ensnaring, as Inconsisting, as Pre-engaging or what ever else Mr. Comy will call it.

inconsolable (ɪnkən'səʊləb(ə)l), *a.* [ad. L. *inconsōlābilis*, f. *in-* (IN-^{3}) + *consōlābilis* CONSOLABLE. Cf. F. *inconsolable* (1611 in Cotgr., but *inconsolablement* is found earlier).

In poetry formerly sometimes stressed *in'consolable* (quots. 1596, 1754); but Bailey 1730 has *incon'solable*.]

Not admitting of consolation or solace; that cannot be consoled, alleviated, or assuaged.

a. Of grief, trouble, etc.

1596 FITZ-GEFFRAY *Sir F. Drake* (1881) 97 And hath by death receiv'd an overthrowe, Vnto the worlds inconsolable woe. **1627-77** FELTHAM *Resolves* II. lxxi. 311 Sins being the work of darkness, we prefer the inconsolable darkness before the pleasure of the brightest Ray. **1746-7** HERVEY *Medit.* (1818) 180 This unallayed and inconsolable anguish of our all-gracious Master. **1754** BLACKLOCK *Elegy Constantia* (R.), Impell'd by deep inconsolable grief, She breathes her soft, her melancholy strain. **1862** *Sat. Rev.* 8 Feb. 153 Inconsolable woe seemed to depress the Ministry—decent grief was stamped on the faces of the Opposition. **1870** MACDUFF *Mem. Patmos* xxiii. (1871) 318 Indulging in a wild and inconsolable lament.

b. Of persons: Disconsolate.

1677 LADY CHAWORTH in *12th Rep. Hist. MSS. Comm.* App. v. 44 The Duchesse is inconsolable, but the Duke bears it lyke a great man. **1710** ADDISON *Tatler* No. 152 ¶6 They were all Three inconsolable for his Absence. **1848** C. BRONTË *J. Eyre* xiii, Was he so very fond of his brother as to be still inconsolable for his loss? **1881** STEVENSON *Virg. Puerisque* 138, I dare say the sick man is not very inconsolable when he receives sentence of banishment.

absol. **1799** MRS. JANE WEST *Tale of Times* I. 20 The mortal dart of woe in the bosom of the fair inconsolable.

Hence **incon,sola'bility**, **incon'solableness**, the condition of being inconsolable; **incon'solably** *adv.*, in an inconsolable manner.

1727 BAILEY vol. II, Inconsolably. *Ibid.*, Inconsolableness. **1752** JOHNSON *Rambler* No. 191 ¶3 A letter from Mr. Trip..about absence and inconsoleableness, and ardour and irresistible passion, and eternal constancy. *a* **1857** D. JERROLD *John Applejohn* Wks. 1864 III. xviii. 386 John wandered inconsolably backwards and forwards. **1858** DE QUINCEY *Autobiog. Sk.* Wks. II. 313 *note*, The poor unhappy goddess seemed to be eternally aground on this Goodwin Sand of inconsolability. **1879** R. T. SMITH *Basil the Great* xii. 182 Sometimes they laugh incessantly and sometimes lament inconsolably.

inconsolate (ɪn'kɒnsələt), *a. rare.* [f. IN-^{3} + CONSOLATE *a.*; cf. F. *inconsolé* (18th c.), Pg. *inconsolado*.] Unconsoled, disconsolate. Hence **in'consolately** *adv.*, disconsolately.

a **1656** BP. HALL *Serm. Gal.* ii. 20 (R.) Honors, titles, treasures, which will at the last leave you inconsolately sorrowfull. **1882** LD. ACTON in *Academy* 9 Dec. 407 The Despot of Cremona dying inconsolate.

inconsonance (ɪn'kɒnsənəns). [f. INCONSONANT (after *consonance*): see -ANCE.] Want of consonance or agreement; inharmoniousness.

1811 REES *Cycl.*, *Inconsonance*, in Music, is of the same import nearly with dissonance, or a jarring and unpleasant sound. **1817** COLERIDGE *Biog. Lit.* (1870) 67, I presumed that this was a possible conception (*i.e.* that it involved no logical inconsonance). **1849** R. I. WILBERFORCE *Holy Bapt.* (1850) 135 To judge respecting the consonance or inconsonance of the means employed.

†in'consonancy. *Obs. rare.* [f. as prec.; see -ANCY.] = prec.

1650 A. A. *Reply Sanderson* 3 The like inconsonancies hath he to this purpose. **1669** W. SIMPSON *Hydrol. Chym.* 37, I have made animadversions upon all his five ingredients shewing the inconsonancy and inconsistency of them.

inconsonant (ɪn'kɒnsənənt), *a.* [f. IN-^{3} + CONSONANT *a.*] Not consonant or agreeable *to* (†*unto*); not agreeing or harmonizing *with*.

1658 SIR T. BROWNE *Hydriot.* 36 They carried them out of the world with their feet forward, not inconsonant unto reason. **1677** HALE *Prim. Orig. Man.* III. iii. 260 A Fiction utterly inconsonant to the whole Method of Nature. **1763** SCRAFTON *Indostan* (1770) 77 These words were too inconsonant to his schemes, to be followed by actions. **1836** LYTTON *Athens* (1837) I. 398 A tradition far from inconsonant with the manners of the time, or the heroism of the sex. **1883** *Century Mag.* XXV. 912 The spell that wars With aught inconsonant to heart or eye.

Hence **in'consonantly** *adv.* (Webster, 1856).

†inconspicable, *a. Obs. rare*$^{-1}$. [f. IN-^{3} + CONSPICABLE.] Invisible.

a **1652** J. SMITH *Sel. Disc.* v. i. (1821) 136 Though God hath copied forth his own perfections in this conspicable and sensible world,..yet the most clear and distinct copy of himself could be imparted to none else but to intelligible and inconspicable natures.

inconspicuous (ɪnkən'spɪkju:əs), *a.* [f. late L. *inconspicu-us* + -OUS; see IN-^{3} and CONSPICUOUS.]

†1. That cannot be seen; invisible. *Obs.*

1624 [implied in INCONSPICUOUSNESS 1]. **1660** BOYLE *New Exp. Phys. Mech.* xvii. 128 Those lesser and inconspicuous parcels of Air. **1678** CUDWORTH *Intell. Syst.* I. iv. §18. 333 The Life or Soul's passing into the Invisible or Inconspicuous. **1708** *Brit. Apollo* No. 72. 2/1 The Moon, while in Conjunction with the Sun, is Inconspicuous. **1751-73** JORTIN *Eccl. Hist.* (R.), Socrates in Xenophon..says that the Deity is inconspicuous.

†b. Not discernible to the mental eye. *Obs.*

1648 BOYLE *Seraph. Love* (1660) 18 Their greatest Accomplishments compar'd to His Perfections..are..as inconspicuous as the faint Qualities of more ordinary Persons. **1713** BERKELEY *Guardian* No. 70 ¶2 The joint beauty of the whole or the distinct use of its parts were inconspicuous. **1793** T. TAYLOR *Orat. Julian* 122 *note*, The occult art by which they were fabricated..was inconspicuous.

2. Not readily seen or noticed; not prominent or striking in appearance or character.

1828 WEBSTER, *Inconspicuous*..2. Not conspicuous. **1835** SIR J. ROSS *Narr. 2nd Voy.* xvii. 266 There was an inconspicuous aurora. **1854** HOOKER *Himal. Jrnls.* II. xxiv. 170 In inconspicuous scattered tufts. **1866** GEO. ELIOT *F. Holt* xlv, A veil drawn down gave her a sufficiently inconspicuous appearance. **1886** SWINBURNE *Misc.* 24 Shakespeare who led an inconspicuous life.

b. *spec.* in *Bot.* Of flowers, when small, green, or of pale colour.

1845 LINDLEY *Sch. Bot.* iv. (1858) 40 Flowers usually racemose, very often small and inconspicuous. **1863** BATES *Nat. Amazon* I. 70 The majority of forest-trees in equatorial Brazil have small and inconspicuous flowers. **1880** C. R. MARKHAM *Peruv. Bark* xxii. 238 A wide-spreading melastomaceous plant, with inconspicuous flowers.

Hence **incon'spicuously** *adv.* †invisibly (*obs.*); so as not to be readily perceived.

1661 BOYLE *Spring Air* (1682) 95 The particles of air which..inconspicuously lurk within the Bladder. **1893** *Christian at Work* (N.Y.) 13 Apr., This Chamber has..shared not inconspicuously in the history..[of] both church and state.

incon'spicuousness. [f. prec. + -NESS.]

†1. The quality or state of being invisible. *Obs.*

1624 ABP. ABBOTT *Visib. True Ch.* 16 This paucitie of beleeuers, and inconspicuousnes of his Church. *a* **1691** BOYLE *Man's Ignorance Uses Nat. Things* i. Wks. 1772 III. 472 The inconspicuousness of those stars.

2. The quality of not being prominent to notice.

1881 J. G. BARNARD in *Smith. Contrib. Knowl.* No. 310. 15 The inconspicuousness of this tide in our actual oceans. **1882** G. ALLEN in *Nature* 17 Aug. 372 Perhaps its very inconspicuousness saves it from the obtrusive visits of undesirable insect guests. **1883** H. DRUMMOND *Nat. Law in Spir. W.* i. II. (1884) 47 The assumed invisibility of inconspicuousness of the old Laws.

†incon'spiring, *ppl. a. Obs.* [f. IN-^{3} + CONSPIRING *ppl. a.*] Not concurring in purpose or aim; without unity of plot or aim.

1678 CUDWORTH *Intell. Syst.* I. iv. §24. 411 Incoherent and Inconspiring, like an Ill-agreeing Drama, botch'd up of Many Impertinent Intersertions.

†in'constance. *Obs.* [a. F. *inconstance* (13th c.), ad. L. *inconstantia*, n. of quality f. *inconstānt-em* INCONSTANT: see -ANCE.]

1. Fickleness of conduct: = INCONSTANCY 1.

c **1386** CHAUCER *Sompn. T.* 250 What nedeth yow diuerse freres seche?.. Youre inconstance is youre confusioun. *c* **1450** tr. *De Imitatione* I. xiii. 14 The begynnyng of all temptacions is inconstance of herte & litel trust in god. **1485** CAXTON *Chas. Gt.* 112 Sortybrant, which knewe the mutabylyte of wymmen & thynconstaunce. **1549** *Compl. Scot.* iv. 30 That terme youthed suld be vndirstandin for ignorance ande inconstance. **1660** tr. *Amyraldus' Treat. conc. Relig.* II. ix. 288 The inconstance and imbecillity of man. **1712** BLACKMORE *Creation* 314 From fair to fair with gay inconstance rove.

2. Mutability of things: = INCONSTANCY 2.

1509 BARCLAY *Shyp of Folys* (1874) II. 240 It lytell auayleth..A whyle to lyue well in suche inconstance. **1569** SPENSER *Visions of Bellay* xi. in *Theat. Worldlings*, Wearie to see th' inconstance of the heauens. **1603** HOLLAND *Plutarch's Mor.* 421 (R.) The uncertainty and inconstance of mutable fortune.

3. Inconsistency: = INCONSTANCY 3

1529 More *Dyaloge* IV. iii. 103 a/2 Whan he chaungeth so often, and wryteth euer the longer, the more contrary.. But I pray you how excuseth he hys inconstaunce [*Wks.* (1557) inconstauncie]?

inconstancy (ɪn'kɒnstənsɪ). [ad. L. *inconstāntia*; see prec. and -ANCY.] Want of constancy.

1. Of persons (or things personified, as Fortune): Fickleness of conduct or purpose; changeableness of character or disposition; unsteadfastness. Also, with *pl.*, an instance of this.

1526 *Pilgr. Perf.* (W. de W. 1531) 90 b, Inconsideration or neglygence, inconstancy or vnstablenes. **1590** Spenser *F.Q.* I. iv. 1 For unto knight there is no greater shame Then lightnesse and inconstancie in love. **1601** Holland *Pliny* II. 600 Willing after a sort to play at Fortunes game.. and in some measure to satisfie her inconstancie. **1663** Cowley *Verses & Ess., Disc. Cromwell* (1669) 54 Art thou the Country which didst hate, And mock the French Inconstancy? **1713** Swift in *Four C. Eng. Lett.* 165 You have triumphed.. by the steadiness of your temper, over the inconstancy and caprice of your friends. **1740** Cheyne *Regimen* 167 Unaccountable Terrors, Panics, Inconstancies. **1894** Sir E. Sullivan *Woman* 47 How you excuse, and even praise, the inconstancy of a woman who throws over another man for you.

2. Of things or events: Mutability, variability; irregularity; absence of uniformity.

1613 Purchas *Pilgrimage* (1614) 13 The silent Moone.. constant image of the worlds inconstancie, which it never seeth twice with the same face. **1645** Boate *Irel. Nat. Hist.* (1652) 165 It is never dry weather two or three dayes together. Which inconstancy and wetness of the weather [etc.]. **1726** Leoni *Alberti's Archit.* I. 101/2 The inconstancy of the air is what spoils every thing. **1825** McCulloch *Pol. Econ.* III. ii. 240 The wages of labour, in different employments, vary with the constancy and inconstancy of employment. **1885** J. Martineau *Types Eth. Th.* I. 421 The inconstancy of his [Comte's] analysis of the human capacities and instincts.

†**b.** Variation, difference. *Obs.*

1646 J. Gregory *Notes & Obs.* (1650) 64 The Armenian Translation rendreth, 'And Pharaoh called Joseph Fesuut'. .. This is all the inconstancy of reading I could observe.

†**3.** Inconsistency (in statements, etc.); an instance of this. *Obs.*

1557 [see INCONSTANCE 3]. **1565** Jewel *Repl. Harding* (1611) 412 He seemeth not to consider the inconstancie, and folly of his owne tale. **1605** Bacon *Adv. Learn.* II. x. §10 Let a man look into their [phisitians'] prescripts and ministrations, and he shall finde them but inconstancies.

¶**4.** Erron. for INCONTINENCY. *Obs.*

1581 Marbeck *Bk. of Notes* 799 Some doe gather of this place, that Paule did mortifie in himself the fire of inconstancy, by long fasting. **1607** Topsell *Four-f. Beasts* (1658) 204 The bladder of a female Kid drunk in powder, helpeth the inconstancy of urine. **1623** Cockeram, *Inconstancie*, vnchastnes.

inconstant (ɪn'kɒnstənt), *a.* (*sb.*) [a. F. *inconstant* (1372 in Hatz.-Darm.), ad. L. *inconstāntem*, f. *in-* (IN-^{3}) + *constānt-em* CONSTANT.] Not constant.

1. Of persons, or their character, actions, etc.: Not steadfast; fickle, changeable.

1402 Hoccleve *Letter of Cupid* 101 She.. ys fals and inconstant and hath no feythe. **1508** Dunbar *Tua mariit wemen* 260 Be constant in ȝour gouernance, and counterfeit gud maneris, Thought ȝe be kene, inconstant, & cruell of mynd. **1590** Spenser *F.Q.* I. iv. 26 Inconstant man, that loued all he saw, And lusted after all that he did loue. **1624** Capt. Smith *Virginia* II. 30 They are inconstant in every thing but what feare constraineth them to keepe. **1776** Gibbon *Decl. & F.* x. I. 278 It is difficult to paint the light, the various, the inconstant character of Gallienus. **1844** Ld. Brougham *Brit. Const.* App. iii. (1862) 461 The fickle, inconstant, volatile temper of the people.

2. Of things: Frequently changing or altering; mutable, variable, irregular.

1526 *Pilgr. Perf.* (W. de W. 1531) 7 b, What is more frayle, more inconstaunt & mutable than is the wyll of man? **1592** Shaks. *Rom. & Jul.* II. ii. 109 O sweare not by the Moone, th' inconstant Moone, That monethly changes in her circle Orbe. **1602** Marston *Ant. & Mel.* I. Wks. 1856 I. 16 Sayling some two monthes with inconstant winds. **1684** *Contempl. State Man* I. ii. (1699) 12 All things on this side Heaven are inconstant and transitory. **1833** Lyell *Princ. Geol.* III. 43 Mineral and organic characters, although often inconstant, may.. enable us to establish the contemporaneous origin of formations in distant countries. **1875** Poste *Gaius* Pref. (ed. 2) 8 The orthography of the Veronese MS. is extremely inconstant.

†**b.** Of the eyes: Unsteady, shifting. *Obs.*

1598 Hakluyt *Voy.* I. 21 They [the Tartars] be hardie and strong.. their eye-browes extending from their fore-heads downe to their noses, their eies inconstant and blacke, their countenances writhen and terrible.

†**3.** Inconsistent *with*. *Obs.*

1642 Sir E. Dering *Sp. on Relig.* 61 Episcopacy is incompatible and inconstant with the authority of a secular jurisdiction.

B. *sb.* An inconstant person or thing. (Cf. F. *un inconstant*.)

1647 Cowley *Mistress* lxiii. (*heading*) The Inconstant. **1703** Farquhar (*title*) The Inconstant; or the way to win him. **1703** Motteux *Prol.* 28 ibid., This night we hope you'll an Inconstant bear. **1794** W. Curtis *Bot. Mag.* No. 218 The Disandra varies extremely in the number of its stamina.. few such inconstants exist. **1840** Mrs. F. Trollope *Widow Married* xxxiv, Either from his being a gambler, or an inconstant.

inconstantly (ɪn'kɒnstəntlɪ), *adv.* [f. prec. + -LY^{2}.] In an inconstant manner, variably, with fickleness, inconsistently.

1549 Coverdale, etc. *Erasm. Par. Gal.* 7 Why art thou now become vnlike thy selfe, why doest thou inconstantly withdrawe the from diner? **1647** Cowley *Mistr.*, *Monopoly* iv, They flutter still about, inconstantlie. *a* **1720** Sheffield (Dk. Buckhm.) *Wks.* (1753) II. 196 Divine power does nothing irregular, or inconstantly. **1757** Warburton *Rem. Hume* xiv. Wks. 1811 XII. 366 A modern often thinks.. inconstantly.

†**in'constantness.** *Obs.* [f. as prec. + -NESS.] Inconstancy.

a **1562** Cavendish *Wolsey* (1893) 286 The inconstantnes of prynces favour. **1575** Churchyard *Chippes* (1817) 132 To terrifie the stubborn stomacks and inconstantnesse of proud people. **1727** in Bailey (vol. II).

incon'struable, *a.* *rare.* [f. IN-^{3} + CONSTRUABLE.] That cannot be construed.

1874 H. R. Reynolds *John Bapt.* v. §2. 325 It may be pronounced.. inconstruable to exact thought.

†**incon'suete,** *a.* *Obs. rare.* [ad. L. *inconsuēt-us* unaccustomed, f. *in-* (IN-^{3}) + *consuētus* CONSUETE.] Unusual, unaccustomed.

1432–50 tr. *Higden* (Rolls) III. 437 As for that inconsuete message. *Ibid.* IV. 395 Ȝiffenge to theym singuler prerogatives, and inconsuete of the noble dignities of Rome.

†**incon'sult,** *a.* *Obs. rare*$^{-1}$. [ad. L. *inconsult-us* unconsulted, unadvised, f. *in-* (IN-^{3}) + *consultus*: see CONSULT *v.* Cf. obs. F. *inconsulte.*] Inconsiderate, unadvised, unreflecting.

1652 Gaule *Magastrom.* 135 Rude sensuall appetites, meer animal affections, and inconsult.

incon'sultable, *a.* *rare.* [In-^{3}.] Incapable of being consulted.

1888 Rye *Records & Record Search.* iv. 39 The King's Silver Books.. owing to damage done them by fire are inconsultable until that [reign] of George I.

†**incon'sulted,** *a.* *Obs. rare.* [f. L. *inconsult-us* (see INCONSULT) + -ED^{1}. Cf. F. *inconsulté.*]

1. = INCONSULT.

1533 Bellenden *Livy* III. (1822) 237 Ye.. ar like ane vane cumpany of pepill inconsultit and fulische.

2. Unconsulted, not asked (cf. L. *inconsulto senatu*, etc.).

1529 in Burnet *Hist. Ref.* II. 98 Ne do by himself any thing notable therein.. the said Emperor first inconsulted, or not consenting thereunto.

inconsumable (ɪnkən'sjuːməb(ə)l), *a.* [IN-^{3}.]

1. Incapable of being consumed by fire, etc.

1646 Sir T. Browne *Pseud. Ep.* III. xiv. 140 Named Asbeston.. whereof by Art were weaved napkins, shirts, and coats inconsumable by fire. **1774** Goldsm. *Nat. Hist.* (1862) II. II. iii. 401 (*Salamander*) The idle report of its being inconsumable in fire, has caused many of these poor animals to be burnt. **1821** Shelley *Epipsychid.* 579 Ever still Burning, yet ever inconsumable. **1875** F. I. Scudamore *Day Dreams* 31 An inconsumable candle, which diminished not, no matter how long it was lighted.

2. *Pol. Econ.* Of which it is not the object or purpose to be consumed in use.

1785 Paley *Mor. Philos.* III. i. ix. (1830) 104 When the identical loan is to be returned, as a book, a horse, a harpsichord, it is called inconsumable. **1884** L. Groulund *Coop. Commw.* i. 28 The inconsumable things, like machinery, leather, coin.

Hence **incon'sumably** *adv.* (Wright, 1855).

†**incon'sumed,** *a.* *Obs. rare*$^{-1}$. [f. IN-^{3} + *consumed*, pa. pple. of CONSUME *v.*] Unconsumed, uncorrupted.

1450–1530 *Myrr. our Ladye* 309 Ioye thou, for thoughe thou be deade, yet thow abydest inconsumed.

†**incon'summate,** *a.* *Obs. rare.* [ad. late L. *inconsummāt-us*: see IN-^{3} and CONSUMMATE.] Not consummated or completed; unfinished.

a **1641** Bp. Mountagu *Acts & Mon.* (1642) 32 The other Iesus, son of Iosedec, left things as imperfect and inconsummate. **1678** Cudworth *Intell. Syst.* I. v. 648 Nor did the Nature of things take begining from inconsummate and imperfect things. **1695** Ld. Preston *Boeth.* III. 134 For Nature doth not derive her Origine from things diminished and inconsummate.

Hence †**incon'summateness** (Webster, 1828).

†**incon'sumptible,** *a.* *Obs.* [a. obs. F. *inconsumptible*, *-somptible*, or ad. late L. *inconsumptibilis*, f. *in-* (IN-^{3}) + *consumptibilis* CONSUMPTIBLE.] Incapable of being consumed.

1579 Fulke *Heskins' Parl.* 50 The maister did set before his disciples the inconsumptible meate. *c* **1610** *Lives Wom. Saints* 33 It [the cross] is diuided to allmoste innumerable receyuers of it daylie, yet still whole to those that adore it, and all this inconsumptible integritie hath it [etc.]. **1644** Digby *Nat. Bodies* vii. (1645) 64 They believe such fires to feed upon nothing; and consequently, to be inconsumptible and perpetuall. **1708** Motteux *Rabelais* v. xli. (1737) 172 They were full of burning Water.. inconsumptible.

†**incon'sutile,** *a.* *Obs. rare.* [ad. late L. *inconsūtilis* (Vulg., *John* xix. 23) not sewed together, without seam, f. *in-* (IN-^{3}) + *consūtilis* CONSUTILE, f. *consuĕre, consūt-* to sew together.] Disagreeing, incongruous (like 'a piece of new cloth sewed on an old garment', *Matt.* ix. 16).

c **1450** *Mirour Saluacioun* 3205 Marie didde onne hire sons cote inconsutyle with out semyng. **1657** Gaule *Sapient. Just.* 42 What perhaps may be congruously spoken betwixt one particular man and another is very inconsutile to be said betwixt Adam and all Mankind.

†**incontaina'bility.** *Obs.* [f. IN-^{3} + CONTAINABLE + -ITY.] Incapability of being contained.

1644 Prynne & Walker *Fiennes's Trial* 65 For his horse and foot, incontainability in the Castle, in Case he had been forced to retire into it.

incontaminable (ɪnkən'tæmɪnəb(ə)l), *a.* [ad. eccl. L. *incontāminābilis*: see IN-^{3} and CONTAMINABLE.] Incapable of being contaminated.

1846 Trench *Mirac.* x. (1862) 221 He.. incontaminable Himself, feared not the contamination of a touch.

incon'taminate, *a.* [ad. L. *incontāminātus*, f. *in-* (IN-^{3}) + *contāminātus* CONTAMINATE *ppl. a.*] Uncontaminated, undefiled, unaffected by any corruption.

1508 Fisher 7 *Penit. Ps.* cxxx. Wks. (1876) 228 It is the very innocent and precious blode of the incontamynate lambe. **1664** H. More *Myst. Iniq.* Apol. 563 Ye that phansy your selves.. the onely sound and incontaminate part of our Nation. **1844** W. Kay in tr. *Fleury's Eccl. Hist.* III. 341 *note*, The essential light mixes not with other matter, but is incontaminate, incapable of being united.. with any other substance.

Hence **incon'taminateness** (Craig, 1847).

†**incon'taminated,** *a.* *Obs. rare*$^{-1}$. [f. as prec. + -ED^{1}.] = INCONTAMINATE.

1654 Cokaine *Dianea* I. 55 Knowing him of an incontaminated goodness, he would have prevented him with chastisement.

incon'temptible, *a.* *rare.* [IN-^{3}.] Not to be despised.

1742 Johnson *Debates in Parl.* (1787) II. 108 New arguments equally conclusive and incontemptible.

†**incon'tentable,** *a.* *Obs. rare*$^{-1}$. [IN-^{3}.] Not contentable; not to be satisfied; or perh. Not to be contained or bounded.

1720 Welton *Suffer. Son of God* II. xiv. 393 O Happy Spirits, whom the Vision.. of this Heavenly Redeemer furnishes with that Incontentable Variety of Bliss.

†**inconten'tation.** *Obs. rare.* [f. IN-^{3} + CONTENTATION.] Dissatisfaction, discontent.

1860 in Worcester, citing Goodwin.

incon,testa'bility. *rare.* [f. next: see -ITY. Cf. F. *incontestabilité.*] The quality of being incontestable; an indisputable fact.

1862 Wraxall *Hugo's 'Misérables'* v. xxviii. (1877) 17 Under the pressure of this incomprehensible incontestability he felt his brain cracking. **1864** in Webster.

incontestable (ɪnkən'tɛstəb(ə)l), *a.* (Also erroneously -ible.) [a. F. *incontestable* (= Sp. *incontestable*, It. *incontestabile*), f. *in-* (IN-^{3}) + *contestable* CONTESTABLE.] That cannot be contested or disputed; indisputable, unquestionable, incontrovertible.

1673 Temple *Let. to Dk. Florence* Wks. 1731 II. 287 Your Judgment is with me incontestable. **1748** *Anson's Voy.* I. iii. 33 This alone would be.. an incontestible proof of the service, which the Nation hath thence received. **1825** Scott *Betrothed* i, Her beauty was incontestable. **1885** Sir J. W. Chitty in *Law Rep.* 29 Chanc. Div. 992, I hold that the evidence is altogether incontestible.

Hence **incon'testableness.**

1727 Bailey vol. II, *Incontestibleness.* **1864** Webster, *Incontestableness.* **1895** *Blackw. Mag.* July 171 One instance .. exceeds all others in definition and incontestableness.

incontestably (ɪnkɒn'tɛstəblɪ), *adv.* (Also erron. -ibly.) [f. prec. + -LY^{2}.] Unquestionably, indisputably, indubitably.

a **1711** Ken *Hymns Evang.* Poet. Wks. 1721 I. 180 Rising from Death, was an appropriate sign Of Power most incontestably Divine. **1794** G. Adams *Nat. & Exp. Philos.* IV. xxxviii. 50 The annual motion of the earth is incontestibly proved by observation. **1873** Symonds *Grk. Poets* vii. 230 Euripides incontestably displays the quality of radiancy.

†**incon'tested,** *a.* *Obs.* [IN-^{3}.] Not contested, uncontested; undisputed.

1712 Addison *Spect.* No. 543 ⁋4, I think we may lay this down as an incontested Principle, that Chance never acts in a perpetual Uniformity and Consistence with it self. **1757–8** Smollett *Hist. Eng.* (1800) II. 158 These assertions were supported by many incontested facts. **1794** J. Williams *Crying Epistle* 55 Her mind was incorruptible, her wisdom incontested.

incontestible, erron. form of INCONTESTABLE.

†**incon'tiguous,** *a.* *Obs. rare.* [f. late L. *incontigu-us* (f. *in-* (IN-^{3}) + *contiguus* CONTIGUOUS) + -OUS.] Not in contact or touching one another; unconnected.

1660 Boyle *New Exp. Phys. Mech.* xxiv. 193 Small Bracelets, consisting of equally little incontiguous Beads. **1685** Cotton tr. *Montaigne* I. 293 The way of speaking that

I love is..free from affectation, irregular, incontiguous and bold, where every piece makes up an entire body.

Hence †**incon'tiguously** *adv.* (Wright, 1855).

incontinence (ɪnˈkɒntɪnəns). Also 4–6 incontynence. [a. F. *incontinence* (12th c.) or ad. L. *incontinēntia*, n. of quality f. *incontinēnt-em*: see IN-[3] and CONTINENT *a.*]

1. Want of continence or self-restraint; inability to contain or retain: **a.** With reference to the bodily appetites, esp. the sexual passion: Unchastity.

1382 WYCLIF *1 Cor.* vii. 5 Eft turne ȝe aȝen in to the same thing, lest Sathanas tempte ȝou for ȝoure incontynence. *c* **1400** MAUNDEV. (1839) xiv. 161 Often tyme..the gode Dyamande lesethe his vertue, be synne and for Incontynence of him that berethe it. **1533** MORE *Apol.* ix. Wks. 866/1, I doe not allowe, but obhorre incontinence in sacred professed persones. **1624** MASSINGER *Renegado* IV. ii, Any virgin..convicted of corporal looseness and incontinence. **1784** COWPER *Task* I. 699 Such London is, by taste and wealth proclaim'd The fairest capital of all the world, By riot and incontinence the worst. **1873** SYMONDS *Grk. Poets* vi. 169 Handsome youths are admonished by Pindar to beware of lawlessness and shun incontinence.

b. In general sense. (Const. *of.*)

1836 HOR. SMITH *Tin Trump.* (1876) 342 He who labours under an incontinence of speech, seldom gets the better of his complaint. **1850** L. HUNT *Autobiog.* I. v. 202 His laughter would follow his tears with a happy incontinence. **1858–65** CARLYLE *Fredk. Gt.* XI. iii, [They] do not waste themselves by incontinence of tongue. **1881** SIR T. MARTIN *Horace, Odes* I. xviii, Transparent as crystal, that shows In its babbling incontinence all that it knows.

2. *Path.* Inability to retain a natural evacuation, esp. ***incontinence of urine*** (= L. *incontinentia urinæ*, in Pliny.)

1754–64 SMELLIE *Midwif.* I. 162 The woman commonly labours under an incontinence of urine. **1874** VAN BUREN *Dis. Genit. Org.* 229 Incontinence, like retention, is a symptom, and not a disease.

†**in'continency.** *Obs.* [ad. L. *incontinēntia*: see prec. and -ENCY.] The quality of being incontinent.

1. a. = INCONTINENCE 1.

1485 *Act 1 Hen. VII*, c. 4 Avoutrie fornicacion inceste or eny other flesshely incontinency. **1526** TINDALE *1 Cor.* vii. 5 Come agayne to the same thynge lest Satan tempt you for youre incontinency. *a* **1682** SIR T. BROWNE *Tracts* (1684) 63 The one accused Susanna of incontinency under a Πρῖνος, or Ever-green Oak. **1732** NEAL *Hist. Purit.* I. 415 Such as shall ..be convicted of..any fleshly Incontinency.

b. = INCONTINENCE 1 b.

c **1715** SWIFT *Inquiry Queen's Last Ministry* i. Wks. 1841 I. 504/1 As the earl was too reserved, so perhaps the other was too free, not from any incontinency of talk, but from the mere contempt of multiplying secrets.

2. *Path.* = INCONTINENCE 2.

[Cf. quot. 1607 s.v. INCONSTANCY 4.]

1789 W. BUCHAN *Dom. Med.* (1790) 531 Suppression and incontinency of urine.

incontinent (ɪnˈkɒntɪnənt), *a.* (*sb.*) [a. F. *incontinent* (14th c.) or ad. L. *incontinēnt-em*, f. *in-* (IN-[3]) + *continēnt-* CONTINENT.]

A. *adj.* **1.** Not continent; wanting in self-restraint: chiefly with reference to sexual appetite.

c **1380** *Minor Poems fr. Vernon MS.* (1892) 138 Of an incontinent monk. *c* **1450** *St. Cuthbert* (Surtees) 7037 þat nane presume, incontinent, To sacre þe haly sacrament. **1526** *Pilgr. Perf.* (W. de W. 1531) 95 He is so incontynent & vnchaste, yᵗ his mynde is blynde. **1613** PURCHAS *Pilgrimage* (1614) 882 It was death for any to be found false and incontinent. **1767** FAWKES *Theocritus* i. Note cvii. (R.), The mistress of Daphnis upbraiding him for his incontinent passion. **1857** GLADSTONE *Glean.* VI. liv. 83 Origen treats the remarriage during the consort's life as forbidden by Scripture; yet thinks it may be conceded, with qualification to the infirmity of incontinent men.

2. Unable to contain, retain, or keep back. Usually const. *of*.

1641 MILTON *Ch. Govt.* II. iii, Although I have given it the name of a liquid thing, yet it is not incontinent to bound itself, as humid things are. **1660** —— *Free Commw.* Wks. (1851) 438 Incontinent of Secrets, if any be imparted to them. *a* **1680** BUTLER *Rem.* (1759) II. 446 A Prodigal..is very loose and incontinent of his Coin, and lets it fly, like Jupiter, in a Shower. **1725** POPE *Odyss.* XIX. 79 Melantho.. Renewed the attack, incontinent of spleen. **1865** *Sat. Rev.* 5 Aug. 167/1 Underlings incontinent of tongue often reveal.. the policy of their masters.

3. Unable to retain natural evacuations.

1828 in WEBSTER. **1901** G. B. SHAW *Admirable Bashville* II. i. 309 To begin my life a speechless babe, hairless, incontinent, Hobbling upon all fours, a nurse's nuisance. **1973** *Times* 11 June 14/2 Mrs Jones is doubly incontinent and vomits several times a day.

B. as *sb.* An unchaste person.

1598 B. JONSON *Ev. Man in Hum.* IV. viii, O, old incontinent, dost thou not shame When all thy powers in chastity are spent To have a mind so hot?

Hence **in'continentness** (Bailey vol. II, 1727).

incontinent (ɪnˈkɒntɪnənt), *adv.* (*a.*) *arch.* Also 5–6 en-, -tynent, -tenent. [a. F. *incontinent* (14th c. = Sp., It. *incontinente*), ad. late L. *in continēnti* (sc. *tempore*) in continuous time, without any interval. The early variant *encontinent* corresponds to earlier OF. *encontenant*, Prov. *encontenen.*] Straightway, forthwith, at once, immediately, without delay; = INCONTINENTLY *adv.*[2]

[**1432–50** tr. *Higden* (Rolls) V. 393 Where he diede incontinenti after that he hade seide so.]

1425 *Sc. Acts Jas. I* (1597) §51 The partie sal be challenged incontinent of the Kingis peace breaking. *c* **1440** *Generydes* 1571 Whanne they were come, anon incontynent Generydes was brought owt of the Iayle. *Ibid.* 1769 Thanne spake Lucas anon encontinent. *a* **1450** *Knt. de la Tour* (1868) 130 She was incontenent iuged vnto the dethe. **1523** LD. BERNERS *Froiss.* I. xiv. 14 They entred encontynent into theyr shippes, to passe the see. **1559** MORWYNG *Evonym.* 12 A water may be made which shall incontenent breake the stone in the bladdar. **1609** SKENE *Reg. Maj.* II. xl. 36 Heires being of lawfull age, incontinent after the deceis of their predicessours they may enter to their heretage. *c* **1611** CHAPMAN *Iliad* XXIV. 299 This charge incontinent He put in practice. **1719** D'URFEY *Pills* (1872) III. 326 Behind the Cloth the Friar went, And was in the Well incontinent. **1818** SCOTT *Hrt. Midl.* xxi, The Lords will be here incontinent, and proceed *instanter* to trial. **1840** BARHAM *Ingol. Leg.* Ser. I. *Leech Folkestone*, Place thyself incontinent in yonder bath.

b. as *adj.* (*nonce-use*) Immediate

1840 BARHAM *Ingol. Leg.* Ser. I, *Leech Folkestone*, Hath any one a smoky chimney?—here is an incontinent cure.

in'continently, *adv.*[1] [f. INCONTINENT *a.* + -LY[2].] In an incontinent manner; loosely, unchastely.

1552 HULOET, Incontinently, *solute.* **1598** BARCKLEY *Felic. Man* (1631) 611 It is an unseemly thing..to live delicately, loosely, or incontinently. **1655** FULLER *Ch. Hist.* III. vii. §28 Queen Isabel..living incontinently with R. Mortimer. **1755** JOHNSON, *Incontinently*, unchastely; without restraint of the appetites.

incontinently (ɪnˈkɒntɪnəntlɪ), *adv.*[2] *arch.* [f. INCONTINENT *adv.* + -LY[2].] Straightway, at once, immediately; = INCONTINENT *adv.*

1484 CAXTON *Fables of Æsop* v. v, Incontynently as the dogges perceyued and sawe the foxe and the catte, they beganne to renne vpon them. **1542–3** *Act 34 & 35 Hen. VIII*, c. 14 §4 The said clerke..shall incontinentlie without delaie certifie the saide names. **1633** T. STAFFORD *Pac. Hib.* II. x. (1810) 337 Sir Charles incontinently dispatched a Horseman with Letters to the President. **1761** STERNE *Tr. Shandy* IV. xxvii, The effect of which was this, that he leapt incontinently up. **1844** EMERSON *Lect., Young American* Wks. (Bohn) II. 297 If one of the flock [of wolves]..so much as limp, the rest eat him up incontinently. **1876** C. M. DAVIES *Unorth. Lond.* (ed. 2) 426 My cheery friend.. presented me incontinently to the lecturer.

inconti'nuity. *rare.* [IN-[3].] The quality or fact of being incontinuous; absence or breach of continuity.

1865 *Athenæum* No. 1959. 648/3 Incoherencies and incontinuities.

incontinuous (ɪnkənˈtɪnjuːəs), *a. rare.* [IN-[3].] Not continuous; discontinuous.

1862 R. H. PATTERSON *Ess. Hist. & Art* 68 They become imperceptible to the ear, in the low notes by the vibrations becoming too dull and incontinuous. **1892** STEVENSON *Across the Plains* 230 All brought down to the same faint residuum as a last night's dream to some incontinuous images.

†**incon'tracted**, *a. Obs. rare.* [IN-[3].] Not contracted; uncontracted.

1725 BLACKWALL *Sacr. Class.* I. 228 (T.) This dialect uses the incontracted termination both in nouns and verbs.

incontractile (ɪnkənˈtræktɪl, -aɪl), *a.* [IN-[3].] Not contractile; incapable of contraction.

1822–34 *Good's Study Med.* (ed. 4) I. 670 The pupil [was] dilated and incontractile. *Ibid.* II. 648 The muscular fibres are equally loose and incontractile.

incontraction (ɪnkənˈtrækʃən). [IN-[3].] The fact of not contracting; failure to contract; noncontraction.

1803 *Med. Jrnl.* X. 2 On the Incontraction of an Artery.

†**incontra'dictable**, *a. Obs.* (Also -ible.) [f. IN-[3] + CONTRADICT + -ABLE: known much earlier than *contradictable.*] That cannot be contradicted or gainsaid.

1624 CAPT. SMITH *Virginia* III. ii. 44 This incontradictable reason will shew them plainely they are too ill advised to nourish such ill conceits. **1630** —— *Trav. & Adv.* 13 Many incontradictible perswading reasons.

†**in'contrair**, *adv.* and *prep. Sc. Obs.* Also -are, -ar. [f. IN *prep.* + CONTRAIR *sb.*; cf. the fuller phrases *in the contrair* (*of*), *in our contrair*, etc.]

a. as *advb. phr.* or *adv.* (followed by a preposition): In opposition *to*, in spite *of*.

c **1480** HENRYSON *Mor. Fab.* 37 This hound of hell, Deuored hes my Lambe..in contrair to your cry. **1535** STEWART *Cron. Scot.* III. 145 Incontrair than of all his lordis will.

b. as *prep.* In opposition to, contrary to; against.

1484 *Sc. Acts Jas. III* (1814) 166 Impetraciouns made in the Court of Rome in contrare our souuerane lordis privilege. **1513** DOUGLAS *Æneis* VII. viii. *heading*, How Alecto persuadit has Turnus To move battale incontrar Latinus. **1558** KENNEDIE *Compend. Tract.* in *Wodrow Soc. Misc.* (1844) I. 119 Abominabyll heresyis incontrar our faith. **1560** ROLLAND *Crt. Venus* Prol. 205 [It is als] incontrair his Complexioun [As ane f]asert to fecht with ane Falcoun.

†**in'contrary**, *adv. Obs. rare*[−1]. [f. IN *prep.* + CONTRARY *sb.* An AF. *encontrarie* is quoted by Godefroy from the *Conquest of Ireland.*] In opposition, contrary (*to*): = prec. b.

1488–9 *Act 4 Hen. VII*, c. 11 Forfeiture of the double value of all the Wolles bought..incontrarie to this ordenaunce.

†**incon'tributive**, *a. Obs. rare.* [IN-[3].] Not contributive; that does not contribute.

1667 WATERHOUSE *Fire Lond.* 170 Proprietors which now are incontributive to the Publique Charge.

incontrollable (ɪnkənˈtrəʊləb(ə)l), *a.* [IN-[3]. Cf. F. *incontrôlable* (Littré).]

1. That cannot be controlled, checked, restrained, or authoritatively regulated; uncontrollable.

1599 SANDYS *Europae Spec.* (1605) L iij b, Their not erring and incontroleable lord of Rome. **1625** BP. MONTAGU *App. Cæsar* v. 153 Solyman, Amurath, and others, challenging absolute, irresistable, incontrouleable power to set up, pull downe, order, alter, and dispose the world, and all things in the world, at pleasure. **1652** J. HALL *Height Eloq.* p. lxxxi, They breed up incontroulable Tyrants over their souls. **1744** HARRIS *Three Treat.* III. II. (1765) 232 Fated in that Order of incontroulable Events. **1820** SCOTT *Abbot* iii, A character..by nature bold, impetuous, and incontrollable. **1844** STANLEY *Arnold* (1845) I. iv. 196 An incontrollable desire to give vent to the thoughts that were struggling within him.

†**2.** That cannot be interfered with or altered in any way; fixed, unchangeable. *Obs.*

1605 TIMME *Quersit.* II. iv. 116 In gold..there is a certaine incontrollable in incorruptible composition. **1646** SIR T. BROWNE *Pseud. Ep.* VI. x. 322 Of colours in generall..no man hath yet beheld the true nature, or positively set downe their incontroulable causes.

†**3.** Incontrovertible, unquestionable. *Obs.*

c **1645** HOWELL *Lett.* (1650) I. 477 Writings..handed over to posterity as incontroulable truths for so many ages. **1646** SIR T. BROWNE *Pseud. Ep.* IV. xii. 214 These were delivered by the Evangelist, and carry no doubt an incontroulable conformity into the intention of his delivery.

Hence **incon'trollably** *adv.* (*a*) Without control; unrestrainedly; †(*b*) Incontrovertibly, fixedly.

1646 SIR T. BROWNE *Pseud. Ep.* IV. xii. 218 Being not incontroulably determined, at what time to begin, whether at conception, animation, or exclusion. *a* **1716** SOUTH *Serm.* VIII. i. (R.), For, as a man thinks or desires in his heart, such indeed he is, for then most truly, because most incontroulably, he acts himself. **1800** T. JEFFERSON *Writ.* (1859) IV. 344 The abuses which would be incontrolably committed.

†**incon'trolled**, *a. Obs.* [IN-[3]. Cf. F. *incontrôlé* (Littré).] Not controlled; unchecked; not interfered with.

1650 HOWELL *For. Trav.* iii. (Arb.) 24 There is no compleat and incontrouled comfort.

incontrovertible (ɪnkɒntrəˈvɜːtɪb(ə)l), *a.* [IN-[3].] That cannot be controverted; incontestable, indisputable, indubitable.

1646 SIR T. BROWNE *Pseud. Ep.* VII. xiii. 365 Lastly, the thing it selfe whereon the opinion dependeth..is not incontrovertible; and for my own part, I remaine unsatisfied therein. **1793** BEDDOES *Math. Evid.* 152 When a theory is established by incontrovertible evidence, the usual mode of hostility is to dispute the author's claim to discovery. **1798** MALTHUS *Popul.* (1817) II. 65 The increase of population since 1780 is incontrovertible. **1873** BLACK *Pr. Thule* xvii, Absolute and incontrovertible truth.

Hence **incontroverti'bility, incontro'vertibleness**, the quality of being incontrovertible.

1775 ASH, *Incontrovertibility* (*s.* perhaps not sufficiently authorized, from *incontrovertible*), the state of being incontrovertible. **1837** SIR F. PALGRAVE *Merch. & Friar* (1844) 121 Cases of flagrant delict,..required no other trial than the publicity or incontrovertibleness of the fact.

incontro'vertibly, *adv.* [f. prec. + -LY[2].] In an incontrovertible manner; without controversy, beyond dispute, indisputably.

1646 SIR T. BROWNE *Pseud. Ep.* VI. i. 278 For the Hebrew, it is incontrovertibly the primitive and surest text to rely on. **1712** in Somers *Tracts* II. 184 That Great-Britain is incontrovertibly more powerful than this State. **1845** LD. CAMPBELL *Chancellors* (1857) III. lxvii. 303 It was then shown very distinctly and incontrovertibly that none of the charges amounted to treason. **1886** SIDGWICK *Hist. Ethics* iv. 248 It is not to be regarded as absolutely and incontrovertibly valid.

in contumaciam: see IN *Lat. prep.*

†**incon'tunded**, *a. Obs.* [IN-[3].] Not bruised or pounded.

1599 A. M. tr. *Gabelhouer's Bk. Physicke* 51/2 Ligate a little incontundede Safferne in a little linnen cloth, soacke it 3 dayes in a little whyte wyne.

inconvenience (ɪnkənˈviːnɪəns), *sb.* [a. OF. *inconvenience* (mod.F. *inconvenance*), ad. late L. *inconvenientia* inconsistency, n. of quality f. *inconvenient-em* INCONVENIENT: see -ENCE. Cf. ILLCONVENIENCE.] The fact or quality of being inconvenient.

†**1.** Want of agreement; incongruity, disagreement; inconsistency with reason or rule, absurdity; with *pl.* An instance of this; an inconsistency; an absurdity. *Obs.*

c **1400** *Beryn* 2576 That I may bet perseyve al inconvenience Dout, pro contra, and ambiguity. **1526** *Pilgr.*

Perf. (W. de W. 1531) 194 Yet it is no inconvenyence y^t his holy mother & other sayntes be as particular meanes bytwene vs & god. **a 1536** TINDALE *Doctr. Treat.* (Parker Soc. 1848) 380 That Christ was made man and died: also bread, which seemeth to some a great inconvenience. **1587** GOLDING *De Mornay* i. 12 By these inconveniences they conclude, that there is no God at all. **1610** A. COOKE *Pope Joan* in *Harl. Misc.* (Malham) IV. 77 *Protestant.* What mean you by the inconvenience of their testimonies? *Papist.* Their disagreeing one with another. **a 1619** FOTHERBY *Atheom.* II. iii. §2 (1622) 215 Yet can he not be the cause of himselfe, for the fore-named inconueniences. **1706** tr. *Dupin's Eccl. Hist. 16th C.* II. v. 45 Francis Maryon believ'd there was no Inconvenience in saying, That some of it [Christ's blood] staid here below.

†**b.** Unsuitableness, unfitness. *Obs.*

1413 *Pilgr. Sowle* (Caxton 1483) IV. ii. 58 Adam was nought well disposyd to etyng of this appel for inconuenyence of the season in whiche he receyued it. **a 1600** HOOKER (J.), They plead against the inconvenience, not the unlawfulness of popish apparel. **1684** R. WALLER *Nat. Exper.* 74 To avoid this inconvenience of the Screws.

†**2.** Moral or ethical unsuitableness; unbecoming or unseemly behaviour; impropriety; with *pl.*, an unseemly act, an impropriety, an offence. *Obs.*

c **1460** *Play Sacram.* 897 Agaynst god yf ye haue wroght eny Inconuenyence. **1509** BARCLAY *Shyp of Folys* (1874) I. 51 Howe youthe which is nat norysshed in doctryne, In age is gyuen vnto al Inconuenyence. **1547** *Homilies* I. *Agst. Contention* I. (1859) 135 They fall.. sometime from hot words to further inconvenience. **1560** BIBLE (Genev.) *Numbers, Argt.*, That either they fall not to such inconueniences, or else return to him quickly by true repentance.

†**3.** Harm, injury, mischief; misfortune, trouble. *Obs.* (passing into 4).

14.. *Proverbs of Good Counsel* 82 in *Q. Eliz. Acad.* (1869) 70 Yf þou be trobyllyd with ynconvenyens, Arme þ^e alway with Inward pacyens. **1509** HAWES *Past. Pleas.* x. (Percy Soc.) 36 To dysnull myschefe and inconvenyence, They made our lawes wyth grete diligence. **1651** HOBBES *Leviath.* II. xviii. 94 They that live under the government of Democracy,.. attribute all the inconvenience to that forme of Commonwealth. **1653** HOLCROFT *Procopius* I. *Goth. Wars* 20 Beneventum standing high, and over against Dalmatia, shares in the inconvenience of this wind. **1695** WOODWARD *Nat. Hist. Earth* v. (1723) 264 The Inconvenience would not have stop'd there.

†**b.** with *pl.* A mischief, an injury; an untoward occurrence, a misfortune. *Obs.* (passing into 4 b).

c **1489** CAXTON *Sonnes of Aymon* i. 33, I haue grete fere that some inconuenyence be happed vnto him. **1584** POWEL *Lloyd's Cambria* 95 Whereof grew a great inconuenience and slaughter. **1608** ARMIN *Nest Ninn.* (1842) 15 Rapine, ruine, and a thousand inconveniences, follow. **1736** BUTLER *Anal.* I. iii. Wks. 1874 I. 57 Often infamy and external inconveniences are the public consequences of vice as vice. **1796** C. MARSHALL *Gard.* ii. (1813) 21 It is yet unable to bear the inconveniences of the weather.

†**c.** Technically distinguished from *mischief*: see quot. *Obs.*

1622 MALYNES *Anc. Law-Merch.* 161 It is better to suffer a mischiefe than an inconuenience; the mischiefe being attributed to one or some particular persons, and the inconuenience to the whole Common-wealth in generall. **a 1709** ATKYNS *Parl. & Pol. Tracts* (1734) 199 By a Mischief is meant, when one Man or some few men suffer by the Hardship of a Law, which Law is yet useful for the Publick. But an Inconvenience is to have a publick Law disobeyed or broken, or an Offence to go unpunished.

4. The quality or condition of being inconvenient; want of adaptation to personal requirement or ease; trouble, discomfort, disadvantage; incommodity.

1653 WALTON *Angler* Table, In this Discourse.. I have not observed a method, which.. may be some inconvenience to the Reader. **1783** MORELL *Ainsworth's Lat. Dict.* IV. s.v. *Tithonus*, That Aurora made him immortal, but could not take from him the inconvenience of old age. **1837** DICKENS *Pickw.* xxvii, She could have spared him without the smallest inconvenience. **1885** *Daily News* 21 Dec. 5/1 The long delay.. has already led to considerable public inconvenience.

b. with *pl.* An inconvenient circumstance; something that interferes with ease or comfort, or causes trouble; a disadvantage, a discomfort.

1578 T. N. tr. *Conq. W. India* 30 The letter being written, there was found an inconvenience, which was, they knew not how to carrye the letter secretly. **1641** WILKINS *Math. Magick* I. ix. (1648) 59 The chief inconvenience of this instrument is, that, in a short space it will be screwed unto its full length. **1732** ARBUTHNOT *Rules of Diet* 296 They have only one Inconvenience, that they create Thirst. **1818** CRUISE *Digest* (ed. 2) II. 327 This rule was originally.. intended to avoid the inconveniences which might arise by admitting an interval, when there should be no tenant of the freehold to do the services to the lord. **1884** *Manch. Exam.* 2 May 4/7 The necessity of taking out passports would be a serious inconvenience to foreign traders.

inconvenience (ɪnkən'viːnɪəns), *v.* [f. prec. sb.] *trans.* To cause inconvenience to; to put to inconvenience; to incommode, trouble.

a **1656** HALES *Gold. Rem.* I. (1673) 49 For it is not the variety of opinions, but our own perverse wills.. which hath so inconvenienced the church. **1674** tr. *Scheffer's Lapland* 90 That they may.. not be inconvenienced with the weight of these blankets. **1797** SOUTHEY *Lett.* (1856) I. 40, I instantly quitted the university, that my uncle might no longer be inconvenienced by me. **1842** S. LOVER *Handy Andy* i. 9 The inconvenienced party had only to say [etc.]. **1876** T. HARDY *Ethelberta* (1890) 369 Be content to let her keep her position without inconveniencing her by your intrusions or complaints.

inconveniency (ɪnkən'viːnɪənsɪ). Now *rare.* [ad. L. *inconvenientia*: see prec. sb. and -ENCY.]

†**1.** = INCONVENIENCE *sb.* 1. *Obs.*

a **1533** FRITH *Wks.* 141 (R.) Of this text should follow two inconueniencies, if the sacrament were the naturall body of Christ. **1662** STILLINGFL. *Orig. Sacr.* I. vi. §8 Thus every way, this opinion.. is pressed with inconveniencies. **a 1682** SIR T. BROWNE *Let. to Friend* in *Hydriot.* etc. (1736) 56 Though some wondered at this Position, yet I saw no Inconveniency in it.

†**2.** = INCONVENIENCE *sb.* 2. *Obs.*

1610 HEALEY *St. Aug. Citie of God* XXII. xxiii. (1620) 846 Lest desire of reuenge should draw vs to inconueniencie. **1747** CHESTERF. *Lett.* (1792) I. cxxxiii. 355, I should have avoided many follies and inconveniencies, which undirected youth run me into.

†**3.** = INCONVENIENCE *sb.* 3. *Obs.*

1553 Q. MARY *Proclam. Coins* in Strype *Eccl. Mem.* (1721) III. App. v. 8 In no wyse can longer suffer the same inconueniencie. **1669** PENN *No Cross* xiv. §7 Insensible of the Inconveniency that attends the like Follies. **1706** MRS. CENTLIVRE *Basset-Table* v, Now you discover what inconveniency your gaming has brought you into.

†**b.** = INCONVENIENCE *sb.* 3 b. *Obs.*

a **1450** *Knt. de la Tour* (1868) 98 To saie no thinge in the presence of the peple vnto his displesaunce, for doute of mani gret Inconueniencys. **1543** GRAFTON *Contn. Harding* 567 That some inconueniencie or cause of strife should chaunce. **1647** SPRIGGE *Anglia Rediv.* I. vi. (1854) 56 He might have prevented that inconveniency which fell out. **a 1722** LISLE *Husb.* (1752) 90 For fear of a worse inconveniency.

4. = INCONVENIENCE *sb.* 4.

1552 HULOET, Inconueniencye, *importunitas.* **a 1628** F. GREVILLE *Sidney* (1652) 64 To weigh the immortall wisdom in even scales with mortall conveniency or inconveniency. **1658–9** *Burton's Diary* (1828) III. 363 Your question is not of conveniency or inconveniency, but of right. **1776** ADAM SMITH *W.N.* (1869) II. IV. i. 9 If money is wanted, barter will supply its place, though with a good deal of inconveniency. **1838** DICKENS *Nich. Nick.* xxxviii, There's inconveniency in it, but the novelty gives it a sort of relish.

b. = INCONVENIENCE *sb.* 4 b.

1640 QUARLES *Enchirid.* III. 53 Cast one eye upon the Inconveniencies, as well as the other upon the Conveniencies. **1746** WESLEY *Princ. Methodist* 31 More Inconveniencies may arise from the latter than from the former. **1818** JAS. MILL *Brit. India* II. v. ix. 697 The lending of money to the Nabob of Arcot.. had given rise to many inconveniencies.

c. *concr.* Applied humorously to an incommodious conveyance: cf. CONVENIENCY 6 d. (*nonce-use.*)

1877 LOWELL *Lett.* (1894) II. xiii. 225 This leather inconveniency will be at the door in half an hour.

inconvenient (ɪnkən'viːnɪənt), *a.* and *sb.* [a. F. *inconvénient* (13th c. in Hatz-Darm.), ad. L. *inconvenient-em*, f. *in-* (IN-³) + *convenient-em* agreement, according, CONVENIENT.]

A. *adj.* †**1.** Not agreeing or consonant; discordant, incongruous; inconsistent with reason or rule, absurd. *Obs.*

1398 TREVISA *Barth. De P.R.* VIII. xxviii. (Bodl. MS.), þanne it is nouȝt in conueniente to sette þat twei bodies bene ifeere in one place ȝif one of ham is sotel and formal.. of þat oþer material and vnperfite. **1552** HULOET, Inconuenient, abhorrynge, discordynge.. *absurdus.* **1570** LEVINS *Manip.* 68/43 Inconvenient, *incongruus.* **1635** PAGITT *Christianogr.* III. (1636) 40 In which booke many things.. were found inconvenient, and contrary to the true faith. **1674** OWEN *Holy Spirit* (1693) 57 Nothing is ascribed unto him that is unreasonable, inconvenient unto him in the Discharge of his Office.

†**2.** Not befitting the case or circumstances; unsuitable, unmeet, inappropriate, out of place. *Obs.*

c **1460** FORTESCUE *Abs. & Lim. Mon.* ix. (1885) 128 That diuerse lordis off Englande haue also moch livelode off thair owne, as than shall remayne in the kynges handes ffor his extraordinarie charges; wich were inconvenient, and wold be to the kynge right dredefull. **1552** HULOET, Inconuenient tyme, *intempestas.* **1600** SHAKS. *A.Y.L.* v. ii. 73 If it appeare not inconuenient to you. **1681** CHETHAM *Angler's Vade-m.* xli. (1689) 307 Because the Pike is so noble a Fish.. it's not inconvenient if I.. make a more particular Discourse of him. **1840** R. M. MCCHEYNE in *Mem.* (1872) 449 It will make the Syren Songs of this world inconvenient.

†**b.** Const. *for, to.* *Obs.*

c **1400** *Lanfranc's Cirurg.* 85 An inconuenient medicyn to þat membre. **1651** J. GOODWIN *Redempt. Redeemed* i. §5 Which signification is no ways inconvenient for this place. **1655** MOUFET & BENNET *Health's Improv.* (1746) 177 No Meat so wholesome as Pheasant-pouts; but to strong Stomachs it is inconvenientest. **1692** LOCKE *Educ.* §159 The reading of the whole Scripture indifferently, is.. very inconvenient for Children.

†**3.** Morally or ethically unsuitable; unbecoming in manner; unseemly, improper. *Obs.*

1494 FABYAN *Chron.* VI. cxcviii. 204 He walowed in lechery, giuynge hym to all vicious and inconuenyent lyfe of his body. **1542** *Procl. Hen. VIII* 22 July in Warton *Hist. Eng. Poetry* liv. (1840) III. 267 Boyes do singe masse, and preache in the pulpitt, with such other vnfittinge and inconuenient vsages. **a 1694** TILLOTSON *Serm.* xxii. (1742) II. 77 It is very inconvenient to say, that they who were to teach the precepts of Christ to others, did themselves break them by inspiration.

4. Not conducive to ease of action or condition; unfavourable to comfort; incommodious, troublesome, embarrassing, disadvantageous, awkward. (The current sense.)

1651 HOBBES *Leviath.* II. xxvi. 147 The people of Rome grew so numerous, as it was inconvenient to assemble them. **1706** PHILLIPS, *Inconvenient*, not convenient, troublesome, cumbersome. **1777** SHERIDAN *Trip Scarb.* II. i, If it be not inconvenient to you, he'll come and wait upon you. **1852** HAWTHORNE *Blithedale Rom.* xvi, This species of nervous sympathy.. was yet found rather inconvenient in its practical operations. **1870** DICKENS *E. Drood* xviii, We have a good choice of inconvenient lodgings in the town.

B. *sb.* That which is inconvenient.

†**1.** Something discordant, an incongruity, an inconsistency; something inconsistent with reason, an absurdity. *Obs.*

c **1374** CHAUCER *Boeth.* v. pr. iii. 123 (Camb. MS.) And yit ther folweth a noother inconuenyent of the whiche ther ne may ben thoght no moore felonos ne moore wykke, and þat is this, þat [etc.]. **1387–8** T. USK *Test. Love* III. iii. (Skeat) I. 77, I wene that none inconuenient shalt thou finde betwene Goddes forweting, and libertie of arbitrement; wherfore, I wote well thei maie stande togider. **1449** PECOCK *Repr.* I. xv. 81 Noon inconvenient is thouȝ God ordeyned the seid resoun.

†**2.** Something morally unfitting; an unseemly or unbecoming act; an impropriety, an abuse.

1460 CAPGRAVE *Chron.* (1858) 279 Aftir the batayle ful schamefully the Walsch women cutte of mennes membris, and put hem in her mouthis that were ded; and many othir inconvenientis ded thei that tyme. **1483** CAXTON *Cato* 3 b, The Synnes and inconuenientes that comen of playeng. **1523** FITZHERB. *Surv.* 26 b, The whiche mesemeth is the grettest inconuenyent that nowe is suffred by the lawe. **1538** BALE *Thre Lawes* 61 Proudenesse ye abhorre with lyke inconuenyentes.

†**3.** A troublesome or untoward circumstance; a misfortune, a mishap; an inconvenience. *Obs.*

c **1400** *Apol. Loll.* 79 þis inconuenient mai not be voydid. **1432–50** tr. *Higden* (Rolls) VIII. 469 Somme inconvenientes wolde folowe with ynne schorte space, bothe to hym and to the realme. **1475** *Bk. Noblesse* (Roxb.) 33 Here is yet noone so gret inconvenient of aventure ne mysfortune falle at this tyme, but that it hathe be seene fallen er now. **1526** *Pilgr. Perf.* (1531) 57 And so by these meanes thou shalte.. eschewe many sclaunders and inconvenientes. **1610** J. MELVILL *Diary* (Wodrow Soc.) 532 Eschewing any danger or inconvenient quhilk may be likelie to fall out. **1645** BOATE *Irel. Nat. Hist.* (1652) 65 In her mouth, she is incumbred with severall inconvenients.

†**inconvenientise.** *Obs. rare.* [f. prec. + -ISE. (Cf. *franchise.*)] = INCONVENIENCE 4 b.

1528 PAYNEL *Salerne's Regim.* B j b, Many other inconuenientises.. groweth and chanceth throughe excesse of meates and drynkes. *Ibid.* B ij, [This] ingendreth many inconuenientises in the body.

incon'veniently, *adv.* [f. INCONVENIENT *a.* + -LY².] In an inconvenient manner.

†**1.** Unsuitably, inappropriately; unbecomingly, improperly; inconsistently, incongruously. *Obs.*

1509 BARCLAY *Shyp Folys* Argt., This present Boke myght haue ben callyd nat inconuenyently the Satyr. **1549** LATIMER *5th Serm. bef. Edw. VI* (Arb.) 147 One wyl say, peraduenture, you speake vnsemelye, and inconuenientlye, so to be agaynste the offycers. **1552** HULOET, Inconuenientlye, or dishonestly, or contrary to reason, *absurde.* Inconuenientlye, or out of due tyme, *intempestiue.*

2. With inconvenience, trouble, or discomfort; uncomfortably, incommodiously.

a **1656** BP. HALL *Mourners in Sion* (R.), There is many an holy soul that dwels inconveniently, in a crazy, tottering, ruinous cottage. **1665** G. HAVERS *P. della Valle's Trav. E. India* 111 We stay'd under a great Tree.. spent this night inconveniently and supper-less. **1717** BERKELEY *Jrnl. Tour Italy* 2 June, Wks. 1871 IV. 559 Inconveniently cold for several hours this morning. **1837** DICKENS *Pickw.* xxxv, I am afraid you'll find it inconveniently large. **1876** GEO. ELIOT *Dan. Der.* xii, Things may turn out inconveniently after all.

†**incon'venientness.** *Obs. rare.* [f. as prec. + -NESS.] The quality of being inconvenient, inconvenience; in quot. 1616 unsuitableness.

1616 SURFL. & MARKH. *Country Farme* 529 If the inconuenientnesse of the place vvill not suffer you to cast them into squares, then make them somewhat more long. **1727** in BAILEY vol. II.

inconversable (ɪnkən'vɜːsəb(ə)l), *a.* ? *Obs.* Also erron. -ible. [f. IN-³ + CONVERSE *v.* + -ABLE; cf. Sp. *inconversable* (Guevara, 1539) and CONVERSABLE.] Not conversable; †unsociable (*obs.*); not disposed to converse, uncommunicative.

1577 HELLOWES *Gueuara's Chron.* 2 If he be inconuersible, they abhorre him [*orig.* si es inconuersable aborrescenle]. **1611** COTGR., *Insociable*, vnsociable, vncompanable, inconuersible. **1668** H. MORE *Div. Dial.* I. ii. (1713) 3 He is a Person very inconversable. **1706** *Reflex. upon Ridicule* 39 They are regarded as inconversable, rough hewn, rude and phantastical. **1720** DE FOE *Capt. Singleton* xv. (1840) 254 They fled from us, and were altogether inconversible.

Hence **incon'versableness** (Bailey vol. II, 1727).

inconversant (ɪn'kɒnvəsənt), *a.* *rare.* [IN-³.] Not conversant; not versed *in* or familiar *with.*

1800–19 G. SHAW *Zool.* III. 99 (L.) A person inconversant in natural history. **1836** SIR W. HAMILTON *Discuss., Stud. Math.* (1852) 311 Though himself not inconversant with these.. he did not perceive of what utility they could be.

inconversi'bility, *rare.* [f. IN-³ + CONVERSIBILITY; cf. L. *inconversiblis*, F.

inconversible.] Incapability of being converted (*into* something else); inconvertibility.

1784 MANN in *Lett. Lit. Men* (Camden) 427 M. Lavoisier, who has been combating these many years past in favour of the inconversibility of Water into any thing else.

†**incon'version.** *Obs. rare.* [IN-³.] Unconverted or unregenerate condition.

1633 BP. HALL *Hard Texts, N.T.* 210 Sinne hath in the time of your inconversion beene but of sleight account.

†**incon'verted,** *a. Obs.* [IN-³.] Not converted; not turned or changed; unconverted.

1646 SIR T. BROWNE *Pseud. Ep.* II. vi. 98 The bird not able to digest the fruit whereon she feedeth, from her inconverted muting. *Ibid.* III. x. 128 Wheresoever they rested remaining inconverted, and possessing one point of the Compasse, whilst the wind perhaps hath passed the two and thirty.

inconvertible (ɪnkən'vɜːtɪb(ə)l), *a.* (and *sb.*) [IN-³; perh. after F. *inconvertible* (1546 in Hatz.-Darm.) or late L. *inconvertibilis* unchanging.] Not convertible; incapable of being converted.

A. *adj.* **1.** Incapable of being changed into anything else; †*spec.* incapable of being assimilated, indigestible (cf. CONVERTIBLE 5 b).

1646 SIR T. BROWNE *Pseud. Ep.* II. v. 85 It..taketh leave of the permeant parts..and accompanieth the inconvertible portion unto the siege. **1652** BENLOWES *Theoph.* Ded. 22 The Immaculate Earth of the Humanity, Inseparable, Inconfusible, Inconvertible.

2. a. Incapable of being exchanged for one another, or transposed each into the place of the other; not interchangeable. Usually of terms: Not equivalent or synonymous.

1706 PHILLIPS, *Inconvertible* (in *Philos.*), that cannot be transposed, changed, or altered; as *inconvertible Terms.* **1864** BOWEN *Logic* v. 113 Genus and Accident inconvertible with the Subject.

b. *Logic.* Of a proposition: That cannot be converted (see CONVERT *v.* 5 b, CONVERSION 4).

1847 A. DE MORGAN *Formal Logic* iv. 58 The universal affirmative..and the particular negative..are not necessarily convertible, and are generally called *inconvertible.* **1849** W. THOMSON *Outl. Laws of Thought* (ed. 2) liii. 216 The judgment O is usually considered inconvertible by the ordinary method. **1857** W. SPALDING in *Encycl. Brit.* XIII. 606/1 They hold O to be inconvertible. **1864** BOWEN *Logic* vii. 204. **1875** ABP. THOMSON *Laws Th.* §85. 155 The judgment O is usually considered inconvertible by the ordinary method.

3. Incapable of being exchanged for something else. *spec.* of paper money, That cannot be converted into specie.

1833 HT. MARTINEAU *Berkeley the Banker* I. vi. 120 Inconvertible bank paper would have been everywhere refused. **1848** MILL *Pol. Econ.* III. xiii. §2 (1876) 330 An inconvertible currency, regulated by the price of bullion, would conform exactly in all its variations, to a convertible one. **1866** CRUMP *Banking* ix. 185 This country had what it is to be hoped it will never see again—an inconvertible paper currency.

†**4.** Incapable of being turned away *from. rare.*

1829 LANDOR *Wks.* (1846) II. 220/1 First, we must find the priests; for ours are inconvertible from their crumbling altars.

B. *sb.* A proposition which cannot be converted.

1847 A. DE MORGAN *Formal Logic* iv. 62 As to inconvertibles, contranominal and converse are terms of the same meaning.

Hence **inconverti'bility, incon'vertibleness; incon'vertibly** *adv.*

1727 BAILEY vol. II, *Inconvertibleness.* **1816** BENTHAM *Chrestom.* App. viii, Inconvertibility of Geometry and Algebra. **1833** HT. MARTINEAU *Berkeley the Banker* I. viii. 159 Others..complained of the example of inconvertibility set by the Bank of England. **1856** EMERSON *Eng. Traits* iv. 55 The fixity or inconvertibleness of races, as we see them. **1882** OGILVIE, *Inconvertibly.*

†**incon'victedness.** *Obs. rare.* [f. IN-³ + CONVICTED + -NESS.] The state of not being convicted or convinced. So †**incon'viction,** absence of conviction.

a **1664** H. MORE *Myst. Iniq.* Apol. 557 It is not the Firmness of our Conviction or Inconviction that will warrant an act from becoming sinful, but the perfect Sincerity of the party. *Ibid.*, By this last Objection it is insinuated that I make Inconvictedness of Conscience to excuse from the most hainous crimes.

incon'vincedly, *adv.* [IN-³.] In an unconvinced way; without conviction.

1642 ROGERS *Naaman* 102 Sinne is not alike dwelling in all, but in some men it dwels without a law, ignorantly, inconvincedly. **1658** [see INCONVINCIBLY, quot. 1646].

inconvincible (ɪnkən'vɪnsɪb(ə)l), *a.* (*sb.*) [IN-³.] Incapable of being convinced; not open to conviction.

1674 *Govt. Tongue* XI. §9 (1684) 162 None are so inconvincible as your half-witted people. **1732** BERKELEY *Alciphr.* II. §19 There is nothing so dogmatical and inconvincible as one of these fine things, when it sets up for free-thinking. **1837** CARLYLE *Fr. Rev.* I. v. i, The Commons are inconvincible, the Noblesse and Clergy irrefragably convincing. **1871** RUSKIN *Fors Clav.* v. 14, I am not inconvincible by any kind of evidence.

b. as *sb.* An inconvincible person.

1845 MRS. S. C. HALL *Whiteboy* i. 3 You are one of the 'inconvinceables'.

Hence **inconvinci'bility; incon'vincibly** *adv.*

1646 SIR T. BROWNE *Pseud. Ep.* I. vii. 27 Yet is it not much lesse injurious unto knowledge obstinately and inconvincibly [*ed.* **1658** inconvincedly] to side with any one. **1882** W. M. WILLIAMS *Science in Short Ch.* 55 With all the conservative inconvincibility of a born and bred Englishman.

†**in'cony,** *a. Obs.* Also inconie, in-conie, in conie, inconey, in conye. [A cant word, prevalent about 1600, of unascertained origin.

It appears to have rimed with *money*, cf. CONEY. Suggestions as to its derivation are that it represents F. *inconnu*, or It. *incognito*, unknown; that it is a variation of *uncanny*, *unconny* incautious, etc. (see CANNY); that it is connected with *unco* unknown, strange, etc.; but none of these is free from difficulty.]

? Rare, fine, delicate, pretty, 'nice'.

1588 SHAKS. *L.L.L.* III. i. 136 *Clow.* My sweete ounce of man's flesh, my in-conie Iew. *Ibid.* IV. i. 144 *Clo...* O my troth most sweete iests, most inconie vulgar wit. *c* **1592** MARLOWE *Jew of Malta* IV. v[i.], Let music rumble Whilst I in thy incony lap do tumble. **1599** PORTER *Angry Wom. Abingd.* Hij, O I haue sport in coney I faith. **1602** MIDDLETON *Blurt, Master-Const.* II. ii, It makes you have, O, a most incony body! **1633** B. JONSON *Tale Tub* IV. i, O super-dainty Chanon! Vicar in coney! Make no delay, Miles, but away; And bring the wench and money.

b. *advb.*

1602 *Narcissus* (1893) 122 Hang it yonder, & twill make mee act in conye.

†**in'coop, incoup,** *v. Obs. rare*⁻¹. [f. IN-² + COOP *sb.*¹] *trans.* To coop up, enclose.

1598 SYLVESTER *Du Bartas* II. iv. III. 665 With sudden blindness smites the Syrian Troup, The which in Dothan did him round incoup.

incoordinate (ɪnkəʊ'ɔːdɪnət), *a.* [IN-³.] Not co-ordinate. So **inco'ordinated.**

1885 F. WARNER *Physical Expression* 71 Co-ordinated movements and inco-ordinated movements. **1889** J. M. ROBERTSON *Ess. Crit. Method* 50 The incoördinate character of Mr. Moulton's doctrine fully betrays itself. **1896** *Allbutt's Syst. Med.* I. 899 Disturbed and incoordinate contraction of it's [the heart's] walls. **1911** W. JAMES *Mem. & Stud.* ix. 218 There was no appearance of general dismay and little of chatter or of inco-ordinated excitement.

incoordination (ɪnkəʊɔːdɪ'neɪʃən). [IN-³; cf. F. *incoordination* (*Dict. Acad.* 1878).] Want of co-ordination; *esp.* in *Phys.* in reference to muscular action (see CO-ORDINATION 4).

1876 W. A. HAMMOND *Nerv. Dis.* (ed. 6) 726 A similar incoordination is observable in the right hand. **1878** A. M. HAMILTON *Nerv. Dis.* 171 Incoordination of upper or lower extremities. **1892** W. R. GOWERS *Dis. Nerv. Syst.* I. 454 The incoordination is revealed by the patient's gait, which is distinctly unsteady.

†**in'copious,** *a. Obs. rare*⁻¹. [IN-³.] Not copious; limited, restricted in quantity.

1734 CAREY *Chrononhotonth.* i, The world is too incopious to contain 'em.

incopresentable (ɪnkəʊprɪ'zɛntəb(ə)l), *a.* [f. IN-³ + CO- + PRESENT *v.* + -ABLE.] Incapable of simultaneous presentation (to the senses or intellect). Hence **incopresenta'bility.**

1886 J. WARD in *Encycl. Brit.* XX. 46/2 Just as..a field of sight all blue is incopresentable with one all red. *Ibid.*, Certain sensations or movements are an absolute bar to the simultaneous presentation of other sensations or movements. We cannot see an orange as at once yellow and green, though we can feel it at once as both smooth and cold. .. Such incopresentability or contrariety..occurs only between presentations belonging to the same sense or to the same group of movements.

†**in'copsed,** *ppl. a. Obs. rare*⁻¹. [f. IN-² (or ? IN-³) + COPSE *sb.* + -ED¹.] ? Covered with copsewood.

1614 RALEIGH *Hist. World* I. I. 159 There was no great pleasure in passing into farre countries after the generall Deluge, when the earth lay (as it were) incopsed for 100 or 130 yeares together.

incorage, obs. form of ENCOURAGE.

†**in'cord,** *v. Obs. rare*⁻⁰. [ad. It. *incordare*; cf. next.] (See quot.)

1611 FLORIO, *Incordare*,..to incord or burst as a horse.

†**in'corded,** *ppl. a.* Also 7 encorded. [ad. It. *incordato*: see INCORDING, quot. 1607.] Of a horse: Ruptured; suffering from hernia.

1607 [see INCORDING]. **1611** FLORIO, *Incordato*,..incorded as a horse. *c* **1720** W. GIBSON *Farrier's Dispens.* xii. (1734) 259 When a Horse is incorded or bursten.

†**in'cordiate,** *v. Obs.*⁻⁰. [ad. supposed L. **incordiāre*, inferred from *incordies*, erroneous reading in Plautus *Cist.* I. i. 110 for *mihi cordi est.*]

1623 COCKERAM, *Incordiate*, to put into ones heart. **1656** in BLOUNT *Glossogr.*

†**in'cording,** *vbl. sb. Obs.* [f. INCORD *v.* + -ING¹ (cf. quot. 1607).] Rupture or hernia in a horse.

1598 FLORIO, *Incordatura*, ..the incording or bursting of a horse. **1607** TOPSELL *Four-f. Beasts* (1658) 307 This term, Incording, is borrowed of the Italian word *Incordato*, which in plain English is as much to say as Bursten..The Italians, as I take it, did call it *Incordato*, because the gut follows the string of the stone, called of them *Il cordone*, or *La corda*, whereof *Incordato* seems to be derived with some reason. According to which reason we should call it rather Instringed, then Incorded; for *Corda* doth signifie a string or cord. Notwithstanding, sith that Incording is already received in the stable, I for my part am very well content therewith, minding not to contend against it. **1610** MARKHAM *Masterp.* II. xlix. 292 This incording or burstinesse in horses, is when the rim or thinne filme which holdeth the guts vp in a horses body is broken, so that the guts falleth downe either into the cods of the horse, or into the horses flancke. **1725** BRADLEY *Fam. Dict.* s.v. *Rupture*, Rupture otherwise called Incording or Burstness, a distemper in a horse.

†**in'cornet,** *v. Obs. rare*⁻⁰. [ad. F. *encorneter* (Cotgr.): see IN-².] (See quot.)

1611 COTGR., *Encorneté*, incornetted; put into a horne; wrapped vp, as spice, etc. in a cornet, or coffin.

†**in'cornished,** *ppl. a. Obs. rare*⁻¹. [f. IN-² + *cornish* CORNICE + -ED; after It. *incorniciare* to put a cornice or frame upon, f. *in-* (IN-²) + *cornice* CORNICE.] Furnished with a cornice or cornices.

1645 EVELYN *Diary* 11 Apr., The outer walls..are.. incornish'd with festoons and niches, set with statues from the foundation to the roofe.

incoronate (ɪn'kɒrənət), *a.* [ad. It. *incoronato* or med.L. *incorōnāt-us* (pa. pple. of *incorōnāre* to crown); cf. OF. *encoroner* to crown, and CORONATE.] **a.** Wearing or having a crown; crowned.

1867 LONGF. *Dante, Inferno* IV. liv, I saw hither come a Mighty One, With Sign of victory incoronate. **1887** E. H. PLUMPTRE *Dante, Comm.* II. 347 My Lady fair in heaven incoronate.

b. *Bot.* (See quot.)

1855 MAYNE *Expos. Lex.*, *Incoronatus*, Applied by H. Cassini to the *calathidium* or *anthodium* of the *Synanthereæ*, when all the flowers which constitute it resemble the form of a corol: incoronate.

So **in'coronated** *ppl. a.*

1867 LONGF. *Dante, Parad.* XXIII. 119 Mine eyes did not possess the power of following the incoronated flame.

incoronation (ɪnkɒrə'neɪʃən). [n. of action f. med.L. *incorōnāre* to crown: see prec. Cf. It. *incoronazione* (Florio).] Coronation, crowning.

1470–85 MALORY *Arthur* I. viii, After the incoronacion of hym at the Cyte of Carlyon. **1836** F. MAHONEY *Rel. Father Prout, Songs Italy* ii. (1859) 349 Concerning this solemn incoronation, we have from the pen of an eye witness, Guido d'Arezzo, details [etc.]. **1876** MRS. WHITNEY *Sights & Ins.* II. xii. 426 From the Nativity of the Virgin to her Assumption and Incoronation.

†**in'corpor,** *v. Obs. rare.* [ad. L. *incorporā-re* (see INCORPORATE): cf. ENCORPORE, F. *encorporer.*]

1. *trans.* To incorporate.

1398 TREVISA *Barth. De P.R.* III. xiv. (1495) 59 The vertue retentiua kepyth the fode that is pured, and sendyth to all the lymmes, and incorporyth, and makyth it like. **1492** *Acta Dom. Conc.* 259/2 A confirmatioune incorporand a charter of selling of the landis of Schethynrawak.

2. *intr.* = INCORPORATE *v.* 6.

a **1618** SYLVESTER *All's not Gold that Glisters* xvi, O where is then the Holy Flock! Call'd in one Hope, built on one Rock, Into our Faith incorporing?

in'corporable, *a. rare.* [f. as prec. + -ABLE.] Capable of being incorporated.

1607 *Schol. Disc. agst. Antichr.* I. ii. 102 They were incorporable into the bread and wine to make one banquet with them. **1899** *Daily News* 19 Sept. 6/2 A great part of the town supposed to be excluded from the Municipal Corporations Act of 1835 did not really exist. Chelsea, Knightsbridge..and Mile-end were not really incorporable.

†**in'corporal,** *a.* (*sb.*) *Obs.* [ad.L. *incorporālis*, f. *in-* IN-³) + *corporālis* CORPORAL: cf. F. *incorporel*, It. *incorporale.*] = INCORPOREAL; immaterial; insubstantial.

1551 GARDINER *Explic. Transubs.* 109 (R.) The soule of man hath his end and terme & spiritual alteration, incorporall, to be regenerate the sonne of God. **1581** MARBECK *Bk. of Notes* 385 His mans nature, which should be forthwith aduaunced to immortall and incorporall glorie. **1603** HOLLAND *Plutarch's Mor.* 1337 No lesse impossible is it to apprehend, that of bodies having no soule any should moove of themselves to an incorporall place, and having no difference of situation. **1646** H. LAWRENCE *Comm. Angels* 9 If you aske..whether the Angells have bodies, or are altogether incorporall.

B. *sb.* An incorporeal thing or place. *rare*⁻¹.

1678 CUDWORTH *Intell. Syst.* I. v. 821 But if it be demanded, when the Soul goes out of this Body, whether it be carried into any Corporal Places, or to Incorporals like to Corporals [etc.].

Hence †**in'corporally,** 'without matter, immaterially' (J.). †**in'corporalness** = next (Bailey vol. II, 1727).

†**in'corporality.** *Obs.* [ad. late L. *incorporālitās*: see prec. and -ITY. Cf. F. *incorporalité.*] The state or quality of being incorporeal.

1601 DEACON & WALKER *Spirits & Divels* 8, Whatsoeuer is incorporall, that same is euery where, because vbiquity is the cause of incorporality. **1678** CUDWORTH *Intell. Syst.* I. v. 801 Incorporality is free from all Custody or Imprisonment, as also devoid of Pain and Pleasure. **1777** PRIESTLEY *Matt. & Spir.* (1782) I. xix. 219 Austin..learned of the philosophers the incorporality of God.

in'corporate, *a.* (*sb.*) *rare.* [ad. rare L. *incorporāt-us* not embodied (Claud. Mamertus, 470), f. *in-* (IN-[3]) + *corporātus* CORPORATE.]

1. Without body or material substance; incorporeal, unembodied.

1540 MORYSINE *Vives' Introd. Wysd.* G j b, The more thou transposeste thy selfe from thinges corporall unto thinges incorporate, the more godlye lyfe shalte thou leade. **1598** BARCKLEY *Felic. Man* (1631) 366 For besides the incorporate world, that is above all the rest..there are three bodily worlds coupled together. *a* **1618** RALEIGH in Gutch *Coll. Cur.* I. 79 Inheritance incorporate, or invisible. **1661** G. RUST *Origen's Opin.* in *Phenix* (1721) I. 31 And so there be brought into light Spirits incorporate. *a* **1849** POE *Silence*, There are some qualities—some incorporate things, That have a double life.

¶**2.** 'Not incorporated; not existing as a corporation; as an incorporate banking association or other society' (Webster, 1864).

Hence in later Dicts., but prob. an error.

†**B.** as *sb.* Something which is incorporeal. *Obs.*

c **1532** DU WES *Introd. Fr.* in Palsgr. 1057 In the whiche all maner shape and effigiation doth shyne clerely, so well corporates as incorporates.

incorporate (ɪn'kɔːpərət), *ppl. a.* [ad. late L. *incorporāt-us*, pa. pple. of *incorporāre*: see the vb.] Formerly used as *pa. pple.* = incorporated.

I. 1. United in one body; combined in one mass or substance. *lit.* and *fig.* Now *rare.*

a **1533** LD. BERNERS *Gold. Bk. M. Aurel.* xv, And the vertues wel incorporate, nourishe many enuious. *c* **1586** C'TESS PEMBROKE *Ps. David* CXXXV. iii, The reaking vapors rise: Then high in cloudes incorporate they stand. **1592** SHAKS. *Ven. & Ad.* 540 Her armes do lend his necke a sweet imbrace, Incorporate then they seeme, face growes to face. **1604** E.G. *D'Acosta's Hist. Indies* IV. xii. 243 Alwaies turning and stirring the mettall, to the end it may be well incorporate. **1752** YOUNG *Brothers* IV. i, The friend of Rome?—That severs you for ever; Tho' most incorporate and strongly knit. **1852** H. ROGERS *Ecl. Faith* (1853) 2 The incorporate life of father and son.

b. Const. *into*, *in*, *with*, †*to*. (Cf. the verb.)

1387 TREVISA *Higden* (Rolls) I. 329 Hibernia..was of olde tyme incorporat [*Harl. MS.* concorporate, L. *concorporata*] in to þe lordschippe of Bretayne, so seiþ Giraldus. **1398** —— *Barth. De P.R.* X. v. (Tollem. MS.), Leye [flame] fondeþ to meue upwarde, and draweþ fro þe neþer parties upwarde to þe whiche he is incorporate. **1502** *Ord. Crysten Men* (W. de W. 1506) I. iv. 40 Incorporat and unyed with holy chirche. **1526** *Pilgr. Perf.* (W. de W. 1531) 186 b, To be incorporate in hym, as one of the membres of his misticall body. **1541** R. COPLAND *Guydon's Quest. Chirurg.*, Oyntementes..made of yͤ powdre of dragons blode,..encorporate with whyte of an egge. **1601** SHAKS. *Jul. C.* I. iii. 135 It is Caska, one incorporate To our Attempts. **1626** BACON *Sylva* §411 Drinke incorporate with Flesh, or Roots..will nourish more easily, than Meat and Drinke taken seuerally. **1837–9** HALLAM *Hist. Lit.* (1847) I. xi. §67. 139 This science is incorporate in all the books of the doctors of the church. **1850** TENNYSON *In Mem.* ii, Gazing on thee, sullen tree,..I seem to fail from out my blood And grow incorporate into thee. *a* **1864** J. D. BURNS *Mem. & Rem.* (1879) 363 Some beloved object which seemed to be one and incorporate with their living selves.

2. Of a company, association, etc.: Formally constituted as a corporation. (Cf. CORPORATE *a.* 4.) Also of persons: United in a corporation.

1480 *Bury Wills* (Camden) 58 Whan so euer the colage of prestis of Bury be incorporat and have a maister, presydent, or other reuler [etc.]. **1540** *Act. 32 Hen. VIII*, c. 42 All personnes of the said company nowe incorporate by this present acte. **1592** WEST *1st Pt. Symbol.* I. §46 Guildes, fraternities, fellowships and companies incorporate. **1633** T. STAFFORD *Pac. Hib.* I. vi. (1810) 78 Conducted to the next incorporate Towne. **1671** *True Non-conf.* 11, I finde the keeping of the Lords Covenant..injoined to the People of Israel, as one body incorporat. **1863** H. COX *Instit.* III. ix. 730 The province of the incorporate municipal governments. **1877** RAYMOND *Statist. Mines & Mining* 64 An incorporate company, having its principal place of business at the town of Gold Run.

†**b.** Of persons: Associated or admitted to fellowship with others, as members of the same corporation. *Obs.*

1590 SHAKS. *Com. Err.* II. ii. 124 Estranged from thy selfe..being strange to me: That vndiuidable Incorporate Am better then thy deere selfes better part. **1605** CAMDEN *Rem.* (1637) 17 The Welshmen our neighbours, or rather our incorporate countrimen, both by approved allegeance and law. **1684** BAXTER *Theol. Dial.* 2 You make your self and all these parties, incorporate Members of the Church of England.

†**c.** *transf.* That constitutes a close connexion (cf. INCORPORATING *ppl. a.* b). *Obs.*

1599 SHAKS. *Hen. V*, V. ii. 394 To make diuorce of their incorporate League. **1765** BLACKSTONE *Comm.* I. 98 *note*, In such an *incorporate union* (which is well distinguished by a very learned prelate from a *foederate alliance*)..the two contracting states are totally annihilated..and a third arises from their conjunction.

II. 3. Having a bodily form; embodied.

1398 TREVISA *Barth. De P.R.* X. vii. (Bodl. MS.), Colle is fuyre incorporat in deede. **1450–1530** *Myrr. our Ladye* 298 The beyng worde of the hiest hathe suffered to be incorporate, takynge a body. **1878** GEO. ELIOT *Coll. Breakf. P.* 424 Ideals never yet incorporate.

incorporate (ɪn'kɔːpəreɪt), *v.* Also 5 **incorperate**, 6–7 **encorporate**. [f. late L. *incorporāt-*, ppl. stem of *incorporāre* to embody, include, f. *in-* (IN-[2]) + *corporāre* to form into a body, CORPORATE *v.*]

I. *trans.* **1.** To combine or unite into one body or uniform substance; to mix or blend thoroughly together (a number of different things or one thing *with* another).

a. material substances.

1544 PHAER *Regim. Lyfe* (1553) F j b, Take..tosted bread, and moist it in wine and incorporate it with pouder of mastyke. **1660** BOYLE *New Exp. Phys. Mech.* Proem 11 A melted Cement, made of Pitch, Rosin, and Wood-ashes, well incorporated. **1678** *Phil. Trans.* XII. 950 Tinn, for the most part, is incorporated with the Stone, or is found in it. **1772–84** COOK *Voy.* (1790) V. 1551 Stirring up the several ingredients, till they were perfectly incorporated. **1848** MILL *Pol. Econ.* I. xii. §2 (1876) 110 Manure..carefully mixed and incorporated with the Soil. **1879** *Cassell's Techn. Educ.* IV. 71/1 Equal parts of oat, wheat, barley, and bean meals, and the whole..incorporated by stirring.

b. *transf.* and *fig.*

1592 SHAKS. *Rom. & Jul.* II. vi. 37 You shall not stay alone, Till holy Church incorporate two in one. **1643** MILTON *Divorce* II. xvi, That the fit union of their souls be such as may even incorporate them to love and amity. **1646** H. LAWRENCE *Comm. Angells* 185 Incorporate your selves with that which is good, make your self one with it. **1684** J. LACY *Sir H. Buffoon* I. Dram. Wks. (1875) 225 An Atheist and a Wit are incorporated, and like man and wife become one flesh. **1825** J. NEAL *Bro. Jonathan* III. 242 That which incorporates their being for ever and ever. **1841** MYERS *Cath. Th.* III. §8. 27 At what period, they were incorporated into a Sacred Canon, is..unknown. **1847–8** H. MILLER *First Impr.* vi. (1859) 89 When the geological vocabulary shall have become better incorporated than at present with the language of our common literature.

2. a. To put into or include in the body or substance of something else; to put (one thing) in or into another so as to form one body or integral whole; to embody, include. Const. *in*, *into*, †*to*.

1398 TREVISA *Barth. De P.R.* XIX. xix. (1495) 875 Clerenesse incorporatyd in that blacke makith it meene and temporat. **1579** FULKE *Heskins' Parl.* 234 This breade and this cuppe..shall assure you, that you are truely incorporated into my bodie. **1598** BARCKLEY *Felic. Man* v. (1603) 542 As though they would incorporate their soule to their body. **1601** HOLLAND *Pliny* II. 365 Some there be who incorporat the said head [of a swallow] within white wax, and therewith annoint the forehead. **1794** PALEY *Evid.* I. i. (1817) 31 The religion of that age was not merely allied to the state; it was incorporated into it. **1843** J. CLASON *Serm.* vii. 126 We eat and drink—what is taken by us enters into and is incorporated in our systems. **1876** MOZLEY *Univ. Serm.* i. (1877) 5 What are the doctrines which the Roman Church will thus incorporate into her teaching?

b. To take in or include as a part or parts of itself (*esp.* of literary material); to absorb.

1824 DIBDIN *Libr. Comp.* 538 The best edition, incorporating all the works of the author. **1861** STANLEY *East. Ch.* viii. (1869) 271 The Koran incorporates some of the earlier Jewish, Christian, and Arabian traditions. **1890** *Law Times Rep.* LXIII. 732/1 The Act of 1885 expressly incorporated sect. 28 of the Act of 1878.

†**c.** To take or absorb into the body. *Obs. rare.*

1653 WALTON *Angler* vi. 139 By the wormes remaining in that box an hour..they had incorporated a kind of smel that was irresistibly attractive.

3. a. To combine or form into a society or organization; *esp.* to constitute as a legal corporation.

c **1460** FORTESCUE *Abs. & Lim. Mon.* ii. (1885) 111 Whan Nembroth..made and incorperate the first realme. **1534** MORE *Treat. on Passion* Wks. 1348/2 Christ..doth..incorporate all christen folke and hys owne body to gether in one corporacyon mistical. **1540** *Act 32 Hen. VIII*, c. 42 Whiche company of Barbours be incorporated to sue and be sued by the name of Maistres or Governours of the mistery and commynaltie of the Barbours of London. **1693** LUTTRELL *Brief Rel.* (1857) III. 176 A charter is past to incorporate the lord Shandois, Mr. Neal, and Mr. Thomas Wharton, in working of mines, and refining of oare, &c. **1732** POPE, etc. *Art Sinking* xvi. 81 It is propos'd, that the two Theatres be incorporated into one company. **1890** GROSS *Gild Merch.* I. 146 The staplers of a town were generally incorporated as a company or fraternity.

b. To admit (a person) as member of a company or association; to receive or adopt into a corporation or body politic. *spec.* To admit a graduate of another university *ad eundem*. (Const. *into*, *in*, rarely †*unto*, *with*.)

1530 PALSGR. 590/2, I incorporate a man, I make him of crafte or faculte to be sworne to it. **1634** *Sir T. Herbert Trav.* 78 Hee had incorporated himselfe unto another people. **1649** *Alcoran* 401 Giving freedom to such prisoners as would embrace his Law, [he] encorporated them into his Army. **1679** WOOD *Life* (O.H.S.) II. 465, I heard at Weston that the vice-chancellor of Oxford, Dr. Fell, has denied Oates his incorporating D.D... Oates sent word to the vice-chancellor, that 'he would come and wait on him..for his degree'. But they denied him—that is, if he was Doctor of Divinity at Salamanca they would incorporate him. **1691** —— *Ath. Oxon.* II. 688 This year Richard Crashaw of Cambridge was incorporated. **1707** HEARNE *Collect.* 21 Mar. (O.H.S.) II. 1 Yesterday was incorporated A.M. Mr. Stevens. **1712** E. COOKE *Voy. S. Sea* 295 The Indians given to Spaniards, should be set free, and incorporated in the Crown. **1861** STANLEY *East. Ch.* xi. (1869) 336 He made a point of compelling all foreigners to..incorporate themselves into the Russian nation by baptism.

4. To furnish with a body; to give bodily shape to; to embody. *rare.*

1623 BP. ANDREWES *Serm.* (ed. 18) 269 The incorporating Christ, the ordaining Him a body. *a* **1688** CUDWORTH *Immut. Mor.* (1731) 145 Certain crasse, palpable, and Corporeal Images, to incorporate those abstracted Cogitations in. **1831** CARLYLE *Sart. Res.* II. v, Some actual Air-maiden, incorporated into tangibility and reality.

II. *intr.* To incorporate itself or become incorporated.

5. Of one thing: To unite or combine with something else so as to form one body. Const. *with*, rarely *into*.

1594 PLAT *Jewell-ho., New sorts Soyle* 6 Salt..by solution being very apt to incorporate therewith, consumeth all the putrified vapors or parts thereof. **1681** FLAVEL *Meth. Grace* xxvi. 452 Grace can no more incorporate with sin, than oyle with water. *a* **1716** SOUTH *Serm.* (1717) IV. 22 He must have mastered his Notions, till they even incorporate into his Mind. **1799** G. SMITH *Laboratory* II. 137 In three or four weeks time the bud will incorporate. **1809** MALKIN *Gil Blas* VI. i. ¶2 A rivulet..meandering..to incorporate with the waters of Guadalaviar. **1831** BREWSTER *Nat. Magic* vi. (1833) 150 The Water will gradually incorporate with the Syrup.

6. a. Of two or more things: To unite so as to form one body; to grow into each other; to form an intimate union (*lit.* and *fig.*). ? *Obs.*

1625 BACON *Ess., Unity Relig.* (Arb.) 431 Truth and Falshood..are like the Iron and Clay, in the toes of Nabucadnezars Image; They may Cleaue, but they will not Incorporate. **1674** GREW *Disc. Nat. Mixture* v. Inst. 2 §4 Take good Oyl of Vitriol and drop it upon Oyl of Anise-seeds; and they will forthwith incorporate together. **1732** BERKELEY *Alciphr.* III. iii, They unite and incorporate into families, clubs, parties and Commonwealths, by mutual Sympathy. **1797** DOWNING *Disord. Horned Cattle* 32 Beat them with a spoon until they incorporate and become a white paste.

†**b.** To copulate. *Obs. rare.*

1622 MASSINGER & DEKKER *Virg.-Mart.* III. iii, Worse than the noise of a scolding oysterwench, or two cats incorporating.

in'corporated, *ppl. a.* [f. prec. + -ED[1].]

1. United into one body; combined.

1599 MINSHEU *Sp. Dict.*, *Incorporado*, incorporated, made into one body. **1712** BLACKMORE *Creation* 298 Now flows in one incorporated flood. **1806** HUTTON *Course Math.* I. 174 To obtain the incorporated or united mass.

2. Constituted as a legal or formal corporation (cf. INCORPORATE *ppl. a.* 2).

1677 YARRANTON *Eng. Improv.* 182 The Incorporated Companies of Weavers, Pin-Makers [etc.]. **1776** ADAM SMITH *W.N.* I. x. II. (1869) I. 137 In many large incorporated towns no tolerable workmen are to be found. **1837** HT. MARTINEAU *Soc. Amer.* III. App. 335 There were about 20 incorporated academies in the State [of Vermont], where young men were fitted for college. **1884** H. SPENCER in *Contemp. Rev.* XLVI. 29 This holds of an incorporated nation as much as of an incorporated company.

3. Included as part of a whole.

1715 NELSON *Addr. Pers. Qual.* 197 An incorporated Member of His Body. **1818** JAS. MILL *Brit. India* II. v. ix. 714 The government of India was made totally dependant upon the minister, and became in fact an incorporated part of his administration.

†**4.** Embodied. *Obs. rare.*

1644 DIGBY *Mans Soul* (1645) 11 An incorporated soule..can looke upon but one single definite place. **1751** JOHNSON *Rambler* No. 110 ¶5 Incorporated minds will always feel some inclination towards exterior acts, and ritual observances.

Hence **in'corporatedness**.

1727 BAILEY vol. II, *Incorporatedness*, the State or Condition of being incorporated, or the unitedness of one Thing with another.

in'corporating, *vbl. sb.* [f. as prec. + -ING[1].]

1. The action of combining into one body (in trans. sense).

1579–80 NORTH *Plutarch* (1595) 78 This diuision was an incorporating, and an vniting of the whole together. **1645** PAGITT *Heresiogr.* (1661) 50 The Lords sign of his..receiving of us into the Church, and incorporating of us into Christ.

b. *spec.* The process of combining the ingredients of gunpowder, so as to produce a homogeneous compound. Also *attrib.*, as ***incorporating mill***.

1869 *Daily News* 19 Aug., The explosion, which originated in one of the incorporating mills, was caused by a workman disobeying the rules. **1883** *Pall Mall G.* 17 Feb. 9/2 The incorporating mills of the Kennal Gunpowder Company's Works, near Penryn, were blown up yesterday. **1881** GREENER *Gun* 311 The incorporating is one of the most dangerous processes.

2. The action of uniting into a society or association (in intr. sense); = INCORPORATION 2.

1651 HOBBES *Leviath.* II. xxii. 119 The End of their Incorporating, is to make their gaine the greater. **1689** tr. *Buchanan's De Jure Regni apud Scotos* 8 You do not then make utility..to be the cause..of men's incorporating in political Societies.

in'corporating, *ppl. a.* [f. as prec. + -ING[2].] That incorporates, or unites into one body.

1611 COTGR., *Incorporant*, incorporating, ioyning in one bodie. **1645** MILTON *Tetrach.* Wks. (1847) 189/2 The most intimate and incorporating duties of Love and embracement. **1746** JAMES *Introd. Moufet & Bennet's Health's Improv.* 64 The tender and fresh Parts of Plants abound with Water, and..Salts..To the Mixture of which, with a moderate oily and vegetable Fluid, is owing their incorporating and dissolving Juice.

b. ***incorporating union***, a union which combines two or more states, etc. under one government, or converts separate bodies into one corporation. (Orig. said of the Union

between England and Scotland in 1707.) So also *Incorporating Act*.

1706 LUTTRELL *Brief Rel.* (1857) VI. 105 The parliament had read 5 or 6 addresses against an incorporating union with England. **1707** *Vulpone* 18 They had changed their Notion of an Incorporating Union into that of a Federal one. **1813** M. CUTLER in *Life, Jrnls. & Corr.* (1888) II. 320, I shall send you..our Incorporating Act and Constitution. **1825** T. JEFFERSON *Autobiog.* Wks. 1859 I. 32 He distinguished between an incorporating and a federal union. **1871** *Pall Mall G.* 12 Jan., It is hopeless to expect an incorporating union of all the seven provinces [of Australia] at present.

c. Of languages: Combining several parts of speech (e.g. verb and objects, etc.) in one word: cf. INCORPORATION 1 b.

1859 MAX MÜLLER *Sc. Lang.* (1871) I. 371 A fourth class, sometimes called polysynthetic or incorporating, including most of the American languages. **1875** WHITNEY *Life Lang.* xii. 260 This common mode of structure..is called the polysynthetic, or incorporating.

incorporation (ɪnkɔːpəˈreɪʃən). [ad. late L. *incorporātiōn-em*, n. of action from *incorporāre* to INCORPORATE. Cf. F. *incorporation* (15th c.).]

1. a. The action of incorporating two or more things, or one thing *with* (*in*, *into*, †*to*) another; the process or condition of being so incorporated; union in or into one body.

1398 TREVISA *Barth. De P.R.* x. vii. (Bodl. MS.), Fuyre by his incorporacion and onyng to gretter and þikker parties of erþelich matere..is iholde byneþe by a certeyne violence of kinde. **1579** FULKE *Heskins' Parl.* 267 Our drinking is as it were a certeine incorporation in him. **1612** T. TAYLOR *Comm. Titus* iii. 5 Such as haue receiued inuisible incorporation into Christs bodie. **1641** FRENCH *Distill.* i. (1651) 11 *Incorporation*, is a mixtion of a dry and moist body together, so as to make an uniform masse of them. **1718** QUINCY *Compl. Disp.* 35 Incorporation, thus term'd in Pharmacy, is employed in bringing and joining together, by the Interposition of a third Body. **1765** HUTCHINSON (*title*) The History of the Colony of Massachusetts Bay from the first settlement thereof in 1628 until its incorporation with the Colony of Plimouth. **1812** G. CHALMERS *Dom. Econ. Gt. Brit.* 95 The incorporation of two independent legislatures has proved equally advantageous to both countries. **1861** STANLEY *East. Ch.* ix. (1869) 285 The gradual incorporation of Russia into the commonwealth of Western nations. **1881** WESCOTT & HORT *Grk. N.T.* Introd. §12 The incorporation of various readings noted in the margin.

b. *Philol.* The combination of two or more parts of speech in one word, as when the object or complement of a verb is inserted between its stem and termination so that the whole forms one word: cf. INCORPORATING *ppl. a.* c.

1874 SAYCE *Compar. Philol.* i. 22 The Basque verb presents the phenomenon of incorporation to an astonishing degree.

2. a. The action or process of forming into a community or corporation; *esp.* the formation of a legal corporation or body politic.

c **1460** FORTESCUE *Abs. & Lim. Mon.* ii. (1885) 112 This incorperacion, institucion, and onynge of hem self into a reaume. **1513–14** *Act 5 Hen. VIII*, c. 6 The forsaid Citie of London, from the tyme of their firste Incorporacion. **1640–4** in Rushw. *Hist. Coll.* III. (1692) I. 154 The Patent for the Incorporation of the Parish Clerks. **1819** J. MARSHALL *Const. Opin.* (1839) 195 The charter of incorporation was granted at his instance.

†**b.** The document creating or legalizing a corporation; a charter. *Obs.*

a **1600** in *Eng. Gilds* 302 A new incorporacion wᶜʰ the saide company of Taylors had procured from the kinge. **1605** BACON *Adv. Learn.* I. vii. §6 Adrian spent his whole reign..in a..survey of the Roman empire..granting new franchises and incorporations.

c. The action of incorporating (cf. INCORPORATE *v.* 3 b) into another university.

1966 *Rep. Comm. Inquiry Univ. Oxf.* I. 404 Degrees in absence and by incorporation.

3. An incorporated society or company; = CORPORATION.

1530 in W. H. Turner *Select. Rec. Oxford* 85 To have of them an incorporacion..and to have a Master and Warden of there Crafte. **1570–6** LAMBARDE *Peramb. Kent* (1826) 169 At Courtopstrete they do yet reserve a Mace and a Horne assured badges of an incorporation. **1631** GOUGE *God's Arrows* III. §11. 206 Vniversities, Innes of Court, Incorporations, Companies, and other such like Societies. **1776** ADAM SMITH *W.N.* v. i. (1869) II. 382 The clergy of every established church constitute a great incorporation. **1822** SCOTT *Nigel* ix, An eminent member of the Goldsmiths' Incorporation. **1879** H. GEORGE *Progr. & Pov.* III. iv, Railroad companies and other incorporations.

4. Embodiment; an embodied realization. *rare.*

1645 M. CASAUBON *Orig. Temp. Evils* 2 That opinion of the ancientest Philosophers..that the Soules of men had a subsistence long before their incorporation. **1647** H. MORE *Poems* 229 The self-form'd soul may work without Incorporation. **1866** GEO. ELIOT *F. Holt* xvi, He thought he saw a very troublesome, vigorous incorporation of that nonsense [enthusiasm] in Felix. **1884** J. RAE *Contemp. Socialism* 233 Schmoller..offers us no other incorporation of his dogma.

Hence (*nonce-wds.*) †**incorpo'rationer**, a member of an incorporation; **incorpo'rationist**, one who favours or supports incorporation.

1594 NASHE *Unfort. Trav.* E j, At the townes end met him the burgers and dunsticall incorporationers of Wittenberg. **1888** *Daily News* 31 Oct. 7/1 The great struggle centres in striving to obtain a majority of incorporationists in the council.

incorporative (ɪnˈkɔːpərətɪv), *a.* [f. INCORPORATE *v.* + -IVE.] Characterized by or tending to incorporation.

1592 LYLY *Galathea* II. iii, We call those spirits that are the grounds of our arte, and as it were the metals more incorporative for domination. **1716** M. DAVIES *Athen. Brit.* II. 424 The same true infinite God and truly finite Man,..Temporally and Humanly Communicative and Incorporative. **1824** *Westm. Rev.* II. 420 The incorporative union of two sovereignties under a common head.

incorporator (ɪnˈkɔːpəreɪtə(r)). [agent-n. in L. form, from INCORPORATE.]

1. One who incorporates or combines into one body or substance.

1829 *Blackw. Mag.* XXV. 89 These compound incorporators of sour fruit, sugar, and brandy.

2. One who takes part in the formation of an incorporated company; *spec.* (*U.S.*) 'one of the persons named in an act of incorporation; one of the original members of an incorporated body or company' (*Cent. Dict.*).

1883 *Harper's Mag.* Nov. 938/2 The first incorporators were not practical railroad men. **1883** *American* VII. 174 The incorporators of the Chain of Rocks Bridge Company. **1887** *Pall Mall G.* 5 Nov. 6/1 Obliged to have a majority of the incorporators United States citizens.

3. A member of one University who is incorporated in another (cf. quots. 1679–1707 in INCORPORATE *v.* 3 b).

1887 J. FOSTER *Prospectus Alumni Oxon.*, I have arranged to include also in my work all honorary and nominal members of the University, as well as Incorporators.

incorporatorship (ɪnˈkɔːpəreɪtəʃɪp). [INCORPORATOR 2.] The position of an incorporator.

1873 'MARK TWAIN' & WARNER *Gilded Age* xlii, It would be more money in my pocket, in the end, than my brother-in-law will get out of that incorporatorship, fat as it is.

†**in'corporature.** *Obs. rare*⁻⁰. [f. L. type **incorporātūra*, f. *incorporāre*: see INCORPORATE and -URE; cf. CORPORATURE.] = INCORPORATION.

1570 LEVINS *Manip.* 192/14 Incorporature, *incorporatio*.

in corpore: see IN *Lat. prep.*

incorporeal (ɪnkɔːˈpɔəriːəl), *a.* (*sb.*) Also 6 -iall. [f. L. *incorpore-us* (Macrobius *c* 400) without body + -AL¹: cf. CORPOREAL.] Not corporeal.

A. *adj.* **1.** Having no bodily or material structure; not composed of matter; immaterial.

1532 MORE *Confut. Tindale* Wks. 387/2 God may make the bodyly corporall water able to worke vpon the vnbodyed incorporiall soule. **1577** HANMER *Anc. Eccl. Hist.* (1619) 190 A Nature incorruptible, incorporeall, free from earthly Matter. **1651** BAXTER *Inf. Bapt.* Apol. 2 Corporeal signs cannot work or make an impression upon incorporeal souls. **1713** BARTELETT *Guardian* No. 130 ¶20 They are not actuated by any incorporeal being or spirit. **1838–9** HALLAM *Hist. Lit.* II. II. iii. §9. 104 Two active incorporeal principles, heat and cold. **1875** JOWETT *Plato* (ed. 2) I. 403 It has been argued that the soul is invisible and incorporeal.

2. Of, pertaining to, or characteristic of immaterial beings.

1667 MILTON *P.L.* VIII. 37 The sedentarie Earth,..receaves, As Tribute such a sumless journey brought Of incorporeal speed, her warmth and light. **1811** W. R. SPENCER *Poems* 200 Thy taste's quick glance of incorporeal sight. **1859** I. TAYLOR *Logic in Theol.* 133 The incorporeal liberty of angelic existences!

3. *Law.* Having no material existence in itself, but attaching as a right or profit to some actual thing; esp. ***incorporeal hereditament*** (see quots.).

1628 COKE *On Litt.* 9 a, Grant, Concessio, is properly of things incorporeall, which as hath been said) cannot passe without Deed. **1767** BLACKSTONE *Comm.* II. iii. 20 An incorporeal hereditament is a right issuing out of a thing corporate (whether real or personal) or concerning, or annexed to, or exercisible within, the same. **1802–12** BENTHAM *Rat. Jud. Evid.* (1827) II. 555 *note*, Property called incorporeal, such as an annuity. **1844** WILLIAMS *Real Prop.* (1877) 11 A house is corporeal, but the annual rent payable for its occupation is incorporeal.

4. In which the body is not (primarily) affected or concerned.

1887 GIFFEN *Pres. Addr. Econ. Sc. Sect. Brit. Assoc.*, Numbers employed in..what may be called incorporeal functions—that is, as teachers, artists, and the like.

B. *sb.* (*pl.*) Things incorporeal.

1628 FELTHAM *Resolves* II. lxix. 195 Nor is it onely true in Materials and Substances; but even in Spirits, in Incorporeals. **1678** CUDWORTH *Intell. Syst.* I. v. 776 That Incorporeals are in No Place. **1793** T. TAYLOR tr. *Plato* Introd. Timaeus 395 The divine nature..cannot be seen through the telescope, and incorporeals are not to be viewed with a microscopic eye. **1880** MUIRHEAD *Gaius* II. §28 It is manifest that incorporeals are incapable of transfer by delivery.

Hence †**incor'porealism**, the doctrine or belief that incorporeal spirit or substance exists. †**incor'porealist**, one who holds this view. **incorpore'ality**, the quality of being incorporeal, incorporeity. †**incor'porealize** *v. intr.*, to maintain the theory of incorporeal existence.

1678 CUDWORTH *Intell. Syst.* I. i. §22. 21 We pass to Pythagoras..it is well known..that he was a professed Incorporealist. *Ibid.* §26. 27 So..did all the other ancient Atomists..joyn Theology and Incorporealism with their Atomical Physiology. *Ibid.* §33. 40 The same persons did..theologize or incorporealize, asserting souls to be a substance really distinct from matter. **1846** GEO. ELIOT tr. *Strauss' Life Jesus* II. 268 The idea that demons shunned incorporeality.

incor'poreally, *adv.* [f. prec. + -LY².] In incorporeal fashion; immaterially.

1626 BACON *Sylva* §700 It is Sound alone, that doth immediately, and incorporeally, affect most. **1678** CUDWORTH *Intell. Syst.* I. iv. §15. 280 There is One God..incorporeally and invisibly present in all things, and pervading them. **1865** DICKENS *Mut. Fr.* III. xiv, Possibly the wooden countenance of Mr. Silas Wegg was incorporeally before him at those moments. **1886** FARRAR *Hist. Interpret.* 288 Christ had ascended incorporeally to the Father.

incorporeity¹ (ɪnkɔːpəˈriːɪtɪ). Also 7 *erron.* -iety. [f. med.L. type **incorporeitās*, f. *incorpore-us* INCORPOREAL: see -ITY; cf. CORPOREITY.]

1. The quality or state of being incorporeal; immateriality; with *pl.*, an incorporeal attribute or quality.

1601 DEACON & WALKER *Spirits & Divels* 89 An omnipresence, or (if so I may speake) an incorporeity, is truely in God. **1647** H. MORE *Song of Soul* II. ii. III. Argt., The souls incorporeitie From powers rationall We prove. *Ibid.* II. iii. I. iii, But still new mists he casts before our eyes, And now derides our prov'd incorporeities. **1660** R. COKE *Justice Vind.* 12 The outward senses apprehend only the corporiety or substance of things..but the understanding only the incorporiety of things so seen. **1744** BERKELEY *Siris* §270 Incommunicable attributes of the Deity..such as infinity, immutability, indivisibility, incorporeity. **1840–9** SIR J. STEPHEN *Eccl. Biog.* (1850) II. 421 The notion that, after death, man was to pass into a state of pure incorporeity.

b. In legal sense; see INCORPOREAL 3.

a **1735** MADOX in Gross *Gild Merch.* (1890) I. 104 One general Figurative notion of Incorporeity hath produced many fictions.

2. An incorporeal entity. *rare.*

1743 J. ELLIS *Knowl. Div. Things* (1811) 394 The first stumbling block was..to conceive an incorporeity, anything entirely void of matter.

†**incorpo'reity**². *nonce-wd.* [f. INCORPOR-ATE *v.*, after prec.] The quality of being incorporated.

1768–74 TUCKER *Lt. Nat.* (1834) II. 189 The merchants became a Bank and South Sea Company, and the six hundred fighting men a regiment, by having incorporeity and regimentality introduced among them.

†**incor'poreous**, *a. Obs.* [f. L. *incorpore-us* (see INCORPOREAL) + -OUS] = INCORPOREAL 1.

1638 RAWLEY tr. *Bacon's Life & Death* (1650) 64 The Reasonable Soule: which is Incorporeous and Divine. **1683** E. HOOKER *Pref. Pordage's Mystic Div.* 103 *note*, There must be..in the passions..some kind of spiritualitie, otherwise incorporeous things could never by these be made as objects of their election.

†**incorpo'rificated**, *a. Obs. rare*⁻¹. [f. IN-³ + *corporificate* (= CORPORIFY q.v.) + -ED¹.] Unembodied; not fixed as a specific substance.

1641 FRENCH *Distill.* v. (1651) 163 The esurine salt being incorporificated is farre more active..then when it hath received its body by becoming a specificated salt.

incorpsed (ɪnˈkɔːpst), *a. rare.* Also 7 en-. [f. IN-² CORPSE *sb.* + -ED².] Made into one body (with something); incorporated.

1602 SHAKS. *Ham.* IV. vii. 88 (2nd Qo., 1604) He grew vnto his seate, And to such wondrous dooing brought his horse, As had he beene incorp'st [*so all Qos.*: *folios* encorps't; *edd. from Pope* incorps'd] and demy natur'd With the braue Beast. **1828** J. WILSON in *Blackw. Mag.* XXIII. 132 The dominion o' the man is lost, and the superior incorpsed with the inferior nature. **1881** W. G. PALGRAVE in *Macm. Mag.* XLV. 33 A fairy structure in a fairy land; itself incorpsed..like Shakespeare's good horseman, into that on and amid which it is placed.

incorrect (ɪnkəˈrɛkt), *a.* [ad. L. *incorrect-us*: see IN-³ and CORRECT; cf. also F. *incorrect* (1421 in Hatz.-Darm.).]

†**1.** Uncorrected; not corrected or amended; unchastened. *Obs.*

1432–50 tr. *Higden* (Rolls) III. 73 So the yere stode as incorrecte from that tyme vn to the tymes of Iulius Cesar. **1435** MISYN *Fire of Love* 56 þe synar awdyr þa leef [either they leave] incorrect, or if [þai] correc or snyb þe synnar, with so grete scharpnes & ferisnes þai speke [etc.]. **1602** SHAKS. *Ham.* I. ii. 95 To perseuer In obstinate Condolement, is a course Of impious stubbornesse... It shewes a will most incorrect to Heauen.

2. Of a book: Uncorrected for the press; containing many scribal or typographical errors.

c **1484** CAXTON *Cant. Tales* (ed. 2) Pref., Of whyche bookes so incorrecte was one broughte to me vi. yere passyd. **1774** WARTON *Eng. Poetry* lvi. (1840) III. 290, I have a most incorrect black lettered copy in duodecimo. **1850** L. HUNT *Autobiogr.* vii. 136 The plays of Shakespeare..the incorrectest publication that ever issued from the press.

3. Of style, action, etc.: Not in conformity with a recognized standard; improper, faulty.

1672 DRYDEN *Def. Epil. Conq. Granada*, The Wit of the last Age was yet more incorrect than their Language. **1735** POPE *Prol. Sat.* 45 The piece, you think, is incorrect? why, take it, I'm all submission, what you'd have it, make it. **1834** MEDWIN *Angler in Wales* I. 100 According to the immortal Brummel, it is highly incorrect to be helped a second time to soup. **1883** C. J. WILLS *Mod. Persia* 96 A practice that was considered incorrect.

4. Of a statement, etc.: Not in accordance with fact; erroneous, inaccurate.

1828 WEBSTER, *Incorrect*,..2 Not according to truth; inaccurate; as, an incorrect statement, narration or calculation. **1858** CARLYLE *Fredk. Gt.* I. v. 43 This is the.. account; incorrect in some unessential particulars. **1860** TYNDALL *Glac.* II. xxvi. 373, I had reason to believe that this statement was incorrect. **1881** SHORTHOUSE *J. Inglesant* ii. (1883) 22 That lazy facility which always gives a meaning, though often an incorrect one.

†**inco'rrected**, *a. Obs. rare*$^{-1}$. [IN-^{3}; cf. prec.] Not corrected or amended.

1646 SIR T. BROWNE *Pseud. Ep.* I. iii 8 Being so illiterate in point of intellect, and their sence so incorrected.

Hence †**inco'rrectedness**.

1681 R. FLEMING *Fulfill. Script.* (1801) I. App. 420 From the incorrectedness of the first impression.

†**inco'rrection.** *Obs. rare.* [IN-^{3}; cf. F. *incorrection* incorrect character (1512 in Hatz.).]

1. The action of making incorrect.

1598 FLORIO, *Scorrettione*, an incorrection or marring of any thing.

2. The condition of being uncorrected.

1649 ARNWAY *Tablet* (1661) 9 (T.), The unbridled swing or incorrection of ill nature maketh one odious.

3. Incorrectness, faultiness.

1788 H. WALPOLE *Lett.*, *Poetic Epochs*, When, after acts of barbarism and incorrection, a master or two produce models [of poetry] formed by purity and taste.

incorrectitude (ɪnkə'rɛktɪtjuːd). *rare.* [f. IN-^{3} + CORRECTITUDE.] The state of being in the wrong in one's conduct or opinions; incorrectness.

1898 *Westm. Gaz.* 4 Oct. 2/2 We are certain that it is not wise to adopt this position of positive incorrectitude. *Ibid.* 10 Nov. 2/3 He is brought round to own the incorrectitude of calling Mr. Gladstone a spider. **1947** *New Biol.* III. 163 It furnishes an everyday illustration of the incorrectitude of regarding different species as being necessarily intersterile.

incorrectly (ɪnkə'rɛktlɪ), *adv.* [f. INCORRECT *a.* + -LY^2.] In an incorrect manner; erroneously.

1611 COTGR., *Incorrectement*, incorrectly, faultily, corruptly. **1756–7** tr. *Keysler's Trav.* (1760) III. 12 The latter [inscription] which has been incorrectly printed before, is as follows. **1855** MACAULAY *Hist. Eng.* xv. III. 602 A Latin word endorsed on the back of the indictment was incorrectly spelt. **1884** J. RAE *Contemp. Socialism* 247 Two important economical changes..which he incorrectly ascribes to the political revolution at the end of last century.

incorrectness (ɪnkə'rɛktnɪs). [f. as prec. + -NESS.] The quality of being incorrect.

1672 DRYDEN *Def. Epil. Conq. Granada*, The Incorrectness of his [Fletcher's] Language. **1749** HURD *Comm. Horace Ars Poet.* 240–51 (R.) An incorrectness and want of care in the Roman writers. **1821** LAMB *Elia* Ser. I. *Imperf. Symp.*, A great deal of incorrectness and inadvertency..creeps into ordinary conversation. **1864** BOWEN *Logic* ix. 267 It is more difficult to weave invalid but specious arguments, knowing their incorrectness.

b. An instance of this; a mistake, error, fault.

a **1771** GRAY *Lett.* I. 139 (Cent.) Several incorrectnesses have been altered in the printing. **1774** WARTON *Hist. Eng. Poetry* Diss. iii. p. lxvii, Many of these petty incorrectnesses are not, however, to be imputed to Froissart. **1829** W. IRVING in *Life & Lett.* (1864) II. 378, I feel certain that there must be many incorrectnesses in my writings. **1838–9** HALLAM *Hist. Lit.* IV. IV. vi. §18. 268 Even his incorrectnesses are often but sacrifices required by good taste.

incorre'spondence. *rare.* [IN-^{3}.] Want of correspondence or harmony.

1667 WATERHOUSE *Fire Lond.* 162 Trade being like a Scale, in motion up and down..upon such incorrespondence, if not insolvency, must acquiesse. **1820** COLERIDGE *Let. to J. H. Green* 25 May in *Lett.* (1895) 708 The repaired organs might from intimate in-correspondence be the causes of torture and madness.

incorre'spondency. *rare.* [IN-^{3}.] = prec.

1817 COLERIDGE *Biog. Lit.* xviii. (1870) 185 The frequent incorrespondency of his diction to his metre. **1845** J. MARTINEAU *Church & State* in *Ess.* (1891) II. 30 Who can fail to observe the healthy and natural tendency of this incorrespondency to right itself?

†**incorre'spondent**, *a. Obs. rare.* [IN-^{3}.] Not corresponding; not in agreement or harmony.

1599 SANDY'S *Europæ Spec.* (1632) 199 A like or at leastwise not incorrespondent forme of Church government. **1667** WATERHOUSE *Fire Lond.* 10 Convulsions, incorrespondent to their general designment.

incorre'sponding, *a.* [IN-^{3}.] Not corresponding; = prec.

a **1834** COLERIDGE is cited by Worcester.

incorrigibility (ɪnˌkɒrɪdʒɪ'bɪlɪtɪ). [f. next + -ITY; cf. F. *incorrigibilité* (1694 in Dict. Acad.).] The quality of being incorrigible: **a.** of being evil beyond correction; **b.** of not being liable or open to correction; of not being open to proof or disproof. So **in'corrigibilist**, one who adheres to an incorrigible theory.

a **1631** DONNE *Serm.* xxxvi. 336 There is an incorrigibility in which when the reproofe cannot lead the Will it must draw blood. **1643** PRYNNE *Sov. Power Parl.* App. 149 The absolute Soveraignty..irresistibilitie, incorrigibility of the Kings of Iudah and Israel by their whole States, Congregations [etc.]. **1740** WARBURTON *Div. Legat.* V. i. Wks. 1811 V. 16 If the corrigibility of a bad soil perfectly agreed with the end of the Dispensation..the incorrigibility of it was as well fitted to the mean. **1881** *Law Rep.* 6 Prob. Div. 169 Drunkenness,..crime..incorrigibility. **1956** E. H. HUTTEN *Lang. Mod. Physics* vi. 226 To ascribe absolute incorrigibility to them [*sc.* sentences] is misleading since it suggests that they are never questioned within any context. **1966** *Amer. Philos. Q.* III. 101/2 The supposed incorrigibility of first person pain reports. *Ibid.*, Part of the guile of the incorrigibilist is not to disclose which reasons.. he is prepared to take into account as relevant.

incorrigible (ɪn'kɒrɪdʒɪb(ə)l), *a.* (*sb.*) Forms: 4 **incorygibile**, 5 **-corigibyll**, **-corrygyble**, 6– **incorrigible**, (6 **-ibill**, **-yble**). [a. F. *incorrigible* (1334 in Hatz.-Darm.), or ad. L. *incorrigibilis* (Seneca), f. *in-* (IN-^{3}) + **corrigibilis* CORRIGIBLE, f. *corrigĕre* to correct: see -IBLE.]

A. *adj.* Incapable of being corrected or amended.

1. Bad or depraved beyond correction or reform: of persons, their habits, etc.

a **1340** HAMPOLE *Psalter* xiii. 5 Incorygibile malice vndire þe lippes of þaim. **1482** *Monk of Evesham* (Arb.) 68 Y hadde wende they had be incorrygyble. **1583** BABINGTON *Commandm.* iii. (1637) 28 Then is the partie..incorrigible, and past all hope of amendment in mans eyes. **1655** R. YOUNGE *Agst. Drunkards* 6 An habituated, infatuated, incorrigible, cauterized Drunkard. **1710** STEELE *Tatler* No. 231 ¶1 Many ill Habits..which, after we have indulged our selves in them, become incorrigible. **1788** *Disinterested Love* I. 95, I found you incorrigible to my remonstrances. *c* **1850** *Arab. Nts.* (Rtldg.) 527 His father continually chastised him, yet still Aladdin remained incorrigible.

†**2.** Of something faulty or defective: That cannot be improved or set right. Of disease: Incurable.

1540–1 ELYOT *Image Gov.* 5 The most miserable astate of the weale publyke, and as it semed incorrigible. **1668** H. MORE *Div. Dial.* I. xxxviii. (1713) 85 The loss is many times irrecoverable, and the inconvenience incorrigible. **1740** WARBURTON *Div. Legat.* V. i. Wks. 1811 V. 16 The soil of Judea was absolutely incorrigible. **1804** ABERNETHY *Surgical Obs.* 45 A malignant ulcer, which..was incorrigible by any medical means employed.

3. Not liable or open to correction; so good that it cannot be improved. Also, not verifiable; that cannot be proved false.

1611 R. PEAKE tr. *Serlio's 3rd Bk. Archit.* A b, The Reader being well instructed..may, without any further labour, make a good and incorrigible peece of worke. **1946** A. J. AYER *Lang., Truth & Logic* (ed. 2) 10 What may be said to verify them [*sc.* basic propositions] conclusively is the occurrence of the experience to which they uniquely refer. .. Propositions of this kind are 'incorrigible'..it is impossible to be mistaken about them except in a verbal sense. **1956** —— *Probl. Knowl.* 54 These experiential statements..are taken as basic because they are held to be 'incorrigible'. *Ibid.* 55 Experiential statements are not incorrigible in the sense that once they have been discovered to be true they cannot subsequently be denied.

B. *sb.* **1.** One who is incorrigible.

1746 W. HORSLEY *Fool* (1748) I. 245 The Man is an Incorrigible; all gentle Rebukes are lost upon him. **1828** P. CUNNINGHAM *N.S. Wales* (ed. 3) II. 279 Lazy incorrigibles, ready to resume their thievish practices again.

2. Something not open to verification.

1936 H. H. PRICE *Truth & Corrigibility* 28 Innumerable judgements..will have to be admitted as incorrigibles.

in'corrigibleness. [f. prec. + -NESS.] The quality of being incorrigible.

a **1631** DONNE in *Select.* (1840) 96 There is the mark of his incorrigibleness, and so of his irrecouerableness, that he cannot weep. **1702** WAGSTAFF *Pres. St. Jacobitism* 4 The not being convinc'd by them argues the utmost degree of Incorrigibleness. **1860** PUSEY *Min. Proph.* 195 On account of the incorrigibleness of the people, the wise and the prophets would be silent.

incorrigibly (ɪn'kɒrɪdʒɪblɪ), *adv.* [f. as prec. + -LY^2.] In an incorrigible manner; beyond the possibility of amendment; obstinately, stubbornly. Also in sense of INCORRIGIBLE *a.* 3.

1610 BP. CARLETON *Jurisd.* 290 If hee persist therein incorrigibly, it is nothing inconuenient for the Church to depart from him. **1748** FIELDING *Jacobite's Jrnl.* No. 34 ¶8 The writers of those papers were so incorrigibly dull. **1810** SYD. SMITH *Wks.* (1867) I. 189 A few boys are incorrigibly idle, and a few incorrigibly eager for knowledge. **1956** A. J. AYER *Probl. Knowl.* 56 Such conditions as make it reasonable for me to claim that the statement is incorrigibly known.

†**inco'rroborated**, *a. Obs. rare.* [IN-^{3}.] Uncorroborated.

1784 *New Spectator* No. 17. 3/2 An incorroborated charge of treason.

incorrodible (ɪnkə'rəʊdɪb(ə)l), *a.* [IN-^{3}.] Incapable of being corroded.

1855 *Cornwall* 217 As compared with iron, it [copper] is remarkably incorrodible. **1897** *Rev. of Rev.* Oct. 429 Aluminum is practically incorrodible.

inco'rrosive, *a. rare.* [IN-^{3}.] Not corrosive; having no tendency to corrosion.

1871 *Echo* 6 Jan., Porcelain teeth, when carefully manufactured,..are low in price, they are incorrosive.

incorrumptibiletee, obs. variant of INCORRUPTIBILITY.

incorrupt (ɪnkə'rʌpt), *a.* Now *rare.* [ad. L. *incorrupt-us*, f. *in-* (IN-^{3}) + *corruptus* CORRUPT *a.*] Not corrupt; free from corruption.

1. Of organic matter: Free from decomposition or putrefaction; not decayed or rotten; not infected by that which causes decay; sound.

1387 TREVISA *Higden* (Rolls) VII. 149 Was i-founde..þe body of Pallantes, unroten and incorupt. **1432–50** tr. *Higden* (Rolls) I. 365 Where the bodies of men neither rote neither be beriedde, but lye with-owte incorrupte. **1598** HAKLUYT *Voy.* I. 11 When hee had seene with his eyes, and handled with his hands the incorrupt body of the foresaid King and Martyr, a sudden feare came vpon him. **1667** MILTON *P.L.* XI. 56 Sin, that first Distemperd all things, and of incorrupt Corrupted. **1676** HOBBES *Iliad* XIX. 36 And dropt Ambrosia into his nose, To keep his body incorrupt and sweet.

†**b.** Incapable of corruption; incorruptible.

a **1520** BARCLAY *Jugurth* A iv, The mynde and soule beynge incorrupt, eternal,..ruleth and weldeth al thynges.

2. Not debased or perverted; pure, sound.

1550 CRANMER *Defence* 116 b, The first churche of the Apostles..was moste pure and incorrupte. **1579** LYLY *Euphues* (Arb.) 151 That he be..brought vp in such a place as is incorrupt, both for the ayre and manners. **1653** MILTON *Hirelings* Wks. (1851) 374 The incorruptest Council of those Waldenses, or first Reformers.

b. Of the text of books, languages, etc.: Unaffected by error or corruption.

1624 BEDELL *Lett.* vi. 99 The quotations..are taken, *ad verbum*, out of those bookes which are incorrupt. **1676** tr. *Guillatiere's Voy. Athens* 149 Their Language at Athens is the most pure and incorrupt of all the Cities in Greece. **1873** H. ROGERS *Orig. Bible* vii. (1875) 260 To preserve the text incorrupt.

3. Morally uncorrupted; pure in life; *esp.* faithful and upright in the discharge of duty, not to be bribed or led into wrong-doing.

1545 JOYE *Exp. Dan.* vii. (R.), The most juste and incorrupt juge. **1669** MILTON *Free Commw.* Wks. (1847) 448/2 Such a king, who..may have no vicious favourite, may hearken only to the wisest and incorruptest of his Parlament. *a* **1797** H. WALPOLE *Mem. Geo. II*, I. 373 We have no succession of incorrupt senators. **1858** POLSON *Law & L.* 92 Dr. Parr has observed, that to say of a judge that he was incorrupt was hardly to eulogize him.

inco'rrupt, *v. rare.* [f. prec. adj.] *trans.* To render incorrupt; to preserve from corruption.

[**1550** VERON *Godly Sayings* (1846) 47 He that will live.. let hym beleve, let him be incorrupted & quyckened.] **1890** TALMAGE *Fr. Manger to Throne* 304 That purity which incorrupts the corruptible.

†**incorrup'tarian.** *Obs. nonce-wd.* [f. prec. adj. + -ARIAN.] One who holds the world to be incorruptible or not liable to decay.

1690 T. BURNET *Th. Earth* III. 23 Porphyry..had the same principles with these æternalists in the text, or, if I may so call them, incorruptarians, and thought the world never had, nor ever would undergo any change.

†**inco'rrupted**, *a. Obs.* [IN-^{3}.] Not corrupted.

1. Not decayed or putrefied; = INCORRUPT 1.

1593 *Rites & Mon. Ch. Durh.* (Surtees) 86 Not onely his bodie was hole and incorrupted, but the vestments wherin his bodie laie..freshe, saife and not consumed. **1646** SIR T. BROWNE *Pseud. Ep.* III. xxv. 172 A speciall proprietie in the flesh of Peacocks rost or boiled, to preserve a long time incorrupted, hath been the assertion of many.

2. Free from corruption, debasement, or perversion; = INCORRUPT 2.

1590 SPENSER *F.Q.* I. xi. 47 That soile, where all good things did grow,..As incorrupted Nature did them sow. **1638** CHILLINGW. *Relig. Prot.* I. iii. §27. 141 How shall I be assured, that the Scriptures are incorrupted in these places? **1664** H. MORE *Myst. Iniq.* 274 The incorrupted Christianity being once made the Religion of the Empire.

3. Uncorrupted in morals, virtue, chastity, devotion to duty, etc.; = INCORRUPT. 3.

1529 MORE *Dyaloge* 123 b/2 They shall..commende yᵉ thyngys whych now theyr incorrupted conscyence abhorreth. **1589** PUTTENHAM *Eng. Poesie* III. xxiv. (Arb.) 299 [It becomes] Priests to be sober and sad..a Iudge to be incorrupted. **1652** GAULE *Magastrom.* 259 Upon this condition, that they should sacrifice an incorrupted virgin. **1654** tr. *Martini's Conq. China* 156 One onely City..which was governed by an incorrupted Tartar, refused to submit. **1768** BOSWELL *Corsica* (ed. 2) 363, I found in him the incorrupted virtues of the brave islander.

Hence †**inco'rruptedness**. *rare*$^{-1}$.

1653 VAUGHAN *Life T. Jackson* in *J.'s Wks.* (1844) I. p. xl, A sure and honourable argument of the incorruptedness of that place.

incorrupti'bility. Also 5 incorrumpt-. [ad. late L. *incorruptibilitas* (Tertullian), f. *incorruptibilis* INCORRUPTIBLE: see -ITY. So F. *incorruptibilité* (1570 in Hatz.-Darm.).]

1. The quality of being physically incorruptible, or not subject to decomposition or decay.

1460–70 *Bk. Quintessence* 7 þe vertu of brennynge watir is sich þat..it holdiþ incorrumptibiletee and an euene heete. **1526** TINDALE *1 Cor.* xv. 54 When this corruptible hath put on incorruptibilite. **1605** TIMME *Quersit.* II. iv. 116 The incorruptibilitie of gold maketh it the best medicine. **1713** BERKELEY *Hylas & Phil.* III. Wks. 1871 I. 354 The being of a God, and incorruptibility of the soul, those great articles of religion. **1874** J. H. BLUNT *Dict. Sects* 38/2 The Aphthartodocetae attributed to our Lord's Body.. incorruptibility.

2. The quality of being morally incorruptible; invincible honesty or uprightness.
1830 MISS MITFORD *Village* Ser. IV. (1863) 238 A guardian of the purity of the corporation, and the incorruptibility of the vestry. **1849** GROTE *Greece* II. lxiv. (1862) V. 477 An established reputation for..incorruptibility.

incorruptible (ɪnkə'rʌptɪb(ə)l). *a.* (*sb.*) [a. F. *incorruptible* (Oresme 14th c.) or ad. late L. *incorruptibilis* (Tertullian), f. *in-* (IN-³) + *corruptibilis* CORRUPTIBLE.]
1. Incapable of undergoing physical corruption; that cannot decay or perish; everlasting, eternal.
a **1340** HAMPOLE *Psalter* xci. 12 He sall be incoruptibil.. in heuen. **1398** TREVISA *Barth. De P.R.* III. xiii. (1495) 56 The resonable soule is euerlastynge incorruptyble and may not dey. **1526** TINDALE *1 Cor.* xv. 52 The trompe shall blowe and the deed shall ryse incorruptible. **1555** EDEN *Decades* 334 *margin*, Golde is incorruptible. **1651** J. GOODWIN *Redempt. Redeemed* iv. §31. 64 Though all the individuals of a species be corruptible..yet the species it self remaines incorruptible. **1786** tr. *Beckford's Vathek* (1834) 91 Beds of incorruptible cedar. **1830** TENNYSON *Deserted House* v, Life and Thought..in a city glorious..have bought A mansion incorruptible. **1886** SIDGWICK *Hist. Ethics* ii. 86 The blessed and incorruptible has no troubles of its own, and causes none to others.
2. Incapable of being morally corrupted; that cannot be perverted or bribed.
1667 MILTON *P.L.* IX. 298 Suppos'd Not incorruptible of Faith, not prooff Against temptation. *a* **1704** T. BROWN *Praise Poverty* Wks. 1730 I. 101 Incorruptible abstinence and honesty. **1734** tr. *Rollin's Anc. Hist.* (1827) VIII. XIX. v. 163 Invincible and incorruptible by money. **1837** CARLYLE *Fr. Rev.* III. II. v, Till all the Convention..had almost indicted the Incorruptible there on the spot. *Ibid.* v. v, Robespierre himself..opens his incorruptible lips copiously in the Jacobins Hall. **1870** DICKENS *E. Drood* ix, A man of incorruptible integrity.
3. as *sb.* (*pl.*) An ancient Christian sect, the Aphthartodocetæ, who maintained the incorruptibility of the body of Jesus Christ.
1727-41 CHAMBERS *Cycl.*, *Incorruptibles, incorruptibiles*, the name of a sect which sprang out of the Eutychians. Their distinguishing tenet was, That the body of Jesus Christ was incorruptible. **1853** M. KELLY tr. *Gosselin's Pope Mid. Ages* I. 89 The edict of Justinian in favour of the sect called the Incorruptibles.

inco'rruptibleness. [f. prec. + -NESS.] The quality of being incorruptible; incorruptibility.
1398 TREVISA *Barth. De P.R.* VIII. ii. (Bodl. MS.), Pureness and incorruptiblenes of mater. **1579** FULKE *Heskins' Parl.* 211 Wicked men are not made..partakers of incorruptiblenesse. **1658** GURNALL *Chr. in Arm.* verse 14 xvi. (1669) 64/1 So much a Soul hath of Heavens purity and incorruptibleness, as it hath of Sincerity. **1685** BOYLE *Enq. Notion Nat.* iv. 114 The incorruptibleness and immutability of the heavenly bodies.

inco'rruptibly, *adv.* [f. as prec. + -LY².] In an incorruptible manner; in a way not subject to corruption.
1579 FULKE *Heskins' Parl.* 351 Which worde of God feedeth them that are corruptible incorruptibly. **1805** SOUTHEY *Madoc* I. xv, The dead, In royal grave-clothes habited..with precious gums and spice Fragrant, and incorruptibly preserved.

incorruption (ɪnkə'rʌpʃən). *arch.* [a. F. *incorruption* (12th c.) or ad. late L. *incorruptiōn-em* (Tertullian), f. *in-* (IN-³) + *corruptiōn-em*. CORRUPTION.]
1. Freedom from physical corruption or decay; incorrupt condition. Now *arch.* and only in reference to 1 Cor. xv. 42, etc.
1526 TINDALE *1 Cor.* xv. 42 Hit is sowen in corrupcion and ryseth in incorrupcion. **1558** BP. WATSON *Sev. Sacram.* xvi. 101 Oure synnes shall kyndle oure payne, and incorruption of bodye and soule shall without ende continue the same. **1611** BIBLE *Wisd.* vi. 18–19 The giuing heed vnto her lawes, is the assurance of incorruption. And incorruption maketh vs neere vnto God. **1646** SIR T. BROWNE *Pseud. Ep.* III. xxv. 172 The same preservation, or rather incorruption, we have observed in the flesh of Turkeys, Capons, Hares, Partridge, Venison, suspended freely in the ayre. **1747** WESLEY *Prim. Physic* (1762) 3 Cloathed in Body as well as in Soul with Immortality and Incorruption. **1871** W. B. POPE *Fernley Lect.* 155 Its incorruption and sinlessness were imparted 'by the indwelling of the Holy Ghost'.
†**2.** Freedom from corrupt conduct; uprightness and honesty. *Obs.*
1600 HOLLAND *Livy* XLVI. 1235 L. Æmylius Paulus.. whose incorruption and abstinence from the publicke treasure was such that [etc.]. **1677** *Govt. Venice* 192 Ancient Senators eminent for Incorruption and good Oeconomie.
†**3.** Of texts: Freedom from erroneous alterations; purity. *Obs.*
1638 CHILLINGW. *Relig. Prot.* I. iii. §27. 141 For the incorruption of Scripture, I know no rationall assurance we can have of it. **1662** STILLINGFL. *Orig. Sacr.* III. iv. §9 The controversie between the present Hebrew Copies and the LXX. in point of integrity and incorruption.

†**inco'rruptive,** *a. Obs. rare*⁻¹. [f. IN-³ + CORRUPTIVE; cf. late L. *incorruptīvus* (Jerome).] Incorruptible, not liable to decay.
1744 AKENSIDE *Pleas. Imag.* I. 435 Round her brow To twine the wreathe of incorruptive praise.

inco'rruptly, *adv.* [f. INCORRUPT *a.* + -LY².] In an incorrupt manner; purely; uprightly.
a **1583** in Strype *Life Grindal* (1710) II. App vii. 71 Whether your Bishop and his Chancellour, commissaries, and all other his officers, do minister Justice indifferently, and incorruptly to all Her Majesty's Subjects. **1612** T. TAYLOR *Comm. Titus* i. 14 If it be purely and incorruptly preached. **1641** MILTON *Ch. Govt.* I. i, Observation will shew us many deep counsellers of state and judges to demean themselves incorruptly in the setl'd course of affaires.

inco'rruptness. [f. as prec. + -NESS.] The quality of being incorrupt, in its various senses.
1695 WOODWARD *Nat. Hist. Earth* II. (1723) 107 Integrity and Incorruptness of Manners. **1771** *Antiq. Sarisb.* 2 The incorruptness and general use of the old British [tongue], before the coming of the Romans and Saxons. **1775** DE LOLME *Eng. Const.* II. vi. (1784) 245 They have, in the discharge of their function, shown an incorruptness. **1876** BANCROFT *Hist. U.S.* V. xlvii. 62 With the faults of pride, inflexibility, and dilatoriness, he also had incorruptness. **1881** WESTCOTT & HORT *Grk. N.T.* II. App. 46 A suspicion as to the incorruptness of the existing MSS.

incorteyn, obs. form of ENCURTAIN *v.*

†**in'costive,** *a. Obs. rare*⁻¹. [? f. IN-² + COSTIVE.] = COSTIVE.
1570 LEVINS *Manip.* 153/43 These folowing..doo rather signifie passiuely: as, Incostiue, *stipatus ventre*.

†**in'counselable,** *a. Obs. rare*⁻¹. [IN-³.] Not open to counsel; unwilling to be advised.
1552 LYNDESAY *Monarche* 2558 Gyf he ȝit remanith obstinat And to the holy kirk Incounsolable [*v.r.* inconsalabill].

incounter, -traunce, -trie, obs. ff. ENCOUNTER, etc.

in-country ('ɪn'kʌntrɪ). [f. IN *adv.* 12 d + COUNTRY.] **1.** *Sc.* The inland country, the interior; the mainland as opposed to the outlying isles; the country within reach of the capital and centre of civilization, as distinguished from outlying districts.
1565 MARY Q. SCOTS *Let.* 23 Aug. in Keith *Hist. Scot.* (1734) 313 Oure Rebellis he retiterate thame to the In-cuntre, the suffering quhairof is na wayis to us honourabil. **1596** DALRYMPLE tr. *Leslie's Hist. Scot.* I. 2 Before I begin the historie of the Inne cuntrey, I wil first..descriue the quarteris and boundes of Scotland. *a* **1639** SPOTTISWOOD *Hist. Ch. Scot.* VI. 412 In the Isles and High-lands were likewise great Troubles: nor was In-country more quiet.
2. Used *attrib.*: in the country; in a contextually specified country. Cf. IN *prep.* 18.
a **1953** DYLAN THOMAS *Prospect of Sea* (1955) 9 Between the incountry fields and the incoming sea. **1963** *Times* 6 Feb. 6/7 Cornwall..has agreed to give all technical assistance that is needed on payment by the Scillies of travelling and subsistence expenses, and to charge for the use of its educational and welfare institutions at the 'in-country' instead of the 'out-country' rate. **1966** *N.Y. Times* 1 May IV. 3 In South Vietnam, in what is called in Saigon the 'in-country' war, development efforts have been concentrated upon types of weapons best utilized in jungles and rice paddies. **1969** *Daily Tel.* 20 Nov. 5/3, 2,500 American Marines are to leave South Vietnam..over a five-day period starting from today. This will reduce America's 'in-country' military strength to 484,000 troops. **1973** *Ibid.* 13 Mar. 5/2 American in-country troop strength [in Vietnam] stands at 7,170 men.

incoup, *v.*: see INCOOP.

†**incouple,** *v. Obs. rare*⁻⁰. [f. IN² + COUPLE.] *trans.* To couple together.
1611 FLORIO, *Incoppiare*, to incouple.

incourage, -ment, etc., obs. ff. ENCOURAGE, etc.
1550 NICOLL *Thucyd.* 69 (R.) The othere rulers, through the requeste & incouragement of the Megariens, wolde assaye to take the port of Athens.

incourcion, obs. form of INCURSION.

†**incourse.** *Obs. rare.* Also 5 yn-. [ad. L. *incursus* (see INCURSE), with assimilation to *concourse*, *recourse*, or to OF. *encours*, *incours* (14th c. in Godef.).] Running in; inflow, inrush; assault, attack.
a **1440** *Ps. xci* in *Found. St. Bartholomew's* (E.E.T.S.) 8 Thou schalt nat drede for the nyghte drede..ne for the yncourse [L. *ab incursu*] and myddday devyl. **1578** BANISTER *Hist. Man* v. 81 Nothyng resisteth the incourse therof into the intrels. **1668** CULPEPPER & COLE *Barthol. Anat.* Man. I. ii. 306 Its Substance is exceeding thin, but..very compact, lest they should break by a strong incourse of the blood.

incourtaine, obs. form of ENCURTAIN *v.*

in'courteously, *adv.* [IN-³.] Uncourteously, impolitely.
1859 MACAULAY in Trevelyan *Life* II. 367, I was.. unwilling to act incourteously towards a person who to me personally had shown the most marked civility.

†**incouth,** scribal var. of UNCOUTH, strange.
c **1340** *Cursor M.* 16541 (Laud MS.) To bery ynne incouþe [*other MSS.* vncuth] men that to that Cite sought.

†**in'covenanted,** *ppl. a. Obs. rare*⁻¹. [IN-².] Brought into covenant.
1656 S. WINTER *Serm.* 23 The children of believing parents are incovenanted, therefore they are to be sealed with the initial seal of the covenant.

†**in'covenanting,** *a. Obs. rare*⁻¹. [IN-³: see COVENANT *v.* 4.] Not covenanting; not signing the Covenant.
1640 in Rushw. *Hist. Coll.* III. (1692) I. 384 Act anent incovenanting Patrons.

incover, variant of ENCOVER *v.*

†**in'coverable,** *a. Obs. rare*⁻¹. [f. IN-³ + **coverable*, f. COVER *v.*²] Irrecoverable, irrevocable.
1526 *Wills & Inv. N.C.* (Surtees 1835) 107, I sir Thomas foster..maks my last and incoverable will and testament in maner & forme following.

incradle, obs. form of ENCRADLE *v.*

†**in'crafty,** *a. Obs. rare*⁻¹. [Erroneous form for UNCRAFTY, with IN-³.] Unskilful, stupid.
a **1520** BARCLAY *Jugurth* A vj b, Nor he gaue nat hymselfe to be corrupte with lust nor incrafty slouthe.

incrash ('ɪnkræʃ). *rare.* [f. IN-¹ + CRASH.] A crashing in; a breaking in with a crash.
1861 *Macm. Mag.* III. 327 No..trace of the murderous incrash of the ball which had slain him.

incrasion: see INCRASSION.

†**in'crassant,** *a.* and *sb. Obs.* [ad. L. *incrassānt-em*, pres. pple. of *incrassāre*: see next.]
A. *adj.* Thickening: said of medicines supposed to thicken the 'humours'.
B. *sb.* An 'incrassant' medicine or preparation.
1678 SALMON *Pharm. Lond.* VI. ii. 814 *Incrassant*, such as make thin humors thick. **1810** REES *Cycl.* s.v., *Incrassants*, or *incrassating medicines*..of the old writers..such medicines as were imagined to condense or thicken the blood and humours.

incrassate (ɪn'kræsət), *a.* [ad. L. *incrassātus*, pa. pple. of *incrassāre*: see next.]
†**1.** Thickened (in consistence); condensed. *Obs.*
1608 WILLET *Hexapla Exod.* 121 The aire..was incrassate and thickned. **1685** BAXTER *Paraphr. N. Test.* Heb. xi. 3 That Earth is but incrassate Humor, and Humor (or Water) incrassate Air, and Air incrassate Fire, and Fire incrassate vegetative Spirit, and that incrassate intellectual Spirit.
†**2.** *fig.* Of the mind: Dulled, made gross. *Obs.*
1659 HAMMOND *On Ps.* cxix. 70 Their heart is incrassate and grosse. *a* **1660** —— *Serm.* Wks. 1684 IV. xiv. 657 Their understandings were so gross within them, being fatned and incrassate with magical phantasms.
3. *Zool.* and *Bot.* Of a thickened or swollen form.
1760 J. LEE *Introd. Bot.* (1765) 225 The Peduncle or Flower-stalk..is said to be..Incrassate, thickened towards the Flower. **1826** KIRBY & SP. *Entomol.* IV. 260 *Incrassate*, disproportionably thick in part. *Ibid.* 294 Margin.. Incrassate, when the margin is disproportionably thick. **1847** J. HARDY in *Proc. Berw. Nat. Club* II. No. 5. 248 Antennæ short, incrassate. **1856-8** W. CLARK *Van der Hoeven's Zool.* I. 382 Femora often incrassate.

incrassate (ɪn'kræseɪt), *v.* [f. L. *incrassāt-*, ppl. stem of *incrassāre* to thicken, f. *in-* (IN-²) + *crassāre* to make thick, f. *crassus* CRASS.]
1. *trans.* To thicken in consistence; to condense, inspissate. Now *rare*.
1601 HOLLAND *Pliny* II. 255 The nature of the seed is astringent: it doth incrassat and thicken humors. **1658** SIR T. BROWNE *Hydriot.* 23 Liquors, which time hath incrassated into gellies. **1709** BLAIR in *Phil. Trans.* XXVII. 74 That does not hinder its Blood from being incrassated by Cold and bad Dyet. **1864** ALGER *Future Life* I. i. 8 Incrassated and clogged with vapors and steams.
b. *absol.*
1601 HOLLAND *Pliny* II. 194 That [gum]..is of a stronger operation to thicken and incrassat. **1718** QUINCY *Compl. Disp.* 96 'Tis reckon'd to cool and incrassate.
†**c.** *intr.* To grow thick, to become condensed.
1733 CHEYNE *Eng. Malady* I. iii. §7 (1734) 21 These naturally subtile Parts..incrassate and grow clumsy.
†**2.** *fig.* To make gross (the mind, etc.); to dull, stupefy. *Obs.*
a **1660** HAMMOND *Serm.* Wks. 1684 IV. xiii. 651 Their spirits fatned and incrassated within them. **1666** SPURSTOWE *Spir. Chym.* Pref. (1668) 6 Men that have incrassated their souls.
†**3.** To thicken in sound: see INCRASSATED b.
4. To thicken in form: see INCRASSATED a.
Hence **in'crassating** *vbl. sb.* and *ppl. a.*
1620 VENNER *Via Recta* viii. 170 Some meats..are of an attenuating and soluble faculty..; and some of an incrassating, and an astringent. **1732** ARBUTHNOT *Rules of Diet* 265 In the Case of incrassating or thickening. **1767** GOOCH *Treat. Wounds* I. 179 Of a cooling, incrassating, and agglutinating nature. **1771** J. S. *Le Dran's Observ. Surg.* (ed. 4) Dict., *Pachuntica*, incrassating Medicines.

incrassated (ɪn'kræseɪtɪd), *ppl. a.* [f. prec. + -ED¹.] **a.** Thickened: esp. in *Zool.* and *Bot.* = INCRASSATE *a.* 3.
1657-83 EVELYN *Hist. Relig.* (1850) I. 143 The angels.. also lost their celestial natures,..and, becoming more incrassated, were thereby..penetrable by that fire prepared

for the devil and his angels. **1806** GALPINE *Brit. Bot.* 309 Siliques bent backward, flat, linear: with an incrassated margin. **1816** KIRBY & SP. *Entomol.* (1843) I. 94 Its four posterior thighs are incrassated. **1857** BERKELEY *Cryptog. Botany* §207. 218 The fruit consists of incrassated cells springing vertically from the frond.

†**b.** Thickened in sound: used as = aspirated.

1668 WILKINS *Real Char.* 367 V Consonant: 'Tis of the same power which is commonly ascribed to B asperated, or rather incrassated. So the Western Jews pronounce their Letter (ב) when not Dageshated. **1691** RAY *Acc. Err.* in *Words* 156 The sound we give to *V* Consonant, which is nothing else but *B* aspirated or incrassated or *Bh.*

incrassation (ɪnkræ'seɪʃən). [n. of action f. L. *incrassāre*: see INCRASSATE *v.*]

1. The action of incrassating, or condition of being incrassated; thickening, condensation.

1633 HART *Diet of Diseased* I. xiv. 48 Lettice..too much thickneth the blood, and..breeds an incrassation in the opticke spirits. **1686** GOAD *Celest. Bodies* I. ix. 31 Ice becomes fixed by Incrassation. **1786** T. ARNOLD *Observ. Insanity* II. 76 Induration, incrassation and partial ossification of one or both membranes of the brain. **1822–34** *Good's Study Med.* (ed. 4) II. 247 This incrassation is traced chiefly in the colon.

b. *concr.* A thickened growth or formation.

1822–34 *Good's Study Med.* (ed. 4) I. 302 The rectum.. was..so indurated as to render it difficult to say whether the incrassation should be called flesh or cartilage.

†**2.** Phonetic 'thickening'; applied by Wilkins to aspiration. *Obs.*

1668 WILKINS *Real Char.* 367 (F)..seems to be such an incrassation of the Letter (P) as (V) is of (B). 'Tis answerable to the Greek (Φ).

incrassative (ɪn'kræsətɪv), *a.* and *sb.* ? *Obs.* [f. L. *incrassāt-*, ppl. stem of *incrassāre* (INCRASSATE) + -IVE.]

A. *adj.* Having the quality of 'incrassating' or thickening the 'humours'. **B.** *sb.* A medicine or preparation having this property.

1666 HARVEY *Morb. Angl.* (J.), Incrassatives to thicken the blood. **1853** E. HAMILTON *Flora Homœop* II. 68 Its juice is very congealing, incrassative, and desiccative.

in'crassion, perverted form for INCRASSATION (sense 1), (for the sake of the rime).

a **1618** SYLVESTER *Tobacco Battered* 454 Also it fries and dries away the Bloud..by whose incrassion [*v.r.* incrasion] The vitall spirits in an unwonted fashion Are bay'd and barred of their passage due Through all the veins.

†'**incre**, *a.* *Sc.* *Obs.* [Of uncertain origin: see ENKERLY.] Earnest, fervent, eager, hearty.

c **1375** *Sc. Leg. Saints, Mathou* 425 In-kyre luf he had god til. *Ibid., Laurentius* 585 þis martyre þane with incre wil He prayt helpe to sende hyme til. *Ibid., Placidas* 101 Placydas with incre wil Presit fast to cum hym til.

†'**increly** *adv.* (also **inkir-**, **inkyr-**, **encre-**, ENKERLY, q.v.), earnestly, fervently, eagerly, heartily.

c **1375** *Sc. Leg. Saints, Petrus* 181 And luffit Criste mar Increly þan þe laf did, Richt fastly. *Ibid., Egypciane* 1368 He lowit god inwartly, And gret rycht sare inkyrly. *Ibid., Andreas* 48 Bot he for þame yhet prayt bane, Sa increly. **1513** DOUGLAS *Æneis* VI. i. 122 The Kyng hymself than inkirly from his hart Maid this orisone.

†**increable**, *a.* *rare*⁻⁰. [f. IN-³ + CREABLE.] Incapable of being created. Hence **increa'bility**, incapability of being (or having been) created.

1668 H. MORE *Div. Dial.* Schol. (1713) 558 The Increability of the external World from eternity.

increasable (ɪn'kri:səb(ə)l), *a.* Also 6–7 **en-**, 6–9 **increaseable**, 8 **increasible**. [f. INCREASE *v.* + -ABLE.] Capable of being increased; susceptible of increase.

1534 MORE *Treat. Passion* Introd., Wks. 1270/2 Their full and perfit, and not encreceable blisse. **1611** COTGR., *Multipliable*, multipliable, increaseable. **1733** TULL *Horse-Hoing Husb.* 17 So is.. this Pasture Increasible *ad Infinitum*. **1735** LAW *Enquiry* i. (R.), But if we could once suppose an end of these, they would be no longer increasable. **1806** W. TAYLOR in *Ann. Rev.* IV. 38 To grant the lands to individuals at a low quit-rent, increasable at definite periods. **1857** RUSKIN *Pol. Econ. Art* i. 30 A certain quantity of art-intellect is born annually..not increaseable by a single grain.

Hence **in'creasableness**, capacity of being increased; **in'creasably** *adv.* (in quot. = increasingly).

1579 TWYNE *Phisicke agst. Fort.* I. xxiv. 33a, The madnesse of men increaseably putteth it in practise. **1678** CUDWORTH *Intell. Syst.* I. v. 766 Indefinite encreasableness of body and space seems to be mistaken for a positive infinity thereof. **1735** LAW *Enquiry* i. (R.), We find an indefinite increasableness of some of our ideas, an impossibility of supposing any end of them.

†**in'creasal**. *Obs. rare.* [f. INCREASE *v.* + -AL¹ 4.] = INCREASE *sb.*: in quot., Profit.

1601–2 FULBECKE *2nd Pt. Parall.* 36 If the executors doe merchaundize with the goodes of the testator, the increasall of them shall bee assets in their hands.

increase (ɪn'kri:s), *v.* Forms: α. 4–5 **encres(se**, **encrees(e**, **encreesse**, **encresce**, 4–6 **encrese**, **encrece**, (5 **encresche**), 5–6 **encreace**, 6 **encreas**, (7 *pa. pple.* **encrest**), 5–9 **encrease**. β. 5 **increase**, **increasse**, 5–6 **increse**, (*Sc.*) **incress**, 5 (6 *Sc.*) **incres**, 6 **increace**, (*Sc.*) **incresce**, 6– **increase**. [a. AF. *encres-*, *encress-* (infl. *encresse*, *encressent*) = OF. *encreis(s)-*, stem of *encreistre*, later *encroistre*:—L. *incrēscĕre* to increase, f. *in-* (IN-²) + *crēscĕre* to grow. In later use, the prefix is assimilated to L.; the *ea* represents ME. open *ē*.]

I. Intransitive senses.

1. To become greater in size, amount, duration, or degree; to be enlarged, extended, or intensified; to wax, grow.

α. **13..** *E.E. Allit. P.* A. 958 Þer glory & blysse schal euer encres. *c* **1380** WYCLIF *Serm.* Sel. Wks. I. 19 Goostly feeste shulde encreese. *c* **1386** CHAUCER *Clerk's Prol.* 50 The Poo.. That Estward ay encresseth in his cours. **1398** TREVISA *Barth. De P.R.* v. lxiii. (Bodl. MS.), Þe more þe fatnes encreseþ and waxiþ. **1594** SHAKS. *Rich. III*, IV. iii. 48 Still his power encreaseth. **1628** SIR W. MURE *Spir. Hymne* 101 Without thee, Lord,..Heaven's glorious courts had neere encrest [*rimes* blest, invest, prest, rest, addrest]. **1774** GOLDSM. *Nat. Hist.* (1776) I. 76 In mines..the cold seems to encrease from the mouth as we descend. **1825** LINGARD *Hist. Eng.* VI. 3 As the danger of the queen encreased.

β. *c* **1440** *Promp. Parv.* 261/1 Increse, or grow or wax more. *c* **1460** *Towneley Myst.* viii. 177 Thare comforth shall euer increasse [*rimes* peasse, seasse, measse]. *a* **1553** UDALL *Royster D.* IV. iii. (Arb.) 65 In case this strife increace. **1567** *Gude & Godlie B.* (S.T.S.) 83 Quhilk ay incressis moir and moir. **1662** STILLINGFL. *Orig. Sacr.* III. iii. §8 As corruption increased in the world. **1736** BUTLER *Anal.* I. i. (1884) 23 Drowsiness, increasing till it ends in sound sleep. **1864** TENNYSON *Victim* iii, His beauty still with his years increased.

2. To grow in numbers, become more numerous or frequent, to multiply; *esp.* by propagation.

α. *c* **1315** SHOREHAM 72 No stren may non encressy Wythoute flesches loste. **1377** LANGL. *P. Pl.* B. XI. 389 And bad euery creature in his kynde encrees. **1526** *Pilgr. Perf.* (W. de W. 1531) 86 Many small graynes of corne may growe and encrease to fyll a great garner. **1642** ROGERS *Naaman* 557 Hypocrites encrease. **1722** DE FOE *Plague* (1884) 11 The Burials encreased. **1798** FERRIAR *Illustr. Sterne* i. 4 Materials have encreased on my hands.

β. **1530** PALSGR. 590/2 It is a straunge thynge that one grayne shulde increase thurty. **1590** SPENSER *F.Q.* III. vi. 34 The mighty word,..That bad them to increase and multiply. **1667** MILTON *P.L.* IV. 748 Our Maker bids increase, who bids abstain But our Destroyer, foe to God and Man? **1727–38** GAY *Fables* I. xxxix. 29 He feels no joy, his cares increase. **1855** TENNYSON *Maud* III. ii, And watch her harvest ripen, her herd increase.

3. To become greater *in* some specified quality or respect; to grow or advance *in*.

1388 WYCLIF *Acts* xvi. 5 The chirches..encreseden in noumbre eche dai. **1513** BRADSHAW *St. Werburge* I. 1705 Dayly encreasynge in worshyp and renowne. **1526** TINDALE *Luke* ii. 52 Iesus increased in wisdom and age, and in favoure with god and man. **1567** *Gude & Godlie B.* (S.T.S.) 146 Lat vs incres in lufe of the. **1662** STILLINGFL. *Orig. Sacr.* III. iv. §12 Daily increasing in numbers and power. **1814** MISS O'KEEFE *Zenobia* II. 112 He became subject to His parents and encreased in stature and in wisdom. **1871** L. MORRIS *Songs two Worlds* Ser. I. *Rich & Wise* (1872) 100 In wit and wealth do I increase.

4. In pregnant sense: To advance in wealth, fortune, power, influence, etc.; to grow richer, more prosperous, or more powerful; to thrive more and more; to prosper. *Obs.* or *arch.*

1388 WYCLIF *Matt.* xxv. 29 To euery man that hath me schal ȝyue, and he schal encreese. **1486** *Bk. St. Albans* C vij a, She shall encrece myghtely. **1526** TINDALE *John* iii. 30 He must increace: and I muste decreace. **1625** BACON *Ess., Riches* (Arb.) 237 He cannot but encrease mainely. **1722** DE FOE *Col. Jack* (1840) 168, I began to increase visibly; I had a large quantity of land cured.

5. *Lat. Gram.* Of a noun or adjective: To have one syllable more in the genitive than in the nominative; the word is said to *increase short* or *long* according as the vowel of this syllable (i.e. the last syllable of the stem, preceding the case-ending) is short or long.

1612 [implied in INCREASER 4]. **1669** MILTON *Accedence, Nouns*, Such [nouns of third declension] as increase not in the genitive are generally feminine, as *nubes nubis*. **1871** *Pub. School Latin Primer* §29. 14 *Merces, merges, quies, seges*, Though their Genitives increase. **1875** W. SMITH *Smaller Lat. Gram.* §144. 84 *Es* increasing short in Genitive.

II. Transitive senses.

6. a. To cause to wax or grow; to make greater in amount or degree; to augment, enlarge, extend, intensify.

α. **13..** *K. Alis.* 1437 His ost he encresed with six thousynd Of noble knyghtis. *c* **1386** CHAUCER *Knt.'s T.* 457 And yet encresseth this al my penaunce. *c* **1491** CAXTON *Chast. Goddes Chyld.* 69 Ryches encreaseth auaryce in a couetous man as drinke encreseth thurst in a man that hathe the dropesie. **1579** LYLY *Euphues* (Arb.) 97 It encreaseth my sorrow and thy shame. **1611** BIBLE *Lev.* xxv. 16 Thou shalt encrease the price thereof. **1747** WESLEY *Prim. Physic* (1762) 57 It may be encreased or lessened according to the strength of the Patient. **1822** IMISON *Sc. & Art* II. 37 The combustion will proceed with a splendour much encreased.

β. *c* **1440** *Promp. Parv.* 261/1 Incresyn, or moryn, *augeo*. *c* **1450** *Cov. Myst.* xxxii. (Shaks. Soc.) 326 Now is my care wel more incressyd! [*rime* dressyd]. *a* **1553** UDALL *Royster D.* Prol. (Arb.) 10 Mirth increaseth amitie. **1611** BIBLE *Eccl.* i. 18 Hee that increaseth knowledge, increaseth sorrow. **1732** ARBUTHNOT *Rules of Diet* 262 Such things as increase its Velocity. **1878** JEVONS *Prim. Pol. Econ.* 73 Wages are increased by increasing the produce of labour, not by decreasing the produce.

b. (See quot. 1957.)

1840 J. GAUGAIN *Lady's Assistant* 96 Increase a stitch on each wire, by knitting the last stitch in the common way; knit it again from the back part of the loop (this is the way to increase without making a hole). **1872** *Young Englishwoman* Nov. 607/1 The increasing and decreasing may..take place at the ends or in the middle of the work. In increasing in the middle, the increase is effected by taking up stitches. **1944** A. THIRKELL *Headmistress* iii. 60 They..had to take off all the stitches and unravel back to where they ought to have begun increasing and pick up all the stitches again. **1957** M. B. PICKEN *Fashion Dict.* 182/2 *Increase*, in knitting, crocheting, tatting, etc., to add to number of stitches in row, pattern, or round so as to enlarge the piece. **1971** *Vogue's Guide to Crochet* 14 Increasing a stitch means adding a stitch, and decreasing a stitch means losing it. *Ibid.*, Care must be taken not to decrease or increase in such a way as to leave an uneven edge.

7. a. To make more numerous, augment the number of, multiply.

1382 WYCLIF *Ecclus.* I. 24 That encreside oure daȝes fro the wombe of oure moder. *c* **1386** CHAUCER *Melib.* ¶774 Sweete wordes multiplien and encreesen [*v.r.* encrescen] freendes. **1552** *Bk. Com. Prayer, Litany*, Encrease the fruites of the yearth. **1611** BIBLE *Jer.* xxix. 6 Take ye wiues ..that ye may bee increased there. **1788** COWPER *Negro's Compl.* i, To increase a stranger's treasures.

†**b.** To make fruitful; to cause to yield increase. *Obs. nonce-use.*

1697 DRYDEN *Virg. Georg.* I. 27 Come all ye Gods and Goddesses that wear The rural Honours, and increase the Year.

8. To make greater *in* some specified quality or respect. Const. *in*, also formerly *with.* Now *rare* or *Obs.*

1421 SIR. H. LUTTRELL in Ellis *Orig. Lett.* Ser. II. I. 86, I pray unto God of hys grace encresce ȝow in worship, prosperite, and perfit ioye. **1526** TINDALE *Rev.* iii. 17 Thou sayst thou arte riche and incresyd with goddes, and haste nede off nothinge. **1700** DRYDEN *Iliad* I. 372 Believe a friend with thrice your years increas'd.

9. In pregnant sense: To make more wealthy, prosperous, or powerful; to enrich or advance; to cause to thrive; to promote. *Obs.* or *arch.* (cf. INCREASER 2).

c **1380** WYCLIF *Wks.* (1880) 369 Þe clergy in alle þese poyntis ben encresyd. *c* **1430** LYDG. *Minor Poems* (Percy Soc.) 5 His mortalle foon to oppressen and bere adoune, And him to encresin as Cristis champion. **1545** ASCHAM *Toxoph.* To Gentlm. Eng. (Arb.) 18 Cicero..increased the latine tounge after another sorte. **1607** SHAKS. *Cor.* IV. v. 235 This peace is nothing, but to rust Iron, encrease Taylors, and breed Ballad-makers.

increase ('ɪnkri:s, *formerly* ɪn'kri:s), *sb.* Forms: see the verb. [f. prec. vb.

The shifting of the stress is recent. Todd remarks 'the accent..has, in modern times, been often placed on the first syllable, by way of so distinguishing the substantive from the verb'. '*Increase* appears in Walker 1791, Perry 1805. Some later dicts. have both *in'crease* and '*increase*: so in Tennyson.]

I. The action of increasing.

1. a. The action, process, or fact of becoming or making greater; augmentation, growth, enlargement, extension.

α. *c* **1374** CHAUCER *Troylus* IV. 1229 (1257) It nys but foly and encres of peyne. *c* **1386** —— *Prol.* 275 Sownynge alway thencrees of his wynnyng. *c* **1430** LYDG. in *Pol. Rel. & L. Poems* 27 Is none so gret encrese Of worldly tresowre as for to lyve in pease. **1526** *Pilgr. Perf.* (W. de W. 1531) 4 Augmentacyon and encrease of meryte. **1602** SHAKS. *Ham.* I. ii. 144 As if encrease of Appetite had growne By what it fed on. **1751** JOHNSON *Rambler* No. 93 ¶1 Opinions which the progress of his studies and the encrease of his knowledge oblige him to resign.

β. *c* **1440** *Promp. Parv.* 139 Encres, or incres, ..*augmentacio*. **1508** DUNBAR *Flyting w. Kennedie* 21 Incres of sorrow, sklander, and evill name. **1597** HOOKER *Eccl. Pol.* v. xi. §2 As God gaue increase to his Church. **1674** PLAYFORD *Skill Mus.* I. vii. 24 Notes of Augmentation or Increase. **1700** DRYDEN *Flower & Leaf* 595 For things of tender kind, for pleasure made Shoot up with swift increase, and sudden are decay'd. **1870** E. PEACOCK *Ralf Skirl.* I. 6 With increase of business came increase of expense.

†**b.** *spec.* The rising of the tide, or of the waters of a river; the advance of daylight from sunrise to noon; the waxing of the moon. *Obs.*

1555 EDEN *Decades* 119 They see the seas by increase and decrease to flowe and reflowe. **1600** SURFLET *Countrie Farme* II. liv. 381 In the increase of the day, that is to saie, about nine or tenne a clocke in the morning. **1613** PURCHAS *Pilgrimage* (1614) 564 The Land of Egypt doth not onely owe the fertilitie, but herselfe also, unto the slimie encrease of Nilus. **1626** BACON *Sylva* §892 Seeds will grow soonest, And Haire, and Nailes, and Hedges, and Herbs, Cut, &c. will grow soonest, if they be Set, or Cut, in the Increase of the Moone. **1665** BOYLE *Occas. Refl.* (1848) 55 Oysters, and other Shell-fish, are observ'd to thrive at the Increase of the Moon, though her Light be unattended with Heat.

2. The becoming more numerous or frequent; growth in numbers; multiplication. **a.** *gen.*

1390 GOWER *Conf.* III. 283 [Moab and Ammon], as it is founde, Cam afterward to great encres. **1579** LYLY *Euphues* (Arb.) 114 Deuise..howe the encrease of them may encrease thy profite. **1662** STILLINGFL. *Orig. Sacr.* III. iv. §13 We can have no reason to think, that..none of them [Sem's posterity] went further off, which necesity would put them upon because of their great increase. **1768** GOLDSM. *Good-n. Man* I. i, The encrease and progress of earthquakes. **1849** MACAULAY *Hist. Eng.* iii. I. 284 The increase of the people has been great in every part of the kingdom.

b. *spec.* The multiplication of a family or race of men or animals; the production of offspring; reproduction, procreation, propagation, breeding.

1390 GOWER *Conf.* III. 277 In whom was gete netheles Of worldes folk the first encres. **1538** STARKEY *England* I. iii. 98 Few men study the increse of bestys and catayl. **1605** SHAKS.

Lear I. iv. 301 Drie vp in her the Organs of increase. **1682** DRYDEN *Mac Fl.* 8 Blest with issue of a large increase. **1842** TENNYSON *Edwin Morris* 44 God made the woman for the man, And for the good and increase of the world.

c. The fruitful multiplication of plants or crops.

1698 G. THOMAS *Penns. & W. New Jersey* (*title-p.*), The Richness of the Soil..the prodigious Encrease of Corn. **1794** S. WILLIAMS *Vermont* 79 Trees and plants derive their nourishment and increase. **1850** TENNYSON *In Mem.* xlvi, The fruitful hours of still increase.

3. Phr. ***on the increase*** (in senses 1, 2): Increasing, becoming greater or more frequent.

1752 HUME *Ess. & Treat.* (1777) I. 51 The power of the crown..is rather on the encrease. **1858** CARLYLE *Fredk. Gt.* II. viii. I. 100 Brandenburg was..always rather on the increase than otherwise. **1884** *Times* (weekly ed.) 26 Sept. 3/4 The use of the telephone is generally on the increase in most parts of the Continent.

†**4.** *spec.* Growth in wealth, prosperity, honour, or influence; advancement, progress. *Obs.*

c **1385** CHAUCER *L.G.W.* 1087 (*Dido*) Al the worshippe and encres That I may goodly doon yow. **1450** Q. MARGARET in *Four C. Eng. Lett.* 8 We, desiryng th' encres, furtherance, and preferring of oure said squire. **1513** MORE in Grafton *Chron.* (1568) II. 793 To take upon him the..governaunce of this realme, to the welth and increase of the same. **1638** F. JUNIUS *Paint. of Ancients* 112 Upon some she bestowed honour, force, and increase. **1718** WATTS *Ps.* cxxii, The man that seeks thy peace, And wishes thine increse, A thousand blessings on him rest. **1719** W. WOOD *Surv. Trade* 57 It is manifest, we have not diminish'd in our Encrease by Foreign Trade, from 1688 to this Time.

II. The result or product of increasing.

5. a. The result of increasing; an increased amount, addition, increment.

1382 WYCLIF *2 Macc.* ix. 11 By alle momentis his sorewis takynge encresis [L. *augmenta*]. *c* **1400** *Cato's Mor.* 40 in *Cursor M.* App., Kepe hit wiþ encrese. *c* **1440** *Promp. Parv.* 261/1 Incres, *incrementum.* **1593** SHAKS. *2 Hen. VI*, III. ii. 292 Thou wilt but adde encrease vnto my Wrath. **1810** WELLINGTON in Gurw. *Desp.* (1838) V. 508 The increase of expense occasioned by the increased subsidy to the Portuguese Government, and by the increase of our own army. **1878** JEVONS *Prim. Pol. Econ.* 69 Working men think that, when their wages are raised, the increase comes out of the pockets of their employers.

b. (See INCREASE *v.* 6 b.)

1872 [see INCREASE *v.* 6 b]. **1971** M. HAMILTON-HUNT tr. *Mon Tricot Knitting Dict.* 20 An increase is the method of making an extra or supplementary stitch in the course of the work... The single increases are known as simple increases. .. Double increases are used for darts, etc.

6. Offspring, progeny, brood (of men or animals). Properly collective: also *poet.*, of an individual = Offspring, child.

1552 HULOET, Increase of cattell, *fœtura.* **1607** SHAKS. *Cor.* III. iii. 114 My deere Wiue's Estimate, her wombes encrease. **1611** BIBLE *1 Sam.* ii. 33 And all the increase of thine house shall die in the floure of their age. **1674** tr. *Scheffer's Lapland* 128 The two Rain-deers..as likewise their increase, which sometimes comes to a considerable number. **1688** DRYDEN *Brit. Rediv.* 208 Iove's increase, who from his brain was born. *a* **1717** ADDISON tr. *Ovid* Wks. 1753 I. 199 Only five Of all the vast increase were left alive.

7. a. That which grows or is produced from the earth; vegetable produce, crops. Also formerly in *pl.* (*rare*). *arch.*

1535 COVERDALE *Ps.* lxvi[i]. 6 That the earth maye bringe forth hir increase. **1535** —— *1 Macc.* xiv. 8 The trees gaue their frute and encreace. *c* **1585** in Capt. Smith *Virginia* I. (1624) 4 Beyond are many isles full of fruits and other Naturall increases. *c* **1600** SHAKS. *Sonn.* xcvii, The teeming autumn, big with rich increase. **1695** WOODWARD *Nat. Hist. Earth* I. (1723) 60 The Earth did not then teem forth its Encrease. **1710** PRIDEAUX *Orig. Tithes* i. 8 Abel brought as much of his encrease.

b. *transf.* That which breeds in or is produced by, any region, as fish in the sea (cf. 'the harvest of the deep'). *rare.*

1559 W. CUNNINGHAM *Cosmogr. Glasse* Ded. A ij, Behold ..the Seas with her merveilous increse. **1687** DRYDEN *Hind & P.* III. 1248 All the wild increase of woods and fields [i.e. birds], And who in rocks aloof, and who in steeples builds.

c. (Chiefly *fig.* from 7). The product, result, or 'fruit' of any action; a literary production (quot. 1589); that which is obtained or gained, profit; interest on money.

1560 BIBLE (Genev.) *Lev.* xxv. 37 Thou shalt not..lend him thy vitailes for increase. **1584** R. SCOT *Discov. Witchcr.* XIV. viii. (1886) 312 They doo [lose] their increase and their principall. **1589** NASHE *Pref. Greene's Menaphon* (Arb.) 17 George Peele..whose first encrease, the Arraignement of Paris, might plead to your opinions, his pregnant dexteritie of wit. **1703** MOXON *Mech. Exerc.* 241 All kinds of Flints.. are hard to burn..because a great part of its increase goes away by a kind of Glass.

increased (ɪnˈkriːst), *ppl. a.* [f. INCREASE *v.* + -ED[1].] Made or become greater, augmented, multiplied, etc.: see the verb.

1552 HULOET, Increased, *auctus.* **1790** HAN. MORE *Relig. Fash. World* (1792) 3 The increased profligacy of the common people. **1846** GREENER *Sc. Gunnery* 374 Occasioned by the increased speed. **1885** *Daily News* 21 Dec. 1/5 Increased facilities for Residence, Travel and Occupation.

increasedly (ɪnˈkriːsɪdlɪ), *adv. rare.* [f. prec. + -LY[2].] In an increased degree; to a greater amount or extent.

1823 *Examiner* 490/1 Encreasedly entitled to public favour. **1840** GLADSTONE *Ch. Princ.* 174 The hope of reward is more exalted than the fear of punishment..and increasedly so, as our conception of the reward approximates to that of St. John.

†**inˈcreaseful**, *a. Obs. rare.* [f. INCREASE *sb.* + -FUL.] Full of increase; productive, fruitful.

1593 SHAKS. *Lucr.* 958 To cheare the Plowman with increasefull crops. **1599** R. LINCHE *Anc. Fict.* M iij, It becommeth more rich, fertile, and increasefull.

increasement (ɪnˈkriːsmənt). Now *rare.* Also 4–7 en-. [f. INCREASE *v.* + -MENT.]

1. The action or process of increasing; growth, augmentation; multiplication: = INCREASE *sb.* 1, 2.

1509 BP. FISHER *Fun. Serm. C'tess Richmond* Wks. (1876) 292 Neuertheles by maryage & adioynyng of other blode, it toke some encreasement. **1545** RAYNOLD *Byrth Mankynde* I The encreasement of the chyld in her wombe. **1592** WYRLEY *Armorie, Ld. Chandos* 60 Him sicknes took with sharpe incresment sore. **1609** R. BARNERD *Faithf. Shepheard* Ep. Ded. 5 A mite in a great Treasurie is small in shew for encreasement thereunto. **1646** TRAPP *Comm. John* xvi. 22 He hides his love oft, as Joseph did, out of increasement of love. **1651** tr. *De las-Coveras' Hist. Don Fenise* 101 The ease they would give him turneth into the encreasement of his paines.

2. That by which something is increased; an increment, addition, augmentation; progeny; produce: = INCREASE *sb.* 5–7.

1389 in *Eng. Gilds* (1870) 79 To brynge yᵉ catelle wᵗ yᵉ encresement. **1561** T. NORTON *Calvin's Inst.* II. 140 With so much greater encreacementes of reuelation he did day by day more brightly shew it. **1612** W. SHUTE tr. *Fougasses' Venice* i. 6 The buildings since then, ought rather to be called encreasements, as made..by little and little. **1878** *Law Rep.* 4 Com. Pleas 442 Where the encroachment of a river was so gradual that..it could not be perceived, the increasement was got to the owner of the river.

increaser (ɪnˈkriːsə(r)). [f. INCREASE *v.* + -ER[1].] One who or that which increases.

1. One who or that which augments or makes greater; an agent that causes something to grow, a 'breeder' (*of* something).

1528 PAYNEL *Salerne's Regim.* H, This strange wyne is special encreacer of the spiritis. **1572** BOSSEWELL *Armorie* II. 124 Luna, the riper and encreaser of fruites. **1624** CAPT. SMITH *Virginia* IV. 155 These crosses and losses were no small increasers of his malady. **1756** BURKE *Vind. Nat. Soc.* Wks. 1842 I. 6 Such a nurse and increaser of blessings. **1893** J. J. MODI in Barrows *Parlt. Relig.* II. 901 Ahura-Mazda,.. He is the creator as well as the destroyer, the increaser as well as the decreaser.

2. One who advances or promotes. *Obs.* or *arch.*

1618 BEAUM. & FL. *Valentin.* v. viii, A lover, and encreaser of his people. **1631** WEEVER *Anc. Fun. Mon.* 384 Honourable increasers, Rulers and preseruers of all such matters which conduce to Christian pietie. **1851** SIR F. PALGRAVE *Norm. & Eng.* I. 258 The Epithet..Encreaser of the Empire. **1858** CARLYLE *Fredk. Gt.* II. ix. I. 101 A notable increaser of his House.

†**3.** (With qualifying adj.) An animal or plant that multiplies (greatly, etc.). *Obs.*

1665 REA *Flora* 96 The Virginia spider wort is a great increaser, and thereby growes common in almost every garden. **1704** *Collect. Voy. & Trav.* III. 46/1 The greatest Encreasers are the Guanaco's. **1727** BRADLEY *Fam. Dict.* s.v. *Hollow-root*, They are great increasers even in any Soil, but like Sandy best.

†**4.** *Lat. Gram.* A noun that 'increases' in the genitive: see INCREASE *v.* 5. *Obs.*

1612 BRINSLEY *Lud. Lit.* 139 *Puer pueri*, is a graue increaser, and therefore of the Masculine Gender.

increasible, obs. form of INCREASABLE.

increasing (ɪnˈkriːsɪŋ), *vbl. sb.* [f. INCREASE *v.* + -ING[1].]

1. The action of the verb INCREASE; increase, augmentation, enlargement, growth, etc.

c **1340** HAMPOLE *Prose Tr.* 25 That þei shuld oo tyme yevene hem..to the werkes of actiffe liffe in profitt of her encresynge. **1382** WYCLIF *Eph.* iv. 16 Of whom alle the body ..makith encresynge of the body. **1552** ABP. HAMILTON *Catech.* (1884) 36 He promissis incressing of grace and vertew. **1586** W. WEBBE *Eng. Poetrie* (Arb.) 89 Artes haue their increasinges euen as other things, beeing naturall. **1620** SANDERSON *Twelve Serm.* (1632) 113 The..encreasing of the body to the edifying it selfe in loue. **1703** MAUNDRELL *Journ. Jerus.* 8 A Benediction and a Virtue of encreasing. **1850** JOHN BROWN *Disc. our Lord* (1852) I. ii. 60 Not near approaches to satisfaction but increasings of the capacity. **1872** [see INCREASE *v.* 6 b]. **1932** D. C. MINTER *Mod. Needlecraft* 70/1 *Increasing*... After knitting a stitch..knit again into back of same loop. **1972** *Where* May/June 133/1 There has been a 78 per cent increasing in the principal venereal diseases, that is to say gonorrhoea, syphilis and chancroid.

†**2.** The result of this action: Increase, produce.

1382 WYCLIF *2 Cor.* ix. 10 He schal multiplie ȝoure seed, and make moche the encresyngis of fruytis of ȝoure riȝtwysnesse. **1483** *Cath. Angl.* 114 An Encresynge, ..*incrementum.* **1644** DIGBY *Mans Soule* (1645) 33 Abridging them of their naturall encreasings.

inˈcreasing, *ppl. a.* [f. as prec. + -ING[2].] That increases; growing, augmenting, enlarging, etc.: see the verb. Esp. in ***law of increasing return***(*s*): the observed fact that in certain manufactures and industries the expenditure of labour or capital up to a certain point produces a more than proportionate corresponding return. Cf. DIMINISHING *ppl. a.* 1 b.

1597 SHAKS. *2 Hen. IV*, I. ii. 205 Haue you not..a decreasing leg, an incresing belly? **1677** HALE *Prim. Orig. Man.* II. ix. 208 Fishes are infinitely more numerous or increasing than Beasts or Birds. **1752** HUME *Ess. & Treat.* (1777) I. 49 The encreasing luxury of the nation. **1849** MACAULAY *Hist. Eng.* viii. II. 484 A pier and a haven.. insufficient for the increasing traffic. **1890** A. MARSHALL *Princ. Econ.* I. IV. xiii. 379 While the part which Nature plays in production conforms to the Law of Diminishing Return, the part which man plays conforms to the Law of Increasing Return. **1925** S. E. THOMAS *Elem. Econ.* x. 114 The Law of Increasing Returns..states that the expansion of an industry, in which there is no dearth of the necessary agents of production, tends to be accompanied by increasing returns.

inˈcreasingly, *adv.* [f. prec. + -LY[2].] In an increasing degree, or at an increasing rate; growingly; more and more.

c **1380** WYCLIF *Sel. Wks.* III. 33 He echide encreessingli hise servauntis. **1620** THOMAS *Lat. Dict.*, *Auctim*,.. increasingly. **1858** FROUDE *Hist. Eng.* III. xii. 27 Finding his position increasingly uneasy. **1885** *Spectator* 18 July 949/1 As time goes on it becomes increasingly difficult to find good investments.

increˈatable, *a. rare*⁻⁰. [f. IN-[3] + CREATABLE.] Incapable of being created. Hence **increatability** (ɪnkriːeɪtəˈbɪlɪtɪ), incapability of being created.

1888 MRS. SPENDER *Kept Secret* III. ii. 29 The indestructibility and increatability of matter.

increate (ɪnkriːˈeɪt), *a.* [ad. med.L. *increātus*, f. *in-* (IN-[3]) + *creātus* created.] Not created, uncreated: said of divine beings or attributes.

1412–20 LYDG. *Chron. Troy* I. vi, Myghty Ioue eterne and increat. **1435** MISYN *Fire Love* 6 þe warmnes of charite increate or vnwroght. *c* **1544** *Golden Litany* in Maskell *Mon. Rit.* II. 245 Lorde god, by thy increate ande vndiuidid trinite: haue mercy on vs. **1667** MILTON *P.L.* III. 6 Hail, holy Light!.. Bright effluence of bright essence increate. **1679** L. ADDISON *First State Mahumedism* 48 The Alcoran was not the Increate word of God. **1849** THOREAU *Week Concord* Monday 158 The Creator is still behind increate.

Hence **increˈately** *adv.*

1833 J. H. NEWMAN *Arians* ii. §4 (1876) 181 In process of time, a distinction was made between ἀγένητος and ἀγέννητος, (*increate* and *ingenerate*),..so that the Son might be said to be ἀγενήτως γεννητός (*increately generate*).

†**increˈated**, *ppl. a. Obs.* [f. as prec. + -ED[1] 2.] Uncreated; = INCREATE *a.*

1552 HULOET, Increated, *increatus.* **1609** BIBLE (Douay.) *Wisd.* viii. *comm.*, God, the increated wisdom is infinite. **1697** BP. PATRICK *Comm. Exod.* xxiii. 20 Not a created Angel, but an increated vis: the Eternal Son of God. **1702** ECHARD *Eccl. Hist.* (1710) 514 Hermogenes..was the first Christian that maintained matter to be increated and eternal. **1721** R. KEITH tr. *T. à Kempis' Solil. Soul* i, How shalt thou be able to dive into that which is increated?

†**increˈation.** *Obs. rare.* [f. INCREATE *a.*: see -ATION.] The condition of being uncreated.

1753 CHAMBERS *Cycl. Supp.* s.v. *Alcoran*, This eternity and increation of the alcoran has occasioned vehement disputes.

increative (ɪnkriːˈeɪtɪv), *a.* [IN-[3].] Not creative; incapable of creating.

1877 FAIRBAIRN *Stud. Philos. Relig.* 238 Nature informed with mind helps to form its lives in its life, receives that she may give ideas and images of beauty: but alone she is increative. **1880** —— *Stud. Life Christ* Introd. (1881) 27 It was fundamentally increative, radically infertile.

incredibility (ɪnkrɛdɪˈbɪlɪtɪ). [ad. L. *incrēdibilitās*, f. *incrēdibilis* INCREDIBLE; cf. F. *incrédibilité* (1690 in Furetiere).]

1. The quality or fact of being incredibile; a thing that cannot be believed; an incredible notion or circumstance.

1613 PURCHAS *Pilgrimage* I. ii. 12 *note*, He to salve his incredibilitie, deviseth a motion both of the Earth and of the Starres. **1664** H. MORE *Myst. Iniq.* 133 The number of these either Delusions or Incredibilities. *a* **1674** CLARENDON *Hist. Reb.* XI. §228 The incredibility or monstrousness of such a kind of proceeding. **1764** HARMER *Observ.* XV. i. 39 The seeming incredibility of the account Josephus gives. **1883** FROUDE *Short Stud.* IV. II. vi. 250 The intellect rose in protest, and declared that incredibilities should not be taught any longer.

2. The fact or quality of being incredulous. *rare.*

1882 *Standard* No. 17942. 5 [They] have become convinced that incredibility is no longer justifiable.

incredible (ɪnˈkrɛdɪb(ə)l), *a.* (*sb.*) Also 6 increadible. [ad. L. *incrēdibilis* unbelievable, unbelieving, f. *in-* (IN-[3]) + *crēdibilis* CREDIBLE: cf. obs. F. *incrédible* (16th c. in Godef.).]

1. Not credible: that cannot be believed; beyond belief.

1412–20 LYDG. *Chron. Troy* IV. xxx, For incredible was.. To se howe he through his great myght The Grekes put proudely to the flyght. **1539** BIBLE (Great) *Acts* xxvi. 8 Why shulde it be thought a thynge incredyble vnto you, that God shuld rayse agayne the deed? **1613** PURCHAS *Pilgrimage* (1614) 503 Pliny reports things more incredible. **1736** BUTLER *Anal.* I. I. (1884) 33 There is nothing incredible in the general doctrine of religion. **1860** TYNDALL *Glac.* II. ix. 269 The assertion that a glacier moves must appear.. startling and incredible. **1871** L. STEPHEN *Playgr. Europe* x.

(1894) 226 The small nucleus of fact round which so many incredible stories have gathered.

b. In weakened sense: Such as it is difficult to believe in the possibility of, or to realize; said esp. of a quantity, quality, number, etc., of a degree beyond what one would *a priori* have conceived as possible; inconceivable, exceedingly great.

1482 *Monk of Evesham* (Arb.) 33 An inestymable and incredibulle swetenes of ioyfull conforte. **1559** W. CUNNINGHAM *Cosmogr. Glasse* 176 Ther are iij. mountaines of an incredible height. **1579** LYLY *Euphues* (Arb.) 72 Euphues was surprised with such increadible joye at this straunge event that he had almost sounded. **1655** FULLER *Ch. Hist.* I. v. §4 It is incredible, how speedily and generally the Infection spread by his preaching. **1777** BURKE *Corr.* (1844) II. 147 These stories do incredible mischief. **1856** KANE *Arct. Expl.* II. xiv. 144 Off they sprang with incredible swiftness. **1856** EMERSON *Eng. Traits, 1st Visit* Wks. (Bohn) II. 7 The incredible sums paid in one year by the great booksellers for puffing.

c. Of a person. *rare.*

1802–12 BENTHAM *Ration. Jud. Evid.* (1827) II. 67 Unless you maintain that the same man is credible or incredible, honest or dishonest, according as [etc.]. *Ibid.* v. 83 He was heard; yes; but upon what occasion? On the occasion on which he is deemed incredible?

†**2.** Unbelieving. *Obs. rare.*

1557 NORTH tr. *Gueuara's Diall Pr.* 191 a/1 Incredible of that is told him. **1624** JACKSON *Serm. Introd. Knowl. Jesus* §29 Their relations of it are so plain..that the incrediblest Gentiles of that age were inexcusable. **1640** WALTON *Life Donne* 26 The incredible reader may find in the Sacred Story that Samuel did appear to Saul even after his death. **1761** L. HOWARD *Hist. Bible, 2 Kings* vii. *note,* This incredible nobleman saw the plenty but did not partake of it.

B. as *sb.* An incredible thing. (Chiefly *pl.*)

1610 HEALEY *St. Aug. Citie of God* XXII. viii. (1620) 825 This incredible thing which was not seene, was confirmed by other incredibles which were seene.

Hence **in'credibleness**, incredibility.

1611 FLORIO, *Incredibilità,* incrediblenesse. **1613** PURCHAS *Pilgrimage* I. ii. 12 The quantitie and the swiftnesse is much more after the former then after this latter opinion, which doth better salue the incrediblenesse thereof. **1668** M. CASAUBON *Credul. & Incred.* 180 (T.) The very strangeness, or incredibleness of the story. **1706** PHILLIPS, *Incredibility* or *Incredibleness.*

incredibly (ɪn'krɛdɪblɪ), *adv.* [f. prec. + -LY[2].] In an incredible manner or degree, in a way or to an extent that is impossible or very difficult to believe; to an extent that one would not have believed possible; exceedingly, extremely.

c **1500** *Three Kings Sons* 99 He had seen hem do in armes that day yncredibly. **1538** LELAND *Itin.* IV. 124 Leofric.. adorned it with Gould and Sylver incredibly. **1656** COWLEY *Pindar. Odes, Praise Pindar* notes i, Pindar was incredibly admired and honoured among the Ancients. **1794** SULLIVAN *View Nat.* I. 372 Unless..we should suppose it to be incredibly condensed. **1858** CARLYLE *Fredk. Gt.* III. i. 140 In an incredibly short period, mutiny was quenched.

†**increditable** (ɪn'krɛdɪtəb(ə)l), *a. Obs.* [IN-[3].] Not creditable; discreditable, bringing discredit.

1695 COLLIER *Ess. Mor. Subj.* II. (1702) 136, I own 'tis difficulty removed, and increditable into the bargain. **1732** *Gentl. Instructed* (ed. 10) 145 (D.) Hypocrisy and dissimulation are always increditable.

†**in'credited**, *a. Obs. rare.* [IN-[3].] Not credited, disbelieved.

c **1633** ADAMS *Serm. Gal.* v. 9 Wks. 1862 II. 354[Hazael] was brought to this self-incredited mischief; as impossible as at first he judged it.

†**in'credule**, *a.* (*sb.*) *Sc. Obs.* Also -uil. [a. F. *incrédule* unbelieving, incredible (Froissart, 14th c.), ad. L. *incrēdulus*, f. *in-* (IN-[3]) + *crēdulus* believing, easy of belief, CREDULOUS.] Incredulous. **b.** as *sb.* An incredulous person.

1549 *Compl. Scot.* iii. 27 Til extinct that false seid ande that incredule generatione. **1590** A. HUME *Hymns* (1832) 12 Increduils hence ga hide you hie.

incredulity (ɪnkrɪ'djuːlɪtɪ). [Late ME., a. F. *incrédulité*, ad. L. *incrēdulitāt-em*, n. of quality f. *incrēdulus* INCREDULOUS.]

1. A disbelieving frame of mind; unreadiness or unwillingness to believe (statements, etc.); disbelief.

1430 LYDG. *St. Margarete* 249 And fynal cause of thi mortal distresse Is thi wilful incredulite. *c* **1460** in *Pol. Rel. & L. Poems* 112 Gayne thomas Indes incredulite. **1533** EDEN *Treat. Newe Ind.* (Arb.) 7 The sodeyn straungenes.. shal not..gender in thee incredulitie [*printed* incrudelitie]. **1672** WILKINS *Nat. Relig.* II. ix. (R.), There is nothing so wild and extravagant, to which men may not expose themselves by such a kind of nice and scrupulous incredulity. **1742** JARVIS *Quix.* II. I. xiv. (1885) 57 Here is my sword, which shall make incredulity itself believe. **1762–71** H. WALPOLE *Vertue's Anecd. Paint.* (1786) III. 66 The altar-piece in the chapel is the best piece I ever saw of his; the subject, the incredulity of St. Thomas. **1870** DICKENS *E. Drood* vii, Mr. Crisparkle looked in his face, with some incredulity. **1875** JOWETT *Plato* (ed. 2) I. 183 The greatness of their professions does arouse in his mind a temporary incredulity.

†**2.** Want of religious faith; unbelief. *Obs.*

1532 MORE *Confut. Tindale* Wks. 713/1 Nor no sinne can damne him but onely incredulitie, that is to say lacke of beliefe. **1560–1** *1st Bk. Discipl. Ch. Scot.* xiv. (1836) 77 Every one that dyeth departeth either in the faith of Christ or..in incredulity. **1619** SANDERSON *Twelve Serm.* (1632) 7 When the Faith of a true beleever is sore shaken with temptations of incredulitie and distrust.

†**3.** = INCREDIBILITY. *Obs.*

1607 MARKHAM *Caval.* III. (1617) 3 Others tell vs other tales, of as much incredulity, of the Horses of Scithia, Greece, and Barbary.

incredulous (ɪn'krɛdjʊləs), *a.* [f. L. *incrēdul-us.* (see INCREDULE) + -OUS.]

1. Unbelieving; not ready to believe; sceptical. Formerly used of religious unbelief, but no longer applicable in that sense. Const. *of*, rarely †*to*.

1579 LYLY *Euphues* (Arb.) 164 Harken what they [Scriptures] say of such as be altogether incredulous. **1582** N. T. (Rhem.) *John* iii. 36 He that is incredulous to the Sonne, shal not see life. **1615** LATHAM *Falconry* (1633) 84, I am altogether incredulous of it, and do know that no man in the world can maintaine it. **1651** HOBBES *Leviath.* III. xxxvii. 235 It was not..that the end of Miracles was not to convert incredulous men to Christ. **1791** COWPER *Odyss.* XIV. 475 Thou hast, in truth, a most incredulous mind. **1829** LANDOR *Wks.* (1846) I. 425/2 They call it philosophical to be incredulous on holy things. **1836** ALISON *Europe* xxxi. §2 (1849–50) V. 299 They were ignorant or incredulous of the rapid change.

b. Of action, etc.: Indicating or prompted by incredulity.

1613 PURCHAS *Pilgrimage* (1614) 223, I perceive by your incredulous smiles, you will scarce beleeve. **1864** TENNYSON *En. Ard.* 854 The woman gave A half-incredulous, half-hysterical cry.

†**2.** Not to be believed; = INCREDIBLE. *Obs.*

1601 SHAKS. *Twel. N.* III. iv. 88 No obstacle, no incredulous or vnsafe circumstance. **1631** WEEVER *Anc. Fun. Mon.* 554 Miracles..will be thought incredulous in this age. **1646** SIR T. BROWNE *Pseud. Ep.* VII. xviii. 380 Unto some it hath seemed incredulous what Herodotus reporteth of the great Army of Xerxes. **1649** BLITHE *Eng. Improv. Impr.* (1653) 142 They..make such vast Improvements, as to raising Corn and Grass also, as is incredulous. **1750** WARBURTON *Julian* Wks. (1811) VIII. 207 The crosses on the garments..must appear a very incredulous circumstance.

†**b.** as *adv.* = INCREDIBLY. *Obs.*

1533 BONNER *Let. to Hen. VIII* in Burnet *Hist. Ref.* (1715) III. Collect. Records 38 The Pope, whos Sight is incredulous quick, eyed me, and that divers tymes.

Hence **in'credulousness**, incredulity.

1727 in BAILEY vol. II. **1755** in JOHNSON.

incredulously (ɪn'krɛdjʊləslɪ), *adv.* [f. prec. + -LY[2].] In an incredulous manner; with incredulity.

1800 MRS. HERVEY *Mourtray Fam.* IV. 199 She shook her head, incredulously. **1863** MISS BRADDON *Eleanor's Vict.* I. i. 9 The Englishman looked almost incredulously at his animated companion.

†**in'creep**, *v. Obs.* [f. IN *adv.* + CREEP *v.*: see IN-*prefix*[1].] *intr.* To creep in. So **'in,creeper**; **'in,creeping** *vbl. sb.* and *ppl. a.* (see IN *adv.* 11 a, c, e).

13.. *K. Alis.* 2168 Now rist grete tabour betyng.. Launces breche and increpyng. *c* **1420** in *Pol. Rel. & L. Poems* 210 So bryth, so gloriouce, þe sonne increppe, His schynyng merkes here bodi bare. **1607** TOPSELL *Four-f. Beasts* (1658) 563 The Epithets hereof [Weasel] are, fearfull, in-creeper, and swift, and beside these I finde not any materiall, or worthy to be rehearsed. **1892** *Chicago Advance* 29 Sept., The increeping tide of worldliness. **1896** *Edin. Rev.* Apr. 352 The most fair-seeming ceremonies were not without their increeping element of moral declension.

†**'incremable**, *a. Obs. rare.* [f. L. type **incremābilis*, f. *in-* (IN-[3]) + L. *cremāre* to burn, consume by fire + -ABLE.] That cannot be burnt or consumed by fire; incombustible.

1646 SIR T. BROWNE *Pseud. Ep.* III. xiv. 140 They conceive that from the skin of the Salamander, these incremable pieces are composed. **1658** —— *Hydriot.* 28 Incombustible sheets made with a texture of Asbestos, incremable flax, or Salamanders wool.

incremation (ɪnkriː'meɪʃən). Now *rare* or *Obs.* [f. IN-[2] + CREMATION, f. L. type **incremāre*: see prec.] Burning, esp. of a dead body; = CREMATION (which is now the usual word).

1826 J. WILSON *Noct. Ambr.* Wks. 1855 I. 107, I hope you will improve that department not withstanding your order of incremation. **1849** THACKERAY *Pendennis* II. iv, 'Shall we take him to the publisher's or make an *auto-da-fé* of him?' 'I don't see what is the good of incremation', Warrington said. **1851** MADDEN *Shrines O. & N. World* I. 44 The mode of incremation which was most followed by the Greeks. **1866** HUXLEY *Preh. Rem. Caithn.* 127 Cistic tombs..constructed according to the customs of incremation. **1870** *Echo* 4 Nov., An article on Incremation as opposed to Interment, is worthy of attention, the case made out being one of considerable strength.

increment ('ɪnkrɪmənt). [ad. L. *incrēmentum* increase, means of growth, f. stem of *incrē-scĕre* to INCREASE: see -MENT. (So F. *incrément*, 18th c.)]

1. a. The action or process of increasing or becoming greater, or (with *pl.*) a particular case or instance of this; increase, augmentation, growth.

c **1425** *Found. St. Bartholomew's* (E.E.T.S) 29 The desirid helth by certeyne incrementys began to come Ageyne. *c* **1450** *Mirour Saluacioun* 2979 Joseph a son growing or increment [*v.r.* encrees] is for to say. **1570–6** LAMBARDE *Peramb. Kent* (1826) 379 It was beaten..into the heades of the common people..that the Roode (for Crucifix) of this church, did by certaine increments continually wax and growe. **1649** JER. TAYLOR *Gt. Exemp.* II. §11. 144 They prayed..that Christ's kingdome upon earth might have its proper increment. **1650** BULWER *Anthropomet.* xvii. 171 The increment of the Nails is very natural. **1762** KAMES *Elem. Crit.* ii. §6 (1833) 53 Our emotions are never instantaneous..[they] have different periods of birth and increment. **1835** KIRBY *Hab. & Inst. Anim.* II. xvii. 218 We add daily increments to our knowledge and science. **1861** BERESF. HOPE *Eng. Cathedr. 19th C.* viii. 264 A standing proof of the increment of dignity which conspicuous height gives to a town construction. **1884** BOWER & SCOTT *De Bary's Phaner.* 532 Woody plants..in which the limit of the annual increment of growth is sharply defined by the layer of periderm formed at [the] outer side [of the cortex] .

†**b.** Increase of prosperity; advancement: cf. INCREASE *v.* 4, *sb.* 4. *Obs.* or *arch.*

1609 HOLLAND *Amm. Marcell.* XIV. xi. 27 Turning to and fro, as she knoweth full well, the weights of increments and detriments both, of risings and fallings. **1667** WATERHOUSE *Fire Lond.* 70 Celebrated benefactors to Londons Clergy, and Religious Increment. **1858** CARLYLE *Fredk. Gt.* II. IX. i. 396 Majesty, by way of increment to Hacke..has lately made him 'Master of the Hunt'.

c. The waxing of the moon: *spec.* in *Heraldry.*

1610 GUILLIM *Heraldry* III. iii. (1611) 91 According to the divers apparitions of the Moone hath she her divers denominations in Heraldrie; as her increment in her increase. **1688** R. HOLME *Armoury* II. 21/2. **1864** BOUTELL *Her. Hist. & Pop.* xi. 71 She is Increscent, or in Increment, when her horns point to the dexter.

d. *Rhet.* 'An advancing from weaker to stronger expressions, an ascending towards a climax': = L. *incrēmentum* in Quintilian (Lewis & Short).

[**1657** J. SMITH *Myst. Rhet.* 132 *Incrementum*..is a form of speech which by degrees ascends to the top of something, or rather above the top, that is, when we make our speech grow and increase by an orderly placing of words, making the later word alwayes exceed the former in the force of signification ..It is a kind of a Climax.] **1753** CHAMBERS *Cycl. Supp., Increment*..in rhetoric, a species of climax, which rises from the lowest to the highest. **1864** WEBSTER, *Increment*..4. (*Rhet.*) An amplification without strict climax, as in the following passage: 'Finally, brethen, whatsoever things are true......' Phil. iv. 8. [**1893** *Funk's Stand. Dict., Increment* ..5. *Rhet.* A form of discourse that consists in repeating with increasing emphasis an already emphatic statement, as in 'he is a parricide—a parricide, I say; do you hear? a parricide!']

†**2.** *transf.* Something that helps or promotes growth: **a.** A support for a growing plant; **b.** Nourishment. *Obs.*

c **1420** *Pallad. on Husb.* I. 189 Stakis longe ar vynys increment. **1708** J. PHILLIPS *Cyder* (1807) 84 The loosen'd roots then drink Large increment.

†**3.** Produce: cf. INCREASE *sb.* 7. *Obs. rare.*

1593 *Bacchus Bountie* in *Harl. Misc.* (Malh.) II. 273 He promised to honour the eating thereof with the best increments of his overflowing tunne.

4. a. Amount of increase; an amount or portion added to a thing so as to increase it, an addition; an amount gained, profit.

unearned increment: see UNEARNED.

1631 BRATHWAIT *Whimzies, Traveller* 93 Should hee cast up his accompts..hee would finde his decrements great, his increments small. **1640–4** SIR E. DERING in Rushw. *Hist. Coll.* III. (1692) I. 293 In fewer Words than this Additional Increment, now offered to your Bill. **1794** HERON *Inform. Powers at War,* The annual increment of the Population. **1861** *7th Rep. Postmaster Gen.* 20 Annual increments of salaries and wages. **1865** MILL *Pol. Econ.* v. ii. §5 (ed. 6), I see no objection to declaring that the future increment of rent should be liable to special taxation. **1875** B. W. RICHARDSON *Dis. Mod. Life* vi. 96 The increment of heat which proves fatal is from 11° to 12° Fahr. above the natural temperature of the animal. **1890** MORLEY *Sp. Ho. Comm.,* The question of unearned increment will have to be faced before many years are over. **1892** *Rep. Sel. Com. on Town Holdings* p. xxv, The person who has benefited by the unearned increment in the value of the land.

b. *Math.* and *Physics.* A small (or sometimes infinitesimal) amount by which a variable quantity increases (*e.g.* in a given small time); *spec.* the increase (positive or negative) of a function due to a small increase (esp. of unity) in the variable, as in the ***Method of Increments***, now called the Calculus of Finite Differences (see DIFFERENCE *sb.* 2 b).

[**1715** B. TAYLOR (*title*) Methodus Incrementorum.] **1721** BAILEY, *Increment*, in *Algebra*, signifies the infinitely small increase of a line in Fluxions, growing bigger by Motion. **1743** EMERSON *Fluxions* 2 The indefinitely small Portions of the Fluent which are generated in any indefinitely small Portions of Time are called *Moments* or *Increments*. **1748** HARTLEY *Observ. Man* I. iii. 352 The Supposition that Fluxions are not Increments, but relative Nothings. **1763** EMERSON *Meth. Increm.* Pref. 4 The Inventor of the Method of Increments was the learned Dr. Taylor. **1803** J. WOOD *Princ. Mech.* vii. 134 Equal increments of velocity are always generated in equal times. **1834** MRS. SOMERVILLE *Connect. Phys. Sc.* x. (1849) 80 The sum of all these increments of velocity..would in time become perceptible. **1879** THOMSON & TAIT *Nat. Phil.* I. I. §28 Acceleration of velocity..is said to be uniform when the velocity receives equal increments in equal times.

c. *Forestry.* The increase in the quantity of wood produced by a tree or group of trees during a limited period; the value of this increase. Also *attrib.*, as **increment borer** [tr. G. *zuwachsbohrer* (M. R. Pressler *Zur Forstzuwachskunde* (1868) 19], a kind of auger with a hollow bit, used to measure the

magnitude of this increase in individual trees, by removing a piece of wood in which annual rings can be examined; **increment boring**, the cylinder of wood removed from a tree by an increment borer.

1889 W. SCHLICH *Man. Forestry* I. ii. 167 The increment laid on by an individual tree does not by itself govern the increment produced per acre, because the latter is represented by the increment per tree, multiplied by the number of trees per acre. **1895** *Ibid.* III. i. 13 In the case of standing trees, the measurements are made with Pressler's Increment Borer. **1905** *Terms Forestry & Logging* (U.S. Dept. Agric. Bureau Forestry) 14 *Increment*, the volume or value of wood produced during a given period by the growth of a tree or of a stand. **1938** WEAVER & CLEMENTS *Plant Ecol.* (ed. 2) ii. 34 The increment borer.. removes a small core of wood from circumference to center, without injuring the tree. **1942** *Amer. Jrnl. Bot.* XXIX. 553/2 (*caption*) An increment boring from a butt treated western red cedar pole. **1967** T. E. AVERY *Forest Measurements* xii. 210 In climates where tree growth is characterized by annual rings, ages of standing trees are usually determined by extracting a radial core of wood with an increment borer. **1972** N. D. G. JAMES *Arboriculturalist's Compan.* xiv. 159 In forestry the measurement and calculation of increment can be of considerable economic importance.

5. A quantity obtained from another by increase or addition. Const. *of*. (*rare.*)

1864 BOWEN *Logic* xii. 410 Each term may be an increment of its predecessor by the addition of a constant quantity. **1865** GROTE *Plato* I. i. 11 *note*, All [numbers] above ten were multiples and increments of ten.

6. *attrib.* and *Comb.*

1909 [see BUDGET *v.* c]. **1909–10** *Act 10 Edw. VII* c. 8 §2 (1) The increment value of any land shall be deemed to be the amount (if any) by which the site value of the land, on the occasion on which increment value duty is to be collected.., exceeds the original site value of the land as ascertained in accordance with the general provisions of this Part of this Act as to valuation. **1971** *Jrnl. Gen. Psychol.* Jan. 68 At a 30-msec interval the difference threshold for a *decrease* in pulse interval would be 30 msec, while the difference threshold for an *increase* in pulse interval would be five msec. These two types of difference thresholds will be referred to as decrement and increment thresholds, respectively.

incremental (ɪnkrɪˈmɛntəl), *a.* [f. prec. + -AL^{1}.] Of or relating to an increment or increments (usually in the mathematical sense, 4 b: in quot. 1882, Relating to growth).

1715 *Phil. Trans.* XXIX. 312 The Principles of the New Incremental Method. **1791** WARING *ibid.* LXXXI. 157 The same principles may be applied to the resolution of algebraical, fluxional, incremental, &c. equations. **1882** QUAIN *Anat.* (ed. 9) II. 552 Lines.. seen in sections of the dry tooth, conforming in direction with the lamination just spoken of (*incremental lines*, Salter). **1885** *Bookseller* Sept. 886/2 The exclusion of the rule of subtraction, and the substitution of incremental or complementary addition.

†**incremenˈtation.** *Obs. rare.* [n. of action f. med.L. *incrēmentāre* to give the increase, f. *incrēmentum* INCREMENT: see -ATION.] Production of growth or increase; means of promoting growth.

c **1420** *Pallad. on Husb.* XII. 294 In Marche and September putacioun To chasten is incrementacioun.

†**ˈincrepate**, *v.* *Obs.* [f. L. *increpāt-*, ppl. stem of *increpāre* to make a noise at, scold, chide, f. *in-* (IN-^{2}) + *crepāre* to make a noise, creak, etc.] *trans.* To chide, rebuke, reprove.

1570 LEVINS *Manip.* 40/33 To Increpate, *increpare.* **1657** W. MORICE *Coena quasi Κοινὴ* Def. xvi. 284 He increpates not the Church-governors for admitting such. **1657** REEVE *God's Plea* 18 He is eager upon a cruel bent, but God doth increpate, and interrogate him.

increpation (ɪnkrɪˈpeɪʃən). *Obs.* or *arch.* [ad. L. *increpātiōn-em* (Tertullian), n. of action from *increpāre* to INCREPATE. Cf. OF. *increpacion*, *-ation* (Oresme, 14th c.).] Chiding, reproof, rebuke: with *pl.* a reproof or rebuke.

1502 *Ord. Crysten Men* (W. de W. 1506) IV. xxix. 330 By thretenynges, & by increpacyons. *c* **1540** tr. *Pol. Verg. Eng. Hist.* (Camden) I. 180 Throughe the holsome precepte and increpations of Annas. **1605** G. POWEL *Refut. Epist. by Puritan-Papist* 33 They.. disswaded them, some-times by milde admonitions, and sometimes by seuerer increpations. *a* **1716** SOUTH *Twelve Serm.* (1717) III. 422 The Thunder of that dreadfull Increpation.. 'Friend, how camest thou in hither, not having a Wedding-garment?' **1868** MILMAN *St. Paul's* 82 Edw. III had promulgated a tremendous increpation against the Dean and Chapter.

†**inˈcrepatively**, *adv.* *Obs. rare.* [f. late L. *increpātīvē*, OF. *en-*, *increpativement*, f. L. **increpātīvus*, OF. *increpatif*, *-ive* scolding, reproachful: see -LY^{2}.] Chidingly, reproachfully; with scolding.

1483 CAXTON *Gold. Leg.* 425 b/2 And as saint powle that to the synnars shewed him Increpatyfly.

†**inˈcrepatory**, *a.* *Obs.* [ad. late L. *increpātōri-us* (Sidonius), f. ppl. stem of *increpāre* to INCREPATE: see -ORY.] Rebuking, reproving.

1645 T. COLEMAN *Hopes Deferred* 1 His answer hath two parts; one increpatory.. the other directory.

incres(s, incresce, obs. forms of INCREASE.

increscent (ɪnˈkrɛsənt), *a.* and *sb.* Also 6–7 incressant, -ent. [ad. L. *incrēscent-em*, pres. pple. of *incrēscĕre* to INCREASE: see -ENT. In the form *incressant*, a. AF. *incressant* = OF. *encreissant* pres. pple.]

A. *adj.* Increasing, becoming greater. Chiefly of the moon (esp. in *Heraldry*): Waxing, in her increment.

1658 PHILLIPS, *Incressant*, resembling the Moon not come to the full, a term in Heraldry. **1822** *Blackw. Mag.* XI. 669 The first is on the wane; the third is not increscent. **1854** H. MILLER *Sch. & Schm.* xii. (1857) 260 Every object stood out clear, though cold, in the increscent light of morning. **1872** TENNYSON *Gareth* 518 The good Queen.. sent, Between the increscent and decrescent moon, Arms for her son.

B. *sb.* (Chiefly *Her.*) The moon in her increment, represented as a crescent with the horns towards the dexter side. (Opp. to *decrescent.*)

1572 BOSSEWELL *Armorie* 11 An Incressante is the moone from the pryme, till after the firste quarter. **1661** MORGAN *Sph. Gentry* I. iv. 45 Or, an Incressant vert. **1691** *Lond. Gaz.* No. 2674/4 A Cross Moline between 2 Increscents and 2 Decrescents. **1864** BOUTELL *Her. Hist. & Pop.* xv. §8 (ed. 3) 198 *Or*, on a fesse *arg.*, three increscents of the field.

†**increst** (ɪnˈkrɛst), *v.* *Obs. rare.* Also en-. [f. IN-^{2}, EN-^{1} + CREST *sb.*] *trans.* To furnish or adorn with or as with a crest; to crest (*with*).

1611 FLORIO, *Increstamento*, an encresting. *Ibid.*, *Increstare*, to encrest. *Ibid.*, *Incimierato*, crested or encrested. **1616** DRUMM. OF HAWTH. *Sonn.* I. xiii, Two foaming billows.. did their tops with coral red increst.

incretionary (ɪnˈkriːʃənərɪ), *a.* [f. **incretion* (f. L. *in-* IN-^{2}) + *crēscĕre* to grow) + -ARY: cf. *concretionary*.] (See quot.)

1874 DAWKINS *Cave Hunt.* ii. 57 Their mineral contents .. have been deposited on the sides of the cavity by the same 'incretionary' action. *Ibid.*, I have used the term incretionary as implying an accumulation of mineral matter from the circumference of a cavity towards its centre, as in the case of an agate.

incriminate (ɪnˈkrɪmɪneɪt), *v.* [f. ppl. stem of med.L. *incrīmināre* to accuse, f. *in-* (IN-^{2}) + *crīmināre* to CRIMINATE; perh. partly due to F. *incriminer* (1791 in Hatz.-Darm.).] *trans.* To charge with a crime; to involve in an accusation or charge.

1730–6 BAILEY (folio), To *Incriminate*, to recriminate. **1828** WEBSTER, *Incriminate*, to accuse; to charge with a crime or fault. **1862** WRAXALL *Hugo's 'Misérables'* V. xi, Their theory is incriminated. **1874** SYMONDS *Sk. Italy & Greece* (1898) I. xi. 220 It would be wrong to incriminate the Order of S. Francis by any suspicion. **1885** *Manch. Exam.* 6 June 5/3 Evidence which will incriminate others while it clears themselves.

Hence **inˈcriminated**, **inˈcriminating** *ppl. adjs.*

1858 *Times* 27 Nov. 8/2 Any incriminated phrase of Montalembert's pamphlet. **1863** KINGLAKE *Crimea* I. xiv. 231 This Maupas, or de Maupas.. deliberately offered to arrange that incriminating papers.. should be secretly placed in the houses of the men whom he wanted to have accused. **1875** STUBBS *Const. Hist.* III. xix. 343 If the ordinary claimed the incriminated clerk. **1882** TRAILL *Sterne* iv. 40 An excuse for the incriminated passage.

incrimination (ɪnkrɪmɪˈneɪʃən). *rare.* [n. of action f. med.L *incrīmināre*: see prec. Cf. F. *incrimination* (Littré).] The action of charging with a crime, or involving in a charge; the fact or condition of being so charged or involved.

1651 BIGGS *New Disp.* ¶212 Their incrimination and arraignement may appear by the verdict. **1827–39** DE QUINCEY *Murder* Postscr., One other fact.. became more.. important than many stronger circumstances of incrimination.. that the shoes of the murderer.. creaked as he walked. **1846** MRS. GORE *Eng. Char.* (1852) 84 To incrimination follows recrimination.

inˈcriminator. *rare.* [agent-n. in L. form, from INCRIMINATE.] One who incriminates; an accuser.

1846 LANDOR *Imag. Conv.* Wks. II. 13 Yet our judges.. our incriminators, firmly believe in the transcendent excellence of those works.

incriminatory (ɪnˈkrɪmɪnətərɪ), *a.* [f. as INCRIMINATE + -ORY.] Tending to incriminate.

1861 *Times* 10 July, That an incriminatory report of an Election Commission shall be followed by a suspension of elective rights for five years. **1890** *Ibid.* 15 Dec. 5/3 The quantity of documents and cipher manuscripts seized.. furnished the authorities with much incriminatory evidence.

†**inˈcriminous**, *a.* *Obs. rare*$^{-0}$. [IN-^{3}.] Not criminous; innocent.

1623 COCKERAM II, Faultlesse, *Inculpable, Incriminous.*

inˈcrimsoned, *ppl. a.* *rare.* = ENCRIMSONED.

1831 TRELAWNEY *Adv. Younger Son* I. 328 Kissing his incrimsoned hands and eyes. **1861** DICKENS *Gt. Expect.* xii, Various stages of puffy and incrimsoned countenance.

inˈcrispated, *ppl. a. rare.* [f. L. *incrispāt-us*, pa. pple. of *incrispāre* (Tertull. *Idol.* 8, with variant *incrustare*), f. *in-* IN-^{2}) + *crispāre* to curl, wrinkle: see CRISPATE.] Stiffly curled, wrinkled.

1747 tr. *Astruc's Fevers* 182 They are incrispated, and each fibre tense, like the chord of a musical instrument. **1922** JOYCE *Ulysses* 695 Incrispated black hairs.

incroach, -ment, incroatch, incroch(e, obs. ff. ENCROACH, -MENT.

incronicle, obs. f. ENCHRONICLE.

†**inˈcrook**, *v.* *Obs. rare.* [f. IN-^{1} + CROOK *v.*, after L. *incurvāre*, which it translates.] *trans.* To crook, bend, or incurve.

a **1340** HAMPOLE *Psalter* lxviii. 28 Mirkid be thaire eghen .. & þe bak of þaim ay inkroke. *Ibid.* Cant. 509 Inkrokid are þe hillis of þe warld. **1382** WYCLIF *Rom.* xi. 10 Be the y3en of hem maad derke.. and incroke algatis the bak of hem [*Ps.* lxviii. 8 the rig of hem.. crooke thou in].

†**inˈcrossed**, *ppl. a.* *Obs. rare*$^{-1}$. [f. IN-^{2} (= EN-^{1}) + CROSS *v.*] Crossed over each other.

1605 DANIEL *Queen's Arcadia* II. i, His Arms incross'd, his Head down on one Side.

‖**inˈcrotchet**, *v. rare.* Also en-. [f. IN-^{2}, EN-^{1} + CROTCHET *sb.*] *trans.* To enclose within crotchets or brackets.

1806 SOUTHEY *Lett.* (1856) I. 397 He will.. encrotchet [] thus what Hyems has to copy. *a* **1834** COLERIDGE in *Athenæum* (1893) 2 Sept. 322/3 Truly lyric as are all the lines incrotcheted.

†**inˈcrouching**, *ppl. a.* *Obs. rare*$^{-1}$. [? f. IN-^{1} + CROUCH *v.*] Crouching in, cringing, fawning.

1593 G. FLETCHER *Licia* To Rdr., As a man may sooner feel us to flatter by our incrouching eloquence than suspect it from the ear.

in-crowd: see IN *a.* 2 b.

‖**incroyable** (ɛ̃krwajabl). [F. *incroyable* incredible, f. *in-* (IN-^{3}) + *croi-re*, *croy-ant* to believe (:—L. *crēdĕre*) + *-able* (see -BLE).] A contemporary name for the French fop or dandy of the period of the Directory.

The term seems to have originated in 1795; acc. to Littré, it had reference not only to the extravagant dress of the fops, but also to their frequent use of the phrase '*C'est vraiment incroyable*'.

1797 H. SWINBURNE *Let.* in *Crts. Eur. close last Cent.* (1841) II. 181 The men were clean, many in English dresses, but there were also a good many *extravagants*, or *incroyables*. **1831** CARLYLE *Sart. Res.* I. ix, Wert thou not, at one period of life, a Buck, or Blood, or Macaroni, or Incroyable, or Dandy, or by whatever name.. such phenomenon is distinguished? **1887** *Westm. Rev.* Nov. 947 The republican young man of fashion, the *incroyable.*

†**inˈcruciated**, *a.* *Obs. rare*$^{-1}$. [IN-^{3}; see CRUCIATE *v.*] Not tormented; untortured.

1627–77 FELTHAM *Resolves* II. xxxi. 223 His Ignorance gave him.. a kind of innocence, whereby might have passed away his life incruciated without the sense of so fatal misfortunes.

incruciˈation. *Anat.* [f. IN-^{2} + CRUCIATION.] 'A crossing of fibres; same as *decussation*' (*Syd. Soc. Lex.* 1886).

1855 MAYNE *Expos. Lex.*, *Incruciatio*.., the decussation or crossing of the fibres of the optic nerve: incruciation.

†**ˈincruent**, *a.* *Obs. rare.* [ad. L. *incruent-us*, f. *in-* (IN-^{3}) + *cruentus* bloody, CRUENT. Cf. obs. F. *incruent* (16th c.).] Bloodless; not attended with shedding of blood.

1624 FISHER in F. White *Repl. Fisher* 463 So should.. the Eucharist be a bloudie Sacrifice, and not incruent as the Fathers tearme it. **1660** WATERHOUSE *Arms & Arm.* 209 For incruent Victories are least offensive to God and man.

So †**incruˈental**, †**incruˈentous** *adjs.* (cf. CRUENTOUS).

1674 BREVINT *Saul at Endor* 408 He musters out as many places as he can find, that make any mention of Liturgy, Oblation, Holy Victime, Incruental Sacrifice, and Mass. **1675** BURTHOGGE *Causa Dei* 302 To offer his Devotions on an Incruentous Altar. *a* **1706** EVELYN *Sylva* (1776) 369 Garlands of the leaves and blossoms [of Myrtles] impaled the brows of Incruentous victors at Ovations.

incrust, etc., variants of ENCRUST, etc.

†**inˈcrustament.** *Obs. rare.* [ad. It. *incrostamento* 'a pargeting or rough casting' (Florio), L. type **incrustāmentum*, from *incrustāre* to incrust.] = INCRUSTATION 2.

1538 LELAND *Itin.* V. 7 There were founde a late.. certeyne paintid Incrustamentes hard by the Castel.

incrustate (ɪnˈkrʌstət), *ppl. a.* (*Erron.* -crustrate.) [ad. L. *incrustāt-us*, pa. pple. of *incrustāre*, f. *in-* (IN-^{2}) + *crustāre*, f. *crusta* CRUST.]

†**1.** Formed or hardened into a crust. *Obs.*

1626 BACON *Sylva* §99 The Finer Part will bee turned into Aire, and the Grosser sticke as it were baked, and incrustate vpon the Sides of the Vessell. **1674** GREW *Nat. Mixture* v. Inst. ii. §8 The top of the unresolved Salt will be incrustate, or as it were frosted over. **1731** TULL *Horse-Hoing Husb.* (1733) 64 If Land sown with Wheat be not Ho'd, its Surface is soon Incrustate.

2. Enveloped with a crust or solid superficial layer of matter: cf. CRUSTATE. *Obs.* exc. *Bot.*

1671 *Phil. Trans.* VI. 3017 A cherry-stone round about incrustrate with stony matter. **1866** *Treas. Bot.* 621/1 *Incrustate*,.. coated with earthy matter.

3. *Bot.* (See quot.)

1855 MAYNE *Expos. Lex.*, *Incrustatus*,.. applied to a seed and pericarp when they adhere one to the other with so

much force that they seem to form an entire body: incrustate. **1866** in *Treas. Bot.* 621.

4. *Zool.* and *Bot.* Having the form of a crust, as a polyzoan or a lichen; *spec.* Of or pertaining to the *Incrustata*, a division of cyclostomatous Polyzoa.

incrustate (ɪn'krʌsteɪt), *v.* Now *rare.* Also en-; *erron.* -crustrate. [f. L. *incrustāt-*, ppl. stem of *incrustāre*: see prec.]

1. To cover with a crust or hardened coating, as of deposited or crystallized matter, rust, scum, etc. = ENCRUST 2.

1570 LEVINS *Manip.* 40/34 To Incrustate, *incrustare.* **1620** VENNER *Via Recta* vi. 106 Couered ouer and incrustated.. with sugar, which we..call Candied Ginger. **1682** H. MORE *Annot. Glanvill's Lux O.* 142 To let its Central Fire to incrustate it self into a Terrella. **1713** DERHAM *Phys.-Theol.* 64 *note*, Vast Stones, which..are incrustated with this Sparry, Stalactical Substance. **1794** G. ADAMS *Nat. & Exp. Philos.* II. App. xiv. 127 The copper in precipitating will.. incrustate the nail with pure copper. **1811** PINKERTON *Petral.* I. 519 Encrustrating various objects, as birds' nests, plants, leaves, &c.

†**2.** In the arts: **a.** To cover with an ornamental layer after the manner of a natural incrustation: = ENCRUST 1. **b.** To attach as or like an incrustation.

1727–41 CHAMBERS *Cycl.*, *Incrusted*, or *Incrustated Column*, is a column consisting of several pieces or slips of some precious marble, masticated or cemented around a mould of brick, or other material. **1764** HARMER *Observ.* VIII. iii. 99 The art of incrustating buildings with it [marble]. *Ibid.* XL. vi. 304 The figures are incrustrated like the cyphers on the dial-plates of watches.

Hence **in'crustated, in'crustating** *ppl. adjs.*

1659 H. MORE *Immort. Soul* (1662) 196 They make their peculiar Vortex..from Pole to Pole, and thread an incrustated Star. **1712** *Phil. Trans.* XXVII. 520 The encrustated Particles which stick to the Skin. **1758** J. S. *Le Dran's Observ. Surg.* (1771) 259, I took off a Quantity of incrustated Gravel with the *Currette.* **1884** *Pall Mall G.*, *Extra* 24 July 2/2 Encrustated papers, luminous paint, &c. **1885** J. CROLL *Climate & Cosmol.* xi. 187 Masses of calcareous tufa which have been formed upon the borders of incrustating springs.

incrustation (ɪnkrʌ'steɪʃən). Also en-. [ad. late L. *incrustātiōn-em*, n. of action from *incrustāre* to INCRUSTATE; cf. F. *incrustation* (16th c.).]

1. The action of encrusting; the formation of a crust, the fact or condition of being encrusted.

1656 BLOUNT *Glossogr.*, *Incrustation*, a pargetting, rough-casting. **1658** PHILLIPS, *Incrustation*, a making or becomeing hard on the outside, like a crust, a rough-casting, or pargetting. **1764** HARMER *Observ.* VIII. iii. 97 The incrustation of their walls with the most exquisite marbles. **1769** CROKER *Dict.*, *Incrustation*, in Surgery, the induction of a crust or Eschar upon any part. **1846** DANA *Zooph.* (1848) 500 The branches formed by incrustation are sometimes six inches long. **1853** RUSKIN *Stones Ven.* II. iv. §24 The incrustation of brick with more precious materials. **1874** SYMONDS *Sk. Italy & Greece* 251 Had the whole church been finished as it was designed, it would have presented one splendid though bizarre effect of incrustation. **1923** *Daily Mail* 24 Jan. 6 The heavy encrustation of swollen buds on every twig.

2. An outer hard layer or crust of some fine or costly material placed over a rough or common substance, *esp.* a facing of marble or other precious stone on a building.

1644 EVELYN *Diary* 7 Mar., A Chapell..all of jasper, with several incrustations of marble in the inside. *Ibid.* 17 Nov., The walls..are cover'd with antiq incrustations of history. **1726** LEONI tr. *Alberti's Archit.* I. 33/2 Alabaster..cut with a Saw into large thin pieces, extremely convenient for Incrustations. **1838** G. DOWNES *Lett. Cont. Countries* I. 338 An incrustation, consisting of small segments of white and black marble, gives these edifices a motley appearance. **1880** C. E. NORTON *Church-build. Mid. Ages* ii. 54 The whole surface..was to be covered with precious incrustations of mosaic or of marble.

†**b.** *fig.* An adventitious ornament. *Obs.*

1607 *Schol. Disc. agst. Antichr.* I. ii. 66 The old popishe ceremonies..are, as it were, an Incrustation both vnlawful and vnseemly. **1644** J. GOODWIN *Innoc. Triumph.* To Rdr. (1645) 3 What incrustations, and misrepresentations of opinions, sayings, practises, actions. **1740** WARBURTON *Div. Legat.* IV. iv. Wks. 1811 IV. 181 Every age adorned it with additional superstitions; so that at length the old foundation became quite lost in these new incrustations.

3. A crust or hard coating formed naturally on the surface of an object; *esp.* a calcareous or crystalline concretion or deposit.

1671 J. WEBSTER *Metallogr.* xxxix. 359 We shall find an Incrustation upon the out-side of the moss and leaves. **1751** JOHNSON *Rambler* No. 166 ⁋3 Like unpolished gems, of which none but the artist knows the intrinsick value, till their..incrustations are rubbed away. **1830** SIR T. D. LAUDER *Floods Moray in 1829* (ed. 2) 234 Stalactitic incrustations, formed by the evaporation of water, holding calcareous matter in solution. **1878** HUXLEY *Physiogr.* 202 This siliceous matter is deposited around the mouth of the hole as an incrustation.

b. *fig.* An accretion of habit, etc. compared to a hard crust formed over and around an object.

1806 FELLOWES tr. *Milton's 2nd Defence* 230 There are.. many evil incrustations about your heart. **1833** L. RITCHIE *Wand. by Loire* 215 Her really warm heart..was frozen over by a thin incrustation of vanity. *a* **1864** J. D. BURNS *Mem. & Rem.* (1879) 364 The pure simplicities of His Word..get overlaid with earthly incrustations. **1869** J. MARTINEAU *Ess.* II. 397 Hidden under the incrustations of sense and evil habit. **1920** H. G. WELLS *Outl. Hist.* 271/2 There was no effective prohibition of superstitious practices..and supplementary worships. At an early stage [of Buddhism] a process of encrustation began. **1957** V. W. TURNER *Schism & Continuity in Afr. Soc.* vi. 197 Each core..in a village may have a number of classificatory encrustations.

4. A hard dry formation on the surface of the body; a scab of eschar (cf. CRUST *sb.* 3).

1656 BLOUNT *Glossogr.*, *Incrustation*,..a crustiness, or thick scabbedness. **1800** *Med. Jrnl.* IV. 2 A slight incrustation was formed on the vesicle. **1875** H. WALTON *Dis. Eye* 729 The incrustations which adhere to the cuticle. **1897** *Allbutt's Syst. Med.* II. 195 Such is the course of the ordinary small-pox papule through the several stages of macule, papule, vesicle, pustule, and incrustation.

†**in'crustative.** *Obs. rare*$^{-1}$. [f. INCRUSTATE *v.* + -IVE.] A substance that tends to form incrustations.

1765 *Universal Mag.* XXXVII. 355/2 Incrustatives and exsiccatives, as myrrh, aloes.

incrusted, incrusting: see ENCRUSTED, ENCRUSTING.

†**in'crystal,** *v. Obs.* Also en-. [f. IN-[2] + CRYSTAL *sb.*]

1. *trans.* (and *intr.*) To turn into crystal, to CRYSTALLIZE.

1611 FLORIO, *Inchristallire*, to encristall, or become cristall.

2. To enclose in crystal.

1648 HERRICK *Hesper.*, *Hour-glass*, That Houre-glasse.. With water fill'd..The humour was..But lovers tears inchristalled. **1664** POWER *Exp. Philos.* I. 35, I have artificially frozen all the said Liquor into a mass of Ice, wherein all these Animals it seemed lay incrystalled.

Hence **in'crystalled** *ppl. a.*, crystallized.

a **1649** DRUMM. OF HAWTH. *Poems* Wks. (1711) 29 The next enchristall'd light Submits to Him its beams; And He doth trace the height Of that fair lamp.

in'crystaˌllizable, *a. rare*$^{-1}$. [IN-[3].] Incapable of being crystallized; uncrystallizable.

1807 T. THOMSON *Chem.* (ed. 3) II. 578 This salt is tasteless, incrystallizable by art, insoluble in water.

incuba, *nonce-wd.*, factitious fem. of INCUBUS.

1708 *Brit. Apollo* No. 45. 1/2 There being in nature no other Incubusses or Incuba's.

incubate ('ɪnkju:beɪt), *v.* [f. L. *incubāt-* (more commonly *incubit-*: see INCUBITURE), ppl. stem of *incubā-re* to lie on, to hatch, f. *in-* (IN-[2]) + *cubā-re* to lie: see -ATE[3].]

1. a. *trans.* To sit upon (eggs) in order to hatch them; to hatch (eggs) by sitting upon them or by some equivalent process.

1721 BAILEY, To *incubate*, to brood or hover over, to lie or set upon as a Hen. **1730–6** *Ibid.* (folio), *Incubated*, brooded or hovered over, as by a Bird on her Eggs or Nest. **1782** A. MONRO *Compar. Anat.* (ed. 3) 61 They are incubated by the heat of the Sun. **1788** JENNER in *Phil. Trans.* LXXVIII. 229 Respecting the Cuckoo: why..it should not build a nest, incubate its eggs? **1849–52** TODD *Cycl. Anat.* IV. 974/1 The egg..had been incubated six days. **1855** OWEN *Comp. Anat. Vertebr.* viii. (L.), Still fewer [fishes] nidificate and incubate their ova.

b. *fig.* To brood upon.

1641 J. JACKSON *True Evang. T.* III. 179 Gods Spirit.. must incubate, and brood both, to make them fruitfull.

2. a. *intr.* To sit upon eggs, to brood.

1755 JOHNSON, To *Incubate*, v.n., to sit upon eggs. **1788** JENNER in *Phil. Trans.* LXXVIII. 230 Many of the birds which incubate have stomachs analogous to those of Cuckoos. **1874** E. COUES *Birds N.W.* 41 The one that is incubating flutters up with loud cries of distress.

b. *fig.* To brood.

1660 tr. *Amyraldus' Treat. conc. Relig.* III. viii. 476 The Spirit of God gently incubated on the World. *a* **1847** MACVEY NAPIER in *Sel. Corr.* (1879) 508, I wrote this while incubating on my Bills in Edinburgh.

3. a. *intr. Path.* Of a disease: To pass through the process of INCUBATION, q.v. 3. **b.** *trans. Biol.* To place in an incubator (for developing bacteria); to maintain at a constant degree of warmth that will favour growth or continued survival (e.g. of micro-organisms); more widely, to maintain under given conditions in a controlled or artificial environment.

1896 *Allbutt's Syst. Med.* I. 805 The tubes are capped, shaken and incubated for twenty-four hours. **1912** *Jrnl. Exper. Med.* XVI. 171 One volume of a 5 per cent. suspension of erythrocytes in isotonic salt solution was mixed with two volumes of serum in capillary pipettes. The pipettes were incubated at 38°C for two hours and then put in an ice box for twenty-four hours. **1938** [see INCUBATION 5]. **1947** *Growth* XI. 232 The ability to ferment galactose occurs exclusively in cells that have been grown on galactose, or have been incubated in a galactose solution for a few hours. **1948** *Biochem. Jrnl.* XLIII. 538/2 The requisite amount of homogenate..is then added and incubated at 37° for 1 hr. **1962** HARRIS & GRUBER in A. Pirie *Lens Metabolism Rel. Cataract* 373 The second method of study has been that of incubating the lens under various conditions at 37°C for a period of time prior to analysis. **1969** *Clin. Sci.* XXXVII. 99 The diffusion of glucose and potassium between erythrocytes and their medium was impaired when the red cells were packed by centrifugation and incubated for 48 hr without agitation. *Ibid.* 409 Rat liver slices were incubated in serum obtained from normal volunteers and from uraemic patients. **1970** *Sci. Jrnl.* May 19/3 The inoculated samples were incubated for up to 27 days at various temperatures—0°, 5°, 10° and 20°C. **1970** *Biol. Abstr.* LI. 11404/2 By incubating the seeds for 8 days at 15 C and then for 3 days at 25 C in a non-sterilized soil coming from a rice field..seed resistance to rotting may be estimated. **1971** *Nature* 19 Nov. 154/1 Because uterine secretions are slightly alkaline, a copper strip was incubated for 18 h in *p*H 8 carbonate buffer.

Hence **'incubated** *ppl. a.*, **'incubating** *vbl. sb.* and *ppl. a.*

1730–6 [see sense 1]. **1835–6** TODD *Cycl. Anat.* I. 673/1 The vascular area of the incubated egg. **1878** *Masque Poets* 216 By its own law..The incubated egg unfolded. **1890** *Daily News* 21 Nov. 3/2 Dr. Koch's lymph..is prepared in an incubating stove within a space which is hermetically sealed and sterilized.

incubate ('ɪnkju:beɪt), *sb.* [f. the vb. + -ATE[3], after *filtrate*, *precipitate*, etc.] A preparation, or material, that has been incubated.

1959 *Jrnl. Amer. Chem. Soc.* LXXXI. 4109/2 Aldosterone was the most abundant steroid found in incubates of adrenals from the American bullfrog, *Rana catesbeiana.* **1972** *Nature* 22 Dec. 470/2 Biosynthesized ^{14}C-labelled 11 KT was detectable in the control but not in the Cd-damaged tissue incubate. **1973** *Biochem. Jrnl.* CXXXI. 406/2 The incubates were extracted with equal volumes of ethyl acetate.

incubation (ɪnkju:'beɪʃən). [ad. L. *incubātiōn-em* brooding, n. of action f. *incubāre* to brood.]

1. The action of sitting on eggs in order to hatch them; the hatching of eggs by sitting on them. More widely, the protection of its eggs by an animal, or the provision of conditions that favour their development. Also, the embryonic development of an animal within an egg.

artificial incubation, hatching of eggs by artificial heat.

1646 SIR T. BROWNE *Pseud. Ep.* III. vii. 120 Incubation alters not the species..as evidently appeares in the eggs of Ducks or Partridges hatched under a Hen. *a* **1711** KEN *Hymnotheo* Poet. Wks. 1721 III. 304 Her Incubations by Degrees dispence Parts, Form, Life, Motion, Nutriment and Sense, Till they full grown, their Prisons open fling. **1835–6** R. B. TODD *Cycl. Anat. & Physiol.* I. 785/2 When the process of incubation begins [in the crayfish] the surface of the yolk is first seen to become covered with star-like or serrated spots. **1845** DARWIN *Voy. Nat.* v. (1879) 91 Each cock bird will have its fair share in the labour of incubation. **1870** ROLLESTON *Anim. Life* Introd. 50 Observed in..the incubation of the Python. **1891** W. N. LANE *Poultry Farming* 4 Artificial incubation is a cheaper method of hatching than the natural one. **1905** J. WYMAN in D. S. Jordan *Guide to Study of Fishes* I. xi. 170 Among the Siluroid fishes of Guiana there are several species, which, at certain seasons of the year, have their mouths and bronchial cavities filled either with eggs or young, and, as is believed, for the purpose of incubation. **1931** J. R. NORMAN *Hist. Fishes* xvi. 320 The period of incubation [of ray eggs] lasts from four and a half to nearly fifteen months. **1960** T. H. WATERMAN *Physiol. Crustacea* I. xiii. 440 As in female vertebrates, the ovary of the crustaceans..secretes a hormone which prepares the mother for incubation. **1962** K. F. LAGLER et al. *Ichthyol.* x. 299 To carry egg protection to its highest degree, some fishes have evolved various types of internal incubation or gestation. *Ibid.*, In a Brazilian catfish..the male parent develops an enlarged lower lip to form a pouch in which labial incubation of the eggs takes place.

2. *transf.* and *fig.* Applied esp. to the 'brooding' or 'moving' of the Divine Spirit over the face of the chaos at the Creation (Gen. i. 2).

1614 RALEIGH *Hist. World* I. (1634) 5 Whether that motion..and operation, were by incubation, or how else, the manner is onely knowne to God. **1677** HALE *Prim. Orig. Man.* III. i. 247 Some assign a natural determined Cause of the first production of Mankind, namely, the due preparation of the fat and slimy Earth after a long incubation of Waters. *a* **1679** GURNALL in Spurgeon *Treas. Dav.* Ps. cxix. 130 He who, by his incubation upon the waters of the creation, hatched that rude mass into the beautiful form we now see. **1731** TULL *Horse-Hoing Husb.* (1733) 25 Many of the Pores or Interstices close up during the Seed's Incubation and hatching in the Ground. **1796** BURKE *Regic. Peace* ii. Wks. VIII. 258 The Dutch Republicks were hatched and cherished under the same incubation. **1856** EMERSON *Eng. Traits* xiv. (1857) 235 The mind became fruitful as by the incubation of the Holy Ghost. **1878** SEELEY *Stein* III. 437 The Middle Ages..were the age..if not actually of the greatest painting and poetry, yet of the incubation of both.

3. *Path.* The process or phase through which the germs of disease pass between contagion or inoculation and the development of the first symptoms.

period of incubation, the space of time occupied by this process, which varies greatly for different diseases, and in different circumstances.

1835 G. GREGORY *Theo. & Pract. Med.* I. vi. (ed. 4) 81 *Period of incubation*..The interval which elapses between exposure to malaria and the invasion of disease is liable to some variety. *Ibid.* II. v. 149 Sometimes a degree of catarrhal affection is present throughout the whole term of incubation. **1876** tr. *Wagner's Gen. Pathol.* 137 The period of incubation of cholera lasts at least one week. **1885** *Daily News* 30 Oct. 3/3 The period of incubation, i.e., the time from the infliction of the bite till the disease shows itself, is stated..to vary from 12 days..to one year and upwards, the average being from 44 to 75 days.

4. *Gr. Antiq.* The practice of sleeping in a temple or sacred place for oracular purposes.

1871 TYLOR *Prim. Cult.* II. 111 This place was celebrated for the worship of Æsculapius, in whose temple incubation, *i.e.* sleeping for oracular dreams, was practised. **1884** *Encycl. Brit.* XVII. 808.

5. The process, or an instance, of incubating anything, in a controlled or artificial environment (see INCUBATE *v.* 3 b).

1928 *Jrnl. Amer. Med. Assoc.* 3 Nov. 1338/1 The maturity-provoking hormone is definitely somewhat more stable to incubation in the presence of acid. **1938** *Biochem. Jrnl.* XXXII. 450 Batches of 100 flasks of Czapek-Dox solution..were sown with..*Helminthosporium leersii*..and incubated in the dark at 24°. The rate of growth was slow and incubation was continued for 90 days... The mycelium was separated by filtration. **1969** *Clin. Sci.* XXXVII. 409 Incubation of slices in uraemic serum had no effect upon glycogenolysis or on glycogen synthesis, but utilisation of glucose was inhibited. *Ibid.* 410 Slices from the same animal served for incubations both with uraemic and with control sera. **1971** *Nature* 19 Nov. 154/1 An 18 h incubation of a copper strip in 2·5 ml. of saline solution alone yielded a Cu^{2+} concentration of 4 × 10^{-5} M.

6. *attrib.* and *Comb.* ***incubation drive, -fever, -period, -process***; **incubation-patch**, an area of the ventral surface of a bird's body that swells and loses its feathers during the incubation of eggs, as a way of providing them with the necessary warmth; usu. called a ***brood-patch***.

1953 N. TINBERGEN *Herring Gull's World* xvii. 155 It is likely that his birds, by being robbed so often, had on the average a lower incubation-drive than our birds. **1954** D. A. BANNERMAN *Birds Brit. Isles* III. 133 Colonel Meiklejohn suggests that this cock may have been suffering from incubation fever and built the nest to satisfy its craving. **1952** J. FISHER *Fulmar* iv. 95 Fulmars have only a single incubation-patch, into which two eggs could probably not fit. **1879** *St. George's Hosp. Rep.* IX. 712 In this case..the incubation period was two days. **1896** *Allbutt's Syst. Med.* I. 539 A specific bacillus which, introduced by feeding into mice, produces..illness and death after a definite incubation period. **1926** H. M. KYLE *Biol. Fishes* 392/1 (*index*) Incubation period. **1940** *Jrnl. Biol. Chem.* CXXXIV. 250 In a prolonged incubation period there was observed nearly complete hydrolysis. **1943** *Biol. Abstr.* XVII. 2253/2 Av. incubation period was 380 hrs. at about 15·5°C [for the tide-pool cottid]. **1961** E. CAMERON *Cockroach* ii. 24 The incubation period [of *Periplaneta americana*] is a fairly long one, and varies a good deal according to the temperature, and the relative humidity of the environment. **1969** A. BELLAIRS *Life of Reptiles* II. x. 444 The incubation period of eggs, from the time of fertilisation to that of hatching, is exceedingly variable. **1973** *Nature* 30 Mar. 329/2 Following a 24 h incubation period, the medium and cells which had not stuck to the well surface were decanted. **1858–65** CARLYLE *Fredk. Gt.* XII. xi. IV. 262 The incubation-process may have uses for some of us!

Hence **incu'bational** *a.*, of or connected with incubation.

1849–52 TODD *Cycl. Anat.* IV. 1209/1 The cloaca..serves as a kind of incubational..pouch.

incubative (ˈɪnkjuːbeɪtɪv), *a.* [f. L. *incubāt-*, ppl. stem (see INCUBATE) + -IVE.]

1. Of, pertaining to, or characteristic of the incubation of oviparous animals.

1859 HELPS *Friends in C.* Ser. II. II. xi. 285 A beautiful thing is the incubative, the pre-maternal instinct.

2. *Path.* Of or pertaining to the incubation of disease; characterized by incubation.

1835 G. GREGORY *Theo. & Pract. Med.* II. v. (ed. 4) 149 The circumstance of the initiatory catarrhal fever, being viewed, or not, as constituting part of the incubative stage. **1851–9** BRYSON in *Man. Sci. Enq.* 248 Its incubative period —the time which the infectious germs when separated from their source will retain their productiveness. **1869** E. A. PARKES *Pract. Hygiene* (ed. 3) 477 The incubative period [of yellow fever] is longer than usually supposed.

incubator (ˈɪnkjuːbeɪtə(r)). [a. L. *incubātor*, agent-n. f. *incubāre* to lie in or on.]

1. a. A bird which incubates or sits on eggs; a sitting bird. Also, any of certain other animals having particular patterns of behaviour to keep their eggs at a higher temperature than the surrounding environment. **b.** *fig.* One who sits brooding.

1858 DE QUINCEY *Language* Wks. IX. 81 The Hebrew.. sitting..as incubator over the awful germs of the spiritualities that connect man with the unseen worlds. **1969** A. BELLAIRS *Life of Reptiles* II. ix. 430 Of the six or more species which have acquired the brooding habit, only the Indian python is now known on good evidence to be a true incubator.

2. a. An apparatus for hatching birds by artificial heat.

1857 *Cottage Gardener* 4 Aug. 274/2 An incubator is an unprofitable machine..It is a good hatcher..but the chickens cannot be reared. **1879** JEFFERIES *Wild Life in S.C.* 188 The heat of the manure-heap acts as an incubator [to snakes' eggs]. **1884** *Health Exhib. Catal.* 119/1 A Series of Thermostatic Incubators..for the artificial hatching of eggs.

b. An apparatus for rearing children born prematurely.

1896 *Westm. Gaz.* 1 June 4/1 One of the incubators, or foster mothers, by means of which the lives of..little ones prematurely born into the world have been saved.

3. An apparatus for the artficial development of bacteria.

1896 *Allbutt's Syst. Med.* I. 805 These [test-tubes] are capped and kept at 37° in the incubators for twenty-four hours.

4. *fig.* and *transf.* A breeder, author, source.

1864 *Daily Tel.* 6 Sept., His mind is only an incubator for hatching lewdness. **1897** L. A. THURSTON *Handbk. Annex. Hawaii* 35 An incubator of international friction.

5. *Comb.* **incubator-bird** *Austral.* = MEGAPODE, MEGAPOD.

[**1896** F. G. AFLALO *Sk. Nat. Hist. Austral.* 152 These most interesting birds do not incubate their eggs... for instead..we find them deposited in a perfectly planned, thoroughly heated incubator.] **1943** C. BARRETT *Austral. Animal Bk.* xvii. 148 There are numerous species of Megapodes... All are 'incubator-birds', burying their large eggs in huge nest-mounds, to be incubated by the heat generated by decaying vegetation, or by solar heat. **1963** *Times* 12 Mar. (Austral. Suppl.) p. x/7 There are several kinds of megapode or incubator-birds in Australia, of which the best-known is the lowan or mallee-hen.

incubatory (ˈɪnkjuːbeɪtərɪ), *a.* [f. L. *incubāt-* (see INCUBATE) + -ORY.] Of or pertaining to incubation; incubative.

1877 HUXLEY *Anat. Inv. Anim.* x. 622 For distinction's sake the incubatory pouch may be termed the ovicyst. **1879** —— *Hume* v. 110 The incubatory instinct of a bird.

†**in'cube**, *v. Obs. nonce-wd.* [f. IN-² + CUBE *sb.*¹] *trans.* To infix like a cube.

1641 MILTON *Ch. Govt.* I. vi, Prelaty..must be faine to inglobe or incube her selfe among the Presbyters.

†**'incubee.** *Obs.* A distortion of INCUBUS; used as a term of reprobation. (Cf. INCUBY.)

1614 B. JONSON *Barth. Fair* II. ii, Where's my pipe now? not fill'd? thou errant Incubee. [Said to a servant.]

†**in'cubiture.** *Obs.* [f. L. *incubit-* (ppl. stem of *incubāre* to INCUBATE) + -URE, as if from L. type **incubitūra*.] Brooding; = INCUBATION 1.

1653 H. MORE *Antid. Ath.* II. xi. (1712) 72 Aldrovandus rejects that Fable of..her [the Bird of Paradise's] Incubiture on the back of the Male. **1706** PHILLIPS, *Incubation* or *Incubiture*, a Philosophical Term for brooding or sitting upon Eggs as Birds do. **1743** J. ELLIS *Divine Things* 153 (T.) The incubiture of the female upon the back of the male.

†**'incubo.** *Obs. rare.* [a. L. *incubo* a spirit that lies on a treasure to guard it, f. *incubā-re* to brood over.] A covetous man, who broods over or jealously guards his wealth.

1607 WALKINGTON *Opt. Glass* 45 The covetous *Incuboes* of the world. *a* **1625** BOYS *Wks.* (1630) 129 Like a brood goose, or a hen that sits; Incubo (for so the Latines terme him) hee keepes his nest and sits as it were brooding.

incubous (ˈɪnkjuːbəs), *a. Bot.* [f. L. *incubā-re* to lie on + -OUS.] (See quots.).

1857 BERKELEY *Cryptog. Botany* §489. 444 The leaves [of some Liverworts] are disposed after two different plans, according to which they have received the name succubous or incubous. In the former case they are disposed in a spiral which turns from left to right, and consequently the anterior border of each inferior leaf is covered by the posterior border of that immediately above. In the latter, the spiral turns from right to left, and the anterior border of each inferior leaf covers the posterior border of the leaf placed immediately above it. **1880** GRAY *Struct. Bot.* (ed. 6) 416/2 *Incubous*, the tip of one leaf or other part lying flat over the base of the next above it.

‖**incubus** (ˈɪnkjuːbəs). Also 6 *Sc.* **incobus.** Pl. **incubi** (-baɪ); also 7–9 **incubuses**, 8 **incubus's**, **incubusses**, (9 **incubus**). [late L. *incubus* (Augustine) = cl. L. *incubo* nightmare; in the middle ages often represented as a malignant demon who lay upon men and women; f. L. *incubāre* to lie upon. Cf. F. *incube* (14th c. in Hatz.-Darm.).]

1. A feigned evil spirit or demon (originating in personified representations of the nightmare) supposed to descend upon persons in their sleep, and especially to seek carnal intercourse with women. In the Middle Ages, their existence was recognized by the ecclesiastical and civil law.

c **1205** LAY. 15783 Heo beoð ihaten ful iwis incubii demones..monine mon on sweuene ofte heo swencheð. *c* **1330** R. BRUNNE *Chron. Wace* (Rolls) 8088 Þise spyrites do women schame; Incuby demones ys cald þer name, ffendes in bedde..þat many woman han forlayn. *c* **1386** CHAUCER *Wife's T.* 24 Wommen may go saufly vp and doun..Ther is noon oother Incubus but he And he ne wol doon hem but dishonour. **1387** TREVISA *Higden* (Rolls) I. 419 That fend þat gooþ a nyȝt, Wommen wel ofte to begile, Incubus hatte be ryȝt. **1535** STEWART *Cron. Scot.* II. 221 Marling also wes in tha samin dais Into Britane..Ane incobus with subtill sorcerie. **1584** R. SCOT *Discov. Witchcr.* II. ix. (1886) 26 They [witches] use venerie with a divell called Incubus. **1624** MASSINGER *Parl. Love* II. ii, I'll sooner clasp an incubus, or hug A fork-tongued adder. **1671** MILTON *P.R.* II. 152 Belial, the dissolutest spirit that fell, The sensualest, and, after Asmodai, The fleshliest incubus. **1801** W. TAYLOR in *Monthly Mag.* XII. 421 Angels, Incubusses, Saints jostle in his song. **1865** TYLOR *Early Hist. Man.* i. 7 The evil demons who trouble people in their sleep, the Incubi and Succubi.

attrib. *a* **1652** J. SMITH *Sel. Disc.* x. 501 He that allows himself in any sin..does..entertain an incubus dæmon. **1674** *Govt. Tongue* v. §2. 120 A sort of incubus brats, the infamous progenies of the lying spirit.

2. A feeling of oppression during sleep, as of some heavy weight on the chest and stomach; the nightmare.

1561 HOLLYBUSH *Hom. Apoth.* 10 a, The disease called Incubus that is the Mare whych is a sycknesse or fantasye oppressinge a man in his slepe. **1602** MARSTON *Antonio's Rev.* IV. iv, Then death, like to a stifling incubus, Lie on my bosome. **1621** BURTON *Anat. Mel.* I. ii. III. ii, Such as are troubled with Incubus, or witch ridden, as we call it, if they lie on their backs. **1753** J. BOND (*title*) Essay on the Incubus or Night-mare. *a* **1834** LAMB *Hypochond.* 30 Night-riding Incubi Troubling the fantasy. *a* **1862** BUCKLE *Civiliz.* (1869) III. v. 472 The dire superstition which sits like an incubus upon them.

3. A person or thing that weighs upon and oppresses like a nightmare.

1648–9 C. WALKER *Relat. & Observ.* 17 Looke to it therefore, ye state Incubi. **1653** MILTON *Hirelings* Wks. (1851) 369 The many years preaching of such an Incumbent, I may say, such an Incubus oft-times. **1653** GAUDEN *Hierasp.* To Rdr. 5 Worldly designes..are..the Incubusses of Conscience. **1829** I. TAYLOR *Enthus.* x. 262 The church of England..fainting under the incubus of false doctrine, and a secular spirit. **1865** LIVINGSTONE *Zambesi* Pref. 10 The great fact that the Americans have rid themselves of the incubus of slavery. **1875** MᶜLAREN *Serm.* Ser. II. vi. 123 Free from the incubus of evil habits.

4. *Entom.* Name of a parasitic genus of hymenopterous insects.

†**'incuby.** *Sc. Obs.* A perversion of *incubus*, or its plural *incubi*; = INCUBUS.

1508 DUNBAR *Poems* vi. 3, I, Maister Andro Kennedy.. Gottin with sum incuby, Or with sum freir infatuatus.

incudal (ˈɪnkjuːdəl, ɪnˈkjuːdəl), *a.* [f. L. *incus, incudem* anvil + -AL.] Of or pertaining to the incus.

1890 in BILLINGS *Med. Dict.*

incudate (ˈɪnkjuːdeɪt, ɪnˈkjuːdət), *a.* [f. as prec. + -ATE².] In rotifers, designating a type of mastax in which the mallei are reduced or absent and the rami enlarged and curved.

1886 HUDSON & GOSSE *Rotifera* I. iii. 29 The typical trophi may, then, be named as follows..Incudate. Mallei evanescent; rami highly developed into a curved forceps. **1896** M. HARTOG in *Cambr. Nat. Hist.* II. viii. 211 In Asplanchnidæ the rami are large and hooked, constituting the 'incudate' mastax. **1967** P. A. MEGLITSCH *Invertebr. Zool.* viii. 263 (*caption*) Lateral and dorsal views of incudate trophi.

incudo- (ɪnˈkjuːdəʊ), before a vowel **incud-**, combining form of INCUS 1, in terms denoting the association of the incus with another part, as ***incudo-malleal, incudo-stapedial, incudo-tympanic*** adjs.

1884 P. MCBRIDE *Guide to Study of Ear Dis.* Plate I (*heading*) Long process of the Incus, incudo-stapedial joint and posterior ramus of the stapes. **1894** GOULD *Dict. Med.* 608/1 Incudo-... In composition, signifying relationship to the incus. I.-malleal... I.-orbicular... I.-stapedial... I.-tympanic. **1908** *Practitioner* Jan. 123 The lax membrane resting upon the inner tympanic wall and incudo-stapedial articulation. **1943** FISCHER & WOLFSON *Inner Ear* v. 191 The capsule of the incudo-malleolar joint is divided [in the operation described]. **1967** *Coll. Papers Surg. Mayo Clinic* LVIII. 373 The most common ossicular injury sustained during stapedectomy is dislocation of the incudomalleal joint.

in cuerpo: see CUERPO.

†**in'culcate**, *ppl. a. Obs.* [ad. L. *inculcātus*, pa. pple. of *inculcāre*: see next.] Inculcated, taught. (Const. as *pa. pple.* or *adj.*)

1608 WILLET *Hexapla Exod.* 308 Wee had neede to haue the word of God often inculcate and beaten vpon vs. **1643** SIR J. SPELMAN *Case of Affairs* 22 The duty which..hath both by Law and Christian Religion been inculcate to him. **1647** H. MORE *Poems* 154 Phansie? that's so swayd..By botched inculcate paradigms made By senses dictate. **1653** —— *Conject. Cabbal.* (1662) 175 Long inculcate Precepts.. mistaken for connate Principles.

inculcate (ˈɪnkəlkeɪt, ɪnˈkʌlkeɪt), *v.* [f. L. *inculcāt-*, ppl. stem of *inculcāre* to stamp in with the heel, tread in, cram in, press in, impress upon (the mind), f. *in-* (IN-²) + *calcāre* to tread, f. *calc-, calx* heel. As to the pronunciation, see CONTEMPLATE.]

1. *trans.* To endeavour to force (a thing) into or impress (it) on the mind of another by emphatic admonition, or by persistent repetition; to urge on the mind, esp. as a principle, an opinion, or a matter of belief; to teach forcibly. Const. *upon, on*; †formerly *in, into, unto, to.*

1550 COVERDALE *Spir. Perle* xxviii. O iv, This practyse dyd the holy elect of god in the olde time not onli inculcate and teach with words, but also expresse and performe in dede. **1559** BP. SCOT *Sp.* in Strype *Ann. Ref.* (1824) I. II. App. vii. 418 The aucthoritie of the bisshoppe of Rome.. some inculcate against us, as a matter of great weight. **1594** HOOKER *Eccl. Pol.* III. xi. §11 That commandement which Christ did so often inculcate vnto Peter. **1633** T. STAFFORD *Pac. Hib.* II. iii. (1810) 251 Yet was not hee ashamed..to inculcate into the eares of the Pope..that shee was more tyranicall than Pharaoh. **1678** R. BARCLAY *Apol. Quakers* VII. viii. 225 He presses this exhortation upon them, and inculcates it three times. **1700** PRIOR *Carmen Sec.* 165 And still the Sire inculcate to his Son, Transmissive Lessons of the King's Renown. **1736** BUTLER *Anal.* II. i. 142 A standing Admonition, to remind them of it, and inculcate it upon them. **1741** MIDDLETON *Cicero* xii. II. 518 This is the notion that he inculcates everywhere of true glory. **1768–74** TUCKER *Lt. Nat.* (1834) I. 210 The moralist will begin with striving to inculcate this desire of happiness into himself and others as deeply as possible. **1792** *Anecd. W. Pitt* II. xxxv. 263 These three words..deserve to be inculcated in our minds. **1792** BURKE *Corr.* (1844) IV. 3 You cannot too often inculcate to your chief friends, that this affair..cannot possibly be the work of a single day. **1802** MAR. EDGEWORTH *Moral T.* (1816) I. xi. 89 An opinion..difficult to inculcate upon the minds of others. **1809** *Susan* I. 155 The conception ..had inculcated itself..into her mind. **1866** FELTON *Anc. & Mod. Gr.* II. I. iii. 47 All these teachers inculcate..the

duties of order, obedience and fidelity, on the slaves. **1874** Green *Short Hist.* viii. §2 These..inculcated passive obedience to the monarch as a religious obligation.

†**2.** To tread upon, trample, press with the feet.

1597 A. M. tr. *Guillemeau's Fr. Chirurg.* *iij, The earth which with our feete we inculcate and treade one. **1657** Tomlinson *Renou's Disp.* III. II. v. 127 A certain Cloth..is often dipped and inculcated [L. *inculcatur*] in a fit Emplaister already made up.

†**inculcatedly**, *adv. Obs. rare*$^{-1}$. [f. *inculcated* pa. pple. of prec. + -LY^{2}.] By inculcation; by impressive repetition.

1681 H. More *Exp. Dan.* ii. 47 The Son of man is a Title which Christ so inculcatedly assumes to himself.

inculcating (see the vb.), *vbl. sb.* [f. INCULCATE *v.* + -ING^{1}.] The action of inculcation; impressive repetition.

1593 Nashe *Christ's T.* (1613) 50 With dismall crying, and vociferatiue inculcating vnto her. *a* **1614** Donne *Βιαθανατος* (1644) 35 The often iteration, and specious but sophisticate inculcatings of Law, and Nature, and Reason, and God. *c* **1645** Howell *Lett.* II. lxix, To use so many iterations, inculcatings, and tautologies..is no good manners in moral Philosophy.

inculcation (ɪnkʌl'keɪʃən). [ad. late L. *inculcātiōn-em*, n. of action f. *inculcāre* to INCULCATE. Cf. F. *inculcation* (16th c.).] The action of impressing on the mind by forcible admonition or frequent repetition; the emphatic or persistent teaching *of* something.

1553 T. Wilson *Rhet.* 94, I wil not trouble the reader with double inculcation, and twyse tellyng of one tale. **1601** R. Johnson *Kingd. & Commw.* (1603) 254 He evermore laboreth with often inculcations, to infixe this most firmely in his mind. **1751** Johnson *Rambler* No. 151 ¶8 The days that are to follow must pass in the inculcation of precepts already collected, and assertion of tenets already received. **1805** Foster *Ess.* I. ii. 17 The constant inculcation of truth. **1844** Stanley *Arnold* I. iv. 186 His works were not merely the inculcations of particular truths, but the expression of his whole mind. **1866** G. Macdonald *Ann. Q. Neighb.* xxxiii. (1878) 588 Action is more powerful than speech in the inculcation of religion.

†**in'culcative**, *a. Obs. rare.* [f. L. *inculcāt-*, ppl. stem (see INCULCATE *v.*) + -IVE.] Tending to inculcate; of the nature of inculcation; impressive.

1626 W. Fenner *Hidden Manna* (1652) 2 Bare teaching will not availe neither; but there must be a speciall inculcative teaching. *a* **1677** Manton *Serm. Ps.* cxix. verse 48 Wks. 1872 VII. 20 When you have heard the word.. apply it to yourselves by serious inculcative thoughts.

inculcator ('ɪnkʌlkeɪtə(r), ɪn'kʌlk-). [agent-n. in L. form from INCULCATE. (Cf. late L. *inculcātor*, used by Tertullian in literal sense.)] One who inculcates.

1675 Boyle *Consid. Reconcil. Reason & Relig.* I. viii. Wks. 1772 IV. 183 Des Cartes himself..has been the greatest example and inculcator of this suspension [of assent]. **1890** *Temple-Bar Mag.* Sept. 91 He was an inculcator of muscular Christianity.

in'culcatory, *a. rare.* [f. INCULCATE *v.* + -ORY.] Fitted or tending to inculcate; characterized by inculcation.

a **1887** M. Hopkins *Discuss. Yng. Men* 233 (Cent.) As typical and inculcatory, nothing could have been more admirable than these sacrifices. **1889** J. M. Robertson *Ess. Crit. Method* 69 A matter of native bias, length of habit, and inculcatory, belike painful, preparation.

†**in'culk**, *v. Obs.* [ad. L. *inculc-āre* to INCULCATE: perh. immed. after F. *inculquer* (1549 in Hatz.-Darm.).] *trans.* = INCULCATE *v.*

1528 in Burnet *Hist. Ref.* II. 85 To inculke unto Him the said Points and Considerations. **1537** *Inst. Chr. Man* F vij b, These thynges..shoulde be continually taughte and inculked into the eares of all true christen people. **1562** Bp. Gardiner *Let. to Somerset* in Foxe *A. & M.* (1563) 740 Yf your Grace thinke not yourselfe encombred with my babling and inculking. **1576** Newton *Lemnie's Complex.* (1633) 34 Which sentence Saint Paul..went about to inculke into the minde of the Athenians.

†**in'culp**, *v. Obs. rare*$^{-1}$. [ad. L. *inculp-āre* to INCULPATE, perh. after F. *inculper* (Cotgr. 1611).] *trans.* = INCULPATE *v.*

1612 Shelton *Quix.* II. vi. I. 108 For, if Chrysostomes impatience and head-long desire slew him, why should mine honest proceeding and care be inculped therewithall?

inculpable (ɪn'kʌlpəb(ə)l), *a.* Now *rare.* [ad. late L. *inculpābilis*, f. *in-* (IN-^{3}) + *culpābilis* CULPABLE.] Not culpable; blameless; free from blame.

1491 Caxton *Vitas Patr.* (W. de W. 1495) I. Prol. 1 b/1 They knewe not that ony euyll were done in the worlde, ne also what synne was: But they were all utterly Inculpable. **1540-1** Elyot *Image Gov.* 31 Suche personages as neuer were infamed with any vice notable, and whose lyues be inculpable. **1649** Jer. Taylor *Gt. Exemp.* I. v. 153 Little more then sins of pure and inculpable ignorance. **1730** Franklin *Ess.* Wks. 1840 II. 56 If his error is inevitable, or such as..he could not help, he is inculpable. **1858** Faber *Spir. Confer.* (1870) 160 There are inculpable unrealities to which bodily weakness exposes us.

Hence **inculpa'bility** = next.

1765 G. Canning *Patriotism* in *Sch. Satire* (1802) 326 Pitying Justice tacks, in their defence, Inculpability to want of sense.

in'culpableness. [f. prec. + -NESS.] Blamelessness.

1548 Udall *Erasm. Par. Luke* xi. 111 The puritie consisteth in the inculpablenesse and innocencie of the herte. **1684** Sharp *Disc. conc. Conscience* 29 The great thing ..is the Culpableness or Inculpableness; the Faultiness or Innocence of the mistake.

in'culpably, *adv.* [f. as prec. + -LY^{2}.] Blamelessly, innocently.

1536 Latimer *Serm. & Rem.* (Parker Soc.) 377 Though I am not altogether so scrupulous, yet I would it were done inculpably and duly. **1649** Jer. Taylor *Gt. Exemp.* II. viii. 81 God will accept the will for the deed when the externall act is inculpably out of our powers. **1685** *Case Doubting Conscience* 96 A man may very innocently and inculpably be Ignorant of it. **1864** Manning *Let. to Pusey* 14 The Church teaches that men may be inculpably out of its pale.

†**in'culpate**, *a. Obs. rare.* [ad. L. *inculpātus*, f. *in-* (IN-^{3}) + *culpātus*, pa. pple. of *culpāre* to blame.] Unblamed, blameless, inculpable.

1612 T. James *Jesuit's Downf.* 14 Every Iesuit takes vpon him to be an illuminate, an inculpate guider of soules. **1647** Jer. Taylor *Lib. Proph.* xi. 171 Causes of Errour in the exercise of Reason which are inculpate in themselves.

inculpate ('ɪnkʌlpeɪt, ɪn'kʌlpeɪt), *v.* [f. med. L. *inculpāt-*, ppl. stem of *inculpāre*, f. *in-* (IN-^{2}) + *culpāre* to blame; cf. *exculpate*. As to the pronunciation, see CONTEMPLATE.]

1. *trans.* To bring a charge against; to accuse; to blame, find fault with.

1799 S. Turner *Anglo-Sax.* I. III. iii. 173 Gildas inculpates him for having destroyed his uncle. **1833** I. Taylor *Fanat.* vi. 185 We should be slow to inculpate motives. **1846** De Quincey *Glance Wks. Mackintosh* Wks. XIII. 65 The poor lady could have had no rational motive for inculpating herself.

2. To involve in a charge; to incriminate.

1839-40 W. Irving *Wolfert's R.* (1855) 257 De Mille.. confessed to a plot to murder the broker,..and inculpated the Count in the crime. **1897** Mary Kingsley *W. Africa* 427 Attempting to exculpate himself and inculpate Dr. Nassau for not having told him one was necessary.

Hence **inculpated, inculpating** *ppl. adjs.*

1837 Carlyle *Fr. Rev.* III. III. ix, Will not perhaps the inculpated Deputies consent to withdraw voluntarily? **1864** *Daily Tel.* 8 June, Major-General Dix..was..ordered forthwith to stop the further publication of the inculpated newspapers. **1892** *Pall Mall G.* 15 Mar. 2/3, I think it is generally felt that the inculpating lie is more serious than the exculpating falsehood.

inculpation (ɪnkʌl'peɪʃən). [n. of action f. INCULPATE: see -ATION. Cf. F. *inculpation* (1752 in Hatz.-Darm.).] The action of inculpating; blame, censure, incrimination.

1798 Sir M. Eden in *Ld. Auckland's Corr.* (1862) III. 389, I should be sorry to have my career terminate in a manner that will be interpreted as an inculpation of me. **1836** Sir W. Hamilton *Discuss., Stud. Math.* (1852) 266 As to the inculpation of the Metaphysicians—why was Locke not mentioned in place of Hume? **1850** Grote *Greece* II. lxv. VIII. 299 In this assembly the most bitter inculpations were put forth against the Athenians. **1871** Freeman *Hist. Ess.* Ser. I. xi. 329 We do not think him equally successful in his inculpation of the Confederates.

b. *transf.* Blame, fault. *rare.*

1822 Byron *Werner* II. i, I should rather lay The inculpation on the Hungarian.

inculpative (ɪn'kʌlpətɪv), *a.* [f. L. *inculpāt-*, ppl. stem (see INCULPATE *v.*) + -IVE.] = next.

1802 Syd. Smith *Lett.* iii, With the inculpative part of your criticisms on mine I very much agree. **1802-12** Bentham *Ration. Evid.* Wks. 1843 VII. 17 The incidents by which the conclusiveness of an inculpative presumption may be proved.

inculpatory (ɪn'kʌlpətərɪ), *a.* [f. as prec. + -ORY.] Tending to inculpate or incriminate; attributing fault or blame.

1837 Carlyle *Fr. Rev.* III. III. ii, From the Southern Cities come addresses of an almost inculpatory character. **1844** H. H. Wilson *Brit. India* II. 495 The second of the inculpatory letters. **1885** J. Martineau *Types Eth. Th.* II. 158 A very sufficient vocabulary of inculpatory words.

incult (ɪn'kʌlt), *a.* Now *rare.* Also 7 **inculte**. [ad. L. *incultus*, f. *in-* (IN-^{3}) + *cultus*, pa. pple. of *colĕre* to cultivate. Cf. F. *inculte* (15–16th c.).]

1. Uncultivated, untilled, in a state of natural wildness.

1621 Burton *Anat. Mel.* II. iii. III. (1651) 326 Germany then, saith Tacitus, was incult and horrid, now full of magnificent Cities. **1730-46** Thomson *Autumn* 884 Her forests huge, Incult, robust, and tall. **1864** Sala *Diary in Amer.* (1865) I. xii. 340 There were no trees, hedgerows, gardens visible. All was incult and horrid—without form and void.

2. Unpolished, untrimmed, inartistic, rude.

1599 A. M. tr. *Gabelhouer's Bk. Physicke* Transl. to Rdr. 1, I hope, and trust the most curteous Reader will accept.. this my most inculte and vntilled labour. **1611** W. Sclater *Key* (1629) 114 Eyther incult and horrid stones or unshapen and rude matter. **1669** Boyle *Contn. New Exp.* II. Pref. (1682) 9 The reading of so incult and unpolite a Rhapsodie. *a* **1851** Mary Wollstonecraft (Webster), His style is diffuse and incult. **1887** Saintsbury *Hist. Elizab. Lit.* iii. (1890) 60 The miscellaneous..writers, who, incult and formless as their work was, at least maintained the literary tradition.

3. Of persons, their manners, etc.: Wanting in culture or refinement; inelegant, rough, coarse.

1621 Burton *Anat. Mel.* To Rdr. 56 Let them be rude, stupid, ignorant, incult. **1671** F. Phillips *Reg. Necess.* 8 In the more incult and fierce behaviour of our English and Saxon Ancestors. **1862** Symonds in *Life* (1895) I. 208 She saw his coarseness at once. He is incult, but clever. **1891** C. Wordsworth *Ann. Early Life* ii. 145 His [Neander's] appearance was very incult.

†**in'cultivate**, *a. Obs.* [f. IN-^{3} + L. *cultīvāt-us*, pa. pple. of *cultīvāre* to CULTIVATE. Cf. F. *incultivé* (16th c.).] = next.

1661 Glanvill *Van. Dogm.* xii. 115 As they did of old upon the Barbarism of the incultivate Heathen. *Ibid.* xvii. 165 The modern Retainers to the Stagirite have spent their sweat and pains upon the most litigious parts of his Philosophy; while those, that find less play for the contending Genius, are incultivate. **1806** Anna Seward *Lett.* (1811) VI. 284 Nothing but the understanding and the heart are left incultivate.

†**in'cultivated**, *a. Obs.* [IN-^{3}.] Uncultivated; uncultured; unpolished, rude.

1665 Sir T. Herbert *Trav.* (1677) 380 (T.) The soil although incultivated, so full of vigour that it procreates without seed. **1682** Evats *Grotius' War & Peace* 85 If there be..any Land that is desart and incultivated. **1694** G. Daniel *Trinarch., Hen. IV*, cccxxii, Where Minds incultivated, feed their owne Thistles of Rage, to boast the highest growne. **1716** M. Davies *Athen. Brit.* III. *Crit. Hist.* 7 More like Verbose..Catechists, or even Exorcists, than well educated Scholars..in their incultivated Exarations.

inculti'vation. *rare.* [IN-^{3}.] Want of cultivation; uncultivated condition.

1784 J. Berrington *Hist. Abeillard* 108 (T.) In that state of incultivation which nature in her luxuriant fancies loves to form.

†**in'culture.** *Obs. rare.* [IN-^{3}.] Want of culture or cultivation.

1627-77 Feltham *Resolves* II. xlix. 257 The Inculture of the World would perish it into a Wilderness, should not the Activeness of Commerce make it an universal City. **1653** *Consid. Dissolv. Crt. Chancery* 48 The smallnesse of Commerce, paucity, poverty, and inculture of people. **1867** C. J. Smith *Syn. & Anton., Agriculture,*..Fallowness. Inculture.

†**in'cumb**, *v. Obs. rare.* [ad. L. *incumb-ĕre*: see INCUMBENT *a.*]

1. *intr.* To be incumbent; to lie upon something.

1629 [see INCUMBING *ppl. a.*].

2. To lie down; to succumb, yield.

1656 S. H. *Gold. Law* 24, I am too weak and brittle to deal with you, so chuse rather to Incumbe, then try it out with such a Combatant.

incumb, obs. form of INCOME.

†**in'cumbence.** *Obs.* [f. INCUMBENT: see next and -ENCE.] **a.** The fact of being incumbent; an overhanging or impending. **b.** A matter that is incumbent; a duty or obligation.

1677 Hale *Contempl.* II. 227 When the Necessity and Fear, and Incumbence of Evil is removed [etc.]. **1681** Burthogge *An Argument* (1684) 18 Which Duty and Incumbence, and the Consequentialness of it from the Covenant, is [etc.]. **1700** Rycaut *Contn. Knolles' Hist. Turks* III. 131 The next care and incumbence of the Generals was to provide Winter-quarters. **1768** *Woman of Honor* III. 137 The education of his only son..he held too sacred an incumbence to trust to any one but himself.

incumbency (ɪn'kʌmbənsɪ). [f. INCUMBENT: see -ENCY.]

1. The condition of lying or pressing upon something; brooding; a spiritual brooding or over-shadowing. Now *rare* or *Obs.*

1651 *Raleigh's Ghost* 226 The sacred Writ..being writen by the peculiar incumbency and direction of the holy Ghost. **1663** *Flagellum or O. Cromwell* (1672) 124 And the addle eggs put under the chill incumbency of other wildfoul. **1805** Wordsw. *Prelude* III. 116 Felt Incumbencies more awful, visitings Of the Upholder of the tranquil soul.

b. With *an* and *pl.*: That which is incumbent; an incumbent weight or mass.

1679 Evelyn *Sylva* I. iii. (ed. 3) 25 We find them [some trees] more fragil, and not so well qualified to support great incumbencies and weights. **1687** *Phil. Trans.* XVI. 456 It becomes altogether unfit for strong Incumbencies, or other robust Uses. **1889** *Cornh. Mag.* Mar. 269 The stream is choked with its compact incumbency of snow.

2. The quality of being incumbent as a duty; an incumbent duty or obligation. Now *rare.*

a **1608** Donne *Let. Sir H. G.* in *Lett.* (1651) 71 The duties of a man, of a friend, of a husband, of a father, and all the incumbencies of a family. **1667** *Lond. Gaz.* No. 159/2, I have thought it an Incumbency both upon my Place and Duty, to represent to Your Majesty the Scandal, that will be given to all the World. **1798** T. Chalmers *Posth. Wks.* (1849) VI. 9 They will there recognise the doctrines which it is incumbent on them to believe, and..the sources of this incumbency. **1799** Washington *Lett.* Writ. 1893 XIV. 184, I feel an incumbency to inform you, that another copy of that letter has been either surreptitiously obtained, or fabricated. **1846** Grote *Greece* II. iv. II. 423 The celebration of the Olympic games thus became numbered among the incumbencies of Elis. **1868** Browning *Ring & Bk.* x. 363 Speaks or keeps silence, as himself sees fit, Without the least incumbency to lie.

3. The position or office of an incumbent; now only *Eccl.* (or *transf.* from this). Also, the sphere in which an incumbent exercises his functions, and the period during which the office is held.
*c*1656 BRAMHALL *Replic.* v. 202 The Pope having instituted one man into a Bishoprick, cannot during his incumbency give the joint government of his Church to another. 1657 HOWELL *Londinop.* 18 There be many things that concern the incumbency of the Conservator of so noble a River. 1681 BURNET *Hist. Ref.* II. Pref. (R.), They have now the same right by their incumbency that they then had. 1841 W. SPALDING *Italy & It. Isl.* II. 37 This bishop's incumbency falls under the reign of Alexander Severus. 1851 GLADSTONE *Glean.* VI. lxi. 41 Inviting the clergy of the various incumbencies..to frame..lists. 1886 *Law Times' Rep.* LIII. 708/1 [He] has..retired from his incumbency and given up his benefice. 1895 *Daily News* 12 July 5/2 With the present incumbency of the Board of Trade, there is no knowing what may happen.

incumbent (ɪn'kʌmbənt), *sb.* [ad. L. *incumbent-em*: see next. The use of the term in senses 1 and 2 is peculiar to English, and app. belongs to a med.L. sense of L. *incumbĕre* = 'obtinere, possidere, ut est apud Jurisconsultos' (Du Cange).]

1. The holder of an ecclesiastical benefice.
1425 *Rolls Parlt.* IV. 306/1 As if the Benefice were voide, be dethe of yencumbent of ye same. 1534 *Act 26 Hen. VIII*, c. 3 §17 Any incumbent of any of the dignitees, benefices, or promocions spirituall afore especified. 1573 *Wills & Inv. N.C.* (Surtees 1835) I. 392 Also I giue to ye Incombent two cowbords a sidbord an almerie. 1641 *Termes de la Ley* s.v., Who is..called the Incumbent of that Church, because he doth bend all his study to the discharge of the cure there. 1739 WHITEFIELD in *Life & Jrnls.* (1756) 147 The Incumbent lent me the Church. 1784 J. POTTER *Virtuous Villagers* II. 137 The present incumbent on the living..is..in a dangerous state of illness. 1818 CRUISE *Digest* (ed. 2) IV. 17 Every parson, vicar, or other incumbent of any ecclesiastical benefice, is enabled to exchange parsonage houses and glebe lands, with the consent of the patron and bishop, for other houses and lands. 1876 GEO. ELIOT *Dan. Der.* xxiv, An incumbent of this diocese.

2. In general sense: The holder of any office.
1672 MARVELL *Reh. Transp.* I. 243 They [kings] are the Incumbents of whole Kingdoms, and the Rectorship of the ..People..rests upon them. 1700 ASTRY tr. *Saavedra-Faxardo* II. 21 'Tis necessary besides to settle a competent Salary upon each Office, such as the incumbent may live handsomely upon. *a*1832 BENTHAM *Offic. Aptitude* Wks. 1843 V. 339 Who is there that does not know, that the value of an office to the incumbent is directly as the emolument, and inversely as the labour? *a*1852 WEBSTER *Wks.* (1877) II. 49 We protest against doctrines which regard offices as created for the sake of incumbents. 1884 *Law Times* LXXVII. 1/2 The incumbents, for the time being, of the various coronerships. 1904 W. OSLER *Aequanimitas* v. 82 His son..held the chair for nearly the same length of time, and the remainder of the period has been covered by the occupancy of John Goodsir, and his successor..the present incumbent. 1940 W. FAULKNER *Hamlet* I. iii. 61 They had waited about the store to see what would happen when he arrived who..must have still believed himself the incumbent. *Ibid.* II. i. 95 The incumbent, the Professor at that time, was an old man. 1966 P. GREEN tr. *Escarpit's Novel Computer* vii. 92 The training division of A.I.M.R. was still at Brive, and boasted a general manager's office; but the incumbent was in fact a low-ranking deputy-manager. 1971 *Nature* 17 Sept. p. x (Advt.), Applications are invited for the Harry Bolus Chair of Botany... It is required that the incumbent should promote work in both experimental and field botany. 1972 *Daily Tel.* 29 Nov. 8 The victory by Mr James Conway..in a ballot for general secretary of the Engineering Union is being challenged... Mr Conway, the incumbent, received 169,806 votes.

3. One who leans *over* something. *nonce-use.*
1719 *Free-Thinker* No. 143 ¶5 Indocil Incumbents over Folios.

incumbent (ɪn'kʌmbənt), *a.* [ad. L. *incumbent-em*, pres. pple. of *incumbĕre* to lie upon, to lean or press upon, to apply oneself to, etc., f. *in-* (IN-²) + *cumbĕre* to lie: cf. CUMBENT.]

1. a. That lies, leans, rests, or presses with its weight upon something else. Const. *on.*
1624 WOTTON *Archit.* in *Reliq.* (1672) 61 Two Incumbent Figures gracefully leaning upon it towards one another. 1667 MILTON *P.L.* I. 226 With expanded wings he stears his flight Aloft, incumbent on the dusky Air. 1782 PENNANT *Journ. fr. Chester to Lond.* 88 His figure..is engraven on the incumbent alabaster slab. 1825 J. NICHOLSON *Operat. Mech* 96 The wheel, with its incumbent apparatus, weighs about 20 tons. 1853 LYTTON *My Novel* v. iv, Rising from his incumbent posture. 1853 HERSCHEL *Pop. Lect. Sc.* iv. §18 (1873) 156 It goes to add to the weight incumbent on the polar.
fig. 1781 GIBBON *Decl. & F.* xxx. III. 161 The nations.. must have pressed with incumbent weight on the confines of Germany. 1862 MERIVALE *Rom. Emp.* (1865) III. xxvi. 230 All support was withdrawn, and the incumbent mass of the conquerors rushed headlong over the bodies of their adversaries.

b. *poet.* Of things which lean or hang *over* something else: also of darkness, breaking waves, etc.
1719 YOUNG *Paraphr. Job* Wks. 1757 I. 207 Death's in-most chambers didst Thou ever see?..and wade To the black portal thro' th' incumbent shade? 1728–46 THOMSON *Spring* 41 Incumbent o'er the shining shore The master leans. 1740 SOMERVILLE *Hobbinol* I 209 Like some huge Rock he stands, That breaks th' incumbent Waves. 1810 SOUTHEY *Kehama* XXI. i, The Ship shot through the incumbent night. 1810 SCOTT *Lady of L.* III. xxvi, Many a rock..in random ruin piled..frowned incumbent o'er the spot.

2. *spec.* a. *Physics.* Of air, fluid, or other weight, with reference to the downward pressure exerted by it.
1660 BOYLE *New Exp. Phys. Mech.* ii. 38 The Atmosphere incumbent upon the upper part of the same key or stopple. 1794 G. ADAMS *Nat. & Exp. Philos.* I. 53 The lower air presses the palm of the hand as much upwards, as the incumbent column presses the back part downwards. 1831 LARDNER *Pneumat.* iii. 243 The elasticity of the air which surrounds us is equal to the weight of the incumbent atmosphere.

b. *Geol.* Overlying and resting (upon); superimposed, superincumbent, as a stratum.
1789 MILLS in *Phil. Trans.* LXXX. 79 The whole is incumbent on regular basalt pillars, of various dimensions. 1811 PINKERTON *Petral* I. 569 Coal sometimes contains.. crystals of calcareous spar, perhaps infiltrated from incumbent limestone. 1839 MURCHISON *Silur. Syst.* I. xxxi. 411 The Lower Ludlow shale or mudstone is as uniformly incumbent on the Wenlock limestone. 1874 LYELL *Elem. Geol.* xiii. 190 The shells of the Incumbent yellow sand of the same territory.

c. *Bot.* Said of an *anther* when it lies flat against the inner side of the filament; of *cotyledons* when the back of one is applied to the radicle.
1760 J. LEE *Introd. Bot.* II. xix. (1765) 112 The Antheræ incumbent. 1830 LINDLEY *Nat. Syst. Bot.* 38 Anthers incumbent, with contiguous lobes. 1851 BALFOUR *Bot.* §601. 288 The cotyledons are applied to each other by their faces, and the radicle is folded on their back, so as to be dorsal, and the cotyledons are incumbent. 1872 OLIVER *Elem. Bot.* II. 139 Compare. Sisymbrium, with the radicle curved over the back of one of the cotyledons (incumbent).

d. *Entom.* Applied to wings which at rest lie horizontally upon the body, as those of most moths.
1826 KIRBY & SP. *Entomol.* IV. 337 *Incumbent*..wings which when at rest cover the back of the insect. 1856–8 W. CLARK *Van der Hoeven's Zool.* I. 321 Wings incumbent.

e. *Zool.* Of hairs, spines, etc.: Lying along the surface on which they grow.

f. *Ornith.* Of the hallux or hind toe of a bird: Resting on the ground or other support with its whole length, its insertion being on a level with the anterior toes (*Cent. Dict.*).

3. a. Resting or falling upon a person as a duty or obligation. Const. *on, upon,* (also †*to*).
1567 in Row *Hist. Kirk* (Wodrow Soc.) 35 The host of God..shall doe all incumbent to them for the establishing of the true religion. 1637–50 Row *ibid.* 344 The first thing incumbent to be done there was to have deposed and excommunicat their Lordships. 1653 CROMWELL *Sp.* 4 July in *Carlyle*, That there was a duty incumbent upon us. 1713 BERKELEY *Hylas & Phil.* III. Wks. 1871 I. 348 It would still be incumbent on you to shew those words were not taken in the vulgar acceptation. 1851 GLADSTONE *Glean.* IV. i. 1, I have come home with a deep sense of the duty incumbent upon me. 1865 *Reader* 14 Jan. 39/1 Our author thinks that it is the incumbent duty of England to promote emigration to such a country.

†b. Falling as a charge or pecuniary liability.
1670 G. H. *Hist. Cardinals* I. I. 23 As to debts, obligations, and incumbent charges, they speak not a word. 1776 ADAM SMITH *W.N.* (1869) I. Introd. 4 Defraying the expenses incumbent on the whole society.

†c. Resting or vested as a right. *Obs.*
1652 *Persuasive to Compliance* 13 The decision of all controversies lay incumbent in the person of the King onely.

†4. Weighing upon the mind or feelings. *Obs.*
1651 HOBBES *Leviath.* II. xxvii. 155 Ambition, and Covetousnesse are Passions..that are perpetually incumbent, and pressing. 1711 SHAFTESB. *Charac.* (1737) II. I. ii. §3. 30 Things are no less active and incumbent on the Mind, at all Seasons, and even when the real Objects themselves are absent.

†5. Impending, imminent, threatening. *Obs.*
1646 BP. MAXWELL *Burd. Issach.* in *Phenix* (1708) II. 295 God's Judgments are incumbent and imminent upon Church and Kingdom. 1682 EVATS *Grotius' War & Peace* 82 When the danger incumbent is past, restitution is to be made, if we are able. 1793 GOUV. MORRIS in Sparks *Life & Writ.* (1832) II. 383 The proselytes will return to their original sentiments as soon as the incumbent terror is removed.

†6. Bending or applying one's energies to some work; closely occupied with something. Const. *on* (*upon*), *over, to. Obs.*
1548 UDALL *Erasm. Par. Luke* xix. 149 a, Lowe men spiritually are suche, as are incumbent and dooe rest on filthie or vile and transitory thynges. 1650 BULWER *Anthropomet.* 78 What she is most incumbent upon, and which she alwayes beholds, are those things which appertain to action and utility. 1668 CLARENDON *Vindicat.* Tracts (1727) 39 Everybody remembers the multiplicity of business the king was incumbent to at that time. 1814 SCOTT *Wav.* (ed. 1) iii, He was losing for ever the opportunity of acquiring habits of firm and incumbent [*later edd.* assiduous] application.

7. †a. In occupation of a benefice; holding the position of an incumbent. Const. *on. Obs.*
1604 N. D. *3rd Pt. Three Convers. Eng.* 193 He had byn depriued..from a certayne benefice, that he vnjustly..was incumbent vpon. 1655 FULLER *Ch. Hist.* II. ii. §68 Parishes ..places bounded in regard of the Profits from the people therein, payable onely to a Pastour incumbent there. *a*1661 —— *Worthies* (1840) III. 210 He was never incumbent on any living with cure of souls.

b. Occupying or having the tenure of any post or position.
1972 *Nature* 28 Apr. 417/2 The incumbent head of the Institute of Theoretical Astronomy would..expect to have more than an equal say in the appointment of his partner. 1972 *Science* 22 Sept. 1087/3 The MSU trustees.. appointed the Pontiac school's incumbent dean..to be dean of the College of Osteopathic Medicine at MSU. 1973 *Sci. Amer.* Mar. 43 (Advt.), Well beyond buffhood is the incumbent partisan of astronomy's cause at the Kodak Research Laboratories.

Hence **in'cumbently** *adv. rare*, in an incumbent manner, after the manner of an incumbent weight.
1817 J. SCOTT *Paris Revisit.* (ed. 4) 229 A duty..which presses most incumbently on all those who stand by the wheel that shapes the course of the state.

in'cumbentess. *nonce-wd.* [f. INCUMBENT *sb.* + -ESS.] A female incumbent or occupant.
1760 H. WALPOLE *Lett. H. Mann* (1833) III. 371 The ancient barony of Clinton, which is fallen to her by the death of the last incumbentess.

incumber, variant of ENCUMBER.

†**in'cumbing,** *ppl. a. Obs.* [f. INCUMB *v.* + -ING².] Lying upon, overlying; = INCUMBENT *a.* 1.
1629 SIR W. MURE *True Crucif.* 563 Crusht downe with weight of Gods incumbing wrath.

†**incum'bition.** *Obs. rare*⁻¹. [n. of action, irreg. f. L. *incumbĕre* (of which the ppl. stem *incubit-* gave L. *incubitiōn-em*).] The action of lying or pressing upon. (In quot. *fig.*)
1759 STERNE *Tr. Shandy* II. iii, The souls of connoisseurs themselves by long friction and incumbition, have the happiness at length to get all be-virtu'd.

incumbrance, etc., var. ENCUMBRANCE, etc.

incummiscibility: see INCOMMISCIBILITY.

incunable (ɪn'kjuːnəb(ə)l). [a. F. *incunable*, ad. L. **incunābulum*: see next.] A book printed in the infancy of the art. Chiefly in *pl.* = next, 2.
1886 P. FITZGERALD *Book Fancier* 32 Concerning the incunables or cradle books. 1886 LANG *Books & Bookmen* (1887) 133 Incunables! for you I sigh. 1894 *Month* May 116 One of the early 'Incunables' or 'Fifteeners'.

‖**incunabula** (ɪnkjuː'næbjʊlə), *sb. pl.* [L. *incūnābula* (neut. pl.) swaddling-clothes, hence cradle, and *fig.* childhood, beginning, origin, f. *cūnæ* cradle.]

1. The earliest stages or first traces in the development of anything.
1824 DE QUINCEY *Falsif. Hist. Eng.* Wks. 1890 IX. 300 Here they fancy that they can detect the *incunabula* of the revolutionary spirit. 1832 —— *Charlemagne* ibid. V. 361 Here, too, we behold in their incunabula..the existing kingdoms of Christendom. 1864 J. MARTINEAU *Ess., Rev.* etc. (1891) II. 476 The Gospel is silent respecting the incunabula of the Master's life.

2. (With sing. *incunabulum*): Books produced in the infancy of the art of printing; *spec.* those printed before 1500.
1861 NEALE *Notes Dalmatia* etc. i. 9 What are Incunabula? you ask. It is the name that Germans give to books printed before 1500. 1866 *Sat. Rev.* 21 Sept. 305 The facsimile of a most interesting 'incunabulum'. 1885 *Even. Standard* 11 Apr. 1/1 'Tall' copies and 'large paper' copies, incunabula and Elzevirs.

3. *Ornith.* The breeding-places of a species of bird.

Hence **incu'nabular** *a.*, of or pertaining to early printed books.
1889 *Athenæum* 15 June 752/1 Each paragraph.. decorated with an imposing and quite incunabular ¶.

incunabulist (ɪnkjuː'næbjʊlɪst). [f. INCUNABULA *sb. pl.* 2 + -IST.] One who collects or is interested in incunabula.
1921 S. GASELEE in *Library* Sept. 135 To all incunabulists it [*sc.* the letter *H*] is almost indissociably the abbreviation for Hain's *Repertorium*. 1928 *Ibid.* Sept. 162 The incunabulist has to stop at the threshold of the year 1501. 1949 F. BOWERS *Princ. Bibliogr. Descr.* ix. 339 Incunabulists view the information in colophons with suspicion until it is checked by other evidence. 1970 *Times Lit. Suppl.* 14 Aug. 906/2 It is well known from the work of the incunabulists that the typographical equipment of a fifteenth-century printer was identifiably unique.

incur (ɪn'kɜː(r)), *v.* Also 5–7 incur(r(e, 7 -cure, 6–7 encurr(e. [ad. L. *incurr-ĕre* to run (into, towards, against), f. *in-* (IN-²) + *currĕre* to run: cf. OF. *encorre, -courre*, mod.F. *encourir*.]

I. *intr.* †1. To run, flow, fall, or come *to* or *into*; to fall (within a period of time, the scope of an argument, etc.). *Obs.*
1536 *Art. Insurgents* in Froude *Hist. Eng.* III. 157 *note*, We humbly beseech..that the Lady Mary may be made legitimate, and the former statute therein annulled, for the danger if the title might incur to the crown of Scotland. 1619 USSHER *Lett.* (1686) 69 The beginning of Dhilkarnain ..certainly doth incurr *in annum periodi Julianae* 4402. *c*1620 A. HUME *Brit. Tongue* xi. 33 Becaus sum nounes incurre into adverbes, let us alsoe noat their differences. 1625 BACON *Ess., Envy* (Arb.) 513 For it..commeth oftner into their remembrance, and incurreth likewise more into the note of others. 1652 BP. HALL *Invis. World* I. §7 These graces do incur into each other, and are not possible to be severed. 1677 HALE *Prim. Orig. Man.* 146 Kircherus in the first Book of his Egyptian Antiquities..supposeth the first 15 Dynasties to have incurred before the Flood.

†**b.** To come in so as to meet the eye, the observation, etc; to occur. *Obs.*

1626 BACON *Sylva* §98 They are Inuisible, and incurre not to the Eie. **1681** EVELYN *Corr.* 27 Sept. in *Mem.* (1819) II. 215 If any thing incurr to you of Curious.. you will greately oblige that Assembly of Virtuosi in communicating any productions of the places you trauell thro'. **1692** SOUTH 12 *Serm.* (1697) I. 317 According to the different Quality of External Objects that incurr into the Senses.

c. To devolve or accrue; to supervene.

1786 T. JEFFERSON *Writ.* (1859) I. 546 The principal, with the interest incurring before and after the war. **1818** CRUISE *Digest* (ed. 2) III. 17 No lapse incurs by the non-presentation of the patron, within six months.

†**2.** To run *into* (danger, etc.); to render oneself liable *to* (damage). *Obs.*

1530–1 *Act 22 Hen. VIII*, c. 15 Other spyrituall persones ..haue fallen and incurred into dyuers daungers of his lawes. **1533** SIR W. FITZWILLIAM in Ellis *Orig. Lett.* Ser. I. II. 28 All suche pore people as shulde receyve her said Maundy shulde encurre to farre in daungier of.. Lawes, and of High Treason. **1620** SHELTON *Quix.* III. xiii. 82 God deliver me..out of this dangerous Profession of being a Squire, into which I have this second time, incurr'd.

II. *trans.*

†**3.** To run into; to move or pass into, on, or against; to come upon, meet with. *Obs.*

1599 A. M. tr. *Gabelhouer's Bk. Physicke* Ded., Whose beaten footepath, your..Maiestyes..persone doth so incurre. *a* **1677** BARROW *Serm.* (1687) I. viii. 92 He that is no longer affected with a benefit than it incurrs the sense, and suffers not it self to be disregarded. *a* **1680** BUTLER *Rem.* (1759) I. 205 Those imported from the East, Where first they were incurr'd, are held the best.

4. To run or fall into (some consequence, usually undesirable or injurious); to become through one's own action liable or subject to; to bring upon oneself.

1535 STEWART *Cron. Scot.* II. 699 And so this Robert incurrit greit skayth, And frustrat war than of tha kinrikis bayth. **1579** LYLY *Euphues* (Arb.) 54, I should haue.. incurred the suspicion of fraud. **1604** SHAKS. *Oth.* III. iii. 67 His Trespasse..is not almost a fault T' encurre a priuate checke. **1667** MILTON *P.L.* x. 15 They, not obeying, Incurr'd, what could they less, the penaltie. **1751** JOHNSON *Rambler* No. 155 ¶1 No weakness of the human mind has more frequently incurred animadversion. **1795** BURKE *Th. Scarcity* Wks. 1842 II. 253 All the expence is incurred gratis. **1812** H. & J. SMITH *Rej. Addr.* x. (1873) 91 Disseminating falsehood without incurring favour. **1838** LYTTON *Calderon* ii. 65, I owe you the greatest debt one man can incur to another. **1841** ELPHINSTONE *Hist. Ind.* I. 581 He incurred the displeasure of his sovereign. **1867** FREEMAN *Norm. Conq.* I. v. 366 A fine..was incurred in ordinary cases. **1885** J. MARTINEAU *Types Eth. Th.* II. 48 Feelings which incur..our disgust or complacency.

†**b.** Obsolete constructions. *Obs.*

c **1430** LYDG. *Min. Poems* (Percy Soc.) 141 The tenthe part fro God yif thou withdrawe, Thou muste incurre.. To been accursyd by rigour of the lawe. **1726** AMHERST *Terræ Fil.* Pref. 20 He has attempted this change, without incurring upon himself that obloquy and clamour, which usually attend such innovations.

†**5.** To cause to be incurred; to bring *on* or *upon* (some one); to entail. *Obs.*

1627 HAKEWILL *Apol.* IV. xii. §5 (1630) 472 The Apostles warinesse in not naming it expressely, lest thereby he should incurre hatred against the Christian Professours and Religion. **1747** *Adv. Kidnapped Orphan* 201 The pusillanimous behaviour of the lieutenant..incurred on him the contempt of the whole corps. **1784** *Laura & Augustus* III. 28 This sickness has necessarily incurred expences, which we are unable to bear.

Hence **incurred** (ɪn'kɜːd) *ppl. a.*; **incurring** (ɪn'kɜːrɪŋ) *vbl. sb.* and *ppl. a.*

1599 MINSHEU *Sp. Dict.*, *Incurrimiento*, running into, falling into, incurring. **1644** MILTON *Judgm. Bucer* xl, Not death but the incurring of notorious infamy. **1836** W. IRVING *Astoria* III. 181 The interior trade, which they pronounced unequal to the expenses incurred. *a* **1890** J. BROWN *Serm.* (1892) 120 The recklessly incurred..debt.

incurability (ɪnkjʊərə'bɪlɪtɪ). [f. next: see -ITY; cf. F. *incurabilité*.] The quality of being incurable; incurableness.

1630 H. R. *Mythomystes* 2 To helpe on these diseases to incurability. **1664** POWER *Exp. Philos.* III. 187 The incurability of Cancers and Quartans. **1761** CANTWELL in *Phil. Trans.* LII. 520 That the incurability proceeded from ..some other distemper complicated with the cataract. **1868** FARRAR *Seekers* Concl. (1875) 330 The supposed incurability of evil.

incurable (ɪn'kjʊərəb(ə)l), *a.* (*sb.*) [a. OF. *incurable* (13–14th c. in Hatz.-Darm.), ad. L. *incūrābilis*, f. *in-* (IN-³) + *cūrābilis* CURABLE.]

1. That cannot be cured; incapable of being healed by medicine or medical skill.

a **1340** HAMPOLE *Psalter* Cant. 520 Venym of snakis incurabil. **1382** WYCLIF *2 Macc.* ix. 5 But the Lord God of Yrael..smote hym with a wound incurable. *c* **1386** CHAUCER *Monk's T.* 610 God..him..smoot With invisible wounde, ay incurable. **1480** CAXTON *Chron. Eng.* cci. 183 The mormal..be hald Incurable. **1533** MORE *Apol.* xii. Wks. 870/2 For healthe of the whole bodye, cutte and cast of the incurable cancred partes therefro. **1715** NELSON *Addr. Pers. Qual.* 210 We have not, for instance, a Hospital for the Incurable. **1846** TRENCH *Mirac.* x. (1862) 216 The disease.. was incurable by the art and skill of man.

2. *transf.* and *fig.* Not admitting of remedy, correction, or reformation.

1377 LANGL. *P. Pl.* B. XIII. 13 How þat lewed men ben ladde..þorugh vnkonnynge curatoures to incurable peynes. **1560** JEWEL *Serm. bef. Queen, Ps.* lxix. 9, That yet before the faulte be incurable, there may be some redresse. **1595** SHAKS. *John* V. i. 16 Present medcine must be ministred, Or ouerthrow incureable ensues. **1665** GLANVILL *Def. Van. Dogm.* 82 The Transcripts were full of errour and incurable defects. **1725** BERKELEY *Propos. Suppl. Ch. Plant.* Wks. III. 226 Ignorance is not so incurable as error. **1855** MACAULAY *Hist. Eng.* xx. IV. 386 The faults of James's head and heart were incurable. **1879** JEFFERIES *Wild Life in S. Co.* x. 203 Wasps are incurable drunkards.

B. *sb.* A person suffering from an incurable disease. Usually in *pl.*

1652 HOWELL tr. *Giraffi's Rev. Naples* II. 131 They burnt the Monastery of Santa Maria, together with the Hospital of the Incurables. *a* **1745** SWIFT (J.), If idiots and lunaticks cannot be found, incurables may be taken into the hospital. **1766** CHESTERF. *Lett.* 1 Aug. (1774) IV. 245 To withdraw in the fulness of his powers..from the House of Commons.. and to go into that Hospital of Incurables, the House of Lords. **1778** *Eng. Gazetteer* (ed. 2) s.v. *Southwark*, This hospital..is said to be for incurables, *i.e.* for such as are turned out of other hospitals for any ailments that are incurable (except lunacy). **1816** SOUTHEY in *Q. Rev.* XIV. 353 To leave a country which, like a lunatic hospital, contained only fools and incurables.

incurableness (ɪn'kjʊərəb(ə)lnɪs). [f. prec. + -NESS.] The quality of being incurable.

1612–15 BP. HALL *Contempl.*, *N.T.* IV. vii, The.. incurablenesse of her disease both sent her to seek Christ, and moved Christ to her cure. **1807** *Med. Jrnl.* XVII. 362 The incurableness of the complaint. **1817** BENTHAM *Plan Parl. Ref.* Introd. 199 The incurableness of the disorder, and the consequently incurable corruptness of Honourable House.

incurably (ɪn'kjʊərəblɪ), *adv.* [f. as prec. + -LY².] In an incurable manner or condition; to an incurable degree.

1529 MORE *Suppl. Soulys* Wks. 322/1 Some other whose body is so incurablye corrupted that they shall walter and tolter. **1649** BP. HALL *Cases Consc.* vi. (R.), If any man shall fraudulently sell an horse, which he knows secretly and incurably diseased, to another for sound. **1763** J. BROWN *Poetry & Mus.* xii. 212 The French Language is..void of Harmony and Variety, and incurably discordant. **1847–8** H. MILLER *First Impr.* i. (1857) 4 Of all great losses and misfortunes, his [the hero's] master achievement—the taking of a nation—is the greatest and most incurably calamitous. **1856** FROUDE *Hist. Eng.* I. 285 Incurably given as they were to fighting in the best ordered times.

†**incurie.** *Obs. rare.* [a. F. *incurie* (Cotgr.), ad. L. *incūria* carelessness, f. *in-* (IN-³) + *cūra* care.] Carelessness.

c **1540** tr. *Pol. Verg. Eng. Hist.* (Camden) I. 301 There varienge bothe in places and menns names.. I thought good to advertise..that their incurie may not be a blemishe to our historie. **1623** COCKERAM, *Incurie*, carelesnesse.

incuriosity (ɪnkjʊərɪ'ɒsɪtɪ). [f. INCURIOUS: cf. CURIOSITY, F. *incuriosité*.] The quality or fact of being incurious, or without curiosity.

1. The quality of being subjectively incurious; want or absence of care; want of curiosity or interest in things.

1603 FLORIO *Montaigne* III. xiii. (1632) 605 How soft, how gentle, and how sound a pillow is ignorance and incuriosity to rest a well composed head upon. **1659** H. L'ESTRANGE *Alliance Div. Off.* 25 Lest by chance, either through ignorance or incuriosity, heterodox and unsound tenets be vented. **1752** WARBURTON *Serm.* Wks. 1811 IX. i. 1 But his [Pilate's] incuriosity or indifference, when Truth was offered to be laid before him as a private man,..shews him in a light much less excusable. **1821** LAMB *Elia* Ser. I. *Old & New Schoolm.*, I alone should stand unterrified, from sheer incuriosity and want of observation. **1857** BUCKLE *Civiliz.* I. vii. 398 Books..from the general incuriosity of the people found but few readers.

2. The quality of being objectively incurious, or not carefully composed; homeliness, inelegance.

1661 *Papers on Alter. Prayer Bk.* 38 God heareth not Prayers, for the Rhetorick, and handsome Cadencies, and neatnesse of Expression, but will bear..with some Incuriosity of words.

†**b.** quasi-*concr.* An inelegant or careless trait.

1651 JER. TAYLOR *Serm. for Year* I. xv. 195 Thinking all things become a good man; even his gestures and little incuriosities.

incurious (ɪn'kjʊərɪəs), *a.* [ad. L. *incūriōs-us* careless, unconcerned, negligent, not done with care, f. *in-* (IN-³) + *cūriōsus* careful, CURIOUS; cf. F. *incurieux*. In sense 7, app. f. IN-³ + CURIOUS.]

I. Subjectively.

1. Without care or concern: **a.** Not bestowing care; careless, negligent, heedless. **b.** Free from care or apprehension; not anxious, untroubled. *arch.* (Constr. *of*.)

1570 LEVINS *Manip.* 226/6 Incuriouse, *incuriosus*. *a* **1619** FOTHERBY *Atheom.* (1622) 270 Can we think that the Providence..should be so supinely incurious as to slight and neglect the falling of Kingdoms? **1647** JER. TAYLOR *Lib. Proph.* Ep. Ded. 15 It would be hard to say that such Physitians are incurious of their Patients. **1647** CLARENDON *Hist. Reb.* VII. §231 In his Cloaths and Habit,..he was not now only incurious, but too negligent. **1670** MAYNWARING *Vita Sana* xv. 132 In a threefold manner the Soul..is incurious of the wellfare of the Body. **1737** L. CLARKE *Hist. Bible* (1740) II. *Gosp.* VI. 157 But they, incurious of those hell torments Judas felt. **1861** LYTTON & FANE *Tannhäuser* 92 He wander'd forth, incurious of the way.

2. Not desirous of obtaining knowledge, information, or news; uninquisitive, uninquiring, indifferent; devoid of curiosity.

1613–18 DANIEL *Coll. Hist. Eng.* (1626) 2 So incurious were they of further knowledg then what concerned their trade. *a* **1614** DONNE *Βιαθανατος* 205 Papias the Disciple of Saint John, whose times cannot be thought ignorant or incurious of Judas' History. **1774** J. BRYANT *Mythol.* I. 155 There surely was never a nation so incurious and indifferent about truth. **1836** J. H. NEWMAN *Par. Serm.* (1837) III. xii. 188, I am speaking of those of us who have learned to reflect, ..not of the incurious or illiterate. **1842** LYTTON *Zanoni* 29 Not with the absent brow and incurious air of students. **1883** *Century Mag.* XXV. 692/1 Cecil was..incurious about the..lives and character of her two comrades.

3. Not careful in observation; heedless, inattentive, careless.

1691 RAY *Creation* I. (1692) 45 Exposed to the Eyes and notice of the more careless and incurious Observer. **1713** DERHAM *Phys.-Theol.* (1749) II. 15 *note*, By an incurious view, it rather regrateth, than pleaseth the eye. **1762** B. STILLINGFL. tr. *Swed. Nat. Hist.* in *Misc. Tr.* 359 *note*, It is a notion which prevails commonly that cows eat the crow-foot..This shews how very incurious the country people are in relation to things they are every day conversant with. **1812** J. J. HENRY *Camp. agst. Quebec* 223 Resembles the latter, in the bark and leaf so much, that an incurious eye might be deceived. **1848** R. I. WILBERFORCE *Incarnation* v. (1852) 99 He discerns the full meaning of what had at first fallen idly on his incurious ear.

†**4.** Not minute or careful in estimating; not precise or fastidious; not particular; uncritical; undiscriminating. *Obs.*

1645 BP. HALL *Remedy Discontents* 116 The meek spirit is incurious; and..takes his load from God (as the Camel from his Master) upon his knees. **1648** HERRICK *Hesper.*, *Wake*, Players..Base in action as in clothes; Yet with strutts they will please The incurious villages. **1728** VANBR. & CIB. *Prov. Husb.* Epil., The greatest Blessing Heav'n e'er sent, Is in a Spouse, Incurious and Content. **1749** *Power Pros. Numbers* 5 Many modern Writers..are so very incurious in this Point, that provided there be Grammar and Thought they seem concerned for nothing else.

II. Objectively.

†**5.** Not carefully or exquisitely prepared, made, composed, or done; plain, homely, coarse.

1608–33 BP. HALL *Medit. & Vows, Love Christ* §10 Canst Thou, O blessed Saviour, be so taken with the incurious and homely features of thy faithful ones? *Ibid.*, *Sight Raven* (1851) 74 No doubt, Elijah's stomach was often up before that his incurious diet came. **1615** T. ADAMS *Black Devil* 47 It [the house] is not sluttish, for it is swept; it is not incurious, for it is garnished. **1691** tr. *Emilianne's Frauds Rom. Monks* 114 The Angel-Limner must have been but a Blockhead and Bungler at his Art, to draw such rude and incurious Stroaks. **1824** DIBDIN *Libr. Comp.* 535 This solid piece of not incurious Sculpture.

†**6.** Not elaborate, or abstruse; simple. *Obs.*

1664 JER. TAYLOR *Dissuas. Popery* 21 They establish no doctrine, neither curious nor incurious.

7. Unworthy of careful notice, not remarkable, uninteresting, deficient in interest; not curious. (Esp. in negative forms of expression.)

1747 GOULD *Eng. Ants* 71 The Manner of the Process is not incurious. **1776** TWISS *Tour Irel.* 71 The inscriptions.. have never been published, and are not incurious. **1824** DIBDIN *Libr. Comp.* 589 The author of several very rare and not incurious pieces of poetry.

incuriously (ɪn'kjʊərɪəslɪ), *adv.* [f. prec. + -LY².] In an incurious manner; carelessly; without care, concern, or close attention.

1603 FLORIO *Montaigne* III. xiii, These..who so slackly and incuriously receive their good fortune. **1654** H. L'ESTRANGE *Chas. I* (1655) 56 Subize..surprised the Isle of Rhe, then incuriously guarded. **1735–8** BOLINGBROKE *On Parties* xix. (T.), In such an age..public accounts [will be] rarely or incuriously inspected. **1874** SYMONDS *Sk. Italy & Greece* (1898) I. i. 18 You take it for a stone cross..and you pass it by incuriously.

incuriousness (ɪn'kjʊərɪəsnɪs). [f. as prec. + -NESS.] The quality of being incurious; = INCURIOSITY 1.

1610 BP. HALL *Apol. Brownists* §6 Maruell at this silent and sociable incuriousnesse. **1649** JER. TAYLOR *Gt. Exemp.* III. xv. 83 Jesus found his apostles asleep, gently chiding their incuriousnesse. **1751** CHESTERF. *Lett.* (1792) III. cclxvii. 222 How many are there..who, from laziness, inattention, and incuriousness, will not so much as ask for it. **1877** R. F. BURTON in *Athenæum* 3 Nov. 569/1 Signor Romolo Gessi..neglected, with true unscientific incuriousness, to land at the southernmost extremity.

incurl, variant of ENCURL *v.*

in-curl ('ɪnkɜːl). *Curling.* [f. IN *adv.* + CURL *sb.*] = INTURN *sb.* 4.

1903 *Westm. Gaz.* 31 Jan. 3/1 The secret of the game is to be able to play the 'out-curl or in-curl' as the skip may direct.

†**in'curment.** *Obs. rare.* [f. INCUR + -MENT.] The action of incurring.

1647 M. HUDSON *Div. Right Govt.* II. iv. 90 The voluntary incurment of a more criminous guilt. *Ibid.* x. 159 The incurment of the guilt of damnation.

incurrable (ɪn'kɜːrəb(ə)l), *a.* [f. INCUR + -ABLE.] Liable to be incurred.

1812 L. HUNT in *Examiner* 11 May 290/1 Hardships incurrable from a dispute between this country and America.

incurrage, obs. form of ENCOURAGE.

incurrence (ɪn'kʌrəns). [f. INCURRENT: see -ENCE.] The action or fact of incurring: **a.** The

entrance of sensations or impressions. **b.** The running into liabilities.

a **1656** BP. HALL *Wks.* (1837–9) V. 421 (D.) No more.. than we can open our eyes at noon-day without an incurrence and admission of an outward light. **1659** STANLEY *Hist. Philos.* XI. (1701) 465/2 Cogitation is made by incurrence of Images. **1831** MRS. GORE in *Fraser's Mag.* IV. 14 Further expenditure forced upon her incurrence. **1892** *Current Hist.* (Detroit) Dec. 226/1 A barrier against the incurrence of new or altered foreign complications.

incurrent (ɪnˈkʌrənt), *a.* [ad. L. *incurrent-em*, pres. pple. of *incurrĕre* to run in: see INCUR and -ENT.] Running in; penetrating into the interior; †falling within (a period).

1563–87 FOXE *A. & M.* (1684) 824/1 Seeing we have comprehended.. the most principal matters in his time incurrent. **1851–6** WOODWARD *Mollusca* 139 *Ampullaria globosa*,.. Animal with a long incurrent syphon, formed by the left neck-lappet. **1884** *Stud. Biol. Lab. Johns Hopkins* III. 39 Running down the middle of the triangular plate is the central string of tissue, the rachis, and at its end the incurrent blood-vessel.

†**inˈcursant**, *a. Obs. rare*⁻¹. [ad. L. *incursānt-em*, pres. pple. of *incursāre*, freq. of *incurrĕre* to run in.] (?) Running into each other, meeting.

1657 TOMLINSON *Renou's Disp.* 401* The stone Amiantus, which consists of many incursant Lines.

†**incurˈsation.** *Obs. rare.* [ad. late L. *incursātiōn-em*, n. of action f. *incursā-re*: see prec.] = INCURSION.

1659 H. MORE *Immort. Soul* III. x. (1662) 186 Taking away this Panick fear of the incursations and molestations of these Aëreal Inhabitants.

†**incurse.** *Obs. rare.* [ad. L. *incurs-us*, f. ppl. stem of *incurrĕre* to INCUR: cf. INCOURSE.]

1. = INCURSION 2.

1543–4 *Act 35 Hen. VIII*, c. 12 The same Scottes.. make diuers and sundry incurses, inuasions.. and depopulations in this his realme. **1597** *Sc. Acts Jas. VI* (1816) IV. 163/2 The samyn landis and Iles wilbe in perrell and hazard of Incurss of the hieland and brokin men. **1642** R. CARPENTER *Experience* II. xi. 219 Every sally or incurse of Temptation.

2. The running of anything into another, so as to join or fall into it.

1578 BANISTER *Hist. Man.* I. 15 Through which hole, a braunch of the viij conjugation taketh direct incurse into these Muscles.

incursion (ɪnˈkɜːʃən). Also 6 incurtion, incourcion, encursion. [ad. L. *incursiōn-em*, n. of action f. *incurrĕre* to INCUR: cf. F. *incursion* (14th c. in Hatz.-Darm.).]

1. The action of running in or of running against.

1615 CROOKE *Body of Man* 174 As the winde it passeth and repasseth at his pleasure, vnseene, but not vnfelt; for the force and incursion thereof is not without a kinde of violence. **1678** CUDWORTH *Intell. Syst.* I. v. 761 The Democriticks and Epicureans did.. suppose, all humane Cogitations to be Caused.. by the Incursion of Corporeal Atoms upon the Thinker. **1760** JOHNSON *Idler* No. 103 ¶8 The inevitable incursion of new images. **1885** *Law Times* LXXX. 133/2 The cargo was damaged by the incursion of sea-water through a hole in a pipe.

2. A hostile inroad or invasion; esp. one of sudden and hasty character; a sudden attack.

1432–50 tr. *Higden* (Rolls) I. 363 That other is expownede to the incursion of deuelles. **1494** FABYAN *Chron.* v. lxxxiii. 61 And the Saxons.. shuld defende the lande from Incursion of all Enemyes. **1555** W. WATREMAN *Fardle Facions* Pref. 8 To auoied the inuasion of beastes, and menne of straunge borders.. with commune aide to withstande suche encursions. **1591** HORSEY *Trav.* (Hakluyt Soc.) 158 He had continuall warrs with the Crimme Tartor, who did sore anoye him.. with their yearly incourcions. **1671** MILTON *P.R.* III. 301 Against the Scythian, whose incursions wild Haue wasted Sogdiana. **1776** GIBBON *Decl. & F.* (1869) I. i. 20 Their incursions were frequently repelled and chastised. **1828** SCOTT *F.M. Perth* xiv, There had been repeated incursions of the Highlanders into the very town of Perth. **1885** J. MARTINEAU *Types Eth. Th.* II. 24 The consequences become.. terrible like an incursion of wild beasts.

b. *transf.* and *fig.*

1640 BP. REYNOLDS *Passions* xxviii. 296 It least of all suffers the Incursion of grosser Passions. **1660** JER. TAYLOR *Worthy Commun.* I. v. 103 We give too much way to the daily incursions of the smaller irregularities of our lives. **1700** DRYDEN *Ceyx & Alcyone* 471 To the neighbouring mole she strode, Rais'd there to break th' incursions of the flood. **1794** PALEY *Evid.* II. vi. (1817) 135 The sudden and critical incursion of the disease. **1860** TYNDALL *Glac.* I. iv. 34 An embankment.. to defend the land from the incursions of the river.

†**c.** *sins of daily incursion*: the small sins which make daily inroads upon a holy life. Cf. quot. 1660 in b. *Obs.*

a **1655** VINES *Lord's Supp.* (1677) 236 Quotidian sins of daily incursion. **1709** *Brit. Apollo* II. No. 67. 1/1 Lesser Miscarriages.. stil'd by the Casuists, Sins of Daily Incursion are Inseparable to Frail Mortality. **1737** WATERLAND *Eucharist* 558 Sins of daily Incursion, such as are ordinarily consistent with a prevailing Love of God, and Love of our Neighbour.

†**3.** The action of incurring (blame or liability).

1610 HEALEY *St. Aug. Citie of God* XV. xv. (1620) 521 Who dare affirme how many they were, without incursion of rashnes?

inˈcursionist. [f. INCURSION + -IST, after *excursionist*.] One who makes an incursion or inroad; an invader. (*Humorous.*)

1883 *Blackw. Mag.* July 111 To be hunted from post to pillar in one's own house by surging floods of independent incursionists. **1892** *Illustr. Lond. News* 17 Sept. 374/1 These incursionists will leave some of their cash to fructify in British pockets. **1898** W. P. GARRISON *New Gulliver* 33 The building.. contained.. along with skeletons of the monkey incursionists, others of the Yahoos.

incursive (ɪnˈkɜːsɪv), *a.* [f. L. *incurs-*, ppl. stem of *incurrĕre* to run in + -IVE.] Given to making incursions; aggressive, invasive.

1592 R. D. *Hypnerotomachia* 66 Shee is malignant, frowarde, disdainefull, with unstable incursyve passions. **1771** GOLDSM. *Hist. Eng.* IV. 61 The forces he had to combat were incursive, barbarous, and shy. *a* **1774** —— *Surv. Exp. Philos.* (1776) II. 331 All the parts oppose their united repelling power, to meet the incursive rays. **1880** *Time* II. 159 In the good old times of feud and petty incursive warfare.

incurtain, -teyn, obs. var. of ENCURTAIN *v.*

incurvate (ɪnˈkɜːvət), *ppl. a.* [ad. L. *incurvāt-us*, pa. pple. of *incurvāre* to INCURVE.] = INCURVED.

1647 H. MORE *Song of Soul* II. App. xc, Their [comets'] widend beards this aire so broad doth strow Incurvate. **17..** *Hue & Cry Dr. S—ft* in Somers *Tracts* I. 390 How does Man (a tender Twig) grow stubborn, incurvate, deformed. **1776–88** J. LEE *Introd. Bot.* Explan. Terms 380 The trunk or stem.. Direction.. *Incurvatus*, incurvate, bending inwards. **1846** DANA *Zooph.* (1848) 578 Large.. spreading ramose, incurvate.

incurvate (ɪnˈkɜːveɪt, ˈɪn-), *v.* [f. L. *incurvāt-*, ppl. stem of *incurvāre* to INCURVE. App. first in pa. pple., f. as prec. + -ED.]

1. *trans.* To bring into a curved shape; to bend from a straight line or form; to curve, to crook; now, *spec.*, to bend or curve inwards.

1578 BANISTER *Hist. Man* I. 34 Obliquely stretching and incurvated. **1623** COCKERAM *Eng. Dict.* II, To *Bow*, Incuruate, Incline. **1650** BULWER *Anthropomet.* 190 By their constant and foolish Fasciation.. the Bones may be incurvated. **1714** DERHAM *Astro-Theol.* I. ii. *note*, A Micrometer.. which would incurvate the rays one way. **1822–34** *Good's Study Med.* (ed. 4) III. 438 The muscles are thrown into a rigid and permanent spasm, not incurvating the body as in.. tetanus.

fig. **1643** SIR T. BROWNE *Relig. Med.* I. §42 Age doth not rectifie, but incurvate our natures. **1691** E. TAYLOR *Behmen's Theos. Phil.* 64 Decorateth or incurvateth his Mind towards Good or Evil.

†**2.** *intr.* To take or have a curved form; to curve, to bend or bow. *Obs.*

1647 LILLY *Chr. Astrol.* xvi. 99 The Body.. not very straight, but incurvating somewhat with the Head. *a* **1697** AUBREY *Lives, Denham* (1898) I. 220 He was of the tallest, but a little incurvetting at his shoulders.

incurvated (ɪnˈkɜːveɪtɪd), *ppl. a.* [f. prec. + -ED¹.] Bent into, or having, a curved form; curved, crooked; *spec.* curved inwards.

1665 MANLEY *Grotius' Low C. Warres* 310 Fortified with a strong incurvated Rampire. **1755** B. MARTIN *Mag. Arts & Sc.* 320 A long incurvated Glass-tube. **1776** CAVALLO in *Phil. Trans.* LXVI. 408 The cord of the incurvated string. **1822–34** *Good's Study Med.* (ed. 4) I. 72 In extreme debility and emaciation, with stiff incurvated limbs.

incurvation (ɪnkɜːˈveɪʃən). [ad. L. *incurvātiōn-em*, n. of action from *incurvāre* to INCURVE.]

1. The action or process of bringing into or assuming a curved form; curving, bending; with *pl.* an instance of this.

1608 HIERON *Defence* III. 156 All incurvation and bowing of the body unto Images. **1612–15** BP. HALL *Contempl., O.T.* XXI. v, That so stiffens the knees of Mordecai that death is more easie to him then their incurvation. **1713** DERHAM *Phys.-Theol.* v. ii. 326 Firmly braced with Muscles and Tendons, for easy incurvations of the Body. **1831** BREWSTER *Newton* (1855) I. vii. 152 The incurvation or bending of a ray of light, incident on such a surface.

†**b.** *spec.* Bowing in reverence or worship. *Obs.*

1607 *Schol. Disc. agst. Antichr.* II. v. 7 Must incurvation towards the East be still continued? **1664** H. MORE *Myst. Iniq.* I. xi. 36 Thou shalt not doe the service of Incurvation, nor any other Religious service to them. **1702** C. MATHER *Magn. Chr.* IV. ii. (1852) 48 It is a peice of cabalistical magic to make an incurvation at the sound of this name.

2. The condition of being bent; curved formation, curvature; an instance of this, a curve or bend.

1647 H. MORE *Song of Soul* II. App. lxxxv, How can the suns rays that be transmisse Through these loose knots in Comets, well expresse Their beards or curld tayls utmost incurvation? **1697** POTTER *Antiq. Greece* III. iv. (1715) 42 The Incurvation of the Scythian Bow, which.. was so great as to form a Half-Moon. **1797** *Monthly Mag.* III. 222 In the incurvation of the spine. **1802–3** tr. *Pallas's Trav.* (1812) I. 179 Extending nearly in a straight line.. without following the incurvations. **1885** GOODALE *Phys. Bot.* (1892) 346 The incurvation [of the leaf] lasts for only a day or two.

fig. **1660** FULLER *Mixt Contempl.* (1841) 168 Some will say that the weight of heavy taxes have caused this crookedness .. Our mutual malice and animosities.. have caused this incurvation. **1765** BLACKSTONE *Comm.* I. ii. 172 *note*, The incurvations of practice are then the most notorious, when compared with the rectitude of the rule.

3. A curving inwards, or the condition of being curved inwards.

1822–34 *Good's Study Med.* (ed. 4) II. 58 It [whitlow] is also occasioned by an incurvation of the nails. **1866** A. FLINT *Princ. Med.* (1880) 202 Bulbous enlargement of the ends of the fingers, with incurvation of the nails, forming what are called clubbed fingers. **1875** DARWIN *Insectiv. Pl.* xvi. 372 There was decided incurvation.

incurvature (ɪnˈkɜːvətjʊə(r)). *rare.* [f. L. *incurvāt-*, ppl. stem of *incurvāre* to INCURVE: cf. L. *curvātūra* curvature, and see -URE.] A curving inwards; an inward curvature or bend.

1809 KENDALL *Trav.* I. ii. 8 Its actual sea-board is rendered much more considerable, by the incurvatures of small bays and inlets. **1888** *Nature* 9 Aug. 359/1 The greater incurvature of the wind in rear than in front of hurricanes in the Southern Indian Ocean.

incurve (ɪnˈkɜːv), *v.* [ad. L. *incurvā-re* to bend in, bow, crook, curve, f. *in-* (IN-²) + *curvāre* to crook, bend, CURVE, *curvus* crooked, bent.]

1. *trans.* To bend into a curved form, to curve (= INCURVATE *v.* 1); in mod. use, To curve or bend (something) inwards.

1610 HOLLAND *Camden's Brit.* I. 651 The Sea now retyring South-ward: and with a mighty Compasse and sundry baies incurving the shores. **1660** J. LLOYD *Prim. Episc.* 51 Come.. to the Cup of his blood, not entending thy hands, but incurving them. **1735** SOMERVILLE *Chase* IV. 426 Yon hollow Trunk, That with its hoary Head incurv'd salutes The passing Wave. **1866** NEALE *Sequences & Hymns* 146 The mountains, incurving themselves round the City. **1880** in *Nature* XXI. 357 The steel having been violently rent and incurved.

2. *intr.* To take or have a curved form; to curve or bend inwards.

1704 GREW *Museum* (L.), Towards its extremity the spine protrudes, and afterwards incurves. **1848** CLOUGH *Amours de Voyage* III. 301 Those fair open fields that incurve to thy beautiful hollow.

Hence **inˈcurving** *vbl. sb.* and *ppl. a.*

1865 *Intell. Observ.* No. 47. 339 The spiral incurving of the wind. **1880** WARREN *Book-plates* iv. 31 The incurving of the shell-work. **1884** *Science* Jan. 42 To find the direction of the storm-centre, we must know the incurving angle of the wind's spiral.

incurve (ˈɪnkɜːv), *sb.* [f. INCURVE *v.*] In baseball and softball, the bending or curving of a ball inwards (i.e. across the front of the batter); the course of such a ball; a ball pitched so as to curve to the right.

1886 H. CHADWICK *Art of Pitching & Fielding* 14 It is essential to change the direction of the curve from an 'out-curve' to an 'in-curve'. **1906** *Spalding's Base Ball Guide* 112 An In-curve.. is a ball which curves in towards the batsman as he stands in his position. **1949** M. WADLOW in Smalley & Dennis *Official Softball—Track & Field Guide* 17 To throw an incurve, the ball is held in the same manner as for the fast ball.

incurved (ɪnˈkɜːvd), *ppl. a.* [f. INCURVE *v.* + -ED¹. Taken as representing L. *incurvus* bent, crooked.] Bent into or having a curved form; curved, crooked; in mod. use, Curved or bent inwards, having an inward curvature. (Now chiefly in *Zool.* and *Bot.*)

1623 COCKERAM, *Incurued*, bowed. **1763** WOLFE in *Phil. Trans.* LIV. 95 They have all sharp black incurved claws. **1816** W. SMITH *Strata Ident.* 22 This thick Strata contains large incurved oysters. **1826** KIRBY & SP. *Entomol.* III. xxxi. 253 The head projects into a long incurved obtuse horn. **1852** DANA *Crust.* I. 252 The spiniform teeth.. a little incurved. **1879** LUBBOCK *Sci. Lect.* i. 5 In the genus Pinguicula.. the leaves are concave with incurved margins. **1880** *Daily News* 3 Nov. 3/8 The incurved varieties [of chrysanthemums] from China. **1895** *Ibid.* 4 Nov. 3/3 The classes for cut flowers comprised Japanese, incurved, reflexed, anemone, and pompon anemone varieties.

incurvetting: see INCURVATE *v.* 2, quot. 1697.

†**inˈcurvity.** *Obs.* [f. L. *incurv-us* bent, crooked + -ITY: cf. L. *curvitās* crookedness, CURVITY.] The quality of being incurved; inward curvature.

1646 SIR T. BROWNE *Pseud. Ep.* v. ii. 235 Men best expressed their velocity by incurvity, and under some figure of a bowe. **1668–9** —— *Wks.* (1848) III. 512 The little incurvitie at the upper end of the upper bill, and small recurvitie of the lower.

‖**incus** (ˈɪŋkəs). *Anat.* and *Zool.* [L. *incūs*, *incūd-em* anvil, f. *incūd-ĕre*: see INCUSE *v.*²]

1. The middle one of the three small bones of the ear (*malleus*, *incus*, and *stapes*), to which the sonorous vibrations are conveyed from the *malleus* or 'hammer': = ANVIL 3 b.

1669 HOLDER *Elem. Speech* 162 The Malleus lies along fixed to the Tympanum; and on the other end is joyned to the Incus by a double or Ginglymoid joynt. **1787** HUNTER in *Phil. Trans.* LXXVII. 434 The incus is attached by a small process to the tympanum, and is suspended between the malleus and stapes. **1856** TODD & BOWMAN *Phys. Anat.* II. 70 The incus is shaped not unlike a molar tooth.

2. A part of the 'trophi' or mouth-apparatus in *Rotifera*, upon which the two mallei work.

1877 HUXLEY *Anat. Inv. Anim.* iv. 188 The contraction of the muscular masses, to which the mallei are attached, causes the free ends of the latter to work backwards and forwards upon the incus. **1888** ROLLESTON & JACKSON *Anim. Life* 633 The mouth [in Rotifera] leads into an œsophagus, followed.. usually directly by a muscular pharynx or mastax containing the chitinous jaw-apparatus or 'trophi'. These consist of two hammer-like bodies, the mallei, which work

against an incus or anvil.. The incus [consists] of two pieces, rami, borne upon a single piece, the fulcrum.

incuse (ɪn'kju:z), *a.* and *sb.* [ad. L. *incūs-us*, pa. pple. of *incūdĕre*: see INCUSE *v.*[2] The sb. use corresponds to F. *incuse* (1692 in Hatz.-Darm.).]

A. *adj.* Hammered or stamped in: said of a figure or impression upon a coin or the like.

1818 R. P. KNIGHT *Symbolic Lang.* (1876) 64 In the centre of an incuse square. **1825-7** HONE *Every-day Bk.* II. 497 The carving is incuse. **1879** LUBBOCK in *19th Cent.* VI. 795 On the one side is an incuse square or punch mark. **1886** *Athenæum* 27 Mar. 426/3 Mr. T. Jones communicated a paper on the rare didrachm with the owl on the obverse and incuse square diagonally divided on the reverse.

B. *sb.* A figure stamped in; an impression in intaglio upon a coin, etc.

1818 R. P. KNIGHT *Symbolic Lang.* (1876) 63 Antiquaries have supposed this incuse to be merely the impression of something put under the coin to make it receive the stroke of the die more steadily. **1868** G. STEPHENS *Runic Mon.* II. 508 The incuse is visible on the back, and this is occasionally a great help when a particular rune has been injured on the front, for we can thus trace it more or less sharply on the other side, so leaflike is the metal. **1879** H. PHILLIPS *Notes Coins* 7 The head of Proserpine in an incuse surrounded by dolphins.

†**incuse**, *v.*[1] *Obs. rare*$^{-0}$. [ad. L. *incūsāre* to accuse, find fault with, f. *in-* (IN-[2]) + *causa* occasion, CAUSE, *causārī* to take occasion of, plead, debate: cf. ACCUSE *v.*] To accuse. So †**incusation**, accusation.

1570 LEVINS *Manip.* 195/5 To incuse, *incusare.* **1623** COCKERAM, *Incusation*, blaming. **1658** PHILLIPS, *Incusation*, a blaming or accusing.

incuse (ɪn'kju:z), *v.*[2] [f. L. *incūs-*, ppl. stem of *incūd-ĕre* to forge with the hammer, work on the anvil (*incūs*).] *trans.* To impress by stamping; to mark with an impressed figure. Chiefly in pa. pple. (or ppl. adj.) **in'cused**.

1864 in WEBSTER. **1876** HUMPHREYS *Coin-Coll. Man.* iv. 37 The reverse is incused with the impress of an amphora. **1879** H. PHILLIPS *Addit. Notes Coins* 13 There are specimens of Sybaris and Metapentum, in Magna Grecia, known as the *incused coinage*.

†**incuss**, *v. Obs.* Also 6 *Sc.* incus. [f. L. *incuss-*, ppl. stem of *incutĕre* to strike into, strike upon, INCUTE, f. *in-* (IN-[2]) + *quatĕre* to shake, strike, dash. Cf. CONCUSS, DISCUSS.] *trans.* To strike in, impress; to strike (terror, etc.) into the mind; to inspire a person with (some feeling).

1527 *St. Papers Hen. VIII*, I. 280 Whereby no litle terrour and feare shalbe incussed unto thEmperialles. **1533** BELLENDEN *Livy* 88 (Jam.) That he micht incus be his deith the samin terroure to the Latinis. **1613** DANIEL *Coll. Hist. Eng.* 11 The first events are those which incussed a dauntingnesse or daring.

†**in'cussion**. *Obs. rare.* Also 7 *erron.* incusion. [ad. L. *incussiōn-em*, n. of action from *incutĕre*: see INCUSS *v.*] A striking or dashing against something; collision, impact.

1615 CROOKE *Body of Man* 591 The better to resist outward injuries and violent incusions of the ayre. **1658** PHILLIPS, *Incussion*, a violent shaking, or dashing against any thing. [In ed. 1706 marked *Obs.*]

incut ('ɪnkʌt), *ppl. a.* [f. IN *adv.* 11 b + CUT *ppl. a.*] Set in by or as if by cutting; *spec.* in *Printing*, inserted in a space left in the outside of the text instead of in the margin; also called *cut-in*.

1888 JACOBI *Printers' Vocab.*, *Incut notes*, side-notes which are let into the text, instead of being in the margin. **1973** C. BONINGTON *Next Horizon* viii. 114 All the climbing [on the Avon Gorge] is similar: balancing up on sloping holds, using small, incut ledges for hand-holds, [etc.].

†**in'cute**, *v. Obs.* [ad. L. *incut-ĕre* to strike into: see INCUSS *v.*] *trans.* To strike in: = INCUSS.

1542 BECON *Christm. Banq.* in *Early Wks.* (Parker Soc.) 63 This doth incute and beat into our hearts the fear of God. —— *Potat. Lent* ibid. 101 Secondly, it incuteth and beateth into our hearts a shamefacedness, whereby we are so ashamed of our faults.

'**in,cutting**, *vbl. sb. rare.* [See IN *adv.* C. 3.] A cutting in, or the opening made thereby; incision.

1598 FLORIO, *Incisione*, an incision, an incutting, a gash [etc.]. **1611** COTGR., *Taillé d' espargne*, ..the incutting being filled with enamell, and the work set out, or appearing among it, in gold &c.

incypyent, obs. (erron.) form of INSIPIENT.

incyse, obs. form of INCISE.

in'cysted, obs. form of ENCYSTED. So †**in'cystated** in same sense (cf. ENCYSTATION).

1728 RUTTY in *Phil. Trans.* XXXV. 565 This Tumour proved a Congeries of incystated Abcesses..of different Sizes. **1738** A. STUART *Ibid.* XL. 328 Small incysted pultaceous and cretaceous Tumours. **1791** HOME *Ibid.* LXXXI. 97 All preceded by the same kind of incysted tumours.

Ind (ɪnd). Forms: 3-6 Ynde, (4 Yngde), 4-9 Inde, 5 Yende, Ynd, 7- Ind. [a. F. *Inde*:—L. *India* (cf. *Afric*, *Greece*): see INDIA.]

1. An earlier name of the country now called INDIA; sometimes applied to Asia or the East. Now *archaic* and *poetic*.

a **1225** *Ancr. R.* 342 Deorewurðe ouer alle gold hordes, and ouer alle ȝimstones of ynde. **13..** *K. Alis.* 4843 In the londe of Ynde thou mighth lere Nyne thousynde folk of selcouth manere. *c* **1386** CHAUCER *Clerk's T.* 1143 And sklendre wyues, fieble as in bataille, Beth egre as is a tygre yond in Ynde. **1519** *Interl. Four Elem.*, This sayde north parte is callyd Europa And this south parte callyd affrica This eest parte is callyd ynde But this newe landes founde lately Ben callyd america. **1535** COVERDALE *1 Macc.* vi. 37 Euery Elephante was couered with a stronge tower of wod ..& within it was a man of Inde to rule the beest. **1621** QUARLES *Div. Poems, Esther* 1, Whose Kingdome was to East, and West confin'd, And stretcht from Ethiopia unto Ind. **1821** BYRON *Sardan.* I. ii. 151 Who conquer'd this same golden realm of Ind. **1823** —— *Juan* XII. ix, From Ceylon, Inde, or far Cathay. **1871** R. ELLIS *Catullus* xi. 2 Whether your Catullus attain to farthest Ind.

†**b.** *pl.* (Cf. INDIES.) *Obs.*

c **1400** *Three Kings Cologne* 40 þer be iij. Indes of þe whyche þes iij. lordes were kynges; and all þes londes & kyngdoms for þe more partye be yles. **1558** W. WARDE tr. *Alexis' Secr.* I. 108 b (Stanf.) Dowe or paste of Borace.. broughte lately oute of the Indes.

c. With qualification = (East or West) Indies; formerly also the *less* and the *great Ind* = Hindustan and the East Indies or the East generally.

c **1375** *Sc. Leg. Saints, Thomas* 441 In hest [= highest; L. *superiorem*] ynde, or he fane, he went, & þar throw ferlys schan. *c* **1400** MAUNDEV. *Trav.* Prol. (Roxb.) 3 Thurgh.. Amazon, Inde þe lesse and þe mare, a grete party. *c* **1450** CAMPEDEN *Sidrac* in Warton *Hist. Eng. Poetry* (1840) II. 306 *note*, His londe lay be grete Inde, Bectorye hight hit as we fynde. **1600** SHAKS. *A.Y.L.* III. ii. 93 From the east to westerne Inde No iewel is like Rosalinde.

†**2.** *pl.* Indians, natives of India. *Obs.*

c **1380** WYCLIF *Sel. Wks.* III. 341 Jewis and Sarasynes, Grekis and Yngdis. **1398** TREVISA *Barth. De P.R.* XVIII. xli. (MS. Bodl.), The Elephaunte hatte Elephas..but þe Indes [**1495** Yndes] clepiþ hym Barro. *c* **1400** tr. *Secreta Secret.*, *Gov. Lordsh.* (E.E.T.S.) 67 Of whom of philosophers þe bigynnynge of Philosophye hadden Indes, Grecys, Percys and latyns. **1526** *Pilgr. Perf.* (W. de W. 1531) 37 What sholde be the ende of the warre..bytwene hym and the yndes.

†**3.** The Indian language. *Obs. rare.*

a **1400-50** *Alexander* 5012 Scho begynes all in grew & endis in ynde.

4. *attrib.* and *Comb.*

1430-40 LYDG. *Bochas* IX. xxxviii. 217 b, Inde stones vpon their golden tresses. **1433** —— *St. Edmund* I. 873 Of gold and stonys ynde. **1856** MRS. BROWNING *Aur. Leigh* V. Poems 1890 VI. 189 An Ind-born man.

ind, indigo: see INDE.

ind-, *Chem.*: see INDI-, INDO-.

-ind, -inde, obs. ME. ending of pres. pple.: see -ING[2].

‖**indaba** (ɪn'dɑ:bə). [Zulu *in-daba* subject, topic, matter, affair, business, doing, f. nominal inflex *in-* + stem *daba* (pl. *izin-daba* affairs, communications, news).] A communication or transaction of affairs, a conference or consultation between or with South African natives.

1894 *Pall Mall G.* 26 Dec. 3/2 A message was therefore conveyed..to the King, inviting Umtassa to come in to an indaba at Umtali. **1896** *Westm. Gaz.* 30 Mar. 5/1 They will then attack Gimgem's kraal, where the chief Ulimo is holding an indaba, or consultation. **1896** *Daily News* 31 Aug. 3/1 The Indunas, after the final indaba, returned to the hills with the professed intention of consulting their brethren.

†**inda'gacious**, *a. Obs. rare.* [f. stem of L. *indāgā-re* (see next) + -ACIOUS.] Given to search or investigation.

1653 R. SANDERS *Physiogn.* 270 The business requires that we be indagacious and exact in the least punct of the measure thereof.

indagate ('ɪndəgeɪt), *v.* ? *Obs.* [f. L. *indāgāt-*, ppl. stem of *indāgāre* to trace out, search into, investigate.] *trans.* To search into, investigate.

1623 COCKERAM, *Indagate*, to search. **1633** J. FOSBROKE *Six Serm.* Ep. Ded., To indigate and search out the drift and scope of the Spirit of God. **1677** CARY *Chronol.* II. i, I. xiii. 126 How from them should we indagate the time of his Expulsion? **1829** LANDOR *Wks.* (1846) I. 470/1 We talk of indagating, of investigating. **1867** MUSGRAVE *Nooks Old France* I. ix. 293 They indagate the history of a hundred and fifty years.

indagation (ɪndə'geɪʃən). ? *Obs.* [ad. L. *indāgātion-em*, n. of action f. *indāgāre*: see prec.; cf. It. *indagatione* (Florio).] The action of searching or tracking out; investigation.

1589 NASHE *Anat. Absurd.* 38 The indagation of the truth. **1590** BARROUGH *Meth. Physick* (1639) Pref. 1 The painfull indagation of the secrets of nature. **1664** EVELYN *Sylva* 95 See also with what accurateness the Society constantly proceeds in all their Indagations, and Experiments. **1772** NUGENT tr. *Hist. Friar Gerund* II. 341 Having mocked our most diligent and exquisite indagation. **1839** BAILEY *Festus* xix. (1848) 200 By indagation of supremest spheres Material and spiritual.

†**indagative**, *a.* ? *Obs.* [f. L. *indāgāt-* (see INDAGATE) + -IVE.] Characterized by searching or investigating; in quot., inclined to seek.

1642 JER. TAYLOR *Episc.* §49 The Church might not be ambitious, or indagative of such imployment.

indagator ('ɪndəgeɪtə(r)). Now *rare.* [a. L. *indāgātor*, agent-n. from *indāgāre* to INDAGATE; cf. obs. F. *indagateur* (Cotgr.).] A searcher, investigator, inquirer.

1620 VENNER *Via Recta* iii. 62 Not sensible, but to the curious Indagator and Obseruer of things. **1653** H. MORE *Conject. Cabbal.* (1662) 155 To pretend to be more accurate Indagators into matters of Religion. **1742** YOUNG *Nt. Th.* v. 748 Awake, ye curious indagators! fond Of knowing all, but what avails you known. **1849** JEFFREY *Let.* in Cockburn *Life* II. ccvii, Unreadable for all but the indefatigable indagators of transcendental truths. **1884** *Athenæum* 9 Feb. 187/3 Being too extensive and obstructed for a solitary non-resident indagator.

indagatory ('ɪndəgeɪtərɪ), *a. rare.* [f. L. *indāgāt-* (see INDAGATE) + -ORY.] Pertaining to or of the nature of investigation.

1855 G. MUSGRAVE *Ramble Normandy* 312 In classical studies, their [the Germans'] indagatory research and laborious analysis have long since placed them in the first rank of Scholiasts. **1861** —— *By-Roads* 285.

†**inda'gatrix**. *Obs. rare.* In 7 indig-. (Cf. quot. 1633 in INDAGATE *v.*) [a. L. *indāgātrix*, fem. of *indāgātor*.] A female searcher or investigator.

1653 R. SANDERS *Physiogn.* 269 The soul, the indigatrix of all things.

indaign, variant of INDEIGN *v. Obs.*

indamage, -dammage, obs. var. ENDAMAGE.

indamine ('ɪndəmi:n). *Chem.* [f. IND(O-[2] + AMINE.] A blue dye, $NH_2 \cdot C_6H_4 \cdot N$: C_6H_4:NH (also called *phenylene blue*); also, any of the derivatives of this compound, which form a group of blue and green dyes now important only as intermediates for safranine dyes.

1888 *Jrnl. Chem. Soc.* LIV. 949 (*heading*) Indamines and indophenols. **1903** C. SALTER tr. *G. von Georgievics's Chem. Dye-Stuffs* 265 When di-p.-amidodiphenylamine is oxidised with potassium bichromate, there is formed a blue dye-stuff, known as Indamine or Phenylene Blue... From this are derived a whole group of dye-stuffs, which are, therefore, named 'Indamines'. **1961** L. F. & M. FIESER *Adv. Org. Chem.* xxvi. 852 The highly pigmented N-phenyl derivatives of quinonimine and quinonediimine, indophenol and indamine, are relatively stable, crystallizable substances.

indamnifie, obs. form of INDEMNIFY.

indanger, -daunger, obs. var. ENDANGER *v.*

indanthrene ('ɪndənθri:n). Also Indanthren(e. [f. INDO-[2] + ANTHR(A- + -ENE.] **a.** (With lower-case initial.) Indanthrone, $C_{28}H_{14}N_2O_4$ (in quot. 1921 used for the oxygen-free parent compound, $C_{28}H_{18}N_2$: cf. quot. 1920 s.v. INDANTHRONE). **b.** (Usu. with capital initial.) Any of a large and important class of vat dyes derived from or containing indanthrone or other compounds based on the anthraquinone nucleus.

Indanthren(e) has been registered as a proprietary term in Great Britain.

1901 *Trade Marks Jrnl.* 23 Oct. 1063 Indanthrene. **1901** *Jrnl. Soc. Dyers & Colourists* XVII. *facing* p. 302 Indanthrene X is a blue paste insoluble in water. *Ibid.*, Indanthrene S is a coppery coloured paste which is soluble in hot water. **1903** *Jrnl. Chem. Soc.* LXXXIV. I. 446 The substance 'A', of the German Patent 135407,..can be purified by dissolving it in concentrated sulphuric acid and allowing the solution to gradually absorb water; well-formed, blue needles separate which, in the case of 'Indanthrene C', have the composition $C_{28}H_{10}O_4N_2Br_2$, and, in the case of indanthrene itself, the composition $C_{28}H_{12}O_4$ N_2. **1920** [see FLAVANTHRONE]. **1920** [see INDANTHRONE]. **1921** E. DE B. BARNETT *Anthracene & Anthraquinone* xvi. 342 The first cyclic azine of the anthraquinone series to be prepared was *trans. bisang.*-anthraquinonedihydro azine. This was placed on the market under the name Indanthrene Blue, and the name 'indanthrene' has come into general use in the literature. The word ' indanthrene', however, is a registered trade name (B.A.S.F.) and is applied to many vat dyes which are not azines. Indanthrene Blue is an anthraquinone derivative and ketonic in structure, and in order to denote its ketonic nature the name should terminate in -one. In the following pages, therefore, the word 'indanthrone' is used to denote the ketonic hydroazine, indanthrene (without a capital) being used for the parent, oxygen free hydroazine (*trans. bisang.*-dihydroanthrazine). Where 'Indanthrene' is used as a registered trade name it is spelt with a capital. **1922** *Trade Marks Jrnl.* 8 Nov. 2019 Indanthren. **1952** K. VENKATARAMAN *Chem. Synthetic Dyes* II. xxx. 861 With the amalgamation of the German dyemakers into the IG in 1924, Indanthrene was adopted as the group name for vat dyes with the maximum all-round fastness. **1961** [see FLAVANTHRONE]. **1971** R. L. M. ALLEN *Colour Chem.* x. 163 If hydroxyl groups are introduced into the molecule of Indanthren Yellow GK in positions 4 and 8 the shade becomes violet; this product is manufactured as Indanthren Brilliant Violet BBK.

indanthrone ('ɪndənθrəʊn). *Chem.* [f. INDANTHR(ENE + -ONE.] **a.** A blue compound, $C_{28}H_{14}N_2O_4$, which is composed of two anthraquinone nuclei linked by two imino-groups and is the parent compound of an important group of vat dyes. **b.** Any of the derivatives of this compound.

1920 F. A. MASON tr. *G. von Georgievic's Text-bk. Dye Chem.* (ed. 2) 449 Indanthrene (or more correctly *Indanthrone*, which expresses the quinoid character of the compound, whereas the name generally used would correspond to an oxygen-free compound) is a dianthraquinone-dihydroazine. **1921** [see INDANTHRENE]. **1921** E. DE B. BARNETT *Anthracene & Anthraquinone* xvi. 343 By far the most important method of obtaining the indanthrones is by fusing the β-aminoanthraquinones with caustic alkali. **1954** I. L. FINAR *Org. Chem.* (ed. 2) I. xxxi. 689 Indanthrone (Indanthrene Blue R; Bohn, 1901) is prepared by fusing 2-amino-anthraquinone with potassium hydroxide in the presence of potassium chlorate or nitrate at 250°. **1959** *Jrnl. Amer. Chem. Soc.* LXXXI. 3762/2 Strong amide resonance contributes greatly to the resonance hybrid of the indanthrones.

†**in'dare**, *v. Obs. rare.* Also 7 en-. [f. IN-² (= EN-) + DARE *v.*] *trans.* To inspire with daring; to incite, provoke.

1599 *Life More* in Wordsw. *Eccl. Biog.* (1853) II. 139 Considering that if he should there in his owne presence, receaue any overthrowe, it would..indare them to attempt the like or greater matters. **1611** FLORIO, *Inardire*, to endare, to enhardie.

†**in'darken**, variant of ENDARKEN *v.*

1628 FELTHAM *Resolves* II. xxii. 74 As if the breath which the child lost, had disclouded his indarkned heart.

indart (ɪn'dɑːt), *v.* Also 6–7 en-. [f. IN-¹ + DART *v.*] *trans.* To dart in.

1598 SHAKS. *Rom. & Jul.* I. iii. 98 (2nd Qo.) No more deepe will I endart [*so later Qos. and Fos.; ed. Theobald* (1733) indart] mine eye, Then your consent giues strength to make [it] flie. **1882** H. SCOTT HOLLAND *Logic & Life* (1885) 263 In the light of his indarted splendour..evil reveals the full horror of its..deformity.

indazole ('ɪndəzəʊl). *Chem.* [ad. G. *indazol* (Fischer & Kuzel 1883, in *Ann. d. Chem.* CCXXI. 264), f. *indol* INDOLE *sb.*: see AZO- and -OLE.] **a.** A colourless crystalline compound, $C_7H_6N_2$, in which a benzene ring is fused to a pyrazole ring. **b.** Any of the derivatives of this compound.

1884 *Jrnl. Chem. Soc.* XLVI. 441 Indazole crystallises in colourless needles. **1967** KATRITZKY & LAGOWSKI *Princ. Heterocyclic Chem.* 138 Indazole is the trivial name for the benzopyrazole nucleus. *Ibid.* 140 Certain *o*-toluenediazonium salts cyclize spontaneously to indazoles.

†**inde.** *Obs.* Also 4 ind, 4–5 ynde. [a. F. *inde*, AF. *ynde*, ad. L. **indium* = *indicum*, lit. Indian, as subst. indigo.] A blue dye obtained from India, now called INDIGO; the colour of this, or a fabric dyed with it.

a **1300** *Cursor M.* 9920 þe toiþer heu neist for to find, Es al o bleu, men cals Ind [*v.r.* ynde]. *c* **1320** *Cast. Love* 712 Seþþen abouten þat oþer heuȝ So is inde and eke bleu [*orig.* Si rest e ynde, e blui]. **14..** *Anc. Cookery* in *Househ. Ord.* (1790) 434 Colour hit wyth ynde. **1581** *Act 23 Eliz.* c. 9 §3 Grounded..with Woad and Anele, *alias* blue Inde. **1658** [see INDEBAUDIAS below].

b. *attrib.* or as *adj.* Blue. *inde carde*: cf. CARDE *sb.*

1359–60 *Durham Acc. Rolls* (Surtees) II. 384 In duabus peciis de indekarde. **1360–61** *Ibid.* 385 Et in vj vln. de inedecard. *c* **1400** MAUNDEV. (Roxb.) vii. 25 His back es ynde colour. **1433** LYDG. *St. Edmund* Prol. 49 This other standard, feeld stable off colour ynde. **14..** *Voc.* in Wr.-Wülcker 588/23 *Jacinctinus*, ynde colour.

Hence †**indebaudias (Inde Baunias)**, indigo.

1573 *Art of Limming* 4 Indebaudias of it self maketh a darke and sad blacke. **1634** PEACHAM *Gentl. Exerc.* I. xxiii. 80 Take Indebaudias and grinde it with the water of Litmose, if you will have it deepe, but if light, grinde it with fine Ceruse. **1658** PHILLIPS, *Inde*,..a certain Mineral wherwith they use to paint or die of a blew colour, called also Indico. .. It is of two sorts, English Inde, and Inde Baunias.

indear, -ment, obs. var. ENDEAR, -MENT.

indeavour, obs. variant of ENDEAVOUR.

†**inde'bilitate**, *a. Obs. rare*⁻¹. [ad. med.L. *indēbilitāt-us*: see IN-² and DEBILITATE *a.*] Debilitated, enfeebled.

1529 *Will of Prymar* (Somerset Ho.), Indebilitate of body. So †**inde'bilitated** *a.*

1696 W. COWPER in *Phil. Trans.* XIX. 302 Of these extravagant Pains she was much eased,..but never the less continued much indebilitated.

†**in'debt**, *ppl. a. Obs. rare.* In 6 indett, endebt. [Short for INDEBTED; cf. DEBT *ppl. a.*] Indebted.

1504 *Bury Wills* (Camden) 95 All my good ffrendes soullys that I am bownd or indett to pray for. **1642** *Perkins' Prof. Bk.* ii. §180. 79 If a man by his Obligation doth acknowledge himselfe to be endebt unto the Obligee.

in'debt, *v.* Now *rare.* [Inferred from INDEBTED; perh. after F. *endetter* (*endebter*) in same sense.]

1. *trans.* To bring under monetary obligation; to involve in debt. (In quots. *refl.*)

1586 T. B. *La Primaud. Fr. Acad.* (1589) 206 After he had indebted himselfe in seven hundred and fiftie thousand crownes. **1603** HOLLAND *Plutarch's Mor.* 209 One indebteth himselfe for to build a sumptuous and stately house.

2. To bring under an obligation of any kind.

1603 DANIEL *Panegyr.* Wks. (1717) 340 Thy Fortune hath indebted thee to none. *a* **1639** W. WHATELEY *Prototypes* II. xxiv. (1640) 13 Bee they not benefits indebting us to God in many praises? **1672** PENN *Spir. Truth Vind.* 114 We would not indebt our selves to his Favour. **1875** RUSKIN *Fors Clav.* V. lviii. 285 If it borrow at all, it is at least in honour bound to borrow from living men, and not indebt itself to its own unborn brats.

indebted (ɪn'dɛtɪd), *ppl. a.* Forms: α. 3 andetted, 4–6 endetted, (4 -id, 5 -yd); β. 5 indettydd, 6 -detted, 6– indebted. [ME. *endetted*, after OF. *endetté*, pa. pple. of *endetter* to involve in debt, f. *en-* (EN-) + *dette* DEBT *sb.*; cf. Pr. *endeptar*, *-deutar*, Sp. *endeudar*, It. (and med.L.) *indebitāre*. In the 15–16th c. the prefix was assimilated to IN-² and the radical to DEBT *sb.*]

1. Under obligation on account of money borrowed; owing money; in dept.

α. *c* **1386** CHAUCER *Can. Yeom. Prol. & T.* 181 Yit I am endetted so therby Of gold, that I haue borwed trewely. **1422** T. HOSTEL in Ellis *Orig. Lett.* Ser. II. I. 96 He being.. now falle to greet age and poverty: gretly endetted. **1494** FABYAN *Chron.* VII. 653 He..after longe beynge in Westmynster as a seyntwary man..dyed there, beynge greatly endettyd vnto many parsonys. **1542–3** *Act 34 & 35 Hen. VIII*, c. 4 Anie person..endebted to anie such offendour.

β. **1483** *Cath. Angl.* 195/2 Indettydd. **1512** *Act 4 Hen. VIII*, c. 18 §15 Persones so indetted..to be utterly acquyted & discharged therof. **1579–80** NORTH *Plutarch* (1595) 162 Hee beganne to flatter the common people, and specially those that were indebted. **1761–2** HUME *Hist. Eng.* (1806) IV. lxiii. 709 Notwithstanding the supplies voted him, his treasury was still very empty and very much indebted. **1885** TAIT *Prop. Matter* iv. §63. 51 If he over-draws..he is to that amount indebted to the bank.

†**b.** *to be indebted*, to owe (so much).

1601 R. JOHNSON *Kingd. & Commw.* (1603) 17 [He] left his sonnes indebted 30. millions of crownes, and without credite amongst the merchants. **1755** J. SHEBBEARE *Lydia* (1769) II. 292 Jenkin Williams..lent him the money he was indebted. **1784** R. BAGE *Barham Downs* II. 158, I am indebted..to your Lordship an answer. **1797** MARY ROBINSON *Walsingham* III. 187 To this infamous associate I was indebted thirty pounds.

2. Under obligation to another on account of some liability incurred or claim unsatisfied; liable for some omission of duty, an unfulfilled promise, etc.; bound. *Obs.* or *arch.*

a **1225** *Ancr. R.* 126 þu ert andetted touward me swuðe mid sunnen. *c* **1380** WYCLIF *Sel. Wks.* III. 352 Ech man is endettid to God, as ech man is endettid to oþir, to helpe him algatis goostli and bodili. **1557** N. T. (Genev.) *Luke* xi. 4 And forgeue vs our synnes; for euen we forgeue euery man that is indebted to vs. **1575–85** ABP. SANDYS *Serm.* (1841) 202 The flock is indebted to their pastor, to honour and to reverence him as their father. **1608–33** BP. HALL *Medit. & Vows* (1656) 114 When I have promised, I am indebted; and debts may be claimed, must be paid. **1667** MILTON *P.L.* III. 235 He her aide Can never seek, once dead in sins and lost; Attonement for himself or offering meet, Indebted and undon, hath none to bring.

3. Under obligation to another for favours or services received; owing gratitude; beholden.

1561 tr. *Calvin's Foure Godlye Serm.* ii. D v, If we be so endetted and bounde to god. **1590** GREENE *Menaphon* (Arb.) 63 Then, sir, haue I mistooke your honestie, and am lesse indebted to your courtesie. **1660** WILLSFORD *Scales Comm.* Pref. A vij, All the others have nothing to glory in, but how Princes and States are indebted to them. **1777** PRIESTLEY *Matt. & Spir.* (1782) I. xiv. 157 For this observation I am indebted to an ingenious and worthy friend. **1847** MARRYAT *Childr. N. Forest* viii, They were indebted to him for the situation they hold now in the forest.

b. Of things.

1613 PURCHAS *Pilgrimage* (1614) 430 Paulus that renowned Venetian to whom our Relations are so much indebted. **1732** POPE, etc. *Art Sinking* ii. 11 To such as these ..our Art has been often infinitely indebted. **1843** PRESCOTT *Mexico* (1850) I. 54 The Aztec mythology..was much indebted, as I have noticed, to the priests.

indebtedness (ɪn'dɛtɪdnɪs). [f. prec. + -NESS.]

1. The condition of being indebted or in debt.

1828 in WEBSTER. **1848** MILL *Pol. Econ.* II. vi. §2. I. 307 The indebtedness of the proprietors in the flourishing cantons of Zurich 'borders on the incredible'. **1861** GOSCHEN *For. Exch.* 9 It is above all things necessary to form a clear view of what is meant by international indebtedness.

b. The extent to which one is indebted; the sum owed; the actual debt.

1862 SALA *Ship Chandler* (L.), Perhaps..this vast sum is in payment of Master Edward's indebtedness. **1867** *Times* 4 June, The indebtedness of the bankrupt amounted to £1,382. **1889** *Ibid.* (weekly ed.) 27 Dec. 5/4 The indebtedness of the Municipal Corporation of Belfast is only £777,733.

2. The condition of being under obligation for services, etc., rendered.

1647 TRAPP *Exp. Epistles* Ep. Ded. A iij a, To professe my deep indebtednesse unto You, for Your many fatherly favours. **1893** SIR R. BALL *Story of Sun* 26, I am glad to acknowledge my indebtedness to these papers. **1897** MARY KINGSLEY *W. Africa* 9 The indebtedness which all African travellers have to the white residents in Africa.

indebtment (ɪn'dɛtmənt). *rare.* [f. as prec. + -MENT; app. after F. *endettement* (*endebtement*, Cotgr. 1611).] The state of being indebted; indebtedness.

1650 BP. HALL *Balm Gil.* (R.), Fear thou a worse prison if thou wilt needs wilfully liue and dye in a just indebtment, when thou maiest be at once free and honest. **1813** T. JEFFERSON *Writ.* (1830) IV. 198 It is, at the same time, a salutary curb on the spirit of war and indebtment. **1815** *Ibid.* 254, I feel my portion of indebtment to the reverend author. **1862** R. H. PATTERSON *Ess. Hist. & Art* 71 The work of one to whom we love to be indebted, and still more to proclaim our indebtment.

†**in'decence.** *Obs. rare.* [f. INDECENT (see -ENCE): perh. a. F. *indécence* (16th c.).] Unbecomingness, impropriety: = INDECENCY 1.

1714 BURNET *Hist. Ref.* III. Introd. (R.), I was indeed amazed to find a poor harmless woman..so carried to an indecence of barbarity. **1740** tr. *De Mouhy's Fort. Country Maid* (1741) II. 93 To commit such an Indecence. *a* **1797** H. WALPOLE *Mem. Geo. III* (1845) I. viii. 122 Stating to Barré the indecence of treating an infirm and much older man with such licence.

indecency (ɪn'diːsənsɪ). [ad. L. *indecentia*, n. of quality f. *indecent-em*: see next and -ENCY.] The quality of being indecent.

1. Unseemliness, unbecomingness; unbecoming or outrageous conduct.

1589 PUTTENHAM *Eng. Poesie* III. xxiii. (Arb.) 279 As rude and vnciuill speaches carry a marueilous great indecencie, so doe sometimes those that be ouermuch affected and nice. **1650** BULWER *Anthropomet.* 126 An act not only of indecency, but of injustice and ingratitude against God and Nature. **1702** *Eng. Theophrast.* 104 We must not be too familiar with Inferiors by reason of indecency. *a* **1814** LD. N. SPENCER in *Ld. Auckland's Corr.* (1862) III. 261 The indecency of excluding and proscribing the English at the same time that other strangers are received. **1849** MACAULAY *Hist. Eng.* iv. I. 453 The disgrace which the barbarity and indecency of so great a functionary brought upon the administration of justice.

b. With *an* and *pl.* An instance of this; an unbecoming or unseemly action, trait, etc.

1639 FULLER *Holy War* III. ii. (1647) 112 These Bishops.. were fain to descend to many indecencies and indignities to support themselves. **1650** HOBBES *Answ. Pref. Gondibert* Wks. (1840) IV. 454 Of the indecencies of an heroic poem, the most remarkable are those that show disproportion either between the persons and their actions, or between the manners of the poet and the poem. **1675** TRAHERNE *Chr. Ethics* 422 A discontented mind..throws a man into all the indecencies of avarice, ambition [etc.].

†**2.** Uncomeliness of form. *Obs.*

1598 SYLVESTER *Du Bartas* II. II. i. *Ark* 567 Th' unpleasing blemish of deformed marks; As lips too great, or hollownesse of eyes, Or sinking nose, or such indecencies. **1648** HERRICK *Hesper.*, *To Perenna*, When I thy parts runne ore, I can't espie In any one, the least indecencie.

3. A condition which offends against personal delicacy or the recognized standards of propriety; immodesty; a quality savouring of obscenity.

1692 E. WALKER *Epictetus' Mor.* xli, If vain, or frivolous the Converse be, Or seem to savour of Indecency, Alter the Subject. **1779–81** JOHNSON *L.P.*, *Addison* Wks. III. 84 No greater felicity can genius attain than that of having purified intellectual pleasure, separated mirth from in-decency and wit from licentiousness. **1802** J. BOWLES (*title*) Modern Female Manners, as distinguished by In-difference to Character, and Indecency of Dress. **1871** DARWIN *Desc. Man* I. iv. (ed. 2) 119 The hatred of indecency..is a modern virtue.

b. With *an* and *pl.* Something indecent; *esp.* an indecent act, an offence against decency.

1774 WARTON *Hist. Eng. Poetry* xvi. (1840) II. 190 Various freedoms and indecencies unsuitable to the sex. **1790** BEATTIE *Moral Sc.* I. ii. §5 (R.) Profane talkers, lewd jesters, and they who, by speech or writing, present to the ear or to the eye of modesty any of the indecencies I allude to, are pests of society. **1885** *Law Times Rep.* LII. 317/1 That is an indecency which could not have been intended.

indecent (ɪn'diːsənt), *a.* [a. F. *indécent* (14th c.), or ad. L. *indecent-em*, f. *in-* (IN-³) + *decent-* DECENT.]

1. Unbecoming; highly unsuitable or inappropriate (†*to*); contrary to the fitness of things; in extremely bad taste; unseemly.

1563–87 FOXE *A. & M.* (1684) III. 94 It is not..indecent to thy Justice. **1589** PUTTENHAM *Eng. Poesie* III. xxiv. (Arb.) 283 The Philosophers [action was] disproportionable both to his profession and calling and therefore indecent. *a* **1674** CLARENDON *Hist. Reb.* x. §44 This so positive Declaration of the Prince..made all farther Arguments..not only useless but indecent. **1779–81** JOHNSON *Lives*, *Sydenham* Wks. IV. 500 He never betrayed any indecent impatience, or unmanly dejection. **1839** KEIGHTLEY *Hist. Eng.* II. 82 With indecent haste she gave him her hand. **1879** FROUDE *Cæsar* xx. 345 It is indecent to owe money to a political antagonist.

†**2.** Uncomely, inelegant in form. *Obs.*

1590 SPENSER *F.Q.* II. ix. 1 Of all Gods workes..There is no one more faire and excellent, Then is mans body.. Whiles it is kept in sober gouernment; But none then it more fowle and indecent, Distempered through misrule and passions bace. **1671** BLAGRAVE *Astrol. Physic* 77 His thighs lean, his feet and knees indecent. **1705** J. LOGAN in *Pa. Hist. Soc. Mem.* X. 57 To correct that much..would render it too indecent and ungrateful to the eye. **1743** tr. *Heister's Surg.* 190 They usually occasion indecent Cicatrices.

3. Offending against the recognized standards of propriety and delicacy; highly indelicate, immodest; suggesting or tending to obscenity.

1613 J. CHAMBERLAIN in *Crt. & Times Jas. I* (1848) I. 273 If you knew what indecent words have passed in the course of this suit, you would excuse me and think me modest. **1676**

tr. *Guillatiere's Voy. Athens* 267 Their Dances were lascivious, their Gestures indecent, and their Songs immodest. **1751** EARL ORRERY *Remarks Swift* (1752) 21 The many filthy ideas, and indecent expressions (I mean indecent in point of cleanliness and delicacy) that will be found throughout his works. **1768** STERNE *Sent. Journ.* (1778) II. 65 (*Passport*), I have something within me which cannot bear the shock of the least indecent insinuation. **1883** C. J. WILLS *Mod. Persia* 322 The costume of the women.. is now, when carried to the extreme of the fashion, highly indecent. **1965** *Times* 17 Feb. 17/2 After verdict and before sentence, while the jury were still in court, they had come to the conclusion that neither the films nor the brochure were obscene, but had concluded that they were indecent.

4. Special collocations: ***indecent assault***: an assault (sense 3) of a sexual nature, but not involving rape or attempted rape; used *colloq.* as a euphemism for rape (Webster, 1934); ***indecent exposure*** (see EXPOSURE 1 f).

1861 *Act 24 & 25 Vict.* c. 100 §52 Whosoever shall be convicted of any indecent Assault upon any Female..shall be liable..to be imprisoned for any Term not exceeding Two Years, with or without Hard Labour. *Ibid.* §62 Whosoever..shall be guilty..of any indecent Assault upon any Male Person, shall be guilty of a Misdemeanor. **1938** J. CURTIS *They drive by Night* xvii. 190 You want to get pinched for indecent assault, do you? **1956** *Act 4 & 5 Eliz. II* c. 69 §14 It is an offence, subject to the exception mentioned in subsection (3) of this section, for a person to make an indecent assault on a woman. *Ibid.* §15 It is an offence for a person to make an indecent assault on a man. **1969** C. ALLEN *Textbk. Psychosexual Disorders* (ed. 2) xxii. 458 The Act does not provide a definition of 'indecent assault'... In the majority of cases a man..has, without invitation, put his hand up the clothing of an unsuspecting female. **1974** *Guardian* 24 Jan. 7/3 Mr Breredon, at present serving four years for two cases of indecent assault.

Hence **in'decentness**, indecency (Bailey vol. II, 1727).

indecently (ɪn'diːsəntlɪ), *adv.* [f. prec. + -LY^{2}.] In an indecent manner; unbecomingly, indelicately, immodestly.

1589 PUTTENHAM *Eng. Poesie* III. xxiii. (Arb.) 269 If they fall out decently..all is well, if indecently, and to the eares and myndes misliking..all is amisse. **1660** R. COKE *Power & Subj.* 161 Let there be no vain speech, nor anything indecently done. **1723–4** SWIFT *To Stella* 13 Mar., When indecently I rave, When out my brutish passions break. **1771** FLETCHER *Checks* Wks. 1795 II. 211, I enquired into the cause of the dissatisfaction he had so indecently expressed. **1849** THACKERAY *Pendennis* vii, A stout fellow-passenger..kept him awake by snoring indecently. **1961** NEW ENG. BIBLE *Rom.* i. 27 Males behave indecently with males. **1970** *Times* 8 Jan. 2/8 As she walked along a lonely path..a boy threw her to the ground, indecently assaulted her and stabbed her.

indeciduate (ɪndɪ'sɪdjuːət), *a. Zool.* [IN-^{3}.] Not deciduate, as a placenta; not having a decidua; belonging to the *Indeciduata*, or non-deciduate mammals (a division comprising the Ruminantia, Edentata, and Cetacea).

1879 tr. *De Quatrefages' Hum. Spec.* 109 Man, apes, bats, insectivora, and rodents, form a natural group to which..no indeciduate mammals can be admitted.

indeciduous (ɪndɪ'sɪdjuːəs), *a.* Also 7 indiciduous. [IN-^{3}.]

†**1.** Not liable to fall off or be shed; permanently attached. *Obs.*

1646 SIR T. BROWNE *Pseud. Ep.* V. xxi. 269 The statua of the Sun was framed with rayes about the head, which were the indiciduous and unshaven locks of Apollo. **1656** in BLOUNT *Glossogr.*

2. *Bot.* Of a leaf; Not falling off at a definite time of the year; not deciduous. Of a tree or plant: Not losing the leaves annually; evergreen.

1755 JOHNSON, *Indeciduous*,..used of trees that do not shed their leaves in winter. **1828** WEBSTER, *Indeciduous*, not falling, as the leaves of trees in autumn. **1836** LANDOR *Peric. & Asp.* Wks. 1846 II. 385/2 There are no indeciduous plants, Aspasia! the greater part lose their leaves in winter, the rest in summer.

†**in'decimable**, *a. Obs. rare.* [f. IN-^{3} + L. *decimā-re* to tithe, DECIMATE + -ABLE. Cf. med.L. *indecimātus* not tithed.] (See quot.)

1642 COKE *Inst.* II. 490 What things be indecimable by the Law, and ought not to pay tithe. **1670** in BLOUNT *Law Dict.* [Hence in later Dicts.]

indecipherable (ɪndɪ'saɪfərəb(ə)l), *a.* [IN-^{3}.] Incapable of being deciphered or made out.

1802 T. JEFFERSON *Writ.* (1830) III. 491 A cipher..which ..is the most indecipherable..of any I have ever known. **1853** RUSKIN *Stones Ven.* II. iii. §35. 50 Nor are the original features of the rest of the edifice altogether indecipherable. **1886** A. EVANS in *Archæol.* XLIX. 143 A few words were indecipherable.

Hence **inde,ciphera'bility**, **inde'cipherableness**.

1806 W. TAYLOR in Robberds *Mem.* II. 127 The indecypherableness of the story. **1894** *Westm. Gaz.* 13 Sept. 8/2 Downright indecipherability [of handwriting].

indecision (ɪndɪ'sɪʒən). [a. F. *indécision* (1611 in Cotgr.); see IN-^{3} and DECISION.] Want of decision; inability to decide or to make up one's mind; a wavering between possible courses of action; hesitation.

a **1763** SHENSTONE *Ess.* (1765) 208 The term indecision, in a man's character, implies an idea very nicely different from that of irresolution; yet it has a tendency to produce it. **1791** BOSWELL *Johnson* 17 Apr. an. 1778, I talked of the strange indecision of mind, and imbecility of the common occurrences of life, which we may observe in some people. **1828** D'ISRAELI *Chas. I*, I. x. 290 A character of hopeless indecision is fatal to military success. **1868** FREEMAN *Norm. Conq.* (1876) II. App. 529 His indecision, his unwillingness to accept the crown..cause delay.

indecisive (ɪndɪ'saɪsɪv), *a.* [IN-^{3}.]

1. Not decisive; not such as to decide or settle (a question, contest, etc.); inconclusive.

1726 BERKELEY *Let. to T. Prior* 12 Nov. in Fraser *Life* iv. (1871) 137 The observations you have sent are..so ambiguous and indecisive as to puzzle only. **1798** W. TAYLOR in *Monthly Mag.* V. 4 An indecisive passage of Deuteronomy. **1855** MACAULAY *Hist. Eng.* xix. IV. 275 On the Upper Rhine..an indecisive predatory war was carried on. **1878** DOWDEN *Stud. Lit.* 134 In place of truth he found only a conflict of indecisive reasonings.

2. Characterized by indecision; undecided; hesitating; irresolute.

1787 T. JEFFERSON *Writ.* (1859) II. 155 An honester man cannot be found, nor a slower, nor a more indecisive one. **1824** W. TAYLOR in *Monthly Rev.* CIII. 32 Somewhat indecisive about his future place of residence. **1843** MOZLEY *Ess., Ld. Strafford* (1878) I. 75 Perplexed and indecisive whether to go forwards or backwards.

3. Uncertain, doubtful; not definite, indistinct.

1816 J. SCOTT *Vis. Paris* (ed. 5) 339 As if on purpose to render indecisive..the hope of that immortality which is one of the noblest prerogatives of our being. **1822–34** *Good's Study Med.* I. 341 As there is much obscurity in this disease, its medical treatment is indecisive. **1874** T. HARDY *Far fr. Mad. Crowd* II. i. 15 A contrasting prospect eastward, in the shape of indecisive and palpitating stars.

Hence **inde'cisively** *adv.*

1828 in WEBSTER. **1869** M. PATTISON *Serm.* (1885) 180 Whether Christian or deist, or wavering indecisively between the two. *Mod.* The first day's struggle had ended indecisively.

indecisiveness (ɪndɪ'saɪsɪvnɪs). [f. prec. + -NESS.] The quality of being indecisive.

1793 W. ROBERTS *Looker-on* No. 50 ¶3 The indecisiveness of battles; the formalities of encounter. **1809–10** COLERIDGE *Friend* (1837) II. 193 Indecisiveness of character..is almost always associated with benevolence. **1864** J. H. NEWMAN *Apol.* 168–9, I saw..a patent fulfilment of all that I had surmised as to their vagueness and indecisiveness.

†**inde'clarable**, *a. Obs. rare*$^{-1}$. [IN-^{3}.] Incapable of being declared.

1610 HEALEY *Vives' Comm. St. Aug. Citie of God* (1620) 372 Plato mentions the Father and the Sonne expressly, indeed the third he thought was indeclareable.

indeclinable (ɪndɪ'klaɪnəb(ə)l), *a.* (*sb.*) [a. F. *indéclinable* (15th c.), ad. L. *indeclīnābilis* unchangeable, grammatically indeclinable: see IN-^{3} and DECLINABLE.]

†**1.** Incapable of declining, or being caused to decline; undeviating, unchangeable, fixed, constant.

1432–50 tr. *Higden* (Rolls) IV. 25 This Fabricius is as indeclinable [**1387** TREVISA 'hardere to be i-torned'] from honeste as the sonne from his naturalle cowrse. **1623** COCKERAM, *Indeclinable*, constant. **1637** R. HUMPHREY tr. *St. Ambrose* Pref., Stoicks [maintain]..the indeclinable order of things.

†**2.** That cannot be turned aside from or shunned; unavoidable, inevitable (cf. DECLINE *v.* 12). *Obs.*

1658 PHILLIPS, *Indeclinable*, not to be declined, or shun'd. **1660** JER. TAYLOR *Duct. Dubit.* I. ii. rule 7 §9 For the avoiding of a greater evil which is otherwise indeclinable.

3. *Gram.* Incapable of being declined grammatically; having no inflexions.

1530 PALSGR. Introd. 37 For the knowledge of theyr partes indeclynable remyttyng the lernar to the seconde boke. **1668** WILKINS *Real Char.* 353 The other Particles are not capable of Inflexion..and therefore may be stiled indeclinable or invariable. **1748** WESLEY *Eng. Gram.* ii. 18 All Adjectives are indeclinable, having no variation either of Gender, Case, or Number. **1877** MOULTON tr. *Winer's N.T. Gram.* II. §10. 2 Many Hebrew proper names are treated as indeclinable in the LXX. and the N.T.

B. as *sb.* An indeclinable word.

1530 PALSGR. 370 Al numeralles of this sorte be indeclynables. **1761** CHURCHILL *Rosciad* 784 [He] stands alone in indeclinables; Conjunction, preposition, adverb, join To stamp new vigour on the nervous line. **1786–1805** TOOKE *Purley* 251 All the Indeclinables except the Adverb, we have already considered. **1897** F. HALL in *Nation* (N.Y.) LXIV. 396/2 As regards the hinges of language, indeclinables.

Hence **inde'clinableness**, the quality of being inevitable or irresistible.

1648 JENKYN *Blind Guide* iv. 79 The invincibility, certainty, and indeclinablenesse of the worke of grace upon the will.

indeclinably (ɪndɪ'klaɪnəblɪ), *adv.* [f. prec. + -LY^{2}.] In an indeclinable manner:

†**a.** Undeviatingly. †**b.** Unavoidably, irresistibly. **c.** As an indeclinable word.

1624 BP. MOUNTAGU *Immed. Address* 140 The Angels.. did euer indeclineably Behold the face of God in glory. **1625** —— *App. Cæsar* II. i. 111 To follow indeclinably..the Discipline of the Church of England. **1648** JENKYN *Blind Guide* iv. 79 You give your owne interpretation of working invincibly and indeclinably upon the will. *a* **1677** MANTON *Twenty Serm.* vi. Wks. 1871 II. 235 The apostle prays that God would form and set their hearts straight, that they may be more indeclinably fixed towards God. **1864** WEBSTER, *Indeclinably*, without variation of termination. **1877** *Fraser's Mag.* XV. 171 The forms ending in *-um* were employed indeclinably.

indecom'ponible, *a. rare.* [f. IN-^{3} + DECOMPONIBLE.] = next.

1809–10 COLERIDGE *Friend* (1818) III. 173 The assumed indecomponible substances of the Laboratory. **1821** —— in *Blackw. Mag.* X. 246 Existence is a simple intuition, underived and indecomponible. **1844** *N. Brit. Rev.* II. 76 An indecomponible substance accidentally discovered.

indecomposable (ɪndiːkəm'pəʊzəb(ə)l), *a.* [IN-^{3}: cf. F. *indécomposable* (Voltaire, 1738).] Incapable of being decomposed or resolved into constituent elements.

1807 R. KIRWAN *Logick* I. III. v. 212 It has been laid down ..that water was an element, and that elements were indecomposable. **1812** SIR H. DAVY *Chem. Philos.* 291 A compound in-soluble in water, indecomposable by acid or alkaline solutions. **1860** FARRAR *Orig. Lang.* v. 97 Words which are primitive, indecomposible, and irreducible. *a* **1862** BUCKLE *Civiliz.* (1869) III. v. 359 Other faculties, which being original and indecomposable, resist all inductive treatment. **1868** LOCKYER *Guillemin's Heavens* (ed. 3) 435 Among the many nebulæ, indecomposable into stars. **1968** P. A. P. MORAN *Introd. Probability Theory* ix. 406 A distribution containing all its probability concentrated at two points is indecomposable. **1971** POWELL & HIGMAN *Finite Simple Groups* iii. 140 A root system Δ with base Π is *indecomposable* if it is impossible to split up Π into two non-empty subsets which are orthogonal to each other.

Hence **,indecomposa'bility**.

1950 *Mathematical Rev.* May 377/1 (*title*) Proof of the indecomposability of a certain graph. **1968** P. A. P. MORAN *Introd. Probability Theory* ix. 409 We now consider an example of the indecomposability of absolutely continuous distributions.

indecorous (ɪndɪ'kɔərəs, -'dɛkərəs), *a.* [f. L. *indecōr-us* (see IN-^{3} and DECOROUS) + -OUS: or ad. late L. *indecorōsus*. For the pronunciation see DECOROUS.]

†**1.** Unbecoming, inappropriate. *Obs.*

1680 [implied in INDECOROUSNESS]. **1692** RAY *Dissol. World* III. xii. (1732) 441 It seems to me indecorous and unsuitable to the Person and Majesty of God.

2. Contrary to, or wanting, decorum or propriety of behaviour; in bad taste.

1682 *Enq. Elect. Sheriffs* 46 Their Actions are infinitely more indecorous, unreasonable, and silly. **1790** BURKE *Army Estim.* Wks. 1878 III. 280 At his time of life..it was useless and indecorous to attempt any thing by mere struggle. **1832** G. DOWNES *Lett. Cont. Countries* I. 76 The demeanour of both sexes was strikingly indecorous—a harsher epithet would be unjust. **1856** KANE *Arct. Expl.* II. xiv. 139 Among savages especially haste is indecorous. **1877** J. D. CHAMBERS *Div. Worship* 305 The indecorous habit of overlapping one part of the Office by another.

b. Immodest, indecent. *rare.*

1829 MACAULAY *Ess., Southey's Colloq. Soc.* (1851) I. 113 Drapery was put on indecorous statues.

Hence **indecorously** *adv.*, in an indecorous manner, without decorum.

1818 in TODD. **1873** BURTON *Hist. Scot.* VI. lxvi. 62 The religious squabbles which so indecorously disturbed the latter years of the reign of King James. **1885** *Law Rep.* 14 Queen's Bench Div. 683 The oath was not taken indecorously, improperly, or without order.

indecorousness (see prec.). [f. prec. + -NESS.]

†**1.** Inappropriateness. *Obs.*

1680 H. DODWELL *Disc. Sanchoniatho's Phœnician Hist.* (1691) 102 The indecorousness of their Allegories to their Deities.

2. The quality of being indecorous; violation of propriety or decorum.

1762 STERNE *Let. to Garrick*, Crebillon..has agreed to write to me an expostulatory letter on the indecorousness of 'Tristram Shandy'. **1811** *Ann. Reg.* Chron. 108 He never fails to dwell with censurable indecorousness on the illness of our venerable Sovereign. **1842** DICKENS *Lett.* (ed. 2) I. 62, I have seen none of that greediness and indecorousness on which travellers have laid so much emphasis.

indecorum (ɪndɪ'kɔərəm). [a. L. *indecōrum*, subst. use of neut. sing. of *indecōrus* INDECOROUS; cf. DECORUM.]

1. An indecorous or unbecoming action or proceeding; an impropriety, a violation of the rules of behaviour proper to the sex, age, or character of the actor.

1575 GASCOIGNE *Instr. Eng. Verse* (Arb.) 32 To entermingle merie iests in a serious matter is an *Indecorum*. **1594** J. DICKENSON *Arisbas* (1878) 91 If any Decorum be omitted, or Indecorum committed, I can not otherwise excuse it. **1659** *Gentl. Calling* VI. xiii. 433 They will not be guilty of such an Indecorum. **1709** STEELE *Tatler* No. 109 ¶1 It may be thought an Indecorum that I visit a Man. **1828** CARLYLE *Werner* in *Misc. Ess.* (1888) I. 74 It was a much coarser curiosity..which the dissipated man, by successive indecorums occasioned. **1849** GROTE *Greece* II. lv. (1862) V. 52 This was a flagrant indecorum, and known violation of the order of the festival.

2. The quality of being indecorous; lack of decorum; impropriety, now esp. of behaviour.

1664 H. MORE *Myst. Iniq.* Apol. 542 It is little detriment or Indecorum for them to use so well a limited indulgence. **1677** HALE *Prim. Orig. Man.* 60 Upon a bare Moral account of the *indecorum*, unreasonableness, unseasonableness or utter unfitness of the thing it self. **1742** JARVIS *Quix.* II. II. xxii. (1885) 88 A woman suffers more..by public indecorum than by secret wantonness. **1771** BURKE *Corr.*

(1844) I. 324 The charge is not..for *indecorum*, or indiscretion, but for *falsehood*. **1823** Scott *Quentin D.* xvi, The adroit manner in which he apologized for the acts of indecorum committed by their attendant.

†**b.** Inelegance, unhandsomeness. *Obs. rare.*
1597 A. M. *Guillemeau's Fr. Chirurg.* 47/2 The patient might be mutilate, and without greate indecorum or deformity, should not be able to goe.

indeed (ɪnˈdiːd), *adv. phrase.* Forms: see deed *sb.* [f. in *prep.* + deed *sb.* (5 b and 5 c): down to 1600 commonly written as two words, as still in the stronger *in very deed.*]

1. In actual fact, in reality, in truth; really, truly, assuredly, positively.
c **1330** R. Brunne *Chron. Wace* (Rolls) 7591 Þat was þe firste wassail in dede. *c* **1340** *Cursor M.* 10160 (Trin.) Of him we wol oure story rede For worþiest hit is in dede. **1430–40** Lydg. *Bochas* ix. iii. (MS. Bodl. 263) 408/2 In al his book, he had afforn nat seen A mor woful creature, in deede. **1526** Tindale *Luke* xxiv. 34 The lorde is risen in dede and hath apered to Simon. **1610** Shaks. *Temp.* i. ii. 96 My trust.. which had indeede no limit. **1766** Goldsm. *Vic. W.* iv, When Sunday came it was indeed a day of finery. **1816** J. Wilson *City of Plague* ii. i. 37, I hear thy voice, And know that I indeed am motherless. **1878** Hutton *Scott* iv. 37 He was, indeed, a man of iron nerve.

b. Freq. placed after a word in order to emphasize it: hence, with sb. = actual, real, true, genuine; with adj. or adv. = really and truly. (The adj. is often preceded by *very*.)
1575 Fleming *Virg. Bucol.* x. 1 O Arethusa, graunt this labour be my last indeede. **1611** Bible *John* i. 47 Behold an Israelite indeed [Tindale a ryght Israelite] in whom is no guile. **1638** F. Junius *Paint. of Ancients* 236 Our discourse is not about ordinary workmen, but wee doe rather speake of such men as are Painters indeed, that is, men of excellent wittes and great. **1653** Walton *Angler* xi. 218, I marry Sir, this is Musick indeed, this has cheered my heart. **1742** Jarvis *Quix.* ii. i. i. (1885) 14 'Marvellous indeed!' said the priest. **1816** J. Wilson *City of Plague* i. i. 163 My hours of sleep are now but few indeed. **1848** B. Lefroy in *State Trials* (N.S.) VI. 695, I should be very glad indeed to find that I had mistaken altogether the drift of that defence. **1876–7** L. Morris *Epic Hades, Phaedra*, Amid the crowd of youths He showed a Prince indeed.

2. In reality, in real nature or essence, opposed to what is merely external or apparent.
1412–20 Lydg. *Chron. Troy* i. v. (MS. Digby 230), There was oone enclosed in her herte And anoþir in hir chere declared For maidens han ofte siþes spared To shewe oute þt þei desire in dede. **1526** *Pilgr. Perf.* (W. de W. 1531) 143 Rather make it seme lesse incomparably than it is in deede. *a* **1568** Ascham *Scholem.* Pref. (Arb.) 18 The Scholehouse should be in deede, as it is called by name, the house of playe and pleasure. **1649** Milton *Eikon.* Pref., Like those captive women who bewail'd the death of Patroclus in out-ward show, but indeed their own condition. **1692** E. Walker *Epictetus' Mor.* v, That which I see, Is not indeed that which it seems to be. **1876–7** L. Morris *Epic Hades, Marsyas* 88 The Muses' Eyes, who were indeed Women, though god-like.

†**b.** In an adversative clause, emphasizing the real fact or reason in opposition to that which is false. *Obs.*
1596 Dalrymple tr. *Leslie's Hist. Scot.* I. 33 The schirrefdome..of Perth is not litle, bot ample indede and large. **1610** Shaks. *Temp.* ii. i. 54 *Gon.* How lush and lusty the grasse lookes? How greene? *Ant.* The ground indeed is tawny. **1611** Bible *Transl. Pref.* 2 [He] was iudged to be no man at armes (though in deed he excelled in feates of chiualrie). **1613** Purchas *Pilgrimage* (1614) 90 Whereas that rednesse ariseth indeed of the winds, which..carry..red Earth or Minium.

3. Used in a clause which confirms and amplifies a previous statement: In point of fact, as a matter of fact.
1535 Joye *Apol. Tindale* 42 And in dead I brought the same texte agenst him. **1601** R. Johnson *Kingd. & Commw.* (1603) 78 Their disposition (as indeed almost all the rest of the Germans) very honest. **1662** *Bk. Com. Prayer* Pref., Of the Church of England, or indeed of the whole Catholick Church of Christ. **1710** Hearne *Collect.* III. 16 There is a very large Preface, but silly, and plainly shews the Author to be a Whigg, and indeed a fool. **1854** Mrs. Jameson *Bk. of Th.* (1877) 117 What do we know of the mystery of..child-life? What, indeed, do we know of any life? **1885** Rider Haggard *K. Solomon's Mines* 32, I am..a cautious man, indeed a timid one.

4. With concessive force (usually followed by an adversative clause) = It is true, it must be admitted.
1563 W. Fulke *Meteors* (1640) 8 Indeed sometimes it may be so, but..it is not so alwayes, nor yet most commonly. *a* **1568** Ascham *Scholem.* i. (Arb.) 32 These ye will say, be fond scholemasters..They be fond in deede, but surelie ouermany soch be found euerie where. **1711** Steele *Spect.* No. 95 ¶3 Grief and Weeping are indeed frequent Companions, but, I believe, never in their highest Excesses. **1828** Scott *F.M. Perth* v, She blushed deeply indeed, but there was more than maiden's shame in her face. **1894** Fowler *Adamnan* Introd. 81 Latin, not classical indeed, but good of its kind.

5. In dialogue, used to emphasize the reply (affirmative or negative) to a question or remark: e.g. 'Yes, indeed!', 'No, indeed!'
1583 Stubbes *Anat. Abus.* ii. (1882) 89 Is not that your meaning? That is my meaning indeed. **1591** Shaks. *Two Gent.* ii. iv. 9 *Sil.* Seruant, you are sad. *Val.* Indeed, Madam. I seeme so. **1734** Carey *Chrononhoton.* ii, *Queen.* Away! 'you flatter me. *1st Lady.* We don't indeed. **1875** Jowett *Plato* (ed. 2) I. 19 Can you tell me? Indeed I cannot. **1885** *Punch* 19 Dec. 298/1 'But you don't mean to tell me you're the secretary of all these companies?' 'Indeed I do, my dear fellow'.

b. Used in echoing the question asked by another speaker.
1766 Goldsm. *Vic. W.* vii, 'Who knows how this may end?' 'Aye, who knows that indeed!' answered I. **1826** Disraeli *Viv. Grey* ii. xv, 'Who is this Mr. Grey?' 'Who, indeed!'

6. Interrogatively = 'Is it so?' 'Really?'
1598 Shaks. *Merry W.* iv. ii. 15 *Mis. P.* Whose at home besides your selfe? *Mis. F.* Why, none but mine owne people. *Mis. P.* Indeed? *Mis. F.* No, certainly. **1604** —— *Oth.* iii. iii. 101 *Ia.* I did not thinke he had bin acquainted with hir. *O.* O yes, and went betweene vs very oft. *Ia.* Indeed? *O.* Indeed? I indeed. Discern'st thou ought in that? **1710** Steele *Tatler* No. 171 ¶3, I go no further than, Say you so, Sir? Indeed! Heyday! **1870** Dickens *E. Drood* xviii, 'That's Jarsper's'. 'Indeed?' said Mr. Datchery.

7. As an interjection, expressing (according to the intonation) irony, contempt, amazement, incredulity, or the like.
1834 Medwin *Angler in Wales* I. 181 This is the Angler in Wales, indeed! exclaims some fair reader. **1837** Dickens *Pickw.* xxvi, 'Ah', said Sam, 'to be sure; that's the question.' 'Question, indeed', retorted Mrs. Cluppins. 'she'd question him, if she'd my spirit.' **1866** Ruskin *Wild Olive* (ed. 2) 91, I think such and such a thing might be desirable..a damask curtain or so at the windows. 'Ah', says my employer, 'damask curtains indeed! That's all very fine'. **1875** Jowett *Plato* (ed. 2) I. 219 'O, indeed', I said, 'what a wonderful thing, and what a great blessing!'

8. ***indeed and indeed***, really and truly. *colloq.*
1673 Wycherley *Gentl. Dancing-M.* iii. i. Wks. (Rtldg.) 52/2 Indeed, and indeed, father, my aunt puts me quite out. *Ibid.* iv. i. 54/2 Indeed and indeed, father, I shall not have him. **1840** Dickens *Barn. Rudge* xxii, She said that indeed and indeed Miss Dolly might take pattern by her blessed mother. **187.** W. S. Gilbert *Distant Shore*, O say that I love him indeed and indeed!

indeedy (ɪnˈdiːdɪ, ɪnˈdɪdɪ), *adv. colloq.* (orig. *U.S.*). [f. indeed *adv. phr.* + -y *suffix*[6].] Used as an emphatic affirmative (or negative), esp. after *yes* (or *no*): indeed, certainly.
1856 *Knickerbocker* XLVIII. 620 'Is thy eye not opened?' 'Yes, indeedy,' says I. **1872** 'Mark Twain' *Roughing It* 336 He never shook his mother... No indeedy..he looked after her and took care of her. **1932** W. Cather *Obscure Destinies* 165 I'd like to, powerful well, Mrs. Harris. I would, indeedy. **1961** *Sunday Times* 26 Mar. 13/1 He's also got two episcopal rings—'One's a spare I can use for the washing-up.' Yes, indeedy. **1965** N. Freeling *Criminal Conversation* i. ix. 62 'People always lie to policemen.' 'Yes indeedy.' **1966** 'D. Shannon' *With a Vengeance* xi. 147 'A little lower than the angels,' he said. 'Yes indeedy.' **1967** J. Porter *Chinks in Curtain* xii. 124 Yes, indeedy! That was a good question. **1970** L. Sanders *Anderson Tapes* xxviii. 73 No, indeedy.

indeere, obs. form of endear.

†**indeˈfailable**, *a. Obs.* [f. in-[3] + defail *v.* + -able. Cf. obs. F. adv. *indefalliblement* 'indefailably' (15th c. in Godef.).] Not liable to fail.
1693 Beverley *True St. Gosp. Truth* 32 All is in Connexion, and inseparable Concatenation, and indefailable Certainty to the Elect. **1701** —— *Glory of Grace* 15 Such a Communication of Holiness, as should be unchangeable, or indefailable.

indeˌfatigaˈbility, [f. next: see -ity.] The quality of being indefatigable; incapability of being wearied; unremitting diligence or perseverance.
a **1634** Isaackson in Fuller *Abel Rediv., Andrewes* (1651) **iij b, His Indefatigability in Study cannot be paralleld. **1802** Mar. Edgeworth *Moral T.* (1816) I. vi. 37 All the manly virtues, were inseparably connected with pedestrian indefatigability. **1862** C. Stretton *Chequered Life* II. 100 Every one is conversant with the indefatigability of the ant.

indefatigable (ɪndɪˈfætɪgəb(ə)l), *a.* [a. obs. F. *indéfatigable* (15–16th c. in Godef.), ad. L. *indēfatīgābil-is*, f. *in-* (in-[3]) + *dēfatīgāre* to wear out: see -ble.] Incapable of being wearied; that cannot be tired out; unwearied, untiring, unremitting in labour or effort. **a.** Of persons or things personified.
1586 [implied in indefatigably]. **1611** Cotgr., *Indefatigable*, indefatigable, vnweariable, vntirable, not to be toyled out. *a* **1635** Naunton *Fragm. Reg.* (Arb.) 49 He was an indefatigable Reader, whether by Sea or Land. **1667** Milton *P.L.* ii. 408 Upborn with indefatigable wings Over the vast abrupt. **1711** Addison *Spect.* No. 115 ¶6 My Friend Sir Roger has been an indefatigable Man in Business of this kind. **1781** Gibbon *Decl. & F.* xxix. III. 111 Active and indefatigable in the pursuit of revenge. **1847** Grote *Greece* ii. xlvi. (1862) IV. 108 He was indefatigable in his attention to public business. **1858** Gladstone *Homer* II. ii. 137 The indefatigable students of Germany.

b. Of qualities or actions.
1621 Burton *Anat. Mel.* iii. iv. i. i. (1651) 635 An indefatigable love and beauty. **1646** Sir T. Browne *Pseud. Ep.* i. viii. 31 A man of great eloquence, and industry indefatigable. **1781** Gibbon *Decl. & F.* xviii. (1869) I. 476 His diligence was indefatigable. **1855** Milman *Lat. Chr.* vii. vi. (1864) IV. 178 The Hermit..with indefatigable restlessness went from province to province.

indeˈfatigableness. [f. prec. + -ness.] The quality of being indefatigable.
1653 Waterhouse *Apol. Learn.* 231 (L.) Dost thou thus repay thy teachers for their pains, care, study, indefatigableness? **1755** Carte *Hist. Eng.* IV. 300 He.. pursued them with the greatest perseverance and indefatigableness imaginable till he lost his life. **1830** *Edin. Rev.* LI. 505 Adams was a representative..of the sturdy indefatigableness..of New England.

indeˈfatigably, *adv.* [f. as prec. + -ly[2].] In an indefatigable manner; unweariedly; with unremitting perseverance.
1586 W. Webbe *Eng. Poetrie* (Arb.) 34 Master Arthur Golding..which..trauelleth as yet indefatigably, and is addicted without society, by his continuall laboure, to profit this nation and speeche in all kind of good learning. **1682** Dryden *Pref. Relig. Laici* Wks. (Globe) 185 A man indefatigably zealous in the service of the Church. **1748** *Anson's Voy.* iii. v. 336 We laboured indefatigably in getting in our water. **1887** Ruskin *Præterita* II. 413 Indefatigably carrying his little daguerreotype box up everywhere.

†**indefatiˈgation**. *Obs.* [f. in-[3] + defatigation.] The condition of being unwearied.
a **1646** J. Gregory *Posthuma, Terrestr. Globe* (1650) 267 The Arabian Geographers..holding themselvs not to bee inferior..either to the indefatigation or Skill of the Greek Geographers.

indefeasible (ɪndɪˈfiːzɪb(ə)l), *a.* Forms: 6 indiffeasable, 6–7 indefecible, 7–8 -feasable, -feisible, 8 -feazable, -fiezable, 7– indefeasible. [f. in-[3] + defeasible; cf. It. *indeffessibile* (Florio).] Not defeasible; not liable to be 'defeated', made void, or done away with; that cannot be forfeited.
1548 Ld. Somerset *Epist. Scots* A v in *Compl. Scot.* (1872) App. iii. 239 By mariage..one bloude..is made of two, and an indefecible right geuen of bothe to one, without the destruction and abolishing of either. *a* **1600** Hooker *Eccl. Pol.* viii. ii. §8 All those things are utterly void, they make him no indefeasible estate, the inheritor by blood may dispossess him. **1661–98** South *12 Serm.* III. 18 He, who gives a Being..has an Indefeasible claim to whatsoever the said Being so Given..either is, or has, or can Possibly do. **1670** Blount *Law Dict.* s.v., A good and indefeisible estate. **1735–8** Bolingbroke *On Parties* 101 If it be not proved to be something more than human, it will hardly be proved indefiezable. **1859** Mill *Liberty* i. 19 The great writers.. have mostly asserted freedom of conscience as an indefeasible right. **1873** Symonds *Grk. Poets* xii. 414 Beauty is the true province of the Greeks, their indefeasible domain.

Hence **indefeasiˈbility**, **indeˈfeasibleness**, the quality or character of being indefeasible.
1755 Carte *Hist. Eng.* IV. 2 The indefeasableness of the succession seems to be a natural consequence of its being a lineal one. **1828** Webster s.v., The indefeasibility of a title. **1843** Mill *Logic* iii. v. §1 There are very few [uniformities] which have any, even apparent, pretension to this rigorous indefeasibility. **1885** *Law Times* LXXIX. 332/2 There are limits to this indefeasibility of title.

indefeasibly (ɪndɪˈfiːzɪblɪ), *adv.* [f. prec. + -ly[2]] In an indefeasible manner; so as to be indefeasible.
1540 *Act 32 Hen. VIII*, c. 42 §1 By the same name peasably quietly and indiffeasably, shall have, possesse, and enjoye, to them and to their successours for ever all suche landis and tenementis. **1719** De Foe *Crusoe* i. vii, I was.. Lord of all this Country indefeasibly. **1831** Carlyle *Sart. Res.* iii. iv, Venerable to me is the hard Hand; crooked, coarse; wherein..lies a cunning virtue, indefeasibly royal, as of the Sceptre of this Planet.

†**indeˈfeatable**, *a. Obs.* Also -ible. [f. in-[3] + defeat *v.*] Incapable of being defeated or undone; indefeasible; indefectible. Hence **indefeataˈbility** (-ibility).
(Possibly in quot. 1643 an error for *indefeasable, -ible*, in 1755 for next two words.)
1643 T. Warmstry *Answ. W. Bridges conc. War* 15 That indefeatable power, and that incorruptible wisdome that is in God himselfe. **1755** Carte *Hist. Eng.* IV. 53 Those [controversies] about free will,..predestination and reprobation, grace irresistible and indefeatible. *Ibid.* 55 The decisions of this factious synod [of Dort] in favour..of the irresistibility and indefeatibility of grace.

indefectibility (ɪndɪfɛktɪˈbɪlɪtɪ). [f. next: see -ity. Cf. F. *indéfectibilité* (17th c. in Hatz.-Darm.).] The quality of being indefectible; exemption from liability to failure or decay.
1624 Bp. Hall *True Peace-Maker* Wks. (1627) 541 Hee alone hath infallibility and indefectibilitie. **1644** Digby *Man's Soul* vi. (1645) 68 These Propositions..have in themselves an indefectibility insuperable. **1726** J. Trapp *Popery* i. 50 There is no Promise of Indefectibility made by our Saviour to any particular church. **1882** Farrar *Early Chr.* I. 383 That [controversy] which raged between Calvinists and Arminians on the 'indefectibility of grace'.

indefectible (ɪndɪˈfɛktɪb(ə)l), *a.* [f. in-[3] + defectible, prob. after F. *indéfectible* (1582 in Hatz.-Darm.), or med.L. *indefectibiliter* adv. (Du Cange).] Not defectible.

1. Not liable to failure, defect, or decay; unfailing; that cannot fall short, come to an end, or be done away.
1659 Pearson *Creed* viii. (1866) 476, I believe this infinite and Eternal Spirit to be..of perfect and indefectible holiness in himself. **1676** Marvell *Mr. Smirke* 46 When the Greek Church is excommunicate by the Roman..what and where then was the Catholick Church, that was indefectible and against which the Gates of Hell did not prevail? **1736** Chandler *Hist. Persec.* 273 The burning, and not consuming bush, signifies the indefectible splendor of the church. **1842** Manning *Serm., Falling fr. Baptismal Grace* (1848) I. 36 Some beguile themselves by the dream that they magnify the mercies of God, in contending that the gifts of

grace are indefectible. **1887** FAIRBAIRN IN *Congregat. Rev.* May 426 The system that made grace most absolute made the saints most indefectible.

2. Not subject to defect; faultless.

1833 J. H. NEWMAN *Arians* II. v. (1876) 231 At first Arianism had not scrupled to admit the peccable nature of the Son, but it soon.. avowed that, in matter of fact, He was indefectible. **1852** H. ROGERS *Ecl. Faith* (1853) 403 An indefectible wisdom on one point.

Hence **inde'fectibly** *adv.*, without capability of failure.

1837 J. H. NEWMAN *Proph. Off. Ch.* 394 The faith committed to the Church is represented.. as clearly proclaimed, indefectibly maintained, and universally acknowledged.

indefective (ɪndɪ'fɛktɪv), *a.* ? *Obs.* [f. IN-^{3} + DEFECTIVE: cf. med.L. *indēfectīv-us* (15th c. in Du Cange).] Not defective; free from defect; faultless, flawless.

a **1641** BP. MOUNTAGU *Acts & Mon.* (1642) 5 Charity indefective in this.. life, and in the world to come everlasting life. **1659** PEARSON *Creed* (1839) 93 God is of himself infinitely glorious, because his perfections are absolute, his excellencies indefective. **1670** SOUTH *12 Serm.* (1698) III. 118 A Covenant promising Life upon Condition of absolute indefective obedience. **1708** FALCONAR in Hearne *Collect.* 19 Sept. (O.H.S.) II. 131 Everlasting and indefective happines. **1717** CROXALL *Ovid, Met.* VI. (R.), Seven are my daughters, of a form divine, With seven fair sons, an indefective line.

†**inde'fectuous**, *a. Obs. rare*$^{-0}$. [f. IN-^{3} + DEFECTUOUS: cf. obs. F. *indeffectueux* (16th c. in Godef.).] = prec. Hence †**inde'fectuousness**.

a **1687** H. MORE in Norris *The. Love* (1688) 153 Those terms *Totum* and *Omne*.. may signify either the Entireness, Indefectuousness or Perfection of the thing they are pronounced of.

†**inde'fendable, -ible**, *a. Obs.* [f. IN-^{3} + DEFENDABLE. Cf. F. *indéfendable* (Molière, 17th c.).] Incapable of being defended; indefensible.

1671 *True Nonconf.* 424 You hereby plainly acknowledge that Religion is not indefendible, except by meer subjects, against their Soveraign.

indefensible (ɪndɪ'fɛnsɪb(ə)l), *a.* [f. IN-^{3} + DEFENSIBLE. Cf. F. *indéfensible* (Montaigne, 16th c.).] Not defensible; admitting of no defence.

1. Incapable of being defended by force of arms.

1569 STOCKER tr. *Diod. Sic.* II. xxx. 82 They did forsake the indefensible small townes and villages. **1682** BURNET *Rights Princes* Pref. 11 By an obstinate keeping of an indefensible piece of Ground. **1849** JAMES *Woodman* iv, Their great extent rendered them indefensible against the means of escalade. **1884** *Spectator* 4 Oct. 1290/1 The town of itself is nearly indefensible.

2. Incapable of being defended in argument, maintained, or vindicated; unjustifiable, inexcusable.

1529 MORE *Dyaloge* I. Wks. 151/1 His proude foly, in the defence of his indefensible errour. *a* **1614** DONNE *Βιαθανατος* (1644) 123 Of which I perceive not any kinde to be more obnoxious, or indefensible then that.. so common with our Delinquents to stand mute at the Barre. **1745** WESLEY *Answ. Ch.* 5 Those Expressions.. of our own Countrymen, are utterly indefensible. **1799** KIRWAN *Geol. Ess.* 65 This hypothesis is as indefensible as the foregoing. **1849** COBDEN *Speeches* 35 It is manifestly unjust and indefensible, that you should tax the people of this country for the expenses of our colonies. **1883** FROUDE *Short Stud.* IV. I. iii. 34 To risk the peace of the Church in so indefensible a quarrel seemed obstinate folly.

Hence **indefensi'bility, inde'fensibleness**, the quality or character of being indefensible; **inde'fensibly** *adv.*, in an indefensible manner, so as not to admit of defence.

1690 J. MACKENZIE *Siege London-Derry* 21/2 Collonel Lundy.. spoke so discouragingly.. concerning the indefensibleness of the place. **1776** MICKLE tr. *Camoens' Lusiad* IX. Note 32 (R.) Some of the terms of expression are still indefensibly indelicate. **1823** BENTHAM *Not Paul* 216 The utter indefensibility of the design. **1876** GEO. ELIOT *Dan. Der.* xxix, The indefensibleness of her marriage. **1891** LOUNSBURY *Stud. Chaucer* I. Introd. 20 The evidence.. seems to me sufficient to show the idefensibility of any such position.

†**inde'fensive**, *a. Obs.* [f. IN-^{3} + DEFENSIVE (sense 1 c).] Incapable of making defence; defenceless.

1586 FERNE *Blaz. Gentrie* To Gentl. Inner Temp., Thus, if I had to alledge no other reason in the defence of this my action.. Yet were I not left indefensiue. **1634** SIR T. HERBERT *Trav.* 78 Turkes and Persians, both whom in all occasions were insulting over them, because indefensive and without government. *Ibid.* 337 The sword awes the indefensive villager.

indeferent, obs. form of INDIFFERENT.

†**inde'fesse**, *a. Obs.* [ad. L. *indēfess-us*, f. *in-* (IN-^{3}) + *dēfessus* wearied, tired (*dē-* down, etc. + *fessus* weary, tired).] Unwearied, untiring.

1621 BP. MOUNTAGU *Diatribæ* 512 The learned Grammarian Didymus, for his Indefesse paynes in reading and writing, surnamed, Iron-side, or heart of Oke.

†**inde'ficiency.** *Obs.* [f. next: see -ENCY.] The quality or character of being indeficient or unfailing; unfailingness.

1614 JACKSON *Creed* III. vii. §2 *note*, Their readinesse to defend the indeficiencie of his faith.. argues, they must of necessitie holde, that the Popes faith doth neuer faile. **1666** TILLOTSON *Rule Faith* III. §6 Wks. 1742 IV. 690 The indeficiency of oral tradition. **1732** STACKHOUSE *Hist. Bible* IV. i. (T. Suppl.), He [God] took care of their meat and drink, and indeficiency of their clothing.

†**indeficient** (ɪndɪ'fɪʃənt), *a. Obs.* [a. OF. *indéficient* (15th c. in Godef.), ad. L. *indēficient-em*, f. *in-* (IN-^{3}) + *dēficient-em* DEFICIENT.] Unfailing, exhaustless, unceasing.

1508 DUNBAR *Poems* vii. 25 Welcum oure indeficient adiutorie, That evir our Naceoun helpit in thare neyd. **1526** *Pilgr. Perf.* (W. de W. 1531) 170b, Euer fresshe and newe, indefycyent and neuer faylyng. **1604** T. WRIGHT *Passions* VI. 308 Whence-from proceedeth the indeficient regular.. beating of the pulse. **1656** JEANES *Fuln. Christ* 229 He hath .. an indeficient fullnesse, an inexhaustible fountaine. **1695** J. SAGE *Article* Wks. 1844 I. 366 There is Sermon upon Sermon,—indeficient Sermoning, till the Congregation within the Church is dissolved. **1851** TRENCH *Poems* 75 The Lamb His people feeds from indeficient streams.

Hence †**inde'ficiently** *adv.*, unfailingly.

1622 PRESTON *Godly Man's Inquis.* ii. 49 Trees of the Lords planting continue their fruits indeficiently, neither doe their leaues drop off.

indefinability (ɪndɪfaɪnə'bɪlɪtɪ). *Logic.* [f. INDEFINABLE *a.* (*sb.*) + -ITY.] The quality of being indefinable; incapability of definition in simpler or more fundamental terms.

1903 B. RUSSELL *Princ. Math.* §80 The point which is chiefly important.. is the indefinability of propositional functions. **1908** W. R. B. GIBSON *Probl. Logic* 82 The indefinability of the proper name. **1936** *Mind* XLV. 101 He proceeds to consider the nature of such good, criticising Dr. Moore's theory of indefinability.

indefinable (ɪndɪ'faɪnəb(ə)l), *a.* and *sb.* [f. IN-^{3} + DEFINABLE.] **A.** *adj.* That cannot be defined or exactly described; not susceptible of definition.

1810 tr. *Mad. Cottin's Chevalier de Versenai* I. 194 That secret and indefinable instinct. **1822** LAMB *Elia* Ser. I. *Roast Pig*, O call it not fat! but an indefinable sweetness growing up to it. **1830** D'ISRAELI *Chas. I*, III. xiii. 269 An obscure and indefinable line. **1863** GEO. ELIOT *Romola* xxii, Something as indefinable as the changes in the morning twilight. **1867** MISS BRADDON *Rupert Godwin* I. i. 2 Every look, every movement was instinct with that indefinable grace for which we can find no better name than good breeding.

B. *sb.* An indefinable person or thing.

1810 tr. *Mad. Cottin's Chev. de Versenai* I. 164 That woman is one of your indefinables. **1904** *Mind* XIII. 132 On the indefinables of philosophy, especially, much new light is thrown by M. Couturat's labours. **1927** F. A. LINDEMANN in R. J. S. McDowall *The Mind* 137 Though the so-called physical laws will be in general consistent with reality, there is no certainty that the indefinables employed in their statement.. have any fundamental significance beyond their appeal to the mental preferences.. of the physicist. *Ibid.* 139 The commonest indefinables used in physics are space and time. **1932** —— *Physical Significance of Quantum Theory* 12 The indefinables upon which all our thought processes depend. *Ibid.* 14 The three indefinables commonly used in physics are length, time, and mass. **1948** *Mind* LVII. 409 What we ignored was the less exact and less elegant work of insuring that the defining but undefined general terms upon which our explanations finally depended were themselves understood. The application of these indefinables we knew could be explained only by examples but the work of providing and arranging those examples and surrounding them with comment bringing out their interconnexions we could not bring ourselves to do. **1963** *Times* 26 Jan. 4/7 Halewyn declares his allegiance to evil and gallops away to his destruction; his talk is a series of verbal conjuring tricks with indefinables.

Hence **inde'finableness**; **inde'finably** *adv.*

1847 CRAIG, *Indefinably*. **1849** THACKERAY *Pendennis* II. ix, The expression in Captain Costigan's eye.. was.. indefinably humourous. **1889** *Harper's Mag.* Dec. 118/1 It has a vaporous indefinableness that leaves it a riddle.

†**indefinible.** *a. Obs. rare*$^{-1}$. [f. IN-^{3} + L. **dēfīnībilis*, f. *dēfīnīre* to set bounds, bound, limit: see DEFINE *v.*] Incapable of being limited; illimitable.

1652 BENLOWES *Theoph.* Ded. 22 The Empyræan flame of the Divinity, Indefinible, Interminable, Ineffable.

indefinite (ɪn'dɛfɪnɪt), *a.* (*sb.*) Also 6 **indiffynit(e, -yte, indiffinite, indyfinyte**, 7 **indifinite, indefinit.** [ad. L. *indēfīnīt-us*, f. *in-* (IN-^{3}) + *dēfīnīt-us* DEFINITE. Cf. F. *indéfini* (Montaigne, 16th c.).] Undefined, unlimited: the opposite of DEFINITE.

I. *generally.*

1. Without distinct limitation of being or character; having no clearly defined or determined character: indeterminate, vague, undefined.

1561 T. NORTON *Calvin's Inst.* I. xiii. (1634) 46 When there is simple and indefinite mention made of God, this name belongeth no lesse to the Sonne and to the Holy Ghost, than to the Father. **1616** BULLOKAR, *Indifinite*, not precisely exprest; vndefined. **1651** BAXTER *Inf. Bapt.* 76 Some generall indefinite promises. **1722** *Wodrow Corr.* (1843) II. 678 Your address is likewise a little indefinite; but I send this at a venture as you direct. **1818** HALLAM *Mid. Ages* (1878) II. viii. II. 329 Those indefinite aspirations for the laws of Edward the Confessor were changed into a steady regard for the Great Charter. **1875–6** W. B. POPE *Compend. Theol.* (1881) 656 The indefinite use of the term Sacrament in the early church. **1885** S. COX *Exposit.* Ser. I. v. 66 A fine, though indefinite, emotion.

2. Of undetermined extent, amount, or number; unlimited.

1594 NASHE *Unfort. Trav.* 46 Peace to thy Ghost, and yet me thinkes so indefinite a spirit should haue no peace or intermission of paines. **1625** BACON *Ess., Usury* (Arb.) 546 Let these Licensed Lenders be in Number Indefinite. **1842** GROVE *Corr. Phys. Forces* 86 Thus oxygen and hydrogen.. will remain unaltered for an indefinite period. **1852** ROBERTSON *Serm.* Ser. III. xii. 150 With respect to our moral and spiritual capacities, we remark that they are not only indefinite but absolutely infinite. **1877** E. R. CONDER *Bas. Faith* ii. 67 That is *indefinite* which has, or may have, a limit, but whose limit cannot be ascertained. **1884** J. RAE *Contemp. Socialism* 100 Commodities that admitted of indefinite multiplication.

†**b.** Formerly, sometimes, Extending beyond any assignable limits; boundless, infinite. *Obs.*

1664 POWER *Exp. Philos.* Pref. 17 The process of Art is indefinite, and who can set a non-ultra to her endevours? **1745** W. THOMPSON *Sickness* v. (R.), Indefinite and omnipresent God, Inhabiting eternity! shall dust, Shall ashes, dare presume to sing of thee?

II. *specifically* (in various technical uses).

3. *Grammar.*

a. Applied to various adjectives, pronominal words, and adverbs, which do not define or determine the actual person or thing, the place, time, or manner, to which they refer; as *any, other, some, such, somewhere, anyhow, otherwise*, etc.: esp. in ***indefinite article***, a name for the individualizing adjective *a, an* (A *adj.*^{2}), or its equivalents in other languages.

b. Applied to those tenses or inflexions of verbs which merely denote an action taking place at some time (past, present, or future), without specifying whether it is continuous or complete (thus distinguished from both *imperfect* and *perfect*), e.g. the Greek aorist and the English simple past; in French grammar formerly (as by Palsgrave) to the simple past tense corresponding to these, now called *past* or *preterite definite*; in modern French, *past* or *preterite indefinite* is applied to the compound tense corresponding to that called *perfect* in English, e.g. *il a parlé*, he has spoken. **c.** In the Slavonic verb formerly applied to one of the branches or aspects. **d.** Sometimes applied, in German and Old English grammar, to that declension of the adjective which is used when it is preceded by the indefinite article, possessive adjective, pronouns, etc: the *strong* declension of the adj.

1530 PALSGR. Introd. 32 The indiffynite indicatyve of the thyrde conjugation endeth ever in *S. Ibid.* 84 The indiffinite tens, as *je parlay*, I spake. *Ibid.* 382 To knowe therfore howe and whan the frenche men use their preter imparfyte tence, and whan their indiffynyte tence, whiche name I borowe of the grekes, for they have a tence whiche they call *aoristus*, that is to say, *indifinitus*, whiche moche resembleth this tence in the frenche tonghe. **1727** BAILEY vol. II, *Indefinite Pronouns.* **1727–41** CHAMBERS *Cycl.* s.v. *Article*, The article *a* is said to be *indefinite*, because applied to names taken in their more general, and confused signification. **1827** J. HEARD *Gram. Russ. Lang.* v. §1. 141 There are four branches: the *indefinite*, the *perfect*, the *semelfactive*, and the *iterative*. The *indefinite* expresses the action indeterminately with regard to its completion; as [*on trogal*], he moved. **1874** R. MORRIS *Chaucer's Prol.* etc. (Clar. Press Ser.) Introd. 33 Adjectives, like the modern German, have two forms—Definite and Indefinite. **1877** MOULTON tr. *Winer's Gram. N.T.* III. §25. 2 The indefinite pronoun *τις, τι*, is joined to abstract nouns.

4. *Logic.* Applied to propositions in which the subject has no mark of quantity; not distinguishing between 'some' and 'all'.

1773 REID *Aristotle's Log.* ii. §6 Wks. II. 692/2 A proposition is called indefinite when there is no mark either of universality or particularity annexed to the subject: thus, 'Man is of few days' is an indefinite proposition. **1864** BOWEN *Logic* v. 122 The logicians formerly distinguished another Class of judgments as *Indefinite*, meaning those in which the Subject, having no sign or predesignation of Quantity affixed to it, is not expressly declared to be either Universal, Singular, or Particular. Thus, *Elephants are sagacious animals*;—*Learned men are to be found at Oxford.* **1887** FOWLER *Deduct. Logic* iii. (ed. 9) 29 'Indefinite' or 'indesignate' propositions, as they are called, i.e. propositions in which the subject, being a common term, is not quantified, are inadmissible in Logic.

5. *Bot.* **a.** Said of inflorescence in which the central axis grows indefinitely in length, producing a succession of lateral branches bearing flower-buds (or of sessile flower-buds) which open successively from the lowest upwards; also called *centripetal* or *indeterminate*. **b.** Sometimes similarly applied to fibrovascular bundles which grow indefinitely, so that the stem increases in thickness, as in 'Exogens' or Dicotyledons. **c.** Said of the stamens or other parts of the flower when numerous and not clearly multiples of the number of the petals, etc.

1845 LINDLEY *Sch. Bot.* iv. (1858) 25 Stamens indefinite; that is to say, more numerous than can be easily counted. **1849** BALFOUR *Man. Bot.* §77 The vascular bundles [in exogens], from their mode of development in an indefinite manner externally, have been called *exogenous*; and for the same reason, Schlieden has denominated them *Indefinite*. *Ibid.* §472 The ovules are very numerous or indefinite. **1876** HOOKER *Botany Primer* 46 Called *indefinite*, because the axis goes on elongating after the first flower opens. **1880** GRAY *Struct. Bot.* v. (ed. 6) 144 The kinds of Inflorescence.. are all reducible to two types.. viz. Indefinite and Definite, or .. Indeterminate and Determinate. Each may be.. simple or compound.

B. *sb.* (ellipt. uses of the adj.) An indefinite thing, word, statement, etc.; something of indefinite nature or meaning, or which cannot be definitely specified, described, or classed.

1591 PERCIVALL *Sp. Dict.* F a, Aduerbs commonly gouerne an Indicatiue Moode: saue that where Interrogatiues are changed into Indefinites they haue some time a Subiunctiue. **1625** BACON *Ess., Dispatch* (Arb.) 248/1 That Negative is more pregnant of direction, then an indefinite. **1865** *Pall Mall G.* 16 Aug. 10/1 A table of the occupations of the people after a new classification..I. 'Professionals'..II. 'Domestics'..III. Commercials; IV. Agriculturists..V. Industrials..VI. Indefinites, that is, general labourers, gentlemen of means, and paupers, with a few others not open to classification.

Hence †**in'definite** *v. Obs.* (*nonce-wd.*), in phr. ***to indefinite it*** = to act or speak indefinitely. **in'definitism** (*nonce-wd.*), indefinite character.

1656 S. H. *Gold. Law* 76 If we indefinite it, when we should demonstrate, and universalize it. **1855** DORA GREENWELL *Present Heaven* (1861) 103 The vague spirituality or rather indefinitism of our ideas.

indefinitely (ɪn'dɛfɪnɪtlɪ), *adv.* [f. prec. + -LY².] In an indefinite manner or degree.

1. Without definition or limitation to a particular thing, case, time, etc.; indeterminately, vaguely.

1471 [see INDETERMINABLY]. **1530** PALSGR. Introd. 32 Other thre dyvers tymes, imparfytly past, indiffynitly past, and more than parfytly past. **1561** T. NORTON *Calvin's Inst.* I. 37 So oft as we do indefinitely speake of the name of God, we meane no lesse the Sonn and the Holy ghost than the Father. **1635** J. GORE *Well-doing* 3 A preacher..delivers his message indefinitely to the whole assembly. **1858** CARLYLE *Fredk. Gt.* I. iv, She had felt herself indefinitely unwell. **1863** MRS. CARLYLE *Lett.* III. 168 They pressed me to come to them..and I promised indefinitely that I would.

2. To an indefinite amount or extent; without specified or assignable limit or end; unlimitedly.

1621 BURTON *Anat. Mel.* II. iii. 111, 'Tis a fortune which some indefinitely preferre before prosperity. **1664** POWER *Exp. Philos.* Pref. 10 Motion also may be indefinitely swift or slow. **1697** DAMPIER *Voy.* I. 94 The Pacifick Sea..from 30 to about 4 deg. south latitude, and from the American shore westward indefinitely. **1833** MISS MITFORD in L'Estrange *Life* III. i. 6 Life is too short..for an alienation indefinitely prolonged. **1868** FREEMAN *Norm. Conq.* II. App. 540 It would be easy to prolong the list indefinitely.

indefiniteness (ɪn'dɛfɪnɪtnɪs). [f. as prec. + -NESS.] The quality of being indefinite; want of definiteness; indeterminateness, vagueness.

1589 PUTTENHAM *Eng. Poesie* II. xi. (Arb.) 111 The Roundell or Spheare..for his indefinitenesse hauing no speciall place of beginning nor end. **1623** BP. HALL *Best Bargaine* Wks. (1648) 476 The indefinitenesse of the charge implies a generallity. **1797** *Monthly Mag.* III. 201 That pernicious looseness and indefiniteness of speech, which prevail so generally. **1880** E. WHITE *Cert. Relig.* 34 There is now and then an Oriental indefiniteness as to method. **1885** SPURGEON *Treas. Dav.* cxxxii. 10 The fault of most prayers is their indefiniteness.

indefinition (ɪndɛfɪ'nɪʃən). [f. IN-³ + DEFINITION.] A condition of being indefinite, of lacking definition.

1888 *Pall Mall Gaz.* 14 Nov. 5/1 This negative quality of indefinition leaves a sense of uncertainty. **1940** BLUNDEN *Poems 1930–40* 57 About the stern defining phrase A gay indefinition plays. **1958** C. RABIN in *Aspects of Translation* 128 Turkish or Arabic with marking 'individuation + indefinition' rather than definition.

indefinitive (ɪndɪ'fɪnɪtɪv), *a. rare.* [f. IN-³ + DEFINITIVE.] Not definitive; not characterized by definition or limitation; indeterminate, indefinite.

1598 BARRET *Theor. Warres* V. i. 125 From the point of the first Trauesse next adioyning, is drawne an indefinitiue line. **1850** J. H. NEWMAN *Diffic. Anglic.* 82 A school of opinion..fixed in its principles, indefinitive and progressive in their range.

Hence **inde'finitively** *adv.*, without definition or limitation; **inde'finitiveness**, vagueness.

1621 SANDERSON *Twelve Serm.* (1637) 59 Ordinarily in our Sermons we indefinitively condemne as evill, swearing, and gaming for money. **1795** *Ann. Reg.* App. Chron. 92 They are all elected for two years, and may be immediately and indefinitively re-elected. *a* **1849** POE *Marginalia* Wks. 1864 III. 587 If the author did not deliberately propose to himself a suggestive indefinitiveness of meaning.

indefinito- (ɪndɛfɪ'naɪtəʊ), comb. form from L. *indēfīnītus* INDEFINITE; as in ***indefinito-definite*** adj., applied by Sir W. Hamilton to propositions predicated of the greater part or more than half.

1847 SIR W. HAMILTON *Let. De Morgan* 43 Indefinito-definites, To UI, YO, last we come; And that affirms, and this denies, Of more, most (half plus some). *Ibid.* 44 [Propositions] 1. Definite; 2. Indefinito-definite; 3. Semi-definite; 4. Indefinite.

indefinitude (ɪndɪ'fɪnɪtjuːd). [f. IN-³ + DEFINITUDE (or f. INDEFINITE after *definitude*).]

†**1.** The condition of having no known or assignable limit; undefined or undefinable number or amount. *Obs.*

1677 HALE *Prim. Orig. Man.* II. iv. 157 They arise to a strange and prodigious multitude, if not indefinitude, by their various Positions, Combinations, and Conjunctions.

2. Want of definiteness or precision; indefiniteness, undefined state.

1827 G. BEAUCLERK *Journ. Marocco* Ded., Until it has arrived at years of discretion..an indefinitude of age both in books and men. **1833** SIR W. HAMILTON *Discuss., Eng. Treat. Logic* (1853) 146 The vacillation or indefinitude of Aristotle himself in regard to the number of the modes. **1854** R. G. LATHAM *Native Races Russian Emp.* 248 They are measures of the extent to which the author who uses them eschews indefinitude.

indefinity (ɪndɪ'fɪnɪtɪ). *rare.* [f. INDEFINITE, after *infinity*: see -ITY.]

†**1.** = prec. 1. *Obs.*

1623 COCKERAM II, Endlesnes, *indifinity*. **1678** CUDWORTH *Intell. Syst.* Contents (I. v. 643) This potential Infinity or Indefinity of Body, seems to be mistaken for an actual Infinity of Space.

2. = prec. 2.

a **1734** NORTH *Exam.* I. iii. §38 (1740) 144 He can..come off, upon the Ambiguity or Indefinity of his Expressions. **1882** *Fraser's Mag.* XXV. 487 Branch lines..only to be entered upon after the ominous 'change' to whose convenient indefinity the porter stentoriously invites us.

indeflectible (ɪndɪ'flɛktɪb(ə)l), *a.* [f. IN-³ + **deflectible*, f. DEFLECT *v.* + -IBLE.] Incapable of being deflected or turned from a straight course.

1883 F. W. POTTER *Gambetta* in *French Celebr.* 28 Proclaiming in a single voice his indeflectible fidelity. **1884** *Fortn. Rev.* May 569 All unite in one undeviating and indeflectible direction.

†**inde'flexible**, *a. Obs. rare.* [IN-³.] = prec.

a **1641** BP. MOUNTAGU *Acts & Mon.* (1642) 122 Indeflexible subjection to Gods will.

†**inde'flore**, *a. Obs.* [Arbitrary f. IN-³ + stem of L. *dēflōrā-re* to DEFLOWER; for *indeflored* or *indeflorit*.] Not deflowered; chaste, inviolate.

1500–20 DUNBAR *Poems* lxxxv. 55 Implore, adore, thow indeflore, To mak our oddis evyne.

†**inde'flourishing**, *a. Obs.* [f. IN-³ + pres. pple. of DEFLOURISH *v.*] Not ceasing to flourish, unfading: cf. DEFLOURISH 2.

1610 G. FLETCHER *Christ's Vict.* I. xlvi, Ros'd all in liuely crimson ar thy cheeks, Whear beawties indeflourishing abide.

indeformable (ɪndɪ'fɔːməb(ə)l), *a.* [IN-³.] Not deformable; incapable of being 'deformed' or put out of shape.

1880 MINCHIN *Statics* (ed. 2) 13 In nature there are no such things as rigid bodies. For a great many practical matters there are bodies which may be treated as if they were rigid or indeformable.

indegent, indegest: see INDIGENT, etc.

indehiscent (ɪndɪ'hɪsənt), *a. Bot.* [IN-³.] Not dehiscent: said of fruits that do not split open when mature, but retain the seed till they decay.

1832 LINDLEY *Introd. Bot.* I. ii. 179 Cells one-seeded, indehiscent, dry, perfectly close at all times. **1841** MRS. LOUDON *1st Bk. Bot.* (1845) 25 Most of the kerneled fruits are indehiscent, and, if left to nature, must decay before they can liberate the seed. **1871** H. MACMILLAN *True Vine* 158 The fruit of the vine is indehiscent. **1872** OLIVER *Elem. Bot.* I. vii. 95 Syncarpous fruits..which are dry and indehiscent, that is, which do not open, but liberate the seed by decay, as the fruit of the Hazel, you may simply call nuts.

Hence **inde'hiscence**, the quality of being indehiscent.

1847 in CRAIG.

†**indeign**, *v. Obs. rare.* In 4 indeyne, 5 indaign. [A form intermediate between ENDEIGN and INDIGN; q.v.]

1. *intr.* To be indignant or angry.

1382 WYCLIF *Gen.* xviii. 30 Y biseche thee, he seith, ne indeyne thow, Lord, if I speke.

2. *trans.* To disdain, despise.

1483 CAXTON *Cato* C j b, Thou myghtest lese theyr loue and be indaigned of them.

†**inde'layed**, *a. Obs.* [IN-³.] Not delayed or put off; immediate.

1523 *St. Papers Hen. VIII*, VI. 118 If this overture shall not mowe take effect, indelaied order must be geven by His Majeste for the raysing and setting furthe of an armye. **1564** Q. ELIZ. in *Abp. Parker's Corr.* (Parker Soc.) 227 We will that you shall duly inform us thereof, to the end we may give indelayed order for the same.

†**inde'layedly**, *adv. Obs.* [f. prec. + -LY².] Without delay; immediately.

1535 HEN. VIII *Let. Earl Sussex* 17 Apr., We..wol Therfore and command you..that ye indelavedly do apprehend and take them. **1563–87** FOXE *A. & M.* (1596) 262/1 That he indelaiedlie..should prepare himselfe to be gone out of the realme. **1579** *Sc. Acts Jas. VI*, c. 70 Presentlie and indilayitlie upoun thair apprehensioun or convictioun..he or sche sall be put and haldin in the stokkis. *c* **1600** *Gowrie's Conspir.* in *Select. Harl. Misc.* (1793) 192 Verie miscontent that indelaiedlie he raid not to Sanct-Iohnstoun.

indeleble, -ebly, obs. ff. INDELIBLE, -IBLY.

inde'lectable, *a. rare.* [IN-³: cf. obs. F. *indelectable* (Godef.).] Unpleasant, disagreeable.

1748 RICHARDSON *Clarissa* lxxi. (1811) VIII. 327 Stiffened and starched..into dry and indelectable affectation. **1806** *Edin. Rev.* Oct. 109 His remarks upon this indelectable attendant.

†**in,delega'bility**. *Obs. rare*⁻¹. [f. IN-³ + DELEGABLE + -ITY. Cf. F. *indélégable* (Littré).] Incapability of being delegated.

1695 J. SAGE *Article* etc. Wks. 1844 I. 75 Is such a delegation consistent with our author's position about the indevolvibility or indelegability of such a power?

indeliable, obs. form of INDELIBLE.

indeliberate (ɪndɪ'lɪbərət), *a.* [IN-³: cf. F. *indélibéré* (17th c.).]

†**1.** Of persons, their qualities, etc.: Wanting in deliberation; inconsiderate; hasty or rash. *Obs.*

a **1617** BAYNE *On Eph.* (1658) 100 This may rebuke rash, indeliberate, and self-willed persons. **1652** GAULE *Magastrom.* 22 He reprooves..their indeliberate rashness. *a* **1677** MANTON *Twenty Serm.* xv. Wks. 1871 II. 333 There is a will natural and indeliberate, and a will deliberate and elective.

2. Of actions: Done without deliberation or forethought; not carefully considered or planned beforehand. Also of thoughts, words, etc.: Unpremeditated, spontaneous. Now *rare*.

1655 BP. BRAMHALL *Def. true Liberty* 37, I distinguish between free acts and voluntary acts. The former are always deliberate, the latter may be indeliberate. **1680** H. DODWELL *Two Lett. Advice* (1691) 96 Indeliberate actions are not capable of affectation. *a* **1711** KEN *Psyche* Poet. Wks. 1721 IV. 162 She felt a sudden indelib'rate Thought, Which strange Conviction in her Spirit wrought. **1896** *Academy* 12 Dec. 535/2 Short, insignificant, prattling, indeliberate letters.

†**inde'liberated**, *a.* [IN-³.] = prec. (sense 2).

a **1663** BRAMHALL (J.), Actions proceeding from blandishments, or sweet persuasions, if they be indeliberated, as in children..are not presently free actions.

inde'liberately, *adv. rare.* [f. INDELIBERATE + -LY².] Without deliberation or premeditation; unintentionally, involuntarily.

1681 KETTLEWELL *Chr. Obed.* (1715) 340 What we have been wont to do by long practice, we do as easily, as quickly, and as indeliberately, as we do those things which flow from the necessity of our very nature itself. **1700** R. PEARSON *Naaman Vindic.* 44 They might be..forced Ignorantly, or indeliberately to Worship..the Pagan Idols.

inde'liberateness. *rare.* [f. as prec. + -NESS.] Absence of deliberate intention.

1681 KETTLEWELL *Chr. Obed.* (1715) 345 That indeliberateness in sinning, which ariseth from an habit and custom of sin..doth not in any wise lessen or excuse a sinful action.

indelibe'ration. Now *rare.* [See INDELIBERATE and -ATION. (So mod.F. *indélibération* (Littré).] Want of deliberation or forethought.

a **1614** DONNE *Βιαθανατος* (1644) 31 Any mortall sinne..proceeding from indeliberation. **1646** JER. TAYLOR *Apol. Liturgy* Pref. §11 She should have no Liturgy at all, but the worship of God be left to the managing of chance and indeliberation and a petulant fancy. **1681** KETTLEWELL *Chr. Obed.* (1715) 561 They, who scarce ever sin wilfully at all, or very rarely, are wont most frequently through indeliberation and unadvisedness to miscarry. **1854** FABER *Growth in Holiness* iii. (1872) 45 Eagerness, anxiety..indeliberation..are all fatal to recollection.

indeli'bility. *rare.* Also -ebility. [f. next: see -ITY.] The quality of being indelible.

1804 HORSLEY *Speeches Parlt.* (1813) 421 The indelebility of the sacred character was a principle in the Church of Rome. **1891** *Daily News* 1 July 5/6 The ink..lost its ancient indelibility. **1896** *Blackw. Mag.* May 683 This indelibility of tribal types.

indelible (ɪn'dɛlɪb(ə)l), *a.* Also 6–7 indeleble, (7–9 indeliable). [In 16–17th c. *indeleble*, ad. L. *indēlēbilis*, f. *in-* (IN-³) + *dēlēbilis* DELIBLE; cf. F. *indélébile*, *-leble* (16th c.). The termination has been assimilated to -IBLE.]

That cannot be deleted, blotted out, or effaced; ineffaceable, permanent.

a. of a material mark, stain, etc. or of the substance which makes these, as ***indelible ink***; also ***indelible pencil***.

1579 FULKE *Heskins' Parl.* 422 Before he..hath his indeleble character scraped out of his handes and fingers endes. **1613** PURCHAS *Pilgrimage* (1614) 850 The women paint their faces with indeleble lines. **1650** BULWER *Anthropomet.* Pref., Pricking the same with Needles, then they take Indeliable tincture. **1656** BLOUNT *Glossogr.*, Indeleble. **1658** PHILLIPS, Indelible. **1772–84** COOK *Voy.* (1790) I. 92 This operation, called by the natives Tattaowing..leaves an indelible mark on the skin. **1816** J. SMITH *Panorama Sc. & Art* II. 783 Indelible Ink for marking Linen, &c. **1885** *Encycl. Brit.* XVIII. 490/2 In the indelible and copying pencils which have come into use in recent years, the colouring matter is an aniline preparation mixed with clay and gum. **1916** *Daily Colonist* (Victoria, B.C.) 23 July 9/1 All the newspaper offices in San Francisco yesterday received a communication written in Roman scrip [*sic*] with an indelible pencil, many of the words being heavily underscored. **1961** *Lebende Sprachen* VI. 69/2 Indelible pencil, der Tintenstift.

fig. **1825** T. JEFFERSON *Autobiog.* Wks. 1859 I. 49 Nature, habit, opinion have drawn indelible lines of distinction between them.

b. of a stain on character or reputation, infamy, disgrace, etc.

1529 MORE *Suppl. Soulys* Wks. 322/1 So deadly poisoned wᵗ sin, yᵗ their spottes bene indelible & their filthines

vnpurgeable. **1624** SANDERSON *Serm.* (1637) 432 Branded with an indeleble note of infamy. **1647** WARD *Simp. Cobler* 20 Accursed with indelible infamy. **1756** C. LUCAS *Ess. Waters* III. 284 This would be an unpardonable, an indelible reproach. **1887** BOWEN *Virg. Æneid* v. 198 This victory gain.. and preserve us from shame's indelible stain.

c. of a mark, stamp, or character impressed upon anything; *spec.* of the spiritual character which, according to various sections of the Christian Church, is held to be impressed or conferred by some of the sacraments.

1532 MORE *Confut. Barnes* VIII. Wks. 745/1 With the indelible caracter and badge of baptisme receiued into hys liuerey and hys holy houshold. **1638** CHILLINGW. *Relig. Prot.* I. vi. §39. 358 We shall then consider whether your indelible Character bee any reality. **1711** G. CARY *Phys. Phylastick.* 416 This Divine Power is what the School men and Church call an Indelible Character. **1871** DARWIN *Desc. Man* II. xxi. 405 Man still bears in his bodily frame the indelible stamp of his lowly origin. **1875** MANNING *Mission H. Ghost* i. 21 To all eternity they will bear the mark of their regeneration, the indelible character stamped upon them at the font.

d. of an impression on the mind; also of a feeling.

a **1631** DONNE *Lett.* (1651) 271, I have so many and so indeleble impressions of your favour to me. **1697** EVELYN *Numism.* viii. 265 Most grateful and indelible Sense of a long and intire Friendship. **1830** D'ISRAELI *Chas. I*, III. iii. 29 Charles had retained too indelible a recollection of the past. **1847** DISRAELI *Tancred* II. ii, Such an event makes an indelible impression.

†**e.** of a title, right, or the like: Indefeasible.

c **1645** HOWELL *Lett.* (1650) I. IV. viii. 186 They shall be only Keepers of the Great Seal, which for title and office are deposable; but they say the Lord Chancellor's title is indelible. **1769** BLACKSTONE *Comm.* IV. i. 3 The indelible rights of mankind.

Hence **in'delibleness**, the quality of being indelible, incapability of being blotted out or destroyed.

1654–66 EARL ORRERY *Parthenissa* (1676) 401 The indelibleness of the impressions of Youth. [In mod. Dicts.]

indelibly (ɪn'dɛlɪblɪ), *adv.* [f. prec. + -LY[2].] In an indelible manner; so as not to be blotted out or effaced.

1611 SPEED *Hist. Gt. Brit.* VII. x. 253 The murderesse Quendrid.. hath left her name indelebly stained with his innocent bloud. **1659** E. REYNOLDS in Eliot *Gosp. New-Eng.* A iij b, These premises are indelebly written in the minds of men by nature. **1750** JOHNSON *Rambler* No. 54 ¶11 Our crime.. is indelibly recorded, and the stamp of fate is fixed upon it. **1858** FROUDE *Hist. Eng.* III. xvii. 524 He had left the print of his individual genius stamped indelibly.. into the constitution of the country.

indelicacy (ɪn'dɛlɪkəsɪ). [IN-[3]: see next and -ACY.] Want of delicacy; want of a nice sense of propriety, refinement, or good taste; coarseness of character, manners, etc.

1712 STEELE *Spect.* No. 286 ¶1 Your Papers would be chargeable with something worse than Indelicacy, they would be Immoral. **1766** COLE in Ellis *Orig. Lett.* Ser. II. IV. 486, I hope you will pardon the indelicacy of the expression. **1774** GOLDSM. *Nat. Hist.* (1776) III. 177 The indelicacy of this animal [the pig] is.. rather in our apprehensions than in its nature. **1818** JAS. MILL *Brit. India* (1826) I. 398 The indelicacy of the Hindus. **1856** FROUDE *Hist. Eng.* I. 316 That indelicacy which was the singular blemish of his character.

indelicate (ɪn'dɛlɪkət), *a.* [IN-[3]. Cf. F. *indélicat* (1812 in Hatz.-Darm.).]

1. Wanting in, or offensive to, a sense of delicacy or propriety; coarse, unrefined; bordering upon what is immodest or indecent.

1742 RICHARDSON *Pamela* IV. 42 Don't think to let me lose my beloved Wife and have an indelicate Nurse put upon me instead of her. **1774** WARTON *Hist. Eng. Poetry* xxx. (1840) II. 447 Their manners were too indelicate to be shocked at any indecency. **1804** W. TENNANT *Ind. Recreat.* (ed. 2) I. 274 Who bandied about amongst each other the coarsest ribbaldry, and most indelicate sarcasms. **1846** GROTE *Greece* I. i. I. 15 A cast of fancy more coarse and indelicate than the Homeric.

†**b.** Used as *sb. Obs.*

1742 RICHARDSON *Pamela* xxxv. III. 342 These Gentlemen, the very best of them, are such Indelicates! *Ibid.* IV. Let. xiv. 82 What strange indelicates do these writers of tragedy often make of our sex!

2. Wanting in fine tact or nice regard to the feelings and tastes of others.

1800 MRS. HERVEY *Mourtray Fam.* IV. 102 She felt that, under the present circumstances, it would be indelicate to attempt more. **1849** MACAULAY *Hist. Eng.* iv. I. 462 It was apprehended that such indelicate greediness might disgust the benefactor.

3. Of food: Coarse. *Obs.*

1750 COVENTRY *Pompey Litt.* (1752) 101 The coarse fare he met with.. were but indelicate morsels to one who had formerly lived on ragouts and fricassees. **1777** G. FORSTER *Voy. round World* II. 224 Time makes these indelicate viands acceptable and delicious to their taste.

Hence **in'delicately** *adv.*, without delicacy.

1800 MRS HERVEY *Mourtray Fam.* III. 71 To throw herself, most indelicately, into the arms of a gamester, a profligate, a man of no birth. **1816** SCOTT *Let. to Byron* 5 Jan., The indiscreet zeal of the friend, who.. has injudiciously and, as she thinks, indelicately brought into view circumstances of private attention.

indeligence, variant of INDILIGENCE, *Obs.*

†**in'delve**, *v. Obs. rare*$^{-1}$. [f. IN-[1] + DELVE, after L. *infodĕre*.] *trans.* To dig in, to bury.

1382 WYCLIF *Gen.* xxxv. 4 Thei ȝyuen to hym alle alyen goddis that thei hadden.. and he indeluede hem vndur a theribynte.

†**in'demn**, *a. Obs. rare*$^{-1}$. In 6 indempne. [a. F. *indemne* (in 16th c. also *indempne*), ad. L. *indemnis*, f. *in-* (IN-[3]) + *damnum* loss, damage.] Free from or clear of loss or hurt.

1526 SIR R. WINGFIELD *Let. to Wolsey* (*MS. Cott. Galba B.* 14 lf. 3 b) The sayde kynge hath bownde hymsylff to save themperour indempne agaynste the kynges highnes of alle thingis.

indemn (ɪn'dɛm), *v. rare*$^{-1}$. [See INDEMN *a.*] *absol.* To indemnify.

1906 HARDY *Dynasts* II. I. viii. 177 To your ally, the Tsar, I must refer you... He can indemn.

†**in'demned**, *a. Obs. rare*$^{-0}$. [f. INDEMN *a.* + -ED[1], after F. *indemné*, pa. pple. of *indemner* to indemnify]. = INDEMN *a.*

1552 HULOET, Indempned. *indemnis.* **1570** LEVINS *Manip.* 49/36 Indemned.

indemnification (ɪn,dɛmnɪfɪ'keɪʃən). [f. INDEMNIFY: see -FICATION.]

1. The action of compensating for actual loss or damage sustained; also the fact of being compensated; *concr.* the payment made with this object.

1732 LEDIARD *Sethos* II. IX. 335 The only security we have left for our indemnification, is in our prisoners. **1765** BLACKSTONE *Comm.* I. i. 139 Giving him a full indemnification and equivalent for the injury thereby sustained. **1789** BENTHAM *Princ. Legisl.* xiii. §3 The party injured loses all hope of indemnification. **1844** H. H. WILSON *Brit. India* III. 145 The unwillingness to pay a money indemnification was so insuperable.. that the British Commissioners were induced to lower their demand.

b. The action of compensating for trouble, annoyance, etc.; *concr.* the recompense so rendered.

1774 WARTON *Hist. Eng. Poetry* ix. I. 294 The Franciscans.. enjoyed from the popes the privilege of distributing indulgences, a valuable idemnification for their voluntary poverty. **1839** DE QUINCEY *Recoll. Lakes* Wks. 1862 II. 97 Not likely to accept.. gorgeous philosophy.. as an indemnification for irregular performance of public duties.

†**2.** 'Security against loss or penalty' (J.); indemnity. *Obs.*

in'demnifi,cator. *rare.* [agent-n. in Latin form, f. INDEMNIFY.] One who indemnifies.

1802–12 BENTHAM *Ration. Judic. Evid.* (1827) V. 493 The common vouchee or indemnificator general, in the Common Pleas.

in'demnifi,catory, *a. rare.* [f. INDEMNIFY: see -ORY.] Pertaining or tending to idemnification.

1875 POSTE *Gaius* III. (ed. 2) 397 Where the actions on delict are purely indemnificatory.

indemnified, -fier: see under next.

indemnify (ɪn'dɛmnɪfaɪ), *v.*[1] Also 7 **indempnifie, -damnifie.** [f. L. *indemn-is* INDEMN + -FY.]

1. *trans.* To preserve, protect, or keep free *from*, secure *against* (any hurt, harm, or loss); to secure against legal responsibility *for* past or future actions or events; to give an indemnity to.

1611 COTGR., *Indemniser*, to.. indamnifie. **1651** BIGGS *New Disp.* ¶217 Save harmles and keep indempnified. **1665** J. WEBB *Stone-Heng* (1725) 153 An Asylum, to which any of them flying remain'd indemnified for whatever Delict committed. **1712** ARBUTHNOT *John Bull* II. iv, Why must the rest of the Tradesmen be.. indemnified from charges? **1769** BLACKSTONE *Comm.* IV. xi. 142 The fact indemnified the peace officers and their assistants, if they killed any of the mob in endeavouring to suppress such riot. **1855** MACAULAY *Hist. Eng.* xxi. IV. 554 An Act.. providing that, if Cook would make.. a true and full discovery, he should be indemnified for the crimes which he might confess. **1870** *Standard* 12 Nov., On entering into partnership in 1860 he was indemnified against liability on previously overdrawn accounts. **1884** J. RAE *Contemp. Socialism* 376 A sound system of working class insurance must be devised, which shall indemnify them against all the accidents and reverses of life.

2. To compensate (a person, etc.) *for* loss suffered, expenses incurred, etc.

1693 *Mem. Ct. Teckely* III. 2 That they who formerly possessed Employments, should be indempnified for the Loss of their Posts. **1771** ROBERTSON *Hist. Amer.* (1778) II. VI. 226 The plunder of the countries they invaded served to indemnify them for what they had expended in equipping themselves for the service. **1847** MRS. A. KERR *Hist. Servia* xx. 377 It was left to the Sultan to indemnify his vassals for their loss. **1847** MARRYAT *Childr. N. Forest* i, [They] indemnified themselves for the nonpayment of their salaries by killing the deer for sale and for their own subsistence. **1866** FELTON *Anc. & Mod. Gr.* II. II. vii. 395 They.. indemnified themselves by extortions from their unhappy subjects.

b. To compensate *for* disadvantages, annoyances, hardships, etc.

1707 *Reflex. upon Ridicule* 121 You ought to indemnify others for the Uneasiness you give them. **1836** MACGILLIVRAY tr. *Humboldt's Trav.* xxv. 376 The high price of provisions indemnifies the cultivator for the hard life. **1856** GRINDON *Life* xiv. (1875) 173 However long and dreary may be the winter, we are always indemnified by the spring. **1766** BURKE *Corr.* (1844) I. 110 This is one way of indemnifying one's self for the plainness of one's habit. **1863** MRS. OLIPHANT *Salem Ch.* iii. 40 She somehow appeared.. to indemnify herself for her privations.

†**3.** To compensate, make up for. *Obs. rare.*

1750 BEAWES *Lex Mercat.* (1752) 3 Two advantages.. indemnified this defect.

Hence **in'demnified, in'demnifying** *ppl. adjs.* Also **in'demnifier**, one who indemnifies.

1769 BLACKSTONE *Comm.* IV. xi. 143 There is the like indemnifying clause, in case any of the mob be.. killed in the endeavour to disperse them. **1817–18** COBBETT *Resid. U.S.* (1822) 341, I am doing my best to repay this country for the protection which it has given me against our indemnified tyrants. **1882** LD. BLACKBURN in *Law Rep.* 7 App. Cases 339 The amount which the indemnifier is bound to pay.

†**in'demnify**, *v.*[2] *Obs. rare.* Also **en-**. [f. IN-[2] + DAMNIFY, with vowel assimilated to INDEMN.] *trans.* To hurt, harm.

1583 STOCKER *Hist. Civ. Warres Lowe C.* I. 63 a, He.. did not believe that his Maiestie by this occasion coulde any way be endemnified. **1593** LODGE *William Longbeard* E ij, What harme the Rhodians haue doone thee, that thou so much indemnifiest them?

indemnitee (ɪndɛmnɪ'tiː). *U.S.* [irreg. f. INDEMNITY: see -EE.] 'The person to whom indemnity or promise of indemnity is given.' So **in'demni,tor**, the person who undertakes to indemnify another against loss or liability.

In recent American dictionaries.

indemnity[1] (ɪn'dɛmnɪtɪ). Also 5–7 **indempn-**, 6 **indimn-**; 5–6 **-te**, 6–7 **-tie.** [a. F. *indemnité* (1367 in Hatz.-Darm.), ad. late L. *indemnitās*, *-tātem*, n. of condition f. *indemnis* INDEMN.

The order of the senses is obscure; an early use of sense 3, otherwise unexemplified, appears in 3 c.]

1. Security or protection against contingent hurt, damage, or loss; safety. *spec.* (see quot. 1834).

1467 *Paston Lett.* No. 575 II. 307, I entende noon other but in als meche as in me is to se your indempnyte. **1533** MORE *Debell. Salem* Wks. 970/1 Vpon complaint made to the kynge and hys counsayle.. thei would prouide sufficiently for thindemnity of the wytnes in that behalfe. **1548** HALL *Chron., Edw. IV*, 216 The citiezens.. began maturely to consult, what parte they should folow for their most indempnite. **1642** in Clarendon *Hist. Reb.* IV. §164 The Indemnity of the Rights and Priviledges of Parliament. **1681** FLAVEL *Righteous Mans Refuge* 208 Gods unchangeableness is his peoples indempnity. **1796** BURKE *Regic. Peace* iv. Wks. IX. 61 They assure you.. that they will give you nothing in the name of indemnity or security, or for any other purpose. **1834** MACCULLOCH *Dict. Commerce* I. 682 Indemnity is where one person secures another from responsibility against any particular event. **1858** LD. ST. LEONARDS *Handy-Bk. Prop. Law* xxi. 148 You will, of course, be entitled to an indemnity against any demand which still binds you; for example, future rent under a lease to the testator. **1879** LUBBOCK *Addr. Pol. & Educ.* viii, 148 Insurance ought to be a contract of indemnity.

2. A legal exemption from the penalties or liabilities incurred by any course of action.

1670 COTTON *Espernon* I. III. 122 An indempnity, and oblivion of all pass'd unkindnesses. **1703** DK. QUEENSBERRY in Ellis *Orig. Lett.* Ser. II. IV. 238 To secure their friends there would be a General Indemnity past. **1761** HUME *Hist. Eng.* I. ix. 201 All his vassals who had entered into confederacy with Richard, should receive an indemnity for the offence. **1767** BLACKSTONE *Comm.* II. xxxi. 483 Besides this allowance, he has also an indemnity granted him, of being free and discharged for ever from all debts owing by him at the time he became a bankrupt; even though judgment shall have been obtained against him. *a* **1862** BUCKLE *Civiliz.* (1869) III. iii. 145 Receiving beforehand an indemnity for every excess.

b. ***Act*** (or ***Bill***) ***of Indemnity***, an act of Parliament or other authority granting exemption from the penalties attaching to any unconstitutional or illegal proceeding. Also *fig.*

Such an act used, previously to the general act of 31 & 32 Vict., c. 72 §16, to be passed annually for the relief of those who had failed to take the necessary oaths of office. In *Eng. Hist.* the term is specifically applied to the Acts of 1660 and 1690, exempting those who had taken arms or acted against Charles II and William III respectively, from the penal consequences of their former deeds.

1647 FULLER *Good Th. in Worse T.* (1841) 106 So shall I have an act of indemnity before he can enter his action against me. **1648** D. JENKINS *Wks.* 79 The Army by an Act of Indemnity free themselves from all those dangers, which an Ordinance can no more do then repeale all the Lawes of the Land. **1672** MARVELL *Reh. Transp.* I. 94 He therefore carried the Act of Oblivion and Indempnity thorow. **1793** BURKE *Rem. Policy Allies* Wks. 1842 I. 603 A valuable friend.. asked me what I thought of acts of general indemnity and oblivion, as a means of settling France. **1827** HALLAM *Const. Hist.* (1876) III. xv. 112 They retained the bill of indemnity in the commons. **1836** H. COLERIDGE *North. Worthies* (1852) I. 19 The Act of Indemnity and the trial of the regicides transpired before the commencement of the correspondence.

3. Compensation for loss or damage incurred; indemnification.

1793 LD. AUCKLAND *Corr.* (1861) III. 13 The reasonableness of furnishing some indemnity to the Dutch by the cession of Lillo and Leifenshock. **1825** BENTHAM *Ration. Rew.* 138 When an individual is only indemnified, he is not rewarded: reward.. begins when indemnity is complete. **1849** MACAULAY *Hist. Eng.* ii. I. 157 The Cavaliers very naturally demanded indemnity for all that they had suffered.

b. A sum paid by way of compensation.

1872 YEATS *Growth Comm.* 216 The vigour of Cromwell eventually compelled the Dutch to pay an indemnity of 1,000,000 guilders. **1876** FAWCETT *Pol. Econ.* (ed. 5) I. iv. 32 Within four years, France had to pay to Germany a war indemnity of £240,000,000.

†**c.** *spec.* (in early use). A payment made to the archdeacon in compensation for the loss of his induction money, and also to the bishop in lieu of his institution fees, when a church was impropriated to an abbey or college. *Obs.*

1542-3 *Act 34 & 35 Hen. VIII*, c. 19 §1 Diuers pencions, porcions, corrodies, indimnities, sinodies, proxies and other profites. **1545** *Instr. to Cromwell* in *Cott. MS. Cleop.* F. 1 lf. 85 Pensions or Indemnities be thes, whan a churche is Impropered to an abbay or a coleage, then the Archedeacon for euer lesithe his induction money, and in recompens of that he shall haue yerly oute of the saide benefice so Improperede xijd. or ijs. for a yerly pension more or lesse.. euyn so episcopus conseruatur Indemnis and hathe a lyke pension for his Indemnitie, in the lewe of his Institucion.

4. *attrib.*, as ***indemnity bill, loan, money.***

1818 *Gen. Hist.* in *Ann. Reg.* 36/1 The third reading of the indemnity bill occurred on March 5th. **1867** *Homeward Mail* 16 Nov. 954/2 The indemnity money paid after the destruction of the Old Factory gardens. **1897** *Daily News* 17 Sept. 5/7 The Powers, it is believed, will guarantee the indemnity loan.

†**in'demnity**[2]. *Obs. rare.* Also 6 endemnitee. [ad. OF. *indampnité* (1433 in Hatz.-Darm.), f. *in-* (IN-[2]) + L. *damnum* loss, damage; for the vowel cf. INDEMNIFY *v.*[2]] Damage, hurt, injury.

1556 J. HEYWOOD *Spider & F.* xxxi. 12 Which growth.. of kinred, not of enmitee, Did I (in you) by ingrate endemnitee Doute here:..I were a beaste. *c* **1629** LAYTON *Syon's Plea* To Rdr., We doe not read of greater Persecution, higher indignitie and Indemnity done upon Gods People..than in this our Iland.

indemni'zation. *rare.* [a. F. *indemnisation*, n. of action from *indemniser*: see next.] = INDEMNIFICATION 2.

1836 *Tait's Mag.* III. 651 To be indebted for the indemnization of my creditors to some other grocer's daughter. **1845** *For. Q. Rev.* XXXIV. 281 He spent two vexatious years in the sorry business of secularization and indemnization, which the peace of Luneville had left as a legacy to diplomatists.

†**in'demnize,** *v. Obs. rare*[−0]. [a. F. *indemnise-r* (1598 in Hatz.-Darm.), f. *indemne* INDEMN.] *trans.* To indemnify.

1611 COTGR., *Indemniser*, to indemnize, or indamnifie.

inde,monstra'bility. *rare.* [f. next: see -ITY.] The quality of being indemonstrable; incapability of being demonstrated.

1789 T. TAYLOR *Proclus' Comm.* II. 2 Principles in simplicity, indemonstrability, and self-evidence, should excel things posterior to principles. **1847** DE QUINCEY *Protestantism* Wks. VIII. 108 Kant was the first person, and perhaps the last, that ever undertook formally to demonstrate the indemonstrability of God.

indemonstrable (ɪndɪ'mɒnstrəb(ə)l), *a.* [IN-[3]: cf. F. *indémonstrable* (Littré).] Incapable of being demonstrated or proved. (Said *esp.* of primary or axiomatic truths, principles, etc.)

1570 BILLINGSLEY *Euclid* I. i. 9 The first principles and grounds, which are indemonstrable. *a* **1619** FOTHERBY *Atheom.* I. i. §4 (1622) 6 The first and most ancient principle, and therefore of all other the most indemonstrable. **1785** REID *Intell. Powers* VI. vii. (1803) II. 388 We find likewise some of the axioms of geometry mentioned by Aristotle as axioms, and as indemonstrable principles of mathematical reasoning. **1867** *Contemp. Rev.* VI. 447 Let us give up endeavouring to demonstrate the indemonstrable. **1877** E. CAIRD *Philos. Kant* I. 139 Certain primary conceptions or indemonstrable material principles of truth.

Hence **inde'monstrableness**, incapability of being demonstrated; **inde'monstrably** *adv.*

1654 WARREN *Unbelievers* 195 Which indemonstrably sheweth the instrumentality of this grace. **1727** BAILEY (vol. II), *Indemonstrableness.*

†**in'den,** *v. Obs. rare.* Also 7 en-. [f. IN-[2] + DEN *sb.*[1]] *trans.* To put into a den.

1598 FLORIO, *Intanare*, to indenne, to put, enter, go, or creepe into a caue or denne. **1611** *Ibid.*, *Incauernare*,..to endenne. **1664** FULLARTON *Turtle Dove*, Ierome was stoned, and Daniel was indened. Amos was rent. Paul by the sword did end.

†**indencion.** *Obs. rare*[−1]. [Erroneous form for *indensation*: see INDENSE.] A rendering dense, a thickening.

1547 BOORDE *Brev. Health* cxlviii. 54 The one [fever] doth come by the indencion or thyckenes of bloude.

indene ('ɪndiːn). *Chem.* [f. IND(O-[2] + -ENE, or as a contraction of INDONAPHTHENE.]

1. a. = INDONAPHTHENE (which name *indene* has completely superseded). **b.** Any of the derivatives of this compound.

1888 *Jrnl. Chem. Soc.* LIV. 1303 (*heading*) Indene-derivatives. **1892** E. F. SMITH tr. *V. von Richter's Chem. Carbon Compounds* (ed. 2) 903 The formation of the carboxyl derivatives of indene..proceeds in a manner analogous to the formation of alkyl indenes. **1956** RODD & VAN ALPHEN in E. H. Rodd *Chem. Carbon Compounds* IIIB. xx. 1260 (*heading*) Substituted indenes. **1968** L. K. ARNOLD *Introd. Plastics* ix. 111 Coumarone and indene, found in certain coal tar fractions, are polymerized to produce resins which range from those liquid at room temperature to others melting at 300° F.

2. Special Comb.: **indene resin**, any thermoplastic resin made from indene; usually = *coumarone-indene resin.*

1900 *Jrnl. Chem. Soc.* LXXVIII. I. 657 The indene resin decomposes at 290–340°. **1947** [see COUMARONE b].

†**inde'niable,** *a. Obs. rare.* [IN-[3].] That cannot be denied; undeniable.

1621 BP. MOUNTAGU *Diatribæ* 82 Maine and indeniable consequences. **1652** FRENCH *Yorksh. Spa* iii. 38 Their indeniable testimony.

†**inde'nied,** *a. Obs. rare*[−1]. [IN-[3].] Not denied; undenied.

1624 BP. MOUNTAGU *Gagg* 17 By necessary consequence, and indenied it is but you have tied yourselfe..unto expresse words.

indenize, -ation, etc.: see ENDENIZE, etc.

1749 MARTIN *New Eng. Dict.* Introd. Eng. Tongue 17 Many words and terms in these arts have also been indenized.

inde'nominable, *a. rare*[−1]. [IN-[3].] That cannot be named; unnameable.

1647 WARD *Simp. Cobler* 28 An indenominable Quæmalry of overturcas'd things.

†**in'densate,** *a. Obs. rare*[−1]. [ad. L. type **indensāt-us*, pa. pple. of **indensā-re*: see next, and cf. DENSATE *v.*] Rendered dense; thickened.

1599 R. LINCHE *Anc. Fict.* N, The aire becommeth indensate and grosse.

†**in'dense,** *v. Obs. rare*[−1]. [ad. L. type **indensā-re*, f. *in-* (IN-[2]) + *densā-re* to make thick, f. *densus* DENSE.] *trans.* To make dense or thick.

1576 NEWTON *Lemnie's Complex.* (1633) 118 Vnctions and Frictions..indense the body, that the ayre and windes should not batter and damnifie it.

indent (ɪn'dɛnt), *v.*[1] Also 5–6 endent. [ad. F. *endenter* (Ph. de Thaun, 12th c.) 'to snip, notch, iag on the edges' (Cotgr.), L. type **indentā-re* (med.L. and It. *indentare*), f. *in-* (IN-[2]) + **dentā-re* to furnish with teeth, f. *dens, dent-em* tooth; cf. *dentātus* DENTATE.]

I. In general sense.

1. *trans.* To make a tooth-like incision or incisions in the edge or border of; to notch or jag; now, chiefly, to give a zigzag or strongly seriate outline to.

c **1430** *Pilgr. Lyf Manhode* II. cxlviii. (1869) 135 She.. fyled myn yren and endented it. *c* **1440** *Ipomydon* 1641 A barbor he callyd,..And shove hym bothe byhynd and before, Queyntly endentyd, oute and in. **1523** FITZHERB. *Husb.* §23 Take hede that thy mower mow clene and holde downe the hynder hand of his sith, that he do not endent the grasse. **1866** TATE *Brit. Mollusks* iv. 120 The jaw..is marked with five longitudinal ribs which indent the edges of the plate.

b. To form a deep recess or recesses in (a coast-line, etc.); to penetrate deeply. Also *transf.*

1555 EDEN *Decades* III. ix. 138 It is eaten and indented with two goulfes. **1612** DRAYTON *Poly-olb.* i. 5 Those armes of sea..By their meandred creeks indenting of that land. **1773** JOHNSON *Lett. to Mrs. Thrale* 21 Sept. ¶17 It is an island..so much indented by inlets of the sea that there is no part of it removed from the water more than six miles. **1777** COOK *2nd Voy.* III. xii. (R.), The coast..seemed to be indented into creeks and projecting points. **1831** CARLYLE *Sart. Res.* I. iv, Each part [of the book] overlaps, and indents, and indeed runs quite through the other. **1855** MACAULAY *Hist. Eng.* xviii. IV. 191 Lochleven, an arm of the sea which deeply indents the western coast of Scotland.

c. *intr.* To recede or form a recess.

1784 J. BARRY in *Lect. Paint.* iii. (1848) 145 The forms are angular, as well where they indent or fall in as where they swell out. **1856** GROTE *Greece* II. App. XII. 667 At the spot here mentioned, the gulf indents eastward.

II. To indent a document, and senses thence arising.

2. *trans.* To sever the two halves of a document, drawn up in duplicate, by a toothed, zigzag, or wavy line, so that the two parts exactly tally with each other; to cut the top or edge of two or more copies of a legal document in such an exactly corresponding shape; hence, to draw up (a document) in two or more exactly corresponding copies.

This was done in the case of a deed, covenant, agreement, etc. in which two or more parties had an interest, so that one copy was retained by each party; the genuineness of these could be subsequently proved by the coincidence of their indented margins. See INDENTURE *sb.* 2.

1385 [see INDENTED *ppl. a.*[1] 3]. **1413** *Exam. Oldcastle* in Arb. *Garner* VI. 133 His Belief, which was indented and taken to the Clergy, and set up in diuers open places. **1473** WARKW. *Chron.* 10 Alle this poyntment aforeseide were wrytene, indentyde, and sealede. **1526** *Pilgr. Perf.* (1531) 85 All thynges..that thou hast promysed to god, & be conteyned in thyne obligacyon, endented bytwene god & thy soule. **1557** *Order Hospitalls* Dvj b, An Inventorie.. shall be Indented, th' one part thereof to remaine in your custodie, and the other in the custodie of the persons charged. **1622** CALLIS *Stat. Sewers* (1647) 232 All other Laws and Ordinances of Sewers..which be but in parchment, and not Indented, or which be indented also, if not sealed, continue in force no longer then that Commission continueth by the power whereof they were made. **1624** CAPT. SMITH *Virginia* VI. 229 Contracted with me by articles indented vnder our hands. **1735** *Col. Rec. Pennsylv.* III. 601 Articles of Agreement Indented Made, Concluded and Agreed upon at Philadelphia. **1767** BLACKSTONE *Comm.* II. xx. 295 If a deed be made by more parties than one, there ought to be regularly as many copies of it as there are parties, and each should be cut or indented (formerly in acute angles *instar dentium*, but at present in a waving line) on the top or side, to tally or correspond with the other; which deed, so made, is called an indenture. **1809** R. LANGFORD *Introd. Trade* 103 When a deed begins *This Indenture*, it must actually be indented, that is, must be cut or scalloped at the top, otherwise it will be a Deed-poll. [This is no longer so: cf. quot. 1845 in INDENTURE *sb.* 2.]

†**3.** *intr.* To enter into an engagement by indentures; hence, to make a formal or express agreement; to covenant (*with* a person *for* a thing); to engage. Also *fig. Obs.*

1489 W. PASTON in *P. Lett.* No. 908 III. 351 My Lorde of Northethombyrland..hath endentyd with the Kynge for the kepynge owt of the Schottys and warrynge on them. **1541** *Act 33 Hen. VIII*, c. 22 The said maister of the wardes and liueries..shall haue power..to couenaunt and indent with euery person..for his..liuerie. **1561** T. NORTON *Calvin's Inst.* III. 301 Many..do nothing but indent with God vpon a certaine condicion, and binde him to the lawes of their couenanting. **1642** FULLER *Holy & Prof. St.* v. iii. 367 At last she indents downright with the devil. He is to find her some toies for a time, and to have her soul in exchange. **1655** —— *Ch. Hist.* II. iv. §23 Thus would I have Ecclesiasticall and civil Historians indent about the Bounds, and Limits of their Subjects. **1700** J. BROME *Trav. Eng. Scot.* III. (1707) 176 The Servants..do usually indent with their Masters, when they hire them. **1705** STANHOPE *Paraphr.* I. 139 The Persons baptized by John, did also undertake some new conditions, and indent in some Privileges. *a* **1734** NORTH *Exam.* III. viii. §38 (1740) 612 Courage did not serve them to refuse delivering over the Goals by Indenture to North and Rich, as the Way is; nor to indent with their own Anti-Sherriffs. **1759** GOLDSM. *Pres. St. Pol. Learning* xi. Wks. (1854) II. 50, I fire with indignation when I see persons wholly destitute of education and genius indent to the press, and thus turn book-makers.

†**b.** with *subord. cl.* or *inf.* expressing purpose.

1462 *Paston Lett.* No. 453. II. 104 He hathe endented with the owners of the schip what daye it schulbe redy. **1480** *Howard Househ. Bks.* (Roxb.) 9, I, Iohn lord Howard, endented with the King my sovrain Lord to do him servisse opon the see. **1585** ABP. SANDYS *Serm.* xiv. §26 (Parker Soc.) 276 He indented not what reward he should have. **1643** S. MARSHALL *Letter* 7 Suppose a free man indents with another to be his servant in some ingenious employment. *a* **1661** FULLER *Worthies* (1840) III. 366 [She] indented with her husband that her heritable issue should assume her surname. **1715** RAMSAY *Christ's Kirk Gr.* II. iii, Till this time towmond I'se indent Our claiths of dirt will sa'r.

†**4.** *trans.* **a.** To contract for, bind oneself to, or promise, by or as by making indentures; to covenant, stipulate, agree about, promise. *Obs.*

a **1555** BRADFORD *Hurt Hearing Mass* Wks. (Parker Soc.) 318 We should take it no less than idolatry or image-service, whatsoever thing is indented by man, saint, or angel, and not by him, concerning his worship and service. **1600** HOLLAND *Livy* VII. xli. 279 He would not indent ought for his owne securitie. **1607** *Schol. Disc. agst. Antichr.* I. ii. 72 Euen as Paul indented an imitation of Iewish rites when he shaued his head at Cenchrea. **1631** R. H. *Arraignm. Whole Creature* x. §1. 74 They indent golden Mountaines, but pay chirping Myce.

†**b.** To engage (a person) as a servant, etc. by or as by indentures; = INDENTURE *v.* 2. *Obs.*

1758 [see INDENTED *ppl. a.*[1] 4]. **1787** BURNS *Let. to Moore* 2 Aug., I was thinking of indenting myself, for want of money to procure my passage. **1804** J. GRAHAME *Sabbath* (1839) 17/2 To indent one's person for life, is a tremendous engagement.

5. *intr.* To make out a written order with a duplicate or counterfoil; hence, to make a requisition *on* or *upon* a person *for* a thing. (Orig. an Anglo-Indian use.) In later usage also to draw *upon* (a source of supply). Cf. INDENT *sb.*[1] 4.

1829 *Bengalee* 136 Could it prove of any service..to offer part of the accommodation for his stores? but at all events, he might indent freely on hers, on their arrival. **1837** MACAULAY in *Life & Lett.* (1880) I. 469, I have indented largely, to use our Indian official term,) for the requisite books. **1851** F. HALL in *Benares Mag.* VI. 719 *note*, Shefta's work..is indented upon, by the Maulawi, without stint and without acknowledgement. **1859** LANG *Wand. India* 277 Other magistrates had been indented upon (as magistrates very frequently were, when ladies were nervous and travelling with only an ayah). **1882** SALA in *Illustr. Lond. News* 30 Sept. 343 The medical officers are unable to 'indent' on the commissariat or ordnance stores for newspapers. **1888** *Pall Mall G.* 9 Mar. 14/1 [quoting Indian paper] The salt tax has at last been indented upon for covering the deficit in our Budget.

6. *trans. Comm.* To order by an indent: to order a supply of (a commodity). Cf. INDENT *sb.*[1] 5.

1897 *Westm. Gaz.* 2 Mar. 10/1 On what principle do you work in indenting books from England? **1899** *Ibid.* 27 Feb. 2/2 A short time ago Mr. Kinder indented 20,000 tons of Welsh coal.

III. In other literal and technical senses.

7. *trans.* To make an incision in (a board, etc.), for the purpose of mortising or dovetailing; to join or joint together by this method.

(Although the evidence for the sense is late, it appears very early in INDENTING *vbl. sb.*[1] 2 and INDENTURE *sb.* 1 b.)

1741 A. MONRO *Anat. Bones* (ed. 3) 71 Each of these bony Pieces is indented into the larger Bones. **1805-17** R. JAMESON *Char. Min.* (ed. 3) 154 The ranges are indented into each other. **1811** *Self Instructor* 135 In wainscoting, the dimensions are taken..indenting the string where the plane goes. **1825** J. NICHOLSON *Operat. Mechanic* 588 Boards can

be connected together at any given angle..by indenting them together. 1844 H. ROGERS *Introd. Burke's Wks.* 65 He put together a piece of joinery, so crossly indented and whimsically dove-tailed. 1876 GWILT *Archit.* Gloss., *Indented*, toothed together, that is, with a projection fitted to a recess.

b. ***indent in***, to mortise in, joint in with art: in quot. *fig.*

1639 DRUMM. OF HAWTH. *Char. Anagram* Wks. (1711) 231 An anagram..fitly cometh in mostly in the conclusion, but so that it appeareth not indented in, but of it self naturally.

8. *Printing.* To set back (from the margin of the column of writing or type) the beginning of (one or more lines), as a means of marking a new paragraph, of exhibiting verse, etc.; to begin (a line or a succession of lines) with a blank space.

1676 MOXON *Print Lett.* 11 You must indent your Line four Spaces at least. 1791 BOSWELL *Johnson* May an. 1748 Indenting the notes into text. 1824 J. JOHNSON *Typogr.* II. vi. 137 Authors should always make the beginning of a new paragraph conspicuous to the compositor, by indenting the first line of it far enough.

absol. 1884 SOUTHWARD *Pract. Print.* (ed. 2) 87 To set out a paragraph in this style, the compositor would be told to 'run out and indent'.

†**9.** *intr.* To move in a zigzag or indented line; to turn or bend from side to side in one's course; to double. *Obs.*

1565 GOLDING *Ovid's Met.* VII. (1593) 177 But doubling and indenting still avoids his enimies lips. 1592 SHAKS. *Ven. & Ad.* 704 Then shalt thou see the dew-bedabbled wretch Turn, and return, indenting with the way. 1607 TOPSELL *Four-f. Beasts* (1658) 176 It windeth or indenteth like a Serpents figure. 1643 MILTON *Divorce* II. xiv, To limit and levell out the direct way from vice to vertue..not winding or indenting so much as to the right hand of fair pretences.

†**b.** *trans.* ***to indent the way***: in same sense.

1612 W. PARKES *Curtaine-Dr.* (1876) 57 To see light-headed drunkennesse indent the way from side to side. 1622 J. TAYLOR (Water P.) *Water Cormor.* Wks. (1630) III. 5/1 From side to side he staggered as he went, As if he reeling did the way indent.

indent (ɪn'dɛnt), *v.*² Also 4–5 (*inf.* and *pa. pple.*) endent(e. [f. IN-² + DENT *v.*

Although this is, at least in its radical part, etymologically distinct from INDENT *v.*¹, the two are in actual use (and perh. have always been) consciously regarded not as distinct words, but only as senses or uses of the same word, the difference between them in their primary signification being much less than that between actual senses of INDENT *v.*¹. This blending is even more apparent in the derivatives, such as *indentation*, *indenture*, which owe their form entirely to the Romanic INDENT *v.*¹, but have senses derived from both verbs.]

I. †**1.** *trans.* To inlay, set, emboss; = DENT *v.* 3.

13.. *E.E. Allit. P.* A. 1011 þe topasye twynne how þe nente endent. ?*a*1400 *Morte Arth.* 3298 His dyademe was droppede downe, dubbyde with stonys, Endente alle with diamawndis. *c*1400 MAUNDEV. (Roxb. xxiii. 106 þe greece.. es all of precious stanes, endentid with gold. *c*1435 *Torr. Portugal* 227 Towrres Endentyd with presyos stonys, Schynyng ase crystall clere. ?*c*1475 *Sqr. lowe Degre* 788 Your sensours shall be of golde, Endent with asure many a folde. *a*1649 DRUMM. OF HAWTH. *Poems* 129 A Glasse Indent'd with Gems. 1730 A. GORDON *Maffei's Amphith.* 368 The Marble..in which he imagin'd precious Stones were indented. *Ibid.* 371 Small Streaks and Pieces of other Metal..are nicely indented and interspersed on the Statue.

fig. 13.. *E.E. Allit. P.* A. 628 Anon þe day with derk endente, þe myȝt of deth dotz to enclyne.

II. 2. *trans.* To form as a dint, dent, or depression; to strike or force inwards so as to form a dent or hollow; to impress.

*c*1400 *Beryn* 1851 Thus Iangelyng to ech othir, endenting euery pase, They entrid both in-to the hall. 1613 PURCHAS *Pilgrimage* (1614) 83 A huge Dragon..divided the earth, as he went seeking to hide... Thus did he indent a passsage for this River. 1641 *Rhode Island Colon. Rec.* (1856) I. 115 A Manual Seale shall be provided for the State..in the Liess or Bond, this motto indented: *Amor vincet omnia.* 1693 DRYDEN *Juvenal* vi. (1697) 123 Deep Scars were seen indented on his Breast. 1725 POPE *Odyss.* XIX. 267 Deep in the neck his fangs indent their hold. 1769 *Chron.* in *Ann. Reg.* 160/2 Having his name indented only on a tin plate and not painted on his cart. 1851 J. D. MACLAREN in *Mem.* (1861) 213 [These] leave their footsteps deeply indented. 1877 LL. JEWITT *Half-ho. Eng. Antiq.* 83 Lines produced by indenting a twisted thong into the soft clay.

fig. 1613 PURCHAS *Pilgrimage* (1614) 31 Among all the Lessons which Nature hath taught, this is the deepliest indented. 1655 FULLER *Ch. Hist.* II. iv. §17 The Danish Garrisons lay so indented in the Heart of the Land. 1822–34 *Good's Study Med.* (ed. 4) II. 422 Properties..which if not peculiar to the plague are indented upon it far more strikingly, than upon any other disease.

3. To make a dint or dints in the surface of (a thing) with or as with a blow; to mark with a surface hollow, or depression; to dint or dent.

*c*1586 C'TESS PEMBROKE *Ps.* CV. v, Ioseph..Whose feete.. fretting irons did indent. 1653 J. HALL *Paradoxes* 114 A countenance Savage with bristles or indented with scars. 1725 POPE *Odyss.* XIX. 37 Shields indented deep in glorious wars. 1736 S. WESLEY *Battle of Sexes* 154 Furrows deep indent his batter'd arms. 1824 LANDOR *Imag. Conv.* Wks. 1846 I. 184/1 Although the sabre does not penetrate the metal, it indents it so deeply as to produce the same effect. 1837 DICKENS *Pickw.* xvi, Mr. Pickwick..indenting his pillow with a tremendous blow.

fig. 1798–9 LAMB *Corr.* (1870) 107 Many a little thing which..seemed scarce to indent my notice now presses painfully on my remembrance.

4. *intr.* To receive or take an indentation; to become indented or furrowed.

1653 A. WILSON *Jas. I.* 161 His countenance had indented with Age before he was old. 1774 GOLDSM. *Nat. Hist.* (1776) VII. 55 The oyster..breeds a large shell, and the shell itself indents to receive its impression.

indent (ɪn'dɛnt, 'ɪndɛnt), *sb.*¹ [f. INDENT *v.*¹]

I. 1. An incision in the edge of a thing; a deep recess, strictly of angular form; an indentation.

1596 SHAKS. *1 Hen. IV*, III. i. 104 It [the Trent] shall not winde with such a deepe indent, To rob me of so rich a Bottome here. 1627 SPEED *England* xviii. §2 The whole in Circumference, traced by the compasse of her many indents, one hundred twentie and eight miles. 1779 FORREST *Voy. N. Guinea* 268 A cut, or an indent into the coral rocks, about a hundred foot broad. 1807 J. JOHNSON *Oriental Voy.* 40 Simmon's Bay, a cove or indent on the western shore. 1867 OUIDA *Idalia* xxix, The cliff..rose aloft, curving inward and shaping one of the many indents of the irregular southern coast.

2. *Printing.* The blank space or set-in at the commencement of a paragraph: = INDENTION 2.

1884 in *Cassell's Encycl. Dict.*

II. 3. = INDENTURE *sb.* 2: in various senses.

1589 PUTTENHAM *Eng. Poesie* III. xxiv. (Arb.) 299 In negotiating with princes we ought to seeke their fauour.. and not..to trafficke with them by way of indent or condition. *a*1605 R. BANNATYNE *Jrnl.* (1806) 346 To mak it as it were a contract, to be subscryvit be both the parteis; or rather everie partie to subscryve thair awin part of the indent. 1710 *New Hampsh. Provinc. Papers* (1868) II. 623 You will call them over by the Indent of the Engineer left when he received them. 1724 S. SEWALL *Diary* 1 Feb. (1882) III. 330 The Coroner shewed me the Indent of the Jury. 1820 in P. Warung *Tales Old Regime* (1897) 167 The indent having been examined, this certifies seven years have elapsed since sentence of Transportation..was passed. 1897 *Ibid.* 146 Make a note, Mr. Comptroller, to ascertain how it is that the ship's indent was so imperfect.

b. A certificate of a money claim or the like; *spec.* an indented certificate issued by the U.S. Government, or by a state government, at the end of the War of Independence, for the principal or interest due on the public debt. *Obs.* exc. *Hist.*

1788 M. CUTLER in *Life, Jrnls. & Corr.* (1888) I. 381 Adventurers who have paid for shares are exceedingly pressing for the Indents, which are to be returned to them. 1798 BAY *Amer. Law Rep.* (1809) I. 121 An indented certificate (of loan) commonly called a general indent of the State of South Carolina. 1809 J. MARSHALL *Const. Opin.* (1839) 124 The indents issued upon them [state bonds] for interest, were drawn by David Rittenhouse.

4. An official requisition for stores. (Originally by a convenanted servant of the E. Ind. Company.)

1799 WELLINGTON *Let. to Lieut. Col. Harness* in Gurw. *Desp.* (1837) I. 46, I have desired the commissary of supply to be prepared at Bangalore to answer your indents for every thing that you will want. 1803 —— *Let. to Sec. Gov.* 18 Apr., Specifying in the indent the contents of the loads. *Ibid.*, I shall countersign these indents. 1871 *Daily News* 21 Sept., Any regimental quartermaster, through the simple medium of an indent, can in any emergency obtain a supply of provisions out of this. 1892 *Pall Mall G.* 15 Nov. 2/1 Indents were made on the Medical Department for quantities which soon nearly exhausted the stores at its command.

5. *Comm.* An order for goods, esp. one sent to England from abroad.

1800 *Asiat. Ann. Reg., Proc. Parl.* 27/1 From the ready sale, the governments abroad were induced to add considerably to their indents. 1879 *Commercial Let.*, We enclose an indent of stationery. 1883 *Manch. Exam.* 30 Nov. 4/5 The sudden fall in sterling exchange has checked dealers in sending home indents to any extent. 1891 *Times* 9 Oct. 9/3 Indents come home at rather better figures owing to supplies abroad being light.

indent ('ɪndɛnt), *sb.*² [f. INDENT *v.*²] A dint or depression in the surface of anything, made by a knock or blow; an indentation; hence, any depression, hollow, or furrow in a surface.

1690 LEYBOURN *Curs. Math.* 454 b, If a Spherical Body had..here and there some irregular indents made in it. 1781 THOMPSON in *Phil. Trans.* LXXI. 254 Its surface was full of small indents. 1868 *Daily Tel.* 3 July, This shot made an indent of 4·5 inches, and drove the 12 by 5-inch supports out between two and three inches. 1876 HUMPHREYS *Coin-Coll. Man.* ii. 11 On the other [side of the coin] merely the indent formed by the punch used to drive the metal into the die. 1897 *Allbutt's Syst. Med.* IV. 356 A superficial unevenness in the shape of scattered indents or depressions.

fig. 1874 HELPS *Soc. Press.* vi. (1875) 77 Character..has deeper indents in it than are made by any of the adventitious circumstances that you have adduced.

indentation (ɪndɛn'teɪʃən). [In form, n. of action f. INDENT *v.*¹ (see -ATION); but in sense derived also from INDENT *v.*²]

I. Senses from INDENT *v.*¹

1. The action of indenting; the condition of being indented or having the edge cut into tooth-like notches or angular incisions; denticulation; toothing.

1836 *Penny Cycl.* V. 247/1 The form of leaves..margin, the manner of their indentation, and the nature of the leaf-stalk. 1858 GLENNY *Gard. Every-day Bk.* 65/2 If the edge be smooth, with no indentation, and pefectly circular. 1877 F. HEATH *Fern W.* 22 The indentation assuming various shapes, often being deeply incised.

2. with *an* and *pl.* A cut, notch, or angular incision in the margin of anything; a deep recess in a coast-line, or the like; a series of incisions; a zigzag moulding, etc.

*a*1728 WOODWARD (J.), The margins do not terminate in a streight line, but are indented; each indentation being continued in a small ridge, to the indentation that answers it on the opposite margin. 1796 MORSE *Amer. Geog.* II. 101 The opposite Welsh coast is broken by various bays and indentations. 1806 *Med. Jrnl.* XV. 69 Leaves oblong, on short leaf-stalks, blunt, wing cleft, with indentations. 1853 KANE *Grinnell Exp.* xxii. (1856) 170 Captain Austin.. entered the same little indentation in which five of us were moored before. *a*1862 BUCKLE *Misc. Wks.* (1872) I. 302 The Greek coast is full of indentations.

3. *Printing.* = INDENTION 2.

1864 WEBSTER s.v., Common indentation..hanging indentation. 1884 SOUTHWARD *Pract. Print.* 86 The first line of the paragraph..is shorter than the two following, there being a widespace at the beginning of it. This is called an indentation.

II. Sense from INDENT *v.*²

4. The action of impressing so as to form a dent or dint; the dent, hollow, or depression thus formed; any deep and decided depression in a surface.

1847 JAMES *Convict* ii, On the summit of one of the most elevated points..there was a little indentation. 1861 *Times* 11 July, Injurious compression of a soft, moist soil, by the indentation of its wheels. 1880 BASTIAN *Brain* 115 The extent of its surface is further increased by the existence of numerous superficial folds or indentations.

5. Special Comb.: **indentation hardness**, hardness as determined by one of the indentation tests; **indentation test**, any of various tests for determining the hardness of a solid by making an indentation in a sample under standard conditions and measuring either its size or the distance travelled by the indenter.

1918 *Proc. Inst. Mech. Engin.* Oct.–Dec. 487 Researches on indentation hardness. 1956 B. W. MOTT *Micro-Indentation Hardness Testing* i. 9 The general definition of indentation hardness..is the ratio of the load applied to the surface area of the indentation. 1968 D. A. SMITH *Addition Polymers* x. 447 The testing of fabricated polymer components..may include evaluation of tensile stress-strain and flexural properties.., indentation hardness, and the examination of the effects of temperature on rigidity. 1897 *Min. Proc. Inst. Civil Engin.* CXXIX. 334 (*heading*) A new indentation test for determining the hardness of metals. 1956 B. W. MOTT *Micro-Indentation Hardness Testing* i. 2, (1) Static indentation test: A steady load is applied to an indenter..and the hardness is calculated from the area or depth of indentation produced. (2) Dynamic indentation test: A ball, cone or a number of small spheres is allowed to fall from a definite height and the hardness number is obtained from the dimensions of the indentation and the energy of the impact.

indented (ɪn'dɛntɪd), *ppl. a.*¹ [f. INDENT *v.*¹ + -ED¹.]

1. Having the edge or margin deeply cut with angular incisions; deeply, strongly, or coarsely serrated along the margin.

*c*1440 *Promp. Parv.* 261/1 Indentyd, *indentatus*. 1551 TURNER *Herbal* I. A v b, Acanthium is a kynde of thystel indented after the fashion of branke vrsin. *Ibid.* B j b, One of them hath leues lyk a plain tre, and depely endentyd. 1601 HOLLAND *Pliny* I. 307 All [beasts] that haue teeth indented in like saws, be naturally devourers of flesh. 1628 MILTON *Vacat. Exerc.* 94 Trent, who, like some earth-born giant, spreads His thirty arms along the indented meads. 1653 H. COGAN tr. *Pinto's Trav.* xxxiv. 135 Banners of white damask, deeply indented. 1664 POWER *Exp. Philos.* I. 14 She had two Claws..which were indented, or made Saw-wise on the inside. 1715 DESAGULIERS *Fires Impr.* 127 Plates of Tin.. indented along their length. 1851 D. WILSON *Preh. Ann.* (1863) II. IV. i. 200 The inlets of their indented coast. 1877 F. HEATH *Fern W.* 22 Sometimes the leafy portion, though undivided, has its margin beautifully cut in, or indented.

b. Having a serrated or zigzag figure, direction, or course, as a line, wall, moulding, path, etc.; constructed with salient and re-entrant angles, as a battery, parapet, etc.

1600 SHAKS. *A.Y.L.* IV. iii. 113 A green and guilded snake ..with indented glides, did slip away. 1660 BOYLE *New Exp. Phys. Mech.* xxiv. 193 A wavering or wrigling motion, whereby they describ'd an indented Line. 1667 MILTON *P.L.* IX. 496 The Enemie of Mankind, enclos'd In Serpent ..toward Eve Address'd his way, not with indented wave,.. but on his reare. 1706 PHILLIPS (ed. Kersey), *Indented Line*, (in *Fortif.*) a Line running in and out like the Teeth of a Saw: often us'd on the bank of the Counterscarp upon a River or Sea-Coast. *c*1710 CELIA FIENNES *Diary* (1888) 72 There is one walke all ye length of the Garden..it is indented in and out in Corners. 1802–19 REES *Cycl.* s.v. *Redens*, Redens, redans, or redant in Fortification. A kind of work indented in form of the teeth of a saw... It is also called saw work and indented work. 1834–47 J. S. MACAULAY *Field Fortif.* (1851) 15 Some authors recommend an indented parapet to obtain fire on the salient angles of works. 1853 STOCQUELER *Milit. Encycl.*, *Indented Line*, in fortification, is a serrated line, forming several angles, so that one side defends another. The faces are longer than the flanks. 1875 PARKER *Gloss. Archit.* (ed. 4) 158 The other favourite mouldings of the Norman style, are..the Indented [etc.].

2. *Her.* Of an ordinary, etc.: Having a series of similar indentations or notches.

In the *Bk. St. Albans* on Heraldry, what is now called 'embattled' is represented and described as 'indentit', while 'irrasit' is used to describe the modern indented figure; in Guillim, however, the description of 'indented' shows it to bear the current meaning.

?*a*1400 *Morte Arth.* 2053 A derfe schelde, endenttyd with sable With a dragone engowschede. 1470–85 MALORY *Arthur* IX. xxxvi, His sheld..was endented with whyte and black. 1486 *Bk. St. Albans, Her.* D iij, Qvarterit armys.. calde indentit for .ij. colowris oon in to an othir by the maner of teth ar indentit. 1523 LD. BERNERS *Froiss.* (1812) I. lx. 81 His baner..was goules, a sheffe, syluer, thre cheuorns in the

sheffe, bordred syluer indented. **1611** GUILLIM *Heraldry* I. v. 18 He beareth Gules a bordure indented Argent. *Ibid.* This bordure is said to be indented, because it seemeth to be composed (as it were) of teeth. **1725** BRADLEY *Fam. Dict.*, *Indented*, a Term in Heraldry, when the Out-Line of a Bordure, Ordinary, &c. is in the Form of the Teeth of a Saw. **1864** BOUTELL *Her. Hist. & Pop.* xii. 84 *Indented*, having a serrated border line.

3. Of a legal document: Cut zigzag or wavy at the top or edge; having counterparts severed by a zigzag line; *esp.* in ***deed*** (***bill***, etc.) ***indented*** (as opposed to DEED POLL) = INDENTURE *sb.* 2. Cf. med.L. *chartæ* (*scripturæ*, etc.) *indentatæ*.

1385 (May 15) *Award betw. Robert Earl of Fyfe and John of Logy*, To the wytnes of the qwylkis al and syndry in thir endentyt lettrys contenyt, tyl ilke parte of the forsayde endenturis I hafe put my Cele. **1424** *E.E. Wills* (1882) 62 Made by dede endented. **1432–50** tr. *Higden* (Rolls) VIII. 432 Seales were not putte to wrytnges indentede that the kynge of Ynglonde scholde have all londes of the duchery off Aquitanny. **1440** *Walsall Rules* c. 17 in Gross *Gild Merch.* (1890) II. 249 The olde Masters of the Gylde shall by byll indented..delyver to the newe Masters alle the money, plate [etc.]. **1494** FABYAN *Chron.* v. cxxxii. 116 He there in yᵗ presence made his testament, yᵗ before he had causyd to be written in .iiii. sondrye skynnes endentyd, to be rad, & than sealyd wᵗ certeyne of theyr sealis, wherof yᵗ one he wyllid to be kept in the tresory of Seynt Denys. **1523** FITZHERB. *Surv.* 20 There is no maner of estates made of free lande by polle dede or dede indented. **1679** BEDLOE *Popish Plot* 11 They were both parties to the same Indented Articles. **1706** PHILLIPS, *Deed Indented*, or *Indenture*, a Writing cut with Dents or Notches on the top or side; which consists of two or more Parts, and wherein 'tis express'd, That the Parties concerned have interchangeably, or severally set their Hands and Seals to every Part of it. **1747** CARTE *Hist. Eng.* I. 581 There were three indented copies made. **1765** BLACKSTONE *Comm.* I. xi. 426 Apprentices..are usually bound for a term of years, by deed indented, or indentures, to serve their masters, and be maintained and instructed by them. **1818** CRUISE *Digest* (ed. 2) IV. 10 Deeds are divided into two sorts; deeds poll, or cut in a straight line; and deeds indented. **1845** [see INDENTURE 2].

4. Bound or engaged by an indenture or formal covenant: = INDENTURED I.

1758 *Acc. Micmakis & Maracheets* 105 He had been an indented servant in New England. **1771** SMOLLETT *Humph. Cl.*, *Let. to Mrs. Gwyllim* 28 Apr., What between his willfullness and his waste, his trumps and his frenzy, I lead the life of an indented slave. **1788** WESLEY *Wks.* (1872) VII. 79 Indented servants, who are legally engaged to remain with you for a term of years. **1810** *Public Notice, Sydney, Australia* 21 July (Morris) A ship..with female convicts, whom it is..the Governor's intention to distribute among the settlers, as indented servants. **1864** SALA in *Daily Tel.* 24 Sept., These miserable bondsmen—these indented apprentices to the great planter, Death. **1882** FISKE in *Harper's Mag.* Dec. 114/2 There were a few indented white servants.

5. *Printing.* Of a line of writing or printing: Set in, so as to break the line of the margin. See INDENT *v.*^{1} 8.

1840 MRS. BROWNING *Lett. R. H. Horne* (1877) I. xxi. 123, I am sorry you do not print the stanzas with the indented lines.

indented (ɪnˈdɛntɪd), *ppl. a.*^{2} [f. INDENT *v.*^{2} + -ED^1.] Impressed, struck, or dinted in, so as to make a depression or hollow in a surface.

1635 BRATHWAIT *Arcad. Pr.* 123 With an indented pace ..[he] addressed himselfe with best speed he could towards Themista. **1834** LYTTON *Pompeii* II. i, Their eyes..fixed on the bloody throat of the one, and the indented talons of the other.

b. Marked with sharp depressions on the surface, as if caused by the dint of some instrument.

Hence **inˈdentedly** *adv.*, by indentation; in intaglio.

1753 CHAMBERS *Cycl. Supp.* s.v. *Camaieu*, Any kind of gem, whereon figures may be engraven either indentedly, or *in relievo*.

indentee (ɪndɛnˈtiː), *a. Her.* [ad. F. *endenté*, ad. med.L. *indentātus*, pa. pple. of *indentāre*: see INDENT *v.*^{1}] (See quots.)

1727–41 CHAMBERS *Cycl.*, *Indented, indentee*,..when the outline of a bordure, ordinary, etc. is notched, in form of the teeth of a saw. **1828** BERRY *Encycl. Herald.* I, *Indentée*, having indents not joined to each other, but set apart, as *indentée borderwise*, called by the French a *bordure canelée*, and *dentelée of each point*.

indenter^1 (ɪnˈdɛntə(r)). [f. INDENT *v.*^{1} + -ER^1.] One who indents, covenants, or orders by indent.

1660 HEXHAM, *Een bespreker*,..a Conditioner, or an Indenter. **1897** *Manch. Guard.* 25 Oct., Cases..where goods indented for..are now wanted for delivery, the indenters coolly offering to pay at the guaranteed rate.

indenter^2 (ɪnˈdɛntə(r)). Also -or. [f. INDENT *v.*^{2} + -ER^1, -OR.] Something that produces indentations; *spec.* a small hard sphere, pyramid, or similar object used for producing an indentation in a solid (as in an indentation test).

1929 *Proc. Inst. Mech. Engin.* I. 384 If only a fraction of the attention..had been devoted to the economical production of high quality cones or pyramids as indenters, they would now be in a more satisfactory position with regard to hardness testing. **1948** SPIELMANN & ELFORD *Road Making & Administration* (ed. 2) VII. 265 Indenters, Crimpers, and Key Cutters are no longer manufactured. **1950** *Engineering* 4 Aug. 102/3 Mechanical testing..includes..measurement of the shape of impressions made by Knoop hardness indenters. **1966** *Nature* 28 May 879/1 A hard steel indenter (sphere, cone, or pyramid) was pressed with a known load for a specified time on to the surface of a smooth block of ice. **1971** B. SCHARF *Engin. & its Lang.* iv. 23 All three are indentation tests in which a weighted steel ball or other 'indentor' is applied to the test piece. The hardness is assessed according to the size of the impression (Brinell and Vickers) or the travel of the indentor (Rockwell).

indentilly (ɪnˈdɛntɪlɪ), *a. Her.* Also -illey, -elly. [Corrupted from OF. *endentelé* f. *en-* (IN-^{2}) + *dentelé* DENTELATED.] (See quots.)

1828 BERRY *Encycl. Herald.* I, *Indentilley*, having long indents, somewhat resembling piles conjoined, as a fesse indentilley at the bottom... These kind of indents are, in old authors upon heraldry, sometimes blazoned *indented per long*, meaning with long indents. **1889** ELVIN *Dict. Her.*, *Indentelly*, indented Perlong, with notches much deeper than usual.

indenting (ɪnˈdɛntɪŋ), *vbl. sb.*^{1} [f. INDENT *v.*^{1} + -ING^1.] The action of INDENT *v.*^{1}, or the result produced by this.

1. = INDENTATION I and 2.

c **1386** CHAUCER *Pars. T.* ⁋343 The cost of embrowdynge, the degise, endentynge, barrynge..and semblable wast of cloth in vanitee. *c* **1440** *Promp. Parv.* 261/1 Indentynge, *indentacio*. **1551** TURNER *Herbal* I. I v a, In forme and indentyng of the leafe, lyke vnto an oke leafe. **1608** WILLET *Hexapla Exod.* 614 To carue a graue with incisions and indenting. **1650** FULLER *Pisgah* IV. iii. 44 They removed not foreright, but with many flexures and indentings. **1787** G. WHITE *Selborne* v. (1789) 12 The outline, in all its curves and indentings, does not comprise less than thirty miles. **1797** *Encycl. Brit.* II. 437/2 Neither of these..take notice of any indentings in the curve..which divides the illuminated part from the dark in the disk of Venus.

b. *Her.* (Cf. INDENTED *ppl. a.*^{1} 2.)

1486 *Bk. St. Albans, Her.* C vj a, This engraylyng is no propur langage aftir the sight of thys cros: bot rather an endentyng as truth is. **1611** GUILLIM *Heraldry* I. v. (1660) 28 Every of these Indentings, entring into the Field, lessen and take away some part of them as they goe.

†**2.** Mortising; a mortise joint: see INDENT *v.*^{1} 7.

1382 WYCLIF *1 Chron.* xxii. 3 And myche yren..to endentyngis [Vulg. *ad commissuras*] and ioynyngis Dauid made redy.

3. The making of an INDENTURE (2) or INDENT (*sb.*^{1} 3–5).

1488 in *Naval Acc. Hen. VII* (1896) 33 In makyng of.. Rekennynges of pursers of shipps indentyng with diuers persons & other muniments. **1618** E. ELTON *Rom.* vii. (1622) 115 By way of restipulation or indenting with them againe. **1655** FULLER *Ch. Hist.* II. ii. §40 Though there be no indenting, and conditional capitulating with God (who is to be taken on any terms). **1808** PENSON in H. A. Page *De Quincey* (1877) I. vii. 137, I must insist on your indenting on my funds.

indenting (ɪnˈdɛntɪŋ), *vbl. sb.*^{2} [f. INDENT *v.*^{2} + -ING^1.] The action of INDENT *v.*^{2}, or the result produced by this.

1. = INDENTATION 4.

1580 HOLLYBAND *Treas. Fr. Tong*, *Eschancrure*, an indenting. **1606** SYLVESTER II. iv. II. *Magnificence* 59 Hils were not seen but for the Vales betwixt The deep indentings artificiall mixt. **1693** *Phil. Trans.* XVII. 955, I conclude, that these Indentings are the places where the Scarf-skin is most united to the Skin underneath it. **1746** BADCOCK *ibid.* XLIV. 168 The only Part of the Flower which appears with a Hollow or Indenting on its Top.

†**2.** Inlaying or embossing; inlaid work. *Obs.*

1730 A. GORDON *Maffei's Amphith.* 371 Ornamenting Works of Metal..by Indenting and In-laying. *Ibid.* These Indentings are of a reddish kind of Copper.

inˈdenting, *ppl. a.* [f. INDENT *v.*^{2} + -ING^2.] That indents or makes indentations on a surface.

1831 J. HOLLAND *Manuf. Metal* I. 274 The contrivance of what are called indenting cylinders.

indention (ɪnˈdɛnʃən). [Irregularly formed from INDENT *v.*^{1}, instead of *indentation*; but in sense derived also from INDENT *v.*^{2}]

I. From INDENT *v.*^{1}

1. = INDENTATION I and 2.

1763 *Nat. Hist.* in *Ann. Reg.* 66/1 They are..smooth, thick, and without indention at the edge. **1814** SCOTT *Diary Voy.* 16 Aug. in *Lockhart*, The bay is formed by a deep indention in the mainland. **1861** HULME tr. *Moquin-Tandon* II. III. ii. 119 A lamina of bone folded upon itself so as to form three indentions on the outer edge. **1870** F. R. WILSON *Ch. Lindisf.* 126 Each indention [is] enriched with bead ornament.

2. The indenting of a line in printing or writing; the leaving of a blank space at the beginning of a line at the commencement of a new paragraph, etc.; the blank space so left. See INDENT *v.*^{1} 8.

Hanging or ***reverse indention***, the projection of the first line of a paragraph, etc., beyond the vertical line of those that follow.

1824 J. JOHNSON *Typogr.* II. 136 The mere indention of an m [is] scarcely perceptible in a long line. **1884** SOUTHWARD *Pract. Print.* (ed. 2) 87 The whole would be a 'hanging indention', because part of the first line would hang over the succeeding ones.

II. From INDENT *v.*^{2}

3. A dent or dint: = INDENTATION 4.

1839 CHATTO *Wood Engraving* 564 It will make a small indention in the [wood] block, and occasion a white or grey speck in the impressions.

†**inˈdentment.** *Obs.* [f. INDENT *v.*^{1} + -MENT: cf. F. *endentement*.]

1. Indentation (of the edge of anything).

1671 GREW *Anat. Pl.* v. §4 Yet is the top of the Empalement indented also; that the Indentments, by being lapp'd over the Leaves before their expansion, may then protect them. **1713** in *Connect. Colon. Rec.* (1870) V. 389 There must be new cut on this larger plate, the words on the indentment at the head of each bill.

2. An indenture, covenant.

1597–8 BP. HALL *Sat.* IV. ii. (T.), The brabling neighbours on him call For counsel in some crabbed case of law, Or some indentments, or some bond to draw. **1599** NASHE *Lenten Stuffe* (1871) 99 With this indentment and caution, that, though there be neither rhyme nor reason in it ..they..shall supply it with either. **1611** SPEED *Hist. Gt. Brit.* IX. viii. §14. 540 Sundry great Lords of eyther side were by indentment of Writing, made sureties to the counterpart.

indentor (ɪnˈdɛntə(r)). *Comm.* [f. INDENT *v.*^{1} 6 + -OR.] One who indents or writes an order for goods.

1883 *Manch. Exam.* 30 Nov. 4/5 There have been heavy arrivals [at Bombay] on account of native indentors. **1886** *Daily News* 24 Sept. 2/3 All other circumstances remaining the same the indentor from India pays more or less gold according to the state of the exchange.

indentor^2, var. INDENTER^2.

indenture (ɪnˈdɛntjʊə(r)), *sb.* Forms: 4–6 endentur(e, 5 -or, -our, 7 -er; 5–6 indentour, 6 -er, 5– indenture. [In form (ME. *endenture*) a. OF. *endenteure* (later *-ure*) indentation, furnishing with teeth, f. L. type **indentātūra*, f. **indentāt-*, ppl. stem of **indentā-re* INDENT *v.*^{1}: cf. L. *dentāt-us* DENTATE, and see -URE. But in sense, representing also INDENT *v.*^{2}]

I. Senses derived from INDENT *v.*^{1}

1. The action of indenting or notching a thing on the edge; an angular notch, indentation, or incision in the edge or border of anything.

1671 GREW *Anat. Pl.* i. §45 The Lobes of the Seed, have both a little Indenture. **1686** PLOT *Staffordsh.* 239 Which counterchanging of the ridges make the indentures on the sides. **1692** RAY *Dissol. World* II. iv. (1732) 138 Some serrate with small teeth others with great indentures. **1723** CHAMBERS tr. *Le Clerc's Treat. Archit.* I. 96 A little Indenture or Retreat, BC, not exceeding a Minute in depth. **1763** WINTHROP in *Phil. Trans.* LIX. 506 The Sun's limb, undulating..made it somewhat difficult to judge when the indenture, formed by the Planet upon it, intirely ceased. **1818** SCOTT *Rob Roy* xxxvi, This noble lake..spreads its base around the indentures and promontories of a fair and fertile land. **1865** SWINBURNE *Poems & Ball.*, *Cameo* 11 Till lips and teeth bite in their sharp indenture. **1883** HOLDER in *Harper's Mag.* Jan. 181/1 Those who..linger along the indentures of rocky shores on summer nights.

†**b.** Jointing by means of notches or indentations: cf. INDENTING *vbl. sb.*^{1} 2. *Obs.*

13.. *E.E. Allit. P.* B. 313 Þenne cleme hit [the ark] with clay comly with-inne & al þe endentur dryuen daube withouten.

2. A deed between two or more parties with mutual covenants, executed in two or more copies, all having their tops or edges correspondingly indented or serrated for identification and security. Hence, A deed or sealed agreement or contract between two or more parties, without special reference to its form.

Originally both copies were written on one piece of parchment or paper, and then cut asunder in a serrated or sinuous line, so that when brought together again at any time, the two edges exactly tallied and showed that they were parts of one and the same original document: hence the expression 'pair of indentures'. Occasionally a word, sentence, or figure was engrossed on the space where they were divided, as in the space between a bank cheque and its counterfoil.

(The earliest sense, and app. of Eng. or Anglo-Fr. origin.)

[**1304** *Rolls of Parlt.* I. 164/2 Et fiat Indentura inter ipsum & Coronatorem. **1339** *Ibid.* II. 107/2 Sous certeynes Condicions comprises es Endentures sur ceo faites, et enseales.] **1375** BARBOUR *Bruce* I. 513 The barownys thus acordyt ar, and that Ilk nycht writyn war Thair Endenturis, and aythis maid. *Ibid.* 565 Bot the Endentur till hym gaf he, That soune schawyt the Iniquite. **1423** SIR T. ROKEBY in Ellis *Orig. Lett.* Ser. II. I. 97 Als it, be hys endenture made, betwix the forsayd noble kyng and the forsayd Thomas Rokeby, pleinli appiers. **1480** CAXTON *Chron. Eng.* cxlviii, 127 The fourme of accord..was in a payr of Endentures and they put her seales vnto that one part, and they that comen in the kynges name putt her seales to that other part of endentures. **1494** FABYAN *Chron.* VII. 441 [He] concludyd a peace atwene the Kynge & the Scottis, & causyd to be delyuered vnto theym the Chartyr or Endenture called Ragman, with many other thynges. **1534** MORE *Comf. agst. Trib.* III. Wks. 1228/2 You deuyse as it were indentures betwene God and you, what thing you will doe for him, and what thing you wyll not doe. **1592** WEST *1st Pt. Symbol.* §101. **1596** SHAKS. *1 Hen. IV*, III. i. 80 And our Indentures Tripartite are drawne: Which being sealed enterchangeably ..Tomorrow, Cousin Percy, you and I, And my good Lord of Worcester, will set forth. **1598** HAKLUYT *Voy.* I. 164 One part of which indentures remaineth in the custodie of the English ambassadors, and the other part in the hands of the commissioners of Prussia. **1628** COKE *On Litt.* I. 229 a, If a deed beginneth, *Hæc Indentura*, &c. and in troth the Parchment or Paper is not indented, this is no indenture, because words cannot make it indented..It may be an Indenture without words, but not by words without

indenting. **1706** [see INDENTED[1] 3]. **1767** [see INDENT *v.*[1] 2]. **1844** WILLIAMS *Real Prop.* (1877) 150 Deeds are divided into two kinds, Deeds poll and Indentures. **1845** *Act 8 & 9 Vict.* c. 106 §5 A deed executed after the said first day of October 1845, purporting to be an indenture, shall have the effect of an indenture, although not actually indented.

b. *spec.* The contract by which an apprentice is bound to the master who undertakes to teach him a trade; also the contract by which a person binds himself to service in the colonies, etc.

to take up one's indentures, to receive the indenture back from the master in evidence of the completion of apprenticeship or service.

1463 *Bury Wills* (Camden) 16 He to haue his indentour of his prentished yᵉ whiche I hadde in kepyng. **1542–3** *Act 34 & 35 Hen. VIII*, c. 18 The same indentures of apprentisehode, shall comprehende like couenauntes. *a* **1635** NAUNTON *Fragm. Reg.* (Arb.) 14 Fortune calling to mind, that the time of her servitude was expired, gave up her Indentures. **1745** *De Foe's Eng. Tradesman* i. (1841) I. 8 An apprentice who has served faithfully and diligently, ought to claim it as a debt to his indentures. *Ibid.* xii. (1841) I. 87 They who contract matrimony should forfeit their indentures. **1822** J. FLINT *Lett. Amer.* 98 The indenture of the boy expires when he is twenty-one years of age. **1822** SCOTT *Nigel* xxxv, I have broke my indenture, and I think of running my country. **1862** *Lond. Rev.* 23 Aug. 165 By the terms of the indenture, the Coolie agrees to serve the planter for three years, receiving the same rate of wages as is paid to the unindentured labourer. **1865** CARLYLE *Fredk. Gt.* IX. xi, He is now out of his Apprentice-ship; entitled to take up his Indentures.

c. An official or formal list, inventory, certificate, etc., prepared (orig. in duplicate) for purposes of control, as a voucher, etc., and properly authenticated.

[**1300** *Indenture* in *Nat. MSS. Scot.* II. No. 10 Indentura de nominibus equitum et peditum commorancium in municione castri de Edenborghe a .xxvij.ᵒ die Nouembris anno regni Regis Edwardi .xxix.ᵒ.]

1420 *E.E. Wills* (1882) 45 Thys endenture makyth mencion of þe goodes þat I..3yve to sertayn personis. **1497** in *Naval Acc. Hen. VII* (1896) 82 The said Retorne must accord with the Indentures of Shipping of the same. **1570–4** BP. COX *Injunctions*, Whether your Ministers kepe their Registers of Maryages buryalles and christenynges well and orderly, and to present the copie of them once a yere by indenture, to the Ordinarie or his officers. **1651** N. BACON *Disc. Govt. Eng.* II. xiv. (1739) 77 The names of the persons elected..shall be returned by Indenture between the Sheriff and the Elizors. **1707** CHAMBERLAYNE *St. Gt. Brit.* II. xvi. 225 (*List Officers Navy*) Surveyor..whose Office is..to..estimate the Value of Repairs by Indenture. **1846** MACCULLOCH *Acc. Brit. Empire* (1854) II. 319 The election of scholars [at Eton] takes place every year..The usual number admitted on what is termed the indenture [i.e. between King's Coll. and Eton], at each election, is twenty-four. [This ceased in 1871.] **1875** STUBBS *Const. Hist.* III. xix. 362 The persons arrested are to be delivered to the ordinaries by indenture to be made within ten days of the arrest.

d. *fig.* Contract, mutual engagement.

1540 MORYSINE *Vives' Introd. Wysd.* G vij, We haue by indenture of Jesu..that they shall lacke nothinge whiche seke..the kyngdome of God. **1589** NASHE *Almond for Parrat* 3 My soule being the cittie, whereof the deuill is made free by endenture. **1595** SHAKS. *John* II. i. 20 This zelous kisse, As seale to this indenture of my loue. **1624** QUARLES *Div. Poems*, *Job* (1717) 210 My heart hath past Indentures with mine eye, Not to behold a Maid. *a* **1677** MANTON *Serm. Ps. cxix.* cxxxiii. Wks. 1872 VIII. 251 God's covenant..this mutual and interchangeable indenture.

†**3.** A zigzag line; a zigzag course; a doubling.

1598 I. M. *Seruingmans Comf.* (1868) 138 He turned his Cattle from Plough to Pasture, making Indentures all along the ditches. [**1608** TOPSELL *Serpents* (1658) 743 He must not run directly forward, but winde to and fro, crooking like an Indenture.] **1611** COTGR., *Bricoller*,..to reele, stagger, or make indentures, in going. **1672** MARVELL *Reh. Transp.* I. 146 He makes Indentures on each side of the way wheresoever he goes. **1781** W. BLANE *Ess. Hunting* (1788) 45 It must never be expected that the indentures of the Hare can be well covered, or her doubles struck off.

II. Senses derived from INDENT *v.*[2]

†**4.** An inlaying or embossing. *Obs.*

1664 POWER *Exp. Philos.* I. 7 Her eye is indented all over with a pure Emerauld-green, and all latticed or chequered with dimples..which makes the Indentures look more pleasantly.

5. A hollow or depression in a surface; = INDENTATION *sb.* 4.

1793 SMEATON *Edystone L.* §245 Little indentures upon the surface of the courses. **1822** *New Monthly Mag.* VI. 334 Furrows..left by the indentures of vessels' bottoms. **1872** LE FANU *In a Glass Darkly* I. 201 He pointed to a deep indenture, as if caused by a heavy pressure.

III. 6. *attrib.* and *Comb.* (from I.), as †**indenture English**, the language of legal deeds; ***indenture-fashion***, ***indenture-wise*** adv.

a **1568** ASCHAM *Scholem.* II. (Arb.) 111 As if a wise man would take Halles Cronicle, where moch good matter is quite marde with Indenture Englishe, and first change strange and inkhorne tearmes into proper and commonlie vsed wordes. **1598** FLORIO, *Filicare*, to notch about the edges, as ferne is, or indenter wise. **1613** PURCHAS *Pilgrimage* (1614) 542 Their Crisses or Daggers are two foote long waved Indenture fashion, and poysoned.

in'denture, *v.* [f. INDENTURE *sb.*, in several unconnected senses, related to both verbs INDENT.]

I. From INDENTURE *sb.* 2 (INDENT *v.*[1]).

†**1.** *intr.* To enter into an indenture; to covenant. *Obs.*

1658 R. FRANCK *North. Mem.* (1821) 79 Hee's but slipt to the bottom to recruit himself and indenture with stones to oblige their protection.

2. *trans.* To bind by indentures, esp. as an apprentice or servant.

1676 MARVELL *Mr. Smirke* I iij b, A good Christian will not, cannot atturn and indenture his conscience over; to be Represented by others. **1808** W. TAYLOR in *Monthly Mag.* XXVI. 111 Men..too deficient in skill, or industry, or character, to be employed or indentured by the profession. **1834** HT. MARTINEAU *Moral* II. 77 The plan of indenturing servants to colonial settlers. **1884** *Daily News* 13 Oct. 4/8 Mr. Cole..was indentured as a clerk or writer to Mr., afterwards Sir Francis, Palgrave.

II. From INDENTURE *sb.* 3.

†**3.** *intr.* To move in a zigzag line; to zigzag. *Obs.*

1631 BRATHWAIT *Whimzies*, *Wine-soaker* 102 Indenturing along in some blinde alley, hee terribly affrights the passenger if hee meete any: for hee coasts here and there, as if it were Saint Anthonies fire, or some *ignis fatuus*. **1635** HEYWOOD *Hierarch.* 134 (L.) They took Their staves in hand, and at the good man strook: But, by indenturing, still the good man 'scap'd.

III. From INDENTURE *sb.* 5. (INDENT *v.*[2])

4. *trans.* To make an indentation in; to indent, furrow.

c **1770** WOTY *Autumnal Song* (T.), Age may creep on, and indenture the brow. **1854** DOBELL *Balder* v. 32 Immemorial plains Indentured where the furrows fill with flowers As with a Tyrian rain.

Hence **in'denturing** *vbl. sb.*

a **1632** T. TAYLOR *God's Judgem.* II. vii. (1642) 108 Two Gallants..overtaken with Wine..loath..to take the benefit of a light, because their indenturing should not be observed. **1898** in *Westm. Gaz.* 7 Jan. 3/1 The Imperial sanction had been given to the indenturing of the Bechuana rebels.

indentured (ɪn'dɛntjʊəd), *ppl. a.* [f. INDENTURE *v.* + -ED[1].]

1. Bound by indentures, esp. as an apprentice or servant.

1757 in W. Thompson *R.N. Advoc.* 6 George Woods, Eastcheap, Indentured Master. **1806** SURR *Winter in Lond.* (ed. 3) III. 241 An attorney at Oxford, who..consented to receive me as his indentured clerk. **1808** W. TAYLOR in *Monthly Mag.* XXVI. 111 Indentured bond-slaves are shipped from Liverpool and Glasgow, for Canada, and independent North-America, in considerable numbers. **1882** *Daily News* 17 Mar. 5/3 The employment of indentured labourers [coolies] from India. **1952** S. SELVON *Brighter Sun* v. 72 He had come from India to work as an indentured labourer on the white man's plantations. **1961** [see EAST INDIAN *sb.* 2]. **1969** S. M. SADEEK *Windswept & Other Stories* 29 My grand parents were indentured immigrants, never-the-less pioneers.

2. Indented, having the border incised.

1885 *Pall Mall G.* 17 Apr. 6/1 The three towns on the densely timbered, deeply indentured Vancouver Island.

†**in'denturely**, *adv.* [f. INDENTURE *sb.* + -LY[2].] In the way of an indenture, by making indentures.

1525 *Sc. Acts Jas. V* (1814) 302 (Jam.) That all gudis and artilyery..sall be put in the handis of the provest of Abirdene..be auctentick Inuentore indentourly maid.

indentureship (ɪn'dɛntjʊəʃɪp). *rare.* [f. INDENTURE *sb.* 2 b + -SHIP.] The position of being indentured as an apprentice, servant, etc.

1878 *Daily News* 7 Jan. 5/2 Misgivings as to the expediency of extending the indentureship system, which in other colonies has notoriously provoked grave scandals. **1882–3** S. M. JACKSON in Schaff *Encycl. Relig. Knowl.* 1252 A few months of indentureship to a shoemaker.

'**indentwise**, *adv.* [f. INDENT *sb.*[1] + -WISE.] After the form of an indenture, with a counterpart.

1758 J. BLAKE *Plan Mar. Syst.* 8 The sheet is then to be cut in the middle, from top to bottom, indentwise. **1758** *Act 32 Geo. II*, c. 10 §38 Which two Columns..shall be joined with some Flourish or Device, through which the outermost Tickets may be cut off Indentwise.

†**inde'partable**, *a. Obs.* [IN-[3].] That cannot be parted or separated; inseparable. So †**inde'parted** *a.*, not parted or separated.

1393 LANGL. *P. Pl.* C. XIX. 27 Thei by-tokneþ..þe trinite ..Thre persons in-departable. **1434** MISYN *Mend. Life* 126 O lufe indepartyd, o lufe singulere. **1435** —— *Fire of Love* 123 Luf truly is indepartyd qwhen..þe mynde is kyndyld and to criste with þoght vndepartyd draws.

†**inde'pend**, *v. Obs. nonce-wd.* [f. IN-[3] + DEPEND, after *independent*: cf. also *independing*.] *intr.* ? To be independent, or to profess Independency.

1649 G. DANIEL *Trinarch.*, *Rich. II*, xcviii, And Newer Lights, old Rights may vilepend; But wee must All be fixt or Independ.

independable (ɪndɪ'pɛndəb(ə)l), *a.* [f. IN-[3] + DEPENDABLE *a.*] Not dependable; untrustworthy; not to be depended *upon*.

1802 BENTHAM *Let.* 27–30 June in *Works* (1843) X. 388/1 All Frenchmen are independable upon. **1897** *Geogr. Jrnl.* Feb. 122 This lady is..capricious, independable, and exacting. **1921** S. GRAHAM *Europe* xvii. 210 English action is so sluggish and so independable.

independence (ɪndɪ'pɛndəns). Also 8 -ance. [f. INDEPENDENT: see -ENCE; or f. IN-[3] + DEPENDENCE. Cf. F. *indépendance* (1630 in Hatz.-Darm.), It. *independenza* (Florio, 1611).]

1. a. The condition or quality of being independent; the fact of not depending on another (with various shades of meaning: see the adj.); exemption from external control or support; freedom from subjection, or from the influence of others; individual liberty of thought or action. Rarely in bad sense: Want of subjection to rightful authority, insubordination.

Declaration of Independence: see DECLARATION 6.

1640 BP. HALL *Humble Remonstr.* (R.), Some..can be content to admit of an orderly subordination of severall parishes to presbyteries, and those again to synods; others are all for a parochiall absolutenesse and independence. **1750** SHENSTONE *Eleg.* ix. 50 The charms of independence let us sing. *c* **1760** SMOLLETT *Ode to Indep.* I Thy spirit, Independence, let me share! Lord of the lion-heart and eagle-eye. **1764** GOLDSM. *Trav.* 339 That independence Britons prize too high, Keeps man from man, and breaks the social tie. **1775** (28 Nov.) in W. H. Foote *Sk. North Carol.* (1846) 43 Resolved, That the delegates from this colony, in Continental Congress, be empowered to concur with the delegates of the other colonies, in declaring independence, and in forming foreign alliances. **1783** BURKE *Rep. India* Wks. 1842 II. 50 That general spirit of disobedience and independence, which has..prevailed in the government of Bengal. **1831** CARLYLE *Sart. Res.* III. v, Independence, in all kinds, is rebellion. *a* **1850** CALHOUN *Wks.* (1874) IV. 329 It is one great defect in the character of the public men of America, that there is that real want of independence. **1856** FROUDE *Hist. Eng.* (1858) I. ii. 161 Their national independence was respected. **1873** L. FERGUSON *Disc.* 130 He denuded himself of His original Self-completeness and independence. **1875** STUBBS *Const. Hist.* III. xviii. 38 The proud independence of the Percies was becoming..a source of danger. **1876** TAIT *Rec. Adv. Phys. Sc.* xiii. (ed. 2) 319 The mobility and perfect independence of the various particles of..gases. **1885** *Daily News* 21 Dec. 5/1 A..scheme for conceding legislative independence on purely Irish subjects to Ireland. **1895** 'IAN MACLAREN' *Auld Lang Syne* 273 (*A Servant Lass*) If she didna sit up at nicht makin' the bairns' claithes, and work in the fields a' day tae earn their schulin', an' a' tae keep her independence, as they ca't.

b. Const. *on*, *upon*, *of*, rarely *from*.

1657–83 EVELYN *Hist. Relig.* (1850) I. 235 Her independence from the body. **1761** HUME *Hist. Eng.* I. App. ii. 260 The dignified clergy..pretended to a total independence on the State. **1768** *New Hampsh. Prov. Pap.* (1873) VII. 250 The House of Burgesses..have therefore thought proper to represent..That they do not affect independence of their parent Kingdom. **1771** GOLDSM. *Hist. Eng.* I. 229 A pretence of independence upon secular power. **1852** HAWTHORNE *Blithedale Rom.* xix, Our habitual independence of conventional rules. **1867** FREEMAN *Norm. Conq.* I. iii. 159 The independence of the English Crown upon any foreign superior. **1896** BRYCE in *Century Mag.* June 250 A..convention, signed at Bloemfontein in February, 1854, declared the independence from the British crown of the inhabitants of the country..between the Orange and Vaal rivers.

c. Corresp. to INDEPENDENT *a.* 3 d.

1902 *Bull. Amer. Math. Soc.* VIII. 296 No attempt seems to have been made to prove the independence of the postulates employed to define a group. **1941** O. HELMER tr. *Tarski's Introd. Logic* §56. 194 (*heading*) Independence of the axioms of the simplified system. **1954** I. M. COPI *Symbolic Logic* vi. 179 The axioms of a deductive system are said to be independent (or to exhibit independence) if no one of them can be derived as a theorem from the others. **1955** A. N. PRIOR *Formal Logic* 233 This is the method regularly used for establishing the 'independence' of the axioms in a given set, i.e. for showing that no axiom in the set is superfluous, in the sense of being derivable from the others as a theorem. **1956** J. H. WOODGER tr. *Tarski's Logic, Semantics, Metamath.* 390 On account of the non-ramifiability the independence proof for such sentences cannot be carried out..by an interpretation in logic. **1962** W. & M. KNEALE *Devel. of Logic* xii. 692 Bernays..turned to investigate the independence of the axioms of the calculus of propositions in *Principia Mathematica*.

2. *concr.* A competency: = INDEPENDENCY 3 d.

1815 JANE AUSTEN *Emma* I. iv, As early as most men can afford to marry, who are not born to an independence. **1837** DICKENS *Pickw.* viii, She possessed that most desirable of all requisites, a small independence. **1849** THACKERAY *Pendennis* xxviii, You are heir to a little independence. **1874** DASENT *Half a Life* II. 41 He was an old man who..had made an independence.

3. *attrib.* and *Comb.*

Independence Day, July 4, the day on which, in 1776, the Declaration of Independence was made; celebrated annually in the United States as a national holiday; also *transf.*

1791 J. HILTZHEIMER *Diary* 4 July (1893) 170 This being Independence Day, the Governor invited several of the neighbors to dine with him. **1860** BARTLETT *Dict. Amer.*, *Independence Day*. **1875** *Graphic* 10 July 30/3 As the Fourth of July fell this year on a Sunday, 'Independence Day' was observed by the Americans resident in London on Monday, the 5th inst., who dined together at the Crystal Palace. **1894** *Pop. Sci. Monthly* XLIV. 481 These independence-loving, self-governing mountaineers. **1898** *Daily News* 7 Sept. 5/7 To offer..inducements to the independence party to co-operate. **1967** R. LOWELL *Near Ocean* 17 Another summer! Our Independence Day Parade, all innocence Of children's costumes, helps resist The communist and socialist. **1970** M. SLATER *Caribbean Cooking* 45 Strangers to the islands may well be taken by surprise on..Independence Day. **1972** *Times* 9 Oct. (Nigeria Suppl.) p. i/6 In his Independence Day speech last week General Gowon disclosed that the census would take place..next year.

independency (ɪndɪ'pɛndənsɪ). Also 7–8 -ancy. [f. as prec. + -ENCY.]

1. = prec. 1. Now *rare.*

1611 FLORIO, *Independensa*, independencie. **1645** H. MARTEN (*title*) The Independency of England Maintained

against the Scottish Commissioners. **1646** Sir T. Browne *Pseud. Ep.* I. iii. 12 The independency of their causes, and contingency in their events. **1647** May *Hist. Parl.* I. v. 55 The independency of that kingdome. *a* **1670** Rust *Disc. Truth* (1682) 185 Then will God be determined in his actions from something without himself, which is to take away his independency and self-sufficiency. **1737** Pope *Hor. Ep.* I. vii. 70 'Give me', I cry'd, (enough for me) 'My Bread, and Independency!' **1748** Chesterf. *Lett.* (1792) II. cxlv. 20 The Seven United Provinces; whose independency was first allowed by Spain at the treaty of Munster. **1775** J. Adams in *Fam. Lett.* (1876) 66 Suspicions entertained of designs of independency; an American republic. **1790** Bewick *Hist. Quadrup.* (1807) 1 The wild and extensive plains..where he [the horse] ranges without controul, in a state of entire independency. **1829** I. Taylor *Enthus.* iii. (1867) 55 Reason as well as faith..demands that we deny independency to whatever is created. **1884** *Pall Mall G.* 16 Feb. 8/2 Urged to maintain the independency of Zulu territory.

b. Const. *on, upon, of*, rarely *from*.

1624 F. White *Repl. Fisher* 450 In an extasie there is alienation and independencie of the spirit vpon the sences. **1630** Prynne *Anti-Armin.* 94 The freenesse of Gods Election, and its in-dependancy on any fore-seene faith. **1642** G. Eglisham *Forerunner Revenge* in *Select. Harl. Misc.* (1793) 371 In regard..of my independency from the accused. **1668** Pepys *Diary* (1877) V. 433 In opposition to, or at least independency of, the Duke of York. **1796** Morse *Amer. Geog.* I. 256 A desirable degree of independency on British and other foreign manufactures. **1841–4** Emerson *Essays* Ser. I. ix. (1876) 217 Its independency of those limitations which circumscribe us on every hand.

2. That system of ecclesiastical polity in which each local congregation of believers is held to be a church independent of any external authority: = congregationalism 1.

The prevailing name in England, in the 17th century, for this form of church government, but not favoured in New England (see quot. 1648, and congregational 3), and in modern use (other than historical) largely displaced by *Congregationalism*.

1642 Sir E. Dering *Sp. on Relig.* xvi. 82 That new-borne Bastard, Independency. **1648** J. Cotton *Way Congreg. Ch.* (New Eng.) 11 Nor is Independency a fit name of the way of our Churches. For in some respects it is too strait, and in others too large. **1648** C. Walker (*title*) The History of Independency. **1694** *Provid. God* 95 Those they then called Puritans..were divided about Church-Government, some for Presbytery and others for Independency. **1733** Neal *Hist. Purit.* II. 107 His [Robinson's] peculiar sentiments of Church discipline, since known by the name of Independancy. **1872** G. H. Curteis *Bampton Lect.* ii. 41 The cradle in which Independency was nurtured was the Non-Conforming Puritanism of the sixteenth century.

3. *concr.* **a.** *pl.* Independent things; things unrelated to each other.

1659 Bp. Walton *Consid. Considered* 9 The whole being 'rudis indigestaque moles', a confused heap of Independencies. [A pun on sense 2.]

b. An independent or autonomous state. (Cf. dependency 4 c.)

1818 Jas. Mill *Brit. India* II. v. ii. 355 Of these independencies, the most important..was that..which..included the whole of the vast province, or region of Berar. **1847** Grote *Greece* II. xxv. IV. 16 Many petty independencies, small towns, and villages.

c. A person of independent means.

1866 Carlyle *Edw. Irving* 125 Expecting to be flattered like an independency, as well as paid like an innkeeper.

d. A competency; a fortune which renders it unnecessary for the possessor to earn his living: = prec. 2.

1748 Richardson *Clarissa* (1811) I. xiii. 87, I, who never designed to take advantage of the independency bequeathed me. **1804** W. Tennant *Ind. Recreat.* (ed. 2) I. 286 Men..who leave their native country with the sole view of acquiring an independency. **1886** *L'pool Daily Post* 5 Mar. 4/5 The deceased had something in the nature of an independency, however modest.

independent (ɪndɪˈpɛndənt), *a.* and *sb.* Also 7–8 **-ant.** [f. in-[3] + dependent: cf. F. *indépendant* (*c* 1600 in Hatz.-Darm.), It. *independente* (Florio, 1598).] Not dependent.

A. *adj.*

1. a. Not depending upon the authority of another, not in a position of subordination or subjection; not subject to external control or rule; self-governing, autonomous, free.

1611 H. Jacob *Declar. & Plainer Open.* 13 [Each congregation is] an entire and independent body-politic, endued with power immediately under and from Christ. **1651** Hobbes *Leviath.* II. xxix. 172 It is not one independent Common-wealth, but three independent Factions. **1774** J. Bryant *Mythol.* II. 40 Attica..was divided into..independant hamlets. **1776** Adam Smith *W.N.* I. viii. (1869) I. 73 An independent workman, such as a weaver or shoemaker. **1882** Mrs. Pitman *Mission L. Greece & Pal.* 37 In 1829, Greece was acknowledged as an independent state, having its own king and government. **1885** J. Martineau *Types Eth. Th.* II. 10 The theory of an autonomous or independent conscience.

b. Const. *of* (formerly *on, upon, from*).

1651 Hobbes *Govt. & Soc.* xv. §18. 258 An opinion, that there is any man endued with a Soveraignty independent from God. **1680** Morden *Geog. Rect., Brit. Isles* (1685) 15 These Islands..were first possessed by divers People, independent one upon the other. **1705** Addison *Italy* 489 The Town of St. Gaul is a little Protestant Republick, wholly independent of the Abbot. **1776** (13 June) *Amherst Rec.* (1884) 70/1 Voted—That should the Honourable Congress, for the safety of the united Colonies in America: Declare them Independant of the Kingdom of Great-Britain; We..solemnly engage with our lives and fortunes to support them in the measure. **1785** T. Balguy *Disc.* 115 It has been said..that the church is independent on the state.

2. (with capital *I.*) Belonging or adhering to that form of ecclesiastical polity called independency (q.v., sense 2): = congregational 3.

Also applied to that political party in the 17th century of which the Independent churches formed the chief element.

[**1611**: see 1.] **1642** T. Lechford *Pl. Dealing or News fr. New Eng.* 79 The Congregationall independent government, whereof I have had some experience. **1653** W. Dell *Tryal Spir.* 82 Sydrach Simpson, one of the first Pastors of an Independant Congregation in England. *a* **1654** Selden *Table-t.* (Arb.) 57 Both the Independant man, and the Presbyterian man do equally exclude the Civil Power, though after a different manner. **1660** R. Coke *Power & Subj.* 262 The Army, commanded by Oliver Cromwell, turned out the Rump of the Long Parliament which headed the Independent party. *a* **1674** Clarendon *Hist. Rebell.* VIII. §259 The Independent party (for so they were now [1645] contented to be call'd, in opposition to the other which was styled Presbyterian). **1676** W. Hubbard *Happiness of People* 35 Why else doe wee in New England..practise the discipline of them called Independant, or Congregational Churches? **1712** Addison *Spect.* No. 494 ¶1 A very famous independent minister. **1766** Entick *London* IV. 8 There is an Independent meeting-house. **1831** (*title*) Declaration of the Faith, Order and Discipline of the Congregational or Independent Dissenters. **1872** G. H. Curteis *Bampton Lect.* ii. 40 The Independent system does not concern itself with either Ritual or Doctrine.

3. Not depending on something else for its existence, validity, efficiency, operation, or some other attribute; not contingent on or conditioned by anything else. **a.** Const. as in sense 1.

1614 Jackson *Creed* III. xxix. §6 His faith [is] no otherwise independent of any externall proposall then ours is. **1646** H. Lawrence *Comm. Angells* 73 The will is independent upon all created power, both in its operation and in its being. **1659** Pearson *Creed* (1682) I. 31 A Being of itself and independent from any other. **1692** Bentley *Boyle Lect.* 69 An incorporeal substance independent from matter. **1709** Steele *Tatler* No. 54 ¶1 Beauty and Merit are Things real, and independent on Taste and Opinion. **1772** Priestley *Inst. Relig.* (1782) I. 276 They cannot be considered as independent of one another. **1790** Paley *Horæ Paul.* I. ¶13 The instances are independent of one another. **1816** Playfair *Nat. Phil.* II. 323 This is quite independent of the figure of the Earth, and would be the same though the Earth were truly spherical. **1885** S. Cox *Exposit.* Ser. I. ix. 107 An argument..wholly independent of the teaching of the Scripture.

b. *simply.* Not depending upon the existence or action of others, or of each other; existing, acting, conducted, or obtained in a way apart from and unaffected by others, as ***independent action, inquiry, investigation, conclusion, results, account, record, information, evidence***; ***independent suspension***; also of the agent, as ***independent investigator, observer, witness***, etc.

1790 Paley *Horæ Paul.* I. ¶6 No danger of confounding the production with original history, or of mistaking it for an independent authority. *Ibid.* IV. No. iv, It is the junction of two conclusions, deduced from independent sources. *Ibid.* V. No. ii, Two records..manifestly independent, that is manifestly written without any participation of intelligence. **1865** Earle *Two Saxon Chron.* Introd. 37 Some of the independent entries of C countenance its Abingdon origin. *Ibid.* 45 Other independent annals about the same date, e.g. 1031, 1032, 1043, argue the presence of such a source. **1867** Freeman *Norm. Conq.* I. vi. 510 Something is proved when two independent narratives agree. **1872** Watts *Dict. Chem.* II. 779 Scheeler's investigation..comprised another independent discovery of oxygen gas. **1879** J. A. H. Murray *Synopsis Horæ Paul.* 10 Here four independent witnesses, none of which give all the facts, confirm and supplement each other. *Ibid.* 14 Have we any independent information connecting Erastus with Corinth? **1885** Tait *Prop. Matter* iii. §33 Air is made up of separate and independent particles. *a* **1900** *Mod.* An independent inquiry has been instituted by the Local Board of Health. The work is the result of independent research. **1930** *Engineering* 7 Feb. 162/3 A special chapter on independent suspension systems. **1963** R. F. Webb *Motorist's Dict.* 135 *Independent suspension*, a form of suspension where each wheel is completely independent of the others and no connecting axle beams are used. **1973** *Country Life* 15 Dec. 1581/2 For absolute comfort and stability at very high speeds there is all round independent suspension.

c. Often used adverbially in phr. ***independent of*** (†*on*, †*from*) = Independently of, apart from, without regard to, irrespective of.

1690 Locke *Hum. Und.* III. v. §5 Put together in the Mind, independent from any original Patterns in Nature. **1748** *Anson's Voy.* III. ii. 311 Independent of that attachment which all mankind have ever shown to the places of their birth..there were few countries more worthy to be regretted. *a* **1871** Grote *Eth. Fragm.* i. (1876) 20 We pursue the one and avoid the other quite independent of regard to the feelings of others.

d. Of one of a set of equations, axioms, or quantities in respect of the others: incapable of being expressed in terms of, or of being derived or deduced from, the others; hence applied to a set of axioms, etc., all of which have this property; ***linearly independent***, (of each of a set of equations or quantities) incapable of being expressed as a linear combination of the others, i.e. satisfying no relation of the form $a_1x_1 + a_2x_2 + \ldots + a_nx_n = 0$ (where x_i are the quantities and a_i arbitrary constants) unless $a_1 = a_2 = \ldots = a_n = 0$.

1740 N. Sanderson *Elem. Algebra* I. II. 105 If a problem be justly proposed, it ought to have as many independent conditions..as there are unknown quantities to be discovered by them. **1798** J. Wood *Elem. Algebra* (ed. 2) 73 These equations must also be independent, that is, not deducible one from another. **1875** *Encycl. Brit.* I. 541/1 A problem is limited when the conditions furnish just as many independent equations as there are unknown quantities to be determined: if there be fewer, the problem is indeterminate; but if there be more, the problem in general admits of no solution. **1885** [see Legendre]. **1902** *Trans. Amer. Math. Soc.* III. 142 Hilbert states..that his body of axioms consists of independent axioms, that is, that no one of the axioms is logically deducible from the remaining axioms. **1931** L. J. Rouse *College Algebra* v. 69 The equations $2x + y = 5$ and $x - y = 4$ cannot be reduced to the same form and are therefore independent. **1941** O. Helmer tr. *Tarski's Introd. Logic* §39. 131 We strive to arrive at an axiom system which does not contain a single superfluous statement..which can be derived from the remaining axioms... An axiom system of this kind is called independent (or a system of mutually independent axioms). **1944** A. Church *Introd. Math. Logic* I. i. 25 An axiom of a logistic system is said to be independent if, in the system whose axioms and rules consist of all axioms and rules of the original system except that one, the suppressed axiom is not a theorem. **1959** G. & R. C. James *Math. Dict.* 107/1 The numbers 3 and π are linearly independent with respect to rational numbers, since $a_1 \cdot 3 + a_2 \cdot \pi$ can not be zero if a_1 and a_2 are rational numbers, not both zero. Since $-1 \cdot 3 + (3/\pi)\pi = 0$, 3 and π are linearly dependent with respect to real numbers. **1961** Powell & Crasemann *Quantum Mech.* v. 117 Two solutions of Eq. (5–47) (or, more generally, any two functions of *x*) are linearly independent if the equation $C_1\psi_1 + C_2\psi_2 = 0$ cannot be satisfied identically in *x* for any choice of the constants C_1 and C_2 except $C_1 = C_2 = 0$. *Ibid.* 118 To linearly independent solutions, ψ_1 and ψ_2, are a complete set in the sense that every solution of Eq. (5–47) can be expressed as a linear combination of ψ_1 and ψ_2. **1965** Hughes and Londey *Elem. Formal Logic* xviii. 132 Since A_4 is non-independent, the axiom set for PM could be reduced by one. But no further reduction of this sort is possible; neither A1 nor A2 nor A3 nor A5 is a consequence of the other three under Substitution and Detachment, and these four are therefore said to be independent axioms.

4. Not dependent or having to rely on another for support or supplies. **a.** Const. as in sense 1.

1670 R. Coke *Disc. Trade* Pref., While other Creatures live free and Independent from one another, only Man stands in need and help of another. *a* **1788** N. Cotton *Fables, Bee, Ant & Spar.*, Who..Are independent of the great, Nor know the wants of pride and state. **1837** Lytton *E. Maltrav.* I. xii, He was thus made independent of his father. **1880** Shorthouse *J. Inglesant* ii. (1883) 18 His father had left him so considerable a fortune that he was independent of any profession.

b. *simply.* (*a*) Not dependent on any one else for one's living; (*b*) not needing to earn one's livelihood; possessing a competency.

1732 Law *Serious C.* x. (ed. 2) 142 He hath chosen to be idle and independant in the world. **1786** Burns *Ep. Yng. Friend* vii, Gather gear by ev'ry wile That's justify'd by Honor..for the glorious privilege Of being independent. **1802** Mar. Edgeworth *Moral T.* (1816) I. i. 7 He was really independent, because he had learnt how to support himself either by the labours of his head or of his hands. **1847** C. Brontë *J. Eyre* xvii, She [a servant] has saved enough to keep her independent if she liked to leave. **1893** *Westm. Gaz.* 10 Apr. 5/2 A room occupied by an independent elderly gentleman.

transf. **1784** Cowper *Task* IV. 409 A dry but independent crust, hard earned And eaten with a sigh.

c. *transf.* Sufficient to make one independent; constituting a competency.

c **1790** Imison *Sch. Art* I. 215 The prices..being..out of the reach of any, but such as are possessed of independent fortunes. **1837** Dickens *Pickw.* xxxiv, A gentleman of considerable independent property. **1885** *Daily News* 3 Oct. 4/6 A person of independent means.

5. a. Not depending on others for the formation of opinions or guidance of conduct; not influenced or biased by the opinions of others; thinking or acting, or disposed to think or act, for oneself. (Of persons, their dispositions, etc.)

1735–8 Bolingbroke *On Parties* 9 On this Foundation all the reasonable, independent Whigs and Tories unite. **1771** Smollett *Humph. Cl.* 26 June, I believed there was not a more independent and incorruptible member in the house. **1795** Burns *For a' that* iii, The man of independent mind, He looks and laughs at a' that. **1849** Cobden *Speeches* 52 An independent and energetic man who will vote as he pleases. **1852** Hawthorne *Blithedale Rom.* xix, A person capable of taking an independent stand. **1861** Geo. Eliot *Silas M.* i. 10 This would have been an effort of independent thought such as he had never known. **1889** *Daily News* 28 June 5/2 Perhaps the best *bon-mot* attributed to the late Lord Derby is his definition of an independent politician as 'a politician who cannot be depended on'.

b. Used in the names of various political or other parties, as ***Independent Republicans*** (U.S.: see B. 2 b); ***Independent Labour Party*** (abbrev. I.L.P.: see I. III): the title of the political organization founded at Bradford in January 1893 by James Keir Hardie as an offshoot of the Social Democratic Federation, for the support of parliamentary candidates of approved socialistic views; orig. as opp. the Conservative and Liberal parties, later distinct from the Labour Party; also in the names of newspapers, as the *Cambridge Independent Press*.

c **1888** *Scottish Labour Party Manifesto* in M. Beer *Hist. Brit. Socialism* (1920) II. xv. 300 The formation of a distinct, separate, and *Independent Labour Party*. **1902**

Encycl. Brit. XXXII. 668/2 Attempts had been made to influence politics directly by means of an Independent Labour Party..which bound itself to support only candidates of sound socialist views. **1922** *Ibid.* XXXII. 507/1 The Labour party..included the Independent Labour party and the Fabian Society and one or two smaller Socialist bodies. **1953** D. E. BUTLER *Electoral Syst. in Brit.* II. v. 154 The total of 5 [members of parliament from outside the three major parties] for 1935 is made up of 4 Independent Labour Party members from Glasgow—where a substantial part of the Labour party had split away—and 1 Communist. **1955** *Times* 24 May 14/3 An election manifesto issued last night by the Independent Labour Party reaffirms the party's belief that workers' control 'is an essential part of Socialism'. **1971** BUTLER & PINTO-DUSCHINSKY *Brit. Gen. Election 1970* v. 112 The failure of those other traditional spokesmen of the left, the Independent Labour party and the Socialist Party of Great Britain, was still more complete.

c. Also (with some colouring of 4), Refusing to be under obligation to others; having a self-respect which declines unearned assistance.

Mod. The widow has a hard struggle, but is very independent, and refuses all pecuniary aid. He is too independent to accept as a favour what he cannot earn by his own exertions.

d. Of schools: receiving no grant from the government and not subject to the control of a local authority.

1944 *Act 7 & 8 Geo. VI* c. 31 §70 The Minister shall appoint one of his officers to be Registrar of Independent (i.e. private) Schools. **1957** *Encycl. Brit.* VII. 989/1 The Independent Schools association..; its official publication is the *Independent School.* **1966** *Rep. Comm. Inquiry Univ. Oxf.* II. 45 Independent schools are subdivided into independent boarding and independent day schools according to whether the majority of pupils were boarders or day pupils.

e. ***Independent Television (Authority)*** (abbrev. I.T.A., I.T.V.: see I. III): a corporation, independent of direct government control, engaged in commercial television broadcasting in Great Britain; also, the channel carrying their programmes; renamed in 1972 the ***Independent Broadcasting Authority*** (abbrev. I.B.A.: see I. III), and widened to include commercial radio broadcasting.

1954 *Act 2 & 3 Eliz. II* c. 55 §1 There shall be an authority, to be called the Independent Television Authority..whose function shall be to provide, in accordance with the provisions of this Act, and for the period of ten years from the passing of this Act, television broadcasting services, additional to those of the British Broadcasting Corporation. **1958** *Times Lit. Suppl.* 15 Aug. p. xl/1, This brings sharply into the picture the B.B.C.'s rival, Independent Television. **1959** *Chambers's Encycl.* XI. 349/2 (*heading*) Independent Television Authority. *Ibid.*, This corporation is controlled by directors appointed by the government and leases facilities to privately financed companies, which draw their revenues from advertisements. **1960** *B.B.C. Handbk.* 165 The Postmaster General issued a broadcasting licence, for television only, at a later stage to the Independent Television Authority, which was set up under the Television Act of 1954. **1971** [see *I.B.A.* s.v. I. III]. **1973** *Times* 13 Dec. 4/5 The Independent Broadcasting Authority will hold meetings today..about advertising which will be lost as a result of the shorter hours of transmission announced yesterday. *Ibid.* 15 Dec. 2 BBC and independent television agreed last night to spread their closing hours.

6. a. *Math.* Not depending upon another for its value. ***independent variable***: a quantity whose variation does not depend on that of another.

1852 TODHUNTER *Diff. Calc.* i. §1 Frequently when we are considering two or more variables it is in our power to fix upon whichever we please as the independent variable. **1873** B. WILLIAMSON *Diff. Calc.* (ed. 2) i. §2 [If *u*, *v*, *w*, be functions of *x*], *x* is said to be the *independent* variable, to which any value may be assigned at pleasure; and *u*, *v*, *w*, are called *dependent* variables, as their values depend on that of *x*. **1892** J. EDWARDS *Diff. Calc.* i. §5 An Independent variable is one which may take up any arbitrary value that may be assigned to it.

b. ***independent float***: in Critical Path Analysis, the amount of 'float' or leeway in any one activity which can occur without affecting the timing of the whole operation.

1963 R. E. MCGARRAH *Production & Logistics Managem.* viii. 211 'Independent float' pertains to those non-critical activities whose leeway is not affected by the starting or completion time of its preceding or succeeding activities. **1964** K. G. LOCKYER *Introd. Critical Path Analysis* v. 48 *Independent float*, the time by which an activity can expand without affecting any other activity either previous or subsequent. **1967** A. BATTERSBY *Network Analysis* (ed. 2) App. 4. 335 *Independent float* is so called because it is what remains if all proceeding jobs finish as late as possible and all succeeding jobs begin as early as possible. **1967** S. WOODGATE in Wills & Yearsley *Handbk. Managem. Technol.* 80 Independent float is the minimum spare time available under any condition, i.e. either early or late. **1968** *Gloss. Terms Project Network Analysis* (*B.S.I.*) 8 *Independent float*, earliest date of succeeding event minus latest date of preceding event minus activity duration. (If negative, the independent float is taken as zero.)

7. *Comb.* ***independent seconds (watch)***: see quots.

1837 DICKENS *Pickw.* xxviii, A kind, excellent, independent-spirited..man. *a* **1877** KNIGHT *Dict. Mech.* II. 1179/1 *Independent seconds-watch*, a watch in which the action of the center seconds-hand is independent of the regular going works of the watch.... For great nicety in timing, quarter and fifth second watches are now made. **1890** BOLDREWOOD *Col. Reformer* (1891) 143 A certain independent-minded young lady friend. **1962** E. BRUTON *Dict. Clocks & Watches* 93 *Independent seconds*, clock or watch with seconds hand..which jumps from one second to the next, i.e. it is dead beat.

B. *sb.*

1. An adherent of Independency; a member or adherent of an Independent church; a Congregationalist.

Also *Hist.* a member of the Independent party in the 17th century: see A. 2.

1644 (*title*) Apologetical Narration of the Independents. **1646** (29 Aug.) in *Hamilton Pap.* (Camden) 113 Cheesely says the Independents intend not to demaund the King. **1692** WASHINGTON tr. *Milton's Def. Pop.* Pref., They that we call independents..hold, that no classes or synods have a superiority over any particular church. **1710** STEELE & ADDISON *Tatler* No. 257 ¶12 Camaronians, Muggletonians, Brownists, Independents, Masonites, Camisars, and the like. **1870** ROGERS *Hist. Gleanings* II. 74 In modern times the credit of being the first to advocate the doctrine of toleration must be shared between the Independents and Quakers. **1884** STOUGHTON *Relig. Eng.* I. 236 The old historic name of Independent began [at the beginning of the 19th century] to be merged in that of Congregationalist.

2. a. A person or thing that is independent (in various senses). *nonce-uses.*

1675 OGILBY *Brit.* Pref. 2 Roads we have divided into Independants, such as commence actually at London [etc.]. **1742** YOUNG *Nt. Th.* II. 332 That awful Independent on Tomorrow!.. Whose Yesterdays look backward with a Smile. **1886** *Daily News* 4 June 5/2 There is a school of independents in domestic service, as there is in literature.

b. A person who acts (in politics, art, etc.) independently of any organized party; also, a member of any organized party called ***Independent*** (see A. 5 b).

1808 PIKE *Sources Mississ.* III. App. (1810) 50 Twenty thousand auxiliaries from the United States..joined to the independents of the country [Texas]. **1888** BRYCE *Amer. Commw.* II. III. lvi. 379 The Independent Republicans.. Independents, or Mugwumps. **1896** A. HILLIER in *Daily News* 16 Jan. 6/3 If later painters arrived at more harmonious results..the Independents have still the glory of being the bold hussars of the vanguard, the Jacobins of the revolution in art which has since been accomplished throughout all Europe.

c. A frequent name of a newspaper, as the *New York Independent* (cf. A. 5 b).

1837 DICKENS *Pickw.* xiii, That disgraceful and dastardly journal, the [Eatanswill] Independent. **1855** THACKERAY *Newcomes* liv, He endeavoured to be civil to the 'Newcome Independent'..as well as to the 'Newcome Sentinel'.

Hence †**inde'pendented** *ppl. a. Obs.* (*nonce-wd.*), made independent, formed according to Independency. †**inde'pendentish** *a.*, having a flavour of Independency.

1653 R. BAILLIE *Disswas. Vind.* (1655) 44 Presbyterian water, exceedingly weakened with Independentish ingredients. **1659** GAUDEN *Tears Ch.* 43 The new titles..of bodyed and congregated, associated or independented and new-fangled Churches.

inde'pendentism. [f. INDEPENDENT + -ISM.]

†**1.** = INDEPENDENCY 2. *Obs.*

1653 R. BAILLIE *Disswas. Vind.* (1655) 44, I love not Episcopal principles, neither Independentisme. **1659** GAUDEN *Tears Ch.* 564 Anabaptisme, or Presbyterisme, or Independentisme..rudely justled Episcopacy out of the Church of England. **1665** J. LIVINGSTONE *Mem. Charact.* in *Sel. Biog.* (1845) I. 335 He marvellously refuted Independentisme. **1827** AIKMAN *Hist. Scot.* IV. VII. 84 They opposed every approach to independentism.

2. The principles of any party called *Independent.*

independently (ɪndɪ'pɛndəntlɪ), *adv.* [f. INDEPENDENT *a.* + -LY[2].] In an independent manner; without dependence on another person or thing, or on each other; apart from or without regard to the action of others.

1651 J. GOODWIN *Redemption Red.* i. §10 Second causes.. do not perform, what..they do perform, independently, and of themselves. **1849** T. R. BIRKS *Horæ Apostol.* Pref., My own conclusions were formed independently. *Ibid.*, The dates to which I have been independently led agree very nearly with those adopted in the Literary History. **1860** TYNDALL *Glac.* I. xxv. 186 Mr. Wills..made the same observation independently. **1876** GEO. ELIOT *Dan. Der.* xxiii, She can hardly earn her own poor bread independently. **1886** FARRAR *Hist. Interpret.* 403 He examined the Canon as independently as Luther had done. *Mod.* The two parts of the mechanism work independently.

b. With *of* (formerly *on*, *upon*, *from*): In a way independent of; without regard to; apart from.

1659 PEARSON *Creed* (1845) 485 *note*, Independently from this place, we have proved, that the Holy Spirit is a person. **1678** CUDWORTH *Intell. Syst.* I. iv. §7. 199 They Maintained Matter to exist Independently upon God. *a* **1700** DRYDEN (J.), Dispose lights and shadows, without finishing every thing independently the one of the other. **1707** S. CLARKE *3rd & 4th Def.* (1712) 7, Parts, existing distinctly and independently from each other. **1824** L. MURRAY *Eng. Gram.* (ed. 5) I. 274 The infinitive mood is often made absolute, or used independently on the rest of the sentence. **1867** TROLLOPE *Chron. Barset* II. li. 76 So that he might work at his canvas independently of his model. **1884** J. RAE *Contemp. Socialism* 165 Utility can confer value independently of labour.

†**inde'pending,** *a. Obs.* [f. IN-[3] + DEPENDING *ppl. a.*: cf. INDEPEND *v.*] = INDEPENDENT *a.*

1604 T. WRIGHT *Passions* VI. 301 The soule..being immortall, and independing of the body. **1627** HAKEWILL *Apol.* II. v. (1630) 82 A Soveraigne and independing power. **1650** B. SPENCER (*title*) Chrysomeson, a Golden Mean.. wherein all Seekers..may find the True Religion, independing on Man's Invention. **1652** BP. HALL *Invis. World* II. §1 An independing and selfsubsisting agent. **1675** OGILBY *Brit., Post-Roads Eng.*, The..Roads..are Reduc'd to these 6 Independing Itineraries.

†**inde'plorable,** *a. Obs. rare*[-0]. [IN-[3].]

1623 COCKERAM I I, Not to be Lamented, *Indeplorable.*

inde'posable, *a. rare.* [IN-[3].] That cannot be deposed.

1673 STILLINGFL. *Serm.* 5 *Nov.* (L.), That doctrine which makes princes indeposable by the pope.

†**in'depravate,** *a. Obs.* [ad. L. *indēprāvātus*, f. *in-* (IN-[3]) + *dēprāvātus* depraved, corrupted, DEPRAVATE.] Not depraved; uncorrupted, pure.

1609 J. DAVIES *Holy Roode* (1876) 28 (D.) O let these Wounds, these Woundes indeprauate, Be holy Sanctuaries for my whole Man.

†**in'deprecable,** *a. Obs. rare*[-0]. [ad. L. *indēprecābil-is* that cannot be averted by prayer, f. *in-* (IN-[3]) + *dēprecābilis* DEPRECABLE.]

1623 COCKERAM, *Indeprecable*, that will not be entreated. **1656** in BLOUNT *Glossogr.* **1658** in PHILLIPS, etc.

†**indepre'hensible,** *a. Obs.* [ad. L. *indēprehensibilis* not to be seized or caught (Quintil.), f. *in-* (IN-[3]) + *dēprehendĕre* to seize, catch, DEPREHEND: see -IBLE.] Incapable of being mentally apprehended or detected; undiscoverable.

1633 T. MORTON *Discharge* 174 (T.) A case perplexed and indeprehensible. **1652** GAULE *Magastrom.* 142 To presume his errour indeprehensible.

indeprivable (ɪndɪ'praɪvəb(ə)l), *a.* Now *rare.* [f. IN-[3] + DEPRIVABLE.]

1. Of which one cannot be deprived; incapable of being taken away; inalienable.

1744 HARRIS *Three Treat.* III. I. (1765) 121 The Sovereign Good..should..be durable, self-derived, and (if I may use the Expression) indeprivable. *Ibid.* II. 192 Rectitude of Conduct is a Good Indeprivable. **1789** MRS. PIOZZI *Journ. France* I. 126 The advantages of blood..may surely be deemed indeprivable. **1835** GRESWELL *Parables* II. 59 So pure, so valuable, and so indeprivable.

2. That cannot be deprived of something. *rare*[-0].

1828 WEBSTER, *Indeprivable*, that cannot be deprived. [Hence in later Dicts.]

Hence **indepriva'bility**, the quality of being indeprivable or inalienable.

1789 MRS. PIOZZI *Journ. France* I. 125 James Harris tells us, that virtue answers to the character of indeprivability.

in-depth *attrib.*: see DEPTH I. 3 c.

inder, -ly, -more, -ward: see INNER, -LY, etc.

inderborite (ɪndə'bɔəraɪt). *Min.* [f. *Inder*, the name of a lake in Kazakhstan + BOR(ON + -ITE[1].] A colourless to white hydrated borate of calcium and magnesium, $CaMgB_6O_{11}.11H_2O$.

1941 G. S. GORSHKOV in *Compt. Rend.* (*Doklady*) *de l'Acad. des Sci. de l'URSS* XXXIII. 255 The new mineral is an analogon of hydroboracite and has been named inderborite after the place of finding. **1967** E. L. MUETTERTIES *Chem. Boron & its Compounds* iii. 188 The binary salt minerals, in the system $CaO.MgO.B_2o_3.H_2o$ (hydroboracite and inderborite) are probable derivatives of the colemanite-meyerhofferite trimer.

inderite ('ɪndəraɪt). *Min.* [f. as prec. + -ITE[1].] A colourless hydrated magnesium borate, $Mg_2B_6O_{11}.15H_2O$.

1937 BOLDYREVA & YEGOROVA in *Mat. Central Sci. Investig. Geol. Prospecting Inst.* (U.S.S.R.) Gen. Ser. No. 2. 52 Inderite, a new hydrated magnesium borate—$Mg_2B_6O_{11}.15H_2O$ has been found in the Kzyl-Tau deposit (Western Kasakhstan, Inder Mountains) in the form of fine white, sometimes slightly pinkish kidney-shaped nodules. **1946** *Amer. Mineralogist* XXXI. 71 A second occurrence of inderite ($Mg_2B_6O_{11}.15H_2O$)..has been discovered. **1967** E. L. MUETTERTIES *Chem. Boron & its Compounds* iii. 161 NMR analyses have been performed on the minerals inderite, $Mg_2B_6O_{11}.15H_2O$..borax..and tincalconite.

†**inderkins.** *Obs. rare*[-1]. Some kind of fabric: see quot.

1696 J. F. *Merchant's Ware-ho.* 25 Inderkins, which is a sort of Cloth of no great use in this Town, only proper for Towels, it is a coarse narrow Cloth which comes from Hamborough..it is made of the worst of Hemp.

indescriba'bility. [f. next: see -ITY.] Incapacity of being described; also (with *an* and *pl.*) something that cannot be described.

1824 *Examiner* 456/2 In ably conveying the assumed hoyden, and falling somewhat short of critical conception in the indescribabilities. **1843** CARLYLE *Past & Pr.* I. ii, A fearful indescribability. **1864** SALA in *Daily Tel.* 21 Sept., I have now done my best to describe what..I may term the indescribability of Transatlantic warfare.

indescribable (ɪndɪ'skraɪbəb(ə)l), *a.* (*sb.*) [IN-[3].]

1. That cannot be described; that does not admit of exact description; indefinite, vague.

1794 W. CURTIS *Bot. Mag.* No. 254 That indescribable something, called by Linnæus the Nectary. **1833** HT. MARTINEAU *Cinnamon & Pearls* i. 16 Various sacred indescribable articles were scattered around. **1862** MRS. OLIPHANT *Last Mortimers* I. xii, His voice..had..an

occasional indescribable note which reminded me of some other voice.

2. That transcends description; too great, beautiful, etc. to be adequately described.

1796 MORSE *Amer. Geog.* I. 613 The rapture of the spectator is really indescribable. **1817** COBBETT *Pol. Reg.* XLII. 366 A Funding System has never existed in any country, without producing indescribable misery. **1880** HAUGHTON *Phys. Geog.* v. 240 Its waters break with indescribable fury.

B. *sb.* **1.** *pl.* Things of which no description can be given.

1839 MARRYAT *Diary Amer.* Ser. I. I. 105 Pine-apples, boiled hams, pies, puddings, barley-sugar, and many other indescribables. **1890** *Boy's Own-Paper* 1 Feb. 278/3, I had to fish out [from a bath] about twenty long-named indescribables that had committed suicide during the night.

2. *humorous slang* (orig. *euphemism*). Trousers (cf. *inexpressibles*, *unmentionables*).

1794 *Sporting Mag.* III. 221 That hebdomodal display of Foppery, Frivolity, and Fashion, has already begun to sport its vernal variety of indescribables. **1837** DICKENS *Pickw.* xvi, Mr. Trotter..gave four distinct slaps on the pocket of his mulberry indescribables.

Hence **inde'scribableness**, the quality of being indescribable. *rare.*

1880–1 CHEYNE *Isaiah* (1884) I. 92 His sense of their indescribableness.

indescribably (ɪndɪ'skraɪbəblɪ), *adv.* [f. prec. + -LY².] In a manner incapable of being described or transcending description.

1795 tr. *Moritz' Trav. Eng.* (1886) 101 How indescribably beautiful was this evening and this walk. **1875** LYELL *Princ. Geol.* II. III. xxvii. 65 The quantity..is said to have been indescribably great.

inde'script, *a. rare.* [IN-³.] Undescribed.

1854 DOBELL *Balder* xxiv. 162 Some ethereal colour indescript.

inde'scriptive, *a. rare*⁻⁰. [IN-³.] 'Not descriptive or containing just description' (Webster, 1828).

indesert (ɪndɪ'zɜːt). Now *rare.* [f. IN-³ + DESERT *sb.*¹] Absence of desert; want of merit; the fact or character of being undeserving.

1646 G. DANIEL *Poems* Wks. 1878 I. 80 Let the giddie Rout give weight and poise To Indesert. **1672** PENN *Spirit of Truth Vind.* 97 This much in Answer to his Cavills, whose Emptiness might have been enough to sound out their own indesert of any. **1709** STEELE *Tatler* No. 69 ¶1 A Man in Power who can..raise obscure Merit, and discountenance successful Indesert. **1861** GOULBURN *Pers. Relig.* IV. iv. (1870) 282 To relieve them without any remarkable indesert on their part.

b. *pl.* Demerits, faults.

1612 SHELTON *Quix.* III. xiii. 264 What indeserts did this wench commit. **1711** ADDISON *Spect.* No. 256 ¶1 All those who..were once looked on as his Equals, are apt to think the Fame of his Merits a Reflexion on their own Indeserts.

indesignate (ɪn'dɛsɪgnət), *a. Logic.* [f. IN-³ + DESIGNATE *ppl. a.* (see quot. 1844).] Not quantified, indefinite. Also *absol.* as *sb.*

1844 HAMILTON *Reid* 692 The term *indefinite* ought to be discarded in this relation, and replaced by *indesignate*. **1852** —— *Discuss.* App. ii. 601 The Indesignate is thought, either precisely, as whole or as part, or vaguely, as the one or the other, unknown which, but the worse always presumed. **1865** MILL *Exam. Hamilton* xxii. (1872) 511 *note*, The Indesignate is..often not thought in any relation of quantity at all. **1866** FOWLER *Deduct. Logic* (1869) 29 'Indefinite' or 'indesignate' propositions..in which the subject, being a common term, is not quantified.

†**in'desinence.** *Obs. rare*⁻¹. [IN-³: cf. INDESINENT, DESINENCE.] Want of proper ending.

1593 NASHE 4 *Lett. Confut.* 68 In a verse..a leake of indesinence as a leake in a shippe, must needly be stopt, with what matter soever.

†**in'desinency.** *Obs. rare*⁻¹. [f. next: see -ENCY.] Unending continuance; perpetuity.

1657 REEVE *God's Plea* 239 Oh what a diuturnity and indesinency of bliss might there be, even from generation to generation.

†**in'desinent,** *a. Obs.* [ad. late L. *indēsinent-em*: see IN-³ and DESINENT.] Unceasing, incessant, perpetual.

1601 DENT *Pathw. Heaven* 174 What indesinent paines and unwearied labour, this silly creature [the ant] taketh. **1641** FRENCH *Distill.* vi. (1651) 174 The foure elements by their indesinent motion cast forth a Sperme. **1799** E. DU BOIS *Piece Fam. Biog.* I. 131 He made up for this loss by an indesinent application to his snuff-box.

†**in'desinently,** *adv. Obs.* [f. prec. + -LY².] Without ceasing or interruption; incessantly; continuously.

1651 J. GOODWIN *Redemption Red.* iv. §19 These things are not there..either past or to come, but indesinently and as present. *a* **1677** BARROW *Serm.* I. vi. 70 'Αδιαλείπτως, that is, indesinently, or continually. **1756** AMORY *J. Buncle* (1825) I. 191 Reason must confess a miraculous power indesinently and variously put forth in our bodies.

†**inde'sirable,** *a.* [IN-³.] Undesirable.

1846 WORCESTER cites *Month. Anth.*

†**'Indess.** *Obs. rare.* [f. IND + -ESS.] A female (American) Indian.

1672 JOSSELYN *New Eng. Rarities* 49 Of the Moss that grows at the roots of the white Oak the Indesses make a strong decoction. **1674** —— *Voy. New Eng.* 133 Another time two Indians and an Indess came running into our house.

indestructi'bility. [f. next: see -ITY. Cf. F. *indestructibilité* (1737 in Hatz.-Darm.).] The quality of being indestructible; incapability of being destroyed.

1671 J. WEBSTER *Metallogr.* iv. 78 There is therefore in Mercury itself..the nearest cause or reason of indestructibility. **1829** I. TAYLOR *Enthus.* x. 261 Proof of the indestructibility and victorious power of Christianity. *a* **1862** BUCKLE *Misc. Wks.* (1872) I. 16 To the magnificent doctrine of the indestructibility of matter, we are now adding..one of the indestructibility of force. **1883** H. DRUMMOND *Nat. Law in Spir. W.* (ed. 2) 236 The philosophical thesis of the immateriality or indestructibility of the human soul.

indestructible (ɪndɪ'strʌktɪb(ə)l), *a.* (and *sb.*) [IN-³: see DESTRUCTIBLE. Cf. F. *indestructible* (17–18th c.).] That cannot be destroyed; incapable of destruction. Used *subst.* An indestructible thing.

1674 BOYLE *Excell. Theol.* I. i. 27 The soul..is a simple substance and yet as real a substance as matter itself, which yet the adversaries affirm to be indestructible. **1768–74** TUCKER *Lt. Nat.* II. xxxviii. §9. 480 The individuality of his [man's] perceptive part rendering it indestructible by all natural powers. **1794** in G. Adams *Nat. & Exp. Philos.* I. App. 524 [Carbon] is indestructible by any agent except fire in the open air. **1816** J. SCOTT *Vis. Paris* (ed. 5) 337 The bones, the most indestructible part of the human frame. *a* **1861** T. WINTHROP *Life in Open Air* (1863) 17 My pair of these indestructible [*sc.* socks] will outlast my last legs. **1876** TAIT *Rec. Adv. Phys. Sc.*, *Force* (1885) 366 Energy is indestructible—it is changed from one form to another, and so on, but never altered in quantity. **1880** J. ROSS *Hist. Corea* x. 332 The things used in the evening sacrifice are to be removed,..but spirits and indestructibles may remain. **1898** G. MEREDITH *Odes French Hist.* 76 Refreshful chatter, laughter, gailiard songs. So like Earth's indestructible they were.

Hence **inde'structibleness**, the quality of being indestructible; indestructibility. **inde'structibly** *adv.*, in an indestructible way.

1831 CARLYLE *Sart. Res.* II. ii, How indestructibly the good grows and propagates itself. **1844** DISRAELI *Coningsby* VII. ii, The indestructibleness of its [the Church's] principles. **1865** *Sat. Rev.* 11 Feb. 160/2 Their most transient blunders and follies are embalmed indestructibly in print. **1870** E. WHITE *Life in Christ* IV. xxiv. (1878) 378 The thought of the indestructibleness of the wicked in the fires of hell.

inde'tectable, *a.* Also -ible. [IN-³.] Not detectable; incapable of being detected.

1853 *Fraser's Mag.* XLVII. 98 What was then an exception, easily checked, has now become an indetectible system. **1869** E. A. PARKES *Pract. Hygiene* (ed. 3) 78 When mixed even in large quantity with water, [they] are indetectable by the senses. **1930** W. DE LA MARE *On the Edge* 207 In hope of detecting that shadow's indetectible motion! **1961** D. G. JAMES *Matthew Arnold* i. 27 There always remained in him something evasive and indetectable.

indeterminable (ɪndɪ'tɜːmɪnəb(ə)l), *a.* (*sb.*) [ad. L. *indēterminābilis* (Tertullian): see DETERMINABLE. Cf. F. *indéterminable* (1753 in Hatz.-Darm.).] Not determinable.

†**1.** Incapable of being limited or bounded in respect of range, number, etc. *Obs. rare.*

1486 *Bk. St. Albans, Her.* A v, Ther ben ix. vices contrari to gentilmen of the wiche v. ben indetermynable and iiij determynable. The v indetermynable ben theys: oon to be full of slowthe in his werris [etc.]. **1649** JER. TAYLOR *Gt. Exemp.* I. Ad sect. 3 §11 His memory is indeterminable and unalterable, ever remembring to do us good. **1690** LOCKE *Hum. Und.* II. xvii. §11 Conceiving ourselves to be, as it were, in the center [of space], we do on all sides pursue those indeterminable lines of number.

2. Of disputes, difficulties, etc.: Incapable of being decided or settled.

1611 SPEED *Hist. Gt. Brit.* IX. xvi. §87. 846 In Monarchies ..where lineall succession is the rule of inheritance, there somtimes fal out as great and as indeterminable difficulties, as where Election designeth the Successor. **1651** HOBBES *Govt. & Soc.* xvii. §27. 334 The controversies which rise among them will become innumerable, and indeterminable. **1841** MYERS *Cath. Th.* IV. §32. 333 Were the whole question to be determined by the old Testament alone, it would be at present for us indeterminable.

3. Incapable of being definitely fixed or ascertained.

1646 SIR T. BROWNE *Pseud. Ep.* VI. i. 273 As its [the world's] period is inscrutable, so is its nativity indeterminable. **1798** W. MAVOR *Brit. Tourists* V. 31 Veins of rock run into the sea to an indeterminable distance. **1881** WESTCOTT & HORT *Grk. N.T.* Introd. §13 The gain or loss ..is from the nature of the case indeterminable.

b. *Nat. Hist.* Of which the species, or place in classification, cannot be determined.

1848 OWEN in *Times* 11 Nov., Of any large marine nondescript or indeterminable monster they [the museums of Scandinavia] cannot shew a trace.

B. as *sb.* An indeterminable point or problem.

1646 SIR T. BROWNE *Pseud. Ep.* VII. i. 340 To condemne such indeterminables, unto him that demanded on what hand Venus was wounded, the Philosopher thought it a sufficient resolution to reinquire upon what leg King Philip halted.

Hence **inde'terminableness**, the quality of being indeterminable.

In mod. Dicts.

inde'terminably, *adv. rare.* [In sense 1, f. IN-³ + DETERMINABLY; in 2, f. prec. + -LY².]

†**1.** In an indefinite manner: cf. DETERMINABLY *adv.*

1471 FORTESCUE *Wks.* (1869) I. 533 Our lorde sayde.. indiffinytely or indetermynably that she [woman] shulde be vnder the power and lordshipp of man.

2. In an indeterminable manner.

1846 WORCESTER, *Indeterminably*, in an indeterminable manner. *Dr. Allen.*

inde'terminacy. [f. next: see -ACY.]

a. The quality of being indeterminate; want of determinateness or definiteness.

1649 BP. REYNOLDS *Hosea* vi. 72 Such an indifferency and indeterminacy in the manner of working. **1879** THOMSON & TAIT *Nat. Phil.* I. I. §337 The linear transformation ceases to be wholly determinate; but the degree or degrees of indeterminacy which supervene is the reverse of embarrassing. **1892** *Nation* (N.Y.) 27 Oct. 324/2 Vagueness is an indeterminacy in the limits of the application of an idea. **1919** J. M. KEYNES *Econ. Consequences Peace* v. 208 The Allies recognised the inconvenience of the indeterminacy of the burden laid upon Germany. **1947** P. A. M. DIRAC *Princ. Quantum Mech.* (ed. 3) i. 4 There is an unavoidable indeterminacy in the calculation of observational results, the theory enabling us to calculate in general only the probability of our obtaining a particular result when we make an observation. **1953** C. F. HOCKETT in Saporta & Bastian *Psycholinguistics* (1961) 46/1 Thus, if there is no indeterminacy, no element of choice, there can be no transmission of information. **1962** *Listener* 15 Feb. 290/1 Most murderers are now subject to a higher degree of indeterminacy in their sentence than would be the case with those who were given the maximum sentence which I am canvassing. *Ibid.* 27 Sept. 472/2 Contemporary composers such as Stockhausen are often attacked for their deliberate indeterminacy—a word which has become a technical term. **1963** D. A. FIRMAGE *Fund. Theory of Struct.* v. 118 To determine the degree of indeterminacy..remove reaction components one at a time and see if the structure is stable against all possible forces. **1971** *Archivum Linguisticum* II. 50 It will be seen that the inclusion of a single additional item serves to reduce in some measure the indeterminacy we have noted as attending the parts and the whole of words.

b. Physics. ***principle of indeterminacy*** (or ***indeterminacy principle***) = *uncertainty principle.*

1928 A. S. EDDINGTON *Nature Physical World* x. 220 It was Heisenberg again who set in motion the new development in the summer of 1927, and the consequences were further elucidated by Bohr. The outcome of it is a fundamental general principle which seems to rank in importance with the principle of relativity. I shall here call it the 'principle of indeterminacy'. The gist of it can be stated as follows: a particle may have position or it may have velocity but it cannot in any exact sense have both. **1938** W. S. MAUGHAM *Summing Up* 289 Of late the Principle of Indeterminacy, by bringing to view certain events to which apparently no causes can be assigned, has cast a doubt on the universal efficacy of those laws upon which science has hitherto been based. **1959** *Listener* 1 Oct. 519/1 Heisenberg's principle of indeterminacy showed that the process of observing could affect the observation. **1964** D. ROSENTHAL *Introd. Properties Metals* iv. 68 There is the unavoidable lack of resolution caused by the interaction between waves and particles and deriving from the fundamental behavior of matter and energy (the indeterminacy principle). **1971** *Physics Bull.* June 329/2 It led Heisenberg to formulate his principle of indeterminacy, postulating that a measurement of one property of an entity, such as its momentum, involved an inevitable uncertainty in our knowledge of the conjugate property, such as its position.

indeterminate (ɪndɪ'tɜːmɪnət), *a.* (*sb.*). [ad. L. *indēterminā̆t-us* (Tertullian): see DETERMINATE. Cf. F. *indeterminé* (14th c., Oresme).] Not determined; undetermined.

†**1.** Not definitely set down; undetermined: cf. DETERMINATE *pa. pple. Obs.*

c **1391** CHAUCER *Astrol.* II. §17 To knowe the verrey degree of any maner sterre..thow he be indeterminat in thin astralabie.

2. a. Not fixed in extent, number, character or nature; left uncertain as to limits of extent, number, etc.; of uncertain size or character; indefinite, indistinct, uncertain.

1603 HOLLAND *Plutarch's Mor.* 1334 This indeterminate and troublesome infinity. **1651** HOBBES *Leviath.* II. xxviii. 163 An indeterminate, that is to say, an arbitrary Punishment. **1662** STILLINGFL. *Orig. Sacr.* III. ii. §9 Numenius..condemns all those, as not understanding Pythagoras, who attribute to him the production of the indeterminate Hyle. **1722** WOLLASTON *Relig. Nat.* ii. 33 For time, as well as space, is capable of indeterminate division. **1774** J. BRYANT *Mythol.* I. 226 Can we believe that they would..choose for a characteristic what was so general and indeterminate? **1782** MARTYN *Geog. Mag.* I. 728 Empires of great extent but indeterminate limits. **1805–17** R. JAMESON *Char. Min.* (ed. 3) 109 The eight or nine sided prisms afford only accidental or indeterminate varieties. **1831** R. KNOX *Cloquet's Anat.* 702 This artery gives off twigs of indeterminate number. **1885** J. MARTINEAU *Types Eth. Th.* II. 6 Would it be better..to blur into an indeterminate mess perception, reasoning, imagination, passion?

b. Of statements, thoughts, words, etc.: Not clear and definite; wanting in precision; vague.

1774 J. BRYANT *Mythol.* I. 498 His account is very indeterminate and obscure. **1874** JEVONS *Princ. Sc.* I. 49 Some is an indeterminate adjective; it implies unknown qualities..but gives no hint as to their nature. **1878** C.

STANFORD *Symb. Christ* iii. 69 Too often the term 'Angel' has for us a cloudy and indeterminate meaning.

c. *Math.* Of a quantity: Not limited to a fixed value or number of values. (Also *absol.* as *sb.*) Of a problem: Having an unlimited number of solutions. Also (in *Engin.*), of a structure or its stresses, = *hyperstatic* adj. (s.v. HYPER- IV): usu. qualified by *statically*.

indeterminate analysis, the branch of analysis which deals with the solution of indeterminate problems; ***method of i. coefficients*** (more properly of ***undetermined coefficients***), a method of analysis invented by Descartes; ***i. equation***, an equation in which the unknown quantities are indeterminate; ***i. form***, a form consisting of two indeterminate quantities; ***i. series***, a series whose terms proceed by the powers of an indeterminate quantity.

1706 PHILLIPS s.v. *Problem*, Such an one as is capable of an infinite number of different solutions..is..called an indeterminate Problem. **1795** HUTTON *Math. Dict.* s.v. *Series, Indeterminate Series* is one whose terms proceed by the powers of an indeterminate quantity *x*. **1806** —— *Course Math.* I. 131 It is obvious..that questions of this sort admit of a great variety of answers..These kinds of questions are called by algebraists indeterminate or unlimited problems. **1812–16** PLAYFAIR *Nat. Phil.* (1819) I. 27 No one of them can be indeterminate, or can admit of innumerable values, otherwise V itself would be indeterminate. **1816** tr. *Lacroix's Diff. & Int. Calculus* 143 We may take the successive differentials, by making those of the two indeterminates, which are considered as functions of the third, vary at the same time. **1841** J. R. YOUNG *Math. Dissert.* ii. 34 The equation..becomes indeterminate, and capable of an infinite number of different values. **1882** MINCHIN *Unipl. Kinem.* 211 At each of these points the value of ψ is indeterminate. **1905** I. HIROI (*title*) The statically-indeterminate stresses in frames commonly used for bridges. **1919** PIPPARD & PRITCHARD *Aeroplane Struct.* xxii. 280 The principle of Least Work..enables the engineer to find the stresses in structures which are statically indeterminate, i.e. in structures with too many members. **1926** PARCEL & MANEY *Elem. Treat. Statically Indeterminate Stresses* p. v, This book has grown out of the authors' needs in teaching the subject of Indeterminate Structures during the past fifteen years. **1963** D. A. FIRMAGE *Fund. Theory of Struct.* v. 118 A truss can..be determinate, indeterminate, or unstable with respect to the system of bars. **1964** J. H. FAUPEL *Engin. Design* ii. 130 In a statically indeterminate system the basic equations of statics (ΣF and $\Sigma M = 0$) are insufficient for obtaining a solution.

d. *Bot.* (*a*) = INDEFINITE 5 a; (*b*) of æstivation: see quot. 1880.

1842 BRANDE *Dict. Sci., Lit.* etc., *Indeterminate*,..when a stem is never terminated by a flower, nor has its growth stopped by any other organic cause. **1880** GRAY *Struct. Bot.* iv. §2. 134 The æstivation is said to be Open or Indeterminate, when the parts do not come into contact in the bud, so as to cover those within. The most familiar case is that of the petals of Mignonette.

e. ***indeterminate sentence***, a sentence in a criminal case which leaves the prisoner's release dependent on his conduct and on the probability of his amendment; ***indeterminate vowel***, the 'obscure' vowel (ə), mid-mixed-wide; = SHEVA 2.

1873 E. C. WINES *Rep. Internat. Penitentiary Congr. 1872* xxxviii. 273 It is extremely doubtful whether society will, or could, ever become reconciled to so great a change on the sudden as that from determinate to wholly indeterminate sentences. **1888** KING & COOKSON *Princ. Sound & Inflexion Gr. & Latin* 70 The same indeterminate vowel appears in Sk., where it is called a *svarabhakti* vowel. **1894** W. M. LINDSAY *Latin Lang.* 257 The obscure or indeterminate vowel (like the Hebrew shᵉva). **1962** *Listener* 15 Feb. 290/1 Indeterminate sentences have been common in western Europe and the United States for some time. **1972** *N.Y. Law Jrnl.* 14 Nov. 6/5 People, &c., v. Manuel Santos—Indeterminate sentence.

3. Not fixed or established; uncertain.

1626 BACON *Sylva* §698 The Insecta haue Voluntarie Motion.. And whereas some of the Ancients haue said, that their Motion is Indeterminate, and their Imagination Indefinite, it is negligently obserued. **1838** PRESCOTT *Ferd. & Is.* (1846) I. vi. 268 The place of its sittings, before indeterminate..was fixed at Valladolid. **1842** POE *Marie Roget* Wks. 1864 I. 233 The period of their rising is, and necessarily must be indeterminate. **1876** GEO. ELIOT *Dan. Der.* vii, It [harvest] lies all underground, with an indeterminate future.

4. Not settled or decided; left doubtful.

1656 STANLEY *Hist. Philos.* v. (1701) 191/2 Indeterminate is that which is in our Power, and to which part soever it enclineth, will be true or false. **1678** MARVELL *Def. Howe* Wks. 1875 IV. 201 So it will be too if God be to determine it, indeterminate till he have determined it. **1783** MARTYN *Geog. Mag.* II. 65 This court, where the law is silent or indeterminate, has a decisive voice. **1872** YEATS *Growth Comm.* 216 Meanwhile several millions sterlng had been wasted by both companies in indeterminate conflicts.

5. Not determined by motives (regarded as external forces); acting freely.

1836 J. GILBERT *Chr. Atonem.* iv. (1852) 98 This characteristic of moral action, its indeterminate working. *a* **1871** GROTE *Eth. Fragm.* ii, In positive morality, the mandate is conceived as emanating from an indeterminate superior.

indeterminately (ɪndɪ'tɜːmɪnətlɪ), *adv.* [f. prec. + -LY^2.] In an indeterminate manner.

1. Without precision; indefinitely; vaguely.

1571 GOLDING *Calvin on Ps.* lviii. 12 To speake indeterminately, as it were of a multitude. **1628** T. SPENCER *Logick* 168 This word some..doth designe an vniversall, or common terme indeterminately. **1726** AYLIFFE *Parergon* 350 A Libel is not valid, if the Demand or Petition therein containd be deduced and set forth indeterminately. **1835** I. TAYLOR *Spir. Despot.* iv. 166 No writer of the age of Cyprian uses the words bishop, presbyter, and deacon so indeterminately or so abstractedly as do the apostles.

†**2.** Without specification or selection; indifferently. *Obs.*

1677 HALE *Prim. Orig. Man.* I. iv. 106 Whether we subduct that Number of Ten out of the last Generations of Men, or out of Generations a thousand years since, or indeterminately out of the whole Collection [etc.]. **1704** NORRIS *Ideal World* II. iii. 150 All knowledge must be immediate or mediate indeterminately. *a* **1761** LAW *Th. Relig.* III. ii. (R.), The worst and most dreadful part of the sentence..which denounced death absolutely and indeterminately.

3. Without deciding or settling a question. *rare.*

Based on It. *indeterminatamente* in the title of Galileo's *Dialogo* (1632): the English transl. of 1661 renders it 'impartially and indefinitely'.

1841 BREWSTER *Mart. Sc.* v. 81 Galileo's work..[in which] he discusses, indeterminately and firmly, the arguments proposed on both sides.

inde'terminateness. [f. as prec. + -NESS.] The quality of being indeterminate; vagueness, indefiniteness, want of exactness, etc.

1644 DIGBY *Mans Soul* (1645) 58 To draw..from indeterminatenesse and confusion to a clarity and determination. **1816** BENTHAM *Chrestom.* 249 This deficiency, in respect or preciseness, is among the unavoidable results, of the indeterminateness..attached to the names in common use. **1879** H. SPENCER *Data Ethics* ix. 154 To the double indeterminateness of the end has to be added the indeterminateness of the means.

indetermination (ɪndɪtɜːmɪ'neɪʃən). [f. INDETERMINATE: see -ATION. Cf. F. *indétermination* (1651 in Hatz.-Darm.).] Absence or want of determination; the fact or condition of being undetermined; unsettledness.

1649 JER. TAYLOR *Gt. Exemp.* I. §7. 107 The indetermination of her [the Virgin's] thoughts was a trouble great as the passion of her love. **1660** —— *Duct. Dubit.* IV. i. I. §5 In moral and spiritual things, liberty and indetermination are weakness. **1749** BOLINGBROKE *Patriot.* 243 His whole management..was contrived to keep up a kind of general indetermination in the party about the succession. **1838** *Blackw. Mag.* XLIV. 545 While this indetermination continues, the power of choice remains inoperative. **1860** FARRAR *Orig. Lang.* viii. 166 The earliest languages are marked by exuberance, indetermination.

b. The fact of being indeterminate as a quantity, a problem, or the like.

1789 T. TAYLOR *Proclus' Comm.* II. 32 Such things as are properly denominated problems, ought to avoid indetermination, and not to be of the number of things capable of infinite variation.

†**c.** An indeterminate number or quantity. *Obs.*

a **1619** FOTHERBY *Atheom.* II. x. §4 (1622) 309 All wholes, all parts, all termes, and all indeterminations.

indetermined (ɪndɪ'tɜːmɪnd), *a.* Now *rare.* [f. IN-^{3} + DETERMINED *ppl. a.*] Not determined, UNDETERMINED.

1. Not definitely fixed, settled, decided, or ascertained; having no definite or clearly-marked character.

1611 SPEED *Hist. Gt. Brit.* IX. vi. §90. 507/1 The Westerne Princes..wrapt and knotted in mutuall suspitions and quarrels indetermined. **1641** R. GREVILLE (Ld. BROOKE) *Eng. Episc.* I. x. 56 Most of their Tenets were so much indetermined, that scarce any of them knew what he was to hold and beleeve. **1735–6** H. BROOKE *Univ. Beauty* v. 5 The Eternal Height of indetermin'd space! **1764** REID *Inquiry* I. i. 47 The word impression as used by Hume is for the most part a vague and indetermined expression. **1864** BOWEN *Logic* iv. 60 What..has no qualities attributed to it, though attributable, is said to be indetermined.

†**2.** Not determined to a certain course of action.

1628 T. SPENCER *Logick* 219 Mans will is a facultie free, and indetermined vnto one. **1660** tr. *Amyraldus' Treat. conc. Relig.* II. ii. 180 He will become poised between contrary probabilities, and indetermin'd (as they speak) not knowing on which side to propend. *a* **1670** RUST *Disc. Truth* (1682) 190 We have natures so indetermined to what is good.

†**3.** *Math.* = INDETERMINATE 2 c. *Obs.*

1706 W. JONES *Syn. Palmar. Matheseos* 137 Here 'tis plain, the Question is Indetermined. **1740** CHEYNE *Regimen* 220–1 Indetermin'd Problems in Algebra. **1743** EMERSON *Fluxions* 2 Those Quantities that are continually changing their Value are called *variable* or *indetermin'd Quantities*.

indeterminism (ɪndɪ'tɜːmɪnɪz(ə)m). [f. IN-^{3} + DETERMINISM (see quot. 1874).]

1. The philosophical theory that human action is not necessarily determined by motives, but is to some extent free.

1874 W. G. WARD in *Dublin Rev.* Apr., Mr. Mill..calls his theory 'determinism'; we will call our own, therefore, by the name of 'indeterminism'. **1882–3** F. L. PATTON in Schaff *Encycl. Relig. Knowl.* III. 2525/1 According to the tenets of indeterminism, there is no way of having a free choice, except through an infinite series of choices, or else through a theory that makes all choices fortuitous. **1886** SIDGWICK *Hist. Ethics* iv. 250 In Clarke's system..Indeterminism is no doubt a cardinal notion.

2. = INDETERMINACY.

1928 *Chem. Rev.* V. 472 Because of the ambiguity resulting from the Heisenberg indeterminism principle, the future of a dynamical system can never be predicted with certainty. **1957** *Encycl. Brit.* XV. 680/1 Because *h* is so small, the indeterminism caused by the uncertainty principle is of no consequence in ordinary experience. **1969** R. B. FULLER *Operating Man. Spaceship Earth* v. 65 Heisenberg's principle of 'indeterminism' which recognized the experimental discovery that the act of measuring always alters that which was being measured turns experience into a continuous and never-repeatable evolutionary scenario.

inde'terminist. [f. IN-^{3} + DETERMINIST.] One who holds the doctrine of indeterminism. Also *attrib.* = **indetermi'nistic** *a.*, of or pertaining to the doctrine of indeterminism.

1880 W. L. COURTNEY *Epicurus* in *Hellenica* (1880) 257 Epicurus was not..an Indeterminist: he was an opponent of Fatalism, not of Determinism. *a* **1882** T. H. GREEN *Prol. Ethics* II. i. (1883) 93 The question commonly debated..between 'determinists' and 'indeterminists';..whether there is, or is not, a possibility of unmotived willing. **1902** W. R. B. GIBSON in H. Sturt *Personal Idealism* III. 160 The Indeterminist, like the Britisher, is king of his own castle, and woe to the combatant who fights the battles of Freedom within that..enclosure. Of such a kind is the indeterministic challenge of Professor James. **1903** A. E. TAYLOR *Elem. Metaphysics* IV. iv. 376 The essence of the indeterminist position is the denial of the principle affirmed alike by the doctrine of self-determination and, in an unintelligent travesty, by the determinist theory that conduct results from the reaction of 'character' upon circumstances. **1907** W. JAMES *Pragmatism* 117 The chaplet of my days tumbles into a cast of disconnected beads as soon as the thread of inner necessity is drawn out by the preposterous indeterminist doctrine. **1925** A. G. HOGG *Redemption from this World* 243 Bushnell, accepting a very indeterministic type of libertarianism, postulates an unresolved plurality of 'powers' or uncaused causes. **1936** *Times Lit. Suppl.* 11 Jan. 38/4 A very lucid exposition of the indeterminist philosophy. **1940** *Mind* XLIX. 465 An erroneous belief that acceptance of the new 'indeterministic' view of physical law would make it less likely that the sun would rise tomorrow. **1969** *Adv. Hydroscience* V. 102 Indeterministic models would exclude those possessing deterministic and probabilistic properties.

indett, obs. form of INDEBT.

†**in'devil**, *v. Obs. rare.* Also **en-**. [f. IN-^{2} (EN-) + DEVIL *sb.*] *trans.* To possess with a devil; esp. in pa. pple. **in'devilled**.

1604 PARSONS *3rd Pt. Three Convers. Eng.* 279 They were indeuilled, superdeuilled, and thorowdeuilled. **1611** FLORIO, *Indemoniare*, to endiuell, to possesse one with some diuell or euill spirit. **1624** GEE *Foot out of Snare* 52 There was one M. Blewes..and one M. Fowell..of whom either were or seemed to bee indiuelled.

†**inde'virginate**, *a. Obs. rare.* [IN-^{3}.] Undeflowered. Also *fig.* Unsullied.

1616 CHAPMAN *Homer's Hymn to Venus* (R.), Pallas, the seede of Ægis-bearing Joue; Who still liues indeuirginate. **1822** T. G. WAINEWRIGHT *Ess. & Crit.* (1880) 294 Those plump shoulders, that bosom indevirginate.

indevoir, obs. Sc. form of ENDEAVOUR *v.*

†**indevolvi'bility.** *Obs. rare*$^{-1}$. [f. ***indevolvible*** (f. IN-^{3} + DEVOLVE *v.* + -IBLE) + -ITY.] Incapability of being devolved on another.

1695 [see INDELEGABILITY].

indevor, obs. form of ENDEAVOUR *sb.* and *v.*

†**inde'vote**, *a. Obs. rare*$^{-1}$. [ad. late L. *indēvōtus*, f. *in-* (IN-^{3}) + *dēvōtus* DEVOTE *a.*: cf. F. *indévot* (15th c.).] = INDEVOUT.

a **1742** BENTLEY *Corr.* (1842) I. 7 They give no good account of the other little book. There are so many of the same arguments, and so indevote an age.

†**inde'voted**, *a. Obs.* [f. IN-^{3} + DEVOTED *a.*] Not devoted or attached; disaffected or disloyal.

1647 CLARENDON *Hist. Reb.* II. §102 By which husbandry all the rich families of England..were exceedingly incensed, and even indevoted to the Crown. *a* **1674** —— *Surv. Leviath.* (1676) 158 To curb and subdue that Clergy that was indevoted to him. **1759** HURD *Dial. Retirem.* Note (R.), Some persons indevoted to the excellent chancellor.

indevotion (ɪndɪ'vəʊʃən). [f. IN-^{3} + DEVOTION: cf. F. *indévotion* (1584, L. *indēvōtio*).] Want of devotion; indevout feeling or conduct.

1526 *Pilgr. Perf.* (W. de W. 1531) 139 Cese not fro prayer ..by yᵉ reason of suche drynes or indeuocyon. **1614** T. ADAMS *Devils Banquet* 21 The chilling and killing cold of our Indevotion. **1649** JER. TAYLOR *Gt. Exemp.* I. Ad §8. 116 The example may entice us on a little further, then the customes of the world or our own indevotions would engage us. **1756** W. DODD *Fasting* (ed. 2) 11 Spiritual vices, such as.. indevotion and deadness in prayer. **1866** *Ch. Times* 17 Nov. 382/4 The sloth and indevotion of the clergy.

inde'votional, *a.* [IN-^{3}.] Not devotional.

1865 MISS YONGE *Clever Wom. Fam.* 79 One deemed praise..the prime object of his ministry; the other found the performance indevotional, and raved that education should be sacrificed to wretched music.

indevout (ɪndɪ'vaʊt), *a.* [f. IN-^{3} + DEVOUT. (In first quot. transl. L. *indēvōtus*: see INDEVOTE.)] Not devout, irreverent, irreligious.

c **1450** tr. *De Imitatione* III. xxxviii. 108 þou shalt be founden..now deuoute, now indeuoute [**1502** ATKYNSON *ibid.*, vndeuout]. **1645** BP. HALL *Remedy Discontents* 158 Under which, a praying soule can no more miscary, then an indevout soule can enjoy safety. **1770** J. BARETTI *Journ. to Genoa* III. lviii. 98 No lady here misses hearing mass every day..if she did..she would be considered as indevout. **1855** MAURICE *Learn. & Work.* vi. 181 Brought together by what in our thoughtless, indevout language we call accidents.

Hence **inde'voutly** *adv.*, **inde'voutness**.

1694 KETTLEWELL *Comp. Persecuted* 48 Thy pure Worship and Service had been..carelessly and indevoutly attended. 1842 MANNING *Serm., Worlaly Affect.* (1848) I. 68 The indevoutness of your present prayers.

indew, obs. form of ENDUE.

indewly, variant of INDULY.

index (ˈɪndɛks), *sb.* Pl. **indexes** (also 7 **index's**) and **indices** (ˈɪndɪsiːz). [a. L. *index, indic-em*, pl. *indicēs*, the forefinger, an informer, sign, inscription, f. *in-* (IN-[2]) + **dic-* to point out: see INDICATE. Cf. F. *index* (16th c.).

In current use the plural is *indices* in senses 8, 9, and usually in other senses except 5, in which *indexes* is usual.]

1. The fore-finger: so called because used in pointing. Now chiefly *Anat.*

Also, in *Comp. Anat.*, the corresponding digit of the fore-limb of a quadruped, or of the wing of a bird.

1398 TREVISA *Barth. De P.R.* v. xxix. (1495) 140 The seconde fyngre hyght *Index*..for by hym is moche shewynges made. 1594 PLAT *Jewell-ho.* III. 43 The *index* or forfinger of your right hand. 1620 SKELTON *Quix.* IV. iv. 27 He..clapt the *Index* of his right Hand upon his Nose and Eye-brows. 1644 BULWER *Chiron.* 79 Both the Indexes joyn'd, and pyramidically advanced. 1758 J. S. *Le Dran's Observ. Surg.* (1771) 269, I thrust the Index of my Left-Hand into the Cavity. 1825 *Sporting Mag.* XVII. 36 Our hero longed to have his index upon the trigger. 1844 MRS. BROWNING *Lady Geraldine* xxx, And the left hand's index droppeth from the lips upon the cheek. 1893 NEWTON *Dict. Birds* 459 *Index*..in Birds always the best developed of the digits of the fore-limb.

2. a. A piece of wood, metal, or the like, which serves as a pointer; *esp.* in scientific instruments, a pointer which moves along a graduated scale (or which is itself fixed while a graduated scale moves across its extremity) so as to indicate movements or measurements. Cf. INDEX *v.* 5.

1594 PLAT *Jewell-ho.* III. 11 Let there be a sharpe *index*, that may point vpon a table of wood. 1613 M. RIDLEY *Magn. Bodies* 115 So that his broad Index..may be set to point out the degrees of the altitude of the pole. 1667 R. TOWNELEY in *Phil. Trans.* II. 458 Marking above 40,000 Divisions in a Foot, by the help of two *Indexes*. 1715 DESAGULIERS *Fires Impr.* 121 To know at sight in what manner the Holes are open..have an Index which takes up but little room. 1726 tr. *Gregory's Astron.* I. 263 Having brought the Place of the Sun to the Meridian, bring the Index to twelve a Clock. 1727-41 CHAMBERS *Cycl., Index of a Globe*, is a little style fitted on to the north-pole and turning with it, pointing to certain divisions in the hour-circle. 1833 J. HOLLAND *Manuf. Metal* II. 296 The graduated arch passes through the loop, until the index on the edge of the loop is opposite zero. 1860 TYNDALL *Glac.* I. xxv. 190 The magnet to arrange the index of the thermometer. 1863 J. WATSON *Theory & Pract. Art of Weaving* vi. 209 After the wheel is turned, the next process is to divide its circumference into as many divisions as will make up the number of teeth required; this is done by an index which is fixed on the spindle of the lathe. 1879 J. J. HOLTZAPFFEL *Turning & Mech. Manipulation* IV. v. 118 The index, is a steel spring or rod terminating in a point, which is inserted in any required series of holes, in any of the circles of the division plate, to retain the mandrel for the time, at rest, in certain relative positions. For example, to divide the work into 12 parts; the point of the index is placed successively in the holes 8. 16. 24. 32. etc. of the 96 circle..and while the mandrel is arrested at these points, the work is marked.

b. The arm of a surveying instrument; an alidade.

1571 DIGGES *Pantom.* G. iij, Laye the line fiduciall of your index vppon the beginning of the degrees in your Quadrant. 1682 *Providence Rec.* (1894) VI. 80, 2 sights for sirveiors worke belonging to an Jndex. 1712 J. JAMES tr. *Le Blond's Gardening* 81 Two Rulers or Indexes, one immoveable.. and the other moveable. 1793 SMEATON *Edystone L.* §97 To the index of the Theodolite was screwed a ruler..this index-ruler being carried horizontally round..the index would mark the degree and minute of the circle in which it is placed. 1807 HUTTON *Course Math.* II. 54 An index, which is a brass two-foot scale, with either a small telescope, or open sights set perpendicularly on the ends. These sights and one edge of the index are in the same plane, and that is called the fiducial edge of the index.

3. a. The hand of a clock or watch; also, the style or gnomon of a sun-dial. Now *rare.*

1594 BLUNDEVIL *Exerc.* III. II. x. (1636) 390 Untill the Index do justly touch the prick of some perfect houre. 1623 FEATLY *Fisher catch'd* O ij*, No man can perceiue the index in a Watch, or finger in a Diall to wagge or stirre. 1677 HALE *Prim. Orig. Man.* IV. iv. 324 If I should see a curious Watch ..and should observe the exact disposition of the Spring, the String, the Wheels, the Ballance, the Index. 1817 T. L. PEACOCK *Melincourt* xxxii, There was a sun-dial in the centre of the court; the sun shone on the brazen plate, and the shadow of the index fell on the line of noon. 1822 IMISON *Sc. & Art* I. 87 The showing the time is contrived by the motion of the indices or hands on the dial-plate.

fig. 1635 SWAN *Spec. M.* ii. §2 (1643) 31 The Sunne (who is the Index of time, by whose revolution we account for years). 1742 YOUNG *Nt. Th.* IX. 1324 Pointing out Life's rapid..flight, With such an Index fair, as none can miss.

b. *slang.* The nose (cf. GNOMON 1 c); or ? 'the face' (Farmer; cf. DIAL *sb.* 6 c).

1817 *Sporting Mag.* L. 53 He put in a sharp blow on the bridge of Randall's nose, so that it pinked the index of Paddy in an instant. 1818 *Ibid.* (N.S.) II. 280 The handy work of Martin upon his opponent's index was now apparent. 1828 EGAN *Finish to Tom & Jerry* 48 (Farmer) Kind-hearted Sue! Bless her pretty index. [Cf. 4 b, quot. 1616.]

4. a. That which serves to direct or point *to* a particular fact or conclusion; a guiding principle.

1598 DRAYTON *Heroic. Ep.* I. 103 Lest when my lisping guiltie Tongue should hault, My Lookes might prove the Index to my Fault. 1640 LAUD *Let. to Chas. I* in *Biblioth. Reg.* 41 This is the only index to us whereby that the blessing of God is present with you. 1747 *Scheme Equip. Men of War* 26 His Services would be Indexes denoting his Merit. *c* 1750 SHENSTONE *Elegies* ii. 36 And readers call their lost attention home Led by that index where true genius shines. 1803 JANE PORTER *Thaddeus* viii. (1831) 76 His uniform being black, he needed no other index than his pale and mournful countenance to announce that he was chief mourner. 1859 HOLLAND *Gold F.* i. 13 The proverbs of a nation furnish the index to its spirit and the result of its civilization. 1888 BRYCE *Amer. Commw.* II. xxxviii. 52 They [amendments] are so instructive..as an index to present tendencies of American democracy. 1880 *Nature* 19 Sept., One of the first indices to the solution of the question lies in the situation of the oil-bearing regions.

b. A sign, token, or indication *of* something.

1607 TOPSELL *Four-f. Beasts* 151 The square and flat Nose is the best signe and index thereof. 1616 R. C. *Times Whistle* ii. 632 Man is to man a subject of deceite; And that olde saying is vntrue 'the face Is index of the heart'. 1677 GALE *Crt. Gentiles* II. III. 193 Diodorus saith that Isis was wont to appear by night and to inject dreams..giving manifest indices of her presence. 1779 J. MOORE *View Soc. Fr.* (1789) I. xlii. 363 A sensible manly countenance..the true index of his character. 1878 HUXLEY *Physiogr.* 211 A raised beach is therefore an index of elevation of the land. 1887 STEVENSON *Misadv. J. Nicholson* i. 3 His son's empty guffaws..struck him with pain as the indices of a weak mind.

5. †**a.** A table of contents prefixed to a book, a brief list or summary of the matters treated in it, an argument; also, a preface, prologue. *Obs.* **b.** An alphabetical list, placed (usually) at the end of a book, of the names, subjects, etc. occurring in it, with indication of the places in which they occur.

One work may have several indexes, e.g. an index of names of persons and places, of subjects, of words, etc. For these the Latin phrases *index nominum, locorum, rerum, verborum* are often employed as headings.

[1578 LYTE *Dodoens* (heading), Index Latinorum nominum. *Ibid.*, Index appellationum et nomenclaturarum omnium Stirpium [etc.]. *Ibid.*, The Englishe Table conteyning the names and syrnames [etc.].] 1580 FLEMING in *Baret's Alv.* Aaaaj, Which words, though expressed in this Index, are notwithstanding omitted..in this Aluearie. *Ibid.* Nnnn ij (*heading*), A briefe note touching the Prouerbiall Index. *Ibid.*, Such Prouerbes as we haue.. reduced into an Abecedarie Index or Table. *a* 1593 MARLOWE *Hero & Leand.* II. 129 As an index to a book So to his mind was young Leander's look. 1604 SHAKS. *Oth.* II. i. 263 An Index and obscure prologue to the History of Lust. 1606 —— *Tr. & Cr.* I. iii. 343 In such Indexes, although small prickes To their subsequent Volumes [etc.]. 1632 MASSINGER & FIELD *Fatal Dowry* IV. i, The index tells us the contents of stories, and directs to the particular chapters. 1699 BENTLEY *Phal.* Pref. 79 No Learning..no Knowledge in Books, except Index's and Vocabularies. [1750-1 JOHNSON *Let. to Richardson* 9 Mar. in *Boswell*, I wish you would add an index rerum, that when the reader recollects any incident, he may easily find it.] 1858 CARLYLE *Fredk. Gt.* I. i. §3. 9 Books..which want all things, even an Index. [1888 *Athenæum* 28 Jan. 112/3 The Royalist Composition Papers..of which Mr. Phillimore supplies a capital *index nominum*.]

fig. 1641 HINDE *J. Bruen* xviii. 57 He became as a very profitable Index to the family, to call to minde what they had learned. 1663 J. SPENCER *Prodigies* (1665) 71 God hath appointed..all the labors of Nature, as a kind of Indices to this great Volume of the World. *a* 1680 BUTLER *Rem.* (1759) II. 188 He is but an Index of Things and Words, that can direct where they are to be spoken with, but no further.

†**c.** A reference list. *Obs.*

1660 WILLSFORD *Scales Comm.* 209 Some men of very great Commerce and trading keep a Kalender, Register, or an Alphabeticall Index, of the names of Men, Wares, Ships. *a* 1734 NORTH *Lives* (1826) I. 12 The master employed him to make an alphabetical index of all the verbs neuter.

d. *Computers.* A set of items each of which specifies one of the records of a file and contains information about its address.

1962 *Gloss. Terms Automatic Data Processing* (*B.S.I.*) 27 *Index*, a sequence or array of items with keys, used to identify or locate records. 1970 O. DOPPING *Computers & Data Processing* xvi. 261 The index can contain the addresses of all individual records, but if the file is ordered, it is usually more economic to make the index cruder. 1971 R. L. BOYES et al. *Introd. Electronic Computing* viii. 201 An index is simply a shorthand substitute for the original information and is used to assist in the location of a given record... The general form of an index..will contain these two items: 1. The index term. This is the shorthand description of a stored record... 2. Record identification or location. This may be a document number or the physical address of the record described by the index term.

6. a. *spec.* (short for *Index librorum prohibitorum*). The list, published by authority, of books which Roman Catholics are forbidden to read, or may read only in expurgated editions.

Rules for the formation of such an Index (*Regulæ Indicis*) were formulated by the Council of Trent, in accordance with which an *Index librorum prohibitorum* (Index of prohibited books) was published by authority of Pius IV in 1564, and, with an Appendix, by Clement VIII in 1596; new editions, augmented with the names of later authors and books, have been published from time to time down to the present. This is the official 'Index'. In its current form, it is a list, not only of works entirely prohibited to the faithful, but also of works not to be read, unless or until they are corrected (*nisi* or *donec corrigantur*); in the case of the latter, the portions to be deleted or altered are sometimes indicated.

(In first quot., short for *Index expurgatorius*: see b.)

1613 PURCHAS *Pilgrimage* (1614) 90 L. Vives..when he telleth tales out of Schoole, the good mans tongue is shortned, and their Index purgeth out that wherewith hee seeketh to purge their leaven. 1640 SIR E. DERING *Sp. on Relig.* 23 Nov. iii. 7 The Roman Index is better then are our English Licences. 1676 MARVELL *Mr. Smirke* 10 We seem to have got an Expurgatory Press, though not an Index. 1791-1823 D'ISRAELI *Cur. Lit., Licensers of Press*, The simple Index is a list of condemned books which are never to be opened. 1839 [see CONGREGATION 10]. 1857 CHURCH *Misc. Writ.* (1891) I. 79 They [Montaigne's Essays] were.. put in the Index. 1886 FARRAR *Hist. Interpret.* 320 His [Erasmus's] Colloquies were burnt in Spain and put on the Index at Rome.

fig. 1882 *Spectator* 7 Oct. 1289 She..read by stealth Shakespeare, at that time on the Index of a religiously narrow village opinion.

b. ‖ ***index expurgatorius*** (Lat.), ***Expurgatory Index***, an authoritative specification of the passages to be expunged or altered in works otherwise permitted. Also *transf.* and *fig.*

The *Regulæ* of the Council of Trent provided for the expurgation of such books, and in accordance therewith an *Index Expurgatorius* was printed at Antwerp, under the authority of Philip II, in 1571 (reprints of which are referred to in quot. 1611), another under the authority of the Inquisitor General Quiroga at Madrid in 1584 (see quot. 1625), and others with the same or similar titles in various Roman Catholic states. A bull of Sixtus V (1585-90) also authorized the Cardinals chosen to deal with prohibited books to prepare 'indices expurgatorios'. Such a work on a large scale was commenced at Rome 1607 (Bergamo 1608), with the title 'Indicis librorum expurgandorum in studiosorum gratiam confecti Tomus I., in quo 50 auctorum libri præ cæteris desiderati emendantur, per F. Jo. Mariam Brasichell., Sacri Palatii Apostol. Magistrum'. This (which never proceeded beyond the first volume) is the work referred to in quot. 1620. (See, on the whole subject, Rev. J. Mendham *Account of the Indexes, both prohibitory and expurgatory*, 1826, *Literary Policy of the Church of Rome*, 1830 and 1844). In English use, the name *Index Expurgatorius* has often been applied to the *Index librorum prohibitorum* (cf. quot. 1845), especially in transf. and fig. uses.

1611 CORYAT *Crudities* 521 The *Index expurgatorius* printed at Geneua and Strasbourg. 1620 BRENT tr. *Sarpi's Counc. Trent* (1676) 875 In the year 1607, they printed in Rome with publick authority, a Book intituled *Index Expurgatorius*. 1625 USSHER *Answ. to Jesuit* 513 Their old Expurgatory Index..set out by Cardinall Quiroga. 1691 T. BROWNE *Reas. Mr. Bays*, etc. 13 (Stanf.) To prevent, Sir, all storms that might have issued from that quarter, I presently set me up an *Index expurgatorius*. 1788 H. WALPOLE *Remin.* v. 42, I acquainted him with it..why he had been put into the queen's *Index expurgatorius*. 1845 THACKERAY *Pict. Gossip* in *Misc. Ess.* (1885) 260 Knowing well that *Fraser's Magazine* is eagerly read at Rome, and not..excluded in the *Index Expurgatorius*.

†**7. a.** *Music.* = DIRECT *sb.* 2. *Obs.*

1597 MORLEY *Introd. Mus.* 20 *Phi.* What is that which you haue set at the end of the Verse? *Ma.* It is called an Index or director; for looke in what place it standeth, in that place doth the first note of the next Verse stand. 1869 NUTTALL *Dict. Sci. Terms* 189 *Index*..in music, a character or director at the end of a stave to direct to the first note of the next stave.

b. *Printing.* = HAND 18 b. ?*Obs.*

1727 W. MATHER *Yng. Man's Comp.* 38 Index is a Note like a Hand, with the Forefinger pointing out at something that is remarkable, thus ☛. 1807 CRABBE *Library* 186 Till every former note and comment known, They mark'd the spacious margin with their own; Minute corrections proved their studious care; The little index, pointing, told us where.

8. *Math.* **a.** *Alg.* A number or other symbol placed above and to the right of a quantity to denote a power or root: = EXPONENT 2 a.

An ***integral index***, as in x^2, denotes a power; a ***fractional index***, as in $x^{\frac{1}{2}}$, a root; a ***negative index***, the reciprocal of a power, as x^{-2} = unity divided by x^2.

1674 JEAKE *Arith.* (1696) 191 Mark their Indices, or how many degrees the Number you would produce is removed from the Root, as whether it be second, third, fourth, etc. 1748 HARTLEY *Observ. Man.* I. iii. 279 Algebraic Signs for Addition, Subtraction, Indexes, Coefficients. 1810 HUTTON *Course Math.* I. 163 So 3 is the index of the cube or 3d power, and..$\frac{1}{3}$ is the index of the cube root. 1859 BARN. SMITH *Arith. & Algebra* (ed. 6) 198 The figures 2, 3,..*m*, denoting the number of factors which produce the powers, are called Indices.

†**b.** The integral part, or characteristic, of a logarithm. *Obs.*

1678 PHILLIPS (ed. 4) s.v., In Logarithmical Arithmetick Index is that which represents the distance of the first figure of any whole number from Unity. 1727-41 CHAMBERS *Cycl.*, *Index*, in arithmetic, is the same with what is otherwise called the characteristic, or exponent of a logarithm. 1795 HUTTON *Math. Dict.* II. 46/1 The Index is also called the Characteristic of the Logarithms, and is always an integer, either positive or negative, or else = 0. 1828 J. H. MOORE *Pract. Navig.* (ed. 20) 25 Whatever index you make represent unity, omit it in the sum of the indices.

c. Applied to the number which is characteristic of a particular member, or group of members, of a class of geometrical or algebraical concepts; as the index of a point, line, or plane, relatively to a quadric surface. ***discriminantal index***: see DISCRIMINANTAL.

d. *Computers.* A quantity which is fixed in relation to the set of operations laid down by a program but which assumes a prescribed sequence of values as the program is run; *spec.* (*a*) one held in an index register and used to modify the addresses of instructions; (*b*) one in a DO statement (in Fortran) or a FOR statement (in Algol) that is used to control the number of repetitions of a sequence of instructions. Freq. *attrib.*, esp. denoting the

portion of an instruction specifying the appropriate index register (see also *index register* in 11 below).

1957 D. D. McCracken *Digital Computer Programming* viii. 99 Instructions which call for an index to be added are written with the one or two following the address. **1959** J. W. Carr in E. M. Grabbe et al. *Handbk. Automation, Computation & Control* II. ii. 51 When the values of the bound variables (usually indices) that assume a sequence of different values during the course of a problem solution change.. such variables are changed in actual, although not notational value. By a change in such an index, therefore, no change is made in the flow diagram notation, although the actual value of free or floating variables will change. *Ibid.* 55 Many artificial instruction codes.. use such index registers to speed up hand programming. A certain portion of every instruction word is used to designate just how that particular instruction is to be modified with respect to one or more such special locations, which have been filled with specified values of an index. **1961** Leeds & Weinberg *Computer Programming Fund.* vi. 177 Flow diagrams will be generally easier to follow if we can represent our control logic in enumerative terminology. To do this we make use of an index rather than an actual computed quantity on the flow diagram to show the count. **1962** Y. Chu *Digital Computer Design Fund.* xii. 454 The amount of change of an address, called the index value, is stored in an index register. *Ibid.*, The number in the index field [of an instruction] designates the index register selected. **1962** Huskey & Korn *Computer Handbk.* xx. 29 The index is not always added, so there is an address modifier.. which determines whether the index is to be added to the address or not. **1966** B. A. M. Moon *Computer Programming* vii. 117 Within the range of the DO no statement is permitted which alters the value of the index. **1969** V. J. Calderbank *Course on Programming in FORTRAN IV* iv. 36 The DO statement automatically causes execution of all the statements following it up to and including the statement labelled *n* for values of *i* from m_1 in steps of m_3... The counter *i* is sometimes referred to as the index of the loop. **1969** Index bit [see INDEX *v.* 6]. **1969** C. W. Gear *Computer Organization & Programming* ii. 53 There are four items of information to be specified—the start of the loop in memory (X), the initial value of the index (0), the increment (1), and the end condition on the index (999). **1970** O. Dopping *Computers & Data Processing* vi. 101 The character.. in the last position means that the content of the corresponding index register is to be added to the address... The last position of the instruction can be called the 'index tag'.

e. *Computers.* One of a continuous sequence of numbers each of which specifies one of an ordered set of items.

1962 R. V. Oakford *Introd. Electronic Data Processing Equipment* iv. 101 Assume that 15 independent quantities are stored in memory registers 0016 through 0030 and that another 15 independent quantities are stored in registers 0031 through 0045. The location of the *i*th register in the first set may be designated as A_i, while that of the second set may be designated as B_i; then *i* can be considered as an index that assumes the values 1, 2, 3,..., 14, 15. Thus A_i is equal to 0016. **1972** H. S. Stone *Introd. Computer Organization* vi. 120 The FORTRAN statement DIMENSION x(100) creates an array named x with 100 elements such that the first has index 1 and the last has index 100.

9. In various sciences, a number or formula expressing some property, form, ratio, etc. of the thing in question.

a. *Optics.* ***index of refraction*** or ***refractive index*** (of a medium), the ratio between the sines of the angles of incidence and refraction of a ray of light passing from some medium (usually air) into the given medium.

1829 *Hand-bk. Nat. Philos., Optics* ii. 4 The number 1.336, which regulates the refraction of water, is called its index, or exponent, or co-efficient of refraction, and sometimes its refractive power. **1871** Tyndall *Fragm. Sc.* (1879) I. xi. 340 The media must possess different refractive indices.

b. In *Craniometry*, A formula expressing the ratio of one diameter or other dimension of the skull to another, as ***alveolar*** or ***basilar***, ***cephalic***, ***facial***, ***gnathic***, ***nasal***, ***orbital***, ***vertical index***. Also, generally, in *Anthropometry*, The ratio of two dimensions of an organ or part to each other.

1866 Huxley *Preh. Rem. Caithn.* 83 The term *cephalic index*.. indicates the ratio of the extreme transverse to the extreme longitudinal diameter of a skull, the latter measurement being taken as unity. **1882** Quain *Anat.* (ed. 9) I. 82 The proportion of this [the height of the skull] to the length.. is the index of height. *Ibid.* 83 The nasal index of Broca. *Ibid.*, The orbital index is the ratio of the vertical height of the base of the orbit to the transverse width.

c. *Cryst.* Each of the three (or, in Bravais' notation, four) whole numbers which define the position of a face of a crystal.

1868 Dana *Min.* Introd. 28 Miller.. uses the letters *h*, *l*, *k*, as 'indices' referring to the axes. **1878** Gurney *Crystallogr.* 18 The three numbers *h*, *k*, and *l* are called the indices of the plane, and the three together *hkl* is called its symbol. **1895** Story-Maskelyne *Crystallogr.* 472 The introduction of the fourth index [in Bravais' notation].

d. *Dynamics.* ***index of friction***, the coefficient of friction: see COEFFICIENT 2 b.

e. *Econ.* A number showing the variation (increase or decrease) in the prices or value of some specified set of goods, shares, etc., since a chosen 'base' period (often represented by the number 100), as a retail price index, a cost-of-living index, etc. Cf. Dow-Jones.

1886 *Rep. Brit. Assoc. Adv. Sci. 1885* 872 The index for quantity is the same as that for value in the standard year (1883); that for 1884 is arrived at by dividing the value index by the price index, and is shown in the last column. **1922** *Encycl. Brit.* XXX. 759/1 Suppose that the modification of diet (margarine instead of butter, decrease of sugar and eggs and increase of other foods) reduces the food index to 260, .. and the index is 200 instead of 305. **1927** [see COST *sb.*[2] 1 e]. **1942** J. R. Hicks *Social Framework* xv. 160 The most famous of all British index-numbers is the cost-of-living index published by the Ministry of Labour. The basket of goods on which this index is based is supposed to be that consumed in a week by a representative working-class family. It is thus an index of very fundamental importance. .. It covers a large part of the field which would be covered by the ideal index which we should desire to have for measuring the national income in real terms. **1955** *Times* 31 Aug. 9/3 Their members have expressed lack of confidence in the index as a measurement of their living costs. **1958** *Spectator* 22 Aug. 261/2 Industrial equity shares touched bottom—161·5 for the index. **1969** *Daily Tel.* 13 June 3 The index would have dropped say 12 points, War Loan would have continued its downhill march. **1972** *Accountant* 28 Sept. 398/1 When the heaviest Index fall in a day is accompanied by a reduction in the number of Stock Exchange recorded bargains to under 8,000, it can only be assumed that the vast bulk of the 8,000 deals was the same selling way. **1973** *Daily Tel.* 12 Apr. 21/3 The provisional price index of goods manufactured for the home market rose by just over 0·25 p.c., compared with 0·5 p.c. in both January and February.

10. [f. INDEX *v.* 5.] A movement from one predetermined position to another during the indexing of a work-piece.

1962 G. H. DeGroat *Metalworking Automation* v. 120 (*caption*) Another 'homemade' automated machine is this eight-spindle Boremattic with two banks of four spindles each. This one bores, chamfers, and grooves servo valve bodies, finishing two parts per index at 100 pieces per hour. **1964** *Automobile Engineer* LIV. 200/2 After each index, the table is positively locked.

11. *attrib.* and *Comb.*, as ***index-face***, ***-maker***, ***-making***, ***-map***, ***-point***, ***-ruler***; ***index arm***, ***crank***, ***pin***, ***spindle*** (all parts of an index head or used in indexing (sense 2)); also **index-arm** = sense 2 b; **index board**, a type of heavy paper as used for index cards; **index card**, a card for a card-index file; **index centre** *Engin.*, each of the centres (sense 5) that support work for indexing; **index circle** *Engin.*, one of the circles of holes on an index plate; **index constituency**, a constituency in which the result of an election is considered a good indication of the state of parties in the country; **index-correction**, a correction for index-error; **index-digit** = sense 1; **index-error**, the constant error in the reading of a mathematical instrument, due to the zero of the index not being exactly adjusted to that of the limb; **index figure** *Econ.* = sense 9 e above; **index-finger**, (*a*) = sense 1; (*b*) = sense 2; **index fossil** = *guide fossil* (GUIDE *sb.* 14); **index-gauge**, a measuring instrument in which the distance between the measuring-points is shown by an index; **index-glass**, a mirror at the fixed point of the index-arm in an astronomical or surveying instrument, from which the light is reflected to the horizon-glass; **index-hand** = senses 2 and 3; **index head** *Engin.*, an attachment used with a milling machine or gear-cutting machine that holds the work and enables it to be readily and accurately indexed between successive operations; **index horizon** *Geol.*, a horizon distinguished by certain groups of fossils found within it, or other characteristics which make it an indicator of a particular stratigraphic position; **index-hunter**, one who acquires information by consulting indexes; so **index-hunting**; **index-knowledge**, **index-learning**, information gained by means of indexes, superficial knowledge; **index law** (*Alg.*): see quot. 1859; **index-linked** *a.*, designating bonds, pensions, etc., of which the value is adjusted according to the level of the cost-of-living index or some other economic indicator; cf. INDEXATION; also [as back-formation] **index-link** *v. trans.*, to make dependent on such an index; **index-linking** *vbl. sb.*; **index machine**, a machine for fancy-weaving, being a modification of the Jacquard loom; **index map**, a relatively small-scale map which is so marked as to act as an index to a series of more detailed maps; **index number**, (*a*) = sense 9 e above; (*b*) a number in an index; *spec.* the registration number of a motor vehicle; **index-pip**, a miniature indication of the denomination of a playing-card, placed in the left-hand corner for convenience in sorting; **index plate**, (*a*) (see quot. 1825); (*b*) *Engin.*, a disc that contains regularly spaced holes arranged in concentric circles, which represent different divisions of a circle and determine the possible angular positions of work being indexed; (*c*) a plate bearing the registration number of a motor vehicle; **index-raker** = *index-hunter*; **index register** *Computers*, a register whose contents may be added to or subtracted from the address portion of an instruction before the instruction is executed and then (by means of a second instruction) increased or decreased by a prescribed amount, so enabling the first instruction to be used for a series of identical operations on a series of different operands.

1879 Newcomb & Holden *Astron.* 92 The *index-arm carries the index-glass. **1919** H. Thompson *Mod. Engin. Workshop Pract.* xi. 173 By turning this index arm and spindle, motion is given to the worm and worm-wheel. **1937** E. J. Labarre *Dict. Paper* 160/1 **Index board* or *Bristol* also termed Fourdrinier Bristol is (1) (card-) board resembling a heavy ledger specially adapted for this purpose... (2) also a size of board 30½" × 25½". **1962** F. T. Day *Introd. to Paper* 116/2 Index boards are made in white and tints with an even and well-finished surface... Stock size is 20½ in. × 35½ in., also cut sizes. **1928** *Funk's Stand. Dict.*, *Index card. **1947** *Partisan Rev.* XIV. 469 He placed the books down on the main desk, stuck the envelope of index cards and cross-references under his arm and walked out. **1971** *Jrnl. Gen. Psychol.* LXXXV. 52 *S*s were supplied with 3 × 5 inch white unlined index cards. *a* **1884** Knight *Dict. Mech.* Suppl. 434/1 The tool-post can be removed from the sliding table, and *index centers, milling vise, or any milling fixture put on, required for milling. **1913** *Lockwood's Dict. Mech. Engin.* (ed. 4) 439 *Index centres*, the head, and the tail stock between which work is carried to be pitched or indexed. **1953** L. E. Doyle *Metal Machining* ix. 214 Index centers provide means for spacing cuts accurately around a workpiece. **1902** *Internat. Library of Technol.* II. §15. 23 For convenience of measuring fractional parts of a turn of different values, as $\frac{3}{8}$ of a turn, $\frac{5}{17}$ of a turn,.. etc., the index plate is provided with several concentric *index circles, each circle having a different number of holes. **1950** J. Martin in A. W. Judge *Machine Tools & Operations* III. iii. 142 In ordinary plain indexing, the use of 30 holes in a 42-hole index circle would give 42/30 × 40 = 56 divisions in work. **1888** *Pall Mall G.* 13 Nov. 4/1 Aston Manor is not only a Midland constituency, but it is emphatically an *index constituency. **1905** T. R. Shaw *Machine Tools* vi. 415 Forty revolutions of the *index crank are required to make one complete revolution of the spindle. **1964** S. Crawford *Basic Engin. Processes* vi. 172 Indirect Indexing... When using this method of indexing the worm is permanently engaged with the worm wheel, and the workpiece is rotated by means of the index-crank. **1843–55** Owen *Anat. Vertebr.* (L.), The Pottos.. offer an anomaly, in the fore-hand, by the stunted phalanges of the *index digit. **1851–9** Airy in *Man. Sci. Enq.* 1 The *index-error of the sextant must be carefully ascertained. **1875** Bedford *Sailor's Pocket Bk.* v. (ed. 2) 152 Taking the angles off and on the arc, adding them together, and dividing by 2, gives an angle free of index error. **1664** Butler *Hud.* II. iii. 284 Quote Moles and Spots, on any place O' th' body, by the *Index-face. **1927** *Index figure [see COSTING *vbl. sb.*]. **1930** *Engineering* 3 Jan. 23/3 The index figure of 100 being given to Great Britain in both cases. **1849** Thackeray *Pendennis* II. i, Jeames simply pointed with his *index finger to the individual. **1875** Routledge *Discov.* (1876) 12 The index-finger and graduated scale are seen, protected by a glass plate. **1900** C. R. Eastman tr. *Zittel's Text-bk. Palaeontol.* I. 4 Having determined the chronological succession of the clastic rocks by means of their super-imposition and their characteristic or *index-fossils, they may be divided up into still smaller series. **1933** R. C. Moore *Historical Geol.* xiv. 186 In precise correlation of fossil-bearing strata it is important to recognize and differentiate species that appear only in a given bed, or a short succession of beds, for the occurrence of the same species elsewhere points to equivalence in age of the containing strata. Such fossils may be termed *index fossils*. **1968** J. R. Beerbower *Search for Past* (ed. 2) viii. 207 Relatively few groups of organisms provide most of the index fossils. **1773** *Gentl. Mag.* XLIII. 390 The *index-glass being bent by the brass frame that contains it. **1828** J. H. Moore *Pract. Navig.* (ed. 20) 152 If the arch seen direct, together with its reflected image, appear to be in one line, the Index-glass is truly adjusted. **1742** Pope *Dunc.* IV. 140 A Spectre rose, whose *index-hand Held forth the virtue of the dreadful wand. **1812** Woodhouse *Astron.* viii. 53 The index-hand of the sidereal clock. **1902** *Index head [see INDEXING *vbl. sb.* 2]. **1923** R. C. H. Heck *Mechanics of Machinery: Mechanism* v. 234 Indexing is done mostly on the milling machine and on gear cutting machines. For general service a distinct appliance called the index head is used. **1961** L. E. Doyle et al. *Manuf. Processes* xxiv. 586 A dividing or index head is a mechanical device for dividing a circle accurately into equal parts. **1956** W. Edwards in D. L. Linton *Sheffield* 13 No marine horizons are known, but a widespread *index-horizon with *Euestheria*, the Low '*Estheria*' Band, overlies a split-off lower leaf of the Silkstone Coal. **1969** Bennison & Wright *Geol. Hist. Brit. Isles* ix. 224 The marine horizons (called marine bands) are sometimes of great lateral extent and act as vitally important index horizons. **1751** Smollett *Per. Pic.* xlii. (1779) II. 57 He rated him in his own mind as a mere *index-hunter. **1699** Bentley *Phal.* xii. 381 Mr. B. declares more than once, that he despises the mean Employment of *Index-hunting. **1859** Boole *Different. Equations* 373 The *index law, expressed by the equation $m^a m^b = m^{a+b}$. **1728** Pope *Dunc.* I. 279 How *index-learning turns no student pale, Yet holds the eel of science by the tail. **1974** *Daily Tel.* 8 Aug. 6/2 If it becomes necessary.. to *index-link a large proportion of their deposits some form of index linking of mortgages would have to be considered. **1975** *Economist* 4 Jan. 67 The Shah has long advocated that oil prices.. should be index-linked, preferably to the prices of 20 to 30 key commodities. **1984** *Which?* Jan. 3/1 They may also have persuaded you to swap to a new-for-old policy, and they've probably index-linked the amount you're insured for. **1970** *Guardian Weekly* 14 Nov. 9/5 The scope for cutting any kind of tax is therefore limited unless some incentive to save can be invented. An *index-linked bond might provide such an incentive. **1976** *Listener* 15 Jan. 41/1 There are more than one would think, in the private sector, who also have index-linked pensions. **1986** *Economist* 3 May 31/2 Index-linked capital from Nationwide building society is financing an Oxford scheme for the homeless. **1974** *Daily Tel.* 14 June 19/8 *Index-linking is one of a number of propositions being considered by the Government to attract and retain

National Savings. **1985** *Investors Chron.* 8–14 Nov. 33/2 The 3rd issue..pay a tax-free compound rate of 3.54 per cent over five years, on top of index-linking of capital. **1831** MACAULAY *Johnson* Misc. 1860 II. 273 Starving pamphleteers and *index-makers. **1869** DUNKIN *Midn. Sky* 1 The assistance of the corresponding *index-maps. **1932** *Discovery* May 153/1 As large a selection of the recorded information as the smaller scales will carry is issued on the standard scale of one inch, and with further selection and reduction, on the ½ inch scale of the 'index map'. **1875** W. S. JEVONS *Money & Mechanism of Exchange* xxv. 332 A table containing the Total *Index Number of prices, or the arithmetical sum of the numbers expressing the ratios of the prices of many commodities to the average prices of the same commodities in the years 1845–50. **1886** *Rep. Brit. Assoc. Adv. Sci. 1885* 871 The index number for the price of each article in 1883 is 1 or 100, according to the use or otherwise of the decimal point. **1887** *Encycl. Brit.* XXII. 466/1 The only matter connected with price which it is necessary to refer to here is the theory of the index number. **1893** *Jrnl. Soc. Arts* 3 Feb. 211/2 This total index number.. merged all prices high and low in a single figure. **1900** A. L. BOWLEY *Wages in U.K. in 19th Cent.* xii. 95 (*caption*) Index numbers, showing rate of Change of Wages in the London Building Trades. **1928** J. W. F. ROWE *Wages in Pract. & Theory* 14 Index numbers based on changes in the nominal weekly rates in these industries afford a general guide to the character of wage fluctuations. **1942** [see sense 9e above]. **1966** *McGraw-Hill Encycl. Sci. & Technol.* III. 233/1 The distribution of coal by rank, geologic age, and district is indicated in Fig. 4. The index numbers, which refer to coal districts, are grouped by continent and country in the accompanying list. **1973** *Daily Tel.* 11 July 6/6 He admitted owning a car which had an index number identical to one Miss Mallalieu had noted. **1905** T. R. SHAW *Machine Tools* vi. 413 If the *index pin does not come exactly opposite a hole, there is an adjustment by means of two screws. **1899** *Let. fr. T. De La Rue & Co.*, [For these] Playing Cards, the proper term is 'with *index-pips'. **1825** *Index plate [see *index-point* below]. **1879** *Jrnl. Franklin Inst.* CVIII. 106 The making of practically perfect index plates for gear cutting machines is a different matter from graduating circles for astronomical instruments. **1902** Index plate [see *index circle*]. **1923** R. C. H. HECK *Mechanics of Machinery: Mechanism* v. 235 At the other end of the worm shaft [of the index head] is the index crank C, with handle H and plunger pin Q which can be let into any hole in index plate P. **1950** J. MARTIN in A. W. Judge *Machine Tools & Operations* III. iii. 131 By the use of worm-gearing, the indirect dividing head can space work up to 360 divisions, using standard index plates. **1973** *Daily Tel.* 15 Sept. 2/5 He noticed that the index plates..had been hurriedly removed from another vehicle. **1825** J. NICHOLSON *Operat. Mechanic* 526 A change of place in the *index-point on the graduated arch or index-plate. **1676** R. DIXON *Two Testam.* To Rdr. 15 Not stuffing my Margin, as *Index-Rakers do, with Quotations of Divines, Philosophers, Lawyers, Historians, etc. **1955** R. K. RICHARDS *Arithmetic Operations in Digital Computers* xi. 348 In these machines..each instruction specifies an *index register as well as an operation and an address. For each operation, the number stored in the indicated index register is automatically added to the address, and the sum is then the actual address which is used. **1957, 1970** Index register [see INDEXING *vbl. sb.* 3]. **1970** O. DOPPING *Computers & Data Processing* vi. 101 In most modern computers address modification and counting is facilitated by index registers. **1793** *Index-ruler [see 2b above]. *a* **1884** KNIGHT *Dict. Mech.* Suppl. 494/2 The centers are shown..attached to the *index-spindle.

index (ˈɪndɛks), *v.* [f. prec. sb.]

1. a. *trans.* To furnish (a book, etc.) with an index. Also *transf.* (cf. INDEX *sb.* 5d).

1720 *Wodrow Corr.* (1843) II. 522 Since the Letters are not indexed, I cannot point out all the places. *a* **1832** SCOTT in *Lockhart* xvii, There were always huge piles of materials to be arranged, sifted, and indexed. **1851** CARLYLE *Sterling* II. ii. (1872) 103 Sterling's Letters..a large collection of which now lies before me, duly copied and indexed. **1885** *Law Times* LXXIX. 159/1 The contents are exceedingly well indexed. **1969** C. W. GEAR *Computer Organization & Programming* vi. 242 Each time that a file was completed, the system would index it; that is, its name would be placed in a table of file names..with an indication of where it was physically located. **1969** P. B. JORDAIN *Condensed Computer Encycl.* 242 If the cylinder index becomes too long, a master index may be created to index it.

b. To furnish (the parts of a diagram) with different symbols to facilitate identification in the accompanying description.

1894 *Harper's Mag.* Mar. 552/1 The accompanying diagram of an abstract flower, the various parts being indexed.

2. To enter (a word, name, etc.) in an index.

1761 *Descr. S. Carolina* Pref., Every material Fact or Circumstance in this Description is indexed under its proper Head. **1848** *Fraser's Mag.* XXXVIII. 364 In many German universities the Amber Witch was indexed as a criminal law book.

3. To place on the Index: see INDEX *sb.* 6.

1791–1823 D'ISRAELI *Cur. Lit.*, *Licensers of Press*, While the Catholic crossed himself at every title, the heretic would purchase no book which had not been indexed.

4. To serve as an index of, to indicate. Also *to index out*, to point out.

1788 BURNS *His face with smile* 4 High as they hang with creaking din To index out the Country Inn. **1862** R. H. PATTERSON *Ess. Hist. & Art* 350 These changes indexed the general turning of the European intellect from Mind to Matter, and from Man to Nature. **1885** *Century Mag.* XXIX. 683/2 A slender, bony negro-man; whose iron-gray wool and wrinkled face indexed his age at near seventy years.

5. *Engin.* **a.** *trans.* (Cf. quot. 1879 s.v. INDEX *sb.* 2.) To rotate (work to be machined, or a machine part) through a given aliquot part of a complete turn; to position in accordance with intermittent motion of this kind; hence, to transfer or move from one predetermined position to another in order that different locations may be machined or different operations performed. (Cf. INDEXING *vbl. sb.* 2.)

1902 [implied in INDEXING *vbl. sb.* 2]. **1913** [see *index centre* s.v. INDEX *sb.* 11]. **1936** COLVIN & STANLEY *Drilling & Surfacing Pract.* xxii. 242 Turning the indexing crank without this geared connection indexes the spindle in any desired number of graduations, or parts of a circle. **1951** H. C. TOWN in *Gen. Engin. Workshop Pract.* (ed. 2) iii. 112/2 A spring-loaded plunger..locates the turret in any one of four positions... To index the turret, the ball handle is revolved and the screw lifts the turret clear of the locating plunger, so that it can be rotated to the next..position, and then locked in position. **1953** L. E. DOYLE *Metal Machining* ix. 214 The workpiece is turned by means of the worm and wheel and is indexed by the pin that registers in holes in the face of the worm wheel. *Ibid.* xiii. 298 On a dividing head with a 40 to 1 ratio, one full turn of the crank is needed to index a 40 tooth gear from one tooth space to the next. **1959** *Machinery* XCIV. 511/2 Spacing of the holes axially along the length of the rod is accomplished by indexing the rod vertically in 0·026-in. steps by means of an accurate lead-screw. **1966** *McGraw-Hill Encycl. Sci. & Technol.* VII. 407/2 When the turret [of the lathe] is indexed for successive operations, the saddle acts as a guide for the ram in its strokes to and from the work.

b. *trans.* To produce or obtain (a desired number of divisions or operations) by indexing.

1900 *Machinery* (N.Y.) Nov. 88/2 For indexing prime numbers we must use other than the one-hole basis. **1923** R. C. H. HECK *Mechanics of Machinery: Mechanism* v. 237 The test or criterion of ability to index any number *n* is expressed by putting Eq. (89) into the form $c = 40 \times h/n$. **1936** COLVIN & STANLEY *Drilling & Surfacing Pract.* xxii. 242 The index sector is a great convenience in counting holes to index the required number of divisions. **1961** L. E. DOYLE et al. *Manuf. Processes* xxiv. 587 Several means are available for indexing numbers not obtainable with standard plain indexing, especially large numbers.

c. *intr.* To move or travel during indexing.

1901 *Machinery* (N.Y.) Jan. 147/1 To divide into 91 parts, index forward, on the front side of the plate, six spaces on the 39 circle; then index forward on the back of the plate, 14 spaces on the 49 circle. **1953** L. E. DOYLE *Metal Machining* xiii. 298 The crank must be turned $40 \div 36 = 1\frac{4}{36} = 1\frac{1}{9}$ turns to index from one space to another on the gear. **1966** *McGraw-Hill Encycl. Sci. & Technol.* VII. 409/1 A horizontal, circular table holding the rotating chucks indexes under the vertical spindles with a different operation being performed at each station. **1968** BOOTHROYD & REDFORD *Mechanized Assembly* ii. 8 With continuous transfer the work carriers are moving at constant speed whilst the workheads index backwards and forwards. *Ibid.* 13 Reciprocation of the transfer bar over a distance equal to the spacing of the workheads will cause the work carriers to index between the workheads.

6. *Computers.* To modify (an instruction or its address) by causing the contents of a specified index register to be added to the address before the instruction is executed; to provide with a number that brings about such modification; also, to carry out (a repetitive sequence of operations) by this means.

1962 Y. CHU *Digital Computer Design Fund.* xii. 454 Its contents are used to modify the address of the instruction to be indexed. **1962** R. V. OAKFORD *Introd. Electronic Data Processing Equipment* iii. 89 The counter may be added to the operand address of an instruction to index the repeated performance of an operation on a sequence of registers. **1969** C. W. GEAR *Computer Organization & Programming* ii. 52 We can indicate this in our program writing by using Y to mean the unindexed address Y (that is, the index bits are 0) and by using Y,I to mean the address Y indexed by index register I. **1972** BERGMAN & BRUCKNER *Introd. Computers & Computer Programming* vii. 204 Since this instruction is indexed, its effective operand is 000 (operand) + 251 (contents of index register) = 251 (effective operand and address of X1).

Hence **ˈindexer**, one who compiles an index.

1856 WEBSTER, *Indexer.* **1882** FURNIVALL *Forewords to E.E. Wills* 16 May all oppress Indexers hav the like sweet consolement! **1887** *Sat. Rev.* 24 Sept. 418/2 The classifier and indexer of natural objects.

indexation (ɪndɛkˈseɪʃən). *Econ.* [f. INDEX *v.* + -ATION.] An adjustment in rates of payment in money (e.g. wage-rates, bond prices, etc.) to reflect changes in the value of money by means of an index of such changes. Cf. INDEX *sb.* 9e.

1960 *Spectator* 29 Apr. 602 The system of 'indexation' by which wages and prices rose in an officially sponsored spiral. **1972** *Times* 22 July 16/3 If the current rate of inflation continues it will be essential to introduce some form of indexation into the capital gains tax system. **1973** *Daily Tel.* 10 Feb. 31/1 The most likely form of control is by 'indexation' of business leases, which would mean that business rents would be able to rise no faster than the wholesale price index, the cost of living index or such index as the Government cares to regard as a fair indicator of the trend of inflation.

indexed (ˈɪndɛkst), *ppl. a.* [f. INDEX *v.* or *sb.* + -ED.]

1. Furnished with or having an index; entered in an index.

1872 *Daily News* 27 Apr. 3/4 In addition to his indexed ledger, the warder has a large scrap-book.

2. *Her.* Having a book-marker in it.

1885 *Burke's Peerage* 310 [Arms of Sir J. Conroy, bart.] Azure, an ancient book, open, indexed, edged or, a chief embattled of the last.

3. *Computers.* Modified by or executed by means of an index (sense 8d).

1957 D. D. MCCRACKEN *Digital Computer Programming* viii. 98 Examples are presented which compare an indexed loop with the nonindexed form. **1972** M. D. FREEDMAN *Princ. Digital Computer Operation* ii. 23 An indirect address can be indexed. We will illustrate the concept of an indexed indirect address by an example.

indexible (ɪnˈdɛksɪb(ə)l, ˈɪndɛks-), *a.* Also **-able.** [f. INDEX *v.* + -IBLE, -ABLE.] Capable of being indexed.

1951 *Industrial Equipment News* Dec. 100 (*caption*) Indexable Kennametal tip has 4 cutting edges. **1959** C. V. L. SMITH *Electronic Digital Computers* ii. 45 Most type B instructions are 'indexable'. This means that, when any such instruction is executed, the address actually referred to is the address given decreased by the contents of the index register specified by the tag bits. **1966** C. J. SIPPL *Computer Dict. & Handbk.* 145/2 *Index register...* Used with indexible instruction addresses during execution. **1971** *Computers & Humanities* VI. 68 By 'indexible' we mean [to denote] a character string that..is likely to be used as a criterion for selective retrieval and/or sorting.

indexical (ɪnˈdɛksɪkəl), *a.* [irreg. f. INDEX *sb.* + -ICAL.] **a.** Arranged like an index. **b.** Relating or pertaining to an index. **c.** Of the nature of an index or indication.

1828 in WEBSTER. **1866** R. W. SMALL (*title*) The Carrier's Indexical Ready Reckoner. **1884** *American* VIII. 267 Lists of indexes and indexical works. **1893** *Nation* (N.Y.) 11 May 350/3 Indexical defects are so common that the reviewer is in danger of becoming hardened to their seriousness. **1897** *Harper's Mag.* Apr. 744 This is very tame beside the idiomatic Spanish in which it was said, but it is indexical. *a* **1914** C. S. PEIRCE *Coll. Papers* (1932) II. II. iii. 164 Some indices are more or less detailed directions for what the hearer is to do in order to place himself in direct.. connection with the thing meant... Along with such indexical directions of what to do to find the object meant, ought to be classed..*selective* pronouns. *Ibid.*, Other indexical words are prepositions, and prepositional phrases. **1957** *Lingua* VII. 1. 27 Within the same vowel system, diaphonic differences are considerable, and appear to be highly indexical, both socially and regionally, in differentiating accents within England. **1970** *English Studies* LI. 276 Beside these indexical features a medium also has aesthetic properties.

So **inˈdexically** *adv.*, in the manner of an index, alphabetically.

1728 SWIFT *Let. to Pope* 16 July, I would have the names of those scriblers printed indexically at the beginning or end of the poem.

ˈindexing, *vbl. sb.* [f. INDEX *v.* + -ING[1].]

1. The action or process of compiling an index.

1887 *Athenæum* 21 May 667/2 The exhaustive indexing of at least a hundred selected authors.

2. *Engin.* The intermittent rotation of work through aliquot parts of a complete turn in order that some operation may be performed on it at equal angular intervals; also, the movement of work or of a machine part or tool from one predetermined position to another during machining operations.

1902 *Internat. Library of Technol.* II. §15. 21 Direct indexing is done by the aid of an index plate fastened direct to the index-head spindle; that is, the index plate is moved to obtain the divisions. In indirect indexing, the index plate is normally stationary, and the index-head spindle is rotated by the use of suitable gearing. Indirect indexing is divided into..simple and compound indexing. **1930** *Engineering* 30 May 693/3 During the return stroke, indexing of the worm takes place. **1936** COLVIN & STANLEY *Drilling & Surfacing Pract.* xxii. 243 The essential thing to remember in all indexing is that the worm wheel on the spindle has 40 teeth and that the worm is a single thread. This means that for every turn of the crank the spindle is rotated $\frac{1}{40}$ of a revolution. **1957** S. E. RUSINOFF *Manuf. Processes* (ed. 2) xii. 489 In straight in-line indexing, the work piece moves intermittently from one machining station to the next in a straight line; a group of machine tools is assembled into one machine. **1961** L. E. DOYLE et al. *Manuf. Processes* xxiv. 587 Linear indexing may be done on a general-purpose milling machine for such jobs as cutting rack teeth. **1964** S. CRAWFORD *Basic Engin. Processes* vi. 172 When using this method of indexing the number of possible divisions is limited to the three-hole circles available on the front index plate. **1966** *McGraw-Hill Encycl. Sci. & Technol.* VII. 408/1 Turret indexing, actuation of the collet, feeding of stock, and spindle clutch operations are automatic.

3. *Computers.* The automatic increasing or decreasing of the address portion of an instruction, following each execution, by means of an index register, so that a succession of operands is operated on.

1957 D. D. MCCRACKEN *Digital Computer Programming* viii. 106 All we really want from the indexing is the sum of the index register contents and the indicated address. *Ibid.* 109 Locations 1200, 1208, 1216, etc., up to 1272 contain ten numbers... Write a program, using indexing, to compute the sum of the squares of these numbers and store it in 1307. **1961** LEEDS & WEINBERG *Computer Programming Fund.* iv. 101 Many machines have special circuitry designed to facilitate common operations associated with repetition... In mathematics, indexes, or subscripts, are used to keep track of such processes. As an outgrowth of these terms, the words *indexing* and *index arithmetic* have been given to the type of computer instruction which does this job, although indexing may be thought of as a special type of control which also takes over certain tasks of counting from the regular arithmetic instructions. **1970** HULL & DAY *Computers & Probl. Solving* 197/2 Index registers have a second important use in what is called automatic address modification or indexing. This occurs when the address of an instruction is modified, just before the instruction is executed, by having the content of an index register added to it.

4. *attrib.* and *Comb.*, as *indexing pin*; **indexing head** = *index head* (INDEX *sb.* 11).

1901 *Machinery* (N.Y.) Jan. 145/1 A dividing or indexing head.. With the tailstock shown..comprises what is commonly known as a pair of index centers. **1944** *Model Engineer* 17 Aug. 157/1 The method..is a modification of the indexing head of a milling machine. **1960** H. W. PORTER et al. *Machine Shop* (ed. 2) viii. 294 The indexing head.. comes equipped with three index plates. **1964** S. CRAWFORD *Basic Engin. Processes* v. 117 A spring-loaded indexing-pin in the face of the compound-slide accurately locates the post in any one of the four positions.

indexless (ˈɪndɛkslɪs), *a.* [f. INDEX *sb.* + -LESS.] Having no index.

1858 CARLYLE *Fredk. Gt.* VII. viii. II. 272 The date, in these indexless Books, is blown away again. **1889** *Sat. Rev.* 31 Aug. 250/2 Few writers are so indexless in all editions as Hazlitt. **1893** E. COUES in *Hist. Lewis & Clark Exp.* I. p. cxxv, There ought to be a law against indexless books.

Hence ˈ**indexlessness**.

1888 *Amer. Naturalist* Feb. 174 Certainly no reader of the last year's volume of the Gazette can complain, in Carlylean phrase, of its 'indexlessness'.

index'terity. *rare.* [f. IN-[3] + DEXTERITY: cf. F. *indextérité* (Littré), It. *indesterita* (Florio).] Want of dexterity; awkwardness.

1611 FLORIO, *Indesterita*, indexteritie, vnaptnesse. **1647** M. HUDSON *Div. Right Govt.* Ep. Ded. 9 The Husbandman, whose Indexterity hath reaped this sorrie Crop. **1670** G. H. *Hist. Cardinals* II. III. 178 His weakness and indexterity in politick affairs. **1899** *Academy* 19 Aug. 175/2 His indexterity of execution no less disqualifies him.

†**in'dextrous,** *a. Obs. rare*[−1]. [IN-[3].] Void of dexterity; clumsy, awkward.

1684 tr. *Bonet's Merc. Compit.* IX. 329, I have often observed..an indextrous way of making an Issue.

indeyne, variant of INDEIGN, *Obs.*

indfine (ˈɪndfɪnɪ). *Irish Hist.* Also indfhine, innfine. [O.Ir. (mod.Ir. *innfhine*) f. *ind* end + *fine* family, FINE *sb.*[2]] One of the four branches of the Irish clan structure comprising the men most distantly related to the chief. Cf. GEILFINE, IARFINE; the fourth branch is the *derbfine*.

1875 H. S. MAINE *Lect. Early Hist. Inst.* 209 The eldest member of the Iarfine moved into the Indfine; and the eldest member of the Indfine passed out of the organisation altogether. **1893** P. W. JOYCE *Short Hist. Ireland* I. ix. 70 A *Gelfine* organisation when complete consisted of seventeen men all related to each other: ..the *gelfine* group..consisting of five; the *derfine*, the *iarfine*, and the *innfine*, of four each. **1921**, **1967** [see IARFINE].

indi-. *Chem.* [f. L. *Indus*, as root of *indicum*, *indigo*.] A combining element used in naming substances derived from or related to indigo: e.g. *indifulvin*, *indirubin*.

India (ˈɪndɪə). [a. L. *India*, a. Gr. Ἰνδία, f. Ἰνδός the (river) Indus, a. Pers. *hind*, OPers. (Achæmenian) *hiñd'u*, Zend *heñdu*, Skr. *sindhu* 'river', *spec.* the river Indus; hence the region of the Indus, the province Sindh; gradually extended by Persians and Greeks to all the country east of the Indus. OE. had *India* from L.; but the ME. form from Fr. was *Ynde*, *Inde*, IND (cf. *Afric*), now archaic and poetic; the early 16th c. adaptation of L. was *Indie*, INDY (cf. *Italy*, *Germany*), of which the pl. INDIES is still in use. The current use of *India* appears to date from the 16th c., and may partly reflect Spanish, or Portuguese usage.]

1. A large country or territory of southern Asia, lying east of the river Indus and south of the Himalaya mountains (in this restricted sense also called *Hindustan*: see HINDUSTANI); also extended to include the region further east (***Farther*** or ***Further India***), between this and China. See also EAST INDIA.

*c***893** K. ÆLFRED *Oros.* I. i. §6 Ðæt sint India [*Cott. MS.* Indea] ȝemæro..Indus seo ea be westan, and seo Reade Sæ be suþan..On Indea londe is xliiii þeoda. *Ibid.* §10 Of þæm beorȝum þe man hæt Caucasus..þa þe be norþan India sindon. **1519** *Interl. Four Elem.*, This quarter is India minor And this quarter India maior The lande of prester Iohn. **1576** EDEN (*title*) Decade of Voyages. The Navigation and Voyages of Lewes Vertomanus..to the regions of Arabia.. East India, both within and without the Ganges. **1613** PURCHAS *Pilgrimage* (1614) 452 Under the name of *India*, heere we comprehend all that Tract between Indus..on the West, unto China Eastward. **1663** BUTLER *Hud.* I. ii. 283 He spoused in India, Of noble house, a lady gay. **1783** BURKE *Sp. E. I. Bill* Wks. IV. 7 If we are not able to contrive some method of governing India well. **1818** MILL *Brit. India* (1826) V. 533 The same barefaced disregard of truth, which always characterized the natives of India.

†**2.** Formerly applied to America, or some parts of it: see quots., and cf. INDIES, WEST INDIES.

(Mostly reproducing Spanish or Portuguese usage.)

1553 EDEN (*title*) A treatyse of the newe India, with other new founde landes and Ilandes..after the descripcion of Sebastian Munster. **1613** PURCHAS *Pilgrimage* (1614) 451 The name of India, is now applied to all farre-distant Countries, not in the extreeme limits of Asia alone; but even to whole America, through the errour of Columbus..who.. in the Westerne world, thought that they had met with Ophir, and the Indian Regions of the East. *Ibid.* 786 It [Cholollal] was the Citie of most devotion in all India..Eight leagues from Cholollа is the hill Popocatepec, or smoake-hill. **1760–72** tr. *Juan & Ulloa's Voy. S. Amer.* (ed. 3) II. 243 An idea of the fertility of this country..a live beast.. may be purchased for four dollars; a price vastly beneath that in any other part of India.

†**3.** *pl.* = INDIES. *Obs.*

1523 *St. Papers Hen. VIII*, VI. 193 Golde..browght hithir from the Indias. **1548** HALL *Chron., Hen. VIII*, 125 By the labor..of us only Portyngales, the trade to the.. Indias [was] fyrst sought and found. **1604** T. WRIGHT *Passions* VI. 333 In every place, as in the Indiaes..the vse of many seemeth to take away all abuse.

†**4.** Used allusively for a source of wealth. *Obs.*

1613 J. MAY *Declar. Est. Clothing* i. 2 No kingdome whatsoeuer can speake so happily of this benefit [wool]..it may be rightly called, The English India.

5. Short for *India silk*, *paper*, etc.: see 6.

1712–13 STEELE *Guardian* No. 10 ¶5 Celia, whose wrapping-gown is not right India. **1812** H. & J. SMITH *Rej. Addr.*, *Theatre* 104 Where Spitalfields with real India vies. **1885** *Daily News* 21 Dec. 4/4 This celebrated..plate, now ready for issue, signed, India remarque.

6. *attrib.* Belonging or relating to India, Indian; esp. in names of fabrics or other commodities imported from India, as ***India calico***, ***carpet***, ***cloth***, ***cotton***, ***cracker***, ***goods***, ***lake***, ***matting***, ***muslin***, ***satin***, ***shawl***, ***silk***, etc.; also, of or belonging to the East India Company, or to the British Indian Empire or government, as ***India bonds***, ***stock***, etc.; (*East* and *West*) **India Docks**, docks in East London, formerly appropriated to vessels trading with the East and West Indies; † **India House**, the office of the East India Company in London; **India ink** (see INDIAN INK); **India Office**, that department of the British Government which dealt with Indian affairs; **India proof** = *India paper proof*: see INDIA PAPER 1; **India red** = *Indian red* (see INDIAN A. 4 a); **India tag**, a type of tag which is used to fasten papers together and consists of a cord with a small metal bar at either end; † **India wood**, a name for log-wood. See also INDIA PAPER, RUBBER.

1751 SMOLLETT *Per. Pic.* I. i, His money, which he had laid out in Bank stock and *India bonds. **1805** *Times* 7 Nov. 1/1 Stout *India calico, full ell-wide. *c***1702** C. FIENNES *Journeys* (1947) 346 A pladd bed lined with Indian callicoe and an *India carpet on the bed. **1931** A. U. DILLEY *Oriental Rugs & Carpets* Pl. 32 (*caption*) India Carpets of Seventeenth Century from the Palace of the Maharaja at Jaipur. **1817** RAFFLES *Java* (1830) I. 243 The import and export of..*India cloths. **1881** C. C. HARRISON *Woman's Handiwork* III. 176 Scarves of *India cotton worked in tarnished gold. **1779** *Phil. Trans.* LXIX. 413 Those paper matches which the Chinese put into those little squibs, which go by the name of *India crackers. **1773** GOLDSM. *Stoops to Conq.* II. i, Left me by my uncle, the *India director. **1837** *Penny Cycl.* IX. 45 The East *India Docks.. are situated at Blackwall, below the entrance to the West India Docks. **1848** DICKENS *Dombey* ix, Captain Cuttle lived..near the India Docks. **1837** *Lett. fr. Madras* (1843) 95 So, *India-fashion, we took him in to do the best we could for him. **1712** E. COOKE *Voy. S. Sea* 363 Laden with rich *India Goods. **1794** W. WOODFALL (*title*) A Sketch of a Debate at the *India House. **1856** EMERSON *Eng. Traits* x. 165 Scandinavian Thor..sits down at a desk in the India House. **1658** W. SANDERSON *Graphice* 80 The Colour Crimson is most difficult to worke..therefore instead of that, use *India Lake or Russet. **1858** SIMMONDS *Dict. Trade*, **India-matting*, grass or reed mats, made..from *Papyrus corymbosus*. **1885** *Daily News* 21 Dec. 4/5 Tea and *India merchants. **1796** M. EDGEWORTH *Parent's Assistant* (ed. 2) II. 167 Oh, Miss Eden, your beautiful *India muslin! —take care of the chimney sweeper. **1852** E. TWISLETON *Let.* 10 July (1928) ii. 27, I intend to appear in my India muslin. **1929** D. H. LAWRENCE *Pansies* 39 A yard of India muslin is alive with Hindu life. **1869** *Bradshaw's Railway Manual* XXI. 394 Government Director of the Indian Railway Companies, *India Office, Whitehall, S.W. **1880** E. W. HAMILTON *Diary* 24 Apr. (1972) I. 2 Cabinet-making has been going on all day... Lord Hartington [is to go] to the India office. **1885** *Daily News* 22 Sept. 2/1 Industrious at the India Office. **1895** *Ibid.* 26 Feb. 6/3 *India Pale Ale is so called because it was originally made solely with a view to the climate of the East Indies. **1732** J. PEELE *Water-Colours* 42 *India-Red..is helpful for a back Ground. **1822** D. WORDSWORTH *Jrnl.* 23 Sept. (1941) II. 374 The ladies.. wore gorgeously embroidered *India shawls. **1837** DICKENS *Mudfog Papers* (1880) 159 His view of the ladies within being obstructed by the India shawls. **1756** B. FRANKLIN *Writings* (1905) III. 294 When you incline to buy..*India silks. **1816** SCOTT *Antiq.* III. vii. 142 His India silk handkerchief. **1881** C. C. HARRISON *Woman's Handiwork* I. 48 The India silks manufactured for Mr. Louis Tiffany, by a well-known firm in Connecticut, from cocoons imported by themselves. **1769** (*title*) An Address to the Proprietors of *India Stock. **1809** R. LANGFORD *Introd. Trade* 57 *India stock*..is the capital of the East India Company, and is placed under the management of a Court of Directors. **1849** THACKERAY *Pendennis* II. vii, Three stars in India Stock to her name, begad! **1912** *List Articles Authorised to be Supplied by H.M.S.O.*, Tags, Treasury (Insertion), Tags, *India (cross-bar). **1963** R. L. COLLISON *Mod. Business Filing & Archives* ii. 47 The documents are then secured to the file by what is known as a Treasury or India tag—i.e. a cord with a metal tag at each end. **1800** *Asiatic Ann. Reg., Hist. Ind.* 2/1 Hence the mariners employed in the *India trade became confident in their skill. **1727–41** CHAMBERS *Cycl.*, **India Wood*..is taken out of the heart of a large tree growing plentifully in the isles of Jamaica, Campeche, &c.

indiademed (ɪnˈdaɪədɛmd), *ppl. a.* [IN-[1] or [2]; cf. *endiadem* (EN- *pref.*[1] 1 b).] Set in a diadem.

1805 SOUTHEY *Madoc* I. vii, Whereto shall that be liken'd? to what gem Indiadem'd, what flower, what insect's wing?

†**in'dial,** *v. Obs. rare*[−1]. [f. IN-[2] + DIAL *sb.*] *trans.* To record or exhibit on a dial.

1648 EARL WESTMORELAND *Otia Sacra* (1879) 156 The Sun-beams steady Fire, with the Aire Of the inconstant winds Indiall'd are.

indialite (ˈɪndɪəlaɪt). *Min.* [f. INDIA + -LITE.] The hexagonal dimorph of cordierite.

1954 MIYASHIRO & IIYAMA in *Proc. Japan Acad.* XXX. 746 The present paper is concerned with the finding of a new hexagonal mineral from Bokaro coalfield, India, (Mg, $Fe^{+2})_2Al_4Si_5O_{18}$ in composition, polymorphic with cordierite. This mineral has hitherto been identified as cordierite; but..it is a distinct species, to which the name 'indialite' is proposed. **1972** M. H. BATTEY *Mineral. for Students* 254/1 Indialite, a dimorph of cordierite, is isostructural with beryl.

Indiaman (ˈɪndɪəmən). Pl. **-men.** [f. INDIA + MAN, as in *man of war*, etc.] A ship engaged in the trade with India; *spec.* a ship of large tonnage belonging to the East India Company.

1709 [see EAST INDIA]. **1712** E. COOKE *Voy. S. Sea* 452 The Donegal India-Man gave us seven, which we all return'd. **1748** *Anson's Voy.* III. vii. 365 The French pretending their India-men to be Men of War. **1772** *Ann. Reg., Chron.* 65 On the private trade of an homeward bound India-man. **1844** H. H. WILSON *Brit. India* I. 323 From time to time valuable Indiamen fell into their hands.

Indian (ˈɪndɪən), *a.* and *sb.* Also 5 Yndeen, 6 Indyan, 7 Indean. [f. INDIA: cf. -AN.]

A. *adj.* **1. a.** Belonging or relating to India, or the East Indies, or to the British Indian Empire; native to India.

Formerly, sometimes, more vaguely = Oriental, Asiatic.

*c***1566** J. ALDAY tr. *Boaystuau's Theat. World* D ij, An Indian Philosopher named Diphileus. **1596** SHAKS. *Merch. V.* III. ii. 99 The beautious scarfe, Vailing an Indian beautie. **1667** MILTON *P.L.* III. 436 Toward the Springs Of Ganges or Hydaspes, Indian streams. **1734** SALE *Koran* Prelim. Disc. §1 Alexander the Great, after his return from his Indian expedition. **1793** W. ROBERTS *Looker-on* No. 57 ¶11 Of China..the Emperor and other Indian monarchs. **1839** *Lett. fr. Madras* (1843) 283 That is the grand Indian sorrow —the necessity of parting with one's children. **1882** *Garden* 11 Mar. 171/1 The unrivalled collection of Indian Rhododendrons in the temperate house at Kew. **1893** ANNA BUCKLAND *Our Nat. Inst.* 109 The Indian Budget is brought into the English House of Commons every year and submitted to its approval.

b. Of Indian manufacture, material, or pattern.

1673 DRYDEN *Marr. à la Mode* III. i. Wks. 1883 IV. 304 That word shall be mine too, and my last Indian gown thine for 't. *c***1702** Indian Calico [see *India carpet*]. **1715** *Lond. Gaz.* No. 5367/4 Robert Sutton..Indian Gown-Seller. **1718** J. STEUART *Letter-Bk.* (1915) 64, I doe not mean you should goe to the expense of bying Indian chints. *c***1793** JANE AUSTEN *Volume First* (1933) 9 Your sentiments so nobly expressed on the different excellencies of Indian & English Muslins. **1794** A. YOUNG *Trav. France* (ed. 2) I. xix. 548 They print a great quantity of Indian callicoes. **1798** Indian shawl [see SHAWL *sb.* 2]. **1825** HONE *Every-day Bk.* I. 967 Flowered Indian gowns, formerly in use with schoolmasters. **1830** M. EDGEWORTH *Let.* 13 Dec. (1971) 449, I have..laid out fifteen guineas on—an Indian shawl. **1851** J. F. ROYLE *On Culture & Commerce of Cotton in India* I. 22 Indian cotton is well known to have certain good qualities of its own. **1863** A. J. MUNBY *Diary* 12 May in D. Hudson *Munby* (1972) 160 Curtains of old Indian chintz. **1873** C. M. YONGE *Pillars of House* IV. xlii. 218 Cherry cleared her large sofa, and covered him up with her Indian silk quilt. **1876** GEO. ELIOT *Dan. Der.* xxi, An Indian shawl over her arm. **1879** *Queen* 1 Mar. (Advt.), An entirely new under garment successfully introduced in Silk, Merino, Gauze Merino, and Indian Gauze. **1898** A. BENNETT *Man From North* xxviii. 241 Its square of Indian carpet over Indian matting. **1910** *Encycl. Brit.* VII. 258/1 The Indian cottons are usually of short staple. **1937** J. LAVER *Taste & Fashion* xii. 178 A combination chemise and knickers of Indian gauze. **1938** *Decorative Art* 83 A modern Indian rug in green. **1971** *Habitat Catal.* 76/2 Indian cotton durries.. simple tough cotton rugs. **1974** 'G. BLACK' *Golden Cockatrice* xi. 190 Blood had reached an Indian rug.

2. Belonging or relating to the race of original inhabitants of America and the West Indies (cf. INDIA 2, INDIES 1); occas. with reference to the endurance of tortures and hardship by North American Indians. ***Indian house***, a wigwam.

*a***1618** SYLVESTER *Tobacco Battered* 19 (That which now no Ingle wants) Indian Tobacco. **1634** *Relat. Ld. Baltimore's Plant.* (1865) 17 The Indian houses are all built heere in a long halfe Ouall. **1637** T. MORTON *New Eng. Canaan* (1883) 198 A small sized Choffe that eateth the Indian maisze. **1657** R. LIGON *Barbadoes* (1673) 55 This Indian Maid..fell in love with him, and hid him close from her Countrymen. **1716** B. CHURCH *Hist. Philip's War* (1867) II. 112 In ranging the Woods found several Indian-houses, their fires being just out, but no Indians. **1737** J. WESLEY *Let.* 22 July (1931) I. 225 When..He shall have chosen one or more to magnify Him,..not with a stoical or Indian indifference, but blessing and praying for their murderers. **1798** I. ALLEN *Hist. Vermont* 34 To give an Indian whoop and raise their ambuscade. **1817** COLERIDGE *Biogr. Lit.* I. x. 185 Three week's truly Indian perseverance in tracking us. **1822** WORDSWORTH *Eccl. Sk.* 67 The shrouded Body, to the Soul's command, Answering with more than Indian fortitude. **1855** LONGF. *Hiaw.* Introd. 86 Listen to this Indian Legend, To this Song of Hiawatha! **1888** M. A. GREEN *Springfield* (Mass.) 3 It was, in fact, an Indian trail centre. **1916** C. A. EASTMAN *From Deep Woods to Civilization* iii. 32 He took out his Bible and hymn-book printed in the Indian tongue. **1931** F. J. STIMSON *My United States* i. 4 Indian camps were not unusual in the vacant lots outlying Dubuque. **1934** *Beaver* June 9 When word came that they had landed, I left the living room for the Indian shop. **1940** W. FAULKNER *Hamlet* II. 98 A man who was not

thin so much as actually gaunt, with straight black hair.. and high Indian cheekbones. **1942** *Chicago Tribune* 24 Nov. 12/3 This stone marks the site of an ancient Indian village and chipping station. **1966** *Oxf. Compan. Amer. Hist.* 405/2 Since Indian tribes acted as buffer states between French and British colonies and were invaluable allies in time of war, colonial governors always sought to make treaties of friendship with the Indians. **1969** *Islander* (Victoria, B.C.) 5 Oct. 10/3 An Indian express was sent ahead to Fort Colville. **1970** D. BROWN *Bury my Heart at Wounded Knee* ii. 15 Many of the Mexicans had Indian blood. **1971** *Times* 30 Sept. 12/3 There has been a resurgence of interest in the Indians..partly (among the young) to embrace aspects of Indian life on behalf of the counter-culture. **1971** *Times* 15 Oct. 14/4 Dr. Robert Euler..has directed salvage archeology at prehistoric Indian sites in the area to be mined. **1973** *Freedomways* XIII. 81 The book is rich with examples of Indian culture and social life as practiced by the Oglala.

3. Made of Indian corn or Maize, as ***Indian bread*** (see also 4 b), ***Indian meal***, ***Indian dumpling***.

1635 *Mass. Col. Rec.* (1853) I. 140 Noe person whatsoeuer shall from henceforth transport any Indean corne or meale out of this jurisdiccon, till the nexte harvest. **1672** SIR W. TALBOT in F. L. Hawks *Hist. N. Carolina* (1858) II. 45 Who, at our setting out, laughed at my provision of Indian-meal. **1751** J. BARTRAM *Observ. Trav. Pennsylv.*, etc. 60 Last of all was served a great bowl, full of Indian dumplings, of new soft corn, cut or scraped off the ear. **1775** *Connect. Col. Rec.* (1890) XV. 16 Half a pint of rice or a pint of indian meal. **1897** WILLIS *Man. Flower. Plants* II. 395 The grain [of maize] is made into flour, *Indian meal*.

4. In names of various natural and artificial products **a.** of India or the East Indies (sense 1), or so originally supposed: **Indian almond**, a large tree (*Terminalia Catappa*), the seeds of which resemble almonds; **Indian antelope** = *black-buck* (BLACK *a.* 19); †**Indian ass**, a fabulous animal like a unicorn; **Indian berry** = COCCULUS INDICUS, or the plant (*Anamirta Cocculus*) which yields this; **Indian blue**, a name for indigo (cf. INDY *blue*); **Indian cane**, a name for the Bamboo; **Indian club**, a heavy club shaped somewhat like a large bottle, for use in gymnastic exercises; hence ***Indian-clubber***; †**Indian cock**, an old name for the turkey (cf. *cock of Ind*, COCK *sb.*[1] 10, F. *coq d'Inde*, and synonymous names in other European languages: prob. by some confusion; the bird being a native of North America); **Indian crocus**, a name for the dwarf orchids of the subgenus *Pleione* (genus *Cœlogyne*), having large bright-coloured flowers which appear before the leaves (as in the crocus) or after the leaves have fallen; **Indian elephant**, the smaller of the two existing species of elephant, *Elephas maximus*; **Indian English**, the form of English used by inhabitants of India for whom English is not a native language; cf. BABU; **Indian eye**, name for a species of pink (*Dianthus plumarius*), from the eye-shaped marking on the corolla; **Indian fire**, a composition of sulphur, realgar, and nitre, burning with a brilliant white flame, used as a signal-light; **Indian geranium**, name for a grass of the genus *Andropogon*, which yields a fragrant oil used in perfumery; †**Indian grass**, an old name of silkworm gut used by anglers; (see also in b below); **Indian hay** *U.S. slang*, marijuana; **Indian head** (see quot. 1957[2]); **Indian heart**, a plant of the genus *Cardiospermum*, esp. *C. Corindum* (see *heartseed*, s.v. HEART *sb.* 56 b); **Indian hemp**: see HEMP 5 (see also in b below); **Indian hog**, a name of the Babiroussa; †**Indian house**, a shop for the sale of Indian goods; **Indian ivy**, a climbing plant of the genus *Scindapsus* (N.O. *Araceæ*); **Indian leaf**, the aromatic leaf of a species of *Cinnamomum*; **Indian light** = BENGAL *light*; **Indian lotus**, an aquatic plant, *Nelumbo nucifera*, native to Asia, and bearing fragrant white or pink flowers; also called Egyptian or sacred lotus; †**Indian mouse** = ICHNEUMON 1; †**Indian nut**, the coco-nut; **Indian oak**, a name for the teak-tree (*Treas. Bot.* 1866); **Indian Ocean**, the ocean lying to the south of India, extending from the east coast of Africa to the Malay Archipelago; **Indian oil**, in phrase *to anoint with I. o.*, to 'tip' with gold; †**Indian rat** = *Indian mouse*; **Indian red**, a red pigment orig. obtained from the East Indies in the form of an earth containing oxide of iron; now prepared artificially by roasting iron sulphate (Ure *Dict. Arts* (1875) II. 890); **Indian reed** = next (*Treas. Bot.* 1866): (see also in b below); **Indian shot**, name for the plant *Canna indica* (N.O. *Marantaceæ*), from its round hard black seeds; **Indian tea**, tea grown in India or Sri Lanka, especially in Assam and the Darjeeling district; cf. sense 4 b below; **Indian walnut**, a name for the Candleberry-tree (*Aleurites triloba*), from the form of its seeds (*Treas. Bot.* 1866); †**Indian weed** = *Indian grass*; (see also in b below); **Indian work**, Indian handicraft, *spec.* drawn-thread work on muslin; **Indian yellow**, a bright yellow pigment obtained from India: see quot.

1887 MOLONEY *Forestry W. Afr.* 351 **Indian Almond*.. Large tree... The bark and leaves yield a black pigment, used by the Indians to dye their teeth. **1888** *Indian Antilope [see *black-buck* (BLACK *a.* 19)]. **1964** E. P. WALKER et al. *Mammals of World* II. 1457/1 Blackbucks, Indian Antelopes... This animal occasionally lives in herds of several hundred members. **1594** BLUNDEVIL *Exerc.* v. x. (1636) 553 The Unicorne is found in Æthiopia, like as the *Indian Asse is found in India, which hath like-wise one only horne in his forehead. **1765** CROKER, etc. *Dict. Arts & Sc.*, *Indian Berry, *Cocculus Indicus*. **1828** WEBSTER, *Indian Berry*, a plant of the genus Menispermum. **1578** LYTE *Dodoens* IV. liv. 531 The Cane of Inde, or ye *Indian Cane is of the kind of Reedes, very high, long, great, and strong. **1857** *Chambers' Inform. People* II. 674/1 *Indian Club Exercises.. The main object is to expand the chest, and increase the power of the arms. **1891** *Harper's Mag.* July 177/1 A more persevering dumb-beller and *Indian-clubber never was. **1638** tr. *Bacon's Life & Death* (1651) 10 The *Indian-Cock, commonly called the Turkey-Cock. **1882** *Garden* 30 Sept. 304/1 *Indian Crocuses..are now among the gayest occupants of Orchid houses. **1607** TOPSELL *Four-f. Beasts* 192 The *Indian Elephants are greatest, strongest, and tallest. **1965** D. MORRIS *Mammals* 338 Smaller than the African Elephant, the bull Indian Elephant rarely reaches 10 feet high at the shoulder. **1907** G. C. WHITWORTH (*title*) *Indian English: an examination of the errors of idiom made by Indians in writing English. **1934** R. C. GOFFIN in *S.P.E. Tract* XLI. 31 We have touched on the preference of Indian English for the archaic in vocabulary and phrase. **1971** *Shankar's Weekly* (Delhi) 4 Apr. 22/3 The best of Indian English et al you gave. **1573** TUSSER *Husb.* xliii. (1878) 96 *Indian eie, sowe in May, or set in slips in March. **1875** *Ure's Dict. Arts* II. 890 **Indian fire*..is composed of 7 parts of sulphur, 2 of realgar, and 24 of nitre. **1696** *Lond. Gaz.* No. 3206/4 Angle-Rods made of Foreign Dogwood..also the best new *Indian Grass, and all other sorts of Fishing Tackle. **1769** G. WHITE *Selborne* xxii. (1789) 63 Your account of the Indian-grass was entertaining.. Inquiring.. what they supposed that part of their tackle to be made of? they replied 'of the intestines of a silkworm'. **1939** *Jrnl. Amer. Med. Assoc.* 1 July 4/1 In America the name marihuana..is used. It has numerous picturesque names, such as muggles, reefers, Mary Warner, *Indian hay, the weed and tea. **1969** *Sci. Amer.* Dec. 17 In the U.S. it [*sc.* marijuana] is variously called the weed, stuff, Indian hay,.. and other names. **1911** *Daily Colonist* (Victoria, B.C.) 9 Apr. 24/2 New Wash Dress Materials in Muslins.. *Indian head and Linen Suitings. **1957** M. MCCARTHY *Memories Catholic Girlhood* vi. 117 Blue Indianhead 20 yds. **1957** M. B. PICKEN *Fashion Dict.* 183/1 *Indian head*, trade name for sturdy, firm, cotton material of linen-weave, made in many lovely colors. Used for work, play, and sports clothing and for home furnishings. **1884** MILLER *Plant-n.*, *Cardiospermum Corindum*, Heart-seed, *Indian Heart. **1876** B. W. RICHARDSON *Dis. Mod. Life* xii. 324 The ancient Scythian.. threw the seed of the *Indian hemp on the hot stones and then inhaled the narcotic vapour. **1897** *Allbutt's Syst. Med.* II. 900 It is stated by the 'Indian Hemp Drug Commission' of 1893–94 that 'its moderate use has no physical, mental, or moral ill-effects whatever'. **1774** GOLDSM. *Nat. Hist.* (1776) III. 192 The Babyrouessa, or *Indian Hog. **1783** ROWE *Ulyss.* Epil. 28 There are no *Indian Houses to drop in And fancy Stuffs and chuse a pretty Screen. **1765** CROKER, etc. *Dict. Arts & Sc.*, *Indian Leaf, *Malabathrum*,..the leaf of a tree brought from the East-Indies. **1884** MILLER *Plant-n.*, *Cinnamomum Malabathrum*, Indian, or Malabar, Leaf. **1787** *Phil. Trans.* LXXVII. 214 The *Indian lights are alternately exhibited. **1901** L. H. BAILEY *Cycl. Amer. Hort.* III. 1065/1 (*caption*) The *Indian Lotus, Nelumbium speciosum of the trade, but properly Nelumbo nucifera. **1963** W. BLUNT *Of Flowers & Village* 104 The seeds of the Indian Lotus 'rattle in their sockets like teeth in the jaw-bone of a skull'. **1617** MINSHEU *Ductor*, *Indian Mouse. **1658** PHILLIPS, *Indian Mouse*, a little beast called in Greek Ichneumon. **1613** M. RIDLEY *Magn. Bodies* 67 Cuppes..of Ostridge-egges, *Indian-Nuts, Mace-wood, and Stone. **1653** H. MORE *Antid. Ath.* II. vii. (1712) 61 The famous Indian Nut-Tree, which at once almost affords all the Necessaries of Life. **1727–41** CHAMBERS *Cycl.* s.v. *Ocean*, *Eastern*, or **Indian Ocean*, has its first name from its situation to the east; as its latter from India, the chief country it washes. **1626** L. OWEN *Running Register* 12 Constrained to anoint Pope Paulus Quintus in the fist with *Indian oyle, for his good-will. **1647** TRAPP *Comm. Rom.* xiii. 11 Whiles the Crocodile sleepeth with open mouth, the *Indian rat gets into his stomack, and eateth thorow his entrails. **1753** CHAMBERS *Cycl. Supp.* s.v. *Red*, **Indian Red*, a name used by the colourmen and painters for a kind of purple ochre, brought from the island of Ormus in the Persian gulf. **1882** *Garden* 30 Sept. 289/1 The colour is a clear orange-red, or rather Indian red. **1760** J. LEE *Introd. Bot.* App. (1765) 316/1 *Indian Shot, *Canna*. **1794** MARTYN *Rousseau's Bot.* xi. 117 The seeds..are round, and very hard; whence this plant has the name of Indian shot. **1865** GOSSE *Land & Sea* (1874) 322 The noble, reed-like leaves of the Indian-shot throw up their scarlet spikes. **1884** E. MONEY *Tea Controversy* (ed. 2) 10 A pound of *Indian Tea of any grade will give considerably more infusions of a like strength than a similar pound of Chinese. **1893** *Illustr. London News* 11 Nov. 618/2 Indian tea shipping warehouses. *c* **1938** *Fortnum & Mason Price List* 6 State whether China or Indian Tea is preferred. **1960** *Good Housek. Cookery Bk.* 451/2 Household teas,..are usually full-flavoured blended Indian teas. **1969** *Times* 13 Oct. (India Suppl.) p. x (Advt.), Darjeeling, Assam, Nilgiris. Three of the greatest names in Indian Teas. **1741** *Compl. Fam.-Piece* II. ii. (ed. 3) 333 At most Fishing-Tackle Shops you may have *Indian Weed, which is best to make your lower Link of for either Trout, Bream or Carp. **1865** F. B. PALLISER *Hist. Lace* xxi. 250 There is also a good specimen of that description of drawn muslin lace, commonly known under the name of '*Indian work', but which appears to have been made in various manners. **1882** CAULFEILD & SAWARD *Dict. Needlework* 157/2 Fig. 299 is of a later description of Drawn Work, and would be known as Indian Work, as its foundation is muslin. **1900** E. JACKSON *Hist. Hand-Made Lace* 150 Drawn-work..was known all over Europe as Hamburg Point, Indian work (when executed in muslin). **1920** A. K. ARTHUR *Embroidery Bk.* ix. 90 Some of the elaborately worked pieces of Indian and Persian work, where tinsel braids are freely employed, are things to marvel at. **1866–72** WATTS *Dict. Chem.* IV. 751 Purree serves for the preparation of *Indian yellow, a fine rich durable yellow colour much used both in oil and water-colour painting, and consisting mainly of euxanthate of magnesium. **1874** SCHORLEMMER *Organic Chem.* 414. **1875** *Ure's Dict. Arts* II. 890.

b. of America or the West Indies; chiefly of North America: **Indian agent** (see AGENT *sb.* 4 b); **Indian apple**, a name for the May-apple, *Podophyllum peltatum* (N.O. *Ranunculaceæ*); **Indian arrow**, the shrub *Euonymus atropurpureus*, also called Burning-bush; **Indian awl** (see quot. 1941); **Indian balm**, the purple Trillium or Birth-root (*Trillium erectum* or *T. pendulum*); **Indian bean**, a tree, *Catalpa bignonioides*, N.O *Bignoniaceæ* (Miller *Plant-n.* 1884); **Indian blanket**, orig. a blanket made by or for N. Amer. Indians, often used as a cloak; now also a blanket made in imitation of this; **Indian bread**, †(*a*) a former name for the Cassava, or the bread made from it; (*b*) bread made of Indian corn; **Indian bureau** (or **Bureau**): in N. and S. America, a bureau concerned with the affairs of American Indians; *spec.* in the U.S., the Bureau of Indian Affairs; **Indian chickweed**, the Carpet-weed, *Mollugo*, N.O. *Caryophyllaceæ* (*Treas. Bot.* 1866); **Indian chocolate**, *Geum rivale* and other species, from the colour of their roots (*Treas. Bot.*); cf. CHOCOLATE-*root*; **Indian cress, cresses**, a name for the South American genus *Tropæolum* (now popularly called Nasturtium), from the flavour of the leaves; **Indian cup, cups**, the N. American Pitcher-plant (*Sarracenia*); **Indian currant** = *coral-berry* (CORAL *sb.*[1] 9); **Indian devil**, a N. American name for either the wolverine or the cougar; **Indian's dream**, a N. American fern, *Pellæa atropurpurea*; †**Indian drug**, applied to tobacco (*obs.*); **Indian file**, the same as *single file*, so called because the North American Indians usually march in this order; **Indian gift** (see quot.); so **Indian giver**, one who expects a gift in return; so **Indian giving**; **Indian ginger**, a name for *Asarum canadense*, from the flavour of its root (*Treas. Bot.*); **Indian grass**: see quots.; †**Indian harvest**, the harvest of Indian corn; **Indian hemp**, the common name of *Apocynum cannabinum*, a plant having a fibrous integument used by the North American Indians for the same purposes as hemp (see also a above); **Indian hen**, the American bittern, *Botaurus mugitans* or *B. lentiginosus*; †**Indian herb**, applied to tobacco (*obs.*); **Indian ladder**, 'a ladder made of a small tree by trimming it so as to leave only a few inches of each branch as a support for the foot' (Bartlett *Dict. Amer.* 1860); **Indian lettuce**, a name for *Frasera verticillata* (N.O. *Gentianaceæ*); **Indian mound** [MOUND *sb.*[3] 4 e], in N. America, a mound or earthwork erected in former times by Indians as a burial place, fortification, etc.; **Indian paint**, a N. American perennial herb with reddish sap and thick red-tinted roots; **Indian paint-brush**, a herbaceous plant of the genus *Castilleja*; **Indian path**, a foot-path or track through the woods, such as is made by North American Indians; **Indian pear** *N. Amer.*, a tree or shrub of the genus *Amelanchier*, or its edible fruit, a fleshy red or purple berry; †**Indian pepper**, old name for Capsicum; **Indian physic**, name for *Gillenia trifoliata*, a N. American rosaceous plant with a medicinal root; **Indian pipe**, an American name for *Monotropa uniflora*, a leafless plant with a solitary drooping flower, of a uniform pinkish-white throughout, parasitic on the roots of trees (*Treas. Bot.* 1866); also **Indian pipe-stem**; **Indian plantain**, common name of the genus *Cacalia* of composite plants (*Treas. Bot.*); **Indian poke**, the White Hellebore of N. America, *Veratrum viride* (Webster, 1864); **Indian pony**, a type of pony descended from horses originally brought to America by Spanish colonists; **Indian pudding**, a pudding made with Indian meal, molasses, and suet, a frequent dish in New England; also, the same as *hasty-pudding* (*Cent. Dict.*); **Indian purge**, a species of *Ipomœa* (? *I. pandurata*), the *Mechameck* of North American Indians; **Indian reed**, applied to a blow-pipe such as the N. American Indians use for shooting arrows; (see also in a above); **Indian reservation, reserve** (see RESERVATION 3 b, RESERVE *sb.* 5 b); **Indian**

rice, a North American aquatic grass, *Zizania aquatica*, or one of several similar plants resembling rice; **Indian root**, (*a*) *Indian physic*; (*b*) the American Spikenard, *Aralia racemosa* (*Cent. Dict.*); **Indian shoe**, (*a*) a moccasin; (*b*) an American name for the plant *Cypripedium*, also called Lady's Slipper, from the shape of the flower; **Indian sign(s)**, a (usually faint) track or trail, etc., that reveals the presence of Indians; also a smoke-signal or other signal used by Indians; phr. ***to put*** (or ***have***) ***the Indian sign on*** (someone) (see quot. 1944); † **Indian smoke**, applied to tobacco smoke; † **Indian sun**, old name of the Sunflower (*Helianthus*); **Indian tea**, any one of several N. American plants whose leaves are used to make a drink resembling tea; = *Labrador tea*; **Indian tobacco**, a name for *Lobelia inflata*; also applied to other plants; **Indian turnip**, (*a*) the tuberous root of *Arisæma triphyllum* (N.O. *Araceæ*), or the plant itself; (*b*) the edible tuberous root of a leguminous plant *Psoralea esculenta* (Bartlett *Dict. Amer.* 1860); **Indian weed**, (*a*) see quot. 1687; (*b*) an appellation of tobacco; † **Indian wheat**, an old name for Indian corn.

1766 W. JOHNSON *Let.* 23 Jan. in R. Rogers *Jrnls.* (1883) 216 As Commandant and *Indian Agent, it will be extremely difficult to check him. **1816, 1901** [see AGENT *sb.* 4b]. **1974** A. MACLEAN *Breakheart Pass* iii. 44, I asked the Governor here to appoint me Indian agent for the territory; I settle differences..allocate reservations, try and stop the traffic in guns and whisky. **1847** F. PARKMAN in *Knickerbocker* XXIX. 310 The rich flowers of the *Indian-apple were there in profusion. **1931** W. N. CLUTE *Common Names of Plants* 35 The May-apple (*Podophyllum peltatum*) was known to settlers as Indian apple, but it is really a berry. **1821** G. SIMPSON *Jrnl. Occurrences in Athabasca Dept.* (1938) 142 Awls, *Indian, doz. **1922** *Beaver* July 10/2 It requires but three tools to build a canoe: an axe, a 'crooked knife', and a square or Indian awl. **1941** *Beaver* Sept. 38 *Indian awl*, a square two-ended awl for bark, leather or wood. **1866** *Treas. Bot.* s.v. *Trillium*, The plant [*T. erectum* or *pendulum*] is also called *Indian Balm. **1843** J. TORREY *Flora N.Y.* II. 25 Catalpa. *Indian Bean... About habitations... The Catalpa is more esteemed for ornament than for use. **1933** [see *cigar-tree*]. **1969** T. H. EVERETT *Living Trees of World* 298/2 The Indian-bean has many more flowers in each cluster than the Western catalpa. **1764** in *New Jersey Archives* (1902) 1st Ser. XXIV. 350 There are a blue Great Coat, and an *Indian Blanket missing. **1782** *Quebec Gaz.* 19 Dec. 4/1 For Sale..A Large assortment.. Indian blanket Rugs. **1807** *Salmagundi* 13 Feb. 49 The shawl..thrown over one shoulder, like an Indian blanket. **1927** W. CATHER *Death comes for Archbishop* I. iii. 31 The earth floor was covered with thick Indian blankets; two blankets, very old, and beautiful in design and colour, were hung on the walls like tapestries. **1962** J. BRAINE *Life at Top* xxvi. 278 There's a cigarette burn in my Indian blanket. **1966** *Islander* (Victoria, B.C.) 27 Feb. 7/1 We smelled perfume and talcum from many Indian blankets. **1753** CHAMBERS *Cycl. Supp.*, **Indian-Bread*, see the article *Cassada-Bread*. **1828** WEBSTER, *Indian Bread*, a plant of the genus Jatropha. **1856** G. DAVIS *Hist. Sk. Stockbridge & Southbr.* (Mass.) 179 Skilled in..making rye and Indian bread. **1831** C. ATWATER *Remarks Tour to Prairie du Chien* 142 Taking advantage of frauds committed on the Indians, by persons connected with the *Indian bureau, the Factory system gave place to the present system. **1922** D. H. LAWRENCE *Phoenix II* (1968) 239 The Indian Bureau is supposed to do the cherishing. **1972** *Buenos Aires Herald* 2 Feb. 7/1 Officials of Brazil's Indian Bureau here believe that numerous small tribes of Indians living along the projected new highway have never seen an outsider. **1597** GERARDE *Herbal* II. xiv. (1623) 253 *Indian cresses. **1629** PARKINSON *Paradisi* v. 281 *Nasturtium Indicum*, by which name it is now generally..called, and we thereafter in English, Indian Cresses. **1883** *Gd. Words* Nov. 712/1 Dahlias, fuschias, morning glories and Indian cress. **1837** P. H. GOSSE in E. W. Gosse *Life* (1890) 108 That curious plant, the *Indian cup or pitcher plant (*Sarracenia*). **1785** H. MARSHALL *Arbustrum Amer.* 82 *Lonicera Symphoricarpos*. *Indian Currants, or St. Peter's Wort. This hath a shrubby stalk, which rises from four to five feet high. **1806** LEWIS & CLARK *Orig. Jrnls. Lewis & Clark Expedition* (1905) V. 327 Deep purple berry or the large Cherry of the Current Species which is common... The engagees call it the Indian Current. **1866** [see CURRANT 3]. **1948** *South Sierran* Feb. 2/2 'Indian currant' was also in bloom. **1851** J. S. SPRINGER *Forest Life & Forest Trees* 66 A dangerous specimen of the feline species, known by woodsmen as the '*Indian devil', had prowled from time immemorial. **1901** W. M. THOMPSON *In Maine Woods* 60 The cougar, or 'Indian devil', is sometimes seen. **1937** H. H. LANGTON in P. Campbell *Trav. Interior Parts N. Amer.* 71 The Wolverine..has long been extinct in the province [*sc.* Nova Scotia], where it is remembered as the 'Injun devil'. **1965** *Wildlife Rev.* (Victoria, B.C.) Mar. 19 Cougars, also known as panthers, pumas, catamounts, mountain lions, and Indian devils, are large unspotted cats. **1630** J. TAYLOR (Water P.) *Wks.* (N.), His breath compounded of strong English beere, And th' *Indian drug, would suffer none come neere. **1758** in *Essex Inst. Hist. Coll.* (1881) XVIII. 179 They march'd in *Indian file. **1791** W. BARTRAM *Carolina* 440 Having ranged themselves in regular Indian file, the veteran in the van, and the younger in the rear. **1814** SCOTT *Wav.* xxxviii, The party..moved up the pathway in single or Indian file. **1841** CATLIN *N. Amer. Ind.* (1844) I. xxii. 150 At his heels in 'Indian file', i.e. single file, one following in another's tracks. **1873** G. M. GRANT *Ocean to Ocean* 189 As the line of march had to be in Indian file, we soon exchanged the undemonstrative 'good-bye' with him. **1922** *Beaver* Sept. 6/2 The long camp fire gave sufficient light to see the dancers, who followed one another in Indian file. **1971** *Ceylon Times Weekender* (Colombo) 3 Oct. 5/5 As the family came trotting along towards the crocodile in Indian file, the lean, rangy patriarch was in the lead. **1765** T. HUTCHINSON *Hist. Mass.* I. 469 *note*, An *Indian gift is a proverbial expression, signifying a present for which an equivalent return is expected. **1879** B. F. TAYLOR *Summer-Savory* xxvi. 207 She is glad it [*sc.* the check] is an 'Indian gift', that the conductor did not present it to her outright. **1860** BARTLETT *Dict. Amer.*, **Indian giver*, When an Indian gives any thing, he expects to receive an equivalent, or to have his gift returned. **1892** H. C. BOLTON in *Jrnl. Amer. Folk-Lore* V. 68 If an American child, who has made a small gift to a playmate is indiscreet enough to ask that the gift be returned, he (or she) is immediately accused of being an Indian-giver, or, as it is commonly pronounced Injun-giver. **1904** *N.Y. Herald* 10 Sept. 5 Later he took the position of the 'Indian giver' and wanted the money back. **1939** *Time* 23 Oct. 4/1 Call us Indian-giver. **1965** R. MANHEIM tr. *Grass's Dog Yrs.* I. 12 'You threw my knife.' 'It was my knife. Don't be an Indian giver.' **1971** M. MCCARTHY *Birds of America* 29 He wanted the little violin which Hans, an Indian giver, took back to the store. **1837** W. IRVING *Capt. Bonneville* II. vi. 71 His experience in what is proverbially called '*Indian giving' made him aware that a parting pledge was necessary on his own part. **1962** B. SPOCK *Problems of Parents* (1968) II. 50 The one-year-old who has yelled bloody murder during his physical examination may, ten minutes later.. sweetly hand him a toy and then take it back. This latter trick may look like Indian giving. **1765** T. HUTCHINSON *Hist. Mass.* I. 480 *note*, The natural upland grass of the country commonly called *Indian grass, is poor fodder. **1884** MILLER *Plant-n.*, Grass, Indian, *Sorghum nutans* and *Molinia cœrulea*. **1643** *Mass. Col. Rec.* (1853) II. 37 Two bigger Corts are to be kept there, the one between the English and *Indian harvest, and the other in the spring. **1676** in S. G. Drake *Old Ind. Chron.* (1867) 282 Our Indian Harvest is like to be very Fruitfull, that Grain is now sold at two Shillings Sixpence the Bushell. **1707** *N. Hampsh. Prov. Papers* (1868) II. 566 Which will last till the Indian Harvest is over. **1637** T. MORTON *New Eng. Canaan* (1883) 135 Matts..made of their *Indian hempe. **1794** S. WILLIAMS *Vermont* 71 The Indian Hemp (*asclepias*) may be woven into a fine, and strong thread. **1866** *Treas. Bot.* 80 From the fibrous bark of *A*[*pocynum*] *cannabinum* (commonly called Indian Hemp), and *hypericifolium*, the Indians prepare a substitute for hemp, of which they make twine, bags, fishing-nets, and lines. **1597** *1st Pt. Return fr. Parnass.* I. i. 447 Longe for a rewarde may your witts be warmde with the *Indian herbe. **1791** W. BARTRAM *Carolina* 247 Having provided ourselves with a long snagged sapling, called an *Indian ladder. *Ibid.* 42 A very singular and elegant plant.. called *Indian Lettuce, made its first appearance in these rich vales. **1884** MILLER *Plant-n.*, Lettuce, Indian, *Frasera verticillata*. **1791** in *Mass. Hist. Soc. Coll.* (1794) 1st Ser. III. 24 There is an *Indian mound, the base of which is about three hundred paces round, and rises in a conic form about one hundred feet. **1869** B. HARTE *Luck of Roaring Camp* 186 Cattle and sheep are gathered on Indian Mounds waiting the fate of their companions whose carcases drift by us. **1949** *Illinois State Archaeol. Soc. Jrnl.* Jan. 7/2 When the term, 'Indian Mound', is mentioned, one naturally thinks of a large ceremonial Mound which covers one to three acres of ground and is perhaps five or ten or even 20 feet in height. **1950** *Caribbean Q.* II. II. 24 Scientific excavation of the so-called Indian Mounds has brought to light masses of.. pottery ware, celts. **1803** A. F. M. WILLICH *Domestic Encycl.* (Amer. ed.) IV. 442/1 Sanguinaria Canadensis, called commonly *Puccoon*, blood-wort, red-root, *Indian paint, turmeric. **1931** W. N. CLUTE *Common Names of Plants* 26 The bloodroot..is also called puccoon-root, Indian paint. **1892** *Jrnl. Amer. Folk-Lore* V. 101 *Castilleia coccinea* ..*Indian paint-brush. **1923** 'B. M. BOWER' *Parowan Bonanza* ii. 21 He plucked a bright red 'Indian paint brush' from beside a rock. **1959** *Calgary Herald* 31 July 10/1 There is no finer feature of the autumn landscape in Alberta..than the roadside aster,..Indian paint brush and wild geranium. **1969** *Islander* (Victoria, B.C.) 5 Oct. 7/1 Sometimes the red-orange of the Indian paint-brush was like a blanket spread beneath the pines. **1634** W. WOOD *New Englands Prospect* II. vii. 71 An *Indian path (which seldome is broader than a Cart's rutte). **1793** W. BENTLEY *Diary* 26 Aug. (1907) II. 51 An Indian path was visible through the town from the N.W. corner. **1794** A. THOMAS *Newfoundland Jrnl.* (1968) iv. 63, I shall resume my journey..endeavouring as well as I can to give you an idea of an Indian Path in Newfoundland. **1809** A. HENRY *Trav.* 180 Our only road was a foot-path, or such as, in America, is exclusively termed an *Indian path*. **1939** G. H. EVANS *Pigwacket* 3 To the consideration of this important gateway, through which the old Indian path entered Pigwacket, further attention will be directed. **1796** *Descr. Prince Edward Island* 5 A fruit in this Island, called the *Indian Pear, is very delicious. **1856** W. E. CORMACK *Narr. Journey across Newfoundland* (1874) 19 On the skirts of the forest, and of the marshes, are found..Indian pear [etc.]. **1873** G. M. GRANT *Ocean to Ocean* 156 The sasketoon are simply what are known in Nova Scotia as 'Indian pears'. **1956** T. H. RADDALL *Wings of Night* 12 Then came the long reach of scrub woods, wire birch and poplar mostly, with blossoming clumps of Indian pear, like patches of snow on the slopes. **1578** LYTE *Dodoens* V. lxix. 634 The *Indian Pepper hath square stalkes. **1596** RALEIGH *Discov. Guiana* (1887) 141 All places yield abundance of all sorts of gums, of Indian pepper. **1788** M. CUTLER in *Life*, etc. (1888) II. 285 A plant called *Indian Physic, or Indian Root; it blossoms, I believe, early in the year, for the seed was ripe in August. **1823** J. D. HUNTER *Captiv. N. Amer.* 445 A warm infusion of the Indian physic, or *gillenia trifoliata*. **1822** A. EATON *Man. Bot.* (ed. 3) 357 *Monotropa uniflora*, birds nest, *indian-pipe. **1884** 'C. E. CRADDOCK' *In Tennessee Mts.* I. 60 The ashy Indian pipes silvered the roots of the trees. **1962** *Maclean's Mag.* 10 Mar. 17/1 It was a palely sprouting parasite called Indian pipe, or corpse plant, which extrudes almost overnight from rotting compost and lives only briefly. **1870** *Amer. Naturalist* III. 6 The *Indian Pipestem will be found rarely in low woods. **1758** P. STEVENS *Jrnl.* 13 July in N. D. Mereness *Trav. Amer. Colonies* (1916) 314 He is given us for an *Indian pony in his place. **1865** *Nor'Wester* (Red River Settlement) 21 Sept. 2/3 Our hardy Indian ponies found many purchasers at good prices. **1869** [see BRONCO a]. **1965** D. M. GOODALL *Horses of World* 211 The descendants of these [Spanish] horses, known as Mustangs, migrated through Mexico to the United States, scattering far west and north-west. Some were captured by the Indians and subsequently became Indian ponies. **1771** J. ADAMS *Diary* 10 June, Wks. 1850 II. 276 Just as they had got their *Indian pudding and their pork and greens upon the table. **1809** W. IRVING *Knickerb.* III. i. (1820) 159 He was making his breakfast from a prodigious earthen dish, filled with milk and Indian pudding. **1888** J. Q. BITTINGER *Hist. Haverhill* (N. Hampsh.) 358 The Indian pudding was a great favorite, if we may judge from the frequency with which it made its appearance at meal time. **1687** J. CLAYTON *Virginia* in *Phil. Trans.* XLI. 150 There is another Herb, which they call the **Indian Purge*..It bears yellow Berries round about the Joints: They only make use of the Root of this Plant. **1877** LANIER *Poems, Hard Times Elfland* 88 Bows, arrows, cannon, *Indian reeds. **1819** D. THOMAS *Trav. Western Country* 12 This tract is an *Indian reservation. **1949** *Kansas Hist. Q.* Feb. 2 They learned that Council Grove was situated on an Indian reservation and was not available for settlement. **1954** H. EVANS *Mist on River* 43 She said that this fall or next..she would try to get him into an Indian reservation school. **1792** in *Rep. Bureau Arch. Ontario* (1905) III. 215 Every farm of good land, in that part of the Country, is comprehended within the *Indian reserve. **1818** F. HALL *Trav. Canada & U.S.* 131 The river Credit is an Indian reserve, well stocked with salmon. *a* **1843** [see RESERVE *sb.* 5b *attrib.*]. **1958** *Edmonton* (Alberta) *Jrnl.* 18 June 31/7 Conditions on the two Indian reserves have improved greatly. **1822** *Minutes of Council, N. Dept. of Rupert's Land*, in *Publ. Hudson's Bay Rec. Soc.* (1940) III. 22 All the *Indian rice and corn he may collect. **1872** SCHELE DE VERE *Americanisms* 409 The Indians of the Northern regions..depend largely upon..this perennial plant, from whence it is also known as Indian rice. **1933** E. C. JAEGER *California Deserts* xiii. 165 Indian rice (*Oryzopsis hymenoides*) is frequent in porous soils, particularly on blown sand. **1775** A. ADAMS in *J. Adams' Fam. Lett.* (1876) 96, I should be glad of one ounce of *Indian root. **1704** *N. Hampsh. Prov. Papers* (1868) II. 422 For entertaining an Express, and some friend Indians about making *Indian Shoes. **1758** in G. Sheldon *Hist. Deerfield, Mass.* (1895) I. 656 His scoutsmen are destitute of Indian shoes. **1805** P. GASS *Jrnl.* 30 May (1807) 93 We see a great many fresh *Indian tracks or signs as we pass along. **1854** J. R. BARTLETT *Pers. Narr. Explor. Texas* I. iv. 95 They had seen 'Indian sign', and pointed out..the well-known Indian signal of a puff of smoke suddenly rising from the earth. **1866** *Rep. Indian Affairs* (U.S.) 188 On the 19th, proceeding again to the Malheur river, but found no fresh Indian signs. **1873** J. H. BEADLE *Undevel. West* xxxiv. 738, I rode around our camp, a circle of about six miles, looking for Indian signs. **1910** R. GRAU *Business Man in Amusement World* 97 He has also been careful to protect himself against 'the Indian Sign'. **1912** *McClure's Mag.* XXXIX. 235/1 He sure put the Indian sign on Tommy Ryan that time. **1916** *Boy Scouts' Year Bk.* (N.Y.) 93/2 He had proved that the Indian sign wasn't infallible... After all, then, the Indian sign was a kind of superstition. *a* **1918** G. STUART *40 Yrs. on Frontier* (1925) I. 115 Plenty of Indian signs, saw signal fires on the mountains to westward. **1929** *Bookman* Sept. 62/2 Owen Johnson always has had what is known as the 'Indian Sign' on me. I never won a bet from him and never will. **1944** R. F. ADAMS *Western Words* (1945) 83/1 To put the Indian sign on someone meant to hex or curse him with some kind of witchcraft, also to get him where you want him. **1948** V. PALMER *Golconda* x. 79 What silly notions about ourselves we can coddle! I believe the old boy's put the Indian sign on you, Neda. **1973** *Listener* 5 June 6/3 We were riding very high in terms of our legislative programme. We had the Indian sign on the Congress, so to speak. **1626** L. OWEN *Running Register* 50 They spend it all most lewdly in good liquor and *Indian smoake. **1645** G. DANIEL *Poems* Wks. 1878 II. 26 Keep the Round of good Societie, In high-pris'd Indian Smoke. **1578** LYTE *Dodoens* II. xxxiv. 191 The *Indian Sunne, or the golden floure of Perrowe is a plante of such stature and talnesse that..it groweth to the length of thirtene or fouretenne foote. **1709** J. LAWSON *New Voy. Carolina* 91 This plant [*sc.* Yaupon] is the *Indian Tea, us'd and approv'd by all the Savages on the Coast of Carolina. **1771** G. CARTWRIGHT *Jrnl.* 6 Mar. (1792) I. 100 As I judged, that Indian tea was of the same nature with the herbs which are recommended by that author [*sc.* Dr. Brookes], I had some gathered from under the snow in the woods, and gave her a pint of the strong infusion of that plant sweetened with sugar. **1794** A. THOMAS *Newfoundland Jrnl.* (1968) iv. 71, I breakfasted with Mrs Harty on Indian Tea, the growth of Newfoundland. **1925** A. HEMING *Living Forest* 131 The old woodsman infused some of the Indian tea he had gathered. **1938** *Beaver* June 23/1 Light springing feet of youths and maidens would make little impression on the tough bushes of Indian Tea. *a* **1618** *Indian tobacco [see sense 2]. **1851** BALFOUR *Man. Bot.* §924 *Lobelia inflata*, Indian Tobacco.. is used medicinally as a sedative, expectorant, and anti-spasmodic. **1872** SCHELE DE VERE *Americanisms* 415 Indian Tobacco (*Lobelia inflata*), occasionally used instead of tobacco by virtue of its acrid leaves. **1950** C. P. LYONS *Milestones on Mighty Fraser* 89 Indian tobacco..was used by the Thompson Indians from time immemorial. **1806** *Deb. Congress U.S.* 19 Feb. 1142 *Indian turnip, wild carrot, wild onion. **1856** [see TURNIP *sb.* 2b]. **1866** *Treas. Bot.* 90 The Dragon-root, or Indian turnip of America, is the tuber of *A*[*risæma*] *atrorubens*, which furnishes a kind of starch. *Ibid.* 935 *P*[*soralea*] *esculenta* is a native of Wisconsin..and other parts of North-west America, where its tuberous roots, known as Indian or Prairie turnips..form a great part of the food of the indigenous population. **1873** J. MILLER *Life amongst Modocs* x. 128 He [*sc.* winter] cut down the banners of the spring that night, lamb-tongue, Indian turnip and catella. **1894** [see TURNIP *sb.* 2b]. **1911** G. S. PORTER *Harvester* xix. 459 He..brought her samples of ginger leaves, Indian hemp, queen-of-the-meadow, cone-flower, burdock, baneberry, Indian turnip, [etc.]. **1949** *Nature Mag.* Apr. 178 A few of these, like Indian turnip or jack-in-the-pulpit, cowslip and milkweed, may be considered mildly inedible. **1687** J. CLAYTON *Virginia* in *Phil. Trans.* XLI. 145 They have..various very good Wound-herbs, as an Herb commonly called *Indian-weed, which perhaps may be referred to the Valerians. **1889** FARMER *Americanisms*, *Indian weed*, tobacco. **1578** LYTE *Dodoens* IV. x. 464 They do now call this grayne..in English Turkish Corne, or *Indian wheate. **1595** DRAKE *Voy.* (Hakluyt Soc.) 25 An iland, called St. Crusado,..where they had store of hens and Indian wheate for nine weekes. **1634** *Relat. Ld. Baltimore's Plant.* (1865) 21 We haue planted since wee came, as much Maize (or Indian Wheate) as will suffice..much more company than we haue. **1720** DE FOE *Capt. Singleton* ix. (1840) 163 We found some maize, or Indian wheat, which the negro-women planted.

c. For *Indian arrowroot, cucumber, currant, jalap, lake, millet, ochre, ox, pink, ringworm, steel,* etc. see the sbs. See also INDIAN CORN, FIG, INK, SUMMER, in their places as main words: *Indian rubber*: see INDIA RUBBER.

d. *Chess.* (i) ***Indian problem*** (see quots. 1878). Also *ellipt.*

1846 *Chess Player's Chron.* 96 We now publish the names of those amateurs who have sent us the correct solution of our Indian problem. **1878** S. LOYD *Chess Strategy* 96 Its entire difficulty consists in the skill with which the fact of its being an *Indian* is concealed. *Ibid.* 97 The theme of the Indian problem culminates in a stale-mating position, which has been anticipated by preparing an ambush for allowing the defence a move that may expose him to a discovered mate. *Ibid.* 100 The old Indian problem... The leading feature of the problem does not consist in the discovered check, but in the unexpected and apparently useless withdrawal of the two pieces to a remote quarter of the board, the one intersecting the protection of the other so as to allow the adverse King a move. **1913** A. C. WHITE *Sam Loyd* 287 Two of Loyd's best Indians are shown in Nos. 402 and 403.

(ii) Used to denote openings in which a player seeks to control the centre of the board with knights, fianchettoed bishops, etc., rather than by advancing his centre pawns. Now esp. ***Indian defence***, where Black plays thus; also *ellipt.*

King's (or ***Queen's***) ***Indian defence***: an Indian defence in which Black's king's (or queen's) bishop is fianchettoed. See also NIMZO-INDIAN *a.*

1896 H. F. CHESHIRE *Hastings Chess Tournament 1895* 369 Openings,.. Hungarian,.. Indian,.. King's Gambits. **1899** E. E. CUNNINGTON *Mod. Chess Primer* ix. 181 Or Black may play the 'Indian Defence'. **1925** *Chess Budget* I. 117/2 A third case was in a small club tournament with the new form of Indian defence. **1929** *Chess Amateur* XXIII. 202/1 Indian Defence. Played recently in the semi-final of the Three Counties' Championship Tournament. **1942** H. GOLOMBEK *50 Great Games Mod. Chess* 67/1 (*heading*) Queen's Pawn, Queen's Indian Defence. **1950** *Hoyle's Games Modernized* (ed. 20) IV. 410 The Indian Defences (those in which Black does not play P-Q4 at an early stage). *Ibid.* 411 The *Catalan system*—a modern combination of the King's Indian and Queen's gambit. **1958** *Listener* 13 Nov. 803/3 If you favour complications, you are most likely to be suited by the queen's pawn opening and by the Sicilian and King's Indian Defences. **1964** I. A. HOROWITZ *Chess Openings* 638 King's Indian Defense... Introduced in the Leipzig tournament of 1879.

B. *sb.*

1. a. A member of any of the native races of India or the East Indies; an East Indian. †In early use sometimes *spec.* (like Gr.'Ινδός) applied to an elephant-driver or *mahout*: cf. Yule 331/2, 333/2. Now *spec.* (before 1947) a native or inhabitant of the Indian sub-continent and (after 1947) of the Republic of India.

1495 *Trevisa's Barth. De P.R.* XVIII. xlii. (W. de W.) 804 Elyphauntes ben full peryllous in time of generacion and namely the wilde eliphauntes..and therfore the Yndeens [*Bodl. MS.* Indes] hyde theyr tame female eliphauntys. **1548** HALL *Chron., Hen. VIII*, 125 You Portyngales..to the Indyans you cary nothyng but wyne, whiche is hurt to all countreys. **1611** BIBLE *1 Macc.* vi. 37 There were also vpon euery one [elephant] two and thirtie strong men that fought vpon them, besides the Indian that ruled him. **1663** BUTLER *Hud.* I. ii. 587 As Indians with a female Tame Elephant inveigle the male. **1705** (*title*) The Customs of the East Indians, with those of the Jews and other ancient People. **1794** S. WILLIAMS *Vermont* 385 A copper colour denotes the complexion of the Indians of Asia. **1802** BARTOLOMEO *Voy. E. Indies* I. vii, The Indians consider it indecent. **1885** H. J. S. COTTON *New India* ii. 11 The attitude of Englishmen to Indians is not of a character to inspire confidence. **1896** in *Macm. Mag.* Sept. (1906) 820 Purely Indian-raised troops. **1912** E. M. FORSTER *Let.* 25 Dec. in *Hill of Devi* (1953) 17 In the evening we went to the Tennis Club—all Indians—and drove back through the tidy little town. **1923** *Glasgow Herald* 20 Feb. 6 The possible future absorption by Indians of the bulk of Indian Army commissions and military appointments. **1946** J. H. HUTTON *Caste in India* iii. 27 It is the cultivated and educated Bengali who has been probably more than any other Indian the interpreter of the Englishman to the Indian. **1954** *Chambers's Encycl. World Survey* 210/1 Indians have long shown a genuine flair for the parliamentary system of government. **1965** N. C. CHAUDHURI *Continent of Circe* iv. 89 No sensible Indian will have a moment's hesitation in saying which is preferable. **1971** M. EDWARDES *Nehru* xx. 328 The machinery that was to move Lal Bahadur Shastri, a very different sort of Indian, into the office of Prime Minister had already been put in gear.

b. A European, esp. an Englishman, who resides or has resided in India; an Anglo-Indian. Chiefly in ***Old Indian***, ***returned Indian***, and the like.

1751 ELIZA HEYWOOD *Hist. Betsy Thoughtless* III. 254 This young Indian. **1816** ELPHINSTONE in Sir T. E. Colebrooke *Life* (1884) I. 367 (Y.) Our best Indians. In the idleness and obscurity of home they look back with fondness to the country where they have been useful and distinguished. **1829** *Bengalee* 360 A friendliness..to be met with among old Indians. *Ibid.* 450 Bath, and Cheltenham.. At the latter two, so many returned Indians are in the habit of congregating. **1884** *Contemp. Rev.* Feb. 216 We all know that 'advice' is plentiful enough, even the advice of 'old Indians'.

c. One of the indigenous inhabitants of the Philippine Islands; applied esp. to one who has been converted to Christianity.

1697 W. DAMPIER *New Voy. round World* xi. 307 He fell in with these Philippine Islands, and anchored at Luconia; where he warr'd with the native Indians, to bring them in obedience to his master the king of Spain. **1817** J. MCLEOD *Narr. Voy. H.M.S. Alceste Yellow Sea* 171 The religion of the Indians under the immediate control of the Spaniards is Christianity; but at Mindanao and the other islands..it is said to be a mixture of Mahomedanism with..Pagan rites. **1885** *Encycl. Brit.* XVIII. 752/1 Cigars they [*sc.* the Negritos of the Philippines] often smoke with the burning end between the teeth—a practice occasionally observed among the civilized Indians. **1905** F. W. ATKINSON *Philippine Islands* x. 264 The Spaniards used the term Indian in speaking collectively of these seven Christian tribes and the word Filipino in speaking of any one born in the Islands without distinction as to religious belief. **1967** D. MANNIX *Sporting Chance* ii. 35 This outfit was made by the Zubanoan Indians who live in the mountains of Mindanao. **1968** R. NELSON *Philippines* ii. 31 The majority of the people, called Indians by the Spanish, had an olive complexion.

†**d.** A member of one of the indigenous peoples of Australia and New Zealand. *Obs.*

1769 J. BANKS *Jrnl.* 21 Oct. (1896) 191 We applied to our friends the Indians [*sc.* Maoris] for a passage in one of their canoes. **1770** *Ibid.* 28 Apr. 264 During this time, a few of the Indians [*sc.* Australian Aboriginals]..remained on the rocks opposite the ship, threatening and menacing with their pikes and swords. **1825** B. FIELD *Geogr. Mem. New South Wales* 437 Some of the Indians have also seriously applied to be allowed convict-labourers..till the maize and cabbage that have been planted to their hands are fit to gather. **1830** A. F. GARDINER *Friend of Australia* xiii. 244 It is the observation of some writers, that the system pursued in Australia for educating the children of the Indians, is not attended with success.

2. a. A member of any of the aboriginal races of America or the West Indies; an American Indian. Also, examples of ***American Indian***. Cf. AMERIND, AMERINDIAN *sbs.*

The Eskimo, in the extreme north, are usually excluded from the term; as are sometimes the Patagonians and Fuegians in the extreme south.

1553 EDEN *Treat. Newe Ind.* (Arb.) 32 They saw certayn Indians gatheringe shel fyshes by the sea bankes. **1607–12** BACON *Ess., Atheism* (Arb.) 334 The Indians of the West have names for theire particuler Godes, though they have noe one name for God. **1632** MASSINGER *City Madam* III. iii, Receive these Indians, lately sent him from Virginia, into your house. **1662** STILLINGFL. *Orig. Sacr.* III. iv. §8 The tradition of the Flood is among the Indians, both in New France, Peru, and other parts. **1736** WESLEY *Let.* xxviii. Wks. XII, They have sent up such traders, both to the Creek and Chicasaw Indians. **1818** JAS. MILL *Brit. India* (1826) I. 397 *note*, The Indians of Peru. **1824** BULLOCK *Six Months Mexico* 78 As we approached Puebla, we met several groups of Indians. **1846** J. HALL *Wilderness & War Path* 1 The life of the American Indian is not so destitute of the interest created by variety of incident, as might be supposed by a casual observation of the habits of this singular race. **1858** LONGF. *M. Standish* I. 50 Now we are ready, I think, for any assault of the Indians. **1879** HARLAN *Eyesight* vi. 78 No one ever heard of a short-sighted Indian. **1926** S. G. INMAN *Probl. in Pan Americanism* ii. 68 The visitor to South America will see nothing more pitiful than the Indians of Peru and Bolivia, descendents of great civilizations now forgotten. **1931** F. J. STIMSON *My United States* xviii. 187 Harvard College was founded in 1636 to teach the Puritans to be preachers and to teach the Indians to be Christians. **1933** *Recent Social Trends in U.S.* (President's Res. Comm. Social Trends) I. xi. 590 Doubts as to the educability of the Indian have been dispelled by the increasing number of those creditably completing college courses and by the measures of mental tests which indicate intelligence of a high rank. **1962** *Canada Month* May 29 North American Indians number more than 500,000: 180,000 in Canada, more than half of whom live in B.C., Saskatchewan, and Ontario, and 350,000 in the U.S. **1963** *Amer. Speech* XXXVIII. 271 The military-like terms might have been introduced by American Indians who went to Haskell after completing their compulsory military service. **1965** J. BALDWIN in *Penguin Dict. Mod. Quots.* (1971) 10/2 It is a great shock at the age of five or six to find that in a world of Gary Coopers you are the Indian. **1965** *Globe & Mail* (Toronto) 26 May 3/4 Those whose names are in a register kept by the federal Indian Affairs Branch are officially Indians; others are not... The Indians have special rights. **1971** D. HEFFRON *Nice Fire & Some Moonpennies* i. 10 Hey ya know, you look like a real Indian with that head-band, you know that? **1971** *Times* 23 Aug. 10/3 In every measurable way Indians are at the bottom of the great American pile. *Ibid.* 10/6 The modern plight of the American Indian is almost entirely traceable to treachery of the white man.

b. ***Red Indian***: one of the aboriginal race of North America; so called from the coppery colour of their skin; also, colloq., *red man, redskin.*

Still used commonly outside N. Amer. but rarely in the U.S.A. and Canada. The *Dict. of Canadianisms* (1967) labels the use 'erroneous' exc. in respect of the extinct Beothuk people in Newfoundland. The usual term in N. Amer. is 'Indian'.

1831 CARLYLE *Sart. Res.* III. vii, A red Indian, hunting by Lake Winnipic. **1887** A. LANG *Bks. & Bookmen* 53 Japanese, Australians, Red Indians, and other distant peoples. **1891** *Trans. R. Soc. Canada* IX. II. 124 The name Red Indians..is the translation of the Micmac name for them, Maquajik, which means redmen or red people. **1897** E. R. YOUNG *On Indian Trail* 11 Romantic missionary work among the red Indians will soon be a thing of the past. **1903** G. B. SHAW *Revolutionist's Handbk.* viii, in *Man & Superman* 212 Museums are set up throughout the country to encourage little children and elderly gentlemen to make collections of corpses preserved in alcohol, and to steal birds' eggs and keep them as the red Indian used to keep scalps. **1922** JOYCE *Ulysses* 760, I hope he hasnt long greasy hair hanging into his eyes or standing up like a red Indian. **1957** *Chronicle-Herald* (Halifax, Nova Scotia) 16 Aug. 29/8 Since then I have always liked the Red Indians. **1964** *Newfoundland Q.* Summer 12/3 The Journal takes us back to pioneer days in Labrador and Newfoundland to a day when the wigwams of the Red Indians could be seen on the shores of Exploits Bay. **1973** *Times* 5 June 8/7 There he is—a voluminously white-clad figure with head-dress..and a face ..which might be that of a Red Indian Chief.

c. One of the 'Indians' in a child's game. Cf. COW-BOY 3 d.

1883 W. W. NEWELL *Games & Songs Amer. Children* i. 26 The players were divided into Indians and hunters, the former uttering their war-cry... The game ended with the extermination of one party or the other. **1941** in R. D. Abrahams *Jump-Rope Rhymes* (1969) 148 One little, two little, three little Indians. Four little, five little, six little Indians, etc. **1969** I. & P. OPIE *Children's Games* v. 181 The attraction of 'Stalking' ('Gang Stalking', 'Shadowing', 'Indians') is that the hunters can become the hunted.

3. Short for *Indian corn.*

1651 *Rec. Dedham* (Mass.) (1892) III. 187 To be paid.. halfe in Indian corne, the Indian when the said Daniell shall demaund. **1664** *Plymouth Col. Rec.* (1855) IV. 72 The barly att four shillings..and the Indian att three shillings the bushell. **1860** BARTLETT *Dict. Amer.* 215 A mixture of the flour of wheat and maize is called *wheat and Indian.*

4. Any one of the languages spoken by American Indians.

1714 S. SEWALL *Diary* 6 Apr. (1879) II. 433 Mr. Mayhew writes a Letter in Indian to Saul. **1857** THOREAU *Maine W.* (1894) 285 Our Indian knew one of them, and fell into conversation with him in Indian. **1894** M. EELLS *Father Eells* 91 A school was also kept in Indian, the lessons being prepared on paper, hung up on the side of the house and read and recited. **1946** T. M. STANWELL-FLETCHER *Driftwood Valley* 114 Be that as it may, I have pronounced and spelled it, just as we do all the various other localities, as it sounds to us in Indian. **1958** *Camsell Arrow* (Edmonton, Alberta) Jan.–Feb. 1 Although [the sisters] are French and the children speak Indian, English is the language of the school.

5. Name of a constellation (*Indus*) lying between Sagittarius and the south pole.

1674 MOXON *Tutor Astron.* I. iii. §10 (ed. 3) 19 Twelve Constellations..posited about the South Pole..2 The Phenix, 3 The Indian, 4 The Peacock. **1860** LOCKYER *Guillemin's Heavens* (ed. 3) 344 The constellation of the Indian.

6. *Comb.*, as ***Indian-like*** adj. and adv.

a **1765** YOUNG *Wks.* (1767) III. 95 (Jod.) 'Behold the Sun!' and, Indianlike, adore. **1851** MAYNE REID *Scalp Hunt.* ii. 16 Their erect, Indian-like carriage in the streets. **1869** T. W. HIGGINSON *Army Life* (1870) 56 An Indian-like knowledge of the country.

7. Short for *Indian tea* (see sense 4 a above).

1748 M. W. MONTAGU *Let.* 17 July (1966) II. 407, I have planted a great deal [of tea] in my Garden, which..has succeeded very well. I cannot say it is as strong as the Indian, but has the advantage of being Fresher and at least unmix'd. **1907** *Yesterday's Shopping* (1969) 1 Tea..[Blend] Congou and Indian. **1933** E. A. ROBERTSON *Ordinary Families* xiii. 278, I ordered fresh tea..and pressed the visitor to make up her mind..whether she preferred Indian or China. **1938** [see CHINA¹ 6]. **1958** J. CANNAN *And be a Villain* i. 39 'Couldn't you find the Earl Grey?'.. Primrose said, 'Indian's better for pulling you together.' **1968** G. BUTLER *Coffin Following* ix. 198 You will take tea? Will you have Indian or China?

Indiana (ɪndɪˈænə). The name of a state in the U.S.A., used esp. *attrib.* to designate objects, etc., from or connected with that state; esp ***Indiana limestone***, an oölitic limestone sometimes known as Bedford limestone.

1858 O. H. SMITH (*title*) Early Indiana trials; and sketches. **1894** *Country Gentlemen's Catal.* 113 Shirts..in our special Indiana Gauze Oxford. **1934** WEBSTER, Indiana limestone. **1947** J. C. RICH *Materials & Methods Sculpture* viii. 219 Indiana limestone can be secured in buff to gray colors and is an attractive, fairly soft, and easily worked stone. **1948** MENCKEN *Amer. Lang.* Suppl. II. 616 An aged Indiana poetaster named John Finley. **1965** *Harper's Bazaar* Feb. 41 Mean black blazer in rubber-proofed Indiana, 7 gns. **1969** R. MAYER *Dict. Art Terms* 193/2 *Indiana limestone*, the limestone most widely used by American sculptors... Bedford Stone is another Indiana limestone.

Indianan: see INDIANIAN.

Indian corn. [INDIAN *a.* 2.] The common name of *Zea Mays*, a North American graminaceous plant, or of the grain produced by it; not known in the wild state, but cultivated by the North American Indians at the time of the discovery of America; an important cereal in the United States and in the warmer parts of the world generally, to which its cultivation has extended. Also called MAIZE, and in U.S. simply CORN. Also *attrib.*

c **1621** W. HILTON *Let.* in Capt. Smith *New Eng. Trials* (Arb.) 261 Better grain cannot be then the Indian corne. **1630** WINTHROP *Let.* in *New Eng.* (1825) I. 379 Though we have not beef and mutton, &c. yet (God be praised)..our Indian corn answers for all. **1642** in *Essex Inst. Hist. Coll.* (1863) V. 219/2 Other poore people shalbe repayed..at the next Indian corne harvest. **1677** W. HUBBARD *Narrative* (1865) II. 56 He propounded it in his Council, that all the West-plantations..should this last Summer be planted with Indian-corn. *a* **1738** W. BYRD *Hist. Dividing Line* (1929) 209 We encampt near one of these Indian Corn Fields, where was excellent Food for our Horses. **1751** J. BARTRAM *Observations Pensilvania to Ontario* 60 This repast consisted of 3 great kettles of Indian corn soop, or thin homony, with dry'd eels and other fish boiled in it. **1778** in *Pennsylvania Mag. Hist. & Biogr.* (1902) XXVI. 32 Went into winter quarters in Newport, in old empty houses..and the food worse,—little bread and that made of rice and Indian corn meal. **1781** S. A. PETERS *Hist. Connecticut* 242 Maize, or

RAFFLES *Java* (1830) I. 108 Indian corn is usually roasted in the ear. **1818** F. HALL *Trav. Canada & U.S.* xxviii. 324 The traveller.. suddenly mounting a little rise, close to a poor cottage with its Indian corn patch.. finds himself opposite to the Capitol of the Federal city. **1856** *Cottage Gardener* 2 Dec. 140/2 Indian corn is bad food for poultry. **1888** W. WHITMAN *November Boughs* 76 On the floor of the big kitchen, toward sundown, would be squatting a circle of twelve or fourteen 'pickaninnies', eating their supper of pudding (Indian corn mush) and milk. **1964** *Cookbk.* (Amer. Heritage) (1967) 163 Indian corn stew.

Indianeer (ɪndɪə'nɪə(r)). *rare.* [f. INDIAN + -EER[1], after *privateer*.] = INDIAMAN.
1846 WORCESTER cites *For. Q. Rev.*

Indianesque (ɪndɪə'nɛsk), *a.* [f. INDIAN *a.* 2.] Of an Indian type.
a **1861** T. WINTHROP *John Brent* (1883) iv. 36 This was the Indianesque Saxon who greeted me. *a* **1861** —— *Canoe & Saddle* (1883) ii. 12 Indianesque, not fully Indian, was her countenance. **1882** J. W. STEELE *Frontier Army Sk.* (1883) 84 In all that is peculiarly Indianesque, she excels her master. **1896** *Month* Jan. 113 Most elaborate and beautiful examples of Indianesque architecture. **1942** *Chicago Tribune* 15 Nov. (Pict. Sect.) 6/2 (*caption*) Indianesque.

Indianess ('ɪndɪənɪs). *nonce-wd.* [f. INDIAN *sb.* + -ESS.] A female Indian; an Indian woman.
1827 G. DARLEY *Sylvia* 89, I might pass for a wild Indianness, and exhibit myself as a pattern of unsophisticated nature.

Indian fig. [INDIAN *a.* 4.]
1. Applied to species of *Opuntia* or Prickly Pear.
1712 Indian fig [see FIG *sb.*[1] 1 c]. **1718** LADY M. W. MONTAGU *Let. to Abbe Conti* 31 July, That plant we call *Indian-fig*.. is an admirable fence, no wild beast being able to pass it. **1797** HOLCROFT tr. *Stolberg's Trav.* (ed. 2) II. lx. 367 The *cactus opuntia*, or Indian fig, grows.. among the rocks. **1830** DISRAELI *Home Lett.* (1885) 54 Surrounded by aloes and Indian figs I could have fancied myself in the Antilles.
2. ***Indian fig-tree.*** **a.** The BANIAN tree.
1594 BLUNDEVIL *Exerc.* v. vii. (1636) 546 The Indian figtree groweth round about Goa.. the fruits are small Figges, and red as blood. *a* **1715** TATE *Cowley* (Mason), The Indian figtree next did much surprise With her strange figure all our deities. **1885** C. J. STONE *Chr. bef. Christ* 93 He perceived a sacred Indian fig-tree.
†**b.** The BANANA. *Obs.*
1613 PURCHAS *Pilgrimage* (1614) 505 The Indian Figgetree: if it may bee called a tree, which is not above a mans height, and within like to a reede.. it hath leaves a fathom long, and three spannes broad.. men beleeve that Adam first transgressed with this fruit.

Indianian (ɪndɪ'ænɪən). Also **Indianan.** [f. INDIANA + -IAN.] A native or inhabitant of Indiana.
1784 T. JEFFERSON *Writings* (1894) III. 401 Should.. the Indianians and Kentuckians take themselves off. **1835** C. F. HOFFMAN *Winter in West* I. 226 The term 'Hooshier',.. has now become a *soubriquet*, that bears nothing invidious with it to the ear even of an Indianian. **1863** W. WHITMAN *Specimen Days* (1882–3) 48 Some unconscious Indianian, or from Ohio or Tennessee. **1877** J. HABBERTON *Jericho Road* x. 97 Small parties of discharged Illinoisans and Indianians had frequently passed through. **1900** *Congress. Rec.* 5 Feb. 1508/2 The nation.. mourns the death of this distinguished soldier, and Indianians feel it as a personal loss. **1944** *Amer. N. & Q.* Mar. 188 Its advertisements.. were answered by a number of Indianans. **1947** *Amer. Speech* XXII. 250 Indianan is now used officially in the State. **1948** MENCKEN *Amer. Lang.* (Suppl.) II. 620 *Hoosier*, at the start, did not signify an Indianan particularly, but any rough fellow of what was then the wild West.

Indian ink. Also **India ink.** A black pigment made in China and Japan, sold in sticks; understood to consist of lampblack made into a paste with a solution of gum and dried. More accurately called *China ink* (CHINA 2 b).
1665 PEPYS *Diary* 5 Nov., Mr. Evelyn, who.. showed me most excellent painting in little, in distemper, Indian incke, water colours. **1667** *Ibid.* 26 Apr., A young man was working in Indian inke the great picture of the King and Queen. **1762–71** H. WALPOLE *Vertue's Anecd. Paint.* (1786) III. 32 His designs.. are in Indian ink, heightened with white. **1848** THACKERAY *Van. Fair* xxxvii, A drawing of the Porter's Lodge at Queen's Crawley, done.. in India ink. **1887** A. LANG *Bks. & Bookmen* 88 It seemed to be sepia, sometimes mixed with a little Indian ink.

Indianism ('ɪndɪənɪz(ə)m). [-ISM.] Action or policy devoted to the interests of Indians; advocacy of (North American) Indians.
1651 W. FRENCH in *Strength out of Weakness* (1652) 37 All the while I went on in Indianisme I was going from God. **1871** *Rep. Indian Affairs* (1872) 181 We were in our original Indianism. **1887** W. TIREBUCK in Longfellow *Hyperion, Kavanagh and Trouvères* Introd. p. xiii, Those who stood between the culture of *Hyperion* and *Kavanagh*, and the wild Indianism of Aimard and Cooper. **1923** *Spectator* 29 Sept. 422/1 In India it works out in unrest.. an exaggerated sense of Indianism—the nationalistic idea. **1950** *Caribbean Q.* II. III. 14 It is in the Antilles, in Cuba and Santo Domingo that one finds the most abundant, and some of the best manifestations of literary Indianism. **1969** *Indo-Asian Culture* Oct. 25 It was after the coming of the Buddha that Indianism travelled fast.

Indianist ('ɪndɪənɪst). [-IST.] **1.** One versed in the languages, history, or customs of India.
1851 F. HALL in *Benares Mag.* V. 22 Whose merits the indolence or indifference of Indianists has.. left uncanvassed. **1869** FARRAR *Fam. Speech* i. (1873) 9 The problems remained unsolved, because the sinologues had known no Sanskrit, and the Indianists had known no Chinese. **1894** *Nation* (N.Y.) 14 June 443/2 The author [W. D. Whitney] was one of the strictest Indianists rather than one of the professed comparative grammarians.
2. *attrib.* or as *adj.* Of or pertaining to American Indians.
1950 *Caribbean Q.* II. III. 14 Perhaps the finest *Indianist* writing was produced in Brazil by Goncalves Dias and José de Alencar. **1960** *Guardian* 22 Nov. 9/6 The new generation of [Mexican] artists and architects were obsessed and inspired by.. their own Indianist past.

indianite ('ɪndɪənaɪt). [-ITE.]
1. *Min.* A variety of ANORTHITE found in India, where it forms the matrix of corundum.
1814 T. ALLAN *Min. Nomen.* 18 (Chester). **1873** *Proc. Amer. Phil. Soc.* XIII. 375 A white, grayish and reddish variety of anorthite, called indianite.
2. Name given to a solution of caoutchouc or indian-rubber. (Cf. *vulcanite*.)
1870 *Eng. Mech.* 11 Mar. 625/3 A solution of caoutchouc (indianite).

Indianization (,ɪndɪənaɪ'zeɪʃən). [f. INDIANIZE *v.* 2 + -ATION.] The process of making Indian in character or composition; *spec.* the replacement of Europeans or other foreigners by native-born Indians in positions of authority.
1918 *Pall Mall Gaz.* 29 June 5/2, I do not expect as large an Indianisation of the central Cabinet as of the provincial Cabinets. **1922** *Q. Rev.* July 142 The more rapid Indianisation of the public services. **1924** J. F. BRYANT (*title*) Gandhi and the Indianisation of the Empire. **1928** *Manch. Guardian Weekly* 29 June 513/1 The Indianisation of the Indian army. **1930** *Times Educ. Suppl.* 1 Mar. 92/4 Quicken the process of 'Indianization' by recruiting the superior services.. in India. **1930** *Economist* 14 June 1322/1 The rapid progress of Indianisation in the 'transferred' fields. **1969** *Eve's Weekly* (Bombay) 20 Dec. 51/1 The Indianisation of the Roman Catholic Church has come to stay in India. **1973** *Black Panther* 5 May 6/1 (*heading*) 'Indianization' at Wounded Knee.

Indianize ('ɪndɪənaɪz), *v.* [-IZE.]
†**1.** *intr.* To act like an Indian; to play the Indian. *Obs.*
1702 C. MATHER *Magn. Chr.* VI. v. (1852) 400 We have shamefully Indianized in all those abominable things.
2. *trans.* To make Indian in character, habits, or appearance. Chiefly in *pa. pple.* So **'Indianized** *ppl. a.*
1702 C. MATHER *Magnalia Christi Americana* VII. 68/2 On March 18. the French with Indians, being half one, half t'other, half Indianized French, and half Frenchified Indians.. fell suddenly upon Salmon Falls. **1782** 'J. H. ST. JOHN DE CRÈVECŒUR' *Lett. from Amer. Farmer* xii. 293 Many an anxious parent.. went to the Indian villages where.. their children had been carried in captivity... They found them so perfectly Indianised, that many knew them no longer. **1829** *Bengalee* 408 Turning from my Indianised friend. **1837** *Lett. fr. Madras* (1843) 117 From having been completely heated through in the summer, I am now pretty well Indianized. **1879** in *S. Sewall's Diary* II. 375 *note*, Competent authorities tell us that.. on this continent, more than one hundred of the whites have been 'Indianized' to each single Indian who has been civilized. **1882** *Standard* No. 17,972. 5 The polite mapmakers have done their best to Indianise the worst of them [place-names given by settlers]. **1924** E. M. FORSTER *Passage to India* xxiv. 225 The invocation of Mrs. Moore continued... The syllables.. became Indianized into Esmiss Esmoor. **1935** *Times* 19 June 7/4 If they really meant to Indianize the Army, did they mean to do it because they thought the Indian Army would be more efficient when it had got rid of British officers, or because they thought it would please the Indian sepoy? **1936** *Discovery* Nov. 337/1 The capital of a great Indianised empire extending over the Malay Peninsula and the islands of Java and Sumatra from the 8th to the 12th century A.D. **1963** *Times* 2 May 15/2 The house party, so to speak, includes an English doctor, an Austrian musician who has become Indianized, and an American sociologist and his wife. **1969** *Eve's Weekly* (Bombay) 20 Dec. 51/4 Their Indianised service is generally well-attended, and very little opposition has been met with.

Indianly, *adv. nonce-wd.* [f. INDIAN *a.* + -LY[2].] In Indian fashion; like an Indian. (In quot. with allusion to tobacco-smoking.)
1599 H. BUTTES *Dyets drie Dinner* P iv, On English foote: wanton Italianly: Go Frenchly: Duchly drink: breath Indianly.

Indianness ('ɪndɪənnɪs). [f. INDIAN *a.* + -NESS.] The quality or state of being Indian, or of displaying Indian characteristics.
1934 A. HUXLEY *Beyond Mexique Bay* 192 He had had.. enough.. education to make him aware of his own Indianness. **1967** *Evening Standard* 20 Sept. 10/1 The Indianness of our summer was largely, I think, the creation of the flower children. **1969** *Guardian* 5 Mar. 7/1 She exploits her Indian-ness where she has met most disapproval. **1970** *New Yorker* 18 Apr. 103 After mastering the meaning of Negritude and *machismo* they would have to grapple with the meaning of Indianness. **1971** *Illustr. Weekly India* 11 Apr. 6/2 That non-Hindu Indians abroad tend to shake off their Indianness.

Indianologist (ɪndɪə'nɒlədʒɪst). [f. INDIAN *sb.* 2.] A student of, or authority on, the American Indian.
1894 *Nation* (N.Y.) 31 May 417/3 His ears, in the view of Indianologists, were a sure mark of aboriginal origin. **1947** *Time* 3 Mar. 37/1 The R.D.C. preferred the route that followed the old telegraph line strung diagonally across the great Brazilian plateau by General Candido Nariano Rondon, a famed Indianologist.

Indian rubber: see INDIA-RUBBER.

Indian summer. [INDIAN *a.* 2.]
a. A period of calm, dry, mild weather, with hazy atmosphere, occurring in the late autumn in the Northern United States. Also *transf.* in other countries.
(The name is generally attributed to the fact that the region in which the meteorological conditions in question were originally noticed was still occupied by the Indians; but other more specific explanations have been essayed. In its origin it appears to have had nothing to do with the glowing autumnal tints of the foliage, with which it is sometimes associated. The actual time of its occurrence and the character of the weather appear also to vary for different regions: see the quots.)
1778 'J. H. ST. JOHN DE CRÈVECŒUR' *Sk. 18th-Cent. Amer.* (1925) 41 It [*sc.* snow] is often preceded by a short interval of smoke and mildness, called the Indian Summer. **1794** E. DENNY *Milit. Jrnl.* (1859) 198, Oct. 13th—Pleasant weather. The Indian summer here [near Presqu' Isle]. Frosty nights. **1804** C. B. BROWN tr. *Volney's View Soil U.S.* 210 A series of fine days are expected near November, which is called the Indian summer [une série de beaux jours, appelés l'été sauvage (*Indian summer*)]. **1812** J. FREEMAN *Serm.* viii. 277–8 *note*, Two or three weeks of fair weather, in which the air is perfectly transparent, and the clouds, which float in a sky of the purest azure, are adorned with brilliant colours... This charming season is called the Indian Summer, a name which is derived from the natives, who believe that it is caused by a wind, which comes immediately from the court of their great and benevolent God Cautantowwit, or the south-western God. **1817** J. BRADBURY *Trav. Amer.* 259 About the beginning or middle of October the Indian summer commences, and is immediately known by the change which takes place in the atmosphere, as it becomes hazy, or what they term smoky. **1824** DODDRIDGE *Notes on Ind. Wars W. Virginia* 266 The smokey time commenced and lasted for a considerable number of days. This was the Indian summer, because it afforded the Indians another opportunity of visiting the settlements with their destructive warfare. **1837** LONGF. *Drift-Wood* Prose Wks. 1886 I. 324 There is.. no long and lingering autumn, pompous with many-coloured leaves and the glow of Indian summers. **1860** O. W. HOLMES *Elsie V.* xiii. (1891) 186 The real forest is hardly still except in the Indian summer. **1878** G. MEREDITH *Let.* 9 Oct. (1970) II. 563 Perhaps you and Mrs. Carr will do us the honour to come and see the Indian summer here. **1887** J. C. MORISON *Service of Man* (1889) 128 The soft autumnal calm, and purple tints as of an Indian summer. **1906** W. MARRIOTT *Hints to Meteorol. Observers* (ed. 6) 66/2 *Indian Summer*, fine weather for a few days about September 30, in North America. **1939** [see GUPTA *a.* and *sb.*]. **1958** HAYWARD & HARARI tr. *Pasternak's Dr. Zhivago* I. iv. 110 The end of a hot golden autumn had turned into an Indian summer. **1960** J. RAE *Custard Boys* I. vi. 69 Meanwhile the Indian summer continued warm and dusty on the trodden earth of the farmyard. **1962** *Sunday Times* 16 Sept. 1/3 An Indian summer in the West Country brought peak holiday traffic jams in Devon yesterday.
fig. **1830** DE QUINCEY *Bentley* Wks. VI. 180 An Indian summer crept stealthily over his closing days. **1899** AUSTIN *Indian Summer*, Long may the Indian Summer of your days Yet linger in the Land you love so well! **1918** GALSWORTHY in *Five Tales* (*title*) The Indian summer of a Forsyte. **1930** V. SACKVILLE-WEST *Edwardians* iii. 100 Meanwhile she was quite content that Sebastian should become tanned in the rays of Sylvia's Indian summer. **1962** N. DEL MAR *Richard Strauss* I. ix. 418 The works of his Indian Summer when, in the last five years of his life, inspiration came to him once more.
b. *attrib.* and *Comb.*
1848 LOWELL (*title*) An Indian-Summer Reverie. **1856** MRS. STOWE *Dred* II. 221 It is a calm, still, Indian summer afternoon. **1883** E. P. ROE in *Harper's Mag.* Dec. 46/1 A perpetual Indian-summer haze of kindliness. **1898** BOLDREWOOD *Rom. Canvass Town* 71 Cool nights, bracing mornings and mild Indian-summer-like days. **1927** M. DE LA ROCHE *Jalna* xvii. 190 The drowsy Indian-summer heat still continued, but the air had become heavier. **1961** M. BEADLE *These Ruins are Inhabited* (1963) vii. 97 Homeward bound in a lackadaisical Indian-summer mood.
Hence **Indian-'summerish** *a. nonce-wd.*
1852 THOREAU *Autumn* (1894) 79 It is a warm, Indian-summerish afternoon.

India paper.
1. A soft absorbent paper of creamy-yellow or pale buff colour, imported from China where it is made, and used for the 'proofs' or first and finest impressions of engravings; for the proofs of copperplate or steel engravings, it is mounted upon ordinary stout paper. The name is sometimes given loosely to other papers of Oriental manufacture, and to European or American imitations. Hence ***India paper proofs*** (also *India proofs*).
The kind of paper referred to in quot. 1768 is uncertain: cf. an earlier letter to Rev. W. Mason of 7th June 1760.
[**1750** WALPOLE *Lett.* (1846) II. 351 Mrs. Frere.. screamed about Indian paper.] **1768** GRAY *Let. to Rev. Norton Nicholls* 3 Feb., Are your India-paper, your Axminster carpets, your sofas and pechés mortels in great forwardness? **1786** *Catal. Print Sale by Greenwood* ('Gulston' Sale) 95, No. 16. Eight illustrious heads, by Houbraken, on India paper, prior to the reign of Queen Elizabeth. *Ibid.* 148, No. 103. 'The Battle of La Hogue', a most beautiful proof on India paper, by Woollett, after West. *Ibid.* 152, No. 83. A remarkable fine impression of the Small Copenal, on India paper. **1817** *Sotheby's Catal. Sale Prints* Feb., No. 640 India paper, proofs. *Ibid.* No. 750 Proof Etchings on India paper. **1842** FRANCIS *Dict. Arts*, etc. s.v. *Paper*, India paper.. comes from China, and is used as a superior article for the same purpose as plate paper. **1864** *Lowndes' Bibl. Man.* 401/2 Cervantes. Don Quixote..

1818 With plates on India paper. *Ibid.* 2829/1 The engravings were originally published separately, India proofs, at £10 10*s.*

2. (*Oxford India paper.*) A very thin tough opaque printing-paper made by the Oxford University Press in imitation of paper from the East, used chiefly for Bibles and Prayer-books. (See *The Periodical* 17 Dec. 1896.)

1875 *Spectator* 28 Aug., India paper of extreme toughness. **1875** *Athenæum* 4 Sept., Tough India paper of exceeding thinness and opacity. **1875** *Guardian* 15 Sept. 1184 We have received from Mr. Henry Frowde, of the Oxford University Press Warehouse, a copy of the Smallest Bible ever produced..printed on tough India paper, of extreme thinness, and wonderfully clear for the size. **1896** *Periodical* 17 Dec., The incidents which led up to the manufacture of the Oxford India Paper.

ˌindia-ˈrubber, india rubber. Also 8–9 Indian rubber.

1. The coagulated juice of certain trees and plants of South America, Africa, the East Indies, etc., which forms a highly elastic and flexible substance, used for rubbing out black lead pencil marks, and for many purposes in the arts and manufactures; also called CAOUTCHOUC, q.v. for earlier notices. In later use shortened to *rubber*.

[**1788–9** HOWARD *New Royal Encycl.*, *Caoutchouc*, in natural history..a very elastic resin..Very useful for erasing the strokes of black lead pencils, and is popularly called rubber, and lead-eater.] **1799** HOOPER *Med. Dict.* s.v., The substance known by the names Indian rubber, Elastic gum, Cayenne resin, Cautchuc..is prepared from the juice of the *Siphonia elastica.* **1802** HENRY in *Phil. Trans.* XCIII. 31 It is attached to the copper pipe, by a tube of Indian rubber. **1812** J. SMYTH *Pract. of Customs* (1821) 113 India Rubber is a substance which oozes out under the form of a vegetable milk, from incisions made in the Syringe Tree of Cayenne. **1817** RAFFLES *Java* (1830) I. 48 The elastic gum, commonly called Indian-rubber. **1837** DICKENS *Pickw.* xv, The unwonted lines..in Mr. Pickwick's clear and open brow, gradually melted away..like the marks of a black-lead pencil beneath the softening influence of India rubber. **1838** T. THOMSON *Chem. Org. Bodies* 694 *Caoutchouc*..is very much used in rubbing out the marks made upon paper by a black-lead pencil; and therefore in this country it is often called *Indian-rubber.* **1861** DU CHAILLU *Equat. Afr.* x. 122 It is a pleasant sight to see a party of natives setting out to gather India-rubber. **1885** TAIT *Properties Matter* v. §99 The rapid passage of gases through unglazed pottery, sheet indiarubber, etc., shows the porosity of these bodies.

2. An overshoe made of india-rubber. *U.S. colloq.* In later use commonly *rubber*.

1840 LONGF. in *Life.* (1891) I. 357 Feet pinched with India-rubbers. **1852** EMILY DICKINSON *Lett.* (1894) I. 141 I'll take my india-rubbers In case the wind should blow.

3. = RUBBER *sb.*[1] 11.

1794 EARL HOWE *Let. to Capt. Sir R. Curtis* 20 Feb. (MS. in Henry E. Huntington Library) f. 1ᵛ, If India Rubbers means pieces of the elastic Gum for rubbing out pencil lines &c., I have enough of that. **1857** M. J. HOLMES *Meadow-Brook* v, Taking my India-rubber, I erased it [*sc.* the writing]. **1910** 'I. HAY' in *Granta* 11 June, He concluded by imploring me as a personal favour to purchase an india-rubber and erase the lot. **1939–40** *Army & Navy Stores Catal.* 376/2 Artists' india-rubber... Kneaded rubber for Pastel, Chalk and Pencil.

4. a. *attrib.* Belonging or relating to india-rubber; made of india-rubber, as ***india-rubber ball, band, bottle, ring, tube***, etc.; yielding india-rubber, as ***india-rubber plant, tree, vine***; devoted to the manufacture of india-rubber, as ***india-rubber works***.

1833 LONGF. *Outre-Mer* Prose Wks. 1886 I. 237 The pale invalid may go about without his umbrella, or his India-rubber walk-in-the-waters. **1837** DICKENS *Pickw.* xxxv, There was one young gentleman in an India-rubber cloak. *Ibid.* xxxvi, Mr. Dowler bounced off the bed as abruptly as an India-rubber ball. [**1852** MRS. GASKELL *Cranford* (1853) v. 82 Indian-rubber rings, which are a sort of deification of string.] **1858** *Cottage Gardener* 14 Dec. 170/2 The shoots of a fine India-rubber plant. **1885** TAIT *Properties Matter* xi. §224 The pulling out of an india-rubber band is almost entirely due to change of form. **1887** MOLONEY *Forestry W. Afr.* 87 The destruction of enormous tracts of india-rubber forest. **1897** *Allbutt's Syst. Med.* II. 948 His experience was gained in the india-rubber works in Paris. *Ibid.* III. 563 When the whole of the wall of the stomach is affected, it forms what is known as the india-rubber bottle stomach. **1939–40** *Army & Navy Stores Catal.* 812/3 Indiarubber rings. For use on hockey sticks.

b. *transf.* Resembling india-rubber; highly elastic and flexible (also *fig.*).

1894 *Daily News* 1 Aug. 5/2 Mr. Morton coming up quite fresh with his indiarubber amendment applicable to the third in the list of Tramway Bills. **1900** *Daily News* 23 July 3/3 (*heading*) An indiarubber enemy. **1929** E. WALLACE (*title*) The india-rubber men. **1929** F. BOWEN *Sea Slang* 72 *India rubber man*, the physical training instructor. **1949** 'M. INNES' *Journeying Boy* vii. 78 Mr. Wambus..is known as the Great Elasto, the India-rubber Man.

5. *Comb.*, as ***india-rubber-bodied, india-rubber-like, india-rubber-tyred*** adjs.

1882 *Daily News* 22 May 2/2 The 'india-rubber-bodied' style of entertainment, recently popularised by the Vokes' and the Girards. **1888** *Pall Mall G.* 22 Aug. 1/2 To cultivate a certain indiarubber-like forbearance and a cool temper. **1896** *Daily News* 23 May 6/3 The whole apparatus..is wheeled to the bedside on an indiarubber tyred trolly.

Hence **ˌindia-ˈrubbered** *ppl. a.*, treated with india-rubber, coated with a solution of india-rubber: **ˌindia-ˈrubbery** *a.*, resembling or having the consistence of india-rubber.

1890 ABNEY *Treat. Photogr.* (ed. 6) 176 An image in pigmented gelatine remains on the india-rubbered paper. **1891** MISS DOWIE *Girl in Karp.* iii. 28 Sheep's cheese is.. elastic or indiarubbery in texture. **1896** HOWELLS *Impressions & Exp.* 36 The rollers..were of an india-rubbery elasticity and consistency.

†**ˈIndiary,** *a. Obs. rare.* [f. INDI-A + -ARY, after *lunary*, etc.] Relating to India, Indian.

1646 SIR T. BROWNE *Pseud. Ep.* I. viii. 30 He wrote the History of Persia, and many narrations of India..his testimony is acceptable in his Indiary relations.

Indic (ˈɪndɪk), *a.*[1] [ad. L. *Indic-us*, a. Gr. Ἰνδικός INDIAN.] Of or belonging to India; Indian, Hindu. Also, designating the Indian branch of the Indo-Iranian languages, including the dead languages Sanskrit, Prakrit, and Pali and the living languages Hindi, Bengali, Marathi, etc.

1877 RAWLINSON *Orig. Nations* vi. (1883) 24 Indic civilization is supposed to have commenced about the same time with Iranic. **1877** A. H. KEANE tr *Hovelacque's Sci. of Lang.* 320 Hindui..Aryan-Indic. **1893** in *Funk's Stand. Dict.* **1909** *Indogerman. Forsch.* XXV. 177 Although the rule is not without exception even in the older Indic and Hellenic documents, it nevertheless holds true in general for the languages claimed. **1911** L. BLOOMFIELD in C. F. Hockett *Leonard Bloomfield Anthol.* (1970) 7 The Indic and the Iranian languages differ greatly in their treatment of the IE. stopped consonants. **1935** A. TOYNBEE *Study of Hist.* (ed. 2) I. 87 And so we have identified the society 'apparented' to the Hindu Society. Let us call it 'Indic'. **1937** *Discovery* Sept. 286 The American School of Indic and Iranian Studies. **1973** *Amer. N. & Q.* 83/1 Eliot began Ph.D. studies at Harvard, majoring jointly in the Indic and Philosophy Departments.

ˈindic, *a.*[2] *Chem.* [f. IND-IN + -IC.] Of indin; in ***indic*** (formerly *indinic*) ***acid***, the hypothetical acid $C_{16}H_{11}N_2O_3$, of which the potassium salt is ***indin-potassium*** or potassium indate.

[**1845** *Penny Cycl.* Suppl. I. 345/2 *Indinic Acid* is formed in combination with potash, yielding black crystals..the indinate of potash is readily decomposed by water..Indinic acid is probably similar in composition to isatic acid.] **1889** ROSCOE & SCHORLEMMER *Chem.* III. v, When Indin ($C_{16}H_{10}N_2O_2$) is treated with concentrated alcoholic potash, it yields the potassium salt of indic acid, $C_{16}H_{11}N_2O_3K$, which forms small black crystals, which are decomposed by water with formation of the original indin. **1892** MORLEY & MUIR *Dict. Chem.* III. s.v. *Indin*, A solution in concentrated alcoholic potash deposits black crystals..probably potassium indate $C_{16}H_{10}KN_2O_3$.

†**ˈindical,** *a. Obs. rare*[−1]. [f. L. *indic-em* INDEX + -AL[1].] Pertaining to an index or indexes.

a **1661** FULLER *Worthies, Norfolk* II. (1662) 256 There is a lazy kind of learning which is onely Indical, when scholars ..nibble but at the tables..neglecting the body of the book.

indican (ˈɪndɪkən). *Chem.* [Named by Schunck 1855, from INDIC-UM + -AN I. 2: see ALLOXAN.] The natural glucoside ($C_{26}H_{31}NO_{17}$) formed in plants which yield indigo, by the decomposition of which indigo-blue is produced; it forms a light-brown syrup, of bitter taste, and slightly acid reaction. **b.** ***indican of urine***: an incorrect name for the potassium salt of indoxyl sulphuric acid, a normal constituent of the urine of animals. Also called *uroxanthin*.

1859 T. A. CARTER in *Edin. Med. Jrnl.* Aug. 119 (*title*) On Indican in the Blood and Urine. *Ibid.* 121 On treating indican with the mineral acid, he [Schunck] found that it was resolved into blue indigo, 'indirubine', 'indifuscine', and a peculiar kind of sugar. **1866** ODLING *Anim. Chem.* 122 Human urine..contains habitually an indigo-yielding substance known as indican, which is probably a glucoside of white or hydrogenised indigo. **1874** SCHORLEMMER *Organ. Chem.* 462. **1878** FOSTER *Phys.* (1884) 768 The indican obtained from urine is not a glucoside. **1889** MORLEY & MUIR *Dict. Chem.* II. 759/2 Indican by heating with dilute acids is resolved into indigo and indiglucin (a sugar). Simultaneously are formed *indirubin* $C_{16}H_{10}N_2O_2$, *indiretin* $C_{18}H_{17}NO_5$ (dark-brown resin, sol. alcohol), *indifulvin* (reddish-yellow resin, insol. alk.), *indihumin* $C_{10}H_9NO_3$ (brown powder, insol. water and alcohol, sol. alk.), *indifuscin* $C_{24}H_{20}N_2O_9$ (analogous to indihumin).

Hence **indicanine** (ˈɪndɪkənaɪn), *Chem.*: see quot.; **indicaˈnuria**, *Path.* presence of indican in excess in the urine.

1865–72 WATTS *Dict. Chem.* III. 248 *Indicanin*, $C_{20}H_{23}NO_{12}$..is produced, together with indiglucin, by the action of aqueous alkalis..on indican. Indicanin is a yellow or brown bitter syrup, soluble in water, alcohol, and ether. **1889** MORLEY & MUIR *Dict. Chem.* II. 759/2 Indicanine. **1897** *Allbutt's Syst. Med.* IV. 200 We occasionally meet with indicanuria.

indicant (ˈɪndɪkənt), *a.* and *sb.* [ad. L. *indicānt-em*. pres. pple. of *indicāre* to INDICATE.]

A. *adj.* That indicates; indicative. ***indicant days***: see quot. 1706.

1607 *Schol. Disc. agst. Antichr.* I. ii. 108 There are words meerely indicant which shew, and signes figuratiue which signifie. **1633** AMES *Agst. Cerem.* II. 340 It is a naturall indicant signe of peace. **1706** PHILLIPS, *Indicant Days* (among Physicians), those Days which signifie that a Crisis or Change in a Disease, will happen on such a Day. **1886** in *Syd. Soc. Lex.*

B. *sb.* (*Med.*) That which indicates the remedy or treatment suitable (cf. INDICATION 1 b).

1623 HART *Arraignm. Ur.* iv. 103 Contraindication is that which primarily and principally doth hinder that which was suggested by the indicant. **1701** GREW *Cosm. Sacra* 66 (L.) A physician..considers first the nature, causes, and symptoms of the disease, as the prime indicants of what he is to do.

Hence †**ˈindicantly** *adv. Obs.*, by indication.

1607 *Schol. Disc. agst. Antichr.* I. ii. 108 A booke teacheth indicantly, not Sacramentally.

†**ˈindicate,** *ppl. a. Obs.* [ad. L. *indicāt-us*, pa. pple. of *indicāre*: see next.] Indicated.

1541 R. COPLAND *Galyen's Terap.* 2 C ij b, I neuer founde curation that was indicate and shewed of the olde vlceres, nor of new.

indicate (ˈɪndɪkeɪt), *v.* [ad. L. *indicāt-*, ppl. stem of *indicāre* to point out, show, mention, etc.; f. *in-* (IN-[2]) + *dicāre* to make known: cf. INDEX.]

1. *trans.* To point out, point to, make known, show (more or less distinctly). In *Med.*, To point out as a remedy or course of treatment. *pass.* Of a course of action, treatment, etc.: to be pointed out or suggested as desirable or necessary. Also *transf.*

1651 WITTIE *Primrose's Pop. Err.* IV. viii. 237 It is an Axiome of Physicians; One thing is indicated or betokened by one... Whatsoever indicates any thing, doth indicate either the conservation or removeall of it selfe. **1661** GLANVILL *Van. Dogm.* v. 42 To suppose a Watch..by the blind bits of Chance..to indicate the hour, day of the Moneth, Tides, age of the Moon, and the like..were the more pardonable absurdity. **1767** GOOCH *Treat. Wounds* I. 381 The patient must submit to a spare, liquid diet, have his body kept open, and lose blood occasionally, as fever, inflammation, &c. shall indicate. *c* **1780** COWPER *Jackdaw* ii, Above the steeple shines a plate, That turns and turns, to indicate From what point blows the weather. **1880** MACCORMAC *Antisept. Surg.* 30 In every case of strangulated hernia..such an operation as this would seem to be indicated. **1880** GEIKIE *Phys. Geog.* ii. §9. 57 Under ordinary circumstances the thermometer indicates 212° as the temperature at which water boils. **1885** *Daily News* 21 Dec. 3/8 The dotted lines indicate the extreme variations. **1886** *Brit. Med. Jrnl.* 17 Apr. 750/1 Recourse to this method is more particularly indicated when the teeth to be replaced are front teeth. **1907** *Lancet* 25 May 1462/1 Considering the great analogy which is presented between syphilis and leprosy..it seemed indicated to try on this patient the treatment by large doses of atoxyl. **1919** WODEHOUSE *Damsel in Distress* xv. 184 Strategy, rather than force, seemed to the curate to be indicated. **1922** W. R. INGE *Lay Thoughts* (1926) 235 Whenever a patient consults a doctor, the latter should always order some drug, even if drugs are not really indicated. **1946** M. PEAKE *Titus Groan* 353 My dear ladies, ..I feel that some hot coffee is indicated, but what do *you* feel? **1971** *Nature* 31 Dec. 557/1 Further investigations of the directions of propagation and the presence of pacemaker function are certainly indicated. **1972** *Sci. Amer.* May 80/2 Periodic measurement of arterial and central venous pressure, blood acidity and dissolved gases may be indicated in the management of patients with heart, kidney, lung or metabolic disorders.

2. a. To point to or towards the presence, existence, or reality of; to be a sign or symptom of, to betoken. Also with obj. clause, expressing a fact.

1706 PHILLIPS, *To Indicate*, to shew or discover; as This high Colour indicates some Inflammation. **1774** BURKE *Corr.* (1844) I. 517 The unusual mode of protesting on the address indicated a vigorous campaign. **1798** FERRIAR *Illustr. Sterne* iv. 102 Large noses..were considered as indicating prudence. **1814** SCOTT *Wav.* xxxi, He..observed symptoms, which indicated a disposition in the Highlanders to take arms. **1833** L. RITCHIE *Wand. by Loire* 186 The masts of some vessels..indicate the proximity of the river. **1860** TYNDALL *Glac.* I. xxvii. 197 There was..no voice of joy to indicate that it was the pleasant Christmas time.

†**b.** *intr.* To point. *Obs. rare.*

1675 R. BURTHOGGE *Causa Dei* 305 A Symbol not obscurely indicating unto Jesus Christ.

3. *trans.* Of persons: To point out, direct attention to. Less usually, in literal sense, To point to with the hand or by gesture.

1808 BENTHAM *Sc. Reform* 69 So, in regard to written or real evidence, A has not the document sought: but he indicates B, who is supposed to have it. **1829** LYTTON *Devereux* I. ii, An admirable plan, but liable to some little exceptions which Sir William will allow me to indicate. **1852** HAWTHORNE *Blithedale Rom.* xi, The course you indicate would certainly be the proper one. **1853** C. BRONTE *Villette* viii, 'Will you go backward or forward?' she said, indicating with her hand, first the small door of the dwelling-house [etc.]. **1885** L. CARROLL *Tangled T.* ii. 9 She drew up the blind, and indicated the back garden.

4. To state or express, *esp.* to express briefly, lightly, or without detail or development; to give an indication of.

1751 HARRIS *Hermes* I. viii. Wks. (1841) 158 If we simply declare or indicate something to be or not to be..this constitutes that mode called the declarative or indicative. **1846** GROTE *Greece* (1869) I. 237 The opinion long ago expressed by Heyne, and even indicated by Burmann. **1846** ELLIS *Elgin Marb.* II. 1 The waves are indicated on the plinth. **1855** BAIN *Senses & Int.* II. i. §6 (1864) 84 My last argument is one that can only be indicated here; the full illustration belongs to a more advanced stage of the exposition.

Hence **ˈindicated, ˈindicating** *ppl. adjs.* *indicated* (*horse-*) *power*, the working power of a steam-engine, shown by the INDICATOR; so ***indicated duty***.

1753 N. TORRIANO *Gangr. Sore Throat* 30 A more indicating Pulse. **1855** MAYNE *Expos. Lex.*, *Indicating Days*, the same as Critical days. **1875** URE *Dict. Arts* II. 812 Nominal horse-power is a conventional mode of describing the dimensions of a steam-engine..and bears no fixed relation to indicated or to effective horse-power. *Ibid.*, The indicated power of different engines usually exceeds the nominal power [etc.]. **1885** *Pall Mall G.* 8 May 8/1 The

demarcation . . of the line of frontier . . as well as the placing of the indicating posts, will be reserved for Commissioners, which the two Governments will furnish with powers for this purpose.

indication (ɪndɪˈkeɪʃən). [a. F. *indication* (Paré, 16th c.), ad. L. *indicātiōn-em* (found only in the sense of 'valuation'), n. of action from *indicāre* to INDICATE.]

1. a. The action of indicating, pointing out, or making known; that in which this is embodied; a hint, suggestion, or piece of information from which more may be inferred.

1626 BACON *Sylva* §479–80 But these are Idle and Ignorant Conceits; And forsake the true Indication of the Causes. **1677** HALE *Prim. Orig. Man.* IV. vi. 340 The configurations and indications of the various Phases of the Moon . . and divers other curious indications of Celestial Motions. **1793** BURKE *Corr.* (1844) IV. 154 His skill consists in . . following the indications given by nature, times, and circumstances. **1866** GEO. ELIOT *F. Holt* xv. (ed. 2) II. 6 The case was nothing short of a heavenly indication. **1885** TAIT *Properties Matter* i. 1 The indications of the senses are always imperfect, and often misleading.

b. *spec.* in *Med.* A suggestion or direction as to the treatment of a disease, derived from the symptoms observed. (App. the earliest use in Eng.)

1541 COPLAND *Galyen's Terap.* 2 B iv b, It is euydent yᵗ none indication is taken of the cause that hath excited and made the vlcere. *Ibid.* 2 C ij b, What is the indicacyon curatyfe taken of olde Sores? **1651** WITTIE *Primrose's Pop. Err.* 43 The use of indications, without which no remedy can be applyed. **1793** BEDDOES *Calculus* 261 It is probable that the true indication of cure in typhus is to restore the oxygene. **1875** H. C. WOOD *Therap.* (1879) 19 The term or expression *indication* for a given remedy, being in constant use, ought to be distinctly understood; by it is meant the pointings of nature, or, in other words, the evident needs of the system.

c. The degree of some physical state, as pressure, temperature, etc., indicated by an instrument, as a barometer, anemometer, thermometer, etc.; the reading of a graduated instrument.

a **1734** NORTH *Lives* (1826) II. 197 Settling the grand affair of the mercurial barometer, and its indications. **1860** TYNDALL *Glac.* II. iii. 245 The effect . . produced was very large as measured by the indications of the instrument. **1871** B. STEWART *Heat* (ed. 2) §82 In comparing an English and a French barometer it is therefore necessary to reduce the indications of each to 32° Fahr.

2. a. A sign, token, or symptom; an expression by sign or token.

1660 H. MORE *Myst. Godl.* V. xv. 175 There are other indications of the beginning of a new Systeme of Prophecies. **1712** STEELE *Spect.* No. 350 ¶2 Modesty is the certain Indication of a great Spirit, and Impudence the Affectation of it. **1749** F. SMITH *Voy. Disc.* II. 16 A Black-Bird was seen . . which was looked on as an Indication that the Geese would soon follow. **1818** CRUISE *Digest* (ed. 2) VI. 563 The will contained indications of such an intention. **1860** MAURY *Phys. Geog. Sea* iii. §158 Perhaps the best indication as to these cold currents, may be derived from the fish of the sea. **1863** LYELL *Antiq. Man* 16 No traces of grain . . nor any other indication that the ancient people had any knowledge of agriculture.

b. *Mining.* Something which indicates the presence of valuable ore, oil, etc. *U.S.*

1855 *Southern Californian* (Los Angeles) 28 Mar. 1/7 Mineral indications in Southern California . . differ in many respects with the mineral indications of the earth's surface in Central, or Northern California. **1862** 'MARK TWAIN' *Lett.* (1917) I. 80 We went and looked at the ledges, and both of them acknowledged that there was nothing in them but good 'indications'. **1873** J. H. BEADLE *Undevel. West* xviii. 326 My comrades are off down the mountain side picking at 'indications', and mapping out the 'run of the country rock'. **1877** B. HARTE *Story of a Mine* 394 Luckily the fertile alluvium of these valleys . . offered no 'indications' to attract the goldseekers. **1948** *Duncan* (Oklahoma) *Daily Banner* 2 July 1/3 The location was one of three staked by the Ohio Oil Co. on indications given by the Palmer No. 1 Leard-Amerada.

indicative (ɪnˈdɪkətɪv, ˈɪndɪkeɪtɪv), *a.* (*sb.*) [ad. F. *indicatif*, *-ive* (Oresme, 14th c.) = Sp., It. *indicativo*, ad. L. *indicātīv-us* (in sense 1 below), f. *indicāt-*: see INDICATE and -IVE. The first pronunciation is that used in sense 1; the second is frequent, though not exclusive, in sense 2, in which it is recognized by Smart, 1836.]

A. *adj.*

1. *Gram.* That points out, states, or declares: applied to that mood of a verb of which the essential function is to state a relation of objective fact between the subject and predicate (as opposed to a relation merely conceived, thought of, or wished, by the speaker).

1530 PALSGR. 84 The indicative mode they use whan they shewe or tell a thyng to be done. **1669** MILTON *Acced. Grammar* Wks. (1851) 447 The Indicative Mood sheweth or declareth, as *laudo* I praise. **1705** HICKERINGILL *Priest-cr.* I. (1721) 16 The original Greek Word, translated *search*, may as well be translated in the Indicative Mood. **1876** MASON *Eng. Gram.* (ed. 21) 62 *note*, In modern English it is getting . . more and more common to use the Indicative Mood in cases where the Subjunctive would be more correct. **1892** SWEET *Eng. Gram.* I. 105 The statement *he comes* is in the 'indicative' mood.

b. Of a form of statement: Having the verb in the indicative mood; assertive of objective fact.

a **1667** JER. TAYLOR *Div. Instit. Office Ministerial* (R.), The instance of Isaac blessing Jacob, which in the several parts was expressed in all forms, indicative, optative, enunciative. **1872** O. SHIPLEY *Gloss. Eccl. Terms* s.v. *Absolvo te*, It is a matter of controversy whether the indicative or the precative form of absolution was the earliest.

2. That indicates, points out, or directs; that hints or suggests. † ***indicative day*** (see quot. and cf. INDICANT *a.*).

1624 F. WHITE *Reply Fisher* 525 It is a Precept indicatiue, or significatiue, what is fit to be done, but not obligant. **1647** LILLY *Chr. Astrol.* xlvii. 292 It was the first Indicative day, wherein the Physician might expect how the disease then would shew it selfe. **1653** R. SANDERS *Physiogn.* 11 The next is called Index, the indicative or demonstrative finger, because with it we point at any thing. **1711** SHAFTESB. *Charac.* VI. iv. (1737) III. 371 That which we . . have already term'd her persuasive or indicative Effort. **1748** RICHARDSON *Clarissa* (1811) I. xii. 73, I shall pass over these whole hundred of his puerile rogueries (although indicative ones I may say). **1865** W. COLLINS *Armadale* IV. v, The lawyer's indicative snuff-box was . . in one of his hands, as he opened the door with the other.

b. Furnishing indications *of*; suggestive *of*.

1663 J. SPENCER *Prodigies* (1665) 315 There are no such indicative Signs of any changes in States and times as mention hath been made of. **1772** *Ann. Reg.* 8/2 These transactions seemed indicative of some such consequences as followed. **1812** SIR H. DAVY *Chem. Philos.* 7 The earlier philosophical work of the Romans, as if indicative of the youth of the people, is marked by power and genius, by boldness and incorrectness. **1882** WESTCOTT *St. John* Introd. 8 The portraiture of the people in the fourth Gospel is no less indicative of its Jewish authorship.

B. *absol.* and as *sb. Gram.* The indicative mood; an instance of this, a verb in the indicative mood.

1530 PALSGR. 99 The first parson singular of the indiffinite tense of the indicative. *a* **1679** POOLE in Spurgeon *Treas. Dav.* Ps. xxv, The infinitive is here thought to be put for the future tense of the indicative. **1870** MOULTON tr. *Winer's Gram. N.T.* III. xli, The indicative denotes the actual, the conjunctive and optative that which is merely possible. **1879** ROBY *Lat. Gram.* II. 235 Principal clauses which contain an indicative or imperative. **1892** SWEET *Eng. Gram.* I. 107 The inflections of the English verb are so scanty that . . the distinction between indicative and subjunctive is very slight.

indicatively (see prec.), *adv.* [f. prec. + -LY².]

1. *Gram.* In the indicative mood.

a **1603** T. CARTWRIGHT *Confut. Rhem. N.T.* (1618) 647 Whether it be turned Imperatiuely or Indicatiuely, it hurteth not us. **1882** WESTCOTT *St. John* viii. 39 If 'do' be taken imperatively in v. 38, the connexion is [etc.]. If it be taken indicatively, then the answer is [etc.].

2. As regards indications given.

a **1711** GREW (J.), These images, formed in the brain, are indicatively of the same species with those of sense.

3. In an indicative manner; so as to point out.

1856 DICKENS *Rogue's Life* ii, I heard her say sweetly and indicatively 'my father'.

indicator (ˈɪndɪkeɪtə(r)). [a. late L. *indicātor*, agent-noun from *indicāre* to INDICATE; cf. F. *indicateur* (1690 in Hatz.-Darm.).]

1. a. One who or that which points out, or directs attention to, something.

1819 (*title*) The indicator. **1831** CARLYLE *Sart. Res.* III. v, We ourselves, restricted to the duty of Indicator, shall forbear commentary. **1855** SINGLETON *Virgil* I. 72 O youth, The indicator of the crooked plough. **1879** FROUDE *Cæsar* ii. 9 Birds . . were celestial indicators of the gods' commands. **1907** *New Pictorial & Descr. Guide to Malvern* 56 Many of the more prominent objects and principal sites may be identified by . . the help afforded by the Indicator, or Toposcope, erected on the summit of the hill. **1927** *Glasgow Herald* 4 June 9 (*headline*) Mountain Indicator. *Ibid.*, The indicator . . points out over ninety places famous in Border song and story. **1967** *Listener* 10 Aug. 167/2 There's a recent book which displays, at a glance, what's distinctive about the scientific analysis of international affairs. It's the *World Handbook of Political and Social Indicators.*

b. *Anat.* The muscle which extends the index or forefinger; the *extensor indicis.*

1696 PHILLIPS, *Indicator*, one of the Muscles extending the Fore-finger. **1782** A. MONRO *Anat. Bones, Nerves, etc.* 191 The tendons of the indicator.

c. In a microscope, A pointer which indicates the position of a special object in the field of view.

1837 GORING & PRITCHARD *Microgr.* 51 It would perhaps be advisable to have the tire of the wheel made broad enough to admit of four sets of divisions, over which the indicator should extend with a sharp edge. **1883** J. HOGG *Microsc.* 191 Finders and Indicators.

d. *Philos.* = *token-reflexive word*; see quots. Also ***indicator-word.***

1951 N. GOODMAN *Struct. Appearance* xi. 290 Roughly speaking, a word is an indicator if . . it names something not named by some replica of the word. . . Among the commonest indicators are the personal indicators, the spatial indicators, and the temporal indicators. Of the personal indicators, an 'I' or 'me' normally refers to its own utterer. **1952** A. J. AYER in *Mind* LXI. 444, I shall refer to predicates instead of properties and to individual signs, to which I shall give the name of indicators, instead of individuals. **1954** *Mind* LXIII. 380 Like Professor Ayer I shall . . speak of indicators and predicates rather than of individuals and properties. **1960** W. V. QUINE *Word & Object* §21. 101 The indicator words: 'this', 'that', 'I', 'you', 'he', 'now', 'here', 'then', 'there', 'today', 'tomorrow'.

2. a. That which serves to indicate or give a suggestion *of* something; an indication *of*.

1666 J. SMITH *Old Age* (ed. 2) 73 They are the true indicators of strength. **1760–72** H. BROOKE *Fool of Qual.* (1809) II. 98 Our silence and our looks were too sure indicators of the fatal tidings. **1860** TYNDALL *Glac.* I. i. 5 The shells became the indicators of an action to which the mass . . had been subjected. **1882** FROUDE *Carlyle* II. 130 They [clothes] were the outward indicators of the inward and spiritual nature.

b. Anything used in a scientific experiment to indicate the presence of a substance or quality, change in a body, etc.; *spec.* (i) a substance which may be added to a solution to indicate whether the concentration of hydrogen ions or of some other ion in the solution is above or below a particular value, esp. by giving different colours for the two conditions.

1842–3 GROVE *Corr. Phys. Forces* (1846) 19 The substance we use as an indicator does not undergo the same physical change as those whose dynamical relations we are examining. *c* **1860** FARADAY *Forces Nat.* v. 129 You need be in no want of indicators to discover the presence of this attraction. **1869** ROSCOE *Chem.* (1871) 25 Solids expand too little and gases too much to be convenient indicators. **1874** *Jrnl. Chem. Soc.* XXVII. 191 (*heading*) Alizarin as an indicator in volumetric analysis. **1902** *Encycl. Brit.* XXVIII. 12/2 Para-nitro-phenol has colourless molecules, but an intensely yellow negative ion. In neutral, and still more in acid solutions, the dissociation of the indicator is practically nothing, and the liquid is colourless. **1930** *Jrnl. Amer. Chem. Soc.* LII. 2347 The use of various organic substances . . as irreversible oxidation-reduction indicators in the titration of trivalent antimony with ceric sulfate was proposed by Rathsberg. **1938** R. E. OESPER tr. *Böttger's Newer Methods Volumetric Chem. Analysis* i. 19 The fluorescent indicators are related to the ordinary acidimetric color indicators. However, a change of the pH value of the solution produces in them no color change, but a fluorescence appears or disappears. **1939** P. J. DURRANT *Gen. & Inorg. Chem.* ix. 214 An indicator may be used for determining the *p*H value of a solution, or for deciding at what stage during an acid-alkali titration the *p*H value of a solution has reached a certain value. **1966** *Ward Lock's Compl. Gardening* v. 78 Certain chemical indicators are available for testing a soil in the field as to its approximate pH. **1970** R. U. BRUMBLAY *First Course Quant. Analysis* vi. 83 Adsorption indicators are organic compounds with rather complex molecules which undergo a change in color due to a slight structural change which occurs when they are adsorbed on the surfaces of colloidal particles.

(ii) An isotope (usually a radioactive one) used as a tracer (see TRACER¹).

1919 [see ISOTOPIC *a.* a]. **1926** R. W. LAWSON tr. *Hevesy & Paneth's Man. Radioactivity* xv. 122 In problems of this kind, where the radio-element is not the object but the agent of the investigation, we say that the radio-elements serve as 'indicators'. **1938** *Ibid.* (ed. 2) xviii. 168 In those rare cases in which inactive isotopes are readily accessible they can be used as indicators in fundamentally the same manner, though other methods of measurement must be used. . . Such experiments have been carried out with deuterium ^{2}D and the oxygen and nitrogen isotopes ^{17}O, and ^{15}N. **1943** *Thorpe's Dict. Appl. Chem.* (ed. 4) VI. 432/1 The hydride of bismuth was discovered by using thorium-C as indicator and causing hydrogen to be generated in an apparatus in which this radioactive indicator had been placed. The gas which escaped was found . . to have radioactive properties. **1956** E. DE B. BARNETT *Mechanism Org. Chem. Reactions* i. 13 The use of an isotopic indicator or tracer often gives useful information as regards mechanism.

c. A geological clue to the presence of gold.

1894 R. A. F. MURRAY in A. W. Howitt *Miners' Handbk.* 5 Where the gold ceases is usually near and above the line of reef or vein whence it was derived. . . 'Indicators' or small veins of pyrites, ironstone, and often thin bands of peculiar slate, intersected by small quartz veins, should . . be carefully looked for. **1943** VON BERNEWITZ & CHELLSON *Handbk. Prospectors* (ed. 4) xvii. 200 A lead-bismuth mineral is an indicator in the Quartzburg district of Idaho. The gold is intimately associated with it, yet free.

d. *Ecology.* A group of plants or animals whose presence acts as a sign of particular environmental conditions. Also *attrib.*

1906 E. W. HILGARD *Soils* 545 Its [*sc.* alkali-heath's] perennial, deep-rooting habit of growth, and flexible, somewhat wiry rootstock, which enables it to persist even in cultivated ground, render it a valuable plant as an alkali indicator. **1920** F. E. CLEMENTS *Plant Indicators* iv. 112 These [areas of disturbance] furnish an enormous amount of indicator material. **1949** W. C. ALLEE et al. *Princ. Animal Ecol.* IV. xxix. 567/2 Typical or characteristic organisms . . are biotic indicators. **1964** J. M. MACLENNAN tr. *Viktorov's Short Guide Geo-Bot. Surveying* vi. 122 The composition, structure, and other features of the plant cover may often serve as indicators of various environmental conditions. **1970** *Nature* 25 July 381/1 They [*sc.* chaetognaths] have also frequently been used as 'indicator species' for water masses.

e. A board or device in a railway station used to indicate the times and platform numbers of arriving and departing trains.

1913 LD. MONKSWELL *Railways Gt. Brit.* iii. 163 A large indicator showing the platform at which each train will depart, is displayed high up on the side of one of the buildings flanking the concourse. **1914** H. M. HALLSWORTH *Elem. Railway Operating* iii. 46 Since there are trains for different destinations frequently departing from the same platform at or about the same time passengers are liable to board the wrong train. This is a danger which must be provided for by suitable indicators. **1961** *Trains Illustr.* Jan. 22/2 (*caption*) The new train indicator board for the Cambridge main line departure platforms. **1972** *Travelling Winter* 43/3 New automatic departure and arrival indicators will be installed. **1973** *Railway Mag.* Mar. 151/2 A new form of train departure indicator is replacing the printed sheets at many stations on BR.

f. In *Cryptography* (see quot.).

1961 SHULMAN & WEINTRAUB *Gloss. Cryptogr.*, *Indicator*, a means of showing a change of key or encipherment, usually with a letter of the alphabet agreed upon in advance.

3. *techn.* A mechanical device or recording instrument which indicates the condition of the apparatus, etc., to which it is attached; e.g.:

a. An instrument which indicates the pressure of steam on the piston of a steam-engine at each portion of its stroke. **b.** In mines: see quot. 1867. **c.** In a blast furnace, a gauge which indicates the proper height of a charge (Knight *Dict. Mech.* 1875). **d.** The dial and mechanism by which messages are indicated in a dial-telegraph. **e.** An instrument which indicates the position at any moment of the cage in the shaft of a mine (Raymond *Mining Gloss.* 1881). **f.** A contrivance in a lending library for showing what books are out or in.

1839 R. S. ROBINSON *Naut. Steam Eng.* 153 A most useful instrument, called an indicator, can be attached to the cylinder, which will point out the exact working state of the engine, how much of the steam is lost between the boiler and cylinder, [etc.]. **1867** *Morning Star* 30 Jan., The barometers in mines are sometimes furnished with an indicator, which tells the furnaceman when it reaches a certain point that he should light up a great fire. **1876** ROUTLEDGE *Discov.* 9 The actual power of a steam engine is ascertained by an instrument called the Indicator. **1876** PREECE & SIVEWRIGHT *Telegraphy* 85 If the pointer in the indicator jumps..the currents are either too strong, or the pointer is too lightly adjusted. **1886** *Leeds Mercury* 20 Jan. 5/4 Causing him to lose sight of the indicator, which would show him the position of the cages in the shaft. **1886** T. GREENWOOD *Public Libraries* (1891) xix. 392 (*Indicators*) There are several methods of showing to the public, by means of the devise called the indicator, what books in a lending department are in use or on the shelves. *Ibid.* 393 [In] 1870 ..Mr. John Elliot, public librarian of Wolverhampton, brought forward his indicator. **1898** MACFARLANE *Libr. Administr.* 208

g. A device fitted to a motor vehicle to indicate an intended change in direction. Cf. *direction indicator*.

Now usu. consisting of two pairs of lights, one pair placed at the front and the other at the rear of a vehicle, that flash on one side or the other when operated by the driver.

1932 [see FLASHING *ppl. a.* 1 c]. **1958** *Observer* 17 Aug. 15/6 Triggers under the steering-wheel work the self-cancelling indicators and the headlamp flasher. **1962** *Which? Car Suppl.* Oct. 133/1 All the indicators' flasher times fell within the legal limits. *Ibid.* 133/2 The rear indicators could be seen from the side. **1973** R. LEWIS *Blood Money* vi. 69 A police car..turned into the gateway, indicator flashing.

4. *Ornith.* A honey-guide, a bird of the genus *Indicator*, or family *Indicatoridæ*; esp. the South African species, *I. Sparmanni*.

First described by Sparrman (1777) who gave it the name of *Cuculus indicator* (Newton *Dict. Birds* 429).

1835 STEEDMAN *Wander. S. Afr.* II. v. 189 The little honey-sucker, or *indicator*, kept fluttering before us with its cry of *cherr, cherr*. *Ibid.* 190 The trunk of a tree over which the indicator was hovering.

5. *Math.* [tr. F. *indicateur* (E. Prouhet 1846, in *Nouv. Ann. de Math.* V. 176).] = TOTIENT.

1919 *Amer. Math. Monthly* XXVI. 290 E. Prouhet.. defined the term indicator of *n* as the number $\phi(n)$ of the positive integers less than *n* and prime to *n*. **1939** H. N. WRIGHT *First Course in Theory of Numbers* i. 11 Other names for $\phi(m)$ are the totient of *m* and the indicator of *m*. **1948** O. ORE *Number Theory* v. 110 We shall consider the problem of finding how many of the numbers $1, 2, 3, \ldots, m-1, m$ are relatively prime to *m*. This number is usually denoted by $\phi(m)$, and it is known as Euler's ϕ-function of *m* because Euler around 1760 for the first time proposed the question and gave its solution. Other names, for instance, indicator or totient have occasionally been used.

6. *attrib.* and *Comb.*, as **indicator-card**, the card on which an indicator-diagram is traced (Webster, 1864); **indicator-cylinder**, the cylinder of a steam-engine indicator; **indicator-diagram**, a figure traced by the indicator of a steam-engine, showing the pressure at different points of the stroke (Webster, 1864); **indicator lamp, light**, a luminous signal indicating operating conditions (see quots. and sense 3 g above); **indicator-muscle** = INDICATOR 1 b; **indicator-pointer**, the pointer in a telegraph indicator; **indicator switch**, a switch for an indicator light; **indicator-telegraph**, a form of telegraph in which the letters of a message are indicated by a pointer on a dial-plate.

1875 KNIGHT *Dict. Mech.* 1180/2 Near the mid-length of the *indicator-cylinder. **1875** R. F. MARTIN tr. *Havrez' Winding Mach.* 77 The mean pressure is most easily deduced from the theoretical *indicator diagram of the half stroke. **1961** *Which?* Dec. 313/2 For most cookers, we found that the *indicator light going out gave a satisfactory indication that the oven was nearly at its steady temperature. .. The *Falco Royalty* had no *indicator lamp. **1962** *Ibid. Car Suppl.* Oct. 133/2 Both front and rear indicator lights were visible from the side in the VW 1500. **1882** QUAIN *Anat.* (ed. 9) I. 224 The *extensor indicis* or *indicator muscle arises from the outer division of the posterior surface of the ulna. **1876** PREECE & SIVEWRIGHT *Telegraphy* 85 If..the *indicator pointer lags behind and drops letters, the currents sent are too weak, or the springs are too stiffly adjusted. **1959** *Motor Manual* (ed. 36) vi. 183 When the *indicator switch is moved, either for a right- or left-hand turn, current is fed to the lamps [etc.]. **1875** KNIGHT *Dict. Mech.* 1182/1 Cooke and Wheatstone's *indicator-telegraph.

indicatory (ˈɪndɪkətərɪ, ˈɪndɪkeɪtərɪ), *a.* [f. L. *indicāt-*, ppl. stem of *indicāre* to INDICATE + -ORY.]

†**1.** *Med.* Serving to indicate the nature or tendency of a disease; symptomatic: cf. INDICANT *a. Obs.*

1590 BARROUGH *Meth. Physick* III. xiii. (1639) 119 If the flux..be indicatory, the signes are rehearsed in another place. **1603** SIR C. HEYDON *Jud. Astrol.* i. 19 Who will say that the Physition in his iudgement by vrine, by indicatorie and criticall daies, by Symptomes and other arguments.. doeth intrude into the secret prouidence of God? **1624** DONNE *Devot.* 347 (T.) The Pharisees pretended, that if they had been in their fathers' days (those indicatory and judicatory, those critical days), they would not have been partakers of the blood of the prophets.

2. Serving to indicate or point out something.

a **1734** NORTH *Lives* (1826) II. 198 Sir Samuel Moreland published..a device to prolong the indicatory space from three inches as in common tubes to a foot or more..This he called a statick barometer. **1824** *Examiner* 471/1 The overture is admirably spirited, indicatory, and impressive. **1871** EARLE *Philol. Eng. Tongue* (1877) § 198 The *la* of Saxon times has none of the indicatory or pointing force which *lo* now has. **1873** SIR C. W. THOMSON *Depths of the Sea* vii. 294 The box which covers the coil and indicatory part of the thermometer.

3. Indicative *of* something.

1798 BELSHAM *Hist. Gt. Brit.* an. 1781 (R.) Great preparations were made..indicatory of an approaching siege. **1821** *Blackw. Mag.* X. 675 The writer alludes to certain physiognomical peculiarities of the writers in the Review, as indicatory of their character.

indicatrix (ɪndɪˈkeɪtrɪks). [mod.L., fem. of INDICATOR: see -TRIX. Cf. DIRECTRIX.]

1. *Geom.* The curve in which a given surface is cut by a plane indefinitely near and parallel to the tangent-plane at any point; so called because it indicates the nature of the curvature of the surface at that point.

1841 J. R. YOUNG *Math. Dissert.* ii. 43 This evanescent curve, the limit of the intersections of the plane with the proposed surface, is that which Dupin calls the *indicatrix*. **1879** THOMSON & TAIT *Nat. Phil.* I. I. § 130 A plane parallel to the tangent plane and very near it cuts the surface in an ellipse, hyperbola, or two parallel straight lines, in the three cases respectively. This section, whose nature informs us as to whether the curvature be synclastic, anticlastic, or cylindrical, at any point, was called by Dupin the *Indicatrix*.

2. ***optical indicatrix***: name given by L. Fletcher to a surface (sphere, spheroid, or ellipsoid) devised to indicate by its geometrical characters the optical characters of rays of light refracted through a crystal of any kind.

1892 L. FLETCHER (*title*) The Optical Indicatrix and the Transmission of Light in Crystals. *Ibid.* 20 To the surface of reference the term *Optical Indicatrix* may be assigned.. The Indicatrix is identical in form with the *ellipsoid of elasticity* of various authors, the *ellipsoid of polarisation* of Cauchy, the *ellipsoid of indices* of MacCullagh, and the *index-ellipsoid* of Liebisch.

‖**indicavit** (ɪndɪˈkeɪvɪt), *sb. Law.* [Substantive use of L. *indicāvit* 'he has pointed out', 3rd sing. perf. ind. of *indicāre* to INDICATE.] A writ of prohibition, by which a suit raised by one ecclesiastic against another on account of tithes, amounting to at least a fourth part of the profits of an advowson, might be removed from the ecclesiastical court to the king's court, at the instance of the patron of the defendant, whose right of patronage would be prejudiced if the plaintiff were successful in the spiritual court.

[**1285** *Statute Westm.* c. 5 Cum per breve Indicavit impediatur rector alicujus ecclesie ad petendum decimas in vicina parochia. **1292** BRITTON v. x. § 11 La prohibicioun del *Indicavit*, a fere suspendre le play en Cristiene court jekes autaunt qe discus soit en nostre court par entre les avowez (etc.).] **1607** in COWEL *Interpr.* **1642** COKE *2nd Inst.* (1671) 489 It appeareth by the ancient Writ..of *Indicavit*..that the right of tithes was tried in the Kings Court. **1768** BLACKSTONE *Comm.* III. vii. 91 If the right of patronage comes at all into dispute..there the ecclesiastical court hath no cognizance, provided the tithes sued for amount to a fourth part of the value of the living, but may be prohibited at the instance of the patron by the king's writ of *indicavit*.

†**'indice.** *Obs. rare.* [a. F. *indice* (1501 in Hatz.-Darm.), or ad. L. *indicium* INDICIUM.] An indication, sign, token.

1636 B. JONSON *Discov.*, *Homeri Ulysses* (Rtldg.) 744/2 Too much talking is ever the indice of a foole. **1645** *City Alarum* 5 An infallible indice of self-emptinesse of worth.

indices, plural of INDEX.

indich, variant of INDITCH, *Obs.*

indicia, plural of INDICIUM.

indicial (ɪnˈdɪʃəl), *a.* [f. INDICI-UM + -AL[1]; but in senses 2 and 3 used as adj. to INDEX.]

1. Of the nature of an indicium; indicative.

a **1849** POE *Lancy* Wks. 1864 III. 380 The renown thus acquired is strongly indicial of his deficiency in that nobler merit.

2. Of the nature or form of an index.

1858 J. P. COLLIER (*title*) Shakespeare's..Poems, edited with copious notes and indicial Glossary.

3. *Ornith.* Of or pertaining to the index-finger.

1895 *Pop. Sci. Monthly* Apr. 764 The claws on the indicial digits of young gallinules are pretty well developed.

†**in'dicible**, *a. Obs.* Also 5 **-dycybylle**, 6 **-dycible**. [a. OF. *indicible* (1480 in Hatz.-Darm.) or ad. med.L. *indicibilis*, f. *in-* (IN-[3]) + *dīcibilis*, f. *dīcĕre* to say: see DICIBLE.] Unspeakable, inexpressible.

1480 CAXTON *Ovid's Met.* XII. xix, It is grete joye and indicible gladnes to all hys enemies. **1482** *Monk of Evesham* (Arb.) 40 Owte of that same fowle ponde bysyly brake a myste of an indycybylle stenche. *c* **1532** DU WES *Introd. Fr.* in *Palsgr.* 1037 To consider and beholde the indicible vertues of the whiche our Lorde..hath..made [you] to shine. **1685** EVELYN *Mrs. Godolphin* (1888) 151 O vnparalell'd loss! O griefe indicible.

indiciduous, obs. form of INDECIDUOUS.

†**in'dicion**[1]. *Obs. rare*$^{-1}$. [a. OF. *indicion*, variant of *indiction* (Godef.).] = INDICTION 3.

c **1532** DU WES *Introd. Fr.* in *Palsgr.* 1079 Indicions that ben made of thre lustres, which ben fyftene yeres.

†**in'dicion**[2]. *Obs. rare.* Also **-dit-**. [irreg. f. L. *indic-* (see INDEX, INDICATE) + -(C)ION, -TION.] = INDICATION, INDICIUM.

1541 COPLAND *Galyen's Terap.* 2 Biij, The prymytyfe cause serueth nothynge to the indicion of curynge, althoughe it be vtyle to the knowledge of the dysease, to them that haue knowen the nature of venymous beastes by vse and experience, and therof taketh curatyfe indicion. **1588** R. PARKE tr. *Mendoza's Hist. China* 85 And if..the Judge do vnderstand by witnesse and by indicions that hee is faultie and culpable. *Ibid.* 379 That is a sufficient indition [etc.].

‖**indicium** (ɪnˈdɪʃɪəm). Pl. indicia. [L. *indicium* sign, mark, etc., f. *indic-*: see INDEX, INDICATE.] An indication, sign, token. Chiefly in *pl.*

1625–6 PURCHAS *Pilgrims* II. x. 1857 Other sufficient *Indicia*, or euidence besides. *Ibid.*, This *Indicium* of this Malefactor. **1675** HANNAH WOOLLEY *Gentlew. Companion* 55 A ridiculous Garb is the most certain indicium of a foolish person. **1776** SIR J. BURROW *Reports K. Bench* IV. 2366 Now where are the *Indicia* or distinguishing marks of Ideas? **1815** SCOTT *Guy M.* x, The corpse afforded no other *indicia* respecting the fate of Kennedy. **1862** SIR G. C. LEWIS *Astron. Anc.* iv. 1 We may perhaps rather wonder that Hipparchus should have succeeded in discovering this truth by means of the far and faint *indicia* which were within his reach.

indico, obs. form of INDIGO.

indicolite (ɪnˈdɪkəlaɪt). *Min.* [f. Gr. ἰνδικό-ν INDIGO + -LITE: named by d'Andrada in 1800.] An indigo-coloured variety of tourmaline.

1808 T. ALLAN *List. Min.* 38 Indicolite..from Uto in Sweden. **1816** CLEVELAND *Min.* 262 *Indicolite*..has an indigo blue color, sometimes so dark, that it appears almost black. **1843** PORTLOCK *Geol.* 213 The Indicolite, of a fine blue colour, occurs in the granite of Donegal.

indict (ɪnˈdaɪt), *v.*[1] Forms: *α.* 4–6 **endyte**, 4–7 **endite**, 6 **endight (endict)**. *β.* 4–9 **indite**, 5 **indyte**, (6 **indyght**, 6–7 **indight**). *γ.* 7– **indict**. [ME. *endite-n*, a. AF. *endite-r* to indict, charge, accuse, corresponds in form to OF. *enditer*, *-ditier*, *-ditter*, answering to a late L. type **indictāre*, f. *in-* (IN-[2]) + *dictāre* to say, declare, DICTATE. But the OF. verb is recorded only in the senses 'make known, indicate, dictate, suggest, compose, write, instruct, inform, prompt, incite' (Godef.), so that the history of the AF. and ME. word is not clear. A corresponding med.L. *indictāre* to indict, accuse, is cited by Du Cange only in English legal use, and seems to be merely the latinized form of the AF. and ME. verb, in accordance with which again the ME. *endite* has been altered to *indite*, and (since 1600) written *indict*, though the spoken word remains *indite*. See also INDITE *v.*

The sense of *endite*, *indict*, may have arisen from L. *indīcĕre* 'to declare publicly', taken as in It. *indicere* 'to denounce' (Florio); but it comes near to a sense of L. *indicāre* to INDICATE, 'to give evidence against'; and it appears as if there had been, in late L. or Romanic, some confusion of the L. verbs *indicāre*, *indīcĕre*, *indictāre*: thus in It., Florio has '*Indicare*, to shew, to declare, to utter; also to endite and accuse, as *Indicere*'; '*Indicere*, to intimate, denounce, manifest, declare;..also to accuse, to appeach or detect'; '*Indittare*, to indite; also as *Indicere*'; '*Indittore*, an inditer, a denouncer; also an intimator'.]

I. 1. *trans.* To bring a charge against; to accuse (a person) *for* (†*of*) a crime, *as* (†*for*) a culprit, esp. by legal process.

[**1278** *Rolls of Parlt.* I. 4/2 Ceus ke sunt enditee par quatre hundredez. **1292** BRITTON I. v. § 8 Il n'i deit estre, car mei endita [he ought not to be upon the jury, because he indicted me].]

α. **1303** R. BRUNNE *Handl. Synne* 1340 What shul we sey of þys dytours..þat for hate a trewman wyl endyte? **1377** LANGL. *P. Pl.* B. XI. 307 Neyther is blamelees þe bisshop ne þe chapleyne, For her eyther is endited. **1393** *Ibid.* C. XVI. 119 Ferly me þynkeþ, Bote dowel endite ȝow, *in die indicii*. **1480** CAXTON *Chron. Eng.* cxciii. 169 Els the man that ought it shold be falsely endyted of forest or of felonye. **1537** WRIOTHESLEY *Chron.* (1875) I. 62 Which too lordes were endighted of highe treason against the Kinge. **1581** J. BELL *Haddon's Answ. Osor.* 111 You must withall endite guiltie of

the same crime, the best and most approved .. interpretours of elder age. **1610** G. FLETCHER *Christ's Vict.* I. xxvi, Justice herself the plaintiffe to endite him.

β. *c* **1440** *Promp. Parv.* 261/1 Indytyd be lawe, for trespace, *indictatus*. **1530** PALSGR. 590/2, I indyte a man by indytement. **1592** WARNER *Alb. Eng.* VIII. xl. (1612) 194 He being then indighted Was hardly found a Felon. **1593** NASHE 4 *Lett. Confut.* 6 Hold vp thy hand G. H. thou art heere indited for an incrocher. **1652** ASHMOLE *Theat. Chem.* 196 Thereof the People will the at Sessions indight. **1678** *Trans. Crt. Spain* 53 Your Majesty might have indited him, or received his Justifications.

γ. *a* **1626** BACON *Max. & Uses Com. Law* (1636) 66 If he bee indicted of felony, or treason. **1640–4** in Rushw. *Hist. Coll.* III. (1692) I. 59 William Coltman .. did indict him at the Sessions at Newgate. **1709** STEELE *Tatler* No. 110 ¶4 One of her Admirers who was indicted upon that very Head. *a* **1713** ELLWOOD *Autobiog.* (1885) 285 They indicted our friends as rioters. **1764** BURN *Poor Laws* 247 If a man be indicted for an assault. **1875** JOWETT *Plato* (ed. 2) V. 325 Let any one who will, indict him on the charge of loving base gains.

2. To make (it) matter of indictment; to charge (a thing). *rare*.

a **1670** HACKET *Cent. Serm.* (1675) 483 That their own infamy should be endited against them to after ages. **1828** SCOTT *F.M. Perth* xxv, It is indited against Simon Glover .. that he hath spoken irreverent discourses.

Hence **in'dicted** *ppl. a.*^{1}, **in'dicting** *vbl. sb.*

c **1440** *Promp. Parv.* 139/2 Endytyd, or indytyd for trespas, *indicatus*. *Ibid.* 140/1 Endytynge (*K.* indytinge) of trespace, *indictacio*. **1529** MORE *Suppl. Soulys* Wks. 290/2 The byshoppe of London was in a greate rage for endyghtynge of certayne curates of extorcyon and incontinencye. **1785** CRABBE *Newspaper* Wks. 1834 II. 124 Rector, doctor, and attorney pause .. on .. Indited roads and rates that still increase.

† **in'dict**, *v.*^{2} *Obs.* Also 7 *erron.* **indight, indite.** [f. L. *indict-*, ppl. stem of *indīcĕre* to declare, proclaim, announce, appoint, f. *in-* (IN-^{2}) + *dīcĕre* to say, tell, declare, etc.: cf. *addict*, *contradict*, *predict*. In OF. *endire*, *indire*, pa. pple. in 16th c. *indict* (Godef.). which may have contributed to the formation of the Eng. word.]

1. To declare authoritatively, announce, proclaim. **a.** To proclaim (a public meeting), convoke or summon (a council, assembly).

1538 *Epist. Hen. VIII* (title-p.), The Kynges Hyghenes owght neyther to sende nor go to the Councill, indicted at Vincence. **1565** HARDING in Jewel *Def. Apol.* (1611) 584 To summon them to the Councel, which the Pope thought good to indict at Trent. **1639** *Chas. I.'s Proclam. Scot.* 2 We were pleased to cause indict a free generall assembly to be holden at Glasgow. **1648** SIR E. NICHOLAS *Let.* in Carte *Ormonde* (1735) III. 584 Cromwell .. stays there to assist in perfecting the business of indighting a new Parliament. **1692** WASHINGTON tr. *Milton's Def. Pop.* viii. Wks. 1848 I. 165 The consuls used to indict a meeting of the senate. **1720** *Wodrow Corr.* (1843) II. 535 The next Assembly is indited to May 11, 1721.

b. To proclaim, announce, or ordain (a religious observance, esp. a solemn fast or festival); to fix or name (a day for a fast or festival).

1590 H. BARROW in *Confer.* iii. 55 You .. solemnlie indict an Eaue, a day, on the one a fast, on the other a solemne feast. **1649** BP. HALL *Cases Consc.* IV. vii. (1654) 357 In some solemne fasts indicted by the Church for some publique humiliation. **1662** GUNNING *Lent Fast* 50 To break .. the Lent indicted to Believers. **1702** C. MATHER *Magn. Chr.* VII. App. (1852) 651 The pastor of the church there indicted a day for prayer with fasting.

c. To declare or proclaim (peace or war).

c **1555** HARPSFIELD *Divorce Hen. VIII* (Camden) 186 The Pope should indicte a general peace among all Christian princes. **1671** EVELYN *Mem.* (1857) III. 229 His Majesty's ministers being recalled from their respective ministries abroad, the war was fully indicted.

¶ **2.** To indicate: cf. INDICTION 6.

1653 R. SANDERS *Physiogn.*, *Moles*, etc. 31 [It] indicts to the native some kindes of strife.

Hence † **in'dicted** *ppl. a.*^{2}

1685 EVELYN *Mrs. Godolphin* 173 (R. Suppl.) Upon indicted fast dayes, how extraordinary were her recesses and devotions on euery Friday.

indict, obs. erron. form of INDITE.

indictable (ɪn'daɪtəb(ə)l), *a.* [f. INDICT *v.*^{1} + -ABLE.]

1. Liable to be indicted or accused of a crime.

1706 PHILLIPS (ed. Kersey), *Indictable*, that may be .. indicted or prosecuted. **1708** *Brit. Apollo* No. 97. 1/2 We stand Indictable of a Non-compliance. **1762** tr. *Busching's Syst. Geog.* V. 310 The abbot .. should not be indictable before any other person than the Emperor. **1817** COBBETT *Wks.* XXXII. 72 These gallant Knights .. are, I think, fairly indictable for an attempt at fraud.

2. That renders one liable to an indictment; on account of which an indictment may be raised.

1721 *Mod. Rep.* X. 336 The keeping of a gaming house is an offence indictable at common law as a nusance. **1768** BLACKSTONE *Comm.* I. ii. (ed. 2) 167 The reasons .. extended equally to every indictable offence. **1860** EMERSON *Cond. Life, Culture* Wks. (Bohn) II. 364 The sufferers parade their miseries, .. reveal their indictable crimes that you may pity them. **1871** BLACKIE *Four Phases* i. 131 Even though the points had been proven, there was no indictable offence.

Hence **in'dictably** *adv.*, so as to be indictable.

1824 DE QUINCEY *Goethe* Wks. 1863 XII. 194 If the novel be German, this is indictably indecent.

† **in'dictament.** *Obs. rare*$^{-1}$. [ad. med.L. *indictāmentum* an accusation, f. *indictāre* = AFr. *enditer* to accuse.] = INDICTMENT.

1523 in W. H. Turner *Select. Rec. Oxford* (1880) 39 All such indictaments as shalbe agaynst him.

indictee (ɪndaɪ'tiː). Also 6–7 **enditee.** [f. INDICT *v.*^{1} + -EE.] A person indicted or charged with a crime.

1581 LAMBARDE *Eiren.* IV. vii. (1588) 517 To certifie an other Record of the acquittall of that Enditee. **1613** SIR H. FINCH *Law* (1636) 404 No enditor be put in enquests vpon the deliuerance of enditees of felonies or trespasse. **1721** *St. German's Doctor & Stud.* 316 The Judges knew of their own knowledge that the Indictee was guilty.

indicter (ɪn'daɪtə(r)). Forms: 5 **indytar**, 6 **endightour, indighter**, 7 **enditor, inditer, indictor**, 7– **indicter.** [a. AF. *enditour*, f. *enditer* to INDICT *v.*^{1}] One who indicts, a formal accuser.

[**1292** BRITTON I. v. §8 Ay presumpcioun de ly et de touz mes enditours, qe, etc. [I presume of him and all my indicters, that, etc.].] *c* **1460** *Towneley Myst.* xx. 24 All fals indytars Quest mangers and Iurers .. Ar welcom to my sight. **1533** MORE *Apol.* xl. Wks. 908/2 Thendightours maye haue euidence geuen them a part, or haue heard of the matter ere they came there. *a* **1535** —— *Wks.* 987 (R.) Maister More saith yet further that vpon indightmentes at Sessions the indighters vse not to shewe ye names of them that gaue them informacion. **1622** BACON *Hen. VII*, 146 (R.) In them [king's suite] .. there passeth a double jurie, the indictors, and the tryors. **1655** FULLER *Ch. Hist.* IX. vi. §51 By Law no man may be Accuser, and Witness; Inditer and Iurer. **1872** *Daily News* 5 Oct. 5 [He] has been accused .. of plagiarism, and occasionally proofs positive have been furnished by his indicters.

indiction (ɪn'dɪkʃən). [ad. L. *indictiōn-em*, noun of action from *indīcĕre* to appoint, announce, INDICT *v.*^{2}, perh. immed. a. OF. *indiction*, *indictiun* (Ph. de Thaun, 12th c.).]

1. The action of ordaining or announcing authoritatively and publicly; an appointment, declaration, proclamation.

1563–87 FOXE *A. & M.* (1596) 642/2 A prorogation is made before the terme is expired and not after, for after, it is rather called an newe indiction or appointment. **1586** FERNE *Blaz. Gentrie* 153 A hereald must be couragious to promulgate the cruell indictions of warres (by his soueraignes commaunde). **1654** H. L'ESTRANGE *Chas. I* (1655) 161 According to the Kings indiction, the Assembly met and sate at Edenburgh. *a* **1714** BURNET *Hist. Ref.* an. 1536 (R.) He agreed that neither he nor they should accept of the indiction of a General Council, but by all mutual consent. **1731** CHANDLER tr. *Limborch's Hist. Inquis.* II. 110 He must take care that the Rectors of the Churches have these Letters of Indiction on Sunday. **1872** W. H. JERVIS *Gallican Ch.* I. ii. 150 The bull of indiction was so worded as to admit the view for which the French contended.

2. The decree or proclamation of the Roman Emperors fixing the valuation on which the property-tax was assessed at the beginning of each period of fifteen years; hence, the tax or subsidy paid on the basis of this assessment. Also *transf.*

1586 FERNE *Blaz. Gentrie* 147 Their indiction or subsedie (called the indiction of fifteene yeares) was payd in this manner. *a* **1626** BP. ANDREWES *Serm.*, *Giving Cæsar his Due* (1661) 735 Besides those other ordinary, the indictions for war (which we call subsidies) are part of *quæ Cæsaris* too. **1781** GIBBON *Decl. & F.* xvii. II. 62 The emperor subscribed with his own hand, and in purple ink, the solemn edict, or indiction, which was fixed up in the principal city of each diocese, during two months previous to the first day of September. And, by a very easy connection of ideas, the word indiction was transferred to the measure of tribute which it prescribed, and to the annual term which it allowed for the payment. **1848** HALLAM *Mid. Ages* II. Note vii. I. 306 The indiction, or land-tax, imposed on the subjects of the Roman empire. **1851** SIR J. STEPHEN *Lect. Hist. Fr.* (1852) I. 25 There was a new assessment, or, as it was called, indiction, every fifteenth year.

3. The fiscal period of fifteen years, instituted by the Emperor Constantine in A.D. 313, and reckoned from the 1st of Sept. 312, which became a usual means of dating ordinary events and transactions, and continued in use as such down through the Middle Ages. Also called ***cycle*** or ***era of indiction*** or ***indictions***.

Besides this, the original or ***Constantinopolitan indiction***, there were also the *Constantinian* (adopted on mistaken grounds in Western Europe) which began on Sept. 24, and the so-called *Roman* or *Pontifical*, beginning with the commencement of the civil year.

1387 TREVISA *Higden* (Rolls) IV. 255 Þe Romayns .. hadde of every lond þat þey hadde i-wonne þre manere tribute in fiftene ȝere, and cleped þe fiftene ȝere Indictioun. **1552** HULOET, Indiction, which is the space of fiftene yeres and used after the church of Rome, *indictio*. **1613** PURCHAS *Pilgrimage* (1614) 127 Computation of times, as amongst the Greekes by Olympiads, and amongst the Romans by Lustra and Indictions. *a* **1656** USSHER *Ann.* (1658) 641. **1702** ECHARD *Eccl. Hist.* (1710) 692 From this year [312] began that noted Æra or period of time called the *Indiction*. **1824** T. TEGG *Chron.* Introd. 17 The Cycle of Indiction .. was established by Constantine A.D. 312; if therefore from any given year of the Christian era 312 be subtracted and the remainder be divided by 15, the year of this cycle will be obtained. **1897** W. M. RAMSAY in *Expositor* Apr. 275 The indictions are not known to have been in use earlier than the fourth century.

b. *transf.* Any similar cycle of years.

1843 PRESCOTT *Mexico* I. iv. (1864) 36 To enable them to specify any particular year, they divided the great cycle into four smaller cycles, or indictions, of thirteen years each.

4. A specified year in the recurring period of fifteen years, counting from A.D. 312–313, indicated by its numerical position in the cycle; the number thus indicating a year.

1387 TREVISA *Higden* (Rolls) IV. 253 After þe concepcioun of Iohn Baptiste, þe sixte monþe, þe fyve and twenty day of Marche, in a Friday, þe tenþe day of the mone, þe twelfþe Inductioun [Higden *Indictione duodecima*; *Harl. transl.* the xii^{the} indiccion], at Nazareth in Galilee, Crist is iconceyved of þe virgine Marie. **1447** BOKENHAM *Seyntys* (Roxb.) 28 The secunde yer of the forseyd pope Sergye, and thwelfte indiccyoun. **1594** BLUNDEVIL *Exerc.* VII. ix. (1636) 661 Adde to the yeere of the Lord given 3, and divide the product thereof by 15, and the remainder shall be the number of the said Indiction. **1657** *North's Plutarch* (1676) Add. Lives 41 [Charlemain] died .. in the year of our Lord eight hundred and fourteen, the seventh Indiction, on the fifth Calends of February. **1710** PRIDEAUX *Orig. Tithes* iv. 178 These things were enacted in the Year of the Incarnation of our Lord 855, in the third Indiction, on the Nones of November. **1861** SCRIVENER *Introd. Crit. N. Test.* 183 *note*, The letter χ is quite illegible, but the Indiction 9 belongs only to A.D. 831, 1131, 1431. **1875** —— *Lect. Text N. Test.* 15 The year of the Greek era, and sometimes the proper Indiction of that year.

† **5.** An ecclesiastical observance authoritatively enjoined, or the period during which it is observed; *esp.* a public fast. *Obs.*

1641 MILTON *Reform.* I. Wks. (1847) 10/1 He that cannot tell of stations and indictions .. shall be counted a lank, shallow, insufficient man. **1665** EVELYN *Corr.* 9 Feb., The Lenten abstinence minds me of another incongruity .. the frequency of our Theatrical pastimes during that Indiction. **1685** —— *Mrs. Godolphin* (1888) 175 Not onely did she fast on dayes of Indiction, and such as the Church enjoynes.

¶ **6.** = INDICATION: cf. INDICT *v.*^{2} 2. *Obs.*

1653 R. SANDERS *Physiogn.*, *Moles* etc. 21 [It] is the indiction of a short life.

indictional (ɪn'dɪkʃənəl), *a.* [f. prec. + -AL^{1}.] Of or pertaining to an indiction or cycle of years.

1701 BEVERLEY *Apoc. Quest.* 8 The rest of the parts of Prophetic Time are not strictly Indictional by themselves, but joyn'd one part with another, fall into Indictions. **1897** W. M. RAMSAY in *Expositor* Apr. 275 The indictional periods of fifteen years.

in dictione (ɪn dɪktɪ'əʊniː), *phr. Logic.* [L. tr. of Gr. παρὰ τὴν λέξιν (Aristotle, *Sophistical Refutations*, ch. 4).] Of fallacies: resulting from the linguistic expression used; due to ambiguity, division, etc. (Opp. EXTRA DICTIONEM *phr.*)

1826 R. WHATELY *Elem. Logic* iii. §1. 135 The division of Fallacies into those in the words *in dictione*, and those in the matter *extra dictionem*, has not been, by any writers hitherto, grounded on any distinct principle. **1847** A. DE MORGAN *Formal Logic* xiii. 241 The Aristotelian system of fallacies contains two subdivisions. In the first, which are *in dictione*, or *in voce*, the mistake is said to consist in the use of words: in the second, which are *extra dictionem*, or *in re*, it is said to be in the matter. **1852** [see EXTRA DICTIONEM *phr.*]. **1870** J. McCOSH *Laws Discursive Thought* III. §82. 172 Fallacies from the days of Aristotle have been logically divided into those *In Dictione* and those *Extra Dictionem*, or, to use a better mode of expression, into those in Form and those in Matter. **1916** H. W. B. JOSEPH *Introd. Logic* (ed. 2) xxvii. 578 The fallacies *in dictione* are so many different forms of error that may arise through the double meanings of language. **1970** [see EXTRA DICTIONEM *phr.*].

indictive (ɪn'dɪktɪv), *a. rare.* [ad. L. *indictīv-us* proclaimed, f. *indīcĕre*: see INDICT *v.*^{2} and -IVE. (In sense 2 from INDICT *v.*^{1})]

† **1.** Proclaimed or appointed by authority. *Obs.*

1656 BLOUNT *Glossogr.*, *Indictive*, that which is declared, appointed, or solemnly uttered, whereunto the people were wont to be called by Proclamation. **1696** KENNETT *Romæ Antiq.* II. x. (R.), The *funus publicum* .. may be sometimes understood as entirely the same with the indictive funeral, and sometimes only as a species of it. **1727–41** CHAMBERS *Cycl.*, *Indictive*, an epithet given to certain feast-days appointed by the Roman magistrates.

2. Accusing, containing an indictment or charge.

1880 'MARK TWAIN' *Tramp Abr.* I. 73 Each sang his indictive narrative in turn.

indictment (ɪn'daɪtmənt). Forms: α. 4–6 **endyte-**, 4–8 **endite-**, 5 **endyt-**, 6 **endyght-**, 6–7 **endightment**. β. 5–6 **indyte-**, 6–8 **indite-**, 7 **indightment**. γ. 6– **indictment**. [a. AF. *enditement*, *-dictement*, f. *enditer* INDICT *v.*^{1}.]

1. The action of indicting or accusing, a formal accusation; *spec.* in *Eng. Law*, the legal process in which a formal accusation is preferred to and presented by a Grand Jury. Hence the phrases ***to bring in*** or ***lay an indictment***, and (of the Grand Jury) ***to find an indictment***.

1303 R. BRUNNE *Handl. Synne* 8915 Ne quest take of endytement Yn holy cherche, oþer ȝerde purseynt. *c* **1440** *Promp. Parv.* 261/2 Indytynge, or indytement for trespas, *indictacio*. **1460** CAPGRAVE *Chron.* (Rolls) 247 The tydingis of this endytment cam to the knowlech of the duke of Glouceter; and he .. swore on the Holy Gospel, that it vas nevyr his purpos, ne his wil, for to purpos no thing ageyn the velfare of the kyng. **1581** LAMBARDE *Eiren.* IV. v. (1588) 484, I take an Enditement to be the Verdite of the Iurors, grounded upon the accusation of a third person. **1645** MILTON *Colast.* Wks. (1851) 356 Who dares bring in such a foul endightment against the divine law. **1682** BUNYAN *Holy*

War vii, Mr. Haughty,.. How sayest thou? Art thou guilty of this indictment or not? *a*1716 SOUTH *Serm.* (1717) III. 512 The Hand-writing against him may be Cancelled in the Court of Heaven, and yet the Enditement run on in the Court of Conscience. 1769 BLACKSTONE *Comm.* IV. xix. 262 When such an indictment is therefore found by a grand jury of freeholders in the king's bench,.. it is to be removed by a writ of *certiorari* into the court of the lord high steward. 1849 JAMES *Woodman* xiii, You plead, my lord, to an indictment I have never laid. 1886 FARRAR *Hist. Interpret.* 309 An even more tremendous indictment against the decadent morality of Rome and her priesthood might be drawn from the writings of Petrarch.

fig. 1645 MILTON *Tetrach.* (1851) 146 Must we against the glory of Gods transcendent love towards us be still the servants of a literall 'indightment'?

b. The legal document containing the charge; 'a written accusation of one or more persons of a crime or misdemeanor, preferred to, and presented upon oath by, a grand jury' (Blackstone). Hence ***to draw* (*up*) *an indictment*.**

1506 W. DE WORDE (*title*) The boke of Justyces of peas the charge with.. all that longyth to ony Justyce to make endytements of haute treason, petyt treason. 1548 HALL *Chron.*, *Hen. VIII*, 86 When thenditement was openly redde, the Duke sayd it is false. 1594 SHAKS. *Rich. III*, III. vi. 1 Here is the Indictment of the good Lord Hastings, Which in a set Hand fairely is engross'd, That it may be to day read o'er in Paules. 1660 SOUTH *Serm.* (1717) IV. 7 Notaries and Journeymen to Courts, to draw up Inditements, Bonds, Leases, Contracts, and the like. 1686 F. SPENCE tr. *Varillas' Ho. Medicis* 15 The Enditement was drawn up. 1855 MACAULAY *Hist. Eng.* xv. (1889) II. 177 A motion in arrest of judgment was instantly made, on the ground that a Latin word endorsed on the back of the indictment was incorrectly spelt. 1883 SIR J. F. STEPHEN *Hist. Crim. Law* I. 274 When they [the grand jury] have heard enough to satisfy themselves that a *prima facie* case is or is not made out against the prisoner, they endorse upon the indictment 'a true bill' or 'no true bill' as the case may be.

fig. 1875 McLAREN *Serm.* Ser. II. vi. 103 The gloomy indictment has been penned by our own hands.

c. *bill of indictment*, the written accusation as preferred to the Grand Jury, before it has been by them either found a true bill, or ignored.

*c*1530 *Star Chamb. Proceed.* in *Proc. Soc. Antiq.* Ser. II. IV. 322 The seid William Trewhitt toke the seid billes of indytement of the seid fyle. 1589 *Pasquil's Return* C iij b, The.. Elders.. had neuer put vppe any Billes of endightment against her the last Parliament. 1678 HALE *Hist. Placit. Cor.* (1736) xxii. II. 157 If a bill of indictment for murder, or other capital offence be presented against A, if upon the hearing the king's evidence.. they are dissatisfied, they [the grand inquest] may return the bill *ignoramus*. 1769 BLACKSTONE *Comm.* IV. xxiii. 301 A presentment.. is the notice taken by a grand jury of any offence from their own knowledge or observation, without any bill of indictment laid before them at the suit of the king. 1818 JAS. MILL *Brit. India* (1826) V. 53 The absurdities with which a bill of indictment is frequently stuffed.

2. *Scots Law.* A form of process by which a criminal is brought to trial at the instance of the Lord Advocate; the formal written charge.

1773 ERSKINE *Just.* IV. iv. §87 The trial of proper crimes by the court of justiciary proceeds either on indictment, which method is generally observed when the accused person to be tried is in prison, or [etc.]. *Ibid.* §89 That part of the indictment.. which contains the ground of the charge against the defender, and the nature and degree of the punishment that he ought to suffer, is called the *libel*. 1861 *Bell's Dict. Law Scot.* 440/2 Where the private party is the principal prosecutor.. it is not in the form of an indictment that he brings his action, but in the form of criminal letters. *Ibid.* 441/1 The indictment is prepared in a syllogistic form, in which the *major proposition* states the nature of the crime .. the *minor proposition* states the offence actually committed .. the *conclusion* is, that on the panel's conviction by the jury, he ought to suffer the punishment inflicted by law on the crime.

†in'dicular, *a. Obs. rare.* [f. L. *indiculus*, *-um*, dim. of INDEX + -AR.] Of the nature of, or containing, a list or catalogue.

1716 M. DAVIES *Athen. Brit.* III. *Conamina Lyr.* Ded., An Indicular Essay upon the Domestick Criticisms and Clerical Characters.. contain'd in his said *Athenæ Britannicæ*.

‖'indicum. *Obs.* [L. *Indicum* (Pliny), ad. Gr. Ἰνδικόν, neut. of Ἰνδικός Indian.] = INDIGO.

1398 TREVISA *Barth. De P.R.* XIX. xxxii. (Bodl. MS.), Indicum is founde in Caues of Inde, ipiȝt in slyme wt fome clemynge to þe slyme & ayrie wiþ wondre medlinge of kinde purpur and of blewe. 1558 WARDE tr. *Alexis' Secr.* I. 89 a, Stiepe the *Indicum* in thicke redde wyne. 1712 tr. *Pomet's Hist. Drugs* I. 91 There is a Meal made of Anil, that is only distinguished from the Indicum.. as being made out of the entire Plant.

indie ('ɪndɪ), colloq. abbrev. of INDEPENDENT *a.* and *sb.* (used esp. in the film industry in the United States).

1942 BERREY & VAN DEN BARK *Amer. Thes. Slang* §217/5 *Indie*, independent. *Ibid.* §587/4 *Indie*, an independently owned theater. *Ibid.* §605/23 *Indie*, an independent exhibitor. 1961 A. BERKMAN *Singers' Gloss. Show Business* 29 *Indie*, independent movie producer. 1962 *Amer. Speech* XXXVII. 149 On names for 'indies'—independent motion picture companies. 1970 *New Yorker* 15 Aug. 65/1 An indie producer met a dope in a bar. An indie producer is an independent producer.

Indies ('ɪndɪz), *sb. pl.* [Plural of *Indie* or INDY, adaptation of L. *India*.]

1. A name given to India and the adjacent regions and islands, and also to those lands of the Western Hemisphere discovered by Europeans in the 15th and 16th centuries, and originally supposed to be part of the former; with the progress of geographical knowledge the two were distinguished as EAST INDIES and WEST INDIES, q.v.

In mod. English use, *Indies* without qualification means the East Indies; and *West Indies* is (in strict use) confined to the group of islands lying to the east of Central America; but, in translations from French, Spanish, or Portuguese, *Indies* often occurs in its 16th c. sense.

1555 EDEN *Decades* 174 All that trauayle into these Indies haue greater respecte to luker and gaynes then diligently to searche the woorkes of nature. *Ibid.* 175 (*heading*) Of the ordinary nauygation from Spayne to the Weste Indies. 1588 T. HICKOCK (*title*) The Voyage and Trauaile of M. Cæsar Frederick.. into the East India, the Indies, and beyond the Indies. 1605 *Jeronimo* in Hazl. *Dodsley* IV. 354 Alas, that Spain cannot of peace Forbear a little coin, the Indies being so near. 1662 STILLINGFL. *Orig. Sacr.* III. iii. §1 Telling men that there are Jewels of inestimable value in the Indies. 1700 TOLAND *Clito* viii. 6 Both Indys gladly will thy Handmaids be. 1856 EMERSON *Eng. Traits* viii. (1857) 140 The English did not calculate the conquest of the Indies.

†2. Used allusively for a region or place yielding great wealth or to which profitable voyages may be made. *Obs.*

1598 SHAKS. *Merry W.* I. iii. 79 They shall be my East and West Indies. 1613 —— *Hen. VIII*, IV. i. 45 Our King ha's all the Indies in his Armes. *c*1640 [SHIRLEY] *Capt. Underwit* II. iii. in Bullen *O. Pl.* II. 353, I am sailing now to my owne Indies, And see the happie Coast, too. *a*1700 B. E. *Dict. Cant. Crew*, *Black-Indies*, Newcastle, from whence the Coals are brought. 1742 JARVIS *Quix.* II. IV. liv, Regarding it [Spain] as their Indies, to which they are certain of making a profitable voyage.

indiffeasable, obs. form of INDEFEASIBLE.

indifference[1] (ɪn'dɪfərəns). Also 6 -aunce. [f. as INDIFFERENCY; see -ENCE. Cf. F. *indifférence* (1629 in Hatz.-Darm.).] The quality of being indifferent.

†1. The making of no difference between conflicting parties; impartiality; = INDIFFERENCY 1.

1533 MORE *Debell. Salem* Wks. 1008/1 He is.. farre fro such indifference & equitie, as ought and must be in the iudges. 1537 in W. H. Turner *Select. Rec. Oxford* 140 Trustyng in yor wysdomes and indifferaunces, and upon the fidelyte ye bere unto us. 1642 *Declar. Lords & Com.* 7 Nov. 3 Reasonable satisfaction shall be made unto them,.. according to Justice and indifference. 1699 BURNET 39 *Art.* ix. (1700) 116 Thus I have set down the different Opinions in this point, with that true Indifference that I intend to observe on such other occasions. *a*1754 FIELDING *Conversation* Wks. 1784 IX. 371 The gentlemen.. are to be seated with as much seeming indifference as possible, unless there be any present whose degrees claim an undoubted precedence.

2. Absence of feeling for or against; hence *esp.* Absence of care for or about a person or thing; want of zeal, interest, concern, or attention; unconcern, apathy. Const. *to*, *towards*.

1659 STANLEY *Hist. Philos.* XII. (1701) 471/2 Eratosthenes relates, That he.. often carried to Market Birds, or.. Pigs to sell, and managed his Houshold-Affairs with the like indifference, insomuch as he is reported to have washed a Sow. 1711 LADY M. W. MONTAGU *Let. to Wortley Montagu* 26 Feb., Your indifference to me does not hinder me from thinking you capable of tenderness. 1749 FIELDING *Tom Jones* I. xi, She behaved to him before company with the highest degree of indifference. 1756 BURKE *Subl. & B.* I. ii, The human mind is often.. in a state neither of pain nor pleasure, which I call a state of indifference. 1828 SCOTT *F.M. Perth* vi, 'Perhaps never, if such be my father's pleasure', continued Conachar, with assumed indifference. 1833 HT. MARTINEAU *Charmed Sea* i. 8 Her indifference was towards her parents, and most who crossed her daily path. 1847 GROTE *Greece* II. xlv. (1862) IV. 56 The feeling towards Athens was rather indifference than hatred. 1848 C. BRONTE *J. Eyre* xiv, A look of complete indifference to his own external appearance.

3. a. Indetermination of the will (cf. INDIFFERENCY 3), or of a body to rest or motion; neutrality.

1728 PEMBERTON *Newton's Philos.* 29 All bodies have such an indifference to rest, or motion, that if once at rest they remain so [etc.]. 1768–74 TUCKER *Lt. Nat.* (1834) I. 66 It will tear up the main foundation whereon they build their doctrine of indifference [of the will], namely, that without it there could be no demerit, and consequently no room for punishment. 1831 LARDNER *Hydrost.* vii. 124 A solid immersed in a liquid may have several distinct positions of equilibrium, instability, and indifference. 1886 W. CUNNINGHAM *St. Austin* iv. 128 The indifference of the human will, its perfect ability to choose this or that.

b. *Psychol.* **indifference point** [tr. G. *indifferenzpunkt*], a position or value between two continua of experience, such as a temperature that is experienced as neither warm nor cold, or a feeling-value that is neither pleasant nor unpleasant.

1887 A. SETH *Hegelianism* ii. 57 Schelling proceeds to define the Absolute as the indifference-point of subject and object. 1890 W. JAMES *Princ. Psychol.* I. xv. 616 An 'Indifference-point'; that is to say.. a time which we tend to estimate as neither longer or shorter than it really is, and away from which, in both directions, errors increase their size. 1901 BALDWIN *Dict. Philos. & Psychol.* I. 533 *Indifference point*,.. the theoretical point at which neither of two contrasted sense or other qualities, which are supposed to depend on the same sort of stimulation, is experienced. 1938 R. S. WOODWORTH *Exper. Psychol.* xviii. 445 The 'indifference point', a phenomenon observed for many years in judgments of magnitude.

†4. a. The quality of being indifferent, or neither decidedly good nor evil (cf. INDIFFERENCY 6). *Obs.*

1690–1 TILLOTSON *Serm.* (1728) I. 355 Conscience is nothing else but the Judgment of a Man's own Mind concerning the Morality of his actions; that is, the Good or Evil, or Indifference of them.

b. 'Passableness; mediocrity; as, *indifference* of quality' (Webster, 1864).

5. Want of difference or distinction between things; = INDIFFERENCY 7.

doctrine of indifference: the doctrine (of certain 12th c. philosophers) that universals are individuals considered in those respects in which they do not differ from other individuals of the same kind.

1656 STANLEY *Hist. Philos.* IV. (1701) 142/1 He asserted Indifference, that there is no difference of things. 1662 GUNNING *Lent Fast* 194 Each one therefore.. is willing through these daies, to keep himself from indifference of meats. 1850 MAURICE *Moral & Met. Philos.* I. 558 We cannot work ourselves into his [Abelard's] passionate feelings against this doctrine of Indifference.

6. The fact of not mattering or making no difference; unimportance; esp. in phrase ***a matter of indifference***; also, an instance of this; a thing or matter of no essential importance.

1644 MILTON *Areop.* (Arb.) 76 Those neighboring differences, or rather indifferences, are what I speak of, whether in some point of doctrine or of discipline. 1683 E. HOOKER *Pref. Pordage's Mystic Div.* 71 What are, as cunningly as commonly, called.. innocent indifferences and orderli decences. 1708 STANHOPE *Paraphr.* (1709) IV. 79 The Necessity or Indifference of observing the Mosaic Rites. 1816 SCOTT *Bl. Dwarf* ii, This would have been a circumstance of great indifference to the experienced sportsman. 1885 *Yorksh. Post* 17 July 4/2 If the possession of the Zulfikar Pass is a matter of such utter indifference to the Ameer [etc.].

7. *Magnetism.* ***indifference point, point of indifference***: 'the middle zone of a magnet where the attractive powers of the two ends neutralise each other' (*Syd. Soc. Lex.* 1886).

8. indifference curve (occas. **line of indifference**) *Econ.*, a graph, the co-ordinates of which are the quantities of alternative goods and services that would leave the consumer indifferent in choosing between them because he judges them of equal value. Also **indifference map** (see quot. 1972).

1881 F. Y. EDGEWORTH *Math. Psychics* I. 21 It is evident that X will step only on one side of a certain line, the *line of indifference*, as it might be called. 1894 —— in *Economic Jrnl.* IV. 426 A curve of constant advantage, or 'indifference-curve'.. representing states for which the advantage to England is no greater than if there had been no trade. 1934 J. R. HICKS in *Economica* I. 53 If there are only two sorts of goods, this scale of preferences can be represented by a diagram of indifference curves... We can take as an 'index' of utility any variable which has the same value all along an indifference curve, and which increases as we proceed from one indifference curve to a higher one. *Ibid.* 61 Take any point *P* on a given indifference-map, and draw the tangent at *P* to the indifference-curve that passes through *P*. 1949 *Mind* LVIII. 197 On a graph, the line which connects these collections is the contour line, or indifference-curve, on which all collections are iso-satisfactory. 1965 *Economist* 7 Aug. 533/1 The analysis deals with indifference curves, contract curves, equi-product curves, and so on. 1969 R. BLACKBURN in Cockburn & Blackburn *Student Power* 169 The economic assumption of profit maximization is validated by the theory that business decisions only reflect the needs ('utility curve' or 'indifference curve') of the sovereign consumer. 1971 A. S. SCHWIER tr. *Pareto's Man. Pol. Econ.* iii. 119 Professor F. Y. Edgeworth.. assumed the existence of *utility*.. and deduced the indifference curves from it... I consider the indifference curves as given, and deduce from them all that is necessary for the theory of equilibrium. 1972 C. GILES et al. *Understanding Econ.* viii. 97 An alternative analysis of consumer behaviour is known as indifference curve analysis. *Ibid.* 99 An indifference map represents a series of indifference curves.

†in'difference[2]. *Obs. rare.* [app. f. IN-[2] + DIFFERENCE, but perh. erroneous; see INDIFFERENT *a.*[2]] Difference.

1502 ARNOLDE *Chron.* (1811) 103 The indifferences of theis obligacions. *Ibid.* 105 Theis ben the indiffrence of ye aquitauncis, the furst is one party of payment. The ij is of ful payment. 1589 NASHE *Pref. Greene's Menaphon* (Arb.) 7 The hunger of our insatiate humorists.. readie to swallowe all draffe without indifference.

in'differenced, *ppl. a. nonce-wd.* [f. INDIFFERENCE[1] + -ED[2]; cf. *iced*, *frosted*.]

indifferenced over, covered over with indifference, having an outward show of indifference.

1748 RICHARDSON *Clarissa* (1811) III. xxxi. 186, I again turned to her, all as indifferenced over as a girl at the first long expected question, who waits for two more.

in'differencist. *nonce-wd.* [f. as prec. + -IST.] One who maintains the indifference or indetermination of the will.

1768 TUCKER *Lt. Nat.* I. vi. §25. 159 If.. merit or demerit extend no further than while the will can act independently, why do your indifferencists ever punish for acts done in consequence of a perverseness already contracted?

indifferency (ɪn'dɪfərənsɪ). Also 6 indyff-, 6–7 indeff-. [ad. L. *indifferentia* (Gellius), n. of

quality from *indifferent-em*: see INDIFFERENT *a.*[1] and -ENCY.] The quality of being indifferent.

I. Of a person or thing, in relation to two or more persons, things, courses, etc.

1. Absence of bias, prejudice, or favour for one side rather than another; impartiality, equity, fairness. Now *rare*.

1534 MORE *Comf. agst. Trib.* III. Wks. 1226/2 Then shall they fall from indifferencye, and mayntayne false maters of theyr friendes. 1548 HALL *Chron., Hen. VI* 177 b, Not as he, which requireth of you favor, parcialitie, or bearyng, but egall right, frendly indifferencie, and trew..justice. *a* 1571 JEWEL *On 2 Thess.* (1611) 122 Marke then, and witnesse of my indifferencie..that I follow not affection, but deale vprightly. 1610 CARLETON *Jurisd.* 131 How can sinceritie and indifferencie bee expected of them, that are aforehand bound by Oath to the Pope? *a* 1670 HACKET *Cent. Serm.* (1675) 11 Mark here the equity and indifferency of the Son of God both to Jew and to barbarian. 1785 PALEY *Mor. Philos.* VI. viii. (1830) 406 The advantage attending the second kind of judicature [where the judge is determined by lot at the time of the trial, and for that turn only] is indifferency. 1832 AUSTIN *Jurispr.* (1873) I. iii. 137 Few of them will pursue it with this requisite 'indifferency' or impartiality.

2. Neutrality of feeling; hence, Absence of active feeling or interest; unconcern, apathy; = INDIFFERENCE 2. Const. *to*, *towards*. Now *rare*.

1625 BP. HALL *Let.* in Neal *Hist. Purit.* (1733) II. 156 How long will you halt in this Indifferency? 1626 DONNE *Serm.* iv. 38 That you are in æquilibrio, in an Evenesse an Indifferency in an Equanimity whether ye die this night or no. 1642 ROGERS *Naaman* 176 Their former love of the word hath turned to indifferency. 1689 HOWE in H. Rogers *Life* ix. (1863) 253 In matters of religion Charles II was sufficiently known to be a prince of great indifferency. 1715 *Wodrow Corr.* (1843) II. 54 The state of things did not bear an indifferency and neutrality. 1722 DE FOE *Col. Jack* (1840) 203, I had a perfect indifferency for the whole sex. 1835 I. TAYLOR *Spir. Despot.* i. 7 To rest in a profligate indifferency to religion. 1836 J. GILBERT *Chr. Atonem.* vii. (1852) 195 Even the least semblance of indifferency towards the decisions of law.

†3. Indetermination of the will; freedom of choice; an equal power to take either of two courses. † ***liberty of indifferency***, freedom from necessity, freedom of the will. *Obs.*

1552 LATIMER *Serm. & Rem.* (1845) 80 We cannot do so here in England; for our indifferency is taken away by a law. *a* 1617 BAYNE *On Eph.* (1658) 144 The indifferency of the inclination in exercise is bound by Gods decree. *a* 1652 J. SMITH *Sel. Disc.* VII. ii. (1821) 316 Upon Adam's first transgression, that grand liberty of indifferency equally to good or evil began first to discover itself. 1690 LOCKE *Hum. Und.* II. xxi. §71 The operative Powers..remaining equally able to operate, or to forbear operating after, as before the Decree of the Will, are in a State, which, if one pleases, may be call'd *Indifferency*. 1699 BURNET *39 Art.* x. (1700) 117 This Indifferency to do or not to do, cannot be the true Notion of Liberty.

4. Of a word: Capability of being applied to different things; neutral or equivocal sense, ambiguity. Now *rare* or *Obs.*

1596 BELL *Surv. Popery* III. xii. 497 To make aduantage of the indifferencie of the word. 1640 FULLER *Joseph's Coat, 1 Cor.* xi. 28 (1867) 77 The seeming indifferency in the English tongue is necessitated in the Greek, Δοκιμαζέτω. 1702 C. MATHER *Magn. Chr.* II. v. (1852) 136 The usage.. seems to have been accommodated unto that indifferency of signification in the terms. 1881 J. C. DOLAN in *Penn. Sch. Jrnl.* XXX. 88 Because of this indifferency, the term *will* has here been used in its most popular sense.

†5. Of a place: Neutrality in point of advantage. **a.** Absence of advantage for either of two opposing sides. *Obs.*

1603 KNOLLES *Hist. Turks* (1621) 592 The Rhodians accounted the Turks as good as vanquished, for that they being so many in number, and in a place of such indifferencie, had not yet prevailed. *Ibid.* 848 The Christians fought at great disadvantage, both for the number of men, and indifferencie of the place.

†b. Equal accessibility for all parties concerned.

a 1645 HABINGTON *Surv. Worc.* in *Proc. Worc. Hist. Soc.* II. 193 An Officer of Armes was joyned in commissyon to consyder the safety and indifferency of theyre place of meetinge.

†6. The condition of being neither good nor bad, pleasant nor unpleasant. *Obs.*

1690 LOCKE *Hum. Und.* II. xxi. §69 'Tis a mistake to think, that men cannot change the Displeasingness or Indifferency that is in Actions into Pleasure and Desire. 1692 —— *Educ.* 75 Though before it were a Thing of Delight or Indifferency.

II. Of two or more things, in their relation to each other or to a person, etc.

7. Want of difference in nature or character; substantial equality or equivalence. Now *rare*.

1568 GRAFTON *Chron.* II. 131 For indifferencye and equalitie of both [buyer and seller].. was ordeyned that [etc.]. 1672 SIR T. BROWNE *Let. Friend* §7 Tho more have perished by violent deaths in the day, yet in natural dissolutions both times may hold an indifferency, at least but contingent inequality. 1809–10 COLERIDGE *Friend* (1865) 27 If the assertor of the indifferency of truth and falsehood in their own natures, attempt to justify his position. 1841–4 EMERSON *Ess.* Ser. I. x. (1876) 251 You have arrived at a fine Pyrrhonism, at an equivalence and indifferency of all actions.

8. Absence of difference in respect of consequence, effect, significance, or importance; the fact of its making no difference, or of being of no consequence or importance either way.

1564 *Brief Exam.* ***, If the indifferencie of these orders hange vpon the vse: then we must loke wherevnto they are ordeyned. 1594 HOOKER *Eccl. Pol.* II. iv. §4 The choice is left to our owne discretion, except a principall bond of some higher dutie remoue the indifferencie that such things haue in themselues. 1637 LAUD *Sp. Star-Chamb.* 14 June 54 The Indifferency of the standing of the Holy Table either way. 1692 WAGSTAFFE *Vind. Carol.* xiii. 88 Ceremonies..how indifferent soever they are in themselves, when they are once commanded, the indifferency ceases. 1882 T. MOZLEY *Remin.* II. cxviii. 331, I still believe..in the indifferency of customs, so long as they do not make void the Divine word.

b. esp. in phrase ***of indifferency***, that is indifferent, unessential, immaterial, unimportant.

1560 BECON *New Catech.* Wks. 1844 II. 300 So far is it off that these missal vestures are now things of indifferency. 1579 FULKE *Refut. Rastell* 781 It is a matter of meere indifferency. 1650 BULWER *Anthropomet.* 56 Haire long or short, thick or thin, more or lesse, is a matter of indifferency. *a* 1673 T. HORTON in Spurgeon *Treas. Dav.* Ps. lxiii. 6 As a place of indifferency; that is, there as well as anywhere besides. 1758 S. HAYWARD *Serm.* iv. 124 It is not a mere matter of speculation, and therefore not a point of indifferency. 1863 J. BROWN *Horæ Subs.* (ed. 3) 127 Religion was no matter of indifferency to him.

†c. A matter of indifference; a non-essential.

1643 SIR T. BROWNE *Relig. Med.* I. §26, I would not perish upon a Ceremony, Politick points, or indifferency. 1668 H. MORE *Div. Dial.* I. xvi. (1713) 36 If it be an Imperfection, it is to be removed... If an Indifferency, it is indifferent whether you remove it or not.

indifferent (ɪnˈdɪfərənt), *a.*[1] (*sb.* and *adv.*) Also 5–6 -deferent, -dyfferent. [a. F. *indifférent* (15th c. in Littré), or ad. L. *indifferent-em* not differing, making no difference, of medium quality, of no consequence, not particular, careless, f. *in-* (IN-[3]) + *different-em* DIFFERENT.]

I. Of a person or thing, in relation to two or more objects, courses, etc.

1. Without difference of inclination; not inclined to prefer one person or thing to another; unbiased, impartial, disinterested, neutral; fair, just, even, even-handed. Const. *to*, *unto* (†*for*). *arch.* **a.** Of persons: esp. ***indifferent judge, critic, reader***.

1387–8 T. USK *Test. Love* I. vii. (Skeat) l. 34 Indifferent folk wil say: 'ye, who is trewe, who is fals, him-selfe knowlegeth the thinges.' 1413 *Pilgr. Sowle* (Caxton) I. ii. (1859) 4 Thou assignest a juge that is nought indifferent, but frend to your partye. 1465 *Paston Lett.* No. 529 II. 38 He choulde be indeferent for bothe partyes acordyng to the lawe. 1502 ARNOLDE *Chron.* (1811) 124 And nether wyll delyuer the sayde goodis to me or to ony other indifferent man. 1523 FITZHERB. *Surv.* 20 The stewarde is bounde by lawe and conscyence to be an indyfferent iudge bytwene the lorde and his tenauntes. *a* 1568 ASCHAM *Scholem.* (Arb.) 133 Trewly, D. Medcalfe was parciall to none: but indifferent to all. 1594 WEST *2nd Pt. Symbol.* §22 Two things seeme necessarie..namely that the arbitrators be sufficient, and indifferent. *a* 1618 RALEIGH *Apol.* 21, I leave to all worthy and indifferent men to judge. 1745 *De Foe's Eng. Tradesman* (1841) II. xxxix. 119 A man who means honestly, is never afraid..to refer all differences to the next unbiassed and indifferent man he meets. 1814 SOUTHEY *Roderick* XXI. Poet. Wks. IX. 194 He the indifferent Judge of all, regards Nations, and hues, and dialects alike. 1844 LD. BROUGHAM *Brit. Const.* xvii. (1862) 260 They dare not go before an impartial judge and indifferent jury.

b. Of a thing, action, etc.; esp. ***indifferent justice***, impartial or even-handed justice.

1494 FABYAN *Chron.* VI. clxiv. 157 Guydyng it with all sobernesse and indifferent iustyce. 1570–6 LAMBARDE *Peramb. Kent* (1826) p. viij, The indifferent and discrete course ye keepe in handling and compounding such controversies. 1612 DAVIES *Why Ireland* etc. (1787) 213 There is no nation..that doth love equal and indifferent justice better than the Irish. 1690 CHILD *Disc. Trade* (1694) 5 Their excise, which is certainly the most equal and indifferent tax in the world. 1721 *St. German's Doctor & Stud.* 312 Methinketh that the law in that point is very good and indifferent. 1882 FARRAR *Early Chr.* II. 34 It even stands as a description of St. James on the indifferent page of the Jewish historian.

2. Not inclined to one thing or course more than to another; having no inclination or feeling for or against a thing; hence, Without interest or feeling in regard to something; unconcerned, unmoved, careless, apathetic, insensible. Const. *to*.

1519 *Interl. Four Elem.* in Hazl. *Dodsley* I. 43 By my troth, I care not greatly, I am indifferent to all company, Whether it be here or there. 1529 MORE *Dyaloge* I. Wks. 165/1 Woulde ye be then indifferent to take the one syde or the other. 1599 SHAKS. *Hen. V*, I. i. 72 *B. Ely*, Doth his Maiestie Incline to it, or no? *B. Cant.* He seems indifferent. 1645 SLINGSBY *Diary* (1836) 145 They..show'd a mind indifferent w[t] way they went, so they followed their General. 1702 FARQUHAR *Twin-Rivals* III. iii, Madam, you appear very indifferent to me to what you were lately. 1757 WARBURTON *Lett.* (1809) 256, I am very indifferent of obligations from that quarter. 1814 SCOTT *Ld. of Isles* III. xvii, These mighty cliffs, that heave on high Their naked brows..Indifferent to the sun or snow. 1836 J. H. NEWMAN *Par. Serm.* (1837) III. iii. 41 He was indifferent, and cared for none of these things. 1849 C. BRONTË *Shirley* xxi, When people are long indifferent to us, we grow indifferent to their indifference. 1868 FREEMAN *Norm. Conq.* (1876) II. x. 504 Not merely indifferent or unfriendly to his cause, but avowedly and bitterly hostile.

†3. Undetermined in regard to impressions, actions, etc.; of neutral disposition; equally apt, disposed, or indisposed *to*. *Obs.*

1538 STARKEY *England* I. ii. 28 The mynd of man fyrst of hyt selfe ys as a clear and pure tabul..apt and indyfferent to receyue al maner of pycturys and image. 1548–77 VICARY *Anat.* iv. (1888) 33 Why he [the brain] is moyst, is, that it should be the more indifferenter and abler to euery thing that shoulde be..gotten into him. 1662 STILLINGFL. *Orig. Sacr.* III. iii. §7 The soul being of such a nature as is indifferent to good or evil. 1690 LOCKE *Hum. Und.* II. xxi. (1695) 141 A man is at Liberty to lift up his Hand to his Head, or let it rest quiet: He is perfectly indifferent to either.

†4. Having a neutral relation *to* (two or more things); impartially pertinent or applicable. *Obs.*

1529 MORE *Dyaloge* II. Wks. 181/1 There might be saide, that it nedeth not to assigne any place, wher the very churche & true christen congregacion is. But sith euery place is indifferent ther vnto [etc.]. 1533 ELYOT *Cast. Helthe* (1539) 36 a, The latyn worde Cereuitia, is indifferent as welle to ale as to biere. 1580 LYLY *Euphues* (Arb.) 271 To liue and to loue well is incident to fewe, but indifferent to all. 1678 CUDWORTH *Intell. Syst.* I. iii. 124 A certain infinite *materia prima*, which was neither air, nor water, nor fire, but indifferent to every thing.

†b. Of a word: Of neutral signification or application; hence, Equivocal, ambiguous; of either gender, common. *Obs.*

a 1533 FRITH *Disput. Purgat.* (1829) 167 Albeit the word of itself were indifferent in the Latin, yet it is not indifferent in the English. 1584 R. W. *Three Ladies Lond.* in Hazl. *Dodsley* VI. 309 You know that *homo* is indifferent. 1622 BACON *Hen. VII*, 11 Chose rather a middle way..and that under covert and indifferent words.

†5. Not more advantageous to one person or party than to another. **a.** Of a place: Neutral in situation, as respects position and accessibility.

1531–2 *Act 23 Hen. VIII*, c. 2 Iayles..shoulde be.. edified in suche townes..as shall be most indifferent for conueiance of prisoners from euery parte of the shire. 1548 HALL *Chron., Edw. IV* 230 If your pleasure shalbe, to have the communicacion in any place, indifferent betwene bothe tharmies. 1593 *Jack Straw* III. in Hazl. *Dodsley* V. 405 If the king would anything with us, Tell him the way is indifferent to meet us. 1655 FULLER *Ch. Hist.* II. ii. §2 An indifferent Place, for mutual Ease, in mid-way betwixt both.

†b. Of a contest: Even, equal, undecided. *Obs.*

c 1611 CHAPMAN *Iliad* XIII. 9 He thought not any one of all the Deities, When his care left th' indifferent field, would aid on either side. 1618 BOLTON *Florus* (1636) 6 The same beasts which carried away the first day cleere, and made the second indifferent, gave away the third past controversie.

†6. Having a neutral quality between excess and defect; not extreme; of medium quality or character. *Obs.*

1523 FITZHERB. *Surv.* (1539) 60 The moste indifferentest mean to make. 1579 LYLY *Euphues* (Arb.) 144 The mind with indifferent labour waxeth more perfect, with [ouer] much studye it is made fruitlesse. 1614 MARKHAM *Cheap Husb.* I. ii. (1668) 26 Make not your career too long..or too short..but competent and indifferent. 1699 DAMPIER *Voy.* II. III. 33 Where there blows a moderate and indifferent Gale between both extreams.

b. Of medium or moderate extent, size, etc.; fairly large; tolerable. *Obs.* or *arch.*

1546 *Yorksh. Chantry Surv.* (Surtees) 482 Of good conversacion and qualities and indifferent lerenyng. 1580 LYLY *Euphues* (Arb.) 408 Indifferent wealth to maintaine his family, expecting al[l] things necessary, nothing superfluous. 1601 R. JOHNSON *Kingd. & Commw.* (1603) 77 Of sheepe they have in some places indifferent store. 1697 DAMPIER *Voy.* I. 96 Two little Islands, each about a mile round, of an indifferent heighth. 1707 *Curios. in Husb. & Gard.* 231, I discover'd them to be compos'd of much Mercury, of an indifferent Quantity of Sulphur, and a little less of fixt Salt.

7. Not definitely possessing either of two opposite qualities; *esp.* (in current use), Neither good nor bad; of neutral quality.

1532 MORE *Confut. Tindale* Wks. 367/1 Those thynges whiche he taketh for indifferent, that is to wit of their nature neither good nor euyl. 1568 TILNEY *Disc. Mariage* B, Tell us, how the indifferent sorte were maried, that were neyther foule, nor fayre, but lovely browne. 1613 PURCHAS *Pilgrimage* (1614) 369 The Chaldeans..in the seven Planets making two good, two bad, three indifferent. *Ibid.* 550 The Earth diversified in aspiring Hills, lowly Vales, equall and indifferent Plaines. 1702 *Eng. Theophrast.* 81 We are to look upon men as indifferent sort of things, neither good nor bad to us but according to our management. 1821 *Blackw. Mag.* VIII. 668 Bards and bardlings, good, bad, and indifferent.

b. Hence, by euphemism: Not particularly good; poor, inferior; rather bad. (Frequently preceded by *but* or *very*.)

1638 F. JUNIUS *Paint. Ancients* 66 The favourable acclamations of them that praise and extoll every indifferent worke. 1647 CLARENDON *Hist. Reb.* VI. §60 After an ill supper, he was shewed an indifferent bed. *a* 1715 BURNET *Own Time* (1766) I. 246 The English interest was managed chiefly by two men of a very indifferent reputation. 1796 JANE AUSTEN *Pride & Prej.* xiv. (1813) 59 Her indifferent state of health unhappily prevents her being in town. 1824 SCOTT *St. Ronan's* xiv, Meg..sipped again, then tried to eat a bit of bread and butter, with very indifferent success. 1878 H. H. GIBBS *Ombre* 20, It is generally more advisable to pass than to play with an indifferent hand.

†c. In poor health, ailing, poorly. *Obs.* or *dial.*

1753 MRS. DELANY *Autobiog.* (1861) III. 244 [She] is but very indifferent, but really looks as pretty as ever. 1779 MISS WILKES *Let.* in *Wilkes' Corr.* (1805) IV. 295, I saw her last night, when she was very indifferent with shortness of breath. 1803 NELSON in Nicolas *Disp.* (1845) V. 455, I have been but very indifferent, but I am much recovered. 1816 JANE AUSTEN *Lett.* (1884) II. 327 Your Mama means to ride

to Speen Hill to-morrow to see the Mrs. Hulberts, who are both very indifferent. **1828** *Craven Dial.* s.v., If I ask a Craven peasant how his wife does, he replies 'indifferent, thank ye'; then I conclude that she is in tolerably good health. But if he tells me that 'she is very indifferent', I am assured she is very ill; or almost in a hopeless state.

8. In scientific use: **a.** Neutral in chemical, electrical, or magnetic quality, as ***indifferent point***. **b.** Undifferentiated, not specialized, as ***indifferent cell, tissue***, etc.

1855 MAYNE *Expos. Lex.*, *Indifferens*..term applied to compound bodies which do not exercise electro-chemical reactions and which do not combine with other bodies: indifferent. **1872** HUXLEY *Physiol.* xii. 272 The material of the body when in this stage of growth is often spoken of as indifferent tissue. **1873** T. H. GREEN *Introd. Pathol.* (ed. 2) 103 These cells, which are usually known as indifferent cells, possess no limiting membrane, but consist of little masses of protoplasm which are almost in close contact with one another. **1886** *Syd. Soc. Lex.*, *Indifferent gases*, gases which when breathed excite no irritation or other unpleasant effect, but in the absence of oxygen are incapable of sustaining life. *Ibid.*, *Indifferent point*, the point of the intrapolar region of an electronised nerve which lies between the anelectrotonic and the catelectrotonic areas. **1890** *Nature* 11 Sept., The mode of renewal of the nails or of the epidermis generally is a good example, each cell commencing its existence in an indifferent form in the deeper layers of the epidermis, and gradually acquiring the adult peculiarities as it approaches the surface. **1896** *Allbutt's Syst. Med.* I. 360 Place the indifferent electrode in a suitable position on the patient.

II. Of two or more things, a thing and its contrary, etc., in relation to each other, to a person, etc.; and in senses thence arising.

†**9.** Not different in character, quality, effect, incidence, etc.; equal, even; identical, the same. *Obs.*

1547 BOORDE *Introd. Knowl.* xxxv. (1870) 210 Latyn, welcome to me!.. For thou art indyfferent here and in euery place. **1549** *Act of Leet* in Sharp *Cov. Myst.* (1825) 184 At the indeferent costs and charges of Mr. Maire and the Shereffs. That is, the Maire to pay the one half, and the Shereffs the other half. **1584** R. SCOT *Discov. Witchcr.* v. ix. (1886) 88 It is indifferent to saie in the English toong; She is a witch; or, She is a wise woman. **1721** *St. German's Doctor & Stud.* 328 He may have meat and drink..and his fellows also at their own costs, or at the indifferent costs of the parties.

10. Not differing in estimation or felt importance; regarded as not mattering either way. ***to be indifferent to***, to make no difference to, to be all the same to.

(The converse of sense 2: we are subjectively indifferent to things which are objectively indifferent to us.)

1513 MORE in Grafton *Chron.* (1568) II. 758 Friend and foe was much what indifferent unto him: where his advauntage grew, he spared no mannes death. **1601** SHAKS. *Jul. C.* I. iii. 115, I am arm'd, And dangers are to me indifferent. **1682** DRYDEN *Medal* Ep. Whigs, 'Tis indifferent to your humble servant, whatever your party says or thinks of him. **1724** A. COLLINS *Gr. Chr. Relig.* 139 It was indifferent to him whether you said Moses was the author of the Pentateuch, or Esdras re'established it. **1743** JOHNSON *Let. to Cave* Aug. in *Boswell*, I would have it understood as wholly indifferent to me. **1768** *Woman of Honor* I. 147 In quality of brother to Lady Harriet..he commands and obtains her utmost respect; but for any thing farther..there is not that man on earth that is more indifferent to her. **1885** J. MARTINEAU *Types Eth. Th.* II. 71 The sentiments of others are indifferent to him.

b. Of no consequence or matter either way; unimportant, immaterial.

1611 BIBLE *Ecclus.* xxvii. 1 Many haue sinned for a smal matter [*marg.* thing indifferent]. **1704** HEARNE *Duct. Hist.* (1714) I. 18 As the differences we speak of are not essential in points of Faith, the Apostles and Fathers..might fairly enough neglect these indifferent Disputes. **1788** PRIESTLEY *Lect. Hist.* III. xiv. 118 The real time of Christ's birth can no more affect the proper use of this system than that of any other indifferent event. **1876** GEO. ELIOT *Dan. Der.* vii, What she herself held in tenderness and reverence had constantly seemed indifferent to Gwendolen. **1885** *Jrnl. Sc.* July 408 It is perfectly indifferent to which race the father or the mother belongs.

c. *spec.* Of an observance or ceremony: That may equally well be done or not done, observed or neglected, etc.; non-essential.

1563 GRINDAL *Rem.* (Parker Soc.) 94 In that meal it shall be indifferent to eat flesh or fish. **1576** ABP. SANDYS *Serm.* (Parker Soc.) 187 Neither would they so uncharitably have judged their brethren in things indifferent. **1689** LOCKE *Toleration* i. Wks. 1727 II. 244 Things in their own Nature indifferent cannot, by any human Authority, be made any Part of the Worship of God. **1705** STANHOPE *Paraphr.* II. 127 By Indifferent are only meant, such as might be either ..done thus or otherwise. **1731** WESLEY *Lett.* xiv. Wks. XII, This rule holds of things indifferent in themselves.

III. 11. *Comb.*, as ***indifferent-looking*** (senses 2, 7), ***-minded*** (sense 1) adjs.

1622 *Relat. Eng. Plantat. Plymouth* in Arber *Story Pilgr. Fathers* (1897) 503 Every indifferent-minded man should be able to say, with father Abraham. 'Take thou, the right-hand; and I will take the left!' **1838** DICKENS *Nich. Nick.* xviii, If she was twice as indifferent-looking, I should be so much the more her friend. **1894** H. NISBET *Bush Girl's Rom.* 70 She was struggling to be calm and indifferent-looking, with a great horror chilling her young heart.

B. *sb.*

†**1.** One who is impartial or disinterested. *Obs.*

c **1570** *Pride & Lowl.* (1841) 17 For of the hyndes or of the paysauntie I feare I should not have indifferents. **1602** *Archpriest. Controv.* (Camden) II. 6 He would have some indifferent joined with them.

2. One who is neutral or unconcerned, esp. in religion or politics; a neutral; an apathetic person.

†Hence, as a *quasi*-proper name, ***John Indifferent***.

1556 J. HEYWOOD *Spider & F.* lxiii. Dd vij b, These indifrentes (or newters) that part most take That strongest is, or strongest like to be. **1589** R. HARVEY *Pl. Perc.* 5 If I vse indifferency, call me not *Iohn Indifferent*. **1624** STRAFFORD *Lett. & Disp.* (1739) I. 23, I was best pleased to hear of that Commodity, being for all the rest John Indifferent. **1633** G. HERBERT *Temple, Method* v, Should Gods eare To such indifferents chained be, Who do not their own motions heare? **1703** *Secr. Policy Jansenists* 119 Why then did not the pretended Indifferents side with the Clergy, the King, the Pope, the whole Church to defend the Faith? **1742** *Lond. Mag.* 614 Indifferents and Absentees are equally abhorrent to our Constitution. **1852** THACKERAY *Esmond* III. x, The indifferents might be counted on to cry King George or King James, according as either should prevail. **1894** *Westm. Gaz.* 20 Nov. 1/2 It is the indifferents, the abstainers, the waverers, and the wobblers who decide elections.

3. *pl.* Things indifferent (see A. 10); non-essentials. *rare.*

1626 SCLATER *Exp. 2 Thess.* (1629) 256 Vaine ianglings about indifferents. **1647** WARD *Simp. Cobler* (1843) 5 To tolerate more than indifferents, is not to deal indifferently with God. **1876** F. H. BRADLEY *Eth. Stud.* Note to Ess. v. 191 Now, where there are no indifferents and no choice between them, rights are never wider than duties.

†**C.** *adv.* = INDIFFERENTLY *adv.* 5. *Obs.*

(Very common *c* 1600–1730.)

1583 HOLLYBAND *Campo di Fior* 117 Me thinkes I understand indifferent well. **1601** HOLLAND *Pliny* II. 497 Indifferent good workemen, but nothing comparable to the other before named. **1602** SHAKS. *Ham.* III. i. 123, I am my selfe indifferent honest. **1620** MARKHAM *Farew. Husb.* II. xv. (1668) 68 Lay upon the Harrows some indifferent heavy piece of wood. **1707** J. CHAMBERLAYNE *St. Gt. Brit.* I. I. iii. 21 The Air is cold, the Soil indifferent fruitful. **1748** F. SMITH *Voy. Disc.* I. 20 An indifferent high Land to N... but to the S. it falleth away very low. **1824** SCOTT *St. Ronan's* iii, He..was supposed to make an indifferent good thing of it. **1826** —— *Woodst.* v, You have seen me act my part indifferent well.

†**in'different**, *a.*² *Obs. rare.* [app. f. IN-², but perh. erroneous: cf. INDIFFERENCE².] Different.

1513 DOUGLAS *Æneis* x. vii. 179 Thayr agis was nocht far indyfferent [L. *nec multum discrepat ætas*]. **1549** *Compl. Scot.* xiii. 107 There naturis and conditions ar as indefferent as is the nature of scheip and voluis. **1644** DIGBY *Nat. Bodies* (1645) 362 This [*Septum lucidum*] is an indifferent body from all the rest that are in the braine.

indiffe'rential, *a.* and *sb. rare.* [IN-³.] **A.** *adj.* Characterized by indifference. **B.** *sb.* A thing indifferent (see INDIFFERENT 10 c); a non-essential.

1818 COLERIDGE in *Lit. Rem.* (1836) III. 172 Driving into wildernesses their Christian brethren for admitted indifferentials. **1836** G. S. FABER *Election* (1842) 52 Some.. it tells us, are neither elected nor reprobated; and..these indifferential individuals either may, or may not, be saved.

indiffe'rentiated, *a. rare.* [IN-³.] Not differentiated; not rendered different in structure, function, or the like; not specialized.

1878 BELL *Gegenbaur's Comp. Anat.* 109 Thus the cellular layer of the ectoderm, in the Hydroid-Polyps, is as yet an indifferentiated organ of sensation.

indifferentism (ɪn'dɪfərəntɪz(ə)m). [f. INDIFFERENT *a.* + -ISM: cf. F. *indifférentisme* (Littré).]

1. A spirit of indifference professed and practised.

1831 CARLYLE *Sart. Res.* II. iv, Often, notwithstanding, was I blamed..for my so-called Hardness, my Indifferentism towards men. **1877** BLACK *Green Past.* i, There are others who have educated themselves into a useful indifferentism or cynicism. **1879** HOWELLS *L. Aroostook* xxiii. 265 A cast-off accent of jaded indifferentism, just touched with displeasure. **1890** BOLDREWOOD *Col. Reformer* (1891) 6 These people either did not know..or, with the absurd indifferentism of Englishmen, did not care.

b. *esp.* The principle that differences of religious belief are of no importance; adiaphorism; absence of zeal or interest in religious matters.

1827 SACK *Let.* in Pusey *Hist. Enq.* (1828) I. p. xiv, It originated with men very far removed from indifferentism. **1828** PUSEY *Ibid.* 59 His anxiety to promote Christian charity converted into indifferentism. **1840** MILMAN *Hist. Chr.* II. 381 The public acts..of Constantine, show how the lofty eclectic indifferentism of the Emperor..gave place to the progressive influence of Christianity. **1845** E. B. BARRETT in *Letters of R. Browning & E. B. Barrett* (1899) I. 240 He has a certain latitudinarianism (not indifferentism) in his life and affections. **1856** R. A. VAUGHAN *Mystics* (1860) I. 59 The signs of a growing toleration or indifferentism meet him on every side.

2. *Metaph.* (See quot.)

1866 MANSELL in *Contemp. Rev.* I. 33 Hence arises a third form of philosophy, which, for want of a better name, we will call *Indifferentism*, as being a system in which the characteristic differences of mind and matter are supposed to disappear, being merged in something higher than both.

3. *Biol.* 'Term originally applied to the condition of the sexual glands at the time of development, when parts of them are common to both sexes' (*Syd. Soc. Lex.* 1886).

in'differentist. [f. as prec. + -IST; cf. F. *indifférentiste* (Littré).] One who professes or practises indifference, neutrality, or unconcern. Also *attrib.* **a.** In religious matters.

1807 SOUTHEY *Espriella's Lett.* II. 36 Into this party all the indifferentists from other sects..naturally fall. **1813** W. TAYLOR in *Monthly Mag.* XXXVI. 232 It was after the expulsion of the Moriscoes that the Spaniards became indifferentists. **1853** CONYBEARE *Ess.*, *Ch. Parties* (1855) 155 Arnold was no indifferentist and his followers have been no Epicureans. **1869** ROSSETTI *Mem. Shelley* p. xxxii, He was ..as so many other people are, a religious indifferentist who acquiesced in what he found established. **1884** *Athenæum* 23 Feb. 244/1 Those Japanese who pretend to any education are almost universally indifferentist agnostics.

b. In politics.

1817 BENTHAM *Parl. Ref. Catech.* Introd. 169 Corruption-eaters, and corruption-hunters, and blind custom led men, and indifferentists. **1879** M. PATTISON *Milton* 121 These political phases were not the acquiescence of a placeman, or indifferentist, in mutations for which he does not care. **1890** G. GISSING *Emancipated* I. 75 Madeline was an indifferentist in politics and on social questions.

c. *generally.*

1866 ALGER *Solit. Nat. & Man* IV. 342 It is obvious that he was never a misanthrope or an indifferentist, but painfully concerned about his fellow-men.

indifferently (ɪn'dɪfərəntlɪ), *adv.* [f. INDIFFERENT *a.* + -LY²; but in earliest use directly based on L. *indifferenter* or F. *indifféremment.*] In an indifferent manner; with indifference.

1. Without difference or distinction; equally, alike, indiscriminately.

c **1374** CHAUCER *Boeth.* v. pr. iii. 122 (Camb. MS.) So þat he wite egaly, as who seyth indifferently, þat thinges mowen ben doon or elles nat ydoon. *c* **1400** *Apol. Loll.* 30 Ilk prest of Crist was callid indifferently prest and bischop. **1549** COVERDALE, etc. *Erasm. Par. Gal.* 12 What lette shoulde there be, why God shoulde not indifferently coumpte all for his chyldren? **1600** HOLLAND *Livy* II. xxxiii. 66 The same yeare died Menenius Agrippa, a man..beloved indifferently [L. *pariter*] of the Senatours and the Commons. **1709** STEELE *Tatler* No. 57 ¶2 All Mankind are indifferently liable to adverse Strokes of Fortune. **1756** BURKE *Subl. & B.* II. ii, They frequently use the same word, to signify indifferently the modes of astonishment or admiration and those of terrour. **1880** GEIKIE *Phys. Geog.* iv. 265 At first we might expect to meet with lakes indifferently on any part of the earth's surface.

†**b.** In a position equally convenient as to distance for all parties. *Obs.*

1655 FULLER *Ch. Hist.* v. ii. §44. 187 A Court is called in the Priory of Dunstable in Bedford-shire, as a favourable place, indifferently distanced.

†**2.** Without bias or prejudice; impartially. *Obs.*

1430–40 LYDG. *Bochas* v. xxx. (1544) 141 Indifferently his domes demeaning Such one is able to be cleped a kyng. **1531–2** *Act 23 Hen. VIII*, c. 5 §5 You..shall trewly and indifferently execute the auctoritie to you geuen. **1548–9** (Mar.) *Bk. Com. Prayer, Commun.*, That they maye truely and indifferently minister iustice. **1617** SIR R. BOYLE *Diary* (1886) I. 165 So many mares as shalbe vallued at lx[li] by two men indifferently to be chose by us bothe. **1737** WESLEY *Wks.* (1872) I. 53, I..was determined to behave indifferently to all, rich or poor, friends or enemies. **1844** LD. BROUGHAM *Brit. Const.* xix. §6 (1862) 351 Twelve men indifferently chosen, and of a station near his own.

3. With indifference or unconcern; calmly, unconcernedly; carelessly.

1573–80 BARET *Alv.* I 128 But if he shall vnderstand..that you take the matter indifferently or quietly [L. *æquo animo*]. **1601** SHAKS. *Jul. C.* I. ii. 87 Set Honor in one eye, and Death i'th other, And I will looke on both indifferently. **1663** PEPYS *Diary* 10 Jan., I answered him [Penn] so indifferently that I think he and I shall be at a distance. **1747** *Gentl. Mag.* Apr., But Lovat's fate indifferently we view, True to no king, to no religion true. **1848** C. BRONTE *J. Eyre* xvii, 'I have not considered the subject', said he indifferently, looking straight before him.

†**4.** Without determination either way; neutrally.

1607 SHAKS. *Cor.* II. ii. 19 If he did not care whether he had their loue, or no, hee waued indifferently, 'twixt doing them neyther good, nor harme. *a* **1716** BLACKALL *Wks.* (1723) I. 53 Whether they be our Friends or our Enemies, or indifferently affected towards us.

5. To some extent, in some degree (as intermediate between *very* or *very much* and *not at all*); moderately, tolerably, fairly; esp. ***indifferently well***, pretty well. (Cf. INDIFFERENT *adv.*) Now *rare.*

c **1540** tr. *Pol. Verg. Eng. Hist.* (Camden) I. 28 That everie man, but indifferentlie skilfull maye perceave the crafte. **1578** BANISTER *Hist. Man* I. 19 A certayne rownd and long Processe, indifferently thicke. **1599** SHAKS. *Hen. V*, II. i. 58, I haue an humor to knocke you indifferently well. **1772–84** COOK *Voy.* (1790) IV. 1227 The churches are not magnificent without; but within are decent, and indifferently ornamented. **1855** PRESCOTT *Philip II*, I. I. ii. 13 French he could speak indifferently well. **1858** CARLYLE *Fredk. Gt.* v. i. II. 57 For reasons indifferently good.

b. Not very well; poorly, badly (usually preceded by *very* or *but*).

1676 tr. *Guillatiere's Voy. Athens* 110 The Wine they provided was indifferently good, but their water was excellent. **1700** S. L. tr. *Fryke's Voy. E. Ind.* 159 He thought I understood my business but very indifferently, since I kept him so long under my hands. **1706–7** FARQUHAR *Beaux Strat.* I. Wks. (Rtldg.) 644/1 We are an inland Town, and indifferently provided with Fish. **1855** PRESCOTT *Philip II*, I. vii. (1857) 114 Montmorency..now took the command, for which his rash and impetuous temper but indifferently

qualified him. **1868** DICKENS *Lett.* (1880) II. 339, I rest very indifferently at night.

in'differentness. [f. as prec. + NESS.] The quality of being indifferent; indifference.

1727 BAILEY vol. II. *Indifferentness*, the having little or no Concern or Affection for; also middle Nature or Quality neither best nor worst.

†**in'differing,** *a. Obs. rare*$^{-1}$. = INDIFFERENT.

a **1694** *Life Matt. Robinson* (ed. Mayor) 57 As to Church ceremonies he was indiffering.

indiffinite, -ynite, obs. ff. INDEFINITE.

indi'ffusible, *a.* [IN-[3].] Not diffusible.

1890 in *Cent. Dict.*

indifulvin (ɪndɪ'fʌlvɪn). *Chem.* [f. INDI- + L. *fulv-us* yellow, FULVOUS + -IN.] A brittle, friable, reddish-yellow resin ($C_{22}H_{20}N_2O_3$) obtained (in two forms) by treating indican with dilute acids.

1865–72 in WATTS *Dict. Chem.* III. 248.

indifuscin (-'fʌsɪn). *Chem.* [f. INDI- + L. *fusc-us* dark, FUSCOUS + -IN.] A brown powder ($C_{24}H_{20}N_2O_9$) obtained from indican and indicanin.

1859 [see INDICAN]. **1865–72** in WATTS *Dict. Chem.* III. 249.

So **indi'fuscone** ($C_{22}H_{20}N_2O_5$) [see -ONE].

indigen, var. of INDIGENE.

‖**in'digena.** Pl. indigenæ. [L. *indigena* native, f. *indu-* in, within + *-gena* from *gen-*, stem of *gignĕre* to produce, beget.] A native, aboriginal; = INDIGENE *sb.*

1591 G. FLETCHER *Russe Commw.* (Hakl. Soc.) 98 As though they were indigenæ, or people bredde upon that very soyle. **1659** HAMMOND *On Ps.* xxxvii. 35 Spreading himself as an indigena flourishing. **1799** W. G. BROWNE *Trav. Africa* etc. xxi. 320 The ordinary maxims of indigenæ are rarely to be entirely disregarded.

indigenal (ɪn'dɪdʒɪnəl), *a.* and *sb.* [f. L. *indigen-a* + -AL[1].] **A.** *adj.* = INDIGENOUS.

1725 H. BOURNE in *Spirit Pub. Jrnls.* (1825) 390 It appears to me to be an indigenal Custom of our own. **1802** *Sporting Mag.* XX. 170 The indigenal British cattle are still extant. **1847** MEDWIN *Shelley* II. 140 Bright auburn hair and eyes, that seem indigenal to, or hereditary in, the fair Venetians.

B. *sb.* A native; = INDIGENE *sb.*

1720 BLAIR in *Phil. Trans.* XXXI. 35, I have not inserted any Plant.. but such as are indigenals in Britain.

†**in'digenary,** *a. Obs.* [f. L. *indigen-a* native + -ARY.] Native; = INDIGENOUS.

1651 BIGGS *New Disp.* ¶288 The indigenary ferment in the stomack. **1653** URQUHART *Rabelais* II. vi, The primeval orgin of my aves and ataves was indigenary of the Lemovick regions [F. *indigène des régions Lemovicques*].

†**in'digenate,** *sb. Obs.* [a. F. *indigénat*, ad. L. type **indigenātus*, f. *indigena* native: see -ATE[1] 1.] The position or status of a native.

1762 tr. *Busching's Syst. Geog.* IV. 138 It was formerly customary that the person who was desirous of obtaining the right of indigenate, or a share in the privileges, must previously pay a certain sum of matriculation or enrollment. **1796** MORSE *Amer. Geog.* II. 27 The law of indigenate, which excludes foreigners, not naturalized, from holding any employment of trust or profit.

†**in'digenate,** *a. Obs. rare.* [app. f. L. *indigen-a* + -ATE[2].] Of native origin.

1775 PLANTA in *Phil. Trans.* LXVI. 139 The domains granted out by them to different indigenate families.

indigence ('ɪndɪdʒəns). Also 5–6 **indygence,** 6 **indigens,** (7 **indygens**). [a. F. *indigence* (13th c. in Littré), ad. L. *indigēntia*, f. *indigēnt-em* INDIGENT: see -ENCE.]

†**1.** The fact or condition of wanting or needing (a thing); want or need *of* something requisite; lack, deficiency; need, requirement.

c **1375** *Sc. Leg. Saints, Egipciane* 319 Grant syne to myn Indigens þi proteccione & defens! **1387–8** T. USK *Test. Love* III. viii, By indigence of goodes.. by right shulde he ben punisshed. ?**14..** *Chester Pl.* (Shaks. Soc.) II. 223 And beestys alle shal.. Nouthir ete nor drynke for noon indigence. **1513** DOUGLAS *Æneis* Prol. 72 Therto perfyte, but ony indigence. *a* **1628** PRESTON *New Covt.* (1634) 25 Mutual indigence knits men together, when they have need one of another. **1678** GALE *Crt. Gentiles* III. 165 Working.. by a particular concurse suitable to the indigence of the mater it workes on. **1775** HARRIS *Philos. Arrangem.* Wks. (1841) 316 Every subordinate being.. is.. subject to wants, (indigence and imperfection being essential to its constitution).

2. *spec.* Want of the means of subsistence; straitened circumstances; poverty, penury, destitution.

c **1386** CHAUCER *Man of Law's T.* 6 Thou most for Indigence Or stele, or begge, or borwe thy dispence. **1444** *Pol. Poems* (Rolls) II. 217 Avaunsyd persownys holde residence Among ther parysshens, make a departysoun Of ther tresours to folk in indigence. **1555** ABP. PARKER *Ps.* xxxiv. 86 God seeth the just in providence.. He them relieveth in indigens. **1603** HOLLAND *Plutarch's Mor.* 1211 This other heere, doth not abandon povertie, nor raseth out the hereditary indigence of his father and house. **1712** STEELE *Spect.* No. 276 ¶1 To tell a rich Man of the Indigence of a Kinsman of his. **1791** BURKE *App. Whigs* Wks. 1842 I. 495 As they had before been reduced from affluence to indigence. **1884** J. RAE *Contemp. Socialism* 414 To have no shoes is a mark of extreme indigence to-day.

b. *personified.*

c **1420** LYDG. *Story Thebes* I. in *Chaucer's Wks.* (1561) 360/2 Treason, Pouert, Indigence and Nede And cruell death, in his rent wede. **1766** GOLDSM. *Vic. W.* xviii, This place, the usual retreat of indigence and frugality. **1858–65** CARLYLE *Fredk. Gt.* XI. i. IV. 7 Under this King Indigence itself may still have something of a human aspect.

†**3.** An instance of want; a want, a need. *Obs.*

c **1416** HOCCLEVE *Min. Poems* (1892) 62 Let your hy worthynesse Oure indigences softne & abate! **1491** CAXTON *Vitas Patr.* (W. de W. 1495) I. xliii. 72 b/1 She endured not oonly grete indigences; But also many rebukes and shames. **1664–94** SOUTH *Twelve Serm.* II. 114 We.. lay before them our Wants and Indigences, and the misery of our Condition.

indigency ('ɪndɪdʒənsɪ). [ad. L. *indigēntia*: see prec. and -ENCY.] The quality or condition of being indigent.

†**1.** Want, deficiency; need; = INDIGENCE 1. *Obs.*

a **1619** FOTHERBY *Atheom.* I. v. §4 (1622) 38 The chiefest tye, and bond of all humane society, is neither reason, nor speech, nor indigency; but religion and piety. *c* **1624** LUSHINGTON *Recant. Serm.* in *Phenix* (1708) II. 492 Man ceaseth to be Man, if we conceive him All-sufficient; God only is so.. Man's Being and his God is Indigency and Want. **1714** FORTESCUE-ALAND *Pref. to Fortescue's Abs. & Lim. Mon.* 12 In the Infancy of the State and Indigency of Laws.

2. *spec.* Want of the means of subsistence; = INDIGENCE 2.

1631 WEEVER *Anc. Fun. Mon.* 255 Great want and indigencie. **1684** T. BURNET *Th. Earth* II. 183 Where there is indigency, there is sollicitude, and distraction, and uneasiness, and fear. **1692** BENTLEY *Boyle Lect.* 38 That the common heathens had such mean apprehensions about the indigency of their gods, it appears plainly.. from Aristophanes's Plutus, and the Dialogues of Lucian. **1906** *Daily Chron.* 25 Sept. 6/7 The Government has set up an Indigency Inquiry Commission. **1924** *Glasgow Herald* 7 Feb. 7 Unemployment and indigency.. existed on a scale that was entirely disproportionate to the size of the white population.

†**3.** with *pl.* A want, a need; = INDIGENCE 3. *Obs.*

1651 J. ROCKET *Chr. Subj.* vii. (1658) 90 Ready to supply their indigencies, to pardon their infirmities. **1713** DERHAM *Phys.-Theol.* x. 459 All which various Methods being so nicely accommodated to the Indigencies of those helpless Vegetables. **1721** R. KEITH tr. *à Kempis' Vall. Lillies* 52 Who is there that is found like to the 'poor (Jesus)' as to all his Indigencies? Verily none.

indigene ('ɪndɪdʒiːn), *a.* and *sb.* Also 7 **-gin(e,** 7–9 **-gen.** [a. F. *indigène* (Rabelais, 16th c.), ad. L. *indigena* native, lit. 'in-born' person, f. *indi-* (*indu-*) ancient deriv. form of *in* prep. + *gen-* stem of *gignĕre*, in passive 'to be born'.]

†**A.** *adj.* Native; = INDIGENOUS. *Obs.*

1598 HAKLUYT *Voy.* I. 491 They were Indigene, or people bred vpon that very soyle. **1675** EVELYN *Terra* (1729) 7 All sorts of Mould, foreign or indigen. **1697** —— *Numism.* ix. 312 The Native, and truly Indigin are generally well shap'd.

B. *sb.* A native.

1664 EVELYN *Sylva* xxiv. 62 The Alaternus.. thrives with us in England, as if it were an Indigene and Natural. **1679** *Ibid.* (ed. 3) xvi. 68 The Birch.. [is] doubtless a proper Indigene of England. **1807** G. CHALMERS *Caledonia* I. I. i. 14 The Goths were indigenes of Scandia. **1817** COLERIDGE *Own Times* (1850) III. 952 One of the true indigens of this planet. **1859** DARWIN *Orig. Spec.* iv. (1873) 89 They differ, moreover, to a large extent, from the indigenes. **1876** H. SPENCER *Princ. Sociol.* (1877) I. 46 The Hill-tribes of India, which are remnants of indigenes planted by the flood of Aryans.

†**indi'genital,** *a. Obs. rare.* [f. L. *indi-* (see prec.) + *genit-us* born + -AL[1]: after L. *indigena, -genus.*] Of indigenous character.

1656 BLOUNT *Glossogr.*, *Indigenital*, born in the same Town or Country; natural. **1674** JEAKE *Arith.* (1696) 89 Greek Measures of capacity may be considered, as Indigenital.. Or, 2. Exotick.

indi'genity. *rare.* [f. L. *indigen-us* adj. (see INDIGENOUS *a.*) + -ITY.] The quality of being indigenous; indigenousness.

1895 *Naturalist* No. 241. 241 Many new species, but mostly of doubtful indigenity, have their line for the first time.

indigenization (ɪnˌdɪdʒɪnaɪ'zeɪʃən). [f. INDIGENOUS *a.* + -IZATION.] The act or process of rendering indigenous or making predominantly native; adaptation or subjection to the influence or dominance of the indigenous inhabitants of a country; *spec.* the increased use of indigenous people in government, employment, etc. Also **in'digenist,** an advocate or supporter of indigenization; also *attrib.* or as *adj.*; **in'digenize** *v. trans.*; **in'digenized** *ppl. a.*

1942 D. FITTS *Anthol. Contemp. Latin-Amer. Poetry* 639 Vasquez is a member of the Puno indigenist school. He scatters Indian words throughout his writing and celebrates the charms of Indian girls. **1944** *Hispania* May 245 In the last twenty years Protestantism in Latin America has gained mainly in the Indian communities where latifundism is strongest... A number of *indigenists* are Protestants. **1949** *Internat. Jrnl. Amer. Ling.* XV. 111, Guatemala is to be congratulated on the activities of its Indigenist Institute. **1951** *Missionary Research Library Occas. Bull.* 14 Feb. 7 It is the fascinating story of an indigenous Church in what is otherwise a 'missionary' land; and its development contains many lessons as to the proper principles of indigenization. **1951** L. THOMPSON *Personality & Govt.* 58 Navaho administration should aim primarily to guide, teach and influence the Navaho by means of indigenized methods to improve their own pattern of living. *Ibid.* 61 It is recommended.. that the Navaho Agency and its services be completely reorganized, decentralized, and indigenized. **1954** *Theology* LVII. 249 Making the Church really indigenous with greater indigenization of leadership as well as support. **1962** *Economist* 21 Apr. 227/1 The process of 'indigenisation', which has narrowed managerial opportunities, is now being steadily extended to technical posts also. **1968** *Listener* 26 Dec. 859/3 The 'indigenist' movement in Haiti and the 'negrist' movement in Cuba. The indigenists, who relied mainly on a European form, the novel, turned back to the study of Voodoo. **1971** G. ANSRE in J. Spencer *Eng. Lang. W. Afr.* 163 The general tendency in word structure seems to have been in the direction of indigenisation, but more knowledge of English and sophistication in its use seems to be reversing things. *Ibid.*, The phonologically indigenised form of the English plural. **1971** *Guardian* 29 Sept. 17/4 The indigenisation policy.. is unlikely to be fully pursued.. because of the shortage of capital needed for Nigerians to take over from foreign concerns. **1971** *Jrnl. Educ. Thought* V. II. 75 An ethnic-sensitive planner would have substituted the legends of their hogan house, their maize-grinding mano (millstone), and other indigenizations. **1973** *Nation Rev.* (Melbourne) III. 31 Aug. 1459/6 She will help to indigenise music education in the schools.

indigenous (ɪn'dɪdʒɪnəs), *a.* [f. late L. *indigen-us* born in a country, native (f. *indigen-a* a native: see INDIGENE) + -OUS.]

1. Born or produced naturally in a land or region; native or belonging naturally *to* (the soil, region, etc.). (Used primarily of aboriginal inhabitants or natural products.)

1646 SIR T. BROWNE *Pseud. Ep.* VI. x. 325 Although.. there bee.. swarmes of Negroes serving under the Spaniard, yet were they all transported from Africa.. and are not indigenous or proper natives of America. **1697** *Phil. Trans.* XIX. 497 This Creature was formerly Common with us in Ireland; and an Indigenous Animal.. universally met with in all parts of the Kingdom. **1791** NEWTE *Tour Eng. & Scot.* 188 In different Highland glens.. where the indigenous sheep are supposed to remain unmixed. **1794** S. WILLIAMS *Vermont* 70 A plant indigenous only to China and Tartary. **1837** WHEWELL *Hist. Induct. Sc.* (1857) I. 212 They had.. been passionately fond of their indigenous poetry. **1868** F. HALL in *Examiner* 11 Apr. 228/3 Compositions which studiously reject all words that are not either Sanskritic or indigenous. **1881** WESTCOTT & HORT *Grk. N.T.* Introd. §118 Hardly any indigenous Syriac theology older than the fourth century has been preserved. **1885** RIDER HAGGARD *K. Solomon's Mines* Introd. 5 The indigenous flora and fauna of Kukuanaland.

b. *transf.* and *fig.* Inborn, innate, native.

a **1864** I. TAYLOR (Webster), Joy and hope are emotions indigenous to the human mind. **1885** J. MARTINEAU *Types Eth. Th.* II. 68 The more we appreciate what *obligation* means, the more shall we rest in the psychologically indigenous character of its conditions.

2. Of, pertaining to, or intended for the natives; 'native', vernacular.

1844 H. H. WILSON *Brit. India* II. 579 Most of the Missionary establishments attempted the formation of an English school in connexion with their indigenous schools.

Hence **in'digenously** *adv.*, in an indigenous manner, as a native growth. **in'digenousness,** the quality of being indigenous or native.

1846 GROTE *Greece* II. iv. II. 403 The Achæans.. belonging indigenously to the peninsula. **1851** G. BLYTH *Remin. Miss. Life* iv. 183 The cotton plant grows indigenously. **1894** *Forum* (U.S.) Mar. 19 Progress is slow, population increasing but slightly, and that indigenously. *Mod.* The plant is recorded from various localities in Scotland, but its indigenousness in the north is doubted.

indigent ('ɪndɪdʒənt), *a.* (*sb.*) Also 5 **indygent(e,** 6 **indigente.** [a. F. *indigent*, ad. L. *indigēnt-em*, pres. pple. of *indigē-re* to lack, want, f. *indu-* (IN-[2]) + *egē-re* to want.]

A. *adj.* **1. a.** Lacking in what is requisite; falling short of the proper measure or standard; wanting, deficient. *arch.* (In quot. 1596, said of the thing wanted.)

1426 LYDG. *De Guil. Pilgr.* 6388 He ys so feble & indygent.. That he knoweth her-off ryht nouht. **1531** ELYOT *Gov.* I. xxii, Whan they be done with suche moderation that nothing in the doinge may be sene superfluous or indigent.. they be maturely doone. **1596** DALRYMPLE tr. *Leslie's Hist. Scot.* I. 40 Quhat ane way abundes with ws, another way inlakes with vs, and is indigent. **1678** CUDWORTH *Intell. Syst.* I. iv. §34. 537 The Divided Parts of the World, taken severally, are but indigent and imperfect things. **1742** GRAY *Odes, Spring* ii, How low, how little are the Proud, How indigent the Great! **1841** EMERSON *Addr., Meth. Nature* Wks. (Bohn) II. 222 Great men do not content us.. There is somewhat indigent and tedious about them.

b. Destitute *of*, void *of*.

1490 CAXTON *Eneydos* 12 The sayd troians myserable semed.. indygent of force. **1535** STEWART *Cron. Scot.* II. 630 Indigent Off meit and drink, quhilk wes thair lyvis fude. **1626** BACON *Sylva* §840 Such Bodies, as.. haue the Tangible Parts Indigent of Moisture. **1663** COWLEY *Ess., Greatness* (1684) 124 They abound with Slaves, but are indigent of Mony. **1788** T. TAYLOR *Proclus* I. 115 Such things as are indigent of matter.. degenerate from the perfection of their essence. **1805** WORDSW. *Prelude* III. 435 Nor indigent of songs warbled from crowds In under-coverts.

†**c.** In need *of*; requiring the aid of. *Obs.*

1589 PUTTENHAM *Eng. Poesie* I. xii. (Arb.) 44 Misconceauing his diuine nature.. Namely to make him ambitious of honour.. and indigent of mans worships. 1660 WILLSFORD *Scales Comm.* Ded. A ij b, Indigent of Protectors for a Convoy. 1702 STEELE *Funeral* II. (1734) 44 How do I see that our Sex is naturally indigent of Protection? 1708 J. PHILIPS *Cyder* II. 81 Oh Albion.. indigent Of nothing from without.

2. *spec.* Lacking the necessaries of life; in needy circumstances; characterized by poverty; poor, needy. Of persons, their condition, etc.

c 1400 *Rom. Rose* 5695 An usurer.. Shal never for richesse riche bee, But evermore pore and indigent. *a* 1420 HOCCLEVE *De Reg. Princ.* 1059 Yfalle in indigent povert. 1483 CAXTON *Gold Leg.* 431/2 To al Indygente he openyd the bosom of myserycorde. 1535 *Suppress. Monast.* (Camden) 104 Refresshing of poore indigent persons. 1599 SHAKS. *Hen. V*, I. i. 16 Indigent faint Soules, past corporall toyle. 1671 J. WEBSTER *Metallogr.* i. 18 The Miners.. being but people of the most indigent sort. 1711 ADDISON *Spect.* No. 177 ¶4 That which goes under the general Name of Charity.. consists in relieving the Indigent. 1762-71 H. WALPOLE *Vertue's Anecd. Paint.* (1786) III. 240 A man of indigent circumstances. 1766 ENTICK *London* IV. 379 An almonry or alms-house for the reception of indigent children. 1844 THIRLWALL *Greece* VIII. 391 The indigent who could only expect relief through.. changes in the distribution of property. 1874 GREEN *Short Hist.* vii. §5. 385 Each town and parish was held responsible for the relief of its indigent and disabled poor.

fig. 1663 COWLEY *Ess., Solitude* (1684) 92 The solitary Life will grow indigent, and be ready to starve without them [books]. *a* 1711 KEN *Div. Love* Wks. (1838) 304 The utmost ardours of a penitential and indigent love.

B. *sb.* An indigent person; one poor and needy.

1563 WINȜET *Four Scoir Thre Quest.* Wks. 1888 I. 115 Kirk landis, anis dedicat to.. feble and waik indigentis. 1739 CIBBER *Apol.* viii. (1756) I. 214 The author of it was a desperate indigent that did it for bread. 1747 HERVEY *Medit., Winter Piece* (1813) 369 The bitter winds plead for the poor indigents. 1903 *Westm. Gaz.* 15 Jan. 6/2 Mr. Chamberlain.. gratefully accepted the offer to provide accommodation for the indigents. 1905 *Daily Chron.* 23 Sept. 5/1 The farmers submitted a lengthy list of subjects for redress, including.. settlements for indigents, &c. 1922 W. S. MAUGHAM *On Chinese Screen* VIII. 37 He was a man whose purse was always open to the indigent. 1972 *N.Y. Law Jrnl.* 31 Oct. 1/5 The Legal Defense Panel administers the program of assistance to indigents who are criminal defendants.

Hence **ˈindigently** *adv.*, in an indigent or destitute manner (Webster, 1856); **ˈindigentness**, indigency (Bailey vol. II, 1727).

†inˈdigerable, *a.* *Obs.* *rare*⁻¹. [a. obs. F. *indigérable* (*a* 1516 in Godef.), f. *in-* (IN-³) + *digér-er* to DIGEST: see -ABLE.] = INDIGESTIBLE.

1599 A. M. tr. *Gabelhouer's Bk. Physicke* 7/1 You must take especiall heede.. of all manner of tarte and indigerable viandes.

†indiˈgest, *a.* (*sb.*) *Obs.* Also 5-6 *Sc.* -de-. [ad. L. *indigest-us* unarranged, confused, not digested, f. *in-* (IN-³) + *dīgest-us*, pa. pple. of *dīgerĕre* to DIGEST. Cf. F. *indigeste* (14th c. in Hatz.-Darm.).] Undigested; crude, immature; shapeless, confused; unarranged.

(Often with reference to Ovid's *Quem dixere chaos, rudis indigestaque moles*, Met. I. 7.)

1398 TREVISA *Barth. De P.R.* XVII. lxxiv. (Addit. MS. 27944) lf. 228/1 Fruyt is first grene and indigest.. but þe vtter hete comforteþ þe Inner hete, and makiþ digestioun in the soure humour, and dissolueth it. 1538 STARKEY *England* II. i. 154 Correctyon of corrupt and indygest humorys ys the chefe poynt. *a* 1572 KNOX *Hist. Ref.* Wks. 1846 I. 133 Then the personis fornamed heard weaping and, as it war ane indigest sound, as it war of prayeris, in the which he continewed neyre ane hour. 1613 W. BROWNE *Brit. Past.* I. ii. (R.), Me thinkes a troubled thought is thus exprest, To be a chaos rude and indigest. 1803 W. TAYLOR in *Ann. Rev.* I. 257 The somewhat rude and indigest mass of his materials. 1806 *Ibid.* IV. 884 The lump of indigest materials industriously provided by a man of letters for the purpose of drawing up a book.

b. *fig.* Of persons: Immature; of crude or hasty character.

1423 JAS. I *Kingis Q.* xiv, Though [sely] ȝouth of nature Indegest, Vnrypit fruyte with windis variable. 1513 DOUGLAS *Æneis* XI. vii. 104 A man nocht indegest, bot wys and cald.

B. *sb.* A shapeless mass.

1595 SHAKS. *John* v. vii. 26 You are borne To set a forme vpon that indigest, Which he hath left so shapelesse and so rude.

indiˈgest, *v.* (*trivial.*) [f. IN-³ + DIGEST *v.* after INDIGESTION.] **a.** *trans.* To fail to digest.

1814 BYRON *Let. to Moore* 9 Apr., Which I swallowed for supper, and *in*digested for I don't know how long. 1882 *Three in Norway* p. xii, One of those people who never indigest anything, but always look, and always are, in perfect health and spirits. 1938 S. BECKETT *Murphy* 81 On this part of himself that I am about to indigest may the Lord have mercy.

b. *intr.* To fail to digest; to fail to be digested.

1857 MRS. GASKELL *Let.* Dec. (1966) 489, I don't see exactly what you do in America. You indigest, all of you, and some of you make money at a great rate. 1863 SALA *Capt. Dangerous* II. ix. 299 He breakfasted very heartily of Minced Veal, which he hoped would not indigest. 1954 W. FAULKNER *Fable* 337 'Then we will starve,' the first said. 'Or indigest,' the third said.

indigested (ɪndɪˈdʒɛstɪd), *a.* [f. INDIGEST *a.* + -ED¹, or f. IN-³ + DIGESTED *ppl. a.*] Not digested; undigested.

1. Not ordered or arranged; without form or arrangement of parts; shapeless, unformed, chaotic.

(Often in expressions echoing Ovid's description of chaos: see INDIGEST *a.*)

1593 SHAKS. *2 Hen. VI*, v. i. 157 Hence heape of wrath, foule indigested lumpe, As crooked in thy manners, as thy shape. 1613 PURCHAS *Pilgrimage* (1614) 7 A rude and indigested Chaos, or confusion of matters. 1677 HALE *Prim. Orig. Man.* IV. ii. 295 The remaining indigested parts of Nature. 1692 BENTLEY *Boyle Lect.* viii. 289 A rude and indigested lump of Atoms. *a* 1794 GIBBON *Misc. Wks.* (1814) I. 42-3 The only principle that darted a ray of light into the indigested chaos. 1884 CHURCH *Bacon* viii. 193 Half his time was spent in collecting huge masses of indigested facts.

fig. 1709 MRS. MANLEY *Secret Mem.* (1736) IV. 175 Boys of the same Age appear crude, indigested, devoted only to Rudeness and Play.

b. Not ordered in the mind; not thought out; ill-considered.

1587 ABP. SANDYS *Serm.* (Parker Soc.) 448 Rude and indigested platforms.. tending not to the reformation, but to the destruction of the church of England. 1667 EVELYN *Mem.* (1857) III. 159, I send you notwithstanding these indigested thoughts, and that attempt upon Cicero, which you enjoined me. 1719 DE FOE *Crusoe* I. i, The wild and indigested Notion of raising my Fortune. 1748 RICHARDSON *Clarissa* (1811) II. xliv. 328 Forgive these indigested self-reasonings. 1867 SWINBURNE *Ess. & Stud.* (1875) 177 This is not a fair or clear judgment: it is indigested and violent and deformed in expression.

2. That has not undergone digestion in the stomach.

1620 VENNER *Via Recta* viii. 186 Causing the meat to passe from the stomacke indigested. 1702 *Aristotle's Sec. Secr.* 58 The Stomach cannot digest the Food, but it remains an indigested Nutriment. 1822-34 *Good's Study Med.* (ed. 4) I. 126 Morsels of indigested fruit.

fig. 1868 GEO. ELIOT *Sp. Gipsy* III. 257 Repentance is the weight Of indigested meals ta'en yesterday.

†b. Suffering from indigestion. *Obs.*

1663 P. HENRY *Diary* (1882) 141 Preacht in the aftern. indigested.

†3. Not purified or rectified by heat; crude, raw.

1624 WOTTON *Archit.* in *Reliq.* (1672) 7 That it [the air] be not indigested for want of Sun.

†4. 'Not brought to suppuration' (J.). *Obs.*

1676 WISEMAN *Surgery* (J.), His wound was indigested and inflamed.

Hence **indiˈgestedness**, undigested condition.

1682 BURNET *Life Hale* (R.), They looked on the Common Law as a study that could not be.. formed into a rational science by reason of the indigestedness of it.

indigestibility (ɪndɪdʒɛstɪˈbɪlɪtɪ). [f. next + -ITY. Cf. F. *indigestibilité*.] The quality of being indigestible.

1847 E. J. SEYMOUR *Severe Dis.* I. 35 Experiments on the comparative digestibility or indigestibility of various articles of diet. 1854 BADHAM *Halieut.* 206 Fish of hard fibre, whales, dolphins, seals, and large old thunny, which last.. come very near to them in indigestibility.

indigestible (ɪndɪˈdʒɛstɪb(ə)l), *a.* (*sb.*) [ad. L. *indīgestibilis*, f. *in-* (IN-³) + *dīgestibilis* DIGESTIBLE.] Incapable of being digested, or difficult to digest; not easily assimilated as food.

1528 PAYNEL *Salerne's Regim.* G b, Wheate sodde is heuy meate and indigestable. 1646 SIR T. BROWNE *Pseud. Ep.* III. xxii. 165 To reduce that indigestible substance into such a forme as may.. enter the cavities, and lesse accessible parts of the body, without corrosion. 1774 GOLDSM. *Nat. Hist.* (1776) VI. 111 Among the ancients the goose was abstained from as totally indigestible. 1813 SIR H. DAVY *Agric. Chem.* (1814) 106 Woody fibre appears to be an indigestible substance. 1896 *Amer. Ann. Deaf* Feb. 73 If you give him his [mental] food in an indigestible and unpalatable form, you take away all his interest in his work.

fig. and *transf.* 1603 FLORIO *Montaigne* I. lvi. (1632) 173 They present us with the state of an indigestible agonie. 1625 PURCHAS *Pilgrims* IV. 1808 Out of the indigestable malice that he had conceiued against Biencourt. 1873 MISS BRADDON *L. Davoren* I. Prol. 6 It's rather a pity that one's friends are reported to be indigestible. 1898 LD. CURZON in *Daily News* 8 Nov. 6/4 He had utilised his time at home by placing a number of solid and thoroughly indigestible volumes upon the library shelves.

B. as *sb.* An indigestible substance.

1841 BRANDE *Chem.* 1410 Hair, feathers, the shells of insects.. belong to the class of absolute indigestibles.

Hence **indiˈgestibleness**, the quality of being indigestible; also †inability to digest (*obs.*).

1626 DONNE *Serm.* iv. 38 Our stomachs are dead in an indigestiblenesse, our feete dead in a lamenesse [etc.]. 1727 BAILEY vol. II, *Indigestibleness*, uncapableness of being digested. *Mod.* Things to be avoided on account of their indigestibleness.

indigestion (ɪndɪˈdʒɛstjən). Also 7 indisgestion. [a. F. *indigestion* (13th c. in Hatz.-Darm.), ad. late L. *indīgestiōn-em*, f. *in-* (IN-³) + *dīgestiōn-em* DIGESTION.]

1. Want of digestion; incapacity of or difficulty in digesting food.

1450-1530 *Myrr. our Ladye* 30 They fele some tyme a maner of payne in the stomacke or in the hed, for lacke of sleape or indygestyon. 1495 *Trevisa's Barth. De P.R.* v. xlii. (W. de W.) 159 By scarsyte of vse of mete and indygestion a gloten desyreth indygeste superfluyte of mete. 1601 HOLLAND *Pliny* II. Explan. Words, *Indigestion*, want of concoction and digestion, by which means many crudities and raw humors are ingendered. 1611 COTGR., *Indigestion*, indisgestion, want of disgestion. *a* 1674 CLARENDON *Surv. Leviath.* (1676) 2 Which manner of diet for the indisgestion Mr. Hobbes himself doth much dislike. *c* 1750 SHENSTONE *Ruined Abbey* 82 Wks. 1764 I. 310 The trivial pain Of transient indigestion. 1858-65 CARLYLE *Fredk. Gt.* XI. viii. (1872) IV. 97 'His Imperial Majesty felt slightly indisposed'—indigestion of mushrooms or whatever it was. 1880 BEALE *Slight Ailm.* 84 Indigestion is learnedly spoken of as dyspepsia. 1896 *Allbutt's Syst. Med.* I. 402 Indigestion of amylaceous food leads to the same [acid dyspepsia].

fig. 1824 LADY GRANVILLE *Lett.* (1894) I. 306 The uncertainty of our future plans, gives me a sort of indigestion of mind which quite disturbs its tranquillity. 1891 *Spectator* 5 Sept., We have eaten so much territory in the decade, that if we do not take care, we shall have indigestion. 1894 *Outing* (U.S.) XXIV. 185/1, I wonder the mixture didn't give him moral indigestion.

b. with *pl.* A case or attack of indigestion.

1702 J. PURCELL *Cholick* (1714) 147 The Cure of the Cholick occasion'd by Crudities and Indigestions of an Acid Nature. 1798 MALTHUS *Popul.* (1878) 22 The disorders arising from indigestions. 1845 JAMES *A. Neil* ii, You will give me an indigestion.

2. Undigested condition; the state of not being reduced to order or brought to maturity; disorder, imperfection. Also, an instance of this condition.

1656 BP. HALL *Occas. Medit.* §38 (1851) 45 In this man's country.. our whiteness would pass.. for an unpleasing indigestion of form. 1870 LOWELL *Study Wind.* 5 Leading him to dwell rather upon the indigestions of the elements than his own.

3. *attrib.* and *Comb.*

1861 *Illustr. Lond. News* 25 May 485/1 Eschewing all indigestion-creating.. delicacies. 1897 *Westm. Gaz.* 2 Dec. 3/2 What with the skate and the cycle, liver pills and indigestion syrups should soon vanish from the land.

indigestive (ɪndɪˈdʒɛstɪv), *a.* [f. IN-³ + DIGESTIVE; cf. obs. F. *indigestif* (Godef.).]

1. Characterized by or suffering from indigestion; tending to indigestion; dyspeptic.

1632 SHERWOOD, Indigestiue, *indigeste*. 1658 R. FRANCK *North. Mem.* (1694) 208 To shave off the foreign Ferment from your crude and Indigestive Ventricle. 1861 DICKENS *Gt. Expect.* xxv, She was a cousin, an indigestive single woman. 1870 —— *E. Drood* x, Disturbed from an indigestive after-dinner sleep.

†2. Not ready to 'digest' or brook offences. *Obs.* (Cf. DIGEST *v.* 6.)

1670 COTTON *Espernon* III. xi. 560 To which indigestive humour of his, his Animosity.. being every day exasperated more and more by new Provocations; he, in the end, was no longer able so to conquer his passion.

†ˈindigete. *Obs. rare.* [ad. L. *indiges, -etis.*] A deified hero regarded as a patron deity of his country.

1549 *Compl. Scot.* To Rdr. 8 Amasis the sycond, quhilk vas the last kyng ande indegete of the egiptiens. *marg.*, Indigetes var goddis of egipt quhilkis hed beene verteouse princes quhen thai lyuit.

indight, obs. var. of INDICT and INDITE.

†inˈdigit, *v.* *Obs. rare.* [ad. L. *indigitāre, -etāre* to INDIGITATE.] = INDIGITATE *v.* 2.

1603 HARSNET *Pop. Impost.* 101 Be sure they were reserued for your owne fingring.. indigiting holy priests.

†indigitament. *Obs.* *rare.* [ad. L. *indigitāmentum*, in pl. *indigitāmenta* books containing the names of the gods and prescribing their ritual, f. *indigitā-re* to INDIGITATE: see -MENT.] An appellation or title by which a deity was (in local or special connexion) known and invoked: see also quot. 1675.

1658 W. BURTON *Itin. Antonin.* 56 The indigitaments of old Deities were often inscribed to Rivers; as Belisama, a name of Minerva, to the River Rible.. as the names of Saints are usually to divers places abroad at this day. 1675 BURTHOGGE *Causa Dei* 253 Reuchlin.. affirmeth that.. their Imprecations, Vows, or Blessings were called Indigitaments.

indigitate (ɪnˈdɪdʒɪteɪt), *v.* [f. ppl. stem of L. *indigitāre, -etāre* to call upon, invoke (a deity), to utter, proclaim, declare; of obscure origin, erroneously associated in 16th c. Latin-Eng. Dictionaries with *digitus* finger, and explained as 'to point out as with the finger'; hence the Eng. use in sense 2. Sense 3 is taken directly from *digitus*.]

†1. *trans.* **a.** To call, to indicate by an appellation or name. **b.** To proclaim, declare. *Obs.*

1623 COCKERAM, *Indigitate*, to call; to shew with pointing the finger. 1653 H. MORE *Conject. Cabbal.* (1713) 77 It is not at all harsh to conceive, that they [the Naiades] may be here indigitated by the name of the Upper Waters. *a* 1670 HACKET *Cent. Serm.* (1675) 600 The Scriptures did indigitate he would rise again the third day. 1680 H. MORE *Apocal. Apoc.* 191 Idolatry is indigitated here by φαρμακεια, Sorcery or Witchcraft, as that whereby it is introduced.

†2. To point out with or as with the finger; to show, indicate, point to. *Obs.*

1623 [see 1]. 1646 SIR T. BROWNE *Pseud. Ep.* I. vi. 21 Juvenall and Perseus were no prophets, although their lines did seeme to indigitate and point at our times. 1649 ROBERTS

Clavis Bibl. 620 To indigitate and point out, as with the finger, John Baptist the first Prophet of the New Testament. **1706** PHILLIPS, *To Indigitate*, to shew, or point at, as it were, with the Finger. **1716** M. DAVIES *Athen. Brit.* III. *On Pal. Angl.* 5 Under the Analogy of *Dialectica* or *Logick*, he indigitates the Anabaptists, Rosacrusians, Capucins, Nominalists, and such like gross and mean Elementary Professors.

3. *intr.* To interlock like the fingers of the two hands; to penetrate each other in this way.

1835-6 TODD *Cycl. Anat.* I. 7/2 These bundles [of fleshy fibres] indigitate with those of the diaphragm.

indigitation (ɪndɪdʒɪ'teɪʃən). [n. of action from L. *indigitā-re* to INDIGITATE: see -ATION.]

†**1.** The action of pointing out or indicating; an indication, demonstration; a declaration. *Obs.*

1644 BULWER *Chirol.* 163 The naturall validity of this indigitation of persons. **1653** H. MORE *Antid. Ath.* II. vii. (1662) 59 Which things I conceive no obscure Indigitation of Providence. **1658** PHILLIPS, *Indigitation*, a pointing at, or shewing with the finger. **1689** S. WILLARD in *Andros Tracts* I. 189 This [taking of an oath upon the Bible] must of necessity be more than the bare Indigitation of the Person, and nothing less than a Religious Application. **1706** PHILLIPS, *Indigitation*, an indigitating, or shewing; a convincing Proof, or plain Demonstration.

2. Computing or conversing by the fingers.

1826 SOUTHEY *Vind. Eccl. Angl.* 77 He wrote also upon indigitation, both as an art of computing by the fingers, and of conversing by them.

3. *Anat.* Interlocking of the fingers of two hands; hence, the mode of junction of muscle and tendon.

1846 T. CALLAWAY *Disloc. & Fractures* (1849) 33 The Serratus magnus..takes its rise by nine indigitations from the eight superior ribs. **1851** E. WILSON *Anat. Vade M.* 217 To show the muscles beneath without interfering with its indigitations with the serratus magnus.

indiglucin (ɪndɪ'gluːsɪn). *Chem.* [f. INDI- + Gr. γλυκ-ύς sweet + -IN.] A light yellow sweet compound or 'sugar', $C_6H_{10}O_6$, one of the constituents of indican.

1865-72 WATTS *Dict. Chem.* III. 250 Schunck has further shown that woad contains indican,..which,..when boiled with acids, splits up into indigo-blue and indiglucin.

indign (ɪn'daɪn), *a.* Now only *poet.* Forms: 5-6 indygne, 5-7 indigne, 6 (9) *Sc.* inding, 6- indign. [a. F. *indigne*, ad. L. *indignus* unworthy, f. *in-* (IN-³) + *dignus* worthy.]

1. Unworthy; undeserving. Const. *of* (*to*, or *inf.*). *arch.*

c **1450** *Chaucer's Clerk's T.* 303 (Petw.) Indigne [*other MSS.* vndigne] and vnworþi Am I to þat [honour] þat ȝe me bede. **1483** CAXTON *Gold. Leg.* 417 b/2 A cursyd foole and Indygne hounde that peruertest the myght of god to enchauntementes. *c* **1489** —— *Sonnes of Aymon* vi. 152, I, Indygne for to speke. —— *Blanchardyn* Ded. 1 Unto the right noble puyssaunt & excellent pryncesse,..Moder vnto ..henry þe seuenth..I, wyllyam caxton, his most Indygne humble subgette and lytil seruaunt, presente this lytyl book. **1491** —— *Vitas Patr.* (W. de W. 1495) II. 243 b/2 To haue mercy of me poore synnar & Indygne of thy grete myserycordye. **1536** BELLENDEN *Cron. Scot.* (1821) I. p. vi, I wes in service with the King;..Clerk of his Comptis, thoucht [= though] I wes inding. **1596** SPENSER *F.Q.* IV. i. 30 She her selfe was of his grace indigne. **1618** *Declar. Demeanour Raleigh* 25 If by new offences hee should make himselfe indigne of former mercies. **1657** W. MORICE *Coena quasi Κοινὴ* Def. xvi. 263 No less is every holy Ordinance [polluted] by an indign Partaker. **1678** PHILLIPS (ed. 4) *List Barbarous Words, Indign*, unworthy. **1819** W. TENNANT *Papistry Storm'd* (1827) 192 Worthy o' you to say and sing, Albeit I be to write inding. **1898** T. HARDY *Wessex Poems* 132 Such scope is granted not my powers indign.

2. Unworthy of or unbefitting the person or circumstances; unbecoming; fraught with shame or dishonour; disgraceful.

1545 JOYE *Exp. Dan.* vi. L vij b, It were the moste indygne and detestable thynge that good lawes shulde bee subjecte and under evill men. **1604** SHAKS. *Oth.* I. iii. 274 All indigne, and base aduersities, make head against my Estimation. **1612** T. TAYLOR *Comm. Titus* iii. 1 This were an indigne thing, and a great blot in his high place. **1683** E. HOOKER *Pref. Pordage's Mystic Div.* 104 *note*, When thei sai their Ave Maries (so praiing for her, which is most indign and injurious). **1830** W. PHILLIPS *Mt. Sinai* II. 615 He freely promises; no guerdon mean, Indign, or scant. **1879** TRENCH *Poems* 38 He..counts it scorn to draw Comfort indign from any meaner thing.

b. Of punishment or suffering: Undeserved.

1747 *Advent. Kidnapped Orphan* 142 The villains who have offered such indign treatment to a worthy youth! **1836** GLADSTONE *On an Infant* viii, Fruition of the immortal prize, Purchased for thee..By agony indign.

†**3.** Indignant, resentful. *Obs. rare.*

1652 GAULE *Magastrom.* 274 Nero, indigne in the fall and losse of so necessary a friend and familiar, took occasion against Peter.

†**in'dign**, *v. Obs.* [a. F. *indigner* (14th c. in Hatz.-Darm.), ad. L. *indignā-rī* to regard as unworthy, to be indignant at, f. *indignus* unworthy: cf. ENDEIGN.]

1. *trans.* To treat with indignity.

1490 CAXTON *Eneydos* xviii. 68 Yarbas, kynge of Gectuses, that I haue so ofte indygned, for to auenge hys Iniuryes, shalle reduce me in-to captyuite.

2. To be indignant at or with; to resent.

1652 GAULE *Magastrom.* 242 Diana, indigning this insolency, raised up a scorpion, that slew him. *Ibid.* 282 He, indigning to be thus dealt withall, quite deserted Christianity. **1657** —— *Sapient. Justif.* 106 He is indigning him in especial, that shall..tax him for it.

in'dignance. *rare.* [f. INDIGNANT: see -ANCE. Cf. med.L. *indignantia*.] The fact or condition of being indignant; indignation.

1590 SPENSER *F.Q.* III. xi. 13 With great indignaunce he that sight forsooke. **1790** A. WILSON in *Poems & Lit. Prose* (1876) II. 30 Fired wi indignance I turned round. **1845** R. W. HAMILTON *Pop. Educ.* x. (ed. 2) 269 We are not scared by ..all this towering indignance, this 'Ercles vein'.

indignancy (ɪn'dɪgnənsɪ). *rare.* [f. INDIGNANT: see prec. and -ANCY.] The quality or state of being indignant; indignation.

1790 G. WALKER *Serm.* II. xx. 100 Mutual indignancy breaks an union which mutual esteem and kindness had tied. **1837** J. BUCHANAN *Comfort in Affliction* vi. (1851) 102 A generous indignancy against whatever was base.

indignant (ɪn'dɪgnənt), *a.* (*sb.*) [ad. L. *indignānt-em*, pres. pple. of *indignā-rī* to regard as unworthy, to be indignant at, f. *indignus* unworthy: see INDIGN *a.* and *v.*] Affected with indignation; provoked to wrath by something regarded as unworthy, unjust, or ungrateful; moved by an emotion of anger mingled with scorn or contempt; 'inflamed at once with anger and disdain' (J.). Said of persons, their feelings, etc.; also *fig.* of things.

1590 SPENSER *F.Q.* III. v. 23 Full of fiers fury and indignant hate To him he turned. **1667** MILTON *P.L.* x. 311 Xerxes..Europe with Asia joyn'd; And scourg'd with many a stroak th' indignant waves. *a* **1735** ARBUTHNOT & POPE (J.), The lustful monster fled, pursued by the valorous and indignant Martin. **1770** GOLDSM. *Des. Vill.* 282 His seat.. Indignant spurns the cottage from the green. **1782** COWPER *Boadicea* i, When the British warrior queen, Bleeding from the Roman rods, Sought, with an indignant mien, Counsel of her country's gods. **1870** DICKENS *E. Drood* viii, He feels indignant that Helena's brother should dispose of him so coolly. **1880** C. R. MARKHAM *Peruv. Bark* 45 He published an indignant pamphlet on the subject of his wrongs.

b. Const. *at*; *with* (a person); †*of* (a thing).

1728-46 THOMSON *Spring* 435 And flies aloft, and flounces round the pool, Indignant of the guile. **1797** MRS. RADCLIFFE *Italian* ii. (1826) 16 Indignant at the slander which affected her name. **1805** ANNA SEWARD *Lett.* (1811) VI. 234, I was too indignant of his cruel neglect of Chatterton. **1858** DICKENS *Lett.* (1880) II. 64 Our men are rather indignant with the Irish crowds. **1858** BUCKLE *Civiliz.* (1873) II. viii. 553 The clergy, indignant at such proceedings, murmured and even threatened.

B. *sb.* An indignant person. *rare.*

1861 *Sat. Rev.* XII. 584/1 These three sets of people—the indignants themselves [etc.].

indignantly (ɪn'dɪgnəntlɪ), *adv.* [-LY².]

†**1.** With indignity. *Obs. rare*⁻¹.

1602 WHITGIFT *Let.* in Strype *Life* (1718) 555 [To others he wrot not, especially the Maior, because he took himself so] indignantly [used by him].

2. In an indignant manner, with indignation.

a **1783** H. BROOKE *Fox-Chase* (R.), Indignantly they feel The clanking lash, and the retorted steel. **1788** GIBBON *Decl. & F.* xxxix. (1869) II. 449 They indignantly supported the restraints of peace and discipline. **1828** D'ISRAELI *Chas. I*, I. ii. 17 The little Prince indignantly flung down the square cap, and trampled on it. **1859** TENNYSON *Vivien* 402 He answer'd half indignantly. **1885** L. CARROLL *Tangled Tale* ii. 9 The landlady indignantly protested.

indignation (ɪndɪg'neɪʃən). Forms: 4-5 indignacioun, 4-6 -cion, 5 -cyoun, indygnacion, -cyon, (endyg-, indignacione), 5-6 indignacyon, 6- indignation. [ad. L. *indignātiōn-em*, n. of action f. *indignā-rī* to regard as unworthy, to be indignant at: see INDIGN *v.*; or immed. a. F. *indignation* (12th c. in Hatz.-Darm.).]

†**1.** The action of counting or treating (a person or thing) as unworthy of regard or notice; disdain, contempt; contemptuous behaviour or treatment.

c **1374** CHAUCER *Boeth.* I. pr. iv. 9 (Camb. MS.), I putte me ayeins the hates and indignaciouns of the accusor Cyprian. *c* **1380** WYCLIF *Wks.* (1880) 204 ȝif þei lyuen in pride of herte for nobeleie of blood..& han indignacion and dispit of oþere pore men or wymmen. ? *a* **1400** *Arthur* 48 At Cayrlyone..he let make þe Rounde table..þat no man schulde sytt aboue other, ne haue indignacioun of hys broþer. *c* **1440** *Jacob's Well* (E.E.T.S.) 76 þe sexte cornere of pride is indignacioun. þat is, whan þou hast dysdeyn of symple folk, & lust noȝt to speke to hem. **1530** PALSGR. 234/1 Indygnation, disdaynyng, *indignation*.

†**b.** Treating with indignity. *Obs.*

1513 BRADSHAW *St. Werburge* I. 3474 Lest the cruell gentils..With pollute hondes full of corrupcion Shulde touche her body by indignation. **1526** *Pilgr. Perf.* (W. de W. 1531) 305 And some with great indignacyon offred thy grace aysell to drynke. **1615** G. SANDYS *Trav.* 131 The face [of the Colossus] is something disfigured by time, or indignation of the Moores, detesting images.

2. Anger at what is regarded as unworthy or wrongful; wrath excited by a sense of wrong to oneself or, especially, to others, or by meanness, injustice, wickedness, or misconduct; righteous or dignified anger; the wrath of a superior.

1382 WYCLIF *Isa.* xxvi. 20 Go, my puple..be hid a litil while, to the tyme that passe myn indignacioun. **1470-85** MALORY *Arthur* I. vi, There were some of the grete lordes had indignacion that Arthur shold be kynge. **1526** TINDALE *Matt.* xxvi. 8 When his disciples saw that, they had indignacion sayinge: what neded this wast? **1601** SHAKS. *Twel. N.* III. iv. 269 His indignation deriues it selfe out of a very computent iniurie. **1651** HOBBES *Leviath.* I. vi. 26 Anger for great hurt done to another, when we conceive the same to be done by Injury, [is called] Indignation. **1729** BUTLER *Serm. Resentm.* Wks. 1874 II. 95 The indignation raised by..injustice, and the desire of having it punished.. is by no means malice. **1784** COWPER *Task* v. 442 That man should thus encroach on fellow man..Moves indignation. **1828** D. STEWART *Act. & Mor. Powers* Wks. 1854-8 VI. 202 When injustice offered to *others* awakens resentment against the transgressor..the emotion we feel is more properly denoted in our language by the word *indignation.* **1858** CARLYLE *Fredk. Gt.* III. x. (1872) I. 198 His indignation knew no bounds. **1865** KINGSLEY *Hereward* xxi. 268 Ivo rode on, boiling over with righteous indignation. **1866** LIDDON *Bampt. Lect.* iv. (1875) 192 We cannot regard with any other sentiment than indignation the propagation of what is known to be false.

fig. **1595** SHAKS. *John* II. i. 212 Ready mounted are they to spit forth Their Iron indignation 'gainst your walles. **1613** PURCHAS *Pilgrimage* (1614) 827 The fresh-water not able further to endure the hot indignation of that now-beleeved Burning-Zone, fled out.

b. Const. *against*, *with* (†*of*, †*upon*) a person; *at* (†*against*, †*of*) an action, etc.

1382 WYCLIF *Dan.* xi. 30 He schal turne aȝen, and schal haue indignacioun aȝens the Testament of seyntuarie. —— *Matt.* xx. 24 And the ten herynge hadden indignacioun of the two bretheren. **1520** *Caxton's Chron. Eng.* v. 4 b/1 The Brytons had indygnacyon of Aloth, and wolde not be to hym attendaunt. **1534** ELYOT *Doctr. Princes* 16 Persons..that.. do envie and have indignacion at them that speake truly. **1605** SHAKS. *Lear* I. ii. 86 To suspend your indignation against my Brother. **1607** TOPSELL *Four-f. Beasts* (1658) 81 Venus had turned a Cat into a beautiful woman..who.. contended with the Goddesse for beauty; in indignation whereof, she returned her to her first nature. **1611** BIBLE *Mal.* i. 4 The people against whom the Lord hath indignation for euer. **1667** MILTON *P.L.* IX. 666 With show of Zeale and Love To Man, and indignation at his wrong. **1843** LYTTON *Last Bar.* IV. vi, I read your generous indignation with our poor Clarence. **1856** FROUDE *Hist. Eng.* (1858) I. ii. 157 So great was the indignation against Wolsey.

†**3.** The turning of the stomach against unwelcome food, etc. *Obs.*

1398 TREVISA *Barth. De P.R.* XVII. xxxiii. (Bodl. MS.), Cardomomum..helpeþ þerfor aȝens..wlatenes and indignacioun of þe stomake. **1668** CULPEPPER & COLE *Barthol. Anat.* I. ix. 20 The Pylorus..being Moderator of Digestion: From the indignation whereof he fetches the cause of the Palsie, and Swimming Dizziness of the Head.

4. *Comb.*, as ***indignation-letter***; **indignation-meeting**, a meeting to express public indignation in reference to some proceeding.

18.. W. IRVING *Knickerb.* (Bartlett), Those indignation meetings set on foot in the time of William the Testy, where men met together to rail at public abuses. **1856** *Sat. Rev.* II. 391/2 Paterfamilias, who writes indignation-letters from Margate to the *Times*. **1861** *Ibid.* 7 Dec. 583 When Liverpool heard of the affair of the Trent, there was what the Yankees call an 'indignation meeting'. **1894** MRS. H. WARD *Marcella* I. 101 His constituents held indignation meetings.

in'dignatory, *a. rare.* [f. L. *indignāt-*, ppl. stem of *indignā-rī* to be indignant + -ORY.] Expressive of indignation.

a **1624** BP. M. SMITH *Serm.* (1632) 27 The question is tentatory (Will you also go away?)..the answer is partly indignatory (Lord, to whom shall we goe?). **1834** *Tait's Mag.* I. 367 He may inflate the indignatory muscles of his mouth.

†**in'digned**, *ppl. a. Obs.* [f. F. *indigné* (L. *indignātus*) pa. pple., with English ending -ED¹ 2: cf. INDIGN *v.*] Excited to indignation, rendered indignant; offended, angry.

1490 CAXTON *Eneydos* xix. 70 The Soule of my fader Anchisis, the whiche..apyereth byfore me..strongely indygned, and ayenste me sore moeued. *Ibid.* xxvii. 96 The see wexed right sore impacyent & indigned. *c* **1500** *Melusine* 262 Ye ne owe to be therfore indigned ayenst vs. **1598** YONG *Diana* 481 Indigned spirits, once at my request Powre foorth your wrath.

†**in'dignify**, *v. Obs.* [f. L. *indign-us* unworthy + -FY: cf. DIGNIFY.] To treat with indignity; to dishonour; to represent as unworthy.

1595 SPENSER *Col. Clout* 583, I deeme it best to hold eternally Their bounteous deeds..Then by discourse them to indignifie. **1611** [TARLTON] *Jests* (1844) 14 The gallant, scorning that a player should take the wall, or so much indignifie him..presently drew his rapier. *a* **1626** BP. ANDREWES 96 *Serm., Holy Ghost* (1661) 482 The Elders of the Jews dignified him [the Centurion, *Luke* vii. 4] highly: but he indignified himself as fast. *a* **1684** LEIGHTON *Comm. 1 Pet.* i. 23 Do children delight to indignify and dishonour their father's name? **1743** E. POSTON *Pratler* (1747) 149 The very Idea..is greatly indignified, even by our aiming or pretending to understand it.

indignity (ɪn'dɪgnɪtɪ). [ad. L. *indignitāt-em*, n. of quality f. *indignus* unworthy, INDIGN; cf. F. *indignité* (15-16th c. in Hatz.-Darm.).]

†**1.** The quality or condition of being unworthy; unworthiness. In *pl.*, Unworthy qualities; undeserving traits. *Obs.*

1589 NASHE *Anat. Absurd.* Ep. Ded. 3 Let my vnschooled indignities conuert themselves to your courtesie. **1589** PUTTENHAM *Eng. Poesie* III. iv. (Arb.) 159 In steade of *indignitie*, yee haue vnworthinesse: and for *penetrate*, we may say *peerce*. *a* **1618** SYLVESTER *Du Bartas* Corona Ded., Accept my Zeale, and pardon mine Indignitie. **1677** GALE *Crt. Gentiles* IV. 154 To suppose that God should fetch the commun rule of his giving or not giving grace, from man's dignitie or indignitie.

†2. The quality or condition of being unbecoming, dishonourable, or disgraceful; want or loss of dignity or honour. **b.** Conduct involving shame or disgrace; a disgraceful act. *Obs.*

1596 SPENSER *F.Q.* v. xi. 63 Fie on the pelfe for which good name is sold, And honour with indignitie debased. *Ibid.* vi. i. 28 'To take defiaunce at a Ladies word' (Quoth he) 'I hold it no indignity'. **1603** H. CROSSE *Vertues Commw.* (1878) 22 When he had ended his office, went againe to his olde labour without indignitie to his person, or derogating ought from his worthinesse. **1671** MILTON *Samson* 411 Foul effeminacy held me yoked Her bond-slave; oh, indignity! oh, blot To honour and religion! **1766** GOLDSM. *Vic. W.* xx, A mind too proud to stoop to such indignities.

3. Unworthy treatment; contemptuous or insolent usage; injury accompanied with insult. With *an* and *pl.*: A slight offered to a person; an act intended to expose a person to contempt; an insult or affront.

1584 R. SCOT *Discov. Witchcr.* v. vii. (1886) 83 They thinke it too great an indignitie for Christ to be made subject to Sathans illusions. **1600** HAKLUYT *Voy.* III. 440 Their contempts and indignities offered to our Countrey and Prince. **1610** SHAKS. *Temp.* III. ii. 42 The poore Monster's my subiect, and he shall not suffer indignity. **1665** MANLEY *Grotius' Low C. Warres* 177 He pretended the Indignities offer'd him by the States were the cause of his departure. **1757** SMOLLETT *Reprisal* II. v, You dare not treat me with indignity. **1873** SYMONDS *Grk. Poets* xi. 356 That a human body should toss, unburied, unhonoured, on the waves, seemed to them the last indignity. **1876** GEO. ELIOT *Dan. Der.* III. xxiii, The mere association of anything like 'indignity' with herself, roused a resentful alarm.

†4. Anger excited by unworthy conduct or treatment; = INDIGNATION 2. *Obs.*

1596 SPENSER *F.Q.* IV. vii. 36 Her noble heart with sight thereof was fild With deepe disdaine, and great indignity. **1650** FULLER *Pisgah* IV. iii. 55 God (as justly he might) took this their affront in high indignity. **1701** SWIFT *Contests Athens & Rome* iii. Wks. 1778 II. 265 That great Roman received the notice with the utmost indignity. **1784** BAGE *Barham Downs* I. 105 My bosom glows with indignity at the remembrance.

† in'dignly, *adv. Obs.* [f. INDIGN *a.* + -LY².] In an indign manner, with indignity; undeservedly; shamefully, ignominiously. *to take indignly*: to take as an insult, be indignant at.

1593 NASHE *Christ's T.* (1613) 136 His iust demerits, indignly, draw vnto him vniust hatred. **1607** *Schol. Disc. agst. Antichr.* I. i. 49 They take nothing more indignly, then to see the least indignity offered against it. **1608–11** BP. HALL *Epist.* II. iii. Wks. (1627) 299 A place, I grant, miserably handled by our aduersaries, and .. indignly torne out of the councels. **1612** T. TAYLOR *Comm. Titus* i. 6 Whence we may gather, how indignely the Lord taketh it. **1659** GAUDEN *Tears Ch. Eng.* 53 Behold how I am faln .. indignly, and almost desperately.

† in'dignous, *a. Obs. rare.* Also erron. **indignious.** [f. L. *indign-us* unworthy + -OUS: see INDIGN *a.*] Unworthy; ignominious.

1611 SPEED *Hist. Gt. Brit.* IX. viii. §36. 553 The most indignious injury, which the Pope meant to obtrude vpon him and his Kingdome. *Ibid.,* A farre more indignous wrong and contumely.

indigo ('ɪndɪgəʊ), *sb.* (*a.*) Forms: α. 6–8 indico. β. (6 endego) 6– indigo. [Occurs from 16th c., in the two forms *indico*, *indigo*, repr. two Romanic forms, from L. *indicum* (Pliny), a. Gr. ἰνδικόν (Dioscorides) the blue Indian dye, lit. 'the Indian (substance)', sb. use of neuter of Ἰνδικός, *Indicus*, Indian, *Indico*, ? from Sp., was the usual form in 16-17th c., and continued into the 18th; *endego* occurs in R. Eden 1555 (from the It. of Ramusio *Itinerario* (Venice, 1550), transl. a Portuguese list of prices at Calicut and Malabar), and *indigo* in the 1598 transl. of Linschoten, from Dutch, app. also of Indo-Portuguese origin; but this form came into general use only after the middle of the 17th c.: cf. also F. *indigo*, 1658 in Hatz.-Darm.

The usual name in the Mediterranean countries, before the Portuguese went to India, was *annil*, *anil*, which came west, through Arabic and Persian, from Sanskrit: see ANIL. But *indaco* occurs in It. in 1390: see *Voc. della Crusca,* s.v.]

A. *sb.* **1. a.** A substance obtained in the form of a blue powder from plants of the genus *Indigofera,* N.O. *Leguminosæ,* and largely used as a blue dye.

It is produced by the decomposition of the glucoside INDICAN, which exists not merely in the indigo-plant, but in woad and various other plants. Its essential constituent is indigo-blue; besides which, however, *commercial* or *crude indigo* contains indigo-red, indigo-brown, and some earthy glutinous matters (indigo-gluten).

α. *a* **1599** HAKLUYT *Voy.* II. 218 There goeth out of Chaul .. great quantity of Indico, Opium, Cotton, Silke. **1616** BULLOKAR, *Indico,* a stone brought out of Turkie, wherewith dyers vse to die blew. **1680** MORDEN *Geog. Rect.,* Mogul (1685) 398 In the Suburbs they make Indico. **1686** *Lond. Gaz.* No. 2186/1, 700 Chests of Indico of Guatimala. **1703** MOXON *Mech. Exerc.* 62 Workmen sometimes grind Indico and Sallad-oyl together. **1755** *Gentl. Mag.* XXV. 201 Indico, or Indigo, is a dye extracted from a plant of the same name. **1788** *New Lond. Mag.* 244 A ship .. freighted with indico, cochineal, and rich stuffs.

β. **1555** EDEN *Decades* 239 Endego to dye silke, trewe and good, the farazuola, Fanan. xxx. [RAMUSIO *Itinerario* (1550)]

348 Endego vero e buono val la farazuola, fanoes xxx.] **1598** W. PHILLIPS tr. *Linschoten's Voy.* I. (Hakluyt Soc.] II. 91 Annil or Indigo by the Gusurates is called Gali, by others Nil. [LINSCHOTEN *Itinerarium* (1596) lxix. 92/2 Van't Annil ofte Indigo. Het Annil, anders Indigo ghenaemt, ende in Gusaratte, *Gali*; van andere *Nil.*] **1665** PEPYS *Diary* 25 Sept., We did agree a bargain of £5000 .. for silk, cinnamon, nutmegs, and indigo. **1690** CHILD *Disc. Trade* (1694) 172 It employs the Nation for its Consumption, with Pepper, Indigo, Calicoes, and several useful Drugs. **1712** tr. *Pomet's Hist. Drugs* I. 90. **1731–7** MILLER *Gard. Dict.* (ed. 3) s.v. *Anil,* Every-body does, or should know, that Indigo is a Dye used to dye Wool, Silk, Cloaths and Stuffs blue. **1813** SIR H. DAVY *Agric. Chem.* (1814) 92 Indigo may be procured from Woad .. by digesting alchohol on it, and evaporating the solution. **1826** HENRY *Elem. Chem.* II. 277 Good indigo has a deep blue colour, inclining to purple, and is destitute both of taste and smell. **1865–72** WATTS *Dict. Chem.* III. 250 Its introduction into Europe as a dye is generally attributed to the Jews, who during the middle ages practised the art of dying with indigo in the Levant. **1889** MORLEY & MUIR *Watts' Dict. Chem.* II. 753/1 The Egyptian mummy cases were certainly dyed with indigo, and it has been employed in India for many thousands of years. **1889–96** G. M'GOWAN *Bernthsen's Organ. Chem.* (ed. 3) 469 In addition to indigo-blue (indigotin), commercial indigo contains indigo-gelatine, indigo-brown, and indigo-red, all of which can be extracted from it by solvents. *Ibid.,* Indigo has been prepared synthetically by Baeyer .. from isatin chloride [etc.].

b. *pl.* (In commercial use.) Sorts or samples of indigo. (But formerly a collective pl., like *ashes, oats, grains, silks.*)

1609 SIR H. MIDDLETON in Beveridge *Hist. India* (1862) I. II. i. 251 Their indicoes and other goods of theirs. **1624** CAPT. SMITH *Virginia* v. 171 There are great abundance of .. Tobacco, Sugarcanes, Indicos, Parsnips. **1821** LAMB *Elia* Ser. I. *Imperf. Symp.,* Hast thee heard how indigos go at the India House? **1875** *Ure's Dict. Arts* II. 903 The Manilla indigos present the marks of the rushes upon which they have been dried.

†c. Used in extended sense for 'dye'. *Obs.*

1703 DAMPIER *Voy.* (1729) III. I. 438 They make a saffron-coloured Indico of the Seed, called Arnatto.

2. a. A plant from which indigo is obtained, INDIGO-PLANT, including several species of *Indigofera.*

Among these are **common** or **East Indian i.,** *Indigofera tinctoria,* **W. Indian i.,** *I. Anil,* **Australian i.,** *I. Australis,* **purple-flowered i.,** *I. floribunda.*

1600 J. PORY tr. *Leo's Africa* II. 268 In this prouince groweth great store of Indico, being an herbe like vnto wilde woad. **1613** PURCHAS *Pilgrimage* (1614) 507 Annil or Indigo growes in Cambaia: the herb is like Rosemary. **1657** R. LIGON *Barbadoes* 24 We found Indico planted, and so well ordered, as it is sold in London at very good rates. **1703** DAMPIER *Voy.* (1729) III. I. 438 White Indico has a white Flower, and the Roots yield a blue Juice. **1813** SIR H. DAVY *Agric. Chem.* iii. (1814) 93 The indigo of commerce is principally brought from America. It is procured from the *Indigofera Argentea* or Wild Indigo, the *Indigofera disperma* or Guatimala Indigo, and the *Indigofera tinctoria* or French Indigo. **1876** HARLEY *Mat. Med.* (ed. 6) 657 Indigo .. is a small shrubby plant indigenous to the tropical parts of the East and West Indies, and Africa. **1881** MRS. C. PRAED *Policy & P.* I. vi. 110 Overgrown with rank grass and creeping indigo.

b. Also, with prefixed word, applied to other plants yielding a blue dye: as **bastard indigo,** an American shrub of the genus *Amorpha;* **Chinese** or **Japanese indigo,** *Polygonum tinctorium;* **Egyptian indigo,** *Tephrosia Apollinea* (*Treas. Bot.* 1866); **false** or **wild indigo** (of *U.S.*), (*a*) the genus *Baptisia* (*Treas. Bot.* 1866); (*b*) = *Bastard Indigo;* **Pegu indigo,** *Marsdenia tinctoria.*

1760 J. LEE *Introd. Bot.* App. (1765) 316/1 Indigo, Bastard, *Amorpha.* **1819** *Pantologia, Amorpha,* Bastard indigo. There are two species, both natives of Carolina: *A. fruticosa* and *A. pubescens.* **1841** MRS. LOUDON *Ladies' Comp. Flower-Gard.* (1846) 159–60 The false Indigo, Amorpha, also belongs to Leguminosæ.

3. The colour yielded by indigo, reckoned by Newton as one of the seven prismatic or primary colours, lying in the spectrum between blue and violet, and now often called *blue-violet* or *violet-blue.*

1622 PEACHAM *Compl. Gent.* xiii. (1634) 136 For a deepe and sad Greene, as in the inmost leaves of Trees, mingle Indico and Pinke. **1658** W. SANDERSON *Graphice* 72 Darkest shadows, you may well set off with sap-green and Indico. **1704** NEWTON *Opticks* 87–8 The Spectrum *pt* formed by the separated rays, did .. appear tinged with this series of colours, violet, indico, blue, green, yellow, orange, red, together with all their intermediate degrees, in a continual succession perpetually varying. *Ibid.* 49 It is scarce to be discovered and perceived by sense, except perhaps in the Indigo and Violet. **1831** BREWSTER *Optics* vii. 67 There will be formed upon the screen .. an oblong Image .. of the Sun, containing seven colours, viz. red, orange, yellow, green, blue, indigo, and violet. **1873** HOLLAND *A. Bonnic.* i. 27, I fancy the family blood has been growing blue for several generations, and perhaps there's a little indigo in me. **1874** SYMONDS *Sk. Italy & Greece* (1898) I. i. 21 The pine-forests on the mountain-sides are of darkest indigo.

B. *adj.* (attrib. use of A. 3.) Of a deep violet-blue colour. Also in comb. to express blended shades, as *indigo-black.*

1856 KANE *Arct. Expl.* II. xxiv. 245 We see its deep indigo horizon. **1878** H. S. WILSON *Alp. Ascents* i. 18 A sky of .. a streaky indigo hue. **1897** MARY KINGSLEY *W. Africa* 550 Sometimes it is wreathed with indigo-black tornado clouds.

C. *attrib.* and *Comb.*

1. Simple attrib. and general Comb., as *indigo factory, plantation, vat; indigo-planter; indigo-bearing, -dyed, -producing, -yielding* adjs.

1887 MOLONEY *Forestry W. Afr.* 151 *Indigo-bearing plants. Ibid.* 144 *Indigo-dyed cotton.* **1838** *Penny Cycl.* XII. 460/2 In the *indigo factories of Bengal it is the custom for the European factors to provide the seed. **1888** J. INGLIS *Tent Life Tigerland* 106 The general tendency on all *indigo plantations is to bring .. ryot and landlord into a much more harmonious state. **1772** J. HABERSHAM *Let.* 12 Aug. in *Coll. Georgia Hist. Soc.* (1904) VI. 202 We have had a great Quantity of Rain fall, which must hurt the *Indigoe Planters. **1849** THACKERAY *Pendennis* xxiv, Amory .. set up as indigo-planter and failed. **1876** HARLEY *Mat. Med.* (ed. 6) 657 It appears that the *indigo-producing constituent is indican. **1765** CROKER, etc. *Dict. Arts & Sc.* s.v., Mr. Hellot describes two *indigo vats with urine. **1865–72** WATTS *Dict. Chem.* III. 250 Woad .. is now used only as an addition to the indigo-vat. **1874** SCHORLEMMER *Org. Chem.* 426 An 'indigo-vat' is prepared by mixing one part of powdered indigo with two parts of ferrous sulphate, three parts of slaked lime and 200 parts of water. **1887** MOLONEY *Forestry W. Afr.* 155 In *indigo-yielding plants our knowledge is indeed very contracted.

2. Special Comb.: **indigo-berry,** a name given to: (*a*) the fruit of *Randia latifolia* and *R. aculeata,* from which a blue dye is obtained; (*b*) that of the South American *Passiflora tuberosa* (*Cent. Dict.* 1890); **indigo-broom,** an American name of Wild or False Indigo; **indigo-brown,** a brown resinous substance, a mixture of indihumin and indiretin, existing in all kinds of commercial indigo; **indigo-carmine,** indigo-disulphonate (sulphindigotate) of sodium or potassium, used for dyeing silk, and as a water-colour; **indigo-copper,** the mineral COVELLINE; **indigo-extract:** see quots.; **indigo-finch** = INDIGO-BIRD; **indigo-gelatine, indigo-gluten,** the glutinous matter found in commercial indigo; **indigo-green,** a green substance obtained from indigo by adding potash to an alcoholic solution of an alkaline hyposulphindigotate (*Ure's Dict. Arts* 1875); **indigo-mill,** a name for the cistern in which indigo is triturated to a fine paste (Knight *Dict. Mech.* 1875); **indigo-purple,** purple obtained from indigo by the action of fused sodium sulphate; **indigo-purpurin, indigo-red,** synonyms of INDIRUBIN; **indigo-snake** (*U.S.*), the gopher-snake, *Spilotes Couperi;* **indigo-sulphate, sulphate of indigo:** see quots.; **indigo-sulphonic** (*popularly* -sulphuric) **acids,** i.e. *indigo monosulphonic* and *indigo disulphonic acids,* products of the action of sulphuric acid on indigo-blue; **indigo weed** = *indigo broom;* **indigo-yellow,** 'a substance produced by heating hyposulphindigotate of calcium with lime-water in contact with air; it is a transparent yellow mass' (Watts *Dict. Chem.* 1865–72).

1866 *Treas. Bot.* 621/1 *Indigo-berry, Randia latifolia.* **1838** *Penny Cycl.* XII. 460/1 According to Berzelius the indigo of commerce .. consists of indigo-blue, indigo-red, *indigo-brown, and a glutinous matter. **1855** MAYNE *Expos. Lex., Indigocarmina,* a term used by some chemists for the purple of indigo, a modification of soluble blue .. *indigocarmine. **1865–72** WATTS *Dict. Chem.* III. 261 Sulphindigotate of potassium occurs in commerce as paste or dry powder, known as precipitated indigo, indigo-carmine, soluble indigo or solid blue .. Sulphindigotate of sodium, also called indigo-carmine, resembles the potassium salt, and is used for similar purposes, but is more soluble in saline solutions. **1868** DANA *Min.* (ed. 5) 83 Covellite, .. *Indigo-Copper. **1875** *Ure's Dict. Arts* III. 914 *Indigo-copper,* the native proto-sulphide of copper. **1874** SCHORLEMMER *Org. Chem.* 427 They [pot. & sod. indigotindisulphonates] are found in commerce under the name of 'indigo-carmine' or '*indigo-extract.' **1889** MORLEY & MUIR *Watts' Dict. Chem.* II. 757/2 By dyeing from a bath of indigo-di-sulphonic acid ('sulphindigotic acid', 'indigo-carmine', or 'indigo-extract'). **1865–72** WATTS *Dict. Chem.* III. 257 To obtain it [indigo-brown], the *indigo-gluten is first removed by treating the indigo with dilute sulphuric .. acid. **1838** *Penny Cycl.* XII. 460/2 This solution of indigotin .. has been called sulphate of indigo. According to Berzelius, it contains *indigo-purple, sulphate of indigo, and hyposulphate of indigo. **1865–72** WATTS *Dict. Chem.* III. 257 *Indigo-purple ...* probably consists of sulphindigotate or sulphophœnicate of sodium. *Ibid.* 261 *Sulphophœnicic acid,* 2C₈H₅NO.SO₃, Indigo-purple, Phœnicin, Sulphopurpuric acid. This acid is formed when sulphuric acid is allowed to act upon indigo for a short time, or not in excess. **1838** *Indigo-red* [see *Indigo-brown* above]. **1881** WATTS *Dict. Chem.* 3rd Supp. 1086 When an aqueous solution of indican is boiled .. and .. then decomposed by acids, [it] yields, no longer indigo blue, but indigo-red, and other products. **1884–5** *Riverside Nat. Hist.* (1888) III. 367 *Spilotes couperi .. is known by the negroes as *indigo or gopher-snake. **1875** *Ure's Dict. Arts* II. 906 The compounds [of indigo-sulphuric or sulphindigotic acid] are called *indigo-sulphates, and are, like the acid, of a dark blue colour... The indigo-sulphates of the alkalis may .. be prepared by steeping wool, previously well cleaned, into the solution in sulphuric acid. **1881** WATTS *Dict. Chem.* 3rd Supp. 1088 A peculiar modification of commercial *indigosulphonic acid (commonly called indigosulphuric acid). **1889** MORLEY & MUIR *Watts' Dict. Chem.* II. 758/1 *Indigo-mono-sulphonic acid,* C₁₆H₉N₂O₂(SO₃H), Phœnicine sulphuric acid: a blue powder formed by allowing to stand some time a mixture of indigo with ordinary sulphuric acid. *Ibid., Indigo-di-sulphonic acid,* C₁₆H₈N₂O₂(SO₃H)₂, Sulphindigotic acid, Cæruline-sulphuric-acid, Indigo-

extract. **1785** *Mem. Amer. Acad. Arts & Sci.* I. 473 *Indigofera*... *Indigoweed... A durable pale blue may be obtained from the leaves and small branches. **1852** *Trans. Mich. Agric. Soc.* III. 197 My timber is generally oak, with some hickory, indigo weed, tea weed. **1884** MILLER *Plant-n.*, Indigo-weed, *Baptisia tinctoria.*

'indigo-,bird. A well-known North American bird, a species of painted finch, *Cyanospiza cyanea*, family *Fringillidæ*, the male of which has the head and upper parts of rich indigo-blue. It is found on the Atlantic slope from Canada southward, and is often kept as a cage-bird.

1864-5 WOOD *Homes without H.* xxix. (1868) 550 The Indigo Bird, or Blue Linnet of America, which derives its name from the hue of its feathers. **1870** LOWELL *Study Wind.* (1886) 17 Till within a fortnight, a pair of indigo-birds would keep up their lively *duo* for an hour together. **1884** ROE *Nat. Ser. Story* viii, That indigo-bird in yonder tree-top. **1898** *Atlantic Monthly* Apr. 462/1 Populous with chats, indigo-birds, wood pewees, wood thrushes, and warblers.

indigo-blue, *sb.* and *a.*

A. *sb.* 1. The blue-violet colour of indigo.

1712 E. COOKE *Voy. S. Sea* 329 The Back of an Indigo Blew. **1796** KIRWAN *Elem. Min.* (ed. 2) I. 27 [Colours] Indigo blue—the deepest, nearly black. **1860** TYNDALL *Glac.* I. xxvii. 196 They appeared of a decided indigo-blue. **1879** ROOD *Chromatics* viii. 93 The original white colour passed rapidly through a greenish blue into a beautiful indigo-blue.

2. The blue colouring matter of indigo, also called *indigotin*, $C_{16}H_{10}N_2O_2$, crystallizing in fine right rhombic prisms of blue colour and metallic lustre; pure indigo.

1838 T. THOMSON *Chem. Org. Bodies* 198 The sublimed sulphite becomes blue when dissolved in water, probably in consequence of a little indigo blue having been carried over. **1865-72** WATTS *Dict. Chem.* III. 250 Schunck has further shown that woad contains indican..which..when boiled with acids splits up into indigo-blue and indiglucin, without the intervention of oxygen. **1875** *Ure's Dict. Arts* II. 907 The value of indigo depends entirely on the quantity of indigo-blue which it contains.

B. *adj.* Of the blue colour of indigo.

1836 MACGILLIVRAY tr. *Humboldt's Trav.* xxii. 309 The surface of the bay was of an indigo-blue or violet tint. **1846** G. E. DAY tr. *Simon's Anim. Chem.* II. 178 Urine containing an excess of this colouring matter..deposits a brownish, blackish, or frequently an indigo-blue sediment.

indi'goferous, *a.* [f. INDIGO + L. *-fer* bearing, -FEROUS.] Bearing or producing indigo.

1813 E. BANCROFT *Philos. Perm. Colours* (ed. 2) I. Introd. 42 The blue procured from indigoferous plants, particularly the woad.

indigogen ('ɪndɪgəʊdʒɛn). *Chem.* [f. INDIGO + -GEN, taken as 'producing'.] An obsolete name for INDIGO-WHITE.

1838 T. THOMSON *Chem. Org. Bodies* 375 Indigogen dissolves in alkalies. **1841** BRANDE *Chem.* 1122 The probable composition of white deoxidized indigo, or indigogene. **1878** KINGZETT *Anim. Chem.* 233 Indigo blue is derived from a colourless constituent of the urine or indigogen.

indigoid ('ɪndɪgɔɪd), *a.* (*sb.*) [a. G. *indigoid* (P. Friedländer 1908, in *Ber. d. Deut. Chem. Ges.* XLI. 773): see INDIGO *sb.* (*a*) and -OID.] Of a dye: similar to indigotin in chemical structure, *spec.* in having another atom or atoms, esp. of sulphur, in place of one or both of the imino-groups. Hence as *sb.*, an indigoid dye.

1908 *Jrnl. Chem. Soc.* XCIV. I. 371 (*heading*) Indigoid dyes. *Ibid.*, The author applies the term 'indigoid' to dyes which are related to indigotin in that the imino-groups of the latter are substituted by a sulphur or other bivalent atom or group. **1939** J. B. CONANT *Chem. Org. Compounds* (rev. ed.) xxx. 560 Indigo, its halogenated derivatives, and certain related compounds of analogous structure are sometimes referred to as the indigoids. **1946** *Biochem. Jrnl.* XL. 669/1 This communication describes the isolation and identification of the indigoid pigments indirubin and indigotin from the acid-treated urine of a case of sprue. **1952** K. VENKATARAMAN *Chem. Synthetic Dyes* II. xxxiii. 1004 Apart from indigo itself, the thio-indigoids constitute a much more important series than the indigoids. **1963** A. J. HALL *Textile Sci.* iv. 178 All these new synthetic dyes related in chemical composition to indigo are classed as indigoid dyes. **1966** KIRK & OTHMER *Encycl. Chem. Technol.* (ed. 2) XI. 562 The nomenclature of the indigoids is based on the indole.., or thionaphthene, part of the molecule.

indigolite, variant of INDICOLITE.

1864 in WEBSTER. **1896** in CHESTER *Dict. Names Min.*

indigometer (ɪndɪ'gɒmɪtə(r)). [f. as prec. + -METER.] An instrument for ascertaining the strength of indigo.

So **indi'gometry**, the art or method of determining the colouring power of indigo.

1828 WEBSTER, *Indigometer.* **1847** CRAIG, *Indigometry.*

indigo-plant. A plant yielding indigo; *spec.* a plant of the genus *Indigofera*: cf. INDIGO 2.

1757 H. BAKER in *Phil. Trans.* XL. 137 (*title*) The Effects of the Opuntia, or Prickly Pear, and of the Indigo Plant. **1779** FORREST *Voy. N. Guinea* 270 In that part of the country, the indigo plant taggum grows abundantly amidst the long grass. **1796** STEDMAN *Surinam* II. xxvii. 303, I shall present the curious with a drawing of the indigo plant. **1870** YEATS *Nat. Hist. Comm.* 216 The indigo plant grows best in the East Indies.

'indigotate. *Chem.* [f. as next + -ATE.] A salt of indigotic acid; a nitrosalicylate.

1838 T. THOMSON *Chem. Org. Bodies* 142 Buff found indigotate of barytes composed of Indigotic acid 10.. Barytes 7.

indigotic (ɪndɪ'gɒtɪk), *a.* [f. as INDIGOTIN + -IC.] Of, pertaining to, or produced from indigo; ***indigotic acid***, $C_7H_5(NO_2)O_3$, prepared by treating indigotin with oxidizing agents; = ANILIC ACID.

1838 T. THOMSON *Chem. Org. Bodies* 141 Indigotic acid has been given in the Chemistry of Inorganic bodies. **1866** ODLING *Anim. Chem.* 121 By boiling indigo for a long time with oxidising agents, and by treating salicic acid with strong nitric acid, we obtain identically the same product, which has received the names of anilic, indigotic, and nitro-salicic acid. **1876** tr. *Schützenberger's Ferment.* 118 We ought to add previously to the yellow indigotic liquid a sufficient quantity of a diluted solution of ammonia.

indigotin ('ɪndɪgəʊtɪn). *Chem.* [f. INDIGO + *t* euphonic (cf. *agiotage*) + -IN.] = INDIGO-BLUE.

1838 *Penny Cycl.* XII. 460/1 When common indigo has been treated with dilute acids, alkalis, and alcohol, the remainder is indigo-blue, or indigotin, or indigo nearly in a state of purity. **1874** SCHORLEMMER *Org. Chem.* 425 Indigotin or indigo-blue, $C_{16}H_{10}N_2O_2$.

b. *attrib.* and *Comb.*, as **indigotin-disulphonic** = *indigo disulphonic*; **indigotin-disulphonate** = *sulphindigotate*: see *indigo-carmine* (INDIGO C. 2).

1874 SCHORLEMMER *Org. Chem.* 427 The filtrate from this acid contains indigotindisulphonic acid (indigo-sulphuric acid), $C_{16}H_8N_2O_2(SO_3H)_2$.—[See quot. for *indigo-extract* (INDIGO C. 2).]

indigo-white. *Chem.* Reduced or deoxidized indigo, $C_{16}H_{12}N_2O_2$, also called *leucindigo*, a white crystalline powder produced by subjecting commercial indigo to the action of a reducing agent, as an alkaline fluid; it is re-converted by oxidation to indigo-blue.

Formerly supposed to exist ready-formed in indigoferous plants (see quot. 1850), (whence the former name INDIGOGEN); but now known to be formed from the natural glucoside, INDICAN, by the agency of a special bacillus.

[**1850** DAUBENY *Atom. Th.* viii. (ed. 2) 237 Indigo is extracted from a variety of plants, in which it exists in a colourless form, constituting what is called white indigo, which becomes blue on exposure to light and air.] **1874** SCHORLEMMER *Org. Chem.* 426 Hydro-indigotin or Indigo-white stands in the same relation to indigotin as hydrazobenzene to azobenzene... Indigo-white is a crystalline white powder. **1875** *Ure's Dict. Arts* II. 907 When an excess of some acid is added to the yellow solution, the indigo-white is precipitated in white or greyish-white flocks.

indihumin (ɪndɪ'hju:mɪn). *Chem.* [f. INDI- + L. *hum-us* soil + -IN.] A product of the decomposition of indican, which occurs with indiretin in indigo-brown: formula $C_{10}H_9NO_3$.

1865-72 WATTS *Dict. Chem.* III. 72. **1889** [see INDICAN].

†**indi'judicable**, *a. Obs. rare.* [IN-[3].] Incapable of being decided. Hence †**indi'judicably** *adv.*

1659 STANLEY *Hist. Philos.* XII. (1701) 485/2 Whether will they say, the controversy is dijudicable..or indijudicable? if indijudicable, it is fit we suspend; for in things indijudicably repugnant, it is not possible to assert.

†**indike**, *v. Obs. rare*[−1]. [a. F. *indique-r* to INDICATE.] = INDICATE *v.* 1.

1541 R. COPLAND *Galyen's Terapeut.* 2 D ij b, The which wold indyke the curacyon.

†**indi'latable**, *a. Obs. rare*[−0]. [IN-[3].] Not dilatable. Hence †**indilata'bility**, incapability of being dilated or distended.

1783 POTT *Chirurg. Wks.* II. 169 Who can tell what may be the consequence of..this indilatability of the skin?

†**indi'lately**, *adv. Sc. Obs.* Also 6-7 **indilatlie**, **-laitlie**. [f. IN-[3] + *dilate*, Sc. pa. pple. of DILATE *v.*[1] to delay + -LY[2].] Without delay; immediately, forthwith.

1572 in Calderwood *Hist. Kirk* (Wodrow Soc.) III. 181 We require you indilatlie, upon the recept heereof to proceed to your election. **1579** *Sc. Acts Jas. VI* (1814) III. 138/2 The refuiss or inhabilite of ony persone..to pay þe saidis panes respectiue, presentlie and indilaitlie.

†**in'dilatory**, *a. Obs. rare*[−1]. [IN-[3].] Not dilatory; expeditious.

1654 tr. *Cornwallis' Let. to Sp. King* in *Cabala* Supp. 105 Since you have firmed..new orders..you would be pleased in like manner to give them a new form of indilatory execution.

indileucin (ɪndɪ'l(j)u:sɪn). *Chem.* [f. INDI- + Gr. λευκ-ός white + -IN.] A substance, $C_{16}H_{22}N_2O$, obtained, in colourless glistening needles, by reduction of indirubin with zinc-dust and acetic acid.

1889 MORLEY & MUIR *Watts' Dict. Chem.* II. 760/1.

†**in'diligence**. *Obs.* [ad. L. *indiligentia*, f. *in-* (IN-[3]) + *diligentia* DILIGENCE.]

1. Want of diligence or application; inconstancy or negligence in effort; indolence, sloth.

1496 *Sc. Acts Jas. IV* (1814) II. 238/2 Gif thai be notit of Indeligence of sleuth þarin, þat þai be punyst be þe kingis gude grace. **1604** EDMONDS *Observ. Cæsar's Comm.* 61 The armie was distressed for want of corne by reason of the povertie of the Boij and the indiligence of the Hedui. **1658** PHILLIPS, *Indiligence*, want of diligence, sloth.

2. Want of attention; heedlessness, carelessness.

1636 B. JONSON *Discov.*, *De optimo scriptore* Wks. (Rtldg.) 760/1 Is it not as great an indignity, that an excellent conceit and capacity, by the indiligence of an idle tongue, should be disgrac'd? **1651** JER. TAYLOR *Serm. for Year* I. iii. 38 It is with much errour and great indiligence usually taught in this question, that [etc.].

†**in'diligent**, *a. Obs.* [ad. L. *indīligent-em*, f. *in-* (IN-[3]) + *dīligent-em* attentive, careful; cf. F. *indiligent* (Montaigne, 16th c.).]

1. Not diligent; idle, slothful.

1633 BP. HALL *Hard Texts, N.T.* 50 So is the unfaithfull and indiligent man apt to lay the fault upon his Maker. **1670** EVELYN *Corr.* 20 Jan., I easily believe his Majestie will neither believe the time long nor me altogether indilligent, if he do not receive this Historie so soone as otherwise he might have expected.

2. Inattentive, heedless, careless.

1549 CHALONER *Erasm. on Folly* P iij a, They are indiligent remembrerers what is written in many places of scripture concerning theyr duties. *a* **1617** BAYNE *On Coloss.* i.-ii. (1634) 119 There is such an indiligent carelesnesse that we let them hang in the ayre. **1658** W. BURTON *Itin. Anton.* 26 As will easily appear to the not indiligent Reader of Beda. **1738** WARBURTON *Div. Legat.* I. 22 The most indiligent observer.

Hence †**in'diligently** *adv.*, without diligence.

a **1631** DONNE *Serm.* c. IV. 309 Let us..not pray, not preach, not hear, slackly..suddenly, unadvisedly, extemporally, occasionally, indiligently. *a* **1656** BP. HALL *Rem. Wks.*, *Specialities* (1660) 5 After I had spent some years (not altogether indiligently) under the ferule of such Masters. **1775** E. HARWOOD *Classics* Pref. 11 (Jod.), I have not indiligently revised the whole.

†**in'dim**, *v. Obs. rare*[−1]. [f. IN-[2] + DIM *v.*] *trans.* To make or render dim; to dim.

a **1520** BARCLAY *Jugurth* (Pynson, ed. 2) 76 a, That the ayre therwith was indymed.

indi'mensible, *a. rare*[−1]. [f. IN-[3] + *dimensible* from DIMENSE *v.*] That cannot be measured or reduced to measure.

1844 W. H. MILL *Serm. Tempt. Christ* Notes 161 Things in themselves unmixable are mingled..the Eternal with time, the Indimensible with measure.

indi'mensional, *a. rare*[−1]. [IN-[3].] Not dimensional; having no dimensions.

1875 TAIT in *Gd. Words* No. 1. 20 One of the most singular facts presented to the human mind is the Indimensional character of space.

†**indi'minishable**, *a. Obs. rare.* [IN-[3].] That cannot be diminished or lessened.

1641 MILTON *Reform.* II. (1851) 52 To slight and brave the indiminishable Majestie of our highest Court, the Law-giving and Sacred Parliament. **1799** DAVY in T. Beddoes *Contrib. Phys. & Med. Knowledge* 79 A gas or gases indiminishable by nitrous oxyd. *Ibid.* 167 *note.*

indin ('ɪndɪn). *Chem.* [f. IND-, indigo- + -IN.] A crystalline substance of a beautiful rose-colour, isomeric with indigo-blue.

1845 *Penny Cycl.* Suppl. I. 345/2 *Indin* is prepared by the action of potash on sulphesathyde.. It is isomeric with white indigo. **1865-72** WATTS *Dict. Chem.* III. 265 Indin forms a deep rose-coloured powder, or fine microscopic needles, insoluble in water.

b. *Comb.*: **indin-potassium** ($C_{16}H_{11}N_2O_2K$), the potassium salt of indic acid; ***indinsulphuric acid***, ***indinsulphate***, etc. Also, as a second element in *dibromindin*, *dichlorindin*, *hydrindin*, *nitrindin*, compounds of indin with bromine, chlorine, etc.

1865-72 WATTS *Dict. Chem.* III. 265 *Indin-potassium*.. may be prepared..by warming indin moistened with alcohol, and dissolving it in strong alcoholic potash. *Ibid.* 267 A hot solution of indinsulphuric acid mixed with excess of a potassium-salt..deposits the indinsulphate on cooling in interlaced needles of a dark-red colour. *Ibid.* 268 The barium-salt evaporated down with hydrochloric or sulphuric acid, is converted into indinsulphate of barium.

Hence **in'dinic** *a.*, obs. synonym of INDIC *a.* q.v.

inding, Sc. variant of INDIGN.

Indio ('ɪndɪəʊ). [Sp. and Pg.] A member of one of various indigenous peoples of America and E. Asia in those areas formerly subject to Spain or Portugal; *spec.* (*a*) in Brazil and Mexico, an Indian, distinguished as an ***Indio bravo***, if he had retained his independence, and ***Indio manso*** or ***Indio fidele***, if he had come under European domination; (*b*) = INDIAN *sb.* 1 c. Also **Indiano**.

1836 *Penny Cycl.* V. 365/1 All the aborigines, who lead an independent and roving life, are called in Brazil Indianos bravos, or Gentios, in contradistinction to the Indianos mansos (domesticated Indians), who have settled among, or in the neighbourhood of the Europeans. **1839** *Ibid.* XV. 158/1 The Indios Bravos generally live on the produce of the chase. **1840** *Ibid.* XVIII. 88/1 The mountains [of the Philippines] were occupied by a black race, which..was called by the Spaniards, Negritos or Aetas, while the Malays

were called Indios. **1860** MAYNE REID *Odd People* 43 The 'Indios bravos',..a phrase used throughout all Spanish America to distinguish those tribes..who refused obedience to Spanish tyranny, and who preserve..their native independence and freedom. In contradistinction to the 'Indios bravos' are the 'Indios mansos', or 'tame Indians'. *Ibid.* 44 The true son of the forest—the 'Indio bravo'. **1883** *Encycl. Brit.* XVI. 218/2 The great majority of the *Indios fideles*, mestizoes, and creoles still adhere at least outwardly to the Roman Church. **1901** [see MORO²]. **1969** J. MANDER *Static Society* i. 28 The apparent orthodoxy of the Guatemalan *indio* may conceal the most bizarre Christian-pagan syncretism. **1970** OJEDA & CASTRO tr. *Marche's Luzon & Palawan* v. 60 The *indios* are far from giving up the plow of their fathers.

† **in'dip**, *v. Obs.* Also endip. [f. IN-¹ + DIP *v.* Cf. Du. *indippen.*] *trans.* To dip in.

1596 R. L[INCHE] *Diella, Don Diego* (1877) 82 Sacred Pymplæides endip my quill Within the holy waters of your spring. **1610** G. FLETCHER *Christ's Tri.* II. xi, Whose garment was before indipt in blood. **1631** *Celestina* VI. 77 That poyson..wherewith that cruel shot of Cupid hath it's sharpe point deepely indipped.

Hence † **in'dipping** *vbl. sb.*

a **1564** BECON *Cert. Art. Chr. Relig. in Prayers*, etc. (Parker Soc.) 415 Julius the pope..doth utterly forbid such intinction or indipping, and commandeth that the cup should severally be taken by itself.

indirect (ɪndɪ'rɛkt, -daɪ'rɛkt), *a.* [a. F. *indirect* (1364 in Godef. *Compl.*) or ad. L. *indīrectus* (Quintilian), f. *in-* (IN-³) + *dīrectus* DIRECT.] Not direct.

1. a. Of a way, path, or course: Not straight; crooked, devious; also of a movement: Oblique. (Chiefly *fig.*, often with suggestion of b.)

1474 CAXTON *Chesse* IV. I [lf. 66] The quene foloweth..to a place indirect in the maner of a rook in to the black poynt tofore the physicien [Cessoles (ed. 1505, h I): *Ad locum indirectum ad modum Rochi in quadro nigro ante medicum*]. **1595** C. MIDDLETON *Swimming* 8 Unorderly labouring in the water, they by the indirect mooving of their bodyes pull downe themselves. **1597** SHAKS. *2 Hen. IV*, IV. v. 185 Heauen knowes..By what by-pathes, and indirect crook'd-ways I met this Crowne. **1638** SUCKLING *Aglaura* I. i. (1646) 6 The indirect way's the nearest. **1667** MILTON *P.L.* XI. 631 O pittie and shame, that they..should turn aside to tread Paths indirect, or in the midway faint! **1762** CHURCHILL *Ghost* 702 By ways oblique and indirect.

b. Of actions or feelings: Not straightforward and honest; not fair and open; 'crooked', deceitful, corrupt. (Also of persons: see DIRECT *a.* 5 b.)

1570 *Act 13 Eliz.* c. 20 §1 Livings..may not by corrupt and indirect Dealings be transferred to other Uses. **1604** SHAKS. *Oth.* I. iii. 111 Did you, by indirect and forced courses Subdue, and poyson this yong Maides affections? *a* **1653** GOUGE *Comm. Hebr.* xiii. 5 Whatsoever is by force or fraud, by stealing, lying, or any other indirect course gotten, is an effect of covetousnesse. **1696** PHILLIPS, *Indirect*, said of a thing done by ill Practice, or under-hand Dealing, or by foul means, contrary to Law and Custom. **1708** *Lond. Gaz.* No. 4422/7 One of Her Majesty's..Secretaries of State receiv'd a Letter..promising discovery of several indirect Practices. **1727** SWIFT *Poison. E. Curll* Wks. 1755 III. I. 150, I do sincerely pray forgiveness for those indirect methods I have pursued in inventing new titles to old books, putting authors' names to things they never saw, &c.

c. Of a succession, title, etc.: Not descending or derived in a straight line.

1596 SHAKS. *1 Hen. IV*, IV. iii. 105 His Title, the which wee finde Too indirect, for long continuance.

d. *indirect lighting* (see quot. 1925).

1925 *Gloss. Terms Illum. & Photom.* (B.S.I.) 8 *Indirect lighting*, a system of lighting in which the greater part of the luminous flux reaches the area to be illuminated only after reflection from a ceiling or other object external to the fitting. **1933** *Archit. Rev.* LXXIV. 214 Indirect lighting is housed in a specially designed reflector abutting against a mirror which reflects and doubles it. **1969** *Bodl. Libr. Rec.* VIII. 117 This lighting is not only sufficient for reading, but is diffused to give adequate indirect lighting to the immediate surroundings.

2. a. Not taking the straight or nearest course to the end in view; not going straight to the point; not acting or exercised with direct force; round-about. *spec.* **indirect aggression**, aggression by one nation by other than military means; so **indirect aggressor**; **indirect evidence** = *circumstantial evidence* (CIRCUMSTANTIAL *a.* 1); **indirect rule**, a system of government in which the governed people retain certain administrative and legal, etc., powers.

1584 R. SCOT *Discov. Witchcr.* II. iii. (1886) 19 All maner of waies are to be used, direct and indirect. **1665** BOYLE *Occas. Refl.* Introd. Pref. (1848) 32 To condemn Figurative and Indirect ways of conveying ev'n Serious and Sacred matters, is to forget How often Christ himself made use of Parables. **1720** WATERLAND *Eight Serm.* 237 The implicite or indirect proofs I shall but briefly mention. **1783** WATSON *Philip II* (1793) I. III. 381 To agree to such an indirect form of expression, as might not alarm the pride..of the Spaniards. **1824** T. STARKIE *Pract. Treat. Law of Evidence* I. III. 478 These positions lead immediately to an inquiry into the nature and force of indirect or circumstantial evidence. **1865** TYLOR *Early Hist. Man.* i. 4 The place of direct records has to be supplied, in great measure, by indirect evidence. **1922** F. D. LUGARD *Dual Mandate Brit. Trop. Afr.* x. 199 The Governor of the Gold Coast.. observed: 'The chiefs are keenly appreciative of our policy of indirect rule, and of the full powers they retain under their native institutions.' **1928** —— (title) Representative forms of government and 'indirect rule' in British Africa. *Ibid.* 19, I propose in this chapter to discuss..'Indirect

Rule'—though 'Dependent Rule' would seem a more suitable term,—more especially in..the conditions of tropical Africa. **1931** *Economist* 28 Mar. 667/2 He [*sc.* Sir Donald Cameron]..submitted that this dream would be shattered if the policy, inaugurated in Tanganyika in 1925, of developing that territory on the lines of indirect rule by the mandatory and direct economic production by the natives were allowed to develop. **1939** H. NICOLSON *Diary* 20 July (1966) 406 The Ambassador is..so interested in convincing them how right is the Soviet definition of 'indirect aggression' that he forgets to offer them any tea. **1940** B. WARD *Russian Foreign Policy* 28 Mutual guarantees, the definition of indirect aggression—all these were trivial points compared with the principal obstacle, the Polish guarantee. **1957** P. WORSLEY *Trumpet shall Sound* 261 This became particularly urgent, when..the growing inadequacy of direct methods of rule..brought about the introduction of Indirect Rule in many territories. **1958** *Hansard Commons* 16 July 1245 The question is one of perverting nationalist feelings and perverting those who wish to overthrow the established order of society so that they serve to further indirect aggression. **1958** *Listener* 7 Aug. 185/1 Much has been said about President Nasser's propaganda machine, which has given rise to a new term, 'indirect aggression', which in Western eyes, it seems, may now be held as justification for military intervention. **1958** *Spectator* 8 Aug. 184/3 Nor was this member of the Baghdad Pact the only indirect aggressor against France. **1959** JOWITT *Dict. Eng. Law* II. 960/1 *Indirect evidence*, proof of collateral circumstances from which a fact in controversy, not directly attested by witnesses or documents, may be inferred. **1959** *Spectator* 21 Aug. 236/2 The invention of 'indirect rule', the system of governing a territory by allowing the existing tribal authorities to continue to administer tribal law under the restraint of a British Resident. **1962** *Listener* 18 Oct. 593/2 The legacy of Britain's policy of indirect rule in this Region of Nigeria is clearly visible in the comparatively static nature of these societies.

b. *Logic.* (See quots., and DIRECT *a.* 4 c.)

1727-41 CHAMBERS *Cycl.*, *Indirect Modes*, of syllogisms, in logic, are the five last modes of the first figure..It is the conversion of the conclusion which renders the modes indirect. **1828** WHATELY *Rhet.* I. ii. §1 in *Encycl. Metrop.* 258/1 Either the Premiss of an opponent or his Conclusion may be disproved, either in the Direct or in the Indirect Method; i.e. either by proving the truth of the Contradictory, or by showing that an absurd Conclusion may fairly be deduced from the Proposition in question. **1860** ABP. THOMSON *Laws Th.* §127. 271 Showing that something impossible or absurd follows from contradicting our conclusion is called indirect demonstration. **1864** BOWEN *Logic* v. 141 Indirect..predication was..that..in which the species was predicated of the genus [etc.]. *Ibid.* vii. 201 If we exclude the Fourth Figure altogether, considering Bramantip, Camenes, &c. as indirect Moods of the First, there are but fourteen direct Moods. **1891** [see DIRECT *a.* 4 c]. **1896** WELTON *Manual of Logic* (ed. 2) IV. iv. §128 I. 358 Reduction is indirect when a new syllogism is formed which establishes the validity of the original conclusion by showing the illegitimacy of its Contradictory.

c. *Pol. Econ.* Of taxation: Not levied directly upon the person on whom it ultimately falls, but charged in some other way, esp. upon the production or importation of articles of use or consumption, the price of which is thereby augmented to the consumer, who thus pays the tax in the form of increased price. Cf. DIRECT *a.* 6 e.

1801 A. HAMILTON *Wks.* (1886) VII. 192 That which is called the direct tax..was always insisted upon by them as preferable to taxes of the indirect kind. **1845** [see DIRECT *a.* 6 e]. **1868** ROGERS *Pol. Econ.* xxii. (1876) 287 The greater part of the taxes raised in this and in most other civilised countries are known as indirect. They consist in the levy of imposts on articles of consumption [etc.]. **1884** J. RAE *Contemp. Socialism* i. 37 Customs and indirect taxation of different kinds.

d. *Metallurgy.* Designating a process by which wrought iron or steel is obtained from the ore through the intermediate stage of pig iron (the usual method).

1869 H. S. OSBORN *Metall. Iron & Steel* II. ii. 274 In ancient times iron was extracted from the ore as malleable iron. This is called the direct, in contra-distinction to the present method of producing cast iron and afterward malleable, which latter is called the indirect method. **1967** W. H. DENNIS *Found. Iron & Steel Metall.* i. 13 Gradually a technique was developed of removing the derived impurities... This process was designated fining..and resulted in wrought iron... The method involved a two-stage process: (a) Reduction of iron ore to make pig iron, and (b) remelting and purifying the pig iron to make wrought iron and hence was an indirect process in contrast to the former direct process of producing iron blooms from the ore in one stage.

e. *indirect address* (*Computing*): an address (ADDRESS *sb.* 7 b) which specifies the location of information about the address of an operand, rather than the location of the operand itself; cf. *direct address* s.v. DIRECT *a.* 7 i; so *indirect addressing* vbl. sb.

1959 *Jrnl. Assoc. Computing Machinery* Apr. 130 The 709 has built-in indirect addressing; i.e., the address field can specify the location of a location rather than the location of an operand. **1960** *Datamation* Sept.-Oct. 33/1 Whenever an indirect address is specified, it selects another half-word in which is contained another address. **1970** O. DOPPING *Computers & Data Processing* vi. 105 One can say that the contrary of immediate addressing is indirect addressing, which can be used in certain computers and denoted by a tag in the instruction. **1979** *Sci. Amer.* Apr. 75/3 In another method, called indirect addressing, the address given in a program specifies not the actual location of the desired data but a register or a memory cell where the address will be found. **1980** C. S. FRENCH *Computer Sci.* xxiv. 181 If the second address is yet a further indirect address then the address is called a multi-level address.

3. *Gram.* † **a.** *indirect relation*, the syntactical relation between two words which are not in full grammatical concord.

1393 LANGL. *P. Pl.* C. IV. 344 Quaþ þe kynge to conscience, 'knowen ich wolde What is relacion rect and indyrect after..for englisch was it neuere'. *Ibid.* 365 Thus is relacion rect ryht as adiectif and substantif A-cordeþ in alle kyndes with his antecedent. Indirect pyng ys as ho so coueited Alle kynne kynde to knowe and to folwe, With-oute [case] to cacche [to] and come to boþe numbres.

b. Of speech or narration: Put in a reported form, not in the speaker's own words, but with the changes of pronouns, persons, tenses, etc. which conform it to the point of view of the reporter; oblique: opposed to DIRECT *a.* 6 b.

The idioms of different languages differ widely in respect to indirect construction. In English, indirect sentences are usually introduced by *that* or *if*, expressed or understood. Thus, a speaker's actual words 'I will not go unless you use force', are reported indirectly, by the person addressed, as 'he said [that] he would not go unless I used force', by a third party as 'he told X. [that] he would not go, unless he (X.) used force'. The question 'Do you know me?' becomes, in indirect narration, 'He asked me if I knew him', and 'he asked X. if he knew him'.

1866 MASON *Eng. Gram.* (ed. 7) 111 In such sentences.. the dependent clauses are indirect questions. **1866** W. E. JELF *Grk. Gram.* (ed. 4) §886 II. 627 Indirect interrog. sentences. **1870-7** MOULTON tr. *Winer's N.T. Gram.* III. §60. 9 When words spoken by others are quoted, they are not, as a rule, brought into the structure of the sentence in the indirect construction. **1879** ROBY *Lat. Gram.* II. 342 When a statement, question [etc.] is reported in a form which makes it dependent in construction on some such words as *said*, the language is said to be oblique or indirect.

c. *indirect object* (see quots.).

1879 ROBY *Lat. Gram.* II. 54 The indirect object is the person (or thing) affected by the occurrence of an action.. although not directly or primarily acted on. **1881** MASON *Eng. Gram.* (ed. 24) 149 The Indirect Object of a verb denotes that which is indirectly affected by an action, but is not the immediate object or product of it, as 'Give *him* the book', 'Make *me* a coat'.

d. *indirect passive*, a passive verb having for its subject the indirect object of the active voice, as *I was told it*; *he was refused admittance*; *the mayor is given power and authority* (see GIVE *v.* 2); also, a passive voice formed on an intransitive verb construed with a preposition, the prepositional object becoming the subject of the passive verb, while the preposition becomes adverbial, as *they have spoken to him, he has been spoken to*; *many run after her, she is much run after*.

4. a. Not directly aimed at or attained; not immediately resulting from an action or cause.

1823 SCOTT *Peveril* xxxix, He is one who will neither seek an indirect advantage by a specious road, nor take an evil path to gain a real good purpose. **1849** MACAULAY *Hist. Eng.* vi. II. 95 He could not bring himself to sacrifice..his salary of eight thousand pounds a year, and the far larger indirect emoluments of his office. **1875** JOWETT *Plato* (ed. 2) III. 9 Happiness is not the direct aim, but the indirect consequence of the good government.

b. *Biol.* Of nuclear or cell division: mitotic.

[**1879** W. FLEMMING in *Arch. f. path. Anat. u. Physiol.* LXXVII. 3 Bei anderen..Fällen..lassen sich Bilder, die anscheinend einer directen Kerntheilung entsprachen, einer indirecten (s.u.) zudeuten.] **1880** *Jrnl. R. Microsc. Soc.* III. 51 In discussing the changes undergone by the nucleus in cell-division, Professor W. Flemming distinguishes two methods of division which have been described by various observers, the direct and the indirect. **1888** [see AMITOTIC *a.*]. **1909** J. R. GREEN *Hist. Bot.* II. i. 181 The terms indirect, and direct, nuclear division were introduced by Flemming in 1879, and were long in favour. **1925** E. B. WILSON *Cell* (ed. 3) ii. 116 Mitosis (indirect division).

5. Of or pertaining to the work and expenses which cannot be apportioned to any particular job or undertaking, pertaining to overhead charges and subsidiary work. (Cf. DIRECT *a.* 6 f.)

1903, 1922 [see DIRECT *a.* 6 f]. **1925** R. J. H. RYALL *Primer of Costing* 49 Labour may be employed in..repairing machinery..or in supervising the direct workers... Such labour is classified as Indirect Labour. **1966** *New Statesman* 19 Aug. 256/1 The Americans..are more inclined to lay down precise standards for the number of indirect workers who ought to be employed in a particular location. **1974** *Times* 4 Feb. 15/4 Its first offer..covers..some 4,300 'indirect' workers—men who service the production areas —in the body plant.

6. *indirect fire*, gunfire aimed at a target which cannot be seen (see quot. 1918).

1879 *Man. Siege & Garrison Artill. Exerc.* I. 23 Indirect or curved fire from guns or howitzers. *Ibid.* 24 Breaching by indirect fire would, as a rule, be by demolition and not by the formation of regular cuts. **1918** E. S. FARROW *Dict. Mil. Terms* 309 *Indirect Fire*, when the target cannot be seen, and guns are aimed by means of calculations, from map, or by bearings. *Indirect Laying Fire*, when the gun is laid for direction on an aiming point or on aiming points and elevation adjusted by sight clinometer. **1962** *Ordnance Technical Terminol.* (U.S. Army Ordnance School) (AD 660 112) 162/2 *Indirect fire*, gunfire delivered at a target that cannot be seen from the gun position or firing ship.

indi'rected, *a. rare.* [IN-³.] Not directed or guided.

1601 CORNWALLYES *Disc. Seneca* (1631) 71 Have fixed their indirected steppes upon Arts unprofitable. **1819** CRABBE *Tales of Hall* IV. 228, I pray'd in heart an indirected prayer.

indirection (ɪndɪˈrɛkʃən). [f. INDIRECT, after DIRECTION.]

1. Indirect movement or action; a devious or circuitous course to some end; round-about means or method. ***by indirection***, by indirect means, indirectly.

1602 SHAKS. *Ham.* II. i. 65 And thus doe we..By indirections finde directions out. **1634** FORD *P. Warbeck* III. iii, If king James, By any indirection, should perceive My coming near your court, I doubt the issue Of my employment. **1673** S. C. *Art of Complaisance* 73 These were the effects of real merit and virtue, which still sheds a luster on the rest, and not of indirection. **1856** EMERSON *Eng. Traits* xiii. 211 Oxford also has its merits... Whether in course or by indirection,..education according to the English notion of it is arrived at. **1879** J. BURROUGHS *Locusts & W. Honey* (1884) 100 The weather is..to be understood, not by rule, but by subtle signs and indirections. **1888** *Q. Rev.* Oct. 407 As is always the case with good critics, Mr. Arnold worked more by indirection and suggestion than by sheer delivery of judgment.

b. In literal sense: An indirect or devious way.

1858 HAWTHORNE *Fr. & It. Jrnls.* (1872) I. 16 Through some other indirections we at last found the Rue Bergère.

2. Want of straightforwardness in action; an act, or practice, which is not straightforward and honest; deceit; malpractice.

1595 SHAKS. *John* III. i. 276 The better Act of purposes mistooke, Is to mistake again, though indirect, Yet indirection thereby growes direct, And falshood, falshood cures. **1601** —— *Jul. C.* IV. iii. 75 To wring From the hard hands of Peazants, their vile trash By any indirection. **1710** *Tatler* No. 191 ¶1 The Indirection and Artifice which is used among Men. **1834** MAR. EDGEWORTH *Helen* (Rtldg.) 106 To no vile indirections will I stoop. **1895** *Rev. of Rev.* Aug. 138 He hated diplomatic indirections, or, to speak bluntly, lying.

indirectly (ɪndɪˈrɛktlɪ, -daɪˈrɛkt-), *adv.* Also 6 indyrectly. [f. INDIRECT + -LY^2; in early use perh. f. IN-^{3} + DIRECTLY.] In an indirect way or manner; not directly.

1. Not in a straight line or with a straight course; circuitously: obliquely. Now *rare*.

1474 CAXTON *Chesse* [lf. 67] The quene..[may go] on the right side tofore the alphyn & secondly on the lift syde where the knyght is & thirdly Indirectly vnto the black poynt tofore the phisicien [CESSOLES (ed. 1505, h 1 b): *Tercio indirectum: ad locum nigrum & uacuum ante medicum*]. **1503** HAWES *Examp. Virt.* xiv. 6 Entrynge theyr houses of the .xii. synes Some indyrectly and some by dyrecte lynes. **1563** W. FULKE *Meteors* (1640) 4 b, In places where the beames are cast indirectly and obliquely. **1596** *Edward III*, I. i. 2 You are the lineal watchman of our peace, And John of Valois indirectly climbs. **1831** BREWSTER *Nat. Magic* ii. (1833) 15 All objects seen indirectly are seen indistinctly.

†**b.** By crooked methods; wrongfully, unfairly, dishonestly. *Obs.*

1580 HOLLYBAND *Treas. Fr. Tong, Apposter*, to suborne, to appointe some body to saye or doe indirectlye. **1599** SHAKS. *Hen. V*, II. iv. 94 He bids you then resigne Your Crowne and Kingdome, indirectly held From him. **1603** HOLLAND *Plutarch's Mor.* 937 Unto whom this imputation was laid, that by corruption he had caried away the prize, and indirectly obteined the victorie.

†**c.** Not to the point, evasively. *Obs.*

1596 SHAKS. *1 Hen. IV*, I. iii. 66 This bald, vnioynted Chat of his..Made me to answer indirectly. **1603** —— *Meas. for M.* IV. vi. 1 To speak so indirectly I am loath, I would say the truth, but to accuse him so That is your part. **1673** DRYDEN *Marr. à la Mode* II. i, You answer sawcily, and indirectly: What Interest can you pretend in her? **1712** ADDISON *Spect.* No. 305 ¶11 The other is to answer him indirectly, and, if possible, to turn off the Question.

2. By indirect action, means, connexion, agency, or instrumentality; through some intervening person or thing; mediately.

1477 EARL RIVERS (Caxton) *Dictes* 56 The lyf Jugeth inderectly amongis the dede. **1526** *Pilgr. Perf.* (W. de W. 1531) 165 Eyther immediatly or mediatly, that is to say, without meane, or by some meane, directly or indirectly. **1590** SWINBURNE *Testaments* 199 Whereof any person is not capable directly or by himselfe, he is not capable thereof, indirectly or by an other. **1655** SIR E. NICHOLAS in *N. Papers* (Camden) II. 172 Tell vs freely whether..Tom Chichly holds any correspondence directly or indirectly with Secretarie Nich. **1776** ADAM SMITH *W.N.* V. ii. II. (1869) II. 466 The state not knowing how to tax, directly and proportionably, the revenue of its subjects, endeavours to tax it indirectly by taxing their expense, which, it is supposed, will in most cases be nearly in proportion to their revenue. **1885** TAIT *Prop. Matter* iii. §34. 26 Its weight, except indirectly through friction, has nothing to do with it.

b. Not in express terms; by suggestion or implication.

1594 SHAKS. *Rich. III*, IV. iv. 225 Whose hand soeuer lanch'd their tender hearts, Thy head (all indirectly) gaue direction. **1613** WITHER *Abuses* IV. in *Juvenilia* (1633) 26 If to the Father they dispraise the Sonne, It shall be slily indirectly done. **1875** JOWETT *Plato* (ed. 2) IV. 230 The question..has been already asked and indirectly answered in the Meno. **1882** WESTCOTT *St. John* Introd. 5 What then is the evidence which the fourth Gospel itself bears to its authorship, first indirectly, and next directly?

3. *Gram.* In or by indirect or oblique oration (see INDIRECT *a.* 3 b).

1877 MOULTON tr. *Winer's N.T. Gram.* III. §60. 2 When a writer has begun by quoting words indirectly, he will frequently pass very quickly into the *oratio directa*.

indirectness (ˌɪndɪˈrɛktnɪs, -daɪˈrɛkt-). [f. INDIRECT *a.* + -NESS.] The quality of being indirect; want of directness or straightforwardness.

1628 WITHER *Brit. Rememb.* VII. 1581 Is thy Sov'raynes path Unequall? or is't rather thine which hath Such indirectnesse? **1654** W. MOUNTAGUE *Devout Ess.* II. vii. §5. 142 The maligners of this doctrine of Purgatorie, have methinks, us'd a worse kind of indirectness in their exposure of it. **1790** PALEY *Horæ Paul.* i. 4 This very indirectness and subtlety is that which gives force and propriety to the example. **1821–30** LD. COCKBURN *Mem.* iii. (1874) 140 Indirectness was..entirely foreign to his manly nature.

indiretin (ɪndɪˈriːtɪn). *Chem.* [f. INDI- + Gr. ῥητίνη resin + -IN.] A dark-brown shining resin, $C_{18}H_{17}NO_5$, one of the components of indigo-brown, obtained by decomposition of indican.

1865–72 WATTS *Dict. Chem.* III. 248 The indiretin which still remains in solution is separated by ammonia. **1889** [see INDICAN].

indirubin (ɪndɪˈruːbɪn). *Chem.* [f. INDI- + L. *rub-er* red + -IN.] A substance, isomeric with indigo-blue, obtained by decomposition of indican, crystallizing in long purple metallic-shining needles. Also called *indigo-purpurin* and *indigo-red.*

1859 [see INDICAN]. **1865–72** WATTS *Dict. Chem.* III. 249 On..exposing the filtrate to the air, a purple-red deposit is formed, consisting of indirubin. **1881** *Nature* XXIV. 230 The red isomeride of indigo-blue, Indirubin..possesses a splendid red colour, but has little or no tinctorial power. **1889** MORLEY & MUIR *Watts' Dict. Chem.* II. 759/2 When fresh indican solution is mixed with strong acid and boiled, only indigo and indiglucin are obtained, but if the indican solution is previously boiled for a short time indirubin is also formed.

†**indi'scerned**, *a. Obs. rare*$^{-1}$. [IN-^{3}.] Not discerned, indistinct.

1652 GAULE *Magastrom.* 166 The study and search.. proves very confused, indiscerned, unsafe, and pernicious.

indiscerni'bility. [f. INDISCERNIBLE *a.*: see -ITY.] The quality or condition of being indiscernible.

1878 S. H. HODGSON *Philos. of Reflection* II. 140 Indiscernibility in point of content is therefore the final test of truth in concrete reasoning. **1892** W. WALLACE tr. *Hegel's Logic* (ed. 2) 417 The principle of individuation or indiscernibility is: 'If two individuals were perfectly alike [etc.]'. **1936** *Mind* XLV. 245 This latter kind of immediacy is unmediatedness, or indiscernibility of any mediation. **1953** W. V. QUINE *From Logical Point of View* viii. 139 One of the fundamental principles governing identity is that of *substitutivity*—or, as it might well be called, that of *indiscernibility of identicals.* **1955** A. N. PRIOR *Formal Logic* 264 Even if we do not admit..the 'identity of indiscernibles', we must admit the indiscernibility of identicals. **1962** W. & M. KNEALE *Devel. of Logic* x. 604, $x = y \supset (fx \supset fy)$ may perhaps be called the principle of the indiscernibility of identicals. **1973** A. QUINTON *Nature of Things* vi. 153 The indiscernibility of dreams..does not cast doubt on necessary truths.

indiscernible (ɪndɪˈzɜːnɪb(ə)l, -ˈsɜːn-), *a.* and *sb.* Also 7 -able. [f. IN-^{3} + DISCERNIBLE: cf. F. *indiscernable* (1582 in Hatz.-Darm.).]

A. *adj.* **1.** Incapable of being discerned by the senses or intellect; imperceptible; undiscoverable.

1635 SWAN *Spec. M.* v. §2 (1643) 148 Dew..falleth down in very small and indiscernible drops. **1640** W. CRABTRIE in *Phil. Trans.* XXVII. 283 The light of the Sun..doth make it..indiscernable. **1664** POWER *Exp. Philos.* I. 18 An Animal ..whose whole bulk to the bare eye is quite indiscernable. **1754** SHERLOCK *Disc.* (1759) I. 63 His Wisdom and Holiness, and even his Mercy, are as indiscernible as his Justice. **1853** READE *Chr. Johnstone* 34 A rapid look, indiscernible by male eye. **1879** CHR. G. ROSSETTI *Seek & F.* 192 Be the stars at a given moment discernible or indiscernible by our vision.

2. That cannot be distinguished (*from* something else); indistinguishable. *Obs.* or *arch.*

1646 SIR T. BROWNE *Pseud. Ep.* III. xxv. 176 That red and sanguineous humor..affording in linnen or paper an indiscernable tincture from blood. **1825** WATERTON *Wand. S. Amer.* I. (1887) 79 The mountains gradually retire..till they are indiscernible from the clouds in which they are involved.

B. *sb.* **1.** A thing (animal, etc.) that cannot be discerned by the senses.

1835 KIRBY *Hab. & Inst. Anim.* (1852) I. 162 The infusories, or as they have been also called *animalcules, microscopic animals, acrita* or indiscernibles.

2. *Metaph.* A thing that cannot be distinguished from some other thing or things.

identity of indiscernibles: the doctrine that things cannot exist together as separate entities unless they have different attributes.

1717 S. CLARKE *Leibnitz' 5th Paper* 173 The Supposition of two Indiscernibles, such as two Pieces of Matter perfectly alike, seems indeed to be possible in abstract Terms. **1877** E. CAIRD *Philos. Kant* Introd. v. 82 Where there is no difference, there is no activity, and hence no substance or individuality. This is the meaning of the celebrated 'identity of indiscernibles'. **1882** *Sat. Rev.* 11 Mar. 289 Mr. Gladstone, whose ingenuity in detecting the non-identity of indiscernibles..has been sharpened by this matter to a preternatural degree.

Hence **indi'scernibleness**, the quality of being indiscernible; **indi'scernibly** *adv.*, in an indiscernible manner, imperceptibly.

1643 T. GOODWIN *Child of Night* 61 He is able indiscernibly to communicate all his false reasonings. **1648** HAMMOND *Serm.* iv. Wks. 1684 IV. 494, I should have shew'd you also the indiscernibleness (to the eye of man) of the difference of these distant states. **1821** DE QUINCEY *Richter* Wks. 1860 XIV. 117 The pathetic and the humorous ..melt indiscernibly into each other. **1885** *Sat. Rev.* 30 May 717 The human mind is seldom found in such a state of indiscernibleness.

†**indi'scerning**, *a. Obs. rare.* [IN-^{3}.] Not discerning.

1660 N. INGELO *Bentivolio & Urania* (1682) II. 126 That so many varieties..should rise out of Matter by a blind scuffle of indiscerning Principles, is..an absurd Phancy.

†**indi'scerpible**, *a. Obs.* [f. IN-^{3} + DISCERPIBLE.] = INDISCERPTIBLE.

1659 H. MORE *Immort. Soul* (1662) 111 A Soul..is a Spirit, and therefore of an Indivisible, that is, of an Indiscerpible, Essence. **1662** GLANVILL *Lux Orient.* iv. (1682) 35 The soul, which is immortal and indiscerpible. **1703** KELSEY *Serm.* 224 Some Philosophers make it [the Soul] a Substance indiscerpible, that it cannot be divided. **1722** WOLLASTON *Relig. Nat.* ix. 189 That there should be atoms, whose parts are..indiscerpible. **1837–9** HALLAM *Hist. Lit.* III. III. iii. §63 If..we could know the internal structure of one primary atom, and could tell..through what constant laws its component, though indiscerpible, molecules, the atoms of atoms, attract, retain, and repel each other.

Hence †**indiscerpi'bility**, †**indi'scerpibleness**, the quality of being indiscerpible; †**indi'scerpibly** *adv.*, in an indiscerpible manner.

1659 H. MORE *Immort. Soul* Pref. (1662) 7 Endowing it with such Attributes as are essential to it, as Indiscerpibility is to the Soul of Man. **1678** CUDWORTH *Intell. Syst.* Contents (I. v. 833) Something..extended otherwise than Body, so as to be penetrable thereof, and indiscerpibly one with itself and self-active. **1682** H. MORE *Annot. Glanvill's Lux O.* 222 An Indiscerpibleness not arising from thinner and thinner parts of matter. **1721** BAILEY, *Indiscerpibility*, a being inseperable.

indiscerptible (ɪndɪˈsɜːptɪb(ə)l), *a.* [f. IN-^{3} + DISCERPTIBLE.] Incapable of being divided into parts; not destructible by dissolution of parts.

1736 BUTLER *Anal.* I. i. Wks. 1874 I. 21 There is no.. reason to think death to be the dissolution..of the living being, even though it should not be absolutely indiscerptible. **1759** JOHNSON *Rasselas* xlvii, A power impassive and indiscerptible. *a* **1848** R. W. HAMILTON *Rew. & Punishm.* v. (1853) 216 The soul has no parts to be separated: in Butler's phrase, it is indiscerptible. **1880** PRITCHARD in *Churchman* No. 5. 330 Definite groups or clusters of indiscerptible atoms are associated, we believe, into molecules.

Hence **indiscerpti'bility**, **indi'scerptibleness**, the quality of being indiscerptible; **indi'scerptibly** *adv.*

1755 JOHNSON, *Indiscerptibility*, incapability of dissolution. **1775** ASH, *Indiscerptibleness.* **1825** R. P. WARD *Tremaine* III. ix. 83 The indiscerptibility of thought..is, in truth, the great argument which goes to the bottom of the proof *à priori.* **1855** DE QUINCEY in 'H. A. Page' *Life* (1877) II. xviii. 128 Its indiscerptibility or non-liability to violent separation.

indisciplinable (ɪnˈdɪsɪplɪnəb(ə)l), *a.* [f. IN-^{3} + DISCIPLINABLE: cf. F. *indisciplinable* (1580 in Hatz.-Darm.).] Incapable of being disciplined; not amenable to discipline; intractable.

1600 ABP. ABBOT *Exp. Jonah* 354 Their rudeness and indisciplinable barbarisme. *a* **1652** J. SMITH *Sel. Disc.* iv. 85 Sense..which is the most indisciplinable thing that may be. *a* **1676** HALE *Provis. Poor* Pref. (Mason), Necessity renders men of phlegmatic and dull natures stupid and indisciplinable. **1793** W. GODWIN *Enq. conc. Polit. Justice* 304, 311. **1814** SHELLEY *Review Hogg* (1886) 27 His great though indisciplinable energies.

†**in'disciplinate**, *a. Obs. rare.* [ad. late L. *indisciplīnāt-us*, f. *in-* (IN-^{3}) + *disciplīnāt-us* DISCIPLINATE: cf. F. *indiscipliné.*] Not disciplined; not subjected to discipline.

c **1450** tr. *De Imitatione* II. iii. 43 Harde & ouerthwart men indisciplinate & contrariouse. **1579** J. FIELD tr. *Calvin's Serm.* Ded., An indisciplinate kinde of life.

†**indiscipli'nation.** *Obs. rare*$^{-1}$. [ad. late L. *indisciplīnātiōn-em*, f. *in-* (IN-^{3}) + *disciplīnātiōn-em* DISCIPLINATION.] Non-subjection to discipline; undisciplined conduct.

c **1450** tr. *De Imitatione* III. xii. 80 Lest þou engendre sclaundre in oþir þoruȝ indisciplinacion.

indiscipline (ɪnˈdɪsɪplɪn). [f. IN-^{3} + DISCIPLINE, or a. F. *indiscipline* (1762 in Hatz.-Darm.).] Absence or lack of discipline; want of the order imposed by constituted (*esp.* military) authority upon a body of persons amenable to it; want of the order and method acquired by training.

1783 J. ADAMS *Wks.* (1854) IX. 517 To venture upon a piece of indiscipline, in order to secure a tolerable peace. **1792** GOUV. MORRIS in Sparks *Life & Writ.* (1832) II. 175 My former letters have mentioned the indiscipline of the French armies. **1812** WELLINGTON in Gurw. *Desp.* (1838) IX. 604 The habits of indiscipline and insubordination are such, that even those corps..are in as bad a state. **1884** *Guardian* 21 May 769 Indiscipline in the Church of England. **1887** T. HARDY *Woodlanders* II. xvii. 310 Mental indiscipline hindered her from beginning her conversation.

†**indi'sconsolate**, *a. Obs. rare.* [IN-^{3}.] Not disconsolate.

1647 W. BROWNE tr. *Gomberville's Polexander* IV. i. 164 [They] would not have been so indisconsolate, but onely for taking off Iphidamantus discontent.

indiscoverable (ɪndɪˈskʌvərəb(ə)l), *a.* [f. IN-³ + DISCOVERABLE.] Not discoverable; not to be found out; undiscoverable.

1640 QUARLES *Enchirid.* I. (1641) 74 To keepe his own designs indiscoverable to his Enemy. **1704** NORRIS *Ideal World* II. iii. 177 Conclusions of great importance to be known, and otherwise perhaps indiscoverable. **1889** SWINBURNE *Study Ben Jonson* 21 The artist, the scholar..is as indiscoverable as the spontaneous humourist or poet.

Hence **indiˈscoverably** *adv.*

1669 *Addr. hopeful yng. Gentry Eng.* 80 An old stout Carrack..lost by its old indiscoverably growing leakages.

†**indiscovered,** *a. Obs. rare*⁻¹. [IN-³.] Not discovered; undiscovered.

1663 COWLEY *Verses sev. Occas., Ode Drake's Chair* iv, Lanch forth into an indiscovered Sea.

†**indiˈscovery.** *Obs. rare.* [f. IN-³.] Non-discovery; failure to discover or find out.

1629 N. CARPENTER *Achitophel* I. 8 The indiscovery of such mens natures causeth..their worst actions to carry the best construction. **1646** SIR T. BROWNE *Pseud. Ep.* VI. xii. 338 The collaterall verity, may unto reasonable speculations, requite the capitall indiscovery.

indiscreet (ɪndɪˈskriːt), *a.* Forms: 5 indys-, 5–7 indiscrete, 6 *Sc.* -creit, (7 -creete), 6– -creet. [prob. a. F. *indiscret, -crète* (though this is cited only of 16th c. in Hatz.-Darm.) = It., Sp. *indiscreto*; or directly ad. L. *indiscrētus*, in a late or med.L. sense: see note to DISCREET *a.* The direct repr. of the L. word in its classical sense is INDISCRETE.] Not discreet, without discretion.

†**1.** Without discernment or sound judgement. *Obs.*

1413 *Pilgr. Sowle* (Caxton 1483) III. viii. 55 So haue they ben forfaren with indiscrete sorowe, as was cursyd Cayn the fyrst borne child. **1432–50** tr. *Higden* (Rolls) I. 319 Indiscrete men supposede hym to haue the wynde in his guernaile and powere. *c* **1450** MYRC 825 Leste indyscrete hys prest were Hys confessyone for to here. *c* **1611** CHAPMAN *Iliad.* II. (1884) 36 O Priam! thou art always pleased with indiscreet advice. **1617** CORNWALLYES *Ess., Praise Rich. III* (ed. 2) C iij, The partiall writings of indiscreet chroniclers. **1675** BOYLE *Reconcil. Reason & Relig.* I. i. Wks. 1772 IV. 158 There are others, who, out of an indiscrete devotion, are so solicitous to increase the number and the wonderfulness of mysteries.

2. Injudicious or imprudent in speech or action; inconsiderate; unadvised, unwary.

1588 SHAKS. *L.L.L.* IV. ii. 31 It would ill become me to be vaine, indiscreet, or a foole. **1656** *Nicholas Papers* III. 280 That it may bee knowen where to lay the blame of so indiscreete, if not malicious, a reporte. **1661** BAXTER *Mor. Prognost.* I. ¶84. 17 The younger, and indiscreeter passionate sort. *a* **1715** BURNET *Own Time* (1766) I. 369 The indiscreetest and wildest creature that ever was in a court. **1742** JARVIS *Quix.* II. lxxii, By his indiscreet zeal the object would be lost. **1857** RUSKIN *Pol. Econ. Art* i. (1868) 35 You may do much harm by indiscreet praise and by indiscreet blame. **1876** GEO. ELIOT *Dan. Der.* iii, The younger sister had been indiscreet..in her marriages.

3. *Sc.* Uncivil, impolite.

1727 P. WALKER *Life Peden* To Rdr. (1728) 4 Others..gave me indiscreet, upbraiding Language, calling me a vile old Apostate. **1824** MISS FERRIER *Inher.* (1882) I. 225, 'I think I never saw so ill-bred a man'. 'I can't just say that, Bell', said her mother, 'I'm sure he was nowise indiscreet'.

Hence **indiˈscreetness**, the quality of being indiscreet, indiscretion.

1658 A Fox *Wurtz' Surg.* I. iii. 11 Through this rashness and indiscreetness most dangerous and worst symptoms are caused. **1852** DICKENS *Bleak Ho.* liv, I'm surprised at the indiscreetness you commit.

indiscreetly (ɪndɪˈskriːtlɪ), *adv.* [f. prec. + -LY².]

1. In an indiscreet manner; with or through want of discernment, judgement, or prudence.

c **1450** tr. *De Imitatione* III. viii. 74 Somme indiscretly for grace of deuocion haue destroied hemself. **1535** *Act 27 Hen. VIII*, c. 10 §1 They..doo many times dispose indiscretely and vnaduisedly their landes and inheritances. **1634** MASSINGER *Very Woman* I. i. Wks. (Rtldg.) 368/2 'Twas done indiscreetly. **1749** FIELDING *Tom Jones* XIII. viii, It should be a warning to all persons (says she, looking at her daughters) how they marry indiscreetly. **1825** BENTHAM *Ration. Rew.* Wks. 1843 II. 210 Astonished that legislators have so indiscreetly multiplied the operations which tend to weaken its [veracity's] influence.

2. *Sc.* Uncivilly, impolitely.

1637–50 ROW *Hist. Kirk* (Wodrow Soc.) 312, I hope you will not use me so indiscreetlie as did one Mr David Calderwood when I was coming out of Scotland.

indiscrete (ɪndɪˈskriːt), *a.* Also 7 indiscreet. [ad. L. *indiscrēt-us* unseparated, undistinguished: see IN-³ and DISCRETE, and cf. the differentiated INDISCREET.]

†**1.** Not distinctly separate or distinguishable from contiguous objects or parts. *Obs.*

1608 TOPSELL *Serpents* (1658) 629 The Ammodyte, indiscreet on the Land [*indiscretus arenis*], Doth hold the colour of the burning sand. **1661** LOVELL *Hist. Anim. & Min.* Introd., The round crustates, *sc.* the Cancri, have..an in-discrete head.

2. Not divided into distinct parts.

1782 POWNALL *Antiq.* 132 (T.) A chaos, in which the terrestrial elements were all in an indiscrete mass of confused matter. **1883** SIR M. MONIER-WILLIAMS *Relig. Th. & Life India* 13 Next all was water, all a chaos indiscrete. **1893** FAIRBAIRN *Christ in Mod. Theol.* II. II. iii. 409 The Absolute is not Substance homogeneous and indiscrete.

Hence **indiˈscretely** *adv.*, without separation or division.

1698 *Phil. Trans.* XX. 463 As for Method, there is none at all..the Species being promiscuously and indiscreetly placed as they came to Hand.

indiscretion (ɪndɪˈskrɛʃən). Forms: 4 indiscrecyone, 5 indyscrecioun, 6 indiscression, -cretione, 6– indiscretion. [a. F. *indiscrétion* (12–13th c. in Hatz.-Darm.), ad. late L. *indiscrētiōn-em*, f. *in-* (IN-³) + *discrētiōn-em* DISCRETION.]

1. Want of discretion; the fact of being indiscreet; in early use, chiefly, want of discernment or discrimination; in later, want of judgement in speech or action; injudicious, unguarded, or unwary conduct; imprudence.

c **1340** HAMPOLE *Prose Tr.* 18 He sall neuer erre by fantasye, ne by indiscrecyone. *c* **1450** *Pol. Poems* (Rolls) II. 242 Vengeaunce and wrathe in an hastyvyte, Wyth an unstedefast speryte of indyscrecioun. **1502** ATKYNSON tr. *De Imitatione* I. viii. 159 They be theyr indiscression & euyl maners..discomfort and hurte those they wene to helpe & comforte. **1592** DANIEL *Compl. Rosamond* Wks. (1717) 39 Happy liv'd I, whilst Parents Eye did guide The Indiscretion of my feeble Ways. **1602** SHAKS. *Ham.* v. ii. 8 Our indiscretion sometimes serues vs well, When our deare plots do paule. **1645** in Ellis *Orig. Lett.* Ser. I. III. 318 Prince Rupert was absolved and cleared from any disloyalty or treason, in the rendering of Bristol; but not of Indiscretion. **1697** DAMPIER *Voy.* I. 128 Thus our hopes perished by the indiscretion of one foolish fellow. **1751** JOHNSON *Rambler* No. 167 ¶5 Granting what only the indiscretion of her kindness enabled him to withhold. **1825** W. OXBERRY *Dram. Biog.* III. 43 When and where the first act of indiscretion (this is the holiday term for vice) occurred, we know not. **1855** MACAULAY *Hist. Eng.* xvii. IV. 21 In spite of calumny for which their own indiscretion had perhaps furnished some ground.

2. An indiscreet or imprudent act or step. (Sometimes a euphemism for a transgression of social morality: cf. 1825 in 1.) Also, an accidental or ('calculated indiscretion') a supposedly accidental revelation of an official secret, etc.

1601 R. JOHNSON *Kingd. & Commw.* (1603) 82 It were an equall indiscretion, to estimate a mannes worth, either by their body or apparell. **1718** LADY M. W. MONTAGU *Lett. to C'tess [Bristol]* (1887) I. 238 They suffer sometimes for their indiscretions in a very severe manner. **1739** CIBBER *Apol.* (1756) I. 57 A lady..whose female indiscretions had occasion'd her family to abandon her. **1752** [see INFANCY 2]. **1840** MACAULAY *Ess., Ranke* (1854) II. 146 A youth, guilty only of an indiscretion. **1929** T. S. ELIOT *Dante* 63 The *Vita Nuova* is neither a 'confession' nor an 'indiscretion' in the modern sense. **1930** [see CALCULATED *ppl. a.* 1]. **1931** *Economist* 5 Dec. 1066/1 Socialist 'indiscretions'..took the form of the publication of certain alleged confidential information as to advances to French banks and foreign Governments from the French Treasury. **1955** *Bull. Atomic Sci.* Mar. 84/2 We have useful men denied the opportunity to contribute to our scientific efforts because of their youthful indiscretions. **1961** *Spectator* 26 May 742/1 He is psychologically indiscretion-prone.

3. *Sc.* Incivility, want of politeness, rudeness.

1825–80 in JAMIESON.

indiˈscretionary, *a. nonce-wd.* [f. prec., after DISCRETIONARY.] Of or pertaining to indiscretion.

1841 LEVER *C. O'Malley* xxxvi. 202 With a most indiscretionary power over the cellar.

†**indiˈscriminally,** *adv. Obs. rare*⁻¹. [f. IN-³ + L. *discrīmināl-is* serving to divide or separate + -LY²; with erron. application.] = INDISCRIMINATELY.

1665 BOYLE *Occas. Refl.* IV. xvii. 109 She vouchsafes to discourse indiscriminally with all commers that Talk to her.

†**indiˈscriminancy.** *rare.* [f. IN-³ + DISCRIMINANT: see -ANCY.] Undiscriminating quality.

1890 *Universal Rev.* 15 Oct. 306 It..strikes with sunlike indiscriminancy 'the just and the unjust'.

indiscriminate (ɪndɪˈskrɪmɪnət), *a.* [f. IN-³ + DISCRIMINATE.] Not discriminate.

1. Of things: Not marked by discrimination or discernment; done without making distinctions; confused, promiscuous.

1649 JER. TAYLOR *Gt. Exemp.* ix. §2 Before he gave to him an indiscriminate testimony. **1755** *Connoisseur* No. 58 ¶1 The inconveniences arising from the indiscriminate power lodged in our Press-gangs. **1777** PRIESTLEY *Matt. & Spir.* (1782) I. xvii. 199 They lay aside this indiscriminate vengeance. **1838** THIRLWALL *Greece* II. xiv. 195 Otanes..commanded an indiscriminate slaughter without regard to age or to place. **1862** STANLEY *Jew. Ch.* (1877) I. xviii. 346 Partisans who are loud in indiscriminate censure and applause. **1876** GREEN *Stray Stud.* 23 The indiscriminate almsgiving which has done so much to create and encourage pauperism.

2. Of persons or agents: Undiscriminating, not exercising discrimination; making no distinctions.

1792 *Anecd. W. Pitt* III. xlii. 120 The indiscriminate hand of vengeance has lumped together innocent and guilty. **1808** *Sketches of Character* (1813) I. 200 You are too indiscriminate in your partiality for them. **1840** MISS MITFORD in L'Estrange *Life* (1870) III. vii. 107 Without being one of his indiscriminate admirers, I like parts of his books.

3. quasi-*adv.* = INDISCRIMINATELY.

1597–8 BP. HALL *Sat.* v. iii. (T.), Could ever wise man wish, in good estate, The use of all things indiscriminate?

Hence **indiˈscriminateness**, the quality of being indiscriminate.

1879 MCCARTHY *Own Times* I. ix. 183 Measures to mitigate the rigour and to correct the indiscriminateness of the death punishment. **1890** *Spectator* 13 Dec. 866/2 No word can be denuded of its true utility by fatuous indiscriminateness of application.

indiscriminated (ɪndɪˈskrɪmɪneɪtɪd), *a.* [f. IN-³ + DISCRIMINATED *ppl. a.*] Not discriminated or distinguished from one another; indiscriminate.

1669 *Addr. hopeful yng. Gentry Eng.* 33 Supposing those many indiscriminated..Heads to have had but one common parent. *a* **1715** BURNET *Own Time* (1766) I. 273 To keep themselves united, and either to set on an indiscriminated toleration, or a general prosecution; for so we love to soften the harsh word of persecution.

indiscriminately (ɪndɪˈskrɪmɪnətlɪ), *adv.* [f. INDISCRIMINATE + -LY².] In an indiscriminate manner; without distinction; promiscuously; without the exercise of discrimination.

1652 GAULE *Magastrom.* 179 Divines, Historians, and Poets thus speak of them indiscriminately. **1654** JER. TAYLOR *Real Pres.* i. (R.), A cloud of fire, majesty, and secrecy indiscriminately mixt together. **1774** PENNANT *Tour Scotl. in* 1772, 252 Not to shelter indiscriminately every offender. **1774** J. BRYANT *Mythol.* I. p. x, To distinguish the various people..of whom writers have so generally and indiscriminately spoken. **1824** L. MURRAY *Eng. Gram.* (ed. 5) I. 412 The stress is laid on long and short syllables indiscriminately. **1875** JOWETT *Plato* (ed. 2) I. 126 They praise indiscriminately all their goods, without knowing what are really beneficial or hurtful.

indiscriminating (ɪndɪˈskrɪmɪneɪtɪŋ), *a.* [f. IN-³ + DISCRIMINATING *ppl. a.*] Not discriminating; that does not make or recognize distinctions; undiscriminating.

1754–67 BALLY (Mason), That indiscriminating floods should spare A chosen few. **1776** BENTHAM *Fragm. Govt.* Wks. 1843 I. 229 A hasty and indiscriminating condemner of what is established, may expose himself to contempt. **1860** MILL *Repr. Govt.* (1865) 23/1 Too lavish and indiscriminating beneficence.

Hence **indiˈscriminatingly** *adv.*, in an indiscriminating manner, without discrimination.

1824 *New Monthly Mag.* X. 105 Complaints made indiscriminatingly against authors. **1887** *Spectator* 23 July 995/2 A comparison which has been made too indiscriminatingly of late.

indiscrimination (ɪndɪskrɪmɪˈneɪʃən). [f. IN-³ + DISCRIMINATION.] The fact of not discriminating or making distinctions; the condition of not being discriminated; absence of distinction; want of discrimination or discernment.

1649 JER. TAYLOR *Gt. Exemp.* I. §6. 97 Since God had hindered him [Herod] from the executions of a distinguishing sword he resolved to send a sword of indiscrimination and confusion. **1659** HAMMOND *On Ps.* xcii. 9 What ever indiscrimination there appears between them here in this world. **1796** S. HORSLEY *Serm.* (1812) I. 240 The like indiscrimination may prevail in higher orders. **1876** LOWELL *Among my Bks.* Ser. II. 325 As far indeed is his 'Lamia' from the lavish indiscrimination of 'Endymion'. **1894** *Westm. Gaz.* 16 Nov. 3/2 In spite of her indiscrimination and lack of sound judgment, which has alienated many.

indiscriminative (ɪndɪˈskrɪmɪnətɪv), *a.* [f. IN-³ + DISCRIMINATIVE.] Not discriminative; not characterized by, or inclined to, discrimination.

1854 *Tait's Mag.* XXI. 168 Conscious of..weaknesses, arising..from excessive but..indiscriminative strength. **1880** SWINBURNE *Introd. Collins* in *T. H. Ward's Eng. Poets* III. 279 That sweeping violence of indiscriminative depreciation.

†**indiˈscriminatively,** *adv. Obs.* [f. IN-³ + DISCRIMINATIVE + -LY².] Without exercise of discrimination; indiscriminately.

1684 HOCKIN *God's Decrees* 316 The Almighty hath..indiscriminatively ascertain'd future happiness to every one. **1715** M. DAVIES *Athen. Brit.* I. Contents Zz ij b, Lavishing of their Lashes and Encomiums..Indiscriminatively, rather than impartially.

†**indiˈscussed,** *a. Obs. rare.* [f. IN-³ + DISCUSSED *ppl. a.*] Not discussed; undiscussed.

1534 WHITINTON *Tullyes Offices* III. (1540) 116 He promysed to wryte of thre maners of delyberacions, and lefte the thyrde indiscussed. *a* **1631** DONNE *Lett. to Sir H. Goodeere* in *Poems*, etc. (1633) 359 Upon reasons light in themselves or indiscussed in mee.

indiˈscussible, *a.* Also -able. [f. IN-³ + DISCUSSIBLE.] Incapable of being discussed.

1893 *Nation* (N.Y.) 24 Aug. 134/1 The letter..must be accepted as the sole and indiscussable rule by which all Catholics must be guided on the question involved. **1898** SWINBURNE in *Westm. Gaz.* 15 Nov. 10/1 The noble passion and the noble pathos of its greater parts are alike indiscussible and irresistible.

indiscutable (ɪndɪˈskjuːtəb(ə)l), *a.* [f. IN-³: see DISCUTABLE *a.* Cf. F. *indiscutable* indisputable.] = INDISCUSSIBLE *a.*

1933 *Proc. Brit. Acad.* XVIII. 171 In every field, a writer may without injustice give plain warning to the world that

he regards certain questions as ultimate and indiscutable. **1959** *Encounter* XII. iv. 53 The book is *indiscutable*.

† **indis'graced**, *a. Obs. rare*$^{-1}$. [f. IN-^{3} + DISGRACED *ppl. a.*] Not disgraced; undisgraced.

1606 MARSTON *Sophonisba* II. ii, Our troopes of horse make indisgrac'd retraite; Trot easie off; not poore.

† **'Indish**, *a. Obs.* [f. IND + -ISH: cf. *Engl-ish, Scott-ish, Span-ish*, etc.] = INDIAN *a.*

1548 TURNER *Names of Herbs*, Indishe peper, *Capsicum annuum*. *c* **1550** LLOYD *Treas. Health* (1585) F ij, For the webbe and cloudines in y^{e} eyes, take & stampe indisshe Peper, and put to it y^{e} ioyce of a Fenel rote. **1599** HAKLUYT *Voy.* II. II. 71 A great many catchpoules with rods of Indish canes dragged on the ground. **1599** H. BUTTES *Dyets drie Dinner* Aa iv, And smoke Tobaccos antidot..With Indish ayre, like to Cameleon, fed. **1601** HOLLAND *Pliny* I. 235 The biggest and most monstrous creature in the Indish Ocean.

† **in'dish**, *v. Obs. rare.* Also en-. [f. IN-^{1} or ^{2} + DISH *sb.*] *trans.* To put into a dish.

1611 FLORIO, *Impiattare*, to endish. *Ibid.*, *Inscudellare*, to indish, to put into dishes.

indi'spellable, *a. rare.* [f. IN-^{3} + **dispellable*, from DISPEL *v.*] Incapable of being dispelled.

1817 BENTHAM *Ch. of Eng.* (1818) 122 *note*, Note the essential and utterly indispellable obscurity of the subjects themselves.

indispensa'bility. [f. next + -ITY.] The quality or fact of being indispensable.

1. Incapability of dispensation. (See INDISPENSABLE, 1, 2.)

a **1648** LD. HERBERT *Henry VIII* (1683) 401 The indispensability of the first Marriage. **1660** JER. TAYLOR *Duct. Dubit.* II. iii. rule 11 §1 The indispensability of the natural laws, which are the main constituent parts of the evangelical.

2. Incapability of being dispensed with or done without. (See INDISPENSABLE 3.)

1793 HOLCROFT *Lavater's Physiog.* vi. 41 Of all earth's creatures, man alone rejoices in his indispensability. **1827** HALLAM *Const. Hist.* (1876) I. vii. 395 Preaching the divine right, as it is called, or absolute indispensability, of episcopacy. **1861** MILL *Utilit.* v. 81 Recognised indispensability becomes a moral necessity, analogous to physical.

indispensable (ɪndɪ'spɛnsəb(ə)l), *a.* (*sb.*) [ad. med.L. *indispensābil-is*, f. *in-* (IN-^{3}) + *dispensābilis* DISPENSABLE: cf. F. *indispensable* (17th c. in Hatz.-Darm.).] **A.** *adj.* Not dispensable; not to be dispensed, or dispensed with. (See also, in senses 1 and 2, UNDISPENSABLE.)

† **1.** Not subject to ecclesiastical dispensation; that cannot be permitted, allowed, or condoned, by suspension or relaxation of a law or canon. (Cf. DISPENSABLE 1.) *Obs.*

1533 CRANMER in Ellis *Orig. Lett.* Ser. I. II. 36, I gave finall Sentance therin, howe it was indispensable for the Pope to lycense any suche marieges. *c* **1555** HARPSFIELD *Divorce Hen. VIII* (Camden) 121 There were also two doctors of divinity..that thought the case was indispensable. **1638** CHILLINGW. *Relig. Prot.* I. vi. §39. 359 Whether the Popes irregularities if he should chance to incurre any, be indispensable? **1654** BP. HALL *Cases Consc.* Addit. i. 399 [He] absolutely condemnes this marriage as incestuous and indispensable.

2. Of a law, obligation, duty, etc.: That cannot be dispensed with, remitted, set aside, disregarded, or neglected. Also † ***indispensable with***.

1653 H. MORE *Conject. Cabbal.* (1662) 162 The indispensable dictates of the divine Light. **1655** FULLER *Ch. Hist.* v. ii. §18 A Book of Cranmers penning, proving Gods Law indispensable with, by the Pope. *a* **1677** BARROW *Serm.* (1687) I. viii. 100 He..hath by settled rules and indispensable promises obliged himself to requite them. *a* **1714** BURNET *Hist. Ref.* an. 1532 (R.) Those few that were about the pope, thought the prohibition of such marriages was only positive, and might be dispensed with by the pope: whereas all other learned men thought the law was moral and indispensable. *a* **1732** ATTERBURY *Serm. 1 Cor.* xv. 19 (Seager) A great and indispensable duty. **1736** BUTLER *Anal.* II. i. Wks. 1874 I. 170 Our obligations to obey all God's commands..are absolute and indispensable. **1781** GIBBON *Decl. & F.* xxx. III. 142 The citizens, and subjects, had purchased an exemption from the indispensable duty of defending their country. **1818** JAS. MILL *Brit. India* Pref. 24, I lay under an indispensable obligation to be faithful.

3. That cannot be dispensed with or done without; absolutely necessary or requisite. Const. *to*, *for*.

1696 PHILLIPS, *Indispensable*, that is of Absolute Necessity. **1707** ADDISON *Pres. State War* (Seager), There are few perhaps that will not think the maintaining a settled body of numerous forces indispensable for the safety of our country. **1793** HOLCROFT *Lavater's Physiog.* xvi. 82 The knowledge of anatomy is indispensable to him. **1829** SIR W. NAPIER *Penins. War* VIII. II. 268 To attack Victor, it was indispensable to concert operations with Cuesta. **1831** CARLYLE *Sart. Res.* (1858) 139 Thou toilest for the altogether indispensable, for daily bread. **1845** M^{c}CULLOCH *Taxation* Introd. (1852) 19 The articles on which they are imposed are rarely, if ever, indispensable. **1874** SYMONDS *Sk. Italy & Greece* (1898) I. x. 195 Physical exercises..were indispensable to a young Italian soldier. **1883** FROUDE *Short Stud.* IV. v. 336 Courage and character..are the conditions indispensable for national leaders. **1899** *Brit. Weekly* 13 July 230/3 There are many ways of getting on in the City, but none apparently in which a silk hat is not indispensable.

B. *sb.* **a.** An indispensable thing or person; one that cannot be done without.

1681 H. MORE *Exp. Dan.* Pref. 77 The Indispensables of Christian Religion. **1720** MRS. MANLEY *Power of Love* VI. (1741) 317 To buy your Highness necessary Linnen, and those Indispensables that belong to young Women. **1823** J. D. HUNTER *Captiv. N. Amer.* 324 Their equipments and stores amount merely to indispensables. **1895** *Westm. Gaz.* 17 Jan. 2/1 He pays the 'indispensables', like engine-drivers, a fancy wage, to seduce them from loyalty to the poorly paid workers in the poorer grades. **1901** *Ibid.* 12 Dec. 3/1 An indispensable to the complete success of the lace blouse is a chiffon lining. **1965** *Austral. Women's Weekly* 20 Jan. 25 Inevitably in a life of constant moving one picks up indispensables.

† **b.** A kind of small satchel or bag worn by women instead of a pocket. (F. *indispensable*, Littré.) See *N. & Q.* 9th Ser. IV. 310. *Obs.*

1800 (12 Feb.) GILLRAY *Print* (repr. scene French Milliner's), A number of disputes having arisen in the Beau Monde, respecting the exact situation of ladies Indispensibles (or New Invented Pockets). **1806** C. K. SHARPE *Corr.* (1888) I. 265 Rows of pretty peeresses, who sat eating sandwiches from silk indispensables [at Lord Melville's trial].

c. *pl.* (*colloq. euphemism.*) Trousers.

a **1828** J. BERNARD *Retrospections Stage* (1830) II. iv. 116 Black silk indispensables, and stockings. **1841** J. T. HEWLETT *Parish Clerk* I. 156 Manufacture broadcloth..into coats, waistcoats, and indispensibles. **1842** *Comic Almanack* June (Farmer), He slapped his hand against his yellow leather indispensables. **1884** *Manch. Exam.* 1 Nov. 5/6 A pair of native-cut indispensables.

indi'spensableness. [f. prec. + -NESS.] The quality of being indispensable: **a.** incapability of dispensation or of being set aside; **b.** inability to be done without; absolute necessity.

1654 HAMMOND *Fundamentals* xii. §2 Of Indispensableness of Oaths. **1712** BERKELEY *Pass. Obed.* §26 The indispensableness of the negative precepts of the law of nature. **1833** COLERIDGE *Table-t.* 7 Jan., A deep sense of the indispensableness of a holy life. **1882** *Times* 26 May 9 It is a tribute to the sense of his indispensableness at present to France.

indi'spensably, *adv.* [f. as prec. + -LY^{2}.] In an indispensable manner: † **a.** without possibility of dispensation or remission; **b.** without possibility of being dispensed with or done without.

a. *c* **1645** HOWELL *Lett.* (1650) II. 58 Under penalty of a forfeiture which is to be indispensably payed. *a* **1677** MANTON *Serm. Ps.* cxix. verse 142 Wks. 1872 IX. 11 The law of God immutably and indispensably bindeth all men. **1767** MRS. ELIZ. CARTER *Mem.* (1816) I. 389 This declaration, which I thought myself indispensably engaged to make. **1837–9** HALLAM *Hist. Lit.* III. iv. §126 Grotius.. determines that subjects are indispensably bound not to serve in a war which they conceive to be clearly unjust.

b. **1664–94** SOUTH *Twelve Serm.* II. 152 Devotion, and Affection, is indispensably required in Prayer. *a* **1708** BEVERIDGE *Thes. Theol.* (1710) I. 47 The understanding the principles of religion is indispensably necessary to salvation. **1745** WESLEY *Answ. Ch.* 19 In order to this, nothing is indispensably required, but Repentance, or Conviction of Sin. **1879** *Cassell's Techn. Educ.* I. 239 Robbing the soil of the sun's heat, which is so indispensably requisite.

† **indi'spensible**, *a.* (*sb.*) *Obs.* [f. IN-^{3} + DISPENSIBLE, q.v.] = INDISPENSABLE.

1662 STILLINGFL. *Orig. Sacr.* III. iii. §5 The indispensible obligation which was in the nature of man to obey whatever his Maker did command him. **1692** LOCKE *Educ.* Pref., I think it every man's indispensible duty. **1792** *Anecd. W. Pitt* II. xxiii. 89 The corruption of Parliament..is become an indispensible part of the mechanism of Government. **1800–41** [see INDISPENSABLE *sb.* b, c].

Hence † **indi'spensibleness**, † **indi'spensibly** *adv.*

1649 *Bounds Publ. Obed.* 44 If I..be..still indispensibly obliged by it. **1681** FLAVEL *Meth. Grace* xxvi. 443 The indispensibleness and necessity thereof. **1710** STEELE *Tatler* No. 159 ¶5 A longer Letter..which I am indispensibly obliged to answer. **1768** BOSWELL *Corsica* Introd. (ed. 2) 1 Liberty..is indispensibly necessary to our happiness. **1860** GEN. P. THOMPSON *Audi Alt.* III. ciii. 9 On the indispensibleness of Slavery to the West India interest.

† **indi'spersed**, *a. Obs. rare.* [f. IN-^{3} + DISPERSED *ppl. a.*] Not dispersed or scattered; undispersed.

1647 H. MORE *Song of Soul* II. ii. II. ix, Indispers'd, quick, close with self-union. *Ibid.* II. iii. II. xxxv, But indisperst is this bright Majesty. **1686** PLOT *Staffordsh.* 22 While the Meteor remains compact and indisperst.

† **indi'spersion.** *Obs. rare*$^{-1}$. [f. IN-^{3} + DISPERSION.] Undispersed condition.

1647 H. MORE *Song of Soul* III. III. xvii, The soul is of such subtlety, And close collectednesse, indispersion.

† **indi'spertible**, *a. Obs. rare.* [ad. late L. *indispertībilis* indivisible, f. *in-* (IN-^{3}) + *dispertīre* to divide.] Indivisible.

a **1641** BP. MOUNTAGU *Acts & Mon.* (1642) 413 Gods eternity..is an indivisible, indispertible Duration, Continuance, or Being all at once in act without succession.

indispose (ɪndɪ'spəʊz), *v.* [f. IN-^{3} + DISPOSE *v.*; perh. orig. a back-formation from next.]

1. To put out of the proper condition or 'disposition' for some action or result; to render unfit or incapable (*to do* something, or *for* something); to disqualify, incapacitate.

1657 S. PURCHAS *Pol. Flying-Ins.* 113 Dust (much more ashes) will..so fur their dew-clawed feet, that it will indispose them to flye. **1672** WILKINS *Nat. Relig.* 33 That prejudice..and their ignorance of His divine commission and high calling, did indispose them for an equal judgment of things, and render them unteachable. **1674** *Govt. Tongue* viii. §12. 149 He so indisposes the soil, that no future seeds can ever take root. **1710** NORRIS *Chr. Prud.* vii. 310 Rather assisting than indisposing a man to be a good Christian. **1863** E. FITZGERALD *Lett.* (1889) I. 291 Not to get one's Sleep..indisposes one more or less for the Day.

2. To affect with bodily indisposition, put out of health, disorder. (Chiefly in *pa. pple.*; see INDISPOSED, 4.)

1694 WOOD *Life* 31 Dec. (O.H.S.) III. 475 This hard winter of 1694 hath strangley indisposed my body. **1714** ADDISON *Spect.* No. 582 ¶1 The Small-Pox..after having indisposed you for a time, never returns again. **1726** G. ROBERTS *4 Years Voy.* 333 He was a little indisposed by a Fall that he had received. **1821** *Examiner* 156/2 Varney causes the Countess to swallow a medicine to indispose her.

3. To affect with mental indisposition, disincline, render averse or unwilling. Const. *to*, or with *inf.*; rarely *towards*, *from*.

1692 LOCKE *Educ.* §21 You are now..to indispose him to those Inconveniences as much as you can. **1709** *Tatler* No. 90 ¶5 A Scene written with so great Strength of Imagination, indisposed me from farther reading. **1798** MALTHUS *Popul.* III. x. (1806) II. 262 *note*, Indisposing landlords to let long leases of farms. **1817** J. SCOTT *Paris Revisit.* (ed. 4) 309 The miseries of the revolution, succeeded..by..an imperial despotism, had totally indisposed the people towards any interference with politics. **1889** *Spectator* 16 Mar., An annual summons would indispose everybody to employ Reserve-men, and therefore destroy the force.

4. To cause to be unfavourably disposed; to make unfriendly, set at variance. (Now unusual.)

1748 CHESTERF. *Lett.* (1792) II. clxvi. 108 Polemical conversations.. certainly do indispose, for a time, the contending parties towards each other. **1779** F. HERVEY *Nav. Hist.* II. 103 The declamations of the pulpit, indisposed the minds of men towards each other, and propagated the blind rage of party. **1788** A. HAMILTON *Federalist* No. 83 II. 337 The capricious operation of so dissimilar a method of trial..is of itself sufficient to indispose every well regulated judgment towards it. **1815** W. TAYLOR in *Monthly Rev.* LXX. 462 The licentious passages might have indisposed the censors of the Inquisition. **1848** LD. MALMESBURY *Mem. Ex-minister* (1884) I. 209 She had long indisposed the whole kingdom against her.

5. To undo a physical tendency or inclination in; to render not liable or subject (*to* something).

1822–34 *Good's Study Med.* (ed. 4) IV. 347 A constitutional or superinduced hebetude of the muscular coat of the bladder, so as to indispose it to inflammation. **1830** COLERIDGE *Table-t.* 23 May, Inoculation..has so entered into the constitution, as to indispose it to infection under the most accumulated and intense contagion.

indisposed (ɪndɪ'spəʊzd), *ppl. a.* [f. IN-^{3} + DISPOSED *ppl. a.* Cf. F. *indisposé* (1442 in Godef.), *indispost* (16th c.), late L. *indispositus*. In later use taken as pa. pple. of prec.]

† **1.** Not put in order, not properly arranged or prepared; unorganized; hence out of order, disordered, disorganized. In quots. 1425 (in reference to death), Not prepared for, for which one has not made the proper dispositions or preparations: = med.L. *indispositus*. *Obs.*

c **1425** *Orolog. Sapient.* v. in *Anglia* X. 361/17 þat I falle not in suche peryl of indisposid deth. *Ibid.* 364/22, I haue so litil fors taken of indisposed deth. **1598** FLORIO, *Indisposto*, indisposed, vnlustie, crazed, weake, without order, disordred. **1661** COWLEY *Ess.*, *Cromwell* Wks. 1710 II. 652 The indispos'd and long tormented Commonwealth. **1691** RAY *Creation* II. (1692) 74 Creation being not only a Production of a Thing out of Nothing, but also out of indisposed Matter. *Ibid.* 75 Whatever Agent can introduce a Form into indisposed Matter.

† **2.** Not properly fitted, unfitted, unqualified. Cf. INDISPOSITION 1. *Obs. rare.*

c **1449** PECOCK *Repr.* III. v. 308 In indisposid persoones, bi her vndisposicioun..thei ben..occasiouns of vicis. **1646** SIR T. BROWNE *Pseud. Ep.* I. iii. (1650) 6 They are farther indisposed ever to attain unto truth. *Ibid.* I. v. 14 There are not onely particular men, but whole nations indisposed for learning.

† **3.** Of evil disposition or condition; evilly disposed or inclined; ill-conditioned; also, of the weather, in a bad state, bad (cf. OF. *indisposition du temps*, Godef.). *Obs.*

1481 *Surtees Misc.* (1888) 44 Indisposed personnes onely of malice have..troubled hyme. **1490** CAXTON *Eneydos* xviii. 67 In this harde wedder of wynter..ye see full of tempest.. and the tyme alle indisposed more than euer it was. **1597** J. KING *On Jonas* 90 All carelesse, dissolute, indisposed persons.

4. In a disordered bodily condition; out of health; ill, unwell. (Usually implying a slight degree of ill health.) Mostly predicative.

1598 [see 1]. **1605** SHAKS. *Lear* II. iv. 112 To take the indispos'd and sickly fit, For the sound man. **1623** MASSINGER *Dk. Milan* III. ii, If I am sought for, Say I am indisposed. **1653** H. COGAN tr. *Pinto's Trav.* xliv. 175 The Captain..found himself much indisposed in his health. **1670** TEMPLE *Let. to Ld. Berkeley* Wks. 1731 II. 217 The first is like Diet, but the other like Exercise, to an indisposed Body. **1712** STEELE *Spect.* No. 284 ¶1 She..professes Sickness..and acts all things with an indisposed Air. **1749** FIELDING *Tom Jones* v. vii, Mr. Allworthy had been for some days indisposed with a cold. **1832** LANDER *Adv. Niger* III.

xx. 233 Six of her crew, who had been ill of fever, and are still indisposed.

5. Not disposed or 'in the mind', disinclined, unwilling, averse (*to*, or *to do* something).

1646 CROMWELL *Let. Bridget Ireton* 25 Oct. in *Carlyle*, I write not to thy husband; partly to avoid trouble,..partly because I am myself indisposed at this time, having some other considerations. *a* **1665** J. GOODWIN *Filled w. the Spirit* (1867) 281 Hardhearted and indisposed unto acts of bounty. **1812** CRABBE *Tales* xviii, Unfit to rule and indisposed to please. **1885** *Law Times* LXXVIII. 212/2 The learned judge might have been less indisposed to stay the execution.

6. Not of friendly disposition; not favourably disposed or inclined (*towards*); unfriendly; unfavourable. (Now somewhat *rare*.)

1647 CLARENDON *Hist. Rebel.* I. §190 The king..was sufficiently indisposed towards the persons or the principles of Mr. Calvin's disciples. **1793** GOUV. MORRIS in Sparks *Life & Writ.* (1832) II. 382 The people are already indisposed, and only kept under by fear of instant death. **1844** NAPIER *Conq. Scinde* II. viii. (1845) 469 Lord Ellenborough..was already indisposed towards him.

7. Not having a physical inclination or tendency; not liable or subject.

1646 SIR T. BROWNE *Pseud. Ep.* II. i. (1659) 40 Salinous spirits..which do assimilate all bodies not indisposed for their impressions. **1790** WEDGWOOD in *Phil. Trans.* LXXX. 312 The saturated marine solution is indisposed to crystallize.

†**8.** Not disposed of or bestowed. *Obs. rare.*

1694 SOUTHERNE *Fatal Marriage* I. ii, When yet a Virgin, free, and indisposed.

indi'sposedness. Now *rare* or *Obs.* [f. prec. + -NESS.] The condition of being indisposed; indisposition.

†**1.** Want of arrangement, disorder. *Obs.*

a **1677** BARROW *Serm.* Wks. 1716 III. 384 Who can fansy how out of..Confusion and Indisposedness the World could be created?

2. Want of adaptation; unfitness.

a **1684** LEIGHTON *Comm.* I *Pet.* ii. I A child hath in it a reasonable soul, and yet by the indisposedness of the body.. it is so bound up that its difference from the beasts..is not so apparent as afterwards.

3. Disordered state of health; bodily indisposition.

1654 WHITLOCK *Zootomia* 500 Dulnesse, drowsinesse, or indisposednesse of head, or stomach. *c* **1655** P. HENRY in *Life* in *M. Henry's Wks.* (1835) II. 619 My very great indisposedness in point of health. **1683** TRYON *Way to Health* 70 For this..causeth a heavy indisposedness through the whole Body.

4. Mental indisposition; disinclination, unwillingness.

1651 BP. HALL *Susurrium* §73 Not that we should in the midst of a sensible indisposedness of heart fall suddainly into a fashionable devotion. **1656** BAXTER *Reformed Pastor* (1862) 234 Our own darkness, dulness and indisposedness to duty. **1685** *Col. Rec. Pennsylv.* I. 156 [They] declared their utter Indisposedness thereunto. *a* **1691** FLAVEL *Sea-Deliv.* (1754) 182 The indisposedness of the Master that evening both to meat and sleep.

indisposition (ɪndɪspə'zɪʃən). [f. IN-³ + DISPOSITION: cf. F. *indisposition* (15th c. in Littré).] The fact or condition of being indisposed.

†**1.** Want of adaptation to some purpose, or to the circumstances of the case; unfitness, unsuitableness; incapacity, inability. *Obs.*

1440 *Manifesto Dk. Gloucester* (Pat. Roll 18 Hen. VI, 111), Thyndisposicion of my said Lords adversary, that he neither hath wisdom nor discretion to govern himself, but must be led for defaut of natural reason. **1529** WOLSEY in Ellis *Orig. Lett.* Ser. I. II. 12 Supplying myn indyssposcycon and lack of wyt. **1612** BREREWOOD *Lang. & Relig.* xxv. 216 By reason of the indisposition of Libanus, in most places, for frequent habitation. **1663** BOYLE *Usef. Exp. Nat. Philos.* II. v. ii. 126 If we examine other plants..and observe..their disposedness or indisposition to yield spirits or oyls by fermentation. **1750** tr. *Leonardus' Mirr. Stones* 31 A bad Commixture sometimes happens..from the indisposition of the hot or cold agent, and sometimes from the unfitness of the place.

†**2.** Want of apt arrangement or orderly placing; displacement or misplacement; disorder, chaotic condition. *Obs.*

1598 FLORIO, *Indispositione*, indisposition, vnlustines, crasednes, weakenes, disorder. **1605** WILLET *Hexapla Gen.* 353 Difficult trauaile..may be caused..by the greatnes of the infant, or the indisposition thereof in the wombe. **1677** HALE *Prim. Orig. Man.* 293 The disposition, or rather indisposition of this Matter, dark, stupid, and unactive.

3. Disordered bodily condition; ill health, illness, ailment; esp. of a slight or passing character.

1598 [see 2]. **1600** HOLLAND *Livy* 1189 That indisposition of his hee set on fire with untemperate drinking of wine. **1627** *Lisander & Cal.* I. 4 Lisander's indisposition proceeded from the unholesome ayre of the citie. **1677** HALE *Prim. Orig. Man.* To Rdr. 3 A long indisposition of Health hath much hindred and interrupted me. **1739** (*title*) The Ladies' Physical Directory, or a Treatise of all the Weaknesse, Indispositions, and Diseases peculiar to the Female Sex, from Eleven Years to the Age of Fifty or upwards. **1788** COWPER *Wks.* (1837) XV. 198, I shall be happy to hear that my friend Joseph has recovered entirely from his late indisposition, which I was informed was gout. **1855** MACAULAY *Hist. Eng.* xxi. IV. 543 The father of the bridegroom was detained in London by indisposition.

4. The state of not being mentally disposed, or 'in the mind' (*to* something, or *to do* something); disinclination, unwillingness.

1594 HOOKER *Eccl. Pol.* III. i. §10 The indisposition..of the Church of Rome to reform herself. **1607** SHAKS. *Timon* II. ii. 139 Perchance some single vantages you tooke, When my indisposition put you backe. *a* **1628** PRESTON *Saint's Daily Exerc.* (1629) 74 A great indisposition to prayer. **1705** STANHOPE *Paraphr.* III. 31 To correct and sweeten the Tempers of Men, and to bring them off from these Indispositions. **1804** CASTLEREAGH in Owen *Mrq. Wellesley's Desp.* (1877) 252 He declined the proposal evidently from indisposition to receive a British force within his dominions.

5. The state of being unfavourably disposed *to* or *towards* a person or thing; aversion.

1647 CLARENDON *Hist. Reb.* I. §32 This Indisposition of the King towards the Duke was exceedingly encreased and aggravated. **1780** BURKE *Let. to T. Burgh* 5 Jan., I had conceived that an indisposition to the interests of Ireland had never been my characteristical fault. **1898** *Westm. Gaz.* 24 June 3/2 Was it from indisposition towards the Colonial Secretary?

6. Want of physical inclination or tendency; the condition of not being liable or subject.

Mod. The two substances showed an indisposition to combine.

indisputable (ɪn'dɪspjuːtəb(ə)l, ɪndɪ'spjuːtəb(ə)l), *a.* [ad. late L. *indisputābilis* (Cassiodorus), f. *in-* (IN-³) + *disputābilis*, DISPUTABLE.]

1. That cannot be disputed; unquestionable.

1551 ROBINSON tr. *More's Utopia* I. (1895) 91 [That] whiche with good and iust Judges is of greater force than all lawes be, the Kynges indisputable prerogatiue. **1643** SIR T. BROWNE *Relig. Med.* I. §29 Great and indisputable miracle, the cessation of Oracles. **1790** BURKE *Fr. Rev.* Wks. V. 74 The Revolution was made to preserve our ancient, indisputable laws and liberties. **1883** FROUDE *Short Stud.* IV. II. iii. 192 One of those persons of indisputable genius who was likely to make a mark upon his time.

†**2.** Undisputing. *Obs. rare.*

1742 RICHARDSON *Pamela* IV. 74 'My Lady commands so or so'..are sure to meet with an indisputable Obedience.

Hence **indisputa'bility**, **indisputableness**, the character or fact of being indisputable.

1727 BAILEY vol. II, *Indisputableness*,.. unquestionableness, so great Certainty, as not to be argued against. **1856** RUSKIN *Mod. Paint.* IV. v. xix. §32 People shut their eyes to the dark indisputableness of the facts in front of them. **1880** A. ARNOLD *Free Land* 207 It may be stated with a considerable degree of indisputability.

indisputably (see prec.), *adv.* [f. prec. + -LY².] In an indisputable way; without possibility of dispute; unquestionably.

1646 SIR T. BROWNE *Pseud. Ep.* III. xii. 251 Nor is it indisputably certaine what manner of death she dyed. **1719** STEELE *Old Whig* 287 The property of the house of peers will indisputably surmount that of the house of commons. **1755** YOUNG *Centaur* i. Wks. 1757 IV. 127 The more it is disputed, the more indisputably will it shine. **1879** FROUDE *Cæsar* xi. 139 The list..contained the names of none but those who were indisputably guilty.

†**indi'sputed**, *a. Obs.* [IN-³.] Not disputed; undisputed, unquestioned.

1643 SIR T. BROWNE *Relig. Med.* I. §15 *Natura nihil agit frustra*, is the only indisputed Axiome in Philosophy. **1733** SWIFT *On Poetry* 303 His indisputed rights extend Through all the lane, from end to end. **1804** EARL LAUDERD. *Publ. Wealth* Advt. 8 They are assumed as indisputed and incontrovertible.

indi'sseverable, *a. rare.* [f. IN-³ + *disseverable*, f. DISSEVER + -ABLE.] That cannot be dissevered, indivisible.

a **1641** BP. MOUNTAGU *Acts & Mon.* (1642) 25 The true, actuall, indisseverable union hypostaticall of God and Man, in one Christ. **1950** A. L. ROWSE *England of Elizabeth* p. viii, We next have to tackle the Church, not as a system of belief, but as a social institution—indeed as the whole of society regarded from one aspect, inextricably entwined with secular life at every level, indisseverable from it.

Hence **indi'sseverably** *adv.*, indivisibly.

1586 *Will of Spenser* in Grosart *Spenser's Wks.* I. p. xvii, All other thinges..shall be indyseverablie occupied betwixt my wyfe and..my..sone. **1935** W. DE LA MARE *Early One Morning* 5 The fresh and virgin waters are so rapidly and indisseverably involved with the rest. **1952** *Scottish Jrnl. Theol.* V. 307 For [Bouyer] as for Preiss eschatology and Christology are woven indisseverably together as the background of ethics.

†**indi'ssimulable**, *a. Obs. rare*⁻⁰. [IN-³.] 'That cannot be dissembled' (BAILEY vol. II, 1727).

†**in'dissipable**, *a. Obs.* [IN-³.] That cannot be dissipated.

1657–83 EVELYN *Hist. Relig.* (1850) I. 182 The Soul..is indissipable otherwise than by a total annihilation. **1661** G. RUST *Origen's Opin.* in *Phenix* (1721) I. 54 The Souls of Brutes are Spirits..and remain undiminishable and indissipable in their intire Substances.

indissociable (ɪndɪ'səʊʃ(ɪ)əb(ə)l), *a.* [IN-³: cf. eccl. L. *indissociābilis*.] Incapable of being dissociated.

1855 H. SPENCER *Princ. Psychol.* (1872) I. IV. viii. 476 States of consciousness once separate become indissociable.

indissolubility (ɪn,dɪsəl-, ɪndɪ,sɒljuː'bɪlɪtɪ). [f. next: see -ITY.] The quality of being indissoluble.

1. Incapability of being decomposed or disintegrated (or of being disunited, as parts or elements).

a **1704** LOCKE (J.), From whence steel has its firmness, and the parts of a diamond their hardness and indissolubility. **1748** HARTLEY *Observ. Man* II. iv. 427 The Happiness of the Good is denoted by Incorruption, Indissolubility.

†**2.** Incapability of being dissolved in a liquid; insolubility. *Obs.*

1768–74 TUCKER *Lt. Nat.* (1834) I. 92 The whole complex of gold..malleability, ductility, specific gravity, dissolubility in aqua regia, and indissolubility in all other menstruums. **1794** SULLIVAN *View Nat.* I. 258 The effervescence and indissolubility of many of them in the vitriolic acid.

3. Of a connexion or obligation: Incapability of being dissolved, undone, or broken; perpetuity of binding force. (The prevailing sense.)

1677 HALE *Prim. Orig. Man.* IV. iii. 313 Upon the breach of that Condition were either utterly lost, as the indissolubility of the Union of the Composition. **1748** HARTLEY *Observ. Man* II. iii. 232 The Indissolubility of the Marriage Bond. **1830** MACKINTOSH *Eth. Philos.* Wks. 1846 I. 195 The best writers of Mr. Bentham's school overlook the indissolubility of these associations. **1884** *Contemp. Rev.* Feb. 262 Christianity..setting upon monogamy the seals of sanctity and indissolubility.

indissoluble (ɪn'dɪsəljuːb(ə)l, ɪndɪ'sɒljuːb(ə)l), *a.* [ad. L. *indissolūbil-is*: see IN-³ and DISSOLUBLE.] Not dissoluble; that cannot be dissolved.

1. That cannot be dissolved into its elements or particles; incapable of being decomposed or disintegrated; that cannot be destroyed, put an end to, or abolished; indestructible.

a **1568** COVERDALE *Hope Faithf.* xvi. (1574) 134 Which spiritual body (that is incorruptible, indissoluble and immortall) we haue receiued of Christ our Lorde. **1610** HOLLAND *Camden's Brit.* I. 519 Well fenced with an indissoluble wall. **1794** SULLIVAN *View Nat.* I. 109 Atoms, as being the first matter, must also be indissoluble, in order to their being incorruptible. **1822–34** *Good's Study Med.* (ed. 4) I. 44 Some of the drying-earths, employed as cements ..which harden into an indissoluble plate or mass under water.

b. That cannot be separated or disunited, as an element, from the whole. *rare.*

1840 CARLYLE *Heroes* iii. (1872) 94 Not a leaf rotting on the highway but is indissoluble portion of solar and stellar systems.

†**2.** That cannot be dissolved in a liquid (see DISSOLVE 2 b). *Obs.* (Replaced by INSOLUBLE.)

1666 BOYLE *Orig. Formes & Qual.* (1667) 41 Indissoluble in Aqua fortis. **1758** REID tr. *Macquer's Chym.* I. 142 It is mild, unctuous, indissoluble in spirits of wine. **1794** G. ADAMS *Nat. & Exp. Philos.* I. xi. 487 The clear liquid then should be carefully poured off..from any indissoluble sediment that may remain.

b. That cannot be melted or liquefied (see DISSOLVE 2 a); not fusible. ? *Obs.*

1751 JOHNSON *Rambler* No. 174 ¶4 Some bodies, indissoluble by heat, can set the furnace and crucible at defiance. **1826** SCOTT *Letter to Lady Davy* 6 Feb. in *Lockhart*, That direful chemist never put into his crucible a more indissoluble piece of stuff.

3. Of something that binds, as a chain, knot, etc., or (usually) *fig.* of a 'tie', connexion, 'bond', obligation, etc.: That cannot be dissolved, undone, or broken; firm, stable, perpetually binding or lasting. (The prevailing sense.)

1542 HEN. VIII *Declar. Scots* B ij b, In his wordes he professeth an indissoluble amitie. **1548** UDALL, etc. *Erasm. Par. Matt* xix. (R.), The indissoluble knot of the manne and of the wyfe. **1605** SHAKS. *Macb.* III. i. 17 A most indissoluble tye. **1695** LD. PRESTON *Boeth.* IV. 194 This binds together the Actions and Fortunes of Men by an indissoluble Connection of Causes. **1777** PRIESTLEY *Disc. Philos. Necess.* II. 17 There are persons who admit this indissoluble chain of circumstances. **1833** MRS. BROWNING *Prometh. Bound* Wks. 1850 I. 139 With links Indissoluble of adamantine chains. **1879** STAINER *Music of Bible* 3 The natural and indissoluble link between music and rhythm.

4. That cannot be dissolved, as an assembly or association.

1649 MILTON *Eikon.* v, If..he..were so loath to bestow a Parlament once in three yeare,..was it likely..he should bestow willingly on this Parlament an indissoluble sitting?

5. That cannot be solved or explained; inexplicable, insoluble. *rare.*

1868 *Pref. Digby's Voy. Medit.* 35 An indissoluble riddle.

indissolubleness (see prec.). [f. prec. + -NESS.] The quality of being indissoluble; indissolubility.

1656 W. D. tr. *Comenius' Gate Lat. Unl.* ¶71 The Earth, hardened to indissolubleness, is a stone. **1685** BOYLE *Enq. Notion Nat.* vi. 209 The indissolubleness of the alcalisate salt, that is one of the two ingredients of glass. **1699** BURNET *39 Art.* xxv. (1700) 289 This doctrine of the Indissolubleness of Marriage..was never settled in any Council before that of Trent. **1863** GEO. ELIOT *Romola* III. xv, In her marriage..she had ceased to see the mystic union which is its own guarantee of indissolubleness, had ceased even to see the obligation of a voluntary pledge.

indissolubly (ɪn'dɪsəljuːblɪ, ɪndɪ'sɒljʊblɪ), *adv.* [f. as prec. + -LY².] In an indissoluble manner; so as to be incapable of being dissolved; in the

way of firm or perpetual connexion; inseparably.

1538 LELAND *Itin.* VII. 141 The old Walles..made of Britons Brikes, very large and great Flynt set togyther almost indissolubely with morters made of smaule Pybble. **1622** PRESTON *Godly Man's Inquis.* ii. 50 It knits vs indissolublie to the Lord. **1667** MILTON *P.L.* VI. 69 On they move Indissolubly firm. **1754** EDWARDS *Freed. Will* I. iv. 22 A previous Bias and Inclination..may be so powerful that the Act of the Will may be certainly and Indissolubly connected therewith. **1797** MRS. RADCLIFFE *Italian* xvi, She considered herself as indissolubly bound by that promise as if it had been given at the altar. **1855** LYNCH *Rivulet* XXXIX. iii, Fair peace shall be to truth at last..Wedded indissolubly fast. **1870** EMERSON *Soc. & Solit., Farming* Wks. (Bohn) III. 57 Early marriages and the number of births are indissolubly connected with abundance of food.

indissolute (ɪn'dɪsəl(j)uːt), *a. rare.* [In[3] + DISSOLUTE *a.*: cf. late L. *indissolūt-us* (Boethius).] Undissolved, unbroken.

1834 SIR H. TAYLOR *1st Pt. Artevelde* III. iii, Where is that indissolute chain Which to thy anchor'd mandaments eterne The floating soul shall grapple!

†**indi'ssolvable**, *a.* (*sb.*) *Obs.* Also 7 -ible. [IN-[3].] Incapable of being dissolved.

1. Incapable of being disintegrated, destroyed, or abolished; = INDISSOLUBLE 1.

1660 R. COKE *Justice Vind.* 47 Mr. Hobbs outruns the Constable, and makes the King or Civitas..indissolvable by that power that made him. **1701** NORRIS *Ideal World* II. ii. 55 A substance really distinct from matter, must likewise of necessity be indissolvable. *a* **1711** KEN *Hymnotheo* Poet. Wks. 1721 III. 300 They of no disagreeing Parts consist: Immortal, indissolvable abide, What has no parts, Time never can divide.

2. Insoluble in a liquid; = INDISSOLUBLE 2.

1676 BOYLE *Exper. Orig. Qualities* II. vii, We found it as indissolvable in aqua regis too. **1698** NORRIS *Pract. Disc.* IV. 176 Like a Medicine wrapt up in an indissolvible Vehicle. **1774** *Westm. Mag.* II. 315 The indissolvable earthy residuum.

b. Infusible; = INDISSOLUBLE 2 b.

1650 SIR T. BROWNE *Pseud. Ep.* II. i. (1658) 60 The softer veins of Chrystal remain indissolvable in scorching territories. **1684** T. BURNET *Th. Earth* II. 79 There is no terrestrial body indissolvable to fire.

3. Of a tie, connexion, obligation, etc.: = INDISSOLUBLE 3.

1531 *Dial. on Laws Eng.* I. xxvi. (1638) 47 That bond of Matrimony was indissolvable. **1649** BP. REYNOLDS *Hosea* vi. 63 There is a necessary and indissolvable dependence of all second causes upon the first. **1681** FLAVEL *Meth. Grace* ii. 27 This [conjugal] union is not indissolvable, but may and must be broken by death. **1701** NORRIS *Ideal World* I. ii. 67 The union of their ideas appears so indissolvible, that we find we have it not in our power to disunite them in our thoughts. **1788** *Lond. Mag.* 429 There, indeed, friendships were happy and unions indissolvable.

4. Of an assembly, etc.; = INDISSOLUBLE 4.

1643 *Cunning Plot to divide Parlt.* 10 This Parliament.. was..made indissolvable without its own consent.

5. Insoluble, inexplicable; = INDISSOLUBLE 5.

1637 JACKSON *2nd Serm. 2 Chron.* vi. 39–40 Wks. 1844 VI. 40 The unsearchable ways of God's wisdom, or his indissolvable contrivances of extraordinary success. **1643** SIR T. BROWNE *Relig. Med.* II. §9 There are not onely diseases incurable in Physick, but cases indissolvable in Laws.

b. as *sb.* Something insoluble or inexplicable.

1661 GLANVILL *Van. Dogm.* v. 53 The composition of bodies, whether it be of divisibles or indivisibles, is a question which must be rank'd with the indissolvibles.

Hence †**indissolva'bility**, †**indi'ssolvableness** = INDISSOLUBILITY; †**indi'ssolvably** *adv.* = INDISSOLUBLY.

1659 *Army's Plea pres. Practice* 22 All that may be said with reference to the Parliament..the indissolvableness of them without their own consent. **1667** WATERHOUSE *Fire Lond.* 135 They unite into an indissolvability of affection. **1673** *Lady's Call.* I. v. ⁋67. 54 Only that he may the more indissolvably unite, yea incorporate himself with us.

†**indi'ssolved**, *a. Obs.* [IN-[3].] Not dissolved; undissolved.

1626 in Rushw. *Hist. Coll.* (1659) I. 320 While the said Peace was continuing, and the said Treaties indissolved.

indi'ssuadable, *a. rare*$^{-0}$. [f. IN-[3] + *dissuadable*, f. DISSUADE *v.* + -ABLE.] That cannot be dissuaded; inexorable. Hence **indi'ssuadably** *adv.*, inexorably.

a **1894** STEVENSON *Weir of Hermiston* vi. (1896) 178 Fate.. obscure, lawless, august, moving indissuadably in the affairs of Christian men.

†**in'distance**. *Obs.* [ad. med.L. *indistāntia*, f. *indistāns* (see INDISTANT *a.*): cf. IN-[3] and DISTANCE.] The quality or character of being 'indistant'. So †**in'distancy**, in same sense.

1624 F. WHITE *Repl. Fisher* 439 They make nothing for corporall presence by indistance of place. **1656** JEANES *Fuln. Christ* 137 The..Lutherans from the inseparability, and indistance of the union, betwixt the two natures, plead for the coextension of the manhood, with the Godhead. **1659** PEARSON *Creed* v. (1870) 421 If not by way of circumscription, as proper bodies are, yet by way of determination and indistancy.

in distans: see IN *Lat. prep.*

†**in'distant**, *a. Obs.* [ad. late or med.L. *indistāns, -stāntem*, tr. Gr. ἀδιάστατος: see IN-[3] and DISTANT.

In L. the adv. *indistānter* occurs in Priscian and Ammianus; the adj. *indistāns* (with the sb. *indistāntia*) in a 13th c. grammarian quoted in Thurot *Doctrines grammaticales du moyen âge*, 187, and in William of Moerbeka's transl. of Proclus *De decem dubitat.* (col. 85, Cousin), and Ficinus' transl. of Plotinus (ed. Oxon. I. 88). (Prof. I. Bywater.)]

1. Not distant, not separated by an interval; without break or interval, continuous.

1644 DIGBY *Nat. Bodies* v. (1645) 43 The very nature of quantity uniteth any two parts that are indistant from one another. **1647** H. MORE *Song of Soul* Notes 336 Eternity hath all the world in an indivisible indistant way at once. **1674** OWEN *Holy Spirit* (1693) 51 To be present with them, or indistant from them. **1788** T. TAYLOR *Proclus* I. 91 Whatever form contains occultly, and in an indistant manner, is produced into the phantasy subsisting with intervals, divisibly and expanded.

2. Without material extension.

1678 CUDWORTH *Intell. Syst.* I. iv. 416 The Generality of those other Ancients who asserted Incorporeal Substance, did suppose it likewise to be Unextended, they dividing Substances (as we learn from Philo) into διαστηματικαί, και ἀδιάστατοι οὐσιαι, Distant and Indistant, or Extended and Unextended Substances. *Ibid.* I. v. 774 In like manner Simplicius..writeth thus: τὸ δὲ τοιοῦτον ἀμερὲς εὐθὺς ἀνάγκη εἶναι και ἀδιάστατον, μεριστὸν γὰρ καὶ διάστατον ὑπάρχον, οὐ δύναται [κ.τ.λ.], because what is such, must of necessity be indivisible, and indistant; for where it divisible, and distant, it could not all of it be conjoined with its whole self [etc.].

Hence †**in'distantly** *adv.* [f. prec. + -LY[2], repr. L. *indistānter* (see above), Gr. ἀδιαστάτως.]

1656 JEANES *Fuln. Christ* 137 Divines..affirme, that the manhood, and the person of the word are united, not onely inseparably but also indistantly, therefore one of them is not distant from the other. **1678** CUDWORTH *Intell. Syst.* I. v. 776 (transl. fr. Porphyrius) The corporeal world is distantly present to the Intelligible (or the Deity); and that is indivisibly and indistantly [ἀδιαστάτως] present with the world.

indistinct (ɪndɪ'stɪŋkt), *a.* (*sb.*) [ad. L. *indistinct-us*, f. *in-* (IN-[3]) + *distinctus* distinguished, DISTINCT: cf. F. *indistinct* (1549 in R. Estienne).]

1. Not distinct or distinguished from each other, or from something else; not kept separate or apart in the mind or perception; not clearly defined or marked off.

(In quot. 1871 with mixture of sense 'Not distinguished or celebrated, without distinction': cf DISTINCT *a.* 5.)

1604 T. WRIGHT *Passions* v. §4. 199 What shall I say of.. three sacred persons in Trinitie, distinguished really, and yet indistinct essentially? **1612** SELDEN *Illustr. Drayton's Poly-olb.* i. (R.), The Gauls, Cimmerians and Celts, under indistinct names,..over-ran Italy, Greece, and part of Asia. **1658** PHILLIPS, *Indistinct*, not distinguisht or known one from another. [**1871** RUSKIN *Fors Clav.* ix. 12 The rest of the candidates for distinction, finding themselves, after all their work, still indistinct, think it must be the fault of the police, and are riotous accordingly.]

2. In active sense, of judgement or action: Not distinguishing between different things; undiscriminating, indiscriminate. Now *rare* or *Obs.*

1650 SIR T. BROWNE *Pseud. Ep.* III. xxv. (ed. 2) 144 Some in an indistinct voracity eating almost any, others out of a timorous preopinion refraining very many. **1794** GIFFORD *Baviad* 74 Fools who, unconscious of the critic's laws, Rain in such show'rs their indistinct applause. **1875** JOWETT *Plato* (ed. 2) V. 15 The use of the relative and antecedent is more indistinct..than in the other writings of Plato.

3. Not seen or heard so as to be clearly distinguished or discerned, or to present a clear distinction of parts; confused, blurred; hence, faint, dim, obscure. (Also *transf.*, *e.g.* from speech to the speaker.)

1589 PUTTENHAM *Eng. Poesie* II. iv. [v.] (Arb.) 87 The most laudable languages are alwaies most plaine and distinct, and the barbarous most confuse and indistinct. **1726–46** THOMSON *Winter* 632 The city swarms intense. The public haunt, Full of each theme, and warm with mixt discourse, Hums indistinct. **1764** REID *Inquiry* vi. §22 (R.) According as they are more distant..their minute parts become more indistinct, and their outline less accurately defined. **1839** LONGF. *Hyperion* II. iii, The objects around them grew indistinct in the fading twilight. **1844** H. H. WILSON *Brit. India* I. 247 He.. was awakened by the indistinct noise of the approaching multitude. **1887** *Nature* 21 Apr. 581/1 The *Oldhamia* is often indistinct.

b. Of the act of perception or mental impression, or a faculty by which something is perceived.

1526 *Pilgr. Perf.* (W. de W. 1531) 186 But this fayth..was not sufficyent: for it was imperfyte & indistincte. **1780** T. FRANCKLIN tr. *Lucian, True Hist.* (1887) 135 We had a view, but confused and indistinct, of the Island of Dreams. **1781** COWPER *Conversat.* 539 Their views indeed were indistinct and dim. **1875** JOWETT *Plato* (ed. 2) III. 275, I have an indistinct recollection of his mentioning a complex Cretic rhythm.

c. as *sb.* Something indistinctly perceived. *rare.*

1880 G. MEREDITH *Tragic Com.* (1881) 173 The woman who had become the radiant indistinct in his desiring mind was one whom he knew to be of a shivery steadfastness.

†**indi'stinctible**, *a. Obs. rare.* [f. IN-[3] + *distinctible*, f. L. *distinct-*, ppl. stem of *distinguĕre* to distinguish + -IBLE.] Undistinguishable.

1774 WARTON *Hist. Eng. Poetry* (1840) I. Diss. iii. 176 A favourite old romance is founded on the indistinctible likeness of two of Charlemagne's knights, Amys and Amelion.

indistinction (ɪndɪ'stɪŋkʃən). Now *rare.* [f. IN-[3] + DISTINCTION, after *indistinct.*]

1. The fact of not distinguishing or making distinctions; failure to perceive or make a difference.

1624 BP. MOUNTAGU *Gagg* 31 Such variety and difference is in traditions which this Hudler confoundeth to deceive his Novice with indistinctions. **1768** *Woman of Honor* II. 107 That scandalous indistinction between the worthy and the worthless. **1876** STEVENSON *Charles of Orleans* Wks. 1894 II. 263 Was it always one woman? or are there a dozen here immortalised in cold indistinction?

2. The condition or fact of not being distinct or different; absence of distinguishing qualities or characteristics; undistinguishableness.

1644 JESSOP *Angel of Eph.* 7 Sundry Divines..doe prove the Identitie and Indistinction of Bishops and Presbyters both in name and Office in sacred Writ. **1654** JER. TAYLOR *Real Pres.* 220 In a body there cannot be indistinction of parts, but each must possesse his own portion of parts. **1824** LAMB *Elia* Ser. II. *Blakesmoor in H——Shire*, I was astonished at the indistinction of everything. Where had stood the great gates? What bounded the Court-yard? Whereabout did the outhouses commence?

†**3.** Indistinctness, obscurity, dimness. *Obs.*

1651 BIGGS *New Disp.* ⁋77 The indistinction, confusion and perpetuall turbulency of our Œconomy. **1693** SOUTH *Twelve Serm.* (1698) III. 62 His whole Soul is nothing but Night, and Confusion, Darkness, and Indistinction. *a* **1774** HARTE *Charit. Mason* (R.), Wild indistinction did their place supply; Half heard, half lost, th' imperfect accents die. **1795** MASON *Ch. Mus.* ii. 96 The numerous Composers who succeeded Tallis..rather increased than diminished this indistinction of the words, by introducing more elaborate harmonies.

4. Absence of distinction or eminence; obscurity. *nonce-use.*

1865 *Athenæum* No. 1969. 105/1 Persons of distinction or in-distinction.

indistinctive (ɪndɪ'stɪŋktɪv), *a.* [f. IN-[3] + DISTINCTIVE, after *indistinct.*] Not distinctive.

1. Not distinguishing; undiscriminating.

1699–1881 [implied in INDISTINCTIVELY].

2. Without distinctive character or features; not markedly different from others.

1846 POE *Kirkland* Wks. 1864 III. 38 In person rather short and slight; features indistinctive. **1861** *Sat. Rev.* 25 May 541 The hills, of New Red-Sandstone, are low and indistinctive,—the streams slow and sluggish. *a* **1864** HAWTHORNE *Amer. Note-Bks.* (1879) I. 183 The blue and indistinctive scene.

indi'stinctively, *adv.* [f. prec. + -LY[2]: cf. *distinctively.*] In an indistinctive manner; without distinction; indifferently, indiscriminately.

1699 LD. TARBUT in *Pepys' Diary* VI. 191 That men, women, and children, indistinctively, were subject to it. **1845** *Blackw. Mag.* LVII. 398 The whole Essay addresses itself to two descriptions of persons—to those who *will be* critics, and to those who *will be* poets. Both are here addressed, and indistinctively. **1881** *Contemp. Rev.* June 897 Pastimes in which nobles and patricians indistinctively took part.

indi'stinctiveness. [f. as prec. + -NESS.]

1. Incapacity for distinguishing or making distinctions.

a **1859** DE QUINCEY cited in Worcester *Suppl.* 1881.

2. Want of distinctive character; indistinctness.

1837 *For. Q. Rev.* XIX. 401 The might that gave shape to confusion, defined indistinctiveness, and portrayed the very void of the soul.

indi'stinctly, *adv.* [f. INDISTINCT *a.* (or its L. original) + -LY[2]: repr. L. *indistincte.*]

†**1.** In such a way as not to distinguish or make a difference between things, persons, or cases; without distinction; indifferently, indiscriminately.

c **1420** *Pallad. on Husb.* III. 1064 The herid blake, in colde contre the hoor, And euery hugh to haue in places warme, Is indistincly good, and may not harme. **1526** *Pilgr. Perf.* (W. de W. 1531) 189 In yᵉ first article..is conteyned & included indistinctly all yᵗ we byleue expresly of god in hymselfe. **1656** BRAMHALL *Replic.* 32 But I am far from concluding all indistinctly. **1726** AYLIFFE *Parergon* 370 After the year of Probation, when this Habit is common and indistinctly given to Novices and Persons profess'd.

2. Not clearly to the perception, discernment, or understanding; confusedly, obscurely, dimly.

1580 HOLLYBAND *Treas. Fr. Tong*, *Confusément*, confusedly, indistinctly. **1677** HALE *Prim. Orig. Man.* I. ii. 46 The phantasie..Compounds those Images into some things not unlike Propositions, though confusedly and indistinctly. **1764** REID *Inquiry* vi. §22 (R.) When the object is removed beyond the farthest limit of distinct vision, it will be seen indistinctly. **1826** FOSTER in *Life & Corr.* (1846) II. 78 Articulate more indistinctly than formerly. **1862** TROLLOPE *Orley F.* xiii. 105 The black unwelcome guest, the spectre of coming evil, had ever been present to her; but she had seen it indistinctly. **1863** H. COX *Instit.* III. iv. 639

Their earliest constitution and functions are..very indistinctly traceable.

indi'stinctness. [f. as prec. + -NESS.] The quality or condition of being indistinct; obscurity, dimness. (In reference to either sensuous or mental perception.) **a.** As a quality of the object: Incapability of being clearly perceived or understood.

a **1727** NEWTON (J.), According to the indistinctness of this picture [in the bottom of the eye], the object will appear confused. **1785** REID *Intell. Powers* v. ii. (1803) 123 If we attend to the cause of this indistinctness, we shall find, that it is not owing to their being general terms, but to this, that there is no definition of them that has authority. **1827** WHATELY *Logic* (1845) Introd. 33 The ambiguity or indistinctness of Terms. **1880** E. WHITE *Cert. Relig.* 35 There is a certain indistinctness in her outlines.

b. As a quality of perception or thought: cf. INDISTINCT 3 b.

1783 BLAIR *Rhetoric* x. I. 186 The obscurity which reigns so much among many metaphysical writers is, for the most part, owing to the indistinctness of their own conceptions. **1783** JOHNSON *Lett. to Mrs. Thrale* 19 June, I felt a confusion and indistinctness in my head, which lasted I suppose about half a minute. **1837** WHEWELL *Hist. Induct. Sc.* (1857) I. 185 The indistinctness of thought which is so fatal a feature in the intellect of the stationary period.

indistinguishable (ɪndɪ'stɪŋgwɪʃəb(ə)l), *a.* [IN-³.] Not distinguishable; that cannot be distinguished.

1. a. Incapable of being discriminated or recognized as different *from* something else, or from each other; of which the difference cannot be perceived. Also as *sb.*

1658 SIR T. BROWNE *Gard. Cyrus* iii. 51 The true seeds of Cypresse and Rampions are indistinguishable by old eyes. **1847** LEWES *Hist. Philos.* (1867) II. 359 The simultaneousness of the two sensations renders them indistinguishable. **1882** G. ALLEN in *Knowledge* No. 19. 403 So after a short time they became as indistinguishable from the true Celts, as Normans and Danes in England have become indistinguishable from the rest of the community. **1903** *Daily Chron.* 24 Nov. 4/5 All this contention and uncertainty might be avoided if we abolished..the artificial distinction between two indistinguishables. **1949** H. W. B. JOSEPH *Lect. Philos. Leibniz* ii. 23 There will be a perpetual substitution of indistinguishables.

b. *transf.* Of which the parts are not distinguishable; of indeterminate shape or structure.

This is perh. the meaning in the Shaks. quot., where the word is used of Thersites, ? in reference to his deformity.

1606 SHAKS. *Tr. & Cr.* v. i. 33 You ruinous But, you whorson indistinguishable Curre. **1873** BLACK *Pr. Thule* (1874) 1 The sea and the air and the sky seemed to be one indistinguishable mass of whirling and hurrying vapour.

2. That cannot be clearly perceived (by the senses or the mind); not discernible; imperceptible.

1642 *Answ. Observ. agst. King* 10 The Scales of the Votes dancing indistinguishable whether they leane. **1809–10** COLERIDGE *Friend* (1837) III. 110 The silent and.. indistinguishable lapse of time. **1822–34** *Good's Study Med.* (ed. 4) I. 527 The pulse of the arteries of a paralytic arm was quite indistinguishable. **1847** J. WILSON *Chr. North* (1857) I. 244 Indistinguishable to the eye.

Hence **indistinguisha'bility**, **indi'stinguishableness**, the quality or character of being indistinguishable.

1731 BAILEY vol. II, *Indistinguishableness*..uncapableness to be distinguished. **1855** H. SPENCER *Princ. Psychol.* (1872) II. VI. vi. 52 The true interpretation of equality is indistinguishableness. **1885** F. TEMPLE *Relat. Relig. & Sc.* ii. 41 Here we mean a different thing by the word *same.* We mean indistinguishability. **1891** *Monist* I. 488 Shading off from perfect likeness or indistinguishableness to just recognisable affinity.

indi'stinguishably, *adv.* [f. prec. + -LY².]

†**1.** Without distinguishing; indiscriminately.

1689 *Proc. Pres. Parl. Justified* 5 All who cherish Resentments of this kind I dare not indistinguishably condemn.

2. So as to be indistinguishable; so that the difference cannot be perceived.

1825 COLERIDGE *Aids Refl.* (1858) I. App. C. 404 They likewise pass into each other so indistinguishably, that the whole order forms a very network. **1873** SYMONDS *Grk. Poets* ii. 44 Empedocles lived at a time when poetry and fact were indistinguishably mingled.

indi'stinguished, *a.* Now *rare.* [IN-³.] Not distinguished; undistinguished.

1605 SHAKS. *Lear* IV. vi. 278 Oh indistinguish'd space of Womans will, A plot vpon her vertuous Husbands life, And the exchange my Brother. **1646** SIR T. BROWNE *Pseud. Ep.* III. xxiv. 171 In that indistinguisht masse, all things seemed one. **1884** *Congreg. Year Bk.* 52 The common and indistinguished life of man.

†**indi'stinguishing,** *a. Obs.* [IN-³.] Not distinguishing; undiscriminating.

1828 WEBSTER, *Indistinguishing,* making no difference; as, indistinguishing liberalities. *Johnson.*

indistributable (ɪndɪ'strɪbju:təb(ə)l), *a.* [IN-³.] That cannot be distributed: see DISTRIBUTE *v.*

1847 SIR W. HAMILTON *Let. De Morgan* 43 The rule of the Logicians, that the middle term should be once at least distributed (or indistributable)..is untrue. **1879** H. SPENCER *Data Ethics* xiii. 236 Since that..cannot be happiness itself which is indistributable.

indisturbable (ɪndɪ'stɜ:bəb(ə)l), *a.* [f. IN-³ + *disturbable*, f. DISTURB *v.* + -ABLE.] Incapable of being disturbed.

1660 H. MORE *Myst. Godl.* 268 The true and indisturbable kingdome, full of all..heavenly Beautifulness. **1885** S. COX *Expos.* Ser. I. vii. 85 The quiet and indisturbable depths of a soul stayed on God.

indisturbance (ɪndɪ'stɜ:bəns). Now *rare.* [f. IN-³ + DISTURBANCE.] Absence of disturbance; undisturbed condition; quietness, tranquillity.

1659 STANLEY *Hist. Philos.* XI. (1701) 459/1 You..neither perceive, through want of knowledge, the bounds of Indisturbance and Perturbation. *a* **1677** BARROW *Serm. Govt. Tongue* in *Beauties Barrow* (1846) 52 Speaking ill upon presumption of secrecy, and thence of indisturbance and impunity. **1770** BEATTIE *Ess. Truth* III. ii. (1811) 274 We are told that the end of Scepticism, as it was taught by Pyrrho ..was to obtain indisturbance. **1866** FERRIER *Grk. Philos.* I. xv. 469 Perceiving our ignorance to be inevitable, we shall live in a state of..mental indisturbance.

†**indi'sturbed,** *a. Obs.* [IN-³.] Not disturbed; undisturbed.

1660 N. INGELO *Bentivolio & Urania* (1682) II. 150 Notwithstanding the indisturbed temper of the Divine Nature. **1686** PLOT *Staffordsh.* 20 Others of the same kind being wholly indisturbed.

†**in'ditch,** *v. Obs.* Also 6 **endich,** 7 **indich.** [f. IN-¹ or ² + DITCH *sb.*]

1. *trans.* To cast into or bury in (or as in) a ditch.

1597 BP. HALL *Sat.* III. ii, Wert thou inditched in great secrecie; Where as no passenger might curse thy dust, Nor dogs sepulchrall sate their gnawing lust. **1630** J. TAYLOR (Water P.) *Wks.* I. 64/2 One was cast dead into the Thames ..drawne with a Boat and a rope downe some part of the Riuer, and dragged to shore and indiched.

2. To enclose or surround with a ditch; to entrench.

1598 FLORIO, *Affossare,* to dike, to ditch or moate about, to make trenches or dikes, to endich. **1610** HOLLAND *Camden's Brit.* I. 212 The Danes..raised as it is thought certaine trenches: whereof one is called Maumbury being an acre indiched.

indite (ɪn'daɪt), *v.* Forms: *α.* 4–6 **endyte,** 4–9 **endite,** (5 **enditt,** 6 **endight, -dyt,** 6–7 *erron.* **endict).** *β.* 5–6 **indyte,** 6 **indight, -dyt(t,** (**-ditie**), 6– **indite,** (6–8 *erron.* **indict).** See also ADYTE. [a. OF. *enditer, -ditier, -ditter*:—L. type **indictāre*, f. *in-* (IN-²) + *dictāre* to declare, dictate, compose in words, freq. of *dīcĕre* to say. The same word orig. as INDICT, but retaining the French form of the radical part.]

†**1.** *trans.* To utter, suggest, or inspire a form of words which is to be repeated or written down; = DICTATE *v.* 1. Also *absol. Obs.*

α. *c* **1374** CHAUCER *Boeth.* I. met. i. 1 (Camb. MS.) Rendynge Muses of poetes enditen to me thinges to ben writen and drery vers. **1450–1530** *Myrr. our Ladye* 16 The holy gost endited the rewle hymselfe by his holy mouthe to saynt Birgit. **1483** CAXTON *Gold. Leg.* 267/1 As he endyted the lettre..and another monk wrote hit. **1600** HOLLAND *Livy* XXXI. ix. (1609) 778 The Consull pronounced the vow according to the very same forme of words (as the high priest endited and spake before him). **1639** FULLER *Holy War* v. ii. (1647) 231 In this case their words are endited not from their heart but outward limbes. **1815** T. JEFFERSON *Writ.* (1830) IV. 251 English newspapers endited or endowed by the Castlereaghs or the Cannings.

β. *c* **1440** *Promp. Parv.* 139/2 Endytyn, or indytyn scripture and feyre speche, *dicto.* **1483** *Cath. Angl.* 195/2 To Indyte, *dictare, jndictare.* **1586** T. B. *La Primaud. Fr. Acad.* I. (1594) 84 Iulius Cæsar..would indight a letter to one of his secretaries. *a* **1633** AUSTIN *Medit.* (1635) 160 That..I may alwaies beleeve what the Spirit of Love hath Indited, and the beloved Disciple hath written. **1657** SPARROW *Bk. Com. Prayer* 94 The Common Prayers which were indicted or denounced by the voice of the Deacon. **1717** PRIOR *To the Earl of Oxford* 4 Smiling, bid her freely write What her happy thoughts indite. **1727** W. MATHER *Yng. Man's Comp.* Pref., Canonical Scripture, which is indicted by the Holy Ghost.

†**2.** To enjoin as a law, precept, or maxim; = DICTATE *v.* 2. *Obs.*

1413 *Pilgr. Sowle* (Caxton 1483) IV. vii. 61 Iustyce ne maye nought endyten this sentence that this shold be due. **1594** CAREW *Huarte's Exam. Wits* v. (1596) 66 Out of one consideration endicted to them by their Schoolemaister, they will gather a hundred. **1633** BP. HALL *Hard Texts, N.T.* 299 God himselfe..hath indited these things to us. **1709** POPE *Ess. Crit.* I. 92 Hear how learn'd Greece her useful rules endites, When to repress and when indulge our flights.

b. To dictate to, enjoin (a person).

c **1399** *Pol. Poems* (Rolls) II. 15 Noght only to my king of pes y write, Bot to these othre princes cristene alle, That ech of hem his oghne herte endite. **1582–8** *Hist. Jas. VI* (1804) 5 Shoe constraint nane of her subiects to exercise in religion utherwayes than thair conscience indytit thame.

3. To put into words, compose (a poem, tale, speech, etc.); to give a literary or rhetorical form to (words, an address); to express or describe in a literary composition.

α. *a* **1340** HAMPOLE *Psalter, Cant.* 499 Anna..made þis psalme enditand it. *c* **1374** CHAUCER *Troylus* I. 6 Thesiphone þow helpe me for tendite This woful vers. *a* **1420** HOCCLEVE *De Reg. Princ.* 1854 Endite in Latyne or in Frensshe thy grief clere. **1508** DUNBAR *Gold. Targe* 64 Quho could wele endyte How all the feldis..Depaynt war brycht. **1534** MORE *Comf. agst. Trib.* III. Wks. 1223/1 He hadde deuised his artycles so wysely, and endicted the[m] so well. **1575** LANEHAM *Let.* (1871) 35 The ditty in miter so aptly endighted to the matter. **1659** HAMMOND *On Ps.* lxxiv. (*title*) The Seventy Fourth Psalm..seems to have been endited under the captivity. *a* **1670** HACKET *Abp. Williams* I. (1692) 118 That which comes to the institute I handle was thus endicted. **1692** W. LOWTH *Vind.* (1699) 8 Unless..God cannot order a Book to be writ in as Intelligible a manner, as men can endite it.

β. **1501** DOUGLAS *Pal. Hon.* III. i, Ye musis nine..caus me dewlie till indite this storie. **1555** J. PROCTOR *Wyat's Reb.* Ded., Moving others to indict and pen stories. *c* **1560** A. SCOTT *Poems* xiii. 8 Sum thame delytis till indyte Fair facound speich. **1611** BIBLE *Ps.* xlv. 1 My heart is inditing a good matter. **1667** MILTON *P.L.* IX. 27 Not sedulous by Nature to indite Warrs, hitherto the onely Argument Heroic deem'd. *c* **1706** PRIOR *Her Right Name* 21 Old Homer only could indite Their vagrant grace and soft delight. *a* **1800** COWPER *Ode to Apollo* 3 Luckless brains, That..Indite much metre with much pains, And little or no meaning. **1847** DISRAELI *Tancred* III. iv, Men far too well acquainted with their subject to indite such tales of the Philistines as these!

b. *absol.* or *intr.*

1377 LANGL. *P. Pl.* B. xv. 367 For is none of þis newe clerkes..þat can versifye faire ne formalich enditen. *c* **1386** CHAUCER *Knt.'s T.* 1883 Of this bataille I wol namoore endite. **1447** BOKENHAM *Seyntys* Introd. (Roxb.) 3 The matere wych I wyl of wryte Althow but rudely I kun endyte. **1514** BARCLAY *Cyt. & Uplondyshm.* (Percy Soc.) p. lxii, Of gay matters to sing & to endite. **1687** WALLER *On his Divine Poems* 2 The subject made us able to indite. **1742** SHENSTONE *Schoolmistress* 167 Sigh'd as he sung and did in tears indite.

4. *trans.* To put into written words, write, pen (a letter, etc.); to inscribe, set down, or enter in writing. In later use, passing into 3, the 'wording' being more thought of than the actual writing.

1340–70 *Alex. & Dind.* 181 þanne let þe lordliche king lettres endite. **1481** CAXTON *Reynard* (Arb.) 51 Saye that ye your self haue made the lettre and endited it. **1509** HAWES *Past. Pleas.* xxx. (Percy Soc.) 149 Whan for my selfe she did so well indite, As I shall shew..The gentyll fourme and tenour of her letter. **1548** HALL *Chron., Edw. IV,* 227 A letter of diffiance, bothe for the stile and the pennyng excellently endited. **1588** J. MELLIS *Briefe Instr.* Eiij b, Thus yee shall indight the parcell of the Journall into the Debitor, that is on the left hand. **1672** MARVELL *Reh. Transp.* I. 4 He may..be improved to endite Tickets for the Bear-garden. **1745** *De Foe's Eng. Tradesman* ii. (1841) I. 11 The young Man's learning how to indite his letters in a tradesman's style. **1870** DISRAELI *Lothair* lxix. 367 He would probably find that functionary inditing a private letter to the English Secretary of State.

¶**5.** *Catachr.* **a.** for *invite*; **b.** for *inscribe. Obs.*

1592 SHAKS. *Rom. & Jul.* II. iv. 135 She will endite him to some Supper. **1597** —— *2 Hen. IV,* II. i. 30 Hee is indited to dinner to the Lubbars head in Lombard street. **1793** J. WILLIAMS *Life Ld. Barrymore* 115, I will not indite his sepulchre with that adulatory language.

Hence **in'dited** *ppl. a.*

c **1440** *Promp. Parv.* 139/2 Endytyd (*K.* or inditvd) as scripture and speche, *dictatus.* **1575** LANEHAM *Let.* (1871) 46 Her wel endighted dialog. **1597** HOOKER *Eccl. Pol.* v. xxxviii. §2 The Prophet Dauid..left behind him..a number of diuinely endited Poems. **1626** W. FENNER *Hidden Manna* (1652) 10 An indited Epistle, which an unskilful Ideot.. cannot read.

†**in'dite,** *sb. Sc. Obs.* In 6 en-, indite, en-, indyte. [f. INDITE *v.*: cf. DITE *sb.*¹]

1. The action or faculty of inditing.

1508 DUNBAR *Gold. Targe* 270 This Ile before was bare, and desolate Off rhetorike, or lusty fresch endyte. —— *Flyting w. Kennedie* 109 Thow hes full littill feill of fair indyte. **1573** *Satir. Poems Reform.* xxxix. 324 My dull indyte can not direct my pen.

2. Style of composing, literary style; also, the thing indited, a composition; esp. a poem.

1501 DOUGLAS *Pal. Hon., Envoy* iii, Thy barrant termis, and thy vile indite Sall not be mine. **1513** —— *Æneis* Pref. 2 Laude, honor, prasingis, thankis infynite To the, and thi dulce ornate fresch endite Mast reuerend Virgill. **1552** LYNDESAY *Monarche* 6335 All gentyll Redaris hertlye I Implore For tyll excuse my rurall rude Indyte. **1567** *Satir. Poems Reform.* iii. 212 In poetrie I traist ȝow be na barne, Quhilk dois reheirs the Poetis auld indyte. **1570** *Ibid.* xx. 7 Desyring all, baith greit and small..Not for to wyte my rude Indyte.

indite, obs. or archaic form of INDICT *v.*

inditement (ɪn'daɪtmənt). *Obs.* or *arch.* (Also 7 **indictment.**) [f. INDITE *v.* + -MENT. Cf. OF. *enditement, -dictement* suggestion, instigation (Wace, 12th c.).] The action of composing in prose or verse; composition.

1567 DRANT *Horace, Ep.* Ded. *iij, No potentate of all the world..hath more fayre inditements to his commendation. *a* **1635** NAUNTON *Fragm. Reg.* (Arb.) 56 His Secretaries did little for him by the way of Inditement, wherein they could seldome please him, he was so facete and choice in his phrase and stile. *a* **1639** WOTTON *Ps.* civ, May..both harp and voice In sweet indictment of thy hymns rejoyce. **1805** W. TAYLOR in *Monthly Mag.* XIX. 328 The Ecclesiasticus.. was actually in the process of composition or inditement. **1806** —— in *Ann. Rev.* IV. 604 They gave up these long undertakings, as likely to outlast the spirit, the rapture, the enthusiasm, of enditement.

inditement, obs. form of INDICTMENT.

inditer (ɪn'daɪtə(r)). Forms: *α.* 4 **enditour,** 5 **-dytour,** 5–9 **-diter,** 7 **-ditor, -dighter,** (8 *erron.* **endicter.** *β.* 5 **indyter,** 6 **-dytor,** 6–7 **-dighter,** 6– **inditer.** [ME. (and ? AF.) *enditour* (L. type **indictātōr-em*), f. *endite,* INDITE *v.* + agent-

suffix *-our*, *-or*, passing at length into -ER: cf. DITER.] One who indites; one who composes or dictates a literary work, speech, or letter; an author, writer, composer.

α. **1387** TREVISA *Higden* (Rolls) IV. 173 In his tyme Plautus Latinus, þe grete Pompeus his enditour and faire speker, Libertus þe doctour, florischeþ at Rome [L. *Cujus diebus Plautus Latinus rhetor, magni Pompeii libertus, doctor Romæ claruit*]. **1390** GOWER *Conf.* II. 82 Enditours Of old cronique and eke auctours. **1483** *Cath. Angl.* 115/1 An Enditer, *dictator, indictator.* *a* **1586** SIDNEY *Arcadia* (1622) 267 [He] presented his Letters, desiring Amphialus, that.. he would consider that he was onely the bearer, and not the enditer. **1645** MILTON *Colast.* Wks. (1851) 364 The basest and the hungriest endighter. **1664–94** SOUTH *Twelve Serm.* II. 142 It is the simplicity of the Heart, and not of the Head, that is the best Enditer of our Petitions. **1717** J. FOX *Wanderer* (1718) 46, I could hardly with-hold my Compassion from the fair Endicter [of the Fiction]. **1813** W. TAYLOR in *Monthly Mag.* XXXV. 215 This Memoir.. must have had Joseph for its main compiler, enditer, or author. **1815** W. H. IRELAND *Scribbleomania* 47 The feeling enditer of Sympathy's tale.

β. **1483** *Cath. Angl.* 195/2 An Indyter of lettirs, *dictator.* **1579** FULKE *Ref. Rastel* 734 Bookes of holy scripture, the indighters of which.. be not knowne. **1617** COLLINS *Def. Bp. Ely* II. vi. 249 We know the inditer, though we doubt of the penman. **1754** RICHARDSON *Grandison* (1781) VI. xxxvi. 245 You will think your ward very bold to address you by Letter: especially as she is a very poor inditer. **1876** BANCROFT *Hist. U.S.* IV. xxvii. 518 Jonas Clark, the bold inditer of patriotic state papers.

inditer, obs. form of INDICTER.

inditing (ɪnˈdaɪtɪŋ), *vbl. sb.* [f. INDITE *v.* + -ING[1].] **a.** The action of the verb INDITE; composition. **b.** A thing indited, a literary composition, a treatise, poem, letter, etc.

1340–70 *Alex. & Dind.* 243 Dereworþe dindimus þe enditinge hurde. **1388** WYCLIF *2nd Prol. Job*, Fro the begynnyng of the volume vnto the woordis of Job, anent the Ebruys the enditing is prose. *c* **1400** tr. *Secreta Secret., Gov. Lordsh.* (E.E.T.S.) 106 Þe endytynge ys þe body and þe writynge ys þe clethynge of wordys and spekynge. **1500–20** DUNBAR *Poems* lix. 15 He hes indorsit myn indytting With versis off his [awin] hand vrytting. **1553** T. WILSON *Rhet.* 172 There are three maner of stiles or inditynges. **1579** G. HARVEY *Letter-bk.* (Camden) 76 Affectinge the comendation of an eloquent.. style by overcurious and statelye enditinge. **1604** ARMIN in *Nest Ninn.* (1842) Introd., The Booke of her owne indighting. **1708** *Brit. Apollo* No. 20. 3/1 For Letters and Writings, Of other's Indicting. **1749** FIELDING *Tom Jones* XVIII. x, It was all his own invention, and the letter of his inditing.

indition: see INDICION[2].

inˈditress. *rare.* [f. INDITER + -ESS.] A female inditer.

1822 *Blackw. Mag.* XII. 657 Was there to be a virtual *non-imprimatur* in force against our songstresses, romance-inditresses, tragedianesses, sonneteeresses, or other 'buildresses of the lofty rhyme'?

†**inˈditure.** *Obs. rare*$^{-1}$. [f. *indite*, INDICT *v.* + -URE.] = INDICTMENT.

1614 T. KENNEY in *Lismore Papers* Ser. II. (1887) I. 202 Being twise indited, by twoe seuerall inditures, I was cleared of both.

indium (ˈɪndɪəm). *Chem.* [f. radical of *ind-icum* INDIGO + *-ium*, after *sodium*, etc.; in reference to the two indigo lines which form the characteristic spectrum of the metal.] A soft silver-white metal of extreme rarity, occurring in association with zinc and other metals; discovered by Reich and Richter in 1863, by means of spectrum analysis, in the zinc-blende of Freiberg. Symbol In.

1864 LYELL *Inaug. Addr.* in *Reader* 17 Sept. 358 A fourth metal named indium, from its indigo-coloured band, was detected by Professor Richter of Freiberg in Saxony in a zinc ore of the Hartz. **1874** tr. *Lommel's Light* 114 The blue light of Indium undergoes a still stronger refraction than that of Thallium. **1882** *Nature* No. 639. 290 He finds that indium is like some other metals in not coming under the often-accepted rule that pure metals have a change of coefficient of resistance with temperature.

b. *attrib.*, as ***indium bromide*** (In Br), ***indium chloride***, ***monochloride*** (In Cl), ***dichloride*** ($InCl_2$), ***trichloride*** ($InCl_3$); ***indium iodide***, ***oxide***, ***hydroxide***; ***indium salts***, etc.

1897 ROSCOE & SCHORLEMMER *Chem.* II. 609 *Indium Oxide* In_2O_3 is a pale yellow powder. *Ibid.* 611 *Indium Ammonium Alum*.. is deposited in well-defined regular octohedra.

indivertible (ɪndɪˈvɜːtɪb(ə)l), *a.* [f. IN-[3] + *divertible*, f. DIVERT *v.* + -IBLE.] Incapable of being diverted or turned aside.

1821 LAMB *Elia* Ser. I. *Old Benchers I.T.*, Indivertible from his way as a moving column. **1874** G. MACDONALD *Malcolm* (1875) III. xiii. 176 The indivertible guardian of his morals.

Hence **indiˈvertibly** *adv.*, in a way that cannot be turned aside.

1853 *Tait's Mag.* XX. 267 Its recent history, its greatness all associate it intimately and indivertibly with the German 'Fatherland'. **1868** H. BUSHNELL *Serm. Living Subj.* 186 We are all saying, the young man eagerly, the old man indivertibly, the same thing.

†**indiˈvertive,** *a.* *Obs. rare*$^{-1}$. [f. IN-[3] + DIVERTIVE.] Not divertive; not of an amusing or entertaining character or tendency.

1700 J. BROME *Trav. Eng., Scot.* Ded. Ep. (1707) 3 Something which may not prove altogether indivertive.

†**indiˈvestible,** *a.* *Obs. rare*$^{-1}$. [f. IN-[3] + *divestible*, f. DIVEST + -IBLE.] Of which one cannot divest oneself.

a **1631** DONNE *Serm.* cvi. IV. 433 Being under an invincible ignorance and indivestible Scruples.

†**indiˈvid.** *Obs.* Abbreviation of INDIVIDUAL.

1677 T. HARVEY tr. *Owen's Epigr.* (N.), Why want none tasting, touching? 'cause of these That th' individ, this guards the species. **1843** [see BURG 2].

†**indiˈvidable,** *a.* *Obs.* [IN-[3].] Not dividable, indivisible.

The exact sense in the Shaks. quotation is uncertain. Schmidt says 'Not to be distinguished by a particular appellation'; Aldis Wright, 'Where the unity of place is observed'.

1602 SHAKS. *Ham.* II. ii. 418 (Qos, 2–3, 1604–5) Scene indeuidible [*Qos.* 4–6 (1611–37) indeuidable; *Folios* indiuible] or Poem vnlimited. **1602** R. DOLMAN tr. *La Primaud. Fr. Acad.* (1618) III. xi. 663 Democritus, and Diodorus affirme, that before all things, there were certen Atomoes, or litle indiuidable bodies [etc.]. **1625** GILL *Sacr. Philos.* I. 32 One individeable and peculiar being cannot belong to more than one, as the being of Thomas cannot be the very same being which is of Peter or Iohn. **1637** EARL MONMOUTH tr. *Malvezzi's Romulus & Tarquin* 149 A point which in the abstract is individable.

†**indiˈvided,** *a.* *Obs.* [IN-[3].] Undivided.

1563 WINȜET *Four Scoir Thre Quest.* Wks. 1888 I. 84 Christe realie thair præsent (quhilk ane indiuidit.. euiry Christiane.. ressauis). **1579** FULKE *Heskins' Parl.* 147 He remained whole in that his indiuided vnity with his father. **1647** H. MORE *Song of Soul* II. ii. II. xxxi, One individed faculty. **1695** BP. PATRICK *Comm. Gen.* xviii. 2. 299 A Representation of the blessed individed Trinity.

individual (ɪndɪˈvɪdjuːəl), *a.* and *sb.* Also 5 indyvyduall. [f. med.L. *indīviduāl-is*, f. *indīvidu-us* indivisible, inseparable (see INDIVIDUUM) + -AL[1]: cf. F. *individuel* (16th c.), It. *individuale*. (*Formæ individuales* occurs in Adhelard of Bath, *c* 1115 (Haureau *Philos. Scolast.* I. 349); the adv. *indīviduāliter* in Abelard *Epist.* I. ii. 5.)]

A. *adj.* †**1.** One in substance or essence; forming an indivisible entity; indivisible. *Obs.*

c **1425** *Found. St. Bartholomew's* (E.E.T.S.) 11 To the.. glorie of the hye and indyuyduall Trynyte. *a* **1619** FOTHERBY *Atheom.* I. vii. §1 (1622) 50 Some make their god of Atomes, and indiuidual moates: some of diuidual numbers; as Epicurus, and Pythagoras. **1623** WHITBOURNE *Newfoundland* 56 In the name of the holy and indiuiduall Trinitie. **1641** MILTON *Animadv.* ii, This untheologicall Remonstrant would divide the individuall Catholicke Church into severall Republicks. **1678** CUDWORTH *Intell. Syst.* I. iv. §36. 611 It would be liable to misinterpretation, and to be taken, in the Sabellian sense, for that which hath one and the same singular and individual essence.

†**2.** That cannot be separated; inseparable. *Obs.*

c **1600** *Timon* I. ii. (1842) 6 Where ere thou go'st I still will folowe thee An indiuiduall mate. **1623** COCKERAM, *Indiuiduall*, not to bee parted, as man and wife. *c* **1645** HOWELL *Lett.* I. III. ix, He.. is an individual Companion to the King. **1667** MILTON *P.L.* IV. 486 To have thee by my side Henceforth an individual solace dear.

3. a. Existing as a separate indivisible entity; numerically one, single. **b.** Single, as distinct from others of the same kind; particular, special. Also *absol.* in phr. †*in the individual*, in the particular case: opposed to *in the general* (GENERAL *a.* 11 d).

1613 JACKSON *Creed* II. v. §5 Whether things indifferent in the general, or vnto many.. be indifferent in the indiuiduall, to this or that particular man. **1651** BAXTER *Inf. Bapt.* 25 The whole Church must be so sanctified; therefore the individuall members. **1690** LOCKE *Hum. Und.* III. vi. §3 Our Idea of any individual Man would be.. far different. **1729** BUTLER *Serm. Hum. Nat.* iii. Wks. 1874 II. 31 Every man in his physical nature is one individual single agent. **1786** BURKE *W. Hastings* Wks. 1842 II. 227 All powers delegated from the board to any individual servant of the company. **1793** A. HAMILTON *Wks.* (1886) VII. 75 Settlement of Accounts between the United and Individual States. **1833** L. RITCHIE *Wand. by Loire* 23 The traveller takes it [the château] for a town rather than an individual edifice. **1856** FROUDE *Hist. Eng.* (1858) II. viii. 244 A determination in each individual man to go his own way. **1896** DK. ARGYLL *Philos. Belief* 74 It is not in the use of individual words, alone, that this principle of explanation is adopted.

†**c.** Expressing self-identity: Identical, self-same, very same. *Obs.*

1633 PRYNNE *Histriomastix* 177 To sport themselves with those individuall sinnes upon the Stage, which the parties.. are condoling now in Hell? **1641** J. JACKSON *True Evang. T.* II. 130 Polycarpus, Bishop of Smirna, and some say that Individuall Angell of the Church of Smirna, whereunto the second of those seven Asiatique Epistles are written. **1655** MRQ. WORCESTER *Cent. Inv.* §1 Seals.. setting down.. the individual place where anything was sealed. **1681–6** J. SCOTT *Chr. Life* (1747) III. 228 That this Remnant still continued the same individual Kingdom of Christ with the former, tho' very much reformed and improved. **1701** WALLIS in Hearne *Collect.* 24 July an. 1705 (O.H.S.) I. 15 Which I do believe to be this individual Book. **1753** SMOLLETT *Ct. Fathom* (1784) 178/1 They were communicated to her by the nun, who was no other than the individual Wilhelmina. **1804** CHARLOTTE SMITH *Conversations* I. 132 It is more probable that the individual insect in question had been produced this Summer.

4. Distinguished from others by attributes of its own; marked by a peculiar and striking character.

1646 SIR T. BROWNE *Pseud. Ep.* I. v. 19 A man should be something that men are not, and individuall in somewhat beside his proper nature. **1894** *Harper's Mag.* Mar. 494 He is so quaint and so individual in his views. **1897** *Brit. Weekly* 27 May 97 In him Nonconformity has lost one of her most conspicuous and individual figures.

5. a. Of, pertaining or peculiar to, a single person or thing, or some one member of a class; characteristic of an individual.

1605 BACON *Adv. Learn.* I. iii. §4 As touching the Manners of learned men, it is a thing personall and individuall. **1712** S. CLARKE *Def. Immateriality Soul* 13 The sole Reason urged.. why a System of Matter cannot have a Power of Thinking or an Individual Consciousness. **1777** BURKE *Addr. to King* Wks. 1842 II. 395 We,.. several of the peers of the realm, and several members of the house of commons.. do in our individual capacity,.. beg leave [etc.]. **1838–42** ARNOLD *Hist. Rome* xliii. III. 64 Our tendency is to admire individual greatness far more than national. **1859** DARWIN *Orig. Spec.* ii. (1878) 34 The many slight differences which appear in the offspring from the same parents.. may be called individual differences. **1859** MILL *Liberty* i. (1864) 3/2 There is a limit to the legitimate interference of collective opinion with individual independence. **1862** RUSKIN *Unto this Last* iv. (1880) 169 All effectual advancement.. must be by individual, not public effort.

b. ***individual name*** (†***word***), ***judgement*** (see quots.).

1641 MILTON *Animadv.* xiii, It is no individuall word, but a Collective. **1843** MILL *Logic* I. ii. §3 An individual or singular name is a name which is only capable of being truly affirmed, in the same sense, of one thing. **1864** BOWEN *Logic* v. 122 A Singular or Individual Judgment, in which a Predicate is affirmed of one thing, or of a class of things taken as one whole. **1871** *Public Sch. Lat. Gram.* 23 Nouns or Names are Individual or Proper.. which can only be applied to single persons, places, or objects.

c. Intended to serve one person; designed to contain one portion.

1889 *Cent. Dict.* s.v., An individual salt-cellar [colloq.]. **1895** *Montgomery Ward Catal.* 531/2 Individual Butter Plates. **1911** *Daily Colonist* (Victoria, B.C.) 22 Apr. 2/1 (Advt.), Table Necessities.. Cut Glass Individual Salts, up from 35¢. **1948** *Good Housek. Cookery Bk.* 454 Use small individual moulds if you want jellies in a hurry. **1951** *Catal. of Exhibits, South Bank Exhib., Festival of Britain* 52/2 Individual casserole in heat-resisting glassware. **1965** T. FITZGIBBON *Art Brit. Cooking* 203 If made in individual small moulds they [*sc.* canary puddings] are called 'Castle Puddings'. **1970** K. GILES *Death in Church* i. 20 Node.. dug his fork into the individual pudding.

d. *Psychol.* Relating or pertaining to the study of individuals, as opposed to that of a group or society. Also used to denote A. Adler's method of analytical psychology.

1898 *Amer. Jrnl. Psychol.* X. 329 The systematic consideration of the problems grouped under the name of 'Individual Psychology' is of but recent date. Indeed, the only treatment of the whole subject for its own sake is that contained in a paper published in 1895, by Mm. Binet and Henri. *Ibid.* 330 Individual Psychology, on the contrary, studies those psychical processes which vary from one individual to another. **1917** GLUECK & LIND tr. *Adler's Neurotic Constitution* (1921) p. v, An empiric basis is made use of in comparative individual-psychology for the purpose of establishing a fictive standard of normality in order to enable one to measure and compare with it grades of deviation from it. **1933** T. S. ELIOT *Use of Poetry* 17, I cannot accept any such theory which is erected upon purely individual-psychological foundations. **1933** W. J. H. SPROTT tr. *Freud's New Introd. Lect. Psycho-Anal.* xxxiv. 180 In reality Individual Psychology has very little to do with analysis, but.. lives a sort of parasitic existence at its expense..; we cannot assent to any interference with its correct application as meaning the opposite of Group Psychology. **1951** E. E. EVANS-PRITCHARD *Social Anthropol.* iii. 45 There are various and particular objections to each of these successive attempts to explain social facts by individual psychology. **1959** L. RADL in Adler & Deutsch *Ess. Individual Psychol.* 162 At this point the close similarity between the Existentialist doctrine and Individual Psychology once again becomes strikingly apparent.

e. individual variable *Logic*, a variable that ranges over individuals. Cf. sense B. *sb.* 2 b.

1937 A. SMEATON tr. *Carnap's Logical Syntax of Lang.* 195 A ^0v is called an individual variable. **1952** P. F. STRAWSON *Introd. Logical Theory* v. 130 To the variable '*x*' and other variables of the same type.. we give the name 'individual variables'. **1954** I. M. COPI *Symbolic Logic* iv. 67 The small letter '*x*'—called an 'individual variable'—is a mere *place marker* which serves to indicate where an individual constant may be written for a singular proposition to result. **1965** HUGHES & LONDEY *Elem. Formal Logic* xxiii. 169 We shall call such variables individual-variables (meaning thereby, of course, not that the variables are themselves individuals—whatever that might mean—but that they stand indifferently for the names of individual things).

B. *sb.*

†**1.** *pl.* Inseparable things: see A. 2. *Obs.*

1627 FELTHAM *Resolves* I. xix. (1628) 17 Humanity and Miserie are alwayes paralels: sometimes indiuiduals. **1661** —— *Lusoria* (1696) 44 They are here Individuals, for no Demonstrance of Duty or Authority can distinguish them.

2. a. A single object or thing, or a group of things forming a single complex idea, and regarded as a unit; a single member of a natural class, collective group, or number.

1605 TIMME *Quersit.* I. iv. 17 We shall thoroughly discuss and ransacke euery particular indiuiduall in his kinde. **1700** DRYDEN *Palamon & A.* III. 1056 That individuals die, his

will ordains; The propagated species still remains. **1715–20** POPE *Iliad* Pref., We see each circumstance of art and individual of nature summoned together by the extent and fecundity of his imagination. **1850** R. G. CUMMING *Hunter's Life S. Afr.* (ed.2) I. 269 *note*, I have not unfrequently met with herds [of giraffes] containing thirty individuals. **1868** ROGERS *Pol. Econ.* vi. (1876) 54 It makes no difference whether the individual be a numerical unit, or an aggregate unit, as a partnership, company, or corporation of traffickers.

b. *Logic* and *Metaph.* An object which is determined by properties peculiar to itself and cannot be subdivided into others of the same kind; *spec.* in *Logic*: An object included in a species, as a species is in a genus. See INDIVIDUUM.

1628 T. SPENCER *Logick* 44 It is not possible to know vntill wee come vnto indiuiduals..vntill we ataine vnto those things which doe not admit division. **1658** PHILLIPS s.v., An individual..in Logick..signifies that which cannot be divided into more of the same name or nature, and is by some called Singulare. **1727–41** CHAMBERS *Cycl.* s.v., The usual division in logic is made into genera..those genera into species, and those species into individuals. **1833** J. H. NEWMAN *Arians* II. iv. (1876) 185 Οὐσία..being, substance ..'that which has existence in itself, independent of every thing else to constitute it': that is, an individual. **1858** WHEWELL *Hist. Sci. Ideas* (ed. 3) II. 148 (L.) Our idea of an individual is, that it is a whole composed of parts, which are not similar to the whole, and have not an independent existence, while the whole has an independent existence and a definite form. **1860** ABP. THOMSON *Laws Th.* §56. 86 An individual is that which cannot be divided without ceasing to be what it is.

c. *Zool.* and *Bot.* A single member of a species; a single specimen of an animal or plant.

1859 DARWIN *Orig. Spec.* ii. (1873) 34 No one supposes that all the individuals of the same species are cast in the same actual mould. **1880** GRAY *Struct. Bot.* ix. §1. 315 Individuals are the units of the series which constitute species..Each individual is an independent organism, of which the component parts are reciprocally means and ends. **1885** GOODALE *Phys. Bot.* (1892) 425 In scientific as well as popular language the term *individual* is commonly applied to each and every plant.

d. *Biol.* An organism regarded as having a separate existence.

Sometimes used specifically of a single member of a colony of organisms, (as a leaf-bud, or a polyp of a cœlenterate); by others defined as 'the whole product of a single fertilized ovum'; more strictly: an organism detached from other organisms, composed of coherent parts, and capable of independent life.

1776 WITHERING *Brit. Plants* (1796) I. 159 Blossom general, regular. Individuals of 1 petal, tubular. **1847** CARPENTER *Zool.* §46 In the Polypes..a number of individuals, each capable (like a leaf-bud) of living by itself, are arranged on one common plant-like structure. **1864** H. SPENCER *Princ. Biol.* §74 I. 207 A biological Individual is any concrete whole having a structure which enables it, when placed in appropriate conditions, to continuously adjust its internal relations to external relations, so as to maintain the equilibrium of its functions. **1870** NICHOLSON *Zool.* 25 In zoological language, an individual is defined as 'equal to the total result of a single ovum'. **1888** ROLLESTON & JACKSON *Anim. Life* 231 The proglottides..are supposed to be produced..by posterior germination of the scolex, from which they are detached in many instances either singly or in groups..But the facts do not appear to necessitate the view that the proglottis is an individual.

3. a. A single human being, as opposed to Society, the Family, etc.

1626 J. YATES *Ibis ad Caesarem* II. 12 *margin*, The Prophet saith not, God saw euery particular man in his bloud, or had compassion to say to euery Indiuiduall, *Thou shalt liue.* **1641** J. JACKSON *True Evang. T.* III. 213 Peace..is the very supporter of Individualls, Families, Churches, Commonwealths. **1776** ADAM SMITH *W.N.* (1869) I. Introd. 2 Among the savage nations of hunters and fishers, every individual..is..employed in useful labour. **1868** M. PATTISON *Academ. Org.* v. 141 We are most jealous of the rights of individuals, and careless of the common welfare. **1899** J. MONRO GIBSON in *Expositor* Feb. 144 It will not be as Churches but as individuals that we shall all stand before the Judgment seat of Christ.

b. Without any notion of contrast or relation to a class or group: A human being, a person. (Now chiefly as a colloquial vulgarism, or as a term of disparagement.)

1742 JOHNSON *Debates* (1787) II. 172 Only one individual was injured by another. **1771** GOLDSM. *Hist. Eng.* III. 125 These she bequeathed to different individuals. **1781** S. PETERS *Hist. Conn.* 74 The People of Massachusetts.. conceived the idea of exalting an individual of their own Province. **1828** SCOTT *F.M. Perth* xxiv, The three individuals entered the boat with great precaution. **1856** KANE *Arct. Expl.* II. x. 111 The individual whom I desired to meet. **1888** F. HUME *Mad. Midas* I. Prol., He appeared to be an exceedingly unpleasant individual.

†**4.** Short for *individual person*; person, personality, self. *Obs.*

1655 SIR E. NICHOLAS in *N. Papers* (Camden) 305 As to what concerns my owne poore indiuiduall, I am armed against all euents and deffy fortune to her teeth. **1678** CUDWORTH *Intell. Syst.* I. v. 674 They could not propagate their kind by generation, as neither indeed preserve their own individuals. **1771** SMOLLETT *Humph. Cl.* 15 July, A transient compliment made to his own individual in particular, or to his country in general. **1774** LEE *Let. to Burke* B's Corr. 1844 I. 513 Even the appearance of their individuals is totally changed since I first knew them. **1800** GODWIN in C. Kegan Paul *W. Godwin* (1876) II. 5 Driven back..to consider of my own miserable individual.

individu'alic, *a.* *nonce-word.* [f. prec. + -IC.] Denoting individuals.

1824 J. GILCHRIST *Etym. Interpreter* 72 It [English] has.. too many generic, and too few specific and individualic, terms. *Ibid.* 129.

individualism (ɪndɪˈvɪdjuːəlɪz(ə)m). [a. F. *individualisme* (f. med.L. *individuāl-is* INDIVIDUAL + *-isme*, -ISM); or f. INDIVIDUAL + -ISM.]

1. Self-centred feeling or conduct as a principle; a mode of life in which the individual pursues his own ends or follows out his own ideas; free and independent individual action or thought; egoism.

1827 L. T. REDE *Road to Stage* 59, I beg to disclaim, in these observations, any individualism; several talented persons may be found connected with such establishments. **1835** H. REEVE tr. *De Tocqueville's Democr. in Amer.* II. II. ii. (1840) III. 203 Individualism is a novel expression, to which a novel idea has given birth..Individualism is a mature and calm feeling, which disposes each member of the community to sever himself from the mass of his fellow-creatures, and to draw apart with his family and friends. **1840** GLADSTONE *Ch. Princ.* 98 It is too closely connected with our individualism in religion. **1856** KINGSLEY *Misc.*, *Hours w. Mystics* I. 351 He is not tempted by it to selfish individualism, or contemplative isolation, as long as he is true to the old Mosaic belief. **1873** M. ARNOLD *Lit. & Dogma* (1876) 312 It is the consecration of absolute individualism.

2. The social theory which advocates the free and independent action of the individual, as opposed to communistic methods of organization and state interference. Opposed to COLLECTIVISM and SOCIALISM.

1851 MILL in *Westm. Rev.* LVI. 87 Socialism as long as it attacks the existing individualism, is easily triumphant. **1884** J. RAE *Contemp. Socialism* 209 Socialism and individualism are merely two contrary general principles, ideals, or methods, which may be employed to regulate the constitution of economical society. **1890** WESTCOTT in *Guardian* 8 Oct. 1581/1 Individualism regards humanity as made up of disconnected or warring atoms: Socialism regards it as an organic whole, a vital unity formed by the combination of contributory members mutually interdependent.

3. *Metaph.* The doctrine that the individual is a self-determined whole, and that any larger whole is merely an aggregate of individuals, which, if they act upon each other at all do so only externally.

1877 E. CAIRD *Philos. Kant* iv. 71 Is such a more adequate philosophy to be found in the idealistic individualism of Leibnitz?

4. = INDIVIDUALITY 2, 3.

1854 *Blackw. Mag.* LXXV. 66 Their ideas of God did not possess that individualism and personality which so remarkably characterised those of the Hebrews. **1870** EMERSON *Soc. & Solit.* viii. 173 A person of commanding individualism will answer it as Rochester does. **1885** *Harper's Mag.* Mar. 520/2 The individualism which is aimed at by architects.

5. An individual peculiarity; e.g. a manuscript reading peculiar to an individual scribe or copyist.

1881 WESTCOTT & HORT *Grk. N.T.* II. 232 Singular readings which are mere individualisms, so to speak, originating with the scribe or one of his immediate predecessors.

6. *Bot.* [ad. G. *individualismus* (K. von Tubeuf *Pflanzenkrankheiten* (1895) I. ii. 102).] A type of symbiosis in which the product of the relationship differs from either of the component organisms. Now *rare.*

1897 A. SCHNEIDER in *Minnesota Bot. Stud.* I. 944 The best known and perhaps the most typical form of complete individualism is represented by the higher lichens. **1913** *Mycologia* V. 102 It is supposed that the relationship is becoming closer and closer, and that finally it will be so intimate that neither symbiont will be able to live independently. Then will the individualism be perfect. **1967** P. GRAY *Dict. Biol. Sci.* 268/1 *Individualism*, a type of symbiosis, in which the aggregate differs from any of its components. A lichen is a case in point.

individualist (ɪndɪˈvɪdjuːəlɪst). [f. INDIVIDUAL + -IST; cf. F. *individualiste.*]

1. One who pursues an independent or egoistic course in thought or action.

1840 GLADSTONE *Ch. Princ.* 131 The sentiment of the catholic is better, and its besetting danger less, than those of the individualist in religion. **1856** KINGSLEY *Misc.*, *Hours w. Mystics* I. 351 The Pharisee becomes a selfish individualist just because he has forgotten this. **1883** BEARD *Reformation* vi. 189 The Anabaptists were the individualists of the Reformation.

2. An adherent of the social theory of Individualism. (See also quot. 1891.)

1876 FAWCETT *Pol. Econ.* (ed. 5) II. x. 275 It is maintained by the individualists that if a great number of manufactories and other trading establishments were brought into connection with the Wholesale Society, the business would become far too extensive and complicated to be properly managed. **1888** *Pall Mall G.* 10 Sept. 3/2 To hold the scales between individualists and Socialists. **1891** BEATRICE POTTER *Coop. Movem. Gt. Brit.* 75 The term *Individualist* has been used within the Cooperative movement for the last twenty years to denote that school of Cooperators who insist that each separate manufacturing establishment shall be governed (if possible owned) by those who work therein; the profits being divided among the working proprietors. Opposed to *Federalist.* **1896** *Times* 30 Jan. 8 If the individualists are to hold their own against the encroachments of the State.

3. *attrib.* or as *adj.* = INDIVIDUALISTIC.

1871 MORLEY *Crit. Misc.* Ser. I. 341 Owing to the supremacy in European thought of the individualist ideas which Christianity carried in with it. **1885** *Contemp. Rev.* June 903 He condemns Liberalism because it is individualist. **1892** *Times* 14 Oct. 7/2 The traditions of French workmen are strongly individualist, and they have not been in a hurry to enter into combinations. *Ibid.* 26 Nov. 9/2 The cautious individualist development of colonization in Australia or North America.

individualistic (ɪndɪˌvɪdjuːəˈlɪstɪk), *a.* [f. prec. + -IC.] Of or pertaining to individualism or individualists; characterized by individualism.

1874 SIDGWICK *Meth. Ethics* v. 262 Individualistic ideal. **1879** MORLEY *Burke* 172 That reaction..into which the Revolution drove many of the finest minds of the next generation by showing the supposed consequences of pure individualistic rationalism. **1893** G. ALLEN *Scallywag* III. 190 The opinion of others has a vast effect upon even the most individualistic amongst us. **1897** BRYCE *Impress. S. Africa* 156 They [Boers] were self-reliant and individualistic to excess.

individualistically (ˌɪndɪvɪdjuːəˈlɪstɪkəlɪ), *adv.* [f. INDIVIDUALISTIC *a.*: see -ICALLY.] In an individualistic manner; from the individualistic standpoint.

1894 *Internat. Jrnl. Ethics* Oct. 42 The trumpery decorations of the present-day individualistically arrayed establishment. **1922** A. G. HOGG *Redemption from this World* 245 In India the problem has been conceived individualistically, while by the Hebrews it was..conceived socially. **1925** *Contemp. Rev.* Aug. 234 They find themselves at variance of purpose with other [*sic*] less individualistically inclined. **1938** R. G. COLLINGWOOD *Princ. Art* xiv. 324 This activity..is performed not only by the man whom we individualistically call the artist, but partly by all the other artists..'influencing' him.

individuality (ɪndɪvɪdjuːˈælɪtɪ). [f. as INDIVIDUALISTIC *a.* + -ITY: cf. F. *individualité.*]

1. The state or quality of being indivisible or inseparable; indivisibility, inseparability. **b.** An indivisible or inseparable entity.

1645 MILTON *Tetrach.* (1851) 165 These words also inferre that there ought to be an individuality in Mariage. **1833** J. H. NEWMAN *Arians* II. iii. (1876) 171 As though He were so derived from the simple Unity of God as..to inhere within that ineffable individuality. **1864** —— *Apol.* App. 61 When the eternal foes are so intermingled and interfused that to human eyes they seem to coalesce into a multitude of individualities.

2. The fact or condition of existing as an individual; separate and continuous existence.

1658 SIR T. BROWNE *Hydriot* iii. 19 But the soul subsisting, other matter clothed with due accidents, may salve the individuality. *a* **1735** ARBUTHNOT (J.), He would tell his instructor..that individuality could hardly be predicated of any man. **1802** PALEY *Nat. Theol.* xxvii. (1819) 482 Consciousness carries identity and individuality along with it through all changes of form or of visible qualities. **1876** J. P. NORRIS *Rudim. Theol.* I. iv. 72 Individuality is essential to our idea of a person.

b. The action or position of the individual members of a society.

1796 BURKE *Regic. Peace* ii. Wks. VIII. 253 To them the will, the wish, the want, the liberty, the toil, the blood of individuals is as nothing. Individuality is left out of their scheme of government. The state is all in all.

3. The aggregate of properties peculiar to an individual; the sum of the attributes which distinguish an object from others of the same kind; individual character. **b.** Idiosyncrasy; strongly marked individual character.

1614 SELDEN *Titles Hon.* 117 Appietas and Lentulitas, For the indiuidualite, as it were of Appius and Lentulus, or Patauinitas for Liuies stile. **1628** T. SPENCER *Logick* 196 A man is a living Creature, mortall, and capable of learning. In this sentence, man abstracted from individualitie..is described. **1792** MARY WOLLSTONECR. *Rights Wom.* iv. 151 The spring-tide of life over, we look for soberer sense in the face;..expecting to see individuality of character. **1866** A. FLINT *Princ. Med.* (1880) 18 The circumstances which give to the different diseases their individuality. **1874** GREEN *Short Hist.* viii. §10. 585 The Puritan individuality is nowhere so overpowering as in Milton. **1875** JOWETT *Plato* (ed. 2) V. 21 In every man's writings there is something like himself and unlike others, which gives individuality.

c. *pl.* Individual characteristics.

1647 H. MORE *Poems* 126 The soul..Against the law of Corporeities, It doth devest them both of time and place, And of all individualities. **1862** BURTON *Bk. Hunter* (1863) 16 All identically the same in edition and minor individualities. **1871** R. H. HUTTON *Ess.* II. 304 Mere individualities of taste and talent and temper.

4. a. An individual thing. **b.** An individual personality.

1775 JOHNSON *Lett. to Mrs. Thrale* 26 July, Here sit poor I, with nothing but my own solitary individuality. **1859** B'NESS BUNSEN in Hare *Life* (1879) II. iv. 245 That little cherished individuality, though ever so young, lives on. **1862** DANA *Man. Geol.* 759 In what respects the earth is an individuality. **1863** MRS. C. CLARKE *Shaks. Char.* vi. 150 Jack Falstaff, that most unique and fine of individualities.

5. *Phrenology.* The faculty of knowing objects as mere substances or existences; the supposed 'organ' of this faculty.

1828 G. COMBE *Const. Man* 72 Individuality and Eventuality, or the powers of observing things that exist and occurrences.

individualization (ɪndɪˌvɪdjuːəlaɪˈzeɪʃən). [f. next + -ATION.] The action of individualizing; the fact or condition of being individualized: in various senses of the vb.; see next.

1746 W. HORSLEY *Fool* (1748) I. 195 A Nation, or Community, is a Number of Individuals assembled under one Kind of Government, for the mutual Benefit of each other; from which.. in Proportion as they deviate, they fall into a Kind of Individualisation again. **1817** COLERIDGE *Biog. Lit.* 217 In a poem, the characters of which, amid the strongest individualization, must still remain representative. **1823** BENTHAM *Not Paul* 24 Towards the individualization of the portion of space some approach is made: the town being foreknown.. the street is particularized. **1845** STODDART in *Encycl. Metrop.* 67/1 When this process of individualization is effected by a separate word, we call that word an Article. **1854** OWEN *Skel. & Teeth* in *Orr's Circ. Sc., Organ. Nat.* I. 301 This individualization of the teeth is eminently significative of the high grade of organization of the animals manifesting it. **1876** H. SPENCER *Princ. Sociol.* III. ix. (1879) 777 The division presupposed by individualization of property cannot be carried far without appliances which savage life does not furnish.

individualize (ɪndɪˈvɪdjuːəlaɪz), *v.* [f. INDIVIDUAL + -IZE.]

1. *trans.* To render individual or give an individual character to; to characterize by distinctive marks or qualities; to mark out or distinguish from other persons or things.

1637 GILLESPIE *Eng. Pop. Cerem.* IV. ii. 5 In morall actions, *modus adjectus is principium individuationis*, and nothing else doth individualize a morall action. **1805** N. DRAKE *Ess. Tatler* (L.), The peculiarities which individualize and distinguish the humour of Addison. **1834** L. RITCHIE *Wand. by Seine* 61 Every element.. every class of objects recognisable by the senses, individualised into a god. **1835** J. H. NEWMAN *Par. Serm.* (1837) III. xi. 162 The natural effect.. of pain and fear, is to individualize us in our own minds. **1840** MILMAN *Hist. Chr.* III. 374 The Church stood, as it were, individualised, by the side of the other social impersonation, the State. **1851** MANSEL *Prolegom. Log.* i. (1860) 25 To have a valid conception of a horse.. I must also be able to combine these attributes in a representative *image*; that is, to *individualize* them. **1863** MRS. C. CLARKE *Shaks. Char.* i. 5 The inferior agents are individualised with a minuteness of surpassing truth to nature.

absol. *a* **1834** COLERIDGE in *Fraser's Mag.* (1835) XII. 494 Life, in the sense here meant.. may be defined—'tendency to individualise'. **1865** LOWELL *Scotch the Snake* Prose Wks. 1890 V. 242 The more we can individualize and personify, the more lively our sympathy.

2. To point out, mention, notice, or consider, individually; to specify, particularize. Also *absol.*

1656 S. H. *Gold. Law* 100 Many.. men, worthy of honour, which I may not individualize. **1807** *Ann. Reg.* 251 Without individualizing any, it was a virtual declaration of hostility against every neutral power. **1823** *Examiner* 658/2 We may revert to this subject, in which case we shall individualize a little more than we have now done. **1840** DE QUINCEY *Style* II. Wks. 1860 XI. 239 The.. general functions of the article definite.. are first, to individualize [etc.]. **1849** ROBERTSON *Serm.* Ser. I. x. 152 We feel that God sympathises and individualizes.

3. To appropriate to the use of an individual. *rare.*

1863 HAWTHORNE *Our Old Home* (1883) I. 264, I a little grudged the tracts [of land] that have been filched away, so to speak, and individualized by thriving citizens.

Hence **indi'vidualized** *ppl. a.*, rendered individual; marked by distinctive characteristics. **indi'vidualizer**, one that individualizes.

1825 COLERIDGE *Aids Refl.* (1848) I. 327 The distinct and individualized agency that by the given combinations utters and bespeaks its presence. *a* **1834** —— *Lit. Rem.* (1836) II. 102 Their different combinations and subordinations were in fact the individualizers of men. **1854** J. SCOFFERN in *Orr's Circ. Sc., Chem.* 49 Lithium is the least individualised alkaline metal. **1892** *Monist* II. 298 Law became an *individualista*—or, individualiser.

individualizing (ɪndɪˈvɪdjuːəˌlaɪzɪŋ), *ppl. a.* [f. prec. + -ING[2].] That individualizes.

1830 COLERIDGE in Mrs. H. Sandford *Th. Poole & Friends* (1888) II. 321 This is not.. the most individualizing trait of our friend's character. **1833** LAMB *Elia* Ser. II. *Barrenness Imag. Fac. Mod. Art*, That individualising property, which should keep the subject.. distinct in feature from every other subject. **1865** GROTE *Plato* I. i. 38 The individualising influences arising from the body.. overpowered this kindred with the universal.

Hence **indi'vidua,lizingly** *adv.*, in an individualizing manner.

1873 PATRICK tr. *Keil's Jeremiah* I. ii. 57 People in the two opposite regions of the world are individualizingly mentioned instead of all peoples.

individually (ɪndɪˈvɪdjuːəlɪ), *adv.* [f. INDIVIDUAL + -LY[2].] In an individual manner.

†**1.** Indivisibly; inseparably, undividedly. *Obs.*

1597 HOOKER *Eccl. Pol.* V. lvi. §2 How should that subsist solitarily by it selfe which hath no substance, but indiuidually the very same whereby others subsist with it? **1613** PURCHAS *Pilgrimage* (1614) 3 The persons which all have that one being, and every of which have all that being, which in itselfe is individually one. **1627** HAKEWILL *Apol.* (1630) 283 An attribute.. individually proper to the Godhead, and incommunicable to any created substance.

2. In individual identity; as one and the same person or thing. ***individually the same***, identically the same, the self-same. ? *Obs.*

1624 GATAKER *Transubst.* 48 One thing is said to be another, which cannot be individually or specifically the same. **1656** tr. *Hobbes' Elem. Philos.* Wks. 1839 I. 137 Whensoever the name, by which it is asked whether a thing be the same it was, is given it for the matter only, then, if the matter be the same, the thing also is individually the same; as the water, which was in the sea, is the same which is afterwards in the cloud. **1748** H. WALPOLE *Lett. H. Mann* (1834) II. 219, I have received the Eagle's head; the lid is broken off individually in the same spot with the original.

b. ***individually different***: different as individuals (though they may be identical in species).

1824 L. MURRAY *Eng. Gram.* (ed. 5) I. 257 The definite article is likewise used to distinguish between things, which are individually different, but have one generic name. **1864** BOWEN *Logic* iv. 92 Two things may be said to be.. individually or numerically different, when they do not constitute one and the same reality.

3. Personally; as a single person distinct from others; in an individual capacity.

1660 R. COKE *Power & Subj.* 54 There are many things so inherent in the Prince individually, that they are incommunicable to any other. **1781** W. BLANE *Ess. Hunting* Pref. (1788) 8 *note*, Impossible for him, who is not individually free and independent, to be politically so. **1840** MISS MITFORD in L'Estrange *Life* (1870) III. vii. 108 To me individually it would be a great release to be quit of the trouble and expense of the garden.

4. In an individual or distinctive manner; as single persons or things, singly; each by each, one by one: opposed to *collectively*.

1641 'SMECTYMNUUS' *Vind. Answ.* xiii. 129 To whom as to individuall persons such care and offices were individually intrusted. **1659** *Gentl. Calling* (1696) 9 Not only to those Exercises which belong indifferently to their whole species, but to those also for which they are individually qualified. **1776** ADAM SMITH *W.N.* V. i. i. (1869) I. 282 That army was superior, in which the soldiers had, each individually, the greatest skill and dexterity. **1830** MARRYAT *King's Own* i, Whether we act in a body or individually. **1859** HAWTHORNE *Fr. & It. Jrnls.* II. 300 Moss plants too minute to be seen individually, but making the whole tree green. **1881** JOWETT *Thucyd.* I. 122 The sacrifice which they collectively made was individually repaid to them. **1896** C. LLOYD MORGAN *Habit & Inst.* 346 There is little or no evidence of individually acquired habits in man becoming instinctive through heredity.

indi'viduate, *ppl. a.* [ad. med.L. *indīviduāt-us*, pa. pple. of *indīviduā-re*: see next; but, in sense, partly representing L. *indīviduus*.]

†**1.** Undivided, indivisible, inseparable. *Obs.*

1621 BRATHWAIT *Nat. Emb., Blasphemie* (1877) 34 Touching the Indiuiduate essence of God. **1630** —— *Eng. Gentlem.* (1641) 34 Mildenesse is a quality so inherent, or more properly individuate to a gentleman. *Ibid.* 165 A friend, being indeed a mans second selfe, or rather an individuate companion to himselfe. **1751** *Student* II. 311 (T.) O Thou, the third in that eternal trine, In individuate unity divine!

2. = INDIVIDUATED 1. *arch.*

1606 FORD *Honor Tri.* (Shaks. Soc.) 24 Bewty matched with the indiuiduat adjunct, unsoyled constancy. **1609** R. BARNERD *Faithf. Shepheard* 31 If the places agree not to one indiuiduate thing.. there is no contradiction betweene them. **1681** BAXTER *Acc. Sherlocke* vi. 216 Perhaps you think that as Averrhois thought all Souls are one, individuate only by receptive matter [etc.].

individuate (ɪndɪˈvɪdjuːeɪt), *v.* [f. med.L. *indīviduāre* or obs. F. *individuer* to render individual, f. L. *indīvidu-us*: cf. prec. and -ATE[3].] To render individual.

1. *trans.* To form into an individual or distinct entity; to give individual organization or form to.

1646 SIR T. BROWNE *Pseud. Ep.* VI. i. 274 There was a seminality and contracted Adam in the rib, which by the information of a soule, was individuated into Eve. **1653** H. MORE *Antid. Ath.* II. ix. (1662) 66 Life being individuated into such infinite numbers that have their distinct sense and pleasure. **1681-6** J. SCOTT *Chr. Life* (1747) III. 385 That which individuates any Society, or makes it a distinct Body from all other Societies, is the Charter or Law upon which it is founded. **1864** D. G. MITCHELL *Sev. Stor.* 9 This symbolism of language which individuates a man's private memories.

2. To give an individual character to; to distinguish from others of the same species; to individualize; to single out.

1614 [see INDIVIDUATING below]. **1641** J. JACKSON *True Evang. T.* II. 156 Circumstances individuate actions. **1661** RUST *Origen's Opin.* in *Phenix* (1721) I. 74 Such Peculiarities as individuate Peter and Paul, as to their Bodies. **1732** BERKELEY *Alciphr.* VII. §5 In Peter, James, and John, you may observe in each a certain collection of Stature, Figure, Colour, and other peculiar Properties, by which they are known asunder, distinguished from all other Men, and if I may so say, individuated. **1802** COURTIER *Pleas. Solit.* 13 The heart, that loves its object to select, To individuate. **1827** HARE *Guesses* Ser. I. (1873) 111 That in which he differs and is distinguisht from other men, is his individuality, and individuates or individualizes him.

†**3.** To appropriate to an individual. *Obs. rare.*

1641 TRAPP *Theol. Theol.* 207 Neither [do they] individuate the same to themselves. **1646** —— *Comm. John* xx. 28 This is true faith indeed, that individuates God, and appropriates him to itself. **1647** —— *Comm. Gal.* ii. 20 True faith individuateth Christ, and appropriateth him to a mans self.

Hence **indi'viduating** *vbl. sb.* and *ppl. a.*

1614 SELDEN *Titles Hon.* Pref. Biv, It's thought, that, in the Seed are alwaies potentially seuerall indiuiduating Qualities deriu'd from diuers of the neere Ancestors. **1677** HALE *Prim. Orig. Man.* IV. iv. 323 In the separating or individuating of these Elements. **1678** CUDWORTH *Intell. Syst.* I. iv. §36. 602 Peculiar notes and properties or individuating circumstances. **1835** GRESWELL *Parables* V. I. 208 Other individuating marks of distinction. **1954** A. J. AYER *Philos. Ess.* i. 22 In ordinary speech, expressions which I have classified as indicators do the work of individuating.

individuated (ɪndɪˈvɪdjuːeɪtɪd), *ppl. a.* [f. INDIVIDUATE *v.* or *ppl. a.* + -ED[1].]

1. a. Rendered individual; individualized.

1823 DE QUINCEY *Language* Wks. 1860 IX. 126 The Hebrew has scarcely any individuated words. **1862** H. SPENCER *First Princ.* II. xiv. §107 (1875) 308 A simultaneous increase of combination among such individuated portions.

b. Denoting a person who has been through the process of individuation (see INDIVIDUATION 1 b).

1959 *Times Lit. Suppl.* 6 Feb. 73/1 The 'Individuated' man of Jungian analytical psychology, released from the destructive contradictions within humanity, bears a startling resemblance to the 'new man' of the Pauline Epistles, released from the bondage of sin. **1973** J. SINGER *Boundaries of Soul* xiii. 330 The wresting of consciousness, of self-awareness, from the tendency to become submerged in the mass, is the task of the individuated person.

†**2.** = INDIVIDUATE *ppl. a.* 1. *Obs.*

1698 NORRIS *Treat. Sev. Subj.* 37 All the Perfection belonging to that Individuated Nature.

individuation (ɪndɪˌvɪdjuːˈeɪʃən). [ad. med.L. *indīviduātiōn-em*, n. of action f. *indīviduā-re*: see INDIVIDUATE *v.*]

1. a. The action or process of individuating or rendering individual; that of distinguishing as an individual. *spec.* in Scholastic Philosophy, The process leading to individual existence, as distinct from that of the species.

principle of individuation (= med.L. *principium individuationis*): the principle through which the individual is constituted or comes into being. In Scholastic Philosophy this was variously held to be Form (by most Realists); Matter (by the Nominalists); and Matter as limited in the individual (by Albertus Magnus and Thomas Aquinas).

1628 T. SPENCER *Logick* 43 The matter is the principium of individuation, saith Thomas.. And againe, the essence is restrained vnto one individuall thing by the matter. *a* **1638** TWISSE in *Mede's Wks.* (1672) IV. lxxiv. 855 Natural actions require Time and Place for the performance of them, the unity whereof together with the unity of the subject necessarily concur to the individuation of them, if I remember aright my old Philosophy. *a* **1640** JACKSON *Creed* X. xii. §3 The root of individuation or distinction of one particular person from another was wholly from the matter, not from the form. **1664** H. MORE *Myst. Iniq.* 506 Agreeable to the sense of several considerable Philosophers and School-men.. who contend that Individuation is from the Form onely, and that the Matter and Suppositum is individuated from it. **1704** SWIFT *T. Tub* ix, Effects of so vast a difference.. as to be the sole point of individuation between Alexander the Great, Jack of Leyden, and Monsieur Des Cartes. **1729** BUTLER *Serm. Hum. Nat.* iii. Wks. 1874 II. 31 *note*, The inward frame of man considered as a system or constitution: whose several parts are united, not by a physical principle of individuation, but by the respects they have to each other. **1732** BERKELEY *Alciphr.* VII. §11 None but those who had nicely examined, and cou'd themselves explain, the Principle of Individuation in Man, or untie the Knots and answer the Objections, which may be raised even about Humane Personal Identity. **1817** COLERIDGE *Biog. Lit.* 175 Essence, in its primary signification, means the principle of individuation, the inmost principle of the possibility of any thing, as that particular thing. **1855** H. SPENCER *Induct. Biol.* III. iii. 353 (L.) Schelling defines life as the tendency to individuation. **1869** FARRAR *Fam. Speech* iii. 92 He never got to the idealisation, or even the individuation, of words.

b. *Psychol.* In the analytical psychology of Jung, the process by which consciousness and the collective unconscious of the psyche are integrated and wholeness of the individual self is established; also *attrib.*, as ***individuation process***.

1909 W. A. HAUSSMANN tr. *Nietzsche's Birth of Tragedy* 121 Apollo stands before me as the transfiguring genius of the *principium individuationis* through which alone the redemption in appearance is to be truly attained, while by the mystical cheer of Dionysius the spell of the individuation is broken, and the way lies open to the Mothers of Being. **1923** H. G. BAYNES tr. *Jung's Psychol. Types* xi. 561 Individuation, therefore, is a process of differentiation, having for its goal the development of the individual personality. **1948** G. ADLER *Stud. Analytical Psychol.* i. 3 The process of psychic growth and maturation, that is the process of integration and individuation, presents the individual with widely different situations and tasks according to the particular point he has reached in life. **1955** I. FLETCHER in J. Wain *Interpretations* 156 In its detail, the poem resembles what might be described in Jungian terms as an attempt at 'individuation', a harmonious relation between the components of the self. **1959** D. COX *Jung & St. Paul* xii. 341 Justification by Faith precedes all advance towards a full life whereas Individuation crowns an advance which has already taken place. **1973** J. SINGER *Boundaries of Soul* i. 8, I sat before the examiner and the two experts for my oral examination on The Individuation Process, which is the essence of analysis.

†**2.** Undivided character or condition; oneness.

1654 H. L'ESTRANGE *Chas. I* (1655) 8 It cannot be denied, but unity and individuation of perswasion in all points of sacred truths, were to be wished between married couples.

3. The condition of being an individual; separate and continuous existence as a single indivisible object; individuality, personal identity.

1642 H. MORE *Song of Soul* II. iii. II. xix, Fine spunne glittering silk crumpled in one Changeth not 'ts individuation From what it was, when it was gaily spread In fluttering winds. **1660** —— *Myst. Godl.* VI. iv. 223 It being most certain there is no stable Personality of a man but what is in his Soul, (for if the Body be Essential to this numerical Identity, a grown man has not the same individuation he had when he was Christned). **1722** WOLLASTON *Relig. Nat.* v. 75 We are severally conscious to our selves of the individuation and distinction of our own minds from all other. **1725** WATTS *Logic* I. vi. §6 What is the principle of individuation? Or what is it that makes any one thing the same as it was some time before?

4. An individualized condition.

1648 W. SCLATER, Jr. in *W. Sclater's Malachi* (1650) Ep. Ded., It gives them al their several natures, or distinct individuations. **1852** A. BALLOU *Spirit Manifest.* i. 16 Each spirit is an individuation of Spirit-substance, combined with and interiorating a corresponding individuation of Matter.

5. a. *Biol.* The sum of the processes on which the life of the individual depends.

1867 H. SPENCER *Princ. Biol.* §327. II. 409 Grouping under the word Individuation all processes by which individual life is completed and maintained. **1871** DARWIN *Desc. Man* I. viii. 318 Mr. Herbert Spencer has shown..that with all organisms a ratio exists between what he calls individuation and genesis.

b. The unification of parts or forces necessary to constitute an individual or organic unity.

1881 MIVART *Cat* 376 Such an animal..is really the theatre of some unifying power which synthesizes its varied activities, dominates its forces, and is a principle of individuation. **1889** —— *Truth* 390 Without the presence of some immaterial principle of individuation, our different mental acts..could not be united so as to constitute an act of judgment.

c. *Bot.* [tr. G. *individualismus* (K. von Tubeuf *Pflanzenkrankheiten* (1895) I. ii. 102).] = INDIVIDUALISM 6.

1897 W. G. SMITH tr. *Tubeuf's Dis. Plants* viii. 87 This unification of two living beings into an individual whole, I have designated 'Individuation'.

indi'viduative, *a.* *rare*$^{-1}$. [f. ppl. stem of med.L. *indīviduā-re* to INDIVIDUATE + -IVE.] Tending to individuation; individualizing.

1862 BURTON *Bk. Hunter* 224 The eighteenth century having been an age of individuative, the nineteenth necessarily became an age of associative..development.

indi'viduator. *rare.* [agent-n. in L. form, from med.L. *indīviduā-re* to INDIVIDUATE.] One who or that which individuates.

1643 DIGBY *Observ. Browne's Relig. Med.* (1659) 52 He is composed of the same Individual Matter; for it hath the same Distinguisher and Individuator, to wit, the same Forme or Soul.

†**indi'viduify,** *v.* *Obs.* *rare*$^{-1}$. [f. L. *indīvidu-us* (see INDIVIDUUM) + -FY.] *trans.* To mark out as a separate individual; to individualize.

a **1661** FULLER *Worthies* I. (1662) 46 The Statute of Additions, was made in the first of King Henry the fifth, to Individuifie (as I may say) and separate persons from those of the same name.

†**indi'viduism.** *Obs.* *rare*$^{-1}$. [f. L. *indīvidu-us* (see INDIVIDUUM) + -ISM.] Individuality.

1825 *Sporting Mag.* XVI. 404 Knowing no reason why a state of individuism should not prevail.

†**indivi'duity.** *Obs.* [ad. med.L. *indīviduitāt-em* individuality, f. L. *indīvidu-us* (see next); cf. F. *individuité* (16–17th c. in Hatz.-Darm.).]

1. The quality or character of being indivisible.

1611 COTGR., *Individuité*, indiuiduitie, inseperablenesse. **1632** I. L. *Womens Rights* 63 The consummation and indiuiduitie of marriage. **1695** LD. PRESTON *Boeth.* IV. 193 The further it departs from the middle Individuity of the Point, so much the more Space it doth fill.

2. The quality of being individually owned.

1605 DANIEL *Queen's Arcadia* Wks. (1717) 182 No Tenures, but a customary Hold..Common, without Individuity.

3. The quality that constitutes an individual, whether as distinct from other individuals, or as continuously indentical with itself.

1650 FULLER *Pisgah* II. III. vi. 422 Gods unintermitted service..preserving the individuity, or oneness of this Temple with the former. **1656** tr. *Hobbes' Elem. Philos.* Wks. 1839 I. 135 Some place individuity in the unity of matter; others in the unity of form; and one says it consists in the unity of the aggregate of all the accidents together.

†**indi'viduous,** *a.* *Obs.* *rare.* [f. L. *indīvidu-us* not divided, indivisible + -OUS: see INDIVIDUUM.] Of undivided nature; indivisible.

1642 H. MORE *Song of Soul* II. iii. II. xxv, That thing is individuous, Whatever can into it self reflect, Such is the soul as hath been prov'd by us Before. **1647** *Ibid.* III. App. lxxxv, But I elsewhere, I think, do gainly prove That souls of beasts, by reasons nothing scant, Be individuous. *Ibid.* lxxxvi, But if mens souls be individuous, How can they ought from their own substance shed?

‖**individuum** (ɪndɪ'vɪdjuːəm). Pl. -a, -ums. [L. *indīviduum* an indivisible particle, an atom, in med.L., an individual, esp. a member of a species; subst. use of neut. sing. of *indīviduus* undivided, indivisible, inseparable, f. *in-* IN-^{3}) + *dīviduus* divisible, DIVIDUOUS, f. *dīvidĕre* to divide. Treated as a Latin word in senses 1–2; but in 3 as naturalized, with pl. *-ums.*]

1. That which cannot be divided; the indivisible; an indivisible entity.

1599 MARSTON *Sco. Villanie* I. ii. 177 Almighty men, that can their maker make, And force his sacred bodie..to be gnawne..Diuiding *indiuiduum* really. **1609** *Ev. Woman in Hum.* v. i. Hiij, Linke her to thy soule, Deuide not *indiuidium*, be her and shee thee. **1616** BULLOKAR, *Indiuiduum*, that which cannot bee diuided. **1754** SHERLOCK *Disc.* (1764) I. 203 The Learned made the Soul alone to be the perfect Individuum.

†**b.** An atom. *Obs.*

1656 BLOUNT *Glossogr.*, *Individuum*, one singular thing; that which cannot be divided, a body inseparable, a Moat. **1706** PHILLIPS, An *Individual* or *Individuum*, (in *Philos.*) a Body or Particle so small that it cannot be divided, which is otherwise call'd an *Atome*.

2. *Logic.* A member of a species; = INDIVIDUAL *sb.* 1 b.

individuum vagum: something indicated as an individual, without specific identification.

1555 RIDLEY *Lord's Supper* Wks. (Parker Soc.) 24 And therefore he [Duns] calleth this pronoun demonstrative 'this', *individuum vagum*, that is, a wandering proper name. **1610** D. CARLETON in *Crt. & Times Jas. I* (1848) I. 124 When we ask the question, 'Why this objection may not as well hold in every private bill of this kind?' they answer that, 'individua, by name, do no hurt to the general'. **1652** GAULE *Magastrom.* 230 In the forehead of the image let be written the name of the species, or individuum, which the image represents. **1727** POPE *Mem. M. Scriblerus* I. vii. Wks. 1751 VI. 131 From particular propositions nothing can be concluded, because the *Individua vaga* are..barren.

3. An individual person or thing; = INDIVIDUAL *sb.* 2, 3.

1591 SYLVESTER *Du Bartas* I. v. 843 That so each Kinde may last immortally, Though th' *Indiuiduum* pass successively. **1618** M. BARET *Horsemanship* I. 98 In horses, though there be many differences of the *indiuiduums*..yet the expert Horseman..can reforme their rebellion. **1646** J. HALL *Poems* I. 23 Why would she choose her Priests to be Such *Individuums* as ye? Such Insecta's? **1656** STANLEY *Hist. Philos.* VI. (1701) 253/2 A continual succession of many individuums of the same species. **1659** BP. WALTON *Consid. Considered* in Todd *Mem.* II. 80 Is not a man the same *individuum*, when his hair is cut or his nails pared, that he was before? **1745** BAKER *Don Quix.* II. VI. v. 206 He had the misfortune to appear in my Eyes the most horrid Individuum of human Race.

†**indi'vinable,** *a.* *Obs.* *rare.* [IN-^{3}.] Not divinable; incapable of being divined.

1603 FLORIO *Montaigne* III. ii, There are secret and indivinable parts in the objects men doe handle.

†**indi'vine,** *a.* *Obs.* *rare.* [IN-^{3}.] Not divine; unholy.

1603 J. DAVIES *Microcosm.* (1876) 57 (D.) His brother Clarence..He did rebaptize in a butt of wine..A Turkish providence most indivine.

†**indi'vinity.** *Obs.* *rare.* [IN-^{3}: cf. mod.F. *indivinité.*] Want of divinity, absence of divine character.

1646 SIR T. BROWNE *Pseud. Ep.* I. x. 41 How openly did he [the Devil] betray his Indivinity unto Craesus, who being ruined by his Amphibologie, and expostulating with him..received no higher answer, then the excuse of his impotency upon the contradiction of fate.

†**indi'vise,** *a.* *Obs.* *rare*$^{-1}$. [ad. L. *indīvīs-us* undivided, f. *in-* (IN-^{3}) + *dīvīsus* divided, DIVISE.] Undivided.

1677 GALE *Crt. Gentiles* IV. 255 Those things, whose essential notion is indivise and inseparable, are most one and simple.

indivisibility (ɪndɪvɪzɪ'bɪlɪtɪ). [f. next: see -ITY. Cf. F. *indivisibilité* (1516 in Godef.), It. *indivisibilità.*] The quality or condition of being indivisible.

1647 H. MORE *Song of Soul* II. ii. III. xix, Now shall the indivisibilitie Of the souls virtues make an argument. **1662** STILLINGFL. *Orig. Sacr.* III. ii. §15 The solidity and indivisibility of these angled Atoms. **1775** DE LOLME *Eng. Const.* II. xvii. (1784) 256 The solidity and indivisibility of the power of the crown. **1878** MORLEY *Condorcet* 63 Conspiring against the unity and indivisibility of the Republic.

indivisible (ɪndɪ'vɪzɪb(ə)l), *a.* and *sb.* Also 4–6 with y for i; (7–9 *erron.* -able, 8 -viseable). [ad. late L. *indīvīsibilis*, f. *in-* (IN-^{3}) + *dīvīsibilis* DIVISIBLE. Cf. F. *indivisible* (13–14th c. in Hatz.-Darm.).]

A. *adj.* Not divisible; incapable of being divided (actually, or in thought); incapable of being distributed among a number; †incapable of being separated or detached, inseparable (*obs.*).

c **1380** WYCLIF *Serm.* Sel. Wks. I. 197 Ech þing þat God contynneþ is maad of partis indyvysible. **1526** *Pilgr. Perf.* (W. de W. 1531) 190 Fayth is a supernaturall lyght, & therfore it is indiuysyble. **1553** GARDINER *True Obed.* 43 (R.) [In] all thynges which he created, spake, or did, he was alwaies, together with the Holy Ghost, the indiuisible worker, (one substaunce of the three persons in diuinitie.) **1638** F. JUNIUS *Paint. of Ancients* 164 They carried him every where along as an indivisible companion. **1651** HOBBES *Govt. & Soc.* ix. §1. 135 Dominion (that is) supreme power is indivisible, insomuch as no man can serve two Masters. **1656** tr. *Hobbes' Elem. Philos.* Wks. 1839 I. 313 Besides, equality and inequality are found out often by the division of the two quantities into parts which are considered as indivisable; as Cavallerius Bonaventura has done in our time, and Archimedes often. **1694** SOUTH *Twelve Serm.* III. 304 Who can resolve..the Difficulties about the Composition of a continued Quantity, as whether it is Compounded of Parts Divisible or Indivisible? *a* **1711** KEN *Hymns Festiv.* Poet. Wks. 1721 I. 218 A thousand Years is but one Day In God's Indivisible Ray. **1837–9** HALLAM *Hist. Lit.* III. iii. §86 The consciousness of a self within, a percipient indivisible Ego. **1853** W. GREGORY *Inorg. Chem.* (ed. 3) 21 According to the atomic hypothesis..matter is composed of certain minute, indivisible particles, or atoms; and consequently cannot be divided infinitely. **1870** *Daily News* 11 Nov., M. Gent..calls on the Marseillais in the name of the Republic one and indivisible, to carry on the war without truce or mercy.

B. *sb.* That which is indivisible; an infinitely small particle or quantity.

method of indivisibles: a method of calculating areas, volumes, etc. based on the conception of indivisibles, published by Bonaventura Cavalieri in 1635. (Cf. quot. 1656 in A.)

1644 DIGBY *Man's Soul* (1645) 140 One instant or indivisible of time. **1647** H. MORE *Philos. Poems* 376 If quantity consists of Indivisibles or Atoms. **1656** HOBBES 6 *Less.* Wks. 1845 VII. 301 The method of indivisibles, invented by Bonaventura. **1664** POWER *Exp. Philos.* Pref. 7 The very Atoms and their reputed Indivisibles and least realities of Matter. **1721** BAILEY, *Indivisibles*, (in Geometry), are such Elements or Principles, as any Body or Figure, may be supposed to be ultimately resolved into. **1837–9** HALLAM *Hist. Lit.* III. III. viii. §11. 400 Galileo trod in the steps of Kepler, and..became conversant with indivisibles.

Hence **indi'visibleness**, indivisibility.

1648 W. MOUNTAGUE *Devout Ess.* I. ii. §2. 19 In which the intire Trinity doth reside, the Son of God in Person, the Holy Ghost or Spirit of God by Character and impression, and consequently God the Father by the indivisibleness of his essence from their presences. **1682** H. MORE *Annot. Glanvill's Lux O.* 220 We will conclude with Mr. Baxter's Conceit of the Indivisibleness of a Spirit.

indivisibly (ɪndɪ'vɪzɪblɪ), *adv.* [f. prec. + -LY^2.] In an indivisible manner; inseparably; in a manner not admitting of division.

1552 HULOET, Indiuisiblye, *indiuidue.* **1598** BARCKLEY *Felic. Man* VI. (1603) 611 Christian charitie which is indivisiblie joyned with true religion. *a* **1711** KEN *Hymnarium* Poet. Wks. 1721 II. 21 The Infinite is ne'er confin'd to Place, Indivisibly fills all real Space. **1849** DE QUINCEY *Eng. Mailcoach* II. Wks. 1890 XIII. 304 Light does not tread upon the steps of light more indivisibly. **1882** FARRAR *Early Chr.* II. 352 The Divine became Human, and dwelt in our Humanity indivisibly.

indivision (ɪndɪ'vɪʒən). [ad. late L. *indīvīsiōn-em* (Boethius): see IN-^{3} and DIVISION; cf. F. *indivision* (16th c. in Hatz.-Darm.).] Absence of division; undivided condition.

1624 F. WHITE *Repl. Fisher* 410 The body of Christ in heauen, is not ioyned to the sacramentall body, by continuation or indiuision. **1654** JER. TAYLOR *Real Pres.* 226 Bellarmine..sayes there is a double indivision or unity of being: an intrinsecal and an extrinsecal, a local, and an essential. **1875** MAINE *Hist. Inst.* vii. 194 The land had remained in a state of indivision during several generations.

†**indi'visive,** *a.* *Obs.* *rare.* [IN-^{3}.] Indivisible.

1657–83 EVELYN *Hist. Relig.* (1850) I. 162 Its [the Soul's] immortal and indivisive nature.

†**indi'vulsion.** *Obs.* *rare*$^{-1}$. [IN-^{3}; cf. L. *indīvulsus* not torn asunder (Macrobius).] Absence of separation; unsevered condition.

a **1638** MEDE *Wks.* (1672) I. xxxvi. 192 The Water ascends upward, the Aire downward, against nature, to maintain the connexion and indivulsion of the parts of the world.

†**indi'vulsive,** *a.* *Obs.* *rare*$^{-0}$. [IN-^{3}.] Characterized by not tearing or being torn asunder. Hence †**indi'vulsively** *adv.*, inseparably.

1678 CUDWORTH *Intell. Syst.* I. iv. §36. 566 The..highest of souls..are so near a kin to that Highest Good of all that they do naturally and indivulsively cleave to the same.

†**'indling,** *a.* *Sc.* var. of EYNDLING, jealous.

1600 J. MELVILL *Diary* (Wodrow Soc.) 355 God, who was holy, angry and indling.

Indo-^{1} ('ɪndəʊ), combining form of Gr. Ἰνδός, L. *Indus* (cf. Gr. Ἰνδο-σκυθία Scythia of the Indies, Indian Scythia), employed in modern compounds, in which it qualifies another word, substantive or adjective, or denotes the combination of Indian with some other characteristic (chiefly ethnological); as ***Indo-Arabian***, ***-Arabic***, ***-Austral***, ***British***, ***-Briton***, ***-English***, ***-heathenish***, ***-human***, ***-Mohammedan***, ***-Portuguese***; **Indo-Abyssinian** *a.*, of or pertaining to both the Dravidians of India and the Hamites of north-east Africa; also as *sb.*, one of these peoples; **Indo-African** *a.*, of or pertaining to India and Africa, *spec.* applied to a supposed former continent now covered by the Indian Ocean; relating to Indians and Africans in South Africa; **Indo-Anglian** *a.*, of or pertaining to literature in English written by Indian authors; also as *sb.*, a writer of such literature; **Indo-Aryan**, Aryan of or in India, or modified by native Indian characters; so **Indo-Celtic**, a term used by some for Indo-Germanic

and Indo-European, emphasizing the position of Celtic as the most western member of the linguistic family; **Indo-Chinese**, belonging to Further India, or the region between India and China, sometimes called **Indo-China**; **Indo-Egyptian**, **-Greek**, Egyptian or Greek influenced by Indian; **Indo-Hittite** (see quot. 1930); **Indo-Malayan** *a.*, pertaining to India and Malaya; *spec.*, denoting an ethnological region comprising Sri Lanka, the Malay peninsula, and Malayan islands; **Indo-Oceanic** *a.*, pertaining to the East Indian islands and the islands of the Pacific Ocean; **Indo-Pacific** *a.*, relating to the Indian Ocean and the adjacent parts of the Pacific Ocean; also, relating to the group of languages, usually called Malayo-Polynesian, spoken in the islands of these waters; **Indo-Pakistan**, **-Pakistani** *adjs.*, pertaining to India and Pakistan or to their inhabitants; also **Indo-Pak** colloq. abbrev.; **Indo-Saracenic** *a.*, pertaining to the products of mixed Indian and Saracenic origin; **Indo-Scythian**, **-Scythic** *adjs.*, pertaining to India and Scythia; also as *sb.*, also **Indo-Scyth**, a person from these regions; **Indo-Spanish**, Spanish modified by (American) Indian; **Indo-Teutonic** (*rare*) = INDO-GERMANIC. See also INDO-EUROPEAN, -GERMANIC.

1896 A. H. KEANE *Ethnol.* viii. 170 Again, what is to be made of the expression '*Indo-Abyssinian', or even 'Abyssinian' at all as an ethnical term. *Ibid.* x. 229 Considerable sections of the *Indo-African Continent.. must have persisted far into the tertiary epoch. *Ibid.* xii. 295 It is admitted by all ethnologists that Asia is the original home of the Mongolic division, a fact which harmonises with the view that the vanished Indo-African Continent was the cradle of mankind. **1971** *Illustr. Weekly India* 18 Apr. 24/3 Dr Naicker and Dr Dadoo forged an Indo-African political alliance. **1883** in K. R. Srinivasa Iyengar *Indian Writing in English* (1962) i. 3 *Indo-Anglian. **1935** A. R. CHIDA (*title*) Anthology of Indo-Anglian Verse. **1943** K. R. SRINIVASA IYENGAR (*title*) Indo-Anglian literature. **1962** *Times Lit. Suppl.* 10 Aug. 596/3 Authors such as R. K. Narayan, Dom Moraes, Balachandra Rajan (now called 'Indo-Anglians') find their public in the West, rather than inside India itself. **1969** *Sunday Standard* (Bombay) 3 Aug. (Mag. Sect.) p. vii/7 Anita Desai is one of the most competent amongst the small band of Indo-Anglian novelists who have successfully established that a branch of English literature can grow and flourish as well in India as .. in Australia or Canada. **1884** *Encycl. Brit.* XVII. 627/1 In Europe, before the introduction of the algorithm or full *Indo-Arabic system with the zero. **1850** H. TORRENS in *Jrnl. Asiat. Soc. Bengal* 1 In the *Indo-Arian researches, we see the suggestion and first discovery with Prinsep. **1881** *Athenæum* 9 Apr. 494/3 A new work..on the history, language, literature, customs, dress, &c., of the early Indo-Aryans. *Ibid.* 23 Apr. 553/3 The largest section of the population is the Kho, a high Indo-Aryan type. **1896** A. H. KEANE *Ethnol.* x. 226 The..possible fusion of Melanochroid Caucasic (South Indian) and Austral Negro blood at a remote epoch in some now perhaps submerged *Indo-Austral region. **1954** G. S. RAO (*title*) Indian words in English: a study in *Indo-British cultural and linguistic relations. **1831** J. GOLDINGHAM in Southey *Life Andrew Bell* (1844) III. 697 Some of the most respectable *Indo-Britons. **1862** BEVERIDGE *Hist. India* III. VIII. iv. 394 An Indo-Briton of the name of Campbell. **1884** *Indo-Celtic [see INDO-EUROPEAN 1]. **1886** *Q. Rev.* Jan. 211 The name *Indo-China was an invention of that versatile and fiery spirit John Leyden. **1898** *Westm. Gaz.* 29 June 3/2 Such an end of the ..Siamese problem will be regretted by few who understand the inner track of affairs in the Indo-China peninsula. **1842** PRICHARD *Nat. Hist. Man* xxiii. (1845) 240 Others approximate to the *Indo-Chinese form. **1933** BLOOMFIELD *Language* 69 The great Indo-Chinese (or Sino-Tibetan) family consists of three branches. **1951** 'J. WYNDHAM' *Day of Triffids* ii. 42 Its first occurrence..took place in Indo-China... But..the Indo-Chinese specimen can have had no great lead. **1953** M. POWYS *Lace & Lace-Making* iv. 18 Indo-Chinese Venise, 20th century. The Indo-Chinese industry shows more originality in design. **1969** N. FREELING *Tsing-Boum* xiii. 90 Our Indochinese adventure finished shortly afterwards. **1861** J. G. SHEPPARD *Fall Rome* xii. 675 He indicates an original source purely Greek, another Indo-Greek, another *Indo-Egyptian. **1837** SIR G. C. LEWIS *Lett.* (1870) 73 The history of *Indo-English Administration. **1887** SKEAT *Princ. Eng. Etym.* I. §84 The Indo-English family of languages. **1886** W. J. TUCKER *E. Europe* 341 The second [hymn]..can easily be traced to its *Indo-heathenish source. **1930** E. H. STURTEVANT in J. T. Hatfield et al. *Curme Vol. Ling. Stud.* 142 We now know that Hittite broke away from the parent stock long before the other historic languages did and that we must thus consider Hittite and primitive IE as parallel offshoots of an earlier language, which we may call *Indo-Hittite. **1964** S. K. CHATTERJI in D. Abercrombie et al. *Daniel Jones* 407 Primitive Indo-European, as it had evolved out of the earlier primitive Indo-Hittite. **1964** R. H. ROBINS *Gen. Ling.* 305 Scholars differ as to whether it [*sc.* Hittite] is an I-E language or a representative of a collateral branch forming with I-E a yet more inclusive Indo-hittite family. **1845** DARWIN *Voy. Nat.* xvi. (1873) 371 Within the *Indo-human period. **1864** *N. & Q.* 3rd Ser. VI. 142/2 *Indo-Mahomedan folk-lore. **1869** *Indo-Malayan [see AUSTRO-[2]]. **1875** *Encycl. Brit.* II. 696/2 The Indo-Malayan peninsula and Archipelago. **1936** *Discovery* Jan. 21/2 Of Indo-Malayan origin. **1896** A. H. KEANE *Ethnol.* xii. 326 *margin*, *Indo-Oceanic linguistic relations. **1877** *Encycl. Brit.* VII. 280/2 The Oriental or *Indo-Pacific marine region. **1880** *Ibid.* XII. 680/2 The eastward extension of the Indo-Pacific fauna. **1885** *Ibid.* XIX. 422/2 Indo-Pacific Races of Men. **1965** *Punch* 27 Jan. 116/1 Fearing that *Indo-Pak hostilities would break out along the border of the North End road. **1967** L. DEIGHTON *London Dossier* 44 Most Indo-Pak restaurants have Pakistani owners, red velvet wallpaper, stars on the ceiling and undrinkable coffee. **1971** *Illustr. Weekly India* 18 Apr. 20/2 Sub-continental peace and prosperity would appear to be prime requisites for discouraging Chinese intention [*sic*] being diverted from South-East Asia to the Indo-Pak sub-continent. **1955** *Times* 2 Aug. 5/5 Calcutta business men have generally welcomed devaluation of the Pakistan rupee as removing a main obstacle to *Indo-Pakistan trade. **1968** *Times* (Pakistan Suppl.) 6 Apr. p. viii/3 The tiger population in the Indo-Pakistan subcontinent in the 1920s was 40,000; by 1966 it had fallen to 2,800. **1958** *Oxf. Univ. Gaz.* 23 Apr. 893 The taxonomy and zoo-geography of some groups of *Indo-Pakistani birds. **1969** *Capital* (Calcutta) 27 Feb. 353/2 In contrast, 1967–68 was the year which came immediately after the two worst years of drought in living memory coupled with the Indo-Pakistani war. **1970** P. OLIVER *Savannah Syncopators* 14 [Gunther Schuller] considers it 'worth mentioning that Indo-Pakistani music is divided into six principal modes, three of which—afternoon modes—are nothing but the blues scale'. **1886** YULE & BURNELL *Hobson-Jobson* Introd. 24 The *Indo-Portuguese Patois. *Ibid.*, The Indo-Portuguese New Testament. **1887** KIPLING *From Sea to Sea* (1899) I. iv. 31 A wonder of carven white stone of the *Indo-Saracenic style. **1908** H. CRAIK *Impressions India* ii. 16 Our great grandfathers..attempting no flimsy imitations in the Indo-Saracenic style. **1959** *Chamber's Encycl.* VII. 464/2 The Indo-Saracenic style which may be seen in centres of Mohammedan culture throughout northern India. **1841** M. ELPHINSTONE *Hist. India* I. 474 Coins of the latter nation [*sc.* the Hindus] have been found, bearing nearly the same relation to those of the *Indo-Scythians that theirs did to the coins of the Greeks. **1884** *Encycl. Brit.* XVII. 660/2 The Indo-Scythian class..is fixed approximately to periods by finds in which aurei occur ranging from the earlier Roman emperors to the Antonines. **1961** H. W. BAILEY (*title*) Indo-Scythian studies: being Khotanese texts, volume IV. *Ibid.* 18 It will be possible for the historian of India to speak with more intimate knowledge of the Sakas, whom we call also the Indo-Scyths, the rulers of north India for some four hundred years. **1853** H. N. HUMPHREYS *Coin Collector's Manual* II. 706/2 *Indo-Scythic kings. **1891** *Times* 8 Jan. 9/2 In Paraguay [etc.]..the mass of the population is *Indo-Spanish. **1850** H. L. MANSEL *Lett., Lect. & Rev.* (1873) 11 A more extensive examination of the *Indo-Teutonic languages. **1855** MILMAN *Lat. Chr.* XIV. vii. VI. 527 Indo-Teutonic languages. **1938** *Burlington Mag.* Nov. 231/1 The primeval ways of the 'Indo-Teutonic North'.

indo-[2]. *Chem.* Before a vowel **ind-**. [f. Gr. Ἰνδός, L. *Indus*, as root of *indicum*, INDIGO.] A formative of names of various compound bodies related to indigo, or belonging to the INDOLE group: see INDOGEN, INDONE, INDOPHANE, INDOXYL, etc.

Indo-[3] ('ɪndəʊ), combining form of *Indus*, a river of the northern part of the Indian subcontinent, as in **Indo-Gan'getic** *a.*, of or pertaining to the Indus and the Ganges.

1880 *Encycl. Brit.* XII. 735/2 The Indo-Gangetic Plain covers an area of about 300,000 square miles. **1925** J. JOLY *Surface-Hist. Earth* vii. 126 The vast sedimentary collections of the Indo-Gangetic plain. **1969** *Pioneer* (Lucknow) 13 Aug. 6/4 The IIT is located on the Indo-Gangetic plain, ten kilometres west of Kanpur.

indoaniline (ɪndəʊ'ænɪliːn). *Chem.* [f. INDO-[2] + ANILINE.]

a. A violet dye, $O{:}C_6H_4{:}N{\cdot}C_6H_4{\cdot}NH_2$. **b.** Any of the derivatives of this compound.

1886 *Jrnl. Chem. Soc.* L. 146 (*heading*) Indophenol and indoaniline. **1952** K. VENKATARAMAN *Chem. Synthetic Dyes* II. xxv. 763 Alkaline hydrolysis leads to the indophenols, sometimes called indoaniline to distinguish them from the 'true indophenols'. **1958** PACKER & VAUGHAN *Mod. Approach Org. Chem.* xix. 645 Thus aniline gives..dyestuffs such as indoaniline and the aniline blacks.

†**indoce**, var. of ENDOSS *v. Obs.*, to endorse.

1500–20 DUNBAR *Poems* xxxviii. 7 Chryst with his blud our ransonis dois indoce. *Ibid.* xlii. 103 Matremony..The band of freindschip hes indost, Betuix Bewty and the presoneir.

indochinite (ɪndəʊ'tʃaɪnaɪt). *Geol.* [f. *Indo-China* (s.v. INDO-[1]) + -ITE[1].] Any tektite from the tektite field of Indo-China.

1940 *Pop. Astron.* XLVIII. 44 The most typical indochinite specimens occur in South China and northern and central Indo-China. **1961**, **1964** [see JAVAITE]. **1969** *New Scientist* 30 Oct. 237/1 We obtain an age of the order of 0·7 m.y. for an indochinite.

†**indoci'bility**. *Obs.* [f. next + -ITY.] Incapability of being taught; unteachableness.

1607 TOPSELL *Four-f. Beasts* (1658) 21 Making a man with an Asses head to signifie impudency, shamelessness, and indocibility. **1837–9** HALLAM *Hist. Lit.* (1847) II. 486 A different fault is indocibility, or difficulty of being taught.

†**in'docible**, *a. Obs.* [ad. late L. *indocibilis*, or f. IN-[3] + DOCIBLE.] Incapable of being taught or instructed; unteachable. Also ***indocible of***.

1555 EDEN *Decades* (Arb.) 52 Be not indocible lyke Tygers and dragons. **1666** SANCROFT *Lex Ignea* 10 Our indocible and unteachable Humor. **1768–74** TUCKER *Lt. Nat.* (1834) II. 142 It renders him indocible of that most useful science of ignorance.

Hence †**in'docibleness**.

1647 JER. TAYLOR *Lib. Proph.* ii. 25 Out of pevishnesse and indociblenesse of disposition. **1678–9** FOULKES *Alarm Sinn.* 31 The ignorance or indocibleness of some of the People.

indocile (ɪn'dəʊsaɪl, -'dɒsɪl), *a.* [a. F. *indocile* (15th c.), or ad. L. *indocilis*, f. *in-* (IN-[3]) + *docilis* DOCILE.] Unwilling or unapt to be taught; not readily submitting to instruction or guidance; intractable.

1603 FLORIO *Montaigne* I. xx. (1632) 43 Men have reason to checke the indocile libertie of this member. **1692** BENTLEY *Boyle Lect.* 13 Indocil intractable fools, whose stolidity can baffle all arguments, and be proof against demonstration it self. **1794** GODWIN *Cal. Williams* 15 He had been indocile and restive to the pedant who held the office of his tutor. **1852** THACKERAY *Esmond* II. i, We are indocile to put up with grief, however. **1884** RUSKIN *Pleas. Eng.* 20 The Lombards..were sternly indocile.

Hence **in'docileness**, indocility (Bailey 1727).

indocility (ɪndəʊ'sɪlɪtɪ). [f. prec. + -ITY; perh. after F. *indocilité* (16th c.) or L. *indocilitās*.] Indocile character or nature; intractableness, unruliness.

1648 W. MOUNTAGUE *Devout Ess.* I. Pref. a iv b, For Humane Nature..is well charactered in the stiffness and indocility of the Pharisees. *a* **1656** BP. HALL *St. Paul's Combat* (T.), To have left us in their miserable darkness and indocility. **1785** J. ADAMS *Wks.* (1854) IX. 537 Ireland, I think, stands between us and evil. Her indocility may have changed the plans of the cabinet. **1873** HAMERTON *Intell. Life* II. ii. (1875) 54 Many of us..were remarkable for our indocility in boyhood.

†**indock**, *v. Obs. nonce-wd.* To put in dock, to dock: in quot. *fig.* (in *pa. pple.*) Intently fixed, 'anchored'.

1611 *Coryat's Crudities* Panegyr. Verses h ij, Nimble Tom ..Whose minde on trauels still indockt Eates Obseruations by the eyes, Hath spu'd a booke of Crudities, Which Vulcans forge will not concoct.

†**in'doct**, *a. Obs. rare*[−1]. [ad. L. *indoct-us*: cf. DOCT.] Untaught, not learned.

1677 T. HARVEY *Owen's Epigr.* (N.), Sick stomachs much receive, not much concoct; So thou know'st much, I know, yet art indoct.

indoctrinate (ɪn'dɒktrɪneɪt), *v.* Also 7, 9 **en-**. [f. L. type **indoctrīnāre*, *-ināt-* (see DOCTRINATE), prob. used in med. or mod.L.: cf. It. *indottrinare* (Florio), Pr. *endoctrinar*, F. *endoctriner* (12th c. in Littré).]

1. a. *trans.* To imbue with learning, to teach.

1626 JACKSON *Creed* VIII. xii. §6 This will not indoctrinate him to know the extremities of the stone so perfectly as his meanest patient doth. **1652–62** HEYLIN *Cosmogr.* II. (1682) 128 They are altogether unlearned, even the Priests meanly indoctrinated. **1677** *Govt. Venice* 144 Young Gentlemen, who..are received into the Colledg to be indoctrinated. **1820** SCOTT *Monast.* xix, It shall be my part so to indoctrinate him, as to convince him what is due..to your lordship. **1865** LIVINGSTONE *Zambesi* xxv. 513 No pains whatever are taken to indoctrinate the adults of the tribe.

b. To instruct *in* a subject, principle, etc.

1656 H. MORE *Enthus. Tri.* 21 Manes..left a sect behind him indoctrinated in all licentious and filthy principles. *a* **1661** FULLER *Worthies* (1840) II. 312 The lord treasurer Burleigh..was indoctrinated by a cobbler in the true tanning of leather. **1858** SEARS *Athan.* III. v. 291 His mind had become thoroughly indoctrinated in the tenets of his sect. **1876** C. GEIKIE *Christ* xxxv. (1879) 417 He rather trained their spiritual character than indoctrinated them in systematic theology.

c. To imbue *with* a doctrine, idea, or opinion. *spec.* To imbue with Communist ideas, etc. (cf. INDOCTRINATION).

1832 *Blackw. Mag.* XXXII. 438 The little town having long before been handsomely endoctrinated with philosophy..and the solemn and sworn belief that every Frenchman..was perfectly competent to judge of politics. **1861** M. ARNOLD *Pop. Educ. France* 59 Fully indoctrinated with a sense of the magnitude of their office. **1874** CARPENTER *Ment. Phys.* I. iii. (1879) 130 It has been the writer's object..to indoctrinate the Reader with that idea [etc.]. **1945** MENCKEN *Amer. Lang.* Suppl. I. 306 The *reds* who emerged from hiding on the establishment of the *entente* cordiale with Russia in 1940..have revived and propagated..*to indoctrinate*, [etc.]. **1958** *Times* 22 May 6/4 It was his duty to indoctrinate leading coders who were proceeding abroad. **1958** *Oxford Mail* 5 June 6/8 Robert Ford, the English wireless operator 'indoctrinated' by the Chinese in Tibet.

d. To bring *into* a knowledge of something.

1841–4 EMERSON *Ess., Spir. Laws* Wks. (Bohn) I. 62 If a teacher have any opinion which he wishes to conceal, his pupils will become as fully indoctrinated into that as into any which he publishes. **1862** GOULBURN *Pers. Relig.* 274 May He indoctrinate us into it.

2. To teach, inculcate (a subject, etc.). *rare.*

1800 T. GREEN *Extracts* (1810) 209 The Adventures of St. Leon..do not indoctrinate the unsatisfactory nature of boundless opulence and immortal youth. **1868** M. PATTISON *Academ. Org.* v. 308 The philosophical sciences can only be indoctrinated by a master.

Hence **in'doctrinated** *ppl. a.*; **in'doctrinating** *vbl. sb.* and *ppl. a.*

1642 MILTON *Apol. Smect.* i, To expresse his indoctrinating power in what sort him best seem'd. **1644** —— *Educ.* (1780) 183 Then will be required a speciall reinforcement of constant and sound endoctrinating to set them right and firm. **1870** ANDERSON *Missions Amer. Bd.* IV. xlv. 471 Churches..each with its indoctrinated native pastor.

indoctrination (ɪn,dɒktrɪ'neɪʃən). [n. of action from prec.] Instruction; formal teaching. Also *spec.*, the 'instruction' of prisoners of war, etc., in Communist doctrines, ideas, etc.; = BRAINWASHING.

1646 SIR T. BROWNE *Pseud. Ep.* I. vii. 25 Postulates, very accommodable unto Junior indoctrinations. **1668** H. MORE *Div. Dial.* IV. ix. (1713) 309 His Indoctrinations touching the Centre of the Soul in the Heart. **1842** *Tait's Mag.* IX. 751 A science to be understood by the indoctrination of the understanding. **1865** M. PATTISON *Serm.* 123 The positivist knows of no other education than indoctrination. **1935** *Nature* 11 May 801/1 Freedom or indoctrination: an enduring dilemma of Education. **1950** *Ann. Reg. 1949* 188 Communist underground activities..'subversion' and indoctrination. **1955** *Treatm. Brit. P.O.W.'s in Korea* (H.M.S.O.) 8 The political education of prisoners in the North Korean camps was not, however, confined to oral indoctrination. **1956** W. H. WHYTE *Organization Man* (1957) i. 9, I will then pick up the organization man in college, follow him through his initial indoctrination in organization life, and explore the impact of the group way upon him. **1958** *Times* 22 May 6/4 Men on the course would attend an indoctrination meeting.

in'doctrinator. [agent-n. in L. form from INDOCTRINATE: see -OR.] One who indoctrinates.

1889 in *Cent. Dict.* **1952** [see BRAINWASHING]. **1973** *Listener* 20 Dec. 845 The Armed Forces in the Soviet Union ..act as the indoctrinators of the young.

indoctrinatory (ɪn'dɒktrɪ,neɪtərɪ), *a.* [f. INDOCTRINAT(E *v.* + -ORY[2].] That indoctrinates; relating or pertaining to indoctrination.

1953 E. E. CUMMINGS *Let.* 27 Mar. (1969) 223 Having kept my ears & eyes open, I am unaware that 'tis thanks to the indoctrinatory efforts of this gruesome gang of do-gooders that Russia is a worldpower. **1965** J. B. WILSON *Logic & Sexual Morality* 137 The simpler method..is indoctrinatory.

†**in'doctrine,** *v. Obs.* Also 5–7 en-. [ME. *endoctrine*, a. OF. *endoctrine-r* (12th c. in Littré), f. *en-* = L. *in-* + *doctrine*, parallel to Pr. *endoctrinar*, It. *indottrinare*, L. type **indoctrīnāre*; the prefix at length conformed to Latin type: see IN-[2].] *trans.* To teach, instruct; = INDOCTRINATE.

α. *a* **1450** *Knt. de la Tour* (1868) 112 For to norisshe orphelyns and for to endoctrine hem in vertu and science. **1483** CAXTON *Cato* A v b, To teche and endoctryne hyr all good condicions. *a* **1533** LD. BERNERS *Gold. Bk. M. Aurel.* (1546) Ee iij b, Olde wyse men ought to endoctrine the yonge people. **1633** J. DONE *Hist. Septuagint* 2 This Ptolomeus Philadelphus was endoctrined in the Science of good letters by Strabo.

β. **1509** HAWES *Past. Pleas.* 28 Sayeng she wolde in her goodly scyence In short space me so well indoctryne. **1549** *Compl. Scot.* To Rdr. 14 To disput ande tyl indoctryne the maneir of the veyris ande of the batellis. **1624** GEE *Foot out of Snare* v. 29 It plaseth God..to indoctrine the innocent, to refute the insolent. **1820** SCOTT *Monast.* xiv, That all-to-be-unparalleled volume..which indoctrines the rude in civility.

in'doctrinize, *v. rare.* [f. *indoctrine* or *indoctrinate* + -IZE; cf. DOCTRINIZE.] *trans.* = INDOCTRINATE 1. Hence **in,doctrini'zation.**

1861 THORNBURY *Turner* (1862) I. 19 Turner..there received..both health and learning—being at once oxygenized and indoctrinized. **1887** *New Princeton Rev.* Jan. 32 All that remains for specific indoctrinization may easily be left to the Sabbath-schools and the churches.

,Indo-Euro'pean, *a.* and *sb.* [f. INDO-[1] + EUROPEAN.]

A. *adj.* **a.** Common to India and Europe; applied to the great family or class of cognate languages (also called INDO-GERMANIC and ARYAN, q.v.) spoken over the greater part of Europe and extending into Asia as far as northern India, and to the race or its divisions characterized by the use of one or other of these languages.

The earliest name for this family of languages, and, both from priority of date and superior fitness of expression, having greater claims than INDO-GERMANIC.

1814 [DR. T. YOUNG] in *Q. Rev.* X. 255 (*Adelung's Mithridates*) Another ancient and extensive class of languages, united by a greater number of resemblances than can well be altogether accidental, may be denominated the Indo-european, comprehending the Indian, the West Asiatic, and almost all the European languages. *Ibid.* 256 Classes and Families..II. Indoeuropean: Sanscrit, Median, Arabian, Greek, German, Celtic, Latin, Cantabrian, Sclavic. **1815** [DR. T. D. WHITAKER] *Ibid.* XIV. 97 (*Hermes Scythicus*) Of the five classes which we denominated Monosyllabic, Indoeuropean, Tataric, African, and American, the first two only are to be considered as constituted according to correct philological principles. **1826** PRICHARD *Phys. Hist. Mankind* v. i. 491 By some the term of Indo-European, by others that of Indo-German dialects, has been applied to the whole class of idioms which are found to be thus allied. The former of these terms is preferable to the latter, and indeed to any other, as being the most general. **1831** —— *Eastern Origin Celtic Nat.* 20 Adelung and Murray have regarded the Celtic as a branch of the Indo-European stock. **1841** LATHAM *Eng. Lang.* i. 3 That the Celtic languages were Indo-European has lately been demonstrated by Dr. Prichard. **1871** MORRIS *Hist. Outl. Eng. Accid.* (1873) 6 The Indo-European family comprehends nearly all the languages of Europe, and all those Indian dialects which have sprung from the old Hindu language (Sanskrit). **1877** PAPILLON *Man. Compar. Philol.* (ed. 2) 12 The original home of the Indo-European or Aryan nations. *Ibid.*, The position of an Indo-European people. **1884** RHYS *Celtic Britain* I The great group of nations which has been variously called Aryan, Indo-European, Indo-Germanic, Indo-Celtic, and Japhetic.

b. Pertaining or belonging to the Indo-European family of languages or peoples, as ***Indo-European root, philology, culture,*** etc.

B. *sb.* **1.** A member of the Indo-European race; an Aryan.

1871 MORRIS *Hist. Outl. Eng. Accid.* 10 The language of the primitive Indo-Europeans had its local varieties or dialects.

2. An Indianized European. *rare.*

1825 HEBER *Jrnl.* (1828) II. 343 One of these Indo-Europeans is an old Colonel, of French extraction, but completely Indian in colour, dress, language, and ideas.

Hence **,Indo-Euro'peanist**, a person who studies the Indo-European family of languages.

1927 *Mod. Philology* Nov. 217 This fallacy was possible because most Indo-Europeanists spoke a Germanic language and knew Latin and Greek from school and Sanskrit from grammars ultimately based on Panini. **1951** *Archivum Linguisticum* III. 114 Both Sapir and Bloomfield —who are at present usually identified with work in exotic languages—began as Indo-Europeanists. **1969** *Language* XLV. 249 The weight of this evidence seems to have persuaded a majority of Indo-Europeanists that Sievers-Edgerton's Law is a valid hypothesis.

Indogæan (ɪndəʊ'dʒiːən, -'giːən), *a.* [f. mod.L. *Indogæa*, f. INDO-[1] + Gr. γαῖα the earth + -AN.] Of or pertaining to *Indogæa*, the zoological region (also called *Indian*) comprising India, China, the Eastern Peninsula, and the Indo-malayan archipelago, as far as Wallace's line.

1885 GILL in *Proc. Biol. Soc. Washington* II. 17 We see reason for admitting nine primary divisions of the earth's inland surface characterised by major associations of animals... (3) The Indogaean. *Ibid.* 19 The Indogaean realm. **1899** W. L. & P. L. SCLATER *Geog. Mammals.*

indogen ('ɪndəʊdʒɛn). *Chem.* [f. INDO-[2] + -GEN I.] A name for the group $C_6H_4\langle{}^{CO}_{NH}\rangle C=$ the double molecule of which (di-indogen) constitutes indigo-blue. Hence **indo'genic** *a.* in *i. acid* = indoxylic acid. **in'dogenide**, a compound of indogen with another radical, as *indogenide of benzoic aldehyde*, or of *pyruric acid*. Indigo-blue is the indogenide of pseudo-isatin, or di-indogen.

1886 *Syd. Soc. Lex.*, Indogen. **1892** MORLEY & MUIR *Dict. Chem.* III. 7 Indoxyl forms condensation products, called indogenides, with bodies containing a CO group.

,Indo-'German, *a. rare.* = next.

1826 [see INDO-EUROPEAN *a.*] **1847** PRICHARD *Rep. Brit. Assoc.* 241 The Indo-European, sometimes termed Indo-German, and, by late writers, Arian or Iranian languages. **1880** EARLE *Philol. Eng. Tongue* §262 These forms are an indelible feature of all Indo-German tongues.

,Indo-Ger'manic, *a.* [f. INDO-[1] + GERMANIC, ad. Ger. *indogermanisch.*] = INDO-EUROPEAN *a.*, ARYAN *a.*

('Indo-Germanic' is a term of later introduction than 'Indo-European', and of German origin, appearing first, so far as yet traced (see Gustav Meyer in *Indoger. Forschungen* II. 125–130), in Klaproth *Asia Polyglotta*, 1823. With Klaproth it seems to have been a kind of abbreviation of the expression (used by him in an earlier work) 'die grosse Indisch-Medisch-Sclavisch-Germanische Völkerkette, die vom Ganges bis zu den Britannischen Inseln reicht', naming the two extreme members of the ethnological 'chain'. When Celtic was shown to be a still more extreme member of the same series, 'indogermanisch' lost its appropriateness, and some scholars tried to substitute *indokeltisch*, 'Indo-Celtic', in Fr. *indo-celtique*, while others, as Bopp in his *Vergleichende Grammatik*, gave preference to the more comprehensive *indoeuropäisch*, the equivalents to which, INDO-EUROPEAN, *indo-européen*, were also favoured in Great Britain and France. But the employment of 'indogermanisch' on the title-page of Pott's *Etymologische Forschungen auf dem Gebiete der indogermanischen Sprachen* (1833–36) popularized this term in Germany, whence under the influence of German textbooks, or of teachers trained in Germany, it came into English use, and was, in the 19th c., probably more used than 'Indo-European'.)

1835 [DR. ROSEN] in *Q. Jrnl. Educ.* Apr. 332 (*Review of Pott*), The family of the Indo-Germanic languages may, according to Mr. Pott, be divided into five branches. **1839** *Penny Cycl.* XIII. 308/2 The following table taken from Pott's *Etymologische Forschungen* contains a list of the principal transformations of letters in some of the Indo-Germanic languages. **1848** LATHAM *Eng. Lang.* (ed. 2) iv. §31 Until the Celtic was shown by Dr. Prichard to have the same affinities with the Latin, Greek,..Sanskrit, and Zend, as those tongues had with each other, the class in question was called Indo-Germanic; since, up to that time, the Germanic languages had formed its western limit. **1866** *Cornh. Mag.* Nov. 631 The highest forms of Indo-Germanic culture. **1877** PAPILLON *Man. Compar. Philol.* (ed. 2) 10 The name Indo-Germanic, employed by many German scholars, is hardly comprehensive enough of the European branch of the family.

Hence **,Indo-'Germanist**, a student of Indo-Germanic philology.

1889 MAYHEW in *Academy* 17 Aug. 104/3, I hardly think that any Indo-Germanist would be found at the present day to favour such an hypothesis. **1896** LLOYD *Ibid.* 7 Mar. 203/1 A *Phonetik* for Indogermanists.

†**in'dogged,** *a. Obs. rare*[−0]. [f. IN-[2] + *dog.*]

1611 FLORIO, *Incanito*, indogged, become currish.

[**indoice**, error for INDORE *v.*]

indoin ('ɪndəʊɪn). *Chem.* [f. INDO-[2] + -IN.] A blue dye-stuff, $C_{32}H_{20}N_4O_5$, related to indigo.

1884 in *Cassell's Encycl. Dict.* **1890** MORLEY & MUIR *Dict. Chem.* II. 760/2.

,Indo-I'ranian, *a.* and *sb.* [f. INDO-[1] + IRANIAN *a.* and *sb.*] **A.** *adj.* Of or pertaining to both India and Iran; *spec.* designating a division of the Indo-European languages comprising the Indian and Iranian branches. **B.** *sb.* **a.** The Indo-Iranian languages collectively. **b.** A member of the Indo-Iranian people.

1876 T. L. PAPILLON *Man. Compar. Philol. Gr. & Latin Inflections* ii. 10 The term *Aryan*..employed..by some in the more restricted sense of *Indo-Iranian*, i.e. to denote the Asiatic sub-division of the Indo-European family. **1885** *Encycl. Brit.* XVIII. 606/1 Indo-Iranian frontier. **1888** KING & COOKSON *Princ. Sound & Inflexion Gr. & Lat.* 26 The term 'Aryan' or better 'Arian' is also applied in a more restricted sense to the Indo-Iranian group. **1895** A. MENZIES *Hist. Relig.* xxi. 380 How the Indo-Iranian religion was developed in India. **1921** E. SAPIR *Lang.* ix. 212 The peculiar, dull vowel..is entirely wanting in Germanic, Greek, Armenian, and Indo-Iranian, the nearest Indo-European congeners of Slavic. **1959** *Chambers's Encycl.* VII. 699/2 Iranian languages have developed from Indo-Iranian, one of the eastern descendants of the Indo-European parent language. The first appearance of Indo-Iranians is traced to the middle of the 2nd millennium B.C.

†**'Indois.** *Obs. rare.* In 4–5 yndoys. [a. OF. *Indois*: cf. GREGOIS.] **a.** The language of India. **b.** *pl.* Indians.

a **1400–50** *Alexander* 5009 þe son-tre..Entris in with yndoyes, & endis in Greke. *Ibid.* 5072 þis titill was of twa tongis tane out & grauen, Of Ebru & of yndoys. *c* **1400** tr. *Secreta Secret., Gov. Lordsh.* 83 Aftyr þe ordre and þe craft of gregeys, of yndoys, & of hem of Perse.

indole ('ɪndəʊl), *sb. Chem.* Also (*improp.*) **indol.** [f. IND(O-[2] + -OLE, from L. *oleum* oil. (Not *-ol*, as indole has not the structure of an alcohol.)] **a.** A crystallizable substance (C_8H_7N), called also *ketole*, formed in large shining colourless laminæ, having a peculiar but not very powerful odour; it is obtained artificially by reduction of indigo-blue, and occurs in small quantities in human excrement. The pl. *indoles* is applied to alkylated derivatives of indole.

indole group, a name for the group including indole, isatin, indigo, and related compounds and derivatives.

1869 ROSCOE *Chem.* 390 Indol is a crystalline substance which forms the starting-point of the indigo series. **1872** WATTS *Dict. Chem.* VI. 733 Indol, C_8H_7N..may be regarded as the nucleus of the indigo-group. **1881** *Ibid.* 3rd Suppl. II. 1089 The clear ethereal solution leaves on distillation a reddish oil with the characteristic smell of indole. **1886** *Syd. Soc. Lex.* s.v., Indol..when fused with potash forms aniline, and when in solution forms with ozone indigo-blue. **1892** MORLEY & MUIR *Dict. Chem.*, Indole.

b. Comb.: ***indoleacetic acid***, any of the seven isomeric acetic acid derivatives, $C_8H_6N{\cdot}CH_2COOH$, of indole; *esp.* the one having the acetic acid side-chain substituted in the 3- (or β-) position, which is an important natural growth hormone in plants.

1886 *Jrnl. Chem. Soc.* L. 806 Methylindoleacetic acid, $NH\langle{}^{C_6H_4}_{CMe}\rangle C.CH_2.COOH$, is prepared by heating phenylhydrazinelevulinic acid..with zinc chloride. **1957** *New Biol.* XXIII. 17 Among the naturally occurring auxins, β-indoleacetic acid is widely, if not perhaps universally, distributed in the higher plants. **1958** *Plant Physiol.* XXXIII. 317 (*table*) Relative activity of indole-4-acetic acid (I-4-AA) on Avena coleoptile sections, and test for interaction with indole-3-acetic acid.

†**indole,** *a. Obs. rare*[−1]. [ad. med.L. *indol-us*, f. *in-* (IN-[3]) + *dolus* guile.] Guileless.

1549 *Compl. Scot.* xv. 126 His 3ongest sone beniemyn vas indole and innocent.

indolence ('ɪndələns). [a. F. *indolence* (16th c.), or directly ad. L. *indolēntia* freedom from pain, insensibility (Cicero), n. of quality f. *in-* (IN-[3]) + *dolēnt-em*, pres. pple. of *dolēre* to be pained.]

†**1.** Insensibility or indifference to pain; want of feeling. *Obs.*

1603 HOLLAND *Plutarch's Mor.* 69 Clemencie and Mildnesse, [they say it is the meane] betweene senselesse Indolence and Crueltie. **1706** [see INDOLENCY 1]. **1723** *Pres. State Russia* I. 153 A Russian values neither Life nor Death, and undergoes capital Punishment with unparalleled Indolence.

†**2.** Freedom from pain; a state of rest or ease, in which neither pain nor pleasure is felt. *Obs.*

1656 STANLEY *Hist. Philos.* IV. (1701) 135/1 Indolence, which Epicurus held, they esteem not pleasure, nor want of pleasure..for Indolence is like the state of a sleeping Man. **1702** S. PARKER tr. *Cicero's De Finibus* ii. 56 D'you know, said I, what Hieronymus Rhodius has allotted for the *Summum Bonum*? I know, said Torquatus, he resolves it into *Nihil dolere*, Mere Indolence. **1713** BERKELEY *Hylas & Phil.* I. Wks. 1871 I. 269, I could rather call it an indolence. It seems to be nothing more than a privation of both pain and pleasure. **1751** EARL ORRERY *Remarks Swift* (1752) 113 That tranquility of mind, and indolence of body which he made his chief ends.

b. *Path.* Absence of pain (in a tumour: cf. INDOLENT 1).

1758 J. S. *Le Dran's Obs. Surg.* (1771) 219 The Pain or Indolence of the Tumour indicates the Quality of the Contents.

3. The disposition to avoid trouble; love of ease; laziness, slothfulness, sluggishness.

1710 STEELE *Tatler* No. 132 ¶1 Heavy honest Men, with whom I have passed many Hours with much Indolence. **1784** JOHNSON *Let. to Langton* 12 July, That voluntary debility which modern language is content to term indolence. **1816** SCOTT *Fam. Lett.* 14 Nov. (1894) I. xii. 376 He is one of the many many hundreds in whom indolence has strangled genius. **1844** H. H. WILSON *Brit. India* I. 23 Passing his days in indolence and indulgence. **1878** R. W. DALE *Lect. Preach.* iii. 63 Some men fail as preachers through intellectual indolence.

† **'indolency.** *Obs.* [ad. L. *indolentia*: see prec. and -ENCY.]

1. = INDOLENCE 1.

[**1577** tr. *Bullinger's Decades* (1592) 301 The vnsauerie opinion of the Stoickes, touching their *Indolentia* or lacke of greefe.] **1622** DONNE *Serm.* xvi. 159 He wept not inordinately, but he came nearer Excesse then Indolency. **1662** H. MORE *Enthus. Tri.* 42 That affected, and not altogether unattainable power of Indolency amongst the Heathen. **1706** PHILLIPS, *Indolence*, or *Indolency*, a being insensible of Pain or Grief.

2. = INDOLENCE 2.

1603 FLORIO *Montaigne* II. xii. (1632) 275 The sect of Philosophie, that hath most preferred sensualitie, hath also placed the same but to indolencie or unfeeling of paine. **1689** POPPLE tr. *Locke's 1st Let. Toleration* 6 Civil Interests I call Life, Liberty, Health, and Indolency of Body. **1690** LOCKE *Hum. Und.* II. xx. §10 Despair..sometime producing uneasiness or pain sometimes rest and indolency.

3. = INDOLENCE 3.

1741 MIDDLETON *Cicero* I. i. 48 The indolency of his ancestors.

indolent ('ɪndəʊlənt), *a.* (*sb.*) [ad. late L. *indolēnt-em* (Jerome: 'dicamus ἀπηλγηκότες indolentes sive indolorios'), f. *in-* (IN-³) + *dolēns* grieving, DOLENT. Cf. F. *indolent* (16–17th c.).]

1. *Path.* Causing no pain, painless; esp. in ***indolent tumour, ulcer***.

1663 BOYLE *Usef. Exp. Nat. Philos.* II. i. 25 Curing of cancers..by the outward application of an indolent powder. **1713** R. RUSSELL in *Phil. Trans.* XXVIII. 277 An Indolent Tumour in her Breast. **1783** POTT *Chirurg. Wks.* II. 286 As he lay on his back, it was perfectly indolent; but in an erect posture..he complained of pain. **1804** ABERNETHY *Surg. Obs.* 58, I was led to inquire further, whether the surface might not be sometimes irritable and sometimes indolent. **1861** HULME tr. *Moquin-Tandon* II. III. iii. 133 Ceratum Cantharidis..is used to..stimulate issues and indolent ulcers.

† **b.** *loosely.* Of a pain: Very slight. *Obs.*

1758 J. S. *Le Dran's Observ. Surg.* (1771) 155 He felt an indolent Pain on the Shoulder.

2. Of persons, their disposition, action, etc.: Averse to toil or exertion; slothful, lazy, idle.

1710 STEELE *Tatler* No. 132 ¶4 A good-natured indolent Man. **1711** ADDISON *Spect.* No. 5 ¶1 To gratifie the Senses, and keep up an indolent Attention in the Audience. **1744** H. WALPOLE *Lett. H. Mann* (1834) I. xciv. 324, I am naturally indolent and without application to any kind of business. **1839** LONGF. *Hyperion* I. vi, An easy and indolent disposition. **1885** S. COX *Exposit.* Ser. I. ix. 112 [To] rouse the indolent and indifferent.

transf. **1839** LONGF. *Hyperion* III. i, Through the meadow winds the river—careless, indolent.

† **B.** *sb.* An indolent person. *Obs.*

1720 *Humourist* 49 The Indolent remains in Suspense and Anguish. **1810** *Splendid Follies* I. 144 'Yes, yes, I see her', replied the fair indolent.

Hence **'indolentness** (Bailey vol. II, 1727).

indolently ('ɪndəlɛntlɪ), *adv.* [f. prec. + -LY².] In an indolent or lazy manner.

a **1719** ADDISON (J.), While lull'd by sound, and undisturb'd by wit, Calm and serene you indolently sit. **1762** GOLDSM. *Cit. W.* xiv, I perceived a little shrivelled creature indolently reclined on a sofa. **1871** R. ELLIS *Catullus* iv. 25 Indolently now She rusts, a life in autumn. **1885** *Leeds Mercury* 31 Jan. 6/5 If..we indolently decide to do nothing at all, we shall soon see the result.

‖ **indoles** ('ɪndəʊliːz). *rare.* [L. *indolēs*, f. *indu-* in, within + **ol-* to grow (the stem found in ABOLISH, ADOLESCENT, ADULT). Cf. OF. *indole*, Sp. *indole*.] Innate quality or character.

1673 O. WALKER *Educ.* ix. 93 He must be treated as the Brachmans did their children, whose *indoles* they disliked. **1677** HALE *Prim. Orig. Man.* II. iv. 160 Such is the *indoles* of the Humane Nature, where it is not strangely over-grown with Barbarousness. **1882** *Q. Rev.* July 214 Every language has its own 'indoles'.

indolic (ɪn'dəʊlɪk), *a.* [f. INDOL(E *sb.* + -IC.] † **1.** *Med.* Designating a type of chronic excessive intestinal putrefaction. *Obs. rare.*

1907 C. A. HERTER *Common Bacterial Infections Digestive Tract* 279 The proposed classification recognizes three types of putrefaction which are common: the first may be called the Indolic Type,..the second.. may be designated the Saccharo-butyric Type... In the third group..we find associated the characters of the indolic and the saccharo-butyric types of decomposition. **1909** *Practitioner* Feb. 227 They remark that there are three types of chronic excessive intestinal putrefaction:—(1) The indolic type, occurring in the small as well as the large intestine. In this type large quantities of indol are produced, and the stool is usually alkaline.

2. *Chem.* Containing, composed of, or characteristic of indole.

1949 *Jrnl. Biol. Chem.* CLXXX. 966 There is, then, little doubt that the empirical formula of the indolic base portion of the complex..is $C_{10}H_{14}O_2N_2$. **1958** *Jrnl. Amer. Chem. Soc.* LXXX. 126/1 The ultraviolet absorption spectrum.. was recognized to be indolic. **1971** *Nature* 7 May 25/1 Indolic substances have been clearly implicated in some conditions..which are often accompanied by mental disturbances.

indoline ('ɪndəʊlaɪn). *Chem.* [f. INDOLE + -INE.] A polymer of indole, $C_{16}H_{14}N_2$, formed by heating leucindigo with barium hydrate, zinc-dust, and water, crystallizing in long bright yellow needles.

1884 in *Cassell's Encycl. Dict.* **1892** in MORLEY & MUIR *Dict. Chem.* II. 760.

Indological (ɪndəʊ'lɒdʒɪkəl), *a.* [f. INDOLOG(Y + -ICAL.] Of or pertaining to Indology.

1950 *Austral. Outlook* Mar. 46 They formed the so-called 'ethical group' mainly centred at the Indological Faculty of the University of Leyden. **1957** *Contrib. Indian Sociol.* I. 14 The difficulty in Indological studies in general is that of discovering..the 'whole'. **1958** *Oxf. Mag.* 13 Mar. 368/1 Studies aspiring to be called 'indological', however, demand some knowledge of Sanskrit. **1964** *Language* XL. 114 His interests covered a broad..range of Indological subjects. **1971** *Illustr. Weekly India* 11 Apr. 35/1 The University of Kiel..had been a centre of Indological studies for over a century and a half.

Indologist (ɪn'dɒlədʒɪst). [f. INDOLOG(Y + -IST.] A student of Indology.

1904 M. DE Z. WICKREMASINGHE in *Epigraphia Zeylanica* I. I. p. vi, The thanks of all Indologists are due to the Ceylon Government. **1928** *Spectator* 7 Apr. 535/1 Indologists at once recognized the importance of this ample..collection of material for their studies. **1929** A. STEIN *On Alexander's Track to Indus* xii. 89 M. Sylvain Lévi, the eminent French Indologist. **1957** P. WORSLEY *Trumpet shall Sound* 224 The explanation of this absence of millenarism from Hindu India..can only be attempted by an Indologist. **1971** *Illustr. Weekly India* 11 Apr. 35/1 Hermann Jacobi (1850–1937) is remembered with great reverence by indologists as a pioneer in the field of Jain and Prakrit studies.

Indology (ɪn'dɒlədʒɪ). [f. INDO-¹ + -LOGY.] The study of Indian history, literature, philosophy, etc.

1888 *Trübner's Monthly List* Oct. 134 There is not a single branch of Indology—with, perhaps, the single exception of Vedic studies—which will not gain very considerably by its publication. **1895** *Atlantic Monthly* Mar. 399.

So **Indo'logian**, a student of Indology.

1897 A. DRUCKER tr. *Ihering's Evol. Aryan* 20 The endeavour of Indologians to attribute the highest possible degree of civilization to the mother-nation.

indolyl ('ɪndəlaɪl, -ɪl). *Chem.* [f. INDOL(E *sb.* + -YL.] Any of the seven isomeric univalent radicals derived from indole by removal of a hydrogen atom; freq. as a word-forming element.

1907 *Jrnl. Chem. Soc.* XCII. I. 737 Acidification of the solution precipitates α-benzoylaminoindolylacrylic acid. **1926**, etc. [see INDOLYLACETIC *a.*]. **1937** *Chem. Abstr.* XXXI. 9489/1 Indolyl C_8H_6N—(from indole, 7 isomers). **1949** *Jrnl. Biol. Chem.* CLXXX. 966 If we subtract the formula for the indolyl group (C_8H_6N), the number of atoms which must still be put into place is very few, $C_2H_8O_2N$. **1972** W. J. HOULIHAN *Indoles* II. iv. 87, 4-Indolylisoprene has been prepared by the use of the Wittig reaction.

indolylacetic (ɪndəlaɪl-, ɪndəlɪlə'siːtɪk), *a.* *Chem.* [f. prec. + ACETIC *a.*] ***indolylacetic acid*** = *indoleacetic acid.*

1926 *Chem. Abstr.* XX. 759 Boiled 6 hrs. with 20‰ KOH it [*sc.* β-indolylacetonitrile] gives 84% β-indolylacetic acid. **1937** *Discovery* June 174/1 It [*sc.* hetero-auxin] is an acid, β-indolyl-acetic acid, and can now be bought as crystals and used for growth hormone experiments. **1972** L. J. AUDUS *Plant Growth Substances* (ed. 3) I. iii. 74 IAA (indol-3yl-acetic) is the most active, indol-1yl-acetic..and indol-2yl-acetic..are less active but indol-4yl-acetic..has very low activity indeed.

† **in'domable**, *a.* *Obs. rare.* [ad. L. *indomābilis*, f. *in-* (IN-³) + *domābilis* tameable, f. *domāre* to tame. Cf. OF. *indomable*.] Untameable.

c **1450** *Mirour Saluacioun* 5062 The Egle indomable thow reclamed at the fulle **1623** COCKERAM, *Indomable*, not to bee tamed. **1656** in BLOUNT *Glossogr.* **1728** MORGAN *Algiers* I. iii. 47 Inhabitants, no less indomable than the very Leopards it breeds.

Hence † **in'domableness** (Bailey vol. II, 1727).

indomage, obs. var. of ENDAMAGE *v.*

indomethacin (ɪndəʊ'mɛθəsɪn). *Pharm.* [f. INDO(LE *sb.* METH(YL + AC(ETIC *a.* (words which occur in the systematic name: see quot. 1963¹) + -IN¹.] A yellowish-white powdery indole derivative, $C_{19}H_{16}NO_4Cl$, which has anti-inflammatory, anti-pyretic, and analgesic properties and has been given orally in the treatment of rheumatoid arthritis, gout, and similar conditions.

1963 T. Y. SHEN et al. in *Jrnl. Amer. Chem. Soc.* LXXXV. 488/2 We wish to report a new class of anti-inflammatory and antipyretic agents, substituted indole acetic and propionic acids... One member of the series, 1-(*p*-chlorobenzoyl)-5-methoxy-2-methylindole-3-acetic acid.., designated as indomethacin, has demonstrated a high degree of anti-inflammatory activity. **1963** *New Scientist* 10 Oct. 103/2 One patient, aged 73, had had arthritis for 30 years and was bed-ridden with inflamed joints and a temperature. Within three days of being given indomethacin the temperature fell to normal and pain was relieved. **1968** *Clin. Pharmacol. & Therapeutics* IX. 94 Indomethacin may be useful in treating other..rheumatic diseases, but as yet few comparisons with other standard therapies have been made. The drug has severe side effects and should be used with caution. **1971** *New Scientist* 24 June 745/2 This..might well eliminate the gastrointestinal side-effects of drugs such as indomethacin used to treat rheumatoid diseases.

indomitable (ɪn'dɒmɪtəb(ə)l), *a.* [ad. late L. *indomitābilis*, f. *in-* (IN-³) + *domitāre* to tame: see DOMITABLE.]

1. That cannot be tamed; untameable. ? *Obs.*

1634 SIR T. HERBERT *Trav.* 13 The inhabitants so indomitable. **1653** A. WILSON *Jas. I*, 162 Indomitable Spirits by gentle usage may be tamed and brought to obedience.

b. Of temper and the like: passing into 2.

1828 SCOTT *F.M. Perth* ix, Personal qualities of wisdom and valour, mingled with indomitable pride. **1828** D'ISRAELI *Chas. I*, II. ii. 40 The genius of Richelieu alone could at once subdue an indomitable aristocracy. **1874** GREEN *Short Hist.* vii. §1. 347 The temper of the man remained indomitable as ever.

2. Of persons, etc.: That cannot be overcome or subdued by labour, difficulties, or opposition; unyielding; stubbornly persistent or resolute. Usually approbative. (The ordinary use.)

1830 CARLYLE *Misc.* (1857) II. 133 A rugged, deep-rooted, indomitable strength. **1856** KANE *Arct. Expl.* II. xiv. 145 The natives, as indomitable as their dogs, made the entire circuit of Dallas Bay. **1865** LIVINGSTONE *Zambesi* xxi. 427 He has by indomitable energy overcome obstacles under which most persons would have sunk. **1873** SMILES *Huguenots Fr.* I. vi. (1881) 100 They were alike indomitable and obstinate in their assertion of the rights of conscience.

Hence **indomita'bility, in'domitableness**, the quality of being indomitable.

1851 SIR F. PALGRAVE *Norm. & Eng.* I. 311 This young prince..obtained singular importance through his spirit, his indomitability. **1860** PUSEY *Min. Proph.* 116 Joel exhibits the indomitableness of the locusts, how nothing checks, nothing retards them.

indomitably (ɪn'dɒmɪtəblɪ), *adv.* [f. prec. + -LY².] Resolutely, stubbornly, unyieldingly.

1837 EMERSON, *Addr., Amer. Schol.* Wks. (Bohn) II. 189 If the single man plant himself indomitably on his instincts, and there abide, the huge world will come round to him. **1856** FROUDE *Hist. Eng.* (1858) I. ii. 119 Both had imperious tempers, and both were indomitably obstinate.

† **in'domite**, *a.* *Obs.* *rare*⁻¹. [ad. L. *indomit-us*, f. *in-* (IN-³) + *domitus*, pa. pple. of *domāre* to tame.] Untamed, savage.

1617 J. SALKELD *Treat. Paradise* 122 (L.) No tiger so fierce ..no not any creature, so indomite, but that it was subject to man's dominion, while man were subject to his Lord and Maker.

† **in'domptable**, *a.* *Obs.* *rare*⁻¹. [a. F. *indomptable* (1420 in Hatz.-Darm.), f. *in-* (IN-³) + *dompter* to tame:—L. *domit-āre*.]

= INDOMITABLE.

1653 H. COGAN tr. *Pinto's Trav.* lii. 208 Emperor of the indomptable [*ed.* 1663 indomitable] Forces of the Elephants of the Earth.

indonaphthene (-'næfθiːn). *Chem.* [f. INDO-² + NAPHTHENE.] The hydrocarbon C_9H_8, or $C_6H_4\langle{}^{CH}_{CH_2}\rangle CH$, a clear colourless oil, present in coal-tar; also called *indene*.

'indone. *Chem.* [f. IND(O-² + -ONE.] The ketone $C_6H_4\langle{}^{CO}_{CH}\rangle CH$, which may also be viewed as the anhydride of di-oxy-indonaphthene.

Indonesian (ɪndəʊ'niːʃ(ɪ)ən), *a.* and *sb.* [f. INDO-¹ + Gr. νῆσ-ος island + -IAN.] **a.** *adj.* (*a*) Of or belonging to the East Indian islands; *spec.* pertaining to those Malay inhabitants of these islands who approximate to an Indian type. (*b*) (Also as *sb.*) (Of, relating to, or designating) the western branch of the Malayo-Polynesian family of languages; (*c*) Of or pertaining to the federal republic of Indonesia. **b.** *sb.* (*a*) An inhabitant of the East Indian islands; *spec.* a member of this branch of the Malay race. (*b*) A native or inhabitant of Indonesia.

The national language of Indonesia is now called *Bahasa Indonesia*.

1850 J. R. LOGAN in *Jrnl. Indian Archipelago* IV. 254, I prefer the purely geographical term Indonesia..for the Indian Islands or the Indian Archipelago. We thus get Indonesian for Indian Archipelagian or Archipelagic, and Indonesians for Indian Archipelagians or Indian Islanders. *Ibid.* 441 The partially negro character which the Polynesian or Indonesian community has acquired. *Ibid.* 446 In the Indonesian languages everything beyond the mere surface resolved itself into their phonology. **1851** *Ibid.* V. 214 In W. Indonesian the final vowels and consonants are in general in about equal proportions. **1881** *Nature* XXIII. 249 That fair element in Malaysia which Dr. Hamy proposes to group as Indonesians. **1891** *Athenæum* 10 Oct. 485/1 Interesting aspects or phenomena in Indonesian ethnology and folk-

lore. **1895** *Edin. Rev.* Oct. 516 The dark Indonesian race. *Ibid.*, The Malagasy are Indonesians. **1932** W. L. GRAFF *Lang.* iii. 151 In Indonesian the infix *-um-* gives the radical a verbal active meaning. **1933** L. BLOOMFIELD *Lang.* iv. 71 The Malayan (or Indonesian) branch includes Malay... Further, it embraces the languages of the great islands of the East, such as Formosan, Javanese, [etc.]. **1948** D. WEHL *Birth of Indonesia* xii. 177 The Netherlands Government.. could not but feel that they had been interrupted in the very act of bringing to birth the Indonesian Commonwealth. *Ibid.*, Two years of conflict between the Netherlands and the Indonesian Republic had ended. **1950** THEIMER & CAMPBELL *Encycl. World Politics* 228/1 Sovereignty was transferred to the Indonesian government on 27 December 1949. **1958** *Listener* 4 Dec. 914/1 The Indonesians.. write their common language, Bahasa Malay, in Roman letters. **1968** M. CALDWELL *Indonesia* i. 23 The decision to promote a national language—*Bahasa Indonesia*—was taken at an All-Indonesia Youth Congress in 1928, and thereafter enthusiastically forwarded by Indonesian intellectuals and leaders. **1973** 'I. DRUMMOND' *Jaws of Watchdog* iii. 35 He found himself dancing with the little wife of an Indonesian diplomat... [He] stayed with his Indonesian until ten. **1973** D. MAY *Laughter in Djakarta* i. 13 He had worked furiously ..learning Indonesian.

indoona, var. INDUNA.

indoor, in-door (ˈɪnˌdɔə(r)), *a.* (*adv.*) [For earlier *within-door* (Bacon), phrase taken attrib.: cf. next. In early use generally hyphened.]

A. *adj.* **1. a.** Pertaining to the interior of a house or other building; situated or carried on within doors or under cover. (Opposed to *out-door*.) *spec.* Of amusements, games, etc., occurring or played indoors.

1711 SHAFTESB. *Charac.* (1737) II. 430 One admires musick and paintings, cabinet-curiositys, and in-door ornaments. **1774** FOOTE *Cozeners* I. Wks. 1799 II. 158 He.. does.. more in-door christenings than any three of the cloth. **1813** SCOTT *Let. to Joanna Baillie* 12 Sept. in *Lockhart*, The indoor work does not please me as well. **1847** C. BRONTË *Jane Eyre* II. iii. 61 In-door amusements.. became more lively and varied, in consequence of the stop put to out-door gaiety. **1856** KANE *Arct. Expl.* II. xxix. 296 Gradually accustoming ourselves to indoor life and habits. **1863** THACKERAY *Virginians* xxvi. 178, I don't care for indoor games much.. but I.. long to see a good English hunting-field. **1865** C. M. YONGE *Clever Woman* II. vii. 135 'How is Conrade?' 'Quite himself. Up to a prodigious amount of indoor croquet.' **1873** *Young Englishwoman* Mar. 154/2 Can you recommend me.. any indoor games suitable for young children, and the words used. **1883** C. J. WILLS *Mod. Persia* 131 Part of the universal indoor dress of the Persian women. **1890** *Harper's Weekly* 8 Mar. 179/4 In-door baseball has not the slightest resemblance to parlor croquet. **1897** *Illustr. London News* 13 Nov. 710/3 (Advt.), Puff billiards. The latest and most amusing in-door game yet produced. **1921** *Daily Colonist* (Victoria, B.C.) 22 Oct. 10/1 Several upsets featured the play in the Canadian indoor tennis championships here yesterday. **1925** A. HUXLEY *Those Barren Leaves* I. vii. 70 'When all is said, is there a better indoor sport [than philosophy]?..' 'Possibly not... But the point is, aren't there better occupations for a man of sense than indoor sports, even the best of indoor sports?' **1926** R. MACAULAY *Crewe Train* II. iv. 88 Have you always hated indoor games? **1948** J. BETJEMAN *Sel. Poems* 35 (*title*) Indoor games near Newbury. **1949** *Daily Ardmoreite* (Ardmore, Okla.) 23 Feb. 18/2 The explosive charge.. occupies a sphere of three or four inches—about the size of an indoor baseball. **1951** E. COXHEAD *One Green Bottle* ii. 54 Baiting Harry was.. one of Johnny Hollinger's favourite indoor sports. **1965** J. SYMONS *Belting Inheritance* iii. 51 The sort of indoor cricket that you play on paper by picking words out of a book. **1972** *Country Life* 23 Nov. 1424/2 Miniature Croquet Sets... Great indoor game for family and friends. **1972** R. PERRY *Fall Guy* iv. 71 We once again indulged in the oldest of indoor sports.

b. Within the workhouse or poorhouse.

1864 *Times* 24 Dec., The State, with its vast revenue of Poor-rates, its capacious workhouses.. its indoor and out-door poor. **1876** FAWCETT *Pol. Econ.* (ed. 5) p. xxxi. (Contents), The in-door relief given in London is a charge upon the whole metropolis.

2. *transf.* In an inward position or direction.

1874 J. H. COLLINS *Metal Mining* 93 The water is raised in the lower or drawing lift by the up or 'in-door' stroke of the engine. *Ibid.* 98 The piston-rod, which is attached.. to the inner or 'in-door' end.. of the great beam.

B. *adv.* = INDOORS.

1884 TENNYSON *Becket* II. ii, They are plagues enough in-door.

So (*nonce-wds.*) **in'doorness**, the essence of being indoors; **in'doory** *a.*, preferring to remain indoors.

1934 G. B. SHAW *Village Wooing* 120 My mother was that indoory that she grudged having to go out and do her marketing. **1949** E. BOWEN *Heat of Day* vi. 103 The concentrated indoorness of the lounge was made.. greater rather than less by the number of exits.

indoors, in-doors (ˌɪnˈdɔəz), *adv.* [Orig. two words, repr. earlier *within doors* (see DOOR 5): sometimes hyphened.] Within or into a house, etc.; under cover. (Opposed to *out-of-doors*.)

18.. L. HUNT *To Grasshopper & Cricket*, In doors and out, summer and winter. **1832** HT. MARTINEAU *Demerara* iii. 29 Would they step in-doors and rest. **1872** BLACK *Adv. Phaeton* ix, Tita rose and said we must go indoors. **1885** MABEL COLLINS *Prettiest Woman* xii, I am sure she lives indoors too much.

†**b.** *attrib.* = INDOOR *adj. Obs.*

1799 WASHINGTON *Writ.* (1893) XIV. 229 There are many sorts of in-doors work, which can be executed in Hail, Rain, or Snow, as well as in sunshine.

indophane (ˈɪndəʊfeɪn). *Chem.* [f. INDO-² + Gr. -φανης appearing.] A condensation product, $C_{22}H_{10}N_4O_4$, a blue substance resembling indigo.

1875 WATTS *Dict. Chem.* VII. 669 Pure dry indophane is of a violet colour, and has a beautiful green metallic lustre.

indophenin (-ˈfiːnɪn). *Chem.* [f. INDO-² + Gr. φαίν-ειν to show, appear + -IN.] A condensation product, $C_{12}H_7NOS$, formed by shaking isatin with sulphuric acid and benzene that contains thiophene; obtained as a blue powder exhibiting when rubbed a coppery lustre, or in small needles.

1892 in MORLEY & MUIR *Dict. Chem.* III. 7. **1896** G. M'GOWAN tr. *Bernthsen's Organ. Chem.* (ed. 3) 331 The formation of the blue colouring matter Indophenin.

indophenol (-ˈfiːnɒl). *Chem.* [f. INDO-² + PHENOL.] A coal-tar colour used in dyeing, produced by the simultaneous oxidation of a phenol and a paradiamine; one of its commercial forms is *naphthol blue*.

1892 in MORLEY & MUIR *Dict. Chem.* III. 7.

Indophile (ˈɪndəʊfɪl, -faɪl). [f. INDO-¹ + Gr. φίλος lover, friend.] A lover or champion of the natives and interests of India.

1865 *Pall Mall G.* 19 Sept. 10/1 Sir Fitzroy Kelly comes out.. as an Indophile of the most exalted disinterestedness.

Hence **In'dophilism**, partiality for the natives or interests of India; **In'dophilist** = INDOPHILE.

1897 *Westm. Gaz.* 22 Sept. 2/3 [He] was held up as a type of the Indophilists whose educational theories have had a bad influence on the natives.

†**in'dore**, var. of ENDORE *v.*, *Obs.*, to glaze with yolk of egg, etc.

a **1655** SIR T. MAYERNE *Archimag. Anglo-Gall.* cxxiv. (1658) 79 Take some Potters moulds.. and indore [*pr.* indove] them over with a little melted butter. **1688** R. HOLME *Armoury* III. 83/1 *Indoice* [error for *Indorre*], is to rub the in-side of the Coffin of a Pie, with Butter very thin.

in'dorsable, *a.* Another form of ENDORSABLE: cf. INDORSE.

1704–1809 [see ENDORSABLE].

†**in'dorsate**, *pa. pple. Sc. Obs.* [ad. med.L. *indorsātus*, pa. pple. of *indorsāre*, taken as = Sc. *indorsit*.] Indorsed.

c **1470** HENRYSON *Mor. Fab.* VI. (*Sheep & Dog*) iv, The rauin, as to his office weill effeird, Indorsate hes the write.

indorsation (ɪndɔːˈseɪʃən). [n. of action from INDORSE *v.*: chiefly Sc.; see quot. 1849.] The action of indorsing, indorsement.

1540 *Sc. Acts Jas. V* (1597) c. 74 That na indorsation sall haue faith.. bot they that ar signed with the saids signettes. **1656** BLOUNT *Glossogr.*, *Indorsation*, an indorsing; or a bearing, or laying on the back. **1752** LOUTHIAN *Form of Process* (ed. 2) 175 The Indorsations, certifying, that every thing required of him by the said Writs, was done. **1766** W. GORDON *Gen. Counting-ho.* 339 The indorser.. remits it to his correspondent, with an indorsation or transference of property. **1816** SCOTT *Antiq.* xv, Ancient Indorsation of Letters of Importance. **1849** GILBART *Banking* (ed. 5) 20 Should we say indorsement or indorsation? In England, we always use the word indorsement.. In Scotland, the term more generally used is indorsation. **1892** STEVENSON & L. OSBOURNE *Wrecker* (ed. 2) 170 This hearty indorsation clinched the proposal. **1892** *Annual Rep. Exam. Papers Inst. Bankers Scotl.* 46 What effect can be given to endorsation of a Deposit Receipt to a third party?

in'dorse, *v.* Another form of ENDORSE *v.*, q.v. Etymologically, *indorse* is the fully latinized type (conformed to med.L. *indorsāre*), while *endorse* is a partially latinized form of the earlier ME. *endoss*, OF. *endosser*.

1547–1893 [see ENDORSE *v.* 1 β].

indorsee (ˌɪndɔːˈsiː). [f. prec. + -EE.] One in whose favour a note or bill is indorsed: see ENDORSEE.

1754–1888 [see ENDORSEE].

in'dorsement. [Another form of ENDORSEMENT: see INDORSE *v.*] The action of indorsing a document; the signature or writing on the back of such document; *spec.* that by which a bill or cheque is made payable to another person.

1586–1866 [see ENDORSEMENT].

in'dorser. Also 8 -or. [Another form of ENDORSER: see INDORSE *v.*] One who indorses a bill or document.

1743–1849 [see ENDORSER]. **1766** [see INDORSATION]. **1849**, **1866** [see ENDORSEE].

indoss (*pa. pple.* indost): see ENDOSS *v.*

†**in'dot**, *v.*, var. of ENDOTE *v. Obs.*, to endow.

1520 *Charters, etc. Peebles* (1872) 50 The said Schir Patrik sall indot gyf and infeft certane landis.. in honor of God.

†**indotate**, *v. Obs. rare*⁻¹. [f. ppl. stem of L. *indōtāre* to endow. Cf. DOTATE.] *trans.* To dower.

1647 LILLY *Chr. Astrol.* clxxxv. 815 The Profectionall Revolution having the Signe of the seventh ascending.. giveth hopes of Marriage (if indotated), and strong caution to be carefull of trusting Martiall men.

†**in'doubtable**, *a. Obs. rare*⁻¹. [IN-³.] That cannot be doubted; indubitable.

1557 N. T. (Genev.) Ep. *iv, Jesus Christ was declared by certeyn and indoubtable testimonies to be him, and no nother, yᵗ shulde come.

†**in'doubted**, *a. Obs. rare.* Also *Sc.* 6 **-doutit**, 7 **-dowtit**. [IN-³.] Undoubted.

1467 *Paston Lett.* No. 575 II. 306 He thynkyth in-doubted that William Worcetre shuld not be unremembred of this. **1563** WINȜET *Four Scoir Thre Quest.* Wks. 1888 I. 66 We dar .. embrace the samin as the indoutit veritie. **1598** J. RACSTER *Answ. Alabaster* 6 The Apostles were the in-doubted and authentical scribes of the Holy Ghost.

Hence †**in'doubtedly** *adv.* (also **in'doubtly**), undoubtedly.

1563 WINȜET *Four Scoir Thre Quest.* Wks. 1888 I. 132 Ȝour fatheris afoir ȝou hes bein men haifand indoutitlie the samin giftis. **1606** *Sc. Acts Jas. VI* (1816) IV. 291 The Infinite commoditie and contentment, quhilk Indowtlie they sall ressaue be the same.

indow, -ment, obs. forms of ENDOW, -MENT.

indoxyl (ɪnˈdɒksɪl). *Chem.* [f. INDO-² + OXYL.] A brownish oil, C_8H_7NO, isomeric with oxindole, formed, with evolution of carbonic acid gas, when indoxylic acid is heated above its melting point; it is converted by oxidation into indigo-blue.

Hence **indo'xylic** *a.*, in *i. acid*, $C_9H_7NO_3$, a white crystalline precipitate, slightly soluble in water, and converted by air or oxidizing agents into indigo-blue: its salts are **in'doxylates.**

1886 *Syd. Soc. Lex.*, Indoxyl. **1896** *Allbutt's Syst. Med.* I. 899 Albuminous [urine] and containing indoxyl and casts. **1897** *Ibid.* IV. 287 The most important of these are the indoxyl and skatoxyl sulphates of potash.

indraft: see INDRAUGHT.

†**in'dragon**, *v. Obs. rare.* Also 7 en-. [f. IN-² + DRAGON *sb.*; cf. It. *indragare*, *indracare* (Florio, 1598).] *trans.* To convert into a dragon, invest with the form or character of a dragon.

1611 FLORIO, *Indracato*, endragoned, become a Dragon. *a* **1711** KEN *Hymnotheo* Poet. Wks. 1721 III. 208 Lucifer now in-dragon'd swell'd with Pride.

†**indrape**, *v. Obs.* [f. IN-² + DRAPE *v.* Cf. It. *indrappare* to put into clothes, OF. *endraper* to drape.] *trans.* To make into cloth; to weave.

1622 MALYNES *Anc. Law-Merch.* 56 An Epitome of all former Acts concerning the indraping of Wools. **1636** STRAFFORD *Lett.* (1739) II. 19 So long as they did not indrape their own Wools. **1778** *Phil. Surv. S. Irel.* 344 Suffering Ireland to indrap her own wool. **1843** MOZLEY *Ess.*, *Ld. Strafford* I. 42 England at present indraped Irish wools.

indraught, indraft (ˈɪndrɑːft, -æ-). [f. IN *adv.* 11 d + DRAUGHT: cf. *indrawn*, etc., and *draw in*, DRAW *v.* 82.]

1. The act of drawing in; inward attraction.

1682 SIR T. BROWNE *Chr. Mor.* III. §22 Having been long tossed in the ocean of this world, he will by that time feel the in-draught of another, unto which this seems but preparatory. **1697** DAMPIER *Voy.* I. 289 The Dutch call that part of this Coast, the Land of Indraught, (as if it magnetically drew Ships too fast to it). **1749** F. SMITH *Voy. Disc.* II. 267 Being also dubious as to the Indraught of the Fall, the Boats came to an Anchor. **1751** SMOLLETT *Per. Pic.* (1779) I. xviii. 166 Better be sucked into the gulph of Florida, than once get into the indraught of a woman. **1891** *Daily News* 7 Sept. 6/5 The indraft of the towns is irresistible, and usually in silence, but with decision, and 'for good', the capable young men abandon country labour.

2. An inward flow, stream, or current, as of water or air; *esp.* a current setting towards the land or up an estuary, etc.; a draught of air into a confined space; an influx, inrush.

1594 BLUNDEVIL *Exerc.* VII. liv. (1636) 744 The Sea wil flow more by one point of the Compasse in the spring-tides, .. in every River, that hath any indraft. **1598** HAKLUYT *Voy.* I. 122 Hee sayd that those foure Indraughts were drawne into an inward gulfe or whirlepoole, with so great a force, that the ships which once entred therein, could by no meanes be driuen backe againe. **1622** SIR R. HAWKINS *Voy. S. Sea* (1847) 141 In some bayes, where are great in-draughts, it [the tide] higheth eight or ten foote. **1719** DE FOE *Crusoe* I. iii, To avoid the Indraft of the Bay or Gulf of Mexico. **1794** G. ADAMS *Nat. & Exp. Philos.* I. iv. 102 The larger the fire, the sharper is the indraught of the air. **1853** KANE *Grinnell Exp.* vii. (1856) 54 The Esquimaux, too,.. assert the existence of a well-marked indraft. **1858** MAURY *Phys. Geog. Sea* v. §283 These indraughts are known as monsoons at sea; on the land, as the prevailing winds of the season.

b. *transf.* and *fig.*

1638 SIR R. COTTON *Abstr. Rec. Tower* 24 To abate the mighty indraught of Forraine Manufactures. **1851** RUSKIN *Stones Ven.* I. App. viii. 360 This indraught of the Lombard energies upon the Byzantine rest, like a wild north wind descending into a space of rarified atmosphere.

†**3.** A place where the water flows into the land; an inlet; an inward passage. *Obs.*

1570–6 LAMBARDE *Peramb. Kent* (1826) 234 Which betokeneth an Indraught (or Inlett) of water into the lande, out of, and besides the maine course, of the Sea, or of a River. **1665–6** *Phil. Trans.* I. 284 They have also vast In-draughts of some hundred Miles within Land. **1677** PLOT *Oxfordsh.* 30 The one..is received by a rocky subterraneous indraught, and appears no more. **1706** PHILLIPS, *Indraught*, a Gulph or Bay that runs in between two Lands.

†**b.** *fig.* 'Inlet; passage inwards' (J.). *Obs.*

a **1626** BACON (J.), Navigable rivers are indraughts to attain wealth.

4. Revenue, income; 'toll or duty collected at a port' (Jam.). *Sc. Obs.* [Cf. Sw. *indrägt* revenue, income, rent.]

1633 *Sc. Acts Chas. I* (1814) V. 93 Grantit..the port and harberie of the said burgh of Bruntiland callit the port of grace with the indraucht thairof and prymegilt of all shipes coming to the said port.

indraw (ɪn'drɔː), *v.* [f. IN-^{1} + DRAW *v.*] *trans.* To draw in.

See also M.E.D. *indrauen.*

1883 R. JEFFERIES *Story of my Heart* vii. 116 It is lying beside the immortals, in-drawing the life of the ocean, the earth, and the sun. **1887** G. MEREDITH *Ballads & Poems* 62 Fearful.. All their breath indrew. **1905** J. THORNTON in T. Stephens *Child & Religion* ix. 316 He [*sc.* Christ] 'indraws', and stores up in the interiors of the child's spirit all the good affections of innocence. **1911** W. OWEN *Let.* 17 Sept. (1967) 82 Depend upon it, whichever Fire indraws me, I shall.. come out unscathed.

'indraw, *sb. rare.* [f. IN *adv.* 11 d + DRAW *sb.*] The act of drawing in.

1899 A. C. LYALL *Asiatic Stud.* 2nd Ser. vii. 380 There has always been an indraw from the cool uplands..into the low-lying fertile regions.

indrawal ('ɪn,drɔːəl). *rare.* [f. IN *adv.* + DRAW *v.* + -AL^{1}, after *withdrawal.*] The act of drawing in: = INDRAUGHT 1.

1869 BLACKMORE *Lorna D.* viii. (1889) 50 Centred (as it might be) with a bottomless indrawal. **1884** PROCTOR in *Gd. Words* 110 The indrawal of water below the sea-floor.

indrawing ('ɪn,drɔːɪŋ), *vbl. sb.* [IN *adv.* 11 c.] The action of drawing in.

1398 TREVISA *Barth. De P.R.* III. xv[i]. (Add. MS. 27944) lf. 23/1 þe kepinge of þe kinde hete is a temperat indrawinge of coold aier. **1904** R. J. FARRER *Garden of Asia* xvi. 147 The frock-coated officials..bow with ceremonious reverence and indrawings of the breath. **1904** F. LYNDE *Grafters* xxii. 280 His smile was a mere indrawing of the lips.

'in,drawing, *ppl. a.* [IN *adv.* 11 a.] That draws in or inward.

1598 HAKLUYT *Voy.* I. 122 Purposely described all the Northerne Islands, with the indrawing seas. **1886** C. A. YOUNG in *New Princeton Rev.* Jan. 51 The moon is continually moving faster and faster, as if upon an indrawing spiral which ultimately would precipitate her upon the earth. **1892** TENNYSON *St. Telemachus*, Borne along by that full stream of men, Like some old wreck on some indrawing sea.

indrawn, *ppl. a.* [IN *adv.* 11 b.] Drawn in. **a.** as *adj.*, or before sb. ('ɪndrɔːn). Also *fig.*

1751 ELIZA HEYWOOD *Betsy Thoughtless* IV. 168 He stood undistinguished in the circle..with a kind of an indrawn reserve. **1810** SOUTHEY *Kehama* IV. v, She saw the start and shudder, She heard the in-drawn groan. **1856** MRS. BROWNING *Aur. Leigh* VI. 627 And then with indrawn steady utterance said. **1959** *Times* 10 Dec. 15/2 The father, quiet and indrawn. **1965** *New Statesman* 27 Aug. 298/2 His [*sc.* P. Maxwell Davies's] early, very Viennese *Piano Pieces*..have an indrawn intensity which we can accept as characteristic only in the light of later events.

b. as *pple.*, or after sb. (ɪn'drɔːn).

1865 SWINBURNE *Atalanta* 1336 With chin aslant indrawn to a tightening throat. **1878** B. TAYLOR *Deukalion* II. v. 91 With sight indrawn he sat, And seemed to listen.

†**in'dread,** *v. Obs. rare*$^{-1}$. [f. IN-^{1} + DREAD *v.* (Cf. *adread*, OE. *ondrǽdan.*)] To dread inwardly; to feel an inward or secret dread.

1584 HUDSON *Du Bartas' Judith* I. 57 So Isaaks sonnes indreading for to feel This tyrant, who pursued them at the heel, Dissundring fled.

†**in'drench,** *v. Obs.* Also 6–7 en-. [f. IN-^{2}, EN-^{1} + DRENCH *v.*] *trans.* To 'drench' or drown in something; to immerse. (Cf. DRENCH *v.* 2, 6.) Also *fig.*

1593 NASHE *Christ's T.* (1613) 44 My soule..will.. endrench mee in..dolour. **1606** SHAKS. *Tr. & Cr.* I. i. 51 Reply not in how many Fadomes deepe They lye indrench'd. **1609** JONES *Musicall Dreame* (T.), If in this flesh, where thou indrench'd dost lie, Poore soule, thou canst reare up thy limed wings. **1741** FENNING *Dict.*, *Indrench*, to soak; to drown.

‖**indri** ('ɪndrɪ). Also **indris**. [An erroneous application of the Malagasy exclamation *indry!* 'lo! behold!', or *indry izy!* 'there he is!', mistaken by the French naturalist Sonnerat for the name of the animal, when first seen by him *c* 1780: the only Malagasy name is *babakoto.* See quot. 1893.] A name given to the BABACOOTE, a lemurine animal of Madagascar (*Indris* or *Lichanotus brevicaudatus*), living in trees, with soft woolly hair, very long hind legs and very short tail.

1839 *Penny Cycl.* XIII. 461/2 The Indris are inhabitants of Madagascar. **1863** HUXLEY *Man's Place Nat.* II. 72 In that remarkable lemurine form, the Indri (*Lichanotus*), the leg is about as long as the spinal column, while the arm is not more than $\frac{11}{18}$ of its length. **1890** *Daily News* 5 Jan. 2/6 The avahi is still more nearly related to the indri, of which there is not a specimen in the Zoo. **1893** J. SIBREE in *Antananarivo Ann.* V. 83 Their native name is *Bàbakòto*, literally 'father-child' (or '-boy'), not *Indri*, as said by Sonnerat, who discovered the species.

†**'indried,** *ppl. a. Obs.* [IN *adv.* 11 b. ? transl. G. *eingetrocknet.*] Dried inwardly, desiccated.

1527 ANDREW *Brunswyke's Distyll. Waters* L vj, The same water is good for them that have an indryed nature and dystroyed.

indrunk ('ɪndrʌŋk), *ppl. a. rare.* [IN *adv.* 11 b.] Drunk in, imbibed.

1662 J. SPARROW tr. *Behme's Rem. Wks., 1st Apol. Balth. Tylcken* 23 It giveth forth that indrunk meek Spirit.

†**in'drunken,** *v. Obs.* In 4 in-dronkenen. [f. IN-^{1} + DRUNKEN *v.*, after L. *inēbriāre.*] *trans.* To make drunken, inebriate: in quot. *fig.*

a **1300** *E.E.Ps.* lxiv. 11 [lxv. 10] Brokes of it indronkenand [Vulg. *rivos ejus inebrians*].

indubious (ɪn'djuːbɪəs), *a.* [f. IN-^{3} + DUBIOUS; perh. after L. *indubius* not doubtful, certain.]

1. Not admitting of doubt; certain, clear, indubitable. Now *rare.*

1624 T. JAMES in *Ussher's Lett.* (1686) 319 The Decretals ..will make the matter indubious. **1753** SHUCKFORD *Creation* Pref. 73 To keep clear and indubious the Articles of our Faith. **1808** J. BARLOW *Columb.* VIII. 315 Gives each effect its own indubious cause. **1840** CLOUGH *Amours de Voyage* (1874) 238 Am I not free to attend for the ripe and indubious instinct?

†**2.** Feeling no doubt; free from doubt. *Obs.*

1665 G. HARVEY *Advice agst. Plague* 14 Hence appears the vulgar vanity, reposing an indubious confidence in a spoonful or two of those ordinary Antipestilential spirits.

Hence **in'dubiously** *adv.*, not doubtfully; clearly, certainly.

1642 SIR E. DERING *Sp. on Relig.* xvi. 75 Epistles that are indubiously his. *a* **1670** HACKET *Abp. Williams* I. (1692) 38 They that..were ripe and weighty in their answers, were indubiously designed to some place of credit and profit.

indubitable (ɪn'djuːbɪtəb(ə)l), *a.* (*sb.*) [a. F. *indubitable* (16th c.), or ad. L. *indubitābilis*: see IN-^{3} and DUBITABLE.] **a.** That cannot be doubted; perfectly certain or evident.

1625 CONWAY in *Howell's Lett.* I. IV. vii, Prince Charles, his rightful and indubitable Heir. **1678** CUDWORTH *Intell. Syst.* I. v. 716 Whensoever any thing is thus necessarily inferred, from what is undeniable and indubitable, this is a Demonstration. **1725** WATTS *Logic* II. ii. §7 Those Propositions, which contain the most certain and indubitable Truths. **1775** JOHNSON *Tax. no Tyr.* 13 That the Americans are able to bear taxation, is indubitable. **1871** BLACKIE *Four Phases* I. 127 Evidence of the most distinct and indubitable description.

b. *absol.* as *sb.* An indubitable thing or fact.

1733 WATTS *Philos. Ess.* Pref. ¶6 A few Indubitables.

Hence **in'dubitableness**, the quality of being without any doubt. Also **indubita'bility** = INDUBITABLENESS.

1727 in BAILEY vol. II. **1849** *Fraser's Mag.* XL. 522 Receiving indubitableness, not from this world, but..from the sure and certain truth of the life to come. **1933** *Mind* XLII. 531 Even if Husserl's argument concerning the indubitability of transcendental selves be granted, it does not follow [etc.]. **1946** *Nature* 10 Aug. 185/2 There remains a residuum of indubitability consisting of our sensations themselves and the ultimate elements of rational necessity.

indubitably (ɪn'djuːbɪtəblɪ), *adv.* [f. prec. + -LY^{2}.] Beyond the possibility of doubt; unquestionably; without any doubt.

1624 WOTTON *Archit.* in *Reliq.* (1672) 34 There will indubitably result from either a gracefull and harmonious contentment to the Eye. **1646** SIR T. BROWNE *Pseud. Ep.* VII. xviii. 382 Whereunto neither can we indubitably assent. **1761** STERNE *Tr. Shandy* III. xx, Parts..indubitably both made and fitted to go together. **1873** M. ARNOLD *Lit. & Dogma* (1876) 198 The way of the Eternal was most indubitably a way of peace and joy.

†**in'dubitate,** *a. Obs.* [ad. L. *indubitāt-us*, f. *in-* (IN-^{3}) + *dubitāt-us*, pa. pple. of *dubitāre* to DOUBT.] Undoubted, certain.

1480 CAXTON *Chron. Eng.* ccxlix. (1482) 318 Eugenye the fourth was pesybly chosen in rome by the Cardynals, and was very and indubytate pope. **1494** FABYAN *Chron.* V. cxxiii. 101 He shuld there shewe and proue yᵗ he was the indubitat sone of yᵉ first Clothayre. **1548** HALL *Chron., Hen. V* 73 The very indubitate heyre general to the crowne of Fraunce. **1678** CUDWORTH *Intell. Syst.* I. iv. §16. 281 Such Monuments of Pagan Antiquity, as are altogether unsuspected and indubitate.

Hence †**in'dubitately** *adv.*, undoubtedly, unquestionably, without doubt.

1538 LELAND *Itin.* I. 92 Howbeit the hole Chirch that now standith indubitately was made sins the Conquest. **1661** GLANVILL *Van. Dogm.* xxiii. 227 They..are indubitately assur'd of the Truth, and comparative excellency of their receptions.

†**in'dubitate,** *v.*^{1} *Obs. rare.* [f. IN-^{2} + L. *dubitāt-us* doubted: see prec.] *trans.* To render doubtful or uncertain; to call in question.

1646 SIR T. BROWNE *Pseud. Ep.* I. x. 42 He [the Devil] would make men beleeve there is no such creature as himselfe..and contriveth accordingly many wayes to conceale or indubitate his existency. **1660** tr. *Amyraldus' Treat. conc. Relig.* III. ix. 502 He..might with good reason be judg'd troublesome and impertinent for indubitating a thing of so constant credit.

†**in'dubitate,** *v.*^{2} *Obs. rare*$^{-0}$. [f. IN-^{3} + L. *dubitāre* to doubt; cf. DUBITATE *v.*] 'To doubt nothing at all' (Cockeram, 1623).

†**indubi'tation.** *Obs. rare*$^{-0}$. [IN-^{3}.] 'A not doubting, a yielding for certain' (Phillips, 1658).

in'dubitatively, *adv. rare.* [IN-^{3}.] Indubitably.

a **1853** WARDLAW *Lect. James* xii. (1869) 186 A case most clearly and indubitatively decisive of the point. **1898** W. J. LOCKE *Idols* 284 But it was for her happiness. Indubitatively.

induce (ɪn'djuːs), *v.* Forms: α. 4–8 enduce, 6 enduse. β. 5– induce, (6 induse, induice). [ad. L. *indūcĕre* to lead into, to introduce, etc., f. *in-* (IN-^{2}) + *dūcĕre* to lead. In early use the prefix was commonly assimilated to that of OF. *enduire* (pres. subj. *enduise*): see ENDUE. The L. verb developed a number of special senses, some of which are represented by obsolete uses in English.]

1. *trans.* To lead (a person), by persuasion or some influence or motive that acts upon the will, *to* (†*into*, †*unto*) some action, condition, belief, etc.; to lead on, move, influence, prevail upon (any one) *to do* something. **a.** Of persons, personal action, influence, etc.

α. *c* **1375** *Sc. Leg. Saints, Egipciane* 562 Al vthyr als, þat I mycht enduce to þat foly. *Ibid., Baptista* 773 þe caynis bruthire..with cristine wes enducyt sa þat he baptysme can haly ta. **1494** FABYAN *Chron.* V. xcvii. 71 She lafte nat to enduce and tourne her Lord to the faith in all that she myght. **1523** LD. BERNERS *Froiss.* I. cclxxii. 408 He..sayd, he wolde go himselfe to Angolesme to the prince, and to the lordes that be ther, trustyng to..enduse them. **1533** MORE *Answ. Poysoned Bk.* Wks. 1044/2 To enduce theym the better to the beliefe of his great kindnes. **1633** T. STAFFORD *Pac. Hib.* II. xxiii. (1810) 432 Willingly enduced for just respects, to disengage themselves.

β. *c* **1440** *Jacob's Well* (E.E.T.S.) 199 Ful perylous it is to inducyn & steryn an-oþer to synne. **1480** CAXTON *Chron. Eng.* VI. (1520) 67 b/1 He induced the noble men to swere that..they sholde chese Octavianus his sone pope. **1490** —— *Eneydos* xxiv. 90 She can not by no wyse induce herselfe to gyue a reste vnto her eyen by a lityll slepe. **1531** ELYOT *Gov.* I. v, To induce them in-to a contention with their inferiour companions. **1551** ROBINSON tr. *More's Utopia* II. ix. (1895) 272 If he coulde not by fayre and gentle speche induce them vnto his opinion. **1607** SHAKS. *Cor.* I. ix. 16, I haue done as you haue done..Induc'd as you haue beene. **1613** PURCHAS *Pilgrimage* (1614) 159 Hee perswaded them for the space of a whole yeare..and at last induced them to leave their riches..and to follow him. **1647** CLARENDON *Hist. Reb.* I. §3, I have the more willingly induced myself to this unequal task, out of the hope of contributing somewhat to that blessed end. **1679** *Animadv. Sp. 5 Jesuits* 20 That Prince..who induces his Subjects into Heresie. **1793** BURKE *Conduct Minority* Wks. 1842 I. 620 To induce us to this, Mr. Fox laboured hard to make it appear [etc.]. **1839** BAILEY *Festus* xvii. (1852) 223 Where is the spirit which induced me here? **1864** LOWELL *Fireside Trav.* 266 To induce settlers upon territory of such uninhabitable quality. **1878** R. W. DALE *Lect. Preach.* ix. 279 You should try by gentle means to induce the people to make a change.

b. Of things, circumstances, or considerations. (Also *absol.*, without personal object expressed.)

1430–40 LYDG. *Bochas* VI. i. (1554) 145 b, People of Grece, of Rome and of Chartage..Were indused by swetenes of language To haue together their conversacion. **1513** MORE in Grafton *Chron.* (1568) II. 778 The thing that enduced him to be..one of the speciallest contrivers of all this horrible treason. *c* **1530** *Pol. Rel. & L. Poems* (1866) 31 Let necessite induce the therto. **1581** J. BELL *Haddon's Answ. Osor.* 76 Many men were wonderfully enriched by your Canons: but very fewe enduced to have any especiall regarde to feare God by yᵉ knowledge of them. **1607** ROWLANDS *Guy Warw.* 74 There to be buried where he had been born, Was all the cause that did induce him back. **1654** GATAKER *Disc. Apol.* 73, I make no doubt, but that manie Points and Practises in Poperie..induce millions unto Atheism. **1662** STILLINGFL. *Orig. Sacr.* III. i. §1 If I have not a soul of an immortal nature, there can bee no sufficient..motive inducing to it [religion]. **1720** WATERLAND *Eight Serm.* 254 Where an Argument is drawn from the natural and necessary Perfections of God, to induce us to some faint resemblance and imitation of them. **1796** H. HUNTER tr. *St.-Pierre's Stud. Nat.* (1799) II. 263 These considerations induce me to believe [etc.]. **1871** YEATS *Techn. Hist. Comm.* 427 The demands for food, clothing, fuel and shelter have induced men to labour.

†**c.** *ellipt.* To lead to the belief or opinion (*that*); to persuade. *Obs. rare.*

1655 in Hartlib *Ref. Commw. Bees* 21 And that out of Kine, either strangled, or otherwise dying, and so lying abroad, exposed to the influence of the Heavens, Bees naturally will not spring, I am induced.

2. a. To bring in, introduce (a practice, condition, state of things, custom, law, etc.). Const. *into. Obs.* or blended with 4.

1401 *Pol. Poems* (Rolls) II. 51 Ȝour daliaunce inducit ire and envie. **1432–50** tr. *Higden* (Rolls) I. 251 From the cite made unto clx. yere folowenge was movede noo diuorce. The firste man inducenge hit was callede Carbilius. **1485**

Paston Lett. No. 883 III. 318 The seid Henry Tidder.. entendith also..to enduce and establisse newe lawes and ordenaunces amongez the Kynggs seid subjetts. **1548** HALL *Chron., Hen. V* 65 b, He doubted not but by his onely meanes, peace should be induced. **1589** PUTTENHAM *Eng. Poesie* II. xii[i.]. (Arb.) 127 By some leasurable trauell it were no hard matter to induce all their auncient feete into vse with vs. **1630** WADSWORTH *Pilgr.* iii. 30 The first that induced this Order of Nunnes, was Father Gerard. *a* **1652** BROME *Love sick Court* v. iii, If you think it meet, I will induce The practise of it presently. **1802** PALEY *Nat. Theol.* iv. (1819) 50 Occasional irregularities may subsist in a considerable degree, without inducing any doubt into the question. **1836** SIR W. HAMILTON *Discuss., Stud. Math.* (1852) 269 To induce that numb rigidity into our intellectual life.

†**b.** To introduce, insert (a material thing).

c **1420** *Pallad. on Husb.* VI. 80 Into a potte of erthe enduce a floure Vppon his bough doun bounden ther to dwelle.

†**c.** To introduce, bring in, present (a person).

1534 MORE *Comf. agst. Trib.* II. Wks. 1196/2 S. James exhorteth men yᵗ they shall in their bodely sickenes induce the priestes. **1605** B. JONSON *Masque Blackness* Wks. (Rtldg.) 544/2 These [Oceanus and Niger] induced the masquers, which were twelve nymphs. *a* **1652** BROME *Queen & Concubine* I. iii, My last command, which was Never to see the court till I induc'd you.

†**d.** To introduce or bring in as a character or speaker in a literary work. *Obs.*

1484 CAXTON *Fables of Æsop* Pref., Esope..induceth the byrdes, the trees and the beestes spekynge. **1534** WHITINTON *Tullyes Offices* III. (1540) 135 Tully..induceth two of Socrates secte of dyuers opinyons. **1558** KNOX *First Blast* (Arb.) 24 In an other place he induceth God speaking to the woman in this sorte. **1613** PURCHAS *Pilgrimage* (1614) 250 The rest are all delivered as the wordes of God; hee being induced as speaker. *a* **1744** POPE (J.), The poet may be seen inducing his personages in the first Iliad.

†**e.** To introduce, bring in, bring forward, by way of illustration or argument; to adduce, quote.

1433 LYDG. *S. Fremund* 70 Now purposyng..[to] Induce a story longyng to this mater. **1523** SKELTON *Garl. Laurel* 94 Ovyde was bannisshed for his skill And many mo whome I cowde enduce. **1563–87** FOXE *A. & M.* (1684) II. 44/2 Long it were to induce here all Prophesies that be read in Histories. **1581** *Satir. Poems Reform.* xliii. 89 Sum auld exemples heir I man induce, To bring my purpose to more speciall. **1605** VERSTEGAN *Dec. Intell.* i. (1628) 10 All which may enduce sufficient reasons to thinke him their first chiefe. **1646** SIR T. BROWNE *Pseud. Ep.* III. xxv. §3. 173 To exprobrate their Stupiditie, he induceth the providence of Storkes. Now if the bird had been unknown, the illustration had been obscure.

†**3. a.** To introduce or bring (a person) into the knowledge of something; to initiate, instruct. *Obs.*

c **1477** CAXTON *Jason* 70 b, The sage and wisemen shal enduce and teche the rude peple and harde of entendement. **1483** —— *Gold. Leg.* 333/2 He was..wel lerned and enduced in the sacrefyses and werkes of the temple. **1511–12** *Act 3 Hen. VIII*, c. 3 §1 Every man hauynge..men children.. shall provyde..a bowe and ij shaftes to enduse and lern theym and bryng them uppe in shotyng.

†**b.** To introduce *to* a subject or study; to initiate *into*; to habituate or accustom *to*. *Obs.*

1490 CAXTON *Eneydos* xxi. 77, I requyre only that he putte this thyng in delaye, for a certayn Space of tyme, Duryng the whiche I may induce my self to sorow. **1534** MORE *Treat. Passion* Wks. 1330/1 Inducyng them into the communyon of the Sacramentes. **1556** WITHALS *Dict.* Prol., A thinge written by me to induce children to the latin tongue. **1561** DAUS tr. *Bullinger on Apoc.* Pref. (1573) 1 The holy Ghost beyng sent to his Apostles, induced them into all truthe.

4. a. To bring about, bring on, produce, cause, give rise to. Now widespread in technical contexts, freq. with a concrete or material obj. rather than an abstract one.

1413 *Pilgr. Sowle* (Caxton 1483) v. xiv. 107 Euery thyng that werketh naturelly..enduceth the fourme of it seluen. **1432–50** tr. *Higden* (Rolls) I. 73 That grauntede, that place scholde induce otherwhile the eclipse of the moone. **1523** FITZHERB. *Husb.* §164 If thou forgyue not the wronge done vnto the..thou enduces goddes curse to fall vpon yᵉ. **1555** EDEN *Decades* 267 The Scythian wyll accuse the Romane heauen as induceinge feuers. **1676** HALE *Contempl.* I. 334 There are two things that induce the loss of friends. **1710** PRIDEAUX *Orig. Tithes* i. 7 This induceth a necessity of coming to a positive institution. **1780** HARRIS *Philol. Enq.* Wks. (1841) 462, I mean gentle walking without inducing fatigue. **1831** BREWSTER *Optics* xxviii. 241 The phenomena are related to the shape of the mass in which the change is induced. **1859** LANG *Wand. India* 355 Agricultural improvement would induce lasting and increasing prosperity of the cultivating classes. **1874** CARPENTER *Ment. Phys.* I. i. §27 (1879) 27 Such automatic states..may be artificially induced. **1928** *Biol. Abstr.* II. 686/2 In the early gastrula stage the whole quadrant lying above the blastopore is capable of inducing formation of a new embryonic axis. **1931** J. NEEDHAM *Chem. Embryol.* I. 579 A piece of the brain of a free-swimming larva would still induce a medullary plate in the early embryo. **1941** *Jrnl. Nat. Cancer Inst.* (U.S.) II. 199/2 Whether carbon tetrachloride is the active agent in inducing hepatomas in mice or whether these tumors are merely the result of hepatic damage caused by carbon tetrachloride awaits further study. **1947** *Growth* XI. 228 Fifty-two compounds..were tested for their activity in inducing pectinase production. **1953** *Cold Spring Harbor Symp. Quant. Biol.* XVIII. 101/2 The transition from the prophage to the vegetative state can therefore be induced with a probability of nearly 1. **1968** *Ann. Rev. Nuclear Sci.* XVIII. 343 (*heading*) Compound nuclear reactions induced by heavy ions. **1969** *Times* 9 June 2/1 How then do D.N.A. viruses induce interferon in the cell? **1971** tr. *S.E. Bresler's Introd. Molecular Biol.* v. 487 The existence of compounds that repress and induce the formation of enzymes provides direct evidence that regulatory mechanisms are present. **1973** *Nature* 12 Jan. 132/1 Bachem..induced cataracts in guinea-pigs and rabbits with ultraviolet light. **1973** *Ibid.* 9 Feb. 367/1 Whereas ^{224}Ra with a short 3·8 day half life induces in man chiefly osteosarcomas, ^{226}Ra with a half life of 1,620 years induces both osteo and fibrosarcomas.

b. *spec.* To produce (an electric current or magnetic state) by induction: see INDUCTION 10.

1777 T. CAVALLO *Compl. Treat. Electr.* IV. iv. 384 The action of these plates depends upon a principle long ago discovered, viz. the power that an excited electric has to induce a contrary Electricity in a body brought within its sphere of action. **1812** [see INDUCED *ppl. a.* 1 a]. **1832** [see INDUCTION 10]. **1839** G. BIRD *Nat. Philos.* 266 A current traversing a wire induces a secondary one in a wire parallel to it. **1855** H. M. NOAD *Man. Electr.* I. 44 The electricity of *e* induces a change in the electric state of *dc*. **1892** S. P. THOMPSON *Dynamo-Elect. Mach.* (ed. 4) 30 To induce currents in a conductor, there must be a relative motion between conductor and magnet, of such a kind as to alter the number of lines of force embraced in the circuit.

c. To bring on as a state or condition. Const. *upon.*

1857–8 SEARS *Athan.* xi. 97 This dim and sleepy life is induced upon us that we may not know at the beginning all that we are. **1863** E. V. NEALE *Anal. Th. & Nat.* 65 We induce upon the new individual the result of our observation of past individuals.

d. To initiate (labour) artificially. Cf. INDUCTION 9.

1852 *Lancet* 2 Oct. 297/2 Under these circumstances, a new method of inducing premature labour..cannot fail of being recognised by obstetricians as a great boon. **1916** G. P. SHEARS *Obstetrics* xxvi. 573 Manual dilatation is not in itself a method of inducing labor, but it is sometimes most valuable in accelerating the progress of labor. **1968** D. C. BETHEA *Introd. Maternity Nursing* ix. 121 The mother who is to have labor induced may feel uneasy... She is likely to want to know if her labor will be longer, harder, or more painful because it is induced.

e. *Biol.* To cause (a bacterium containing a prophage) to begin the lytic cycle.

Quots. 1950, 1951 illustrate the origin of this use in sense 4 a (*induce* = produce, cause).

[**1950** A. LWOFF et al. in *Ann. de l'Inst. Pasteur* LXXIX. 833 Nous avons induit la lyse de la totalité des bactéries d'une culture de *B. megatherium*. **1951** *Jrnl. Bacteriol.* LXII. 317 Maturation from prophage into phage can be induced in every bacterium of a culture of K12 by irradiation with small doses of ultraviolet rays (Lwoff effect).] **1953** *Cold Spring Harbor Symp. Quant. Biol.* XVIII. 104/1 In order to be induced to the same extent, cultures of *B. megatherium* in minimal medium require a dose of ultraviolet light 20 times greater than cultures in yeast extract. **1959** JACOB & WOLLMAN in Burnet & Stanley *Viruses* II. ix. 332 When..inducible lysogenic bacteria are first induced and then infected with an adequate multiplicity of a mutant of the homologous phage, each bacterium releases particles of the prophage as well as of the mutant type. **1962** *Nature* 24 Nov. 783/2 Certain antitumour agents are capable of inducing lysogenic bacteria. **1970** *Jrnl. Virol.* V. 240/2 When an intermediate amount of mitomycin C (1 μg/ml) was also used to induce the culture in addition to thymine deprivation, the production of PBLB was almost doubled.

†**5.** To lead to (something) as a conclusion or inference; to lead one to infer; to suggest, imply. *Obs.*

1481 CAXTON *Tulle on Old Age* A v (R. Suppl.), Notable examples to induce the soul to be perpetuel and most lyght and parfyght. **1581** SAVILE *Tacitus, Agricola* (1622) 188 The coloured countenances of the Silures..seeme to induce, that the old Spaniards passed the Sea and possessed those places. **1601** R. JOHNSON *Kingd. & Commw.* (1603) 58 Which are reasons sufficient to induce, that in his gulfe..he hath small means to rig out any. ? *a* **1624** SWINBURNE *Spousals* (1686) 72 The sixth Limitation is, When as by common use of Speech the words induce Matrimony. **1646** SIR T. BROWNE *Pseud. Ep.* IV. x. 201 That an unsavoury odour is gentilitious or nationall unto the Jews,..we cannot well concede, nor will the information of reason or sense induce it.

6. To infer; *esp.* in recent use, to infer by reasoning from particular facts to general principles; to derive as an induction.

1563 W. FULKE *Meteors* II. (1655) 34 If it were lawfull to reason of this sort we might enduce them to betoken not only these few things, but all other things that chance in the world. **1583** FULKE *Defence* xii. (Parker Soc.) 424 He hath already given you a sufficient reason to induce, that the apostle speaketh not of faith as generally as of knowledge. **1667** *Decay Chr. Piety* viii. ¶41 'Twould be hard to discern, how from different premisses the same conclusion should be induced. **1855** MISS COBBE *Intuit. Mor.* 45 *note*, We obtain a multitude of contingent truths..and from these we induce the general proposition. **1888** *Science* Dec. 304 From a sufficient number of results a proposition or law is induced.

†**7.** To draw (something) on or over; to put on or overspread as a covering or the like. Const. *on, upon, over. Obs.*

1567 DRANT *Horace, Ep.* xvi. E viij, Beduske my fraude withe cloudes, my sinnes, Induce on theym a night. **1588** J. READ *Compend. Method* 69 Dura mater, which had begun.. to induce flesh, had induced so beyond all measure [etc.]. **1667** MILTON *P.L.* VI. 408 Now Night her course began, and over Heav'n Inducing darkness, grateful truce impos'd. **1708** J. PHILIPS *Cyder* I. (R.), There are, who, fondly studious of increase, Rich foreign mould on their ill-natur'd land Induce laborious. **1784** COWPER *Task* I. 32 And o'er the seat, with plenteous wadding stuff'd, Induc'd a splendid cover.

induceable, obs. variant of INDUCIBLE.

induced (ɪn'djuːst), *ppl. a.* [f. INDUCE *v.* + -ED¹.]

1. a. Brought on, caused, or produced, by attraction, persuasion, etc. (see esp. INDUCE *v.* 4 b); ***induced current***, an electric current excited by INDUCTION (sense 10). Also, affected by induction as ***induced magnet***. More widely (in sense 4 of the vb.), caused or brought into being artificially or by some extraneous agent or process; not spontaneous (cf. INDUCTION 9).

1611 COTGR., *Meu*,..also induced, inclined, persuaded. **1652** NEEDHAM tr. *Selden's Mare Cl.* 21 Som deriving the Dominion of the Republick over the Sea from Custom, som from prescription, others from an induced subjection. **1812** SIR H. DAVY *Chem. Philos.* 133 The conductor, which is thus affected by induced electricity. **1830** HERSCHEL *Stud. Nat. Phil.* 324 The phenomena of the communication of magnetism and what is called its induced state, alone remain unaccounted for. **1852** GROVE *Contrib. Sc.* in *Corr. Phys. Forces* (1874) 359 The ordinary plan for producing an induced current. **1874** CARPENTER *Ment. Phys.* I. ix. §2 (1879) 393 The essential feature..of natural and induced Reverie. **1922** C. C. VAN BLARCOM *Obstetr. Nursing* xiii. 309 Induced abortion applies to the termination of pregnancy before the child is viable,..and is performed solely in the interests of the mother, as the fetus is always lost. **1929** *Biol. Abstr.* III. 1495/2 The distal skeleton of the induced limbs might be normal. **1941** *Jrnl. Nat. Cancer Inst.* II. 198/2 The incidence of spontaneous hepatomas..is decidely below that of the induced tumors in our experimental animals. **1947** *Growth* XI. 225 (*heading*) The occurrence of substrate-induced enzyme formation. **1960** B. I. BALINSKY *Introd. Embryol.* vi. 168 In other experiments the whole of the induced neural tube was developed exclusively from host tissue. **1962** H. D. BUSH *Atomic & Nucl. Physics* v. 105 (*heading*) Induced nuclear transmutations. **1970** G. K. WOODGATE *Elem. Atomic Struct.* iii. 32 Three radiation processes are postulated: spontaneous emission,.. absorption,..and induced emission.

b. ***induced (radio)activity***, radioactivity brought about in otherwise non-radioactive material by its transformation under bombardment or irradiation or by the proximity of radioactive material.

[**1899** P. & M. CURIE in *Compt. Rend.* CXXIX. 714 Nous avons constaté que les rayons émis par ces matières, en agissant sur des substances inactives, peuvent leur communiquer la radioactivité, et que cette radioactivité induite persiste pendant un temps assez long.] **1900** RUTHERFORD in *Phil. Mag.* XLIX. 169 Two or three layers of ordinary foolscap-paper completely cut off the ordinary radiation given out by thorium compounds, but do not much diminish the amount of induced radio-activity. **1904** F. SODDY *Radio-Activity* ii. 33 With the power of a radio-active element to produce a radio-active emanation is bound up its power to impart radio-activity to objects in the neighbourhood. Rutherford discovered this property for the thorium emanation, and designated it the excited activity. M. and Mme. Curie..called it the induced activity. **1913** [see EXCITED *ppl. a.* 2 d]. **1926** R. W. LAWSON tr. *Hevesy & Paneth's Man. Radioactivity* viii. 90 Before the material nature of the active deposit had been recognised, it was customary to call the activity acquired by bodies that had been in contact with emanation by the name of 'induced activity'. **1963** B. FOZARD *Instrumentation Nucl. Reactors* i. 7 When the irradiated material is removed from the neutron flux the induced activity is measured. **1966** *McGraw-Hill Encycl. Sci. & Technol.* XI. 277/2 The yield of any induced radioactivity is the initial rate of production of the activity under the particular conditions of nuclear bombardment.

2. *Biol.* Of a bacterium: that has been induced (see INDUCE *v.* 4 e).

1951 *Jrnl. Bacteriol.* LXII. 305 The induced bacteria double in length and thickness..between irradiation and lysis. **1963** G. S. STENT *Molecular Biol. Bacterial Viruses* xii. 312 There is little doubt..that the phages are liberated by lysis of the induced lysogenic cells. **1970** *Jrnl. Virol.* V. 244/2 After mitomycin C treatment, DNA continues to be synthesized by the induced bacterium.

3. Special comb.: ***induced drag***, that part of the drag on an aircraft or aerofoil which arises from the development of lift; ***induced draught***, a draught towards a fan or other device that draws air through a furnace, up a chimney, etc.; ***induced reaction***, a chemical reaction that is accelerated by the presence of an inductor (see INDUCTOR 4) that reacts with one of the reactants.

1926 H. GLAUERT *Elem. Aerofoil & Airscrew Theory* x. 132 The lift force is..inclined backwards at the small angle ..and therefore gives a component in the direction of the drag force. This component is called the *induced drag, since it is caused by the induced velocity of the trailing vortices. **1931**, **1948** [see DRAG *sb.* 7 e]. **1962** F. I. ORDWAY et al. *Basic Astronautics* viii. 340 There are three basic types of aerodynamics drag: skin-friction drag, form drag, and induced drag. **1887** W. A. MARTIN in *Trans. Soc. Engin. 1886* 117 In comparing the three systems, of ordinary draught, forced draught, and the author's *induced draught,..it is necessary to say [etc.]. **1894** *Westm. Gaz.* 29 Dec. 3/2 The other improvement is that of induced—instead of forced—draught. **1971** *Sci. Amer.* May 73/3 In a forced-draft [cooling] tower the fan is at the bottom and pushes the air up through the tower; in an induced-draft tower the fan is at the top and pulls the air up. **1903** *Jrnl. Chem. Soc.* LXXXIV. II. 277 The reaction between bromic and sulphurous acids is the primary spontaneous reaction; and that between bromic and arsenious acids is the secondary *induced reaction. **1917** *Ibid.* CXI. I. 702 In all the experiments on induced reactions recorded above, the oxidising agents take part and are themselves reduced during the chemical change. **1964** J. R. PARTINGTON *Hist. Chem.* IV. vi. 194 Closely related to the subject of autoxidation is that of induced reactions.

inducement (ɪn'djuːsmənt). Also 7–8 **en-**. [f. as prec. + -MENT.]

†**1.** The action of inducing or moving by persuasion or influence. *Obs.*

1601 SHAKS. *All's Well* III. ii. 91 A verie tainted fellow, and full of wickednesse, My sonne corrupts a well deriued nature With his inducement. **1648** MILTON *Observ. Art.*

Peace Wks. (1851) 569 And this in all likelihood by the inducement and instigation of these Representers.

2. That which induces; something attractive by which a person is led on or persuaded to action.

1594 SHAKS. *Rich. III*, IV. iv. 279 If this inducement moue her not to loue Send her a Letter of thy Noble deeds. **1632** A. GROSSE (*title*) Sweet and Sowle-Perswading inducements, leading unto Christ. **1687** DRYDEN *Hind & P.* II. 673 Coarse diet, and a short repast..were weak inducements to the taste Of one so nicely bred. **1746** MELMOTH tr. *Pliny's Lett.* I. xii, Corellius had many inducements to be fond of life. **1779** F. HERVEY *Nav. Hist.* II. 129 As an enducement for people to bring them in their cash, these goldsmiths paid at the rate of fourpence a day per cent. **1818** JAS. MILL *Brit. India* II. v. vi. 579 Nor can the pleasure of exercising unbounded sway..be justly regarded as a feeble inducement. **1867** SMILES *Huguenots Eng.* Pref. (1880) 6 The English kings..held out repeated inducements to foreign artisans to come over and settle in this country.

†**b.** More widely: Any ground or reason which leads or inclines one to a belief or course of action; a moving cause; an incentive. *Obs.*

1594 HOOKER *Eccl. Pol.* II. v. §7 Many inducements besides Scripture may lead me to that, which if Scripture be against, they all..are of no value, yet otherwise are strong and effectual to persuade. **1601** R. JOHNSON *Kingd. & Commw.* (1603) 175 These reasons I take to be a sufficient inducement to beleeve these reports. **1691** T. H[ALE] *Acc. New Invent.* 11 Grounded this their sentence upon no other Inducements..than the particulars of Complaint accompanying the said Report.

†**c.** Something that leads to a result; an operative cause. *Obs.*

1605 BACON *Adv. Learn.* I. vii. §6 It pleased God..to use the curiosity of this emperor as an inducement to the peace of his Church in those days.

†**3.** A preamble or introduction to a book or subject. *Obs.*

1605 BACON *Adv. Learn.* II. xxiii. §6 Formal speakers, that study more about prefaces and inducements, than upon the conclusions and issues of speech. *a* **1617** HIERON *Wks.* (1619) II. 446 An introduction and inducement to that which is now to bee taught.

b. *Law.* (See quot. 1891).

1792 in Addison *Pennsylv. Rep.* (1800) 37 (Porter *v.* Brown), The date of the bond is immaterial and the bond itself but matter of inducement. **1891** W. B. ODGERS *Pleading*, Matters of inducement are Introductory averments stating who the parties are, how connected and other surrounding circumstances leading up to the matter in dispute, but not stating such matter.

†**4.** A leading on to some conclusion or inference; that which leads to a conclusion. *Obs.*

1646 SIR T. BROWNE *Pseud. Ep.* I. vii. 25 Having received the probable inducements of truth, we become emancipated from testimoniall engagements, and are to erect upon the surer base of reason. *Ibid.*, It carrieth not, with it, the reasonable inducements of knowledge.

inducer (ɪn'djuːsə(r)). [f. as prec. + -ER¹.]

1. One who or that which induces, persuades, or leads on (*to* some act, conduct, opinion, etc.).

1554 MARTIN *Marr. Priests* C iij b (T.), How can he be a mete perswader or inducer of the people to widowheade, which hath himselfe been often maried? **1624** R. B. in *F. White's Repl. Fisher* App. 25 Euerie thing that is the first Inducer to beleeue is not by and by..the principall Motiue. *a* **1716** SOUTH *Serm.* (1744) VIII. iv. 85 As if he [God] were the great impeller and inducer of men to sin. **1799** E. DU BOIS *Piece Fam. Biog.* III. 159 Grief is perhaps a greater inducer to invoke the muse than joy.

2. a. One who or that which introduces or brings in or on (some state or condition). *rare* except in scientific contexts.

a **1631** DONNE *Serm.* ciii. I. 387 And yet..this Messenger of Satan was..a forerunner and some kind of inducer of that Grace which was sufficient for him. **1833** MRS. BROWNING *Prometh. Bound* Wks. 1850 I. 160, I..devised for them Number, the inducer of philosophies. **1970** *Sci. Jrnl.* June 70/1 Corticine favours the development of the cortex and inhibits the medulla while medullarine has the opposite effect. These inducers, as they are called, also impose ovogonial or spermatogonial development upon the germ cells. **1971** *New Scientist* 24 June 745/2 Consistency is maintained by several indications..that prostaglandins are potent inducers of fever. **1971** *Sci. Amer.* July 27/3 The search for inducers..turned up many different kinds of substances that stimulated interferon production in animals. These included bacteria, parasites, viruses, polysaccharides, ..and other substances.

b. *Biochem.* Any substance (freq. the substrate of the enzyme concerned) whose presence results in (increased) production of an enzyme. (Cf. INDUCTION 9c.)

1953 [see INDUCTION 9c]. **1959** *Jrnl. Molecular Biol.* I. 175 When inducer is added at this stage, enzyme synthesis is resumed. **1971** J. Z. YOUNG *Introd. Study Man* iii. 54 The action of the inducer (lactose) is to inactivate the repressor.

†**in'duces**, *sb. pl. Obs. rare*⁻¹. [a. OF. *induces*, ad. L. *indūciæ*: see next.] Respite, truce.

1490 CAXTON *Eneydos* viii. 34 She..demaunded Induces and space of thre monethes, In which tyme she sholde doo her dylygence for to accomplysshe alle theyr wylles.

‖**induciæ** (ɪn'djuːsiiː, -ʃiiː), *sb. pl. Sc. Law.* [L. *indūciæ, -dūtiæ* truce, delay, *indūciæ legālēs* legal delay.] The space of time intervening between the citation of a defendant and the day fixed for his appearance in the action or process.

1752 J. LOUTHIAN *Form of Process* (ed. 2) 256 Such *induciæ* as the Sheriff shall think proper. **1861** W. BELL *Dict. Law Scot.* 443/1 The *induciæ* of criminal letters and indictments are fifteen days. **1868** *Act 31 & 32 Vict.* c. 100 §14 All summonses..may proceed on seven days warning or induciæ where the defender is within Scotland.

†**in'duciary**, *a. Obs. rare.* [ad. med.L. *indūciāri-us*, f. *indūciæ*: see prec.] 'Pertaining to truce or league' (Blount *Glossogr.* 1656).

inducibility (ɪndjuːsɪ'bɪlɪtɪ). [f. INDUCIBLE *a.*: see -IBILITY.] The property or state of being inducible; *spec.* in *Biochem.* (see INDUCIBLE *a.* 1 c).

1953 COHN, MONOD, et al. in *Nature* 12 Dec. 1096/2 Thus 'constitutivity' and 'inducibility' are properties of enzyme-forming systems, not of enzymes *per se*, and can be used as significant expressions only in a biological frame of reference, not in a chemical one. It should be stressed that the notions of constitutivity and inducibility are relative, not absolute; in any given biological system, a certain fraction of a particular enzyme-forming capacity may be constitutive, the remaining fraction inducible. For the sake of convenience, one may wish to refer to 'an induced enzyme' or to 'a constitutive enzyme'; but it should always be kept in mind that these are shorthand expressions for 'an enzyme the formation of which is largely or entirely inducible (or constitutive) in the particular organism concerned'. **1959** *Jrnl. Molecular Biol.* I. 165 (*heading*) The genetic control and cytoplasmic expression of 'inducibility' in the synthesis of β-galactosidase by *E. coli.* **1965** M. DEUTSCH in B. B. Wolman *Scientific Psychol.* 513 Inducibility provides the basis for normative control of individual behavior in the cooperative situation. **1972** *Science* 20 Oct. 315/2 The inducibility of [the enzyme system] AHH shows genetic variation in the mouse.

in'ducible, *a.* Also 7 -ceable. [f. INDUCE *v.* + -IBLE.]

1. a. Capable of being brought on, brought about, or caused.

a **1677** BARROW *Serm.* Wks. 1686 III. ix. 99 Subject to all the changes, inducible from the restless commotions of outward causes affecting and altering sense. **1958** *Times* 7 Nov. 7/7 This [*sc.* 'vigour tolerance'] is attributed to factors such as increased weight or improved biochemical conditions, inducible as a strain characteristic to be found in extremes of environmental conditions. **1973** *Nature* 6 July 6/1 In the case of adjuvant arthritis—inducible in rats by remote injection of water-in-oil emulsion incorporating killed mycobacteria.

b. *Biol.* Of a bacterium: capable of being induced (INDUCE *v.* 4 e).

1953 *Cold Spring Harbor Symp. Quant. Biol.* XVIII. 102/1 A growing culture of inducible lysogenic bacteria. **1959** JACOB & WOLLMAN in Burnet & Stanley *Viruses* II. ix. 328 Within the same bacterial species, both inducible and non-inducible strains can be isolated.

c. *Biochem.* Of an enzyme or enzyme system: produced in response to the presence of an appropriate inducer.

1953 [see INDUCTION 9c]. **1966** E. R. M. KAY *Biochem.* xxvii. 353 Some enzymes appear only when a special, but nevertheless necessary energy source is provided, as in the case of β-galactosidase formation. Such enzymes are called 'inducible' enzymes. **1971** *Nature* 19 Nov. 135/1 In the inducible regulatory system of mammals, hormones rather than substrates..serve as inducers.

†**2.** Capable of being inferred. *Obs. rare.*

1643 SIR T. BROWNE *Relig. Med.* I. §48 Many things are true in Divinity, which are neither inducible by reason, nor confirmable by sense. **1646** —— *Pseud. Ep.* VI. vi. 303 That the extream and remote parts of the earth were in this time inhabited, is also induceable from the like Testimonies.

in'ducing, *vbl. sb.* [f. as prec. + -ING¹.] The action of the verb INDUCE. **a.** Persuading. **b.** Bringing about.

c **1375** *Sc. Leg. Saints, Baptista* 265 Endusing makis men to pennance for þare syne to do. **1548–67** THOMAS *Ital. Dict.*, *Indezzamento*, an enducing, perswasion, or entisement. **1626** BACON *Sylva* §304 The Causes for the Accelerating of Clarification, in generall, and the Enducing of it. **1887** SAYER tr. *Dante, Convito* II. xiv. 83 The inducing of perfection in the things so inclined.

in'ducing, *ppl. a.* [f. as. prec. + -ING².]

1. That induces, persuades, or leads on.

1606 BIRNIE *Kirk-Buriall* xix, He did punishe..the seducing serpent with a curse, the inducing Eua with a crosse of subjection. **1640** BASTWICK *Lord Bps.* viii. H iij b, The prime inducing cause to that beleif. **1700** *Col. Rec. Pennsylv.* II. 10 That being the Inducing reason at first to Settle the Town where it now is.

†**2.** Introductory, preliminary. *Obs.*

1605 BACON *Adv. Learn.* II. Ded. §15 But the inducing part of the latter (which is the survey of learning) may be set forward.

3. Producing electric or magnetic effects by induction.

1837 *Penny Cycl.* IX. 343/1 Hence the directions of the inducing and induced currents are contrary. **1870** TYNDALL *Lect. Electr.* 15 Its attracted electricity is held captive by the inducing electrified body. **1870** R. M. FERGUSON *Electr.* 7 If the inducing magnet be strong enough, the induced magnet ..can induce a bar like itself..to become a magnet.

4. That induces or brings about; causing induction (see INDUCTION 9).

1931 J. NEEDHAM *Chem. Embryol.* I. 579 Regeneration of the adult amphibian lens takes place under the inducing influence of the retina. **1947** *Growth* XI. 237 Each of these two closely related compounds induced within the same cells the formation of different enzyme systems, each completely specific towards the inducing agent. **1950** L. G. BARTH tr. *Brachet's Chem. Embryol.* x. 345 (*heading*) Metabolism of the organization center and chemical nature of the inducing substance. **1966** E. R. M. KAY *Biochem.* xxvii. 354 One form [of repressor] is active as a repressor, but combines with an inducer if present in the form of an inducing substrate, thereby becoming an inactive form so that the structural gene may form 'messenger' RNA normally. **1968** M. W. STRICKBERGER *Genetics* xix. 401 The 'inducing' trigger that produces lysis in lysogenic strains.. involves a change in the activity of the phage from a quiescent prophage state to a proliferative vegetative state.

in'ducive, *a. rare.* [f. INDUCE *v.* + -IVE; cf. CONDUCIVE.] Tending to induce.

1611 FLORIO, *Indottiuo*, induciue, perswasiue. **1757** MRS. ELIZ. GRIFFITH *Lett. Henry & Frances* (1767) II. 187 That pleasing opinion, so flattering to the dignity of human nature, and so inducive to its ethicks. **1886** MISS LINSKILL *Haven under Hill* II. xi. 137 Soft murmuring sounds.. inducive of quiet hoping and trusting.

†**in'duct**, *ppl. a. Obs. rare.* Also 5 en-. [ad. L. *inductus*, pa. pple. of *indūcĕre* to INDUCE.]

a. Induced. **b.** Initiated, instructed. **c.** Introduced.

1460 CAPGRAVE *Chron.* (Rolls) 308 Jon..vas loth to resine; but be the emperoure he vas induct that he schuld do it. **1481** CAXTON *Godefroy* cxcv. 286 In his harnoys and armes wel enducte and acustomed, that it semed that hit greued ne coste hym nothyng to bere them. **1545** *Primer Hen. VIII* (Prayers), Grant..that, all the course of my life being led in holiness and purity, I may be induct at last into the everlasting rest.

induct (ɪn'dʌkt), *v.* [f. L. *induct-*, ppl. stem of *indūcĕre* to INDUCE.]

1. a. *trans. Eccl.* To introduce formally into possession of a benefice or living, to install. (See INDUCTION 4.)

c **1380** WYCLIF *Wks.* (1880) 450 Instuyng wiþ inducting & many oþere mannus lawis weren not to charge, but riȝt offiss þat þis curat shulde do. **1495** FABYAN *Chron.* VII. 455 That no man..shuld present or inducte any suche persone or persones that so by the pope were promoted. **1531** *Dial. on Laws Eng.* II. xxvi. (1638) 111 If he be able, then the Bishop to admit him, institute him, & induct him. **1667** *Answ. Quest. out of North* 7 By Instituting and Inducting Parsons and Vicars to Benefices when they fall. **1712** PRIDEAUX *Direct. Ch.-wardens* (ed. 4) 25 Every Vicar, when he is inducted into the Church, takes possession of the Body of the Church. **1846** HAWTHORNE *Mosses* II. vii. 123 Lately he has taken orders, and been inducted to a small country living.

b. To introduce into office, to install.

1548 HALL *Chron., Hen. VII* 17 b, Then John..woulde in all haste have rydden to induct the French kyng as their sovereigne lorde. **1820** SCOTT *Monast.* xix, Thy knee, my son—that we may, with our own hand..induct thee into office. **1828** WEBSTER s.v., In the United States, certain civil officers and presidents of colleges, are inducted into office with appropriate ceremonies.

c. To place or install in a seat, room, etc.

1706–7 FARQUHAR *Beaux' Strat.* II. ii, Then I, Sir, tips me the Verger with half a Crown; he pockets the Simony, and Inducts me into the best Pue in the Church. **1826** SCOTT *Woodst.* i, Inducting himself into the pulpit without further ceremony. **1840** DICKENS *Barn. Rudge* lx, Hugh and his two friends..were received with signal marks of approbation, and inducted into the most honourable seats.

2. a. To lead, conduct *into* (*lit.* and *fig.*). *rare.*

1600 HOLLAND *Livy* 1029 So soone as any one is inducted and brought in thither, she or he is delivered to the priests as a very sacrifice to be killed. **1861** *Crt. Life at Naples* 239 She led the way to the galleria, into which she first inducted the visitor. **1876** *World* V. No. 106. 11, I was inducted into error last week in stating [etc.]. **1881** STEVENSON *Virg. Puerisque* 155 Thus gradually inducted into the slumber of death.

b. To lead in (before a court). *rare.*

1834 LYTTON *Pompeii* IV. vii, They say the crime is of so extraordinary a nature, that the senate itself must adjudge it; and so the lictors are to induct him formally.

3. a. To introduce (*to*); to initiate (*into*).

1603 HOLLAND *Plutarch's Mor.* 461 There was a sacrificer or priest named Philippus, who inducted and professed men in the ceremoniall religion of Orpheus. **1833** LAMB *Elia* Ser. II. *Wedding*, [At weddings] I feel a sort of cousinship for the season. I am inducted into degrees of affinity. **1845** J. SAUNDERS *Cab. Pict. Eng. Life, Chaucer* 23 The master of the inn..inducts us into all its hidden mysteries. **1848** THACKERAY *Van. Fair* lvi, The pleasures to which the footman inducted him.

b. *U.S.* To bring into military service.

1934 WEBSTER, *Induct*, to enroll for military service in compliance with a draft law, as the selective service act of 1917. **1940** *Congress. Rec.* 6 Sept. 11675/2 Men..who are voluntarily inducted pursuant to this act. *Ibid.* 11676/1 The word 'inducted' I maintain means any of them [service men] because they are taken in... They are inducted either after they volunteer or after they are conscripted. **1967** *Boston Sunday Herald* 26 Mar. II. 7/7 Muhammad (Clay) was to be inducted—supposed to be inducted—into the Army April 11.

†**4.** To bring in, introduce (a custom). *Obs.*

1615 G. SANDYS *Trav.* 24 The ceremonies in the gathering hereof were first inducted by the Venetians. *Ibid.* 85 Who use extreme unction, as inducted by Saint James.

5. *absol.* To form an induction; to infer by induction. *rare.*

1832 WHEWELL in *Todhunter's Acc. Whewell's Writ.* (1876) II. 141 The conceptions which must exist in the mind in order to get by induction a law from a collection of facts; and the impossibility of inducting or even of collecting without this.

6. *Electr.* = INDUCE *v.* 4 b. See INDUCTING *ppl. a.*

in'ductance. [f. prec. (sense 6) + -ANCE.]

1. a. That property of a circuit or device by virtue of which any variation in the current flowing through it induces an e.m.f. in the

circuit itself (self-inductance) or in another conductor (mutual inductance): without qualification usu. the former. Also, the magnitude of this, as measured by the ratio of an induced e.m.f. to the rate of change of the inducing current.

1886 O. HEAVISIDE in *Electrician* 12 Feb. 271 Conductivity and conductance are mathematically related in the same manner (except as regards 4π) as inductivity and what it is naturally suggested to call Inductance. The Inductance of a circuit is what is now called its coefficient of self-induction... When the mutual coefficient of induction of two circuits is to be referred to, it will of course be the mutual inductance. **1888** *Science* July 18 The term commonly employed to denote the electrical inertia-like effect is 'self-induction', which is becoming gradually shortened to inductance. **1889** J. A. FLEMING *Alternate Current Transformer* I. ii. 42 The..inductance of a circuit is, speaking generally, a quality of it in virtue of which a finite and steady electromotive force applied to it cannot at once generate in it the full current.., and when the electromotive force is withdrawn time is required for the current strength to fall to zero. **1928** STERLING & KRUSE *Radio Manual* i. 20 The inductance of a circuit conductor, coil or of any apparatus is a property of that thing just as resistance is one of its properties. **1943** C. L. BOLTZ *Basic Radio* v. 88 In most radio work the only inductance anywhere worth considering is certainly that in coils. Nevertheless we must not forget that any conductor whatever has some inductance. *Ibid.* 90 Two coils have inductances of 2H and 4H. If they are coupled together so that only 50 per cent. of the flux is linked with all the turns, what is the value of the mutual inductance? **1957** *Encycl. Brit.* VIII. 293/2 When direct current is used, the inductance has no effect while the current is steady, but it delays the establishment of current when the circuit is first completed. **1962** CORSON & LORRAIN *Introd. Electromagn. Fields* vi. 232 In rationalized m.k.s. units, inductance is measured in webers/ampere, or in henrys. *Ibid.* 233 We shall now..calculate the self-inductance of a long solenoid..and the mutual inductance between two coaxial solenoids. **1964** GOODIER & MEYNELL *Electr.* iv. 49 A circuit will have an inductance of 1 henry if a current in it changing at the rate of 1 ampere per second induces an e.m.f. of 1 volt.

b. = INDUCTOR 3 d.

1908 J. A. FLEMING *Elem. Man. Radiotelegr.* ii. 66 One form which the inductance may take is that of a loop of one or a few turns of insulated wire. **1928** STERLING & KRUSE *Radio Manual* i. 20 The most commonly employed inductance at radio frequencies consists of a single layer coil wound as an air core solenoid. **1962** D. F. SHAW *Introd. Electronics* i. 9 The coupling between inductances may reach a value close to unity if they share a ferro-magnetic core.

2. Special Comb.: **inductance coil**, an inductor (sense 3 d) in the form of a loop or coil.

1902 *Encycl. Brit.* XXXIII. 232/1 The Slaby-Arco arrangement consists at the transmitting end of an *inductance coil elevated above the ground; one end of this coil is connected to the earth..and the other end to a condenser, the opposite terminal of which is connected to one secondary terminal of an induction coil. **1923** E. W. MARCHANT *Radio Telegr.* iv. 38 The coherer may, in a simple circuit, be conveniently placed across the inductance coil.

†**in'ductative**, *a. Obs. rare*$^{-1}$. [f. L. *induct-*, ppl. stem (see INDUCT) + -ATIVE.] Tending to lead or be led *into* something.

1387-8 T. USK *Test. Love* II. xiii. (Skeat) l. 48 Naturell goodnesse of euery substaunce, is nothing els than his substaunciall beyng, whiche is icleaped goodnesse, after comparison that he hath to his firste goodnesse, so as it is inductatife by meanes into the firste goodnesse.

inductee (ɪndʌk'tiː). *U.S.* [-EE[1].] A person inducted into military service. Also *transf.*

1941 *Ann. Reg. 1940* 278 The Act provides that no 'inductee' may be required to serve outside the Western Hemisphere. **1956** W. H. WHYTE *Organization Man* (1957) v. 58 Universal organization training..so effectively emphasises the group spirit that there is little danger that inductees will be subverted into rebelliousness. **1958** S. ELLIN *Eighth Circle* (1959) II. xii. 137 You sound like an army doctor asking an inductee about his sex life.

inducteous (ɪn'dʌktiːəs), *a.* [irreg. f. INDUCT *v.* + -EOUS.] Rendered electro-polar by induction.

1855 H. M. NOAD *Man. Electr.* I. 54 The originally active body is called the *inductric*, and that under its influence the *inducteous*; thus, in the last figure, A is the inductric and C the inducteous body.

inductile (ɪn'dʌktɪl, -aɪl), *a.* [IN-[3]: cf. F. *inductile* (Littré).] Not ductile; not pliable; unyielding to influences.

1736 LD. HERVEY *Mem. Geo. II*, I. 57 The stuff she had to work with was so stubborn and so inductile. **1827** J. FEARN in E. H. Barker *Parriana* (1828) I. 568 The human mind becomes extremely inductile to the pressure of any new evidence. **1828** WEBSTER, *Inductile*, not capable of being drawn into threads, as a metal. **1855** H. SPENCER *Princ. Psychol.* (1872) II. VI. xii. 156 Of bodies that resist in different modes..we have..the Ductile and Inductile. **1891** F. W. ROBINSON *Her Love & His Life* I. III. ix. 278 A man of honour,..but inductile, unimaginative, hard.

Hence **induc'tility**, the quality of being inductile (so F. *inductilité*).

1828 in WEBSTER.

in'ducting, *vbl. sb.* [f. INDUCT *v.* + -ING[1].]

1. *Eccl.* The action of introducing into, or putting in formal possession of, a benefice.

c **1380** [see INDUCT *v.* 1]. **1575-85** ABP. SANDYS *Serm.* (Parker Soc.) 241 The bestowing of benefices, the presenting, instituting, and inducting of pastors. **1684** BAXTER *Par. Congreg.* 28 Do all Independents assume the power of Ordination,..instituting, inducting?

2. The making of inductions or inferences.

1818 JAS. MILL *Brit. India* Pref. 15 Powers of combination, discrimination,..inferring, inducting, philosophizing in short.

in'ducting, *ppl. a.* [f. as prec. + -ING[2].] That induces or causes induction.

1839 G. BIRD *Nat. Philos.* 173 Evidence..that the intervening dielectric, air, has its particles of electricity arranged in a manner analogous to those of the conductor.. by the inducting influence of the glass tube.

induction (ɪn'dʌkʃən). Also 5-6 **inducцyon**, (6 **enduction**). [a. F. *induction* (14th c.) or ad. L. *inductiōn-em*, n. of action from *indūcĕre* to INDUCE.]

†**1.** The action of inducing by persuasion; inducement. *Obs.*

1490 CAXTON *Eneydos* xii. 44 The incitacyons moeued by naturell dylection, whiche commen of thy self, with out ony othre induction. *Ibid.* xxix. 113 There was som deceptyon or frawdulent induction that hath made her to condescende therunto. **1588** ALLEN *Admon.* 5 Not the pope alone but God himselfe suerly, & other the most zelous & mightiest princes in Christendom by his Induction.

2. The action of introducing to, or initiating in, the knowledge of something; the process of being initiated; introduction, initiation.

1526 *Pilgr. Perf.* (1531) 25 b, Of these iii examples we may take a general inducсyon or informacyon to our sayd iourney. **1531** ELYOT *Gov.* I. xxii, The principal cause of this my little enterprise is to declare an Induction or mean how children..may be trayned into the waye of vertue. **1600** HOLLAND *Livy* 379 A strange kind of induction and institution of the souldiours, binding them to take their oth, ..as if they were to take orders in some holy mysteries. **1724** DE FOE *Mem. Cavalier* (1840) 59, I have never yet seen any service, and must have my induction some time or other. **1877** BLACK *Green Past.* xli, Society is vastly more concerned in the induction of its youthful members into these branches of culture than it is in teaching them to bawl harmoniously.

attrib. **1962** *B.B.C. Handbk.* 162 Induction courses were also continued during the year for all senior members of staff joining the Corporation to acquaint them with its purpose, organization, and basic procedures. **1962** E. GODFREY *Retail Selling & Organization* xi. 121 It may be very useful to provide a special week or fortnight of induction training for them [*sc.* juniors]. **1965** *New Statesman* 30 Apr. 678/3 The organisation of refresher or induction courses. **1966** *Ibid.* 14 Jan. 49/1 Many firms run so-called 'induction' classes for new entrants, teaching them something about the company and its welfare provisions, perhaps giving them a brief run-down on the reasons for deductions from their wage packets, and even occasionally dealing with safety and hygiene.

3. a. That which introduces or leads on or in *to* something; an introduction. Now *rare.*

c **1540** *Four P.P.* in Hazl. *Dodsley* I. 355 Comparing that life for the best Induction to your endless rest. **1556** J. HEYWOOD *Spider & F.* liv. 12 Enter the path..One depe enduction wherto..Is to flee rash deedes rashlie done. **1631** CHAPMAN *Cæsar & Pompey* Plays 1873 III. 149 This prepares a good induction to the change of fortune. **1646** BUCK *Rich. III* 118 (T.) An induction to those succeeding evils which pursued that inconsiderate marriage. **1894** BLACKMORE *Perlycross* 15 An old-fashioned Inn... This.. was not in the Parson's opinion a pleasing induction to the lych-gate.

b. An introductory statement; a preface, preamble, or introduction (to a book or the like). *arch.*

1533 MORE *Answ. Poysoned Bk.* Wks. 1094/1 In the .xi. leafe he hath an other argument, towarde whyche he maketh a blynde inducсion before. **1559** T. SACKVILLE *The Induction to Mirrour for Magistrates.* **1607** BEAUM. & FL. *Woman-Hater* Prol., Inductions are out of date, and a prologue in verse is as stale as a black velvet cloak. **1645** MILTON *Colast.* Wks. (1851) 362 That which hee takes for the second Argument..is no argument, but an induction to those that follow. **1875** A. W. WARD *Eng. Dram. Lit.* I. Introd. 11 In the form of a Prologue or..by means of a separate Induction, or even by an inductive Dumb-show.

†**c.** The initial step in any undertaking. *Obs.*

1574 SHAKS. *Rich. III*, I. i. 32 Plots haue I laide, Inductions dangerous,..To set my Brother Clarence and the King In deadly hate, the one against the other. **1596** — *1 Hen. IV*, III. i. 2 These promises are faire, the parties sure, And our induction full of prosperous hope.

†**d.** A leading on or gradual transition from one thing to another. *Obs.*

1638 F. JUNIUS *Paint. of Ancients* 281 [In a centaur] the horse..turneth from the one into the other as by a quiet and insensible induction.

†**e.** *Music.* (See quot.) *Obs.*

1597 MORLEY *Introd. Mus.* 92 Here they set downe certaine obseruations, which they termed Inductions.. euerie proportion whole, is called the Induction to that which it maketh being broken. As tripla being broken in the more prolation will make Nonupla, and so is tripla the Induction to nonupla.

4. a. *Eccl.* The action of formally introducing a clergyman into possession of the church to which he has been presented and instituted, together with all rights, profits, etc. pertaining to it.

c **1380** WYCLIF *Wks.* (1880) 248 For institucion and inducсion he schal ȝeue moche of þis god þat is pore mennus to bischopis officers, archdekenes & officialis. **1583** STUBBES *Anat. Abus.* II. (1882) 81 At the time of their initiation, institution, induction and admission. **1660** R. COKE *Power & Subj.* 21 The division of all parishes..the right of institution and induction..were all originally of the King's foundation and donation. **1765** BLACKSTONE *Comm.* I. xi. 307 The method of becoming a parson or vicar is much the same. To both there are four requisites necessary: holy orders; presentation; institution; and induction. **1875** GLADSTONE *Glean.* VI. lii. 228 He had indeed received a formal induction..from the arch priest of Cavriana.

b. In Presbyterian churches: The placing of a minister already ordained in a new pastoral charge. (Distinguished from *ordination.*)

1871 SIR H. MONCRIEFF *Pract. F.C. of Scot.* (1877) 269 The Presbytery resolved to loose him from his present charge and translate him to—,..and they request that Reverend Court to give them notice of his Induction when it takes place. *Ibid.* 270 Edict previous to Ordination or Induction.

c. *gen.* The formal introduction to an office, position, or possession; installation. (Cf. ENDUE *v.* 1.)

1460 CAPGRAVE *Chron.* (Rolls) 301 Ve send oure special legates to trete..of the restitucion, and the real inducсioune of the duchy of Gian. **1828** WEBSTER s.v., Induction is applied to the introduction of officers only when certain oaths are to be administered or other formalitites are to be observed, which are intended to confer authority or give dignity to the office. In the United States it is applied to the formal introduction of civil officers, and the higher officers of colleges.

d. *U.S.* Introduction into military service (cf. INDUCT *v.* 3 b). Also *attrib.*

1934 in WEBSTER. **1940** *Congress. Rec.* 6 Sept. 11676/1 Any person..shall be afforded an opportunity to volunteer for induction. **1951** *N.Y. Herald-Tribune* 26 Dec. 11/3 You label this procedure of impressing R.O.K. Army members into your army as voluntary induction... It is nothing more than forced induction, impressment. **1967** *Boston Sunday Herald* 26 Mar. II. 7/7 Clay has been ordered to appear for induction in the Army on April 11. **1973** C. HIMES *Black on Black* 209 Here is your induction papers... I hope the army likes you bettern I does. **1973** *Times Lit. Suppl.* 19 Oct. 1269/1 One summer the dreaded Induction Notice comes and he goes to war.

5. The action of introducing or bringing in (a person, custom, etc.). *rare.*

1604 DEKKER *King's Entert.* Wks. 1873 I. 271 The induction of such a person, might pass very currant. **1610** HEALEY *St. Aug. Citie of God* II. xiii. (1620) 66 Such things as our Gods themselues doe make sacred, by their owne expresse induction of those plaies into our customes. **1612** WOODALL *Pref. Surg. Mate* Wks. (1653) 9 The Knowledge and use of all such medicines..as were of his production and induction. **1802** LAMB *J. Woodvil* IV. ii, Therefore, without much induction of superfluous words, I attach you..of high treason.

6. The bringing forward, adducing, or enumerating *of* a number of separate facts, particulars, etc., esp. for the purpose of proving a general statement.

1551 GARDINER *Explic., Transubst.* 125 (R.) For the auctour of this booke concludeth solemly thus by induction of the premisses, that euen so the bodye of Christe was after thascension chaunged into the godly substaunce. **1624** BEDELL *Lett.* iii. 57 The rest of your induction of Arch-bishops, Bishops, and whole Clergie.., &c. is but a needlesse pompe of words. **1631** GOUGE *God's Arrows* IV. §3. 377 It may further be proved by that induction of particulars tending to this purpose which God himselfe bringeth in. **1655** FULLER *Ch. Hist.* II. vi. §42 That the Doctrine remained still sound and entire..will appeare by an Induction of the dominative Controversies. **1794** PALEY *Evid.* I. ix. (1817) 168 The persuasion produced by this species of evidence depends upon a view and induction of the particulars which compose it. **1842** H. ROGERS *Introd. Burke's Wks.* I. 40 It is valuable rather as a most extensive induction of facts, than as an instance of their successful application.

7. *Logic.* **a.** The process of inferring a general law or principle from the observation of particular instances (opposed to DEDUCTION, q.v.).

[Directly representing L. *inductio* (Cicero), rendering Gr. ἐπαγωγή (Aristotle), in same sense.]

1553 T. WILSON *Rhet.* 111 We mighte heape many men together, and prove by large rehersall, any thyng that we would, the whiche of the logicians is called induction. **1613** PURCHAS *Pilgrimage* (1614) Ep. Ded. ¶iii, Others may hence learne by that most laborious, though not most learned Argument of Induction, two lessons fitting these times. **1656** STANLEY *Hist. Philos.* v. (1701) 182/1 Induction is every method of reason which proceedeth either from like to like or from singulars to generals. **1734** BERKELEY *Analyst* §19 You must take up with Induction, and bid adieu to Demonstration. **1812-16** PLAYFAIR *Nat. Phil.* I. 2 It is from induction that all certain and accurate knowledge of the laws of nature is derived. *a* **1862** BUCKLE *Misc. Wks.* I. 41 Logic, considered as a science, is solely concerned with induction; and the business of induction is to arrive at causes. **1876** FOWLER *Induct. Logic* (ed. 3) Pref., Induction..may or may not employ hypothesis, but what is essential to it is the inference from the particular to the general, from the known to the unknown.

b. An act or instance of induction; the result of this; a conclusion derived from induction; formerly used in the wider sense of 'inference'.

c **1440** CAPGRAVE *Life St. Kath.* v. 1923 The hill in whiche god ȝaf the wrytyn lawe On-to the Iewes, ledeth to that perfeccyon Of crystis gospell..Paule in his bookis maketh swyche inducсyon; He seyth it longeth to Ierusalem as in seruage With alle his children heere in pylgremage. *c* **1530** L. COX *Rhet.* (1899) 49 He treateth of the fourme of Sillogismes, Enthimemes and Inductions. **1587** GOLDING *De Mornay* xxvi. 396 We would haue [God] to vse Inductions as Plato doth, or Syllogismes as Aristotle doth. **1697** tr. *Burgersdicius his Logic* II. xi. 46 In an induction.. it's proved that animals void of bile are long-liv'd, because a man, a horse, an ass, &c., are long-liv'd. **1727-41** CHAMBERS *Cycl.* s.v., The conclusion of a syllogism, is an induction made from the premises. **1833** HT. MARTINEAU *Briery Creek* iv. 86 They look..into the evidence of circumstance, and learn to make an induction for themselves. **1868** W. R. GREG *Lit. & Social Judgm.* 313 The

contrast between his wide inductions and the apparently flimsy foundation on which they are made to rest. **1869** Fowler *Induct. Logic* i. 1 [This] is an inference of that particular character which is called an Inductive Inference or an Induction.

8. *Math.* (See quot. 1875.)

1838 *Penny Cycl.* XII. 466/1 An instance of mathematical induction occurs in every equation of differences, in every recurring series, &c. **1875** Todhunter *Algebra* (ed. 7) xxxiii. §484 The method of mathematical induction may be thus described: We prove that if a theorem is true in one case, whatever that case may be, it is true in another case which we may call the *next* case; we prove by trial that the theorem *is* true in a certain case; hence it is true in the next case, and hence in the next to that, and so on; hence it must be true in every case after that with which we began.

9. a. The action of bringing on, bringing into existence or operation, producing, causing. Chiefly *Med. spec.* Induction of labour.

1660 Stanley *Hist. Philos.* ix. (1701) 403/2 The induction of sickness is the expulsion of health. **1835** I. Taylor *Spir. Despot.* iii. 108 The gradual induction of political, ecclesiastical and moral changes. **1840** *Lancet* 7 Nov. 225/1 (*heading*) Induction of premature labour. **1865** *Reader* 1 Apr. 374/3 Abuse of tobacco is far more operative in the induction of this paralysis than alcohol. **1877** Erichsen *Surg.* I. 23 The time required for the induction of the anaesthetic state varies. **1916** G. P. Shears *Obstetrics* xxvi. 567 By the induction of abortion is meant the artificial interruption of pregnancy during the first twenty-eight weeks; i.e., before the fœtus becomes viable. The artificial interruption of pregnancy at any subsequent period is known as the induction of labor. **1962** *Lancet* 6 Jan. 6/2 The failure-rate was decidedly high when induction of labour was started after the calculated date for confinement had passed. **1968** D. C. Bethea *Introd. Maternity Nursing* ix. 120 Inductions may also be done for the convenience of the mother and/or the doctor.

b. *Embryol.* The determination of the development or differentiation of an embryonic region into a particular morphogenetic pattern by the influence or activity of another embryonic region; an instance of this.

1928 *Biol. Abstr.* II. 686/2 In the small yolk-plug stage both the median and paramedian parts of the posterior $\frac{2}{3}$ of the gut roof are capable of induction. **1935** *Discovery* May 136/2 If..an organisation centre is grafted out of its usual place in an egg into new surroundings it will cause those new surroundings to develop into a complete embryo or complete organ. This 'induction' of a new embryo involves both sorts of embryological change; the production of new sorts of tissues..and the arrangement of those tissues. **1950** L. G. Barth tr. *Brachet's Chem. Embryol.* x. 397 The middle layer..gave good inductions in 16 per cent of the cases. **1958** B. M. Patten *Found. Embryol.* vi. 134 Experimental studies ..have yielded extraordinarily interesting information as to the way one part of a developing embryo may influence the differentiation of other parts. When this occurs it is spoken of as induction. **1960** B. I. Balinsky *Introd. Embryol.* vi. 169 The result may be expressed as a percentage of successful inductions. **1962** T. W. Torrey *Morphogenesis Vertebr.* xviii. 481 Neural induction has been shown to occur in vertebrates other than amphibians.

c. *Biochem.* An increase in the rate at which an enzyme is synthesized by a cell (esp. in a micro-organism), or the initiation of its synthesis, as a result of the exposure of the cell to some specific substance (the inducer).

1947 *Growth* XI. 242 Where the enzymes have not been obtained in pure crystalline state.., the evidence must come mainly from a study of the specificity of the phenomenon of induction. **1951** *Biochim. & Biophys. Acta* VII. 599 These observations are incompatible with all hypotheses which imply that the induction is connected..with the activity of the enzyme. **1953** Cohn, Monod et al. in *Nature* 12 Dec. 1096/1 It might prove unpractical to abandon the use of the term 'enzyme adaptation' altogether at this stage; but we should like to suggest that..a more accurate and significant terminology be employed. We therefore propose the following terms and designations; previously used terms are placed in parenthesis. A relative increase in the rate of synthesis of a specific apoenzyme resulting from exposure to a chemical substance is an 'enzyme induction' (enzyme adaptation). Any substance thus inducing enzyme synthesis is an enzyme 'inducer'. An enzyme-forming system which can be so activated by an exogenous inducer is 'inducible', and the enzyme so formed is 'induced' (adaptive). Although many compounds can act both as inducer and substrate, the terms are not equivalent. Certain substrates for induced enzymes are not inducers, while some inducers cannot function as substrates of the enzymes the formation of which they elicit. **1966** E. R. M. Kay *Biochem.* xxvii. 357 By many mechanisms of feedback control, repression, and induction, enzyme levels can be regulated in accord with the metabolic demands of the cell. **1971** *Nature* 26 Nov. 177/2 Substrate induction of enzymes (that is, their synthesis in response to the presence of their substrates) is now commonplace in microorganisms and not infrequent in higher animals.

d. *Biol.* The initiation of the lytic cycle in a bacterium carrying a prophage; the process of inducing a bacterium that contains a prophage.

[**1950** A. Lwoff et al. in *Ann. de l'Inst. Pasteur* LXXIX. 817 Entre l'induction et la libération du bactériophage, il s'écoule de quarante-cinq à quatre-vingts minutes. **1951** *Jrnl. Bacteriol.* LXII. 302 High titer stocks of this phage were obtained from K12 by induction of phage production with UV (the Lwoff effect).] *Ibid.* 304 The plaque count rises..to a number equal to the colony count before induction. **1953** *Cold Spring Harbor Symp. Quant. Biol.* XVIII. 101/2 In 1950, Lwoff, Siminovitch and Kjeldgaard showed that..irradiation of cultures of lysogenic *Bacillus megatherium* with ultraviolet light greatly increased the proportion of bacteria producing phage... This phenomenon is called induction. **1959** Jacob & Wollman in Burnet & Stanley *Viruses* II. ix. 326 It makes it possible to compare phage development in the same phage-bacterium system, whether after infection of sensitive bacteria, or after induction of lysogenic bacteria. **1959** *Jrnl. Molecular Biol.* I. 177 When the reverse mating (♂ non-lysogenic × ♀ λ-lysogenic) is performed, zygotic induction does not occur. **1968** Echols & Joyner in H. Fraenkel-Conrat *Molecular Basis Virol.* vi. 557 The treatments which produce induction of wild-type prophages are rather diverse (e.g., UV irradiation, growth in mitomycin C, thymine deprivation of a thymine requiring bacterium).

10. *Electr.* and *Magnetism.* **a.** The action of inducing or bringing about an electric or magnetic state in a body by the proximity (without actual contact) of an electrified or magnetized body.

The terms *induce* and *induction* were originally employed apparently to avoid the use of terms involving any theory of the nature of the action involved. The medium of communication was later held to be, as in the case of other forms of energy, the intervening ether.

electrodynamic or ***voltaic induction***, the production of an electric current (*induced current*) by the influence of another independent electric current. ***electromagnetic induction***, the production of a state of magnetic polarity in a body near or round which an electric or galvanic current passes, or the generation of an electric current by the action of a magnet (the latter called by Faraday, more properly, *magneto-electric induction*). ***electrostatic induction***, the production of an electrical charge upon a body by the influence of a neighbouring body charged with statical electricity, as exemplified in Volta's electrophorus. ***magnetic induction***, the production of magnetic properties in iron or other substances when placed in a magnetic field, as when a bar of soft iron is magnetized by a neighbouring magnet. ***mutual induction***, the reaction of two electric circuits upon each other; ***self-induction***, the reaction of different parts of the same circuit upon one another.

1801 *Encycl. Brit.* Suppl. I. 572/2 (*marginal note*) A neutral body attracted, because rendered electrical by induction. **1812** Sir H. Davy *Chem. Philos.* 132 To produce a succession of effects both conductors must be brought near bodies connected with the ground, which gain the opposite state, in consequence of what may be called *induction*. **1830** Herschel *Stud. Nat. Phil.* 329 The communication of magnetism from the earth to a magnetic body, or from one magnetic body to another, is performed by a process to which the name of *induction* has been given. **1832** Faraday *Exp. Researches* §1 in *Phil. Trans.* 125 The power which electricity of tension possesses of causing an opposite electrical state in its vicinity has been expressed by the general term Induction; which, as it has been received into scientific language, may also with propriety be used in the same general sense to express the power which electric currents may possess of inducing any particular state upon matter in their immediate neighbourhood. *Ibid.* §58. 139, I propose to call the agency thus exerted by ordinary magnets, *magneto-electric* or *magnelectric* induction. §59 The only difference which powerfully strikes the attention as existing between volta-electric and magneto-electric induction, is the suddenness of the former, and the sensible time required by the latter. **1870** Tyndall *Lect. Electr.* 14 This forcible separation of the two fluids of a neutral conductor, by the mere proximity of an electrified body, is called *electric induction*. Bodies in this state are also said to be electrified by *influence*. **1892** S. P. Thompson *Dynamo-Elect. Mach.* (ed. 4) 83 We know that every electric current possesses a property sometimes called 'electric inertia', sometimes called 'self-induction', by virtue of which it tends to go on, and that it is in the current's own magnetic field that this inertia of self-induction resides. *Ibid.* 102 Mutual induction between adjacent parts is of enormous importance in alternate current machines.

b. (Also ***magnetic induction***.) Magnetic flux or (more commonly) flux density, by virtue of which an electric current experiences a magnetic force; as flux density, it is a vector quantity whose magnitude at any point is the magnetic force exerted per unit length on a conductor carrying unit current in the direction that gives rise to the maximum force, and whose direction is normal to those of the current and the force. Also (***electric induction***), electric flux or flux density, = displacement 2d (now somewhat *rare*). ***line of induction***, one of the imaginary lines conceived as representing, by their direction and number, the induction at each point throughout a region.

The C.G.S. unit of magnetic induction (flux density) is the gauss; in the International System of Units the tesla (= 10,000 gauss) is used.

1855 J. C. Maxwell in *Trans. Cambr. Philos. Soc.* (1864) X. 49 The unit cells in this case are portions of space in which unit of magnetic quantity is produced by unity [*sic*] of magnetizing force. The length of a cell is therefore inversely as the intensity of the magnetizing force, and its section is inversely as the quantity of magnetic induction at that point. *Ibid.* 50 If a closed conductor move transversely to the lines of magnetic induction..there will be no current. **1861** —— in *Phil. Mag.* XXI. 168 The total amount of magnetic induction through a closed surface surrounding the pole of a magnet, depends entirely on the strength of that pole. **1873** —— *Treat. Electr. & Magn.* I. i. ii. 77 If *dS* is the element of the surface, the electric displacement through *dS* will be ..$KR \cos \epsilon\, dS/4\pi$. Since we do not at present consider any dielectric except air, $K = 1$. We may..avoid introducing at this stage the theory of electric displacement, by calling $R \cos \epsilon\, dS$ the Induction through the element *dS*. *Ibid* 85 We have used the phrase Lines of Force because it has been used by Faraday and others. In strictness, however, these lines should be called Lines of Electric Induction. *Ibid.* II. iii. ii. 24 The three vectors, the magnetization $\mathfrak{I}$, the magnetic force $\mathfrak{H}$, and the magnetic induction $\mathfrak{B}$ are connected by the vector equation $\mathfrak{B} = \mathfrak{H} + 4\pi\mathfrak{I}$. **1879** *Encycl. Brit.* VIII. 75/2 For 'number of lines of force' may of course be substituted the equivalent expressions, 'induction through the circuit', or 'surface integral of magnetic induction'. **1885** O. Heaviside in *Electrician* 4 Sept. 311/1 There is a definite magnitude called by Maxwell 'the magnetic induction', which may well be called simply 'the induction'. *Ibid.* 311/2 We pass to electric displacement, the analogue of magnetic induction (noting by the way that it had better not be called the electric induction..but be called the displacement). **1922** Glazebrook *Dict. Appl. Physics* II. 449/2 *Magnetic flux*, the total amount of magnetic induction through a circuit, measured by the number of lines of induction which are linked with the circuit. **1925** F. B. Pidduck *Treat. Electr.* (ed. 2) iii. 96 It is of some importance..to inquire what happens when the polarisation is not proportional to the electric force. We now require two vectors, P, E, not in general parallel to each other, to express the state of the medium at any point... If we define a vector $D = E + 4\pi P$, $\mathrm{div}\, D = 0$. The vector D is called the electric induction. **1938** G. P. Harnwell *Princ. Electr. & Electromagn.* ix. 278 By analogy with the introduction of the electric field E in electrostatics it is convenient to introduce a vector B, known as the magnetic induction, which determines the force on a current element. The element of induction is defined by the equation $dF_1 = i_1\, dl_1 \times B_2$. **1957** B. I. & B. Bleaney *Electr. & Magn.* v. 116 Both a magnet and a current-carrying coil are said to produce a magnetic induction B, which exerts forces on other coils or magnets. *Ibid.* 128 With a magnetic pole, H is the force vector, while the introduction of a uniform magnetic medium throughout the whole of space leaves the magnetic induction B due to a pole unchanged. In the case of a current, B is the force vector and introduction of a magnetic medium leaves H unchanged. If the magnetizable matter does not fill the whole of space, then it is the surface integral of B, the total normal induction, which remains unchanged in magnetostatics. **1962** Corson & Lorrain *Introd. Electromagn. Fields* v. 179 If the current *I* is distributed in space with a current density J amperes/meter^2, then *I* becomes *J da* and must be put under the integral sign... Thus, in the general case, the magnetic induction B at a point in space is given by $B = (\mu_0/4\pi)\int_\tau (J \times r_1)/r^2 d\tau$, where the integration is carried out over any volume τ which includes all the currents.

11. *Grammar.* (See quot.)

1860 Haldeman *Anal. Orthogr.* ix. 52 Induction is the influence of larger classes of words on smaller ones, causing uniformity and regularity in Grammatical inflections.

12. *Chem.* (See quot.)

1857 Bunsen & Roscoe in *Phil. Trans. R. Soc.* CXLVII. 381 The act by which the resistance to combination is diminished, and the combining power thus brought into greater activity, we call Chemical Induction. **1892** Morley & Muir *Dict. Chem.* III. 8/1 When H and Cl are mixed in equal volumes and exposed to sunlight, a measurable time elapses before chemical change begins. Bunsen and Roscoe, who examined this phenomenon, regard the mixture as resisting chemical change, and they used the term *induction* to express the gradual overcoming of this resistance. The term has also been used by Wright, who noticed a similar phenomenon in the reduction of metallic oxides by CO and H.

13. *attrib.* and *Comb.*, as (sense 10) ***induction apparatus, current, machine, shock, spark***; also **induction accelerator** = betatron; **induction-balance**, an electrical apparatus so contrived that the currents induced in the secondary wires of two induction-coils balance each other; **induction-bridge**, a form of induction-balance arranged on the principle of a Wheatstone's bridge; **induction coil**, an apparatus for producing electric currents by induction, consisting of two separated coils of wire generally surrounding a soft-iron core, the primary coil being connected with an external source of electricity, and having an arrangement for causing the electric current to vary in intensity, the effect of which is to produce a current of different character in the other or secondary coil; a coil in which an electric current is induced; an inductance coil; *Teleph.*, a transformer in a telephone comprising two coils with a common core; **induction compass** = *inductor compass*; **induction furnace**, a furnace for melting metal by means of induction heating; **induction generator**, an induction motor driven at a greater speed than its synchronous speed, so that it acts as a generator; **induction hardening**, hardening of ferrous metal by means of induction heating followed by quenching; **induction heater**, an apparatus for the induction heating of objects; **induction heating**, in which an alternating current is made to induce heating currents in the substance or object to be heated or (less commonly) in its container; **induction motor**, an a.c. electric motor in which the torque or force is due to the interaction between a moving magnetic field produced by stationary primary windings and currents induced by this field in moving secondary conductors; (sense 12) **induction period** *Chem.*, the time elapsing between the initiation of a chemical reaction and the production of detectable amounts of the product or products; (sense 3) **induction-pipe**, the pipe through which the live steam is introduced into the cylinder of a steam-engine; **induction-port**, the opening by which steam passes from the steam-chest into the cylinder; **induction valve**, the valve which controls the passage of steam into the cylinder.

1940 D. W. Kerst in *Physical Rev.* LVIII. 841/2 Of several suggestions which have been made for naming the apparatus, *induction accelerator seems to be the shortest descriptive one. **1958** Condon & Odishaw *Handbk. Physics* ix. ix. 154/2 To make this device practical, it is necessary

only to restrain the beam to a closed path around the flux and to maintain it in a stable orbit over some thousands of revolutions. Credit for the solution of the latter problem goes to D. W. Kerst, who built the first successful induction accelerator or 'betatron' in 1940. **1855–7** H. M. NOAD *Man. Electr.* II. 728 The *induction apparatus as at present constructed by M. Ruhmkorff is shown in Fig. 395. **1879** D. E. HUGHES in *Proc. R. Soc.* XXIX. 56 M. Dove.. constructed an *induction balance, wherein two separate induction coils, each having its primary and secondary coils, were joined together in such a manner that the induced current in one coil was made to neutralize the induced current in the opposite coil, thus forming an induction-balance, to which he gave the name of *differential inductor*. *Ibid.*, I have obtained a perfect induction balance which.. allows us to obtain direct comparative measures of the force or disturbance produced by the introduction of any metal or conductor. **1889** FLEMING *Alternate Current Transformer* 247 Lord Rayleigh found it more convenient.. to slightly alter the arrangement of the induction balance.. B and I are a battery and interrupter, T is a telephone in the 'bridge'. **1837** *Mag. Pop. Sci.* III. 110 A lever has also been applied to move.. the *induction-coil up and down along two magnetic bars. **1855–7** NOAD *Man. Electr.* II. 728 In 1851, M. Ruhmkorff of Paris brought the induction-coil to a far greater degree of perfection than it had hitherto attained by paying the greatest possible attention to the insulation of the secondary wire. **1876** PREECE & SIVEWRIGHT *Telegraphy* 262 Each globe or tube ought to be tested from time to time with an induction-coil, or some other generator of electricity of high potential. **1885** R. S. CULLEY *Handbk. Pract. Telegr.* (ed. 8) IX. 328 The current from the battery does not itself pass out to line, but through a local circuit formed by the primary wire of an induction coil. This coil has a core made of soft iron wires,.. and is wound with two wires one over the other... Every variation of the battery current in the primary, produces a corresponding current in the secondary, but of a much higher potential; this last goes out to line, and acts on the distant receiver. *Ibid.* 329 The microphone, induction coil and battery, form the sending portion of the telephone. **1891** J. W. URQUHART *Dynamo Construction* 9 (*caption*) The induction coils combined with the field magnet. **1896** *Allbutt's Syst. Med.* I. 351, I shall speak of electrostatic methods, of treatment by the battery current, and of treatment by the induction coil current. **1943** A. L. ALBERT *Fund. Telephony* vii. 142 When the receiver is removed.. the battery causes direct current to flow through the transmitter and the primary of the transformer, often called in telephony an induction coil. **1966** *McGraw-Hill Encycl. Sci. & Technol.* VII. 72/2 Still another type of induction coil, called a reactor, is really a one-winding transformer designed to produce a definite voltage drop for a given current. **1925** *Mech. Engin.* XLVII. 796/2 Since to keep on the correct course it is only necessary to keep the pointer of the *induction compass indicator on zero, it is easier to read than the magnetic compass. **1931** B. JONES *Avigation* ii. 18 The induction compass is a distant-reading magnetic compass, the part indicating the heading to the pilot being at a considerable distance from the part affected by the earth's magnetism. **1881** MAXWELL *Electr. & Magn.* II. 408 This diffusion and decay of the *induction-current is a phenomenon precisely analogous to the diffusion of heat. **1875** BENNETT & DYER tr. *Sachs' Bot.* 689 Weak induction-currents act on the sensitive parts of the leaves of *Mimosa*.. like concussion or contact. **1906** A. HIORTH *Brit. Pat.* 28,960 (*heading*) Improved electrical *induction furnace with electrodes. **1951** G. R. BASHFORTH *Manuf. Iron & Steel* II. ix. 251 When.. it was decided to dispense with the iron core of the early induction furnaces, it was necessary to increase the frequency of the current in the primary coil. **1904** G. T. HANCHETT *Alternating Currents* xiv. 173 The *induction generator cannot generate its own magnetizing current, but must receive a reaction from the line which will permit the magnetizing current of displaced phase to flow in its fields. **1952** G. V. MUELLER *Alternating Current Machines* viii. 284 In an induction generator driven above synchronous speed with a negative slip.. the rotor conductors are moving faster than the magnetic field of the stator. **1941** *Metals & Alloys* Nov. 687/1 *Induction hardening has been applied to the surface of certain steel parts for modern tractor and road-building machinery. **1968** E. N. SIMONS *Outl. Metall.* III. ii. 142 The three main forms of surface hardening steel parts are carburizing, cyaniding, and nitriding... There are also the processes of flame hardening and induction hardening. **1919** *Electr. World* 29 Mar. 634/1 (*heading*) High-power-factor *induction heaters. **1930** *Engineering* 9 May 611/2 The electric resistance [heaters].. heated the chilled surface of the roll and were not so good as the induction heaters, which generated heat within the body of the roll. **1919** H. P. TIEMANN *Iron & Steel* (ed. 2) 153 Induction furnace (*induction heating). **1937** *Metals & Alloys* May 149/1 Applications of induction heating.. now being installed.. include.. hardening of metal surfaces by quenching after induction heating. **1954** J. W. CABLE *Induction & Dielectric Heating* xii. 319 Many types of furnaces use induction heating as an indirect source of heat... Installations using graphite crucibles, which extract energy from the magnetic field and transfer it to the charge, fall in this general classification. **1959** *Engineering* 13 Feb. 210/1 Plastics to plastics welding is most easily performed by high frequency induction heating. **1962** G. R. BASHFORTH *Manuf. Iron & Steel* (ed. 2) IV. ii. 58 Induction heating differs from the conventional methods of heating metallic components by virtue of the fact that the heat is generated within the material itself without the surface of the material coming into contact with the heating media. **1896** *Westm. Gaz.* 7 May 8/2 A small Wimshurst *induction machine. **1897** *Electrician* 17 Sept. 688/1 (*heading*) A 400 H.P. *induction motor. **1918** P. KEMP *Alternating Current Electr. Engin.* xxvi. 394 On account of the fact that it must run at a speed rather less than that of synchronism, the induction motor is sometimes termed an asynchronous motor. **1962** *Newnes Conc. Encycl. Electr. Engin.* 492/1 In its basic form the induction motor is essentially a constant-speed motor: the variation in speed from no load to full load when running normally near synchronous speed is only a few per cent. **1971** E. R. LAITHWAITE *Linear Electr. Motors* i. 7 (*caption*) Imaginary process of unrolling a conventional motor to obtain a linear induction motor. **1973** *Nature* 9 Feb. 359/2 It is now feasible both to levitate and to propel a hovertrain using only a linear induction motor. **1902** *Proc. R. Soc.* LXX. 74 The *induction and deduction periods follow as a necessity from the same general thermodynamic conceptions. **1924** H. S. TAYLOR *Treat. Physical Chem.* II. xviii. 1219 The induction period was not a function of the oxygen content of the gas—this only retarded the reaction velocity. **1953** FROST & PEARSON *Kinetics & Mechanism* viii. 156 The duration of the induction period, arbitrarily taken as the time to reach the point of inflection on the C [*sc.* concentration of product] versus *t* [*sc.* time] curve.. is easily seen to be equal to the time for B [*sc.* concentration of intermediate] to reach its maximum value. **1970** Induction period [see INHIBITION 3 b]. **1875** BENNETT & DYER tr. *Sachs' Bot.* 689 The number of *induction-shocks.. appears to have no considerable influence on the action. **1878** FOSTER *Phys.* I. ii. §2. 46 Induction-shocks, or at least galvanic currents in some form or other. **1865** *Intell. Observ.* No. 36. 389 When the *induction spark is taken in air. **1870** PROCTOR *Other Worlds* xii. 280 The spectrum of the induction spark. **1847** *Rep. Comm. Patents 1846* (U.S.) 87 The *induction valve is then closed, and an expansion valve simultaneously opened. **1859** RANKINE *Steam-Engine* (1861) 480 The admission and discharge of the steam take place through openings near the ends of the cylinder called 'ports', connected with passages called 'nozzles', which are opened and closed by induction and eduction valves.

in'ductional, *a.* [f. prec. + -AL[1].] Of, pertaining to, or of the nature of induction.

1829 *Blackw. Mag.* XXVI. 621 The leading facts upon which his inductional argument is founded.

inductionist (ɪn'dʌkʃənɪst). [f. INDUCTION + -IST.] An adherent of inductive methods in philosophy or science. Cf. INDUCTIVISM.

1893 in *Funk's Stand. Dict.* *a* **1915** J. C. WILSON *Statement & Inference* (1926) II. IV. i. 589 Now clearly the argument is demonstrative, and the inductionists in their opposition of induction to deduction would be obliged to call it deduction.

inductionless (ɪn'dʌkʃənlɪs), *a.* *Electr.* [f. INDUCTION + -LESS.] Possessing no inductance.

1902 *Encycl. Brit.* XXX. 600/1 The wattmeter can best be standardized by employing it to measure the known power taken up in an inductionless circuit, such as a bank of incandescent lamps. **1908** J. SKELTON tr. *Kolbe's Introd. Electr.* II. vi. 347 The self-induction is thus almost entirely stopped (inductionless winding).

†**in'ductious,** *a.* *Obs. rare*$^{-1}$. [f. INDUCTION: see -OUS.] Persuasive; seductive.

1620 FORD *Linea V.* (Shaks. Soc.) 60 Flatterie to publique persons is not more inductious on the one side, then enuie on the other is vigilant.

in'ductive, *sb.* [ad. L. *inductīvum*, neut. sing. of *inductīvus*: see next.] †**1.** An inducement, incentive. *Obs. rare.*

a **1420** HOCCLEVE *De Reg. Princ.* 453 Me thynkyth this a verray inductif Vnto stelthe. **1657** W. MORICE *Coena quasi Κοινὴ* Def. xxviii. 278 The same reason.. may become also an inductive to their expulsion from Ecclesiastick Communion. **1683** E. HOOKER *Pref. Pordage's Mystic Div.* 92 These reasons, grounds, persuasives, motives, or, if you please, inductives and incentives.

2. = INDUCTIONIST. *rare.*

1877 F. H. LAING *Ld. Bacon's 'Philosophy' Examined* xii. 110 The inductives themselves are forced.. to employ.. all these words, which perpetually occur in their writings.

inductive (ɪn'dʌktɪv), *a.* [ad. L. *inductīv-us* (Priscian), f. *induct-*, ppl. stem of *indūcĕre*: see INDUCE and -IVE. Cf. F. *inductif, -ive* (14th c. in Godef.).]

1. Leading on (*to* some action, etc.); inducing.

1607 *Schol. Disc. agst. Antichr.* II. vi. 56 An active scandall is not only given by a purpose to drawe to sinne, but also when hauing no intent a man doth that, which of it selfe is inductiue to it. **1667** MILTON *P.L.* XI. 519 To serve ungovern'd appetite.. a brutish vice, Inductive mainly to the sin of Eve. **1825** in *Law Rep.* 9 App. Cases 329/1 The inductive cause and primary object of granting the obligation was to secure an annuity to Jean Knox.

†**2.** Productive *of*, giving rise to. *Obs.*

1613 T. MILLES tr. *Mexia's, etc. Treas. Anc. & Mod. T.* 957/1 Wee know and perceiue it [air] to be the operatiue and inductiue Instrument, of the vertue of life. **1677** HALE *Prim. Orig. Man* II. i. 132 Probable and inductive of Credibility, though not of Science or Infallibility. **1772** *Junius Lett.* lxviii. 343 Circumstances inductive of a doubt, whether the prisoner be guilty or innocent.

3. Caused by induction; of induced nature or origin. *rare.*

1827 COLEBROOKE *Misc. Ess.* (1837) I. 371 Its activity is not of its essence, but inductive through its organs.

4. *Logic.* **a.** Of the nature of, based upon, or characterized by the use of induction, or reasoning from particular facts to general principles.

1764 REID *Inquiry* vi. §24 (R.) Upon this principle of our constitution.. all inductive reasoning, and all our reasoning from analogy is grounded. **1828** MILL in *Westm. Rev.* IX. 140 They talk in high-flown language, not always conveying very precise ideas, of a supposed system of *inductive* logic, which is to supersede the syllogistic, and really to accomplish still more than the other even attempts. *Ibid.* 150 An inductive logic would be highly useful as a supplement to the syllogistic logic, not to supersede it. **1830** HERSCHEL *Stud. Nat. Phil.* 104 The whole of natural philosophy consists entirely of a series of inductive generalizations. **1837** WHEWELL (*titlwhat ise*) History of the Inductive Sciences. **1864** BOWEN *Logic* viii. 262 In Inductive reasoning, the parts are first stated, and what is predicated of them is also predicated of the whole they constitute. **1865** —— *Auguste Comte* 58 Comte's determined abstinence from the word and the idea of Cause, had much to do with his inability to conceive an Inductive Logic. **1869** FOWLER (*title*) The Elements of Inductive Logic. **1874** DARWIN in *Life & Lett.* (1887) III. 193 My mind is so fixed by the inductive method, that I cannot appreciate deductive reasoning. **1934** A. C. EWING *Idealism* iv. 170 An inductive logic which dispenses with such arguments. **1964** F. BOWERS *Bibliogr. & Textual Crit.* II. i. 36, I am aware that *inductive* and *deductive* as applied to reasoning have acquired philosophical half-lights that may in the end cause a subtle mind to deny that there is any difference between them. **1964** E. MENDELSON *Introd. Math. Logic* 9 In the course of this deduction, P (n, y_1,..., yk) is called the inductive hypothesis.

b. Of persons: Using the method of induction.

1764 REID *Inquiry* vi. §9. 150 He planned out much work for his followers who call themselves inductive philosophers. **1842** N. B. WARD *Closed Cases Pl.* iii. (1852) 68 The inductive mind of a Davy or a Faraday. **1871** TYLOR *Prim. Cult.* I. 4 This man's observation may have been as narrow as his inferences are crude and prejudiced, but nevertheless he has been an inductive philosopher more than forty years without knowing it.

c. With reference to ethics (see quots.).

1861 MILL *Utilit.* i. 3 What may be termed the inductive school of Ethics.. according to it, right and wrong as well as truth and falsehood are questions of observation and experience. **1869** LECKY *Europ. Mor.* I. i. 3 The other [theory of morals] as the Epicurean, the inductive, the utilitarian or the selfish.

5. a. Of the nature of, pertaining to, or due to electric or magnetic induction. Also ***inductive coupling***, coupling between two electric circuits or devices that is due to their mutual inductance; so ***inductive-coupled*** adj., coupled in this way; ***inductive reactance***, reactance due to inductance.

1832 FARADAY in *Phil. Trans. R. Soc.* CXXII. 137 The inductive force was of course greater. **1849** MRS. SOMERVILLE *Connex. Phys. Sc.* (ed. 8) xxviii. 314 The inductive process may be indefinitely modified by the various circumstances of the quantity and intensity of the electricity. **1871** TYNDALL *Fragm. Sc.* (1879) I. xv. 410 When.. good hard magnets act on each other from a sufficient distance, the inductive action practically vanishes. **1879** G. PRESCOTT *Sp. Telephone* 86 *note*, The phenomenon of inductive retardation in long ocean cables. **1907** Inductive coupling [see *direct coupling* s.v. DIRECT *a.* 7]. **1911** *Whittaker's Electr. Engineer's Pocket-Bk.* (ed. 3) 124 The two may be added algebraically, the capacity reactance being considered as opposite in sign to the inductive reactance. **1913** A. F. COLLINS *Man. Wireless Telegr.* (ed. 3) vii. 126 (*heading*) Diagram of an inductive-coupled resonator. **1954** E. MOLLOY *Radio & Television Engineer's Ref. Bk.* vii. 7 Figs. 7 and 8, with closely-coupled inductive or direct coupling, give no harmonic voltage reduction in the aerial circuit other than that afforded by the aerial loading coil. **1960** E. HUGHES *Electr. Technol.* xi. 339 The inductive reactance is proportional to the frequency. **1966** *McGraw-Hill Encycl. Sci. & Technol.* III. 521/1 Inductive-coupled circuits have a common magnetic flux linking the two circuits.

b. Possessing inductance.

1902 *Encycl. Brit.* XXX. 599/2 In series with the inductive circuit another non-inductive circuit is joined. **1920** *Whittaker's Electr. Engineer's Pocket-Bk.* (ed. 4) 129 The current through an inductive circuit of negligible resistance lags 90° behind the impressed e.m.f. **1962** [see CAPACITIVE *a.*].

6. Introductory.

1868 *Act 31 & 32 Vict.* c. 101 Sched. (B) No. 1, After the inductive and dispositive clauses, the deed may proceed thus [etc.]. **1875** [see INDUCTION 3 b].

7. *Embryol.* Of, pertaining to, or producing induction (sense 9 b).

1931 J. NEEDHAM *Chem. Embryol.* I. 578 The inductive power of the cells of the dorsal lip is not abolished by drying them. **1962** SAXÉN & TOIVONEN *Primary Embryonic Induction* i. 7 The blastoporal lip of an early gastrula, and that part of an older one, have qualitatively different inductive properties. *Ibid.*, Until 1932, the real nature of the inductive action presented an enigma. **1967** T. W. TORREY *Morphogenesis Vertebr.* (ed. 2) xviii. 359/1 When extracts are treated with proteolytic enzymes, inductive ability is destroyed.

8. Comb. ***inductive-minded*** adj.

1905 W. JAMES in *Mind* XIV. 191 The one condition of understanding humanism is to become inductive-minded oneself, to drop vigorous definitions, and follow lines of least resistance 'on the whole'.

Hence **in'ductiveness**, the quality of being inductive.

c **1820** FABER *Eight Dissert.* VI. vi. (1845) II. 54 Understanding the conjunction in its common import of inductiveness. *a* **1866** J. GROTE *Exam. Utilit. Philos.* xvii. (1870) 260 Such inductiveness therefore as there is in utilitarianism.

in'ductively, *adv.* [f. prec. + -LY[2].]

1. By inductive reasoning.

a **1716** SOUTH *Serm.* (1744) VIII. vii. 197 This I shall make appear inductively, by recounting the several ends and intents, to which.. it may be designed. **1800** *Med. Jrnl.* IV. 487 No sufficient documents have yet been furnished, either experimentally, inductively, or analogically. **1881** SEELEY *Bonaparte* in *Macm. Mag.* XLIV. 165/2 My desire is to see this question.. treated inductively and without ungrounded assumptions.

2. By electric induction.

1848 W. S. HARRIS *Rudimentary Electr.* iii. 52 The cover, being insulated, does not take up the electricity of the plate, but is acted upon inductively. **1870** R. M. FERGUSON *Electr.* 12 The two magnets.. act inductively on each other and so lessen the conjoint power. **1879** G. PRESCOTT *Sp. Telephone* 22 The current pulsations, which are inductively produced by the vibrations of the diaphragms. **1892** S. P. THOMPSON

Dynamo-Elect. Mach. (ed. 4) 101 In disk armatures of the.. Wallace-Farmer type, each of the parallel coils acted inductively on its neighbour.

inductivism (ɪn'dʌktɪvɪz(ə)m). [f. INDUCTIVE *a.* + -ISM.] The preference for, use of, or belief in the superiority of, inductive as opposed to deductive methods; the belief that scientific laws can be inferred from observational evidence. Opp. DEDUCTIVISM.

a **1866** J. GROTE *Treat. Moral Ideals* (1876) xviii. 425 The matter is complex..on account of the exceeding inappropriateness of the assumption of inductivism for anything in its way so idealist as Utilitarianism is. **1951** *Mind* LX. 43 Professor Popper..attacks frequently what he calls 'observationalism' or 'inductivism'. **1956** E. H. HUTTEN *Lang. Mod. Physics* vi. 229 If we take induction as a psychological process of discovery and, at the same time, as a logical method of proof, we end up with an insoluble problem... Neither Hume's scepticism nor Mill's belief in the uniformity of nature are solutions of the inductive problem, but rather they are attempts to banish a riddle. There is, to-day, an ever-increasing number of philosophers as well as of scientists who reject this inductivism, and they advise us to drop the term 'induction' altogether when describing scientific method. **1959** K. R. POPPER *Logic Sci. Discovery* I. i. 30 The view that a hypothesis can only be empirically *tested*..might be called 'deductivism', in contrast to 'inductivism'. **1962** [see DEDUCTIVISM]. **1965** J. W. N. WATKINS *Hobbes's Syst. Ideas* ii. 34 (*heading*) Repudiation of inductivism. **1972** A. J. AYER *Probability & Evidence* iii. 74 Popper..explicitly rejects what he calls inductivism. **1972** *Nature* 10 Nov. 110/1 The author then delineates in turn three theories of the logical structure of science—inductivism, Popperian falsificationism and positivism.

inductivist (ɪn'dʌktɪvɪst), *sb.* and *a.* [f. INDUCTIVE *a.* + -IST.]

A. *sb.* One who follows or upholds inductivism or inductive methods; one who holds that the method of science is inductive. Cf. prec. word.

1940 K. R. POPPER in *Mind* XLIX. 421 Jeans was.. originally an inductivist, that is, he thought that theories are obtained from experience by some more or less simple procedure. **1962** *Listener* 22 Mar. 513/2 The kind of sociologist whom Sartre despises, the cautious inductivist, collects facts but has no theoretical equipment to understand them. **1968** A. J. AYER *Origins Pragmatism* 99 The inductivist was having a run of failures. **1968** J. J. C. SMART *Between Sci. & Philos.* vi. 196 The inductivists, who wish to justify inductive procedures.

B. *adj.* Of, pertaining to, or employing inductivism or inductive methods; implying that the method of science is inductive.

1945 *Mind* LIV. 3 Certain 'inductivist' accounts of scientific procedure seem to assume that relevant evidence, or relevant data, can be collected in the context of an inquiry prior to the formulation of any hypothesis. **1956** E. H. HUTTEN *Lang. Mod. Physics* vi. 268 To believe that we learn by induction is part of the inductivist myth which identifies a psychological process with a logical method. **1960** E. H. GOMBRICH *Art & Illusion* ix. 321 This inductivist ideal of pure observation has proved a mirage in science no less than in art. **1968** J. J. C. SMART *Between Sci. & Philos.* vii. 247 It is doubtful..whether such an inductivist account of geometry will do.

inductivity (ɪndʌk'tɪvɪtɪ). [f. INDUCTIVE + -ITY.] Inductive quality; power or capacity for magnetic induction.

1888 HEAVISIDE in *Philos. Mag.* Ser. v. XXVI. 367 When the inductivities are equal, there is a material simplification.

inducto- (ɪn'dʌktəʊ), used as a combining form of INDUCTION, in forming names of some electric apparatus or processes, as **inductometer** (-'ɒmɪtə(r)), an instrument for ascertaining the force of electrical induction. **in'ductoscope**, an instrument for detecting induction. **in'ductoscript**, a figure produced on a photographic plate by means of an electric discharge from the object, usually by an induction-coil; the process of obtaining such figures.

1839 FARADAY *Exp. Researches* I. 416, I beg to propose for it..the name of *Differential Inductometer*. **1892** F. J. SMITH in *Proc. Physical Soc.* XI. 353 The inductoscript is a name I venture to propose as it somewhat suggests the nature of the process. **1893** *Times* 11 May 6/1 The Rev. F. J. Smith's inductoscript..By its means figures and pictures are made by placing the object to be reproduced in contact with an ordinary photographic plate placed upon a conducting sheet of metal.

inductomeric (ɪn,dʌktə'mɛrɪk), *a. Chem.* [f. INDUCTO- + *-meric* as in ELECTROMERIC *a.*] Of, pertaining to, or designating the ability of an atom or group to become polarized along a saturated bond by an external electric field (e.g. that of another molecule).

1933 C. K. INGOLD in *Jrnl. Chem. Soc.* 1124 It cannot be doubted that a counterpart of two coexisting polarisations obtains also for polarisability effects, and that an inductive polarisability or inductomeric effect completes the scheme annexed. **1943** A. E. REMICK *Electronic Interpretations Org. Chem.* v. 61 The extent to which the inductomeric effect is called into play..will depend on the strength of the polarizing field and on the polarizability of the bond in question. **1953** C. K. INGOLD *Struct. & Mech. Org. Chem.* ii. 72 By inductomeric polarisability is understood the polarisability which atoms and groups in saturated combination exhibit along the lines of their bonds... For isoelectronic atoms with completed valency shells, inductomeric polarisability thus depends on electro-negativity. **1956** E. DE B. BARNETT *Mechanism Org. Chem. Reactions* i. 4 If a powerful electron-repelling group such as a hydroxyl ion approaches a hydrogen atom of a nitromethane molecule..the resulting inductomeric effect is so great that a hydrogen atom is completely protonized. **1959** E. S. GOULD *Mechanism & Struct. Org. Chem.* vii. 208 A number of workers..prefer to differentiate inductive influences in reactants and products from those electronic shifts that occur in the activated complex as a result of the electrical demands of one reagent on another. The former are termed inductive effects, the latter inductomeric effects.

inductor (ɪn'dʌktə(r)). [a. L. *inductor*, agent-n. from *indūcĕre*, INDUCT *v.*]

1. One who introduces or initiates. *rare.*

1652 BROME *City Wit* v. Wks. 1873 I. 364 *Try.* Who should act and personate these?.. *Sar.* I'le play the Inductor, and then we are all fitted. **1841** L. HUNT *Seer* II. (1864) 28 Inductor of ladies and gentlemen into the shapely and salutary art of dancing.

2. One who inducts a clergyman to a benefice.

1726 AYLIFFE *Parergon* 283 If Inductors received more than this on the Score of such Induction..they were..to incur a Suspension *ab officio*. **1818** CRUISE *Digest* (ed. 2) III. 15 After which the inductor opens the door, and puts the clerk into the church, who usually tolls the bell to make his induction public, and known to the parishioners; after this the inductor endorses a certificate of the induction on the mandate, which is witnessed by the persons present.

3. a. Any part of an electric apparatus which acts inductively on another. *Esp.* one which induces an e.m.f. or current in another part (as in an inductor alternator).

1867 W. THOMSON in *Proc. R. Soc.* XVI. 67 To stems connected with the inside coatings of two Leyden phials are connected [cylindrical] metal pieces, which..I shall call inductors and receivers. *Ibid.* 68 Suppose now a small positive charge of electricity be given to the first jar. Its inductor electrifies negatively each drop of water breaking away in its centre from the continuous uninsulated water above. **1881** MAXWELL *Electr. & Magn.* I. 295 The moveable conductors are called Carriers, and the fixed ones may be called Inductors, Receivers, and Regenerators. **1892** *Electrician* 13 May 37/2 Electric currents are produced by revolving the magnetic inductors in proximity to the magnet. **1909** R. B. WHITMAN *Motor-Car Princ.* (rev. ed.) 320 The Remy magneto is of this type, and Fig. 17 is a diagram of the revolving core, or inductor, with the coil surrounding it. **1915** W. H. ECCLES *Wireless Telegr.* 204 This alternator is of the inductor type... The inductor or rotor is a chrome-nickel steel disc about a foot diameter with 300 slots cut $\frac{1}{2}$ in. apart near its edge. **1941** A. W. JUDGE *Aircraft Engines* II. ix. 338 The polar inductor magneto has stationary magnets as well as coils, and the changes of magnetic flux are obtained by rotating soft-iron inductors between the poles of the magnets. **1956** D. WARBURTON-BROWN *Induction Heating Pract.* i. 8 In any induction heating arrangement there are three main components, namely: (a) a high-frequency generator; (b) a work-coil or inductor; (c) a work-piece.

attrib. **1891** *Times* 2 Oct. 3/2 In the machinery hall they show the Kingdon inductor dynamo, a most efficient and interesting machine.

b. A conductor or device in which an e.m.f. or current is induced; **earth inductor**, a device for investigating the earth's magnetic field, consisting essentially of a coil of wire that can be rapidly turned about an axis in its own plane so that a current is induced in it proportional to the component of the field normal to the axis of rotation.

1837 tr. Gauss in *Mag. Pop. Sci.* III. 109 A few weeks ago I had my inductor increased again, (from 3527 to about 6800 convolutions,) and now its effects are much stronger. The sensations it produces by the current being transmitted through the body..are not only very perceptible, but, when the inductor is rapidly moved, painful almost beyond endurance. **1883** E. ATKINSON tr. *Ganot's Elem. Treat. Physics* (ed. 11) x. vi. 852 The inductor itself..consists of a drum-shaped frame of soft iron wire covered with a layer of insulating material, and fixed to an axle which..is rotated. .. Machines of this class give continuous currents, but alternators..are also constructed. **1883** *Encycl. Brit.* XV. 240/2 This is the principle of Weber's 'earth inductor', by means of which the horizontal and vertical components of the earth's force can be measured, and in consequence the declination and inclination determined. **1901** SHELDON & MASON *Dynamo Electr. Machinery* iii. 45 By inductor is meant that part of the winding conductor which lies on the face of the armature that sweeps past the pole pieces, and.. in which E.M.F. is induced. **1940** R. R. LAWRENCE *Princ. Alternating-Current Machinery* (ed. 3) i. 1 Any direct-current generator, with the exception of the unipolar generator, is in fact an alternator in which the alternating voltage set up in the armature inductors is rectified by means of a commutator. **1966** *McGraw-Hill Encycl. Sci. & Technol.* IV. 338/2 The earth inductor has almost completely supplanted the dip circle throughout the world for precise measurement of magnetic inclination. **1973** *Sci. Amer.* Feb. 101/2 A unipolar inductor is a magnetized metal sphere. One terminal of an external circuit is attached to one of the sphere's poles of rotation and the other terminal is a stationary brush in contact with the sphere's equator. When the sphere is spun, a galvanometer in the circuit registers the passage of an electric current.

c. An induction coil (Ruhmkorff coil).

1872 J. & C. LASSELL tr. *Schellen's Spectrum Analysis* xxx. 157 By connecting the binding screws 1, 2 on one side with the inductor, and on the other side..with the platinum wire *b* of the first vessel, and a_2 of the last vessel,..the electric current may be made to pass through all the liquids. **1904** *Electr. World & Engin.* XLIV. 513/2 A very imposing view ..is given by the seven induction coils arranged upon steps in the centre of the cabinet, beginning at the bottom, with an inductor giving a 40-inch spark and ending at the top with one of 10-inch spark.

d. A device (commonly a coil) possessing inductance or used on account of its inductance.

1928 STERLING & KRUSE *Radio Manual* i. 20 Iron Core Inductance.—This form of inductor is made by winding many turns of wire on an iron core. **1950** K. HENNEY *Radio Engin. Handbk.* (ed. 4) iii. 124 Straight wires are used as inductors in h-f applications where the inductance must be very low. **1963** WILLIAMS & PRIGMORE *Electr. Engin.* v. 129 A standard mutual inductor..can be made by winding coil No. 1 on a long straight core and winding No. 2 round the mid-portion of No. 1.

4. *Chem.* Any substance which while reacting with one substance (the 'actor') increases the rate at which this reacts with a second substance (the 'acceptor'); a substance that has an accelerating effect on a reaction but differs from a catalyst in being consumed.

1903 *Jrnl. Chem. Soc.* LXXXIV. II. 277 The substance taking part in both these reactions..is termed the 'actor'; the substance taking part only in the primary reaction..is the 'inductor'; the substance taking part only in the secondary reaction is the 'acceptor'. **1918** *Chem. Abstr.* XII. 111 A number of reduction reactions which take place at ordinary temps. in sunlight, fail to proceed even at more elevated temps. in the dark. The reactions may be induced to take place in the dark by the addition of small amts. of certain oxidizing agents ('inductors'). **1937** *Thorpe's Dict. Appl. Chem.* (ed. 4) I. 12/2 *Acceptor*, a substance..which normally is not oxidised by oxygen (or reduced by hydrogen) but is oxidised (or reduced) when in presence of another substance termed the inductor..which itself is undergoing oxidation (or reduction) by a third substance the actor. **1966** A. G. SYKES *Kinetics Inorg. Reactions* ix. 205 Arsenite ions are..effective in inducing the reaction between Cr^{VI} and iodide, and, at high iodide concentrations, a ratio of two equivalents of iodide to one of the inductor are likewise involved.

5. *Embryol.* A region of an embryo, or a substance produced by such a region, capable of causing induction (sense 9 b).

1929 *Biol. Abstr.* III. 1495/2 The action of the inductor, whatever it be, manifests itself in the activation of a supernumerary embryonic field. **1946** L. B. AREY *Developmental Anat.* (ed. 5) ix. 163 The specific, morphogenetic effect brought about by a chemical stimulus transmitted from one embryonic part to another is known as an induction or evocation. The part exerting this influence is an inductor or organizer, and the chemical substance emitted is an evocator. **1963** E. J. W. BARRINGTON *Introd. Gen. & Compar. Endocrinol.* vi. 152 Germ cells that enter the cortex become female, those that enter the medulla become male, and in embryological terminology these two regions are said to act respectively as female and male inductors. **1967** T. W. TORREY *Morphogenesis Vertebr.* (ed. 2) xviii. 359/1 An inherent difficulty in the identification of the 'natural' inductor lies in the minute amount available for analysis.

6. Special Comb.: **inductor alternator**, an alternator in which both armature and field windings are stationary, the current being produced by the periodic variation in the magnetic flux through the armature windings as successive teeth of a rotating inductor pass by; **(earth-)inductor compass**, any of various kinds of compass in which the earth's magnetic field is made to induce in a coil an electric current whose strength depends on the relative orientation of the coil to the field; **inductor generator** = *inductor alternator*.

1893 W. P. MAYCOCK *Electr. Lighting* II. viii. 239 Kingdon's *Inductor Alternator. **1940** R. R. LAWRENCE *Princ. Alternating-Current Machinery* (ed. 3) 3 An inductor alternator is usually characterized by large armature reaction, relatively high magnetic density, small air gap and greater weight than alternators of the other types. The difficulties in the design of a satisfactory inductor alternator have caused this type of alternator to go out of use. **1965** J. HINDMARSH *Electr. Machines* viii. 482 Another special case of single-phase generator is the inductor alternator used to provide high-frequency supplies in the range 1000 to 10,000 cycles/sec for use in induction furnaces. Here, all the windings are on the stator. **1922** *Rep. U.S. Nat. Advisory Comm. Aeronaut.* No. 128. 44 The earth *inductor compass ..was developed by Dr. Paul R. Heyl and Dr. Lyman J. Briggs of the Bureau of Standards. **1926** *Encycl. Brit.* Suppl. I. 19/2 The earth inductor compass, developed in America, depends upon the measurement of the electromotive force induced by the earth's magnetic field in a coil rotating about a vertical axis. **1927** LINDBERGH in *Sci. Monthly* XXV. 91/1, I also had a magnetic compass; but it was the inductor compass which guided me so faithfully that I hit the Irish coast... The inductor compass was so accurate that I really needed no other guide. **1931** M. F. SCHOEFFEL in P. V. H. Weems *Air Navigation* vii. 93 Although the armature of an inductor compass is gyroscopic, yet, since it is also pendulous, it tends to..bank with the plane. **1943** REDPATH & COBURN *Air Transport Navigation* iv. 80 The principle of the inductor compass is to generate electric currents utilizing the earth's magnetic field to operate suitable indicating instruments in the cockpit. **1958** *Van Nostrand's Sci. Encycl.* (ed. 3) 386/2 The earth-inductor compass was designed..for use on aircraft, but has been rendered obsolete by the aperiodic and gyro-flux-gate instruments. **1940** *Chambers's Techn. Dict.* 446/1 *Inductor generator. **1957** *Encycl. Brit.* VIII. 148/1 For a given number of poles and a given speed of rotation, an inductor generator delivers twice the frequency of the present common types of A.C. generators. In the early years of radio telegraphy the inductor generator was the best source of the frequencies required.

inductorium (ɪndʌkˈtɔərɪəm). [mod.L., neut. of late L. *inductōrius* INDUCTORY: see -ORIUM. (L. had *inductōrium* in the sense 'covering': see INDUCE *v.* 7).] A name for the induction-coil as adapted for the display of the electric spark.

1875 in KNIGHT *Dict. Mech.* 1182/2. **1877** ROSENTHAL *Muscles & Nerves* 36 An apparatus of this kind is called a sliding inductorium. **1881** *Sci. American* XLIV. 388 This is the foundation of what is now called induction coils or inductoriums.

in'ductory, *a.* [ad. late L. *inductōri-us*, in Augustine in sense 'leading on, misleading', f. *indūcĕre, induct-*: see -ORY.] Leading in; introductory.

1632 C. DOWNING *State Eccles. Kingd.* (1634) 70 [They] are not Lawes inductory of a new, but declaratorie of the ancient authoritie of our Prince. **1831** *Fraser's Mag.* III. 513 Having made these admissions for the sake of candour, and done that justice to the administration of Lord Grey which their inductory conduct deserves [etc.].

†in'ductric, *a. Electr. Obs.* [irreg. f. INDUCTION, after *electric*.] Operating by induction.

1855 NOAD *Man. Electr.* I. 54 [see INDUCTEOUS]. *Ibid.* 725 The manner in which this machine acts will be clearly understood by reference to the general principles of *volta-inductric* action. **1855** MAYNE *Expos. Lex., Inductric*, a term synonymous with..inducing. *Inductric Contraction*, a term for that contraction of the muscles, obtained without employing the electric current for its production.

So **in'ductrical** *a.* = prec. (Webster, 1864).

indue, variant of ENDUE, q.v.

induellar, -er, obs. Sc. forms of INDWELLER.

induement, var. of ENDUEMENT, *Obs.*

induire, obs. Sc. form of ENDURE.

†indu'ition. *Obs. rare.* [irreg. f. L. *indu-ĕre* (ppl. stem *indūt-*).] Putting on (of a garment).

1584 R. SCOT *Discov. Witchcr.* xv. xxiv. (1886) 371 Item, there must be..communion, and induition of the surplis.

†in'dulcate, *v. Obs. rare.* Also 7 **indulciate.** [f. ppl. stem of L. *indulcāre* to sweeten, f. *in-* (IN-²) + *dulcāre* to sweeten, *dulcis* sweet.] *trans.* To sweeten. Hence **†indul'cation** (indulciation), sweetening.

1628 FELTHAM *Resolves* II. [i] xli. 123 A friendly warre doth indulciate the insuing cloze. **1661** —— *On St. Luke* (1696) 323 The secret sweetness that gratifies and indulciates all his spirits. **1656** BLOUNT *Glossogr., Indulcate, Indulciate*, to make sweet. **1658** PHILLIPS, *Indulcation* or *Indulciation*, a sweetning, a making sweet.

indulge (ɪnˈdʌldʒ), *v.* Also 8 **endulge.** [ad. L. *indulgē-re* (intr. with dative) to be courteous or complaisant, to be kind or indulgent, to yield, give oneself up (to), indulge in; (with acc. and dat.) to bestow as a favour, to concede, grant, allow. The verb was adopted in 17th c. in several of the L. senses, the way having been prepared by the earlier use of *indulgence, indulgent*.]

I. Transitive.

1. a. To treat (a person) with such favour, kindness, or complaisance as he has no claim to, but desires or likes; to gratify by compliance, or by absence of restraint or strictness; to humour by yielding to the wishes of. (The personal obj. represents L. dative.) Const. *in*.

1660 R. COKE *Power & Subj.* 116 King Charles had not the same Reason of State to indulge the House of Commons. **1661** MARVELL *Corr.* xxi. Wks. 1872–5 II. 55 In the matter of your two companyes..he is willing to indulge you. **1749** WESLEY *Hymn, 'Jesu, thou Sovereign Lord'*, Indulge us, Lord, in this request. **1852** MRS. STOWE *Uncle Tom's C.* xvi, The fact is, St. Clare indulges every creature under this roof but his own wife.

b. *refl.* To give free course to one's inclination or liking; to gratify oneself, take one's pleasure. Const. *in* (†in first quot. *to*: cf. 7).

1659 HAMMOND *On Ps.* ciii. 14 [They] do not indulge themselves to any deliberate sin. **1736** BUTLER *Anal.* Introd., Wks. 1874 I. 7 There are some, who..indulge themselves in vain and idle speculations. **1802** MAR. EDGEWORTH *Moral T.* (1816) I. xviii. 147 Pleasing anticipations in which he indulged himself. **1887** BOWEN *Virg. Æneid* II. 776 Why so fain to indulge thee in this wild passion of woe?

c. To favour or gratify (a person) *with* something given or granted.

1790 W. WRIGHTE *Grotesque Archit.* 9 The author hopes he may be indulged with observing, that he hath..seen a fine piece of water in the park. **1800** *Asiat. Ann. Reg., Proc. E. Ind. Ho.* 146/1 Mr. Henchman gave notice of a motion..to indulge Mr. Dundas, during his life, with the house in Downing Street.

d. *fig.*

1697 DRYDEN *Virg. Georg.* III. 320 Indulge his Growth, and his gaunt Sides supply. **1710** STEELE *Tatler* No. 175 ¶1, I have allowed Tale-Bearers to indulge the Intervals of my Female Patients. **1752** YOUNG *Brothers* I. i, The sword by both too much indulg'd in blood. **1951** AUDEN *Nones* (1952) 39 How jocular the bells as They Indulge the peccant shore.

2. To grant an indulgence, privilege, or dispensation to: see INDULGENCE II.

1662 GUNNING *Lent Fast* 57 In holy Lent the Lord hath indulged these two weekly daies [Saturday, and Lord's day]. **1673** SIR W. COVENTRY *Sp. Ho. Commons* 14 Feb. in *Grey's Debates* 1667–94 II. 30 Some are for indulging Protestant Subjects only, and some for extending it to Catholic subjects. **1682–1816** [see INDULGED 2]. *a* **1832** MACKINTOSH *Revol. of 1688*, Wks. 1846 II. 161 A Declaration for indulging Nonconformists in matters ecclesiastical.

3. To gratify (a desire or inclination); to give free course to, give way to, yield to, give oneself up to. Sometimes in weaker sense: To entertain, cherish, foster.

1656 BLOUNT *Glossogr.* Pref. 3 To indulge my own fancy, I began to compile this work. **1697** DRYDEN *Virg. Georg.* I. 408 Saylors..crown their Vessels, then indulge their Ease. **1777** WATSON *Philip II* (1839) 465 Delusive hopes which he had long fondly indulged. **1781** GIBBON *Decl. & F.* xxxiii. (1869) II. 252 He indulged the sterner passions of anger and revenge. **1874** GREEN *Short Hist.* iii. §5. 140 The fall of Hubert de Burgh enabled him to indulge his preference for aliens.

4. To bestow or grant (something) as a favour, or as a matter of free grace; to allow or concede as an indulgence. Const. *unto, to, indirect obj.* Now *rare*.

In passive, ***something must be indulged to*** = some indulgence must be shown to.

1638 F. JUNIUS *Paint. of Ancients* 164 He indulged unto you, O Lysippe, to conceive him great. *Ibid.* 337 Somthing must be indulged unto the wits of great Masters..onely that we doe excuse small mistakes in them. **1647** CLARENDON *Hist. Reb.* I. §32 In this the Duke resumed the same impetuosity he had so much indulged to Himself in the debate of the journey. **1648** E. SPARKE in *J. Shute's Sarah & Hagar* a iv a, Scarce indulging himself necessary Relaxations. **1650** FULLER *Pisgah* II. v. 126 On Benhadads feigned submission he indulged life unto him. **1709** STRYPE *Ann. Ref.* (1824) I. xviii. 338 In the conclusion of the Queen's letters patents, where she indulged the Colleges that liberty. **1774** S. HALLIFAX *Anal. Rom. Civ. Law* Pref. (1795) 11 A Valuable privilege is likewise indulged to Graduates in this faculty. **1870** LOWELL *Among my Bks.* Ser. I. (1873) 182 In the utterance of great passions, something must be indulged to the extravagance of Nature.

5. *Comm.* To grant an indulgence on (a bill); to allow (a person) an extension of the time within which a bill is to be met. Cf. INDULGENCE 5.

1766 W. GORDON *Gen. Counting-ho.* 341 An inland bill may be indulged before protesting. **1827** CHITTY *Bills of Exchange* (ed. 7) 298 Though the giving time to an acceptor or indorser, will thus in general discharge all subsequent indorsers, who would be entitled to resort to the party indulged, the giving time to a subsequent indorser, will not discharge a prior indorser.

II. Intransitive.

†6. ***indulge to***: to grant indulgence *to*, to give free course to, give way to, gratify (a propensity, etc. = 3; rarely, a person = 1). Orig. = L. intr. use with dative; but in later use coinciding in sense with *indulge in* (7). Also with *indirect passive*. *Obs.*

1646 H. LAWRENCE *Comm. Angells* 124 By a soft and delicate life, by indulgeing to bodily things. **1647** CLARENDON *Hist. Reb.* I. §130 He indulged still too much to those importunate and insatiate appetites. **1674** *Govt. Tongue* VI. §5. 124 There lies sure no obligations upon any man, to wrong himself, to indulge to another. **1738–41** WARBURTON *Div. Legat.* (1758–65) III. 334 By indulging too much to abstract speculation. **1790** G. WALKER *Serm.* II. xxii. 149 Indulging to a worldly spirit at the throne of grace.

7. ***indulge in*** (ellipt. for *indulge oneself in*, 1 b): To give free course to one's inclination for; to gratify one's desire or appetite for; to take one's pleasure freely in (an action, course of conduct, etc., or a material luxury). †In first quot., to dwell with pleasure *on*. Also with *indirect passive*.

1706 ESTCOURT *Fair Examp.* v. i. 58 While my transported Soul indulges on the Thought. **1763** MRS. BROOKE *Lady J. Mandeville* (1782) II. 189 The tears we shed are charming, we even indulge in them. *a* **1784** JOHNSON (Webster 1828), Most men are more willing to indulge in easy vices, than to practice laborious virtues. **1837** DICKENS *Pickw.* xlv, Any little amusement in which he could indulge. **1842** A. COMBE *Physiol. Digestion* (ed. 4) 210 Bodily exercise and exposure to the open air are more indulged in. **1876** GEO. ELIOT *Dan. Der.* II. xiv. I. 268 Some of the gentlemen strolled a little and indulged in a cigar. **1883** C. J. WILLS *Mod. Persia* 96 Card-playing..is only indulged in by the less reputable of the community.

8. To gratify a desire, appetite, etc.; to take one's pleasure; *spec.* to 'partake', i.e. (too) freely of intoxicants (*colloq.*).

a **1718** T. PARNELL *Poems on Several Occasions* (1722) 125 Wretch that I was! I might have warn'd the Dame, Yet sat indulging as the Danger came. **1953** P. C. BERG *Dict. New Words* 96/2 *Indulge*, to take alcoholic liquors without restraint. **1973** P. O'DONNELL *Silver Mistress* xv. 250 Tarrant..took out his cigar case. He had not indulged all night.

Hence **indulgeable** (ɪnˈdʌldʒəb(ə)l) *a.*, fit to be indulged; **†in'dulgement** = INDULGENCE.

1691 WOOD *Ath. Oxon.* II. 381 Giving himself the liberty of too frequent indulgments. **1791** *Gentl. Mag.* 20/2 He was qualified by law, as well as indulgeable in reason and equity, for non-residence. *a* **1846** *Penny Mag.* cited in WORCESTER for *Indulgment*.

indulged (ɪnˈdʌldʒd), *ppl. a.* [f. prec. + -ED¹.]

1. Gratified or favoured by compliance; humoured, etc. (see the verb).

1736 BUTLER *Anal.* II. vi. 300 If there be a strong bias within, suppose from indulged passion, to favour the deceit. **1831** KEBLE *Serm.* v. (1848) 107 Partaking in other men's sins, merely by brooding over them in fancy, with anything like indulged approbation or sympathy.

2. That has received or accepted an Indulgence; in *Sc. Hist.* applied to those Presbyterian ministers, who, in the reigns of Charles II and James II, were licensed to hold services under certain conditions: see INDULGENCE 4.

1682 *Sec. Plea Nonconf.* 37 When His Majesty was moved to grant an Indulgence, the indulged were to give their Names, and their Places. **1693** *Apol. Clergy Scot.* 105 Mr. Rate, then Minister of Dundee, an Indulg'd Presbyterian. **1816** SCOTT *Old Mort.* v, My uncle..is of opinion that we enjoy a reasonable freedom of conscience under the indulged clergymen.

indulgence (ɪnˈdʌldʒəns), *sb.* [a. F. *indulgence* (12th c. in Littré), or ad. L. *indulgēntia* indulgence, complaisance, fondness, remission, f. *indulgēnt-em* INDULGENT: see -ENCE.]

I. General senses.

1. The action of indulging (a person), or the fact of being indulgent; gratification of another's desire or humour; favouring forbearance or relaxation of restraint. Sometimes dyslogistic: Fond humouring, over-lenient treatment.

1382 WYCLIF *Isa.* lxiii. 9 In his loue and in his indulgence he aȝeen boȝte them, and bar hem. *c* **1386** CHAUCER *Wife's Prol.* 84 And for to been a wyf he yaf me leue Of Indulgence. **1604** R. CAWDREY *Table Alph., Indulgence*, sufferance, too gentle intreating. **1610** SHAKS. *Temp.* Epil. 20 As you from crimes would pardon'd be, Let your Indulgence set me free. **1625** FLETCHER, etc. *Fair Maid of Inn* I. i, Some sons Complain of too much rigour in their mothers; I of too much indulgence. **1667** MILTON *P.L.* IX. 1186 Left to her self.. Shee first his weak indulgence will accuse. **1718** *Freethinker* No. 152 ¶11 The first Failure of every Man calls for Indulgence. **1800** *Asiat. Ann. Reg., Proc. E. Ind. Ho.* 90/2 He would not trespass any longer upon the indulgence of the proprietors. **1837** HT. MARTINEAU *Soc. Amer.* III. 106 Indulgence is given her as a substitute for justice. **1863** H. COX *Instit.* I. ix. 137 Where a member, by the indulgence of the House, is permitted to make personal explanations.

b. with *an* and *pl.* An instance of this; an act of indulging; a licence, favour, or privilege granted. (See also II.)

1591 SHAKS. *1 Hen. VI*, I. iii. 35 Stand back..Thou that giu'st Whores Indulgences to sinne. **1664** EVELYN *Sylva* 110 One Mʳ Christopher Darell..of Nudigate, that had a particular Indulgence for the cutting of his Woods at pleasure, though a great Iron-Master. **1712** STEELE *Spect.* No. 545 ¶14 To prepare the Indulgences necessary to this Lady and her Retinue, in advancing the Interests of the Roman Catholic Religion in those Kingdoms. **1849** MACAULAY *Hist. Eng.* x. II. 599 He ordered them to be removed to a more commodious apartment and supplied with every indulgence.

2. The action of indulging (desire, inclination, etc.); the yielding to or gratification of some propensity (const. *of, in,* formerly *to*); the action of indulging *in* some practice, luxury, etc.

1638 F. JUNIUS *Paint. of Ancients* 206 Passions: in which heate doth..more than diligence. Provided onely, That this indulgence doe not deceive us. **1665** BOYLE *Occas. Refl.* IV. xix. (1848) 283 And a full Table..tempt him..to Indulgence to his Appetite, prejudicial to his Health. **1769–72** *Junius Lett.* Pref. 10 The indulgence of private malice. **1843** J. CLASON *Serm.* v. 80 Our continued indulgence in Sin. **1885** S. COX *Expos.* Ser. I. iv. 49 Excessive indulgence of natural appetite and desire.

b. *absol.* The practice or habit of indulging or giving way to one's inclinations; self-gratification, self-indulgence. With *an* and *pl.* A particular act or habit of self-gratification; something indulged in, a luxury.

1649 SIR R. TEMPEST *Entert. Solit.* 5 (T.) The loosenesses and indulgences of this age..bear a proportion with the religion of the Ottomans. **1726** LAW *Chr. Perfect.* ii. 42 A Separation of our Souls from worldly Tempers, vain Indulgences, and unnecessary Cares. **1732** —— *Serious C.* iv. (ed. 2) 54 To grow Rich, that he may live in figure and indulgence. **1818** MRS. SHELLEY *Frankenst.* ii. (1865) 46 The time at length arrives, when grief is rather an indulgence than a necessity. **1835** T. WALKER *Original* viii. (1887) 87 The people..spent their earnings on eating and drinking and other indulgences. **1860** EMERSON *Cond. Life, Considerations* Wks. (Bohn) II. 419 Human nature is prone to indulgence.

II. Specific and technical senses (from 1 b).

3. *R.C. Ch.* **a.** 'A remission of the punishment which is still due to sin after sacramental absolution, this remission being valid in the court of conscience and before God, and being made by an application of the treasure of the Church on the part of a lawful superior' (Amort, quoted in *Catholic Dict.* s.v.).

1362 LANGL. *P. Pl.* A. VIII. 156 And diuinede þat Dowel Indulgence [*B & C texts*, Indulgences] passede, Bienals and Trienals and Busschopes lettres. **1377** *Ibid.* B. XVII. 253 And purchace al þe pardoun of Pampiloun & Rome, And indulgences ynowe. *c* **1380** WYCLIF *Sel. Wks.* III. 345 Many heresies as of assoilingis and indulgencis, and cursyngis, wiþ feyned pardons. *c* **1400** *Apol. Loll.* 9 If it be askid weþer þe pope selle indulgencs and merits of seynts. **1570–6** LAMBARDE *Peramb. Kent* (1826) 300 For confirmation wherof, I will make you partaker of a Popish Indulgence (or pardon, as they termed it) made under the seale of the brotherhead of this house. **1667** MILTON *P.L.* III. 492 Then might ye see..Indulgences, Dispenses, Pardons, Bulls, The sport of Winds. **1717** BERKELEY *Tour Italy* 9 Jan., An indulgence of above six thousand years was got by a visit to

that church on any ordinary day. **1769** ROBERTSON *Chas. V* II. (1826) III. 307 Among others he had recourse to a sale of Indulgences. **1839** KEIGHTLEY *Hist. Eng.* I. 418 He might also ..by paying money, or, by visiting some place of devotion obtain an indulgence to exempt him from the punishment due to one or more of his transgressions. **1885** *Catholic Dict.* (ed. 3) 440. *Ibid.* 444 Divisions of Indulgences.—Plenary remit all, partial a portion, of the temporal punishment due to sin—*e.g.*, an indulgence of forty days, as much as would have been atoned for by forty days of canonical penance.. Indulgences may be temporal —*i.e.* granted only for a time; or again perpetual or indefinite, which last till revoked.. Personal indulgences are those granted to particular persons.. Local indulgences may be gained only in a particular place.. Real indulgences are those attached to crucifixes, medals, etc.

†**b.** Formerly in sense: Remission of sin. *Obs.*

1377 LANGL. *P. Pl.* B. VII. 56 Whan þai drawen on to deye, and Indulgences wolde haue, Her pardoun is ful petit at her partyng hennes. *c* **1425** *Found. St. Bartholomew's* (E.E.T.S.) 3 That he myghte obteyne parfite and plenere pardoun and indulgence of his synnes..he decreid yn hym self to go to the courte of Rome. *c* **1430** *Pilgr. Lyf Manhode* (1869) 52 In þe tenthe þe.. communioun of þe seyntes, and þe indulgence of sinne bi cristenynge and penaunce.

c. Loosely used for an authoritative relaxation of ecclesiastical law or obligation, properly called DISPENSATION (sense 8).

a **1680** BUTLER *Rem.* (1759) I. 243 Your wise and cautious Consciences Are free to take what Course they please; Have plenary Indulgence to dispose At Pleasure, of the strictest Vows.

4. *Eng.* and *Sc. Hist.* Applied (*a*) to the grant or offer to Nonconformists, in the reigns of Charles II and James II, of certain religious liberties as special favours, but not as legal rights; also (*b*) to the licence offered during the same reigns to Presbyterian ministers in Scotland to hold services on various conditions, such as receiving collation from the bishops, recognition of the King's ecclesiastical supremacy, etc.

Declaration of Indulgence, a royal proclamation offering such religious liberties: esp. applied to that of Charles II in 1672 (withdrawn the following year), and that of James II in 1687 and 1688, which was one of the circumstances that precipitated the Revolution. In Scotland there were five Indulgences, two under Charles II in 1669 and 1672, and three under James II in 1687.

a. [**1668** J. OWEN (*title*) Indulgence and Toleration considered, in a Letter to a person of Honour; with a Peace Offering, in an Apology and Humble Plea for Indulgence and Liberty of Conscience.] **1672-3** CHAS. II. *Sp. at Opening Parlt.* 4 Feb. 3 Some few days before I Declared the War, I put forth My Declaration for Indulgence to Dissenters, and have hitherto found a good Effect of it. *Ibid.* 4 And in the whole Course of this Indulgence, I do not intend that it shall in any way Prejudice the Church, but I will support its Rights, and It in its full Power. **1675** VILLIERS (Dk. Buckhm.) *Speech* 16 Nov., Wks. (1752) 165 My humble motion therefore.. is, that you would give leave to bring in a bill of indulgence to all protestant dissenters. **1687** (4 Apr.) JAS. II *Declar. Lib. Consc.*, To the end that all Our Loving Subjects may receive and enjoy the full Benefit and Advantage of Our Gracious Indulgence hereby intended. **1688** (27 Apr.) *Ibid.*, Ever since we granted this Indulgence [that of 1687], We have made it Our principal Care to see it preserved without Distinction, as we are encouraged to do daily by multitudes of Addresses. **1827** HALLAM *Const. Hist.* (1876) III. xiv. 78 [The clergy] were driven to extremity by the order of May 4, 1688, to read the declaration of indulgence in their churches. *a* **1832** MACKINTOSH *Revol. of* 1688, Wks. 1846 II. 112 The difficulty of proposing to confine such an indulgence to one class of dissidents, and the policy of moving for a general toleration, which it would be as much the interests of Presbyterians as of Catholics to promote. **1849** MACAULAY *Hist. Eng.* ii. I. 177 He knew..it would be impossible to grant liberty of worship to the professors of that [R.C.] religion without extending the same indulgence to Protestant dissenters.

b. **1681** J. BAIRDY (*title*) Balm from Gilead; or the differences about the indulgences stated and impleaded, in a Letter to the People of Scotland. **1687** JAS. II in Hetherington *Hist. Ch. Scotl.* (1842) 518 We allow and tolerate the moderate Presbyterians to meet in their private houses and there to hear all such ministers as have or are willing to accept of our Indulgence. **1721** WODROW *Suffer. Ch. Scotl.* I. II. iii. 291 In June or July this year [1668] the Earl of Tweddale called for some of the Presbyterian Ministers who were under their Hidings, and made proposals to them anent some Favour and Indulgence he hoped might be procured for them in Scotland. **1816** SCOTT *Old Mort.* v, This indulgence, as it was called, made a great schism among the presbyterians, and those who accepted of it were severely censured by the more rigid sectaries. *Ibid.*, 'Of all the baits with which the devil has fished for souls in these days of blood and darkness, that Black Indulgence has been the most destructive.' **1849** MACAULAY *Hist. Eng.* ii. I. 185 Presbyterian divines who had consented to accept from the government a half toleration, known by the name of the Indulgence.

5. *Comm.* An extension, made as a favour, of the time within which a bill of exchange or a debt is to be paid.

1827 CHITTY *Bills of Exchange* (ed. 7) 292 If a holder agree to give indulgence for a certain period of time to any one of the parties to a bill, this takes away his right to call upon that party for payment before the period expires. **1891** BYLES *Treat. Law Bills Exchange* (ed. 15) 328 No indulgence to an acceptor or other prior party will discharge an indorser, if the indorser previously consent to it.

III. 6. *attrib.* and *Comb.*

1895 *Daily News* 6 Oct. 3/3 A native boy, to whom the captain had given an indulgence passage from Tamatave. **1897** *Q. Rev.* July 41 Undermining such moral ideals as the indulgence-mongers had left among them.

in'dulgence, *v.* [f. prec. sb.]

†**1.** *trans.* To grant or permit as an indulgence or favour: = INDULGE 4. *Obs.*

1599 NASHE *Lenten Stuffe* 2 If..it were lawfully indulgenst me freely to aduocate my owne astrology.

2. *R.C. Ch.* To attach an indulgence to (a particular act or object): see prec. 3 a, and INDULGENCED.

1866 J. H. NEWMAN *Let. to Pusey* (ed. 2) 106 There is one collection of Devotions.. which.. consists of prayers of very various kinds which have been indulgenced by the Popes. **1885** *Catholic Dict.* (ed. 3) 444 Large and often plenary indulgences are attached to the recitation of short prayers.. and to the use of blessed crosses, medals, etc... Other acts of piety—*e.g.* examination of conscience, hearing sermons, visiting the Blessed Sacrament—are also largely indulgenced. **1891** J. BRITTEN *Lay Help* 5 [The Catholic Truth Society] is indulgenced by the Holy See.

indulgenced (ɪn'dʌldʒənst), *ppl. a. R.C. Ch.* [f. prec. sb. or vb. + -ED.] Having an indulgence attached to it; applied to prayers, material objects, etc., the use of which is declared to convey an indulgence.

1841 W. PALMER *Second Let. to Wiseman* 14 The whole paraphernalia of indulgenced rites, objects, and prayers. **1854** FABER *Growth in Holiness* xv. (1872) 287 The use of indulgenced devotions is almost an infallible test of a good Catholic. **1879** LITTLEDALE *Plain Reas.* xxv. (1884) 76 Of the crowd of religious books in use in Italy, many of them indulgenced, there is scarcely one which treats of the life and teaching of Christ. **188.** (*titles of R.C. leaflets*), Indulgenced Prayers for Souls in Purgatory.. Indulgenced Prayers for the Rosary of the Holy Souls.

†**in'dulgencer.** *Obs. rare.* [f. INDULGENCE *v.* + -ER.] One who is authorized to grant indulgences; = INDULGENTIARY.

1647 TRAPP *Comm. Rev.* xviii. 11 The Popes Indulgencers, and other officers of his Exchequer.

indulgenciaries: see INDULGENTIARY.

indulgency (ɪn'dʌldʒənsɪ). Now *rare.* [ad. L. *indulgēntia*: see INDULGENCE *sb.* and -ENCY.]

1. The quality or practice of being indulgent; indulgent disposition or action; = INDULGENCE *sb.* 1.

1547 *Act 1 Edw. VI*, c. 12 §1 Great clemencye and indulgencye.. rather.. then exacte severitie and justice to be shewed. *a* **1635** NAUNTON *Fragm. Reg.* (Arb.) 51 The first was, a violent indulgencie of the Queen (which is incident to old age..) towards this Lord. **1659** *Burton's Diary* (1828) IV. 395 We used all acts of indulgency to them. **1663** COWLEY *Verses & Ess.*, '*A Tower of Brass*' v, Thrice happy He To whom the wise indulgency of Heaven, With sparing hand, but just enough has given. **1704** D'URFEY *Royal Converts* Tales, etc. 247 Tortur'd twixt Indulgency and Rage. **1806-7** J. BERESFORD *Miseries Hum. Life* (1826) I. Introd., As the crown of all its indulgency.

b. An indulgence; = INDULGENCE *sb.* 1 b.

1768-74 TUCKER *Lt. Nat.* II. xxiv. (1834) I. 505 Indulgencies.. granted in condescension to our infirmity. **1811** *Ora & Juliet* I. 101 This person.. distributed her indulgencies.. according to the price that was paid for them.

2. = INDULGENCE *sb.* 2.

1691-8 NORRIS *Pract. Disc.* IV. 321 You should be very sparing and indifferent in the indulgency of your Passions. **1889** STEVENSON *Master of B.* 263, I warn you, my lord, against this indulgency of evil feeling.

b. = INDULGENCE *sb.* 2 b.

1688 NORRIS *Theory Love* (1694) 141 That Sort of Corporal Indulgency, which is emphatically call'd Sensuality. **1748** *Anson's Voy.* II. xiii. 278 An amicable well frequented port.. abounding with the conveniencies and indulgencies of a civilized life. **1827** J. F. COOPER *Prairie* I. i. 14 Thousands.. broke up from the enjoyment of their hard earned indulgencies. **1878** FR. A. KEMBLE *Rec. of Girlhood* I. iii. 90 Meantime, the poetical studies, or rather indulgencies of home, had ceased.

†**3.** = INDULGENCE *sb.* 3. *Obs.*

1670 G. H. *Hist. Cardinals* I. I. 11 They receive Indulgencies. **1708** MOTTEUX *Rabelais* IV. xxix. (1737) 119 Swarming with Pardons, Indulgencies, and Stations. **1789** BURNEY *Hist. Mus.* III. i. 32 *note*, Luther began to preach against indulgencies 1517. **1845** S. AUSTIN tr. *Ranke's Hist. Ref.* III. 519 The communes.. were vainly reminded how much their masses and indulgencies had heretofore cost them.

indulgent (ɪn'dʌldʒənt), *a.* (*sb.*) [ad. L. *indulgent-em*, pres. pple. of *indulgēre* to INDULGE. Cf. F. *indulgent* (16th c. in Hatz.-Darm.).]

1. That indulges or tends to indulge; disposed to gratify by compliance with desire or humour, or to overlook faults or failings; showing or ready to show favour or leniency; disinclined to exercise strictness, severity, or restraint: a quality of superiors or such as have the power to refuse compliance. Often in dyslogistic sense, Not exercising (as parent or superior) due restraint, too forbearing, weakly lenient. Const. *to*, †*unto*.

1509 FISHER *Fun. Serm. C'tess Richmond* Wks. (1876) 298 Oftentymes in scrypture the.. faders maketh lamentable exclamacyons, agaynste almyghtye god, for that he semeth, to be more indulgent and fauourable vnto the wycked persone then vnto the good lyuer. **1606** SHAKS. *Ant. & Cl.* I. iv. 16 You are too indulgent. *a* **1680** WALLER (J.), Hereafter such in thy behalf shall be Th' indulgent censure of posterity. **1683** *Brit. Spec.* 12 Nature, like an indulgent Mother has furnished it [Britain] with so great abundance of all things, necessary for the Life of Man. **1710** STEELE *Tatler* No. 271 ¶7 The indulgent Readers Most Obliged, Most Obedient, Humble Servant, Richard Steele. **1732** BERKELEY *Alciphr.* III. §15 The present age is very indulgent to everything that aims at profane raillery. **1839** KEIGHTLEY *Hist. Eng.* II. 84 The best and most indulgent of landlords. **1849** MACAULAY *Hist. Eng.* ii. I. 170 His favourite vices were precisely those to which the Puritans were least indulgent.

b. *fig.* of things.

1697 DRYDEN *Virg. Past.* x. 94 Not tho' beneath the Thracian Clime we freeze; Or Italy's indulgent Heav'n forego. **1762-72** SIR W. JONES *Poems, Arcadia* (1777) 106 Kind Vanity their want of art supplies, And gives indulgent what the Muse denies. *c* **1860** W. ALLINGHAM in *Sonn. of Century* ii, Tenderer in its moods Than any joy indulgent summer dealt.

†**2.** Indulging or disposed to indulge oneself or one's own inclinations; SELF-INDULGENT. *Obs.*

1572 [implied in INDULGENTLY 2]. **1697** DRYDEN *Æneid* v. 936 The feeble old, indulgent of their ease. **1705** STANHOPE *Paraphr.* II. 192 A Satisfaction, to which all the Pleasures of the most indulgent Epicure are as nothing.

†**B.** as *sb.* An easy chair. *Obs.*

1825 R. P. WARD *Tremaine* II. i. 1 His chair, which was what the upholsterers call an Indulgent (a great deal too indulgent for study).

Hence **in'dulgentness** (Bailey vol. II, 1727).

†**indul'gential,** *a. Obs.* [f. L. *indulgēntia* INDULGENCE + -AL[1]. Cf. *penitential.*] Of or pertaining to indulgences: see INDULGENCE *sb.* 3 a.

1674 BREVINT *Saul at Endor* x. (T.), You are fitted with rare indulgential privileges.

†**indul'gentiary.** *Obs.* Also -enciary. [f. L. *indulgēntia* INDULGENCE + -ARY.] A dealer in or seller of indulgences.

1577 tr. *Bullinger's Decades* (1592) 587 What shall we say of the very Indulgenciaries, and the Pope himselfe whose hirelings they bee? **1617** COLLINS *Def. Bp. Ely* II. x. 458 The Pardon-mongers, and Indulgentiaries, were not reformed, but extinguished.

indulgently (ɪn'dʌldʒəntlɪ), *adv.* [-LY[2].]

1. In an indulgent manner; with indulgence or disposition to humour; kindly, favourably, leniently; without strictness or severity.

a **1611** BEAUM. & FL. *Tri. Love* i, My mother, father, And uncle, love me most indulgently, Being the only branch of all their stocks. **1748** RICHARDSON *Clarissa* (1811) I. xvi. 102 Being thus indulgently put into employment, [I] soon recovered myself. **1884** *Manch. Exam.* 8 May 5/3 Not in the humour to listen indulgently to an invitation to lay out fifty thousand pounds on another public park.

†**2.** With indulgence of one's own inclinations; self-indulgently. *Obs.*

1572 tr. *Buchanan's Detection* (London ed.) Hiij a, Indulgently following the wantonnes of hyr wealth. **1647** HAMMOND *Power of Keys* iv. 112 To live indulgently in sin. **1659** —— *On Ps.* cxix. 7 As long as I live in any sin indulgently.

indulger (ɪn'dʌldʒə(r)). [f. INDULGE *v.* + -ER[1].] One who indulges. **a.** One who treats (a person or thing) with indulgence: see INDULGE *v.* 1.

1659 A. BROME *On R. Brome's Com.* 6 These issues of thy brain, Of all th' Indulgers of the Comick strain Deserve applause. **1693** YALDEN *Ode St. Cecilia* Poet. Wks. (1833) 34 Music's the soft indulger of the mind, The kind diverter of our care. **1826** E. IRVING *Babylon* II. VII. 240 Ye in-tolerant indulgers of heresy, and the arch-heretic!

b. One who indulges or gives way to (a desire, inclination, etc.): see INDULGE *v.* 3.

1648 W. MOUNTAGUE *Devout Ess.* I. xiii. §5 (R.) And if.. the severest watchers of their nature have task hard enough, what shall be hoped of the indulgers of it? **1705** STANHOPE *Paraphr.* III. 322 Indulgers of those Lusts which every baptized Believer hath solemnly renounced.

c. One who indulges *in* (some practice): see INDULGE *v.* 7.

1827 HONE *Every-day Bk.* II. 12 Illustrated by portraits of some of the indulgers. **1850** McCOSH *Div. Govt.* (1852) 206 An indulger in fine sentiment.

†**in'dulgiate,** *v. Obs. rare.* [irreg. f. INDULGE or L. *indulgēre* + -ATE[3].] *trans.* = INDULGE *v.*

1615 G. SANDYS *Trav.* IV. 293 More for profit, then to indulgiate his gluttony. **1628** FELTHAM *Resolves* II. [i.] xlvii. 139 Too much indulgiating of the flesh. **1656** in BLOUNT *Glossogr.*

indulging (ɪn'dʌldʒɪŋ), *ppl. a.* [f. INDULGE *v.* + -ING[2].] That indulges; indulgent; that indulges in some practice. Hence **in'dulgingly** *adv.*

[**1707** NORRIS *Treat. Humility* vi. 237 Every nice, humoursome, self-indulging fancy.] **1740** tr. *De Mouhy's Fortunate Country Maid* (1741) II. 178 No wonder my Mother was so indulging. **1786** tr. *Beckford's Vathek* (1868) 58 Bababalouk perceived his pupils indulgingly expanding their arms. **1816** J. SCOTT *Vis. Paris* (ed. 5) 198 It is perfectly well understood, both by the husband and society, and the indulging party is not severely treated by either. **1883** *Pall Mall G.* 19 Nov. 12/2 Calmly, lovingly, and indulgingly trusting to God's providence.

induline ('ɪndjuːlaɪn). *Chem.* [f. IND(O-[2] + *-ul-*, dimin. + -INE.] A general name for a series of compounds related to aniline, yielding blue-black, blue, and greyish dyes, known in commerce as nigrosine, violaniline, Elberfeld blue, aniline grey, etc.: see quot.

1882 *Athenæum* 30 Dec. 902/2 'Induline' is a term applied to all coloured compounds formed by the action of amidoazo

compounds on the hydrochlorides of aromatic amines with elimination of ammonia. **1892** in MORLEY & MUIR *Dict. Chem.* III. 8/2.

indult (ɪn'dʌlt), *sb.* [a. F. *indult* (15–16th c.), or ad. L. *indultum* indulgence, permission, favour, privilege, subst. use of neuter of *indultus*, pa. pple. of *indulgēre* to INDULGE.]

†**1.** A special privilege granted by authority; a licence or permission. *Obs.* in *gen.* sense.

1535 STEWART *Cron. Scot.* III. 548 Ane fre indult of euerie falt and cryme. **1625** SANDERSON *Serm.* (1681) I. 121 From the free and voluntary indult of temporal princes.

2. *R.C.Ch.* 'A licence or permission granted by the Pope, whether to a corporation or to an individual, authorising something to be done which the common law of the Church does not sanction' (*Catholic Dict.*).

1536 BELLENDEN *Cron. Scot.* (1821) II. 327 At this time, mony indultis and privilegis war grantit be the Paip. **1635** PAGITT *Christianogr.* (1653) 259 The summes of money which the pope receiveth for Firstfruits, Palls, Indulgences, Buls, Confessionals, Indults.. Dispensations.. cannot be counted. **1688** *Lond. Gaz.* No. 2389/3 By vertue of an Apostolical Indult of Eligibility previously granted him. **1718** in Earl Stanhope *Hist. Eng.* II. p. lxxviii, The indult granted the Pretender for the nomination of Irish bishops. **1858** FABER tr. *Life Xavier* 202 He had an indult from the Holy See, authorizing him to say the Office of three lessons, which is considerably shorter than that which is common to ecclesiastics. **1885** *Catholic Dict.* (ed. 3) s.v., A familiar instance is that of the Lenten indults, by which the Pope authorises the bishops, according to the circumstances of different countries, to dispense more or less with the rigour of the canons as to the quadragesimal fast. In former times indults chiefly related to the patronage of church dignities and benefices.

3. = INDULTO 2.

In mod. Dicts.

†**in'dult,** *v. Obs. rare.* [f. *indult-*, ppl. stem of L. *indulgēre* to INDULGE.] *trans.* To grant as a privilege or favour: = INDULGE *v.* 4.

1612 G. BUCK *3rd Univ. Eng.* xlviii. in *Stow's Ann.* (1615) 988/2 Colledges, Athenæes, houses, and schooles, founded and.. endowed with lands, and reuenewes by the auncient Kinges and Princes of this land.. and vnto them royall priuiledges indulted.

[**indultif, -tyf,** error for *inductyf*: see INDUCTIVE *sb.*, quot. *a* 1420.]

‖**indulto** (in'dulto). [Sp. and Pg. *indulto*, exemption, privilege, licence:—L. *indultum* INDULT.]

†**1.** = INDULT *sb.* 1, 2. *Obs.*

1645 *Treaty w. Spain* in C. King *Brit. Merch.* (1721) III. 132 Other Favours and Indulto's, which the King.. granted you. **1753** *Scots. Mag.* Jan. 10/1 In virtue of an indulto granted by the Pope. **1765** *Hist. Europe* in *Ann. Reg.* (1766) 19/1 That all slaves should be made free, by an indulto general. **1813** *Examiner* 1 Mar. 131/2 In conformity with the Concordat, and by virtue of the present indulto.

2. *Hist.* A duty paid to the King of Spain or Portugal on imported goods; a licence-duty.

1691 *Lond. Gaz.* No. 2722/3 The Galeons had not yet been permitted to unlade, because the Indulto to be paid to the King was not settled. **1697** *Ibid.* No. 3276/1 An indulta of 4 per Cent. is laid upon the Silver and other Merchandizes brought home in the Flota. **1739** CIBBER *Apol.* (1756) I. 291 An indulto was laid of one third out of the profits of every benefit for the proper use and behoof of the patent. **1772** *Weekly Mag.* 7 May 188/1 The King had laid an indulto of 33 per cent on all kinds of merchandise.

‖**in'dultum.** [L.: see INDULT.] = INDULT.

1640 SOMNER *Antiq. Canterb.* 310 The Archbishops forenoted indultums or grants made to this Archdeacon.

†**in'duly,** *adv. Obs.* In 5 indewly. [IN-[3].] Unduly.

1484 CAXTON *Curiall* 11 Herof foloweth that we lese by good right that whyche we Iuge to our self, and that we dar demande indewly.

†**indument.** *Obs.* [In branch I, ad. L. *indument-um* garment, clothing, f. *induĕre* to put on. (The L. is also in current scientific use: see sense 2.) In branch II = ENDUEMENT, ENDOWMENT.]

I. ('*indument.*)

1. Clothing, investiture; an article of clothing, a garment, robe, vesture.

1494 FABYAN *Chron.* VII. ccxxi. 243 This palle is an indument that euery archebysshop must haue.. and is a thynge of whyte lyke to the bredeth of a Stole. **1586** FERNE *Blaz. Gentrie* 338 The conquered shall forfeit to the victor all his robes or indumentes of honour. **1609** BELL *Theoph. & Remig.* 2 He caused.. the papall induments to be taken away. **1640** BP. REYNOLDS *Passions* xxxvi. 435 Their Lives and Substance [of animals were given to man] to Aliment, Indument, Ornament or any other use.

fig. **1589** NASHE *Almond for Parrat* 3 That thou sholdst adorne thy false dealing with the induments of discipline. **1684** HOCKIN *Gods Decrees* 176 The wedding garment.. must be understood of the inward sanctity and indument of the heart.

b. *fig.* A material body or form, regarded as the investiture of the soul.

1592 NASHE *P. Penilesse* (Shaks. Soc.) 83 Spirits.. although in their proper essence they are incorporal, yet can they take upon them the induments of any living bodies whatsoever. **1678** CUDWORTH *Intell. Syst.* I. iv. §36. 565 Ancient Christian Writers concurred with Origen herein, that the Highest Created Spirits were no Naked and Abstract Minds, but Souls cloathed with some Corporeal Indument.

2. *Nat. Hist.* A covering, as of hair, feathers, etc.; an investment, integument; an investing membrane. (Also in Lat. form *indumentum.*)

1578 BANISTER *Hist. Man* VIII. 100 [The] Pia Mater.. with which indument the brayne and Cerebellum are nearely clad. **1864** WEBSTER, *Indument* (*Zool.*), plumage; feathers. [**1880** GRAY *Struct. Bot.* (ed. 6) 416/2 *Indumentum*, any hairy covering or pubescence which forms a coating.]

II. (*in'dument.*)

3. The action of investing or fact of being invested with some quality or attribute; also the quality or attribute with which something is invested; = ENDUEMENT.

1527 *St. Papers Hen. VIII*, I. 243 For the parilite of your mutual indumentes, both of grace and nature. **1583** STUBBES *Anat. Abus.* I. (1877) 42 Without the induments of vertue, whereto only al reuerence is due. **1659** H. MORE *Immort. Soul* (1662) 31 It is as easy a thing for him to.. indue it [a creature] with what other Properties he pleases.. which induments being immediately united [etc.].

4. = ENDOWMENT.

1602–3 SIR E. STANHOPE *Will* in Willis & Clark *Cambridge* (1886) II. 672 The Benefactors who haue given anie yearelie perpetuitie of maintenaunce to that Colledg.. together with the perticuler induments which they have so yearelie given.

indumentum (ɪndjʊ'mɛntəm). *Bot.* Pl. **-ta.** [a. L. *indumentum*; see INDUMENT.] The covering of hairs on part of a plant, esp. when dense, e.g. the covering of the lower surface of the leaves of many species of rhododendron. Cf. INDUMENT 2.

1847 J. LINDLEY *Elem. Bot.* (ed. 5) p. xlix, Indumentum: The hairy covering of plants, of whatever kind. **1858** A. GRAY *Introd. Struct. & Syst. Bot.* (ed. 5) 537/1 Indumentum: any hairiness or downy covering. **1930** J. B. STEVENSON *Species of Rhododendron* 364 Under surface [of leaves of *R. eriogynum*] at first clad with a thin white flaking stellate indumentum easily rubbed off and quickly falling away. **1950** J. M. COWAN *Rhododendron Leaf* i. 1 On looking at the leaves of Rhododendrons, it will be seen that the under surface is often clothed with a hairy or scale-like covering, now loose and of a fine texture like a spider's web, now dense and compact like a thick felt or wool, now a mere sprinkling of brownish dots on a green background. This leaf covering, which is very variable, is known as the indumentum. **1963** DAVIS & HEYWOOD *Princ. Angiosperm Taxon.* v. 155 To be of use for critical discrimination, indumentum must, of course, be described in detail, each type of hair present (and its disposition) being separately recorded. **1970** *Watsonia* VIII. 104 *H[ieracium] termifrons* occurs in two well-marked forms differing in shape of head and indumentum of the phyllaries. **1972** *Biol. Abstr.* LIV. 68/1 *X[imenia] caffra* differs from *X. americana* in that a dense or sparse indumentum is often present.

‖**induna** (ɪn'du:nə). Also 9 **tuna,** 9– **indoona.** [Zulu *in-duna* officer of state or army under the chief, f. nominal inflex *in-* + stem *duna* (pl. *izin-duna*): cf. *i-duna* (pl. *ama-duna*) male, sire, lord, person of consequence having land and people under him.] **a.** An officer under the king or chief of the Zulus, Matabele, and other South African tribes.

1835 A. SMITH *Diary* 19 June (1940) II. 79 Masalacatzie has two grades among his chiefs, viz.: *numzan* and *tuna*, the former the highest. **1837** F. OWEN *Diary* (1926) 28 A regiment is stationed at each town under several Indoonas or Captains. *Ibid.* 60 The King.. was seated in his hut on a chair: his Indoonas were also present. *a* **1875** F. OATES *Matabele Land* (1889) 83 They call it [baobab tree] the 'indunas' tree; for here the indunas from the neighbouring kraals are wont to sit and drink beer when any thing particular is on hand. **1889** *Pall Mall G.* 7 Mar. 6/3 Her Majesty talked some time with the indunas. **1897** *Rev. of Rev.* 21 Lobengula's indunas are to have £60 a year and a horse each. **1955** E. A. RITTER *Shaka Zulu* xiii, These [soldiers] were now harangued for a considerable time by their fighting *indunas* or officers and given a discourse on new tactics. **1971** *Daily Dispatch* (S. Afr.) 24 May 1 In the Libode district unoccupied huts were set on fire by tribesmen. Recently a headman and his induna in the district were murdered.

b. *transf.* A person, especially a black person, in authority; a pundit.

1953 P. LANHAM *Blanket Boy's Moon* II. iv. 116 A big factory, where he had obtained the job of *Induna* or head-boy. **1953** F. ROBB *Sea Hunters* iv. 28 On deck.. Ndwe, the Induna or bossboy, heaved on the vang and centred the boom over the gaping hatchway. **1970** *News/Check* (S. Afr.) 4 Sept. 9 This followed the attack on the Press by rugby induna Dr. Danie Craven for blowing up the incidents of rough play in the second Test. **1970** W. SMITH *Gold Mine* xxix. 72 The Old One, the Shangaan Induna, lived in a Company house. **1971** in *Towards Dict. S. Afr. Eng.* 42 They have an induna there to hold you down while they X-ray you.

Hence **in'dunaship,** the office or dignity of an induna.

1955 in M. Gluckman *Judicial Process among Barotse* iii. 87 This is indunaship—this is ruling.

indungeon, var. of ENDUNGEON *v.*

†**induperator.** *Obs. rare.* [a. L. *induperātor*, old form (with prefix *indu-* for *in-*) of *imperātor*.] = IMPERATOR.

1599 NASHE *Lenten Stuffe* 22 This monarchall fludy Induperator [the herring]. **1660** TRAPP *Comm. Jer.* li. 27 Thus God the great *Induperator* bespeaketh the Medes and Persians as his field-officers.

induplicate (ɪn'dju:plɪkət), *a. Bot.* [f. IN-[2] + DUPLICATE.] Folded or rolled in at the edges, without overlapping: said of leaves and petals in vernation or æstivation.

1830 LINDLEY *Nat. Syst. Bot.* 69 The æstivation of Franklandia is induplicate, according to Mr. Brown. **1835** —— *Introd. Bot.* (1848) II. 375 *Induplicate*, having the margins bent abruptly inwards, and the external face of these edges applied to each other without any twisting. **1857** HENFREY *Bot.* 71 Valvate buds.. *induplicate vernation.* **1896** HENSLOW *Wild Fl.* 154 The four lobes of the corolla are valvate in bud, having the edges induplicate or folded inwards.

induplication (ɪndju:plɪ'keɪʃən). [f. IN-[2] + DUPLICATION; prob. suggested by prec.] Folding or doubling in; an example of this.

1874 BARKER tr. *Frey's Histol. & Histochem.* §212. 389 The whole induplication is enclosed in a transparent structureless membrane. **1879** tr. *Semper's Anim. Life* 12 In every case where such organs have ceased to be superficial on the skin by its induplication.

indupli'cative, *a. Bot.* [f. INDUPLICATE + -IVE: cf. DUPLICATIVE.] = INDUPLICATE.

1864 in WEBSTER (citing GRAY). **1866** in *Treas. Bot.*

in'durable, *a.*[1] *rare.* [ad. med.L. *indūrābilis*, f. *in-* (IN-[3]) + *dūrābilis* DURABLE.] Not durable; not enduring or lasting.

c **1450** tr. *De Imitatione* III. xxvii. 97 Rauisshe me & delyuere from all indurable comfort of creatures. **1899** *Hub* 28 Oct. 822/1 Soft wood blocks are.. insanitary and indurable.

†**in'durable,** *a.*[2] *Obs. rare*[−1]. [f. IN-[3] + DURABLE (sense 4).] Unendurable, unbearable.

1607 TOPSELL *Four-f. Beasts* 567 An extreame and almost indurable inflammation and burning, through all the parts of the body.

indurable, -durance, etc., obs. ff. ENDURABLE, ENDURANCE, etc.

†**in'durand,** obs. Sc. f. ENDURING *prep.*, during.

1490 *Act. Dom. Concil.* 172 (Jam.) Indurand the tyme of the ward of the samyn. **1549** *Compl. Scot.* To Rdr. 18 Indurand the schort tyme of this oure fragil peregrinatione.

†**in'durant,** *ppl. a.* (*sb.*) *Obs. rare.* [ad.L. *indūrānt-em*, pres. pple. of *indūrāre*: see ENDURE.]

1. Lasting, continuing long.

1611 SPEED *Hist. Gt. Brit.* IX. 547 His wilde speeches.. some by errour alledge as cause of his indurant durance.

2. Of medicines: Having the quality of hardening. Also as *sb.* An indurating medicine.

1678 SALMON *Pharmac. Lond.* VI. ii. 814 *Indurant*, such as coagulate, congeal or harden. **1721** BAILEY, *Indurants*, hardening Medicines.

indu'rascent, *a. Bot. rare.* [ad. L. type **indūrāscent-em* (*indūrescĕre* is found in post-Aug. Latin), inceptive form from *indūrāre* to INDURATE.] 'Hardening by degrees' (*Treas. Bot.* 1866).

indurate ('ɪndjʊrət), *ppl. a.* Now *rare.* Also 5–6 en-. [ad. L. *indūrāt-us*, pa. pple. of *indūrāre* to make hard, f. *in-* (IN-[2]) + *dūrus* hard: see ENDURE. Formerly stressed *in'durate.*]

1. Of things: Made hard, hardened. Now *rare.*

1530 TINDALE *Answ. More* Wks. (Parker Soc.) III. 13 As the nature of those hard and indurate adamant stones is, to draw all to them. **1555** EDEN *Decades* 273 Haddockes or hakes indurate and dryed with coulde. **1607** TOPSELL *Four-f. Beasts* (1658) 339 A little above the hoofs.. there are indurate and hardned thick skins. **1621** BURTON *Anat. Mel.* II. v. I. vi. (1651) 397 Avoid at all times indurate salt.. meat. **1870** HOOKER *Stud. Flora* 315 Beta.. Calyx urceolate, base indurate in fruit.

2. Of persons, their character, feelings, etc.: Morally hardened, rendered callous; also, fixed in determination, stubborn, obstinate. Now *rare.*

Often of the heart, referring to the phrase *induratum est cor Pharaonis* (Pharaoh's heart was hardened) in the Vulgate (*Exod.* vii. 13, 22).

c **1425** *Orolog. Sapient.* vii. in *Anglia* X. 388/24 To hem þat haue her vndirstondynge blyndet, and hir affeccyon indurate & hardnet. **1426** LYDG. *De Guil. Pilgr.* 4070 Hertys that be obstynat With synnes olde, ek indurat, And fulfyllyd with vnclennesse. **1581** J. BELL *Haddon's Answ. Osor.* 497 b, Whereby we are taught to eschew the company of endurate heretyques after once or twise admonition. **1598** ROWLANDS *Betraying of Christ* 15 My heart's indurate, hardned, vnrelenting. **1667** *Answ. West North* 14 They are as indurat as Pharaoh. **1855** *Fraser's Mag.* LI. 170 Nothing but indurate cynicism.. can account for it.

†**b.** Physically hardened; rendered hardy or capable of enduring hardships. *Obs.*

1555 EDEN *Decades* 253 They are indurate to abyde coulde, hunger and laboure.

†**c.** *fig.* Of conditions and the like. *Obs.*

1558 WARDE tr. *Alexis' Secr.* (1568) 24 b, If the griefe be so indurate and hardened that it will not be healed by the aforesaid remedies. **1635** N. R. *Camden's Hist. Eliz.* III. ann. 26. 256 To ease the indurate passion of the spleene.

indurate ('ɪndjʊreɪt), *v.* [f. L. *indūrāt-*, ppl. stem of *indūrāre*: see prec. Formerly stressed *in'durate*.]

1. *trans.* To make (a substance) hard; to harden.

1594 PLAT *Jewell-ho.* I. 23 Which water..doth indurate and congeale it self with such things as doo happen to bee mixed with it. **1597** A. M. tr. *Guillemeau's Fr. Chirurg.* 4/1 The same syde and the stomacke beginne to be induratede and harde. **1675** EVELYN *Terra* (1729) 10 Divers waters, not only indurate, and petrify other substances [etc.]. **1706** PHILLIPS s.v., The Sun indurates Clay. **1856** MRS. BROWNING *Aur. Leigh* IV. 358 The very heat of burning youth applied To indurate forms and systems. **1865** MERIVALE *Rom. Emp.* lxiii. VIII. 28 The deep alluvial soil of the Danubian Valley was indurated by frost.

b. To make hardy; to inure.

c **1575** HOOKER *Life Sir P. Carew* in *Archæol.* XXVIII. 148 Yf fortytude..doe also indurate the bodye to abyde all labors. **1879** TOURGEE *Fool's Err.* xx. 114 They [slaves] had been indurated to want, exposure and toil. **1890** *Spectator* 4 Jan., They are hardier and more indurated against the indifference or ridicule of the world.

2. To harden (the heart, etc.); to render callous or unfeeling; to make stubborn or obstinate.

1538 LATIMER *Serm. & Rem.* (Parker Soc.) 392 More like to indurate than to mollify. **1584** R. SCOT *Discov. Witchcr.* XIII. xviii. (1886) 257 God indeed performed the other actions, to indurate Pharao. **1635** BRATHWAIT *Arcad. Pr.* 118 Sharp doomes indurate natures most relenting. **1801** H. M. WILLIAMS *Sk. Fr. Rep.* I. ii. 13 It is the curse of revolutionary calamities to indurate the heart. **1891** FARRAR *Darkness & Dawn* I. 318 That such a spectacle..should indurate still further the callosity of hardened hearts.

3. *intr.* Of things: To become or grow hard.

1626 BACON *Sylva* §796 This sheweth that Bodies doe..by the Coldnesse of the Quick-siluer, Indurate. **1646** SIR T. BROWNE *Pseud. Ep.* II. v. 91 That plants and ligneous bodies may indurate under water..we have experiment in Coralline. **1804** ABERNETHY *Surg. Obs.* 149 The disposition [of the sore] to indurate is greater. **1831** LYTTON *Godolphin* xxi, The drops that trickle within the cavern harden, yet brighten into spars as they indurate. **1898** J. HUTCHINSON *Archives Surg.* IX. 113 The one begins by an ulcer which indurates, the other begins by an induration which ulcerates.

b. Of a custom: To become fixed or inveterate.

1865 PUSEY *Eirenicon* 30 (tr. from Latin) And now, through custom, or, rather, corruption, it has indurated, that a mass..is bought and sold by a blind people and by wicked simoniacal priests. **1881** *Times* 10 Feb. 9/5 The prescription will soon grow, and begin to indurate.

indurated ('ɪndjʊreɪtɪd), *ppl. a.* [f. prec.]

1. Of substances: Made hard, hardened (esp. *Geol.* of clay, marl, etc.).

1677 PLOT *Oxfordsh.* 141 The outward crust of these is somtimes only an indurated chalk. *c* **1720** W. GIBSON *Farrier's Guide* II. xlviii. (1738) 176 They so often degenerate into those indurated and hard excrescences. **1794** MARTYN *Rousseau's Bot.* xxix. 456 These have..one seed within the indurated calyx. **1799** KIRWAN *Geol. Ess.* 299 Two beds of indurated clay. **1847–8** H. MILLER *First Impr.* iii. (1857) 33 Solid deposits of indurated sandstone.

2. Of the heart, feelings, etc.: Rendered callous or stubborn.

1604 T. WRIGHT *Passions* 349 A hard indurated heart may resist the sweete calling of God. **1764** GOLDSM. *Traveller* 232 Love's and friendship's finely pointed dart Fall blunted from each indurated heart. **1811** J. ADAMS *Wks.* (1854) IX. 635 Indurated stoic as I am. **1866** *Sat. Rev.* 21 Apr. 466/1 It is by hitting on some fresh power within us, that habits, however indurated, are now and then broken or dissolved.

†**in'durately,** *adv.* *Obs. rare.* In 6 en-. [f. INDURATE *ppl. a.* + -LY[2].] Stubbornly.

1553 BALE *Gardiner's 'De vera Obed.'* B ij, If thy hearte be not endurately locked and cast vp from discerning the truthe.

†**in'durateness.** *Obs. rare.* [f. as prec. + -NESS.] The quality of being indurate or spiritually hardened.

1537 *Inst. Chr. Man, Creed* in *Formul. Faith* (1856) 59 Eyther for their infidelitie or for their induratenes.

'indurating, *ppl. a.* [f. INDURATE *v.* + -ING[2].] That hardens or makes hard.

1855 tr. *Wedl's Path. Hist.* I. i. 10 As indurating agents, alcohol, dilute chromic and nitric acids..have already been mentioned. **1895** T. WATTS in *Athenæum* 5 Jan. 17/1 The indurating effects of a selfish religiosity never withered her soul.

induration (ɪndjʊ'reɪʃən). Also 6 en-. [a. F. *induration* (14th c.), or ad. med.L. *indūrātiōn-em*, n. of action f. *indūrāre* to INDURATE.]

1. The action of hardening; the process of being hardened or becoming hard; also, hardened condition. Now chiefly in *Geol.* and *Path.*

c **1386** CHAUCER *Can. Yeom. Prol.* 302 Of bodies mollificacion And also of hire induracion. **1471** RIPLEY *Comp. Alch.* VI. i. in Ashm. (1652) 161 It ys of soft thyngs Induracyon. **1584** R. SCOT *Discov. Witchcr.* XIV. i. (1886) 294 Mysticall termes of art; as (for a tast)..mollifications and indurations of bodies. **1646** SIR T. BROWNE *Pseud. Ep.* II. i. 50 Wee usually ascribe their induration to cold. **1783** POTT *Chirurg. Wks.* II. 198 The induration, enlargement, or other morbid affection of such parts. **1855** *Cornwall* 81 The elvans have mostly a common mineral character, though of very variable degrees of induration.

attrib. **1898** J. HUTCHINSON *Archives Surg.* IX. 113 A new induration form of large size and exactly like a primary Hunterian sore.

b. A hardened formation or mass.

1809 *Med. Jrnl.* XXI. 281, I have found on opening these subjects, remarkable indurations in the brain.

c. Hardened condition of body; ability to endure hardships.

1827 J. F. COOPER *Prairie* I. i. 23 His whole figure had attained an appearance of induration.

2. A hardening of character or feeling; obstinacy, stubbornness; callousness, want of feeling.

1493 *Festivall* (W. de W. 1515) 128 b, Askynge Ihesu forgyuenes of her enduracyon & obstynacy. **1550** BALE *Image Both Ch.* D iij b, In her place shall stande up the sinagoge of Sathan, with blyndnesse and induracion. **1651** C. CARTWRIGHT *Cert. Relig.* I. 230 He saves the elect by mercy, and damnes the Reprobate by induration. *a* **1732** ATTERBURY *Matt.* xxvii. 25 (Seager) The hand of God is in it, and some degree of a judicial induration. **1873** *Mem. T. Finlayson* 181 To what a degree of induration and searedness must you have brought yourself.

†**b.** A hardening influence. *Obs.*

1583 STUBBES *Anat. Abus.* II. (1882) 114 A hinderaunce to manie in comming to the Gospel, and an induration to the papists, hardning their hearts.

indurative ('ɪndjʊreɪtɪv), *a.* Also 6 en-. [f. L. *indūrāt-* (see INDURATE *v.*) + -IVE.] Of hardening tendency or quality.

1592 LYLY *Galathea* II. iii, Bellowes mollificative and endurative. **1863** *Sat. Rev.* XV. 622/1 The habit of analysis and self-examination has also a great indurative effect. **1873** T. H. GREEN *Introd. Pathol.* (ed. 2) 255 When..an endocarditis is the precursor of the indurative process. **1882** *Quain's Med. Dict.* 255/2 Indurative changes in the solid viscera lead to venous obstruction.

†**in'duratize,** *v.* *Obs. nonce-wd.* [f. INDURATE *ppl. a.* + -IZE.] *trans.* To harden (the heart).

1598 TOFTE *Alba* (1880) 86 Thy hart gainst me, not still induratize, But my sad thoughts in me retranquillize.

†**in'dure,** obs. form of ENDURE *v.* = INDURATE.

c **1450** *Mirour Saluacioun* 387 Whi god Pharaos hert wald in malice indure. **1535** *Goodly Primer* in *3 Prim. Hen. VIII* (1848) 222 Make soft our hard hearts..which be indured & hardened. **1578–1600** [see ENDURE *v.* 1].

Hence †**in'dured** (Sc. *in'durit*) *ppl. a.*, hardened, indurate; whence †**in'duritness** (*Sc.*), hardened condition, induration.

1558 KENNEDIE *Comp. Tract.* in *Wodrow Soc. Misc.* (1844) I. 144 The indurit opinioun quhilk he consavis. *Ibid.* 161 Geve thow wyll manteyne, with pertinacitie and induritnes, ane wickit opinion. **1563** *Ressoning Crosraguell & Knox* C iij a (Jam.), His induretnes and pertinacitie. **1567** *Gude & Godlie B.* (S.T.S.) 148 Indurit ignorance hes slaine Thy hart, and put vs to greit paine. *a* **1598** ROLLOCK *Lect. Hist. Passion* iv. Wks. (Wodrow Soc.) II. 63 What avails it to speak to an indured heart?

†**in'during,** variant of ENDURING *prep.*, *Obs.*

1450–70 *Golagros & Gaw.* 405 Na nane sa doughty of deid, induring his daw. **1524–1650** [see ENDURING *prep.*].

Indus ('ɪndəs). *Astron.* [L.] = INDIAN *sb.* 5.

1838 *Penny Cycl.* XII. 467/1. **1910** *Encycl. Brit.* VII. 13/1 Johann Bayer, a German astronomer..published a *Uranometria* in 1603, in which twelve constellations, all in the southern hemisphere, were added to Ptolemy's forty-eight, viz. Apis (or Musca) (Bee),..Indus (Indian), [etc.]. **1964** D. H. MENZEL *Field Guide Stars & Planets* iv. 113 Indus (the Indian). Although the name is masculine, Flamsteed drew a female figure.

indusial (ɪn'dju:zɪəl), *a.* *Geol.* [f. INDUSI-UM + -AL[1].] Containing, or composed of, indusia or larva-cases; in ***indusial limestone*** (see quots.).

1833 LYELL *Princ. Geol.* III. 232 There is another remarkable form of fresh-water limestone in Auvergne, called 'indusial', from the cases, or *indusiæ*, of the larvæ of Phryganea, great heaps of which have been encrusted, as they lay, by hard travertin, and formed into a rock. **1851** RICHARDSON *Geol.* (1855) 375 These indusial limestones form but a portion of the strata of the district.

indusiate (ɪn'dju:zɪət), *ppl. a.* *Bot.* [ad. L. *indūsiāt-us*: see INDUSIUM and -ATE[2] 2.] Furnished or covered with an indusium.

1830 LINDLEY *Nat. Syst. Bot.* 188 Monopetalous dicotyledons, with..an indusiate stigma. **1875** BENNETT & DYER tr. *Sachs' Bot.* 395 A resemblance..between the sporocarp of Salvinia and the indusiate sorus of this family of Ferns.

in'dusiated, *ppl. a.* *rare.* [f. as prec. + -ED[1].]

1. 'Cloathed with a petticoat, waste-coat, or shirt' (Blount *Glossogr.* 1656).

2. *Bot.* = INDUSIATE.

1864 in WEBSTER.

indusiform (ɪn'dju:zɪfɔ:m), *a.* *Bot.* Also -iiform. [f. INDUSI-UM + -FORM.] Having the form or shape of an indusium.

1857 BERKELEY *Cryptog. Bot.* §603 The sori are produced on exserted concave indusiiform marginal lobes. **1866** JOHN SMITH *Ferns Brit. & For.* (1879) 82 Sori round..furnished with indusiform laciniate scales.

indusioid (ɪn'dju:zɪɔɪd), *a.* *Bot.* [f. as prec. + -OID.] Resembling an indusium.

1866 J. SMITH *Ferns Brit. & For.* (1879) 87 Sori oblong-linear, marginal, furnished with indusioid stipitate squamæ.

‖**indusium** (ɪn'dju:zɪəm). Pl. -ia. [L. *indūsium* a tunic, app. f. *induĕre* to put on: see ENDUE.]

1. *Anat.* **a.** The amnion of the fœtus.

1706 in PHILLIPS. **1855** RAMSBOTHAM *Obstetr. Med.* 43 Besides the peritoneal coat,—indusium—they possess beneath it another,—their proper tunic.

b. Also *erron.* **induseum.** The thin layer of grey matter covering the upper surface of the corpus callosum. In full ***indusium*** (or ***induseum***) ***griseum***.

1890 BILLINGS *Med. Dict.* I. 693/2 Indusium griseum. **1908** *Quain's Elem. Anat.* (ed. 11) III. I. 401 The lateral striæ are similar, but their corresponding grey matter is even more rudimentary than the indusium. **1948** A. BRODAL *Neurol. Anat.* x. 330 Smaller contingents [of fibres] appear to reach it from the induseum griseum. **1963** ZEMAN & INNES *Craigie's Neuroanat. Rat* (ed. 2) vii. 147 The rest [of the hippocampal formation] curves around it and becomes continuous with the indusium. **1966** HASSLER & STEPHAN *Evolution of Forebrain* 104 The supracallosal gyrus (or induseum griseum).

2. *Bot.* **a.** The membranous shield or scale covering the sorus or fruit-cluster of a fern.

1807 J. E. SMITH *Phys. Bot.* 248 My learned friends Willdenow and Swartz have judged otherwise, calling this membrane the *indusium*, or covering; which seems to me altogether superfluous. **1851** T. MOORE *Brit. Ferns & Allies* (1864) 12 The *indusium*..is mostly a thin transparent membranous scale of the same general form as the sorus itself. **1875** BENNETT & DYER tr. *Sachs' Bot.* 356 The whole sorus is very generally covered by an excrescence of the epidermis, the true *Indusium*: in other cases the false indusium consists of an outgrowth of the tissue of the leaf itself.

b. A collection of hairs united into a sort of cup, and inclosing the stigma in the *Goodeniaceæ*.

1830 LINDLEY *Nat. Syst. Bot.* 186 Campanulas have not the fringed indusium which terminates the style of Goodeniaceæ, and surrounds their stigma.

3. *Entom.* The case or covering of a larva.

1832 LYELL *Princ. Geol.* II. 246 The Indusia, or cases of the larvæ of Phryganea. **1865** PAGE *Handbk. Geol.* (ed. 2) 256 The *indusium* or case of the caddis-worm.

industrial (ɪn'dʌstrɪəl), *a.* and *sb.* [Occurs in end of 16th c.; then app. not till late in 18th. The early instances, as well as 15th c. F. *industrial*, appear to be independent formations from L. *industria* + -AL[1]. In the 19th c. the word appears as an adaptation of mod.F. *industriel* (*Dict. Acad.* 1835), f. *industrie* + *-el* = -AL[1] 1.]

A. *adj.* **a.** Pertaining to, or of the nature of, industry or productive labour; resulting from industry. Of persons: Engaged in or connected with an industry or industries.

industrial accession, additional value given to property by labour expended on it (see ACCESSION 7). †***industrial fruits***, fruits grown or cultivated by human industry (so obs. F. *fruits industriaux, -eux*).

1590 SWINBURNE *Testaments* VII. §10 (1640) 135 Of fruits, some bee Industriall, and some Naturall. By Industriall, I meane suche as bee sowne in the ground by mans industry, in hope..to be reaped with increase ere long. *Ibid.* 136. **1774** S. HALLIFAX *Anal. Rom. Civ. Law* (1795) 24 Industrial Accessions are 1. Specification, or producing a new form from another's materials [etc.]. **1830** W. THOMPSON *Pract. Direct. Estab. Commun.* p. iii, The whole of the industrial operations of society [*Note.* From the French 'of or belonging to industry']. **1841** F. VESEY *Decl. Eng. Lang.* 82 *Industrial*, a French word, said to mean mechanical: lately adopted by the English newspapers. **1848** MILL *Pol. Econ.* I. iii. §3 The industrial capacities of human beings. **1860** MOTLEY *Netherl.* (1868) I. viii. 489 Such of the industrial classes as could leave the place had wandered away to Holland and England.

b. ***industrial school***: A school for teaching one or more branches of industry (cf. *school of industry*, INDUSTRY 4 b); *spec.* a school established for the compulsory attendance of neglected children, where, besides being boarded (or lodged and boarded) and being taught the ordinary elementary subjects, they are instructed in some industry or trade; a school of this kind in which the children are boarded or partially boarded but not lodged is more distinctively called a ***day industrial school***.

1853 (*title*) Industrial Schools the Means for Decreasing Juvenile Crime. **1857** *Act 20 & 21 Vict.* c. 48 §3 The Committee of..Council on Education may, upon the Application of the Managers of any School in which Industrial Training is provided, and in which Children are fed as well as taught..grant a Certificate..and thenceforth the School shall be a Certified Industrial School. **1876** *Act 39 & 40 Vict.* c. 79 §16 A school in which industrial training, elementary education, and one or more meals a day, but not lodging, are provided..to be a certified day industrial school.

c. Of a quality suitable for industrial use.

1904 GOODCHILD & TWENEY *Technol. & Sci. Dict.*, *Industrial soaps*, a term used to describe that class of soap used for special purposes, such as ox gall soap, which is useful for scouring woollen goods and cleaning carpets, soap for silk dyers, fulling soap, etc. **1904** *Chemist & Druggist* LXV. 852/2 Industrial Alcohol Committee..appointed to inquire into the use of duty-free alcohol for industrial purposes. **1905** *Ibid.* LXVI. 630/2 There is only one way in which the influence of the spirit-duties can be satisfactorily counteracted in favour of industrial alcohol. **1906** *Act 6 Edw. VII* c. 20 §4 The expression 'industrial methylated spirits' means any methylated spirits (other than mineralized methylated spirits) which are intended for use in any art or manufacture within the United Kingdom. **1968** J. IRONSIDE *Fashion Alphabet* 89 *Industrial*, applied to

special fabrics or garments specially designed for use in particular industries.

d. Characterized by highly developed industries.

1911 C. G. ROBERTSON *Eng. under Hanoverians* II. iv. 346 Napoleon..failed to see that he fought not with a nation of shopkeepers—a commercial State—but with a nation of capitalists and artisans—an industrial State. **1948** S. LILLEY *Men, Machines & Hist.* vi. 72 England was transformed from one of the most backward to one of the most rapidly advancing commercial and industrial countries of Europe. **1953** J. D. BERNAL *Sci. & Industry in 19th Cent.* vi. 171 Only the industrial countries of Europe and the newly industrialized parts of America contributed to modern science.

e. In specific uses.

industrial accident, an accident occurring in the course of one's employment, esp. in a factory; ***industrial action***, action such as a strike, a go-slow, working to rule, etc., taken by industrial or other workers; ***industrial archæology***, the study of the equipment and workings of industry of former times; so ***industrial archæologist***; ***industrial art***, art applied to the design of industrial products; so ***industrial artist***; ***industrial assurance***, a form of life assurance for industrial workers, mainly to cover funeral costs, with premiums payable in small regular instalments; ***industrial court***, a court for the settlement of industrial disputes; ***industrial design***, design as applied to industrial products; so ***industrial designer***; ***industrial disease***, a disease contracted in the course of one's employment, esp. in a factory; ***industrial dispute***, a dispute between employers and employees; ***industrial espionage***, spying directed towards discovering the secrets of a rival industrial company, manufacturer, etc.; ***industrial estate***, an area of land devoted to factories and other industrial enterprises; ***industrial fatigue***, fatigue in industrial workers; ***industrial frequency*** (see quot. 1940); ***industrial injury***, an injury occurring in the course of one's employment, esp. in a factory; ***industrial insurance***, (*a*) = *industrial assurance*; (*b*) insurance for industrial workers against injury or absence from work; ***industrial park*** (chiefly N. Amer.) = *industrial estate*; ***industrial proletariat***, the section of the proletariat that is employed in industrial work; ***industrial property***, the collective name applied to commercial rights derived from patents, designs, trade marks, etc.; ***industrial psychology***, psychology as applied to all aspects of human involvement in industry; so ***industrial phychologist***; ***industrial relations***, relationships between employers and employees; ***industrial revolution***, a rapid development in industry; *spec.* (freq. with capital initials) the development which took place in England in the late eighteenth and early nineteenth centuries, chiefly owing to the introduction of new or improved machinery and large-scale production methods; ***industrial spy***, a person engaged in industrial espionage; ***industrial union***, a union of all workers in an industry irrespective of their craft or occupation; so ***industrial unionism, unionist***; ***Industrial Workers of the World***, a labour organization advocating syndicalism which enjoyed its greatest support in the western United States during the early twentieth century.

1910 *Encycl. Brit.* IX. 361/1 By a law of..1910, *Sweden* adopted the principle of the personal liability of the employer for *industrial accidents. **1922** *Ibid.* XXXI. 698/1 The former has legalized deductions for hospital benefits on approval of the Industrial Accident Commission. **1968** *Brit. Med. Bull.* XXIV. 256/1 A 40-year-old man with a history of several industrial accidents..presented after a fall at work. **1971** *Times* 17 Mar. 1/8 The Times regrets that, in common with other national newspapers, it will probably be unable to publish tomorrow because of *industrial action. **1972** *Guardian* 15 June 26/1, I fear..that if you imprison individual dockers we are going to get full scale industrial action. **1954** M. RIX in *Country Life* 28 Oct. 1501/1 This canal..has a special interest for industrial archæologists. **1951** *History Today* July 59/2 The most fascinating subject of all is what might be called the *industrial archaeology of the area. **1971** K. HUDSON (*title*) A guide to the industrial archaeology of Europe. **1850** *Punch* 29 June 10 Mind where you fix your show... Where Fashion rides and drives House not *industrial Art, But 'mid the busy hives Right in the City's heart. **1851** *Illustr. Lond. News* 21 June 605/3 Premiums for works of industrial art were offered. **1863** J. B. WARING (*title*) Masterpieces of industrial art and sculpture at the International Exhibition, 1862. **1902** *Encycl. Brit.* XXV. 687/1 The awakening of interest in industrial art—sharply separated by pedantic classification from fine art—which began about the middle of the 19th century. **1930** *Times* 7 May 11/4 Industrial Artists. An Association is to be formed of artists engaged in industry. **1896** *Act 59 & 60 Vict.* c. 26 (*title*) Collecting Societies and *Industrial Assurance Companies Act. **1920** *Rep. Industr. Assurance Comp.* (Cmd. 614) 2 The business of Industrial Assurance consists in the assurance of small sums, payable for the most part on the death of the life assured, in consideration of the payment of weekly premiums. **1935** *Economist* 2 Mar. 497/2 Following the terrible disaster at the Gresford Colliery, a sum of £10,000 was paid to some 200 families under industrial assurance policies. **1919** *Act 9 & 10 Geo. V* c. 69 §14 This Act may be cited as the *Industrial Courts Act, 1919. **1973** *Listener* 15 Nov. 660/1 The leaders of the AUEW see their own refusal to recognise the Industrial Court as part of the historic struggle of trade-unionists for the rights of the working man. **1934** H. READ (*title*) Art and industry, the principles of *industrial design. **1967** L. B. ARCHER in Wills & Yearsley *Handbk. Managem. Technol.* 122 There is a range of products in which aesthetic appearance and convenience in use are very important, such as in furniture, domestic appliances, and office machinery. Design of this kind is called 'industrial design'. **1940** H. VAN DOREN *Industr. Design* 27 *Industrial designers who take their work seriously cannot afford to play the prima donna. **1972** F. MACCARTHY *All Things Bright & Beautiful* 147 The hero of the piece was the industrial designer. **1906** *Act 6 Edw. VII* c. 58 §8 (*heading*) Application of act to *industrial diseases. **1974** *Guardian* 20 Mar. 1/8 A working class Yorkshire family, whose father contracts cancer through an industrial disease. **1907** *Times* 1 Feb. 4/5 The Minister of Labour [in Canada] has brought in an *Industrial Disputes Investigation Act, which provides for the constitution of conciliation boards. **1973** *Times* 13 Dec. 18/8 Men for whom wage claims and industrial disputes are tools to be used in.. the destruction of the existing political order. **1962** L. DEIGHTON *Ipcress File* viii. 52 His reports concern *industrial espionage. **1972** K. BENTON *Spy in Chancery* ii. 22 He runs an industrial espionage service. **1953** P. C. BERG *Dict. New Words* 96/2 **Industrial estate*, a trading estate. **1972** M. JONES *Life on Dole* ix. 68 The Council declared this property to be an industrial estate. **1974** *Times* 14 Jan. 2/5 A secondary modern school on an industrial estate. **1914** *Rep. Brit. Assoc. Adv. Sci.* 176 What increase..has occurred in general morbidity in recent years, and to what extent this can be ascribed to *industrial fatigue. **1950** *Chambers's Encycl.* VII. 543/1 In 1918 the Industrial Fatigue Research Board was formed. **1940** *Chambers's Techn. Dict.* 446/1 **Industrial frequency*, a term used to denote the frequency of the alternating current used for ordinary industrial purposes, usually 50 or 60 cycles. **1958** *Engineering* 14 Mar. 341/1 Two [railway] systems..which are able to utilise widely spaced substations and light overhead conductors, are the Swedish system at $16\frac{2}{3}$ cycles, and the French (and now British) system at industrial frequency (50 cycles) and 25 kV. **1933** M. CORRELL in *U.S. Women's Bureau Bull.* No. 102 (*title*) *Industrial injuries to women in 1928 and 1929. **1940** *Bull. U.S. Bureau of Labor Statistics* No. 667. p. ix, Efficient accident prevention can be promoted by administrators of workmen's compensation laws by prescribing types of reports to be submitted in cases of industrial injuries which can be used in analyzing accident causes. **1946** *Industr. Welfare & Personnel Managem.* XXVIII. 214 Important changes in Industrial Law have taken place recently as a result of such measures as the Industrial Injuries Act (which supersedes the Workmen's Compensation Acts). **1971** *Morning Star* 8 Apr. 3 Industrial injuries, on average, had been halved. **1911** *Encycl. Brit.* XIV. 671/2 The system of *industrial insurance was introduced into the United States in 1876. **1920** S. & B. WEBB *Hist. Trade Unionism* (rev. ed.) ix. 507 The life assurance agents—principally those employed in 'industrial' insurance—number 100,000. **1920** *Rep. Industr. Assurance Comp.* (Cmd. 614) 3 There is little thought for the development of industrial insurance upon the sound economic lines by which it might become a valuable instrument. **1955** *Barron's Nat. Business & Financial Weekly* 10 Oct. 13 (*title*) *Industrial parks; planned factory districts are attracting more customers. *Ibid.* 15/3 The combined shopping center and industrial park. **1957** *Urban Land* Apr. 5/2 Several questions indicated a strong local interest in the development of industrial parks as a means of stimulating development. The Panel stated that such parks are becoming increasingly popular and effective in attracting the smaller manufacturing plants and distribution warehouses. **1963** *Amer. City* July 95/2 The new industrial park..offers the prospective industry a tract of graded land located on a wide, paved and landscaped boulevard. The attractive 'price of admission' also includes curbs, gutters and storm drains, water and sewer mains, gas, electric and telephone lines and access to railroad sidings. **1972** *Evening Telegram* (St. John's, Newfoundland) 5 Aug. 10/1 Murray and Davis Properties Ltd. has announced the opening of their new..building..in the industrial park area. **1887** F. K. WISCHNEWETZKY tr. *Engels's Condition of Working-Class in Eng.* i. 15 (*heading*) The *Industrial Proletariat. **1930** G. B. SHAW *John Bull's Other Island* Pref., in *Wks.* XI. 71 The growing political power of the industrial proletariat organized in trade unions. **1972** G. WIGG *George Wigg* i. 23 The tiny red brick houses, typical of the growth of an industrial proletariat. **1884** in Hertslet *Treaties* (1890) XVII. 408 The International Convention for the Protection of *Industrial Property, concluded at Paris on the 20th March, 1883. **1952** LAUTERPACHT & OPPENHEIM *Internat. Law* (ed. 7) II. II. ii. 330 Enemy assets..are to be returned —with the important exception of industrial property (*i.e.*, patents, designs, trade marks and trade names, etc.). **1921** J. DREVER *Psychol. of Industry* iv. 46 Even when the factors affecting industrial efficiency and success are physical, the work of the *industrial psychologist may still be valuable in tracing out the physiological and psychological results of physical conditions. **1936** *Discovery* Sept. 279 There are too many salients in the front line of social progress and it is the duty of the industrial psychologist to smooth these away. **1964** M. ARGYLE *Psychol. & Social Probl.* viii. 114 It is one of the major tasks confronting industrial psychologists today to discover ways of organizing such work that will make it an acceptable human activity. **1971** A. K. KORMAN *Industr. & Organizational Psychol.* i. 12 The industrial psychologist.. continues to be actively concerned with the..techniques and methods which will increase the effectiveness of manpower utilization in the modern organization both from the company's and from the individual's point of view. [**1913** H. MÜNSTERBERG (*title*) Psychology and industrial efficiency.] **1917** B. MUSCIO (*title*) Lectures on *industrial psychology. **1932** *Discovery* Nov. 374/1 Industrial psychology is an awkward term for the improvement of the human factor in industry, but its value is unquestionable. **1970** D. P. SCHULTZ *Psychol. & Industry* i. 1 The field of industrial psychology includes a complex of activities covering all facets of the relationship between man and his work. **1904** S. A. BARNETT et al. in H. Barnett *Canon Barnett* (1918) II. xli. 258 Luxury..leads to cruelty in our *industrial relations. **1972** *Times* 4 May 4/1 Members of Parliament are likely to be given greater latitude by the Speaker in discussing..matters that have been brought before the Industrial Relations Court. **1973** *Listener* 25 Oct. 553/3 There were no shop-stewards, solicitors or industrial relations managers present. *Ibid.* 15 Nov. 660/2 The Labour Party is committed to the repeal of the Industrial Relations Act. **1848** MILL *Pol. Econ.* II. III. xvii. 119 The opening of a foreign trade..sometimes works a complete *industrial revolution in a country whose resources were previously undeveloped. **1884** A. TOYNBEE (*title*) Lectures on the Industrial Revolution in England. **1911** C. G. ROBERTSON *Eng. under Hanoverians* II. iv. 341 The manufacturer of the Industrial Revolution is the modern master who provides capital, owns his mill or factory,..and creates and maintains a market. **1938** H. GRANVILLE-BARKER *Quality* 3 We sometimes refer to the Industrial Revolution as if it were a thing of the past. **1957** G. E. WRIGHT *Biblical Archaeol.* viii. 120/2 The Philistine defeat..meant *an industrial revolution*. Philistine power was broken and the secret of the iron smelting process became common property. **1973** *Guardian* 4 June 9/6 It is no good being nostalgic for society before the Industrial Revolution. **1959** K. VONNEGUT *Sirens of Titan* (1962) iii. 73 He..had a superb system of *industrial spies. **1972** G. LYALL *Blame the Dead* xii. 77 This letter..would be a useful guide to any industrial spy trying to penetrate your organisation. **1923** J. D. HACKETT in *Managem. Engin.* May 344/1 **Industrial union*, a union of all workers within a plant or within an industry, irrespective of occupation or craft, and outside the control of the employer. **1928** *Britain's Industr. Future* (Liberal Industr. Inquiry) III. xiv. §3. 155 The Industrial Unions are a modern development, inspired by the idea of enabling all the workers in an industry..to present a united front against their employers. **1937, 1950** Industrial union [see HORIZONTAL *a.* 3 d]. **1905** *Socialist* Oct. 4/3 *Industrial Unionism is the name applied to that form of trades unionism which has sprung into existence as a direct outgrowth of modern industrial conditions under which whole industries are practically owned and controlled by capitalists through the medium of a trust or combine. **1912** [see SYNDICALISM]. **1920** S. & B. WEBB *Hist. Trade Unionism* (rev. ed.) ix. 659 The revolutionary Industrial Unionism and Syndicalism preached by James Connolly and Tom Mann..between 1905 and 1912 did not commend itself to the officials of the Trade Unions. **1905** *Socialist* Oct. 4/3 The *Industrial Unionist calls upon the workers to organise in a manner consistent with the economic conditions with which they are surrounded... The plan of the industrial unionist..calls for the joining of all in the one national body of the industry. **1917** G. HARVEY *Industr. Unionism & Mining Industry* v. 148 Analysis of the Arrangement of Industries (based on Industrial Unionist literature). **1905** *Industrial Workers of the World: Constitution & By-Laws* 4 This Organization shall be known as 'The *Industrial Workers of the World'... And shall be composed of thirteen International Departments, subdivided in industrial unions of closely kindred industries..for representation in the departmental administration. **1912** *Century Mag.* July 473/1 Counsels of violence were emphatically rejected, despite the opposition of the ideas of the Industrial Workers of the World. **1920, 1957** [see *I.W.W.* (I. III)]. **1962** G. WOODCOCK *Anarchism* xiv. 466 After 1905 the anarchists who were interested in labor organization tended to join the Industrial Workers of the World.

B. *sb.* **1.** One engaged in industrial pursuits.

1865 *Pall Mall G.* 16 Aug. 10/1 Commercials.. Agriculturists..Industrials. **1887** *Ibid.* 20 Jan. 12/1 A place in which the home-keeping industrial could find out all he wants to know about colonial industry. **1894** *Lancaster* (Pa.) *Morn. News* 16 May, A band of Western 'Industrials' received..an offer of £1.40 per day and per man to work on a railroad contract. **1899** *Q. Rev.* Jan. 10 To him it appears a matter of course..that nobles and industrials should be fighting.

2. *pl.* Shares in a joint-stock industrial enterprise.

1894 *Daily News* 21 Sept. 3/6 There was no general tone to the market, which—excluding Industrials—appears for the present to have reached a state of equilibrium. **1898** *Westm. Gaz.* 2 Mar. 8/3 There is always plenty of money awaiting investment in sound industrials.

3. A joint-stock industrial enterprise.

1908 *Westm. Gaz.* 20 Jan. 11/1 A Colonial Industrial. The prospectus of the Vryheid (Natal) Railway, Coal, and Iron Company, Limited, has now made its appearance. **1909** *Ibid.* 3 June 13/4 A large falling off is shown in the earnings of that well-known industrial, Wm. Cory and Son.

Hence **in'dustrially** *adv.*, in respect of industry; **in'dustrialness**, the quality of being industrial.

a **1846** *For. Q. Rev.* cited in Worcester for *Industrially*. **1858** SIMMONDS *Dict. Trade* 203/1 Those identified with the manufacturing pursuits, or producing arts, are said to be industrially employed. **1876** H. SPENCER *Princ. Sociol.* (1877) I. 756 Simple tribes which are exceptional in their industrialness. **1879** *Ibid.* III. ix. 711 Decrease of militancy and increase of industrialness. **1883** *American* VI. 37 No country which keeps a large fraction of its people under arms, can compete industrially with countries like England and America.

in'dustrialism. [f. prec. + -ISM. Cf. F. *industrialisme* (Littré).] A system of things arising from or involving the existence of great industries; the organization of industrial occupations.

1831 CARLYLE *Sart. Res.* II. iv, Preparing us, by indirect but sure methods, Industrialism and the Government of the Wisest. **1844** MARY HENNELL *Soc. Syst.* 201 The anarchy of civilized industrialism. **1869** SEELEY *Lect. & Ess.* i. 18 Poets sang of a golden age returned, and they hymned industrialism in exquisite language. **1880** *Academy* 24 Jan. 59/1 Ceremony..dies away among industrial societies, and among those classes which industrialism has produced.

in'dustrialist. [f. as prec. + -IST. Cf. F. *industrialiste* (Littré).]

1. One engaged in, or connected with, industrial occupations; a worker or manufacturer.

1864 *Times* 23 Mar., The well-to-do industrialists, and the landowners. **1869** M. ARNOLD *Cult. & An.* (1882) 235 Industrialists in search of gentility. **1884** *Pall Mall G.* 25 Aug. 4/1 When once men have begun to be divided definitely into industrialists and fighters [etc.].

2. *attrib.* or *adj.* Characterized by or engaged in industrialism.

1886 *Encycl. Brit.* XXI. 197/2 What Saint-Simon desired ..was an industrialist state directed by modern science.

industrialization (ɪnˌdʌstrɪəlaɪˈzeɪʃən). [f. INDUSTRIALIZE *v.* + -ATION.] The process of industrializing or fact of being industrialized; also, the conversion of an organization into an industry.

1906 *Westm. Gaz.* 26 Oct. 2/1 A creed..that commends itself to all whom the 'industrialisation' of American politics has revolted. **1911** G. H. MAIR *Eng. Lit.: Mod.* ix. 225 If we want a picture of the great fact of modern Scotland, its industrialisation, it is to Galt we must go. **1923** *19th Cent.* Jan. 47 It is easy to obtain an exaggerated idea of the pace at which the industrialisation of the country by means of indigenous agency is taking place. **1928** *Daily Tel.* 20 Mar. 12/6 The present rulers of Russia have staked everything upon the policy of industrialisation under State auspices. **1953** *Encounter* Oct. 78/2 The process of industrialisation produces certain social types. **1963** P. TRENCH in *Industrialized Building Syst. & Components* Oct. 10/1 It must be some ten years ago that Roger Watters..and I first talked industrialisation. I can't remember who coined the word—it may well have been neither of us... It is now the U word. *Ibid.* 10/2 Industrialisation as a process must cover everything from the use of ready mixed concrete through modular co-ordination to the closed proprietary building system. It is in fact too wide a term to be of real use but since we have no other to describe the change in the nature of building which is going on we must accept it. **1969** *Observer* 12 Jan. 9/2 Art education is a safeguard against over-organisation, industrialisation, bureaucratisation and dehumanisation. **1969** H. A. FREY tr. *Schmidt & Testa's Syst. Building* 34/2 *Industrialization of building* in the proper sense, and in contrast to building rationalization, has to do not only with selected operations, but comprises the entire construction process from the planning stage to execution. **1973** *Listener* 20 Dec. 857 Industrialisation played a big part in the drive to paint the map pink.

in'dustrialize, *v.* [f. as INDUSTRIAL *a.* + -IZE.] **a.** *trans.* To affect with or devote to industrialism; to occupy or organize industrially.

1882 [implied at INDUSTRIALIZED *ppl. a.* a] **1886** *Pall Mall G.* 8 Sept. 4/1 Professor Foxwell..spoke ominously of 'industrializing' the villages and making markets near the agriculturists. **1888** [implied at INDUSTRIALIZED *ppl. a.* a]

b. *intr.* To become industrial.

1965 D. E. C. EVERSLEY in Glass & Eversley *Population in Hist.* ii. 60 Countries which did not industrialize shared in this process because they began to act as granaries for areas not self-sufficient in food. **1971** *Daily Tel.* 16 Oct. 10/4 The pace at which it [*sc.* Australia] is being forced to industrialize is turning large sections of the wide brown land into a polluted wasteland.

Hence **in'dustrializing** *vbl. sb.* and *ppl. a.*

1925 *Glasgow Herald* 16 Nov. 9 It appears to be the general conclusion that any industrialising schemes apart from the water-power projects cannot succeed. **1959** *Daily Tel.* 10 Mar. 13/1 Fairly good industrial production increases occurred in new industrialising countries like Pakistan, the Philippines, Formosa and South Korea. **1967** *Economist* 10 June 1105/3 Rapidly mounting food deficits are one sign of an industrialising society. **1971** A. SHONFIELD in A. Bullock *20th Cent.* 326/1 The end of colonial empires would start a race with the newly industrializing nations in which the Old World would soon be overtaken.

industrialized, *ppl. a.* [f. INDUSTRIALIZE *v.* + -ED.] **a.** Affected by industrialism.

1882 *Cornh. Mag.* Dec. 736 Our modern desecrated and industrialised England. **1888** *New Princeton Rev.* May 328 Contempt of civilians, patronage of 'trades-people', survive from the middle-age..with a persistence that strikes our industrialized sense as puerile.

b. ***industrialized building***, building in which industrial methods are employed, esp. prefabrication, mechanization, and standardization. Hence applied to buildings built in accordance with such methods.

1963 *Daily Tel.* 4 Feb. 18 Prefabricated units developed under 'industrialised building' methods will be made available to small as well as big builders. **1963** *Ibid.* 2 May 14 The suggestion is that spare shipbuilding capacity should be turned over to the manufacture of component parts for industrialised housing. **1963** *Industrialised Building Syst. & Components* Oct. 5 Industrialised building is not the mere substitution of prefabrication for traditional methods or the adoption of 'systems'. We see it as the application of modern industrial methods to the planning and execution of construction projects. **1965** R. B. WHITE *Prefabrication* III. vi. 302 'Industrialized' building, or 'system' building,..is usually taken to mean a considerable degree of prefabrication. **1967** *Times Rev. Industry* Feb. 23/2 The National Building Agency..suggests that the number of industrialized houses in the public sector should be increased to at least 165,000. **1968** *New Scientist* 23 May 388 Industrialized buildings by their nature are less continuous than traditional structures. The degree of continuity depends on the techniques adopted to join together the prefabricated units.

†in'dustriate, *v. Obs. rare*⁻¹. [f. F. *industrier* + -ATE³ 6: cf. *s'industrier* 'to labour, indeauour, bestirre himselfe' (Cotgr.).] *refl.* To use one's industry, to make diligent endeavour.

1613 SHERLEY *Trav. Persia* 2 It was..a weaknesse in my judgement, which, notwithstanding, I ever industriated my selfe to make perfect.

industrious (ɪnˈdʌstrɪəs), *a.* [ad. L. (post-class.) *industriōsus* (f. *industria* industry: see -OUS), or its Fr. repr. *industrieux* (1503 in Hatz.-Darm.). Cf. also L. *industrius* diligent.] Characterized by industry.

†1. Characterized by or showing intelligent or skilful work; skilful, able, clever, ingenious. (Of agents, their actions, etc.). *Obs.*

[Cf. **1538** ELYOT *Dict.*, *Industrius*, He that is wytty and actyue.]

1523 [implied in INDUSTRIOUSLY 1]. **1531** ELYOT *Gov.* I. xxiii, They that be called Industrious, do moste craftily and depely understande in all affaires what is expedient, and by what meanes and wayes they maye sonest exploite them. And those thinges in whome other men trauayle, a person industrious lightly and with facilitie spedeth, and fyndeth newe wayes and meanes to bringe to effecte that he desireth. **1549** *Compl. Scot.* Ep. Queen 6 Be that industreus martial act, he renforsit the toune vitht victualis. **1555** EDEN *Decades* 338 The industrious and subtyle art of partyng gold from new syluer. **1594** T. B. *La Primaud. Fr. Acad.* II. 411 Are there many creatures although greater in substance, that yet haue such industrious & ingenious natures, as these litle beasts [bees] haue? **1595** SHAKS. *John* II. i. 376 They gape and point At your industrious Scenes and acts of death. **1601** R. JOHNSON *Kingd. & Commw.* (1603) 178 Adversitie ripeneth the looser, and maketh him warie and industrious. **1657** W. RAND tr. *Gassendi's Peiresc* II. 76 That the Ancients were so industrious, that they made no Vessel, which did not contain a set measure, and a certain weight. **1679** G. R. tr. *Boaystuau's Theat. World* II. 308 Another composed a compleat Ship..so industrious that a Bee might hide or cover it under his Wings. **1687** DRYDEN *Hind & P.* II. 571 Industrious of the needle and the chart, They run full sail to their Japonian mart.

2. Characterized by or showing application, endeavour, or effort; painstaking, zealous, attentive, careful. Const. *in* (†*after, of, to*) some matter, *to do* something.

1552 HULOET, Industrious, *peruigil.* **1596** SHAKS. *1 Hen. IV*, I. i. 62 Heere is a deere and true industrious friend, Sir Walter Blunt, new lighted from his Horse. **1596** SPENSER *State Irel.* Wks. (Globe) 626/1 Industrious to seeke out the trueth of these thinges. **1608** MIDDLETON *Trick to catch old one* II. i, His uncle [is] very industrious to beguile the widow and make up the match. **1613** PURCHAS *Pilgrimage* (1614) 51 More industrious in humane inventions, then religious devotions. **1644** MILTON *Educ.* Wks. (1847) 98/2 Those people who have at any time been most industrious after wisdom. **1659** HAMMOND *On Ps.* cx. 1 Some others..are most industrious to evade it. **1667** MILTON *P.L.* II. 116 His thoughts were low; To vice industrious, but to Nobler deeds Timorous and slothful. **1693** G. STEPNEY in *Dryden's Juvenal* viii. (1697) 220 He was Industrious to be esteem'd the best Musitian of his Age. **1699** BENTLEY *Phal.* Pref. 11 Considering with what industrious Malice the false Story had been spread over England. **1699** DRYDEN *To John Driden* 53 Industrious of the common good. **1725** POPE *Odyss.* VIII. 82 Before his eyes the purple vest he drew, Industrious to conceal the falling dew. **1741** MIDDLETON *Cicero* II. viii. 176 Very industrious in recommending it. **1761** HUME *Hist. Eng.* III. li. 116 Hollis was so industrious to continue his meritorious distress, that when one offered to bail him he would not yield.

†3. Characterized by or showing design or purpose: intentional, designed, purposed, voluntary.

1629 N. CARPENTER *Achit.* 8 It was the part of a shamelesse Cham to bee an industrious spectator of his fathers nakednesse. **1652** J. WRIGHT tr. *Camus' Nature's Paradox* 290 By industrious excuses (purposely invented) hee had sharpen'd the desire of his Auditours. **1654** H. L'ESTRANGE *Chas. I* (1655) 183 Some there are suspect this mistake to have been not involuntary but industrious in him. **1668** H. MORE *Div. Dial.* (J.), The industrious perforation of the tendons of the second joints of fingers and toes, draw the tendons of the third joints through. **1691** T. H[ALE] *Acc. New Invent.* 90 An industrious Omission..of the Principal Point of Care. **1817** G. S. FABER *Eight Dissert.* (1845) I. 269 His [Elijah's] industrious affectation of the wilderness.

4. Characterized by or showing assiduous and steady work; full of work; diligent, laborious, hard-working. (The prevailing sense.)

1591 SPENSER *Muiopotmos* 122 Who beeing..more industrious, gathered more store Of the fields honour than the others best. **1611** BIBLE *1 Kings* xi. 28 Solomon seeing the young man that he was industrious [*marg.*, *Heb.* did worke]. **1683** ROBINSON in *Ray's Corr.* (1848) 132 We have been very industrious since our coming to Paris. **1725** DE FOE *Voy. round World* (1840) 263 Soil well cultivated by the poor industrious Chilians. **1764** GOLDSM. *Trav.* 299 Industrious habits in each bosom reign. **1782** COWPER *Heroism* 69 Yet man, laborious man, by slow degrees.. Plies all the sinews of industrious toil. **1864** J. WALKER *Faithf. Ministry* 207 The most pious man ought to be the most industrious. **1892** JAS. BROWN *Serm.* 207 Industrious poverty becomes a nobler thing than idle wealth.

5. = INDUSTRIAL *a. rare.*

1825 MCCULLOCH *Pol. Econ.* Introd. 45 Those who are engaged in industrious undertakings. **1845** —— *Taxation* II. v. (1852) 207 Such improvements..in the arts as will enable industrious undertakings to be carried on with a much less expenditure of fuel.

industriously (ɪnˈdʌstrɪəslɪ), *adv.* [f. prec. + -LY².] In an industrious manner.

†1. With intelligent or skilful work; skilfully, cleverly, ingeniously. *Obs.*

1523 SKELTON *Garl. Laurel* 851 The noble Pamphila.. Habillimentis royall founde out industriously. **1647** W. BROWNE tr. *Polexander* I. 26 The first part was full of little Chambers, so industriously built that they seemed to be cut out of the Rocke it selfe. *Ibid.* 28 The seeling was of a hollow mirror, made of many Venice glasses, so industriously joyned together, that [etc.].

2. With painstaking work; carefully, studiously, zealously, persistently; often in bad sense: with evil pertinacity.

1575–85 ABP. SANDYS *Serm.* (Parker Soc.) 212 Let us cast off all hinderances, and strive industriously unto that salvation which is set before us. **1670** CLARENDON *Contempl. Ps.* Tracts (1727) 608 The rankest pleasures which are industriously applied to the corruption of human nature. **1709** ADDISON *Tatler* No. 96 ¶3 It has been industriously given out..that John Partridge is dead. *Ibid.* ¶7 Several have industriously spread abroad, That I am in Partnership with Charles Lilly. **1716** S. SEWALL *Diary* 5 Oct. (1882) III. 105 Govr., Lt. Govr. laid their hands on the Bible, and kiss'd it very industriously. **1796** MORSE *Amer. Geog.* II. 437 A notion industriously propagated by the Romish clergy. **1871** MORLEY *Voltaire* (1886) 8 Industriously shouting the cry of a church. **1883** GILMOUR *Mongols* xviii. 212 In the act of disrobing, prayers are said most industriously.

†3. Of set purpose; with design; intentionally, designedly. (= L. *de industria.*) *Obs.*

1611 SHAKS. *Wint. T.* I. ii. 256 If industriously I play'd the Foole, it was my negligence, Not weighing well the end. **1642** HOWELL *For. Trav.* (Arb.) 30 But here, shee seemes to have industriously, and of set purpose studied it. **1674** T. TURNOR *Case Bankers & Creditors* Concl. 33 There be many things which possibly I have forgot, and some things which I have perhaps industriously omitted. **1774** J. BRYANT *Mythol.* II. 431 His horns are industriously so placed as to form two lunettes. **1816** G. S. FABER *Orig. Pagan Idolatry* III. 244 The three pyramids of Egypt have been industriously built upon the first hill between Cairo and the western bank of the Nile.

4. With steady application to work; diligently, assiduously, laboriously.

1611 COTGR. *Industrieusement*, industriously; diligently.. laboriously. **1663** COWLEY *Verses & Ess.*, *Ode Orinda's Poems*, But thou industriously hast sow'd and till'd The fair, and fruitful field. **1781** W. BLANE *Ess. Hunt.* Pref. (1788) 10 If he..chuses to be idly busy rather than industriously so. **1859** SMILES *Self-Help* ii. 41 He worked away industriously employing a few hands.

in'dustriousness. [f. as prec. + -NESS.] The quality of being industrious: = INDUSTRY 3.

1591 SAVILE *Tacitus, Hist.* II. xc. 106 Extolling his own industriousnesse and temperancy. **1619** SCLATER *Exp. 2 Thess.* (1630) 393 The Pismire can teach the Sluggard prouidence, and industriousnesse. **1818** HALLAM *Mid. Ages* (1872) II. 269 The characteristic independence and industriousness of our nation. **1881** H. SPENCER tr. *Pop. Sci. Monthly* Nov. 1 Industrialism is not to be confounded with industriousness.

†in'dustrous, *a. Obs. rare.* Variant of INDUSTRIOUS. So **†in'dustrously** *adv.*

1606 G. W[OODCOCKE] tr. *Hist. Ivstine* 84 b, Painefull and industrous souldiors. **1635** HEYWOOD *Hierarch.* IV. 214 The Second to the Third is like industrous, And as degreed, 'tis more and more illustrous. **1721** *Lond. Gaz.* No. 5932/2 All which..were industrously set on Fire.

industry (ˈɪndəstrɪ). [a. F. *industrie* (14th c.), or ad. L. *industria* diligence, 'a vertue comprehendynge bothe study and diligence' (Elyot *Dict.* 1538).]

†1. Intelligent or clever working; skill, ingenuity, dexterity, or cleverness in doing anything.

1494 FABYAN *Chron.* I. xiii. (1533) 7 b, Saynge that the foresayd hote bathes were made by the industrye, or made of the industry of Iulius cesar. **1531** ELYOT *Gov.* I. xxiii, Industrie hath nat ben so longe tyme used in the englisshe tonge as Prouidence; wherfore it is the more straunge, and requireth the more plaine exposition. It is a qualitie procedyng of witte and experience, by the whiche a man perceyueth quickly, inuenteth fresshly, and counsayleth spedily. *c* **1566** J. ALDAY tr. *Boaystuau's Theat. World* C viij, With what industrie do they [ants] make theyr little holes, of the which the comming in is not straight, for feare that other beasts come not in. *Ibid.* D ij b, The Cuckowe..[has] the industrie to espie where other Birdes make their nestes, and there layth hir egges. **1597** A. M. tr. *Guillemeau's Fr. Chirurg.* 12 b/1 There is a certayne industrye in the depressione of the trepane. **1613** PURCHAS *Pilgrimage* (1614) 521 [They] have no..weapons, but certaine swords: and are without all industry for fishing and navigation.

†2. An application of skill, cleverness, or craft; a device, contrivance; a crafty expedient. *Obs.*

c **1477** CAXTON *Jason* 93 b, I shal deliuere to him the industrie and teche him how he shal wynne the flees of golde. **1555** EDEN *Decades* 84 Nature was not sollicitate to brynge furthe suche greate fluds by this so smaule industry. **1560** WHITEHORNE *Arte Warre* (1588) 94 The first industrie is, to make the walles crooked, and full of tourninges, and of receiptes. **1596** DALRYMPLE tr. *Leslie's Hist. Scot.* VII. 33 Sche, as was reported, suddenlie thairefter dies, be industrie of the gouernour. **1613** PURCHAS *Pilgrimage* (1614) 885 To make the Computation of their yeere certaine, they used this industrie. **1621** BURTON *Anat. Mel.* II. i. II. (1651) 222 All the physick we can use, art, excellent industry, is to no purpose without calling upon God.

3. Diligence or assiduity in the performance of any task, or in any effort; close and steady

application to the business in hand; exertion, effort.

1531 ELYOT *Gov.* III. xxiii, That slouthe and dulnesse beynge plucked from them by Industrie, they be induced unto the continuall acte. **1576** GASCOIGNE *Steele Gl.* Ded. (Arb.) 44 These examples are sufficient to proue that by industrie and diligence any perfection may be attained. **1681** LUTTRELL *Brief Rel.* (1857) I. 62 It consumed but one house, being quenched by the great industry of the people. **1741** MIDDLETON *Cicero* II. x. 416 A story, kept up for some days with great industry. **1792** *Anecd. W. Pitt* I. i. 3 The present publication is the effect of industry, not of ability. **1863** FROUDE *Hist. Eng.* VIII. 91 In a few well chosen sentences she complimented the students on their industry.

4. a. Systematic work or labour; habitual employment in some useful work, now esp. in the productive arts or manufactures. (This, with 5, is the prevalent sense.)

1611 SHAKS. *Cymb.* III. vi. 31 The sweat of industry would dry, and dye But for the end it workes too. **1699** DAMPIER *Voy.* II. I. 141 Those who can turn their hands to any thing besides drudgery, live well enough by their industry. **1764** BURN *Poor Laws* 151 A man that has been bred up in the trade of begging, will never, unless compelled, fall to industry. **1776** ADAM SMITH *W.N.* II. iii. (1869) II. 338 The funds destined for the maintenance of industry are much greater in proportion..than they were two or three centuries ago. **1843** CARLYLE *Past & Pr.* IV. iv, The Leaders of Industry..are virtually the Captains of the World. **1863** FAWCETT *Pol. Econ.* II. v. 198 When industry is conducted by other combinations than those of employers and employed.

b. ***house of industry***, a workhouse. ***school*** **(†*college*) *of industry***, a school in which various industrial occupations are taught; an industrial school.

1696 J. BELLERS (*title*) Proposals for raising a College of Industry for all useful Trades and Husbandry. **1773** R. POTTER (*title*) Observations on the Poor Laws, on the Present State of the Poor, and on Houses of Industry. **1782** *Phil. Trans.* LXXII. 366 In the month of June, 1777, several years after the House of Industry has been built. **1789** (*title*) Plan of the Sunday Schools and School of Industry established in the City of Bath. **1882** MRS. PITMAN *Mission L. Greece & Pal.* 68 She said that she was most of all pleased with the school of industry, because it was confined to the poor.

5. a. A particular form or branch of productive labour; a trade or manufacture.

c **1566** J. ALDAY tr. *Boaystuau's Theat. World* C iv b, Spinners or Spiders..have a much better grace..in their industries, for there is no knots in their workings, nor wast. **1621** G. SANDYS tr. *Ovid's Met.* II. (1626) 32 The Thunderer then..finding nothing there by fire decay'd; He Earth, and humane industries suruay'd. **1741** JOHNSON *Debates Parl.* (1787) I. 278 To maintain themselves by a more honest and useful industry. **1844** DISRAELI *Coningsby* II. i, The rights and properties of our national industries. **1883** *Athenæum* 8 Sept. 309/2 An industry that has lately sprung up in the United States concerned in the production of galvanised iron cornices for architectural purposes. **1883** C. J. WILLS *Mod. Persia* 360 They knit socks as long as daylight lasts; some widows even maintain a family by this industry.

b. *Archæol.* A collection of prehistoric implements of the same age found at an archæological site and used as evidence of the original technique of working; also, the technique so revealed.

1911 *Jrnl. R. Anthrop. Inst.* 458 (*title*) On the classification of British Stone-Age industries. **1952** [see GRAVETTIAN *a.* and *sb.*]. **1959** J. D. CLARK *Prehist. S. Afr.* ii. 39 A single living or workshop site where a number of specimens all of the same age are associated is called an 'industry', while the term 'culture' is usually employed to describe a number of 'industries' all of the same type, and of which the distribution is more than purely local.

c. Preceded by a personal name or the like: scholarly or diligent work devoted to the study of a particular author or subject; also, the practice of a profitable occupation.

1965 *New Statesman* 9 Apr. 575/1 The Pindar industry began fairly early in antiquity, as we can still see in the surviving scholia. **1966** *Listener* 10 Nov. 685/1 The Shakespeare industry..is a very old one; I have an eighteenth-century snuffbox made from Shakespeare's mulberry tree. **1969** *Daily Tel.* 24 Apr. 22/3 The way to tackle 'Ulysses' is to plunge into it headfirst,..which is what we all had to do before the Joyce industry began. *Ibid.* 5 Aug. 14/2 The brisk pick-up of business in the abortion industry has greatly alarmed many people.

†**6.** ***of industry***, on purpose, intentionally (after L. *de* or *ex industria*). *Obs. rare.*

1613 CHAPMAN *Revenge Bussy D'Ambois* II. D ij a, Romes Brutus is reuiu'd in him, Whom hee of industry doth imitate. *Ibid.* III. F ij b, When Homer made Achilles passionate,..He did compose it all of industrie, To let men see, that [etc.]. **1648** MILTON *Tenure Kings* 4 A dissembl'd piety fain'd of industry to begett new discord.

7. Comb. ***industry-wide*** adj.

1946 *Nature* 30 Nov. 797/1 Research should mainly be on an industry-wide basis, and for the benefit of the industry as a whole. **1958** *Listener* 24 July 116/2 It is possible to preserve industry-wide bargaining. **1971** *Publishers' Weekly* 2 Aug. 43/3 The American National Standards, Inc., the official agency for certifying industry-wide standards in the United States.

Hence **'industrying** [-ING¹], practice of an industry. *nonce-wd.*

1865 CARLYLE *Fredk. Gt.* XVIII. v. (1872) VII. 182 An eye-sorrow, they, with their commerce, their weavings and industryings, to Austrian Papists, who cannot weave or trade.

†**in'dute**, *ppl. a. Obs. rare*⁻¹. [ad. L. *indūt-us*, pa. pple. of *induĕre*: see ENDUE.] Clothed, endued.

c **1450** *Cov. Myst.* xxi. (Shaks. Soc.) 204 Clothe the in clennes, with vertu be indute.

†**in'dution.** ? Endowment (f. INDUE = ENDOW).

1580 LYLY *Euphues* F iv, They [bees] vse as great wit by indution, and Arte by workmanship, as euer man hath or can.

indutive (ɪn'djuːtɪv), *a. Bot.* [f. L. *indūt-*, ppl. stem of *induĕre* (see next) + -IVE.] Of seeds: Having the usual integument or covering (*Syd. Soc. Lex.* 1886).

†**induviæ** (ɪn'djuːviiː), *sb. pl. Bot.* [L. *induviæ* clothes, clothing, f. *induĕre* to put on.] (See quot.)

1835 LINDLEY *Introd. Bot.* (1848) I. 242 The withered remains of leaves which not being articulated with the stem cannot fall off but decay upon it have been called..induviæ, the part so covered is said to be induviate.

Hence **in'duvial**, *a. Bot.*

1855 MAYNE *Expos. Lex.*, *Induvialis*,..applied by Mirbel, to a calyx when it persists and covers the fruit..induvial.

in'duviate, *a. Bot.* [f. prec. + -ATE².] Clothed with induviæ (q.v.).

1835 [see INDUVIÆ]. **1855** in MAYNE *Expos. Lex.* **1870** BENTLEY *Bot.* 127 The stem is said to be induviate.

induyr(e, obs. form of ENDURE *v.*

indw, obs. form of ENDUE, ENDOW.

c **1440** *Promp. Parv.* 261/2 Indwyn, and yeve warysone, *doto. Ibid.*, Indwynge, *dotacio.*

indwell (ˌɪn'dwɛl), *v.* Pa. t. and pple. **indwelt.** [f. IN-¹ + DWELL; in Wyclif rendering L. *inhabitāre.*]

1. *trans.* To dwell in, inhabit, occupy as a dwelling; also *fig.* To live in, occupy, or possess, as a spirit or principle may inhabit a body.

1382 WYCLIF *Ps.* xxxvi[i]. 3 Hope in the Lord, and do goodnesse; and indwelle thou [Vulg. *inhabita*] the erthe. **17..** *Fumbler's Rant* in Herd *Collect. Sc. Songs* (1776) II. 46 We aw him nought but a grey groat, Thy off'ring for the house we in-dwell. **1839** BAILEY *Festus* xiii. (1848) 120 Living clouds Indwelt by warrior souls. **1871** BLACKIE *Four Phases* I. 94 The Intelligence which indwelleth the whole of things. **1882** H. SCOTT HOLLAND *Logic & Life* (1885) 124 The body..which man's spirit takes and inhabits..and indwells.

2. *intr.* To dwell, abide, have one's abode (*in*). Also *fig.*

1382 WYCLIF *Job* x. 22 Wher shadewe of deth, and noon order, but fulli indwellith euere durende orrour. **1649** ROBERTS *Clavis Bibl.* Introd. ii. 31 Let the word of Christ indwell in you richly in all wisdome. Not *be*, but *dwell* with you: not *dwell with you*, but *dwell in you*, yea *indwell in you*. **1846** TRENCH *Mirac.* Introd. (1862) 37 He is not asking for a power not indwelling in Him. **1861** J. G. SHEPPARD *Fall Rome* xiii. 692 The secret principle of life indwelling in its formal type.

Hence **'inˌdwelt** *ppl. a.* (the pa. pple. is *indwelt*).

1855 MILMAN *Lat. Chr.* XIV. ii. (1864) IX. 56 The Holy Ghost became a Dove, not as a symbol, but as a constantly indwelt form.

indweller, in-dweller ('ɪnˌdwɛlə(r)). [f. IN *adv.* 11 e + DWELLER: cf. prec. In Wyclif rendering L. *inhabitāns*, *inhabitātor.*] One who dwells or lives in a place; an inhabitant. Also *fig.*

1382 WYCLIF *Ps.* xxxii[i]. 8 Of hym forsothe first ben togidere moued alle the indwelleris the world [Vulg. *omnes inhabitantes orbem*]. —— *Zeph.* ii. 5 Y shal distruye thee, so that an yndweller be not [Vulg. *ut non sit inhabitator*]. **1535** COVERDALE *2 Chron.* xx. 20 Herken vnto me O Iuda, & ye indwellers of Ierusalem. **1593** *Interl. Droichis Pt. Play* 22 in *Dunbar's Poems* (1893) 315 Prowest, baillies, officeris, And honerable induellaris, Marchandis and familiaris Of all this fair towne. **1608–33** BP. HALL *Occas. Medit.* §110 A house ready to fall on the head of the indweller. **1618** E. ELTON *Rom.* vii. (1622) 351 The corruption of nature..is still an in-dweller in them. **1855** PUSEY *Doctr. Real Presence* Note S. 84 We may receive the good Lord as our indweller. **1860** GEN. P. THOMPSON *Audi Alt.* III. cxvii. 54 If France could..with the assent of the in-dwellers, rejoin the Rhenish provinces.

b. A mere resident; a sojourner.

1535 COVERDALE *Gen.* xxiii. 4, I am a straunger and an indweller amonge you. **1826** SCOTT *Jrnl.* 29 June, I have been so long a citizen of Edinburgh, now an indweller only. **1835** J. P. KENNEDY *Horse Shoe R.* xiii. (1860) 150 He was an in-dweller at the homestead.

indwelling ('ɪnˌdwɛlɪŋ), *vbl. sb.* [f. IN *adv.* 11 c + DWELLING *vbl. sb.*: cf. INDWELL *v.* In Wyclif rendering L. *inhabitātio.*] The action of dwelling in a place; residence. Usually *fig.*: *esp.* The abiding of God or the Divine Spirit in the heart or soul.

1382 WYCLIF *Wisd.* ix. 15 Ertheli indwelling [Vulg. *inhabitatio*] presseth doun the wit. *c* **1449** PECOCK *Repr.* III. ii. 282 Indwelling is no more than an vsing. **1675** TRAHERNE *Chr. Ethics* 133 By the indwelling of God all objects are infused, and contained within. **1680** T. LAWSON *Mite into Treas.* 18 Her Voice, her Prayers, her Praises, arising from Divine indwellings. **1848** R. I. WILBERFORCE *Incarnation* xi. (1852) 275 This passage..they interpreted of an immediate in-dwelling of Godhead in the whole body of mankind. **1887** J. S. BANKS *Chr. Doctr.* II. iv. 210 Sin in its guilt and indwelling is defilement.

'inˌdwelling, in-dwelling, *ppl. a.* [f. IN *adv.* 11 a + DWELLING *ppl. a.*] **a.** That dwells within, inhabits, occupies, or possesses. Usually *fig.*

14.. *Chalmerlain Ayr* i. in *Sc. Stat.* I, Alswele induellande as furth duelland. **1646** P. BULKELEY *Gospel Covt.* IV. 319 It was not any indwelling power within themselves, by which they did them [those great works]. **1799** HAN. MORE *Fem. Educ.* (ed. 4) I. 264 So religion is not an occasional act, but an indwelling principle..from which indeed every act derives all its life. **1880** E. WHITE *Cert. Relig.* 87 An assurance..of the indwelling presence of God. **1885** CLODD *Myths & Dr.* II. vi. 180 The patient is kept without food so as to starve out the indwelling enemy.

b. *Med.* Of a catheter, electrode, or other device: more or less permanently fixed in position either within the body or leading from the interior to the exterior of the body.

1932 DORLAND & MILLER *Med. Dict.* (ed. 16) 252/1 Indwelling catheter. **1962** *Lancet* 5 May 950/1 Infection nearly always followed on drainage by indwelling catheter. **1964** *Ibid.* 26 Dec. 1349/1 All the very immature babies..were fed from birth by indwelling tubes. **1968** *Jrnl. Thoracic & Cardiovasc. Surg.* LV. 555 (*heading*) Thoracic duct cannulation in the dog: a study of thrombotic occlusion of indwelling cannulas. **1972** *Amer. Jrnl. Physical Med.* LI. 113 (*title*) Electromyographic study of the anterolateral abdominal musculature utilizing indwelling electrodes.

Hence **in'dwellingness**, the quality of indwelling.

†**indwir**, obs. Sc. form of ENDURE *v.*

1571 *Satir. Poems Reform.* xxvii. 50 Thatt freindschip..langest will indwir.

†**Indy, Indie.** *Obs.* [ad. L. *India*: cf. *Italy*, *Sicily*, *Germany*, *Tuscany*, etc. The pl. INDIES, q.v., is still in use.] = INDIA. Also *attrib.*

1578 LYTE *Dodoens* v. lxix. 634 Large Pepper of Indie. **1599** HAKLUYT *Voy.* II. II. 81 The Indie-writers make mention of sundry great cities in this Iland. **1647** H. MORE *Philos. Poems* 181 Indie, Egypt, Arabie.

b. indy blue, the dye INDIGO, or its colour.

1509 HAWES *Past. Pleas.* XVIII. (Percy Soc.) 80 A fayre and goodly garment, Of most fyne velvet, al of Indy blewe. *a* **1529** SKELTON *'Knoledge, aquayntance'* 17 Saphyre of sadnes, enuayned with indy blew.

indycyble, indyfferency, indygence, indygn, etc.: see INDICIBLE, etc.

†**'ine**, *prep. Obs.* [An early ME. formation found in southern dialects from 1175 to 1340, when still in regular use in Kentish. Of uncertain formation: see below.] = IN *prep.*, in its various uses.

c **1175** *Lamb. Hom.* 49 Alse þeos men doð þe liggeð inne eubruche and ine glutenerie and ine manaðas. *Ibid.* 73 Of ileue spek ure drihten ine þe hali godspel. *Ibid.* 75 His halie fif wunden þa he þolede for us ine þe halie rode. *c* **1200** *Trin. Coll. Hom.* 185 Ine þe lond of ierusalem. *a* **1225** *Ancr. R.* 20 Hwen ȝe vesteð ine winter..& ine sumer. *Ibid.* 54 Þer heo lei ine prisune. *Ibid.* 64 Spellunge and smecchunge beoð ine muðe boðe, ase sihðe is iðen eien. *a* **1225** *Juliana* 12 As þeo þet ine godd hire hope hefde. *a* **1250** *Owl & Night.* 962 Theȝ hit bo ful ine nest þine. *c* **1250** *Meid. Maregrete* xlix, Hef up þi fot a littel, þat ine myn necke stond. *c* **1315** SHOREHAM 7 Godes body ine forme of bred. *Ibid.* 146 Foȝeles, fisches ine the depe. **1340** *Ayenb.* 7 Þe ilke þet dispendeþ þane zonday ..ine zenne and ine hordom and in oþre zennes aye God. *Ibid.* 167 Þe salamandre þet leueþ ine þe uere. *Ibid.* 220 Þet child lyerneþ ine his yeȝeþe, he hit wyle healde ine his elde. *Ibid.* 262 Yblissed þou ine wymen.

b. In sense 'INTO'.

c **1175** *Lamb. Hom.* 143 Þe heðene, þe erites..sculen beon iwarpen ine eche pine. *c* **1315** SHOREHAM 6 That man ne falle ine wanhope. *c* **1340** *Ayenb.* 25 Þis hire todelþ ine þry. *Ibid.* 185 Þe angel..þet com ine erþe, þe uor to rede.

¶ In northern dialects, and in later use, *ine*, *yne* appear to be only scribal variants of IN, *yn*, *prep.* or *adv.*

a **1300** *Cursor M.* 941 (Gött.) Yon tre þat lijf was ine [*Cott.* þat lijf es in]. *Ibid.* 9674 (Gött.) Noe..in þat schipp allone was ine. *c* **1400** *Ywaine & Gaw.* 760 A pot with riche wine, And a pece to fil it yne.

[*Note.* In the dialects in which it occurs, *ine* is the regular word for *in* preposition. The 12–13th c. documents in which it is used have also *i* in the connexions *i þe*, *i þen*, *i þis*, *i þet*, *i þine*, etc.; but these do not appear in the *Ayenbite* 14th c. *Ine* has been viewed as an extension of the prep. IN with an inorganic *e*, and as a weakened or simplified form of INNE; there are difficulties, historical or phonetic, in either view, though the latter is perhaps the less objectionable. *Inne* and *ine* are found side by side in the Lambeth Homilies.]

-ine, *suffix*¹, forming adjs., repr. L. *-īnus*, *-īna*, *-īnum*, added to names of persons, animals, or material things, and to some other words, with the sense 'of' or 'pertaining to', 'of the nature of', represented in Fr. by *-in* masc., *-ine* fem., in Eng. now usually by *-ine*, formerly and still exceptionally by *-in*. Examples are L. *adulterīnus* adulterine, *anserīnus* anserine, *asinīnus* asinine, *canīnus* canine, *dīvīnus* divine, *fēminīnus* feminine, *genuīnus* genuine, *lībertīnus* libertine, *marīnus* marine, *masculīnus* masculine, *supīnus* supine; in some cases with blending of a previous suffix, as *clandestīnus* clandestine, *intestīnus* intestine, *mātūtīnus* matutine, *vespertīnus* vespertine. Also from proper names, as *Alpīnus* Alpine, *Capitōlīnus* Capitoline, *Latīnus* Latin (*formerly* Latine), *Sāturnīnus*

Saturnine, *Tarentīnus* Tarentine. On the pattern of these, adjs. have continued to be freely formed in the Romanic langs. and in English, as in *Algerine, Caroline, Florentine, Socotrine*; and the termination is now greatly used in Natural History, in forming adjs., with or without L. type, on the names of genera, as *acarine, accipitrine, bovine, caprine, equine, feline, hystricine, murine, passerine*. In these Natural History adjs. the pronunciation is (-aɪn), usually unstressed; but in other words it is very various, depending upon the length of time the word has been in English, the channel through which it came, the place of the stress, and other circumstances: cf. *divine, supine* ('-aɪn), *marine* (-'iːn), *feminine, genuine* (-ɪn), *aquiline, bovine, leonine, alkaline* (-aɪn), and see the history of the individual words.

-ine, *suffix*², forming adjs., repr. L. *-īnus*, a. Gr. *-ινος*, from names of minerals, plants, etc., or (in a few words) of L. origin, having, in Romanic and Eng., the same sense and the same forms, as -INE¹; as *adamantin-us* adamantine, *amethystinus* amethystine, *corallinus* coralline, *crystallinus* crystalline, *hyacinthinus* hyacinthine, *pristinus* pristine. The etymological and historical pronunciation was (-ɪn), e.g. ('prɪstɪn), (ædə'mæntɪn); but, from the spelling *-ine*, and the attraction of words in -INE¹, there is now a strong tendency to lengthen the *i* in *crystalline* (-aɪn), etc.

-ine, *suffix*³, forming sbs., repr. F. *-ine*, L. *-īna*, Gr. *-ῑνη*, forming feminine titles, as in Gr. *ἡρωΐνη*, L. *hērōīna*, F. *héroine* heroine. With this the Ger. *landgräfin, markgräfin*, Du. *landgravin, markgravin* (the suffix of which is orig. the same as -EN² 1), have fallen together in French and in Eng., as *landgravine, margravine*.

-ine, *suffix*⁴, forming sbs., repr. F. *-ine* (*-in*), L. *-īna* (*-īnus*), in origin identical with -INE¹. In L., *-īna* formed feminine abstracts from verbs, as *rapīna* rapine, *ruīna* ruin, and from agent-nouns, as *disciplīna* discipline, *doctrīna* doctrine, *medicīna* medicine; also sbs. from other sources, as *fascīna* fascine, *resīna* resin, *ūrīna* urine. The adjs. in *-īnus, -īna* were also used subst., as in *concubīnus, -īna* concubine, *lupīnus* lupine, and esp. in proper names, as *Antōnīnus* Antonine, *Augustīnus* Augustine, *Constantīnus* Constantine, *Crispīnus* Crispin, *Justīnus* Justin, *Agrippīna, Constantīna*, etc. The English form of those in *-īna* (through Fr., or on the Fr. type) is *-ine*, occasionally in early words reduced to *-in*; those in *-īnus* give F. and Eng. *-in*, but in Eng. often *-ine*.

Formations of this type were multiplied in late L. and Romanic, e.g. *famīna* famine, F. *routine*; in Romanic this suffix (It., Sp. *-ino, -ina*, F. *-in, -ine*) is greatly used in forming names of derived substances, similative appellations, diminutives, etc. Many of these have come into English, in the F. form *-ine* (-'iːn), which has consequently become a formative element, freely used in forming the names of derivative products, and of things supposed to be derived from, resemble, imitate, or commemorate those from which they are named, and thus in the trade-names of new varieties of fabrics, cosmetics, patent medicines, and proprietary articles generally, e.g. *dentine, osseine, nectarine, brilliantine, grenadine, albertine, victorine*, etc. Feminine personal names of Romanic origin in *-ina* sometimes retain that form, but often take *-ine* (-ɪn or -'iːn) after Fr., as *Caroline* (now -aɪn), *Catherine, Ernestine, Josephine*.

-ine, *suffix*⁵, *Chem.*, in origin an offshoot of -INE⁴, as occurring in the names of some derived substances: see GELATIN, -INE. At first used unsystematically in forming names of extractive principles and chemical derivatives of various kinds; also, in the English names given early in the 19th century to the four elements *chlorine, fluorine, iodine, bromine* (in F. *chlore, fluor, iode, brome*). In all these, but especially in the names of extractive principles, the ending *-ine* was by some reduced to *-in*, thus *gelatine* or *gelatin, aconitine* or *aconitin, chlorine* or *chlorin*. In recent systematic nomenclature the two forms have been differentiated, *-ine* being now used (1) in forming names of alkaloids and basic substances, as *aconitine, cocaïne, nicotine, strychnine*, etc., which are thus distinguished from names of neutral substances, proteids, etc., in *-in* (see -IN¹); and (2) in Hofmann's systematic names of hydrocarbons of the form C_nH_{2n-2}, as *ethine* or acetylene, C_2H_2, *propine* or allylene, C_3H_4, etc. These latter are not much used. In the names of the elements, and some other substances, not belonging to any of the classes named, *-ine* is retained (though *chlorin, fluorin*, etc., appear in some American books). In popular and commercial use, the ending *-ine* is still current in the names of some substances for which systematic nomenclature requires *-in*: see -IN¹.

-ine has been used by some authors to form the names of minerals; but in later systematic use, esp. by Dana, this is changed, in names of species, into *-ite*: thus *chalcosine, erythrine*, in Dana *chalcocite, erythrite*. *-ine* is also used systematically to form the names of certain six-membered monocyclic compounds having a nitrogen atom in the ring, as *azine*. Cf. -IN¹.

1928 *Jrnl. Amer. Chem. Soc.* L. 3078 In the field of six-membered [heterocyclic] rings are found names corresponding to the above systematic names for five-membered [heterocyclic] rings, but with the suffix *-ine* or *-in* replacing -ole (or -ol), as: triazine, oxazine, thiodiazine, dioxin (the latter being non-nitrogenous). Thus the ending -ine (or -in), although regarded as properly the ending for bases, has a specific sense in which it indicates a six-membered ring. **1940** in PATTERSON & CAPELL *Ring Index* 21. **1957** [see -IN¹].

in-earnestness (ɪn'ɜːnɪstnɪs). *rare*⁻¹. [f. IN *prep.* + EARNESTNESS; cf. EARNEST *sb.*¹ 2a.] Seriousness, serious intention.

1879 G. M. HOPKINS *Lett. to R. Bridges* (1955) 89, I do avoid them [*sc.* inversions], because they weaken..the earnestness or in-earnestness of the utterance.

inearth (ɪ'nɜːθ), *v.* [f. IN-¹ + EARTH *sb.* Cf. med.L. *interrāre*, F. *enterrer*.]

1. *trans.* To bury in the earth, to inter. Chiefly *poetical*.

1801 SOUTHEY *Thalaba* I. xxii. 20 The Ethiop..Detects the ebony..deep-inearth'd. **1805** —— *Madoc* iii. Poet. Wks. (1853) 320/2 Refusing rest, Till I had seen in holy ground inearth'd My poor lost brother. **1849** H. MAYO *Pop. Superst.* (1851) 54 The body..that had been rudely inearthed after violent death. **1880** *Contemp. Rev.* Mar. 431 The Founder and his mate Were here inearthed.

2. To render 'earthy' or earthly. *rare*.

1863 PUSEY *Oxford Lenten Serm.* ix. 12 What in us was lofty, lowered: what was in the image of the heavenly, inearthed.

ineaw, var. form of ENEW *v.*, *Obs.*

inebriacy (ɪ'niːbrɪəsɪ). *rare.* [f. INEBRIATE *a.*: see -ACY.] The condition of an inebriate; the habit of drunkenness.

1876 *Christian Union* 27 Dec. (Cent.), No faith in any remedy for inebriacy, except as an aid to..strong purpose.

inebriant (ɪ'niːbrɪənt), *a.* and *sb.* [ad. L. *inēbriānt-em*, pres. pple. of *inēbriāre* to INEBRIATE. Cf. OF. *inébriant* (15th c. in Godef.).] **a.** *adj.* That inebriates; intoxicating. **b.** *sb.* An inebriating substance or agent; an intoxicant.

1819 *Pantologia* s.v., Inebriants..are properly divided into native and artificial. **1828** WEBSTER, *Inebriant*, intoxicating. **1859** R. F. BURTON *Centr. Afr.* in *Jrnl. Geog. Soc.* XXIX. 224 The favourite inebriant is tembo or palm-toddy. **1897** *Allbutt's Syst. Med.* III. 435 Among the inebriants alcohol may cause..an intensely red colour [of the interior of the stomach].

inebriate (ɪ'niːbrɪət), *ppl. a.* and *sb.* [ad. L. *inēbriāt-us*, pa. pple. of *inēbriāre*: see next.]

A. *ppl. a.* Inebriated, drunken; intoxicated (*lit.* and *fig.*). Often const. as *pa. pple.*

1497 BP. ALCOCK *Mons Perfect.* Biij, Peter as a man inebryat in the loue of god. **1548** UDALL *Erasm. Par.* Pref. 5 a, We myghte haue ben so inebriate wᵗ our unestimable felicitie. *Ibid., Luke* ix. 98 Thus spake Peter as a man inebriate and made drounken with the swetenesse of this vision. **1742** YOUNG *Nt. Th.* III. 20 Inebriate at fair Fortune's fountain-head, And reeling through the wilderness of joy. **1805** SOUTHEY *Ball. & Metr. T.* Poet. Wks. VI. 48 Inebriate with the deep delight, Dim grew the Pilgrim's swimming sight. **1844** SIR W. NAPIER *Conq. Scinde* II. i. (1845) 227 Inebriate, luxurious Princes.

B. *sb.* An intoxicated person; *esp.* a person addicted to drunkenness, a habitual drunkard.

1794-6 E. DARWIN *Zoon.* (1801) I. 365 This vertigo also continues, when the inebriate lies in his bed, in the dark. **1864** *Soc. Sc. Rev.* I. 419 We learn that an Asylum for Inebriates has been opened at Binghampton. **1898** *Westm. Gaz.* 26 Apr. 2/1 When questions were over, the Home Secretary introduced his Habitual Inebriates Bill.

inebriate (ɪ'niːbrɪeɪt), *v.* [f. prec., or ppl. stem of L. *inēbriāre* to inebriate, intoxicate, f. *in-* (IN-²) + *ēbriāre* to intoxicate, f. *ēbrius* drunk.]

1. *trans.* To make drunk; to intoxicate. Also *absol.*

1555 EDEN *Decades* 259 Such stronge drinkes as are of force to inebriate. **1601** HOLLAND *Pliny* II. 152 Sweet wines do not so much inebriate and ouerturne the brain, as others. **1744** BERKELEY *Siris* §217 The luminous spirit lodged in the native balsam of pines..is of a nature so mild..as to warm without heating, to cheer but not inebriate. **1784** COWPER *Task* IV. 40 While..the cups That cheer but not inebriate, wait on each. **1894** *Cornh. Mag.* Mar. 300 Mr. Tasker's tendency to inebriate himself.

2. *transf.* and *fig.* **a.** To intoxicate in mind or feeling; to excite or stupefy, as with liquor.

1497 BP. ALCOCK *Mons Perfect.* B iij, It inebriate them so yᵗ they were made by it oblyvyous of all worldly things. **1577** NORTHBROOKE *Dicing* (Shaks. Soc.) 13 Securitie in wealth and prosperity, which doth inebriate the mindes of men. **1640** HABINGTON *Castara* III. (Arb.) 128 O you! whom your Creators sight Inebriates with delight! **1640-1** LD. J. DIGBY *Sp. in Ho. Comm.* 9 Feb. 10 Christs discipline hath beene adulterated,..the whole Church inebriated by the Prelates. **1728-9** BERKELEY *Serm. Rom.* viii. 13 Wks. 1871 IV. 632 Curb..every passion, each whereof inebriates and obfuscates no less than drink and meat. **1860** PUSEY *Min. Proph.* 105 A spiritual drunkenness, inebriating the soul, as strong drink doth the body. **1878** DISRAELI *Sp.* 28 July, A sophistical rhetorician, inebriated with the exuberance of his own verbosity.

†**b.** To refresh as with drink; to water, drench, moisten. *Obs.*

1609 BIBLE (Douay) *Ps.* lxiv. 10 [lxv. 9] Thou hast visited the earth, and hast inebriated [Vulg. *inebriasti*] it. **1624** GATAKER *Transubst.* 72 The Chalice is our Saviours blood to cleanse and inebriate devout Soules. **1649** ROBERTS *Clavis Bibl.* 83 With bloud I will inebriate Mine arrows.

†**3.** *intr.* To become intoxicated. *Obs. rare.*

1626 BACON *Sylva* §703 Great Quantities of Fish..when they come into the Fresh Water, do inebriate and turn vp their Bellies, So as you may take them with your Hand [cf. quot. 1615 in INEBRIATED 1].

i'nebriated, *ppl. a.* [f. prec. + -ED¹.]

1. Intoxicated, drunken.

1615 G. SANDYS *Trav.* 29 Fish of sundry kinds..meeting with the fresh, as if inebriated, turne vp their bellies, and are taken. **1646** SIR T. BROWNE *Pseud. Ep.* IV. vii. 196 As may be observed in the lifting or supporting of persons inebriated. **1839** H. ROGERS *Ess.* (1874) II. iii. 148 To be 'drunk' is vulgar; but if a man be simply 'intoxicated' or 'inebriated', it is comparatively venial.

2. *transf.* and *fig.*: see prec. 2.

1609 BIBLE (Douay) *1 Macc.* xvi. *comm.*, To be inebriated signifieth no more but to be replenished with drinke competently, or abundantly, without excesse. *a* **1647** CRASHAW *Wks.* (Grosart) 319 A sweet inebriated extasy. **1830** D'ISRAELI *Chas. I*, III. vii. 154 When that genius becomes inebriated by the flattery it receives.

i'nebriating, *ppl. a.* [f. as prec. + -ING².] That inebriates; intoxicating. *lit.* and *fig.*

1609 BIBLE (Douay) *Ps.* xxii[i]. 5 Thou hast fatted my head with oyle; and my chalice inebriating how goodlie is it! **1613** PURCHAS *Pilgrimage* VII. ix. §3 (1614) 698 Strong and inebriating wine. **1748** HARTLEY *Observ. Man* II. ii. 106 The fermenting and inebriating Quality of vegetable Juices. **1806** SURR *Winter in Lond.* III. 130 Flying from reflection to inebriating pleasures. **1841** LANE *Arab. Nts.* I. 18 Wine and all inebriating liquors are strictly forbidden.

inebriation (ɪniːbrɪ'eɪʃən). [ad. L. *inēbriātiōnem* (Augustine), n. of action from *inēbriāre* to INEBRIATE. Cf. OF. *inebriation, -acion* (15th c. in Godef.).] The action of inebriating, or condition of being inebriated; intoxication, drunkenness.

1646 SIR T. BROWNE *Pseud. Ep.* V. xxi. 270 Unexpected inebriation from the unknowne effects of wine. *a* **1682** —— *Tracts* 25 Some generous strong sweet wine, wherein more especially lay the power of inebriation. **1791** NEWTE *Tour Eng. & Scot.* 171 He is computed to have drank, during the period of his inebriation, half a century, a quart of gin or whisky per day. **1860** PUSEY *Min. Proph.* 489 Through inebriation the mind of those who drink is changed.

b. *fig.* Intoxication of the mind or feelings; extravagant exhilaration, excitement, or emotion, such as to cause loss of mental or moral steadiness.

1526 *Pilgr. Perf.* (W. de W. 1531) 291 This inebriacyon or heuenly dronkennesse of the spiryte. **1638** BAKER tr. *Balzac's Lett.* (1654) IV. 4 Such inebriations of the spirit.. Philosophie hath observ'd in extraordinary successes. **1828** MACAULAY *Ess., Hallam* (1851) I. 82 They did not preserve him from the inebriation of prosperity. **1886** SYMONDS *Renaiss. It., Cath. React.* (1898) VII. ix. 76 The inebriation of the Renaissance..pulses through all his utterances.

†**i'nebriative**, *a. Obs.* [f. L. *inēbriāt-*, ppl. stem of *inēbriāre* to INEBRIATE + -IVE. Cf. F. *inébriatif, -ive* (Oresme, 14th c.).] Having the quality of inebriating, intoxicating; of or pertaining to inebriation.

1615 T. ADAMS *Blacke Devill* 31 Those that drinke wines ..with inebriative delight. *a* **1625** BOYS *Wks.* (1629–30) 525 A man taking an inebriatiue potion. **1628** GAULE *Pract. The.* (1629) 294 Potions (whether inebriatiue, soporatiue, or stupefying).

inebriety (ɪnɪ'braɪɪtɪ). [f. IN-² + EBRIETY (L. *ēbrietās*), after INEBRIATE, etc.] The state or habit of being inebriated; drunkenness, intoxication, inebriation; now chiefly applied to habitual drunkenness, esp. when regarded as a disease.

1801 *Med. Jrnl.* V. 99 Driven to the slower suicide of habitual inebriety. **1817** LADY MORGAN *France* I. 68 (Jod.) In the desperation of poverty and inebriety. **1826** DISRAELI *Viv. Grey* VI. i, How ludicrous is the incipient inebriety of a man who wears spectacles! **1860** DICKENS *Uncomm. Trav.* x, His mistress was sometimes overtaken by inebriety. **1893** *Arena* Mar. 452 Inebriety is a disease of the nervous system, just like epilepsy, chorea, or insanity.

b. *fig.*: cf. INEBRIATION b.

1786 tr. *Beckford's Vathek* (1868) 59 In the inebriety of youthful spirits. **1829** I. TAYLOR *Enthus.* IX. 233 An habitual inebriety of the imagination.

inebriism (ɪ'ni:brɪɪz(ə)m). [f. stem of *inebri-ate*, etc. + -ISM.] The scientific study of inebriety.

1886 *Alien. & Neurol.* VII. 716 A permanent contribution to the subject of Inebriism.

inebrious (ɪ'ni:brɪəs), *a. rare.* Also 5 **enebriouse**. [f. L. type **inēbriōsus* or F. **in-*, **enebrieux*, after L. *ēbriōsus* (see EBRIOUS), with prefix *in-* as in INEBRIATE, etc.]

†**1.** Inebriating, intoxicating. (In quot. 1450 *fig.*: cf. INEBRIATE *v.* 2.) *Obs.*

c **1450** *Mirour Saluacioun* 1052 Y^t virgine gloriouse Bering this vigne of wyne thus wele enebriouse. *a* **1704** T. BROWN *Wks.* (1760) IV. 331 (R.) And with inebrious fumes distract our brains.

2. Inebriated, drunken; addicted to drunkenness.

1837 *Tait's Mag.* IV. 676 Did no inebrious Pontiff stand Hiccupping, to ask for thee..A jovial benedicite? **1862** JEAFFRESON *Bk. abt. Doctors* xxvii. 320 Sailors..retain a decided preference for an inebrious to a sober surgeon.

†**ine'bulliated**, *a. Obs.* [f. IN-³ + *ebulliated*, EBULLIATE *v.*] Not boiled.

1599 A. M. tr. *Gabelhouer's Bk. Physicke* 26/1 A draught of inebulliated iuyce of greene peasen. *Ibid.* 28/2 Take a good Capone, which hath binne choackede, and overcrammed, but inebulliatede.

†**in-eche**, *v.* in *ineched*, perhaps rather, as in the MSS., two words, *in eched*, added in: see ECHE *v.*

c **1374** CHAUCER *Troylus* III. 1280 (1329) (Campsall MS.) And yf þat I at loues reuerence Haue ony word In eched for þe beste [*16th c. edd.* ineched]. **1658** PHILLIPS, *Ineched* (old word), put in.

ineconomic (ɪni:kə'nɒmɪk), *a.* [IN-³.] Not economic; not according to (political) economy.

1852 *Q. Rev.* Sept. 360 The in-economic prejudice against them on the score of their causing a diminution of employment. **1897** *Westm. Gaz.* 25 Oct. 5/2 A screw propeller works at a very great ineconomic disadvantage when working so near the surface.

ine'conomy. [IN-³.] Want of economy; waste of power, resources, etc.

1897 C. D. HASKINS in *Let. to Editor* 1 Sept. **1899** *Boston* (U.S.) *Gen. Electric Co., Bulletin* 30 Aug., The function of the Street Railway Meter is to record the exact amount of energy used per trip by each car..Attention is at once directed to ineconomy in any part of the system.

†**in'edge**, *v. Obs.* [f. IN-¹ + EDGE *v.*] *trans.* To edge in, get in edgeways or surreptitiously.

1563-87 FOXE *A. & M.* (1684) I. 607/2 Occupying him thus busily to inedge such Sentences to maintain his Errors.

inedible (ɪn'ɛdɪb(ə)l), *a.* [IN-³.] Not edible; unfit to be eaten.

1822-34 *Good's Study Med.* (ed. 4) I. 218 Inedible fungi mistaken for esculent mushrooms. **1855** BAILEY *Mystic* 31 The inedible fruit of immortality.

Hence **inedi'bility**, the quality of being inedible.

1882 A. R. WALLACE in *Nature* XXVI. 87/2 Various degrees of inedibility in butterflies. **1887** *Athenæum* 12 Mar. 357/1 In tracing the inedibility through the stages it was found that no inedible imago was edible in the larval stage.

†**in'edifying**, *a. Obs.* [IN-³.] Not edifying.

1659 H. L'ESTRANGE *Alliance Div. Off.* vi. 181 Latin, a Language very inedifying to a non-intelligent people. *Ibid.* 184 Declining nice, thorny and inedifying disputes.

‖**inédit** (inedi). [Fr.; cf. INEDITA.] An unpublished work. Also *fig.*, something secret or unrevealed.

1910 *Encycl. Brit.* XII. 231/1 The inner, undiscovered, minute truths of contemporary existence, the *inédit* of life. **1922** A. E. HOUSMAN *Let.* 25 Oct. (1971) 206, I know you bibliophiles and your passion for *l'inédit* regardless of merit. **1958** *Times Lit. Suppl.* 18 Apr. 212/4 Harmon is not an unknown figure, nor his journal strictly an 'inédit'. *Ibid.* 17 Oct. 592/2 There are magazines anxious for *inédits*.

inedita (ɪn'ɛdɪtə). [mod.L., neuter pl. of L. *inēditus*, f. *in-* IN-³ + *editus*, pa. pple. of *edĕre* to give out, EDIT *v.*] Unpublished writings.

1886 *Encycl. Brit.* XXI. 141/1 The luminous exposition of the grammar and the happy choice of the pieces in the chrestomathy..all inedita. **1948** *Mind* LVII. 522 Scholars ..brought to light a number of *inedita* and checked..his writings.

inedited (ɪn'ɛdɪtɪd). *a.* [IN-³. Cf. L. *inēditus* not made known.] Not edited.

a. Not published; unpublished.

1776 BURNEY *Hist. Mus.* (1789) I. Pref. 6 Manuscript information, and inedited materials from foreign countries. **1837** SIR F. PALGRAVE *Merch. & Friar* Ded. (1844) 11 An inedited epistle addressed to one Anselm, preserved or buried in the Bodleian. **1855** LEWES *Goethe* I. IV. ii. 334 Her letters, still extant although inedited.

b. Not described in any published work.

1760 SWINTON in *Phil. Trans.* LI. 856 All which singularities..will perhaps intitle the medal I am considering to the denomination of an inedited Coin. **1834** J. Y. AKERMAN (*title*) Rare and Inedited Roman Coins.

c. Published without editorial alteration or suppression.

1865 MAFFEI *Brigand Life* II. 226 In this document, inedited, and written with the frankness of a soldier. **1884** *American* VIII. 217 The newspaper portrait of an author, with 'inedited' anecdotes of him.

ineducability (ɪn,ɛdjʊkə'bɪlɪtɪ). [f. INEDUCABLE *a.* + -ITY.] The condition of being ineducable.

1918 *Dial* (Chicago) 23 May 492 Carlyle in despair over the ineducability of nineteenth-century minds. **1927** CARR-SAUNDERS & JONES *Survey Social Struct. Eng. & Wales* 214 The criterion of mental deficiency for adults..is social inefficiency, while for children..it is ineducability. **1964** M. CRITCHLEY *Developmental Dyslexia* xiii. 77 Perhaps the patient and his parents have resigned themselves to a state of hopeless ineducability, and no longer importune doctors and teachers.

ineducable (ɪn'ɛdjʊkəb(ə)l), *a.* [IN-³.] Not educable; incapable of being educated.

1884 *Pop. Sci. Monthly* Dec. 272 He is childish..in intellect, and ineducable beyond the first standard. **1895** *Forum* (N.Y.) May 350 A 'practical short-cut' by which uneducated or ineducable men are helped to the rewards of knowledge or skill.

inedu'cation. *rare.* [IN-³.] Want of education, uneducated condition.

1803 W. TAYLOR in *Ann. Rev.* I. 396 There is a polished public to please, to whom the blunders of ineducation, or the coarseness of underbreeding can find no access.

inée (i:'neɪ). Also **onage, onaye**. [Fr., ad. Fang *ene*, Mpongwe *onai*.] An arrow-poison made from the seed of *Strophanthus hispidus*.

1874 LINDLEY & MOORE *Treas. Bot.* II. Suppl. 1323/1 *Onaye* or *onage*..also called Inée and Kombé. **1887** *Encycl. Brit.* XXII. 608/1 The inée or onaye poison of the Gaboon, the kombé poison of equatorial North Africa,..are.. derived from members of this genus.

ineffability (ɪnɛfə'bɪlɪtɪ). [f. next: see -ITY.] The quality of being ineffable; unspeakableness.

1628 GAULE *Pract. The.* (1629) 51 Amazed at the incomprehensiblenesse and ineffabilitie of such his Birth and Being. **1652** BENLOWES *Theoph.* XIII. xlvii. 241 With joyes ineffabilitie. **1721** in BAILEY. **1755** in JOHNSON; and in mod. Dicts. **1902** W. JAMES *Var. Relig. Exper.* xvi. 381 *Ineffability*... *Noetic quality*... These two characters will entitle any state to be called mystical, in the sense in which I use the word. **1922** JOYCE *Ulysses* 709 The supernatural character of Judaic scripture: the ineffability of the tetragrammaton: the sanctity of the sabbath. **1961** M. LASKI *Ecstasy* xxii. 243 When *ineffable*, etc. is attached to a noun, 'supreme of its kind'..seems always to be implied. The *ineffability* device is particularly common among religious writers.

ineffable (ɪn'ɛfəb(ə)l), *a.* (*sb.*) [a. F. *ineffable* (14th c. in Hatz.-Darm.), ad. L. *ineffābilis* unutterable, f. *in-* (IN-³) + *effābilis*: see EFFABLE.]

A. *adj.* **1. a.** That cannot be expressed or described in language; too great for words; transcending expression; unspeakable, unutterable, inexpressible.

c **1450** *Mirour Saluacioun* 1679 O godde of hiegh pitee inmense and ineffable. **1526** TINDALE *2 Cor.* ix. 15 Thankes be vnto God for his ineffable gyfte. **1559** *Primer in Priv. Prayers* (1851) 109, I stedfastly trust in thine ineffable mercy. **1650** BULWER *Anthropomet.* 104 Setting forth his ineffable wisdome. **1709** *Tatler* No. 81 ¶4 The Virgin.. smiled with an ineffable Grace at their Meeting, and retired. **1826** DISRAELI *Viv. Grey* V. vii, A form of such ineffable and sparkling grace. **1871** H. AINSWORTH *Tower Hill* I. ii, 'Go to, knave!' cried Henry, with a look of ineffable disgust. **1887** BOWEN *Virg. Æneid* II. 3 'Tis an ineffable anguish again thou bidd'st me renew.

b. Applied to a person.

1832 THIRLWALL in *Philolog. Museum* I. 492 A thoroughly bad citizen, as well as an ineffable fool. **1961** WEBSTER, Ineffable bungler. **1969** *Spectator* 14 Mar. 325/3 The ineffable Mr. George Thomson.

2. That must not be uttered; †not to be disclosed or made known (*obs.*).

1597 A. M. tr. *Guillemeau's Fr. Chirurg.* 47 b/1 A secreate and ineffable venoume or poyson. **1608** WILLET *Hexapla Exod.* 39 The name of Iehouah is ineffable, and not to be vttered. **1744** GRAY *Let.* in *Poems* (1775) 177 If I may be permitted to pronounce..that ineffable Octogrammaton.. Laziness. **1864** BROWNING *Abt Vogler* ix, To whom turn I but to thee, the ineffable Name?

†**3.** That cannot be uttered or pronounced; unpronounceable. *Obs. rare.*

1638 SIR T. HERBERT *Trav.* (ed. 2) 18 Pliny confesses.. That their names and Townes were ineffable. **1686** *Observ. Chinese Char.* in *Misc. Cur.* (1708) III. 225 The single Strokes may be taken for single ineffable Letters as are the Consonants.

†**4.** *Math.* That cannot be expressed in terms of rational quantities; irrational, surd. *Obs.*

1706 PHILLIPS, *Ineffable Numbers*, the same as Surd Numbers. **1709-29** V. MANDEY *Syst. Math., Geom.* 137 Rational or Effable Magnitudes, are those whose Proportions may be exprest by certain Numbers: Irrational or Ineffable, are the contrary.

B. *sb.* (*colloq.*)

1. *pl.* Trousers. (A humorous euphemism: cf. *inexpressibles, unmentionables.*)

1823 *New Monthly Mag.* VIII. 337 Our lower garments, or Ineffables, sit but awkwardly. **1867** W. CORY *Lett. & Jrnls.* (1897) 196 Shoes off, ineffables tucked up.

2. One not to be mentioned or named; an anonymous journalist, etc.; an 'unutterable' swell.

1859 SALA *Tw. round Clock* (1861) 31 The 'Times' has its secrets by this time..it holds them all fast now, admitting none to its confidence but the Ineffables, the printers, and the ever-throbbing steam-engine. **1861** *Illustr. Lond. News* 15 June 549/1 Two white-hatted and pegtopped ineffables.

ineffableness (ɪn'ɛfəb(ə)lnɪs). [f. prec. + -NESS.] The quality of being ineffable; unspeakableness. (In quot. 1883 want of the power of utterance.)

1681 H. MORE *Exp. Dan.* iii. 75 The ineffableness and unutterableness of the admirable union. **1883** MELVILLE BELL in *Nature* XXVII. 531/2 In some quarters.. Ineffableness is held to indicate grasp of thought; taciturnity to be the cloak of profundity.

ineffably (ɪn'ɛfəblɪ), *adv.* [f. as prec. + -LY².] In an ineffable manner, or to an ineffable extent or degree; inexpressibly, unspeakably, unutterably.

1550 CRANMER *Answ. Gardiner* 371 (T.) So dyd the divinity ineffably put itselfe into the visible sacrament. **1667** MILTON *P.L.* VI. 721 He all his Father full exprest Ineffably into his face receiv'd. **1707-8** BERKELEY *Serm. 2 Tim.* i. 10 Wks. 1871 IV. 601 A good so ineffably, so inconceivably great. **1873** HOLLAND *A. Bonnic.* i. 29 A name which was ineffably sacred to him.

ineffaceable (ɪnɪ'feɪsəb(ə)l), *a.* [f. IN-³ + EFFACE + -ABLE. Cf. F. *ineffaçable* (1564 in Hatz.-Darm.).] That cannot be effaced, obliterated, or blotted out; indelible. (*lit.* and *fig.*)

1804 W. TAYLOR in *Ann. Rev.* II. 219 The ineffacable horrors and disgraceful excesses of the promoters and quellers of the Wexford insurrection. **1807** SOUTHEY *Lett.* (1856) II. 25 The everlasting and ineffaceable infamy of bombarding Copenhagen. **1858** HAWTHORNE *Fr. & It. Jrnls.* I. 87 The nail-marks in the hands and feet of Jesus, ineffaceable, even after he had passed into bliss and glory. **1879** FARRAR *St. Paul* (1883) 52 That ineffaceable impression produced by His very aspect.

Hence **ineffacea'bility**, the quality of being ineffaceable; **ine'ffaceably** *adv.*, in an ineffaceable manner, indelibly.

1814 SOUTHEY *Roderick* x. Poet. Wks. IX. 99 On his fame The Ethiop dye, fixed ineffaceably, For ever will abide. **1832** *Fraser's Mag.* V. 510 The hideous brand of interested apostacy..ineffaceably imprinted on his forehead. *a* **1878** MRS. GROTE in Lady Eastlake *Life* vii. (1880) 145 The curious fact of the ineffaceability of the Jews. **1893** LOUISA TWINING *Recoll.* 58 The ineffaceability of early impressions.

ineffectible (ɪnɪ'fɛktɪb(ə)l), *a. rare.* Also **-able**. [f. IN-³ + EFFECTIBLE (or its elements).]

†**1.** Not capable of producing the effect; ineffectual, ineffective. *Obs.*

1649 BP. HALL *Cases Consc.* III. ii. (1654) 175 Superstitious acts, done by meanes altogether in themselves ineffectable, and unwarrantable.

†**2.** Not to be effected by ordinary or natural means; supernatural. *Obs.*

a **1656** BP. HALL *Soul's Farew.* 7 He, in an ineffectible manner, communicates himself to blessed spirits, both angels and men, and that very vision is no less to them than beatifical.

3. That cannot be effected or carried out; impracticable.

1806 *Monthly Mag.* XXII. 210/1 To reduce implicitly.. pronunciation to orthography, or orthography to pronunciation, is ineffectible.

Hence **ine'ffectibly** (**-ably**) *adv.*, in an ineffectible manner: see sense 2.

1658 MANTON *Exp. Jude* verse 25 Wks. 1871 V. 372 For as Christ, the wisdom of the Father, was eternally and ineffectably begotten in the divine essence, so they worshipped a..goddess of wisdom, and feigned that she was begotten by Jupiter, of his own brain.

ineffective (ɪnɪ'fɛktɪv), *a.* (*sb.*) [f. IN-³ + EFFECTIVE.]

1. Of such a nature as not to produce any, or the intended, effect; insufficient; hence, without effect, ineffectual; inoperative.

1651 BIGGS *New Disp.* ¶264 Other grievous and ineffective remedies. **1706** PHILLIPS, *Ineffective*, or *Ineffectual*, that has no effect, vain, fruitless. *a* **1808** HURD *Serm.* Wks. III. xxxv. (R.), How faint and partial and ineffective his best virtues. **1844** H. H. WILSON *Brit. India* III. 81 The Burmas, after one or two ineffective discharges, fled from the approach of the storming party. **1898** A. W. W. DALE *Life R. W. Dale* v. 114 Any public appeal, he felt, would be injudicious and ineffective.

2. Of a person: Not able to effect or accomplish anything; inefficient; not fit for work or service.

1653 JER. TAYLOR *Serm. for Year* I. xiii. 165 Vertue hates weak and ineffective minds, and tame easie prosecutions. **1814** SOUTHEY *Roderick* XXIII. Poet. Wks. IX. 218 Weak childhood there and ineffective age In the chambers of the rock were placed secure. **1897** *Westm. Gaz.* 29 Apr. 3/1 The community..has a special duty to the old, the weak, and the ineffective.

3. Wanting in artistic effect.

1858 HAWTHORNE *Fr. & It. Jrnls.* I. 182 The architecture ..is very ineffective. **1879** *Cassell's Techn. Educ.* VII. 26 The height..would render very fine work altogether ineffective.

B. *sb.* An ineffective person; one unfit for work or service.

1856 GROTE *Greece* II. xciii. XII. 213 Leaving under guard ..the baggage, the prisoners and the ineffectives. **1878** BOSW. SMITH *Carthage* 397 Having restored discipline by clearing his camp of the ineffectives.

ineffectively (ɪnɪ'fɛktɪvlɪ), *adv.* [f. prec. + -LY^2.] In an ineffective manner; without effect or result; fruitlessly.

1655 JER. TAYLOR *Unum Necess.* vii. §5. 479 Still it contended, but ineffectively for the most part. **1675** *Art Contentm.* VIII. §3. 216 He..will be like Sestorius's soldier, who ineffectively tugg'd at the horses tail to get it off at once, when he that pull'd it hair by hair, quickly did it. **1881** STEVENSON *Virg. Puerisque* 163 A career..which was so fitfully pursued, and which is now so ineffectively to end.

ineffectiveness (ɪnɪ'fɛktɪvnɪs). [f. as prec. + -NESS.] The quality of being ineffective.

1865 *Sat. Rev.* 7 Oct. 461/1 Another great cause of the ineffectiveness of modern sermons. **1867** BARRY *Sir C. Barry* viii. 276 The meagre ineffectiveness of our older buildings.

ineffectual (ɪnɪ'fɛktjʊəl), *a.* [f. IN-^{3} + EFFECTUAL: perh. from a med.L. or OF. corresp. form.] **a.** Not effectual. Of efforts, attempts, or actions: Without effect; unable to produce the intended effect; unavailing, unsuccessful, fruitless.

c **1425** *Foundat. St. Bartholomew's* (E.E.T.S.) 10 Yneffectualle these prayers myght nat be, whoes auctor ys the Apostle, whois gracyous herer was God. **1631** GOUGE *God's Arrows* III. §21. 220 We observe meanes to be wanting or to be ineffectuall. **1665** BOYLE *Occas. Refl.* Ded., Your Commands can Prevail..where those of Others would have been wholly Ineffectual. *a* **1704** T. BROWN *Satire Antients* Wks. 1730 I. 25 All his efforts were ineffectual. **1790** GIBBON *Misc. Wks.* (1814) V. 173 The title was vain, the grant ineffectual. **1821** J. Q. ADAMS in C. Davies *Metr. Syst.* III. (1871) 85 In England..the statute-books are filled with ineffectual attempts of the legislature to establish uniformity. **1841** BREWSTER *Mart. Sc.* i. (1856) 7 When he found his reasoning ineffectual, he appealed to direct experiment.

b. Of things: Not producing the usual or expected effect; weak or tame in effect. (Often in allusions to Shakspere's 'uneffectual fire', *Ham.* I. v. 90.)

1784 COWPER *Task* v. 7 His [the sun's] slanting ray Slides ineffectual down the snowy vale. **1856** KANE *Arct. Expl.* I. xxxii. 451 The phosphorescence was not unlike the ineffectual fire of the glow-worm. **1856** MRS. BROWNING *Aur. Leigh* II. (1857) 76, I..there confronted at my chamber-door, A white face,—shivering, ineffectual lips. **1876** OUIDA *Winter City* v. 95 She smiled a little, and let the cigarette pale its ineffectual fire and die out.

c. Of a person: That does not effect the ends for which he exists; that is a failure. Also as *sb.*

1865 M. ARNOLD *Ess. Crit.* iii. (1875) 124 The passive and ineffectual Uranus of Keats's poem. **1896** MRS. CAFFYN *Quaker Grandmother* 142 In everything she had become ineffectual. Work had lost its savour, prayer its creative atmosphere. **1897** T. HODGKIN *Chas. Gt.* 90 Pope Stephen III., the Sicilian, a weak and ineffectual man. **1925** G. GREENE *Babbling April* 4 You snobbish intellectual, Suburban ineffectual, Can't you feel that shimmy in the air?

ineffectuality (ɪnɪfɛktjuː'ælɪtɪ). [f. prec. + -ITY.] The condition or fact of being ineffectual; *concr.* something ineffectual (quot. 1838).

1670 G. H. *Hist. Cardinals* III. II. 256 Seeing the ineffectuality of his words,..he held his peace. **1838** CARLYLE *Misc., Scott* (1872) VI. 32 Lope de Vega..plays at best in the eyes of some few as a vague aurora-borealis, and brilliant ineffectuality. **1870** FROUDE *Hist. Eng.* Concl. XII. 543 With their ineffectuality, their simony, and their worldliness, they brought themselves and their office into contempt.

ineffectually (ɪnɪ'fɛktjʊəlɪ), *adv.* [f. as prec. + -LY^2.] In an ineffectual manner; without producing the intended effect or result; unavailingly, fruitlessly, in vain.

c **1610** SIR J. MELVIL *Mem.* (1735) 390 Which being done by the said Earl ineffectually. *a* **1693** LUDLOW *Mem.* I. 145 (R.) It had been besieged for about two months ineffectually by the Scotts. **1800** MRS. HERVEY *Mourtray Fam.* I. 243 Having ineffectually exerted all her eloquence to shake Emma's resolution. **1860** MILL *Repr. Govt.* (1865) 137/2 Even the Spanish Government did this, sincerely and earnestly, though ineffectually.

ineffectualness (ɪnɪ'fɛktjʊəlnɪs). [f. as prec. + -NESS.] The quality or character of being ineffectual; failure to produce the intended effect.

1650 WEEKES *Truth's Confl.* ii. 42 These phrases..of Effectualness and Ineffectualness, are not plainly understood. **1663** BOYLE *Usef. Exp. Nat. Philos.* II. v. xx. 302 The ineffectualnesse of our vulgar medicines. **1752** CARTE *Hist. Eng.* III. 442 Acquainting her with his son's design and the ineffectualness of his own remonstrances. **1880** CHEYNE *Isaiah* I. 143 It is the violence, not the ineffectualness, of the attack which needs emphasising.

† **ine'ffectuate**, *v. Obs.* [f. stem of *ineffectu-al*, *ineffectu-ous* + -ATE, after *effectuate*: cf. F. *ineffectué* uneffected.] *trans.* To render ineffectual.

1633 T. ADAMS *Exp. 2 Peter* ii. 14 It [covetousness] ineffectuates the instruments of salvation.

ineffervescence (ɪnɛfə'vɛsəns). *rare.* [IN-^{3}.] The fact of not effervescing; absence of effervescence. So **ineffer'vescent** *a.* (*rare*$^{-0}$), having the quality of not effervescing; **ineffer'vescible** *a.* (*rare*$^{-0}$), incapable of effervescing; **ineffervesci'bility**, incapability of effervescing.

1794 KIRWAN *Min.* I. 199 Porcelain Clay is distinguished, from..Marls, by colour, fineness, ineffervescence with acids. *Ibid.* 201 Indurated lithomarga is distinguished from ..marls, by its fineness and ineffervescibility. **1828** WEBSTER, *Ineffervescent*..*Ineffervescible.* **1850** MANSEL *Lett.* (1873) 16 Substances ineffervescent in themselves.

† **i'nefficace**, *a. Obs. rare*$^{-0}$. [a. F. *inefficace*, ad. L. *inefficāc-em*: cf. EFFICACE.] = next.

1570 LEVINS *Manip.* 7/24 Inefficace, *inefficax.*

inefficacious (ɪnɛfɪ'keɪʃəs), *a.* [f. IN-^{3} + EFFICACIOUS: repr. L. *inefficāx*, *-cācem*, F. *inefficace.*] Of a remedy, treatment, course of action, etc.: Not efficacious; without efficacy.

1658 MANTON *Exp. Jude* verse 5 Wks. 1871 V. 178 The devils assent..is not a naked and inefficacious assent, but such as causeth horror and tremblings. **1769** *Town & Country Mag.* Sept. 473/1 His remedy proved inefficacious. **1842** DICKENS *Amer. Notes* (1850) 135/2 The precaution.. is quite inefficacious. **1875** POSTE *Gaius* III. (ed. 2) 387 It did not inevitably follow that his contract was inefficacious.

ineffi'caciously, *adv.* [f. prec. + -LY^2.] Ineffectually, unsuccessfully.

1727 BAILEY vol. II, *Ineffectually, Inefficaciously,* fruitlessly, to no Purpose. **1795** *Chron.* in *Ann. Reg.* 10 He exerted himself, however inefficaciously, in the cause of parliamentary reform.

ineffi'caciousness. [f. as prec. + -NESS.] The quality of being inefficacious; inefficacy.

1646 H. LAWRENCE *Comm. Angells* 67 That the inefficatiousnesse of grace is as well discovered by this, because even the Saints are sometimes overcome. **1678** *Lively Orac.* VIII. §3. 310 To this we may probably impute that strange inefficaciousness we see of the word. **1721** [see next].

inefficacity (ɪnɛfɪ'kæsɪtɪ). [ad. F. *inefficacité* (16th c. in Hatz.-Darm.): cf. IN-^{3} and EFFICACITY.] = prec.

1721 BAILEY, *Inefficacity*.. inefficaciousness, want of Force or Virtue. **1886** DICEY *Case agst. Home Rule* 76 [He] attributes the inefficacity of laws passed by the Imperial Parliament to their coming before Irishmen in a foreign garb.

inefficacy (ɪn'ɛfɪkəsɪ). [ad. late L. *inefficācia*, f. *inefficāx*, *-cācem*: cf. IN-^{3} and EFFICACY.] Want of efficacy; failure or incapacity to produce the effect proposed or desired.

1612–15 BP. HALL *Contempl., O.T.* XIX. viii, No marvell if carnall mindes despise the foolishnesse of preaching..the seeming inefficacy of censures. **1688** BOYLE *Final Causes Nat. Things* II. 84 The inefficacy of the burning fiery furnace on Daniel's three companions. **1751** JOHNSON *Rambler* No. 87 ¶3 The inefficacy of advice is usually the fault of the counsellor. **1849** LONGF. *Kavanagh* vi, The unintentional allusion to the inefficacy of his prayers.

† **ine'fficience.** *Obs. rare.* [f. as INEFFICIENT + -ENCE: cf. EFFICIENCE.] = next.

1797 ANNA SEWARD *Lett.* (1811) IV. 377 What does it prove but the inefficience of an inert majority, opposed to the active struggles of a party, less numerous by two-thirds?

inefficiency (ɪnɪ'fɪʃənsɪ). [f. as next + -ENCY: cf. EFFICIENCY.] Want of efficiency; inability or failure to accomplish something; ineffectiveness, inefficient character.

1749 CHESTERF. *Lett.* (1774) II. 187 Venice..owes its security to its neutrality and inefficiency. *a* **1761** LAW *The. Relig.* II. (R.), Numerous texts affirm this total insensibility and inefficiency of all such entities in the most absolute terms. **1817** B. R. HAYDON in *Four C. Eng. Lett.* 474 Relapsing for a time to languid inefficiency. **1878** LECKY *Eng. in 18th C.* II. viii. 504 The scandalous inefficiency of the Government of Lewis XV.

inefficient (ɪnɪ'fɪʃənt), *a.* (*sb.*) [f. IN-^{3} + EFFICIENT.] Not efficient; failing to produce, or incapable of producing, the desired effect; ineffective. Of a person: Not effecting or accomplishing something; deficient in the ability or industry required for what one has to do; not fully capable.

1750 CHESTERF. *Lett.* (1774) II. 337 He is as insipid in his pleasure, as inefficient in every thing else. **1804** W. TENNANT *Ind. Recreat.* II. 240 Ploughs..of a more awkward, and inefficient structure than those I have already described. **1833** HT. MARTINEAU *Berkeley the Banker* I. viii. 165 When the law was found inefficient the punishment was increased. **1839** KEIGHTLEY *Hist. Eng.* II. 75 He..rarely promoted an inefficient person. **1879** H. GEORGE *Progr. & Pov.* IX. ii. (1881) 398 Poorly paid labor, is inefficient labor.

B. *sb.* An inefficient person.

1898 *Times* 16 Dec. 7/6 Ill-born, ill-fed, ill-housed, ill-clad, many of them at best are poor animals, and 'inefficients' by birth or degeneration.

ine'fficiently, *adv.* [f. prec. + -LY^2.] In an inefficient manner; in a way that does not effect its purpose; ineffectively.

1828 in WEBSTER. **1835** T. WALKER *Original* i. (1887) 17 The art of government is the most difficult of all arts..and it is the most inefficiently practised. **1879** *Cassell's Techn. Educ.* VI. 403/2, I fear that I have very feebly enforced and very inefficiently illustrated the true principles on which works of furniture should be constructed.

† **ine'ffigiate**, *a. Obs. rare*$^{-1}$. [ad. L. *ineffigiāt-us*, f. *in-* (IN-^{3}) + *effigiātus* fashioned: see EFFIGIATE.] Unfashioned.

1657 tr. *Crollius' Philos. Ref.* I. 58 The first matter was a kind of ineffigiate confused Essence, which Phylosophers call the Chaos and Hylen, or Mother of the world.

† **i'neffrenate**, *a. Obs. rare*$^{-1}$. [ad. late L. *ineffrēnāt-us* unbridled, f. *in-* (? IN-^{2}) + *effrēnātus* unbridled.] Unbridled.

1581 STUBBES *Two wunderfull Examp.* in *Shaks. Soc. Papers* (1849) IV. 82 So are the people ineffrenate, peruerse in each degree.

† **i'neffugible**, *a. Obs. rare*$^{-0}$. [ad. L. *ineffugibilis* inevitable, f. *in-* (IN-^{3}) + **effugibilis*, f. *effugĕ-re* to flee from, avoid.] Inevitable.

1656 BLOUNT *Glossogr.*, *Ineffugible*, inevitable, not to be avoided.

ineffulgent (ɪnɪ'fʌldʒənt), *a. rare.* [IN-^{3}.] Not effulgent; wanting brilliance.

1824 *Examiner* 138/2 No ineffulgent suns.

† **inegal**, *a. Obs.* [a. F. *inégal* (Oresme, 14th c.) f. *in-* (IN-^{3}) + *égal* equal, EGALL, after L. *inæquālis* INEQUAL.] Unequal.

1484 CAXTON *Chivalry* 82 Pryde is a vyce of Inequalyte or to be inegal to other and not lyke.

inegalitarian (ɪnɪgælɪ'tɛərɪən), *a.* and *sb.* [f. IN-^{3} + EGALITARIAN *a.* (and *sb.*).] **A.** *adj.* Favouring, pertaining to, or marked by inequality. **B.** *sb.* One who denies or opposes equality between persons, = INEQUALITARIAN.

1955 T. H. PEAR *Eng. Social Differences* x. 211 The views of fervent English egalitarians and inegalitarians. **1961** *Guardian* 1 May 6/7 Madame Lefauchaux is dealing with their inegalitarian deficiencies. **1971** P. WORSTHORNE *Socialist Myth* ix. 219 The forces of democracy, *in practice*, compel society towards a shape that is highly inegalitarian. **1972** *Guardian* 15 June 14/5 The present distribution of financial aid [for housing]..is highly inegalitarian in its effects. **1972** *Daily Tel.* (Colour Suppl.) 24 Nov. 20/1 Paradoxically, Australia has a most remarkably inegalitarian educational system.

Hence **inegali'tarianism**.

1966 *Economist* 15 Oct. p. xxviii/1 This increased the inegalitarianism of what rapidly became a very inegalitarian German tax system. **1971** P. WORSTHORNE *Socialist Myth* v. 70 The Labour party has come to terms with the economic purpose of inegalitarianism.

† **i'neger**, *v. Obs. rare*$^{-1}$. [f. IN-^{2} + *eger* EAGER: corresp. to OF. *enaigr-ir*, *enegrir* to render sharp, irritate, envenom.] *trans.* To make eager or keen, to excite.

1657 S. PURCHAS *Pol. Flying-Ins.* II. 306 He is inegered with thirsty greedinesse for pardon and grace.

† **i-'nehleche**, *v. Obs.* [OE. *ʒenealæcan* f. *nealæcan*; see NEHLECHE.] To draw near, approach.

971 *Blickl. Hom.* 199 þa ne dorstan hie þære stowe ʒenealæcan. *Ibid.* 243 Hi ne dorston hine ʒenealæcan. *c* **1175** *Lamb. Hom.* 111 Summe lauerdes inehlecheð gode þurh heore lauer(d)scipe.

i-neiled, ME. pa. pple. of NAIL *v.*

inelaborate (ɪnɪ'læbərət), *a.* [IN-^{3}. Cf. obs. F. *inelaboré* (1605 in Godef.).] Not elaborate; not having much labour expended on it; simple or slight in workmanship.

1650 BULWER *Anthropomet.* 60 Crasse and excrementitious humours about the forepart of their Brain, which should make their faces more inelaborate and confused. **1747** WARBURTON *Shaks. Cymb.* v. v. 165 (Jod.) What Shakespeare meant by 'brief nature', inelaborate, hasty, and careless as to the elegance of form in respect of art. **1814** JEFFREY in *Mem. Moore* (1853) II. 16 One little piece of yours, however short and inelaborate. **1864** C. CLARKE *Box for Season* I. 122 Miss Markby's style was decidedly inelaborate.

Hence **ine'laborately** *adv.*, in a way void of elaboration.

1824 LANDOR *Imag. Conv.* Wks. 1846 I. 205 In regard to Herodotus, his style I consider as..the most simply and inelaborately harmonious, of any author in any language.

† **ine'laborate**, *v. Obs. rare*$^{-0}$. [f. IN-^{2} + ELABORATE.] = ELABORATE *v.*

1623 COCKERAM, *Inelaborate*, to doe a thing curiously.

inelaborated (ɪnɪ'læbəreɪtɪd), *a.* [IN-^{3}.] Not elaborated, not laboriously worked out; not thoroughly formed by natural or chemical process.

1623 COCKERAM *Eng. Dict.* II, Not Curiously done, *Inelaborated.* **1822–34** *Good's Study Med.* (ed. 4) IV. 368 Their weakened and relaxed condition allowed the serous or more liquid parts of the blood to pass off..in a crude and inelaborated form.

inelastic (ɪnɪ'læstɪk), *a.* [f. IN-^{3} + ELASTIC.]

1. a. Not elastic; void of elasticity or springiness, whether from rigidity or plastic quality; not yielding to a strain and springing back to its normal condition on the removal of the strain.

inelastic fluids, a name for liquids, as being void of 'elasticity' in the older sense (see ELASTIC A. 2): cf. *elastic fluids* s.v. ELASTIC A. 3.

1748 HARTLEY *Observ. Man* I. i. 87 The Excess of Softness, which renders the medullary Substance totally inelastic as to Sense. **1780** CHESTON in *Phil. Trans.* LXX. 328 Its cavity was above half filled with a firm inelastic substance. **1826** HENRY *Elem. Chem.* I. 245 Common or inelastic fluids are capable of remaining in contact with each other for a long time without admixture. **1863** TYNDALL *Heat* vii. 175 The principle of conservation holds equally good with elastic and inelastic bodies.

b. Of a collision (esp. between sub-atomic particles), or the scattering of one particle by another: involving a reduction in the total kinetic energy of the particles or bodies that come together, or a change in their internal energies.

1847 L. D. B. GORDON tr. *Weisbach's Princ. Mech. Machinery & Engin.* I. IV. iv. 302 The vis viva lost by inelastic impacts is equivalent to the sum of the products of the masses and the squares of their loss or gain in velocity. *Ibid.* 310 These two general formula [*sic*] also embrace the laws of perfectly elastic and perfectly inelastic impact. **1907** J. H. JEANS *Theoret. Mech.* ix. 238 When the contact between the surfaces of two bodies is of such a nature that they do not rebound at all after impact, it is said to be perfectly inelastic. **1938** *Physical Rev.* LIII. 795/1 The results of experiments on the inelastic scattering of such fast neutrons are especially suitable for theoretical investigation because the number of excited states in which the nucleus may be left when the neutron is reemitted will be large enough to make statistical considerations valid. **1942** *Ibid.* LXI. 129/1 The scattering of fast neutrons by nuclei is at least partly inelastic in the case of medium and heavy masses like Fe, Ag, and Pb. **1958** W. K. MANSFIELD *Elem. Nucl. Physics* iv. 30 The compound nucleus formed in inelastic collisions disposes of its surplus energy, the kinetic energy and binding energy of the incident neutron, by several different processes involving the ejection of particles or radiation from the nucleus. *Ibid.* 33 For inelastic scattering to occur the neutron must have sufficient energy to leave the target nucleus in an excited state. **1962** *Gloss. Terms Nucl. Sci.* (*B.S.I.*) 103 In inelastic scattering the scattered particle or photon loses energy by exciting the struck nucleus. **1966** J. HARWOOD *Introd. Mech.* xi. 138 A collision between two balls of lead or putty would be inelastic.

2. *fig.* **a.** That does not expand and contract in accordance with circumstance or need; unyielding.

1867 *Spectator* 29 June 713/2 The House of Lords show not firmness and independence, but inelastic obstinacy and obstructiveness, in such a vote. **1871** ALABASTER *Wheel of Law* p. lvii, Buddhism does not seem to be inelastic or unsuitable to civilization. **1894** *Westm. Gaz.* 5 June 6/1 The aggregate of the bank notes in active circulation is equally unchangeable and inelastic.

b. *Econ.* Varying less than in proportion to changes in price; (more loosely) unresponsive to changes in price: applied either to demand (for commodities, money, labour, etc.) or to supply.

1890 A. MARSHALL *Princ. Econ.* III. iii. 167 There may be ..violent changes..in the price of a thing which is not necessary, if it is perishable and the demand for it is inelastic. **1913** *Q. Rev.* Oct. 520 The demand for gas is comparatively inelastic. **1925** S. E. THOMAS *Elem. Econ.* iv. 37 Demand is said to be elastic when a rise or fall in the price causes a more than proportionate rise in the amount demanded. On the other hand, demand is said to be inelastic when a fall or rise in price causes relatively little rise or fall in the amount demanded. **1969** D. C. HAGUE *Managerial Econ.* II. iii. 57 Demand at all of these numerical elasticities less than one is often described as being inelastic. **1973** *Lancet* 14 Apr. 815/1 Russell found that the demand for cigarettes is inelastic... This means that if prices rise by 1% demand falls, but by an amount less than 1%; total revenue from taxation would then increase just as long as demand remained inelastic.

inelastically (ɪnɪˈlæstɪkəlɪ), *adv.* [f. prec.: see -ICALLY.] In a manner characteristic of inelastic bodies; with a reduction in the total kinetic energy.

1938 *Physical Rev.* LIII. 796/1 Inelastically scattered neutrons. **1942** J. D. STRANATHAN *'Particles' of Mod. Physics* vi. 229 It is possible that a few atoms..may occasionally collide inelastically, that one atom may spend a part of its kinetic energy in raising the electron of another atom to a higher energy level. **1966** D. G. BRANDON *Mod. Techniques Metallogr.* 112 It introduces a proportion of inelastically scattered electrons into the transmitted beam. **1969** *Physics Bull.* Mar. 86/2 The primary electron transfers an amount of energy V_0 to the atom and then leaves again, being observed externally as an inelastically reflected electron of energy $V_p—V_0$.

inelasticate (ɪnɪˈlæstɪkeɪt), *v.* [f. INELASTIC *a.* + -ATE³.] *trans.* To render inelastic.

1875 *Ure's Dict. Arts* I. 701 These threads must be deprived of their elasticity before they can be made subservient to..textile manufacture. Each thread [of caoutchouc] is *inelasticated* individually in the act of reeling, by the tenter boy or girl pressing it between the moist thumb and finger..Thread thus *inelasticated* has a specific gravity of 0·948732.

inelasticity (ˌɪnɪlæˈstɪsɪtɪ, ɪniːlæs-). [IN-³.] Absence of elasticity; a condition the reverse of elastic; rigidity.

1828 in WEBSTER. **1881** *Spectator* 26 Mar. 407/2 The inelasticity of highly elaborate instincts among the lower insects. **1883** *19th Cent.* May 742 No blind uniformity, no unintelligent inelasticity. **1925** S. E. THOMAS *Elem. Econ.* iv. 37 The Elasticity and Inelasticity of Demand. **1929** *Ibid.* (ed. 4) 51 Even in the case of necessaries, the degree of inelasticity may vary considerably.

inelegance (ɪnˈɛlɪgəns). [f. INELEGANT: see -ANCE, and cf. F. *inélégance* (1525 in Hatz.-Darm.).] The fact or quality of being inelegant; want of refined grace of form or manner; clumsiness; an instance of this.

1726 G. ROBERTS *4 Years Voy.* Ded. A iij b, Pardon the Inelegance, &c. of this unpolish'd Essay. **1779–81** JOHNSON *L.P.*, *Watts* Wks. IV. 184 Whatever they had among them before, whether of learning or acuteness, was commonly obscured and blunted by coarseness, and inelegance of style. **1837–9** HALLAM *Hist. Lit.* I. vi. §26 Their intemperance, their coarseness, their inelegance, their scurrility..are not compensated..by any impressive eloquence.

inelegancy (ɪnˈɛlɪgənsɪ). [f. next: see -ANCY.] The quality of being inelegant; = INELEGANCE.

1727 in BAILEY vol. II. **1732** BERKELEY *Alciphr.* v. §19 Whatever futility there may be in their notions, or inelegancy in their language. **1887** *Spectator* 29 Oct. 1460 Those literary inelegancies which seem the besetting sins of lady-novelists.

inelegant (ɪnˈɛlɪgənt), *a.* [a. F. *inélégant* (15–16th c. in Hatz.-Darm.), ad. L. *inēlegānt-em*, f. *in-* (IN-³) + *ēlegānt-em* ELEGANT.] Not elegant.

1. Wanting in grace of form or manner; ungraceful; unrefined; clumsy, coarse, unpolished.

1570 LEVINS *Manip.* 26/5 Inelegant, *inelegans*. **1623** COCKERAM, *Inelegant*, not decked, rough. **1753** HOGARTH *Anal. Beauty* vi. 31 When the forms..are inelegant, that is, when they are composed of unvaried lines. **1768** BOSWELL *Corsica* (ed. 2) 23 The church of St. John in this city, by no means an inelegant building. **1827** LYTTON *Pelham* viii. 21 Vincent's somewhat inelegant person.

b. *esp.* of language and literary stlye.

1509 BARCLAY *Shyp of Folys* (1874) I. 7 A maner of wrytinge nat inelegant. **1755** *World* No. 106 (1823) III. 8 If the dispute be about a Greek word, and he pronounces it to be inelegant. **1779–81** JOHNSON *L.P.*, *Rochester* Wks. II. 199 His imitation of Horace on Lucilius is not inelegant. **1824** L. MURRAY *Eng. Gram.* (ed. 5) I. 293 Such expressions..are very inelegant, and do not suit the idiom of our language.

†**c.** Not of delicate taste or flavour. *Obs.*

1708 J. PHILIPS *Cyder* I. 49 Ample Fruit..pleasing to Sight, But to the Tongue inelegant and flat.

d. Of a medical preparation: cf. ELEGANT 5 b.

1876 BARTHOLOW *Mat. Med.* (1879) 150 The decoction, although officinal, is inelegant and faulty.

2. Wanting in æsthetic refinement or delicacy.

a. Of things.

1667 MILTON *P.L.* v. 335 Order, so contriv'd as not to mix Tastes, not well joyned, inelegant. **1712** STEELE *Spect.* No. 521 ¶4 Fort Knock has occasioned several very perplexed and inelegant Heats and Animosities. **1736** BOLINGBROKE *Patriot.* (1749) 13 They wander about from one object to another, of vain curiosity, or inelegant pleasure. **1834** LYTTON *Pompeii* 245 [It was] thought inelegant among the Romans to entertain less than three or more than nine at their banquets. **1840** MACAULAY *Ess.*, *Ranke* (1851) II. 138 Letters and the fine arts undoubtedly owe much to this not inelegant sloth.

†**b.** Of persons. *Obs.*

1735 SOMERVILLE *Chase* I. 59 What remains On living Coals they broil, inelegant Of Taste. **1756** *Connoisseur* No. 130 ¶2, I am..the unfortunate wife of that inelegant (I had almost said insensible) husband. **1782** V. KNOX *Ess.* (1819) II. cxvii. 293 A common and inelegant spectator.

3. (*nonce-use* from late L.) Not in harmony with the main body of the Law.

1832 AUSTIN *Jurispr.* (1879) II. xxx. 552 This want of harmony or consistency with the great bulk of the system the Roman Lawyers denote..'inelegantia juris'. Now the Canon or Civil Laws (as they obtain in England) may be singular or inelegant but they are not less portions of the general law.

Hence **in'elegantness**, inelegancy (Bailey vol. II. 1727).

inelegantly (ɪnˈɛlɪgəntlɪ), *adv.* [f. prec. + -LY².] In an inelegant manner; ungracefully, clumsily.

1667 SOUTH *Serm.* (1698) III. x. 477 He was not so much buryed, as..deposited in the Grave for a small inconsiderable space; So that even in this respect he may not inelegantly be said to have tasted of Death. **1779–81** JOHNSON *L.P.*, *Milton* Wks. II. 154 Comus..is a drama in the epick style, inelegantly splendid, and tediously instructive. **1860** EMERSON *Cond. Life* viii. (1861) 169 The cat and the deer cannot move or sit inelegantly. **1871** RUSKIN *Fors Clav.* I. iv. 20 We fight inelegantly as well as expensively, with machines instead of bow and spear.

inelevable (ɪnˈɛlɪvəb(ə)l), *a.* [IN-³.] Not elevable; incapable of being elevated or raised.

1806 SOUTHEY in *Ann. Rev.* IV. 582 He is said to have expressed..his opinion that Rome..was inelevable.

ineligibility (ɪnˌɛlɪdʒɪˈbɪlɪtɪ). [f. next: see -ITY.] The quality or fact of being ineligible.

1795 *Fortnight's Ramble* 88 To them I thus object, on the score of their ineligibility. **1805** *East's Rep.* V. 215 The supposed ineligibility of a bailiff to be elected mayor. **1828** WEBSTER, *Ineligibility*..2. State or quality of not being worthy of choice. **1884** *Manch. Exam.* 7 Aug. 4/5 The amendment..declaring the ineligibility of all monarchical pretenders as candidates for the Presidency of the Republic.

ineligible (ɪnˈɛlɪdʒɪb(ə)l), *a.* [f. IN-³ + ELIGIBLE: cf. F. *inéligible* (1752 in Hatz.-Darm.).]

1. Incapable of being elected; legally or officially disqualified for election to an office or position.

1770 JOHNSON *False Alarm* Wks. X. 144 The votes given to a man ineligible being given in vain, the highest number of an eligible candidate becomes a majority. **1825** T. JEFFERSON *Autobiog.* Wks. 1859 I. 80 My wish..was that the President should be elected for seven years, and be ineligible afterwards. **1861** O'CURRY *Lect. MS. Materials* 252 He was dumb, and therefore..ineligible to be made a king.

b. Hence, Unfit, or considered unfit, to be chosen; unworthy of choice.

1828 WEBSTER, *Ineligible*..2. Not worthy to be chosen or preferred. **1862** TROLLOPE *Orley F.* lii, As a son-in-law he was quite ineligible. *Mod.* Altogether ineligible as a permanent residence.

†**2.** Of actions, etc.: Such as one would not choose to do; inexpedient; undesirable. *Obs.*

1779 R. HOWE in Sparks *Corr. Amer. Rev.* (1853) II. 321 He reports that storming them, at present, would be ineligible. **1793** SMEATON *Edystone L.* Contents 9 [It was] ineligible to take a greater time in the whole than formerly. **1797** T. JEFFERSON *Writ.* (1859) IV. 155 If there be any circumstance which might render its delivery ineligible, you may return it to me.

B. *absol.* with *pl.* as *sb.* One not eligible as a suitor or a husband.

1896 *Westm. Gaz.* 11 May 2/3 Archibald Rolles, an ineligible, declares his love to Margaretta Ridout, a penniless girl. **1898** *Ibid.* 25 May 3/2 Mothers of marriageable daughters..sometimes lament that eligible men as a class are so much less agreeable than the ineligibles.

Hence **in'eligibly** *adv.*, in an ineligible manner; **in'eligibleness** = INELIGIBILITY.

1846 WORCESTER, Ineligibly. *Dr. Allen.* **1872** *Daily News* 2 Sept., The camp of the Army Corps headquarters, ineligibly situated..if military conditions are regarded. **1881** *Ibid.* 4 Mar. 9/3 Unless experience of this latter place tends to show its ineligibleness for sanitary reasons.

ineliminable (ɪnɪˈlɪmɪnəb(ə)l), *a.* [IN-³.] Incapable of being eliminated.

1875 *N. Amer. Rev.* CXX. 108 The number of laborers is an ineliminable element in the problem.

ineloquence (ɪnˈɛləkwəns). [IN-³.] Want of eloquence; the quality of being ineloquent; (in Carlyle) the reverse of eloquence or speaking out; silence.

1843 CARLYLE *Past & Pr.* II. xi, The Lord Abbot's eloquence is less admirable than his *in*eloquence, his great invaluable 'talent of silence'. **1894** SIR H. IRVING in *Daily News* 3 Dec. 6/7 We..feel keenly the ineloquence of finite words to express our emotions.

ineloquent (ɪnˈɛləkwənt), *a.* [f. IN-³ + ELOQUENT: cf. F. *inéloquent* (16th c. in Littré).] Not eloquent, void of eloquence.

c **1530** L. COX *Rhet.* (1899) 42 The audyence falleth, for werynes of his ineloquent langage, fast on slepe. **1667** MILTON *P.L.* VIII. 219 Nor are thy lips ungraceful, Sire of men, Nor tongue ineloquent. **1818** SOUTHEY in *Q. Rev.* XIX. 52 He quotes the old man's honest and not ineloquent exhortation. **1843** CARLYLE *Past & Pr.* III. v, The ineloquent Brindley, behold he has chained seas together.

Hence **in'eloquently** *adv.*, in an ineloquent manner; without eloquence.

1828 in WEBSTER. **1865** J. HULLAH *Transit. Period Music* 119 Rameau..declared, very ineloquently no doubt, but very decisively, that it was the work of two hands, the one an artist, the other an utter ignoramus.

ineluctable (ɪnɪˈlʌktəb(ə)l), *a.* Also 7 -ible. [ad. L. *inēluctābil-is*, f. *in-* (IN-³) + *ēluctābil-is*, f. *ēluctā-rī* to struggle out. Cf. F. *inéluctable* (15th c. in Hatz.-Darm.).] From which one cannot escape by struggling; not to be escaped from.

1623 COCKERAM, *Ineluctable*, not to bee ouercome by any paines. **1629** JACKSON *Creed* VI. II. xx. §2 The titles of fate were anciently..unavoidable, insuperable, inflexible, ineluctable. **1659** PEARSON *Creed* 495 As if the damnation of all sinners now were ineluctable and eternall. **1765** *Hist. Eur.* in *Ann. Reg.* 3/1 That trouble and confusion which must probably attend these ineluctable events. **1880** SWINBURNE *Thalassius* 222 All glories of all storms of the air that fell, Prone, ineluctable. **1888** MRS. H. WARD *R. Elsmere* IV. xxix. 366 She and he were alike helpless—both struggling in the grip of some force outside themselves, inexorable, ineluctable.

Hence **ine'luctably** *adv.*, irresistibly, so that one cannot escape from its grip. Also **inelucta'bility**, the condition of being ineluctable.

1657 T. PEIRCE *God's Decrees* 62 That..doth prevail upon the will not ineluctably, but infallibly. **1922** JOYCE *Ulysses* 214 That lies in space which I in time must come to, ineluctably. **1939** —— *Finnegans Wake* I. 120 Those throne open doubleyous..reminding uus ineluctably of nature at her naturalest. **1943** *Mind* LII. 11 The limitation of the ability of a man to achieve salvation..may be, and often is, hypostasized to seeming ineluctability.

ineludible (ɪnɪˈl(j)uːdɪb(ə)l), *a.* Also -able. [IN-³.] That cannot be eluded or escaped.

1662 GLANVILL *Lux Orient.* ii. 18 An opinion, so very obnoxious..should not be admitted but upon..ineludable [1682 ineludible] demonstrations. **1787** BENTHAM *Panopt.* Let. xxi. (1791) 126 Doubts..whether it would be advisable ..to give such herculean and ineludible strength to the gripe of power? **1846** HAWTHORNE *Mosses* I. ii. 34 The ineludible gripe, in which mortality clutches the highest and purest of earthly mould. **1882** G. MACDONALD *Castle Warlock* xviii. 104 Making up his mind to the ineludible.

Hence **ine'ludibly** *adv.*, in an ineludible manner.

1893 *National Observer* 20 May 9/1 Persisted in stubbornly, unchangeably, ineludably.

†inˌemana'bility. *Obs. rare*$^{-1}$. [f. IN-^{3} + L. *ēmānābil-is*, f. *ēmānā-re* to EMANATE.] The attribute of not originating by emanation.

a **1656** HALES *Gold. Rem.* (1688) 327 The..properties are ..innascibility and inemanability..these belong to the Father.

inembryonate (ɪn'ɛmbrɪənət), *a. Biol.* [IN-^{3}.] Not embryonate; having no embryo.

1846 WORCESTER cites REID. **1855** MAYNE *Expos. Lex.*, *Inembryonatus*, having no embryo, germ, or corculum; inembryonate.

†ine'mendable, *a. Obs. rare.* [ad. L. *inēmendābilis* that cannot be amended or improved; (in Laws of Cnut and Hen. I, in sense 'that cannot be remedied by a fine', Du Cange); f. *in-* (IN-^{3}) + *ēmendābilis* amendable, EMENDABLE.] Incapable of being emended; incurable.

1532 MORE *Confut. Tindale* Wks. 569/2 In auoyding of their sedicious trouble, and for the repressyng of theyr inemendable malice. **1708** KERSEY s.v., [In old Times] such a Crime was said to be inemendable, as could not be atoned for by a Fine. **1721** in BAILEY.

Hence **†ine'mendableness** (Bailey, 1727).

†inemitie, obs. Sc. form of ENMITY.

a **1572** KNOX *Hist. Ref.* (1847) I. 147 This inemitie [*ed.* 1732 inamitie] was judged mortall, and without all hope of reconciliatioun.

inemotivity (ˌɪnɪməʊ'tɪvɪtɪ). [f. IN-^{3} + EMOTIVITY.] Lack of emotional sensibility.

1894 W. JAMES in *Psychol. Rev.* I. 529 M. Sollier thinks.. that in complete *inemotivity* the visceral reactions themselves do not take place. **1902** —— in *Encycl. Brit.* XXXII. 66/1 We must remember that the patient's inemotivity may have been a co-ordinate result with the anæsthesia of his neural lesions, and not the anæsthesia's mere effect.

in'emulous, *a. rare*$^{-1}$. [IN-^{3}.] Not emulous; without emulation; not envious *of* (fame, power, or the like).

1789 E. DARWIN *Bot. Gard.* II. (1791) 80 He treads, inemulous of fame or wealth, Profuse of toil, and prodigal of health.

inemye, obs. form of ENEMY: see INIMI.

in'enarrable, *a.* [a. F. *inénarrable* (14th c. in Hatz.-Darm.), ad. L. *inēnarrābil-is*, f. *in-* (IN-^{3}) + *ēnarrābilis*, f. *ēnarrā-re* to narrate. Cf. ENARRABLE.] That cannot be narrated, told, or declared; indescribable, unspeakable.

c **1450** *Mirour Saluacioun* 4329 So grete is the payne of helle and so inenarrable. **1508** FISHER *7 Penit. Ps.* cii. Wks. (1876) 138 He is the profoundyte of thyn inenarrable wysdome. *Ibid.* 196 Whose goodnes is inenarrable and euerlastynge. *c* **1611** CHAPMAN *Iliad* II. 422 The princes then, and nauie that did bring These so inenarrable troopes, and all their soyles, I sing. **1616** —— *Homer's Hymns, Hercules* (1858) 104 And who..through all the sea was sent, And Earth's inenarrable continent. **1628** JACKSON *Worthy Churchman* 25 An inenarrable hardnesse is the first and chiefe quality of the Diamond. **1716** M. DAVIES *Athen. Brit.* II. 424 That sacred..Mystery of the Holy Trinity is ineffable and inenarrable by any Creature. **1730** BAILEY (folio), *Inena'rrable.* **1914** R. BROOKE *Coll. Poems* (1918) 18 The inenarrable godhead of delight. **1923** A. HUXLEY *Antic Hay* xv. 213 Those Mohammedan ecstasies that last..six hundred inenarrable years apiece. **1936** —— *Eyeless in Gaza* xlvii. 525 The scent of the flowers was like the brief and inenarrable revelation of something more than earthly. **1967** *Listener* 5 Jan. 37/3 The music has an inenarrable greatness which quite transcends the occasion of its composition.

Hence **†inenarrableness.**

1727 BAILEY vol. II, *Inena'rrableness*, Unspeakableness.

†i'nence, i'nent, obs. forms of ANENT *prep.*

13.. *Cursor M.* 23011 (Edin.) Saint austin says inent þat dai Es nan can godis consail sai.

inenchyma (ɪ'nɛŋkɪmə). *Bot.* [f. Gr. ἴς, ἰν- fibre + ἔγχυμα infusion.] Fibrocellular tissue, the cells of which resemble spiral vessels.

1851 BALFOUR *Bot.* §11. 5 When united, they [fibrous cells] form fibro-cellular tissue or Inenchyma.

inenergetic (ɪnɛnə'dʒɛtɪk), *a. rare.* [IN-^{3}.] Not energetic; without energy.

1826 COLERIDGE *Lett., Convers.*, etc. (1836) I. Let. viii. 47 The energetic or inenergetic state of the minds of men.

†ine'nodable, *a. Obs. rare*$^{-0}$. [f. IN-^{3} + L. *ēnōdābil-is*, f. *ēnodā-re* to ENODATE.] That cannot be untied or unravelled.

1623 COCKERAM, *Inenodable*, not to bee vnknit. **1721** BAILEY, *Inenodable*, not to be untied or explained.

Hence **ine'nodableness**, 'uncapableness of being unloosed, untied, or explicated' (Bailey vol. II, 1727).

ine'nubilable, *a. rare.* [f. IN-^{3} + L. *ēnūbil-āre* to make clear (see ENUBILATE *v.*) + -ABLE.] That cannot be cleared of clouds or mist, or (*fig.*) of obscurity; indistinct; inexplicable.

1903 *Sat. Rev.* 7 Feb. 169/1 This business of the avalanche is treated by the critics as something quite inenubilable. **1911** BEERBOHM *Zuleika D.* xii. 191 There is nothing in England to be matched with what lurks in the vapours of these meadows, and in the shadows of these spires—that mysterious, inenubilable spirit, spirit of Oxford.

inept (ɪ'nɛpt), *a.* [ad. L. *ineptus* unsuited, absurd, foolish, f. *in-* (IN-^{3}) + *aptus* APT: perh. immed. a. F. *inepte* (14th c. in Hatz.-Darm.).]

1. Not adapted or adaptable; not suited *for* (†*to*) a purpose; without aptitude; unsuitable, unfit. *arch.*

1603 FLORIO *Montaigne* I. xxxix. (1632) 126 A manner peculiar unto myself, inept to all publike Negotiations. **1651** HOBBES *Leviath.* II. xxv. 134 The differences between *apt* and *inept* Counsellours. **1692** RAY *Dissol. World* 142 The Air ..would contain but few nitrous Particles, and so be inept to maintain the Fire. *a* **1734** NORTH *Exam.* I. ii. §67 (1740) 65 The Parliament then in being..by all Experiments was found inept for the great Designs of the Faction. **1810** BENTHAM *Packing* (1821) 268 Not to wrest power out of the hands of present possessors, but to render them somewhat less generally and flagrantly inept than at present for..the exercise of it. **1895** *Cornh. Mag.* Oct. 380 Else the lawyers of the land were singularly inept when our soldiers and sailors were at their best.

b. Not suited to the occasion; not adapted to circumstances; out of place, inappropriate.

1675 BAXTER *Cath. Theol.* I. I. 49 If they mean Negative Propositions, it's true, but inept. **1858** J. MARTINEAU *Stud. Chr.* 121 If the doctrine were true, could anything be more inept than an allusion to it in this place? **1883** *Law Times Rep.* XLIX. 555/1 He has merely used inept words which do not affect the preceding absolute gift.

2. Absurd; wanting in reason or judgement; silly, foolish.

1604 JAS. I *Counterbl.* (Arb.) 102 As to the Proposition, That because the braines are colde and moist, therefore things that are hote and drie are best for them, it is an inept consequence. **1653** H. MORE *Antid. Ath.* I. xi. (1662) 34 So soft and moistened by Drunkenness and excess, as to make the Understanding inept and sottish in its Operations. **1710** *Brit. Apollo* III. No. 81. 2/2 She look'd on you as an Inept Animal. **1888** R. F. BURTON in *Academy* 20 Oct. 249/3 This policy of meddle and muddle, this ineptest interference with local administration for party purposes.

3. *Law.* Void, of no effect.

1818 SCOTT *Hrt. Midl.* xxiii, Extrajudicial confession.. was totally inept, and void of all strength and effect from the beginning. —— *Br. Lamm.* xxvii, As a transaction *inter minores*..the engagement was inept, and void in law. **1882–3** in Schaff *Encycl. Relig. Knowl.* III. 2515/1 Edward III. died ..and so the bull to the king became inept.

inepticality (ɪnɛptɪ'kælɪtɪ). *rare.* [f. INEPT *a.* + -ICAL + -ITY.] = INEPTITUDE.

1923 E. E. CUMMINGS *Let.* 15 Sept. (1969) 102 A friend of mine called 'Slater' 'Brown', looks not too much like J. Christ and has attacks of total inepticality and is a very pleasant person.

ineptitude (ɪ'nɛptɪtjuːd). [ad. L. *ineptitūdo*, n. of quality f. *ineptus* INEPT: see -TUDE. Cf. obs. F. *ineptitude* (15th c. in Godef.).] The quality of being inept.

1. Want of aptitude; inaptness, unsuitableness, unfitness *to* or *for* something; incapacity.

1615 CROOKE *Body of Man* 507 A ineptitude to learne [sheweth] a drie and a hard braine. **1640** WILKINS *New Planet* II. (1684) 115 There is in it, and so likewise in the other Planets, an ineptitude to motion. *c* **1645** HOWELL *Lett.* I. I. ix. 17 A strong conjecture of the aptnesse or ineptitude of ones capacity. **1710** STEELE *Tatler* No. 203 ¶1 That Ineptitude for Society, which is frequently the Fault of us Scholars. **1885** *N. & Q.* 6th Ser. XI. 110/1 An endeavour to imitate phonetically the Red Indian name of the plant..a process for which the French usually show an extraordinary ineptitude.

2. Want of mental capacity; folly, silliness. With *an* and *pl.*: A foolish act or remark.

1656 BLOUNT *Glossogr.*, *Ineptitude*, unaptness, fondness, foolishness, trifling, vainness. **1675** BAXTER *Cath. Theol.* II. II. 42 Here are a multitude of Errors or Ineptitudes together. **1832** CARLYLE *Misc.* (1857) III. 55 [He] lived no day of his life without doing and saying more than one pretentious ineptitude. **1885** *Spectator* 18 July 948/1 This..goes far to justify Buckle's strictures on the ineptitude of statesmen.

ineptly (ɪ'nɛptlɪ), *adv.* [f. INEPT + -LY^2.] In an inept manner; unfitly, unsuitably; foolishly.

(The first example (which comes second-hand from Brian Twyne's transcript *c* 1620–24) may be an isolated occurrence after L. *inepte*, F. *ineptement*, 1380 in Godef.)

1523 HEN. VIII *Let. to Bayliffe of Oxford* 18 Oct., Twyne MSS. XIII. 259 (cf. Turner *Rec. Oxf.* 42) All common welth there is ineptly permytted to fall into extreme ruyne and decay. **1611** COTGR., *Ineptement*, ineptly, vnaptly. **1612** J. COTTA *Disc. Dang. Pract. Phys.* I. vii. 54 Ineptly and injuriously may the illusion of fancy..be made snares for the innocent. **1653** H. MORE *Antid. Ath.* I. x. (1662) 31 Though it be done never so ineptly and foolishly. **1691** RAY *Creation* II. (1692) 22 The Crystalline Humor of the Eye which they [the Peripatetics] ineptly fansied to be the immediate Organ of Vision. **1886** TRAILL *Shaftesbury* (1888) 89 A subtle note of ironical compassion, as of a rat who was leaving the sinking ship, for a rat who has ineptly selected the same moment for joining it.

ineptness (ɪ'nɛptnɪs). [f. INEPT + -NESS.] The quality of being inept.

1. = INEPTITUDE 1.

1633 W. STRUTHER *True Happines* 66 An universall ineptnesse, both in soul and bodie to any good office. **1661** G. RUST *Origen's Opin.* in *Phenix* (1721) I. 24 An utter ineptness to all things worthy of a Man. **1722** WOLLASTON *Relig. Nat.* IX. vii. (Seager), The ineptness of matter has been well considered.

2. = INEPTITUDE 2.

1877 SPARROW *Serm.* xiii. 173 They rebuke the multitude for the grossness and ineptness of their views. **1892** *Times* 28 Apr. 5/1 Able, thanks to the ineptness of the prosecution, to transform the prisoner's dock into a Tribune from which he preached Anarchy.

†inequa'bility. *Obs. rare*$^{-1}$. [f. IN-^{3} + EQUABILITY: perh. directly ad. late L. *inæquābilitās*, f. *inæquābilis* INEQUABLE.] Want of equability or uniformity.

1581 J. BELL *Haddon's Answ. Osor.* 403b, Upon what grew this inequabilitie and parcialitie of dispensation.

inequable (ɪn'iːk-, -'ɛkwəb(ə)l), *a.* [ad. L. *inæquābil-is* uneven, f. *in-* (IN-^{3}) + *æquābil-is* EQUABLE.] Uneven, not uniform.

1717 J. KEILL *Anim. Œcon.* (1738) 64 The middle Velocity, either equable or inequable. **1721** in BAILEY. **1924** *Glasgow Herald* 21 Nov. 11 The inequable incidence of the regulations. **1926** A. E. ELLIS *Brit. Snails* 31 An important obstacle in the way of fresh-water colonization is the inequable temperature of rivers and lakes.

Hence **in'equableness** (Bailey vol. II, 1727).

inequal (ɪn'iːkwəl), *a.* [ad. L. *inæquāl-is*, f. *in-* (IN-^{3}) + *æquāl-is* EQUAL: cf. OF. *inequal* (Oresme, 14th c.), mod.F. *inégal.*] = UNEQUAL. (The earlier formation; now *arch.* exc. as in b.)

Its earliest use appears to have been in *inequal hours*, the hours formed by dividing the natural day or night into twelve equal parts, the length of which therefore varied according to the time of the year, the hours of the day being also unequal to the hours of the night, except at the equinoxes.

c **1386** CHAUCER *Knt.'s T.* 1413 The thridde houre inequal that Palamon Bigan to Venus temple for to gon Vp roos the sonne. *c* **1391** —— *Astrol.* II. §10 Thise howris inequalis ben cleped howres of planetts..þe howr in-equal of the day with þe howr inequal of the nyght contenen 30 degrees. **1539** TONSTALL *Serm. Palm Sund.* (1823) 7 The father bygatte hym not inequalle to hym selfe. **1577** HARRISON *England* II. ix. (1877) I. 192 The Dane law..of all the rest the most inequall and intollerable. **1588** A. KING tr. *Canisius' Catech.* I iij, ȝow haiff..ye place of ye sone euery day according to ye astronomicall calculation of his middle or æqual motion, for seing ye præcise reconing of his inæqual or trew motion do varie euery ȝere [etc.]. *a* **1681** SIR G. WHARTON *Æquation of Time* Wks. (1683) 101 Seeing that Inequal days cannot be the measure of equal motions, it is requisite that those Inequal days be converted to equal. **1711** HEARNE *Collect.* III. 268 Inequal Distributions were made. **1741** SHENSTONE *Judgm. Hercules* 486 Welcome all toils th' inequal Fates decree. **1831** BREWSTER *Newton* (1855) I. iv. 82 An image..which..would be..more or less elongated and coloured, if the two refracting angles were more or less inequal.

b. Of a surface: Uneven.

1661 LOVELL *Hist. Anim. & Min.* 319 The ventricles.. their inward superficies is inequall with caruncles. **1890** *Cent. Dict.*, *Inequal*. 2. In *entom.*, covered with irregular elevations and depressions: said of a surface.

Hence **in'equally** *adv.*, in an unequal manner; **in'equalness**, inequality (Bailey vol. II. 1727).

1661 LOVELL *Hist. Anim. & Min.* 288 The field Spiders eaten or drunk doe inequally affect the whole body by heate, cold, horror, and itching. **1675** R. BURTHOGGE *Causa Dei* 172 He doth inequally dispense it.

inequalitarian (ɪnɪkwɒlɪ'tɛərɪən). *rare.* [f. INEQUALITY, after EQUALITARIAN.] One who holds the principle of the innate inequality of mankind. Also as *adj.*

1878 GLADSTONE *Glean.* (1879) I. 234 In practice they [the English people] are what I may call determined inequalitarians. —— in *Newman Hall's Autobiog.* (1898) 276, I coined a word to express my opinion. I said I was an 'Inequalitarian'. I believe more and more in Heredity. Qualities are inherited. **1949** *Mind* LVIII. 207 Consider an inequalitarian society in which there are rich people who buy 'luxuries' and poor people who buy only 'necessities'. **1966** *Punch* 13 Apr. 521/2 The ritualistically observed Sunday is inequalitarian... While the rich can enjoy their private swimming-pools..and so on, the poorer elements are denied access even to the inadequate public amenities.

inequality (ɪnɪ'kwɒlɪtɪ). [a. OF. *inequalité*, 14th c. in Littré (= mod.F. *inégalité*), ad. med.L. *inæquālitās*, f. *inæquālis* INEQUAL.] The state or condition of being unequal; want of equality.

1. Want of equality between persons or things; disparity: **a.** in respect of magnitude, quantity, number, intensity, or other physical quality.

1531 ELYOT *Gov.* III. i, Iustyce commutatiue..onely consideryngе the inequalitie, wherby the one thynge excedeth the other, indeuoureth to brynge them bothe to an equalitie. **1597** MORLEY *Introd. Mus.* 27 Proportion of inæqualitie is, when two things of vnequall quantitie are compared togither. **1674** BOYLE *Excell. Theol.* II. iv. 177 It remains doubtful, whether the differing sizes [of the fixed stars]..proceed from a real inequality of bulk, or onely from an inequality of distance. **1776** ADAM SMITH *W.N.* (1869) I. I. x. II. 119 Inequalities in the wages of labour and profits of stock. **1825** J. NICHOLSON *Operat. Mechanic* 430 Should the inequality of tension be occasioned by any original inequality of thickness in the strands. **1858** FROUDE *Hist. Eng.* III. xiii. 94 The growing inequality of fortunes had broken through this useful custom.

b. In respect of dignity, rank, or circumstances: Social disparity; the fact of occupying a more or a less advantageous position.

1484 CAXTON *Chivalry* 82 Pryde is a vyce of Inequalyte or to be inegal to other and not lyke. **1583** STUBBES *Anat. Abus.* II. (1882) 103 The apostles..amongst whom was no

superiority, inequalitie, or principallitie at all. **1603** KNOLLES *Hist. Turks* (1638) 135 Betwixt Othoman and her was great inequality..she was (as she said) but meanly born, and therefore was not to expect so great a match. **1791** BOSWELL *Johnson* 13 Apr. an. 1773, She wondered how he could reconcile..his notions of inequality and subordination with wishing well to all mankind. **1802** MAR. EDGEWORTH *Moral T.* (1816) I. i. 1 The inequality between the rich and the poor shocked him.

c. In respect of excellence, power, or adequacy. Also, A condition of superiority or inferiority in relation to something, *esp.* the condition of being unequal *to* a task, insufficiency, inadequacy.

1553 EDEN *Treat. Newe Ind.* Ded. (Arb.) 5 There seemed too me no lesse inequalitye betwene the tytle and the booke, then if a man woulde professe to wryte of Englande, and entreated onelye of Trumpington. **1694** SOUTH *Twelve Serm.* (1698) III. 265 The Nature of the Things themselves, which are the Subject matter of the Christian Religion.. Their surpassing Greatness and Inequality to the mind of Man. **1708** MRS. CENTLIVRE *Busie Body* Ded., Conscious of the Inequality of a Female Pen to so Masculine an Attempt. **1777** WATSON *Philip II* (1793) II. XIV. 233 When she considered the inequality of the dispute between him and the Flemings. **1899** CHEYNE in *Expositor* Apr. 258 There are no doubt stylistic inequalities in the different Psalms.

2. †**a.** Of persons: Unequal treatment of others; unfair dealing, unfairness, partiality. **b.** Or things: Want of due proportion, uneven distribution. With *an* and *pl.*, an instance of this.

1538 STARKEY *England* II. ii. 183 The chefe..cause of al sedycyon..that ys to say, the inequalyte of dystrybutyon of the commyn offyceys. **1552** LATIMER *5th Serm. Lord's Prayer* Wks. (Parker Soc.) I. 399 What meaneth God by this inequality, that he giveth to some an hundred pound; unto this man five thousand pound; unto this man in a manner nothing at all? **1675** TRAHERNE *Chr. Ethics* 478 If we shall not be liberal to one another, it is a strange inequality. **1740** WARBURTON *Div. Legat.* V. iv. Wks. 1811 V. 145 We sometimes find men complaining of inequalities in events, which were indeed the effects of a most equal Providence. **1858** BRIGHT *Sp. Reform* 27 Oct. (1876) 281, I could show you inequalities as great and scandalous in the manner in which the income-tax..presses upon the owners of the soil and those engaged in professions and trades chiefly carried on in towns.

3. Want of uniformity in a thing, person, or process; unevenness, irregularity, variableness: **a.** in surface or outline. With *an* and *pl.*: an irregularity of surface or outline; a rise or fall of the ground.

1607 TOPSELL *Four-f. Beasts* (1658) 330 The roughness and inequality of the place grieved, one part being higher then another. **1645** BOATE *Irel. Nat. Hist.* (1652) 5 The inequality of the coast, and of the great Bayes and Forelands. **1691** RAY *Creation* II. (1692) 109 To find out the side towards which the inequality of the ground might more easily permit it to rowl its shell. **1801** W. COXE *Tour Monmouth.* I. 117 The distant country is broken into fine inequalities of hill and dale. **1874** SYMONDS *Sk. Italy & Greece* (1898) I. i. 4 These inequalities in the surface of the earth which we call Alps. **1878** HUXLEY *Physiogr.* 135 The water soon finds out some slight inequalities of surface.

b. in motion, action, or condition; in duration or recurrence; in rate or proportion; in manner, quality, degree, or other respect in which a thing is liable to variation. With *an* and *pl.*: an instance of such unevenness.

1626 BACON *Sylva* §700 Inequality [of sounds], not Stayed vpon, but Passing, is rather an Encrease of Sweetnesse. **1638** F. JUNIUS *Paint. of Ancients* 316 Whatsoever doth not hang well together, bewrayeth it selfe ..by an inequalitie of colour. **1671** SALMON *Syn. Med.* II. xlvi. 308 The inequality of the Pulse continuing is an evil sign. **1748** *Anson's Voy.* I. viii. 77 These tempests..were yet rendered more mischievous to us by their inequality, and the deceitful intervals which they at some-times afforded. **1753** HANWAY *Trav.* (1762) II. II. ii. 76 The inequality of our climate. **1797** COLERIDGE in Jos. Cottle *Early Recoll.* (1837) I. 250 In Wordsworth there are no inequalities. **1815** W. H. IRELAND *Scribbleomania* 55 *note*, The inequalities observable both in his style and versification. **1833** N. ARNOTT *Physics* (ed. 5) II. 9 Owing merely to an inequality of temperature.

4. *Astron.* A deviation from uniformity in the motion of a heavenly body.

The older astronomers reckoned four inequalities, two common to planets and the moon, and two confined to the moon. ***first inequality***: that which is due to the eccentricity of the orbit, and the acceleration of motion at a planet's perihelion or the moon's perigee. ***second inequality***: that which arises from the obliquity of the direction of the planet's motion to the radius vector of its orbit; = EVECTION. ***third inequality***: = VARIATION (of the moon). ***fourth inequality***: that due to the more rapid motion of the moon when the earth is in perihelion; also called ***annual inequality*** or ***annual equation***. Later astronomers have discovered several others, as ***parallactic inequality*** (see quot. 1867–76); ***periodic inequality***, the comparatively short recurring orbital perturbation due to the attraction of another body, as the great inequality of Jupiter and Saturn.

1690 LEYBOURN *Curs. Math.* 758 The second Inequality of the Moon is explained by a little Circle. **1726** tr. *Gregory's Astron.* I. 427 By any single observation of a Planet..to clear it of its Second Inequality, and find its Distance from the Sun. **1728** PEMBERTON *Newton's Philos.* 228 Sir Isaac Newton has computed the very quantity of many of the moon's inequalities. **1816** PLAYFAIR *Nat. Phil.* II. 277 Besides these two great inequalities, there are ten others..to which Jupiter is subject. **1831** BREWSTER *Newton* (1855) I. xi. 262 The annual inequality of the moon depending on the position of the earth in its orbit. **1833** HERSCHEL *Astron.* xi. 347 An irregularity, which is well known to astronomers by the name of the great inequality of Jupiter and Saturn. **1867–76** CHAMBERS *Astron.* I. vii. (ed. 3) 80 The *Variation*.. was the first lunar inequality explained by Sir I. Newton on the theory of gravitation. *Ibid.*, The *Parallactic Inequality* arises from the sensible difference in the disturbing influence exerted by the Sun on the Moon, according as the latter is in that part of its orbit nearest to, or most removed from, the Sun. *Ibid.*, The *Secular Acceleration* of the Moon's mean motion..This inequality was detected by Halley in 1693. *Ibid.* 81 Hansen elucidated, a few years ago, two other inequalities in the Moon's motion, due, the one directly and the other indirectly, to the influence of Venus.

5. *Math.* **a.** The relation between quantities that are unequal in value or magnitude. ***sign of inequality***, either of the signs > ('is greater than') and < ('is less than'). **b.** An expression of this relation, consisting of two unequal quantities connected by either of these signs: distinguished from *equation*.

1875 TODHUNTER *Algebra* (ed. 7) li. §674 If the signs of all the terms of an inequality be changed the sign of inequality must be reversed.

inequation (ɪnɪˈkweɪʃən). [f. L. *inæquāt-us* unequal, after EQUATION.] A formula expressing inequality; = INEQUALITY 5 b.

1855 H. SPENCER *Princ. Psychol.* (1872) II. 16 To consider the case of inequations. *Ibid.* VI. iii. 29 The inequation expresses a relation in which the second quantity bears a greater ratio to the first.

inˈequi-, combining element, in sense 'unequal', 'unequally'; not of L. formation (the negative of L. *æquus* being *inīquus*), but f. IN-³ + EQUI-: usually in words that are the negatives of *equi-* words, as *equidistant*, *inequidistant*, but also forming negative compounds without corresponding positive forms. The following are examples of both classes:

inˌequiˈaxed, inˌequiˈaxial *a.* [AXE, AXIAL], having unequal axes. **inˌequiˈcostate** *a.* [COSTATE], unequally ribbed, as a shell or seed (Mayne, 1855). **inˌequiˈdistant** *a.*, not equidistant. **inˌequiˈlibrity**, want of equilibrium. **inˌequiˈlobate, iˈnequilobed** *a.*, having unequal lobes. **inˌequipoˈtential** *a.*, not equipotential; so **inˌequipotentiˈality**, inequality of potential, as at different points on the surface of a glacier.

1862 G. P. SCROPE *Volcanos* 107 Where the component *inequiaxed crystals or scales are disposed conformably. **1879** RUTLEY *Study Rocks* iv. 35 When *inequiaxial, arranged with their longer axes parallel with the lamination. **1677** PLOT *Oxfordsh.* 268 Three *inequidistant arched ribs of stone. **1788** T. TAYLOR *Proclus* I. 78 Another operates with weights, the motion of which is reckoned to be the cause of *inequilibrity. **1855** MAYNE *Expos. Lex.*, *Inequilobate. **1872** NICHOLSON *Palæont.* 328 In the Glyptolæmus..the tail is *inequilobed.

inequilateral (ɪniːkwɪˈlætərəl), *a.* [f. IN-³ + EQUILATERAL. Cf. F. *inéquilatéral.*] Having unequal sides; unequal-sided.

inequilateral shell: one in which a transverse line drawn through the apex of the umbo divides the valve into two unequal and unsymmetrical parts.

1662 J. BARGRAVE *Pope Alex. VII* (1867) 123 Several rude pieces of mountain chrystall..amongst which there is one.. sexangular, inaequilateral, cylindrical, pyramidical. **1830** BREWSTER *Edin. Cycl.* VII. I. 91/2 Shell transverse, inequilateral, inequivalved. **1854** WOODWARD *Mollusca* II. 246 The Bivalves are all more or less inequilateral, the anterior being usually much shorter than the posterior side. **1880** GRAY *Struct. Bot.* III. iv. 106 Inæquilateral Leaves, being unsymmetrical by the much greater development of one side... This is illustrated in the whole genus Begonia.

So †**inequilater** *a.* [cf. F. *inéquilatère*], †**iˌnequiˈlaterous** *a.* = prec.

1614 T. BEDWELL *Nat. Geom. Numbers* i. 7 An inequilater parallelogramme. **1855** MAYNE, Inequilaterous.

in equilibrio: see EQUILIBRIUM 3.

inequitable (ɪnˈɛkwɪtəb(ə)l), *a.*¹ [f. IN-³ + EQUITABLE: cf. F. *inéquitable.*] Not equitable; characterized by want of equity or fairness; unfair, unjust.

1667 *Decay Chr. Piety* 64 The way of Process men take in this affair is so inequitable as certainly presages the partiality of the sentence. **1753** JOHNSON *Adventurer* No. 62 ¶8 Nothing is more inequitable than that one man should suffer for the crimes of another. **1768–74** TUCKER *Lt. Nat.* (1834) II. 273 A spiritual pride, making them censorious, inequitable, turning everything to the worst side. **1790** BURKE *Fr. Rev.* Wks. V. 252 The proportions seemed not inequitable. **1879** H. GEORGE *Progr. & Pov.* VII. i. (1881) 306 The inequitable division of wealth.

Hence **inˈequitably** *adv.*, in an inequitable manner, unfairly, unjustly.

1842 DE QUINCEY *Cicero* Wks. 1857 VII. 207 As a commander-in-chief, Pompey was known to have been inequitably fortunate. **1880** MUIRHEAD *Gaius* IV. §126 It sometimes happens that an exception, which *prima facie* seems just enough, will yet bear inequitably upon the pursuer.

†**iˈnequitable**, *a.*² *Obs. rare*⁻⁰. [ad. L. *inequitābil-is*, f. *in-* (IN-³) + *equitābil-is* ridable, f. *equitā-re*: see next.] That cannot be ridden through.

1623 COCKERAM, *Inequitable*, not to bee rid through. Hence in BLOUNT, PHILLIPS, etc.

†**iˈnequitate**, *v. Obs. rare*⁻¹. [f. ppl. stem of L. *inequitā-re* to ride on or over, f. *in-* (IN-²) + *equitā-re* to ride, f. *eques, equit-em* horseman, f. *equus* horse.] *trans.* To ride over or through; hence, to pervade, permeate.

1653 H. MORE *Conject. Cabbal.* ii. §7 The World of Life, which is everywhere nigh at hand, and does very throngly inequitate the moist and unctuous Aire.

inequity (ɪnˈɛkwɪtɪ). [IN-³. (The corresp. L. formation was *inīquitās* INIQUITY.)] Want of equity or justice; the fact or quality of being unfair; unfairness, partiality.

1556 J. HEYWOOD *Spider & F.* lvii. 10 Equite, in all things ..is a vertew pewre. Inequite, for wrong, no waie can make. **1682** SCARLETT *Exchanges* Pref. A ij, To discern between the justice and injustice, the equity and inequity of these Exchanges. **1876** BANCROFT *Hist. U.S.* VI. Index 614 Many of her statesmen confess its inequity and inexpediency. **1886** SYMONDS *Sidney* iii. 48 The inequity and the political imprudence of freeing great nobles from burdens.

b. with *pl.* An unfair or unjust matter or action.

1857 J. PULSFORD *Quiet Hours* i. §1 Thine iniquities are *in-equities.* **1884** H. SPENCER in *Contemp. Rev.* July 38 Our system of Equity, introduced..to make up for the short-comings of Common-law, or rectify its inequities.

ineˈquivalence. [f. IN-³ + EQUIVALENCE *sb.*] Lack of equivalence.

1879 A. MACFARLANE *Princ. Algebra of Logic* 53 (*heading*) The signs of inequivalence > and <.

ineˈquivalent, *a.* *rare.* [IN-³.] Not of equal value; unequalled in value, matchless.

1568 NORTH tr. *Gueuara's Diall. Pr.* (1619) 712/1 Beeing inequiualent in estate or degree to them. **1610** *Chester's Tri., Britain* 2 Whose boundlesse glories inequivalent Doe so reflect on Fames oriental wings. **1954** I. M. COPI *Symbolic Logic* v. 127 A similar pair of inequivalent propositions may be written as [etc.].

inequivalve (ɪnˈiːkwɪvælv), *a.* *Conch.* [f. INEQUI- + VALVE.] Having valves of unequal size.

1776 PENNANT *Zool.* IV. 108 *Anomia*, bivalve, inequivalve. **1851** RICHARDSON *Geol.* viii. 243 If one valve is larger than the other, it is said to be inequivalve. **1888** ROLLESTON & JACKSON *Anim. Life* 125 The valves of the shell are inequivalve in the *Ostreidae*, one valve being smaller than the other.

So **inˈequivalved, inˌequiˈvalvular** *a.* = prec.

1816 W. SMITH *Strata Ident.* 30 Six species of inequivalved Bivalves. **1835–6** TODD *Cycl. Anat.* I. 710/1 When one of the valves is larger than the other, it is of course inequivalved. **1828** WEBSTER, *Inequivalvular.*

†**ineˈquivocal**, *a.* *Obs. rare*⁻¹. [IN-³.] Not equivocal, unequivocal.

1779 *Hist. Eur.* in *Ann. Reg.* (1780) 146/2 A recent transaction from which the minister and he must from thence forward stand upon the most inequivocal terms.

ineradicable (ɪnɪˈrædɪkəb(ə)l), *a.* [IN-³.] Incapable of being eradicated or rooted out. Also *fig.*

1818 BYRON *Ch. Har.* IV. cxxvi, This ineradicable taint of sin. **1821** SHELLEY *Prometh. Unb.* I. 175 And in the corn.. Teemed ineradicable poisonous weeds. **1840** BARHAM *Ingol. Leg.*, *Spectre of Tapp.*, An ineradicable bloodstain on the oaken stair. **1882** FARRAR *Early Chr.* II. 340 But prejudice fortified by custom is almost ineradicable.

Hence **ineˈradicably** *adv.*, in an ineradicable manner.

1829 LANDOR *Imag. Conv.* Wks. 1846 II. 22/2 A winged word hath stuck ineradicably in a million hearts. **1867** MORLEY in *Fortn. Rev.* July 48 The lapse of a century and a half gave time for the spirit of independence to grow ineradicably into the national character.

inerasable (ɪnɪˈreɪsəb(ə)l, -ˈreɪz-), *a.* Also -ible. [IN-³.] That cannot be erased, expunged, or effaced. Hence **ineˈrasably (-ibly)** *adv.*

1811 SHELLEY *St. Irvyne* iv. Pr. Wks. 1888 I. 160 What man of honour needs a moment's rumination to discover what nature has so inerasibly implanted in his bosom—the sense of right and wrong? **1811** —— *Let.* 17 May (1964) I. 90 Nor do I think her Xtianity of the most inerasible nature. **1812** —— *Proposals* ibid. 280 Men whose names are inerasable from the records of Liberty. **1885** L. SAUNDERS *R. Boyle* ii. 34 An ink perfectly inerasable.

†**inergetic** (ɪnəˈdʒɛtɪk), *a. Obs. rare.* [f. IN-³ + (EN)ERGETIC.] = next.

1807 'CERVANTES HOGG' [E. S. Barrett] *Rising Sun* III. 49 His whole administration was weak, inergetic, and uninvigorating. **1852** TUPPER *Proverb. Philos.* 403 Until spirit be infused, the organism lieth inergetic.

†**inerˈgetical**, *a. Obs. rare.* [f. IN-³ + (EN)-ERGETICAL.] Without energy; inactive, sluggish.

a **1691** BOYLE *Hist. Air* xiii. (1692) 72 Those eminent Stars and Planets..are not to be considered by us as sluggish inergetical Bodies. **1706** PHILLIPS, *Inergetical Bodies or Particles*, such as are unactive and sluggish.

Hence †**inerˈgetically** *adv.*, *Obs.*

1727 BAILEY vol. II, *Inergetically*, sluggishly, unactively.

inerm (ɪˈnɜːm), *a.* *Bot.* [ad. L. *inerm-is* unarmed, f. *in-* (IN-³) + *arma* arms, armour. Cf. F. *inerme* (1798 in Hatz.-Darm.).] Destitute of prickles or thorns; unarmed.

1760 J. LEE *Introd. Bot.* III. v. (1765) 180 Leaves, in respect to their Margin, are..Inerm, unarmed or smooth:

which is opposed to Spinose. **1886** *Syd. Soc. Lex.*, *Inerm*, without spikes, prickles, or the like; unarmed.

inermous (ɪ'nɜːməs), *a.* *Bot.* [f. as prec. + -OUS.] = prec.

1828 in WEBSTER; and in recent Dicts.

inerrability (ɪnɛrə'bɪlɪtɪ). [f. next: see -ITY.] Freedom from liability to err; infallibility.

1627 H. BURTON *Baiting Pope's Bull* 84 You are perswaded of the Popes inerrability. **1790** SIBLY *Occult Sci.* (1792) I. 51 A standing memorial of the inerrability and truth of this science. **1829** *Sporting Mag.* XXIV. 105, I wish we could experience the inerrability of the press. **1878** GLADSTONE *Glean.* (1879) III. 260 If we are to believe in the inerrability of a person, or a body of persons.

inerrable (ɪn'ɛrəb(ə)l), *a.* [ad. L. (post-class.) *inerrābilis*, f. *in-* (IN-³) + *errāre* to err.]

Incapable of erring; not liable to err; exempt from the possibility of error; infallible, unerring.

1613 JACKSON *Creed* II. xxiv. §6, Such a facile, inerrable rule as the Papists haue framed for direction in points of faith. **1687** BURNET *Six Papers, Answ. New Test Ch. Eng. Loyalty* 34 We do not pretend that we are Inerrable in this Point. **1715** M. DAVIES *Athen. Brit.* I. 240 The Scripture-Letter, as the inerrable Standard of their Morals and Discipline. **1839** J. ROGERS *Antipopopr.* II. ii. §12. 142 No man or men on the globe compose a tribunal from whose inerrable decision we may not appeal. **1879** BARING-GOULD *Germany* II. 177 Catholic Christianity rested on an inerrable Church as the teacher of truth.

Hence **in'errableness** = INERRABILITY; **in'errably** *adv.*, in an inerrable manner, infallibly.

1620 BP. HALL *Hon. Mar. Clergy* Answ. Advt., The inerrablenesse of Councels, whether particular, confirmed by the pope, or generall. **1654** HAMMOND *Fundamentals* xii. §2 The infallibility, and inerrableness, which is assumed, and inclosed by the Romish church. **1672** PENN *Spirit Truth Vind.* 40 To this end God gives it to . . his Church, that in Doctrine, Life and Government she may inerrably be guided. **1877** PATMORE *Unknown Eros* (1890) I Many speak wisely, some inerrably.

inerrancy (ɪn'ɛrənsɪ). [f. as INERRANT *a.*: see -ANCY.] The quality or condition of being inerrant or unerring; freedom from error.

1818-34 HORNE *Introd. Crit. Stud. Script.* (ed. 7) II. II. 81 Absolute inerrancy is impracticable in any printed book. **1865** PUSEY *Eiren.* 326 The old Ultramontane doctrine of the inerrancy of the Pope, i.e. that of his preservation from error. **1880** *19th Cent.* Sept. 429 The superstition . . which magnifies the wisdom of our ancestors into inerrancy.

inerrant (ɪn'ɛrənt), *a.* [f. L. *inerrānt-em*, f. *in-* (IN-³) + *errānt-em*, pr. pple. of *errāre* to err or wander.]

†**1.** *Astron.* Of a star: Fixed; not 'wandering' as a planet. *Obs.*

1652 GAULE *Magastrom.* xxvi, The sunne . . after which the moon, and, beneath these, the rest, errant and inerrant.

2. That does not err; free from error; unerring.

1837 *Fraser's Mag.* XV. 368 The same inerrant pen winds up this . . in the emphatic terms, 'which is idolatry'. **1868** E. S. FFOULKES *Church's Creed or Crown's Creed?* 20 Whether absolutely inerrant or not in matters of faith.

inerratic (ɪnɛ'rætɪk), *a.* [IN-³.] Not erratic or wandering; fixed (as a star); following a fixed course.

1655 STANLEY *Hist. Philos.* I. (1701) 11/2 He fixed a great company of inerratick Stars. **1793** T. TAYLOR tr. *Sallust*, etc. vii. 34 The inerratic sphere commences its motion from the east. **1797** *Monthly Mag.* III. 511 The inerratic circle . . comprehends the seven spheres in which the stars are placed. **1822** T. TAYLOR *Apuleius* 334 An inerratic course.

†**in'erring**, *a.* *Obs.* *rare*⁻¹. [IN-³.] = UNERRING. So †**in'erringly** *adv.*, unerringly.

1645 HOWELL *Twelve Treat.* (1661) 328 They think they have an inerring spirit, and that their Diall must needs go tru, howsoever the Sun goes. **1755** JOHNSON, *Inerringly*. [J. quotes Glanvill (*Sceps. Sci.* vii. 34), 'that matter should frame itself so inerringly', but in the first edition (1661, v. 45) the word is 'absolutely', and in the 1665 ed. 'unerringly'.]

inerroneous (ɪnɛ'rəʊniːəs), *a.* *rare*. [IN-³.] Not erroneous, without error or mistake.

1880 R. G. WHITE *Every-Day Eng.* 127 There are many thoughtful, although not inerroneous students of the subject.

inert (ɪ'nɜːt), *a.* [ad. L. *inert-em* unskilled, inactive, sluggish, f. *in-* (IN-³) + *art-em* ART: cf. F. *inerte* (16th c. in Hatz.-Darm.).]

1. a. Of matter and material things: Having no inherent power of action, motion, or resistance; inactive, inanimate; having the property of INERTIA.

1647 H. MORE *Immort. Soul* I. iv. vii. 104 Poore naked substance . . dull, slight, Inert, unactive. **1710** BERKELEY *Princ. Hum. Knowl.* §69 Matter is said to be passive and inert, and so cannot be an agent or efficient cause. **1774** GOLDSM. *Nat. Hist.* (1776) VIII. 199 An opinion, that all nature was animated, that . . even the most inert mass of matter, was endued with life and sensation. **1830** HERSCHEL *Stud. Nat. Phil.* §234 To say that matter is inert, or has *inertia*, . . is only to say that the cause is expended in producing its effect. **1864** BOWEN *Logic* vii. 211 If matter is essentially inert, every change in it must be produced by mind.

fig. **1820** HAZLITT *Lect. Dram. Lit.* 15 The inert mass of accumulated prejudices. **1857** BUCKLE *Civiliz.* I. vii. 307 Knowledge is not an inert and passive principle, which comes to us, whether we will or no.

b. Without active chemical, physiological, or other properties; neutral.

1800 *Med. Jrnl.* III. 432 Fumigations may . . be serviceable in rendering contagious matter inert. **1850** DAUBENY *Atom. Th.* ii. (ed. 2) 54 One of them, for instance, might possess acid properties, the other be tasteless and inert. **1864** H. SPENCER *Biol.* I. 4 Carbon . . is totally inert at ordinary heats. **1879** *Cassell's Techn. Educ.* III. 1 The collodion film is inert, and plays no actual part in the production of a picture.

c. ***inert gas***: (*a*) As an ordinary use of the adj. with *gas*: any gas that is (relatively) inert. (*b*) Usu. as (***the***) ***inert gases*** (now apprehended as a special collocation, analogous to the terms *alkaline earths* and *rare earths*): any of the elements of group 0 of the periodic table, viz. helium, neon, argon, krypton, xenon, and radon, all of which are colourless, odourless, and tasteless gases which were formerly thought to be completely unreactive chemically, forming no compounds (though compounds of some of the gases are now known). Cf. *noble gas*.

(*a*) **1885** W. MACGREGOR *Gas Engines* v. 127 Nitrogen retards the combustion of hydrogen and that of carbonic oxide... The inert gas at the same time lowers the temperature of combustion. **1911** *Encycl. Brit.* XIX. 715/1 Nitrogen is a very inert gas: it will neither burn nor support the combustion of ordinary combustibles. **1966** *McGraw-Hill Encycl. Sci. & Technol.* V. 553/2 The gas contains about 27% carbon monoxide and over 70% of inert gases (CO_2 and N_2), giving it the lowest heating value . . of any of the commercially used fuel gases. **1973** *Sci. Amer.* Dec. 22/3 The flywheel and the generator-motor would operate in an atmosphere of inert gas (hydrogen or helium).

(*b*) [**1898** W. CROOKES in *Proc. R. Soc.* LXIII. 411 Professor Ramsay and Mr. Travers have discovered two other inert gases accompanying argon in the atmosphere. These are called Neon and Metargon.] **1902** G. S. NEWTH *Text-bk. Inorg. Chem.* (ed. 9) II. iv. 232 This property of nitrogen of uniting directly with magnesium was utilised in effecting the separation of the nitrogen of the air from the small quantities of argon and other 'inert gases' contained in the atmosphere. **1927** J. W. MELLOR *Comprehensive Treat. Inorg. & Theoret. Chem.* VII. xlviii. 906 The five gases—helium, neon, argon, krypton, and xenon—are colourless, and without odour. They are chemically indifferent and are hence called the inert gases or the rare gases, or the noble gases of the atm. **1939** H. J. REICH *Theory & Applications Electron Tubes* xi. 396 An external electrode may also be used to initiate breakdown of a mercury pool tube containing a small amount of inert gas. **1950** N. V. SIDGWICK *Chem. Elements* I. 10 Apart from the molecular ions occurring in the gas, there is in no case satisfactory evidence of the existence of chemical compounds of any of the inert gases. **1961** G. A. COOK *Argon, Helium & Rare Gases* I. i. 1 Unlike the atoms of oxygen, nitrogen, and some of the common gaseous elements, the atoms of the inert gases do not combine to form stable diatomic molecules. **1962** *Proc. Chem. Soc.* 218/2 Although inert-gas clathrates have been described, this compound [*sc.* xenon hexafluoroplatinate (v), $Xe^{+}[PtF_6]^{-}$] is believed to be the first xenon charge-transfer compound which is stable at room temperatures.

2. Of persons, animals, and (*transf.*) moving things: Inactive, sluggish, slow, not inclined for or capable of action. Also of mental faculties.

1774 BURKE *Corr.* (1844) I. 479 He is of that inert and undecided temper, that I fear he will not prevail on himself to pursue his point with vigour. **1809** W. IRVING *Knickerb.* (1861) 151 He was, in fact, . . neither tranquil and inert . . nor restless and fidgetting. **1834** MRS. SOMERVILLE *Connect. Phys. Sc.* xxvi. (1849) 284 In some places the subterraneous fires are in the highest state of activity, in some they are inert. **1849** BRIGHT *Sp. Ireland* 2 Apr. (1876) 171 He is rather timid as a Minister and inert as a statesman. **1851** CARPENTER *Man. Phys.* (ed. 2) 334 It contains sufficient oxygen to stimulate the nervous and muscular systems of these comparatively inert animals. **1855** H. SPENCER *Princ. Psychol.* (1872) I. I. i. 5 As we ascend from creatures that are inert to creatures that are vivacious. **1859** DICKENS *Lett.* 19 Oct. (1880) II. 104 The deadest and most utterly inert little town in the British dominions.

‖**inertia** (ɪ'nɜːʃɪə). [The L., = want of art or skill, unskilfulness; inactivity, f. *iners*, *inert-em* INERT. The L. term was introduced into Physics by Kepler.]

1. a. *Physics.* That property of matter by virtue of which it continues in its existing state, whether of rest or of uniform motion in a straight line, unless that state is altered by an external force. Originally used as L., and also called *vis inertiæ* (force of inertia).

centre of inertia, moment of inertia, product of inertia: see CENTRE, MOMENT, PRODUCT.

[**1687** NEWTON *Principia* Def. III, Materiæ vis insita est potentia resistendi . . neque differt quicquam ab inertia Massæ. **1706** PHILLIPS (ed. Kersey) *Vis insita Materiæ* or *Vis Inertiæ*, is the bare Power of Resistance only, by which every Body . . endeavours to continue in that State in which it is, either of Rest or Motion.]

1713 DERHAM *Phys.-Theol.* I. v. 33 The cause of the resistance of all Fluids is partly from the Friction of the parts of the Fluid, partly from the Inertia thereof. **1756** BLAKE in *Phil. Trans.* LI. 2 By the principles of Mechanics, the Inertia of any bodies revolving about a Center is as the quantities of matter into the squares of the Brachia. **1803** J. WOOD *Princ. Mech.* i. 8 Inactivity may be considered . . as that quality by which it resists any such change. In this . . sense it is usually called the *force of inactivity*, the *inertia*, or the *vis inertiæ*. **1879** THOMSON & TAIT *Nat. Phil.* I. I. §216 The Inertia of matter is proportional to the quantity of matter in the body. **1882** MINCHIN *Unipl. Kinemat.* 107 The force of inertia of a moving particle, in any direction, is the product of its mass and its component of acceleration in that direction.

fig. **1843** J. MARTINEAU *Chr. Life* (1867) 106 The inertia of a massive civilization. **1851** GLADSTONE *Glean.* VI. xxxiv. 22 That bias . . in favour of trusting to the force of inertia, to the chapter of accidents.

b. ***electric inertia***, a term applied to the resistance offered by a circuit to sudden changes of current, due to self- or mutual induction, or both. ***magnetic inertia***, that property of a magnetic substance which prevents its being instantaneously magnetized or demagnetized.

1886 HEAVISIDE *Electr. Papers* II. 60 The inertia, in the electro-magnetic case, is that of the magnetic field, not of the electricity. **1892** [see INDUCTION 10].

c. *Photogr.* The exposure corresponding to the inertia point, from which the Hurter and Driffield speed of an emulsion may be calculated.

c **1886** F. HURTER in W. B. Ferguson *Photogr. Res. Hurter & Driffield* (1920) 12 Supposing that a source of diffuse white light of intensity one acting directly upon a plate needed a time *t* to so far alter a bromide of silver gelatine film on that plate that an impenetrable black deposit of silver was caused upon it on development... That time *t* . . measures the inertia of the plate. **1888** HURTER & DRIFFIELD *Brit. Pat.* 5545, Upon one of the fixed pair of scales . . we mark what we call and hereinafter define as the 'inertia' or slowness of the plate. **1899** C. F. TOWNSEND *Chem. for Photographers* (ed. 2) iv. 73 Several of the dots are in a straight line; this is the period of correct exposure. The straight line is prolonged to meet the base line, and the number read off, which gives the 'inertia' of the plate. **1927** C. B. NEBLETTE *Photogr.* ix. 238 The inertia is an inverse measure of the speed of the plate: that is to say, a slow plate has a high inertia while a rapid plate has a low inertia. *Ibid.*, The precise significance of the inertia as a measure of speed is somewhat difficult to define. The exposure which it represents is not the 'threshold exposure' (the minimum exposure necessary to produce a measurable density) nor does it indicate the maximum [?*read* minimum] exposure which will give proper rendering of the gradations of the subject, but an exposure somewhere between these extremes. **1955** E. F. TEAL tr. *Lobel & Dubois's Sensitometry* 96 Characteristic curves are drawn for a range of development times using a developer containing no restraining bromide. The straight line portions of the curves intersect on the log exposure axis at *E*, called the inertia point. Distance *OE* is the inertia *i* and the H. & D. speed is defined as 34/*i*, *i* being measured in log candle-metre-seconds.

2. *transf.* Inactivity; disinclination to act or exert oneself; inertness, sloth, apathy.

1822-56 DE QUINCEY *Confess.* (1862) 212 Tranquillity that seemed no product of inertia. **1837** CARLYLE *Fr. Rev.* I. v. ii, By wise inertia, and wise cessation of inertia, great victory has been gained. **1868** M. PATTISON *Academ. Org.* v. 148 An aimless inertia, an Oriental lassitude of habit, are not seldom seen to be the consequence of high philosophical training.

3. Special Comb.: **inertia governor** *Engin.*, a governor which operates by virtue of both centrifugal force and inertia (1934 in Webster); **inertia point** *Photogr.*, the point in which the straight-line portion of the characteristic curve cuts the horizontal (log exposure) axis when produced; **inertia reel** *Motoring*, a reel which enables a safety belt looped around it to be self-adjusting, esp. in ***inertia reel*** (***safety***) ***belt***; also the belt served by the reel; **inertia selling**, the supply of goods to persons who have not requested them, in the hope that the recipients will not take the necessary action to refuse them; **inertia starter** *Aeronaut.*, a starter (STARTER 7) which utilizes the energy stored in a flywheel.

1907 SHEPPARD & MEES *Investigations Theory Photogr. Process* II. vi. 221 The reciprocity failure may be considered to start at much the same point relatively to the *inertia points in the two plates. **1955** [see sense 1 c above]. **1957** K. M. HORNSBY *Sensitometry in Pract.* ii. 9 Hurter and Driffield regarded the inertia point as a fixed characteristic of the emulsion, and they used it as a criterion by which to specify the sensitivity of emulsions. This criterion is not now recognised as an unchangeable characteristic of the emulsion since . . fog will shift it to the left . . and a developer containing bromide does not give a constant inertia point for all development times. **1962** *Daily Tel.* 14 Aug. 16/6 The webbing runs off a small *inertia reel mounted at the foot of the door pillar. **1962** *B.S.I. News* Dec. 10/1 With the exception of inertia-reel models . . all the belts on display seemed to bear a Kite-mark label. **1968** *Economist* 6 July 49/2 Not so usual are inertia reel belts, the sort that are always held at the correct tension (many injuries to wearers of seat belts may arise because they were too loose). **1970** *Motoring Which?* Apr. 43/2 Daimler V-8 250 . . radio (with power operated aerial), automatic (inertia reel) safety belts; two years old. **1971** *Guardian* 25 Jan. 7/7 Spaghetti belts are replaced by inertia reels. **1968** *Times* 25 Apr. 14/3 Mrs. Butler . . asked if the President of the Board of Trade would take powers to control *inertia selling campaigns... She deplores this exploitation of inertia sales promotion... It will be difficult for people who are subjected to inertia selling. **1970** *Times* 13 Jan. 4/6 The Daily Mail reported on the banning . . of inertia selling advertisements... Inertia selling was the practice by which companies sent unsolicited goods, then pestered people for payment if they were not returned. **1970** *New Statesman* 13 Feb. 217/1 Now the Consumer Council is urging another dairy monopolist to abandon the practice of slipping homogenised milk, at 1d extra on to doorsteps . . , and billing for it if it is accepted. The company denies that this is inertia selling, but does it matter what you call it? **1972** *Guardian* 14 Oct. 1/4 Disreputable trading practices which victimize the

housewife. Among these are 'inertia selling' and 'pyramid selling'. **1929** *Flight* 7 Mar. 181 (*title*) *Inertia starters for aero engines. **1931** D. GARNETT *Grasshoppers Come* 89 He.. got the engine to fire with the inertia starter. **1958** *Times* 1 July p. iv/5 Simms Motor Units Ltd. have entered a Tensec inertia starter which enables Diesel engines to be started by hand with the minimum effort.

inertial (ɪˈnɜːʃ(ɪ)əl), *a.* [f. prec. + -AL^1.] **1. a.** Of, pertaining to, or of the nature of inertia.

1849 *Fraser's Mag.* XL. 609 A weight of inertial resistance.

b. Applied to a frame of reference in which Newton's first law of motion holds, i.e. a frame in which a body continues in a state of rest or of uniform motion in a straight line unless that state is altered by an external force.

1887 *Mind* Jan. 151 The subsidiary conceptions which he puts forward of 'the inertial system, the inertial scale, inertial rotation, and inertial rest'. **1914** L. SILBERSTEIN *Theory of Relativity* i. 5 The 'fixed-stars' system of reference... We will call [this]..following the modern habit, the inertial system, or sometimes, also, the Newtonian system of reference. **1918** A. S. EDDINGTON *Rep. Relativity Theory Gravitation* viii. 83 The measurement of the rotation of the earth detects something of the nature of a fundamental frame of reference—at least in the part of space accessible to observation. We shall call this the 'inertial frame'. **1924** *Physical Rev.* XXIII. 543 Lange and Mach have done much to spread a relative conception of motion. Lange introduced the name 'inertial system'. **1952** C. MØLLER *Theory of Relativity* ii. 36 The concept of simultaneity between two events in different space points consequently has an exact meaning only in relation to a given inertial system. **1953** E. T. WHITTAKER *Hist. Theories Aether & Electr.* II. v. 159 In Einstein's general theory, the velocity of light at any place has always the value *c* with respect to any inertial frame of reference for this neighbourhood. **1959** J. AHARONI *Special Theory Relativity* i. 3 Let *K* be an inertial frame of reference, then, according to the principle of relativity, in every set of axes *x′*, *y′*, *z′* which moves along a straight line and with constant velocity relative to *K* it is equally possible to adjust the clocks as in *K*, and all the frames of reference so obtained are inertial and are completely equivalent to each other not only with respect to the law of inertia, but also with respect to any other law or physical relation. **1970** *Nature* 17 Oct. 273/1 The experimental observation, by Michelson and Morley and others, of the isotropic constant velocity of light in inertial frames.

2. Special collocations: ***inertial guidance***, (automatic) control of the course of a vehicle or vessel by a system employing the principle of inertial navigation; ***inertial mass***, mass as measured by the ratio of the force on a body to the resulting rate of change of its momentum; cf. *gravitational mass*; ***inertial navigation***, navigation in which the course of a vehicle or vessel is calculated automatically by a computer, without the need for external observations or equipment, from its acceleration at each successive moment, this being measured by accelerometers whose orientation is gyroscopically controlled; ***inertial system***, (*a*) (see sense b above); (*b*) a system for carrying out inertial guidance.

1955 *Aviation Age* Jan. 28 (*heading*) Dependable *inertial guidance systems can be found. **1956** *Time* 30 Jan. 40/1 One [guiding system]..is 'inertial guidance'. Its heart is a subtle instrument that senses every force that acts on the flying missile... This information goes to a computer. **1958** *Economist* 16 Aug. 521/1 Navigation under the ice requires a further modern development—inertial guidance to replace conventional types of navigational aid which become unreliable near the pole or under water. **1962** F. I. ORDWAY et al. *Basic Astronautics* ix. 383 The heart of the inertial guidance system is the stabilized platform with its gyroscopes and accelerometers. **1920** R. W. LAWSON tr. *Einstein's Relativity* xix. 65 If now, as we find from experience, the acceleration is to be independent of the nature and condition of the body and always the same for a given gravitational field, then the ratio of the gravitational to the *inertial mass must likewise be the same for all bodies. **1955** Inertial mass [see *gravitational mass*]. **1954** *Aviation Age* Sept. 34/2 The idea of 'absolute' guidance—which evolves rather naturally from advanced work in *inertial navigation—is startlingly promising. **1957** *Sci. News Let.* 27 Apr. 259/1 Inertial navigation is of particular importance to the military because it is jam-proof. **1969** *New Scientist* 28 Aug. 418/2 Inertial navigation systems..depend..on the fact that an acceleration integrated twice, gives distance run and therefore position. **1952** K. W. GATLAND *Development of Guided Missile* iii. 56 Attempts are being made to develop the *inertial system, e.g., the technique used in the A-4 rocket. **1962** F. I. ORDWAY et al. *Basic Astronautics* ix. 385 A possible solution to the problem of overcoming accumulated error over long flight times is an inertial system supervised by a continuous series of fixes on celestial bodies. **1970** *New Scientist* 1 Jan. 22/2 The inertial system, already tested by BOAC during some 500 hours of flying, has been working *en route* with an average error of only one nautical mile an hour.

inertialess (ɪˈnɜːʃ(ɪ)əlɪs), *a.* [f. INERTIA + -LESS.] Having no inertia; responding instantaneously to any change in the forces acting on it.

1927 *Jrnl. Franklin Inst.* CCIV. 592 This correction.. causes the servo-mechanism to deliver the position which an ideal inertialess watthour meter would have. **1933** [see ICONOSCOPE 2]. **1937** *Discovery* Nov. 329/1 These beams of inertialess particles are regulated in large vacuum tubes. **1961** G. MILLERSON *Technique Television Production* ii. 19 A small gun in the camera-tube generates a continuous beam of electrical particles (electrons). This fine inertialess 'pointer' explores the charge pattern on the camera-tube screen. **1971** *Physics Bull.* July 402/1 Amongst potential advantages of laser machining are the following: (1) Light is inertialess; hence high 'tool' velocities with very rapid stopping and starting becomes [*sic*] possible.

inertially (ɪˈnɜːʃ(ɪ)əlɪ), *adv.* [f. INERTIAL *a.* + -LY^2.] By means of or as a result of inertia or inertial forces.

1957 *Astronautics* Dec. 27/1 (*title*) Servo considerations in an inertially stabilized reference system utilizing air-bearing gyros. **1971** *Sci. Amer.* June 21/1 Energy-releasing fusion reactions..can be initiated and to some extent controlled within an 'inertially confined' plasma. **1971** *Ibid.* Dec. 57/1 The catalyst is inertially removed from the product vapors in a cyclone separator.

inertion (ɪˈnɜːʃən). [irreg. f. INERT, perh. on analogy of *exert, exertion*.] Inert condition; inertness; inactivity; sloth.

1756 P. BROWNE *Jamaica* 121 Weaknesses of the stomach and viscera proceeding from cold or inertion. **1798** WEBBE in Owen *Mrq. Wellesley's Desp.* (1877) 5 Our inertion during the contest. **1814** D'ISRAELI *Quarrels Auth.* (1867) 220 Mortified with the inertion of public curiosity. **1837** SIR W. HAMILTON *Metaph.* xliv. (1870) II. 478 A natural proneness to inertion in man. **1889** BROWNING *Rephan* xxii, Tranquillity that lulls Not lashes inertion.

†**iˈnertious,** *a. Obs. rare*$^{-0}$. [f. L. *inertia* + -OUS.] Inert. Hence †**iˈnertiously** *adv.*, idly.

1611 SPEED *Hist. Gt. Brit.* VI. xiv. (1623) 90 His youth.. inertiously consumed in lasciviousness and penurie.

†**iˈnertitude.** *Obs. rare*$^{-0}$. [ad. med.L. *inertitūdo*, f. L. *inert-em* INERT.] = INERTNESS.

1656 BLOUNT *Glossogr.*, *Inertitude*, slothfulness, dulness, without Science or any craft. **1828** WEBSTER cites GOOD.

inertly (ɪˈnɜːtlɪ), *adv.* [f. INERT + -LY^2.] In an inert or inactive manner; inactively; idly.

1742 POPE *Dunc.* IV. 7 Ye Pow'rs!.. To whom Time bears me on his rapid wing, Suspend awhile your Force inertly strong, Then take at once the Poet and the Song. **1837** WHEWELL *Hist. Induct. Sc.* II. VI. i. §3 The more a heavy body recedes from the beginning, or approaches the end of violent motion, the slower and more inertly it goes. **1863** MRS. H. WOOD *Verner's Pride* I. xi. 114 Her small white hands rested inertly upon her pink dress.

inertness (ɪˈnɜːtnɪs). [f. as prec. + -NESS.] The quality or fact of being inert; inactivity; inactive or inoperative condition or character.

1661 GLANVILL *Van. Dogmat.* v. (R.), So long and deep a swoon as is absolute insensibility and inertnesse. **1710** BERKELEY *Princ. Hum. Knowl.* I. § 25 The very being of an idea implies passiveness and inertness in it. **1793** BURKE *Policy Allies* Wks. VII. 195 It is not humanity, but laziness and inertness of mind. **1836** J. M. GULLY *Magendie's Formul.* (ed. 2) 102 Perceiving this inertness, I myself took a teaspoonful of the tincture: nothing ensued upon it. **1855** H. SPENCER *Princ. Psychol.* (1872) I. I. v. 91 A greater inertness of the nerve-centres. *a* **1862** BUCKLE *Civiliz.* (1869) III. v. 394 The great enemy of Knowledge is not error, but inertness. **1878** HUXLEY *Physiogr.* 81 Nitrogen is remarkable for its inertness.

b. = INERTIA 1.

1768–74 TUCKER *Lt. Nat.* (1834) I. 305 Others..style the perseverance of body either in motion or rest a 'force or power of inertness'. **1830** HERSCHEL *Stud. Nat. Phil.* §234 Matter..presents us with two general qualities..activity and inertness.

†**iˈnerty.** *Obs. rare*$^{-0}$. [ad. L. INERTIA: cf. F. *inertie* (14th c. in Hatz.-Darm.).] = prec.

1623 COCKERAM, *Inertie*, slothfulnesse.

ineruˈbescent, *a. rare.* [IN-^{3}.] Unblushing, shameless.

1788 *New Lond. Mag.* 515 She..proved so inerubescent as to render..absurd all those exaggerations in her favour.

inerudite (ɪnˈɛruːdaɪt), *a.* [ad. L. *inērudīt-us*, f. *in-* (IN-^{3}) + *ērudīt-us* ERUDITE.] Not erudite; unlearned, uninstructed.

1801 LAMB *Ess., Curious Fragm.*, Verbose, inerudite, and not sufficiently abounding in authorities. **1816** BENTHAM *Chrestom.* App. §19 Wks. 1843 VIII. 124 The primæval or inerudite analysis:—a logical analysis performed upon physical wholes. **1889** LANCIANI *Anc. Rome* i. 4 The simple and inerudite imagination of the Middle Ages.

Hence **inˈeruditely** *adv.*, in an inerudite manner.

1851 SARA COLERIDGE *Mem. & Lett.* II. 421 It is a great pity that a good poem..should begin so carelessly and ineruditely.

†**ineruˈdition.** *Obs. rare*$^{-1}$. [ad. late L. *inerudītiōn-em* (Vulgate): see IN-^{3} and ERUDITION; cf. F. *inérudition* (Littré).] Want of erudition; unlearned condition.

1685 COTTON tr. *Montaigne* I. 241, I..being too conscious of my own inerudition to be able to instruct others.

inescapable (ɪnɪˈskeɪpəb(ə)l), *a.* [IN-^{3}.] That cannot be escaped or avoided; inevitable.

1792 BURNS *Let. to Cunningham* 10 Sept., An inescapable and inexorable hell, expanding its leviathan jaws for the vast residue of mortals! **1865** RUSKIN *Sesame* 113 To lead us.. with their winged power, and guide us, with their inescapable eyes. **1872** W. R. GREG *Enigmas Life* vi. 239 The inescapable conclusion from all this ratiocination. **1895** S. P. THOMPSON *Elem. Less. Electr.* p. ix, The views which the inescapable logic of facts drove Maxwell..to adopt.

absol. **1896** J. L. ALLEN *Kentucky Cardinal* 17 Is it this flight from the inescapable..that makes the singing of the redbird thoughtful and plaintive?

inescapably (ɪnɪˈskeɪpəblɪ), *adv.* [f. INESCAPABLE *a.* + -LY^2.] Inevitably; undeniably. Also **inescapaˈbility**, inevitability, undeniableness.

1881 *Academy* 24 Dec. 468/2 The single word 'inescapably' (i.e., inevitably)..has crept in we know not how. **1945** *Mind* LIV. 210 Thus the inescapability of some sort of realism is proved once again! **1963** *Times* 24 May 13/7 The very clarity and inescapability of the story which the landscape tells has helped to create the beginnings of a will to remedy these evils.

†**iˈnescate,** *v. Obs.* [f. ppl. stem of L. *inescā-re* to allure with bait, f. *in-* (IN-^{2}) + *esca* food, bait.] *trans.* To allure with or as with a bait; to entice.

1602 F. HERING *Anatomyes* 15 Thus they inescate and circumvent poore silly Soules. **1628** PRYNNE *Love-lockes* 2 A Baite..to Inescate, and Inamour others with vs. **1721** in BAILEY.

Hence †**iˈnescating** *ppl. a.*, enticing, alluring.

1633 PRYNNE *1st Pt. Histrio-M.* v. x. 289 All the inescating lust-inflaming solicitations..that either human pravity or Satans policie can invent.

†**ineˈscation.** *Obs.* [ad. late L. *inescātiōn-em* (Augustine), n. of action f. *inescā-re* to INESCATE.]

1. The action of attracting with a bait; alluring; an enticement or allurement.

1645 USSHER *Body Div.* (1647) 324 Inescation and enticing of the heart with delight. **1692** HALLYWELL *Excell. Mor. Virt.* 107 The Deceitful Allurements and Inescations of Flesh and Blood.

2. (See quots.)

1678 PHILLIPS (ed. 4), *Inescation*,..also a kind of transplantation. **1730–6** BAILEY (fol.), *Inescation* (with some pretenders to Physick), a kind of transplantation used in curing some diseases. It is done by impregnating a proper medium or vehicle with some of the mumia or vital spirit of the patient, and giving it to some animal to eat. It is pretended that the animal unites and assimilates that mumia with it self, imbibing its vicious qualities, by which means the person..is restored to health.

iˈnescatory, *a. rare*$^{-1}$. [f. ppl. stem of L. *inescā-re* (see INESCATE) + -ORY. Cf. med.L. *inescātorium* allurement.] Of or pertaining to baiting; adapted to bait.

1825–43 T. D. FOSBROOKE *Encycl. Antiq.* I. 390/1 Pollux mentions mouse-traps, inescatory traps, and others with snares.

inescaturation, erron. f. INEXSATURATION.

†**inesˈchewable,** *a. Obs.* [f. IN-^{3} + **eschewable* from ESCHEW *v.*] That cannot be eschewed, unavoidable.

1412–20 LYDG. *Chron. Troy* II. xix. (MS. Digby 230) lf. 91/1 Nor come so fer for to fecche ageyn The quene Eleyne ..With outen harmes now in eschewable.

inesculent (ɪnˈɛskjʊlənt), *a.* [IN-^{3}.] Not esculent, not used for food; inedible.

1831 T. L. PEACOCK *Crotchet Castle* ii. (1887) 29, I care not a rush (or any other aquatic and inesculent vegetable) who or what sucks up either the water or the infection.

inescutcheon (ɪnɪˈskʌtʃən). *Her.* Forms: see ESCUTCHEON. [f. IN *adv.* + ESCUTCHEON.] An escutcheon of pretence, or other small escutcheon, charged on a larger escutcheon; in the case of a baronet, an escutcheon borne in chief and charged with the red hand of Ulster. Cf. ESCUTCHEON 1 c.

1610 GUILLIM *Heraldry* II. vii. (1611) 65 The Inescocheon is an ordinarie formed of a threefold line, representing the shape of the escocheon..This Escocheon is sometimes tearmed an Escocheon of Pretence. **1612** in Selden *Titles Hon.* (1614) 358 The Baronets and their descendants shall and may beare either in a Canton in their Coat of Armes, or in an Inscutcheon at their election, the Armes of Vlster. **1614** CAMDEN *Rem.* 193 An Inschocheon of Armes may haue place amongst Augmentations, which is the Armes of a wife being an heire generall, inserted in the centre or middle of her Husbands Coates after he hath issue by her, to manifest the apparent right of her inheritance transmissible to his and her issue. **1725** BRADLEY *Fam. Dict.* s.v., He bears Ermine, an Inescutcheon. **1897** *Westm. Gaz.* 2 July 2/3 The Duke of Saxe-Coburg and Gotha..bears the Royal Arms of England (with the 'differences' as previously assigned to him in this country) on an inescutcheon upon the arms of Saxony.

inesite (ˈaɪnɪsaɪt). *Min.* [Named 1887, f. Gr. ἶνες fibres + -ITE.] Hydrous silicate of manganese and calcium, found in flesh-coloured fibrous masses.

1889 *Amer. Jrnl. Sc.* Ser. III. XXXVII. 500 *Inesite.*

†**inespecial,** obs. erroneous writing of the phrase *in especial*, especially: see ESPECIAL *a.* 4.

1568 GRAFTON *Chron.* II. 478 None of his counsail durst once speake unto him, and inespeciall the Ladie Michell his wife..was in great feare to be forsaken.

†**ineˈspecially,** *adv. Obs.* [f. phr. *in especial* (see prec.) + -LY^2; also found as two words *in especially*.] In an especial manner; especially.

1557 NORTH tr. *Gueuara's Diall Pr.* 92 a/1 The women, and in especially greate ladies, knew not [etc.]. **1563** GOLDING *Cæsar* (1565) 213 As..to torne hys jorney into Province, he thoght it behoved him not at the time so to do ..but inespecially for that he was sore afraid for Labienus.

1572 BOSSEWELL *Armorie* II. 25 b, Inespecially they must be so ordered at theire funerals. **1633** FORD *Love's Sacr.* I. ii, I vow myself your servant; only yours, inespecially yours.

in esse: see ESSE 1.

†**in'essence.** *Obs. rare*$^{-0}$. [IN-^{3}.]
1623 COCKERAM II, The not Being of a thing, *Inexistence, Inessence.*

†**in-essent,** *a. Obs. rare*$^{-1}$. [f. IN *adv.* + L. *essens, essent-em*, assumed pres. pple. of *esse* to be.] That is within.
1628 FELTHAM *Resolves* II. [I.] lxxxviii. 254 When the ayre is thus moued, it comes by degrees to the eare . . and [is] by that in-essent Ayre, carried to the Auditory nerue.

inessential (ɪnɪ'sɛnʃəl), *a.* (*sb.*) [IN-^{3}.]
A. *adj.* **1.** Devoid of essence; unsubstantial, immaterial.
1677 GALE *Crt. Gentiles* IV. 237 Of these Names [of the Deity] some are negative, signifying that Superessential Being: as, inessential, without time, independent. **1754** ARMSTRONG *Forced Marriage* V. xi, Are you not a ghost then? . . as inessential As the vain rainbow? **1813** SHELLEY *Q. Mab* VII. 71 His inessential figure cast no shade Upon the golden floor. **1818** —— *Rev. Islam* I. xxv, When life and thought Sprang forth, they burst the womb of inessential Nought.
2. Not essential, not of the essence of a thing; not necessary or indispensable to the constitution or existence of any thing.
1836 MACGILLIVRAY tr. *Humboldt's Trav.* xviii. 264 To consider man as inessential to the order of nature. **1849** RUSKIN *Sev. Lamps* ii. §19. 50 Ornament is an extravagant and inessential thing. **1886** SYMONDS *Renaiss. It., Cath. React.* (1898) VII. viii. 6 Details so insignificant as to be inessential.
B. *sb.* That which is inessential.
1778 BENTHAM *View Hard-Labour Bill* §45 Wks. 1843 IV. 24 An anxious attention to the inessentials and externals of religion. **1825** *Engl. Life* II. 265 She yields to me in what she terms *inessentials*. **1902** *Daily Chron.* 22 Apr. 3/3 If we ignore the inessentials of place, costume, speech and employment, friendship is the same to-day as it has been for a myriad of yesterdays. **1927** *Observer* 22 May 8 Stripped of its inessentials (which are too roughly handled) his story comes down to this [etc.]. **1960** J. BETJEMAN *Summoned by Bells* 96 All the inessentials of the Faith.

inessentiality (ɪnɪˌsɛnʃɪ'ælɪtɪ). [f. prec. + -ITY.] The quality of being inessential.
1890 J. H. STIRLING *Gifford Lect.* 306 Contingency in this sense is inessentiality, adventitiousness, extrinsicality.

inessive (ɪ'nɛsɪv), *a. Gram.* [irreg. f. L. *inesse* to be in or at (f. *in-* (IN-^{2}) + *esse* to be) + -IVE.] Denoting the place in which a thing is; locative.
1886 I. TAYLOR in *N. & Q.* 7th Ser. I. 422/2 The suffix *-itan* or *-etan* . . is the sign of the inessive or locative case in Basque. **1896** *Edin. Rev.* Jan. 84 [In Finnish] The student must remember the nominative, partitive, genitive, inessive . . and instructive.

†**inˌestima'bility.** *Obs. rare*$^{-1}$. [f. next + -ITY.] The quality or fact of being inestimable.
1678 CUDWORTH *Intell. Syst.* I. iv. §14. 241 Do you think that you are able to determine, what Length or Quantity of Time there hath been since Cities . . first began? . . there is a kind of Infinity and Inestimability of this time.

inestimable (ɪn'ɛstɪməb(ə)l), *a.* (*sb.*) [a. F. *inestimable* (14th c. in Hatz.-Darm.), ad. L. *inæstimābilis*, f. *in-* (IN-^{3}) + *æstimābilis* ESTIMABLE.]
1. Incapable of being estimated; that cannot be reckoned up or computed; too great, profound, or intense to be estimated.
c **1374** CHAUCER *Boeth.* v. pr. iii. 123 (Camb. MS.) The gerdon of þe dyuyne grace which þat is inestymable. þat is to seyn þat it is so gret þat it ne may nat ben ful ypreysyd. **1482** *Monk of Evesham* (Arb.) 40 On tothyr syde of the forseyde hye hylle was so grete and inestymable coolde that ys to seye of snowe and Hayle. **1555** EDEN *Decades* 253 With great ingeniousnesse and inestimable pacience these nations haue ouercome much greeter difficulties. **1601** R. JOHNSON *Kingd. & Commw.* 185 The number of oxen . . and prisoners was inestimable. **1722** DE FOE *Mem. Cavalier* (1840) 47 The wealth consumed was inestimable. **1875** JOWETT *Plato* (ed. 2) I. 81 A companion of inestimable value for young men at their age.
b. Too precious to be estimated; of surpassing value or excellence; priceless; invaluable.
1579 B. G[ARTER] (*title*) New Yeares Gifte, dedicated to the Pope's Holiness . . in recompence of divers singular and inestimable Reliques sent into England. **1594** SHAKS. *Rich. III*, I. iv. 27 Wedges of Gold, great Anchors, heapes of Pearle, Inestimable Stones, vnvalewed Iewels. **1635–56** COWLEY *Davideis* III. 1002 At last th' inestimable Hour was come, To lead his Conqu'ring Prey in Triumph home. **1771** BURKE *Prosecut. Libels* Wks. 1842 II. 492 This charter, the inestimable monument of English freedom. **1827** LYTTON *Pelham* xvi, He would have been inestimable as an undertaker. **1879** M. ARNOLD *Ess., Democr.* 37 Of one inestimable part of liberty, liberty of thought, the middle class has been the principal champion.
†**2.** quasi-*adv.* = INESTIMABLY. *Obs.*
c **1460** FORTESCUE *Abs. & Lim. Mon.* vii. (1885) 125 This charge woll all wey be grete, and so inestimable grete, þat [etc.]. **1581** W. STAFFORD *Exam. Compl.* ii. (1876) 67, I hearde wise men say, that the Queenes highnesse Father did winne inestimable great summes by the alteration of the Coyne.
3. [f. IN-^{3} + ESTIMABLE.] Unworthy of esteem. *rare.*
1811 *Henry & Isabella* II. 210 None but the inestimable would offer insolence.

B. as *sb.* A person of inestimable merit.
1727 FIELDING *Love in Sev. Masques* I. i. Wks. 1882 VIII. 12 But have I never seen this inestimable?
Hence **in'estimableness** (Bailey vol. II, 1727).

inestimably (ɪn'ɛstɪməblɪ), *adv.* [f. prec. + -LY^{2}.] In an inestimable manner or degree.
1526 *Pilgr. Perf.* (W. de W. 1531) 179 b, Whiche . . thus confoundeth yᵉ devyll . . & delyteth aungell & man inestimably. **1647** H. MORE *Song of Soul* III. iii. vii, So Paul and John that into Patmos went, Heard and saw things inestimably excellent. **1824** SCOTT *Fam. Lett.* 4 June II. 206 Poor Byron's loss will be inestimably felt by the Greeks. **1860** MILL *Repr. Govt.* (1865) 17/1 Their religion . . gave existence to an inestimably precious unorganized institution —the Order . . of Prophets.

†**i'nestimal,** *a. Obs. rare*$^{-1}$. = INESTIMABLE.
1678 *Yng. Man's Call.* 318 Consider the inestimal joys prepared for them, who . . have . . triumpht over all the powers of darkness, hell, death, and damnation.

†**in'estimate,** *a. Obs. rare*$^{-1}$. [f. IN-^{3} + ESTIMATE *pa. pple.*] = INESTIMABLE.
1614 ROWLANDS *Fooles Bolt* 34 No mins a hap inestimate, Thou hast wrought me a freemans life, By taking hence my sculding wife.

†**i'nestuate,** *v. Obs. rare*$^{-0}$. [f. ppl. stem of L. *inæstuā-re* to foam or boil in, f. *in-* (IN-^{2}) + *æstuā-re* to be hot, boil, f. *æstus* heat.]
1656 BLOUNT *Glossogr.*, *Inestuate*, to be very hot, to boil vehemently.

ineuch, ineugh, inewch, obs. Sc. ff. ENOUGH.

ineunt ('ɪnɪʌnt), *a.* and *sb.* [ad. L. *ineunt-em* entering, beginning, pres. pple. of *inī-re* to go in, enter, f. *in-* (IN-^{2}) + *ī-re* to go.]
A. *adj.* Entering.
1836–7 SIR W. HAMILTON *Metaph.* xli. II. 423 In place of two energies, an immanent and a transeunt, we may competently suppose three,—an ineunt, an immanent, and a transeunt . . The ineunt energy might be considered as an act of mind, directed upon objects in order to know them.
B. *sb.* A point of a curve. Also ***ineunt-point.***
1859 CAYLEY *6th Mem. Quantics* §185 Instead of the term point of a curve, it will be convenient to use the term 'ineunt' of the curve. The line through two consecutive ineunts of the curve is the tangent at the ineunt.

ineuphonious (ɪnju:'fəʊnɪəs), *a.* [f. IN-^{3} + EUPHONIOUS *a.*] Not euphonious.
1887 *Lancaster* (Pennsylvania) *Daily Examiner* 7 Apr., The name is too remote, too foreign and too ineuphonious. **1921** *Public Opinion* 15 July 62/3 Their own ineuphonious patois . . communicates its harshness to the voice itself. **1927** *Brit. Weekly* 14 July 337/3 In spite of the . . drawback of a somewhat formless, ineuphonious style.

ine'vadible, *a. rare*$^{-0}$. [f. IN-^{3} + *evadible*, EVADABLE.] = INEVASIBLE. Hence **ine'vadibly** *adv.*, in a way not to be evaded.
1842 DE QUINCEY *Philos. Herodotus* Wks. 1858 IX. 201 For us, who know its truth, and how inevadibly it must have haunted for months the Egyptians.

†**inevan'gelic,** *a. Obs. rare*$^{-0}$. [IN-^{3}.] Not evangelical; unevangelical. Hence †**inevan'gelicly** *adv.*, unevangelically.
1683 E. HOOKER *Pref. Pordage's Mystic Div.* 19 Superstitiously supercilious, immoraly obstreperous and most inevangelicly malevolous.

inevasible (ɪnɪ'veɪzɪb(ə)l), *a.* [IN-^{3}.] Not evasible; that cannot be evaded.
1846 WORCESTER cites *Eclectic Rev.* **1880** MRS. WHITNEY *Odd or Even?* xl. 49 There were absolute verities of life presented there that were tangible, inevasible.

inevictable (ɪnɪ'vɪktəb(ə)l), *a. rare.* [IN-^{3}.] That cannot be evicted. Hence **ine'victably** *adv.*
1895 W. STEVENS *Let.* 23 July (1967) 6 Some unnameable smathering of greasy fritters, . . and of course the inevictable applesauce. **1954** W. FAULKNER *Fable* (1955) 155 The scarlet-spurting stump inevictably aloft. *Ibid.* 166 The inevictable establishment in coeval space of the sum of his past.

inevidence (ɪn'ɛvɪdəns). Now *rare.* [IN-^{3}. Cf. mod.F. *inévidence* (Littré).] Lack of evidence; the fact of being inevident.
†**1.** Want of evidence or manifestation (*of* something). *Obs.*
a **1654** H. BINNING *Comm. Princ. Chr. Relig.* Wks. 1839 I. 69 It is not so much the inevidence of marks and fruits that makes them doubt. **1667** FLAVEL *Saint Indeed* (1754) 102 The hiding of God's face, the prevalency of corruption, and the inevidence of grace. **1698** NORRIS *Pract. Disc.* (1707) IV. 146 When Faith is said . . to be of inevident things, the Meaning is not of an absolute but of a Relative inevidence.
†**2.** Uncertainty. *Obs.*
1658 BP. REYNOLDS *Van. Creature* Wks. (1677) 6 He opposeth the life of God, to the vanity and uncertainty, the word is, to the Inevidence of Riches. *a* **1677** BARROW *Serm.* (1687) I. xxxi. 449 Charge them . . that they be not high-minded, nor trust in uncertain riches (ἐπὶ πλούτου ἀδηλότητι in the obscurity or inevidence of riches). [Cf. 1 Tim. vi. 17.]
3. The condition of not being evident or clearly discernible; want of clearness, obscurity. *rare.*
1671 FLAVEL *Fount. of Life* xxi. 63 If thou . . hast gone . . mourning and lamenting because of the Inevidence and Cloudiness of thy Interest in Him. **1681** —— *Meth. Grace* vii. 139 It may come to from the inevidence of the premises.

1817 COLERIDGE *Biog. Lit.* I. 269 *note*, This is clear by the inevidence of the converse.

inevident (ɪn'ɛvɪdənt), *a.* Now *rare.* [ad. late L. *inēvident-em* (Boeth.): see IN-^{3} and EVIDENT: cf. F. *inévident* (Littré).] Not evident, not manifest; lacking evidence; not clear or obvious, obscure.
1614 JACKSON *Creed* III. xxxii. Contn. 1st Bk., (*tr.* Valentia) Seeing aswell the diuine reuelations, as the Churches infallible proposall are obscure and ineuident [orig. *obscuræ et ineuidentes*]. *a* **1623** W. PEMBLE *Wks.* (1635) 94 Knowledge is an assent to things evident, Beliefe an assent to things inevident. *a* **1656** BP. HALL *Rem. Wks.* (1660) 267 Our Schoolmen make distinction of a certainty, evident, and inevident. *a* **1755** BP. CONYBEARE *Serm.* II. viii. (T.), An undoubting assent to those things which are of themselves inevident. *Mod. Newspaper*, A mysterious widening out and flow in the skirt, the cause whereof is beautifully inevident.

inevitability (ɪnˌɛvɪtə'bɪlɪtɪ). [f. next: see -ITY. Cf. mod.F. *inévitabilité.*] The quality of being inevitable; inevitableness. Also with *an* and *pl.* An instance of this.
1649 JER. TAYLOR *Gt. Exemp.* Ad §vi. ¶6 Ambition . . falls under the inevitability of such Accidents which either could not be foreseen or not prevented. **1675** WOODHEAD, etc. *Paraphr. Paul* 25 This inevitability of sinning. **1847** MRS. TROLLOPE *Three Cousins* (Railw. ed.) 47 By the help of that effectual mind-strengthener inevitability, the Bishop bore this 'contretems' rather better than his lady expected. **1871** R. H. HUTTON *Ess.* (1880) II. *Goethe* 25 He was already beginning to accommodate himself to all inevitabilities.

inevitable (ɪn'ɛvɪtəb(ə)l), *a.* (and *sb.*) [ad. L. *inēvītābilis* unavoidable, f. *in-* (IN-^{3}) + *ēvītābilis* EVITABLE, f. *ēvītāre* to avoid. Cf. F. *inévitable* (1549 in R. Estienne).] **a.** That cannot be avoided; not admitting of escape or evasion; unavoidable. In extended use: that cannot fail or is bound to occur, appear, be used, etc.; that is inherent (in) or naturally belongs *to* (see also quot. 1893).
c **1430** *Life St. Kath.* (1884) 52 My body whyche aftur þe ineuitable lawe of nature abydeth to be resolued in to deþ. *c* **1510** BARCLAY *Mirr. Gd. Manners* (1570) Div, What should he dread of deathe? it is ineuitable, The generall duetie and tribute of nature. **1606** SHAKS. *Ant. & Cl.* IV. xiv. 65 When I should see behinde me Th' ineuitable prosecution of disgrace and horror. **1676** W. ROW *Contn. Blair's Autobiog.* x. (1848) 212 There was an inevitable necessity laid upon them. **1750** GRAY *Elegy* 35 All . . Await alike th' inevitable hour. **1795** SOUTHEY *Joan of Arc* x. 508 [He] then beholds the inevitable shark Close on him open-mouthed. **1838** THIRLWALL *Greece* V. xl. 122 A battle became inevitable. **1860** TYNDALL *Glac.* I. ii. 10 The conclusion seems inevitable that the mountain is sinking by its own weight. **1879** F. W. FARRAR *Life St. Paul* Pref., The English version . . only requires the removal of errors which were inevitable to the age in which it was executed. **1893** *Funk's Stand. Dict.*, *Inevitable* . . jocularly, customary; usual; as, the *inevitable* row with the cabman; the *inevitable* hash for breakfast. **1932** *N. & Q.* 6 Feb. 107/1 Illustrations of French wit; . . of the 'inevitable' phrase, that gift to the world past all praise. **1932** H. READ in H. J. & H. Massingham *Great Victorians* 400 Patmore, at this stage of his inspiration, was no inevitable poet. **1974** *Daily Tel.* (Colour Suppl.) 4 Jan. 19/3 Walter Harris was awarded a light diet of prunes, apricots, grapefruit, broth, and the inevitable yoghurt.
b. *absol.* and as *sb.* ***the inevitable***, that which is inevitable, what cannot be avoided or escaped. Also (with *an* or *pl.*), an inevitable fact, event, truth, etc.; a person who, or thing which, is necessarily chosen or employed.
1850 CARLYLE *Latter-d. Pamph.* iv. 16 Our one interest in such Government is, that it would be kind enough to cease and go its ways, before the inevitable arrive. **1887** LOWELL *Democr.* 16 There is no good in arguing with the inevitable. **1888** W. WHITMAN in *Century Mag.* (1911) Dec. 255/1 Grant was one of the inevitables: he always arrived; he was as invincible as a law. **1901** *Westm. Gaz.* 24 Apr. 4/2 Here at length are some true inevitables. **1903** *Ibid.* 28 Aug. 3/2 After the Canadian Arch it was only an 'inevitable' that there should be a rush to the Dominion. **1927** *Observer* 17 July 9/4 A further twenty volumes of Everyman's Library. . . The 'Areopagitica' was another of the inevitables. **1936** L. C. DOUGLAS *White Banners* viii. 167 Paul greeted them amiably, exchanged the inevitables with the comely Mrs. Edmunds [etc.]. **1965** *Listener* 22 July 112/2 It seemed that it was only a matter of time before . . the United States would bow gracefully to the inevitable.

inevitableness (ɪn'ɛvɪtəblnɪs). [f. prec. + -NESS.] The quality or condition of being inevitable or unavoidable.
1626 DONNE *Serm.* lxxviii. 801 Whatsoever the Prophets say . . yet they meane not thee nor doe thou assume it in inevitablenesse upon thyselfe. **1695** H. DODWELL *Def. Vind. Deprived Bishops* 96 Why can they not see the inevitableness of the same Consequences? **1857** TOULMIN SMITH *Parish* 132 The certainty and inevitableness of the result are what is needed in order that the true sense of responsibility may exist. **1879** CHR. ROSSETTI *Seek & F.* 204 To express the inevitableness of human suffering.

inevitably (ɪn'ɛvɪtəblɪ), *adv.* [f. as prec. + -LY^{2}.] In an inevitable manner; unavoidably.
1447 BOKENHAM *Seyntys* (Roxb.) 33 Allas quoth he evene as a straunger . . Inevytabylly I must deyin here. **1594** HOOKER *Eccl. Pol.* Pref. ii. §6 All good men were now ineuitably certaine to be trampled under foot. **1667** MILTON *P.L.* VIII. 330 For know, The day thou eat'st thereof . . inevitably thou shalt dye; From that day mortal. **1862** H.

SPENCER *First Princ.* II. vii. §65 (1875) 196 Uniformity of law thus follows inevitably from the persistence of force.

inew, obs. Sc. form of ENOW pl. of *enough.*

†**inew**, var. of ENEW *v. Obs.* Hence †**i'newing** *vbl. sb.*, driving into water.
1596 HARINGTON *Metam. Ajax* (1814) 47 The fine phrase of inewing a woodcock.

†**inewch**, variant of *ineuch*, ENOUGH.

inexact (ɪnɛg'zækt), *a.* [IN-^{3}. Cf. F. *inexact* (1701 in Hatz.-Darm.).] Not exact; not strictly correct or precise; also, not strict or rigorous.
1828 WEBSTER, *Inexact*, not exact; not precisely correct or true. **1837** WHEWELL *Hist. Induct. Sc.* (1857) I. 83 This statement of the ancient writer is inexact. **1875** JOWETT *Plato* (ed. 2) III. 390 The enquiry was continued in..a very inexact manner. **1883** *Longm. Mag.* Apr. 620 The records of an anemometer on the top of a house are, from their very nature, inexact.
b. Of a person: Characterized by inexactness of knowledge, statement, etc.
1849 MACAULAY *Hist. Eng.* vii. II. 178 *note*, Burnet was far indeed from being the most inexact writer of his time. **1875** WHITNEY *Life Lang.* viii. 150 Inexact thinkers.

inexactitude (ɪnɛg'zæktɪtjuːd). [IN-^{3}. Cf. F. *inexactitude* (1701 in Hatz.-Darm.).] The quality or character of being inexact; want of exactitude, accuracy, or precision; inexactness. Also (with *pl.*), an instance of this; an inaccuracy.
1786 T. JEFFERSON *Writ.* (1859) II. 48 Further enquiry.. has satisfied me of the inexactitude of this information. **1865** CARLYLE *Fredk. Gt.* XVI. x. (1872) VI. 261 The King..never pardons any fault which tends to inexactitude in the Military Service. **1869** J. MARTINEAU *Ess.* II. 83 The author's inexactitude of thought and expression. **1875** POSTE *Gaius* III. (ed. 2) 481 This..must be regarded as an inexactitude of Ulpian. **1881** *Times* 11 Apr. 5/3 There may be inexactitudes of detail in the document.

ine'xactly, *adv.* [f. INEXACT + -LY^2.] In an inexact or inaccurate manner; not with perfect correctness.
1849 MACAULAY *Hist. Eng.* vii. (1858) II. 421 He [William of Orange] spoke and wrote French, English, and German, inelegantly, it is true, and inexactly, but fluently and intelligibly. **1875** WHITNEY *Life Lang.* 34 All through the life-long process of learning one's 'mother-tongue', one is liable to apprehend wrongly, and to reproduce inexactly.

inexactness (ɪnɛg'zæktnɪs). [f. as prec. + -NESS.] The quality of being inexact; want of precision; inaccuracy. Also with *an* and *pl.*: An instance of this.
1828 WEBSTER, *Inexactness*, incorrectness; want of precision. **1841** MYERS *Cath. Th.* III. §25. 92 An..instance of literal inexactness in the Gospel narratives. **1846** LANDOR *Imag. Conv.* Wks. I. 75/1 They do exclude wit, which sometimes shows inexactnesses where measurement would be tardy and incommodious. **1899** *Q. Rev.* Jan. 113 To sweep it [language] away because of its inadequacy and inexactness would be to sweep away the thoughts which it has more or less inadequately preserved.

inexaturable, -rate: see INEXSAT-.

†**in'excellence**. *Obs. rare*$^{-1}$. [IN-^{3}.] Want of excellence; the opposite of excellence. So †**in'excellency**.
1590 MARLOWE *2nd Pt. Tamburl.* V. iii, Blush, heaven, to lose the honour of thy name..And let no baseness in thy haughty breast Sustain a shame of such inexcellence [*v.r.* inexcellencie].

inexcitability (ɪnɛk,saɪtə'bɪlɪtɪ). *rare.* [f. next: see -ITY.] The quality of being unexcitable; constitutional calmness.
1864 in WEBSTER. **1876** T. HARDY *Ethelberta* xxviii. (1890) 201 She had set him down to be a man whose external inexcitability owed nothing to self-repression.

inexcitable (ɪnɛk'saɪtəb(ə)l), *a. rare.* [In sense 1 (stressed *i'nexcitable*), ad. L. *inexcitābilis*, f. *in-* (IN-^{3}) + *excitābilis*; in 2, f. IN-^{3} + EXCITABLE.]
†**1.** From which one cannot be roused. *Obs.* (Cf. Seneca *Epist.* lxxxiii. 13 *somnus inexcitabilis.*)
1616 CHAPMAN *Homer's Wks., Hymn Venus* N ij, What pleasure..letts Humor steepe Thy lidds, in this inexcitable sleepe? **1651** T. STANLEY *Poems, Moschus* 48 A long obscure inexcitable sleep.
2. Not excitable; not liable to excitement.
1828 in WEBSTER. **1846** LANDOR *Imag. Conv.* Wks. I. 68/1 Animosities [have grown] tame, inert, and inexcitable.

inex'cludible, *a. rare*$^{-1}$. [IN-^{3}.] That cannot be excluded.
1816 BENTHAM *Chrestom.* App. §12 Wks. 1843 VIII. 109 By the derivation, and thence by the inexcludible import, of the word *between.*

inexclusively (ɪnɛk'skluːsɪvlɪ), *adv.* [IN-^{3}.] Not exclusively; so as not to exclude others.
1789 BENTHAM *Princ. Legisl.* viii. §8 When an incident is directly intentional it may either be exclusively so or inexclusively. **1822** *New Monthly Mag.* IV. 314 Every theatre should possess inexclusively the right to represent the ancient dramatic authors.

†**inex'cogitable**, *a. Obs. rare*$^{-1}$. [ad. L. *inexcōgitābilis* incomprehensible, f. *in-* (IN-^{3}) + *excōgitābilis* EXCOGITABLE.] Incapable of being excogitated; inconceivable, incogitable.
1599 R. LINCHE *Fount. Anc. Fict.*, That vnspeakable wisdome and inexcogitable care. **1721** in BAILEY.

inexco'mmunicable, *a. rare.* [IN-^{3}.] That cannot be excommunicated.
1610 DONNE *Pseudo-Mart.* 39 So may they prodigally extend the name and priviledge of inexcommunicable Locusts to many in the other orders. **1617** COLLINS *Def. Bp. Ely* II. x. 531 A multitude is inexcommunicable.

†**inex'cult**, *a. Obs. rare*$^{-0}$. [ad. L. *inexcultus*, f. *in-* (IN-^{3}) + *excultus* cultivated, polished.]
1623 COCKERAM, *Inexcult*, rude, not polisht.

inex'cursive, *a. rare.* [IN-^{3}.] Not excursive; incapable of a wide range of flight.
1837 LANDOR *Pentameron* Wks. 1846 II. 353/2 Allegory had few attractions for me: believing it to be the delight, in general, of idle, frivolous, inexcursive minds.

inex,cusa'bility. *rare.* [f. next: see -ITY.] = INEXCUSABLENESS.
1888 R. F. LITTLEDALE in *Academy* 8 Dec. 368 In his eyes the worst of all the sins committed by the Leaguers in history, surpassing murder itself in criminality and inexcusability, was breaking up the Harkhallow hunt.

inexcusable (ɪnɛk'skjuːzəb(ə)l), *a.* [ad. L. *inexcūsābilis*, f. *in-* (IN-^{3}) + *excūsābilis* EXCUSABLE. Cf. F. *inexcusable* (1474 in Hatz.-Darm.).] Not excusable; incapable of being excused or justified.
a. Of persons.
1526 TINDALE *Rom.* ii. 1 Therfore arte thou inexcusable [Vulg. *inexcusabilis*; WYCLIF vnexcusable] o man. **1548** LD. SOMERSET *Epist. Scots* B j b, Nothyng should be left, of our part vnoffered, nothyng of your part vnrefused, whereby you might bee inexcusable. **1662** STILLINGFL. *Orig. Sacr.* III. i. §13 Those Philosophers who questioned the existence of a Deity..were not so inexcusable therein, as our Modern Atheists. **1775** BURKE *Sp. Concil. Amer.* Wks. III. 37, I should be inexcusable in coming after such a person with any detail.
b. Of conduct or actions.
1555 EDEN *Decades* Pref. (Arb.) 55 Howe muche I saye shall this sounde vnto owre reproche and inexcusable slothfulnesse and negligence. **1645** CHAS. I. in Ellis *Orig. Lett.* Ser. I. III. 313 The strange and most inexcusable deliverye upp of the Castle and Fort of Bristoll. **1712** STEELE *Spect.* No. 284 ⁋2 It is inexcusable in Men to come where they have no Business. **1829** LYTTON *Disowned* xliv, He made no reply to the inexcusable affront he had received. **1871** BLACKIE *Four Phases* I. 131 To condemn an honest thinker to death for simple heterodoxy..was altogether inexcusable.

inex'cusableness. [f. prec. + -NESS.] The quality of being inexcusable.
1612–15 BP. HALL *Contempl., O.T.* xx. i, If God had not meant the inexcusablenesse of Jehoram. **1684** J. GOODMAN *Old Relig.* (1848) 93 The inexcusableness of a total and final omission of it. *a* **1716** SOUTH *Serm.* (1737) II. vii. 263 Their inexcusableness is stated upon the supposition of this very thing; That they knew God, but for all that, did not glorify him as God.

inexcusably (ɪnɛk'skjuːzəblɪ), *adv.* [f. as prec. + -LY^2.] In an inexcusable or unjustifiable manner.
1587 HARMAR tr. *Beza's Serm.* 35 (T.) Behold here wherein Eve, and after her Adam, did fail inexcusably. **1638** CHILLINGW. *Relig. Prot.* I. iii. §3. 129 Who..is more inexcusably guilty, for the omission of any duty; they that either haue no meanes to doe it,..or they which professe to haue..means to doe it? **1785** SARAH FIELDING *Ophelia* II. vi, I should have thought myself inexcusably ungrateful. **1875** WHITNEY *Life Lang.* viii. 139 Here is an inexcusably gross misrepresentation.

inex'cussable, -ible, *a. rare*$^{-0}$. [f. IN-^{3} + EXCUSSABLE.] That cannot be shaken out or off. Hence **inex'cussably (-ibly)** *adv.*, in an inexcussable manner, so as not to be shaken out.
1816 T. L. PEACOCK *Headlong Hall* xi, Grasped..firmly and inexcussibly in the hands.

†**in'execrable**, *a. Obs. rare.* In quot. 1594, a misprint for *inexorable*; in quot. 1596, Folios 3 and 4, and some mod. edd. have *inexorable*; but some would retain *inexecrable* in the sense, or as an intensive, of EXECRABLE.
1594 CONSTABLE *Diana* VIII. i, Though shee protests the faithfullest severitie, inexecrable beautie is inflicting. **1596** SHAKS. *Merch. V.* IV. i. 128 O be thou damn'd, inexecrable dogge, And for thy life let iustice be accus'd.

inexecutable (ɪnɛk'sɛkjuːtəb(ə)l), *a.* [f. IN-^{3} + EXECUTABLE. Cf. F. *inexécutable* (a neologism in 1726, Hatz.-Darm.).] That cannot be executed.
1833 *Q. Rev.* XLIX. 555 They are the creatures of circumstances—the victims of their own inexecutable system of government. **1837** CARLYLE *Fr. Rev.* II. v. v, The King has accepted this Constitution..and executes it in the hope mainly that it will be found inexecutable. **1861** M. ARNOLD *Pop. Educ. France* 19 But the arbitrary and violent provisions of this edict made it inexecutable.

inexecution (ɪnɛksɪ'kjuːʃən). [IN-^{3}. Cf. F. *inexécution* (*c* 1600 in Hatz.-Darm.).] Lack or neglect of execution; the fact or condition of not being executed; non-execution, non-performance.
1681 NEVILE *Plato Rediv.* 161 Complaints of the Inexecution of the Law. **1720** OZELL *Vertot's Rom. Rep.* I. I. 55 If..any one of my Fellow-Citizens still condemns me for the Inexecution of my Word, I willingly put [etc.]. **1805** T. JEFFERSON *Writ.* (1830) IV. 35 His inexecution of orders baffled that effort. **1825** BENTHAM *Ration. Rew.* 188 Blackstone complains of their inexecution. He did not perceive that a law which is not executed is ridiculous.

inexertion (ɪnɛg'zɜːʃən). [IN-^{3}.] Want of exertion; failure to exert (oneself) or exercise (a power or faculty); inaction.
1794–6 E. DARWIN *Zoon.* (1801) IV. 360 A temporary inexertion of the brain. **1829** D. O'CONNELL in *Bentham's Wks.* (1843) XI. 21, I give myself six or seven weeks here of comparative mental inexertion. **1886** *Daily News* 13 Oct. 5/6 Those form two reasons for past inexertion against bad laws in agricultural Wales.

inex'halable, *a. rare*$^{-1}$. [IN-^{3}.] Not exhalable; that cannot be exhaled or evaporated.
1650 SIR T. BROWNE *Pseud. Ep.* III. xxviii. 151 A new laid egge..contains a greater stock of humid parts; which must be evaporated, before the heat can bring the inexhalable parts into consistence.

†**ine'xhaurible**, *a. Obs. rare*$^{-0}$. [f. IN-^{3} + L. *exhaurīre* to exhaust: see -IBLE.] = INEXHAUSTIBLE. So †**inexhauri'bility**.
1656 BLOUNT *Glossogr.*, *Inexhauribility*, a disability to draw out or empty. *Charleton.* **1658–78** PHILLIPS, *Inexhaustible*, or *Inexhaurible*, not to be drawn out or emptied ['*Inexhaurible*' omitted in 1696–1706].

†**ine'xhaust**, *a. Obs.* [ad. L. *inexhaustus*, f. *in-* (IN-^{3}) + *exhaustus* EXHAUST *ppl. a.*] = next.
1612 T. TAYLOR *Comm. Titus* iii. 4 God the inexhaust fountaine of all goodnes. **1615** SIR E. HOBY *Curry-combe* i. 68 It must be an inexhaust treasure indeed, that can stop a Popelings mouth. *a* **1665** GOODWIN *Filled w. the Spirit* (1867) 325 An inexhaust abyss of all excellency.

inexhausted (ɪnɛg'zɔːstɪd), *a.* [IN-^{3}.] Not exhausted; unexhausted.
1626 SCLATER *Comm. 2 Thess.* (1629) 91 That they stand so long inexhausted is..by the word of God supporting them. *a* **1652** J. SMITH *Sel. Disc.* v. 168 Emanations of that inexhausted light which is above. **1711** ADDISON *Spect.* No. 111 ⁋9 Inexhausted Sources of Perfection. **1846** TRENCH *Mirac.* xvi. (1862) 273 Himself..the inexhausted and inexhaustible source of all life.
Hence **ine'xhaustedly** *adv.*, without exhaustion.
1684 T. BURNET *Th. Earth* II. xi. 313 A third Glass that pierceth further still makes new discoveries of Stars; and so forwards indefinitely and inexhaustedly for any thing we know.

inexhaustibility (ɪnɛg,zɔːstɪ'bɪlɪtɪ). [f. next: see -ITY.] The quality of being inexhaustible; inexhaustibleness.
1834 *Fraser's Mag.* X. 437 Can a poet control the exhaustion of the heart better than through the inexhaustibility of the human fancy? **1865** CARLYLE *Fredk. Gt.* XVI. xi. (1872) VI. 272 A dexterity, felicity, inexhaustibility of laughing mockery and light banter.

inexhaustible (ɪnɛg'zɔːstɪb(ə)l), *a.* Also 8–9 -able. [IN-^{3}. Cf. OF. *inexhaustible* (15–16th c. in Godef.).] Not exhaustible.
1. Incapable of being exhausted, consumed, or spent; exhaustless.
a **1631** DONNE in *Select.* (1840) 65 A free pardon by the incorruptible..and inexhaustible blood of Christ Jesus. **1656** COWLEY *Misc.* Pref. *ad fin.*, Employing all her inexhaustible Riches of Wit and Eloquence. **1732** BERKELEY *Alciphr.* II. §14 If you had an inexhaustible fund of gold and silver. **1766** PENNANT *Zool.* (1768) I. Pref. 4 Our inexhaustable strata of coal. **1823** J. BADCOCK *Dom. Amusem.* 179 The most inexhaustable supply. **1873** HAMERTON *Intell. Life* XII. iii, A noble loch in its inexhaustible loveliness.
2. Of a receptacle or vessel: Incapable of being exhausted or emptied of contents.
inexhaustible bottle: a toy used by conjurors, and others; it consists of an opaque bottle containing within it generally five small phials, which communicate with the exterior by five small holes; each phial has also a small neck which passes up into the neck of the bottle; the phials are filled with different liquors, any of which may at will be allowed to pour out by opening the proper hole and letting in air.
1601 R. JOHNSON *Kingd. & Commw.* (1603) 40 The corne and provision of the inexhaustible garners of Apulia, Sicil, Sardinia. **1646** J. HALL *Horæ Vac.* 182 Rather free of their countenance then purse, which as it cannot be inexhaustible, so [etc.]. **1709** ADDISON *Tatler* No. 119 ⁋1 The present Age by the Invention of Glasses, opened a new and inexhaustible Magazine of Rarities.
3. Of a person or his attributes: Incapable of being exhausted or worn out in strength or vigour.
1762 GIBBON *Jrnl.* 23 Sept., He has inexhaustible spirits. **1842** LYTTON *Zanoni* 24 The inexhaustible Paisiello, charmed with her performance. **1848** A. B. LONGSTREET *Georgia Scenes* 207 They [mountaineers] are, however, almost inexhaustible by toil. **1870** DISRAELI *Lothair* liii. 288 Berwick is at Biarritz, an inexhaustible intriguer.

inexhaustibleness (ɪnɛg'zɔːstɪb(ə)lnɪs). [f. prec. + -NESS.] The quality of being inexhaustible.
1727 in BAILEY vol. II. **1827** HARE *Guesses* Ser. I. (1873) 175 A stream of love, the purity and inexhaustibleness of which betokened its heavenly origin. **1845** THORPE tr.

Lappenberg's Anglo-Sax. Kings II. 22 This inexhaustibleness of the enemy was particularly felt by England. **1862** BURTON *Bk. Hunter* (1863) 322 No one can grapple with history without feeling its inexhaustibleness.

ine'xhaustibly, *adv.* [f. as prec. + -LY^{2}.] In an inexhaustible manner or degree.

1694 F. BRAGGE *Disc. Parables* XIII. 427 A patron so inexhaustibly full. *a* **1716** SOUTH *Serm.* X. x. (R.), A cup never to be drank off, inexhaustibly full, inconceivably bitter. **1836** *Fraser's Mag.* XIV. 513 Iron, hemp, wood, are hers inexhaustibly.

inexhaustive (ɪnɛg'zɔːstɪv), *a.* [IN-^{3}.] Not exhaustive.

1. = INEXHAUSTIBLE; exhaustless.

1728-46 THOMSON *Spring* 478 Ah, where find words.. whose power..may perfume my lays With that fine oil, those aromatic gales, That inexhaustive flow continual round? **1799** SOUTHEY *Eng. Eclogues* Poet. Wks. III. 166 Contemplate..What inexhaustive springs of public wealth The vast design required. **1838** *Fraser's Mag.* XVIII. 525 The sea..nourishes an inexhaustive store of shells.

2. That does not exhaust the subject dealt with.

1865 *Pall Mall G.* 24 May 11 It [a book] is admittedly desultory and inexhaustive.

Hence **ine'xhaustively** *adv.*, in an inexhaustive manner; inexhaustibly; in a way that does not exhaust the matter.

1882 SEELEY *Nat. Relig.* 122 Occupation for the thought so inexhaustively interesting.

ine'xhaustless, *a.* [Erroneous formation, due to confusion of *inexhausted* (or *inexhaustible*) and *exhaustless.*] Unexhausted, exhaustless.

1739 G. OGLE *Gualtherus & Griselda* 60 Her Strength of Soul..a pure but in-exhaustless Store! **1805** MRS. BURKE *Secret of Cavern* II. 240 Possessing an inexhaustless source of entertainment within themselves. **1867** BAILEY *Univ. Hymn* 6 Who showers, On spiritual and natural world alike, His inexhaustless good.

inexigible (ɪn'ɛksɪdʒɪb(ə)l), *a.* [IN-^{3}. So mod.F. *inexigible.*] That cannot be exacted.

1818 BENTHAM *Ch. Eng.* 280 Turn now to those [duties] of imperfect obligation—the inexigible services so often distinguished and explained.

inexist (ˌɪnɛg'zɪst), *v.* [f. IN *adv.* + EXIST *v.*: see INEXISTENT *a.*^{1}] *intr.* To exist or have its being *in* something else. Hence **ine'xisting** *ppl. a.*, inexistent, inherent.

1678 CUDWORTH *Intell. Syst.* I. i. §31. 38 Nothing can be made ἐκ μηδενὸς ἐνυπάρχοντος ἢ προϋπάρχοντος, from nothing either inexisting or preexisting. *Ibid.* iv. §32. 500 How can that which is created coexist with the Ingenit God? how much less can it inexist in Him? **1768-74** TUCKER *Lt. Nat.* (1834) II. 189 The roundness inexists in the clay, and the thought of it inexists in my understanding. **1855** PUSEY *Doctr. Real Presence* Note S. 647 The inexisting Wisdom of God the Father. **1874** —— *Lent. Serm.* 427 See the Ever-blessed Trinity, Each Person..inexisting in the Other.

inexistence^{1} (ɪnɛg'zɪstəns). [f. IN-^{2} + EXISTENCE: see INEXISTENT *a.*^{1} and -ENCE.] The fact or condition of existing in something; inherence.

1635 PAGITT *Christianogr.* 134 By reason of their mutuall inexistence. **1654** WARREN *Unbelievers* 70 There was an inexistence, or being of all men in Adam. **1678** CUDWORTH *Intell. Syst.* I. iv. §36. 559 These three Hypostases or Persons..have a Mutual *Περιχώρησις* and *'Ενύπαρξις*, Inexistence, and Permeation of one another. **1684** BOYLE *Min. Waters* 52 He..may..be also inabled to discover the presence or inexistence of divers other Minerals. **1871** FRASER *Life Berkeley* 422 Separate inexistence in perception is one phase of the dualism of Berkeley.

ine'xistence^{2}. Now *rare.* [f. IN-^{3} + EXISTENCE: see INEXISTENT *a.*^{2} and -ENCE. In mod.F. *inexistence* (Littré).] The fact or condition of not existing; non-existence.

1623 COCKERAM II, The not Being of a thing, *Inexistence, Inessence.* **1648** BOYLE *Seraph. Love* (1660) 68 Our Inexistence..was a condition wherein nothing in us was capable of being a Motive of God's love. **1722** WOLLASTON *Relig. Nat.* iii. 48 *note,* That way, which some Sceptics take to prove the inexistence of truth. **1725** BROOME *On Odyss.* (J.), He calls up the heroes of former ages from a state of inexistence to adorn and diversify his poem. **1830** W. PHILLIPS *Mt. Sinai* II. 422 Till..Death drop stricken on his latest prey, To inexistence starved.

†**ine'xistency**^{1}. *Obs.* [f. IN-^{2} + EXISTENCY: see INEXISTENT *a.*^{1} and -ENCY.] = INEXISTENCE^{1}; also (with *pl.*), something inexistent or inherent (cf. EXISTENCY 2).

1674 BREVINT *Saul at Endor* 382 This Moral Capacity is grown into a true Natural Inexistency or Conjunction. **1768-74** TUCKER *Lt. Nat.* (1834) I. 346 The ancients held forms, ideas, and truths, to be eternal..in the Divine Mind ..They were not God, nor attributes, nor yet distinct substances, but inexistencies in Him: which *inexistency* was a very convenient term, implying something that was both a substance and not a substance, and so carrying the advantages of either.

†**inexistency**^{2}. *Obs.* [f. IN-^{3} + EXISTENCY: see INEXISTENT *a.*^{2} and -ENCY.] = INEXISTENCE^{2}.

1659 STANLEY *Hist. Philos.* XII. (1701) 485/2 The Dogmatists take away Hippocentaures, instancing them as examples of Inexistency.

inexistent (ˌɪnɛg'zɪstənt), *a.*^{1} Also 7 -ant. [ad. late L. *inexistent-em* (Boethius), f. *in-* (IN-^{2}) + *ex(s)istent-em* existing, EXISTENT.] Existing or having its being in something else; inherent.

1553 BALE *Gardiner's De vera Obed.* F ij a, Both scriptures and reasons do alow it [the supreme head of the Church], as a thing inexistent vnto the name of a prince and of a king. **1678** CUDWORTH *Intell. Syst.* I. i. §14. 15 [tr. Aristotle] Empedocles and Democritus..say that Generation is not the Production of any new Entity, but only the Secretion of what was before Inexistant. **1768-74** TUCKER *Lt. Nat.* (1834) II. 190 The ideas of pain, ignorance, doubt..too frequently inexistent in the minds of men.

ine'xistent, *a.*^{2} ?*Obs.* [IN-^{3}. Cf. F. *inexistant* (Littré), med. or mod.L. *inexistens.*] Not existing; having no existence; non-existent. (In quot. 1704, said of a state in which the person is as if non-existent.)

1646 SIR T. BROWNE *Pseud. Ep.* V. xx. 263 They took a liberty to compound and piece together creatures of allowable formes into mixtures inexistent. **1704** STEELE *Lying Lover* V. i, Oh sleep!..Still in thy downy Arms embrace my Friend, Nor loose him from his inexistent Trance.

inexorability (ɪnˌɛksərə'bɪlɪtɪ). [ad. L. *inexōrābilitās*: see next, and -ITY.] The quality or character of being inexorable; incapability of being prevailed upon by entreaty; relentless or rigid severity.

1606 DEKKER *Sev. Sinnes, Shaving* (Arb.) 41 Audacitie: Shifting: Inexorabilitie: and Disquietnesse of mind. **1748** RICHARDSON *Clarissa* (1811) VIII. xi. 58 Violence and fierce wrath, and inexorability. **1847** DISRAELI *Tancred* V. vi, What sublime inexorability in the law! **1874** BUSHNELL *Forgiven. & Law* ii. 141 The dread inexorabilities of justice.

inexorable (ɪn'ɛksərəb(ə)l), *a.* (*sb.*) [ad. L. *inexōrābilis*, f. *in-* (IN-^{3}) + *exōrābilis* that can be entreated, EXORABLE; perh. after F. *inexorable* (15-16th c. in Hatz.-Darm.).] Incapable of being persuaded or moved by entreaty; that cannot be prevailed upon to yield to request, esp. in the way of mercy or indulgence; not to be moved from one's purpose or determination; relentless, rigidly severe. **a.** Of persons, their actions or attributes.

1553 BRENDE *Q. Curtius* 192 (R.) To declare..howe inexorable hee was to such as hee wanne by force. **1592** SHAKS. *Rom. & Jul.* v. iii. 38 More inexorable farre, Then emptie Tygers, or the roaring Sea. **1633** MARMION *True Compan.* IV. v, Your excuse shall prevail; We are not inexorable upon extremity. **1697** DRYDEN *Virg. Georg.* III. 111 Death's inexorable Doom. **1725** DE FOE *Voy. round World* (1840) 231 The Spaniards are..cruel, inexorable, uncharitable, voracious. **1847** DISRAELI *Tancred* I. ii, Her mouth spoke inexorable resolution. **1876** J. PARKER *Paracl.* I. ii. 12 As if the uttermost farthing alone would mitigate the severity of the inexorable demand.

b. *fig.* Of things (chiefly personified).

1600 HOLLAND *Livy* 45 (R.) Lawes..are things deafe and inexorable. **1621** BURTON *Anat. Mel.* I. iv. I. (1651) 213 Lucian said of the gout, she was the queen of diseases, and inexorable. *a* **1720** SHEFFIELD (Dk. Buckhm.) *Wks.* (1753) II. 196 [Destiny] is inflexible and inexorable. **1858** CARLYLE *Fredk. Gt.* I. i. (1872) I. 13 How entirely inexorable is the nature of facts.

B. *sb.* A person who is inexorable.

1748 RICHARDSON *Clarissa* (1811) V. 257 The fair inexorable is actually gone to church with Mrs. Bevis. **1818** SYD. SMITH *Wks.* (1867) I. 238 Two..most beautiful women..who acted..the part of inexorables.

inexorableness. [f. prec. + -NESS.] The quality of being inexorable; inexorability.

1622 DONNE *Serm. 15 Sept.* (1622) 14 An inordinate apprehension of Gods anger, and his inaccessiblenesse, his inexorablenesse. **1659** *Gentl. Calling* v. §20 (1684) 421 There are many..that far outgo him [the Unjust Judge] in inexorableness of temper. **1675** BURTHOGGE *Causa Dei* 84 By reason of their Imbenignity, Inexorableness, and Inclemency.

inexorably (ɪn'ɛksərəblɪ), *adv.* [f. as prec. + -LY^{2}.] In an inexorable manner; so as not to be moved by entreaty; relentlessly.

1610 HEALEY *St. Aug. Citie of God* 178 Coriolanus warring inexorably against his countrey. **1726-46** THOMSON *Winter* 482 To virtue still inexorably firm. **1781** GIBBON *Decl. & F.* xxxviii. (1869) II. 399 Justice inexorably requires the death of a murderer. **1863** GEO. ELIOT *Romola* xvii, He saw her standing inexorably aloof from him.

†**ine'xorbitant,** *a. Obs. rare*$^{-1}$. [? f. IN-^{2} + EXORBITANT; or ? merely an error for the latter.]

1549 *Compl. Scot.* i. 21 The inexorbitant extorsions that it [Rome] committit on the vniuersal varld.

inexpansible (ɪnɛk'spænsɪb(ə)l), *a.* [IN-^{3}.] Not expansible; incapable of being expanded.

1878 MORLEY *Diderot* I. v. 174 Because that superstition was incorporated in a strong and inexpansible social structure.

inexpansive (ɪnɛk'spænsɪv), *a.* [IN-^{3}.] Not expansive.

186. O. W. HOLMES *Hunt after 'Captain'* in *Pages fr. Old Vol. Life* (1891) 48 General Wood still walked the corridors, inexpansive, with Fort McHenry on his shoulders.

inexpectable (ɪnɛk'spɛktəb(ə)l), *a. rare*$^{-1}$. [IN-^{3}.] Not to be expected.

1625 BP. HALL *Serm. Thanksgiving Mortality* Wks. 1837 V. 223 What loud cries did beat on all sides at the gates of heaven! and with what inexpectable, unconceivable mercy were they answered! **1721** in BAILEY.

inex'pectancy. [IN-^{3}.] Absence of expectancy; the condition of not being expectant.

1643 HERLE *Answ. Ferne* 31 Inexpectancy of reward in the discharge of that trust. **1885** E. F. BYRRNE *Entangled* II. II. i. 153 The empty inexpectancy of a vague moment.

inex'pectant, *a.* [IN-^{3}.] Not expectant; devoid of expectation.

1853 C. BRONTË *Villette* xiii, Loverless and inexpectant of love, I was as safe from spies in my heart-poverty, as the beggar from thieves in his destitution of purse. **1894** J. KNIGHT *Garrick* iii. 51 First appearance, before a thin, cold, inexpectant audience.

inexpec'tation. [IN-^{3}.] Absence of expectation; the fact of not expecting.

1627 FELTHAM *Resolves* I. [II.] v. (1628) 5 Three things are there which aggrauate a miserie and make an euill seeme greater then indeed it is: Inexpectation, Vnacquaintance, Want of Preparation. **1946** M. PEAKE *Titus Groan* 390 He had made so rapid and nimble a detour of the stone table that he surprised Steerpike, appearing with such inexpectation beneath the boy's nose.

†**inex'pected,** *a. Obs.* [IN-^{3}. Cf. L. *inexspectātus* in same sense.] Not expected; unexpected, unlooked-for.

a **1586** SIDNEY *Arcadia* IV. (1622) 432 When Pyrocles.. saw his friend Musidorus, with the noble Lady Pamela in that inexpected sort returned. **1628** BP. HALL *Righteous Mammon* Wks. 723 Inexpected fall of markets. **1651** HOWELL *Venice* 127 Which strange and inexpected supply ..bred an amazement.

Hence †**inex'pectedly** *adv.*, unexpectedly; †**inex'pectedness.**

1612 BP. HALL *Contempl., O.T.* XX. iv, How could it bee otherwise, when those great spirits of hers..finde themselves so inexpectedly suppressed. *Ibid.* XXI. vi, The inexpectednesse of pleasing objects makes men many times the more acceptable. **1645** —— *Remedy Discontents* 150 Comming inexpectedly to his Country-House. **1651** HOWELL *Venice* 125 The Turks, passing by the Galeasses, were inexpectedly torn by their great shot.

†**in'expedible,** *a. Obs. rare*$^{-0}$. [ad. late L. *inexpedībilis*, f. *in-* (IN-^{3}) + **expedībilis*, from *expedīre*: see EXPEDE.]

1721 BAILEY, *Inexpedible*, cumbersome, that one cannot rid himself of.

inexpedience (ɪnɛk'spiːdɪəns). Now *rare.* [See next and -ENCE.] = next.

1608 BP. HALL *Char. Virtues & V., Envious* 170 Not for any incommoditie or inexpedience. **1653** DICKSON *Psalms* Pref. to Vol. II. (1834) I. p. vii, The inexpedience of keeping me in bonds. **1831** SOUTHEY in *Q. Rev.* XLIV. 115 An argument to prove the inexpedience of the punishment.

inexpediency (ɪnɛk'spiːdɪənsɪ). [f. IN-^{3} + EXPEDIENCY; or f. INEXPEDIENT: see -ENCY.] The quality of being inexpedient; disadvantageousness, unadvisableness, impolicy.

1641 (*title*) Certaine Reasons to prove the Unlawfulnesse and Inexpediencie of all Diocesan Episcopacy. *a* **1663** SANDERSON (J.), It concerneth superiours to look well to the expediency and inexpediency of what they enjoin in indifferent things. **1785** PALEY *Mor. Philos.* VI. v. (1827) 110/1 It is not the rigour, but the inexpediency of laws and acts of authority, which makes them tyrannical. **1845** MCCULLOCH *Taxation* II. xii. (1852) 390 The inexpediency of attempting to raise any considerable revenue by means of income-taxes.

inexpedient (ɪnɛk'spiːdɪənt), *a.* [f. IN-^{3} + EXPEDIENT.] Not expedient; not advantageous, useful, or suitable in the circumstances; unprofitable, unadvisable, impolitic.

1608 BP. HALL *Char. Virtues & V., Flatterer* 117 If hee grant evill things inexpedient, or crimes errors, he hath yeelded much. *a* **1714** BURNET *Hist. Ref.* an. 1550 (R.), Hooper maintaining, that if it was not unlawful, yet it was highly inexpedient to use those ceremonies. *a* **1808** HURD *Serm.* Wks. VII. xlviii. (R.), They are indeed inexpedient, that is, unprofitable, unadvisable, improper in a great variety of respects. *a* **1832** BENTHAM *Offic. Aptit.* Wks. 1843 V. 297 Nothing could be more correctly lawful: but..few things would be more manifestly inexpedient. **1875** JOWETT *Plato* (ed. 2) I. 148 There are some things which may be inexpedient, and yet I call them good.

Hence **inex'pediently** *adv.*

1856 in WEBSTER.

†**inex'peditate,** *a. Obs. rare.* [IN-^{3}.] Not expeditated.

1644 COKE *On Litt.* IV. (1671) 298 *margin*, A man may claim to have dogs inexpeditate and hounds within the Forest.

inexpellable (ɪnɛk'spɛləb(ə)l), *a. rare.* [f. IN-^{3} + EXPELLABLE *a.*] Incapable of being expelled.

1911 BEERBOHM *Zuleika D.* iii. 33 He loved her, and he could not help seeing her... Inexpellable was her image.

inexpensive (ɪnɛk'spɛnsɪv), *a.* [IN-^{3}.]

1. Not expensive or costly; involving little expense; cheap.

1837 [implied in INEXPENSIVELY]. *a* **1846** *Eclectic Rev.* cited by WORCESTER. **1859** LANG *Wand. India* 185, I resolved upon taking a small bungalow for a short period, and furnishing it in a mild and inexpensive manner. **1896** W. G. WOOLCOMBE *Pract. Work Physics* III. Pref., The apparatus required is inexpensive.

2. Not given to expenditure; not extravagant. **1859** HAWTHORNE *Fr. & It. Jrnls.* II. 273 The Swiss people are frugal and inexpensive in their habits.

inex'pensively, *adv.* [f. prec. + -LY², or f. IN-³ + EXPENSIVELY.] In an inexpensive manner; without much expense; cheaply.

1837 R. B. EDE *Pract. Chem.* 46 The grand secret of Chemistry, to those who would pursue it inexpensively, is the art of working on a minute scale. **1871** TYNDALL *Fragm. Sc.* (1879) I. v. 173 Such water can be softened inexpensively.

inex'pensiveness. [f. as prec. + -NESS.] The quality of being inexpensive; cheapness.

1864 MISS YONGE *Trial* I. 156 Leonard treated its inexpensiveness as a personal matter. **1870** *Eng. Mech.* 18 Mar. 660/2 The advantage..is its simplicity and inexpensiveness.

inexperience (ɪnɛk'spɪərɪəns). [a. F. *inexpérience* (1460 in Godef. *Compl.*), ad. late L. *inexperientia* (Tertull.), f. *in-* (IN-³) + *experientia* EXPERIENCE.] Want of experience; the condition of not having been practically conversant with some department of study or work, or with affairs generally; the want of adequate knowledge or skill resulting from this.

1598 FLORIO, *Inesperientia*, inexperience, vnskilfulnes, vnacquaintance. **1609** DANIEL *Civ. Wars* Wks. (1717) 207 The Inexperience of his Years Made him less skill'd in what was to be done. **1693** DRYDEN *Juvenal* Ded. (1697) 51 Those Failings which are incident to Youth and Inexperience. **1769** *Junius Lett.* xxxv. 156 We..are ready to allow for your inexperience. **1827** LYTTON *Pelham* xlii, An authority to which nothing but the inexperience of the young could accede.

inexperienced (ɪnɛk'spɪərɪənst), *a.* [IN-³.] Not experienced; without experience; having no (or little) experience; lacking the knowledge or skill derived from experience. Const. *in*.

1626 GOUGE *Serm. Dign. Chivalry* §18 Such as for want of former exercising were altogether inexperienced. **1776–96** WITHERING *Brit. Plants* (ed. 3) I. 116 The inexperienced botanist is not likely to encounter them at the commencement of his progress. **1856** KANE *Arct. Expl.* I. xvi. 193 We were not inexperienced in sledging over the ice.

Hence †**inex'periencedness** *Obs. rare*, the state or quality of being inexperienced.

1725 BAILEY *Erasm. Colloq.* (1877) 318 (D.) The damsel has three things to plead in her excuse: the authority of her parents, the persuasion of her friends, and the inexperiencedness of her age.

†**inex'perient,** *a. Obs.* [ad. late L. *inexperiens* (Boethius), f. *in-* (IN-³) + *experiens* EXPERIENT.] Not having experience; = INEXPERIENCED.

1670 G. H. *Hist. Cardinals* III. II. 273 He had but two Nephews..who were young, and inexperient in all kind of Politicks.

inexperi'mental, *a. rare.* [IN-³.] Not founded on experiment.

1798 *Europ. Mag.* in *Spirit Pub. Jrnls.* (1799) II. 93 So wonderfully sagacious is crude and inexperimental theory.

†**inex'perimenting,** *a. Obs. rare.* [f. IN-³ + *experimenting*, pres. pple. of EXPERIMENT *v.* (Cf. F. *inexpérimenté* wanting experience.)] Not in the habit of making experiments; unenterprising.

1746 *Brit. Mag.* 98 The Ignorance, or unactive inexperimenting Spirit of our Manufacturers.

inexpert (ɪn'ɛkspɜːt, ɪnɛk'spɜːt), *a.* (*sb.*) [a. OF. *inexpert, -e* (14–16th c. in Godef.), ad. L. *inexpert-us* untried, unexperienced, f. *in-* (IN-³) + *expertus*: see EXPERT *a.*]

†**1.** Not having experience, without experience; inexperienced, unacquainted. Const. *in, of*. *Obs.*

c **1450** tr. *De Imitatione* III. viii. 74 þei þat biþ ȝit newe & inexperte in þe wey of god. **1526** TINDALE *Heb.* v. 13 Every man that is feed with mylke is inexpert in the worde of rightewesnes. *a* **1621** J. KING in Spurgeon *Treas. Dav.* Ps. xxx. 8 Utterly inexpert of the way into so far a country. **1697** *Col. Rec. Pennsylv.* I. 519 The best of us all being but inexpert in mainie things relating to those affairs. [**1862** LOWELL *Biglow P.* Ser. II. 54 Himself, haply, not inexpert of evil in this particular.]

2. Wanting the readiness, aptitude, or dexterity derived from experience; not expert; unskilled.

1597 A. M. tr. *Guillemeau's Fr. Chirurg.* 5/2 Although that theire Chyrurgian is wholy inexperte. **1612** T. TAYLOR *Comm. Titus* i. 6 They are not vnlike an inexpert musician. **1739** MELMOTH *Fitzosb. Lett.* (1763) 378 Inexpert in the management of this sort of contests. **1808** J. BARLOW *Columb.* VIII. 684 In counsel sage, nor inexpert in arms. **1871** CARLYLE in *Mrs. C.'s Lett.* II. 157 Workmen honest though inexpert.

B. *sb.* [mod., after EXPERT *sb.*] An inexpert or unskilled person; opposed to EXPERT *sb.*

1879 MᶜCARTHY *Own Times* II. xxi. 102 All these made on the mind of the ordinary inexpert a confused impression. **1883** *American* VI. 371 A test examination for experts, a competitive examination for inexperts.

Hence **in'expertly** *adv.*, in an inexpert way, unskilfully; **in'expertness**, unskilfulness, want of expertness or dexterity derived from practice.

1744 H. WALPOLE *Lett. H. Mann* (1834) I. xcv. 328 The French pursued them outsailed them and missed them by their own inexpertness. **1822–34** *Good's Study Med.* (ed. 4) III. 431 In attempting the recovery of those who have been hung, and particularly who have inexpertly hung themselves. **1897** *Atlantic Monthly* LXXIX. 126 Paddling inexpertly through a lake.

inexpertise (ɪnɛkspə'tiːz). [f. IN-³ + EXPERTISE.] Lack of expertise.

1926 *Chicago Even. Post* 12 Nov., It results in part from ignorance of foreign politics and international relations, and from inexpertise in discussing them. **1961** J. SHERWOOD *Half Hunter* vi. 74 The élite were performing their loops and spins in an atmosphere of solemnity and calm, oblivious of the revolving mass of inexpertise around them. **1963** *Times* 9 Mar. 11/3 If one grows impatient in performance, it is more often with vocal than compositorial inexpertise.

inexpiable (ɪn'ɛkspɪəb(ə)l), *a.* [ad. L. *inexpiābilis* inexpiable, implacable, f. *in-* (IN-³) + *expiābilis* EXPIABLE. Cf. F. *inexpiable* (15–16th c. in Godef. *Compl.*).]

1. Of an offence: That cannot be expiated or atoned for; of which the guilt cannot be done away.

1570 LEVINS *Manip.* 4/26 Inexpiable, *inexpiabilis*. **1609** HOLLAND *Amm. Marcell.* XXIX. i. 352 This was in him a fault inexpiable. **1655** STANLEY *Hist. Philos.* III. (1701) 93/2 Such as have used inexpiable deceit to wrong the publick. **1728** YOUNG *Love Fame* VI, Her lover must be sad to please her spleen; His mirth is an inexpiable sin. **1855** MILMAN *Lat. Chr.* XIV. ii. (1864) V. 54 One of the inexpiable offences of the Latin church.

2. Of a feeling, etc.: That cannot be appeased by expiation; implacable, irreconcilable. (Also *transf.* of an action.)

1598 FLORIO, *Inespiabile*, inexpiable,..vnmercifull, deadlie, marble-minded. **1600** HOLLAND *Livy* XXXIII. xlvii. 851 They continued an endlesse and inexpiable warre with him alone still. **1671** MILTON *Samson* 839 To raise in me inexpiable hate. **1792** BURKE *Corr.* (1844) III. 404 Against the nobility and gentry they have waged inexpiable war. **1878** BOSW. SMITH *Carthage* 44 The revolt of the outraged Libyan mercenaries..which is known in history by the name of the 'War without Truce' or the 'Inexpiable war'.

Hence **in'expiableness**, the quality of being inexpiable; **in'expiably** *adv.*, in an inexpiable manner or degree, unpardonably.

1650 R. HOLLINGWORTH *Exerc. Usurp. Powers* 36 The inexpiablenesse of his former facts. **1684** EARL ROSCOMMON *Ess. transl. Verse* Poems (1780) 48 Excursions are inexpiably bad, And 'tis much safer to leave out than add. **1816** SOUTHEY *Ess.* (1832) I. 357 This struggle so inexpiably and ineffaceably disgraceful for France. **1884** *Chr. World* 17 July 543/3 They were inexpiably wronged in the past.

inexpiate (ɪn'ɛkspɪət), *a.* [ad. late L. *inexpiāt-us* (Augustine), f. *in-* (IN-³) + *expiātus*, pa. pple. of *expiāre* to EXPIATE.]

1. Not expiated or atoned for.

1819 *Blackw. Mag.* IV. 733 That mantle of inexpiate dishonour. **1876** SWINBURNE *Erechtheus* 1275 The unclean soul's inexpiate hunted head.

†2. Unappeased: cf. prec. 2. *Obs.*

c **1611** CHAPMAN *Iliad* IX. 493 To rest inexpiate were much too rude a part.

in'expiated, *a. rare.* [IN-³.] = prec. 1.

1836 LYTTON *Athens* (1837) I. 457 The inexpiated sacrilege made a duty of revenge.

inexplainable (ɪnɛk'spleɪnəb(ə)l), *a. rare.* [IN-³.] That cannot be explained; inexplicable.

1623 COCKERAM, *Inexplanable*, that cannot be explaned. **1861** MRS. OLIPHANT *Last Mortimers* VI. xv. (1862) 254 It was a dread, inexplainable pause. **1899** *Daily News* 3 July 7/2 One very curious phenomenon recorded by all the diagrams..is at present wholly inexplainable.

†**i'nexpleble,** *a. Obs.* Also erron. **inexpleable.** [ad. L. *inexplēbilis*, f. *in-* (IN-³) + **explēbilis*, f. *explēre* to fill up: see EXPLETE *v.*] That cannot be filled or satisfied; insatiable.

1569 NEWTON *Cicero's Olde Age* 16 b, Which with such earnest sedulitie and inexpleble greediness I learned or rather snatched unto me. **1656** STANLEY *Hist. Philos.* VIII. (1701) 322/2 An inexpleble desire of that which we want. **1788** D. GILSON *Serm.* 507 That inexpleable desire after what is good and lovely.

Hence †**i'nexplebly** (erron. **inexpleably**) [cf. late L. *inexplēbiliter* (Prosper)], insatiably.

1615 G. SANDYS *Trav.* 9 What were these Harpyes, but flatterers, delators, and the inexpleably covetous?

inexplicability (ɪnˌɛksplɪkə'bɪlɪtɪ). [f. next: see -ITY.] The quality of being inexplicable; incapability of being explained.

1804 W. TAYLOR in *Ann. Rev.* II. 513 The inexplicability of many allusions, especially in Taliesin. **1824** SCOTT *St. Ronan's* xxiii, The inexplicability which seemed to shroud the purposes and conduct of his new ally. **1856** DOVE *Logic Chr. Faith* v. ii. 321 The very appearance of such inexplicability is a portion of the probation.

b. (with *an* and *pl.*) Something inexplicable.

1814 SCOTT *Wav.* xxiii, This is one of the inexplicabilities of human nature. **1865** MASSON *Rec. Brit. Philos.* 393 He has had to assume an inexplicability, an inconceivability, a paradox, as nevertheless a fact.

inexplicable (ɪn'ɛksplɪkəb(ə)l), *a.* (*adv.*) and *sb.* [a. F. *inexplicable* (1486 in Godef. *Compl.*), ad. L. *inexplicābilis* that cannot be unfolded or loosened, f. *in-* (IN-³) + *explicābilis* EXPLICABLE.]

A. *adj.* †**1.** That cannot be unfolded, untwisted, or disentangled; inextricable; very intricate or complex. *Obs.*

1555 EDEN *Decades* Pref. (Arb.) 49 Of the Mazes cauled Labyrinthi..of knottes inexplicable..and dyuers suche other portentous inuentions. **1601** HOLLAND *Pliny* II. 579 Before a man can come to the Labyrinth indeed which is so intricat and inexplicable. **1656** STANLEY *Hist. Philos.* v. (1701) 159/1 He was busied in surveying the inexplicable banks of Nilus..and the winding compass of their Trenches. [**1837** EMERSON *Addr., Amer. Schol.* Wks. (Bohn) II. 175 There is never a beginning, there is never an end, to the inexplicable continuity of this web of God.]

†**b.** as *adv.* = INEXPLICABLY. *Obs.*

1490 CAXTON *Eneydos* xiv. 49 The contynuelle thoughte wherinne she is Inexplycable occupyed.

†**2.** That cannot be 'unfolded' or expressed in words; inexpressible, indescribable. *Obs.*

1502 *Ord. Crysten Men* (W. de W. 1506) v. ii. 363 Flagellacyons and tormentes inexplycables without ende or without releasynge. **1551** RECORDE *Cast. Knowl.* (1556) 97 The inexplicable benefite of knowledge. **1622** MALYNES *Anc. Law-Merch.* 431 The miseries and afflictions of imprisonment are inexplicable and cannot bee conceiued by any that haue not felt or had proofe thereof. **1691** RAY *Creation* I. (1704) 81 Fire..a Subject or Utensil of so various and inexplicable use.

3. That cannot be explained; inscrutable, unintelligible; (in recent use) that cannot be accounted for, unaccountable.

1546 GARDINER *Declar. Joye* (Quarto ed.) 84 b, You turne the matteir so aboute, as it is inexplicable. **1570** BILLINGSLEY *Euclid* x. ix. 239 The matter..obscure and hard, and in a maner inexplicable. **1602** SHAKS. *Ham.* III. ii. 13 Inexplicable dumbe shewes. **1699** BURNET *39 Art.* I. (1700) 37 If God has declared this inexplicable thing concerning himself to us, we are bound to believe it. **1793** BEDDOES *Calculus* 188 Phænomena hitherto inexplicable in the animal and vegetable œconomy. **1828** SCOTT *F.M. Perth* vi, The wooer had begun to hold the refusal of the damsel as somewhat capricious and inexplicable. **1860** MAURY *Phys. Geog. Sea* xiii. (Low) §566 There were, in the depths of the sea, untold wonders, and inexplicable mysteries. **1879** FROUDE *Cæsar* xv. 226 Still more inexplicable was the ingratitude of the aristocracy.

B. *sb.* **1.** Something that cannot be explained. (Usually in *pl.*)

1745 NEEDHAM *Microsc. Disc.* Introd. 5 We may surely reckon it among the Inexplicables. **1864** BOWEN *Logic* ix. 294 Miscellaneous sophisms of so puzzling a character that the old logicians called them the Inexplicables.

2. *pl.* A vulgar euphemism for 'trousers': cf. *inexpressibles*.

1836–7 DICKENS *Sk. Boz* III. 257 He usually wore a brown frock coat without a wrinkle, light inexplicables without a spot.

in'explicableness. [f. prec. + -NESS.] The quality of being inexplicable; inexplicability.

1652 GAULE *Magastrom.* 158 Why are they so confounded at the inexplicableness of the circumstances? **1754** EDWARDS *Freed. Will* II. vii. 64 Not to insist..on the Abstruseness and Inexplicableness of this Distinction. **1862** H. SPENCER *First Princ.* I. iii. §21 The explanation of that which is explicable, does but bring out into greater clearness the inexplicableness of that which remains behind.

in'explicably, *adv.* [f. as prec. + -LY².] In an inexplicable manner: †**a.** Inextricably, very intricately; †**b.** Inexpressibly, indescribably; **c.** Inscrutably, unaccountably.

1629 BP. HALL *Hypocrite* Wks. (1634) 361 What is their case? Surely inexplicably, unconceivably fearefull. **1710** BERKELEY *Princ. Hum. Knowl.* §152 The inexplicably fine machine of an animal or vegetable. **1814** BYRON *Lara* I. xvii, In him inexplicably mix'd appear'd Much to be loved and hated, sought and fear'd. **1822** LAMB *Elia* Ser. I. *Roast Pig*, A bundle of virtues and vices, inexplicably intertwisted. **1865** G. M. HOPKINS *Poems* (1967) 162 Meadows to them inexplicably dear. **1903** G. B. SHAW *Man & Superman* p. x, Inexplicably forcing you to range the hero with his enemy the statue on a transcendent plane. **1922** JOYCE *Ulysses* 680 Was the proposal of asylum accepted? Promptly, inexplicably, with amicability, gratefully it was declined.

inexplicant (ɪn'ɛksplɪkənt), *a. nonce-wd.* [f. IN-³ + L. *explicānt-em*, pres. pple. of *explicāre* to EXPLICATE.] Not explicating or explaining; giving no explanation.

1825 LAMB *Vision of Horns*, Tired with the fruitless chase of inexplicant analogies.

†**inexplicate** (ɪn'ɛksplɪkət), *a. Obs.* [IN-³: cf. late L. *inexplicāt-us* unexplained, *inexplicitus* not unfolded.] Not to be disentangled; very intricate; = INEXPLICABLE 1.

1611 SPEED *Hist. Gt. Brit.* IX. vi. §102. 509 Hee built..an intricate Labyrinth at Woodstocke and therein bestowed this his pearle of esteeme, vnto whose closet (for the inexplicate windings) none could approach but the King himselfe.

†**in'explicate,** *v. Obs. rare*⁻¹. [Loosely or erroneously used for EXPLICATE *v.* 2 a.] *trans.* To disentangle.

1653 E. CHISENHALE *Cath. Hist.* 280 Alexander..doubting if he should not inexplicate it [the Gordian knot] that it might be reputed as an evidence..of his bad fortune to come, with his sword cut it asunder.

inexplicit (ɪnɛk'splɪsɪt), *a.* [IN-³. Cf. L. *inexplicitus* in same sense.] Not explicit; not definitely expressed or expressive; not clear in terms or statement.

1802-12 BENTHAM *Ration. Jud. Evid.* (1827) I. 116 You have yourself, though in an obscure and inexplicit way.. been delivering to me a proposition. **1847** J. HARDY in *Proc. Berw. Nat. Club* II. No. 5. 256 The description..is.. inexplicit. **1886** *Sat. Rev.* 20 Feb. 245 The grumbles were inexplicit and almost inarticulate.

So **inex'plicitly** *adv.*; **inex'plicitness**.

1775 R. CHANDLER *Trav. Greece* (1825) II. 130 Two structures yet remain, either omitted or mentioned inexplicitly by Pausanias. **1869** A. W. POTTS *Lat. Pr. Comp.* (1870) 2 Indistinctness, inexplicitness..were faults which excluded a writer from the list of literary men. **1871-3** EARLE *Philol. Eng. Tongue* (ed. 2) §610 Saying a great deal in brief compass, and with all the entailed consequences of inexplicitness.

inexplorable (ɪnɛk'splɔərəb(ə)l), *a.* [IN-³.] That cannot be explored; inscrutable.

1646 BUCK *Rich. III*, III. 82 It was the Kings owne immoveable and inexplorable doome. **1802-12** BENTHAM *Ration. Jud. Evid.* (1827) IV. 1 A blind inexplorable labyrinth. **1834** WILSON *Dissert. Reasonableness Chr.* viii. 171 The inexplorable infinity of his grace.

inexplosive (ɪnɛk'spləʊsɪv), *a.* [IN-³.] Not explosive; not liable to or capable of explosion.

1867 HOWELLS *Venet. Life* (ed. 2) xvii, To enjoy themselves in the mild, inexplosive fashion [*ed.* 1, 1866 unexplosive manner] which seems to satisfy Italian nature. **1884** *American* VIII. 38 The inexplosive materials of which dynamite is compounded.

inexposable (ɪnɛk'spəʊzəb(ə)l), *a.* *rare*⁻¹. [f. IN-³ + *exposable*, from EXPOSE *v.* + -ABLE.] Not capable of being, or liable to be, exposed.

1618 T. ADAMS *Serm. Rage Oppress.* Wks. 1861 I. 83 Those whom nature or art, strength or sleight, have made inexposable to easy ruin, may pass unmolested.

inex'posure (ɪnɛk'spəʊʒ(j)ʊə(r)). *rare*⁻¹. [IN-³.] 'A state of not being exposed'.

1828 WEBSTER cites *Med. Repos.*

inex'press, *a.* *rare*⁻¹. [IN-³.] Not definitely expressed; not explicit: cf. EXPRESS *a.* 3.

1871 MORLEY *Crit. Misc.* 277 Great work enough has been done..by men whose recognition was informal and inexpress.

inex'pressed, *a.* *rare.* [IN-³.] Unexpressed.

1821 T. G. WAINEWRIGHT *Ess. & Crit.* (1880) 186 For the inexpressed purpose of deforming [etc.].

inexpressible (ɪnɛk'sprɛsɪb(ə)l), *a.* and *sb.* [IN-³.]

A. *adj.* That cannot be expressed in words; unutterable, unspeakable, indescribable. (Often as an emotional intensive: cf. *ineffable.*)

1625 DONNE *Serm.* iii. 22 Thou shalt feele the Ioy of his third birth in thy soul most inexpressible this day. **1667** MILTON *P.L.* VIII. 113 Ere mid-day arriv'd In Eden, distance inexpressible By Numbers that have name. **1711** ADDISON *Spect.* No. 159 ⁋8, I gazed with inexpressible Pleasure on these happy Islands. **1802** MAR. EDGEWORTH *Moral T.* (1816) I. 224-5 It is with inexpressible concern, that I find myself called upon..to be the accuser of such a man. **1860** TYNDALL *Glac.* I. xxiii. 166 Its seclusion gives it an inexpressible charm.

B. *sb.* **1.** Something inexpressible. (In quot. 1846 with punning allusion to next sense.)

1652 BENLOWES *Theoph.* II. vi. 24 Praise best doth Inexpressibles expresse. **1846** MRS. GORE *Eng. Char.* (1852) 73 A pair of standard footmen seems to be the real pair of inexpressibles.

2. *pl.* (*colloq.*) Breeches or trousers. (Orig. euphemistic: cf. *ineffables*, *inexplicables*, *unmentionables.*)

1790 WOLCOTT (P. Pindar) *Rowland for Oliver* Wks. 1795 II. 154 (Farmer) I've heard, that breeches, petticoats, and smock, Give to thy modest mind a grievous shock, And that thy brain (so lucky its device) Christ'neth them inexpressibles, so nice. **1793** GIBBON *Let.* 11 Nov. **1800** HELEN BEDINGFELD in *Jerningham Lett.* (1896) I. 196 A pair of old *inexpressibles*..contained seven thousand Guineas!.. deposited in so vulgar a Garment. **1809** *Farmers' Mag.* X. 500 A fine lady can talk about her lover's inexpressibles, when she would faint to hear of his breeches. **1875** *Spectator* (Melbourne) 12 June 64/1 The episcopal inexpressibles.. for obvious reasons will be unsuited to lay legs.

Hence **inexpressi'bility**, **inex'pressibleness**, the quality of being inexpressible.

1727 BAILEY vol. II, *Inexpressibleness.* **1826-7** DE QUINCEY *Lessing* Wks. 1859 XIII. 249, I do not admit the inexpressibility of paternal grief. **1869** SPURGEON *Treas. Dav.* Ps. xxi. 1 Our joy should have some sort of inexpressibleness in it.

inexpressibly (ɪnɛk'sprɛsɪblɪ), *adv.* [f. prec. + -LY².] In an inexpressible manner or degree; beyond expression; unutterably, unspeakably, indescribably. (Often as an emotional intensive.)

a **1660** HAMMOND (J.), God will protect and reward all his faithful servants in a manner and measure inexpressibly abundant. **1711** STEELE *Spect.* No. 75 ⁋8 Something so inexpressibly Graceful in his Words and Actions. *a* **1797** H. WALPOLE *Mem. Geo. II* (1847) I. vii. 212 The King was inexpressibly alarmed. **1860** TYNDALL *Glac.* I. ii. 17 The final echos being inexpressibly soft and pure. **1875** W. COLLINS *Q. of Hearts* 21 You terrify me so inexpressibly that I shall be glad to get rid of you.

inex'pression. *nonce-wd.* [IN-³.] Want or absence of expression.

1796 COLERIDGE *Let. to Thelwall* 19 Nov. in *Lett.* (1895) 180 'Tis a mere carcass of a face; flat, flabby, and expressive chiefly of inexpression.

inexpressive (ɪnɛk'sprɛsɪv), *a.* [IN-³. Cf. F. *inexpressif* (15th c. in Godef.).]

1. = INEXPRESSIBLE. *arch.* (In modern writers prob. in imitation of Shaks. *A.Y.L.* III. ii. 10, or Milton *Lycidas* 176, where *unexpressive* is the word.)

1652 BENLOWES *Theoph.* V. xxxix. 72 On the Vision inexpressive rayes did wait. **1744** AKENSIDE *Pleas. Imag.* I. 124 Then the inexpressive strain Diffuses its inchantment. **1794** MATHIAS *Purs. Lit.* (1798) 298 To mortal ken he dares unveil The inexpressive form in semblance frail. **1856** MRS. BROWNING *Aur. Leigh* VII. 730 Those soft-winged eyes ..'Twixt trembling lids of inexpressive joy. **1866** J. H. NEWMAN *Gerontius* (1874) 14, I feel in me An inexpressive lightness and a sense Of freedom.

2. Not expressive; not expressing a meaning, feeling, character, etc.; wanting in expression.

1744 AKENSIDE *Pleas. Imag.* III. 285 To behold, in lifeless things, The inexpressive semblance of himself, Of thought and passion. **1761** LLOYD *Prol. Hecuba* (R.), O! glorious times, when actors thus could strike, Expressive, inexpressive, all alike! **1791** ROBERTSON *India* App. 280 Finished in a stile considerably superior to the hard inexpressive manner of the Egyptians. **1834** MEDWIN *Angler in Wales* I. 239 His features are inexpressive of intellect. **1846** MRS. GORE *Eng. Char.* (1852) 152 That blank and inexpressive vacuity, which an able diplomatist is careful to assume as a vizard. *c* **1860** FABER *Old Labourer* x, His inexpressive eye.

inex'pressively, *adv.* [f. prec. + -LY².]

1. Inexpressibly, indescribably. *Obs.* or *arch.*

1809 *Susan* I. 217 The notes were wild, but inexpressively sweet. **1840** POE *Pit & Pendulum* Wks. 1864 I. 319, I felt very—oh, inexpressively, sick and weak.

2. Not expressively; without expressive power.

1823 BENTHAM *Not Paul* 236 The name, so inexpressively rendered, in the English, by the word *Deacons.* **1893** *Athenæum* 27 May 663/3 The idea here is a good one; but how inexpressively..it is indicated!

inex'pressiveness. [f. as prec. + -NESS.] The quality of being inexpressive; want of expressiveness.

1816 BENTHAM *Chrestom.* Table i. Wks. 1843 VIII. 40 The fictitiousness, and hence the inexpressiveness, or rather the misexpressiveness, of the language. **1833** HOOK *Parson's Daughter* (1847) 260 A countenance of immovable inexpressiveness. **1881** H. JAMES *Portr. Lady* liv, Pity for the poor woman's inexpressiveness, her want of regret, of disappointment, came back to her.

†**in'exprimable**, *a.* *Obs.* *rare.* [a. F. *inexprimable* (16th c. in H. Estienne), f. *in-* (IN-³) + *exprimer* to express.] Inexpressible.

a **1577** GASCOIGNE *Hearbes, Weedes*, etc. Wks. (1587) 236 A louer being charged with inexprimable ioyes.

inexpugnable (ɪnɛk'spʌgnəb(ə)l), *a.* [a. F. *inexpugnable* (14th c. in Littré *Suppl.*), ad. L. *inexpugnābilis*, f. *in-* (IN-³) + *expugnābilis* EXPUGNABLE.] That cannot be taken by assault or storm; incapable of being overcome, subdued, or overthrown by force; impregnable, invincible.

a. *lit.* of a fortress, an army, etc.

1490 CAXTON *Eneydos* Prol. 10 Troye the graunte, and many other places stronge and inexpugnable haue ben besieged sharpely & assayled. **1533** MORE *Answ. Poysoned Bk.* Wks. 1062/1 How the inexpugnable walles of Jerico were ouerthrowen. **1540-1** ELYOT *Image Gov.* (1556) 23 The inexpugnable armies prepared against hym. **1658** *Hist. Christina Queen of Swedland* 292 The Castle of Besen.. seated on a craggy mountain, which renders it inexpugnable. **1787** *Hist. Eur.* in *Ann. Reg.* 79/2 Convinced at length..that this empire was inexpugnable. **1849** GROTE *Greece* II. lix. V. 249 Syracuse..had not only become inexpugnable, but had assumed the aggressive.

b. *fig.* of a statement, argument, principle, desire, disposition, quality, condition, etc., or of a person in reference to his principles or disposition: That cannot be overthrown or overcome.

a **1535** MORE *Agst. Tyndall* II. Wks. 662 By some of hys own argumentes..he..maketh it rather more strong, and proueth it playn inexpugnable. **1590** BARROUGH *Meth. Physick* I. xv. (1639) 24 An inexpugnable desire of sleeping. **1662** GUNNING *Lent Fast* 218 By Fasting, the three Children also were found..inexpugnable by the Babylonians. *a* **1734** NORTH *Exam.* III. vi. §85 The inexpugnable good Will of the Parliament at that Time was the Preservation of the King. **1865** MILL *Exam. Hamilton* 34 His arguments seem to me very far from inexpugnable. **1894** MRS. H. WARD *Marcella* II. 4 A certain inexpugnable dignity surrounded him.

Hence **inexpugna'bility**, **inex'pugnableness**, the quality of being inexpugnable, impregnability; also **inex'pugnably** *adv.*, impregnably, invincibly.

1653 H. MORE *Conject. Cabbal.* App. (1662) V. V. 122 Incompossibility and Incommensurability that is inexpugnably lodged up in the perverse and unreclaimable *Hyle.* **1727** BAILEY vol. II, *Inexpugnableness.* **1821** CRAIG *Lect. Drawing* viii. 437 Fixing those transactions inexpugnably in your minds. **1865** CARLYLE *Fredk. Gt.* XV. v. (1872) VI. 3 What silent courage, or private inexpugnability of mind, was in him. **1871** MORLEY *Crit. Misc.* 140 He was..persuaded of the general justice and inexpugnableness of the orthodox system. **1881** STEVENSON in *Longm. Mag.* Apr. 680 Of one thing I am inexpugnably assured.

†**inexpugnate**, *a.* *Obs.* *rare*⁻¹. [ad. L. *inexpugnāt-us* unconquered: see IN-³ and EXPUGNAT.] Unconquered.

1632 LITHGOW *Trav.* I. 6 Then gnashing Spirits That howling waile, Hells inexpugnat merits: Where's all your gentry?

inexpungible, -geable (ɪnɛk'spʌndʒɪb(ə)l, -əb(ə)l), *a.* [f. IN-³ + **expungible*, f. EXPUNGE *v.*] That cannot be expunged or obliterated; indelible.

1888 R. DOWLING *Miracle Gold* III. xxxiv. 135 With inexpungeable features of the dwarf sharp limned upon his smarting sight. **1896** *Chicago Advance* 20 Feb. 264/3 The law is on the statute book of human thought, inexpungible.

†**i'nexputable**, *a.* *Obs.* *rare*⁻⁰. [ad. L. *inexputābilis* incalculable, f. *in-* (IN-³) + *exputāre* to reckon: see -BLE.]

1623 COCKERAM, *Inexputable*, not to bee numbred.

inexquisite (ɪn'ɛkskwɪzɪt), *a.* *rare.* [f. IN-³ + EXQUISITE *a.*] Not exquisite.

1922 JOYCE *Ulysses* 264 The bar where bald stood by sister gold, inexquisite contrast.

†**inex'saturable, inexat-**, *a.* *Obs.* *rare*⁻⁰. [ad. L. *inexsaturābilis* (*inexatur-*), f. *in-* (IN-³) + *exsaturābilis*, f. *exsaturāre* to EXSATURATE.] Incapable of being satisfied; insatiable.

1656 BLOUNT *Glossogr.*, *Inexaturable.*

†**inex'saturated, inexaturated**, *a.* *Obs.* *rare*⁻⁰. [IN-³: see EXSATURATE.]

1658 PHILLIPS, *Inexaturated*, not to be filled or satisfied, of an unsatiable appetite.

†**inex'superable**, *a.* *Obs.* *rare.* [ad. L. *inexsuperābilis*: see IN-³ and EXSUPERABLE.] That cannot be overcome.

1623 COCKERAM, *Inexuperable*, not to bee passed ouer. **1656** BLOUNT *Glossogr.*, *Inexuperable*, that cannot be passed or overcome, invincible. **1659** H. MORE *Immort. Soul* I. ix. (1662) 37 [His] inexuperable confidence of the truth of the Conclusion.

in'extant, *a.* *rare.* [IN-³.] Not extant; no longer existing.

1831 *Fraser's Mag.* IV. 541 The poem..is supposed to have for its basis one yet older, and for some time inextant.

inex'tended, *a.* *rare.* [IN-³.] Unextended; without extension.

1739 WATTS *Proof Separate State* i, If they suppose it [the soul] to be inextended, or to have no parts or quantity, I confess I can have no manner of idea of the existence or possibility of such an inextended being without consciousness or active power. **1897** M. DZIEWICKI *Wyclif's 'De Logica'* (Wyclif Soc.) III. Introd. 19 Even Averrhoës' position, viz., that they exist, but with less intensity of being, would be contrary to the system of inextended points. *Ibid.* 33 Movement indeed, though inextended in itself, is extended in the body which moves.

†**inex'tensed**, *a.* *Obs.* *rare*⁻¹. [f. med. or mod.L. *inextens-us* (f. *in-* (IN-³) + *extensus* EXTENSE *a.*) + -ED¹.] Without extension.

1604 T. WRIGHT *Passions* VI. 300 How can the Soule extend itselfe thorow the whole body, being a Spirit indivisible, inextensed?

inextensi'bility. *rare.* [f. next: see -ITY. Cf. F. *inextensibilité* (Littré).] The quality of being inextensible.

1829 *Nat. Philos.* I. *Mechanics* II. viii. 32 (U.K.S.) This power of transmitting pressure in the direction of its length, is not owing to the flexibility of the rope, but to its inextensibility. **1847-9** TODD *Cycl. Anat.* IV. 512/2 Its inextensibility admirably adapting it to..mere passive resistance. **1876** *Encycl. Brit.* IV. 448.

inextensible (ɪnɛk'stɛnsɪb(ə)l), *a.* [IN-³; cf. F. *inextensible* (Buffon).] Not extensible; incapable of extension; that cannot be stretched or drawn out in length.

1840 LARDNER *Geom.* 307 A heavy body..attached to a flexible and inextensible string. **1853** J. H. JELLETT (*title*) On the Properties of Inextensible Surfaces. **1881** *Athenæum* 2 July 16/3 He starts with the assumption that the density of the luminiferous ether is constant (in other words that the ether is inextensible and incompressible).

inextension (ɪnɛk'stɛnʃən). *rare.* [IN-³.] Want of extension; unextended state.

1827 J. FEARN in E. H. Barker *Parriana* (1828) I. 632 The inextension of the mind.

inex'tensive, *a.* *rare.* [IN-³.] Not extensive, small.

1890 *Scots Observer* 25 Jan. 269/1 The public..will no doubt clamour for his inextensive volume.

in extenso: see IN *Lat. prep.*

inex'terminable, *a.* *rare.* [ad. L. (post-class.) *inextermĭnābilis*: see IN-³ and EXTERMINABLE.]

†**1.** Having no possible end; interminable, endless. *Obs.* *rare.*

1586 A. DAY *Eng. Secretary* I. (1625) 145 Continuall, nay rather inexterminable vowes..unto your services. **1668** H.

MORE *Div. Dial.* II. Contents Ll va, That there is an ever-anticipative Eternity and inexterminable Amplitude that are proper to the Deity onely.

2. 'That cannot be exterminated.'

a **1828** RUSH cited in WEBSTER.

inex'tinct, *a. rare.* [ad. L. *inexstinct-us* (Ovid): cf. IN-^{3} and EXTINCT.] Unextinguished.

1623 COCKERAM, *Inextinct, Inextinguable*, not to bee quenched. **1823** J. WILSON *Trials Marg. Lyndsay* xxxi, In which he had not supposed such a capacity of love had yet remained inextinct. **1832** *Fraser's Mag.* VI. 402 Man's high hope and inextinct desire.

†**inex'tinguible**, *a. Obs.* [a. F. *inextinguible* (15th c. in Hatz.-Darm.), or ad. L. *inexstinguibilis*: see IN-^{3} and EXTINGUIBLE.] = next.

1412-20 LYDG. *Chron. Troy* III. xxviii. (MS. Digby) lf. 134/1 þat was by crafte made in extinguible For it ne myȝt ..Neiþer be queynt wᵗ winde, tempest, ne reyn. **1502** ATKYNSON tr. *De Imitatione* III. lxiii. 256 They brenne in soule with the ardoure of inextynguyble charyte. **1594** *Mirr. Policy* 186 The inextinguible fire of ciuile war. **1604** T. WRIGHT *Passions* VI. 325 Those inextinguible flames of infernall fernaces. **1677** GALE *Crt. Gentiles* IV. 142 This infinite inextinguible thirst after terrene goods.

inextinguishable (ɪnɛk'stɪŋgwɪʃəb(ə)l), *a.* [f. IN-^{3} + EXTINGUISHABLE.] That cannot be extinguished (in various senses of the verb); unquenchable, indestructible, etc.

In 'inextinguishable laughter', an echo of the Homeric ἄσβεστος γέλως, Iliad I. 599.

1509 HAWES *Past. Pleas.* xlv. (Percy Soc.) 218 In heaven and hell I am continually Withouten ende to be inextinguissible. **1661** MORGAN *Sph. Gentry* I. iv. 40 And to shew his inextinguishable light and heat they used to maintain a perpetual fire upon their altars. **1667** MILTON *P.L.* VI. 217 So..together rush'd Both Battels maine, with ruinous assault And inextinguishable rage. **1791** COWPER *Iliad* I. 739 Heav'n rang with laughter inextinguishable. **1815** SCOTT *Guy M.* ii, The efforts of the professor..were totally inadequate to restrain the inextinguishable laughter of the students. **1816** SOUTHEY in *Q. Rev.* XVI. 239 An impulse of..the most inextinguishable hope was excited in every heart. **1833** LAMB *Elia* Ser. II. (1860) 387 What an inextinguishable titter that time spared not celestial visages. **1861** MAINE *Anc. Law* v. (1876) 126 Primitive law considers the..family groups, as perpetual and inextinguishable.

Hence **inex'tinguishableness** (Bailey vol. II, 1727); **inex'tinguishably** *adv.*

1821 SHELLEY *Epipsych.* 82 The Moon Burns, inextinguishably beautiful. **1883** *Harper's Mag.* Aug. 464/2 She burst out crying inextinguishably.

inex'tinguished, *a.* [IN-^{3}.] Not extinguished: still burning; unextinguished.

1746-7 HERVEY *Medit.* (1818) 174 Ye Stars, that beam with inextinguished brilliancy through the midnight sky. **1823** J. WILSON *Trials Marg. Lyndsay* xliii, That feeling, perhaps, had inextinguished love below it. **1863** BATES *Nat. Amazon* ix. (1864) 271 Having found the inextinguished fire of their last encampment.

inextirpable (ɪnɛk'stɜːpəb(ə)l), *a.* [ad. L. *inexstirpābilis* (Pliny), f. *in-* (IN-^{3}) + *exstirpāre* to EXTIRPATE: cf. F. *inextirpable* (15-16th c.)] That cannot be extirpated or entirely rooted out.

1623 in COCKERAM. **1673** O. WALKER *Educ.* i. 11 All these, indulged and accustomed, grow stronger, and at last inextirpable. **1838** CHALMERS *Wks.* XII. 137 An inextirpable disease.

Hence **inex'tirpableness** (Bailey vol. II, 1727).

†**inex'tollible**, *a. Obs. rare* [f. IN-^{3} + **extollible* from EXTOL *v.*] That cannot be extolled.

1772 NUGENT *Hist. Friar Gerund* II. 337 Our inextollible Friar Gerund remained alone.

in extremis: see IN *Lat. prep.*

in,extrica'bility. *rare.* [f. next: see -ITY. Cf. F. *inextricabilité* (Littré).] The quality or state of being inextricable. Also with *an* and *pl.* An instance of this, a situation, etc. from which one cannot extricate oneself.

1834 H. O'BRIEN *Round Towers Irel.* 444 Taking them, as his clue, into a labyrinth of inextricability. **1847** MEDWIN *Shelley* I. 187 Spain has emancipated herself from the inextricability of the chain. **1865** CARLYLE *Fredk. Gt.* XX. x. (1872) IX. 186 He..fell partly..into drinking, as the solution of his inextricabilities.

inextricable (ɪn'ɛkstrɪkəb(ə)l), *a.* [ad. L. *inextrīcābilis* that cannot be disentangled or disengaged, from which one cannot disengage oneself, inexplicable (f. *in-* (IN-^{3}) + *extrīcāre* to EXTRICATE); perh. immed. a. F. *inextricable* (15th c. in Hatz.-Darm.).]

1. From which one cannot extricate oneself; esp. so intricate or complicated that no means of exit can be discovered.

a. Of places, esp. a labyrinth or maze. Also *fig.*

1555 EDEN *Decades* 260 It causeth marysshes and quamyres inextricable and dangerous both for horse and man. **1572** BOSSEWELL *Armorie* II. 49 Of the Labyrynthe, or of th' obscure and inextricable buyldinge which Minos.. caused Dedalus..to make. **1603** KNOLLES *Hist. Turks* (1638) 95 The cuts and channels..winding in and out with a thousand inextricable twinings, inclosed them. **1720** WATERLAND *Eight Serm.* 268 Lest..we..lose our selves in inextricable Mazes. **1818** JAS. MILL *Brit. India* II. IV. i. 54 A road among the woods which they would have found inextricable.

b. Of a state or condition: That cannot be escaped or got free from.

1576 FLEMING *Panopl. Epist.* 161 [They] cast themselves ..into millions of..daungers in manner inextricable. **1626** JACKSON *Creed* VIII. viii. §2 The crooked by-paths which tend to death, and inextricable misery. **1667** MILTON *P.L.* v. 528 God..ordaind thy will By nature free, not overrul'd by Fate Inextricable, or strict necessity. **1712** E. COOKE *Voy. S. Sea* 241 That he should run himself into inextricable Danger by going on. **1858** HAWTHORNE *Fr. & It. Jrnls.* I. 136 The Laocoön..is such a type of human beings, struggling with an inextricable trouble.

2. Of a knot, coil, etc.: That cannot be unravelled, disentangled, or untied. Also *transf.*

1610 B. JONSON *Alch.* v. ii, To deceive him..that would break Such an inextricable tie as ours was. **1728** VENEER *Sincere Penit.* Pref. 7 Compassed about by the strongest and most inextricable bonds of iniquity. **1829** SCOTT *Guy M.* Introd., The knot of the accursed sophistry became more inextricable in appearance, at least to the prey whom its meshes surrounded.

b. Of a grasp: That cannot be loosened or detached.

1847 J. WILSON *Chr. North* (1857) I. 138 Catching an inextricable hold of every wall they can reach.

†3. Of a problem: Incapable of being solved.

1613 PURCHAS *Pilgrimage* (1614) 147 The Scribes..in certaine niceties, and scrupulous questions, sometimes inextricable. **1660** WILLSFORD *Scales Comm.* 138 An exact proportion betwixt the Diameter and Circumference is inextricable to Art. **1664** H. MORE *Myst. Iniq.* 215 A Problem too curious to enquire into, but not altogether inextricable.

4. Intricately involved, confused, or perplexed; incapable of being cleared up or put straight.

1655 FULLER *Ch. Hist.* II. v. §3 In this Story there is an inextricable Errour in point of Chronology. **1675** BAXTER *Cath. Theol.* II. I. 157 If this be Nature with you, you cast your self into inextricable difficulties to know what you say. **1748** *Anson's Voy.* III. ix. 394 To embroil his Commodore in an inextricable squabble with the Chinese Government. **1849** MACAULAY *Hist. Eng.* ii. I. 159 The ecclesiastical polity of the realm was in inextricable confusion.

5. Intricate, elaborate, exquisitely wrought. *rare.*

1691 RAY *Creation* II. (1692) 93 What force and strength was requisite, there being in them such inextricable Perfection [a transl. of Pliny's phrase, *inextricabilis perfectio*]. **1799** HAN. MORE *Fem. Educ.* (ed. 4) I. 34 A net of such exquisite art and inextricable workmanship. **1851** RUSKIN *Stones Ven.* (1874) I. 328 The inextricable richness of the fully developed Gothic jamb and arch.

Hence **in'extricableness**.

1624 DONNE *Devotions* 122 There is no perplexity in thee, my God, no inextricablenesse in thee. **1727** in BAILEY vol. II.

inextricably (ɪn'ɛkstrɪkəblɪ), *adv.* [f. prec. + -LY^{2}.] In an inextricable manner; beyond all possibility of being disentangled or extricated.

1598 DRAYTON *Rosamond to K. Henry* Annot., Vaults arched and walled with brick and stone, almost inextricably wound one within another. **1692** RAY *Dissol. World* 134 The Sun may be so inextricably inveloped by the maculæ, that he may quite lose his light. **1725** POPE *Odyss.* VIII. 342 Th' intangling snares deny (Inextricably firm) the pow'r to fly. **1830** D'ISRAELI *Chas. I*, III. xii. 268 Politics was now inextricably connected with religion. **1887** J. S. BANKS *Man. Chr. Doctr.* II. iii. 178 In the Roman teaching..truth and error are subtly and inextricably interwoven.

†**in'extricate**, *a. Obs. rare*$^{-1}$. [f. IN-^{3} + L. *extrīcāt-us* pa. pple.: see EXTRICATE *v.*] Not to be disentangled; involved, tangled, intricate.

1615 CHAPMAN *Odyss.* XI. 389 But the equal fate Of God withstood his stealth; inextricate Imprisoning bands.

inexuperable, variant of INEXSUPERABLE.

†**ineye** (ɪ'naɪ), *v. Obs.* Also 5 **eneye**. [f. IN-^{2} (EN-) + EYE, after L. *inoculāre*.] *trans.* To put an eye or bud into (the bark of a tree); to inoculate, to propagate by inoculation; = BUD *v.* 5.

c **1420** *Pallad. on Husb.* VIII. 53 The figtre now teneye hit is no wronge. **1708** J. PHILIPS *Cyder* I. 21 Let sage experience teach thee all the Arts Of Grafting and In-eyeing.

†**in'fabricated**, *a. Obs. rare*$^{-0}$. [IN-^{3}.] Not fabricated, unwrought.

1623 COCKERAM, *Infabricated*, Vnwrought. **1721** BAILEY, *Infabricated*, not well wrought, rough. **1775** ASH, *Infabricated*, slightly put together. **1828** in WEBSTER.

inface ('ɪnfeɪs). *Geomorphol.* Also **in-face**. [See quot. 1896.] The steep scarp-face of a cuesta.

1896 W. M. DAVIS in *Science* 15 May 732/2 The surrounding rims of harder stratified rocks offer interesting examples of outer slope and inface, with inner subsequent valleys, all in concentric circular arrangement. [*Note*] The invention of this excellent term, the abbreviation of 'inward facing escarpment', should be credited to Mr. L. C. Glenn, of Darlington, S.C. **1939** A. K. LOBECK *Geomorphol.* xiii. 451 Each cuesta has a steep inface and a gentle back slope, down the dip of the beds. **1954** W. D. THORNBURY *Princ. Geomorphol.* v. 133 One of the common regional expressions of gently or moderately dipping rock is the cuesta. This has an abrupt escarpment or in-face on the up-dip side and a more gentle backslope or dip slope extending in the direction of the regional dip.

†**infa'cilitate**, *v. Obs. rare*$^{-1}$. [f. IN-^{3} + FACILITATE *v.*] *trans.* To render difficult.

1649 BLITHE *Eng. Improv. Impr.* ix. (1653) 50 The discovery of some of those hindrances or rubs that either hinder or infacilitate this work of Fen-drayning.

infædation, obs. erron. form of INFEUDATION.

†**in'failable**, *a. Obs.* Also 7 **infaillible**. [IN-^{3}. Partly, at least, a. F. *infaillible* (15th c.).] Not liable to fail; unfailing; reliable; infallible.

1561 EDEN *Arte of Nauig.* Pref. ℂℂ ij, Certain infaileable sygnes and tokens of the same. *Ibid.* A ij b, Infaylable principles. **1631** DENISON *Heav. Banq.* 47 Liuely and infaillible signes of the presence of Christ. *Ibid.* 106 A few ..infaillible markes, wherby we may know whether wee haue receiued Christ.

infair: see INFARE *sb.*

infaisable, obs. form of INFEASIBLE.

†**in'faithful**, *a. Obs. rare*$^{-0}$. [IN-^{3}.] = UNFAITHFUL. Hence †**in'faithfulness**.

1688 NORRIS *Theory Love* 164 It oftentimes receives a Denomination from the sensuality, but never from the injustice, infaithfulness, or the like.

infall ('ɪnfɔːl). [f. IN *adv.* 11 d + FALL *sb.*; = Ger. *einfall*, Du. *inval*, hostile incursion.]

1. An inroad, attack, incursion, or descent *upon* an army, town, etc., or *into* a country. Now *rare*.

1645 CROMWELL *Let.* 25 Apr. in *Carlyle*, A party of the Earl of Northampton's Regiment..came to make an infall upon me. **1647** CLARENDON *Hist. Reb.* VII. §322 The garrison at Hull had many strong infalls into the country. **1679** in Wodrow *Hist. Suffer. Ch. Scot.* (1722) II. 54 At the Infal upon Glasgow. **1894** ATKINSON *Old Whitby* 67 The piratical, predatory raids or infalls—we can hardly dignify them by calling them invasions—from the side of the sea.

2. The place where the water enters a reservoir, canal, etc. Cf. *outfall*.

1863 *Daily Tel.* 6 Apr., The puddling was not put in for about 300 feet at the infall, and about 150 feet at the outfall, the ground forming, in fact, a natural bank.

3. The falling of a stream, road, etc. into another; junction, confluence.

1895 CROCKETT *Men of Moss Hags* xlvii. 334 It was near the infall of the road from Loch Dee that we first got sight of those we sought.

4. a. (A) falling upon or into (esp. a planet) from an outside source.

1899 *Edin. Rev.* Oct. 328 The waning atmospheric stock of carbon is reinforced by meteoric infalls. **1961** *New Scientist* 23 Feb. 465/3 Cosmic infall dust..would also provide a source of very finely divided ferrous material [on the moon]. **1969** *Nature* 20 Dec. 1160/1 Relative to the galactic gas the average velocity of infall would be about 500 km s^{-1}. **1971** I. G. GASS et al. *Understanding Earth* iii. 67/2 At present the energy of infall of a meteorite or a space rocket is very large.

b. Material that falls or has fallen.

1960 *New Scientist* 18 Feb. 387/2 There is..some evidence of it in the spectra of comets, and fragments from these continue to form part of the meteoroidal infall. **1962** F. I. ORDWAY et al. *Basic Astronautics* v. 188 On airless worlds surface materials may be..mixed with cosmic infall, including meteoritic debris.

†**infa'llacious**, *a. Obs. rare.* [IN-^{3}.] Not fallacious or deceptive.

1677 GREW *Exp. Solut. Salts* i. §10 In..this Experiment, two things, to render it infallacious, are to be noted.

infallen ('ɪn,fɔːlən), *ppl. a.* [f. IN *adv.* 11 b + FALLEN.] That has fallen in. Cf. FALL *v.* 58 b.

1882 *B'ham Weekly Post* 8 Apr. 3/4 Due to the covering up by the infallen rock of certain submarine cavities.

infallibilism (ɪn'fælɪbɪlɪz(ə)m). [f. as next + -ISM.] The principle of the infallibility of some person or thing, esp. of the Pope.

1870 *Sat. Rev.* 2 Apr. 443 The present Archbishop of Westminster..having learnt infallibilism at Rome,..was put over the heads of English Catholics by the Pope, against their will. **1895** BOYD CARPENTER *Lect. Preach.* 200, I would not have any of you..climb into the seat of smug and self-satisfied infallibilism.

infallibilist (ɪn'fælɪbɪlɪst). Also **-blist**. [f. L. *infallibil-is* INFALLIBLE + -IST.] One who believes in or upholds the infallibility of some person or thing, esp. (in reference to the Vatican Council) that of the Pope.

1870 *Pall Mall G.* 10 Feb., The Infallibists are said to be now moving swiftly and surely towards their goal. **1873** MORLEY *Rousseau* II. xiv. 274 The presumptuousness of all varieties of theological infallibilists. **1879** *19th Cent.* No. 32. 670 Hieronymus Porcius, the Infallibilist, wrote maintaining the doctrine of the Papal infallibility. **1894** *Academy* 25 Aug. 127/3 The position of a negative dogmatist is assumed to differ fundamentally from that of a theological or scientific infallibilist.

b. *attrib.* or as *adj.*

1875 PUSEY 2 Jan. in Liddon *Life* (1897) IV. xi. 279 The whole extreme Ritualist party is practically infallibilist. 'We will not retreat; because we are certainly right.'

Hence **infallibi'listic** *a.*, of or pertaining to an infallibilist.

1890 *Microcosm* Mar. 90 Any other acknowledgment would be fatal to its infallibilistic pretensions [i.e. those of the Papacy].

infallibility (ɪnfælɪˈbɪlɪtɪ). [f. as INFALLIBLE + -ITY; repr. med.L. *infallibilitās*, obs. F. *infallibilité* (Franç. de Sales *c* 1600, in Godef. *Compl.*).]

1. The quality or fact of being infallible or exempt from liability to err.

1611 COTGR., *Infallibilité*, infallibilitie, or infalliblenesse; certainetie, assurance. **1611** BIBLE *Transl. Pref.* 8 Men.. priuiledged with the priuiledge of infallibilitie. **1624** GATAKER *Transubst.* 110 The Pope sitting in his Chaire,.. may yet erre for all his infallibility so much and so oft bragged of. **1662** STILLINGFL. *Orig. Sacr.* II. i. §2 [The evidences] will likewise prove the undoubted certainty and infallibility of those writings. **1791** MRS. RADCLIFFE *Rom. Forest* xii, A striking instance of the infallibility of my judgment. **1870** *Sat. Rev.* 2 Apr. 443 Roman Catholics in this country acquired all their civil rights on the strength of their reiterated declarations that Papal infallibility was no doctrine of their church. **1875** MANNING *Mission H. Ghost* xi. 301 That which we call infallibility is nothing but this: the Church cannot err from the path of revealed truth.

b. ***His Infallibility***, a title given to the Pope; also, a mock title.

1834 *Oxf. Univ. Mag.* I. 121 The day before the Pope expired, the startling announcement came forth 'His Infallibility is delirious'. **1886** *Pall Mall G.* 19 June 1/1 An *ex cathedrâ* utterance from his Infallibility of Midlothian.

c. An infallible person. *rare.*

1886 SIR F. H. DOYLE *Remin.* 49 Youthful infallibilities of the normal Arnoldian type.

2. The quality of being unfailing or not liable to fail; unfailing certainty.

a **1631** DONNE in *Select.* (1840) 188 Thy light shall grow up, from a fair hope, to a modest assurance and infallibility, that that light shall never go out. **1640** HOWELL *Dodona's Gr.* 67 Puff'd up with such a certitude and infallibilitie of hopes and presumptions, that..there were Bonefires alreadie made. **1856** KANE *Arct. Expl.* I. xviii. 216 The prestige of a gun with a savage is in his notion of its infallibility.

†**infalliˈbilityship.** *Obs.* [f. prec. + -SHIP.] A mock title given to one who claims infallibility, *spec.* to the Pope.

1679 in Hone *Every-day Bk.* I. 1490 The crafty devil leaving his infallibilityship in the lurch. **1683** E. FOWLER *Resol. Symbolizing with Ch. Rome* 34 [If] his Infallibilityship had judg'd Impartially of Errors and Superstitions. **1709** J. JOHNSON *Clergym. Vade M.* II. 264 His Infallibility-ship owns it to be true.

infallible (ɪnˈfælɪb(ə)l), *a.* (*sb.*) Also 5–6 **infal(l)yble, 6 -abil, -able, -iable.** [ad. med.L. *infallibilis* (in Bæda), f. *in-* (IN-³) + *fallibilis* FALLIBLE. Cf. F. *infaillible* (15th c. in Hatz.-Darm.); also INFAILABLE.] Not fallible.

1. Of persons, their judgements, etc.: Not liable to be deceived or mistaken; incapable of erring.

1491 CAXTON *Vitas Patr.* (W. de W. 1495) I. Prol. 1 a/1 Blessyd be god our souerayn creatour & dyrectour Infallyble. **1529** MORE *Dyaloge* I. Wks. 169/1 The infallible authoritie of the church in yᵗ god techeth it euery trueth requisite to yᵉ necessitie of mans saluacion. **1643** SIR T. BROWNE *Relig. Med.* II. §9 If General Councells may erre, I doe not see why particular Courts should be infallible. **1651** C. CARTWRIGHT *Cert. Relig.* I. 113 If the Popes authority be so great, and his judgement so infallible. **1771** *Junius Lett.* xlviii. 252 Parliaments are not infallible. **1870** JEVONS *Elem. Logic* i. 8 As well might a man claim to be immortal in his body as infallible in his mind. **1875** JOWETT *Plato* (ed. 2) III. 209 You admitted that the ruler was not infallible and might be mistaken.

2. Of things: Not liable to fail, unfailing.

a. Not liable to prove false, erroneous, or mistaken; that unfailingly holds good.

1526 *Pilgr. Perf.* (W. de W. 1531) 23 b, Our lorde to wytnesse in his blessed promesse, whiche is infalyble. **1559** W. CUNNINGHAM *Cosmogr. Glasse* 57 Th' infallible rules of Arithmetik and Geometrie. **1577** VAUTROUILLIER *Luther on Ep. Gal.* 158 It foloweth by an infallible consequence. **1654** tr. *Scudery's Curia Pol.* 73 That Maxime is infallible, that what is just, is honourable. **1748** *Anson's Voy.* II. ix. 228 The height of the mountains was itself an infallible mark of the harbour. **1764** REID *Inquiry* i. §8. 104 This justly entitles her to my..confidence, till I find infallible proofs of her infidelity. **1883** H. DRUMMOND *Nat. Law in Spir. W.* (ed. 2) 361 An infallible standard is a temptation to a mechanical faith.

b. Not liable to fail in its action or operation.

1711 STEELE *Spect.* No. 134 ⁋2 You..offer an infallible Cure of Vice and Folly, for the Price of one Penny. **1712** ARBUTHNOT *John Bull* I. ix, An infallible ointment and plaister. **1801** *Med. Jrnl.* V. 244 The one being often liable to fail, while the other is in its nature almost infallible. **1854** H. H. WILSON tr. *Rig-veda* II. 288 May she sew her work with an infallible needle. **1881** MRS. R. T. COOKE *Somebody's Neighbors* 64 (Cent.) He..mended china with an infallible cement.

c. That cannot fail to be, or to come; certain.

1601 SHAKS. *All's Well* I. i. 150 To accuse your Mothers; which is most infallible disobedience. **1611** SPEED *Hist. Gt. Brit.* VI. lv. (1623) 199 A Forme infallible to bee of the Britaine's Coines. **1843** CARLYLE *Past & Pr.* I. v, One of the infalliblest fruits of Unwisdom.

B. *sb.* One who or that which is infallible.

1816 G. S. FABER *Orig. Pagan Idol.* III. 333 What heretic shall presume to decide between these two discordant Infallibles? **1830** GALT *Lawrie T.* I. ii. (1849) 4 Some proposed one kind of infallible, and some another. **1858** O. W. HOLMES *Aut. Breakf.-t.* vii. (1891) 172 A point of difference between an infallible and a heretic.

Hence †**inˈfallible** *v. trans.*, to render infallibly certain; also †**inˈfallibleship** = INFALLIBILITY 1 b.

1613 JACKSON *Creed* II. xxix. §4 His infallible-ship heares no farther in matters *de facto* then meaner men. **1656** S. H. *Gold. Law* 1 We wil first begin with Scripture Arguments the better to infallible it. *Ibid.*, We will next pursue it with right Reason which will selfly infallible it.

inˈfallibleness. [f. prec. + -NESS.] The quality of being infallible; infallibility.

a **1586** SIDNEY *Arcadia* (1622) 12 Nothing but fancie, wherein there must either be vanitie, or infalliblenesse. **1640** BP. HALL *Episc.* II. §22. 210 In the infalliblenesse of their judgement. **1870** RUSKIN *Lect. Art* iii. 74 [Its] infallibleness ..as a proof of every other good power.

infalliblist: see INFALLIBILIST.

infallibly (ɪnˈfælɪblɪ), *adv.* [f. INFALLIBLE *a.* + -LY².] In an infallible manner.

1. Without fail or liability to prove false; most certainly, indubitably.

1502 *Ord. Crysten Men* (W. de W. 1506) V. vii. 422 The which ryght derely the blyssed Ihesu Cryste unto us hathe conquered and promysed infayllybly. *a* **1529** SKELTON *Replyc.* 364 With me ye must consent And infallibly agre Of necessyte. *c* **1532** DU WES *Introd. Fr.* in Palsgr. 1048 Infallibly, madame, the mater is to hyghe for my symplenesse. **1653** WALTON *Angler* ii. 53 He will infallibly take the bait, and you will be as sure to catch him. **1726** SWIFT *Gulliver* I. v, Mine eyes..I should have infallibly lost, if I had not suddenly thought of an expedient. **1844** LD. BROUGHAM *Brit. Const.* viii. (1862) 106 The Sovereign would infallibly take part with the privileged orders.

2. Without liability to err or be mistaken; unerringly.

1597 HOOKER *Eccl. Pol.* V. lviii. §1 That the one might infallibly teach what the other doe most assuredly bring to pass. **1690** LOCKE *Hum. Und.* III. ix. (1695) 277 Though every thing said in the Text be infallibly true, yet the Reader may be..very fallible in the understanding of it. **1707** HICKERINGILL *Priest-cr.* II. i. 5 Pope Sixtus V. afterwards infallibly said, That [etc.]. **1860** PUSEY *Min. Proph.* 321 To learn..that He, the Infallible Truth, will teach them infallibly. **1875** H. C. WOOD *Therap.* (1879) 428 Bile..is to be recognized..more infallibly by testing with the proper reagents.

†**inˈfallid**, *a. Obs.* [f. IN-³ + (app.) an assumed *fallid or L. *fallid-us, from *fallĕre*, bearing the same analogy to *fallible* that *horrid* does to *horrible*.] That does not fail or prove false; = INFALLIBLE 2.

1635 HEYWOOD *Hierarch.* V. 308 Infallid testimonies of the wisedome and power of the Almighty. *a* **1639** WEBSTER *Appius & V.* II. iii, Upon my infallid evidence, You may pronounce the sentence on my side. **1639** G. DANIEL *Ecclus.* xxxvii. 87 He gives infallid rules Of Knowledge.

infalling (ˈɪnˌfɔːlɪŋ), *sb.* [IN *adv.* 11 c.] A falling in; †an invasion (*obs.*).

1676 W. ROW *Contn. Blair's Autobiog.* x. (1848) 250 The young laird of Swintoun, who before the infalling was suspected to favour the enemy. **1826** E. IRVING *Babylon* II. VIII. 303 Preparatory for the in-falling of an outward power.

infalling (ˈɪnˌfɔːlɪŋ), *a.* Also **in-falling.** [IN *adv.* 11 a.] Falling into or towards something (specified or understood).

1954 J. R. R. TOLKIEN *Two Towers* IV. iv. 259 They washed themselves and drank their fill at the in-falling freshet. **1969** *Nature* 20 Dec. 1160/1 The gravitational field of the galaxy, as well as the infalling gas from the universe, will sweep the halo clouds back into the galactic layer. **1971** I. G. GASS et al. *Understanding Earth* iii. 67/2 As the Earth grew and its gravitational attraction became greater so the energy released by an infalling body increased.

†**infaˈmation.** *Obs.* [a. f. *infamation* (1359 *-acion*, in Godef.), ad. L. *infāmātiōn-em*, n. of action f. *infāmāre*: see INFAME *v.*] The action of holding up to infamy; the spreading of an ill report; defamation.

1533 MORE *Apol.* xlv. Wks. 915/2 He bryngeth in as you see, his charitable infamacion of the cleargies crueltie, making men wene it wer so. **1563–87** FOXE *A. & M.* (1684) II. 123/2 The nature of the Church hath ever been to suffer ..slanderous reports and infamation by the malignant Adversaries. **1651** *Life Father Sarpi* (1676) 50 Some such pestiferous Pens..have..infected the World with impostures and infamations of those, whose works they were neither able to extinguish nor confute.

†**ˈinfamator.** *Obs. rare*⁻¹. [Agent-noun in L. form from L. *infāmāre*: see INFAME *v.*] One who defames; a slanderer.

1571 in Calderwood *Hist. Kirk* (Wodrow Soc.) III. 37 Suche as impugne proclamatioun of bannes cheeflie by imfamie, and prove not, lett them be punished..as infamators.

inˈfamatory, *a. rare.* [ad. med.L. *infāmātōri-us*, f. ppl. stem of L. *infāmāre*: see -ORY.]

†**a.** = DEFAMATORY (*obs.*). **b.** Bringing infamy.

1612 T. JAMES *Jesuits' Downf.* 58 These Libels, the contents whereof were wholly infamatory. **1620** SHELTON *Quix.* III. i. 12, I have not heard of infamatory Verse against the Lady Angelica. **1880** MUIRHEAD *Gaius* IV. §182 *note*, The reference to the infamatory result of compromise of a claim *ex delicto* is in the edict *de infamia*.

†**inˈfame**, *sb.*¹ *Obs.* Also 4 **enfame.** [a. OF. *infame, enfame*:—late L. *infāmium* (Isidore v. xxxvii. 26) = L. *infāmia* INFAMY.] = INFAMY.

1387–8 T. USK *Test. Love* I. vi. (Skeat) l. 6 Comenly the people wol lye and bringe aboute soche enfame. *Ibid.* 49 But infame that goeth alwaie tofore, and praising worship by any cause folowyng after, maketh to rise thilke honour, in double of wealth, and that quencheth the spotte of the firste enfame. **1413** HOCCLEVE *Piteous Compl. Soul* 258 Yit am I nought of this oppinion, To couere so be excusacion Of this infame, the malise of my synne. **1570** *Satir. Poems Reform.* x. 131 Than come dishonour and Infame, our fais, And brocht in ane to reule with raggit clais. **1616** J. LANE *Contn. Sqr.'s T.* xi. 74 And conscient fault thear wears owne willfull shame, Wheare reason playd false to right iust infame.

†**inˈfame**, *a.* (*sb.*²) *Obs.* [a. F. *infâme* (1356 in Hatz.-Darm.), ad. L. *infām-is* of ill fame, infamous, f. *in-* (IN-³) + *fāma* fame, report.] = INFAMOUS.

1555–86 *Satir. Poems Reform.* xxxvi. 124 That fals and degenerat seid Of Douglassis fals, wratchit, and infame. *a* **1572** KNOX *Hist. Ref.* I. Wks. 1846 I. 81 Whosoever war produced for witnesses war admitted, how suspitious and infame that ever thei ware. **1609** SKENE *Reg. Maj.* Table 82 Infame persones are all they quha are convicted of perjurie, vpon ane Assise. *Ibid.*, He is infame, quha reveales the secret of the gilde. *a* **1711** KEN *Hymns Festiv.* Poet. Wks. 1721 I. 274 Long had the Galilæan Name Been reprobated and infame. *a* **1734** NORTH *Exam.* I. iii. §34 (1740) 142 A scandalous, infame State Libel.

B. *sb.* [absol. use of adj. as in Fr.] An infamous person; one branded with infamy.

1550 BALE *Eng. Votaries* II. K iv, He shoulde be..made an infame or be put to the open reproch of all men.

infame (ɪnˈfeɪm), *v. arch.* Also 5–6 **enfame.** [a. F. *infame-r*, ad. L. *infāmāre* to render infamous, f. *infāmis*: see prec.]

1. *trans.* To render infamous; to brand with infamy or dishonour; to hold up to infamy; to reprobate. *arch.*

1413 HOCCLEVE *Piteous Compl. Soul* 252 Thi sone him banysshed from heuen blisse, as for enfamed; he and alle his. *c* **1477** CAXTON *Jason* 10 Shal I murder Jason..nay..for treuly for as moche as I sholde be enfamed. **1577–87** HOLINSHED *Chron.* I. 66/2 Because he..somewhat persecuted the christians, he was infamed by writers. **1598** BARCKLEY *Felic. Man* III. (1603) 271 Quintus Hortensius.. is infamed by historians, because he looked in a glasse when he made him ready. *a* **1718** PENN *Tracts* Wks. 1726 I. 611 This inhuman Practice will infame your Government. **1826** C. BUTLER *Vind. Bk. Rom. Cath. Ch.* 116 Why then do you infame Doctor Lingard for his not mentioning it? *Ibid.* 127 If we are to be infamed, let it be by the production of facts. **1897** CREIGHTON *Papacy* V. VI. v. 147 He infamed good works as though they were not meritorious.

†**2.** To spread an ill report of; to defame. *Obs.*

1483 CAXTON *Gold. Leg.* 181/2 She that enfamed the servaunte of god was taken and vexyd wyth a deuyl. **1529** MORE *Dyaloge* I. 19 a/2 No such faynyd wonders shulde enfame goddes very myracles. *a* **1533** LD. BERNERS *Gold. Bk. M. Aurel.* (1546) Ll vij b, To the entente to couer their owne infamy, they infame all other that bee good. **1604** T. WRIGHT *Passions* V. §4. 279 If the Iudge or Iustice of peace infame any person called before them vniustly, the iniury is almost doubled.

†**3.** To accuse of something infamous. *Obs.*

1531 ELYOT *Gov.* II. vii, Infamynge hym to be a man without charitie. **1536** *Rem. Sedition* 8 Is there any nation, that hath been more enfamed of barbarous conditions, than the Scythes? **1550** BALE *Eng. Votaries* II. L vj b, She was afore that, infamed of lyghte conuersacyon. **1571** CAMPION *Hist. Irel.* II. vi. (1633) 87 Hee infamed the said Prior, as an abettour and favourer of Arnolds heresie. **1797** *R. Burn's Eccl. Law* (ed. 6) III. 275 Ecclesiastical judges shall not compel any to come to purgation at the suggestion of their apparitors, unless they be infamed by grave and good men.

Hence **inˈfaming** *vbl. sb.* and *ppl. a.*

1535 E. HARVEL in Ellis *Orig. Lett.* Ser. II. II. 74 The infaming of our Nacion with the vehementist words they cowde use. **1599** JAS. I *Βασιλ. Δωρον* (1682) 25 The infaming and making odious of the parent is the readiest way to bring the sonne in contempt. **1611** COTGR., *Charivaris*,..an infamous (or infaming) ballade sung by an armed troupe vnder the window.

inˈfamed, *ppl. a. arch.* [f. prec. vb. + -ED¹.] Made or become infamous; branded with infamy.

1480 CAXTON *Chron. Eng.* IV. (1520) 39/1 Here was the fyrst that ever the chyrche of Rome had an infamed pope. **1536** BELLENDEN *Cron. Scot.* (1821) I. 176 He waistit al the public rentis..in his infamit lust. *a* **1619** FOTHERBY *Atheom.* I. x. §4 (1622) 102 Theodorus, the most infamed of the Atheists. **1663** *Flagellum or O. Cromwell* (ed. 2) 8 For Drinking..and the like outrages of licentious youth, none so infam'd as this young Tarquin.

†**b.** Legally pronounced or held infamous. *Obs.*

1529 MORE *Dyaloge* III. iii. 72 a/1 [That] the lawe made by the chyrche, sholde..admytte and receyue a persone infamed. *a* **1572** KNOX *Hist. Ref.* Wks. 1846 I. 277 Abused by the flattery of sick ane infamet person of the law and mensworne apostate. **1577** NORTHBROOKE *Dicing* (1843) 134 Whosoeuer vsed diceplaying was taken..and holden as infamed persons.

c. *Her.* (= F. *infamé.*) Applied to a lion or other beast figured without a tail; = DEFAMED 2.

1780 in EDMONDSON *Heraldry* II. Gloss. **1828** in BERRY *Encycl. Herald.* I. **1889** ELVIN *Dict. Her.* Plate 26, Defamed, Defame, or Infamed.

† **in'famer.** *Obs. rare.* Also 6 -our. [f. as prec. + -ER[1].] One who brings infamy; a defamer.
a **1533** LD. BERNERS *Gold. Bk. M. Aurel.* (1546) Gg viij b, Nor Rome shall not repute theim..for augmentours of the commonwealth, but infamours and robbers of clemency. **1601** CHESTER *Love's Mart., K. Arthur* cvi, That vniust Mordred, Mischiefes Nourisher, Times bad infamer.

infamili'arity. *rare.* [IN-[3].] = UNFAMILIARITY.
1866 *Edin. Rev.* Apr. 575 Whether something is to be allowed for a Norfolk man's infamiliarity with natural beauty.

† **in'famity.** *Sc. Obs.* [a. OF. *infameté* infamy, f. *infame* INFAME *a.*: see -ITY.] = INFAMY 3.
1493 *Acta Audit.* 176 (Jam.) Vnder the pain of periure & infamite. **1543** *Aberdeen Reg.* (Jam.), Infamite & periure.

infamize ('ɪnfəmaɪz), *v.* [f. L. *infāmis* INFAME *a.* + -IZE.]
1. *trans.* To render infamous; to brand with infamy; to stigmatize *with*; = INFAME *v.* 1.
1596 NASHE *Saffron Walden* 37 Another age..may baffull and infamize my name when I am in heauen. **1817** COLERIDGE *Zapoyla* I. i. 141 Riotous slanderers leagued To infamize the name of the king's brother With a lie black as hell. **1848** MILL *Pol. Econ.* v. x. §2 (1876) 560/1 The moral sense of mankind very rightly infamizes those who resist an otherwise just claim on the ground of usury.
b. To render infamous in law.
1827 MILL in *Bentham's Rat. Jud. Evid.* V. 746 All persons..who have suffered any afflictive or infamizing punishment. **1832** AUSTIN *Jurispr.* (1873) I. xxiii. 472 Certain obligations..are sanctioned by penalties which are purely infamising: by a declaration pronounced by competent authority, that the party shall be held infamous or merits infamy. **1865** MILL in *Westm. Rev.* XXVIII. 18.
2. To defame; = INFAME *v.* 2.
1598 SYLVESTER *Du Bartas* II. ii. I. *Noah* 577 Cham that impudently view'd His Fathers shame, and..thus began To imfamize the poor old drunken man. **1651** *Life Father Sarpi* (1676) 74 This Cardinal did always use to infamise the Father for his publisht Writings with odious appellations. **1817** COLERIDGE *Own Times* (1850) III. 957 Who infamizes another man as an Apostate and Renegado. **1831** *Examiner* 449/2 How is the claim to be stated without infamizing the claimant?
Hence **'infamizing** *vbl. sb.* and *ppl. a.* (see sense 1 b); also **'infamizer**, a defamer.
1592 G. HARVEY *Pierce's Super.* (1593) 180 Vnlineall vsurpers of iudgement, infamizers of vice. **1827-32** Infamizing [see 1 b above]. **1841** GEN. P. THOMPSON *Exerc.* (1842) VI. 197 Whatever baseness, whatever cruelty, whatever infamizing of the national character [etc.].

† **in'famonize,** *v.* [A perversion of *infamize.*]
1588 SHAKS. *L.L.L.* v. ii. 684 *Braggart* (*Armado*). Dost thou infamonize me among Potentates?

infamous ('ɪnfəməs), *a.* Also 5 **enfamouse,** (4 **infamis, -es**). [Corresponds to rare OF. *infameux*, med.L. *infāmōsus* = L. *infāmis*: cf. L. *fāmōsus*, F. *fameux*, Eng. *famous*. Formerly stressed *in'famous* (still in Bailey 1730, but Milton has *'infamous*). The L. form *infamis*, also *infames*, occurs in early use.]
1. Of ill fame or repute; famed or notorious *for* badness of any kind; notoriously evil, wicked, or vile; held in infamy or public disgrace.
a. of persons, their attributes, etc.
1533 MORE *Debell. Salem* ii. Wks. 935/1 [This] should but make..both partes more infamouse, amonge such other.. as would be glad and reioice to here much euill spoken of them both. *c* **1590** MARLOWE *Faust.* ii. 33, I fear he is fallen into that damned art for which they two are infamous through the world. **1611** BIBLE *Ezek.* xxii. 5 Those that be neere..shall mocke thee which art infamous, and much vexed. **1684** *Contempl. St. Man* I. ix. (1699) 103 Set before thy Eyes Christ Crucified upon Mount Calvary; if a Man more Infamous be imaginable. **1734** tr. *Rollin's Anc. Hist.* xx. i. IX. 7 Perseus was utterly infamous for his crimes. **1844** THIRLWALL *Greece* lx. VIII. 11 He appears to have been more infamous for sacrilege than for bloodshed.
b. of things.
c **1380** WYCLIF *Serm.* Sel. Wks. I. 271 No man liȝtiþ a lanterne in derknesse, and puttiþ it in oon of þes two infamous [*MS. Douce* 321 famous] places: neþer in hid place ne undir a bushel. **1398** TREVISA *Barth. De P.R.* XIX. cxvii. (Add. MS. 27944) lf. 326/2 þis nombre..is in-fames among som men, for, by þe nombre of tweyne we beþ departed fro oon, and so þis nombre is acompted tokne..of departyng. **1570-6** LAMBARDE *Peramb. Kent* (1826) 245 No lesse infortunate, but much more infamous to this countrie, was the time of the second muster here. **1650** FULLER *Pisgah* II. xii. 253 The high-way betwixt Jericho and Jerusalem is infamous for theeving. **1667** PRIMATT *City & C. Build.* 10 Salisbury Plain, and divers other places..famous for curious air, and as infamous for their barrenness. **1777** ROBERTSON *Hist. Amer.* (1778) II. VI. 155 An island, infamous for the most unhealthy climate in that region of America. **1838** THIRLWALL *Greece* II. xv. 281 A part of the Coast, infamous in ancient times, under the name of Cœla (the Hollows).
2. Deserving of infamy; of shameful badness, vileness, or abominableness; of a character or quality deserving utter reprobation. (One of the strongest adjectives of detestation.) **a.** of persons, etc.
c **1489** CAXTON *Blanchardyn* xlvi. 178 O thou ryght enfamouse churle and olde myschaunte! **1590** SPENSER *F.Q.* I. xii. 27 False erraunt knight, infamous, and forswore. **1605** SYLVESTER *Du Bartas* II. iii. IV. *Captains* 1082 A Sink of Filth, where ay th' infamousest Most bold and busie, are esteemed best. **1711** ADDISON *Spect.* No. 126 ¶3 Infamous Hypocrites, that are for promoting their own Advantage, under Colour of the Publick Good. **1841** LANE *Arab. Nts.* I. 108 Thou liest, thou infamous woman.
b. of things.
1555 EDEN *Decades* 208 The nobilitie..repute it infamous to ioyne with any of base parentage. **1586** MARLOWE *1st Pt. Tamburl.* v. ii, Then is there left..no hope of end To our infamous, monstrous slaveries. **1671** MILTON *Samson* 417 My former servitude, ignoble, Unmanly, ignominious, infamous. **1703** MAUNDRELL *Journ. Jerus.* (1732) 106 Detest the very ground on which was acted such an infamous Treachery. **1858** *Act 21 & 22 Vict.* c. 90 §29 Any registered medical practitioner..guilty of infamous conduct in any professional respect. **1869** E. A. PARKES *Pract. Hygiene* 561 The sanitary conditions..were, without exception, infamous.
3. *Law.* Of a person: Deprived of all or certain of the rights of a citizen, in consequence of conviction of certain crimes.
An infamous person is, until he has served his sentence, disqualified for any public appointment, any public pension or allowance, the right to sit in Parliament or exercise any franchise. He is permanently disqualified (unless restored by a free pardon) from serving as a juror; and, down to 1844, was incapacitated from giving evidence in a court of law.
[**1395** *Remonstrance* (1851) 87 And thei that ben forsworen opinli, ben infamis, and worthi to be priuid of alle beneficis.] **1548** *Act 2 & 3 Edw. VI*, c. 15 §1 Everie Person so conspiring..for the third offence shall..be taken as a man infamous and his sayinge deposicions or oathe not to be credyted at anye tyme in any matters of judgement. **1551** *Sc. Acts Mary* (1597) c. 19 Infamous persons, never able to bruik office, honour, dignitie, nor benefice in time to-cum. **1651** W. G. tr. *Cowel's Inst.* 278 They [perjurers] were to be committed to Prison, and for ever rendered so infamous, that they were deprived of the benefit of the Lawes, and their Testimonies never to be admitted in any Cause. **1707** J. CHAMBERLAYNE *St. Gt. Brit.* III. viii. (*Punishments*) 339 They are condemned to lose the Franchise or Freedom of the Law, that is, become Infamous, and of no Credit. **1726** AYLIFFE *Parergon* 55 Persons that are Infamous, or branded with any Note of Infamy,..are *ipso Jure* forbidden to be Advocates. **1768** BLACKSTONE *Comm.* III. xxiii. 370 Infamous persons are such as may be challenged as jurors, *propter delictum.* **1841** ELPHINSTONE *Hist. Ind.* I. 59 Infamous persons..with others disqualified on slighter grounds, are in the first instance excluded from giving testimony.
b. Of a crime or punishment: Involving or entailing infamy.
infamous crime was chiefly applied to abominable and disgusting crimes, as sodomy and kindred offences: see the Larceny Act of 1861, sect. 46. In U.S., 'in general, an offence punishable in a state prison'.
c **1555** HARPSFIELD *Divorce Hen. VIII* (Camden) 255 And so had two wives at once, which is by the civil law a thing infamous. *c* **1780** *Constit. U.S.* Amendm. v, No person shall be held to answer for a capital or otherwise infamous crime, unless on a presentment or indictment of a grand jury. **1785** PALEY *Mor. Philos.* VI. ix. (1830) 444 Infamous punishments are mismanaged in this country, with respect both to the crimes and the criminals. **1861** *Act 24 & 25 Vict.* c. 96 §46 *margin*, 'Infamous crime' defined. **1863** BRIGHT *Sp., Amer.* 26 Mar. (1876) 128 A conspiracy whose fundamental institution..is declared to be felony and infamous by the statutes of their Country. **1870** *Act 33 & 34 Vict.* c. 77 §10 No man who has been or shall be attainted of any treason or felony, or convicted of any crime that is infamous, unless he shall have obtained a free pardon..is or shall be qualified to serve on juries or inquests. **1897** *Bouvier's Law Dict.* (U.S.) s.v., The..doctrine..that imprisonment in a state prison or a penitentiary with or without hard labour was an infamous punishment. *Mod. Newsp.* A warrant being issued against him for an infamous crime, he fled the country.

'infamously, *adv.* [f. prec. + -LY[2].] In an infamous manner or degree; with infamy.
1611 FLORIO, *Infamemente*, infamously. **1621-51** BURTON *Anat. Mel.* I. iv. 1, Two melancholy brethren, that made away with themselves, and for so foul a fact, were accordingly censured, to be infamously buried. **1666** *More News fr. Rome* (title-p.), According to the account of that infamously famous man, Dr. Lee. **1718** LADY M. W. MONTAGU *Let. to C'tess Bristol* 10 Apr., They are bought and sold as publicly and more infamously in all our Christian great Cities. **1728** MORGAN *Algiers* I. iv. 160 He was in a Condition to listen to the Insinuations of the Infamously famous Count Julian.
b. In a manner or degree deserving of infamy or utter reprobation; disgracefully, atrociously, detestably. (A very strong adverb of reprobation.)
1695 DRYDEN tr. *Du Fresnoy* (J.), That poem was infamously bad. **1741** MIDDLETON *Cicero* I. vi. 404 The second..infamously betrayed him. **1800** MRS. HERVEY *Mourtray Fam.* I. v. 180 He is a horrid brute, and uses Mrs. Lenmer infamously. **1886** W. J. TUCKER *E. Europe* 98 His own class considered itself infamously outraged.

'infamousness. [f. as prec. + -NESS.] The quality of being infamous; infamy.
1647 CLARENDON *Hist. Reb.* IV. §131 The Infamousness of the Charge against him. **1675** J. SMITH *Chr. Relig. App.* I. 17 His Daughter and Niece, being for their infamousness, thrust by his own Decree into exile.

† **infamouze,** *v. Obs. rare*$^{-1}$. [irreg. f. INFAMOUS *a.*] *trans.* To make infamous.
1628 SIR S. D'EWES *Jrnl.* (1783) 44 Some wit, to infamouze the rare confidence of Mr. Felton, in that he fledd not..framed [etc.].

infamy ('ɪnfəmɪ). [a. F. *infamie* (14th c. in Hatz.-Darm.), which took the place of earlier OF. *infame*, ad. L. *infāmia*, f. *infāmis* INFAME *a.*]
1. Evil fame or reputation; scandalous repute; public reproach, shame, or disgrace.
1473 *Rolls of Parlt.* VI. 69/2 Nowe there remayneth no colour or matere of argument to the hurt or infamye of the same right and title. **1490** CAXTON *Eneydos* xxvi. 93 Thou hast dyuerted my honour in-to dishonest infamye. **1553** EDEN *Treat. Newe Ind.* (Arb.) 21 She should incurre most vyle infamie. *a* **1633** AUSTIN *Medit.* (1635) 160 He not onely saw Christ in glory betweene Moses and Elias..But he saw him also in Infamy betweene two theeves. **1783** WATSON *Philip III* (1839) 67 The young baron de Harmont involved himself in ruin and infamy, by surrendering it[Grave]. **1867** FREEMAN *Norm. Conq.* (1876) I. v. 274 Two caitiffs..whose names are handed down to infamy.
b. with *an* and *pl.* An instance of this: in quot. 1611 *transf.* an object of public reproach.
1526 *Pilgr. Perf.* (W. de W. 1531) 114 To suffre all.. aduersite: As..persecucyons, temptacyons, & infamyes or shames. **1598** GRENEWEY *Tacitus' Ann.* I. xi. (1622) 21 Now was the time to blot out the infamies of their former conspiracies. **1611** BIBLE *Ezek.* xxxvi. 3 Ye are taken vp in the lips of talkers, and are an infamy of the people.
2. The quality or character of being infamous or of shameful vileness; (with *pl.*) an infamous or utterly disgraceful act.
1513 MORE *Rich. III* Wks. 65/2 With which infami he wold not haue his honoure stayned for anye crowne. *a* **1680** BUTLER *Rem.* (1759) I. 154 As if it were an Infamy To live, when he was doom'd to die. **1776** GIBBON *Decl. & F.* x. (1869) I. 196 The infamy of the peace was more deeply and more sensibly felt. **1819** SHELLEY *Cenci* IV. i. 81 Thro' infamies unheard of among men. **1859** WRAXALL tr. *R. Houdin* v. 53 For the honour of my family let not this proof of my infamy be found here.
3. *Law.* The loss of all or certain of the rights of a citizen, consequent on conviction of certain crimes: see INFAMOUS 3. (Cf. INFAMITY.)
1609 SKENE *Reg. Maj.* I. xiv, [Perjured jurors] sall tyne the benefite of the law, and of the land, and sall incurre the paine of infamie. **1702** *Levinz's Reports* III. 426 It is said, That Pillery although it infers Infamy by the Common Law, yet by the Canon and Civil Law..does not import Infamy except the cause for which it is inflicted be infamous.

† **'infance.** *Obs. rare.* In 4 en-, **infaunce.** [a. OF. *enfance*, *-aunce* (mod.F. *enfance*):—L. *infāntia*: see next.] = next.
c **1400** *Rom. Rose* 4288 In hir enfaunce. *Ibid.* 5006 The foly dedis of hir infaunce.

infancy ('ɪnfənsɪ). [ad. L. *infāntia* inability to speak, childhood, f. *infānt-em* INFANT *sb.*[1]: see -ANCY.]
1. The condition of being an infant; the earliest period of human life, early childhood, babyhood.
1494 FABYAN *Chron.* III. lviii. 38 This was from his Infancy norysshed and brought vp among the Romaynes. **1531** ELYOT *Gov.* I. v, Hit shall be expedient that a noble mannes sonne, in his infancie, haue with hym continually onely suche as may accustome hym by litle and litle to speake pure and elegant latin. **1594** SHAKS. *Rich. III*, IV. iv. 168 A greeuous burthen was thy Birth to me, Tetchy and wayward was thy Infancie. **1671** MILTON *P.R.* IV. 508 Seldom have I ceased to eye Thy infancy, thy childhood, and thy youth. **1692** LOCKE *Educ.* §1 The little, or almost insensible impressions on our tender infancies, have very important and lasting consequences. **1736** BUTLER *Anal.* I. i. Wks. 1874 I. 13 The helpless imperfect state of infancy. **1803-6** WORDSW. *Intimations* v, Heaven lies about us in our infancy. **1871** *Educ. Times* 1 June 49 The child begins to emerge from the state which is properly called infancy; in truth, he is no longer an infant, for he is no longer speechless. **1874** FARRAR *Christ* ii, In the Arabic Gospel of the Infancy, Simeon recognizes Jesus because he sees Him shining like a pillar of light in His mother's arms.
b. *transf.* Second childhood, dotage.
1697 DRYDEN *Virg. Georg.* Ded., An insipid Manhood, and a stupid old Infancy.
2. *Law.* The condition of being a minor; the period of life during which a person remains under guardianship (extending, in common law, to the end of the twenty-first year); minority, nonage.
1658 GRIMSTONE tr. *Croke's Rep., Jas. I* (1791) 320 Debt brought upon a lease for years..The defendant in bar pleaded infancy at the time of the lease made. **1752** SIR C. VINER *Cancelled Will* 1 July, I give to the Chancellor and University of Oxford (to whom I think myself in some measure obliged to make some Amends for my Indiscretions there in my Infancy). **1755** JOHNSON, *Infancy.* 2. Civil infancy, extended by the English law to one and twenty years. **1769** BLACKSTONE *Comm.* IV. 22 We will consider the case of infancy, or nonage. **1786** BURKE *W. Hastings* Wks. 1842 II. 215 The ministerial party at Poona, who held and exercised the regency of that state in the infancy of the peshwa. **1818** CRUISE *Digest* (ed. 2) III. 34 It [the right of advowson] was not vested in a guardian in socage, nor was he accountable for any presentation made during the infancy of his ward. *Mod.* The defendant pleaded infancy, the goods having been supplied before he was of age.
3. *fig.* The earliest period in the history of anything capable of development; the initial and rudimentary stage in any process of growth.
1555 EDEN *Decades* Pref. (Arb.) 56 He wrought miracles.. euen in thinfancie of faythe. **1633** P. FLETCHER *Purple Isl.* I. xlix, Thrice happy was the worlds first infancie. **1677** YARRANTON *Eng. Improv.* 62 There will be such advantage given to the Linen Manufacture in its Infancy. **1772** PRIESTLEY *Inst. Relig.* (1782) I. 143 Our present being is but the infancy of man. **1872** RAYMOND *Statist. Mines & Mining* 185 Our quartz interests are in their infancy. **1875** JOWETT *Plato* (ed. 2) IV. 229 In the infancy of logic, a form of thought has to be invented.
4. *concr.* (chiefly *rhetorical.*) Childhood as embodied in living examples; infants collectively.
1598 SHAKS. *Merry W.* v. v. 56 Sleepe she as sound as carelesse infancie. **1606** —— *Tr. & Cr.* II. ii. 105 Soft

infancie, that nothing can but cry. **1781** COWPER *Charity* 48 Nor age nor infancy could find thee there. **1813** SHELLEY *Q. Mab* II. 152 Old age and infancy Promiscuous perished. **1860** GEN. P. THOMPSON *Audi Alt.* III. cvi. 17 When tender infancy evinces needless terror at cow, or dog, or shaggy goat.

†**5.** In etymological sense: Inability or unwillingness to speak; speechlessness; silence. *Obs.*

1641 MILTON *Ch. Govt.* II. Introd., Dare not now to say or do anything better than thy former sloth and infancy. **1670** —— *Hist. Eng.* v. Wks. (1851) 202 So darkly do the Saxon Annals deliver thir meaning with more then wonted infancy.

†**in'fand,** *a. Obs.* exc. as *nonce-wd.* [ad. L. *infānd-us* unspeakable, abominable, f. *in-* (IN-^{3}) + *fānd-us*, gerundive of *fā-rī to speak.*] = next.

1608 BP. J. KING *Serm.* 5 Nov. 18 Rome..the *Coluuies* and common sewer of all infande wickednesse. **1678** CUDWORTH *Intell. Syst.* I. iv. §14. 240 They ought by all means possible to hide and conceal that opinion (as infand and detestable). **1889** *Sat. Rev.* 2 Mar. 245/1 The Society.. has caused dolours infand [cf. Virgil *infandos dolores*] to Gladstonians.

†**in'fandous,** *a. Obs.* [f. as prec. + -OUS.] Unspeakable, not to be spoken of; nefarious.

1644 HOWELL *Twelve Treat.* (1661) 135 With what infandous blasphemies have Pulpits rung! *c* **1645** —— *Lett.* I. v. xii. (1655) 209 This infandous custom of Swearing.. reigns in England lately more than any where else. **1658** PHILLIPS, *Infandous*,..monstrously wicked and hainous. **1686** GOAD *Celest. Bodies* III. iii. 466 To give some.. warning of such Infandous Cataclysmes, Pictures, and Assurances of Noah's Floud. **1708** HEARNE *Collect.* (O.H.S.) II. 93 Hang'd for most infandous Crimes.

†**'infang,** *sb. Sc. Obs.* Abbrev. of INFANGTHIEF.

1549 *Compl. Scot.* xiii. 106 The grit familiarite that Inglis men and Scottis hes hed on baith the boirdours..in marchandeis in..out fang and in fang, ilk ane amang vtheris. **1828** SCOTT *F.M. Perth* iv, Would you have us now yield up our rights and immunities, our outfang and infang, our hand-habend..and our blood-suits?

†**'infang,** *v. Sc. Obs.* [f. IN-^{1} + FANG *v.*] *trans.* To take in, haul in.

1513 DOUGLAS *Æneis* v. Prol. 30 Himself infangis the le scheit of the saill.

†**in'fanglement.** *Obs. rare.* [f. IN-^{2} + FANGLE *v.*^{2} + -MENT.] A scheme, machination.

1745 RICHARDSON *Grandison* VI. xxv. 143 Neither you nor your niece know how..to go out of the common femality path, when you get a man into your gin, however superior he is to common infanglements, and low chicanery.

†**'infang,thief.** *Old Eng. Law. Obs.* Forms: 1–2 **infangenþeof,** 3 **infangen(e)-, infangethef,** 4–6 **infangthef, -e,** (6 **infanthef, infanketheiff),** 7 **infangtheefe, -theif(e),** 9 *Hist.* **infangthief.** Also *erron.* 6–7 **infang-,** 8 **infangentheft.** [OE. *infangenþéof*, f. IN *adv.* + *fangen*, pa. pple. of *fōn* to seize (see FANG *v.*) + *þéof* THIEF; *lit.* 'thief seized within'.]

Jurisdiction over a thief apprehended within the manor or territorial limits to which the privilege was attached; the right of the lord of a manor to try and to amerce a thief caught within its limits.

According to the 13th c. 'Laws of Edward the Confessor', the criminal must be the lord's 'own thief', i.e. his own man or tenant; and, according to Bracton, must further be caught in the act, or in possession of the thing stolen; the latter provision also appears in the 16th c. Scotch statements of Balfour and Skene. The Latin formula for 'infangen þéof and útfangen þéof' was 'cum furis comprehensione intus et foris'.

1020 in Earle *Land Charters* (1888) 233 Ic cyðe eow þæt ic hæbbe ȝeunnen him þæt he beo his saca & socne wyrðe, & griðbryces & hamsocne & forstealles & infangenes þeofes. *a* **1066** *Ibid.* 343 Ic cyðe eow ðæt ic habbe ȝeȝeofen Criste.. and Ælfwine abbod into Rameseȝe saca and socna, tol and team, and infangenðeof. **12..** *Laws Edw. Conf.* c. 22 Quid sit soche, et sache, et tol, et theam, et infangenthef. *Ibid.* §4 De infangeneþef. Justitia cognoscentis latronis sua est de homine suo, si captus fuerit super terram suam. *c* **1250** *Gloss.* in *Rel. Ant.* I. 33 Infangenethef, *Larum pris ens nostre tere. c* **1250** BRACTON III. ii. xxxv, Et dicitur infangethef, latro captus in terra alicujus, de hominibus suis propriis, seysitus latrocino. **1292** BRITTON I. xvi. §1 Qe, tauntost soint pris et en la Court le seignur del fee si il eit la fraunchise de Infangenthef..soint menez en jugement. *c* **1350** HIGDEN *Polychron.* (Rolls) II. 94 Infangthef, pelfinde inward [*v.r.* pelfande in warde], id est infra suum capere reum, Gallice, dedeinz le soen attachement de laroun [*Harl.* (2261) *transl.* Infanthef pelfynde inwarde, that is to say, to take a gilty man within his lordeschippe, in Frenche, dedeins le soen atachemente de laron]. **1535** *Act 27 Hen. VIII*, c. 26 §23 Lordes Marches..shall have within..their said Lordeshippes..Wayff Straiff Infanthef Outfanthef Treasoure Troves. *a* **1600** *Balfour's Practicks* (1754) 39 Thair is sum Baronis quha hes privilege and libertie of infang thift and outfang thift, quha thairfoir hes power to sit and give dome..upon all theives tane and apprehendit in manifest thift [SKENE *Quon. Attach.* ch. c., vpon ane man, taken within their fredome, saised with manifest thift] sic as hand-havand and back-beirand, within thair baronie. *a* **1657** SIR W. MURE *Hist. Rowallane* Wks. (S.T.S.) II. 241 The Mures..were possessours of the estate & lieveing of Rowallane..infeft cum furca et fossa, sock et sack, thole et theam, infang theif et outfang theif. **1832** SIR F. PALGRAVE *Eng. Commw.* vii, At the Conquest, the Lords of Township had a right called the Right of Infang Thief, or summary punishment of criminals taken in open delict. **1839** KEMBLE *Cod. Dipl.* Introd. xlv. **1895** POLLOCK & MAITLAND *Hist. Eng. Law* I. 628 The criminal justice of the boroughs [*c* 1272] seems seldom to have stretched to any higher point than that of infangthief and utfangthief, in other words, the punishment of criminals caught in the act.

infant ('ɪnfənt), *sb.*^{1} (*a.*) Forms: 4–5 **enfaunt, infaunt,** 6 **enfant, infante,** (7 **inphant**), 6– **infant.** [a. OF. *enfant, -aunt* (F. *enfant*, Pr. *enfan*, Sp., Pg., It. *infante*) child:—L. *infāns, infānt-em* child, sb. use of *infāns* unable to speak, f. *in-* (IN-^{3}) + *fāns*, pres. pple. of *fā-rī* to speak. Aphetized FAUNT.]

1. a. A child during the earliest period of life (or still unborn); now most usually applied to a child in arms, a babe; but often extended to include any child under seven years of age (cf. *infant-class*, INFANT-SCHOOL); in early use (esp. when transl. L. *infāns*, or F. *enfant*) used in the wider sense of 'child', and thus passing into the legal sense 2.

1382 WYCLIF *Zech.* viii. 5 And streetis of the citee shuln be fulfillid with infauntis [1388 ȝonge children] and maydens, pleyinge in the stretis of it. —— *1 John* ii. 14, I wrijte to ȝou, infauntis [*gloss* or ȝonge children], for ȝe han knowe the fadir. *c* **1440** *Gesta Rom.* I. xlviii. 209 (Harl. MS.) Gothe swyftly..to the house of the forster,..and takithe of him the litle Infaunt, that his wyf this nyght chylded. *c* **1450** *Bk. Curtasye* 141 in *Babees Bk.* (1868) 303 Yf that þou be a ȝong enfaunt, And thenke þo scoles for to haunt. **1582** N.T. (Rhem.) *Luke* xviii. 15 They brought vnto him infants also, that he might touche them. **1594** T. B. *La Primaud. Fr. Acad.* II. 397 The burthen..hath sense & feeling about the sixe and thirtieth day, and from that time forward it is called an infant. But as yet it is voyde of motion. **1600** SHAKS. *A.Y.L.* II. vii. 143 The Infant, Mewling, and puking in the Nurses armes. **1655** MILTON *Sonn.*, *Massacre Piedmont*, The bloody Piemontese, that rolled Mother with infant down the rocks. **1710** PARNELL *Hermit* 151 The closed cradle where an infant slept. **1818** CRUISE *Digest* XXVIII. xvii. (ed. 2) 469 It was held that a devise to an infant *in ventre matris*,..was good, which began with an allowance for the birth of a posthumous child. **1850** TENNYSON *In Mem.* liv, An infant crying in the night: An infant crying for the light: And with no language but a cry.

b. *fig.* One who is a 'child', or very young beginner, in some department.

1526 *Pilgr. Perf.* (W. de W. 1531) 12b, They were ledde by Moyses as yonge infantes and tender babes in fayth. **1594** PLAT *Jewell-ho.*, *New sorts Soyle* 9 Whereby all those that be the true infantes of Art, may receive a full light into Nature. **1899** *N.B. Daily Mail* 16 Feb. 5 As every political infant cannot fail to recognise, the whole question was.. unconnected with party politics.

c. *transf.* A thing newly come into existence, or in its earliest stage.

c **1586** C'TESS PEMBROKE *Ps.* XCVI. vi, Leavy infants of the wood. **1602** SHAKS. *Ham.* I. iii. 39 The Canker Galls, the Infants of the Spring. **1608** HIERON *Defence* III. 139 Reputed an infant and a novelty, rather then an antiquity. **1890** BOLDREWOOD *Col. Reformer* (1891) 215 The.. questioning of old Paul..seemed adverse to the Utopian infant.

2. A person under (legal) age; a minor. In common law, one who has not completed his or her twenty-first year; in the case of a ruler, one who has not reached the age at which he becomes constitutionally capable of exercising sovereignty.

[**1376** *Rolls of Parlt.* II. 342/2 La Fyn ou Note se leva tan qe come l'Enfant estoit deinz age.] **1513** MORE in Grafton *Chron.* (1568) II. 774, I may require it for hym, except the lawe geve the infaunt a guarden onely for his goods. **1601** F. TATE *Househ. Ord. Edw. II* §25 (1876) 17 The infantes which happen to be the kinges wardes, shal have wages, and liverees, and al other necessaries, according to their estate. **1603** OWEN *Pembrokesh.* (1890) 19 [He] was governed by tutours beinge an inphant. **1624** COKE *On Litt.* 2b, An infant or *minor* (whom we call any that is under the age of 21 yeares). **1642** tr. *Perkins' Prof. Bk.* x. §684. 295 An enfant who is a feoffee shall give notice, and an enfant who is Lord shall take notice. **1765** BLACKSTONE *Comm.* I. 460 The privileges and disabilities of an infant, or one under age and subject to guardianship. **1786** W. THOMSON *Philip III* (1839) 249 Mary de Medicis sole regent of France during the minority of her son, an infant in the ninth year of his age. **1858** LD. ST. LEONARDS *Handy Bk. Prop. Law* xiii. 81 Although..until a recent period an infant might have appointed a guardian to his children by deed or will, yet it seems that he can no longer do so by will.

fig. **1692** WASHINGTON tr. *Milton's Def. Pop.* Wks. 1738 I. 521 The Judges..swear, that they will do nothing judicially, but according to Law, though the King by Word, or Mandate, or Letters under his own Seal, should command the contrary. Hence it is that the King is often said in our Law to be an Infant; and to possess his Rights and Dignities, as a Child or a Ward does his.

†**3.** A youth of noble or gentle birth. Cf. INFANT *sb.*^{2}, CHILD 5. *Obs.*

1590 SPENSER *F.Q.* II. viii. 56 To whom the Infant thus: 'Fayre sir, what need Good turnes be counted as a servile bond?' **1596** *Ibid.* VI. viii. 25 The Infant [Arthur] hearkned wisely to her tale. **1600** FAIRFAX *Tasso* XVI. xxxiv, The noble Infant [Rinaldo] stood a space Confused, speechless.

4. Humorously applied to various productions of exceptional size, strength, etc. (See quots.)

1832 *Brighton Gazette* in Blew *Brighton & its Coaches* (1893) 187 Mr. Walter Hancock's steam-carriage, the 'Infant', was on the way from London to this place on an experimental trip. **1874** *Graphic* 5 Dec. 538/1 The heaviest gun now actually in position, commonly called the Woolwich Infant,..weighs 35 tons. **1888** *Pall Mall G.* 6 June 2/2 The speciality of Woolwich is its big guns, its now famous and historic 'infants'.

5. *attrib.* (or *adj.*) (When appositive or attrib., often equivalent to an adj. = *infantile, infantine.*)

a. *appositive.* That is an infant or like an infant, as ***infant angel, God, heir, king, martyr, poor, prodigy, warrior,*** etc.

1595 DANIEL *Civ. Wars* I. xxxiv, Kingdomes euer suffer this distresse, For one or manie, guide the infant king. **1596** SHAKS. *1 Hen. IV*, III. ii. 113 The Hotspur Mars, in swathing Clothes, This Infant Warrior. **1629** MILTON *Hymn Christ's Nativ.* 16 A present to the Infant God. **1678** DRYDEN & LEE *Œdipus* IV. i, All the riches That empire could bestow.. Upon its infant heir. **1692** WASHINGTON tr. *Milton's Def. Pop.* xii. (1851) 241 A poor indigent King, surrounded with so many Infant-Priests and Doctors. *a* **1704** T. BROWN *Praise Drunkenness* Wks. 1730 I. 37 Cheeks like those the Painters give to infant-angels. **1720** WELTON *Suffer. Son of God* I. ix. 231 Thou wouldst not suffer those Infant-Martyrs..to endure so much as Thy Self. **1831** [see PRODIGY 3c]. **1872** J. A. H. MURRAY *Complaynt of Scotl.* Introd. viii, Of the three centuries of Scottish history [1300–1600]..nearly a century and a half were occupied by the reigns of infant sovereigns. **1874** FARRAR *Christ* ii, The recognition of the Infant Saviour by Simeon and Anna. *a* **1900** *Mod.* The presentation of the infant Jesus in the temple. **1924** R. M. OGDEN tr. *Koffka's Growth of Mind* ii. §4. 49 Infant-prodigies who fail to live up to their early promise. **1939** F. PRATT *Secret & Urgent* i. 25 He was Jean François Champollion, an infant prodigy.

b. *appositive* (or *adj.*). In its earliest stage, newly existing, ungrown, undeveloped, nascent, incipient, as ***infant blossom, civilization, code, colony, commerce, community, convert, fruit, industry*** (see quot. 1914), ***letters, navy, sorrow, spring, world,*** etc.

1593 SHAKS. *Lucr.* 1096 Old woes, not infant sorrows, bear them mild. **1671** GREW *Anat. Pl.* I. vi. §2 Upon observation of a young and Infant-Apple. **1707** J. ARCHDALE *Carolina* 23 Vast expence upon such an Infant Colony. **1728** POPE *Dunc.* III. 95 The soil that arts and infant letters bore. **1779** F. HERVEY *Nav. Hist.* II. 144 Of all the infant settlements in America, New-England alone..acknowledged the authority of the commonwealth. **1784** COWPER *Tiroc.* 43 Spring hangs her infant blossoms on the trees. **1796** BURKE *Regic. Peace* i. Wks. VIII. 154 The ruin of commerce and the almost total extinction of an infant credit. **1820** KEATS *Hyperion* I. 26 She was a Goddess of the infant world. **1861** M. PATTISON *Ess.* (1889) I. 43 The unequal contest..of England's infant navy against the..supremacy of the Hanseatic Confederacy. **1870** *Congress. Globe* App. 29 Mar. 240/3 But, argue our defenders of monopoly, let us protect our infant industries, and when they have grown to manhood..they will need no further protection. **1906** *Daily Chron.* 17 Oct. 6/5 The argument for Protection there is not at all the infant-industry argument. **1914** *Cycl. Amer. Govt.* II. 176 *Infant Industry.* This term is applied to the need of protecting new industries in order to give them opportunity to compete with older foreign establishments.

6. *attrib.* (or *adj.*). Of or belonging to an infant or infants, proper to or intended for an infant or infants; childlike; childish; infantile, as ***infant bands, blood, breath, class, cradle, eye, gaud, state, softness, weakness, welfare, years,*** etc. **infant mistress**, a woman teacher of infants at an elementary school; **infant mortality**, the death of infants, *spec.* of those less than a year old. Also INFANT-SCHOOL, q.v.

c **1586** C'TESS PEMBROKE *Ps.* LXXI. ix, By thee from infant cradle Taught. **1599** SHAKS. *Hen. V*, Epil. 9 Henry the Sixt, in Infant Bands crown'd King. **1651–3** JER. TAYLOR *Serm. for Year* (1678) 282 Though it be a shame to us to need such allectives and infant-gauds. **1671** MILTON *P.R.* II. 78 The murderous king..who sought his life, and missing filled With infant blood the streets of Bethlehem. *a* **1711** KEN *Hymns Festiv.* Poet. Wks. 1721 I. 386 You in their Infant-age, To tender them engage. **1720** WELTON *Suffer. Son of God* I. viii. 190 Even thro' Thy Infant-State, I behold Thy Majesty. *Ibid.* iv. 76 That Infant-Weakness which Thou took'st upon Thee! **1792** S. ROGERS *Pleas. Mem.* II. 392 The joys and sorrows of our infant-years. **1877** W. R. ALGER *Life Edwin Forrest* I. 147 The rate of infant mortality may be reduced to one per cent of its present murderous average. **1918** *79th Ann. Rep. Registrar-General 1916* (Cd. 8869) 35 Infant welfare organisations might well devote special attention to the first days of the life of illegitimate children. **1921** *N.Z. Educ. Gaz.* 1 Nov. 12/2 (Advt.), *Infant-mistress*—South Wellington (Grade VII G): £310–£320. **1922** *Encycl. Brit.* XXX. 650/2 *Infant Welfare Centres.*—The first task has been to coördinate the work at the Infant Centre and the visitation of the mothers in their own homes. *a* **1930** D. H. LAWRENCE *Phoenix II* (1968) 18 Last week the infant mistress did not come up, so I was alone. **1939** M. SPRING RICE *Working-Class Wives* p. vii, The high rates of infant mortality..in the early years of the present century. *Ibid.*, Better methods of mothercraft through the influence of the Infant Welfare Centre. **1962** *Guardian* 9 Mar. 8/2 The orders might contain..infant welfare foods (distributed as a voluntary service). **1963** B. PEARSON *Coal Flat* iii. 48 'The first infant mistress's job that's going,' she thought.

7. *Comb.* as **infant-baptism**, the baptism of infants, pædobaptism; ***infant-queller; infant-killing, -sprinkling; infant-feeding*** adj.; also ***infant-like*** adj. and adv.

1674 N. FAIRFAX *Bulk & Selv.* 51 A blind man, who had been so from his *Infant-baptism. **1680** ALLEN *Peace & Unity* 49 Churches Founded in Infant-Baptism, are not to be held Communion with. **1897** *Westm. Gaz.* 19 Jan. 12/2 The *infant-feeding competition represents the..ceaseless intrigues in Court circles. **1611** COTGR., *Infanticide*, child-murthering, *infant-killing. **1607** SHAKS. *Cor.* II. i. 41 Your abilities are to *infant-like, for dooing much alone. **1678** CUDWORTH *Intell. Syst.* I. v. 689 Produced, not in a mature and adult but an infant-like weak and tender state. *a* **1641** BP. MOUNTAGU *Acts & Mon.* (1642) 386 Herod..the *infant queller. **1655** SANDERSON *Serm.* II. Pref. 7 Where

are your lay-presbyters, your classes, &c. to be found in scripture? Where your steeple-houses?.. Your *infant-sprinklings?

infant ('ɪnfənt), *sb.*² [ad. Sp., Pg. *infante*: perh. through F. *infant* (1407 in Hatz.-Darm.): see INFANTE.] A prince or princess of Spain or Portugal: = INFANTE, INFANTA.

1555 EDEN *Decades* 349 Don Lewes thinfant & brother to the kynge of Portugale. **1594** PARSONS *Confer. Success.* II. viii. 181 The two duchesses..daughters..of the lord Edward infant of Portugal. **1614** SELDEN *Titles Hon.* 179 The Infant and heir of Spain..had the title of Prince of Asturias. **1631** HEYWOOD *Eng. Eliz.* (1641) 1 A match was concluded betwixt Prince Arthur..and the Infant Katharine, daughter to the King of Spain. **1753** *Scots Mag.* Jan. 12/1 The Infant Don Philip. **1838** LYTTON *Calderon* i, The craft of the king was satisfied by the device of placing about the person of the Infant one devoted to himself.

† **'infant**, *v. Obs.* Also 5 **enfaunt**. [a. F. *enfanter* (12th c.) f. *enfant*, INFANT *sb.*¹] *trans.* To bring forth (a child), to give birth to. Also *fig.*

1483 CAXTON *Gold. Leg.* 128/2 The place in whych the vyrgyne marye enfaunted and childed Jhesu cryst. **1584** SOUTHERNE in Puttenham *Eng. Poesie* III. xxii. (Arb.) 260 An ingenious inuention, infanted with pleasant trauaille. **1610** G. FLETCHER *Christ's Vict.* I. lxxx, But newely he was infanted, And yet alreadie he was sought to die. **1641** MILTON *Reform.* II. (1851) 42 This worthy Motto, No Bishop, no King is of the same batch, and infanted out of the same feares. **1642** —— *Apol. Smect.* xi.

‖**infanta** (ɪn'fantə). [Sp., Pg., fem. of INFANTE.] **1.** A daughter of the king and queen of Spain or Portugal; *spec.* the eldest daughter who is not heir to the throne.

1601 *Imp. Consid. Sec. Priests* (1675) 82 He might..intitle the King of Spain and the Infanta his Daughter to the Crown..of England. **1687** *Lond. Gaz.* No. 2221/7 A Marriage is Treating between the Prince of Tuscany and the Infanta of Portugal. **1704** *Ibid.* No. 3989/2 Some of the Infantes his Sons, and both the Infanta's his Daughters, have been ill. **1832** W. IRVING *Alhambra* II. 130 The tower of the Infantas, once the residence of the three beautiful Moorish princesses, partook of the general desolation.

†**2.** *transf.* and *fig.* Applied analogously or fancifully to other young ladies. *Obs.*

1611 SPEED *Hist. Gt. Brit.* IX. xvii. §108. 876 In the meanewhile Ladie Elizabeth the Infanta of England was in the French Court vsually called Madame the Daulphin. **1616** B. JONSON *Devil an Ass* IV. i. Wks. (Rtldg.) 363/1 The very infanta of the giants. **1632** MASSINGER & FIELD *Fatal Dowry* IV. i, O that I were the infanta queen of Europe! **1750** H. WALPOLE *Lett. to Mann* 31 Jan., Lady Catherine grew frightened, lest her infanta [her daughter] should vex herself sick. **1751** SMOLLETT *Per. Pic.* lxxxvii, Meanwhile the infanta [a girl] herself..promised to keep a stricter guard for the future.

¶ See also INFANTE.

‖**infan'tado**, app. a grandiose erroneous extension of *infante*.

1659 RUSHW. *Hist. Coll.* I. 113 He had rather go home and cast himself at his Masters feet and mercy..then be Duke or Infantado of Spain.

'infantage. *rare*⁻¹. [f. INFANT *sb.*¹ + -AGE *suffix*, associated in sense with AGE *sb.*: cf. *barnage*, *nonage*.] = INFANCY.

1866 *Cornh. Mag.* XIII. 437 Rude, provisional rules, only absolutely obligatory during the infantage of men.

‖**infante** (in'fante). (Also 7 *erron.* **infanta.**) [Sp., Pg. *infante*:—L. *infānt-em* INFANT *sb.*¹] A son of the king and queen of Spain or Portugal other than the heir to the throne (who is called *principe*); *spec.* the second son.

Sometimes erroneously applied to the heir to the throne.

1555 EDEN *Decades* 242 The conquest of Affryke..began where the infante of Portugale Don Henrique..dyd begynne to enlarge it. **1615** BEDWELL *Arab. Trudg.*, *Sherif*, The Heire apparant: the Dolphin, they call him in France: the Infanta, in Spaine. **1668** DAVENANT *Man's the Master* II. i. Wks. 1874 V. 30 You remember the triumphs at Burgos for the first Infante. **1704** [see INFANTA 1]. **1715** *Lond. Gaz.* No. 5337/1 The King, the Queen..and the two Infantes continue at Aranjuez.

infanteer (ɪnfən'tɪə(r)). *slang.* [f. INFANT(RY + -EER.] An infantryman.

1944 J. H. FULLARTON *Troop Target* xxiii. 174 A lone infanteer..watched it all from a slit trench. **1961** *Guardian* 14 Nov. 8/3 Did he and his fellow-Gunners never talk of Guardees or Infanteers?

infanthood ('ɪnfənthʊd). [f. INFANT *sb.*¹ + -HOOD.] = INFANCY.

1862 MISS MULOCK *Mistr. & Maid* xxiv, Master Henry was not a remarkable specimen of infanthood. **1893** *Columbus* (Ohio) *Disp.* 5 Oct., The unspeakable terrors of an infanthood where every other child about him showed only the face of a harassing ogre.

†**in'fantical**, *a. Obs. rare*⁻¹. [f. INFANT *sb.*¹ + -ICAL.] Of or pertaining to infants.

1601 DEACON & WALKER *Spirits & Divels* 236 These Exorcizings..are either archicall, apostolicall, ecclesiasticall, or infanticall [for the timely expelling of spirits and divels from out of newly borne infants, before their admission to baptisme].

in'fanti,cidal, *a.* [f. INFANTICIDE² + -AL¹.] Of, pertaining to, or practising infanticide.

1835 in BOOTH *Analyt. Dict.* **1852** *Fraser's Mag.* XLVI. 86 Laying violent infanticidal hands upon biscuit babies. **1873** W. E. MARSHALL *Phrenol. among Todas* xxiii. 191 Probably, no nation can justly escape the charge of being descended of infanticidal ancestors.

infanticide¹ (ɪn'fæntɪsaɪd). [a. F. *infanticide* (16th c. in Hatz.-Darm.), ad. late L. *infānticīda*, f. *infānt-em* INFANT *sb.*¹ + *cædĕre*, *-cīdĕre* to kill: see -CIDE 1.] One who kills an infant.

1680 POTTER *Christophalgia* 52 (T.) Christians accounted those to be infanticides..who did but only expose their own infants. **1834** *Blackw. Mag.* XXXVI. 360/2 The regicide [Lady Macbeth] lied against herself, in saying that under any circumstances she could have been an infanticide.

attrib. **1856** *Sat. Rev.* II. 336/1 An infanticide mother.

infanticide² (ɪn'fæntɪsaɪd). [a. F. *infanticide* (Cotgr. 1611), ad. late L. *infānticīd-ium* (Tertull.), f. *infānt-em* INFANT *sb.*¹: see prec. and -CIDE 2.] The killing of infants, *esp.* the custom of killing new-born infants, which prevailed in primitive societies, and was common in the ancient world.

1656 BLOUNT *Glossogr.*, *Infanticide*, a slaying or killing of Infants, child-murthering; such was that of Herod. *a* **1779** WARBURTON *Div. Legat.* IX. ii. Wks. 1811 VI. 285 The madness did not cease to rage till it terminated in Infanticide, or in offering up to their grim idols..the Children of their bowels. **1809** SOUTHEY in *Q. Rev.* II. 58 Pomarre has..promised the missionaries to abolish infanticide and human sacrifices. **1869** LECKY *Europ. Mor.* iv. II. 27 Infanticide..was..admitted among the Greeks, being sanctioned, and in some cases enjoined..by the ideal legislations of Plato and Aristotle, and by the actual legislations of Lycurgus and Solon. **1897** *Westm. Rev.* June 290 The exigencies of primitive savage life made daughters a source of weakness to the tribe, and accordingly female infanticide was largely practised.

b. *spec.* The crime of murdering an infant after its birth, perpetrated by or with the consent of its parents, esp. the mother.

1789 BENTHAM *Legisl.* xiii. §6 *Infanticide*, that is to say homicide committed upon a new born child with the consent of its father and mother. **1888** *Pall Mall G.* 21 Sept. 1/2 For 86 cases of murder and 77 of infanticide only 72 persons were committed for trial. **1890** *Standard* 20 Feb., If, then, it were made practically impossible for them to hide the fact of their shame..we must face the probability of a considerable increase of infanticide.

infanticipate (ɪnfæn'tɪsɪpeɪt), *v.* Chiefly *U.S.* [f. INFANT *sb.*¹ 1 + ANT)ICIPATE *v.*] *intr.* To be in the state of expecting a child. Hence **infan'ticipating** *ppl. a.* and *vbl. sb.*

1934 W. WINCHELL in *News & Post* (Baltimore) 28 May 10/1 The J. Clark Baldwin, 3ds,..are infanticipating. **1941** in *Amer. Speech* (1942) XVII. 271/2 'Storkettes' for 'infanticipating' friends of yours. **1961** *N.Z. Listener* 8 Sept. 34/4 Although I agree that 'infanticipating' will be very hard to rival. **1963** *New Musical Express* 10 May 12/1 Frank Sinatra jnr. dating actress Jana Taylor... Infanticipating—singer Gene McDaniels' wife.

Hence **infantici'pation**, the state of expecting a child; the child that is *in utero*.

1934 W. WINCHELL in *News & Post* (Baltimore) 2 July 8/2 The Alan Mowbray infanticipation is due in late October. **1939** in *Amer. Speech* (1940) XV. 218/1 Cameraman Leonard Smith shot Miss O'Sullivan behind fern fronds, through leafy screens, at respectful distances, permitted his camera to drop no hint of her..infanticipation.

infantile ('ɪnfəntaɪl, -tɪl), *a.* [ad. late L. *infāntil-is*, f. *infānt-em* INFANT *sb.*¹: cf. F. *infantile* (16th c. in Hatz.-Darm.).] **1. a.** Of or pertaining to an infant, infants, or infancy; belonging to a person when an infant; existing in its infancy or earliest stage of development.

1696 BROOKHOUSE *Temple Open.* 13 All this time, Monarchy was as a Beast in its Infantile State. **1713** DERHAM *Phys. Theol.* VIII. vi. (1727) 390 The Fly lies all the Winter in these Balls in its Infantile State. **1753** N. TORRIANO *Midwifry* 5 We are obliged to them for their tender Care of the infantile Age. **1800** *Med. Jrnl.* III. 293 Medical men..who are often consulted on infantile diseases. **1806** SURR *Winter in Lond.* I. 260 The interest which his story first impressed upon her infantile imagination. **1864** *Spectator* 24 Dec. 1476 The rapid growth of infantile literature.

b. Of the character of an infant; infant-like.

1772 PRIESTLEY *Inst. Relig.* (1782) II. 117 Consider the infantile state of the first man. **1875** EMERSON *Lett. & Soc. Aims* ix. 220 In the savage man, thought is infantile.

2. *Geol.* Of a landscape: in the earliest stage of the cycle of erosion. Of a land form or feature: characteristic of such a landscape.

1885 *Proc. Amer. Assoc. Adv. Sci.* XXXIII. 429 Just as the surface of the deposit rises above its base-level of erosion ..a smooth, unbroken plain is revealed... The smoothness of the surface and the shallow lakes are indeed truly infantile features, retained only during the earliest life of the plain, and soon lost in its further development. **1941** C. A. COTTON *Landscape* xvii. 191 The theoretical distinction between 'infantile' forms developing on a peneplain as it is slowly uplifted and the 'senile' forms it exhibited before uplift was first made by Walther Penck. **1968** R. W. FAIRBRIDGE *Encycl. Geomorphol.* 1110/2 Initial or infantile (i.e., uneroded) forms of mountains composed of such materials have indeed had no real existence, because they have been destroyed while relatively slow or intermittent upheaval has been in progress.

3. Special collocations: ***infantile mortality*** = *infant mortality*; ***infantile paralysis***, poliomyelitis (which affects chiefly the young).

1859 W. MOORE (*title*) On *infantile mortality, and the establishment of hospitals for sick children. **1901** *Daily Chron.* 14 Nov. 5/5 In England the term 'infantile' mortality applies only to the deaths of children under one year of age. **1911** G. B. SHAW *Getting Married* 135 The high birth-rate of the very poor is counterbalanced by a huge infantile-mortality in the slums. **1843** *Lancet* 27 May 301/1 There is a disease of very considerable frequency—I mean *infantile paralysis—to which, I think, so much attention has not been given as its importance merits. **1916** *Daily Colonist* (Victoria, B.C.) 5 July 1/2 Twenty-five children died from the epidemic of infantile paralysis..during the 24 hours ending at 6 o'clock tonight. **1955** *Sci. News Let.* 16 Apr. 242/2 No matter how it is called, poliomyelitis, infantile paralysis, or polio for short, it is a scourge that has long been a crippler and killer. **1957** *Economist* 7 Sept. 847/1 Experience with the Salk vaccine during the past two years has convinced the National Foundation for Infantile Paralysis that the enemy is in full retreat.

infantilism (ɪn'fæntɪlɪz(ə)m). *Path.* [prob. ad. F. *infantilisme*: see INFANTILE *a.* and -ISM.] Infantile or childish condition; *spec.* **a.** The state or condition of being physically undeveloped. **b.** *Psychol.* A condition in which infantile behaviour patterns persist, owing to some emotional repression in early life, and are dominant over more appropriate reactions.

[**1871** F. V. FANEAU DE LA COUR (*title*) Du féminisme et de l'infantilisme chez les tuberculeux.] **1895** W. D. MORRISON in Lombroso & Ferrero *Female Offender* Introd. p. xvi, Sexual peculiarities, such as feminism in men, mascul[in]ism in women, and infantilism in both. **1897** tr. *T. Ribot's Psychol. of Emotions* 422 The formula which.. sums up and explains the unstable is this: psychological infantilism. *Ibid.*, The term infantilism is equally applicable to the congenital and the acquired forms. The former have never left their childhood behind, the latter return to it. **1903** *Lancet* 30 May 1526/1 A case of Infantilism in a child, aged ten years, who had not grown since four years old. Her weight was 26 pounds and her height was three feet. **1909** ROBERTSON & MACKENZIE tr. *Tanzi's Text-bk. Mental Dis.* xxii. 670 There is then an arrest of the genetic instinct at the infantile stage—an erotic infantilism. **1924** J. RIVIERE et al. tr. *Freud's Coll. Papers* I. xiv. 277 The 'infantile sexual traumas' were in a sense supplanted by the 'infantilism' of the sexuality in these cases. **1924** W. B. SELBIE *Psychol. Relig.* xv. 297 The worship of God is a form of infantilism, and survives because it meets a certain elementary need and satisfies the sense of dependence which man never altogether loses. **1943** S. R. SLAVSON *Introd. Group Therapy* vii. 224 Children whose parents are in conflict with each other are not only fixed in their infantilism as a result, but use it to exploit the two parents. **1950** R. H. WILLIAMS *Textbk. Endocrinol.* ii. 49 Gonadal hypoplasia with dwarfism..is sometimes referred to as infantilism or the Lorain-Lévi syndrome. **1953** A. W. SPENCE *Clin. Endocrinol.* xli. 495 The word 'infantilism' was first used in medical literature by Lorain (1871) when he wrote the preface of the thesis of one of his pupils, Faneau de la Cour, on feminism and infantilism in tuberculous patients. **1962** R. H. WILLIAMS *Textbk. Endocrinol.* (ed. 3) xv. 933 The differentiation of persistent sexual infantilism from constitutionally delayed adolescence.

infantilistic (ɪn,fæntɪ'lɪstɪk), *a.* [f. INFANTILE *a.* + -ISTIC.] Pertaining to, exhibiting or characterized by infantilism; abnormally immature.

1930 C. G. SELIGMAN *Races Afr.* ii. 51 Rather should they be considered to represent an early human type 'infantilistic' both physically and mentally. **1936** *Discovery* June 167/2 Negritos, a pygmy, infantilistic, dark-skinned type.

infan'tility. [f. INFANTILE *a.* + -ITY. Cf. It. *infantilità* (Florio).] The fact or quality of being infantile. Also, an instance of infantile behaviour.

1631 J. BURGES *Answ. Rejoined* 544 Christ..knoweth our infantility, and disdained not to speake with vs..after a childlike fashion. **1919** M. K. BRADBY *Psycho-Anal.* iii. 31 In these [*sc.* unreasoned convictions] we shall find his kinship with the primitive and with his own infantility. **1921** *Discovery* May 133/2 Its chief characteristics [*sc.* of the 'Personal Unconscious'] are its infantility and its compensatory character. **1928** *Daily Tel.* 28 Aug. 5/2 With amazing veracity and power, Tolstoy portrays all that infantility of the Russian race. **1930** A. HUXLEY *Brief Candles* 66 He laughed at every naïveté or impertinence she uttered..and..led her on into fresh infantilities.

infantilization (ɪn,fæntɪlaɪ'zeɪʃən). [f. INFANTIL(E *a.* + -IZATION.] The action of prolonging or perpetuating a state of infancy.

1939 *Nature* 25 Feb. 325/2 Following Bolk's thesis of infantilization he would regard man as the permanent baby amongst mammals. **1943** D. M. LEVY *Maternal Overprotection* iv. 53 Infantilization consists in the performance of activities in the care of a child beyond the time when such activities usually occur. **1970** G. GREER *Female Eunuch* 98 In pushing the masochistic role as the proper role for woman, psychology reinforces the infantilization which has gone on ever since she was born. **1971** JONAS & KLEIN (*title*) Man-child: a study of the infantilization of man.

Hence **in'fantilized** *ppl. a.*, made the object of infantilization; **in'fantilizing** *vbl. sb.* and *ppl. a.*

1943 S. R. SLAVSON *Introd. Group Therapy* i. 8 The period of forbearance on the part of the group therapists is much shorter with pampered and infantilized children. **1943** D. LEVY *Maternal Overprotection* v. 73 Maternal overprotection becomes largely an infantilizing process. **1965** *Listener* 29 Apr. 626/2 In this context, the infantilizing mother, who holds herself ever indispensable, is a kind of murderer.

infantine ('ɪnfəntaɪn), *a.* [a. F. *infantin*, *-ine* (Cotgr. 1611), var. of *enfantin*, *-ine* (12–13th c.

in Hatz.-Darm.): see INFANT *sb.*[1] and -INE[1].] = INFANTILE I.

1603 FLORIO *Montaigne* I. xi. (1632) 20 A demy-God.. with an infantine face, yet fraught with an aged-like wisedome. **1633** P. FLETCHER *Purple Isl.* I. viii, These infantine beginnings gently bear. **1757** BURKE *Abridgem. Eng. Hist.* II. iii. (R.), A degree of credulity next to infantine. **1818** SHELLEY *Rev. Islam* II. xxii, What wert thou then? A child most infantine [*rime* divine]. —— *Euganean Hills* 322 Autumn's evening meets me soon, Leading the infantine moon. **1862** CARLYLE *Fredk. Gt.* IX. vii. (1872) III. 132 The countenance.. is so innocent and infantine, you would think this head belonged to a child of twelve. **1871** BROWNING *Pr. Hohenst.* 1848 Genius has somewhat of the infantine: But of the childish, not a touch or taint Except through self-will.

Hence **'infantinely** *adv.*, in an infantine manner.

1833 MILL *Lett.* (1910) I. 77 A man singularly free.. from self-consciousness; simple, graceful, at times almost infantinely playful.

†**'infantize,** *v. Obs. rare*[−1]. [f. INFANT *sb.*[1] + -IZE.] = INFANT *v.* (In quot. *fig.*)

1619 *Time's Storehouse* 899 (L.) Significant words.. explicite, and (as a man may say) do infantize and produce the conceptions of man.

†**'infantly,** *a. Obs. rare*[−1]. [f. INFANT *sb.*[1] + -LY[1].] Infant-like, childlike.

c **1618** FLETCHER *Q. Corinth* III. i, He utters such single matter in so infantly a voice.

†**infantment.** *Obs. rare.* Also 5 enfante-. [a. F. *enfantement* (12th c. in Hatz.-Darm.), f. *enfanter* to INFANT: see -MENT.] Child-bearing; childbed, confinement. Also, Offspring.

1483 CAXTON *Gold. Leg.* 260b/1 Where thou arte thenfantemente or fruyte of my wombe. *c* **1566** J. ALDAY tr. *Boaystuau's Theat. World* D vj b *note*, Hippo, in his booke of infantments. **1597** LOWE *Chirurg.* (1634) To Rdr., Such other things.. in the Treatise of the helpe of Women in their Infantment.

infan'tocracy. *nonce-wd.* [f. INFANT *sb.*[1]: see -CRACY.] The rule of an infant.

1850 MISS MULOCK *Domest. Stor.* (1862) 284 Your infantocracy is the most absolute government under the sun.

infan'tolatry. *nonce-wd.* [f. INFANT *sb.*[1] + Gr. λατρεία worship, -LATRY; after IDOLATRY, MARIOLATRY, etc.] Infant worship; babyolatry.

1882 MISS BRADDON *Mt. Royal* II. x. 215 Infantolatry is a feminine attribute.

infantry ('ɪnfəntrɪ). Also 6–7 -terie, -ery, 7 -trie, (-ree). [a. F. *infanterie*, ad. It. (Sp., Pg.) *infanteria* foot-soldiery, f. *infante* a youth, foot-soldier:—L. *infāntem* INFANT *sb.*[1] For the development of the It. *infante* cf. the apocopated form *fante* 'a man or woman seruant or attendant; also, a footman or soldier seruing on foot; also the knaue or varlet at cards' (Florio); cf. also the history of *footman, groom, knave, knight, lad*, etc. By Sylvester stressed (ɪn'fæntərɪ). Sense 2 is from INFANT *sb.*[1] sense 1.]

1. The body of foot-soldiers; foot-soldiers collectively; that part of an army which consists of men who march and manœuvre on foot and are armed with small arms, now a rifle.

mounted infantry, soldiers who are mounted for the sake of transit, but who fight on foot. (Cf. DRAGOON in original sense.)

1579 FENTON *Guicciard.* (1618) 256 Which rendred the infantery of Italy infamous through all Europe. **16..** SYLVESTER *Bethulia's Rescue* II. 428 Covering far and nigh, The Plains with Horse, Hills with Infanterie. **1605** *Play Stucley* 2626 in Simpson *Sch. Shaks.* (1878) I. 263 All Portingales brave Infantries slain. **1612** BACON *Ess., Greatn. Kingd.* (Arb.) 476 Take away the middle people, and you take away the infantery, which is the nerue of an Armie. **1667** MILTON *P.L.* I. 575 That small infantry Warr'd on by Cranes. **1709** STEELE & ADDISON *Tatler* No. 18 ¶6 The private Gentlemen of the Infantry will be able to shift for themselves. **1847** JAMES *Convict* xvi, A small but compact body of infantry advanced at the charge with fixed bayonets. **1856** STANLEY *Sinai & Pal.* ii. 133 The Israelites were a nation of infantry.

fig. **1598** B. JONSON *Ev. Man in Hum.* II. ii, Your poor infantry, your decayed, ruinous, worm-eaten gentlemen of the round.

2. Infants collectively, or as a body. Now *jocular*.

1613–16 W. BROWNE *Brit. Past.* II. i, No carefull nurse would wet her watchfull eye When any pang should gripe her infantry. **1634** A. HUISH *Hymn*, All glorie, laud, and praise to Thee, Christ our Redeemer and our King; To whom the youngly infantree Did their devout hosanna sing. **1663** NEEDHAM *Disc. Schools* 2 The little dirty Infantry, which swarms up and down in Alleys and Lanes. **1701** C. WOLLEY *Jrnl. New York* (1860) 58 If the case be so, the minors and infantry of the best Families might wish they had been born in Kent. **1847** *Blackw. Mag.* LXII. 264/1 The swarms of bare-legged and flaxen-haired infantry. **1863** *Reader* 1 Aug. 100 There was one A.B.C. book, or pretty nearly one, for the whole 'infantry' of the country.

3. *attrib.*, as ***infantry brigade, corps, regiment***, etc.

1813 WELLINGTON *Let. to Sir G. Collier* 19 Aug. in Gurw. *Desp.* XI. 15 A letter.. directing that the Infantry now in the horse ships at Bilbao may be removed to the Infantry ships. **1897** *Daily News* 15 Mar. 6/5 The Mounted Infantry Corps, now an established and highly valued arm of the Service.

'infantryman. A soldier of an infantry regiment.

1883 E. O'DONOVAN *Story of Merv* x. 107 The few infantrymen, with their cumbrous old muzzle-loading rifles. **1891** *Pall Mall G.* 21 Sept. 5/1 The infantrymen of the four regiments, as they passed.. looked rather distressed.

'infant-'school. A school for infants, a school organized for the instruction and training of young children (usually under seven years of age). Also ***infants*** (or ***infants'***) ***school***.

The usual form is now ***infant school***.

1824 S. WILDERSPIN *Importance Educating Infant Poor* 33 Rules to be observed by the Parents of Children admitted into the Spitalfields Infant School. *Ibid.* 50 An infant school may be regarded.. as a combination of the school and nursery. **1833** HT. MARTINEAU *Loom & Lugger* II. ii. 42 He often thought of taking him to the infant school. **1839** [see COLERIDGIAN *a.* and *sb.*]. **1841** *Penny Cycl.* XLI. 38/2 The real founder of Infant-Schools appears to have been the Pastor Oberlin. *Ibid.*, Mr. Owen was the first Englishman to establish an infant-school on a large scale.. at New Lanark in Scotland.. in the year 1818. **1921** MENCKEN *Amer. Lang.* (rev. ed.) 120 An English boy whose father is unable to pay for his education goes first into a *babies' class*.. in a *primary* or *infants'* school. **1945** *Guide Educ. Syst. Eng. & Wales* (Min. Educ.) 59 *Infants School* (*Infants Department*), primary school for children of about 5 to 7 years, including in some cases classes for children of 3 and 4. **1969** I. & P. OPIE *Children's Games* xii. 331 Even beyond Infant School the girls sometimes play 'Mothers and Fathers'.

infarce, -se, variants of ENFARCE *v. Obs.*

†**in'farciate,** *v. Obs. rare.* In 7 infartiate. [irreg. f. L. *infarcīre* (see next) + -ATE[3].] *trans.* To stuff in.

1657 TOMLINSON *Renou's Disp.* III. iv. 124 As it were filling up or infartiating.

infarct (ɪn'fɑːkt), *sb. Path.* [ad. med. or mod.L. *infarctus*, f. ppl. stem of *infarcire*: see next.] A portion of tissue that has become stuffed with extravasated blood, serum, or other matter; the substance of an infarction.

1873 T. H. GREEN *Introd. Path.* (ed. 2) 340 The tract of tissue.. which is more or less extensively infiltrated with blood, is known as a hæmorrhagic infarct. **1879** *St. George's Hosp. Rep.* IX. 409 Scattered congestions and a few infarcts were found in the lungs.

infarct (ɪn'fɑːkt), *v. Path.* [f. L. *infarct-* (more correctly *infart-*), ppl. stem of *infarcīre*, f. *in-* (IN-[2]) + *farcīre* to stuff.] *trans.* To stuff up or obstruct (a vessel, organ, etc.); to affect with infarction. Hence **in'farcted** *ppl. a.*

1822–34 *Good's Study Med.* (ed. 4) IV. 315 One or more of the abdominal organs, considerably infarcted and enlarged. **1889** *Lancet* 12 Jan. 64 The result of inflammation in infarcted areas.

infarction (ɪn'fɑːkʃən). *Path.* [n. of action from L. *infarcīre*: see prec.] The action of stuffing up or condition of being stuffed up, obstruction; *concr.* the substance with which a vessel or other part is stuffed up, or a portion of tissue thus affected (= INFARCT *sb.*). Now usually restricted to morbid conditions of the tissues resulting from obstruction of the circulation, as by an embolus.

1689 G. HARVEY *Curing Dis. by Expect.* iv. 19 The Humours.. will be compacted into.. most obstinate Infarctions. **1710** T. FULLER *Pharm. Extemp.* 334 They.. expedite pulmonary Infarctions. **1747** tr. *Astruc's Fevers* 114 The plenitude and infarction of the capillary arteries. **1822–34** *Good's Study Med.* (ed. 4) IV. 290 Infarction of the abdominal viscera. **1885–8** FAGGE & PYE-SMITH *Princ. Med.* (ed. 2) I. 181 Infarctions of the spleen are.. not infrequently found after death from enteric fever.

†**in'fardel, -dle,** *v. Obs. rare*[−0]. [f. IN-[2] + FARDEL *sb.*[1], after It. *infardell-āre*; cf. OF. *enfardeler*.] *trans.* To make into, or pack up in, a 'fardel' or bundle.

1611 FLORIO, *Infardellare*, to infardle, or bundle vp.

infare ('ɪnfɛə(r)), *sb.* Forms: 1 **infær, innfær,** 1–2 **infer,** 2 **infar,** 4, 9 **infair,** 7– **infare,** (9 **infar**). [OE. *innfær*, f. *inn*, IN adv. 11 d + *fær* going, journey, expedition, FARE *sb.*[1], f. *faran* to go.]

†**1.** (OE. and early ME.) **a.** The act of going in; entrance. **b.** An entrance, entry, way in. *Obs.*

a **1000** *Ags. Gloss.* in Wr.-Wülcker 230/15 *Ex aditis, ex ingressibus*, of inferum. *c* **1000** ÆLFRIC *Gen.* iii. 24 Þa ᵹesette God æt þam infære engla hyrdrædene and fyren swurd. —— *Hom.* I. 178 He ᵹewite fram urum heortum mid þam innfære ᵹehæft, mid þam þe he inn-afaren wæs and us ᵹehæfte. *a* **1175** *Cott. Hom.* 231 He haueð ȝerimed rihtwisan mannan infer to his rice.

2. a. *Sc., north. dial.*, and *U.S.* A feast or entertainment given on entering a new house; *esp.* at the reception of a bride in her new home. Also *transf.*

1375 BARBOUR *Bruce* XVI. 340 For he thoucht for till mak Infair, And till mak gud cher till his men. *a* **1670** SPALDING *Troub. Chas. I* (1792) II. 54 Upon the 25th of October he brought over his wife to his own house in the Oldtown, where there was a goodly infare. **1744** J. MACSPARRAN *Diary* (1899) 18 Dr. Hazard and Betty Gardiner went to.. Billy Hazard's weding. They are both gone again.. to the Infair. **1794** in *Amer. Pioneer* II. 223 An Infair was given to-day by Mason, to a fellow named Kuykendall, who had.. run off with Mason's daughter.. a few weeks ago. **1801** JOANNA BAILLIE in A. Whitelaw *Bk. Scot. Song* 73/1 At bridal and infare I've braced me wi pride. **1818** *Edin. Mag.* Nov. 414 The day after the wedding is the *infare*.. the company is less numerous, and the dinner is commonly the scraps that were left at the wedding-feast. **1847** PORTER *Big Bear*, etc. 162 (Farmer), I hurried home to put up.. some turkies to fatten for the infare. **1872** SCHELE DE VERE *Americanisms* 236 The minister is said to settle,.. a ceremony which.. in many churches is made the occasion of much ceremony, called an installation or infare, because resembling an old-fashioned wedding festival. **1887** *Harper's Mag.* Apr. 730/1 The wedding and the infair were attended.. by Wiley.

b. *Comb.* **infare-cake,** a cake of shortbread broken over the bride's head on crossing the threshold of her new home.

1884 C. ROGERS *Soc. Life Scotl.* I. iii. 118 The custom of the infar-cake had its origin in the rite of Confarreation whereby the Romans constituted matrimony.

†**in'fare,** *v. Obs.* [OE. *inn-, infaran*, f. *inn*, IN *adv.* + *faran* to go: cf. OFris. *in-fara*, Du. *invaren*, Ger. *einfahren* (with separable pref.: see IN-[1]). Orig. two words, and so usually written.] *intr.* To go in, to enter.

c **1000** *Ags. Gosp.* John iii. 5 Ne mæᵹ he in faran on ᵹodes rice. *c* **1000** ÆLFRIC *Saints' Lives* (E.E.T.S.) x. 27 þæt he ælmessan under-fencge æt þam infarendum [*v.r.* inn farendum]. *a* **1400** *Sir Perc.* 1538 The portere was redy thare, Lete the knyghtis in fare.

infarre, obs. variant of INFER.

†**in'fascinate,** *v. Obs. rare.* [IN-[2].] *trans.* To fascinate; to draw in by fascination.

1687 MRS. BEHN *Emperor of Moon* II. i, That bright Nymph that had infascinated, charm'd and conquer'd the mighty Emperor Iredonozor.

†**in'fashionable,** *a. Obs. rare.* [IN-[3].] Unfashionable.

1635 SHIRLEY *Coronation* I. i, His rich cloaths [may] be discomplexion'd With bloud, beside the infashionable slashes. **1787** *Mirror* 88 An infashionable wretch cannot, nor will not, be acceptable.

infat, variant of ENFAT *v. Obs.*

†**in'fatigable,** *a. Obs.* [a. F. *infatigable* (15–16th c. in Hatz.-Darm.), ad. L. *infatīgābilis*, f. *in-* (IN-[3]) + *fatīgābilis* FATIGABLE.] Incapable of being wearied; untiring, INDEFATIGABLE.

c **1510** MORE *Picus* Wks. 15/1 With much watch and infatigable trauaile. **1591** R. TURNBULL *St. James* 207 Albeit the deuill be infatigable, and neuer wearied. **1677** GALE *Crt. Gentiles* III. 144 An infatigable and invincible champion of Free-grace against Free-wil. **1713** *Lond. Gaz.* No. 5122/3 The infatigable Application of Your Ministry.

Hence †**infatiga'bility,** †**in'fatigably** *adv.*

1652 KIRKMAN *Clerio & Lozia* 70 Those perceptive eyes which are infatigably open to behold thy actions. **1709** *Brit. Apollo* II. No. 64. 2/2 Incessant Infatigability hath render'd Thee.. Verbose.

infatuate (ɪn'fætjuːət), *ppl. a.* (and *sb.*) Also 6 **enfatuate, infatuat.** [ad. L. *infatuāt-us*, pa. pple. of *infatuāre*: see next.] = INFATUATED. Hence as *sb.*, an infatuated person.

1471 RIPLEY *Comp. Alch.* I. xiii. in Ashm. (1652) 132 Soe many one doth whych bene infatuate. *c* **1510** BARCLAY *Mirr. Gd. Manners* (1570) F vj, Gasing on the ground as one infatuate. *a* **1529** SKELTON *Sp. Parrot* 377 The dull abusyd brayne The enfatuate fantasie. **1584** R. SCOT *Discov. Witchcr.* XVI. v. (1886) 403 What man.. will be so infatuate as to beleeve these lies? **1619** W. SCLATER *Exp. 1 Thess.* (1630) 223. **1724** R. WELTON *Subst. Chr. Faith* 443 The holy prophet mourns the infatuate stupidity of that people. **1884** JESSOPP in *19th Cent.* Mar. 405 He often exhibits an infatuate attachment for it. **1934** *sb.* in WEBSTER. **1949** *Scrutiny* XVI. 210 The earlier criticism of *Antony and Cleopatra* tended to stress the down-fall of the soldier in the middle-aged infatuate.

infatuate (ɪn'fætjuːeɪt), *v.* Also 7 **en-**. [f. prec., or L. *infatuāt-*, ppl. stem of *infatuāre* to make a fool of, infatuate, f. *in-* (IN-[2]) + *fatuus* foolish, fatuous.]

†**1.** *trans.* To turn (counsels, etc.) into folly, to reduce to foolishness, exhibit the foolishness of; to confound, frustrate, bring to nought. *Obs.*

1533 TINDALE *Supper of Lord* Wks. (Parker Soc.) III. 234 God hath infatuated your high subtle wisdom. **1655** R. YOUNGE *Agst. Drunkards* (1863) 16 That I have unmasked their faces, is to infatuate their purpose. **1683** *Lond. Gaz.* No. 1856/5 That the Divine Wisdom may infatuate the Plots, baffle the Enterprizes of all Traiterous Conspirators. **1724** R. WELTON *Subst. Chr. Faith* 139 He prays that God would infatuate their counsels.

2. To make (a person) utterly foolish or fatuous; to affect with extreme and unreasoning folly; to inspire or possess with an extravagant passion.

a **1567** ? COVERDALE *Carrying of Cross* iv. Wks. (Parker Soc.) II. 241 Therefore doth God justly infatuate them, and maketh them foolish. **1621** BURTON *Anat. Mel.* I. ii. III. xiii, Those two maine plagues.. of humane kind, Wine and Women, which haue infatuated and besotted Myriades of people. *a* **1631** DONNE *6 Serm.* (1634) ii. 40 We shall be enfatuated in our counsels. **1712** STEELE *Spect.* No. 278 ¶1 He has so infatuated her with his Jargon, that [etc.]. **1791** BOSWELL *Johnson* (1831) III. 525 He partook of the short-lived joy that infatuated the public. **1860** EMERSON *Cond. Life, Fate* Wks. (Bohn) II. 325 All the toys that infatuate men.. are the selfsame thing, with a new gauze or two of illusion overlaid.

absol. 1633 T. Adams *Exp. 2 Peter* i. 6 He..can turn bread into stones; and make wine infatuate, not exhilarate. 1755 Young *Centaur* ii. Wks. 1757 IV. 136 Heaven infatuates, when it determines to destroy.

†3. To stupefy (the senses). *Obs. rare.*
1712 tr. *Pomet's Hist. Drugs* I. 138 The chiefest Things they are us'd for, is to infatuate Birds.

infatuated (ɪnˈfætjuːeɪtɪd), *ppl. a.* [f. prec. + -ED^1.] Made or become utterly foolish; possessed with an extravagantly foolish passion; besotted.
1642 Fuller *Holy & Prof. St.* v. viii. 389 He may grow so infatuated as to conceive himself..a sincere Saint. 1756 Ld. Barrington in Ellis *Orig. Lett.* Ser. ii. IV. 383 Alas! they were as infatuated as their chief. 1778 Burke *Corr.* (1844) II. 210 What the infatuated ministry may do, I know not; but our infatuated House of Commons..have begun a new war in America. 1863 Mrs. Oliphant *Salem Ch.* v. 94 The infatuated young man made no effort of resistance, but hugged the enchanted chain.
Hence **inˈfatuatedly** *adv.*, in a way as if infatuated; with excessive folly; madly.
1833 *Blackw. Mag.* XXXIII. 439 Infatuatedly addicted to attempts..which..would prove fatal. 1889 *Times* 26 Feb. 9/2 The government had infatuatedly made themselves the dupes and accessories of..an imposture and a plot.

inˈfatuating, *ppl. a.* [f. as prec. + -ING^2.] That infatuates or renders foolish.
c 1565 T. Robinson *Mary Magd.* i. 468 The poynted Beame, th' infatuatinge Fire, The Northern Comœts and yᵉ painted Ire. 1660 J. Sharp in *Lauderd. Papers* (Camden) I. 56 Infatuating and ruining distempers. *a* 1708 Beveridge *Thes. Theol.* (1711) III. 346 Uncleanness..is an infatuating sin. 1858 Froude *Hist. Eng.* III. xii. 19 They had ascribed the king's conduct to the infatuating beauty of this lady.

infatuation (ɪnfætjuːˈeɪʃən). [n. of action from L. *infatuāre* to INFATUATE; cf. F. *infatuation* (*c* 1700 in Littré).] The action of infatuating, or condition of being infatuated; a making or becoming fatuous; possession with extravagant folly; an extravagantly foolish or unreasoning passion.
1649 Bp. Hall *Cases Consc.* iii. i, Free from all the uncleanness of diabolical infatuation. 1718 *Freethinker* No. 77 ¶6 The Infatuation of the Enthusiast, sets him above the Fear of Death. 1751 Johnson *Rambler* No. 169 ¶14 Authors and lovers always suffer some infatuation, from which only absence can set them free. 1815 Jane Austen *Emma* i. viii, Your infatuation about that girl blinds you. 1882 Miss Braddon *Mt. Royal* I. iii. 97 There never was a more obvious case of mutual infatuation.

infatuator (ɪnˈfætjuːeɪtə(r)). [agent-n. in L. form from INFATUATE *v.*: see -OR.] One who or that which infatuates.
1888 Lady Hardy *Dangerous Exper.* III. i. 9 Are we to have the pleasure of seeing Jessie's infatuator tomorrow?

infauna (ˈɪnfɔːnə). [ad. Da. *ifauna* (C. G. J. Petersen 1913, in *Beretn. f. d. Danske biol. Station* XXI. (in *Fiskeri-Beretn.* 1912) 15), f. IN-^{2} + FAUNA.] A collective term for animals that live just beneath the surface of the sea bed.
1914, 1964 [see EPIFAUNA]. 1969 G. Vevers tr. *Friedrich's Marine Biol.* v. 254 The infauna, that is the animals living in the substrate, is either liberosessile, semisessile, or more or less motile.

infaust (ɪnˈfɔːst), *a. rare.* [ad. L. *infaust-us* unlucky, perh. through F. *infauste* (Cotgr. 1611).] Unlucky, unfortunate, ill-omened.
1658 Phillips, *Infaust*, or *Infaustous*, unlucky, unfortunate. 1668 Charleton *Ephes. & Cimm. Matrons* ii. 17 Dismal and infaust visions. 1708 Motteux *Rabelais* v. (1737) 231 O most infaust who optates there to live! 1848 Lytton *Caxtons* ii. vii. xxvi, It was an infaust and sinister augury. 1870 Lowell *Study Wind.* 303 Taurus, whose infaust aspect may be supposed to preside over the makers of bulls and blunders.
So †**inˈfausting** *vbl. sb.* (*rare*$^{-1}$), a rendering 'infaust', a boding of ill luck; †**inˈfaustous** *a.* (*rare*$^{-0}$) = INFAUST.
1622 Bacon *Hen. VII* 196 Hee did withall bring a kind of Malediction and Infausting upon the Marriage, as an ill Prognosticke. 1656 Blount *Glossogr.*, *Infaustous*, unlucky, unfortunate, dismal. 1658 in Phillips.

†**inˈfavour, -or,** *v. Obs.* [f. IN-^{2} + FAVOUR *sb.*: cf. ENFAVOUR in EN- *pref.*^{1} 2.] *trans.* To bring into favour; to ingratiate.
1628 Feltham *Resolves* ii. [i.] lxxxix. 257 But it is to be wondred at, how Repentance can againe infavour vs with an offended God.

†**infavourable,** *a. Obs. rare*$^{-0}$. [IN-^{3}. Cf. L. *infavōrābilis.*]
1721 Bailey, *Infavourable*, not to be favoured [1730-6 (folio) *adds*, also severe].

†**infeable,** obs. form of ENFEEBLE *v.*
1552 Huloet, *Infeable, Infeabled.*

†**infeaffe,** obs. form of ENFEOFF.
1589 Nashe *Anat. Absurd.* B iij b, Might the name of the Church infeaffe them in the Kingdom of Christ.

infeasiˈbility. [f. next + -ITY.] The quality of being infeasible or impracticable.
1655 Fuller *Ch. Hist.* iii. v. §42 Thus not King Iames, but the infeacibility of the thing they petitioned for..gave the denyall to their Petition. 1781 S. Peters *Hist. Conn.* 11 There is an infeasibility in this supposition. 1806 Lamb *Let. to Rickman* Wks. (1840) 80 Let the infeasibility be as great as you will. 1955 *Bull. Atomic Sci.* Mar. 78/2 That such a development is not now in sight does not offer conclusive proof of technical infeasibility. 1965 H. I. Ansoff *Corporate Strategy* (1968) viii. 130 This example is based on an actual diversification history in which the infeasibility was not recognized.

infeasible (ɪnˈfiːzəb(ə)l), *a.* Now *rare.* Also 6 **-faisible,** 7 **-fesible, -fe(a)cible,** 7-9 **-feasable.** [f. IN-^{3} + FEASIBLE. Cf. F. *infaisable* (17th c. in Hatz.-Darm.).] Incapable of being accomplished or carried out; impracticable, impossible.
1533 *St. Papers Hen. VIII*, VII. 497 Ye shall say that ye remember ye herd Hym say oones, He wold neuer conclude that mariage, but to do Us good, whiche is nowe infaisible. 1646 Sir T. Browne *Pseud. Ep.* iii. xii. 135 Which secrets, although extreamly difficult, and *tantum non* infesible, yet are they not impossible. 1665 Glanvill *Scepsis Sci.* xiv. 80 But this is so difficult; and..so almost infeasable. 1678 Butler *Hud.* iii. iii. 391 Therefore I hold no Course s' infecible As this of force to win the Jezabel. 1704 tr. *Boccalini's Lett. fr. Apollo* I. 194 Judging the Attempt infeasable. 1827 Hallam *Const. Hist.* (1876) III. xiv. 70 Designs which the rising spirit of the nation rendered utterly infeasible. 1881 *19th Cent.* No. 48. 239 They pronounced it not only infeasible, but of very doubtful benefit, even could it be carried out.
Hence **inˈfeasibleness** = INFEASIBILITY.
1654 W. Mountague *Devout Ess.* ii. vi. §3. 117 He began the work; and being disabus'd in point of the infeasableness, pursu'd his task, and perfected it.

†**inˈfeather,** *v. Obs.* Also en-. [IN-^{2} = EN-^{1}.] *trans.* To furnish with feathers, to feather.
1611 Florio, *Impennare*, to enfeather, to enplume. *Ibid.*, *Inpennacchiare*, to infeather, to inplume.

†**inˈfect,** *a. Obs. rare.* [ad. L. *infect-us*, f. *in-* (IN-^{3}) + *facĕre* to make.] Incomplete, imperfect.
1398 Trevisa *Barth. De P.R.* xvii. ii. (Add. MS. 27944) lf. 212/1 Grene is þe myddil colour bitwene reed, þat comeþ of the accioun and worchyng of perfyt hete and bytwen white þat comeþ of infecte.

†**infect,** *ppl. a. Obs.* Also 4-6 **enfect(e.** [a. F. *infect* (Oresme, 14th c.), or ad. L. *infect-us*, pa. pple. of *inficĕre*: see next. The spelling with *en-* was rather English than French. OF. had also *infaict, -fait, -fet, enfait* (f. *infaire*: see next), whence ME. *enfeit* (*c* 1400 *Three Kings Cologne* 124).] = INFECTED: Often construed as pa. pple. of next.
1. Affected materially, usually detrimentally; hence (*a*) dimmed, (*b*) stained, polluted, (*c*) made invalid, (*d*) exhausted.
c 1374 Chaucer *Boeth.* iv. met. v. 103 (Camb. MS.) Why þat the hornes of the fulle Moene wexen paale & Infect by bowndes of the derke nyht. 1382 Wyclif *2 Macc.* xii. 15 The pool of stondynge water..infect [*gloss* or meyned] with blood was seen to flowe. *c* 1386 Chaucer *Prol.* 320 So greet a purchasour was nowher noon Al was fee symple to hym in effect His purchasyng myghte nat been infect [*v.r.* enfect]. *c* 1420 *Pallad. on Husb.* i. 294 A gret labour is to correcte A moold in this maner that is enfecte.
2. Tainted *with* disease or organic corruption.
1382 Wyclif *Lev.* xiii. 48 A..skynne, if it were infect with whijt or reed wemme, it shal be holdun a lepre. *c* 1440 *Jacob's Well* (E.E.T.S.) 5 Corrupt watyr, stynkynge and infecte, of which watyr ȝif þou drynke or vse, þou schalt be enpoysonyd. 1518 in W. H. Turner *Select. Rec. Oxford* (1880) 18 As well from London as from other infect places. 1525 Ld. Berners *Froiss.* II. cv. [ci.] 306 Dyuers that were enfecte with sickenesse..coulde not scape the peryle of dethe. 1540 *Act 32 Hen. VIII*, c. 13 §7 Any hors gelding or mare infect with scabbe or mange.
b. Of a disease: Caused by infection.
1541 R. Copland *Guydon's Quest. Chirurg.*, *Maner exam. lazares* Q ij b, Scantly the chylde scapeth lepry, or to be scalled, or tached with suche infecte dyseases.
3. Tainted or contaminated *with* some fault, defect, or vice, with evil habit, false doctrine, etc. Also, culpably involved *in*, guilty *of*.
c 1380 Wyclif *Wks.* (1880) 379 We may se..how þe clergi is wondirfulle enfect wiþ symonye & heresie. 1496 *Dives & Paup.* (W. de W.) vi. x. 248/1 Woman was lesse infecte in the fyrste pryuaricacyon than was man. 1497 Bp. Alcock *Mons Perfect.* D iij, Infecte of ydolatry in worshyppynge fals goddes. *c* 1586 C'tess Pembroke *Ps.* cvi. x, Their sonns, with fathers fault infect. *a* 1612 Harington *Brief View Ch.* 54 (T.) A blinded eye, a closed ear, A hand with bribe infect. 1617 *Machivell's Dogge* in Farr *S.P. Jas. I* (1848) 204 Heale the infect of sinne with oyle of grace.
b. *simply.* Morally corrupted; contaminated; infected with sedition.
c 1400 Lydg. *Æsop's Fab.* iii. 140 A false witnesse hath his avauntage With mowth infect alwey to do damage. 1509 Barclay *Shyp of Folys* (1874) I. 5 Holsom medicyne which gaue vnto infect myndes frutful doctryne and norisshinge. 1606 Shaks. *Tr. & Cr.* i. iii. 187 And in the imitation of these twaine..many are infect. 1607 Tourneur *Rev. Trag.* iv. iii, For whose infect perswasions I could scarce Kneele out my prayers.

infect (ɪnˈfɛkt), *v.* Also 4-6 **enfect(e,** 6 *Sc.* **infeck;** 4-5 *pa. tense and pple.* **in-, enfecte.** [ad. L. *infect-*, ppl. stem of *inficĕre* to dip in, stain, taint, impregnate, spoil, etc., f. *in-* (IN-^{2}) + *facĕre* to make, do, put. Cf. F. *infecter* (16th c.); in older Fr. the popular form was *in-, enfaire*, with pa. pple. *in-, enfait* (see prec.).] To imbue a person or thing *with* certain (esp. bad) qualities; said either of the personal or material agent.
1. *trans.* To affect, influence, or imbue with some quality or property by immersion or infusion.
†a. To dye, tinge, colour, stain. *Obs.*
1495 *Trevisa's Barth. De P.R.* xvi. xxxvii. (W. de W.), Electrum receyueth sone colour and hewe in what manere a man woll and so it is soone enfected [*MSS.* infecte]..wyth Percyl. 1623 Lisle *Ælfric on O. & N. Test.* Ded. xxvi, Nor shall we more with artificiall hew, Infect our fells, by teaching them to faine What Nature gaue not. 1633 P. Fletcher *Purple Isl.* ii. xvii, His native beautie is a lilie white, Which still some other colour'd stream infecteth. 1691 Ray *Creation* ii. (1692) 23 To those that have the Jaundice..objects appear of that same Color wherewith their Eyes are infected.
b. To impregnate or imbue with some qualifying substance, or active principle, as poison, or salt; to taint. *Obs.* or *rare.*
1553 Eden *Treat. Newe Ind.* (Arb.) 23 They vse also to infect theyr arrowes with venime. 1563 W. Fulke *Meteors* (1640) 64 b, Salt..is first generated in the earth, after commeth the water of the Sea, and is infected with it. 1601 Holland *Pliny* I. 44 The nature of the earth infecteth the waters, as it were, with some strong medicine. 1613 Purchas *Pilgrimage* (1614) 646 He tempered a poyson for that purpose, with which a weapon infected, drawing never so little bloud, did kill. 1680 Boyle *Scept. Chem.* i. 68 Upon the unluting the Vessels it infected the Room with a scarce supportable stink. 1853 Kane *Grinnell Exp.* xxxiii. (1856) 288 Our snow-water has been infected for the past month by a very perceptible flavor and odor of musk.
†2. To affect injuriously or unpleasantly; to spoil or corrupt by noxious influence, admixture, or alloy; to adulterate. *Obs.*
c 1420 *Pallad. on Husb.* vi. 177 Att Mayes eende a solar is to paue, And rather [earlier] not, lest frostis hit enfecte. 1563 W. Fulke *Meteors* (1640) 67 Copper..giveth way to corruption, being infected with that greene minerall Copperas. 1576 Gascoigne *Steele Gl.* (Arb.) 80 When pewterers infect no Tin with leade. 1590 Lodge *Euphues Gold. Leg.* (ed. Collier) 100 The synople tree, whose blossomes delight the smell, and whose fruit infects the taste. 1599 B. Jonson *Ev. Man out of Hum.* Epil. 8 Our cities torrent (bent t'infect The hallow'd bowels of the silver Thames). 1693 Dryden tr. *Persius* vi. 91 Our sweating Hinds their Sallads, now, defile, Infecting homely Herbs with fragrant Oil.
3. To impregnate or taint with deleterious qualities; to fill (the air, etc.) with noxious corruption or the germs of disease; to render injurious to health.
c 1375 *Sc. Leg. Saints, George* 51 A serpent fel..þat of his aynd infect þe ayre. 1483 Caxton *Gold. Leg.* 415 b/2 A dragon right venomous..whiche enfected soo the place that nothyng grewe aboute hym. 1542 Boorde *Dyetary* iii. (1870) 236 Many thynges doth infect, putryfye, and corrupteth the ayre. 1599 Shaks. *Much Ado* ii. i. 257 If her breath were as terrible as [her] terminations, there were no liuing neere her, she would infect to the north starre. 1635 Swan *Spec. M.* v. §2 (1643) 122 The matter of lightning..is much infected, and therefore hurteth where it entereth. 1717 Lady M. W. Montagu *Let. to Miss Sara Chiswell* 1 Apr., There are many that escape it [the plague]; neither is the air ever infected. 1885 S. Cox *Expos.* Ser. i. ii. 23 The carcase would but rot and fester and infect the air.
fig. *c* 1400 *Destr. Troy* 936 He Enfecte the ffirmament with his felle noise.
4. To affect (a person, animal, or part of the body) with disease; to communicate a morbific virus or noxious germs so as to generate disease; to act upon by infection or contagion. Also *absol.*
c 1386 Chaucer *Manciple's Prol.* 39 Hoold cloos thy mouth..Thy cursed breeth infecte wole vs alle. 1483 Caxton *Gold. Leg.* 262 b/2 All they that were vexed and seke and the fyre of pestylence had infected. 1538 Bale *Thre Lawes* 286 The ayre whych geueth breathe, Sumtyme infecteth to deathe. 1548 Hall *Chron., Hen. VIII* 176 b, Neither he nor the quene nor none of their company was enfected of yᵉ disease. 1628 Wither *Brit. Rememb.* ii. 449 Right so, this Plague..infects (At such or such a distance) ev'ry one. 1697 Dryden *Virg. Georg.* iii. 671 The Causes and the Signs shall next be told, Of ev'ry Sickness that infects the Fold. 1722 De Foe *Plague* 37 Persons infected with plague. 1845 Budd *Dis. Liver* 309 The lungs were infected, as well as the liver.
b. *transf.* and *fig.* Used of influences whose operation or effect is (expressly or by implication) compared to that of an infectious disease.
c 1385 Chaucer *L.G.W.* 2242 *Philomela*, ȝit lestyth the venym of so longe ago That it enfectyth [*v.r.* infecteth] hym that wele [*v.r.* wyll] beholde The storye of Therius. *c* 1421 Hoccleve *Complaint* 235 This grevous venyme that had enfectyd and wildyd my brayne. 1548 Hall *Chron., Hen. VII* 30 She compassed, ymagened, and invented how..to infect his whole realme with a pestiferous discorde. 1697 Dryden *Æneid* ii. 733 With a Son's death t'infect a Father's sight. 1784 Cowper *Task* v. 606 All the plagues with which his sins Infect his happiest moments. 1821 Shelley *Prometh. Unb.* iii. iv. 148 The wretch crept a vampire among men, Infecting all with his own hideous ill.
5. To taint with moral corruption; to deprave; to exert a bad influence upon character or habits.
c 1374 Chaucer *Boeth.* iv. pr. iii. 94 (Camb. MS.) The vtteriste wikkednesse..ne defowleth ne entechcheth nat hem oonly but infectyth and enuenymeth hem gretly. *c* 1460 J. Russell *Bk. Nurture* 1249 Now, good god, graunt vs grace oure sowles neuer to Infecte! 1482 *Monk of Evesham* (Arb.) 69 With her wyckydnes they haue al moste enfecte

and cumbrid alle the howse. **1535** STEWART *Cron. Scot.* II. 245 He wes..Infectit far with auerice that syn. **1574** G. SCOTT in Farr *S.P. Eliz.* (1845) II. 522 Rome is a cage of birdes uncleane,..Few errours haue the Church infect, That dyd not there begynne. **1667** MILTON *P.L.* x. 608 Till I in Man residing,..His thoughts, his looks, words, actions all infect, And season him thy last and sweetest prey. **1751** JOHNSON *Rambler* No. 155 ¶12 Indolence is..one of the vices from which those whom it infects are seldom reformed. **1833** CRUSE *Eusebius* II. i. 50 These, after the manner of their founder,..infected those with the greatest corruption.

6. To taint with crime; to involve in crime or its penalties.

1580 LYLY *Euphues* (Arb.) 314 If any English-man be infected with any mysdemeanour. **1602** FULBECKE *1st Pt. Parall.* 79 If one say to an other that he is infected of the robbery and murder lately committed and smels of the murder, an action vpon the case will lye for these wordes. **1651** W. G. tr. *Cowel's Inst.* 271 Moreover the Issue of Felons is so infected, that they are excluded from all hope or possibility of succeeding in the Inheritances of their Ancestors, which otherwise should have descended to them. **1828** in WEBSTER; hence in mod. Dicts.

b. *Internat. Law.* To taint or contaminate with illegality; to involve (a ship or cargo) in the seizure or forfeiture to which contraband or prohibited goods, or an enemy's ship, are liable. Cf. INFECTION 8, INFECTIOUS 6.

a **1758** SIR GEO. LEE in F. T. Pratt *Law of Contraband* (1867) 170 Soap and potashes are not contraband, but as they belong to the same owners..they by law are liable to confiscation by being infected by the contraband. **1879** WOOLSEY tr. *Treaty of Utrecht* in *Introd. Internat. Law* (ed. 5) §198. 342 The ship itself, as well as the other goods found therein, are to be esteemed free, neither may they be detained on pretense of their being, as it were, infected by the prohibited goods.

7. To imbue with an opinion or belief, esp. a pernicious one, as heresy or seditious views; †formerly sometimes used in a good or neutral sense. Also said of the opinion, etc.

1483 CAXTON *Gold. Leg.* 232/2 Whan the heresye of the arryans had enfected al Italye. **1494** FABYAN *Chron.* v. cxxxiii. 117 Y[e] cursyd secte of y[t] detestable & false prophete Machomet..hath enfectyd .ii. pryncypall partis of y[e] worlde. **1559** J. WHYTE *Serm.* in Strype *Ann. Ref.* (1824) I. vii. 154 Books..full of pestilent doctrines, blasphemy and heresy, to infect the people. **1588** *Marprel. Epist.* (Arb.) 24 Being infected by him with the true knowledge of the gospell. **1660** *Trial Regic.* 55 The end of your Speech is nothing, but to infect the People. **1782** PRIESTLEY *Corrupt. Chr.* I. I. 23 Philosophical opinions..had then begun to infect the Jews. **1882** J. H. BLUNT *Ref. Ch. Eng.* II. 226 These foreign religionists had infected their English friends ..with their opinions.

8. To affect (a person) with some feeling, esp. by force of influence or example. Also of feelings: To seize upon, take hold of.

1595 SHAKS. *John* IV. iii. 69 A holy Vow..Neuer to taste the pleasures of the world, Neuer to be infected with delight. **1611** —— *Wint. T.* I. ii. 262 'Twas a feare Which oft infects the wisest. **1667** MILTON *P.L.* I. 453 The Love-tale Infected Sions daughters with like heat. **1765** H. WALPOLE *Otranto* ii. (1798) 33 Your terrors, I suppose, have infected me. **1828** SCOTT *F.M. Perth* xxxiv, The frenzy of rage and despair, infected next the minstrels. **1885** MABEL COLLINS *Prettiest Woman* vii, Her gaiety infected him.

9. To affect or influence with some quality, or by the introduction of some extraneous element.

1605 BACON *Adv. Learn.* I. v. §7 Men have used to infect their meditations, opinions, and doctrines, with some conceits which they have most admired. *a* **1680** BUTLER *Rem.* (1759) II. 217 His Muse is not inspired but infected with another Man's Fancy. **1750** JOHNSON *Rambler* No. 71 ¶9 Forgetfulness of the fragility of life has remarkably infected the students of monuments. **1883** FROUDE *Short Stud.* IV. I. v. 56 The enthusiasm of the biographers for their master and his cause infects every line of their narratives.

b. *spec.* Of a sound: To affect and alter the quality of a sound in a neighbouring syllable, as takes place especially in the Celtic languages. (Cf. INFECTION 11.)

(Introduced in L. form *inficere* by Zeuss *Gram. Celt.* I. 3.)

1872 [see INFECTED 4]. **1885** STOKES in *Trans. Philol. Soc.* 179 [Final] *-a* (Indo-Eur. *ā*) is lost, but infects a following consonant and breaks a preceding *i* or *u*. *Ibid.* 205 Toneless or grave *e* becomes *a* or *i*, or (after infecting a previous vowel) is lost.

†10. To infest, beset noisomely. *Obs.* [So F. *infecter* in La Fontaine and Buffon (Littré).]

1547 BOORDE *Brev. Health* §119 It is kynd of spirites, the which doth infect and trouble men when they be in theyr beddes slepynge. **1607** TOPSELL *Four-f. Beasts* (1658) 177 Foxes are annoyed with many enemies..the small flies, called Gnats, do much trouble and infect them. **1654** H. L'ESTRANGE *Chas. I* (1655) 130 His coasts were..infected with Pickroons, Turks, and Dunkirk-Pirats to the great dammage of traffique. **1712** W. ROGERS *Voy.* (1718) 319 Much infected with serpents, moskittos, and other insects.

†11. *intr.* To become infected (in various senses).

c **1420** *Pallad. on Husb.* XI. 350 Lest they [wines] enfecte is ferther now to trete. **1500-20** DUNBAR *Poems* xxxv. 30 Thir terrible monsteris sall togidder thrist..Quhill all the air infeck of thair pysoun. *a* **1529** SKELTON *Image Ipocr.* IV. 2 Nowe with sondry sectes The world sore infectes. **1589** COGAN *Haven Health* (1636) 318 All infected in a manner at one instant, by reason of a dampe or mist which arose. **1597** MONTGOMERY *Cherrie & Slae* 1354 Luke quhat laiks for his releif Or furder he infeck.

in'fectant, *a. rare.* [f. INFECT *v.* (or its source) + -ANT[1]: cf. F. *infectant* (Littré).] Infecting; causing infection.

1867 *Pall Mall G.* No. 813. 1001/1 Uniformity of infectant power.

infected (ɪn'fɛktɪd), *ppl. a.* [f. as prec. + -ED[1].]

1. Tainted with disease or infectious properties. **a.** Of a thing or place, the air, etc.; †also formerly of pestilence.

1480 CAXTON *Chron. Eng.* ccxxviii, The pestylence was so enfected & so haboundant..that unnethe there were left lyvyng folk to burye hem that were dede. **1542** BOORDE *Dyetary* xxvii. (1870) 290 Strawe & rushes..cast out of a howse infectyd. **1549** *Compl. Scot.* vi. 38 Al..caliginus fumis & infekkit vapours..hed bene generit. **1666** W. BOGHURST *Loimogr.* (1894) 64 More have received the disease from infected Linen than infected Woollen. **1730** SOUTHALL *Bugs* 34 Coming from infected Houses. **1897** HUGHES *Medit. Fever* ii. 91 Isolated agricultural villages, never visited by the inhabitants of the infected towns.

b. Of persons or animals, the body or its parts, the mind, etc.

1597 A. M. tr. *Guillemeau's Fr. Chirurg.* 37 b/1 The whole infectede and spoylede parte swelleth. **1600** SHAKS. *A.Y.L.* II. vii. 60, I will..Cleanse the foule bodie of th' infected world, If they will patiently receiue my medicine. **1605** —— *Macb.* v. i. 80 Infected mindes To their deafe pillowes will discharge their Secrets. **1693** W. BOWLES in *Dryden's Juvenal* v. (1697) 102 All round from him, as from th'infected run. **1722** DE FOE *Plague* 43 To remove either his sound or his infected people. **1798** W. BLAIR *Soldier's Friend* 67. **1828** SCOTT *F.M. Perth* xxvii, It is no light thing to be shunned by the worthy as an infected patient.

†2. Evilly affected or contaminated in respect of moral character, opinions, etc. Also of sin. *Obs.*

1570 in Strype *Ann. Ref.* (1824) I. II. lvii. 370 The tyranny of such infected members, as..might have imprisoned a number of good subjects. **1590** SPENSER *F.Q.* I. x. 25 Inward corruption and infected sin. **1638** *Div. & Pol. Observ.* 26 Mens former flocking to Sermons in Infected places.

†3. Discoloured; stained; tinged. *Obs.*

1701 ADDISON *Let. fr. Italy* 23 Hoary Albula's infected tide. **1713** YOUNG *Last Day* III. 68 Yet still some thin remains of fear and doubt, Th' infected brightness of their joy pollute.

4. *Celtic Gram.* Altered in sound by the influence of a neighbouring sound: see INFECT *v.* 9 b.

[**1853** ZEUSS *Gram. Celt.* I. 2 Certis collocationis legibus pulsi transeant in alios sonos secundarios, qui dici possunt alterati vel infecti.] **1872** STOKES *Goidelica* 112 Infected *g, d, t* are dropped, as in *bri(gh)te, blie(dh)nec..be(th)ad.* *Mod.* The *ai* of *faidh*, and *i* of *fir* are instances of infected vowels.

Hence **in'fectedness**, the condition of being infected (in quot., with disease).

1882 *Quain's Med. Dict.* (Cent.), The infectedness of the patient is first made known..by..general pyrexia.

in'fecter. ? *Obs.* [f. INFECT *v.* + -ER[1].] One who infects; = INFECTOR.

1509 BARCLAY *Shyp of Folys* (1874) I. 56 Lousers of loue, and infecters of Charite, Unworthy ar to lyue here at large. **1765** JOHNSON *Note Shaks. Timon* IV. iii, This alludes to an opinion in former times, generally prevalent, that the venereal infection transmitted to another, left the infecter free.

in'fectible, *a. rare.* [f. INFECT *v.* + -IBLE.] Capable of being infected.

1612-15 BP. HALL *Contempl., N.T.* IV. xvi, It was not possibly infectible, nor any way obnoxious to the danger of others sin.

in'fecting, *vbl. sb.* [f. as prec. + -ING[1].] The action of the verb INFECT, in various senses.

1480 CAXTON *Chron. Eng.* ccxxxii. (1482) 249 A sikenes that men callyd the pokkes slowe both men and women thurgh hir enfectyng. **1508** KENNEDIE *Flyting w. Dunbar* 487 For fyling and infecking of the aire. **1613** *Nottingham Rec.* IV. 308 For kepinge a skebed horse, to the infectinge of his nebores horses. **1722** DE FOE *Plague* (1884) 256 This infecting and being infected..is evident.

in'fecting, *ppl. a.* [f. as prec. + -ING[2].] That infects: in senses of the vb.

1590 GREENE *Orl. Fur.* Wks. (Rtldg.) 107/1 To sting thee with infecting jealousy. *a* **1653** GOUGE *Comm. Heb.* xii. 8 Afflictions are as a rasor..to let out the putrifying infecting matter. **1883** M'SWINEY tr. *Windisch's Irish Gram.* §18 The infecting or attenuating vowel (invariably an *i*), either takes its place beside the vowel of the foregoing syllable, or has wholly extruded it. **1897** *Allbutt's Syst. Med.* IV. 419 Infecting virus being conveyed by the veins or lymphatics.

infection (ɪn'fɛkʃən). Also 5-6 **en-**. [a. F. *infection* (13-14th c.), ad. late L. *infectiōn-em* (in St. Gregory in sense 'infection, contagion' of poison, heresy), n. of action from *inficĕre* to INFECT. (The *en-* form appears to be without French precedent.)]

†1. The action or process of affecting injuriously, or the fact of being so affected; corrupted or diseased condition. *Obs.*

1398 TREVISA *Barth. De P.R.* VII. xvi[i]. (Add. MS. 27944) lf. 84/1 If it [rheum in the eyes] is euel I-kept, þerof leueþ a litil mole and infeccioun. *c* **1400** *Lanfranc's Cirurg.* 116 Þe ventriclis of þe brayn..ben of so greet nobilitie, þouȝ þat þer be neuere so litil infeccioun..þei ben depriued of her heelþe. **1557** PAYNEL *Barclay's Jugurth* 31 Thyrdly ye infeccion of Justice whiche is no wher here among us, but clene exyled from our cytie. **1563** W. FULKE *Meteors* (1640) 65 b, Gold never corrupteth by rust, because it is pure from poysonous infection. **1621** BURTON *Anat. Mel.* I. i. III. i. (1651) 31 [Melancholy] a privation or infection of the middle cell of the Head.

†2. Contamination or corruption of air or water, rendering it apt or liable to generate or propagate disease; a morbific condition or quality of the atmosphere, etc. *Obs.*

1412-20 LYDG. *Chron. Troy* I. vi. (1555), The enfection of theyr troubled eyre, He hath vanquished. **1548** HALL *Chron., Edw. IV* 232 What with savor of burnynge of townes, and infeccion of the ayre, corrupted by the multitude of dead carcases. **1625** K. LONG tr. *Barclay's Argenis* III. ii. 154 For the bodies of the enemies, lest by the Aires infection, they should after their death prove hurtfull [etc.]. **1747** *Gentl. Mag.* 480, I have long been of opinion, that the plague itself is caused by the air's being full of invisible animalcula, to which it owes its infection. **1801** *Med. Jrnl.* V. 146 Dr. Tissott..observes, that the Small-pox ..does not propagate itself so much by contagion as by an infection of the air.

3. The agency, substance, germ, or principle by which an infectious disease is communicated or transmitted; morbific influence.

1412-20 LYDG. *Chron. Troy* I. ii. (1555), He was so full of foul coruption, and eke so dredeful of infection. *c* **1477** CAXTON *Jason* 75, I coude not so fast flee but that the terrible dragon cast upon me a gobet of the most detestable infeccion that neuer was. **1542** BOORDE *Dyetary* xxvii. (1870) 290 The syckenes is taken with the sauour of a mans clothes..for the infection wyl lye and hange longe in clothes. **1601** R. JOHNSON *Kingd. & Commw.* (1603) 114 Even the houses and their ruins are receptakles of infection, and matter of corruption. **1722** DE FOE *Plague* 124 The infection may be in the very air. **1794** MRS. RADCLIFFE *Myst. Udolpho* i, She had..taken the infection during her attendance upon him. **1855** MACAULAY *Hist. Eng.* xx. IV. 530 Towards the end of the year 1694..At length the infection spread to the palace, and reached the young and blooming Queen. **1871** B. TAYLOR *Faust* (1875) I. xix. 174 Seek protection As from a corpse that breeds infection.

b. *pl.* Morbific influences, principles, or germs.

1533 ELYOT *Cast. Helthe* (1539) 24 In a tyme of pestilence, if one beinge fastynge, doo chewe some of the leaues [of sorrel]..it meruaylously preserueth from infections. **1610** SHAKS. *Temp.* II. ii. 1 All the infections that the Sunne suckes vp From Bogs, Fens, Flats, on Prosper fall, and make him By ynch-meale a disease. **1885** S. COX *Expos.* Ser. I. ii. 26 That the air may be freed from poisonous infections.

4. The communication of disease, esp. by the agency of the atmosphere or water (hence, in strict use, distinguished from *contagion*, which implies communication by actual contact); the action or process of infecting; the fact of being infected.

1548 HALL *Chron., Hen. VIII* 64 The kyng..kept no solempne Christmas, willyng to have no resort for feare of infeccion. **1618** LATHAM *2nd Bk. Falconry* xxviii. 129 The Rye, the Cramp, and the Craye..the best way will be for the keeper euermore to bee mindfull and carefull to preuent their infection, before any of them hath laid holde, or seazed on his Hawke. **1751** JOHNSON *Rambler* No. 174 ¶14 As a man suspected of infection is refused admission into cities. **1804** *Med. Jrnl.* XII. 327 Whatever is observed in the artificial infection by inoculation, holds true in the natural infection. **1860** FLOR. NIGHTINGALE *Nursing* ii. (1861) 29 True nursing knows nothing of infection, except to prevent it.

5. Disease caused by infection; an infectious disease; a plague, epidemic, pestilence; †formerly sometimes, A disease, a seizure with disease.

1563 BALDWIN in *Mirr. Mag.* Ccj b, God him selfe will fyght with enfections and erthquakes. **1576** FLEMING *Panopl. Epist.* 238 *note*, Lecherie..loathsome for the foule infections which it breedeth: as the spanishe pocke [etc.]. **1577** EARL LEICESTER in Ellis *Orig. Lett.* Ser. I. II. 273 The infection in Oxford and the Country falleth out to be onely at the Assizes gotten. **1593** NASHE *4 Lett. Conf.* 50 There would more gentle Readers die of a merrie mortality..than there haue done of this last infection. **1680-90** TEMPLE *Ess., Learning* Wks. 1731 I. 169 As an Infection that rises in a Town, first falls upon Children or weak Constitutions. **1725** DE FOE *Voy. round World* (1840) 26 We were crowded together enough to bring an infection among us. **1789** W. BUCHAN *Dom. Med.* (1790) 493 Sometimes indeed a slight infection may be carried off in a few days, by bathing the parts in warm milk and water. **1844** THIRLWALL *Greece* lxvi. VIII. 429 He found himself shunned in public places as an infection.

6. Moral contamination; vitiation of character or habits by evil influences; an instance of this.

a **1529** SKELTON *Bk. 3 Fooles*, Lechery..is..full of enfeccion and bytterness, for it distayneth the soule of man. **1582** in *Lett. Lit. Men* (Camden) 67 Heathen Poets..from which the youth of the realme doth rather receive infection in manners than advancement in virtue. **1697** tr. *Dupin's Eccl. Hist.* II. 76 The Cares and Affairs of the World.. corrupt Men by an Infection, that is almost unavoidable. **1794** GIFFORD *Baviad* 345 If yet there be One bosom from this vile infection free. **1828** W. SEWELL *Oxf. Prize Ess.* 46 We dread the infection of mean and degraded objects.

7. Corruption of faith or loyalty by heretical or seditious principles; communication of harmful opinions or beliefs.

1529 MORE *Dyaloge* I. 29 b, Bringynge vp of some newe fangell heresies to the infeccion of our olde faythe. **1548** HALL *Chron., Hen. VII* 36 b, Contamynate wyth that sedicious infeccion. **1665** MANLEY *Grotius' Low C. Warres* 465 This man, by the infection of the Earl of Leicesters party, was carryed so far [etc.]. **1719** YOUNG *Busiris* II. i, Thou hast a heart that swells with loyalty, And throws off the infection of these times. **1796** MORSE *Amer. Geog.* I. 444 A regard for the public peace, and for the preservation of the church of Christ from infection.

8. *Internat. Law.* Contamination by illegality; the communication to a ship or cargo of liability to seizure, from association with hostile or contraband cargo, etc. (cf. INFECT *v.* 6 b).

1879 WOOLSEY *Introd. Internat. Law* (ed. 5) §189 In 1744 . . a regulation freed neutral ships from the infection of the hostile cargo.

9. The 'catching' and diffusive influence or operation of example, sympathy, and the like, in the communication of feelings or impulses from one to another; = CONTAGION 5.

1616 R. C. *Times' Whistle* III. 1098 The infection Of thy high leveld thoughts lets thee not see The ougly face of thy deformity. *c* **1630** MILTON *Passion* 55 And I . . Might think the infection of my sorrows loud Had got a race of mourners on some pregnant cloud. **1715–20** POPE *Iliad* VI. 645 There, while her tears deplored the godlike man, Through all her train the soft infection ran. **1873** BLACK *Pr. Thule* xiv, The infection of his warm and poetic enthusiasm.

†**10.** The process of moistening, colouring, etc. by immersion or infusion (cf. INFECT *v.* 1). *Obs. rare.*

1657 TOMLINSON *Renou's Disp.* 59 Tincture or infection is neere akin to humectation. **1686** GOAD *Celest. Bodies* I. ii. 7, I find Fire to spit at the infection of Salt or Water.

11. *Celtic Gram.* Alteration of a sound under the influence of a neighbouring sound.

[Cf. **1853** ZEUSS *Gramm. Celtica* I. 3 Evolutione quam nos dicemus infectionem.]

1872 STOKES *Goidelica* 112 As to infection of the initials. Of vocalic infection, or, as Irish grammarians call it 'aspiration'. . . Of nasal infection of tenues, or, as Irish grammarians call it, eclipsis. **1883** M'SWINEY tr. *Windisch's Irish Gram.* §16 The purity of the vowels undergoes infection or alteration, owing to the influence the vowels of the neighbouring syllables exercise over each other. *Ibid.* §17 Infection takes place most frequently by means of the slender vowels.

¶**12.** Humorously misused for *affection*, liking.

1596 SHAKS. *Merch. V.* II. ii. 133 He hath a great infection sir, as one would say, to serue. **1598** —— *Merry W.* II. ii. 120 Her husband has a maruellous infection to the little Page.

13. *attrib.* and *Comb.*

1896 *Allbutt's Syst. Med.* I. 215 Infection experiments carried out upon animals. *Ibid.* 538 The toxic products of the infection-carriers.

in'fectionist. *rare.* [f. prec. + -IST.] One who lays stress upon infection as a cause of disease.

1836 E. HOWARD *R. Reefer* xxxvii, The appeal was unfortunate, both for the appealer and the doctor. The latter was an infectionist. **1865** *Pall Mall G.* 18 Aug. 9/2 An ardent 'infectionist', says that, in the very same quarter of London, those who used the Southwark and Vauxhall Company's water . . died at the rate of seventy-one to every ten thousand houses. **1865** *Intell. Observer* No. 44. 128 The ultra contagionist or infectionist.

infectious (ɪn'fɛkʃəs), *a.* [f. INFECT-ION + -IOUS; cf. mod.F. *infectieux*. An earlier formation after L. *infectu-s* was INFECTUOUS.]

1. a. Having the quality or power of communicating disease by infection; infecting with disease; pestilential, unhealthy.

1542 BOORDE *Dyetary* xxvii. (1870) 290 Whan the Plages of the Pestylence or the swetynge syckenes is in a towne or countree . . the people doth fle from the contagious and infectious ayre. *Ibid.*, In such infectious tyme. **1602** MARSTON *Antonio's Rev.* IV. iii, Why permit you now such scum . . to . . taint the ayre With his infectious breath? **1774** GOLDSM. *Nat. Hist.* I. 195 It would seem that the predominance of any one vapour . . becomes infectious, and that we owe the salubrity of the air to the variety of its mixture. **1829** LYTTON *Devereux* II. ii, There is something infectious in the atmosphere. **1838** *Penny Cycl.* XII. 470/2 The infectious qualities of substances which cannot be conveniently washed.

†**b.** Poisonous. *Obs. rare*$^{-1}$.

1658 ROWLAND *Moufet's Theat. Ins.* 909 On the trees . . there growes a kinde of infectious honey. The which poyson being drank makes men stupid, and out of their wits.

2. a. Of diseases: Apt to be communicated or received by infection; liable to be transmitted from one person to another by means of air or water (in strict use, distinguished from CONTAGIOUS, q.v.).

1592 SHAKS. *Rom. & Jul.* v. ii. 10 In a house Where the infectious pestilence did raigne. **1610** BP. HALL *Recoll. Treat.* (1614) 754 Leprosie or plague . . diseases, not more deadly then infectious. **1683** BURNET tr. *More's Utopia* (1684) 93 That such of them as are sick of infectious Diseases, may be kept so far from the rest, that there can be no danger of Contagion. **1790** BEATSON *Nav. & Mil. Mem.* II. 13 The fever was highly infectious, and swept off great numbers. **1897** *Allbutt's Syst. Med.* II. 252 Its virus is incapable of diffusion in the atmosphere, and . . consequently it is contagious only and not infectious also.

b. *transf.* Of or for infectious diseases.

1887 *Pall Mall G.* 5 Oct. 9/1 Typhoid is prevalent . . and several cases are now being treated at the infectious hospital. **1894** *Lancet* 3 Nov. 1064 The infectious hospital is that of St. Ladislaus.

c. In the names of various diseases, as ***infectious hepatitis***, an acute infectious virus disease characterized by hepatitis and jaundice; ***infectious mononucleosis***, an acute disease (also called glandular fever) chiefly affecting young adults, characterized by fever, swelling of the lymph nodes, and leucocytosis.

1920 SPRUNT & EVANS in *Bull. Johns Hopkins Hosp.* XXXI. 410 (*heading*) Mononuclear leucocytosis in reaction to acute infections ('infectious mononucleosis'). **1945** *Amer. Jrnl. Med. Sci.* CCX. 561 (*heading*) Homologous serum hepatitis and infectious (epidemic) hepatitis. **1970** PASSMORE & ROBSON *Compan. Med. Stud.* II. xviii. 117/1 Infectious hepatitis is usually spread by faecal contamination from a patient or convalescent carrier of the disease. **1970** A. J. ZUCKERMAN *Virus Dis. Liver* xiii. 149 Infectious mononucleosis is an endemic disease affecting principally adolescents and young adults.

†**3.** Infected with disease. *Obs.*

1542 BOORDE *Dyetary* xvii. (1870) 290 The syckenes is taken with the sauour of a mans clothes the which hath vysyted the infectious howse. **1604** SHAKS. *Oth.* IV. i. 21 It comes ore my memorie As doth the Rauen o're the infectious [*Qos.* infected] house Boading to all. **1618** ROWLANDS *Sacr. Mem. Mirac.* 41 Are there not ten infectious creatures cleane, Of whom this poore Samaria stranger, meane, Onely returns? **1727** BRADLEY *Fam. Dict.* s.v. *Canker*, Incorporate the whole together with Vinegar . . and rubbing the infectious Place therewith, it will cure them.

4. Tending or liable to infect or contaminate character, morals, etc. Now *rare*.

1547–64 BAULDWIN *Mor. Philos.* (Palfr.) To Rdr., That pestilent and most infectious canker, idlenesse. **1685** BAXTER *Paraphr. N.T., Matt.* xviii. 15, etc., To keep Christians from the snare and the shame of infectious and wicked Associates. **1742** YOUNG *Nt. Th.* v. 142 The world's infectious; few bring back at eve, Immaculate, the manners of the morn.

5. Of actions, emotions, etc.: Having the quality of spreading from one to another; 'catching', contagious.

a **1611** BEAUM. & FL. *Maid's Trag.* I. i, She carries with her an infectious grief, That strikes all her beholders. **1700** DRYDEN *Palamon & Arc.* II. 313 Through the bright quire th' infectious virtue ran. All dropt their tears. **1828** WHATELY *Rhet.* in *Encycl. Metrop.* 300/1 Almost every one is aware of the infectious nature of any emotion excited in a large assembly. **1866** G. MACDONALD *Ann. Q. Neighb.* xi. (1878) 200 How hearty and infectious his laughter! **1899** *Nation* (N.Y.) 12 Oct. 275/2 An infectious good humour and urbanity.

6. *Internat. Law.* Tainting with illegality (said of contraband or hostile goods in their effect on the rest of a cargo, or on the ship); cf. INFECT *v.* 6 b.

1878 KENT *Internat. Law* ix. (ed. 2) 339 Contraband articles are said to be of an infectious nature, and they contaminate the whole cargo belonging to the same owners.

in'fectiously, *adv.* [f. prec. + -LY².] In an infectious manner; so as to infect; as if infected.

1606 SHAKS. *Tr. & Cr.* II. ii. 59 The will dotes that is inclineable To what infectiously it selfe affects, Without some image of th' affected merit. **1612–15** BP. HALL *Contempl., O.T.* XVIII. iii, The surest way is to keep aloof from the infectiously wicked. **1638** SIR T. HERBERT *Trav.* (ed. 2) 60 The ditch . . which too oft smels infectiously. **1896** *Chicago Advance* 15 Oct. 516 Glasgow's famous hospital for the infectiously diseased.

in'fectiousness. [f. as prec. + -NESS.] The quality of being infectious.

1619 W. SCLATER *Exp. 1 Thess.* (1630) 223 Seeing the infectiousnesse of the pestilence or leprosie in others. **1685** BOYLE *Salub. Air* iii. 89 Sometimes the plague ceases, or at least very notably abates of its infectiousness and malignity, in far less time. **1748** HARTLEY *Observ. Man* I. iv. 489 The Infectiousness of our Tempers and Dispositions. **1878** T. BRYANT *Pract. Surg.* I. 136 Some classification of the partially infectious tumours by their kinds of infectiousness may be agreed upon.

infective (ɪn'fɛktɪv), *a.* [ad. L. *infectīvus* (in cl.L. in neut. pl. *infectīva* dyes): see INFECT *v.* and -IVE. Cf. OF. *infectif, -ive* (Godefroy). The word seems to have gone out of use *c* 1700, but has recently been revived in medical use.]

†**1.** Having the quality of affecting injuriously or tainting. Const. *of*. *Obs. rare.*

1398 TREVISA *Barth. De P.R.* XVII. lxxv. (Tollem. MS.), Hit is sone greuid with colde eyer, with hayle, with rayne, with euel dewe and infectyue [*ex rore . . infectivo*]. *c* **1420** *Pallad. on Husb.* IX. 14 Al other donge is infectif of wynys.

2. a. Having the quality of infecting with disease, or of spreading disease by infection; infectious.

1398 TREVISA *Barth. De P.R.* XVIII. lxv[i]. (Add. MS. 27944) lf. 291/1 His [a lion's] breþ stynkeþ and is infectiue, and infecteþ oþre þinges, and his bitynge is dedliche and venemous. *c* **1485** *Digby Myst.* IV. 368 To wash away corrupcion of wondes infectyfe. **1502** ATKYNSON tr. *De Imitatione* III. xlv. 233 Truly vayne glory is an infectyue pestylens. **1523** LD. BERNERS *Froiss.* I. ccxxxix. 347 They bare with full great trouble the heate, and the infectyue ayre of the countrey of Spaygne. **1562** TURNER *Baths* 2 a, If he be sieke in a smitting or infective disease. **1583** BABINGTON *Commandm.* iii. (1637) 27 Some pestilent thing of an infective operation. **1616** SURFL. & MARKH. *Country Farme* 428 This Oyle of Oates . . expelleth out of the bodie all manner of venimous and infectiue humours. **1867** *Pall Mall G.* No. 813. 1001/1 The infective power of the poison. **1881** *Nature* XXIV. 373/2 Prof. Klebs . . declared the infective quality to be due to the presence of a microphyte. **1883** *St. James's Gaz.* 29 Nov., The infective matter shown to exist in the blood serum. **1895** PARKES *Health* 30 The prevention of infective diseases.

b. ***infective hepatitis*** = *infectious hepatitis.*

1939 G. M. FINDLAY et al. in *Trans. R. Soc. Trop. Med. & Hygiene* XXXII. 578 To those cases where the jaundice is associated with sensitivity phenomena the term 'allergic jaundice' might be applied, while for those in which hepatitis is the primary lesion 'epidemic' or possibly 'infective hepatitis' is probably preferable to the name 'common infective hepatic jaundice' used by Rolleston and McNee (1929). **1959** [see HEPATITIS]. **1971** *New Scientist* 25 Mar. 676/1 Infective hepatitis . . results from liver cell damage caused by a virus (or viruses) usually taken in with food or drink, and picked up from the faeces of an already infected person.

3. Producing or spreading moral infection.

1576 FLEMING *Panopl. Epist.* 269 The desire of vertue . . though it be excessive, yet is it not noisome, yet is it not hurtful, yet is it not infective. **1602** W. BURTON *Anat. Belial* 161 Some in their wanton and light behaviour are . . infective to the weaker Christians. **1627–77** FELTHAM *Resolves* II. lxx. 309. **1899** *Expositor* Mar. 182 Sin is not only cumulative but infective.

†**4.** Producing an emotion, feeling, etc. by infection. *Obs.*

a **1586** SIDNEY (J.), True love, well considered, hath an infective power. **1626** BACON *Sylva* §945 Feare and Shame are likewise Infectiue; for wee see that the Starting of one will make another ready to Start: And when one Man is out of Countenance in a Company, others doe likewise Blush in his behalfe. **1703** FARQUHAR *Inconstant* IV. iv, There, there, behold an object that's infective; I cannot view her, but I am as mad as she.

Hence **in'fectiveness, infec'tivity,** the quality of being infectious.

1871 *Daily News* 16 Aug., Cholera has a certain peculiar infectiveness of its own. **1881** *Nature* XXIV. 373/2 The fatal infectiveness of crude tubercular matter. **1882** G. F. DOWDESWELL in *Jrnl. Microsc. Sc.* Jan. 67 There is . . considerable uncertainty in the infectivity of such blood. **1897** *Allbutt's Syst. Med.* II. 186 The virus may be carried from a small-pox hospital by the air a considerable distance without losing its infectivity.

infector (ɪn'fɛktə(r)). [a. L. *infector*, agent-n. f. *inficĕre* to INFECT.] One who infects; one who causes or spreads infection.

1580 *Godly Admonition* in *Liturg. Serv. Q. Eliz.* (Parker Soc.) 574 Infectors to others by their evil example. **1768** STERNE *Sent. Journ.* (1775) I. 63 (*Gloves*) They are communicated and caught so instantaneously, that you can scarce say which party is the infector. **1868** W. HOWITT in *Pall Mall G.* 12 Dec. 5 How is it possible to avoid a general infection with . . infectors riding and running all over the land?

†**in'fectory,** *a. Obs.* [ad. L. *infectōri-us*: see prec. and -ORY.] Having the property of dyeing.

1657 TOMLINSON *Renou's Disp.* 283 Grain, which is vulgarly called Scarlet dye, or infectory grain.

in'fectress. *rare.* [f. INFECTOR: see -ESS.] A female infector.

1860 PUSEY *Min. Proph.* 301 How Lachish came first to apostatise and to be the infectress of Judah, Scripture does not tell.

‖**infectum** (ɪn'fɛktəm). [L. (Varro *De Lingua Latina* IX. xcvii).] (See quot. 1954².)

1954 L. R. PALMER *Latin Lang.* II. ix. 266 In Latin the three aspects of the IE. verb were reduced to two, for the verbal system shows a contrast only between the *infectum* and the *perfectum*. **1954** PEI & GAYNOR *Dict. Ling.* 100 *Infectum*, the aspectual category introduced by the Roman grammarian Varro (1st century B.C.), including the present, preterit and simple future tenses. **1965** *Amer. Speech* XL. 113 The infectum verbal form.

†**in'fectuous,** *a. Obs.* [f. L. (post-class.) *infectu-s* (*u*-stem) dyeing + -OUS; cf. OF. *infectueux* (1381 in Godef.). Cf. AFFECTUOUS, DEFECTUOUS.]

= INFECTIOUS.

1495 *Trevisa's Barth. De P.R.* XVIII. lxvi. (W. de W.), The brethe of a lyon stynketh and is ryght infectuous [*MSS.* infectiue] and contagyous. **1530** RASTELL *Bk. Purgat.* III. vii. 3 Nature shall expulse those infectuos humours. **1567** MAPLET *Gr. Forest* 52 Venemous and infectuous Plants. *a* **1626** BACON *New Alt.* Sylva, etc. (1676) 243 The nature of the sickness of our men was not infectuous. **1747** *Col. Rec. Pennsylv.* V. 106 There was a very infectuous Distemper.

†**in'fecture.** *Obs. rare*$^{-1}$. [f. INFECT *v.* + -URE.] The action of infecting; infection.

1580 H. GIFFORD *Gilloflowers* (1875) 142 The cause of my sadnes at length I coniecture, Is loue with his madnes, that breedes this infecture.

infecund (ɪn'fɛkʌnd), *a.* [ad. L. *infēcund-us* f. *in-* (IN-³) + *fēcundus* FECUND; cf. F. *infécond* (15th c.). Formerly *infe'cund* (so in J.).] Not fecund, prolific, or fruitful; barren, unproductive.

c **1420** *Pallad. on Husb.* I. 667 Tak noon [pheasants] but of oon yeer; for, infecounde Are old. **1664** EVELYN *Sylva* 51 That little infecund part of the seed. *a* **1770** SMART *Hop Gard.* I. Poems (1810) 37/1 The next Is arid, fetid, infecund, and gross. **1885** E. F. BYRRNE *Entangled* II. II. viii. 255 How cold, infecund, and unpromising.

in'fecundated, *a.* [IN-³.] Unfertilized; not impregnated.

1864 *Intell. Observ.* No. 32. 138 The infecundated ovum.

infecundity (ɪnfɪ'kʌndɪtɪ). [ad. L. *infēcunditās*: see INFECUND and -ITY. Cf. F. *infécondité* (14th c.).] Unfruitfulness; barrenness. *lit.* and *fig.*

1605 WILLET *Hexapla Gen.* 313 Shee grieued rather at her owne infecunditie or barrennesse. **1774** GOLDSM. *Nat. Hist.* II. 308 Diminish the number of the other by infecundity. **1818** SOUTHEY in *Q. Rev.* XVIII. 30 What he calls the invincible infecundity of the Spaniards in epic poetry. **1823** LINGARD *Hist. Eng.* VI. 250 The infecundity of Anne . . had hitherto disappointed the king's most anxious wish to provide for the succession to the throne.

†**infe'cundous**, *a.* *Obs. rare*$^{-1}$. [f. L. *infēcund-us* INFECUND + -OUS.] = INFECUND.

1661 GLANVILL *Van. Dogm.* xix. 179 That the Aristotelian Physiology cannot boast itself the proper Author of any one Invention is prægnant evidence of its infecundous deficiency.

infeeble, obs. form of ENFEEBLE *v.*

in-feed ('ɪnfi:d). Also **infeed**. [IN *adv.* 11 d.] **a.** The action or process of supplying a machine; *spec.* in centreless grinding, movement of the work-piece part-way into the space between the two wheels followed by its withdrawal, in contrast to its passage right through. **b.** A mechanism that carries out this process. Freq. *attrib.*

1901 *Manning, Maxwell & Moore Catal.* 636 The upper in-feed tool is fluted. **1926** *Automotive Industries* 2 Sept. 385 The back carriage has only a straight in-feed and no longitudinal motion except for setting tools. **1937** COLVIN & STANLEY *Grinding Pract.* v. 80 Work having shoulders or heads..is ground by the infeed method. **1960** *Times Rev. Industry* Sept. 39/3 Two independently variable rates of in-feed are provided. **1964** S. CRAWFORD *Basic Engin. Processes* vii. 190 At the end of each traverse the wheel is fed in towards the work..; this movement is referred to as in-feed, and it controls reduction of work diameter. **1968** *Gloss. Terms Offset Lithogr. Printing (B.S.I.)* 35 *In-feed roller*, a roller aiding or controlling the forward movement of a sheet to the printing or other processing units. **1971** *Timber Trades Jrnl.* 14 Aug. 57/2 On model KDK 36, with an electric infeed, the speeds are 36 and 72 ft/min.

infeft (ɪn'fɛft), *v.* *Sc. Law.* Pa. t. and pa. pple. **infeft**, rarely **infefted**. [Sc. form of ENFEOFF; the final *t* appears to be the suffix of the pa. pple., taken as belonging to the stem.] *trans.* To invest with heritable property; to ENFEOFF.

1462 in Sir W. Fraser *Douglas Bk.* (1885) III. 91, I am infeft heretabli be the saide erle in the laundis of Corsrig [etc.]. **1498** —— *Melvilles of Melville* (1890) III. 52 The said John Gowrlay, elder, sal infeft with chartyr and possessioune al and haill his landis of Cargowre to the said Johne Gowrlay, younger. **1520** *Charters, &c., Peebles* (1872) 50 The said Schir Patrik sall indot gyf and infeft certane landis..in honor of God. **1609** SKENE *Reg. Maj.*, *Act Alex. II*, 19 And gif the lands are halden of the king: the Schiref sall infeft the buyer be ane precept, quha buyes them. *a* **1700** *Burd Isbel & Sir Patrick* xliv. in Child *Ballads* VIII. cclvii. B. (1892) 422/1, I would infeft your son this day In third part o your land. **1862** J. R. MACDUFF *Sunsets Hebr. Mount.* 186. **1893** *Dict. Nat. Biog.* XXXIII. 76 On his infefting his brother William in the lands of Cairnie.

Hence **in'feft** *sb. rare.* = next.

1893 *Dict. Nat. Biog.* XXXIII. 76 On 3 June 1566 Andrew received a new infeft of the earldom.

in'feftment. *Sc. Law.* [f. prec. + -MENT.] The action or fact of infefting; 'the act of giving symbolical possession of heritable property, the legal evidence of which is an instrument of sasine' (Bell *Dict. Law Scot.*); ENFEOFFMENT.

infeftment in security, temporary infeftment of a creditor, to secure payment of a debt. ***infeftment of relief***, a similar security to relieve a cautioner from his engagement. (Bell.)

1456 in Sir W. Fraser *Wemyss of Wemyss* (1888) II. 74 Twychyng the infeftments of the said landis. **1489** *Sc. Acts Jas. IV*, c. 12 And to eschew all circumvencionns & dissatis That has bene done to the Kingis hienes be bringing of diuerse Signaturis Infeftmentis donacions giftis. **1535** STEWART *Cron. Scot.* II. 358 Fyftene abbais..He foundit hes with riche infeftment ilkane. *a* **1572** KNOX *Hist. Ref.* Wks. 1846 I. 356 That the same [town] may be guyded and reulled frelie, as it was befoir, be the Baillies and Counsale, conforme to thair infeftmentis gevin to thame be the ancient and maist excellent Kingis of this realme. **1617** in W. McIlwraith *Guide Wigtownsh.* (1875) 90 The said burgh is now erect, made, and constitute and creat in ane free burgh of barony by us and our infeftment. **1832** AUSTIN *Jurispr.* (1873) I. xiv. 392 The word *infeftment*, or *investiture*, properly applies to the personal title completed by the sasine: but is sometimes applied to the sasine as distinct from the personal title, where, as it sometimes happens, they conflict. **1861** BELL *Dict. Law Scot.* 444 By the Infeftment Act, 8 and 9 Vict. c. 35, 1845, infeftment may be effectually obtained by producing to the notary-public the warrants of sasine and relative writs..and by expeding and recording in the appropriate register an instrument of sasine [etc.]. **1884** *Law Rep.* 9 App. Cases 305 The trustee's infeftment in the heritable estate was recorded in the register of sasines at Glasgow.

infelicific (ɪnfi:lɪ'sɪfɪk), *a.* *Ethics.* [f. L. *infēlīx*, *infēlīci-* unhappy, after FELICIFIC.] Productive of unhappiness.

1874 SIDGWICK *Meth. Ethics* (1877) 371 *note*, It will be convenient to use the terms 'felicific' and 'infelicific' for 'productive of happiness' and the reverse. *Ibid.* 423 The breach of any moral rule is *pro tanto* infelicific from its injurious effects on moral habits generally. **1890** M. MACMILLAN *Promotion Happiness* i. 3 The infelicific consequences which would result to them from the knowledge of our better fortunes.

†**infe'licious**, *a.* *Obs.* [f. as prec. + -OUS: cf. FELICIOUS.] Unhappy, unfortunate, unlucky.

1597 A. M. tr. *Guillemeau's Fr. Chirurg.* *iv, Those are esteemed infelicioufe and vnfortunate. **1669** COKAINE *Ovid* 136 Paid we not that duty To excellent Ovid's infelicious end.

infelicitate (ɪnfɪ'lɪsɪteɪt), *v. rare.* [f. ppl. stem of L. *infēlīcitāre*, f. *infēlīcitās* INFELICITY: cf. *felicitate.*] *trans.* To make unhappy.

1654 COKAINE *Dianea* II. 161 The Gods be praised, that hereafter my life cannot infelicitate any.

infelicitous (ɪnfɪ'lɪsɪtəs), *a.* [f. IN-^{3} + FELICITOUS: cf. next.] Unhappy, unfortunate; *esp.* not happily suited to the occasion or circumstances; not apt or appropriate: the opposite of FELICITOUS.

1835 I. TAYLOR *Spir. Despot.* ix. 386 Prompted to deny with indignation the allegation of their infelicitous position. **1857** *Fraser's Mag.* LVI. 600 He..conceived the infelicitous idea of making an abridged translation. **1876** GEO. ELIOT *Dan. Der.* xxxvi. 79 The infelicitous wife who had produced nothing but daughters. **1884** *Spectator* 4 Oct. 1290/1 His illustration..is singularly infelicitous.

Hence **infe'licitously** *adv.*, unhappily, inaptly.

a **1834** COLERIDGE *Church & State* (1839) 192 The second power..commonly but most infelicitously called irritability. **1841** H. F. CHORLEY *Music & Manners* (1844) III. 251 [It] dramatised the solemn text not infelicitously.

infelicity (ɪnfɪ'lɪsɪtɪ). [ad. L. *infēlīcitās*, f. *infēlīx* unhappy: cf. obs. F. *infélicité* (15th c.).]

1. The state of being unhappy or unfortunate; an unhappy condition or state of affairs; unhappiness, misery; bad fortune, ill luck, misfortune.

1382 WYCLIF *2 Macc.* viii. 35 Nychanore..cam to Antioche, hauynge heiȝist infelicitee [*gloss* or most wretchidnesse], of the deeth of his oost. *c* **1450** tr. *De Imitatione* III. xxiii. 92, I morne and bere myn infelicite wiþ sorowe. **1568** GRAFTON *Chron.* II. 350 For so is your power depoverished, and Lordes and great men brought to infelicitee. **1652–62** HEYLIN *Cosmogr.* To Rdr. 1 Being, by the unhappiness of my Destiny, or the infelicity of the Times, deprived of my Preferments. **1759** JOHNSON *Rasselas* xxviii, You surely conclude too hastily from the infelicity of marriage against its institution. **1825** LAMB *Elia* Ser. II. *Barbara S——*, That pure infelicity which accompanies some people in their walk through life.

b. A particular case or instance of bad fortune; an unfortunate circumstance or event; a misfortune; a cause or source of unhappiness.

1577 FENTON *Gold. Epist.* 2 When God administereth to vs diseases, sorowes, deaths, and infelicities. **1651** HOBBES *Govt. & Soc.* x. §16. 163 The government comes to be administred in a Democraticall manner, and..thence arise those infelicities which for the most part accompany the Dominion of the People. **1682** H. MORE *Annot. Glanvill's Lux O.* 189 It is the infelicity of too many, that they are ignorant. **1732** NEAL *Hist. Purit.* I. 81 So that his death was not an Infelicity to the Church. **1891** *Spectator* 7 Mar., These infelicities of travel were of frequent occurrence, and endured with cheerfulness.

2. The quality of not being happily suited to the occasion or circumstances; unlucky inaptness or inappropriateness; with *pl.* an unhappily inappropriate expression or detail of style.

1617 HALES *Gold. Rem.* (1673) 10 With how great infelicity or incongruity soever it be. **1659** HAMMOND *On Ps.* cxx. *heading paraphr.*, A complaint of the infelicity of such companions. **1823** LAMB *Elia* Ser. I. *Oxf. in Vac.*, Peradventure the Epiphany, by some periodical infelicity, would, once in six years, merge in a Sabbath. **1879** CHURCH *Spenser* 33 The beginnings of that great critical literature, which in England, in spite of much infelicity, has only been second to the poetry which it judged. *Mod.* A work marred by its infelicities of style.

infelonious (ɪnfɪ'ləʊnɪəs), *a.* *nonce-wd.* [IN-^{3}.] Not felonious; not of the nature of felony.

1876 GEO. ELIOT *Dan. Der.* I. iii, The thought of that infelonious murder [of a canary] had always made her wince.

infelt, *ppl. a.* [f. IN *adv.* 11 b + FELT *ppl. a.*] Felt within; inwardly felt or experienced.

a **1586** SIDNEY *Astr. & Stella* lxi, Who indeed infelt affection beares. **1774** *Westm. Mag.* II. 93 Dice can no infelt bliss impart. **1894** J. R. ILLINGWORTH *Personality* viii. (1895) 194 Its infelt capacity for intercourse with God.

infeminine (ɪn'fɛmɪnɪn), *a.* *rare.* [IN-^{3}.] Not feminine; unwomanly.

1879 G. MEREDITH *Egoist* III. 30 There's my flat confession, and highly infeminine it is.

†**in'fence**, *v.* *Obs.* Also 7 **en-**. [f. IN-^{1} or ^{2} + FENCE *v.*] *trans.* To inclose in, or as in, a fence; to fence in. Hence †**in'fenced** *ppl. a.*

1613–18 DANIEL *Coll. Hist. Eng.* (1626) 158 The ill administration of Iustice..threw open agayne..this ill infensed closure. **1652** BENLOWES *Theoph.* V. xi, Tomes full of mystick characters enfense Those seas of blisse!

†**infenci'bility**. *Obs. rare.* [f. IN-^{3} + FENCIBLE + -ITY.] The condition of not being 'fencible'; unfitness for defensive military service.

1652 URQUHART *Jewel* Wks. (1834) 252 Then were these very same men whom they had formerly cast, either for malignancy or infencibility, inrolled in their troups.

†**in'fense**, *a.* *Obs. rare.* [ad. L. *infensus* hostile, inimical.] Hostile, inimical.

a **1641** BP. MOUNTAGU *Acts & Mon.* (1642) 470 The Iewes as infense to the Samaritans as they to them. **1680** CALDERWOOD in Hickes *Spir. Popery* 30 A most infense Enemy to the Purity of Religion.

†**in'fensive**, *a.* *Obs. rare.* [f. L. *infens-us* (see prec.) + -IVE; cf. *defensive*, *offensive*.] = prec.

1596 DALRYMPLE tr. *Leslie's Hist. Scot.* IV. 256 This King was verie infensiue to the Regentis and Gouernouris.

infeodate, -ation: see INFEUDATE, -ATION.

infeof(f, -ment, obs. ff. ENFEOFF, -MENT.

infer (ɪn'fɜ:(r)), *v.* Also (6 infarre, enferre), 6–7 inferre, 7–8 inferr. Inflected **inferred**, etc. [ad. L. *inferre* to bear, bring, or carry in, to inflict, make (war), to cause, occasion, to introduce; in med.L., to infer; f. *in-* (IN-^{2}) + *ferre* to bear. Cf. F. *inférer* to allege, show, infer (16th c.).]

†**1. a.** *trans.* To bring on, bring about, induce, occasion, cause, procure; to bring *upon* (a person, etc.), to inflict; to wage (war) *upon*. *Obs.*

c **1540** BOORDE *The boke for to Lerne* C iv a, Immoderat slepe..doth induce and infarre [**1542** —— *Dyetary* viii. (1870) 245 infer] breuyte of lyfe. **1543–4** *Act 35 Hen. VIII*, c. 12 The same frenche kyng..hathe inferred and done vnto his maiestie..intollerable displeasures. **1566** PAINTER *Pal. Pleas.* I. B ij b, Determined by common accorde, to inferre warres vppon the Romaines. **1576** FLEMING *Panopl. Epist.* 160 If any wound be inferred with force of forreigne weapon. **1589** NASHE *Almond for Parrat* 11 b, A wicked mind..eyther meditates the iniuries which he is about to inferre, or feares some reproch to be inferred by others. **1594** SHAKS. *Rich. III*, IV. iv. 343 Inferre faire Englands peace by this Alliance. **1596** SPENSER *F.Q.* VI. viii. 31 Faire Serena; who..fled fast away, afeard Of villany to be to her inferd. **1640** BP. REYNOLDS *Passions* iii. 16. **1697** POTTER *Antiq. Greece* I. xxvi. (1715) 178 He who wilfully infers Damage, shall refund twice as much. **1754** EDWARDS *Freed. Will* II. xii. 123 If absolute Decrees are inconsistent with Man's Liberty as a moral Agent..it is not on account of any Necessity which absolute Decrees infer.

†**b.** To confer, bestow. *Obs.*

1571 CAMPION *Hist. Irel.* (1633) 45 That the Metropolitanes See was inferred upon meere lay persons of the blood royall. **1589** NASHE *Anat. Absurd.* Epist. ¶ iij, What ever content felicitie or Fortune may enferre. **1614** RALEIGH *Hist. World* I. II. 363 That this honour might bee inferred on some one of the bloud and race of their ancient King.

†**c.** with *compl.* To cause to be; to make, render. *Obs. rare.*

1667 MILTON *P.L.* VII. 116 To glorifie the Maker, and inferr Thee also happier.

†**2.** To bring in, introduce (in discourse or writing); to mention, report, relate, tell; to bring forward (as an argument, etc.), adduce, allege. (With *simple obj.*, or more rarely *obj. cl.*) *Obs.*

1526 SKELTON *Magnyf.* 61 Somewhat I could enferre Your consayte to debarre. **1584** R. SCOT *Discov. Witchcr.* XIII. vii. (1886) 245 The Jasper stone, touching which..I have inferred Marbodeus his verses. **1593** SHAKS. *3 Hen. VI*, II. ii. 44 Full well hath Clifford plaid the Orator, Inferring arguments of mighty force. **1607** *Drewill's Arraignm.* in *Harl. Misc.* (Malh.) III. 60 This oath..hauing beene..read ..he was required to alleadge or inferre against any part thereof what he colde. *a* **1668** DAVENANT *Play House* Wks. (1673) 103 Towards the conclusion, it infers the Voyages of the English thither, and the amity of the Nations towards them. **1710** PRIDEAUX *Orig. Tithes* iii. 152 *note*, The Canon of the Council of Friuli..is too long to be here at full inferred.

3. a. To bring in or 'draw' as a conclusion; *spec.* in *Logic*, To derive by a process of reasoning, whether inductive or deductive, from something known or assumed; to accept from evidence or premisses; to deduce, conclude. (With *simple obj.* or *obj. cl.*)

1529 MORE *Dyaloge* I. Wks. 147/1 Wherupon is inferred eftsone al that the messenger wold haue fled fro by force. **1568** in H. Campbell *Love Lett. Mary Q. Scots* (1824) 18 They inferred upon a letter of her own hand that there was another meane..devised to kill the king. **1584** FENNER *Def. Ministers* (1587) 3 Because the strength of a consequence doeth hange..vppon..the necessitie of the illation, let vs marke what hee inferreth. **1624** SANDERSON *Twelve Serm.* (1632) 468 We should from the premisses inferre something for our farther use. **1717** PRIOR *Alma* III. 312 What I never meant Don't you infer. **1738** WARBURTON *Div. Legat.* II. 225 From this State of Antiquity I would inferr these two Things. **1843** MILL *Logic* (1856) Introd. §4 The truths known by intuition are the original premises from which all others are inferred. **1867** FREEMAN *Norm. Conq.* (1876) I. vi. 423 Cnut hastily inferred that they had deserted. **1871** B. STEWART *Heat* §13 It will be inferred from what we have said that [etc.].

b. *absol.* To draw a conclusion or inference; to reason from one thing to another.

1577 VAUTROUILLIER *Luther on Ep. Gal.* 155 Reason hearing this, by and by doth thus inferre: Then God gaue the lawe in vaine. **1634** MILTON *Comus* 408 I do not, Brother, Infer, as if I thought my Sister's state Secure. **1769** BURKE *Late St. Nation* 76 These reasonings, which infer from the many restraints under which we have already laid America, to our right to lay it under still more..are conclusive..as to right; but the very reverse as to policy and practice. **1828** WHATELY *Rhet.* in *Encycl. Metrop.* 242/1 To *infer* is to be regarded as the proper office of the Philosopher; —to *prove*, of the Advocate. **1876** JEVONS *Logic Prim.* 12 When we thus learn one fact from other facts, we infer or reason, and we do this in the mind.

4. To lead to (something) as a conclusion; to involve as a consequence; to imply. (Said of a fact or statement; sometimes, of the person who makes the statement.)

This use is widely considered to be incorrect, esp. with a person as the subject.

c **1530** MORE *Answ. Frith* Wks. 840/2 The fyrste parte is not the proofe of the second, but rather contrary wyse, the seconde inferreth well yᵉ fyrst. **1581** MULCASTER *Positions* xliii. (1887) 277 Socrates findes a good scholer which in naturall relation inferreth a good maister. **1633** EARL MANCH. *Al Mondo* (1636) 110 Solomon saying that the day of death was better than the day of birth, inferred that there was a faire way of doing well. **1667** MILTON *P.L.* VIII. 91 Consider first, that Great or Bright inferrs not Excellence. **1736** BUTLER *Anal.* I. vii. Wks. 1874 I. 134 These assertions..would infer nothing more than that it might have been better. **1813** J. S. STANHOPE in A. M. W. Pickering *Mem.* (1902) II. 377 He said nothing that could in any way infer the necessity of a retreat of the allies. **1814** SCOTT *Waverley* II. xviii. 284 They are..more benign in demeanour than their physiognomy or aspect might infer. **1818** JAS. MILL *Brit. India* II. v. vi. 583 Yet, what did the proposition of the Governor-General to the Council infer? **1884** *Academy* 10 May 327 Socrates argued that a statue inferred the existence of a sculptor. **1946** M. PEAKE *Titus Groan* 373 That he had fulfilled his intention of inveigling his enemy to the place of his own choosing must surely infer that the initiative once again lay with him. **1969** BENNISON & WRIGHT *Geol. Hist. Brit. Isles* i. 5 A. Holmes deprecated the use of the term 'Absolute' age as inferring an accuracy which is unwarranted. **1970** *Private Eye* 2 Jan. 12, I can't stand fellers who infer things about good clean-living Australian sheilahs. **1973** *Daily Tel.* 30 June 14, I have seen references..to the watering of Ascot racecourse, inferring that the water has been taken from public mains at a time when economy is being urged on all consumers.

†**5.** To carry to the grave, to bury (= L. *inferre*). *Obs. rare.* (But perh. the word is *interred.*)

c **1555** HARPSFIELD *Divorce Hen. VIII* (Camden) 200 Her dead corpse was carried to Peterborough and there inferred.

†**6.** To carry in, insert; to figure as inserted or projecting *into*. *Obs. rare.*

1572 BOSSEWELL *Armorie* II. 27 Engrayled..because two colors, or any mettal or colour, be gradately inferred one into the other, that no partition, but onely the Purflue, maie be seene betwene them.

infer: see INFARE *sb.*

inferable, -ible (ɪnˈfɜːrəb(ə)l, ˈɪnfərɪb(ə)l), *a.* See also INFERRIBLE. [f. INFER *v.*, on the pattern of *preferable*, *referable*, from the corresp. Fr. words; but there is no F. *inférable*; L. analogy would require *inferible*; both L. and Fr. analogy, with the example of *preferable*, *referable*, *transferable*, require the stress to be on the first syllable; the pronunciation (ɪnˈfɜːrəb(ə)l), which is that of most dictionaries, would require the spelling *inferrable*: see INFERRIBLE.] That may be inferred or drawn as a conclusion; deducible.

1755 JOHNSON, *Inferible* [citing SIR T. BROWNE who has INFERRIBLE]. **1791** BURKE *App. Whigs* Wks. VI. 129 That an Argument is inferable from these premisses. **1807** G. CHALMERS *Caledonia* I. II. ii. 251 The fact is inferible, from..the informations of Ptolemy. **1811** SHELLEY *Let. to Godwin* in Dowden *Shelley* (1886) I. v. 218, I see no reason hence inferable which should alter my wishes. **1860** H. SPENCER *Phys. Laughter* Ess. 1891 II. 463 The fact, alike inferable *a priori* and illustrated in experience. **1875** WHITNEY *Life Lang.* xiv. 290 The inferable beginnings of human language-making.

inferably (ˈɪnfərəblɪ), *adv.* [f. INFERABLE *a.* + -LY².] By inference; = INFERRIBLY *adv.*

1903 *Harvard Psychol. Stud.* I. 340 The extent of this differentiation—and inferably the definition of rhythmical synthesis—corresponds to the reported musical aptitudes of the subjects.

inferd, obs.: see FERD *sb.*¹

†**in fere, in fer**, *adv. phr.*, in company: see FERE *sb.*² 2.

inference (ˈɪnfərəns). [ad. med.L. *inferentia* (Abelard *Œuvr. inéd.* ed. Cousin, 325, 328) (cf. It. *inferenza* 'an inference, an implying', Florio 1611), f. *inferent-em*, pr. pple. of *inferre* to INFER: used instead of cl. L. *illātio*.]

1. a. The action or process of inferring; the drawing of a conclusion from known or assumed facts or statements; *esp.* in *Logic*, the forming of a conclusion from data or premisses, either by inductive or deductive methods; reasoning from something known or assumed to something else which follows from it; = ILLATION. Also (with *pl.*), a particular act of inferring; the logical form in which this is expressed.

In English, the word appears first in the general sense, not as a term of formal Logic. In Logical treatises, it is found first applied to the deductive process of the syllogism, and its conclusion (*mediate inference*); its application to the inferring of a conclusion from a single proposition by conversion, opposition, permutation, or the like (*immediate inference*), and its use in the logic of induction (*inductive inference*) appear later, and are not accepted by all logicians. On the other hand, some restrict the term to induction, and deny that either a syllogism or an immediate inference can properly be called an inference.

1594 HOOKER *Eccl. Pol.* III. xi. §10 These are but weake and feeble disputes for the inference of that Conclusion which is intended. **1605** *Lond. Prodigal* III. ii, 'Tis merely unsound unprofitable idle inference. **1643** MILTON *Divorce* II. ix, 'Therefore shall a man cleave to his wife'..which we see is no absolute command, but with an inference, *Therefore.* **1736** BUTLER *Analogy* II. vi. 308 Religion is..a matter of deduction and inference. **1803** LD. ELDON in *Vesey's Rep.* VIII. 436 That is too thin an evidence of intention to afford much inference. **1827** WHATELY *Logic* IV, The Province of Reasoning. iii. (*heading*), Of Inference and Proof. **1837–8** SIR W. HAMILTON *Logic* xv. (1860) I. 279 Inference or illation, indicates the carrying out into the last proposition what was virtually contained in the antecedent judgements. *Ibid.* II. App. 255 There are various Immediate Inferences of one proposition from another..The first of these is *Conversion.* **1843** MILL *Logic* II. i. §3 Cases of inference in the proper acceptation of the term, those in which we set out from known truths, to arrive at others really distinct from them. *Ibid.* IV. i. §2 In almost every act of our perceiving faculties, observation and inference are intimately blended. **1864** BOWEN *Logic* vi. 148 Inference or Reasoning is that act of Pure Thought whereby one Judgment is derived from another, or from two others. **1866** FOWLER *Deduct. Logic* III. i. (1869) 70 In any inference, we argue either to something already implied in the premisses or not: if the latter, the inference is inductive, if the former deductive. If the deductive inference contain only a single premiss, it is immediate; if it contain two premisses, and the conclusion be drawn from these jointly, it is mediate, and is called a syllogism. **1874** STUBBS *Const. Hist.* I. i. 2 This..is not a matter of inference. It is a recorded fact of history.

b. *inference rule*, in a system of logic: any rule permitting inferences of a specified form.

1962 CLARK & WELSH *Introd. Logic* ii. 93 We lay down the following cluster of inference rules. **1964** KALISH & MONTAGUE *Logic* 14 From the second and third lines of the derivation we may infer 'Q' by means of an inference rule. **1965** B. MATES *Elem. Logic* vi. 93 We need a reasonably small group of simple inference-rules.

2. That which is inferred, a conclusion drawn from data or premisses. Also, an implication; the conclusion that one is intended to draw. Cf. INFER *v.* 4.

1612 BACON *Ess., Judicature* (Arb.) 452 Iudges must beware of hard constructions and strained inferences. **1692** SOUTH *12 Serm.* (1697) I. 479, I shall draw some usefull Inferences, by way of Application, from the Premises. **1724** WATTS *Logic* Introd. Wks. 1813 VII. 315 These inferences, or conclusions, are the effects of reasoning, and the three propositions, taken all altogether, are called syllogism or argument. **1788** REID *Aristotle's Log.* vi. §1. 128 When a child first draws an inference, or perceives the force of an inference drawn by another, we may call this the birth of reason. **1828** MACAULAY *Ess., Hallam* (1851) I. 55 When it wishes to avoid a disagreeable inference from an admitted proposition. **1843** MILL *Logic* Introd. §5 To draw inferences has been said to be the great business of life. **1876** GLADSTONE *Homeric Synchr.* 69 The natural inference is that the wheel was just beginning to be known. **1933** D. L. SAYERS *Hangman's Holiday* 147 'I don't know if you realise, Mr. Egg,' observed the inspector, 'the bearing, or, as I might say, the inference of what you said just now.' **1972** P. H. KOCHER *Master of Middle-Earth* (1973) v. 82 These four are named 'first', with the inference that they deserve priority. **1973** *Daily Tel.* (Colour Suppl.) 5 Oct. 7/2 The main inference of the propaganda is that unless we adopt the metric system Britain will lose export orders.

†**3.** That which a thing leads to or brings in its train. *Obs. rare.*

1673 *Lady's Calling* I. i. §16 This is evident enough if we look only on the meer surface of the crime [Drunkenness]; but if we dive farther into its inferences and adherencies, the affirmation is yet more irrefragable.

ˈ**inferencer.** *nonce-wd.* [f. prec. + -ER¹.] One who draws an inference.

1738 MRS. DELANY *Life & Corr.* (1861) II. 13 The character you give me of the Inferencer has raised my esteem of him.

inferential (ɪnfəˈrɛnʃəl), *a.* [f. med.L. *inferentia* + -AL¹.] Of or pertaining to inference; involving or depending on inference; of the nature of inference.

1657 GAULE *Sapient. Justif.* 16 But was this inferential motive heedlesly escaped? **1804** W. TAYLOR in *Ann. Rev.* II. 323 The speculations of hypothetical and inferential reasoning. **1813–21** BENTHAM *Ontol.* Wks. 1843 VIII. 195 An inferential entity, is an entity which, in these times at least, is not made known to human beings in general, by the testimony of sense, but of the existence of which the persuasion is produced by reflection. **1854** R. G. LATHAM *Native Races Russian Emp.* 109 The belief was, probably, inferential. **1885** G. ALLEN *Darwin* viii. 137 Minute inferential proofs which hardly admit of deliberate condensation.

Hence (*nonce-wds.*) **infeˈrentialism**, a theory involving or depending on (mere) inference (as distinguished from direct observation or conclusive demonstration); **infeˈrentialist**, an advocate of such a theory.

1874 MᶜCOSH *Scot. Philos.* xliv. (1875) 334 Brown's doctrine can scarcely be called idealism. It might more appropriately be called inferentialism. **1891** *Athenæum* 8 Aug. 196/3 That the inferentialists will give up the contest, is not to be expected.

inferentially (ɪnfəˈrɛnʃəlɪ), *adv.* [f. prec. + -LY².] In an inferential manner; in the way of, or by means of, inference. Sometimes qualifying the whole clause or statement: = as an inference, as may be inferred.

1691 BEVERLEY *Thousand Yrs. Kingd.* 23 From whence He Inferentially Goes on upon the Supposition [etc.]. **1852** WASHN. WILKS *Hist. Half Cent.* 337 Inferentially, had the natural rate of increase been followed, the population would have been two millions more than at present. **1884** *Manch. Exam.* 2 Dec. 5/2 That women had no souls, and inferentially no brains. **1895** F. HALL *Two Trifles* 9, I am inferentially assigned an equality with the poor creature.

†**inˈferial**, *a. Obs.* [cf. OF. *inferial* low-lying, in low position (applied to hell), prob. repr. a med.L. **inferiālis*, f. L. *inferus* low, or *inferius* adv. lower. (L. had *inferiālis* funeral, f. *inferiæ* sacrifices in honour of the dead, f. *inferī* those of the infernal regions, the dead; whence sense 2.)]

1. Low in position, low-lying; situated below, lower, nether; = INFERIOR A. 1; *spec.* belonging to this lower world, mundane, sublunary.

1432–50 tr. *Higden* (Rolls) I. 151 After that is Cilicia..The nowbleste cite off theyme alle was Tharsis, more inferialle towarde the see. **1509** HAWES *Past. Pleas.* XXII. (1845) 104 And the second day..The waters above he did devide aryght, From the erthely waters which are inferiall. **1519** *Four Elements* in Hazl. *Dodsley* I. 9 Men..Disputing of high creatures celestial..And know not these visible things inferial. **1542** BOORDE *Dyetary* x. (1870) 253 Strayne the vpper parte..and cast the inferyall parte awaye.

b. Of planets: = INFERIOR A. 5 a.

a **1545** BOORDE *Pronost.* Prol. in *Introd. Knowl.* (1870) Forewords 25 The son..illumynatynge as wel the inferyal planetes as yᵉ superyal planetes.

2. (See quot.) *rare*⁻⁰.

1656 BLOUNT *Glossogr.*, *Inferial*, belonging to Funeral Obsequies. **1658** in PHILLIPS.

inferior (ɪnˈfɪərɪə(r)), *a.* and *sb.* Also 6 **-oure**, 6–8 **-our**. [a. L. *inferĭor* lower, comp. of *inferus* low. Cf. F. *inférieur*, 16th c. in Littré (also rare *inferiore*, 15th c.). (The 16–17th c. spelling *inferiour* followed words from AF. *-our*, F. *-eur*.)] Lower: opposed in all senses to *superior*, and often antithetical to it in designating pairs of things, as 'superior and inferior courts of law'.

A. *adj.*

1. Lower in position; situated below, or farther down than, something else; nether; subjacent. (Now chiefly in technical use; see also senses 3–8.)

1432–50 tr. *Higden* (Rolls) I. 255 The inferior Germany, towarde the weste, is abowte the floode callede Renus. **1517** *Domesday Inclos.* I. 257 A messuage in Tynton inferior belongyng to John Richerdson. **1563** T. GALE *Enchirid.* 13 a (Stanf.), The inferior ventricle receyuing the liuer, stomacke, splene, kidneyes. *a* **1631** DONNE *Epigr.* (1652) 98 Here the swoln sea views the inferiour ground. **1751** FALCONER *To Pr. of Wales* 59 The soul..sails incumbent on inferior night. **1812** SIR H. DAVY *Chem. Philos.* 97 The heated elastic matter must remain longer in contact with the inferior than with the superior portion. **1830** LYELL *Princ. Geol.* I. 297 The result would be the same if, the swiftness being equal, the inferior current had only a fourth of the volume of the superior. **1862** DANA *Man. Geology* v. 576 The old Glacial drift..being observed in several places as an inferior deposit.

b. Const. *to* (that which is higher). *rare.*

1571 DIGGES *Pantom.* I. xvii. E iij b, So that the vent or end..be inferior to the Fountaine whence it is deriued.

2. Lower in the stream of time; later. (Cf. DESCEND *v.* 5, DOWN *adv.* 15.)

1641 *Vind. Smectymnuus* vii. 90 The Bishops of inferior times. **1894** *Daily News* 20 Dec. 6/2 The year which has been chosen as the inferior limit.

3. Lower in degree, rank, importance, quality, amount, or other respect; of less value or consideration; lesser; subordinate.

1531 ELYOT *Gov.* I. i, In hym [man] shulde be no lasse prouidence of god declared than in the inferiour creatures. **1548** HALL *Chron., Edw. IV* 241 b, The chief of his nobilitie..beside merchauntes, and other inferior persones. **1606** G. W[OODCOCKE] tr. *Hist. Ivstine* 38 The basest of their retinue, and the inferriour of their friends. **1607** NORDEN *Surv. Dial.* A vj, Revenues..brought in..by the labours of inferiour tenants. **1613** PURCHAS *Pilgrimage* (1614) 822 The people worship the Sunne..the Moone also..but in an inferiour degree. **1754** ERSKINE *Princ. Sc. Law* (1809) 13 Inferior courts are those whose sentences are subject to the review of the supreme courts. **1756** BURKE *Vind. Nat. Soc.* Wks. I. 11 The body, or, as some love to call it, our inferiour nature. **1878** STEWART & TAIT *Unseen Univ.* iv. §146. 150 To obtain at least an inferior limit to the density of the ether.

b. With *to* (†*unto*); = lower than, less than, not so good or great as; unequal to.

1535 COVERDALE *Job* xiii. 2 Nether am I inferior vnto you. **1535** JOYE *Apol. Tindale* (Arb.) 29 A man farre inferior vnto them both in lerning, iugement, and vertew. **1638** SIR T. HERBERT *Trav.* (ed. 2) 20 The noyse not inferiour to a Cannon. **1706** H. MAULE *Hist. Picts* in *Misc. Scot.* I. 8 It had been nothing inferiour to them in beauty and profit. **1768** BOSWELL *Corsica* Introd. (ed. 2) 9, I feel myself inferiour to the task. **1841** MYERS *Cath. Th.* III. §48. 180 How inferior is it [the Koran] to any preceptive or prophetic portion of even the Hebrew Scriptures.

†**c.** With other constructions. *Obs. rare.*

1539 TONSTALL *Serm. Palm Sund.* (1823) 7 He was made inferiour vnder angels. **1553** EDEN *Treat. Newe Ind.* (Arb.) 15 The Elephant is a beast..little inferiour from humaine sense.

4. In a positive or absolute sense (admitting comparison with *more* and *most*): Of low degree, rank, etc.; in mod. use esp. in reference to quality: Of no great value or excellence; comparatively bad, poor, mean.

(In early instances, *more inferior* may be regarded simply as a double comparative = *inferior*.)

1531 ELYOT *Gov.* I. i, Begynnyng at the moste inferior or base, and assendynge upwarde. **1699** GARTH *Dispens.* II. 17 I'le calmly stoop to more inferiour things. **1714** FORTESCUE-ALAND *Pref. Fortescue's Abs. & Lim. Mon.* 34 It [English Law] provides for the Security and Happiness of every Individual, tho' never so inferior. *a* **1745** SWIFT (Seager), The black A more inferiour station seeks, Leaving the fiery red behind. **1806** SURR *Winter in Lond.* I. 265 The hand..did but its duty, and must have done the same thing..for

the most inferior of his fellow creatures. **1868** J. H. BLUNT *Ref. Ch. Eng.* I. 413 Richard Masters.. was too inferior a man to deal properly with such an outbreak. **1878** GLADSTONE *Primer Homer* 14 The country with which he shows so inferior an acquaintance.

b. *adverbially.* In a lower position.

1597 tr. *Guillemeau's Fr. Chirurg.* 22/2 It is situated more inferior, wher all the fibers of the Scrotum doe end.

5. *Astron.* **a.** Applied to those planets (Venus and Mercury) whose orbits lie within that of the earth (originally, according to the Ptolemaic astronomy, as having their spheres below that of the sun). **b.** ***inferior conjunction***: see CONJUNCTION 3. **c.** ***inferior meridian***: that part of the celestial meridian which lies below the pole; so ***inferior passage*** (of the meridian), etc.

1658 PHILLIPS s.v., *Inferiour* Planets are those which are placed below the Globe of the Sun. **1787** BONNYCASTLE *Astron.* ii. 26 The two first, because they move within the earth's orbit, are called inferior planets. **1833** HERSCHEL *Astron.* viii. 253 The inferior conjunction will happen when .. the planet has reached a point between the sun and earth. **1834** MRS. SOMERVILLE *Connex. Phys. Sc.* xiii. (1849) 105 Once under the superior and once under the inferior meridian. **1854** MOSELEY *Astron.* x. (ed. 4) 47 Let the altitude of the star be observed.. at the time of its inferior passage.

6. *Bot.* Growing below some other part or organ; said of the calyx when growing below or free from the (*superior*) ovary, and of the ovary when adherent to the sides of the (*superior*) calyx so as to be below the lobes of it.

[**1765** LEE *Introd. Bot.* Gloss., *Inferus flos*, Flowers whose Receptacle are situated below the Germen.] **1785** MARTYN *Rousseau's Bot.* v. 55 The greater number of plants.. have the germ inclosed within the flower; these are called inferior flowers as inclosing or being below the germ. **1830** LINDLEY *Nat. Syst. Bot.* Introd. 25 The difference between a superior and inferior calyx consists only in the cohesion of that organ with the ovarium in the one case, and its separation from it in another. **1857** HENFREY *Bot.* §285 The Bacca, or true berry, differs from the *nuculanium* only in being inferior, so that it is crowned by the withered teeth of the calyx. **1880** GRAY *Struct. Bot.* (ed. 6) 416/2 An inferior ovary is one with adnate or superior calyx.

7. *Anat.* and *Zool.* Applied to parts or organs situated below others of the same kind (distinguished as *superior*), or below the usual or normal position.

[**1563**: see 1.] **1826** KIRBY & SP. *Entomol.* IV. 314 Eyes.. Inferior.. When they are placed on the lower side of the head. *Ibid.* 336 Wings.. Inferior. The posterior wings are so denominated if the anterior wings, when at rest, are placed upon them. **1840** E. WILSON *Anat. Vade M.* (1842) 39 The Inferior Maxillary Bone.—The lower jaw is the arch of bone which contains the inferior teeth. *Ibid.* 349 The inferior Vena Cava is formed by the union of the two common iliac veins. **1878** FOSTER *Phys.* III. i. 392 The latter degenerate from the inferior cervical ganglion below upwards to the superior cervical ganglion above.

8. *Printing.* Applied to small letters or figures cast or made to range at the bottom of the ordinary letters, in a line of type, as in H_2, C_nH_{2n-2}.

1888 JACOBI *Printers' Vocab.*, *Inferior Letters*, small letters which are cast on the lower part of the body, e.g. $_{a\,e\,i\,o\,u}$—the reverse of 'superior' letters— $^{a\,e\,i\,o\,u}$.

B. *sb.*

1. A person inferior to another (in rank, or in some respect specified or implied); one who ranks below another; one of less consideration, attainments, etc.; a subordinate. (Commonly with possessive pronoun; cf. BETTER A. 7.)

1502 ATKYNSON tr. *De Imitatione* III. xxiv. 217 He may nat very worthely exalte hym selfe aboue other ne vylypende his inferyoure or the poore. *c* **1530** L. COX *Rhet.* (1899) 46 Superyours whiche haue power to make lawes to the inferiours. **1573** G. HARVEY *Letter-bk.* (Camden) 4, I have not shoun mi self so surli towards mi inferiors. **1613** PURCHAS *Pilgrimage* (1614) 524 The Governours have absolute rule over their inferiours. **1754** SHERLOCK *Disc.* (1759) I. xiii. 344 Love towards Inferiors is Courtesy and Condescension. **1876** MOZLEY *Univ. Serm.* ix. (1877) 194 He finds out how much harder it is to be fair to an equal than ever so generous to an inferior.

2. A thing inferior to another; something of less amount, subordinate importance, etc.; †also formerly (in *pl.*), things of this lower world, sublunary affairs or events (cf. INFERIAL 1).

1589 PUTTENHAM *Eng. Poesie* II. xiv. [xv.] (Arb.) 137 All aboue the number of three are but compounded of their inferiours. **1591** SYLVESTER *Du Bartas* I. iv. 461 And such is he, that doth affirm the Stars To have no force on these inferiours. **1658** tr. *Porta's Nat. Magic* I. viii. 13 Whosoever is rightly seen in all these things, he will ascribe all these inferiours to the stars as their causes. **1871** M. COLLINS *Mrq. & Merch.* I. viii. 247 The.. Manor.. had been the manorial inferior of the lords of Ashridge.

3. *Printing.* An inferior letter: see A. 8.

1884 SOUTHWARD *Pract. Printing* (ed. 2) 17 The distinction between ordinary letters and superiors or inferiors is found in the unusually large white space at the top or bottom of them respectively.

inferiority (ɪnfɪərɪˈɒrɪtɪ). [f. L. type **inferiōritās* (see INFERIOR and -ITY), prob. in med.L., cf. Sp. *inferioridad* (Minsheu, 1599), It. *inferiorità* (Florio, 1611), F. *infériorité* (Oudin, 1642).]

1. The quality or condition of being inferior; lower position or state:

a. in degree, rank, quality, amount, etc.

1599 MINSHEU *Sp. Dict.*, *Inferioridad*, inferioritie, the lower part. **1611** FLORIO, *Inferiorita*, inferioritie, a lower state. **1641** BP. HALL *Def. Humb. Remonstr.* 124 A superiority and inferiority betweene Officers of different kindes, will not prove a superiority and inferiority betweene Officers of the same kinde. **1751** JOHNSON *Rambler* No. 149 ¶10, I may feel the stings of inferiority. **1830** LYELL *Princ. Geol.* I. 110 The inferiority of heat in the temperate and arctic zones south of the line. **1856** MACAULAY *Biog.* (1867) 69 [Goldsmith] was painfully sensible of his inferiority in conversation. **1886** RUSKIN *Præterita* I. xi. 345 With these farther inferiorities to Davie.

b. in local position. *rare.*

1833 LYELL *Princ. Geol.* III. 208 The inferiority of the Blaye limestone to the Miocene strata.

2. *attrib.* and *Comb.* **inferiority complex**, generalized and unrealistic feelings of inadequacy caused by a person's reactions to actual or supposed inferiority in one sphere, sometimes compensated for by aggressive self-assertion; *colloq.*, exaggerated feelings of personal inadequacy; also ***inferiority feeling***.

1922 A. G. TANSLEY *New Psychol.* (rev. ed.) xix. 214 Thus the '*inferiority complex' may account for a whole series of well-known human traits. **1924** C. MACKENZIE *Heavenly Ladder* xxiii. 288, I could psycho-analyse all Bloomsbury now. They all suffer from an inferiority complex. Either they feel themselves intellectually inferior to Newton or physically inferior to Sandow or morally inferior to Christ. **1925** *N.Y. Times* 20 Sept. IX. 12/2 Those psychic disturbances which Freudians attribute to repressed sex impulse Adler attributes to a deficiency in the mechanism of self-assertion—to the 'inferiority complex', which today is on the tongue of thousands who have no idea of what they are talking about. *Ibid.* 12/3 Dr. Adler replied: 'Individual psychology holds that the most important key to the understanding of both personal and mass problems is the so-called sense of inferiority, or inferiority complex, and its consequences.' **1926** W. MCDOUGALL *Outl. Abnormal Psychol.* xxvii. 436 The inferiority complex is an important factor in some neurotics. **1933** W. J. H. SPROTT tr. *Freud's New Introd. Lect. Psycho-Anal.* 88 A writer who brings in the expression 'inferiority-complex' thinks he has satisfied all the demands of psycho-analysis... As a matter of fact the phrase ' inferiority-complex' is hardly ever used in psycho-analysis. **1947** N. L. MUNN *Psychol.* xi. 224/2 Alfred Adler ..popularized the terms 'inferiority and superiority complex' which are regarded as outcomes of, respectively, unsuccessful and successful exploitation of the 'will to power'. **1954** L. CARMICHAEL *Manual of Child. Psychol.* (ed. 2) xviii. 1118/2 Such a child.. will develop an inferiority complex and will soon slow down in his attempts to cope with his environment. **1974** *Daily Tel.* 9 Mar. 15/3 Mrs Thompson seemed to have an inferiority complex. Strangers were made to feel unwelcome. **1934** H. C. WARREN *Dict. Psychol.* 137/2 *Inferiority feeling. **1937** C. DAY LEWIS *Starting Point* I. ii. 32 I'd not be sure that I wasn't doing it from false motives—from envy.. or inferiority-feeling. **1961** J. A. C. BROWN *Freud & Post-Freudians* iii. 39 In order to compensate for inferiority feelings, each child develops.. his own particular strategy.

in'feriorize, *v. rare.* [f. INFERIOR + -IZE.] *trans.* To make inferior. (In quot. *absol.*)

a **1834** COLERIDGE *Lit. Rem.* (1838) IV. 238, I would avoid the inferiorizing consequences by a stricter rendering of the εἰ μὴ ὁ Πατήρ.

inferiorly (ɪnˈfɪərɪəlɪ), *adv.* [f. INFERIOR *a.* + -LY².] In an inferior position or degree.

1. In a lower position; further down; below, beneath; on the lower part or side.

1556 J. HEYWOOD *Spider & F.* lxxxviii. 110 Spiders are plaste a boue superiorlie, And flies beneth them plaste inferiorlie. **1597** A. M. tr. *Guillemeau's Fr. Chirurg.* 16 b/2 A little stone-drawer, superiorly hollowe.. and inferiorlye like vnto a hoocke. **1841** T. R. JONES *Anim. Kingd.* 664 Inferiorly, each plate of whalebone is terminated by a broad fringe of horny fibres resembling hair. **1885** H. O. FORBES *Natur. Wander.* 369 Bordered inferiorly by a light band.

2. In a lower degree, subordinately; to a less extent; with a low degree of excellence, comparatively badly, poorly.

1605 VERSTEGAN *Dec. Intell.* x. (1628) 320 More inferiorly it is a deputy or officer vnder some noble man. **1838** JOHN MARTIN *Rem.*, *Ess.* IV. 316 Born partly, or, if you will, say chiefly, by God, but partly also, however inferiorly, by man. **1873** BROWNING *Red Cott. Nt.-cap* IV. 762 Artist-preference For work complete, inferiorly proposed, To incompletion, though it aim aright.

†in'feriorness. *Obs. rare.* [f. as prec. + -NESS.] The quality of being inferior; inferiority.

1674 A. G. *Quest. Oath Alleg.* To Rdr. 2, I hop'd my inferiourness in number would not be able to work me any great prejudice. **1727** in BAILEY vol. II.

†in'ferious, *a. Obs. rare.* [f. as INFERI-AL + -OUS.] = INFERIOR.

1607 *Schol. Disc. agst. Antichr.* I. ii. 76 As if a seruant should.. take the right hand of him, because of old that was the inferious place. **1642** *Soveraignty Kings* title-p., This was spoken Principally and Peculiarly of Kings, and not of inferious subjects.

inferme, etc., obs. form of INFIRM, etc.

†in'ferment. *Obs. rare.* [f. INFER *v.* + -MENT.] The action of inferring; citation; inference.

1593 BILSON *Govt. Christ's Ch.* 297, I have cleared the inferments of both places before.

†infermen'tation. *Obs. rare.* [IN-³.] Absence of fermentation; unfermented condition.

1608 *Disput. Kneeling Sacram.* 49 The circumstance of the Evening, and of the infermentation belonged peculiarly to the feast of the Passover, and of the unleavened bread.

†infer'mented, *a. Obs.* [IN-³.] Unfermented.

1732 ARBUTHNOT *Rules of Diet* 409 A Diet of farinaceous Substances infermented, as of Pudding.

infern (ɪnˈfɜːn), *a. poet. rare.* [ad. L. *infernus* situated below, lower, infernal; in Dunbar perh. immed. from OF. *inferne*.] = INFERNAL.

1500–20 DUNBAR *Poems* lxxxv. 7 Our tern inferne for to dispern, Helpe rialest rosyne. **1802** COURTIER *Solitude* 19 To reconnoitre the infern abode Of sheer philosophist.

infernal (ɪnˈfɜːnəl), *a.* and *sb.* [a. F. *infernal* (from 12th c. in Littré), ad. L. *infernāl-is* of the realms below, infernal, f. *infernus* adj. situated below, subterranean, of the lower regions, whence *infernī* the shades, *inferna* the lower regions, and, in later (Christian) use, *infernus* sb. masc. 'hell'.]

A. *adj.*

1. Of or belonging to the world or 'regions' below, i.e. to the realm of the dead in ancient mythology, or the abode of evil spirits in Jewish and Christian belief; of, pertaining or relating to, hell.

c **1374** CHAUCER *Troylus* IV. 1515 (1543) And this on euery god celestial.. On euery Nymphe and deite infernal. *c* **1485** *Digby Myst.* II. 412 The myȝte prince of the partes infernall. **1555** EDEN *Decades* 325 To open a way to the courte of infernal Pluto. **1563** *Homilies* II. *Rebellion* II. (1859) 567 The miserable captives and vile slaves of that infernal tyrant Satan. **1601** HOLLAND *Pliny* I. 3 The infernall powers beneath. **1629** MILTON *Nativity* xxvi, The flocking shadows pale Troop to the infernal jail. **1703** POPE *Thebais* 411 By the black infernal Styx I swear. **1774** GOLDSM. *Nat. Hist.* (1776) II. 141 To ascribe this strange production to the operations of an infernal agent. **1828** SCOTT *F. M. Perth* xxxii, The most abhorred fiend in the infernal regions is sent to torment me.

2. Of the character, or having some of the attributes of hell; like that of hell; hellish.

1562 BULLEYN *Def. agst. Sickness, Bk. Sicke Men* 79 a, God deliuer us all, from soche infernall plagues from henceforthe. **1634** SIR T. HERBERT *Trav.* 119 The forty load of Toback.. fired, whose black vapour upon free-cost, gave the whole City infernall incense, two whole dayes. *a* **1691** BOYLE *Hist. Air* (1692) 157 The heat of the island Suaquena, Gregory used to call, infernal. **1858** KINGSLEY *Lett.* I. (1878) 21 The infernal hiss and crackle of the flame.

3. Of the nature of the inhabitants of hell; diabolical, fiendish, devilish.

1603 KNOLLES *Hist. Turks* (1638) 101 The Sultan.. carried with an infernall fury, defaced and most shamefully polluted the sepulchre of our blessed Sauior. **1660** MILTON *Free Commw.* Wks. (1851) 445 The Language of thir infernal Pamphlets. **1725** DE FOE *Voy. round World* (1840) 48 An infernal project of the second mate's. **1756–7** tr. *Keysler's Trav.* (1760) III. 37 Tophana.. is still living in prison here, and few foreigners leave Naples without seeing this infernal hag. **1827–35** WILLIS *Wife's Appeal* 20 Voltaire, With an infernal sneer upon his lips. **1848** W. H. KELLY tr. *L. Blanc's Hist. Ten Years* I. 607 An infernal plot, it was said, had been formed;.. miscreants went about, poisoning food, wine, and the water of the fountains.

4. **†a.** ***infernal stone***: an old name for lunar caustic. *Obs.*

1706 PHILLIPS, *Infernal Stone*, a sort of Caustick.. so call'd from the exquisite Pain it causes in the Operation; it is the same with Silver Cautery. **1758** REID tr. *Macquer's Chym.* I. 53 They are used by Surgeons, under the title of *Lapis infernalis*, Infernal Stone, or Silver Caustic. **1855** MAYNE *Expos. Lex.*, *Lapis Infernalis*, the infernal stone, a term for the caustic potash.

b. ***infernal machine***: an apparatus (usually disguised as some familiar and harmless object) contrived to produce an explosion for the criminal destruction of life or property; formerly, an explosive apparatus used in military operations.

[**1769** FALCONER *Dict. Marine* (1789) F iv, Amidst the confusion occasioned by this infernal apparatus.] **1810** *Naval Chron.* XXIII. 137 The infernal machine which was let off at St. Malo had no effect. **1816** W. WARDEN *Lett. fr. St. Helena* (ed. 4) 169 He [Napoleon] still retains his original belief in the contrivance of the Infernal Machine. **1863** CHAMBERS *Bk. of Days* I. 109/1 It was the third time that what the French call an Infernal Machine was used in the streets of Paris. **1880** MCCARTHY *Own Times* IV. liv. 154 Some rudely constructed infernal-machine was flung into his bedroom at midnight.

c. ***infernal fig***: a name for *Argemone mexicana*, a plant of the poppy tribe, with acrid seeds.

1760 J. LEE *Introd. Bot.* (1788) 339 Infernal Fig, *Argemone*. **1866** *Treas. Bot.*, Fig, Devil's or Infernal.

5. *colloq.* As a term of strong execration or condemnation: 'Confounded', execrable, detestable.

1764 FOOTE *Patron* III. (1781) 64 *Bever*... The infamy of being the author [of the play]. *Juliet*. What, is it bad, then? *Bever*. Bad! most infernal! **1775** SHERIDAN *Duenna* III. i, Well, it is the most unaccountable affair! 'sdeath! there is certainly some infernal mystery in it. **1866** MRS. RIDDELL *Race for Wealth* xv. (Tauchn.) 159 Her father boxed her ears, and told her not to make such an infernal fool of herself. **1897** MARY KINGSLEY *W. Africa* 213 His white trader friends told him not to be such an infernal ass.

B. *sb.*

1. An inhabitant of the infernal regions, or of hell; an infernal deity; a fiend, devil. (Usually in *pl.*)

1582 N.T. (Rhem.) *Phil.* ii. 10 That in the name of Iesus every knee bowe of the celestials, terrestrials, and infernals. **1613** HEYWOOD *Braz. Age* Wks. 1874 III. 217 Vnmanacle the fiends, and make a passage Free for the Infernals. *c* **1790** COWPER *Notes Milton's P.L.* I. 114 To invent speeches for these Infernals so well adapted to their character. **1833** I. TAYLOR *Fanat.* i. 6 Outlaw of humanity, and offspring, as he [the persecutor] seems of infernals.

†2. *pl.* The infernal regions. *Obs.*

1613 HEYWOOD *Silv. Age* Wks. 1874 III. 158 And with my club Worke my free passage (maugre all the fiends) Through these infernals. **1673** DRYDEN *Marr. à la Mode* v. i, And let me die, but I'll follow you to the infernals, till you pity me.

3. *transf.* **a.** A person of fiendish character.

1748 RICHARDSON *Clarissa* (1811) III. 387 They are a set of infernals. **1788** J. MAY *Jrnl. & Lett.* (1873) 42 Only three days agone, some of the infernals [Indians] killed a white man.

†b. A thing of infernal character; in later use, short for *infernal machine* (see A. 4 b). *Obs.*

1610 *Histrio-m.* II. 219 *Ush.* One of you answer the names of your playes. *Post*.. A russet coat and a knaves cap (an Infernal). **1779** *Hist. Eur.* in *Ann. Reg.* 87/2 That no mercy ought to be shewn to them, and if the infernals could be employed against them he should approve of that measure. **1809** *Naval Chron.* XXII. 203 Rockets, infernals, fire-devils.

Hence (*nonce-wds.*) **in'fernalism**, infernal system, practice, or character; **in'fernalness**, infernality (Bailey vol. II, 1727); **in'fernalry**, a haunt of 'infernals'; **in'fernalship**, the personality of an 'infernal'.

1607 DEKKER *Knt.'s Conjur.* (1842) 16 Had his Infernalship ben arrested to any action how great soeuer ..(the Diuell scornes to be nonsuited) he would haue answered that too. **1864** E. SARGENT *Peculiar* II. 219 A noble people..manfully fighting the great battle of humanity against such infernalism as this. **1871** CARLYLE in *Mrs. Carlyle's Lett.* III. 199 Cockneydom with its slums, enchanted aperies and infernalries. **1888** *Voice* (N.Y.) 20 Dec., In its plenary infernalism the rumseller's license implies the following contract.

infernality (ɪnfəˈnælɪtɪ). [f. prec. + -ITY.]

1. The quality of being infernal, or an instance of this; hellishness, diabolicalness; a diabolical act or characteristic.

1805 FOSTER *Ess.* (1844) 256 The Mexican abominations and infernalities have already received from us their epic tribute. **1862** *Sat. Rev.* 629 An old philosopher, we are told, is right—that every Frenchwoman has a certain 'dose of infernality'.

†2. The infernal world and its occupants. *Obs.*

1593 NASHE *Christ's T.* (1613) 33, I would haue fought for them, with hell, the diuell, and al infernality.

infernalize (ɪnˈfɜːnəlaɪz), *v.* [f. INFERNAL *a.* + -IZE.] *trans.* To render infernal; to imbue with a hellish disposition or character.

1817 COLERIDGE *Own Times* (1850) III. 961 To *infernalize* human nature, by poisoning the very sources of morality and peace. *c* **1875** in Miss Cobbe *Life* (1894) II. 219 [Scenes which, as Colonel Leigh said], 'infernalise a whole generation'.

infernally (ɪnˈfɜːnəlɪ), *adv.* [f. as prec. + -LY².] In an infernal manner, hellishly, diabolically. Usually *colloq.* To an 'infernal' extent, 'confoundedly', detestably.

1638 SIR T. HERBERT *Trav.* (ed. 2) 275 An act so infernally devillish, that all Persia cursed him. *a* **1670** HACKET *Abp. Williams* I. (1693) 211 All this I perceive is infernally false. **1831** LYTTON *Godolphin* 14 You lost infernally last night. **1874** HATTON *Clytie* (ed. 10) 211 'It is infernally lonely here', whined Ransford.

‖**inferno** (ɪnˈfɜːnəʊ). [It. *inferno*:—late L. *infernus* hell (Ambrose).] Hell; a place of torment or misery compared to hell; a place likened in some respect to the *Inferno* of Dante's *Divine Comedy*.

1834 MEDWIN *Angler in Wales* I. 24 The passage to what some, who attribute to Byron a cloven foot, might call his *inferno*. **1839** CARLYLE *Chartism* iv. (1858) 23 This black unluminous unheeded Inferno and Prisonhouse of souls in pain. **1889** RUSKIN *Præterita* III. i. 27 Rossetti..was really not an Englishman, but a great Italian tormented in the Inferno of London.

infero- (ˌɪnfərəʊ), modern combining form of L. *inferus* low (see INFERIOR), used in scientific terms (chiefly *Zool.*) to designate parts situated low down or on the under side; as **infero-an'terior** *a.*, situated below and in front; **infero-'frontal** *a.*, in the lower part of the forehead; **infero-'lateral** *a.*, below and on one side; **infero-'median** *a.*, in the middle of the under side; **infero-po'sterior** *a.*, below and behind.

1849 DANA *Geol.* App. i. (1850) 701 From the beak to the *infero-anterior margin. **1864** HUXLEY in *Reader* 19 Mar. 364/3 The lateral excavation of the *infero-frontal region. **1877** —— *Anat. Inv. Anim.* vi. 322 The *infero-lateral parietes of the stomach are strengthened by a number of other plates and bars. *Ibid.* vi. 316 The lamella which forms the *infero-median region of the rostrum. **1852** DANA *Crust.* II. 1273 Dorsal and *infero-posterior margin minutely denticulate. *Ibid.* 871 Palm *infero-subapical.

inferobranch (ˈɪnfərəʊˌbræŋk). *Zool.* [f. INFERO- + L. *branchiæ* gills: cf. mod.L. *Inferobranchiata.*] One of the order or sub-order *Inferobranchiata* of gastropod molluscs, originally comprising those in which the gills are situated under the projecting border of the mantle, now extended to include allied forms without gills. So **ˌinfero'branchian**, **ˌinfero'branchiate** *adjs.*, belonging to the *Inferobranchiata*; *sbs.* = INFEROBRANCH.

1836–9 TODD *Cycl. Anat.* II. 411/2 Met with in the.. Inferobranchiate..orders. **1847** CRAIG, *Inferobranchians.* **1851–6** WOODWARD *Mollusca* 34 In some of the Gasteropoda, the respiratory organs form tufts..protected by a fold of the mantle, as in the inferobranchs and tectibranchs of Cuvier.

inferrability (ɪnfɜːrəˈbɪlɪtɪ). Also **inferability**. [f. INFERRABLE *a.* + -ITY: see INFERRIBLE *a.*] = INFERRIBILITY.

1914 C. D. BROAD *Perception* ii. 128 This inferrability of one attribute from another. **1924** W. E. JOHNSON *Logic* III. viii. 104 The term 'one—one correspondence' is understood as equivalent to reciprocal inferability.

inferred (ɪnˈfɜːrd), *ppl. a.* [f. INFER *v.* + -ED.]

†a. Brought in, brought on, inflicted (*obs.*). **b.** Derived by inference.

1592 GREENE *Upst. Courtier* in *Harl. Misc.* (Malh.) II. 228 That when they have wasted what their fathers left them by pride, they may grow sparing and humble by inferred pouerty. **1690** LOCKE *Hum. Und.* IV. xvii. (R.), To see or suppose such a connection of the two ideas of the inferred proposition. **1866** FOWLER *Deduct. Logic* iii. §1 (1869) 81 The inferred proposition being virtually contained in the propositions from which it is inferred.

inferrible, -able (ɪnˈfɜːrɪb(ə)l, -əb(ə)l), *a.* See also INFERABLE. [f. INFER *v.* + -ABLE: the spelling *inferrible* is of mongrel character between the analogical L. **inferibilis* with single *r*, and the analogical English *in'ferrable* with *rr*, as in *inferring*: see -BLE.] That may be inferred; deducible.

1646 SIR T. BROWNE *Pseud. Ep.* I. iv. 13 Conclusions no way inferrible from their premises. **1681** BOYLE *Contn. Exper. Spring Air* II. III. ix, From this experiment..it seems to be inferrible, that [etc.]. **1843** MILL *Logic* II. iii. §5 (1856) I. 223 A general proposition, every tittle of which is legitimately inferrible from our premises. **1881** *N. Amer. Rev.* CXXXII. 308 It is fairly inferrable from these ambiguous declarations..that they are neither of them really in favor of the proposed reformation.

Hence **inferri'bility**, capability of being inferred.

1843 MILL *Logic* I. iv. §3 (1856) 91 What is asserted is.. the inferribility of the one from the other.

inferribly (ɪnˈfɜːrɪblɪ), *adv. rare.* [f. INFERRIBLE *a.* + -LY².] By inference. (Cf. INFERABLY *adv.*)

1905 J. M. ROBERTSON *Did Shakes. write Titus Andron.?* 198 It would inferribly be his latest play, as it has 69 double-endings to 461 lines of blank verse. **1913** —— *Baconian Heresy* 18 When they were written we know not..but it was inferribly before 1623.

inferring (ɪnˈfɜːrɪŋ), *vbl. sb.* [f. INFER *v.* + -ING¹.] The action of the vb. INFER; the drawing of inferences.

1571 GOLDING *Calvin on Ps.* v. 8 After the manner of inferring, in this wyse. **1827** WHATELY *Logic* IV. iii. §1 (1846) 310 Reasoning comprehends Inferring and Proving.

in'ferring, *ppl. a.* [f. as prec. + -ING².] That infers, that draws inferences. Hence **in'ferringly** *adv.*, in the way of inference, in an inferential sense.

1571 GOLDING *Calvin on Ps.* lxxi. 17 The particle (Nam) is taken inferringly. **1890** *Athenæum* 12 Apr. 463/2 That tendency, impulse or belief which makes man an inferring being.

infertile (ɪnˈfɜːtɪl, -taɪl), *a.* Also 6 -ille, 7 -il. [a. F. *infertile* (1488 in Hatz.-Darm.), ad. late L. *infertilis*, f. *in-* (IN-³) + *fertilis* FERTILE.] Not fertile; unfruitful, unproductive, barren, sterile.

1597 A.M. tr. *Guillemeau's Fr. Chirurg.* *iv b, To sowe the same in an infertille grownde. **1611** SPEED *Theat. Gt. Brit.* xliii. (1614) 85/1 The soile..being so full of infertile places, which the Northern Englishmen call Moores. **1753** HANWAY *Trav.* (1762) I. III. xi. 181 A defect..in one man, could render only one woman infertile. **1868** DARWIN *Plants & Anim.* (1875) II. 130 Animals and plants, when removed from their natural conditions, are often rendered in some degree infertile or completely barren. **1869** RAWLINSON *Anc. Hist.* 54 The most infertile of the four Continents.

Hence **in'fertilely** *adv.*, in an infertile manner (Craig, 1847); **in'fertileness** (Bailey vol. II, 1727) = next.

infertility (ɪnfəˈtɪlɪtɪ). [a. late L. *infertilitās*, f. *infertilis*: see prec. and -ITY: cf. F. *infertilité* (15–16th c. in Godef. *Compl.*).] The quality or condition of being infertile; unfruitfulness, unproductiveness, barrenness.

1610 W. FOLKINGHAM *Art of Survey* I. iii. 7 The Minerals ..shall Counteruaile the infertilitie of Soile. **1677** HALE *Prim. Orig. Man.* II. ix. 214 Commonly the same distemperature of the Air that occasioned the Plague, occasioned also the infertility or noxiousness of the Soil. **1847** LEWES *Hist. Philos.* (1867) I. p. lxii, This immunity from error accompanies an infertility of knowledge. **1859** DARWIN *Orig. Spec.* ix. (1878) 248 Individuals which happened to be endowed..with mutual infertility.

†in'fesse, *v. Obs. rare*⁻⁰. [f. IN-² + FESSE.] To place a heraldic charge in fesse.

1611 FLORIO, *Infasciare*,..to infesse in armory.

†in'fest, *sb. Obs.* Used (in pl.) by Turberville to render L. *inferiæ*, funeral offerings or expiations.

1567 TURBERV. tr. *Ovid, Heroid.* xii. K vij, O wronged Syre reioyce: ye men of Colche Be glad: and of my brothers ghost receiue Th' infests.

†in'fest, *a. Obs.* [ad. L. *infest-us* unsafe, hostile. But in sense 2 perh. short for *infested.*]

1. Hostile. Const. *to, against, towards.*

1513 DOUGLAS *Æneis* XI. iii. 51 Drances, that had full gret envy At ȝyng Turnus, all way to him infest. **1548** HALL *Chron., Hen. V* (1809) 65 Now approched the fortunate faire daie to the Englishmen and the infest and unlucky daie to the French Nobilitee. **1612** T. JAMES *Jesuit's Downf.* 30 The Iesuits proued no lesse infest foes against the late Princesse. **1641** J. JACKSON *True Evang. T.* I. 23 Two great and signall Historians give in evidence against him, how infest an enemy he was to Christians.

2. Molested, attacked. *rare*⁻¹.

1601 R. JOHNSON *Kingd. & Commw.* (1603) 177 While time passeth, the neighbouring nations provide (if not infest) for their owne safetie.

†in'fest, *v.*¹ *Obs. rare*⁻¹. [f. IN-¹ + *fest*, FAST *v.*¹, after L. *infigĕre.*] *trans.* To fasten or fix in something.

a **1340** HAMPOLE *Psalter* lxviii. 18 Out take me of þe lare þat i be not infestid [L. *ne infigar*].

infest (ɪnˈfɛst), *v.*² [a. F. *infester* (1390 in Hatz.-Darm.), or ad. L. *infestāre* to assail, molest, f. *infestus* unsafe, hostile.]

1. *trans.* To attack, assail, annoy, or trouble (a person or thing) in a persistent manner; to molest by repeated attacks; to harass. Said **a.** Of persons, animals, hurtful things. Now *rare.*

1477 SIR J. PASTON in *P. Lett.* No. 797 III. 191, I shalle nott trowble ner infete [? *read* infeste] them therein. **1533** BELLENDEN *Livy* II. (1822) 130, I sal never infest nor trubil you ony forthir with sic desiris. **1548** HALL *Chron., Hen. V* 38 Outward enemitie or foreyn hostilitie not halfe so muche infested, greved or troubled the valiaunt Brittons as their owne. **1563–87** FOXE *A. & M.* (1684) I. 229/2 He sought all manner of ways to infest the Emperor. **1646** GAULE *Cases Consc.* 38 The Divell now infesting them, if they grow slacke to infest others. **1647** CLARENDON *Hist. Reb.* I. §198 They would not have endured..the Rain and the Wind to infest them. **1726** LEONI *Alberti's Archit.* I. 70/1 Deep roads.. unsafe upon account of the ground which lies above them, from whence any enemy may be prodigiously infested. **1846** LANDOR *Imag. Conv.* Wks. II. 9, I am infested and persecuted and worried to death by duns. **1850** NEALE *Med. Hymns* (1867) 160 Cold and sorrow Him infest.

†b. Of diseases, perverse opinions, errors, etc.; (sometimes confused with INFECT, sense 4). *Obs.*

1542 BOORDE *Dyetary* xxxii. (1870) 294 The syckness wyll infeste [*v.r.* infecte] them more there than in any other place. **1590** SPENSER *F.Q.* I. xi. 6 That mightie rage Wherewith the martiall troupes thou doest infest, And hartes of great Heroes doest enrage. **1650** BULWER *Anthropomet.* 189 Their children are more rarely infested with this infirmity. **1732** ARBUTHNOT *Rules of Diet* (J.), No disease infests mankind more terrible in its symptoms and effects. *a* **1754** FIELDING *Covent Gard. Jrnl.* Wks. 1784 X. 64 That complication of political diseases which infests the nation.

2. To trouble (a country or place) with hostile attacks; to visit persistently or in large numbers for purposes of destruction or plunder; to haunt with evil intent, so as to render unsafe or unpleasant; to swarm in or about, so as to be troublesome. Said of persons (e.g. robbers, pirates), animals (e.g. wolves, vermin, insects), diseases or other evils.

1602 WARNER *Alb. Eng.* Epit. (1612) 368 England.. dilacerate and infested aswell by the Saxons themselues as by the Danes. **1613** PURCHAS *Pilgrimage* (1614) 610 The Turkish Pyrats, which..infested al those Seas. **1615** G. SANDYS *Trav.* 38 The plague for the most part miserably infesteth this City. **1651** C. CARTWRIGHT *Cert. Relig.* To Rdr., Popery is the grand evill that doth infest the Church. **1697** DRYDEN *Virg. Georg.* IV. 358 Wasps infest the Camp with loud Alarms. **1718** BP. NICOLSON in Ellis *Orig. Lett.* Ser. II. IV. 318 A country said to be much infested with a set of barbarous and pilfering Tories. **1765** A. DICKSON *Treat. Agric.* I. xiii. (ed. 2) 106 Some [weeds]..infest the land that is in tillage, and others the land that is in grass. **1796** SCOTT *Chase* note, An aerial hunter, who infested the forest of Fountainebleau. **1863** LYELL *Antiq. Man* 207 Over lands covered with glaciers, or over seas infested with icebergs.

Hence **in'fested** *ppl. a.*, **in'festing** *vbl. sb.* and *ppl. a.*

1676 tr. *Guillatiere's Voy. Athens* 39 This way of infesting of Ships is ordinary among them. **1881** *Daily News* 14 Sept. 3/1 A clearance of infesting borders, hedges, and poor timber is wanted. **1893** *Jrnl. R. Agric. Soc.* Dec. 821 Infested barley heads present a very characteristic appearance.

†in'festance. *Obs. rare.* [a. OF. *infestance.*] = INFESTATION.

1490 CAXTON *Eneydos* xxi. 76 Infestaunce obprobre ne vytupere [Fr. *nulle infestance ne opprobre ne de raison*] to anchises..were neuer doon of my behalue.

† **in'festant**, *a. Obs. rare.* [ad. L. *infestānt-em*, pres. pple. of *infestāre* to INFEST: see -ANT. Cf. OF. *infestant* (Godef.).] Infesting.

1659 H. MORE *Immort. Soul* II. xvi, That this facilitates their condition of appearing, is evident from that known recourse these infestant Spirits have to their dead Bodies.

infestation (ɪnfɛ'steɪʃən). [ad. late L. *infestātiōn-em* (Tertullian), n. of action from *infestāre* to INFEST; cf. F. *infestation* (14th c. in Godef.).] The action of infesting, assailing, harassing, or persistently molesting; now used esp. of insects which attack plants, grain, etc. in large swarms. Also, with *an* and *pl.* An assault or attack of this kind. Also, the state or condition of being infested.

1536 BELLENDEN *Cron. Scot.* (1821) II. 187 The Scottis sal perpetuallie rejose al boundis of Northumbirland, but ony infestatioun of Inglismen, in times cuming. **1563–87** FOXE *A. & M.* (1684) I. 567/1 Wheresoever that Water is sprinkled, all vexation or infestation of the unclean Spirit should avoid. **1637** R. HUMPHREY tr. *St. Ambrose* I. 37 In the time of infestation of the Arrian heresie. **1695** KENNETT *Par. Antiq.* iii. 9 The guard of our Sea-coasts from the infestation of Northern Pirats. **1751** LAVINGTON *Enthus. Method. & Papists* II. iii. (1754) 152 The Diabolical Infestations, and surprizing Contagions.. were all among the Nuns. **1851** SIR F. PALGRAVE *Norm. & Eng.* I. 136 The external enemies possessed a power of infestation which could not be quelled. **1881** MISS ORMEROD *Injurious Insects, Prev. & Rem.* (1890) 248 The infestation did much harm in young Fir woods. **1895** *Times* 8 Oct. 2/6 The world-wide referee on entomological infestations.

† **in'fested**, *ppl. a.*[1] *Obs. rare.* Also 6 en-. [? f. INFEST *v.*[1]; but perh. confused with INFESTERED.] Infixed, rooted, inveterate.

1536 *Act 27 Hen. VIII*, c. 28 Preamb., By a cursed Custome soo rooted and enfested. **1591** SPENSER *Muiopot.* 354 That olde Enfested grudge. **1598** HAKLUYT *Voy.* I. 161 (R.) Only one man died of a maladie inueterate, and long infested.

infested, *ppl. a.*[2]: see under INFEST *v.*[2]

in'fester, *sb. rare.* [f. INFEST *v.*[2] + -ER[1].] One who, or that which, infests.

1791 COWPER *Odyss.* XXII. 348 The gadfly, infester fell Of beeves. **1826** KIRBY & SP. *Entomol.* IV. 208 Their insect infesters.. are confined to the Orders Strepsiptera [etc.].

† **in'fester**, *v. Obs. rare.* Also 7 en-. [f. IN-[2] + FESTER *v.*] *trans.* To render (a sore) festered, to cause to rankle. Also *fig.* Chiefly in **in-, enfestered** *ppl. a.*, festered, inveterate.

1563–87 FOXE *A. & M.* (1596) 1193/1 The long coloured peruerse obstinacy, and infestered hatred of this double faced dissembler. **1594** J. RADFORD *Truth in Relig.* To Rdr., Olde infestred diseases must be cured with sharpe medicines. **1609** J. DAVIES *Holy Roode* (1876) 16 Whiche His enfestered sores exulcerates. **1611** FLORIO, *Inrancorare*, to enrancor, to enfester.

† **in'festious**, *a. Obs.* [irreg. f. L. *infest-us* (INFEST *a.*) or INFEST *v.*[2], after adjs. in *-ious*; cf. *infectious*, etc.] Hostile, inimical, troublesome.

1597 LYLY *Wom. in Moone* IV. i. 191 Detested falsor! that to Stesias' eyes Art more infestious then the basiliske. **1601** R. JOHNSON *Kingd. & Commw.* (1603) 234 The king of Adel is his no lesse infestious enimy. **1632** LE GRYS tr. *Velleius Paterc.* 201 A Citizen was slaine then whom there had none lived more pernicious to the Commonwealth, nor more infestious to honest men. **1709** SACHEVERELL *Serm. 5 Nov.* 23 Like Growing Mischiefs, or Infestious Plagues.

† **in'festive**, *a.*[1] *Obs. rare.* [f. INFEST *v.*[2] + -IVE.] Tending to infest; troublesome, annoying.

1563–87 FOXE *A. & M.* (1596) 277/1 Yet was he.. to him a most secret and infestive enimie. **1602** WARNER *Alb. Eng.* Epit. (1612) 356 When their owne ciuill warres were most intestine, and the Barbarians most infestiue to their Empire. *c* **1611** CHAPMAN *Iliad* VIII. 151, I will all their ships inflame, with whose infestive smoke.. the conquer'd Greeks shall choke. **1704** CIBBER *Careless Husb.* Prol., The Garden of the Mind To no infestive Weed's so inclined, As the rank Pride.

† **in'festive**, *a.*[2] *Obs. rare*[-0]. [ad. L. *infestīv-us* not pleasant (Gellius): see IN-[3] and FESTIVE.]

'Without mirth or pleasantness.'

1623 in COCKERAM. **1656** in BLOUNT *Glossogr.*

So **infe'stivity** (*rare*), absence of festivity; dullness.

1727 in BAILEY vol. II. **1755** in JOHNSON. **1855** ANNE MANNING *O. Chels. Bun-ho.* [in 18th c. style] xiii. 211, I was quite wicked to be secretly complaining merely because of the infestivity. **1882** T. HARDY *Two on a Tower* I. vi. 121 Lady Constantine's life of infestivity.

in'festment. *rare.* [f. INFEST *v.*[2] + -MENT.] The action of infesting; infestation.

1819 W. S. ROSE *Lett.* I. 288 The infestment of the roads by banditti. **1822–34** *Good's Study Med.* (ed. 4) IV. 505 Infestment of the common louse, chiefly inhabiting the head of uncleanly children.

† **in'festuous**, *a. Obs.* [irreg. f. L. *infest-us* (INFEST *a.*) or INFEST *v.*[2], after adjs. in *-uous*: cf. INFECTUOUS.] = INFESTIOUS.

1593 NASHE *Christ's T.* (1613) 64 There fell such an infestuous vnsaciable famine amongst them. **1604** *Supplic. Masse Priests* § 1 The two Kingdomes (which not seldome in former times have beene much infestuous one to the other). **1630** *R. Johnson's Kingd. & Commw.* 426 Baduini.. alike infestuous to neighbour and traveller. **1712** *H. More's Antid. Ath.* I. viii. Schol. 151 The infestuous shafts of the accurate and sharp Wits.

Hence † **in'festuously** *adv. Obs.*

1604 *Supplic. Masse Priests* § 39 In driving away divels also from the places they most infestuously haunted.

† **'in,fetching**, *vbl. sb. Obs. rare*[-1]. [IN *adv.* 11 c.] A bringing in; introduction.

1535 LYNDESAY *Satyre* 2650 The infetching of Iustice airis, Exercit mair for couetice Then for the punisching of vyce.

infetter, obs. variant of ENFETTER *v.*

† **in'feudate**, *a. Obs.* In 8 infeodate. [ad. med.L. *infeudāt-us*, pa. pple. of *infeudāre*: see next.] Of tithes: Granted to laymen (cf. F. *dîmes inféodées*).

1706 tr. *Dupin's Eccl. Hist.* II. v. 89 That the Rights of Regales and infeodate Tithes would be overturned.

infeudation (ɪnfjuː'deɪʃən). *Law.* Also 5–8 **infeodation**, (8 *erron.* **infæd-**). [ad. med.L. *infeudātiōn-em*, n. of action f. *infeudāre*, f. *in-* (IN-[2]) + *feudum*: see FEUD *sb.*[2], FEE *sb.*[2] Cf. F. *inféodation*, formerly *infeudation* (1393 in Hatz.-Darm.).]

1. a. The granting of an estate to be held in fee; enfeoffment. **b.** ***infeudation of tithes***, the granting of tithes to laymen.

1473–4 *Acc. Ld. H. Treas. Scotl.* I. 5 Item componit with Adame Mure for a new infeodacione of his landis.. to be haldin of the King in warde and relef. **1682** EVATS *Grotius War & Peace* 119 Under Alienation is deservedly comprised even Infeudations, under penalty of confiscation for breach of Faith, given to the Lord of the Feoff. **1695** KENNETT *Par. Antiq.* ix. 441 This appropriation and infeodation of Tithes and Glebe, was the meer innovation of Popery. **1710** PRIDEAUX *Orig. Tithes* iii. 162 Alienations or Infædations of Tithes. **1767** BLACKSTONE *Comm.* II. iii. 27 A decree of the council of Lateran held A.D. 1179.. prohibited what was called the infeodation of tithes, or their being granted to mere laymen. **1861** MAINE *Anc. Law* ix. 365 A person wishing to engraft himself on the brotherhood [of vassals] by commendation or infeudation came to a distinct understanding [with the lord] as to the conditions on which he was to be admitted. **1874** STUBBS *Const. Hist.* I. ix. 252 *note*, The infeudation of benefices and transfer of magisterial jurisdictions to the landowners.

2. A deed by which lands or tithes are granted in fee, a deed of enfeoffment.

1647 N. BACON *Disc. Govt. Eng.* I. 50 Which shews that the Demesnes of the Crown were holden sacred.. and herewith concur all the Saxon infeodations. **1767** BLACKSTONE *Comm.* II. iv. 53 *Dedi et concessi*; which are still the operative words in our modern infeodations or deeds of feoffment.

infibred (ɪn'faɪbəd), *a. rare.* [f. IN-[2] + FIBRE *sb.*] Wrought into the fibre; engrained.

1879 J. D. LONG *Æneid* VI. 953 Not every pest infibred in our wretched lives, Is sloughed.

infibulate (ɪn'fɪbjuːleɪt), *v. rare.* [f. ppl. stem of L. *infibulāre*, f. *in-* (IN-[2]) + *fibula* a clasp, pin, FIBULA. Cf. FIBULATE.] *trans.* To fasten with a clasp or buckle. Hence **in'fibulated** *ppl. a.*, fastened with a clasp (see next).

1623 COCKERAM, *Infibulate*, to buckle. **1721** in BAILEY. **1847** DE QUINCEY *Sir W. Hamilton* Wks. 1890 V. 326 Hooks and eyes.. that are fitted to infibulate him... *Infibulate* cannot be a plagiarism, because I never saw the word before; and, in fact, I have this moment invented it. **1850** LEITCH tr. *C. O. Müller's Anc. Art* § 425 (ed. 2) 611 Caricature of an infibulated citharœdus.

infibulation (ɪn,fɪbjuː'leɪʃən). [n. of action f. INFIBULATE *v.*, perh. after F. *infibulation* (16th c. in Godef.).] The action of infibulating; *spec.* the fastening of the sexual organs with a fibula or clasp.

1650 BULWER *Anthropomet.* 202 This art of Infibulation, or buttoning up the Prepuce with a Brasse or Silver-button. **1770** *Monthly Rev.* 531 Infibulation, an operation performed on young boys and singers by the Romans, who used it as a muzzle to human incontinence. **1782** WESLEY *Wks.* (1872) XIII. 454 He will enlarge upon virginity, impotence, castration, infibulation (never heard of before in England). **1798** MALTHUS *Popul.* (1806) I. v. 79 The Abbé Raynal speaking.. of islanders in general says, 'It is among these people that we trace the origin of.. Anthropophagy, the castration of males, the infibulation of females, late marriages, the consecration of virginity, etc. **1872** W. W. READE *Martyrdom Man* 448 Premature unions among children were forbidden, and sometimes prevented by infibulation.

† **in'ficche**, *v. Obs. rare.* [f. IN-[2] + FICCHE *v.*, after L. *infīgĕre*.] *trans.* To fix, make fast.

1382 WYCLIF *Ps.* xxxvii[i]. 3 [2] For thin arwis ben in ficchid to me [Vulg. *infixæ mihi*]. *Ibid.* lxviii. 3 [lxix. 2], I am inficchid [Vulg. *infixus*] in the slim of the depthe.

infi'cete, *a. rare.* [ad. L. *inficēt-us*, f. *in-* (IN-[3]) + *facētus* FACETE.] Unfacetious; not witty.

1830 *Westm. Rev.* XII. 277 Childish matter.. very inficete and unprofitable to peruse. **1831** PEACOCK *Crotchet Castle* vi. (1887) 77 *Mr. E.* Sir, you are very facetious at my expense. *Dr. F.* Sir, you have been very unfacetious, very inficete at mine.

† **in'ficial**, *a. Obs. rare*[-0]. [ad. L. *inficiālis*, more correctly *infitiālis*, f. *infitiæ* denial, f. *in-* (IN-[3]) + *fatērī* to confess.] 'That pertaineth to denial, negative' (Blount *Glossogr.* 1656).

† **in'ficiate**, *v. Obs. rare*[-0]. [f. L. *inficiāt-*, *infitiāt-*, ppl. stem of *infitiārī* to deny, f. *infitiæ*: see prec.] *trans.* To deny.

1611 COTGR., *Denier*, to denie, disaffirm, inficiate, say nay vnto. **1623** COCKERAM II, To Deny.., *Abnegate, Infic[i]ate.*

Hence † **infici'ation** [ad. L. *inficiātiōn-em*], denial; † **in'ficiative**, † **in'ficiatory** *adjs.*, pertaining to, or of the nature of, denial.

1611 COTGR., *Deniement*, a deniall, denying, inficiation, disaffirming, saying nay vnto. *Ibid.*, *Negatif*, negatiue, inficiatiue, denying. *Ibid.*, *Negatoire*, negatorie, inficiatorie, denying. **1656** BLOUNT *Glossogr.*, *Inficiation, Inficiatory.*

† **in'ficient**, *a. Obs. rare.* [ad. L. *inficient-em* that does nothing, f. *in-* (IN-[3]) + *facient-em* doing.] Of no effect, ineffective.

1609 *Ev. Woman in Hum.* II. i. in Bullen *O. Pl.* IV, To erect A towre of Sand on the uncertain surge, Or any thing that were more inficient.

† **in'ficious**, *a. Obs. rare*[-1]. [f. L. *inficiæ*, *infitiæ* denial (see INFICIAL) + -OUS.] Given to denying.

1623 *Something Written by Accid. Blacke Friers* 4 When.. we are to deale with such Antagonists, and inficious aduersaries, wee may well vse the language of Canaan.

† **in'fide**, *a. Obs. rare*[-1]. [ad. L. *infīdus*, f. *in-* (IN-[3]) + *fīdus* faithful.] Faithless, dishonest, treacherous.

1663 *Flagellum or O. Cromwell* (ed. 2) 4 The Elements of Language and principals of Religion, both which he studied with the same indifference, and infide and fallacious endevour.

infidel ('ɪnfɪdəl), *sb.* and *a.* Forms: 5–6 infydele, (5 yn-), -fidele, 6 infydel(l, -fidell, -fedel, 6– infidel. [a. OF. *infidèle* (15–16th c. in Hatz.-Darm.), ad. L. *infidēl-is* unfaithful, (in eccl. writers) unbelieving, f. *in-* (IN-[3]) + *fidēlis* faithful, FIDELE.]

A. *sb.* † **1.** One who does not believe in (what the speaker holds to be) the true religion; an 'unbeliever'. *Obs.*

1526 TINDALE *2 Cor.* vi. 15 What parte hath he that beleveth with an infidele? [So all 16–17th c. versions; WYCLIF (1382) with vnfeithful, or hethene, (1388) the vnfeithful; 1881 *R.V.* an unbeliever]. —— *1 Tim.* v. 8 The same denyeth the fayth, and is worsse then an infydell [so all 16th c. versions; WYCLIF (1388) an vnfeithful man; *R.V.* an unbeliever].

2. In specific applications: **a.** From a Christian point of view: An adherent of a religion opposed to Christianity; esp. a Muhammadan, a Saracen (the earliest sense in Eng.); also (more rarely), applied to a Jew, or a pagan. Now chiefly *Hist.*

1470–85 MALORY *Arthur* V. ii, Two honderd sarasyns or Infydeles. **1494** FABYAN *Chron.* VII. 301 If any thynge be done to honoure of the Cristen, and reproche of infydelys, it is most lykely to be done by vs. **1548** HALL *Chron., Hen. VII* 23 b, The Moores or Mawritane nacion, beyng infideles and unchristened people. **1548–9** (Mar.) *Bk. Com. Prayer* (Coll. Good Friday), Haue mercy upon all Jewes, Turkes, Infidels, and heretikes. **1596** SHAKS. *Merch. V.* IV. i. 334 A Daniel, Iew, Now infidell I haue thee on the hip. **1677** W. HUBBARD *Narrative* (1865) I. 98 Finding no Indians, so secure were they, that they ventured along further to find the Infidels at their chief Town. **1725** DE FOE *Voy. round World* (1840) 280 Propagating the Christian faith among infidels. **1828** SCOTT *F. M. Perth* xxxi, Such services.. gave the infidels possession of Spain. **1847** MRS. A. KERR *Hist. Servia* 14 He.. did not hesitate to call even infidels—the Osmanli Turks.. to his assistance.

b. From a non-Christian (esp. Jewish or Muhammadan) point of view: = Gentile, Giaour, etc.

1534 MORE *Comf. agst. Trib.* I. Wks. 1159/1 [Solomon] takinge to wyfe amonge other, such as were infidels. **1613** PURCHAS *Pilgrimage* (1614) 301 The Meizin.. prayeth God to inspire the Christians, Jewes, Greekes, and generally all Infidels to turne to their Law. **1671** MILTON *Samson* 221, I sought to wed The daughter of an infidel. **1841** LANE *Arab. Nts.* I. 62 A slave, among Muslims, is either a person taken captive in war, or carried off by force, and being at the time of capture an infidel.

3. A disbeliever in religion or divine revelation generally; especially one in a Christian land who professedly rejects or denies the divine origin and authority of Christianity; a professed unbeliever. Usually a term of opprobrium.

1526 *Pilgr. Perf.* (W. de W. 1531) 218 b, I shall not syt with wycked infydeles that hath no fayth. **1552** HULOET, Infydele, *atheos.* **1625** JACKSON *Creed* V. § 1 Every atheist is an infidel; so is not every infidel an atheist. **1630** PRYNNE *Anti-Armin.* 132 There are many Infidels, and vnbeleeuers in the world who haue no faith at all. **1709** STEELE *Tatler* No. 111 ¶ 4, I love to consider an Infidel, whether distinguished by the Title of Deist, Atheist, or Free-thinker. **1772** *Junius Lett.* lxviii. 335 Some men are bigoted in politics, who are infidels in religion. **1857** BUCKLE *Civiliz.* I. vii. 335 He not only peremptorily affirms the reality of witches, but he says that those who deny their existence are not merely infidels but atheists.

4. In general sense: One who does not believe in something specified; an unbeliever. Const. *in*, † *to*, † *against*. (Freq. *fig.* from sense 3).

1606 WARNER *Alb. Eng.* XIV. lxxxviii. 359 Not to be Fortunes Infidels, but better times to hope. **1716** ADDISON *Freeholder* No. 14 ¶ 4 A Tory, who is the greatest Believer in

what is improbable, is the greatest Infidel in what is certain. **1720** De Foe *Life Duncan Campbell* (1841) 44 If many do remain infidels to my relations. **1748** Richardson *Clarissa* (1811) III. ix. 67 She must be an infidel against all reason and appearances, if I do not banish even the shadow of mistrust from her heart. **1858** Hawthorne *Fr. & It. Jrnls.* II. 12 Spiritual communications, as regards which Mrs. Browning is a believer, and her husband an infidel. **1884** *World* 20 Aug. 5/1 The truth is that [he] is a political infidel.

†**5.** One who is unfaithful to some duty. *Obs. nonce-use* (with allusion to 1 *Tim.* v. 8: see sense 1).

1655 Fuller *Ch. Hist.* v. v. §31 One so faithfull to his Servants, cannot be suspected for an Infidel in not providing for his family, of his own children.

B. *adj.* (including appositive or attributive uses of the substantive.)

1. Of persons: Unbelieving; adhering to a false religion; pagan, heathen, etc. (Cf. the sb.)

[**1480** Caxton *Chron. Eng.* ccliv. (1482) 328 The Cyte of Constantynople.. was taken by the turkes infydeles.] **1551** Cranmer *Answ. Gardiner* 369 You haue written what you dreamed in your sleape, rather then what you learned of any author catholyke or infidele. **1651** Hobbes *Govt. & Soc.* iv. §16. 66 Saint Paul.. reprehends the Corinthians.. for going to Law one with another before infidell Judges. **1718** Lady M. W. Montagu *Let. to C'tess [Bristol]* Lett. (1887) I. 239 Her infidel lover was.. fond of her. **1821** Shelley *Hellas* 244 Are there.. No infidel children to impale on spears? **1839** Keightley *Hist. Eng.* II. 26 Desiring her to go to the infidel King.

†**b.** Incredulous, sceptical. *Obs. rare.*

1607 Topsell *Four-f. Beasts* (1658) 495 Wonders in our own Nation.. for which other Nations account us as great liers.. as these Infidel fools do them. **1704** Hearne *Duct. Hist.* (1714) I. 400 Of their Skil in Magick much is spoken in Ancient Writers, but for our Part we are Infidel as to that Power, and therefore shall pass it over.

2. Of things, actions, views, etc.: Of, pertaining to, or characteristic of, infidels or infidelity.

1742 Young *Nt. Th.* i. 109 Why wanders wretched Thought their Tombs around, In infidel Distress? **1773** Burke *Sp. Prot. Dissenters* Wks. 1842 II. 473 The author has collected in a body the whole of the infidel code. **1784** Cowper *Task* i. 740 Through profane and infidel contempt Of holy writ. **1837** Ht. Martineau *Soc. in Amer.* III. 257 The clergy complain of the enormous spread of bold books, from the infidel tract to the latest handling of the miracle question.

infi'delic, *a. rare.* [f. prec. + -ic (? after *evangelic*).] Pertaining or related to the views or opinions of infidels. So also **infi'delical** *a.*

1802 Coleridge *Unpubl. Lett. to J. P. Estlin* (Bright 1884) 95 The infidelical argument from Christian wars.. is childish. **1864** *Bookseller's Catal.*, This volume, for its infidelical principles, has rendered him infamously popular. **1882** *Homil. Monthly* July 596 Let Spiritualism free itself from its immoral and infidelic tendencies.

†**infi'delious,** *a. Obs. rare.* [f. L. *infidēli-s* (see infidel) + -ous. Cf. fidelious.] **a.** Unfaithful. **b.** Unbelieving; infidel; of the nature of infidelity; characteristic of infidels.

1581 Andreson *Serm. Paules Crosse* 18 Good and euil ones.. faithful and infidelious, holy and hypocriticall. **1648** W. Bridge *England saved with a Notwithstanding* 26 That infidelious, hereticall, apostatizing Princes and Governours are to be deposed and excommunicated by the Pope. **1652** Gaule *Magastrom.* 163 A paganish and infidelious scandall at good things happening to bad men here.

Hence †**infi'deliously** *adv. Obs.*, perfidiously.

1614 Raleigh *Hist. World* 339 Which citie.. another of the Ptolemies infideliously wrested from his sonne in law Alexander.

'infidelism. *nonce-wd.* [f. infidel + -ism.] A system based on unbelief in religion.

a **1834** Coleridge *Lit. Rem.* (1838) IV. 231 To suppose that the exposure of the folly and falsehood of one form of Infidelism would cure or prevent Infidelity.

infidelity (ɪnfɪ'dɛlɪtɪ). [ad. L. *infidēlitās* unfaithfulness, n. of quality from *infidēlis* infidel. Cf. F. *infidélité* (12th c. in Hatz.-Darm.).]

1. Want of faith; unbelief in religious matters, esp. disbelief in the truth or evidences of Christianity; the attitude of an infidel.

1509 Barclay *Shyp of Folys* (1874) II. 188 Nowe shall I touche wretches of mysbyleue, Expressynge theyr foly by theyr infydelyte. **1529** More *Dyaloge* i. Wks. 158/1 The stubburnes and obstynate infidelite of the Jewes. **1577** Vautrouillier *Luther on Ep. Gal.* 20 Not fained or trifling sinnes, but such as are against the first table: to wit, greet infidelitie, douting [etc.]. **1678** Cudworth *Intell. Syst.* i. iv. §15. 278 Let us for the present yield thus much to your Infidelity and grant that Christ was but an ordinary man. **1755** Young *Centaur* i. Wks. 1757 IV. 106 Infidelity lets loose the rein to Pleasure, and gives it an ample range. **1814** Chalmers *Evid. Chr. Revel.* Advt. 5 The external testimony of Christianity.. leaves infidelity without excuse. **1875** Manning *Mission H. Ghost* iv. 110 Infidelity is the proper opposite of faith.

†**b.** Muhammadanism; Heathenism (cf. infidel *sb.* 2). *Obs. rare.*

1603 Knolles *Hist. Turks* Introd., Whose grieuous groanings vnder the heauy yoke of infidelity no tongue is able to expresse. **1613** Purchas *Pilgrimage* (1614) 746 That thy Virgin Truth, by Virginian Plantation, or Northerly Discovery, may triumph in her conquests of Indian Infidelity.

†**c.** An infidel opinion or practice. *Obs. rare.*

1542-5 Brinklow *Lament.* (1874) 80 Which thinge aboue all other infidelityes shall be our dampnacion. **1652** Gaule *Magastrom.* xxvi, Yea, they fear not to teach most pernicious heresies and infidelities.

2. In general sense: Disbelief, incredulity.

1579 Lyly *Euphues* (Arb.) 171, I meane not to wast winde in prouing that, which thine infidelytie will not permit thee to beleeue. **1642** Fuller *Holy & Prof. St.* iv. xviii. 335 After his death, how did men struggle to keep him alive in their reports?.. partly out of infidelity that his death could be true. **1853** Kane *Grinnell Exp.* xxxvi. (1856) 325, I am, I fear, heterodox almost to infidelity as to the direct action of remedies.

3. Unfaithfulness or disloyalty to a person, e.g. to a sovereign, lord, master, friend, lover; esp., in mod. use, to a husband or wife, called more fully ***conjugal infidelity***.

1529 Latimer *Serm. Card* i, The king, seeing the great infidelity of this person, dischargeth this man of his office. **1548** Hall *Chron., Hen. VI* 128b, The Duke.. sente his letters to the kyng of Englande.. to purge and excuse himselfe, of his untruth and infidelitie. **1598** Barckley *Felic. Man* (1631) 636 Martiall finding the infidelitie and inconstancie of love and friendship giveth this counsell. **1673** R. Head *Canting Acad.* 120 A remarkable casual revenge on Tradewells infidelity. **1676** tr. *Guillatiere's Voy. Athens* 243 When Theseus, after his infidelity to Ariana, stole away Hellen. **1700** 'Castamore' (*title*) Conjugium Languens; or, the Natural, Civil, and Religious Mischiefs arising from conjugal infidelity and impunity. **1749** Fielding *Tom Jones* xviii. x, I told her.. that you had never been guilty of a single instance of infidelity to her since your seeing her in town. **1856** Froude *Hist. Eng.* xi. (Cab. ed.) II. 357 Whether provoked or not by infidelity on the part of Henry, [Anne's] own conduct had been singularly questionable. **1877** S. Cox *Salv. Mundi* Pref. 11 Any man's infidelity to his convictions.

b. With *an* and *pl.*: An instance or act of such unfaithfulness.

1714 *Spectator* No. 624 ¶5 The Infidelities on the one Part between the two Sexes, and the Caprices on the other. **1739** Cibber *Apol.* (1756) I. 95 That scene of Alexander, where the heroe throws himself at the feet of Statira for pardon of his past infidelities. **1876** Geo. Eliot *Dan. Der.* lxiii, When his mother accused him of being in love with a Jewess, any evasion seemed an infidelity.

†**4.** Untrustworthiness; an instance of this. *rare.*

1777 Burke *Let. to Fox* Wks. 1842 II. 389 My opinion of the infidelity of that conveyance [the post] hindered me from being particular. **1785** Jefferson *Let. to Izard* 26 Sept. in *Corr.* (1829) I. 325 The infidelities of the post offices, both of England and France, are not unknown to you.

'infidelize, *v.* [f. infidel + -ize.]

1. *trans.* To render infidel.

1836 *Blackw. Mag.* XL. 591 The work of infidelizing a country is then more than half done. **1847** Medwin *Shelley* II. 219 To infidelize the world.

2. *intr.* To play the infidel, profess infidelity.

1876 G. Meredith *Beauch. Career* III. i. 18 We shall see him.. infidelizing, republicanizing, scandalizing his class and his country.

'infidelly, *adv. rare.* [f. infidel *a.* + -ly².] In an infidel or unbelieving way.

1844 *Fraser's Mag.* XXIX. 143 By this education the religious nature of man is turned.. by a fried against himself to consume him! —— Infidelly-religious, revolutionary principles!

†**infidous,** *a. Obs. rare.* [f. L. *infīd-us* + -ous; cf. infide.] Unfaithful; faithless.

1656 in Blount *Glossogr.* **1657** Tomlinson *Renou's Disp.* 572 Tabaxir, which his infidous Interpreter Clusius calls his Spodium.

infield, in-field ('ɪnfiːld), *sb.* and *adv.* [f. in *adv.* + field *sb.*]

A. *sb.* **1. a.** The land of a farm which lies around or near the homestead, as opposed to the outlying parts, which are usually on higher ground and may consist of moorland; hence, arable land as opposed to pasture; land regularly manured and cropped. ***infield and outfield***, a system of husbandry which confines manuring and tillage to the infield land.

1733 P. Lindsay *Interest Scot.* 37 When we break up one Field for Tillage, if we left out another for Hay or Pasture in good Condition, the unfrugal Practice of Outfield and Infield would be at an End, every Part of a Farm would in its Turn produce equally plentiful Crops of Grain or Grass. **1765** A. Dickson *Treat. Agric.* (ed. 2) 109 *note*, The arable land in Scotland is divided into infield and outfield. The infield is the land upon which, from time immemorial, the whole dung made in the farm has been laid. **1820** Scott *Monast.* i, The part of the township properly arable, and kept as such continually under the plough, was called *in-field*. **1848** Hepburn in *Proc. Berw. Nat. Club* II. No. 6. 272 The wretched system of agriculture, called *infield* and *outfield*, which prevailed throughout the greater part of last century. **1856** Olmsted *Slave States* 270 The cultivated land was divided into 'in-fields' and 'out-fields'; the former, being those nearest the central establishment, received all the manure that was made, and were planted with tobacco.

b. *attrib.*, as ***infield corn, ground, land.*** (This was prob. the original use.)

1606 *Sc. Acts Jas. VI*, c. 8 (Jam.) The croft infield corne [to be teynded] at ane tyme, the beere at ane vther tyme, and the outfield corne at the third tyme. **1765** A. Dickson *Treat. Agric.* (ed. 2) 465 All land called infield land, has a mixture of this kind of soil in its composition. **1791** *Act 31 Geo. III*, c. 92 *title*, An Act for.. inclosing a certain large open Tract of Land within the Manor of Holy Island.. and for extinguishing the Right of Common upon the ancient Infield Lands within the said Island. *a* **1800** in *Edinb. Rev.* CLXVIII. 196 The rich infield ground produced spontaneously rib-grass, white, yellow, and red clover. **1820** Scott *Monast.* xiii, There was but a trifling quantity of arable or infield land attached to it.

2. A field adjacent to the farmhouse or grange; a home field.

1875 Sir G. W. Dasent *Vikings* II. 165 As they left the in-fields, near the grange [etc.].

3. *Baseball.* **a.** That part of the field enclosed within the base-lines; the diamond. **b.** The four fielders placed on the boundaries of the in-field, i.e. the three base-men and the short-stop.

1867 H. Chadwick *Base Ball Player's Bk. Reference* 138 The In-Field.—That portion of the field within the base lines. **1897** *Encycl. Sport* I. 76/1 Short Stop.. is also called upon to back up all the positions of the in-field. **1906** *Spalding's Base Ball Guide* 15 The 'infield' team comprising the three base players and short stop. **1912** C. Mathewson *Pitching in a Pinch* ii. 23 Devoe beat out an infield hit. **1970** *New Yorker* 3 Oct. 32/1 Soon there will be nobody around who remembers muddy infields.

4. *Cricket.* **a.** The part of the playing area near the wicket; *collect.*, the fieldsmen stationed there (as opposed to the outfield *sb.*). **b.** = infieldsman.

1898 G. Giffen *With Bat & Ball* vii. 99 In the in-field the soil had been well watered and was fairly hard... But what of the out-field? *Ibid.* xi. 188 He is a brilliant in-field. **1954** A. G. Moyes *Austral. Batsmen* iii. 46 Few bowlers.. relish seeing the ball flying back over their heads, forcing them to weaken the in-field to stop the fours. **1960** E. W. Swanton *W. Indies Revisited* vii. 167 May's in-field was spread so deep for Sobers as to invite him to take a single almost anywhere.

5. *U.S.* The area enclosed by a race-track. Also *attrib.*

1923 E. Hemingway *Three Stories & Ten Poems* 36 You could see them [*sc.* horses] way off across the infield all in a bunch starting on the first swing like a lot of little toy horses. **1929** —— *Farewell to Arms* xx. 138 We.. walked across the infield and then across the smooth thick turf of the course to the paddock. **1934** in B. A. Botkin *Treas. S. Folklore* (1949) ii. iv. 404 His cry is echoed by a mighty 'They're off' from the packed stands and the infield crowd. *Ibid.* 407 They buried Black Gold there in the infield of the track. **1966** *Publ. Amer. Dial. Soc.* 1964 xlii. 6 *Infield*, area inside the racing course.

B. *adv.* In or towards the centre of a playing-field.

1959 *Times* 18 Feb. 5/1 Evans.. came infield and burst through the centre. **1960** V. Jenkins *Lions Down Under* viii. 116 A brilliant try by Malcolm Thomas, who ran down the touch-line.. before cutting in-field to touch down under the posts.

in'field, *v.* [f. in-² + field *sb.* Cf. *impark.*] *trans.* 'To inclose, as a field' (Webster, 1856).

infielder, in-fielder ('ɪn,fiːldə(r)). [f. infield *sb.* + -er¹.] **1.** *Baseball.* One of the players on the in-field.

1867 H. Chadwick *Base Ball Player's Bk. of Ref.* 138 The in-fielders include the first six players of a nine. **1897** *Encycl. Sport* I. 76/2 Third Baseman.. must be more on the alert.. than the other in-fielders. **1905** *McClure's Mag.* June 123/2 Hutchinson, an in-fielder, had played in the same league with Johnson. **1967** *Boston Sunday Herald* (TV Mag.) 7-13 May 12/1 He hit a line drive right at the pile of baseballs, causing them to scatter in all directions. Every infielder came up with a different ball.

2. *Cricket.* = next.

1927 M. A. Noble *Those 'Ashes'* 193 Macartney.. was going very quickly, picking out the gaps in the field or lofting the ball over the heads of the in-fielders. **1930** C. V. Grimmett *Getting Wickets* ii. 49 When a new batsman comes in, have your in-fielders close enough to save the singles.

in-fieldsman ('ɪn,fiːldzmən). *Cricket.* [f. in *adv.* + fieldsman.] A fieldsman placed close to the wicket.

1910 *Westm. Gaz.* 19 Mar. 18/1 If the ball got past the in-fieldsmen there were men on the boundary to save the four. **1928** *Daily Tel.* 17 July 17/5 Nor was Freeman the only bowler who had his infieldsman too far away.

in fieri: see fieri.

in'fight, *v.* [f. in-¹ + fight *v.*, after L. *impugnāre.*] †**1.** *trans.* To fight against, attack, assail. *Obs. rare.*

a **1300** *E.E. Psalter* xxxiv. 1 Over-come þe in-fightand me [L. *impugnantes*, OE. ða on-fehtendan]. *Ibid.* cxix. 7 Þai in-faght [L. *impugnabant*] me self-willi.

2. To fight or box at close quarters; also *fig.* and *transf.* (cf. next).

1916 J. B. Cooper *Coo-oo-ee* xi. 156 Jack glued his chin to his chest and 'smothered', watching his opportunity to in-fight. **1966** T. Pynchon *Crying of Lot 49* vi. 164 We face this anarchy of jealous German princes, hundreds of them scheming, counter-scheming, infighting.

'in-,fighting, *vbl. sb.* [f. in *adv.* + fighting *vbl. sb.*] In pugilism: Fighting or boxing at close quarters; the practice of getting close up to an opponent: cf. quot. 1812 in in *adv.* 3. So **'in-,fighter,** a boxer who practises this method. Also *fig.* and *transf.*

1812 *Sporting Mag.* XXXIX. 19 It would not be too much to denominate him as good an in-fighter. **1816** *Ibid.* XLVII. 256 The combat lasted one hour and fifty minutes all at in-fighting. **1886** D. C. Murray *1st Person Sing.* xxviii. 201 There are otherwise admirable boxers who know nothing of what is called 'in-fighting'... Once get inside the guard and

they go to pieces. **1907** J. London *Iron Heel* ii. 38 He was unused to this fierce 'infighting', as Ernest called it. **1928** L. Woolley *Sumerians* ii. 52 Two [spears] have plain butts and are intended for in-fighting. **1930** H. G. Wells *Autocracy of Mr. Parham* iv. i. 274 The temperament and tradition of both navies disposed them for attack and in-fighting. **1936** G. B. Shaw *Millionairess* iv. 193 *Epifania*. You are two stone heavier than I; and I cannot keep my head at infighting as you can. **1960** Auden *Homage to Clio* 79 Untrained in a ruthless Verbal in-fighting. **1970** W. Smith *Gold Mine* xxxi. 78 She would use even the dirtiest in-fighting to see that Rod was not overlooked. **1972** *Listener* 24 Aug. 241/1 The cheerful in-fighting that characterizes intellectual exchange between clinician and medical scientist. **1973** *Time* 25 June 38/2 Inside the Politburo, he is known as a tough infighter.

†**in'figure**, *v. Obs. rare.* [f. L. type **infigūrāre* (see in-² and figure *v.*) = OF. *enfigurer*, It. *infigurare*.]

1. *trans.* To represent in or by a figure or emblem.

1606 Holland *Sueton.* 81 *marg.*, Doues [are] consecrate to Venus from whence the Iulij are descended. By them therefore..was infigured perpetuall felicitie to that name and familie. **1621** Lady M. Wroth *Urania* 274 Your dearest selfe remaines infigured in my chastest breast.

2. To give figure or form to.

1611 Florio, *Infigurare*, to infigure, to shapen.

in'figured, *ppl. a.* Also en-. [f. in-², en-¹ + figured. Cf. F. *infiguré*.] Marked or adorned with figures.

1611 Cotgr., *Infiguré*, infigured, figured. *a* **1649** Drumm. of Hawth. *Poems* Wks. (1711) 38/1 Like world's bright eye [the sun], That once each year surveyes all earth and sky,.. Hurries to both the poles, and moveth even In the infigur'd circle of the heaven. **1774** *Poetry* in *Ann. Reg.* 211 Behold The tissued vestment of enfigur'd gold.

infile, obs. variant of enfile *v.*

infill (ɪn'fɪl), *v.* [f. in-¹ + fill *v.*] *trans.* To fill within or internally. Also *intr.*

1880 Mrs. Whitney *Odd or Even?* ix. 79 Pure atmosphere and the glory that infilled it. **1888** J. Ellis *New Christianity* ii. 42 The nobler works of God, which are infilled with life to every fibre. **1958** *Antiquity* XXXII. 110 This had been infilled with weathered flints. **1971** *Farmer & Stockbreeder* 23 Feb. 39/1 He is renovating the drainage system, in-filling and levelling, so 230 acres can be ploughed. **1971** P. Gresswell *Environment* 133 It is possible to 'infill' between two distant houses. **1972** *Daily Tel.* 23 May 15/4 Get the outline first, with basic shrubs... Then 'infill' with smaller shrubs and roses. **1973** *Nature* 23 Mar. 227/1 Channels, cut by streams rejuvenated during regression of the sea, have been infilled by alluvial and terrestrial clastics.

infill ('ɪnfɪl), *sb.* = infilling *vbl. sb.* (various senses).

1939 *Geogr. Jrnl.* Jan. 56 While it is not theoretically impossible for great stretches of the present flood-plain to have been formerly aggraded..followed by removal of the infil [*sic*]..such an explanation involves difficulties. **1958** *Antiquity* XXXII. 110 The basis of the infill of the enclosure. **1958** *Archit. Rev.* CXXIII. 10/2 Infill panels of brick, precast concrete or coloured glass. **1966** J. S. Cox *Illustr. Dict. Hairdressing* 83/1 *Infill*, (1) The dressed hair enclosed within a specified area. (2) Knotting hair within a specified area. **1969** *New Scientist* 15 May 352/3 Sound absorbing infill is there primarily for heat and fire resistance. **1970** *Observer* 15 Mar. 7/6 Local landowners..stand to make small fortunes out of selling their acres to the infill excavators. *Ibid.*, Welsh infill could not be used on the M4. **1971** *New Scientist* 6 May 317/1 The full four-runway airport will undoubtedly need more infill than could be provided from..dredging.

infilled ('ɪnˌfɪld), *ppl. a.* [in *adv.* 11 b: see *fill in.*] Filled in, filled up (of a vacant space).

1849 Murchison *Siluria* i. (1867) 10 Orthoceratites,.. known to be the infilled borings of Annelids and small Crustacea. **1887** *Geol. Mag.* 89 The impressions have been produced by the infilled tracks and burrowings of marine animals.

'**inˌfilling**, *vbl. sb.* [in *adv.* 11 c: cf. prec.] The action of filling in (a vacant space); that which is used to fill up a hole or cavity. Also *fig.*

1871 S. Sharp in *Archæol.* XLIII. 122 The fragments [of pottery]..were wheeled away and buried with the infilling. **1880** *Libr. Univ. Knowl.* (U.S.) VI. 584 Various theories have been proposed to account for the infilling of mineral veins. **1895** J. MacNeil *Spirit-Filled Life* xiv. 100 The Lord Jesus is prepared to grant us a fresh Infilling, a 'refilling' of The Holy Ghost. **1958** *Times Rev. Industry* May 46/1 Aluminium curtain walling in conjunction with a steel framed building..reduces labour charges..incurred by the use of the normal masonry infilling. **1961** *Guardian* 27 May 5/5 In its earliest forms, watercolour was little more than an infilling for sketches in ink and bistre. **1962** *Listener* 1 Feb. 228/3 Those coloured earths which in French gardens so often provide the infilling for *broderies*. **1970** *Cabinet Maker & Retail Furnisher* 30 Oct. 201/2 Infillings of horse hair.. and hand-springing are used exclusively. **1972** L. Alcock *By South Cadbury* viii. 178 A plausible reconstruction of the building would suggest an infilling of wattle and daub for the walls.

b. *spec.* in *Town Planning.*

1943 Forshaw & Abercrombie *County of London Plan* 35 Five types of units of dispersed industrial population: i. Infilling of gaps in incomplete schemes within the County. **1944** P. Abercrombie *Greater London Plan 1944* 35 A rounding off of the communities by infilling on the backlands and vacant frontages. **1964** *Daily Tel.* 17 Mar. 23/2 No part of his plan could possibly be regarded as infilling. By which they meant one or at most two houses pushed into existing gaps. **1971** P. Gresswell *Environment* 134 Infilling in villages is in many cases both inevitable and desirable. **1974** *Times* 5 Feb. 10 New building, other than infilling, was more extensive on the mainland.

in'film, *v.* [f. in-² + film *v.*] *trans.* 'To cover with a film; to coat thinly' (Webster, 1864).

infilter (ɪn'fɪltə(r)), *v.* [f. in *adv.* + filter *v.*, or ad. F. *infiltre-r* (Paré, 16th c.).] *trans.* = infiltrate *v.* 3.

a **1846** *Med. Jrnl.* cited in Worcester. **1875** Lyell *Princ. Geol.* I. ii. xvi. 364 The congelation of water infiltered into the porous mass. **1879** Rutley *Study Rocks* xiv. 287 The amygdaloids of calcspar which have been infiltered into the vesicles and crevices in basalts, long after their solidification.

infiltrate ('ɪnfɪltreɪt, ɪn'fɪltreɪt), *v.* [f. in-² + filtrate *v.*, perh. after F. *infiltrer* (Paré, 16th c.).]

1. *trans.* To introduce by filtration; to cause (a fluid) to permeate through pores or interstices.

1758 J. S. *Le Dran's Observ. Surg.* (1771) 83 In most of these Abscesses, the Pus seemed rather to be infiltrated than deposited. **1811** Pinkerton *Petral.* I. 537 Sands..which, by means of a calcareous juice which the sea infiltrates at that spot, harden gradually. **1854** tr. *Lamartine's Mem. Celebr. Char.* II. *Milton* 5 The air of Naples, which infiltrated itself through his veins. **1866** Rogers *Agric. & Prices* I. xv. 293 The tissues becoming disorganized, and the blood thereupon being infiltrated into them, dark blotches appear on the skin.

fig. **1876** Jas. Grant *One of the '600'* vi. 51 Love steals into the nature..infiltrating its sentiments..through every crevice of the being. **1885** R. W. Dixon *Hist. Ch. Eng.* III. 354 Into the body of..ancient matter he skilfully infiltrated a leaven of spurious additions.

2. To pass into or permeate by filtration; to pass through the pores or interstices of (a substance). Freq. in pass. ***infiltrated with*** (rarely ***by***).

1758 J. S. *Le Dran's Observ. Surg.* (1771) 141 Purulent Serum..with which the Parts were infiltrated. **1867** J. Hogg *Microsc.* i. ii. 67 As this infiltrates the osseous substance. **1869** *Eng. Mech.* 10 Dec. 294/2 The blood.. infiltrates the loose tissue. **1878** Huxley *Physiogr.* 225 Carbonized remains, often infiltrated with mineral matter.

fig. **1884** *Expositor* Dec. 457 Abstractions infiltrated with analogical conceptions.

3. *intr.* To pass through or into a substance by filtration; to percolate through pores or interstices.

1828 in Webster. **1851** Carpenter *Man. Phys.* (ed. 2) 362 The watery part of the blood from the small vessels..may either infiltrate into the areolar tissue, or it may be poured into some neighbouring serous cavity. **1856** Mrs. Browning *Aur. Leigh* ii. 1059 Death's black dust.. Infiltrated through every secret fold Of this sealed letter.

fig. **1858** J. Martineau *Stud. Chr.* 24 The Greek element of thought..infiltrating through the theosophy of Alexandria. **1861** Sir J. K. Shuttleworth *Let. to Earl Granville* 51 Education infiltrates from the upper and governing classes to the lower.

4. *Mil. trans.* and *intr.* To penetrate (enemy lines) by the gradual or surreptitious movement of small numbers of troops; to move (one's own troops) surreptitiously into the enemy's lines. Also *fig.*, esp. for the purpose of political subversion.

1934 in Webster. **1944** *Times* 1 Apr. 8/1 Skilfully infiltrating through the chain of Japanese outposts and garrisons, the force penetrated hostile territory as far as the Shan States. **1956** A. H. Compton *Atomic Quest* 125 Some of its branches had been infiltrated by Communists. **1958** [see fifth column]. **1972** *Daily Tel.* (Colour Suppl.) 21 Jan. 27/1 There CIA agents succeeded in infiltrating several of its groups. **1972** *Daily Tel.* 30 Mar. 4/6 Terrorist groups started infiltrating from neighbouring African States. **1972** *Sunday Express* 21 May 17/5 Security men fear that Moscow would take the chance to infiltrate agents into Britain. **1972** *Daily Tel.* 19 June 2/1, I was paid..about £500 for infiltrating the IRA network in London. **1974** *Ibid.* (Colour Suppl.) 1 Mar. 7/2 Equally insidious is the way in which Communists..are infiltrated into the sphere of education.

in'filtrate, *sb.* [f. prec.: cf. filtrate *sb.*] An infiltrated substance; an infiltration.

In mod. Dicts.

infiltrated ('ɪn-, ɪn'fɪltreɪtɪd), *ppl. a.* [f. prec. vb. + -ed¹.] **a.** Permeated with some substance.

1868 W. B. Carpenter in *Sci. Opin.* (1869) 6 Jan. 175/1 The infiltrated condition of those [sponges] previously obtained. **1879** *St. George's Hosp. Rep.* IX. 305 Free incisions into infiltrated parts.

b. Introduced by infiltration.

1873 T. H. Green *Introd. Pathol.* (ed. 2) 58 The pressure exercised by the infiltrated fat produces considerable anæmia of the organ. **1884** Bower & Scott *De Bary's Phaner.* 106 This thickening of the membrane contains..a large quantity of calcium carbonate..as a homogeneous infiltrated mass.

fig. **1876** Geo. Eliot *Dan. Der.* iv. xxviii, All the infiltrated influences of disregarded religious teaching.

infiltrating, *ppl. a.* [f. as prec. + -ing².] That infiltrates; percolating, permeating.

1849 Dana *Geol.* v. (1850) 317 The infiltrating fluid may have contained silica. **1872** —— *Corals* ii. 155 The agency of infiltrating waters. **1884** Bower & Scott *De Bary's Phaner.* 509 The origin of the infiltrating substances.

infiltration (ɪnfɪl'treɪʃən). [n. of action from infiltrate *v.*; perh. a. F. *infiltration* (16th c.).]

1. The action or process of infiltrating; percolation. **a.** In *Physics* and *Geol.*, of water or mineral substances in solution.

1796 Kirwan *Elem. Min.* (ed. 2) I. 427 The percolation or infiltration of the particles. *Ibid.* 428 The infiltration of sea-water through lavas. **1822** J. Flint *Lett. Amer.* 102 The soil is..broken on the surface by funnel-shaped hollows... These inverted cones are evidently excavated by the infiltration of water. **1851-6** Woodward *Mollusca* 74 The phragmocone..owes its preservation to the infiltration of calc-spar. **1876** Page *Adv. Text-bk. Geol.* iii. 70 Waters of infiltration always contain less or more of these Salts.

b. *Physiol.* and *Path.*, of fluids (esp. blood or fat) which penetrate the tissues.

1853 Kane *Grinnell Exp.* xvii. (1856) 129 The infiltration of fatty matter is rather alarming. **1866** A. Flint *Princ. Med.* (1880) 54 Infiltration is a term ordinarily applied to the deposition of some material in or between the tissue-elements. **1874** Van Buren *Dis. Genit. Org.* 6 Contusions involving the urethra may lead to infiltration of urine.

c. *fig.* of immaterial elements or influences, as ideas, opinions, etc.

1840 Mill *Diss. & Disc.* (1859) I. *Bentham* 374 Principle after principle of those propounded by him is..making its way by infiltration into the understandings most shut against his influence. **1867** —— *Inaug. Addr. St. Andrews* (People's ed.) 8 Reason..is beginning to find its way by gradual infiltration even into English schools. **1875** Maine *Hist. Inst.* viii. 235 The infiltration of tribal ideas.

d. The gradual penetration of one people into another.

1904 *Westm. Gaz.* 14 Nov. 5/1 In the interior of the Empire the French work of gradual 'infiltration' will proceed by not less efficacious means. **1927** Peake & Fleure *Priests & Kings* 54 As time went on there seems to have been an ever-increasing infiltration of Southern Steppe-folk from the desert. **1930** J. L. Myres *Who were the Greeks?* ii. 55 The southward infiltration of Albanian and Slav into districts formerly Romanized.

e. *Mil.* The gradual or surreptitious penetration of enemy lines by small numbers of troops.

1930 *Economist* 16 Aug. 313/1 They thus succeeded..in reaching the outlying quarters of Peshawar, albeit in small numbers, by a process of nocturnal 'infiltration'. **1933** B. H. L. Hart *Future of Infantry* 27 We profited from the lesson taught us by the remarkable success, at our expense, of the new infiltration or soft spot tactics in..1918. **1967** *N.Y. Times* (Internat. Ed.) 11-12 Feb. 1/6 At a background briefing early in November, the American command made available infiltration figures covering the year through Sept. 30.

f. *fig.* (Cf. infiltrate *v.* 4.)

1940 *Economist* 15 June 1036/1 The Nazis have developed the technique of infiltration to such a pitch that [etc.]. **1941** *Ann. Reg. 1940* 209 Great uneasiness was caused in the country by the infiltration..of thousands of able-bodied young Germans in the guise of tourists. **1949** Koestler *Promise & Fulfilment* ii. v. 281, I wonder whether an American don is the right match for the propaganda and infiltration experts of the Soviet Union. **1958** *Times* 20 Jan. 5/7 Alleged Communist infiltration into the Oxford branch of the National Union of Railwaymen. **1973** P. Evans *Bodyguard Man* v. 44 You're an ex-Special Branch man, supposedly a professional at infiltration techniques.

2. The action of infiltrating a substance with something; the process, fact, or condition of being infiltrated or permeated; esp. in *Path.*

1830 Herschel *Stud. Nat. Phil.* 61 Fluids..keep the country in a constant state of infiltration from below upwards. **1873** T. H. Green *Introd. Pathol.* (ed. 2) 51 Fatty Infiltration—which is often described as 'fatty degeneration'—consists in the infiltration of the tissues with fat, which is deposited in them from the blood.

3. An infiltrated deposit.

a **1812** Kirwan (Webster 1828) Calcareous infiltrations filling the cavities of other stones. **1815** Bakewell *Introd. Geol.* 21 This he attributes to a calcareous infiltration. **1898** J. Hutchinson *Archives Surg.* IX. 317 The cells composing the infiltration are round or oval in shape.

fig. **1882** Child *Ballads* i. xv. 179/2 This passage is clearly an infiltration from a different story.

4. *attrib.* and *Comb.* **infiltration anæsthesia**, anæsthetization of an area by the injection into it of a local anæsthetic; **infiltration capacity**, the maximum rate at which soil in a given condition can absorb water; **infiltration rate**, the rate at which soil absorbs water; infiltration capacity.

1897 *Med. Rec.* LI. 44/1 (*heading*) The method of *infiltration anæsthesia: its technique and..advantages. *Ibid.* 45/2 Cocaine anæsthesia lasting from two to five minutes, infiltration anæsthesia from fifteen to twenty minutes. **1958** J. H. Burn *Lect. Notes Pharmacol.* (ed. 5) 56 Lignocaine..is a useful anaesthetic for producing nerve block and for infiltration anaesthesia. **1933** R. E. Horton in *Trans. Amer. Geophysical Union* XIV. 446 '*Infiltration-capacity' will be used to describe the maximum rate at which rain can be absorbed by a given soil when in a given condition. **1952** *Proc. Soil Sci. Soc. Amer.* XVI. 85/2 The term 'infiltration capacity'..has been an object of some controversy because it implies that an extensity is involved, whereas an intensity such as *infiltration rate* would be more apt. **1882** Geikie *Text-bk. Geol.* ii. ii. 72 The relation.. between these *infiltration products and the decomposition of the surrounding mass. **1940** *Proc. Soil Sci. Soc. Amer.* V. 400/2 It is unfortunate that the terms 'infiltration-capacity' and '*infiltration rates' have sometimes been confused... There may be an infinite variety of rates but there is only one capacity at a particular time for a particular soil. **1952** *Ibid.* XVI. 88/1 Infiltration rate (soil). The maximum rate at which soil, in a given condition at a given time, can absorb rain. **1957** *Soil Sci.* LXXXVII. 338 After infiltration begins, increasing the initial moisture content reduces the

infiltration rate. **1881** RAYMOND *Mining Gloss.*, **Infiltration-theory*, the theory that a vein was filled by the infiltration of mineral solutions. **1888** *Times* in *Pall Mall G.* 1 Oct. 4/1 This infiltration theory had necessarily to come under Mr. Judd's consideration.

in'filtrative, *a. rare.* [f. as prec. + -IVE.] Of the nature of, or productive of, infiltration.

1856 KANE *Arct. Expl.* I. xx. 242 The expansion of the ice after the contraction of low temperatures, and the infiltrative or endosmometric changes thus induced.

infiltrator ('ɪnfɪltreɪtə(r)). [f. INFILTRATE *v.* + -OR.] One who infiltrates (esp. in sense 4 of the vb.).

1944 *Infantry Jrnl.* (U.S.) May 28 Our men had orders not to leave the lines in case of any infiltration, because our rear elements would take care of the infiltrators. **1949** KOESTLER *Promise & Fulfilment* I. xv. 165 Arab infiltrators from neighbouring countries were exercising 'considerable administrative control' in Samaria. **1953** *Wall St. Jrnl.* 1 Sept. 1/3 Police already have arrested nearly 4,000 infiltrators from the Soviet zone. **1957** L. F. R. WILLIAMS *State of Israel* x. 200 The 'economic infiltrators' who slip across [the frontier] to harvest crops on fields once their own. **1959** *Economist* 27 June 1154/1 The much greater confidence existing at Standard between union officials, shop stewards and the rank and file..is always the first target of communist infiltrators on the spot. **1970** *Guardian* 2 May 11/5 The Mekong..seldom poses problems to Communist infiltrators. They cross by raft or skiff at night.

infiltrometer (ɪnfɪl'trɒmɪtə(r)). [f. INFILTR(ATION + -OMETER.] An apparatus for measuring the rate at which soil can absorb water.

1940 P. B. ROWE *Construction, Operation & Use of North Fork Infiltrometer* (U.S. Dept. Agric.) 1 Laboratory tests of the infiltrometer and the infiltration studies in which it has been employed since it was first developed in 1934 indicate that it affords a practical and reliable means of measuring the infiltration capacity of soils under natural field conditions. **1955** R. K. FREVERT et al. *Soil & Water Conservation Engin.* iii. 47 Infiltrometers using simulated rainfall cover areas varying from less than 2 to nearly 500 square feet. **1971** *Agronomy Jrnl.* LXIII. 306/2 Ring infiltrometer tests were made in the spring and fall.

‖**infima species** ('ɪnfɪmə 'spiːʃiːz). Pl. **infimæ species.** [f. L. *infima* nom. fem. of *infimus* lowest (see INFIMOUS *a.*) + SPECIES *sb.*] The lowest species of a classification or division; *concr.*, an 'infimous' person (? *obs.*).

1645 J. HOWELL *Lett.* I. xii. 23 Being contented to be the *infima species*, the lowest in the predicament of your frends. **1843** MILL *Logic* II. III. xxii. 134 Such generalizations.. ought to be grounded upon an examination of all the *infimæ species* comprehended in them. **1961** T. LANDAU *Encycl. Librarianship* (ed. 2) 283/1 Any one species may, in its turn, be capable of further division into species, when for that purpose it becomes a genus—and so on down to the most minute species required, the *infima species*.

†**'infimate,** *sb. Obs. rare.* [ad. L. *īnfimāt-is* (Plautus) one of the lowest, f. *infimus* lowest, INFIMOUS; after OPTIMATE.] One of the lowest class.

1733 TULL *Horse-Hoing Husb.* Pref. 7 He will not suffer, that the Possessors of Land shall be trampled on by Servants and Labourers, or other Infimates of the Country.

†**'infimate,** *v. Obs. rare.* [f. ppl. stem of L. *infimāre* to make low, f. *infim-us* lowest, INFIMOUS.] *trans.* To make low or base; to degrade, debase. Hence **infimating** *ppl. a.*, debasing.

a **1641** BP. MOUNTAGU *Acts & Mon.* (1642) 394 Popular novellising factionists and infimating sectaries..who through colour of piety trouble all.

in'fimity. *nonce-wd.* [ad. L. *infimitās* lowness, f. *infim-us*; see next; in mod.F. *infimité*.] The quality of being 'infimous'; *concr.* an 'infimous' person.

1885 *Sat. Rev.* 28 Mar. 410/2 Mediocrities, or rather infimities, like those who crowd the French chamber.

†**'infimous,** *a. Obs.* [f. L. *infimus* (superl. of *inferus*) lowest + -OUS.] Very low or base; basest.

1613 DANIEL *Coll. Hist. Eng.* 172 A man risen by subtletie and his tongue from infimous condition. **1627** W. SCLATER *Exp. 2 Thess.* (1629) 159 They vowed to suffer losse, I say not of life, but of the infimous goods of fortune, for the cause of the Gospel. **1663** WOOD *Life* 15 June (O.H.S.) I. 476 A yong heire, who valuing not his father's labours, because of his ignorance, put most of his papers..to infimous uses.

infimum (ɪn'faɪməm). *Math.* [L., = lowest part, neut. of *infimus* lowest (see INFIMA SPECIES).] The largest number that is less than or equal to each of a given set of real numbers; an analogous quantity for a subset of any other ordered set.

1940 G. BIRKHOFF *Lattice Theory* ii. 16 We shall use the words 'supremum' and 'sup' synonymously with l.u.b.; similarly, we shall use 'infimum', and 'inf', and 'common part' synonymously with gr.l.b. **1949** S. LEFSCHETZ *Introd. Topology* i. 27 We shall also use on occasion the supremum and infimum of a nonvoid set *A* of real numbers, written sup *A*, inf *A*. **1964** W. J. PERVIN *Found. Gen. Topology* i. 15 In the natural ordering for the set of natural numbers, 2 is the infimum of the set of even numbers. In the case of the ordering < 1, 3, 5, . . . ; . . . , 6, 4, 2 >, there is no infimum to the set of even numbers even though they are bounded below. *Ibid.*, The rational numbers ordered by size are not order-complete, since the subset consisting of all rationals which are positive and have squares greater than 2 does not have an infimum, even though it is bounded below by 0. **1968** E. T. COPSON *Metric Spaces* i. 14 The infimum of a subset *A* is its greatest lower bound, and is denoted by inf *A*.

†**in'final,** *a. Obs. rare.* [f. IN-[3] + L. *fīn-is* end + -AL[1]: cf. *final*.] = INFINITE.

1503 HAWES *Examp. Virt.* v. xxxi, Wo worth infynall payne and dystresse. **1509** —— *Past. Pleas.* xlv. (Percy Soc.) 219 Praye to thy swete sonne whiche is infinall.

in fine, *adv. phr.* Finally, in short, to sum up: see FINE *sb.*[1]

infinitant (ɪn'fɪnɪtənt), *a. Logic.* [ad. Schol.L. *infīnītāns*, pres. pple. of *infīnītāre* to INFINITATE.] That infinitates; applied to a sign of negation when joined to a term. See INFINITE *a.* 8.

infinitary (ɪn'fɪnɪtərɪ), *a. Math.* [= Ger. *infinitär*, as in *infinitärkalkul* 'infinitary calculus' (Du Bois Raymond): see -ARY[1].] Relating to infinity, or to an infinite value of a quantity; as ***infinitary property*** of a function, i.e. one which the function has when the variable becomes infinite.

infinitate (ɪn'fɪnɪteɪt), *v.* [f. ppl. stem of Schol.L. *infīnītāre* (Abelard *Dialectica*, Wks., Paris 1836, 225), f. *infīnīt-us* INFINITE: see -ATE[3].] *trans.* To render infinite; in *Logic*, to make (a positive concept, term, or predicate) 'infinite' (see INFINITE *a.* 8) or indefinite in extent, by prefixing a negative. Hence **in'finitated** *ppl. a.*

1864 BOWEN *Logic* vi. 152 Either *A*, or its Infinitated correlative, *not-A*, must belong to everything, and must include everything. *Ibid.* 153 A negative Judgment can always be changed in Form to an affirmative, or an affirmative to a negative, simply by Infinitating one of its Terms, or by dropping its Infinitation. **1867** ATWATER *Logic* 61 Hence such purely Negative Conceptions are sometimes classed by logicians as Infinitated Conceptions.

infinitation (ɪnfɪnɪ'teɪʃən). *Logic.* [ad. Schol.L. *infīnītātio* (Abelard *Dialectica* 225), n. of action from *infīnītāre*: see prec.] The action of infinitating or making 'infinite'; the condition of being infinitated; hence, applied to one of the forms of immediate inference, also called *permutation* or *obversion*, in which one term, usually the predicate, of the original proposition is made negative.

1652 URQUHART *Jewel* Wks. (1834) 205 For the affirmation, negation, and infinitation of propositions. **1864** [see prec.]. **1867** FOWLER *Deduct. Logic* III. ii. 77 The same inference is sometimes called Infinitation, from the Nomen Infinitum, or, more properly, Nomen Indefinitum (not-Y, as the contradictory of Y), which is employed as the predicate. **1867** ATWATER *Logic* 71 [Division] must not be *a priori*, or by Infinitation.

infinite ('ɪnfɪnɪt), *a.* (*adv.*) and *sb.* Forms: 4-6 infynyt(e, 4-7 infinit, (5 infenite, 6 infinyte, infynit(e, *Sc.* infineit), 4- infinite. [ad. L. *infīnīt-us* unbounded, unlimited, f. *in-* (IN-[3]) + *fīnīt-us* FINITE; perh. orig. through OF. *infinit, -ite* (13th c. in Hatz.-Darm.), later *infini* (Oresme, 14th c.). In hymns sometimes rimed with (-aɪt).]

A. *adj.*

1. a. Having no limit or end (real or assignable); boundless, unlimited, endless; immeasurably great in extent, duration, or other respect. Chiefly of God or His attributes; also of space, time, etc., in which it passes into the mathematical use (4 b).

1413 *Pilgr. Sowle* (Caxton) v. i. (1859) 71 The largenes therof may not be comprehended by thought of mannes wytte; for it is Infynyte. **1477** EARL RIVERS (Caxton) *Dictes* 1 Releued by thynfynyte grace & goodnes of our said lord. **1535** COVERDALE *Ps.* cxlvi[i]. 5 Greate is oure Lorde, and greate is his power, yee his wyszdome is infinite. **1557** N. T. (Genev.) Ep. *iij, That he might shewe more manifestly his goodnes and infinit mercie among men. **1651** HOBBES *Leviath.* I. iii. (1886) 22 No man can have in his mind an image of infinite magnitude; nor conceive infinite swiftness, infinite time, or infinite force, or infinite power. **1754** EDWARDS *Freed. Will* I. iv. 22 That Power is not Infinite; and so goes not beyond certain Limits. **1811** HEBER *Hymn*, Lord of mercy and of might..Maker, Teacher, Infinite; Jesus, hear and save! **1849** FROUDE *Nemesis Faith* 130 The doctrine of the infinite divisibility of matter must be called in to help you in your dividings. **1860** TYNDALL *Glac.* I. ii. 15 An infinite series of images of the candle will be seen.

b. In loose or hyperbolical sense: Indefinitely or exceedingly great; exceeding measurement or calculation; immense, vast.

c **1385** CHAUCER *L.G.W.* 1675 *Hypsip.*, Why lykede me.. of thyn tunge the infynyt graciousnesse. *c* **1440** *Gesta Rom.* I. xxxii. 122 (Harl. MS.) He shulde wed hir with goodis infinite. **1527** R. THORNE in Hakluyt *Voy.* (1589) 255 Infinite number of Iewes that were expelled out of Castill. **1596** SHAKS. *Merch. V.* I. i. 114 Gratiano speakes an infinite deale of nothing. **1602** —— *Ham.* II. ii. 316 What a piece of worke is a man! how Noble in Reason? how infinite in faculty? **1748** *Anson's Voy.* Introd., Of infinite importance to the commercial and sea-faring part of mankind. **1857** MAURICE *Ep. St. John* xvii. 281 We owe them infinite thanks for it. **1865** R. W. DALE *Jew. Temp.* xxi. (1877) 233 A truth this of infinite importance.

†**c.** Occupying an indefinitely long time; immensely long, very tedious, 'endless'. (Used predicatively, with inf. or with personal subj.: cf. *long*.) *Obs.*

1575-85 ABP. SANDYS *Serm.* (Parker Soc.) 26 It were infinite to recite what huge sums of money they have.. gathered. **1608** TOPSELL *Serpents* (1658) 667 All which..I will (lest I should seem to be infinite) passe over with silence. **1620** E. BLOUNT *Horæ Subs.* 363, I dare walke no farther in this Labyrinth, for feare of growing too infinite. **1638** CHILLINGW. *Relig. Prot.* I. ii. §116. 97 Lastly, not to be infinite, it is taught by Mr. Knot himselfe, not in one page only..but all his Book over.

d. *infinite regress* (see quots.).

1836-7 [see REGRESS *sb.* 1 *fig.*]. **1934** A. C. EWING *Idealism* iv. 149 If we once view relations as terms we are involved in Bradley's infinite regress. **1946** P. HARRISON *Oxf. Marmalade* I. iii. 27 George's criterion of niceness, however, might be described as an infinite regress. Every girl he met was nice, until he met another, and she was nicer. **1968** E. H. GOMBRICH *Art & Illusion* (ed. 3) ix. 268 Are we not led into what philosophers call an infinite regress, the explanation of one thing in terms of an earlier which again needs the same type of explanation? **1973** A. QUINTON *Nature of Things* 109 The concept of an axiom..solves the problem of the infinite regress of justification.

2. with *sb. pl.* Unlimited or indefinitely great in number; innumerable, very many, 'no end of'. Now *arch.* or *rare.*

c **1386** CHAUCER *Knt.'s T.* 1969 Infinite been the sorwes and the teeres Of olde folk and eek of tendre yeeres. **1483** CAXTON *Cato* I ij, Many and Infynyte euyles and inconuenientes. **1555** EDEN *Decades* 88 Not onely..infinite hundredes and legions but also myriades of men. **1556** *Aurelio & Isab.* (1608) L j, She and heir ladeis shedde infinite teares. **1611** BIBLE *Transl. Pref.* 5 Now the Latine Translations were too many to be all good, for they were infinite. **1668** HALE *Pref. Rolle's Abridgm.* b ij, Infinite other Instances of like nature may be given. **1709** ADDISON *Tatler* No. 119 ¶2 There are infinite Parts in the smallest Portion of Matter. **1775** HARRIS *Philos. Arrangem.* Wks. (1841) 265 Thus there are..infinite ways of being vicious, though but one of being virtuous. **1858** CARLYLE *Fredk. Gt.* III. xviii. (1872) I. 253 The Swedes..found infinite 'pigs, near Insterburg'.

†**3.** Indefinite in nature, meaning, etc.; indeterminate. *Obs.*

1520 WHITINTON *Vulg.* (1527) 6 Nownes infinyte as *quisquis, quicunque.* **1553** T. WILSON *Rhet.* 1 Either it is an infinite question and without ende, or els it is definite and comprehended within some ende. **1663** J. SPENCER *Prodigies* (1665) 111 It is a blind, confused, infinite, giddy thing.

4. *Math.* †**a.** Having no determined limit; of indefinite length or magnitude. *Obs.*

1660 BARROW *Euclid* I. xii, Upon an infinite right line. *Ibid.* xxii, From the infinite line DE.

b. Of a quantity or magnitude: Having no limit; greater than any assignable quantity or magnitude (opp. to *finite*). Of a line or surface: Extending indefinitely without limit, and not returning into itself at any finite distance (opp. to *closed*).

1692 HALLEY in *Phil. Trans.* No. 195 (*title*) Of the several Species of Infinite Quantity, and of the Proportions they bear to one another. **1743** EMERSON *Fluxions* 277 To find the Force wherewith an infinite Solid, plain on one Side Ll, attracts a Corpuscle placed at C. **1836** DE MORGAN *Calculus* Elem. Illustr. 61 When we say, $a + \frac{1}{x}$ is equal to *a* when *x* is infinite, we only mean that as *x* is increased $a + \frac{1}{x}$ becomes nearer to *a* and may be made as near to it as we please, if *x* may be as great as we please. **1840** LARDNER *Geometry* 278 When the ellipse becomes a parabola, the further focus will be removed to an infinite distance. **1869** TODHUNTER *Plane Trigon.* (ed. 4) iv. §58 As the angle increases from 0 to 90° the tangent increases from 0 without limit, so that by taking an angle sufficiently near to 90° we can make the tangent as great as we please; this is usually expressed for the sake of abbreviation thus, *the tangent of 90° is infinite.* **1875** —— *Algebra* (ed. 7) lii. §706 The number of prime numbers is infinite. **1885** WATSON & BURBURY *Math. The. Electr. & Magn.* I. 4 If *u* become infinite at any point within *S*, we cannot include in the integration the point at which the infinite value occurs.

c. *infinite series*: a series of quantities or expressions which may be indefinitely continued without ever coming to an end (but may or may not have a finite value or 'limit' to which it approaches as more and more terms are taken: see CONVERGING 2, DIVERGENT 4). So ***infinite decimal.***

1706 W. JONES *Syn. Palmar. Matheseos* 44 The Operation may either be terminated..or else continued on in an Infinite Series. **1763** EMERSON *Increments* p. vi, The Method of Increments will help us to this term, either expressed in finite quantities, or by an infinite series. **1796** HUTTON *Math. Dict.* s.v., *Infinite Decimals*, such as do not terminate, but go on without end. **1875** TODHUNTER *Algebra* (ed. 7) xl. §557 An infinite series in which all the terms are of the same sign is divergent if each term is greater than some assigned finite quantity, however small.

5. *Mus.* Applied to a form of musical structure which can be repeated infinitely.

1869 OUSELEY *Counterp.* xv. 105 If [the canon] is made continually to recur to the beginning, so as never to come to a regular close, it is called Infinite, or Circular. **1876** STAINER & BARRETT *Dict. Mus. Terms* s.v. *Canon*, The above is also an *infinite* canon, because, anyone having such a remarkable desire as to play it for ever, could do so. **1880** GROVE *Dict. Mus.* s.v. *Canon*, Many canons lead back to the

beginning and thus become 'circular' or 'infinite'. **1959** *Collins Mus. Encycl.* s.v. *Canon*, If.. each part, on coming to the end of the melody, goes back to the beginning again and repeats, the result is a 'perpetual' or 'infinite' canon.

6. *Law.* ***distress infinite***: see DISTRESS *sb.* 3 b.

1495 *Act 11 Hen. VII* c. 24 §1 In the same atteynte there shalbe awarded ageynst the petite Jurie the party and the graund Jury somons and resomons and distres infynyte. **1531–2** *Act 23 Hen. VIII*, c. 3 §1. **1641, 1768** [see DISTRESS *sb.* 3 b]. **1882** *Scriven's Copyholds* (ed. 6) vi. §2. 227 The proper remedy for neglect of suit of court, as well as for refusal to do fealty, was a distress infinite of the beasts or other personal property of the defaulter.

7. *Gram.* Applied to those parts of the verb which are not limited by person or number; viz. those verbal sbs. and adjs. which have certain verbal properties, the Infinitive 'Mood', Gerunds, Supines, and Participles. Opposed to *finite*.

1871 ROBY *Lat. Gram.* II. xvi. 183 The forms of the verb proper are often called collectively the Finite Verb; the verbal nouns above named are sometimes called the Infinite Verb. **1871** *Publ. Sch. Lat. Gram.* §35 The forms of the Verb Infinite are not limited by Mood and Person. It comprises ..(1) The Infinitive, a Verbal Substantive: as, *amare*, to love ..(2) Participles, which are Verbal Adjectives.

8. *Logic.* A rendering of Schol.L. *infinitus*, applied to a negative term, etc.; infinitated.

1860 SIR W. HAMILTON *Logic* xiv. I. 253 Aristotle denominated the negative terms, such as *non-B*, *non-homo*, *non-albus*, etc., ὀνομαnα ἀόριστα, literally indefinite nouns. Boethius however unhappily translated..ἀόριστος by the Latin *infinitus*. The Schoolmen..thus called the ὀνόματα ἀόριστα..*nomina infinita*: and the *non-* they styled the *particula infinitans*.

†**B.** *adv.* = INFINITELY: usually in hyperbolical sense = very greatly. *Obs.*

1526 *Pilgr. Perf.* (W. de W. 1531) 298 Infinyte ryche in glory. **1642** ROGERS *Naaman* 616 Are there not infinite many passages in thy life? **1658** W. SANDERSON *Graphice* 60 Nature is so infinite various in the Colours and shadows of the face. **1673** DRYDEN *Marr. à la Mode* I. i, I set a good face upon the matter, and am infinite fond of her before company.

C. *absol.* or as *sb.*

1. That which is infinite, or has no limit; an infinite being, thing, quantity, extent, etc. Now almost always in sing. with *the*; esp. as a designation of the Deity or the absolute Being.

1587 GOLDING *De Mornay* ii. 14 Two infinites cannot be abidden, no nor imagined together,.. therefore, as there must neede s be one Infinite, so must there be but onely one. *a* **1711** KEN *Hymnarium* Poet. Wks. 1721 II. 1 No Rival Infinite could share thy Throne, There no more Infinites can be but one. **1712** *H. More's Antid. Ath.* I. viii. Schol. 151 Since every part of an Infinite is infinite, there may be supposed something more infinite than an Infinite. **1830** HERSCHEL *Stud. Nat. Phil.* §106 The telescope and the microscope laid open the infinite in both directions. **1843** J. MARTINEAU *Chr. Life* (1867) 455 The Presence-chamber of the Infinite. **1856** VAUGHAN *Mystics* (1860) I. 44 Hindoo mysticism.. aims at ultimate absorption in the Infinite.

2. In hyperbolical use: An exceedingly large amount or number; a very great quantity or multitude; very much or many; 'no end'.

†**a.** *absol.* (from A. 2: always in plural sense.) *Obs.*

a **1568** ASCHAM *Scholem.* I. (Arb.) 69 Infinite shall be made cold in Religion by your example. **1577** NORTHBROOKE *Dicing* (1843) 170 Infinite from thence haue returned home vnchast. **1656** RIDGLEY *Pract. Physick* 120 Infinite have been cured by it.

†**b.** Const. *of*, with no defining word prefixed.

1591 SHAKS. *Two Gent.* II. vii. 70 A thousand oathes, an Ocean of his teares, And instances of infinite of Loue. **1613** PURCHAS *Pilgrimage* IV. xvi. (1614) 428 There are infinite of Frier-like companions passing to and fro. **1661** PEPYS *Diary* 1 June, There was infinite of new cakes placed. **1677** YARRANTON *Eng. Improv.* 115 Down the Elb to Hamborough, is sent infinite of Corn. **1697** CONGREVE *Mourn. Bride* IV. i, No term, no bound, but infinite of woe.

c. With article or other defining word prefixed; usually const. *of*. Formerly also in *pl.* (cf. mod. colloq. *lots*, *heaps*, *oceans*).

1563 WINȜET *Wks.* (1890) II. 64 Thow may se an infinit of exemplis. **1595** MARKHAM *Sir R. Grinvile* xciii, Shee lesse great shot in infinets did hide. **1611** HEYWOOD *Gold. Age* III. i. Wks. 1874 III. 36 We haue assembled infinites of men. **1615** J. WRIGHT *Acc. Lady J. Grey* in *Phenix* (1708) II. 28 She brought forth her Increase in such abundance of Infinites, that the least of her Excellencys were impossible to be circumscrib'd. **1647** R. STAPYLTON *Juvenal* 279 The ibes, that kill infinites of serpents. **1662** GLANVILL *Lux Orient.* Pref. (1682) 10 What an infinite of Books are written upon almost all subjects. **1748** F. SMITH *Voy. Disc.* I. 188 You have an Infinite to lose, should you be defeated. **1856** RUSKIN *Mod. Paint.* IV. v. i. §3 That Calais tower has an infinite of symbolism in it.

†**3.** Phr. ***in infinite, to infinite***, = L. *in* or *ad infinitum* (see INFINITUM); endlessly. *Obs.*

a **1631** DONNE *Elegy to Lady Bedford* Poems (1633) 299 Diffus'd, and spread in infinite. **1651** *Life Father Sarpi* (1676) 71 Mischiefs have their terminations, but fears go in infinite. **1651** JER. TAYLOR *Serm. for Year* I. vii. 87 And so on to infinite.

4. *Math.* An infinite quantity: see A. 4 b.

Different orders of infinites are distinguished, each infinitely greater than the preceding: cf. INFINITESIMAL B. 1.

1656 HOBBES *Consid. Wallis* Wks. 1845 VII. 446 This arguing of infinites is but the ambition of school-boys. **1677** PLOT *Oxfordsh.* 288 Dr. John Wallis.. first demonstrated the impossibility of squaring the Circle, Arithmetically,.. having apply'd his method of Infinites in order thereunto. **1692** HALLEY in *Phil. Trans.* XVII. 556 That among themselves each of those Species of Infinites are in given Proportions, is what I now intend to make plain. **1706** W. JONES *Syn. Palmar. Matheseos* 205 Of Infinites 'tis hence plain, that some are equal, others unequal. **1710** BERKELEY *Princ. Hum. Knowl.* §130 Of late the speculations about Infinites have.. grown to such strange notions, as have occasioned no small scruples and disputes among the geometers. **1831** BREWSTER *Newton* (1855) II. xvii. 127 He then proceeds to correct an error of Dr. Bentley's in supposing that all infinites are equal. **1858** BUCKLE *Civiliz.* (1869) II. iv. 190 The geometry of infinites applied to the ordinates and tangents of curves. **1864** PLUCKER *New Geom. Space* in *Phil. Trans.* (1865) 727 The number of rays constituting a configuration, a congruency, a complex and space, are infinites of first, second, third, and fourth order. **1864** *Reader* 21 May 657 The symbol $\frac{1}{0}$, the infinite of common algebra, represents an extreme of infinite.

'infinite, *v. rare.* [f. INFINITE *a.*]

†**1.** *to infinite it*: to proceed to an 'infinite' or indefinite extent. *Obs. nonce-use.*

1656 S. H. *Gold. Law* 72 Suppose that any King.. should .. Solomon-like, infinite it in Wives and Concubines.

2. *trans.* To render infinite; to infinitate.

1868 H. BUSHNELL *Serm. Living Subj.* 105 They are creatures to be somehow infinited, to be eternized in their continuance of good. **1868** *Contemp. Rev.* VIII. 617 Those very elements of diversity by which.. spirit in its last individual forms infinites and unifies the manifold.

infinitely ('ınfınıtlı), *adv.* [-LY².]

1. In an infinite degree, or to an infinite extent; without limit or end; boundlessly.

1413 *Pilgr. Sowle* (Caxton 1483) v. xiv. 109 The trouthe of the hooly trynyte passeth infynytely al that may be said. **1587** GOLDING *De Mornay* iv. 47 Considering his effects; howbeit in such sort as that we must think infinitely of him. **1651** HOBBES *Leviath.* III. xxxviii. 248 God, who is infinitely more mercifull then men. **1777** PRIESTLEY *Matt. & Spir.* (1782) I. iii. 38 Every particle of matter is infinitely divisible. **1899** *Expositor* Feb. 92 There is a power working within us .. that is infinitely wiser, stronger and better than ourselves. *Mod.* We conceive of space as extending infinitely in all directions.

b. In loose or hyperbolical sense: To an indefinitely great extent; beyond measurement or calculation; exceedingly, immensely, vastly.

1584 R. SCOT *Discov. Witchcr.* VI. iv. (1886) 95 He grew infinitlie rich. **1596** SHAKS. *Merch. V.* V. i. 135 This is the man, this is Anthonio, To whom I am so infinitely bound. **1673** TEMPLE *Observ. United Prov.* Wks. 1731 I. 66 They buy infinitely, but 'tis to sell again. **1717** STEELE in *Four C. Eng. Lett.* 173 Dear Prue—I have yours of the 14th, and am infinitely obliged to you for the length of it. **1827** MAGINN *Red-nosed Lieut.*, I like the blonde.. infinitely. **1868** G. DUFF *Pol. Surv.* 49 The Turkish population is infinitely more harshly used than the Christian, as regards exactions.

†**2.** Without determinate limit or end; to an indefinite distance or extent; indefinitely. *Obs.*

c **1430** *Art Nombryng* (E.E.T.S.) 3 And so infynytly mvltiplying by these .3. 10, 100, 1000. **1555** EDEN *Decades* 254 Which he knewe.. to reach infinitely towarde the north-east. **1597** MORLEY *Introd. Mus.* 6 The Keyes.. may be continued infinitely. **1625** BACON *Ess., Empire* (Arb.) 297 It being not possible for them to goe forward infinitely. **1638** F. JUNIUS *Paint. of Ancients* 344 Even so the mind.. runneth on infinitly, remembring all what is to be remembred. **1695** LD. PRESTON *Boeth.* III. 135 Wherefore that we may not infinitely produce our Reasons.

†**3.** In an indefinite manner or sense; indefinitely, indeterminately, generally. (In quot. 1530, = in the infinitive mood.) *Obs.*

1530 PALSGR. 352 And infynitely: *je ne scay que pencer*. **1574** tr. *Marlorat's Apocalips* 8 The number of seuen is put infinitely. **1591** R. TURNBULL *St. James* 3 b, In this sence infinitely is 'seruant' taken in holy Scripture, meaning all such as serue God in profession of religion.

4. *Math.* To an infinite extent or amount; without limit.

infinitely small = INFINITESIMAL; so ***infinitely near, to diminish infinitely***, etc.

1692 HALLEY in *Phil. Trans.* XVII. 556 A Line infinitely long. **1704** [see INFINITESIMAL A. 2]. **1710** BERKELEY *Princ. Hum. Knowl.* §123 No finite extension contains innumerable parts or is infinitely divisible. **1740** CHEYNE *Regimen* 294 Between an infinitly small, and an infinitly great part of the Diameter of an infinit Circle. **1743** EMERSON *Fluxions* 279 Draw the Axis.. and the Ordinates.. infinitely near. **1796** HUTTON *Math. Dict.* s.v., The mean proportional between infinitely great, and infinitely little, is finite. **1828** —— *Course Math.* II. 103 The centre of a parabola is infinitely distant from the vertex. **1873** B. WILLIAMSON *Diff. Calc.* (ed. 2) i. §5 When the increment is supposed infinitely small, it is called a differential.

'infiniteness. Now *rare.* [f. as prec. + -NESS.] The quality or condition of being infinite; infinitude, infinity. **a.** Boundlessness, illimitableness.

1534 WHITYNTON *Tullies Offices* I. D, To the entent we maye auoyde that infynytenesse of Ennius [who recommended giving charity to all], that degree is nygher that is of the same kynne. **1552** HULOET, Infynytenes, *apiria*. **1561** T. NORTON *Calvin's Inst.* II. xv. (1634) 232 They which by faith perceive what he is, have comprehended the whole infinitenesse of heavenly good things. **1608** A. WILLET *Hexapla Exod.* 39 Shewing his.. perfection, goodnesse, infinitenes. **1645** USSHER *Body Div.* (1647) 36 What is Infinitenesse? It is an essentiall property of God, whereby all things in his essence are signified to be without measure and quantity. **1700** D. PHILLIPS *Proteus Rediv.* 11 The Schools talk of the Infiniteness of Space. **1813** SHELLEY *Q. Mab* VIII. 206 The thoughts that rise In time-destroying infiniteness. **1894** MRS. FR. ELLIOT *Rom. Gossip* v. 162 There was infiniteness in the look-out over a boundless sea.

b. Indefiniteness of amount or number; usually in hyperbolical sense: The state of being exceedingly great or numerous; immensity, vastness; immense quantity or number.

1579 J. JONES *Preserv. of Bodie & Soule* Ep. Ded. 2 The infinitenesse of creatures doeth declare the power. **1612** BREREWOOD *Lang. & Relig.* x. 85 Very few in respect of that infiniteness of people, wherewith Ægypt doth and ever did abound. **1633** FORD *Love's Sacr.* IV. i, More base in the infiniteness of her sensuality than corruption can infect. **1654** COKAINE *Dianea* II. 124 Complaining on the infinitenesse of his Miseries.

infinitesimal (ınfını'tɛsıməl), *sb.* and *a.* Also *erron.* -ess-. [f. mod.L. *infinītesim-us*, f. L. *infinīt-us* (cf. *cent-esimus* hundredth, *mill-esimus* thousandth): cf. F. *infinitésime* (1752 in *Dict. Trévoux*), *infinitésimal* (1762 in *Dict. Acad.*).

The form. of the mod.L. word shows that it was orig. meant as an *ordinal*, viz. the 'infiniteth' in order, that which is at an infinite distance from the first; but the ordinals are also used to name fractions, e.g. hundredth (part), $\frac{1}{100}$, thousandth (part) $\frac{1}{1000}$; hence, *infinitesima pars*, *infinitesimal part* or *infinitesimal*, came to mean unity divided by infinity, $\left(\frac{1}{\infty}\right)$, and thus an infinitely small part or quantity. Although essentially an adj., our earliest example shows the word used absolutely as a sb.]

A. *sb.* (or *absolutely*.)

†**1.** As ordinal: The 'infiniteth' member of a series. *Obs. rare.*

1655 H. MORE *App. Antid. Ath.* xiii. 391 But for us whose capacities are finite, if we would venture to name a *first* in infinite succession, we should call it πρῶτον ἀπειραστὸν, *the first infinitessimal*, and acknowledge our selves unable to go through, our understandings being finite.

2. a. (Chiefly *Math.*) As a fraction or fractional quantity. The inverse or reciprocal of an infinite quantity; †an infinitely small fraction or part *of* anything (*obs.*). Hence **b.** (*Math.*) An infinitely small quantity or amount, a quantity less than any assignable quantity.

Chiefly used of the infinitesimal differences or *differentials* treated of in the differential and integral calculus: see DIFFERENTIAL A. 3, B. 1 a. Mathematicians distinguish different orders of infinitesimals; thus, if we make x infinite, $\frac{1}{x}$ is an infinitesimal of the first order, $\frac{1}{x^2}$ $\left(\text{being infinitely less than } \frac{1}{x}\right)$ an infinitesimal of the second order, and so on.

[**1704** HAYES *Fluxions* 1 These infinitely little Parts of an infinitely little Part of a given Quantity are.. called *Infinitesimæ Infinitesimarum* or Fluxions of Fluxions.] **1706** DITTON *Fluxions* 20 Let m denote an infinite Quantity, d any finite one; then is $\frac{d}{m}$ the Infinitesimal of d, according to Mr. Nieuwentyt. **1710** BERKELEY *Princ. Hum. Knowl.* §130 Some .. not content with holding that finite lines may be divided into an infinite number of parts, do yet farther maintain that each of these infinitesimals is itself subdivisible into an infinity of other parts or infinitesimals of a second order, and so on *ad infinitum*. These, I say, assert there are infinitesimals of infinitesimals of infinitesimals, etc., without ever coming to an end. **1745** NEEDHAM *Microsc. Disc.* Introd. 3 A little Ant-hill.. would appear to its Inhabitants .. an Infinitesimal of the terraqueous Globe.

b. 1734 BERKELEY *Analyst* §6 An infinite succession of infinitesimals, each infinitely less than the foregoing. **1743** *Phil. Trans.* XLII. 349 In the Method of Infinitesimals, the Element, by which any Quantity increases or decreases, is supposed to become infinitely small. **1816** tr. *Lacroix's Diff. & Int. Calculus* 78 A very simple explanation of the various orders of infinitesimals admitted by Leibnitz. **1831** HIND *Princ. Differ. Calc.* 116 The method of Infinitesimals adopted by Leibnitz as the foundation of his Differential Calculus. **1873** B. WILLIAMSON *Diff. Calculus* (ed. 2) ii. §36.

3. In loose or hyperbolical use: An extremely small quantity or amount; something excessively minute or insignificant.

1840 HOOD *Up Rhine* 255 Hahnemann, having hit on the advantage of small doses, never rested till he had reduced them to infinitesimals. **1854** EMERSON *Lett. & Soc. Aims, Resources* Wks. (Bohn) III. 197 What power does Nature not owe to her duration of amassing infinitesimals into cosmical forces!

B. *adj.*

1. (Chiefly *Math.*) **a.** Infinitely or indefinitely small; smaller than any assignable fraction or magnitude. (Correlative to *infinite*, and, with it, opposed to *finite*.) **b.** *transf.* Relating to infinitesimal quantities; esp. in ***infinitesimal calculus***, a name for the differential and integral calculuses considered as one (corresponding to the direct and inverse methods of fluxions).

1710 BERKELEY *Princ. Hum. Knowl.* §132 It will not be found.. necessary to make use of or conceive infinitesimal parts of finite lines. **1770** HORSLEY in *Phil. Trans.* LX. 435 *note*, The infinitesimal segments of that line. **1801** W. DICKSON (*title*) Reflections on the Infinitesimal Calculus. From the French of Carnot, with Notes. **1862** H. SPENCER *First Princ.* I. iii. §17 (1875) 57 It is quite possible to think of its motion as diminishing insensibly until it becomes infinitesimal. **1871** TYNDALL *Fragm. Sc.* (1879) I. ii. 58 The aqueous vapour it contains is of almost infinitesimal amount.

2. In loose or hyperbolical use (cf. A. 3): Too small to be measured or reckoned; extremely minute or insignificant.

1733 CHEYNE *Eng. Malady* III. iv. (1734) 337, I was not reduc'd to such extreme Weakness, that infinitesimal Errors, could do great Hurt. **1748** HARTLEY *Observ. Man* I. iii. 393 An Obstruction of the infinitesimal Vessels of the Nervous System. **1830** LYELL *Princ. Geol.* I. 474 No river

can push forward its delta without raising the level of the whole ocean, although in an infinitesimal degree. **1831** CARLYLE *Sart. Res.* II. ix. (1858) 120 Were it but the pitifullest infinitesimal fraction of a Product, produce it in God's name! **1884** *Times* (weekly ed.) 19 Sept. 6/4 Each infinitesimal right of grazing..had to be surveyed, examined into.

Hence **infini'tesimalist**, one who supports the method of infinitesimals (sense A. 2); **infinitesi'mality**, an infinitesimally small matter; **infini'tesimalness**, infinitesimal smallness.

1863 [see MOMENTARIAN]. **1867** *Gd. Words* 801/1 The infinitesimality (I am sorry to have to coin a word) of his influence. **1895** *Columbus* (O.) *Disp.* 17 Oct. 11/3 It is well sometimes to let the mind dwell on such infinitesimalities. **1897** *N.Y. Voice* 8 July 2/3 This infinitesimalness of the Church practise. **1937** *Mind* XLVI. 227 Berkeley's penetrating criticism of the postulates of the fluxionists and infinitesimalists of his day.

infinitesimally (ɪnfɪnɪ'tɛsɪməlɪ), *adv.* [f. prec. + -LY².] In an infinitesimal degree: almost always qualifying *small.* (But in quots. 1801, 1814, used for: To an infinite extent, infinitely.)

1801 W. TAYLOR in *Monthly Mag.* XI. 648 Herder is a vague sweeping declaimer, who multiplies metaphors infinitesimally. **1814** *Ibid.* XXXVIII. 212 So infinitesimally various are nature's shades of hue. **1850** GROVE *Corr. Phys. Forces* (ed. 2) 51 Cases where infinitesimally small quantities of matter are acted on. **1875** WHITNEY *Life Lang.* iv. 66 These differ, at the utmost, only infinitesimally in articulating position from *i* and *u*. **1885** *Manch. Exam.* 26 Oct. 5/1 Corroborative evidence of this nature..reduces the chance of mistake to an infinitesimally small fraction.

infiniteth, *a. Math. nonce-wd.* [f. INFINITE + -TH¹, termination of ordinal numerals.] Used as the ordinal numeral corresponding to *infinite*; ***infiniteth power***, that power obtained by multiplying a quantity by itself an infinite number of times. (infinitieth, from *infinity*, is now current in oral use.)

1708 E. HALLEY *Demonstr. Anal. Logar. Tang.* in *Misc. Cur.* II. 28 If a Table of Logarithm Tangents be made by extraction of the root of the Infiniteth power, whose Index is the length of the arch you put for Unity.

infinitinomial (ɪnfɪnaɪtɪ'nəʊmɪəl), *a.* and *sb. Math. rare.* [f. L. *infinīt-us* INFINITE, after *binomial*, *multinomial.*] **A.** *adj.* Consisting of an infinite number of terms; **B.** *sb.* An expression of this nature.

1706 W. JONES *Syn. Palmar. Matheseos* A iv, The General Theorems for Extracting the Root of any Binomial or Infinitinomial Power. **1763** EMERSON *Increments* 78 The infinitinomial 1 + *By* + *Cy*² &c. is to be raised to the *m*th power.

†**infi'nition.** *Obs. rare*⁻¹. [ad. L. *infīnītiōn-em* boundlessness, infinity, f. *in-* (IN-³) + *fīnītiōn-em* ending, FINITION.] Infinited or infinitated condition.

a **1618** J. DAVIES *Wittes Pilgr.* etc. (1878) 23 For what ioy is so great but the conceipt Of falling to his Infinition (Of blacke Non-essence) will confound it streight?

infinitism (ɪn'fɪnɪtɪz(ə)m). [f. INFINITE *a.* + -ISM.] The belief that God, or the world, is infinite; or that there is an actual infinite. So **in'finitist**, an exponent or adherent of infinitism; also *attrib.* or as *adj.*

1897, 1900 Infinitist [see FINITIST *sb.*]. **1902** W. JAMES *Var. Relig. Exper.* 525 He [*sc.* God] is assumed..to be 'infinite'... Nevertheless..religious experience..cannot be cited as unequivocally supporting the infinitist belief. **1922** Infinitism [see FINITISM].

infinitival (ɪn,fɪnɪ'taɪvəl), *a. Gram.* [f. L. *infīnītīv-us* (see next) + -AL¹.] Of or belonging to the infinitive.

1869 FARRAR *Fam. Speech* ii. 46 *Esse*..the infinitival form of the verb 'to be'. **1877** F. HALL *Eng. Adject. in -able* 47 To all verbs..from the Anglo-Saxon, to all based on the uncorrupted infinitival stems of Latin verbs of the first conjugation, and to all substantives..we annex *-able* only.

Hence **infini'tivally** *adv.*, after the manner of the infinitive.

1882 F. HALL in *Amer. Jrnl. Philol.* III. 297 (*heading*) On the English Perfect Participle used Infinitivally.

infinitive (ɪn'fɪnɪtɪv), *a.* and *sb.* Also 5 **infenitife.** [ad. L. *infīnītīv-us* unlimited, indefinite, infinitive, f. *in-* (IN-³) + *fīnītīv-us* defining, definite. Cf. F. *infinitif*, *-ive* (14–15th c.).]

A. *adj.*

1. *Gram.* The name of that form of a verb which expresses simply the notion of the verb without predicating it of any subject. Usually classed as a 'mood', though strictly a substantive with certain verbal functions, esp. those of governing an object, and being qualified by an adverb.

(Called by Quintilian and Priscian *infinitus modus*, by Diomedes *infinitivus* 'because it has not definite persons and numbers, whence it has also been called by some, *impersonativus* and *insignativus*'. In the short grammar of Dionysius Thrax (B.C. 80), it is called ἀπαρέμφατος, i.e. without modification of sense, unmodified.)

In modern Eng., the infinitive has the simple uninflected form of the verb; agreeing in this respect with the imperative, and (except in the verb *be*), with the first pers. sing., and the whole plural, of the present indicative. In OE., the infinitive had (in the nom.-acc. case) the suffix *-an*, ME. *-en*, *-e*; it had also a dative form in *-anne*, ME., *-enne*, *-ene*, *-en*, *-e*. The latter is sometimes fancifully called by modern grammarians, the *gerundial* or *gerundive infinitive*, as answering in some of its functions to the Latin gerund or gerundive. (It answers more to the L. supine.) The OE. nom.-acc. infinitive is the source of the (now less frequent) simple infinitive, as in 'we saw him *come*', 'they need not *come*'. The dative-infinitive is formally the source of the infinitive with *to*, and functionally the origin of this in such uses as 'he went *to see* the fight' ('*infinitive of purpose*'), 'it was easy *to see*' ('*adverbial infinitive*'); but *to* is now prefixed also to the nom.-acc. infinitive, where OE. had the simple form in *-an*, as in '*to see* is to believe', 'he likes *to see* it'. See TO *prep.*

1520 WHITINTON *Vulg.* (1527) 3 *Quis, qui*, is..gouerned ..somtyme of yᵉ infinytyue mode folowynge. **1530** PALSGR. 84 The infinitive mode whiche they use whan we use to put *to* before a verbe. **1580** HOLLYBAND *Treas. Fr. Tong*, Firste I doe specifie th' Infinitiue mode, *Aimer*, to loue: *Courir*, to run. **1668** WILKINS *Real Char.* IV. vi. 445 That which is called the Infinitive Mode, should according to the true Analogy of that speech be stiled a Participle Substantive. **1876** MASON *Eng. Gram.* (ed. 21) §191 The preposition *to* is not an essential part of the infinitive mood, nor an invariable sign of it. **1889** MORFILL *Gram. Russian Lang.* 37 There are three moods, the infinitive, indicative, and imperative. *Ibid.* 39 Each verb has two stems, firstly, the infinitive stem, and, secondly, the present stem.

†**2.** ? Infinite, endless: in quot. as *adv.* Without end, in perpetuity. *Obs. rare.*

c **1470** HARDING *Chron.* CV. 5 To Peter and Pole he graunted infenitife The Roome pence then of all Englande, As Flores saieth, as I can vnderstande.

B. *sb.*

1. *Gram.* The infinitive 'mood' or form of a verb.

cleft or ***split infinitive***, an infinitive with an adverb between *to* and the verbal part, as in 'to carefully search'. ***gerundial infinitive***: see under A. 1.

1530 PALSGR. Introd. 31 His preterit participle, and his present infynityve. **1676** tr. *Guillatiere's Voy. Athens* 32 [*Lingua franca*] an ill favour'd kind of Italian that makes use of the Infinitive of every Verb, to express all the Tenses and Moods. **1751** HARRIS *Hermes* I. viii. (1786) 163 The Latin and modern Grammarians have called Verbs under this Mode, from this their indefinite Nature, *Infinitives.* **1871** ROBY *Lat. Gram.* II. xvi. 183 Two indeclinable substantives, called *Infinitives* (or the Infinitive Mood). **1871** MORRIS *Hist. Outl. Eng. Accidence* §290 The infinitive had a dative form expressed by the suffix *-e*, and governed by the preposition *to.* This is sometimes called the *gerundial* infinitive: it is also equivalent to Lat. *supines. Ibid.*, The dative infinitive assumed the form of the simple infinitive as early as the twelfth century. **1892** SWEET *New Eng. Gram.* §293 The infinitive, which is a noun-verbal, has nothing in common with the moods of finite verbs. **1893** F. HALL in *Nation* (N.Y.) LVI. 274/2 My paper on the cleft infinitive, printed in the *American Journal of Philology.* **1897** *Academy* 3 Apr. 371/2 Are our critics aware that Byron is the father of their *split infinitive*? 'To slowly trace', says the noble poet, 'the forest's shady scene'.

†**2.** An infinite or endless amount: an infinity.

1595 MARKHAM *Sir R. Grinvile* (Ded. Earl Sussex), Great Lord, to whom infinitiues of fame Flock like night starres about the siluer Moone. *Ibid.* C, Fie, that infinitiues of forces can, Nor may effect what one conceit fulfills.

3. *attrib.* and *Comb.*, as ***infinitive-adjunct***, ***-splitter***, ***-splitting***.

1957 R. W. ZANDVOORT *Handbk. Eng. Gram.* I. i. 9 In the fourth example the infinitive stands in apposition to the noun; in the fifth the *infinitive adjunct is semi-adverbial. **1927** *Glasgow Herald* 1 Nov. 8/7 A competition..to discover the most distinguished *infinitive-splitters. **1926** FOWLER *Mod. Eng. Usage* 447/1 They were obsessed by fear of *infinitive-splitting.

infinitively (ɪn'fɪnɪtɪvlɪ), *adv.* [-LY².]

1. *Gram.* In the infinitive mood.

1711 J. GREENWOOD *Eng. Gram.* 211 The verb put infinitively, that is, with 'to' before it, often tells what it is, does, or suffers. **1879** WHITNEY *Sanskrit Gram.* 382 The few infinitively used words of this formation have a weak root-form.

†**2.** Infinitely. *Obs. rare.*

1726 in H. Campbell *Love Lett. Mary Q. Scots* (1824) 32 His presence would have been of infinitively more service than that of Morton. *Ibid.* 33, I write to you with infinitively more tranquillity of mind.

infinitize ('ɪnfɪnɪtaɪz), *v.* [f. INFINITE *a.* + -IZE.] *trans.* To render infinite. Also as *vbl. sb.*

1913 E. UNDERHILL *Mystic Way* 62 They aspire to infinitise life and to define infinity. **1930** [see FINITIZE *v.*].

infinito- (ɪnfɪ'naɪtəʊ), combining form from L. *infinīt-us* INFINITE, used in the sense 'infinitely, to an infinite degree': as in ***infinito-infinitesimal*** adj. (used by Hartley to describe what is now called 'an infinitesimal of the second degree'); so ***infinito-infinitely*** adv. Also loosely in sense 'infinite and', as in ***infinito-absolute***.

1748 HARTLEY *Observ. Man* II. i. 14 If the Balance be infinitely in favour of each, God will be infinitely benevolent to each, and infinito-infinitely to the whole System. *Ibid.* iii. 330 If F be infinitesimal, L will be infinito-infinitesimal. **1829** SIR W. HAMILTON *Discuss.* (1852) 1 Cousin's Doctrine of the Infinito-Absolute.

infinitude (ɪn'fɪnɪtjuːd). [f. L. type **infīnītūdo*, prob. in med. or mod.L. (after *multitūdo*, *magnitūdo*, etc.). Cotgrave, 1611, has the corresp. F. *infinitude* = *infinité*, and Florio has It. *infinitudine* 'infinitenesse, endlesnesse'. Cf. FINITUDE, which has no It. or Fr. equivalent, and may have been formed after this; also the later DEFINITUDE.]

1. The quality or attribute of being infinite; boundlessness. Also in hyperbolical sense: Immensity, vastness (cf. INFINITE A. 1 b).

1641 MILTON *Reform.* II. (1851) 68 Thou, the third Subsistence of Divine Infinitude, illumining Spirit, the joy and solace of created Things. **1677** HALE *Prim. Orig. Man.* I. vi. 117, I remove Infinitude from what I find to be necessarily finite. **1744** HARRIS *Three Treat.* III. II. (1765) 226 Where the Telescope that can descry, to what Infinitude Wisdom extends. **1807** W. TAYLOR in *Ann. Rev.* V. 549 The best arguments..for the infinitude of Deity. **1890** GARNETT *Milton* 157 The universe fatigues with its infinitude.

2. (with *pl.*) Something that is infinite (or, by hyperbole, indefinitely great); a boundless (or vast) extent, space, amount, number, etc.; infinity.

1667 MILTON *P.L.* VII. 168 Boundless the Deep, because I am who fill Infinitude, nor vacuous the space. **1762** STERNE *Tr. Shandy* V. xxiv, There was that infinitude of oddities in him. **1847** E. FITZGERALD *Lett.* I. 181 Science..unrolls a greater Epic than the Iliad; the history of the World, the infinitudes of Space and Time! **1859** DARWIN *Orig. Spec.* iv. (1873) 101 The form of each depends on an infinitude of complex relations.

‖**infinitum** (ɪnfɪ'naɪtəm). [L.: = INFINITE; also as sb.] = INFINITY; an infinitude, an endless amount or number: see AD INFINITUM, and *in infinitum* s.v. IN *Lat. prep.* 5.

1682 CREECH *Lucretius* (1683) II. 63 Those must be begun From others, and so to *infinitum* on. **1737** *Gaudentio di Lucca* 210 These People must in process of Time encrease to an Infinitum.

infinituple (ɪn'fɪnɪtjuːp(ə)l), *a. nonce-wd.* [f. L. *infinītus* INFINITE, after *centuple*, etc.] Infinitely as much or many; an infinite number of times (something else).

1722 WOLLASTON *Relig. Nat.* v. 85 If the comparison could be made, I verily believe these would be found to be almost infinituple of the other.

infinity (ɪn'fɪnɪtɪ). Also 4–5 -te, 5–6 -tie. [a. F. *infinité* (13th c. in Hatz.-Darm.), ad. L. *infīnītās* endlessness, boundlessness, infinity, f. *infīnītus*: see -ITY.]

1. The quality or attribute of being infinite or having no limit; boundlessness, illimitableness (esp. as an attribute of Deity).

c **1374** CHAUCER *Boeth.* v. pr. vi. 134 (Camb. MS.) Al thogh þat the lyf of it be strechched with infinite of tyme, yit algates nis it no swych thing. *c* **1435** MISYN *Fire Love* 14 In þe infenite of gode meruaile and worschip, with-oute begynyng all-myghti clerely scheuys. **1532** MORE *Confut. Tindale* Wks. 636/1 One whose eternity passeth al time, and whose infinity passeth all nombre, that is almightye God himselfe. **1647** COWLEY *Mistr.*, Constant iii, What, alas can be Added to that which hath Infinity Both in Extent and Quality? **1690** LOCKE *Hum. Und.* II. xxiii. §35 It is Infinity, which, joined to our Ideas of Existence, Power, Knowledge, &c. makes that complex Idea, whereby we represent to our selves the best we can, the supreme Being. *a* **1774** GOLDSM. *Surv. Exp. Philos.* (1776) II. 94 Wherever the doctrines of infinity enter into philosophy, knowledge ceases, and we talk at random. **1875** JOWETT *Plato* IV. 9 Of that positive infinity, or infinite reality, which we attribute to God, he had no conception.

2. Something that is infinite; infinite extent, amount, duration, etc.; a boundless space or expanse; an endless or unlimited time. (In quot. 1682 the Infinite Being, the Deity.)

1377 LANGL. *P. Pl.* B. XIII. 127–8 One pieres þe plough-man..seith þat dowel and dobet aren two infinites, Whiche infinites, with a feith fynden oute dobest, Which shal saue mannes soule. *a* **1618** RALEIGH (J.), There cannot be more infinities than one; for one of them would limit the other. **1682** DRYDEN *Relig. Laici* 93 Darest thou, poor worm, offend Infinity? **1845** DARWIN *Voy. Nat.* i. (1879) 12 Any power, acting for a time short of infinity. **1846** RUSKIN *Mod. Paint.* I. II. III. iii. §25 The greatest number is no nearer infinity than the least, if it be definite number. **1856** MASSON *Ess.* iii. 62 They did not tenant all space, but only that upper and illuminated part of infinity called Heaven. **1865** M. ARNOLD *Ess. Crit.* ix. 297 For all his sweetness and serenity, however, man's point of life 'between two infinities' (of that expression Marcus Aurelius is the real owner) was to him anything but a Happy Island.

3. a. In hyperbolical use (from 1 and 2): Immensity, vastness; an indefinitely great amount or number, an exceeding multitude, 'no end' (*of*). [A frequent sense in OF.]

c **1375** *Sc. Leg. Saints, George* 321 þe king þane ane infinite Of gret tresore gert offere be To george. **1581** MULCASTER *Positions* xxxvi. (1887) 134 Whether all children be to be set to schoole or no, without repressing the infinitie of multitude. **1634** W. TIRWHYT tr. *Balzac's Lett.* (vol. I.) 168 By meanes of an infinity of rules and maximes. **1681** NEVILE *Plato Rediv.* 102 He gives daily charitable audience to an Infinity of poor people. **1756** BURKE *Subl. & B.* III. iv, An infinity of observations of this kind are to be found in the writings and conversations of many. **1875** JOWETT *Plato* (ed. 2) III. 390 When little things are elaborated with an infinity of pains.

b. Phr. ***to infinity*** (= L. *ad* or *in infinitum*): to an 'infinite' extent, 'endlessly', without limit.

1640 tr. *Verdere's Romant of Rom.* I. 27 Loving him to infinity, I almost died at the first news of his sicknes. **1772** BURKE *Sp. Acts Uniform.* Wks. 1842 II. 466 You may delight yourselves in varying to infinity the fashion of them. **1825** MCCULLOCH *Pol. Econ.* II. iv. 189 The multiplication of such commodities to infinity, could never occasion a glut.

4. a. *Math.* Infinite quantity (see INFINITE A. 4c): denoted by the symbol ∞. Also, an infinite number (*of* something; quot. 1831).

1692 HALLEY in *Phil. Trans.* XVII. 556 The whole..is the summ of the beginning and ceasing Infinity, or as I may say of Infinity *a parte ante* and *a parte post*, which is analogous to Eternity in time or Duration. **1831** BREWSTER *Newton* (1855) II. xiv. 21 The curve which should cut at right angles an infinity of curves of a given nature. **1855** MACAULAY *Hist. Eng.* xx. IV. 496 To say..that a hundred was five times infinity. **1859** HALLIWELL *Evid. Chr.* 14 In modern science, there is a symbol used to express infinity. **1880** *Encycl. Brit.* XI. 138 In this treatise [Nova Stereometria Doliorum, 1615] he [Kepler] introduced for the first time the name and notion of 'infinity' into the language of geometry.

b. *Geom.* Infinite distance, or that portion or region of space which is infinitely distant: usually in phr. ***at infinity***. In *Photogr.* also used of any distance, or the range of distances, at which an object is effectively in focus when the lens is set for the greatest possible distance.

1867 SUTTON & DAWSON *Dict. Photogr.* 122 In every lens there is..a certain distance of a near object from it, between which and infinity all objects are in equally good focus. **1873** B. WILLIAMSON *Diff. Calculus* xiii. §192 A system of parallel lines may be considered as meeting in the same point at infinity. *Ibid.* §195 The ordinary parabola..[has] the line at infinity for an asymptote. **1885** LEUDESDORF *Cremona's Proj. Geom.* 221 Suppose the four tangents to be parallel in pairs ..then one diagonal will pass to infinity. **1910** *Photogr. for Beginners* (Country Life Ltd.) ii. 13 These are called 'fixed focus' cameras, and the lens is 'set at Infinity', which means that, provided the object to be photographed is not *nearer* the camera than, say, twenty feet, everything in the picture will appear sharp. **1929** R. H. GOODSALL *Beginner's Guide Photogr.* v. 22 The next thing is to adjust the lens to correct focus... All subjects over 100 feet away will be at 'infinity', smaller distances are marked on the scale. **1939** J. M. BLAIR *Pract. & Theoret. Photogr.* ix. 89 The hyperfocal distance is the least distance at which a lens may be focussed when objects at infinity are still in focus. **1950** G. L. WAKEFIELD *Your Camera Lens & Shutter* ii. 27 In photography, an object at 100 feet away from the lens would be normally considered as being at infinity. Infinity cannot be rigidly defined in the photographic sense, but it becomes a greater distance as the focal length of the lens increases. **1974** *Trafford Catal.* Spring & Summer 890/1 Kodak 100 pocket camera outfit. Fine 3-element lens gives sharp colourful prints or slides from 4 ft. to infinity.

†**in'fire** *v.*, obs. var. ENFIRE, to fire, enflame.

a **1661** HOLYDAY *Juvenal* 131 Corrupting their impure imaginations and infiring their desires.

infirm (ɪn'fɜːm), *a.* [ad. L. *infirm-us* weak, feeble, etc., f. *in-* (IN-[3]) + *firmus* FIRM. Cf. F. *infirme* (16–17th c., earlier *enferme*, *enfer*, etc.), Sp. *enfermo*, It. *infermo*.]

1. a. Of things: Not firm or strong; weak, unsound; esp. unable to resist pressure or weight, giving way easily, frail, 'shaky', feeble. Now *rare*.

c **1374** CHAUCER *Boeth.* v. met. ii. 119 (Camb. MS.) The sonne..ne may..nat by the Infirme lyht of his beemes, brekyn or percen the inward entrailes of the erthe. **1624** J. HEWES *Surv. Eng. Tongue* A iv, Those that build on sandie or infirme ground. **1638** CHILLINGW. *Relig. Prot.* I. i. §8. 36 A building cannot be stable, if any of the necessary pillars thereof be infirme and instable. **1703** R. SAVAGE *Lett. Antients* ii. 20 The World..in its Infancy..form'd an infirm Orb. **1726** LEONI *Alberti's Archit.* I. 40/2 Ground, tho it does resist the Pick-axe,..may..be infirm. **1824** SCOTT *Redgauntlet* Let. xiii, The still more infirm state of his under-garments.

b. *transf.* Of arguments, titles, etc.: Weak, invalid; unsound. Now *rare*.

1557 N. T. (Genev.) Ep. *iv, The Newe Testament..is so named in respect of yᵉ Olde, the which..was in it selfe infirme and vnperfect. **1653** MILTON *Hirelings* 82 The reason which they themselves bring..becomes alike infirme and absurd. **1662** STILLINGFL. *Orig. Sacr.* III. ii. §10 This opinion..was built on the same infirm conclusions. **1844** LD. BROUGHAM *Brit. Const.* xiv. (1862) 198 The infirm title of the House of Lancaster during the earlier portion of the period. **1952** *Mind* LXI. 83 Clearly the argument is infirm.

2. a. Of persons, with reference to physical condition: Not strong and healthy; physically weak or feeble, esp. through age; hence freq. ***old*** (or ***aged***) ***and infirm***. Also *transf.* of age.

1605 SHAKS. *Lear* I. i. 302 The vnruly way-wardnesse, that infirme and cholericke yeares bring with them. *Ibid.* III. ii. 20 A poore, infirme, weake, and dispis'd old man. **1693** TEMPLE *Mem. fr. Peace* 1679 (R.) The present elector is old and infirm, and has, for some years past, deceived the world by living so long. **1727** GAY *Fables* I. xxxi. 6 With secret ills at home he pines, And, like infirm old age, declines. **1773** *Observ. State Poor* 83 The aged and infirm who have settled habitations. **1805** SCOTT *Last Minstrel*, The minstrel was infirm and old. **1832** HT. MARTINEAU *Ella of Gar.* i. 8 Their father had been growing infirm for many years. **1846** McCULLOCH *Acc. Brit. Empire* (1854) I. 691 Allowance being made for old and infirm persons, children, &c.

b. Of parts of the body. (†In early use: unhealthy, diseased).

1601 SHAKS. *All's Well* II. i. 170 What is infirme, from your sound parts shall flie. **1643** J. STEER tr. *Exp. Chyrurg.* vii. 29 If the offended part be the arme or the leg, begin at the infirme part. **1819** SHELLEY *Prometh. Unb.* IV. 565 If, with infirm hand, Eternity..should free The serpent [etc.].

†**c.** *absolutely.* = INVALID *sb.* *Obs. rare.*

1711 *Light to Blind* in *10th Rep. Hist. MSS. Comm.* App. v. 184 The royal infirm is fully possessed of..patience at the shortness of his life.

3. Of persons, with reference to the mind: Not firm or strong in character or purpose; weak, frail, irresolute. Also of the mind, judgement, etc.

1526 *Pilgr. Perf.* (W. de W. 1531) 80b, It is a token of an infyrme and weyke herte, the subgette to discusse the commaundement of his prelate. **1605** SHAKS. *Macb.* II. ii. 52 Infirme of purpose: Giue me the Daggers. **1641** MILTON *Ch. Govt.* I. vi, Let us think it worth the examining for the love of infirmer Christians. **1667** —— *P.L.* x. 956 That on my head all might be visited, Thy frailty and infirmer Sex forgiv'n. **1784** COWPER *Task* III. 44 Too infirm, Or too incautious, to preserve thy sweets. **1841** DISRAELI *Amen. Lit.* (1859) II. 129 His judgment was the infirmest of his faculties. **1850** HT. MARTINEAU *Hist. Peace* II. v. ix. 344 He was..infirm of purpose.

infirm (ɪn'fɜːm), *v.* Now *rare.* Also 5 **inferm.** [ad. L. *infirmāre* to weaken, invalidate, etc., f. *infirmus* INFIRM *a.*; cf. F. *infirmer* (Oresme, 14th c.; earlier *enfermer*), Sp. *enfermar*, It. *infermare*.] To make infirm.

†**1.** *trans.* To make physically infirm or frail; to weaken, impair the strength of. *Obs.*

1555 BRADFORD *Let.* in Foxe *A. & M.* (1684) III. 287/2 If they be strong, you do what you can to infirm their strength. **1583** STUBBES *Anat. Abus.* I. (1877) 95 It infirmeth the sinewes. **1646** SIR T. BROWNE *Pseud. Ep.* IV. v. 188 Herein the spleene is injustly introduced to invigorate the sinister side, which being dilated it would rather infirme and debilitate.

transf. **1635** CHAPMAN & SHIRLEY *Chabot* v. iii, Those distempers that infirm my blood And spirits. **1646** SIR T. BROWNE *Pseud. Ep.* I. v. 18 Our understandings being eclipsed, as well as our tempers infirmed, we must betake our selves to wayes of reparation. **1650** W. BROUGH *Sacr. Princ.* (1659) 475 Nature is vanquisht..her faculties infirm'd.

†**2.** To weaken (belief), impair the force of (an argument, reason, proof, etc.); to make less firm or certain; to render doubtful or questionable. *Obs.*

c **1449** PECOCK *Repr.* II. vi. 175 Thou infirmyst and feblist bi a greet deel the Euydencis which thou hast & holdist aȝens the hauyng & the using of ymagis. **1563** WINȜET *Four Scoir Thre Quest.* Wks. 1888 I. 58 To infirm and adnull his awin cause rather than to strenthe the samin. **1605** BACON *Adv. Learn.* II. xiv. §6 Socrates..professing to affirme nothing, but to infirme that which was affirmed by another. **1677** HALE *Prim. Orig. Man.* I. vi. 124 The Reason herein given doth not at all infirm the important Reason against the Eternity of Mankind.

3. To invalidate (a law, custom, privilege, etc.); to declare invalid, call in question. Now *rare*.

1558 KNOX *First Blast* (Arb.) 22 This is a speciall lawe.. whose sentence, lest it shulde be violated, infirmed, or made weake, women are commanded to be in silence. **1590** SWINBURNE *Testaments* 127 The vnhonest condition..doth either presently confirme or infirme the effect of the disposition. **1642** SIR E. DERING *Sp. on Relig.* 27, I will neither inveigh upon them as unnamed Commissioners, nor infirme them as the work of a dead Convocation. **1644** LAUD *Wks.* (1854) IV. 103 Mr. Vassal..desired the Lords he might have reparation, which altogether in law infirms that which he testified. **1890** *Times* 19 Feb. 5/4 The bad faith of the Habsburgs could not infirm Magyar rights.

Hence **in'firming** *vbl. sb.*

1612 T. TAYLOR *Comm. Titus* i. 9 Tending to the conuerting and confirming of the tractable; or else the infirming and weakening of false doctrine. **1639** LD. DIGBY, etc. *Lett. conc. Relig.* iv. (1651) 58 To your infirming of those Ancient Authorities..it will be sufficient to put you in minde that [etc.].

infirmarer (ɪn'fɜːmərə(r)). *Hist.* Also 5 **enfermerere**, 9 **-firmerer**. [a. OF. *enfermerier* (Godef.), app. f. *enfermerie* INFIRMARY, but see -ER[1] 3. The usual OF. form was *enfermier* (mod.F. *infirmier*) ENFERMER (see also FERMERER).] In mediæval monasteries, the person who had charge of the infirmary; the infirmarian.

c **1430** *Pilgr. Lyf Manhode* IV. lx. (1869) 205 And heerfore hath grace dieu maad me enfermerere in þis place. **1432–50** tr. *Higden* (Rolls) VII. 403 Noo man schalle absente hym from servyce, neiþer go furthe after complyn, but the infirmarer, celerer and hostiler. **1794** W. TINDAL *Evesham* 110 Which..the Infirmerar receives to the value of three marks annually. **1802** FOSBROOKE *Brit. Monachism* xix. (1843) 135 The Abbot..was to appoint such a person Infirmarer as might be able..to receive the confession of the sick. **1884** *19th Cent.* Jan. 112 At Evesham the sacristan, the chamberlain and the infirmarer were allowed forage and the keep of one horse.

So **in'firmaress** [-ESS[1]], a female infirmarer.

1802 FOSBROOKE *Brit. Monachism* xix. (1843) 135 The Infirmaress had a Lay-sister as an assistant. **1896** LINA ECHENSTEIN *Woman under Monast.* 416 There is the prioress ..the chambress, the infimaress, the portress and others.

infirmarian (ɪnfə'mɛərɪən). [f. INFIRMAR-Y + -IAN.] One who has charge of an infirmary and of the patients there, esp. in a monastic establishment or as a member of a religious order.

1669 WOODHEAD *St. Teresa* II. xvi. 114 In all her sickness ..she did neither more nor less, but as the Infirmarian would have her. **1858** FABER tr. *Xavier's Life* 47 He was their doctor, infirmarian, comforter, father, servant. **1871** *Pall Mall G.* 15 Feb. 7 A small passage communicated with each carriage, so that the surgeon and infirmarians could go to and fro between the sick beds and the kitchen.

infirmary (ɪn'fɜːmərɪ). Also 7 **-firmery**, **(-irie)**, **-fermery**. [ad. med.L. *infirmāria*, f. *infirmus* INFIRM *a.*: see -ARY[1] B. 3. The obs. forms perh. repr. F. *infirmerie* (earlier *enfermerie*, etc.) = Sp. *enfermeria*, It. *infermeria*. The ME. aphetized form was FERMERY, q.v.]

1. A building or part of a building for the treatment of the sick or wounded; a hospital; esp. the sick-quarters in a religious establishment, a school, workhouse, or other institution.

In the 18th c., the common name for a public hospital: see HOSPITAL *sb.* 3. Nearly all such institutions in English provincial towns had originally this name, which is still retained in many cases, e.g. the Royal Infirmary, Edinburgh, the Royal Infirmary, Liverpool, the Radcliffe Infirmary, Oxford, etc.

1625 BACON *Ess., Building* (Arb.) 552 You must fore-see, that one of them, be for an Infirmary, if the Prince, or any Speciall Person should be Sicke. **1666** PEPYS *Diary* 29 Jan., He entertained me with discourse of an Infirmary which he hath projected for the sick and wounded seamen. **1722** DE FOE *Col. Jack* (1840) 274 She was carried to the infirmary, so they call it in the religious houses in Italy, where the sick nuns or friars are carried. **1748** BUTLER *Serm. Gov. Lond. Infirm.* Wks. 1874 II. 307 There is..a necessity, in such a city as this [London], for public infirmaries. **1772–84** COOK *Voy.* (1790) I. 15 The taste of the convents, especially of the Franciscans is better..The Infirmary also is a piece of good architecture. **1806** *Med. Jrnl.* XV. 47 She was..admitted an out-patient, and her friends had directions given them to attend at the Infirmary on proper days for medicines. **1838** DICKENS *O. Twist* xxiii, This is the port wine, ma'am, that the board ordered for the infirmary. **1855** MACAULAY *Hist. Eng.* xviii. IV. 243 There was not then, in the whole realm, a single infirmary supported by voluntary contribution.

fig. **1648** EARL WESTMORELAND *Otia Sacra* (1879) 27 Man is Bethesda, and 's five Senses be Porches unto that great Infermery, Where divers cures are sought for. **1649** JER. TAYLOR *Gt. Exemp.* I. v. 151 Those are the persons of Christs infirmary, whose restitution and reduction to a state of life and health was his great design.

†**2.** A house for rearing delicate plants; a conservatory. *Obs. rare.*

1707 SLOANE *Jamaica* I. Pref., By means of Stoves and Infirmaries, many of them have come to greater perfection, than in any part of Europe.

3. *attrib.* and *Comb.*

1758 J. S. *Le Dran's Observ. Surg.* (1771) 100, I ordered the Infirmary-Keeper to bring him into the Ward. **1816** in A.C. Hutchison *Pract. Obs. Surg.* (1826) 161 He was detected by the vigilance of the Infirmary serjeant.

†**in'firmat**, *pa. pple. Sc. Obs. rare.* [as if from a verb **infirmate*: cf. OF. *enfermer* to affirm, confirm.] Confirmed, made certain.

1487 *Burgh Rec. Aberdeen* (1844) I. 43 Quhilkis thingis, gif thai be infirmat of verite, ar richt displesand.

†**in'firmate**, *v. Obs.* rare^{-1}. [f. L. *infirmāt-*, ppl. stem of *infirmāre* to INFIRM.] *trans.* To weaken, invalidate.

1657 TOMLINSON *Renou's Disp.* 378 He will never be able to infirmate or disprove the authority of such grave men.

infirmation (ɪnfə'meɪʃən). *rare.* [ad. L. *infirmātiōn-em*, n. of action f. *infirmāre* to INFIRM; cf. F. *infirmation* (1520 in Hatz.-Darm.).] The action of weakening or invalidating (evidence).

1808 BENTHAM *Sc. Reform* 72 The testimony of each witness operating either in confirmation or infirmation of that of the rest. *a* **1812** —— *Ration. Judic. Evid.* (1827) V. 128 For infirmation, or even for confirmation..it may still have its use. **1953** W. V. QUINE *From Logical Point of View* ii. 37 Method of empirical confirmation or infirmation.

infirmative (ɪn'fɜːmətɪv), *a.* (*sb.*) *rare.* [a. F. *infirmatif*, *-ive*: see INFIRMATE *v.* and -IVE, -ATIVE.] Tending to weaken or invalidate.

b. *sb.* That which tends to weaken.

1611 COTGR., *Infirmatif*,..infirmatiue; weakening, infeebling; disanulling, disallowing. *a* **1812** BENTHAM *Ration. Judic. Evid.* (1827) III. 14 Any such disprobabilizing fact..may be termed an infirmative fact. *Ibid.* 173 No other infirmatives seem applicable.

†**in'firmatory**, *sb. Obs. rare.* [ad. med.L. *infirmātōri-um*, f. *infirmus* INFIRM: cf. INFIRMITORY.] = INFIRMARY.

1598 STOW *Surv.* xxxv. (1603) 319 Peter de Heliland made the infirmatorie. *a* **1641** BP. MOUNTAGU *Acts & Mon.* (1642) 438 If any bee sick, hee is carried into the Infirmatory. **1678** PHILLIPS (ed. 4) App. *Infirmatorie*, or *Infirmary*.

†**in'firmatory**, *a. Obs.* rare^{-1}. [f. L. *infirmāt-*, ppl. stem of *infirmāre* to INFIRM + -ORY.] Tending to make infirm or invalidate.

1726 AYLIFFE *Parergon* 492 Such a Sentence ought to be pronounc'd..as is neither Confirmatory, nor Infirmatory.

infirmed (ɪn'fɜːmd), *ppl. a.* [f. INFIRM *v.* + -ED[1].] Rendered infirm; affected with infirmity.

1552 HULOET, Infyrmed, *infirmus*. **1583** STUBBES *Anat. Abus.* II. (1882) 53 Euerie man..is suffered to exercise the misterie of phisick, and surgerie..to the diseased, and infirmed persons. **1647** LILLY *Chr. Astrol.* xliv. 266 If the Disease be not chronick,..you shall find great alteration in the Disease and party infirmed. *c* **1785** *J. Thompson's Man* 14 Apish, ugly, saucy, infirmed, diseased.

infirmerer, variant of INFIRMARER *Obs.*

†**in'firmited**, *ppl. a. Obs.* [? for *infirmated*, f. INFIRMATE *v.*, or after *infirmity*.] = INFIRMED.
1616 EARL CUMBERLD. in Whitaker *Craven* (1812) 291, I grow much into yeares, and am something infirmited.

†**in'firmitory**. *Obs. rare.* [ad. med.L. *infirmitōrium*, var. of *infirmātōrium*: cf. INFIRMATORY *sb.*] = INFIRMARY 1.
1538 LELAND *Itin.* V. 82 The Fratry and Infirmitory be now mere Ruines. **1645** EVELYN *Diary* 25 Jan., The Infirmitory [at Rome] where the sick lay was paved with various colour'd marbles.

infirmity (ɪn'fɜːmɪtɪ). [ad. L. *infirmitāt-em*, n. of quality f. *infirm-us* INFIRM *a.* (see -ITY). Cf. F. *infirmité* (15th c. in Hatz.-Darm.), earlier *enfermeté*.] The condition of being infirm.
1. Weakness or want of strength; lack of power to do something; inability. Also with *pl.* an instance or case of this.
1382 WYCLIF *2 Cor.* xi. 30, I shal glorie in tho thingis that ben of myn infirmyte [*gloss* or freelte]. *Ibid.* xii. 5 For sich maner thing I schal glorie: forsothe for me no thing, no but in myn infirmitees. **1447** BOKENHAM *Seyntys* (Roxb.) 6, I durst not hastyly assente hym to, Weel knowyng myn owyn infyrmyte. **1590** SPENSER *F.Q.* III. vii. 33 Him he saw still stronger grow through strife, And him selfe weaker through infirmity. **1664–94** SOUTH *Twelve Serm.* II. 131 All Abortion is from Infirmity and Defect. **1796** BURKE *Let. Noble Ld.* Wks. VIII. 7 When I could no longer hurt them, the revolutionists have trampled on my infirmity. **1880** *Mem. J. Legge* 131 Weaker men feel the confidence that infirmity reposes in strength.
b. Of an argument or title: Want of validity.
a **1614** DONNE *Βιαθανατος* (1644) 21 What infirmity soever my reasons may have, yet I have comfort in Tresmegistus Axiome. **1647** N. BACON *Disc. Govt. Eng.* I. lxii. (1739) 126 Kings..knew no such infirmity in that manner of conveyance, as is pretended. **1888** LD. BRAMWELL in *Law Rep.*, 13 App. Cases 345 They had notice of the infirmity of the title of those from whom they claimed.
2. Physical weakness, debility, frailty, feebleness of body, resulting from some constitutional defect, disease, or (now mostly) old age.
1375 BARBOUR *Bruce* xx. 244 The kyngis Infermite Woxe mair & mair. *c* **1375** *Sc. Leg. Saints, Bartholomew* 20 Fulis trewit wele þat he þame heylyt of Infyrmyte. *c* **1440** *Gesta Rom.* xi. 35 (Harl. MS.) The lawe is I-sette for hem þat ben made blinde by infirmite, or by þe will of god. **1508** DUNBAR *Poems* iv. 3, I..am trublit now with gret seiknes, And feblit with infirmitie. **1601** SHAKS. *Twel. N.* I. v. 82 Infirmity that decaies the wise, doth euer make the better foole. **1796** BURKE *Corr.* (1844) IV. 413 If infirmity had not the trick of assuring to itself strange privileges, and having them allowed by the good-nature of others. **1838** LYTTON *Leila* I. ii, When age and infirmity broke the iron sceptre of the king. **1871** R. ELLIS *Catullus* lxiv. 305 To a tremor of age their gray infirmity rocking.
†**b.** Unhealthiness. *Obs. rare.*
1481 CAXTON *Godfrey* 218 Thenne deuysed the barons that they wold remeue for thynfyrmyte of the place.
3. A special form or variety of bodily (or mental) weakness; †an illness, disease (*obs.*); now, esp., a failing in one or other of the faculties or senses.
1382 WYCLIF *1 Tim.* v. 23 Use a litil wyn for thi stomak, and thin ofte falling infirmytees. *a* **1400–50** *Alexander* 5581 Slike a fell infirmite was in his hors bunden..þat he for bale dies. *c* **1440** *Gesta Rom.* xx. 69 (Harl. MS.) If I myght bathe in blode of goetis, I shulde be hole of this infirmite. **1540** *Act 32 Hen. VIII*, c. 42 §3 The pestilence, great pockes & such other contagious infirmityes. **1656** RIDGLEY *Pract. Physick* 84 If from the Liver or the Spleen, there are signs of their Infirmities. **1712** tr. *Pomet's Hist. Drugs* I. 179 This gum is us'd..for several Infirmities of the Lungs. **1790** COWPER *Wks.* (1837) XV. 222 The voice of the Almighty can in one moment cure me of this mental infirmity. **1791** *Gentl. Mag.* 22/2 A gentleman, aged 50, who felt the infirmities of age at an earlier period than most do. **1875** JOWETT *Plato* (ed. 2) III. 372 He is a little deaf and has a similar infirmity in sight.
†**b.** A noxious vegetative growth. *Obs. rare.*
1597 GERARDE *Herbal* I. xvii. §1. 22 The first groweth in gardens and arable grounds, as an infirmitie and plague of the fields. **1759** tr. *Duhamel's Husb.* I. viii. (1762) 25 Produce nothing but moss and cankerous infirmities.
4. Weakness of character; moral weakness or frailty; inability to maintain a high moral standard or to resist natural inclinations.
1382 WYCLIF *Rom.* vi. 19 The infirmite [*gloss* or vnstabilnesse] of ȝoure fleisch. *Ibid.* viii. 26 The spirit helpith oure infirmyte [*gloss* or vnstedefastnesse]. **1414** BRAMPTON *Penit. Ps* xxi. (Percy Soc.) 9, I synne al day, for I am frele; It is mannys infirmyte. **1581** LAMBARDE *Eiren.* IV. xxi. (1588) 624 Erring by infirmitie they are not altogether unworthie of pardon. **1614** BP. HALL *Recoll. Treat.* 1037, I see that forty daies talk with God cannot bereave a man of passionate infirmity. **1783** BURKE *Rep. Aff. India* Wks. 1842 II. 63 Some degree of ostentation is not extremely blamable. It is human infirmity at the worst. **1873** BURTON *Hist. Scot.* liii. V. 38 The head of the house..was a byword for infirmity of purpose.
b. With *an* and *pl.* A weakness, flaw, defect in a person's character.
1382 WYCLIF *Heb.* iv. 15 We han not a byschop, that may not..haue compassioun to oure infirmytees. **1526** *Pilgr. Perf.* (W. de W. 1531) 9b, The which cureth, releueth & heleth all defautes & spirituall infirmytees. **1637** MILTON *Lycidas* 71 Fame is the spur that the clear spirit doth raise (That last infirmity of noble mind). **1712** ARBUTHNOT *John Bull* II. iv, I know the infirmity of our family; we are apt to play the boon companion. **1871** R. W. DALE *Commandm.* iii. 82 It is easy enough..to discover grave infirmities and faults in most Christian people.

†**in'firmize**, *v. Obs. rare.* [f. INFIRM *a.* + -IZE.] *trans.* To render infirm.
1751 R. SHIRRA *Rem.* (1850) 66 The Word was made flesh, infirmized.

infirmly (ɪn'fɜːmlɪ), *adv.* [f. INFIRM *a.* + -LY^2.] In an infirm manner; weakly, feebly, insecurely.
1615 G. SANDYS *Trav.* 38 Infirmely walled; yet great, if you comprehend the suburbs therewith. **1662** STILLINGFL. *Orig. Sacr.* III. iv. §2 So weakly grounded and infirmly proved an opinion. **1727** SWIFT *Gulliver* IV. vii, I walked infirmly on my hinder feet. **1816** WORDSW. *French Army in Russia* i, A withered bough, Infirmly grasped within a palsied hand. **1849** RUSKIN *Sev. Lamps* 2 The same infirmly balanced liability to the prevalence of the lower part over the higher.

in'firmness. Now *rare.* [f. as prec. + -NESS.] The quality of being infirm (in various senses); weakness, feebleness, frailty, infirmity.
1602 WARNER *Alb. Eng.* XII. lxxv. (1612) 313 A Friend should not, nor you will I, in this Infirmnes flye. **1655** OUGHTRED in Rigaud *Corr. Sci. Men* (1841) I. 87 So far as..the infirmness of my healh, and the greatness of my age..would permit. **1663** BOYLE *Exp. Hist. Colours* I. v. Wks. 1772 I. 695 The infirmness and insufficiency of the common peripatetick doctrine. **1680** *Lond. Gaz.* No. 1485/4 On account of his infirmness of Body.

infissile (ɪn'fɪsɪl), *a. rare.* [IN-^{3}.] Not fissile; that cannot be split.
1855 H. SPENCER *Princ. Psychol.* II. xi. 210 Of bodies that resist in different modes..we have the Fissile and Infissile.

†**in'fistulate**, *v. Obs. rare.* [f. IN-^{2} + FISTULATE *v.*; after med.L. *infistulātus* (OF. *enfistulé*) or It. *infistolare*.] **a.** *intr.* To become a fistula.
b. *trans.* To convert into a fistula.
1611 FLORIO, *Infistolare*, to infistulate, to fester. **1631** *Celestina* VI. 77 Doe not infistulate your wound.
Hence †**in'fistulated** *ppl. a.*; †**infistu'lation**.
1611 FLORIO, *Infistolatione*, an Infistulation. **1706** PHILLIPS, *Infistulated*, turned to, or full of Fistula's.

†**in'fit**, *a. Obs. rare*$^{-1}$. [IN-^{3}.] Unfit.
a **1626** BP. ANDREWES *96 Serm., Holy Ghost* (1661) 453 To such men, such simple men,..a full infit and indisposed matter to receive it.

'**infit**, *v. U.S. local.* [f. IN *adv.* + FIT *v.*, after *outfit*.] *trans.* To furnish (a seaman) with things required on shore. Hence '**infitter**.
1887 *Fisheries U.S.* V. II. 226 The merchant is as anxious to 'infit' as he was to 'outfit' him, but the man must now bring an order from the agent or owner of the vessel. *Ibid.*, The outfitters are also 'infitters', that is, they furnish the men with such supplies and articles of clothing as they may need when the vessel returns.

'**infix**, *sb.* [f. L. *infix-*: see next; after *affix*, *prefix*, *suffix*.]
†**1.** A fixing in, fixed position resulting from firm insertion. *Obs.*
1611 BARKSTED *Hiren* (1876) 93 Forecast the Basis he shall rest vpon, Whose firme infixe thunders nor winds can shake.
2. *Gram.* A modifying element inserted in the body of a word, instead of being prefixed or suffixed to the stem.
1881 *Nature* XXIII. 271/1 The arguments establishing the..connection of the Cambojan and Malayan languages..based on the principle of modifying infixes. **1883** *Athenæum* 24 Mar. 381/1 Some voices [in Semitic languages] are found made by what appear at first sight to be infixes. **1887** MAX MÜLLER in *Fortn. Rev.* May 709 A certain number of formal elements, called suffixes, prefixes, and infixes.

infix (ɪn'fɪks), *v.* Also 7–9 **en-**. [Partly f. L. *infix-*, ppl. stem of *infigĕre* to fix or fasten in, imprint, impress, or OF. *infixer* (Godef.); partly f. IN-^{1} or ^{2} + FIX *v.*]
1. *trans.* To fix or fasten (one thing) *in* (another); to implant or insert firmly.
1502 ATKYNSON tr. *De Imitatione* I. xii. 161 To returne vs to god; in whom if we wolde feruently infixe our selfe, it shulde nat be great nede to seke outwarde consolacions. **1533** MORE *Answ. Poysoned Bk.* Wks. 1114/1 Therfore hath he..suffered hymselfe..to be touched and eaten, and yᵉ very teeth to be infixed into his flesh. **1578** BANISTER *Hist. Man* I. 14 So much [of the teeth] as is infixed within the Goummes to be perfect sensible. **1650** BULWER *Anthropomet.* 169 Infixing their Nailes in the Fronts of them, they claw off the skin. **1774** GOLDSM. *Nat. Hist.* (1776) IV. 145 The animal cannot infix one tooth without all the rest accompanying its motions. **1809** tr. *Mad. Cottin's Amelia Mansfield* I. 109 Whether it is not there that vice enfixes, in silence, her most envenomed stings. **1820** MATURIN *Melmoth* (1892) III. xxx. 213 Daggers..which those who wish me to live would not willingly see infixed.
b. *fig.* (of non-material action.)
1509 BARCLAY *Shyp of Folys* (1874) II. 16 O noble Princes..Infix your myndes to vertue and prudence. **1595** SHAKS. *John* II. i. 502, I do protest I neuer lou'd my selfe Till now infixed I beheld my selfe, Drawne in the flattering table of her eie. **1822** LAMB *Elia* Ser. II. *Confess. Drunkard*, The vices which they introduced, and the habits they infixed. **1875** E. WHITE *Life in Christ* II. xiii. (1878) 148 So deeply is this habit of thought infixed in modern readers, that [etc.].
†**c.** To affix. *Obs.*
1577–87 HOLINSHED *Chron.* III. 887/1 He vsed the seruice of secretaries in all the letters he wrote to him, infixing nothing of his owne hand but the subscription.
d. To fix or fasten on something.
1601 SHAKS. *All's Well* v. iii. 47 Where the impression of mine eye enfixing, Contempt his scornfull Perspectiue did lend me. **1843** E. JONES *Sens. & Event* 199 And we can wait thee, Death, our eyes enfixed Firmly there.
2. To fix (a fact, etc.) *in* the mind or memory, so as to cause a deep impression; to impress.
1542 BECON *Potation Lent* in *Early Wks.* (Parker Soc.) 120 Grant..that we..may so infix in our breasts his most bitter death. **1642** FULLER *Holy & Prof. St.* III. x. 175 First soundly infix in thy mind what thou desirest to remember. **1751** JOHNSON *Rambler* No. 147 ¶5 The care with which he shewed all the companions of his early years how strongly they were infixed in his memory. **1889** *Macm. Mag.* Aug. 301/2 These thoughts were but infixed more deeply.
3. *Gram.* To insert (a formative element) in the body of a word: cf. INFIX *sb.* 2.
1868, 1883 [implied in INFIXING below].
Hence **infixed** *ppl. a.*, **in'fixing** *vbl. sb.* and *ppl. a.*
1552 HULOET, Infyxed,..*infixus*. **1634** T. JOHNSON *Parey's Chirurg.* IX. v. (1678) 218 According as the Body infixed is either hard or easie to be found. **1755** JOHNSON, *Implantation*,..the act of enfixing or settling. **1860** RUSKIN *Mod. Paint.* V. IX. ix. §24 Death with the taunting word, and burning grasp, and infixed sting. **1868** MAX MÜLLER *Stratific. Lang.* 22 The infixing or incapsulating languages are but a variety of the affixing class. **1883** *Amer. Jrnl. Philol.* 347 Of the infixing of a letter between the first and third radical there seems to be no sure proof.

infixation (ɪnfɪk'seɪʃən). *Gram.* [f. INFIX *v.* + -ATION.] The action of infixing; the state of being infixed.
1921 E. SAPIR *Lang.* iv. 76 A peculiarly interesting type of infixation is found in the Siouan languages, in which certain verbs insert the pronominal elements into the very body of the radical element. **1964** E. BACH *Introd. Transformational Gram.* iii. 48 And the infixation of the object marker..should be brought about by a low-level rule in the grammar.

infixion (ɪn'fɪkʃən). *rare.* [n. of action from INFIX *v.*, after L. type **infixiōn-em*.] The action of infixing; the condition of being infixed.
1651 STANLEY *Poems* 150 The first [type of cross is] when to one single piece of wood there is affixion or infixion. **1885** SIEVERS in *Encycl. Brit.* XVIII. 789/2 The infixion of a nasal in the formation of tense-stems.

†**in'flagon**, *v. Obs. rare*$^{-0}$. [IN-^{2}.] *trans.* To put into a flagon.
1611 FLORIO, *Infiascare*, to inflagon, to inflaske.

inflamable, obs. variant of INFLAMMABLE.

inflame (ɪn'fleɪm), *v.* Forms: α. 4 **enflaumme**, 4–5 **-flaume**, **-flawme**, **-flamme**, 5 **-fla(u)mbe**, 5–9 **enflame**. β. 4 **inflaume**, 4–6 **-flamme**, 6 **-flambe**, 5– **inflame**. [ME. a. OF. *enflammer*, *-flamber*, *-flamer* = Sp. *inflamar*, It. *infiammare*:—L. *inflammāre*, f. *in-* (IN-^{2}) + *flamma* FLAME. From the 16th c. the prefix has usually been *in-*, and the radical has the same phonetic history as FLAME *sb.* and *v.*]
I. *trans.* **1.** To cause to blaze or burst into flames; to set ablaze; to set on fire; to kindle.
1382 WYCLIF *Mal.* iv. 1 Alle proude men..shuln be stobil; and the day cummynge shal enflawme hem. **1413** *Pilgr. Sowle* (Caxton) II. lx. (1859) 58 Of wexe ne of matche ..ther cometh neuer stynke, but yf that it be fyrst enflammed with fyre. **1582–8** *Hist. Jas. VI* (1804) 9 They ..kendlit thair traine of gwn powder quhilk inflamit the timber of the haill hous. **1626** BACON *Sylva* §361 It is Heat, rather than Flame, which neuerthelesse is sufficient to Enflame the Oyl. **1631** HEYWOOD *Eng. Eliz.* (1641) 176 *marg.*, Gardiner had inflamed many Martyrs, and hath now his body inflamed. **1769** FALCONER *Dict. Marine* (1789) Cc iv b, The fuse..inflames the powder. **1826** HENRY *Elem. Chem.* I. 237 Action of platinum in inflaming hydrogen gas. **1850** ROBERTSON *Serm.* Ser. III. viii. 104 Fire will inflame straw.
fig. **1595** SHAKS. *John* v. i. 7 Vse all your power To stop their marches 'fore we are enflam'd: Our discontented Counties doe reuolt.
b. *transf.* To light up or redden as if with flame; to 'fire'.
c **1477** CAXTON *Jason* 73 Certayn oxen or bulles of fyre so grete that they enflamed alle the region of the ayer. **1697** DRYDEN *Virg. Georg.* IV. 577, I will my self conduct thee on thy Way, When next the Southing Sun inflames the Day. **1822** SHELLEY *Chas. I*, I. 119 The torches Inflame the night to the eastward. **1892** C. HAVILAND in *Pall Mall G.* 8 Aug. 3/1 The red, reflected sky Inflames the river, tints the trees.
2. *fig.* To set on fire with passion, strong feeling, or desire; to excite passionately.
a **1340** HAMPOLE *Psalter* civ. 18 þe worde of oure lord enflaummyd him. *c* **1375** *Sc. Leg. Saints, George* 567 Hou dacyane..wes inflammyt of yre & tene. *c* **1400** MAUNDEV. (Roxb.) Pref. 2 Pride enuy and couetise has so enflaumbed þe hertes. *c* **1449** PECOCK *Repr.* III. viii. 330 The wil is heet and inflamyd into loue. **1560** A. L. tr. *Calvin's Foure Serm. Songe Ezech.* iii. 61 If we be not then enflamed to praise him with full mouth. *a* **1572** KNOX *Hist. Ref.* Wks. 1846 I. 361 The multitud easelie inflambed gave the alarme. **1663** BUTLER *Hud.* I. iii. 242 Honour, Revenge, Contempt and Shame Did equally their Breasts enflame. **1726** LEONI tr. *Alberti's Archit.* III. 18/1 Having their minds enflamed with passion. **1752** HUME *Ess. & Treat.* (1777) I. 69 Court and country-party enflamed into a civil war by an unhappy concurrence of circumstances. **1845** S. AUSTIN *Ranke's Hist. Ref.* III. 215 The warning..had served only to enflame Suleiman with fresh ardour to seek him out. **1867** SMILES *Huguenots Eng.* iii. (1880) 40 [They] did their utmost to inflame the minds of the people against the heretics.
b. To fire, kindle, rouse (passion, etc.).
c **1340** HAMPOLE *Prose Tr.* 2 It inflawmes þe affeccyone. **1573–80** BARET *Alv.* I 141 His anger was inflamed againe. **1732** in *Swift's Lett.* (1766) II. 267 The motive that inflamed

his passions upon that subject [Religion]. **1838** PRESCOTT *Ferd. & Is.* (1846) II. xviii. 162 The reports..of the first adventurers had inflamed the cupidity of many.

3. To heat, make hot; *esp.* to raise (the body or blood) to a feverish or morbid heat; to excite inflammation in.

1530 PALSGR. 534/2 His lyver is al enflamed with drinkyng of hote wynes. **1589** COGAN *Haven Health* ccxvii. (1636) 238 White wine inflameth or heateth least of all wines. **1599** H. BUTTES *Dyets drie Dinner* N viij b, Hurtes..hot constitutions, by inflaming the inward parts, and blood. **1665** SIR T. HERBERT *Trav.* (1677) 282, I put some of the wood into my mouth and chewed it;..for half an hour my mouth was inflamed as if I had taken so much Vitrol. **1712–14** POPE *Rape Lock* IV. 69 If e'er thy Gnome could..Like Citron-waters matrons cheeks inflame. **1775** R. CHANDLER *Trav. Asia M.* (1825) I. 340 We had..wooden lattices to admit the air, while cool; and with shutters to exclude it, when inflamed. **1847** TENNYSON *Princ.* I. 59, I saw my father's face Grow long and troubled..Inflamed with wrath. **1897** FLOR. MARRYAT *Blood Vampire* xv, Her eyes were inflamed with crying.

b. Of a stimulant. (Uniting senses 2 and 3.)

1560 BIBLE (Genev.) *Isa.* v. 11 Wo vnto them, that rise vp early to followe drunkennes, and to them that continue vntil night, til the wine do inflame them. *a* **1586** SIR H. SIDNEY in *Ussher's Lett.* (1686) App. 23 Lest, being enforced to drink [wine] upon the sudden, you should find your self enflamed. **1678** R. L'ESTRANGE *Seneca's Mor.* (1702) 320 Others are enflam'd by Wine. **1850** ROBERTSON *Serm.* Ser. III. ix. 116 Stimulants like wine inflame the senses.

4. To add heat or fuel to, to aggravate, augment in violence, exacerbate.

1607 HIERON *Wks.* I. 353 How happy might I bee, if..I might either enkindle this desire, where hitherto it hath not beene, or might enflame it or adde heate vnto it, where it is? **1706** COLLIER *Reply Filmer* (1730) 415 The Repetition of an ill Thing heightens the Degree, and inflames the Guilt. **1709** ADDISON *Tatler* No. 123 ⁋3 This Stream..rather inflamed than quenched their Thirst. **1818** JAS. MILL *Brit. India* II. v. v. 540 The customary disputes were renewed and inflamed. **1879** FARRAR *St. Paul* (1883) 679 Had he any right to inflame an existing animosity?

†**b.** To augment (a price, or amount charged).

1672 PETTY *Pol. Anat.* (1692) 351 The interest must inflame the price of Irish commodities. **1696** STANHOPE *Chr. Pattern* (1711) 187 Beware lest this busy and malicious impertinence do not inflame the reckoning. **1773** GOLDSM. *Stoops to Conq.* II. i, We passengers are to be taxed to pay all these fineries. I have often seen a good side-board,..though not actually put in the bill, inflame a reckoning confoundedly.

II. *intr.* **5.** To burst into flame; to catch fire.

†**b.** *transf.* To become very hot (*obs.*).

1638 SIR T. HERBERT *Trav.* (ed. 2) 296 Long becalmed, whereby the ayre inflam'd, and Sea gave a fierie reflection. **1783** *Phil. Trans.* LXXIII. 227 When the metal is red-hot, it melts and inflames instantaneously. **1794** G. ADAMS *Nat. & Exp. Philos.* I. xii. 493 It does not inflame, unless mixed with atmospherical or with vital air. **1812** SIR H. DAVY *Chem. Philos.* 89 By the friction of solids..the axle trees of carriages sometimes inflame. **1871** TYNDALL *Fragm. Sc.* (1879) I. iii. 85 It first smokes and then violently inflames.

6. To become hot or excited with passion; to glow with ardour of feeling.

1559 *Mirr. Mag., Jack Cade* xiii, I therby enflamed much the more. **1621** QUARLES *Div. Poems, Esther* vi, Their fell disdaine..inflam'd. **1824** CARLYLE *Schiller* App. ii. (1872) 272, I know how soon your noble heart inflames when sympathy and humanity appeal to it.

7. To become inflamed under the action of disease or stimulants; to be affected with inflammation.

1607 TOPSELL *Four-f. Beasts* (1658) 176 Sometime the liver of the Fox inflameth. **1737** BRACKEN *Farriery Impr.* (1757) II. 162 The Fibres will not fret or inflame as soon. **1753** N. TORRIANO *Gangr. Sore Throat* 126 The Blister inflamed to a great Degree. **1755** *Man* x. 3 Their high blood being apt to inflame with wine. **1892** *Argosy* Mar. 181 He was compelled to drink sparingly lest his head should inflame. **1898** J. HUTCHINSON *Archives Surg.* IX. 313 The patches do not ulcerate or inflame.

inflameable, obs. variant of INFLAMMABLE.

inflamed (ɪn'fleɪmd), *ppl. a.* [f. INFLAME *v.* + -ED[1].]

1. Set on fire, kindled, burning, blazing, in flames. Now *rare*.

1603 FLORIO *Montaigne* (1634) 300 Archimedes..saith, the Sunne is a God of enflamed yron. *c* **1611** CHAPMAN *Iliad* VIII. L iij b, I had conceipt, we should haue made retreate, By light of the inflamed fleet. **1774** J. BRYANT *Mythol.* I. p. xix, It appears to have been an hollow and inflamed mountain. **1858** GREENER *Gunnery* 261 The degree of heat in the inflamed fluid. **1876** T. HARDY *Ethelberta* (1890) 37 A huge inflamed sun was breasting the horizon of a wide sheet of sea.

b. *Her.* Depicted as in flames; flamant.

1610 GUILLIM *Heraldry* III. iv. (1660) 118 The Field is, Or, a Mountain Azure, inflamed, Proper. **1864** BOUTELL *Her. Hist. & Pop.* xxi. §9 (ed. 3) 365 An antique Roman lamp or, inflamed ppr.

2. Enkindled, fired in mind or feeling; fervent, glowing.

1526 *Pilgr. Perf.* (W. de W. 1531) 97 [He] with moost enflamed charite prayed for them. **1579** FENTON *Guicciard.* 190 The Duke of Myllan..nourished an inflamed desire to assubject it to him self. **1710** NORRIS *Chr. Prud.* i. 15 How we come to have such an inflamed Propension to sensible good is another question. **1746–7** HERVEY *Medit.* (1818) 51 What suitable returns of inflamed and adoring devotion can we make to the Holy One of God?

b. Passionately excited; hot with anger; enraged.

1612–32 DELONEY *Thomas of Reading* in Thoms *E.E. Prose Rom.* (1858) I. 104 Neither Hodgekins nor Martin could intreat their inflamed Oast to let him downe. **1797** MRS. RADCLIFFE *Italian* ii, They parted mutually inflamed.

3. Affected with feverish or morbid inflammation; red or swollen from inflammation.

1599 H. BUTTES *Dyets drie Dinner* G ij b, [It] very much helpes an inflamed stomacke. **1789** W. BUCHAN *Dom. Med.* (1790) 495 An emollient clyster, which..will serve as a fomentation to the inflamed parts. **1860** TYNDALL *Glac.* I. xi. 85 Our guide's eyes were..greatly inflamed.

Hence **in'flamedly** *adv. rare*, in an inflamed or excited manner; hotly, fervently.

1637 BASTWICK *Litany* I. 1 My affections began..more inflamedlier to loue the place of permanent and glorious immortality.

inflamer (ɪn'fleɪmə(r)). [f. INFLAME *v.* + -ER[1].] One who or that which inflames or kindles; an exciter, arouser, instigator. (Chiefly in bad sense.)

1609 BP. W. BARLOW *Answ. Nameless Cath.* 364 The originall nourishing inflamers, which minister the rechaffment to these disloyal attempts. *a* **1631** DONNE *Ess. Divinity* (1651) 191 Ceremonies, the cement and mortar of all Exterior, and often the inflamer of interior Religion. **1655** FULLER *Ch. Hist.* IV. i. §23 The inflamer of this rebellion. **1711** ADDISON *Spect.* No. 185 ⁋4 Interest is likewise a great Inflamer, and sets a Man on Persecution under the colour of Zeal. **1750** WARBURTON *Julian* Wks. 1811 VIII. 228 Inflamers of their master's follies. **1852** GROTE *Greece* II. lxxvi. X. 82 Accordingly I seize this man Ismenias as the great inflamer of war. **1881** *Daily News* 17 Feb. 5/2 The inflamers of public hatred against the Jews.

b. That which causes heat or inflammation (in the blood, etc.).

1747 BERKELEY *Tar-water for Cattle* Wks. III. 490, I knew that tar-water was cordial and diaphoretic, and yet no inflamer.

inflaming (ɪn'fleɪmɪŋ), *vbl. sb.* [f. INFLAME *v.* + -ING[1].] The action of the verb INFLAME; inflammation.

1450–1530 *Myrr. our Ladye* 16 All hys herte was enflaumed to the loue of god, wherof after that fulfyllynge and enflaumynge..he broughte fourthe the wordes and the notes. **1547** BOORDE *Brev. Health* ccxix. 75 If there be any inflamyngs in the breste. **1613** T. MILLES tr. *Mexia's* etc. *Treas. Anc. & Mod. T.* I. 15/1 By the Seraphicall enflaming, which is something neere to this divine Fire.

in'flaming, *ppl. a.* [f. as prec. + -ING[2].] That inflames; in various senses of the vb.

1562 A. BROOKE *Romeus & Jul.* 231 In wait lay warlike Love..Till now she had escaped his sharp inflaming dart. **1595** SHAKS. *John* III. i. 340, I am burn'd vp with inflaming wrath. **1709** ADDISON *Tatler* No. 148 ⁋3 The inflaming kind of Diet which is so much in Fashion. **1742** RICHARDSON *Pamela* IV. 82 How unnatural in some, how inflameing in others, are the Descriptions of it! **1789** W. BUCHAN *Dom. Med.* (1790) 547 Dosed with wine, punch,..or some other hot and inflaming liquors. **1864** H. SPENCER *Illustr. Univ. Progr.* 118 The poles of a galvanic battery..will give off, the one an inflammable and the other an inflaming gas.

Hence **in'flamingly** *adv.*, in an inflaming or exciting manner.

1612 CHAPMAN *Widdowes T.* Plays 1873 III. 50 He does become it [the character of Hymen] most enflamingly. **1731** A. HILL *Adv. Poets* Ep. 8 The Warlike Images, so inflamingly touch'd, in the Great Kinds of Poetry.

inflammability (ɪnflæmə'bɪlɪtɪ). [f. next: see -ITY. So F. *inflammabilité* (Buffon).]

a. The quality of being inflammable; †an inflammable. Cf. FLAMMABILITY

1646 SIR T. BROWNE *Pseud. Ep.* III. xxi. 161 If the ambient air be impregnate with subtile inflamabilities, and such as are of quick accension. **1674** BOYLE *Grounds Corpusc. Philos.* 25 Sulphur..owes its inflammability to the convention of yet more simple and primary corpuscles. **1831** BREWSTER *Optics* iii. 26 The high absolute refractive power of oil of cassia..indicates the great inflammability of its ingredients. **1966** WALLACE & WILKINSON *Res. Burns* 634 Standards of non-inflammability to which textile fabrics must conform. **1968** E. MILLER *Textiles* vi. 133 The necessity for some form of treatment which would reduce inflammability risk in fabrics has been on record since the seventeenth century at least.

b. *fig.* Excitableness of temperament.

1787 JEFFERSON *Let. to Madison* 30 Jan. in *Corr.* (1829) II. 90 He has one foible, an excessive inflammability of temper. **1858–62** CARLYLE *Fredk. Gt.* IX. x. (1872) III. 166 This royal Young Gentleman, with his vanities, ambitions, inexperiences, plentiful inflammabilities. **1863** MARY HOWITT *F. Bremer's Greece* I. viii. 264, I had thus an opportunity of witnessing Greek inflammability during parliamentary discussion.

inflammable (ɪn'flæməb(ə)l), *a.* (*sb.*) Also 7 **inflamable**, 7–8 **inflameable**. [repr. L. type **inflammābilis*, f. *inflammāre* (see INFLAME and -BLE); perh. immediately from F. *inflammable* (Cotgr. 1611). The 17–18th c. *inflamable*, *inflameable*, was app. an Eng. formation on the vb.: cf. *blam(e)able*.]

A. *adj.* **1.** Capable of being inflamed or set on fire; susceptible of combustion; easily set on fire. Cf. FLAMMABLE *a.*

inflammable air (***light i. a.***), a name formerly given to hydrogen gas; ***heavy inflammable air***, carburetted hydrogen or fire-damp.

1605 TIMME *Quersit.* I. xiii. 54 The sulphurous substance and inflamable matter. **1646** SIR T. BROWNE *Pseud. Ep.* II. v. 87 Brimstone is a Minerall body of fat and inflamable parts. **1673–4** GREW *Veget. Trunks* iv. §4 A volatile and inflammable Spirit. **1674** PETTY *Disc. Dupl. Proportion* 93 In what proportions several Liquors contein more or less of inflameable or ardent parts. **1736** *Phil. Trans.* Abr. VIII. 77 (*heading*) Experiments on Inflammable Air. **1779** Inflammable gas [see GAS *sb.*[1] 2]. **1789** AUSTIN in *Phil. Trans.* LXXX. 54, I therefore attempted to decompose the heavy inflammable air by means of sulphur, which readily unites with the light inflammable air in a condensed state, and with it forms hepatic air. **1791** [see HYDROGEN]. **1871** ROSCOE *Chem.* 322 Alcohol is very inflammable. **1878** HUXLEY *Physiogr.* 103 This is the gas which was formerly known as inflammable air, and is now called hydrogen. **1962** MUIR & BARCLAY *Burns & their Treatm.* Foreword, It is unfortunate that children and the elderly should bear the brunt of our apparent unwillingness to..elaborate methods of rendering clothing less inflammable. **1968** *Which?* Mar. 92 Recently..the Toilet Preparations Federation recommended to their members that inflammable hair preparations should carry a warning. **1968** E. GALE *From Fibres to Fabrics* xiv. 151 To render fabrics non-inflammable, they may be treated with mineral salts. **1972** *Sci. Amer.* Mar. 54/3 If a resulting spark has enough energy inflammables are ignited and explosions are set off.

2. Easily fired or roused to excitement; excitable, hasty-tempered, passionate.

1800 MRS. HERVEY *Mourtray Fam.* II. 222 Henry..was, moreover, of so violent and inflammable a temper, that half a word was sufficient..to set his blood boiling. **1836** LYTTON *Athens* (1837) I. 442 That lively, high-souled, sensitive, and inflammable people. **1845** FORD *Handbk. Spain* I. 65 Their disposition is very sanguine and inflammable.

3. Of disease: Inflammatory. *rare.*

a **1862** BUCKLE *Misc. Wks.* (1872) I. 405 The inhabitants are little liable to inflammable disease.

B. *sb.* An inflammable substance. (Chiefly in *pl.*) Also *fig.*

1770 CRONSTEDT in *Monthly Rev.* 312 Inflammables, which can be dissolved in oils but not in waters. **1794** KIRWAN *Min.* I. 1 The Mineral Kingdom is usually divided into four parts; 1. Earths and Stones. 2. Salts. 3. Inflammables. 4. Metallic Substances. **1807** 'CERVANTES HOGG' *Rising Sun* I. 141 There may be some inflammables [women] here, for all that. **1894** *Daily News* 7 Apr. 5/8 An alarming fire broke out amongst some cargo, consisting of hay, timber, and other inflammables.

Hence **in'flammableness**, the quality of being inflammable; **in'flammably** *adv.*, in an inflammable manner.

1680 BOYLE *Scept. Chem.* v. 318 They ascribe..to sulphur, as well Odours as inflameableness. **1727** BAILEY vol. II, *Inflameableness* [*ed.* **1731** inflammableness], capableness of being inflamed or set on Fire. **1817** J. SCOTT *Paris Revisit.* (ed. 4) 393 A light, ill-informed, inflammably-constituted public mind. **1830** GODWIN *Cloudesley* II. ii. 29 Partly by the inflammableness of his disposition in that respect. **1922** JOYCE *Ulysses* 716 The same concupiscence, inflammably transmitted first with alarm, then with understanding.

†**in'flammate**, *a. Obs. rare.* [ad. L. *inflammāt-us*, pa. pple. of *inflammāre*.] Inflamed.

c **1450** tr. *De Imitatione* I. xiv. 16 God wol haue us parfitly suget to him, & by loue inflammate passe all maner mannys reson. **1590** BARROUGH *Meth. Physick* II. ix. (1639) 84 If the skins which be joyned all the length of the breast within be inflammate, then [etc.].

inflammation (ɪnflə'meɪʃən). Also 6–7 **inflamation**. [ad. L. *inflammātiōn-em*, n. of action f. *inflammāre* to set on fire: cf. F. *inflammation*, 14th c. in Littré in sense 2, 16th c. in sense 3: these senses were also in L.]

1. The action of inflaming; setting on fire or catching fire; the condition of being in flames, conflagration.

1563 W. FULKE *Meteors* (1640) 31 A thick Exhalation, violently moved out of a cloud, without inflammation or burning. **1626** BACON *Sylva* §366 We will first therefore speake..of Bodies Enflamed, wholly, and immediatly, without any Wieke to helpe the Inflammation. **1650** FULLER *Pisgah* II. xiii. 269 More proper it had been, that such an inflammation [that of the Cities of the Plain] should have left an Etna, Hecla or Vesuvius behinde it. **1794** J. HUTTON *Philos. Light* 185 These different substances require very different degrees of heat, in order to excite their inflammation. **1833** BREWSTER *Nat. Magic* xiii. 313 One of the commonest experiments..is that of producing inflammation by mixing two fluids perfectly cold. **1854** J. SCOFFERN in *Orr's Circ. Sc., Chem.* 230 The inflammation of a gas by electricity.

†**b.** *concr.* Something in flames or on fire; a blazing body or appearance. *Obs.*

1563 W. FULKE *Meteors* (1640) 27 If lightning or any other inflamation be in the upper part of these clouds. **1620** MELTON *Astrolog.* 31 Another will foretell of Lightning and Thunder..when there are no such Inflamations seene. **1760–72** tr. *Juan & Ulloa's Voy.* (ed. 3) I. 443 One of these inflammations [meteors], of a very extraordinary largeness, was seen at Quito whilst we were there.

2. The action of inflaming mentally, of firing the mind, passions, senses, etc. (in quot. 1597 with liquor); the condition of being so inflamed; excitement, fervour. Also, with *an* and *pl.*, an instance of this.

1597 SHAKS. *2 Hen. IV*, IV. iii. 103 They are generally Fooles, and Cowards; which some of vs should be too, but for inflamation. **1609–38** HEYWOOD *Lucrece* Wks. 1874 V. 184 Our hearts with inflammations burne. **1627** F. E. *Hist. Edw. II* (1680) 24 Their Bodies were divided, but their Affections meet with a higher Inflammation. **1777** BURKE *Addr. to King* Wks. 1842 II. 397 The means of calming a people in a state of extreme inflammation. **1818** JAS. MILL *Brit. India* II. IV. vii. 250 The combustion..was soon

communicated to the rest, whose bosoms were perfectly prepared for inflammation.

†**b.** An incitement; a kindling of devotion. *Obs.*

1597 Hooker *Eccl. Pol.* v. xxxiv. §1 The minde..taketh euerywhere new inflammations to pray.

3. *Path.* A morbid process affecting some organ or part of the body, characterized by excessive heat, swelling, pain, and redness; also, a particular instance or occurrence of this.

1533 Elyot *Cast. Helthe* II. xxx. (1541) 47 b, Much sleepe augmenteth heate, more than is necessary, wherby hot fumes and inflamacions are often ingendred. **1543** Traheron *Vigo's Chirurg.* 26 b/1 The patient complayned of great payne and heate, and inflammation. **1611** Bible *Lev.* xiii. 28 If the bright spot stay in his place, and spread not in the skin,..it is an inflammation of the burning. **1732** Arbuthnot *Rules of Diet* i. 249 It is reckoned good in Inflammations of the Bowels. **1813** J. Thomson *Lect. Inflam.* 39 The term Inflammation has long been employed by medical men, to denote the existence of an unusual degree of redness, pain, heat, and swelling, in any of the textures or organs of which the human body is composed. **1879** Harlan *Eyesight* v. 54 The most common disease of the eye is inflammation of the conjunctiva.

†**4.** Augmentation of price or charge: cf. inflame 4 b. *Obs.*

1821 Byron *Juan* III. xxxv, That climax of all human ills, The inflammation of his weekly bills.

inflammative (ɪnˈflæmətɪv), *a.* and *sb. rare.* [f. L. type **inflammātīv-us* (perh. in med.L.: cf. obs. F. *inflammatif, -ive,* 15–16th c. in Godef.), f. ppl. stem of L. *inflammāre* to inflame: see -ive.]

A. *adj.* = inflammatory *a.*

1730–6 Bailey (fol.), *Inflammative,* of an inflaming nature or quality. **1760–72** tr. *Juan & Ulloa's Voy.* (ed. 3) I. 270 Their favourite liquor is brandy, brought also from Lima, and is less inflammative than rum.

B. *sb.* = inflammatory *sb.*

1685 Ken *Serm.* in *Life* (1854) I. 260 That powerful inflammative and preservative of love which Daniel had. *a* **1711** —— *Div. Love* Wks. (1838) 329 O my crucified God, thou sovereign inflammative of love. —— *Philothea* Poet. Wks. 1721 IV. 415 God, in whom all Inflammatives unite, Which can our Love excite.

inflammatory (ɪnˈflæmətərɪ), *a.* and *sb.* [f. L. type **inflammātōri-us* (perh. in mod.L.: cf. F. *inflammatoire,* 1722 in Hatz.-Darm.): see inflammative *a.* and *sb.* and -ory.]

A. *adj.*

†**1.** Of, pertaining to, characterized by, or causing an inflamed or blazing condition. *Obs.*

1757 W. Thompson *R.N. Advoc.* 44 They can also tell what use those inflammatory Combustibles..are of. **1796** Morse *Amer. Geog.* II. 572 The chief of the natural curiosities..is the burning phenomenon, and its inflammatory neighbourhood [Naphtha Springs, near Baku].

2. Tending to inflame with desire or passion; of a nature to rouse passion, anger, or animosity. (Now usually in a bad sense.)

a **1711** Ken *Hymnarium* Poet. Wks. 1721 II. 13, I felt a darted heav'nly Flame..Thus an inflammatory Ray Devour'd my Heart, dry'd all my Tears away. **1767** *Junius Lett.* ii. 11 People..read the poisonous and inflammatory libels. **1776** Gibbon *Decl. & F.* (1869) I. vi. 121 The inflammatory powers of art were summoned to his aid. **1834** Pringle *Afr. Sk.* v. 193 Inflammatory speeches were delivered. *a* **1862** Buckle *Civiliz.* (1869) III. ii. 97 They used the most inflammatory language.

b. Characterized by excitement or passion.

1874 Motley *Barneveld* I. i. 45 Such an inflammatory age.

3. That tends to heat or inflame the blood; exciting the brain or senses; stimulating.

1733 Cheyne *Eng. Malady* II. iii. §4 (1734) 140 Without leaving that..Depression behind it..like Brandy or inflammatory Spirits. **1794** S. Williams *Vermont* 159 Everything which was astringent stimulating and inflammatory. **1805** W. Saunders *Min. Waters* 144 The high activity of Buxton water, and its inflammatory tendency.

4. *Path.* Of the nature of, pertaining to, indicative of, or characterized by inflammation or an inflamed condition of the body.

1732 Arbuthnot *Rules of Diet* 278 In inflammatory Distempers..the Strength may be diminished. **1799** Lear *Let. Presid. U.S.* in *Sir J. Sinclair's Corr.* (1831) II. 32 His [General Washington's] disorder was an inflammatory sore throat, which proceeded from a cold. **1800** *Med. Jrnl.* IV. 420 The rapid progress of the inflammatory symptoms. **1876** Duhring *Dis. Skin* 42 Papules may or may not be inflammatory.

B. *sb.* An inflammatory agent; that which inflames, excites, or rouses strong feeling or passion.

1681 H. More *Exp. Dan.* vi. 159 Her beauty being such an Inflammatory to love. **1759** Franklin *Ess.* Wks. 1840 III. 262 The assembly chose only to glance at the inflammatories thrown in their way.

Hence **inˈflammatorily** *adv.*, in an inflammatory manner.

1840 Dickens *Let.* 2 Oct. (1969) II. 131 Yours inflammatorily and despondingly Charles Dickens. **1887** *Illustr. Lond. News* 12 Mar. 282/2 An inflammatorily religious harangue.

†**inˈflask,** *v. Obs. rare*$^{-0}$. [f. in-² + flask *sb.*] *trans.* To put into a flask.

1611 Florio, *Inflascare,* to inflagon, to inflaske.

inflatable (ɪnˈfleɪtəb(ə)l), *a.* and *sb.* Also **inflateable.** [f. inflate *v.* + -able.]

A. *adj.* Capable of being inflated, blown out, or distended with air or gas.

1878 *Gentl. Mag.* May 603 This craft was made of caoutchouc, inflatable, and weighed 300 lbs. **1884** *Pall Mall G.* 23 Sept. 6/1 Inflatable collars..which will support them in the water. **1897** *Daily News* 19 Feb. 3/5 The defendants, an American firm, use an inner inflateable tube and cover.

B. *sb.* An object, e.g. a dinghy, a toy, etc., which is capable of being inflated.

1954 *Official Directory—American Toy Fair* 46 Phonographs, inflatables, swimming accessories, [etc.]. **1962** *Engineering* 3 Aug. 151 No less than 17,000 Allied aircrew lives were saved by inflatables. **1970** *Guardian* 30 July 9/6 Mark Fisher..and Simon Connolly..are now preparing a DIY inflatable dome kit to order... It makes up into an inflatable 12 ft in diameter by 8 ft high. **1971** A. Bullock *20th Cent.* 245/1 The sculptor has a variety of..plastics with which to make inflatables or multiples. **1971** *New Scientist* 27 Apr. 284/3 Inflatables help children move without fear. **1971** *Ink* 12 June 11/4 Children's Rights Day: Action Space with inflatables and events. **1973** *New Society* 11 Jan. 70/2 A huge plastic inflatable for people to jump around on.

inflatant (ɪnˈfleɪtənt). *rare*$^{-1}$. [f. as prec. + -ant¹.] That which inflates; an inflating agent.

1888 *Pall Mall G.* 31 May 5/1 The use of this inflatant [coal-gas] limits military ballooning considerably.

inflate (ɪnˈfleɪt), *ppl. a.* Now *rare* or *Obs.* [ad. L. *inflāt-us* blown into, filled by blowing, puffed up, pa. pple. of *inflāre*: see next.] = inflated. (Usually construed as pa. pple.)

c **1480** Henryson *Test. Cres.* 463 Nocht is your famous laud and hy honour Bot wind inflat in uther mennis eiris. **1502** Atkinson tr. *De Imitatione* III. xxxv. 224 That thou be nat inflate by pryde & lyft up aboue thy selfe. **1526** *Pilgr. Perf.* (W. de W. 1531) 88 b, That our scyence or connynge ..make vs not inflate with pryde. **1620** T. Scott *God & King* (1633) 4 With eyes staring, countenance red and inflate. **1760** J. Lee *Introd. Bot.* I. xv. (1765) 39 The Pericarpium..varies..in being Turbinate..Inflate, puffed, as in Cardiospermum and Staphylæa. **1833** I. Taylor *Fanat.* vi. 201 The perpetrator is inflate with the persuasion of himself being a demigod in goodness.

inflate (ɪnˈfleɪt), *v.* Also 7 **en-.** [f. L. *inflāt-,* ppl. stem of *inflāre,* f. *in-* (in-²) + *flāre* to blow. For the pa. pple., *inflate* was in early use: see prec.]

1. *trans.* To blow out or distend with wind or air; to fill (a cavity of the body, a balloon, etc.) with air or gas; also *absol.* of food, to cause flatulence.

1533 Elyot *Cast. Helthe* II. vii. (1541) 22 b, They do inflate the stomacke, and cause head ache. **1589** Cogan *Haven Health* ix. (1636) 33 If they [pease] be eaten in the Husks, they be hurtfull, and doe inflate. *a* **1612** Harington *Salerne's Regim.* (1634) 34 Yet the dry figges enflate not so much. **1620** Venner *Via Recta* vii. 120 They..fill the stomacke with winde, and inflate the melt. **1789** W. Buchan *Dom. Med.* (1790) 455 The bowels are inflated with wind. **1834** J. Forbes *Laennec's Dis. Chest* (ed. 4) 159 We must inflate the lung, pass a ligature above the affected part, and then dry it in the open air. **1868** Darwin *Anim. & Pl.* I. v. 138 The habit of slightly inflating the crop is common to all domestic pigeons. **1871** Roscoe *Chem.* 31 We can calculate the weight of zinc and sulphuric acid needed to inflate a balloon of the capacity of 150 cubic metres with hydrogen. **1887** Bowen *Virg. Æneid* v. 32 A following gale, Risen from the west, inflates with a favouring breath their sail.

fig. **1818** Jas. Mill *Brit. India* II. v. vi. 566 The supposed dignity of a King's Court..inflated the pretensions of the Judges. **1870** R. W. Dale *Week-day Serm.* iv. 81 Honest approbation seldom inflates vanity.

2. To puff up (a person) *with* (also †*by*) high spirits, pride, etc.; to elate. Also *absol.*

[**1502**: see inflate *ppl. a.*] **1530** Palsgr. 591/1 Connynge inflateth excepte a man have grace withall. *a* **1618** J. Davies *Wit's Pilgr.* P ij (T.), Envy..Will not admit, that art herself should show By others' fingers; but the mind inflates. *a* **1797** H. Walpole in *Walpoliana* (ed. 2) I. cxxxv. (*Innocent XI*) 111 Castlemain, the ambassador, was inflated with his master's infatuation. **1803** Jane Porter *Thaddeus* Pref., Character that prosperity could not inflate, nor adversity depress. **1873** L. Ferguson *Disc.* 254 Talk about learning may inflate with pride.

3. To dilate, distend, or swell; to enlarge unduly.

a **1705** Ray (J.), That the muscles are inflated in time of rest. **1768–74** Tucker *Lt. Nat.* (1834) I. 547 We work upon certain unknown nerves, they inflate the muscles. **1782** J. Scott *Ess. Paint.* Poems 303 When Passion's tumults in the bosom rise, Inflate the features, and enrage the eyes. **1822–34** *Good's Study Med.* (ed. 4) II. 630 The whole body was emaciated, the eyebrows inflated.

4. To swell or expand artificially or unduly; to expand beyond proper or natural limits; to raise above the amount or value which sound commercial principles would fix. Also *intr.*, to resort to, exhibit, or produce (monetary) inflation.

1843 Sir R. Peel in *Croker Papers* Apr. (1884), Commerce, inflated by extravagant speculation..demands some remedy. **1844** Emerson *Yng. American* Wks. (Bohn) II. 298 We inflate our paper currency. **1887** B. F. Cowen in Vincent *You & I, Business Integr.* 641 (Funk), The want of integrity in business has inflated the stocks of our large corporations. **1940** *Economist* 27 Jan. 136/1 The most direct ..method of inflating, if it cannot be avoided, would..be the deliberate creation of additional credit. **1965** *New Statesman* 31 Dec. 1021/1 Even if *all* countries inflated at the same rate, some problems would remain. **1971** *Sunday Times* 24 Oct. 44/6 More recently..all types of Southern property have been inflating faster than anywhere in the country. **1973** *Time* 25 June 23/2 In the supermarket.. prices have been inflating at an annual rate of 25% or more.

Hence **inˈflating** *vbl. sb.* and *ppl. a.*; whence **inˈflatingly** *adv.*, in an inflating manner (Webster, 1856); also **inˈflater, -or,** one who or that which inflates or puffs up (*lit.* and *fig.*); *spec.* an air-pump for inflating pneumatic cushions, tyres, etc.

1533 Elyot *Cast. Helthe* (1541) 10 b, Meates inflatynge or wyndye: Beanes, Lupines [etc.]. **1807** Crabbe *Par. Reg.* II. Poems 1834 II. 183 In vain, they come, she feels th'inflating grief. **1884** *American* VIII. 84 The clamor of contending inflaters and wreckers at the stock exchange. **1896** *Westm. Gaz.* 19 May 2/1 As soon as it is ready, and the gas made, the balloon will be inflated. The inflating, it is calculated, will take three days. **1899** *Mod. Newspaper,* Immediately the tyre becomes slack when riding..the inflator responds, without any aid from the rider.

inflated (ɪnˈfleɪtɪd), *ppl. a.* [f. prec. + -ed¹.]

1. Puffed out or swollen by air or gas; in quot. 1700, 'filled with wind'.

1681 tr. *Willis' Rem. Med. Wks.* Vocab., *Inflated,* blown or puffed up as a bladder with wind. **1700** Dryden *Fables, Cock & Fox* 750 They chas'd the murderous Fox, With brazen trumpets, and inflated box. **1841** Orderson *Creol.* xiii. 137 Up rose with inflated majesty the gaseous globe. **1853** Sir H. Douglas *Milit. Bridges* (ed. 3) 223 Bridges on ..air-tight cases, and inflated skins.

2. Of language: Full of empty rhetoric; turgid, bombastic.

1652 Cogan tr. *Scudery's Ibrahim* Pref. A v b, A narrative stile ought not to be too much inflated, no more than that of ordinary conversations. **1774** Goldsm. *Nat. Hist.* (1862) I. vii. 34 The account he gives of it is long and inflated. **1788** Mad. D'Arblay *Diary* 2 Aug., I did not in general like Akenside's odes..I thought they were too inflated. **1867** Freeman *Norm. Conq.* I. iii. 145 Are these titles..mere pieces of inflated rhetoric?

3. Swollen, expanded, or dilated with hollow interior, as if by inflation.

1726–46 Thomson *Winter* 166 Now th' inflated wave Straining they scale. **1776–96** Withering *Brit. Plants* (ed. 3) III. 134 Calyx egg-shaped, inflated. **1828** Stark *Elem. Nat. Hist.* II. 384 Abdomen inflated and vesicular. **1880** Gray *Struct. Bot.* (ed. 6) 416/2 *Inflated,* bladdery.

4. Puffed up or elated with vanity, or false notions.

1784 Cowper *Task* v. 268 Inflated and astrut with self-conceit, He gulps the windy diet. **1790** Cath. Graham *Lett. Educ.* 69 Knight errantry was the effect of an inflated imagination. **1818** Jas. Mill *Brit. India* II. iv. vi. 228 The inflated conceptions diffused among their countrymen of the riches of India. **1868** Gladstone *Juv. Mundi* ii. (1869) 63 In his [Thersites'] short speech, of which an inflated presumption is the principal mark.

5. Raised or enhanced in price by speculation or other artificial and temporary causes.

1881 Gladstone *Sp. Leeds* 7 Oct., Exported at an inflated state of prices that could not possibly be maintained. **1899** *Morning Herald* 28 June 4/3 There was an unnatural and an unhealthy inflated value put upon land.

Hence **inˈflatedness,** the quality of being inflated.

1867 C. J. Smith *Syn. & Antonyms* s.v. *Altiloquence,* Turgidity, Inflatedness. **1890** *Spectator* 29 Mar., Illimitable obtuseness to the bathos of moral and intellectual inflatedness.

inflatile (ɪnˈfleɪtɪl), *a.* [ad. late L. *inflātil-is* (Cassiodorus) of or for blowing: see -ile. Cf. obs. F. *inflatil* (16th c. in Godef.).] Of a musical instrument: Sounded by blowing.

1776 Hawkins *Hist. Music* I. II. ix. 243 The general division of musical instruments is into three classes, the pulsatile, tensile, and inflatile. **1891** *Athenæum* 19 Sept. 390/3 The drum, the flute, and the lyre, as types respectively of percussive, inflatile, and pulsatile instruments.

inflation (ɪnˈfleɪʃən). [ad. L. *inflātiōn-em,* n. of action f. *inflāre* to inflate. Cf. obs. F. *inflation, -flacion,* etc. (15th c. in Godef.).]

1. The action of inflating or distending with air or gas.

1601 Holland *Pliny* Explan. Words, *Inflation,* swelling or puffing vp with winde. **1646** Sir T. Browne *Pseud. Ep.* IV. vi. 194 Whereby..the putrifying parts do suffer a turgescence and inflation, and becomming airy and spumous..ascend unto the surface of the water. **1802** *Med. Jrnl.* VIII. 338 Having separated by inflation, the skin and muscles of one of the posterior extremities of a frog. *Mod.* The inflation of military balloons with hydrogen instead of coal-gas.

2. The condition of being inflated with air or gas, or of being distended or swollen as if with air.

a **1340** Hampole *Psalter* l. 8 It purges þe longes of inflacioun. *c* **1420** *Pallad. on Husb.* XI. 504 This condyment is esy and iocounde Wherof inflacioun shal noon redounde. *c* **1550** Lloyd *Treas. Health* (1585) F viij A julep of Roses is good for the inflation of the longes. **1646** Sir T. Browne *Pseud. Ep.* III. xxi. 162 The inflation or swelling of the body made in this animal upon inspiration or drawing in its breath. **1732** Arbuthnot *Rules of Diet* 294 Winds coming upwards, Inflations and Tumours of the Belly are signs of a phlegmatick Constitution. **1845** Darwin *Voy. Nat.* i. (1879) 14 By the inflation of its body, the papillae with which the skin is covered, become erect and pointed.

3. The condition of being puffed up with vanity, pride, or baseless notions.

1526 *Pilgr. Perf.* (1531) 34 Singular inflacyons & elacyons of the mynde. **1658** BAXTER *Saving Faith* vii. 54 The undoubted fruit of this Doctrine received, would be the inflation of audacious, fiery, fantastick spirited men. **1844** H. H. WILSON *Brit. India* I. 69 The inflation of Holkar's ambition with the hope that [etc.]. **1883** FROUDE *Short Stud.* IV. II. i. 172 The words well convey the inflation with which the Catholic revivalists were going to their work.

4. The quality of language or style when it is swollen with big or pompous words; turgidity, bombast.

1603 HOLLAND *Plutarch's Mor.* 1199 A tragicall pompe, and swelling inflation of words. **1791** W. BEAUMONT tr. *Barthelemi's Trav. Anacharsis Greece* (1796) I. p. vi, A style which to an English reader will appear to border on inflation and bombast. **1824** DIBDIN *Libr. Comp.* 713 Conceits were the then fashion of the age, as inflation and obscurity are now.

†**5.** Of a plague: Spread, extension (cf. DILATATION 2); or (?) increase of virulence. *Obs. rare.*

1536 BELLENDEN *Cron. Scot.* (1821) II. 444 This pest rais with sa terribill inflation, that ilk man that tuk it deceissit within two dayis efter.

6. Great or undue expansion or enlargement; increase beyond proper limits; esp. of prices, the issue of paper money, etc. *spec.* An undue increase in the quantity of money in relation to the goods available for purchase; (in lay use) an inordinate rise in prices.

1838 D. D. BARNARD *Speeches & Rep.* 195 The property pledge can have no tendency whatever to prevent an inflation of the currency. **1841** in X. D. MacLeod *Biogr. F. Wood* (1856) 75 We have been periodically visited by panics, revulsions, and distresses, inflations and reäctions. **1863** W. S. JEVONS *Serious Fall in Value of Gold* i. 13 The inflation of credit must be checked by the well defined boundary of available capital. *Ibid.* 14 A revulsion occasioned by a failure of the national capital must cause.. a collapse of credit, and of any inflation of prices due to credit. *Ibid.* 25 It is impossible to account for this permanent change [in prices] by any excessive speculation, inflation of currency, or credit. **1864** WEBSTER, *Inflation*.. 4 Undue expansion or increase, from over-issue;—said of currency. **1870** W. W. FOWLER *Ten Yrs. Wall St.* 315 Used ten thousand shares of the new stock to load up the bulls at these inflation prices. **1874** *N. Y. Tribune* 26 Nov. 5 An Inflation Party [has been organized] reaffirming, in effect, the financial plank of the Indiana Independents. **1878** *N. Amer. Rev.* CXXVI. 156 Despite the illegal inflation authorized by President Grant. **1885** *Manch. Exam.* 18 Mar. 5/1 The never-failing tendency to a needless inflation of our armaments. **1887** JESSOPP *Arcady* ii. 62 The inflation of prices brought with it a speculative mania. **1922** *Encycl. Brit.* XXX. 984/1 Inflation had the effect of reducing the pre-war unit of value. **1949** *Times* 10 Sept. 5/6 Inflation is used to describe the situation in any country where there is an excess of currency and credit in relation to the work to be done, an excess of purchasing power and effective demand in relation to its goods available, with prices and wages, and prices again, rising in consequence. **1967** *Economist* 16 Dec. 1143/3 That fearsome thing called 'inflation psychology' is taking hold. **1972** *Accountant* 5 Oct. 434/5 He made a plea for a Dutch recommendation on inflation accounting in external reporting. **1973** *Sun* 18 Jan. 16 The Premier named inflation as public enemy No. 1.

7. Inspiration, afflatus. *rare.*

1835 I. TAYLOR *Spir. Despot.* iii. 87 The opinion that the priests and priestesses of the oracular temples were nothing more than involuntary subjects of the divine inflation.

8. inflation-proof, *v. trans.*, to protect from the effects of monetary inflation; so ***inflation-proofing***; **inflation-rubber**, a removable rubber sleeve inside each teat cup of a milking machine which, as it is rhythmically inflated and deflated, squeezes the cow's teats; also ellipt. *inflation*.

1973 *Times* 26 Nov. 14/6 The Chancellor could profitably devote the budget.. to inflation-proofing those of our laws and institutions which have been created on the false assumption that monetary values are constant. *Ibid.* 27 Nov. 18/6 Neither of them enjoys any automatic inflation-proofing beyond the moment of their retirement. **1974** *Guardian* 23 Jan. 10/1 The cuts affect universities in three ways: delayed building, a loss of inflation-proofing in current spending, and doubt about student grants. **1950** *N.Z. Jrnl. Agric.* Feb. 114/2 Old rubberware such as used inflations must never be allowed to accumulate.. close to the dairy. *Ibid.* Oct. 301/3 Inflation rubbers give quicker milking if they retain their tension. **1960** B. CRUMP *Good Keen Man* 102 His bellowing discourse on the good and bad brands of inflation-rubbers for milking machines.

inflationary (ɪnˈfleɪʃənərɪ), *a.* [f. INFLATION + -ARY[1].] Of, pertaining to, characterized by, or involving (monetary) inflation.

1920 *Glasgow Herald* 21 Aug. 7 The transition from an inflationary to a deflationary period in prices. **1921** *Spectator* 28 May 677/1 The enormous Government loans, with their inflationary influence. **1930** *Time & Tide* 1 Nov. 1356 France is uneasy about the inflationary effects of the gold she has collected. **1931** *Economist* 12 Dec. 1118/1 Progressive depreciation of sterling.. would.. make the beginning of an all-round inflationary spiral a certainty. **1943** *Ann. Reg. 1942* 31 Increases in basic wages had not been of a kind calculated to produce the inflationary spiral. **1945** WEBSTER Add., *Inflationary gap*, the gap between an increasing purchasing power, that is, money available for spending, and a shrinking or static supply of civilian goods available for purchase, which as it widens sets in motion an inflationary spiral. **1970** T. LUPTON *Managem. & Social Sci.* (ed. 2) ii. 46 The inflationary pressure generated by collective bargaining at the workplace in conditions of full employment.

inflationism (ɪnˈfleɪʃənɪz(ə)m). [f. as prec. + -ISM.] The condition or fact of being inflated; the policy of inflating the currency. Also *transf.* and *fig.*

1919 J. M. KEYNES *Econ. Consequences Peace* 223 The inflationism of the currency systems of Europe has proceeded to extraordinary lengths. **1930** *New Statesman* 9 Aug. 572/2 The book is a tract against inflationism. **1938** C. CONNOLLY *Enemies of Promise* ix. 93 The deflationary activities of the Cambridge critics..have replaced the inflationism of Bloomsbury. **1973** *Spectator* 3 Mar. 280/3 His real enemy is not the dialectical materialism of the Marxist militants but the dialectical inflationism of the Tories' own monetary policy.

inflationist (ɪnˈfleɪʃənɪst). [f. INFLATION + -IST.] One who advocates inflation; *spec.* in *U.S.*, and hence elsewhere, one who advocates an increase of the paper currency as beneficial to trade. Also *attrib.*

1876 *N. Amer. Rev.* CXXIII. 451 The election of Gilden would spike the whole inflationist battery. **1889** *Times* 5 Mar. 9/2 Originally distrusted as an inflationist, he showed considerable skill in conducting the refunding operations.

†**inˈflative**, *a. Obs.* [ad. mod.L. *inflātīv-us* (cf. obs. F. *inflatif, -ive*, 15th c. in Godef.), f. ppl. stem of L. *inflāre* to INFLATE: see -IVE.] Of inflating quality or tendency.

1528 PAYNEL *Salerne's Regim.* P ij, The substance of all pulse is inflatiue [L. *inflativa*] and harde of digestion. **1612** WOODALL *Surg. Mate* Wks. (1653) 22* The inflative instrument, for giving of a fumous medicine. **1658** ROWLAND *Moufet's Theat. Ins.* 925 The distilled water of common Wasps.. applied to the belly it makes it swell as if it had the Dropsie.. it may be concluded that their venome is exceeding hot and inflative.

‖**inflatus** (ɪnˈfleɪtəs). [L. *inflātus* a blowing into, inspiration; cf. INFLATION.] A blowing or breathing into; inflation; inspiration, afflatus.

a **1861** MRS. BROWNING (Webster 1864), The divine breath that blows the nostrils out To ineffable inflatus.

inflect (ɪnˈflɛkt), *v.* [ad. L. *inflect-ĕre*, f. *in-* (IN-[2]) + *flectĕre* to bend.]

1. *trans.* To bend inwards; to bend into a curve or angle; hence, simply, to bend, to curve.

c **1425** *Found. St. Bartholomew's* (E.E.T.S.) 5 Whan he from so grete an highnesse wolde inflecte and bowe downe his yie to the lower party donward, he behelde an horrible pytte. **1578** BANISTER *Hist. Man* I. 24 These [cartilages] occupying the meane space betwixt the ribbes and brest bone, are by expiration inflected. **1665** GLANVILL *Scepsis Sci.* viii. 44 It cannot be apprehended but that the line be inflected if some parts of it move faster than others. **1712** BLACKMORE *Creation* I. (1736) 11 To a determin'd distance they ascend, And there inflect their course, and downward tend. **1732** ARBUTHNOT *Rules of Diet* 410 They must be inflected to that side where the Muscle pulls strongest. **1804** C. B. BROWN tr. *Volney's View Soil U.S.* 134 The course of a general wind is often inflected, from 30 to 80 degrees, by the hollow of a river, a ridge of hills [etc.]. **1875** DARWIN *Insectiv. Pl.* ii. 22 All the tentacles were soon energetically inflected.

b. *fig.* To bend, incline, dispose.

c **1555** HARPSFIELD *Divorce Hen. VIII* (Camden) 174 Ruth by no means could be inflected.. to break company from her mother-in-law. **1624** GEE *Foot out of Snare* 17 Inflecting, fashioning and refashioning their religion according to the will and wantonness of them. **1657** W. MORICE *Coena quasi Κοινὴ* Pref. 2 A gentle suppling and inflecting them to pay their Tythes. **1804** W. TAYLOR in *Ann. Rev.* II. 276 That memoir of Turgot's which.. is at this time still inflecting toward itself the new as it did the old authorities.

†**2.** *Optics.* To bend in or deflect (rays of light) in passing the edge of an opaque body or through a narrow aperture; to DIFFRACT. *Obs.*

1704 NEWTON *Optics* (J), Are they [rays of light] not reflected, refracted, and inflected by one and the same principle, acting variously in various circumstances? **1727-41** CHAMBERS *Cycl.* s.v. *Ray*, Sir Isaac Newton suspects they [light-rays] may have..a power of being inflected, or bent, by the action of distant bodies. **1811** [see DEFLECT *v.* 2 b].

3. *Gram.* To vary the termination (of a word) in order to express different grammatical relations.

1668 WILKINS *Real Char.* 449 As to the inflexions of Adjectives by the degrees of comparison.. those which are inflected through all degrees, have several irregularities in the manner of it. **1747** JOHNSON *Plan Dict.* Wks. 1787 IX. 178 We are to examine..how they [words] are inflected through their various terminations. **1871** *Public Sch. Lat. Gram.* §14. 22 Flexion, or Stem-flexion, is the method of inflecting a Stem, that is, of making such changes in its form as may indicate changes in its meaning and use.

4. To modulate (the voice); *spec.* in *Music*, to flatten or sharpen (a note) by a chromatic semitone.

1828 WEBSTER, *Inflect*.. 3. To modulate, as the voice. **1867** MACFARREN *Harmony* i. 5 With the Greeks, it allowed of no notes inflected by sharps or flats. **1889** PROUT *Harmony* xii. §274 Whenever a modulation takes place, the note inflected by an accidental is regarded as belonging to the key in which it is diatonic.

Hence **inˈflecting** *ppl. a.*, that inflects.

1666 *Phil. Trans.* I. 242 The Air light, and clear without inflecting parts. **1831** BREWSTER *Newton* (1855) I. ix. 200 He ascribes it [inflexion] to the variable density of the ether within and without the inflecting body.

inflectable (ɪnˈflɛktəb(ə)l), *a. Gram.* [f. INFLECT *v.* 3 + -ABLE.] Capable of being inflected.

1958 W. N. FRANCIS *Struct. Amer. Eng.* 594 *Noun*,..a lexical word which..is inflectable with the plural and possessive inflections (*-es*) and (*'s*). **1963** F. G. LOUNSBURY in S. Koch *Psychol.* VI. 563 The determination of the particular form of an inflectable word. **1965** *English Studies* XLVI. 30 An inflectable possessive pronoun.

inflected (ɪnˈflɛktɪd), *ppl. a.* [f. INFLECT *v.* + -ED[1].]

1. Bent or curved; bent inwards.

1646 SIR T. BROWNE *Pseud. Ep.* III. i. 105 Galen.. commends unto us..not to lye directly, or at length, but somewhat inflected, that the muscles may be at rest. **1796** H. BROUGHAM in *Phil. Trans.* LXXXVI. 228 The angle.. which the inflected ray makes with the line drawn [etc.]. **1847** LEWES *Hist. Philos.* (1867) I. 82, I here sit in an inflected position. **1870** ROLLESTON *Anim. Life* Introd. 48 The angle of the lower jaw is almost always inflected. **1875** DARWIN *Insectiv. Pl.* vii. 165 All the tentacles except three inflected or sub-inflected.

2. *Gram.* Of a word: Varied in the terminations to express varied grammatical relations. Of a language: Characterized by grammatical inflexion.

1775 in ASH. **1865** TYLOR *Early Hist. Man.* iv. 64 Inflected languages such as Latin. **1871** EARLE *Philol. Eng. Tongue* §30 The essence of an inflected language is, to express by modifications of form that which an uninflected language expresses by arrangements of words.

3. ***inflected arch***: an arch having the curve of its flanks reversed near the crown, so as to terminate in an acute angle. (Knight *Dict. Mech.* 1875).

Hence **inˈflectedness**, the state or condition of being inflected.

1811-31 BENTHAM *Univ. Gram.* Introd., Wks. 1843 VIII. 341 Sparingly inflectedness and copiously inflectedness, as applied to language.

inflection: see INFLEXION.

inflective (ɪnˈflɛktɪv), *a.* [f. INFLECT *v.* + -IVE; in mod.F. *inflectif*.]

1. Having the quality of inflecting; tending to inflect.

1666 *Phil. Trans.* I. 240 The Inflective veins of the Air (if I may so call those parts, which..have a greater or less Refractive power than the Air next adjoyning). **1713** DERHAM *Phys.-Theol.* 13 *note*, Although this inflective Quality of the Air be a great Incumbrance and Confusion of Astronomical Observations.

2. Pertaining to or characterized by grammatical inflexion.

1799 W. TAYLOR in *Monthly Rev.* XXVIII. 569 Inflective and derivative syllables. **1875** WHITNEY *Life Lang.* vi. 104 The glories of a completely inflective language. **1885** CLODD *Myths & Dr.* I. iv. 76 Their language had passed into the inflective or highest stage.

inflector (ɪnˈflɛktə(r)). *rare*[−1]. [f. INFLECT *v.* + -OR.] That which inflects or bends. (In quot. *attrib.*)

1851 RICHARDSON *Geol.* viii. 273 Propulsion through the water.. by the action of the inflector muscles of the tail.

†**inˈfledged**, *a. Obs.* [IN-[3].] = UNFLEDGED.

a **1661** FULLER *Worthies, Barksh.* I. (1662) 97 He therein made nests for many birds; which otherwise, being either infledged or maimed, must have been exposed to wind and weather.

†**inˈfleeing**, *vbl. sb. Obs. rare*[−1]. [f. IN-[1] + FLEEING.] A place to flee into; a refuge.

a **1300** *E.E. Psalter* cxliii[i]. 2 Mi merci and in-fleing mine, Mi helper and leser mine.

inflesh, obs. form of ENFLESH *v.*

ˈ**inflex**, *sb.* [ad. L. *inflexus* (*u*-stem), synonymous with *inflexio* INFLEXION.] In the grammar of the Bantu languages, the particle prefixed to a root, to form a noun, which has functions similar to those of inflexional suffixes in the Aryan and Semitic languages. (Also called *prefix* or *initial*.)

1859 COLENSO *First Steps Zulu-Kafir* ii. 4 Every Zulu noun consists of two parts, the *root* and the *inflex*, the latter being a small particle, which is set before the root, forming with it the complete noun... We give the name of inflex to this initial particle, because, by changes of it, certain modifications of the noun are effected, as they are in Latin and Greek, by means of terminal particles.. Thus..in the Zulu word *umuntu*, person, the root is *ntu*, and the inflex *umu*, which is changed to *aba* for the plural, and the whole word becomes *abantu*, people.

†**inˈflex**, *a. Bot. Obs. rare.* [ad. L. *inflex-us*, pa. pple. of *inflectĕre* to INFLECT.] = INFLEXED.

1753 CHAMBERS *Cycl. Supp.* s.v. *Leaf*, *Inflex Leaf*, that which in growing from its base, turns its point again toward the plant. **1794** MARTYN *Rousseau's Bot.* xvii. 234 The petals are inflex, or bent upwards at the end.

inflexed (ɪnˈflɛkst), *ppl. a.* [f. as prec. + -ED[1].] Bent inwards; incurved.

1661 FELTHAM *Disc. Luke* xiv. 20 Wks. (1677) 361 Davids right-heartedness became inflex'd and crooked. **1708** J. PHILIPS *Cyder* II. 69 Suffice it to provide a brazen tube Inflext. **1735** H. BROOKE *Univ. Beauty* II. 265 Thy grand machine.. There most direct where seeming most inflex'd. **1816** KIRBY & SP. *Entomol.* (1843) II. 255 The tail..is furnished with an inflexed fork..usually bent under the

body. **1830** LINDLEY *Nat. Syst. Bot.* 59. **1872** OLIVER *Elem. Bot.* II. 182 The apices of the petals are often inflexed.

inflexibility[1] (ɪnˌflɛksɪˈbɪlɪtɪ). [f. INFLEXIBLE[1] + -ITY, perh. after F. *inflexibilité* (1611 in Hatz.-Darm.).] The quality or condition of being inflexible; incapability of being bent; unyielding stiffness, rigidity; firmness of purpose, obstinacy.

1611 FLORIO, *Inflessibilita*, inflexibilitie. **1706** in PHILLIPS. *c* **1730** A. BAXTER *Enq. Nat. Soul* II. 125 (T.) Against the 'inertia' of matter, or the inflexibility of mechanism. **1742** FIELDING *J. Andrews* IV. v, The squire, who knew her inflexibility, interrupted her. **1818** SCOTT *Rob Roy* xxiii, His features arranged into the utmost inflexibility of expression. **1873** L. FERGUSON *Disc.* 218 Mere inflexibility of purpose is not necessarily an excellence. **1876** tr. *Wagner's Gen. Pathol.* 337 Bone..cannot swell, in consequence of its inflexibility.

inflexibility[2]: see INFLEXIBLE[2].

inflexible (ɪnˈflɛksɪb(ə)l), *a.*[1] [ad. L. *inflexibil-is*, f. *in-* (IN-[3]) + *flexibilis* FLEXIBLE: cf. F. *inflexible* (13–14th c. in Littré).] Not flexible.

1. Incapable of being bent; unbendable; not pliant; rigid, stiff.

c **1400** *Lanfranc's Cirurg.* I. ii. 24 If þat he [the ligament] hadde be inflexible as a boon..oon lyme myȝte not han meued wiþouten anoþer. **1545** JOYE *Exp. Dan.* vi. (R.), Of this thing is the king's scepter a very apt signe and token, in that it is ferme and inflexible. **1607** TOPSELL *Four-f. Beasts* (1658) 153 His trunck..is crooked, gristly, and inflexible, at the root next to the nose. **1725** POPE *Odyss.* XXI. 188 The bow inflexible resists their pain. **1728** PEMBERTON *Newton's Philos.* 63 If two equal bodies..be hung at the extremities of an inflexible rod. **1892** *Strand Mag.* Dec. 652/1 An ivory-handled knife with a very delicate inflexible blade.

2. Unbending in temper or purpose; not to be turned from a purpose by persuasion or argument; immovable, inexorable.

1398 TREVISA *Barth. De P.R.* II. viii. (Add. MS. 27,944 lf. 15/1) He is inflexible, stedfast, and faileþ not. **1460** CAPGRAVE *Chron.* (Rolls) 168 The bischop vas inflexibil. **1542** N. UDALL in *Lett. Lit. Men* (Camden) 6 Not to bee inexorable nor inflexible towardes me your poor servant. **1694** KETTLEWELL *Comp. Persecuted* 145 Fill me with an inflexible Integrity and Constancy in my Duty. **1716** LADY M. W. MONTAGU *Let. to C'tess Mar* 21 Nov., She..remains still inflexible, either to threats or promises. **1777** WATSON *Philip II*, XVI. (1839) 329 Sebastian adhered to his purpose with inflexible obstinacy. **1855** MACAULAY *Hist. Eng.* xvi. III. 727 Billop, though courteous, was inflexible.

3. Unalterable, rigidly fixed.

1693 SOUTH *Twelve Serm.* (1698) III. 84 To make it the Rigid Inflexible Rule, which it is to Judge by. **1871** NAPHEYS *Prev. & Cure Dis.* I. viii. 220 Nature's laws are more inflexible than iron. **1885** S. COX *Exposit.* Ser. I. ii. 20 The moral order of the universe is as inflexible as the physical order.

†**inflexible**, *a.*[2] *Obs. rare.* [f. L. *inflex-* (see INFLEX *a.*) + -IBLE.] Capable of being inflected; in *Optics* diffrangible. Hence †**inflexiˈbility**.

1432–50 tr. *Higden* (Rolls) III. 405 Hym semede his herte to be more inflexible [L. *inflecti*] to melody then to chevallery. **1796** H. BROUGHAM in *Phil. Trans.* LXXXVI. 233 Wherefore I conclude that the rays of the sun's light differ in degree of inflexibility, and that those which are least refrangible are most inflexible. **1857** H. LLOYD *Wave-Theory Light* (ed. 2) §95 Supposing that the rays which differ in refrangibility differ also in inflexibility.

inˈflexibleness. *rare.* [f. INFLEXIBLE[1] + -NESS.] = INFLEXIBILITY[1].

a **1617** HIERON *Wks.* (1619) II. 372 For the inflexiblenesse of it [man's heart], I shewed you erewhile..of what a stony qualitie it is. *a* **1688** W. CLAGETT *17 Serm.* (1699) 449 The inflexibleness of true doctrine.

inflexibly (ɪnˈflɛksɪblɪ), *adv.* [f. as prec. + -LY[2].] In an inflexible manner; rigidly, firmly, obstinately; unalterably.

1534 MORE *Comf. agst. Trib.* II. xvi. Wks. 1194/1 Inflexibly set vpon the purpose to destroy himself. **1647** BP. HALL *Christ Myst.* (R.), We know him indeed to be infinitely and inflexibly just. **1776** GIBBON *Decl. & F.* xvi. (1869) I. 382 The payment of this tribute was inflexibly refused. **1856** KANE *Arct. Expl.* I. xxiv. 310 As far as we could see, it [the ice] remained inflexibly solid.

inflexion, inflection (ɪnˈflɛkʃən). [ad. L. *inflexiōn-em*, n. of action f. *inflectĕre* (ppl. stem *inflex-*) to INFLECT. Cf. F. *inflexion* (14th c. in Godef. *Compl.*). As to the spelling cf. CONNEXION, DEFLEXION.]

1. The action of inflecting or bending, or, more particularly, of bending in or towards itself.

1531 ELYOT *Gov.* I. xx, A..crafty daunser, which in his daunse coulde imagine the inflexions of the serpente. **1646** SIR T. BROWNE *Pseud. Ep.* III. i. 104 They conceive there may be a progression or advancement made in motion without the inflexion of parts. **1756** BURKE *Subl. & B.* III. xxii, There is required a small inflexion of the body. **1837** WHEWELL *Hist. Induct. Sc.* (1857) II. 61 The inflexion of a direct motion into a curve. **1875** DARWIN *Insectiv. Pl.* vii. 172 Sufficient to cause the inflection of a single tentacle.

b. The condition of being inflected or bent; *concr.* a bending, bend, curvature, or angle.

1658 SIR T. BROWNE *Gard. Cyrus* ii. 45 The Labyrinth of Crete, built upon a long quadrate, containing five large squares, communicating by right inflections, terminating in the centre of the middle square, and lodging of the Minotaur. **1662** STILLINGFL. *Orig. Sacr.* III. i. §16 The several inflections of the joynts serve for all kind of figures. **1771** SMOLLETT *Humph. Cl.* 18 July, Let. to Lewis, [The] view..varied..according to the inflexions of the road. **1802** PLAYFAIR *Illustr. Hutton. Th.* 213 The section..of this ridge is highly instructive, from the great disturbance of the primary strata, and the variety of their inflexions. **1837** BREWSTER *Magnet.* 234 This singular inflexion of the magnetic equator in the South Sea. **1856** WOODWARD *Mollusca* 301 Ligament contained in a spoon-shaped inflection.

c. *fig.* A mental or moral bending or turning.

1597 HOOKER *Eccl. Pol.* v. xxxviii. §1 The very steps and inflections euery way..of all passions whereunto the mind is subject. **1774** J. BRYANT *Mythol.* I. 190 The allusion will not be..obtained by undue inflexions or distortions. **1890** BOLDREWOOD *Col. Reformer* (1891) 158 Even in..self-analysis men are not infrequently insincere and evasive... Were the moral processes incapable of such inflections [etc.].

†**2.** *Optics.* The bending of a ray of light, at the edge of a body, into the geometrical shadow. Now called DIFFRACTION. *Obs.*

1704 NEWTON (*title*) Opticks: or a Treatise of the Reflections, Refractions, Inflections and Colours of Light. **1728** PEMBERTON *Newton's Philos.* 377 These shadows are also observed to be bordered with colours. This our author calls the inflection of light. **1796** H. BROUGHAM in *Phil. Trans.* LXXXVI. 228 If a ray passes within a certain distance of any body, it is bent inwards; this we shall call Inflection. **1831** BREWSTER *Newton* (1855) I. ix. 194 There is an inflexion of light differing both from refraction and reflexion, and seeming to depend upon the unequal density of the constituent parts of the ray. **1865–72** WATTS *Dict. Chem.* III. 601 s.v. *Light*, These effects, formerly known as Inflection, and now called Diffraction.

3. *Geom.* Change of curvature from convex to concave at a particular point on a curve; the point at which this takes place is called ***a point of inflexion*** (or shortly ***an inflexion***); at such a point the moving tangent to the curve becomes stationary, the direction of its angular motion being changed; hence *inflexion* is also applied to such a stationary tangent itself, or to the analogous stationary osculating plane (***plane inflexion***) in a non-plane curve.

1721 BAILEY, *Inflection Point of a Curve* is the Point where a Curve begins to bend back again a contrary Way. **1743** EMERSON *Fluxions* 144 The Point of Inflexion or contrary Flexure is that Point which separates the convex from the concave Part of the Curve. **1882** MINCHIN *Unipl. Kinemat.* 100 Points on this circle are therefore points of inflexion on the roulettes to which they give rise; and the circle is hence called the *Circle of Inflexions*. **1886** A. G. GREENHILL *Diff. & Integr. Calc.* 240 At a point of inflexion the curve crosses the tangent.

4. *Gram.* The modification of the form of a word to express the different grammatical relations into which it may enter; including the declension of substantives, adjectives and pronouns, the conjugation of verbs, the comparison of adjectives and adverbs (but some treat the last under Derivation or Word-formation).

1668 WILKINS *Real Char.* 297 The rules which are proper and peculiar to any one Language..about the Inflexion of words, and the Government of cases. *Ibid.* 453 Varro..doth not there design to give an account of the just number of words in the Latin, but only to shew the great variety [of words] which is made by the Inflexion and Composition of Verbs. **1876** MASON *Eng. Gram.* (ed. 21) 27 The process of forming the different cases of a noun is called inflection.

b. *concr.* An inflected form of a word; also, the inflexional suffix or element.

1668 WILKINS *Real Char.* 21 Rules for all such Grammatical Derivations and Inflexions. **1841** ELPHINSTONE *Hist. Ind.* I. 277 It has now been demonstrated by means of a comparison of the inflexions. **1871** ROBY *Lat. Gram.* II. xviii. 189 The indicative mood contains no special inflexions to distinguish it. **1874** SWEET *Hist. Eng. Sounds* 160 Old English is the period of full inflections..Middle English of levelled inflections..and Modern English of lost inflections. **1876** MASON *Eng. Gram.* (ed. 21) 29 This power of treating an inflected form or a complex phrase as though it were a single declinable word, and adding inflections to it, is very remarkable in English.

5. Modulation of the voice; in speaking or singing: a change in the pitch or tone of the voice.

a **1600** HOOKER (J.), The motion of his body and the inflection of his voice. **1783** BLAIR *Rhet.* vi. I. 108 With regard to inflexions of voice, these are so natural, that, to some nations, it has appeared easier to express different ideas, by varying the tone with which they pronounced the same word, than to contrive words for all their ideas. **1795** MASON *Ch. Mus.* i. 59 It does neither so easily and generally admit, nor so variously introduce those accentual inflexions which they love to employ. **1839–40** W. IRVING *Wolfert's R.* (1855) 51 Such melodious sounds and exquisite inflexions could only be produced by organs of the most delicate flexibility. **1880** GROVE *Dict. Mus.* II. 765/2 A series of Inflections usually described by modern writers as the 'Gregorian Tones'. **1883** F. M. PEARD *Contrad.* I. 10 There was an inflection in her voice which suggested command.

Hence **inˈflexionless (inflectionless)** *a.*, void of inflexion or modulation.

1878 J. A. H. MURRAY in *Encycl. Brit.* VIII. 398 The language had at length reached the all but inflexionless state which it now presents. **1888** MRS. SPENDER *Kept Secret* III. xiii. 225 His voice was subdued and inflectionless.

inflexional, inflectional (ɪnˈflɛkʃənəl), *a.* [f. prec. + -AL[1].] **1.** Pertaining to or characterized by grammatical inflexion.

1832 J. C. HARE in *Philol. Museum* I. 656 That disposition ..to shorten inflexional terminations. **1860** FARRAR *Orig. Lang.* 185 *note*, Pott's formula for the morphological classification of languages was that they are 'isolating' 'agglutinative', and 'inflectional'. **1875** WHITNEY *Life Lang.* vi. 107 It does not lose what it once possessed in the way of inflectional apparatus. **1876** FREEMAN *Norm. Conq.* V. xxv. 509 Had no Norman ever set foot on our shores, the inflexional Old-English would still have passed, sooner or later, into the non-inflexional modern English.

2. *Geom.* Of or pertaining to a point of inflexion.

1862 G. SALMON *Treat. Analytic Geom. Three Dimensions* x. 182 We shall call the two lines which meet the surface in three coincident points, the inflexional tangents at the point. **1926** S. GANGULI *Theory Plane Curves* (ed. 2) II. i. 32 Through each point there pass four lines, each of which passes through two..points of inflexion. These lines are called inflexional lines. **1966** J. H. CADWELL *Topics in Recreational Math.* x. 100 Still more special is an inflectional tangent which both touches and crosses a curve.

Hence **inˈflexionally (inˈflectionally)** *adv.*, in regard to inflexion.

1885 G. BADEN-POWELL in *Contemp. Rev.* Oct., The Bushman language is classed inflectionally with the Basque, Finn [etc.].

†**inˈflexity.** *Obs. rare*$^{-1}$. [f. L. *inflex-us* inflected + -ITY, after FLEXITY.] Of rays of light: The quality of being inflected: see INFLECT *v.* 2.

1797 BROUGHAM in *Phil. Trans.* LXXXVII. 360 We may, therefore, say that the rays of light differ in degree of refrangity, reflexity, and flexity, comprehending inflexity and deflexity.

inflexive (ɪnˈflɛksɪv), *a.*[1] *rare*$^{-0}$. [f. L. *inflex-*, ppl. stem of *inflectĕre* to INFLECT + -IVE.] = INFLECTIVE.

1890 in *Cent. Dict.*

†**inflexive**, *a.*[2] *Obs. rare*$^{-1}$. [f. IN-[3] + FLEXIVE.] Not flexive; inflexible.

1616 CHAPMAN *Homer's Hymns, Mars* 35 And to beare safe, the burthen vndergone Of Foes inflexiue, and inhumane hates.

†**inˈflexure.** *Obs. rare.* [f. L. *inflex-*, ppl. stem of *inflectĕre*, after FLEXURE.] A bend, curve, or turn inwards: = INFLEXION 1 b.

1578 BANISTER *Hist. Man* v. 74 It lightly obtaineth aboue the lower part of the splene certaine foldes, or inflexures. **1658** SIR T. BROWNE *Gard. Cyrus* iii. 52 The contrivance of nature is singular in the opening and shutting of Bindeweeds, performed by five inflexures.

†**inflict**, *ppl. a.* *Obs. rare.* [ad. L. *inflict-us*, pa. pple. of *inflīgĕre*: see next.] Inflicted.

1526 *Pilgr. Perf.* (W. de W. 1531) 182 b, Thou art..free from all malediccyon and opprobry, inflycte to woman for synne.

inflict (ɪnˈflɪkt), *v.* [f. L. *inflict-*, ppl. stem of *inflīgĕre* to dash or strike (one thing on or against another), to inflict (punishment).]

1. *trans.* To lay on as a stroke, blow, or wound; to impose as something that must be suffered or endured; to cause to be borne.

1593 SHAKS. *2 Hen. VI*, III. i. 377 No paine they can inflict vpon him Will make him say, I mou'd him to those Armes. —— *Lucr.* 1630 Lasting shame On thee and thine this night I will inflict. **1596** SPENSER *F.Q.* VI. viii. 22 For revengement of those wrongfull smarts, Which I to others did inflict afore. **1611** BIBLE *2 Cor.* ii. 6 This punishment, which was inflicted of many. **1651** HOBBES *Leviath.* II. xxvii. 153 A penalty..hath been usually inflicted in the like cases. **1711** *Light for Blind* in *10th Rep. Hist. MSS. Comm.* App. v. 195 Tho' Cromwell had been dead, yett justice was inflicted on his corps. **1774** GOLDSM. *Nat. Hist.* (1776) VII. 210 [The rattle-snake] inflicts its wound in a moment; then parts, and inflicts a second wound. **1863** FR. A. KEMBLE *Resid. in Georgia* 42 Each driver is allowed to inflict a dozen lashes. **1873** L. FERGUSON *Disc.* 197 The suffering was not wantonly inflicted.

b. To impose something unwelcome. (Often jocular.)

1809 BYRON *Bards & Rev.* Argt., Wks. (1846) 422 *note*, Master Southey hath inflicted three poems..on the public. **1833** L. RITCHIE *Wand. by Loire* 129 In Prussia, where the order of the great Frederick suffices equally well to inflict a spouse and the bastinado! **1875** JOWETT *Plato* I. 51 Your father is pleased to inflict many lords and masters on you.

2. With inverted construction: To afflict, assail, trouble (a person) *with* something painful or disagreeable. (Now *rare*, and only in sense 1 b.)

1566 PAINTER *Pal. Pleas.* (1890) II. 30 The wycked villaine inflicted her bodye with manifold wounds. **1608** SHAKS. *Per.* v. i. 61 The most just gods For every graff would send a caterpillar, And so inflict [*mod. edd.* afflict] our province. **1652** COKAINE tr. *Calprenede's Cassandra* I. 36 Oroondates..began to be deeply inflicted with it. **1883** *Macm. Mag.* XLVIII. 130 We should be inflicted with less ..twaddle and useless verbosity.

Hence **inˈflicted** *ppl. a.*; **inˈflicting** *vbl. sb.* and *ppl. a.*

1598 FLORIO, *Inflitto*, stroken violently, inflicted, smitten against. **1611** *Ibid.*, *Inflittione*, an infliction or inflicting. **1631** GOUGE *God's Arrows* I. §1 The inflicting cause [of the plague] was the Lord. **1652** S. S. *Secretaries Stud.* 202, I hope time wil..weaken these inflictings. **1848** BUCKLEY

Homer's Iliad 267 His soul fled in haste through the inflicted wound.

in'flictable, *a.* [f. prec. + -ABLE.] That can or may be inflicted.

1810 BENTHAM *Packing* (1821) 164 An offence called a contempt of Court, and the punishment inflictable for that offence. **1888** *Pall Mall G.* 8 June 4/2 The smallest fine inflictable by law for the particular offence was 40*s.*

in'flicter, -or. [f. as prec. + -ER^1, -OR. *Inflictor* is according to the L. type from *inflīgĕre*.] One who inflicts, in senses of the vb. (Usually const. *of* the thing inflicted.)

1605 WILLET *Hexapla Gen.* 191 God the authour of all good things..as also the inflicter of all such punishments. **1672-5** COMBER *Comp. Temple* (1702) 497 The Jews generally did believe Satan was the Inflicter of all Diseases. **1748** RICHARDSON *Clarissa* (1811) IV. 213 If it so please the all-gracious Inflictor. **1836** E. HOWARD *R. Reefer* xlvii, The inflicter of my wound. **1892** ZANGWILL *Big Bow Myst.* 26 How the inflictor of the wound got in or out.

infliction (ɪn'flɪkʃən). [ad. late L. *inflictiōn-em*, n. of action f. *inflīgĕre* to INFLICT. Cf. F. *infliction* (1486 in Godef. *Compl.*).] The action of inflicting (pain, punishment, annoyance, etc.); in quot. 1603, the fact of being inflicted.

1534 MORE *Comf. agst. Trib.* III. Wks. 1216/2 The terror and infliccion of intollerable payne and torment. **1603** SHAKS. *Meas. for M.* I. iii. 28 Our Decrees, Dead to infliction, to themselues are dead. **1651** HOBBES *Leviath.* II. xxviii. 163 In declared Hostility, all infliction of evill is lawfull. **1794** SULLIVAN *View Nat.* II. 19 The infliction of such exemplary punishment. **1832** LEWIS *Use & Ab. Pol. Terms* i. 17 To punish..by the infliction of pain.

b. An instance of this; something inflicted, as pain, punishment, etc., or in weaker sense, an annoyance, a nuisance, a 'visitation'.

1586 MARLOWE *1st Pt. Tamburl.* v. ii, Our expressless bann'd inflictions. **1665** BOYLE *Occas. Refl.* (1848) 58 Distress'd by such Persecutions, as seem to be Divine Inflictions. **1834** HT. MARTINEAU *Farrers* ii. 21 He was aware that few inflictions could be so dreadful to his father. **1870** MISS BRIDGMAN *R. Lynne* II. x. 213 What an infliction he must be!

inflictive (ɪn'flɪktɪv), *a.* [f. L. type **inflictīv-us* (cf. F. *inflictif, -ive*, Cotgr. 1611), f. ppl. stem of *inflīg-ĕre*: see -IVE.] Tending to inflict; pertaining to infliction.

1611 COTGR., *Inflictif*,..inflictiue, inflicting; or, of property to inflict. **1643** HERLE *Answ. Ferne* 36 Nor have they any inflictive power on his person. **1753** HERVEY *Dial.* I. 10 (Jod.) This will be still more inflictive to an ingenuous mind. **1779** WHITEHEAD *Ode his Majesty's Birth-day*, Like her own oak..Ev'n from the steel's inflictive sting, New force she gains. **1831** MOORE *Poet. Wks.* II. 339 Without the aid Of that inflictive process, tuning.

inflight ('ɪnflaɪt), *a.* Also **in-flight.** [f. IN *prep.* 18 + FLIGHT *sb.*^{1}] Within or during a flight.

1945 *This Week Mag.* 25 Mar. 20/3 The Air Transport Command furnished quarters..and provided another 2,000,000 'inflight' meals. **1952** *N.Y. Times* 21 Dec. X27/3 Thousands of in-flight refueling operations have been completed without a single accident. **1964** *Punch* 11 Nov. 712/2 World airlines..are offering..in-flight movies and TV. **1969** *Sunday Times* (Colour Suppl.) 17 Aug. 18/3 There are six big screens for the inflight movies which no American airline can now do without. **1972** *Lebende Sprachen* XVII. 72/1 By the spring of 1970 in-flight results should be available for comparison with wind-tunnel predictions.

inflood (ɪn'flʌd), *v.* [f. IN-^{1} or ^{2} + FLOOD *v.*] *intr.* To flow in, to enter as a flood. Hence **in'flooding** *vbl. sb.*

1855 SINGLETON *Virgil* I. 119 The Sea Venting its choler in prodigious roars, Where doth the Julian billow boom afar, The deep in-flooding. **1885** STEVENSON *Pr. Otto* III. i. (1895) 215 She..saw far before her the silent inflooding of the day.

inflorescence (ɪnflɒ'rɛsəns). *Bot.* [ad. mod.L. *inflōrēscentia* (Linnæus), f. L. *inflōrēscĕre* to come into flower: see IN-^{2} and FLORESCENCE. Cf. F. *inflorescence* (1792 in Hatz.-Darm.).]

1. The mode in which the flowers of a plant are arranged in relation to the axis and to each other; the flowering system.

1760 J. LEE *Introd. Bot.* (1765) 217 Inflorescence is the manner in which the Flowers are fastened to the Plant by the Peduncle. *Ibid.* 224 Inflorescence affords the truest, and in most Genera the most elegant Distinction. **1794** MARTYN *Rousseau's Bot.* xix. 272. **1830** LINDLEY *Nat. Syst. Bot.* 134 Flowers often with a centrifugal inflorescence. **1872** OLIVER *Elem. Bot.* I. vii. 82 It is convenient to speak of the Flowering System, or mode of arrangement of the flowers of plants, as the *Inflorescence*. **1880** GRAY *Struct. Bot.* v. (ed. 6) 141 *Inflorescence*, a term which would literally denote the time of flower-bearing, was applied by Linnæus to the mode, that is, to the disposition of blossoms on the axis and as respects their arrangement with regard to each other. Anthotaxy..is a better term.

b. The collective flower or blossom of a plant.

1851 *Beck's Florist* 128 There they produce their brilliant inflorescence amid a variety of Passion-flowers, Bromelias, and Ferns. **1854** HOOKER *Himal. Jrnls.* I. ii. 52 In mass, the inflorescence resembles sheets of flame. **1857** HENFREY *Bot.* §115 The solitary flower, or the connected system of flowers arising from one point, is called the inflorescence. **1884** ROE *Nat. Ser. Story* vii, There are few objects of more exquisite ..beauty than this inflorescence.

2. The process of flowering or coming into flower; blossoming. Also *fig.*

1800 *Asiatic Ann. Reg., Misc. Tr.* 271/2 No leaves during inflorescence. **1846** J. BAXTER *Libr. Pract. Agric.* (ed. 4) I. 358 Early flowering grasses..at their period of inflorescence. **1885** O. W. HOLMES in *Century Mag.* XXX. 488 Those who are just coming into their time of inflorescence.

inflow ('ɪnfləʊ), *sb.* [f. IN *adv.* 11 d + FLOW *sb.*^{1}] The action or fact of flowing in; that which flows in; = INFLUX. *lit.* and *fig.*

1839 BAILEY *Festus* xix. (1852) 292 In the belief that through them came Vast spiritual inflow. **1865** *Cornh. Mag.* Aug. 182 A door is opened..to the inflow of much solid gain. **1865** *Reader* 11 Feb. 161/3 The extraordinary inflow of Europeans, Americans and Chinese. **1875** LYELL *Princ. Geol.* I. II. xx. 498 In the depths of the Straits..it is less interfered with..by the surface inflow. **1881** P. BROOKS *Candle of Lord* 225 Tell me..the real nature of your friend's influence, the inflow of his life on yours. **1897** *Allbutt's Syst. Med.* III. 746 The blood must be maintained at a normal standard by a regular inflow of nutritive material.

attrib. **1890** *Anthony's Photogr. Bull.* III. 390 Securely tying the rubber pipe..to the reservoir inflow pipe.

inflow (ɪn'fləʊ), *v.* [f. IN-^{1} + FLOW *v.*]

†1. *intr. Astrol.* To flow in; to exert astral influence; = INFLUE *v. Obs.*

1652 GAULE *Magastrom.* 93 Either the stars doe inflow and impress..or not. *a* **1670** HACKET *Abp. Williams* II. (1692) 150 The vertue of such and such a star..they hold to be propitious, in-flowing into the life and death of men.

2. To flow in.

1882 H. SCOTT HOLLAND *Logic & Life* (1885) 204 The forces set loose by that Divine affection unceasingly inflow, inrush, invigorate.

†3. *trans.* To cause to flow in. *Obs.*

1651 HOBBES *Leviath.* (1839) 70 What is the meaning of these words, The first cause does not necessarily inflow any thing into the second.

Hence **†'inflowed** *ppl. a.*, that has flowed in.

1676 WISEMAN *Chirurg. Treat.* I. iii. 16 Either of these [prescriptions]..will..dry up the inflowed Humour.

inflowering (ɪn'flaʊərɪŋ). [f. IN-^{2} + FLOWER *v.* + -ING^1, after F. *enfleurage*.] A process whereby the aroma of flowers is extracted, the essential oils being absorbed in fixed oils and fatty substances.

1885 PIESSE in *Encycl. Brit.* XVIII. 526/2 Certain flowers ..do not yield their attars by distillation..In these cases the odours are secured by the processes of inflowering (enfleurage), or by maceration.

inflowing ('ɪn,fləʊɪŋ), *vbl. sb.* [IN *adv.* 11 c.] The action or fact of flowing in; inflow, influx.

1450-1530 *Myrr. our Ladye* 198 The inflowynge of this flowde. **1561** T. NORTON *Calvin's Inst.* I. 53 The soule is of the essence of God, or a secrete inflowing of Godhead. **1842** R. M. McCHEYNE in *Mem.* (1878) 402 The engrafting of the branch is good, the inflowing of the sap good, but the fruit is the end in view. **1878** HUXLEY *Physiogr.* xx. 345 Yet this inflowing does not take the shape of a due north wind.

'inflowing, *ppl. a.* [IN *adv.* 11 a.] That flows in.

1611 FLORIO, *Infruente*, influent, inflowing. **1840** CLOUGH *Amours de Voy.* v. 4 A city that fringes the curve of the inflowing waters. **1855-8** MAURY *Phys. Geog.* iv. §231 The circle of inflowing air is gradually enlarged. **1871** *Daily News* 13 Sept., Researches..made into the inflowing and outflowing currents of the Baltic and the Mediterranean.

†'influct. *Obs. rare*$^{-1}$. [f. IN-^{2} + L. *fluctus* flowing, flow, flood; after *influĕre* to flow in.] = INFLUX; inflow.

1675 BAXTER *Cath. Theol.* I. II. 8 No habits immutably fix without the Influct of the Holy Ghost.

†influe, *v. Obs. rare.* [a. F. *influer* (14–15th c. in Godef.), ad. L. *influĕre* to flow in: see INFLUENCE.] *intr.* To shed astral influence: = INFLOW *v.* 1.

1541 R. COPLAND *Guydon's Quest. Chirurg.*, *Lazares* Qijb, Some constellacion that influed equally vpon a kynred, and specyally on them that dwelt togyder.

Hence **†'influing** *vbl. sb.* = INFLUENCE 2.

a **1618** SYLVESTER *Job Triumph.* IV. 451 Canst thou restrain the pleasant influing Of Pleiades the ushers of the spring?

influence ('ɪnflu:əns), *sb.* [a. F. *influence* (13th c. in Hatz.-Darm.) emanation from the stars (also inflow of water; affluence) = Pr. and Sp. *influencia*, It. *influenza*, late or med.L. *influentia* f. L. *influent-em*, pr. pple. of *influĕre* to flow in. The astrological sense (corresp. to late L. *influxus* (*stellarum*) 'astral influence', 4th c. in Firmicus) was common in med.L.: cf. Pico di Mirandola *adv. Astrologos* iii. 5. Sense 4 was already established in Scholastic Lat.: Aquinas (*c* 1260) has *influentia causæ* (Prof. Bywater).]

†1. The action or fact of flowing in; inflowing, inflow, influx: said of the action of water and other fluids, and of immaterial things conceived of as flowing in. Also *concr.* flowing matter. *Obs.*

1546 *Mem. Ripon* (Surtees) III. 28 At suche tymes as the Inhabitantes of the sam town cannot com to the paroche church for the Influence of water when the water here is bigge. **1577-87** HARRISON *England* in *Holinshed's Chron.* I. 77 The Towie..taketh in the influences of diverse waters in one chanell. **1655** E. TERRY *Voy. E. Ind.* 98 In the.. branches of those Trees they make incisions..under which they hang Pots..to preserve the influence which issues out of them in a large quantity in the night-season. **1677** HALE *Prim. Orig. Man.* II. iv. 158 The Phantasie..of Man, which is various, according to those various Temperaments that have ingredience and influence into him. **1702** *Eng. Theophrast.* 250 The sources of Conquests like those of great Rivers are generally obscure, until their streams increasing by the influence of others, make mighty inundations.

2. a. *spec.* in *Astrol.* The supposed flowing or streaming from the stars or heavens of an etherial fluid acting upon the character and destiny of men, and affecting sublunary things generally. In later times gradually viewed less literally, as an exercise of power or 'virtue', or of an occult force, and in late use chiefly a poetical or humorous reflex of earlier notions.

c **1374** CHAUCER *Troylus* III. 569 (618) O, Influences of þise heuenes hye. Soth is þat vnder god ye ben oure hierdes. **1398** TREVISA *Barth. De P.R.* XVI. lxxv. (Tollem. MS.), Stones beþ diuerse in virtu and in kynde; also influence of heauen comeþ into þer place, and prenteþ þerin þe effectes þerof. *c* **1430** LYDG. *Compl. Bl. Knt.* 630 O goddesse immortall..do thy diligence, To let the streames of thine influence Descend down. **1483** CAXTON *Cato* E vb, The synne whyche I haue doon ageynst myn owne wylle and by the influence of the planette on whiche I am borne. **1490** —— *Eneydos* xxiv. 89 The sterres..by their coniunctions and moeuynge and influences celestyalle, that sygnyfye and denounce the dysposycion secret of the deuine prouydence. **1555** EDEN *Decades* 94 In the nyght, the mone and other coulde planettes: but in the daye the soone and other hotte planettes doo chiefely exercise theyr influence. **1560** BIBLE (Genev.) *Job* xxxviii. 31 Canst thou restraine [1611 bind] the sweete influences [*R.V.* the cluster] of the Pleiades? [COVERD. Hast thou brought ye vij starres together?] **1590** SPENSER *F.Q.* I. viii. 42 What euill starre On you hath frownd, and pourd his influence bad? **1602** SHAKS. *Ham.* I. i. 119. **1610** —— *Temp.* I. ii. 182. **1625** BACON *Ess., Envy* (Arb.) 511 The Astrologers call the euill Influences of the Starrs, Euill Aspects. **1658** EARL MONMOUTH tr. *Paruta's Wars of Cyprus* 199 This maligne influence of the Heavens. **1667** MILTON *P.L.* VII. 375 The Pleiades before him danc'd, Shedding sweet influence. **1704** STEELE *Lying Lover* II. (1747) 40 The Sun to me shed Influence in vain. **1752** BURKE *Corr.* (1844) I. 27 They say the sun sends down much the same influences whenever he comes into the same signs. **1813** SHELLEY *Q. Mab* I. 114 Stars! Your balmiest influence shed! **1887** RUSKIN *Præterita* II. xi. 391 One of the leaden influences on me of the planet Saturn.

b. *transf.* The exercise of personal power by human beings, figured as something of the same nature as astral influence. Now only *poet.*

1439 LYDG. *Lyfe St. Albon* (1534) A ij, I stande in hope his influence shall shyne My tremblyng penne by grace to enlumyne. **1509** HAWES *Past. Pleas.* v. (Percy Soc.) 23, I set my mynde wyth percyng influence To lerne her scyence, the fyrst famous arte. **1591** SHAKS. *Two Gent.* III. i. 183 If I be not by her faire influence Foster'd, illumin'd, cherish'd, kept aliue. **1613** PURCHAS *Pilgrimage* (1614) Ep. Ded. ¶iij, To eclipse your Gracious aspect and influence unto our Church and State. **1632** MILTON *L'Allegro* 122 Store of ladies, whose bright eyes Rain influence, and judge the prize. **1673** GREW *Anat. Roots* Ded., The Vintage of the whole, will depend much upon the continued Influence of your Beams. **1805** COLERIDGE *Sibyl. Leaves* II. 226 The truly great Have all one age, and from one visible space Shed influence.

†c. Disposition, nature, or temperament, as held to be the result of astral influence. *Obs.*

14.. *Songs Costume* (Percy Soc.) 53 Charbonclys..Shewe in darknesse lyght..By ther natural heuenly influence. **1601** R. JOHNSON *Kingd. & Commw.* (1603) 60, Germans and Bohemians, nations by influence heavie, slowe. **1647** N. BACON *Disc. Govt. Eng.* I. lvi. (1739) 102 And yet..they were not always of such sad influence, but had their *lucida intervalla*. **1663** GERBIER *Counsel* C v b, Neither is it naturall to all those, which are born under one Constellation, to have like Influences.

†3. The inflowing, immission, or infusion (*into* a person or thing) of any kind of divine, spiritual, moral, immaterial, or secret power or principle; that which thus flows in or is infused. *Obs.* (Passing into 4 or 5.)

c **1430** LYDG. *Min. Poems* (Percy Soc.) 16 Wateris..Oute of wellis of oure Saviour, Wiche have vertu to curen alle langueres, Be influence of her grete swettness. **1494** FABYAN *Chron.* II. xxxi. 24 They thought y^t Juno that Goddesse, had by her influence, gyuen that grace vnto ye Ganders. **1532** MORE *Confut. Tindale* Wks. 387/1, I think that god gaue an influence of his power into that plaster, wherby he cured hys yien. **1597** HOOKER *Eccl. Pol.* v. lvi. §5 God hath his influence into the very essence of all things..All things are therefore partakers of God, they are his offspring, his influence is in them. **1611** BIBLE *Wisd.* vii. 25 She is the breath of the power of God, and a pure influence flowing from the glory of the Almighty. **1623** AILESBURY *Serm.* (1624) 1 The vnknowne God, whose influence to all his Creatures was made knowne by the Poet. **1667** MILTON *P.L.* v. 695 So spake the false Arch-Angel, and infus'd Bad influence into th' unwarie brest Of his Associate. **1677** HALE *Prim. Orig. Man.* I. v. 111 An eternal Creation of them by Almighty God, and an unintermitted Influence from him to support them.

4. a. The exertion of action of which the operation is unseen or insensible (or perceptible only in its effects), by one person or thing upon another; the action thus exercised. Orig. const. *into* (cf. 3); now *on, upon, in.* ***undue influence***: see UNDUE.

physical influence (mod.L. *influxus physicus*), the direct action of matter upon mind, and mind upon matter, as a doctrine of metaphysics: see quot. 1836 7.

1588 SHAKS. *L.L.L.* v. ii. 869 A gibing spirit, Whose influence is begot of that loose grace, Which shallow laughing hearers giue to fooles. **1605** BACON *Adv. Learn.* II. xxiii. §3 The Wisdom of conversation..hath..an influence also into business and government. **1628** T. SPENCER *Logick* 36 A Physicall operation is a reall influence into the effect. **1646** J. HALL *Horæ Vac.* 177 Examples of Great ones..have

. . a great influence on manners. **1672** Temple *Ess., Orig. & Nat. Govt.* Misc. (1681) 45 The Nature of Man seems to be . . varied . . by the force and influence of the several climates where they are born and bred. **1680** H. Dodwell *Two Lett. Advice* (1691) 166 The main design of those Sciences, and their influence in Divinity. **1725** De Foe *Voy. round World* (1840) 172 The reason . . why the magnetic influence directs to the poles. **1751** Johnson *Rambler* No. 141 ¶3 Before they had much influence on my thoughts. **1833** N. Arnott *Physics* (ed. 5) II. 125 Heat has powerful influence also on animated nature, both vegetable and animal. **1836–7** Sir W. Hamilton *Lect. Metaph.* xvi. (1859) I. 306 The fourth hypothesis is that of Physical Influence (*Influxus Physicus*). On this doctrine, external objects affect our senses, and the organic motion they determine is communicated to the brain. The brain acts upon the soul, and the soul has an idea, —a perception. **1845** McCulloch *Taxation* I. ii. (1852) 85 The land tax would . . have comparatively little influence in preventing or retarding improvements. **1863** H. Cox *Instit.* I. viii. 116 The offence of undue influence . . includes the use of force, or threatening any damage or loss, or practising any intimidation against a voter. **1876** Mozley *Univ. Serm.* xiii. (1877) 237 The Ephesian crowd that shouted 'Great is Diana of the Ephesians', was under the influence of a religious zeal. **1879** Lubbock *Sci. Lect.* ii. 31 Neither plants nor insects would be what they are, but for the influence which each has exercised on the other.

†**b.** Bearing, relation. (Const. *into.*) *Obs.*

1672 Evelyn *Corr.* 17 Sept., I would . . be glad to know, what light your Lordship can give me out of the letters and dispatches of my Lord Holles, Mr. Coventrie, and Sir Gilbert Talbot, which have all of them an influence into that affaire.

c. ***under the influence***: affected by alcoholic liquor; intoxicated, drunk.

[**1866** Mayne Reid *Headless Horseman* xix. 110 If not absolutely intoxicated, it could be seen that the ex-officer of volunteers was under the influence of drink.] **1879** 'Mark Twain' *Lett.* (1917) I. 367 Nobody got in the least degree 'under the influence', and we had a pleasant time. **1922** Joyce *Ulysses* 297 Lowest blackguard in Dublin when he's under the influence. **1925** Wodehouse *Carry on, Jeeves!* vii. 159 Boat-Race Night. Then, if ever, you will see Bertram under the influence. **1940** L. A. G. Strong *Sun on Water* 77 If a man under the influence tries to give you too much, sure, you slip it back into his pocket when he isn't looking. **1960** H. & M. Williams *Double Yolk* in *Plays of Year* XXI. 47 The police sergeant . . asked if I'd been drinking. . . I'd had a drink—and then he said I must go to the station with him, as he'd have to charge me with driving under the influence.

5. The capacity or faculty of producing effects by insensible or invisible means, without the employment of material force, or the exercise of formal authority; ascendancy of a person or social group; moral power *over* or *with* a person; ascendancy, sway, control, or authority, not formally or overtly expressed.

1652 Heylin *Cosmogr.* iv. 113 It is probable . . that those of New England . . were of like influence also amongst the Natives. **1769** Robertson *Chas. V*, vi. Wks. 1826 IV. 117 The vast influence which the order of Jesuits acquired. **1771** *Junius Lett.* xlv. 243 The influence of the crown naturally makes a septennial parliament dependent. **1775** Johnson *Journ. West. Isl., Ostig* 202 The laird . . cannot extend his personal influence to all his tenants. **1786** Burke *Art. Hastings* Wks. 1842 II. 140 Engaging . . that no British influence shall be employed within his dominions. **1814** Jane Austen *Mansf. Park* xiii. (1846) 90 She has no influence with . . my sisters that could be of any use. **1888** Bryce *Amer. Commw.* III. lxxxviii. 177 This position gave him a vast amount of 'influence' which he continued to use for his own advantage. **1898** Lugard in *Daily News* 7 Mar. 7/2 When the partition of Africa began in and subsequent to 1885, the hitherto unknown principle of spheres of influence was introduced into international custom in order to avoid dangerous complications between European nations. *Mod.* He owed his position to influence, not to merit. Have you any influence with any of the electors?

6. A thing (or person) that exercises action or power of a non-material or unexpressed kind.

1736 Butler *Anal.* ii. vii. Wks. 1874 I. 260 These prejudices . . are to be considered as influences of a like kind to enthusiasm. **1873** Hamerton *Intell. Life* i. iv. (1876) 23 Musical studies, the most powerful of softening influences. **1888** W. D. Lighthall *Yng. Seigneur* 9 He was an influence in the Dominion Legislature.

7. *Electr.* = induction 10.

[**1767** Priestley *Hist. Electricity* 247 The electric fluid, when there is a redundancy of it in any body, repels the electric fluid in any other body, when they are brought within the sphere of each other's influence.] **1870** Tyndall *Lect. Electr.* 14 This forcible separation of the two fluids of a neutral conductor, by the mere proximity of an electrified body, is called *electric induction*. Bodies in this state are also said to be electrified by *influence*. **1883** E. Atkinson tr. *Mascart & Joubert's Electr. & Magn.* §301 I. 289 This is magnetisation by influence, or induced magnetisation.

8. *attrib.* and *Comb.*, as ***influence-rich*** adj.; **influence line** *Engin.*, a graph showing how the resultant moment, stress, or other quantity at a given point of a structure varies with the position of the applied (constant) load producing it; **influence machine** (*Electr.*), an induction-machine; **influence pedlar** (or **peddler**) *U.S.* (see quot. 1968); hence ***influence peddling***.

1902 *Encycl. Brit.* XXVI. 377/1 In dealing with the action of travelling loads much assistance may be obtained by using a line termed an influence line. Such a line has for abscissa the distance of a load from one end of a girder, and for ordinate the bending moment or shear at any given section, or on any member, due to that load. **1936** Pippard & Baker *Analysis Engin. Struct.* xiv. 319 We shall consider the truss shown in Fig. 14.18 and find the influence line for the force in a diagonal bracing member as a load rolls along the bottom chord. **1972** R. C. Coates et al. *Structural Analysis* ii. 51 A bending moment diagram (shear force diagram) shows graphically the value of the bending moment (shear force) at *all* sections of a beam under a force whose position is *fixed*; an influence line for bending moment (shear force) shows graphically the value of the bending moment (shear force) at a *single* section for *all* possible positions of a movable force. **1889** *Anthony's Photogr. Bull.* II. 286 An instantaneous photograph, taken . . by a spark from a Holtz or other influence machine. **1890** *Pall Mall G.* 16 July 3/1 Mr. Wimshurst, the inventor of the influence machine. **1949** *N.Y. Times* 14 Aug. E7/5 The Investigations subcommittee of the Senate Committee on Expenditures in the Executive Departments which is inquiring into the activities of the 'five percenters' and the 'influence peddlers' has discovered that selling influence may be unethical, but it is not always illegal. **1968** W. Safire *New Lang. Politics* 204/2 *Influence pedlar*, one who has, or claims to have, the contacts and 'pull' supposedly necessary to get government contracts and favors from public officials, for a fee. **1971** *Wall St. Jrnl.* 20 July W1/3 The acknowledged dealer in stolen securities said part of the £100,000 he paid went to Nathan Voloshen, a convicted Washington influence peddler. **1972** *N.Y. Times* 22 Sept. 43 In 1956 a Senate investigation showed that Mr. Chotiner was engaged in influence peddling. **1850** Tennyson *In Mem.* lxxx, Influence-rich to soothe and save.

influence (ˈɪnfluːəns), *v.* [f. prec. Cf. mod.F. *influencer* (1792 in Hatz.-Darm.).]

1. *trans.* To exert influence upon, to affect by influence. **a.** To affect the mind or action of; to move or induce by influence; sometimes esp. to move by improper or undue influence. (Often with advb. extension, defining the nature or object of the influence.)

1658 Cromwell *Sp.* 25 Jan. in *Carlyle*, He [the Pope] influences all the Powers, all the Princes of Europe to this very thing. **1676** Newton in Rigaud *Corr. Sci. Men* (1841) II. 385 As if I influenced the press in what concerns Mr. Linus and me. **1712** Addison *Spect.* No. 357 ¶9 The Representation . . is wonderfully contriv'd to influence the Reader with Pity and Compassion. **1816** A. C. Hutchison *Pract. Obs. Surg.* (1826) 310 The very little prospect . . of any termination to hostilities . . certainly influenced the men to desert in greater numbers. **1853** J. H. Newman *Hist. Sk.* (1876) II. ii. ii. 250 In his political course he was more or less influenced by a sense of duty. **1856** Sir B. Brodie *Psychol. Inq.* I. iii. 94 As the brain may influence the mind, so may the mind influence the brain. **1883** Froude *Short Stud.* IV. i. iv. 51 Could he see the pope in person, he thought that he could influence him. **1883** C. J. Wills *Mod. Persia* 180 In the opinion of judges, whose fiat is possibly influenced. **1891** E. W. Bemis in *Chautauquan* 605 (Funk) Expenditures to 'influence' city council.

b. To affect the condition of, to have an effect on.

1661 Glanvill *Van. Dogm.* xiii. 125 The Senses, Phancy, and what we call Reason it self, being thus influenc'd by the Bodies temperament, and little better then indications of it. **1704** Newton *Optics* (J.), These experiments . . are not influenced by the weight or pressure of the atmosphere. *a* **1715** Burnet *Own Time* (1823) I. 448 This natural heat is influenced by frequent excesses in drinking. **1768** Sterne *Sent. Journ.* (1775) I. 6 (*The Monk* i.), The same causes . . which influence the tides themselves. **1832** G. R. Porter *Porcelain & Gl.* xii. 267 The specific gravity of glass is influenced by the degree of heat to which it has been exposed during its vitrification. **1844** Ld. Brougham *Brit. Const.* Introd. (1862) 20 The Sovereign can influence the conduct of public affairs. **1860** Tyndall *Glac.* i. ii. 12 Being less influenced by the atmospheric resistance.

2. *intr.* To exert influence; to work influentially *on*, *upon* a person or thing (*obs.*). Now only as an absol. use of 1 a.

1670 Eachard *Cont. Clergy* 34 A thing that . . infects the whole life, and influences upon most actions. **1675** Sharp *Wks.* (1754) I. ii. 41 It [religion] influenceth upon us, in order to the making us more useful. **1755** J. Shebbeare *Lydia* (1769) II. 83 So little did the virtues of his mother . . influence on his mind and behaviour. **1756** Foote *Eng. fr. Paris* ii. Wks. 1799 I. 118 Canst thou . . suppose thy frippery dress . . could influence beyond the borders of a brothel? **1897** *Daily News* 21 June 2/7 The Queen no longer rules; but she influences.

†**3.** *trans.* To cause to flow in; to infuse, inspire, instil. *Obs.*

1691 tr. *Emilianne's Observ.* 317 The Clergy . . in Revenge influence a double Corruption upon the Seculars. **1701** in *N. Jersey Archives* (1881) II. 378 The long Experience . . had of the Justice and Veracity of Coll. Hamilton, ought to have influenced a Beliefe of what he related to Us. **1705** in W. S. Perry *Hist. Coll. Amer. Col. Ch.* I. 105, I cannot but be ashamed . . that the Gospel should have influenced no better principles into your hearts.

Hence **ˈinfluenced**, **ˈinfluencing** *ppl. adjs.*

1709 Mrs. D. Manley *Secret Mem.* (1736) IV. 244 His Almighty influencing Spirit. **1718** Prior *Power* 667 By whose kind power and influencing care The various creatures move, and live, and are. **1818** Cobbett *Pol. Reg.* XXXIII. 99 To shew what a set of influenced and insignificant things now have the power to ruin and enslave us. **1850** Daubeny *Atom. The.* ix. (ed. 2) 310 An ample margin seems to be still left for other influencing causes.

influenceable (ˈɪnfluːənsəb(ə)l), *a.* [f. prec. + -able.] Capable of being influenced.

1859 *Life Eben Henderson* iv. 200 All hearts are influenceable from above. **1970** G. Greer *Female Eunuch* 94 Deutsch . . drew an extraordinary picture of woman as the ideal life-companion. . . 'They seem to be easily influenceable.'

influencer (ˈɪnfluːənsə(r)). [f. as prec. + -er[1].] One who or that which influences.

1664 H. More *Myst. Iniq.* 473 The head and influencer of the whole Church. **1775** Mad. D'Arblay *Early Diary* (1889) II. 103 Known as the chief influencer of her conduct. **1826** E. Irving *Babylon* I. iv. 309 The chief and sovereign influencers of the destinies of men. *a* **1866** J. Grote *Exam. Utilit. Philos.* x. (1870) 167 Honour is one of the most powerful influencers of human nature.

†**influenciary.** *Obs. rare.* [f. med.L. *influentia* influence + -ary[1].] One who or that which possesses or exercises influence.

1659 H. More *Immort. Soul* i. xiii. (1662) 51 The other Influenciaries hold the same power of the Heavens as these.

influencing (ˈɪnfluːənsɪŋ), *vbl. sb.* [f. influence *v.* + -ing[1].] The action of the verb influence; exertion of influence.

1754 P. H. *Hiberniad* i. 5 The Horrors of Oppression . . uninterruptedly defeat all influencing of the Climate. **1810** Southey *Kehama* xviii. x, Though all other things Were subject to the starry influencings. **1886** Dowden *Shelley* I. 533 Its ['Alastor's'] influencings upon us are like those of the autumnal wind.

influencive (ˈɪnfluːənsɪv), *a. rare.* Also **-sive.** [irreg. f. influence *v.* or L. *influens* pr. pple. + -ive: app. due to Coleridge.] Having the quality of influencing; influential.

1809 Coleridge *Ess. Own Times* (1850) 616 Many of the most distinguished and influencive of the patriotic party were zealous Catholics. *Ibid.* 643 A widely influensive Morning Paper. **1820** —— *Lett., Convers.* etc. I. Let. xv. 157 Savagely as I have been injured by one of the two influensive Reviews. **1842** Sara Coleridge *Mem. & Lett.* I. 259 She was a most impressive influencive person. **1857** Choate *Eloq. Revol. Periods* in *Addr.* (1878) 168 How influencive and inevitable the sympathy.

†**ˈinfluency.** *Obs. rare.* [ad. med.L. *influentia*: see influence and -ency.] = influence *sb.*

1641 French *Distill.* vi. (1651) 177 That dark body . . that is interposed betwixt the philosophicall Sunne and Moone, and keeps off the influencies of the one from the other. *Ibid.* 189 Crude gold is . . most fit to receive the influencies of the Sun.

influent (ˈɪnfluːənt), *a.* (*sb.*) [ad. L. *influent-em*, pres. pple. of *influĕre* to flow in: cf. F. *influent* (16th c. in Godef. *Compl.*).]

A. *adj.* **1. a.** Flowing in (in early use in astrological sense).

1471 Ripley *Comp. Alch.* Ep. iii. in Ashm. (1652) 114 Phebus it smiteth with his Heate influent. **1513** Douglas *Æneis* xii. Prol. 42 [The sun] Defundand fra hys sege etheriall Glaid influent aspectis celicall. **1607** Topsell *Four-f. Beasts* (1658) 113 By [wearing] them the afflicted place receiveth a double relief; first, it resisteth the influent humors. **1635** Heywood *Hierarch.* v. 274 Stars, luminous and cleare . . full of influent vertue. *a* **1705** Ray *Creation* ii. (1714) 277 The refluent Blood . . is a Pondus to the influent Blood. *a* **1800** Cowper tr. *Milton's Elegies* i. 9 Where Thames, with influent tide, My native city laves. **1883** *Harper's Mag.* Oct. 713/2 One of the influent streams.

b. *transf.* and *fig.*

c **1445** Lydg. *Testament* in *Min. Poems* (1840) 241, I now purpoose, by thy grace influent, To write a tretys. *c* **1485** *Digby Myst.* (1882) iii. 1096 þe hey and nobyll Inflventt grace of . . Iesus. **1739** J. Huxham *Fevers* ii. (1750) 26 The Constitution of the Solids and Fluids . . may be so far depressed as to bring on the low Influent, or slow nervous Fever. **1839** Bailey *Festus* xix. (1852) 277 Born Of effluent or influent Deity. **1890** J. Pulsford *Loyalty to Christ* I. 331 Living through God's influent life.

2. Exercising celestial or astral influence or occult power. *arch.*

1430–40 Lydg. *Bochas* ix. Envoye, An heuenli signe bi Influent pourueiaunce Sent from aboue to shewe Edwardis riht. **1613** Heywood *Braz. Age* Wks. 1874 III. 217 If the Moones spheare can any helpe infuse, Or any influent Starre. **1615** Chapman *Odyss.* Ep. Ded. 46 As th' influent stone . . Lifts high the heavy iron. **1856** Mrs. Browning *Aur. Leigh* i. 625 Multitudinous mountains . . panting from their full deep hearts Beneath the influent heavens. **1922** T. Hardy *Late Lyrics* 93 No influent star endeared me, Unknown, unrecked, unproved!

†**3.** Exercising (mental, moral, or physical) influence *on*, *upon*; influential. *Obs.*

1632 Lithgow *Trav.* 89 So tumultuous were the disordered Souldiers, and the occasions of revenge and quarrellings so influent. **1654** W. Mountague *Devout Ess.* ii. ix. §2. 174 [Humility] is more operative and influent upon others, then any other vertue. **1655** Fuller *Ch. Hist.* viii. iii. §6, I finde no office . . assigned unto Dr. Cox . . who was vertually influent upon all. **1657** W. Morice *Coena quasi Κοινὴ* Def. xiii. 178 The old may have the same effects influent on our times.

B. *sb.* **1.** A river or stream which flows into another or into a lake; a tributary, an affluent.

1859 R. F. Burton *Centr. Afr.* in *Jrnl. Geog. Soc.* XXIX. 116 The Rumuma river . . a southern influent or a bifurcation of the Mukondokwa. **1881** *Academy* 21 May 366/3 One of the largest influents of the Zambesi.

2. *Ecology.* An organism which affects the ecological balance of a plant or animal community.

1926 V. E. Shelford in *Ecology* VII. 389 Professor [F. E.] Clements kindly suggested the term influent to cover those organisms which have important relations in the biotic balance and interaction. **1935** [see biome]. **1938** Weaver & Clements *Plant Ecol.* (ed. 2) xviii. 478 It is more convenient to employ a distinct term and call them [*sc.* animals] influents in reference to their abundance and corresponding importance.

influential (ɪnfluːˈɛnʃəl), *a.* (*sb.*) [f. med.L. *influentia* influence + -al[1].]

A. *adj.* †**1. a.** *Astrol.* Possessing or exercising the influence formerly attributed to the stars; of,

pertaining to, or of the nature of astral 'influence'. *Obs.*

1570 DEE *Math. Pref.* biiijb, Mans body, and all other Elementall bodies, are altered, disposed, ordred..by the Influentiall working of the Sunne, Mone, and the other Starres and Planets. **1648** JENKYN *Blind Guide* i. 14 Shining not like a sweetly influentiall star, but flashing like an angry bloody Comet. **1652** GAULE *Magastrom.* 137 Potentiall influxes, influentiall proclivities, seminall dispositions. **1664** POWER *Exp. Philos.* II. 99 Atmosphaerical Air..is a mixt Body of Luminous and Magnetical Effluviums, powdred with the influential Atoms of Heaven from above.

†**b.** *transf.* Exercising, caused by, or of the nature of supernatural or spiritual influence; working by mysterious or hidden processes. *Obs.*

1643 T. CASE *3 Serm.* (1644) 32 The more full and sweet influentiall manifestations of his [God's] presence among them. *a* **1711** KEN *Preparatives* Poet. Wks. 1721 IV. 23 His Unction's influential Force. **1745** W. THOMPSON *Sickness* II. 652 Thy influential vigour reinspires This feeble frame.

2. Having or exerting influence, power, or effect. Const. *on*; †formerly *unto, upon, to, towards, of.*

1655 S. ASHE *Fun. Serm. 18th June* 28 The whole City, unto which he was profitably influentiall. **1655–62** GURNALL *Chr. in Arm.* (1669) 336/1 It seems to be superadded as a generall Duty influentiall upon all the pieces [of armour] fore-named. *a* **1677** BARROW *Pope's Suprem.* (1687) 140 Hurtful errours, influential on practice. **1679** JENISON *Popish Plot* 13, I was willing so far to consult their safety, as not to be influential to their prejudice, by any act of mine. **1720** WELTON *Suffer. Son of God* I. xi. 279 The Disposition of our Hearts being..Influential toward the Bent and Bias of our Judgments. **1757–8** *Herald* II. xxii. 97 All the qualities..should be blended together in our minds and hearts, and made influential of our opinions and practices. **1892** JAS. BROWN *Serm.* 163 A motive influential on life.

3. Having, possessing, or characterized by great influence or power; powerful.

a. Of persons.

a **1734** NORTH *Exam.* (1740) 550 He was of such an ouer-ruling Genius..as enabled him to be very influential among the Citisens. **1787** A. HAMILTON *Wks.* (1886) VII. 14 Fay, and Ira Allen, two of the most influential individuals in that country. **1829** GEN. P. THOMPSON *Exerc.* (1842) I. 170 The large and influential portion of the English nation. **1833** COLERIDGE *Table-t.* 8 Apr., He [Burke] would have been more influential if he had less surpassed his contemporaries. **1868** E. EDWARDS *Raleigh* I. xvii. 348 Grey's family connections were numerous and influential.

b. Of things.

a **1734** NORTH *Exam.* (1740) 518 So influential are Faction and Prejudice, in Matters of Justice. **1757–8** *Herald* I. viii. 121 More ceremony, and a greater regard for forms..are..influential principles in every other kingdom of Europe. **1833** HERSCHEL *Astron.* iii. 111 Any error which may affect the astronomical determination of a star's altitude will be especially influential. **1852** H. SPENCER *Ess., Phil. Style* (1891) II. 334 However influential the precepts thus dogmatically expressed, they would be much more influential if reduced to something like scientific ordination. **1860** MILL *Repr. Govt.* (1865) 6/1 To make these various elements of power politically influential, they must be organized.

absol. **1830** *Westm. Rev.* XII. 291 Mr. Moore's general system of acquiescence with the influential in all its forms.

4. Of, pertaining to, of the nature of, or working by influence. *rare.*

1795 COLERIDGE *Plot Discov.* 28 Nov. 43 The Liberty of the Press (a power resident in the people) gives us an influential sovereignty.

B. *sb.* An influential person.

1831 *Westm. Rev.* XV. 224 Comparison..between the fashionables of England and the influentials in France. **1837** W. DYOTT *Diary* 16 July (1907) II. 257 And was there strongly entreated by the influentials in the South Division of the county to allow himself to be put in nomination with Lord Ingestre for the south. **1899** 'MARK TWAIN' in *Forum* (N.Y.) Mar. 29 It was their official duty to entertain the influentials after some sort of fashion. **1957** R. K. MERTON *Social Theory* (rev. ed.) 128 Two types of influentials—the local and the cosmopolitan. **1965** D. V. GLASS in Glass & Eversley *Population in Hist.* i. 19 Manuals of domestic medicine, intended not only..for the practitioner but also for the clergy and for other local 'influentials'.

influentiality (-ʃɪ'ælɪtɪ). *rare.* [f. prec. + -ITY.] The quality of being influential; an instance or example of this; *concr.* an influential personage.

1840 CARLYLE *Heroes* vi. (1872) 206 Keep your red-tape clerks, your influentialities, your important businesses. **1848** W. E. FORSTER in Wemyss Reid *Life* (1888) I. 239 No influentiality likes to give tickets over the mob.

influentially (ɪnflu:'ɛnʃəlɪ), *adv.* [f. as prec. + -LY[2].]

†**1.** *Astrol.* With astral or stellar influence. *Obs.*

1652 GAULE *Magastrom.* 97 Why the starres should be more notable for influentially operating and efficaciously inclining at the point of the edition, parturition, or birth. **1682** SIR T. BROWNE *Chr. Mor.* III. §3 Look upon opinions as thou doest upon the moon..Embrace not the opacous and blind side of Opinions, but that which looks most Luciferously and influentially unto Goodness.

2. In the way of influence; in such a way as to exercise or exert influence.

1670 PENN *Case Lib. Consc.* 28 Plenty..will be converted into Poverty by the Destruction of so many thousand Families..and that not only to the Sufferers, but influentially to all the rest. **1821** *Examiner* 706/1 His temper was practically and influentially Norman. **1841** MYERS *Cath. Th.* III. §36. 132 The Revelation..is such that its sum and substance may be influentially conveyed to men in any language under heaven.

3. By persons of influence.

1870 *Daily News* 9 Sept. 2 The following gentlemen have been influentially invited to allow themselves to be put in nomination.

4. *Electricity.* By induction: cf. INFLUENCE *sb.* 7.

1792 *Phil. Trans.* LXXXII. 233 During this time, the rod was only electrified with its own electricity, or what has been termed influentially electrified.

influenza (ɪnflu:'ɛnzə). [a. It. *influenza*, lit. 'influence':—med.L. *influentia*: see INFLUENCE.

It. *influenza* has the various senses of Eng. *influence*; but has, besides, developed (app. from the notion of 'astral' or 'occult influence') that of 'visitation' or 'outbreak' *of* any epidemic disease which assails many people at the same time and place (e.g. *influenza di catarro, influenza di febbre scarlattina*), a sense known as early as 1504; hence, absolutely, 'an epidemic'; in 1743 applied specifically to 'the epidemic' (called also *la grippe*) which then raged in Italy, and spread over Europe generally, and for which the Italian word (anglicized in pronunciation) became the English specific name.]

A specific febrile zymotic disorder, highly contagious, and occurring for the most part in widespread epidemics. Its symptoms and sequelæ are extremely variable, but generally include rapid prostration and severe catarrh. The mortality is not high in proportion to the numbers attacked.

The term has been also applied loosely to any severe catarrh of the respiratory mucous membrane, esp. to a 'cold in the head' with running at the nose, sometimes called an *influenza-cold*. This use was frequent in the interval between the epidemic of 1847–8, and that which began in 1889, during which period no true influenza visited Great Britain.

1743 *Lond. Mag.* 145 News from Rome of a contagious Distemper raging there, call'd the *Influenza*. **1743** MANN *Let. to Walpole* 12 Feb. in Doran '*Mann*' *& Manners* (1876) I. vi. 144 Everybody [in Rome] is ill of the *Influenza*, and many die. **1750** J. HUXHAM *Fevers* ii. (ed. 2) 20 The catarrhal Fever, which spread through all Europe under the Name of *Influenza* in the Spring 1743, frequently became pleuritic or peripneumonic. **1762** MRS. MONTAGU in Doran *Lady of last Cent.* (1873) 133 Mr. Montagu..had been much pulled down by the fashionable cold called *l'influenza*. **1770** FOOTE *Lame Lover* I. Wks. 1799 II. 62 Confin'd to bed two days with the *new influenza*. **1801** NELSON 5 June in Nicolas *Disp.* (1845) IV. 403 Sir Thomas Graves is still very ill..In the St. George we have got the Influenza. **1803** DUNCAN *Ann. Med. for 1802* II. II. 480 The Influenza as it has appeared in Edinburgh in 1803..has extended itself at different periods for near a thousand years past over almost the whole of Europe. **1831** COL. HAWKER *Diary* (1893) II. 29 Very unwell with the influenza that has, more or less, affected everyone this season. **1843** R. J. GRAVES *Lect. Clin. Med.* xxv. 543 In the portion of the nineteenth century already elapsed four influenzas have already occurred, viz., in 1803, 1831, 1834, and 1837. **1852** THEO. THOMPSON *Ann. Influenza* 2 In 1510, the first well described and widely prevalent epidemic of Influenza appeared. **1886** FAGGE & PYE-SMITH *Princ. Med.* (ed. 2) I. 1018 The practice, so common among the higher classes in this country, of designating as influenza any catarrhal attack that happens to be painful and distressing. **1892** F. A. DIXEY *Epidemic Influenza* 1 During the first twenty-two weeks of 1890, 599 deaths were returned in London as primarily due to influenza..[but] the tale of victims direct or indirect of this destructive malady cannot have fallen far short of 2800 for London alone.

b. A communicable disease of horses, characterized by shivering and fever, affection of the respiratory organs, and great weakness.

1872 LONGF. in *Life* (1891) III. 209 An influenza is raging among the horses.

c. *fig.* Applied to a mental or commercial epidemic; a prevalent craze; an attack of some general state of prostration.

1774 J. BRYANT *Mythol.* I. 199 The learned Michaelis..says, that it [the attempt to derive all words from Hebrew] is the reigning influenza, to which all are liable, who make the Hebrew their principal study. **1784** GOUV. MORRIS in Sparks *Life & Writ.* (1832) I. 268 The present influenza is the banko-mania. **1785** MRS. A. M. BENNETT *Juv. Indiscretions* (1786) I. 153 Mr. Downes was certainly smitten with Lavinia Orthodox, but not with the matrimonial influenza. **1834** SOUTHEY *Doctor* xxiv. (1862) 56 Such preachers have never failed to appear during the prevalence of any religious influenza. **1891** *Daily News* 29 June 2/2 Some months ago the markets were said to be suffering from financial influenza.

d. *attrib.* and *Comb.*, as ***influenza bacillus***, etc.; **influenza-cold**, a severe cold with symptoms resembling those of influenza.

1891 C. CREIGHTON *Hist. Epidem.* 570 A pure and unmistakable epidemic of influenza-cold. **1896** *Daily News* 15 July 5/3 More than one bacillus, closely allied to the influenza bacillus, but differing from it in some biological and microscopical features, has been found in seven out of eight cases of 'influenza cold'. **1896** *Allbutt's Syst. Med.* I. 681 In some of these [patches of solid lung] the influenza bacillus has been found, thus shewing the disease in truth to be influenzal pneumonia. *Ibid.* 684 The chief characteristic of this influenza smell was its overpowering nastiness.

Hence **in'fluenzaed, -a'd,** †**influ'enzacized** *adjs.*, attacked by influenza; **influ'enzaish** *a.*, having some of the qualities of influenza; **influ'enzal, influ'enzic** *adjs.*, of or pertaining to influenza, characterized by influenza; **influ'enzally** *adv.*, in an influenzal manner; **influ'enzoid** *a.*, resembling or allied to influenza.

1803 *Med. Jrnl.* IX. 518 The *influenzal* epidemic of the present period, in no instance, loses either its catarrhal form or nature. **1825** *Sporting Mag.* XVI. 354 Dependent on an influenzal state of the atmosphere. **1836** J. MITFORD in *Lett. & Remin.* (1891) 51, I was so influenza'd when your letter came, that I thought of nothing but warming pans. **1841** R. OASTLER *Fleet Papers* I. No. 14. 105 The atmosphere is gloomy—and I am influenzaish. **1849** *Lond. Jrnl.* 9 June 212/2 The comfort and the consolation of the influenzacised florist. **1857** DUNGLISON *Med. Lex.* 497 *Influenzoid*..Resembling influenza.—Dr. T. Thompson. **1887** *Standard* 17 June, The influenzic attack is disappearing. **1892** *Nation* (N.Y.) 14 Apr. 281/2 His Eminence Cardinal Sanfelice, is 'influenzaed', as is about every third person in Naples. **1897** *Brit. Med. Jrnl.* 20 Mar. 744/1 Ill influenzally. **1955** *Sci. News Let.* 19 Mar. 190/2 Meningitis may also be caused by a germ called Hemophilus influenzae. This form is called influenzal meningitis, but has nothing to do with influenza. **1969** *Daily Tel.* 18 Dec. 15/3 There had been a sharp increase this month in influenzal-type illness in South-East England. **1972** *Ibid.* 20 Jan. 7 A total of 180 people died during the week ending Jan. 7 from influenza and influenzal pneumonia.

†**'influous,** *a. Obs. rare*$^{-1}$. [f. late L. *influ-us* flowing in (f. *influ-ĕre* to flow in) + -OUS: see INFLUENCE.] Shedding (astral) influence.

1662 J. CHANDLER *Van Helmont's Oriat.* 26 In the bowels, the planetary Spirits do most shine forth, even as also, in the whole influous Archeus, the courses and forces of the Firmament do appear.

influx ('ɪnflʌks). [a. F. *influx* (1547 in Godef.), or ad. late L. *influxus*, f. *influĕre* to flow in, f. *in-* (IN-[2]) + *fluĕre* to flow.]

1. The act or fact of flowing in; an inflow, as of a physical fluid, water, air, light, heat, spiritual or immaterial influence into the soul, etc.

1626 BACON *Sylva* Cent. x. Pref., Whether there be..any such Transmission and Influx of Immateriate Vertues. **1659** PEARSON *Creed* (1839) 143 God did command the use of such anointing oil..that by it the person anointed might be made fit to receive the divine influx. *a* **1691** BOYLE *Strange Reports* I. viii. Wks. 1772 V. 608 When the great springtides come roaring over those shoals..the first influx is irresistible by such vessels as use that port. **1707** FLOYER *Physic. Pulse-Watch* 19 The Heart of it self is like a Muscle, and contracts its Fibres by the Influx of Animal Spirits. **1823** RUTTER *Fonthill* 34 The lofty windows to the west admit a strong influx of light. **1860** PUSEY *Min. Proph.* 89 God..has removed all hindrance to the influx of His grace.

b. The flowing of a river or stream *into* another river, a lake, or the sea; the point at which this takes place, the mouth of a river.

1652 HEYLIN *Cosmogr.* IV. 110 Rivers..a mile and an half broad at the mouth or influx. **1675** OGILBY *Brit.* 20 The Kennet, near its Influx into the Thames. **1778** *Eng. Gazetteer* (ed. 2), *Torksey*, near the influx of the Fosdyke into the Trent. **1846** MCCULLOCH *Acc. Brit. Empire* (1854) I. 33 From Wallingford, a little below the influx of the Thame, the river flows almost due south.

2. *transf.* The flowing or continuous ingression of persons or things into some place or sphere.

1652 KIRKMAN *Clerio & Lozia* 77 There were railes round about to hinder the influx of unruly people. **1771** JOHNSON *Falkland Isl.* ¶5 The Spaniards, who..discovered America ..surprized and terrified Europe by a sudden and unexampled influx of riches. **1775** —— *Journ. West. Isl., St. Andrews* 8 A people..who..suffered no dilution of their zeal through the gradual influx of new opinions. **1848** MILL *Pol. Econ.* III. xxi. §1 (1876) 375 Imported commodities have possibly risen in price, from the influx of money into foreign countries. **1871** EARLE *Philol. Eng. Tongue* §420 The influx of Greek..and its general adoption into scientific terminology. **1888** BRYCE *Amer. Commw.* II. xlviii. 234 The influx of settlers from the Slave States.

†**3.** = INFLUENCE 2. [So *influxus stellarum* in Firmicus *c* 340.] *Obs.*

1626 BACON *Sylva* §907 Not by Formes, or Celestiall Influxes (as is vainly taught and received), but by the Primitiue Nature of Matter, and the Seeds of Things. **1642** HOWELL *For. Trav.* (Arb.) 36 That dominion, which the Starres have over the sensuall appetite, which together with the Will, are..incited..by their influxes. **1650** —— *Giraffi's Rev. Naples* I. 106 He escap'd the influxes of Heaven, and advanc'd himself in despight of the malignant stars.

†**4.** = INFLUENCE 3–5. *Obs.*

physical influx: see INFLUENCE 4

1644 HUNTON *Vind. Treat. Monarchy* v. 39 Have not the Houses an Authoritative Concurrence and Influx into that businesse? **1650** BAXTER *Saints' R.* I. Ded., The nature of the Divine Influx on the Will in the working of Grace. **1681** CHETHAM *Angler's Vade-m.* xxxviii. §14 (1689) 251 By heats and droughts..though those two do not much concern Sea-fish..yet they have a great influx upon Rivers, Ponds and Lakes. *a* **1703** BURKITT *On N. T., Rom.* ix. 18 God did not harden Pharaoh's heart by any positive act or influx upon it, by infusing any evil into it.

†**'influxed,** *a. Obs. rare.* [f. L. *influx-us*, pa. pple. of *influĕre* to flow in + -ED[1].] That has flowed in.

1684 tr. *Bonet's Merc. Compit.* x. 368 They stop the passing out of the influxed humours. **1710** T. FULLER *Pharm. Extemp.* 183 It..presseth out the influx'd Phlegm.

in'fluxible, *a. rare.* Also **-able**. [IN-[3].] Not fluxible; not liable to flux or change.

1871 FRASER *Life Berkeley* x. 392 The flux of sense-given phenomena, contrasted with the supposed influxable nature of external things.

So **in'fluxibly** *adv. rare*, without flux or change.

1677 GALE *Crt. Gentiles* IV. 253 The Son who always, eternally, influxibly, impassibly is begotten of the Father.

influxion (ɪnˈflʌkʃən). Now *rare*. [ad. late L. *influxiōn-em*, f. *influĕre* to flow in: cf. F. *influxion* (1549 in Godef.).]

1. The action of flowing in, inflow, influx.
1605 BACON *Adv. Learn.* II. xi. §2 The retyring of the minde within it selfe, is the state which is most susceptible of diuine influxions. **1638** A. READ *Chirurg.* ix. 67 To stay the influxion of more blood. **1650** BULWER *Anthropomet.* 233 The Brain was weakned, being deprived of the influxion of the vital spirits. **1789** T. TAYLOR *Proclus* II. 269 It is requisite to banish all influxions externally, before the phantastic spirit can superinduce the divinity. **1885** HOLDEN *Anat.* 735 (Cent.) Preserve the brain from those sudden influxions of blood to which it would..be..exposed.

†**2.** = INFLUENCE 2. *Obs.*
a **1641** BP. MOUNTAGU *Acts & Mon.* (1642) 122 The Stars of the Firmament..communicate influxion, two ways especially and for our purpose. **1642** HOWELL *For. Trav.* (Arb.) 35 Although we should acknowledge that the Celestiall bodies by their influxions, do domineere over Sublunary creatures.

†**inˈfluxious**, *a.* *Obs.* *rare*⁻¹. [f. prec.: see -OUS.] Characterized by influxion; shedding (astral) influence.
1644 HOWELL *Eng. Teares* (1645) 175 Men will be men, while there is a world, and as long as the Moon hath an influxious power to make impressions upon their humours.

†**inˈfluxive**, *a.* *Obs.* [f. L. *influx-*, ppl. stem of *influĕre* to flow in + -IVE.] Infusing or communicating influence; influential.
1624 F. WHITE *Reply Fisher* 362 Shee may rightly be called the Queene of Heauen, yea, and of Earth; for shee hath preheminencie and influxiue vertue ouer all. **1642** HOLDSWORTH *Inaug. Serm.* 9 He is the influxive head, who both governs the whole bodie, and every member. **1657** W. MORICE *Coena quasi Κοινή* Def. xvi. 292 A Communion with wicked men..had been more influxive and apt to pollute at the Sacrament.

Hence †**inˈfluxively** *adv.*, by influxion.
1856 in WEBSTER.

info (ˈɪnfəʊ), colloq. abbrev. of INFORMATION.
1913 *Sat. Even. Post* 15 Feb. 8/2, I can slip you the info. **1925** WODEHOUSE *Sam the Sudden* xiii. 93 So you've only to pool your info' to bring home the bacon? **1954** 'N. BLAKE' *Whisper in Gloom* ii. 29 Then we pass the info. to the police, and they raid the joint. **1968** J. C. HOLMES *Nothing More to Declare* 28 Legman..the walking dossier of scandalous info about the sex habits of politicians. **1971** *New Scientist* 9 Sept. 582 (*heading*) Generating info for schools.

in-foal (ˈɪnfəʊl), *a.* [attrib. use of phrase *in foal*: see IN *prep.* 10 b.] That is in foal.
1929 *Chilean Rev.* No. 31. 59/1 To prevent joint-ill in foals, these stations feed a teaspoonful of potassium iodide crystals twice per month to each in-foal mare. **1948** *Vet. Rec.* 25 Dec. 679/1 The in-foal mares were run out during the day until near to foaling.

†**infœˈdation.** *Obs.* *rare*⁻¹. [ad. L. type **infœdātiōn-em*, f. *in-* (IN-²) + *fœdāre* to defile, f. *œdus* foul.] Defilement.
1661 FELTHAM *Disc. Luke* xiv. 20 Wks. (1677) 363 But voluptuous men (besides the Infœdations of Sensuality) are usually both proud and covetous also.

†ˈ**infold**, *sb.*¹ *Obs.* [f. IN-¹ or ² + FOLD *sb.*³: INFOLDING, and ENFOLD *sb.*]

1. A convolution.
1578 [see ENFOLD *sb.*]. **1701** C. WOLLEY *Jrnl. N. York* (1860) 41 First of the thick Guts, which by reason of its divers infolds and turnings seems to have no end.

2. The folding in of a part; a fold.
a **1641** BP. MOUNTAGU *Acts & Mon.* (1642) 303 A by-stander..observed an infold in his upper garment, and supposing the letter might be folded up therein, opened it.

ˈ**inˌfold**, *sb.*² *rare.* [f. IN *adv.* + FOLD *sb.*²] A fold or small field near a farm-house.
1860 G. H. K. in *Vac. Tour.* 128 A rude enclosure near his house, which separated the infolds from the outfolds of his small farm.

†**inˈfold**, *v.*¹, †**inˈfolded**, *ppl. a.*, obs. varr. of ENFOLD *v.*¹, to envelop, enclose, contain, etc., ENFOLDED *ppl. a.*

†**inˈfold**, *v.*², obs. var. of ENFOLD *v.*², to shut up in, or as in, a fold.

infolded, *ppl. a.* [IN *adv.* 11 b. Stressed ˈ*in-folded* before a sb.; *in-*ˈ*folded* after it or in predicate.] Folded in; having the margin turned inward with a fold.
1871 DARWIN in *Life & Lett.* (1887) III. 140 The infolded part of the human ear. **1875** —— *Insectiv. Pl.* xiv. 324 As the rim is infolded. **1880** *Plain Hints Needlework* 36 Then let each child buttonhole-stitch the infolded edge of her lesson-piece. **1882** VINES *Sachs' Bot.* 950 The cambium layer..becomes deeply infolded where it extends inwards.

ˈ**inˌfolding**, *vbl. sb.* [IN *adv.* 11 c.] A folding in, a turning in with a fold.
1873 MIVART *Elem. Anat.* ix. 372 Infoldings of the surface of the organ. **1897** *Allbutt's Syst. Med.* II. 1122 Microscopically they consist of hypertrophic ingrowths rather than infoldings of the cuticle. **1898** P. MANSON *Trop. Diseases* xxxii. 499 The cylindrical appearance of the worm is produced by the lateral infolding of the two sides of what would otherwise be a flat body.

†**inˈfoliate**, *v.* *Obs.* *rare*⁻¹. Also 7 -folliat. [f. L. type **infoliāre*, f. IN-² + *folium* leaf, perh. after It. *infogliare* 'to enleafe or grow greene' (Florio). See -ATE³, and cf. FOLIATE *v.* 3.] *intr.* To put on leaves, to become leafy.
1640 HOWELL *Dodona's Gr.* (1645) 167 Long may his fruitful Vine infolliat and clasp about him. **1656** BLOUNT *Glossogr.* (citing Howell), *Infoliate*,..to be full of leaves, to be enleaved or wrapt with leaves.

†**infoliˈation.** *Obs.* *rare*⁻¹. [f. as prec. + -ATION; cf. FOLIATION.] (See quot.)
1577 B. GOOGE *Heresbach's Husb.* (1586) 90 b, Another waie..is to take a verie fruitefull stocke..and him after the maner of other trees they graffe by infolliation.

inˈfolio. *rare.* [f. *in folio* (see FOLIO), prob. after F. *in-folio.*] A folio volume. Also *attrib.*
1835 *Fraser's Mag.* XII. 457 Where huge infolios and ponderous tomes Build up Divinity's dark arsenal. **1897** W. J. LOCKE *Derelicts* xx. 346 She..took up a great in-folio black-letter.

†**inˈfollowing**, *vbl. sb.* *Obs.* *rare*⁻¹. [f. IN-¹ + FOLLOWING, after L. *insectātio.*] A reproving or censuring.
1382 WYCLIF *Ecclus.* xxxii. 23 In his infolewingis [*v.r.* folewingus; 1388 suyngis] he shal ben vndernome [L. *suis insectationibus arguetur*].

†**inˈfonded**, *ppl. a.* *Obs.* *rare*⁻¹. [f. IN-¹ + *fonded*, pa. pple. of FOND *v.*] Infatuated.
1567 TURBERV. tr. *Ovid's Ep.* A vij b, My selfe (least thou shouldst want at neede a Barck to leaue my lande) Infonded [*v.r.* infounded] did repaire the shippes that ragged lay on sande.

infooted (ˈɪnˌfʊtɪd), *a.* *rare.* [f. IN *adv.* 13 + FOOT *sb.* + -ED²; cf. *inkneed*, *intoed.*] Having the feet turned inwards.
1899 *N. & Q.* 9th Ser. IV. 31/1 Infooted folk are called 'twilly-toed', for each foot in turn makes a 'twirl' or half-circular movement at each step.

inforce, -ly, -ment, -forcer: see ENFORCE, etc.

Inforciat, obs. form of INFORTIATE.

†**inˈforcive**, var. of ENFORCIVE *a.* *Obs.* Hence †**inˈforcively** *adv.*, by force, under compulsion.
1604 MARSTON *Malcontent* To Rdr., One thing afflicts me, to think that scenes, invented merely to be spoken, should be inforcively published to be read.

†**inˈfordable**, *a.* *Obs.* *rare*⁻¹. [IN-³.] Not fordable; that cannot be forded.
1600 DYMMOK *Ireland* (1843) 35 Those [foot and horse] were rayned in sight of our army, devided from yt by an infordable ryver.

†**inˈfore**, *prep.* *Obs.* *rare*⁻¹. [? alteration of AFORE.] = BEFORE.
1607 WALKINGTON *Opt. Glass* 18 Like torrents of mellifluous snow infore th' Sun, His sacred Hippocrene gins to runne.

inforest, variant of ENFOREST *v.* *Obs.*

†**inforeˈstation.** *Obs.* *rare.* [n. of action f. med.L. *inforestāre* to convert into forest: see -ATION.] = AFFORESTATION.
1677 F. SANDFORD *Geneal. Hist. Kings Eng.* 89 Great Fines exacted of the possessors of Inforrestations.

inform (ɪnˈfɔːm), *a.* [a. F. *informe* (15th–16th c. in Godef. *Compl.*), ad. L. *informis* shapeless, deformed, f. *in-* (IN-³) + *forma* FORM.]

1. Having no definite or regular form; unshapen, misshapen, deformed. *arch.*
1555 EDEN *Decades* 261 The damme with continuall lyckynge by lyttle and lyttle figurethe the informe byrthe. **1633** HART *Diet of Diseased* III. xxviii. 344 Metamorphosing the whole man into an informe monster. **1660** JER. TAYLOR *Duct. Dubit.* IV. i. rule 3 §14 Not if it [the fœtus] was inform and unshapen. **1681** COTTON *Wond. Peak* Poet. Wks. (1765) 342 Bleak Crags, and naked Hills, And the whole Prospect so inform and rude. **1888** R. BUCHANAN *City of Dream* XI. 227 Moloch and Baal, two shapes Inform and monstrous.

2. Without form; formless; of the nature of matter unendowed with 'form' or the informing principle: see FORM *sb.* 4, INFORM *v.* 3.
1654 VILVAIN *Theorem. Theol.* i. 25 An inform lump..without a Soul is neither Man nor Beast. **1656** STANLEY *Hist. Philos.* v. (1701) 208/1 Nature in it self inform, when it receives form from God is the Angelick Mind. **1681** WHARTON *Disc. Soul World* Wks. (1683) 648 God is Light, in which there is no Darkness; that is Form wherein there is nothing Inform. **1707** NORRIS *Treat. Humility* iv. 166 In the old creation we read of a void and inform mass. **1881** BLACKIE *Lay Serm.* v. 170 His transforming energy triumphs..over the inform domain of the unfruitful clod.

b. *inform* (also *informed, informal*) *faith* (*fides informis*), in Scholastic Theology, faith that is not informed, vitalized or animated by charity (which is said to be the 'form' or formative principle of faith). Cf. INFORMED *a.* 1.
[Cf. Thomas Aquinas *Summa* 2-2, q. 4, etc.; Petrus Lombardus 3. sent. dist. 23. lit. C.]
a **1656** BP. HALL *Rem. Wks.* (1660) 269 Every faith makes not an effectual calling;..there is an inform, there is a counterfeit Faith.

inform (ɪnˈfɔːm), *v.* Forms: α. 4–6 enfourme, 4–7 enforme, 5 enfoorme, 7–8 enform. β. 4–6 infowrme, 4–7 informe, 5–6 infourme, 6– inform. [a. OF. *enformer*, *-fourmer* (mod.F. *informer*), ad. L. *informāre* to give form to, shape, fashion, form an idea of, describe, f. *in-* (IN-²) + *forma* FORM. The Latin form of the prefix became common (as in F.) in the 16th c., and prevailed after 1600.

The primary sense had undergone various developments in ancient and med.Latin, and in French, before the word appeared in Eng.; hence the chronology of the senses in Eng. does not agree with the logical order. In general, branches I and III were in ancient L.; II was a Scholastic L. offshoot from I; IV was app. an Eng. offshoot from III, with the thing taught made the object, instead of the person taught.]

I. To give form to, put into form or shape.

†**1. a.** *trans.* To put into (material) form or shape; to form, shape, frame, mould, fashion. *Obs.*
1590 SPENSER *F.Q.* III. vi. 8 Infinite shapes of creatures..Informed in the mud on which the Sunne hath shynd. **1621** BURTON *Anat. Mel.* II. iii. v. (1651) 345 If he found her, he may as happily find another; if he made her..he may as cheap inform another. **1643** SIR T. BROWNE *Relig. Med.* I. §35 And so Omniety informed Nullity into an Essence.

†**b.** To put into proper form or order, to arrange; to compose (a writing). *Obs.* †*to enforme the pes* (OF. *enformer la pais*), to compose or make peace.
c **1330** R. BRUNNE *Chron.* (1810) 285 Þider..com þe tresorere..þat had bien messengere With þe Cardinalle forto enforme þe pes. **1382** WYCLIF *1 Chron.* xii. 33 Of Zabulon that..stoden in the scheltrun, enfourmed in armys of batail. *a* **1400–50** *Alexander* 2751 A pistill he enfourmes, Wrate a writt of his will, so sendis to his princes. **1523** LD. BERNERS *Froiss.* I. xxxix. 53 He enformed his somones, and sent..to kepe the towne and fronters..agaynst his ennemies. *c* **1646** CRASHAW *Poems, Music's Duel* 87 Awakes his lute, and 'gainst the fight to come Informs it. **1654–66** LD. ORRERY *Parthenissa* (1676) 763 By that time I had informed these Resolutions, and dispatched these Expresses.

†**c.** To delineate, sketch, describe. (A Latin sense.) *Obs.*
1615 CHAPMAN *Odyss.* I. 1 The man, O Muse, inform, that many a way Wound with his wisdom to his wished stay.

†**2.** *intr.* To take form; to form or be formed; to appear in a visible shape. *Obs.*
1588 A. KING tr. *Canisius' Catech.* 223 The Charitie of God is powred forth in thair hartes..and informes or inhæres in the same. **1605** SHAKS. *Macb.* II. i. 48 It is the bloody Businesse, which informes Thus to mine Eyes. **1652** *News fr. Lowe-Countr.* 1 When, first, the first confused Masse Did, from its mish mash medley, passe To those four segregated forms, Whose re-commixture now informs.

II. To give 'form' or formative principle to: see FORM *sb.* 4. (From Scholastic L. *informare*: Petrus Lombardus, etc.)

3. a. *trans.* To give 'form', formative principle, or determinative character to; hence, to stamp, impress, imbue, or impregnate *with* some specific quality or attribute; *esp.* to impart some pervading, active, or vital quality to, to imbue *with* a 'spirit'; to fill or affect (the mind or heart) *with* a feeling, thought, etc.; to inspire, animate.

(The first quot. may belong to b; the second appears to contain the sense 'to furnish with a practical example, to illustrate'.)
c **1380** WYCLIF *Sel. Wks.* I. 115 Þus bi greetnesse of feiþ enfourmed wiþ charite ben siche soulis maad hool. *c* **1425** *St. Christina* xv. in *Anglia* VIII. 125/25 At þat he schewed wiþ ensaumpil, wee enforme hit þat wee haue seyde, wiþ a dede of Cristyne. **1607** SHAKS. *Cor.* v. iii. 71 The God of Souldiers..informe Thy thoughts with Noblenesse. **1646** SIR T. BROWNE *Pseud. Ep.* II. ii. 61 If an iron be touched before..it admits not this magneticall impression, as being already informed by the Load-stone. **1711** ADDISON *Spect.* No. 13 ¶6 Could they..inform their Faces with as significant Looks and Passions. **1758** BLACKSTONE *Study of Law* in *Comm.* (1765) I. 37 [To] inform them with a desire to be still better acquainted with the laws and constitution of their country. **1842** TENNYSON *Day-Dream, Sleeping Beauty* ii, Her constant beauty doth inform Stillness with love, and day with light. **1861** MILL *Utilit.* ii. 32 The Christian religion is fitted to inform the hearts and minds of mankind with a spirit which should enable them to find for themselves what is right.

b. Said of the quality or principle: To be the 'form' or formative principle of; to give a thing its essential quality or character, to make it what it is; to pervade as a spirit, inspire, animate.
1432–50 tr. *Higden* (Rolls) I. 33 When feithe and grace of sacramentes informede the life of theyme [Cristen men]. **1605** CHAPMAN *Al Fooles* I. i, Without loue..All vertues borne in men lye buried, For loue informes them as the Sunne dothe colours. **1667** MILTON *P.L.* III. 593 Not all parts like, but all alike informd With radiant light, as glowing Iron with fire. **1771** *Muse in Miniature* 144 This scull might once contain Some rich materials for the lofty strain, Enform'd, enrapt with more than mortal fire. **1814** CARY *Dante, Paradise* VII. 132 The elements..and what of them is made, Are by created virtue inform'd. **1821** SHELLEY *Prometh. Unb.* I. 249 Speak the words which I would hear, Although no thought inform thine empty voice. **1871** MATILDA BETHAM-EDWARDS *Sylvestres* II. ii. 38 Even in..happy England the spirit of caste informs the very breath and life of the nation.

c. *spec.* Of a soul or life: To impart life or spirit to; to inspire, animate, actuate.
1606 BRYSKETT *Civ. Life* 129 His opinion..that the soules were created in a certaine number, to the end they might informe so many bodies. *c* **1611** CHAPMAN *Iliad* XXII. 311 A soul of iron informs thee. **1643** SIR T. BROWNE *Relig. Med.*

I. §12 If one Soul were so perfect as to inform three distinct Bodies, that were a petty Trinity. **1677** GALE *Crt. Gentiles* III. 105 Plotinus and Hermes Trismegistus tel us 'that Images were made as bodies to be informed by Ghosts as with souls'. **1700** PRIOR *Carmen Sec.* 403 Long as Breath informs this fleeting Frame. **1805** WORDSW. *Prelude* IV. 167 How the immortal soul with God-like power Informs, creates, and thaws the deepest sleep That time can lay upon her. **1878** B. TAYLOR *Pr. Deukalion* II. iv. 81 By one soul Informed.

III. To give form to the mind, to discipline, instruct, teach (a person), to furnish with knowledge.

4. *trans.* **a.** To form, mould, or train (the mind, character, etc.), esp. by imparting learning or instruction; hence, To impart instruction to (a person), to instruct, teach (in general sense); †to advise (quot. 1330). Now *rare.*

c **1330** R. BRUNNE *Chron.* (1810) 315 Þo ilk men so wise suld go, and enforme zour kynges, Withouten mo justise or trauaile of oþer lordynges. *a* **1340** HAMPOLE *Psalter* xxxi. 10 Vndirstandynge i sall gif till þe, and i sall enfourme þe [*instruam te*]. *c* **1440** *Promp. Parv.* 261/2 Informyn, or techyn, *informo, instruo.* *c* **1450** tr. *De Imitatione* III. vi. 70 Visite me, lorde, ofte tymes, & enforme wiþ disciplines of konnyng. **1514** BARCLAY *Cyt. & Uplondyshm.* (Percy Soc.) p. lxxii, His sight infourmeth the rude and ignorant. **1526** TINDALE *1 Cor.* ii. 16 For who knoweth the mynde of the lorde, other who shall informe hym? **1589** NASHE *Almond for Parrat* 10 a, The nouice that comes to be informed, desireth to enforme others, before he bee enformed himselfe. **1621** BURTON *Anat. Mel.* I. ii. IV. ii. (1651) 145 That leaves his son to a covetous Schoolemaster to be informed. **1794** GIFFORD *Baviad* 270 So may thy varied verse, from age to age Inform the simple, and delight the sage. **1824** G. W. DOANE *Hymn, 'Thou art the Way'* ii, Thou only canst inform the mind. **1878** MORLEY *J. De Maistre* in *Crit. Misc.* 137 To guide and inform an universal conscience.

†**b.** To train or discipline in some particular course of action; to instruct in some particular subject, doctrine, etc.; to teach how to do something. Const. *of, to, in, with,* or with *infin.* or *subord. clause. Obs.*

c **1320** R. BRUNNE *Medit.* 238 In þe secunde þou mayst se How he enformed hem yn charyte. *c* **1374** CHAUCER *Boeth.* I. pr. iii. 6 (Camb. MS.) Oonly for they weeren enformyd of myne maneres. *c* **1375** *Sc. Leg. Saints, Nycholas* 55 His fadir .. Gert informe hyme besyly In liberale hartis sutely. **1382** WYCLIF *Dan.* xii. 3 Thei that lernen [*gloss* or enfourmen] manye to riȝtwijsnesse. *c* **1400** *Destr. Troy* III. *heading,* Medea enformed Iason to get the ffless of Golde. *a* **1529** SKELTON *Replyc.* Wks. 1843 I. 209 They were but febly enformed in maister Porphiris problemes. **1529** MORE *Dyaloge* I. Wks. 132/2 He nedeth not our aduice to enforme hym what thing were sufficient occasion to worke hys wonders for. **1589** PUTTENHAM *Eng. Poesie* I. xxvi. (Arb.) 67 Musicians .. by good admonitions enformed them to the frugall and thriftie life all the rest of their dayes. **1607** HIERON *Wks.* (1624) I. 334 First, to teach vs to eschew Euill, and then to enforme vs how to doe good. **1736** BUTLER *Analogy* II. viii. 393 Nor are we informed by nature, in future contingencies and accidents.

†**c.** To give instructions or directions for action; to instruct, direct, bid (*to do* something). *Obs.*

c **1380** WYCLIF *Sel. Wks.* III. 351 And þei enformen þer cuntreis to holde stifli wiþ þer pope. **1390** GOWER *Conf.* III. 229 To done as he was last enformed. *c* **1449** PECOCK *Repr.* I. xiii. 66 Enformyng and tising ther to vnsufficient[l]i leerned clerkis. **1645** PAGITT *Heresiogr.* (1661) 201 But, the voice from Heaven enformed him otherwise. Bade him, Rise, kill, eat. **1740** SHENSTONE *Judgm. Hercules* 268 And gentle zephyrs .. For thy repose inform .. Their streams to murmur and their winds to sigh.

†**d.** To direct, guide. *Obs.*

1634 MILTON *Comus* 180 Where else Shall I inform my unacquainted feet, In the blind mazes of this tangled wood? **1671** —— *Samson* 335 If old respect .. hither hath informed Your younger feet. **1846** KEBLE *Lyra Innoc.* (1873) 129 Strange powers their course inform.

5. a. To impart knowledge of some particular fact or occurrence to (a person); to tell (one) of or acquaint (one) with something; to apprise. Const. *of, about, on,* or with subordinate clause; rarely †*with,* †*in,* or *second object.* The prevailing modern sense.

c **1386** CHAUCER *Sqr.'s T.* 327 Enformed whan the kyng was of that knyght. *c* **1400** *Destr. Troy* 3011 He was enformyt before of þat fre lady, þat ho to Castor .. accounttid was euon, And to Pollux, pure suster. **1529** MORE in *Four C. Eng. Lett.* 11, I am enfourmed by my son Heron of the loss of our barnes. **1548** HALL *Chron., Hen. VIII* 141 b, Some have enformed me that my realme was never so riche. **1651** BAXTER *Inf. Bapt.* 116 They were enformed that Paul taught the dispersed Jews not to circumcise their children. **1655** FULLER *Ch. Hist.* IX. ii. §34, I have for that cause informed the Bishop of Dublin with all mine occurrences. **1713** ADDISON *Cato* V. i. 24 This in a moment brings me to an end; But this informs me I shall never die. **1718** LADY M. W. MONTAGU *Let. to Mrs. Thistlethwayte* 4 Jan., I would gladly be informed of the news among you. **1775** SHERIDAN *Rivals* Pref. p. viii, For on subjects on which the mind has been much informed, invention is slow of exerting itself. **1787** *William of Normandy* II. 10 Soon were they informed the deceitful cause. **1841** D'ISRAELI *Amen. Lit.* (1867) 360 Ascham informs us that .. Elizabeth understood Greek better than the canons of Windsor. **1841** LANE *Arab. Nts.* I. 85 He informed him who he was. **1860** TYNDALL *Glac.* I. ii. 13 We were informed of the descent of an avalanche by the sound. **1863** G. MACDONALD *D. Elginbrod* III. iii. x. 170 Do not hesitate to inform us on all possible subjects. **1880** DISRAELI *Endymion* II. lxi. 255 It must be a mind .. fairly informed on the questions involved in the wealth of nations. **1888** MRS. H. WARD *R. Elsmere* III. xliii. 254 The Frenchman .. had been informed about him. **1944** P. CHEYNEY *They never say When* xi. 172 It seems an amazing thing that you didn't inform someone about this. **1963** S. BRORSTRÖM *Increasing Frequency Preposition 'About'* VIII. 323 'Inform *about*' is an accepted construction in sentences like 'Did he *inform* you *about* it?', 'I wasn't *informed about* it', i.e. in sentences where the preposition is followed by *it.*

b. *spec.* To furnish (a magistrate or the like) with accusatory information *against* a person. (Cf. INFORMATION 4, 5.)

1526 TINDALE *Acts* xxiv. 1 Ananias .. with senioures, and with a certayne oratour named Tartullus, .. enfourmed the ruelar agaynst Paul.

c. With quoted words as object.

1877 *My Mother-in-Law* xii. 112 'Baby is not very well, Charlie,' Bessie informed me. **1881** MRS. J. H. RIDDELL *Senior Partner* I. xiv. 290 'Ye're out of your mind, Janet,' Mr. McCullagh informed her.

6. *refl.* [= F. *s'informer*] (from 4 and 5). To gain knowledge, instruction, or information; to acquaint oneself with something; to get to know, to learn. Const. as in 4 and 5.

1611 SHAKS. *Wint. T.* II. i. 167 Informe your selues, We neede no more of your aduice. **1623** GOUGE *Serm. Extent God's Provid.* §15 The Bishop of London .. sent to me to inform myself thorowly of the whole businesse. **1697** DAMPIER *Voy.* I. 114 They confessed that they came purposely to view our Ship, and .. to inform themselves what we were. **1747** in *Col. Rec. Pennsylv.* (1851) V. 84 To inform myself how you do and what passes among the Indians. **1775** C. JOHNSTON *Pilgrim* 208 The motive .. was to inform myself particularly in the laws. **1861** M. PATTISON *Ess.* (1889) I. 36 Edward .. requires his ambassador to observe the young prince, and to inform himself of his character and disposition.

7. *absol.* or *intr.* †**a.** To give information; to report. *Obs.*

1605 SHAKS. *Macb.* I. v. 34 Is not thy Master with him? who, wer't so, Would haue inform'd for preparation. **1656** STANLEY *Hist. Philos.* IV. (1701) 134/1 They held that the Senses inform not always truly. **1683** LUTTRELL *Brief Rel.* (1857) I. 287 Letters from Hungary inform of the good news of the emperors forces .. haveing taken Gran.

b. To lay or exhibit an information, bring a charge or complaint (*against,* rarely *on*).

1586 A. DAY *Eng. Secretary* II. (1625) 122 Sinisterly to speake, or otherwise to enforme against them. **1588–9** *Act 31 Eliz.* c. 5 §3 Any suche officers of recorde, as have .. heretofore laufullye used to exhibite informacions, or sue upon penall lawes .. may informe and pursue in that behalfe, as they might have done before the making of this Acte. **1605** SHAKS. *Lear* IV. ii. 93 'Twas he inform'd against him. **1766** GOLDSM. *Vic. W.* xxi, Even though it may benefit the public, you must not inform against him. **1809** R. LANGFORD *Introd. Trade* 9 Parties have reason to fear being informed against. **1884** SIR J. C. DAY in *Law Rep.* 14 Q. Bench Div. 201 It seems to me doubtful whether the Crown can appoint anybody to go into Court and inform other than the Attorney General. **1889** BOLDREWOOD *Robbery under Arms* xxiv, Somebody had informed on the man.

IV. To instruct in (a thing), impart the knowledge of, make known.

†**8.** *trans.* To impart the knowledge of (a subject, doctrine, method of action, etc.); to give instruction in, to teach. **a.** To inform *a person a thing. Obs.*

1390 GOWER *Conf.* I. 132, I woll sue What thing, that ye me woll enforme. *c* **1394** *P. Pl. Crede* 272 Knowest þou ouȝt .. a creatour on erþe, þat coude me my Crede teche and trewliche enfourme. *c* **1450** *Merlin* 5 And so he taught and enformed hem here creaunce and feith. **1529** in *Vicary's Anat.* (1888) App. xiv. 252 No persone .. shall enfourme or teche eny Foren, other than hys Apprentyce, eny poynte of his Crafte. **1621** BURTON *Anat. Mel.* I. i. I. i. (1651) 3 These chastisements are inflicted upon us .. to informe and teach us wisdome.

†**b.** To inform *a thing. Obs.*

a **1340** HAMPOLE *Psalter* Prol. 3 The sange of psalmes .. quemes god, it enformes perfytnes, it dos away and distroys noy and angire of saule. *c* **1374** CHAUCER *Boeth.* I. pr. iv. 13 (Addit. MS.) Certis thou enfourmedist [*Camb. MS.* conformedest] .. þis sentence, þat is to seyne þat commune þinges or comunabletes weren blysful yif [etc.]. **1377** LANGL. *P. Pl.* B. xv. 548 Al for to enforme þe faith in fele contreyes. **1589** PUTTENHAM *Eng. Poesie* I. xviii. (Arb.) 53 These Eglogues came after to containe and enforme morall discipline. **1605** BACON *Adv. Learn.* II. vi. §1 The bounds of this knowledge are, that it sufficeth to convince atheism, but not to inform religion.

†**9.** To impart the knowledge of (a fact or occurrence); to make known, report, relate, tell.

a. To inform *a person a thing*: To let *him* know *a thing, that something is,* etc. *Obs.*

Here the personal object may be viewed as a dative: cf. the constr. with *to* in b. The thing told may in passive construction be expressed by the pronoun *it* introducing a subordinate clause ('it was informed me that ..'); this is distinguished from the construction with subordinate clause in 5, in that the passive form of the latter has the person as subject ('I was informed that ..').

c **1400** MAUNDEV. (1839) viii. 82 He commanded .. to enforme me pleynly alle the Mysteries of Every place. **1470–85** MALORY *Arthur* VI. vii, For as it is enformed me thou .. hast done grete despyte and shame vnto knyghtes of the round table. **1523** LD. BERNERS *Froiss.* I. cclv. 378 The vicount of Rochechoart was had in suspecte; for it was enfourmed the prince, howe he wolde turne frenche. **1548** HALL *Chron., Hen. VIII* 61 It is informed us that your young and ryotous people will ryse. **1765** COLMAN tr. *Terence* 170 Did not you inform him The bent of my affections? **1797** SOUTHEY *Lett.* (1856) I. 46 My mother will inform you my town direction as soon as I have one. **1810** *Ho. Lancaster* I. 149, I am compelled to inform you the reason of the meeting.

†**b.** To inform *a thing* (*to* a person). Sometimes *spec.* To make known or tell as an informer or accuser. *Obs.*

a **1533** LD. BERNERS *Gold. Bk. M. Aurel.* (1546) M iij, It shulde be informed to the senate. **1557** NORTH tr. *Gueuara's Diall Pr.* 134 b, The sonne informed the quarel to the Phylosopher. *a* **1586** SIDNEY *Arcadia* V. (1674) 461 Whatsoever hath been informed, was my fault. **1601** SHAKS. *All's Well* IV. i. 91 Haply thou mayst informe Something to saue thy life. *a* **1616** BEAUM. & FL. *Bl. Brother* III. i, What affairs inform these out-cries? **1635** LAUD *Wks.* (1853) V. 336 My lord the bishop informs that that county is very full of impropriations. **1655** SIR E. NICHOLAS in *N. Papers* (Camden) II. 311 Admitting .. all to bee true which hee hath informed, can there bee a greater act of baseness then to betray a confident? **1681** BURNET *Hist. Ref.* II. 67 It being informed to the Council, that Gardiner had written to some of that Board. **1711** *Light to Blind* in *10th Rep. Hist. MSS. Comm.* App. v. 142 A deserter came from the English army into the town, and informed that there was eight pieces of battering-cannon .. on the roade from Dublin. **1753** POCOCKE *Descr. East* I. 119 My servant talk'd .. as if he was a spy, and had inform'd what presents I had made.

†**in'formable,** *a. Obs. rare*$^{-1}$. [f. INFORM *v.* or med.L. *informāre*: cf. OF. *informateur* inquisitor, *information de vie et mœurs* inquest into life and manners, also INFORMATION *sb.* 5.] In the character of an inquisitor (?) or an accuser.

c **1485** *Digby Myst.* (1882) v. 540 At his deth I [Lucifer] shall appere informable, Shewyng hym all hys synnys abhomynable, Prevyng his soule dampnable.

informal (ɪnˈfɔːməl), *a.* [IN-^{3}.] Not formal.

1. a. Not done or made according to a recognized or prescribed form; not observing forms; not according to order; irregular; unofficial, disorderly.

1608 BACON *Sp. Union Laws* in *Resuscitatio* (1661) 24 If our Laws, and proceedings, be too Prolixe and Formall, it may be theirs are too informall and Summary. **1649** BP. GUTHRIE *Mem.* (1702) 61 His Majesty's Warrant sent to them for prorogation was so informal, that it could not subsist in Law. **1774** BP. HALLIFAX *Anal. Rom. Civil Law* (1795) 36 Soldiers and Sailors, in England, have the Privilege of making Informal Testaments. **1786** BURKE *Charge agst. W. Hastings* III. iv, The said Hastings .. did .. send to the Rajah a charge in writing, which, though informal and irregular, may be reduced to four articles. **1823** LAMB *Elia* Ser. II. Pref., The informal habit of his mind, joined to an inveterate impediment of speech, forbade him to be an orator. **1836** W. IRVING *Astoria* III. 255 He accordingly made an informal overture to the President of the United States .. through Mr. Gallatin, offering to renew his enterprise. **1874** GREEN *Short Hist.* iii. §2. 119 In a previous though informal gathering .. the convent had already chosen its sub-prior .. as Archbishop.

b. Done, performed, etc. without formality or ceremony; unceremonious.

1828 WEBSTER, *Informal* .. 2 Not in the usual manner; not according to custom; as, an informal visit. **1864** *Ibid.*, *Informal,* without ceremony. **1881** *Confess. frivolous Girl* 174 That word *informal* is one of the deadliest foes to higher civilization. It is only a synonyme for free-and-easy. **1883** *Harper's Mag.* Oct. 652/1 His breakfast was a very informal meal.

c. *N.Z.* and *Austral.* Of a vote or voting-paper: not in due form, spoilt, invalid.

1957 *Wanganui Herald* 2 Dec. 5/2 (*table*) *Cotterill* 6121 *Mrs MacLean* 4626 *Marks* 3167. There were 39 informal votes on the preliminary count. **1965** *Parliamentary Handbk. Austral.* 359 Victoria, 1951. No. on Rolls, 1,388,116. No. who Voted, 1,332,339. No. of Informal Ballot-papers, 90,887. **1966** *Official Year Bk. Western Austral.* 105 Number of Informal Ballot Papers, 922.

d. Pertaining to or in respect of the non-compulsory admission of a patient to a mental hospital, esp. by his or her own volition.

1959 *Act 7 & 8 Eliz. II* c. 72 §5 (*heading*) Informal admission of patients. *Ibid.*, Whenever possible admission and treatment should be on an informal basis and .. compulsion should only be resorted to where it is absolutely essential in the interests of the patient and for his safety or that of the public. **1964** B. ACKNER *Handbk. Psychiatric Nurses* (ed. 9) 3 The Mental Health Act of 1959 .. permitted mentally ill patients to be admitted on an 'informal' basis without any documentation. **1968** K. O'HARA *Bird-Cage* vii. 65 'I don't understand this about informal patients.' 'It should have been explained to you. We don't call it certification now, but we do still need powers to protect patients from themselves.' **1970** *Times* 9 Sept. 16/6 (Advt.), Is there a Christian community who would accept a maladjusted 29-year-old girl? She is an informal patient in a mental hospital. **1972** *Guardian* 11 Aug. 11/3 An informal patient can sign for himself; the next of kin of a detained patient must give his permission.

†**2.** ? Disordered in mind. *Obs.* (Cf. FORMAL 4 c.)

1603 SHAKS. *Meas. for M.* V. i. 236, I doe perceiue These poore informall women, are no more But instruments of some more mightier member That sets them on.

†**3.** = INFORM *a.* 2 b: tr. L. *informis. Obs.*

1826 K. DIGBY *Broadst. Hon.* II. (1846) 319 That which Lewis Grenadensis calls the living faith, that which is joined with love, in opposition to the informal or dead faith which is without love.

informality (ɪnfɔːˈmælɪtɪ). [f. prec. + -ITY.] The quality or fact of being informal; absence of formality; with *an* and *pl.* An instance of this, an informal act or proceeding.

1597 MORLEY *Introd. Mus.* 75 In the first and second notes you rise as though it were a close, causing a great informalitie of closing, when you shoulde but begin. **1686** CLARENDON

Lett., To Ld. Treas. I. 125 (T.), I thought the informality was, that . . it was not countersigned by you. **1783** WATSON *Philip III* (1793) I. III. 307 The defects and informalities complained of must have been entirely owing to carelessness. **1865** PUSEY *Truth Eng. Ch.* 265 The informality or mistake of altering the common Creed.

informally (ɪnˈfɔːməlɪ), *adv.* [f. as prec. + -LY².] In an informal way; not according to the regular or prescribed form, unofficially; without form or ceremony, unceremoniously.

1800 *Admir. Desp.* 29 Mar. in Nicolas *Disp. Nelson* (1845) IV. 217 *note*, Passports . . which may have been in the interval (however informally) granted. **1828** SCOTT *F.M. Perth* x, The dispensation from Rome was informally granted. **1882** EARL DERBY in *Standard* 5 Jan. 2/3 The House must do formally what after all it now does informally —it must fix a period when debate shall close. **1883** OUIDA *Wanda* I. 193 A chance acquaintance made quite informally.

†**inˈformance.** *Obs. rare.* [f. L. *informā-re* to INFORM: see -ANCE.] Information.

1628 GAULE *Pract. The.* (1629) 315 We search Registers . . for our more Informance, for our better Assurance.

informant (ɪnˈfɔːmənt), *a.* and *sb.* [f. L. *informānt-em*, pres. pple. of *informāre* to INFORM; in mod.F. *informant.*]

A. *adj. Metaph.* 'Informing'; giving form; actuating: see INFORM *v.* 3.

1890 in *Cent. Dict.*

B. *sb.*

†1. That which 'informs', animates, or actuates.

1661 GLANVILL *Van. Dogm.* xvi. 153 The matter can be actuated at once but by a single Informant.

2. a. One who informs or tells a person of some fact or occurrence; one who gives information.

1693 *Col. Rec. Pennsylv.* I. 396 The informant, Polycarpus Rose, saith, That about 5 weeks since [etc.]. **1699** BENTLEY *Phal.* Pref. 13 A Third Informant, who over heard some Discourse of mine. **1742** RICHARDSON *Pamela* IV. 204 But, dear Sir, your Knowledge of the Informants makes nothing at all as to the Truth of the Information. **1826** J. W. CROKER in *C. Papers* 20 Mar. (1884), You have heard the whole story from day to day by better informants.

b. *Law.* One who lays an information against a person; an 'informer'.

1783 BURKE *Aff. India* (R.), It was the last evidence of the kind. The informant was hanged. **1848** *Act 11 & 12 Vict.* c. 43 §10 The matter of such information shall be substantiated by the oath or affirmation of the informant. **1865** *Act 28 & 29 Vict.* c. 104 §6 An English information, exhibited . . in the name of Her Majesty's Attorney General . . as the informant.

c. A person from whom a linguist, anthropologist, etc., elicits information about language, dialect, culture, etc. Used esp. in *Dialect Geography*. Also *attrib.*

1889 A. J. ELLIS *On Early Eng. Pronunc.* V. 2 Where I was unable to obtain vivâ voce or palaeotypic information, I had the same difficulty as before in interpreting the informants' orthography. **1902** *Amer. Anthropologist* IV. 732 To quote the words of my Indian informant, 'the ceremonies of the other shrines were like branches of this shrine'. **1917** *Internat. Jrnl. Amer. Ling.* I. i. 1 They were obtained by dictation from a few informants. **1933** L. BLOOMFIELD *Lang.* xix. 324 The forms were collected in each case from a single informant by means of a questionnaire of some two-thousand words and phrases. **1936** *West Virginia Univ. Stud.* I. 51 The first requirement is that both potential informants be natives. **1943** *Language* XIX. i. 42 The language must be learned from the lips of a native informant, whose sole function is to talk in his own language. **1944** *Amer. Speech* Apr. 135 The danger inherent in partial reporting, especially when based on . . inadequate informant work. **1953** J. B. CARROLL *Study of Lang.* vi. 173 A linguistic scientist . . directed the class-room teaching process and used native informants as models for drill purposes. **1963** J. LYONS *Structural Semantics* iv. 76 The linguist can satisfy himself . . by going around and exasperating several tobacconists with his 'informant-technique'. **1964** R. H. ROBINS *Gen. Ling.* ix. 355 The informant is not a teacher, nor a linguist; he is simply a native speaker of the language willing to help the linguist in his work. **1971** D. CRYSTAL *Ling.* Interlude 137 These characteristics of the informant sample would have to be made . . explicit.

in forma pauperis: see IN *Lat. prep.*

†**inˈformate**, *v. Obs. rare.* [f. ppl. stem of L. *informāre* to INFORM, in the Scholastic sense.] *trans.* To give 'form' to; = INFORM *v.* 3.

1627 JACKSON *Creed* XII. ii. §3 'Acervus' . . an heap or congest of bodies homogeneal and contiguous, but not informated by one and the same form, not animated by one and the same soul or spirit.

informatics (ɪnfəˈmætɪks). [tr. Russ. *informátika* (A. I. Mikhailov et al. 1966, in *Nauchno-tekhnicheskaya Informatsiya* XII. 35), f. INFORMATION: see -ICS.] (See quot. 1967.) Cf. *information science* (INFORMATION 8). Hence **inforˈmatical** *a.*, **informaˈtician**.

1967 *FID News Bull.* XVII. 73/2 *Informatics* is the discipline of science which investigates the structure and properties (not specific content) of scientific information, as well as the regularities of scientific information activity, its theory, history, methodology and organization. **1970** *Times* 2 Sept. 9 It was agreed . . that an introduction to Informatics should form an integral part of general education. **1972** *Jrnl. Librarianship* IV. 177 The name Informatics satisfies several criteria for the designation of a new discipline. *Ibid.*, Other terms can be derived from it, such as Informatician for a person who is engaged in activities in this field . . and the adjective informatical, to describe the attributes of the field. **1973** *Times Lit. Suppl.* 28 Sept. 1133/1 The problem falls into two parts: the preparation of decisions, which is a matter of informatics, and the making of the decisions themselves, which is a matter of 'politics'.

information (ɪnfəˈmeɪʃən). Forms: α. 4–6 **enformacion**, (**-ioun**, **-ione**, **-yon**), 6–7 **enformation**. β. 4–6 **informacion**, (**-ioun**, **-yon**), 6– **information**. [a. OF. *enformacion*, *informacion* (mod.F. *information*), ad. L. *informātiōn-em* outline, concept, idea, in med.Schol.L. the action of 'informing' matter, n. of action from *informāre* to INFORM. Conformed to the L. spelling in 16th c. The L. sb. had a very restricted use; the Eng. senses represent all the senses of the verb; but the chronological appearance of these does not accord with the logical order.]

I. 1. a. The action of informing (in sense 4 of the verb); formation or moulding of the mind or character, training, instruction, teaching; communication of instructive knowledge. Now *rare* or *Obs.*

1387 TREVISA *Higden* (Rolls) VI. 33 þere is i-write þat fyve bookes com doun from heven for informacioun of mankynde. **1390** GOWER *Conf.* III. 145 A tale, which is evident Of trouthe in commendacion, Toward their enformacion. **1450–1530** *Myrr. our Ladye* 140 Athanasius . . made thys psalme . . to comforte and enformacion of them that were in trew byleue. **1526** TINDALE *Eph.* vi. 4 Brynge them vppe with the norter and informacion off the lorde. **1597** HOOKER *Eccl. Pol.* v. xx. §11 Their [apocryphal books'] fitnesse for the publique information of life and manners. **1663** J. SPENCER *Prodigies* (1665) 20 To lead them to the light by a faithful information of their Judgments. **1736** BUTLER *Anal.* II. vii. 357 Our reason and affections, which God has given us for the information of our judgment and the conduct of our lives. **1813** JEFFERSON *Writ.* (1830) IV. 182 The book I have read with extreme satisfaction and information.

†**b.** with *an* and *pl.* An item of training; an instruction. *Obs.*

c **1386** CHAUCER *Melib.* ¶904 Whanne Melibee hadde herd the grete skiles and resons of Dame Prudence, and hire wise informacions and techynges. **1553** GRIMALDE *Cicero's Offices* Ep., Paines taking here to enriche themselves, with enformations of vertue. **1760** LAW *Spir. Prayer* I. 12 A most kind and loving information given by the God of love to his new-born offspring.

†**c.** Divine instruction, inspiration. *Obs.*

14.. *Circumcision* in *Tundale's Vis.* (1843) 96 A prophete by holy enformacion. **1526** *Pilgr. Perf.* (W. de W. 1531) 199 The holy apostles makyng this Crede by the instinccyon & informacyon of the holy goost. **1559** *Primer* in *Priv. Prayers* (1851) 30 O God, which by the information of the Holy Ghost hast instructed the hearts of thy faithful.

d. Capacity of informing; instructiveness. *rare.*

1712 J. HENLEY in *Spect.* No. 518 ¶7 With a Number of Circumstances of equal Consequence and Information.

2. The action of informing (in sense 5 of the verb); communication of the knowledge or 'news' of some fact or occurrence; the action of telling or fact of being told of something.

1390 GOWER *Conf.* III. 66 This night for enformation Ye shall have an avision. *c* **1400** MAUNDEV. (1839) v. 60, I haue vndirstonden be informacioun, that his lampe quencheþe. **1513** MORE in Grafton *Chron.* (1568) II. 759 This I have by credible informacion learned. **1555** EDEN *Decades* To Rdr. (Arb.) 50 The autoure . . hath seene a greate parte him selfe . . and gathered the residewe partly by information. **1664–94** SOUTH *Twelve Serm.* II. 113 By way of Information or Notification of the Thing to Him. **1794** PALEY *Evid.* (1825) II. 318 Difficulties always attend imperfect information. **1843** BORROW *Bible in Spain* xlix. 282/1 For your information, however, I will tell you that it is not.

3. a. Knowledge communicated concerning some particular fact, subject, or event; that of which one is apprised or told; intelligence, news. *spec.* contrasted with *data*.

c **1450** LYDG. & BURGH *Secrees* 1695 Ferthere to geve the Enformacioun, Of mustard whyte the seed is profitable. **1464** J. GRESHAM in *Paston Lett.* No. 482 II. 144, I have spoken onto Catesby, and delyvered hym your enfromacion. **1555** EDEN *Decades* 63 Muche otherwyse then Zamudius information. **1662** STILLINGFL. *Orig. Sacr.* II. ii. §1 That he have sufficient information concerning the things he undertakes to write of. **1727** SWIFT *Gulliver* III. ii, It was necessary to give the reader this information. **1895** *Law Times Rep.* LXXIII. 651/1 If the underwriters wanted to know more, they ought to have asked for information. **1970** [see DATUM 1 d]. **1970** O. DOPPING *Computers & Data Processing* i. 14 In administrative data processing, a distinction is sometimes made between data and information by calling raw facts in great quantity 'data', and using the word 'information' for highly concentrated and improved data derived from the raw facts.

attrib. **1890** M. TOWNSEND *U.S.* Pref. 1 The mass of curious facts, coincidences, and information-items from which this book is evolved. **1891** *Daily News* 2 Oct. 4/7 Information agent at the German Exhibition.

†**b.** with *an* and *pl.* An item of information or intelligence; a fact or circumstance of which one is told. In earlier use, An account, relation, narrative (*of* something). *Obs.*

1527 R. THORNE in Hakluyt *Voy.* (1589) 252 An information of the parts of the world discouered by him. *a* **1533** LD. BERNERS *Gold. Bk. M. Aurel.* (1546) Ll viij b, I . . haue herde of the a longe informacion. **1624** (*title*) A Briefe information of the Affaires of the Palatinate. **1666** MARVELL *Corr.* Wks. 1872–5 II. 190 Many informations are daily brought in to the two Committees about the Fire of London. **1724** SWIFT *Drapier's Lett.* Wks. 1755 V. II. 61 All the assistance I had, were some informations from an eminent person. **1748** CHESTERF. *Lett.* (1792) I. 327 The informations I have lately received in your favour from Mr. Harte. **1845** CARLYLE *Schiller* (ed. 2) Pref., Great changes in our notions, informations, in our relations to the Life of Schiller.

c. Separated from, or without the implication of, reference to a person informed: that which inheres in one of two or more alternative sequences, arrangements, etc., that produce different responses in something, and which is capable of being stored in, transferred by, and communicated to inanimate things.

Information in this sense may at the same time be, or be regarded as, information in the following sense.

1937 *Discovery* Nov. 329/1 The whole difficulty resides in the amount of definition in the [television] picture, or, as the engineers put it, the amount of information to be transmitted in a given time. **1944** *Jrnl. Sci. Instrum.* XXI. 133/2 Information is conveyed to the machine by means of punched cards. **1953** J. C. ECCLES *Neurophysiol. Basis Mind* i. 1 We may say that all 'information' is conveyed in the nervous system in the form of coded arrangements of nerve impulses. **1953** WATSON & CRICK in *Nature* 30 May 965/2 In a long molecule many different permutations are possible, and it therefore seems likely that the precise sequence of the bases is the code which carries the genetical information. **1958** *Spectator* 4 July 22/3 The complex molecules carrying genetic information from one generation to the next. **1961** *New Scientist* 26 Jan. 201/2 The colour information is added to a conventional black-and-white signal on an amplitude and phase modulated sub-carrier located in the vision band. **1962** *Listener* 10 May 817/2 The fertilized ovum of a particular animal is not, in any obvious way, like that animal; yet its development will proceed along certain lines only. It contains the information characteristic of that particular kind of animal. **1962** *Times* 5 July 15/7 A disc is apt to give slightly inferior quality towards the centre, where the information is more crowded. **1971** R. M. DOWBEN *Cell Biol.* v. 97 Genetically transmitted information precisely determines the amino acid composition of all proteins synthesized by each cell.

d. As a mathematically defined quantity (see quots.); now *esp.* one which represents the degree of choice exercised in the selection or formation of one particular symbol, sequence, message, etc., out of a number of possible ones, and which is defined logarithmically in terms of the statistical probabilities of occurrence of the symbol or the elements of the message.

The latter sense (introduced by Shannon, quot. 1948², though foreshadowed earlier) is that used in information theory, where information is usually regarded as synonymous with entropy.

1925 R. A. FISHER in *Proc. Cambr. Philos. Soc.* XXII. 709 What we have spoken of as the intrinsic accuracy of an error curve may equally be conceived as the amount of information in a single observation belonging to such a distribution. *Ibid.* 710 If p is the probability of an observation falling into any one class, the amount of information in the sample is $S\{(\partial m/\partial\theta)^2/m\}$ where $m = np$, is the expectation in any one class [and θ is the parameter]. **1928** R. V. L. HARTLEY in *Bell Syst. Techn. Jrnl.* VII. 540 What we have done then is to take as our practical measure of information the logarithm of the number of possible symbol sequences. *Ibid.* 541 The information associated with 100 characters will be 500 log 2. **1935** R. A. FISHER in *Jrnl. R. Statistical Soc.* XCVIII. 47 One could, therefore, develop a mathematical theory of quantity of information from these properties as postulates, and this would be a normal mathematical procedure. *Ibid.*, As a mathematical quantity information is strikingly similar to entropy in the mathematical theory of thermo-dynamics. **1948** N. WIENER *Cybernetics* iii. 76 Thus a reasonable measure of the amount of information associated with the curve $f_1(x)$ is:

$$\int_{-\infty}^{\infty} (\log_2 f_1(x)) f_1(x)\, dx.$$

The quantity we here define as amount of information is the negative of the quantity usually defined as entropy in similar situations. The definition . . is not the one given by R. A. Fisher for statistical problems, although it is a statistical definition. **1948** C. E. SHANNON in *Bell Syst. Techn. Jrnl.* XXVII. 392 We have represented a discrete information source as a Markoff process. Can we define a quantity which will measure, in some sense, how much information is 'produced' by such a process, or better, at what rate information is produced? Suppose we have a set of possible events whose probabilities of occurrence are $p_1, p_2, \ldots, p_n$. These probabilities are known but that is all we know concerning which event will occur. Can we find a measure of how much 'choice' is involved in the selection of the event or of how uncertain we are of the outcome? If there is such a measure, say $H(p_1, p_2, \ldots, p_n)$, it is reasonable to require of it the following properties: [etc.]. *Ibid.* 394 We shall call $H = -\Sigma p_i \log p_i$ the entropy of the set of probabilities $p_1 \ldots, p_n$. . . The quantity H has a number of interesting properties which further substantiate it as a reasonable measure of choice or information. **1949** W. WEAVER in Shannon & Weaver *Math. Theory Communication* 99 The word *information*, in this theory, is used in a special sense that must not be confused with its ordinary usage. In particular, information must not be confused with meaning. In fact, two messages, one of which is heavily loaded with meaning and the other of which is pure nonsense, can be exactly equivalent, from the present viewpoint, as regards information. *Ibid.* 100 Information in communication theory relates not so much to what you *do* say, as to what you *could* say. That is, information is a measure of one's freedom of choice when one selects a message. **1953** D. GABOR in W. Jackson *Communication Theory* i. 2 'Information' in the exact sense of communication theory is far more restricted than the vague concept which goes by this name in everyday life. It may also be mentioned that this definition has nothing to do with the value of information. It is a measure

of the minimum effort or cost by which the message can be transmitted, not of its importance or consequences. **1953** J. B. CARROLL *Study of Lang.* vii. 200 Information (in the special sense required in communication theory) may be measured in bits. **1953** C. F. HOCKETT in Saporta & Bastian *Psycholinguistics* (1961) 45/2 The keynote of the quantification of information is the matter of choice of any message, for actual transmission at a given time, from a fixed repertory of possible messages. **1956** L. BRILLOUIN *Sci. & Information Theory* p. x, Information is a function of the ratio of the number of possible answers before and after, and we choose a logarithmic law in order to insure additivity of the information contained in independent situations... This definition cannot distinguish between information of great importance and a piece of news of no great value for the person who receives it. **1957** KENDALL & BUCKLAND *Dict. Statistical Terms* 138 In a specialised sense in the theory of estimation, the amount of information about a parameter θ from a sample of n independent observations drawn at random from a population with a frequency function $f(x, \theta)$ is defined as

$$nE(\partial \log f/\partial\theta)^2 \equiv n \int_{-\infty}^{\infty} (\partial \log f(x, \theta)/\partial\theta)^2 f(x, \theta)dx.$$

1968 J. LYONS *Introd. Theoret. Ling.* ii. 84 Another important statistical notion has to do with the amount of *information* carried by a linguistic unit in a given context; and this also is determined by (or is generally held to be determined by) its frequency or occurrence in that context. **1968** P. A. P. MORAN *Introd. Probability Theory* i. 53 In statistical theory 'information' is usually 'information about a particular parameter' of a probability distribution, and is measured by the reciprocal of the square of the standard deviation of some estimator of that parameter. **1970** O. DOPPING *Computers & Data Processing* i. 19 Any language with different frequency of occurrence of different symbols has less information per symbol than another (hypothetical) language with the same number of symbol values but with equal probability of occurrence of them all.

4. The action of informing against, charging, or accusing (a person).

(Originally the general sense whence 5 arises; now *Obs.*, exc. as transf. from 5: cf. also 6.)

1480 CAXTON *Chron. Eng.* ccxliii. (1482) 288 A grete part of the peple..weren in grete errour and grutchyng ayenst the kyng thurgh Informacyon of lyes and fals lesyng that this Serle has made. **1535** JOYE *Apol. Tindale* (Arb.) 24 Besydis this condempnacion of me by hearsaye or enformacion of hys faccyon. **1550** CROWLEY (*title*) An informacion and Peticion agaynst the oppressours of the pore Commons of this Realme. **1565** GOLDING *Cæsar* 16 Here vppon hee called Dumnorix aside..laying before him what informations were put vp against him. **1613** SHAKS. *Hen. VIII*, v. iii. 110 In seeking tales and Informations Against this man.

5. *spec.* in *Eng. Law.* **a.** A complaint or charge against a person lodged with or presented to a court or magistrate, in order to the institution of criminal proceedings without formal indictment.

The original object of this procedure was to dispense with the previous finding of a grand jury. Criminal informations are laid (*a*) in any criminal court, partly at suit of the Crown, partly at suit of an individual, to enforce a penalty under a penal statute (the penalty being paid partly to the use of the Crown, partly to the informer); (*b*) in the Queen's Bench Division, in the name of the Crown alone, being either *ex officio* informations for misdemeanours dangerous to the government, e.g. seditious libel, or informations filed by the Master of the Crown Office, on the complaint of a private individual, for gross misdemeanours; (*c*) before a Justice of Peace, in matters that may be dealt with summarily, being a statement of the facts by the prosecutor, verbally or in writing, with or without oath. Most of these uses exist also in the law of the United States, where the most common sense is 'An official criminal charge presented, usually, by the prosecuting officers of the state, without the interposition of a grand jury'.

1629 in Cobbett *State Trials* (1809) III. 300 This matter [against Elliot, Hollis and Valentine] is brought in this court by way of Information, where it ought to be by way of Indictment. **1898** *Encycl. Laws Eng.* (Renton) VI. 446 The distinction between an Information and an Indictment is that an Indictment is an accusation found by the oath of twelve men.., whereas an Information is only the allegation of the officer who exhibits it.

(*a*) **1467–8** *Rolls of Parlt.* V. 633/1 That..every such Infourmer..be admitted to sue for the Kyng and hym self Actions..uppon the same by Enformation to be ȝeven or made in eny of the seid Courtes. **1523** *Act 14 & 15 Hen. VIII*, c. 1 The person..that will first sue for the same, by originall of dette, bill, plainte, or informacion, in any of the kynges courtes. **1647** MAY *Hist. Parl.* I. i. 13 They were also vexed with informations in inferiour Courts; where they were sentenced, and fined for matters done in Parliament. **1742** JOHNSON *Deb. Parlt.* (1787) II. 407 The prospect of raising money by detecting their practices incited many to turn information into a trade. **1769** BLACKSTONE *Comm.* IV. xxiii. (1809) 308 **1838** DICKENS *O. Twist* liii, The gentleman being accommodated with threepennyworth of brandy to restore her, lays an information next day, and pockets half the penalty. **1875** T. S. PRITCHARD *Quarter Sess. Pract.* iv. §4. 173 Prosecutions by information at the quarter sessions can only be instituted in cases where, by a penal statute, an informer is allowed to take this course to recover the penalty; but this proceeding is generally disused.

(*b*) **1482** *Rolls Parlt.* VI. 208/1 If the Kyngs Attourney Generall of his said Duchie..put a Bill into eny of the Kyngs Courtes by wey of enformation..the Justices of the same Court..shall have power [etc.]. **1537** *Act 28 Hen. VIII* in Bolton *Stat. Irel.* (1621) 167 And that the kings suit by writ, bill, plaint, enditement, and enformation in that behalfe be commenced. **1588–9** *Act 31 Eliz.* c. 5 §3 Suche officer[s] of recorde as have in respecte of their offices heretofore laufullye used to exhibite informacions or sue upon penall lawes. **1769** BLACKSTONE *Comm.* IV. xxiii. §3 (1809) 309 The objects of the other species of informations, filed by the master of the crown-office upon the complaint or relation of a private subject, are any gross and notorious misdemesnors, riots, batteries, libels, and other immoralities of an atrocious kind, not peculiarly tending to disturb the government. **1803** MACKINTOSH *Def. Peltier* Wks. 1846 III. 291 No prosecutions,—no Criminal Informations followed the liberty and the boldness of the language then employed. **1827** HALLAM *Const. Hist.* (1876) II. viii. 4 The attorney-general..exhibited an information against Sir John Eliot for words uttered in the house. **1883** SIR J. F. STEPHEN *Hist. Crim. Law Eng.* ix. I. 294 A criminal information..may be preferred only for misdemeanours, and only by the Attorney or Solicitor General, or by the Master of the Crown Office acting under the orders of the Queen's Bench Division, upon a motion made in open court.

(*c*) **1733** J. HARVEY (*title*) Orders, Warrants, Informations, and variety of Precedents for Justices of the Peace. **1802** MAR. EDGEWORTH *Moral T.* (1816) I. xv. 122 A magistrate, with whom informations had been lodged. **1897** C. M. ATKINSON *Magistrate's Ann. Pract.* ii. 22 The mode of commencing proceedings before justices of the peace is by preferring a complaint or an information..[It] is called an *information* when it is the foundation for summary proceedings of a criminal nature, which are followed either by a conviction or an acquittal.

b. A complaint of the Crown in respect of some civil claim, in the form of a statement of the facts by the attorney general or other proper officer, either *ex officio*, or on the relation or report of a private individual.

Civil informations are or have been laid: †(*a*) in Chancery, on behalf of the crown or government, or of those of whom the crown has custody, as Idiots (*obs.*); (*b*) in the Exchequer, under the equitable jurisdiction of the court (called ***English information*** from its resemblance to a complaint in equity formerly called an English bill); now transferred to the Queen's Bench Division; (*c*) at Common Law, for Intrusion or trespass on crown lands; Purpresture or encroachment on crown or public lands; *in personam*, for money due to the crown; *in rem*, for goods, derelicts, etc. belonging to the crown, and for default in payment of excise duties.

1624 *Act 21 Jas. I*, c. 14 (*title*) An Act to admit the Subject to plead the General Issue in Informations of Intrusion brought on the Kings behalf, and to retain his possession till Trial. **1768** BLACKSTONE *Comm.* III. xvii. (1809) 261 An information on behalf of the crown, filed in the exchequer by the king's attorney general. **1819** WIGHTWICK *Rep.* 167 *marg.*, The Prince of Wales may file an English information of intrusion by his Attorney General, for lands parcel of the Dutchy of Cornwall. **1838** MEESON & WELSBY *Rep.* II. 23 An information of intrusion, to recover possession of certain encroachments on the wastes of the Crown. **1865** *Act 28 & 29 Vict.* c. 104 §6 An information, styled an English information, exhibited in the Court of Exchequer. **1883** *Rules Sup. Crt.* I. i, All actions which..were commenced by bill or information in the High Court of Chancery..shall be instituted in the High Court of Justice by a proceeding to be called an action. **1888** *Daily News* 4 Dec. 5/2 By an exercise of the Royal prerogative an ancient method of procedure, known as an English information, is adopted for the settlement of these foreshore disputes between the Crown and its subjects.

c. ***information quo warranto*** (superseding the ancient Writ of *Quo warranto*): the step by which proceedings are commenced to remedy the usurpation of an office or franchise.

1765 BLACKSTONE *Comm.* I. xviii. (1809) 485 An information in the nature of a writ of *quo warranto*, to enquire by what warrant the members now exercise their corporate power. **1827** HALLAM *Const. Hist.* (1876) II. xii. 453 An information, as it is called, quo warranto, was accordingly brought into the court of King's bench against the corporation.

6. In other legal systems.

a. In *Civil Law.* (See quot.)

1774 BP. HALLIFAX *Anal. Rom. Civil Law* (1795) 125 Informations are arguments urged before the Judge by the Advocates on both sides, after the Pleadings and Proofs are concluded. **1863** H. COX *Instit.* II. iv. 404.

b. In *Scots Law.* (*a*) in Civil Procedure: A written argument upon a case ordered either by a Lord Ordinary in the Court of Session when reporting the case to the Inner House (*obs.*), or by the Court of Justiciary in a case where difficult questions of law or relevancy are raised before it (now *rare*). (*b*) in Criminal Procedure: A statement or complaint in writing in which a person is specifically charged with a criminal offence, upon which a warrant of commitment to gaol for trial may proceed.

1681 STAIR *Inst. Law Scot.* IV. xxxix. 14 (1832) 690 All informations and bills relating to interlocutors given, or to be given. **1701** *Sc. Acts Will. III*, c. 6 Enacts and ordains that all Informers shall signe their Informations. **1752** J. LOUTHIAN *Form of Process* (ed. 2) 102 The Clerk..reads the Prosecutor's Information, with the Information on or Answers thereto for the Pannel, off the Book; and after all is read, the Preses resumes the Heads of the Information and Answers to the Lords, and desires their Opinion. **1754** ERSKINE *Princ. Sc. Law* (1828) IV. iv. §85 No person can be imprisoned in order to trial for any crime, without a warrant in writing, expressing the cause, and proceeding upon a signed information. **1768** in D. Hume *Comm. Law Sc.* II. x. §4 In the information on the part of the pannel very alarming consequences are endeavoured to be grafted on the doctrine pled in behalf of the prosecutor in this case.

c. Applied also to similar proceedings in foreign systems of judicature, ancient or modern.

1601 R. JOHNSON *Kingd. & Commw.* (1603) 57 [He] is forced to answer presently to the information of his adversarie if he be present. **1625** *Gonsalvio's Sp. Inquis.* 1 Whensoeuer any denunciation (as they terme it) or rather information is giuen against any person..the Inquisitors accustomably vse this kind of practice. **1770** LANGHORNE *Plutarch* (1879) II. 909/2 The information was first laid under the archonship of Chœrondas. **1781** GIBBON *Decl. & F.* xvii. II. 60 The terrors of a malicious information, which might select them as the accomplices, or even as the witnesses, perhaps, of an imaginary crime, perpetually hung over the heads of the principal citizens of the Roman world. **1875** JOWETT *Plato* (ed. 2) III. 107 Then follow informations and convictions for treason.

II. †**7.** The action of 'informing' with some active or essential quality (see INFORM *v.* 3); the giving of a form or character to something; inspiration, animation (*e.g.* of the body by the soul).

1646 SIR T. BROWNE *Pseud. Ep.* VI. i. 274 There was a seminality and contracted Adam in the rib, which by the information of a soule, was individuated into Eve. **1669** CLARENDON *Ess.* Tracts (1727) 117 That..no information of pride may enter into us to make us believe that we are better than other men. **1701** NORRIS *Ideal World* II. ii. 72 To be always in a separate state would be violent and unnatural to spirits made apt for the information of bodies, to which therefore they would naturally require to be united. **1870** EMERSON *Soc. & Solit., Works & Days* Wks. (Bohn) III. 65 There does not seem any limit to these new informations of the same Spirit that made the elements at first.

III. 8. *attrib.* and *Comb.*, as ***information content, desk, explosion*** [EXPLOSION 4 b], ***flow, gap*** [GAP *sb.*[1] 6 a], ***office, service, storage, system, transfer, work***; ***information-carrying, -gathering*** (so ***gatherer***), ***-giving, -seeking*** vbl. sbs. and ppl. adjs.; **information bureau**, an office where information is given and questions are answered; also *fig.*; **information officer**, a person engaged in the provision of specialized information; **information processing**, the processing of information so as to yield new or more useful information; data processing; **information retrieval**, the tracing of information stored in books, computers, or other collections of reference material; **information revolution**, the increase in the availability of information and the changes in the ways it is stored and disseminated that have occurred through the use of computers; **information room** (see quot. 1958); **information science**, (that branch of knowledge which is concerned with) the procedures by which information, esp. that relating to technical or scientific subjects, is stored, retrieved, and disseminated; hence **information scientist**, a person employed in providing an information service, or one who studies the methods used to do so; **information technology**, the branch of technology concerned with the dissemination, processing, and storage of information, esp. by means of computers. Also INFORMATION THEORY.

1922 E. WALLACE *Flying Fifty-Five* vii. 44 Well, Jebson. ..You're a pretty fine *information bureau! You told me that Patience hadn't a ghost of a chance. **1926** *Aslib Prospectus*, The objects of the Association are..to develop the usefulness and efficiency of special libraries and information bureaux under whatever title they may function. **1968** *Listener* 4 July 31/3 The information bureau of the Disabled Living Activities Group. **1962** *Science Survey* IV. 68 The *information-carrying capacity of a wave depends directly on the frequency. **1971** J. Z. YOUNG *Introd. Study Man* p. v, The spectacular recent information that biochemistry has provided about the large molecules in the body, and especially about the information-carrying properties of the nucleic acids. **1928** *Bell Syst. Techn. Jrnl.* VII. 541 For example, in the Baudot System..the number *s* of primary symbols is..2 and the *information content of one selection is log 2. **1937** J. C. WILSON *Television Engin.* xii. 426 The information-content of a television image has been evaluated solely from the point of view of what is transmitted. **1965** *Language* XLI. 385 This decomposition, or normal form, is of special interest because of various correlations with vocabulary, information-content, etc. **1967** *Economist* 11 Nov. 627/3 A national Referral Centre for Science and Technology is trying to build up a world-wide '*information desk' for advice on where and how to obtain information. **1973** D. MACKENZIE *Postscript to Dead Let.* 23, I..put the key in an envelope marked *to be called for* and left it at the Information Desk. **1964** *New Statesman* 13 Mar. 396/2 The 'population explosion' has collided with the '*information explosion'. Vastly more people and more kinds of people are chasing vastly more information about more kinds of things. **1972** *Jrnl. Librarianship* IV. 161 The advent of ISR roughly coincided with the first commercial applications of computers and it was then thought that very rapid handling of coded data was all that was needed to cope with the 'information explosion'. **1953** C. F. HOCKETT in Saporta & Bastian *Psycholinguistics* (1961) 64/1 Energy flow is power; *information-flow is entropy; money-flow (at least in one direction) is income. **1965** H. I. ANSOFF *Corporate Strategy* (1968) i. 19 Product-market characteristics create operating needs, and these, in turn, determine the structure of authority, responsibility, work flows, and information flows within the firm. **1969** *Daily Tel.* 11 Jan. 12/8 Bold human causes..will not be served by ignoring the new technologies which space research is encouraging; and Britain would be well advised to close the *information gap which seems to be developing. **1971** K. HOPKINS *Hong Kong* iii. 95 Mr. Woo's speech was an example of the many and repeated expressions of concern by members of the public and of Government about a so-called 'information gap' between Government and the people. **1964** M. MCLUHAN *Understanding Media* (1967) II. xxviii. 302 Man the food-gatherer reappears incongruously as *information-gatherer. **1971** J. Z. YOUNG *Introd. Study Man* xxiv. 317 One of man's many paradoxes is that although with him each individual organism is more important than in other animals as an information-gatherer for the species, yet his manner of life

is largely controlled by his fellows. **1964** M. McLuhan *Understanding Media* (1967) II. xiv. 149 In the age of instant information man..assumes the role of *information-gathering. **1967** Cox & Grose *Organiz. Bibliogr. Rec. by Computer* 70 A subject-specialist studies the information needs and information-gathering habits of a group of teachers. **1908** *Westm. Gaz.* 1 July 6/3 The first products of Canada, states one of the numerous *information-giving tablets, are worth thirty million dollars a year. **1927** J. Adams *Errors in School* iv. 122 Instruction must be distinguished from mere information-giving. **1890** W. Booth *In Darkest Eng.* App. p. xiv, We shall also be glad, through the *information office of Labour Department, to give you..further information. **1918** E. S. Farrow *Dict. Mil. Terms* 310 *Information officers..send to their own commanders all information of military importance to them. **1935** *Aslib Rep. Proc. 12th Conf.* 38 (*heading*) B. Fullman... (Information Officer, British Non-Ferrous Metals Research Association). **1947** *Jrnl. Documentation* II. 240, I am not a librarian at all; I am not even a trained information officer. **1970** *Aslib Proc.* XXII. ix. p. ii (Advt.), Vacancy for Scientific Information Officer at the Commonwealth Forestry Bureau. **1958** *Automation* Mar. 65 (*heading*) *Information processing. **1959** *Unesco Bull. Libr.* XIII. 226 Nearly 2,000 electronic computer experts took part in the International Conference on Information Processing organized by Unesco in Paris from 15 to 20 June. **1964** T. W. McRae *Impact of Computers on Accounting* vii. 190 Even today few companies segregate 'information processing' or even 'data processing' under a separate cost head. **1970** O. Dopping *Computers & Data Processing* i. 11 Many speak of the advent of mechanized information processing as the second industrial revolution. *Ibid.* 15 When both input and output are data, that is, digital information consisting of a great number of records in standardized layout, the information processing is usually called data processing. **1950** C. N. Mooers *Theory Digital Handling Non-Numerical Information* (*Zator Techn. Bull.* No. 48) 5 The requirements of *information retrieval, of finding information whose location or very existence is a-priori unknown, now requires that it be possible by some efficient technique to specify a selection of complexes Cj by means of *any* set or combination of descriptors chosen in *any* way from the vocabulary ((a$_j$)). **1958** *Listener* 11 Dec. 983/1 Only a week or two ago there was a conference on information retrieval in Washington. **1963** *Publishers' Weekly* 23 Sept. 34/2 At the Oxford store, the feature which so far has attracted the most attention is the free bibliographical information retrieval service. **1963** *Cambr. Rev.* 12 Oct. 24/1 A book miscatalogued..is a book lost: and they [*sc.* librarians] thereby justify greater and greater expenditure on more and more elaborate systems of 'information retrieval'. **1972** *Computers & Humanities* VII. 61 Prof. D. Raj Reddy offers a set of exercises in statistics, natural language processing, language translation, poetry concordance, and information retrieval to interested readers. **1969** *SIAM Jrnl. Appl. Math.* XVII. 1203 The recent advent of large scale, high-speed computers has produced a '*information revolution'. **1983** *Listener* 23 June 22/1 Societies are about to become divided between inner-city poor and small-town rich—a new Two Nations created by the information revolution. **1934** J. Moylan *Scotland Yard* (ed. 2) v. 132 At Scotland Yard there are *Information and Operation Rooms from which the wireless cars are directed. **1940** R. Morrish *Police & Crime-Detection* ii. 28 Every Force has its 'Information Room', to which members of the public should report by telephone anything suspicious. **1958** A. Garfitt *Bk. for Police* I. iii. 77 An Information Room is established at some [police] headquarters and is the centre through which information, particularly as to crime and suspected crime, can be disseminated by wireless, teleprinter or telephone. **1970** P. Laurie *Scotland Yard* i. 16 The first floor carries the electronic complexities of the Information Room. **1960** *Computers & Automation* IX. 39/2 Moore School of Electrical Engineering, University of Pennsylvania... Prof. Saul Gorn, Chairman, Computer and *Information Sciences Curriculum. **1962** *Conf. on Training Science Information Specialists 1961–62* (Georgia Inst. Technol.) 115 Information science..investigates the properties and behavior of information, the forces governing the flow of information, and the means of processing information for optimum accessibility and usability. **1963** *Library Jrnl.* LXXXVIII. 4161/1 The information sciences are conceived as: 1) the study of the properties, structure, and transmission of specialized knowledge; and 2) the development of methods for its useful organization and dissemination. **1971** C. W. Hanson *Introd. Science-Information Work* 2 'Information science' can be used to imply..the exploitation of scientific and technical information of all kinds... On the other hand, it is often used to imply the application of science and technology..to handling information generally. **1958** *Nature* 4 Jan. 20/1 A meeting will be held on January 23..to discuss terms of inauguration of an Institute of *Information Scientists. The aims of the proposed Institute would include the promotion of high standards in scientific and technical information work, the promotion of educational courses, and the establishment of qualifications for those engaged in such information work. **1963** *Aslib Proc.* XV. 100 These are post-graduate courses for those about to become information scientists. **1972** *Jrnl. Librarianship* IV. 169 The American protagonists of IS generally say that people involved in this science should be called information scientists. **1956** J. Klein *Study of Groups* x. 140 The whole elaborate process of *information-seeking, evaluation and decision. **1935** E. S. Hedges in *Aslib Rep. Proc. 12th Conf.* 35 An *information service which distributes in-coming information to interested quarters can be more effective than one which merely renders the information available on request. **1950** *N.Y. Times* 20 Apr. 1/8 Mr. Kolarek..has been in Czechoslovakia since September, 1945, serving first as assistant and later as chief press attache and information service director. **1968** B. E. Holm *How to manage your Information* iii. 55 The Dow Chemical Company is one of the many organizations which provides information services to its engineers. **1950** *Information storage [see *information transfer* below]. **1972** *Jrnl. Librarianship* IV. 161 Somewhat later, it was realized that, to 'retrieve' information from a place, it obviously had to be stored prior to the retrieval, so the term was augmented to 'Information storage and retrieval' (ISR). **1953** C. F. Hockett in Saporta & Bastian *Psycholinguistics* (1961) 64/2 If it is necessary to maintain

some analogy between an *information-system and a power-system, then entropy can better be compared to voltage. **1964** T. W. McRae *Impact of Computers on Accounting* iii. 82 The objective of an information system..is to note all of the events happening within the organization being controlled, to extract those events which require to be reported and to report them to the controlling authority fast enough for compensating action to be possible. **1969** D. C. Hague *Managerial Econ.* i. 18 The information system [of a firm].. will be partly a rather mechanical system for providing routine reports about things like production, costs, sales or profits. It will also be partly a much less formal arrangement whereby those within the firm pass on information..to those who need it. **1958** Leavitt & Whisler in *Harvard Business Rev.* XXXVI. 41/1 The new technology does not yet have a single established name. We shall call it *information technology. **1979** *London Rev. Bks.* 25 Oct. 21/1 Attali is a French economist..who writes..studies of, for example, music (*Bruits*) and information technology. **1984** *Nat. Westminster Bank Q. Rev.* Aug. 13 The development of cable television was made possible by the convergence of telecommunications and computing technology (..generally known in Britain as information technology). **1950** *Amer. Scientist* XXXVIII. 278/2 A consideration of the effects of information storage and *information transfer on physical, chemical, biological, psychological, and sociological systems..may help in understanding and predicting many of the aspects of our universe. **1964** G. H. Haggis et al. *Introd. Molecular Biol.* x. 279 Each operator with its associated structural genes forms a coordinated unit of information-transfer to which Jacob and Monod have given the name *operon*. **1935** B. Fullman in *Aslib Rep. Proc. 12th Conf.* 38 Organised *information work is at present only in its infancy. **1959** *Aslib Proc.* XI. 290 The role of the textbook in technical information work is usually a fundamental one. **1972** *Jrnl. Librarianship* IV. 111 (inside front cover), The *Journal of Librarianship* is an independent quarterly journal dealing with all aspects of library and information work.

informational (ɪnfəˈmeɪʃənəl), *a.* [f. prec. + -AL¹.] Of or pertaining to information; conveying information.

1810 Bentham *Elem. Packing* (1821) 142 *note*, The sub-pœna'd interpreter of informational innuendoes. **1882** *Times* 21 Nov. 10 They [addresses] were nearly always informational. **1898** *Pop. Sci. Monthly* LIII. 781 How little value I place upon the informational results. **1967** M. McLuhan *Medium is Massage* 138 Subtle electric informational media. **1971** *Nature* 2 July 66/2 The 'monogenomic' viroplast consists of viral genome, informational RNA, a complex of specific viral enzymes and structural proteins. **1971** *Jrnl. Gen. Psychol.* LXXXV. 207 Innovative substitutions of informational types of thinking in psychology. **1972** *Jrnl. Social Psychol.* LXXXVI. 111 The influence of interpersonal evaluations may result from their informational value for the individual.

informationally (ɪnfəˈmeɪʃənəlɪ), *adv.* [f. INFORMATIONAL *a.* + -LY².] As regards information.

1964 Y. R. Chao in D. Abercrombie et al. *Daniel Jones* 41 Those aspects of speech which are informationally important but often acoustically weak. **1965** *Math. in Biol. & Med.* (*Med. Res. Council*) IV. 133 Here is a system [*sc.* the nervous system of higher animals] that reacts more reliably and predictably to informationally rich stimuli than to 'simple' ones. **1973** *Physics Bull.* May 281/1 Informationally, the incident speech signal requires about 50,000 bit/s to specify it.

informationless (ɪnfəˈmeɪʃənlɪs), *a.* [f. INFORMATION + -LESS.] Without information; carrying or conveying no information.

1965 [see DROPPABLE *a.*].

information theory. [See INFORMATION 3 d.] The quantitative theory, based on a precise definition of information and on the theory of probability, of the coding and transmission of signals and information.

1950 D. M. MacKay in *Phil. Mag.* Mar. 290 (*heading*) The formalisation of information theory. **1950** W. G. Tuller in *Trans. Amer. Inst. Electr. Engin.* LXIX. 1612/1 The statistical theory of communications, developed over the past few years and often called information theory, can be of real assistance in the design of communication systems. **1950** L. Brillouin in *Amer. Scientist* XXXVIII. 594 (*heading*) Thermodynamics and information theory. **1955** H. Quastler *Information Theory in Psychol.* I. 8 It is basic to information theory that any event is evaluated against the background of the whole class of events which could have happened. Information theory proposes to measure the effect of operations by which a particular selection is made out of a range of possibilities. Choice, specification, discrimination, recognition, are examples of such operations. **1960** E. Delavenay *Introd. Machine Transl.* 131 The statistical study of language in so-called information theory bears mainly on the frequency of reference of graphemes and phonemes. **1961** *New Scientist* 26 Jan. 200/2 Normal television amplitude modulation of a carrier takes no advantage of the fact that the rate of change of picture content is relatively slow, and that because of this much redundant information is continuously transmitted at the cost of considerable bandwidth. Unfortunately no system of television picture transmission has yet been devised which is more logical from an information theory point of view and does not also require a complex computing apparatus in the receiver. **1962** J. R. Pierce *Symbols, Signals & Noise* vi. 107 The two great triumphs of information theory are establishing the channel capacity and, in particular, the number of binary digits required to transmit information from a particular source and showing that a noisy communication channel has an information rate in bits per character or bits per second up to which errorless transmission is possible despite the noise. **1964** M. A. K. Halliday et al. *Ling. Sci.* I. iv. 104 Information theory, which has a place in the quantitative description of a language, implies nothing about the relative efficiency of languages or the effectiveness of language activity. **1968**

Unesco Bull. Libr. XXII. 62 When Shannon and Weaver evolved their information theory, they..were guilty of an unfortunate use of terminology. They were concerned, of course, not with a theory of information but a theory of signals, the message-carrying capacity of a symbol, a telephone wire, or any other medium or channel of communication. **1970** O. Dopping *Computers & Data Processing* i. 21 Information theory deals largely with what happens when a random interference ('noise') is superimposed on the desired signal. **1972** *Jrnl. Librarianship* IV. 164 It is worth noting that Shannon never referred to his theory as an 'Information theory'.

Hence **information theorist.**

1953 C. F. Hockett in Saporta & Bastian *Psycholinguistics* (1961) 57/1 Neither the information theorist nor the linguist would claim that codes (*d*) and (*d'*) are identifiable with code (*a*) in quite the same way as codes (*b*) and (*c*). **1972** J. L. Dillard *Black English* i. 25 Research on the degree of intelligibility between the white man's English and Black English would be an expensive proposition... Ideally,..not only linguists but also anthropologists, psychologists, and an information theorist should be involved.

informative (ɪnˈfɔːmətɪv), *a.* [f. L. *informāt-* ppl. stem of *informāre* (cf. INFORMATE) + -IVE, perh. after a med.L. *informātīvus.*] Having the quality of informing, in various senses.

1. That informs or gives 'form' (to matter); that imparts an active quality, or inspires with life; animative. ? *Obs.*

1647 H. More *Song of Soul* II. i. II. xxiv, Many put out their force informative In their ethereall corporeity, Devoid of heterogeneall organity. *a* **1652** J. Smith *Sel. Disc.* iv. viii. (1821) 114 That definition which he gives of the soul, wherein he seems to make it nothing else..but an entelechia or informative thing, which spends all its virtue upon that matter which it informs. **1656** Jeanes *Mixt. Schol. Div.* 81 If we consider this union effective, so it regards the whole Trinity; if terminative, so the sonne; if informative, so the humanity of Christ alone.

2. a. Having the quality of imparting knowledge or communicating information; instructive.

1655 Fuller *Ch. Hist.* x. i. Ded., The most informative Histories to Posterity..are such as were written by the Eye-witnesses thereof. **1665** Boyle *Occas. Refl.* III. vi. (1848) 44 Ways and Methods, whereby to make the Objects we consider informative to us. *c* **1819** Coleridge in *Rem.* (1836) II. 211 The preparation informative of the audience is just as much as was precisely necessary. **1858** Ruskin *Arrows of Chace* (1880) I. 186 All art employed in decoration should be informative.

b. *Bridge.* = INFORMATORY *a.* b.

1921 A. E. M. Foster *Auction Bridge made Clear* 105 There is an 'informative' double which some English players adopt... It is the double of a bid of one of a suit. **1925** —— *Auction Bridge Play & Probl.* 53 Thus Z bids 'one No Trumps' and A doubles informatively... The informative Re-double is never left in. **1931** —— *Auction Bridge made Clear* (rev.) 103 It is no longer an 'informative' double, but a 'business' double.

3. *Law.* Of the nature of or relating to legal information (sense 5).

1626 *Impeachm. Dk. Buckhm.* (Camden) 70 The informative Proofes, the Sentence..in the Admiralty Court. **1639** Gentilis tr. *Servita's Inquis.* (1676) 854 The thirteenth Chapter..treats of Informative Processes, which are to be sent into other places.

inˈformatively, *adv.* [f. prec. + -LY².] In an informative manner: **a.** With regard to the impartation of life or some essential quality (? *obs.*). **b.** By way of information or communication of knowledge. **c.** *Bridge.* (See INFORMATIVE *a.* 2 b).

1656 Jeanes *Fuln. Christ* 139 But now if we consider it informatively, in regard of information, or inhesion..so it is seated in the humane nature, that is not every where, but onely in heaven, at the right hand of God. **1822** *Blackw. Mag.* XI. 7 Informatively for the reader, I make known the following. **1925** [see INFORMATIVE *a.* 2 b].

informativeness (ɪnˈfɔːmətɪvnɪs). [f. INFORMATIVE *a.* + -NESS.] The quality or condition of being informative.

1924 C. Mackenzie *Old Men of Sea* v. 68 With the words Mr. Harper managed to assume as air of such bland informativeness that..his attitude reminded me of a conjurer who entreats a member of the audience to mount the stage. **1942** *Mind* LI. 60 It has been shown that the informativeness of memory plays a double part in the process of proof. **1955** *Essays in Crit.* V. 369 One of their number would write with such moral informativeness that he would catch up with Shakespeare.

†inforˈmator. *Obs. rare.* [a. late L. *informātor* (Tertullian), agent-n. from *informāre* to INFORM; cf. obs. F. *informateur*.] An instructor, a teacher; = INFORMER 1.

1651 Barksdale *Nympha Libethris* II. vi, No reward hath He That is an Informator of School-free. Did I perhaps a School unlicens'd teach..I should then at their Feasts, my fingers lick.

informatorily (ɪnˈfɔːmətərɪlɪ), *adv. Bridge.* [f. INFORMATORY *a.* + -LY².] Informatively; in order to give information. Cf. next.

1928 *Observer* 29 Apr. 25 We should be placed in the ridiculous position that a player could not double informatorily, just because he happened to hold the suit that has been called against him. **1928** *Daily Express* 23 July 4 Unless you are prepared for any answer partner may make, do not double informatorily. **1929** W. Buller *Reflections Bridge Player* 178 Do you double two of a suit informatorily?

informatory (ɪn'fɔːmətərɪ), *a.* [f. L. *informāt-* (see INFORMATOR) + -ORY.]

a. = INFORMATIVE 2.

1881 MASSON *De Quincey* xi. 138 Any kind of useful, or, as they are beginning to call it, 'informatory', printed matter. **1883** *Fortn. Rev.* 1 Sept. 391 The volume is gossipy but instructive, always informatory. **1889** J. M. ROBERTSON *Ess. Crit. Meth.* 202 They are often of great informatory value.

b. Bridge: ***informatory double***, a double which is intended to give information to one's partner, as distinct from a 'business double' which is for the purpose of scoring penalty points. So ***informatory pass***.

1926 FOSTER & HERVEY *Auction Bridge Informatory Doubles* 82 This Informatory Pass would be made against (say) a Spade bid on such a hand as [etc.]. **1927** [see BUSINESS 21 d]. **1929** W. BULLER *Reflections Bridge Player* 176 'The Informatory Double' is not strictly *set* convention. **1950** *Hoyle's Games Modernized* (ed. 20) 55 If a player holds a good hand against a call of 1 of a suit, but is without sufficient strength or length in any other suit to justify him in overbidding, he doubles the original call. This is known as the *informatory double* (or *informatory raise*). **1964** G. F. HERVEY *Handbk. Card Games* 161 When a player has bid one of a suit, it is usually better for the opponent to make an informatory or take-out double rather than a weak overbid. An informatory double is a request to partner to bid his best suit.

†**in'formed,** *a. Obs.* [f. IN-^{3} + FORMED, after L. *informis* or F. *informe.*]

1. Of faith: = INFORM *a.* 2 b.

(This was an awkward use, suggesting the pa. pple. of INFORM *v.* 3, which would have the opposite meaning. Cf. UNINFORMED, UNFORMED.)

1526 *Pilgr. Perf.* (W. de W. 1531) 190 Fayth informed, al though it be imperfyte yet..it is fayth. *Ibid.* 186 b, But then fayth is an informed fayth, or a derke fayth. **1630** LENNARD tr. *Charron's Wisd.* II. v. §8 (1670) 262 A belief..such as the Scripture calleth historical, is diabolical, dead, informed, unprofitable.

2. Unformed; imperfectly formed.

1635 SWAN *Spec. M.* iii. §2 (1643) 47 An informed light, which on the fourth day had its perfect form. **1686** PLOT *Staffordsh.* 190 The latter [rushes] having a pith altogether inform'd.

3. *Astron.* Applied to stars not formed into a constellation or forming part of one.

1696 PHILLIPS (ed. 5), *Informed Stars*, such of the Fix'd Stars as are not rang'd under any Constellation or Form.

Hence †**in'formedly** *adv.*^{1}, imperfectly, in an incomplete form.

1670–98 LASSELS *Voy. Italy* I. 107 It was begun in marble by Michael Angelo, but informidly; and so left by him.

informed (ɪn'fɔːmd, *poet.* ɪn'fɔːmɪd), *ppl. a.* [f. INFORM *v.* + -ED^{1}.]

†**1.** Put into form, formed, fashioned. *Obs.*

1596 SPENSER *Hymn Hon. Beautie* 167 Doe still preserve your first informed grace, Whose shadow yet shynes in your beauteous face.

2. Instructed; having knowledge of or acquaintance with facts; educated, enlightened, intelligent.

1549 RECORDE *Gr. Artes* Pref. to Edw. VI (1640) A iij, When they consider that informed reason was the onely instrument. **1753** CHESTERF. *Lett.* (1792) IV. 34 Whenever you are in company with informed and knowing people. **1780** BURKE *Sp. Econ. Ref.* Wks. III. 343 There is nothing ..that does not lie within the reach of an informed understanding. **1805** W. TAYLOR in *Ann. Rev.* III. 322 The theoretical and presumptive reasonings of this informed author. **1897** *Westm. Gaz.* 13 July 6/3 Eliciting an informed and shrewd opinion upon an outlook so depressing.

b. Now usually in ***well-informed, ill-informed***.

c **1440** *Gesta Rom.* I. lxxviii. 396 (Add. MS.) A woman moste fayre, and wise in good werkes, wele Enfourmyd, and deuoute. **1614** RALEIGH *Hist. World* III. (1634) 83 To measure honour or dishonour by the assurance of his well-informed conscience. **1824** LANDOR *Imag. Conv.* Wks. 1846 I. 138/2, I have observed among the well informed and the ill informed nearly the same quantity of infirmities and follies. **1855** MACAULAY *Hist. Eng.* xviii. IV. 186 Not.. known in the best informed circles of London.

Hence **in'formedly** *adv.*^{2}, instructedly.

1642 J. JACKSON *Bk. Conscience* 48 A Conscience informedly strong. **1922** *Times Lit. Suppl.* 10 Aug. 516/3 He deals briefly, but informedly, with the innumerable West African tribes. **1938** *Ibid.* 3 Sept. 573/2 There is in existence no other book dealing so thoroughly and so informedly with the problems of deafness.

in'formedness. [f. INFORMED *ppl. a.* + -NESS.] The fact or quality of being informed; knowledgeableness.

1946 *Scrutiny* XIII. IV. 268 The sheer informedness about society..impresses us with its range. **1960** C. DAY LEWIS *Buried Day* x. 221, I came to rely more and more.. upon the good sense, the informedness and seriousness of Charles Fenby. **1971** D. CRYSTAL *Ling.* i. 11 Topics such as these are..discussed..with varying degrees of informedness.

informer (ɪn'fɔːmə(r)). Forms: 4–7 **enfourmer**, 5 **enformer, -our**, 6 **infourmer, -our**, 6– **informer**. [f. INFORM *v.* + -ER^{1}.] One who or that which informs, in various senses.

†**1.** An instructor, teacher. *Obs.*

1387–8 T. USK *Test. Love* II. ii. (Skeat) l. 87, I am seruaunt of these creatures to me deliuered..not maister, but enfourmer. **1526** TINDALE *Rom.* ii. 20 An informer off them which lacke discrecion. **1565** JEWEL *Def. Apol.* (1611) 86 *Catechistas*, The Informers or Teachers of them that were entring into the faith. **1662** R. MATHEW *Unl. Alch.* §35 Experience which is the truest informer, speaks aloud in this matter also.

2. One who communicates information or intelligence; an informant.

c **1422** HOCCLEVE *Learn to Die* 543 His enformours he wel leeueth. **1665** SIR T. HERBERT *Trav.* (1677) 113 Jackalls.. are the Lions informers. **1737** WHISTON *Josephus, Antiq.* III. xiii, Better have kept close to Josephus than hearken to any of his other authors or informers. **1828** SCOTT *F.M. Perth* xxxiii, He talks no Gaelic, nor had his informer much English, so there may be some mistake in the matter.

3. One who informs against another; one who lays an information; *spec.* one who makes it his business to detect offenders against penal laws and to lay informations against them; also called ***common informer***.

1503–4 *Act 19 Hen. VII*, c. 14 §6 Every such infourmour ..shalbe receyved to sue vppon the seid matter by informacion. **1588–9** *Act 31 Eliz.* c. 5 Divers..daylie unjustlie vexed and disquieted by divers commen informers upon penall statutes. **1591** GREENE *Disc. Coosnage* (1592) 18. *c* **1608** BACON *Certif. touching Penal Laws* Wks. 1879 I. 480 To repress the abuses in common informers, and some clerks and under-ministers, that for common gain partake with them. **1759** ROBERTSON *Hist. Scot.* VI. Wks. 1813 I. 436 Spies and informers were everywhere employed. **1798** BERESFORD in *Ld. Auckland's Corr.* (1862) III. 411 We have ..taken up several persons of family and fortune..and some have turned informers in whom we can rely. **1808** SYD. SMITH *Wks.* (1859) I. 131/2 An informer, whether he is paid by the week..or by the crime..is, in general, a man of a very indifferent character. **1817** SELWYN *Nisi Prius* II. 1148 A penalty..recoverable by common informer in the High Court of Admiralty. **1880** MCCARTHY *Own Times* IV. liii. 149 The man was found guilty on the evidence of an informer.

attrib. **1887** *Pall Mall G.* 16 Aug. 3/1 In the absence of 'informer' evidence the great majority of cases would fail for want of legal proof.

4. One who or that which informs with life, etc. (INFORM *v.* 3); an inspirer, animator, vitalizer.

1727–46 THOMSON *Summer* 104 Thou O Sun!.. Informer of the planetary train, Without whose quickening glance their cumbrous orbs Were brute unlovely mass, inert and dead, And not as now the green abodes of life. **1730** POPE *Prol. Sophonisba* 27 Nature! informer of the Poet's art, Whose force alone can raise or melt the heart.

Hence **in'formership** (*nonce-wd.*), the position or function of an informer.

1612 T. JAMES *Jesuit's Downf.* 65 Parsons had the office of Informership in the English affaires, as well in Spaine as at Rome.

informidable (ɪn'fɔːmɪdəb(ə)l), *a. rare.* [IN-^{3}.] Not formidable; not to be dreaded.

1667 MILTON *P.L.* IX. 486 Of limb Heroic built, though of terrestrial mould; Foe not informidable. **1867** C. J. SMITH *Syn. & Antonyms* s.v. *Awful*, Innocuous. Informidable.

informing (ɪn'fɔːmɪŋ), *vbl. sb.* [f. INFORM *v.* + -ING^{1}.] The action of the verb INFORM, in various senses; instruction, information, etc.

c **1380** WYCLIF *Serm.* Sel. Wks. II. 209 Summe doon folily, for defaute of enformynge. **1382** —— *Wisd.* xix. 15 Who..resceyueden them, that hadden vsid the same enformyngus. **1633** P. FLETCHER *Purple Isl.* VI. xlv, Which back to him with mutuall dutie bears All their informings. **1769** BLACKSTONE *Comm.* IV. xiii. 172 Sharpers; who..if unsuccessful, have it in their power to be still greater gainers by informing.

in'forming, *ppl. a.* [-ING^{2}.] That informs.

1. That imparts 'form', or some determining quality, esp. life or spirit; vitalizing, inspiring, animating: see INFORM *v.* 3.

1635 HAKEWILL *Apol.* V.–VI. 195 Never any Aristotelian.. will acknowledge that the heavens have any informing forme, but that it is a quintessence, a pure body without mixture, or composition of matter and forme. **1659** PEARSON *Creed* (1839) 229 The ancient heretics, who taught that Christ assumed human flesh, but that the Word or his Divinity was unto that body in the place of an informing soul. **1703** ROWE *Fair Penit.* IV. i. 1532 Love was th' informing, active Fire within. **1874** SYMONDS *Sk. Italy & Greece* (1898) I. i. 5 Pantheists..convinced of the omnipresence of the informing mind. **1875** JOWETT *Plato* (ed. 2) III. 166 The informing energy of the human will.

2. Giving or conveying information; instructive; imparting the knowledge of facts. (In quot. 1647 in bad sense; cf. INFORM *v.* 7 b.)

1647 CLARENDON *Contempl. Ps.* Tracts (1727) 506 The busy, mischievous, informing slanderer. *a* **1718** PENN *Tracts* Wks. 1726 I. 718 A seasonable and informing Lecture for our own Times. **1887** *Spectator* 5 Mar. 319/1 Hallam is great not as a literary writer, but as an informing writer.

Hence **in'formingly** *adv.*, in an informing manner, instructively.

1897 *Chicago Advance* 21 Oct. 539/1[He] spoke both inspiringly and informingly of the rise and growth of municipal functions.

informity (ɪn'fɔːmɪtɪ). Now *rare* or *Obs.* [ad. late L. *informitāt-em*, f. *informis*: see INFORM *a.* and -ITY. Cf. F. *informité* (Bossuet, in Littré), It. *informità* (Florio, 1598).] Unformed condition, shapelessness; unshapeliness, deformity.

1598 FLORIO, *Informita*, informitie, shapelesnes. **1615** T. ADAMS *Two Sonnes* 83 The reducing of the old Chaos, and first informitie of things. **1646** SIR T. BROWNE *Pseud. Ep.* I. viii. 32 The informity of Cubbes. **1656** BLOUNT *Glossogr.*, *Informity*,..deformity, want of shape or fashion.

b. *fig.* (in reference to the intellect or manners).

1583 GOLDING *Calvin on Deut.* xiv. 84 We do but bewray the informitie that is in vs. **1622** PEACHAM *Compl. Gent.* 186 You shall finde good Learning..a polisher of inbred rudenesse and our informitie.

informosome (ɪn'fɔːməʊsəʊm). *Biol.* [f. INFORM(ATION + -O + -SOME^{4}.] A cellular particle composed of messenger RNA and associated protein, the latter being thought to protect the messenger RNA from ribonucleases.

1964 A. S. SPIRIN et al. in *Zhurnal Obshchei Biologii* (U.S.S.R.) XXV. 338 mRNA is transferred into the cytoplasm..in the form of specific complexes with protein; these ribonucleoprotein particles, named 'informosomes', were isolated and proved to exist as real complexes. **1971** *Nature* 15 Oct. 448/2 Over the past several years evidence has been accumulated which suggests that messenger RNAs occur in cell nuclei in the form of ribonucleoprotein particles—so-called informosomes.

†**in'formous,** *a. Obs.* [app. f. L. *inform-is* INFORM *a.* + -OUS, but cf. FORMOUS, OF. *formeus*, L. *formōsus*.] Having no definite form, shapeless; of an uncomely form, unshapely.

1610 HOLLAND *Camden's Brit.* I. 267 A man prudently pliable to times..excessive in vaste informous buildings. **1646** SIR T. BROWNE *Pseud. Ep.* III. vi. 116 That a Bear brings forth her young informous and unshapen, which she fashioneth after by licking them over, is an opinion not only vulgar..but hath been of old delivered by ancient Writers. **1701** C. WOLLEY *Jrnl. N. York* (1860) 40.

informulable (ɪn'fɔːmjʊləb(ə)l), *a. nonce-wd.* [f. IN-^{3} + FORMUL-ATE *v.* + -ABLE.] Incapable of being formulated.

1884 *Athenæum* 8 Nov. 587/1 None but a prig would find any satisfaction in..trying to formulate the informulable.

inforrest, variant of ENFOREST, *Obs.*

infors(e, obs. forms of ENFORCE *v.*

Infortiate (ɪn'fɔːʃɪət), *sb. Law. rare.* [ad. med.L. *infortiātum* enforced, strengthened, pa. pple. neut. (used subst.) of *infortiāre* to strengthen, ENFORCE. Cf. F. *infortiat* (Littré).] The middle portion of the Pandects of Justinian, extending from Book xxiv, title 3, to the end of Book xxxviii.

In explanation of the title, Savigny supposes that the Pandects, while known only in imperfect copies, were divided into *Digestum vetus*, *Tres partes* (a fragment so called from its opening words) and *Digestum novum*. When the missing portion was recovered, it filled the gap between *Digestum vetus* and *Tres partes*, the latter of which has since been reckoned a part of the *Infortiatum*.

1560 ROLLAND *Crt. Venus* IV. 14 The Institutis, Digestis, and Angelus, The Inforciat, and Panormitanus. **1883** *Wharton's Law Lexicon* s.v. *Pandects*, That glossator [Odofredus]..informs us, that they had not the Infortiate which was at Rome.

†**in'fortiate,** *ppl. a. Obs.* In 7 **-at**. [ad. L. *infortiāt-us* pa. pple.: see prec.] Enforced. (Const. as pa. pple.)

1601 BP. W. BARLOW *Defence* 96 Were the Law of India and Persia generally infortiat?

in'fortitude. *rare.* [IN-^{3}.] Want of fortitude.

1813 W. TAYLOR in Robberds *Mem.* II. 412 Let us hope it is not out of depression and infortitude that I have been sulky.

†**in'fortunable,** *a. Obs.* [f. INFORTUNE *v.* + -ABLE: cf. FORTUNABLE.] Unfortunate, unlucky.

1432–50 tr. *Higden* (Rolls) VIII. 446 Alle thynges were as infortunable to hym. **1503** HAWES *Examp. Virt.* VII. lviii, Though that a man were infortunable.

†**in'fortunacy.** *Obs.* [f. INFORTUNATE; see -ACY. Cf. *fortunacy*.] The condition of being unfortunate; ill fortune, ill luck.

1571 FORTESCUE *Forrest* 151 b, The Romaines themselves bewept their infortunacie. **1580** LODGE *Forb. & Prisc.* (Shaks. Soc.) 106 Priscerìa..forgetting welnie the infortunacie she was intangeled in, cast her armes about his necke. **1669** *Addr. hopeful yng. Gentry Eng.* 2 So many are found to complain of their peculiar infortunacy.

†**in'fortunage.** *Obs. rare.* [f. INFORTUNE *v.* + -AGE.] Unfortunate condition; affliction.

c **1440** LYDG. *Fortune* in *Harvard Stud.* (1897) V. 193 In thy condicioun of inffortunage, vnstedfast fortune, ther is no confidence.

†**in'fortunate,** *a. Obs.* [ad. L. *infortūnāt-us* (see IN-^{3} and FORTUNATE). Cf. F. *infortuné* (14th c. in Littré), Sp. *infortunado*, It. *infortunato*.] Subject to or marked by ill fortune; unlucky, luckless; UNFORTUNATE. (Of persons, conditions, times, events, etc.)

1390 GOWER *Conf.* III. 375 Yet was he nought infortunate. *c* **1440** *Partonope* 3353 The day infortunate that I was bore. **1548** HALL *Chron., Edw. IV* 239 b, O infortunate brother, for whose lyfe not one creatoure woulde make intercession. **1592–3** in Ellis *Orig. Lett.* Ser. III. IV. 110 Infortunatest peere of Parliament for pouertie that euer was. **1653** H. COGAN tr. *Pinto's Trav.* xxvi. 98 We eleven..seeing the infortunate success of our companions, could do nothing but weep and lament. **1676** MARVELL *Mr. Smirke* Wks. 1875 IV. 11 He took up an unfortunate resolution that he would be witty: infortunate, I say, and no less criminal.

b. *Astrol.* Said of a planet or 'house' when 'afflicted' by some evil or unlucky influence, as by a particular 'aspect', and so causing misfortune.

c **1386** CHAUCER *Man of Law's T.* 204 Infortunat Ascendent tortuous, Of which the lord is helplees falle, allas! Out of his Angle in to the derkeste hous. *c* **1391** —— *Astrol.* II. §4 Yit sein thise Astrologiens, that the assendent, and eke the lord of the assendent, may be shapen for to be fortunat or infortunat. **1585** LUPTON *Thous. Notable Th.* (1675) 30 If . . both the Sun and Moon be in the sixth House infortunate, they that be then born without doubt will be blind. **1671** SALMON *Syn. Med.* I. xxvii. 55 An infortunate Planet in the Ascendent . . always afflicts the Head.

c. Bringing or presaging ill luck; of ill omen, inauspicious.

1552 HULOET, Infortunate dayes to begyn any busynes. **1584** R. SCOT *Discov. Witchcr.* XI. xiv. (1886) 163 When an infortunate beast feedeth on the right side of your waie. **1613** PURCHAS *Pilgrimage* II. xviii. 177 When they have had an infortunate dream.

Hence †**in'fortunately** *adv.*, unfortunately; †**in'fortunateness**, the quality of being unfortunate; ill fortune.

1577–87 HOLINSHED *Chron.* I. 174/2 The death and buriall of Egelred, his wiues . . his infortunatenesse. **1600** HAKLUYT *Voy.* III. 145 The gentleman was so infortunately incumbred with wants. **1607** WALKINGTON *Opt. Glass* xiv. 76 When we dreame of Eagles flying over our heade, it portends infortunatenes. **1682** *Mem. Sir E. Godfrey* 7 (T.) Destructive rocks, upon which most of the unseasoned youth . . do infortunately split.

†**in'fortunate,** *v. Astrol. Obs.* [f. ppl. stem of med.L. *infortūnāre*; see IN-³ and FORTUNATE *v.*] *trans.* To subject to evil or unlucky influence; to render unfortunate; to 'afflict' (a planet, etc. or an event, etc.). Also *absol.*

1585 LUPTON *Thous. Notable Th.* (1675) 16 In whose Nativity Saturn or Mars is in the sixth House, or in the twelfth House, infortunating the Lord of the sixth House. **1651** CULPEPPER *Astrol. Judgem. Dis.* (1658) 110 Venus Lady of the sixth and infortunated by Mars, gives suspitions enough of the French pox. **1790** SIBLY *Occult Sc.* (1792) I. 18 Some heavenly influence that . . fortunateth or infortunateth.

infortune (ɪn'fɔːtjʊn), *sb.* Also 5 yn-, 6 en-. [a. F. *infortune* (Oresme, 14th c.); see IN-³ and FORTUNE. Cf. L. *infortūnium.*]

†**1.** Want of good fortune, success, or prosperity; misfortune, ill fortune, ill luck. *Obs.*

c **1374** CHAUCER *Troylus* III. 1577 (1626) Þe werste kynde of infortune is þis. *c* **1386** —— *Knt.'s T.* 1163 Noght was foryeten by the Infortune of Marte. *c* **1450** LYDG. *Secrees* 913 Be sodeyn Caas Or in necessyte, Or infortunys froward violence. **1491** CAXTON *Vitas Patr.* I. cxxx. (W. de W. 1495) 147 b/2 He shold take his Infortune in pacyence. **1513** BRADSHAW *St. Werburge* II. 1603 A fyre by infortune rose up sodeinly. **1615** CHAPMAN *Odyss.* III. 234 Our long-sustain'd infortune might be freed. **1653** H. COGAN tr. *Pinto's Trav.* lxiv. 262 For my greater infortune, the tempest cast my Brigandine upon the coast of this Country.

†**b.** with *pl.* A piece of ill luck; a misfortune, mishap. *Obs.*

c **1477** CAXTON *Jason* 59 b, We haue had upon the see so many infortunes by tempeste of windes. **1544** PHAER *Pestilence* (1553) K iij b, The lyfe whiche we lead here, is . . subiecte to diseases, infortunes, and calamytyes. **1652** GAULE *Magastrom.* 313 At this the dream-spellers were divided in their divinations; some interpreting it a fortune, some an infortune. **1653** R. SANDERS *Physiogn.* 193 Such lines have the signification of infortunes, and sundry hurtfull falls.

2. *Astrol.* An unfortunate or malevolent planet or aspect; *esp.* each of the planets Saturn and Mars. (Cf. FORTUNE *sb.* 8.)

1632 MASSINGER *City Madam* II. ii, Saturn out of all dignities . . and Venus in the south angle elevated above him . . and free from the malevolent beams of infortunes. **1651** CULPEPPER *Astrol. Judgem. Dis.* (1658) 108 If the sign the Lord of the sixth possesseth, especially if he be an infortune, or a fortune infortunated. **1668** DRYDEN *Even. Love* II. i, The trine aspect of the two infortunes in angular houses. **1671** SALMON *Syn. Med.* I. vi. 16 The Dragons Tail is called in Greek Καταβιβάζων, an Infortune signifying Mischiefs, Scandals, Shame. **1881** PROCTOR *Poetry Astron.* viii. 278 Saturn, the greater Infortune, as Mars himself is the lesser Infortune, of Astrological systems.

†**infortune,** *v. Obs.* [f. prec. Cf. obs. F. *infortuner* (Godef.), f. *infortune* sb.] *trans.* To cause misfortune to, to afflict; in *Astrol.* to 'afflict' (a planet or house) with an unfortunate 'aspect'. So †**infortuned** *ppl. a.*, unfortunate; †**infortuning** *vbl. sb.*

c **1374** CHAUCER *Troylus* IV. 716 (744), I, woful wrecche, and infortuned wight, And born in corsed constellacioun. *c* **1391** —— *Astrol.* II. §4 A fortunat assendent clepen they whan þat no wykkid planete . . is in the hows of the assendent, ne þat no wikked planete haue non aspecte of enemyte vp-on the assendent. . . Fortherouer, they seyn þat the infortunyng of an assendent is the contrarie of thise forseide thinges. **1440** J. SHIRLEY *Dethe K. James* (1818) 20 Then the said Grame, seyng his Kyng and Soveran Lord ynfortuned with so much deseyse, angwesh, and sorowe, wold hafe so levyd, and done hym no more harme.

†**infor'tunity.** *Obs.* [a. OF. *infortunité* (Godef.), ad. late L. *infortūnitās* (Lactantius, Ep. xxix. §9, quoting Aulus Gellius VI. i. 5, where some editors read *importūnitās*). The formation, from L. *infortūnium* (or its sources), was irregular.] Unfortunate condition; misfortune, adversity.

1494 FABYAN *Chron.* VII. 438 Ouer yᵉ noble men that were slayne in Scotlande by his infortunyte. **1548** HALL *Chron.*, *Edw. IV* (1809) 286 Other there be that ascribe his infortunitie onely to the stroke & punishment of God. **1600** HOLLAND *Livy* XLII. lxii. 1152 Considering they are well tamed with the infortunitie of this battell. **1652** GAULE *Magastrom.* 237 If you would know whether your fortunatenesse or infortunity, prosperity or adversity, shall be more, or lesse. **1720** DE FOE *Apparition* 1665 Wks. 1841 XIX. 259 The infortunity of the family.

b. with *pl.* An instance of this, a misfortune.

1477 EARL RIVERS (Caxton) *Dictes* 5 For resistence of the infortunitees that dayly falles in thys worlde. **1548** HALL *Chron., Edw. IV* 247 b, How dolorous . . to remember the chaunces, and infortunites that happened within twoo yere in Englande. **1609** HOLLAND *Amm. Marcell.* XXIV. vii. 258 And . . there happened another no small infortunitie, namely, that the succors which we waited for . . seemed for the causes aforesaid letted and stayd. **1654** COKAINE *Dianea* I. 14 We are all equally made lyable to infortunities. **1656** S. HOLLAND *Zara* (1719) 78.

†**infortuny.** *Obs. rare.* [ad. L. *infortūni-um*, f. *in-* (IN-³) + *fortūna* fortune; cf. INFORTUNE *sb.*] Misfortune.

1432–50 tr. *Higden* (Rolls) I. 245 Not for cause of deuocion or of luffe but for drede of infortuny. *Ibid.* 341 That stokke and kynnerede destroyede by diverse infortuny of batelles and of oper mortalite.

infossous (ɪn'fɒsəs), *a. Bot. rare.* [f. IN-² + FOSSA¹ + -OUS.] (See quot.)

1866 *Treas. Bot.* 622/2 *Infossous*, sunk in anything, as veins in some leaves, leaving a channel, however.

†**in'found,** *v. Obs.* [ad. obs. F. *infond-re, -fundre*, or ad. L. *infundĕre* to pour in (see INFUND); with the form of the radical cf. FOUND *v.*³ and CONFOUND.] *trans.* To pour in; to infuse. (Usually in *fig.* sense.)

c **1420** *Pallad. on Husb.* IV. 510 Mynge askes of vyne and donge, and hem infounde Vnto the roote and they wol be fecounde. *c* **1425** *Found. St. Bartholomew's* (E.E.T.S.) 28 Hete of lyf was ynfowndid to seyr and drye membyrs. **1502** ATKYNSON tr. *De Imitatione* III. lx. 251 Thy holy grace infounded ardently to my hert. **1513** MORE *Rich. III*, Wks. 60/2 The great grace that god giueth & secretly infowndeth in right generacion after the lawes of matrimony. **1589** R. BRUCE *Serm.* (1843) 116 To infound in them this precious love and amitie towards God and their neighbour.

b. To pour *on.*

c **1420** *Pallad. on Husb.* III. 759 Of wynes olde hit is to take dregges . . Infounde hem on thi trees feet and legges.

Hence †**in'founding** *vbl. sb.*, infusion.

1532 MORE *Confut. Tindale* Wks. 383/2 Through faieth to the infounding whereof yᵉ sacrament doth nothing worke. **1557** *Sarum Primer* ℂiv, By infoundinge of thy precious oyle of comforte unto my woundes.

†**in'founded,** *a. Obs. rare*⁻¹. ? Unfounded.

1632 LITHGOW *Trav.* x. 445 The one in quality, and the other in quantity, be extraordinarily infounded.

infounded: see INFONDED, infatuated.

†**in'founder,** *v. Obs.* [a. OF. *enfondre-r* to plunge to the bottom, submerge, swallow up, f. *en-* (IN-²) + *fondrer* to FOUNDER: cf. in another sense ENFOUNDER.] *trans.* To submerge; in *pa. pple.* Submerged, overflowed, flooded.

1505 *Liber Ruber* in H. E. Reynolds *Wells Cathedr.* App. M. (1882) 218 The higheways were so infoundered that the poor tenants and inhabitants [etc.]. **1515** in W. H. Turner *Select. Rec. Oxford* 13 The . . fellowes of Merton College do suffer the lane . . to be surrounded and infoundred.

infourme, infowrme, obs. ff. INFORM *v.*

infra ('ɪnfrə), *adv.* [L.] Below, underneath, further on.

1740 J. GRASSINEAU *Mus. Dict.* 107 Hypo, *infra, below*; this word when joined to the name of any interval or mode, &c. shews that it is lower than it was without, as *Hypo diapason* an octave lower. **1888** *Encycl. Brit.* XXVIII. 702/1 See *infra* in regard to rotary printing. **1888** ROLLESTON & JACKSON *Forms Animal Life* (ed. 2) 459 The cell has been . . supposed by various authorities to be muscular, nervous, or composed of connective tissue. See the original authorities, *infra.* **1955** A. G. DICKENS *Robert Holgate* i. 3 Cf. *infra*, p. 24.

infra- ('ɪnfrə), *prefix*, repr. L. *infrā* adv. and prep. 'below, underneath, beneath' (in med.L. also 'within'), used in numerous recent formations, chiefly adjectival.

This use of *infra-* is scarcely a Latin one, though *infrāforānus* 'situated beneath the forum' occurs in an inscription (Lewis and Short), and *infrāmūrāneus* 'lying within the walls' in Gregory of Tours (Du Cange). Its recent employment is after the analogy of other prepositions; it is regularly opposed to *supra-*, sometimes to *super-*: the second element ought strictly to be one of Latin origin; but it is not always so.

A. In prepositional relation to the sb. represented in second element.

1. Denoting 'below', 'beneath' (i.e. 'lower down than') in respect of local situation or position. Chiefly in terms which are the adjectival representatives of phrases in which L. *infrā* would be followed by a sb. in the accusative, e.g. *infra-axillary* 'that is *infrā axillam*, below the axilla or axil'; *infra-mammary*, 'that is *infrā mammās*, below the breasts'. The majority of these are anatomical terms. In a few cases the second element appears to be a sb., as *infraclavicle*. More rarely *infra-* is simply prefixed to an adj., as *inframedian, infra-red.*

2. Denoting 'below', 'beneath' in respect of status or condition, as *infrabestial* 'lower than bestial', 'beneath the brutes'. In these, *infra-* seems to be directly prefixed to an adjective.

3. Denoting 'within' (as in med.L.), as *inframercurial, -territorial* (see these words below): here the formation is as in 1.

B. In attributive or adverbial relation to the second element: 'lower', 'inferior', 'under-', as *infraconstrictor, infraposition*, etc.

Such compounds can be formed at will when required; the following are the principal ones in use. For the etymology of the second element see the simple words AXILLARY, BESTIAL, CORTICAL, etc.

In most of these compounds, practice varies as to the use of the hyphen; the hyphen is usual when the compound is new, or more or less of a nonce-word, e.g. *infra-red, infra-human, infra-natural*; but it is usually omitted in recognized terms, as *inframaxillary, infrascapular*, except when the following element begins with a vowel, as in *infra-axillary, infra-inguinal, infra-orbital.* It may however be used for the nonce, whenever emphasis is placed either on the prefix, or on the composite character of the word.

†**infra-'annuated** *a.* [L. *annus* year: cf. *superannuated*], below the proper age, too young. ˌ**infra-a'tomic** *a.*, subatomic. *Obs.* **infra-a'xillary** *a.*, (*a*) *Anat.* lying below the axilla or armpit; (*b*) *Bot.* situated below the axil of a leaf or branch. **infra'basal** *Zool.*, any of a series of plates forming a ring beneath the basals in crinoids; also as *adj.* **infra-'bass** *Mus.*, = *sub-bass* (1909 in *Cent. Dict.* Suppl.); also *transf.* **infra'bestial** *a.*, lower than the beasts. **infra'branchial** *a. Zool.*, situated below the branchiæ or gills (*Syd. Soc. Lex.* 1886). **infra'buccal** *a.*, situated below the buccal mass (of a mollusc). **infrace'phalic** *a. Anat.*, situated below the head (*Syd. Soc. Lex.*). **infra-'Christian** *a.*, somewhat less than Christian. **infra'clavicle** = infraclavicular bone. **infracla'vicular** *a. Anat.*, situated below the clavicle or collar-bone, as in ***infraclavicular bone, region*** (see quot. 1879); also as *sb.* = infraclavicular bone. **infracon'strictor** *Anat.*, the lower constrictor muscle of the pharynx. **infra'cortical** *a. Anat.*, situated below the cerebral cortex. **infra'costal** *a. Anat.*, situated beneath the ribs, as in ***infracostal artery, muscles*** (*Syd. Soc. Lex.*). **infraˌdiaphrag'matic** *a. Anat.*, situated below the diaphragm (*ibid.*). **infra'genual** *a.*, under the knee, as in *infragenual bursa.* **infra'glacial** *a.*, subglacial. **infra'glenoid** *a. Anat.*, situated below the glenoid fossa. **infra'glottic** *a. Anat.*, situated below the glottis; also, relating to the parts of the larynx below the glottis. **infra'gular** *a. Anat.*, situated below the gula or throat. **infra'human** *a.*, below the human level. **infra'hyoid** *a. Anat.*, lying below the hyoid bone (*Syd. Soc. Lex.*). **infra-'inguinal** *a. Anat.*, situated below the groin. **infra'labial** *a. Anat.*, situated below the lips. **infra'littoral** *a.*, pertaining to the zone or region of the sea below the littoral region. **infra'mammary** *a. Anat.*, situated below the breasts. **infra'marginal** *a.*, situated beneath the margin or border: *spec.* (*a*) ***inframarginal cell***, an outer cell in the anterior wing of certain aphides, lying behind the marginal cell; (*b*) ***inframarginal convolution***, the superior temporal convolution; (*c*) ***inframarginal shield***, one of the shields between the marginal and plastral in certain chelonians. **infra'maxillary** *Anat.*, (*a*) *a.*, situated below the jaw, as in ***inframaxillary nerve***; (*b*) *sb.*, the lower jaw-bone. **infra'median** *a.*, applied to the zone of the ocean below the median zone: see quot. **inframer'curial** *a. Astron.*, lying within the orbit of the planet Mercury; intramercurial. ˌ**infra-mo'lecular** *a.*, at a level of organization below that of a molecule. **infra'montane** *a.*, situated beneath a mountain. †**infra'mundane** *a.*, lying below the world (Bailey, fol., 1730–6). **infra'natural** *a.*, below what is natural; also as *sb.*; hence **infra'naturalism.** **infra'nodal** *a.*, lying beneath a node or joint in a stem. **infra-oc'cipital** *a. Anat.*, situated under the occiput (*Syd. Soc. Lex.*). **infraœso'phageal** *a. Anat.*, situated under the œsophagus. **infra-'orbital** *a. Anat.*, situated below the orbit of the eye; so also **infra-'orbitar, -'orbitary** *adjs.* **infra-'ordinary** *a.*, below what is ordinary. **infra'papillary** *a. Anat.*, situated below the biliary papilla. **infrapa'tellar** *a. Anat.*, situated below the knee-cap. **infraperi'pherial** *a.*, situated below the periphery. **infra'posed** *a.*, placed below something else [cf. *superposed*]; so

infrapo'sition, the condition of being so placed. **infra'pubian, -pubic** *a. Anat.*, situated below the pubes; sub-pubic. **infra'radular** *a.*, situated under the radula or lingual ribbon of a mollusc. **infra-'rational** *a.*, below what is rational. **infra'renal** *a. Anat.*, situated beneath the kidneys; hence **infra'renally** *adv.* **infra'rimal** *a. Anat.*, situated beyond the rima or opening of the glottis. **infra'scapular** *a. Anat.*, situated below the shoulder-blade. **infra-spe'cific** *a.*, (applied to a category) at a lower taxonomic level than a species. **infra'spinal** *a. Anat.*, situated beneath the spine of the scapula. **infra'spinate** *a.* = prec. **infraspi'nator, -spi'natus** *Anat.*, a muscle of the dorsum of the scapula, arising from the infraspinal fossa; also *attrib.* **infra'spinous** *a.* = *infraspinal*. **infrasta'pedial** *a.*, situated below the axis of the stapes of the middle ear in birds. **infra'sternal** *a. Anat.*, situated below the sternum or breast-bone (*Syd. Soc. Lex.*). **infra'stigmatal** *a. Entom.*, situated below the stigmata or breathing-pores of an insect. **infra'stipular** *a. Bot.*, situated below the stipules in plants. **infra'sutural** *a. Anat.*, situated below the suture. **infra'temporal** *a. Anat.*, situated below the temples (*Syd. Soc. Lex.*). **infraten'torial** *a. Anat.*, situated below the tentorium of the brain. **infrate'rrene** *a.*, situated below the earth, subterranean, hypogean. **infraterri'torial** *a.*, lying within a territory (Webster, 1856). **infratho'racic** *a. Anat.*, situated below the thorax (*Syd. Soc. Lex.*). **infra'tonsillar** *a. Anat.*, situated below the tonsils. **infratrochan'teric** *a. Anat.*, situated below the trochanter (*Syd. Soc. Lex.*). **infra'trochlear** *a. Anat.*, situated beneath the trochlea or pulley of the trochlearis muscle in the eye. **ˌinfra-um'bilical** *a. Anat.*, situated below the umbilicus. **infrava'ginal** *a. Anat.*, situated below the vagina, or its junction with the uterus.

1650 FULLER *Pisgah* v. Ep. Ded. 140, I know it will be objected, that your Lordship is *infraannuated to be the Patron of a Book in the strict acception thereof. **1923** J. S. HUXLEY *Ess. Biologist* i. 55 The *infra-atomic world of electrons. **1966** I. ASIMOV *Fantastic Voyage* viii. 90 It was not merely radioactivity that had to be sensed, but radioactive particles that had themselves been miniaturized; and that, because of their incredibly tiny, infra-atomic size could pass through any ordinary sensor without affecting it. **1858** GRAY *Struct. Bot.* (1880) 416/2 **Infra-axillary*, below the axil. **1862** H. W. FULLER *Dis. Lungs* 4 The infra-axillary [region] has the axillary region for its upper, and the edges of the false ribs for its lower boundary. **1890** *Ann. & Mag. Nat. Hist.* V. 318 The atrophy of *infrabasals is we see a very gradual process. *Ibid.*, The distinction between an infrabasal ring of 5 plates and one of 3, is of far inferior importance. **1962** D. NICHOLS *Echinoderms* ii. 22 In some forms an additional whorl, the infrabasals, is intercalated between the basals and the centro-dorsal. **1958** J. BLISH *Case of Conscience* (1959) II. x. 104 The *infrabass of the buried city's thunder shook the glass in front of him. **1888** J. RICKABY *Mor. Philos.* 267 Writers who..picture primitive mankind as living in this *infrabestial state. **1906** W. R. INGE *Truth & Falsehood in Relig.* ii. 63 It is not justifiable to take examples of *infra-Christian survivals in Christianity, and use them to discredit the religion of Christ. **1917** J. DENNEY *Christian Doctrine of Reconciliation* ii. 51 As an infra-Christian mode of thinking, it sometimes curiously flawed what was otherwise pure Christian truth. **1878** BELL *Gegenbaur's Comp. Anat.* 474 The two lower ones I have shown to be the clavicle and *infra-clavicle. **1839** F. H. RAMADGE *Curability Consumpt.* (1861) 52 The want of clearness in the respiratory murmur was most obvious in the *infraclavicular region of the right side. **1879** KHORY *Princ. Med.* 45 Infra-clavicular [region] extends from below the clavicle down to the lower margin of the third rib. **1890** *Cent. Dict.*, *Infracortical. **1895** *Psychol. Rev.* Mar. 117 In man the consciousness attached to infra-cortical centres is altogether subliminal, if it exist. **1925** *Lancet* 8 Aug. 274/2 Tremor is an involuntary movement belonging to the old motor system (infra-cortical, subpallial). **1858** GRAY *Anat.* 732/2 (Index), *Infra-costal muscles. **1867** *Quain's Elem. Anat.* (ed. 7) I. 243 The subcostal or infracostal muscles are small bundles lying on the inner aspect of the thoracic wall. **1922** JOYCE *Ulysses* 695 A cicatrice in the left infracostal region below the diaphragm. **1894** J. GEIKIE *Gt. Ice Age* (ed. 3) vii. 91 All such *infra- or intra-glacial deposits..occur somewhat partially. **1957** J. K. CHARLESWORTH *Quaternary Era* II. xliv. 1253 The British infraglacial beach, though much narrower than the Norwegian strandflat, marks a steady level of the sea over a considerable time. **1872** COHEN *Dis. Throat* 45 In *infra-glottic laryngoscopy we find the lower surface of these cords to be reddish in color. **1855** KNIGHT *Cycl. Nat. Hist.* III. 65 The under part of the *infra-gular ganglion. **1847** J. WILSON *Lands of Bible* I. iv. 105 The gods of the Egyptian pantheon, human, superhuman, and *infrahuman. **1874** MAHAFFY *Soc. Life Greece* ii. 39 She is rather infra-human than superhuman. **1883** W. ARTHUR *Fernley Lect.* 72 This infra-human thinker, to whom it is hard to turn the eye upward. **1970** *Jrnl. Gen. Psychol.* July 42 Motor responses in infrahuman level. **1972** *Science* 5 May 541/2 Microelectrode recording has shown that tilt detectors in the infrahuman visual system are each turned 20 deg or so on either side of a preferred orientation. **1850** E. FORBES in *Brit. Ass. Rep.* 192 (*title*) The *Infra-littoral Distribution of Marine Invertebrata on the Southern, Western, and Northern Coasts of Britain. **1862** H. W. FULLER *Dis. Lungs* 4 The *infra-mammary [region] is that portion of the anterior surface of the chest which lies below the mammary. **1879** *St. George's Hosp. Rep.* IX. 183 Heaving impulse over left side of chest, strong in inframammary region. **1857** BERKELEY *Cryptog. Bot.* §611. 539 Dictyoxiphium has simple..fronds, *infra-marginal sori. **1872** NICHOLSON *Palæont.* 109 Anus supra-marginal or infra-marginal. **1855** MAYNE *Expos. Lex.*, *Inframaxillaris*, situated under the jaw; *inframaxillary. **1872** HUMPHRY *Myology* 46 The infra-maxillary [nerve]..emerges through a large hole at the front of the base of the suspensorial projection for the jaw. **1865** PAGE *Hand-bk. Geol.* (ed. 2) 468 In the British seas, naturalists (following the late Edward Forbes)..distinguish five belts of depth—viz. 1, the Littoral; 2, Circum-littoral; 3, Median; 4, *Infra-median; and 5, the Abyssal or Deep-sea zone. **1899** *Phil. Mag.* XLVIII. 462 All her [*sc.* Nature's] activities at *infra-molecular degrees of proximity. **1919** A. N. WHITEHEAD *Enquiry Princ. Nat. Knowledge* ii. 18 We may penetrate below the molecule to the electrons and the core which compose it, and thus obtain infra-molecular equations. **1888** *Standard* 13 Feb. 5/2 The Arlberg Tunnel, the latest of these *inframontane engineering efforts. **1851** J. MARTINEAU *Stud. Chr.* (1873) 336 The irresistible tendency of a wholly supernatural religion to produce an *infranatural morality. **1889** F. HALL in *Nation* (N.Y.) XLIX. 412/3 Patronizing a new set of supernaturals, infranaturals, or whatever they may be. **1896** GOLDW. SMITH *Guesses Riddle Exist.* (New Ed.) 28 'Infra-natural', or something implying degradation,..would be the right expression. **1843** *Blackw. Mag.* LIV. 674 The sober supernaturalism of the German has more attractions with us, than the grinning *infra-naturalism of the Frenchman. **1878** A. H. GREEN *Coal* iii. 81 The spaces in question differ altogether in character from the *infra-nodal canals. **1887** L. HEITZMANN tr. *Carl Heitzmann's Anat. Descr. & Topogr.* II. 146 The posterior division of the first cervical nerve, the *infra-occipital nerve. **1880** BASTIAN *Brain* 95 A bilobed *infra-oesophageal ganglion. **1806** *Med. Jrnl.* XV. 230 Dissection of the *infraorbital nerve. **1840** E. WILSON *Anat. Vade M.* (1842) 33 Immediately above the fossa is the infra-orbital foramen,—the termination of the infra-orbital canal, and infra-orbital artery. **1880** GUNTHER *Fishes* 54 The infra-orbital ring of bones consists of several pieces. **1741** A. MONRO *Anat. Nerves* (ed. 3) 133 The *infra-orbitar Branch of the second Branch of the fifth pair of Nerves. **1822–34** *Good's Study Med.* (ed. 4) III. 221 The *infra-orbitary or maxillary branch of nerves. **1802–12** BENTHAM *Ration. Jud. Evid.* (1827) I. 61 A mass or lot of *infra-ordinary or inferior evidence. **1897** *Allbutt's Syst. Med.* III. 723 When the growth is below the biliary papilla, or *infra-papillary, the bile and pancreatic juice tend to regurgitate through the dilated duodenum. **1881** WATSON in *Jrnl. Linn. Soc.* XV. No. 85. 273 With a broadish *infraperipherial chestnut band. **1854** AUSTEN in *Proc. Geol. Soc.* (1855) XI. 116 Terrestrial surface *infraposed to the Drift-gravels. **1839** MURCHISON *Silur. Syst.* I. ii. 25 A similar *infraposition of saliferous marls may be seen at Moss Hill farm. **1853** KANE *Grinnell Exp.* xlii. (1856) 396 The infraposition and superposition of two fluids of differing densities. **1876** GROSS *Dis. Bladder* 133 Termed the *infrapubic puncture. **1885** R. J. H. GIBSON in *Trans. R. Soc. Edinb.* XXXII. 627 On the top of the muscles of the *infraradular sheet there are two ganglia united to each other and to their fellows on the opposite side. **1933** *Mind* XLII. 265 In the concept of life, one may stress either its unconscious, *infra-rational, chaotic fecundity or the conscious order..of its historic manifestations. **1935** *Downside Rev.* LIII. 451 Thus the indefinable element would be irrational in the sense of infra-rational. **1870** ROLLESTON *Anim. Life* 16 The largest of these receptacles are the *infrarenally-placed abdominal air-sacs. **1855** MAYNE *Expos. Lex.*, *Infrascapularis*..*infrascapular. **1879** KHORY *Princ. Med.* 45 Infra-scapular [region], which extends from the angle of the scapula to the lower margin of the thorax below and to the spine behind. **1939** *Entomol. News* L. 198 In practice they propose *infra-specific names—polynomials as well as trinomials—in proper Latin form. **1970** *Watsonia* VIII. 42 The geographical significance of this variation should not be lost sight of and may eventually receive taxonomic recognition at some infra-specific level. **1753** CHAMBERS *Cycl. Supp.* s.v. *Infraspinatus*, The ..*infraspinal cavity, or fossa of the scapula. **1835–6** TODD *Cycl. Anat.* I. 569/2 The spine is..so placed as to divide the dorsum of the scapula into a supra-spinal and infra-spinal depression. **1854** OWEN *Skel. & Teeth* in *Circ. Sc.*, *Organ. Nat.* I. 251 The supraspinal fossa of the scapula is less deep than the infraspinal one. **1855** MAYNE *Expos. Lex.*, *Infraspinatus*, applied to a muscle of the shoulder, ..*infraspinate. **1897** *Allbutt's Syst. Med.* II. 974 Paralysis of the supra and *infra-spinators. **1855** HOLDEN *Hum. Osteol.* (1878) 142 Gives origin to the *infra-spinatus. **1872** MIVART *Elem. Anat.* 154 The infra-spinatus fossa and subscapular fossa together forming its actual outer surface. **1879** KHORY *Princ. Med.* 45 *Infra-spinous [region] to the infra-spinous fossa. **1884** COUES *Key N. Amer. Birds* 154 The stylo-hyal, will join the extra-stapedial plate, and the afterward chondrified band of union will be the **infra-stapedial*. *Ibid.* 186 The stylo-hyal..represented by another claw of the stapes (an *infra*-stapedial element). **1879** KHORY *Princ. Med.* 44 *Infra-sternal [region], that which extends from the third cartilage to the lower end of the sternum. **1880** WATSON in *Jrnl. Linn. Soc.* XV. No. 82. 97 Longitudinal puckerings stretching down from the *infrasutural row of beads. **1897** *Allbutt's Syst. Med.* IV. 309 This [presence of glycosurin] is more especially the case in *infra-tentorial disease. **1853** KANE *Grinnell Exp.* xlviii. (1856) 454 Some of Martin's imaginings of *infraterrene architecture. **1840** G. V. ELLIS *Anat.* 76 Very small filaments from the supra-trochlear..and from the *infra-trochlear. **1875** H. WALTON *Dis. Eye* 726 The nose gets its nerve twigs from the frontal, supra, and infra-trochlear branches. **1900** DORLAND *Med. Dict.* 322/1 *Infra-umbilical. **1906** *Practitioner* Dec. 781 A supra-umbilical and infra-umbilical zone. **1967** *Gray's Anat.* (ed. 34) 641 In its infra-umbilical portion the linea alba is narrow. **1898** G. E. HERMAN *Dis. Women* 121 Elongation of the *infra-vaginal portions of the anterior cervical wall.

infract, *a.*[1] *arch.* [ad. L. *infract-us*, f. *in-* (IN-[3]) + *fractus* broken.] Unbroken; unviolated, unweakened; sound, whole.

1566 GASCOIGNE *Supposes* Wks. (1587) 5 How straight and infract is this line of life. **1592** SYLVESTER *Triumph Faith* III. 23 Martyrs..who..Their faith infract with their own bloods did seal. **1613** HEYWOOD *Silv. Age* III. i, My charme, Which Gods and diuels gaue vnite consent To be infract. **1901** *North Amer. Rev.* Feb. 314 The illusion renews itself in the great moments, but I wish it could be kept infract in the small.

†**infract**, *a.*[2] *Obs.* [ad. L. *infract-us*, pa. pple. of *infringĕre* to INFRINGE.] Broken.

1593 PEELE *Edw. I* Wks. (Rtldg.) 393/1 My sweetest love, an this my infract fortune Could never vaunt her sovereignty. **1603** H. CROSSE *Vertues Commw.* (1878) 25 Subiect to chance and infract fortune.

infract (ɪn'frækt), *v.* [f. L. *infract-*, ppl. stem of *infringĕre* to INFRINGE.] *trans.* To break; to violate, infringe. Chiefly *U.S.*

1798 WASHINGTON *Lett.* Writ. 1893 XIV. 127, I think every nation has a right to establish that form of government, under which it conceives it shall live most happy; provided it infracts no right, or is not dangerous to others. **1808** JEFFERSON *Writ.* (1830) IV. 107 Rights which we considered as infracted. **1819** WIFFEN *Aonian Hours* (1820) 47 Their social bond through centuries survives, Hers homicide infracts in every age. **1833** M. SCOTT *Tom Cringle* xix. (1859) 519 He will never venture to infract the neutrality of the waters. **1890** NICOLAY & HAY *Lincoln* I. xix. 348 It is due to the Constitution, heretofore palpably infracted.

infracted (ɪn'fræktɪd), *ppl. a.* [f. as prec. + -ED[1].] **a.** Broken, interrupted. **b.** *Anat.* Bent suddenly inwards, as if partly broken; geniculated.

1727–46 THOMSON *Summer* 604 Falling fast from gradual slope to slope, With wild infracted course, and lessen'd roar, It gains a safer bed.

†**in'fractible**, *a.*[1] *Obs. rare.* [f. IN-[3] + L. *fract-*, ppl. stem (see FRACT) + -IBLE.] Incapable of being broken in or subdued.

1657 COCKAINE *Obstin. Lady* I. ii. Poems (1669) 307 No surely, nor can I believe that she Ment to enclose a mind infractible Within a body so powerful to subdue.

in'fractible, *a.*[2] *rare.* [f. INFRACT *v.* + -IBLE.] Capable of being infracted or broken.

1846 WORCESTER cites COOKE.

infraction (ɪn'frækʃən). [ad. L. *infractiōn-em*, n. of action f. *infringĕre* to INFRINGE. Cf. F. *infraction* (1250 in Hatz.-Darm.).]

1. The action of fracturing or breaking; *concr.*, a breakage or fracture.

1623 COCKERAM, *Infraction*, a breaking. **1881** *Eng. Mechanic* No. 874. 366/3 The trough gave way at the sides, but the lead of the bullet was clearly injected into the plane of infraction.

2. The action of breaking or infringing (a bond or obligation); breach, violation, infringement.

1673 TEMPLE *Let. to Dk. Ormond* Wks. 1731 I. 125 The Points of Justice must be grounded upon the Infraction of Treaties. **1733** NEAL *Hist. Purit.* II. 558 Evil counsellors which have prevailed with his Majesty to make infractions upon his royal word. **1790** BEATSON *Nav. & Mil. Mem.* I. 246 To oppose the Scots insurgents, was no infraction of the capitulation. **1845** M. PATTISON *Ess.* (1889) I. 17 Bringing him to..trial..for his flagrant infraction of the canon law. **1875** STUBBS *Const. Hist.* II. xiv. 14 His coronation had been a violent infraction of her right.

†**3.** *Optics.* = REFRACTION. *Obs.*

1635 SWAN *Spec. M.* v. §2 (1643) 131 The second [colour of the rainbow] is caused by a more weak infraction. *Ibid.* 133 Neither was the sunne destitute of sparkling raies to make reflection and infraction.

4. *Anat.* An infracted condition.

1882 W. MACCORMAC in Quain *Dict. Med.* 997/2 Very distinct in type from the infractions and extravagant distortions of an osteomalacic skeleton.

infractor (ɪn'fræktə(r)). [a. med.L. *infractor* (Du Cange), agent-n. from *infringĕre* to INFRINGE; cf. F. *infracteur* (1419 in Godef. *Compl.*).] One who breaks or infringes (a bond or obligation); a violator, infringer.

1524 HEN. VIII *Instruct. Pace* in Strype *Eccl. Mem.* I. App. xiii. 29 Infractours of their promises. **1678** MARVELL *Growth Popery* 12 The Infractors and Aggressors of the Peace of Aix la Chapelle. **1767** *Hist. Eur.* in *Ann. Reg.* 22/1 Accusations might be brought against the infractors of those laws. **1823** *Ibid.* 182* Every citizen..may expose any infraction of the constitution, requiring from the competent authority the effective responsibility of the infractors.

infractous (ɪn'fræktəs), *a.* [f. L. *infract-us*, pa. pple. of *infringĕre* (see INFRINGE) + -OUS.] Bent inwards; inflexed.

1866 in *Treas. Bot.*

‖**infra dig.** ('ɪnfrə 'dɪg), *adj. phr.* [Colloquial abbreviation of L. *infrā dignitātem* beneath (one's) dignity: the source of the expression is obscure.] Beneath one's dignity; unbecoming one's position; not consistent with dignity; undignified.

[**1822** HAZLITT *Table-t.* (1885) 287 If the graduates.. express their thoughts in English, it is understood to be *infra dignitatem*.] **1824** SCOTT *Redgauntlet* ch. xi, It would be *infra dig.* in the Provost of this most flourishing and loyal town to associate with Redgauntlet. **1883** C. J. WILLS *Mod. Persia* 312 Few will consent to sing; it is *infra dig.*

infragenual, etc.: see INFRA-.

infragrant (ɪnˈfreɪgrənt), *a.* [IN-³.] Not fragrant; the opposite of fragrant; malodorous.
1813 SYD. SMITH *Let.* in Lady Holland *Life* xii. (1855) I. 411 We shall both be a brown infragrant powder in thirty or forty years. **1842** —— *Let. to L. Horner* Wks. 1859 II. 319/1 He was among the most conspicuous young men in that energetic and infragrant city [Edinburgh].

Infralapsarian (ˌɪnfrəlæpˈsɛərɪən), *sb.* and *a. Theol.* [f. L. *infrā* under, beneath + *laps-us* fall + *-arian*, as in *Trinitarian*, etc.]
A. *sb.* A term applied in the 17th c. to Calvinists holding the view that God's election of some to everlasting life was consequent to his prescience of the Fall of man, or that it contemplated man as already fallen, and was thus a remedial measure: opposed to SUPRALAPSARIAN.
The Supralapsarian view makes Predestination anterior or logically superior to the Fall, and views the creation, fall, and saving of some, as parts of God's eternal purpose. *Infralapsarian* is generally used as synonymous with SUBLAPSARIAN, the earlier and, in English writers, the more usual term. But some distinguish the two, associating *Sublapsarian* with the view that the Fall was foreseen, and *Infralapsarian* with the view that it was permitted, by God.
1731 in BAILEY vol. II. **1756** in BROUGHTON *Hist. Dict. of Relig.* **1775** ASH, *Infralapsarian* s., one who holds that God in the decree of election considered his people as fallen in Adam; a sublapsarian. **1843** J. B. ROBERTSON tr. *Moehler's Symbolism* II. 345 The parties of Supralapsarians and Infralapsarians already stood opposed to each other. **1865** W. G. T. SHEDD *Christ. Doctrine* II. 192 According to the Infra-lapsarians, the decree to create men, and that they shall apostatize, are prior to that of election and reprobation. Election supposes apostasy as a fact.
B. *adj.* Of or pertaining to the Infralapsarians or their doctrine.
1775 ASH, *Infralapsarian* adj., Belonging to the scheme or doctrine of the Infralapsarians. **1860** GARDNER *Faiths of World* II. 135/1 Hagenbach alleges that the synod of Dort approved of the Infralapsarian scheme. **1865** W. G. T. SHEDD *Christ. Doctrine* II. 192 Beza..had adopted the *supra-lapsarian* statement of the doctrine of predestination, which renders the doctrine more austere and repelling than the *infra-lapsarian* representation.
Hence **Infralapˈsarianism**, the doctrine of Infralapsarians.
1847 BUCH tr. *Hagenbach's Hist. Doct.* II. 255. **1865** W. G. T. SHEDD *Christ. Doctrine* II. 193 The Synod of Dort favoured Infra-lapsarianism, in opposition to Gomar, who endeavoured to commit the Synod to Supra-lapsarianism.

inframammary, etc.: see INFRA-.

inframe, variant of ENFRAME *v.*

infranch, -ise, -ment, obs. ff. ENFRANCH, etc.

infrangible (ɪnˈfrændʒɪb(ə)l), *a.* [f. IN-³ + FRANGIBLE; cf. OF. *infrangible* (15th c.).]
1. That cannot be broken; unbreakable.
1597 A. M. tr. *Guillemeau's Fr. Chirurg.* 14 b/1 Shee [a needle] ought to be stiffe, smooth and infrangible. **1603** HOLLAND *Plutarch* 807 He that nameth an Atome, saith as much, as infrangible, impassible, and without vacuitie. **1715–20** POPE *Iliad* XIII. 57 And link'd their fetlocks with a golden band, Infrangible, immortal. **1849** ROBERTSON *Serm.* Ser. I. v. 70 No iron bar is absolutely infrangible.
fig. **1686** H. MORE *Real Presence* 39 The solid, steady, and infrangible Wisdom of God. **1837** HOWITT *Rur. Life* II. vi. (1862) 160 An enchanted forest, bearing the spell of an infrangible silence.
2. That cannot be infringed; inviolable.
1834 SIR W. HAMILTON *Discuss.* (1852) 376 Firm and infrangible compacts, which sometimes last for generations.
Hence **infrangiˈbility, inˈfrangibleness**, the quality of being infrangible; **inˈfrangibly** *adv.*, in an infrangible manner, so as to be unbreakable.
1727 BAILEY vol. II, *Infrangibleness*, uncapableness of being broken. **1828** *Blackw. Mag.* XXIV. 118 The band which bound them all infrangibly together. **1899** *Month* Aug. 146 The infrangibility of the seal of confession.

infranodal to **infravaginal**: see INFRA-.

infra-red (ɪnfrəˈrɛd), *a.* and *sb.* Also as one word (without hyphen). [f. INFRA- + RED *a.* and *sb.*] **A.** *adj.* **1.** Lying beyond the red end of the visible spectrum: the epithet of electromagnetic radiation (and of the part of the spectrum containing it) which has a wavelength greater than that of red light (about 0·7–0·8 microns) and (in modern use) less than that of the shortest microwaves (of the order of 1000 microns, i.e. 1 mm.); it is invisible, and most of the radiation from bodies below red heat is emitted in this form.
1881 *Nature* XXV. 162 The infra-red end of the spectrum. **1896** *Allbutt's Syst. Med.* I. 254 All portions of the spectrum powerfully affect the microbes except the red and the infra-red rays. **1926** *Encycl. Brit.* I. 946/2 Extending beyond the red end of the visible spectrum there are 9 octaves of infra-red radiation overlapping with very short Hertzian waves... A. Glacolewa-Arkadiewa..has created Hertzian waves of only 0·082 mm. in wave length. **1929** *Punch's Almanack for 1930* 4 Nov. p. xxxvii (Advt.), These are like the health-giving rays of heat emitted by the sun—those short infra-red rays that..enfold you with their beneficial warmth. **1932** HARDY & PERRIN *Princ. Optics* xi. 234 Photographs of landscapes taken by infrared light have the general appearance of night scenes because the sky appears dark and the high reflectance of chlorophyl gives foliage the appearance of intense local lighting... Photographs of extremely distant objects are made possible by infrared light because of its greater penetration through atmospheric haze. **1935** *Practitioners Libr. Med. & Surg.* VIII. I. viii. 168 Infra-red radiation..produces the sensation of heat when it comes in contact with the body. This form of radiant energy is produced..by any heated body. **1939** *Jrnl. R. Aeronaut. Soc.* XLIII. 1012 Heating elements such as the steam radiator, which does not glow, emit infra-red energy of long wave-lengths (far infra-red). The filament lamp, like the sun, is a source of near infra-red energy. This is the portion of the spectrum which lies chiefly in the wave-lengths slightly longer than the red visible radiation. **1957** *House & Garden* Dec. 99 An electric Rotary Spit that automatically turns joints, steaks, chops, or poultry under penetrating infra-red heat.
2. a. Involving, producing, or pertaining to infra-red radiation or its use.
1910 *Photogr. Jrnl.* Oct. 320 The idea of photographing landscapes through the infra-red screen. *Ibid.* 330 In the infra-red photograph the shadows are practically black and the sky is very dark. **1929** *Brit. Jrnl. Photogr.* 29 Mar. 183/2 By comparing the results of ordinary photography..with those of infra-red photography. **1935** *Practitioners Libr. Med. & Surg.* VIII. I. viii. 169 The wavelength used in infra-red therapy is not of particular importance. It is mainly a determining factor in the penetration or the depth which the heat reaches. **1951** MRAK & MACKINNEY in M. B. Jacobs *Chem. & Technol. Food & Food Products* (ed. 2) III. xxxiii. 1787 Infrared lamps have been installed in a plant for natural dried cod to reduce the moisture from about 60 to 43%. **1954** 'J. CHRISTOPHER' *22nd Century* 197 He went through to the kitchen, switched the infra-red heater off and collected his breakfast. **1963** F. C. WEBB *Biochem. Engin.* xvii. 482 Small catering-size infra-red heaters are in limited use for grilling. **1968** *Times* 9 Dec. 7/2 Infra-red galaxies.. are just one of several types of cosmic objects being studied in the booming new science of infra-red astronomy.
b. Sensitive to infra-red radiation.
1932 *Discovery* Sept. 292/1 These infra-red plates are not as a rule made sensitive to the green and orange, although they retain their sensitivity to blue. **1938** *Encycl. Brit. Bk. Yr. 1938* 500/1 New films for aerial photography included a fast infra-red film. **1961** *Daily Mail* 20 July 6/3 Midas picks up a rocket by detecting the intense heat of its exhaust flame with an infra-red eye. **1973** *Daily Tel.* (Colour Suppl.) 11 May 44/3 Another student..wants the astronauts to photograph volcanoes with infra-red film which records temperature differences on the Earth rather than grades of light.
B. *ellipt.* as *sb.* The infra-red part of the spectrum; ***near, far infra-red***, the part close to, or far from, the visible spectrum.
1881 *Phil. Mag.* XI. 167 Experiments supposed to prove the existence of lines in the infra-red. **1887** *Encycl. Brit.* XXII. 376/1 Becquerel finds lines in the infra-red at 11,420. **1923** GLAZEBROOK *Dict. Appl. Physics* IV. 533/2 Such solids as rock-salt have a very strong absorption band for light in the far infra-red. **1937** JENKINS & WHITE *Fund. Optics* i. 13 On the long-wavelength side of the visible lies the infrared, which may be said to merge into the radio waves at about 4 × 10^{-2} cm. **1960** CONN & AVERY *Infrared Methods* p. v, By restricting attention to the range from 1 to 25μ we have limited the interest to the 'near infrared' but even this embraces a range of some four to five octaves. **1966** HOUGHTON & SMITH *Infra-Red Physics* i. 1 The infra-red is that region of the electromagnetic spectrum which lies between the visible and microwave regions, i.e. between wavelengths of about 8000 Å (= 0·8 μ) and 1 mm. **1973** *Sci. Amer.* Feb. 89/2 The laser's output was in the infrared.

infrasonic (ɪnfrəˈsɒnɪk), *a.* Also **infra-sonic**. [f. INFRA- + SONIC *a.*, after *supersonic*, *ultrasonic*, as tr. F. *infra-sonore* (E. Esclangon 1925, in *Mém. de l'Artillerie Française* IV. 647).]
A. *adj.* **1.** Of, pertaining to, or designating sound waves or vibrations having a frequency below the audible range (i.e. less than 15–30 Hz).
1927 E. G. RICHARDSON *Sound* x. 236 The lower pitch limit is about 16 vibrations per second. Slow vibrations.. remain unperceived as tones if their rate of pulsation falls below this limit... Such 'infra-sonic' waves have been extensively studied by Esclangon. **1945** *Electronic Engin.* XVII. 328/3 These will not run well..at infra-sonic frequencies. **1960** *McGraw-Hill Encycl. Sci. & Technol.* XII. 506/1 Many problems in vibration, oceanography, seismology, and the dynamic behavior of elastic materials are analyzed by treating the phenomenon being studied as sound waves of infrasonic frequency. **1965** *Aerospace Med.* XXXVI. 817/2 It has been estimated that the very large super boosters of the future..will produce their maximum noise energy in the infrasonic range (below 20 cps). **1965** T. N. DAVIS in W. N. Hess *Space Sci.* v. 227 Infrasonic waves with periods ranging from 10–110 seconds are observed at auroral and middle latitudes. These appear only on nights of moderate or strong auroral activity.
2. Designating speeds below that of sound; subsonic. *rare*⁻¹.
1942 *Jrnl. R. Aeronaut. Soc.* XLVI. 85 Equations of general application are derived, proving that both for infrasonic and for ultrasonic (supersonic) velocities, an extremum of the cross-section is possible.

infrasound (ˈɪnfrəsaʊnd). [f. INFRA- + SOUND *sb.*³, tr. F. *infra-son* (1906 in Robert).] Sound, or a sound, of infrasonic frequency.
1930 A. B. WOOD *Textbk. Sound* II 213 The 'ondes de bouche' (from the mouth of the gun) consists principally of waves of very low frequency (of the order 1 p.p.s.), described by Esclangon as Infra-Sounds. **1965** *Aerospace Med.* XXXVI. 824/1 Very low sonic frequency noise and moderate levels of infrasound are commonly encountered in conventional aerospace operations. **1970** B. W. ALDISS *Moment of Eclipse* 66 This was infrasound. The plant was emitting slow air vibrations at less than ten hertz. **1971** *Observer* 28 Nov. 3/1 Many cars and lorries travelling at sustained high speeds produce such intense levels of low-frequency noise or 'infrasound' inside them that drivers can experience symptoms very similar to those produced by heavy drinking. *Ibid.*, In a wide range of passenger cars travelling at motorway speeds the sound energy is largely concentrated as intense infrasounds—most of which can be felt rather than heard.

infrastructure (ˈɪnfrəˌstrʌktjʊə(r)). [Fr. (1875 in Robert), f. INFRA- + STRUCTURE *sb.*] A collective term for the subordinate parts of an undertaking; substructure, foundation; *spec.* the permanent installations forming a basis for military operations, as airfields, naval bases, training establishments, etc.
1927 *Chambers's Jrnl.* 14 May 374/2 The tunnels, bridges, culverts, and 'infrastructure' work generally of the Ax to Bourg-Madame line have been completed. **1950** W. S. CHURCHILL in *Hansard Commons* CDLXXVI. 2145 In this Debate we have had the usual jargon about 'the infrastructure of a supra-national authority'. **1951** *European Rev.* Oct. 2/1 This new term 'infrastructure'..denotes fixed military facilities such as airfields, base installations and transport systems. **1956** D. NOAKES tr. *Hodeir's Jazz* 197 What I call the infrastructure is the regularly produced two- or four-beat meter (2/2 or 4/4 measure) that characterizes any jazz performance. **1957** T. KILMARTIN tr. *Aron's Opium of Intellectuals* iv. 133 Thirty years ago, the dominant school of thought in the Soviet Union undertook..the task of analysing the infrastructure of society. **1960** *Times* 9 Dec. 14/2 Part of the Nato infrastructure programme. **1971** *Inside Kenya Today* Mar. 15/1 A.I.D. assistance will be focused on Vihiga Division and will..upgrade the infrastructure of roads and other social services. **1971** J. SPENCER *Eng. Lang. W. Afr.* 31 A very complex infrastructure of scores of vernacular languages.
So **ˌinfraˈstructural** *a.*
1963 *Economist* 13 Apr. 130/2 Very low interest rates..for various forms of infrastructural development. **1967** *Ibid.* 23 Sept. 1104/2 Big, infrastructural programmes—the building of dams, power stations, roads, railways, harbours and airports.

†**inˈfree**, *a. Sc. Obs. rare*⁻¹. [IN-³.] Not having the freedom of a borough or city; unfree.
1584 *Burgh Rec. Glasgow* (Rec. Soc.) I. 114 Infre pakeris and pelaris.

†**inˈfrenate**, *v. Obs. rare*⁻⁰. [f. ppl. stem of L. *infrēnāre* to bridle.] *trans.* To bridle.
1623 COCKERAM II, To Bridle a horse, *Infrænate, Capistrate.*

†**infreˈnation.** *Obs. rare*⁻⁰. [f. IN-³ + L. *frēnātiōn-em* bridling; see prec. (Perh. a misunderstanding of Tertullian's *infrēnātio* restraining.)] Unruliness (Cockeram, 1623).

†**inˈfrendiate**, *v. Obs. rare*⁻⁰. [irreg. f. L. *infrendēre, -ĕre.*] To gnash the teeth.
1623 COCKERAM II, To gnash the Teeth, *Infrendiate.*

infrequence (ɪnˈfriːkwəns). *rare.* [f. as next: see -ENCE. Cf. F. *infréquence* (Littré).] = next.
1644 BP. HALL *Free Prisoner* §4 (R.) Is it solitude and infrequence of visitation? **1897** *Westm. Gaz.* 8 Apr. 2/1 Dancing is no mark of London's lightheartedness, but from its infrequence a tribute to its children's gloomy, colourless lives.

infrequency (ɪnˈfriːkwənsɪ). [ad. L. *infrequentia*, n. of quality f. *infrequent-em*: see next and -ENCY.] The state of being infrequent.
†**1.** The fact or condition of being unfrequented; uncrowded state or condition; also, Small attendance; paucity, fewness. *Obs.*
1600 HOLLAND *Livy* XXXIX. xviii. 1034 By occasion of the same infrequencie [*eadem solitudo*] (for that they whose names were presented, neither made answere nor could be found). **1603** —— *Plutarch* 1326 It was the solitude and infrequency of the place that brought the dragon thither, rather than the dragon that caused the said desert solitarinesse. **1615** G. SANDYS *Trav.* 61 Answerable to his small dependancie, and infrequencie of suters. **1658** W. BURTON *Itin. Anton.* 161 The infrequency..of that brave bold Legion, whose bands and troups were not full as then, by reason of absences by leave.
2. The fact or condition of being of infrequent occurrence or of recurring at wide intervals; uncommonness, rarity.
1677 PLOT *Oxfordsh.* 4 The infrequency of the thing (they never happening but at or near the Moons full). **1718** *Wodrow Corr.* (1843) II. 369 The accounts..of the infrequency of public baptism among us. **1776** GIBBON *Decl. & F.* xii. I. 338 The infrequency of marriage, and the ruin of agriculture, affected the principles of population. **1823** LAMB *Elia* Ser. II. *Old China*, The relish of such exhibitions must be in proportion to the infrequency of going. **1880** FLINT *Princ. Med.* 167 The infrequency of gangrene is shown by its having occurred in but one of 133 cases.

infrequent (ɪnˈfriːkwənt), *a.* [ad. L. *infrequent-em*, f. *in-* (IN-³) + *frequent-em* FREQUENT. Cf. F. *infréquent* (Littré).] Not frequent.
†**1.** Not much resorted to or practised; little used; unaccustomed, uncommon. *Obs.*
1531 ELYOT *Gov.* I. xxi, Mater..infrequent, or seldome herde of them that haue nat radde very many autors in greke and latine. *Ibid.* III. xxii, Frugalite, the acte wherof is at this day..infrequent or out of use amonge all sortes of men.
†**2.** Not crowded; thinly peopled, occupied, or filled. *Obs. rare.*

1681 *Whole Duty Nations* 15 A Neighbourhood, whether it be the more populous of Cities.. or the more infrequent of Villages.

3. Not occurring often, happening rarely; recurring at wide intervals of time.

1612–15 BP. HALL *Contempl., N.T.* III. v, It is not so infrequent for a multitude to conspire in evill. **1622** —— *Deceit Appearance* Wks. (1648) 455 A poore conscionable Christian.. cooling his infrequent pleasures with sighs, and saucing them with teares. **1756** JOHNSON *Abr. Eng. Dict.* Pref. ¶2 Words of infrequent occurrence. **1876** MISS YONGE *Womankind* viii. 56 The treat should be sufficiently infrequent to be a real subject of anticipation.

b. Qualifying an agent-noun: That does something seldom or infrequently.

1722 WOLLASTON *Relig. Nat.* I. v. (1724) 18 A sparing and infrequent worshiper of the Deity. **1881** *World* 28 Dec., The rare and infrequent rustic visitor to London.

4. Occurring or met with at wide distances apart; not plentiful; rather few and far between.

a **1682** SIR T. BROWNE *Tracts* 81 The Myrtle.. no rare or infrequent Plant among them. **1858** *Sat. Rev.* 20 Nov. 501/2 Globigerina is comparatively infrequent. **1884** *Harper's Mag.* Aug. 370/1 These windows are small and infrequent.

b. *Zool.* and *Bot.* Of spines, punctures, glands, etc.: Thinly or sparsely planted; distantly placed.

† **infre'quented,** *a. Obs. rare.* [IN-^{3}. Cf. F. *infrequenté* (1575 in Hatz.-Darm.), L. *infrequentātus.*] Not frequented; unfrequented.

1675 OGILBY *Brit.* Pref. 2 Many of these ways.. are grown infrequented. *Ibid.* (1698) 29 Being chiefly mountainous and infrequented.

infrequently (ɪn'friːkwəntlɪ), *adv.* [IN-^{3}.] Not frequently; somewhat rarely, seldom. Now chiefly in ***not infrequently*** = rather frequently.

1673 *Lady's Calling* I. v. §64 [They] come so infrequently as if they thought it a very arbitrary matter whether they come or no. **1779** WILKES *Corr.* (1805) V. 208 Not infrequently a ray of truth pierces the Stygian gloom. **1876** GLADSTONE *Homeric Synchr.* 46 With respect to stone, it very infrequently appears in Homer. **1876** FAWCETT *Pol. Econ.* II. v. (ed. 5) 159 Farmers not infrequently insure their crops against.. hail-storms.

† **in'fresh,** *v. Obs. rare*$^{-1}$. [f. IN-^{2} + FRESH *v.*] *trans.* To make fresh; to freshen.

1635 PERSON *Varieties* I. 20 Lakes.. ever infreshed with streames of fresh springs which flow and run into them.

† **in'friar,** *v. Obs. rare*$^{-0}$. [f. IN-^{2} + FRIAR.] *trans.* To make into a friar; *refl.* to become a friar.

1611 FLORIO, *Infratarsi*, to infrier himselfe.

† **infriate,** *v. Obs. rare*$^{-0}$. [f. ppl. stem of L. *infriāre* to break or rub down.] To crumble (Cockeram, 1623).

† **'infricate,** *v. Obs. rare*$^{-0}$. [f. ppl. stem of L. *infricāre* to rub in.] *trans.* To rub in or on (Cockeram, 1623).

† **infrication.** *Obs. rare*$^{-1}$. [n. of action f. L. *infricāre*: see prec.] = next.

1578 BANISTER *Hist. Man* v. 64 Nature hath endewed [the skin] with an infinite number of pores.. and [by] infrication, these manifestly do shew them selues. **1658** [see next].

infriction (ɪn'frɪkʃən). [ad. L. *infrictiōn-em* (doubtful reading in Celsus VIII. xi): see FRICTION.] The action of rubbing in.

1656 BLOUNT *Glossogr.*, *Infriction*, a rubbing in, a chafing. **1658** PHILLIPS, *Infriction*, or *Infrication*, a rubbing or chafing in. **1721** in BAILEY. **1886** *Syd. Soc. Lex.*, *Infriction*, .. the rubbing into the skin of an ointment. **1888** *Med. News* July 101 The inflammation, he said, set in after the fourth infriction.

† **in'frigidate,** *a. Obs. rare*$^{-1}$. [ad. late L. *infrīgidāt-us*, pa. pple. of *infrīgidāre*: see next.] Made or become cold; chilled, cooled down.

1483 CAXTON *Gold. Leg.* 166b/1 Thenne he whiche was Infrigydate and colde.. was made al hole by the brennyng hete of angre.

infrigidate (ɪn'frɪdʒɪdeɪt), *v.* Now *rare.* [f. ppl. stem of late L. *infrīgidāre* to make cold, f. *in-* (IN-^{2}) + *frīgidus* cold, FRIGID. Cf. obs. F. *infrigider* (Godef.).] *trans.* To make cold or frigid; to chill, cool.

1545 RAYNOLD *Byrth Mankynde* III. iii. (1634) 174 Such hearbes, the which haue power to infrigidate and coole. *c* **1610** SIR C. HEYDON *Astrol. Disc.* (1650) 20 It is not the essence thereof either to heat or infrigidate. **1686** GOAD *Celest. Bodies* I. ix. 35 That Room is the cooler for the walls sake, the Emanation from thence infrigidating the place. **1885** G. MEREDITH *Diana* I. xiii. 269 A congenial atmosphere; which, however, she infrigidated by her overflow of exclamatory wonderment.

Hence **in'frigidating** *vbl. sb.* and *ppl. a.*

1650 ASHMOLE *Chym. Collect.* 77 Therefore make it Cold, for then is manifest the hidden, and the Manifest by infrigidating is hid. **1665–6** *Phil. Trans.* I. 256, I have made infrigidating Mixtures with Sal Armoniack.

infrigidation (ɪnfrɪdʒɪ'deɪʃən). [ad. late L. *infrīgidātiōn-em*, n. of action from *infrīgidāre*: see prec. Cf. OF. *infrigidation* (14th c. in Godef.).] The action of cooling or condition of being cooled, refrigeration.

1590 BARROUGH *Meth. Physick* VII. xi. (1639) 399 If.. we think that there be greater need of infrigidation and cooling. **1686** GOAD *Celest. Bodies* I. ix. 30 All Infrigidation is performed by transfusion of a Spirit, as Rooms are cool by strewing of Herbs, Flags, and Aspersion of sweet Water. **1709** STEELE *Tatler* No. 126 ¶2 She had also the Power of communicating it [the spirit of continency] to all who beheld her. This the Scoffers of those Days called, The Gift of Infrigidation. **1886** in *Syd. Soc. Lex.*

† **in'frigidative,** *a.* and *sb. Obs.* [f. L. *infrīgidāt-* (see INFRIGIDATE *v.*) + -IVE. Cf. OF. *infrigidatif, -ive* (15th c. in Godef.).] **a.** *adj.* Cooling.

b. *sb.* A cooling agent.

1541 R. COPLAND *Guydon's Formul.* Riij b, Medycyns that be colde, dyssycatyues, & infrigidatyues. **1543** TRAHERON *Vigo's Chirurg.* II. iii. 18 It taketh awaye the malignite procedynge of thynges, that are infrigidative and do greatlye coole. **1599** A. M. tr. *Gabelhouer's Bk. Physicke* 248/1 An infrigidative for inflamede and exulceratinge Brestes.

infringe (ɪn'frɪndʒ), *v.*^{1} Also 6 **enfring, infrynge,** 6–7 **infring.** [ad. L. *infring-ĕre* to break, injure, damage, make void, f. *in-* (IN-^{2}) + *frangĕre* to break.]

† **1.** *trans.* To break, shatter (*rare* in physical sense); to break down, crush, destroy; to foil, defeat, frustrate; to cancel, invalidate. *Obs.*

1543 GRAFTON *Contn. Harding* 465 Yᵉ duke.. woulde haue maried lady Mary.. which mariage yᵉ kyng did infringe & stoppe. **1548** HALL *Chron., Hen. VIII* 219 She.. did all that she could to infringe the determinacion of the said Universities and clergie. **1603** KNOLLES *Hist. Turks* (1621) 1016 How the Turkes were to be resisted, and their attempts infringed. **1621** G. SANDYS *Ovid's Met.* XII. (1626) 249 [He] trotting in a round, Infring'd the aire with this disdainefull sound. **1632** QUARLES *Div. Fancies* vii. (1660) 5 It is a potent Science that infringes Strong Prison doors; and heaves them from their hinges. **1637** R. HUMPHREY tr. *St. Ambrose* Pref., The three-fold cable is not easily infringed. **1671** MILTON *P.R.* I. 62 If so we can, and by the head Broken be not intended all our power To be infring'd.

2. To commit a breach or infraction of (a law, obligation, right, etc.); to violate or break (an oath, pledge, treaty, etc.); to transgress, contravene.

1533 in Gross *Gild Merch.* II. 73 Whatsooewer brothir or brethir attempte to infring or breke this sayde lawe. **1548** HALL *Chron., Hen. VII* 22 And least.. the Damosell.. woulde not consent too hym for offending her conscience and infringyng her promes. **1588** SHAKS. *L.L.L.* IV. iii. 144 Ioue for your Loue would infringe an oath. **1647** CLARENDON *Hist. Reb.* II. §69 The undoubted Fundamental priviledge of the Commons in Parliament, that all Supplies should have their rise and beginning from Them.. had never been infringed, or violated, or so much as questioned. **1715–20** POPE *Iliad* IV. 94 The proud Trojans first infringe the peace. **1769** BLACKSTONE *Comm.* IV. vi. 88 The crime [coining] itself is made a species of high treason; as being a breach of allegiance, by infringing the king's prerogative. **1844** H. H. WILSON *Brit. India* III. 7 The editor.. having infringed the regulations to which the press had been subjected by the Government. **1855** MACAULAY *Hist. Eng.* xiii. III. 287 Those privileges of the people which the Stuarts had illegally infringed. **1898** *Westm. Gaz.* 4 May 9/3 With regard to the second alleged infringing tyre.. the judge held that it infringed neither the Welch nor the Clincher patent.

† **3.** To refute; to contradict, deny. *Obs.*

1590 SWINBURNE *Testaments* 264 This conclusion, that the later dooth infringe the former, is diuersly enlarged. **1601–2** FULBECKE *1st Pt. Parall.* 65 This may suffice to infringe that which you haue deliuered. **1660** H. MORE *Myst. Godl.* V. xvii. 200 Nor do those Expressions.. at all infringe the Truth we have declared.

† **4.** To break the force or diminish the strength of; to weaken, enfeeble, impair; to mitigate. *Obs.*

1604 R. CAWDREY *Table Alph.*, *Infringe*,.. to make weake, or feeble. **1620** VENNER *Via Recta* viii. 171 They doe.. oppresse a weake stomacke, and infringe the naturall heat. **1684** tr. *Bonet's Merc. Compit.* XIV. 481 Such [medicines] as concentrate and infringe Acids, such as.. Corals, Chalk. **1694** SALMON *Bate's Disp.* (1715) 533/2 It will yet much more infringe the corrosive Quality of the remaining Acid Spirits.

5. *intr.* To break in or encroach *on* or *upon.*

1760–72 H. BROOKE *Fool of Qual.* (1809) III. 51 Judges.. are yet intimidated from infringing, by any sentence, on the laws and constitution of these realms. **1772–84** COOK *Voy.* (1790) I. 147 They did not infringe upon this boundary for some time. **1774** JEFFERSON *Autobiog.* App. Wks. 1859 I. 141 Let no act be passed by any one legislature, which may infringe on the rights and liberties of another. **1868** FARRAR *Silence & V.* viii. (1875) 137 Never let pleasure infringe on the domain of duty.

Hence **in'fringed** *ppl. a.*; **in'fringing** *vbl. sb.* and *ppl. a.*

c **1555** HARPSFIELD *Divorce Hen. VIII* (Camden) 146 This case.. nothing tendeth to the infringing of any honour or service. **1771** GOLDSM. *Hist. Eng.* I. 370 The subject of his infringed pretensions. **1897** *Daily News* 3 Nov. 2/1 The Incandescent Gas Light Company has spent enormous sums.. in proceedings against unscrupulous dealers and importers of infringing mantles. **1898** *Daily Chron.* 14 Oct. 5/3 Let there be no talk to us of infringed rights.

† **in'fringe,** *v.*^{2} *Obs. rare*$^{-0}$. [IN-^{2}.] *trans.* To furnish with a fringe.

1598 FLORIO, *Infrangiare*, to infringe, or decke with fringe.

infringement (ɪn'frɪndʒmənt). [f. INFRINGE *v.*^{1} + -MENT.] The act or fact of infringing.

1. A breaking or breach (*of* a law, obligation, right, etc.); breach, violation.

Frequent in ***infringement of copyright*** or ***patent.***

1628 WITHER *Brit. Rememb.* II. 973 Which on his Justice may infringement bring. **1654** H. L'ESTRANGE *Chas. I* (1655) 61 The imbarque and stay of our ships at Blay by Lewes.. was an infringement of the League. **1716** ADDISON *Freeholder* No. 14 *ad fin.*, It [is].. a great Infringement of the Liberties of the Subject. **1861** W. FAIRBAIRN *Addr. Brit. Assoc.*, Watt was harassed by infringements of his patent, and lawsuits for the maintenance of his rights. **1878** LECKY *Eng. in 18th C.* II. vii. 285 Resenting every attempt at equality as a kind of infringement of the laws of nature.

b. A breaking in, encroachment, or intrusion.

1673 [R. LEIGH] *Transp. Reh.* 108 They are manifest infringments on our liberty. **1741** BUTLER *Serm. Ho. Lords* Wks. 1874 II. 263 Licentiousness is.. a present infringement upon liberty. **1837** HT. MARTINEAU *Soc. Amer.* III. 238 There is in this respect a dreadful infringement on human rights.

† **2.** Refutation; contradiction. *Obs.*

1593 NASHE *4 Lett. Confut.* 42 If you haue anie new infringement to destitute the inditement of forgerie that I bring against you. **1664** H. MORE *Myst. Iniq.* vi. 15 Nor does the verb being in the plural number make any infringement to this Truth.

in'fringent, *a. Med.* [ad. L. *infringent-em*, pres. pple. of *infringĕre* to INFRINGE.] Of a medicine: Rendering milder; = CORRIGENT.

1886 in *Syd. Soc. Lex.*

infringer (ɪn'frɪndʒə(r)). [f. INFRINGE *v.* + -ER^{1}.] One who infringes (in the various senses of the verb); a violator.

1541 *Act 33 Hen. VIII*, c. 10 §1 To correcte and punyshe the Infringers and contemners thereof. **1655** FULLER *Ch. Hist.* IV. iv. §19 He.. having formerly.. appeared a great Patron of Sanctuaries, and a severe punisher of the unjust infringers thereof. **1738** WARBURTON *Div. Legat.* I. II. iv. 225 Infringers of the Duties of Imperfect Obligation. **1878** THURSTON *Hist. Steam-Eng.* 110 Watt claimed that Hornblower.. was an infringer upon his patents. **1887** *Law Times* LXXXII. 260/2 The alleged infringer of a patent is often more sinned against than sinning.

† **in'fringible,** *a. Obs.* Also **-eable.** [var. of INFRANGIBLE with vowel conformed to L. *infringĕre.* Cf. obs. F. *infringible* (Rabelais, 16th c.).]

1. That cannot be infringed or broken; unbreakable, inviolable, indissoluble.

1548 HALL *Chron., Hen. V* 36b, The Frenche nacion not remembryng this infringible law, deposed.. the very heyre male.. and set up in trone this Pepyn. *Ibid., Edw. IV* 242b, In hope of continual peace, and infringible amitie. **1605** BRETON *Olde Man's Lesson* (1879) 13 Hauing betwixt themselues sealed with their hands the infringible band of Faith and Troth in the heart.. hee tooke leaue of his faire lady. **1642** G. EGLISHAM *Forerunner Revenge* 6 Your Majesty's most royall word, which should be inviolable, your hand and seale which should be infringeable.

b. Rarely of things material: Unbreakable.

1600 R. CAWDRAY *Treas. Similies* 305 To trap within the infringible net of his indignation.

2. Irrefragable, irrefutable.

1581 J. BELL *Haddon's Answ. Osor.* 266 And first of all commeth to hand an infringible Argument of Osorius. **1629** SYMMER *Spir. Posie* I. i. 6 The equity of the dependencie of the latter upon the former, is infringible.

infructescence (ɪnfrʌk'tesəns). *Bot. rare.* [a. F. *infructescence* (G. de St. Pierre, 1870), f. IN-^{2} + L. *fructus* fruit, after *inflorescence.*] Name for an aggregate fruit, bearing the same relation to a simple fruit that inflorescence does to a single flower.

1876 HOOKER *Botany Primer* 80 Aggregate fruits or infructescences.

infructiferous (ɪnfrʌk'tɪfərəs), *a. rare.* [f. late L. *infructifer-us* + -OUS: see IN-^{3} and FRUCTIFEROUS.] Not bearing fruit: in quots. of a disease: Not eruptive, or having the eruption imperfect or suppressed.

1822–34 *Good's Study Med.* (ed. 4) II. 404 In the Barbary plague.. the first and second of the two varieties.. the fructiferous and the infructiferous, were intermixed. *Ibid.* 409 In the.. infructiferous variety it was extremely difficult to distinguish between the one [fever] and the other.

infructuose (ɪn,frʌktjuː'əʊs), *a.* [ad. L. *infructuōsus* unfruitful, fruitless: see IN-^{3} and FRUCTUOSE.] Not producing fruit, unfruitful, unprofitable; = INFRUCTUOUS.

1727 BAILEY vol. II, *Infructuose*, unfruitful. **1879** FARRAR *St. Paul* I. 128 These more intellectual Jews were not content with an infructuose Rabbinism.

Hence **infructu'osity**, unfruitfulness, sterility.

1859 *Sat. Rev.* VII. 553/2 The immobility and infructuosity of the parasitic plants which flourish best in the rereward of the Eastern Counties.

infructuous (ɪn'frʌktjuːəs), *a.* [f. as prec.: see IN-^{3} and FRUCTUOUS, and cf. F. *infructueux* (14th c. in Godef. *Compl.*).]

1. Not bearing fruit: unfruitful, barren.

1615 T. ADAMS *Blacke Devill* 48 Even infructuous barrennesse brought Christs curse on the figge tree. **1860** I. TAYLOR *Spir. Hebr. Poetry* (1873) 77 It is these [wild flowers].. that because they are infructuous, are spared by

marauding bands. **1860** FARRAR *Orig. Lang.* (1865) 62 The intellect..would otherwise remain infructuous.

2. Unproductive of good results; fruitless.

1615 T. ADAMS *Lycanthropy* Wks. 1862 II. 120 The wolf living is like Rumney Marsh: *hyeme malus, æstate molestus, nunquam bonus*... Thus every way is this wolf infructuous. **1822** *Blackw. Mag.* XII. 526 [He] is verging towards fatuity from incessant and infructuous exertions. **1884** FAIRBAIRN in *Contemp. Rev.* 357 There are no controversies so wearisome and infructuous as our ecclesiastical.

Hence **in'fructuously** *adv.*, unfruitfully.

1876 C. M. DAVIES *Unorth. Lond.* (ed. 2) 160 Mr. Peacock's cooperage..around which I found I had been infructuously describing a circle. **1887** *N. Amer. Rev.* July 36 He [the actor] soon found that his art was infructuously employed in obtaining applause.

†**in'frugal,** *a. Obs.* [IN-³.] Not frugal; wasteful.

1684 J. GOODMAN *Winter Even. Confer.* (1720) 21 (L.) What should betray them to such infrugal expences of time. **1770** *New Dispens.* 628 This infrugal and injudicious composition.

infru'giferous, *a.* [IN-³.] Not bearing fruit.

1727 BAILEY vol. II, *Infrugiferous*, bearing no Fruit. **1856** in WEBSTER; and in later Dicts.

†**infrunite,** *a. Obs. rare.* [ad. L. (post-Aug.) *infrūnītus* tasteless, senseless, f. *in-* (IN-³) + *frūnisci* to enjoy.] Senseless, silly.

1657 TOMLINSON *Renou's Disp.* Pref., Every Gentleman who is not sottish or infrunite. **1716** M. DAVIES *Athen. Brit.* II. 278 The few Ficulnean Arguments and Infrunite Pamphlets of the Nestorian Arianism and Arian Eutychianism.

infrustrable (ɪn'frʌstrəb(ə)l), *a. rare.* [f. IN-³ + FRUSTRABLE. Cf. obs. F. *infrustrable* (16th c. in Godef.).] Not frustrable; that cannot be frustrated or rendered ineffectual.

1677 GALE *Crt. Gentiles* IV. 354 A wil universally efficacious, infrustrable, indefectible, and necessary in causing. **1892** N. SMYTH *Chr. Ethics* I. iii. 158 A moral order no less infrustrable, and as universal in its dominion.

Hence **in'frustrably** *adv.*, irresistibly.

1861 W. CUNNINGHAM *Theol. Reform.* (1862) 560 The preservation of the whole ship's company..was infallibly and infrustrably certain.

in'fucate, *v. rare*⁻⁰. [f. ppl. stem of L. *infūcāre* (in pa. pple. *infūcātus*); see IN-² and FUCATE *v.*] *trans.* To colour or paint (the face).

1623 COCKERAM, *Infucate*, to paint, to colour. **1676** COLES, *Infucate*, artificially to colour or paint (the face, etc.). **1828** in WEBSTER. Hence in recent Dicts.

Hence †**infu'cation.** *Obs. rare*⁻⁰.

1658 PHILLIPS, *Infucation*, a laying on of drugs, or artificial colours upon the face.

†**in'fude,** *v. Obs.* Pa. t. in 5 infude. [irreg. f. L. *infundĕre*, perf. *infūdī*: see INFUND and INFOUND. Cf. *defude, diffude, effude*.]

1. *trans.* To pour in, infuse; also, to pour (*on*).

1526 *Pilgr. Perf.* (W. de W. 1531) 185 b, He..infudeth or putteth into the soule the admyrable lyght of grace. **1531** ELYOT *Gov.* III. xxiii, God almyghtie infuded Sapience into the Memorye of man. **1566** PAINTER *Pal. Pleas.* I. 78 The same bloude infudeth himselfe into the vpper partes. **1599** tr. *Gabelhouer's Bk. Physicke* 330/2 Let this stande a night, and a daye, then power it of, & infude other water theron.

2. To infuse or inspire (a person) *with*.

c **1460** *Towneley Myst.* xi. 89 Grete well all oure kyn of bloode, That lord, that the with grace infude, he saue all in this place.

‖**infula** ('ɪnfjuːlə). [L. (in sense 1).]

1. *Roman Antiq.* A slightly twisted flock or fillet of red and white wool, worn on the forehead by priests, worshippers, and suppliants, or similarly placed on victims for sacrifice, and used in other ways as a religious symbol.

1727-41 CHAMBERS *Cycl.*, *Infula*, a name antiently given to one of the pontifical ornaments worn on the head. *Ibid.*, The difference between the diadem and the infula consisted in this, that the diadem was flat and broad, and the infula rounded and twisted. **1869** W. SMITH *Dict. Gr. & Rom. Antiq.*, At Roman marriages the bride, who carried wool upon a distaff in the procession, fixed it as an infula upon the door-case of her future husband on entering the house.

2. *Eccl.* Each of the two lappets or ribbons of a bishop's mitre. Also in *Her.*

In med.L. applied also to a chasuble, and in some mediaeval glossaries explained as a mitre or other covering for the head; see Du Cange.

1610 GUILLIM *Heraldry* IV. ii. (1611) 192 This kind of infula or Miter, is worne by the antichristian prelate of Rome. **1848** MRS. JAMESON *Sacr. & Leg. Art* (1850) 404 The infulæ, two bands or lappets, depending from the mitre behind, distinguish the bishop from the abbot. **1882** CUSSANS *Her.* xiv. (ed. 3) 180 From within the circle [of a mitre] depend two *Vittæ*, *Infulæ*, or ribbons of purple fringed at the ends with gold.

†'**infule.** *Obs.* [ad. L. *infula*.] = INFULA 1.

1581 SAVILE *Tacitus, Hist.* III. xxxi. (1591) 132 [They] then hung out ouer the walles their sacred veles and infules. **1600** HOLLAND *Livy* XXX. xxxvi. 765 There met him a ship of the Carthaginians, garnished with infules, ribbands, and white flags of peace. **1606** —— *Sueton.* 126 This man..hee caused to be dight with sacred hearbs, and adorned with Infules, like a sacrifice.

infulminate (ɪn'fʌlmɪneɪt), *v. rare.* [f. IN-² + FULMINATE.] *trans.* To render thunderous.

1808 J. BARLOW *Columb.* III. 20 Where..suns infulminate the stormful sky.

infumate, *v. rare*⁻⁰. [f. ppl. stem of L. *infūmāre* (Pliny), f. *in-* (IN-²) + *fūmāre* to smoke, f. *fūmus* smoke.] *trans.* To smoke (a thing), to dry by smoking. Hence **infumated** *ppl. a.* Also **infu'mation.**

1721 BAILEY, *Infumation*, a drying in the Smoak. **1727** *Ibid.* vol. II, *Infumated*, smoked, dried in the smoke. **1847** CRAIG, *Infumate*, to dry in the smoke.

†**in'fume,** *v.* Var. of ENFUME *v.*

†**in'fund,** *v. Obs.* [ad. L. *infund-ĕre* to pour in, f. *in-* (IN-²) + *fundĕre* to pour. Cf. INFOUND, INFUDE, INFUSE.]

1. *trans.* To pour in; to infuse; to shed, pour (*on*).

1514 *Fruyte Redempcyon* (W. de W.) A iij, Infunde grace, kyndle loue. **1536** BELLENDEN *Cron. Scot.* (1821) II. 207 The kingis servandis..fand the wichis infunding certane liquor on the image. **1559** *Primer* in *Priv. Prayers* (1851) 110 By infunding thy precious oil of comfort into my wounds. **1579** FULKE *Heskins' Parl.* 53 The diuine essens infundeth it selfe in the sacrament. **1611** SPEED *Hist. Gt. Brit.* IX. xviii. (1623) 918 The great grace that God giueth and secretly infundeth.

2. To steep; = INFUSE *v.* 4.

1657 TOMLINSON *Renou's Disp.* 59 Medicaments are infunded, humected and macerated.

†**infundible.** *Obs. rare*⁻¹. [ad. L. *infundibulum*: see below.] A funnel.

1657 TOMLINSON *Renou's Disp.* 481 Infundibles, and many more, which the Apothecary will not use once in a year.

infundibular (ɪnfʌn'dɪbjʊlə(r)), *a.* [f. L. type **infundibulār-is*, f. *infundibulum*: see below and -AR.] Funnel-shaped; infundibuliform.

1795 HOME in *Phil. Trans.* LXXXV. 227 The uterus itself is..infundibular in its shape. **1809** *Ibid.* XCIX. 212 The bladder..opens externally by an infundibular process. **1841-71** T. R. JONES *Anim. Kingd.* (ed. 4) 71 The cell..is seen to be continued inwards by a membranous infundibular prolongation of its margin.

infundibulate (ɪnfʌn'dɪbjʊlət), *a.* [f. INFUNDIBUL-UM + -ATE¹.]

1. Having an infundibulum.

infundibulate Polyzoa, marine Polyzoans, having the cell-mouth circular and funnel-shaped, corresponding to the group Gymnolæmata (Webster, 1864).

2. Funnel-shaped; infundibuliform.

1864 in WEBSTER; hence in later Dicts.

infundibuliform (ɪnfʌn'dɪbjʊlɪfɔːm), *a.* [ad. mod.L. *infundibuliformis*: see next and -FORM.] Funnel-shaped.

[**1708** KERSEY, *Infundibuliformis* (among Herbalists), any Flower that is shap'd like a Funnel.] **1752** SIR J. HILL *Hist. Anim.* 292 The ventral fins coalesce at their extremities, and form a single, oblong hollow, and, in some degree, infundibuliform fin. **1753** CHAMBERS *Cycl. Supp.*, *Infundibuliform* Flowers, or funnel-fashioned flower,..one of the kinds of monopetalous or one-leav'd flowers..having a narrow tube at one end, and a wide mouth at the other. **1791** W. BARTRAM *Carolina* 104 The flowers are very large, infundibuliform, of a pale incarnate colour. **1846** DANA *Zooph.* (1848) 216 Cells..infundibuliform,.. multilamellate.

‖**infundibulum** (ɪnfʌn'dɪbjʊləm). [L., = funnel, f. *infundĕre* to pour in, INFUND + *-bulum*, suffix forming names of instruments.]

†1. A funnel. *Obs. rare*⁻⁰.

1706 PHILLIPS, *Infundibulum* (Lat.), a Tunnel, or Funnel, for the pouring off Liquors into Vessels.

2. *Anat.* Applied to various funnel-shaped cavities or structures of the body.

infundibulum of the brain (*i. cerebri*), a funnel-shaped prolongation downwards and forwards of the third ventricle of the brain, at the extremity of which is the pituitary body. ***i. of the cochlea***, the thin plate of bone, shaped like half a funnel, under the cupola of the cochlea of the ear. ***i. of the ethmoid bone***, the sinuous canal connecting the frontal sinus with the middle meatus of the nose. ***i. of the Fallopian tube***, the fimbriated end of this. ***i. of the heart***, the *conus arteriosus* or conical upper part of the right ventricle. ***infundibula of the kidney***, the two or three main divisions of the pelvis of the kidney, formed by the confluence of the calyces. ***i. of the lungs***, the funnel-shaped sacs in which the air-passages terminate.

[**1706** PHILLIPS, *Infundibulum Cerebri*,..the Brain-Tunnel.] **1799** HOOPER *Med. Dict.*, *Infundibulum of the Brain*, a canal that proceeds from the vulva of the brain to the pituitary gland in the sella turcica. **1883** MARTIN & MOALE *Vertebr. Dissect.* 153 The *infundibulum*, a prolongation of gray matter from the floor of the third ventricle. **1894** *Field* 9 June 850/3 There being no cavity or infundibulum in the incisors of the ox, there is no mark to be worn out.

b. *Zool.* (*a*) 'A tubular organ in the Cephalopoda through which the water is driven from the gills'. (*b*) 'The gastric cavity of Ctenophora with which the œsophageal tube communicates' (*Syd. Soc. Lex.*). (*c*) The dilated upper extremity of the oviduct of a bird.

1877 HUXLEY *Anat. Inv. Anim.* iii. 172 On opposite sides of the infundibulum a canal is given off towards the middle of each half of the body.

†**in'funeral,** *v. Obs. rare*⁻¹. [f. IN-² + FUNERAL *sb.* or *v.*] *trans.* To entomb.

1610 G. FLETCHER *Christ's Vict.* I. lxvi, Disconsolat (As though her flesh did but infunerall Her buried ghost) she in an arbour sat..weeping her cursed state.

infurcation (ɪnfɜː'keɪʃən). [f. IN-² + L. *furca* fork: cf. FURCATION.] 'A forked expansion' (Craig, 1847).

in'furiant, *sb.* [f. pr. ppl. stem of med.L. *infuriāre*: see INFURIATE *v.*] Something that infuriates; an object, fact, condition, etc., which excites to anger or passion.

1953 K. AMIS *Lucky Jim* viii. 87 The sight of Welch's 'bag' and fishing-hat on a nearby chair, normally a certain infuriant, only made him hum his Welch tune. **1960** *Guardian* 7 Dec. 8/3 There would be a reasonable chance of the races working happily together if only the infuriant of Federation were removed.

infuriate (ɪn'fjʊərɪət), *a.* [ad. med.L. *infuriāt-us*, pa. pple. of *infuriāre*, f. *in-* (IN-²) + *furiāre* to madden, enrage, f. *furia* FURY. Cf. It. *infuriare* to grow into fury or rage (Florio).]

Excited to fury; maddened; full of fury; enraged, raging, frantic, furious. (Of persons and their actions, animals, etc.; *fig.* of things.)

1667 MILTON *P.L.* VI. 486 Hollow Engins long and round Thick-rammd, at th' other bore with touch of fire Dilated and infuriate. **1727-46** THOMSON *Summer* 1096 Th' infuriate hil that shoots the pillar'd flame. **1730-46** —— *Autumn* 39 Inflam'd, beyond the most infuriate wrath Of the worst monster that e'er roamed the waste. **1824** DIBDIN *Libr. Comp.* 594 The infuriate and unrelenting opponent of Nash. **1862** MERIVALE *Rom. Emp.* xxiv. (1865) III. 114 The Roman people..were so infuriate against Caesar's destroyers.

Hence **in'furiately** *adv.*, in an infuriate manner, furiously.

1879 G. MEREDITH *Egoist* I. vii. 121. **1896** A. MORRISON *Child Jago* 134 Billy Leary fought and battered infuriately.

infuriate (ɪn'fjʊərɪeɪt), *v.* [f. ppl. stem of med.L. *infuriāre* to madden; see prec.] *trans.* To fill with fury; to render furious or mad with anger; to provoke to fury or fierce passion; to enrage.

1667 *Decay Chr. Piety* xii. 322 Like those curles of entangled snakes with which Erinnys is said to have infuriated Athemas and Ino. **1870** DICKENS *E. Drood* viii, This insulting allusion to his dark skin infuriates Neville.

Hence **in'furiating** *ppl. a.*; **in'furiatingly** *adv.*; also **infuri'ation**, the action of maddening, infuriated condition.

1851 KINGSLEY *Yeast* i. (1853) 17 He rolled about like a tipsy man..to the utter infuriation of Shiver-the-timbers. **1885** LUCAS MALET *Col. Enderby's Wife* (ed. 3) III. VI. i. 61 He was so infuriatingly calm. **1891** MISS DOWIE *Girl in Karp.* 166, I looked back and saw the painter making cigarettes..It was infuriating!

infuriated (ɪn'fjʊərɪeɪtɪd), *ppl. a.* [f. prec. + -ED¹.] Provoked to fury; maddened with passion; furiously enraged.

1796 BURKE *Regic. Peace* ii. Wks. VIII. 238 They tore the reputation of the clergy to pieces by their infuriated declamations and invectives. **1832** *Blackw. Mag.* XXXII. 965 Not an infuriate, observe, but an infuriated mob—rendered infuriate. **1848** MRS. JAMESON *Sacr. & Leg. Art* (1850) 316 Whereupon he was condemned to death, and stoned by the infuriated people.

†**in'furnace,** *v. Obs. rare*⁻¹. [f. IN-² + FURNACE.] *trans.* To place in a furnace.

1621 G. SANDYS *Ovid's Met.* VII. (1626) 129 As puluer'd flints, infurnest vnder ground, By sprinkled water fire conceiue.

infurþe, in *with infurþe*: see WITHINFORTH.

infuscate (ɪn'fʌskət), *a.* [ad. L. *infuscāt-us*, pa. pple.: see next.] Clouded or darkened.

1826 KIRBY & SP. *Entomol.* IV. 292 *Infuscate*, when a colour is darkened by the superinduction of a brownish shade or cloud.

†**in'fuscate,** *v. Obs.* [f. ppl. stem of L. *infuscā-re*, f. *in-* (IN-²) + *fuscāre*, f. *fuscus* dark-brown, dusky.] *trans.* To make dark-coloured or dusky; to darken. Hence **in'fuscated** *ppl. a.*

1650 tr. *Caussin's Ang. Peace* 90 The eternall City..was infuscated with the sooty vapours of a brutish Warre. **1727** BAILEY vol. II, *Infuscated*, made obscure, dark, black, etc.

†**infu'scation.** *Obs. rare*⁻⁰. [n. of action from L. *infuscāre*: see prec.] The action of darkening; darkened or dusky condition.

1658 PHILLIPS, *Infuscation*, a making dark or dusky. **1755** in JOHNSON; and in mod. Dicts.

†**in'fuse,** *sb. Obs.* [ad. L. *infūs-us* a pouring in, f. ppl. stem of *infundĕre*: see INFUSE *v.*] = INFUSION.

1568 TURNER *Herbal* III. 47 In the infuse they are taken from iii aureis [= $1\frac{1}{2}$ drams each] untill sixe. **1596** SPENSER *Hymn Heav. Love* 47 Some little drop of thy celestiall dew, That may my rymes with sweet infuse embrew.

†**in'fuse**, *a. Obs.* [a. F. *infus*, *-e* (13th c. in Hatz.-Darm.), ad. L. *infūsus*, pa. pple. of *infundĕre* to pour in: see next.] = INFUSED.

1502 *Ord. Crysten Men* I. v. (W. de W. 1506) 48 There ben thre vertues theologales & infuses. That is to knowe fayth, charyte, & hope, the whiche ben called infuses, for that yᵉ whan yᵉ soule is puryfyed by baptem from orygynall synne god createth & putteth these thre vertues in the soule. *c* **1540** in *Vicary's Anat.* (1888) App. ix. 220 Take malvesie and white wyne, of eche a pynte, and styrre all these to-guether, and lett them stande infuse two or thre dayes.

infuse (ɪn'fjuːz), *v.* Also 6 en-. [f. L. *infūs-*, ppl. stem of *infundĕre* to pour in (see INFUND), or a. F. *infuser* (15–16th c. in Hatz.-Darm.).]

1. *trans.* To pour in: †to pour (a liquid) *into* a place or vessel (*obs.*); to introduce (a liquid ingredient).

1432–50 tr. *Higden* (Rolls) I. 61 The occean infusede in to diuerse places. *a* **1625** SIR W. MURE *Misc. Poems* xx. 14 Tho springs and founts infuis thair liquid stoir. **1637** HEYWOOD *Dial.* ii. Wks. 1874 VI. 128 'Tis of great consequence, what is infus'd Into a Vessell when it first is vs'd. **1713** STEELE *Guardian* No. 142 ⁋3 The one as greedily sucks in the poison, as the other industriously infuses it. **1726** SWIFT *Gulliver* I. i, By the force of that soporiferous medicine infused into my liquor. **1815** W. H. IRELAND *Scribbleomania* 70 The..charm of nobility infused its balsam as an ingredient into the dose of criticism. **1908** *Amer. Jrnl. Physiol.* XXI. 144 Saline was infused into a vein. **1972** *Sci. Amer.* May 75/1 Intravenous feeding had its beginning in 1843, when the French physiologist Claude Bernard infused sugar solutions into the veins of animals.

2. *transf.* and *fig.* **a.** To introduce as by pouring; to instil, insinuate. Used spec. of the work of God in the imparting of grace, and of nature in the implanting of innate knowledge. Const. *into* (*in*, †*to*).

1526 *Pilgr. Perf.* (W. de W. 1531) 104 b, This holy gyfte of pite..is infused in to the soule of man or woman with grace. **1583** STANYHURST *Æneis* I. (Arb.) 40 Venus enfuseth sweet sleepe to the partye resembled. **1588** SHAKS. *Tit. A.* I. i. 461 These words, these lookes, Infuse new life in me. **1605** JAMES I *Gunpowder Plot* in *Harl. Misc.* (Malh.) III. 11 All knowledge must be either infused or acquired. **1642** GATAKER *Transubst.* 129 Infants have an habite of faith infused into them in Baptisme. **1781** GIBBON *Decl. & F.* xviii. (1869) I. 476 He infused his own intrepid spirit into the troops. **1858** BUCKLE *Civiliz.* (1873) II. viii. 560 He..as far as he was able, infused new life into the old universities.

refl. **1551** GARDINER *Explic.* 127 b, The diuinite ineffably infused it selfe in to the visible Sacrament. **1596** SHAKS. *Merch. V.* IV. i. 132. **1855** PUSEY *Doctr. Real Presence* Note S. 659 Consider how He abideth in us..infusing Himself into our bodies.

†**b.** To instil or try to instil a notion or belief.

1548 HALL *Chron.*, *Hen. VI* 158 b, Infusyng and puttyng into mens heades..his right to yᵉ crown. **1623** *Dk. Buckhm.'s Narrative* in Rushw. *Hist. Coll.* (1659) I. 122 Gondomar privately infused to the Prince his Highness.. That the Duke was in heart..a Roman Catholick. *a* **1715** BURNET *Own Time* I. 31 They..took care to infuse it into all people..that all was done to make way for Popery.

†**3.** To pour *on* or *upon*; to shed, diffuse. *Obs.*

c **1420** *Pallad. on Husb.* III. 755 Yf ofte vppon the rootes as they stonde, The boles galle enfusid be. **1591** SHAKS. *1 Hen. VI*, I. ii. 85 With those cleare Rayes, which shee infus'd on me, That beautie am I blest with, which you may see. **1601** HOLLAND *Pliny* II. 351 The white of an egg..ought to be infused, or spread vpon the foresaid wooll, with the pouder of Frankincense. *a* **1672** STERRY *2nd Posth. Vol.* (1680) 323 Choice Meats infuse all their pleasant Tastes and Relishes distinctly upon the curious Palate of the Eater.

4. a. To steep or drench (a plant, etc.) in a liquid, so as to extract its soluble properties; to macerate.

1533 ELYOT *Cast. Helthe* (1541) 58 a, Reubarbarum by it selfe from two drammes unto foure, infused or stiped in lycour, from iiii drammes unto viii. **1593** HYLL *Art Garden.* 126 To make Artichocks..grow sweet in tast, infuse the seeds before, in either milke, with hony, or in water with sugar, or els in pleasant wine. **1646** SIR T. BROWNE *Pseud. Ep.* VI. xii. 337 The filings of Iron infused in vinegar, will with a decoction of galles make good Inke, without any copperose at all. **1756** C. LUCAS *Ess. Waters* I. 82 They infuse the ashes of burned vegetables in their water. **1830** M. DONOVAN *Dom. Econ.* I. 293 Strawberry or Raspberry Wine Bruise six gallons of either fruit; press out the juice; on the marc pour seven gallons of water; infuse for twelve hours, and press out the liquor. **1890** BARRIE *Little Minister* (1892) 261 While I am infusing my tea.

†**b.** To dissolve or melt. *Obs.*

1607 TOPSELL *Four-f. Beasts* (1658) 322 Take of mel rosatum, oyl of roses, wax, and turpentine, of each, like quantity: infuse them all on the fire together.

c. *intr.* To undergo the process of infusion or maceration.

1615 LATHAM *Falconry* (1633) 105 You must prouide some distilled water of endiue, and succorie..and into the same put a slice of rubarbe to infuse. **1799** G. SMITH *Laboratory* II. 397 Leave it to infuse till the next day. **1885** R. BUCHANAN *Annan Water* vii, 'The pot's infusing at the kitchen fire, and I'll fetch it in mysel'.

5. With inverted constr.: To affect or act upon (a liquid) by steeping some soluble substance in it; hence, to imbue or inspire (a person or thing) *with* some infused quality. In wider use, to impregnate, pervade, imbue (*with* some quality, opinion, etc.).

1560 *Proud wyues Pater noster* 529 in Hazl. *E.P.P.* IV. 176 Infuse vs with grace, Lorde, in contynaunce. **1592** SHAKS. *Ven. & Ad.* 928 Infusing them with dreadfull prophecies. **1602** MARSTON *Antonio's Rev.* IV. iv, Would I had some poyson to infuse it with. **1610** SHAKS. *Temp.* I. ii. 154 Thou didst smile, Infused with a fortitude from heauen. **1626** BACON *Sylva* (J.), Drink, infused with flesh, will nourish faster and easier than meat and drink together. **1871** L. STEPHEN *Playgr. Europe* v. II. 305 The excessive difficulty of infusing young mountaineers with a proper sense of responsibility. **1900** *Westm. Gaz.* 29 Jan. 1/3 The cant with which the political history of the war is infused and suffused. **1928** *Observer* 5 Feb. 11/4 The splendid camaraderie and corporate spirit which infuse a newspaper staff.

Hence **in'fusing** *vbl. sb.*

1598 FLORIO, *Infusura*, an infusing. **1680–90** TEMPLE *Ess.*, *Health* Misc. 1701 III. 193 The Physician..whose greatest Skill perhaps often lies in the infusing of Hopes.

infused (ɪn'fjuːzd), *ppl. a.* [f. prec. + -ED[1].]

1. Poured in, instilled: *spec.* imparted by divine influence, or by nature. *lit.* and *fig.*

1577 VAUTROUILLIER *Luther on Ep. Gal.* 63 For that worke he poureth into him charitie, which they call charitie infused. **1598** FLORIO, *Infuso*, infused, melted, powred in. **1607–12** BACON *Ess.*, *Cust. & Educ.* (Arb.) 366/1 Mens.. speaches [are] according to theire learninges and infused opinions. **1662** EVELYN *Chalcogr.* (1769) 24 Nor do we think that his [Adam's] unhappy fall did so much concern his rare and infused habits. **1811** *Monthly Mag.* XXXIV. 403 The.. lungs..were totally black from infused blood into the hair cells. **1891** CHURCH *Oxford Movem.* xvii. 307 A doctrine.. which substituted a fictitious and imputed righteousness for an inherent and infused and real one.

2. Steeped in liquid so as to impart its qualities.

1707 *Curios. in Husb. & Gard.* 144 Cover it with good Brandy four Inches above the infus'd Matter. **1853** SOYER *Pantroph.* 92 Ginger is taken infused as a drink.

Hence **in'fusedly** *adv.*, in an infused manner.

1620 GRANGER *Div. Logike* 59 The receptacle of adjuncts inherent..ingendred naturally, infusedly, habitually in it.

infuser (ɪn'fjuːzə(r)). [f. INFUSE *v.* + -ER[1].]

1. One who infuses or pours in. Chiefly *fig.*

1598 FLORIO, *Infonditore*, an infuser, a melter, a powrer in. **1615** J. WHITE *Serm.* 33 Thou o blessed Trinitie, the sole infuser of grace. **1828** *Mirror* V. 334/2 The infuser of joy in our home. **1868** MISS YONGE *Pupils St. John* xvii. 278 James of Nisibis was the great infuser of this spirit.

2. A vessel for making infusions; †*spec.* a retort.

1688 R. HOLME *Armoury* III. 398/1 An Infuser, or a Glass Body with a long Neck..also termed a Distillatory. **1899** *Advt.*, Tea Infuser, Patent, White China.

infusibility[1] (ɪnfjuːzɪ'bɪlɪtɪ). [f. INFUSIBLE *a.*[1]: see -ITY, and cf. F. *infusibilité* (18th c. in Hatz.-Darm.).] The quality or fact of being infusible; incapability of being fused or melted.

1796 KIRWAN *Elem. Min.* (ed. 2) I. 42 The calcination, infusibility or fusibility, at different degrees measured by Mr. Wedgwood's Pyrometer. **1816** CLEAVELAND *Min.* 264 It differs from feldspar by its greater hardness and its infusibility. **1831** CARLYLE *Ess.*, *Schiller* (1872) III. 95 To the last, there is a stiffness in him, a certain infusibility.

infusible (ɪn'fjuːzɪb(ə)l), *a.*[1] [f. IN-[3] + FUSIBLE. Cf. F. *infusible* (1760 in Hatz.-Darm.).] Not fusible; incapable of being fused or melted.

1555 EDEN *Decades* 341 An earthye substaunce infusible and not able to bee molten. **1650** SIR T. BROWNE *Pseud. Ep.* II. i. (1659) 40 Vitrification is..a fusion of the salt and earth ..wherein the fusible salt draws the earth and infusible part into one continuum. **1796** KIRWAN *Elem. Min.* (ed. 2) I. 6 Pure lime, except placed in clay, is infusible. **1870** J. YEATS *Nat. Hist. Comm.* 112 The infusible and rare metal platinum.

fig. **1877** OWEN *Mrq. Wellesley's Desp.* Introd. 44 The beauty of the style, unimpaired..by the amalgam of infusible Orientalisms.

Hence **in'fusibleness**, the quality of being infusible.

In recent Dicts.

in'fusible, *a.*[2] *rare*⁻¹. [ad. L. type **infūsibilis*, f. ppl. stem of L. *infundĕre* to pour in: see INFUSE.] Capable of being infused.

a **1660** HAMMOND (J.), The doctrines being infusible into all.

Hence **infusi'bility**[2].

1828 in WEBSTER; and in mod. Dicts.

in'fusile, *a. rare.* [f. IN-[3] + FUSILE.] Not fusile; not having the quality of fusing.

1825 COLERIDGE in *Lit. Rem.* (1836) II. 347 The uncombining and infusile genius of our language.

infusion (ɪn'fjuːʒən). [a. F. *infusion* (13th c. in Hatz.-Darm.), or immediately ad. L. *infūsiōn-em*, n. of action f. *infundĕre* to pour in: see INFUSE.]

1. The action of pouring in (a liquid), or fact of being poured in; that which is poured in. Now chiefly *fig.*, as in 'the infusion of new blood', which passes into 5.

1532 MORE *Confut. Tindale* Wks. 491/2 Our sauiour himselfe..did put water in to wyne, thoughe there was no mencion made therof in the writing, no more then there was of diuers other thynges..Of whych thynges this infusion of water is one. **1594** T. B. *La Primaud. Fr. Acad.* I. Ep. Ded., When Gods will is to have His children nourished with the ..unmingled milke of His word, dare man use the infusion of water, to the weakening of them? **1709** STEELE *Tatler* No. 131 ⁋7 Another [cyder], with a less quantity of the same infusion, would rise into a dark purple. *a* **1716** SOUTH *Twelve Serm.* (1717) VI. 396 We all know, that we may infuse, what we will into an empty Vessel, but a full one has no room for a farther Infusion. **1853** J. H. NEWMAN *Hist. Sk.* (1876) II. I. iv. 216 The continual infusion into it of new blood to perform its functions.

b. *spec.* in *Surg.* Injection: see quots.

1601 HOLLAND *Pliny* II. Explan. Words, *Infusion* signifieth the conueiance of some medicinable liquour into the body by clystre or other instrument. **1886** *Syd. Soc. Lex.*, *Infusion*,..in Surgery, the act of introducing medicinal substances into the veins by means of the Infusor, or into these or other cavities, or into the parenchyma of organs, by hydrostatic pressure.

2. The action of infusing some principle, quality, or idea, into the mind, soul, or heart; esp. the imparting of *a priori* ideas or of divine grace: see quots. 1857, 1875.

c **1450** tr. *De Imitatione* II. xii. 56 In þe crosse is infusion of hevenly swetnes. **1526** *Pilgr. Perf.* (W. de W. 1531) 149 Whiche inspiracyon..is none other but a infusyon of a spiritual grace. **1622** T. SCOTT *Belg. Pismire* 41 Neither hath he his art altogether by infusion, but by instruction, and experience. **1675** BROOKS *Gold. Key* Wks. 1867 V. 231 How is Christ made righteousness to the believer? Not by infusion, but imputation; not by putting righteousness into him, but by putting a righteousness upon him. **1727–46** THOMSON *Spring* 587 No sooner grows The soft infusion prevalent and wide, Than, all alive, at once their joy o'erflows In music unconfin'd. **1857** T. E. WEBB *Intellectualism Locke* iii. 47 The doctrine of Infusion—the doctrine which regarded our *a priori* Ideas as infused into the Intellect by an act of God. **1875** MANNING *Mission H. Ghost* v. 135 This lifelong increase of charity in the soul is wrought..by gift and infusion on God's part.

†**b.** Insidious suggestion, insinuation. *Obs.*

a **1635** NAUNTON *Fragm. Reg.* (Arb.) 52 The greater error of the two (though unwillingly) I am constrained to impose on my Lord of Essex, or rather on his youth;..But, to omitthat of infusion [etc.]. **1647** CLARENDON *Hist. Reb.* I. §143 By the infusions he made into King James..he did all he could to discountenance that Party. **1756** JOHNSON *Life Browne* Wks. IV. 595 Not watchful against the power of his infusions. **1769** ROBERTSON *Chas. V*, III. VII. 41 [They] contributed by their infusions [*later edd.* suggestions] to sour and disgust him still more.

†**c.** Infused temperament; character imparted by nature. *Obs. rare.* Cf. INFUSIONISM.

1602 SHAKS. *Ham.* V. ii. 122 His infusion of such dearth and rareness.

†**3.** The action of pouring or shedding forth; that which is poured forth; outpouring, effusion. *Obs.*

1563 W. FULKE *Meteors* (1571) 39 Possidonius..saide, it [the milky way] is the infusion of the heate of sterres.

4. The process of pouring water over a substance, or steeping the substance in water, in order to impregnate the liquid with its properties or virtues. †Formerly, also, the dissolving of a salt or other soluble substance.

1573 TWYNE *Æneid* XII. Mmj b, The same [Dittany] Dame Venus thyther bringes, And into water vessels bright it secretly she flinges, And makes therof Infusion [*later edd.* steeping] large, the vertue forth to take. **1612** WOODALL *Surg. Mate* Wks. (1653) 272 Infusion is the preparation of medicaments, cut or bruised in some humidity convenient for the purpose, a lesser or longer time. **1653** WALTON *Angler* vi. 139 Oil of Ivy-berries, made by expression or infusion. **1676** GREW *Exp. Solut. Salts* i. §28 Not only in the Infusion of several Ingredients together, but of any one singly, that such a proportion thereof to the Menstruum be not exceeded. **1707** *Curios. in Husb. & Gard.* 122 After this Time of Infusion, separate the Water from the Substances. **1831** J. DAVIES *Manual Mat. Med.* 37 By infusion, that is, by pouring a liquid, more or less heated, on the substance from which we wish to extract the remedial principles.

b. A dilute liquid extract obtained from a substance by soaking it with, or steeping it in, water; also any water containing dissolved organic (esp. vegetable) matter, such as that in which *Infusoria* are found.

c **1550** LLOYD *Treas. Health*, *Aphorisms Hippocrites* C v, The infusion of hyera healeth the melancolike paynes of the head. **1626** BACON *Sylva* §18 For the Preparations of Medicines and other Infusions. **1684** BOYLE *Porousn. Anim. Bod.* iii. 26 Clothes or spunges wetted in Infusion of Tobacco. **1789** W. BUCHAN *Dom. Med.* (1790) 311 An infusion of the bark, or other bitters, in small wine,..may be drank for some time. **1826** HENRY *Elem. Chem.* II. 520 If the colour of the infusion tend too much to purple, it may be amended by a drop or two of solution of pure ammonia. **1828** STARK *Elem. Nat. Hist.* II. 451 *M*[*onas*] *termo*,.. Found in vegetable and animal infusions. **1869** tr. *Pouchet's Universe* (1871) 9 Many of these creatures do not live in infusions, but on the contrary, inhabit the sea and fresh water. **1871** TYNDALL *Fragm. Sc.* (1879) II. xiii. 295 The infusions continued unchanged for months.

5. The action of infusing or introducing a modifying element or new characteristic; an infused element, admixture, tincture.

1626 BACON *Sylva* §805 The Aire (no doubt) receiueth great Tincture and Infusion from the Earth. **1727** SWIFT *Let. Eng. Tongue* Wks. 1755 II. I. 187 During the usurpation, such an infusion of enthusiastic jargon prevailed in every writing. **1788** BURKE *Corr.* (1844) III. 82 Too great an infusion of various and heterogeneous opinions may embarrass that decision. **1822** LAMB *Elia* Ser. I. *Some Old Actors*, He..was a gentleman with a slight infusion of the footman. **1881** WESTCOTT & HORT *Grk. N.T.* II. Introd. §193 Absence of all the ancient texts..with an increasing infusion of the late Syrian readings.

6. The action of pouring on water in baptism, as opposed to *immersion*; = AFFUSION.

1751–73 JORTIN *Eccl. Hist.* (R.), Baptism by infusion began to be introduced in cold climates. **1879** W. HEPWORTH in *Encycl. Brit.* IX. 361/2 Originally used only for sick or infirm persons, the method of baptism by infusion became gradually the established practice.

7. *attrib.*, as **infusion-jar**: see quot.

1886 *Syd. Soc. Lex.*, *Infusion jar*, an apparatus in which to prepare an infusion;..an earthenware jug containing a strainer on which to receive the material to be dealt with.

infusionism (ɪnˈfjuːʒənɪz(ə)m). [f. prec. + -ISM.] The doctrine that the soul is a divine emanation, infused into the body at conception or birth.

1884 in *Cassell's Encycl. Dict.*

So **inˈfusionist**, an adherent of this doctrine.

1893 MYERS *Sc. & Future Life* 59 Infusionists have held that the soul pre-existed elsewhere, but was infused into the body at some given moment.

infusive (ɪnˈfjuːsɪv), *a.* [f. L. *infūs-*, ppl. stem of L. *infundĕre* to pour in + -IVE.]

1. Having the quality or power of infusing.

1728–46 THOMSON *Spring* 867 Still let my song a nobler note assume, And sing th' infusive force of Spring on Man. **1879** FARRAR *St. Paul* (1883) 315 The infusive virulence of sins which..strike their venom and infix their cancer into the soul.

†**2.** Characterized by being naturally or divinely infused (see INFUSION 2); innate. *Obs.*

1630 BRATHWAIT *Eng. Gentlem.* 30 To treat of the Dispositions of mens mindes, it is strange to see what difference appeares in them (even by natural and infusive motion).

infusor (ɪnˈfjuːzə(r), -sə(r)). [a. L. *infūsor*, agent-n. f. *infundĕre* to pour in: see INFUSE.] One who or that which infuses; *spec.*: see quot.

1886 *Syd. Soc. Lex.*, *Infusor*,..an instrument proposed by Hunter for the introduction of blood or other nutritive substances into the tissues. It consists of an open glass tube ..[with] an india-rubber tube..to which is attached a hollow metallic needle containing 45 or 50 apertures.

‖**infusoria** (ɪnfjuːˈsɔərɪə), *sb. pl.* [Neuter pl. (sc. *animalcula*) of mod.L. *infūsōrius* INFUSORY; in Ger. *infusorien*, F. *infusoires*: the name *animalcula infusoria* was first used by Ledermuller of Nürnberg, 1760–63.]

A class of Protozoa, comprising ciliated, tentaculate, and flagellate animalcula, essentially unicellular, free-swimming, or sedentary; so called because found in infusions of decaying animal or vegetable matter.

Originally, as constituted by O.F. Müller, the *Infusoria* comprehended an assemblage of minute, usually microscopic, organisms, of many diverse kinds, including some now classed as vegetables, as the *Diatomaceæ* and the *Desmidiaceæ*. As now limited, the *Infusoria* are Protozoa characterized by a half-liquid endosarc, a firm cortical ectosarc, an outer membraneous cuticle, a mouth and anus, and a contractile vesicle which injects fluid. They were regarded by Huxley as a primary group in the animal kingdom.

[**1765** WISSBERG (*title*) Observationes de Animalculis Infusoriis. (8vo Göttingen). **1786** O. F. MÜLLER (*title*) Animalcula Infusoria fluviatilia et marina (4to Havniæ et Leipzig).] **1787** G. ADAMS *Ess. Microsc.* (1798) 416 The animalcula infusoria take their name from their being found in all kinds either of vegetable or animal infusions. **1798** F. KANMACHER *ibid.* 428 *note*, Nor is the celerity of the various species of animalcula infusoria less deserving of admiration. **1819** *Pantologia*, *Infusoria*, an order of the class vermes; consisting of minute, simple animalcules, seldom visible to the naked eye. **1832** LYELL *Princ. Geol.* II. 12 Why are there still such multitudes of infusoria and polypes, or of confervæ and other cryptogamic plants? **1834** A. PRITCHARD (*title*) A History of the Infusoria. **1845** DARWIN *Voy. Nat.* i. (1879) 5 Professor Ehrenberg finds that this dust consists in great part of infusoria with siliceous shields. **1880** W. SAVILLE KENT (*title*) A Manual of the Infusoria, including a description of all known Flagellate, Ciliate, and Tentaculiferous Protozoa.

infusorial (ɪnfjuːˈsɔərɪəl), *a.* [f. prec. + -AL¹.] Of or pertaining to the Infusoria; consisting of or formed by Infusoria.

1846 in WORCESTER. **1851–6** WOODWARD *Mollusca* i. 4 Commencing with the Infusorial monad, we may ascend.. by a succession of closely allied forms, to the sea-urchin and holothuria. **1853** KANE *Grinnell Exp.* xviii. 139 The.. remarkable infusorial dust on the coast of Africa. **1869** E. A. PARKES *Pract. Hygiene* (ed. 3) 358 To check the growth of fungoid or infusorial organisms. **1871** TYNDALL *Fragm. Sc.* (1879) I. v. 176 You find the putrefying substance swarming with infusorial life. **1876** PAGE *Adv. Text-bk. Geol.* xix. 363 Among the most remarkable features of foreign tertiaries are the infusorial and foraminiferal strata. **1882** GEIKIE *Text-bk. Geol.* III. II. iii. §3. 461 'Infusorial' earth and 'tripoli powder' consist mainly of frustules and fragmentary debris of diatoms which have accumulated on the bottoms of lacustrine areas.

infusorian (ɪnfjuːˈsɔərɪən), *a.* and *sb.* [f. as prec. + -AN.]

A. *adj.* Of or pertaining to the Infusoria.

1859 TODD *Cycl. Anat.* V. 8/1 A spherical infusorian animalcule. **1872** NICHOLSON *Palæont.* 59 The large and universally-distributed class of the Infusorian Animalcules.

B. *sb.* A member of the Infusoria.

1859 TODD *Cycl. Anat.* V. 7/2 An aperture..formed in the wall of the infusorian. **1877** W. THOMSON *Voy. Challenger* I. iii. 186 One of the Spirula shells was covered with a beautiful stalked infusorian.

infusoriform (ɪnfjuːˈsɔərɪfɔːm), *a.* [f. as prec. + -FORM. repr. G. *infusorienartig* infusorian-like (A. Kölliker 1849, in *Ber. von der k. zootomischen Anstalt zu Würzburg* II. 61).] Having the form of an infusorian. Usu. *spec.* designating or pertaining to a stage in the life-cycle of species of the order Dicyemida (phylum Mesozoa), which comprises parasites of certain cephalopods.

1877 HUXLEY *Anat. Inv. Anim.* xi. 654 The embryos are of two kinds, the one vermiform, the other infusoriform. **1877** *Q. Jrnl. Microsc. Sci.* XVII. 143 The infusoriform embryo probably distributes the species by transmitting the parasite from one cephalopod to another. **1883** *Mitt. Zool. Station zu Neapel* IV. 41 The infusoriform embryos desert the parent before the development of vermiform embryos begins. **1940** L. H. HYMAN *Invertebrates* I. iv. 236 The infusoriform stage is an asexual larva. **1964** T. C. CHENG *Biol. Animal Parasites* vii. 179/1 The infusoriform larvae escape from the parent rhombogen and leave the host. **1967** H. W. & L. R. LEVI tr. *Kaestner's Invertebr. Zool.* I. ii. 21 Only after fertilization do the ova detach, each developing into a short, egg-shaped dispersing infusoriform dicyemid.

infusorigen (ɪnfjuːˈsɔərɪdʒɪn). *Zool.* [f. *infusori-* (repr. INFUSORIFORM *a.*) + -GEN.] A hermaphroditic group of cells formed within a rhombogen during the life-cycle of species of the order Dicyemida (phylum Mesozoa) and giving rise to infusoriform larvæ.

1883 C. O. WHITMAN in *Mitt. Zool. Station zu Neapel* IV. 38 The entire cell-group may be called the Infusorigen, a term used by Van Beneden as a synonym for Rhomb gen. *Ibid.* 39 There arise in the course of the history of every Infusorigen two nuclei. **1940** L. H. HYMAN *Invertebrates* I. iv. 239 After having given off a succession of pseudo-eggs, the infusorigens degenerate. **1964** T. C. CHENG *Biol. Animal Parasites* vii. 179/1 Most authorities on the Mesozoa now agree that infusorigens are hermaphrodites. **1972** *Sci. Amer.* Dec. 95/3 Some of the axoblasts, instead of developing into vermiform embryos, develop into a structure that remains within the axial cell of the adult vermiform and may be thought of as a hermaphroditic gonad. The term infusorigen has been applied to this structure, which in a sense is the only organ the Mesozoa possess.

infusorioid (ɪnfjuːˈsɔərɪɔɪd), *a.* [f. INFUSORI(A *sb. pl.* + -OID.] Resembling an infusorian.

1853 A. HENFREY tr. *Braun's Phenomenon of Rejuvenescence in Nature* 281 Active, Infusorioid structures ..occur not unfrequently in the interior of decaying cells of green fresh-water Algæ.

‖**infusorium** (ɪnfjuːˈsɔərɪəm). [mod.L., sing. of INFUSORIA. Cf. F. *infusoire*.] An individual animalcule of the Infusoria.

1876 LANKESTER *Hist. Creation* I. i. 8 The coming into existence of a natural body, for example, of a crystal, a fungus, an infusorium, depends merely upon the different particles, which had before existed in a certain form or combination. **1879** H. SPENCER *Data Ethics* ii. 10 An infusorium swims randomly about.

infusory (ɪnˈfjuːsərɪ), *a.* and *sb.* [ad. L. type *infūsōrius, f. *infūs-*, ppl. stem of *infundĕre* to pour in: see -ORY.]

A. *adj.* †**1.** Of or pertaining to (surgical) infusion or injection. *Obs.*

1684 tr. *Bonet's Merc. Compit.* XI. 374 An Epistle.. concerning Transfusion of bloud, and infusory Chirurgery.

2. = INFUSORIAL.

1826 GOOD *Bk. Nat.* II. 20 The fifth or infusory order of worms, comprehends those minute and simple animalcules which are seldom capable of being traced, except by a microscope. **1855** H. SPENCER *Princ. Psychol.* (1872) I. III. ii. 298 The infusory animalcule.

B. *sb.* A member of the Infusoria.

1835 KIRBY *Hab. & Inst. Anim.* I. ii. 135 Those that are termed Infusories; because they are usually found in infusions of various substances. **1857** GOSSE *Creation* 227 It was a swimming Infusory with a broad ciliated disk. **1863** *Possibil. Creation* 219 Nature appears to have taken as much pains with the humblest infusory as with the stateliest camelopard.

ing (ɪŋ). *local.* Forms: 5 enge, 5–6 ynge, 6 yng, 7– ing(e. [a. ON. *eng* f., *enge*, *engi* neut. (Da. *eng*, Sw. *äng*), meadow, meadow-land; co-radicate with OHG. *angar*, MHG. *anger* grass land, meadow-land. (Not recorded in OE.)] A common name in the north of England, and in some other parts, for a meadow; esp. one by the side of a river and more or less swampy or subject to inundation.

1483 *Cath. Angl.* 115/1 Enge, *vbi* a medew. **1494** in *Ripon Ch. Acts* (Surtees) 261 Elsay ynges. **1583** *Ibid.* 381 A lease of Swilinge yng; the lease of Bushop yng. **1626** *Quarter Sessions Rec.* III. (North Riding Rec. Soc.) 14 A common waie for leading corne and haie for the inhabitants of Great Broughton from their inges and feildes to the said towne, and for their cariages to the mill. **1663** *MS. Indenture, Barlby, Yks.*, 2 half acres of meadow in the broad ing in Angram. **1793** *Act 33 Geo. III*, c. xci. *title*, An act for dividing..the commons and waste grounds and ings, or meadow grounds, within the township of Knottingley, in the west riding of the county of York. **1828** *Craven Dial.*, *Ing*, a marshy meadow. **1848** C. BRONTË *J. Eyre* ix, Mists as chill as death..rolled down 'ing' and holm till they blended with the frozen fog of the beck. **1851** *Jrnl. R. Agric. Soc.* XII. II. 314 Others [Fens] termed 'ings', belonging to various towns, yet remain (at particular seasons) in a wet condition. **1875** PARISH *Sussex Gloss.*, *Ing*, a common, pasture, or meadow. *c* **1890** *Newspr.*, This morning there is fully 5 ft. of 'fresh' in the Derwent, and the river is still rising. In the ings and marshes of the East Riding the river is over the banks.

b. *attrib.*, as ***ing ground***, ***ing land***.

1641 BEST *Farm. Bks.* (Surtees) 32 In a moist yeare hard-lande-grasse proveth better then carres, or ing-growndes. **1794** *Act Inclosing S. Kelsey* 2 Carr Lands, Ing Lands..and Furze Leas, within the said Manor.

-ing¹, suffix forming verbal derivatives, originally abstract nouns of action, but subsequently developed in various directions: OE. *-ung*, *-ing* = OFris. *-unge*, *-enge*, *-inge*, OS. *-unga* (MLG. and MDu. *-inge*, Du. *-ing*), OHG. *-unga*, *-ung* (MHG. *-unge*, Ger. *-ung*), ON. *-ung* and *-ing*; not known in Gothic:—OTeut. type *-*uŋgā* (and ? *-*iŋgā*) str. fem.; not identified outside Teutonic. In OE. the more usual form was *-ung* (inflected *-unge*), but *-ing* also was frequent, esp. in derivatives from original *ja*-verbs (see Cosijn, *Altwests. Gramm.* II. 21, 22). In early ME., *-ung* rapidly died out, being scarcely found after 1250, and *-ing* (in early ME. *-inge*) became the regular form. In later ME., *-yng* was a frequent scribal variant.

1. The original function of the suffix was to form nouns of action; as *ácsung* ASKING, from *ácsian* to ask, *bíding*, *bodung* preaching, BODING, *céapung*, *-ing* CHEAPING, *cíding*, *-ung* CHIDING, *créopung* CREEPING, *ębbung* EBBING, *féding* FEEDING, *gaderung* GATHERING. These substantives were originally abstract; but even in OE. they often came to express a completed action, a process, habit, or art, as *blętsung*, *-ing* BLESSING, *leornung* LEARNING, *tídung* TIDINGS, *weddung* betrothal, WEDDING, and then admitted a plural; sometimes they became concrete, as in *bedding*, *eardung* dwelling, *offrung* OFFERING, *rynning* rennet, EARNING³. During the ME. period all these uses received greater development, and in the 14th c. the formation became established, esp. in the gerundial use (see 2 below), as an actual or possible derivative of every verb. By later extension, formations of the same kind have been analogically made from substantives (see c, g, below), and, by ellipsis, from adverbs, as *innings*, *offing*, *outing*, *homing* (homecoming); while nonce-words in *-ing* are formed freely on words or phrases of many kinds, e.g. *oh-ing*, *hear-hearing*, *hoo-hooing*, *pshawing*, *yo-hoing* (calling *oh!*, *hear! hear!*, etc.), *how-d'ye-doing* (saying 'how do you do?'); 'I do not believe in all this *pinting*' (having pints of beer).

In current use, verbal substantives in *-ing* may be grouped, as to their sense, under the following heads:

a. Nouns of continuous action or existence, as *crying*, *falling*, *flying*, *kicking*, *living*, *pushing*, *running*, *sleeping*, *speaking*, *striking*, etc. They are distinguished from verbal sbs. of the same form as the verb-stem, as *a cry*, *a fall*, *a kick*, *a push*, *a run*, *a shout*, *a sleep*, etc., in that the latter denote *acts* of momentary or short duration, having a definite beginning and end, and grammatically take *a* and *plural*, while the sbs. in *-ing* imply indefinite duration without reference to beginning or end, and take no plural. Cf. 'a loud *cry*', 'many repeated *cries*', with 'loud and continued *crying*'. A *push* is done at once, but may be repeated as many *pushes*; *pushing* is continuous, there may be 'much', but not 'many' of it.

b. The notion of action may be limited to that of a single or particular occasion, as *a christening*, *a wedding*, *a meeting*, *a sitting*, *a merry-making*, *an outing*. As thus used, the sb. takes a plural: 'three long sittings'.

c. The notion of simple action passes insensibly into that of a process, practice, habit, or art, which may or may not be regarded as in actual exercise; e.g. '*reading* and *writing* are now common acquirements'; so *drawing*, *engraving*, *fencing*, *smoking*, *swimming*. Words of this kind are also formed directly from sbs. which are the names of things used, or persons engaged, in the action: such are *ballooning*, *blackberrying*, *canalling*, *chambering*, *cocking* (cock-fighting), *fowling*, *gardening*, *hopping* (hop-picking), *hurting* (gathering hurts), *nooning*, *nutting*, *sniping*, *buccaneering*, *costering*, *soldiering*, and the like.

d. Hence often transferred to the concrete or material accompaniment or product of the action or process, as 'the paper was covered with *writing*'; so *binding*, *blacking*, *dripping*, *dubbing*, *lightning*, *sewing*, *stitching*, etc.

e. Hence as the designation of a material thing in which the action or its result is concreted or embodied; as '*a writing* was affixed to the wall'; so *a covering*, *holding*, *landing*, *shaving*, *winding* (of a river), etc. A peculiar instance is *a being*, one wherein the attribute of *being* or existence is exemplified, now usually a *living* being.

f. Often used as the collective designation of the substance or material employed in an action or process, as *clothing*, that with which one is clothed; so *bedding*, *carpeting*, *ceiling*, *edging*, *flooring*, *gearing*, *gilding*, *housing*, *lining*, *rigging*, *roofing*, *shipping*, *tackling*, *tiling*, *trimming*, etc.

g. In the preceding group, there is often a sb. of the same form as the verb, with which the noun in *-ing* comes to be closely associated, as in *bed*, *bedding*; *clothes*, *clothing*; *floor*, *flooring*; *rail*, *railing*; *ship*, *shipping*, etc. Hence arise formations in *-ing* from substantives without a corresponding verb; esp. in industrial and commercial language, with the sense of a collection or indefinite mass of the thing or of its material; as *ashlaring*, *coping*, *cornicing*, *costering*, *girdering*, *piping*, *scaffolding*, *tubing*; *bagging*, *quilting*, *sacking*, *sheeting*, *shirting*, *ticking*, *trousering*.

h. In some words the concrete sense appears exclusively, or preferentially, in the plural *-ings*: e.g. *earnings, leavings, sweepings, tidings*; *hangings, innings, moorings, trappings*.

Other exceptional or irregular uses of *-ing* are discussed under the individual words.

The vbl. sb. in *-ing* often forms the second element in a compound. The first element may be a qualifying adv. which in the finite tenses of the vb. formerly stood either before or after it, but in the vbl. sbs. and adjs. regularly preceded, and thus came to be united with these: thus, from *out go* or *go out* came *out going*, now *out-going* or *outgoing*. So *down-sitting, in-being, in-dwelling, off-scouring, up-rising, well-being*. The first element may also be a sb., the direct, indirect, or adverbial object of the verb, as *book-keeping, child-bearing, glass-blowing, house-keeping, sheep-shearing, sea-faring, hand-writing, type-writing*, or merely = a subjective genitive, as *cock-crowing, sun-rising*.

The vbl. sb. often stands in an attributive relation to another sb., as in the *building trade* = the trade *of* building, *drawing materials* = materials *for* drawing, *singing lessons* = lessons *in* singing; when such expressions form established designations, they are regularly hyphened, and pronounced with the stress on the first element, as in *breeding-place, carving-knife, dancing-master, dwelling-house, fowling-piece, laughing-stock, meeting-house, reaping-hook, stumbling-block, spinning-wheel, thanksgiving-day, turning-lathe, walking-stick*, etc. But, when the collocation is only occasional, and the vbl. sb. stands in a simple attributive relation to the following sb., it approaches in function to an adjective, and is liable to be confounded with the pres. pple. (-ING[2]) used adjectivally. The sense generally determines the nature of the collocation; thus, *drawing lessons* are not lessons that draw, but lessons in drawing; *a fainting fit*, not a fit that faints, but a fit of fainting; *a drinking cup*, not a cup that drinks, but a cup for drinking with. A *walking-leaf* is a leaf (so-called) that walks; a *walking-stick* is a stick for walking. But in some cases in which the second element denotes a machine, agency, or agent, it is difficult to say whether the word in *-ing* is the vbl. sb. used attributively, or the present pple. used adjectivally, e.g. *a cutting tool, a bursting charge, an advertising agency*. In accordance with general analogy, such combinations are, as a rule, treated in this dictionary as attrib. uses of the vbl. sb.

2. The most notable development of the vbl. sb. in *-ing* is its use as a gerund, i.e. a substantive with certain verbal functions, particularly those of being qualified by an adverb instead of an adjective, and of governing an object like a verb: e.g. the habit of *speaking loosely* (= loose speaking); he has hopes of *coming back speedily* (= a speedy return); he practises *writing* (= the writing of) *leading articles*; engaged in *building himself a house* (= the building of a house for himself); after *having written a letter* (= the completion of the writing of a letter).

This gerundial use is peculiar to English, of which it is a characteristic and most important feature; it was unknown to OE. and early ME.

The first traces of it as yet pointed out (see R. Blume *Ursprung und Entwickelung des Gerundiums im Englischen*, Bremen 1880) occur *c* 1340 in the Ayenbite of Inwit and in the writings of Richard Rolle of Hampole, in the separation of the adv. in *downcoming, downfalling, ingoing*, etc., and the placing of it after the vbl. sb., *coming down, falling down, going in*, as in the finite verb, *come down, fall down, go in*. This was soon extended to adverbs and adverbial phrases generally, so that it became established that any vbl. sb. could, like the vb. to which it belonged, take an adverbial qualification. In other respects the vbl. sb. at first retained its sb. construction, e.g. *c* **1350** HAMPOLE *Prose Tr.* (E.E.T.S.) 11 'all manere of withdraweynge of oþer men thynges wrangwysely agaynes þaire wyll þat aghte it'.

A generation later, the vbl. sb. is found with a verbal regimen, thus **1377** LANGLAND *P. Pl.* B. XIV. 186 'Confessioun and knowlechyng and crauyng þy mercy Shulde amende vs'; *Ibid.* XIX. 72 'with-outen mercy askynge'. This gerundial construction is very frequent in Wyclif's Bible (1382); and it is significant that he regularly uses it in translating the Latin gerund, while he retains the original substantival construction in rendering a Latin n. of action. Thus, *Exod.* xix. 1 'the thridde moneth of the goyng of Yrael out [*egressionis*] of the loond of Egipte'; but *Heb.* xii. 10 'in receyuynge [*recipiendo*] the halowing of him'; *Mark* iii. 15 'power of heelynge [*curandi*] siknessis, and of castynge out [*ejiciendi*] fendis'. Imitation of the L. gerund was thus app. an influential factor in the development of the Eng. gerundial use of the vbl. sb. Another influence may have been the literal rendering of the Fr. gerund (identical in form with the pr. pple.) after *en*, as in *en venant*, L. *in veniendo*, in coming.

The full development of the gerundial use before 1400 led necessarily to an indefinite increase of vbl. sbs. in *-ing*, since every verb now had one as an actual or potential dependent. In conjunction with the formal identity of gerund and pres. pple. (see -ING[2]), it led also, at a later date, to the introduction of gerundial expressions for the perfect and future tenses, and for the passive voice, coinciding in form with the pples. of the same tenses and voices. Thus SIDNEY *Arcadia* I. (1725) 68 'want of consideration in not *having demanded* thus much'; SPENSER *F.Q.* III. iv. 50 'feare of *being* fowly *shent*'; HOOKER *Eccl. Pol.* I. xi. §2 'by *being* unto God *united*'; SHAKS. *Two Gent.* I. iii. 16 'in *hauing knowne* no trauaile in his youth'; *Tempest* III. i. 19 ''T will weepe for *hauing wearied* you'; *Mod.* 'The news of his *being about to return* home, instead of *having been slain* by the enemy'.

But, although the gerundial use was fully established by 1400, it was a long time before it was distinctly separated from the earlier substantival use. The vbl. sb. has *the* (or equivalent) before it, and *of* (or equivalent) after it; the gerund has neither. A good example of the two constructions side by side, and with identical sense, occurs in Bacon's third Essay: 'Concerning the Meanes of *procuring* Unity: Men must beware, that in *the procuring* .. *of* Religious Unity, they doe not', etc. But, down to the 17th c., mixed constructions were frequent, in which the word in *-ing* had an adjectival qualification with a verbal regimen, or, conversely, an adverbial qualification with the construction of a sb. followed by *of*: thus SIDNEY *Arcadia* I. iv. 15 b, 'to fall to a sodain straitning them'; *Ibid.* I. xii. 56 b, 'by the well choosing of your commandements'.

The gerund still retains one feature of the vbl. sb., viz. that of admitting of a preceding possessive case or possessive pronoun, as in 'after John's behaving so strangely', 'upon my readily granting it'. In the literary language this construction is regularly retained with a pronoun, and very generally with a single personal substantive; but, with names of things, and phraseological or involved denominations, the sign of the possessive began to be dropped already by 1600; thus SHAKS. *Macbeth* I. iii. 44 'By each at once her choppie finger laying Vpon her skinnie lips'. No other treatment is now possible in such constructions as 'in default of one or other being accepted', 'on the general and his staff appearing', 'in the event of your expectations not being at once realized', 'in consequence of much snow having fallen'; and, in current spoken English, the *'s* is commonly omitted with all nouns: thus THACKERAY *Van. Fair* xi. ¶48 'I insist upon Miss Sharp appearing', where 'Miss Sharp's' would now sound pedantic or archaic. Even a pronoun standing before the gerund is put in the objective, in dialect speech; and, when the pronoun is emphatic, this is common in ordinary colloquial English; thus THACKERAY *Esmond* I. 242 'Papa did not care about *them* learning'; —— *Newcomes* 'But who ever heard of them eating an owl?' CHAS. READE *Hard Cash* (1863) II. 332 'That is no excuse for him beating you.' So 'What is the use of *me* speaking?'

In such constructions the objective sb. or pronoun seems to stand in simple apposition to the gerund, the two forming a kind of combined object of the preposition, reminding us of the Greek infinitive with an accusative after a prep., as in μετὰ τὸ παραδοθῆναι τὸν Ιωάννην, 'after John being delivered up'. But in Eng. there has probably been analogical influence from the construction of the pres. pple.: cf., for instance, 'John was digging potatoes', 'Who saw John digging potatoes?', and 'Who ever heard of John (= John's) digging potatoes?'

3. In a few ME. writers, esp. in Wyclif, the form in **-inge, -ynge**, also appears for the Dative Infinitive, OE. *-enne*, ME. *-ene, -en*. Thus Luke xxii. 23 'who it was of hem that was to doynge [*facturus*] this thing.' John vi. 72 'this was to bitraiynge [*traditurus*] him.' In its origin this is a case of phonetic confusion; the OE. *-enne*, confounded with *-ende*, had, like the pres. pple. (see -ING[2]), passed through *-inde* to *-inge, -ynge*.

But it is possible that Wyclif, in using this form to render the L. future participle, actually identified it in sense with the gerund, understanding the first quotation above as if = 'who it was of them that was [destined] to the doing of this thing', which he contracted to the gerundial construction 'to doynge this thing'.

-ing[2], suffix of the present participle, and of adjs. thence derived, or so formed; an alteration of the original OE. *-ende* = OFris., OS. *-and*, OHG. *-ant-i* (*-ent-i, -ont-i*, MHG. *-end-e*, Ger. *-end*), ON. *-and-i* (Sw. *-ande*, Da. *-ende*), Goth. *-and-s, -and-a*, = L. *-ent-*, Gr. *-οντ-*, Skr. *-ant-*.

Already, in later OE., the ppl. *-ende* was often weakened to *-inde*, and this became the regular Southern form of the ending in Early ME. From the end of the 12th c. there was a growing tendency to confuse *-inde*, phonetically or scribally, with *-inge*; this confusion is specially noticeable in MSS. written by Anglo-Norman scribes in the 13th c. The final result was the predominance of the form *-inge*, and its general substitution for *-inde* in the 14th c., although in some works, as the Kentish *Ayenbite* of 1340, the pple. still regularly has *-inde*. In Midland English *-ende* is frequent in Gower, and occasional in Midland writers for some time later; but the southern *-inge, -ynge, -ing*, favoured by Chaucer, Hoccleve, and Lydgate, soon spread over the Midland area, and became the Standard English form. The Northern dialect, on the other hand, in England and Scotland, retained the earlier ending in the form *-ande, -and*, strongly contrasted with the verbal sb. in *-yng, -ing* (*-yne, -ene*). At the present day the two are completely distinct in Northumberland and the Southern Counties of Scotland, although the general mutescence of final *d*, and the change of (-ɪŋ) to (-ɪn), make the difference in most cases only a vowel one: e.g. 'a singan' burd', 'the singin (-ɪn) o' the burds', but 'a gaan bairn' (a going child), 'afore gangin' hame'.

As *-inge* was the proper ending of the vbl. sb. (-ING[1]), it has naturally suggested itself to many that the levelling of the pres. pple. under the same form must have been the result of some contact or confusion of the functions or constructions of the two formations. But investigation has discovered no trace of any such functional or constructional contact in Early ME.; and it is now generally agreed that the confusion was, in its origin, entirely phonetic. On the other hand, the fact that the *forms* had, by the 14th c., become identical, may have been a factor in the development of the gerundial use of the vbl. sb., which began then; and it has certainly influenced the subsequent development of the compound gerundial forms *being made, having made, having been made, being about to go*, etc., which have the same form as the corresponding participles (see -ING[1] 2). The identity of form of pr. pple. and gerund probably also assisted the process whereby, at a later date, such a construction as 'the king went a-hunting', formerly '*on* or *an* huntinge', was shortened to 'the king went hunting', the last word being then taken as the participle; and thus to the shortening of 'the ark was a-building', orig. 'on building', to 'the ark was building',—in which, if 'building' is taken as a pple., it must be explained as a pple. *passive* = being built. To the same cause must be ascribed some of the current constructions of the gerund, and the tendency of the vbl. sb. when used attributively to run together with the pr. pple. used adjectivally, as in *cutting tools*, a *driving wheel* (see -ING[1]).

The termination *-ing* is that of the pres. pple., whether used as part of the verb, or adjectivally; also of adjectives of participial origin or nature, as *cunning, willing, daring, buccaneering, freebooting, non-juring, hulking, lumping, strapping, swingeing*, and of prepositions or adverbs of participial origin, as *concerning, during, excepting, notwithstanding, pending, touching*.

As with the vbl. sb. (-ING[1]), words of participial form and use may be formed on other parts of speech, or on phrases, e.g. *buccaneering* adventurers, sailors *yo-hoing* lustily, *how-d'ye-doing* acquaintances.

-ing[3], a suffix forming derivative masculine sbs., with the sense of 'one belonging to' or 'of the kind of', hence 'one possessed of the quality of', and also as a patronymic = 'one descended from, a son of', and as a diminutive. Found in the same form, or as *-ung*, in the other Teutonic langs. OE. examples are *æþeling* ATHELING, *cyning* KING, *lytling* little one, child, *flýming* fugitive, *hóring* whoremonger; also the patronymics *Æþelwulfing* son of Æthelwulf, *Ecgbrehting, Cerdicing, Wodening*, etc. (OE. Chron. anno 855), *Adaming*, etc. (*Lindisf. Gosp.* Luke iii. 38), and the gentile names *Hoccingas, Iclingas, Centingas* (men of Kent), with the Scriptural *Gomorringas, Moabitingas, Idumingas*, etc. This suffix also formed names of coins, as *pending, penning* PENNY, *scilling* SHILLING, and of fractional parts, as *feorþing* quarter, FARTHING, *teoðung, -ing* tenth, TITHING: so ON. *þriðjung-r* third part, *thriding* RIDING (of Yorkshire).

Among words of various ages with this suffix are *bretheling, bunting, gelding, golding, herring, hilding, sweeting, whiting, wilding*. See also the compound suffix -LING (*-l* + *-ing*).

‖**inga** (ˈɪŋgə). *Bot.* [ad. *ingá, engá*, native name in Brazil (see quot. 1869).]

1. A genus of plants allied to the Mimosa (N.O. *Leguminosæ*), consisting of large shrubs or trees, for the most part native to South America, with red, yellow, or white flowers and pinnate leaves.

1838 *Penny Cycl.* XII. 476/2 *Inga*, a genus of plants.. found in the tropical parts of Asia, Africa, and America. **1869** R. F. BURTON *Highlands of Brazil* II. xii. 172 The name *Ingá* or *Engá* is applied to Mimosas of various species, some bearing an edible legumen.

2. *attrib.* **inga bean**, a species of the genus *Pithecolobium* (*P. dulce*), tribe *Ingeæ*; **inga tree**, a species of Inga (*I. vera*).

1756 P. BROWNE *Jamaica* 253 The Inga Tree or large leafed Sensitive. This shrubby tree is pretty frequent in St. Mary's. **1886** A. H. CHURCH *Food Grains Ind.* 173 *Inga-bean*, a middle sized tree belonging to the natural order Leguminosæ, suborder Mimoseæ.

Inga, obs. form of INCA.

in-ga, variant of INGO *v. Obs.*

†**ingage, -ment**, etc., obs. forms of ENGAGE, -MENT, etc., q.v. for other instances.

1611 COTGR., *Engage*, a pledge, pawne, gage, ingagement. *Ibid.*, *Engageur*, a pledger, ingager, pawner. *Ibid.*, *Engagé*, ingaged, impledged, pawned. *Ibid.*, *Engagement*, a pawning, ingaging, impledging. **1617** MORYSON *Itin.* II. 21 So they feared the ingaging and losse of the Queenes Army. *Ibid.* III. 252 Which made other 7 cantons partners of that ingagement.

†**in'gall**, *v. Obs. rare*$^{-0}$. Also **en-**. [f. IN-[2], EN-[1] + GALL *sb.*[1]] *trans.* To fill or impregnate with gall.

1611 FLORIO, *Affielire*, to engall or enbitter. *Ibid.*, *Infielire*, .. to ingall.

in'gallantry. *rare*. [IN-[3].] The opposite of gallantry; ungallant conduct or behaviour; want of attention to the fair sex.

1805 W. TAYLOR in *Monthly Mag.* XIX. 574 She had solicited Voltaire for a peep, and was eager to punish his ingalantry by a quotation. **1813** —— *Eng. Synonyms* 226, I may felicitate a rival on his marriage with my mistress, when I cannot, without ingallantry, congratulate him.

†**in'galley**, *v. Obs. rare.* [f. IN-[2] + GALLEY *sb.*: cf. *imprison*.] *trans.* To consign to or confine in the galleys.

1595 COPLEY *Wits, Fits, & Fancies* 114 It pleas'd the Iudge in fauour of life to ingalley them for seuen yeers.

ingan (ˈɪŋən). Also -un, -in. [Phonetic development, with *i* as in *mither, brither, hinnie*,

and (ŋ) for (ɲ), as *ring* for *reign*, etc.] Sc. and Eng. dial. form of ONION.

1725 RAMSAY *Gentle Sheph.* II. i. Sang viii, She can mix fu' nice The gusty ingans wi' a curn o' spice. **1818** SCOTT *Rob Roy* xiv, Sae mony royal boroughs yoked on end to end, like ropes of ingans. **1819** —— *Leg. Montrose* ii, Our Spanish colonel, whom I could have blown away like the peeling of an ingan. **1891** *Hartland* (N. Devon) *Gloss.* 77 Taty-ingin.. Seed-ingin.

† **'ingang, -yong.** *Obs.* Also 1 ingong, inngang, 3 inȝeong, 3–4 inȝong, 4 ingonge, 4–5 ingange. [f. IN *adv.* 11 d + GANG *sb.*¹, YONG *sb.* Cf. OHG. *ingang*, Ger. *eingang*, Du. *ingang*.]

1. The act or fact of going in; entrance, entry.

c **900** tr. *Bæda's Hist.* IV. xxv. [xxiv.] (1890) 346 Bi utgonge Israhela folces of Ægypta londe & bi ingonge þæs ȝehatlandes. *c* **1000** *Ags. Ps.* (Th.) cxvii[i]. 19 Soðfæste on þa duru seceað inn-gang. *c* **1205** LAY. 28370 Iherden þa burhweren.. and warnden him inȝeong. *a* **1225** *Ancr. R.* 62 þurh eie þurles deað haueð hire inȝong into þe soule. *a* **1300** *E.E. Psalter* cxx[i]. 8 Laverd yheme þine in-gang and þine out-gang Fra hethen, and in to werld lang. **1377** LANGL. *P. Pl.* B. v. 638 It is ful harde.. for any of ȝow alle To geten ingonge [**1393** C. VIII. 282 ingange] at any gate þere.

2. A way in; an entrance, porch.

a **1225** *Ancr. R.* 206 þe uorrideles þet beoð iwunede ofte to openen þet inȝong & leten in sunne. *a* **1350** *Childh. Jesu* 701 (Mätz.) In a tour starc and strong, þar on nas bote on inȝong. *c* **1440** *Gesta Rom.* I. xlvii. 200 (Harl. MS.) He enterid in to the yerde, & yede in to the In-gange.. and þere he lay al nyght.

† **inga'nnation.** *Obs. rare*⁻¹. [ad. It. *ingannazione*, n. of action from *ingannare* to deceive, f. *inganno* fraud, deceit: see next and -ATION.] Deceiving; deception.

1646 SIR T. BROWNE *Pseud. Ep.* I. iii. 12 Inabilitie to resist such triviall ingannations from others. **1658** PHILLIPS, *Ingannation*, a deceaving.

‖ **inganno** (in'ganno). *Mus.* [It. *inganno* deception, deceit, fraud = Sp. *engaño*, Pg. *engano*, Pr. *engan*, OF. *engan*, *enjan*, *enjain*, a Com. Romanic word of uncertain derivation: see Diez, Mackel, etc.] (See quots.)

1753 CHAMBERS *Cycl. Supp.*, *Inganno*, in the Italian music, is used when the composer, after having done every thing proper for making a close or cadence, instead of so doing places a mark of silence in the place of the final note. **1880** *Grove's Dict. Mus.* II. 3/1 *Inganno*,.. any false or deceptive Cadence, in which the Bass proceeds, from the Dominant, to any other note than the Tonic.

† **ingaol**, obs. f. ENGAOL, ENJAIL, to imprison.

1611 COTGR., *Engeoler*,.. to incage or ingoale.. to lay in gaole. **1632** SHERWOOD, To ingaole, *engeoler*.

ingarland, obs. form of ENGARLAND.

† **in'garnish**, *v.* *Obs. rare.* [f. IN-² + GARNISH *v.*: cf. OF. *engarnir* (14th c. in Godef.).] *trans.* To furnish with means of defence: = GARNISH *v.* 1.

a **1578** LINDESAY (Pitscottie) *Chron. Scot.* (S.T.S.) I. 140 The toune of Roxburght, quhilk the Inglischmen had then ingarnischit with men and munitioun.

ingarrison, obs. form of ENGARRISON.

ingate ('ɪngeɪt), *sb.*¹ (*adv.*) *north. dial.* [f. IN *adv.* 11 d + GATE *sb.*²]

1. The action or faculty of going in or entering; entrance, ingress.

1496 *Will of Yeldham* (Somerset Ho.), Wᵗ free ingate & outegate. **1596** SPENSER *State Irel.* Wks. (Globe) 650/1 One noble parson, whoe.. stoppeth the Ingate of all that evill. **1598** STOW *Surv.* (1754) I. I. xvii. 89/2 All the night following.. the Rebels enjoyed free Ingate and Outgate. **1668** CULPEPPER & COLE *Barthol. Anat.* II. v. 95 It hath five Holes; viz.: for the ingate and outgate of the Vena Cava [etc.]. **1837** CARLYLE *Fr. Rev.* II. v. xii, Perhaps this shut lake, finding no ingate, will retire to its sources again. **1876** *Whitby Gloss.*, *Ingate*, ingress or entrance.

2. A way in, an entrance.

1596 SPENSER *State Irel.* Wks. (Globe) 665/1 Places.. having most convenient.. in-gates to the richest partes of the lande. **1606** *Vestry Bks.* (Surtees) 287 For.. mending the ingate into the church. **1812** J. HODGSON in J. Raine *Mem.* (1857) I. 105 The ingate or entrance from the shaft into the pit. **1865** CARLYLE *Fredk. Gt.* XX. vii. (1872) IX. 135 Batteries commanding every ingate, and under them are Mines.

3. Entrance upon life, a period of time, etc.

1591 SPENSER *Ruines Time* 47 At the ingate of their berth They crying creep out of their mothers woomb. **1596** —— *F.Q.* IV. x. 12 Janus auncient, Which hath in charge the ingate of the yeare.

† **4.** *concr.* That which enters. Usually in *pl.*: Things which enter; ingoings, incomings, imports; also import duties or dues. *Obs.*

1621 *Youghal Council Bk.* (1878) 82 The total of the Ingate amounts to 24*li.* 8*s.* 4*d.* The total of the Outgate, 71*li.* 12*s.* **1646** *Mass. Col. Rec.* (1854) III. 92 So long as our ingate exceeds our outgate, yᵉ ballance.. cann leave vs but litle mony once in yᵉ yeere. **1701** in Picton *L'pool Munic. Rec.* (1883) I. 294 Sandiford.. did take yᵉ tolls of yᵉ Ingates and Outgates. **1714** *Ibid.* II. 44 The Collector of the Ingates and Outgates. **1886** PICTON *Ibid.*, The ingates and outgates .. a sort of octroi levied on all carts with articles of food and provender passing in and out of the town.

† **B.** (?) *adv.* Inwards. *Obs.*

1590 in Picton *L'pool Munic. Rec.* (1883) I. 90 Evrie owner .. shall enter his said Vessell wᵗʰ the Town's Customer of this towne, owte gate and ingate. **1611** *Galway Arch.* in *10th Rep. Hist. MSS. Comm.* App. v. 464 Goodes.. transported either outgate or ingate.

'ingate, *sb.*² *Founding.* [f. IN *adv.* + GATE *sb.*⁴] (See quots.)

1858 SIMMONDS *Dict. Trade*, *Ingate*, an aperture in a mould for pouring in metal; technically called the tedge. **1875** KNIGHT *Dict. Mech.* 1183/1 The ingate is technically called the tedge, gate, geat, or git.

ingather (ˌɪn'gæðə(r)), *v.* Also 6 *Sc.* ingadder. [f. IN *adv.* + GATHER *v.* Cf. MDu. *ingaderen*.] *trans.* To gather in (esp. the harvest). Also *fig.*

c **1575** *Balfour's Practicks* (1754) 24 Gif ony Bischop of this realme deceis, it is leasum to the Vicar generall to tak up, ressave, ingadder, and collect all and sindrie the fruitis, rentis and dewteis pertening *ad mensam episcopi.* **1633** STRAFFORD in Browning *Life* (1891) 145 *note*, I am yet ingathering.. my observations. **1793** DONALDSON *Carse Gowrie* 9 The commencement [of a lease] takes place in some cases at the term of Whitsunday as to the houses and garden, and to the arable land after ingathering the crop. **1891** *Daily News* 23 Oct. 5/8 The Annan.. bringing down.. fragments of ricks, and sheaves of rotten corn, which the good husbandmen have not been able to ingather.

ingathered ('ɪnˌgæðəd), *ppl. a.* [f. IN *adv.* 11 b + GATHERED: cf. INGATHER *v.*] Gathered in.

a. Collected. **b.** Drawn in together, curled in.

1846 TRENCH *Mirac.* xxxi. (1862) 442 *note*, *Καιρὸς τῶν καρπῶν*.. means the time of the ripe fruits, not the time of the ingathered. **1853** RUSKIN *Stones Ven.* III. App. x. 236 It is in disease or in death, by blight, or frost, or poison only, that leaves.. assume this ingathered form. **1886** MRS. MARSHALL *Tower on Cliff* viii. 106 The ingathered harvest.

'inˌgatherer. [f. IN *adv.* 11 e + -ER¹.] One who gathers in.

1883 F. D. HUNTINGTON in J. G. Butler *Bible-Work* I. 298 One Reaper and Ingatherer and Finisher follows them.

ingathering ('ɪnˌgæðərɪŋ), *vbl. sb.* Also 6 yngaderynge. [f. IN *adv.* 11 c + GATHERING *vbl. sb.*: cf. INGATHER *v.*] The action of gathering in or collecting (esp. the harvest); a gathering in, collection. Also *fig.*; applied *spec.* to the congregating of the Jews in Israel.

Feast of Ingathering = Feast of Tabernacles.

1535 COVERDALE *Exod.* xxxiv. 22 The feast of yngaderynge [**1551** ingatherynge] at yᵉ yeares ende. *a* **1555** RIDLEY *Let.* in *Bradford's Wks.* (Parker Soc.) II. 400 Make some ingatherings amongst your neighbours for the relief of them. **1668** R. STEELE *Husbandm. Calling* vi. (1672) 153 The ingathering of his corn. **1799** J. ROBERTSON *Agric. Perth* 92 The ingathering of their hay and corns, [was] executed with a sledge. **1861** *Illustr. Times* 5 Oct. 222 The great ingathering of the hops is completed. **1896** J. F. YOUNGSON *Punjab Mission* xxvii. 257 It resulted in the ingathering of thousands. **1952** S. SPENDER *Learning Laughter* iii. 36 But to-day there is another kind of paradox... This might be called the paradox of the Ingathering. **1964** *Economist* 16 May 703/1 The other chief fact of Israel, politically as well as economically, is the determination to make the in-gathering of Jews.. viable and safe. **1971** *Listener* 14 Jan. 36/3 When Israel became a state on 15 May 1948 the first principle written into its proclamation of independence affirmed that 'the state of Israel will be open to Jewish immigration and the in-gathering of the exiles'. **1973** *Guardian* 12 Mar. 10/3 Young Israelis.. feel no mission to the Jews of the Diaspora. The ingathering of the exiles is a remote slogan.

'inˌgathering, *ppl. a.* [f. IN *adv.* 11 a + GATHERING *ppl. a.*] Gathering in, gathering together.

1887 *Advance* 24 Mar. (Cent.), The ingathering streams are to branch off.. into as many channels to empty the river as had united to fill it.

† **in'gealable**, *a.* *Obs. rare*⁻⁰. [f. IN-³ + GEAL *v.* + -ABLE, prob. after L. *ingelābilis*, var. of *incongelābilis* in Aul. Gell. XVII. viii. 16.] = INCONGEALABLE, not able to freeze (Cockeram, 1623).

Todd (1818) cites the word from Cockeram as *Ingelable*, and mod. Dicts. quote it in this form.

ingear ('ɪnˌgɪə(r)). *Sc. rare.* [f. IN *adv.* 12 a + GEAR *sb.*] Household goods.

1834 H. MILLER *Scenes & Leg.* xxiv. (1857) 350 He died ..possessed of ingear and outgear, and of a very considerable sum of money.

ingein, variant of INGINE, *Obs.*

ingelable: see INGEALABLE.

ingelis, -ish, obs. forms of ENGLISH.

ingem (ɪn'dʒɛm), *v.* Also 7 enjem. [f. IN-², EN-¹ + GEM *sb.*; in most of the quots. rendering It. *ingemmare*.] *trans.* To set with gems; to adorn with, or as with, gems.

1611 FLORIO, *Ingemmare*, to eniem, to eniewell. *a* **1649** DRUMM. OF HAWTH. *Poems* Wks. (1711) 6/2 When clouds engemm'd shew azure, green, and red. **1814** CARY *Dante, Par.* xv. 82 Living topaz! that ingemm'st This precious jewel. **1885** A. J. BUTLER tr. *Dante, Par.* xx. 262 The costly and lucid stones wherewith I saw the sixth light ingemmed.

† **in'geminate**, *ppl. a.* *Obs. rare.* [ad. L. *ingemināt-us*, pa. pple. of *ingemināre*: see next.] Doubled, redoubled; reiterated, repeated.

1637 JACKSON *Serm. Luke* xiii. 5 ⁋ 5 This ingeminate verdict of our Saviours first against the Galileans, secondly against the inhabitants of Ierusalem. **1665–76** REA *Flora* (To Ladies), With scarlet robes appear in state And double ruffs ingeminate.

ingeminate (ɪn'dʒɛmɪneɪt), *v.* Also 6 en-. [f. L. *ingemināt-*, ppl. stem of *ingemināre* to redouble, repeat, f. *in-* (IN-²) + *gemināre* to GEMINATE.]

1. *trans.* To utter (a sound) twice or oftener; to repeat, reiterate (a word, statement, etc.), usually for the purpose of being emphatic or impressive; to emphasize (a fact) by repetition. (Freq. in 17th c.; now chiefly used in echoes of quot. 1647).

1594 *Zepheria* xv, My feares how oft haue I engeminated? Oh black recite of passed miserie. **1621** G. SANDYS *Ovid's Met.* III. (1626) 55 Those threats are deeds: Shee [Echo] yet ingeminates The last of sounds, and what shee heares relates. **1647** CLARENDON *Hist. Reb.* VII. §233 [Falkland] often, after a deep silence and frequent sighs, would with a shrill and sad accent, ingeminate the word, Peace, Peace. *a* **1703** BURKITT *On N.T.*, *1 John* ii. 14 Here we have observable, the enemy described, and the conquest ingeminated. **1883** *Pall Mall G.* 22 Oct. 5/1 But we must ask and ingeminate the inquiry, where is Burns? **1887** *Murray's Mag.* June 730 Thus our Canon ingeminates peace. **1892** *Pall Mall G.* 9 Nov. 1/2 Here comes Mr. Balfour with his olive branch, ingeminating peace.

† **2.** To double (a thing); to repeat (an action). *Obs. rare.*

1625 K. LONG tr. *Barclay's Argenis* IV. x. 272 The woes of your sad state Their doomes deferring shall ingeminate. **1674** JEAKE *Arith.* (1696) 273 The long Names of such Higher Powers, as have the Square or Cube often ingeminated. **1686** GOAD *Celest. Bodies* II. iii. 193 When ever ☿ [Mercury] turning short, happens to ingeminate his Conjunction in less than a Months time [etc.].

† **3.** To couple; to unite in couples. *Obs. rare.*

1609 *Ev. Woman in Hum.* v. i. in Bullen *O. Pl.* IV, Now gallant Bridegroomes, and your lovely Brides, That have ingeminate in endlesse league Your troth-plight hearts.

in'geminated, *ppl. a.* [f. prec. + -ED¹.]

1. Of words, etc.: Reiterated, repeated.

1616 R. CARPENTER *Past. Charge* 55 The like charge doth our Sauior with a thrice ingeminated expostulation, giue vnto Saint Peter. **1673** *Lady's Calling* I. ii. §5 Assaulted.. by ingeminated threatnings of hell and damnations.

2. Of things, feelings, etc.: Doubled, redoubled. *spec.* of a flower (see quot. 1688).

1658 GURNALL *Chr. in Arm.* verse 15 xiii. §1. 426 This ingeminated zeal of Christ for his peoples unity and love. **1665** NEEDHAM *Med. Medicinæ* 68 Renewed and ingeminated Diseases ever appear worst. **1688** R. HOLME *Armoury* II. 67/2 Another kind having the Flower Ingeminated, or Hose in Hose, that is one coming out of another.

ingemination (ɪndʒɛmɪ'neɪʃən). [Noun of action from INGEMINATE *v.*: see -ATION.]

1. The action of repeating or reiterating (a word, statement, etc.); a repetition, a reiteration. *arch.*

1576 FLEMING *Panopl. Epist.* 426 *note*, By the ingemination and twice repeating.. hee signifieth the passion of his minde. *a* **1659** BP. BROWNRIG *Serm.* (1674) I. xii. 160 Such ingeminations will make strong impressions in the hearts of the People. *a* **1703** BURKITT *On N.T.*, *Matt.* xxiii. 39 His ingemination, or doubling of the word, shows the vehemency of Christ's affection.

2. The action or process of doubling (a thing, feeling, etc.); duplication. *rare.*

1644 VICARS *God in Mount* 135 With redoubled and trebled cordiall ingeminations of joy in Soule and Spirit. **1840** DE QUINCEY *Wks.* (1862) X. 161 The iteration and ingemination of a given effect.

ingen, obs. form of ENGINE, INGINE.

ingender, obs. form of ENGENDER.

† **in'genderable**, *a.* *Obs. rare*⁻⁰. [f. *ingender*, ENGENDER + -ABLE. Cf. OF. *engendrable* capable of engendering or being engendered.] Capable of engendering. (In Levins = INGENERABLE *a.*¹)

1552 HULOET, Ingendrable, *genitiuus*. **1570** LEVINS *Manip.* 4/27 Ingenderable, *ingenerabilis*.

† **in'gendered**, *ppl. a.* *Obs. rare*⁻¹. [var. of ENGENDERED.] Inborn; = INGENERATE *ppl. a.*

1596 DALRYMPLE tr. *Leslie's Hist. Scot.* I. 111 A certane ingendired curage.. of the mynd.

ingendrure, var. of ENGENDRURE, *Obs.*

ingene, obs. form of ENGINE.

ingeneer, -er, -ier, obs. forms of ENGINEER.

† **in'gener**, *v.* *Obs.* Also 7 ingenner. [ad. L. *ingenerā-re* to INGENERATE.] = ENGENDER.

1513 DOUGLAS *Æneis* I. i. 48 Jupiter ingenerit Dardanus. **1562** *Burgh Rec. Aberdeen* (1844) I. 343 To ingener discord betuix the craftismen and the fre burgessis of gild. **1607** DEKKER *Knt.'s Conjur.* H ij b, Picking strawes out of poore thatcht houses to build nestes where his twelue pences should ingenner.

†**in,genera'bility**^{1}. *Obs.* [f. INGENERABLE^{1}: see -ITY; cf. It. *ingenerabilità* (Florio), F. *ingénérabilité* (Bayle, in Littré).] The quality of being ingenerable; incapacity of being generated.

1598 FLORIO, *Ingenerabilita*, vnbegetting, ingenerabilitie. **1678** CUDWORTH *Intell. Syst.* I. i. §34. 43 Firmly conclusive ..for Substantial Incorporeal Souls, and their Ingenerability out of the Matter. *a* **1691** BOYLE *Hist. Air* vi. (1692) 18 The Controversy about the Ingenerability (as they speak) or the mutual Transmutation of the Bodies that are called Elementary.

in,genera'bility^{2}. *rare*$^{-0}$. [f. INGENERABLE^{2} + -ITY.] Capability of being generated.

In mod. Dicts.

ingenerable (ɪn'dʒɛnərəb(ə)l), *a.*^{1} Now *rare.* [ad. med.L. *ingenerābilis*: see IN-^{3} and GENERABLE. Cf. F. *ingénérable* (Oresme, 14th c.), It. *ingenerabile* (Florio).] Incapable of being generated. (Chiefly in phrase ***ingenerable and incorruptible***, common in 17th c.)

1398 TREVISA *Barth. De P.R.* VIII. i. (MS. Bodl.) lf. 70/2 þe furste mater of þe whiche þe worlde is kindelich ymade is ingenerable and vncoruptible. **1603** HOLLAND *Plutarch's Mor.* 1031 He thought as much of the world: for full well he knew that eternal it was and ingenerable. **1660** BOYLE *New Exp. Phys. Mech.* xxii. 163 Divers Naturalists esteem the Air ..to be ingenerable and incorruptible. **1794** SULLIVAN *View Nat.* I. 145 It is both ingenerable and indestructible. **1839** BAILEY *Festus* xix. (1852) 284 A high peculiar few,..whose whole position stands Ingenerable by themselves.

Hence **in'generableness** (Bailey vol. II, 1727); **in'generably** *adv.*, in an ingenerable manner.

1678 CUDWORTH *Intell. Syst.* I. i. §29. 35 That Conceit of Anaxagoras, of..Atoms endued with all those several Forms and Qualities of Bodies Ingenerably and Incorruptibly.

in'generable, *a.*^{2} *rare*$^{-0}$. [See INGENERATE *v.* and -ABLE.] Capable of being ingenerated (Annandale *Ogilvie*, 1882). So **in'generableness** (Bailey vol. II, 1727).

ingenerate (ɪn'dʒɛnərət), *a.* [ad. late L. *ingenerātus* (Boethius) 'non generatus, qui per se ipse est': see IN-^{3} and GENERATE *ppl. a.*] Not generated; self-existent.

1656 STANLEY *Hist. Philos.* v. (1701) 182/1 The Soul is moved by it self, therefore the Soul is Incorruptible, Ingenerate, and Immortal. **1678** CUDWORTH *Intell. Syst.* I. iv. §14. 233 Such a God as this, may be..Ingenerate or Vnproduced, and consequently Self-existent. **1833** J. H. NEWMAN *Arians* II. iv. (1876) 181. **1894** H. B. SWETE *Apostles' Creed* iii. 35 The first Synod of Sirmium anathematises those who..identify the Holy Ghost with the Ingenerate God.

ingenerate (ɪn'dʒɛnərət), *ppl. a.* Now *rare.* [ad. L. *ingenerāt-us*, pa. pple. of *ingenerāre*: see next. In early use also as *pa. pple.* of next.]

1. Of character, qualities, etc.: Inborn, innate.

1531 ELYOT *Gov.* III. xxiii, In the soules of men is ingenerate a leme of science. **1540-1** —— *Image Gov.* (1556) 21 b, That gravitie and sternesse, whiche is in you as it were by nature ingenerate. **1581** MULCASTER *Positions* iv. (1887) 23 We did not force them from their ingenerate heat, and naturall stirring, to an vnnaturall stilnesse. **1612** T. JAMES *Jesuit's Downf.* 30 The ingenerate law of all men to bee loyall to their Countrey. *a* **1639** WOTTON *Educ.* in *Reliq.* (1672) 77 Ingenerate and seminal powers. **1882** J. B. STALLO *Concepts Mod. Physics* 290 There is..in every finite part of the world an ingenerate bias from irregularity to regularity.

b. Of diseases or their causes: Born or developed in the system; congenital. *rare.*

1822-34 *Good's Study Med.* (ed. 4) II. 333 We meet with a few scattered cases of it [measles] in almost every month of the year, evidently proving an ingenerate origin. *Ibid.* 482 There are other poisonous irritants which are altogether ingenerate or hereditary.

†**2.** Engendered, begotten (*lit.* and *fig.*). *rare.*

a **1572** KNOX *Hist. Ref.* Wks. 1846 I. 446 Quhairintill great parrellis may be ingenerat to the commoun-weall and libertie thairof. **1583** STUBBES *Anat. Abus.* I. (1877) 28 From the cursed roote of pestiferous Pride do all other euilles sproute, and thereof are ingenerate. *c* **1611** CHAPMAN *Iliad* XVIII. 323 She, reigning queen of Goddesses, and being ingenerate Of one stock with himself.

ingenerate (ɪn'dʒɛnəreɪt), *v.* Now *rare.* [f. ppl. stem of L. *ingenerāre*, f. *in-* (IN-^{2}) *generāre* to GENERATE.] *trans.* To generate within, engender, produce.

1528 FOX *Let. to Gardiner* in Strype *Eccl. Mem.* I. App. xxvi. 77, I..toke occasion to shew..how these opynyons were ingenerated. **1604** T. WRIGHT *Passions* II. i. 55 Inordinate Passions cause and ingenerate in the Soule all those vices which are opposite to prudence. **1674** OWEN *Holy Spirit* (1693) 108 They are the great means whereby all Grace is ingenerated and exercised. **1858** BUSHNELL *Nat. & Supernat.* viii. (1864) 240 God shall be able to ingenerate in him a new, divine state, or principle of action.

†**in'generated**, *a.* *Obs.* *rare*$^{-1}$. [IN-^{3}.] Not generated; ungenerated; = INGENERATE *a.*

1646 SIR T. BROWNE *Pseud. Ep.* I. i. 1 Our first and ingenerated forefathers. **1706** PHILLIPS, *Ingenerated*, not ingender'd, not produc'd by Generation.

in'generated, *ppl. a.* *rare.* [f. INGENERATE *v.* + -ED^{1}.] Inborn, innate; = INGENERATE *ppl. a.*

1677 OTWAY *Cheats Scapin* II. i, The imperfection and corruptness of ingenerated natures. **1822-34** *Good's Study Med.* (ed. 4) II. 566 When it [King's Evil] occurs as a primary or ingenerated affection [etc.].

in'generately, *adv.* *rare*$^{-1}$. [f. INGENERATE *a.* + -LY^{2}.] In an ungenerated manner.

1833 J. H. NEWMAN *Arians* II. v. (1876) 213 Ever generate, ingenerately-generate.

†**in'generateness.** *Obs.* *rare*$^{-1}$. [f. as prec. + -NESS.] Ungenerated condition.

1678 CUDWORTH *Intell. Syst.* I. iv. §14. 250 Himself was the very First..of all the Greeks, who asserted this Ingenerateness or Eternity of the World.

ingeneration (ɪndʒɛnə'reɪʃən). *rare.* [n. of action from INGENERATE *v.*: see -ATION.] The action of ingenerating or engendering.

1652 ASHMOLE *Theat. Chem.* 198 Cause of ingeneration of every body Mettalyne. **1858** BUSHNELL *Nat. & Supernat.* xii. (1864) 374 It is a continuous and living ingeneration of God, who has thus become a divine impulse or quickening in us.

in'generative, *a.* *rare.* [f. INGENERATE *v.* + -IVE.] Ingenerating, engendering.

1877 FAIRBAIRN *Stud. Phil. Relig.* 381 The Purusha, the ungenerated and ingenerative Spirit of the Indian.

†**in'generous**, *a.* *Obs.* *rare.* [IN-^{3}.] Not generous; ungenerous.

a. Of low birth. **b.** Mean-spirited, dastardly.

1621 BRATHWAIT *Nat. Emb.*, *Beggarie* (1877) 43 Sprong of ingenerous bloud. **1635** HEYWOOD *Hierarch.* VI. 394 He neither hath like one ingenerous sayd Nor hath a Lybian barbarisme betrayd. **1684** W. ASPIN *Envious Man's Char.* 24 An envious man takes his advantage of doing us a mischeif when we are least aware of him,..which is most ingenerous in it self, and most deadly in its effects.

†**in'geniary**, *a.* *Obs.* *rare.* [ad. med.L. *ingeniāri-us*, f. L. *ingenium*: see next.] Relating to, or exercising, intellectual skill or contrivance; inventive (as distinguished from operative).

1664 EVELYN *Freart's Archit.* 120 [In Italy] Architects (I mean the Manuary as well as the Ingeniary) have been.. rewarded with Knighthood.

†**in'geniate**, *v.* *Obs.* *rare.* [f. ppl. stem of med.L. *ingeniāre* to contrive, f. L. *ingenium* inborn quality, faculty, genius: cf. F. *ingénier* (14-15th c.).] *trans.* To devise, contrive, plan, design.

1592 DANIEL *Compl. Rosamond* xcvii, Did Nature (for this good) ingeniate To show in thee the glory of her best? **1604** —— *Fun. Poem Earl Devonsh.*, And I must all I can ingeniate To answer for the same.

†**inge'niculate**, *v.* *Obs.* *rare*$^{-0}$. [f. ppl. stem of L. *ingeniculāre*, f. *in-* (IN-^{2}) + *geniculāre* to bend the knee, GENICULATE.]

1623 COCKERAM, *Ingeniculate*,..to bow the knee.

Hence †**ingenicu'lation**.

1658 PHILLIPS, *Ingeniculation*, a bending of the knee.

ingenie, variant of INGENY, *Obs.*

ingenier, obs. form of ENGINEER.

†**ingenio** (ɪn'dʒiːnɪəʊ). *Obs.* Also 7 **ingenewe**. [a. Sp. *ingenio* (in'xenjo) genius, engine (*ingenio de azúcar* sugar-mill):—L. *ingenium* clever thought, invention, in med.L. and Romanic, clever device, machine, engine.] A sugar-mill, sugar-factory, or sugar-works (in the West Indies).

1600 HAKLUYT *Voyages* III. 718 Building his owne Ingenios or sugar-milles. **1613** PURCHAS *Pilgrimage* (1614) 630 His provisions for his Ingenewes or Sugar-gardens. *Ibid.* 732 Oviedo reckons almost thirty Ingenious, the number daily increasing. **1672** W. HUGHES *Amer. Phys.* 30 The Mill, Machine or Ingenio, where they squeeze them. **1722** DE FOE *Col. Jack* (1840) 315 They had an ingenio, that is to say a sugar-house, or sugar-work. **1887** N. D. DAVIS *Cavaliers Barbados* 88 What we now call the Buildings or the Sugar Works, were at first known as the Ingenio.

†**b.** *transf.* A machine or mill for making cider.

1669 WORLIDGE *Syst. Agric.* (1681) 139 These Ingenioes are curiously made by Henry Allen at the Cabinet in Exeter-street..in the Strand. **1676** —— *Cyder* (1691) 98. **1676** *Phil. Trans.* XI. 574 A New invented Ingenio or Mill, for the more expeditious and better making of Cider.

ingeniosity (ɪndʒiːnɪ'ɒsɪtɪ). Now *Obs.* or *rare.* [a. F. *ingéniosité* 'ingeniositie, ingeniousnesse' Cotgr. (16th c. in Godef. *Compl.*), f. L. type **ingeniōsitās*, f. *ingeniōs-us*: see next and -ITY.] The quality of being ingenious; ingenuity.

1607 WALKINGTON *Opt. Glass* 47 Luciane and Juliane, whose very image[s] are to be had in hie repute, for their ingeniosity. **1652-62** HEYLIN *Cosmogr.* IV. (1682) 110 Besides their own natural ingeniosities they have since learned the Civilities and Arts of Europe. **1678** CUDWORTH *Intell. Syst.* I. v. 681 Nature..whose cunning and ingeniosity no art or human opificer can possibly reach to by imitation. **1891** *Sat. Rev.* 8 Aug. 164/2 The distortion of proverbs. Balzac's painters, Schinner and Joseph Bridau, quite gave themselves up to this ingeniosity, for it grows upon one.

ingenious (ɪn'dʒiːnɪəs), *a.* Also 6-7 **en-**. [prob. a. 15th c. F. *ingénieux*, *-euse*, OF. *engeignos*, *-eus*, ad. L. *ingeniōsus* intellectual, talented, clever, ingenious, f. *ingenium* natural quality, character, or capacity; ability, genius, cleverness, a clever thought, an invention: see -OUS.]

I. Senses proper to this word.

†**1.** Having high intellectual capacity; able, talented, possessed of genius. *Obs.* in general sense.

1483 CAXTON *Gold. Leg.* 113/1 He was Ingenyous ayenst the fallace of the deuyl. **1548** HALL *Chron., Edw. IV.* 231 The engenious witte of the Frenche men, excell the dull braynes of Englishmen. **1594** SHAKS. *Rich. III*, III. i. 155 Oh 'tis a perillous Boy, Bold, quicke, ingenious, forward, capable. **1649** LOVELACE *Lucasta* (1864) 9 Temples no less ingenious then Joves. *a* **1704** T. BROWN *Praise Drunkenness* Wks. 1730 I. 35 Wine gives all things, it makes the dull ingenious. **1772** SIR W. JONES *Poems* Pref. (1777) 10 Translated a few years ago from the Persian by a very ingenious gentleman. **1807** T. THOMSON *Chem.* (ed. 3) II. 212 According to the experiments of that ingenious chemist.

†**b.** Of an action, composition, etc.: Showing cleverness, talent, or genius. *Obs.* in general sense: see 3 b.

1509 HAWES *Past. Pleas.* VIII. (Percy Soc.) 31 Then must the mynde werke upon them all, By cours ingenious to rynne dyrectly After theyr thoughtes. *a* **1661** FULLER *Worthies* (1840) II. 425 Freely to follow his own ingenious inclinations. **1711** HEARNE *Collect.* (O.H.S.) III. 255 'Twas a good ingenious Sermon, about Praise. **1809** *Med. Jrnl.* XXI. 321 Some ingenious observations on Purpura, by Dr. Parry.

†**2.** Intelligent, discerning, sensible. *Obs.*

1571 DIGGES *Pantom.* III. viii. Rj b, Wherof to the ingeniouse there need no other Example. *a* **1661** FULLER *Worthies* (1840) III. 201 Especially if some ingenious gentlemen would encourage the industrious gardeners by letting ground on reasonable rates unto them. **1666** BOYLE *Orig. Formes & Qual.* To Rdr., Some Readers even among the ingenioser sort of them will take it up much better. **1733** GENT *Rippon* 46 *note*, Travels of Cyrus..worthy the Perusal of every ingenious Person. **1824** L. MURRAY *Eng. Gram.* (ed. 5) I. 387 Many of the rules and observations respecting Prosody, are taken from 'Sheridan's Art of Reading'; to which book the Compiler refers the ingenious student.

†**b.** Of animals: Intelligent, sagacious. *rare.*

1608 TOPSELL *Serpents* (1658) 604 If there had not been naturally some extraordinary faculty of understanding in this beast..His wisdome would never have sent us to a serpent..but rather to some other ingenious beast, whereof there were great store in the world. **1691** RAY *Creation* I. (1692) 198 The most noble and ingenious Creatures that live there, the Cetaceous kind.

3. Having an aptitude for invention or construction; clever at contriving or making things; skilful. This (with 3 b) is the current use.

Now usually somewhat light or sometimes even depreciative, expressing aptitude for curious device rather than solid inventiveness or skill.

1576 BAKER *Jewell of Health* 8 a, The workman and practiser, howe ingeniouser and better advysed he shall be, so much the more [etc.]. **1638** F. JUNIUS *Paint. of Ancients* 316 The laborious care of an ingenious and industrious artificer. **1668-9** MARVELL *Corr.* Wks. 1872-5 II. 245 Every one will be as ingenious as he can to his own profit. **1703** MOXON *Mech. Exerc.* 57 According to my Observation and common Consent of the most ingenious Workmen. **1798** FERRIAR *Illustr. Sterne* ii. 26 Which several ingenious men have amused themselves by contriving. **1878** JEVONS *Prim. Pol. Econ.* 35 The division of labour leads to invention, because it enables ingenious men to make invention their profession. **1885** S. COX *Expos.* Ser. I. viii. 99 So ingenious are we in tormenting ourselves.

b. Of things, actions, etc.: Showing cleverness of invention or construction; skilfully or curiously contrived or made.

1548 HALL *Chron., Rich. III* 48 Yf no ingenyous remedye coulde be otherwise invented. **1555** EDEN *Decades* To Rdr. (Arb.) 49 Ingenious inuentions of experte artificers. **1634** BRERETON *Trav.* (1844) 2 A most ingenious copperas work erected. **1719** DE FOE *Crusoe* II. v, They made abundance of most ingenious things in wicker-work. **1822** IMISON *Sc. & Art* I. 360 An ingenious contrivance, and well adapted to the purpose. **1860** MAURY *Phys. Geog. Sea* (Low) xiii. §563 The most ingenious and beautiful contrivances for deep-sea soundings were resorted to.

II. Used by confusion for INGENUOUS or L. *ingenuus.*

†**4.** Having or showing a noble disposition, high-minded; honest, candid, open, frank, ingenuous.

1597 HOOKER *Eccl. Pol.* v. lxii. §5. 141 In requitall of which ingenious moderation the rest that withstood them did it in peaceable sort. *c* **1680** BEVERIDGE *Serm.* (1729) I. 527 Our Lord having heard this ingenious confession. **1738** NEAL *Hist. Purit.* IV. 187 If Dr. Hewet had shewn himself an ingenious person, and would have owned..his share in the design against him, he would have spared his life.

†**5.** Well born or bred. *Obs.*

1638 F. JUNIUS *Paint. of Ancients* 286 Neither will any man who hath but a drop of ingenious bloud in his breast, trifle away both his art and time. **1692** WASHINGTON tr. *Milton's Def. Pop.* xii. (1851) 247 All manner of Slavery is scandalous and disgraceful to a freeborn ingenious Person. **1707** J. CHAMBERLAYNE *St. Gt. Brit.* III. xi. 386 (Colleges London) Any other thing that may any way contribute to the Accomplishment of an ingenious Nobleman or Gentleman.

†6. Of employment, education, etc.: Befitting a well-born person; 'liberal'. *Obs.*
1596 SHAKS. *Tam. Shr.* I. i. 9 A course of Learning, and ingenious studies. 1643 S. MARSHALL *Let. Vind. Himself* 7 Suppose a free man indents with another to be his servant in some ingenious employment. 1776 ADAM SMITH *W.N.* I. I. x. I. 125 Education in the ingenious arts and in the liberal professions.

†7. Inborn, innate (= L. *ingenuus*). *Obs. rare.*
1601–2 FULBECKE *1st Pt. Parall.* 58 Curtesie is a free, spontaneal and ingenious quality, to which no inforcement can be used.

ingeniously (ɪn'dʒiːnɪəslɪ), *adv.* [f. prec. + -LY².]
1. In an ingenious manner; cleverly, skilfully; †sagaciously, learnedly (*obs.*); with skilful contrivance.
1548 HALL *Chron., Hen. VII* 27b, When the commissioners were once met, they so ingeniously and effecteously proceded in their great affaires, that they agreed. 1556 J. HEYWOOD *Spider & F.* xxxii. 25 Not being geuen so much ingeniously To lerned iudgement. 1634 SIR T. HERBERT *Trav.* 147 The Quiver and Case, wrought and cut ingeniously. 1678 AUBREY in *Ray's Corr.* (1848) 129 Mr. Merret..hath methodized the laws of England very ingeniously. 1725 POPE *View Iliad & Odyss.* §5 (R.) Homer has ingeniously begun his Odyssey with the transactions at Ithaca, during the absence of Ulysses. 1753 JANE COLLIER (*title*) An Essay on the Art of ingeniously Tormenting. 1869 FREEMAN *Norm. Conq.* III. xiii. 281 A case..in which each fallacy fitted ingeniously into another.
†2. Used, by confusion, for INGENUOUSLY.
1598 FLORIO, *Ingenuamente*, freely, franckly, according to ones conscience, vnconstrained, ingeniously. 1607 SHAKS. *Timon* II. ii. 230 Prythee be not sad, Thou art true, and honest; Ingeniously I speake, No blame belongs to thee. 1692 DRYDEN *St. Euremont's Ess.* 332, I will tell you ingeniously, That it is not mine. 1740 *Col. Rec. Pennsylv.* IV. 464 Is this dealing ingeniously by me? 1765 T. HUTCHINSON *Hist. Mass.* I. i. 147 If they would ingeniously acknowledge their offence they should be forgiven. 1786 S. HASWELL *Victoria* I. 3 Tell me, therefore, ingeniously, whether he has ever entertained you [etc.].

ingeniousness (ɪn'dʒiːnɪəsnɪs). [f. as prec. + -NESS.]
1. The quality of being ingenious; cleverness, ingenuity.
1555 EDEN *Decades* 253 With great ingeniousnesse & inestimable pacience these nations haue ouercome much greater difficulties. *a*1661 FULLER *Worthies* (1662) 79 He shewed as little Ingenuity as Ingeniousnesse, who Cavilled at the Map of Grecia for imperfect, because his Fathers house in Athens was not represented therein. 1679 BURNET *Hist. Ref.* I. 326 The Bishops, wondering at the Ingeniousness and diligence of so poor a man. 1836 *Random Recoll. Ho. Lords* viii. 148 The ingeniousness of his arguments. 1885 *Academy* 22 Aug. 119/3 The paper, however, is well worth reading, owing to its perverse ingeniousness.
†2. Used, by confusion, for INGENUOUSNESS: see INGENIOUS II. *Obs.*
1665 BOYLE *Occas. Refl.* v. ix. 177 The greater appearance of Ingeniousness, as well as Innocence, there is in the practice I am disapproving, the more dangerous it is. 1753 HANWAY *Trav.* (1762) II. XIII. vii. 324 The air with which Osman delivered himself, and the seeming ingeniousness..wrought..an effect upon Arnaud.

†**in'genit, -ite,** *a.*¹ *Obs.* [ad. L. *ingenit-us* inborn, innate, pa. pple. of *ingignĕre* to engender, f. *in-* (IN-²) + *gignĕre* (†*gen-ĕre*) to beget, cause to be born.] Inborn, innate; native, natural.
1604 F. HERING *Modest Def.* 10 Some haue an ingenit propertie of curing their owne poisons. 1649 BULWER *Pathomyot.* I. vi. 28 The Muscles..performe their worke by a certaine ingenit virtue. 1669 GALE *Crt. Gentiles* I. I. iv. 25 There remains in the Syrians an ingenite ardor of Navigation. 1728 EARBERY tr. *Burnet's St. Dead* I. 14 The immortality of the Soul..some will have to be adventitious ..others will have it to be ingenite.

†**ingenit, -ite,** *a.*² *Obs.* [ad. late L. *ingenit-us* unborn, f. *in-* (IN-³) + *genitus* born, pa. pple. of *gignĕre*: see prec.] Not born or begotten; not made or produced; uncreated.
1677 GALE *Crt. Gentiles* II. IV. 253 God is both Father always existing, and ingenite. 1678 CUDWORTH *Intell. Syst.* I. iv. §20. 376 As the Monad is Ingenit or Unmade, it being the Original and Founntain of all Numbers.

ingenital (ɪn'dʒɛnɪtəl), *a. rare*⁻¹. [f. as INGENIT¹, after *congenital*.] Inborn, innate.
1886 GLADSTONE *Irish Quest.* iv. 27 This ingenital defect.

ingenium (ɪn'dʒiːnɪəm). [L., = mind, intellect.] Turn of mind; genius; talent.
1879 W. JAMES *Let.* 10 Oct. in R. B. Perry *Tht. & Char. W. J.* (1935) II. 17 Wundt..certainly is *not* a first-class *ingenium*. 1886 G. MACDONALD *What's Mine's Mine* I. xiii. 225 It [*sc.* a poem] will serve to show something of Ian's youthful *ingenium*. 1920 T. P. NUNN *Education* 205 To school a boy in the tradition of one of these ancient occupations is to ensure (if it suits his *ingenium*) that he will throw himself into his work with spirit. 1921 *Glasgow Herald* 28 Nov. 5 His scientific ingenium was as keen as ever.

†**ingenor, -our.** *Obs.* [See ENGINEER.] A constructor or director of warlike engines: = ENGINEER 2.
1601 W. T. *Ld. Remy's Civ. Consid.* 36 Wherefore the Consull being discontented herewith..sent for the Ingenour, and commanded him to be whipt. 1607 NORDEN *Surv. Dial.* 189 M. William Englebert, an excellent Ingenor.

†**ingent,** *a. Obs.* [ad. L. *ingens, ingent-em* huge, enormous, vast.] Immense, very great.
*c*1450 *Mirour Saluacioun* 668 O ingent magnytude lord blissed mot thow be. 1535 LYNDESAY *Satyre* 3458 That speciall luife ingent God had to man. 1578 BANISTER *Hist. Man* I. 14 The ingent dolours, and tormentes of the teeth.

†**ingen'teel,** *a. Obs.* [IN-³.] Ungenteel.
1658 R. FRANCK *North. Mem.* (1694) p. xviii, Let me flatter my self, that no Gentleman will be so ingenteel to censure my Survey. 1787 *Minor* 29 How ingenteel the sound of Pady, Tady, Norah, Juggy.

†**ingen'tility.** *Obs. rare*⁻¹. [IN-³.] The opposite of gentility: ungentle birth or breeding.
1604 [MIDDLETON] *Father Hubburd's T.* Wks. (Bullen) V. 601 Gold..that throwest the earthen bowl of the world, with the bias the wrong way, to peasantry, baseness, ingentility.

†**in'gentilize,** *v. Obs. rare*⁻⁰. [f. It. *ingentilire* (*ingentilisco*) to make gentle, courteous, or noble (Florio).] = GENTILIZE *v.*¹ 1.
1611 COTGR., *Anobli*, ennobled, made noble, ingentilized, made a gentleman. *Anoblir*, to ennoble, make noble, ingentilize, make a gentleman... *Anoblissement*, an ennobling, or ingentilizing.

†**in'gentle,** *v. Obs. rare*⁻¹. [f. IN-² + GENTLE *a.*, after It. *ingentilire*: cf. prec.] *trans.* To improve (a plant) by cultivation; cf. GENTLE *a.* 4.
1622 BONOEIL *Making Silk* 82 This remoouing and transplanting of wild plants doeth wonderfully mitigate and ingentle them.

†**in'genuated,** *ppl. a. rare*⁻⁰. [f. L. *ingenu-us*: see INGENUOUS.]
1623 COCKERAM, *Ingenuated*, one borne of honest stocke, noble kindred.

ingénue (ǽʒeny). [Fr., fem. of *ingénu* INGENUOUS *a.*] An artless, innocent girl or young woman; also, the representation of such a character on the stage, or the actress who plays the part. Also as *adj.* = INGENUOUS *a.* Hence **ingénueism**.
1848 THACKERAY *Van. Fair* li. 454 When attacked sometimes, Becky had a knack of adopting a demure *ingénue* air, under which she was most dangerous. 1857 G. A. LAWRENCE *Guy Liv.* xxv. 239 Mars herself could hardly play the *ingénues*, when in mature age. 1883 J. HAWTHORNE *Dust* I. viii. 134 Was this lady more or less of a woman of the world than he had imagined? Was there not, after all, something of the *ingénue* about her? 1923 C. MACKENZIE *Seven Ages of Woman* iii. 112 My dear, innocence is a charming and attractive quality; but do not be too *ingénue*. 1930 *Daily Express* 6 Oct. 5/3 French actresses grow in popularity and ingénueism the older they become. 1931 *Times Lit. Suppl.* 5 Mar. 161/4 Her French audiences, still demanding the ingénue, find her enigmatical and disquieting. 1958 *Times* 12 Nov. 3/5 The Nanetta..brings a vibrant line to music more *ingénue* than she suggests. 1967 C. O. SKINNER *Madame Sarah* viii. 171 Every one of them, with the exception of an eighteen-year-old ingénue.. declared to stay. 1973 *Daily Tel.* 16 May 15/2 And we were willing to put up with the quaint tale of the philandering husband and the sweet little ingénue Nanette.

†**in'genuine,** *a.*¹ *Obs. rare.* [f. IN-² + GENUINE, after *ingenuous*.] Genuine.
1661 *Papers on Alter. Prayer Bk.* 126 Whether it be a sign of the right and ingenuine spirit of Religion. 1661 R. L'ESTRANGE *State Divinity* 42 Which Imposition they do not understand to be a sign of the Right and Ingenuine Spirit of Religion.

†**in'genuine,** *a.*² *Obs. rare.* [IN-³.] Not genuine.
1675 R. BURTHOGGE *Causa Dei* 352 A many false, supposititious, and ingenuine [Writings].

ingenuity (ɪndʒɪ'njuːɪtɪ). [ad. L. *ingenuitās* the condition of a free-born man, noble-mindedness, frankness, f. *ingenu-us* INGENUOUS: cf. F. *ingénuité* (16th c. in Hatz.-Darm.), It. *ingenuità* (Florio, 1598), possibly the immediate source. The employment of the word as the abstract sb. from *ingenious* (for *ingeniosity* or **ingeniety*) appears to be confined to Eng. and is connected with the confusion of the two adjs. in the 17th c.: see INGENIOUS II and INGENUOUS 6.]
I. Senses connected with INGENUOUS.
†1. The condition of being free-born; honourable extraction or station. *Obs.*
1598 FLORIO, *Ingenuita*, freedome or free state, ingenuitie, a liberall, free, or honest nature and condition. 1614 SELDEN *Titles Hon.* Pref. C ij, Ingenuitie, not Nobilitie, was designed by the three Names. 1614 RALEIGH *Hist. World* v. iii. §16. 705 Such other tokens of ingenuity for his wife and children as every one did use. 1638 F. JUNIUS *Paint. of Ancients* 254 The noble Art..being forced to seek her bread without any ingenuitie, after the manner of other sordide, mechanike, and mercenarie Arts. 1658 PHILLIPS s.v., Ingenuity is taken for a free condition or state of life.

†b. The quality that befits a free-born person; high or liberal quality (of education); hence, Liberal education, intellectual culture (cf. II). *Obs.*
*a*1661 FULLER *Worthies* (1840) II. 214 He intended it for a seminary of religion and ingenuity. 1662 STILLINGFL. *Orig. Sacr.* II. ii. §1 He [Moses] was brought up in the Court of Ægypt, and..was skilled in all the learning of the Ægyptians; and these.. prove the ingenuity of his education.
†2. Nobility of character or disposition; honourableness, highmindedness, generosity. *Obs.*
1598 [see sense 1]. 1603 FLORIO *Montaigne* II. viii. (1632) 215, I should have loved to have stored their mind with ingenuity and liberty. *a*1638 MEDE *Wks.* (1672) I. xxxii. 161 This word Meekness, whose notion in the Hebrew..is as large well-nigh as Vertue itself..may be expressed, as I think, by Ingenuity, or ingenuous goodness. *a*1716 SOUTH *Twelve Serm.* (1744) II. 247 To injure or offend him that does but wish and desire our good argues little ingenuity.
3. Freedom from dissimulation; honesty, straightforwardness, sincerity; honourable or fair dealing; freedom from reserve, openness, candour, frankness. (Now *rare*, the current word being *ingenuousness*.)
1614 JACKSON *Creed* III. xiii. §11 Melchior Canus,..for a Papist a man of singular ingenuity. 1656 JER. TAYLOR *Deus Justif.* Ep. Ded., When I find that men are angry at my Ingenuity and openness of discourse. *a*1694 TILLOTSON *Serm.* (1743) VII. cxvii. 1960 This is to acknowledge that they were in an error, and mistaken..which few have the ingenuity to own. 1696 PHILLIPS (ed. 5), *Ingenuity*,..a natural Openness and Sincerity always to acknowledge the Truth. 1794 GODWIN *Cal. Williams* 8 An expression of frankness, ingenuity, and unreserve. 1889 STEVENSON *Master of B.* (1896) 188, I told her all with ingenuity, even as it is written here.
II. Senses connected with INGENIOUS.
†4. High or distinguished intellectual capacity; genius, talent, quickness of wit. *Obs.* in general sense: see 6.
1599 B. JONSON *Ev. Man out of Hum.* III. ix, Ingenuitie! I see his ignorance will not suffer him to slander her, which he had done most notably, if he had said wit for ingenuitie, as he meant it. 1639 WOODALL *Wks.* Pref. (1653) 1 May not be so much undervalued as to be ascribed to humane ingenuitie. 1644 H. PARKER *Jus Pop.* 40 It often happens, that the servant has more naturall ingenuity then the master. 1713 WARDER *True Amazons* (ed. 2) 154 If any of more Ingenuity or Leasure, will graft upon this Stock. 1795 MASON *Ch. Mus.* ii. 126 Now it is this learning and ingenuity that I chiefly object to in them.
†b. In *pl.* (of a number of persons). *Obs.*
1628 FELTHAM *Resolves* II. [I.] xlix. 144 No Age, either before or since, could present vs with so many towring Ingenuities. 1648 WOOD *Life* 15 Feb. (O.H.S.) I. 139 May it please your Gravities to admit..a kitten of the Muses.. before your sagacious ingenuities.
†5. Intellectual capacity; intelligence, sense, good judgement; normal condition of the mental faculties; (one's) senses or wits. *Obs.*
1651 BAXTER *Inf. Bapt.* 43 This errour which so strangely bereaves men of common ingenuity! 1665 BOYLE *Occas. Refl.* II. xiii. (1848) 141 He..may very probably lose his Soul, and has most certainly lost his Ingenuity. 1675 tr. *Camden's Hist. Eliz.* III. (1688) 392 A man of good Ingenuity, but not well skilled in Court Arts.
†b. *transf.* A course of action showing good sense or judgement; 'wisdom'. *Obs.*
1657 TRAPP *Comm. Ezra* viii. 22 It is the ingenuity of Saints to study Gods ends more than their own. 1660 MARVELL *Corr.* Wks. 1872–5 II. 18 It will be each man's ingenuity not to grudge an after-payment.
6. Capacity for invention or construction; skill or cleverness in contriving or making something (material or immaterial). Also as attribute of the thing, action, etc.: Skilfulness of contrivance or design. (The current sense.)
1649 BLITHE *Eng. Improv. Impr.* (1653) 101 O Sloth! stand by, & let Ingenuity try a trick or two more. 1664 POWER *Exp. Philos.* I. 76 Men, who could not readily find out the ingenuity of his knavery. 1665 GLANVILL *Def. Vain Dogm.* 67, I acknowledge the ingenuity of Sir Kenelm Digbye's Hypothesis. 1774 PENNANT *Tour Scotl. in 1772*, 145 Such is the ingenuity of our weavers that nothing in their own branch is too hard for them. 1822 HAZLITT *Table-t.* I. ix. 195 Ingenuity is genius in trifles..A clever or ingenious man is one who can do anything well. 1875 JOWETT *Plato* (ed. 2) V. 24 Coincidences too subtle to have been invented by the ingenuity of any imitator.
b. with *an* and *pl.* An ingenious device or contrivance; an artifice.
1650 FRENCH *Distill.* Ded. (1651) A iv, It is pity there is such great encouragement for many empty..arts, and none for this, and such like ingenuities. 1726 G. ROBERTS *4 Years Voy.* 270 They had an Ingenuity peculiar to themselves in splitting the Trees after they felled them. 1829 I. TAYLOR *Enthus.* vii. 177 The kind-hearted schemer..rich in petty ingenuities—always well intentioned and seldom well imagined.

ingenuous (ɪn'dʒɛnjuːəs), *a.* [f. L. *ingenu-us* native, inborn, free-born, having the qualities of a freeman, noble, frank (f. *in-* (IN-²) + *gen-*, stem of *gignĕre* to beget) + -OUS. Cf. F. *ingénu* (13th c. in Godef.).]
1. Of free or honourable birth; free-born. (Chiefly in references to Roman History.)
1638 F. JUNIUS *Paint. of Ancients* 160 It seemeth moreover to have been a priviledge of the ingenuous or free-borne lads onely. 1783 HAILES *Antiq. Chr. Ch.* vi. 192 Caracalla

bestowed the rights of citizenship on all Roman subjects who were of ingenuous birth. **1862** MERIVALE *Rom. Emp.* (1865) V. xl. 57 Augustus allowed the Roman citizens.. to intermarry with freedwomen.. because the females of ingenuous birth were not numerous enough to mate them.

2. Noble in nature, character, or disposition; generous, high-minded. (Of persons, or their dispositions, actions, etc.) *Obs.* or *arch.*

1599 MARSTON *Sco. Villanie* I. Proem., Thou nursing Mother of faire wisdomes lore, Ingenuous Melancholy. **1616** BULLOKAR, *Ingenuous*, gentleman-like. **1631** DENISON *Heav. Banq.* 182 They scoffe him; an iniury hardly indured by any ingenuous man. *a***1661** FULLER *Worthies* (1840) I. 276 His having a prince's mind imprisoned in a poor man's purse rendered him to the contempt of such who were not ingenuous. **1691** RAY *Creation* Ded. 3 To ingenuous Natures, true Honor.. is not the meanest [consideration]. **1788** PRIESTLEY *Lect. Hist.* v. xlvii. 353 Shame is no punishment except upon persons of ingenuous dispositions.

†**b.** Of animals or things: Of high or excellent quality or character; 'noble'. *Obs.*

1607 TOPSELL *Four-f. Beasts* (1658) 101 These [harts] are above all other four-footed Beasts both ingenuous and fearful. **1658** EVELYN *Fr. Gard.* (1675) 257 Pruning off the new setts, and sparing the old, as the most ingenuous and fruitful. **1664** —— *Sylva* (1679) 5 Planted in a more open, free, and ingenuous soil.

†**3.** Befitting a free-born person, or one of honourable station; liberal, high-class. *Obs.*

1611 CORYAT *Crudities* Ep. Ded., These courtly Gentlemen, whose noble parentage, ingenuous education, and vertuous conuersation haue made worthy to be admitted into your Highnesse Court. **1638** F. JUNIUS *Paint. of Ancients* 188 In old time, when naked vertue was yet in esteem.. all kinde of ingenuous arts did flourish. *a***1716** BLACKALL *Wks.* (1723) I. 333 A Person, who.. seems to have good natural Parts, and to have had ingenuous Education. **1757** BURKE *Abridgm. Eng. Hist.* III. ix. Wks. 1842 II. 592 Improved and exalted by.. that great opener of the mind, ingenuous science.

4. Honourably straightforward; open, frank, candid. (The current sense.)

1598 [implied in INGENUOUSLY 1]. **1610** BP. HALL *Apol. Brownists* in *Recoll. Treat.* (1614) 755 You begin to be ingenuous; while you confesse a reformation in the Church of England. **1621** ELSING *Debates Ho. Lords* (Camden) 21 Yf he wyll make an ingenuous confession. **1649** MILTON *Eikon.* xxi, The Damsell of Burgundie, at sight of her own letter, was soon blank, and more ingenuous then to stand outfacing. **1753** HOGARTH *Anal. Beauty* 5, I will be ingenuous enough to confess something of this may be true. **1794** E. HECTOR *Let. to Boswell* 9 Jan. in Boswell *Johnson* an. 1734 *note*, Surely it would be more ingenuous to acknowledge than to persevere. **1855** MACAULAY *Hist. Eng.* xiii. III. 260 The language which he held.. was well weighed and well guarded, but clear and ingenuous.

b. Innocently frank or open; guileless, innocent; artless. (= F. *ingénu*, *-ue*.)

1673 *Heylin's Cosmogr.* IV. 142 The People generally of a modest and ingenuous [1652 ingenious] countenance. **1750** GRAY *Elegy* xviii, To quench the blushes of ingenuous Shame. **1781** W. BLANE *Ess. Hunt.* Pref. (1788) 10 Stories of the young and ingenuous Peasant torn from his weeping Parents, and.. banished. **1877** BLACK *Green Past.* ii, These were fine notions to have got into the head of an ingenuous country maiden. **1887** *Poor Nellie* (1888) 139 His ingenuous eyes opened widely.

†**5.** Native, natural. (*nonce-use*, repr. L. *ingenuus.*) *Obs.*

1856 STANLEY *Sinai & Pal.* xiv. (1858) 460 Before the 'ingenuous rock' had been 'violated by the marble' of Constantine.

¶**6.** In 17th c. frequently misused for *ingenious*: see INGENIOUS 1–3. *Obs.*

1588 SHAKS. *L.L.L.* IV. ii. 80 If their Sonnes be ingennous [*Qo.* 1 ingenous, *Qo.* 2, *Fo.* 3 & 4 ingenuous], they shall want no instruction. *Ibid.* I. ii. 29. **1611** —— *Cymb.* IV. ii. 186 My ingenuous Instrument, (Hearke Polidore) it sounds. **1653** HOLCROFT *Procopius, Vandal Wars* I. 15 John the Cappadocian, a bad man, was ingenuous to find projects for money to the treasury, with the ruine of men. **1663** HEGG *Leg. St. Cuthbert* 42 The art [of illumination of MSS.], I confess, is both ingenuous, and commendable. **1795** *Fate of Sedley* II. 151 A sterile effort of folly and of ingenuous cunning.

ingenuously (ɪnˈdʒɛnju:əslɪ), *adv.* [f. prec. + -LY[2].]

1. In an ingenuous manner; honestly, straightforwardly, openly, frankly, candidly; without dissimulation or reserve.

1598 B. JONSON *Ev. Man in Hum.* IV. v, Tell mee, ingenuously, dost thou affect my sister Bridget, as thou pretend'st? **1611** BIBLE *Transl. Pref.* 5 Sixtus.. and Alphonsus.. doe ingenuously confesse as much. **1662** STILLINGFL. *Orig. Sacr.* I. ii. § 11 Joseph Scaliger plainly gives out, and ingenuously professeth his ignorance. **1759** DILWORTH *Pope* 47 He ingenuously sent them to him in his own handwriting. **1884** *Manch. Exam.* 15 Feb. 5/4 He entered upon a rash enterprise, and conducted it not altogether ingenuously.

†**2.** With the education or culture befitting an honourable station; in the liberal arts; liberally.

1670 R. COKE *Disc. Trade* 74 The Female Sex.. are less bred ingenuously in England, than in France, Spain, Italy, Germany, and the United Netherlands. **1673** *Ess. Educ. Gentlew.* 4 Were a competent number of Schools erected to Educate Ladyes ingenuously, methinks I see how asham'd Men would be of their Ignorance. **1674** tr. *Scheffer's Lapland* 14 Those that are most ingenuously educated in Arts and Letters.

ingenuousness (ɪnˈdʒɛnju:əsnɪs). [f. as prec. + -NESS.]

1. The condition of being free-born; honourableness or gentleness (of birth). *rare.*

1796 MORSE *Amer. Geog.* II. 219 [Burghers in Germany] commonly join to the ingenuousness of their birth the enjoyment of many privileges.

†**2.** Nobility of disposition; generosity. *Obs.*

1611 COTGR., *Ingenuité*, ingenuitie, ingenuousness; noblenesse, franknesse, gallantnesse of humor; an open, honest, franke, or liberall disposition. *a***1687** T. JACOMBE in Spurgeon *Treas. Dav.* Ps. lxxxi. 12 Take heed how you carry yourselves towards him: not only upon ingenuousness, it is base to be unkind to our Guide.

3. Freedom from dissimulation or reserve; straightforwardness, sincerity; openness, frankness, candour.

1611 [see sense 2]. **1721** BAILEY, *Ingenuity, Ingenuousness*, Freedom, Frankness, Sincerity. **1754** RICHARDSON *Grandison* II. xxix. (1781) 268 My ingenuousness shall make atonement for that error. **1794** MRS. RADCLIFFE *Myst. Udolpho* vi, There is something in the ardour and ingenuousness of youth, which is particularly pleasing to the contemplation of an old man. **1812** SIR H. DAVY *Chem. Philos.* 37 He possessed in the highest degree ingenuousness and the love of truth. **1849** MACAULAY *Hist. Eng.* vii, He.. pours out all his thoughts with the ingenuousness of a schoolboy. **1866** LOWELL *Wks.* (1890) II. 256 In Petrarch's [sonnets] all ingenuousness is frittered away into ingenuity.

¶**4.** Used by confusion for *ingeniousness* (= INGENUITY II). *Obs.*

1628 LE GRYS tr. *Barclay's Argenis* 61 The Commonwealth also will flourish with more excellent wits, while Monarchies, as aduerse to ingenuousnesse, will wither. **1642** FULLER *Holy & Prof. St.* II. xix, By his ingenuousness he [a good handicraftsman] leaves his art better than he found it. **1677** GILPIN *Demonol.* (1867) 235 They have not a malicious ingenuousness to prepare themselves without some.. chief mover.

†**ˈingeny.** *Obs.* Also 7 inj-, eng-. [ad. L. *ingenium* innate quality, nature, character, genius, f. *in-* (IN-[2]) + *gen-*, stem of *gign-ĕre* (*gen-ĕre*) to beget, cause to be born.]

1. Mind, intellect, mental faculties; mental tendency, disposition.

*c***1477** CAXTON *Jason* 72 Thou art.. the right oustyll that pollisshith and enlumyneth us and our rude ingenyes. **1583** in Sir J. Melvil *Mem.* (1735) 290 Subtil, secret, and sharp of ingeny. **1607** WALKINGTON *Opt. Glass* 42 A fat belly hath a leane ingenie. **1659** T. PECKE *Parnassi Puerp.* 2 Not Hope, but real Worth doth magnifie The happy Torrent of the Ingenie. **1691** WOOD *Ath. Oxon.* I. 483 A person of great erudition.. and of a most polite ingenie. **1708** MOTTEUX *Rabelais* (1737) V. 230 In which your Ingeny finds Delectation.

b. Distinctive character, nature, or 'spirit' (of a thing): = GENIUS 3 b–e.

1647 SPRIGGE *Anglia Rediv.* IV. vii. (1854) 279 How Oxford, a place of books and colleges, could have been reduced into its gown and peace, but by a motion.. as little destructive, and as suitable to the ingeny of such a place of arts. **1662** J. SPARROW tr. *Behme's Rem. Wks., Complexions* 2 The property and Ingeny or Inclination of the Constellations.

2. Intellectual capacity, mental ability; genius, talent, cleverness, ingenuity.

1474 CAXTON *Chesse* II. ii. (1860) B iv b, The senatours.. commendyd gretly the ingenye and wytte of the chyld. **1596** NASHE *Saffron Walden* 77 *Miserere mei*! what an ingeny is heere? **1602** N. BAXTER *Sidneys Ourania* N ij, Renowned Poets, of highest Ingenie, Shall decke thy tombe with ever-lasting fame. **1662** GLANVILL *Lux Orient.* xiii. (1682) 110 The deaf and dumb have many times.. very remarkable mechanical ingenies. **1697** tr. *Burgersdicius his Logic* II. xix. 92 The scholar may have more ingeny and industry than his master.

†**3.** An invention; a clever contrivance. *Obs. rare.*

1588 R. PARKE tr. *Mendoza's Hist. China* 101 The admirable inuention and the subtill ingenie of printing.

†**inˈgere**, *v. Obs. rare.* [a. F. *ingére-r* (Oresme, 14th c.), or ad. L. *inger-ĕre* to carry in, put or push in, obtrude: see INGEST. The usual Scotch form was INGYRE, q.v.] *refl.* To thrust oneself in, to obtrude oneself, intrude; to presume.

1489 CAXTON *Faytes of A.* III. xxi. 221 Yf it hap that som chapellayn.. goo to werre or that ingereth or putteth hymself forthe.. therto. **1562** WINȜET *Cert. Tractates* ii. Wks. 1888 I. 21 King Ozias, quha in his presumptioun, ingerit him self to offer the brynt sacrifice. **1563** —— *Four Scoir Thre Quest.* ibid. 67 We ingere ws bauldlie.. to propone thir quæstionis folloving.

ingerence (ˈɪndʒərəns). *rare.* [f. L. *ingerĕre* (see INGEST *v.*) + -ENCE. Cf. F. *ingérence.*] Bearing in upon; intrusion; interference.

[**1879** MARQ. SALISBURY in G. Cecil *Life Marq. Salisbury* (1921) II. 356 This is a considerable advance in the direction of 'ingérence' over anything we did either in the case of Rivers Wilson or Romaine.] **1886** *Spectator* 16 Jan. 79 The status of a protected State excludes, of course, all ingerence in the foreign or domestic affairs of the protecting State. **1920** *Edin. Rev.* July 43 It is astonishing to what extent the ingerence of Belgrade is already tolerated.

inˈgerminate, *v.* *rare*$^{-0}$. [IN-[2].] *trans.* To cause to germinate (Worcester, 1860).

†**Ingersollian** (ɪŋgəˈsɒlɪən), *a. Obs.* [f. the name of the American agnostic, Robert Green *Ingersoll* (1833–99) + -IAN.] Imbued with the tenets of R. G. Ingersoll. So **ˈIngersollism**, the doctrines or tenets of Ingersoll.

1883 G. R. WENDLING (*title*) Ingersollism; from a secular point of view. **1892** STEVENSON & OSBOURNE *Wrecker* xi. 179, I don't know if you quite believe in prayer, I'm a bit Ingersollian myself.

†**inˈgert**, *v.*, obs. variant of ENGIRT *v.*

1599 R. LINCHE *Fount. Anc. Fict.* H ij, Close to their bodies is the same ingerted.

ingest (ɪnˈdʒɛst), *v.* [f. L. *ingest-*, ppl. stem of *ingerĕre* to carry in, put or push in, f. *in-* (IN-[2]) + *gerĕre* to carry, bear; cf. *digest*, *egest*.]

†**1.** *trans.* To put in, push in, thrust in. *Obs.*

1617 COLLINS *Def. Bp. Ely* II. viii. 343 When he cannot aspire thether himselfe, he ingests in other partners and compossessioners, he cares not whome.

2. *spec.* To introduce (aliment) into the stomach (or mouth); to take in (food).

1620 VENNER *Via Recta* viii. 164 It is most hurtfull to the body to ingest nourishment vpon nourishment not digested. **1665** G. HARVEY *Advice agst. Plague* 5 Arsenick ingested within the Body.. immediatly effects enormous Vomits. **1709** BLAIR in *Phil. Trans.* XXVII. 98 How can Aliments be ingested into the Mouth, and not pass over by the Larynx? **1848** CARPENTER *Anim. Phys.* i. (1872) 27 A mouth and stomach.. extemporized, as it were on each occasion that aliment is ingested. **1878** BELL *Gegenbaur's Comp. Anat.* 16 At times, indeed, we can see the protoplasm ingesting food.

‖**ingesta** (ɪnˈdʒɛstə), *sb. pl. Phys.* [L. *ingesta*, neut. pl. of *ingestus*, pa. pple. of *ingerĕre*: see prec.] Substances introduced into the body as nourishment; food and drink.

1727 POPE, etc. *M. Scriblerus* I. xiv, The extraordinary quantity of the *Ingesta* and *Egesta* of the people of England. **1805** W. SAUNDERS *Min. Waters* 449 A substance which forms so large a portion of the ingesta, must have a powerful and constant agency upon the animal machine. **1855** H. SPENCER *Princ. Psychol.* (1872) I. II. ix. 274 Inaction, due to deficiency of liquid in the ingesta.

†**ingestar, -ter.** *Obs. rare.* Also ingistera. [ad. It. *inghistara*, *inguistara*, in Florio *enghistara.*] (See quots.)

1611 CORYAT *Crudities* 288 These wines are alwayes brought up.. in certaine great glasses called Ingistera'es that are commonly used in all those cities of Italy that I surveied. **1612** *Trav. Four Englishm.* 29 Euery one that was able, brought.. many bottles or ingesters of exceeding good wine. **1617** MORYSON *Itin.* I. 96 An ingestar of wine (a measure somewhat bigger then the English pint).

ingested (ɪnˈdʒɛstɪd), *ppl. a.* [f. INGEST *v.* + -ED[1].] Taken in (as food).

1646 SIR T. BROWNE *Pseud. Ep.* IV. vii. 196 The grosse ponderosity of the aliment ingested. **1755** FLEMING in *Phil. Trans.* XLIX. 259 Fæces formed out of ingested aliments. *c***1865** *Circ. Sc.* I. 328/1 The essence of the ingested nutriment passes.. into the circulation.

†**inˈgestible**, *a. Obs.* *rare*$^{-0}$. [IN-[3]; cf. L. *ingestābilis* (Pliny).] 'Heavy, hard to be borne' (Cockeram, 1623).

ingestion (ɪnˈdʒɛstjən). [ad. late L. *ingestiōn-em*, n. of action f. *ingerĕre* to INGEST. Cf. mod.F. *ingestion.*] The action of ingesting; the taking in of aliment.

1620 VENNER *Via Recta* viii. 175 The ingestion of too much meat is burthensome and iniurious to all the body. **1665** JER. TAYLOR *Unum Necess.* vii. §1 That Adam was made mortal.. is.. proved by his very eating and drinking.. by ingestion and egestion. **1834** J. FORBES *Laennec's Dis. Chest* (ed. 4) 238 The ingestion of the medicine in an agreeable vehicle. **1858** J. H. BENNET *Nutrition* iv. 86 The ingestion of alcoholic stimulants.. is attended with a feeling of temporary strength.

ingestive (ɪnˈdʒɛstɪv), *a.* [f. INGEST *v.* + -IVE.] Having the function of taking in aliment.

1835-6 TODD *Cycl. Anat.* I. 69/1 Less activity is indicated in the egestive than in the ingestive system. **1877** HUXLEY *Anat. Inv. Anim.* i. 50 The ingestive apertures are numerous secondary pore-like apertures formed by the separation of adjacent cells of the ectoderm and endoderm.

†**ˈinˌgetting**, *vbl. sb. Sc. Obs.* [IN *adv.* 11 c; cf. *get in*, GET *v.* 68 f.] The action of getting in, collecting.

1546 *Sc. Acts Mary* (1814) II. 476 Þe ingetting of the contributioune grantit to þe sete of sessioune. **1597** *Sc. Acts Jas. VI* (1816) IV. 146 The chairges in ingetting of þe samin [tax]. **1640-1** *Kirkcudbr. War-Comm. Min. Bk.* (1855) 138 Assisting of the Collectores and Commissar for ingetting of what is dew to the publict.

Inghamite (ˈɪŋəmaɪt). [f. the surname *Ingham* + -ITE.] A member of the religious body founded about 1740 by Benjamin Ingham (1712–72) of Aberford, near York, on principles akin to those of the Moravians and Methodists. Also *attrib.*

1839 in *Penny Cycl.* XV. 141/1. **1858-60** J. GARDNER *Faiths World* s.v., Remains of the Inghamites are still found in England, but they are a very small body. **1874** J. H. BLUNT *Dict. Sects* s.v., Nine Inghamite chapels [are] enumerated in the Religious Census of 1851.

†**in'giddied**, *ppl. a. Obs. rare*$^{-1}$. [f. IN-^{2} + GIDDY *v.* + -ED^{1}.] Made giddy or unsteady.
1628 FELTHAM *Resolves* II [I.] xxix. 92 He has left vertue ..and is lanched into by-deuices of his owne ingiddyed braine.

†**in'gild**, obs. var. of ENGILD *v.*, to gild.
1598 FLORIO, *Innorare*, to inguilde, to guild.

Ingin. A U.S. colloq. spelling of INDIAN. (Cf. INJUN.)
1683 *Early Rec. Groton, Mass.* (1880) 82 If any Ingins can proue a lagiall [= legal] titall. **1869** B. HARTE *Luck of Roaring Camp* 15 They're mighty rough on strangers, and they worship an Ingin baby. **1870** J. C. DUVAL *Adventures Big-Foot Wallace* xlvi. 303 Whenever he can get to where there's liquor, either the liquor gives out, or he gets 'Ingin drunk'.

ingin, variant of INGAN *dial.*, onion.

inginare, -arie, obs. ff. ENGINEER, ENGINERY.

†**ingine** (ɪn'dʒaɪn). [The usual Sc. form of ENGINE *sb.*, in senses 1 and 2 of that word, q.v. for other examples.] Genius, natural ability, intellect.
1501 DOUGLAS *Pal. Hon.* II. 156 The bounteis of that court dewlie to write War ouir prolixt, transcending mine ingine. **1511** DUNBAR *Poems* lxxvii. 60 Hir for to treit thai sett thair haill ingyne. **1562** WIN3ET *Cert. Tractates* i. Wks. 1888 I. 5 Pure studentis of ryche ingynis. **1596** DALRYMPLE tr. *Leslie's Hist. Scot.* II. 137 Of ane elegant forme, and ane rype Ingine. *c* **1620** SIR W. MURE *Misc. Poems* xx. 11 The puir issues of my weak ingyne. **1819** W. TENNANT *Papistry Storm'd* (1827) 17 And I na help their weak ingyne Wi' my suggestions strang?
Hence †**in'gined** *a.*, minded, disposed. *rare*$^{-1}$.
a **1605** POLWART *Flyting w. Montgomerie* 155 Iacstro, bee better anes inginde, Or I shall flyte against my sell.

ingineer, -er(e, -ier, obs. ff. ENGINEER.

inginous, variant of ENGINOUS *a.*, *Obs.*

ingird, ingirdle: see ENGIRD, ENGIRDLE.

ingire, variant of INGYRE *v.*, *Obs.*

ingirt, variant of ENGIRT *v.*, *Obs.*

†**'in,giver.** *Sc. Obs.* [IN *adv.* 11e; cf. *give in*, GIVE *v.* 59e.] One who gives or hands in (a document, etc.).
1621 *Sc. Acts Jas. VI* (1816) IV. 599 [To] giff vp his Inventar..whiche The Ingevar sall declair to be a trew deid. **1640** *Sc. Acts Chas. I*, V. 291 (Jam.) The ingiveris of the saids articles.

'in,giving, *vbl. sb. rare.* [IN *adv.* 11c: cf. prec.] Giving in, handing in.
1677 W. ROW *Contn. Blair's Autobiog.* x. (1848) 217 After the ingiving of these papers they repaired to Gravesend. **1868** *Act 31 & 32 Vict.* c. 101 §80 Resignation shall be held to be duly made..by the ingiving of the note applying for the charter.

†**in'glamus**, *a. Obs.* var. of ENGLEIMOUS, viscid.
1483 *Cath. Angl.* 195/2 Inglamus, *viscosus.*

Ingland, -londe, obs. forms of ENGLAND.

ingle ('ɪŋg(ə)l, *Sc.* 'ɪŋ(ə)l), *sb.*^{1} Orig. *Sc.* Also 6 ingil(l. [Origin obscure; usually identified with Gael. *aingeal* fire, light; but there are difficulties.]
1. Fire; a fire burning upon the hearth; a house-fire. Now chiefly in *at, by,* or ***round the ingle***.
1508 DUNBAR *Flyting w. Kennedie* 117 Fane at evin for to bring hame a single, Syne rubb it at ane vthir auld wyfis ingle. **1513** DOUGLAS *Æneis* XII. iii. 16 Sum otheris brocht the fontane watter fayr And sum the haly ingill wyth thame bair. *a* **1605** POLWART *Flyting w. Montgom.* 667 Thou sat sa neir the chimney nuik..Fast be the ingle. **1674** RAY *N.C. Words* 26 *Ingle* (Cumb.), fire, a blaze or flame. **1721** RAMSAY *Up in the Air* 2 Now the sun's gane out o' sight Beet the ingle, and snuff the light. **1785** BURNS *Cotter's Sat. Night* iii, His wee bit ingle, blinkin bonilie, His clean hearth-stane. **1820** KEATS *Fancy* 16 Sit thee by the ingle, when The sear faggot blazes bright. **1856** R. A. VAUGHAN *Mystics* (1860) I. 270 With stories such as these..the holy man whiled away our windy March nights by the ingle. **1882** MRS. OLIPHANT *Lit. Hist. Eng.* I. 165 The landlord and all his guests were assembled round the ingle.
¶**2.** Misapplied to an open fireplace.
1841 LYTTON *Nt. & Morn.* v. ii, He settled himself in the ingle, till the guard's horn should arouse him. **1894** HALL CAINE *Manxman* VI. xiii, Cæsar..left Kate as he had found her, crouching by the fire inside the wide ingle of the old hall.
3. *attrib.* and *Comb.*, as **ingle-bench**, a bench beside the fire; **ingle-bred** *a.*, home-bred, untravelled. See also INGLE-CHEEK, -NOOK, -SIDE.
1853 M. ARNOLD *Scholar Gipsy* vi, At some lone ale house in the Berkshire moors, On the warm *ingle-bench, the smock-frocked boors Had found him seated. **1881** ROSSETTI *Ball. & Sonn., Rose Mary* II. xxxii, On the ingle-bench the dead man lay. **1788** PICKEN *Poems* 112 Mony an *ingle-bred auld wife Has baith mair wit an' senses Than me.

ingle, *sb.*^{2} Also 7 eng(h)le, inghle. [Origin unknown: cf. NINGLE.] A boy-favourite (in bad sense); a catamite.
1592 NASHE *Strange News* Wks. (Grosart) II. 277, I am afraid thou wilt make me thy ingle. **1598** FLORIO, *Catamito*, a ganimed, an ingle. **1601** B. JONSON *Poetaster* I. ii, What? shall I have my sonne a stager now? an enghle for players? **1602** MIDDLETON *Blurt, Master-Const.* v. ii, Jove's own ingle, Ganymede. *a* **1610** HEALEY *Theophrastus* (1636) 11 And alwaies sitting by his Ingle courts him. *a* **1683** OLDHAM *Poet. Wks.* (1686) 88 What costs a Rape, or Incest, and how cheap You may an Harlot, or an Ingle keep. **1708** MOTTEUX *Rabelais, Pantagr. Prognost.* v, Those whom Venus is said to rule; as..Ganymedes, Bardachoes, Huflers, Ingles. **1878** SIMPSON tr. *Prodigal Son* I. in Simpson *Sch. Shaks.* II. 93 They lose the bloom of their youth with good-for-nothing companions, or even with whores and ingles. **1926** T. E. LAWRENCE *Seven Pillars* (1935) lxxxi. 448 Abd el Kader called them whoresons, ingle's accidents, sons of a bitch,.. jetting his insults broadcast to the room-full. **1962** H. NICOLSON *Monarchy* v. 94 The Romans were startled by the arrival of this Asian ingle as their Emperor.
¶ Misused for 'Familiar friend', 'chum'.
1821 SCOTT *Kenilw.* iii, 'Ha! my dear friend and ingle, Tony Foster!..have you altogether forgotten your friend, gossip, and playfellow, Michael Lambourne?'

ingle, *sb.*^{3} *local.* [Of doubtful status and derivation.] ? A nook; an angle.
1877 *N.W. Linc. Gloss.*, *Hingles*, the ingles, the corners inside an open chimney. **1890** MORRIS *Glittering Plain* xx, Hallblithe steered toward an ingle of the haven.

†**ingle**, *v. Obs.* [f. INGLE *sb.*^{2}]
1. *trans.* To fondle, caress.
1598 FLORIO, *Zanzerare*, to ingle boies, to play wantonly with boyes against nature. **1599** NASHE *Lenten Stuffe* Ep. Ded. (1871) 15 Hug it, ingle it, kiss it, and cull it now thou hast it. **1601** CHESTER *Love's Mart., Invoc. Poet. Ess.* (1878) 171 And..Ingles his cheeke. *a* **1631** DONNE *Elegy* iv. Poems, etc. (1633) 49 Thy little brethren..those sweet nights..kist, and ingled on thy father's knee.
2. To cajole, wheedle, coax.
1601 B. JONSON *Poetaster* II. ii, I'le presently goe and enghle some broker for a Poets gowne, and bespeak a garland. **1602** MIDDLETON *Blurt, Master-Const.* II. ii, Prithee, Simperina, do not ingle me; do not flatter me, Trivia.
3. *intr.* To fondle *with*.
1611 MIDDLETON & DEKKER *Roaring Girle* IV. Wks. 1873 III. 202 Then deale they vnder hand with vs, and wee must ingle with our husbands a bed.
Hence '**ingling** *vbl. sb.* and *ppl. a.*
1595 T. EDWARDS *Cephalus & Procris* (1878) 43 We'le take more ioy in counting ouer sorrowes, Than Venus gazing on her ingling sparrowes. **1598** E. GILPIN *Skial.* (1878) 3 Insteede of ingling termes for thy good will, Reader fall to, reade, iest, and carpe thy fill. **1610** *Histrio-m.* II. 140 Then we shall have rare ingling at the prodigall child.

ingle-cheek. *Sc.* [f. INGLE *sb.*^{1}] The cheek or jamb of a fireplace.
c **1774** C. KEITH *Farmer's Ha'* iv, They a' drive to the ingle-cheek. **1785** BURNS *Vision* I. iii, There, lanely, by the ingle-cheek, I sat and ey'd the spewing reek. **1899** *Scott. Endeavour* Oct. 2 Sitting on a low stool by the ingle cheek.

ingle-nook. Orig. *Sc.* [f. INGLE *sb.*^{1}] The nook or corner beside the 'ingle'; chimney-corner.
a **1774** FERGUSSON *Poems* (1789) II. 6 (Jam.) The ingle-nook supplies the simmer fields. **1816** SCOTT *Old Mort.* iv, I'll begin with that sulky blue-bonnet in the ingle-nook. **1844** DISRAELI *Coningsby* III. i, There was a comfortable enough looking kitchen; but the ingle nook was full of smokers. **1859** GEO. ELIOT *A. Bede* ii, 'Old Feyther Taft'.. had some time ago gone back to his ingle-nook.

Ingles, variant of INGLIS, *Obs.*

ingle-side. [f. INGLE *sb.*^{1}] A fire-side.
? *a* **1750** *Humble Beggar* x. in Herd *Collect. Sc. Songs* (1776) II. 30 But he was first hame at his ain ingle-side. **1815** SCOTT *Guy M.* xii, It's an auld story now, and every body tells it as we were doing, their ain way by the ingleside. **1887** R. BUCHANAN *Heir of Linne* ii, The farmers welcomed Willie to their inglesides.

ingliding ('ɪnglaɪdɪŋ), *ppl. a. Phonology.* [f. IN *adv.* + GLIDING *ppl. a.*] Gliding towards the central vowel sound (ə), as in words like *air*, *here*, and *poor*, and in U.S. regional pronunciations like *wood* (wʊəd), *bell* (bɛəl), *stem* (stɛəm), *pal* (pæəl); = CENTRING *ppl. a.* Also '**inglide** *sb.*
1948 R. I. McDAVID in *Amer. Speech* XXIII. 203 An apparent tendency to replace the low-country ingliding diphthongs in *date*, *boat* [deᵊt], [boᵊt] with the up-country upgliding type [de·ɪt, bo·ut] also suggests a reversal of the trend in prestige values. **1956** D. W. REED in A. A. Hill *First Texas Conference on Problems of Linguistic Analysis in English* (1962) 3 According to the Trager and Smith analysis there are nine pure vowels—/V/—and nine combinations of vowel and length or inglide. *Ibid.* 93, I think in-glide is a better name than central glide, since in-glide names a direction, central names only an area. **1959** T. H. WETMORE in *Publ. Amer. Dial. Soc.* XXXII. 76 In central Virginia Piedmont..approximately half of the informants have an inglide in the vowel of *pot*. *Ibid.* 112 *Off* with an ingliding diphthong is heard with equal frequency. **1961** KURATH & McDAVID *Pronunc. Eng. in Atlantic States* iii. 101/2 Before voiceless stops, inglides are less common and briefer, and in words of more than one syllable they are infrequent. **1962** *Amer. Speech* XXXVII. 70 Stressed free vowels are upgliding, and all stressed checked vowels are ingliding. **1963** *Ibid.* XXXVIII. 129 An ingliding diphthong [iə]. **1965** *Canad. Jrnl. Linguistics* Fall 64 The free segments are predominantly monophthongal or ingliding. **1972** H. KURATH *Studies in Area Linguistics* vi. 73 Elsewhere ingliding [ɔə~uə] or monophthongal [o~ɔ] are current.

†'**Inglis**, usual 14–16th c. *Sc.* and *north.* form of ENGLISH *a.* and *sb.* Also rarely Ingles(e, -isch, -ise, -ishe, etc.
a **1300** *Cursor M.* 242 Þis ilk bok es translate In to Inglis tong to rede For the loue of Inglis lede. *c* **1470** HENRY *Wallace* I. 351 Inglis clerks in prophecys thai fand [etc.]. **1508** DUNBAR *Gold. Targe* 259 Was thou noucht of oure Inglisch all the lycht? **1513** DOUGLAS *Æneis* I. Prol. 24 Williame Caxtoun, of Inglis natioun, In pross hes prent ane buik of Inglis gros. **1596** DALRYMPLE tr. *Leslie's Hist. Scot.* I. 3 Peple plane ignorant of the Ingles toung. *Ibid.* 82 The Inglise historiographouris. *Ibid.*, The dignitie of the Inglishe name.
So †'**Inglisman**, usual 14–16th c. *north.* and *Sc.* form of ENGLISHMAN. Also **Ingles-, -ise-.**
a **1300** *Cursor M.* 249 To laud and Inglis man i spell. *c* **1425** WYNTOUN *Chron.* VIII. xiii. 19 Gret Despyte þir Inglis men Had at þis Willame Walays þen. **1535** STEWART *Cron. Scot.* 80 Our ald storeis..Tha war distroyit all with Inglismen. **1596** DALRYMPLE tr. *Leslie's Hist. Scot.* I. 85 The Ingles men..vses that ald Saxon toung. *Ibid.* 97 Thair nycht bouris the Inglise men.

Inglishry, obs. form of ENGLISHRY.

inglobate (ɪn'gləʊbət), *a. rare*$^{-1}$. [f. IN-^{2} + GLOBATE *ppl. a.*] Formed into a globe or globular mass.
1852 OTTÉ & PAUL tr. *Humboldt's Cosmos* IV. vii. *Nebulæ* ¶2 If they be vapoury masses, having one or more nebulous nuclei, the various degrees of their condensation suggest the possibility of a process of gradual star-formation from inglobate matter.

inglobe, obs. form of ENGLOBE *v.*

†**in'glomerated**, *ppl. a. Obs. rare*$^{-1}$. [f. L. *inglomerāt-us* (pa. pple of *inglomerāre*; see IN-^{2} and GLOMERATE) + -ED^{1}.] Formed into a rounded mass or heap.
1592 R. D. *Hypnerotomachia* 14 Unto which inglomerated and winding heape of bowelles, there was a convenient comming unto and entrance in.

inglorious (ɪn'glɔərɪəs), *a.* [ad. L. *inglōriōsus* (Pliny): see IN-^{3} and GLORIOUS, and cf. L. *inglōrius*, and F. *inglorieux* (14th c. in Littré).]
1. Not glorious, famous, or renowned; not known to fame; obscure, humble. Now *rare*.
1591 SPENSER *M. Hubberd* 981 Who will not venture life a King to bee, And rather rule..Than dwell in dust inglorious and bace? **1602** *2nd Pt. Return fr. Parnass.* IV. v. (Arb.) 61 Inglorious may they liue, inglorious die, That suffer learning liue in misery. **1671** MILTON *P.R.* III. 42. **1750** GRAY *Elegy* xv, Some mute inglorious Milton here may rest. **1881** STEVENSON *Virg. Puerisque* 120 That mighty place of education, which..turns out yearly many inglorious masters in the Science of the Aspects of Life.
†**b.** Without the glory *of* (something). *rare.*
1788 GIBBON *Decl. & F.* lxiii. (1855) VII. 401 The far greater part were guiltless or inglorious of the deed.
2. Of actions, mode of life, etc.: Bringing no glory or honour (to a person); hence, conferring disgrace, shameful, ignominious.
1573 G. HARVEY *Letter-bk.* (Camden) 41 Which was not so commodious for me..as it was inglorius for them, to ther wunderful greif. **1576** FLEMING *Panopl. Epist.* 161 Neyther let your battell be ingloryous, exempted from noblenesse. **1665** MANLEY *Grotius' Low C. Warres* 824 The King [was] freed from such an inglorious contest. **1776** GIBBON *Decl. & F.* v. (1869) I. 106 The victory over the senate was easy and inglorious. **1849** MACAULAY *Hist. Eng.* ii. I. 191 It involved the country in an inglorious, unprofitable, and interminable war. **1864** BRYCE *Holy Rom. Emp.* xiv. (1875) 224 An inglorious traffic in honours and exemptions.

ingloriously (ɪn'glɔərɪəslɪ), *adv.* [f. prec. + -LY^{2}.] In an inglorious manner, without glory; ignominiously.
1576 FLEMING *Panopl. Epist.* 159 When the successes.. shall be blemished, stayned, and ingloriously defaced. **1615** G. SANDYS *Trav.* I. 46 He reigned eight yeares ingloriously. **1710** SWIFT *On a Broomstick* Wks. 1755 II. I. 180 This single stick, which you now behold ingloriously lying in that neglected corner. **1816** BYRON *Ch. Har.* III. xliv, A sword laid by Which eats into itself, and rusts ingloriously. **1875** JOWETT *Plato* (ed. 2) V. 443 Those who meet their death in this way..shall be buried ingloriously.

ingloriousness (ɪn'glɔərɪəsnɪs). [f. as prec. + -NESS.] The condition or quality of being inglorious; obscurity; ignominy.
1630 DONNE *Serm.* xxv. 249 The ingloriousnesse of having been buried in the dust is recompensed in the glory I rise to. **1654** W. MOUNTAGUE *Devout Ess.* II. i. §2. 9 The Scrutator of this mystery shall be opprest by the ingloriousness of the object. **1661** A. WRIGHT in Spurgeon *Treas. Dav.* Ps. lxii. 7 Let him that walks in the ingloriousness and contempt of the world, contemplate God. **1832** MOORE *Diary* 6 Apr. in *Mem.* (1853) VI. 264 The ingloriousness of such a combat.

inglut, -glutte, obs. forms of ENGLUT *v.*

inglu'tition. *rare.* [n. of action f. late L. *inglūtīre* (Isidore): cf. *glutition, deglutition.*] The action of swallowing.

1803 G. ELLIS *Let. to Scott* 3 Oct. in Lockhart *Scott*, A most formidable drinker whose powers of inglutition.. had procured him a long series of triumphs.

in'gluvial, *a. rare.* [f. next + -AL[1].] Of or pertaining to the ingluvies or crop.

1843 OWEN *Comp. Anat. Inv. Anim.* xvii. 217 In the .. carnivorous Carabidæ, there is a small gizzard, preceded by the usual ingluvial dilatation of the œsophagus.

‖**ingluvies** (ɪn'gluːviːz). *Anat.* [L. *ingluviēs* crop, maw: prob. f. **glŭ-* to swallow.] A dilatation of the œsophagus before it reaches the true stomach; the crop of a bird, the first stomach of a ruminating animal, an insect, etc.

1727–41 CHAMBERS *Cycl.*, *Ingluvies*, Craw, or Crop, a part in granivorous fowls which serves for the immediate reception of the food. **1877** HUXLEY *Anat. Inv. Anim.* vii. 411 The chitinous lining which is continued into it from the ingluvies is greatly thickened. **1884** COUES *Key to N. Amer. Birds* 212 The œsophagus of many birds becomes modified into a special pouch,—the crop or craw, *ingluvies*, where the food is detained to be macerated in a special secretion, before passing on to the true stomach.

ingluvin (ɪn'gluːvɪn). *Med.* [f. INGLUV-IES + -IN.] A preparation from the gizzard of the domestic chicken, used as a tonic and digestive.

1881 *Braithwaite's Retrospect Med.* LXXXIII. 319 Where marked plethora exists, or a full habit of body obtains, the effect of ingluvin is very uncertain. **1898** MARTINDALE & WESTCOTT *Extra Pharmacop.* (ed. 9) 269 Ingluvin had little or no digestive action on coagulated egg-albumen.

†**in'gluvious,** *a. Obs.* [ad. L. *ingluviōs-us* gluttonous, f. *ingluviēs*: see prec. and -OUS. Cf. obs. F. *ingluvieux* (Godef.).] Greedy, gluttonous.

1569 NEWTON *Cicero's Olde Age* 23 b, We must not be too ingluuious, in taking of foode and repaste. *a* **1659** CLEVELAND *Poems, Surv. World* v, What a cold Account of Happiness can here arise From that ingluvious Surfeit of his Eyes?

Hence †**in'gluviously** *adv.*, gluttonously.

1574 NEWTON *Health Mag.* 19 Immoderately dronken and ingluviouslie swilled. **1576** —— *Lemnie's Complex.* (1633) 175 Those.. that have excessively and ingluviously surfeited either in eating or drinking.

†**ingnel,** *a. Obs. rare*[−1]. [a. OF. *ingnel, ignel, inel, isnel*, of Germ. origin; see SNELL.] Quick, swift.

1340 *Ayenb.* 141 Efterward þe milde is wel zuift and wel ingnel.

†**in'go,** *v. Obs.* Forms: see GO. [OE. *ingán* = MHG. *îngân* (G. *eingehen*), Du. *ingaan*, Sw. *ingå*, Da. *indgaa*; see IN-[1] and GO. OE. had also *ingangan* = OHG. *ingangan*, Goth. *inngangan*: see GANG *v.*] *intr.* To go in, to enter.

c **900** tr. *Bæda's Hist.* v. iv. (1890) 394 Þa.. [he] in þes ȝesiðes hus ineode. *c* **1000** *Ags. Gosp.* Matt. xii. 29 Hu mæȝ man ingan on stranges hus. *c* **1250** *Gen. & Ex.* 1068 He boden him bringen ut o-non, Ðo men ðat woren ðidir in gon. *a* **1300** *E.E. Psalter* xlii[i]. 4 To Goddes weved in ga I sal. *Ibid.* cviii. [cix.] 18 Als watre, it in yhede In his inwardes. *a* **1340** HAMPOLE *Psalter* xiv. 2 He þat ingase wiþouten spot. **1382** WYCLIF *Gen.* xxxviii. 16 And he yngoynge to hir, seith, Lat me, that Y goo togidere with thee.

in-goal ('ɪngəʊl). *Rugby Football.* [f. IN *prep.* + GOAL *sb.* 3.] (See quot. 1897.)

1897 *Encycl. Sport* I. 430/2 Those portions of the ground immediately at the ends of the field of play and between the touch-lines, produced to the dead-ball lines, are called in-goal. The goal-lines are in-goal. **1935** [see FAIR *a.* 10 d]. **1960** V. JENKINS *Lions Down Under* xiv. 207 The penalty-try awarded when E. J. Faire obstructed A. J. F. O'Reilly in the in-goal area.

ingoar, variant of ENGORE *v.*[1], *Obs.*

in-'God, *v.* [cf. *engod* (EN- *pref.*[1] B. 2).] *trans.* To deify, make divine; to take into God or into the godhead. So **in-'Godding** *vbl. sb.*

1891 *Church Times* 20 Nov. 1128/1 The Humanity already in-Godded in the Person of the Second Person of the Holy Trinity. **1957** D. L. SAYERS *Further Papers on Dante* 187 Every creature.. possesses a true self which, however much perfected or (in Dante's words) 'in-godded', is never swallowed up or lost in God. **1959** *N. & Q.* July–Aug. 301/2 Dante expounded in the *Comedy* a mystic Way of Affirmation for the 'in-Godding' of man based on the vision of the beloved.

'in,going, *vbl. sb.* Now *rare.* [f. INGO *v.*, or the verbal phrase *go in* (see IN-[1]) + -ING[1].]

1. a. A going in or entering; entrance; passage or way in.

1340 *Ayenb.* 72 Dyaþ is to guodemen ende of alle kueade and gate and inguoynge of alle guode. **1362** LANGL. *P. Pl.* A. VI. 117 Hit is ful hard.. To gete in-goynge [*v.r.* ingange] at þat ȝat. *a* **1400** *Prymer* (1891) 34 Lord kepe þyn ingoynge and thyn outgoynge. **1535** COVERDALE *1 Sam.* xxix. 6 Thy out goynge and ingoynge with me in yᵉ hoost pleaseth me well. **1632** LITHGOW *Trav.* VI. 249 Payed ten Madins of Brasse, the common coine of Jerusalem, for our in-going to that place. **1871** ROSSETTI *Dante at Verona* xiii, The ushers on his path would bend At ingoing as at going out.

b. *Arch.* The recess for a doorway or window.

1859 DONALDSON & GLEN *Specifications* I. 218 Ingoings of all the doors, or other openings in thick walls, to be finished with.. linings. *Ibid.* 270 Ingoings of all the windows.. to be finished with.. linings.

2. The sum paid by a tenant or purchaser for fixtures, etc., on taking over business or other premises.

1905 *Daily Chron.* 4 May, Furniture Business.. for Sale; ..ingoing about £200. **1925** *Daily Tel.* 13 May 19/3 The principal Fully-Licensed Family and Commercial Hotel... Ingoing £1,300.

'in,going, *ppl. a.* [f. as prec. + -ING[2].]

1. That goes in or inwards; that enters.

1825–80 JAMIESON, *Ingaand-mouth*, the mouth of a coal-pit which enters the earth in the horizontal direction. **1833** TENNYSON *Poems, Œnone* 55 Within the green hillside, Under yon whispering tuft of oldest pine, Is an ingoing grotto. **1880** BASTIAN *Brain* 23 They may be, in effect, junctions for in-going impressions or dividing stations for out-going impressions. **1880** *Plain Hints Needlework* 23 The ingoing stitch should.. be parallel to the place where the last came out.

2. Penetrating, thorough.

1928 *Blackw. Mag.* May 645/1 Whether he was quite so ingoing as this would have been is far from sure. **1928** E. C. BUTLER tr. *Grou's Meditations Love of God* p. v, He is very ingoing, and, like every spiritual writer worth his salt, very exacting. **1930** —— *Vatican Council* II. xxviii. 244 To this, the most ingoing question in regard to the Council, a sure answer may be given.

ingonge, variant of INGANG, *Obs.*, entry.

ingorant: see INGRANT.

†**ingor'digious,** *a. Obs. rare*[−1]. [f. It. *ingordigia* greediness (f. *ingordo* greedy) + -OUS.] Greedy, avaricious.

1637 BASTWICK *Litany* I. 19 They are exorbitantly luxurious.. excessiuely ingerdigious [*sic*] and exacting.

Hence †**ingor'digiousness,** greed, avarice.

a **1734** NORTH *Lives* (1890) III. 12 This ingordigiousness of fruit having exhausted our stock.

ingore, variant of ENGORE *v.*[1], *Obs.*

†**in'gorge,** obs. var. of ENGORGE *v.*, to gorge, to fill to excess.

1497 BP. ALCOCK *Mons Perfect.* E ij, They be not ingorged with meete and drynke.

†**in'gorgeous,** *a. Obs. rare*[−1]. [app. f. *ingorge* ENGORGE *v.* + -OUS, after obs. F. *engorgeux* (Cotgr.).] Greedy, insatiable.

1679 T. OATES *Myst. Iniq.* 25, I could produce many Reasons.. to demonstrate what an ingorgeous Ambition the Jesuits have to increase their Greatness.

ingot ('ɪŋgət). Also 4–6 yngot. [Of uncertain origin. Occurs in Chaucer in sense 1; then not till the second half of the 16th c. in sense 2 (though sense 1 is also used in 16–18th c.). French has *lingot* (in sense 2) from 1405 onward; med.L. *lingotus* (1440 in Du Cange), Sp. *lingote*, Pg. *linhota*; all perh. from Fr. See below.

The form *ingold* in Wright's Chaucer (*Can.-Yeom. T.* 656) is a scribal error of MS. Harl. 7334; *ingowe* in Spenser (*F.Q.* II. vii. 5) is either a misprint or a mistaken archaism.]

†**1.** A mould in which metal is cast; an ingot-mould. *Obs.*

c **1386** CHAUCER *Can. Yeom. Prol. & T.* 670 He took the Chalk, and shoope it in the wise Of an Ingot. *Ibid.* 680 And fro the fir he took vp his mateere And in thyngot putte it. **1584** R. SCOT *Discov. Witchcr.* XIV. i. (1886) 294 Mysticall termes of art; as (for a tast) their subliming, amalgaming.. matters combust and coagulat, ingots, tests, &c. [cf. CHAUCER *Can. Yeom. Prol.* 265]. **1613** R. CAWDREY *Table Alph.* (ed. 3), *Ingot*, a wedge of gold, also the trough wherin it is molten. **1683** PETTUS *Fleta Min.* I. (1686) 46 Set the Ingot smooth that the Copper may be no thicker at one end than the other. **1688** R. HOLME *Armoury* III. 306/2 An Ingot or Lingate.. is an Iron, Brass, or Copper Instrument, with an hollow place made in it, to receive and hold any sort of Metal cast into it. **1799** G. SMITH *Laboratory* I. 145 When in fusion, pour it into a flat ingot, and let it cool.

2. A mass (usually oblong or brick-shaped) of cast metal, esp. of gold or silver, and (in modern use) of steel; these last are of various shapes.

1423 *Rolls Parlt.* IV. 22 Item, diverses Yngottes & kakes d'arg[ent], pois[auntz] xxxiii ℔ vii unc'. Item, vi Yngottes d'arg[ent], poisauntz vi ℔ ix unc' di. **1583** STANYHURST *Æneis* I. (Arb.) 29 His wief to hyd treasur he poincted, Where the vnknowne ingots of gould and siluer abounded. **1584** R. SCOT *Discov. Witchcr.* XIV. ii. (1886) 297 A beechen cole, within the which was conveied an ingot of perfect silver. **1590** SPENSER *F.Q.* II. vii. 5 Great heapes of gold.. Of which some were.. new driven, and distent Into great Ingowes [*ed.* **1596** Ingoes] and to wedges square. **1601** HOLLAND *Pliny* II. 464, 15000 wedges or ingots of gold, 35000 lumps or masses of siluer. **1709** STEELE *Tatler* No. 46 ¶2 Not, like a Miser, to gaze only on his Ingots or his Treasures. **1794** SULLIVAN *View Nat.* I. 482 The silver is dried and fused in crucibles to be cast into ingots. **1825** J. NICHOLSON *Operat. Mechanic* 343 The ingots of cast-steel can be drawn into bars one-third of an inch square. **1862** *Fraser's Mag.* Nov. 633 At the present exhibition he [Krupp] shows an ingot of cylindrical form that weighs 20 Tons.

3. *attrib.* and *Comb.*, as ***ingot-copper***, ***-gad***, ***-holder***, ***-mould***, ***-silver***, ***-steel***, etc. **ingot iron**, iron which contains too little carbon to temper and is nearly pure by industrial standards, differing from wrought iron in containing no slag; **ingot stripper**, a machine for separating an ingot from the mould containing it; **ingot structure**, the arrangement of crystals in an ingot.

1877 A. S. HEWISH in Raymond *Statist. Mines & Mining* 363 About 8,000 tons of ingot-copper. **1558–62** PHAER *Æneid* VIII. B b iij, Yngot gaddes with clashing clinckes, In blustryng forges blown. **1887** *Pall Mall G.* 11 Aug. 10/1 Crushed to death by the fall of the ingot-holder, a bar of iron weighing eight tons. **1877** *Trans. Amer. Inst. Mining Engin.* V. 20 Mr. A. L. Holley, Chairman of the International Committee, appointed by the Institute to consider the nomenclature of iron and steel, offered the following report: ... That all compounds of iron with its ordinary ingredients, which have been cast from a fluid state into malleable masses, and which will not sensibly harden by being quenched in water, while at a red heat, shall be called ingot iron. **1938** J. NEWTON *Introd. Metall.* vii. 178 Ingot iron and wrought iron are both very low in carbon, and their physical properties approach those of pure iron. *Ibid.* xvi. 499 Ingot iron is commercially pure iron, with total impurities < 0·10 per cent, which is made by a special basic open-hearth process. **1962** A. G. GUY *Physical Metall. for Engineers* v. 138 Ingot iron in the form of galvanized or enameled sheets is used for such purposes as roofing and siding. **1904** J. W. HALL in Harbord & Hall *Metall. Steel* i. 41 The 'Ingot Stripper' is a most efficient machine.. saving.. all damage to the moulds from sledging to remove the ingots. **1957** CAMP & FRANCIS *Making, Shaping & Treating of Steel* (ed. 7) xv. 295 (*caption*) Schematic representation of the action of an ingot stripper in removing the molds from (left) big-end-down ingots and (right) big-end-up ingots. **1825** J. NICHOLSON *Operat. Mechanic* 759 The metal is poured into an ingot-mould. **1932** E. GREGORY *Metall.* ii. 49 The original ingot structure exerts a profound influence on the behaviour of the material during forging, rolling, etc. **1952** J. WULFF et al. *Metall. for Engineers* xvii. 316 Some knowledge of how steels are melted is useful for interpreting ingot structure.

[*Note.* F. *lingot* is held by some French etymologists to be adopted from Eng., with coalescence of the article, for *l'ingot.* The origin of a term of alchemy (as this evidently was) in Eng., is not *a priori* probable. Also, the only recorded sense of F. *lingot* (which appears frequently in 15th–16th c.) is = our sense 2, while the English *ingot* before 1558 is known only from Chaucer in sense 1: this makes a difficulty, unless it is assumed that sense 2 was also in English during these two centuries, though not yet found. Those who assume an Eng. origin suggest a derivation (not unapt as regards the sense) from *in* adv., and *goten*, ancient pa. pple. of OE. *ȝeótan*, ME. *ȝeoten, ȝeten, yheten*, mod. dial. *yett* to pour, to cast (metal). Here there is the difficulty that the pa. pple. *goten* was conformed to the rest of the vb., as *ȝoten, yhoten, yoten*, before the 14th c.; the hard *g* might perh. have been retained in an old compound, as in the derivative *gote*, 'water-course, gutter, drain', but even in that case we should have expected an original final vowel, giving ME. *ingote.* The existing evidence is thus too contradictory for any certain conclusion.]

Hence '**ingoted** *a.*, furnished with ingots or wealth.

1864 YATES *Broken to Harness* xvii, He's safe to ask no women who are not enormously ingotted. **1875** MISS BRADDON *Hostages to Fortune* I. i. 25 People who trace their lineage as far as Hengist and Horsa are seldom heavily ingotted.

ingotism ('ɪŋgətɪz(ə)m). [f. INGOT + -ISM.] The presence of many large dendritic crystals in an ingot or casting.

1908 H. M. HOWE et al. in *Proc. Amer. Soc. Testing Materials* VIII. 185 By ingotism we mean that extremely coarse structure which exists in unannealed ingots and steel castings. **1925** *Jrnl. Iron & Steel Inst.* CXI. 525 In killed steels the ill effect, if any, of a too high casting heat is pronounced ingotism. **1957** CAMP & FRANCIS *Making, Shaping & Treating of Steel* (ed. 7) xx. 395/2 Ingots exhibiting ingotism tend to crack excessively during rolling unless light drafts are employed for the first few passes in the rolls.

ingrace, obs. form of ENGRACE *v.*

†**in'gracious,** *a. Obs.* [IN-[3].] Ungracious.

1600 HOLLAND *Livy* 41 L. Tarquinius the prowd, and his ingracious wife, and the whole brood of his children. **1606** BIRNIE *Kirk-buriall* v, The ingratious discord.. wil mar al the mirth. **1676** R. DIXON *Two Testam.* 50 How ingracious a thing must it be for a Creature, beloved of God, to refuse the offer of his Grace.

ingradyt, var. of ENGRADED *ppl. a.*, *Obs.*

†**in'graff, in'grafe,** var. ENGRAFF *v.*, *Obs.*

ingraft, obs. variant of ENGRAFT *v.*

†**ingraif,** obs. Sc. form of ENGRAVE *v.*

1562 A. SCOTT *Poems* (S.T.S.) i. 214 Resaif, swaif, and haif, ingraif it here.

ingrail, obs. form of ENGRAIL *v.*

†'**ingrain,** *sb.*[1] *Obs.* [Origin unascertained.] A quarter of a chaldron of coal given in for every five chaldrons purchased.

1730 *Act 3 Geo. II*, c. 26 §10 By ancient Custom in the Port of London, one Chaldron of Coals is allowed in to every Score brought on board Ship.. which is called *Ingrain*; notwithstanding which many Persons dealing in Coals do load the same from on board Ship bare Measure without the aforesaid Ingrain. **1765** *Lond. Chron.* 16 May 470 The action was for not delivering to the buyers the ingrain of two

fives, as metered from on board ship, but took three sacks out of each five.

ingrain, *a.* (*sb.*^{2}) [f. the phrase *in grain*; see GRAIN *sb.*^{1} 10. Now usually stressed *'ingrain* before a sb., *ˌin'grain* after it or in the predicate.]

A. *adj.* **1. a.** Dyed in grain; dyed with fast colours before manufacture; dyed in the fibre; thoroughly dyed.

1766 W. GORDON *Gen. Counting-ho.* 428, 4 pink ingrain calimancoes. **1880** *Plain Hints Needlework* 44, 1 yd. Ingrain marking cotton, No. 100.

b. Applied (chiefly in U.S.) to carpets of the Kidderminster type, in which the pattern goes through and through and appears on both sides, as distinguished from those (such as Axminster or Brussels) in which it appears on the upper surface only.

1836 *Penny Cycl.* 314/1 Kidderminster..carpets, or, as the Americans more descriptively term them, ingrain carpets. **1863** B. TAYLOR *Hannah Thurston* III. 285 Bute had bought a brownish ingrain carpet. **1879** 'E. GARRETT' *House by Works* II. 132, I urge you not to wait till I can exchange this ingrain drugget for a Turkey carpet. **1899** *Corresp.*, Ingrain carpets are generally of inferior quality; but they can be made of very high qualities.

2. a. Of qualities, dispositions, habits, etc.: Inborn, inherent, firmly fixed, inveterate, ingrained.

1852 MRS. STOWE *Uncle Tom's C.* xix. 191 His old court pride..was ingrain, bred in the bone. **1856** MISS YONGE *Daisy Chain* I. xiv. (1879) 137 Too old for changing of ingrain, long-nurtured habits. **1888** T. W. HIGGINSON *Women & Men* 307 The shy graces of character must be something that is ingrain and permanent. **1894** F. ELLIOTT *Rom. Goss.* i. 19 A proof of the ingrain humanity of his soul.

b. Thorough, out-and-out, to the backbone.

1865 *Daily Tel.* 29 May, The most perfect type of the ingrain, hardened criminal.

B. *sb.* **1. a.** 'A name given to yarns, wools, etc., dyed with fast colours before manufacture' (Simmonds *Dict. Trade* 1858). **b.** (*U.S.*) = *ingrain carpet*: see 1 b. (Funk 1893.)

2. That which is ingrain or inherent.

1899 J. MILNE *Romance of Pro-Consul* vi. 49 The natives of the Australian North-West were a fine race physically, and, he judged, had an ingrain of Malay blood. **1918** P. T. FORSYTH *This Life & the Next* v. 55 It is the holy as what might be called the ingrain, the tissue, the physiognomy of eternal love.

ingrain, obs. or arch. variant of ENGRAIN *v.*

ingrained (ɪn'greɪnd), *ppl. a.* [app. orig. a variant of ENGRAINED *ppl. a.*: but now analysed as if from *in* adv. + *grained*: cf. INGRAIN *a.* Stressed *'in-ˌgrained* before a sb., otherwise *ˌin'grained.*] Wrought in the inmost texture; deeply rooted, inveterate.

[**1599** MARSTON *Sco. Villanie* I. iv. 189 Ingrain'd Habits, died with often dips.] **1821** GALT *Ayrsh. Legatees* xxv, Their old ingrained and particular sentiments. **1837** EMERSON *Addr., Amer. Schol.* Wks. (Bohn) II. 182 That great principle of Undulation in nature..deeply ingrained in every atom and every fluid. **1855** SINGLETON *Virgil* II. 142 Their ingrained wickedness is washed away. **1899** *Q. Rev.* Jan. 24 The old ingrained prejudice of his followers.

b. Of persons: Thorough, out-and-out.

[**1630** RUTHERFORD *Lett.* 21 July (1675) III. 156 The bloudy Tongues, crafty Foxes, double ingrained Hypocrites, shall appear as they are before his Majesty.] **1851** MAYHEW *Lond. Labour* I. 329 Many ingrained beggars certainly use the street trade as a cloak for alms-seeking. **1870** LOWELL *Among my Bks.* Ser. I. (1873) 277 He is an ingrained sceptic.

Hence **ingrainedly** (ɪn'greɪnɪdlɪ), ('ɪnˌgreɪndlɪ) *adv.*, in an ingrained manner or degree, thoroughly.

1869 *Athenæum* 16 Oct. 495 Designedly and undesignedly a liar; an utterly ingrainedly untrue creature. **1884** MRS. HOUSTOUN *Caught in Snare* II. xii. 141 She was not ingrainedly selfish. **1893** *Chicago Advance* 25 May, The material to work upon was too ingrainedly bad for even Elizabeth's optimism.

ingram ('ɪŋrəm), *a.* (*sb.*) *Obs.* (exc. *dial.*) Also 6 yngrame, 7 ingrum. A perverted form of IGNORANT, prob. immediately from INGRANT: cf. *vagrom* for *vagrant*.

1553 T. WILSON *Rhet.* 20 A patrone of a benefice wil haue a poore yngrame soule to beare the name of a persone for xx marke. **1570** LEVINS *Manip.* 18/8 Ingrame, *ignarus*. **1596** NASHE *Saffron Walden* 143 Who but an ingram cosset would keepe such a courting of a Curtezan? *c* **1614** BEAUM. & FL. *Wit without Money* v. i, Pray take my fellow Ralph, he has a Psalm Book, I am an ingrum man. **1630** J. TAYLOR *Wks.* (N.), I am no scholler, but altogether unrude, and very ingrum. **1893** *Northumbld. Gloss.*, *Ingram*, ignorant.

B. as *sb.* An ignorant person.

1638 NABBES *Cov. Gard.* III. v, Alas Gentlemen we are very ingrums. **1654** GAYTON *Pleas. Notes* II. ii. 41 Sancho was a very Ingrum as they call him.

Hence †**'ingramness**, ignorance.

1589 *Marprel. Epit.* A ij, You must then beare with my ingramnesse. **1589** *Mar Martine* 8 Beare with his ingramnesse a while, his seasoned wainscot face.

†**ingra'mmatical**, *a. Obs.* [IN-^{3}.] Ungrammatical.

1672 PENN *Spirit of Truth Vind.* 67 This were as ingrammatical altogether.

ingrammaticism (ɪŋgrə'mætɪsɪz(ə)m). *rare.* [IN-^{3}.] An ungrammatical form or construction; a solecism.

1888 *Athenæum* 10 Mar. 304/3 She..remains constant to her quotations and 'ingrammaticisms'.

ingrandize, obs. form of ENGRANDIZE *v.*

†**'ingrant**, *a. Obs.* A perverted form of *ignorant*, through the transitional **ignornant*, *ingorant*, the latter also found: cf. INGRAM.

1597 *1st Pt. Return fr. Parnass.* II. i. 722 The ingorant people that before calde mee Will now call mee William. **1644** QUARLES *Barnabas & B.* Wks. 1880 I. 80/2 That I have been so ingrant in good things, hath been a great heartbreaking to me.

†**in'grapple**, *v. Obs.* Also 8 en-. [f. IN-^{2} + GRAPPLE *v.*] *intr.* and *trans.* To join in grappling; to grapple together.

1597 DANIEL *Civ. Wars* IV. xxxiv, Then shall young Hotspur..Ingrapple [*ed.* **1718** engrapple] with thy sonne. **1599** —— *Let. Octavia* Wks. 1717 I. 83 At whose ingrappling, Neptune's Mantle takes A purple Colour. **1612** DRAYTON *Poly-olb.* xii. 292 Two lyons fierce..at one another flie, And with their armed pawes ingrappled dreadfully. *a* **1661** FULLER *Worthies, Lincolnsh.* II. (1662) 144 A Cub-Foxe..had his head seised on by a mighty Pike, so that neither could free themselves, but were ingrapled together.

ingrassial (ɪn'græsɪəl), *a. Anat.* [f. proper name *Ingrassi-as* + -AL^1.] Of or pertaining to Ingrassias, an Italian anatomist of the sixteenth century, esp. in ***ingrassial bones***, the lesser wings of the sphenoid bone, described by Ingrassias. So **in'grassian** *a.*

1839–47 TODD *Cycl. Anat.* III. 829/2 The ingrassial bones ..are, in the human subject, regarded as portions of the sphenoid. **1890** *Cent. Dict.*, Ingrassian.

ingrate (ɪn'greɪt), *a.* (*sb.*) Also 4 ingrat, 6–7 *Sc.* ingrait. [ad. L. *ingrāt-us* unpleasing, ungrateful, in med.L. also unkind, harsh, angry, f. *in-* (IN-^{3}) + *grātus* pleasing, grateful; perh. originally through F. *ingrat, -ate* (Oresme, 14th c.).] Not grateful.

†**1.** Not pleasing or acceptable to the mind or senses; disagreeable, unpleasant, unwelcome. *Obs.*

1539 TAVERNER *Gard. Wysed.* II. 2 a, I haue marked that thys argument or wrytynge is nat ingrate unto you. *c* **1586** C'TESS PEMBROKE *Ps.* CIV. xiv, This irreligious kinde, Ingrate to God. **1626** BACON *Sylva* § 111 The Causes of that which is Pleasing, or Ingrate to the Hearing, may receiue light by that, which is Pleasing or Ingrate to the Sight. **1665** SIR T. HERBERT *Trav.* (1677) 311 Coho or Coffee..however ingrate or insapory it seems at first, it becomes grate and delicious enough by custom. **1702** SIR J. FLOYER in *Phil. Trans.* XXIII. 1168 Thysselinum is Bitter, Ingrate and Acrid.

†**2.** Not of pleasant or friendly disposition; unfriendly. *Obs.*

1393 LANGL. *P. Pl.* C. XX. 219 Be ingrat [**1377** B. XVII. 253 *ingratus*, v. rr. *ingratis*, ingrat] to þy kynde, The holygost huyreþ þe nat ne helpeth þe. **1547** J. HARRISON *Exhort. Scottes* B iv b, The Britaynes..beeyng..ingrate eche to other..wer..ouercome with outwarde inuasions. **1563** *Mirr. Mag., Somerset* ii, To whom Fortune was ever more ingrate.

3. Not feeling or showing gratitude; ungrateful, unthankful. *arch.*

[**1377** LANGL. *P. Pl.* B. XIV. 169 Of þe good þat þow hem gyuest *ingrati* ben manye.] **1528** GARDINER in Pocock *Rec. Ref.* I. 132 As though he had been the most ingrate man. **1533** ELYOT *Cast. Helthe* (1539) 68 b, Thou shalt al day fynde the chylderne ingrate to their parentes. **1549** *Compl. Scot.* i. 20 To spulȝe al them that ar ingrate of the benefecis of gode. **1567** *Gude & Godlie B.* (S.T.S.) 154 O man, quhome I creat, Quhy art thou sa ingrait? **1627–47** FELTHAM *Resolves* I. xvii. 58 Why should a diswonted unkindnesse make me ingrate for wonted benefits? **1644** BP. MAXWELL *Prerog. Chr. Kings* Ded. 12, I were the ingratest of Christians if I did not acknowledge it. **1676** HOBBES *Iliad* VIII. 618 Must we unto our friends be so ingrate? **1706** LD. LANSDOWNE *Brit. Enchant.* II. i. (R.), See whom you fled, inhuman and ingrate. **1813** SCOTT *Rokeby* III. xxiii, Ingrate in life, in death ingrate. **1865** CARLYLE *Fredk. Gt.* XVIII. x. (1872) VII. 286 Schaffgotsch proved signally traitorous and ingrate.

B. *sb.* An ungrateful person; one who does not feel or show gratitude.

1672 VILLIERS (Dk. Buckhm.) *Rehearsal* I. (Arb.) 41 Let 'em live in ignorance like ingrates. **1775** SHERIDAN *Rivals* IV. ii, Your treachery and deceit, you base ingrate. **1797** NELSON 8 Sept. in Nicolas *Disp.* (1845) II. 442, I should be an ingrate was I not on every occasion to support his honour and glory at all personal risk. **1843** LYTTON *Last of Barons* II. ii, The Neviles are more famous for making ingrates than asking favours. **1892** NEWMAN SMYTH *Chr. Ethics* I. iii. 189 The prodigal comes to himself as an ingrate who has left his Father's house.

†**in'grate**, *v. Obs.* Also en-. [f. IN-^{2}, EN-^{1} + GRATE *v.*^{1} (sense 4).] **a.** *trans.* To treat harshly, oppress, harass. **b.** *intr.* To be harsh or oppressive. Hence **in'grating** *vbl. sb.* and *ppl. a.*

1599 NASHE *Lenten Stuffe* 26 Other engrating vpland cormorants will grunt out it is *Grana paradisi*. **1600** W. WATSON *Decacordon* (1602) 214 To ingrate thus iniuriously both vpon her Maiesties officers and the secular priests as the Iesuites doe. **1600** SURFLET *Countrie Farme* I. vii. 31 To be much exacting and ingrating vpon your farmer, doth oftentimes make him..a meere negligent. **1613** R. CAWDREY *Table Alph.* (ed. 3), *Engrate*, presse vpon. **1628** GAULE *Pract. The.* (1629) 344 He would not long suffer her Ingratings. **1629** —— *Holy Madn.* 410 Whom he hath.. ingrated, spoyled, cheated.

†**in'grateful**, *a. Obs.* [f. IN-^{3} + GRATEFUL: cf. INGRATE.] Not grateful, ungrateful.

1. Not pleasant or acceptable to the mind or senses; displeasing, disagreeable: = INGRATE *a.* 1.

1547–64 BAULDWIN *Mor. Philos.* (Palfr.) 63 It is to be.. imputed as vaine before Him, ingratefull, hurtfull, & voyd. **1694** SALMON *Bate's Dispens.* (1713) 50/1 The Oil is of an ingrateful Odor. **1754** RICHARDSON *Grandison* (1781) II. xxiv. 231 Sir Charles told him: That it was a very ingrateful thing to him to hear his Father spoken slightly of.

2. Unfriendly, harsh. *rare.* (Cf. INGRATE *a.* 2.)

c **1575** TURBERV. *Death Eliz. Arhundle* (R.), If ought my slender skill or writing were of powre, No processe of ingratefull time her vertues should deuour.

3. Not feeling or showing gratitude.

1547–64 BAULDWIN *Mor. Philos.* (Palfr.) 177 Desirous of pleasures, and ingratefull for benefits. **1579** FULKE *Heskins' Parl.* 484 Whiche are sometimes ingratefull to God for his mercies. *a* **1632** CHAPMAN *Alphonsus* Plays 1873 III. 209, I may be thought A most ingrateful wretch unto my Friend. **1759** ROBERTSON *Hist. Scot.* (1761) I. 513 His treatment of the Queen..was unbrotherly and ingrateful. **1913** F. THOMPSON *Works* II. 163 We take ingrateful, for a blinded while, Thine ignorant, sweet smile.

†**in'gratefully**, *adv. Obs.* [f. prec. + -LY^2.] In an ungrateful manner; ungratefully.

1543–4 *Act 35 Hen. VIII*, c. 12 The same Frenche King ..hathe..moost ingratefullye & wrongfullye w^t^drawen.. the dewe..pencion. **1697** DRYDEN tr. *Virgil's Past.* Pref. (1721) 76 Extravagant Heirs..ingratefully deride the good old Gentleman, who left them the Estate. **1711** *Light to Blind* in *10th Rep. Hist. MSS. Comm.* App. v. 114 They ingratefully abandoned him in the tyme of need.

†**in'gratefulness.** *Obs.* [f. as prec. + -NESS.] The quality of being ungrateful; ingratitude.

1570 DEE *Math. Pref.* d iv b, All these thinges, with farder matter of Ingratefulnes. **1619** J. BARLOW *True Guide to Glory* 26 Is not this forgetfulnesse, ingratefulnesse? **1658** CLEVELAND *Rustic Rampant* Wks. (1687) 514 Ingratefulness to his Sacred Head.

†**in'grately**, *adv. Obs.* [f. INGRATE *a.* + -LY^2.] Ungratefully.

1581 *Satir. Poems Reform.* xliii. 110 To his rewarde he [Alcibiades] gat nane vther grace, Ingraitly baneist, to their awin grit skaith. **1585** JAS. I *Ess. Poesie* (Arb.) 29 Will ye then so ingrately make your pen A slaue to sinne, and serue but fleshly men? **1654** VILVAIN *Theorem. Theol.* ii. 50 Why then doo we not rather magnify his Goodnes and Graces.. then ingratly disgrace them?

†**in'grater.** *Obs.* Also -or, -our. [app. with same radical part as REGRATER: perh. a blending of *in-* or *engrosser* and *regrater(-or)*.] A regrater or forestaller.

1583 STUBBES *Anat. Abus.* II. (1882) 45 A sort of ingrators or forestallers, who intercept euerie thing before it come at the market. *Ibid.* 46 These hellishe ingratours, and forestallers make corne and all thinges else deere. **1611** COTGR., *Dardanaire*, a Regrator, Ingrater, Ingrosser; one that buyes, and hoords vp corne..with a purpose to sell it againe when tis growne deere.

ingratiate (ɪn'greɪʃɪeɪt), *v.* Also 7 en-. [app. f. 16th c. It. *ingratiare* 'to engrace', to put in grace, refl. *ingratiarsi* (now *ingraziarsi*) 'to engrace or insinuate himself into favour' (Florio), f. phrase *in grazia* (†*gratia*), L. *in grātiam* into favour.]

†**1.** *trans.* To bring (a person) into favour (*with* any one); to render (him) agreeable (*to* any one).

1641 J. JACKSON *True Evang. T.* I. 49 The Embassador.. to ingratiate his Master with his holinesse, told him [etc.]. **1655** FULLER *Ch. Hist.* IV. iv. §6 All this would not ingratiate this Usurper with them. **1681** FLAVEL *Meth. Grace* xvii. 310 He hath ingratiated us, or brought us into the grace, favour and acceptance of God the Father. **1728** NEWTON *Chronol. Amended* ii. 207 This..might ingratiate Hadad with Pharaoh. **1755** *Man* ix. 4 We shall endeavour..to ingratiate this respectable order with the people.

2. *refl.* To get oneself into favour; to gain grace or favour *with*; to render oneself agreeable *to*.

1622 BACON *Hen. VII* 100 This Taxe..was abolished by Richard the Third..to ingratiate himselfe with the people. **1640** HABINGTON *Castara* III. (Arb.) 115 Should I my selfe ingratiate T' a Princes smile? **1644** JESSOP *Angel of Eph.* 5 That he might the better engratiate himselfe in the eyes of that..Prelate. **1647** CLARENDON *Hist. Reb.* I. §89 If he did not do somewhat to ingratiate himself to the People. **1762–71** H. WALPOLE *Vertue's Anecd. Paint.* (1786) II. 77 Several of the court who ingratiated themselves by offerings of pictures and curiosities. **1853** MACAULAY *Biog., Atterbury* (1867) 16 At the coronation..[he] did his best to ingratiate himself with the royal family.

b. with various pleonastic extensions.

1654 SIR E. NICHOLAS in *N. Papers* (Camden) II. 64 On design to ingratiate himself in the good opinion of the Hugonots of France. *a* **1665** GOODWIN *Filled w. the Spirit* (1867) 385 To ingratiate himself in their affections and good wills. **1713** STEELE *Guardian* No. 14 ¶1 Desirous to ingratiate themselves further into their favour. **1828** P. CUNNINGHAM *N.S. Wales* (ed. 3) II. 195 A convict,—into whose good-will this gentleman had so far..ingratiated himself. **1853** J. H. NEWMAN *Hist. Sk.* (1876) II. II. i. 248

He ingratiated himself still farther in the esteem of the Sicilians.

†**3.** *intr.* (for *refl.*) *Obs.*

1647 TRAPP *Comm. Luke* xvii. 19 Thus gratitude ingratiates with Christ and gets more grace. **1699** BENTLEY *Phal.* xvi. 519 Those, who think to ingratiate with Him by calumniating Me. **1768–74** TUCKER *Lt. Nat.* (1834) II. 314 The methods of civility proper for removing all suspicions of themselves, and ingratiating with whatever company they fall into.

†**4.** *trans.* To make (a thing) pleasant, agreeable, or acceptable (*to* or *with*). *Obs.*

1639 FULLER *Holy War* III. xx. (1647) 142 Such as might more ingratiate with God the persons and prayers of people there assembled. **1656** SIBBES *Confer. Christ & Mary* 11 Things, when wanted, are ingratiated to us, as warmth after cold, and meat after hunger. **1676** TEMPLE *Let. to the King* 3 Mar., Wks. 1720 II. 379 A Clause.. which he thought was put in on purpose to ingratiate it to Your Majesty. *a* **1677** BARROW *Serm.* Wks. 1716 III. 79 Use doth wear out the pleasure which.. Novelty commendeth and ingratiateth. *a* **1748** WATTS *Improv. Mind* II. vi. §1 That he may ingratiate his discourses with their ears.

Hence **in'gratiating** *vbl. sb.* and *ppl. a.*; **in'grati,atingly** *adv.*, in an ingratiating manner, in a way to win favour.

1641 HEYLIN *Hist. Episcopacy* I. (1657) 62 His ingratiating with the Jewes. **1655** FULLER *Church Hist.* x. vi. §29 A Jesuite of excellent Morals, and ingratiating Converse. **1656** *Artif. Handsom.* (1662) 230 The concessions of which ..had been a very great indulgence and ingratiating to women of greatest quality. *a* **1797** H. WALPOLE *Mem. Geo. II* (1847) I. ix. 276 Lord Isla was.. if artful, at least not ingratiating. **1886** *Longm. Mag.* Feb. 423 The.. lad bowed ingratiatingly. **1896** O. SMEATON *Allan Ramsay* i. 11 The ingratiating qualities.. of her father's guest.

ingratiation (ɪngreɪʃɪ'eɪʃən). [n. of action f. INGRATIATE: see -ATION.] The action or process of ingratiating oneself or getting into favour.

1815 *Zeluca* I. 224 His desire of ingratiation was not so ardent as Zeluca's. **1822** W. TAYLOR in *Monthly Mag.* LIV. 493 He had.. cultivated the arts of ingratiation with some sacrifice of the dignity of independence. **1887** STEVENSON *Mem. & Portr.* iv. 70 Daily ear-wigging influential men, for he was a master of ingratiation.

ingratiatory (ɪn'greɪʃɪətərɪ), *a.* [f. INGRATIATE: see -ORY.] That tends to ingratiate.

1865 *Cornh. Mag.* Apr. 399 He spoke with a timid gentleness of tone, an ingratiatory smile. **1881** RUSKIN *Love's Meinie* I. i. 26 You will find one of the robin's very chief ingratiatory faculties is his dainty and delicate movement.

ingratitude (ɪn'grætɪtjuːd). [a. F. *ingratitude* (13th c. in Hatz.-Darm.), ad. late L. *ingrātitūdo* ingratitude, displeasure, n. of quality f. *ingrātus* INGRATE; cf. GRATITUDE.]

1. Want or absence of gratitude; indisposition to acknowledge or reciprocate benefits received; unthankfulness; ungratefulness.

[*a* **1225** *Ancr. R.* 200 Ingratitudo: þesne kundel bret, hwose nis nout icnowen of goddedde, auh telleð lutel þerof, oðer uorȝiteð mid alle.] **1340** *Ayenb.* 18 A vice þet is y-cleped ine clergie: ingratitude: þet is uoryetinge of god and of his guodes. **1477** EARL RIVERS (Caxton) *Dictes* 1 To sette a parte alle ingratitude. **1531** ELYOT *Gov.* II. xiii, The moste damnable vice and moste agayne iustice, in myne oppinion, is ingratitude, commenly called unkyndnesse.. He is unkynde whiche denieth to haue receyued any benefite that in dede he hath receyued. **1607** SHAKS. *Cor.* II. iii. 10 Ingratitude is monstrous, and for the multitude to be ingratefull, were to make a Monster of the multitude. **1675** SOUTH *Serm.* (1737) I. xi. 413. **1796** BURKE *Let. Noble Ld.* Wks. VIII. 51 Ingratitude to benefactors is the first of revolutionary virtues. **1876** MOZLEY *Univ. Serm.* xv. 252 There is perhaps no fault that men think more monstrous in other people than ingratitude.

†**2.** Unpleasant feeling, disagreeableness (between persons); unfriendliness, unkindness. *Obs.*

c **1477** CAXTON *Jason* 41 They ben unkinde and full of ingratitude.. yf they knewe ony thing wherwith they might dishonoure them they wolde do hit. **1548** HALL *Chron., Hen. VII* 13 b, Least it should sowe or kyndle any dissencion or ingratitude betwene the Frenche kyng and him. **1555** EDEN *Decades* 232 *marg.*, The ingrati[t]ude of the Portugales. *c* **1566** J. ALDAY tr. *Boaystuau's Theat. World* E v, There is prepared for him [the child] new sorrow, by the ingratitude of mothers, which are so delicate.. that they will not nourish them.

†**ingra'tuity**. *Obs. rare.* [f. IN-[3] + GRATUITY.] Ungraciousness, unkindness, ingratitude.

1528 in Burnet *Hist. Ref.* II. 36 Rather.. than the King.. should suspect any point of Ingratuyte in him. **1603** J. DAVIES *Microcosmos* Ded. to Pr. Wales ii. (1878) 19, I.. That willingly (to saue thee from annoy Of dire dislike for ingratuitee) Do take vpon me to expresse thy ioy.

†**in'grave**, *v.* *Obs.* Also 6–7 **en-**. [f. IN-[1] or [2] + GRAVE *sb.* or *v.*] *trans.* To put in a grave; to entomb, bury.

α. **1535** STEWART *Cron. Scot.* III. 16 The quhilk bodie.. Ingrauit wes than in ane sepulture. **1683** CHALKHILL *Thealma & Cl.* 167 Shall I think Their cruelty so merciful, to save Her, their ambition strove for to ingrave?

β. **1555** W. WATREMAN *Fardle Facions* App. 336 Lette euin the very ennemie be engraued, and lette no corps lie withoute buriall. **1590** SPENSER *F.Q.* I. x. 42 In seemely sort their corses to engrave. **1633** P. FLETCHER *Elisa* xxvii, Vile headless trunk, why art thou not engraved? **1667** WATERHOUSE *Fire Lond.* 145 Those Lazaritique spirits.. have been of late engraved in cold resolves.

Hence †**in'graved** *ppl. a.*, entombed, buried.

1586 WHETSTONE *Eng. Myrror* 5 The envious committe inhumane outrages upon their ingraved bones. **1608** ARMIN *Nest Ninn.* (1842) 26 Here they lye that gallopt so, In Death's ingraued snare.

†**ingrave, -er, -ery**, obs. ff. ENGRAVE *v.*, etc.

1552 HULOET, Ingrauer. *Ibid.*, Ingrauynge.

†**ingrave**, obs. apocopate form of *ingraven, engraven*, pa. pple. of ENGRAVE *v.*

1513 DOUGLAS *Æneis* v. v. 45 Twa siluer coppis schappin lyk ane bote.. and with figuris ingrave [**1553** engraif].

ingravescence (ɪngrə'vɛsəns). *Med.* [f. next: see -ENCE.] The quality or condition of being ingravescent; increase of gravity or severity.

1822–34 *Good's Study Med.* (ed. 4) I. 689 This desire returned with every returning ingravescence of the fever. **1876** BRISTOWE *Th. & Pract. Med.* (1878) 132 This development of contagium goes on during the whole period of ingravescence.

ingravescent (ɪngrə'vɛsənt), *a.* *Med.* [f. L. *ingravēscent-em*, pr. pple. of *ingravēscĕre* to grow heavy, f. *in-* (IN-[2]) + *gravēscĕre*, f. *gravis* heavy.] Increasing in gravity or severity; growing worse.

1822–34 *Good's Study Med.* (ed. 4) I. 483 Common Asthma. Paroxysm gradual; Ingravescent. **1891** *Lancet* 25 Aug. 954/1 Infective diseases.. like tuberculosis and leprosy, which were persistent and ingravescent, and in no sense self-protective. **1897** *Allbutt's Syst. Med.* II. 923 Ingravescent jaundice gives rise to a series of nervous symptoms.. akin to cholæmic intoxication.

ingravidate (ɪn'grævɪdeɪt), *v.* [f. ppl. stem of late L. *ingravidāre* to make heavy or pregnant, f. *in-* (IN-[2]) + *gravidus* heavy, GRAVID.]

1. *trans.* To load or weigh; to render gravid, to impregnate.

1642 FULLER *Holy & Prof. St.* I. xii. 39 They may.. be so pregnant and ingravidated with lustfull thoughts. **1670** W. SIMPSON *Hydrol. Ess.* 78 Ingravidated with a vitrioline salt. **1698** *Phil. Trans.* XX. 466 [He] tells us how the Country-men ingravidate the Female [Pistachio-tree] with the Flowers of the Male. **1866** ALGER *Solit. Nat. & Man* IV. 381 His receptive and responsive capacity of genius.. ingravidated his utterance as with the weight of worlds.

2. *intr.* To become heavy; to be weighed down.

1657 TOMLINSON *Renou's Disp.* 181 By the cohibition of these dreggs.. the body ingravidates.

†**in'gravidate**, *a.* *Obs. rare*[−1]. [ad. late L. *ingravidāt-us*, pa. pple. of *ingravidāre*: see prec.] Loaded.

1651 BIGGS *New Disp.* ⁋180 To deliver.. the ingravidate ..veins from the Tympany of a Plethora.

ingravidation (ɪngrævɪ'deɪʃən). [n. of action f. prec. vb.: see -ATION.] The action of ingravidating or state of being ingravidated; pregnancy.

1615 CROOKE *Body of Man* 315 All the time of their ingrauidation or in which they go with childe. **1710** T. FULLER *Pharm. Extemp.* 299 The last month of Ingravidation. **1811** HOOPER *Med. Dict.*, *Ingravidation*,.. the same as impregnation, or going with child.

ingrayl, obs. form of ENGRAIL *v.*

†**in'great**, *v.* *Obs.* Also **en-**. [f. IN-[2] + GREAT *a.* Cf. ENGREATEN.] *trans.* To make great, to magnify.

a **1619** FOTHERBY *Atheom.* II. i. §3 (1622) 174 There is, in all things, a desire to dilate, and to ingreat themselues. **1626** SIR C. CORNWALLIS *Disc. Pr. Henry* (1641) 7, I ever after.. found my selfe exceedingly engreated in his favour. **1627** ABP. ABBOT *Narrative* II. in Rushw. *Hist. Coll.* (1659) I. 455 As some are gentle and benign, so some others, to ingreat themselves, might strain more then the string will bear.

†**in'grede**, *v.* *Obs. rare.* [ad. L. *ingred-ī* to enter.] *trans.* To enter into (as an ingredient).

1657 TOMLINSON *Renou's Disp.* Pref., Every Simple which ingredes the Compositions may be dignoted. **1657** *Physical Dict.*, *Ingrede*, go into, or help to make up a medicine.

in'gredience, *sb.* [f. as INGREDIENT: see -ENCE. But, in sense 1, orig. a misspelling of the pl. *ingredients* (cf. ACCIDENCE, INHABITANCE), and subsequently confused with the sing. *ingredient*.]

†**1.** That which enters into a mixture. **a.** The ingredients in a medicine, potion, etc., separately or collectively; or the mixture itself, as containing ingredients. *Obs.*

1526 *Pilgr. Perf.* (W. de W. 1531) 166 The physicyon consyderynge his medecyne or pocyon.. may se in his mynde the dyuerse ingredyence that wente therto. **1533** MORE *Answ. Poysoned Bk.* Wks. 1088/2 Thys plaster.. hath som good ingredience. But it hathe also some deade potycarye drugges putte in it that can do no good. **1605** SHAKS. *Macb.* I. vii. 11 This euen-handed Iustice Commends th' Ingredience of our poyson'd Challice To our owne lips. **1646** S. SHEPPARD *Year Jubilee* 39 An ingredience, which quaft of, might surely destroy the health of both their bodies and souls. **1678** MARVELL *Def. Howe* Wks. 1875 IV. 179 Do I therefore think them equipollent, or that one of them hath not the stronger ingredience? **1694** R. BURTHOGGE *Reason* 167 If there be no ingredience of matter in their making.

fig. **1645** USSHER *Body Div.* (1647) 198 Faith doth not consist in darknesse and ignorance; but Knowledge is of the ingredience of it.

b. (with *pl.*) A single ingredient or element.

1577–87 HOLINSHED *Chron.* II. 13/1 One Theoricus wrote a proper treatise of *Aqua vitæ*.. He declareth the simples and ingrediences thereto belonging. **1589** COGAN *Haven Health* ccxviii. (1636) 250 Ale requireth two ingrediences. **1661** *Sir H. Vane's Politics* 9 All those to receive their proper Ingrediences, or they perfect not the Cure.

2. The fact or process of entering in: **a.** by physical movement; **b.** as an ingredient.

1557 *Sarum Primer, Lauds* B iij, For us in heaven to have ingredience. **1604** R. CAWDREY *Table Alph.*, *Ingresse, Ingredience*, enterance in. **1638** SIBBES *Emanuell* i. 16 Both natures had an ingredience into all the works of mediation. **1677** HALE *Prim. Orig. Man.* II. iv. 158 The Phantasie, Design and Destination of Man, which is various, according to those various Temperaments that have ingredience and influence into him. **1925** A. N. WHITEHEAD *Sci. & Mod. World* (1926) x. 237 This complete ingredience in an occasion, so as to yield the most complete fusion of individual essence with other eternal objects in the formation of the individual emergent occasion, is evidently of its own kind and cannot be defined in terms of anything else. **1955** *Scottish Jrnl. Theol.* VIII. 426 Nor can it [*sc.* history] be seen as a total process given meaning by the ingredience of non-historical reality.

†**in'gredience**, *v.* *Obs. rare.* [f. prec.] *trans.* To introduce as an ingredient; to furnish with ingredients.

1650 ASHMOLE *Chym. Collect.* 30 No unclean Body is ingredienced except one, which is commonly called of the Philosophers, The green Lion. **1822** LAMB *Elia* Ser. I. *Chimneysweepers*, May the descending soot never taint thy costly well-ingredienced soups.

†**in'grediency**. *Obs.* [f. INGREDIENT: cf. INGREDIENCE, and see -ENCY.]

1. = INGREDIENCE 1.

1612 WOODALL *Surg. Mate* Wks. (1653) 345 Those which cannot have all the ingrediency of this composition. **1646** S. BOLTON *Arraignm. Err.* 75 There are but few errours in oure dayes.. but have some ingrediency of truth in them. **1662** R. MATHEW *Unl. Alch.* p. ii, I am sure they know not all the Ingrediencies thereof. *a* **1684** LEIGHTON *Comm. 1 Pet.* v. 4 Pure unmixed glory, without any ingrediency of pride or sinful vanity.

2. = INGREDIENCE 2.

1648 W. BRIDGE *England saved with a Notwithstanding* 27 It [Papistry] destroies your Obedience, by the ingrediency of merits. **1650** WEEKES *Truth's Confl.* ii. 50 There is an ingrediency and concurrence of all the great and glorious Perfections of God. **1668** HOWE *Bless. Righteous* (1825) 192 Think not that sensual pleasure.. can have any ingrediency into.. this state of blessedness. **1695** *Whether Parlt. be not dissolved by Death P'cess Orange* 3 [Parliaments] cannot cease to have an Ingrediency into the Government, without a dissolution of the whole Frame of it.

ingredient (ɪn'griːdɪənt), *a.* and *sb.* [ad. L. *ingredient-em*, pr. pple. of *ingred-ī* to enter, f. *in-* (IN-[2]) + *gradī* to step, go: cf. F. *ingrédient* sb. (1508 in Hatz.-Darm.), which was prob. the immediate source of the sb. in sense 3.]

A. *adj.* That enters in; entering into a thing or place: †**a.** by moving or running in. *Obs.*

1611 FLORIO, *Ingrediente*, ingredient, entring in. *a* **1641** BP. MOUNTAGU *Acts & Mon.* (1642) 115 The course of Gods Spirit is in divers men, different: Either ingredient and insident.. or urgent and impellent. **1668** CULPEPPER & COLE *Barthol. Anat.* I. xvii. 45 The external and common Coat of the ingredient Vessels.

b. as a component part or element. *arch.*

1642 T. LECHFORD *Plain Dealing* (1867) 95 They began about a small trespasse of swine, but it is thought some other matter was ingredient. **1646** SIR T. BROWNE *Pseud. Ep.* III. xxiii. 168 The horne of a Deere is.. ingredient into the confection of Hyacinth. **1663** BUTLER *Hud.* I. ii. 21 Some fierce, deed-doing man, Compos'd of many ingredient valours, Just like the manhood of nine tailors. **1713** BERKELEY *Guardian* No. 83 ⁋1 The generosity that is ingredient in the temper of the soul. **1830** HERSCHEL *Stud. Nat. Phil.* 291 The connection between the external characters of a stone and its ingredient constituents. **1933** *Theology* XXVI. 331 The distinction between the realm of possibility and that of actuality, between 'eternal objects' and the 'actual occasions' into which the eternal objects are ingredient. **1957** G. RYLE in C. A. Mace *Brit. Philos. in Mid-Cent.* 241 He has to declare that his subject-matter consist [*sic*] not of the sentences and their ingredient words in which arguments are expressed [etc.].

B. *sb.* †**1.** One who steps in. *Obs. rare.*

1614 T. ADAMS *Fatal Banquet* i. Wks. 1861 I. 159 If sin.. discovers the green and gay flowers of *delice*, he cries to the ingredients, *Latet anguis in herbâ*,—The serpent lurks there.

†**2.** A thing which enters in or penetrates. *Obs.*

1624 WOTTON *Archit.* in *Reliq.* (1672) 7 [The air] being a perpetual ambient and ingredient.

3. a. Something that enters into the formation of a compound or mixture; a component part, constituent, element. Primarily used of medical compositions and other artificial material mixtures, but also of natural compounds and of things immaterial, actions, conditions, etc.

c **1460** J. RUSSELL *Bk. Nurture* 144 Alle þese ingredyentes, þey ar for ypocras makynge. **1543** TRAHERON *Vigo's Chirurg.* 42 a/2 Thys cerote.. comforteth yᵉ sore place, as it appeareth to hym, that consydereth the ingredientes. **1599** B. JONSON *Cynthia's Rev.* v. ii, What are the ingredients to your fucus? **1601** HOLLAND *Pliny* Explan. Words, *Ingredients*, be those

simples that goe vnto the making of any medicine compound. **1659** GAUDEN *Fun. Serm. Bp. Brownrig* (1660) 124 Stupidity, I told you, is no ingredient in piety. **1680–90** TEMPLE *Ess., Health & Long Life* Wks. 1731 I. 287 Whatever the Spleen is.. it is certainly a very ill Ingredient into any other Disease. **1752** HUME *Pol. Disc.* ii. 25 Human happiness..seems to consist of three ingredients, action, pleasure and indolence. **1784** J. POTTER *Virtuous Villagers* II. 100 These are no inconsiderable ingredients to love and friendship. **1798** MALTHUS *Popul.* (1817) II. 457 The money price of corn..is..the most powerful ingredient in regulating the price of labour. **1838** THIRLWALL *Greece* xxxv. IV. 397 His ambition was quite pure from all sordid ingredients. **1866** ROGERS *Agric. & Prices* I. xxiii. 602 The brass of the Middle Ages was..a mixture of tin and copper, the latter being the larger ingredient in the compound.

†**b.** Chief or main ingredient. *Obs.*

1604 SHAKS. *Oth.* II. iii. 311 Every inordinate cup is unblessed and the ingredient [*Qos.* ingredience] is a devil. **1646** SIR T. BROWNE *Pseud. Ep.* III. xii. 133 We may as firmly conclude, that Diaphœnicon a purging electuary hath some part of the Phœnix for its ingredient.

†**c.** A material. *Obs. rare.*

1691 T. H[ALE] *Acc. New Invent.* 37 The Ingredients employed in that method of Sheathing, are of Forreign growth.

¶ ***ingredients*** occurs as sing. = INGREDIENCE 1 b.

1674 *Essex Papers* (Camden) I. 206 Dulce est Lucrum, etc.; & I finde y[t] Ingredients moves y[e] great ones as well as y[e] Little here. **1688** R. HOLME *Armoury* III. 250/1 The first and more simple Ingredients required in Grammar, is the information and Instruction of Letters.

[**ingree**, erroneous writing of the phrase *in gree* kindly, favourably: see GREE.]

ingrele, -eyl, obs. forms of ENGRAIL *v.*

Ingres (ɛ̃gr). The name of J. A. D. *Ingres* (1780–1867), French painter, used *attrib.* in **Ingres paper** [tr. F. *papier Ingres*], a French mould-made drawing-paper; also used to describe thick mottled paper.

1910 *Winsor & Newton Catal.* in H. Macbeth-Raeburn *Sketchers' Oil Colour Manual* 37 Drawing papers..Ingres paper (imitation Michallet). **1925** V. BLAKE *Way to Sketch* ix. 79 Ingres or Michelet, either white or tinted—say the blue-grey note—is useful for making rather large sketches in Conté or carbon pencil. **1941** [see CONTÉ]. **1968** P. NUTTALL *Picture Framing* ii. 24 There are a wide variety of papers suitable for this purpose [*sc.* mounting], such as..Ingres paper, textured papers, silk wallpaper, marbled papers, and so on.

ingress (ˈɪngrɛs), *sb.* [ad. L. *ingress-us* entering, entrance, f. ppl. stem of *ingredī* to go in, enter, f. *in-* (IN-²) + *gradī* to step, go.]

1. The action or fact of going in or entering. Also, Capacity or right of entrance, esp. in legal phr. ***ingress, egress,*** and ***regress.***

1543–4 *Act 35 Hen. VIII*, c. 10 To haue free ingresse egresse and regresse in to all suche places. **1578** BANISTER *Hist. Man* I. 22 The holes ordayned for the exiture of the Nerues, and ingresse of the vessels of nourishment. **1607** ROGERS *39 Art.* Pref. (1854) 22 Within a year, and little more, after his happy ingress into this kingdom. **1684** BOYLE *Porousn. Anim. & Solid Bod.* vii. 111 Nor is Sulphur the only consistent Body that has this ingress into Metals; for we have found them penetrable by prepared Arsenic. **1767** BLACKSTONE *Comm.* II. ix. 146 The tenant shall have..free ingress, egress, and regress, to cut and carry away the profits. **1818** SCOTT *Hrt. Midl.* vi, A small fee to the keepers would..procure egress and ingress at any time. **1851–6** WOODWARD *Mollusca* 31 The animal has apparently occupied its shell, and prevented the ingress of mud.

b. A place or means of entrance; an entrance.

c **1420** *Pallad. on Husb.* I. 964 Honge hit in thy yatis and ingresse Of hous or toun. **1657** W. RAND tr. *Gassendi's Life Peiresc* II. 13 The Tower of Buquia..stands at the ingress of the Martigian Coast. **1839** DE QUINCEY *Recoll. Lakes* Wks. 1862 II. 4 Running water must force an egress for itself, and, consequently, an ingress for the reader and myself.

c. More fully ***ingress-money***: A payment on entrance into a society, college, etc.; an entrance fee.

1607 in *Hist. Wakefield Gram. Sch.* (1892) 66 Assigninge unto him the whole ingress money of all such as shall be entred schollers under him. **1656** in Willis & Clark *Cambridge* (1886) I. 101 R[d] from Benefactors, Materials, Ingresses, &c. £3650. 10. 11. **1886** *Ibid.* I. 97 From a list of 'Ingresses received' we learn that Mr. Watts occupied 'the corner chamber next King's College Chapel'.

2. The action of entering upon or beginning a thing; a beginning, an attempt; also, The commencement of an action, period, etc. *arch.*

c **1420** *Pallad. on Husb.* IV. 274 Til October from thyn, gresse of this mone, Is coriaunder sowe in fatty lond. **1563–87** FOXE *A. & M.* (1684) III. 1 In the ingress of this foresaid story. *a* **1610** HEALEY *Cebes* (1636) 141 They have forgotten the instruction that Lifes genius gave them at their ingresse. **1622** CALLIS *Stat. Sewers* (1647) 147 Before I shall touch upon the main, I will make an Ingresse to treat of such matters whereby [etc.]. **1898** T. HARDY *Wessex Poems* 146 Since then she comes Oft..at the season's ingresses.

3. a. *Astrol.* The arrival of a planet at that part of the heaven occupied by another planet, or at the ascendant, or the mid-heaven. **b.** *Astron.* The entrance of the sun into a sign of the zodiac. ? *Obs.* **c.** The first contact of an inferior planet with the sun, or of a satellite with its planet, at a transit.

a. 1603 HOLLAND *Plutarch's Mor.* 1304 They solemnize a feast in the new Moone of the moneth Phamenoth, which they call The ingresse or entrance of Osiris to the Moone. **1819** JAS. WILSON *Compl. Dict. Astrol.* 359–60 Active ingresses are those wherein the active stars operate by coming to the places of the significator; and passive ingresses are those wherein the passive stars come to the places of the promittors.

b. 1652 GAULE *Magastrom.* xxvi. I iv a, It is unpossible to finde out the true ingresse of the Sunne into the æquinoctiall points. **1704** HEARNE *Duct. Hist.* (1714) I. 47 At the Sun's ingress into the Sign Leo. **1726** tr. *Gregory's Astron.* I. 225 The beginning of the Day and Night falls upon the Sun's Ingress into the Equinoctial Points.

c. 1751 *Phil. Trans.* XLVII. 160 The whole matter was..to find her [Venus] out a little before her ingress. **1812** WOODHOUSE *Astron.* xxxviii. 378 Instead of observing the mere ingress, they observe the duration of the transit. **1867–77** G. F. CHAMBERS *Astron.* 916. **1868** LOCKYER *Guillemin's Heavens* (ed. 3) 479.

inˈgress, *v. rare.* [f. ppl. stem of L. *ingredī* to enter: see prec.]

1. *intr.* To enter, go in. Now *U.S.*

c **1330** *Arth. & Merl.* 7982 So lyoun doth on dere ingress. *a* **1817** DWIGHT cited by Worcester. **1963** V. NABOKOV *Gift* iii. 178 Boris Ivanovich, horribly smiling, squeezed sideways into the room..then, ingressing entirely, he would shut the door tightly behind him and sit by Fyodor's feet. **1970** N. ARMSTRONG et al. *First on Moon* Gloss. p. xii, *Ingress*, to enter the spacecraft.

†**2.** *trans.* To enter, invade; *spec.* 'to go in to' carnally. *Obs.*

a **1631** DONNE *To C'tess Bedford* Poems, etc. (1633) 89 Yet he as hee bounds seas, will fixe your houres, [Which] pleasure, and delight may not ingresse. —— *Progr. Soul* xxi. ibid. 11 Men, till they tooke laws which made freedome lesse, Their daughters, and their sisters did ingresse, Till now unlawfull, therefore ill.

†**inˈgressance.** *Obs. rare*⁻¹. [irreg. f. L. *ingress-us* entrance + -ANCE.] Entry-money.

1550 LEVER *Serm., Shroudes* (Arb.) 37 It is a wonderous thing to se gentlemen take so great rentes, fynes, and ingressaunce for couetousnes.

ingressant (ɪnˈgrɛsənt), *a. nonce-wd.* [f. ppl. stem of L. *ingredī* to enter + -ANT¹.] Entering, in-going.

1947 AUDEN *Age of Anxiety* (1948) vi. 126 His [*sc.* God's] Good ingressant on our gross occasions Envisages our advance.

ingression (ɪnˈgrɛʃən). [ad. L. *ingressiōn-em*, n. of action f. *ingredī* to enter: see INGRESS. Cf. obs. F. *ingression* (Godef., Littré).] The action of going in or entering; entrance; invasion.

c **1470** HARDING *Chron.* XXXI. i, Pinner then had Logres in gouernaile, And kyng ther of was by wrong ingression. **1509** BARCLAY *Shyp of Folys* (1874) II. 325 It appereth that theyr ingressyon Into relygion, is more for welth and eas. **1633** P. FLETCHER *Elisa* II. xlvi, Unfriendly friends..why do ye strive To barre wisht death from his so just ingression? *a* **1661** FULLER *Worthies, Shropsh.* III. (1662) 2 Sulphur hath ingression into Mettal, and Bitumen none at all. **1738** BOLINGBROKE *Idea Patriot King* ii. 248 If the heart of a prince be not corrupt, these truths will find an easy ingression..to it. **1886** H. W. SMYTH in *Amer. Jrnl. Philol.* VII. 371 Traces are manifest [among critics of the Iliad] of an inclination to suffer the ingression of antique forms.

ingressive (ɪnˈgrɛsɪv), *a.* (*sb.*) [f. L. *ingress-*, ppl. stem of *ingredī* to enter + -IVE: cf. *aggressive*.]

a. Having the character or quality of entering. **b.** *Gram.* Denoting entering upon action, inceptive; also as *sb.*

1649 J. ELLISTONE tr. *Behmen's Epist.* xix. §14 The Divine light is not ingressive (or a light comming into a man from without). **1658** R. FRANCK *North. Mem.* (1694) 300 Such signal Remonstrations (like an ingressive Spirit) strike deep Impressions into my thoughtful Breast. **1885** GILDERSLEEVE in *Amer. Jrnl. Philol.* VI. 71 The sigmatic aorist is decidedly ingressive, and we do not want the ingressive action here. **1931** G. O. CURME *Syntax* xix. 377 The ingressive aspect is often expressed by *begin, commence*, or *start* in connection with an infinitive or gerund or object. *Ibid.* 378 The ingressive idea is often expressed by the ingressives *get, grow, fall, turn, wax*, [etc.]. **1932** *Jrnl. Eng. & Gmc. Philol.* XXXI. 251 The former is called the ingressive aspect: 'He *woke up* (i.e., entered upon the waking state) early.' **1935** [see EFFECTIVE *sb.* 3]. **1961** [see CONCEPTUALISTICALLY *adv.*].

c. *Phonetics.* Of or pertaining to utterances made while breathing in. Also as *sb.*, an ingressive verb or sound.

1943 K. L. PIKE *Phonetics* vi. 88 Sounds thus made are *ingressives* (or *rarefactives*). *Ibid.*, Ingressive lung-air sounds, and clicks, are produced in this way. **1963** *Amer. Speech* XXXVIII. 52 Phonemes..can be produced with an ingressive as well as an egressive air stream. **1969** M. M. FIRESTONE in Halpert & Story *Christmas Mumming in Newfoundland* 66 Some are able to 'talk like a janney'—ingressive utterances at a high pitch. **1972** R. WARDHAUGH *Introd. Ling.* iii. 32 Sometimes ingressive air, that is, air going to the lungs, may also be used. *Ibid.* 36 Ingressives are rare indeed, in English confined perhaps to certain kinds of exclamatory sounds.

Hence **inˈgressiveness**, ingressive quality.

1882–3 TOY in Schaff *Encycl. Relig. Knowl.* 2155 Two forms which denote respectively completedness and ingressiveness of action.

inˈgressively, *adv.* [f. INGRESSIVE *a.* + -LY².] In an ingressive manner.

1921 H. POUTSMA *Characters of Eng. Verb* i. 2 The actions expressed by verbs..may be..(1) indefinitely durative, ..(2) ingressively durative, i.e. with the initial stage of the action more distinctly thought of than the rest. **1928** —— *Gram. Late Mod. Eng.* (ed. 2) I. 2 The combinations into which they [*sc.* copulas] enter are *a*) indefinitely durative, *b*) continuatively durative, or *c*) ingressively durative. **1969** M. M. FIRESTONE in Halpert & Story *Christmas Mumming in Newfoundland* 66 'Yes' and sometimes 'no' are indeed normally uttered ingressively in this area.

†**inˈgressor.** *Obs. rare*⁻¹. [agent-n. from L. *ingredī* to enter: cf. *aggressor*, and OF. *ingresseur* (Godef.).] One who enters; an intruder, an invader.

c **1710** *Light to Blind* in *10th Rep. Hist. MSS. Comm.* App. v. 144 Then they poured in their shott amongst the ingressors from front, right, and left.

†**inˈgressu.** *Law. Obs.* [from L. phr. *de ingressu* 'of entry': cf. next.] An obsolete writ of entry: see quot.

1607 COWELL *Interpr.*, *Ingressu*, is a writ of entrie, that is, whereby a man seeketh entry into lands or tenements; it lyeth in many diuers cases where it hath as many diuersities of formes. **1658** in PHILLIPS. **1670** in BLOUNT *Law Dict.*

‖**inˈgressus.** *Law. Obs.* [L., = 'entrance': see INGRESS.] (See quot.)

1706 PHILLIPS, *Ingressus*,..in a Law-sense, a Relief or Duty which the Heir or Successor at full age anciently paid to the Chief Lord for entring upon the Fee, or Lands that were fallen to him.

ingreve, -grieue, obs. forms of ENGRIEVE.

ingroche, obs. form of ENCROACH *v.*

ingroove, variant of ENGROOVE *v.*

ingrose, ingross(e, -grosser, -grossment, obs. forms of ENGROSS, etc.

†**inˈgrossative.** *Obs. rare*⁻¹. [f. ppl. stem of med.L. *ingrossāre* to thicken (cf. ENGROSS 8), perh. after obs. F. *ingrossatif, -ive* (15–16th c. in Godef.) or a med.L. **ingrossātīvus*.] A medicine for thickening the 'humours': = INCRASSATIVE B.

c **1550** LLOYD *Treas. Health* (1585) I viij, Maturatiues, Ingrossatyues, and Divisiues, as these following.

†**inˈgroten,** *v. Obs. rare.* [f. IN-¹ or ² + GROTEN *v.*: cf. also AGROTE, AGROTEN.] *trans.* To cram with food or drink, to glut.

c **1440** *Promp. Parv.* 215/1 Groton, or ingroton wythe mete or drynke, *ingurgito*. *Ibid.* 261/2 Ingroton wythe mete or drynke, supra in *groton*.

†**inˈground,** *v. Obs. rare.* [f. IN-¹ or ² + GROUND *v.*] *trans.* To fix *into* something as a foundation.

1581 N. WOODES *Confl. Consc.* IV. in Hazl. *Dodsley* VI. 83 So we, which into Christ our Rock are ingrounded.

†**inˈgrounded,** *a. Obs. rare.* [IN-³.] Ungrounded, groundless.

1601 *Archpr. Controv.* (Camden) II. 165 Such ingrounded suspitions as S. N. would engender in his frendes minde.

ˈin-group. [Cf. IN *a.* 2.] A small group of people, within a wider context, whose common interest tends to exclude others; also *attrib.* Hence ***ingroupiness, ingroupness***; **ˈingrouper**, a member of an in-group. Cf. OUT-GROUP.

1907 W. G. SUMNER *Folkways* i. 12 Thus a differentiation arises between ourselves, the we-group, or in-group, and everybody else, or the others-groups, out-groups. **1932** H. BECKER *Syst. Sociol.* II. xi. 182 Members of such groups may indeed manifest a certain loyalty and consideration for all fellow-members, i.e., for the 'in-group'. **1939** *American Imago* Nov. 24 In-groupers must learn to tolerate..anxiety. **1942** *New Statesman* 11 July 26/3 The very progress of civilisation has laid the foundation for a vast extension of in-group mutual dependency and mutual support. **1947** *Partisan Rev.* XIV. 478 The sense of in-groupness of the bohemian intellectual provides a source of psychological security. **1950** B. WOOTTON *Testament Social Sci.* vi. 127 For many primitive peoples..what the sociologist calls the 'in-group' consists of a relatively small tribal community, whereas the Christian is taught..to treat all men as brothers. **1964** M. ARGYLE *Psychol. & Social Probl.* x. 134 It is well known that residential courses are the scene of violent in-group feelings and wild enthusiasm. **1964** *Rev. Eng. Stud.* Aug. 338 Two masterly impersonations: of the shy poet hauled before dons, and of the puzzled philistine, ready with cautious, deflationary, in-group jokes. **1965** *Listener* 4 Mar. 345/2 Mr. Gelber's mixture of sentimentality, in-groupiness, and Village dourness, can be more than a little grating. **1967** J. GARDNER *Madrigal* iii. 65 Cheery as an in-grouper at party time. **1970** *Jrnl. Gen. Psychol.* Oct. 259 An error was considered..ingroup intrusion if the response was a word paired with a similar stimulus. **1971** *Listener* 18 Nov. 674/3 Their closed or in-group speech made me feel out of it. **1972** J. L. DILLARD *Black English* vi. 230 American Blacks are quick to perceive

pronunciation differences on the part of West Indians who migrate to cities like New York and are somewhat slow to accept them into the in-group.

ingrowing ('ɪnˌgrəʊɪŋ), *ppl. a.* [IN *adv.* 11 a.] Growing inwards or within something; *spec.* of a nail: Growing into the flesh.

1869 E. A. PARKES *Pract. Hygiene* (ed. 3) 399 Neglected corns, bunions, or in-growing nails. **1871** H. MACMILLAN *True Vine* iv. (1872) 130 God's word will be.. the *emphutos logos*, the ingrowing word.

So **'ingrowing** *vbl. sb.*

1852 T. J. ASHTON *(title)* Corns, Bunions, and Ingrowing of the Toe-Nail.

ingrown ('ɪngrəʊn), *ppl. a.* [IN *adv.* 11 b.]

a. That has or is grown within something; native, innate (usually of immaterial things).

1670 PETTUS *Fodinae Reg.* v. 5 Particulars of ingrowen Metals and Minerals. **1865** PUSEY *Eiren.* 194 The imperfection ingrown as it were with the soul. **1876** L. MORRIS *Songs Two W.* Ser. III. *Youth of Thought* 25 Art with Language lived ingrown, The cunning hand and golden tongue.

b. Of a nail: That has grown into the flesh.

1878 T. BRYANT *Pract. Surg.* I. 177 In-grown toe-nail is a troublesome affection.

c. *Geol.* Applied to an incised meander having a characteristic asymmetrical cross-section (see quot. 1954) as a result of lateral erosion and movement of the bed as it was being cut.

1914 J. L. RICH in *Jrnl. Geol.* XXII. 470 The In-grown Meander Valley is one whose stream, which may or may not have inherited a meandering course from a previous cycle, has developed such a course or expended its inherited one. Thus, as the stream sunk its channel lower and lower into the bed-rock, the meanders were continually growing or expanding. The term 'in-grown' has been chosen to express this idea. **1954** W. D. THORNBURY *Princ. Geomorphol.* vi. 145 Two types of incised or inclosed meanders are generally recognized: (1) entrenched or intrenched meanders.., which show little or no contrast between the slopes of the two valley sides of a meander curve, and (2) ingrown meanders.., which exhibit pronounced asymmetry of cross profile with under-cut slopes on the outside of the meander curves and slipoff slopes on the inside. **1960** B. W. SPARKS *Geomorphol.* ix. 225 Ingrown meanders are more slowly incised, due to less rapid downcutting or to more resistant rocks.

ingrowth ('ɪngrəʊθ). [IN *adv.* 11 d.]

a. The action of growing inwards. **b.** *concr.* That which grows inwards; a formation due to growth in an inward direction. (Opp. to *outgrowth.*)

1870 ROLLESTON *Anim. Life* 20 Not as yet closed up by ossificatory ingrowth. **1877** HUXLEY *Anat. Inv. Anim.* viii. 482 In these, as in other Invertebrata, the nervous ganglia are modified ingrowths of the epiblast. **1882** VINES *Sachs' Bot.* 14 The cell-walls..are attached externally to the ingrowths of the cell-wall of the mother-cell.

†**in'grudge.** *Obs. rare*$^{-1}$. [? IN-^{2}.] Secret enmity, spite; grudge.

1606 WARNER *Alb. Eng.* XIV. lxxx. 339 Whether fifte Henryes costly warres, or death (he so belou'd) More touched his ingrudge or greefe, a question may be mou'd.

†**'ingruence.** *Obs.* [ad. med.L. *ingruentia* irruption, etc., f. *ingruent-em*: see next and -ENCE.] A coming on, onset, attack.

1626 JACKSON *Creed* VIII. xii. §10 Only by the ingruence of the disease itself. **1673** OLEY *Pref. Jackson's Wks.* (1844) I. 33 The sudden ingruence of a lethargy or apoplexy.

†**ingruent,** *a. Obs.* [f. L. *ingruent-em*, pr. pple. of *ingruĕre* to rush upon, attack: cf. *congruent.*] Coming on, assailing, attacking, invading.

1610 HEALEY *St. Aug. Citie of God* 568 An Arke..lifted from earth by the ingruent force of the waters. *Ibid.* 745 The better to withstand the ingruent warre. **1649** MARBURY *Comm. Habak.* i. 2 They that had wont to stand in the gap, to turn away ingruent judgments.

ingrum, corruption of *ignorant*: see INGRAM.

Ingua, obs. form of INCA.

ingubu (ɪŋ'gu:bəʊ). *S. Afr.* Also 9 **ingoobu, ingouboo, ingubo.** [Nguni; cf. Fanagalo *ngubo*, Bantu-Botatwe *ingubo*, blanket, clothes.] Applied to articles of dress offered for sale to the native inhabitants of Natal.

1833 S. KAY *Trav. Caffraria* i. 37 He maintained that every thing around him, mountains, rivers, grass, cattle, and even his *ingubu*, 'beast-skin garment', proved the truth of what had been said respecting the being of a God. **1837** F. OWEN *Diary* (1926) 25 They [*sc.* the natives] asked in exchange for their fowls, Indian corn and pumpkins, either handkerchiefs, blankets or 'ingubo' i.e. a mantle or carosse. *Ibid.* 77 He..abruptly asked me what was the use of giving all that ingoobu to the children, alluding to the Kilts of Dingareen with which I have clothed the boys. **1860** W. SHAW *Story of Mission in S.-E. Afr.* 406 A Kaffir wears this ingubu, or 'kaross', with the hairy side next to his skin, throwing it over his shoulders, from whence it hangs down to his ancles. **1899** G. RUSSELL *Hist. Old Durban* ix. 187 Cast-off articles of European attire, known to the Natives as 'Ingouboos'.

†**ingudged,** erroneous f. *inguaged* or *ingadged* = ENGAGED *ppl. a.* So **ingudgment.**

1650 in Picton *L'pool Munic. Rec.* (1883) I. 129 His debts and ingudgments. *Ibid.* 130 Wherein the town are ingudged and concerned. **1656** *Ibid.* 177 For y^{e} wch Mr. James Southerne was ingudged.

‖**inguen** ('ɪŋgwɛn). [L.] The groin.

1706 PHILLIPS, *Inguen*, the Groin, or Share. **17..** in J. Thomson *Lect. Inflam.* (1813) 259 A wadd of hard linen cloth, or the like, inside the thigh, a little below the inguen.

inguilty, erroneous form of UNGUILTY.

inguinal ('ɪŋgwɪnəl), *a. Anat.* and *Path.* [ad. L. *inguinālis* (Pliny), f. *inguen, inguin-* the groin: cf. F. *inguinal* (Paré, 16th c.).] Of, belonging to, or situated in the groin.

1681 tr. *Willis' Rem. Med. Wks.* Vocab., *Inguinal*, belonging to the groin. **1757** LAYARD in *Phil. Trans.* L. 531 The parotid, inguinal, or other glands. **1800** *Med. Jrnl.* IV. 39 An incarcerated inguinal hernia. **1878** BELL *Gegenbaur's Comp. Anat.* 422 They [mammæ] form two rows, which.. extend from the Inguinal to the pectoral region.

inguinally ('ɪŋgwɪnəlɪ), *adv.* [f. INGUINAL *a.* + -LY^{2}.] By or in the groin.

1908 *Practitioner* Aug. 255 There are also certain other disadvantages to which the inguinally retained testis is liable. **1966** C. A. W. GUGGISBERG *S.O.S. Rhino* iii. 68 The mammae, two in number, are situated inguinally.

inguino- ('ɪŋgwɪnəʊ), used as combining form of Lat. *inguen, inguin-* (see INGUINAL *a.*): as in **inguino-ab'dominal** *a.*, 'relating to the groin and to the abdomen'; **inguino-'crural** *a.*, 'relating to the groin and to the thigh' (*Syd. Soc. Lex.* 1886); **inguino-cu'taneous** *a.*, relating to the groin and the skin (of the adjoining thigh); **inguino-'scrotal** *a.*, belonging to the groin and the scrotum.

[**1847** CRAIG, *Inguino-cutaneus*, an epithet applied by Chaussier to the anterior branch of the first lumbar nerve.] **1855** MAYNE *Expos. Lex.*, Inguino-cutaneous. **1878** T. BRYANT *Pract. Surg.* I. 680 An inguino-scrotal or labial hernia.

ingulf, etc., variant of ENGULF *v.*, etc.

†**in'gurdge, in'gurge,** obs. ff. ENGORGE *v.*

1631 HEYWOOD *London's Jus Hon.* Wks. 1874 IV. 271 A thousand monsters..gape To ingurdge and swallow you.

ingurgitate (ɪn'gɜ:dʒɪteɪt), *v.* Pa. pple. in 6 **ingurgitate.** [f. ppl. stem of L. *ingurgitāre* to pour in (like a flood), to glut or gorge oneself, f. *in-* (IN-^{2}) + *gurges, gurgit-em* a whirlpool, gulf. Cf. F. *ingurgiter* (Cotgr. 1611).]

1. *trans.* To swallow greedily or immoderately (food, or, in later use esp., drink). Also *fig.*

1570 LEVINS *Manip.* 41/47 Ingurgitate, *ingurgitare.* **1574** NEWTON *Health Mag.* 16 Meate excessively ingurgitate and eaten..commonly engendreth and breedeth cruditie. **1607** TOPSELL *Four-f. Beasts* (1658) 205 To ingurgitate & consume more of Gods creatures. **1657** TOMLINSON *Renou's Disp.* 220 When he had ingurgitated much wine. *a* **1711** KEN *Edmund* Poet. Wks. 1721 II. 83 Those Sots..Flask after Flask ingurgitate, till drown'd In their own Spews they wallow on the Ground. **1822** T. TAYLOR *Apuleius, Philos. Plato* II. 358 To ingurgitate pleasures of every kind. **1855** F. HALL in *Nation* (N.Y.) XL. 257/1 He does not hesitate to ingurgitate, at one brave gulp, all the evil..that is found in the original German.

b. *absol.* To eat or drink to excess; to gormandize, guzzle.

1598 T. BASTARD *Chrestoleros* (1880) 10 Phisition Mirus talkes of saliuation..Who doth ingurgitate, who tussicate. **1621** BURTON *Anat. Mel.* II. ii. I. ii, To eat and ingurgitate beyond all measure, as many doe. **1841** JEFFREY *Let.* in Cockburn *Life* II. clvii, When awake and not ingurgitating, on the whole very good company.

c. To gorge, to cram with food or drink.

1583 STUBBES *Anat. Abus.* I. (1877) 104 Wee must not swill and ingurgitate our stomacks so ful. **1615** T. ADAMS *Spir. Navigator* 15 Cormorants whose gorges have been long ingurgitated with the world.

2. *trans.* To swallow up as a gulf or whirlpool; to engulf. *lit.* and *fig.*

a **1619** FOTHERBY *Atheom.* II. ii. §5 (1622) 206 Let him ingurgitate himselfe neuer so deepe into it. **1644** VICARS *God in Mount* 204 The swelling and swallowing Waves which thought to have ingurgitated and supt us all up. **1787** tr. *Klopstock's Messiah* III. 93 Thus whirlpools..ingurgitate into their gulphs profound the incautious mariner. **1849** E. B. EASTWICK *Dry Leaves* 121 Bankers who pay no interest it is true, but do not absorb and ingurgitate your principal.

†**b.** *intr.* for *refl.* Of a river: To discharge itself into the sea. (Cf. ENGULF 1 b.) *Obs.*

1632 VICARS tr. *Virgil's Æneid* 5 Where swift Simois did ingurgitate.

Hence **in'gurgitated, in'gurgitating** *ppl. adjs.*

1620 VENNER *Via Recta* vi. 102 Mixt sauces.., which of ingurgitating belly-gods are greatly esteemed. **1654** GAYTON *Pleas. Notes* IV. xxv. 284 Sancho had in a short time choak'd himselfe with the ingurgitated reliques and orts of the Canons provision. **1830** *Beauties Thanet* II. 59 Their ingurgitating property is so powerful, that in a few days even the largest vessel driven upon them would be swallowed up. **1851** HAWTHORNE *Ho. Sev. Gables* xx. (1883) 366 A momentary eddy,—very small, as compared with the apparent magnitude of the ingurgitated object.

ingurgitation (ɪngɜ:dʒɪ'teɪʃən). [ad. late L. *ingurgitātiōn-em*, n. of action from *ingurgitāre*: see prec.] The action of ingurgitating.

1. Greedy or immoderate swallowing; excessive eating or drinking; guzzling or swilling.

1530 ELYOT *Gov.* I. xi, I shall exhorte tutours and gouernours of noble chyldren, that they suffre them nat to use ingourgitations of meate or drinke. **1605** BACON *Adv. Learn.* II. x. §7 A large draught and ingurgitation of wine. *a* **1654** SELDEN *Eng. Epin.* iii. §19 Ingurgitation of brain-smoaking liquors. **1794** E. DARWIN *Zoon.* (1801) I. 305 Accustomed to great ingurgitation of spirituous potation. **1837** *New Monthly Mag.* XLIX. 169 The Monday..was.. honoured with a due ingurgitation of collops and eggs.

fig. **1594** *Mirr. Policy* (1599) 191 The wine of worldly wisedome..procureth more ingurgitation then comfort. **1610** HEALEY *St. Aug. Citie of God* 48 Youre mindes being drunke with this continuall ingurgitation of error.

2. The action of swallowing up; engulfment.

1826 *Blackw. Mag.* XIX. 399 A playful prelude to their ingurgitation in that whirlpool—that Corryvrechan—our stomach.

¶**3.** (loosely or erroneously.) A gurgling noise.

1851 HAWTHORNE *Ho. Sev. Gables* viii, When Phœbe heard a certain noise in Judge Pyncheon's throat..when the girl heard this queer and awkward ingurgitation.

Ingush ('ɪnguʃ, ɪn'gʊʃ). Also **Ingoush.** Pl. **Ingoushee, Ingush, Ingushes.** [a. Russ. *Ingúsh*, the name of the former autonomous area of Ingush.] **a.** One of a North Caucasian people, forming the minor part of the population of Checheno-Ingushetia. Also *attrib.* or as *adj.* **b.** The North Caucasic language of this people.

1902 *Encycl. Brit.* XXX. 1/2 The Kabardian aristocracy, who were possessed of feudal rights over the Ossets, the Ingushes, the Abhazes, and the mountain Tatars. **1908** J. F. BADDELEY *Russian Conquest Caucasus* v. 86 The Ingoush elders..[were] summoned to Mozdók. *Ibid.* xxviii. 468 The Russians..decided to gather the Ingoushee..into a few large settlements. **1910** *Encycl. Brit.* V. 548/1 Although the Ingushes speak a Chechen dialect, they have recently been proved to be, anthropologically, quite a distinct race. **1954** PEI & GAYNOR *Dict. Ling.* 101 *Ingush*, a Chechen dialect (Eastern Caucasian group of the North Caucasian family of languages). **1957** [see CHECHEN]. **1958** *Everyman's Encycl.* III. 189/2 A number of peoples (Chechens, Ingushes, Balkars, Karachays, and Kalmyks) were deported from N[orth] C[aucasus] to Central Asia in 1943 for alleged collaboration with the Germans, and only rehabilitated in 1957.

†**in'gustable,** *a. Obs.* Also *erron.* -ible. [ad. L. *ingustābilis* (Pliny) not fit to be tasted, f. *in-* (IN-^{3}) + *gustābilis* GUSTABLE.] Incapable of being tasted; not perceptible by the sense of taste.

1623 COCKERAM, *Ingustible.* **1646** SIR T. BROWNE *Pseud. Ep.* III. xxi. 158 The body of that element is ingustible, void of all sapidity. **1656** STANLEY *Hist. Philos.* VI. (1701) 257/1 The Taste perceiveth that which is gustable, and that which is ingustable.

Ingvaeonic (ɪŋvi:'ɒnɪk), *sb.* Also **Inguaeonic** (-gw-), **Ingweonic.** [f. L. *Ingaeuones* (Tacitus), a Germanic tribe.] From Tacitus's division of the Germanic people into Ingaeuones, Istaeuones and Hermiones, the name applied to the hypothetical language from which the earliest recorded dialects of West Germanic except Old High German descended. Sometimes used synonymously with ANGLO-FRISIAN. Also *attrib.*

[**1907** H. M. CHADWICK *Orig. Eng. Nation* ix. 222 The identification of the Inguaeones with the Anglo-Frisian group rests on the assumption that languages of this type were once spoken in the western Baltic, a hypothesis for which no solid evidence has been produced.] **1933** L. BLOOMFIELD *Lang.* iv. 58 We conclude that English is an offshoot of an *Anglo-Frisian* (or *Ingweonic*) dialect area, which must have been fairly extensive before the migration to Britain. **1939** *Trans. Philol. Soc.* 87 Sporadic cases of *ō* for 'Ingvaeonic' *ā* occur in OSax. **1948** *Neophilologus* XXXII. 176 The pronounced Inguaeonic characteristics of early Low German sources. *Ibid.* 181 The oldest Germanic language of the Dutch area is thus understood to have been primitive Inguaeonic. **1948** *Trans. Philol. Soc. 1947* 14 The original Germanic language of the Low German area was not in any essential matter distinguished from Frisian... In that original state it formed with English a loose unity.. having in a common articulation potentialities for common developments... This loose unity we may call Ingvaeonic. **1959** A. CAMPBELL *Old Eng. Gram.* §4 This West Germanic without Old High German is often called 'Ingvaeonic', because in Tacitus' threefold division of the Germans the Ingvaeones lie near the sea.

ingyn(n)e, obs. ff. ENGINE; var. INGINE.

†**ingynour,** obs. f. ENGINEER, contriver, inventor.

1500–20 DUNBAR *Poems* lxiii. 55 In quintiscence, eik, ingynouris joly, That far can multiplie in folie.

†**in'gyre,** *v.*^{1} *Sc. Obs.* Also 6 **ingire, ingir,** 7 **engyre.** [app. ad. F. *ingére-r*, or L. *ingerĕre* to bring in, thrust (oneself) in: see INGERE.

(The *y* or *i* of the stem vowel is difficult to explain; Jamieson's derivation from L. *gȳrāre* (cf. INGYRE *v.*^{2}) does not seem to be supported by the sense.)]

trans. To introduce forcibly or violently; to thrust in; usually *refl.* to thrust oneself in, obtrude oneself, intrude.

1513 DOUGLAS *Æneis* IX. iv. 136 For nocht thou says sik wordis vane, Ingyrand cacis [that] ar of nane effek. *Ibid.* X. ii. 9 To ingyre him self to Latyn king As mortal fa. 1560–1 *Bk. Discipl. Ch. Scot.* (1621) 76 No man ought to ingyre himselfe, or usurpe this Office without lawfull calling. 1588 A. KING tr. *Canisius' Catech.* 81 b, Yat sho may ingir to the sight, and sensis of the peopl a maist vive repræsentation of our lords death. 1609 SKENE *Reg. Maj.* I. viii. 9 b, Gif he ingired himselfe to that service vndesired. 1647 *Form Ch. Govt.* xxvi, To whom it was not permitted..to ingyre themselves into Ecclesiasticall Communion. *Ibid.* 61 Who.. shall insolently..engyre and obtrude himself upon the Sacrament. 1733 in J. Brown *Life of Fisher* ii. 24 [Pronouncing that he had] engyred [himself into the process not for the vindication of truth but on account of his connection with the delinquent].

Hence †**in'gyring** *ppl. a.*, that thrusts itself upon one.

1638 *Gen. Demands conc. Covt.* 3 We have closed our eyes against a clear and ingyring light.

†**in'gyre,** *v.*² *Obs. rare.* [f. IN-² + L. *gȳrāre* to wheel round, *gȳrus* circle, GYRE.] *trans.*

a. To surround; b. To wind round, to circumgyrate, circumvolve.

1568 C. WATSON *Polyb.* 43 a, It was very dangerous for being ingired, for the Carthaginenses being the greater troupe of horses might easelier environ them disposed so straightly. 1610 *Histrio-m.* II. 335, I have a mistresse whose intangling wit, Will turne and winde more cunning arguments Then could the Crœtan Labyrinth ingyre.

†**inhabile,** *a. Obs.* [a. F. *inhabile*, or ad. L. *inhabilis* incapable, unfit, unable, f. *in-* (IN-³) + *habilis* manageable, suitable, fit, ABLE, HABILE.] Unfit, unable; unqualified.

1727 BAILEY vol. II, *Inhabile*, unmeet, unfit, unwieldy, not nimble. 1745 tr. *Columella's Husb.* XII. i, To the Woman, because Nature had made her inhabile for all these things, she committed the care of domestic affairs. 1830 SCOTT *Demonol.* ix. 299 Extorted confessions, or the evidence of inhabile witnesses.

†**in'habile, in'hable,** *v. Obs. rare.* [f. INHABILE *a.*] *trans.* To render or declare unfit; to disqualify, disable.

1534 in *St. Papers Hen. VIII*, II. 218 [To] inhabill thaym, and every of thaym to receyv or accept anny other. 1542 *Act 33 Hen. VIII* in Bolton *Stat. Irel.* (1621) 192 Nor that any of the said persons being Priests..be inhabled..to marrie or take any wife or wives. 1590 R. BRUCE *Serm. Sacram.* E ij b (Jam.), I speake..of sik fault as inhables the person of the giuer, to be a distributer of the sacrament.

inhabile, obs. form of ENABLE *v.*

†**inha'bilitate,** *v. Obs. rare*⁻¹. [f. L. *inhabilitāt-*, ppl. stem of *inhabilitāre* to declare unfit: cf. INABILITATE *ppl. a.*] *trans.* To render unfit, disqualify.

1670 H. STUBBE *Plus Ultra* 17 Those courses.. inhabilitate them [men's minds] towards those more important but less delightful studies of Law, Policy, and Religion.

†**inha'bility.** *Obs.* Also 6 -ite. [a. F. *inhabilité*, or ad. med.L. *inhabilitās*, f. *inhabilis* unfit, incapable, unable. A doublet of *inability*.]

1. Unfitness, incapacity, disability (for any office).

1488 *Sc. Acts Jas. IV* (1597) §4 And that the Ordinaries dispone vpon their vther benefices, for the inhabilitie of their persones. *c* 1575 *Balfour's Practicks* (1754) 22 Quhilk inhabilitie being alledgit aganis ony Jugeis, Principall or Deputis. 1588 ALLEN *Admon.* 52 The sentence declaratory of Pius Quintus against the said Elizabeth..concerning her illegitimation and vsurpation and inhabillite to the Croune of England. 1670 H. STUBBE *Plus Ultra* 28 If Mr. Cross did urge this otherwise than to try the Intellectuals of Mr. Glanvill (concerning whose Inhability he might be well satisfied). 1757 ERSKINE *Princ. Law Scotl.* IV. ii. §15 (ed. 2) 452 Law allows the party who suspects a witness..to bring evidence of his enmity, or other inhability.

2. = INABILITY, q.v.

inhabit *pa. pple.*: see next.

inhabit (ɪn'hæbɪt), *v.* Forms: α. 4–6 enhabit(e, 5 -yte, -ete. β. 4–7 inhabite, 5 -et(t, -ete, 5–6 -yt(e, 6 inabite, 6– inhabit. *Pa. pple.* en-, inhabited; also 4–7 en-, inhabit, -ite. [a. OF. *enhabiter* (12th c. in Godef.) to dwell, dwell in, ad. L. *inhabitāre*, f. *in-* (IN-²) + *habitāre* to dwell: see HABIT *v.*]

1. *trans.* To dwell in, occupy as an abode; to live permanently or habitually in (a region, element, etc.); to reside in (a country, town, dwelling, etc.). Said of men and animals.

α. *c* 1374 CHAUCER *Boeth.* II. pr. vii. 44 (Camb. MS.) The ferthe partye ys enhabited with lyuynge bestys þat we knowen. *c* 1400 *Destr. Troy* 101 An yle enabit..With a maner of men, mermydons callid. *c* 1477 CAXTON *Jason* 63 b, This cite is enhabited with women without king. *c* 1511 *1st Eng. Bk. Amer.* (Arb.) Introd. 28/1 That other yland is not enhabite.

β. 1390 GOWER *Conf.* I. 324 The citee..Of worthy folk.. Was inhabited here and there. *c* 1400 MAUNDEV. (Roxb.) vii. 23 The land of [Egipte] es lang, bot it es narowe: for men may noȝt inhabit it on brede for desertes. 1559 W. CUNNINGHAM *Cosmogr. Glasse* 174 London..is inhabited with men of everye facultie. 1611 BIBLE *Isa.* lxv. 21 They shall build houses, and inhabit them. 1797 BEWICK *Brit. Birds* (1847) I. 26 This bird inhabits all the northern parts of Europe. 1881 *Athenæum* No. 2777. 97 The pelagic fishes, or those which inhabit the mid ocean.

b. *transf.* (of inanimate things), and *fig.*

1526 *Pilgr. Perf.* (W. de W. 1531) 26 b, More perfyte religyons, whiche be to the seruauntes of god that inhabyte them, as the arke of Noe. 1611 BIBLE *Isa.* lvii. 15 The High and loftie One that inhabiteth eternitie. 1654–66 EARL ORRERY *Parthen.* I Those charms, which in spight of fortunes cruelties, did yet inhabit his face. 1807–8 W. IRVING *Salmag.* xi. (1860) 246 The same echo inhabited the valley.

2. *intr.* To dwell, live; to have one's abode; to abide, lodge. *arch.*

α. *c* 1374 CHAUCER *Boeth.* I. pr. v. 15 (Camb. MS.) Who so þat leteth the wyl for to enhabyte there. 1393 LANGL. *P. Pl.* C. x. 188 Eremites þat en-habiten by þe heye weyes. *c* 1440 *Gesta Rom.* I. xxvii. 102 (Harl. MS.) This knight enhabitid in a woode. 1537 *Act 27 Hen. VIII* in Bolton *Stat. Irel.* (1621) 175 Every person and persons enhabiting within this land.

β. *a* 1400–50 *Alexander* 4020 An Ile, Quare þir Exidraces as Ermets inhabet in caues. 1598 W. PHILLIPS *Linschoten* (1864) 170 In all places of India where the Portugals inabite. 1667 MILTON *P.L.* II. 355 Thither let us bend all our thoughts, to learn What creatures there inhabit. 1796 MORSE *Amer. Geog.* I. 511 The Senecas inhabit on the Chenesee or Genessee river. 1871 BROWNING *Pr. Hohenst.* 1716 But, till notice sound, Inhabit we in ease and opulence!

b. *transf.* and *fig.* To dwell, abide.

1382 WYCLIF *Col.* i. 19 In hym it pleside to gidere al plente for to inhabite. *c* 1430 *Pilgr. Lyf Manhode* I. lxxxviii. (1869) 50 The hous is..lasse than the good that enhabiteth ther inne. *c* 1580 SIDNEY *Ps.* XXXIV. i, In my mouth contynually Inhabit shall his praise. *a* 1619 FLETCHER *Mad Lover* III. iv, Her ey inhabits on him. 1697 DRYDEN *Virg. Past.* IX. 53 See, on the Shoar inhabits purple Spring. 1824 *Westm. Rev.* I. 4 It dignifies every thought that inhabits with it.

†3. *trans.* To occupy or people (a place). *Obs.*

1390 GOWER *Conf.* III. 278 Nations seventy and two, In sondry place eche one of tho [nations] The wide world have enhabited. 1412–20 LYDG. *Chron. Troy* (1555) I. i, Thus gan he praye..His lande tenhabite which standeth desolate. 1613 PURCHAS *Pilgrimage* (1614) 43 The Iberians..dwelt neare to Meotis: certaine Colonies of them inhabited Spaine, and called it Hiberia. 1651 HOBBES *Leviath.* II. xxiv. 131 'Plantations', or 'colonies', which are numbers of men sent out..to inhabit a Forraign Country..void of inhabitants.

†b. To people *with*, to furnish *with* (inhabitants). *Obs.*

c 1400 MAUNDEV. (Roxb.) xii. 52 Þis castell gert Bawdewyne make.. and inhabited it with Cristen men. 1515 in *St. Papers Hen. VIII*, II. 11 He dyd conquyre all the lande,..and dyd inhabyte the same with Englyshe folke. 1579–80 NORTH *Plutarch* (1895) III. 336 Cities..which afterwardes they did inhabite with their owne citizens.

†4. To establish or settle (a person, etc.) in a place, to furnish with a habitation; to locate, house; *refl.* to establish oneself, take up one's abode; *passive*, to be domiciled or resident.

1413 *Pilgr. Sowle* (Caxton 1483) IV. xxxiv. 8 Suche as ben enheryted and enhabyted in the same Countre. 1491 CAXTON *Vitas Patr.* (W. de W. 1495) II. 186 b/1 He..yede his waye to enhabyte him selfe in the deserte within a caue. 1494 FABYAN *Chron.* VI. clv. 143 He after inhabyted them in dyuerse placis of his realme. 1495 *Trevisa's Barth. De P.R.* XVIII. liii. (W. de W.) 812 Amptes..make hepys and hylles in whom they enhabyte themself in. 1496 *Act 12 Hen. VII*, c. 6 The Merchauntes Adventurers inhabite and dwelling in divers parties of this Realme of Englond. 1568 GRAFTON *Chron.* II. 158 Many of the Citizens..voyded the Citie,.. and inhabited themselves in diverse places of the realme. 1600 SHAKS. *A.Y.L.* III. iii. 10 O knowledge ill inhabited, worse then Ioue in a thatch'd house!

†b. *intr.* (for *refl.*) To take up one's abode, settle. *Obs.*

1548 HALL *Chron., Hen. V* 36 After whiche victory certaine souldiers..passed over the water of Sala and there inhabited, betwene the rivers. 1588 PARKE tr. *Mendoza's Hist. China* I. iii. (Hakluyt Soc.) I. 12 Perswaded..that those which did first finde and inhabite in this lande, were the nevewes of Noe.

†c. *fig.* (in *pa. pple.* = (?) Established, located, allotted; addicted, devoted). *Obs.*

c 1374 CHAUCER *Troylus* IV. 415 (443) She þat I serue,.. To whom myn herte enhabit [*v.r.* enabitid] is by right, Shal han me holly hires til þat I dye.

Hence **in'habiting** *ppl. a.*, indwelling.

a 1617 BAYNE *On Coloss.* i. & ii. (1634) 258 Now the inhabiting and the inhabited are not confounded. 1844 W. H. MILL *Serm. Tempt. Christ* ii. 42 To restore this inhabiting Presence to Man.

†**in'habitable,** *a.*¹ *Obs.* [a. F. *inhabitable* (1372 in Hatz.-Darm.), ad. L. *inhabitābilis*, f. *in-* (IN-³) + *habitābilis* HABITABLE.] Not habitable, not adapted to human habitation, uninhabitable.

c 1400 MAUNDEV. (Roxb.) xvii. 78 Beyond Mauritayne.. es a grete cuntree, but it es inhabitable by cause of þe owtrage hete of þe sonne. 1491 CAXTON *Vitas Patr.* (W. de W. 1495) III. xxix. 326 a/1 The londe was inhabytable for the sterylyte & baraynes therof. 1593 SHAKS. *Rich. II*, I. i. 65 Euen to the frozen ridges of the Alpes, Or any other ground inhabitable. 1647 TRAPP *Mellif. Theol.* in *Comm. Ep.* 697 Archimedes..bragged, that he could number the sand in all the world, habitable and inhabitable. 1674 tr. *Scheffer's Lapland* 16 People towards the North, living in a Clime almost inhabitable. 1742 FRANCIS *Horace, Odes* I. iii. 24 Jove has the Realms of Earth in vain Divided by th' inhabitable Main.

b. *catachr.* Uninhabited.

1529 S. FISH *Suppl. Beggers* (E.E.T.S.) 6 These be they that..do let the generation of the people, wherby all the realme..shall be made desert and inhabitable. 1583 STUBBES *Anat. Abus.* II. (1882) 31 In the beginning, before the world was impeopled, men comming into huge and wast places inhabitable. 1609 BIBLE (Douay) *Jer.* xlviii. 9 Her cities shal be desolate and inhabitable.

Hence †**in,habita'bility**¹, the quality of being uninhabitable.

1684 T. BURNET *Th. Earth* I. 266 Nothing seems more remarkable than the inhabitability of the torrid zone, if we consider what a general belief it had amongst the ancients.

inhabitable (ɪn'hæbɪtəb(ə)l), *a.*² [f. INHABIT + -ABLE: cf. late L. *inhabitābilis* (Arnob.).] Capable of being inhabited, occupied, or tenanted.

1601 R. JOHNSON *Kingd. & Commw.* (1603) 181 Lordes of ..all the inhabitable places in that vast Archipelago. *a* 1631 DONNE *Lament. Jeremy* IV. xii, All which live In the inhabitable world. 1654 'PALAEMON' *Friendship* 23 A Soul.. inhabitable by a clear and sublime Friendship. 1794 HERSCHEL in *Phil. Trans.* LXXXV. 68 If stars are suns, and suns are inhabitable, we see at once what an extensive field for animation opens itself to our view. 1877 MRS. OLIPHANT *Makers Flor.* vii. 186 Their new convent was dilapidated, and scarcely inhabitable.

Hence **in,habita'bility**², the quality of being inhabitable; **in'habitableness** (Bailey vol. II).

1865 *Pall Mall G.* 20 May 11 Professor Whewell publishes his *Plurality of Worlds*, arguing against their inhabitability.

†**in'habitance.** *Obs.* Also 5 *erron.* -tauntes, 6 en-. [f. as INHABITANT + -ANCE: cf. HABITANCE.

From the confusion of *inhabitants*, *-tans*, pl. of INHABITANT, with *inhabitance*, came the converse error of *inhabitauntes* for this word.]

1. An inhabiting; inhabitation; residence.

1588 R. PARKE tr. *Mendoza's Hist. China* 409 From this kingdome..to Mazanbique, whereas there is inhabitance of Portingals. 1602 CAREW *Cornwall* 57 a, The ruines yet resting in the wilde Moores, which testifie a former inhabitance. *c* 1630 RISDON *Surv. Devon* §334 (1810) 346 In this parish Cutliffe hath inheritances and inhabitance.

2. A habitation, abode, dwelling.

1482 WARKW. *Chron.* (Camden) 10 Every man to rejoyse his owne lyflode and inhabytauntes. 1555 W. WATREMAN *Fardle Facions* I. i. 24 They ware banysshed that enhabitaunce of pleasure [Paradise]. 1611 BIBLE *Wisd.* xii. 7 A worthy colonie [*marg.* new inhabitance] of Gods children.

inhabitancy (ɪn'hæbɪtənsɪ). [f. INHABITANT: cf. prec. and HABITANCY: see -ANCY.]

1. The fact of inhabiting or of being an inhabitant; occupation by an inhabitant or inhabitants; residence as an inhabitant, *esp.* during a specified period, so as to become entitled to the rights and privileges of a regular inhabitant.

1681 in Somers *Tracts* I. 380 In case of Elections by Inhabitancy; the coming to live in a Place for a small time.. or coming to or taking a House for to serve an Election, doth not give right to vote. 1765 BLACKSTONE *Comm.* I. ix. 362 A legal settlement was declared to be gained by birth, or by inhabitancy, apprenticeship, or service, for forty days. 1814 MRS. J. WEST *Alicia de Lacy* III. 236 They..beheld..that token of inhabitancy and domestic comfort—the smoke of a peat fire. *a* 1848 W. A. BUTLER *Hist. Anc. Philos.* (1856) I. 144 The manhood thus consecrated by the presence and inhabitancy of the Godhead. 1884 GLADSTONE *Sp. Ho. Com.* 28 Feb., A new franchise, which..will be given to persons who are inhabitants, and, in the sense of inhabitancy, who are occupiers.

2. A place of habitation. *rare*⁻¹.

1853 GROTE *Greece* II. xc. XI. 719 The wholesale transportation of reluctant and miserable families from one inhabitancy to another.

inhabitant (ɪn'hæbɪtənt), *a.* and *sb.* Also 5 en-; *sb. pl.* 5–7 -ans, 6 *erron.* -ance. [a. AF. and OF. *inhabitant*, ad. L. *inhabitānt-em*, pr. pple. of *inhabitāre* to INHABIT.]

A. *adj.* Inhabiting, dwelling, resident. *arch.* or *Obs.*, exc. in ***inhabitant householder, occupier***, etc. (where perh. rather an attrib. use of the sb.).

1526 *Pilgr. Perf.* (1531) 61 b, Wherin he myght be inhabytaunt and dwell for euermore. 1531–2 *Act 23 Hen. VIII*, c. 9 §1 Where suche men..ben inhabitant and dwelling. 1625 *Gonsalvio's Sp. Inquis.* 3 Specially if he be there inhabitant. 1724 *Lond. Gaz.* No. 6324/4 John Wicksteed..(formerly..Inhabitant on Horse-lie-down). 1824 MACAULAY *St. Dennis & St. George* Misc. Writ. (Rtldg.) 47 The rates were levied by select vestries of the inhabitant householders. 1897 *Bill for Women's Franchise* (Ho. Comm. 3 Feb.), Every woman who is the inhabitant occupier as owner or tenant of any dwelling-house, tenement, or building within the borough or county where such occupation exists.

B. *sb.* One who inhabits; a human being or animal dwelling in a place; a permanent resident. Const. *of* (†*in*). (In early use only in *pl.*, the *sing.* rarely occurring until late in 16th cent.

In 15–16th c. the pl. was often, as in F., *inhabitans*, which being also spelt *inhabita(u)nce*, was confounded in form with INHABITANCE above.)

[1378 *Act 2 Rich. II*, c. 1 Les enhabitantz et en franchises en ycelles.] 1462 EDW. IV in Ellis *Orig. Lett.* Ser. II. I. 129 All the howsholdars and inhabitaunts within yowre Warde. 1489 CAXTON *Faytes of A.* I. viii. 20 Nethre gold ne siluer nor precyous stones make not the enhabytans to lyue in peas. 1538 STARKEY *England* I. iii. 72 Ruyn and dekey..the wych chefely I attrybute to the lake of inhabytans. 1552 HULOET, Inhabitauntes of a litle walled towne, *castel[lan]i*. 1588 R. PARKE tr. *Mendoza's Hist. China* 345 They did baptise certaine of the inhabitance. 1593 *Tell-Troth's N.Y. Gift* (1876) 42 Holes..vsed..by the inhabitantes of that citie. *Ibid.*, This citie..hath so dispersed her inhabitaunce into

the other partes of the cuntrey. **1594** T. B. *La Primaud. Fr. Acad.* II. 408 If we consider both the house and the inhabitant, wee shall see that [etc.]. **1615** G. SANDYS *Trav.* 217 Frequented with Leopards, Bores, Iaccalls, and such like sauage inhabitants. **1784** R. BAGE *Barham Downs* II. 161, I have been an inhabitant with your Lordship. **1871** FREEMAN *Norm. Conq.* IV. xvii. 11 He had won the land by force..without the good will of a single English-born inhabitant of England.

fig. **1749** FIELDING *Tom Jones* IV. ii, Such was the outside of Sophia; nor was this beautiful frame disgraced by an inhabitant unworthy of it.

b. *U.S.* (See quots.)

1789 *Constit. U.S.* I. §2 No person shall be a representative who shall not..be an inhabitant of that state in which he shall be chosen. **1834** *Congressional Election Cases* 411 An inhabitant of a state within the meaning of the Constitution, is one who is bona fide a member of the State, subject to all the requisitions of its laws, and entitled to all the privileges which they confer. **1883** E. CHANNING *Town & County Govt. Eng. Col. N. Amer.* (1884) 12 To this [parish] meeting all those who had benefit of the things there transacted might come; that is to say, all householders, and all who manured land within the parish. Such were technically termed inhabitants, even though they dwelt in another town.

†**in'habitate**, *pa. pple. Obs. rare*$^{-1}$. [ad. L. *inhabitāt-us*, pa. pple. of *inhabitāre*: see next.] Inhabited.

1432-50 tr. *Higden* (Rolls) I. 341 Giraldus rehersethe and seithe that londe was inhabitate [L. *inhabitata*] firste of Casera.

†**in'habitate**, *v. Obs.* [f. ppl. stem of L. *inhabitāre* to INHABIT.] *trans.* To inhabit.

1600 HOLLAND *Livy* 992 Of all the people which inhabitate Asia, the Gaules are most renowmed for valiance in warre. **1644** DIGBY *Nat. Bodies* xxxviii. (1645) 403 The first discoverers of Islands not inhabitated by men. **1720** MRS. MANLEY *Power of Love* iv. 259 Building Castles in the Air, that could never be inhabitated.

inhabitation (ɪnˌhæbɪ'teɪʃən). Also 6 en-. [ad. late L. *inhabitātiōn-em*, n. of action f. *inhabitāre* to INHABIT. Cf. AF. *enhabitacion* (1483-4 in Godef.).]

1. The action of inhabiting; the fact or condition of being or becoming inhabited.

c **1400** tr. *Secreta Secret., Gov. Lordsh.* (E.E.T.S.) 62 þurgh trew affiance dwellys folk togedre, and þerby ys inhabitacioun in citeez, comunynge to-gedre of ffolke. **1517** *Domesday Inclos.* I. 221 A tenement..ys decayd and fallen down, and non Inabytacyon on yt this xviii yers. **1568** GRAFTON *Chron.* I. 32 The Originall names, and the first inhabitation of this Realme. **1601** R. JOHNSON *Kingd. & Commw.* (1603) 185 By the daily increase of people, the countrey be even pestered with inhabitation. **1773** *Observ. State Poor* 74 Inhabitation for three years, or three months, or three days..will be equally valid for the creation of a parishioner. **1802** PALEY *Nat. Theol.* (1804) 299 Qualifying the animal for that mode of life and inhabitation, to which the structure of its eye confines it. **1856** RUSKIN *Mod. Paint.* IV. v. xix. §31 A pauper or two still inhabiting where inhabitation is possible.

b. *fig.* Spiritual indwelling.

1615 BYFIELD *Expos. Coloss.* (1869) 10 The effects or fruits of it..are: 1. The inhabitation of Christ. **1618** E. ELTON *Exp. Rom.* vii. (1622) 351 Gods children..are not freed from the inhabitation of sinne. **1677** GALE *Crt. Gentiles* IV. 91 The Greek Fathers terme efficacious Grace and our Dependence thereon..the inhabitation of the Holy Spirit. **1841** MYERS *Cath. Th.* xxix. 71 The general inhabitation of the Christian Body by the Christian Spirit.

†**2.** A place of dwelling; an inhabited region or building; an abode, dwelling. *Obs.*

c **1400** *Chron. Eng.* lxxv. in Herrig's *Archiv.* LII. 16 His one foote shall be sette in wike and that othir in london and he shall embrace iij inhabitacouns. **1495** *Trevisa's Barth. De P.R.* XIV. ii. (W. de W.) 465 The erthe is enhabytacion of bodyes that haue lyf. **1515** *Act 7 Hen. VIII*, c. 1 Tythyng houses and other enhabitacyons in any paryshe. **1601** R. JOHNSON *Kingd. & Commw.* (1603) 209 Cusistan the inhabitation of the Susiani. **1639** SIR W. BARCLAY *Lost Lady* I. ii. in Hazl. *Dodsley* XII. 572 When you her know, you will believe, That virtue chose that dark inhabitation.

†**3.** A collection of inhabitants; inhabitants collectively; population; settlement. *Obs. rare.*

(Some understand Milton's use as = Gr. οἰκουμένη the inhabited earth, the world.)

1588 R. PARKE tr. *Mendoza's Hist. China* 329 They came vnto a great inhabitation of Indians. **1671** MILTON *Samson* 1512 Noise call it you, or universal groan, As if the whole inhabitation perished? **1818** *Blackw. Mag.* IV. 328 A Craniopolis like the catacombs, containing so enormous an 'inhabitation', that no regular census has ever been made.

in'habitative, *a.* [f. as INHABITATE + -IVE.] Of or pertaining to inhabitation.

In mod. Dicts.

inhabi'tativeness. *Phrenology.* [f. prec. + -NESS.] = INHABITIVENESS.

1838 S. SMITH *Princ. Phrenol.* 136 If Spurzheim be right, the Dutch and Belgians should be deficient in Concentrativeness or Inhabitativeness. **1850** *Tait's Mag.* XVII. 504 Abnormal development of the organ of inhabitativeness.

†**in'habitator**. *Obs. rare.* [a. late L. *inhabitātor*, agent-noun f. *inhabitāre* to INHABIT.] One who inhabits; an inhabitant.

1432-50 tr. *Higden* (Rolls) I. 101 Syria, callede by that name by Sirus the inhabitator of hit. *Ibid.* 299 That londe towarde Alpes is colde, where the inhabitatores haue swellenges vnder the chynne for the grete habundaunce of waters of snawe beenge there.

†**in'habited**, *a. Obs.* [f. IN-[3] + HABITED *ppl. a.*] Not dwelt in; uninhabited.

1614 BRATHWAIT *Surv. Hist.* (R.), Others..have frequented desarts and inhabited provinces. *a* **1621** BEAUM. & FL. *Thierry & Theod.* III. i, Leave The earth inhabited to people Heaven.

Hence †**in'habitedness**[1], uninhabited condition.

1652-62 HEYLIN *Cosmogr.* III. (1673) 99/1 It hath the name..from the vast Desarts which are in it, and the inhabitedness thereof.

inhabited (ɪn'hæbɪtɪd), *ppl. a.* [f. INHABIT *v.* + -ED[1].] **a.** Dwelt in; having inhabitants.

1570-6 LAMBARDE *Peramb. Kent* (1826) 118 [It] had in it three hundreth and seven houses inhabited. **1665** BOYLE *Occas. Refl.* IV. xiii. (1848) 249 The remotest Parts of the Inhabited World. **1796** SOUTHEY *Lett. fr. Sp. & Portugal* (1799) 132 It can hardly be supposed that a banditti would attack in an inhabited place. **1851** *Act 14 & 15 Vict.* c. 36 §1 The Duties on Inhabited Dwelling Houses..should be assessed and levied according to the annual Value of such Dwelling Houses. **1869** E. A. PARKES *Pract. Hygiene* (ed. 3) 118 Whether the air of inhabited rooms is properly pure.

b. Historiated, e.g. ***inhabited scroll***, an arabesque pattern of foliage in which figures, birds, etc., appear.

1952 D. T. RICE *Eng. Art 871-1100* v. 149 On [a font] at Alphington in Devon there is an inhabited scroll border which suggests the influence of a manuscript of late-eleventh-century type. **1954** M. RICKERT *Painting in Brit.: Middle Ages* ii. 36 This motif..is worked into running scroll patterns enclosing at intervals lively figures of birds and animals—the so-called inhabited scroll. **1959** *Listener* 1 Oct. 538/3 The exuberance of a St. Alban's inhabited scroll. **1970** M. SWANTON *Dream of Rood* 12 The narrower sides of the shaft are more purely decorative, carved with the so-called 'inhabited vine-scroll'. This is a Middle Eastern motif deriving from models like the Ravenna throne.

Hence **in'habitedness**[2], inhabited condition.

In mod. Dicts.

inhabiter (ɪn'hæbɪtə(r)). *arch.* Also 4 en-. [f. INHABIT *v.* + -ER[1].] One who inhabits, an inhabitant; †also (in 16-17th c.) a colonist.

1388 WYCLIF *Gen.* xxiv. 13 The douȝtris of enhabiters [*v.r.* dwelleris] of this citee schulen go out to drawe watir. **1495** *Act 11 Hen. VII*, c. 9 Preamble, Inhabiters and dwellers within the Shires of Northumberland Cumberland and Westmerlond. **1552** HULOET, Inhabiters comminge from farre countreys to dwell here, *coloni*. **1587** GOLDING *De Mornay* xxvi. 404 When they conueyed Inhabiters abroad to people other Countries. **1614** RALEIGH *Hist. World* I. (1634) 87 Nations, which..sought to dis-plant the ancient Inhabiters. **1879** CHR. G. ROSSETTI *Seek & F.* 182 Around the Almighty Redeemer earth and its inhabiters, though weak, rage in impotent rebellion. **1884** G. F. BRAITHWAITE *Salmonidæ Westmorland* ii. 7 This species..is not an inhabiter of our rivers.

inhabiting (ɪn'hæbɪtɪŋ), *vbl. sb.* [f. as prec. + -ING[1].] The action of the verb INHABIT; habitation, dwelling; †a dwelling-place.

a **1400-50** *Alexander* 3736 Oure inhabetting, ser, is in an Ilee [= isle]. **1495** *Trevisa's Barth. De P.R.* XIII. iii. (W. de W.) 442 Wyth his course abowte citees a ryuer..strengthyth them and other dwellynge places of enhabytynge. **1577** HOLINSHED *Chron.* (*title-p.*), The description and Chronicles of England, from the first inhabiting. **1625** PURCHAS *Pilgrims* II. 1140 There is not any City, village or inhabiting, that cometh so near the height of Elana as Toro. **1848** DICKENS *Dombey* iii, The apartments which Mr. Dombey reserved for his own inhabiting.

inhabitiveness (ɪn'hæbɪtɪvnɪs). [f. INHABIT *v.* + -IVE + -NESS.]

1. *Phrenology.* The disposition to remain always in the same abode; attachment to country and home: a faculty to which an 'organ' is allotted by some phrenologists.

(By Combe (*Elem. Phrenol.*, 1824, 28) enlarged in scope and identified with CONCENTRATIVENESS.)

1815 *Edin. Rev.* XXV. 234 To the Order of Feelings..belong the following species..3. *Inhabitiveness.* **1838** S. SMITH *Princ. Phrenol.* 98 These and other considerations have led us to think it extremely probable that the faculty hitherto called Inhabitiveness or Concentrativeness is..the love of continuity, of endurance, of sameness, of permanency of occupation, emotion, feeling, existence. **1842** S. C. HALL *Ireland* II. 398 Perhaps it proceeds from our having 'Inhabitiveness' largely developed. **1854** LOWELL *Cambridge 30 Yrs. Ago* Prose Wks. 1890 I. 51 You know my (what the phrenologists call) inhabitiveness and adhesiveness.

2. The quality of being suited for habitation.

1896 *Daily News* 14 Dec. 6/6 The members always prized in their original locale a certain cosiness and inhabitiveness, which tended to give the Arts Club its peculiar sociality.

†**in'habitor, -our**. *Obs.* Also 5-6 **en-**. [a. AF. **enhabitour*; f. *enhabiter* to INHABIT: see -OUR, -OR.] An inhabitant, inhabiter.

1413 *Pilgr. Sowle* (Caxton) v. i. (1859) 72 The enhabitours of the places. **1519** *Presentm. Juries* in *Surtees Misc.* (1888) 32 The inhabytors of Selby. **1539** BIBLE (Great) *Jer.* xxxiii. 5 The enhabitours of this citie have come to fight against the Chaldees. **1613** PURCHAS *Pilgrimage* (1614) 87 Here and there, as it were sprinkled with miserable Inhabitors. **1637** EARL MONM. tr. *Malvezzi's Rom. & Tarquin* 55 It was not long ere it was replenisht with Inhabitours.

in'habitress. [f. prec. or INHABITER + -ESS.] A female inhabitant.

1601 WEEVER *Mirr. Mart.* A iv b, Th' inhabitresse of foamie Phlegeton. **1616** CHAPMAN *Homer's Hymn Venus* (ad fin.), A Nymph, call'd Calucopides,..an inhabitresse On this thy wood-crownd Hill. **1778** LOWTH *Transl. Isaiah* xii. 6 Cry aloud, and shout for joy, O inhabitress of Sion. **1888** *Eng. Hist. Rev.* III. 106 If the name be of Assyrian origin, it could only be *ramat*—that is, 'the inhabitress'.

inhable, obs. f. ENABLE; var. INHABILE *v.*, *Obs.*

inhære, etc., obs. forms of INHERE, etc.

inhalant (ɪn'heɪlənt), *a.* (*sb.*) *Zool.* Also *erron.* **-ent.** [ad. L. *inhālānt-em*, pr. pple. of *inhālāre* to INHALE. Cf. mod.F. *inhalant*.]

A. *adj.* Inhaling; serving for inhalation; concerned with inhalation.

1825 *Blackw. Mag.* XVII. 326 The numerous inhalent orifices of the absorbent vessels. **1872** NICHOLSON *Palæont.* 67 Very much smaller openings..termed the 'pores', or inhalant apertures. **1875** HUXLEY & MARTIN *Course Elem. Biol.* 105 These 'inhalent' and 'exhalent' currents go on, so long as the animal is alive and the valves are open. **1883** *Harper's Mag.* Jan. 187/2 Their orifices so arranged that the inhalent are upon the outside of the cylinder, and the exhalent upon the inner side. **1935** TWENHOFEL & SHROCK *Invertebr. Paleontol.* ix. 314 In the earliest and most primitive pelecypods..the edges of the mantle are entirely free, but posteriorly they are folded in such a way as to produce an upper exhalant channel separated from a lower inhalant one. **1968** R. D. PURCHON *Biol. Mollusca* iv. 164 *S*[*olen*] *delesserti* can also perform a swimming escape reaction by expulsion of a series of jets of water from the inhalant siphon.

B. *sb.* **1.** An inhalant opening or pore.

1822-34 *Good's Study Med.* (ed. 4) IV. 292 A hundred pounds of fluid have in this manner been absorbed by the inhalents of the skin.

2. An apparatus used for inhaling; a medicinal preparation for inhalation.

In recent Dicts.

†**inhalate**, *v. Obs. rare*$^{-0}$. = INHALE.

1623 COCKERAM, *Inhalate*, to breathe.

inhalation (ɪnhə'leɪʃən). [n. of action f. L. *inhālāre* to INHALE. Cf. F. *inhalation* (1760).]

1. The action, or an act, of inhaling or breathing in; *spec.* inhaling of medicines or anæsthetics in the form of gas or vapour.

1623 COCKERAM, *Inhalation*, a breathing in. **1758** J. MACKENZIE *Health* 286 Our inhalation from the circumambient air is very considerable. **1831** BREWSTER *Nat. Magic* x. (1833) 256 When the inhalation is completed, or the lungs filled. **1832** LYTTON *Eugene A.* I. ii, He took an unusually long inhalation from his pipe. **1836** J. M. GULLY *Magendie's Formul.* (ed. 2) 127 Inhalation of chlorine..has also been recommended. **1869** LECKY *Europ. Mor.* I. i. 166 The medicine of inhalation is still in its infancy. **1875** BENNETT & DYER *Sachs' Bot.* 646 In some flowers and inflorescences the production of carbon dioxide which accompanies the inhalation of oxygen is very energetic.

2. *Med.* A preparation to be inhaled in the form of vapour.

1882 J. C. THOROWGOOD in *Quain's Med. Dict.* 711/1 Oil of turpentine or of pinus silvestris..makes excellent stimulant inhalations in cases of dilated bronchi.

inhalator ('ɪnhəleɪtə(r)). orig. *U.S.* [f. INHALE *v.* + -ATOR.] = INHALER 2.

1929 *Lit. Digest* 30 Mar. 79/2 The most effective arrangement of all is to see that the city fire or police department and the hospital ambulances have inhalators. **1947** *Chicago Tribune* 17 July 32/2 Inside the ambulance is an inhalator. **1949** *Chicago Daily News* 4 May 1/4 (*caption*) [He] is administered oxygen by members of Inhalator Squad 2. **1956** *New Gould Med. Dict.* (ed. 2) 600/2 *Inhalator*..., a device for facilitating the inhalation of a gas or spray. Used for providing oxygen or oxygen-carbon dioxide mixtures for respiration in resuscitation. **1974** J. WAINWRIGHT *Evidence I shall Give* xvi. 61 It was a nasal inhalator..made of white plastic and about the size of a lipstick tube..with a tiny hole at its pointed end.

inhalatorium (ɪnheɪlə'tɔərɪəm). *Med.* Pl. **inhalatoria**. [f. INHALE *v.* after SANATORIUM.] A building or room used for the treatment of respiratory complaints by vaporized medicaments.

1906 *Chambers's Jrnl.* 347/2 In the medical institute called the Inhalatorium special rooms are set apart for the use of patients, who sit for half-an-hour at a time breathing an atmosphere charged with the vapour suited to their special complaints. **1912** *World* 7 May 697/1 The inhalatoria and gurgling-rooms. **1966** *Punch* 2 Feb. 161/2 So heigh-ho for the tap-room, the ambulatory, the graduated walks, the grandiose inhalatorium.

inhale (ɪn'heɪl), *v.* [ad. L. *inhālā-re* to breathe upon, f. *in-* (IN-[2]) + *hālāre* to breathe out, emit as breath. Cf. F. *inhaler* (Littré). The current sense, in Fr. and Eng., has arisen from taking the word as the opposite of *exhale*.]

1. a. *trans.* To breathe in; to draw in by (or as by) breathing; to take into the lungs. Used *spec.* of the taking in of anæsthetics in form of gas or vapour; of tobacco smoke; and *absol.*, as in *do you inhale?*

1725 POPE *Odyss.* IV. 773 But from the breezy deep the blest inhale The fragrant murmurs of the western gale. **1794** MRS. RADCLIFFE *Myst. Udolpho* i, They inhaled the sweet breath of flowers and herbs. **1809** *Med. Jrnl.* XXI. 194 Observing a threatening degree of pulmonary affection to have apparently resulted from incautiously inhaling the distempered vapour of phthisical patients. **1863** TYNDALL *Heat* iii. 54 We are continually inhaling and exhaling atmospheric air. **1878** L. P. MEREDITH *Teeth* 195 She inhaled the gas properly.

absol. **1863** TYNDALL *Heat* iii. 54 When we inhale, the oxygen passes across the cell-walls of the lungs and mixes with the blood. **1933** E. O'NEILL *Ah, Wilderness!* (1934) III. i. 85 Say, you oughtn't to inhale like that! Smoking's awful bad for girls, anyway. **1970** *New Yorker* 17 Oct. 36/3 He reached for a package of Celtique cigarettes, took one, lit it, and inhaled deeply.

b. *fig.*

1791 GIFFORD *Baviad* 187 There, smoking hot, inhale Mit Yenda's strains. **1808** J. BARLOW *Columb.* VI. 381 His fellow chiefs inhale the hero's flame. **1820** LAMB *Elia* Ser. I. *Oxf. in Vac.*, I seem to inhale learning. *a* **1872** MAURICE *Friendship Bks.* iv. (1874) 116 It is a very wonderful operation this, of inhaling opinions, and then of exhaling them again.

2. *loosely.* To absorb (liquid).

1841 A. COMBE *Digestion* (ed. 3) 75 The..venous capillaries [of the stomach]..inhale or absorb fluid, which they carry into the general circulation.

Hence **in'haling** *vbl. sb.* and *ppl. a.*; also **in'halement** = INHALATION.

1820 *Ellen Fitzarthur* p. vi, To breathe with deep inhaling sense The floating odours wafted thence. **1840** *New Monthly Mag.* LVIII. 461 This matin inhalement.. recommended to cousin Dowgate for his troublesome asthma. **1864** *Reader* 5 Nov. 573/3 The inhaling of foul air.

'inhale, *sb. U.S.* [f. the vb.] The action of inhaling (tobacco smoke).

1934 J. O'HARA *Appointment in Samarra* (1935) v. 133 Not holding the cigarette very expertly, but taking appalling inhales. **1954** W. FAULKNER *Fable* 179 Drawing the cigar to life in one slow inhale-exhale. **1959** N. MAILER *Advts. for Myself* (1961) 45 He lit a cigarette, and then after the first couple of inhales, he felt the anger coming back in him.

inhalent, erroneous variant of INHALANT.

inhaler (ɪn'heɪlə(r)). [f. INHALE *v.* + -ER[1].]

1. One who inhales.

1835 WILLIS *Pencillings* II. lix. 162 Inhalers of the oleaginous atmosphere of the stern.

2. A contrivance for inhaling. **a.** An apparatus for administering a medicinal or anæsthetic gas or vapour by inhalation. **b.** An appliance enabling a person to breathe with safety in a deleterious atmosphere or under water; a respirator.

1778 *Projects* in *Ann. Reg.* 127/2 Inhaling warm steams into the lungs; for administering..which he recommends the use of the inhaler, an instrument which he describes. **1836** J. M. GULLY *Magendie's Formul.* (ed. 2) 211 A portion of it may be poured into hot water in a Mudge's inhaler, and the creosoted vapour inspired in the usual manner. **1864** WEBSTER, *Inhaler*..3. A contrivance to protect the lungs from injury by inhaling damp or cold atmospheric air. **1875** KNIGHT *Dict. Mech.* 1184/2 Pilatre des Roziers invented an inhaler for enabling persons to enter places filled with deleterious gases. *Ibid.*, *Inhaler*,..an apparatus to enable a ..diver to work..in water. **1875** H. C. WOOD *Therap.* (1879) 284 Various inhalers have been invented for facilitating the use of ether.

inhame, obs. (prop. Pg.) form of YAM.

inhance, inhanse, obs. ff. ENHANCE *v.*

inharbour, var. ENHARBOUR *v.*, *Obs.*

inharmonic (ɪnhɑː'mɒnɪk), *a.* [IN-[3].] Not harmonic; not in harmony; dissonant, inharmonious; not according to the principles of harmony.

1828 in WEBSTER. **1878** MORLEY *Diderot* II. App. 320 Those inharmonic passages. **1881** BROADHOUSE *Mus. Acoustics* 158 Some qualities of tone whose upper partials are inharmonic.

inhar'monical, *a.* [IN-[3].] Not harmonical. †*inharmonical relation*, or *relation inharmonical*, in *Mus.* the same as *false relation* (obs.).

1674 PLAYFORD *Skill Mus.* (1697) 91 'Tis very Inharmonical, therefore to be avoided. **1706** PHILLIPS, *Relation Inharmonical* (in Musical Composition), a harsh Reflection of Flat against Sharp in a cross Form; viz. when some harsh and displeasing Discord is produc'd in comparing the present Note of another Part. **1875** JOWETT *Plato* (ed. 2) V. 372 It is shocking for a whole harmony to be inharmonical.

inharmonious (ɪnhɑː'məʊnɪəs), *a.* [IN-[3]. Cf. F. *inharmonieux* (Littré).] Not harmonious.

1. Of sound: Not in harmony; sounding disagreeably; discordant, untuneful.

1711 FELTON *Diss. Classics* (1718) 26 Catullus, whom, tho' his Lines be Rough, and his Numbers Inharmonious, I could recommend for the Softness and Delicacy..of his Thoughts. **1784** COWPER *Task* I. 207 Sounds inharmonious in themselves and harsh. **1881** STEVENSON *Virg. Puerisque* 154 No inharmonious prelude to the last quietude and desertion of the grave.

2. Not harmonious in relation, action, or sentiment; disagreeing; conflicting; not in accordance.

1748 HARTLEY *Observ. Man* I. ii. 247 The Contractions of the Ventricles become asynchronous and inharmonious to those of the Auricles. **1846** J. MILLER *Pract. Surg.* v. 154 Squinting..The immediate cause obviously depends on an inharmonious action of the recti muscles. **1879** *Cassell's Techn. Educ.* IV. 230/2 Although they [Chinese works] do not present such a perfect colour-bloom as do the works of India, yet they are never inharmonious. **1899** *Westm. Gaz.* 1 Aug. 2/3 Last Saturday's meeting of the Sliding Scale Committee was singularly inharmonious.

Hence **inhar'moniously** *adv.*; **inhar'moniousness**.

1768-74 TUCKER *Lt. Nat.* I. xiii. (1834) I. 137 They adjudge them one short and the other long, and would be horribly shocked at the inharmoniousness of a verse wherein they should be introduced in each other's places. **1828** WEBSTER, *Inharmoniously*. **1864** SALA in *Daily Tel.* 30 Sept., Some prodigious caricature, in which the heroic and the absurd, the sublime and the vulgar, are inharmoniously but audaciously blended.

inharmony (ɪn'hɑːmənɪ). *rare.* [IN-[3]. Cf. F. *inharmonie* (Littré).] Want of harmony; disharmony, discord.

1799 W. TAYLOR in Robberds *Mem.* I. 257 Your objection to the inharmony of the first line is just. **1867** in Dixon *Spirit. Wives* (1868) II. 235 Seeing so much of domestic inharmony, my mind was made up never to marry.

inhart, variant of ENHEART *v.*, *Obs.*

†**in'hate**, *v. Obs. rare*[−1]. [f. IN-[1] or [2] + HATE *v.*] *trans.* ? To hate inwardly or intensely.

1526 SKELTON *Magnyf.* 2458 Circumspeccyon inhateth all rennynge astray.

inhaul ('ɪnhɔːl). *Naut.* [f. IN *adv.* + HAUL *sb.*] = next.

1860 *Merc. Marine Mag.* VII. 114 Fasten the inhaul and outhaul to the reef cringle. **1882** NARES *Seamanship* (ed. 6) 84 *Trysail inhaul*..the whip is fitted at the end of the inhaul.

inhauler ('ɪnˌhɔːlə(r)). [f. IN *adv.* + HAULER.] An appliance for hauling in; *spec.* (*Naut.*) 'the rope used for hauling in the clue of a boomsail, or jib-traveller' (Smyth *Sailor's Word-bk.*).

1793 SMEATON *Edystone L.* §269 The hook by which the in-hauler guy of the shears was attached, became undone; and in consequence the shears came forward. **1794** *Rigging & Seamanship* I. 223 *Inhauler* makes fast to the traveller.

inhaunce, inhaunse, obs. ff. ENHANCE *v.*

inhaunt, variant of ENHAUNT *v.*, *Obs.*

inhaust (ɪn'hɔːst), *v. rare.* [f. IN-[2] + L. *haust-*, ppl. stem of *haurīre* to draw: cf. *exhaust.*] *trans.* To draw or suck in; to inhale; to imbibe.

1547 BOORDE *Brev. Health* §356. 114b, It may come of some flye inhausted into a mans throte sodeynely. **1848** THACKERAY *Bk. Snobs* xxii, Whilst he was inhausting his smoking tea.

So **inhaustion** (ɪn'hɔːstjən), inhalation.

1854 BRINTON in *Circ. Sc.* (*c* 1865) II. 4/1 Apparatus for the inhaustion or the expulsion of the respiratory gases.

†**'in-having**, *vbl. sb. Sc.* Also **inhawing**. [f. phr. *have in*: see IN *adv.* 11 c, HAVE *v.* 16.] Having or getting in, bringing in (to haven).

1491 *Act. Dom. Concil.* (1839) 203 In þe inhavin of hir in þe port & havin of þe Elye at the Erlis fery. **1541** *Aberd. Reg.* V. 16 (Jam.) The inhawing of the said schip in the Willie gaitt.

inhearing ('ɪnˌhɪərɪŋ). *nonce-wd.* [f. IN *adv.* + HEARING *vbl. sb.*, after *insight.*] The hearing of things inaudible to the outward ear.

1828 J. WILSON in *Blackw. Mag.* XXIV. 686 Who..can think that the cultivation of the mere understanding may ever give an insight, or an inhearing, into such truths of our being? **1834** *Ibid.* XXXVI. 410 To whom was given.. insight and inhearing into the world of light and love.

inhearse, inhearten, inheaven, obs. forms of ENHEARSE, ENHEARTEN, ENHEAVEN.

†**in'hebetate**, *v. Obs. rare*[−1]. In 8 *erron.* **inhebitate**. [IN-[2]: see HEBETATE.] *trans.* To make dull, to blunt. (In quot. *absol.*)

1740 E. BAYNARD *Health* (ed. 6) 16 And then, at distance take the heat, Because it does inhebitate.

†**inheche**. *Obs. rare.* [Known only in Latin context: app. a deriv. of *inhoc*, as if:—OE. *inhóc*, *inhǽce*, *inhéce*, ME. *inheche.*] The ploughing up of fallow for a crop of corn; the piece of land so ploughed up: cf. INHOC.

1274 *Coram Rege*, Hill. 3 Edw. I, m. 17, d, Item quicumque facit inheche, scilicet excolit warectum frumento, ordeo, vel auena, dabit pro qualibet acra unum denarium, excepta una acra quam habere debet quietam.

'inheld, *ppl. a. rare.* [f. IN *adv.* + HELD *ppl. a.*] Held within.

1903 T. HARDY *Dynasts* I. I. vi. 53 His lips with inheld laughter grow deformed.

†**in'helde, -hielde**, *v. Obs. rare*[−1]. [f. IN-[1] + HIELD *v.*] *trans.* To pour in.

c **1374** CHAUCER *Troylus* III. 44 Ye in my nakede herte sentement Inhelde [*v.r.* In hielde, *ed.* 1561 In hilde], and do me shewe of thi swetnesse.

inhell (ɪn'hɛl), *v.* [f. IN-[1] + HELL *sb.*; cf. ENHEAVEN.] *trans.* To put into or confine in hell.

1607 MARSTON *What you Will* IV. i. F iv, She, for whose sake, A man could finde in his heart to in-hell himselfe. **1822** BEDDOES *Bride's Trag.* IV. iii, Aye, thus they sugar o'er the silent dagger..till they've inhelled thy soul. **1839** BAILEY *Festus* xxiii. (1852) 411 These need not be Inhelled for ever.

†**in'herce**, obs. form of ENHEARSE *v.*

1591 SHAKS. *1 Hen. VI*, IV. vii. 45 See where he lyes inherced in the armes Of the most bloody Nursser of his harmes.

†**in'herdance**. *Sc. Obs.* [f. *inherd*, ENHERD, F. *enherdre* to adhere + -ANCE.] Adherence; body of adherents: = ADHERENCY 3.

1448 in *Aberd. Burgh Rec.* (Spald. Cl.) I. 17 In thar helpying and supple with thair inherdance, warr folowaris and makaris of the said soite [= suit].

†**in'herdand**, *ppl. a.* and *sb. Sc. Obs.* [pr. pple. of *inherd* = ENHERD *v.*: see prec. and -AND[1]. Cf. OF. *enherdant* pr. pple. and sb. 'adherent'.] Adhering, adherent.

1513 DOUGLAS *Æneis* X. xiii. 57 Authores, ane of gret Hercules feris..Inherdand to Evander the Archaid.

inhere (ɪn'hɪə(r)), *v.* Also 6 **inhære**. [ad. L. *inhærēre* to stick in or to, adhere to, etc., f. *in-* (IN-[2]) + *hærēre* to stick; cf. *adhere, cohere.*]

1. *intr.* To stick *in*; to be or remain fixed or lodged *in* something. *rare* or *Obs.*

1608 TOPSELL *Serpents* (1658) 594 Little bags of poyson which inhere in their chaps and under their tongues. **1651** *Raleigh's Ghost* 22 These spots do not inhere in the body of the Sun. **1739** 'R. BULL' tr. *Dedekindus' Grobianus* iv. 36 Do Lumps of Meat between thy Teeth inhere? **1796** KIRWAN *Elem. Min.* (ed. 2) I. 338 Stones of one or more species, inhering in another stone. **1804** ABERNETHY *Surg. Obs.* 251 A subtile matter inhering in the brain and nerves.

2. *fig.* To remain or abide *in* something immaterial, as a state or condition; to remain in mystical union with a Divine person. Now *rare* or *Obs.*

a **1617** BAYNE *Eph.* (1658) 123 The third [phrase] noteth Christ the object [and] our inhering in him. **1665** G. HAVERS *P. della Valle's Trav. E. India* 27 The Name Seìàh Selim, tenaciously inhering in the memory of people, remains still to him. **1756** BURKE *Subl. & B.* II. v, So strongly does it inhere in our constitution, that very few are able to conquer it. **1839** BAILEY *Festus* xxiii. (1854) 412 He [Satan] in the Godstate first with all his hosts By fate inhered.

3. To exist, abide, or have its being, as an attribute, quality, etc., *in* a subject or thing; to form an element of, or belong to the intrinsic nature of, something. (The current sense; in earlier use chiefly *Philos.*)

1586 FERNE *Blaz. Gentrie* 293 The insignes thereof which like incidents..or inseparable accidents..doe alwaies inhere, and waite on that office, and dignitie of a kinge. **1624** GATAKER *Transubst.* 173 The accidents of bread and wine remaine without actuall inhering and being in their naturall subject. **1690** LOCKE *Hum. Und.* II. xiii. §19 They who first ran into the Notion of Accidents, as a sort of real Beings that needed something to inhere in. **1739** HUME *Hum. Nat.* I. vi. (1874) I. 324 The particular qualities, which form a substance, are commonly refer'd to an unknown something, in which they are supposed to inhere. **1827** *Gentl. Mag.* XCVII. II. 602 If this sentiment..is found to inhere in a feeling so pure and exalted. **1855** BAIN *Senses & Int.* III. i. §38 (1864) 378 Knowledge and perception inhere in mind alone.

b. To be vested or inherent *in*, as a right, power, function, or the like.

1840 DE QUINCEY *Style* I. Wks. 1860 XI. 188 To an Englishman, the right of occupying the attention of the company seems to inhere in things rather than in persons. **1850** GLADSTONE *Glean.* V. xlviii. 202 The power of order inhering in the Church. **1890** *Century Mag.* 112/1 Where agriculture is dependent upon an artificial supply of water, and where there is more land than can be served by the water, values inhere in water, not in land; the land without the water is without value.

†**c.** *trans.* To pertain to; to be an attribute or prerogative of. *Obs. rare.*

1609 F. GREVIL (Ld. Brooke) *Mustapha* v. Chor. i, Creation, we say, still inheres the crowne.

†**4.** *intr.* To adhere, cleave *to*. *Obs. rare.*

1563 WINȜET *Wks.* (1890) II. 73 Twa certane thingis ar gretumlie and diligentlie to be obseruit, to the quhilkis aluterlie thai suld inhere, quha wald nocht be hæretikis.

†**inhe'reditable**, *a. Obs. rare.* [f. med.L. *inhērēditā-re* to INHERIT, to make (a person) heir to, f. *in-* (IN-[2]) + late L. *hērēditāre* (Vulgate) to receive an inheritance, to inherit + -ABLE.] = HEREDITABLE 2. So †**inhereditament** = HEREDITAMENT 1; †**inhe'reditance** = INHERITANCE; †**inhe'reditary** *a.* = HEREDITARY 1.

1483 *Cath. Angl.* 196/1 An Inhereditance, *hereditas.* **1491** *Act 7 Hen. VII*, c. 2 §5 Their honours Castels Maners londes ..and other their inhereditamentes and possessions. **1503-4** *Act 19 Hen. VII*, c. 40 §1 Londes & tenementes that he..is inhereditable unto as heyr in blood to the same Dame Isabell. **1611** SPEED *Hist. Gt. Brit.* IX. xxiv. §8. 1154 In case the French should challenge Callis as inhereditary vnto the Crowne of France.

inherence (ɪn'hɪərəns). Also 7 **inhærence**. [f. med.L. *inhærentia*, f. *inhærēnt-em* INHERENT: see -ENCE. Cf. F. *inhérence* (14-15th c. in Godef. *Compl.*).] The fact or condition of inhering; the state or quality of being inherent; permanent existence (as of an attribute) *in* a subject; indwelling.

1577 tr. *Bullinger's Decades* (1592) 680 The inward and very substantiall inherence or coequality of the Father and the Son. **1654** JER. TAYLOR *Real Pres.* 211 All the Philosophers..when they divide a substance from an accident, mean by a substance that which can subsist in it self without a subject of inherence. *a* **1716** SOUTH *Twelve Serm.* (1744) II. 238 It is called the light of nature, because of it's general inherence in all men. **1848** R. I. WILBERFORCE *Incarnation* xiv. (1852) 384 What is the merit of the elect

save their inherence in Him, whose perpetual mediation delays the execution of the sentence passed on our common progenitor? **1885** J. MARTINEAU *Types Eth. The.* (1886) I. I. II. iii. 136 This relation of inherence and permanent coexistence in one nature is expressed by the word *attribute*.

inherency (ɪn'hɪərənsɪ). Also 7 **inhærency**. [f. as prec.: see -ENCY.] = prec.; in mod. use chiefly as a quality; also quasi-*concr.*, as ***an inherency of evil*** (nearly = 'inherent evil').

1601 DEACON & WALKER *Spirits & Divels* 36 You cannot congruently conclude from thence any essentiall inherencie of Diuels in the bodies of men. **1647** TRAPP *Comm. Rom.* vii. 18 Corruption is, though dejected from it's regency, yet not ejected from it's inherency. **1706** PHILLIPS, *Inherency*,..the Quality of that which sticks close. **1833** H. COLERIDGE *Poems* I. 35 The fell inherency of sin. **1879** TOURGEE *Fool's Err.* xl. 301 His belief in the equality and inherency of human right.

inherent (ɪn'hɪərənt), *a.* (*sb.*) Also 6–7 **inhærent**. [f. L. *inhærēnt-em*, pr. pple. of *inhærēre* to INHERE. Cf. F. *inhérent* (1599 in Hatz.-Darm.).]

1. Sticking in; fixed, situated, or contained in something (in physical sense). Const. *in*, rarely †*to*. Now *rare* or *Obs.*

1578 BANISTER *Hist. Man* I. 32 Certayne chinkes, to the which are inherent foure tendons. **1664** POWER *Exp. Philos.* III. 169 All the Circles of the Armillary Sphære are really, truly, and naturally inhærent in the Earth. **1756** C. LUCAS *Ess. Waters* III. 297 Let us examine what further proofs of an inherent acid this water gives. **1800** *Med. Jrnl.* III. 581 It destroys the mucilaginous parts inherent to some resins. **1802** *Ibid.* VIII. 335 A peculiar fluid secreted into..or inherent in the substance of the nervous fibres.

2. *fig.* Cleaving fast, remaining, or abiding *in* some thing or person; permanently indwelling. Now *rare* or *Obs.*

1601 DENT *Pathw. Heaven* (1831) 55 This, of all other, is a most inherent sin. **1607** SHAKS. *Cor.* III. ii. 123 Least I..by my Bodies action, teach my Minde A most inherent Basenesse. **1793** SMEATON *Edystone L.* §282 Owing to..the still inherent property of our vessel as a slow sailer, it was not till eight the next morning that we came to..our mooring ground.

3. Existing in something as a permanent attribute or quality; forming an element, esp. a characteristic or essential element of something; belonging to the intrinsic nature of that which is spoken of; indwelling, intrinsic, essential.

1588 FRAUNCE *Lawiers Log.* I. i. 4 b, An argument is either inhærent or fet elsewhere. **1655** FULLER *Ch. Hist.* II. iii. §27 Thus began Corpses to be buried in the Churches, which by degrees brought in much Superstition; especially after degrees of inherent Sanctity were erroneously fixed in the severall parts thereof. **1711** ADDISON *Spect.* No. 215 ¶1 Marble in the Quarry, which shews none of its inherent Beauties, 'till the Skill of the Polisher fetches out the Colours. **1804** ABERNETHY *Surg. Obs.* 12 Whilst it [the tumour] grows by its own inherent powers. **1855** BAIN *Senses & Int.* I. ii. §18 (1864) 54 There is some difficulty in ascertaining how much of the effect is derived and how much inherent. **1886** W. J. TUCKER *E. Europe* 33 Our inherent indolence, our apathy in times of peace is proverbial.

b. Const. *in*; formerly *to*, *unto*.

1622 MALYNES *Anc. Law-Merch.* 3 The said prerogati[u]es doe also appertaine to the Law-merchant as properly inherent vnto commerce. **1633** G. HERBERT *Temple, Faith* ix, When creatures had no reall light Inherent in them. *a* **1635** NAUNTON *Fragm. Reg.* (Arb.) 55 That height of spirit inherent to his House. **1791** BOSWELL *Johnson* Mar. an. 1753, These sufferings were aggravated by the melancholy inherent in his constitution. **1808** CERVANTES HOGG (E. S. Barrett) *Miss-led General* 7 That sweetness of temper which is inherent to himself. **1878** H. IRVING *Stage* 29 The love of acting is inherent in our nature.

4. Vested *in* or attached to a person, office, etc., as a right or privilege.

1628 COKE *On Litt.* I. Pref., Not only by royall descent, and inherent Birthright, but by Rosiall Beauty also, heire to both [Roses]. **1647** CLARENDON *Hist. Reb.* I. §112 Sr Julius Cæsar was then Master of the Rolls, and had inherent in his office, the..disposition of the Six-Clarks places. **1682** BURNET *Rights Princes* Pref. 27 That the Regale is an inherent Right of the Crown. **1788** GIBBON *Decl. & F.* xlix. (1869) III. 110 The legislative authority was inherent in the general assembly. **1891** *Law Rep.* Weekly Notes 68/1 Every Court had an inherent power to allow a person who had invoked its jurisdiction to withdraw his application.

†**B.** *sb.* Something inherent or indwelling. *rare.*

1610 HEALEY *St. Aug. Citie of God* XI. ii, The minde..wherein reason and vnderstanding are naturall inherents.

Hence **in'herentness** (Bailey vol. II, 1727).

inherently (ɪn'hɪərəntlɪ), *adv.* [f. prec. + -LY[2].] In an inherent manner; by inherence; in the way of, or in relation to, an inherent quality or attribute; in inward nature, intrinsically.

1601 DEACON & WALKER *Spirits & Divels* 41 The Diuell doth really, and essentially, enter into, and inherently dwell in the possessed mans minde. **1654** W. CARTER *Covenant of God* 102 We cannot upon certainty affirm of any particular person in the Church that he is inherently holy. **1657–8** *Burton's Diary* (1828) II. 439 The liberties of the free-born people of England, which are inherently in this House. *a* **1708** BEVERIDGE *Thes. Theol.* (1710) I. 128 We are made righteous by Christ, as sinners by Adam inherently. **1837** WHEWELL *Hist. Induct. Sc.* (1857) I. 149 There is nothing inherently improbable in this tradition.

inhering (ɪn'hɪərɪŋ), *ppl. a.* [f. INHERE *v.* + -ING[2].] That inheres; inherent (*lit.* and *fig.*).

1609 J. MELTON *Six-fold Polit.* 35 Tobacco..leaues an inhering stinke in the nostrils and stomackes of the takers. **1789** W. BUCHAN *Dom. Med.* 607 A proper degree of agitation has sometimes loosened the inhering body more effectually than instruments. Thus, a blow on the back has often forced up a substance which stuck in the gullet. **1876** BANCROFT *Hist. U.S.* III. 310 Man was growing aware of the inhering right to the unfettered culture and enjoyment of his whole moral and intellectual being.

inherit (ɪn'hɛrɪt), *v.* Forms: α. 4–5 **enerite**, 4–6 **enheryte**, 4–7 **enherite**, 5–7 **enherit**, 6 **enheret**. β. 5 **ineryte**, **inheritte**, 5–6 **inheryt(e**, **inheret(t**, 6 *Sc.* **inhereit**, 6–7 **inherite**, 6– **inherit**. [a. OF. *enheriter* to put (one) in possession as heir, f. *en-* (EN-[1], IN-[2]) + *heriter* to make (one) heir:—late L. *hērēditāre*: see HERIT *v.* The change of the original sense into that of 'to receive as heir' has also taken place in F. *hériter*.]

†**1.** *trans.* To make heir, put in possession, cause to inherit (*lit.* and *fig.*). *Obs.* (Cf. *disinherit*.)

[**1304** *Year-bk. 32 Edw. I* (Rolls) 165 Pykenot fut enherité de ces tenementz.] **13..** *K. Alis.* 7153 Withynne the walles he made houses,..Of his gentil men he enherited [*Bodley MS.* herited] there, And tho that of the lond ware. **1388** WYCLIF *Ecclus.* xv. 6 God..schal enherite [1382 eritagen] hym with euerlastynge name. **1413** *Pilgr. Sowle* (Caxton 1483) IV. xxx. 80. **1523** LD. BERNERS *Froiss.* I. cxv. 137 To disheryte their naturall lorde and his yssue, to enheryte a stranger. **1593** SHAKS. *Rich. II*, I. i. 85 What doth our Cosin lay to Mowbraies charge? It must be great that can inherite vs So much as of a thought of ill in him.

2. *trans.* To take or receive (property, *esp.* real property, or a right, privilege, rank, or title) as the heir of the former possessor (usually an ancestor), at his decease; to get, or come into possession of, by legal descent or succession.

a **1400–50** *Alexander* 588 Lat him as ayre, quen I am erþed, enherit my landis. *c* **1440** *Promp. Parv.* 261/2 Inheryte, or receyve in herytage (*K.* inerytyn)..., *heredito*. **1513** MORE *Rich. III* (1883) 58 [To] allege bastardy..So that he should seme dishabled to inherite the crowne. **1597** DANIEL *Civ. Wars* VI. xcvii, So much adoe had toyling Fraunce to rend, From vs the right so long inherited. *a* **1719** ADDISON (J.), An estate he had some prospect of inheriting. **1794** MRS. RADCLIFFE *Myst. Udolpho* xx, I inherit it by the female line. **1899** SAYCE *Early Israel* vii. 249 The king inherited his priesthood from him.

fig. **1818** SHELLEY *Rev. Islam* II. vi, All that despair from murdered hope inherits They sought.

b. To derive (a quality or character, physical or mental) from one's progenitors by natural descent; to derive or possess by transmission from parents or ancestry.

1597 SHAKS. *2 Hen. IV*, IV. iii. 128 The cold blood hee did naturally inherite of his Father. **1601** —— *All's Well* I. ii. 22 Youth, thou bear'st thy Fathers face,..Thy Fathers morall parts Maist thou inherit too. **1763** J. BROWN *Poetry & Mus.* xii. 203 Such being the Birth of the modern Opera, no Wonder it inherits the Weakness of its Parent. **1774** GOLDSM. *Nat. Hist.* (1776) II. 238 We find nothing more common..than for children to inherit sometimes even the accidental deformities of their parents. **1841** LANE *Arab. Nts.* I. 127 Whose taste is inherited by the present sovereign. **1868** DARWIN *Anim. & Pl.* II. xii. 1 A variation which is not inherited throws no light on the derivation of species.

c. To receive or have from a predecessor in office. Chiefly *fig.*

1847 TENNYSON *Princ.* IV. 569 He that next inherited the tale, Half-turning to the broken statue, said, 'Sir Ralph has got your colours'. *Mod.* The problems which the present administration has inherited from its predecessors.

3. *transf.* To come into possession of, as one's right or divinely assigned portion; to receive, obtain, have, or hold as one's portion. (Chiefly in biblical and derived uses: see INHERITANCE 4, HEIR 2.)

a **1340** HAMPOLE *Psalter* xxiv. 14 His sede sall enherite þe erthe. —— *Pr. Consc.* 869 When a man Sal dighe he sal enherite þan Wormes and nedders. **1388** WYCLIF *Ecclus.* iv. 14 Thei that holden it [wisdom], schulen enherite lijf. **1526** TINDALE *Matt.* xxv. 34 Come ye blessed children of my father, inheret ye the kyngdome prepared for you from the beginninge of the worlde. **1592** SHAKS. *Rom. & Jul.* I. ii. 30 Such delight..shall you this night Inherit at my house. **1593** —— *Rich. II*, II. i. 83 Gaunt am I for the graue, gaunt as a graue, Whose hollow wombe inherits naught but bones. **1611** BIBLE *Luke* xviii. 18 Good master, what shall I doe to inherit eternall life? **1674** MILTON *Samson* 1012 It is not virtue, wisdom, valour, wit,..That woman's love can win, or long inherit. **1746** C. WESLEY *Hymn*, '*Love divine*', ii, Let us all in thee inherit.

4. To be heir to (a person); to succeed as heir.

a **1533** LD. BERNERS *Gold. Bk. M. Aurel.* (1546) B viij b, The auctoritee that thei had inherityng their fathers. **1721** *St. German's Doctor & Stud.* 38 That the eldest son shall inherit his father. **1832** TENNYSON *Lotos-Eaters* vi, Surely now our household hearths are cold: Our sons inherit us..And we should come like ghosts to trouble joy.

5. *absol.* or *intr.* To succeed as an heir; to come into or take possession of an inheritance.

1533–4 *Act 25 Hen. VIII*, c. 22 §6 That all the issue..shall be..inheritable and inherite accordyng to the..lawes of this realme. **1548** HALL *Chron., Hen. V* 72 b, The issue female may not enherite accordyng to the lawe Salique. **1610** SHAKS. *Temp.* II. ii. 179 The King, and all our company else being dround, wee will inherit here. **1700** TYRRELL *Hist. Eng.* II. 798 His Issue [were] barred from Inheriting. **1841** LANE *Arab. Nts.* I. 19 The children by a wife and those by a concubine slave inherit equally, if the latter be acknowledged by the father.

b. *fig.* †(*a*) To take possession, take up an abode, dwell (*obs.*); (*b*) To derive its being, or some quality or character, *from*.

1600 TOURNEUR *Transf. Metamorph.* i, O where can life celestiall inherit? *a* **1890** CHURCH *Pascal*, etc. (1895) 113 If there is a ministry on earth which in any sense inherits from the apostles. **1891** *Daily News* 10 Feb. 5/1 The music-hall seems beyond redemption. Its traditions are against it; it inherits from the Coal Hole and the Cider Cellars.

Hence **in'herited** *ppl. a.*, **in'heriting** *vbl. sb.* and *ppl. a.*

1622 E. WATERHOUSE *Declar. St. Virginia* title-p., That their lawful heyres..may take order for the inheriting of their lands and estates. **1663** BOYLE *Usef. Exp. Nat. Philos.* II. ii. 44 How madnesse..should not only prove hereditary, but lurk very many yeares in the inheriting person's body. **1797** HOLCROFT *Stolberg's Trav.* (ed. 2) IV. xci. 127 Men who cherished an inherited hatred against each other. **1875** BENNETT & DYER *Sachs' Bot.* 829 The different species of the same genus agree among one another in a number of inherited characters, and are distinguished only by single constant characters.

inheritability (ɪn,hɛrɪtə'bɪlɪtɪ). [f. next: see -ITY.] The quality of being inheritable; capability of being inherited.

1784 JEFFERSON *Corr.* Wks. 1859 I. 337 Such it would be to part with its inheritability, its organization, and its assemblies. **1875** tr. *Schmidt's Desc. & Darw.* 166 The inheritability of morbid tendencies, bodily and mental. **1896** *Speaker* 28 Mar. 346 He was a signal example of the inheritability of acquired characters.

inheritable (ɪn'hɛrɪtəb(ə)l), *a.* Also 5–6 **en-**. [a. AF. *en-*, *inheritable* capable of being made heir, able to inherit, f. *enheriter*: see INHERIT and -ABLE.]

1. Capable of inheriting. **a.** *lit.* Entitled to succeed to property, etc. by legal right.

[**1368** *Act 42 Edw. III*, c. 10 Que les enfantz neez par dela..soient..enheritables de leur heritagee en Engleterre.] **1470** HARDING *Chron.* CXXIII. v, Therle Henry..Deliuered all the castels and citees right To Kyng Wyllyam his brother enheritable. **1535** *Act 27 Hen. VIII*, c. 26 §2 Persons inheritable to any manours landes..or other hereditamentes. **1732** NEAL *Hist. Purit.* I. 76 The marriages..were declared good and valid, and their children inheritable according to law. **1774** BP. S. HALLIFAX *Anal. Rom. Civil Law* (1795) 55 In England..upon deficiency of Inheritable Blood, Lands escheat to the King. **1807** G. CHALMERS *Caledonia* I. II. vi. 307 The daughters were not inheritable to such lands. **1876** DIGBY *Real Prop.* x. §3. 391 The effect of attainder was, as is said, to corrupt the blood so as to render it no longer inheritable.

†**b.** *transf.* and *fig.* Entitled to possess or enjoy something as one's birthright. *Obs.*

1523 in W. H. Turner *Select. Rec. Oxford* (1880) 38 Put from the benefite of the lawes of the Realme whereunto they be inheritable. **1532** MORE *Confut. Tindale* Wks. 731/2 Made inherytable vnto the blesse of heauen. **1581** LAMBARDE *Eiren.* IV. xiii. 539 The auncient libertie of the land, whereunto euery free borne man thinketh himselfe inheritable.

2. Capable of being inherited. **a.** *lit.* That may or can descend by law to an heir: = HERITABLE I.

a **1483** *Liber Niger* in *Househ. Ord.* 74 Till the King's housholds purueyours have taken for the Kinge..with trewe paymentes, according to the Kinges old enheritable prises. **1592** WEST *1st Pt. Symbol.* §39 B, An estate in fee simple, which is, when a man hath lands or other things inheritable, to him and heires for euer. **1683** HICKES *Jovian* 23 It is the *Lex Legum*, or great standing Law of this Inheritable Kingdom. **1786** BURKE *W. Hastings* Wks. 1842 II. 164 That the property of the lands of Bengal is..an inheritable property. **1837** SYD. SMITH in *Q. Rev.* 241 It is clear that the British Crown was in those early days inheritable by females.

b. *fig.* That may be naturally transmitted from parents or ancestry to offspring: = HERITABLE 2.

1828 WEBSTER, *Inheritable*..2. That may be transmitted from the parent to the child; as, inheritable qualities or infirmities. **1859** DARWIN *Orig. Spec.* i. (1872) 9 The number and diversity of inheritable deviations of structure. **1880** A. H. HUTH *Buckle* I. iii. 180 Buckle..had a strong suspicion that superior intellectual power was inheritable.

Hence **in'heritableness**, the quality of being inheritable.

1780 [M. MADAN] *Thelyphthora* II. 162 Laws are made for its regulation, to establish the inheritableness of the issue. **1831** *Examiner* 564/1 The contest against the inheritableness of the peerage arises from a levelling spirit. **1893** H. SPENCER in *Pop. Sci. Monthly* XLIII. 171 If any say that inheritableness is limited to those [characters] arising in a certain way, the onus lies on them of proving that those otherwise arising are not inheritable.

in'heritably, *adv.* [f. prec. + -LY[2].] So as to be inheritable; by inheritance; hereditarily.

1561 T. NORTON *Calvin's Inst.* II. 105 Adams children..by inheritably descending infection, are al borne the bond slaues of sinne. **1611** COTGR., *Heritablement*, inheritably, in fee simple, for euer. *a* **1868** BROUGHAM (O.), He resumed the grants at pleasure, nor ever gave them even for life, much less inheritably.

inheritage (ɪn'hɛrɪtɪdʒ). *rare.* Also 6 **en-**. [f. INHERIT *v.* + -AGE, after HERITAGE.] That which is inherited; a heritage, inheritance.

1557 NORTH tr. *Gueuara's Diall Pr.* 43 b/2 In the end, life is but lone, but death is enheritage. **1591** SPARRY tr. *Cattan's Geomancie* (1599) 68 It signifieth losse of inheritages and of possessions. **1615** G. SANDYS *Trav.* 223 It [Mount Ida] fostereth nothing that is wilde, but hares, red deare, and fallow, and is the inheritage of the *Calargi*. **1811** *Chron.* in *Ann. Reg.* 439 To convey to their minds the inheritage of knowledge and virtue. **1861** MISS BRADDON *Lady Lisle* 27 The weight of this vast inheritage.

†**in'heritament.** *Obs.* Also 5 **enheritemente, enheritamente.** [a. AF. *en-, inheritement*, OF. *enheritement*, f. *enheriter*: see INHERIT and -MENT. Partly conformed to words from L. *-āmentum.*] Inheritable property, hereditament.

[**1397-8** *Act 2 Rich. II*, c. 3 Toutz sez terres..et touz autres enheritementz.] **1463** *Rolls Parlt.* V. 497/2 The seid Londes, Tenements, Rentes, Possessions and Enheritementes. **1483-4** *Act 1 Rich. III*, c. 1 Landes, tenementis, rentis, and services, or other inheritamentes. **1491** *Act 7 Hen. VII*, c. 16 §1 All othre enheritamentes whiche the seid late Duke..forfeited.

inheritance (ɪn'hɛrɪtəns). Forms: see INHERIT; 4-6 **-aunce,** 5- **-ance.** [a. AF. *enheritance* a being admitted as heir, action or fact of inheriting, f. *enheriter*: see INHERIT *v.* and -ANCE.]

I. The action or fact of inheriting.

1. *lit.* Hereditary succession to property, a title, office, etc.; 'a perpetual or continuing right to an estate, invested in a person and his heirs' (Wharton *Law Lex.*).

[**12..** BRITTON *Lois d'Angleterre* lf. 1 a ap. Ste.-Pal. (Godef.), Ceux parolx (ses heires) font l'estate d'enheritance.] **1390** GOWER *Conf.* II. 313 Which of his propre enheritaunce Athenes had in governaunce. **1470-85** MALORY *Arthur* x. xxxiii, The same Castel was hers by ryght enherytaunce. **1548** HALL *Chron., Edw. IV* 227 The realme of Fraunce to him of right, and by lyneall enheritaunce aperteyning. **1617** MORYSON *Itin.* III. 153 Earle of Marre, who..is by inheritance Sheriffe of the County of Sterling. **1767** BLACKSTONE *Comm.* II. i. 12 Rights of inheritance and successions. **1864** BOUTELL *Her. Hist. & Pop.* xiv. 140 This conjoint Inheritance Heraldry sets forth.

2. *transf.* and *fig.* **a.** A coming into, or taking, possession of something, as one's birthright; possession, ownership; right of possession.

1535 COVERDALE *Deut.* iv. 20 But you hath the Lorde taken..that ye shulde be the people of his enheritaunce. **1590** SPENSER *F.Q.* I. iv. 48 To you th' inheritance belonges by right Of brothers prayse, to you eke longes his love. **1602** SHAKS. *Ham.* I. i. 92 A Moity competent..which had return'd To the Inheritance of Fortinbras, Had he bin Vanquisher. **1607** —— *Cor.* III. ii. 68 You will rather shew our generall Lowts, How you can frowne, then spend a fawne vpon 'em, For the inheritance of their loues. ? **1680** H. CARE (*title*) English Liberties, or the free-born Subject's Inheritance.

b. Natural derivation of qualities or characters from parents or ancestry.

1859 DARWIN *Orig. Spec.* v. (1873) 123 These characters may be attributed to inheritance from a common progenitor. **1862** TENNYSON *Idylls* Ded. 31 How should England dreaming of his sons Hope more for these than some inheritance Of such a life, a heart, a mind as thine? **1885** S. COX *Expos.* Ser. I. iii. 30 Our goodness..whether it comes to us by nature, or by inheritance from our parents.

II. That which is inherited; a heritage.

3. a. *lit.* Property, or an estate, which passes by law to the heir on the decease of the possessor.

1473 WARKW. *Chron.* (Camden) 13 Kynge Herry was amitted to his crowne and dignite ageyne, and alle his men to there enherytaunce. **1503-4** *Act 19 Hen. VII*, c. 34 §8 Every suche Woman..[shall] frely enjoye have and possede ..all hir owne inheretaunce. **1553** T. WILSON *Rhet.* (1580) 209 Looke what enheritance came to him..by the death of his owne kinne, and his wifes kinsfolke. **1617** MORYSON *Itin.* III. 248 The whole inheritance would after his death returne to the children of the elder brother. **1770** *Junius Lett.* xxxviii. 191 He [the minister] is the tenant of the day, and has no interest in the inheritance. **1856** OLMSTED *Slave States* 95 Although..a chief part of his inheritance had been in slaves, he had liberated them all.

b. *fig.* Any property, quality, or immaterial possession inherited from ancestors or previous generations.

1611 BEAUM. & FL. *Knight Burn. Pestle* II. ii, My father's blessing, and this little coin Is my inheritance. **17..** SMITH (J.), Oh dear, unhappy babe! must I bequeath thee Only a sad inheritance of woe? **1804** T. CHALMERS *Wks.* (1849) VI. 25 A parent's reputation is a sacred inheritance. **1820** BYRON *Mar. Fal.* II. i, His name, The sole inheritance he left. **1867** SMILES *Huguenots Eng.* i. (1880) 11 Printed books were now part of the inheritance of the human race. **1873** HAMERTON *Intell. Life* I. vi. (1875) 33 Add something to the world's inheritance of knowledge.

4. *transf.* and *fig.* Something that one obtains or comes into possession of by right or divine grant; birthright. In biblical use applied to persons, etc., esp. God's chosen people, as His possession (κλῆρος), and to possessions or blessings, material or spiritual, as received or enjoyed by such persons. (Cf. HERITAGE *sb.* 1 c, 3.)

1535 COVERDALE *Josh.* xiii. 33 The Lorde God of Israel is their enheritaunce. —— *Ps.* ii. 8 Desyre off me, and I shall geue the the Heithen for thine enheritaunce. *Ibid.* xxvii[i]. 9 O helpe thy people, geue thy blessynge vnto thy enheritaunce. **1551** T. WILSON *Logike* (1580) 16 Thereby synnes are forgiven, the inheritance of life everlastyng graunted. **1552** LD. WHARTON in Bp. Nicolson *Leges March.* (1705) 342 The Land Layt called the Debateable Land; and now the *King's Majesties Inheritance.* **1611** BIBLE *Ps.* lxxix. 1 O God, the heathen are come into thine inheritance, thy holy temple haue they defiled. **1871** FREEMAN *Norm. Conq.* IV. xvii. 97 The zealous Primate was driven out of the church..crying aloud as he went that the heathen had come into God's inheritance. **1899** SAYCE *Early Israel* ii. 69 Canaan was the inheritance which the Israelites won for themselves by the sword.

III. 5. *attrib.* and *Comb.*, as ***inheritance tax*** (or ***taxation***), *spec.*, orig. *U.S.*, a tax on inherited property levied on individual beneficiaries, varying according to their degrees of relationship to the testator, rather than on the estate before its distribution.

1841 W. SPALDING *Italy & It. Isl.* I. 101 Caracalla conferred the nominal franchise of Rome on all the provincials, in order to make them liable to the inheritance-tax, and other burdens leviable only on citizens. **1895** E. R. A. SELIGMAN *Ess. Taxation* v. 133 The inheritance tax to-day scarcely needs defence. It is found in almost every country... In the United States..there is now a decided movement toward the progressive inheritance tax. **1903** S. F. WESTON *Princ. Justice in Taxation* viii. 289 We shall not attempt..to discuss the various theories of the inheritance tax. **1911** *Encycl. Brit.* IX. 465/2 The really vital change was the extension in 1894 of the old Probate Duty into a comprehensive impost... This 'Inheritance Tax'—to give it its scientific title—operates as a complementary property tax. **1929** A. COMSTOCK *Taxation in Mod. State* xi. 154 Examples of inheritance taxation may be found in antiquity and in the Middle ages... Since 1914 inheritance taxes have had a less spectacular rôle than income taxes and sales taxes. **1937** M. NEWCOMER in C. Shoup *Stud. Current Tax Probl.* 16 The annual burden of the estate and inheritance taxes has been taken to be the amount of the premium for life insurance sufficient to cover these taxes at death. **1965** *Listener* 2 Dec. 881/2 The positive case for inheritance taxation has become stronger. **1972** *Daily Tel.* 22 Mar. 32/6 This looks a pretty good start towards the possible inheritance tax, in substitution for estate duty.

†**in'heritant,** *sb.* (*a.*). *Obs.* [f. INHERIT *v.* + -ANT[1].] = INHERITOR.

a **1535** MORE *Wks.* (1557) 2 a, Yet maye they not leaue theyr honour to vs as inheritantes, no more then the vertue that themselfe wer honorable for. **1641** J. SHERMAN (*title*) A Treatise concerning Estates Tayle, and Descents of Inheritants.

B. *adj.* Inheriting. (In quot. perh. an error for *inherent.*)

1608 BRETON *Diuine Consid.* B iv, Graces, that essentially do onely dwell, and are inheritant in the diuine nature.

†**in'heritary,** *a. Obs. rare.* = INHERITORY.

1611 SPEED *Hist. Gt. Brit.* IX. xxiv. §37 A man cruell by nature, and claiming an inheritary right of the Prouince of Vlster.

†**inheriteson.** *Obs. rare.* In 5 **enheritesoun.** [Corresponds to an OF. type **enheriteson*:—L. **inhērēditātiōn-em*, f. med.L. *inhērēditāre* to INHERIT: see -ISON.] Inheritance.

1470 HARDING *Chron.* CXXVII. v, Kyng Stephan..His menne thei gaue to their enheritesoun [*ed.* **1543** inheritesoune].

inheritor (ɪn'hɛrɪtə(r)). Forms: see INHERIT; 5-6 **-er,** 6 **-oure,** 5-7 **-our,** 6 **-ar,** 5- **-or.** [The orig. type, as in HERITOR, was prob. *enheriter*, corr. to an OF. **enheritier* (cf. *heritier*), f. *enheriter* to INHERIT. The change of suffix was app. AFr. or Eng., under the influence of agent-nouns, etymologically in *-our*, repr. L. *-ātōrem.*]

1. *lit.* One who inherits, or is heir *to*, an estate, title, etc. on the decease of the former possessor; an heir.

1433 LYDG. *St. Edmund* III. 1464 Pray for th'enherytour off Ingelond and France. **1475** *Bk. Noblesse* (Roxb.) 36 The saide king Edwarde weddid dam Isabel king Charles of Fraunce daughter..enheriter of Fraunce. **1494** FABYAN *Chron.* I. xxii. 17, Iago or Lago..as next Inherytor, was made gouernour of Brytayne. **1538** STARKEY *England* I. iv. 113 They are sure to be inherytarys to a grete porcyon of intaylyd land. **1548** HALL *Chron., Hen. VI* 158 b, Because the kynge was not the true enheritor to the crowne. **1641** MILTON *Ch. Govt.* I. iv, Born inheritors of the dignity. **1791** COWPER *Iliad* IX. 595 Inheritor of all his large demesnes. **1840** DICKENS *Old C. Shop* vii, You became the sole inheritor of the wealth of this rich old hunks.

b. One who inherits a quality or immaterial possession; one who inherits a disease or defect.

a **1533** LD. BERNERS *Huon* clxiii. 640 Huon of Burdeaux, my dere father, the great paines and pouertes that ye were wonte to suffer ye haue left me, now enheryter to the same. **1668** HALE *Pref. Rolle's Abridgm.* c j b, The inheritor of his Father's vertues as well as of his Possessions. **1797** BURKE *Regic. Peace* iii. Wks. VIII. 314 The new emperour, the inheritor of so much glory, and placed in a situation of so much delicacy, and difficulty for the preservation of that inheritance. **1861** BUMSTEAD *Ven. Dis.* (1879) 735 In case of excessive activity of the disease in the first inheritor, it may appear even in the third generation. **1875** WHITNEY *Life Lang.* vii. 119 The inheritors and continuers of a common civilization.

2. *transf.* and *fig.* One who comes into possession of, or is entitled to, something, to be held by him as of lawful right. Often in reference to spiritual possessions: cf. INHERITANCE 4.

c **1440** *Gesta Rom.* II. xxxiii. 352 (Add. MS.) Blissed be the poore of sprite, for enheriters of the kyngdom of heven. **1526** *Pilgr. Perf.* (W. de W. 1531) 69 Called to be enherytours of the celestiall empire. **1548-9** *Bk. Com. Prayer, Catechism*, In my Baptisme, wherein I was made.. the childe of God, and inheritour of the kingdome of heauen. **1594** SHAKS. *Rich. III*, IV. iii. 34 Meane time, but thinke how I may do the good, And be inheritor of thy desire. **1611** BIBLE *Isa.* lxv. 9, I will bring forth a seede out of Iacob, and out of Iudah an inheritour of my mountains. **1837** J. S. B. MONSELL '*God of that glorious gift of Grace*' v, Possessor here of grace and love; Inheritor of Heaven above!

†**in'heritory,** *a. Obs. rare.* [f. prec.: see -ORY.] Descending to an inheritor; hereditary.

1611 SPEED *Theat. Gt. Brit., Scotland* i. §11 These [Counties] are subdivided into Sherifdomes, stewardships and bailiwickes, for the most part inheritory unto honourable families.

inheritress (ɪn'hɛrɪtrɪs). [fem. of *inheriter*, INHERITOR (see -ESS), which has displaced the earlier *inheritrice* (see next).] A female inheritor; an heiress. (Less technical than *inheritrix.*)

1603 HOLLAND *Plutarch's Mor.* 852 A kinswoman of his and cousin germain, an inheritresse. **1640** GLAPTHORNE *Wit in Constable* II. Wks. 1874 I. 181, I was borne Free, an inheritresse to an ample fortune. **1846** TRENCH *Mirac.* xx. (1862) 331 She is a 'daughter of Abraham';..an inheritress, as some understand, of the faith of Abraham. **1855** MILMAN *Lat. Chr.* XIII. x. VI. 233 Joanna II, the inheritress of the name, the throne, the licentiousness, the misfortunes of Joanna I. **1894** MRS. H. WARD *Marcella* I. 4 Marcella Boyce ..inheritress of one of the most ancient names in England.

†**in'heritrice.** *Obs.* Also **en-.** [AFr. adaptation of next: see -TRICE.] = prec.

1513 BRADSHAW *St. Werburge* I. 3282 Of fyue myghty kynges descended lynyally A prynces an enherytryce. **1547** J. HARRISON *Exhort. Scottes* H vj a, He ought of right to mary our Princesse, thinheritrice of yͤ crown of Scotlande. **1607** COWELL *Interpr.* s.v. *Dower*, If she be an inheretrice, her husband holdeth the land but during her life. *a* **1672** WREN in Gutch *Col. Cur.* I. 232 Whom he married to inheritrices, and into the greatest families of the Kingdom.

inheritrix (ɪn'hɛrɪtrɪks). Also 6-7 **enheritrix,** 7 **enheretrix,** 7-8 **inheretrix.** [Latinized fem. of INHERITOR, after L. feminines in *-trix*: cf. HERITRIX. (Its L. type would be **inhērēditātrix.*)] = prec. (The form in technical use.)

[*a* **1481** LITTLETON *Inst.* (ed. Houard) 4 (Godef.) Feme enheritrix de terre en fee simple. *Ibid.* 24 (ibid.) Quecunque que serra inheritrix per force d'un done.] **1531** *Dial. on Laws Eng.* G ij a, One that is an enherytrix of the landes entayled. *a* **1586** SIDNEY *Astr. & Stella*, '*While fauor fed my hope*' iv, The proofe of Beauties worth, th' enheritrix of fame. **1609** BIBLE (Douay) *Num.* xxxvi. *comm.*, In case, an enheretrixe did marrie a man of an other tribe. **1791** *Gentl. Mag.* LXI. II. 924 Both their wives were inheretrixes. **1872** MRS. OLIPHANT *Mem. Montalambert* II. xix. 373 One of his daughters, the inheritrix of much of her father's talent.

inhesion (ɪn'hiːʒən). Also 7-8 **inhæsion.** [ad. late L. *inhæsiōn-em*, n. of action from *inhærēre* to INHERE; cf. *adhesion, cohesion.*] The action or fact of inhering, esp. as a quality or attribute; inherence. ***subject of inhesion***, that in which a quality or attribute inheres.

a **1631** DONNE in *Select.* (1840) 65 The terms of satisfaction in Christ, of acceptation in the Father, of imputation to us, or inhesion in us, are all pious and religious phrases. **1666** BOYLE *Orig. Formes & Qual.* Wks. 1772 III. 17 The nature of a substance consisting in this, that it can subsist of itself without being in any thing else, as in a subject of inhesion. **1773** REID *Aristotle's Log.* i. §3 (1788) 8 A distinction between a subject of predication and a subject of inhesion. **1874** SAYCE *Compar. Philol.* vii. 289 The difference made in formal logic between predication and inhesion in a proposition.

†**in'hesive,** *a. Obs. rare.* [f. L. *inhæs-*, ppl. stem of *inhærēre* to INHERE + -IVE; cf. *adhesive.*] Having the quality of inhering; inherent.

1639 F. ROBERTS *God's Holy Ho.* viii. 58 Inhaesive holinesse is that seasoning and gratious constitution, where with the heart and conscience is inwardly so qualified, by the holy Ghost as disposeth it wholy to the will, honour and glory of almighty God.

Hence †**in'hesively** *adv. Obs.*, inherently. (In quot. 1600, used in a burlesque upon technical terminology.)

c **1600** *Timon* IV. iii, Either aptitudinally and catachrestically, or perpendicularly and inhæsiuely. **1649** FULLER *Just Man's Funeral* 3 Righteous inhesively, having many heavenly graces. **1681** FLAVEL *Meth. Grace* i. 14 The righteousness of Christ..is inhesively in Him, communicatively it becomes ours.

†**in'heyne,** *v. Obs.* [f. IN-[2] (= EN-) + *heyne*, HAIN *v.*[2] (Cf. *en-large.*)] *trans.* To heighten.

c **1475** *Crabhouse Reg.* (1889) 61 She repared the bakhouse an inheyned it.

inhiate ('ɪnhaɪeɪt), *v.* [f. ppl. stem of L. *inhiāre* to gape at or for, f. *in-* (IN-[2]) + *hiāre*: see HIATE.] *intr.* To gape, to open the mouth wide.

1543 BECON *Policy War* in *Early Wks.* (Parker Soc.) 253 How like gaping wolves do many of them inhiate and gape after wicked mammon. **1623** COCKERAM II, To Gape or yawne, *inhiate.* **1873** W. CORY *Lett. & Jrnls.* (1897) 307 The crowd were inhiating and gabbling over the water.

†**inhi'ation.** *Obs. rare.* [ad. late L. *inhiātiōn-em*, n. of action from *inhiāre*: see prec. Cf. It. *inhiatione* (Florio).] The act of gaping *after*, or desiring greedily.

1620 BP. HALL *Hon. Mar. Clergy* I. §4 Who was hee that ..said 'Marriage was a loosing the reynes to luxury, an inhiation after obscene lusts'? *a* **1631** DONNE *Lett.* (1651) 49 A thirst and inhiation after the next life.

inhibit (ɪn'hɪbɪt), *v.* Forms: 5-6 **inhybyte,** (6 **inibbit**), 6- **inhibit.** *Pa. pple.* **inhibited;** also 5-6 **inhibit(e.** [f. L. *inhibit-*, ppl. stem of *inhibēre* to hold in, restrain, hinder, prevent, f. *in-* (IN-[2]) +

habēre to hold. Cf. OF. *inhibir* (later *inhiber*), Sp. *inhibir*, It. *inibire* (Florio *inhibire*).]

1. *trans.* To forbid, prohibit, interdict (a person): esp. as a term of Ecclesiastical Law or practice.

†**a.** *to* do something. Also, rarely, with *that*. (Sometimes with negative in the subord. clause.)

1460 Capgrave *Chron.* 164 In the same time were the Jewis inhibite, that thei schul no more lend no silver to no Christen man. **1533** Bellenden *Livy* v. (1822) 397 The maisteris inhibitis the servandis to have ony cumpany with uncouth men. **1577–87** Holinshed *Chron.* III. 1215/2 Strictlie inhibiting them, that not one of them should once on paine of death looke ouer the wals or rampires. **1600** Holland *Livy* xlii. xxv. 1129 By expresse words he was inhibited to beare armes without his own frontiers. *a* **1670** Hacket *Abp. Williams* ii. (1692) 157 By the same Canon law that forbids clergymen to sentence, they..are more strictly inhibited to give no testimony in causes of blood.

b. *from* doing something; †*from* a thing.

c **1540** *Pilgr. T.* 424 in *Thynne's Animadv.* (1865) App. i. 89 Thes be the prophesys that we shold trust vnto, & not in false lyes that we be inhibyt fro. **1655** Fuller *Ch. Hist.* iii. iii. §5 The said Peckam inhibited all from selling victuals to him or his family. **1747** Carte *Hist. Eng.* I. 502 Anselm.. had inhibited by letters all the bishops of England from assisting at his consecration. **1749** Fielding *Tom Jones* Wks. 1775 II. 238 Partridge was inhibited from that topic which would at first have suggested itself. **1855** Macaulay *Hist. Eng.* xx. IV. 499 A clause was..inserted which inhibited the Bank from advancing money to the Crown without authority from Parliament. **1873** Sir R. Phillimore *Eccl. Law* II. 1345 In the Bishops triennial, as also in regal and metropolitical, visitations, all inferior jurisdictions respectively are inhibited from exercising jurisdiction, during such visitation.

†**c.** To forbid a person a thing. *Obs.*

1599 Sandys *Europæ Spec.* (1632) 108 They..inhibite their partie the reading of Protestant-bookes, and repaire to their Churches. **1641** *Vind. Smectymnuus* xv. 189 Wicked or scandalous livers among them, who were to be inhibited their assemblies. *a* **1648** Ld. Herbert *Hen. VIII* (1683) 13 A Statute..which did inhibit our men other Traffick towards Denmark and Iseland.

d. without const.: *esp.* to forbid (an ecclesiastic) to exercise clerical functions.

1531 Latimer *Serm. & Rem.* (Parker Soc.) 324 He did never inhibit me in my life. **1612** T. Taylor *Comm. Titus* i. 6 The minister here onely inhibited directly. **1633** Bp. Hall *Hard Texts, N.T.* 62 Forbid them not; there is no reason to inhibit them that are well affected to us. **1867** *Morning Star* 19 Sept. 3 Let him [the Archbishop of Canterbury] inhibit the bishop.

2. a. To forbid, prohibit (a thing, action, or practice). Now *rare.*

1494 Fabyan *Chron.* vii. 596 Whan yt wepyn was inhybyted theym, then they toke stonys and plummettes of lede. **1555** R. Taylor in Coverdale *Lett. Mart.* (1564) 175 By S. Paules doctrine, it is the doctrine of deuilles to inhibite matrimony. **1613** Purchas *Pilgrimage* (1614) 225 The Inquisitors have inhibited and taken from them all bookes written on that Theame. **1726** Ayliffe *Parergon* 135 By the novel Constitutions, Burial may not be inhibited or deny'd to any one. **1761–2** Hume *Hist. Eng.* (1806) III. xxxvii. 175 She published a proclamation, by which she inhibited all preaching without a special license. **1821** Lamb *Elia* Ser. i. *My first Play*, At school all play-going was inhibited.

†**b.** with the object expressed by a clause or infinitive phrase (sometimes negative). *Obs.*

1562 Winȝet *Cert. Tractates* i. Wks. 1888 I. 4 The godlye wysedome of thi Maiestie hes be ane edict inhibit ony questioun..to be mouit in this action. **1577–87** Holinshed *Chron.* III. 1184/1 Another proclamation..inhibiting, that from thensefoorth no plaies nor interludes should be exercised, till Alhallowes tide. **1612** Brerewood *Lang. & Relig.* xi. 103 Philosophy..is inhibited to be taught in their universities. **1632** Lithgow *Trav.* iv. 149 The Turkes.. have inhibited that any Christian shall come neare to it.

3. To restrain, check, hinder, prevent, stop. †Also with inf. compl. (*obs.*).

1535 Coverdale *Ezra* v. 5 They were not inhibyte, tyll the matter was brought before Darius, and tyll there came a wrytinge therof agayne. **1601** Holland *Pliny* I. 11 The Planets..are both inhibited by the..Trine aspect of the sun, to hold on a straight and direct course. **1650** Bulwer *Anthropomet.* 47 Coldnesse constipating the pores of the skin, whence the regresse of vapours is inhibited. **1691** Ray *Creation* ii. (1692) 131 That external Sphincter inhibits a too great dilatation of the Gullet. **1816** T. L. Peacock *Headlong Hall* ii, The use of animal food retards, though it cannot materially inhibit, the perfectibility of the species. **1876** Foster *Phys.* i. iii. (1879) 120 The reflex actions of the spinal cord may, by appropriate means, be inhibited.

4. *Psychol.* (See inhibition 4.) Extended from sense 3.

1876 W. James *Coll. Ess. & Rev.* (1920) 30 A representation arises in a mind, but..it is inhibited by another which confronts it. **1943** C. R. Griffith *Princ. Syst. Psychol.* xvi. 596 A strong connection between two elements *a* and *b* inhibits the formation of connections between *a* and some other element *c* or *d*. **1957** Partridge *English gone Wrong* i. 22 *Inhibition* and the adjective *inhibited* and the verb *inhibit* properly denote the restraint that one psychical activity (for instance, thought) imposes upon another (as it might be fear) and also, derivatively, any psychical impediment to the free workings of body or mind or of both; it is this latter sense which has become debased to mean—as if that were a deplorable thing—the dictates of a decent self-restraint and the promptings of a natural modesty.

Hence **in'hibited** *ppl. a.*; **in'hibitedness**; **in'hibiting** *vbl. sb.* and *ppl. a.* (esp. *Psychol.*).

1601 Shaks. *All's Well* i. i. 157 Selfe-loue, which is the most inhibited sinne in the Cannon. **1607** Hieron *Wks.* I. 327 Touching..the inhibiting or forbidding part, the substance of it is contained in this clause, 'let not sinne reigne in your mortall body'. **1608** Willet *Hexapla Exod.* 76 There are two other kinds of inhibiting. **1823** Scott *Peveril* x, The Dobby's Walk was within the inhibited domains of the hall. **1861** W. Bell *Dict. Law Scot.* 446/1 Personal creditors..will be entirely excluded in competition with the inhibiting creditor. **1942** A. L. Rowse *Cornish Childhood* ii. 44 Because of his reserve, his essential inhibitedness. **1961** J. A. Brussel *Layman's Guide Psychiatry* viii. 80 This is best accomplished by removing or modifying the inhibiting factors which have blocked the individual's personality development. **1963** A. Heron *Towards Quaker View of Sex* i. 7 This still repressive and inhibited outlook towards sex. **1967** Hilgard & Atkinson *Introd. Psychol.* (ed. 4) xxii. 556/1 With neurotics who are too inhibited to discuss their feelings spontaneously, more directive methods are usually necessary. **1969** E. Mirel in P. Solomon *Handbk. Psychiatry* xxxii. 389 The 'pathologically shy' children who manifest passivity, inhibited initiative and motor action.

in'hibiter. *rare.* [f. inhibit *v.* + -er[1].] One who inhibits; = inhibitor 1.

1611 Florio, *Inhibitore*, an inhibiter, a forbidder. **1846** *Penny Cycl.* Suppl. II. 81/2 If the inhibition [in Sc. Law] be followed by proceedings to attach the estate at the instance of the other creditors, the inhibiter has a preference over them if the debts have been incurred subsequently to the inhibition.

in'hibitingly, *adv.* [f. inhibiting *ppl. a.* + -ly[2].] In an inhibiting manner.

1941 *Scrutiny* X. 178 The nature and circumstance of the rescue leave each exquisitely and inhibitingly scrupulous about taking advantage of the other's helplessness or chivalry. **1965** *Sat. Rev.* (U.S.) 30 Oct. 91 He has also fought—rigidly, inhibitingly—with his sense of humor.

inhibition (ɪnhɪ'bɪʃən). Also 4–5 -cion(e, 5 ynib-, 5–6 inib-. [a. OF. *inibicion* (13–14th c. in Littré *Suppl.*), later *inhib-*, ad. rare L. *inhibitiōn-em*, n. of action f. *inhibēre* to inhibit.]

1. The action of inhibiting or forbidding; a prohibition (with reference to some act expressed or implied), esp. one formally issued by a person or body possessed of civil or ecclesiastical authority.

c **1375** *Sc. Leg. Saints, Agatha* 188 þane gert he put hire in presone, & mad strat Inhibicione, þat na man access suld hafe. **1387** Trevisa *Higden* (Rolls) VIII. 289 Robert þe archebisshop hadde purchased an inhibicioun of þe pope þat no clerk schulde reward þe kyng of holy chirche goodes. **1483** Caxton *Gold. Leg.* 274/2 He sayd that he ought not to be ordeyned the bisshop lyuyng..& wrote for thynibycion of the general counceylle. **1513** Douglas *Æneis* x. i. 22 Quhat maner discord be this at we se, Expres agane our inhibitioun? **1558** Knox *First Blast* (Arb.) 48 The natiue king made streit inhibition to all his subiectes, that none shuld adhere to this traitor. **1663** J. Spencer *Prodigies* (1665) 165 How ancient the Usage of Divining by such petty occasions was, may appear from that inhibition..'Ye shall not use any Divinations'. **1747** Carte *Hist. Eng.* I. 612 Those extreme measures..which he had hitherto been restrained from taking by the Pope's inhibition. **1837** Foster in *Life & Corr.* (1846) II. 313 Medical inhibition to be out in the night-air. **1888** Bryce *Amer. Commw.* II. xxxvii. 43 It [a state legislature] may be restrained by some inhibition either in the federal Constitution, or in the Constitution of its own State.

2. *spec.* †**a.** In *Eng. Law*, formerly, = prohibition. **b.** In *Eccles. Law*, The order of an ecclesiastical court, stopping proceedings in inferior courts, e.g. the suspension of inferior jurisdictions during the bishop's (or archbishop's) visitation (see inhibit *v.* 1 b, quot. 1873); also, now *esp.*, the command of a bishop or ecclesiastical judge, that a clergyman shall cease from exercising ministerial duty. **c.** In *Sc. Law*, A writ prohibiting a person from contracting a debt which may become a burden on his heritable property; also, a writ passing the Signet, obtained by a husband, to prohibit the giving of credit to his wife; see also quot. 1861.

1532–3 *Act 24 Hen. VIII*, c. 12 §2 Any foreyne inhibitions, appeales..in anye wyse not with standynge. **1543** Bale *Yet a Course* 19 b, The decrees and inhybycyons of my lorde ordynarye of London. **1603** *Constitutions & Canons* §§96–98. **1621** *1st Bk. Discipl. Ch. Scot.* 2 The Assemblie ordaines, that Inhibition shall be made to all and sundry persons, now Serving in the Ministery, who hath not entered into their charges by the order..appointed. **1641** *Termes de la Ley, Inhibition*, is a Writ to inhibite a Judge to proceed further in the cause depending before him... Inhibition is most commonly a Writ issuing forth of a higher Court Christian, to a lower and inferiour, upon an appeale. **1840** *Act 3 & 4 Vict.* c. 86 §14 It shall be lawful for the said bishop at any time to revoke such inhibition. **1846** *Penny Cycl.* Suppl. II. 81/2 The debt on which inhibition may proceed must be founded on some obligatory written document, or established by the decree of a court. **1861** W. Bell *Dict. Law Scot.* 446/2 Inhibition against a Wife. *Ibid.* 447/1 *Inhibition of Tithes* is a writ..by which the titular of teinds is enabled to interrupt the possession of a tenant of the teinds possessing by tacit relocation. **1873** Sir R. Phillimore *Eccl. Law* II. 1345 We find, in the time of Archbishop Winchelsey, a bishop prosecuted for exercising jurisdiction before the relaxation of the inhibition; and in Archbishop Tillotson's time, a bishop suspended, for acting after the inhibition. **1881** *Law Rep.* 6 Queen's Bench Div. 377 The judge issued an inhibition inhibiting the incumbent from the performance of divine service and the exercise of the cure of souls within the diocese for three months.

3. a. The action of preventing, hindering, or checking. Now esp. in *Physiol.* (see quot. 1883).

1621 Burton *Anat. Mel.* i. i. ii. vii, This ligation of senses proceeds from an inhibition of spirits, the way being stopped up by which they should come. **1750** Johnson *Rambler* No. 79 ¶7 It is said that no torture is equal to the inhibition of sleep, long continued. **1883** L. Brunton in *Nature* 1 Mar. 419 By inhibition we mean the arrest of the functions of a structure or organ, by the action upon it of another, while its power to execute those functions is still retained, and can be manifested as soon as the restraining power is removed. **1887** *Fortn. Rev.* May 742 Inhibition in one nervous sphere is often accompanied by dynamogeny in another. **1906** C. S. Sherrington *Integrative Action Nervous Syst.* iii. 84 Classical examples of inhibition are those of the vagus nerve on the heart, and of the *corda tympani* on the blood-vessels of the submaxillary region. **1927** G. V. Anrep tr. *Pavlov's Conditioned Reflexes* iii. 43, I consider it advisable to give a brief description of inhibition of centres as observed in the field of unconditioned reflexes. **1967** R. F. Thompson *Found. Physiol. Psychol.* vii. 168 These more limited hypotheses still imply that inhibition tends to act near the region of the cell body where the spike discharge is initiated.

b. *Chem.* (See quot. 1902[2].)

1902 S. W. Young in *Jrnl. Amer. Chem. Soc.* XXIV. 299, I will..use the word 'inhibition' to cover the phenomena in point. *Ibid.* 302 Inhibition, *i.e.* a marked reduction of the reaction rate under the influence of minute quantities of foreign substances. **1923** [see inhibitory *a.* 2]. **1956** *Nature* 3 Mar. 432/2 Anti-competitive (uncompetitive) inhibition, in which the inhibitor combines with the enzyme-substrate complex but not with the enzyme, has been considered theoretically. **1970** G. Odian *Princ. Polymerization* iii. 221 Polymerization is completely stopped by benzoquinone, a typical inhibitor, during an induction or inhibition period.

4. *Psychol.* A voluntary or involuntary restraint or check that prevents the direct expression of an instinctive impulse; also *colloq.*, in looser use, an inner hindrance to conduct or activity.

1876 W. James *Coll. Ess. & Rev.* (1920) 32 Doubt itself is an active state, one of voluntary inhibition or suspense. **1897** J. Adams *Herbartian Psychol.* 257 It is this work of inhibition that causes the peculiar feeling of effort that marks all voluntary attention as opposed to involuntary. **1916** A. A. Brill tr. *Freud's Wit & its Relation to Unconscious* iv. 206 One cannot possibly consider the amount of the pleasure so great as to believe that it has the power to annul deep-rooted inhibitions and repressions. **1932** E. Bowen *To North* xiv. 141 Blurred by the inhibitions of Pauline, upon which his sister dwelt with such gusto. **1936** *Discovery* Aug. 254/1 To guard against auto-suggestions and personal inhibitions of various kinds. **1965** A. L. Fisher tr. *Merleau-Ponty's Struct. Behaviour* i. 18 That the brain possesses a general power of inhibition would be accepted. **1973** W. J. Burley *Death in Salubrious Place* iii. 56 It was light enough to see the boy's embarrassed shrug. Georgie had no such inhibitions. 'She had a thing about Vince.'

inhi'bitionism. *Psychol.* [f. inhibition + -ism.] (See quot. 1934.) Also *gen.* A tendency towards inhibition.

1934 H. C. Warren *Dict. Psychol.* 138/2 *Inhibitionism*, the view that character is a function of the inhibition of instinctive tendencies. **1952** *Archit. Rev.* CXII. 195/2 For men of his type *fin de siècle* sensitivity and twentieth century inhibitionism are equally abhorrent.

inhibitive (ɪn'hɪbɪtɪv), *a.* (*sb.*) [f. inhibit *v.* + -ive.] That serves or tends to inhibit; inhibitory. Also as *sb.*, An inhibition.

1606 Birnie *Kirk-Buriall* xvi, The Lords lawes are either imperatiues of good or inhibitiues of ill. **1830** W. Phillips *Mt. Sinai* ii. 544 The will inhibitive so late promulged. **1899** W. James *Talks to Teachers* xv. 181 A familiar example of the paralyzing power of scruples is the inhibitive effect of conscientiousness upon conversation. **1902** *Jrnl. Amer. Chem. Soc.* XXIV. 299 An 'inhibitive agent' is then a substance producing an 'inhibition', or having an 'inhibitive effect'. **1944** G. B. Shaw *Everybody's Pol. What's What?* xxiii. 207 He [*sc.* Pavlov] thought he had discovered that reflexes have negative phases as well as positive ones, and can be classed as Excitatory or Inhibitive. **1952** Kirk & Othmer *Encycl. Chem. Technol.* IX. 4 Colloids apparently owe their inhibitive action to their colloidal nature. **1963** A. Heron *Towards Quaker View of Sex* i. 10 The emphasis on morality has so often gone with a cold and inhibitive attitude. **1970** G. F. Newman *Sir, You Bastard* i. 22 Permission was given to live at home provided the distance wasn't inhibitive. **1971** *Mod. Law Rev.* XXXIV. vi. 655 The principal purpose of the Act is inhibitive.

in'hibitor. [agent-n. in L. form f. inhibit *v.*; cf. med.L. *inhibitor*, It. *inhibitore* (Florio, 1611).] **1.** *rare.* One who inhibits. *spec.* in *Sc. Law*, One who takes out an inhibition: see inhibition 2 c.

1868 *Act 31 & 32 Vict.* c. 101 *Sched.* (PP), Notice of letters of inhibition..*A.B.* (insert designation of the inhibitor) against *C.D.* **1886** *Statem. Landlaws by Counc. Inc. Law Soc.* 25 The vendor would simply have to procure the consent of the various inhibitors and persons entering caveats to their removal.

2. a. That which inhibits.

1902 W. James *Varieties Relig. Experience* xi. 265 Danger is for most men the great inhibitor of action. **1908** W. McDougall *Introd. Social Psychol.* iii. 55 [Fear] is thus the great inhibitor of action. **1955** *Sci. Amer.* Apr. 72/2 Many seeds have water-soluble germination inhibitors in their covering. **1973** *Nature* 12 Jan. 140/1 The hydroid may contain a substance which inhibits its nematocysts from discharging and stinging other members of the colony. An occasional hydroid may provide *Pagurus* with such an inhibitor.

b. *Genetics.* A gene whose presence prevents the expression of some other non-allelic gene.

1911 *Jrnl. Genetics* I. 190 The Brown Leghorn..never produces pigmented birds and we..regard it as entirely

without the factor *P*. But it possesses the inhibitor factor *I*. **1911** R. C. PUNNETT *Mendelism* (ed. 3) vii. 70 Probably we ought to regard the beardless as a bearded wheat in which there is an inhibitor that stops the beard from growing. **1925** D. F. JONES *Genetics in Plant & Animal Improvement* iv. 75 A fifth factor, *I*, when present, prevents any color from appearing, no matter what other factors are there. It is called an inhibitor. **1949** F. B. HUTT *Genetics Fowl* vi. 154 The first evidence that the inhibitor of dermal melanin is sex linked was found by Davenport (1906). **1965** J. A. SERRA *Mod. Genetics* I. iii. 60 Inhibitors..completely hinder the manifestation of the gene with which they interact.

c. Any substance which (often in small quantities) slows down or effectively prevents a particular chemical or biochemical process or diminishes the activity of some reactant or catalyst (e.g. in corrosion, the formation of gum in petrol, or enzymic reactants).

1914 S. E. SHEPPARD *Photo-Chem.* vii. 289 The actual inhibitor in the case of ammonia is probably NCl_3. **1924** F. O. RICE in H. S. Taylor *Treat. Physical Chem.* II. xiv. 923 A type of negative catalysis in which the inhibitor combines with one of the reactants to form a molecular compound... The rôle of the inhibitor in all these reactions would therefore be that of a competitor for one of the molecular species undergoing change. **1925** *Jrnl. Soc. Chem. Industry* XLIV. 163 T/1 (*heading*) Water-line corrosion of iron and steel, with special reference to the action of the so-called 'inhibitors' of corrosion. **1935** *Jrnl. R. Aeronaut. Soc.* XXXIX. 791 An attractive method of preventing ice formation..is the use of some form of inhibitor which may be added to the fuel. **1938** W. V. THORPE *Biochem. for Med. Students* x. 130 In many instances the inhibition of an enzyme can be regarded as the result of chemical combination between the enzyme and the inhibitor. **1951** I. L. FINAR *Org. Chem.* I. iii. 44 Gum formation in cracked gasolines is prevented by the addition of inhibitors, which are mainly phenols or aromatic amines. **1962** H. L. KERN et al. in A. Pirie *Lens Metabolism Rel. Cataract* 385 Ouabain is a relatively specific inhibitor of cationic transport. **1962** *Lancet* 27 Jan. 192/1 It seems likely that the tissue activator may be 'unavailable' because an inhibitor is present, but this conclusion must be tentative until more is known about the nature and precise measurement of the inhibitors of fibrinolysis. **1968** R. O. C. NORMAN *Princ. Org. Synthesis* xv. 480 It is advisable to add a small quantity of an inhibitor to the more readily polymerized olefins..to prevent polymerization during storage. **1971** P. J. MCMAHON *Aircraft Propulsion* x. 298 Small quantities of various inhibitors may be used to restrict the rates of reaction in certain places. An inhibitor could for example prevent case temperatures from becoming excessive by cutting down the burning rate of propellants immediately adjacent to the case surface. **1972** *Nature* 18 Feb. 398/2 A generalized metabolic inhibitor..elicited 0% drug response by itself.

inhibitory (in'hibitəri), *a.* Also 5 -ore. [ad. med.L. *inhibitōri-us* (see INHIBIT *v.* and -ORY); in Caxton a. obs. F. *inhibitoire* (15th c. in Godef.).]

1. Of the nature of an inhibition; prohibitory.

1490 CAXTON *Eneydos* xxii. 77 Her feble legacion, the whiche he wold not graunt, by cause that they dyuyne commaundementis inhibytores..were contrarie to the same. **1611** SPEED *Hist. Gt. Brit.* IX. x. §39. 641 The Scots hauing made their way in the Court of Rome, procured inhibitory Letters from the Pope. **1642** SIR E. DERING *Sp. on Relig.* 61 Let therefore this inhibitory Statute against Bishops holding the secular jurisdiction of temporall Lordships stand..irrepealeable. **1701** G. HOOPER *Narr. Lower Ho. Convoc. Vind.* 37 This Original Right of the Archbishop, Inhibitory of our Liberty..is the very Point in Question. **1823** LINGARD *Hist. Eng.* VI. 231 That Clement ..would soon be compelled to issue an inhibitory breve, forbidding all archbishops or bishops, courts or tribunals, to give judgment in the matrimonial cause of Henry against Catharine. **1856** FROUDE *Hist. Eng.* (1858) I. v. 417 An inhibitory mandate was a natural consequence of the conference at Calais.

2. That inhibits or checks anything; producing inhibition. *inhibitory nerve* (*Physiol.*), a nerve of which the stimulation represses or diminishes action.

1855 H. SPENCER *Princ. Psychol.* (1870) I. 64 A system of nerves which diminish action—inhibitory nerves as they are called. **1879** W. JAMES *Coll. Ess. & Rev.* (1920) 129 Positivism takes a middle ground, and with a certain consciousness of the beyond, abruptly refuses by an inhibitory action of the will to think any further. **1882** *Med. Temp. Jrnl.* 97 The hypothesis that alcohol narcotises the inhibitory nerve of the heart. **1883** J. BRUNTON in *Nature* 1 Mar. 420 Several authors have pointed out the analogy between inhibitory phenomena in the animal body and the effects of interference of waves of light or sound. **1901** B. HOLLANDER *Revival of Phrenol.* i. 36 The frontal lobe, as the seat of the reasoning faculty, is an inhibitory apparatus against the lower and more instinctive natural impulses. **1902** *Jrnl. Amer. Chem. Soc.* XXIV. 306 The inhibitory actions in question are quite closely confined to reactions in which free oxygen is involved. **1923** *Jrnl. Physical Chem.* XXVII. 325 The inhibitory power of water in the esterification of acids in alcoholic solutions..represents a complex case of the Titoff type of inhibition. **1944** G. B. SHAW *Everybody's Pol. What's What?* xxiii. 205 Some [*sc.* conditioned reflexes] are too cruel for civilized people to tolerate, and from being what Pavlov calls excitatory have become inhibitory. **1959** *Metabolism* VIII. 101 Calcium gluconate exerted a significant inhibitory effect on insulin degradation.

†**in'hidden,** *ppl. a. Obs.* [IN *adv.* 11 b.] Hidden within.

1674 N. FAIRFAX *Bulk & Selv.* 127 Motion..by its inhidden power..brought on again to a kind of quickness.

†**in'high,** *v. Obs. rare*$^{-0}$. [f. IN-^{1} or ^{2} + HIGH *v.*; cf. ENHIGH.] *trans.* To elevate.

1483 *Cath. Angl.* 196/1 To Inheghe, *allevare, attollere,.. exaltare, extollere.*

---

inhilde, variant of INHELDE *v., Obs.*

inhir, inhirly, obs. forms of INNER, INNERLY.

inhistoricity (ˌɪnhɪstəˈrɪsɪtɪ). *rare.* [IN-^{3}.] Lack of historicity.

1930 C. J. WRIGHT *Miracle in Hist.* 8 The main fact that emerges for our study is that all of these hypotheses postulate a large amount of inhistoricity in the narratives.

†**in'hive,** *v. Obs. rare*$^{-1}$. [IN-^{1} or ^{2}.] *trans.* To put into a hive; to HIVE.

1611 COTGR., *Enrucher,* to inhiue, or put into a hiue. **1622** MABBE tr. *Aleman's Guzman d'Alf.* I. 124 Suffer not these busie Bees of Satan to put honie into them, nor there to swarme and in-hiue themselues.

†**inhoc, -hok(e,** *sb. Obs. rare.* [Of obscure formation. Known only in Lat. charters, where it is also freq. latinized as *inhoka, inhokium.* Kennett conjectures for *hoc, hok,* the sense of Du. *hoek* (MDu. and MLG. *hôk*) 'corner, angle'; but this is not otherwise evidenced in ME. If, however, the term *inheche* is etymologically related, the second element is app. OE. *hóc* 'hook', in same sense.] A term applied in Middle English times to a piece of land (temporarily) inclosed from the fallow and put under cultivation; an inclosure (of this description).

See, as to the use of the term, Vinogradoff *Villainage in England* (1892) 226–8, Kennett *Paroch. Antiq.* Glossary s.v. Kennett's explanation is 'any corner or out-part of a common field ploughed up and sowed (and sometimes fenced off) within that year wherein the rest of the same field lay fallow. It is now called..in Oxfordshire a *hitching.*' But the notion of a *corner* or *out-part* appears to have no other foundation than Kennett's conjectured derivation.

1214 *Sarum Stat.* in Kennett *Par. Antiq.* (1818) Gloss. s.v., Idem canonicus habebit omnes fructus terræ..preter illud inhok, quod ad warettum pertinet. **1268** *Oseney Reg.* ibid., Obligavit se..quod nunquam de dicta pastura.. inhokam faciet in prejudicium dicti abbatis. **1281** *Ibid.* I. 419 Frater Walterus..fieri fecit quoddam inhoc in campo waretabili..per quod Frater Willielmus dicebat se de communi pastura ibidem disseisiri. *a* **1300** *Malmesbury Cart.* (Rolls) II. 186. [**1892** VINOGRADOFF *Villainage in Eng.* 228 A new species of arable—the manured plot under 'inhoc'—came into use, and disturbed the plain arrangement of the old-fashioned three courses.]

Hence †**inhok(e** *v.* (in L. form *inhōkāre*), to inclose and put under crop (part of a fallow).

1265-6 *Gloucester Cart.* (Rolls) III. 36 Et de predicto campo possunt inhokari quolibet secundo anno 40 acre, et valet inde commodum eo anno 10 solidos. **1301** in *Registr. Monast. de Winchelcumba* (1892) 256 Permiserit inhokare. *Ibid.,* Nunquam alias [terras] inhokabunt.

†**in'hogged,** *ppl. a. Obs. rare*$^{-0}$. [IN-^{2}.]

1611 FLORIO, *Inporcito,* inhogged, inswined.

†**in'hold,** *v. Obs.* [f. IN-^{1} + HOLD *v.*]

1. *trans.* To hold within; to contain, enclose.

1614 RALEIGH *Hist. World* I. i. §7 This light..which the Sunne inholdeth and casteth forth. **1628** FELTHAM *Resolves* II. [I.] xxiii. 76, I haue knowne.. a merry face, inhold a discontented soule. *Ibid.* xliii. 128 Who will cast away the whole body of the Beast, because it inheld both guts and ordure?

2. To hold in, keep in, retain.

1726 E. ERSKINE *Serm.* Wks. 1871 I. 185 Grace is not for inholding but for outgiving.

3. *intr.* To contain oneself, refrain or keep *from.*

1655 FULLER *Hist. Camb.* 149, I can hardly inhold from inveighing on his memory.

†**in'holder.** *Obs.* [f. prec., or as prec.]

1. A tenant.

a **1599** SPENSER *F.Q.* VII. vii. 17 If ye please it [the world] into parts divide, And every parts inholders to convent.

2. That which holds or contains.

1660 S. FISHER *Rusticks Alarm* Wks. (1679) 510 Which words Pillar and Ground should not be taken for the Supporter, Upholder or Foundation, nor Inholder of Truth. **1674** N. FAIRFAX *Bulk & Selv.* 148 To think of any other..way of making the body the souls inholder.

inholder, obs. form of INN-HOLDER.

†**inhominious,** *a. Obs. rare*$^{-1}$. [repr. *inhommineuse* of the F. text, app. a distortion of *ignominieuse,* as if from L. *in-* not + *homin-em* man: cf. ABHOMINAL.] ? Ignominious.

1490 CAXTON *Eneydos* xxvii. G iv, She..reputed it to be doon in opprobre and confusion, inhomynouse and full of despyte.

inhomogeneity (ɪnˌhɒməʊdʒɪˈniːɪtɪ). [IN-^{3}.]

1. Something that is not homogeneous with its surroundings; a local irregularity or departure from uniformity.

1899 J. WARD *Naturalism & Agnosticism* I. IV. 117 The former consists of smallest inhomogeneities,—a finely grained structure, as we say in English. **1936** *Jrnl. R. Aeronaut. Soc.* XL. 595 A local slip occurred (owing to a stress-concentration effect at a local inhomogeneity or flaw) in the zone separating the part of the crystal which had slipped from that which had not. **1955** *Jrnl. Brit. Interplanetary Soc.* XIV. 20 Just as the visual twinkling of stars gives information about atmospheric irregularities..so the 'twinkling' of radio stars in radio wave-lengths can show up 'inhomogeneities' in the ionosphere, especially at the top. **1956** *Nature* 10 Mar. 487/1 Crystallographic cracking can be

---

found in such an alloy, although its analysis is complicated by the presence of gross inhomogeneities and intermetallics. **1959** *New Scientist* 22 Jan. 167/1 The solidified ribbon of glass has a certain amount of distortion which cannot be avoided arising from small differences in viscosity due to chemical and thermal inhomogeneities. **1959** *Wiltshire Archaeol. & Nat. Hist. Mag.* LVII. 176 The sensitivity of the [electrical resistivity] method depends on..the size and depth below the surface of the inhomogeneity. **1971** I. G. GASS et al. *Understanding Earth* i. 36/1 Gneissose banding is also developed from original inhomogeneities in the rock such as bedding.

2. The property of being inhomogeneous; lack of homogeneity.

1916 *Sci. Abstr.* A. XIX. 154 The inhomogeneity of the field in the canal-ray tube. **1921** [see GRAININESS]. **1930** *Proc. R. Soc.* A. CXXIX. 221 All the evidence..tends to show that this tail is due, not to initial inhomogeneity of velocity, but to scattering or absorption. **1938** R. W. LAWSON tr. *Hevesy & Paneth's Man. Radioactivity* (ed. 2) xx. 189 The condition of initially complete uniformity in distribution is not satisfied, and it is just this inhomogeneity that is utilized ..for the concentration of the isotopes. **1942** *Jrnl. Biol. Chem.* CXLVI. 459 Further evidence for the inhomogeneity of ferritin is the variability of the iron, phosphorus, and nitrogen content of different crystallized ferritin samples. **1962** *Listener* 12 July 62/3 Information on fundamental crystal size and crystal shape, on lattice strain, on inhomogeneity.

inhomogeneous (ˌɪnhɒməʊˈdʒiːnɪəs), *a.* [IN-^{3}.] Not homogeneous. **a.** Not of uniform nature throughout; composed of diverse constituents; heterogeneous.

1904 *Jrnl. Physical Chem.* VIII. 425 The 58·5 percent alloy is homogeneous when annealed at 720° and quenched. It becomes inhomogeneous..if annealed at 685° and quenched. **1938** R. W. LAWSON tr. *Hevesy & Paneth's Man. Radioactivity* (ed. 2) ii. 34 At the moment of their emission the α-rays from a single radioactive substance all possess the same velocity... As soon as they have traversed a sheet of an absorbing substance, however,..the pencil of rays begins to be inhomogeneous. **1956** *Nature* 25 Feb. 380/2 The relatively great variations are due partly to the inhomogeneous microstructure of the muscular tissue. **1962** CORSON & LORRAIN *Introd. Electromagn. Fields* xi. 400 We shall not attempt here a rigorous discussion of wave propagation in such inhomogeneous media.

b. *Math.* Consisting of terms that are not all of the same degree or dimensions.

1943 MARGENAU & MURPHY *Math. Physics & Chem.* vii. 237 One remarkable feature of an inhomogeneous equation ..is that it may not possess solutions for every value of *k* even though the homogeneous equation, with the same boundary condition, has solutions. **1946** L. BRILLOUIN *Wave Propagation* vi. 109 This is an inhomogeneous differential equation as it stands. **1957** L. Fox *Numerical Solution Two-Point Boundary Probl.* viii. 266 In §5 we solved the approximate finite-difference form of this problem by considering two trial solutions, $y^{(1)}$ and $y^{(2)}$, of which the former satisfied the inhomogeneous finite-difference equations and the correct initial condition, and $y^{(2)}$ satisfied the homogeneous forms..and had initial value zero. **1962** W. B. THOMPSON *Introd. Plasma Physics* iv. 57 Of the two possible choices for pressure, the first leads to slightly simpler results, although it does make eq. (4.5.8) inhomogeneous.

Hence ˌinhomoˈgeneously *adv.,* in an inhomogeneous manner; unevenly, irregularly.

1909 in WEBSTER. **1937** *Q. Jrnl. Geol. Soc.* XCIII. 582 A monomict, inhomogeneously, orientated, heteroaxial quartz-B-tectonite with partial recrystallization. **1966** D. G. BRANDON *Mod. Techniques Metallogr.* i. 4 The difficulty comes when the features of interest are too small to be resolved at a low magnification and too widely or inhomogeneously dispersed to include a representative area ..at a high magnification. **1973** *Sci. Amer.* Dec. 70/3 Owing to the random distribution of impurity ions..the energy levels are inhomogeneously broadened over the volume of the medium.

†**in'honest,** *a. Obs.* [ad. L. *inhonestus,* f. *in-* (IN-^{3}) + *honestus* HONEST; in ME. prob. a. OF. *inhoneste* (Godef.).]

1. Dishonourable, disgraceful, shameful; indecent, vile.

1340 *Ayenb.* 220 þe fole takinges and inhoneste in zenne of lecherie. **1432-50** tr. *Higden* (Rolls) VII. 269 Spekynge to that woman wordes inhoneste. **1520** WHITINTON *Vulg.* (1527) 42 That whiche is inhonest to auoyde vtterly. **1534** — *Tullyes Offices* II. (1540) 83 In that behalfe an inhonest victorie folowed an honest cause. **1599** A. M. tr. *Gabelhouer's Bk. Physicke* 303/1 Haunting of strumpets, or inhoneste Woemen.

2. Void of good manners; ungentlemanly. *rare.*

1534 WHITINTON *Tullyes Offices* I. 65 If any man be aboute to pleade any cause, [and] he studyeth by the way or in walkynge alone..it maye not be reprehended, but if he do this same in bankettynge or at the tauerne, he maye seme inhonest [L. *inhumanus*] bycause he knoweth not tyme.

†**in'honestate,** *v. Obs. rare*$^{-0}$. [f. ppl. stem of L. *inhonestāre,* f. *inhonestus*: see prec.] 'To shame, to dishonest' (Cockeram, 1623).

So †**inhone'station** [late L. *inhonestātio*], 'a shaming or disgracing, a making dishonest' (Phillips, 1658).

†**in'honestly,** *adv. Obs.* [f. INHONEST + -LY^2.] Dishonourably, shamefully, indecently, discreditably.

1340 *Ayenb.* 177 Me zeneʒeþ wel ofte..be fole takinges and inhonesteliche. **1522** R. Fox in Ellis *Orig. Lett.* Ser. II. II. 8 If I shuld sodenly relinquyshe theme, I shuld unresonably & inhonestly disapoynt many maters &

persons. *a* **1572** KNOX *Hist. Ref.* Wks. 1846 I. 109 That he wold not do so foolishlie and inhonestlye, yea, so cruelly and unmercyfullie to the realme of Scotland.

† **in'honesty.** *Obs. rare.* [ad. late L. *inhonestāt-em* (Tertullian): see INHONEST and HONESTY.] The quality of being 'inhonest'; also, that which is 'inhonest', indecent, or filthy.

a **1470** TIPTOFT *Tulle on Friendsh.* (Caxton, 1481) B iv, Therfor lete this now in frendship be confermed that we desire nothinges of his inhoneste. **1509** *Burgh Rec. Edinb.* 27 Sept. (Rec. Soc.) 124 To tak.. of euery flescheour.. for the clengeing of thair inhonestie and filth.. four pennies ilk quarter.

inhonour, variant of ENHONOUR *v.*, *Obs.*

† **in'hood,** *v. Obs. rare*$^{-0}$. [IN-^{2}.]

1611 FLORIO, *Inscuffiare*, to inquoife, to inhood.

† **in'hoop,** *v. Obs. rare*$^{-1}$. [f. IN-^{1} or ^{2} + HOOP *sb.* or *v.*] *trans.* To place or enclose in a hoop, to surround with a hoop.

[**1596** DAVIES *Epigr.* (N.), Cocking in hoopes is now all the play.] **1606** SHAKS. *Ant. & Cl.* II. iii. 38 His Cocks do winne the Battaile still of mine, When it is all to naught: and his Quailes euer Beate mine (in hoopt) at odds.

† **in'horn,** *v. Obs. rare*$^{-0}$. [IN-^{2}.]

1611 FLORIO, *Incornare*, to horne, to inhorne.

† **inhor'tation.** *Obs. rare*$^{-1}$. [n. of action f. L. *inhortārī* to incite.] Instigation.

1502 ARNOLDE *Chron.* (1811) 233 By the inhortacyon and advertisment of a chapleyne off my lady.

inhospitable (ɪn'hɒspɪtəb(ə)l), *a.* [a. OF. *inhospitable* (15–16th c. in Godef.) = It. *inhospitabile*, ad. med. or mod.L. *inhospitābilis* (= L. *inhospitālis*): see IN-^{3} and HOSPITABLE.] Not hospitable.

1. Of persons, their actions, disposition, etc.: Not disposed to welcome and entertain strangers; withholding hospitality from guests or visitors.

1570 LEVINS *Manip.* 4/28 Inhospitable, *inhospitabilis.* **1649** JER. TAYLOR *Gt. Exemp.* III. Sect. xiv. § 18. 47 He found the inhabitants of a little village so inhospitable, as to refuse to give him entertainment. **1671** MILTON *Samson* 989 Jael, who, with inhospitable guile Smote Sisera sleeping, through the temples nailed. **1727** A. HAMILTON *New Acc. E. Ind.* I. iii. 22 The Coast is inhospitable as well as the People. **1800** *Asiat. Ann. Reg., Misc. Tr.* 172/2 But I assured him, that, on account of his inhospitable treatment, he would receive nothing from me. **1832** LYTTON *Eugene A.* I. v, What on earth could make you so inhospitable to your Uncle's guest?

2. *transf.* Of a region, coast, etc.: Not affording or offering shelter or entertainment.

1616 BULLOKAR, *Inhospitable*, harbourles: not fit to entertaine one. **1638** SIR T. HERBERT *Trav.* (ed. 2) 183 Our journey lay sometimes through inhospitable straits. **1667** MILTON *P.L.* XI. 306 All places else Inhospitable appear and desolate. **1748** *Anson's Voy.* I. vi. 57 We.. were now proceeding to an hostile, or at best, a desart and inhospitable coast. **1873** HAMERTON *Intell. Life* III. viii. (1875) 112 The gardeners of an inhospitable climate contend against the natural sunshine of the south. **1880** GEIKIE *Phys. Geog.* iv. 270 Its arid sandy surface stretches for leagues as an inhospitable desert.

Hence **inhospita'bility, in'hospitableness,** the quality or character of being inhospitable.

1641 EVELYN *Diary* 27 Sept., We, impatient of the tyme and inhospitablenesse of the place, sailed again. **1658** PHILLIPS, *Inhospitality*, or *Inhospitability.* **1853** KANE *Grinnell Exp.* xxxviii. (1856) 353 Never leaving this utter destitution, this frigid inhospitableness. **1882–3** SCHAFF *Encycl. Relig. Knowl.* I. 122/1 [Arabia] occupies a very isolated position, partly on account of the inhospitableness of its coasts.

inhospitably (ɪn'hɒspɪtəblɪ), *adv.* [f. prec. + -LY^{2}.] In an inhospitable manner; without or in contravention of hospitality.

1667 MILTON *P.L.* XII. 168 Of guests he makes them slaves, Inhospitably. **1742** FRANCIS *Horace, Ep.* I. xiv. (R.), For what you call inhospitably drear, To me with beauty and delight appear.

† **in'hospital,** *a. Obs.* [ad. L. *inhospitālis*, f. *in-* (IN-^{3}) + *hospitālis* hospitable, HOSPITAL *a.* Cf. OF. *inhospital* (Godef.).] = INHOSPITABLE.

1597–8 BP. HALL *Sat.* IV. v. 98 Or lonely Hermits cage inhospitall. **1608–11** —— *Epist.* V. viii, Some inhospitall sauages make fearful delusions by sorcerie vpon the shore, to fright strangers from landing. **1613** PURCHAS *Pilgrimage* VII. xi. 595 They shewed themselves inhospitall and treacherous. **1615** G. SANDYS *Trav.* I. 27 There being no Innes for entertainment throughout inhospitall Turkie. **1694** R. L'ESTRANGE *Fables* 296 Breach of Faith.. is the most odious Inhospital and inhumane.. of moral offences. *a* **1716** SOUTH *Serm.* (1744) IX. iv. 111 By such an act of inhospital barbarity, as before was unheard of.

Hence † **in'hospitally** *adv.*, inhospitably.

1613 PURCHAS *Pilgrimage* (1614) 482 A Hawke had beene admitted.. which being whole, he inhospitally slew many of these co-hospitall weaker Fowles, and was.. expelled this Bird-Colledge.

† **inhospi'talious,** *a. Obs. rare*$^{-1}$. [irreg. f. L. *inhospitāli-s* (see prec.) + -OUS.] Inhospitable.

1602 WARNER *Alb. Eng.* IX. liii. 240 Inhospitalious, Mutinous, and Hypocrites the best.

inhospitality (ɪnhɒspɪ'tælɪtɪ). [ad. L. *inhospitālitās*, f. *inhospitālis* inhospitable: see above and -ITY. Perh. immed. through F. *inhospitalité* (1530 in Hatz.-Darm.).] The quality or practice of being inhospitable; want of kindness in the reception or entertainment of strangers or visitors.

1570–6 LAMBARDE *Peramb. Kent* (1826) 323 Our naturall inhospitalitie and disdaine of straungers. **1613** PURCHAS *Pilgrimage* (1614) 513 The Seas beare also the names of.. the Euxine by a contrarie appellation, for their inhospitalitie. **1656** STANLEY *Hist. Philos.* VIII. (1701) 323/2 Inhospitality is a vehement opinion,.. that Guests ought to be shunn'd. **1717** BERKELEY *Jrnl. Tour Italy* 1 June Wks. 1871 IV. 557 Their inhospitality in refusing to lodge us. **1845** DARWIN *Voy. Nat.* viii. (1879) 156, I did not meet with even one instance of rudeness or inhospitality. **1894** H. GARDENER *Unoff. Patriot* 122 It was here.. that he learned the inhospitality of the free states to the freed negroes.

inhour ('ɪnaʊə(r)). *Nuclear Science.* [f. *in(verse) hour*: so named because if the reactivity is small it is inversely proportional to the corresponding reactor period (to a first approximation).] A unit for expressing the reactivity of a nuclear reactor, being the reactivity of one having a reactor period of one hour (i.e. in which the neutron flux increases by a factor *e* in one hour).

1947 H. L. ANDERSON et al. in *Physical Rev.* LXXII. 17/1 The unit of [control] rod position was given the name inhour (from 'inverse hour', symbol: ih), with the significance that when the control rod is displaced from the critical position by 1 inhour, the pile will have a period of (very nearly) 1 hour. *Ibid.* 21/2 The inhour is useful as a measure of rod displacement because it is a measure of pile reactivity which is independent of the position of the control rod. **1954** R. STEPHENSON *Introd. Nucl. Engin.* vii. 269 There is no simple relationship between inhours of reactivity and pile period observed. Thus 2 inhours of reactivity do not make the pile period equal to 2 hr, nor do they make the pile period exactly one-half an hour, although for small reactivities the number of inhours is about directly proportional to the reactivity. **1966** D. JAKEMAN *Physics Nucl. Reactors* ix. 340 Equation 9.69 is referred to as the inhour equation and is used to define a unit of reactivity called the inhour. This is the amount of reactivity to give a reactor period of 1 hour and for a U^{235} system is equal to a reactivity of $2{\cdot}62 \times 10^{-5}$.

† **in'house,** *v. Obs. rare*$^{-1}$. [f. IN-^{1} + HOUSE *sb.* or *v.*] *trans.* To house.

1595 MARKHAM *Sir R. Grinvile* (Arb.) 51 And there in-housed with their mother Night, All foure deuise, how heauen and earth to spight.

in-house ('ɪnhaʊs), *a.* and *adv.* [IN *pref.*^{1}]

A. *adj.* Of or pertaining to the internal affairs of a business or institution, etc., as distinguished from its relations with groups or persons external to itself. **B.** *adv.* Internally; without outside assistance.

1956 W. A. HEFLIN *U.S.A.F. Dict.* 268/1 *In-house research*, research done within the Air Force, not by contract. **1966** *Electronics* 14 Nov. 25 Under the new arrangement it's expected that more of the work will be done in-house at the Marshall Space Flight Center. **1967** *Ibid.* 6 Mar. 8/3 Although some electronic equipment makers do produce their own integrated circuits—or at least maintain an in-house capability—most still buy on the open market. **1967** KARCH & BUBER *Offset Processes* iii. 47 The type may be set 'in-house' or obtained from a composition house. **1968** *Lebende Sprachen* XIII. 4/1 A relatively small number of stock microcircuits.. made by outside suppliers or by his own in-house facilities. **1971** *Meta* XVI. 141 The translation assignment came from a large pharmaceutical company with an in-house staff of translators. **1971** *New Scientist* 27 Apr. 251/2 More R and D should be put out to firms, thus further reducing the highly expensive 'in house' staff. **1971** E. F. SCHOETERS in B. de Ferranti *Living with Computer* viii. 67 This does not mean that the day of the in-house computer is coming to an end. **1972** *Science* 5 May 500/3 Postdoctoral fellows, who will be recruited to come to the academy as in-house resident scholars. **1973** R. W. BURCHFIELD in McDavid & Duckert *Lexicogr. in English* 100 Making full use.. of in-house photocopying apparatus.

† **in'household,** *v. Obs. rare*$^{-0}$. [IN-^{1}.] *trans.* To domesticate.

1611 FLORIO, *Infamigliarsi*, to become familiar or to in-houshould himselfe.

inhuman (ɪn'hjuːmən), *a.* (*sb.*) Forms: 5 **inhumayn,** 6–7 **inhumane, -aine,** 7– **inhuman.** [ad. L. *inhūmān-us*, f. *in-* (IN-^{3}) + *hūmānus* HUMAN. In earliest examples app. after F. *inhumain, -aine* (15th c. in Hatz.-Darm.).

The stress was originally, as in F., on the final syllable, but by the close of the 16th c. metrical evidence shows the distinction of *in'human* and *inhu'mane* in verse, though without apparent distinction of meaning. The prose pronunciation was then probably *in'human*, but the spelling *inhumane* was almost invariable till after 1700 (cf. HUMAN, HUMANE). After the spelling *inhuman* came in, the spelling and pronunciation *inhu'mane* became app. very rare. Bailey (after 1730), Johnson, and other 18th c. dictionaries which distinguish *'human* and *hu'mane* in pronunciation and sense, recognize for the negative only *in'human*, and Todd 1818 appears not to have known *inhu'mane*, for he says 'There is now no distinction observed between *inhuman* and *inhumane*: formerly it was *inhumane* with the accent on the last syllable'. Ash 1775 distinguishes '*Inhu'man*, barbarous, cruel, void of compassion', and '*Inhuma'ne*, void of tenderness, unkind (*But not much used*)'. The second entry may refer only to the 17th c. word. None of the 19th c. dictionaries, until quite recently, record *inhumane* (exc. as an obsolete form of *inhuman*). It may therefore be concluded that *inhumane* in current use has been formed afresh on *humane*, in order to provide an exact negative to the latter, and thus a word of milder meaning than *inhuman*. (In treating the two words, we place under INHUMAN all quots. bef. 1600 however spelt, all 17th c. metrical quots. which show the stress on *'hu*, and all 17th c. or later examples spelt *inhuman*.)]

1. Of persons: Not having the qualities proper or natural to a human being; *esp.* destitute of natural kindness or pity; brutal, unfeeling, cruel. Also *fig.* of things.

1481 CAXTON *Godefroy* ccvii. 303 That Inhumayn baylly, whiche was ful of cruelte and of pryde, louyd not the Cristen men. **1548** W. PATTEN *Exped. Scotl.* Pref. b v b, Ye woold neuer shew your selues inhumaine and ingrate towardes hym. **1588** SHAKS. *Tit. A.* V. ii. 178 Her spotlesse Chastity, Inhumaine Traytors, you constrain'd and for'st. **1613–16** W. BROWNE *Brit. Past.* II. i. B ij, What wretch inhumane? or what wilder blood.. Could leaue her so disconsolate? **1697** DRYDEN *Virg. Past.* VIII. 67 Love lent the Sword; the Mother struck the Blow; Inhuman she; but more inhuman thou. —— *Georg.* II. 788 E'er sounding Hammers forg'd th' inhumane Sword. **1725** POPE *Odyss.* VII. 247 We impart To you, the thoughts of no inhuman heart. **1755** *Man* ii. 4 Those who unman themselves, by debasing their nature.. we shall call by the name of inhuman. **1868** *Morn. Star* 25 Feb., The inhuman mother has been taken into custody.

b. Of actions, conduct, etc.: Brutal, savage, barbarous, cruel.

c **1489** CAXTON *Sonnes of Aymon* i. 45 To this inhumayn occysion was come themperoure Charlemayn. **1548** HALL *Chron., Hen. VIII* 90 b, His poore subjectes came with lamentacions and cryes shewyng his grace of the crueltie of the Frenchemen and of their inhumaine dealyng with them. **1613** PURCHAS *Pilgrimage* (1614) 844 Loathing this inhumane feasting with humane flesh. **1641** in Clarendon *Hist. Reb.* IV. § 105 The most Barbarous and Inhumane Cruelties. **1739** THROP *Let. to Swift* 10 Dec., S.'s Lett. 1768 IV. 233 The cruel and inhuman behaviour of that monster. **1840** THIRLWALL *Greece* VII. 301 Apollonides.. set fire to the building: the Five Hundred perished in the flames.. The conduct of Apollonides seems to us inhuman. **1884** PAE *Eustace* 57 Recall the inhuman words, and let us forget that they were uttered.

2. Not pertaining to or in accordance with what is human, in form, nature, intelligence, etc.; not of the ordinary human type.

1568 TILNEY *Disc. Mariage* A vij b, What thing is more inhumane, than for man to contemne that as profane which the eternall hath halowed? **1613** PURCHAS *Pilgrimage* (1614) 900 Of Seales and Sea-monsters, or other more unnaturall and monstrous inhumane shape. **1667** MILTON *P.L.* XI. 511 Can thus Th' Image of God in man.. To such unsightly sufferings be debas't Under inhuman pains? **1838** D. JERROLD *Men of Char., J. Applejohn* xvii, The human and inhuman wonders painted thrice the size of life. **1862** W. W. STORY *Roba di R.* vii. (1864) 131 There is a great deal of human nature in mankind, wherever you go,—except in Paris, perhaps, where Nature is rather inhuman and artificial.

† **B.** as *sb.* A brutal person. *Obs. rare.*

1653 H. COGAN tr. *Pinto's Trav.* x. 30, I had been six and thirty days thus abandoned by these Inhumanes. **1709** MRS. MANLEY *Secr. Mem.* (1736) IV. 158 If your Highness will not rank yourself on the side of those Inhumans. **1755** *Man* xvi. 5 We.. will treat all their despisers as inhumans.

inhumane (ɪnhjuː'meɪn), *a.* Also 7 **-aine.** [ad. L. *inhūmān-us*: see prec. In later use f. IN-^{3} + HUMANE: see note under INHUMAN.]

† **1.** = INHUMAN 1. *Obs.*

(Here are included 17th c. metrical examples which show the stress on *'ane*, and 18th c. prose instances with the spelling *inhumane*, after *inhuman* had become the prevalent spelling. But these latter may possibly have been pronounced *in'human*, and be only archaic retentions of the 17th c. spelling.)

1599 MARSTON *Sco. Villanie* I. ii. 176 That rude law is torne, And disannuld, as too too inhumane, That Lords ore pesants should such seruice straine. **1617** SIR W. MURE *Misc. Poems* xxi. 76 Broyls inhumaine devyding humane harts. **1710** HEARNE *Collect.* III. 30 He was so inhumane to Mrs. Bull.. whom he married that it shorten'd her days. **1726** CAVALLIER *Mem.* III. 180 The Desolation was so great, that the most inhumane Heart would be moved thereat. **1777** ROBERTSON *Hist. Amer.* I. III. 231 He rejected with indignation the idea that any race of men was born to servitude, as irreligious and inhumane.

† **2.** Uncivilized, uncultured, impolite: cf. HUMANE *a.* 2, INHUMANITY 2. *Obs.*

a **1680** BUTLER *Rem.* (1759) I. 125 There's nothing so absurd, or vain, Or barbarous, or inhumane, But if it lay the least Pretence To Piety and Godliness.. Does sacred instantly commence.

3. Not humane; destitute of compassion for misery or suffering in men or animals.

1822 E. PARKER in Dowden *Shelley* II. 487 He would become as humane as he is now inhumane. **1851** LONGF. in *Life* (1891) II. 212 He is to serve up a 'crimped cod'—a most inhumane dish.

Hence **inhu'manely** *adv.*, † (*a*) = INHUMANLY (*obs.*); (*b*) Not humanely, without compassion for suffering (but not with active cruelty).

1598 MARSTON *Pygmal.* II. 144 No Iew, no Turke, would vse a Christian So inhumanely as this Puritan. **1684** GOODMAN *Wint. Even. Conf.* III. (1720) 317 (T.) Whatsoever pretends to be a divine law, and can be made appear to be inhumanely rigorous.. is either no law of his, or at the least is not rightly interpreted.

in'humanism. [IN-^{3}.] Lack of humanism; inhumanity.

1907 W. JAMES *Pragmatism* i. 20 You find empiricism with inhumanism and irreligion. **1933** *Archit. Rev.* LXXIII. 207/2 The dogged enthusiasm of Eric Gill.. undermined the hard-headed business-man's equally dogged belief in the sacrosanct inhumanism of graphic *laissez-faire.* **1960** H. READ *Forms of Things Unknown* xi. 178 The problem is

mass-suffering, mute and absurd: in one word—inhumanism.

inhumani'tarian, *sb.* and *a.* [IN-³.] A. *sb.* One who does not accept the views and practices of humanitarianism. B. *adj.* Not accepting, or disregarding, the views and practices of humanitarianism.

1936 R. FROST *Let.* 25 July (1964) 282, I hate to be done out of it by a hard-boiled inhumanitarian. **1947** *Mind* LVI. 170 The ideals.. which had inspired the French Revolution, have been dexterously transformed into justification of absolute monarchy and inhumanitarian nationalism.

inhumanity (ɪnhjuː'mænɪtɪ). [a. F. *inhumanité* (14th c. in Hatz.-Darm.), or ad. L. *inhūmānitāt-em*, n. of quality f. *inhūmānus* INHUMAN.]

1. The quality of being inhuman or inhumane; want of human feeling and compassion; brutality, barbarous cruelty.

c **1477** CAXTON *Jason* 23, I shall kepe the ryght well.. for to falle in suche inhumanyte or furour. **1556** *Aurelio & Isab.* (1608) L v, What inhumanite suffers that I see the liffinge.. and that I lette [thee] be taken awaie to.. deathe. **1594** T. B. *La Primaud. Fr. Acad.* II. 313 Hardnesse, inhumanitie, crueltie, and all kinde of barbarousnesse. **1675** COCKER *Morals* 55 T' insult, or exult over Misery, Shews baseness mixt with inhumanity. **1785** BURNS *Man was made to mourn* vii, Man's inhumanity to Man Makes countless thousands mourn! **1838** J. MARTIN *Rem., Serm.* v. 134 Inhumanity to any animal.. is manifestly inconsistent with the great law. **1876** MISS BRADDON *J. Haggard's Dau.* I. 17 'And you would see a fellow creature perish', cried Haggard, horrified at this inhumanity.

b. With *an* and *pl.* An instance of this; an inhuman or cruel deed.

1647 WARD *Simp. Cobler* 15 What an Inhumanity it is, to deprive parents of that comfort. **1656** EARL MONM. *Advt. fr. Parnass.* 332 All the inhumanities whereinto we have most imprudently hurryed you. **1798** W. TAYLOR in *Monthly Mag.* VI. 550 Despots are not always obeyed when they command inhumanities. **1893** DK. ARGYLL *Unseen Found. Society* vii. 217 The grosser inhumanities of the past.

†**2.** Want of the politeness or courtesy proper to civilized men. (Cf. HUMANITY 3 a.) *Obs.*

1557 F. SEAGER *Sch. Vertue* 155 in *Babees Bk.* 339 Thy felowes salute In token of loue, Lest of inhumanitie they shall thee reproue. **1613** PURCHAS *Pilgrimage* (1614) 523 It were inhumanitie in us, not to acknowledge a beholdingnesse to them. **1648** *Eikon Bas.* vii. (1824) 48 The rudenesse of those who must make up their want of justice, with inhumanity, and impudence.

in'humanize, *v. rare.* [f. INHUMAN + -IZE.] *trans.* To render inhuman, to make cruel.

1871 *Standard* 5 Jan., Every day brings fresh proofs of the inhumanising effects of war.

†**in'humanlike**, *adv. Obs. rare*⁻¹. [f. INHUMAN + -LIKE.] = next.

1595 *Blanchardyn* v. B j b, The man that so inhumainlike had left him in this distresse.

inhumanly (ɪn'hjuːmənlɪ), *adv.* Forms: see INHUMAN. [f. INHUMAN + -LY².] In an inhuman manner; barbarously, cruelly.

c **1489** CAXTON *Sonnes of Aymon* i. 54 The false enterpryse of Charlemayne.. shalle this daye make me Inhumaynly for to deye. **1586** A. DAY *Eng. Secretary* II. (1625) 32 Having so ingratefully, nay rather inhumanely dealt with me. **1638** COWLEY *Love's Riddle* v. i, I asked her who had used her so inhumanely: She answered, Turkish Pyrates. **1667** MILTON *P.L.* XI. 677 What are these.. who thus deal Death Inhumanly to men? **1683** *Lond. Gaz.* No. 1878/2 That Horrid and Inhumanly-bloody-designed Villany. **1781** GIBBON *Decl. & F.* xxx. (1869) II. 156 Many thousand Christians were inhumanly massacred. **1863** *Dublin Even. Mail* 4 Dec. 4/3 To see.. the negro race inhumanly treated.

in'humanness. *rare.* Forms: see INHUMAN. [f. as prec. + -NESS.] = INHUMANITY.

1649 ROBERTS *Clavis Bibl.* 498 The inhumanenesse of those Syrian Kings. **1727** in BAILEY vol. II. **1895** *Times* 3 Jan. 4/4 With grim inhumanness.

inhumate (ɪn'hjuːmeɪt, 'ɪnhjuːmeɪt), *v. rare.* [f. L. *inhumāt-*, ppl. stem of *inhumāre* to INHUME.] *trans.* To inhume, bury (*lit.* and *fig.*).

1612 WOODALL *Surg. Mate* Wks. (1653) 25* To demonstrate, what too long silence once did inhumate. **1635** HEYWOOD *Hierarch.* IX. 570 Of bodies fifty, not inhumated. **1866** J. B. ROSE tr. *Ovid's Met.* 204 Inhumated were most—but some were cast Unnoted upon pyres. **1871** BLACKIE *Four Phases* I. 151 When he sees my body either burnt or inhumated.

inhumation (ɪnhjuː'meɪʃən). [n. of action f. L. *inhumāre* (see prec. and -ATION). Cf. F. *inhumation* (15–16th c. in Hatz.-Darm.); med.L. had prob. **inhumātio*.]

1. The action or practice of burying in the ground; the fact or condition of being buried; interment, burial of the dead (in quot. 1665 of the living).

1636 BRATHWAIT *Rom. Emp.* 379 The manner of his death and inhumation I read not of. **1658** SIR T. BROWNE *Hydriot.* i. 2 The soberest Nations have rested it two wayes, of simple inhumation and burning. **1665** MANLEY *Grotius' Low C. Warres* 18 Death, by the Sword, was threatned unto Men, and to Women Inhumation, or Burial alive. **1760** BURN *Eccl. Law* (1767) I. 233 (Jod.) The place of inhumation was without the walls. **1851** D. WILSON *Preh. Ann.* (1863) I. iii. 73 Simple inhumation, is the most ancient of all modes of disposing of the dead. **1880** DAWKINS *Early Man* x. 367 Cremation, however, did not altogether abolish the older practice of inhumation.

2. The burying of a thing under ground.

1658 SIR T. BROWNE *Gard. Cyrus* iv. 65 Most plants, though green above-ground, maintain their original white below it.. Green.. [being] separable in many upon ligature or inhumation. **1830** LYELL *Princ. Geol.* I. 353 We must conclude, that the origin of a large part of the covering of Herculaneum was long subsequent to the first inhumation of the place.

fig. **1822** *Blackw. Mag.* XI. 442 We curse it [the revival of letters], as the inhumation of European originality in works of genius for ever. **1824** JAS. MILL in *Westm. Rev.* I. 223 The opposition party had only begun to effect a resurrection from that inhumation which it suffered from the aristocratical terrors engendered by the French revolution.

†**3.** An obsolete chemical process: see quots.

1612 WOODALL *Surg. Mate* Wks. (1653) 272 *Inhumation* is the setting of two pots (the head of the uppermost being very well covered and luted, with his bottome boared full of little pin-holes, and sure fastened to that which is underneath in the ground) and burying them with earth to a certain depth, having a circular fire made for distillatory transudation *per descensum*. **1650** ASHMOLE *Chym. Collect.* 22 And therefore we distill them.. But we doe it sweetly and with inhumation, lest the excessive Fire consume the sought for subtilties.

inhume (ɪn'hjuːm), *v.* Also 8 **enhume.** [ad. L. *inhumāre* (Pliny), f. *in-* (IN-²) + *humus* ground, earth. Cf. F. *inhumer* (1413 in Hatz.-Darm.).]

1. *trans.* To inter, bury (the dead); to lay in the grave.

1616 BULLOKAR *Eng. Exp.*, *Inhume*, to bury. *a* **1626** MIDDLETON *Mayor Queenborough* IV. ii, Here's a storm Able to wake all of our name inhumed. **1715–20** POPE *Iliad* XXI. 376 No hand his bones shall gather, or inhume. **1854** H. MILLER *Sch. & Schm.* xvi. (1857) 369 Not a vestige.. of their bodies occurred in the rocks or soils in which they had been originally inhumed.

fig. **1633** P. FLETCHER *Purple Isl.* II. xxxviii, A whole camps meat he in his gorge inhum'd. **1656** S. HOLLAND *Zara* (1719) 45, I will spare these wretches, and inhume my intended Revenge. *a* **1845** HOOD *Two Swans* xviii, Sorrow.. in gross husks of brutes eternally inhumed. **1873** E. BRENNAN *Witch of Nemi* 63 While life and love are close inhumed by death.

b. *transf.* Of the earth or tomb: To cover (the dead). Also *fig.* ? *Obs.*

1621 G. SANDYS *Ovid's Met.* IV. (1626) 77 Here ghosts descend, whose bodies earth inhume. **1691** WOOD *Ath. Oxon.* I. 576 Th' obscure recesses of this key-cold Tomb, Do Stokeslies ashes, and remains inhume. **1773–83** HOOLE *Orl. Fur.* XI. 242 He op'd his greedy throat that might enhume A horse and horseman in its living tomb!

2. To bury (a thing) in the ground; to cover with soil. Now *rare.*

1621 G. SANDYS *Ovid's Met.* VII. (1626) 130 Those in the turn'd-vp furrowes he inhumes. **1764** GRAINGER *Sugar Cane* I. 256 When best to dig, and when inhume the cane. **1830** LYELL *Princ. Geol.* (1875) I. I. xiv. 316 By which the Cities were inhumed.

Hence **in'humed** *ppl. a.*, buried.

1610 G. FLETCHER *Christ's Vict.* II. lii, This their inhumed soules esteem'd their wealths. **1816** G. S. FABER *Orig. Pagan Idol.* III. 351 He.. forces, by Runic incantation, the inhumed prophetess to utterance.

inhumorous (ɪn'hjuːmərəs), *a.* [f. IN-³ + HUMOROUS *a.*] Not humorous; lacking in humour. So **in'humorously** *adv.*

1898 *Contemp. Rev.* Aug. 194 Burne Jones was sincere in his art, not fanatically or inhumourously, but quietly and subtly. **1920** *Blackw. Mag.* Aug. 138/1 Many Englishmen.. allow themselves to be convinced by hearsay that Scotsmen are inhumorously inclined. **1926** W. J. LOCKE *Old Bridge* II. vi. 78 'Life is real and life is earnest'—but so is the drivelling existence of the inhumorous ant.

inhungre, obs. form of ENHUNGER *v.*

†**in'hurled**, *pa. pple. Obs. rare*⁻¹. [IN *adv.* 11 b.] Hurled or violently driven in.

1583 STANYHURST *Æneis* I. (Arb.) 36 Would God your captayn with sootherne blastpuf inhurled Heere made his arriual.

iniac ('ɪnɪæk), *a. Anat.* [f. INI-ON + -AC. So F. *iniaque* (Littré).] = INIAL.

1886 in *Syd. Soc. Lex.*

iniad ('ɪnɪæd), *adv. Anat.* [f. INI-ON + *-ad*: see DEXTRAD.] In a direction towards the inion.

1803 J. BARCLAY *New Anat. Nomencl.* 165. **1808** WALKER in *Med. Jrnl.* XIX. 397 Movements, which are incoincident, i.e. those which take place iniad and antiniad or backward and forward.

inial ('ɪnɪəl), *a. Anat.* [f. INI-ON + -AL¹.] Of or belonging to the inion.

1808 J. BARCLAY *Muscular Motions* ix. 471 The eye is turned round, so as to describe.. a cone.. whose apex is pointed to the inial aspect. **1814** J. H. WISHART tr. *Scarpa's Hernia* p. xv, The aspect or position of those parts near the *corona* are *coronal*.. and that of those next the *inion*, *inial*.

iniamb, variant of ENJAMB *v.*, *Obs.*

inibbit, obs. form of INHIBIT *v.*

iniciall, inicion, obs. ff. INITIAL, INITION.

inidoneity (ɪnaɪdəʊ'niːɪtɪ). *rare*⁻¹. [IN-³; perh. after a med. or mod.L. **inidōneitās*.] Want of fitness; unfitness.

1894 *Ch. Times* 19 Jan. 75 Townsend was pronounced [in Oct. 1570] incapable of holding a living with cure of souls, inasmuch as he was not a 'clerk' within the meaning of the ecclesiastical, i.e. canon, law. He ought to be deprived for inidoneity, and a fresh vacancy created.

ini'doneous, *a. rare*⁻⁰. [IN-³: prob. after a med.L. **inidōneus*.] Not idoneous; unfit.

1656 in BLOUNT *Glossogr.*

†**'Inigist, Inighist.** *Obs.* [ad. obs. F. *Iniguiste*, *Inigiste*, ad. Sp. *Iñiguista*, f. *Iñigo* obs. or arch. variant of *Ignacio*, Ignatius.] A follower of Ignatius Loyola; a Jesuit.

1686 tr. *Bouhours' Ignatius* IV. 247 The People call'd them Inigists from the Name of Inigo, which in Spanish signifies Ignatius. **1741** tr. *D'Argens' Chinese Lett.* xii. 78 Andrew du Val.. who was intirely devoted to the Inighists.

inigma, obs. form of ENIGMA.

†**ini'maginable**, *a. Obs.* [ad. mod.L. *inimāginābilis* (Erasmus), f. *in-* (IN-³ + *imāginābilis* IMAGINABLE); cf. F. *inimaginable* (16th c., Montaigne).] Unimaginable.

1533 tr. *Erasmus' Com. Crede* T vij b, God is as muche innominable as he is inymaginable and inuisible. **1603** FLORIO *Montaigne* II. xii. (1632) 290 They [heavenly delights] must be thought to be inimaginable. **1698** VANBRUGH *Æsop* I. *ad fin.*, What harmony there is in the words of erudition! The musick of them is inimaginable.

†**inimi, inimy, inymy, inemye, innamy,** obs. Sc. forms of ENEMY. (App. influenced by L. *inimicus*. Still so pronounced in Ireland.)

1423 JAS. I *Kingis Q.* xxiv, Off Inymyis takin and led away We weren all. *Ibid.* clvi, The wyly fox, the wedowis Inemye. **1500–20** DUNBAR *Poems* lxxi. 11 Quhilk is grit plessour to our auld innamy. **1533** GAU *Richt Vay* 94 The deuil.. quhilk is our crwel inimi. **1563** WINȜET *Four Scoir Thre Quest.* Wks. 1888 I. 78 Grete mercy schawin to His inimeis.

†**i'nimic**, *a. Obs. rare*⁻¹. [ad. L. *inimīc-us* unfriendly.] Adverse, harmful, inimical.

1696 LOCKE *Let. to Clarke* 18 May in Fox Bourne *Life* (1876) II. xii. 307 To get off the remainder of my cough before I venture into that inimic air.

i'nimicable, *a. rare.* [f. IN-³ + AMICABLE, after L. *inimicus* enemy, INIMICAL.] = INIMICAL.

1805 E. DE ACTON *Nuns of Desert* I. 118 Self-interest, inimicable to the felicity of others. **1833** *Blackw. Mag.* XXXIV. 236 Slavery is inimicable to the procreation of children.

inimical (ɪ'nɪmɪkəl), *a.* [ad. late L. *inimīcālis* (Sidonius), f. *inimīcus* unfriendly, hostile, an enemy, f. *in-* (IN-³) + *amīcus* friend: see -AL¹.]

1. Having the disposition or temper of an enemy; unfriendly, hostile. Const. *to.*

1678 PHILLIPS (ed. 4) *List Barbarous Words*, *Inimical*, having an enmity against. **1758** RICHARDSON *Corr.* (1804) V. 189 Poor Dr. Clayton! inimical man! Persecutor to his power! **1765** T. HUTCHINSON *Hist. Mass.* I. ii. 324 A prince inimical to civil and religious liberty. **1794** GOUV. MORRIS in Sparks *Life & Writ.* (1832) II. 395 Nine-tenths of the nation are inimical to the government. **1844** LD. BROUGHAM *Brit. Const.* xi. (1862) 158 Their ravages are confined to hostile countries and inimical nations. **1847** LEWES *Hist. Philos.* (1867) I. 24 Equally inimical to democracy and tyranny. **1879** G. MACDONALD *Sir Gibbie* II. iii. 41 The few goats on the mountain were for a time very inimical to him.

2. Adverse or injurious in tendency or influence; harmful, hurtful. Const. *to.*

1643 E. UDALL *Serm.* (1645) 18 The Papists.. slander the doctrine of salvation by faith as inimicall to good works. **1683** TRYON *Way to Health* 185 [Ignorant persons] are diligent to procure such things as are inimical and hurtful to it [health]. **1783** JOHNSON *Lett. to Mrs. Thrale* 3 July, [To] fortify me against the winter, which has been, in modern phrase, of late years very inimical to, Madam, Your [etc.]. **1875** JOWETT *Plato* (ed. 2) III. 169 Practices inimical to health. **1879** D. M. WALLACE *Australas.* xi. 226 Fresh water is very inimical to coral.

Hence **i'nimically** *adv.*, in an inimical or hostile manner; **i'nimicalness** = next.

1651 CULPEPPER *Astrol. Judgem. Dis.* (1658) 26 Accidental inimicalness to Planets, is when they are in square or opposition, &c. the one to the other. Also Inimicalness must needs be in the Signs. **1836** SMART, *Inimically.* **1851** SIR F. PALGRAVE *Norm. & Eng.* I. 99 Danskermen were on their part inimically estranged from their Roman kinsmen. **1872** M. COLLINS *Pr. Clarice* II. viii. 107 Josephine received them not inimically.

inimi'cality. [f. prec. + -ITY.] Unfriendliness, enmity, hostility.

1797 J. BOUCHER *Causes Amer. Rev.* vi. 243 A charge, by which it was hoped the Author's inimicality to America might have been proved. **1887** 'T. GIFT' (Mrs. Boulger) *Victims* I. v. 116 The decided inimicality and resistance showing through all his hostess's attempts at deprecation.

†**inimi'citial**, *a. Obs. rare*⁻⁰. [f. as next + -AL¹.] = INIMICAL.

1656 in BLOUNT *Glossogr.*

†**inimi'citious**, *a. Obs.* Also 7 en-. See also ENEMICITIOUS. [f. L. *inimīcitia* unfriendliness, enmity + -OUS.] Unfriendly, hostile, adverse; = INIMICAL.

1641 J. JACKSON *True Evang. T.* I. 8 The nocent and inimicitious creatures.. first the Wolfe, secondly the Leopard. **1660** R. COKE *Power & Subj.* 100 Gynæcocraty is inimicitious to the law of Nature. **1691** E. TAYLOR *Behmen's Theos. Philos.* i. 1 They become instantly inimicitious and destructive. **1761** STERNE *Tr. Shandy* IV. xxii, To drive the gall.. from the gall-bladder.. of his Majesty's subjects, with all the inimicitious passions which belong to them.

Hence †**inimi'citiously** *adv.*, inimically.

1662 J. SPARROW tr. *Behme's Rem. Wks., 1st Apol. Balth. Tylcken* 1 Venomously, spitefully, hatefully, murtheringly and enimicitiously.

†**i'nimicous,** *a. Obs.* [f. L. *inimīc-us* unfriendly + -OUS.] = INIMICAL.

1597 [implied in INIMICOUSLY below]. **1657** W. MORICE *Coena quasi Κοινὴ* Def. ix. 93 Those that pretend to be inimicous to Episcopacy. **1674** HICKMAN *Quinquart. Hist.* (ed. 2) 58 Not only averse to God, but also inimicous unto God. **1684** tr. *Bonet's Merc. Compit.* VI. 195 A confusion raised in the Bloud and Humours by some inimicous Particles contained in their mass. **1727** S. SWITZER *Pract. Gard.* 192 It is hard to digest, and inimicous to the stomach.

Hence †**inimicously** *adv.*, in an inimicous or inimical manner. *Obs.*

1597 A. M. tr. *Guillemeau's Fr. Chirurg.* 38 b/1 They have agitated most inimicously [*mispr.* inmiciously] this disputatione, the one agaynst the other.

inimitability (ɪnˌɪmɪtəˈbɪlɪtɪ). [f. next: see -ITY. Cf. F. *inimitabilité* (Littré).] The quality of being inimitable.

a **1711** NORRIS (J.), According to the various modes of inimitability or participation. **1800** W. TAYLOR in *Monthly Mag.* X. 320 Delille will question the inimitability of Virgil, —his lyric passages.

inimitable (ɪnˈɪmɪtəb(ə)l), *a.* (*sb.*) [ad. L. *inimitābilis*, f. *in-* (IN-[3]) + *imitābilis* IMITABLE; cf. F. *inimitable* (15–16th c. in Godef. *Compl.*).]

1. Incapable of being imitated; surpassing or defying imitation; without compare; peerless.

1531 ELYOT *Gov.* I. xxiii, For the natiue and inimitable eloquence..he semeth to put all other wryters of like matters to silence. **1603** HOLLAND *Plutarch's Mor.* 922 His stile was thought to be plaine and easie, howbeit, inimitable. **1692** DRYDEN *St. Euremont's Ess.* 122 Such is the Character of Sempronia, in my Judgment inimitable. **1756** C. LUCAS *Ess. Waters* III. 333 [It is] exquisitely performed by the inimitable chemistry of nature. **1843** J. MARTINEAU *Chr. Life* (1867) 86 The inimitable beauties of the lilies of the field. **1899** SAYCE *Early Israel* v. 191 We have an inimitable portrait.

2. Not deserving of imitation; not to be imitated. *rare.*

1798 WASHINGTON *Lett.* Writ. 1893 XIV. 6 My mind..is not a little agitated by the outrageous conduct of France towards the United States, and at the inimitable conduct of its partisans, who aid and abet their measures.

B. as *sb.* An inimitable person.

1748 RICHARDSON *Clarissa* (1811) IV. 274 All matters betwixt me and my fair inimitable.

Hence **in'imitableness**, inimitability.

1660 N. INGELO *Bentivolio & Urania* I. (1682) 99 He prais'd the inimitableness of his Love, that would feed the bodies of his Subjects with his own. **1871** RUSKIN *Fors Clav.* I. ii. 18 We..need not now have been..lecturing..on the inimitableness of the works of Fra Angelico.

inimitably (ɪnˈɪmɪtəblɪ), *adv.* [f. prec. + -LY[2].] In an inimitable manner; in a way or to a degree that cannot be imitated.

1660 N. INGELO *Bentivolio & Urania* II. (1682) 117 It is so inimitably perfect. **1695** LD. PRESTON *Boeth.* I. 29 All-knowing Architect, whose powerful Hand Inimitably fram'd the starry Sky. **1746–7** HERVEY *Medit.* (1818) 113 Fine, inimitably fine, is the texture of the web. **1874** L. STEPHEN *Hours in Library* (1892) I. iii. 102 The language is inimitably clear and pointed.

in'imitative, *a. rare.* [IN-[3].] = INIMITABLE.

1836 J. H. NEWMAN *Lyra Apost.* (1849) 161 The inimitative speech, Which throned thee world's queen.

†**i'nimitie** [a. F. *inimitié*], obs. f. ENMITY.

1533 BELLENDEN *Livy* v. (1822) 414 But ony inimite or mocioun of injuris. *c* **1570** *Pride & Lowl.* (1841) 42 Though on his side were parcialitie, That proved neither of them such anone, As therefore beare to him inimitie. **1642** J. LANGTON in *Lismore Papers* Ser. II. (1888) V. 48 A man quallified with greate inimitie and courage.

inimy, var. of INIMI, *Obs.*, enemy.

†**inin'dustrious,** *a. Obs. rare*$^{-1}$. [IN-[3].] The opposite of industrious; unindustrious.

a **1631** DONNE *Serm.* lxxii. 728 This negligent and lazy man, this in-industrious man.

in infinitum: see IN *Lat. prep.*

ining: see INNING.

†**inin'vestigable,** *a. Obs. rare*$^{-1}$. [ad. eccl.L. *ininvestigābilis* (Tertull.): see IN-[3] and INVESTIGABLE.] That cannot be investigated or traced out.

1604 T. WRIGHT *Passions* v. §4. 203 O God of incomprehensible wisdome and ininuestigable prouidence.

inio- (ˈɪnɪəʊ), also before a vowel **ini-**, combining form of Gr. *ἰνίον* occipital bone, occiput, and of INION[1], used in a few medical terms, as **ˌinien'cephalus** [Gr. *ἐγκέφαλος* brain] = next; also, a monster exhibiting iniencephaly; **ˌinien'cephaly**, an abnormality in which part of the brain protrudes through an opening in the occiput and which is generally accompanied by spina bifida and retroflexion of the spine; so **ˌinience'phalic** *a.*; **ˌinio-gla'bellar** *a.*, extending from the inion to the glabella.

1893 *Trans. Edin. Obstetr. Soc.* XVIII. 227 A sagittal section of an iniencephalic female fœtus. **1958** R. A. WILLIS *Borderland Embryol. & Path.* iv. 158 (*caption*) Paramedian section of the 2-cm. iniencephalic embryo described in the text. [**1836** I. G. SAINT-HILAIRE *Hist. Gén. et Particulière des Anomalies* II. 308 (*heading*) Iniencéphale, *Iniencephalus.*] **1857** DUNGLISON *Dict. Med. Sci.* (rev. ed.) 499/2 *Iniencephalus*, a monster whose encephalon is in great part in the cranium, and in part out of it, behind, and a little beneath the cranium, which is open in its occipital portion. **1905** *Jrnl. Obstetr. & Gynaecol.* VIII. 236 (*heading*) Iniencephalus. **1925** *Surg., Gynecol. & Obstetr.* XLI. 182/2 My own specimen is a large full term female fetus, apparently perfectly developed in every way with the exception of the craniovertebral axis, which shows the characteristic features of iniencephalus. **1951** *Jrnl. Obstetr. & Gynaecol.* LVIII. 463/2 Iniencephalus is a rare condition. [**1836** I. G. SAINT-HILAIRE *Hist. Gén. et Particulière des Anomalies* II. 311 Les trois observations d'iniencéphalie que possède la science suffisent en effet pour fournir les élémens d'une caractéristique exacte.] **1902** *Encycl. Medica* XII. 139 This retroflexion of the foetus is often combined with defective development of the lower part of the occipital bone, when the name iniencephaly is sometimes given to it. **1968** H. KALTER *Teratology Cent. Nervous Syst.* vi. 165 Animals with craniorachischisis sometimes also had iniencephaly. **1803** J. BARCLAY *New Anat. Nomencl.* 146 If lines be drawn between every two of the different aspects, they will constitute the four following diameters: The Dextro-sinistral, the Corono-basilar, the Inio-glabellar, and the Inantinial. **1903** *Science* 30 Oct. 554/2 An inio-glabellar line can be drawn which will correspond very closely to the lower boundary of the cerebrum.

iniomous (ɪnɪˈəʊməs), *a. Ichth.* [f. mod.L. *Iniōmī*, f. Gr. *ἰνί-ον* (see INION) + *ὦμος* shoulder.] Of or pertaining to the *Iniomi*, an order or suborder of physostomous osteous fishes, having the scapular arch not connected with the sides of the cranium, but either impinging upon the nuchal region or else free.

1886 *Science* VII. 374 a (Cent.) The characteristics and families of iniomous fishes.

inion[1] (ˈɪnɪən). *Anat.* [a. Gr. *ἰνίον* nape of the neck.] A ridge of the occiput; *spec.* the external occipital protuberance.

[**1811** HOOPER *Med. Dict.*, *Inion*, the occiput. Blancard says it is the beginning of the spinal marrow: others say it is the back part of the neck.] **1814** [see INIAL]. **1866** HUXLEY *Preh. Rem. Caithn.* 120 The superior scale of the occiput is full, rounded, and prominent; the inion more pronounced than usual in this class of dolichocephalic skulls. **1878** BARTLEY tr. *Topinard's Anthrop.* II. ii. 234.

inion[2], dial. form of ONION.

inioyn(e, obs. form of ENJOIN *v.*

†**i'nique,** *a. Obs.* [a. OF. *inique* (14th c. in Godef.), ad. L. *iniquus* unjust, etc.: see INIQUITY.] Unjust; iniquitous.

1521 *Bradshaw's St. Werburge* 3rd Ball., Geat me suche grace to voyde all synnes inique. **1528** in Burnet *Hist. Ref.* II. 82 To do a thing inique or unjust. **1613** SHERLEY *Trav. Persia* 15 Giue peace to their inique passions. **1730** TULL *Horse-Hoing Husb.* (1733) 256 Their rash Practice, and Judgment more rash and Inique.

†**i'niquitable,** *a. Obs. rare.* [f. IN-[3] + EQUITABLE, after *iniquitous*, *iniquity*, etc.] Unjust; iniquitous. (See also INEQUITABLE.) Hence †**i'niquitably** *adv.*, unjustly.

a **1734** NORTH *Lives* (1826) I. 401 He used to exaggerate the monstrous impudence of counsel that insisted so iniquitably. *Ibid.* 421 Sensible of the prodigious injustice and iniquitable torment. *a* **1734** —— *Exam.* II. v. §31 (1740) 333 Whoever pretended to gainsay or resist an Act of Parliament, although..it may be as iniquitable as any Action of a single Person can be?

iniquitous (ɪˈnɪkwɪtəs), *a.* [f. INIQUIT-Y + -OUS: cf. *felicitous.*] Characterized by or full of iniquity; grossly unjust or unrighteous; wicked.

1726 SWIFT *Gulliver* IV. v, These..precedents, they produce as authorities..to justify the most iniquitous opinions. **1770** *Junius Lett.* xli. 215 *note*, These iniquitous prosecutions cost..six thousand pounds. **1829** SCOTT *Demonol.* vii. 202 The Parliament of Paris had declared the sentence illegal and the judges iniquitous. **1887** RUSKIN *Præterita* II. i. 27 There were many hints in the market about its being iniquitous in price.

i'niquitously, *adv.* [f. prec. + -LY[2].] In an iniquitous manner; with gross injustice; wickedly.

1796 BURKE *Let. Noble Ld.* Wks. VIII. 39 His grants were from the aggregate and consolidated funds of judgments iniquitously legal. **1796** MORSE *Amer. Geog.* II. 559 The East India Company have..very iniquitously, embroiled themselves with the country powers. **1829** LYTTON *Disowned* iv, The name you have so long iniquitously borne.

i'niquitousness. [f. as prec. + -NESS.] The quality of being iniquitous; wickedness.

1870 J. H. NEWMAN *Gram. Assent* I. iv. 74 It needed an organized agitation..to make their acknowledgment of that iniquitousness operative.

iniquity (ɪˈnɪkwɪtɪ). [a. OF. *iniquité* (Oxf. Psalter, 12th c.), ad. L. *iniquitās*, n. of quality f. *iniquus* uneven, unequal, unjust, wrong, wicked, f. *in-* (IN-[3]) + *æquus* equal, just, fair. Cf. EQUITY.]

1. The quality of being unrighteous, or (more often) unrighteous action or conduct; unrighteousness, wickedness, sin; sometimes, esp. in early use, Wrongful or injurious action towards another, infliction of wrong, injury; in mod. use generally connoting gross injustice or public wrong.

13.. *K. Alis.* 132 He thenkith to yeilde him his iniquitè. *c* **1375** *Sc. Leg. Saints, Bertholomeus* 206 Sa sal þis tempil clengit be Of al fylth and Iniquite. *c* **1386** CHAUCER *Knt.'s T.* 82 Creon..That lord is now of Thebes the Citee Fulfild of Ire and of Iniquitee. **1485** CAXTON *Chas. Gt.* 12 Agabondus replenysshed of al inyquyte put to dethe..his broder. **1526** TINDALE *Luke* xiii. 27 Departe from me all ye workers off iniquytie. **1554–9** *Songs & Ball.* (1860) 5 Hys ryghtyusnes ys owr, owr inequyte ys hys. **1596** SPENSER *F.Q.* v. i. 5 Till the world from his perfection fell Into all filth and foule iniquitie. **1651** HOBBES *Leviath.* II. xviii. 90 They that have Soveraigne power, may commit Iniquity. **1777** WATSON *Philip II* (1793) I. x. 391 The iniquity and unrelenting cruelty exercised. **1827** POLLOK *Course T.* v, Leagues, though holy termed..made to under-prop Iniquity, and crush the sacred truth.

b. *pl.* Unrighteous acts or doings, sins; wrongful acts, injuries.

1477 EARL RIVERS (Caxton) *Dictes* 1 In satisfaccoun and recompence of myn Inyquytees and fawtes before don. **1526** TINDALE *Heb.* viii. 12, I wilbe mercifull over their iniquyties. **1665** BOYLE *Occas. Refl.* II. xi. (1848) 133 That this early Death may argue the Measure of his Iniquities exceeding great. *a* **1714** SHARP *Wks.* (1754) II. Serm. i. 7 When their iniquities are at full, he will not fail to repay vengeance into their bosom. **1804** W. TENNANT *Ind. Recreat.* (ed. 2) II. 386 Removing the oppressions and iniquities of the Oude government.

†**2.** Want or violation of equity; injustice, unfairness. *Obs.* exc. as implied in 1.

1587 HARRISON *England* II. xviii. (1877) i. 301 In the measuring of ten quarters,..they lose one through the iniquitie of the bushell. **1651** HOBBES *Govt. & Soc.* iii. §29. 54 Actions may be so diversified by circumstances, and the Civill Law, that what's done with equity at one time, is guilty of iniquity at another. **1748** G. WHITE *Serm.* (MS.), This is their Due,..and therefore 'tis great Iniquity to repay them in any other sort.

3. *Sc. Law.* (See quots.)

1757 ERSKINE *Princ. Scot. Law* (ed. 2) I. ii. §20 A judge is said to commit iniquity, when he either delays justice, or pronounces sentence, in the exercise of his jurisdiction, contrary to law. **1861** W. BELL *Dict. Law Scot.*, *Iniquity*,.. a technical expression, usually applied to the decision of an inferior judge who has decided contrary to law; he is in that case said to have committed iniquity.

4. The name of a comic character or buffoon in the old morality plays, also called the VICE, representing some particular vice, or vice in general.

1594 SHAKS. *Rich. III*, III. i. 82 Thus, like the formall Vice, Iniquitie, I morallize two meanings in one word. **1616** B. JONSON *Devil an Ass* I. i, *Pug.* And lend me but a Vice, to carry with me..Fraud, Or Covetousness, or lady Vanity Or old Iniquity. *Sat.* I'll call him hither. *Enter* Iniquity.

b. As a name for the devil.

1899 *Chamb. Jrnl.* II. 10/2 The evil toon the nine maidens danced to—the very toon that was played by Old Iniquity hisself.

†**5.** Unfavourableness, unfavourable or adverse influence or operation. (A Latinism.) *Obs.*

c **1540** tr. *Pol. Verg. Eng. Hist.* (Camden) I. 31 Lest.. throwghe the iniquitie of time, forgetfullnes shoulde in that poinct prevayle. **1577** HARRISON *England* II. vi. (1877) I. 160 The skilfull workeman dooth redeeme the iniquitie of that element [water]. **1610** HOLLAND *Camden's Brit.* I. 4 The very stones..have yeelded long agoe to the iniquitie of time. *a* **1619** FOTHERBY *Atheom.* II. vii. §3 (1622) 263 They all were destroyed by the iniquitie of Fortune.

†**i'niquous,** *a. Obs.* [f. L. *iniqu-us* (see prec.) + -OUS.] Unjust, unfair; wicked, iniquitous.

1654 EMMOT *North. Blast* 2 A rabble of iniquous persons, not worthy the Saints to interveen. **1682** SIR T. BROWNE *Chr. Mor.* III. §12 Be not Stoically mistaken in the equality of sins, nor commutatively iniquous in the valuation of transgressions. **1711** SHAFTESB. *Charac.* (1737) II. I. II. §3. 32 He cannot in himself be esteem'd iniquous, or unjust. **1724** R. WELTON *Subst. Chr. Faith* 221 That iniquous power, heretofore, attainted the Lord's Anointed.

inirritability (ɪnˌɪrɪtəˈbɪlɪtɪ). [IN-[3].] The quality of not being irritable; insusceptibility to excitement.

1793 BEDDOES *Scurvy* 51 The inirritability of the muscular fibres of the heart. **1817** KITCHINER *Cook's Oracle* (1822) 124 We must increase the stimulus of our aliment as the inirritability of our system increases. **1823** DE QUINCEY *Herder* Wks. XIII. 120 That worst..of all diseases, weariness of daily life, inirritability of the nerves to the common stimulants which life supplies, seized upon him.

inirritable (ɪnˈɪrɪtəb(ə)l), *a.* [IN-[3].] Not irritable or susceptible of excitement; devoid of irritability.

1794–6 E. DARWIN *Zoon.* (1801) I. 439, I suppose when the stomach becomes inirritable, that there is at the same time a deficiency of gastric acid. **1814** SOUTHEY *Lett.* (1856) II. 345 My skin is neither hardened by labour nor inirritable by nature. **1822–34** *Good's Study Med.* (ed. 4) III. 434 In the third..variety the whole system appears to be not so much rendered inirritable to stimulants, as to be suddenly exhausted of its whole stock of nervous power.

inirritant (ɪn'ɪrɪtənt), *a.* and *sb.* [IN-³.]
a. *adj.* Not irritant; not producing irritation.
b. *sb.* An inirritant substance or drug.
1822–34 *Good's Study Med.* (ed. 4) II. 458 A nutritious but inirritant regimen was prescribed. *Ibid.* IV. 231 Inirritants and narcotics may be had recourse to with more advantage.

in'irritative, *a.* ? *Obs.* [IN-³.] Characterized by absence of irritation.
1796 A. DUNCAN *Ann. Med.* I. 214 Inirritative Fever.. Inirritative debility.

inisle, variant of ENISLE *v.*

i-niþered, ME. pa. pple. of NITHER *v.*

initial (ɪ'nɪʃəl), *a.* and *sb.* Also 6 iniciall, inytiall. [ad. L. *initiāl-is*, f. *initi-um* beginning: see -AL¹. In some early instances perh. immed. a. F. *initial, inicial* (13th c. in Godef. *Compl.*).]
A. *adj.*
1. a. Of or pertaining to a beginning; existing at, or constituting, the beginning of some action or process; existing at the outset; primary; sometimes = elementary, rudimentary.
1526 *Pilgr. Perf.* (W. de W. 1531) 73 b, The iniciall feare, that is to say, the feare of good begynners. **1534** WHITINTON *Tullyes Offices* I. (1540) 4 There is..a meane Offyce or inytiall, also a perfyte Offyce. **1665** GLANVILL *Scepsis Sci.* xiv. 95 Our initial age is..capable of any impression from the documents of our Teachers. **1665** EVELYN *Diary* (1827) IV. 138 He is past many initial difficulties. **1789** BELSHAM *Ess.* I. xii. 227 The initial paragraph of Dryden's well-known poem. **1812** PLAYFAIR *Nat. Phil.* (1819) I. 55 The square of the initial velocity. **1833** HERSCHEL *Astron.* iv. 169 The vernal equinox being the initial point of longitudes. **1880** L. STEPHEN *Pope* ii. 58 Pope would seem to have been almost in the initial stage of mental disease.
b. *Math. initial line*: the line from which the angle is reckoned in polar co-ordinates (see CO-ORDINATE B. 2); also called the *axis*.
1844 HYMERS *Int. Calc.* (ed. 3) 195 θ the angle made by ρ with the initial line.
c. *Bot.* Applied to cells from which a mass of tissue is formed by successive division.
1884 BOWER & SCOTT *De Bary's Phaner.* 40 The Initial cell is not the Mother-cell of the stoma, but divides further, once or several times in succession. *Ibid.* 108 This layer of cells, which relatively to the cork-formation may be called the *initial* layer, is the epidermis itself in certain cases of normal development of Dicotyledons. **1885** GOODALE *Phys. Bot.* (1892) 105 The cells from which these primordial layers or masses of nascent tissues arise are known as *initial cells*.
d. Math. ***initial condition***, each of a set of conditions giving the values (***initial values***) of dependent variables or their derivatives for a single set of values of the independent variables.
1834 W. HAMILTON in *Phil. Trans. R. Soc.* CXXIV. [250 No general solution has been obtained assigning (as a complete solution ought to do) $3n$ relations between the n masses.., the $3n$ varying coordinates.., the varying time t, and the $6n$ initial data of the problem, namely, the initial coordinates.., and their initial rates of increase..; the quantities called here initial being those which correspond to the arbitrary origin of time.] *Ibid.* 273 The problem of integrating these [differential] equations consists in proposing to assign, by their means, six relations between the time t, the masses m_1 m_2, the six varying coordinates.. and their initial values and initial rates of increase. **1890** A. R. FORSYTH *Theory Differential Equations* I. iii. 82 He [*sc.* Jacobi] shewed that the introduction of 'initial values' of the variables..renders it possible to take the integrals of the first subsidiary system in a form, which leads immediately to the transformation of the equation. **1902** *Ibid.* IV. i. 4 The conditions, as to the arbitrarily assigned values to be acquired at ζ by w and its derivatives, are called the initial conditions; the values are called the initial values. **1920** H. T. H. PIAGGIO *Elem. Treat. Differential Equations* iv. 53 As t usually denotes time and x and y rectangular coordinates, a condition such as $z = 0$ when $t = 0$ is called an initial condition, while one such as $z = 0$ if $x = 0$, or if $x = l$, or if $y = x$, is called a boundary condition. **1957** L. FOX *Numerical Solution Two-Point Boundary Probl.* i. 5 Boundary-value problems can always be solved in theory, and often in practice, by a combination of initial-value problems, the extra initial conditions being chosen more or less arbitrarily but finally adjusted to satisfy the prescribed boundary conditions. **1968** FOX & MAYERS *Computing Methods for Scientists & Engineers* iii. 30 We need two conditions, and here there are two main possibilities. In the first, giving the so-called initial-value problem, we are provided with two adjacent values y_s and y_{s+1} for some s, or possibly y_s and some linear combination of y_{s-1}, y_s, and y_{s+1}.. The second possibility, giving the so-called boundary-value problem, is the specification say of y_0 and y_n, the values at the two ends of some range.
2. a. Standing at the beginning of a word, paragraph, or division of a book or writing, or of the alphabet: as an *initial letter*.
In old manuscripts frequently, and in modern printing occasionally, the initial letters at the heads of paragraphs or sections are made large and more or less ornamental.
1622 S. WARD *Christ is All in All* (1627) 9 The *A* and *Ω*.. two Letters..the principall, initiall, and finall of the Alphabet. *a* **1714** BURNET *Hist. Ref.* an. 1559 (R.) At the end of every section, the initial letters of his name that had translated it, were printed, as W. E...for Will. Exon. **1762–71** H. WALPOLE *Vertue's Anecd. Paint.* (1786) II. 32 In the initial letter are the portraits of the King sitting on the throne delivering the patent to the Earl [etc.]. **1845** GRAVES *Rom. Law* in *Encycl. Metrop.* 781/1 The work has been usually cited by numbers, not by initial words. **1859** GULLICK & TIMBS *Paint.* 101 Vasari intimates that the initial or large-letter writing was a distinct occupation about 1350.

b. ***initial teaching alphabet***, a 44-letter phonetic alphabet, originally known as the 'Augmented Roman' alphabet, devised by Sir James Pitman (b. 1901) to assist the teaching of reading and writing.
1962 J. A. DOWNING *I.T.A. Reading Exper.* (1964) 14 Sir James Pitman's new Initial Teaching Alphabet..has been evolved from his grandfather's 'Phonotypy' and from the 'Nue Spelling' of the Simplified Spelling Society. **1964** *Daily Tel.* 20 Mar. 19/1 The initial teaching alphabet scheme, in use experimentally for three years to make children read more easily, is to get a Government grant.
B. *sb.* †1. a. An initial stage or element *of* something; a beginning. *Obs.*
a **1655** VINES *Lord's Supp.* (1677) 313 Unregenerate man ..having no initials of true repentance. **1669** W. SIMPSON *Hydrol. Chym.* 81 A seminal or ideal disease, inserted into the very initials of life. **1681** FLAVEL *Meth. Grace* ix. 206 Now it feels the very initials of eternal rest in itself. **1839** BAILEY *Festus* ix. (1852) 122 The initial and conclusion of the world.
†b. An elementary book on some subject of study. *Obs.*
1716 M. DAVIES *Athen. Brit.* III. *Crit. Hist.* 2 Which.. however pretended..to be the easiest and most adapted Initials, yet 'tis certain they are far surpass'd by our Oxford Grammar.
2. a. An initial letter (see A. 2); *esp.* (in *pl.*) the initial letters of a person's name and surname.
1627 USSHER *Lett.* (1686) 383 There being but 22 of them [letters]..without any difference of Initials and Finals. **1735** E. CURLL in *Pope's Lett.* I. Suppl. 24 P. T. are not, I dare say, the true Initials of your Name. **1829** LYTTON *Disowned* v, Honest Folk..don't travel with their initials only. **1858** MASSON *Milton* I. 610 It has not his full name appended to it, but only the initials 'J. M.'
b. *attrib.* Relating to, or carried on by means of, initials.
1735 E. CURLL in *Pope's Lett.* I. Suppl. 24 An Initial Correspondence betwixt E. C. and P. T., and betwixt A. P. and E. C.
c. ***initial-word***, an acronym.
1939 *Jrnl. Inst. Journalists* Jan. 19/3 For one man who says 'London County Council' a thousand say 'Ellceecee', and euphony demands..that this curious initial-word, and L.M.S. and F.J.I., should all be preceded by 'an'.
3. *Mus.* Each of the prescribed notes (usually called ***absolute initials***) on which a Plain-song melody may begin in any given mode.
1880 W. S. ROCKSTRO in Grove *Dict. Mus.* II. 3 The choice of the first note [of a Plain Chaunt Melody] is not left entirely to the Composer's discretion. He can only begin upon one of a series of sounds, selected from the Regular or Conceded Modulations of the Scale..These sounds are called Absolute Initials. Their number varies in different Modes..In the following Table, the letters enclosed in brackets denote the more unusual Initials.
4. *Bot.* An initial cell (cf. A. *adj.* 1 c).
1914 M. DRUMMOND tr. *Haberlandt's Physiol. Plant Anat.* ii. 84 A stratification of the meristem due to the vertical seriation of the initials is sometimes evident. **1938** *Nature* 10 Dec. 1042/2 Douin..has now shown that *P. asplenioides* develops axillary branch initials, the upper developing into normal branches. **1955** *Jrnl. Ecol.* XLIII. 51 Two small.. trees, bearing catkin initials, were transplanted. **1970** RAVEN & CURTIS *Biol. Plants* ii. 129/2 These initials, or growth-initiating cells, appear to surround a group of cells in which no cell division takes place.

initial (ɪ'nɪʃəl), *v.* [f. prec. B. 2.] *trans.* To mark or sign with initials; to put one's initials to or upon. Hence **i'nitialed (-alled)** *ppl. a.*, **i'nitialing (-alling)** *vbl. sb.* and *ppl. a.*
1864 in WEBSTER. **1865** *Daily Tel.* 16 Nov. 7/6 They were initialled by the magistrate. **1866** *Pall Mall G.* 1 Dec. 7 A clerk..initialed it as evidence that the work had been brought home. **1883** HALL CAINE *Cobw. Crit.* iii. 65 An initialed note to an article in the *Edinburgh*. **1884** *Pall Mall G.* 4 Oct. 4/1 The desirability of adopting the initialling system. **1884** SIR E. E. KAY in *Law Times Rep.* LI. 315/1 The deletion was initialed in the margin with the initials of the persons who signed the agreement.

initialese (ɪnɪʃə'liːz). [f. INITIAL *sb.* 2 + -ESE.] Abbreviation by using the initial letters of the words to be shortened.
1955 *Amer. Speech* XXX. 110 In a dinner speech to the National Institute of Social Sciences given in New York in November, 1952..Mr Lovett frankly advocated the convenience of what he called *initialese*, a system of using initials and contractions, in order to save time. **1961** *Engineering* 17 Nov. 654 ASLE is initialese for American Society of Lubrication Engineers. **1962** *Guardian* 31 Jan. 8/2, 2,000-odd abbreviations listed in 'International Initialese'.

initialism (ɪn'ɪʃəlɪzm). [f. INITIAL *sb.* + -ISM.] The use of initials; a significative group of initial letters. Now *spec.* a group of initial letters used as an abbreviation for a name or expression, each letter or part being pronounced separately (contrasted with ACRONYM).
1899 R. THOMAS in *N. & Q.* 9th Ser. III. 103/1 In my 'Handbook' I give an initialism of Mr. Watts's, 'P. P. C. R.' **1928** [see *pseudandry* s.v. PSEUDO- 2 a]. **1965** (*title*) Acronyms and initialisms dictionary (Gale Research Company). **1975** *Globe & Mail* (Toronto) 22 May 10/4 Americanization has also largely done away with periods in acronyms and initialisms. **1979** *Amer. Speech* 1976 LI. 77 KSSU (an initialism of initialisms: KLM (Royal Dutch Airlines), SAS (Scandinavian Airlines System), Swissair, and UTA (Union de Transports Aeriens)). **1981** *Maledicta* V. 95 The acronym..and its cousin, the initialism..are perhaps the newest devices for forming nicknames for ethnic groups.

1984 *Word Ways* XVII. 1. 48 The work consulted by Wolpow distinguishes abbreviations and initialisms.

initialization (ɪnɪʃəlaɪ'zeɪʃən). *Computers.* [f. next + -ATION.] The action or process of initializing; the computer operations involved in this.
1957 D. D. MCCRACKEN *Digital Computer Programming* xiii. 166 The programmer sitting at his desk with no more information than the trace may wish to know what happened in an early section of the program which set up the initialization. **1961** LEEDS & WEINBERG *Computer Programming Fund.* iii. 75 By initialization we mean the program steps which prepare the program to carry out its function. In this instance the initialization would probably correspond to rewinding a magnetic tape to its starting point. **1969** G. B. DAVIS *Computer Data Processing* xii. 271 The general steps for programming a loop are the following: 1. Initialization. 2. Execution. 3. Modification. 4. Test for termination.

initialize (ɪ'nɪʃəlaɪz), *v.* [f. INITIAL *sb.* + -IZE.]
1. *rare.* a. *intr.* To use an initial or initials instead of the full name. b. *trans.* To designate by an initial or initials.
1833 T. HOOK *Widow & Marquess* i, 'Mrs. F.' said Mr. Smith,—it was a way he had of initialising. **1837** *New Monthly Mag.* L. 78 Nobody had successfully initialized, until L. E. L. arose. **1864** *Daily Tel.* 28 June, Messrs. B——, R——, and J—— (I will only initialise them) are already off on their yearly tour.
2. *trans.* (*Computers.*) To set to the value, or put in the condition, appropriate to the start of an operation. Const. *to*.
1957 D. D. MCCRACKEN *Digital Computer Programming* xi. 146 [Instructions] 18 and 19 initialize the address of the instruction with which numbers are brought in from temporary storage. **1961** N. CHAPIN *Programming Computers for Business Applic.* vii. 188 The failure..to initialize the switch would produce errors. **1963** P. M. SHERMAN *Programming & Coding Digital Computers* vii. 124 Another data instruction..is used to 'initialize' the ADD instruction to its initial value. **1972** *Computer Jrnl.* XV. 205/2 To trace from a base point *P*, the trace routine initialises *A* to the address of and *M* to the mode of the object pointed to by *P* and executes the following code.
So **i'nitialist** (*nonce-wd.*), one who signs his initials instead of his full name; **i'nitialized** *ppl. a.*, **i'nitializing** *vbl. sb.* and *ppl. a.*
1823 *Blackw. Mag.* XIV. 438 The blazon-loving herd of dowagers, and the more modest herd of initialists are acquitted with equal ease. **1957** D. D. MCCRACKEN *Digital Computer Programming* vi. 75 The preliminary steps which set up the loop and are not repeated constitute the initializing section of the loop. **1968** P. WEGNER *Programming Lang.* iv. 234 ALGOL contains a small subset of ..initialized identifiers. **1969** MAISEL & WRIGHT *Introd. Electronic Digital Computers* v. 74 Initializing procedures may also provide for such things as changes in the withholding tax rates or the Social Security laws. **1971** K. R. BRITTING *Inertial Navigation Syst. Analysis* i. 1 An appropriately initialized inertial navigation system is capable of continuous determination of vehicle position and velocity without use of external radiation or optical information.

initially (ɪ'nɪʃəlɪ), *adv.* [f. INITIAL *a.* + -LY².] In relation to, or in the way of, a beginning; at the beginning, at the outset, at first.
a **1628** PRESTON *New Covt.* (1634) 361 That upon which all the promises hang initially, is nothing but beleeving. **1674** OWEN *Holy Spirit* (1693) 61 The Minds of Believers are transformed initially into the Image of God. **1847** LEWES *Hist. Philos.* (1857) Introd. 25 We shall find the difference to lie initially [etc.]. **1869** R. A. PROCTOR in *Eng. Mech.* 31 Dec. 372/2 A globe supposed initially at rest.

†**i'nitiament.** *Obs. rare*⁻⁰. [ad. L. *initiāmenta* pl. initiation: cf. It. *initiamenti* 'the first instructions in any kinde of religion, science, or knowledge' (Florio, 1598).] (See quots.)
1727 BAILEY vol. II, *Initiaments*, the first instructions in any kind of Knowledge, Science, etc. **1775** ASH, *Initiament*, a first principle in any art or science.

initiand (ɪ'nɪʃɪænd). [ad. L. *initiandus*, gerundive of *initiāre* INITIATE *v.*: see -AND².] One who is about to be initiated (in quot. 1969, one who initiates).
1915 *Edin. Rev.* Jan. 127 The initiands are taken away from human society, often to a mountain, sometimes to a forest. **1931** K. E. KIRK *Vision of God* 473 A prayer of the initiand follows, in which he addresses the gods. **1969** R. MANHEIM tr. *Corbin's Creative Imagination in Ṣūfism* Introd. 60 To have him as a master and initiand is to be obliged to *be* what he himself *is*.

initiant (ɪ'nɪʃɪənt), *a.* and *sb. rare.* Also 8 *erron.* -ent. [ad. L. *initiānt-em*, pr. pple. of *initiāre* to begin, INITIATE.]
A. *adj.* Beginning, incipient.
1737 BRACKEN *Farriery Impr.* (1757) II. 46 Curing an initient Bone Spavin. *Ibid.* 257 The initient or beginning Cataract.
B. *sb.* An instrument of initiation.
1871 R. ELLIS *Catullus* lxiii. 9 Taborine, the trump that hails thee, Cybele, thy initiant.

initiary (ɪ'nɪʃɪərɪ), *a. rare.* [f. L. *initi-um* beginning + -ARY.] Of or pertaining to a beginning; initial; introductory.
1822–34 *Good's Study Med.* (ed. 4) III. 298 This disease did not proceed beyond these initiary steps. **1885** *Bookseller* 5 Mar. 240/1 The 'Prologes' to each book, and the initiary one, 'W. T. to the Reader', are all duly inserted.

initiate (ɪ'nɪʃɪeɪt), *v.* [f. L. *initiāt-*, ppl. stem of *initiāre* to begin, initiate, f. *initi-um* beginning. Cf. F. *initier* (14th c. in Godef. *Compl.*).]

1. a. *trans.* To begin, commence, enter upon; to introduce, set going, give rise to, originate, 'start' (a course of action, practice, etc.).

1604 R. CAWDREY *Table Alph.*, *Initiate*, to begin, instruct, or enter into. **1611** SPEED *Hist. Gt. Brit.* x. i. §44. 1231 They feared (for the present) to initiate their attempt. *a* **1674** CLARENDON *Life* (1759) III. 554 Many secret Designs only initiated then and not executed till long after. **1855** H. SPENCER *Princ. Psychol.* (1872) I. II. ii. 177 Feelings initiated within the body, including appetites, pains [etc.]. **1872** YEATS *Growth Comm.* 326 This king.. initiated a trade with S. America. **1883** LELY *Wharton's Law-Lex.* (ed. 7) 224 The husband's title to the curtesy is initiated at the birth of issue, and consummated at the death of his wife.

b. *intr.* To take its beginning, commence.

a **1618** SYLVESTER *Mem. Mortality* i, The Grave.. Where, end our Woes; our Joyes initiate. *a* **1681** WHARTON *Festiv. & Fasts* Wks. (1683) 2 The Neomeniæ, or Feasts of New-Moons, Celebrated the First day of every Month, initiating with the New-Moons. **1842** GROVE *Corr. Phys. Forces* 73 While magnetism is thus progressive, some other force is acting, and therefore it does not initiate. **1963** S. TOLANSKY *Introd. Atomic Physics* (ed. 5) xxv. 423 If pure deuterium gas can be raised to a temperature of the order of 500 million degrees C., then a thermonuclear reaction should initiate. **1971** *Nature* 8 Jan. 111/2 Neutrons with incident wave vectors initiating within the cross-hatched area of the example shown satisfy the conditions for diffraction.

2. *trans.* To admit (a person) with proper introductory rites or forms into some society or office, or to knowledge of or participation in some principles or observances, esp. of a secret or occult character; hence more generally, To introduce into acquaintance with something, to instruct in the elements of any subject or practice. Const. *into*, *in* (†*to*).

1603 HOLLAND *Plutarch's Mor.* 1288 Those who are initiated and professed in this divine religion. *a* **1617** BAYNE *On Coloss.* i. and ii. 168 To initiate and to enter men into Christ. *a* **1635** NAUNTON *Fragm. Reg.* (Arb.) 40 My Lord of Essex.. though initiated to Armes, and honoured by the General in the Portugal expedition.. loved him not in sincerity. **1683** DRYDEN *Plutarch* 41 Our author in his old age.. initiated himself in the sacred rites of Delphos. **1704** HEARNE *Duct. Hist.* (1714) I. Pref. 3 In Initiating young Students, nothing is more to be respected than Method. **1759** JOHNSON *Rasselas* viii, At length my father resolved to initiate me in commerce. **1853** LYTTON *My Novel* VIII. xiii, The.. father.. had him frequently at his house—initiated him betimes into his own high-born society. **1875** JOWETT *Plato* (ed. 2) I. 184 He is being initiated into the mysteries of the sophistical ritual. **1878** HUXLEY *Physiogr.* Pref., To initiate young people in the elements of Physical Science.

3. *intr.* **a.** To perform the first rite; to take the initiative. **b.** To undergo or receive initiation.

1725 POPE *Odyss.* III. 564 The king himself initiates to the power; Scatters with quivering hand the sacred flour, And the stream sprinkles. **1896** *Daily News* 16 June 6/3 Initiation into the 'Mysteries' was certainly a source of consolation to many of the greatest spirits of the ancient world. Cicero, who had initiated, said that they enabled man 'to live happily and die with a fairer hope'.

Hence **i'nitiating** *vbl. sb.* = INITIATION (in quot. *attrib.*)

1750 WARBURTON *Julian* Wks. 1811 VIII. 59 *note*, He descended into the initiating cave.

initiate (ɪ'nɪʃɪət), *ppl. a.* and *sb.* [ad. L. *initiāt-us*, pa. pple. of *initiāre* to INITIATE; also treated as pa. pple. of the latter (? as short for *initiated*).]

A. *ppl. a.* = INITIATED.

1. Admitted into some society, office, or position; instructed in some secret knowledge: see INITIATE *v.* 2.

a **1610** HEALEY *Theophrastus* (1636) To Rdr., The Athenians were.. initiate or matriculated into these orders. **1621** BURTON *Anat. Mel.* I. ii. III. xv. (1651) 135 We.. that are initiate Divines. **1742** YOUNG *Nt. Th.* VI. 95 Initiate in the secrets of the skies! **1791** E. DARWIN *Bot. Gard.* I. 89 With pointing finger guides the initiate youth. **1825** COLERIDGE *Aids Refl.* (1848) I. 204 The symbolic meaning was left to be decyphered as before, and sacred to the initiate.

†**b.** *transf.* Pertaining to one newly initiated; of or belonging to a novice or unpractised person.

1605 SHAKS. *Macb.* III. iv. 143 My strange and self-abuse Is the initiate feare, that wants hard vse.

2. Begun, commenced, introduced: see INITIATE *v.* 1. ***tenant by the Curtesy initiate***: see quot. 1767, and cf. INITIATE *v.* 1 (quot. 1883).

1767 BLACKSTONE *Comm.* II. viii. 127 As soon.. as any child was born, the father began to have a permanent interest in the lands,.. and was called tenant by the curtesy initiate. **1855** MILMAN *Lat. Chr.* III. vii. I. 467 This worship [of the Virgin] already more than initiate, contributed.. to the violence with which the Nestorian controversy was agitated.

B. *sb.*

1. A person who has been initiated: see INITIATE *v.* 2. Hence, A beginner, a novice.

1811 COLERIDGE *Ess. Own Times* (1850) 931 The merest initiate in reasoning will reply. **1833** *Fraser's Mag.* VIII. 204 When they see a respectable initiate losing his money. **1839** *Ibid.* XIX. 453 These alchemical initiates still hold themselves singularly high. **1873** HALE *In His Name* viii. 73 The significance of which among the initiates he well knew. **1893** *Nation* (N.Y.) 12 Jan. 32/3 Sulla, Antony, Cicero and his friend Atticus were initiates.

†**2.** ? Something initiated or newly introduced: see INITIATE *v.* 1. *Obs.*

1603 HARSNET *Pop. Impost.* 106 Having many new initiats to advaunce that stood you in more stead.

initiated (ɪ'nɪʃɪeɪtɪd), *ppl. a.* [f. prec. vb. + -ED[1].] **1.** Commenced, originated.

1611 COTGR., *Initie*, initiated, entered into, begun in. **1619** SIR S. D'EWES in *Coll. Life Time Jas. I* (1851) 77, I augmented well the initiated poem. **1865** *Pall Mall G.* 12 Oct. 1 There is no danger of an initiated attack on the part of Austria.

2. That has been admitted into some society, or to the knowledge of some occult teaching or observances; instructed in the elements of something. (Often *absol.* in *pl.* sense; rarely as sb. sing.)

1656 [see INITIATIVE *a.* 2]. **1662** STILLINGFL. *Orig. Sacr.* II. vii. §12 All that were.. fully initiated, might fully understand them. **1673** *True Worsh. God* 55 To be held by all newly Initiated Christians. **1751** BP. LAVINGTON *Enthus. Methodists* (1754) II. 276 There shall not be an Initiator, nor an Initiated, of the Sons or Daughters of Israel. *a* **1831** A. KNOX *Rem.* (1844) I. 60 Certain to be understood only by the initiated. **1897** MARY KINGSLEY *W. Africa* 531 Removal from home and instruction from initiated members.

initiating (ɪ'nɪʃɪeɪtɪŋ), *ppl. a.* [f. as prec. + -ING[2].] That initiates: see the verb.

1651 BAXTER *Inf. Bapt.* 177 To initiate them by Christ's initiating sign. **1751** BP. LAVINGTON *Enthus. Methodists* (1754) II. 276 After parting with their money to the initiating Priests. **1842** GROVE *Corr. Phys. Forces* 52 To commence, then, with electricity as an initiating force.

initiation (ɪnɪʃɪ'eɪʃən). [ad. L. *initiātiōn-em*, n. of action f. *initiāre* to INITIATE. Cf. F. *initiation* (15th c. in Godef. *Compl.*).] The action of initiating, or fact of being initiated.

1. The action of beginning, entering upon, or 'starting' something; the fact of being begun; beginning, commencement, origination.

1641 BRIGHTMAN *Predict.* 3 The Church of Germanie had its initiation or beginning in Martin Luther.. in.. 1517. **1654** H. L'ESTRANGE *Chas. I* (1655) 132 The Parliament.. had granted but one Subsidy since the initiation of King James his reign. **1842** GROVE *Corr. Phys. Forces* 73 We must ever refer them back to some antecedent force.. and therefore the word initiation cannot in strictness apply. **1859** MILL *Liberty* iii. (1865) 39 The initiation of all wise or noble things, comes and must come from individuals; generally at first from some one individual. **1863** H. COX *Instit.* I. vi. 43 Concerned in the initiation of Parliamentary measures.

2. a. Formal introduction by preliminary instruction or initial ceremony into some position, office, or society, or to knowledge of or participation in some principles or observances; hence generally, Admission to the knowledge, or instruction in the elements, of any subject or practice.

1583 STUBBES *Anat. Abus.* II. (1882) 81 At the time of their initiation, institution, induction and admission [into a benefice]. **1610** BP. HALL *Apol. Brownists* §6 In the first of these is required indeede a solemne initiation by baptisme. **1659** *Order in Commons, Bernard Inn* in *N. & Q.* 7th Ser. II. 302/1 Some young Gentlemen of this House have lately had disorderly Meetings which they call 'Initiations'. **1780** JOHNSON *Lett. to Mrs. Thrale* 25 May, Bath is a good place for the initiation of a young lady. **1876** MOZLEY *Univ. Serm.* xvi. (1877) 268 A large school is a most valuable initiation into actual life.

b. *attrib.*, as ***initiation ceremony, fee, process, rite.***

1899 SPENCER & GILLEN *Native Tribes Cent. Austral.* vii. 212 All Australian natives, with rare exceptions, have to pass through some initiation ceremony before being admitted to the secrets of the tribe. **1935** B. MALINOWSKI *Coral Gardens* II. VI. 234 The instruction may take place in the course of initiation ceremonies. **1951** R. FIRTH *Elem. Social Organiz.* ii. 47 Economic, ritual, and recreational affairs.. are often difficult to disentangle within a complex institutional sequence of events, such as an initiation ceremony. **1890** GROSS *Gild Merch.* I. 29 To become a gildsman.. it was necessary to pay certain initiation-fees. **1897** MARY KINGSLEY *W. Africa* 531 They always take a new name, and are supposed by the initiation process to become new beings in the magic wood. **1916** H. B. ALEXANDER *N. Amer. Mythol.* xi. 243 A myth which seems clearly reminiscent of initiation rites. **1937** R. H. LOWIE *Hist. Ethnol. Theory* (1938) xi. 180 Boys' initiation rites probably involve circumcision. **1974** 'S. WOODS' *Done to Death* 186 Tribal initiation rites in one of the Indian reservations in the United States.

initiative (ɪ'nɪʃɪətɪv), *sb.* [a. F. *initiative* (1567 in Hatz.-Darm.), f. as INITIATIVE *a.*]

1. That which initiates, begins, or originates; the first step in some process or enterprise; hence the act, or action, of initiating or taking the first step or lead; beginning, commencement, origination.

on one's own initiative, by one's own origination.

1793 W. GODWIN *Enq. Pol. Justice* IV. viii. 351 A sensation of pain was the initiative, and put my intellectual powers into action. **1809–10** COLERIDGE *Friend* (1837) III. 118 From the absence of the leading thought, which, borrowing a phrase from the nomenclature of legislation, I may not inaptly call the *initiative*. **1818** —— *Method* in *Encycl. Metrop.* (1847) 7 There are many marked differences between Mathematical and Physical studies; but in both a previous act and conception of the Mind, or what we have called an *initiative*, is indispensably necessary, even to the mere semblance of Method. **1858** J. H. NEWMAN *Hist. Sk.* (1873) III. III. iv. 324 Theodoret's visits to Antioch.. were not made on his own initiative. **1882** FARRAR *Early Chr.* II. 505 Men who had followed the noble initiative of St. Paul, and who refused to receive anything from the Gentiles to whom they preached.

b. ***to take the initiative*** (F. *prendre l'initiative*, 1567 in Hatz.-Darm.): to take the lead, make the first step, originate some action.

1856 EMERSON *Eng. Traits, Manners* Wks. (Bohn) II. 46 He has stamina; he can take the initiative in emergencies. **1858** BUCKLE *Civiliz.* (1873) II. viii. 570 No reform can produce real good, unless it is the work of public opinion, and unless the people themselves take the initiative.

2. The power, right, or function of initiating or originating something. Hence to ***possess*** or ***have the initiative.***

1793 W. GODWIN *Enq. Pol. Justice* I. vii. 53 Sensation is of some moment in the affair. It possesses the initiative. *Ibid.* v. xx. 544 The legislative assembly, whether it possesses the initiative, or a power of control only, in executive affairs. **1802** *Morn. Chron.* in *Spirit Pub. Jrnls.* (1803) VI. 302 If.. Mr. Henry Addington is to have the initiative in the Docks. **1842** BRANDE *Dict. Sci.*, etc. s.v., That branch of the legislature to which belongs of right the power to propose measures of a particular class is said to have the initiative with respect to those measures. **1844** LEVER *T. Burke* (1857) II. 113 The initiative lay with you.

b. *spec.*, *Pol. Sci.* The right of a citizen or defined number of citizens, outside the Legislature, to originate legislation, as has been established in some of the Swiss Cantons since 1869–70, and in Switzerland as a Federal Republic since 1874.

1889 ADAMS & CUNNINGHAM *Swiss Confed.* vi. 80 Both Referendum and Initiative are institutions which have grown up gradually in the Cantons, spreading from one to another. **1891** *Speaker* 11 July 36/1 The Initiative, or right of a body of citizens outside the Legislature to initiate proposals for the abolition, alteration, or enactment of laws. **1898** *Hazell's Annual* 643 (Switzerland) The principles of the Referendum and of the Initiative are in force. The latter signifies the right of any 50,000 citizens to demand a direct popular vote on any constitutional question.

initiative (ɪ'nɪʃɪətɪv), *a.* [f. L. *initiāt-*, ppl. stem of *initiāre* to INITIATE + -IVE.]

1. Characterized by initiating; having the function, power, or faculty of beginning or originating something; of or relating to initiation, initiatory.

1642 [implied in INITIATIVELY]. **1795** HEL. M. WILLIAMS *Lett. France* I. i. (Jod.), The initiative term of captivity and death. **1808** BENTHAM *Sc. Reform* 108 Authority, inquisitorial and initiative. **1849** MITCHELL *Battle Summer* (1852) 118 It was initiative, as its makers hoped, to a higher progress. **1874** SYMONDS *Sk. Italy & Greece* (1898) I. i. 5 At the time of Rousseau's greatness the French people were initiative.

†**2.** = INITIATED 2. *Obs.* (Perh. an error.)

1656 BLOUNT *Glossogr.*, *Initiative, Initiated* (*initiatus*), which hath ended his Apprentiship, or is a young beginner in the first Principles; licensed or admitted to.

i'nitiatively, *adv.* [f. prec. adj. + -LY[2].] In the way of initiation or origination.

1642 T. LECHFORD *Plain Dealing* (1867) 5 Some may say, that this power of ruling is but ministerially in the officers, and initiatively, conclusively, and virtually in the people. **1832** in *Mem. Bp. Blomfield* (1863) I. viii. 207 Parliament would probably be jealous of any distinct body legislating, even only initiatively, in Church matters.

initiator (ɪ'nɪʃɪeɪtə(r)). [a. late L. *initiātor* (Tertull.), agent-n. f. *initiāre* to INITIATE.]

a. One who or that which initiates.

1676 COLES, *Initiator*, which doth initiate. **1738** WARBURTON *Div. Legat.* II. iv. Wks. 1811 II. 68 The interpreters of these holy Mysteries, the Hierophants and Initiators. **1822** T. TAYLOR *Apuleius* 276 Initiators into the mysteries. **1847** LEWES *Hist. Philos.* (1853) 125 Regarded as the initiator of a new epoch. **1943** [see ARTICULATOR 4]. **1971** I. F. HANCOCK in J. Spencer *Eng. Lang. W. Afr.* 117 The process of creolising in the direction of a language other than the initiator language of the pidgin form has been rather misleadingly called *relexification*.

b. An explosive or device used to detonate the main charge.

1915 A. MARSHALL *Explosives* xxix. 417 Of all these explosives silver azide, mercury fulminate, and the aldehyde are the only ones that have a sufficiently high acceleration to be of any use as initiators of detonation. **1944** *Compt. Rend. (Doklady) de l'Acad. des Sci. de l'URSS* XLIV. 18 One might naturally expect that the flash-point.. would be lower for the initiators than for secondary explosives. **1962** *Ordnance Technical Terminol.* (U.S. Army Ordnance School) (AD 660112) 164/1 *Initiator*, a device used as the first element of an explosive train, such as a detonator or squib... It generally contains a small quantity of a sensitive explosive. **1964** M. GOWING *Britain & Atomic Energy* ix. 264 His criticism enlivened discussions on bomb assembly, and he participated very actively in the design of the initiator.

c. *Chem.* Any substance which starts a polymerization reaction.

1940 in *Chambers's Techn. Dict.* **1951** FRITH & TUCKETT *Linear Polymers* ii. 50 In any large-scale production of a polymer, catalytic initiation is nearly always used... The word 'catalyst' in this connection is rather a misnomer, as it is almost always destroyed in starting off polymerisation; 'initiator' is less open to objection, but has never really established itself. **1959** CRAM & HAMMOND *Org. Chem.* xxv. 573 There are three principal classes of free-radical initiators: 1. Compounds.. which undergo thermal decomposition... 2. Photosensitizers... 3. Redox systems. **1972** BILLINGHAM & JENKINS in A. D. Jenkins *Polymer Sci.*

I. i. 19 Azo-bis-isobutyronitrile is very frequently used as an initiator for research studies on radical polymerization.

initiatory (ɪ'nɪʃɪətərɪ), *a.* (*sb.*) [f. *initiāt-*, ppl. stem of L. *initiāre* to INITIATE + -ORY.]

1. Such as pertains to or constitutes the beginning or first steps; initial, introductory, opening, first.

1612-15 Bp. HALL *Contempl. O.T.* x. iii, It hath been euer the fashion of God, to exercise his champions with some initiatory incounters. **1710** STEELE *Tatler* No. 234 ¶5, I found.. the principal Defect of our English Discipline to lie in the Initiatory Part. **1823** *Blackw. Mag.* XIV. 545 Prepared for that result by the initiatory sentence. **1875** STUBBS *Const. Hist.* I. iii. 51 The initiatory stage of legal proceedings may well have been gone through.

2. Pertaining or tending to initiation; serving to initiate into some society, or some special knowledge or study: see INITIATE *v.* 2, INITIATION 2.

1632 G. HERBERT *Country Parson* xxiii, He hath gotten to himself some insight in things ordinarily incident and controverted.. By reading some initiatory Treatises in the Law. **1734** A. YOUNG *Idol. Corrupt. Relig.* I. 46 (T.) It being the initiatory rite of their religion. **1740** WARBURTON *Div. Legat.* VI. i. Wks. 1811 V. 291 Which he did by the initiatory Rite of water-baptism. **1833** J. H. NEWMAN *Arians* I. iii. (1875) 53 The Manichees represented the initiatory discipline as founded on a fiction or hypothesis. **1897** MARY KINGSLEY *W. Africa* 532 The girls go into the wood or initiatory hut for a few months before marriage.

B. *sb.* Something that serves to initiate; an initiatory rite.

1675 L. ADDISON *State of Jews* 65 Baptism is a constant initiatory of the Proselyte.

Hence **i'nitiatorily** *adv.*, in an initiatory manner.

1652 SPARKE *Prim. Devot.* (1663) 148 And so sufficiently initiatorily to make good that of the Psalmist, Kings shall bring gifts.

initiatress (ɪ'nɪʃɪeɪtrɪs). [f. INITIATOR + -ESS.] A female initiator.

1861 M. ARNOLD *Pop. Educ. France* Introd. 23 France.. believes the other peoples of Europe to be preparing themselves.. for a like achievement, and.. she is conscious of her power and influence upon them as an initiatress and example.

initiatrix (ɪnɪʃɪ'eɪtrɪks). [a. late L. *initiātrix*, fem. agent-n. f. *initiāre* to INITIATE. Cf. mod.F. *initiatrice*.] = prec.

1850 MAZZINI *Royalty & Repub.* 171, I.. have sacrificed all the joys of life.. to the worship of this one idea of Italy the Initiatrix, of my country, one and free. **1864** *Spectator* 31 Dec. 1510 Italy.. has shrunk from assuming that office of initiatrix of a new order which Mazzini holds it was her duty to fill, and has turned aside to material prosperity.

inition (ɪ'nɪʃən), *rare.* Also 5 -cion. [a. OF. *inition*, *inicion* (Godef.), ad. L. type **initiōn-em*, n. of action f. *inīre* to enter.] Entrance, beginning, initiation.

1463 G. ASHBY *Poems* (E.E.T.S.) 38/817 Vicious men yeve no gladly inicion To gracious werke, ne goode direccion. *a* **1635** NAUNTON *Fragm. Reg.* (Arb.) 53 The inition of my Lords friendship with Mountjoy.

Hence **i'nitionary** *a.*, pertaining to inition or entrance (into a college, etc.).

1865 TROLLOPE *Miss Mackenzie* I. iv. 71 He hesitated, fearing whether he might be able to pass even the initionary gates of Islington.

in-it'selfness. [f. phr. *in itself* (IN *prep.* 23) + -NESS.] The quality or state of being independent of any relation to other entities.

1906 S. S. LAURIE *Synthetica* I. ix. 136 Mere sentience admits of the in-itselfness (which is the for-itselfness) of the object being revealed. **1917** A. S. PRINGLE-PATTISON *Idea of God* xx. 399 It was the aloofness—the in-itselfness, as we might call it—of his [*sc.* Mr. Bradley's] Absolute, which made the stronger impression on contemporary thought.

iniune, iniunge, obs. var. ENJOIN *v.*

iniure, etc.: see INJURE, etc.

injail, injealous: see ENJAIL, ENJEALOUS.

inject (ɪn'dʒɛkt), *v.* [f. L. *inject-*, ppl. stem of *injicĕre* to throw in or on, f. *in-* (IN-²) + *jacĕre* to throw. Cf. F. *injecter* (18th c.).]

1. *trans.* To throw in. †**a.** In general sense. *Obs. rare.*

1611 FLORIO, *Ingettare*, to iniect or cast in. **1623** COCKERAM II, To Cast in, *Inject*. **1646** SIR T. BROWNE *Pseud. Ep.* II. i. 51 As may be observed in Ice injected therein.

b. *spec.* To drive or force (a fluid, etc.) into a passage or cavity, as by means of a syringe, or by some impulsive power; said esp. of the introduction of medicines or other preparations into the cavities or tissues of the body: cf. INJECTION 1 b.

1601 HOLLAND *Pliny* XXVI. xv. 267 It is of great force either applied outwardly or injected inwardly. **1641** WILKINS *Math. Magick* II. i. (1648) 153 The winde-gun, which is charged by the forcible compression of air, being injected through a Syringe. **1684-5** BOYLE *Min. Waters* 109 To guess at the Qualities of the Mineral Waters, as by injecting it into the veins of a Dog, to try whether it will coagulate his Blood, or make it more fluid. **1758** J. S. *Le Dran's Observ. Surg.* (1771) 27, I.. injected Barley Water up the Nose. **1844** DUFTON *Deafness* 91 Injecting warm water into the ear through the Eustachian tube. **1875** KNIGHT *Dict. Mech.* 1185/2 A device for injecting a supply of feed-water into.. a steam-boiler. **1878** HUXLEY *Physiogr.* 193 Lava is then injected into the cracks.

c. *transf.* in scientific contexts: *spec.* (*a*) to introduce or feed (an alternating current or voltage) *into* a circuit or device; (*b*) to introduce (charged atomic or subatomic particles) *into* an accelerator; (*c*) to introduce (charge carriers) *into* a region of a semiconductor device.

1939 *Amat. Radio Handbk.* iii. 43/1 The triode is arranged as an oscillator injecting its oscillations into the common cathode lead of the R.F. pentode. **1945** *Jrnl. Appl. Physics* XVI. 583/1 The electrons are injected with a voltage ranging from 30 to 70 kv and, if allowed to remain in the 66-inch diameter circular orbit for the entire quarter cycle, they circle the magnetic flux about 250,000 times. **1949** RYDER & SHOCKLEY in *Physical Rev.* LXXV. 310/2 When terminal 1 is negative, no holes enter from it and holes injected from terminal 2 are spread over a wide area where their concentration is so small as to produce an inappreciable lowering of resistance. **1950** D. HALLIDAY *Introd. Nucl. Physics* ix. 342 Protons are injected into the cavity at 4-mev energy, from a pressure-type electrostatic generator which serves as an ion source. **1956** L. P. HUNTER *Handbk. Semiconductor Electronics* iii. 10 When such a junction is biased in the forward direction.. electrons (*A*) are injected into the P-type region and holes (*B*) are injected into the N-type region. **1962** *Proc. IRE* L. 1784/2 At any voltage.. there will be excess charge injected into the insulator. **1966** *McGraw-Hill Encycl. Sci. & Technol.* IX. 583/1 Ions are injected into the accelerator by an electrostatic machine. **1968** MARTON & EL-KAREH *Electron Beam & Laser Beam Technol.* 64 The beam formed by the gun is injected into a cylindrical drift tube immersed in a uniform axial magnetic field. **1970** J. EARL *Tuners & Amplifiers* vi. 139 Hum currents can be easily injected into the system with a resulting very loud 'roar' from the loudspeaker. **1972** *Physics Bull.* Mar. 175/2 A high energy electron beam is injected into a CO_2/N_2 mixture to produce uniform volume ionization of the gas [in the laser]. **1973** *Nature* 16 Feb. 444/1 Plutonium isotopes.. have been injected into the stratosphere as a result of atmospheric nuclear weapons tests.

d. *Astronautics.* To put *into* (an) orbit.

1961 C. T. MORROW *Symposium Ballistic Missile & Aerospace Technol.* I. 207 Methods by which a satellite can be injected into the 24-hour equatorial or stationary orbit. **1964** MUELLER & SPANGLER *Communication Satellites* xii. 242 Launch operations.. will probably entail.. a 99 per cent probability for each satellite that it will be injected into orbit, following successful launch of a single booster. **1970** *Sci. Jrnl.* Aug. 10/4 The extra load prevented it from injecting the 260 kilogramme Satellite Test Vehicle (STV) into orbit. **1970** *Nature* 10 Oct. 154/2 Energy considerations make it difficult to consider seriously proposals to inject unwanted material into orbit.

2. *fig.* To 'throw in' or introduce from without with more or less violence or interruption, as a thought or feeling into the mind, a statement into a discourse, etc.; to suggest; to interject. Also (esp. from sense 1 e of INJECTION), to insert, introduce.

1639 SALTMARSH *Policy* 196 Make use of the opportunity offered, and modestly inject the remembrance of your selfe. **1647** FULLER *Good Th. in Worse T.* 73 Our Adversary injects.. bad motions into our hearts. **1654** JER. TAYLOR *Real Pres.* Ep. Ded., To disturb the peace of consciences by troubling the persecuted, and injecting scruples into the infortunate, who suspect every thing. **1776** JOHNSON in *Boswell* 16 Mar., I would have him to inject a little hint now and then, to prevent his being overlooked. **1842** R. M. MᶜCHEYNE in *Mem.* (1872) 405 [Satan] injecting blasphemies and polluted thoughts into their minds. **1865** MOZLEY *Mirac.* vi. 127 A calculating engine injects into a lengthened series of regularly succeeding numbers an insulated deviation. **1950** *N.Y. Times* 20 Apr. 1/6 Senator Harry P. Cain.. sought to inject a note of caution into the debate. **1956** *Britannica Bk. of Year* 493/1 *Inject*, used in the sense of to insert, to interpolate. **1958** *Ann. Reg. 1957* 443 Films of events in the news could be 'injected' directly into the national (London) news bulletin. **1965** *New Statesman* 30 Apr. 696/1 It would inject some urgency into the lives of those.. teams who plod through the season without any real hope of promotion or fear of relegation. **1969** *Listener* 2 Jan. 4/2 The raid injects new factors. **1970** *Nature* 12 Dec. 1019/1 The British government's decision to tighten the purse strings by refusing to inject a large sum of money into either the European Airbus or its rival, the BAC 3-11. **1972** *N.Y. Law Jrnl.* 31 Oct. 15/5 Issues would be injected in the consolidated proceedings which would prejudice the rights of one of the claimants.

3. *transf.* To fill or charge (a cavity, etc., or an animal body) by injection. Const. *with.*

1731 MONRO (*title*) Essay on the Art of Injecting the Vessels of Animals. **1753** CHAMBERS *Cycl. Suppl.* s.v. *Injection*, Many disorders of particular parts are no way curable, unless the parts affected are injected with a proper liquor. **1803** *Med. Jrnl.* IX. 551 An easy and successful method of injecting the auditory organ with metal, in order to exhibit its beautiful and intricate structure. **1844-57** G. BIRD *Urin. Deposits* (ed. 5) 369 The relief.. given.. by injecting the bladder with warm water. **1875** LYELL *Princ. Geol.* I. II. xxv. 629 It is clear that such rents must be injected with melted matter.

†**4.** To throw or cast *on* something. *Obs.*

1599 A. M. tr. *Gabelhouer's Bk. Physicke* 141/2 Iniect the same on hot coales, and sitt therover. **1725** POPE *Odyss.* XI. 322 They yet surround The town with walls, and mound inject on mound.

Hence **in'jecting** *vbl. sb.*

1611 COTGR., *Seringuement*, a squirting; an iniecting. **1877** W. THOMSON *Voy. Challenger* I. i. 16 We are provided with all the necessary apparatus and arrangements.. for dissecting and injecting.

injectable (ɪn'dʒɛktəb(ə)l), *a.* [f. INJECT *v.* + -ABLE.] **1.** Capable of being injected: see INJECT 3.

1830 R. KNOX *Béclard's Anat.* 180 Red and injectable capillary vessels.. are in so small proportion to the uninjectable substance, that [etc.].

2. Suitable for injection into the body. Hence as *sb.*, a substance suitable for injection; *spec.* a drug or medicine that may be injected directly into the bloodstream.

1960 *Antibiotics Ann. 1959-60* 462 Thirty-three gonococcal infections in 31 unselected men have been treated with injectable tetracycline at St. Luke's Clinic. **1967** *N.Y. Times* 1 Aug. 27 The injectables are most often used by persons who formerly took amphetamines orally. **1969** *Daily Tel.* 3 July 23/3 An injectable form of the pill might be more acceptable in developing countries and help to damp down the population explosion. **1970** *Sci. Jrnl.* Aug. 8/3 Pharmacists have voluntarily restricted the supply of injectable amphetamines to hospitals. **1973** *Austral. Humanist* XXVI. 2/1 'Bad news' (he did not explain further) was 'coming up' about Copper 7 and injectables.

injected (ɪn'dʒɛktɪd), *ppl. a.* [f. as prec. + -ED¹.]

1. a. Thrown in, forced in, esp. in a fluid state.

1741 MONRO *Anat.* (ed. 3) 4 The Processes.. are filled with the injected Liquor. **1842** *Penny Cycl.* XXII. 474/2 The injected water and condensed steam-water flowed off into the cistern. **1845** DARWIN *Voy. Nat.* xiv. (1873) 312 The injected axis of plutonic rock. **1897** MARY KINGSLEY *W. Africa* 467 The body is cut open to find in the entrails some sign of the path of the injected witch.

b. In sense corresponding to INJECT *v.* 1 c.

1949 W. SHOCKLEY et al. in *Bell Syst. Techn. Jrnl.* XXVIII. 346 The electronic structure of the germanium is modified in the neighborhood of the emitter point by the presence of the injected holes. **1971** *Solid-State Electronics* XIV. 268/1 The current changes from ohmic to space charge limited when the density of the injected majority carriers exceeds that of the thermally generated ones.

2. Charged with something injected (see INJECT 3); *spec.* in *Path.* Having the capillaries or small vessels distended with blood, bloodshot.

1826 KIRBY & SP. *Entomol.* IV. xxxvii. 7 Resembling blood-vessels as they are seen in injected glands. **1857** DUNGLISON *Med. Lex.* 500 The face and other parts are said to be injected, when the accumulation of blood in the capillary vessels gives them an evident red colour. **1867** J. HOGG *Microsc.* I. i. 6 Upon this disk the injected object is fastened. **1897** *Allbutt's Syst. Med.* III. 963 Patches.. dark, almost black, and surrounded by injected vessels.

injection (ɪn'dʒɛkʃən). [ad. L. *injectiōn-em*, n. of action f. *injicĕre* to INJECT. Cf. F. *injection* (13-14th c. in Littré).]

1. The action of injecting; casting or throwing in. †**a.** In general sense. *Obs. rare.*

1611 COTGR., *Injection*, an injection; a casting in, or vpon. **1626** BACON *Sylva* §327, I wish also, that there be, at some times, an Iniection of some Oyled Substance. **1686** GOAD *Celest. Bodies* II. xiv. 341 'Tis a great Stone which upon injection mudds the Water.

b. *spec.* The action of forcing a fluid, etc. into a passage or cavity, as by means of a syringe, or by some impulsive force; *esp.* the introduction in this way of a liquid or other substance into the vessels or cavities of the body, either for medicinal purposes, or (in a dead body or portion of one) in order to exhibit the structure or preserve the tissues. Also relating to internal-combustion engines: see *fuel injection* s.v. FUEL *sb.* 4 b.

1541 R. COPLAND *Galyen's Terapeut.* 2 H iij, It is also many tymes necessary to make iniection of the medycamentes in the bladder by the yerde. **1625** HART *Anat. Ur.* iv. 69 After the injection of an anodine, or mitigating glister, the paine was much eased. **1668** T. CLAREK (*title*) Observations on the Origin of the Injection into Veins, the Transfusion of Blood [etc.]. **1727-41** CHAMBERS *Cycl.*, *Injection* is also used for the operation of filling the vessels with coloured wax, or any other proper matter, to shew their figures and ramifications. **1799** *Med. Jrnl.* II. 441 The frequent injection of clysters is generally insisted on. **1842** *Penny Cycl.* XXII. 507/2 The most effectual method of condensation is by the injection of cold water into the condenser. **1845** DARWIN *Voy. Nat.* xiv. (1852) 312 This rending and injection would, if repeated often enough.. form a chain of hills. **1894** B. DONKIN tr. *Diesel's Rational Heat Motor* ii. 60 The injection of the combustible powder-dust coal takes place gradually and continuously, during part of the stroke of the piston. **1921** W. H. BERRY *Mod. Motor Car Pract.* i. 32 Mechanical injection would permit of greater power development. **1933** A. W. JUDGE *High Speed Diesel Engines* iii. 25 Advancing.. the moment of injection is equivalent to.. advancing the ignition in petrol engines. **1966** *McGraw-Hill Encycl. Sci. & Technol.* V. 556/1 In a diesel engine, a fuel pump starts injection at the proper engine crank angle and meters the required quantity of fuel through the nozzle.

c. *transf.* in scientific contexts (see INJECT *v.* 1 c).

1945 *Jrnl. Appl. Physics* XVI. 593/2 The electron injection and orbit shift circuits were instantaneous in their action. **1949** RYDER & SHOCKLEY in *Physical Rev.* LXXV. 310/1 Pronounced lowering of resistance can result from transistor action, i.e. the injection of holes into the *N*-type material from a metal contact. **1949** W. SHOCKLEY et al. in *Bell Syst. Techn. Jrnl.* XXVIII. 345 We shall discuss.. evidence that holes are actually introduced into *n*-type germanium by the forward current of an emitter point.. We shall refer to this important process as 'hole injection'. **1950** D. HALLIDAY *Introd. Nucl. Physics* ix. 360 Injection may be done by taking advantage of the necessary radial stability of the betatron orbit. **1952** *Adv. Electronics* IV. 225

A method for the phase control of microwave tubes.. utilizes the injection of power via the output circuit of the oscillator to be controlled. **1958** W. EHRENBERG *Electr. Conduction Semiconductors & Metals* xii. 322 The injection of minority carriers is the basic effect in junction rectifiers and transistors. **1962** *Proc. IRE* L. 1781/1 Under double injection, that is, the simultaneous injection into the insulator of electrons from a cathode and holes from an anode, space-charge limitations are..partially overcome. **1971** *Nature* 9 July 77/1 Cyclotrons have an inherent advantage over tandem Van de Graaffs—there is no need to produce a negative ion for injection. **1971** *Physics Bull.* Aug. 461/1 Such [acoustic] waves are obtained either by deliberate injection from a transducer or by amplifying some of the thermally generated waves already present.

d. *Astronautics.* The placing of a spacecraft in, or its entry into, a particular orbit or trajectory; the time when this occurs; freq. *attrib.*, as **injection point**, the point at which a spacecraft enters a new orbit or trajectory.

1959 *IRE Trans. Military Electronics* III. 150/1 We will assume the vehicle's orbit consists of three phases..: first, escape hyperbola..; second, the sun-centered ellipse controlled only by sun's gravity and using injection conditions taken from the escape hyperbola leaving earth; and third,..the approach hyperbola. *Ibid.* 151/1 The properties of the trajectory after injection. **1960** *Ibid.* IV. 152/1 In order to have zero relative inclination, the injection point must be exactly in the plane of the moon's orbit. **1961** C. T. MORROW *Symposium Ballistic Missile & Aerospace Technol.* I. 208 An initial powered flight phase leads to injection of the vehicle into a coast trajectory. **1963** S. LEES *Air, Space, & Instruments* 100 For each..location there is a readily computable impulsive velocity change (termed the 'injection velocity')..which will place the vehicle in a hyperbolic path with the desired terminal velocity. *Ibid.*, Geographical restrictions tend to limit the choice of injection points. **1966** E. BURGESS *Assault on Moon* iii. 73 A 1 mile error in position at injection can cause a miss of 650 miles.

e. *fig.*

1968 *Listener* 7 Nov. 601/1 Colonel Ojukwu has had sizable injections of capital from European sympathisers. **1970** *Daily Tel.* 7 Oct. 7 An immediate financial injection into the hard-pressed agricultural industry, worth..£54 million, is to be made by the Government. **1972** *Guardian* 22 July 1/8 The report will ask for a massive injection of Government money into the docks industry.

2. *Path.* The fact of being charged with injected matter; injected or blood-shot condition.

1806 *Med. Jrnl.* XV. 469 The injection of the cellular membrane with blood. **1886** *Syd. Soc. Lex.*, *Injection*,..In Pathology, the condition or state of distension of the capillaries with blood. **1887** *Buck's Handbk. Med. Sciences* IV. 660 Massage is contra-indicated when it is found to cause excessive injection, and especially if there be photophobia and lachrymation; and it must not be employed in the presence of iritis.

3. *concr.* That which is injected; *spec.* a liquid or solution injected into an animal body, for medicinal purposes, as an enema, or for preserving the tissues, or displaying the structure by colouring or inflation.

1607 E. GRIMSTONE *tr. Goulart's Mem. Hist.* 93 Then they might see come forth with the said Injection little gobbets of bloud. **1616** BULLOKAR, *Iniection*, a liquor which Surgeons doe squirt into a deepe wound. *c* **1720** W. GIBSON *Farriers' Dispens.* x. (1734) 247. **1830** R. KNOX *Béclard's Anat.* 180 The red injection, which is fine and very penetrating, easily passes from the arteries into the veins, through the intermediate capillary system. **1897** *Allbutt's Syst. Med.* III. 741 The best of all injections for the relief of tympanitic distension is the enema assafœtida.

4. *fig.* The 'throwing in' or active introduction of something from without, as of an idea into the mind, or of a statement into an argument, etc.; that which is so introduced, a suggestion, a hint. (Commonly used in 17th c. of evil thoughts suggested by the devil.) Now *rare*.

1622 T. STOUGHTON *Chr. Sacrif.* ix. 125 The power of Satan, who by iniection of his fiery darts, so weakned the power wherein God had created him. **1632** QUARLES *Div. Fancies* IV. xxxi, Satans Injections are like Weeds that fall Into thy Garden, darted or'e the Wall. **1644** HUNTON *Vindic. Treat. Monarchy* v. 39 Here I answer once for all to this so frequent an injection. **1698** W. CHILCOT *Evil Thoughts* iv. (1851) 26 The devil..may disturb the peace and tranquillity of our consciences, by his wicked injections. **1794** SULLIVAN *View Nat.* V. 201 The metaphysical or physical influence of spirits, suggestions..injections of ideas, Bolingbroke declares he cannot comprehend. **1815** A. BURN *Mem.* (1816) III. 121 Distinguish between the injections of Satan..and the breathings of the Spirit of God.

5. *Math.* Also ***injection map(ping)***. A one-to-one transformation, esp. (formerly) an inclusion.

1950 S. MACLANE in *Bull. Amer. Math. Soc.* LVI. 488 If S is a subgroup of G (notation $S \subset G$), then the injection κ ..of S into G is that homomorphism of S into G with $\kappa(s) = s$ for every $s \in S$. **1963** D. BUSHAW *Elem. Gen. Topology* 147 If X is a subset of Y, the function $j: X \to Y$ defined by $j(x) = x$ is called the injection map from X to Y. The injection map from X to X is called the identity map on X. **1968** E. T. COPSON *Metric Spaces* vii. 86 If the inverse image of each point of E_2 is either empty or consists of a single point of E_1, the mapping $f: E_1 \to E_2$ is said to be an injection or a one-to-one mapping. If $f: E_1 \to E_2$ is an injection, $f(x_1) = f(x_2)$ implies $x_1 = x_2$; and $x_1 \neq x_2$ implies $f(x_1) \neq f(x_2)$.

6. *attrib.* and *Comb.*, as ***injection powder***, ***syringe***, ***theory***; esp. in terms relating to condensing steam-engines in which the steam is condensed by the injection of a jet of cold water, as ***injection-cock***, ***-condenser***, ***-engine***, ***-pipe***, ***-valve***, ***-water***. Also freq. in terms relating to the injection of fuel into the combustion chamber of an internal-combustion engine, as ***injection nozzle***, ***period***, ***pressure***, ***system***, ***time***. Also **injection laser**, a laser in which radiation is produced in a suitably shaped semiconductor crystal by the recombination of electrons and holes at a *p–n* junction as a result of the injection of a large enough number of electrons to produce a population inversion; **injection moulding**, a process for making moulded articles from plastics or other materials by forcing the heat-softened substance through an orifice into a cold, closed mould; hence **injection mould**, **injection-moulded** *ppl. a.*; **injection point** *Astronautics*: see sense 1 d above.

1752 SMEATON in *Phil. Trans.* XLVII. 436 This engine consists of a receiver, a steam and an *injection-cock. **1825** J. NICHOLSON *Operat. Mechanic* 171 The injection cock for allowing a small stream of water to flow into the condenser. **1864** WEBSTER, *Injection condenser. **1842** FRANCIS *Dict. Arts*, *Injection Engine. **1963** *Proc. IEEE* LI. 602/1 (*heading*) Doping of semi-conductors for *injection lasers. **1966** SMITH & SOROKIN *Laser* i. 14 In contrast with the other types of lasers, the injection laser is almost two-dimensional, all the light originating from a region within a few microns of the junction plane. **1970** *New Scientist* 16 July (Telecommunications Suppl.) 16/1 The light emitted from the injection laser depends on the current passed through it. **1945** H. BARRON *Mod. Plastics* xvi. 343 Flash is not formed in a well-made *injection mould. **1947** JOHNSON & DANIELS in P. I. Smith *Pract. Plastics* xiii. 187/1 The second moulding is in thermoplastic resin, injection moulded. **1969** T. C. THORSTENSEN *Pract. Leather Technol.* xv. 250 The expansion of the direct-molded sole and injection molded sole shoe is already placing requirements on the leather with regard to oil content and adhesion. **1932** *Chem. Abstr.* XXVI. 4419 (*heading*) Working plastic substances by the *injection molding process. **1945** H. BARRON *Mod. Plastics* xvi. 344 The essential feature in injection moulding is to force the plastic into the mould at a sufficient speed that the mould is completely filled before the material sets by contact with the cold metal. *Ibid.*, Materials which are nowadays universally fabricated by injection moulding include cellulose acetate,..polystyrene; methyl methacrylate resins, etc. **1967** M. CHANDLER *Ceramics in Mod. World* 10 He [*sc.* the ceramist] now employs shaping methods such as dry-pressing and injection molding, which are not traditional to his craft. **1973** A. PARRISH *Mech. Engineer's Ref. Bk.* xvi. 5 Injection moulding is a particularly important process for producing complex mouldings, primarily from thermoplastic powders or granules but also from thermosetting powders. **1900** B. DONKIN *Text-bk. Gas, Oil, & Air Engines* (ed. 3) xxiii. 416 Connected to the *injection nozzle are two valves, the admission and an overflow. **1946** A. W. JUDGE *Mod. Petrol Engines* viii. 326 For larger cylinders two injection nozzles located on opposite sides of the cylinder would be used to give a better admixture of fuel and air. **1971** B. SCHARF *Engin. & its Lang.* xv. 221 The injection nozzle is normally a spring-loaded needle valve. **1916** A. GARRARD *Gas, Oil, & Petrol Engines* vii. 140 A strong spring tends to keep the valve closed, and a cam on the cam shaft operates..to hold it open during the *injection period. **1934** *Engineering* 3 Aug. 111/2 The fuel pumps.. differ from those fitted on most direct-injection engines in that the termination of the injection period is kept constant, the effective stroke of the pump being varied so as to alter the commencement of the injection period. **1858** SIMMONDS *Dict. Trade*, *Injection-pipe*, a pipe for injecting cold water into the condenser of an engine. **1890** *Daily News* 2 Apr. 2/6 The inflow of water was altogether due to the destruction of the injection-pipes. **1803** *Med. Jrnl.* IX. 189 Shops where '*injection powders' are advertized in the windows. **1930** *Engineering* 11 Apr. 472/1 It was therefore decided to determine the *injection pressure which would give a short injection time, in conjunction with good atomisation. **1941** *Nature* 26 July 105/2 The *injection system, as compared with many present carburettors, has some slight but definite advantages. **1968** C. F. TAYLOR *Internal-Combustion Engine* II. xii. 566 A few Diesel-engine builders design and manufacture their own injection systems. **1881** RAYMOND *Mining Gloss.*, **Injection-theory*, the theory that a vein was filled first with molten mineral. **1930** *Injection time [see *injection pressure* above]. **1875** KNIGHT *Dict. Mech.* s.v., The area of the *injection-valve of a marine steam-engine is stated at one square inch for every 10-horse power. **1916** A. GARRARD *Gas, Oil, & Petrol Engines* vii. 139 Fig. 65 shows the form of injection valve and pulverizer adopted by the majority of makers for all kinds of fuel except the very heaviest crude oils. **1824** R. STUART *Hist. Steam Engine* 68 The cistern, for the supply of *injection water. **1839** R. S. ROBINSON *Naut. Steam Eng.* 59 Over the condenser, and in communication with the air pump is the hot well, into which the condensed steam, mixed with the injection water..is pumped.

injective (ɪn'dʒɛktɪv), *a.* *Math.* [f. INJECT *v.* (or L. *inject-* ppl. stem) + -IVE.] Of the nature of or pertaining to an injection (sense 5).

1952 EILENBERG & STEENROD *Found. Algebraic Topology* i. 8 A set of homomorphisms $i_a: G_a \to G$, $a = 1, \ldots, n$, determine a homomorphism $i: \Sigma^n_{a=1} G_a \to G$... If i is an isomorphism of ΣG_a onto G, then the set $\{i_a\}$ is called an injective representation of G as a direct sum. **1965** J. J. ROTMAN *Theory of Groups* ix. 184 (*heading*) The injective property. **1966** SZE-TSEN HU *Introd. Gen. Topology* i. 8 A function $f: X \to Y$ is said to be one-to-one or injective iff, for every point $y \in Y$, the inverse image $f^{-1}(y)$ is either empty or a singleton.

injector (ɪn'dʒɛktə(r)). [agent-n. f. L. *injicĕre* to INJECT.]

1. a. A contrivance for injecting; an apparatus for injecting water into the boiler of a steam-engine. Also, a device for injecting fuel into the combustion chamber or its intakes in an internal-combustion engine (or into the furnace of a steam engine, quot. 1890).

1744 WARRICK in *Phil. Trans.* XLIII. 16 My Apparatus was, a large *Trois-quarts*..an Injector, capable of containing Two or Three Pints, adapted thereto. **1825** J. NICHOLSON *Operat. Mechanic* 292 The diameter of the piston of the small pump or injector. **1876** ROUTLEDGE *Discov.* 12 The injector is applicable to stationary, locomotive, or marine engines. **1890** W. ROBINSON *Gas & Petroleum Engines* iv. 96 This oil is used to produce steam in stationary boilers. The oil is forced into the furnace in the form of fine spray by steam or compressed air, through injectors, and mixed with the air required for the combustion. **1912** R. B. WHITMAN *Gas-Engine Princ.* v. 72 This pressure vaporizer, or injector, is used on 2-cycle engines, the pressure being obtained from the crank case... An injector of this kind permits the use of kerosene. **1914**, **1962** [see *fuel injector* (FUEL *sb.* 4 b)]. **1932** *Compression Ignition Engines* ix. 115 In some buses run by a big city in the North only three cases of choked injectors have occurred in a year's running. **1947** *Jrnl. Brit. Interplanetary Soc.* VI. 107 The rocket motor can be divided into..the propellant injectors, combustion chamber and expansion nozzle. **1963** *Adv. Space Sci. & Technol.* Suppl. I. 173 In a liquid bipropellant rocket engine the injector serves the same function as the carburetor of a gasoline engine. In addition to atomizing and mixing the liquids, it meters the flow to the combustion chamber.

b. Something that injects (in sense 1 c), e.g. particles into an accelerator, or charge carriers into a semiconductor device.

1945 *Jrnl. Appl. Physics* XVI. 593/2 The polarity of the charge on the capacitors was made so as to make the second ..half-cycle the period of electron acceleration thereby allowing charging of the capacitors in the injector and orbit shift circuits during the first half-cycle. **1953** *Proc. IRE* XLI. 1715/1 The efficiency of the diodes as hole injectors is lower than that usually considered desirable. **1962** [see EMITTER 2]. **1972** *Physics Bull.* Mar. 144/2 The Linac injector is designed to accelerate protons..along its drift tube structure to energies of 19·2 MeV.

2. A person who injects.

1897 *Allbutt's Syst. Med.* II. 895 *note*, All authors agree that withdrawal [of morphine] is more distressing to the injector than to the eater of the drug.

in'jeer, *v.* *Sc.* var. INGERE, INGYRE, to thrust in, obtrude, insinuate.

1820 SCOTT *Abbot* xvii, This is..a stratagem from first to last, to injeer into your confidence some espial of his own.

injelly (ɪn'dʒɛlɪ), *v. rare.* [IN-¹ or ².] *trans.* To set or enclose in jelly.

1842 TENNYSON *Audley Court* 25 A pasty costly-made, Where quail and pigeon, lark and leveret lay, Like fossils of the rock, with golden yolks Imbedded and injellied.

injewel: see ENJEWEL.

injoie, obs. f. ENJOY.

injoin: see ENJOIN.

†**injoint**, *v.*¹ *Obs. rare*⁻¹. [IN-².] *intr.* To unite, join.

1604 SHAKS. *Oth.* I. iii. 35 (1st Qo.) The Ottamites.. Steering with due course toward the Ile of Rhodes, Haue there inioynted with an after Fleete Of 30 saile.

†**in'joint**, *v.*² *Obs. rare*⁻¹. [IN-³.] *trans.* To unjoint, disjoint, disjoin.

1603 HOLLAND *Plutarch's Mor.* 152 The foresaid Bridge by a mightie tempest was injointed and broken.

†**in'jointer, -tre,** *v.* *Obs. rare*⁻¹. [app. f. IN-² + *jointer* JOINTURE.] *trans.* To jointure (a wife); in quot. *fig.*

1654 ? FULLER *Triana* (1664) 44 Don Durio..contented that his Daughter was injointred [*ed.* **1867** en-] in a true affection, consented unto their Marriage.

in-joke ('ɪndʒəʊk). [cf. IN *a.* 2.] A joke enjoyed or appreciated by only a limited group of people. Cf. IN-REFERENCE.

1964 *Economist* 31 Oct. 518/2 Professor Yamey..has published the first independent assessment of the Resale Prices Act..for those who like in-jokes. **1966** *Punch* 4 May 657/1 The dialogue peppered with British upper-class in-joke slang of the most blatant appeal to Lancashire slum-dwellers and Turkish primary schools. **1968** M. ALLINGHAM *Cargo of Eagles* vi. 82 Those who can read between the lines will find some amusement at what are called 'in-jokes' today. **1971** M. BABSON *Cover-up Story* ii. 24 They were laughing at me... It was in-joke laughter, and I was on the outside looking in.

injoy, injoyn(e, obs. ff. ENJOY, ENJOIN *v.*

†**inju'cund**, *a.* *Obs. rare*⁻¹. [ad. L. *injūcundus*, f. *in-* (IN-³) + *jūcundus* pleasant: cf. JOCUND.] Unpleasant, disagreeable.

1657 TOMLINSON *Renou's Disp.* 295 Called Acalyphe because it is injucund to the tact. **1721** in BAILEY.

Hence †**inju'cundly** *adv.* (Bailey vol. II, 1727).

inju'cundity. *rare.* [ad. L. *injūcunditās*, f. *injūcundus*: see prec. and -ITY.] Unpleasantness, disagreeableness.

1623 COCKERAM, *Iniucunditie*, vnpleasantnesse. **1721** in BAILEY. **1755** in JOHNSON. **1822** MRS. E. NATHAN *Langreath* III. 290 Yet have we the injucundity of witnessing that.. their promises are but fabulosities. **1877** PATMORE *Unknown Eros* II. xiv. (1890) 98 The fardel coarse of customary life's Exceeding injucundity.

inˈjudicable, *a. rare*$^{-0}$. [IN-³.] Not cognizable by a judge.
1721 in BAILEY. **1755** in JOHNSON. Hence in mod. Dicts.

injuˈdicial, *a. rare.* [IN-³.] Not judicial. †**a.** Acting without judgement; injudicious. *Obs.* **b.** Not according to the forms of law. **c.** Not proper to or becoming a judge.
1607 S. COLLINS *Serm.* (1608) 59 The clamours of the iniudiciall multitude. **1721** BAILEY, *Injudicial*, not according to judgment. **1755** JOHNSON, *Injudicial*, not according to form of law. **1884** *L'pool Mercury* 21 June 5/5 In a very injudicial spirit..he instituted a comparison between English and American beauty.

injuˈdicially, *adv. rare.* [IN-³.] In an injudicial manner; not judicially.
1632 *Star Chamb. Cases* (Camden) 174, I must lay a fyne of 300li upon Martin for dealing soe iniudicially. **1727** BAILEY vol. II, *Injudicially*, illegally, in a manner not according to Law and Judgment. **1745** ELIZA HAYWOOD *Female Spect.* (1748) III. 234 The Italian red, or any of those injudicially called face-mending stratagems.

injudicious (ɪndʒuːˈdɪʃəs), *a.* [IN-³.] Not judicious.
†**1.** Wanting sound judgement; deficient in the power of judging aright. *Obs.*
1649 BP. HALL *Cases Consc.* III. ix. (R.), You see..how unsafe it is..for an unexpert and injudicious person to meddle with the holy oracles of the Almighty. **1654** WARREN *Unbelievers* C, The hearts of the in-judicious multitude. **1684–90** T. BURNET *Th. Earth* (J.), A philosopher would either think me in jest, or very injudicious, if I took the earth for a body regular in itself, if compared with the rest of the universe. *a* **1694** TILLOTSON (J), A sharp wit may find something in the wisest man, whereby to expose him to the contempt of injudicious people.
2. Not manifesting practical judgement or discretion; showing want of judgement in action, behaviour, etc.; unwise, ill-advised, ill-judged.
1710 STEELE *Tatler* No. 173 ¶1 Our Teachers are also as injudicious in what they put us to learn. **1792** MURPHY *Life Johnson* in *J.'s Wks.* (1816) I. 47 It is painful to be thus obliged to vindicate a man..against an injudicious biographer. **1797** BEWICK *Brit. Birds* (1847) I. 351 Our very unequal and injudicious game laws. **1838** DICKENS *Nich. Nick.* viii, Squeers said what Mrs. Squeers had said was injudicious. **1844** H. H. WILSON *Brit. India* I. 227 An injudicious departure from the practice of negociating with that country through India.

injudiciously (ɪndʒuːˈdɪʃəslɪ), *adv.* [f. prec. + -LY².] In an injudicious manner; in a manner showing want of judgement; unwisely.
1712 STEELE *Spect.* No. 278 ¶5 The Songs of different Authors injudiciously put together. **1790** BEATSON *Nav. & Mil. Mem.* I. 155 The fleets being injudiciously stationed. *Mod.* The time was injudiciously chosen for the attempt.

injudiciousness (ɪndʒuːˈdɪʃəsnɪs). [f. as prec. + -NESS.] The quality of being injudicious; want of judgement; deficiency in practical wisdom.
1648 PRYNNE *Plea for Lords* 36 A manifestation of their injudiciousnesse and folly. **1750** CARTE *Hist. Eng.* II. 309 They seem to have been properly paired for vanity, weakness and injudiciousness. **1880** *Daily Tel.* 2 Dec., Stimulated in wild schemes by the injudiciousness of her friends.

injuir, obs. Sc. form of INJURE.

Injun (ˈɪndʒən). Also Injin. **a.** Colloq. and U.S. dial. form of INDIAN *sb.* 2; also *attrib.* (Cf. INGIN.)
1812 COL. J. COCKE in *Salem Gaz.* 28 Aug. 1/2 The people of Tenessee is antious to have orders commanded out for us to march against the injuns on the Wabash. **1850** MAYNE REID *Rifle Rangers* I. i. 5 Four till one! Injuns!—murder! —help, hyeer! **1853** *Ibid.* (ed. 2) I. iii. 24 Thur's a mighty grist o' venturin', I heern; beats Injun fightin' all holler. **1868** M. I. CARRINGTON *Ab-Sa-Ra-Ka* 83 Better not go *fur.* There is *Injuns* enough lying under wolf skins, or skulking on them cliffs. **1872** [see HEAP *sb.* 4d]. **1889** K. MUNROE *Golden Days* 118 No more attention was paid to the shooting of an 'Injun' than if he were a coyote. **1911** R. D. SAUNDERS *Col. Todhunter* vii. 104 But you're sure about it, too, ain't you? She ain't doin' no Injun-givin' in your case? **1937** [see *Indian devil* s.v. INDIAN *a.* 4b]. **1959** I. & P. OPIE *Lore & Lang. Schoolch.* viii. 134 In the United States such a child, who succumbs to the temptation of wanting back, is termed an 'Injun-giver'. **1973** *Nature* 13 Apr. 485/2 The alternative to receipt of a reprint is a slog through hundreds of miles of Injun territory. **1973** R. THOMAS *If you can't be Good* (1974) iii. 30 She had..long hair..glossy blue-black in color. Injun hair, she called it.
b. In various allusive uses and phrases: ***honest Injun***, honour bright: perh. orig. an assurance of good faith extracted from Indians; ***to play Injun***: to act like an Indian; to avoid being seen or captured; of children playing, to pretend to be Indians.
[**1676** J. TALCOTT *Let.* 8 June in S. Judd *Hist. Hadley* (1905) xv. 169 We sent 27 women and children to Norwich under conduct of some of those we call honest Indians.] **1876** 'MARK TWAIN' *Tom Sawyer* ii, Ben, I'd like to, honest Injun; but [etc.]. **1887** F. ANSTEY *Paleface & Redskin* in *Graphic* 31 Dec. 728/3 'Are you sure..on your honour?' he asked eagerly. 'Honest Injun!' said Lambert. **1887** H. FREDERIC *Seth's Brother's Wife* II. 160 'Is what you've be'n tellin' me here honest? Don't lie to me.' 'Honest Injun,.. every word.' **1891** H. C. BUNNER *Short Sixes* 90 'Hope to die —Honest Injun—cross my breast!' said the boy. **1896** G. B. SHAW *Let.* 8 Sept. in *Ellen Terry & Bernard Shaw* (1931) 54 A thing she would never have done if she had not forgiven him quite thoroughly—honest Injun. **1902** S. E. WHITE *Blazed Trail* xix. 140 'Our compact holds now, honest Injin, doesn't it?' asked the boy anxiously. **1904** 'A. DALE' *Wanted: a Cook* 98 But, Archie, this is all true. It is, honest Injun. **1918** C. E. MULFORD *Man from Bar-20* xiv. 140 So they're combin' th' country an' patrollin'. Hereafter an' henceforth I've got to play Injun for all I'm worth. **1922** F. HAMILTON *P.J.: Secret Service Boy* ii. 85 Bar rot, Mr. Ambrose. Real honest Injun? **1922** JOYCE *Ulysses* 295 'Are you codding?' says I. 'Honest injun,' says Alf. **1950** L. A. G. STRONG *Which I Never* i. 12 'You've invented him.' 'Which I never, sir,..' 'Honest Injun?'

†**inˈjunct**, *a. Obs. rare.* [ad. L. *injunct-us*, pa. pple. of *injungĕre* to ENJOIN.] Enjoined.
1517 in *12th Rep. Hist. MSS. Comm.* App. VII. 6, cccc dayes of perdone of iniuncte penance.

inˈjunct, *v. colloq.* [f. L. *injunct-*, ppl. stem of *injungĕre*: after next.] *trans.* To prohibit or restrain by injunction. Now in somewhat more general use. Hence **inˈjuncted** *ppl. a.*
1872 SCHELE DE VERE *Americanisms* 653 Violent contractions, derived from well-known and well-formed words, like burgled, injuncted, and excurted. **1887** *Ohio St. Jrnl.* (Columbus) 1 Sept., Because Foraker proposed to 'injunct' the return of the rebel flags. **1890** *Daily News* 14 Apr. 3/2 Farmers..were driving up their carts of hay and weighing their produce on the injuncted machine. **1890** in *Pall Mall G.* 19 Feb. 2/2 Stanley..came up to me and said rather grimly, 'I shall have to injunct that little matter of yours'. **1894** *Westm. Gaz.* 14 Dec. 5/3 A man was injuncted from calling a play 'The Fatal Card'. **1900** *Westm. Gaz.* 12 Sept. 2/2 Sir Edward Clarke is very likely right in thinking that the Court would hesitate to injunct a man for pirating his own speech. **1957** *Times* 23 Nov. 3/2 Counsel said that Mr. Fielding wanted the Court to say that as he had first claim on Steele's services he should be injuncted from entering a contract with anyone else. But Steele could not be injuncted from going to South Africa.

injunction (ɪnˈdʒʌŋkʃən). [ad. late L. *injunctiōn-em*, n. of action f. *injungĕre* to ENJOIN: cf. F. *injonction* (1348 in Hatz.-Darm.).]
1. The action of enjoining or authoritatively directing; an authoritative or emphatic admonition or order.
1526 *Pilgr. Perf.* (W. de W. 1531) 92 Theyr commaundementes, statutes, rules, iniunccyons, or other lawes. **1575–85** ABP. SANDYS *Serm.* (Parker Soc.) 238 The prince did his duty, and the priests theirs; he by injunction, and they by execution. **1596** SHAKS. *Merch. V.* II. ix. 17, *Ar.* I am enioynd by oath to obserue three things... *Por.* To these iniunctions euery one doth sweare That comes to hazard for my worthlesse selfe. **1665** BOYLE *Occas. Refl.* IV. xi. (1848) 233 We readily obey the Injunctions of Lawyers and Physitians, as long as we think them Prudently fram'd for our good. **1667** MILTON *P.L.* x. 13 The high Injunction not to taste that Fruit. **1766** GOLDSM. *Vic. W.* x, My wife always let them have a guinea each, but with strict injunctions never to change it. **1791** BOSWELL *Johnson* an. 1744 *note*, The Emphasis should be equally upon *shalt* and *not*, as both concur to form the negative injunction. **1849** MACAULAY *Hist. Eng.* vi. II. 153 In spite of all injunctions of secrecy, the news..had spread fast. **1898** FLOR. MONTGOMERY *Tony* 19 Forgetful of his Mother's parting injunctions.
2. *Law.* A judicial process by which one who is threatening to invade or has invaded the legal or equitable rights of another is restrained from commencing or continuing such wrongful act, or is commanded to restore matters to the position in which they stood previously to his action.
Injunctions were formerly obtained by writ, but now by a judgement or order. They were originally granted only by the Court of Chancery: commonly, to stay one party to an action from continuing that action, if there was an equitable, though not a legal defence thereto. By the Judicature Act of 1873, all divisions of the High Court received full power to grant injunctions. According to their purpose, injunctions are either *restrictive* (restraining) or *mandatory*; as to their force, they are either *interlocutory* (*provisional, temporary, ad interim*), or *perpetual* (*permanent*). (In *Sc. Law*, the equivalent of a restrictive injunction is an INTERDICT.)
1533–4 *Act 25 Hen. VIII*, c. 21 §17 Your highnes..shall haue power..to sende your writte of Iniunction, vnder your great seale, out of your sayde courte of Chauncerie. **1649** FULLER *Just Man's Fun.* 16 He may with an Injunction, out of the Chancery stop their proceedings. **1750** JOHNSON *Rambler* No. 35 ¶13 She is always contriving some improvements of her jointure land, and once tried to procure an injunction to hinder me from felling timber upon it for repairs. **1768** BLACKSTONE *Comm.* (1825) III. 442. **1818** CRUISE *Digest* (ed. 2) II. 256 Special circumstances may arise, which will..induce the Court of Chancery to grant an injunction to stay the proceedings at law. **1883** LELY *Wharton's Law Lex.* (ed. 7) 411/1 By s. 24, subs. (5), of the Judicature Act, 1873, it is enacted that no proceeding in the High Court of Justice, or before the Court of Appeal, shall be restrained by injunction. **1888** LD. LINDLEY in *Law Rep.* 31 Ch. Div. 369 The very first principle of injunction law is that you do not obtain injunctions for actionable wrongs for which damages are the proper remedy.
fig. *a* **1619** DANIEL *To Sir T. Egerton* (R.), Therefore dost thou..by thy provident injunctions stay This never-ending altercation.
†**3.** Conjunction, union. *Obs. rare*$^{-1}$.
1643 MILTON *Divorce* II. ix, It can be but a sorry and ignoble society of life, whose inseparable injunction depends meerly upon flesh and bones.

injunctive (ɪnˈdʒʌŋktɪv), *a.* [f. ppl. stem of L. *injungĕre* to ENJOIN + -IVE. Cf. F. *injonctif.*]
1. Having the character or quality of enjoining.
1624 [implied in INJUNCTIVELY]. **1664** H. MORE *Myst. Iniq., Apol.* 536, I do not mean *Permissive* in counter-distinction to *Injunctive.* *a* **1853** R. WARDLAW *Lect. James* iv. (1869) 66 It is pure in all its precepts, injunctive or prohibitive.
2. *Gram.* Applied to the form of a verb (in Vedic, Hittite, etc.) having secondary personal endings and expressing injunction. Also as *sb.*
1910 A. A. MACDONELL *Vedic Gram.* VII. 316 The unaugmented forms of past tenses used modally, are sometimes called improper subjunctives, but they are more suitably termed injunctives, as they appear to have originally expressed an injunction. **1927** E. A. SONNENSCHEIN *Soul of Grammar* §73 What a pity that no one thought of calling the [subjunctive] mood ἐπιτακτική— a term which would have been translatable by the Latin *iniunctivus*, 'injunctive', i.e. 'enjoining'. **1965** *Language* XLI. 1, *-si* imperatives derive from root injunctives, to which could be suffixed *-i* or *-u* to form imperatives. **1971** F. R. ADRADOS in *Archivum Linguisticum* II. 97 Ambrosini believes that *s* [in Indo-European] was the marker of intransitivity; Pariente calls it an injunctive characteristic. *Ibid.* 99, I think we can ascribe to older Indo-European, verbal forms of a type similar to the injunctive, well attested in Vedic and Hittite.
Hence **inˈjunctively** *adv.*, by way of injunction.
1624 BOLTON *Nero* 233 Actions of life (to whose description an historians penne is iniunctiuely tied).

ˈinjurable, *a.* [f. INJURE *v.* + -ABLE.] Capable of being injured, liable to injury.
1862 MAURICE *Mor. & Met. Philos.* IV. 100 That incorruptible uninjurable and unchangeable which I preferred before the corruptible injurable and changeable.

†**inˈjure**, *sb.* Chiefly *Sc. Obs.* Also 5–6 injur, 6 -juir (-gure). [a. F. *injure* (1266 in Hatz.-Darm.), ad. L. *injūria.*] By-form of INJURY.
c **1374** CHAUCER *Troylus* III. 969 (1018) O Auctor of nature, Is þis an honour to þi deite, That folk vngiltyf suffren here Iniure. *c* **1375** *Sc. Leg. Saints, Baptista* 980 þai ..went to þe emperoure, to plenȝe apone þare fader Iniure. *c* **1450** HOLLAND *Howlat* 921 All the fowlis..plenȝeit to Natur Of this intollerable injur. **1500–20** DUNBAR *Poems* xxiii. 38 Be just and joyws and do to non ingure. **1596** DALRYMPLE tr. *Leslie's Hist. Scot.* I. 101 Thay ar persuadet that..slauchtir and sik iniures be the lawe of God [be] forbidne. *Ibid.* VI. 339 *marg.*, He remittis the iniuir done against him.

injure (ˈɪndʒə(r)), *v.* [Back-formation from INJURY *sb.*; cf. rare OF. *injurer* (13th c. in Godef.). It displaced the earlier verb INJURY between 1580 and 1640.]
1. *trans.* To do injustice or wrong to (a person); to wrong.
1592 SHAKS. *Rom. & Jul.* III. i. 71, I do protest I neuer iniur'd thee. **1594** —— *Rich. III*, I. iii. 56 When haue I iniur'd thee? when done thee wrong? **1609** B. JONSON *Case is Altered* I. ii, I injure him In being thus cold-conceited of his faith. **1611** BIBLE *Gal.* iv. 12, I am as ye are, ye haue not iniured me at all. **1693** CREECH in *Dryden's Juvenal* xiii. (1697) 334 Exalted Socrates! Divinely brave! Injur'd He fell, and dying He forgave. **1718** *Freethinker* No. 59 ¶14 The Wretch, guilty of such Baseness, injures Himself, more than Thee. **1868** BAIN *Ment. & Mor. Sc.* Ethics II. (1875) 494 Can one be injured voluntarily? It seems not, for what a man consents to is not injury. Nor can a person injure himself.
†**2.** To do outrage to (a person) in speech; to speak injuriously to or of; to insult, revile, abuse, slander offensively. *Obs.*
1583 *Leg. Bp. St. Androis* 257 in *Satir. Poems Reform.* xlv, He was stubburne in his talk; Iniurit the elders. **1603** FLORIO *Montaigne* I. xxx. (1632) 105 These prisoners.. outragiously defie and injure them [their keepers] . **1653** URQUHART *Rabelais* I. xxv, The Bun-sellers or Cake-bakers ..did injure them most outragiously, calling them pratling gablers, lickorous gluttons.
3. To do hurt or harm to; to inflict damage or detriment upon; to hurt, harm, damage; to impair in any way.
1586 A. DAY *Eng. Secretary* I. (1625) 140 That she..can become therein more forcible, or lesse injured. **1600** SHAKS. *A.Y.L.* III. v. 9, I would not be thy executioner, I flye thee for I would not iniure thee. **1665** BOYLE *Occas. Refl.* (1848) 379 You must not suffer your charity too much to injure your judgment. **1667** MILTON *P.L.* x. 1057 Least Cold Or Heat should injure us, his timely care Hath unbesaught provided. **1771** *Junius Lett.* lviii 302, I shuld be sorry to injure the character of a man. **1793** ANNA SEWARD *Lett.* (1811) III. 232, I am afraid they will injure their healths. **1859** [see INJURY *sb.* 3]. **1860** TYNDALL *Glac.* I. xxii. 159 He had..injured himself in crossing the Gemmi. **1879** HARLAN *Eyesight* ii. 22 When the eyeball..is injured by the fist, it is always by a blow aimed from beneath.
absol. *a* **1699** TEMPLE (J.), They injure by chance in a crowd, and without a design; then hate always whom they have once injured.
b. *intr.* (for *refl.*) To become injured, to receive injury.
1848 *Jrnl. R. Agric. Soc.* IX. I. 22 The hay being found to injure more rapidly after it has been opened.
Hence **ˈinjuring** *vbl. sb.* and *ppl. a.*
1651 HOBBES *Govt. & Soc.* iii. §4. 38 An injury can be done to no man but him with whom we enter Covenant.. and therefore damaging and injuring are often disjoyn'd. **1877** FURNIVALL *Introd. Leopold Shakspere* 91 So injured friend forgiving meets injuring friend forgiven.

injured (ˈɪndʒəd), *ppl. a.* [f. prec. + -ED¹.]
1. Wronged. Also, Showing a sense of wrong, offended. Esp. in phr. *injured innocence*, the offended attitude of one who is undeservedly

accused of something; freq. with the implication that the accusation is in fact just; also occas. used to designate a person adopting such an attitude.

1634 SIR T. HERBERT *Trav.* 68 Injured King Æta, undone by his subtle Daughter Medæa. **1667** MILTON *P.L.* v. 450 Jealousie.. the injur'd Lovers Hell. **1709** POPE *Ess. Crit.* 693 Erasmus, that great injur'd name, (The glory of the Priesthood and the shame!). **1713** ADDISON *Cato* III. 36 Lucia, thou injur'd Innocence! **1814** JANE AUSTEN *Mansf. Park* i, Mrs. Price, in her turn, was injured and angry. **1827** M. WILMOT *Jrnl.* 3 July in *More Lett.* (1935) 268 She next told us of an act of her benevolence towards a poacher caught in the fact, and perhaps too severely punished... Our Chezy dreadnought..speaks of him as injured Innocence. **1846** G. A. LUNDIE *Miss. Life Samoa* xxx. 229 The injured wife of the transgressing teacher was a native. **1869** TROLLOPE *Phineas Finn* I. xvi. 132 Phineas assumed a look of injured innocence, as though his father was driving him too hard. **1872** BLACK *Adv. Phaeton* iv, 'But it rains!' said Tita to him, in an injured way. *c* **1900** H. A. JONES in M. R. Booth *Eng. Plays of 19th Cent.* (1969) II. 364, I decline to give a certificate of injured innocence to any young person who misses her last train. **1971** J. D. MACDONALD *Seven* (1974) v. 101, I have watched the same game a lot of other times... Just don't give me injured innocence.

2. Hurt, damaged, impaired.

1857 H. H. WILSON tr. *Rig-veda* III. 89 The injured cauldron, leaking, scatters foam. **1899** *Daily News* 20 Dec. 3/4 The official list of killed and injured is as follows. *Mod.* Carrying his injured arm in a sling. The rest of the injured passengers are progressing favourably.

Hence **'injuredly** *adv.*, in an injured or offended manner.

1886 'L. KEITH' (Miss Johnston) *Chilcotes* III. vi. 111 'You're as goading as William Prior', said Stephen injuredly.

injurer ('ɪndʒərə(r)). [f. as prec. + -ER[1].] One who injures.

1595 SHAKS. *John* II. i. 174 Thou monstrous Iniurer of heauen and earth. **1611** FLORIO, *Insultatore*, an insulter,.. a proud iniurer. *c* **1613** MIDDLETON *No Wit like a Woman's* II. iii. 293 O that my heart should feel her wrongs so much, And yet live ignorant of the injurer! **1756** WARBURTON *Let. to Lowth* 12 Oct. (R.), The injurer of your father's memory ..deserved no quarter from you. **1856** MISS YONGE *Daisy Chain* I. xxv. (1879) 261 The injured never hates as much as the injurer.

injuria (ɪn'dʒʊərɪə). *Law.* [L.] An invasion of another's rights; an actionable wrong. Cf. DAMNUM.

1876 *Wharton's Law Lexicon* (ed. 6) 477/1 *Injuria*, injury; a wrongful act done. **1898** *Encycl. Laws Eng.* VI. 485 *Injuria* can only be defined as an infringement of a legal right. **1972** *Times* 23 Feb. 27/8 The jury should be neither encouraged nor allowed to look beyond as generous a solatium as was required for the injuria simply to give effect to feelings of indignation.

†**in'jurier.** *Obs.* [f. INJURY *v.* + -ER[1].] One who injures, an injurer.

1598 J. KEEPER tr. *Romei's Court. Acad.* 168 Such an injurier..is esteemed farre more honorable then is the other. **1598** FLORIO, *Oltraggiatore*, a wronger, a misuser, an iniurier.

injurious (ɪn'dʒʊərɪəs), *a.* [a. F. *injurieux* (14th c. in Hatz.-Darm.), ad. L. *injūriōs-us*, f. *injūria* INJURY.] Fraught with injury; tending to injure: said of actions, and persons committing them.

1. Wrongful; hurtful or prejudicial to the rights of another; wilfully inflicting injury or wrong.

1494 FABYAN *Chron.* VII. 451 We se well that ye entende to perseuyr in your iniuryous withholdynge. **1548** HALL *Chron., Edw. IV* 210 b, Thy kyngdome..could not by very divyne justice, longe contynew in that injurious stocke. **1555** EDEN *Decades* 326 Leaste I bee iniurious to any man in ascrybyng to my selfe the trauayles of other. **1634** W. WOOD *New Eng. Prosp.* (1865) 59 A wronged servant shall have right..from his injurious master. **1704** CIBBER *Careless Husb.* I. sp. i, Was ever Woman's Spirit, by an injurious Husband, broke like mine? **1774** BP. HALLIFAX *Anal. Rom. Civ. Law* (1795) 83 The Injurious Party, besides a Civil, was liable to a Criminal prosecution. **1828** SCOTT *F.M. Perth* xxii, He holds a late royal master of mine in deep hate for some injurious treatment..which he received at his hand. **1871** R. ELLIS *Catullus* lxiv. 75 Gain'd Gortyna's abode, injurious halls of oppression.

2. Wilfully hurtful or offensive in language; contumelious, insulting; calumnious. (Now only of words or speech, and passing into sense 3.)

c **1480** HENRYSON *Test. Cres.* 284 Ane blind goddes hir cald, that micht not see, With slander and defame injurious. **1484** CAXTON *Fables of Æsop* II. xii, The Iniuryous mocquen and scornen the world and geteth many enemyes. *a* **1592** GREENE *Wks.* (1882) II. 219 An injurious Gentleman heere in Saragossa, who with despightfull taunts hath abused the Gentlewomen of Sicillie. **1607** SHAKS. *Cor.* III. iii. 69 Call me their Traitor, thou iniurious Tribune. **1719** DE FOE *Crusoe* I. xviii, Tying his Hands, and giving him injurious Language. [**1726–31** TINDAL *Rapin's Hist. Eng.* (1743) II. XVII. 99 Speaking of Elizabeth in very injurious terms. **1879** FARRAR *St. Paul* (1883) 117 Injurious words had been as far as possible from his thoughts.]

3. Tending to hurt or damage; hurtful, harmful, detrimental, deleterious.

1559 W. CUNNINGHAM *Cosmogr. Glasse* Pref. A iv, This hathe bene to all men profitable, and injurious to no man. **1589** WARNER *Alb. Eng.* II. Prose Add. (1612) 331, I know thee vnwittingly iniurious. **1674** tr. *Scheffer's Lapland* 135 The Martin is not injurious only to the Squirrel, but to both small and great Birds. **1817** W. SELWYN *Law Nisi Prius* (ed. 4) II. 1300 It would be injurious to the public trade of England. **1879** HARLAN *Eyesight* viii. 110 Another equally.. injurious habit is that of reading while lying down.

4. *injurious affection* (Law): a term used of a situation in which part of a person's land is acquired compulsorily under statutory powers and the remaining part is reduced in value, either because it is a smaller piece or because of what has been done on the land compulsorily acquired; also, of other situations in which an owner seeks compensation for the deleterious effect on his property of the exercise of statutory powers; *injurious falsehood* (Law): an actionable falsehood, a false statement claimed to have caused damage to the plaintiff in respect of his office, profession, trade or business, etc.

[**1845** *Act 8 & 9 Vict.* c. 18 The damage, if any, to be sustained by the owner of the lands by reason of the severing of the lands from the other lands of such owner, or otherwise injuriously affecting such lands.] **1867** *Law Rep.* (Queen's Bench) II. 239 The injurious affection of the house by the vibration, smoke, and noise. **1889** *Law Rep.* (Appeal Cases) XIV. 159 The acts complained of as an injurious affection were not done on the land taken. **1909** HALSBURY *Laws Eng.* III. 41 In assessing compensation for..injurious affection all damage that can be reasonably foreseen should be taken into account. **1932** *Act 22 & 23 Geo. V* c. 48 Account shall be taken of any additional injurious affection of the property. **1947** *Act 10 & 11 Geo. VI* c. 48 The compensation (if any) to which that person would be entitled for such injurious affection if the..land were compulsorily acquired. **1965** *Act Eliz. II* c. 56 §10 This section shall be construed as affording in all cases a right to compensation for injurious affection to land. **1971** *Country Life* 6 May 1109/2 A claim for compensation on account of injurious affection is now made under the provisions of sections 7 and 10 of the Compulsory Purchase Act. **1972** *Daily Colonist* (Victoria, B.C.) 10 Feb. 38/3 The report also suggests that the basic formula for compensation [in case of expropriation] be based on the market value of the property expropriated plus damages for 'injurious affection'. **1907** J. W. SALMOND *Law of Torts* xv. 426 The second form of actionable misrepresentation, namely that which we have termed Injurious Falsehood. **1928** *Ibid.* (ed. 7) xv. 582 The most important example of the wrong of injurious falsehood is the use of fraudulent or misleading trade names. **1933** *Law Jrnl. Rep.* CII. 191 A false statement detrimental to the plaintiff's business, but not defamatory, carelessly made in the belief it was true, will not support an action for injurious falsehood. **1955** *Rep. Patent, Design & Trade Mark Cases* (Patent Office) LXXII. 160 The amendment of the writ has been such as to raise the cause of action known as 'injurious falsehood'. **1967** J. G. FLEMING *Introd. Law of Torts* xi. 218 The tort of injurious falsehood, partaking of elements familiar to defamation and deceit. **1973** J. D. HEYDON *Economic Torts* IV. 66 Injurious falsehood. This tort is committed where the defendant maliciously publishes to a third party written or oral falsehoods about the plaintiff in his trade which are calculated to produce and do produce actual damage. **1974** *Trans. Philol. Soc. 1973* 19 The only possibility of action would appear to be in the tort of injurious falsehood, but for a trade-mark proprietor to succeed he would have to show malice on the part of the publishers or editor of the dictionary.

injuriously (ɪn'dʒʊərɪəslɪ), *adv.* [f. prec. + -LY[2].] In an injurious manner.

a. Wrongfully, so as to wrong another.

1561 tr. *Calvin's 4 Godly Serm.* iii. G iij a, If we sholde suppose that he regarded or desyred nothing saue the buildyng..we sholde iudge far a mysse and iniuriously of this most godly and wyse man. **1571** HANMER *Chron. Irel.* (1633) 175 He tooke away by strong hand and injuriously, from an holy Bishop two mannors. **1690** A. BURY in *Wood's Life* 16 Feb. (O.H.S.) III. 325 One of the fellows who..is injuriously, or at least too severely, expelled. **1779–81** JOHNSON *L.P., Pope* Wks. IV. 79 [He] injuriously omitted his predecessor's preface. **1883** *Law Rep. 11* Queen's Bench Div. 597 The censure had been made injuriously and from motives of private malice. **1884** LD. BLACKBURN in *Law Times Rep.* LII. 146/1 They have injuriously, as distinguished from damnously, affected the plaintiff's rights.

b. Hurtfully, harmfully.

1809–10 COLERIDGE *Friend* (1865) 131 No good man communicating what he believes to be truth for the sake of truth..will be found to have acted injuriously to the peace or interests of society. **1818** JAS. MILL *Brit. India* II. v. ii. 367 To affect injuriously the interests of the Company. **1882** *Med. Temp. Jrnl.* LI. 100 Everyone of the individuals..was affected injuriously by the alcohol.

injuriousness (ɪn'dʒʊərɪəsnɪs). [f. as prec. + -NESS.] The quality of being injurious; wrongfulness; hurtfulness, harmfulness.

1648 *Eikon Bas.* ix. (1824) 61 Any propensity..either to injuriousnesse or oppression. **1754** EDWARDS *Freed. Will* III. vii. 185 Desperately inclined to treat his Neighbours with Injuriousness, Contempt and Malignity. **1845** DE QUINCEY *Nat. Temp. Wom.* Wks. 1890 XIV. 271 The injuriousness to enfeebled stomachs of all fluid.

injury ('ɪndʒərɪ), *sb.* [ad. L. *injūria* wrong, hurt, detriment, sb. use of fem. of *injūrius* unjust, wrongful, f. *in-* (IN-[3]) + *jūs, jūr-* right. Cf. AF. *in-*, *enjurie* (Ph. de Thaun).]

1. Wrongful action or treatment; violation or infringement of another's rights; suffering or mischief wilfully and unjustly inflicted. With *an* and *pl.*, A wrongful act; a wrong inflicted or suffered.

1382 WYCLIF *Col.* iii. 25 He that doth iniurie [Vulg. *injuriam*] shal resseyue that that he dide yuele. *c* **1386** CHAUCER *Melib.* ¶845 Ye..han doon grete Iniuries and wronges to me and to my wyf. **1477** EARL RIVERS (Caxton) *Dictes* 19 Ther is no lorde that woll venge the Iniuries don therto. **1509** FISHER *Fun. Serm. C'tess Richmond* Wks. (1876) 291 She was..redy a none to forgete and to forgyue iniuries done vnto her. **1611** BIBLE *Transl. Pref.* 1 By [wholesome laws]..we are bridled..from doing of iniuries. **1627–77** FELTHAM *Resolves* II. xlvi. 248 Injury is properly the willing doing of Injustice to him that is unwilling to receive it. **1729** BUTLER *Serm. Resentment* Wks. 1874 II. 94 Injury, as distinct from harm, may raise sudden anger. **1768** BLACKSTONE *Comm.* III. 2 Private wrongs..are an infringement or privation of the private or civil rights belonging to individuals..and are thereupon frequently termed civil injuries. **1839** KEIGHTLEY *Hist. Eng.* II. 91 It was associated in her mind with her mother's injuries, and her own. **1883** *Wharton's Law Lex.*, *Injury*, any wrong or damage done to another, either in his person, rights, reputation, or property.

†**2.** Intentionally hurtful or offensive speech or words; reviling, insult, calumny; a taunt, an affront. *Obs.* [Cf. F. *injure* = *parole offensante, outrageuse*.]

1514 BARCLAY *Cyt. & Uplondyshm.* (Percy Soc.) 16 This scorfy scoflynge declareth openly Agaynste rurall men, rebuke and injury. **1603** FLORIO *Montaigne* I. xlvi. (1897) II. 185 He began to raile upon them with a thousand injuries. *a* **1626** BACON (J.), He fell to bitter invectives against the French king; and spake all the injuries he could devise of Charles. **1659** D. PELL *Impr. Sea* 107 With the same patience that Chirurgions will [bear] the injuries and blows of mad, and frantick men. **1710** STEELE *Tatler* No. 172 ¶1, I do not mean it an Injury to Women, when I say there is a Sort of Sex in Souls.

3. a. Hurt or loss caused to or sustained by a person or thing; harm, detriment, damage. With *an* and *pl.* An instance of this.

c **1430** *Life St. Kath.* (1884) 39 Wyth oute iniurie of hys godhed he ouercome hym þat..had brought man into synne. **1555** EDEN *Decades* To Rdr. (Arb.) 49 Thiniurie of tyme consumynge all thynges. **1607** TOPSELL *Four-f. Beasts* (1658) 27 Some shepheards in Italy use thereof to make sacks, wherein they wrap themselves from the injury of rain. **1726** LEONI tr. *Alberti's Archit.* I. 45/1 Those parts of the Wall which are near to the ground,..by the alternate injuries of Dust and Wet, are very apt to moulder and rot. **1816** SCOTT *Antiq.* xxx, Having sustained a heavy blow without injury. **1845** *Florist's Jrnl.* 266 Repotting..has been neglected for three or four years without apparent injury to the plants. **1859** *Engineer* VII. 282 Of the cases of injury from causes beyond the passengers' own control, all but twenty-seven were occasioned by collisions between trains, and mostly great numbers were injured at once.

†**b.** *concr.* A bodily wound or sore. *Obs. rare.*

1599 SHAKS. *Hen. V*, III. vi. 129 Wee thought not good to bruise an iniurie, till it were full ripe.

4. *attrib.* and *Comb.*, as *injury-doing*, wrong-doing; ***injury-feigning*** vbl. sb. and ppl. a.; **injury time**, the extra time allowed in a game of football or the like to make up for time spent in attending to injuries.

1567 MAPLET *Gr. Forest* 29 He..began to accuse Nature of Iniurie doing and offence. **1925** J. S. HUXLEY in *Brit. Birds* XIX. 93 The Purple Sandpiper which nests on the.. tundra has an 'injury-feigning' performance which must be hard to beat for elaboration. *Ibid.* 94 In regard to 'injury-feigning' the Avocet is one of the most spectacular of birds. **1932** D. LACK in *Ibis* 282 Injury-feigning is, therefore, assumed to be primarily a partial paralysis due to anxiety. **1948** *Brit. Birds* XLI. 237 The cock several times gave 'lure displays' of the 'injury-feigning' type, creeping away from the dummy with wings dragging and depressed and tail fanned. **1960** *Sunday Times* 18 Dec. 20/1 The winning score ..did not come until the 43rd minute of the second half in what, in the absence of any official designation, is termed 'injury time'. **1971** *New Society* 1 July 24/3 One of the better ideas in the competition is their tie-breaker. If there is a tie the teams play off to an instant death by goals scored from penalties kicked immediately after extra injury-time.

†**'injury,** *v. Obs.* Also (6 injuirie). [a. F. *injurier* (1266 in Hatz.-Darm.), ad. late L. *injūriāre*, f. *injūria* INJURY. Supplanted *c* 1600 by the current INJURE.]

1. *trans.* To wrong; = INJURE 1.

c **1484** *Plumpton Corr.* (Camden) 64 One Robart Walkinham is injuried & wronged of his tennor in Arkenden. **1561** DAUS tr. *Bullinger on Apoc.* (1573) 175 Rome hath spoyled the whole world, and iniuried all nations. **1603** FLORIO *Montaigne* 616 He..should greatly wrong himselfe and injurie me as much. **1651** HOBBES *Leviath.* II. xxii. 119 If any particular member conceive himself injuried by the Body it self.

2. To abuse with words, revile, calumniate; = INJURE 2.

1484 CAXTON *Fables of Æsop* I. xvi, That he be not iniuryed and mocqued of euery one. **1579** TOMSON *Calvin's Serm. Tim.* 1011/2 We must be more greued and tormented at it, then if wee our selues were reuiled and iniuried in most spiteful sort. **1603** FLORIO *Montaigne* I. xlvii. (1897) II. 193 Where occasion brings us neere the enemie, we freely give our souldiers libertie, to..injurie him with all manner of reproaches.

3. To hurt, harm, damage; = INJURE 3.

1579 FULKE *Confut. Sanders* 694 Least the trophee of our victorie by treading vpon..be iniuried. **1630** LORD *Banians* 83 They will not indure to see a fly or worme or anything living injuryed.

Hence †**'injuried** *ppl. a.*, †**'injurying** *vbl. sb.*

1600 J. MUSH in *Archpr. Controv.* (Camden) I. 160 Vnlesse the iniuried freely forgiue. **1604** T. WRIGHT *Passions* 278 The heynousnes of spitefull iniurying.

†**in'just,** *a. Obs.* [a. F. *injuste* (14th c., Oresme), ad. L. *injūstus*, f. *in-* (IN-[3]) + *jūstus* JUST.] Not just; opposed to justice; = UNJUST.

c **1430** LYDG. *Min. Poems, Hors, Shepe, & G.* (Percy Soc.) 120 Injuste promocioune and parcialite. **1491** CAXTON

Vitas Patr. (W. de W. 1495) II. 184 b/2 The wethers represente the Iniuste & wycked. **1598** SPENSER in Grosart *Spenser's Wks.* I. 539 Iniuste and dishonorable meanes. **1646** SIR T. BROWNE *Pseud. Ep.* III. xi. 130 The quarrell of Origen was injust and his conception erroneous. **1711** HEARNE *Collect.* III. 186 Plainly shewing how injust they had been.

injustice (ɪnˈdʒʌstɪs). [a. F. *injustice* (14th c., Oresme), ad. L. *injūstitia*, f. *injūstus* INJUST: cf. JUSTICE.] The opposite of justice; unjust action; wrong; want of equity, unfairness. With *an* and *pl.*, An instance of this; an unjust act.

1390 GOWER *Conf.* III. 246 Speciall misgovernaunce Through covetise and injustice. **1526** *Pilgr. Perf.* (W. de W. 1531) 78 Occasyon to condempne his prelate of iniustyce & iniquite. **1601** in *Archpr. Controv.* (Camden) II. 177 The many iniustices of yor last edict. **1611** BIBLE *Ecclus.* xl. 12 All briberie and iniustice shall be blotted out. **1792** *Anecd. W. Pitt* II. xxix. 141 The Americans have been wronged. They have been driven to madness by injustice. **1839** MISS MITFORD in L'Estrange *Life* (1870) III. vii. 102 The portrait prefixed to his 'Speeches' does him great injustice. **1879** H. SPENCER *Data of Ethics* vii. §45. 122 The class-privileges which make injustices easy.

Hence †**inˈjusticer**, *Obs. nonce-wd.*, an agent or officer of injustice.

a **1618** RALEIGH *Prerog. Parl.* (1628) 27 The Iustices of peace in England haue oppos'd the iniusticers of warre in England.

†**inˈjustifiable**, *a. Obs. rare.* [IN-3. Cf. F. *injustifiable* (Littré).] Incapable of being justified, unjustifiable.

1646 SIR T. BROWNE *Pseud. Ep.* IV. xii. 217 We have no easie reason to doubt, when great and entire Authors shall introduce injustifiable examples. *a* **1714** BURNET *Hist. Ref.* an. 1540 (R.) That injustifiable precedent of passing over so necessary a rule, of giving the partys accused an hearing.

†**inˈjustly**, *adv. Obs.* [f. INJUST + -LY2.] In an unjust manner, unjustly.

1502 *Ord. Crysten Men* (W. de W. 1506) II. ix. 108 To be iniustly the cause of the dethe of our neyghboure. **1633** HALES *Brevis Disquis.* in *Phenix* (1708) II. 340 Either.. your Doctrine is false, or else our Lord Christ injustly requires Impossibilities. *a* **1715** BURNET *Own Time* II. (1725) I. 197 Letting the King see..how injustly they had been misrepresented to him.

injyne, obs. form of ENGINE.

ink (ɪŋk), *sb.*1 Forms: 3–4 enke, (5 enk, henk), 3 inc, 3, 6–7 inck, 4–6 ynk(e, 4–7 inke, (6 incke, 6–7 yncke), 3– ink. [a. OF. *enque* (11th c. in Hatz.-Darm.; in mod.F. *encre*):—late L. *encaustum*, a. Gr. ἔγκαυστον the purple ink used by the Greek and Roman emperors for their signatures, f. ἐγκαίειν to burn in (see ENCAUSTIC). The OF. form retained the Greek accent, while It. *inchiostro* (Old Milanese *incostro*, Diez) is due to the Latin stressing *encauˑstum*, **encauˑstrum*. The word has been adopted in Boh. as *inkoust*, formerly *inkaust*; and in Du. as *inkt* (older *enkt*).]

I. 1. a. The coloured (usually black) fluid ordinarily employed in writing with a pen on paper, parchment, etc. (***writing ink***), or the viscous paste used for a similar purpose in printing (***printing*** or ***printer's ink***).

When the word is used without qualification, the ordinary black writing-fluid is commonly meant. The various kinds of ink are distinguished by their colour, as *black, red, blue, gold ink*, etc.; by the purpose which they serve, as *copying, lithographic, marking, printing* (or *printer's*), *writing ink*; by some special quality, as *indelible, invisible, sympathetic ink*; by the place of manufacture, as *China, Indian Ink*, q.v.

c **1250** *Meid Maregrete* lxi, So boc is writen wid enke. *a* **1300** *Cursor M.* 648 Es nan forsoth wit hert mai think, Ne writer nan mai write wit inc [*Trin. MS.* enke] þe mikel ioy. *a* **1375** *Joseph Arim.* 194 On vche braunche was a word of þreo maner enkes, Gold and Seluer he seis and Asur forsoþe. **1387–8** T. USK *Test. Love* Prol. (Skeat) I. 15 Some.. painten with colours riche and some with vers, as with red inke, and some with coles and chalke. *c* **1400** *Apol. Loll.* 91 We how not to honor þe gospel þus, þat is to sey, þe henk, or þe parchemyn. **1480** CAXTON *Descr. Scotl.* (1520) 1/2 They wolde somtyme..peynt them with ynke or with other peinture or coloure. **1568** GRAFTON *Chron.* II. 637 Guthenbergius,..within .xvj. yeres after did invent the ynke which the Printers now use. **1590** SPENSER *F.Q.* I. i. 22 Deformed monsters, fowle, and blacke as inke. **1638** F. JUNIUS *Paint. of Ancients* 285 Such a thinne kinde of inke or vernish, that it did..darken the.. glasing colours. **1712** tr. *Pomet's Hist. Drugs* I. 142 The Indians dye Skins, and make Ink with them. **1727–41** CHAMBERS *Cycl.* s.v., Indian, or Chinese ink, is an admirable composition..it is not fluid, like our writing inks. *Ibid.*, Printing ink is made of nut-oil, or linseed-oil, turpentine and lamp-black. **1753** *Ibid. Suppl.* s.v., Every sort of liquor with which a person may write so that the letters do not appear till there is some particular means used to give them a colour different from that of the paper, are called by the name of *sympathetic Inks*. **1765** *Dict. Arts & Sc.* s.v., Composition of common black Ink. Preparation of Red Ink from Vermilion. **1796** WITHERING *Brit. Pl.* III. 743 The expressed juice of the petals is a good blue ink. **1819** *Pantologia* s.v. *Ink*, 'Chemical Indelible Ink' sold for the purpose of marking linen. **1829** HOOD *Eug. Aram* xxi, A sluggish water, black as ink, The depth was so extreme. **1855** CARLYLE *Misc., Prinzenraub* (1872) VII. 158 Battles..fought only by ink. **1893** SELOUS *Trav. S.E. Africa* 151 The whole sky on one side of the heavens was as black as ink. **1899** *Brit. Printer* XII. 62 When..type here and there refuses to take ink.

fig. and *transf.* **1548** HALL *Chron., Hen. VII* 48 Yt no person beyng embrued or spotted wt ye ynke of ye abhominable crime, shoulde escape ye peyne. **1677** HORNECK *Gt. Law Consid.* iv. (1704) 198 As if, like *aqua fortis*, it would take out the ink which sin and the devil have cast on their souls in a moment. **1879** J. BURROUGHS *Locusts & W. Honey* 129 The lake was a pool of ink.

b. The black inky liquid secreted by the cuttle-fish and allied cephalopods, and stored in a sac or bladder, from which it is ejected at will so as to cloud the water and assist the animal in its escape from danger.

a **1586** SIDNEY *Arcadia* (1622) 61 The fish called sepia, which being in the net, castes a blacke inke about itselfe, that in the darkenesse thereof it may scape. **1589** tr. *Pasquil's Return* C b, They are the very Spawnes of the fish *Sæpia*,.. where the streame is cleere,..they vomit vp yncke to trouble the waters. **1641** 'SMECTYMNUUS' *Vind. Answ.* v. 62 He deals like the fish Sepia, and casteth out a great deal of black inke before the eyes of the Reader, that so hee may escape without observation. **1815** W. PROUT in Thomson *Ann. Philos.* V. 417 (heading) On the Colouring Matter, or Ink, ejected by the Cuttle Fish. **1847** CARPENTER *Zool.* §880 A very singular secreting organ, which, in the dibranchiate Cephalopods, produces an abundance of a black liquor, commonly termed its *ink*. **1861** HULME tr. *Moquin-Tandon* II. III. ii. 82 A black liquid known as the Ink of the Cuttlefish ..The pigment..known as Roman Sepia, is obtained from this black liquid.

II. *attrib.* and *Comb.*

2. General combinations: **a.** attributive, as ***ink-drop***, ***fever*** (nonce-word), ***-line***, ***-stain***; **b.** objective, as ***ink-carrying***, ***-distributing***, ***-dropping***, ***-wasting*** adjs., ***ink-maker***; **c.** instrumental, as ***ink-blurred***, ***-spotted***, ***-stained***, ***-written*** adjs.; **d.** similative, as ***ink-black***, ***-blue***, ***-coloured***, ***-purple***, adjs.; also ***ink-like*** adj.; ***ink-shine*** v. (nonce-word); **e.** (in Chinese calligraphy, etc.) ***ink-brush***, ***-painting***, ***-sketch***, ***-squeeze***, ***-stick***, ***-study***.

1599 MARSTON *Sco. Villanie* I. iii. 183 What Academick starued Satyrist..with *inke-black fist, Would tosse each muck-heap, for some outcast scraps? **1897** MARY KINGSLEY *W. Africa* 298 Looking blankly at a lake of ink-black slime. **1963** *Times* 16 Feb. 11/6 Baby *ink-blue mussel shells arranged in flower-like clusters with sprays of dried seaweeds in between. **1971** *Guardian* 14 Dec. 9/2 In black, tan, bottle green, honey, and ink blue. **1951** R. FIRTH *Elem. Social Organiz.* v. 164 A traditional Chinese painter works with a definite theory about the use of the *ink-brush. **1875** KNIGHT *Dict. Mech.* 1188/1 The endwise motion of the *ink-distributing rollers. *a* **1847** ELIZA COOK *Room of Household* ii, The *ink-drop may fall. *a* **1649** DRUMM. OF HAWTH. *Poems* Wks. (1711) 16/1 To deadly cypress, and *ink-dropping firrs; Your palms and mirtles change. **1922** T. E. LAWRENCE *Home Lett.* (1954) 355 This long-drawn-out battle over my narrative of the campaigns of Feisal has put an *ink fever into me. I find myself always going about trying to fit words to the sights & sounds in the world outside me. **1605** SYLVESTER *Du Bartas* II. iii. III. *Law* 552 With *Ink-like Rheum the dull Mists' drouzy vapours Quench their home Fires. **1933** W. DE LA MARE *Fleeting* 49 Whose waters..ink-like, ebon,..flow. **1731** W. HALFPENNY *Perspective* 24 Then draw the *Ink Lines..which represents the Top of the Wall. **1598** FLORIO, *Inchiostraro*,..an *inke-maker. **1714** MANDEVILLE *Fab. Bees* (1733) I. 333 The ink-makers..would..offer to choak me with astringents, or drown me in the black liquor. **1805** *Mod. London* 443 Inkmakers, stationers, papermakers. **1925** R. FRY *Chinese Art* 9 Many *ink-paintings ascribed to him [*sc.* Li Lung-mien] are extant, and a few may be originals. *Ibid.* Plate 9 (*caption*) Ink painting on silk. **1954** *Oxf. Jun. Encycl.* XII. 225/1 The greatest master of ink-painting [in Japan] was Sesshū (1420–1506). **1935** E. BOWEN *House in Paris* II. vii. 159 Toppling *ink-purple clouds. **1922** JOYCE *Ulysses* 216 The jet beads of her mantilla *inkshining in the sun. **1906** S. W. BUSHELL *Chinese Art* II. xiii. 136 She [*sc.* the Lady Kuan] was a clever painter of flowers and her rapid *ink sketches of peonies, prunus-flowers and orchids were admirable. **1910** *Brit. Mus. Guide Exhib. Chinese & Japanese Paintings..in Print & Drawing Gallery* 32 But the typical painting of the [Ashikaga] period was the ink-sketch of landscape, bird or flower. **1935** *Burlington Mag.* Oct. 185/2 The illustrations are all line-blocks made from 'rubbings' (or, more correctly, '*ink squeezes'). **1819** *Pantologia* s.v. *Ink*, Lemon-juice, and the juice of sorrel will also remove *ink-stains. **1857** EADIE *J. Kitto* xii. (1861) 418 An *inkstained recluse. **1926** F. B. WIBORG *Printing Ink* ii. 50 The Chinese never used liquid ink... Many *ink-sticks are provided with a rounded notch at the lower end to secure a firmer hold for the finger, while the upper part to be rubbed is rounded. **1935** CHIANG YEE *Chinese Eye* viii. 199 A certain Li T'ing-Kuei of the 'Five dynasties' period supplied all the leading calligraphists with ink-sticks, and he compounded them from ten parts of pine-smoke to three of powdered jade and one of gum. **1939** *Burlington Mag.* Jan. 47/1 Inksticks and experience in making inks. **1936** *Ibid.* Nov. 236/1 Chinese *ink-studies. **1581** SIDNEY *Apol. Poetrie* (Arb.) 71 All, that haue had the euill lucke to reade this *incke-wasting toy of mine.

3. In the names of vessels or receptacles for holding writing or printing ink, as ***ink-bottle***, ***-box***, ***-can***, ***-case***, ***-cup***, ***-dish***, ***-glass***, ***-holder***, ***-reservoir***, ***-tin***. Also INK-HORN, -POT, -STAND, -STANDISH.

1583 HOLLYBAND *Campo di Fior* 333 Hoe boye, reache me that *inke-bottell. **1711** BUDGELL *Spect.* No. 77 ¶9 He writes a Letter, and flings the Sand into the Ink-bottle; he writes a second, and mistakes the Superscription. **1875** A. R. HOPE *My Schoolboy Fr.* 227 He dipped a large pen into his inkbottle. **1640** HOWELL *Dodona's Gr.* (1645) 55 The secretary pour'd the *Ink-box all over the Writings. **1851** *Illustr. Exhib.* 489 The ductor-roller forms one side of an ink-box, from which, as it revolves, it withdraws a portion of ink. **1663** BOYLE *Hist. Colours* II. Exp. ix, I have found pens blacked..when I had a while carried them about me in a silver *ink-case. **1886** STEVENSON *Pr. Otto* II. xiii. 221 Give me the *ink-dish. **1680** V. ALSOP *Misch. Imposit.* 103 If the late change of Ink horns, into *Ink glasses, had but taught us how frail and brittle we all are. **1806–7** J. BERESFORD *Miseries Hum. Life* (1826) VIII. xxiv, Emptying the ink-glass (by mistake for the sand-glass) on a paper which you have just written out fairly. **1703** T. N. *City & C. Purchaser* 194, I saw him Sodder on bottoms to Leaden-stands, or *Ink-holders. **1855** CARLYLE *Prinzenraub* 100 Standing in Luther's room, with Luther's poor old oaken table, oaken inkholder, still there. **1875** KNIGHT *Dict. Mech.* 1187/2 The *ink-reservoir of a printing-press from which the ink is taken by an ink-roller. **1876** PREECE & SIVEWRIGHT *Telegraphy* 73 The ink-reservoir should never be too full, otherwise the apparatus is apt to become clogged with ink.

4. a. Special combinations: **ink-bag**, the bladder-shaped sac in the cuttle-fish and related animals containing the 'ink': see 1 b above; **ink-ball**, (*a*) = BALL *sb.*1 13: see quot. 1884; (*b*) a kind of oak-gall employed in the manufacture of ink; **ink-bench**, the inking-table of a printing machine (Knight *Dict. Mech.* 1875); **ink-block**, in printing, a block or table on which the ink is spread, to be taken up by the rollers or ink-balls; **ink-blot**, a blot of ink; also *fig.*, and *attrib.*, esp. in **ink-blot test** *Psychol.*, a projective test in which the subject's imaginative reactions to a random ink-blot shape are analysed and used as a guide to his personality; also *ellipt.* as *ink-blot*; **ink-brayer** = BRAYER2; **ink-cap**, a fungus of the genus *Coprinus*; **ink-cylinder**, an inking cylinder or roller in a printing machine; †**ink-dabbler**, a scribbler; **ink disease**, a fungal disease caused by species of *Phytophthora*, esp. *P. cambivora*, affecting chestnut and occasionally other trees, making the surface of their roots and sometimes trunks a darker colour; †**ink-divine** (see quot.); **ink-duct**, (*a*) the duct of a cephalopod's ink-bag; (*b*) = *ink-trough*; **ink-eraser**, a piece of prepared caoutchouc, or similar substance, used to erase writing in ink or blots; **ink-feed**, the duct which carries the ink to the nib of a fountain pen; also, the feeding of ink through this duct; **ink-fish**, a cuttle-fish or squid; **ink-fountain** = *ink-trough*; **ink-gland** = *ink-bag*; **ink-jerker** *U.S.*, **-spiller** = *ink-slinger*; **ink-knife**, a blade for controlling the flow of ink from an ink-fountain, or for pressing down the ink; †**ink-man**, the employee in a printing-office who prepares the ink for use; **ink-mirror**, a surface of ink used in clairvoyance in place of a crystal; **ink-mushroom**, a mushroom of the genus *Coprinus*; **ink-nut** = MYROBALAN; **ink-pad**, an inking-pad; **ink-pencil**, a pencil filled with a composition possessing some of the qualities of ink; **ink-plant**, the European shrub *Coriaria myrtifolia*, or New Zealand species *C. thymifolia*; **ink-powder**, the powdered ingredients of ink; **ink-printing**, the process of making photographic prints in common ink; **ink-roller**, an inking-roller; **ink-root**, the root of the American sea-lavender or marsh-rosemary (*Statice Limonium*); **ink-sac** = *ink-bag*; **ink-saucer**, a dark mark (beneath the eye); **ink-slab**, (*a*) the slate or stone slab of an ink-table; (*b*) a container for ink; *spec.* in the Far East, a slab on which ink is mixed ready for writing; **ink-slice**, a broad knife or paddle used for handling printer's ink; **ink-slinger** (orig. *U.S.*), a contemptuous appellation for a professional writer, esp. a reckless writer in the newspaper press; so **ink-slinging**; **ink-spot**, (*a*) a stain of ink; (*b*) a dark spot on the skin; **ink-stone**, (*a*) native copperas or iron-sulphate, used in making ink, (*b*) a slab of stone or slate on which Indian ink is prepared for use by rubbing; **ink-surface**, a surface serving as an ink-table; **ink-table**, in a printing-press, the table or slab on which the ink is distributed by the roller; **ink-tippler** (*nonce-wd.*), one who is constantly using ink, a writer; **ink-trough**, the reservoir containing the ink in a printing machine; **ink-value**, the equivalent in a black-and-white print of a colour in a painting; **ink-wash** *Japanese Painting* (see WASH *sb.*4 4 b); **ink weed** *Austral.* and *N.Z.*, a perennial herb of the genus *Phytolacca*, which bears black berries containing a reddish juice (= POKE *sb.*4 2 a); **ink-well** (see quots.); **ink-wood**, the tree *Hypelate paniculata*, found in S. Florida and the W. Indies; **ink-writer**, a telegraph instrument which records messages in ink.

1835–6 TODD *Cycl. Anat.* I. 536 The *ink-bag probably attains its largest proportional size in the genus *Sepiola*. **1873** DAWSON *Earth & Man* ix. 224 The Belemnite..had ink-bags provided with that wonderfully divided pigment, inimitable by art. **1884** SOUTHWARD *Pract. Print.* (ed. 2) 385 The Printer's *Ink Ball, which is now very seldom used, consists of a semi-globular pad, coated with composition.

1888 *Century Mag.* XXXVI. 765 The juice of poke-berries, compounded with vinegar, or the distillation of a vegetable product known as 'ink balls', usurped the place of ink. **1688** R. HOLME *Armoury* II. iii. 56 Brayer, is a round wooden Rubber..used in the *Inke-block to Bray and Rub Inke. **1727-41** CHAMBERS *Cycl.* s.v. *Printing*, One of these [balls] the pressman takes in each hand, and applying them on the ink-block, to charge them with ink, he [etc.]. **1790** NICHOLSON *Specif. Patent*, O is a cylinder faced with leather and lying across an ink-block. **1841** SAVAGE *Dict. Printing* s.v. *Ink Block*, The introduction of rollers has superseded the use of the ink block, for which has been substituted an inking apparatus. [*a* **1500** ? LYDGATE *Lavenders* 18 Wasshe withe wyne the fervente *ynkes blote.] **1928** J. J. B. MORGAN *Psychol. Abnormal People* iv. 145 The Rorschach test is a special development of the ink-blot test. The ordinary ink-blot test has not yielded very significant results heretofore. Rorschach, some years ago, developed a series of ink-blots which have been more successful than those used previously. **1931** *Psychol. Abstr.* V. 268 An explanation of the use of the Rorschach ink-blot test as a measure of intelligence. **1940** R. S. WOODWORTH *Psychol.* (ed. 12) v. 151 A class of tests sometimes called the 'fantasy tests'... Most used is the inkblot... A variety of things can be seen in such a blot. **1955** *Publ. Amer. Dial. Soc.* XXIV. 13 The interpretation given ink-blots by criminals reveals their unconscious motivations. **1965** *Sun* 20 May 2/2 American military planners are weighing up an 'inkblot' strategy to clear South Vietnam of Communist guerillas. **1967** E. SHORT *Embroidery & Fabric Collage* i. 28 *Ink Blots and Dribbled Paint*. These methods are not as haphazard as they would at first seem as the hand is guided to a great extent by one's intuitive sense of design. **1968** D. RAPAPORT et al. *Diagn. Psychol. Testing* (rev. ed.) ix. 272 From the perceptual point of view it *appears* that the Rorschach inkblots are 'unstructured' perceptual raw material. **1972** *Jrnl. Social Psychol.* Dec. 303 Human movement responses ..may be interpreted as an index of social approach during the administration of an inkblot test. **1887** *Amer. Naturalist* XXI. 553 *Ink-cap (species of Coprinus). **1927** GWYNNE-VAUGHAN & BARNES *Struct. & Devel. Fungi* 301 The genus *Coprinus*, the ink cap, is one of the commonest forms with black spores. **1963** LANGE & HORA *Collins Guide Mushrooms & Toadstools* 136 *Coprinus*—'Ink caps'. Characterised in almost all species by the gradual 'auto-digestion' of the gills, and sometimes the cap, into a black ink-like fluid. **1894** *Brit. Printer* VII. 346 Most rollers in the better machines are driven by the friction of the *ink cylinder. **1598** B. JONSON *Ev. Man in Hum.* v. i, These paper-pedlars! these *ink-dabblers! **1923** *Rev. Appl. Mycol.* II. 188 The so-called '*ink' disease of chestnuts constitutes a serious damper to French sylviculture. **1932** *Forestry* VI. 182 The fungus causing the ink disease of chestnut, has a very wide distribution. **1968** F. G. BROWNE *Pests & Dis. Forest Plantation Trees* II. 915 It [sc. *Phytophthora cambivora*] is one of the pathogens..associated with ink disease, a severe malady of *Castanea*. **1604** S. HIERON *Wks.* I. 533 It is no matter, though the papists continue to call vs in scorne *inke-diuines, because of our close adhering to the holy text. **1835-6** TODD *Cycl. Anat.* I. 530/1 Delicate fasciculi.. intercept the termination of the..*ink-duct. **1883** W. BLADES in *Printers' Reg.* 125/2 The ink-duct at the end, with its roller supplying a small but regular quantity of ink at each revolution. **1881** *Daily News* 1 Mar. 5/1 However long you may boil the tender parts of camel, the *plat*..is no better than so much *ink-eraser. **1907** *Westm. Gaz.* 23 Oct. 11/1 The Patent Spoon-Feed has successfully overcome the *ink-feed difficulty. **1935** *Discovery* Jan. 15/2 He must decide whether to alter the colour of the ink, its consistency, the rate of ink-feed. **1693** *Phil. Trans.* XVII. 855 The Sleave or *Ink-fish, *Lolligo*. **1752** SIR J. HILL *Hist. Anim.* 97 The Ink-fish, or Cuttle-fish..when in danger of being taken, it emits a black liquor like ink out of it's mouth. **1875** KNIGHT *Dict. Mech.* 1798/2 The *ink-fountain and ink-distributing apparatus. **1851-6** WOODWARD *Mollusca* 63 *Ink-gland always present. **1865** *Harper's Mag.* 683/2 This rattle-brained scribbler, this miserable *ink-jerker. **1598** FLORIO, *Inchiostraro*, an *inke-man, an inke-maker. **1619** PURCHAS *Microcosmus* lv. 522 The Printer seemes to muster a great many vnder him; the Founder, Grauer, Cutter, Inke-man, Paper-man, Corrector, Compositor, Presse-men, and others. **1905** E. F. BENSON *Image in Sand* ii, Abdul had.. tried him with the simple experiment of the *ink-mirror, and found him extraordinarily sensitive. **1690** *Lond. Gaz.* No. 2534/4 Holman's London *Ink-Powder,..being the best Ingredients for making the strongest and best black Writing Ink. **1819** *Pantologia* s.v. *Ink*, Ink powder..is nothing else than the substances employed in the composition of common ink, pounded and pulverised. **1825** J. NICHOLSON *Operat. Mechanic* 307 It..remains for a short period in contact with the surface of the *ink-roller.. thereby receiving a portion of ink upon its surface. **1890** W. J. GORDON *Foundry* 181 A series of distributing ink-rollers. **1884** F. M. CRAWFORD *Rom. Singer* I. 3 He had great black eyes, with *ink-saucers under them. **1890** C. T. JACOBI *Printing* 288/2 **Ink slab*, the table on which ink is distributed, either at press or machine. **1895** *Montgomery Ward Catal.* 210/2 Slate ink slabs... 5 inch square with heavy glass cover. **1911** *Encycl. Brit.* XXII. 354/2 A second ..roller conveys the ink from this drum to the distributing table or ink slab. **1938** *Burlington Mag.* Aug. 90/2 The inkslabs and inkstones, so sought after by collectors. **1963** KENNEISON & SPILMAN *Dict. Printing* 100 *Ink slab*, that part of certain printing presses, consisting of a large, flat, steel bed, from which the distributing rollers..take ink. **1969** *Korean Folklore & Classics* I. 23 He..picked up his teacher's ink-slab. **1884** SOUTHWARD *Pract. Print.* (ed. 2) 384 Where very large quantities of ink are required to be spread out on the table, an *ink slice is sometimes used. **1887** W. DOUGLAS *Duelling Days in the Army* 132 Every one on the Paris press seems ready..to fight any other *ink-slinger on the slightest provocation. **1896** *Academy* 7 Nov. 347/2 Only great critics, or impertinent ink slingers, would attempt to appraise their value. **1894** *Daily News* 2 May 6/3 High-bred women who were not given to what modern Americans call '*ink-slinging'. **1896** *Spectator* 7 Nov. 619 There is..no picturesque ink-slinging, as the happy American phrase goes. **1881** *Punch* 10 Sept. 110/2 To think people ain't got more savvy than what these *inkspillers enjoy. **1839** *Mag. Dom. Econ.* IV. 214 *Ink-spots and other stains on silk. **1897** *Allbutt's Syst. Med.* II. 223 If a general erythema [in small-pox] be..accompanied by isolated ink spots it will certainly be fatal. **1825** J. NICHOLSON *Operat. Mechanic* 307 The reciprocating motion of the carriage causes the *ink-table..to receive ink upon its surface from the elastic roller. **1884** SOUTHWARD *Pract. Print.* (ed. 2) 467 As an ink-table for colour work there is nothing equal to white marble. **1892** *Ibid.* (ed. 4) 12 In 'machines'..the ink table always adjoins the type bed, and the rollers are passed over it and on to the type mechanically. **1842** MRS. GORE *Fascin.* 120 Do I look like an old rat that has spent its days in gnawing the classics?.. Am I an *ink tippler? a college sizar? **1818** E. COWPER in Savage *Dict. Print.* (1841) s.v. *Inking Apparatus*, The *ink trough is fixed at one edge of the table. **1890** W. J. GORDON *Foundry* 181 An ink-trough from which the roller..is lifted at every revolution. **1894** *Athenæum* 22 Dec. 867/1 The rendering of what are called the *ink values of Mr. Beardsley's designs..must have been a matter of frequent difficulty. **1936** *Burlington Mag.* Oct. 162/2 The spirited *ink-wash technique. [**1906** T. F. CHEESEMAN *Man. N.Z. Flora* 1085 *Phytolacca octandra*... Ink-plant; Poke-weed.] **1913** *N.Z. Dept. Agric. Jrnl. Agric.* VII. 369 *Inkweed, or pokeweed (*Phytolacca octandra*), is a poisonous plant. **1933** *Bulletin* (Sydney) 15 Nov. 28/4 Inkweed is hard to burn or eradicate if it gets a hold. **1962** N. C. W. BEADLE et al. *Handbk. Vasc. Plants Sydney Distr.* 160 Weed of waste ground. Introd. from Trop. Amer. Ink Weed. *P[hytolacca] octandra*. **1875** KNIGHT *Dict. Mech.* 1188/2 **Ink-well*, an ink-cup adapted to occupy a hole in a desk. **1876** PREECE & SIVEWRIGHT *Telegraphy* 71 While it [the inking disc] just dips into the ink-well it also gently presses against the paper. *Ibid.* 116 Wheatstone's system of automatic telegraphy is that which is used in England..the messages are recorded on an exceedingly delicate form of direct *ink-writer. **1888** T. GRAY in *Encycl. Brit.* XXIII. 119/2 The form of instrument almost universally used in Europe makes the record in ink, and hence is sometimes called the 'ink-writer'.

ink, *sb.*[2] Also 6 ynck, 6-7 inke. [Origin unknown.]

†**1.** *orig.* An iron cross set in the lower face of the upper millstone, and serving to poise it on the spindle which turns it; a mill-rind. As a charge in *Her.* = FER-DE-MOLINE; see also INK-MOLYNE.

1572 BOSSEWELL *Armorie* III. 20 b, The office of an Ynck Molyne, and to what purpose it serueth betwene the Myll stones, is, I thinke, knowne to moste men, but to Myllers especially, who in takinge theire tolle, forget oftentimes the Rule taught them by their myll ynck. **1610** GUILLIM *Heraldry* II. vii. (1611) 70 Perhaps because it resembleth the Inke of a Mill which is evermore Pierced. **1688** R. HOLME *Armoury* III. 341/1 The Inke or Rinde of a Mill. Millers term it in English a Brandret or Mill Rinde. **1727-41** CHAMBERS *Cycl.* s.v. *Fer de Moulin*, The iron-ink, or ink of a mill, which sustains the moving mill-stone.

2. In current use: see quot.

1875 KNIGHT *Dict. Mech.* 1019/2 *Step* or *Ink*, the socket which holds the *toe* of a vertical shaft or spindle.

ink, *sb.*[3]: see INKE.

ink (ɪŋk), *sb.*[4] *Sc.* [var. of ING.] *pl.* Low-lying grassland subject to flooding by spring tides. Also (in *sing.*) *attrib.*

a **1692** A. SYMSON *Large Descr. Galloway* (1823) 138 Down the river, about a mile from the Church..a large plott of fine fir-planting, over-looking a rich ink ground. **1802** *Farmer's Mag.* Aug. 331 Eighty acres..consisted of a rich sea marsh, or *inks*, as we call them here, almost a true level, ..about 4 or 5 acres,..16 inches lower, being a younger marsh, and nothing but what we call ink grass growing upon it. **1824** J. MACTAGGART *Gallovid. Encycl.* 280 *Inks.* On muddy, level shores,..pieces of land over-flowed with spring tides, and not touched by common ones..; on these grow a coarse kind of grass. **1848** *Scottish Jrnl. Topogr.* II. 234/1 *Spurlings* to net in the inks of the Cree. **1899** *Galloway Advertiser* 27 July 1/3 Extent, 240 acres or thereby of Carse Land of excellent quality, together with a very large extent of 'Inks' or Shore Pasture. **1974** *Scottish Field* Apr. 15/4 Some of the sunsets especially, behind the Inks and Wigtown Sands, are as fine as you can see anywhere.

ink (ɪŋk), *v.* Also 6 **enk**. [f. INK *sb.*[1]]

1. a. *trans.* To mark, stain, or smear with or as with ink.

1562 PILKINGTON *Expos. Abdyas* Pref. Aa vij b, Enking their hands in bloude. **1718** LADY M. W. MONTAGU *Let. to Lady Rich* 16 Mar., You may..send letters of passion, friendship..or even of news, without ever inking your fingers. **1755** JOHNSON, *To Ink*, to black or daub with ink: as, his face is all over inked. **1838** DICKENS *Nich. Nick.* viii, There were a couple of long, old, rickety desks, cut and notched, and inked, and damaged in every possible way. **1865** MRS. WHITNEY *Gayworthys* iii. (1879) 39 Grasping the pen close down toward the nib and inking himself profusely.

b. To cover (types, etc.) with ink in order to print from them.

1727-41 CHAMBERS *Cycl.* s.v. *Printing*, The plate sufficiently inked, they first wipe it coarsely over with a foul rag. **1819** *Pantologia* s.v. *Printing*, The cylinder A returns empty, and the cylinder B inked. **1841** *Penny Cycl.* XIX. 18/2 One [man] to ink the types. **1890** W. J. GORDON *Foundry* 190 He seized the semi-liquid glue and with it inked a forme.

2. With adverbs, as ***ink in*** (or ***over***), to go over or trace in ink (lines previously drawn in pencil); ***ink out***, to obliterate with ink; ***ink up***, to cover completely with ink. Also *fig.*

1803 *Lett. Miss Riversdale* I. 319 The Prince took down the notes in pencil..and promised to ink them over for Lady Belfont. **1845** *Athenæum* 18 Jan. 71 The impression is inked up with rollers and printed from in the usual manner of surface-printing. **1881** *Bibliographer* Dec. 8/1 The separate 1525 device..with the objectionable motto inked out. **1884** SOUTHWARD *Pract. Print.* (ed. 2) 398 If the roller has been inked up, it must be carefully scraped with a blunt knife before being used again. **1886** *N. Zealand Herald* 28 May 3/7 Finished drawings, inked in and elaborately coloured. **1892** LD. ROSEBERY in *Daily News* 16 Mar. 3/2 The equity of the case will be met if Mr. Campbell retires with the scrutineers and inks over his pencil. **1929** A. C. & C. EDINGTON *Studio Murder Myst.* iii. 23 It was inked into his mind's eye, so that even when he shut his eyes..he could not shut out that awful picture. **1952** C. DAY LEWIS tr. *Virgil's Aeneid* III. 59 A streaming night inked out The sky. **1959** *Times* 26 Jan. 6/1 The Yeames is a picture surely so inked into the national memory that it would need more than condemnation of its taste to eradicate it.

Hence **inked** (ɪŋkt), *ppl. a.*

1790 NICHOLSON *Specif. Patent*, This motion causes the cylinder B to revolve continually, and consequently to render its inked surface very uniform, by the action of its distributing rollers. **1851** THACKERAY *Eng. Hum.* v. (1876) 316 With inked ruffles, and claret stains on his tarnished lace coat. **1890** W. J. GORDON *Foundry* 216 The hardened gelatin is bitten away on each side of the inked lines.

'ink-,berry. A name given, from their colour or juice, to various berries, and to the shrubs that produce them. **a.** A small shrub of the holly family (*Prinos glaber* or *Ilex glabra*), a native of the Atlantic coast of N. America. **b.** The West Indian indigo-berry (*Randia aculeata*). **c.** The plant *Mollinedia* (or *Kibara*) *macrophylla*, called *Australian* or *Queensland inkberry*. **d. inkberry weed**, the poke weed (*Phytolacca decandra*), a native of the Atlantic coast of N. America and North Africa, the Azores and China; called also, from its purplish-red juice, *red-ink plant*.

c **1850** *Nat. Encycl.* I. 959 *Prinos glaber* is a low handsome shrub, with white flowers and a black fruit; hence it is called, in Jersey, ink-berries. **1880** *Libr. Univ. Knowl.* VIII. 26 Inkberry, *Ilex glabra*, a shrub belonging to the holly family.

†**inke.** *Obs. rare.* Also **ink**. [Derivation unknown.] (See quot.)

1615 LATHAM *Falconry* (1633) 23 Adding unto the inke of a dove as much cleane washt flannell in quantitie, as may make her a reasonable casting. *Ibid.* Explan. Words, *Inke*, whether it be of Partridge, fowle, doues, or any other prey, is the necke from the head to the body. [Hence in later writers and dicts.; in some, as in Phillips 1706, spelt *ink*.]

inken ('ɪŋkən), *a.* Now *rare.* [f. INK *sb.*[1] + -EN[4].] Of ink; written with ink. †***inken divinity*** (see quot. 1698).

1600 O. E. (? M. SUTCLIFFE) *Repl. Libel* II. i. 5 Others call them Inken diuinity, and account them no better then Matter of strife. **1698** *Christ Exalted* Ded. A ij b, A debauched Crew of this Age,..that call the Scriptures an Inken Divinity. **1893** *National Observer* 17 June 120/2 The inken curse was laid upon him;..he was never happy without a pen and something to write upon.

inkennel, variant of ENKENNEL *v.*, *Obs.*

†**'inker**, *pron. Obs.* Forms: 1 **incer, yncer, incyr**, 3 **inker, incker(e, unker**, *Orm.* **ȝunnkerr**. [OE. *incer* of you two, (1) gen. dual of the second pers. pron. THOU: see INC: = Goth. *igqara*, ON. *ykkar*; (2) declinable possessive pronoun = Goth. *igqar*, ON. *ykkarr*. On the ME. *ȝunnkerr*, *unker* see INC.]

1. As *genitive dual*: Of you two. ***either inker***, either of you two; ***inker baþre***, of you both.

c **1050** *Martyrol.* in Cockayne *Shrine* 148 Yncer æȝðer ofslyhð oðerne..and yncer wif beoð on anum dæȝe wudewan. *c* **1200** ORMIN 6183 All þatt ȝho ȝeorneþþ wiþþ skill, To ȝunnkerr baþre gode. *c* **1205** LAY. 32170 þat unker æiðer oðer Luuie swa his broðer. *c* **1230** *Hali Meid.* 31 Swa þat inker eiðer heasci wið oðer. *c* **1300** *Havelok* 1882 Roberd! willam! hware ar ye? Gripeth eþer unker a god tre.

2. as *possess. pron.* Belonging to you two, your.

c **975** *Rushw. Gosp.* Matt. ix. 29 Æfter ȝeleafan incrum ȝeweorðe inc [*c* **1000** *Ags. Gosp.*, Æftyr incrum ȝeleafan; *c* **1160** *Hatton Gosp.*, Æfter yncre ȝeleafen]. *c* **1000** ÆLFRIC *Exod.* x. 17 Biddaþ incerne God, þæt he adrife þisne deaþ fram me. *c* **1205** LAY. 5102 Incker moder inc hateð. *Ibid.* 5623 Ich inckere freond wurðe.

inker ('ɪŋkə(r)), *sb.* [f. INK *v.* + -ER[1].] One who or that which inks.

1. A telegraph-instrument which records the message in ink.

1882 *Daily News* 27 Jan. 2/1 Needle telegraphs, Morse inkers, sounders, and type printers. **1899** *Ibid.* 30 Mar. 5/5 An ordinary Morse inker, or tape-machine.

2. *Printing.* An inking-roller.

1884 SOUTHWARD *Pract. Print.* (ed. 2) 469 Next set in their places the wavers and the inkers. **1890** W. J. GORDON *Foundry* 203 The Marinoni web..with the inkers at the top and bottom. **1898** *Brit. Printer* XI. 281 Three or four inkers ..for distribution on table.

3. A mechanical drawing-pen.

'ink-horn. Forms: see INK *sb.*[1] [f. INK *sb.*[1] + HORN *sb.* 12; cf. obs. Du *inkt-horn, enkt-horen* (Kilian).]

1. A small portable vessel (originally made of a horn) for holding writing-ink: now seldom used. †***to smell of the ink-horn***, to be pedantic; ***term of inkhorn*** = *ink-horn term* 2 b.

1382 WYCLIF *Ezek.* ix. 11 The man that..hadde an enk-horn in his rigge. *c* **1440** *Promp. Parv.* 262/1 Inkehorne, *attramentarium*. **1463** *Mann. & Househ. Exp.* (Roxb.) 229 Item, payd..for a pener and a ynkorne, iij. d. **1474** CAXTON *Chesse* 77 On his gurdel a penner and an ynk-horn. *c* **1570** *Pride & Lowl.* (1841) 30 Ne had they term of ink-horne ne of penne But plaine in speache. **1587** GOLDING *De Mornay* xxvi. 396 Proclamations set foorth in such a stile,..smelling too much of the Inkehorne. **1687** T. BROWN *Saints in*

Uproar Wks. 1730 I. 75 Children don't use to come into the world with their ink-horns and pocket-books about them. **1733** LADY B—z in *Swift's Lett.* (1766) II. 191 Two days ago I washed the mould out of my inkhorn, put fresh ink into it. *c* **1850** *Arab. Nts.* (Rtldg.) 253 He drew from a little writing-case..some paper, a cut cane, and an ink-horn. **1879** MACLEAR *Celts* viii. 133 Literary apparatus, such as waxed tablets, styles, pens, and ink horns.

2. *attrib.* **a.** †**ink-horn fish**, the ink-fish or cuttle-fish; †**ink-horn mate**, **varlet** contemptuous appellations for a scribbler.

1598 *Epulario* Hjb, To dresse an *Inke horne fish, in Latine *Lolligo*. **1635** SWAN *Spec. M.* (1670) 342 The Calamary..Some call him the Ink-horn-fish. **1591** SHAKS. *1 Hen. VI*, III. i. 99 Ere that we will suffer such a Prince..To be disgraced by an *Inke-horne Mate, Wee..all will fight. **1820** LAMB *Elia* Ser. I. 2 *Races Men*, Your sour parochial or state-gatherers,—those *ink-horn varlets, who carry their want of welcome in their faces!

b. **ink-horn term**, a term of the literary language, a learned or bookish word; so also ***ink-horn desire, language, word***. *arch.*

1543 BALE *Yet a Course* 59b, Soche are your Ynkehorne termes. **1589** PUTTENHAM *Eng. Poesie* II. xii[i]. (Arb.) 130 Irreuocable, irradiation, depopulation and such like,..which..were long time despised for inkehorne termes. **1589** GREENE *Menaphon* (Arb.) 51 Wherefore thoughe he had done it of an ink horne desire to be eloquent. **1623** LISLE *Ælfric on O. & N. Test.* Pref. (1638) 16 Faine to stuffe the text with such fustian, such inkehorne termes, as may seem to favour their parts. **1784** HUTTON *Bran New Wark* 6 Inkhorn words, to be honest, we knaw lile abaut. **1871** LOWELL *Study W.* (1886) 330 As if it were a spoken, and not merely an ink-horn language. **1872** MINTO *Eng. Prose Lit.* II. ii. 235 Inkhorn words of Latin origin.

†'**inkhornism.** *Obs. rare.* [f. prec. + -ISM.] A learned or pedantic word or expression; an ink-horn term or phrase.

1597-8 BP. HALL *Sat.* I. viii. 12 Singing his love..In mightiest ink-hornismes he can thither wrest. **1611** COTGR., *Supergurgiter*, to overflow (an Inkhornisme in Rabelais).

So †'**inkhornist**, one who uses ink-horn terms; a pedant. *Obs.*

1592 G. HARVEY *Pierce's Super.* 181, I have seldome read a more garish and pibald stile in any scribling Ink-hornist.

†'**inkhornize**, *v. Obs. rare.* [f. as prec. + -IZE.] *intr.* To use pedantic words. (Also, *to inkhornize it.*) *trans.* To treat to, or assail with, ink-horn terms. Hence †'**inkhornizing** *ppl. a.*; also †'**inkhornizer** = INKHORNIST.

1589 *Pappe w. Hatchet* Bivb, I know a foole that shall so inkhornize you with straunge phrases, that you shall blush at your owne bodges. **1611** COTGR., *Pedantesque*, pedanticall, inkhornizing, pedantlike. *Ibid.*, *Pedantizer*, to pedantize it, or play the Pedant;..also, to inkhornize it.

inkily ('ɪŋkɪlɪ), *adv.* [f. INKY *a.* + -LY².] In an inky manner; like ink.

1894 STEVENSON & OSBOURNE *Ebb-Tide* I. vi. 111 The sea .., inkily blue.

inkindle, obs. variant of ENKINDLE *v.*

inkiness ('ɪŋkɪnɪs). *rare.* [f. INKY *a.* + -NESS.] The quality of being inky.

1611 COTGR., *Encreté*,..inkinesse, or blacknesse. **1853** KANE *Grinnell Exp.* xxvii. (1856) 220 Contrasted with the pure white snow, their waters are black, even to inkyness.

inking ('ɪŋkɪŋ), *vbl. sb.* [f. INK *v.* + -ING¹.] The action of the verb INK; *spec.* the covering of type with ink preparatory to printing.

1818 E. COWPER in Savage *Dict. Print.* (1841) s.v. *Inking Apparatus*, The advantages of this mode of inking are considerable. **1833** J. HOLLAND *Manuf. Metal* II. 233 It [a printing-machine] was found to be too complicated; the inking was defective. **1872** *Daily News* 18 June 5/1 The rending or the inking of a reputation. **1884** *Leeds Mercury* Wkly. Suppl. 15 Nov. 1/1 He succeeded in combining a press with mechanical instead of manual methods of inking.

b. *attrib.* or *Comb.*, chiefly in terms relating to printing, or to those parts of the printing-machine concerned in the process of inking the type, as ***inking-apparatus, -ball, -cylinder, -disk, -pad, -power, -roller, -slab, -table, -trough.*** (Cf. INK *sb.*¹ 4.)

1825 J. NICHOLSON *Operat. Mechanic* 306 Two..systems of *inking apparatus,..adapted to ink their respective forms of types. **1890** W. J. GORDON *Foundry* 190 In 1815 Forster had found the Staffordshire potters dabbing on their patterns with lumps of glue and treacle. He took the mixture and made it into *inking-balls. **1790** NICHOLSON *Specif. Patent*, A is the printing-cylinder..and B is the *inking-cylinder, with its distributing-rollers. **1851** *Illustr. Exhib.* 491 An apparatus similar to the inking cylinder of the platen machine. **1876** PREECE & SIVEWRIGHT *Telegraphy* 71 The position of the *inking disc, with respect to the paper and armature. **1892** SOUTHWARD *Pract. Print.* (ed. 4) 425 The 'Minerva' has its inking disc in two parts. **1790** NICHOLSON *Specif. Patent*, The lever..raises the *inking-piece, which applies itself against one of the distributing-rollers. *Ibid.*, B is the *inking-roller. **1875** KNIGHT *Dict. Mech.* 1188/1 The diagonal arrangement of the inking-roller..is described in Applegath's English patent, 1823. **1841** *Chambers' Inform.* 636/2 The type-carriage and *inking-tables have a reciprocating motion. **1851-3** TOMLINSON *Cycl. Arts* in *Penny Cycl.* 2nd Suppl. (1858) 538/1 As the inking-table..passes the ductor-roller, it receives from it a coating of ink.

inkirly, variant of INCRELY *adv.*

inkish ('ɪŋkɪʃ), *a. rare.* [f. INK *sb.*¹ + -ISH.] Somewhat inky; blackish.

1670 H. STUBBE *Plus Ultra* 95 To pursue the Circulation of the blood there by the injecting of Inkish liquor. **1815** W. H. IRELAND *Scribbleomania* 242 Greeting each imp in his true inkish plight.

inkle (ɪŋk(ə)l), *sb.* Now *rare.* Forms: 6 **ync(h)ull, ynkell, ynkle,** 6–7 **ynckle, inckle,** 6– **incle, inkle.** [Derivation not ascertained.

Du. *enkel*, formerly *enckel*, *inckel* 'single', is suggested by the sound, and it is quite conceivable that this might be applied to a 'narrow' or 'inferior' tape; but historical evidence is wanting. Identity of origin with *lingle* (as conjectured by some) is out of the question.]

1. A kind of linen tape, formerly much used for various purposes.

1541 *Yatton Church-w. Acc.* (Som. Rec. Soc.) 155 For a pece of brode yncull for gyrdyllys..v^d. **1546** *Ibid.* 159 For whyte ynchull to make amyss..j^d. **1567** HARMAN *Caveat* 65 With baskets..on their armes, where in they haue laces, pynnes, nedles, white ynkell. **1616** BEAUM. & FL. *Scornf. Lady* v. iii, My wife is learning now Sir, to weave inkle. **1673** RAY *Journ. Low C.* (1738) I. 41 Here we noted an engine or wheel for the weaving of inkle and tape. **1686** *Lond. Gaz.* No. 2197/4 Lost,..a parcel of Papers,..wrapt and bound about with Red Incle. **1781** W. HARROD *Antiq. Stamford* (1785) II. 438 His shoes were..ty'd with strings of a purple colour,..but whether ribbon, or inkle I know not. **1825** BROCKETT *N.C. Gloss.*, *Inkle*, an inferior kind of tape. **1868** ATKINSON *Cleveland Gloss.*, *Inkle*, a narrow linen fabric, or kind of tape, formerly used for shoe-ties, apron-strings, and the like.

†**b.** A piece, or variety, of inkle. *Obs.*

1607 MARKHAM *Caval.* I. (1617) 58 Take an Incle or Ribband, and measure the Foale when hee is new foaled. **1610** —— *Masterp.* II. iii. 399 Either stitch them together, or with a broad inckle bind them vp. **1611** SHAKS. *Winter's T.* IV. iv. 208 Hee hath Ribbons of all the colours i' th Rainebow; Points..Inckles, Caddysses, Cambrickes, Lawnes. **1639** T. DE GREY *Compl. Horsem.* 141 With an incle or filliting bind the hough. **1733** P. LINDSAY *Interest Scot.* 101 They buy up large Quantities of our fine Linen Yarn,..Yarn of a coarser Staple..for Warp to their wrought Inkles, Fustians and Linsywoolsies.

2. The linen thread or yarn from which inkle is manufactured; usually ***unwrought inkle***.

1545 *Rates Custom-ho.* bvb, Incle the hundreth pounde vnwrought. **1571** *Wills & Inv. N.C.* (Surtees 1835) 361, iij ounces of cotton silk iij^s.—ij ounces of fyne ynkell vj^d. **1583** *Rates Custom-ho.* C vij, Inckle vnwrought called white thred single or double. **1608** SHAKS. *Per.* v. Chor. 8 Marina..with her neeld composes Nature's own shape, of bud, bird, branch, or berry..Her inkle, silk, twin with the rubied cherry. **1714** *Lond. Gaz.* No. 5240/3 Unwrought Incle Imported into this Kingdom. **1813** *Chron.* in *Ann. Reg.* 252/1 Ribbons made of silk mixed with Inkle or cotton. **1875** KNIGHT *Dict. Mech.* 1188/1 Spinel is bleached yarn for the manufacture of the tape, and is known as unwrought inkle. **1879** *Spons' Encycl. Manuf.* I. 590 The majority [of wicks] consist of inkle, a fine flax yarn.

3. *attrib.* and *Comb.*, as ***inkle-house, -loom, -maker, -manufacture, -manufacturer, -points, -roll, string, -wares***; also †**inkle-beggar**, a beggar who sells tape, etc.; **inkle-eloquence**, ? tawdry, shoddy rhetoric; **inkle-weaver**, a weaver of inkle or linen tape; whence the phrase ***as great*** (or ***thick***) ***as inkle-weavers***, extremely intimate (see quot. 1788).

1616 T. ADAMS *Div. Herbal* Wks. 1862 II. 437 From the courtier to the carter, from the lady to the *inkle-beggar, there is this excess. **1774** *Westm. Mag.* II. 453, I have seen a powdered coxcomb of this gawzy make..flatter himself with the power of his *inkle eloquence. **1845** *New Stat. Acc. Scotl.* VI. 157 In 1732 Mr. Harvey brought away from Haerlem two *inkle-looms. *a* **1700** B. E. *Dict. Cant. Crew*, *Cannikin*,..as great as Cup and Cann; or as great as two *Inklemakers. **1805** FORSYTH *Beauties Scotl.* II. 128 Ten tons of linen yarn have been annually consumed in the *inkle manufacture. **1771** SMOLLETT *Humph. Cl.* 3 Sept., Mr. M'Clellan, a rich *inkle-manufacturer. **1603** *Manch. Crt. Leet Rec.* (1885) II. 189 For sale of sackclothe, *inclepoints, Garteringe, Threede, Buttons and oth^r Small wares. **1583** *Rates Custom-ho.* C vij, *Inckle roles the dosen peeces. **1610** MARKHAM *Masterp.* I. xxxiii. 65 Tye vp his eares with a soft *inckle string. **1845** *New Stat. Acc. Scotl.* VI. 157 Glasgow was the first place in Britain where *inkle wares were manufactured. **1691** T. BROWNE *Reasons Mr. Bays changing Relig.* (ed. 2) 15 The *Inkle-weavers..the dealers in Ribbons. **1738** SWIFT *Pol. Convers.* I. 105 She and you were as great as two Inkle-weavers. **1788** COWPER *Let.* 6 May, Wks. 1836 VI. 153 When people are intimate, we say they are as great as two inkle-weavers..inkle-weavers contract intimacies with each other sooner than other people on account of their juxtaposition in weaving of inkle [the inkle-looms being so narrow and close together]. **1874** MRS. H. WOOD *Mast. Greylands* xxxiii. 389 My relatives..and the Greylands' Rest people used to be as thick as inkle-weavers.

inkle (ɪŋk(ə)l), *v. rare.* Also 4 incle. [Origin unascertained: cf. INKLING.]

1. *trans.* To utter or communicate in an undertone or whisper, to hint, give a hint of. In quot. 1340-70 'to inkle the truth', (parenthetically) = to mention or tell the truth, 'sooth to say'. In quots. 1901, 1904 a back-formation from INKLING 2.

1340-70 *Alisaunder* 616 A brem brasen borde bringes hee soone, Imped in iuory, too incle þe truthe. **1901** S. BUTLER *Erewhon Revisited* 42 People like being deceived, but they also like to have an inkling of their own deception, and you never inkle them. **1904** HARDY *Dynasts* I. I. vi. 57 Thou art young, and dost not heed the Cause of things Which some of us have inkled to thee here.

2. *dial.* To get an inkling or notion (of).

[In this sense app. a back-formation from INKLING 3, 4.] **1866** BLACKMORE *Cradock Nowell* xxix. (1883) 153 His marriage settlement and its effects, they could only inkle of. **1868** ATKINSON *Cleveland Gloss.*, *Inkle*. 1. To form notions, guesses or projects..2. To form wishes or inclinations..for this or that gratification, to wit. **1869** BLACKMORE *Lorna D.* lii. (1879) 340 She inkled what it was.

inkless ('ɪŋklɪs), *a.* [f. INK *sb.*¹ + -LESS.] Without ink.

1811 BYRON *Hints fr. Hor.* 599 My inkless pen Shall never blunt its edge. **1899** *Brit. Printer* XII. 231 Several printers have arranged to have machines fitted for electrical inkless printing.

†'**inkleth.** *Obs. rare*$^{-1}$. = next.

1568 LD. SCROPE in Ellis *Orig. Lett.* Ser. I. II. 240 She myght get into France, and that wold hardly be done yf my L. of Murraye have a former ynkleth of her departure thether.

inkling ('ɪŋklɪŋ), *vbl. sb.* Forms: (5 **nyngkiling**), 6 **ink(e)-, inck(e)-, ynk(e)-, inc-, ync-, ing-,** 6–7 **inckling,** 6– **inkling.** [f. INKLE *v.* + -ING¹.]

1. Mentioning in an undertone; a faint or slight mention, report, or rumour; chiefly in phrase ***to hear an inkling*** (***of*** something). *Obs.* exc. *dial.*

(In the first quot. it was the sound of his own name in a whispered communication that Alexander caught.)

a **1400-50** *Alexander* 2968 [Alexander] Herd a nyngkiling of his name, & naytis him to ryse, Buskis him vp at a braide, & fra þe burde rysys. **1533** MORE *Apol.* xxi. Wks. 881/2 The tother had heard an incling whiche yet he belieued not, that this man was not much afore hande. **1548** HALL *Chron.*, *Hen. IV* 25 He was thither come..before the confederates hearde any inkelyng of his marchyng forward. **1576** FLEMING *Panopl. Epist.* 11 There was an ynkling, that it wold not be long er you came. **1600** HOLLAND *Livy* VI. xxv. 235 They had scarcely heard any inkling or rumour of hostilitie. **1658** PHILLIPS, *An Inkling of a matter*, a small rumour or report, as it were a tinckling, or little sound. *a* **1665** J. GOODWIN *Filled w. the Spirit* (1867) 211 They had not so much as heard the least inkling of those blessed tidings. **1755** JOHNSON s.v., The word is derived by Skinner, from *inklincken*, to sound within. This sense is still retained in Scotland: as, I heard not an inkling. [So also in mod. Sc.]

2. A hint, a slight intimation, or suggestion; usually ***to give*** (one) ***an inkling*** (***of*** something).

1513 MORE *Rich. III*, Wks. 38/1 Whyther hee..knewe that hee suche thynge purposed, or otherwyse had anye inkelynge thereof. **1529** —— *Dyaloge* II. Wks. 191/1 But I put case now y^t ye had an inkeling or els a playne warning, y^t some of them were hys enemies. **1548** UDALL, etc. *Erasm. Par. Matt.* xxiii. 110 Geuyng an incklyng of his secound cummyng. **1549** COVERDALE, etc. *Erasm. Par. Thess.* I Signifying vnto them as it were with priuie ynclynges, that there were some among them, whiche were not yet altogether pure. **1553** BRENDE *Q. Curtius* Qj, To the entente no inglynge shoulde appeare of this newe counsaile, he caused it to be proclaimed that the armie should set forwardes the next daye. **1571** CAMPION *Hist. Irel.* II. x. (1633) 133, I have said enough, especially to a learned governour, to whom an inckling were sufficient. **1650** HOWELL *Giraffi's Rev. Naples* I. 77 There were many papers ..wherein there were inklings given. **1682** BUNYAN *Holy War* 287, I have received from this good truth-teller this one inkling further. **1741** RICHARDSON *Pamela* II. 341, I have had some Inkling given me, that you might, if you pleased, augment that Estate. **1865** CARLYLE *Fredk. Gt.* XIII. v. (1872) V. 61 If the least inkling of it ooze out, he shall have right to deny it.

†**b.** An intimation given by a wink or nod. *Obs. rare.*

1598 FLORIO, *Cenno*, a nod, a becke or signe or a glance or touch at any thing, an inkling. *Ibid.*, *Fare d'occhio*, to winke vpon one, to giue a signe with the eyes, to giue an inkling.

3. A hint or slight intimation received; hence, a slight or vague knowledge or notion, however acquired; a suspicion; esp. in phrase ***to have, get an inkling*** (***of*** something).

1546 J. HEYWOOD *Prov.* (1867) 73 He by gesse had got an inklyng Of hir hoord. **1604** T. WRIGHT *Passions* IV. §4. 191 Our memorie is such, that if it conceiue but an inckling of any matter..our understanding followeth it. **1627** SANDERSON *12 Serm.* (1637) 518 Never had..so much as the least inckling of the Doctrine of Salvation. **1755** J. G. COOPER in *World* No. 110 ¶9 The government..begins to entertain an idea, or, as the vulgar phrase it, to have an inkling of the matter. **1765** FOOTE *Commissary* I. Wks. 1799 II. 17 If he gets but an inkling, but the slightest suspicion, our project is marr'd. **1846** J. W. CROKER in *C. Papers* 10 July (1884), Not one of them had the least inkling of the kind of speech he was about to make. **1852** H. ROGERS *Ecl. Faith* (1853) 285 To transform a dim inkling of a truth into an intelligent, vital, conscious recognition of it.

†**b.** A suspicion *of* or *against* a person. *Obs. rare.*

1620 SHELTON *Quix.* III. i. 5 The Chaplain told him, the Rector had an Inckling against him. **1709** STRYPE *Ann. Ref.* (1824) I. xxxviii. 103 By this time they had some inkling of the lord Robert Dudley.

†**c.** ? A vague hope or notion of doing something.

1804 W. TAYLOR in *Ann. Rev.* II. 235 Antijacobinism had ..still some gay hopes to gamble upon, still some inkling to turn up a king.

4. *dial.* An inclination, slight desire. [app. influenced by *incline*, or F. *enclin*.]

1787 GROSE *Prov. Gloss.*, *Inkling*, a desire. N[orth]. **1807** SOUTHEY in Robberds *Mem. W. Taylor* II. 202, I feel inklings to address an ode to the people of Liverpool. **1824** —— *Lett.* (1856) III. 436, I have still an inkling for the west. **1825** BROCKETT *N.C. Gloss.*, *Inckling*, *Inkling*, a desire. **1828** *Craven Dial.*, *Inkling*, a desire. 'I've an inkling to gang to t' fair tomorn'. **1869** *Lonsdale Gloss.*, *Inklin'*, a wish or desire.

†**ink-molyne.** *Obs. rare.* [f. INK *sb.*[2] + *moline* (cf. FER-DE-MOLINE) = F. *moulin* a mill.] = INK *sb.*[2] 1.

1572 BOSSEWELL *Armorie* II. 115 b, He beareth Argent, a Cheuron de Ermines, betweene three Inkes molyn crusule botonie. **1611** COTGR., *Anille*,.. in Blazon; an ink-molyne.

in-kneed ('ɪn'niːd, -ˌniːd), *a.* [f. IN *adv.* 13 + KNEE *sb.* + -ED[2].] Having the legs bent inwards at the knees.

1724 *Auld Rob Morris* in *Ramsay's Tea-t. Misc.* (1733) I. 63 He's out-shin'd, in-knee'd and ringle-ey'd too. **1741** A. MONRO *Anat.* (ed. 3) 277 Weak rickety Children become inkneed. **1836–9** TODD *Cycl. Anat.* II. 168/1 Women.. are naturally more in-kneed than men.

†**in'knit,** *v. Obs. rare*[−1]. [f. IN-[1] + KNIT *v.*] *trans.* To knit up, draw close together.

c **1374** CHAUCER *Troylus* III. 1039 (1088) Ther with þe sorwe so his herte shette That.. euery spirit his vigour ynknette [*v.rr.* inknette, inknitt] So þey astoned & oppressed were.

inknot (ɪn'nɒt), *v. rare.* Also 7 en-. [f. IN-[1] + KNOT *v.*] *trans.* **a.** To include in or with a knot; to tie in. **b.** = INNODATE *v.*

1611 FLORIO, *Incappiare*, to enknot, to ensnare. **1639** FULLER *Holy War* III. xiii. 131 John Stafford Archbishop of Canterbury.. inknotteth that Priest in the greater excommunication that should consecrate *Poculum stanneum.* **1879** J. D. LONG *Æneid* v. 359 The rest [of the wounded snake] Retarded by the wound, delays it there Inknotting knots and twisting round itself.

†**in'know,** *v. Obs. rare*[−1]. [f. IN-[1] + KNOW *v.*, after L. *innōtescĕre.*] *trans.* To take knowledge of.

a **1300** *E.E. Psalter* cxliii[i]. 3 Laverd, whilk es man, for þou in-knew [L. *innotuisti*] him?

inkosi (ɪŋ'kɔʊsɪ). *S. Afr.* Also **enkosi, inkhasi, inkos, inkose(e),** and with capital initial. [Zulu. Cognate forms are found in other Bantu langs. (see quot. 1937); also Bondei, Zegua, Nguru *m-gosi*, Karanga *a-hosi* man, Gogo *mu-gosi* chief.] **a.** The royal title of a Zulu ruler. **b.** A chief, lord; in which sense also used as a title of respect.

[**1824** W. J. BURCHELL *Trav. S. Afr.* II. xiv. 364 The different members of his family, and the *kôsies* or subordinate chieftains, formed round us a circle two or three deep. **1827** G. THOMPSON *Trav. S. Afr.* x. 118 Calling the king, Kousie, which is not his name, but his title, *kousi* signifying king or principal chief in their language.] **1835** A. STEEDMAN *Wanderings S. Afr.* I. x. 256 Among the Zoolahs the title of *Inkose* is solely confined to the principal Chief. **1836** N. ISAACS *Trav. E. Afr.* (1937) II. 245 When the monarch is firmly seated on his throne.. he becomes an absolute king, or 'Inquose'. **1846** J. C. BROWN tr. *Arbousset & Daumas's Narr. Tour N.-E. of Cape Good Hope* (1852) xxvii. 423 As if a Zulu Inkhosi could show clemency! **1899** B. MITFORD *John Ames* x. 96 Policeman he want to see Inkose. **1905** *Westm. Gaz.* 8 June 2/1 All the members of the kraals concerned will.. form,.. with the 'inkosi', his several wives and their brothers and sisters and children and dependent relatives, a formidable audience. **1910** J. BUCHAN *Prester John* xii. 215 Courage, Inkoos; in an hour's time you will be free. **1937** I. SCHAPERA *Bantu-Speaking Tribes S. Afr.* viii. 174 At the head of the whole tribe is the Chief (Nguni, *inkosi*; Shangana-Tonga, *hosi*; Venda, *khosi*; Sotho, *morêna, kxosi*). **1948** A. PATON *Cry Beloved Country* III. ii. 220, I have thought, inkosi, that we should try to keep some of them in this valley.

Hence **inkosikazi** (9 **inquosegose,** etc.), (*a*) the wife of a chief; (*b*) native name for a white married woman.

1835 A. STEEDMAN *Wanderings S. Afr.* I. x. 256 The Chief having many wives.. the sovereignty devolves on the offspring of the *Inkose kosi*, female chieftain, or queen. **1836** N. ISAACS *Trav. E. Afr.* (1937) II. 63 All the inquosegoses were present. **1866** H. ROBERTSON *Mission Life among Zulu-Kafirs* 103 Look, Inkosikazi, here is Mary putting this in my best trowsers. **1878** H. A. ROCHE *On Trek in Transvaal* 246 He [*sc.* the washing Kaffir] acquits himself at his task better than the *Inkosigas* who bungles hers so sadly. **1948** A. PATON *Cry Beloved Country* II. viii. 175 My heart holds a deep sorrow for you, and for the inkosikazi, and for the young inkosikazi, and for the children. **1969** I. VAUGHAN *Last of Sunlit Yrs.* iii. 25 'Nkosikaas,' Moses had asked, 'what sort of a table is this?'

inkpot ('ɪŋkpɒt). [INK *sb.*[1]]

1. A small pot for holding writing-ink.

1553 [see 2]. **1590** LODGE *Euphues' Gold. Leg.* (1592) H iv, They only haue their humours in their inck-pot. **1740** SWIFT *Wks.* (1778) XI. 396, I bequeath to Deane Swift Esq; my large silver standish, consisting of a large silver plate, an ink-pot, a sand-box [etc.]. **1860** EMERSON *Cond. Life, Worship* Wks. (Bohn) II. 393, I am not afraid of falling into my inkpot.

2. *attrib.* **inkpot term** = ink-horn term (see INK-HORN 2 b).

1553 T. WILSON *Rhet.* (1580) 156 A very Caulf that.. thought by his ynke pot termes to get a good Parsonage. **1604** T. WRIGHT *Passions* IV. ii. 141 To vse.. Poetical phrases in prose, or incke-pot tearmes smelleth of affectation.

inkshed ('ɪŋkʃɛd). *humorous.* [f. INK *sb.*[1] + *-shed*, after BLOODSHED.] The shedding or spilling of ink; consumption or waste of ink in writing.

1672 MARVELL *Reh. Transp.* Wks. 1776 II. 58 To spare mine own pains, and prevent ink-shed [etc.]. **1677** W. HUGHES *Man of Sin* III. iii. 94 But to avoid more Ink-shed in these Tales of Blood-shed, let's fall on some that are of a Jocunder Humour. **1759** STERNE *Tr. Shandy* II. ii, Terrible battles, yclept logomachies, have they occasioned and perpetuated with so much gall and ink-shed. **1850** CARLYLE *Latter-d. Pamph.* iii. 17 With no blood-shed.. but with immense beershed and inkshed.

inkstand ('ɪŋkstænd). A stand for holding one or more ink-bottles or ink-glasses (often with a tray or rests for pens, etc.); sometimes applied to an inkspot.

1773 *Lond. Chron.* 7 Sept. 248/3 [In a list of articles made at Soho]. **1776** *Trial Nundocomar* 43/2 The ink-stand was near Bollakey Doss: he dipt his seal on the cushion, and sealed the bond. **1801** MASON, *Inkstand*, an utensil for holding an ink-glass and appendages. **1806–7** J. BERESFORD *Miseries Hum. Life* (1826) VI. 116 It seems as if a spider had dropped into the ink-stand and then crawled all over the paper. **1840** DICKENS *Old C. Shop* v, An inkstand with no ink and the stump of one pen. **1878** HUXLEY *Physiogr.* 69 Ink dries up quickly in a wide-mouthed ink-stand.

†'**ink-ˌstandish.** *Obs.* [f. INK *sb.*[1] + STANDISH (= *stand-dish*).] An inkstand.

c **1730** SAVAGE *Author to be let* Pref. §7 Dick's pen, so often dipped in an ink-standish. **1756** WATSON in *Phil. Trans.* XLIX. 508 In this same place was dug up an ink-standish, with some of the ink. **1818** SCOTT *Br. Lamm.* xxxii, She.. seemed unable.. to dip it in the massive silver ink-standish, which stood full before her. **1833** MARRYAT *P. Simple* xxvi, His lordship then desired me to hand him the paper and inkstandish.

'**inkster.** *nonce-wd.* [f. INK *v.* or *sb.*[1] + -STER.] A scribbler, an inferior writer.

1860 READE *Eighth Commandm.* 343 These inksters are the enemies not only of the country but of the human race.

inky ('ɪŋkɪ), *a.* Also 6 **inckie,** 7 **inkie.** [f. INK *sb.*[1] + -Y.]

1. Of or pertaining to ink; written with ink; using ink; literary. † ***inky divinity***: cf. INKEN.

1581 SIDNEY *Apol. Poetrie* (Arb.) 61 Ouer-mastred by some thoughts, I yeelded an inckie tribute vnto them. **1593** SHAKS. *Rich. II*, II. i. 64 England.. is now bound in with shame, With Inky blottes, and rotten Parchment bonds. **1619** W. SCLATER *Exp. 1 Thess.* (1630) 537 The Scripture read or preached is a dead Letter, Inkie Diuinity. *a* **1688** CUDWORTH *Immut. Mor.* (1731) 185 He will see Heaven, Earth, Sun.. in those Inky Delineations. **1858** HOGG *Life Shelley* II. 163, I enlisted with a special pleader, and fought manfully under his inky banners. **1883** BLACK *Shandon Bells* vii, You haven't been brought up in libraries and inky dens all your life.

2. Abounding with ink, full of ink.

1591 SYLVESTER *Du Bartas* I. v. 87 Th' inky Cuttles, and the Many-feet.

3. As black as ink; extremely black or dark.

1593 NASHE *Christ's T.* (1613) 55 The Moone had.. a blacke inky hood embayling her bright head. **1600** SHAKS. *A.Y.L.* III. v. 46 Your inkie browes, your blacke silke haire. **1709** ADDISON *Tatler* No. 131 ¶9 He took up a little Cruit that was filled with a kind of Inky Juice. **1795** WOLCOTT (P. Pindar) *Pindariana* Wks. 1812 IV. 178 Eternal foe of inky night. **1880** HAUGHTON *Phys. Geog.* v. 235 The largest river in the world takes its most remote origin.. in a little inky tarn. **1888** J. INGLIS *Tent Life Tigerland* 337 Cautiously probing.. the inky, oozy depths in front of him.

4. Of taste, etc.: Resembling that of ink.

1805 W. SAUNDERS *Min. Waters* 325 It has a strong astringent and inky taste.

5. Stained with ink.

1727 BAILEY vol. II, *Inky*, blotted with ink. **1837** DICKENS *Pickw.* xx, One of the gentlemen, in a brown coat and brass buttons, inky drabs, and bluchers. **1894** HALL CAINE *Manxman* v. ii. 285 The fingers of his right hand were then inky up to the first joint.

6. *Comb.*, as ***inky-black, -looking*** adjs.; **inky cap** = *ink-cap* (INK *sb.*[1] 4).

1822–34 *Good's Study Med.* (ed. 4) I. 649 The discharge is sometimes inky-black. **1875** BEDFORD *Sailor's Pocket Bk.* iv. (ed. 2) 86 Small inky-looking clouds foretell rain. [**1891** M. C. COOKE *Brit. Edible Fungi* vi. 47 The 'Inky Mushroom' (*Coprinus atramentarius*) received that name because, when it becomes old, the gills melt away into a thick, black, inky fluid, which may be used as ink.] **1923** J. RAMSBOTTOM *Handbk. Larger Brit. Fungi* 81 One of the chief characteristics of *Coprinus* is the so-called 'deliquescence', which gives the popular name 'inky cap' to these fungi. **1967** W. P. K. FINDLAY *Wayside & Woodland Fungi* 149 (*heading*) *Coprinus*: Inky Caps.

inky ('ɪŋkɪ), *sb.* Colloq. abbrev. of *incandescent lamp.* Also '**inkie.**

1929 *Photoplay* (Chicago) Apr. 31/2 *Inkys*, incandescent lights, the silent lights used for talking pictures in contrast to the old noisy arc lights. **1936** C. B. DEMILLE in *Words* Oct. 6/2 An incandescent lamp is an 'inkie'. **1959** W. S. SHARPS *Dict. Cinematogr.* 103/2 *Inkie* or *Inkie-Dinkie*, a small incandescent lighting unit used for local lighting. **1970** *T.V. Times* (Austral.) 1 Apr. 8/3 Put a Ted Lewis on the Inky Dinky—insert a little, dented, pipe-like piece of tin in front of the small incandescent spot light to diffuse the beam.

‖**inkyo** ('ɪŋkjəʊ). Also **inkiyo.** [Jap., f. *in* (in the) shade, retired + *kyo* to dwell.] In Japan, the act of resigning or renouncing one's office or position; one who has thus abdicated or resigned. Also as *adj.*

1871 A. B. MITFORD *Tales Old Japan* II. 122 *Inkiyô*; abdication. The custom of abdication is common among all classes, from the Emperor down. **1896** L. HEARN *Kokoro* iii. 40 Old men and women likewise—the *inkyô* of the vicinity. *Ibid.* xii. 224 The aged *inkyô*, whose sight and hearing begin to fail, talks cheerily of the impending change that is to provide him with a fresh young body. **1911** B. H. CHAMBERLAIN *Jap. Poetry* 178 Little wonder that heads of families became *inkyo*.. that is, retired from active life as early as possible. **1958** G. B. SANSOM *Hist. Japan to 1334* x. 199 It was common for the head of a great institution or a great house to retire at an early age... This custom, known as Inkyo (which means a sheltered or passive life) has not entirely disappeared.

inky-pinky ('ɪŋkɪ'pɪŋkɪ). *Sc.* Also **inkie-pinkie, inker-pinker,** etc. [Etym. obscure; see *Sc. Nat. Dict.*] Small beer.

The word occurs in versions of the Hallowe'en play *Galatians*; see E. K. Chambers, *English Folk-Play* (1933), 55. There are other senses and forms, on which see the *Sc. Nat. Dict.*

1835 J. MAIDMENT *Galatians* 4 Inky Pinky about seventy or eighty years since was used by the brewers in Stirlingshire to designate the smallest kind of beer. **1842** R. CHAMBERS *Pop. Rhymes Scotl.* 69/2, I have a little bottle of *inker-pinker* in my pocket.

inlace, inlack, var. ENLACE, INLAIK.

†**in'lagary.** *Obs.* [ad. med.L. *inlagāria* (AF. *inlagerie*), f. ME. *inlaȝe* INLAW: see -ARY[1].] The restitution of an outlaw to the benefit and protection of the law; = INLAWRY.

[*c* **1250** BRACTON III. II. xiv, Inlagaria. **1292** BRITTON I. xiv. §1 Inlagerie deit a plusours estre graunté de dreit.] **1607** COWELL *Interpr.*, *Inlagary* (*Inlagatio*), is a restitution of one outlawed to.. the benefit or estate of a subject.

†**inla'gation.** *Obs.* [ad. med.L. *inlagātiōn-em*, n. of action f. *inlagā-re* to INLAW.] = prec.

1656 in BLOUNT *Glossogr.* **1708** *Termes de la Ley*, *Inlagary* or *Inlagation*, is a Restitution of one outlawed to the King's Protection, or to the benefit and condition of a Subject.

inlaid ('ɪnleɪd, ɪn'leɪd), *ppl. a.* [f. INLAY *v.* + -ED[1]; see also *lay in* in LAY *v.*]

†**1.** Laid in, placed or situated within; implanted, fixed within. *Obs.*

1606 *Proc. agst. Late Traitors* 70 His bowels and inlayed parts taken out and burnt. **1611** FLORIO, *Imposto*, in-laid, put in. **1639** FULLER *Holy War* IV. vi. (1647) 178 The inveterate and inlaid hatred (not to be washed off) they bear to the Latines. **1660** —— *Mixt Contempl.* (1841) 174 The warmth of the maid was inlaid, and equally diffused through the whole body.

2. a. Laid or embedded in the surface of a thing, esp. as decorative material in a ground work; ornamented with inserted materials.

1598 FLORIO, *Vermiculato*, wrought with checker work.. in-laid work. **1601** HOLLAND *Pliny* I. 493 Marquetry and other inlaid works. **1756–7** tr. *Keysler's Trav.* (1760) I. 63 The palace is magnificent, abounding with.. tables of inlaid marble. **1883** C. J. WILLS *Mod. Persia* 332 A kind of inlaid work similar to our Tonbridge ware is made in Persia.

fig. **1612** DRAYTON *Poly-olb.* iv. 19 Of all the In-laid Iles her Soueraigne Seuerne keepes, That bathe their amorous breasts within her secret Deepes.

b. Of linoleum or the like: decorated with a design that is set into the surface.

1908 *Westm. Gaz.* 30 May 7/2 The floors will be covered with Greenwich inlaid linoleum. **1959** *Sears, Roebuck Catal.* Spring & Summer 780 Easy-care inlaid vinyl... Toughest plastic used in floorcoverings. *Ibid.* 731 Inlaid linoleum.

3. *dial.* and *slang.* (See quots.)

a **1700** B. E. *Dict. Cant. Crew*, *Inlayed, well inlayed*, at ease in his Fortune, or full of Money. **1828** *Craven Dial.*, *Inlaid*, provided with, laid up in store. 'We're weel inlaid for coals'.

inlaik ('ɪnleɪk, -læk), *sb.* *Sc.* Also 6 **inlak,** 7–8 **inlack,** 6– **inlake.** [f. IN-[1] + *laik*, Sc. form of LACK *sb.*: cf. next.] Lack, want; deficiency; failure.

1500–20 DUNBAR *Poems* xxxiv. 54 The maltman sais, 'I God forsaik.. Gif ony bettir malt may be, And of this kill I haif inlaik.' **1562** WINȜET *Cert. Tractates* i. Wks. 1888 I. 5 Hes not mony throw inlak of techement.. mysknawin thair deuty? **1571** *Sc. Acts Jas. VI*, c. 38 That all persones.. after the decease, decay or inlaik of their said superiours, hald, and sall hald their fewes.. of our Soveraine Lord. *a* **1578** LINDESAY (Pitscottie) *Chron. Scot.* (S.T.S.) I. 14 The king was nocht sufficient to governe the realme for inlaik of aige. **1635** D. DICKSON *Expl. Heb.* viii. 10 The inlacks, or defects, of repentance and fayth. **1720** WODROW *Life R. Bruce* (1843) 27 Through impunity and inlack of justice.

in'laik, *v.* *Sc.* Also 6 **inlak,** (7 **enlaike**), 6– **inlake.** [f. IN-[1] + *laik*, Sc. form of LACK *v.*]

1. *intr.* To lack, to be wanting or deficient; to fail.

1533 BELLENDEN *Livy* I. (1822) 34 Thairfore inlakit xi dayis and vi houris to complete the hail yere. **1535** STEWART *Cron. Scot.* III. 191 All the victuall [that] wes the hous within, Inlaikit fast. **1563–7** BUCHANAN *Reform. St. Andros* Wks. (1892) 10 Geif the principal inlak, the universitie.. sal.. cheiss.. four.. personis to that office. **1637–50** ROW *Hist. Kirk* (Wodrow Soc.) 196 That none of his sheep should be inlaiking. **1820** *Blackw. Mag.* VI. 669 At every word of the grace it [a cup] inlaked an inch.

b. To fail through death; to decease.

c **1575** *Balfour's Practicks* (1754) 333 It micht happin the witnessis to deceis or inlaik. *a* **1651** CALDERWOOD *Hist. Kirk* (Wodrow Soc.) III. 244, I sall enlaike of my present disease. **1785** *Jrnl. fr. Lond.* in R. Forbes *Poems Buchan Dial.* 7 (Jam.), I was fley'd that she had taen the wytenon-fa, an' inlakit afore supper.

2. *trans.* To lack (something requisite for completeness or sufficiency); to be wanting or deficient in; also *absol.*

a **1578** LINDESAY (Pitscottie) *Chron. Scot.* (S.T.S.) I. 19 We inlaik na thing bot hardiment and curraig. **1568** SKEYNE *The Pest* (1860) 15 The patient beand without rest, and ressone inlakand sleip. **1640–1** *Kirkcudbr. War-Comm. Min. Bk.* (1855) 138 Our horss, that are inlacking onlie nyne of

our number. *a* 1774 FERGUSSON *Election* Poems (1845) 42 The gowd that inlakes half-a-crown.

Hence **in'laiking** *vbl. sb.* = INLAIK *sb.*

a 1575 *Diurn. Occurr.* (Bannatyne Club) 191 Thaj.. concludit, that for inlaiking of justice within this realme, necessar it wes to cheis ane regent. **1595** DUNCAN *App. Etymol.* (E.D.S.), *Defectus*, inlaking.

in'lake, *v. rare*⁻¹. [f. IN-¹ or ² + LAKE *sb.*] *trans.* To convert into a lake.

1826 E. IRVING *Babylon* II. VII. 178 The princes of the east, for whose coming Euphrates hath inlaked her mighty stream.

in-lamb (ɪn'læm), *a.* Also **inlamb**. [attrib. use of phrase *in lamb*: cf. INCALF.] Of a ewe: With lamb; pregnant. (In rural use.)

1556 *Richmond. Wills* (Surtees) 155 *note*, An inlambe shepe. **1867** *Gainsb. News* 23 Mar., 170 lambed and inlamb ewes. **1968** J. ARNOLD *Shell Bk. Country Crafts* 90 In-lamb ewes can be accommodated and cared for. **1972** *Country Life* 15 June 1580/1 When grazing is finished the in-lamb ewes are brought indoors.

†**in'lance**, *v. Obs. rare*⁻¹. [f. IN-¹ or ² + LANCE *v.*] *intr.* To thrust a lance.

c **1450** LONELICH *Grail* xiii. 893 Vnder his hawberk Inlawnced he Throwgh the body.

inland ('ɪnlənd, 'ɪnlænd), *sb.*, *a.*, and *adv.* [f. IN *adv.* 12 d + LAND *sb.*¹]

A. *sb.*

1. The inner part of an estate, feudal manor, or farm. †**a.** In OE. and feudal tenure, the land around the mansion occupied by the owner or cultivated for his use, not held by any tenant (cf. DEMESNE 3). **b.** *Sc.* Land cultivated as infield: = *infield land*; see INFIELD.

904 in Earle *Land Charters* (1888) 161 All ðæt inn lond beliȝeð an dic utane. *c* **1000** *Laws of Edgar* II. c. 1 Æȝðer ȝe of þeȝenes in-lande ȝe of ȝeneat-lande. **1235–52** *Rentalia Glaston.* (Som. Rec. Soc.) 134 Idem Persona habet de la Inland iiij^or acras terre. **1437** in Kennett *Par. Antiq.* (1818) II. 324 [Thomas Billyngdon quitted..all right to any common in the pasture or] 'inlandys' [of the said Edmund]. **1473** *Acta Audit.* (1839) 24 He sall haue..vj acris of corne land of Inland, and ij acris of medow at þe side. **1818** HALLAM *Mid. Ages* (1872) II. 373 *note*, The house and inland; all, in short, that is surrounded and bounded by a hedge or fence.

2. *sing.* and *pl.* The interior part of a country, the parts remote from the sea or the borders. †Formerly, also, the inlying districts near the capital and centres of population, as opposed to the remote or outlying wild parts; in Scotch use, also, the mainland as distinct from the outlying isles; = IN-COUNTRY.

1573 *Satir. Poems Reform.* xlii. 158 To God thay ar als deir As ony in the inland heir. *Ibid.* 173 That as weill thay of Mynnie Gof..As..the burghis and Inlandis men. **1599** SHAKS. *Hen. V*, I. ii. 142 They of those Marches..Shall be a Wall sufficient to defend Our in-land from the pilfering Borderers. **1605** VERSTEGAN *Dec. Intell.* ii. (1628) 39 *marg.*, Sea costs more of old time inhabited then the inlands. **1611** SPEED *Hist. Gt. Brit.* IX. iv. §25 Those Flemmings..were now by the King..remoued into Wales..to disburden his In-land of such guests. **1651** WITTIE tr. *Primrose's Pop. Err.* IV. xxxviii. 362 Others that have travailed through the inland of India, doe make no mention of any such creature. **1667** MILTON *P.L.* x. 423 The rest were all Farr to the in land retir'd, about the walls Of Pandæmonium. **1749** F. SMITH *Voy. Disc.* II. 236 The Inland appears to consist of a brown barren Rock. **1842** LYTTON *Zanoni* IV. viii, The rich inlands of the island. **1913** L. V. KELLY *Range Men* 71 Canny men and good traders, built posts in the great inland. **1934** A. RUSSELL *Tramp-Royal in Wild Austral.* iii. 29 The camel.. will long continue to be in many parts, the great utility animal of the Inland. **1941** I. L. IDRIESS *Great Boomerang* xxxi. 235 New cities, new industries, and a great, far-spread population in our inland, where population is needed so urgently. **1969** 'A. GARVE' *Boomerang* ii. 39 Our inland is still very empty country, and a lot of it isn't easily accessible. **1973** *Nation Rev.* (Melbourne) 31 Aug. (Suppl.) 1/1 He enjoys studying the unique wildlife of the inland, and..the people who live and work there.

B. *adj.* (attrib. use of the sb.: hence formerly sometimes hyphened to the following word).

1. **a.** Of or pertaining to the interior part of a country or region; remote from the sea or the border.

inland ice (*sheet*), the ice which forms a permanent cover or ice-cap over most of Greenland; the region over which this ice extends. Hence, more widely, any mass of ice of comparable extent and thickness underlain by rock; *inland sea*, (*a*) a large body of salt water, entirely or nearly severed from the ocean: applied also to large lakes; (*b*) (see quot. 1891).

1557 in Strype *Eccl. Mem.* (1721) III. lix. 447 Whereunto the said inland-men may be induced, seeing the other go forth to adventure their lives for their defence. **1590** SPENSER *F.Q.* II. vi. 10 This wide Inland sea, that hight..the Idle lake. **1601** HOLLAND *Pliny* I. 50 The Firth of Gades.. whereas the Atlanticke Ocean breaking in, is spred into the Inland and Mediterranean seas. **1652–62** HEYLIN *Cosmogr.* IV. (1682) 54 All the In-land Towns in this large Estate. **1670** EACHARD *Cont. Clergy* 47 Although such a sermon may possibly do some good in a coast-town, yet..in an inland-parish, it will do no more than Syriack or Arabick. **1673** TEMPLE *Obs. United Prov.* iv. 134 The Mariners or Schippers, who supply their Ships and Inland-Boats. **1792** GOUV. MORRIS in Sparks *Life & Writ.* (1832) III. 37 Companies for the improvement of our inland navigation. **1853** H. RINK in *Jrnl. R. Geogr. Soc.* XXIII. [149 Let us call the group of peninsulas and islands..the *out-skirts* of the land [*sc.* Greenland], and the compact continent to the E. the *inland*.] *Ibid.* 151 The exclusive origin of the icebergs from the inland ice, through the icy friths, has been mentioned. **1871** A. B. MITFORD *Tales Old Japan* I. 173 *Shikoku*, one of the southern islands separated from the chief island of Japan by the beautiful 'Inland Sea'. **1876** W. E. GRIFFIS *Mikado's Empire* I. v. 55 The 'Inland Sea' (Sêto Uchi) is a name which has been given by foreigners, and adopted by the Japanese, who until modern times had no special name for it as a whole. **1879** MᶜCARTHY *Own Times* II. xxv. 221 A few generations ago Russia was literally an inland state. **1880** *Encycl. Brit.* XI. 166/2 The Danes divide Greenland into two physical divisions—the 'outskirts' and the 'inland ice'. The first comprises the coast-lying land, the latter the interior. **1891** CHAMBERLAIN & MASON *Handbk. Travellers Japan* (ed. 3) 357/2 The Inland Sea is the name given to the water space lying between the Main Island on the North and the islands of Shikoku and Kyūshū on the South. **1895** *Jrnl. Geol.* III. 244 During the climax of the glacial period, when the Scandinavian 'inland-ice' invaded the low grounds of middle Europe, those low grounds supported an Arctic-alpine flora. **1898** *Q. Jrnl. Geol. Soc.* LIV. 200 In addition to these 'inland ice-sheets' there are in Spitsbergen glaciers of the ordinary Alpine type. **1953** G. WILLIAMSON *Changing Greenland* xiv. 167 Six-sevenths of Greenland's 840,000 square miles is locked in the implacable embrace of the Inland Ice. *Ibid.* xx. 254 Before leaving Disko Bay, tourists may..make an excursion to the fringe of the Inland Ice. **1958** G. B. SANSOM *Hist. Japan to 1334* xiv. 300 Before him lay the Inland Sea route to the Straits of Shimonoseki. **1966** T. ARMSTRONG et al. *Illustr. Gloss. Snow & Ice* 27 *Inland ice sheet*, an ice sheet of considerable thickness and more than about 50,000 square km in area, resting on rock. **1969** M. SMEETON *Misty Islands* ii. 19 We entered the Inland Sea through the Hayasui Seto. **1973** *Nature* 5 Oct. 251/2 Although the strong echo from the upper surface of the ice [in Antarctica] shows little variation in strength, the normal bottom echo from inland ice..shows strong fading along the flight line.

†**b.** Having the refinement characteristic of the inlying districts of a country. *Obs.*

1600 SHAKS. *A.Y.L.* III. ii. 363 An olde religious Vnckle of mine..who was in his youth an inland man, one that knew Courtship too well.

2. Carried on or operating within the limits of a country. Opposed to *foreign*, as in ***inland trade, inland bill of exchange.***

inland duty, a duty on inland trade or inland transactions, as the excise and stamp duties. ***inland revenue***, the part of the national revenue consisting of taxes and inland duties.

1546 *St. Papers Hen. VIII*, XI. 75 They cannot spare the corne of the innelonde growthe to be caryed out, for feare of a famyne in thiese partyes. **1682** SCARLETT *Exchanges* 15 The Bill must be paid in the same Sort & Species of Monyes, that the Remitter paid to the Drawer for the Value..these are usually Inland Bills. *a* **1745** SWIFT (J.), A pamphlet printed in England for a general excise or inland duty. **1745** *De Foe's Eng. Tradesman* (1841) I. Introd. 3 Our complete Tradesman ought to understand all the inland trade of England. **1849** FREESE *Comm. Class-bk.* 23 Bills of exchange are either *Inland* bills, or *Foreign* bills. *Inland* bills of exchange, are those which are drawn from one place in a country on another place in the same country, in both of which the same kinds of monies are current..or, drawn by one person on another person in the same place. **1849** *Act 12 & 13 Vict.* c. 1 §1 From and after the passing of this Act the several Persons..now being Commissioners of Excise and Commissioners of Stamps and Taxes respectively shall.. become and be One Consolidated Board of Commissioners, and be called 'The Commissioners of Inland Revenue'. **1895** *Whitaker's Almanack* 164 Inland Revenue Offices, Somerset House. *Ibid.* 165 The Government Laboratory (Inland Revenue Branch). *Mod.* An illicit distillery discovered by the inland revenue officers.

C. *adv.* In or towards the interior or heart of a country, as opposed (*a*) to the coast or border, (*b*) to wild outlying districts.

1600 SHAKS. *A.Y.L.* II. vii. 96 Yet am I in-land bred, And know some nourture. **1784** COOK *3rd Voy.* III. xiii. II. 260 The snow on the rising grounds was thinner spread; and farther inland, there was no appearance of any. **1803–6** WORDSW. *Intimations* ix, In a season of calm weather, Though inland far we be, Our Souls have sight of that immortal sea. **1855** KINGSLEY *Heroes* I. iv. (1868) 48 Perseus feared to go inland, but flew along the shore above the sea.

†**'inlanded**, *a. Obs. rare.* [f. prec. + -ED¹.] Situated in or toward the centre of a land: the opposite of *outlying*.

1611 SPEED *Theat. Gt. Brit.* x. (1614) 19/1 This [Devonshire]..being more inlanded hath more commodious havens for shippings entercourse.

inlander ('ɪnləndə(r)). [f. as prec. + -ER¹.] One who dwells in the interior of a country; an inland inhabitant.

1610 HOLLAND *Camden's Brit.* I. 794 They..attempt to possesse themselves of..the utmost part of the land from out of the Inlanders hands. **1646** SIR T. BROWNE *Pseud. Ep.* VI. i. 274 The same name [*Aborigines*] is also given unto the Inlanders or Midland inhabitants of this Island by Cæsar. **1843** *Standing Rules* (Hudson's Bay Co.) Index, Rations and regales to Inlanders, Scale of. **1867** ATWATER *Logic* 174 If an inlander coming to the sea, observed the phenomenon of the tide. **1933** [see BINGHI, BINGHI]. **1934** A. RUSSELL *Tramp-Royal in Wild Austral.* iii. 33 The amazing feat accomplished by a young inlander. **1935** A. R. EVANS *Reindeer Trek* 179 He had rushed terrified from the spot to tell a tribe of passing Inlanders. **1944** F. CLUNE *Red Heart* 61 Andrew Hume begged his parents to allow him to accompany the famous German inlander. *Ibid.* 72 Several inlanders and explorers had a go. **1968** *Globe & Mail* (Toronto) 13 Feb. 3/3 Hannah Bearskin's parents are Inlanders.

inlandish (ˌɪn'lændɪʃ), *a.* [f. as prec. + -ISH.]

†1. Produced in the land itself; home, domestic, native: opposed to *outlandish*. *Obs.*

1657 REEVE *God's Plea* (T.), Thou art all for inlandish meat, and outlandish sawces.

2. Of or pertaining to the interior of a country; of an inland nature or character.

1849 J. WILSON in *Blackw. Mag.* LXVI. 623 Some other of your outlandish, or inlandish, Lowland or Highland Counties. **1891** *Spectator* 18 July, The great lakes have helped Chicago, and..the fact that they require from the populations that surround them all the seafaring qualities of the English race, will prevent its inhabitants from becoming too inlandish in their habits.

†**in'lap**, *v. Obs.* In 4 **inwlappen**. [f. IN-¹ + ME. (*w*)*lappen* to LAP; rendering L. *involvĕre*, *implicāre*.] *trans.* To enwrap, enfold, involve.

1382 WYCLIF *Ezek.* i. 4 A wynde of tempest..cam fro the north, and a grete cloude, and fyre inwlappynge [**1388** wlappynge in; L. *involvens*]. —— *2 Tim.* ii. 4 No man holdinge knyȝthod to God, inwlappith him silf with worldli nedis. **1435** MISYN *Fire of Love* 100 He allone me holly refreschys & inlappis þat my mynde allone byrnyngly has desiryd.

†**in'lapidate**, *v. Obs. rare.* [f. IN-² + L. *lapidem* stone + -ATE³. Cf. LAPIDATE.] *trans.* To convert into stone, petrify.

1626 BACON *Sylva* §85 There are some Naturall Spring-Waters that will Inlapidate Wood.

inlard, variant of ENLARD *v.*, *Obs.*

inlarge, -ment, etc., obs. var. ENLARGE, etc.

inlasse, obs. form of UNLESS.

†**in'lasting**, *a. Obs. rare*⁻¹. In 4 **-ande**. [f. IN-² + LASTING *ppl. a.*] Lasting on, everlasting.

c **1340** HAMPOLE *Prose Tr.* 3 This name Ihesu..gyffes inlastande ryste.

inlate, obs. form of INLET.

inlaut ('ɪnlaʊt). *Philol.* [G.] A medial or internal sound; a sound which occurs in the middle of a word.

1892 G. DUNN in *Classical Rev.* Feb. 1/2 Latin d as inlaut and auslaut frequently represents Indo-Germanic dh. **1950** E. M. UHLENBECK in E. P. Hamp et al. *Readings in Ling. II* (1966) 251 For the different positions (anlaut, inlaut, auslaut) it must be ascertained separately what phonemes are permissible.

inlaw ('ɪnlɔː), *sb.*¹ *Hist.* Forms: 3 **inlaȝe**, **inlaughe**, 7 **inlagh**, **inlawgh**, 9 **inlaw**. [ME. *inlaȝe*, f. IN-¹ + *laȝe* LAW, after *utlaȝe* outlaw: cf. INLAW *v.*] One who is within the domain and protection of the law: opp. to *outlaw*.

c **1250** *Gloss. Law Terms* in *Rel. Ant.* I. 33 Inlage, *sugest à la lei le rei.* *c* **1250** BRACTON III. II. xi, Non est sub lege i.e. Anglice Inlaughe. **1607** COWELL *Interpr.*, Inlawgh.. signifieth him that is in some frank pledge. **1848** LYTTON *Harold* III. iii, I have the king's grace, and the inlaw's right.

inlaw ('ɪnlɔː), *sb.*² *nonce-wd.* (See quot.)

1880 G. M. HOPKINS *Note-bks. & Papers* (1937) 314 His [*sc.* the universal being's] *inlaw*, the law of his being is unlike mine.

inlaw (ɪn'lɔː), *v. Hist.* Forms: 1 **inlaȝian**, 5 **inlawe**, 7– **inlaw**. [OE. *inlaȝian*, f. IN-¹ + *laȝu* LAW: cf. *útlaȝian* to outlaw.] *trans.* To bring within the authority and protection of the law, to reverse the outlawry of (a person).

c **1000** *Laws of Ethelred* VIII. c. 2 þæt he his aȝenne wer ȝesylle þam cyninge and Criste, and mid þam hine sylfne inlaȝiȝe to bote. *a* **1066** *O.E. Chron.* an. 1050 (MS. C.) Her on þysum ȝere..man ȝe-inlaȝode Sweȝen eorl. *c* **1450** *St. Cuthbert* (Surtees) 7995 Inlawde he was at thre ȝere ende. **1483** *Cath. Angl.* 196/1 To Inlawe. **1622** BACON *Hen. VII*, 12 It should bee a great incongruitie to haue them to make Lawes, who themselues were not Inlawed. **1671** F. PHILLIPS *Reg. Necess.* 265 If any of the Kings Servants should at any time be so indirectly and unduly outlawed, he may by the favour of their Royal Master be inlawed and restored to the benefit and protection of Him and his Laws. **1876** FREEMAN *Norm. Conq.* V. xxiv. 407 When Eadward was to be chosen, when Godwine was to be inlawed, the nation asserted its dormant right. **1898** J. T. FOWLER *Durham Cathedral* 20 Carileph was exiled by William Rufus in 1088, but inlawed in 1091.

Hence **in'lawing** *vbl. sb.*

1874 GREEN *Short Hist.* ii. §2. 65 The scandalous inlawing of such a criminal.

-in-law. [f. IN *prep.* + LAW *sb.*] A phrase appended to names of relationship, as *father*, *mother*, *brother*, *sister*, *son*, etc., to indicate that the relationship is not by nature, but in the eye of the Canon Law, with reference to the degrees of affinity within which marriage is prohibited. These forms can be traced back to the 14th c.: see BROTHER-IN-LAW. Formerly *-in-law* was also used to designate those relationships which are now expressed by *step-*, e.g. *son-in-law* = *step-son*, *father-in-law* = *step-father*; this, though still locally or vulgarly current, is now generally considered a misuse.

In recent colloquial or journalistic phraseology, *in-law* has been humorously used to designate any relative so connected. Hence **in-'lawry**, the position of an 'in-law'; **'in-lawship**, the state of being an in-law.

1894 *Blackw. Mag.* Jan. 24 The position of the 'in-laws' (a happy phrase which is attributed..to her Majesty, than whom no one can be better acquainted with the article) is often not very apt to promote happiness. **1898** *Daily News* 7 Jan. 4/7 'Don't live with them'—with the 'in-laws'. **1898** *Westm. Gaz.* 1 Apr. 1/3 Everyone living is either an 'in-law' himself, and therefore bound to possess corresponding 'in-laws', or his 'in-law' potentiality remains intact. *Ibid.*, 'In-lawry' is the common fate of the entire human race. **1912** D. CANFIELD *Squirrel Cage* I. i. 10 Her mother felt the usual in-law conclusion about her daughter's life. **1926** C. SIDGWICK *Sack & Sugar* i. 9 Eva had invited her future in-laws, male and female, to five o'clock a day or two before her wedding. *Ibid.* vii. 77 He is lost to everyone but his wife and his in-laws. **1939** N. S. COLBY *Remembering* i. 19 Robert's sister Catherine has to mix in-law amenities with adoring love. **1952** A. GRIMBLE *Pattern of Islands* 205 A retired.. policeman, married to a local woman and on a visit to his in-laws. **1954** M. GLUCKMAN in E. E. Evans-Pritchard *Inst. Primitive Society* vi. 69 This immediately established links of in-lawship with people who were, by standards of blood-ties, his enemies. **1957** V. W. TURNER *Schism & Continuity in Afr. Soc.* ix. 258 Links of in-lawship between villages. **1964** GOULD & KOLB *Dict. Social Sci.* 368/1 An indefinite number of affinal relatives or 'in-laws'. **1965** G. MELLY *Owning-Up* xv. 190 He was living with his wife and baby daughter in his in-laws' semi out at Mill Hill. **1970** *Daily Tel.* 8 May 17 How difficult and unnatural are in-law relationships! **1970** G. F. NEWMAN *Sir, You Bastard* iii. 91 His in-laws bought the furniture for the new house. **1972** R. MILNER in W. King *Black Short Story Anthol.* 374 The small salary added to his wife's keeping his in-law landlords quiet as he sweated through his first year of accounting.

'inlawry. [f. INLAW *v.* + -RY: cf. INLAGARY.] Restitution of the domain and protection of the law, reversal of outlawry.

1848 LYTTON *Harold* x. vi, The assembly..which had met for the inlawry of Godwin.

inlay (ɪn'leɪ), *v.* [f. IN-^{1} + LAY *v.*]

†**1.** *trans.* To lay in, or as in, a place of concealment or preservation. *Obs. rare*$^{-1}$.

a **1631** DONNE *Elegies* vii, From the worlds Common having sever'd thee, Inlaid thee, neither to be seen, nor see.

2. To lay or embed (a thing) in the substance of something else so that its surface becomes even or continuous with that of the matrix.

1598 FLORIO, *Inframettere*, to inlay or worke in among other things. **1631** WEEVER *Anc. Fun. Mon.* 18 Inscriptions and Epitaphs, cut, writ, inlaid, or engrauen vpon the Sepulchres. **1793** SMEATON *Edystone L.* §80 The moorstone courses, inlaid into the frame of the building. **1851** WILLMOTT *Pleas. Lit.* xxi. (1857) 137 Horace Walpole's correspondence inlays his own mind in mosaic. **1858** HAWTHORNE *Fr. & It. Jrnls.* II. 75 Other monumental slabs were inlaid with the pavement itself. **1887** BOWEN *Virg. Æneid* I. 167 Facing the deep is a cave inlaid in a precipice.

b. To insert a page of a book, a plate, or a cut, in a space cut in a larger and stouter page, for its preservation, or to enlarge the margin, and thus the whole size.

1810 W. LAING (Bookseller, Edin.) *Catalogue* No. 2722 (Compl. Scot.), The leaves are inlaid, and completed from the new edition. **1872** J. A. H. MURRAY *Compl. Scot.* Introd. 19 The leaves being cut out and 'inlaid' in a large quarto of the size of the large-paper copies of Leyden's reprint. **1892** S. LEE in *Dict. Nat. Biog.* XXIX. 35/2 Book-collectors.. employed him [Ireland] to 'inlay' illustrated books.

3. To furnish or fit (a thing) *with* a substance of a different kind embedded in its surface; to diversify or ornament (a thing) by such insertion of another material disposed in a decorative pattern or design.

1596 SHAKS. *Merch. V.* v. i. 59 Looke how the floore of heauen Is thicke inlayed with pattens of bright gold. **1606** SYLVESTER *Du Bartas* II. iv. II. *Magnificence* 907 A broad rich Baldrick..In-laid with gold. **1674** tr. *Scheffer's Lapland* 101 The lids are of one board, and for ornament often inlaid with Rain-deers bones. **1758** JOHNSON *Idler* No. 96 ¶3 A battle-axe whose handle was inlaid with brass. **1867** LADY HERBERT *Cradle L.* iii. 98 The doors are of tortoise-shell, inlaid with mother-of-pearl.

b. *fig.*

1670 MILTON *Hist. Eng.* VI. Wks. (1851) 297 But these things are..thence borrow'd by the Monks to inlay thir story. *a* **1680** BUTLER *Rem.* (1759) II. 354 His Discourse is inlaid with Oaths. **1813** SCOTT *Trierm.* III. Introd. v, The soft greensward is inlaid With varied moss and thyme.

c. *absol.*

1633 B. JONSON *Tale Tub* v. ii, *Tub.* How long have you studied ingine? *Medlay.* Since I first Join'd, or did in-lay in wit.

d. *transf.* Said of the material embedded; also in *ppl. adj.*, **inlaying**.

1784 COWPER *Task* I. 170 The stream, That, as with molten glass, inlays the vale. **1836** J. W. BOWDEN in *Lyra Apost.* (1849) 193 Tear down th' inlaying gold of Solomon.

inlay ('ɪnleɪ, ɪn'leɪ), *sb.* [f. prec. vb.]

1. The process or art of inlaying. *rare.*

1656 BLOUNT *Glossogr.*, *Inlay*, a term among Joyners, and signifies a laying of coloured wood in Wainscoat-works, Cupboards, &c. **1886** *Pall Mall G.* 26 June 3/1 The inlay of furniture with ivory, and other forms of marquetry.

2. a. Material inlaid or prepared for inlaying; inlaid work.

1697 DAMPIER *Voy.* I. 105 Their Shell..is very thin and clear..'tis used..for inlays, being extraordinary thin. **1725** POPE *Odyss.* XXI. 172 With rich inlay the various floor was graced. **1876** T. HARDY *Ethelberta* (1890) 217 The heavy cupboard doors at the bottom were enriched with inlays of paler wood.

fig. **1667** MILTON *P.L.* IV. 701 The violet, Crocus, and hyacinth, with rich inlay Broidered the ground. **1830** TENNYSON *Recoll. Arab. Nts.* iii, Damask-work, and deep inlay Of braided blooms unmown.

b. *Dentistry.* A filling of gold, porcelain, or other suitable material which is pre-formed to the required shape and then cemented into a cavity.

1888 *Dental Cosmos* XXX. 542 One of the chief obstacles to success..has been the difficulty of exactly fitting the inlay to the tooth. **1921** J. B. PARFITT *Operative Dental Surg.* xix. 175 An 'inlay' is a filling which is constructed outside the patient's mouth and then cemented into place in the tooth cavity. **1963** C. R. COWELL et al. *Inlays, Crowns, & Bridges* ii. 3 Originally gold inlays were prepared by a technique similar to that used for porcelain inlays. **1973** *Which?* Mar. 78/2 Your dentist would not be allowed to fill your mouth with gold inlays when ordinary amalgam fillings would do.

†**3.** The layering of plants. *Obs. rare*$^{-1}$.

1658 SIR T. BROWNE *Gard. Cyrus* 58 The contrivance of Art, in submersions and Inlays, inverting the extremes of the plant, and fetching the root from the top.

4. *Book-binding.* An inner sheet in a gathering.

1877 WINTER JONES in H. B. Wheatley *How to Catalogue* (1889) iv. 169 Each sheet after the first in each gathering being called an inlay.

5. The inlaid edge or inturn in a seam.

1899 *Daily News* 6 July 8/3 There is not enough 'inlay'... Should a ladies' tailor turn out work like that?

6. *attrib.*, as ***inlay work***, inlaid work.

1884 *Sat. Rev.* 14 June 779/2 Some of the inlay work is very fine. **1898** *Daily News* 2 Sept. 5/1 The cheapening of knife handles, billiard balls, inlay work, and pianoforte keys.

inlayer^{1} ('ɪn,leɪə(r)). [f. INLAY *v.* + -ER^{1}.] One who inlays (in senses of the vb.).

1660 BLOOME *Archit.* title-p., Painters, Carvers, In-layers, Antick-Cutters. **1725** BRADLEY *Fam. Dict.* s.v. *Spindle Tree*, The wood of the Spindle Tree is used..by the Inlayer for his Colours. **1881** *Nation* (N.Y.) XXXII. 406 The in-layer who has to frame the text or the print..of the binder.

inlayer^{2} ('ɪn'leɪə(r)). [f. IN *adv.* 12 + LAYER *sb.*] A layer of a material placed within something, an inside layer or sheathing.

1868 J. THOMSON *Hat-making & Felting* 63 The two ends joined by overlapping with a proper inlayer of paper. **1880** *Encycl. Brit.* XI. 519/2 Into each cone of wool or bat an 'inlayer' is now placed to prevent the inside from matting.

inlaying (ɪn'leɪɪŋ), *vbl. sb.* [f. INLAY *v.* + -ING^{1}.] The action of the vb. INLAY, or that which is inlaid.

1. a. The insertion of thin slips of one material within the surface of another for decorative purposes. **b.** A piece of inlaid work. **c.** The mounting of a leaf or engraving in a larger leaf or sheet of paper.

1598 FLORIO, *Tarsia*, a kind of painting, in laying, or setting in of small pieces of wood, Iuorie, horne or bone.. as in tables, chesseboordes and such. **1599** MINSHEU *Span. Dial.* 4/2 It is very curious, and the inlaying of the wood most finely set in. **1644** EVELYN *Diary* 8 Feb., The pavings, inlayings, and incrustations of this Hall are very rich. **1762** DERRICK *Lett.* (1767) II. 66 The inlaying and veneering very beautiful. **1886** T. HARDY *Mayor of Casterbridge* xxii, The little square piano with brass inlayings. **1894** J. T. FOWLER *Adamnan* Pref. 9 The separation, flattening, and inlaying of the consolidated leaves.

fig. **1865** *Sat. Rev.* 26 Aug. 279/2 In her three plays, we meet with natural and apt inlayings of familiar phrases from Shakspeare, Milton, and others.

†**2.** Incorporation, union. *Obs. rare.*

1674 N. FAIRFAX *Bulk & Selv.* 86 It would be no other than one with it, and the nearer any body comes to that plight, the nearer it comes to inlaying or oneness.

3. *attrib.* **inlaying machine**, a machine used in the manufacture of inlaid linoleum; **inlaying-saw** (see quot.).

1908 *Westm. Gaz.* 30 May 7/2 A scheme for increasing the speed at which our inlaying machines are worked. *a* **1877** KNIGHT *Dict. Mech.* II. 1189/2 *Inlaying-saw*, a saw used in piercing stuff for buhl-work.

†**in'lead,** *v.* *Obs.* [f. IN-^{1} + LEAD *v.*, transl. L. *indūcĕre*. (In sense 2 perh. f. IN-^{2} = EN-^{1}.)]

1. *trans.* To lead in, bring in.

c **950** *Lindisf. Gosp.* Matt. vi. 13 Ne inlæd usih in costunge. *a* **1300** *E.E. Psalter* lxxxvii. 8 [lxxxviii. 7] All þi stremes ouer me þou in-ledde. **1382** WYCLIF *Deut.* xxviii. 37 Alle puplis, to the whiche the Lord shal inleede thee.

2. To lead.

c **1560** A. SCOTT *Poems* (S.T.S.) xix. 13 How lang sall I this lyfe inleid, That for hir saik to suffer deid?

'in,leading, *ppl. a.* *rare.* [IN *adv.* 11 a: cf. *lead in.*] That leads in; introductory.

1889 *Pall Mall G.* 20 Nov. 3/2 If any one mayhap should deem this inleading stavelet the loveliest thing in all the tale, we shall not naysay him.

inleague, obs. variant of ENLEAGUE *v.*

†**in'leaguer,** *v.* *Obs. rare*$^{-1}$. [f. IN-^{1} + LEAGUER *sb.*, camp. Cf. the phrases *to lie in leaguer*, *to lie leaguer*, and LEAGUER *v.*] *intr.* To encamp with a besieging or beleaguering force.

1603 HOLLAND *Plutarch's Mor.* 195 Sylla did inleaguer before the citie of Athens, and had not leasure to stay there long and continue the siege.

inleak ('ɪnliːk). [f. IN *adv.* 11 d + LEAK *sb.*] Leakage into the inside of something.

1909 *Cent. Dict.* Suppl., *Inleak*, the leaking of a gas or liquid into an enclosed space or pipe. **1970** *Sci. Jrnl.* Mar. 40/3 Boiloff rate of about 0·2 per cent per day is several times as high as for most above ground insulated tanks, and some frozen earth tanks have failed as a result of excessive heat inleak. **1971** *Physics Bull.* Dec. 722/3 Techniques of constructing large vacuum insulated vessels are well established, but even so the heat inleak (typically a few tens of watts) is such that large closed cycle refrigerators are needed.

'in-leakage. [f. IN *adv.* 11 d + LEAKAGE.] = prec.

1905 *Trans. Inst. Naval Archit.* XLVII. II. 410 It was merely a race between the hand-pump and the in-leakage of water whether she was ever raised to the surface or not. **1963** B. FOZARD *Instrumentation Nucl. Reactors* iv. 40 Thereafter a steady flow of gas sufficient to prevent in-leakage of air is maintained.

†**in'lease,** *v.* *Obs. rare.* [f. IN-^{1} or ^{2} + LEASE.] *trans.* To let on lease.

1608 *Galway Arch.* in *10th Rep. Hist. MSS. Comm.* App. v. 461 Shall not..sell, give, graunt, demyse nor inlease nor to farme let..any manner of landes.

inlease, variant of INLESS *v.* *Obs.*

†**in'leased,** *a.* *Obs. rare*$^{-0}$. [f. IN-^{2} + *lease*, obs. form of LEASH + -ED^{1}.] Ensnared.

1706 PHILLIPS, *Inleased*, or *Enleased*, catch'd in a Gin, a Lease, or Snare. **1721** in BAILEY.

†**'inleck.** *Obs. rare*$^{-1}$. [f. IN-^{1} + *leck*, obs. form of LEAK.] A leak letting water in.

1583 STANYHURST *Æneis* I. (Arb.) 35 Graunt plancks from forrest too clowt oure battered inlecks.

inlegeable, obs. form of ILLEGIBLE.

inleid, Sc. form of INLEAD *v.*, *Obs.*

†**in'less,** *v.* *Obs. rare.* Also 7 **inlease.** [f. IN-^{2} + LESS *a.*] *trans.* To make less, diminish.

1515 BARCLAY *Egloges* iv. (1570) C iv b/1 That..which may hurt or inlesse Thy loued treasure, or minishe thy riches. **1611** SPEED *Hist. Gt. Brit.* IX. xxiv. §142. 1167 Where-through the power of the Word of God might be inleased or diminished.

inlet ('ɪnlɪt), *sb.* Also 4 **inlate.** [f. IN *adv.* 11 d + LET *v.*^{1} Cf. to *let in.*]

1. Letting in, admission. Now *rare.*

a **1300** *Cursor M.* 18078 Þe prince of hell, vndos your yate! Þe king of blis will haf in-late. *c* **1325** *Metr. Hom.* 51 Ful redi sal we haf inlate In to that blis that lastes ay. *a* **1635** NAUNTON *Fragm. Reg.* (Arb.) 57 Demanding his name, she said, Fail you not to come to the Court..And this was his inlet, and the beginnings of his grace. **1655** FULLER *Ch. Hist.* II. v. §51 Had there been a Castle in the place of this Monastery..probably they might have stopped the Danish Invasion at the first Inlet thereof. *a* **1704** T. BROWN *Praise of Poverty* Wks. 1730 I. 101 To gain the easier and unsuspected in-let into his mind and affections. **1774** GOLDSM. *Nat. Hist.* (1776) II. 188, I had already forgotten the light which was my first inlet into life. **1861** LYTTON & FANE *Tannhäuser* 97 Forcing sharp inlet to her throne in Heaven.

2. A way of admission; an entrance.

1624 WOTTON *Archit.* in *Reliq.* (1672) 33 These In-lets of Men and of Light [i.e. doors and windows], I couple together. **1681** LUTTRELL *Brief Rel.* (1857) I. 129 The French Kings troops had entred Cassall, the inlett into Italy. **1774** *Bainton Inclos. Act* 15 Drains, inlets, outlets, and water courses. **1818** LEIGH *New Pict. Lond.* 329 Pall Mall must always be one of the inlets to the west end of the town. **1870** ROLLESTON *Anim. Life* 101 Two venous inlets are seen in the anterior fourth of the upper surface of the heart.

fig. **1662** in Howell *State Trials* (1816) V. 1330 O that we may find death a sweet in-let and a passage to thy blessed arms. **1768** GOLDSM. *Good-n. Man* I. Wks. (Globe) 613/2 An increase of our possessions is but an inlet to new disquietudes. **1833** HT. MARTINEAU *Berkeley the Banker* I. iii. 41 Affected by the establishment of a bank, or by some other inlet of a flood of paper money.

3. A narrow opening by which the water penetrates into the land; a small arm of the sea, an indentation in the sea-coast or the bank of a lake or river; a creek.

1570–6 LAMBARDE *Peramb. Kent* (1826) 234 A thing yet well knowne in Kent, and expressed by the word yenlade or yenlet, which betokeneth an Indraught or Inlett of water into the lande. **1613** PURCHAS *Pilgrimage* (1614) 744 Furnished out the said Henry Hudson, to trie if through any of those Inlets, which Davis saw..any passage might be found to the other Ocean called the South-Sea. **1775** JOHNSON *Journ. West. Isl., Dunvegan*, We landed at Port Re ..The port is made by an inlet of the sea, deep and narrow. **1856** KANE *Arct. Expl.* II. xxvi. 257 The margin of these large fields is almost always broken by inlets of open water.

4. A piece let in or inserted.

1798 I. ALLEN *Hist. Vermont* 3 The whole range is composed of huge rocks confusedly piled on one another, though in many places are large inlets of excellent land. **1858** SIMMONDS *Dict. Trade*, *Inlet*,..inserted materials. **1886** *Pall Mall G.* 17 Dec. 13/2 The inlet into the panel in the upper part of the back of the chair is a photograph of a statue of Hunter.

5. *Anat.* The upper opening into a cavity of the body; used orig. of the pelvis and later of the thorax (both as cavities of the skeleton) and of the larynx.

1828 J. QUAIN *Elem. Anat.* ii. 69 The central line or axis of the inlet, differs very decidedly from that of the outlet;.. both therefore decussate towards the centre of the pelvic cavity. **1906** A. M. BUCHANAN *Manual of Anat.* I. 210 The true pelvis..presents a brim or inlet, a cavity, and an outlet. **1960** E. GARDNER et al. *Anat.* xxix. 339/1 The thoracic cavity communicates with the front of the neck by the superior thoracic aperture, or thoracic inlet. *Ibid.* lxxxii. 938/2 The

inlet or auditus of the larynx..leads from the laryngopharynx into the cavity of the larynx.

6. *attrib.*, as ***inlet area, -cam, -chamber, nipple, -pipe, valve, ventilation.***

1882 *Rep. to Ho. Repr. Prec. Metals U.S.* 584 The inlet valves are screwed into the piston. **1891** *Daily News* 17 Jan. 6/4 The inlet ventilation is by means of fresh-air reservoirs. **1901** L. M. Waterhouse *Conduit Wiring* 56 Metal inlet and outlet nipples. **1903** *Architect* (Suppl.) 24 Apr. 23/2 A 5-inch pipe is carried from the inlet-chamber to the reservoir. **1907** *Westm. Gaz.* 1 Oct. 7/1 Connecting the nozzle to the inlet-pipe of the balloon, the further supply of gas was added to that already within the envelope. **1908** *Ibid.* 9 Jan. 4/1 The inlet-cam being drawn out of position..the inlet-valves become completely closed.

Hence **'inleted** *a.*, having an inlet.

1871 R. Ellis *Catullus* lxiv. 74 When..Theseus Started alert from a beach deep-inleted of Piræus.

inlet ('ɪn,lɛt), *ppl. a.* [f. in *adv.* 11 b + pa. pple. of let *v.*¹: cf. *to let in.*] **1.** Let in, inserted.

1849 Ruskin *Sev. Lamps* iv. §12. 133 A round dot formed by a little inlet circle of serpentine.

2. *Needlework.* Ornamented *with* lace, etc., let in or inserted. So **'inletting** *vbl. sb.*

1901 *Daily Chron.* 31 Aug. 8/3 Flowing skirts inlet with lace. **1904** *Ibid.* 3 May 8/5 The inletting and trimming of a serge or cloth gown with Irish lace is quite usual.

inlet (ɪn'lɛt), *v.* [f. in-¹ + let *v.*¹ Orig. two words = *let in.*] To let in.

†**1.** *trans.* To allow to enter; to admit. *Obs.*

c **1320** *Sir Tristr.* 629 Rohand þo tok he And at þe gate in lete. *a* **1400** *Octouian* 1188 Men openede the gate..He was yn-late. **1627-47** Feltham *Resolves* 163 The minde is then shut up in the borough of the body—none of the Cinque ports of the Isle of Man are then open to in-let any strange disturbers. **1661** —— *Lusoria* xxvii. 25 The first act she [woman] did try Seduc'd Mankind, inletted policy, Taught him a way..To carry murther in a smiling brow.

2. To let in or insert (one thing) in another.

1860 Wraxall tr. *Kohl's Wand. Lake Superior* 6, I may be permitted to inlet here a slight episode in my wigwam building. **1884** A. J. Butler *Anc. Copt. Ch. Egypt* I. iii. 87 All round the framing of the doors tablets of solid ivory..are inlet.

†**'in,letter**, *sb.*¹ *Obs. rare.* [f. in *adv.* 11 e + letter, one who lets or allows.] One who lets in or gives admittance.

1656 Cromwell *Sp.* 17 Sept. in *Carlyle* (1872) IV. 205, I have had some boxes..and rebukes,—on the one hand and on the other; some censuring me for Presbytery; others as an inletter to all the Sects and Heresies of the Nation.

'in-letter, *sb.*² [f. in *adv.* 12 a + letter *sb.*¹ 4.] An incoming letter. Cf. in-basket, in-tray.

1955 C. E. Carrington *Rudyard Kipling* p. vi, Every in-letter was destroyed as soon as it was answered. **1973** *Times Lit. Suppl.* 9 Nov. 1359/1 In-letters, in particular, have been sacrificed: there is only one from Margaret Gillett..as against more than 200 from Smuts to her.

†**in'letter**, *v. Obs. rare*⁻¹. [f. in-² + letter *sb.* or *v.*] *trans.* To inscribe.

1628 Feltham *Resolves* ii. [i.] xlvi. 134 This Sentence might but on them be inletter'd.

†**'in,letting**, *vbl. sb. Obs.* [in *adv.* 11 c.] Letting in, admission.

1660 Boyle *New Exp. Phys. Mech.* xxii. 156 Upon the inletting of this external Air the water was not again impelled to the very top of the tube. **1691** E. Taylor *Behmen's Theos. Philos.* 103 Invaded by the inletting of the four Forms.

inlier ('ɪn,laɪə(r)). *Geol.* [f. in *adv.* 12 + lier, that which lies, after outlier.] (See quot. 1859.)

1859 Page *Handbk. Geol. Terms* (1865) 256 *Inlier*, a term introduced by Mr. Drew, of the Geological Survey, to express the converse of 'outlier'.. 'It means..a space occupied by one formation which is completely surrounded by another that rests upon it'. **1894** *Geol. Mag.* Oct. 460 It is..clearly marked by the Upper Greensand anticline of the Vale of Pewsey, and by the Upper Greensand inliers of Ham and Kingsclere. **1896** *Naturalist* 294 This formation occurs as patches or inliers that are surrounded by Oxford clays.

inlight, var. enlight *v., Obs.* Hence †**in'lighting** *vbl. sb.*, enlightening, enlightenment.

c **1400** tr. *Secreta Secret., Gov. Lordsh.* (E.E.T.S.) 96 Oon of þe stryngthes is a tokenynge..þat glorious god hauys inlightyd of vij strenghes. **1657** Austen *Fruit Trees* ii. 170 Counsells, inlightings..all is in vaine to them.

inlighten, -er, etc., obs. ff. enlighten, etc.

†**in'like, in'liche**, obs. ff. alike, arising perh. from confusing *i-* of *ilike, iliche*, with *in*.

13.. *Cursor M.* 27576 (Cotton Galba) If þai do ill think euer inlike [*Cott.* ilike]. **13..** *E.E. Allit. Poems* A. 602 Þer is vch mon payed inliche Wheþer lyttel oþer much be hys rewarde. *a* **1350** *St. Brice* 167 in Horstm. *Altengl. Leg.* (1881) 157 Þai angerd him ilk day inlike. *a* **1350** *St. Barthol.* 96 ibid. 120 Fully sex and twenty ȝere Lestes it in-like white and clere.

†**inlikewise**, the adv. phr. *in like wise*, in like manner, written conjunctly: see likewise, wise *sb.*, and cf. alikewise.

1542 *Sc. Acts Mary* (1814) 42 (Jam.) My said lord Governour..being inlikviss personalie present.

in limine: see in *Lat. prep.*

'in-line, *sb.* and *a.* Also inline. [f. phr. *in line* (cf. in *prep.* 18).] **A.** *sb. Printing.* (See quot. 1958.) Also *attrib.* or as *adj.* orig. *U.S.*

1923 *Amer. Type Founders Co. Specimen Bk.*, Cheltenham Inline. **1931** Bastien & Freshwater *Printing Types* 133 Erbar Inline... The inline..is a masterpiece of balance and design. **1953** Berry & Johnson *Encycl. Type Faces* 263 Inline fat face capitals and figures. The white line occupies only a small portion of the main strokes. **1958** *Ibid.* (ed. 2) 269 Outline or open letters should be those in which the whole interior of the stroke has been removed, shaded letters those which have a white line running down one side or the other, and Inline letters those with a white line running through the centre of the strokes. **1973** *Publishers Weekly* 1 Jan. 47/1 The third release is Neuland [type-face], which comes in a standard, two outlines, an inline and a black.

B. *adj.* **1.** (Composed of parts) arranged or situated in a line. **a.** Applied to internal-combustion engines in which the cylinders are arranged in one or more rows (in contrast to radial engines); usu. restricted to those in which the cylinders are vertical (so excluding V engines). Also *ellipt.* or as *sb.*

1929 V. W. Pagé *Mod. Aviation Engines* II. xlvi. 1886 Engines of the in-line type and both static and rotary radial two cycle forms continue to receive attention. **1934** *Discovery* Dec. 353/1 The tendency..is to develop..the large in-line engine..composed of four banks of cylinders forming an H, and the corresponding radial engines with two circles of cylinders one immediately behind the other. **1949** I. Katz *Princ. Aircraft Propulsion Machinery* i. 13 The principal cylinder arrangements are: 1. Inline—Single crankshaft, one cylinder bank, one piston per crankpin. 2. Inline-inverted—Inverted version of inline to ease problems of installation and facilitate larger propeller swing in small aircraft. 3. Opposed-cylinder... 4. V... 5. V-inverted [etc.]. **1958** R. D. Blacker *Basic Aeronaut. Sci.* ix. 145/2 In-line engines consist of one or more lines of cylinders placed one behind the other. The rows of cylinders may be arranged in an 'X' or 'V', as well as in a single line. **1961** J. Mackerle *Air-Cooled Motor Engines* x. 200 Twin cylinder engines are arranged in in-line parallel twins, V engines or horizontally opposed. **1969** K. Munson *Pioneer Aircraft 1903–14* 22 Wright Flyer III, *ca.* summer/autumn 1905. *Engine*: one 20 h.p. (approx.) Wright 4-cylinder water-cooled in-line. **1970** *Commercial Motor* 25 Sept. 56/2 A 370 bhp version of the Cummins 335/350 bhp six-cylinder in-line was in production. **1971** P. J. McMahon *Aircraft Propulsion* xi. 312 By the early 1930s..the inline vee..was beginning to offer strong opposition. *Ibid.*, Even though the radial made a comeback..the inline always had this fundamental advantage of a lower frontal area.

b. *gen.*

1961 *Engineering* 24 Nov. 685/1 The plant required for phosphating usually consists of a series of in-line tanks. **1968** *Sci. Jrnl.* Oct. 29/3 Aerial elevation and azimuth are..shown together with range on in-line digital indicators on the control unit.

2. Taking place or situated as an integral part of a continuous, usu. linear, sequence of operations or machines (as in an assembly line); involving or employing such a sequence.

1958 S. E. Rusinoff *Automation in Pract.* xi. 167 In straight in-line indexing, the work piece moves intermittently from one machining station to the next in a straight line. **1967** *Electronics* 6 Mar. 47/1 Production volume of monolithic integrated circuits has reached a point where automatic in-line testing and sorting will pay off in reliability. **1967** *Times Rev. Industry* May 60/2 The accommodation is designed for all the latest production techniques, including automatic inspection, bulk palletisation, in-line decoration and mechanical packing. **1968** Boothroyd & Redford *Mechanized Assembly* ii. 8 An in-line assembly machine is one where the work carriers are transferred in line along a straight slideway. **1971** *Engineering* Apr. 73/1 From the point where the operator selects the proper conductor wires, a portable electro-hydraulic in-line jointing machine..completes the cycle in under 18 seconds. **1971** *Physics Bull.* July 401/2 A typical problem in a steel mill is the in-line measurement of the roundness and diameter of steel rods, which are both hot and vibrating as a consequence of the production process.

3. *Computers.* **a.** Applied to a subroutine that is written, in full, directly into a program wherever it occurs. Now *rare*.

1958 Gotlieb & Hume *High-Speed Data Processing* vi. 107 A subroutine may be incorporated into a routine in either of two ways. If the instruction sequence is of reasonable length it may be inserted directly into place in the routine of which it forms part... A subroutine used in this manner is called an open or in-line subroutine. If a subroutine consists of a long sequence of instructions, or if it must be used in several different places in the routine, it is desirable to store it separately..and enter it by means of a jump.

b. Applied to data processing in which input data are processed in the order in which they are produced or obtained, without being first sorted into batches.

1959 J. Jeenel *Programming for Digital Computers* ix. 419 Random-access storage would permit input data to be processed efficiently in the chronological order in which they arise. This type of processing, which lends itself particularly well to certain commercial applications, is frequently referred to as 'in-line processing', as opposed to 'batch processing'. **1964** T. W. McRae *Impact of Computers on Accounting* i. 17 An in-line processing system updates all of the records on the same run, and the input data do not require sorting.

c. = on-line *a.* 1.

1959 E. M. McCormick *Digital Computer Primer* ix. 135 The input-output equipment of a computer is sometimes referred to as peripheral. If operated and controlled by the computer itself, it is in-line or on-line; if operated independently of the computer, it is off-line. **1971** N. Chapin *Computers* viii. 152 On-line peripheral equipment (or in-line, as it is sometimes called) operates under the direction of the control unit of the automatic computer.

†**in'link**, obs. variant of enlink *v.*

†**in'list**, obs. form of enlist *v.*

1665 Sir T. Herbert *Trav.* (1677) 156 Threbeg inlisted himself under the Turk.

inlive, inliven, obs. ff. enlive, enliven.

†**inlo'cation.** *Obs. rare*⁻¹. [f. in-² + location.] Location within something.

1647 M. Hudson *Div. Right Govt.* i. iv. 41 Thus he [the Devil] entred, and moved, and spoke in the dumb Idols which were the Oracles of the heathen: And so he sometimes acts in the very bodies of dead or murdered men and women: Which he doth, not by way of information, but of inlocation onely.

†**inlock.** *Sc. Obs.* [? for *inn-lock*; cf. Ger. *hausschloss* lock of the main door.] 'A great lock' (Jam.).

1488 *Act. Dom. Conc.* 92 (Jam.) Thre inlokis price iijs. **14..** in *Accts. Ld. High Treas.* Gloss. 421 Pro quatuor magnis seris, dictis inlokkis. **1491** *Ibid.* 184.

inlock, inlodge, var. enlock, enlodge.

in loco: see in *Lat. prep.*

inlook ('ɪnlʊk), *sb.* [f. in *adv.* 11 d + look *sb.*, after outlook.] Looking within, introspection.

18.. Caroline Fox *Jrnl.* (Cent.), A hearty sincere inlook tends..in no manner to self-glorification. **1869** Ruskin *Q. of Air* §135 To all true modesty the necessary business is not inlook, but outlook. *a* **1897** H. Drummond *Ideal Life* (1899) 311 He would begin not in out-look but in in-look.

†**in-'look**, *v. Obs. rare*⁻¹. [f. in-¹ + look *v.* (? after L. *inspicĕre*).] *trans.* To look into, inspect.

a **1649** Drumm. of Hawth. *Poems* Wks. (1711) 31 Thou art Light of Light, An ever-waking Eye still shining bright, In-looking all.

'in-,looker. *rare.* [in *adv.* 11 e.] One who looks into a thing, an inspector.

1587 Golding *De Mornay* xi. 162 In euery of vs he hath his inlookers [F. *inspecteurs*] to chastice vs, in our flesh,..in our minde,..and in our Soules. **1892** B. Hinton *Lord's Return* 52 This world's spectators may be divided into the on-lookers and the in-lookers.

'in-,looking, *vbl. sb. rare.* [in *adv.* 11 c.] Looking within, introspection.

1853 Lynch *Self-Improv.* 50 He who can find time for conscientious in-looking at himself..should be a student of religion.

†**in'lord**, *v. Obs. rare*⁻⁰. [f. in-² + lord *sb.*] *trans.* To make (any one) lord.

1611 Florio, *Insignorirsi*, to inlord, or become Lord, Patron or possessor of any thing. *Ibid.*, *Insignorito*, in-lorded, made or become Lord..or possessor of any thing.

'in-,lot. [f. in *adv.* 12 d + lot *sb.*]

1. A lot or allotment situated within another.

a **1661** Fuller *Worthies* iii. (1662) 166 God in the partage of Palestine..made some Tribes to have In-lots within another.

2. In parts of the United States, originally French, a lot of land in a village large enough for a house, outhouses, and garden (*Cent. Dict.*).

1779 in J. R. Robertson *Petitions Early Inhabitants Kentucky* (1914) 51 [We] pray that every Actual settler..may be entituled to Draw a free lott;..the lotts to consist of half acre in lott and five acre out lott. **1790** in *Amer. Pioneer* (1842) I. 72 Nathaniel Massie doth bind and oblige himself his heirs, &c., to make over and convey..one in-lot in said town. **1819** E. Dana *Geogr. Sk. Western Country* 74 The in-lots 62½ by 87½ feet each, were sold at public auction. **1837** W. Jenkins *Ohio Gazetteer* 109 The regular in-lots are ninety nine feet in front, extending back one hundred and ninety eight feet. **1948** E. N. Dick *Dixie Frontier* 148 The area in and around one of these stations was plotted and each settler could hold one or more 'in lots' or building plots on the townsite and one or more 'out lots' or farming areas.

†**in'loving**, *vbl. sb. Obs. nonce-wd.* [f. love, after *joy, injoy*.] Loving, holding in affection.

1633 W. Struther *True Happines* 124 We shall consider in it two affections..Love and joy: The first is our inloving, the other our injoying of him.

†**in'low**, *v. Obs.* In 3 inloȝen, -loghen. [f. in-¹ + low *v.*, after L. *inflammāre*. Cf. alow *adv.*] *trans.* To set aflame, kindle, inflame.

a **1300** *E.E. Psalter* lxxii[i]. 21 In-lowed es mi hert. *Ibid.* civ. 19 Speche of Laverd, þat was of mighte, In-loghed him, by dai and nighte.

inlure, variant of enlure *v., Obs.*

†**'inly**, *a. Obs.* Also 6 enlyē. [In OE. *in(n)lic*, f. *inn*, in *adv.* + *lic*, -ly¹. But the word is unknown during most of the ME. period, and appears to have been formed anew (perh. from inly *adv.*) in 15th c.] Inward, interior, internal; inwardly felt, heartfelt.

c **900** tr. *Bæda's Hist.* iii. xiii. [xv.] (1890) 198 Se innlica dema [*intimus arbiter*] ælmihtiȝ God. *Ibid.* v. xxii[i]. (1890) 480 Mid inlice hete [*domestico odio*]. **1422** tr. *Secreta Secret., Priv. Priv.* (E.E.T.S.) 204 This erle..roode..into the moste Inli Streynthes of McMahons contre. *c* **1440** Hylton *Scala Perf.* (W. de W. 1494) ii. xxx, Yet are they but outwarde tokens of the Inly grace. **1502** Atkynson tr. *De Imitatione* i. vii, The enlye dysposicyon of every soule. **1588**

SHAKS. *Two Gent.* II. vii. 18 Didst thou but know the inly touch of Loue. **1612** DRAYTON *Poly-olb.* vi. 88 Euer for those inly heats which through your loues they felt.

Hence †'**inlyhede**, inwardness, internal reality.

c **1440** *Jacob's Well* (E.E.T.S.) 171 þat is, inly sorwe for þi synne in þe herte, & no3t in þe chere, feyned outwarde.

inly ('ɪnlɪ), *adv.* Forms: 1 in(n)líce, 3–4 **inliche**, 5– **inly**, (5 *erron.* **endly**). [OE. *in(n)líce*, f. *in(n)líc*: see prec. and -LY[2].] **a.** Inwardly (as opposed to *outwardly*); within, internally; in the heart, spirit, or inner nature; in regard to the inner life or feelings. **b.** In a way that goes to the heart or inmost part; heartily, intimately, closely; fully, thoroughly, extremely.

c **888** K. ÆLFRED tr. *Boeth.* xxxiv. §12 þu miht openlice ongitan þæt ðæt is for inlice good þing þe ealle wuhta.. wilniað to habbanne. *c* **900** tr. *Bæda's Hist.* v. xvii. [xix.] (1890) 464 He.. het, þæt he inlice þam biscope freond wære. *c* **1290** *Beket* 1680 in *S. Eng. Leg.* I. 154 Seint thomas bigan to siche sore: and Inliche wep al-so. **13..** *Guy Warw.* (A.) st. cclxxxi, þe leuedi biheld him inliche, Hou mesays he was, sikerliche. *c* **1374** CHAUCER *Troylus* I. 640 No man may be inly glad I trowe That neuere was yn sorwe or som distresse. *c* **1440** *Generydes* 849 Now who was gladde.. And endly mery but Generydes. *Ibid.* 6698 The fayre mayde Lucidas Right endly was inprentid in his hert. **1579** SPENSER *Sheph. Cal.* May 38 Their fondnesse inly [*gloss* entirely] I pitie. **1591** SYLVESTER *Du Bartas* I. ii. 167 The Substances Inly, or outly, neither win nor leese. **1596** *Edward III*, I. ii. 11 Inly beautify'd With bounty's riches. **1625** GILL *Sacr. Philos.* viii. 143 They.. inly enuy that knowledge which the Christians have. **1715–20** POPE *Iliad* XXIII. 72 Great Pelides, stretch'd along the shore.. Lies inly groaning. **1813** J. MARRIOTT *Hymn 'Thou, whose almighty word'* ii, Thou, who didst come to bring.. Sight to the inly blind. **1838** LYTTON *Alice* XI. ii, Inly resolving not to hazard a second meeting with the Italian. **1847** EMERSON *Poems* (1857) 103 Friends year by year more inly known. **1871** R. ELLIS *Catullus* iv. 12 Oft Cytorus' height With her did inly whisper airy colloquy.

inlying ('ɪn,laɪɪŋ), *vbl. sb. Sc.* [f. IN *adv.* 11 c + LYING *vbl. sb.*: cf. *lie in* in LIE *v.*] Lying in at childbirth, confinement.

1734 KEITH *Hist. Ch. Scot.* 335 The most commodious Place for her Majesty's In-lying. *a* **1805** A. CARLYLE *Autobiog.* 529 Mrs. C. having recovered from her late inlying. **1819** *Edin. Mag.* Mar. 219/2 Attending at 'inlyings', or 'accouchements'.

inlying (,ɪn'laɪɪŋ), *ppl. a.* [IN *adv.* 11 a.] Lying inside; placed or situated in the interior.

1844 *Regul. & Ord. Army* 1 Officers on the Inlying Piquet. **1853** STOCQUELER *Milit. Encycl.* 215 *Inlying Piquets*, detachments told off to remain in camp, but fully accoutred, and ready to turn out instantly on alarm. **1868** SIR H. THOMPSON *Clin. Lect. Dis. Urin. Org.* xiii. (1882) 87 An inlying catheter.. is.. better than frequent catheterism. **1898** A. T. REED in *Advance* (Chicago) 6 Jan. 9/3 There is a place for the evangelist.. in the outlying regions and the inlying regions.

inlymn, variant of ENLIMN *v.*, *Obs.*

inmaculate, obs. form of IMMACULATE *a.*

in-maintenance: see IN *adv.* 12 a.

†'**inmake**. *Obs.* Also 6 **ynmake, inmak**, 7 **inmack**. [f. IN *adv.* 12 a (or perh. orig. INN *sb.* 1) + MAKE *sb.*[1]] A lodger, a person not of the household harboured or lodged; = INMATE *sb.* 1 a.

1537 *Irish Act 28 Hen. VIII* in *Ir. St. at Large* (1765) I. 168 Every person.. which in the harvest season receive or keepe in his or their houses.. any person or persons called ynmakes. **1582** in W. H. Turner *Select. Rec. Oxford* 422 Undertenants commonly called inmakes. **1588** in Picton *L'pool Munic. Rec.* I. 228 Iane Wignall, widow, fined for keeping an Inmake within her house iii[s]. vii[d]. and the Inmake in xij[d]. **1626** *Ibid.*, Wee p'sent the executors.. of Elizabeth Ditchfeild deceased, for harboringe of Inmacks in their backside in their kitchin.

†**in'mantle**, variant of IMMANTLE *v.*

(In some edd. of G. FLETCHER *Christ's Triumph* I. xvi.)

†**in'mask**, *v. Obs.* Also 7 **en-**. [f. IN-[2] + MASK: cf. IMMASK.] *trans.* To cover with or as with a mask, to mask.

1598 MARSTON *Pygmal., To Good Opinion* 118 If thou wilt not with thy Deitie Shade, and inmaske the errors of my pen. **1611** FLORIO, *Inmascherare*, to enmaske.

†**inmasti'cation**. *Obs. rare.* [IN-[1].] Internal mastication, as in the gizzard of a bird or insect.

1705 C. PURSHALL *Mech. Macrocosm* 186 Whose Particles being then not well Digested.. for want of Fermentation, and Inmastication.

inmate ('ɪnmeɪt), *sb.* (*a.*) [f. IN *adv.* 12 a (or perh. orig. INN *sb.* 1) + MATE *sb.*]

1. In relation to other persons: One who is the mate or associate of another or others in the same dwelling; one who dwells with others in a house. (Now *rare.*) In early use, One admitted for a consideration to reside in a house occupied or rented by another; a lodger or subtenant.

In the 16th and 17th c. there were stringent statutes and by-laws against the harbouring of poor persons as 'inmates', subtenants, or lodgers, a practice which tended to increase the number of paupers locally chargeable.

1589 *Act 31 Eliz.* c. 7 §6 There shall not be any Inmate or more Famylies or Housholdes then one, dwellinge or inhabitinge in anye one Cottage. **1597–1602** *Transcript W. Riding Sessions Rolls* (Rec. Ser.) 86 Whosoever.. doth take any Inmate.. shall releefe and keepe them from beggyng. **1601** *Nottingham Rec.* IV. 260 Taking an inmate in to his hous. **1655** STANLEY *Hist. Philos.* I. (1701) 39/1 Bias was of Priene.. some affirm he was rich, others that he had no Estate, but lived as an Inmate. **1676** tr. *Guillatiere's Voy. Athens* 86 In those Countries, the Master and his Cattle are Inmates, and lye higgledy piggledy in the same room. **1690** CHILD *Disc. Trade* (1694) 95 As for the laws against Inmates, and empowering the Parishioners to take security before they suffer any poor person to inhabit amongst them.. I am sure in cities and great towns of trade they are altogether improper, and contrary to the practice of other cities and trading towns abroad. **1832** HT. MARTINEAU *Hill & Valley* iv. 68 Mrs. Sydney inquired whether he was a pleasant inmate and a kind neighbour.

b. Sometimes, One not originally or properly belonging to the place where he dwells; a foreigner, stranger. Often *fig.*

a **1600** HOOKER *Serm. Justif.* §2 *note*, Some critical wits may perhaps half suspect that these two words, *per se*, are inmates. But if the place which they have be their own, their sense can be none other than that which I have given them. **1611** B. JONSON *Catiline* II. ii, He is but a new fellow, An inmate here in Rome (as Catiline calls him). *a* **1682** SIR T. BROWNE *Tracts* (1684) 139 Though the English [language] swell with the inmates of Italian, French, and Latin. **1692** tr. *Sallust* 352 Not an Upstart, an Inn-mate, and but lately admitted to the Privileges of this City.

2. In relation to the house or dwelling-place: An occupant along with others, one of the family or company who occupy a house or other abode; hence sometimes simply = Indweller, inhabitant, occupier. Const. *of.* (*lit.* and *fig.*)

1597 DANIEL *Civ. Wars* VIII. lxxi, Within her brow.. sat scorn; Shame in her cheeks; where also fear became An inmate too. **1613** PURCHAS *Pilgrimage* (1614) 34 Religion which before had bin a privat in-mate in Adams houshold, was now.. publike exercise. *c* **1630** DRUMM. OF HAWTH. *Poems* 22 You inmates of the Woods. **1667** MILTON *P.L.* IX. 495 So spake the Enemie of Mankind, enclos'd In Serpent, Inmate bad. **1674** tr. *Scheffer's Lapland* 115 All the feathered In-mates of the sky. **1784** COWPER *Tiroc.* 892 If thou guard it's [the heart's] sacred chambers sure From vicious inmates and delights impure. **1828** SCOTT *F.M. Perth* xxxvi, It had readily opened its gates to admit the noble lady who was its present inmate. **1834** MEDWIN *Angler in Wales* II. 261 An inmate of a lunatic asylum. **1876** GLADSTONE *Homeric Synchr.* 200 Twelve were married inmates of his palace.

B. *attrib.* or *adj.* That is an inmate (*lit.* or *fig.*); dwelling in the same house with, or in the house of, another; dwelling within, indwelling. ? *Obs.*

1630 SANDERSON *Serm., Ad Mag.* ii. (1681) II. 272 In the famous case of the two inmate Harlots, whereof King Solomon had the hearing. **1667** MILTON *P.L.* XII. 166 A sequent King, who seeks To stop their overgrowth, as inmate guests Too numerous. **1697** DRYDEN *Virg. Georg.* II. 41 Tis usual now, an Inmate Graff to see With insolence invade a Foreign Tree. **1773–83** HOOLE *Orl. Fur.* VI. 210 Unknowing, that beneath thy rugged rind Conceal'd, an inmate spirit lay confin'd. **1806** R. CUMBERLAND *Mem.* (1807) II. 185 The children, who were inmate with me when I settled at Tunbridge Wells.

Hence **inmatecy** ('ɪnmeɪtsɪ) [irreg.: see -CY], the position of an inmate; '**inmated** *ppl. a.*, located as an inmate; '**inmateless** *a.*, without an inmate.

1822–34 *Good's Study Med.* (ed. 4) II. 411 Even those who associated with the sick, were seldom affected unless inmated in their rooms. **1830** J. BADCOCK ['JON BEE'] *Ess. Foote* in *Foote's Wks.* I. p. clxvii. *note*, Thither [to the Fleet-Prison] the Doctor repaired.. and found our laughing philosopher in the usual plight of such an inmatecy, poor and pennyless. **1835** LYTTON *Rienzi* VI. ii, The cottages.. were some shut up.. some open, but seemingly inmateless.

inmateryall, obs. form of IMMATERIAL.

inmeat ('ɪnmi:t). Now *rare* exc. *dial.* Usually in pl. **inmeats**. [f. IN *adv.* 12 c + MEAT *sb.*] Those internal parts or viscera of an animal which are used for food; hence *gen.* Entrails, inwards.

(The first quot. is doubtful: the word may also be read *jumette*, which suits the alliteration but is of unknown meaning.)

[? *a* **1400** *Morte Arth.* 1122 The hott blode of þe hulke unto the hilte rynnez, Ewyne into inmette the gyaunt he hyttez.] **1616** SURFL. & MARKH. *Country Farme* 586 They preserve their inmeats a great deal the better. **1743** MAXWELL *Sel. Trans.* 275 (Jam.) The hide, head, feet, and in-meat, were given for attendance. **1834** SIR H. TAYLOR *Artevelde* II. III. i. Wks. 1864 I. 191 Get thee gone, Or I shall try six inches of my knife On thine own inmeats first. **1877** *N.W. Linc. Gloss.*, *Inmeats*, the edible viscera of pigs, fowls, &c.

in medias res, in memoriam: see IN *Lat. prep.*

in melle: see IMELLE *adv.*

†**inmense**, obs. form of IMMENSE *a.*

c **1450** *Mirour Saluacioun* 1679 O godde of hiegh pitee inmense and ineffable.

in'mesh, var. of ENMESH *v.*, to entangle in the meshes of a net.

1868 F. M. BROWN *For the picture called 'Work'*, For want of work the fiends him soon inmesh!

†**in'mew**, *v. Obs. rare.* [? f. IN-[1] + MEW *v.*] *trans.* ? To IMMEW, to mew or coop up; in quot., app., 'To cause to lie close and keep concealed, as hawk in mew'.

So this and the equivalent *emmew*, in SHAKS. *Meas. for M.* III. i. 91, are explained by the Rt. Hon. D. H. Madden in *Diary of Master William Silence* (1897) 302, Note[2], in opposition to the conjecture of some that the latter is a blundered spelling of ENEW.

a **1625** BEAUM. & FL. *Knt. of Malta* II. ii, I have seen him scale As if a Falcon had run up a trainee, Clashing his warlike pynions, his steel'd curasse, And at his pitch inmew the Town below him.

†**in mid**, *advb. phr.* and *prep. Obs.* [An analytical variant of ME. *on midde, amidde*, AMID.]

A. *adv.* In the middle, in the midst. *in myd among* = AMIDMONG (AMID B. 5).

c **1500** *Lancelot* 3371 In myd among his ennemys. *a* **1555** LYNDESAY *Tragedy* 244 In myd amang his tryumphant Armye.

B. *prep.* Amid, in the middle or centre of.

13.. *E.E. Allit. P.* B. 1677 In mydde þe poynt of his pryde departed he þere. **1375** BARBOUR *Bruce* XII. 576 Axis that rycht scharply schar, In myd the visage met thame thar. *c* **1384** CHAUCER *H. Fame* II. 415 He fyll wete In mydde the se. *a* **1450** *Le Morte Arth.* 2085 In mydde the felde we shall hem byde.

†**in mids**, *advb. phr.* and *prep. Obs.* [A variant of ME. *amiddes, imyddes.*] = AMIDST.

A. *adv.* In the middle, in the midst.

13.. *Gaw. & Gr. Knt.* 167 With gay gaudi of grene, þe golde ay in myddes. *c* **1440** *Jacob's Well* (E.E.T.S.) 191 As þe heued of a schouyll is in-myddes be-twen þe scho & þe handyll.

B. *prep.* In the middle or midst of; amidst.

a **1300** *Cursor M.* 1032 (Gött.) In middes [*Trin.* I mydde; *Cott.* Midward] þat land a welle springes. **13..** *E.E. Allit. P.* A. 739 Euen in myddez my breste hit stode. *a* **1400–50** *Alexander* 1586 (Ashm. MS.) In-myddis þe puple [*Dubl. MS.* in-myddez of þe peple]. *c* **1460** *Towneley Myst.* i. 31 In medys the water. **14..** in Turner *Dom. Archit.* III. 84 In myddys þe halle upon þe flore.

in-migrant ('ɪnmaɪgrənt), *sb.* and *a.* orig. *U.S.* [IN *adv.* 11 e.] **A.** *sb.* One who migrates from one place to another in the same country. **B.** *adj.* Migrating from one place to another in the same country.

1942 *Fortune* Oct. 194 About two-thirds of the 120,000 in-migrants will be without new housing. **1943** *New England Electr. News* Aug. 32 If a demand for the houses exists among the eligible in-migrant workers in a community. **1962** *Amer. Speech* XXXVII. 16 After 1900, the largest number of in-migrants came [to New York] from the Mid-Atlantic states. *Ibid.* 22 The in-migrant Negroes from the South concentrated in their neighborhoods too.., the largest concentration being the Harlem section in uptown Manhattan. **1963** *New Society* 10 Oct. 26/1 In-migrants to Aberdeen contained a much higher proportion of.. university trained women than the native population. **1966** *Publ. Amer. Dial. Soc.* 1964 XLII. 29 Poor in-migrant Southerners.

in-migration ('ɪnmaɪ,greɪʃən). orig. *U.S.* [IN *adv.* 12 a.] The action of moving from one place to another within the same country, e.g. from one state to another in the United States.

1942 *N.Y. Herald Tribune* 17 May N1 An immigration of approximately 3,000 new workers. **1957** *Economist* 28 Sept. 1031/1 Nowadays, with the tide of immigration from Europe a fading memory, American cities are growing by grace of what sociologists call 'in-migration'—movements of people from other parts of the United States. **1971** *Sci. Amer.* July 18/3 Of the 12 states in this region only three.. showed an excess of in-migration over out-migration. **1972** *Real Estate Rev.* Winter 21/1 The heavy in-migration of people from the mainland following the attainment of statehood made the demand for apartment-type housing acute. **1973** *Daily Colonist* (Victoria, B.C.) 11 Oct. 5/1 Land use—controls on highrise development and limits to 'in-migration', the influx of outsiders to the Victoria area.

'**in-milk**, *a.* [attrib. use of phr. *in milk*: cf. MILK *sb.* 1 c.] Of a cow: in a condition to yield milk.

1958 *Times* 11 Dec. 12/7 If an in-milk cow laid down on the grass she was likely to be milked by a hedgehog. **1960** *Farmer & Stockbreeder* 12 Jan. 13/2 Best bid of 108 gs. was made.. for The Pynes Herds' in-milk Jersey heifer, Eastington June.

inmind, variant of IMMIND *v.*, *Obs.*

†**in'miter**, var. *enmitre*: see EN- *prefix*[1] 1 b.

1611 FLORIO, *Infulare*, to inmiter or impale as Bishops be.

inmix (ɪn'mɪks), *v.* [f. IN *adv.* + MIX *v.*] *trans.* and *intr.* = IMMIX *v.*

1892 G. MEREDITH *Sage Enamoured* in *Mod. Love* 99 Then shall those noblest of the earth and sun Inmix unlike to waves on savage sea. *a* **1909** —— *Celt & Saxon* xvi. 237 Celt and Saxon are much inmixed with us. **1931** BELLOC *Ess. Catholic* xvi. 318 It was badly inmixed with motives in no way Catholic.

in-mobill, obs. form of IMMOBILE *a.*

inmoeueable, etc., obs. ff. IMMOVABLE, etc.

†**in-'mong, in-'monges**, *prep. Obs.* [Variants of *imong, imonges* (see YMONG), the initial *i* being app. taken as the prep. and expanded to *in*: see also AMONG.] Among, amongst.

13.. *E.E. Allit. P.* A. 278 And multyplyed mony-fold in-mongez mankynde. *Ibid.* B. 1485 In-mong þe leues.

† **'inmore**, *a.* *Obs. rare.* [f. IN *adv.* + MORE, after *inmost*: see INNER.] Inner, interior.

1610 HOLLAND *Camden's Brit.* I. 131 Of these Angles, some part..passed forward into the inmore quarters of Germanie. *Ibid.* 800 Where they had free entrance..into the inmore parts of England.

inmortal, obs. form of IMMORTAL.

inmost ('ɪnməʊst, -məst), *a.* (*sb.*, *adv.*) Forms: 1 innemest, innemyst, 4 in-mast, in(n)emaste, 4, (6 *Sc.*) inmest, 5 ynmast, 6 ynmost, 4- inmost. [OE. *innemest* (f. **innem-a*, *-e* + *-est*), a double superlative of *inne* IN *adv.*; for the later history of the ending, usual in OE. advs. of place, see -MOST.]

1. *lit.* In reference to spatial position: Situated farthest within, most inward, most remote from the outside.

13.. *Cast. Love* 809 Bote þe inemaste [*v.r.* innemeste] bayle, I wot, Bi-toknep hire holy maidenhod. **1535** COVERDALE *2 Kings* ix. 2 Brynge him in to the ynmost chamber. —— *1 Macc.* ix. 54 Yᵉ walles of the ynmost Sanctuary. **1596** DALRYMPLE tr. *Leslie's Hist. Scot.* x. 331 In the inmest parte of the castel. **1667** MILTON *P.L.* IV. 738 Into thir inmost bower Handed they went. **1713** DERHAM *Phys. Theol.* 4 To penetrate into the inmost Recesses of Nature. *a* **1822** SHELLEY *Hymn to Mercury* xxxi, From the inmost depths of its green glen.

2. *fig.* Of thoughts or feelings, the mind or soul, personal relations, etc.: Most inward or intimate; deepest; closest.

c **897** K. ÆLFRED *Gregory's Past.* xxi. (Sweet) 155 Ealle ða innemestan ȝeðohtas. **1398** TREVISA *Barth. De. P.R.* II. iv. (Add. MS. 27,944), I-rauyschite to þe inmest [*ed.* 1495 innest] contemplacioun of þe sone of god. **1548** UDALL *Erasm. Par. Luke* viii. N vj, In the inmoste affeccion of their hertes. **1667** MILTON *P.L.* I. 168 If I fail not and disturb His inmost counsels from their destind aim. **1818** JAS. MILL *Brit. India* III. VI. i. 2 [He] insinuated himself quickly into his inmost confidence. **1882** FARRAR *Early Chr.* II. 116 To know something of his Master's inmost thoughts.

B. *absol.* or as *sb.* That which is inmost; the inmost part. *lit.* and *fig.* (Rarely in *pl.*)

a **1050** *Liber Scintill.* iv. (1889) 19 Innemyste [*interiora*] his fulle synd facne. *a* **1325** *Prose Psalter* (E.E.T.S.) xlii[i]. 5 In þe in-mast of myn hert. **1382** WYCLIF *Prov.* xxvi. 22 Thei comen thurȝ to the inmostis [**1388** the ynneste thingis] of the herte. *c* **1580** SIDNEY *Ps.* XXVI. ii, Yea, sound my reynes, and inmost of my hart. **1638** FORD *Fancies* II. ii, Be sure To lodge it in the inmost of thy bosom. **1668** H. MORE *Div. Dial.* I. 505 The inmost of the mind. **1856** R. A. VAUGHAN *Mystics* (1860) I. 175 This image and superscription lies in the inmost inmost of the soul.

C. *adv.* Most inwardly. *rare.*

c **1000** ÆLFRIC *Gram.* xxxviii. (Z.) 240 *Intime*, innemest. **1725** POPE *Odyss.* IX. 470 Thro' all their inmost-winding caves.

Hence **'inmostly** *adv.* (*rare*), most inwardly; **'inmostness** (*nonce-wd.*), the inmost essence or nature (cf. *inwardness*).

1674 N. FAIRFAX *Bulk & Selv.* 34 Thoughtsomness setting full as close to the very stamp or inmostness of a thinking Being. **1850** NEALE *Med. Hymns* (1867) 104 How the Virgin Mother's soul Inmostly was grieving. **1889** *Univ. Rev.* Mar. 314 All secrets of Earth They shall inmostly scan.

† **in'mouled**, *ppl. a.* (*sb.*) *Obs.* [f. IN-¹ or ² + MOULD, or F. *moule* mould, *moulé* moulded.] ? Moulded. In quot. *absol.* as *sb.* Moulding.

1548 HALL *Chron., Hen. VIII* 74 The rooffe of the same Closet was siled with woorke of Inmould, gylte with fine Golde and Senapar and Bice.

† **in'move, en'move**, *v.* *Obs.* [f. IN-², EN-¹ + MOVE *v.*] *trans.* To move inwardly, or in the mind; to affect with emotion.

1583 GOLDING *Calvin on Deut.* lxix. 422 Nowe commeth this inmouing of men, or of their own nature? No it is of Gods working in their heartes. **1590** SPENSER *F.Q.* I. ix. 48 The knight was much enmoved with his speach. **1596** FITZ-GEFFRAY *Sir F. Drake* (1881) 58 Honour enmoves her to attempt the flight.

inmutabull, obs. form of IMMUTABLE.

† **inmytee**, obs. f. ENMITY: cf. also INIMITIE.

1423 JAS. I *Kingis Quair* lxxxvii, Sum for dispite and othir Inmytee.

inn (ɪn), *sb.* Forms: 1- inn, 1-7 in, 3-7 inne, (3 hynne, 4 hin), 4-5 yn, 4-6 ine, ynne, (5 hyn, 6 ynn). [OE. *inn* neut.:—OTeut. **innoᵐ*: agreeing, exc. in stem suffix, with ON. *inne*, *inni* (:—OTeut. **innjoᵐ*), f. *inn*, *inne* IN *adv.*]

† **1.** A dwelling-place, habitation, abode, lodging; a house (in relation to its inhabitant).

c **1000** ÆLFRIC *Hom.* I. 110 þaða se steorra glad, and þa tungel-witeȝan ȝelædde, and him ðæs cildes inn ȝebicnode. *c* **1000** *Ags. Gosp.* Matt. xiii. 36 He for let þa ða mæneȝeo and com to his inne [So *c* **1160** *Hatt. Gosp.*]. *c* **1205** LAY. 14263 Hengest..seide þæt he hafde an in iȝarked to-ȝeines him. *a* **1300** *Cursor M.* 4983 (Cott.) þe yongeist..þat þai lefte at þeir fader in [*Gött.* fadris ine]. *c* **1330** R. BRUNNE *Chron.* (1810) 334 Do crie þorgh þe toun, þat non for wele no wo, In strete [*printed* stete] walk vp & doun bot to þer innes go. **1387** TREVISA *Higden* (Rolls) I. 115 In þe side of þe hille was þe yn of Lazarus, of Martha, and of Marie Mawdeleyn; þat toun hiȝt Bethania. **1447** BOKENHAM *Seyntys* (Roxb.) 260 Whan yche man hym dede hyr Hoom to hys yn hym to counforte. **1546** J. HEYWOOD *Prov.* (1867) 10 Restie welth wylth me this wydow to wyn, To let the world wag, and take mine ease in mine in. **1657** HOWELL *Londinop.* 339 Queen Mary gave this House to Nicholas Heth, Archbishop of York, and his successors for ever, to be their Inne or Lodging for their repair to London.

† **b.** *pl.* in sing. sense. (Cf. *lodgings*, *quarters*.)

c **1205** LAY. 14007 þe king..sende to þan innen after al his monnen [*c* **1275** to þeos cnihtes hinne]. *a* **1300** *Cursor M.* 15407 Quar his innes ar to night wel i can yow bring. *Ibid.* 19829 (Edin.) þai saȝ þaim fra, þat innis þare saint petir lai. **1375** BARBOUR *Bruce* II. 1 The bruys went till his Innys swyth. *a* **1400-50** *Alexander* 2920 þis..berne..þat here þus hyndly be þe hand ledis to his Innes. *c* **1470** HENRY *Wallace* IV. 381 For him he gert ane innys graithit be. *c* **1550** LYNDESAY *Descr. Peder Coffeis* ii, For to by hennis reid-wod he rynnis; He lokis thame vp in to his innis. **1603** KNOLLES *Hist. Turks* (1621) 1052 He..came suddenly upon the Turks..compassed about the Innes wherein they lay.

† **2.** Phr. *to take* (*up*) *one's inn* (or *inns*), to take up one's abode, residence, quarters; so, *to have keep* (*one's*) *inn*. *Obs.*

c **1000** ÆLFRIC *Hom.* I. 372 Innan ðam ȝeate þær Petrus inn hæfde. *a* **1300** *Cursor M.* 17650 Wit nichodeme he tok his hin. **1340** *Ayenb.* 195 He zent his messagyers be-uore uor to nime guod in. *c* **1430** *Syr Gener.* (Roxb.) 1476 Here ynnes ther ful sone thei nam. *c* **1450** *Bk. Curtasye* in *Babees Bk.* 308 In no kyn house þat rede mon is..Take neuer þy Innes for no kyn nede. **1581** MULCASTER *Positions* xlii. (1887) 257 If the imperfections which come..from the Elementary schoole would take vp their Inne there, and raunge no further. **1590** SPENSER *F.Q.* I. i. 33 With me ye may take up your In For this same night. **1633** A. H. *Partheneia Sacra* 151 (T.) The phenix will lightly take up his inne no where els.

† **b.** *at inn*: Lodged, housed, resident, put up (in some place specified or implied). *Obs.*

c **1200** ORMIN 12923 þeȝȝ comenn forr to fraȝȝnenn Crist Off whære he wass att inne. *Ibid.* 13088 To lokenn whære he wass att inn. **1297** R. GLOUC. (Rolls) 5998 Wanne at an gode monnes house is men were at inne. **1362** LANGL. *P. Pl.* A. IX. 4 ȝif any wiȝt wiste where do-wel was at Inne. **1553** BRADFORD *Wks.* (Parker Soc.) I. 79 Surely the devil is at inn with you, you are his birds, whom when he hath well fed, he will broach you and eat you, chaw you and champ you. **1592** DEE *Diary* (Camden) 41, I sent a letter..by the wagon-man who is at ynn at the George in Lombard streete.

† **3.** 'Dwelling-place', 'abode', 'place of sojourn', in various figurative uses. *Obs.*

c **1400** *Rom. Rose* 5107 A sory gest..Thou herborest in thine inne The God of Love whan thou let inne. **1535** COVERDALE *Isa.* xxxii. 18 My people shal dwel in the ynnes of peace. **1549** ——, etc. *Erasm. Par. Thess.* 5 The bodie is the dwelling house of the soule and the soule is the Inne of God. **1607** WALKINGTON *Opt. Glass* ii. (1664) 23 Plotin.. blushed often, that his Soul did harbour in so base an Inn, as his Body was. **1615** G. SANDYS *Trav.* 180 Seest thou this tombe hewne in the growing stone? Tis Paula's Inne.

4. A public house kept for the lodging and entertainment of travellers, or of any who wish to use its accommodation; a hostelry or hotel; sometimes, erroneously, a tavern which does not provide lodging.

c **1400** MAUNDEV. (1839) v. 34 Alleweyes men fynden gode innes and all that hem nedeth of Vytaylle. *Ibid.* xxii. 243 Thorgh the desertes..there ben Innes ordeyned be euery iorneye, to resceyue bothe man and hors. *c* **1440** *Promp. Parv.* 260/1 In, of herboroghe.., *hospicium*, *diversorium*. **1534** TINDALE *Luke* ii. 7 She..layed him in a manger, because ther was no roume for them within in the ynne. **1573** G. HARVEY *Letter-bk.* (Camden) 33 Thai carri your letters abrode to the Bear and other commun ins. **1611** BP. HALL *Serm.* v. 51 Like some Inn, that hath a Crown for the sign without..or a Rose upon the post without..or an Angel without. *a* **1763** SHENSTONE *Written at an Inn at Henley* v, Whoe'er has travelled life's dull round..May sigh to think he still has found The warmest welcome at an inn. **1809** KENDALL *Trav.* I. xi. 122 Keeping an inn, or as it is called, a *tavern*. **1845** FORD *Handbk. Spain* I. 21 The Spanish inns..are very much in the same condition as they were in the time of the Romans. **1883** *Law Times* 27 Oct. 432/2 An inn or hotel is an establishment, the proprietor of which undertakes to provide for the entertainment of all comers, especially travellers. **1886** RUSKIN *Præterita* I. 173 We stayed several weeks in Paris, in a quiet family inn.

b. In figurative and allusive uses; *esp.* a temporary lodging as opposed to a permanent abode.

1529 MORE *Dyaloge* I. Wks. 142/1 Our Lord in the parable of the Samaritane, bearing the wounded man into the Inne of his church. **1613** PURCHAS *Pilgrimage* (1614) 566 That Egyptian opinion, esteeming their houses their Innes, and their Sepulchres their eternal habitations. **1647** N. BACON *Disc. Govt. Eng.* I. iii. (1739) 3 To make this Isle to be only an Inn for him to whom it was formerly given for a possession. **1663** BOYLE *Usef. Exp. Nat. Philos.* I. ii. 29 The world is wont to be stiled not unfitly by Divines, The Christian's inne. **1668** DAVENANT *Man's the Master* I. i. Wks. 1874 V. 13 Yes, to the last inn of all travellers, where we shall meet worms instead of fleas. Lovers never rest quietly till they lodge at the sign of the grave. **1814** SCOTT *Ld. of Isles* VI. xxvi, The noble and the slave..the same wild road..trode, To that dark inn, the grave!

5. A lodging-house or house of residence for students (cf. HOSTEL *sb.*¹ 3): now *Obs.*, exc. as retained in the names of buildings orig. so used; see b and c.

In this sense rendering L. *hospitium*, used from early times in the English Universities, as still earlier at Bologna and Paris; OF. *hostel*. The vernacular term *inn* occurs in the proper names of these houses from the 14th, or perhaps the 13th, century.

† **a.** At the Universities. *Obs.* (Preserved till 19th c. in the name of *New Inn Hall*, Oxford.)

[**1214** *Let. Nicholas Bp. Tusculum to Burgenses of Oxford*, Condonetur Scholaribus Oxonie studentibus medietas mercedis Hospitiorum omnium locandorum clericis in eadem villa. *c* **1250** *Statute of Univ. Oxford* (heading), De principalitatibus Hospitiorum et Scholarum.] **1346** *Lett. Pat. of Edw. III*, 5 Aug., De quodam messuagio vocato Take-leysyn. **1438** (9 Sept.) in Anstey *Munim. Acad.* 519-22 Hæc sunt nomina principalium aularum..Principalis aulæ Bekys-yne,..Newels-yne,..Pekwater-yne,..Takleys-ynne. *c* **1460** ROUS *Tabella aularum* (in Wood *City of Oxf.* I. 640) Trillok Yn quod nunc dicitur Novum Hospitium, quia noviter ædificatum. [Called *New Inn*, in New College books, 1542.] **1577** HARRISON *England* II. iii. (1877) I. 87 There are also in Oxford certeine hostels or halls..the liuers in these are verie like to those that are of Ins in the chancerie [**1587** their names also are these so farre as I now remember] Brodegates, Hart hall..S. Marie hall, White hall, New In, Edmond hall. **1655** FULLER *Hist. Camb.* 27 Know also that Inns (whereof onely two, Ovings and St. Pauls) differed onely gradually from Hostles, as being less. **1662** WOOD *City of Oxf.* I. 141 That this inne, which was afterwards, from the said Richard, called Hunsingore Inne, was an eminent receptacle for schollers. [**1877** *Statutes of Univ. Oxf. Commissioners* (1882) 215 Statute for the Union of Balliol College and New Inn Hall.]

b. *Inns of Chancery*: certain houses or sets of buildings in London, originally places of residence and study for students and apprentices of law; also the societies by which they were occupied.

From the 15th or 16th to the 18th c., these were subordinate to the Inns of Court; but they now perform no public function, though several still exist as societies possessing corporate property, the chambers being occupied by solicitors and others.

[**1348** *Will of John Tavie* [Thavye] in Dugdale *Orig. Jurid.* lxv. (1671) 271/1 Totum illud Hospicium [i.e. Thavies' Inn], in quo Apprenticii ad Legem habitare solebant. **1355** *Year-bk. 29 Edw. III*, lf. 47 a, Nous lauons oy souvent entre les apprentices in hostelles. (Cf. *Coke's Repts.* x. (1738) lf. 22 b, inter Apprenticios in Hospitiis Curiæ audivimus.)] **1458** *Short Eng. Chron.* (Camd. 1880, N.S. 28) 71 This yere [Anno xxxvii] was a grete fraye be twene the Cite of London and men of Courte, which were drevyn..from the Standarde in Flete strete to ther innes, the xiii day of Apreill. [*a* **1485** FORTESCUE *De Laud. Leg. Ang.* xlix, Decem hospitia minora..quæ nominantur hospitia Cancellariæ..majora hospitia studii illius, quæ hospitia curiæ appellantur.] **1567** R. MULCASTER ibid. (1660) 113 Ten lesser houses or Innes.. which are called Innes of the Chancery..The greater Innes of the same study called the Innes of Court. **1580** STOW *Annals, 36 Henry VI*, The thirteenth day of Aprill there was a great fray in Fleete streete..the king committed the principall governours of Furnivalls, Cliffords, and Barnardes Inne to prison in the Castle of Hertford. **1670** BLOUNT *Law Dict.*, *Innes of Court*,..these, with the Two Serjants Inns, and Eight Inns of Chancery, do altogether (to use Sir Edward Cokes words) make the most famous University, for Profession of Law onely, or of any one Humane Science in the World. **1809** *Blackstone's Comm.* I. Introd. §1. 26 *note*, The inns of chancery are, Clifford's Inn, Clement's Inn, Lion's Inn, New Inn, Furnival's Inn, Thavies's Inn, Staple's Inn, and Barnard's Inn. These are subordinate to the inns of court; the three first belong to the Inner Temple, the fourth to the Middle Temple, the two next to Lincoln's Inn, and the two last to Gray's Inn. **1883** *Wharton's Law Lex.* (ed. 7), *Inns of Chancery*,..these were formerly preparatory colleges for students, and many entered them before they were admitted into the Inns of Court. They [now] consist chiefly of solicitors, and possess corporate property, hall, chambers, etc., but perform no public functions like the Inns of Court.

c. *Inns of Court*: the four sets of buildings in London (the Inner Temple, the Middle Temple, Lincoln's Inn, and Gray's Inn) belonging to the four legal societies which have the exclusive right of admitting persons to practise at the bar, and hold a course of instruction and examination for that purpose; hence, these four societies themselves. (Formerly also colloq. *inns a court*.)

The distinction of the 'foure principall Innes' of law as Inns of Court, was fully established in the 15th c.: see quot. *a* 1485 in b. But in earlier times, and sometimes later, the name Inns of Court, or its equivalent, seems to have included both the *hospitia majora* and *hospitia minora*: cf. quots. 1355, 1458, and 1580 (referring to the same event) in b, with 1548 and 1597 here.

1396 (June 16) *Inquisitio p. mort. Henry Grey de Wilton*, De Manerio suo de Portpole in Holburne vocato Greysyn. **1427** *Black Booke* (MS.) *of Lincoln's Inn* lf. 13 a, Lyncolnesyn. Manucapcio Sociorum ejusdem Hospicii. **1429-30** *Ibid.* lf. 22 b, Yᵉ Styward of Lyncollysyn. **1436** *Ibid.* lf. 31 a, The felaweshippe of Lyncoll' ynne. *a* **1485** [see b]. **1548** HALL *Chron., Hen. VIII* 241 The .xxiii. daie of February wer foure readers sent for to the Starre Chamber, of every house of the foure principall Innes of Courte one. **1558** FRAUNCE *Lawiers Log.* Ded. ¶ij b, Surely, Sir..it seemeth you came abruptly from a countrey schoole to an Inne of Court. **1597** SHAKS. *2 Hen. IV*, III. ii. 14-15 Hee is at Oxford still, is hee not?.. Hee must then to the Innes of Court shortly: I was once of Clements Inne. **1666** DUGDALE *Orig. Jurid.* (1671) 141/2 These Hostells being Nurseries or Seminaries of the Court, taking their denomination of the end wherefore they were so instituted, were called therefore the *Innes of Court*. **1698** FARQUHAR *Love & Bottle* I. Wks. (Rtldg.) 489/1 You were once an honest fellow; but so long study in the inns may alter a man strangely, as you say. **1710** STEELE *Tatler* No. 186 ¶3 Walking the other Day in a neighbouring Inn of Court. *Ibid.* No. 189 ¶3 Tom, I have bought you Chambers in the Inns of Court. **1711** ADDISON *Spect.* No. 21 ¶4 Many of the Benchers of the several Inns of Court, who seem to be the Dignitaries of the Law. **1883** *Chambers's Encycl.* V. 584 The four inns are each governed by a committee or board, called the benchers, who are generally Queen's counsel or senior counsel. Each inn has also a local habitation, consisting of a large tract of houses or chambers which are in general occupied by barristers..and are a source of great wealth.

attrib. and *Comb.* **1631** LENTON *Leasures* xxix. F iv, A yong Innes a Court Gentleman. **1634** BRERETON *Trav.* (Chetham Soc.) 156 The mayor, a well-bred gentleman, an inns-of-court man. **1655** J. COTGRAVE *Wit's Interpr.* 27 (N.) Much

desired.. by ladies, inns a court gentlemen, and others. **1826** Scott *Woodst.* iv, You are.. an Inns-of-Court-man.

d. ***Serjeants' Inn***: a collegiate building of the now extinct order of Serjeants-at-Law, esp. that in Chancery Lane, sold in 1877.

1646 *Ord. Lords & Com. Presb. Govt.* 14 The classis of the two Serjants Innes. **1841** *Penny Cycl.* XXI. 271/2 The serjeants formerly occupied three inns, or collegiate buildings.. situate in Chancery Lane, Fleet Street, and Holborn. The last, called Scroop's Inn, has long been abandoned, and since the burning down of Serjeants' Inn, Fleet Street.. the serjeants.. have now no other building than Serjeants' Inn, Chancery Lane, which has been lately rebuilt. *Ibid.*, In Serjeants' Inn Hall the judges and serjeants, as members of the Society of Serjeants' Inn, dine together during term-time. **1877** *Law Journal* 3 Mar. 117 Serjeants' Inn was sold on Friday, February 23, for 57,100*l.*, to Mr. Serjeant Cox.. The determination of the judges and serjeants to sell the ancient home of a moribund order was not taken lightly or of mere caprice... We ought to consider that places like Serjeants' Inn have now no sort of practical utility.

¶ Some of the Inns of Chancery and of Court derive their specific names from those of noblemen or persons of quality, whose residence or property they formerly were, and from whom they were at first often rented. It has hence been sometimes assumed that the term *inn* here meant originally 'the town-house or residence' of such nobleman or gentleman, e.g. that 'Lincoln's Inn' meant originally 'the Earl of Lincoln's town-house': but there is no evidence that *inn* ever had any such specific sense (as distinct from its general sense of 'habitation, lodging, house', sense 1), and no proof that any of these houses bore the name ***hospitium*** or *inn*, until it was actually the ***hospitium*** or ***hostel*** of a body of students.

6. *attrib.* and *Comb.*, as ***inn-bill***, ***-door***, ***-gate***, ***-kitchen***, ***-law***, ***-phrase***, ***-play***, ***-stables***, ***-yard***; † **inn-house** = sense 4; **inn-like** *a.* and *adv.*, like an inn. See also INNHOLDER, INNKEEPER.

1855 *Cornwall* 2 It gives no information on posting-houses or horses.. on breakfasts and dinners, on waiters and *inn-bills. **1765** Smollett *Trav.* (1766) II. xli. 258 We stood close by them at the *inndoor. **1755** —— *Quix.* (1803) I. 144 Sancho.. the *inn-gate being thrown wide open, sallied forth. **1694** R. Frankland in *R. Thoresby's Corr.* I. 173 He.. would have sent for my daughter, who was at an *inn-house. **1751** Lady M. Vere in *Lett. C'tess Suffolk* (1824) II. 219 A prodigious house, and furnished *inn-like, two beds in each room. **1838** Dickens *O. Twist* xxxiii, Oliver hurried up the *inn-yard, with a somewhat lighter heart.

inn (ɪn), *v.* Now *rare.* [f. INN *sb.* (In OE. and ME. use often not separable from IN *v.*, q.v.)]

1. *trans.* To lodge, house, find lodging for. *refl.* To lodge oneself, find oneself a lodging.

a **1100** *O.E. Chron.* an. 1048 þa woldon hi innian hi þær heom sylfan ȝelicode. **1297** R. Glouc. (Rolls) 6903 So muche folc þer com, þat me nuste ware hom Inny. *c* **1350** *Will. Palerne* 2479 But eche man al niȝt inned him where he miȝt. *c* **1386** Chaucer *Knt.'s T.* 1334 Whan he had broght hem in to his Citee And Inned hem euerich in his degree. *c* **1410** Love *Bonavent. Sacram. Christ's Body* 126 (Gibbs MS.) Seynt huwe.. was inned for a tyme in a toune þat me clepeþ ioye. *a* **1649** Drumm. of Hawth. *Poems* Wks. (1711) 24 In a poor cottage inn'd, a virgin maid A weakling did Him bear, Who all upbears. **1710** *New Map Trav. High Church Apostle* 7 These Inn'd themselves all Night in Knightsbridge Fields.

b. To put up (a horse) at an inn.

1607 Middleton *Mich. Term* I. i, I have but inn'd my horse.

c. *fig.* (*pass.*) To be lodged or established.

1399 Langl. *Rich. Redeles* III. 135 But here wey is all wronge þer wisdom is ynned. **1633** P. Fletcher *Pisc. Ecl.* VI. xv, A firie beam, And pleasing heat (such as in first of Spring From Sol, inn'd in the Bull, do kindly stream).

2. *intr.* (? for *refl.*) To lodge, find lodging, sojourn; now, to put up (at an inn or hostel).

a **1375** *Joseph Arim.* 166, I haue felauschupe wiþouten.. wel aboute fifti, Boþe wymmen and men þat mote wiþ me Inne. **1563–87** Foxe *A. & M.* (1596) 1554/2 We inned at the signe of the Swan. **1606** *Sir G. Goosecappe* I. iii. in Bullen *O. Pl.* III, I never innd in the Towne but once. **1726** *Brice's Weekly Jrnl.* 18 Feb. 3 John Welch, Cornish Carrier, who formerly Inn'd at the Mermaid in Exon, is now removed to the Bear-Inn. **1885** M. J. Colquhoun *Primus in Indis* I. xiv. 217, I inned at the best house, the Star and Garter.

b. Of a coach: To stop or put up (at an inn).

1748 Richardson *Clarissa* Wks. 1883 VII. 315 The Reading stage-coach, which inns somewhere in Fleet Street. **1775** H. Walpole *Lett.* (1866) VI. 205 You had better send for them where the machine inns. **1834** *New Monthly Mag.* XLI. 175 A Bristol coach which inned at the Red Lion. **1879** E. Walford *Londoniana* II. 61 An account of all the stage coaches.. where they 'inn' and where they 'go out'.

c. *fig.* and *transf.*

1591 Sylvester *Du Bartas* I. ii. 454 So soon as Sol, leaving the gentle Twins, With Cancer, or thirst-panting Leo inns. **1606** Bp. Andrewes *Serm.* II. 205 He.. dwelleth in Christ, and Christ in him; not inneth or sojourneth for a time, but dwelleth continually. **1640** Quarles *Enchirid.* III. 77 If Feare depart from Hope, it travels to Infidelity, and Innes in Despaire. **1839** Bailey *Festus* viii. (1848) 86 Wisdom sometimes inns with ignorance.

inn, obs. form of IN *prep.*, *adv.*, and *v.*

† **i'nnable**, *a.* *Obs.* *rare*$^{-0}$. [ad. L. *innābilis* (Ovid), f. *in-* (IN-^{3}) + *nāre* to swim.]

1658 Phillips, *Innatable*, or *Innable*, not to be swimmed in.

† **innam, -e.** *local.* *Obs.* Also 7 innom, -e. [f. IN *adv.* + ON. *-nám* a taking (in compounds as *land-*, *nes-*, *viðrnám*), f. *nema* to take; cf. OE. *nám* seizure of property as a pledge, f. *niman* to take, NIM *sb.*^{1}.] A piece of ground taken in or inclosed; an intake.

[**1226** *Lincoln Eyre* (Spelman), Innama non capiantur nisi per communem assensum. *c* **1250** *Ceo est Hosebonderie* (in *W. of Henley's Husb.* 1890, 66), E si liad inhom il deit ver quele coture il prent en le inhom. **1344** *Coucher Bk. Selby* (Yorksh. Rec. Soc.) II. 376 Breve villatæ de Keleby tangens innames de Staling[burgh]. **1616** Surfl. & Markh. *Country Farme* 20 He shall.. sow his Oats, either vpon the Innams, which is lande sowne the yeare before, or on the tilth or fallow ground prepared for the purpose. [*a* **1626** *Charter* in SPELMAN *Arch. Gloss.* 383/1 Unum croftum et duas innonias aut inclausuras, vocatas Inholmes.] **1662** Dugdale *Hist. Imbank. & Drain.* (1772) 219 The.. causey from the head thereof towards Kesteven, to the Innome of Doningtone.

b. *Comb.*, as ***innom-barley***.

1674–91 Ray *N.C. Words* 39 *Innom-Barley*, such Barley as is sown the second crop after the Grownd is fallowed.

innammel, obs. form of ENAMEL *v.*

innamorata, -ato, var. (mod.It. spelling) of INAMORATA, -ATO.

innamy, obs. form of ENEMY: see INIMI.

innamyl, obs. form of ENAMEL.

innards ('ɪnədz), *sb. pl.* Dial. and vulgar alteration of *inwards* (see INWARD *a.* and *sb.* B. 1 b) 'entrails'. Now in common *colloq.* use. (Marshall, 1787 (see *E.D.D.*) has only *inwards*.) Also *transf.* and *fig.*, the inside (of anything).

1825 J. Britton *Beauties Wiltshire* III. 375 *Innerds*, the entrails of a hog. **1874** 'S. Beauchamp' *Grantley Grange* I. ii. 29 It's summut i' his innards, or his yud. **1878** Trollope *Is he Popenjoy?* III. i. 7 The Marquis was still in bed. His 'in'ards' had not ceased to be matter of anxiety to Mrs. Walker. **1896** S. Baring-Gould *Dartmoor Idylls* viii. 193 I'm terrible holler in my in'erds. **1903** Kipling *Traffics & Discov.* (1904) 58 There was the cutter's innards spread out like a Fratton pawnbroker's shop. **1921** *Wireless World* 15 Oct. 439/1 The instrument is assembled from a Mk. III ebonite top,.. the parts of an aeroplane 'remote control', etc. .. Its 'innards' were collected from many different firms at all sorts of prices. **1929** G. Mitchell *Mystery of Butcher's Shop* iv. 47 Damned nuisance about the head... He's left us everything else, including the innards. **1932** J. T. Farrell *Young Lonigan* i. 29 His innards made slight noises, as they diligently furthered the process of digesting a juicy beefsteak. **1934** *Mind* XLIII. 234 The music is so bound up with the feelings and impressions of their minds, so spun out of the composers' 'innards', that it.. is inseparable from the feelings and impressions themselves. **1935** *Discovery* May 132/1 The 'innards' of the atom. **1937** *Evening News* 5 Feb. 8/2 The best larder for a good kill was his innards, and the savage's sound logic in over-eating passed down the Middle Ages as Feast Days. **1941** Wyndham Lewis *Let.* 22 Nov. (1963) 310 Next, the true innards of Fascism are uncovered. **1961** *Listener* 16 Nov. 822/3 Here is Hogarth, at thirty-five, exploring the dark innards of the town. **1962** *Ibid.* 8 Mar. 405/2 The whole thing [*sc.* the jury system] can only live so long as we are not allowed to see its innards. **1971** *Physics Bull.* Jan. 27/3 Theoreticians who could not care less about planetary atmospheres but deal purely with the innards of the CO_2 molecule. **1974** *Observer* (Colour Suppl.) 13 Jan. 27/1 The next time I slid the clamp up it wouldn't grip, the sheath of the nylon rope came down with it, and the white innards stretched thin over the lip of rock.

† **i'nnarrable**, *a.* *Obs.* [ad. late L. *innarrābilis*, f. *in-* (IN-^{3}) + *narrābilis*, f. *narrāre* to NARRATE; cf. obs. F. *innarrable* (Godef.).] That cannot be narrated or told; unutterable, indescribable. (Cf. INENARRABLE.)

1552 Lyndesay *Monarche* 6131 The heuinlye sound, quhilk salbe Innarrabyll. **1574** Hellowes *Gueuara's Fam. Ep.* (1584) 363 With innarrable sighes, and teares incomparable.

† **i'nnarrowed**, *ppl. a.* *Obs. rare.* [f. IN-^{1} + NARROWED.] Confined within narrow limits.

1650 *Elegy* in *Gregory's Posthuma*, Though yon' close Anchorite's contracted Shrowd Made his innarrowed Carcass seem a Crowd.

innascibility (ɪnæsɪ'bɪlɪtɪ, ɪnn-). [ad. late L. *innāscibilitās* (Hilary); see next and -ITY. Cf. F. *innascibilité* (Littré).] The attribute of being independent of birth: said of God the Father.

1602 J. Davies *Mirum in Modum* (1878) 17 Innascibility we must admitt The Father. *a* **1656** Hales *Gold. Rem.* (1688) 327 The.. properties are; first innascibility and inemanability.. these belong to the Father. **1678** Cudworth *Intell. Syst.* I. iv. §14. 255 God is the only Ingenerate or Unmade Being.. his very essence is Ingenerability or Innascibility. **1856** Faber *Creator & Creature* II. i. (1886) 110 Who can tell the joy of the Father in His Innascibility?

innascible (ɪ'næsɪb(ə)l, ɪnn-), *a.* [ad. late L. *innāscibilis* (Tertullian), f. *in-* (IN-^{3}) + *nāscibilis*, f. *nāscī* to be born. Cf. F. *innascible* (Littré).] That cannot be born; not subject to the condition of birth: said of God the Father.

1852 Bp. Forbes *Nicene Cr.* 133 He is the unbegotten, the unproduced, the innascible.

† **i'nnatable**, *a.* *Obs.* *rare*$^{-0}$. Also erron. -ible. [f. IN-^{3} + L. *natābilis*, f. *natāre* to swim: cf. INNABLE.] That cannot be swum in.

1623 Cockeram, *Innatible*, not to be swimmed in. **1656** Blount *Glossogr.*, *Innatable*, that cannot be swimmed in.

† **i'nnatant**, *a.* *Obs.* [f. L. *innatānt-em*, pr. pple. of *innatāre*, INNATE *v.*^{2}; cf. NATANT.] Swimming or floating in or upon some liquid.

1657 Tomlinson *Renou's Disp.* 533 Others onely bray and boyl the fruits,.. collecting the innatant spume. **1662** H. Stubbe *Ind. Nectar* iii. 28 Large innatant bodies, resembling a Solution of Fat in Water.

innate ('ɪnneɪt, ɪn'neɪt, ɪ'neɪt), *a.* Also 5 **innat.** [ad. late L. *innātus* (Tertullian), f. *in-* (IN-^{2}) + *nātus*, pa. pple. of *nāscī* to be born.]

1. Existing in a person (or organism) from birth; belonging to the original or essential constitution (of body or mind); inborn, native, natural.

a. Of qualities, principles, etc. (esp. mental).

Opposed to *acquired*, esp. in ***innate ideas***, the nature, character, and even existence of which have been the subject of philosophical dispute, from the times of the Stoics.

a **1420** Hoccleve *De Reg. Princ.* 2130, I am sure that the bookes alle thre Redde hathe & seen your Innat sapience. **1615** G. Sandys *Trav.* 100 Out of an innate hatred greedily pursuing the incounter. *a* **1619** Fotherby *Atheom.* I. iii. §3 (1622) 19 It is innate to all, to owne Their father true, by Nature knowne. **1621** Burton *Anat. Mel.* I. i. II. x. (1676) 17/1 So that in all there be fourteen species of the understanding, of which some are innate.. the other are gotten by doctrine, learning, and use. Plato will have all to be innate. **1690** Locke *Hum. Und.* I. ii. §1 It is an establish'd Opinion amongst some Men, That there are in the Understanding certain Innate Principles.. which the Soul receives in its very first Being, and brings into the World with it. **1692** Bentley *Boyle Lect.* 4 The commonly received notion of an innate idea of God, imprinted upon every soul of man at their creation. **1713** Steele *Englishm.* No. 3. 16 It is below the.. innate Honesty of a true Englishman to enter into a partial Friendship. **1739** Hume *Hum. Nat.* (1874) I. I. i. 316 It has been disputed whether there be any innate ideas, or whether all ideas be derived from sensation and reflexion. **1773** Barrington in *Phil. Trans.* LXIII. 252 Notes in birds are no more innate, than language is in man. **1861** Mill *Utilit.* iii. 45 If.. the moral feelings are not innate, but acquired, they are not for that reason, the less natural. **1868** Farrar *Seekers* I. ii. (1875) 27 But eloquence is a gift as innate as the genius from which it springs.

† **b.** Of inborn material substances or formations. (In quot. 1718 app. misused for 'internal' or 'hidden within'.) *Obs.*

1621 Burton *Anat. Mel.* I. i. II. ii. (1676) 9/1 A humour is a liquid or fluent part of the body.. and is either innate or born with us, or adventitious and acquisite. **1626** Bacon *Sylva* §365 It betrayeth and tolleth forth the Innate and Radicall Moisture. **1660** Boyle *New Exp. Phys. Mech.* Digress. 342 The Pressure of the innate Air in the cavity of the Chest. *a* **1718** Penn *Maxims* Wks. 1726 I. 821 How Nourishment is carried and diffused throughout the Body, by most innate and imperceptible Passages.

c. Of a vegetable formation: Originating within the matrix or the substance of the plant. Of a mineral: Originating within the matrix; native.

1887 W. Phillips *Brit. Discomycetes* 391 *Phacidium Arctostaphyli.* Subgregarious, innate, then erumpent, splitting the epidermis. **1890** *Nature* 6 Feb. 314/1 Diamonds are found in some of the more clayey and pebbly layers, and.. they are innate in the rock.

2. *transf.* Originally or properly existing in the thing spoken of; belonging to the essential nature or constitution of a thing; inherent. ? *Obs.*

1600 Fairfax *Tasso* XVIII. xxxviii, The wood.. Of horrour full, but horrour there innate. **1601** Weever *Mirr. Mart.* A vij, This ayres innate and chiefest qualitie. **1665** *Phil. Trans.* I. 106 All Comets in their innate Motion. **1726** Leoni *Alberti's Archit.* II. 99/1 Of the defects in buildings.. some are innate and owing to the Architect. **1742** Young *Nt. Th.* IX. 1470 Has matter innate motion?

3. *Bot.* Said of a part or organ borne on the apex of another; esp. of an anther that is a direct continuation of the apex of the filament. (Cf. ADNATE 2.)

1830 Lindley *Nat. Syst. Bot.* 61 Anthers, erect, innate. **1857** Henfrey *Elem. Bot.* §202 The anther is attached to the filament in various ways: if the filament runs directly without interruption into the base of the connective, it is said to be innate.

† **innate**, *v.*^{1} *Obs. rare.* [f. prec.] *trans.* **a.** To make innate; to produce or generate within something. **b.** (In Fuller) To imbue or endow by nature (*with* something); usually in *pass.* To be naturally endowed *with*.

1602 Marston *Antonio's Rev.* IV. i. Wks. 1856 I. 117 Wizards.. making curious search For natures secrets, the first innating cause. *a* **1661** Fuller *Worthies* I. (1662) 257 They in this County seem innated with a Genius to study Law. *Ibid.* II. 279 Thus God hath innated every Country with a Peculiar Genius. *Ibid.* IV. 4 A person innated with a publike spirit.

† **i'nnate**, *v.*^{2} *Obs. rare.* [ad. L. *innatāre* to swim in or upon, f. *in-* (IN-^{2}) + *natāre* to swim.] *intr.* To swim or float in or upon something.

1670 H. Stubbe *Plus Ultra* 151 It cast a shadow by its innating on the surface of them.

† **i'nnated**, *a.* *Obs.* [f. L. *innāt-us* INNATE + -ED^{1} 2.] = INNATE *a.* (Frequent *c* 1550–1650.)

1545 Joye *Exp. Dan.* iii. E iv, That innated malyce and roted enuy. **1594** Daniel *Cleopatra* Wks. (1717) 259 That Courage with my Blood and Birth innated. **1601** R. Johnson *Kingd. & Commw.* (1603) 19 The Scots he entertaineth for their innated hatred towards the English.

a **1639** SPOTTISWOOD *Hist. Ch. Scot.* VI. (1677) 364 The innated clemency of the King. **1667** WATERHOUSE *Fire Lond.* 127 Innated instinct of Nature.

i'nnately (see the adj.), *adv.* [f. INNATE *a.* + -LY^2.] By innate character; by birth; by essential nature or constitution; naturally.

1632 J. HAYWARD tr. *Biondi's Eromena* Ep. Ded. A iij b, Finding them so innately habituall, and so constantly permanent in that Sex. **1845** FORD *Handbook Spain* I. 77 The last consolation of the innately noble. **1861** MISS BRADDON *Trail of Serpent* I. i. 8 Natures..so innately wicked.

i'nnateness (see the adj.). [f. as prec. + -NESS.] The quality or fact of being innate. Also in *pl.* innate qualities.

1727 in BAILEY vol. II. **1747** HARTLEY *Enq. Orig. Appet.* I. 51 The innateness of moral principles. **1869** J. HAIG *Symbolism* vi. 56 The innateness of the senses of hearing and seeing. **1876** MRS. WHITNEY *Sights & Ins.* xv. 159 [To] think of what the instincts or innatenesses of this and farther existence, may be.

innatism ('ɪneɪtɪz(ə)m). [f. INNATE *a.* + ISM.] Innate ideas, or belief in them.

1909 in WEBSTER. **1953** *Scottish Jrnl. Theol.* VI. 441 There are discussions on innatism and ontologism.

i'nnative, *a.* Now *rare* or *Obs.* [f. INNATE + -IVE, after NATIVE.] Innate; native.

1513 DOUGLAS *Æneis* I. Prol. 97 Beside his innative polecy, Humanite, curaige, fredome and chevalry. [*comm.*] Innative is als mekil to say as inborn, or that quhilk cumis till ony person be thar natural inclinatioun of kynd, throw thar forbearis. **1652–62** HEYLIN *Cosmogr.* I. (1682) 243 An art so natural and innative to them. **1657** *Lust's Domin.* IV. i. in Hazl. *Dodsley* XIV. 149 All that love, Which by innative duty I did owe her. **1868** LOWELL *Willows* (1869) 263 Some innative weakness there must be.

innato-, used as combining form of L. *innātus* INNATE *a.*, forming adjectives in which it adverbially qualifies the second element, as **i'nnato-e'rumpent**, innate (sense 1 d) and erumpent; **i,nnato-'fibrillose**, covered with innate or adherent fibrils; **i,nnato-'sessile**, innately sessile; **i,nnato-'squamulose**, covered with innate or adherent minute scales.

1857 BERKELEY *Cryptog. Bot.* 313 This genus..seems to me essentially innato-erumpent. **1866** —— in *Intell. Observ.* No. 50. 97 The pileus innato-squamulose. **1886** *Syd. Soc. Lex.*, *Innato-fibrillose*, clad with adherent fibrils. **1887** W. PHILLIPS *Brit. Discomycetes* 199 *Mollisia Cerastiorum.* Gregarious, minute, innato-sessile.

† i'nnatural, *a. Obs.* [ad. late L. *innātūrālis* (Boethius), f. *in-* (IN-^{3}) + *nātūrālis* NATURAL *sb.* Cf. F. *innaturel* (Littré).] Not natural; contrary to nature; unnatural.

c **1400** *Lanfranc's Cirurg.* 203 Colre sum is natural & sum is innatural..Of colre innatural ben. v. maners, as citrina.. adusta, prassina & eruginosa. **1494** FABYAN *Chron.* I. xxvi. 19 For the Innaturall disposicion of the moder y^t so cruelly slewe her owne childe. **1693** DRYDEN *Juvenal* Introd. (1697) 60 They are like the Fruits of the Earth in this innatural Season: The Corn which held up its Head, is spoil'd with Rankness; but the greater part..is laid along.

So **† innatu'rality**, unnaturalness, want of natural affection; **† i'nnaturally** *adv.*, unnaturally, against nature.

1494 FABYAN *Chron.* clvii. 146 She had innaturally slayne hir lorde and husbonde. **1543** GRAFTON *Contn. Harding* 601 This forenamed Iherome..innaturally and falsely dyscouered vnto theim all the bysshoppes and kynges councell. **1579–80** NORTH *Plutarch* (1595) 263 *marg.*, Innaturality amongest kinred [is] infamous. **1611** FLORIO, *Innaturalita*, innaturalitie.

† i'nnaturalize, *v. Obs. rare.* [IN-^{2}.] *trans.* To naturalize within; to convert (a thing) into a natural part of (something); to assimilate.

1685 BAXTER *Paraphr. N.T.*, *James* i. 21 Thus made an innaturaliz'd Word; and so receiv'd and digested, it will save your Souls.

i'nnaturate, *v. rare.* [f. IN-^{2} + L. *nātūra* + -ATE^3.] *trans.* To imbue the nature of (a being) *with* (something).

1849 FROUDE *Nemesis* 167 If those..who..crush the young shootings of the heart, and blight its growth..would but innaturate it with their poison and make it barren for ever!

innavigable (ɪ'nævɪgəb(ə)l, ɪnn-), *a.* [ad. L. *innāvigābilis*, f. *in-* (IN-^{3}) + *nāvigābilis* NAVIGABLE. Cf. F. *innavigable* (16th c. in Littré).] Not navigable; that cannot be navigated. **a.** Of a sea, river, etc.: That cannot be sailed upon, along, or through; impassable for a ship or boat.

1527 R. THORNE in Hakluyt *Voy.* (1589) 257 There is no lande vnhabitable, nor Sea innauigable. **1604** R. CAWDREY *Table Alph.*, *Innauigable*, that cannot be sailed vpon. **1684** T. BURNET *Th. Earth* II. 96 Such a troubled state of the waters, as does not only make the sea innavigable, but also strikes terror into all the maritime inhabitants. **1739** ELIZ. CARTER tr. *Algarotti on 'Newton's Theory'* (1742) I. 86 What the innavigable Ocean was to the Ancients. **1899** *Brit. Weekly* 15 June 158/3 The Thames, choked with hummocks, floes and fields of ice, was innavigable.

b. Of a ship or boat: That cannot be employed in navigation.

1755 MAGENS *Insurances* II. 75 (Ordinances of Middleburg) When a Ship..is rendered innavigable..it is then allowed to abandon such Ship..to the Use of the Assurers.

Hence **i,nnaviga'bility**, **i'nnavigableness**, the quality or condition of being innavigable.

1685 H. MORE *Para. Prophet.* 399 It is not the Innavigableness of the blood..(for so much blood as to sail upon is a monstrous Phancy). **1848** ARNOULD *Mar. Insur.* (1866) I. I. vii. 344 French Jurists confine the 'innavigability' spoken of in the Code, to the single case in which the ship cannot be repaired so as to continue its voyage or keep the sea.

† 'inne, *adv.* and *prep. Obs.* Forms: α. 1–2 innan, 2–3 innen, (2 inna). β. 1–5 inne, (4–5 ynne). [OE. had two derivatives of *in-*: α. OE. *innan* adv. and prep. (of motion and position) with gen., dat., acc., = OS. *innan*, OFris. *inna* adv. and prep. with dat., acc., OHG. *innana*, *innan* adv. and prep. with gen., dat., acc. (MHG., mod.G. *innen*), Goth. *innana*, ON. *innan* adv. and prep. with gen.; β. OE. *inne* adv. of position, = OS., OFris. *inne* adv., Goth. *inna*, ON. *inni* adv., OHG. *inna*, *inni*, *inne* adv. and prep. 'within'. These two words were originally different in sense, *innan* being orig. 'from within', but in late OE. there remained little or no distinction between *innan* and *inne* as adverbs; the main difference being that *inne* was only an adv., while *innan* was both adv. and prep. A few examples of *innan* as prep. are found in 12th c.; and *innen* adv. occurs in Hatton Gospels and Layamon. *Inna* prep. in Lamb. Hom. may be an error for *innan* or *inne*. But the ordinary early ME. form for both adv. and prep. was *inne*, frequent in Southern writings of 12–14th c. It is very rare in the Kentish of Shoreham and the Ayenbite, in which the prep. is regularly *ine*. In northern works, from *Cursor Mundi* onwards, and in Midland works after the time when final *-e* became mute, *inne* (*ynne*) appears to be merely an occasional spelling of *in*.]

A. *adv.* **1.** Of position.

α. **innan, innen**: From within; on the inside, within.

Beowulf (Z.) 2332 Breost innan weoll þeostrum ȝeþoncum. *a* **1000** *Cædmon's Gen.* 1322 (Gr.) ȝeofon-husa mæst..innan and utan eorðan lime ȝefæstnod wið flode. *c* **1000** *Sax. Leechd.* II. 308 Smire mid þa eaȝan innan. *c* **1000** *Ags. Gosp.* Matt. xxiii. 27 Hiȝ synt innan fulle deadra bana. —— Mark vii. 21 Innan of manna heortan yfele ȝeþancas cumað. *c* **1160** *Hatt. G.* ibid., Innen of manne heorten yfele ȝeþances cumæð. *c* **1205** LAY. 21153 þer wes innen igrauen, mid rede golde stauen, an on-licnes deore, of drihtenes moder.

β. **inne**: In, within, inside, in-doors.

c **855** *O.E. Chron.* an. 491 Her Ælle and Cissa..ofsloȝon alle þa þe þær inne eardedon. *c* **893** K. ÆLFRED *Oros.* I. i. §23 þonne þær bið man dead..he lið inne unforbærned. *Ibid.*, Ealle þa hwile þe þæt lic bið inne, þær sceal beon ȝedrync and pleȝa. *c* **900** tr. *Bæda's Hist.* II. ix. [xii.] (1890) 128 Hwæðer he þe ute þe inne wære. *c* **1000** *Sax. Leechd.* II. 352 Sie se drenc þær inne þær se seoca man inne sie. *c* **1050** in Kemble *Cod. Diplom.* IV. 228 On ðam scyran..ðe Ordric abbud hæfð land inne. *a* **1100** *Gerefa* in *Anglia* (1886) IX. 260 ȝe inne ȝe ute. *c* **1175** *Lamb. Hom.* 51 þer wunieð fower cunnes wurmes inne. *a* **1225** *St. Marher.* 10 To beoren me in to his balefule hole þer he wuneð inne. *a* **1225** *Ancr. R.* 160 þe engel wende in to hire,—þeonne heo was inne..al hire one. **1340** *Ayenb.* 203 þer ne may go oute of þe uete, bote zuych ase þer is inne. *c* **1340** *Cursor M.* 1674 (Trin.) Plastre [the timber] wel wiþoute and ynne. *c* **1386** CHAUCER *Monk's T.* 13 Yet fel he for his synne Doun in to helle where he yet is Inne. *c* **1400** MAUNDEV. (1839) xi. 129 The Contree is not worthi Howndes to dwelle inne. *c* **1430** *Syr Tryam.* 167 Of a thyng that now ys ynne. **1460–70** *Bk. Quintessence* I. 9 In which þei ben ynne.

2. Of motion. **inne**: In (to a place). Not in OE. (In later instances, perh. only var. spelling of *in*.)

a **1225** *Ancr. R.* 58 ȝif eni unwrie put were, & best feolle þer inne. *a* **1300** *Cursor M.* 13789, I ne may to þat watir wynne For oþere goon bifore me Inne. **13..** *Coer de L.* 3303 So that ye lat us inne come. *c* **1380** *Sir Ferumb.* 1347 It were ful hard wyþ assaut to comen inne. **1390** GOWER *Conf.* I. 37 Thurgh which division cam inne. *Ibid.* II. 2 Thus bringth he many a meschiefe inne [*rime* beginne]. *a* **1400** *Sir Perc.* 436–7 Thedir inne wille I. He went inne. **1486** *Bk. St. Albans* E ij a, A Rowte of wolues where thay passin inne.

B. *prep.* **1.** Of position: In, within.

α. **innan, innen, (inna)**. (In OE. with gen. or dat., or acc. of time.)

c **897** K. ÆLFRED *Gregory's Past.* xlvii. 359 Innan his ȝeðance. *c* **1000** *Ags. Ps.* (Th.) cxlii[i]. 4 Is me ænge gast innan hreðres. *c* **1000** *Ags. Gosp.* Matt. ix. 10 þa he sæt innan huse [*Lindisf.* in hus; *Rushw.* in huse; *Hatton* innen huse]. *Ibid.* xxi. 12 Ealle þa þe ceapodun innan þam temple [*Lindisf.* in temple, *Rushw.* in þæm temple]. *a* **1100** *O.E. Chron.* an. 789 (Laud MS.) He wæs bebyrȝed..innan þære cyrican. *c* **1175** *Lamb. Hom.* 21 Gif he bidð inna þa sunne, and in þon þonke he is al for-loren. *Ibid.* 27 þe deofel þet to soþe þe rixat in-nan him þet [etc.]. *Ibid.* 43 Innan þan sea weren .vii. bittere uþe.

β. **inne**. (Found esp. at the end of a relative clause, or after its object in verse.) Not in OE.

c **1175** *Lamb. Hom.* 3 þer drihten rad inne þe weye. *Ibid.* 21 He wuneð inne fule sunne. *c* **1200** *Trin. Coll. Hom.* 53 Holie mihtes þe wunieð on hire alse folc inne burh. *c* **1200** ORMIN 3506 And till þatt illke bottle þatt he wollde inne borenn ben. *Ibid.* 19036 Her i þiss Crisstendomess lif þatt Cristess hird iss inne. *c* **1205** LAY. 454 þat Dardanisc kun.. woneð in þisse londe..inne þeowedome. *c* **1290** *Beket* 942 in *S. Eng. Leg.* I. 133 þe furste offize is propre inov: to þe stat þat he was Inne. *c* **1320** *Sir Tristr.* 571 His chawmber he liþ inne. **1362** LANGL. *P. Pl.* A. I. 163 As a Laumpe þat no liht is Inne. *c* **1380** WYCLIF *Serm.* Sel. Wks. II. 222 Poul meneþ bi þis sleep synne þat foolis lyven ynne. *c* **1386** CHAUCER *Prol.* 41 And eek in what array that they were Inne [*rime* bigynne]. *c* **1400** MAUNDEV. (Roxb.) ii. 13 In the Hows, that it is inne. *c* **1420** *Avow. Arth.* xxxiii, Bothe my dethe and my lyfe Is inne the wille of thi wife. *c* **1450** *Merlin* 18 The tyme ..that I was ynne conceyved.

2. Of motion: Into.

α. **innan**. (Only in OE., with acc.)

c **875** *O.E. Chron.* an. 868 Her for se ilca here innan Mierce to Snotengaham. *c* **1000** *Ags. Gosp.* Matt. x. 5 Ne ga ȝe innan samaritana ceastre. *Ibid.* xxi. 21 Ahefe þe upp and feall innan þa sæ.

β. **inne**. (Not in OE.)

c **1175** *Lamb. Hom.* 27 Ne þe deofel mey nefre cumen in-ne him for his gode werkes. *Ibid.* 33 Ne kimeð he nefre inne heoueneriche. *c* **1200** ORMIN 3530 þatt hus þatt bræd is inne don. *a* **1400** *Sir Perc.* 1711 The childe wanne owt of study, That he was inne sett. *c* **1420** *Sir Amadace* (Camden) xxii, Lette the cors go inne his graue.

3. After *believe*: = in, on, upon.

1340–70 *Alex. & Dind.* 597 For loue of þe lord þat we leuen inne. *c* **1400** MAUNDEV. (1839) xv. 166 Thei maken Ymages lyche to tho thinges, that thei han beleeve inne.

inne, obs. f. IN *adv.* and *v.*, INN *sb.* and *v.*

† i'nnebulated, *ppl. a. Her. Obs.* [IN-^{2}: in med.L. *innebulāt-us*.] Having an outline resembling clouds; = NEBULÉ.

1486 *Bk. St. Albans, Her.* D iv b, Theys armys be calde innebulatyd for ij. colowris ar put togedre by the manere of clowdys. **1560–1600** *Satire on Duttons* in *Rel. Ant.* II. 122 For their bravery indented and parted, And for their knavery innebulated.

† i'nnect, *v. Obs. rare.* [ad. L. *innect-ĕre* to tie, fasten, entangle, f. *in-* (IN-^{2}) + *nectĕre* to tie, bind; cf. *annect*.] *trans.* To join together (two things) each within the other; to interlink.

a **1661** FULLER *Worthies*, *Durham* I. (1662) 293 [He] gave (in allusion of his two Bishopricks, which he successively enjoyed) two Annulets innected in his Paternal Coat.

inned (ɪnd), *ppl. a.* [f. IN *v.* + -ED^1.] Taken in, gathered in (as a crop), inclosed, etc.: see IN *v.*

1629 *Drayner Conf.* (1647) B iv b, Neither the bankes of Marsh land nor of other inned grounds. **1640** *Jrnl. Ho. Comm.* II. 68 A Bill declaring the Ancient and Common Law of the Land, concerning Salt-marshes, Inned ground, &c. read the first time. **1854** *Jrnl. R. Agric. Soc.* XV. I. 19 Ward-dykes..to hold off fen-waters from inned grounds.

† i'nnegable, *a. Obs. rare.* [f. IN-^{3} + L. *negā-re* to deny + -ABLE.] Undeniable.

1772 NUGENT *Hist. Friar Gerund* I. 534 The illation is innegable.

inneity (ɪ'niːɪtɪ). *rare.* [ad. mod.F. *innéité* (1810 in Hatz.-Darm.), n. of quality f. *inné* INNATE: see -ITY.] Innateness.

1860 FARRAR *Orig. Lang.* 15 Seeing..that the positive experiment, as well as other considerations, disprove the inneity of language.

innelite ('ɪnəlaɪt). *Min.* [ad. Russ. *innelit* (S. M. Kravchenko), f. *Inneli*, Yakut name for the Inagli river: see -ITE^1.] A yellow-brown complex silicate of barium, near $Ba_4Ti_{3\frac{1}{2}}Si_4O_{18}(OH)_{1\frac{1}{2}}.Na_2SO_4$, found as tabular crystals in pegmatites in the Inagli massif, South Yakutsk, U.S.S.R.

1960 *Geochem.* 741 Innelite—new barium silicate (after S. M. Kravchenko's data). *Ibid.* 745 The RE [*sc.* rare-earth] ratios in the strontium mineral lamprophyllite and the barium mineral innelite are characterized by a high relative content of La (37·64% of the total RE). **1963** *Doklady Earth Sci.* CXLI. 1297/1 Innelite..was discovered in 1957 in aegirite-akermanite-microcline pegmatites of the Inagli massif which occur in dunites. *Ibid.* 1298/1 In comparison with all other known barium silicates, innelite contains the greatest quantity of barium.

inner ('ɪnə(r)), *sb.*^{1} [f. IN *v.* + -ER^1.] One who 'ins', takes in, or reclaims land.

1596 LAMBARDE *Peramb. Kent* (1826) 397 In the yeere 1587 there was an Inning of one thousand acres more, whereof the Inners..enioyed the one halfe and an eight part of the other halfe.

inner ('ɪnə(r)), *a.* (*sb.*^{2}) Forms: 1 innera, innra, inra, 1–3 inre, 3–5 innore, 4 inere 4–5 ynner(e, (4–6 inder), 5 innere, (inhir, ynhir), 4– inner. [OE. *inne(r)r-a*, *in(n)r-a*, *-e* adj. (compar. of *inne*, *inn*, IN *adv.*) = OFris. *inra*, OHG. *innaro*, *innero* (G. *innere*, *innerer*), ON. *innre*, *iðre* (Sw. *inre*, Da. *indre*). With the *d* in ME. cf. THUNDER.

The OE. comparison of *in* was *innerra*, *innemest*; analogical modes of ME. or early mod.E. use were *inner*, *innest*; *innerer*, *innerest*; *innermore*, *innermost*; *inmore*, *inmost*; mod.Eng. uses *inner*, *inmost* and *innermost*. *Inner* is only used attributively, and cannot be followed by *than*, like ordinary comparatives.]

A. *adj.* **1.** Situated more within; more or further inward; interior. Often with a positive force, antithetical, not to *in*, but to *outer*: Situated within or inside; inward; internal.

a. *lit.*, of spatial position.

c **1000** ÆLFRIC *Voc.* in Wr.-Wülcker 149/1 *Liber*, seo inre hrind. *c* **1000** *Leg. St. Swiðun*, etc. (1861) 110 (Bosw.) Se leo ʒewat on ðæt inre westen. *c* **1400** *Lanfranc's Cirurg.* 148 He declineþ into þe ynnere [*v.r.* Innere] partie till þat he peerse þoruȝ þe mydrif. *c* **1400** *Destr. Troy* 749 Þai entrid full evyn into an Inner chamber. **1435** MISYN *Fire of Love* 79 Behald, myn inhir partis has vpbolyd. **1551** RECORDE *Pathw. Knowl.* I. Defin., In a triangle al the angles bee called inner angles. **1590** SPENSER *F.Q.* I. viii. 30 Those were the keyes of every inner dore. **1613** PURCHAS *Pilgrimage* (1614) 507 Cinamom is the inner barke of a tree. **1703** T. N. *City & C. Purchaser* 128 Inner-doors in large Buildings ought to be 3 Foot broad and upwards. **1745** *De Foe's Eng. Tradesman* xxvi. (1841) I. 265 Her inner petticoats, flannel and swan-skin from Salisbury and Wales. **1860** TYNDALL *Glac.* II. xiv. 302 He.. maintains..the opinion, that ice has always an inner temperature lower than zero. **1884** tr. *Lotze's Metaph.* 345 Of the inner movements of things we know nothing.

b. *fig.* Of other limits figured as spatial: More intimate; more central; more hidden or secret.

1480 CAXTON *Chron. Eng.* ccxxv. 230 The ynner loue of the peple was torned in to hate. **1815** SHELLEY *Demon World* 96 From nature's inner shrine, Where gods and fiends in worship bend. **1850** TENNYSON *In Mem.* xlii, Delights.. That stir the spirit's inner deeps. **1875** GEO. ELIOT *Let.* ? 2 Feb. (1956) VI. 121 Because we seclude ourselves from acquaintance that makes us only the more glad to have friends, and you are one of the *inner circle*. **1926** H. CRANE *Let.* 20 June (1965) 262 An 'inner circle' of literary initiates. *a* **1930** D. H. LAWRENCE *Etruscan Places* (1932) iii. 78 Here in the tombs everything is in its sacred or inner-significant aspect. **1973** *Times* 28 May 9/1 It smacks too much of the confidential procedures of an inner circle for many churchmen to feel at ease with it.

c. *transf.* Indistinct or muffled, as if coming from far within. *nonce-use.*

1830 TENNYSON *Dying Swan* i, With an inner voice the river ran.

d. *Music.* Applied to parts or voices intermediate between the highest and lowest of the harmony (also called *middle*).

e. *Printing.* In sheet work, designating the forme containing the type pages from which the inner side of the sheet is printed and including the type page for the second page of the printed sheet.

1755 J. SMITH *Printer's Gram.* 229 (*caption*) The Inner Form of a Sheet in Quarto. **1841** W. SAVAGE *Dict. Art of Printing* 422 *Inner form*, the form that has the second page in it; it is always worked before the outer form, except there be some particular reason to the contrary. **1888** C. T. JACOBI *Printers' Vocab.* 65 *Inner forme*, the pages of type which fall on the inside of a printed sheet in 'sheet' work—the reverse of 'outer' forme. **1892** A. POWELL *Southward's Pract. Printing* (ed. 4) xx. 159 The forme containing the first page is always called by printers the *outside* or *outer* forme, and that containing the second page the *inside* or *inner* forme. **1946** A. MONKMAN in H. Whetton *Pract. Printing & Binding* v. 61/2 So far as the four-page [imposition] schemes are concerned, therefore, it is only necessary to remember that if the job is to be worked as sheet work, pages 1 and 4 will be the outer forme and pages 2 and 3 the inner forme. **1965** *Library* XX. 14 In Table I..the data on choice of forme are abstracted from the list of books, showing for each the number of inner and outer formes printed first... Here is a grand total of 5,338 sheets [printed 1600–1800], of which 3,902, or 73 per cent were printed inner forme first.

f. *inner light*: in Quaker use (see LIGHT *sb.* 7 b and quot. 1957).

1856 R. A. VAUGHAN *Mystics* (1860) II. 217 Fox's inner light does not profess to supersede..the internal light of Revelation. **1909** CHESTERTON *Orthodoxy* v. 135 The Quaker doctrine of the Inner Light. **1957** *Oxf. Dict. Chr. Ch.* 692/1 *Inner light*, the principle of Christian certitude, consisting of inward knowledge or experience of salvation, which is upheld by the Society of Friends.

g. *Phonetics.* Denoting a sound articulated in a part of the mouth nearer the throat than that designated by the unqualified term.

1867 A. M. BELL *Visible Speech* 62 If the breath within the mouth be compressed behind the articulating organs while an *inner closure* is held, a distinct, and in some cases, a powerfully percussive effect will be produced on the abrupt separation of the organs. **1888** H. SWEET *Hist. Eng. Sounds* 5 Most of these [point and blade consonants] admit also of 'inner' and 'outer' varieties.

h. *Inner Circle*: name of one of the lines of the London (underground) railway system.

1869 *Bradshaw's Railway Manual* XXI. 217 Metropolitan District. Incorporated..(29th July, 1864), to construct a series of lines to complete an inner circle of railway north of the Thames. **1882** *Times* 24 July 10/4 The Inner Circle would connect..with the railways south of the Thames. **1884** *Times* 22 Feb. 11/3 As to the Inner Circle line, by the 1st of June, or certainly by the beginning of the second half of the current year, that great work would be finished. **1911** *Encycl. Brit.* XVI. 944/1 This company combines with the Metropolitan District to form the Inner Circle line, which has stations close to all the great railway termini north of the Thames. **1938** G. GREENE *Brighton Rock* IV. iii. 177 He could feel his blood pumped from the heart and moving indifferently back along the arteries like trains on the inner circle. **1966** J. CHAMIER *Cannonball* i. 11 Planes whizzing around a damn sight quicker than the Inner Circle.

i. *inner tube*: in a pneumatic tyre, a separate tube, inside the cover, which is inflated with air.

1895 *Montgomery Ward Catal.* 556/3 Pneumatic Tires.. Inner Tubes complete with valve stem and valve. **1902** *Encycl. Brit.* XXXIII. 535/1 In most tyres for cycles and motor-cars, an inner tube of indiarubber is made separate from the outer cover. **1902** A. C. HARMSWORTH et al. *Motors* x. 223 Half the number of spare covers and inner tubes are required as compared with the requirements when the wheels are of different sizes. **1904** A. B. F. YOUNG *Compl. Motorist* (ed. 2) ix. 250 The piercing of the outer cover and inner tube by a nail or other puncturing agent. **1912** *Motor Manual* (ed. 14) iii. 106 The inner tube has become nipped between one of the security bolts and the cover. **1923** *Michelin Guide Gt. Brit.* (ed. 7) 883 Covers, inner tubes or pneumatic tyres. **1967** N. FREELING *Strike Out* 42 He had done two hundred kilometres a day, on rough country roads with spare inner tubes slung round the neck.

j. *inner Cabinet* (or ***cabinet***): an informal term for a group of decision-making people within a ministerial Cabinet or similar group.

1900 *Westm. Gaz.* 13 Nov. 2/2 No one imagines that this Committee of twenty really decides critical matters of high policy. Those are deputed to the 'inner Cabinet'. **1936** H. NICOLSON *Diary* 24 Feb. (1966) 245 J. H. Thomas..says that our group is not consulted; that there is an inner Cabinet which discuss things between themselves. **1970** *Times* 3 Mar. 2 The meeting was also told that Hebdomadal council, the university's 'inner cabinet', had appointed a committee to listen to the views of the students' elected representatives. **1972** *Guardian* 11 Jan. 20/1 The TUC 'inner cabinet'—the finance and general purposes committee.

k. *inner product* (Math.) [tr. G. *inneres produkt* (H. Grassmann *Die lineale Ausdehnungslehre* (1844) p. XI): so named because an inner product of two vectors is zero unless one has a component 'within' the other, i.e. in its direction]: the sum of the products of corresponding components of two real vectors $(a_1, a_2, \ldots, a_n)$ and $(b_1, b_2, \ldots, b_n)$, i.e. the number $a_1b_1 + A_2b_2 + \ldots + a_nb_n$; in a complex vector space, the number $a_1\bar{b}_1 + A_2\bar{b}_2 + \ldots + a_n\bar{b}_n$, where $\bar{b}_i$ is the complex conjugate number of b_i; (see also quot. 1966).

1920 T. MUIR *Theory of Determinants* III. i. 7 The theorem on the inner product of two magnitudes each of the mth 'Stufe' and consisting of *m* simple factors. **1922** E. H. NEVILLE *Prolegomena Analytical Geom.* IV. i. 192 Let an ordered set of three numbers be called a triplet, and let the number $fp + gq + hr$ be called the inner product of the triplets (f, g, h), (p, q, r). **1941** BIRKHOFF & MACLANE *Survey Mod. Algebra* vii. 181 Physicists often speak of our inner product as a 'scalar product' of two vectors. **1966** A. L. RABENSTEIN *Introd. Ordinary Differential Equations* vi. 156 The inner product of $f(x)$ and $g(x)$ with respect to the weight function $w(x)$ on the interval (a, b) is defined to be $(f, g) = \int_a^b w(x)f(x)g(x)dx$. *Ibid.* 157 If the inner product of $f(x)$ and $g(x)$ is zero,..then $f(x)$ and $g(x)$ are said to be orthogonal with respect to the weight function $w(x)$ on the interval $a < x < b$. **1968** E. T. COPSON *Metric Spaces* ix. 139 In order to avoid confusion between multiplication of a vector by a scalar and the scalar product of two vectors, the scalar product of two vectors is often called their inner product. *Ibid.* 140 A vector space on which an inner product is defined is called an inner product space.

l. *inner quantum number* (Physics) [tr. G. *innere quantenzahl* (A. Sommerfeld 1920, in *Ann. d. Physik* LXIII. 231)]: a quantum number now identified with that of the total angular momentum of an electron, *j* (J II. 6 c).

1923 H. L. BROSE tr. *Sommerfeld's Atomic Struct. & Spectral Lines* vi. 364 If we wish to exclude the forbidden lines by a principle of selection, we must..introduce a new quantum number; we call it the inner quantum number and designate it by n_i. **1926** *Proc. R. Soc.* A. CXI. 84 Each term ..in general will be a multiple term consisting of several members with different values of the 'inner quantum number' *j*. **1967** W. R. HINDMARSH *Atomic Spectra* ii. 18 The regularities of the multiplet structure of spectra were considered in some detail by Sommerfeld... He introduced an 'inner' quantum number to distinguish the various states of a multiplet, and suggested that it may be connected with a property of the electrons in inner shells (the core electrons). The true explanation of the doublet structure of the terms of alkali metal atoms is provided by the concept of electron spin.

m. *inner reserve* (Finance): a secret reserve not disclosed in a balance-sheet and due to an understatement of certain capital assets.

1930 *Daily Express* 16 Aug. 10/1 Former Inner Reserves are now brought from the Assets in which they were hidden and are grouped in an exposed Reserve on the Liability side of the Sheet. **1955** *Times* 10 May 18/5 Your directors have now decided to transfer a part of these inner reserves in order to increase the contingencies reserve.

n. *inner-directed* adj. (Sociol.): a term coined by D. Riesman to designate persons whose behaviour and goals are directed by the standards and ideals which they formed early in life; also postulated as a cultural stage in a society. (See quot. 1950.) Cf. *other-directed* and *tradition-directed* adjs. Hence ***inner direction***.

1950 D. RIESMAN et al. *Lonely Crowd* i. 9 The society of transitional population growth develops in its typical members a social character whose conformity is insured by their tendency to acquire early in life an internalized set of goals. These I shall term inner-directed people and the society in which they live a society dependent on inner-direction. *Ibid.* 16 The inner-directed person becomes capable of maintaining a delicate balance between the demands upon him of his life goal and the buffetings of his external environment. **1959** *Spectator* 4 Sept. 307/2 A criticism renewed by sociology—he [*sc.* C. Wilson in *The Age of Defeat*] seems to imply—can help to renew literature by restoring 'the hero', and 'the hero' will re-accredit in real life the image of the 'inner-directed' man. **1959** *Listener* 3 Sept. 363/2 Mr. Wilson discerns a similar awareness of the difference between 'inner-direction' and 'other-direction' in the existentialist writings of Camus and Sartre. **1961** M. SINGER in B. Kaplan *Studying Personality* 51 The influence of parents and teachers, so vital in the formation of 'inner-direction', is being superseded by the influence of 'peer-groups' and the mass media. **1964** M. ARGYLE *Psychol. & Social Probl.* xv. 186 The life of managers is also changing: as in America the inner-directed individualist is being replaced by the other-directed organization man, who fits in easily with the ideas of others, and subordinates his interests to those of the concern. **1968** P. MCKELLAR *Experience & Behaviour* xi. 288 The capacity to 'go it alone' is characteristic of the inner-directed personality. **1972** *Jrnl. Social Psychol.* LXXXVI. 224 Low authoritarian subjects are more inner-directed.

o. *inner space* [after *outer space*]: (*a*) the regions between the surface of the earth and outer space; (*b*) the regions below the surface of the sea; (*c*) [cf. sense 2] the part of one's mind or personality that is not normally experienced or within one's consciousness.

(*a*) **1958** *Times* 29 Mar. 7/4 We seem to need..names for the parts where the atmosphere is still a drag, where the Earth's gravitation is dominant... Tentatively it might be suggested that these be called..inner space. **1966** I. ASIMOV *Fantastic Voyage* i. 10 We would pile him into an X-52 and rocket him through inner space.

(*b*) **1958** *Times* 7 Oct. 10/3 The Seawolf's [*sc.* a submarine's] captain..had radioed in advance that he considered 'this voyage has proved the feasibility of protracted flights in "inner" space'. **1969** *Sci. Jrnl.* Apr. 64/2 There is a remarkable similarity between many of the problems faced by the astronaut in 'outer space' and those of the aquanaut in 'inner space'.

(*c*) **1958** *Sat. Rev.* (U.S.) 13 Sept. 28/2 Must this inner space continue to be peopled with imaginative dragons of strange color and dropping off places that confine the moral venture to the shallow water of one's own main-land or adjacent islands of narrow self-interest? **1961** 'J. DUNLAP' (*title*) Exploring inner space: personal experiences under LSD-25. **1968** A. DIMENT *Bang Bang Birds* viii. 143 The Indian and Chinese prophets..knew a thing or two about inner space and the turned-on mind. They did it on contemplation though and not mushroom juice. **1969** *Daily Tel.* 20 Feb. 16/7 It is they..who are the investigators of what J. G. Ballard terms 'inner space'—the remoter recesses of man's mind under strange stresses.

p. *inner city*: the central area of a city, esp. regarded as having particular problems of overcrowding, poverty, etc. Also *attrib.* (see sense 6 below). orig. *U.S.*

1968 *Sat. Rev.* (U.S.) 16 Nov. 95 The twin concepts of decentralization and community control of the schools developed in response to the failure of schools in the inner city. **1973** *Black Panther* 17 Mar. 11/1 I'm..interested in getting a little more practical and down to present social policies in the cities, in the inner-cities; the continuing and ever occurring crisis in the inner-cities, where large numbers of people are trapped in a cycle of poverty. **1974** *Times* 19 Jan. 10/2 The problems of the inner city—a work area where almost everyone has gone home.

2. a. Said of the mind or soul (as the more inaccessible or secret, or as the more central or essential part of man, or as distinguished from the external or *outer* world), and of things belonging or relating thereto; hence often = Mental or spiritual.

c **900** tr. *Bæda's Hist.* IV. xiii. (1722) 582 On ðam inneran godum ʒe on ðam uttran. *a* **1050** *Liber Scintill.* ix. (1889) 44 Se inra dema ʒeþanc swyþor þaenne þa word besceawaþ. *a* **1225** *Ancr. R.* 92 Hwo se ȝemeleasliche witeð hire uttre eien, þurh Godes rihtwise dome heo ablindeð in þe inre eien. *a* **1340** HAMPOLE *Psalter* ix. 20 Þat..þe utter man haf noght maistry of þe inere. **1382–1671** [see 3]. **1590** SPENSER *F.Q.* II. vii. 24 But th' Elfin knight with wonder all the way Did feed his eyes, and fild his inner thought. **1813** SHELLEY *Q. Mab* VII. 50 The sense By which thy inner nature was apprised Of outward shows. **1854** GEO. ELIOT tr. *Feuerbach's Essence Christianity* i. 2 The inner life of man is the life which has relation to his species. **1860** J. W. PALMER tr. *Michelet's Love* 118 A feeling that the woman's inner self will not be reached, her soul not attained. **1874** CARPENTER *Ment. Phys.* I. ii. §4 (1879) 120 The Cerebrum,—the instrument of our Psychical or inner life. **1880** W. JAMES *Coll. Ess. & Rev.* (1920) 217 The point of application of the volitional effort always lies within the inner world, being an idea or representation. **1885** J. MARTINEAU *Types Eth. The.* I. I. i. §3. 165 Our own mind we know by what is called the 'Inner Sense' or consciousness. **1886** Inner self [see CLIMATE *sb.* 3 b]. **1899** W. JAMES *Talks to Teachers* ii. 15 There is a stream, a succession of states, or waves, or fields (or of whatever you please to call them), of knowledge, of feeling, of desire, of deliberation, etc., that constantly pass and repass, and that constitute our inner life. **1902** —— *Varieties Relig. Experience* i. 7 Often they [*sc.* religious leaders] have led a discordant inner life, and had melancholy during a part of their career. **1905** A. LANG *Adv. among Books* 122 She [*sc.* Mrs. Radcliffe] delighted in descriptions of scenery, the more romantic the better, and usually drawn entirely from her inner consciousness. **1915** V. W. BROOKS *World of H. G. Wells* v. 106 The force of a work of art does not reside in its 'inner meanings'. **1927** B. RUSSELL *Outl. Philos.* ii. 20 We all have an inner life, open to our own inspection but to no one else's. **1930** *Amer. Jrnl. Psychiatry* 1019 The former is derived from *persona* meaning the essential or inner self. **1944** AUDEN *For Time Being* (1945) 35 The manifestations of the inner life should always remain so easy and habitual. **1952** GERTH & MARTINDALE tr. *Weber's Anc. Judaism* p. xi, He displayed an inner-worldly, stoic attitude in the face of death. **1953** R. G. DAVIS *Ten Mod. Masters* p. xiv, Even a fairy-tale or fantasy must have its inner logic. **1971** *Daily Tel.* 6 Aug. 9/7 This is a girl with an intense inner life. **1974** *Listener* 17 Jan. 76/1 Each [Buddhist monk]..inhabits his private inner world, and yet they're in harmony with each other.

b. *inner speech* (***form***): see quots. Also ***inner linguistic*** (or ***language***) ***form***, ***inner form***.

[**1885** D. G. BRINTON in *Proc. Amer. Philos. Soc.* XXII. iv. 319 Besides the grammatical form of a language, Humboldt recognized another which he called its *internal form*.] **1888** H. A. STRONG tr. *Paul's Princ. Hist. Lang.* xx. 460 The influencing force extends merely to what Humboldt and Steinthal have described as the *inner language form* ('innere

Sprachform'). *Ibid.* 471 A language suffers influence in its *inner linguistic form* principally in the mouths of those who speak it as a foreign tongue. **1901** H. OERTEL *Lect. Study Lang.* i. 64 This is the 'outer speech form', the external, phonetic aspect of the speech symbols. The 'inner speech form' is the definite arrangement of the prelinguistic psychical material into definite groups, the coherence of each group being secured by labelling each with one definite sound-tag. **1930** J. R. FIRTH *Speech* v. 44 The early discussions on inner speech did not touch the bigger question of the extensive motor accompaniment of thought. **1934** WEBSTER, *Inner speech, Psychol.*, use of words or word images in thinking, without audible or visible speaking. *Ibid.*, *Inner speech form* (trans. of G. *innere Sprachform*, used by Humboldt and Steinthal), the mental concept or image associated with a word prior to its use or upon hearing or reading it, as the concept of a quadruped associated with the word 'animal'; abstractly, the quality by which a word evokes such a mental picture. **1970** H. C. SHANDS *Semiotic Approaches to Psychiatry* 10 Inner speech systems are constructed throughout the developmental period in human beings.

3. Phr. ***the inner man***: **a.** The inner or spiritual part of man; the soul or mind. Also, ***the inner woman***.

c **1000** *Ecgbert's Penit.* IV. §63 in Thorpe *Laws* II. 224 Se innra man ðæt is seo sawl. **1382** WYCLIF *Eph.* iii. 16 That he ȝȝyue to ȝou..vertu for to be strengthid by his spirit in the ynnere man [Vulg. *in interiorem hominem*]. **1398** TREVISA *Barth. De P.R.* III. i. (1495) 48 Isidore spekyth..of the inner man and vtter man. **1671** MILTON *P.R.* II. 477 This attracts the soul, Governs the inner man, the nobler part. **1857** TROLLOPE *Barchester T.* III. x. 184 She ate and drank, and as the inner woman was recruited she felt a little more charitable. **1858** HAWTHORNE *Passages from Fr. & It. Note-Bks.* (1871) I. 190 To behave as her inner woman prompts. **1860** FARRAR *Orig. Lang.* i. 32 The living product of the whole inner man. **1892** *Gentlewoman's Bk. Sports* I. 44 After refreshing the inner woman, I was all for trying the Sandhills again.

b. *humorously* (after sense 1): The stomach or "inside', esp. in reference to food.

1856 KANE *Arct. Expl.* II. xx. 204 With my inner man well refreshed with auk-livers, I was soon asleep. **1865** *Day of Rest* Oct. 609 The New Englander, who had been strengthening the inner man during the remarks of the abbé.

4. ***inner barrister, inner post, inner stern-post, Inner Temple***, etc.: see the nouns.

†**5.** *Inner* was formerly sometimes written in combination or hyphened with a sb., where it would now be written separately; e.g. **inner-land**, interior country; **inner-ward**, of a castle (see WARD *sb.*[2]); **innerwit**, internal knowledge (see WIT). *Obs.*

1495 *Trevisa's Barth. De P.R.* III. vi. (W. de W.) 52 Felynge bodyly wytte and ymagynacyon arne sytuate in the soule, that he is onid to the body and yeue it lyfe and Inner-wytte and vtterwytt to perfeccion of the body. **1613** M. RIDLEY *Magn. Bodies* 99 No lesse doth the Needle and Compasse upon the continent and inner-land, decline [etc.].

6. Various phrases used *attrib.*

1908 *Daily Chron.* 22 Jan. 3/3 You may browse at will among the epistles or the notes, feeling that you are always with informed, inner-circle folk. **1909** *Westm. Gaz.* 14 Apr. 10/2 What colour of glass must be used for the front door and inner-court doors? **1927** J. ADAMS *Errors in School* 32 An idea does not merely mean the inner-world equivalent of an outside object. **1953** C. E. BAZELL *Ling. Form* 57 The rare cases of inner-verbal sequence-relevance may be dealt with analogously. **1957** C. HUNT *Guide to Communist Jargon* xxv. 88 According to the *Political Dictionary*, inner-party democracy is the consistent application of the principles of "democratic centralism', though, to be more accurate, it stands for its democratic as opposed to its dominant centralized aspect. **1960** H. EDWARDS *Spirit Healing* vii. 63 Spiritual healers have long known that the origin of organic diseases most often lay in inner-self disharmonies. **1961** *Observer* 8 Oct. 10/3 It is doubtful if Mr. Gaitskell himself had thought through the problem of inner-party democracy. **1964** F. BOWERS *Bibliogr. & Textual Crit.* iv. ii. 112 Any separate small pile of inner-forme sheets. **1968** *Sun* (Baltimore) 4 July A.16/3 A possible explanation of the inner-city language superiority (which had disappeared by the third grade) was, Mrs. Entwisle thought, the unrestricted time which small inner-city children spend in front of television sets. **1970** *New York* 16 Nov. 42/2 From here the city spreads in a wheel-spoke design through seven inner-city black neighborhoods. **1971** *Guardian* 26 Feb. 6/8 Camden's housing problems have often been in the spotlight for revealing inner-city trends. **1972** *Ibid.* 5 Jan. 5/2 The solution to the problem of the inner city child eludes us.

B. *sb.* **a.** That division of a target next outside the bull's-eye: = CENTRE *sb.* 9; or, in some targets, the division immediately outside the centre. **b.** *ellipt.* A shot which strikes this.

1887 *Daily News* 15 July 3/5 Beginning with two inners, he then put together five successive bulls-eyes, and raised his aggregate to within a point of that by which Corporal Soutar won the Bronze Medal last year. **1891** C. JAMES *Rom. Rigmarole* 19 The bygone shot wasn't a bull's-eye; no, only an 'inner'.

† **'inner**, *adv. Obs.* Forms: 1 innor, 3–5 innere, 4 ynnere, 5 inner. [OE. *innor* (compar. of *inn* adv., IN) = OHG. *innor* (MHG. *inner*).] More inwards; further in.

c **1000** ÆLFRIC *Gram.* xxxviii. (Z.) 240 *Intra* wiðinnan, *interius* wiðinnan oððe innor. *c* **1205** LAY. 29282 Swa þe sparewe innere crap. **1399** LANGL. *Rich. Redeles* III. 195 And lete hem pleye in þe porche, and presse non ynnere. *c* **1450** LONELICH *Grail* l. 299 Thanne forth Iosephe Innere wente. **1460** *Lybeaus Disc.* 1771 Lybeauus inner gan pace.

† **'innerer**, *a. Obs. rare.* In 4 inerere. [A double comparative form, f. INNER *a.* + -ER[3]: cf. OHG. *innarôro, innerero*, and superl. INNEREST.]

= INNER: in quot. *absol.* = inner parts.

a **1340** HAMPOLE *Psalter* cviii. 17 Hit entird as watir in his inerere and as oyl in his bonys.

† **'innerest**, *a. Obs.* Forms: 3 (*Orm.*) innresst, 3–4 inrest(e, 4–5 innerest, (-yste), 5 inerest, 6 yndrest. [f. INNER *a.* (q.v.) + EST; cf. OHG. *innarôst* (MHG. *innerest*, G. *innerst*), MDu. *innerst, inrest, inderst*; all which show a superl. formed apparently on a comparative, after the latter had to a certain extent lost its full comparative force.] Innermost, inmost.

c **1200** ORMIN 1017 Biforenn an allterr þat wass Innresst i þþeȝȝre minnstre. *a* **1300** *E.E. Psalter* lxxxv[i.]. 13 Mi saule þou toke fra inreste helle. *c* **1374** CHAUCER *Boeth.* IV. pr. vi. 106 (Camb. MS.) Thilke cercle þat is innerest [*v.r.* inrest], or most with Inne, ioyneth to the symplesse of the Myddel. **1387–8** T. USK *Test. Love* Prol. (Skeat) l. 8 Rude wordes and boistous percen the herte of the herer to the inrest point. **1450–1530** *Myrr. our Ladye* 218 Ioye..in the yndrest bowels of harte. **1483** CAXTON *Gold. Leg.* 55 b/1 He had brought the sheep in to the inneerest part of deserte.

innerly ('ɪnəlɪ), *a. Obs.* exc. *Sc. dial.* Forms: see INNER *a.* [f. INNER *a.* + -LY[1]; cf. MHG. *inner(c)lîch* (G. *innerlich*), MDu. *innerlijk*.]

1. Inner, interior; inward, internal.

1434 MISYN *Mending Life* 118 Of þe inhirliest mergh of our hartis sall rise þe lufe of god. **1435** —— *Fire of Love* 39 Gostely gladnes & inhirly myrth. *Ibid.* 70 Syngand ful fare fro vtward melody to ful inhirly I ha flowne. **1825–80** JAMIESON, *Innerlie*,..situated in the interior of a country.

b. Intimate.

1866 J. BROWN *Horæ Subs.* Ser. III. 286 (Cent.) So mature, so large, and so innerly was his knowledge [etc.].

2. 'Kindly, affectionate, possessing sensibility or compassion' (Jam.).

1824 MACTAGGART *Gallovid. Encycl.*, *Innerly hearted*, of a feeling disposition. **1825–80** JAMIESON s.v., 'She's an innerlie' or 'a very innerlie creature'.

3. In-lying, not exposed; hence, 'Fertile: applied to land' (Jam.).

1868 *Life Hugh Elliott* ii. 73 We live on a drier soil and in a more 'innerlie' country.

Hence **'innerliness**, intimacy, closeness.

1888 MRS. LYNN LINTON in *Pall Mall G.* 2 Oct. 5/1 It was a friendship without the 'innerliness' of true cordiality.

'innerly, *adv. Obs.* or *rare.* Forms: see INNER *a.* [f. INNER *a.* + -LY[2]; cf. MHG. *innerlîche* (Ger. *innerlich*), MDu. *innerlike* (Du. *innerlijk*).]

1. More within (*obs.*); inwardly, internally.

c **1330** R. BRUNNE *Chron. Wace* (Rolls) 3195 Sche tremblede and sykede inderly [*v.r.* inerly]. **1390** GOWER *Conf.* I. 227 Whan she wist it inderly. **1435** MISYN *Fire of Love* 39 With flaume of fyre I am inhirly byrnd. **1555** ABP. PARKER *Ps.* xlv. 133 They shall full nye be brought to hym ....In palace there: most innerly, where kyng hymselfe doth lay. **1617** MORYSON *Itin.* III. 154 Then towards Murrey Frith..more innerly is the Gulfe Vararis. **1674** N. FAIRFAX *Bulk & Selv.* 27 'Tis given out that ghost, as well as the substance of body innerly, is such a thing, as is alwaies the same as much as God is. **1851** S. JUDD *Margaret* II. i. 198 A bunch of the white hardhack, a cream-like flower, innerly blushing. **1917** D. H. LAWRENCE *Look! We have come Through!* 50, I have been so innerly proud, and so long alone, Do not leave me, or I shall break. **1923** —— *Ladybird* 81 If you are true to me, innerly, innerly true, he will not hurt us.

†**2.** Earnestly; intensely, extremely. *Obs.*

c **1330** R. BRUNNE *Chron. Wace* (Rolls) 10843 Arþures folk ....bysoughte God inderly [*v.r.* interly] To graunt Arþur þe maistri. **1382** WYCLIF *Isa.* xxxiv. 6 The swerd of the Lord fulfild is of blod, innerly fattid it is with talȝ of blod of lombis. *c* **1440** *Generydes* 675 For certeyne she was right inderly fayre.

† **innermore** ('ɪnəmɔə(r)), *a.* and *adv. Obs.* exc. *dial.* Forms: 4–7 innermore, (4 innermar(e, inner-mare), 6 ynnermer, *Sc.* innermair, 6 (9 *dial.*) innermer, 8 *dial.* indermore, 9 *dial.* indermer. [f. INNER *a.* (q.v.) and *adv.* + -MORE; after *innermost*: see INNER *a.*]

A. *adj.* Situated more within, inner.

1413 *Pilgr. Sowle* (Caxton) v. i. (1859) 70 Two grete spyeres..in the Innermore of whiche, the sterres were fastned bryght. **1535** COVERDALE *Ezek.* x. 3 The cloude fylled the ynnermer courte. **1545** RAYNOLD *Byrth Mankynde* (1564) 51 A portion of the innermer bottome of the Matrix. **1635** N. R. *Camden's Hist. Eliz.* III. 285 A narrow necke of land betweeen the innermore rock of the haven and the Ocean. **1657** W. RAND tr. *Gassendi's Life Peiresc* II. 96 It seemed..that the hinder and innermore circumduction of the eye was as a Concave-glasse. **1828** *Craven Dial.*, *Innermer*, inner.

fig. **1571** GOLDING *Calvin on Ps.* xl. 9 This innermore and effectual teaching of the Spirit. **1587** —— *De Mornay* xiii. 194 He being neere & innermore to al things than the things themselues are, doth know them most perfectly.

B. *adv.* †**1.** More inward or within. *Obs.*

a **1300** *Cursor M.* 6199 Drightin þam badd drau innermare. *a* **1400** *Sir Perc.* 1233 Wold come none innermare For to kythe what he ware. **1571** *Satir. Poems Reform.* xxvii. 45 Thai will creip innermair.

†**2.** Further on (in a book or writing); 'below'. *Obs.*

1387 TREVISA *Higden* (Rolls) I. 97 As it is inner more i-write [*sicut infra dicitur*]. **1398** —— *Barth. De P.R.* III. xvii. (Tollem. MS.), As it schall be schewid inner more [**1582** hereafter; L. *ut postea patebit*].

innermost ('ɪnəməʊst, -məst), *a.* and *sb.* [f. INNER *a.* (q.v.) + -MOST. Cf. HINDERMOST.]

A. *adj.* Most or furthest within; inmost.

1413 *Pilgr. Sowle* (Caxton) I. xviii. (1859) 19 He knoweth the Innermost of thy thoughtes. **1555** EDEN *Decades* 352 Vppon the innermoste necke to the landewarde is a tufte of trees. **1665** BOYLE *Occas. Refl.* (1848) 32 To pry into the innermost Recesses of mysterious Nature. **1754** RICHARDSON *Grandison* (1781) I. xxxvii. 265 No married woman shall I trust with what lies in the innermost fold of my heart. **1823** SCOTT *Quentin D.* iii, The second inclosure ....commanded by the third and innermost barrier. **1868** J. T. NETTLESHIP *Ess. Browning* i. 48 In the innermost holy of holies.

B. *sb.* That which is innermost; the inmost part.

1674 N. FAIRFAX *Bulk & Selv.* 67 From the innermost or centre to the selvedge. **1794** MATHIAS *Purs. Lit.* (1798) 128 He passed at once to the innermost of the temple, without treading the vestibule. **1860** HAWTHORNE *Marb. Faun* xxxvii. 286 The fire..will have gone into her innermost, and burnt her quite up. **1888** SIR E. ARNOLD *With Sa'di in the Garden*, Utterly wotting all their innermosts, For all to Him is visible.

Hence **'innermostly** *adv. rare.*

1856 MRS. BROWNING *Aur. Leigh* v. 676 His ebon cross worn innermostly.

innerness ('ɪnənɪs). [f. INNER *a.* + -NESS.]

1. Inner or inward quality; inwardness.

1881 PALGRAVE *Vis. Eng.* 159 Not losing innerness in external rite. **1892** GLADSTONE *Impregnable Rock* 159 These and all kindred qualities they develop in what, for want of a better word, I will term their innerness.

2. That which is internal; 'inner consciousness'. *nonce-wd.*

1891 *Sat. Rev.* 8 Aug. 164/2 Dickens cannot have evolved Miss Squeers's letter from his innerness wholly.

innervate (ɪ'nɜːveɪt, ɪnn-), *v. Physiol.* [f. IN-[2] + L. *nerv-us* NERVE + -ATE[3]; cf. *enervate*.] *trans.* To supply (some organ or part) with nerve-force, or with nerves.

1870 ROLLESTON *Anim. Life* 104 The ganglionic mass, whence the jaws and foot-jaws are innervated. **1883** LAUDER BRUNTON in *Nature* 8 Mar. 437 An excellent example..of inhibition occurring in parts innervated by the sympathetic system. **1897** *Allbutt's Syst. Med.* III. 694 The stomach and rectum..are partly innervated directly from the brain and spinal cord.

innervation (ɪnə'veɪʃən). [f. as prec. + -ATION; cf. *enervation*, and mod. F. *innervation* (1878 in *Dict. Acad.*).] **1.** *Physiol.* The action or process of innervating; the fact of being innervated; supply of nerve-force from a nerve-centre to some organ or part by means of nerves; stimulation of some organ by its nerves. Also, the supply of nerve fibres to, or disposition of nerve fibres within, an organ or part.

1832 J. THOMSON *Life W. Cullen* I. 430 The doctrine of Innervation or the Influence of the Nervous System. **1847** tr. *Feuchtersleben's Med. Psychol.* 115 The organic process occasioned by this innervation as it is called..is worthy of observation. **1861** VAN EVRIE *Negroes* 165 His imperfect innervation, his sluggish brain. **1878** HOLBROOK *Hyg. Brain* 16 The medulla is a source of innervation for the heart. **1879** *Jrnl. Physiol.* II. 342 More recently Severini, in his able monograph on the innervation of the blood-vessels, has laid great weight on the contractility of the capillaries. **1908** *Westm. Gaz.* 8 July 2/1 It has been found that the density of the cutaneous innervation—i.e., the number of sensitive nerve terminations in the unit of surface—is greater in small animals than in large. **1910** *Jrnl. R. Microsc. Soc.* 154 Innervation of tympanum.—Agostino Gemelli describes.. the tympanal ramifications (1) of the auriculo-temporal branch of the trigeminal, and (2) of the nerve of Jacobson. **1945** *Amer. Jrnl. Physiol.* CXLIV. 477 It is tacitly assumed that if part of the innervation of a muscle is permanently destroyed, the remaining motor units..continue their normal function. **1967** GARDNER & OSBURN *Struct. Human Body* iv. 121/2 The nerve supply to a muscle is referred to as its innervation.

2. *Psychol.* = KINÆSTHESIS.

1880 W. JAMES in *Anniversary Mem. Boston Soc. Nat. Hist.* 4 Wundt..adopts the term *Innervationsgefühl* to designate the former [*sc.* the feeling of force exerted] in relation to its supposed cause, the efferent discharge. Feelings of innervation have since then become household words in psychological literature. **1898** G. F. STOUT *Man. Psychol.* I. II. vi. 192 According to Bain, there is a direct sense of energy put forth which is independent of any results the putting forth of energy may produce. This peculiar modification of sensory consciousness has been called the sense of effort, or the innervation-sense. **1904** E. B. TITCHENER tr. *Wundt's Princ. Physiol. Psychol.* iii. 57 (*heading*) General principles and problems of a mechanics of innervation. **1924** J. RIVIERE et al. tr. *Freud's Coll. Papers* I. 63 The conversion may be either total or partial, and it proceeds along the line of the motor or sensory innervation that is more or less intimately related to the traumatic experience. **1953** HINSIE & SHATZKY *Psychiatric Dict.* (ed. 2) 667/1 The expressive innervations are involuntary, even though they can be influenced, up to a point, by volition.

innerve (ɪ'nɜːv, ɪnn-), *v.* [f. IN-[2] + NERVE *sb.* or *v.* Cf. mod.F. *innerver* (Littré, *Suppl.*).]

= INNERVATE; also *fig.* to animate. Hence **i'nnerving** *ppl. a.*

1828 in WEBSTER, citing DWIGHT. **1868** BUSHNELL *Serm. Liv. Subj.* 274 Innerving force. **1869** —— *Wom. Suffrage* viii. 167 A different innerving quality. **1880** L. MORRIS *Ode of Life* (ed. 3) 8 The spiritual essence fair Which doth innerve the outward show of things.

inness ('ɪnnɪs). *rare.* [f. IN *adv.* or *a.* + -NESS.] The quality or condition of being *in*

(something). **b.** Inner or internal quality or state.

1866 R. S. Candlish *1 Ep. John* xlv. 512 He is in Him that is true: in Him with a depth and intensity of real inness, that the devout study of a lifetime will not suffice to unfathom. **1867** J. W. Dale *Classic Baptism* (1868) 100 It is the mersion only, the position of inness, which is called for. **1888** Dk. Argyll in *19th Cent.* Jan. 156 Gravitation knows nothing of inness and outness. **1896** *Voice* (N.Y.) 17 Sept., The best representation of the inness of 'things' in this nation that I have seen in years.

† **'innest**, *a. Obs.* [f. IN *adv.* or *a.* + -EST. Cf. ON. *innstr.* See INNER *a.*] Most inward, inmost.

1388 Wyclif *Prov.* xxvi. 22 Tho comen til to the ynneste thingis [**1382** the inmostis] of the herte. **1495** [see INMOST *a.* 2, quot. 1398]. **1532** More *Confut. Tindale* Wks. 628/1 For of yͤ whole world, the innest is as I told you the lowest.

innest (ɪn'nɛst), *v. rare.* Also 7 en-. [IN-[1] or [2].] *trans.* To provide with a nest; to ensconce as in a nest.

1611 Florio, *Innidare*, to ennest, to enroost. *a* **1631** Donne *Paradoxes* (1652) 85 To insinuate and innest it selfe into the body.

innet (ɪn'nɛt), *v. rare.* Also 6 en-. [IN-[1] or [2].] *trans.* To catch or entangle in a net.

c **1586** C'tess Pembroke *Ps.* lxvi. v, For God thou didst our feete innett, And pinching saddles on us sett. **1598** Florio, *Irretare*, to entrap..or take in a net or a ginne, to entramell, to ennet.

† **'inneth.** *Obs.* Forms: 1 innoþ, innaþ, 1–2 inneþ. [OE. *innoð, innað* (? f. *inn, inne*, IN *adv.*) = OHG. *innôdi* (also *innôdili*).] The interior of the body; the inside; *spec.* the womb.

c **888** K. Ælfred *Boeth.* xxii. §1 He werodaþ syðþan he innaþ and biþ swiþe liþe on ðam innoþe. *c* **900** tr. *Bæda's Hist.* iv. xxiv. [xxiii.] (1890) 338 þætte seo adl & þæt sar hwyrfde in hyre innoðas. *c* **1000** *Ags. Gosp.* Mark vii. 23 Ealle þas yfelu of þam innoðe cumað. —— Luke xi. 27 Eadiȝ is se innoð þe þe bær. *c* **1175** *Lamb. Hom.* 83 þe muchele lauerd..bitunde him solue in ane meidenes inneþe. *c* **1200** *Trin. Coll. Hom.* 21 *Ecce concipies* et cetera, þu shalt understonde child on þine innoðe.

† **i'nnew**, *v. Obs. rare.* [f. IN-[1] + NEW: rendering L. *innovāre*. Cf. ENNEW *v.*[1]] *trans.* To renew: = INNOVATE *v.* 1.

1432–50 tr. *Higden* (Rolls) VI. 43 A kynge..whiche shalle innewe alle the londe of Speyne with the lawes of Criste. *Ibid.* VIII. 307 John the xxijti..innewede the vijthe booke of þe Decretalles.

inngendure, obs. form of ENGENDURE.

innholder ('ɪn,həʊldə(r)). Now *rare.* Forms: see INN *sb.* [f. INN *sb.* 4 + HOLDER. Cf. *householder.*] = INNKEEPER.

1464 *Nottingham Rec.* II. 252 Johannes Watson, inhalder. *c* **1510** Barclay *Mirr. Gd. Manners* (1570) G iv, Be thou none Inholder, hosteler nor Taverner. **1587** Harrison *England* ii. iii. (1877) i. 87 Supposing he had serued with some inholder in the stable. **1610** Holland *Camden's Brit.* i. 74 They say that this Lady was at first an Inholder or Hostesse. *a* **1748** Pitt *Imit. Horace, Sat.* ii. vi. (R.), So rov'd wild Buckingham the public jest, Now some innholder's, now a monarch's guest. **1841** Emerson *Misc.* (1855) 258 The very innholders and landlords of the country would muster with fury to their support. **1875** R. J. Hinton *Eng. Radical Leaders* 215 The 'Licensed Victualler's Association', as the Guild or Trades society of inn-holders and keepers of public houses is termed, is a wealthy and powerful body.

inning ('ɪnɪŋ), *vbl. sb.* Also 6–7 ining. [f. IN *v.*, or INN *v.* + -ING[1].]

I. From IN *v.*

† **1.** A putting or getting in; what is put or got in; contents; income. Only OE. *Obs.*

c **888** K. Ælfred *Boeth.* xxxii. §2 Se heofon is betera..and fæȝerra ðonne eall his innung buton monnum anum. **978** in Kemble *Cod. Dipl.* III. 138 Des tunes cyping and seo innung ðara portȝerihta gange into ðere halgan stowe.

2. a. The action of taking in, inclosing, etc.; *esp.* the reclaiming of marsh or flooded land.

c **1530** in Gutch *Coll. Cur.* II. 343 Item deliverid..for the Innyng of the said marshe of Wulwiche..*cl.* **1543–4** *Act 35 Hen. VIII*, c. 9 The recoueringe inclosinge and inninge of.. Wappinge marshe. **1622** Callis *Stat. Sewers* (1824) 94 For inning and safety of their Marshes and Marsh grounds. **1769** *De Foe's Tour Gt. Brit.* I. 186 Rye-Harbour..being.. by the Inning of the Channel and waste Lands..in Danger of being utterly lost. **1852** *Humber Conserv. Act 2038* (15 & 16 *Vict.* c. cxxx. §35) Such inning, gaining, or Reclamation.

b. *pl.* Lands taken in or reclaimed.

1706 Phillips, *Innings*, Lands recovered from the Sea, by draining and banking. **1880** *Archæol. Cantiana* XIII. 189 One of the earliest 'innings' of Walland Marsh, after the Norman Conquest,..has been ever since called Becket's Innings, as this Archbishop has the credit of promoting it.

3. The action of getting in, esp. of crops; ingathering, harvesting.

1522 *MS. Acc. St. John's Hosp., Canterb.*, For caryage & innyng of the seid vij acres [of hay]. **1530** Palsgr. 539/1 He hath ered his lande, God sende hym good innyng. **1662** Gurnall *Chr. in Arm.* Verse 17 vii. §2. 56 The joy of the Husbandman, at the happy inning of his Corn. **1710** D. Hilman *Tusser Rediv.* (1744) 104 (T.) Every one that did any thing towards the inning must now have some reward.

4. a. In *Cricket*, *Baseball*, and similar games (in Great Britain always in *pl.* form **innings**, whether in sing. or pl. sense): That portion of the game played by either side while 'in' or at the bat: cf. IN *adv.* 6 d. In *Cricket* also used of the play of, or score of runs made by, any one batsman during his turn. ***to follow their innings*** (said of one side at cricket) = *to follow on*: see FOLLOW *v.* 19 d.

1735 in H. T. Waghorn *Cricket Scores* (1899) 10 London ..got 67 notches the first innings. **1746** in 'Bat' *Cricketer's Man.* (1850) 80 1st Innings. England. 2nd Innings. **1755** *Game at Cricket* 7 The Bowler shall change [wickets] but once in the same innings. **1770** J. Love *Cricket* 21 Awakened Eccho speaks the Innings o'er, And forty Notches deep indent the Score. **1810** *Sporting Mag.* XXXVI. 194 Won by the former by sixty-two runs at one innings. **1849** *Laws of Cricket* c. 46 in 'Bat' *Cricketer's Man.* 59 The players who go in second shall follow their innings, if they have obtained one hundred runs less than their antagonists. **1856** *Spirit of Times* 6 Dec. 229/1 After the first inning is played, the turn commences at the player who stands next to the one on the list who lost the third hand. **1891** W. G. Grace *Cricket* 216 On five occasions Oxford has won by an innings, whilst Cambridge has done the same thing thrice. **1895** *Nebraska State Jrnl.* 23 June, In the seventh inning Gragg hit for three bases... In the fourth inning Haller got a base on balls. **1955** *Times* 9 May 15/2 Afterwards he played the sort of innings that not surprisingly drives some spectators to distraction. **1968** *Washington Post* 4 July C1/7 The righthanded sinkerballer faced his greatest challenge in the sixth inning.

b. *transf.* (in Great Britain always in *pl.*) The time during which a person, party, principle, etc. is in possession or in power; a term of, or opportunity for, activity of any kind; a turn.

1836 Dickens *Pickw.* (1837) xxiii. 238 It's my innings now, gov'rnor, and as soon as I catches hold o' this here Trotter, I'll have a good 'un. **1855** Thackeray *Newcomes* II. xi. 107 The Marquis not being present, the Baron took his innings. **1870** Miss Bridgman *R. Lynne* I. vi. 81 She's had remarkably good innings, and persons can't expect to live for ever. **1878** W. R. Greg in *19th Cent.* Sept. 395 The new ideas of 'peace, retrenchment and reform' got their innings, and..have ruled the national policy from 1830 till 1875. **1885** *N.Y. Mirror* 23 May 7/3 An Inning for the Lyceum Pupils. **1897** W. H. Thornton *Reminisc. W.-Co. Clergyman* vii. 236 Fortunately I have had most of my innings in happier days.

II. 5. The action of the verb INN; lodging, housing; *concr.* a lodging, dwelling-place.

a **1050** *Liber Scintill.* ii. (1889) 11 On ȝeþances his wununge innunge he ȝearwað criste. **1589** Fleming *Virg. Georg.* iii. 48 The cattell..goes into deserts large Without all inning (housing, fense, shroud, houell, or such like).

Inniskilling (ɪnɪ'skɪlɪŋ). Also **Enniskillen, Enniskilling, Inniskellen, Inniskillen.** The name of the county town of Fermanagh in Northern Ireland, used *attrib.* or *absol.* to designate a regiment originally raised for the defence of that town in 1689. So **Inni'skilliner**, a member of this regiment.

[**1690** A. Hamilton (*title*) A true relation of the actions of the Inniskillingmen, from their first taking up of arms in December, 1688 for the defence of the Protestant religion, and their lives and liberties.] **1715** in E. S. Jackson *Inniskilling Dragoons* (1909) ii. 35 A detachment of Greys and Inniskillings arrived in Edinburgh from Stirling. **1797** *Encycl. Brit.* IX. 243/2 Its [*sc.* Inniskilling's] inhabitants distinguished themselves..in the wars of Ireland at the revolution, out of which a regiment of dragoons, bearing the title of the *Inniskilleners*, was mostly formed. They form the 6th regiment of dragoons in the British Army. **1817** G. Jones *Battle of Waterloo* II. 55 The second heavy brigade of cavalry..consisted of..the 6th, or Inniskillings. **1822** M. Edgeworth *Let.* 11 Feb. (1971) 347 Will you inquire for Wilkie what is put on the caps of the Inniskellen 6th Dragoons... If you know of any Dragoon that would be better than the Inniskillen tell me. **1853** J. H. Stocqueler *Mil. Encycl.* 141/1 *Inniskilliners*, the officers and soldiers of the 6th dragoons and the 27th foot are so called, from the two regiments having been originally raised at Inniskilling, a town of Ulster. **1893** J. C. Ropes *Campaign of Waterloo* xvi. 300 In rear of the left wing..stood the Union brigade.. composed of the Royal Dragoons, the Scots Greys, and the Inniskilling Dragoons. **1968** *Encycl. Brit.* IX. 185/1 At Newtownbutler, in 1689, the Protestant Enniskillen men severely defeated a superior Roman Catholic army of James II and began the victorious tradition of the 'Inniskillings', now represented in the British Army by the Royal Inniskilling Fusiliers and the 5th Royal Inniskilling Dragoon Guards. **1971** G. Blaxland *Regiments Depart* vi. 204 The previous December..the Inniskilling Dragoon Guards were relieved by the 1st Royal Tank Regiment.

innit, vulg. form of *isn't it.*

1959 M. Gilbert *Blood & Judgment* i. 17 That's right, innit? **1962** N. Marsh *Hand in Glove* iv. 105 Dead right, innit? **1965** *Guardian* 3 Apr. 6/3 It's some place to go innit? **1973** J. Wainwright *Touch of Malice* 56 That's a bloody good reason, innit?

† **i'nnitency.** *Obs. rare.* [f. L. *innītent-em*, pr. pple. of *innīt-ī* to lean upon (f. *in-*, IN-[2] + *nītī* to lean, press): see -ENCY.] A leaning, pressing, or resting upon something.

1658 Gurnall *Chr. in Arm.* Verse 16 xi. 586 There is an innitency of his heart on Christ. **1658** Sir T. Browne *Gard. Cyrus* ii. 113 The innitency and stresse being made upon the hypomochlion or fulciment in the decussation.

So † **i'nnitent** *a. Obs. rare*$^{-0}$.

1656 Blount *Glossogr.*, *Innitent*, endeavoring or assaying.

† **i'nnixion.** *Obs. rare.* [n. of action from L. *innītī, innix-*: see prec. and -ION[1].] = prec.

1709 F. Hauksbee *Phys.-Mech. Exp.* v. (1719) 200 The Innixion or Resting of the Parts of the Fluid. **1713** Derham *Phys.-Theol.* v. ii. 327 Keeping the Line of Innixion, and Center of Gravity in due Place and Posture.

innkeeper ('ɪn,kiːpə(r)). Forms: see INN *sb.* [f. INN *sb.* 4 + KEEPER *sb.*] One who keeps an inn or public house for the accommodation of travellers and others; an innholder, a taverner.

1548 Udall *Erasm. Par. Luke* x. Q iij, [He] deliuered thim to his hoste the ynnekeper that he should see the wounded man well attended and kepte. **1596** Shaks. *1 Hen. IV*, iv. ii. 51 The Red-Nose Inne-keeper of Dauintry. **1779** Swinburne *Trav. Spain* xlii. 372 In Spain..the inn-keepers are almost the only well-fed, portly figures to be met with. **1845** Stephen *Comm. Laws Eng.* (1874) II. 84 A common innkeeper—which includes the keeper of every tavern or coffeehouse in which lodging is provided.

fig. **1545** Ascham *Toxoph.* i. (Arb.) 52 Solitariousenes, whyche lurketh in holes and corners, [and] Night an vngratiouse couer of noughtynesse, whyche two thynges be very Inkepers and receyuers of all noughtynesse and noughtye thinges.

Hence **'inn,keeperess**, *rare*, a female innkeeper. So also **'inn,keeping** *sb.*, the keeping of an inn (also *attrib.*); *adj.* that keeps an inn.

1860 G. H. K. in *Vac. Tour.* 121 Anybody who wishes to speculate in the innkeeping line. **1872** Yeats *Techn. Hist. Comm.* 126 The general progress of society rendered inn-keeping increasingly prosperous. **1895** Mrs. Donne *Down Danube* 46 An old peasant Inn-keeperess told us.

innless ('ɪnlɪs), *a.* [f. INN *sb.* + -LESS.] Without an inn or inns.

13.. *Birth Jesus* 510 in Horstm. *Altengl. Leg.* (1875) 88 þer nas non oþer stude þere, Bote þulke þat men to drowe, whan hei inles were. **1845** Ford *Handbk. Spain* i. 29 Hospitality in an hungry inn-less land becomes..a sacred duty. **1885** *Life Sir R. Christison* I. 350 At the innless village of Lower Inveruglas.

inn-melle, var. *in-melle*, IMELLE *Obs.*, among.

innoble, obs. form of ENNOBLE.

† **inno'blesse.** *Obs. rare.* [IN-[3]: perh. F.; cf. *innoble* not noble, ignoble, and *noblesse* nobility.] Want of nobility; ignoble or low rank.

a **1470** Tiptoft *Orat. C. Flaminius* (Caxton) E v b (R. Suppl.), The courage which is pure and free is disposed to take noblesse or innoblesse indifferently.

† **i'nnoblish**, var. ENNOBLISH *Obs.*, to ennoble.

1601 R. Johnson *Kingd. & Commw.* 203 [It] did greatly augment and innoblish this towne.

innocence ('ɪnəsəns). Also 4–5 -ense, 4–6 -ens. [a. F. *innocence* (12th c.), ad. L. *innocentia*: see next and -ENCE.]

I. The quality or fact of being innocent.

1. Freedom from sin, guilt, or moral wrong in general; the state of being untainted with, or unacquainted with, evil; moral purity.

1340 *Ayenb.* 146 Ine þise we onderstondeþ þe innocence þet we ssolle loki þe on a-ye þe oþre. *c* **1380** Wyclif *Sel. Wks.* III. 143 In þo stat of innocense. **1398** Trevisa *Barth. De P.R.* vi. xviii. (1495) 203 Thenne were malyce free, and goodnesse and innocence neuer syker. **1567** *Gude & Godlie B.* (S.T.S.) 70 And he, geue we beleue, hes coste His innocens for our trespas. **1667** Milton *P.L.* ix. 373 Go in thy native innocence; relie On what thou hast of vertue. **1692** South *12 Serm.* (1697) I. 534 How came our first Parents to sin, and to lose their Primitive Innocence? **1770** Goldsm. *Des. Vill.* 5 Dear lovely bowers of innocence and ease. **1850** Lynch *Theo. Trinal* ii. 28 Holiness is innocence made perfect. *a* **1851** Moir *Poems, Message Seth*, For Penitence, However deep it be, brings back not Innocence.

2. Freedom from specific guilt; the fact of not being guilty of that with which one is charged; guiltlessness.

1559 *Mirr. Mag., Dk. Clarence* l, All the worlde dyd know myne innocence. **1613** Shaks. *Hen. VIII*, i. i. 208 It will helpe me nothing To plead mine Innocence; for that dye is on me Which makes my whit'st part, black. **1640** Bp. Hall *Chr. Moder.* (ed. Ward) 37/1 If a Cajetan..shall set favourable states to our controversies, and give justly charitable testimonies to our personal innocences. **1772** *Junius Lett.* lxviii. 336 Where the guilt is doubtful, a presumption of innocence should in general be admitted. **1853** J. H. Newman *Hist. Sk.* (1873) II. i. i. 44 Timour.. protested to the cadhi his innocence of the blood which he had shed.

3. Freedom from cunning or artifice; guilelessness, artlessness, simplicity; hence, want of knowledge or sense, ignorance, silliness.

c **1385** Chaucer *L.G.W.* 1254 *Dido*, O sely wemen [*v.r.* woman] ful of Innocence..What makyth ȝow to men to truste so? *c* **1450** *Merlin* 40 When eny..complayneth to the for the kynges Innocence, and seiden thei wolden thow sholde take vpon the to be kynge. **1589** Nashe *Anat. Absurd.* Ep. Ded. 4 Least their singularitie reflect my simplicitie, their excellence conuict me of innocence. **1611** Shaks. *Wint. T.* v. ii. 70 The Shepheards Sonne..ha's not onely his Innocence (which seemes much) to iustifie him. **1712** Addison *Spect.* No. 299 ⁋2 My little Daughter Harriot.. asked me with a great deal of Innocence, why I never told them of the Generals and Admirals that had been in my Family. **1883** C. J. Wills *Mod. Persia* 70 The servants, who had traded on my innocence and simulated fever.

4. Of things: Harmlessness, innocuousness.

1828 Webster s.v., The innocence of a medicine which can do no harm.

II. *concr.* **5.** An innocent person or thing (in various senses of the adj.). (In quot. 1697 *collect.* Innocent creatures.)

c **1400** Lydg. *Æsop's Fab.* iii. 41 The sely sheepe..Stoode abasshed, ful like an innocence. **1697** Dryden *Virg. Georg.* iv. 745 The Mother Nightingale, Whose Nest some prying Churl had found, and thence, By Stealth, convey'd th' unfeather'd Innocence. **1703** Farquhar *Inconstant* iv. iv,

Stay, my fair innocence! **1777** SHERIDAN *Trip Scarb.* II. i. Wks. (1883) 296 Oh, this is better and better!—[*Aloud*] Well said, Innocence! **1871** TENNYSON *Last Tournament* 31 Take thou the jewels of this dead innocence [a maiden babe].

6. A popular name of *Houstonia cærulea*, a North American plant, with small blue four-cleft flowers, also called Bluet.

1821 W. P. C. BARTON *Flora N. Amer.* I. 119 Fairy-flax-Bluett. Innocence. Venus' Pride. **1863** *Rep. Comm. Agric. 1862* (U.S. Dept. Agric.) 159 The 'Bluets', 'Innocence', 'Dwarf Pink', with, perhaps, some other common name, is one of the prettiest ornaments of our spring meadows. **1892** *Jrnl. Amer. Folk-Lore* V. 97 *Houstonia cœrulea*, innocence. Boston, Mass. **1954** C. J. HYLANDER *Macmillan Wild Flower Bk.* 389 This familiar wild flower, also known as Innocence and Quaker-ladies, is a tufted or matted plant.

innocency (ˈɪnəsənsɪ). Now somewhat *rare* or *arch.* [ad. L. *innocentia*, n. of quality from *innocent-em*: see next and -ENCY.]

1. = prec. 1.

1357 *Lay Folks Catech.* 17 In the state of innocency [*Lamb. MS.* innocence]. *c* **1440** *Gesta Rom.* II. xli. (1838) 405 Mankynde was fyrste [made] in the state of innocencie. **1597** HOOKER *Eccl. Pol.* v. xxxi. §2 At the board..it very well becommeth children's innocencie to pray, and their elders to say Amen. **1634** W. TIRWHYT tr. *Balzac's Lett.* (vol. I.) 76 Our people are not contayned in their primatiue innocency. *a* **1800** J. WARTON *Sappho's Advice* 27 In white and innocency drest, The plainest beauties were the best. **1838** EMERSON *Misc.* (1855) 102 When in innocency, or when, by intellectual perception, he attains to say,—'I love the Right!'

2. = prec. 2.

1513 MORE in Grafton *Chron.* (1568) II. 785 Not suffering the Lordes to speake, and to declare their innocencie. **1542-3** *Act 34 & 35 Hen. VIII* c. 1 Persons..complained on, shalbe admitted to purge and trie..their innocency by other witnesse. **1682** DRYDEN *Pref. Relig. Laici* Wks. (Globe) 188 To declare their innocency in this Plot. **1829** TYTLER *Hist. Scot.* (1864) III. 10 Ready..to surrender his person for the trial of his innocency. **1881** SWINBURNE *Mary Stuart* III. i, Lest I seem To have aught neglected in the full defence Of mine own innocency and honour.

3. = prec. 3.

1494 FABYAN *Chron.* v. lxxxi. 58 Vortiger thenne consyderynge the innocency and myldnesse of the kyng, cast in his mynde howe he myght be kynge hym selfe. **1548** HALL *Chron., Hen. VIII* 244 Suche was his childishe innocencie and feare..he was suche an ignoraunt soule, as knewe not what the affirmyng of an heresie was. **1556** *Aurelio & Isab.* (1608) G vj, Ower innocency and your grete knoleagie makethe to seeme of the liey the trueth.

4. = prec. 4.

1665 BOYLE *Occas. Refl., Disc. Occas. Medit.* IV. v, Good Thoughts..to be gather'd with as much Innocency and Pleasure..as Honey is gather'd by the industrious Bee. **1732** LAW *Serious C.* iv. (ed. 2) 54 His trade, as to him, loses all its innocency.

5. = prec. 5.

1727 DE FOE *Prot. Monast.* 18 Babies, Play-Things, and other pretty Innocencies used of old. **1827** POLLOK *Course T.* VII, Helpless, swaddled innocency.

innocent (ˈɪnəsənt), *a.* and *sb.* Also 4 **innos(s)ent, in-oscente,** 4-6 **innocente, ynnocent,** 5-6 **inocent(e.** [a. F. *innocent*, OF. pl. *-enz, -ens* (Roland, 11th c.), ad. L. *innocēnt-em*, f. *in-* (IN-³) + *nocēnt-em*, pr. pple. of *nocēre* to hurt, injure.]

A. *adj.*

1. a. Of persons: Doing no evil; free from moral wrong, sin, or guilt (in general); pure, unpolluted. Usually (in mod. use always) implying 'unacquainted with evil' (thus freq. of little children; whence passing into sense 5); but formerly sometimes in more general sense (*e.g.* of God or Christ), Sinless, holy.

a **1340** HAMPOLE *Psalter* xvii. 28 With man innocent innocent þou sall be. **1382** WYCLIF *Ps.* xxiii[i]. 4 The innocent in hondis and in clene herte. —— *Heb.* vii. 26 Hooly, innosent, inpolute, departid fro synful men. **1513** MORE *Rich. III*, Wks. 67/1 The lamentable murther of his innocent nephewes, the young king and his tender brother. **1556** *Aurelio & Isab.* (1608) I ij, Be the handes of God was the firste woman createde, innocente, and withoute spotte. **1669** SHADWELL *R. Shepherdess* III. Wks. 1720 I. 257 They are the happiest innocentest people in the world. **1687** A. LOVELL tr. *Thevenot's Trav.* I. 200 Many Innocent Infants, whom the Mothers had hid..were Murdered and Buried there. **1784** COWPER *Task* I. 494 The innocent are gay—the lark is gay. **1851** MAURICE *Patriarchs & Lawg.* ii. (1867) 51 When we say that God made man innocent, What do we mean?

transf. **1500-20** DUNBAR *Poems* ix. 158 Every straik mak throw my hart a stound, That evir did stenȝie thy fair flesche innocent. **1526** *Pilgr. Perf.* (1531) 10 That most innocent body..of the immaculate lambe Jesu Chryst. **1600** SHAKS. *A.Y.L.* II. i. 39 The big round tears Cours'd one another downe his [a stag's] innocent nose In pitteous chase.

b. *fig.* Spotless, stainless.

1629 MILTON *Nativ.* 39 She woos the gentle air To hide her guilty front with innocent snow.

2. a. Free from specific wrong or guilt; that has not committed the particular offence charged or in question; not deserving of the punishment or suffering inflicted; not guilty, guiltless, unoffending. ***innocent blood***, the blood (or life) of the innocent. ***innocent party*** [PARTY *sb.* 11], in matrimonial proceedings, the person adjudged to be innocent.

Since the Divorce Reform Act 1969 the usage has been legally obsolete in England, since that Act abolished the concept of a matrimonial offence as a ground for divorce and substituted for it the concept of irretrievable breakdown of the marriage.

1382 WYCLIF *1 Sam.* xxvi. 9 Who shal stretche his hoond into the crist of the Lord, and shal be innocent? —— *Ps.* xciii[i]. 21 The innocent blod thei shul condempne. **1484** CAXTON *Fables of Alfonce* I Ye shold do grete synne yf ye dyd put this Innocent and gyltles to deth. **1526** TINDALE *Matt.* xxvii. 4, I have synned betraynge the innocent bloud. **1548** HALL *Chron., Hen. VI* 158b, The bloudde of the Innocente man was with his dolorous death, recompensed. **1651** HOBBES *Leviath.* II. xxi. 109 A Soveraign Prince, that putteth to death an Innocent Subject. **1670** MARVELL *Corr.* Wks. 1872-5 II. 350 The Lieutenancy..pick out Hays and Jekill, the innocentest of the whole party, to show their power on. **1729** G. JACOB *New Law-Dict., Divorce*: In Divorces for Adultery, several Acts of Parliament have allowed the Innocent Party to marry again. **1761** HUME *Hist. Eng.* II. xxxvi. 286 Persons not lying under any sense of attainder were still innocent in the eye of the law. **1835** *Tomlins's Law Dict.* (ed. 4) I. (s.v. Divorce), The commissioners appointed by Henry VIII. and Edward VI. ..recommend divorces *à mensa et thoro* to be abolished, and complete divorces to be allowed for adultery, desertion, bad treatment, &c., the innocent party to be allowed to marry again. **1849** MACAULAY *Hist. Eng.* ii. (1871) I. 117 While innocent blood was shedding under the forms of justice. *Ibid.* vi. II. 41 The innocent began to breathe freely, and false accusers to tremble. **1948** J. H. S. BOSSARD *Sociol. of Child Devel.* xvi. 369 One principle usually observed is that custody goes to the so-called innocent party. **1958** *Daily Mail* 3 July 4/8 When are we going to hear the last of that time-worn phrase so beloved of newspaper columnists and the legal profession—'innocent party'? **1959** JOWITT *Dict. Eng. Law* I. 67/2 The Matrimonial Causes Act, 1857.. created a Court for Divorce and Matrimonial Causes.. which would grant to the innocent party a divorce *a mensa et thoro* on the ground of the other's adultery.

transf. **1590** SPENSER *F.Q.* I. ii. 24 Of whose most innocent death When tidings came to mee, unhappy maid.

b. Const. *of* (formerly also *from*).

1513 MORE *Rich. III* (1883) 18, I dare well aunswere for myne vncle Riuers and my brother here, that thei be innocent of any such matters. **1526** TINDALE *Matt.* xxvii. 24, I am innocent of the bloud of this iuste person. **1593** SHAKS. *2 Hen. VI*, III. i. 69 Our Kinsman Gloster is as innocent, From meaning Treason to our Royall Person, As is the sucking Lambe, or harmelesse Doue. **1697** DRYDEN *Virg. Georg.* II. 738 The Peasant, innocent of all these Ills. **1814** CARY *Dante, Paradise* xxv. 105 Innocent of worse intent Than to do fitting honour to the bride. *Mod.* Entirely innocent of the crime with which he was charged.

c. *colloq.* with *of*: Free from; devoid of. (A humorous transference or weakening of prec.)

1706 ADDISON *Rosamond* Prol., The Opera..Enrich'd with songs, but innocent of thought. **1743** WESLEY *Wks.* (1872) I. 428 The Sermon..was quite innocent of meaning. **1834** MEDWIN *Angler in Wales* II. 180 His clothes..were quite innocent of a fit. **1884** J. COLBORNE *Hicks Pasha* 60 The windows are small apertures..innocent of glass.

3. a. Having or showing the simplicity, ignorance, artlessness, or unsuspecting nature of a child or one ignorant of the world; devoid of cunning or artifice; simple, guileless, unsuspecting; hence, artless, naive, ingenuous.

1382 WYCLIF *Prov.* xxii. 3 The innocent passede and is tormentid with harm. *c* **1386** CHAUCER *Clerk's T.* 218 Grisilde of this, god woot, ful Innocent That for hire shapen was al this array. **1390** GOWER *Conf.* III. 169 Ful ofte Deceived ben with wordes softe The kinges, that ben innocent. *c* **1440** *Generydes* 951 Of all this werk the kyng was innocent And of ther falsed no thing perceyuyd. **1535** COVERDALE *Esther* xvi. 6 Which also with false and disceatfull wordes..disceaue and betraye the innocent goodnes of prynces. **1711** STEELE *Spect.* No. 118 ¶3 For all she looks so innocent as it were, take my Word for it she is no Fool. **1859** C. READE *Love me Little* xiv, Shall I tell you your real character?..You are an innocent fox! **1875** A. W. WARD *Eng. Dram. Lit.* I. 7 Chaucer indeed made a very innocent use of the words tragedy and comedy when he applied them simply to poems ending happily or unhappily.

b. Deficient in intelligence or sense; silly, half-witted, imbecile: cf. B. 3b. Now *dial.*

1548 HALL *Chron., Hen. VI* 169 That he was either a childe, which had nede of norice..or an innocent creature, whiche muste be ruled by a tutor. *Ibid., Edw. IV* 210 He was a man of no great wit, suche as men comonly call an Innocent man, neither a foole, neither very wyse. **1688** *Vestry Bks.* (Surtees) 342 To John Dods for keeping the innocent boy, 1*l.* **1706** PHILLIPS, *Innocent*, inoffensive,.. harmless, also simple, or silly. *a* **1825** FORBY *Voc. E. Anglia* s.v., 'An innocent man'..is an extremely common expression for a silly fellow.

4. Of actions, etc.: Free from guilt or moral evil; not arising from or involving any evil intent or motive. Often blending with 5: Producing no morally bad result; morally harmless.

1514 BARCLAY *Cyt. & Uplondyshm.* (Percy Soc.) 19 Ryght so he named men meke & pacyent, His flocke & his shepe, for maners innocent. **1665** BOYLE *Occas. Refl.* IV. xiii. (1848) 258 The Innocentest use that we are wont to make of our time. **1676** tr. *Guillatiere's Voy. Athens* 214 Mahometan Ladies..would come to his House to play their innocent tricks. **1728** FRANKLIN *Ess.* Wks. 1840 II. 3, I think no pleasure innocent, that is to man hurtful. **1848** A. TOD *Disc.* 102, I mean not to condemn innocent hilarity. **1893** SIR J. W. CHITTY in *Law Times Rep.* LXVIII. 429/1 The case..is one, not of innocent misrepresentation, but of fraudulent misrepresentation.

5. a. Of things: Doing no harm; producing no ill effect or result; not injurious; harmless, innocuous. (In *Path.* opposed to *malignant.*)

1662 H. MORE *Philosophical Writings* Pref. Gen. (1712) 20 How innocent and inoffensive that doctrine was in the more pure and intemerate Ages of the Church. **1703** DAMPIER *Voy.* III. 68 A sort of..Calabash or Gourd-kind..It is of a sharp and pleasing Taste, and is very innocent. **1712** BUDGELL *Spect.* No. 283 ¶17 His Powder upon Examination being found very innocent. **1715-20** POPE *Iliad* xv. 547 The shaft with brazen head Fell innocent, and on the dust lay dead. **1758** *Descr. Thames* 207 The Flesh is white, soft, innocent, and nourishing. **1804** ABERNETHY *Surg. Obs.* 94 *note*, Tumours of an innocent nature commonly increase in an equal ratio. **1897** *Allbutt's Syst. Med.* III. 370 Pressure on these nerves in innocent stricture of the gullet is rare.

b. That does not transgress the law; lawful. ***innocent conveyance***, a conveyance which does not have any tortious operation, one which does not create a discontinuance or result in forfeiture.

All conveyances are now innocent by statute in England and in the United States.

1811 E. B. SUGDEN *Gilbert's Law of Uses & Trusts* (ed. 3) 232 A conveyance by lease and release is like a bargain and sale, and covenant to stand seised what is termed an innocent conveyance. **1828** WEBSTER, *Innocent*..4. Lawful; permitted; as, an *innocent* trade. 5. Not contraband; not subject to forfeiture; as, *innocent* goods carried to a belligerent nation. *Kent.* **1841** H. J. STEPHEN *New Comm. Laws Eng.* I. 508 The other conveyances can, in their nature, pass no more than the grantor might lawfully transfer. For this reason, they have received, by way of distinction from a feoffment, (and others now abolished of the like nature,) the appellation of *innocent* conveyances. **1848** WHARTON *Law Lexicon* 322/2 *Innocent conveyances*, a covenant to stand seised, a bargain and sale, and release, so called, because since they convey the actual possession by construction of law only, they do not confer a larger estate in property than the person conveying possesses. **1937** W. S. HOLDSWORTH *Hist. Eng. Law* VII. 357 Both a bargain and sale and a covenant to stand seised were, unlike a feoffment, 'innocent' conveyances.

6. *Comb.*

1621 LADY M. WROTH *Urania* 182 Twas not sillines..that made that innocent-like fashion shew in me. **1799** MALTHUS *Diary* 30 June (1966) 108 He was a remarkably meek & innocent looking man. **1830** TENNYSON *Lilian* ii, So innocent-arch, so cunning-simple. **1838** *Lett. fr. Madras* xxi. (1843) 213 Have you heard of the Cooly Trade? 'Emigration of Hill Coolies to the Mauritius' it is called, and divers other innocent-sounding names. **1842** S. LOVER *Handy Andy* xxiii. 207 He came up quite innocent-like to the corner. **1860** F. & J. GREENWOOD *Under Cloud* III. xiv. 307 The jovial, innocent-hearted actor. **1895** A. W. PINERO *Second Mrs. Tanqueray* I. 42 Paula..is..beautiful, fresh, innocent-looking. **1925** BLUNDEN *Eng. Poems* 19 So innocent-gay was her look. **1955** E. BOWEN *World of Love* xi. 212 Banks were innocent-blue with scabious. **1959** J. L. AUSTIN *Sense & Sensibilia* (1962) i. 4 In philosophy it is often good policy, where one member of a putative pair falls under suspicion, to view the more innocent-seeming party suspiciously as well. **1962** Y. OLSSON in F. Behre *Contrib. Eng. Syntax* 87 Like innocent-looking people, even the most innocent-looking personal pronouns are deeper than one would be led to believe.

B. *sb.* (In 4 *pl.* **innocens, innocenz, -ntz.**)

1. a. An innocent person; one not disposed to do harm, or unacquainted with evil: see A. 1.

[*c* **1200** *Vices & Virtues* 79 Se ðe ne nimð none mede of ða *innocentes*, ðat bien uneilinde menn ðe none manne euel ne willeð.] **13..** *Ipotis* 71 (Vernon MS.) in Horstm. *Altengl. Leg.* (1881) 342 Þe feorþe heuene is gold iliche..To Innocens þat place is diht. *c* **1386** CHAUCER *Sompn. T.* 275 Ye..chiden heere the sely Innocent Youre wyf that is so meke and pacient. **1390** GOWER *Conf.* I. 175 All to deceive an innocent, Whiche woll not be of her assent. **1483** *Cath. Angl.* 196/2 An Innocent, *innocens, innoxius.* **1508** DUNBAR *Tua Mariit Wemen* 267 Be of ȝour luke like innocentis, thoght ȝe haif euill myndis. **1604** SHAKS. *Oth.* v. ii. 199 Thou hast kill'd the sweetest innocent, That ere did lift vp eye. **1711** ADDISON *Spect.* No. 198 ¶1 Like good queen Emma, the pretty Innocent walks blindfold among burning Ploughshares, without being scorched or singed by them. **1873** BROWNING *Red Cott. Nt.-cap* 205 A pair of innocents Who thought their wedded hands not clean enough To touch and leave unsullied their soul's snow!

†**b.** One innocent of a charge, or undeserving of the punishment inflicted; a guiltless person: see A. 2. *Obs.*

c **1340** HAMPOLE *Prose Tr.* 11 Thay are slaers gastely..þat defames men, and þat confoundes innocentys. *c* **1400** tr. *Secreta Secret., Gov. Lordsh.* (E.E.T.S.) 53 To helpe simple men, to vpbere þe defautes of Innocentz. **1526** TINDALE *Matt.* xii. 7 Ye wold never have condemned innocentes. **1631** *Star Chamb. Cases* (Camden) 49 For hope of gaine he had combyned with the Lord Sarsfield to indict, convict, and execute one Philip Bushell, an innocent, for a supposed murther. **1707** J. CHAMBERLAYNE *St. Gt. Brit.* III. viii. 339 Those who shall conspire to indict an Innocent falsely and maliciously of Felony. **1748** RICHARDSON *Clarissa* (1811) IV. 89 You will save from ruin a multitude of innocents.

2. a. *esp.* A young child, as being free from actual sin, or unacquainted with evil (see A. 1); *spec.* in *pl.* (with capital), the young children slain by Herod after the birth of Jesus (Matt. ii. 16), reckoned from early times as Christian martyrs (also called ***the Holy Innocents***).

c **1325** *Lai Le Freine* 164 And help this seli innocent, That it mot y-cristned be. *a* **1340** HAMPOLE *Psalter* ii. 2 Herode, þ^t sloghe þe innocenz. *c* **1400** MAUNDEV. (Roxb.) ix. 36 Vnder þe cloistre..es þe Charnell of þe Innocentz, whare þaire banes lies. **1548** HALL *Chron., Rich. III* 34b, When I was credibly enformed of the death of the .ii. younge innocentes, his awne natural nephewes. **1641** J. JACKSON *True Evang. T.* II. 98 The seventh and last of these innocent creatures, is an innocent indeed, a child. **1704** NELSON *Fest. & Fasts* viii. (1739) 101 The Martyrdom of the Holy Innocents. **1863** KINGSLEY *Water Bab.* v. (1886) 221 They were all there, except, of course, the babes of Bethlehem who were killed by wicked King Herod; for they were taken straight to heaven long ago, as everybody knows, and we call them the Holy Innocents.

b. (*Holy*) ***Innocents' Day***, the 28th of December, observed as a church festival in

commemoration of the slaughter of the Innocents. (Formerly called CHILDERMAS.)

1548-9 (Mar.) *Bk. Com. Prayer, Introits*, etc., The Innocentes Daye. **1658** PHILLIPS, *Innocents day*, the 28 of December..also called Childermas day. **1683** WOOD *Life* (O.H.S.) III. 38 Innocents day..a very cold day. **1828** SCOTT *F.M. Perth* xvi, I can make bodily oath to the bonnets I made for them since last Innocents'.

c. *fig.* in *pl.* (*Parliamentary slang.*) Applied to measures 'sacrificed' at the end of a session for want of time; usually in phr. ***massacre*** or ***slaughter of the innocents***.

1859 *Times* 20 July 7/3 (Farmer) The Leader of the House would have to go through that doleful operation called the massacre of the innocents. **1870** *London Figaro* 6 Aug. (ibid.), So vigorously has the slaughter of the innocents been proceeding that the Appropriation Bill was read a first time in the House of Commons on Wednesday. **1887** *Spectator* 20 Aug., At this period of the Session, amongst the 'innocents', this innocentest of the innocents is not destined to be spared the sacrificial knife.

3. a. A guileless, simple, or unsuspecting person; one devoid of cunning or artifice; hence, **b.** One wanting in ordinary knowledge or intelligence; a simpleton, a silly fellow; a half-wit, an idiot.

c **1386** CHAUCER *Can. Yeom. Prol. & T.* 523 O sely preest, o sely Innocent With coueitise anon thou shalt be blent. **1579** LYLY *Euphues* (Arb.) 98 In body deformed, in minde foolish, an innocent borne. **1593** R. HARVEY *Philad.* 91 That he might do what he list in the kingdome under such an innocent and milksop. **1598** *Faversham Par. Reg.* (MS.), Buryed, Margery, an innocent from the Abby. **1694** R. L'ESTRANGE *Fables* (ed. 6) ccccxxxviii. 475 There was just such another Innocent as this, in my Father's Family. **1706** PHILLIPS, *An Innocent*, an Idiot, or Ninny, a silly, half-witted Person. **1814** SCOTT *Wav.* ix,'He is an innocent, sir', said the butler..Waverley learned..from this colloquy; that in Scotland..a natural fool [was called] an innocent. **1838** JAMES *Robber* vi, The man is a poor innocent whom I have known this many a year.

4. *Herb.* = INNOCENCE 6. *U.S.*

(***Herb***) ***St. Innocent*** (F. *Herbe de S. Innocent* Cotgr.), Knot-grass, *Polygonum aviculare.*

1616 SURFL. & MARKH. *Country Farme* 45 Some doe make in like manner Neck-laces and Bracelets of the hearbe S. Innocent. **1855** 'MARION HARLAND' *Hidden Path* xxxiii. 324 Filling his hat with wild violets, sorrel, and the frail, azure innocents.

†**inno'cential,** *a. Obs. rare.* [f. L. *innocentia* INNOCENCE + -AL^{1}: cf. *inferential, prudential,* etc.] Of, belonging to, or characterized by, innocence; innocent. So †**inno'centious** *a.*; also ††**inno'centive** *a.*

1624 HEYWOOD *Gunaik.* IX. 459 She appeared to him in her former simple and innocentious life. **1627** FELTHAM *Resolves* II. [I.] xii. (1628) 34 There is an innocentiall prouidence, as well as the slynesse of a vulpine craft. *Ibid.* II. xvli. (1677) 299 A man that hath not experienced the Contentments of Innocentiue Piety.

†**'innocen,tize,** *v. Obs. rare.* [f. INNOCENT *sb.* + -IZE, after F. *innocenter* (Cotgr.).] *trans.* 'To breech, whip, lash (on Childermas or Innocents' day), to jerke all such as they can find in bed' (Cotgr.: mentioned as a 'merrie custome' in France.)

1708 MOTTEUX *Rabelais* v. xiv, We will Innocentize your Fopship with a Wannion, you never were so innocentis'd in your days.

innocently ('ɪnəsəntlɪ), *adv.* [f. INNOCENT *a.* + -LY^{2}.] In an innocent manner; without doing, having done, or intending, harm; guiltlessly, harmlessly, guilelessly, artlessly. See the adj.

c **1400** MAUNDEV. (Roxb.) xxxii. 145 Liffand innocently in lewtee and in luffe and charitee. **1526** *Pilgr. Perf.* (W. de W. 1531) 79 Whan they haue..suffred..many obieccions & iniuryes innocently for the loue of Jesu. **1555** EDEN *Decades* 8 Men lyued simplye & innocentlye without inforcement of lawes. **1621** G. SANDYS *Ovid's Met.* IV. (1626) 83 Where the innocently wretched maid Was for her mothers proud impietie..sentenced to die. **1711** STEELE *Spect.* No. 157 ¶6 Let him go before he has innocently suffered. **1712** ADDISON *ibid.* No. 383 ¶1 The Child who went to the Door answered very Innocently, that he did not Lodge there. **1862** STANLEY *Jew. Ch.* (1877) I. ix. 186 What was meant innocently..is taken for a conspiracy, a rebellion. **1885** *Manch. Exam.* 5 May 5/2 They might spend their time less innocently.

b. *fig.* Spotlessly. (Cf. INNOCENT *a.* 1 b.)

1715 tr. *Pancirollus' Rerum Mem.* I. I. xv. 36 The Parian [[marble] is the most innocently white.

†**'innocentness.** *Obs. rare.* [f. as prec. + -NESS.] The quality of being innocent; innocency.

1482 *Monk of Evesham* (Arb.) 72 The pure and clere symplycyte and innocentnes of the very chirc[h]e of god. **1727** BAILY vol. II, *Innocentness*, Guiltlessness, Harmlessness.

innocuity (ɪnəʊ'kjuːɪtɪ). [f. L. *innocu-us* (see next) + -ITY, perh. after F. *innocuité* (1806 in Hatz.-Darm.).] The quality of being innocuous; innocuousness.

1855 *Med. & Surg. Reporter* Mar., Drugs, having no guarantee of their purity or innocuity. **1861** BUMSTEAD *Ven. Dis.* (1879) 431 The innocuity of the milk is proved by the fact, that a mother..may nurse that child with impunity.

innocuous (ɪ'nɒkjuːəs), *a.* [f. L. *innocu-us* (f. *in-*, IN-^{3} + *nocuus* (rare), f. root of *nocēre* to hurt) + -OUS.] Not hurtful or injurious; harmless. In *Zool.* applied *spec.* to the non-venomous snakes (constituting the division *Innocua*).

1598 BARCKLEY *Felic. Man* (1631) 171 The still hours of his innocuous life. **1638** COWLEY *Love's Riddle* II. Wks. (1684) II. 75 To spend the rest of my..days in their innocuous sports. **1641** J. JACKSON *True Evang. T.* II. 107 All these innocuous and harmlesse creatures. **1791** COWPER *Iliad* v. 20 But over Diomedes' left shoulder passed The point innocuous. **1846** RUSKIN *Mod. Paint.* I. Pref. 14 Men have commonly more pleasure in the criticism which hurts than in that which is innocuous. **1861** DELAMER *Kitch. Gard.* 93 Spinach-juice furnishes an innocuous colouring-matter.

i'nnocuously, *adv.* [f. prec. + -LY^{2}.] In an innocuous manner; harmlessly; without doing harm. (In first quot., Without suffering harm.)

1650 SIR T. BROWNE *Pseud. Ep.* (ed. 2) III. xxviii. 152 Whether Quailes..doe innocuously feed upon Hellebore. **1795-1814** WORDSW. *Excurs.* III. 516 A low cottage in a sunny bay, Where the salt sea innocuously breaks. **1837** MACAULAY *Ess., Bacon* (1887) 424 Science..has guided the thunder-bolt innocuously from heaven to earth.

i'nnocuousness. [f. as prec. + -NESS.] The quality of being innocuous; harmlessness.

1644 DIGBY *Nat. Bodies* ix. (1645) 93 That innocuousnesse of the effect. **1845** McCULLOCH *Taxation* I. i. §1 (1852) 57 The land-tax owes its innocuousness partly, no doubt, to its moderation. **1875** H. C. WOOD *Therap.* (1879) 395 Evidence as to the innocuousness and even the therapeutic value of this method.

†**'innodate,** *ppl. a. Obs.* [ad. L. *innōdāt-us*, pa. pple. of *innōdāre*: see next.] Bound up or fastened in a knot; involved in an interdict.

1587 FLEMING *Contn. Holinshed* III. 1363/1 She being excommunicate and deposed, all that doo obeie hir are likewise innodate and accurssed.

†**'innodate,** *v. Obs.* [f. ppl. stem of L. *innōdā-re* to knot in, fasten with a knot, entangle, implicate, f. *in-* (IN-^{2}) + *nōdāre* to knot, f. *nōdus* NODE.] *trans.* To fasten in or with a knot; *spec.* to include or involve in an anathema or interdict: from med.L. *vinculis anathematis innodare* to involve in the bonds of anathema (of frequent occurrence in Charters, Du Cange).

1635 N. R. *Camden's Hist. Eliz.* Introd., The Prelates..fearing lest the Pope should innodate the Realme with his Interdict. *Ibid.* II. an. 13. 124 Pius Quintus..secretly innodated her by his sentence of Anathema. **1655** FULLER *Ch. Hist.* IX. ii. §24 Those which from henceforth obey her are innodated with the anathema.

Hence †**inno'dation** *vbl. sb.*

1731 CHANDLER *Limborch's Hist. Inquis.* II. 13 Let no man dare to infringe, or..to contradict this Page of our Excommunication, Anathematization, Interdict, Innovation, Innodation.

innomb(e)rable: see INNUMBERABLE *a.*, *Obs.*

i'nnominable, *a.* (*sb.*) *arch.* [ad. L. *innōminābil-is*, f. *in-* (IN-^{3}) + *nōminābilis* NOMINABLE.] Incapable of being named or not fit to be named.

1387-8 T. USK *Test. Love* I. ix. (Skeat) I. 55 Of foule thynges innominable. **1533** [see INIMAGINABLE]. **1570** BILLINGSLEY *Euclid.* v. def. IV. 129 The excesse of the one to the other is euer unknowen, and therefore is surd, and innominable. **1625** T. JAMES *Manuduct. Divinity* Ep. Ded., As concerning the manuscripts, they are..innominable as yet. **1839** *Fraser's Mag.* XIX. 626 Those innominable garments, the mere allusion to which is sufficient to shock ears polite. **1839** BAILEY *Festus* xix. (1852) 278 There are innominable depths, Which cannot be revealed of human life.

B. *sb.* in *pl.* (*humorous euphemism*) 'Unmentionables', trousers.

1834-43 SOUTHEY *Doctor* (1847) VII. 606 The lower part of his dress represented innominables and hose in one.

‖**innominata, -tum:** see INNOMINATE 3.

innominate (ɪ'nɒmɪnət), *a.* [ad. late L. *innōmināt-us* (Boethius), f. *in-* (IN-^{3}) + *nōmināt-us* NOMINATE.]

1. Not named, unnamed, anonymous.

1638 SIR T. HERBERT *Trav.* (ed. 2) 306 Zeyloon..was not innominate to the Antients. **1686** GOAD *Celest. Bodies* I. ix. 36 The Spirit called Light or Heat, is Innominate of itself. **1692** RAY *Dissol. World* II. v. (1732) 221 Communicated by an innominate Person. **1847** *Blackw. Mag.* LXI. 630 Better to live for ever innominate in a song. **1898** *19th Cent.* Sept. 304 The infant and still innominate Church.

2. *Roman Law.* Of a contract: Unclassified: see quot. 1818.

1774 BP. HALIFAX *Anal. Rom. Law* (1795) 62 Innominate Contracts were usually ranged under four classes, expressive of the Consideration on which they were founded. 1. *Do ut des.* 2. *Do ut facias.* 3. *Facio ut des.* 4. *Facio ut facias.* **1818** COLEBROOKE *Treat. Oblig. & Contr.* I. 18 Unnamed or innominate contracts are those which had no certain denomination denoting their particular nature. **1875** POSTE *Gaius* III. 372. **1880** MUIRHEAD *Gaius* II. §89 *note.*

3. Anat. ***innominate bone*** (*Os innominatum*), the hip-bone, a union of three original bones: see quot. 1879. ***innominate artery*** (*Arteria innominata*), a large artery given off from the arch of the aorta, just before the left carotid artery. ***innominate vein*** (*Vena innominata*), each of the two veins formed by the junction of the subclavian and the internal jugular veins behind the inner ends of the clavicle.

[**1706** PHILLIPS, *Innominata Ossa*,..the Nameless Bones, two large Bones plac'd on the sides of the *Os Sacrum*.] **1866** HUXLEY *Preh. Rem. Caithn.* 87 The right innominate bone was restored after the model of the left. **1870** ROLLESTON *Anim. Life* Introd. 52 The aorta [in birds] divides after a very short course into three great trunks, by giving off two subequal innominate arteries. **1876** *Trans. Clin. Soc.* IX. 112 The innominate veins were stretched over the sac. **1879** WRIGHT *Anim. Life* 6 Each innominate bone is made up of three bones, ilium, ischium, and pubis.

b. *absol.* as *sb.* (also in L. form *innominatum*, *-ata*): = ***innominate bone, artery,*** or ***vein.***

1879 *St. George's Hosp. Rep.* IX. 407 The first part of the aorta..was greatly dilated..the innominate was also dilated. **1880** *Med. Temp. Jrnl.* July 184 Aneurism of the innominata. **1886** *Syd. Soc. Lex.* s.v., The three parts of the innominate are fused into one bone in Mammals and Birds, in Reptiles there are three separate bones.

†**i'nnominated,** *a. Obs. rare*$^{-1}$. [f. as prec. + -ED^{1}: cf. NOMINATED.] Unnamed, nameless.

1660 H. MORE *Myst. Godl.* III. ii. 60 A discovery out of their own Religion that this innominated Deity was not the True God but the Material world.

in nomine: see IN *Lat. prep.*

innormity, -mous, obs. ff. ENORMITY, -MOUS.

†**inno'tescence.** *Obs. rare*$^{-1}$. [ad. med.L. *innōtēscentia*, f. L. *innōtēscent-em*, pr. pple. of *innōtēscĕre*, inceptive f. *in-* (IN-^{2}) + *nōscere, nōt-* to know.] A becoming known.

1629 DONNE *Serm.* V. cxxv. 254, I shall see it in the face of that God who is all face, all manifestation, all innotescence to me.

‖**inno'tescimus.** *Law. Obs.* [Lat., = we come to know, we have cognizance.] (See quot.)

1670 BLOUNT *Law Dict.*, *Innotescimus*, Letters Patent so called, which are always of a Charter of Feofment or some other Instrument, not of Record; and so called from the words in the Conclusion, *Innotescimus per presentes.* An *Innotescimus* and *Vidimus* are all one.

'innoth, early form of INNETH, the inside.

innouth, var. of INWITH *Obs.*, within.

innovate ('ɪnəʊveɪt), *v.* [f. L. *innovāt-*, ppl. stem of *innovāre* to renew, alter, f. *in-* (IN-^{2}) + *novāre* to make new, f. *novus* new. Cf. F. *innover* (1322 in Godef. *Compl.*).]

†**1.** *trans.* To change (a thing) into something new; to alter; to renew. *Obs.* (*rare* after 1750.)

1561 T. NORTON *Calvin's Inst.* IV. xx. (1634) 737 A desire to innovate all things..moveth troublesome men. **1572** H. MIDDELMORE in Ellis *Orig. Lett.* Ser. II. III. 6 It shulde shewe very daingerous to every State to suffer the same any waye to be innovatyd or alteryd. **1621** G. SANDYS *Ovid's Met.* IV. (1626) 72 Scython who his nature innouates, Now male, now female, by alternate Fates. **1674** BOYLE *Excell. Theol.* I. i. 22 Theology teaches..that this world..shall either be abolished by annihilation, or..be innovated, and, as it were, transfigured. **1751** JOHNSON *Rambler* No. 179 ¶5 Attempts to innovate the constitutional or habitual character. **1818** SCOTT *Rob Roy* xxii, The dictates of my father were..not to be altered, innovated, or even discussed.

2. To bring in (something new) the first time; to introduce as new. *Obs.* exc. in *Comm.*

1548 UDALL *Erasm. Par. Luke* Pref. (R.), If any other do innouate and brynge vp a woorde to me afore not vsed or not hearde, I would not disprayse it. **1592** R. D. *Hypnerotomachia* 57 b, This..table being taken up..there was presently an other innovated, with a cloth of silke. **1656** *Burton's Diary* (1828) I. 98 He was tried in the same way for innovating a new religion. **1666** DRYDEN *Pref. Ann. Mirab.* Wks. (Globe) 41 Some words which I have innovated..upon his Latin. **1735-8** BOLINGBROKE *On Parties* 63 To surrender their old Charters, and accept new ones, under such Limitations and Conditions, as the King thought fit to innovate. **1967** *Times Rev. Industry* Oct. 86/2 Nylon..was first invented in 1928, but not innovated until 1939. **1972** *Physics Bull.* Feb. 67/1 (Advt.), We've been innovating electrometer values like these for over 20 years.

3. *intr.* To bring in or introduce novelties; to make changes *in* something established; to introduce innovations. Sometimes const. *on* or *upon* (also with *indirect passive*). *spec.* in *Comm.*

1597 DANIEL *Civ. Wars* v. lxxvii, Such..who..Hated his might, and glad to innouate. **1651** HOBBES *Govt. & Soc.* v. §5. 78 There are many who supposing themselves wiser then others, endeavour to innovate, and divers Innovators innovate divers wayes. **1658** CROMWELL *Sp.* 20 Jan. in *Carlyle*, Designs..laid to innovate upon the Civil Rights of the Nations, and to innovate in matters of Religion. **1720** WATERLAND *Eight Serm.* 319 They innovated in the Form of Baptism, which was one of the best Fences to the true Faith. **1796** BURKE *Lett. noble Ld.* Wks. VIII. 20 It can-not at this time be too often repeated, line upon line, precept upon precept..to innovate is not to reform. **1853** J. H. NEWMAN *Hist. Sk.* (1873) II. I. iv. 193 Efforts have been made..to innovate on the existing condition of its people. **1877** PUSEY in *Daily Express* 21 May, We the old Tractarians deliberately abstained from innovating in externals. **1965** *New Statesman* 9 Apr. 561/1 There is a willing market to offset a more reluctant British industry, whose failure to innovate fast enough has certainly made the British computer industry less competitive. **1971** *Physics Bull.* Dec. 707/2 The view has been put forward that the very large firms, the dinosaurs of the 20th century, do not truly

innovate and, indeed, may hinder innovation because they are so inflexible.

Hence †'**innovated** *ppl. a.*; '**innovating** *vbl. sb.* and *ppl. a.*

1591 PERCIVALL *Sp. Dict.*, *Inovation*, innouating. **1628** HOBBES *Thucyd.* (1822) 48 Their own innovating confederates. **1635** HAKEWILL *Apol.* v–vi. 338 What use of the elect shall have of the innovated world I.. as yet can not find. **1704** HEARNE *Duct. Hist.* (1714) I. 82 The Holy Professors of true Christianity, who.. oppos'd themselves to the innovated Idolatry and Superstition. **1866** GEO. ELIOT *F. Holt* Introd. 5 An innovating farmer, who talked of Sir Humphrey Davy, had been fairly driven out by popular dislike. **1877** Innovating [see 3 above]. **1972** C. LAYTON *Ten Innovations* I. i. 7 Study is needed of other possible tax incentives for small innovating enterprises. *Ibid.* 12 The small innovating firm crosses a whole series of thresholds as it grows in size.

innovation (ɪnəʊ'veɪʃən). [ad. L. *innovātiōn-em*, n. of action f. *innovāre* to INNOVATE: cf. F. *innovation* (1297 in Hatz.-Darm.).]

1. a. The action of innovating; the introduction of novelties; the alteration of what is established by the introduction of new elements or forms. †Formerly const. *of* (the thing altered or introduced).

1553 BRENDE *Q. Curtius* 221 b, Perdicas, whose ambicious mynde desirous of innouation, was (he sayde) to be preuented in time. **1561** T. NORTON *Calvin's Inst.* Table Contents, It is the duty of private men to obey, and not to make innovation of states after their own will. **1597** HOOKER *Eccl. Pol.* v. xlii. §11 To traduce him as an authour of suspitious innouation. **1614** SELDEN *Titles Hon.* 286 Thanes remained as a distinct name of dignitie, and vanisht not at the innouation of new honors. *a* **1639** WEBSTER *Appius & V.* v. iii, The hydra-headed multitude That only gape for innovation. **1796** BURKE *Corr.* (1844) III. 211 It is a revolt of innovation; and thereby, the very elements of society have been confounded and dissipated. **1824** L. MURRAY *Eng. Gram.* (ed. 5) I. 65 This spirit of innovation has extended itself to other parts of grammar, and especially to the names of the Tenses. **1874** GREEN *Sh. Hist.* vii. §1 Cranmer and his colleagues advanced yet more boldly in the career of innovation.

†**b.** Revolution (= L. *novæ res*). *Obs.*

1596 SHAKS. *1 Hen. IV*, v. i. 78 Poore Discontents, Which gape, and rub the Elbow at the newes Of hurly burly Innouation. **1633** T. STAFFORD *Pac. Hib.* I. xx. (1821) 206 For the same reason of innovation, he besought them to send unto him fiue Lasts of powder with match and lead.

2. a. A change made in the nature or fashion of anything; something newly introduced; a novel practice, method, etc.

1548 *Act 2 & 3 Edw. VI*, c. 1 To staye Innovacions or newe rites. **1641** (*title*) A Discovery of the notorius Proceedings of William Laud, Archbishop of Canterbury, in bringing Innovations into the Church. **1717** J. KEILL *Anim. Oecon.* Pref. (1738) 47 This Attraction.. is no Innovation in Philosophy. **1800** *Asiatic Ann. Reg., Misc. Tr.* 106/1 The tribute you demand from the Hindûs.. is an innovation and an infringement of the laws of Hindustân. *a* **1862** BUCKLE *Civiliz.* (1873) II. viii. 595 To them antiquity is synonymous with wisdom, and every improvement is a dangerous innovation. **1868** FREEMAN *Norm. Conq.* II. viii. 297 The sturdiest champions of Norman innovations.

†**b.** A political revolution; a rebellion or insurrection. (= L. *novæ res.*) *Obs.*

1601 R. JOHNSON *Kingd. & Commw.* (1603) 227 Neither doth he willingly arme them for feare of sedition and innovations. **1726** LEONI *Alberti's Archit.* I. 77/2 A Province so inclined to tumults and innovations.

3. *spec.* in *Sc. Law.* The alteration of an obligation; the substitution of a new obligation for the old: see quot.

1861 W. BELL *Dict. Law Scot.* 450/1 *Innovation*, is a technical expression, signifying the exchange, with the creditor's consent, of one obligation for another; so as to make the second obligation come in the place of the first, and be the only subsisting obligation against the debtor, both the original obligants remaining the same.

4. *Bot.* The formation of a new shoot at the apex of a stem or branch; *esp.* that which takes place at the apex of the thallus or leaf-bearing stem of mosses, the older parts dying off behind; also (with *pl.*) a new shoot thus formed.

1835 LINDLEY *Introd. Bot.* (1848) I. 168 Shoots which have not completed their growth have received the name of *innovations*, a term usually confined to mosses. **1845** *Florist's Jrnl.* 130 The lateral ones.. terminate a two-leaved branch, or innovation, while the central peduncle springs from the apex of the older branch. **1863** BERKELEY *Brit. Mosses* iii. 13 One mode of branching.. is known under the name of innovations. *Ibid.* Gloss. 312 *Innovations*, accessory branches produced generally after the fruit is perfect.

5. *Comm.* The action of introducing a new product into the market; a product newly brought on to the market.

1939 J. A. SCHUMPETER *Business Cycles* I. iii. 84 Innovation is possible without anything we should identify as invention, and invention does not necessarily induce innovation. **1958** J. JEWKES et al. *Sources Invention* ix. 249 It seems impossible to establish scientifically any final conclusion concerning the relation between monopoly and innovation. **1962** E. M. ROGERS *Diffusion of Innovations* v. 124 It matters little whether or not an innovation has a great degree of advantage over the idea it is replacing. What does matter is whether the individual perceives the relative advantage of the innovation. **1967** J. A. ALLEN *Sci. Innovation & Industr. Prosperity* ii. 8 Innovation is the bringing of an invention into widespread, practical use... Invention may thus be construed as the first stage of the much more extensive and complex total process of innovation.

6. innovation trunk, a kind of wardrobe trunk.

1912 *Bag, Portmanteau & Umbrella Trader* 20 Nov. 18/1 The Innovation Trunk Company.. makes a striking show of wardrobe trunks. They also specialise in the refitting of ordinary wardrobes according to their principle. **1913** A. BENNETT *Regent* iii. 83 Many parcels and boxes, comprising diverse items in the equipment of a man-about-town, such as tie-clips and Innovation trunks. **1915** E. PHILLPOTTS *Angel in House* I. 17 Robert and Manservant enter through the main entrance carrying Innovation trunk.

Hence **inno'vational** *a.*, of, pertaining to, or characterized by innovation; also in *Comm.*; **inno'vationist**, one who favours innovations.

1800 W. TAYLOR in *Monthly Mag.* VIII. 684 Writers, who bring against certain philosophic innovationists a clamorous charge of Vandalism. **1817** BENTHAM *Plan Parl. Reform* Introd. 194 A proposition so daring, so innovational. **1873** R. BLACK tr. *Guizot's France* II. xxv. 492 His kingly despotism was new, and, one might almost say, innovational. **1959** J. P. LEWIS *Business Conditions Analysis* v. xxiv. 534 The insights of economics do not illuminate the process of innovation very much... On the optimistic side of the innovational outlook, it can be argued, [etc.]. **1960** L. S. SILK *Research Revolution* iii. 50 In the past, the United States has had three great innovational pushes.

innovative ('ɪnəʊveɪtɪv), *a.* [f. as INNOVATE + -IVE.] Having the character or quality of innovating. (In quot. 1608, revolutionary.) *spec.* in *Comm.* in sense of INNOVATION 5.

1608 DAY *Hum. out of Br.* v. ii. (1860) 68 We ha yet performd but the least part of duetie, Your reinstalment: it rests, that with our bloud We keepe out innouatiue [*printed* innouasiue] violence. **1806** W. TAYLOR in *Ann. Rev.* IV. 239 Persons.. addicted to innovative politics. **1807** —— in *Monthly Rev.* LXXXIII. 91 An affected, innovative, technical strange nomenclature. **1873** F. HALL *Mod. English* 27 Some writers are, as to manner and diction, conservative, while others are innovative. **1970** N. ARMSTRONG et al. *First on Moon* i. 20 The Air Force.. sounded more exciting and more innovative. **1971** *Sci. Amer.* Mar. 14 His division is now involved with.. innovative building processes and systems. **1971** *Times* 6 Sept. 12 (Advt.), Well-known American company is introducing an innovative line of electro-optical measurement systems into the European Machine Tool and Metal Working industries. **1972** *Lebende Sprachen* XVII. 72/2 In order to release scarce manpower for the later phases of the innovative process, including marketing.

Hence '**innovatively** *adv.*, in an innovative manner; involving innovation; '**innovativeness**.

1962 E. M. ROGERS *Diffusion of Innovations* vii. 195 The innovativeness continuum may be divided into adopter categories. *Ibid.* x. 285 The present chapter is an attempt to demonstrate two means of predicting innovativeness. **1971** *Bull. Amer. Assoc. Univ. Professors* Sept. 337 My other two innovatively run courses.. are seemingly as successful as courses could be. **1973** *Black World* Mar. 23 The conventions of folk music might be employed in the traditional manner.. or innovatively, as is Miss Brooks' 'The Sermon on the Warpland'.

innovator ('ɪnəʊveɪtə(r)). Also 7 -er. [a. late L. *innovātor* (Gloss. Cyril.), agent-n. from *innovā-re* to INNOVATE. Cf. F. *innovateur* (1529 in Hatz.-Darm.).] One who innovates; an introducer of novelties or new methods; †a revolutionist.

1598 FLORIO, *Innouatore*, an innouator [**1611** innouater], alterer, disturber or changer. **1607** SHAKS. *Cor.* III. i. 175 My Selfe Attach thee as a Traitorous Innouator: A Foe to' th' publike Weale. **1625** BACON *Ess.*, *Innovations* (Arb.) 526 He that will not apply New Remedies, must expect New Euils: For Time is the greatest Innouatour. **1681** E. SCLATER *Serm. Putney* (ed. 2) 18 Moses was a Tyrant, and Aaron an Innovator. **1768** BOSWELL *Corsica* (ed. 2) 337 Of modern infidels and innovatours, he said 'Sir, these are all vain men'. **1882** G. MATHESON in *Expositor* Aug. 137 He was no innovator on the national faith.

†**b.** A changer or alterer *of* (a thing) by innovation. *Obs.*

1638 BAKER tr. *Balzac's Lett.* (vol. II) 202 There is no longer any.. safety for innovatours of our Language. *a* **1716** SOUTH *Serm.* (J.), Innovators of divine worship.

'**inno,vatory**, *a.* [f. as INNOVATE + -ORY.] Of innovating character or tendency.

1853 MISS SHEPPARD *Ch. Auchester* I. 251 So utterly would they have been spurned as innovatory. **1856** *Chamb. Jrnl.* VI. 401 Inveterate conservatives they are, despising all innovatory ideas. **1868** *Philatelist* II. 74 Modern innovatory improvements. **1965** *Listener* 23 Sept. 464/1 In these with-it days of innovatory cinematic trends. **1967** J. A. ALLEN *Sci. Innovation & Industr. Prosperity* ii. 25 There has been little deliberate innovatory effort over a long period. **1971** *Nature* 2 Apr. 301/3 Historians have been so impressed by the innovatory nature of modern science. **1972** *Physics Bull.* Mar. 151/2 Remembering that the major innovatory phase took place before 1939, most of this gain has resulted from sustained research and development by physicists.

†**i'nnovelty.** *Obs. rare*$^{-1}$. [IN-^{3}.] The quality of not being novel; the opposite of novelty.

1783 J. YOUNG *Crit. Gray's Elegy* (1810) 17 The innovelty of the views represses effusion.

innoxious (ɪ'nɒkʃəs), *a.* [ad. L. *innoxi-us*, f. *in-* (IN-^{3}) + *noxius* NOXIOUS: see -OUS.]

1. Not noxious or hurtful; harmless, innocuous.

1638 F. JUNIUS *Paint. of Ancients* 82 Propounding themselves hereafter an innoxious and happie life. **1703** J. SAVAGE *Lett. Antients* xiii. 70 The Poison Serpents produce remains innoxious to themselves. **1831** TRELAWNEY *Adv. Younger Son* I. 296 Even lions, when surfeited, are innoxious. **1843** SIR J. BOWRING in *Bentham's Wks.* VIII. 140 *note*, Alarm-clocks are innoctious and useful applications of this kind.

†**2.** Innocent, guiltless, blameless. *Obs. rare.*

1623 COCKERAM, *Innoxious*, blamelesse, guiltlesse. **1735** POPE *Prol. Sat.* 395 The good man walk'd innoxious thro' his age. **1794** MATHIAS *Purs. Lit.* (1798) 146 Innoxious man: yet what may truth avail!

innoxiously (ɪ'nɒkʃəslɪ), *adv.* [f. prec. + -LY^{2}.] In an innoxious manner, harmlessly, without evil effects.

1646 SIR T. BROWNE *Pseud. Ep.* VII. xvii. 378 Animals that can innoxiously digest these poisons become antidotall unto the poyson digested. **1816** SCOTT *Antiq.* xiv, I ask nothing of society but the permission of walking innoxiously through the path of life. **1862** G. U. POPE tr. *Dubois' People India* II. xxix. (ed. 2) 222 They stood in extreme awe of their curse, which was believed never to fall innoxiously.

innoxiousness (ɪ'nɒkʃəsnɪs). [f. as prec. + -NESS.] The quality or fact of being innoxious; harmlessness.

1665–6 *Phil. Trans.* I. 385 Some Observations about Insects and their Inoxiousness. **1673** *Ibid.* VIII. Ded. 3 The Innoxiousness of the huge weight of the vast Atmosphere to all Terrestrial inhabitants. **1818** BENTHAM *Parl. Ref. Catech.* (ed. 2) 39 Look to speechifying and writing, and the comparative beneficialness and innoxiousness of the sort of information to be expected from the two sources.

†**i'nnoyandness.** *Obs. rare*$^{-1}$. [f. IN-^{3} + *noyand*, pr. pple. of NOY *v.*, to hurt, annoy + -NESS; after L. *innocentia*.] Innocence.

a **1340** HAMPOLE *Psalter* xxv. 1, I am ingone in myn innoyandnes [*in innocentia mea ingressus sum*].

innoyaunce, obs. form of ANNOYANCE.

†'**innuate**, *v. Obs. rare*$^{-1}$. [irreg. f. L. *innuĕ-re* to intimate: see -ATE^{3} (but perhaps misprint for *insinuate*).] *trans.* To intimate, hint.

c **1611** CHAPMAN *Iliad* XIX. *Comm.*, As if Agamemnon would innuate that, as this sow being splayed is free from Venus, so had he never attempted the dishonour of Briseis.

in nubibus: see IN *Lat. prep.*

†**i'nnubile**, *a. Obs. rare*$^{-1}$. [f. IN-^{3} + NUBILE, L. *nūbilis* marriageable.] Not nubile; not of marriageable age.

1642 G. EGLISHAM *Forerunner Revenge* 12 The Bride was yet innubile.

†**i'nnubilous**, *a. Obs. rare.* [f. L. *innūbilus*, f. *in-* (IN-^{3}) + *nūbilus* NUBILOUS: see -OUS.] Not nubilous or cloudy; cloudless.

1656 BLOUNT *Glossogr.*, *Innubilous*, fair, without clouds, serene. **1708** *Brit. Apollo* No. 33. 2/1 We will.. descend from out Innubilous Empireum.

in nuce: see IN *Lat. prep.*

‖**innuendo** (ɪnju:'ɛndəʊ). Also *erron.* inuendo. Pl. innuendoes, (7–8 -do's, 8–9 -dos). [L., = 'by nodding at, pointing to, meaning, intimating', abl. gerund of *innuĕre* to nod to, signify, mean; in med.L. used to introduce a parenthetic clause.]

I. 1. The med.L. formula used esp. in legal documents to introduce a parenthetical explanation of the precise reference of a preceding noun or pronoun; = meaning, to wit, that is to say.

1564 *Child-Marr.* 123 What-soeuer thinge it is, that knave your sonne—innuendo this deponentes sonne—made it, & brought it to the Church. **1656** BLOUNT *Glossogr.*, *Innuendo*, is a Law term, most used in Declarations and other pleadings.. to declare and design the person or thing which was named incertain before; as to say, he (*innuendo* the Plaintiff) is a Theef. **1701** DE FOE *Let. To How* in *Misc.* (1703) 343 'But when Religion comes to be the Mode of a Country, so many Painted Hypocrites, there's the Word, get into the Church, that Guile is not to be seen till it arrive to Apostacy'. Pray, Sir, who can these Painted Hypocrites refer to, that you should say, *Innuendo*, All those that are not of my Party, or that are not so stingy as I?

II. Hence, as sb.

2. The parenthetical explanation or specification itself; an interpolated or appended explanation of, or construction put upon a word, expression, or passage; *esp.* the injurious meaning or signification alleged to be conveyed by words not *per se* injurious or actionable, which, in an action for libel or slander, is usually introduced into the record and issue by the words 'meaning thereby', after the expressions alleged to have been used.

1701 DE FOE *Let. to How* in *Misc.* 341, I cannot find one Word in the whole Book which can, no, not with the help of an *Innuendo*, be so much as pretended to look that way. **1714** SCROGGS *Courts-Leet* (ed. 3) 196 No *Innuendo* can make such Words actionable. *a* **1715** BURNET *Own Time* II. III. 571 This, by an inuendo, was said to be an evidence to prove, that he [Sidney] was in a plot against the king's life. *a* **1726** GILBERT *Cases Law & Equity* (1760) 116 That to tie up the Meaning of the first Words to Bankruptcy, the Plaintiff had laid an *Innuendo*. **1753** *Stewart's Trial* 72 We have seen doubtful actions by the help of innuendoes construed criminally.

b. The words or expressions thus parenthetically explained, or needing explanation; a blank to be filled up with the name of the person to whom it is alleged to refer.

1755 CHESTERF. in *World* No. 105 ¶11 By publishing the names at full length in your paper, I humbly conceive, said he, that you avoid all the troublesome consequences of *innuendo's*. **1769–72** *Junius Lett.* Pref. 11 He told the jury.. that they had nothing to determine, except the fact of printing and publishing, and whether or no the blanks or inuendoes were properly filled up in the information. **1802** *Edin. Rev.* Oct. 106 An indictment for a libel, with all the *inuendos* filled up.

3. An oblique hint, indirect suggestion; an allusive remark concerning a person or thing, esp. one of a depreciatory kind.

1678 R. L'ESTRANGE *Seneca's Mor.* (1702) 517 His Innuendo's are infinitely more Instructive than his Words at length. **1694** COLLIER *Ess. Mor. Subj.* I. (1709) 39 What a broad *Inuendo* is here upon the Beneficed Clergy? **1732** *Pol. Ballads* (1860) II. 234 For Sir Philip well knows That his *innuendoes* Will serve him no longer in verse or in prose. **1788** BURNS *Let. to Mrs. Dunlop* 13 Nov., They so intoxicated me with their sly insinuations and delicate inuendos of compliment, that if it had not been for a lucky recollection.. I had certainly looked upon myself as a person of no small consequence. **1850** W. IRVING *Goldsmith* xxxi. 305 [He] sought by nods and winks and inuendoes to intimate his authorship. **1855** MOTLEY *Dutch Rep.* II. iv. (1866) 200 The Cardinal omitted nothing in the way of anecdote or inuendo, which could injure the character of the leading nobles.

4. *attrib.* and *Comb.*

1772 *Batchelor* (1773) II. 156 He justly termed it an inuendo resolution. **1807** E. S. BARRETT *Rising Sun* III. 66 That thou wert..exhibited to public scorn, by any innuendo-making Attorney-General.

Hence **innu'endoish** *a.*, having the character of innuendo. *rare.*

1861 G. MEREDITH *Evan Harrington* xxxviii, The Countess's confessional thoughts were all inuendoish, aërial; too delicate to live in our shameless tongue.

innu'endo, *v.* [f. prec. sb.]

1. *intr.* To utter or make innuendoes.

1705 [see INNUENDOING]. **1852** R. S. SURTEES *Sponge's Sp. Tour* (1893) 192 We have heard that there were six old ladies ..innuendoing, nodding, and hinting to their friends, 'that, etc.'. **1896** *Voice* (N.Y.) 8 Oct. 1, I believe that.. it is better for a man to 'say his say' straight, than to kite and innuendo, no matter how sweetly.

2. *trans.* To bring *into* (some position) by making innuendoes.

1757 WARBURTON *Lett.* (1809) 245 The rogues.. would.. inuendo me into some disaffection against the government.

3. To convey by innuendo, to insinuate.

1858 R. S. SURTEES *Ask Mamma* i, [He] would inuendo his own version of the story as dexterously as he could.

4. *Law.* To interpret or construe by attaching an innuendo.

1851 BAGEHOT *Lit. Stud.* (1879) I. 349 They take the other side's article piece by piece, and comment on him, and, as they say in libel cases, *innuendo* him. **1890** LD. KINNEAR in *Times* 6 Feb. 7/6 What is the ground upon which you innuendo the statement in this letter to mean that he was in point of fact given to drink?

Hence **innu'endoing** *ppl. a.*, making innuendoes.

1705 S. WHATELY in W. S. Perry *Hist. Coll. Amer. Col. Ch.* I. 177 His insinuating and Innuendoing methods. **1839–49** SIR J. STEPHEN *Eccl. Biog.* (1850) II. 32 This innuendoing special pleader.

[**innuent,** *a.* Significant. First in Todd (1818), based on a misreading of *inuent* = *invent* in the following.

1628 BURTON *Anat. Mel.* II. ii. IV. 264 He may apply his minde..to Heraldry, Antiquity, inuent Impresses, Emblems, make Epithalamiums [etc.].]

Innuit ('ɪnuːɪt). Also **Inuit.** [ad. Inupik Eskimo *inuit* people, pl. of *inuk* man.] An Eskimo; the Eskimos collectively. Also *attrib.* or as *adj.*

1765 C. DRACHARD in *Ethnohistory* (1972) XIX. 136 They [*sc.* the Labrador Eskimos] also by way of eminence in contra-distinction to the Europeans call themselves Innuit (the Men). **1774** B. LA TROBE *Brief Acct. Mission Esquimaux Indians Labrador* 10 Formerly, they..looked upon the Europeans as upon dogs, giving them the appellation, Kablunets, that is, Barbarians, but called themselves Innuit, which signifies men. **1850** [see ESKIMO *sb.* 1]. **1860** MAYNE REID *Odd People* 88 They [*sc.* the Esquimaux] generally call themselves 'Inuit' (pronounced enn-oo-eet), a word which signifies 'men'. **1864** *Spectator* 31 Dec. 1506 The Innuits believe in a supreme Being called Anguta, whose daughter Sidne is the creator and the tutelary deity of the Innuit people. **1864** C. F. HALL *Life with Esquimaux* I. 122 A highly-intelligent Innuit..was boat-steerer. **1895** [see ESKIMO *sb.* 1]. **1903** J. LONDON *People of Abyss* xxvii. 313 In Alaska, along the banks of the Yukon River, near its mouth, live the Innuit folk. **1919** W. T. GRENFELL *Labrador Doctor* (1920) vii. 140 With the influx of white settlers from Devon and Dorset, Scotland and France the 'Innuits' were driven farther and farther north. **1963** *North* (Ottawa) May–June 34 Without us the Innuit go hungry. **1973** *Sci. Amer.* Sept. 196/3 Nearly 400 sculptors of quality are represented here from the *inuit*.

†**i'nnumberable,** *a. Obs.* Forms: 5–6 **inno(u)mberable,** (**-nowmber-**), **-no(u)mbr-,** 6 **innumberable.** [orig. a. F. *innombrable* (1341 in Hatz.-Darm.), ad. L. *innumerābil-is*: subseq. conformed to *number*.] = INNUMERABLE.

1434 MISYN *Mend. Life* 110 Vicis innowmberabill þai cees not to gedyr. *c* **1450** *Mirour Saluacioun* 58 So were in our lady mary innoumbrable virtus schinyng. **1450–1530** *Myrr. our Ladye* 185 The innomberable company of aungels. **1590** BARROW & GREENWOOD in *Confer.* 43 All the.. innumberable enormous Canons & Constitucions of Antichrist.

Hence †**i'nnumberably** *adv.*

c **1450** *Mirour Saluacioun* 4305 So als crist ouer alle seints is haly innoumbrably.

i,nnumera'bility. [ad. L. *innumerābilitāt-em*, f. *inumerābil-is* INNUMERABLE: cf. obs. F. *innumerableté* (16–17th c. in Hollyband, Cotgr.).] The quality of being innumerable.

1607 TOPSELL *Four-f. Beasts* (1658) 561 There is so great an innumerability of Lybian Oxen, of so great swiftnesse and celerity, that the Hunters are many times deceived in hunting them. *a* **1619** FOTHERBY *Atheom.* (1622) 217 He reiecteth this innumerability of Causes.

innumerable (ɪ'njuːmərəb(ə)l), *a.* [ad. L. *innumerābil-is*, f. *in-* (IN-[3]) + *numerābil-is* NUMERABLE.]

Incapable of being numbered or reckoned; not to be counted for multitude; numberless, countless. Often with exaggerative force.

a. With singular sb.; now only with *host*, *multitude*, and similar collectives.

1340 *Ayenb.* 267 Þe innumerable uelaȝrede of þe holy martires. **1432–50** tr. *Higden* (Rolls) I. 391 Then Vnguste.. was compassede abowte with a innumerable hoste of Briteynes at a felde callede Merc. *c* **1485** *Digby Myst.* (1882) II. 1100 Itt is In-nvmerabyll to expresse,..of my loye how myche itt es. **1509** HAWES *Past. Pleas.* xxxvii. (Percy Soc.) 193 He blew out so much fyre innumerable. **1526** TINDALE *Heb.* xii. 22 But ye are come vnto the mounte Sion..and to an innumerable sight [1611 companie, **1881** innumerable hosts] of angels. **1535** COVERDALE *2 Macc.* iii. 6 The treasury in Ierusalem was full of innumerable money. **1590** SPENSER *F.Q.* II. xii. 35 An innumerable flight Of harmefull fowles. **1606** G. W[OODCOCKE] tr. *Hist. Ivstine* 24 a, By reason of their innumerable greedines. **1613** SHAKS. *Hen. VIII*, III. ii. 326 That you haue sent inumerable substance. *a* **1654** SELDEN *Table-t.*, *King* (Arb.) 62 Twenty pound of Diamonds, which is a sum innumerable. **1718** WATTS *Hymn*, '*Not to the terrors of the Lord*' iii, Behold the innumerable host Of Angels cloth'd in light! **1719** DE FOE *Crusoe* I. xiv, The innumerable crowd of thoughts. **1816** BRYANT *Thanatopsis* 74 So live, that when thy summons comes to join The innumerable caravan [etc.].

transf. **1877** L. MORRIS *Epic Hades* II. 127 The innumerable laughter of the sea [lit. rendering of Æschylus' ἀνήριθμον γέλασμα, the 'many-twinkling smile of Ocean']. **1889** *Harper's Mag.* Apr. 822/2 The grasshoppers spin into mine ear A small innumerable sound.

b. Now usually with pl. sb. (which it often follows).

c **1450** *Craft of Louers* (R.), Precious stones reckened innumerable. **1482** *Monk of Evesham* (Arb.) 76 Eueryche on of hem were ponyshte in peynys innumerable. **1535** COVERDALE *Ps.* xxxix. [xl.] 12 Innumerable troubles are come aboute me. **1563** W. FULKE *Meteors* (1640) 38 b, The milke way.. Democritus.. sayd, that it was nothing else but innumerable little Starres. **1667** MILTON *P.L.* IX. 1089 Ye Cedars, with innumerable boughs. **1725** DE FOE *Voy. round World* (1840) 108 We were sure to meet with islands innumerable. **1836** W. IRVING *Astoria* I. 246 He fell.. pierced with innumerable arrows. **1847** TENNYSON *Princ.* VII. 207 Murmuring of innumerable bees.

c. *absol.* †Formerly sometimes followed by *of*.

1535 TINDALE *Tracy's Test.* 11 Likewise..did innumerable more. **1535** FISHER *Wks.* (1876) 382 When innumerable of soules haue..receyued as much the loue of Christ Iesu. **1545** BRINKLOW *Lament.* (1874) 90 London.. hath..innumerable of poore people. **1561** DAUS tr. *Bullinger on Apoc.* (1573) 103 b, I beleeue that innumerable..haue at length seene the filthines of Papistrie. **1691** RAY *Collect. Words, Acc. Err.* 155 In the words *God, Rod, Horn,* and innumerable the like. **1830** PUSEY *Hist. Inquiry* II. 244 While innumerable profess this religion, only few observe it.

†**d.** *absol.* with *pl.* form. *Obs. rare.*

1796 *Mod. Gulliver's Trav.* 207 There are almost innumerables who say, wish, and hope so. **1807** SOUTHEY *Lett.* (1856) I. 426 He wrote sonnets—a class of poems in which there must be innumerables which are good for nothing.

Hence **i'nnumerably** *adv.*; **i'nnumerableness.**

1561 DAUS tr. *Bullinger on Apoc.* (1573) 80 To esteme the power of kings by the greatnes, hugenes, and innumerablenes of their armyes. **1574** WHITGIFT *Def. Aunsw.* ii. Wks. 1851 I. 241 St. Augustine speaketh of the unreasonable multitude of ceremonies, using these words, *innumerabiliter variantur*, 'are varied innumerably'. **1580** HOLLYBAND *Treas. Fr. Tong*, *Innumerableté*, innumerablenesse. **1653** WALTON *Angler* viii. 162 Where they will breed, they breed innumerably. **1787** GLOVER *Athenaid* XXIX. Poems (1810) 178/2 The light Of sparkling brands, innumerably wav'd.

innumeracy (ɪ'njuːmərəsɪ). [f. IN-[3] + NUMERACY.] The quality or state of being innumerate.

1959 *15 to 18: Rep. Cent. Advisory Council for Educ.* (*Eng.*) (Ministry of Educ.) I. xxv. 271 If his numeracy has stopped short at the usual Fifth Form level, he is in danger of relapsing into innumeracy. **1960** *Times Rev. Industry* June 59/3 Handicap on British business was the 'innumeracy' of the population. **1965** *New Scientist* 5 Aug. 348/1 The word 'innumeracy', to describe an intellectual disability in regard to mathematics (and, by reference, to science) has become one of the vogue words of our time. **1970** *Daily Tel.* 22 Dec. 8 Lord Snow was complaining a decade ago about the vice of innumeracy.

†**i'nnumeral,** *a. Obs.* [ad. L. *innumerāl-is* numberless, f. *in-* (IN-[3]) + *numerālis* of or pertaining to number, NUMERAL.]

= INNUMERABLE.

1585 *Sc. Acts Jas. VI* (1814) III. 422 The Innumerall oppressionis committit aganis hir..familie. **1625** FLETCHER *Nob. Gent.* IV. iii, All his suspitions Which are innumerall.

innumerate (ɪ'njuːmərət), *a.* and *sb.* [f. IN-[3] + NUMERATE *a.*] **A.** *adj.* Unacquainted with the basic principles and ideas of mathematics and science.

1959 *15 to 18: Rep. Cent. Advisory Council for Educ.* (*Eng.*) (Ministry of Educ.) I. xxv. 270 When we say that a historian or a linguist is 'innumerate' we mean that he cannot even begin to understand what scientists and mathematicians are talking about. **1967** *Times Rev. Industry* June 108/3 'Why are so many of us innumerate?' asked Lord Annan... The answer..was quite simple. For years, girls and boys have given up maths at 15 or 16, thus maiming themselves intellectually. **1969** *Physics Bull.* Sept. 383/2 In this short book, intended for the general reader (though not for the innumerate one), a distinguished engineer describes how computers work. **1971** *Daily Tel.* 13 Oct. 2/7 It alleges that one student in every four entering colleges has had no sixth form experience, and that up to one-fifth are 'practically innumerate'.

B. *sb.* One who is innumerate; freq. (with *the*) in *pl.* sense.

1971 *Daily Tel.* 1 Feb. 15 The old gibe that 'you can prove anything with figures' is perhaps not heard so frequently now. It was the classic defence of the innumerate. **1971** *Nature* 2 Apr. 306/1 The conflict is between the technological and the humane, and derives from various related sources: first, the fable that educational research can be a science as pure as classical physics..and finally the innumerate's fascination with statistics. **1972** *Ibid.* 10 Mar. 55/1 At the other extreme stand the recalcitrant innumerate, proclaiming themselves the last defenders of humanism.

†**i'nnumerate,** †**innume'ration,** erroneous ff. ENUMERATE, ENUMERATION.

1611 RICH *Honest. Age* (Percy Soc.) 15 He setteth downe (as it were) by innumeration, so many vanities as for breuities sake I will here omit to speake of. *a* **1649** A. LEIGHTON in Chandler *Hist. Persec.* (1736) 371 To innumerate the rest of your Petitioner's heavy Pressures.

†**i'nnumered,** *a. Obs. rare*$^{-1}$. [A partial adaptation of L. *innumerāt-us*, which would properly give **innumerate*.] Unnumbered, numberless.

1471 RIPLEY *Comp. Alch.* in Ashm. (1652) 118 Benefyts.. ynnumeryd by sapience.

innumerous (ɪ'njuːmərəs), *a. arch.* [ad. late L. *innumerōs-us* countless, f. *in-* (IN-[3]) + *numerōsus* NUMEROUS.]

1. Without number, too numerous to be counted; innumerable, numberless, countless. Now only *poetical* or *rhetorical*.

1536 BELLENDEN *Cron. Scot* Proheme Cosmogr. 329 An syne posseid triumphe innumerus With lang empire, and hie felicitie. **1667** MILTON *P.L.* VII. 455 The Earth obey'd, and strait..teem'd at a Birth Innumerous living Creatures. **1740** DYER *Ruins Rome* 173 Columns innumerous As cedars proud on Canaan's verdant heights. **1855** J. H. NEWMAN *Callista* xv. (1890) 170 At length the huge innumerous mass was put into motion. **1880** W. WATSON *Prince's Quest* (1892) 9 Cool with the presence of innumerous trees, And fountains playing before palaces.

Comb. **1728–46** THOMSON *Spring* 570 All this innumerous-coloured scene of things.

2. Void of metrical or rhythmical number. *rare.*

1886 *Spectator* 6 Nov. 1487 There is sure to be a host of them in rhyme, blank verse, and numerous or innumerous prose.

†**i'nnurtured,** *a. Obs. rare*$^{-1}$. [IN-[3].] Not nurtured or educated; ill educated.

1660 R. COKE *Power & Subj.* 137 Nor is any man better in any kind whatsoever for being innurtured or ignorant.

innutrient (ɪ'njuːtrɪənt), *a.* [IN-[3].] Not nutrient or nourishing, innutritious.

1822–34 *Good's Study Med.* (ed. 4) IV. 36 The appetite is feeble and capricious and shews a desire for the most unaccountable and innutrient substances. **1857** GEO. ELIOT *Sc. Cler. Life, A. Barton* i, They are smooth and innutrient as the summit of the Rev. Amos Barton's head.

innutrition[1] (ɪnjuː'trɪʃən). [IN-[3], or ad. mod.L. *innūtritiōn-em*, f. *in-* (IN-[3]) + *nūtri-re* to nourish.] Lack of nutrition, failure of nourishment. ***innutrition of the bones*** (mod.L. *innūtritio ossium*) = RICKETS.

1796 *Duncan's Ann. Med.* I. 216 *Innutritio ossium*.. Innutrition of the bones. **1822–34** *Good's Study Med.* (ed. 4) I. 372 Many patients..seem..to be carried off by hectic fever, or some other cause of irritation, rather than by actual innutrition. **1879** H. SPENCER *Data Ethics* ii. §4 Ninety-nine in the hundred of these minute animals..disappear either by innutrition or by destruction. *a* **1884** M. PATTISON *Mem.* (1885) 208, I was gradually drawn out of it..by the slow process of innutrition of the religious brain.

†**innu'trition**[2]. *Obs. rare*$^{-0}$. [n. of action f. L. *innūtrīre* to nourish in (something), f. *in-* (IN-[2]) + *nūtrīre* to nourish.]

1656 BLOUNT *Glossogr.*, *Innutrition*, a nourishing or bringing up. **1658** PHILLIPS, *Innutrition*, a nourishing inwardly.

innutritious (ɪnjuː'trɪʃəs), *a.* [IN-[3].] Not nutritious; affording no nourishment. Also *transf.*

1796 SEWARD *Anecd.* I. 174 (Jod.) Masticating some light and innutritious substance. **1809–10** COLERIDGE *Friend* (1818) II. 288 Too scanty and too innutritious food. **1872** HUXLEY *Phys.* vi. 139 The whole purpose of the alimentary apparatus is to separate these proteids, &c. from the innutritious residue. **1893** SELOUS *Trav. S.E. Africa* 109

Living for a long time on very innutritious food. **1905** *Sydney Morning Herald* 15 Feb. 4/6 The..teacher is offered for his mental food these innutritious products as the bread of life. **1916** E. V. LUCAS *Vermilion Box* cxxv. 141 As a rule I have found that the soldier who sits opposite one on railway journeys is an innutritious person, whether he has been to the front or not.

innutritive (ɪ'nju:trɪtɪv), *a.* [IN-³.] Not nutritive; innutritious.
1844 T. J. GRAHAM *Dom. Med.* 363 The chyle, or nutritious part, being absorbed into the blood..while the excrementitious, or innutritive part passes..into the larger bowels.

inny, early ME. infinitive of INN *v.*

ino- ('aɪnəʊ), comb. form of Gr. ἴς, ἰν-ός, ἰν- muscle, fibre, nerve, strength, an element in some mod. scientific terms, chiefly physiological, as *inogen, inolite, inolith*: see these words.

†**ino'bedience.** *Obs.* [a. OF. *inobedience*, or ad. late L. *inobēdientia* (Augustine), f. *in-* (IN-³) + *obœd-, obēdientia* OBEDIENCE: see -ENCE.] The withholding of obedience; = DISOBEDIENCE. (Rare after 1600.)
a **1225** *Ancr. R.* 198 þe vifte hweolp hette Inobedience, þet is, þet child þet ne buhð nout his eldre. **1382** WYCLIF *Rom.* v. 19 By inobedience of o man manye ben ordeyned synneris. *c* **1440** *Gesta Rom.* I. lviii. 242 (Harl. MS.) þerefore late vs obeye in all thinges to god, that we be not dampnid for owr inobedience. **1563** FOXE *A. & M.* 767/1 Notorious and apparant contemptes and other inobediences. **1677** GALE *Crt. Gentiles* III. 131 Clement Alexandrinus..asserted that obedience and inobedience was in our power. **1684** tr. *Bonet's Merc. Compit.* xx. 867 It must be attributed to the inobedience of the Matter.

†**ino'bediency.** *Obs. rare.* [f. late L. *inobēdientia*: see prec. and -ENCY.] Disobedience.
1432-50 tr. *Higden* (Rolls) VI. 123 Winfridus..whom he deposide soone after for inobediency. **1634** in *Antid. Sabbat. Err.* (1636) A iij b, The man..hath..this inobediency punished.

†**ino'bedient,** *a.* and *sb. Obs.* [a. OF. *inobedient*, or ad. late L. *inobēdient-em* (Augustine), f. *in-* (IN-³) + *obœdient-em* OBEDIENT.]
A. *adj.* Withholding obedience; = DISOBEDIENT.
1377 LANGL. *P. Pl.* B. XIII. 282 He bosteth and braggeth with many bolde othes, And in-obedient to ben vndernome of any lyf lyuynge. *c* **1386** CHAUCER *Pars. T.* ¶318 Inobedient is he that disobeyeth for despit to the comandementz of god and to hise souereyns And to his goostly fader. *c* **1430** *Pilgr. Lyf Manhode* I. cxxii. (1869) 65 Wherfore it was neuere afterward rebelle ne inobedient to his comaundement. **1533-4** *Act 25 Hen. VIII*, c. 12 Diuers & sondry wilfull & inobedient subiectes of this realme. *a* **1631** DONNE *Lett. to Sir H. G.* Wks. (Alford) VI. 408 Heretofore the inobedient Puritans and now the over-obedient Papists attempt you. **1805** SOUTHEY *Madoc* II. vi, Irresolute They heard, and inobedient; to obey Fearing, yet fearful to remain.
b. *transf.* Of a thing: = DISOBEDIENT b.
1495 *Trevisa's Barth. De P.R.* XVI. iv. (W. de W.) 554 As longe as bras or laton is medlyd wyth the substaunce of gold, it cleueth alway vnder the hamour and is inobedyent [*MSS.* vnobedient] to take due shape. **1668** CULPEPPER & COLE *Barthol. Anat.* I. xi. 26 By digesting the inobedient Chylus, which could not be tamed, in the Stomach.
B. *sb.* A disobedient or perverse person.
1548 HALL *Chron., Hen. V* 71 Landes gotten or to be gotten and overcome in the name of our said father upon rebelles and inobedientes to hym.
Hence **ino'bediently** *adv.*, in a disobedient manner; disobediently.
1536 LADY MARY in Burnet *Hist. Ref.* I. III. (1679) 206 The Kings Highness my Father, whom I have obstinately and inobediently offended. **1563** FOXE *A. & M.* 712/1 Hath with his eares hard dyuers persons..vnreuerently, inobediently, and not faythfully speake of the kinges maiestye.

†**ino'beisance.** *Obs. rare*⁻¹. In 4 -shaunce. [a. OF. *inobeissance*, f. *in-* (IN-³) + *obeissance* obedience, OBEISANCE.] = INOBEDIENCE.
1382 WYCLIF *Bible, Pref. Ep. Jerome* iii, Redi to vndirȝoken al inobeishaunce.

†**ino'beisant,** *a. Obs. rare.* In 4 -shaunt. [a. OF. *inobeissant*, f. *in-* (IN-³) + *obeissant* obedient, OBEISANT.] Disobedient; = INOBEDIENT.
1382 WYCLIF *Deut.* viii. 20 ȝe shulen perishe, if inobeishaunt ȝe shulen be to the voys of the Lord ȝoure God.

inoble, obs. form of ENNOBLE *v.*

inobli'gality. *nonce-wd.* [f. IN-³ + *obligality* (f. OBLIGAL + -ITY).] The quality of not being obligatory.
a **1663** SANDERSON *Cases Consc.* vii. (1678) 128 The unlawfulness, and consequently the invalidity, or inobligality thereof.

inob'noxious, *a. rare.* [IN-³.] Not obnoxious; not exposed *to*; not offensive, inoffensive.
1659 H. L'ESTRANGE *Alliance Div. Offices* 99 The want of expresse rule..left our Liturgy, in this point, not altogether inobnoxious to exceptions. **1682** NORRIS *Hierocles* 101 The way to live an unenvy'd and inobnoxious life. **1818** BENTHAM *Ch. Eng.* 120 Not to speak of Jews, who..as they write not much, either to attack the establishment or to defend themselves, are comparatively inobnoxious.

inob'scurable, *a. rare.* [ad. late L. *inobscūrābilis* (Tertullian), f. *in-* (IN-³) + *obscūrāre* to OBSCURE; see -ABLE.] That cannot be obscured.
1881 E. MYERS in *Fraser's Mag.* Feb. 195 That inobscurable brilliance..and that keen sentience of the sweet and bitter of human love.

†**inob'sequent,** *a. Obs. rare*⁻¹. [ad. L. *inobsequent-em*, f. *in-* (IN-³) + *obsequent-em* OBSEQUENT.] Unsubmissive, disobedient.
1604 F. HERING *Modest Def.* A iv b, Men, being ill house-doues, haue been very vnruly and inobsequent to the counsell of their Physicians.

inob'sequiousness. *rare*⁻¹. [IN-³.] Want of obsequiousness or deference.
1625 DONNE *Serm.* 3 Apr. 40 There may bee an inobsequiousnesse and an indiligence in the Wife.

inobservable (ɪnɒb'zɜːvəb(ə)l), *a.* Now *rare.* [ad. L. *inobservābilis*, f. *in-* (IN-³) + *observābilis* OBSERVABLE. (So in mod.F.)] Incapable of being observed; not noticeable.
1600 E. BLOUNT tr. *Conestaggio* 179 Men who..expresly to cause disorders, made commaundements inobservable. **1616** BULLOKAR, *Inobseruable*, which cannot be obserued or marked. **1649** J. H. *Motion to Parl. Adv. Learn.* 9 Time hath defaced all the bounds of the Roman conquests, and left them as invisible and inobservable, as the flight of any bird. **1650** R. STAPYLTON *Strada's Low C. Warres* IX. 40 Christ himself, that afforded his presence to the Jews and when he pleased was inobservable.

inobservance (ɪnɒb'zɜːvəns). [a. F. *inobservance* (1534 in Godef. *Compl.*), ad. L. *inobservāntia*; see next and -ANCE.]
1. Failure to observe or notice; inattention, heedlessness.
1611 FLORIO, *Innoseruanza*, inobseruance. **1628** DONNE *Serm.* vi. 52 This which some doe out of slacknesse and in-observance and infirmity, many men..do out of impiety. **1768-74** TUCKER *Lt. Nat.* (1834) I. 529 Inobservance of second causes throws men into all the delusions of superstition and enthusiasm. **1806** *Monthly Mag.* XXI. 385 The drowsy inobservance of Dr. Johnson is no where more conspicuous than in the diversity of his mode of spelling. **1879** FARRAR *St. Paul* I. 20 St. Paul's inobservance of these things..due to the..paramount importance of other thoughts.
2. The not keeping or non-observance of a law, custom, bond, promise, etc.
a **1626** BACON *Judic. Charge*, etc. 16 (T.) The breach and inobservance of certain wholesome and politick laws. **1642** ROGERS *Naaman* 614 Beware of oversight and inobservance of promises. **1740** WARBURTON *Div. Legat.* v. iv. Wks. 1811 V. 121 By considering the effects which the observance or inobservance of it [the Law] would have on mankind. **1837-9** HALLAM *Hist. Lit.* I. I. iv. §69. 313 They justly blame ..his inobservance of propriety. **1888** H. C. LEA *Hist. Inquis.* II. 15 He was taxed by the legate with inobservance of the conditions of the peace.

inobservancy (ɪnɒb'zɜːvənsɪ). *rare.* [ad. L. *inobservāntia*, n. of quality f. *inobservānt-em*; see next, and -ANCY.]
1. Want of attention or notice; = prec. 1.
1677 GILPIN *Demonol.* (1867) 90 Through the weakness and inobservancy of the reprover. **1822** M. A. KELTY *Osmond* II. 39 Even the quiet inobservancy of Mr. Lascelles could scarcely overlook the change.
2. Neglect of observing or keeping; = prec. 2; an instance of this.
1824 SOUTHEY *Bk. of Ch.* (1841) 410 These..were connived at for inobservancies, which in them were harmless, because they did not proceed from a spirit of insubordination.

inobservant (ɪnɒb'zɜːvənt), *a.* [ad. L. *inobservānt-em* unobservant: see IN-³ and OBSERVANT.] That does not observe or notice; unobserving.
1663 J. SPENCER *Prodigies* (1665) 144 [Men are] stupidly inobservant of those rational signs and intimations. **1685** J. SCOTT *Chr. Life* II. 42 Considering what heedless and inobservant Creatures we are. **1768-74** TUCKER *Lt. Nat.* (1834) I. 523 Nor can [God] remain ignorant or inobservant of what impulses He gives. **1847** BUSHNELL *Chr. Nurt.* II. iii. (1861) 273 One must be a very inobservant person, not to have noticed [etc.].
Hence **inob'servantness**, inobservance.
1659 D. PELL *Impr. Sea* 282 For their Cæcity, and inobservantness of the works of God.

inobservation (ɪnɒbzə'veɪʃən). *rare.* [f. IN-³ + OBSERVATION, perh. a. F. *inobservation* (1572 in Godef. *Compl.*).]
†**1.** The non-observance or not keeping *of* a law, promise, etc. *Obs.*
1579 FENTON *Guicciard.* XVII. 974 Themperour being moued with thinobseruation of the French king, would not propounde for a common surety. **1653** HOLCROFT *Procopius, Goth. Wars* III. 82 They call the inobservation of Lawes, Mercy.
2. Want of observation or attention; failure to observe; inobservance.
1727 SHUCKFORD *Creation* 118 (T.) These writers are in all this guilty of the most shamefull inobservation.

†**in'obstinate,** *v. Obs. nonce-wd.* [IN-².] *trans.* To render obstinate, confirm in obstinacy.
1599 SANDYS *Europæ Spec.* (1632) 196 The endlesse and ill fruicts of these contentions..which in-obstinate the Iew, [and] shake the faith of the Christian.

inob'tainable, *a. rare.* [IN-³.] Not obtainable; not to be obtained.
a **1718** PENN *Tracts* Wks. 1726 I. 701 Unity in minute or circumstantial Things, that perhaps is inobtainable. **1735** SEWEL *Dutch Dict.*, *Onverwervelyk*, inobtainable.

inobtrusive (ɪnɒb'truːsɪv), *a. rare.* [IN-³.] Not obtrusive, unobtrusive; modest, retiring.
1796 COLERIDGE *Refl. having left place Retirem.* 23 The inobtrusive song of Happiness. **1804** PARR in *Bentham's Wks.* (1838-43) X. 417/2 He is a very inobtrusive, enlightened..prelate. *a* **1834** COLERIDGE *Shaks. Notes* (1875) 211 Note the inobtrusive..mode of introducing the main character.
Hence **inob'trusively** *adv.*, in an inobtrusive manner; **inob'trusiveness.**
1847 CRAIG, *Inobtrusively*, see Unobtrusively. *Inobtrusiveness*, see Unobtrusiveness.

ino'carpin. *Chem.* [f. mod. Bot.L. *Inocarpus* (f. INO- fibrous + Gr. καρπός fruit) + -IN.] A red colouring matter contained in the juice of *Inocarpus edulis*, a tree of Asia and the E. India islands.
1865-72 in WATTS *Dict. Chem.* III. 274.

†**i'noccate,** *v. Obs. rare*⁻⁰. [f. ppl. stem of L. *inoccāre*, f. *in-* (IN-²) + *occāre* to harrow.]
1623 COCKERAM, *Inoccate*, to harrow the ground.

†**inoc'ciduous,** *a. Obs. rare*⁻⁰. [f. L. *inoccidu-us* never setting + -OUS.] Of a star: Never setting or going down.
1656 BLOUNT *Glossogr.*, *Inocciduous*, that never useth to fall, that never sleeps, that never sets or goes down, as some stars do. *Thom.* **1658** in PHILLIPS.

inoccupation (ɪnɒkjuː'peɪʃən). [IN-³.] Want of occupation; unoccupied condition.
1786 W. THOMSON *Watson's Philip III* (1793) II. VI. 214 The languor of inoccupation..the great curse of human life. **1841** HOR. SMITH *Moneyed Man* III. vi. 154 Aweary..of the inoccupation which allowed my melancholy thoughts to prey upon themselves. **1883** HOLME LEE *Loving & Serving* II. ii. 26 Total inoccupation was very hard upon him.

inoch, obs. form of ENOUGH.

i-nocked, ME. pa. pple. of NOCK *v.*

inoculability (ɪˌnɒkjʊlə'bɪlɪtɪ). [f. next + -ITY. Cf. mod.F. *inoculabilité*.] The quality of being inoculable or communicable by inoculation.
1847-9 TODD *Cycl. Anat.* IV. 124/2 The inoculability of growths has not been maintained except in the instance of cancer. **1876** tr. *Wagner's Gen. Pathol.* (ed. 6) 134 The inoculability of measles and of scarlet fever has not yet been certainly demonstrated. **1898** P. MANSON *Trop. Diseases* xxxvii. 564 This inoculability of boils is apt to be overlooked.

inoculable (ɪ'nɒkjʊləb(ə)l), *a.* [ad. L. type **inoculābil-is*, f. *inoculāre* to INOCULATE: see -ABLE. Cf. F. *inoculable* (Littré).]
a. Of a person: Capable of being infected with a disease by inoculation. **b.** Of a disease: Capable of being communicated or transmitted by inoculation. **c.** Of matter or virus: That may inoculate a person or transmit a disease.
1847-9 TODD *Cycl. Anat.* IV. 114/1 The varieties of pus ..in the Class (B) differ from those in the Class (A) in being inoculable. **1855** *Jrnl. R. Agric. Soc.* XVI. II. 402 The injured or battered ones..are little liable to come in contact with the inoculable matter. **1898** P. MANSON *Trop. Dis.* viii. 144 Plague is a specific, inoculable and otherwise communicable disease.

inoculant (ɪ'nɒkjʊlənt). [f. INOCUL(ATE *v.* + -ANT¹.] A substance suitable for use in inoculation; *spec.* in *Metallurgy*, a substance with which molten metal is inoculated.
1911 *Experiment Station Rec.* XLVII. III. 234 State laws concerning the sale of seeds and legume inoculants. **1944** *Jrnl. Iron & Steel Inst.* CL. 144A The second purpose was to measure the effect of increasing-percentages of steel and varying amounts of inoculants. **1960** *Ibid.* CXCV. 222/1 The use of graphitizing inoculants, usually based on silicides, is described. **1962** A. G. GUY *Physical Metall. for Engineers* v. 149 Typical inoculants are ferrosilicon and calcium-silicon, very small amounts of which are effective in reducing flake size.

inocular (ɪ'nɒkjʊlə(r)), *a. Entom.* [IN-².] Of an antenna: Inserted in a sinus in the inner margin of the compound eye, which thus partly surrounds its base.
1826 KIRBY & SP. *Entomol.* III. xxxiv. 514 In the Capricorn-beetles they [antennæ] may be termed inocular, or placed in a sinus of the eye.

inoculate (ɪ'nɒkjʊleɪt), *v.* Also 5 en-. [f. L. *inoculāt-*, ppl. stem of *inoculāre* to engraft, implant, f. *in-* (IN-²) + *oculus* eye, bud.]
1. a. *trans.* (*Hort.*) To set or insert (an 'eye', bud, or scion) in a plant for propagation; to subject (a plant) to the operation of budding; to

propagate by inoculation; to bud (one plant) *into*, *on*, or *upon* (another).

c **1420** *Pallad. on Husb.* v. 123 Peches han their seson At May Kalendes hem tenoculate. **1589** Fleming *Virg. Georg.* ii. 21 To graft And to inoculat or set yoong imps into the stocke. **1668** R. Steele *Husbandm. Calling* vi. (1672) 166 The crab-tree stock must be cut off, and then into it must the scion be ingraffed and inoculated, before it can be an apple in his orchard. **1707** *Curios. in Husb. & Gard.* 269 A dextrous Hand inoculates a Rose-tree Bud upon an Apple-Stock. **1752** Mrs. Delany *Autobiog. & Corr.* III. 133, I have just inoculated two orange-trees of my own raising. **1838** *Penny Cycl.* XII. 483/1 It is therefore found most advantageous to bud or inoculate them in the summer, when both scion and stock are in the state of equal vegetation.

absol. **1621–51** Burton *Anat. Mel.* ii. ii. iv. 272 Cincinnatus, Cato, Tully.. how have they been pleased.. to prune, plant, inoculate and graft. **1669** Worlidge *Syst. Agric.* (1681) 296 Now begin to Inoculate. **1697** Dryden *Virg. Georg.* ii. 103 Various are the ways to change the state Of Plants, to Bud, to Graff, t' Inoculate.

b. *fig.* To engraft.

1602 Shaks. *Ham.* iii. i. 118 Vertue cannot so innocculate our old stocke, but we shall rellish of it. *a* **1639** Wotton in *Reliq.* (1651) 342 Pompey had one very ignoble custome, to insert, or (as I may term it) to inoculate himself into other mens merits and praises. **1752** Chesterf. *Lett.* (1792) III. ccxciii. 348 You have yet very little experience and knowledge of the world; now I wish to inoculate mine upon you. *a* **1797** H. Walpole *Mem. Geo. II* (1847) I. vi. 188 The Pelhams.. always inoculated private quarrels on affairs of state.

†**2. a.** *transf.* To join or unite by insertion (as the scion is inserted into the stock so as to become one with it). *Obs.*

1647 Trapp *Comm. Mark* xiii. 1 Huge stones and so cunningly cemented, as it were inoculated, the one into the other. **1658** R. Franck *North. Mem.* (1821) 110 This is the rock and that which you see elevated in place and inoculated to it is an artificial fabrick developed.. on the very breast of this prodigious mountain. **1668** Culpepper & Cole *Barthol. Anat.* i. xxxvii. 82 The smallest Twigs of the Branches [of the arteries] are inoculated into the greater.

b. *intr.* To become joined or united with continuity of substance.

1646 Sir T. Browne *Pseud. Ep.* iii. xv. 142 Their Eggs in chaines or links together (which sometime conjoyne and inoculate into each other). *c* **1720** W. Gibson *Farrier's Guide* (1738) i. iv. 42 The fifth pair inoculate with the sixth.

3. a. *trans.* (*Path.*) To engraft or implant (a disease, or the germ or virus) upon an individual, by a process of inoculation (q.v.); to introduce (cells or organisms to be cultured) *into* a culture medium or its container.

1722 *Lond. Gaz.* No. 6040/11 The Experiment of inoculating the Small-Pox upon.. Criminals. **1799** *Med. Jrnl.* I. 323 Knowing that cow-pox has a temporary influence upon small-pox, we can suppress the progress of it by immediately inoculating cow-pox. **1801** E. Darwin *Zoon.* (ed. 3) III. 370 Since the above was first published [1794] the cow-pox.. has been successfully inoculated on the human subject. **1892** *Daily News* 12 Sept. 2/6 A man with a scratch might inoculate the poisonous germ from contact with an infected animal. **1896** *Allbutt's Syst. Med.* I. 95 Virulent anthrax bacilli are inoculated subcutaneously into an ordinary rabbit and into one that has been rendered immune. **1928** L. E. H. Whitby *Med. Bacteriol.* iii. 46 The loop or needle must be sterilized in the flame before being charged with the material to be inoculated. **1939** K. L. Burdon *Med. Microbiol.* xx. 273 At this temperature it [*sc.* agar] is still liquid and yet cool enough so that the organisms to be inoculated will not be killed by its heat. **1964** Wheeler & Volk *Basic Microbiol.* viii. 89/1 The pour-plate method consists of inoculating the mixed culture into a test tube containing melted agar. **1970** Passmore & Robson *Compan. Med. Stud.* II. xviii. 50/1 When bacteria are inoculated into a fresh fluid medium there is little or no increase in their number for a period.

b. To impregnate (a person or animal) with the virus or germs of a disease; *spec.* for the purpose of inducing a milder form of the disease and rendering the subject immune from its ordinary attacks. First used in connexion with small-pox; then with vaccine inoculation; now with contagious or bacterial diseases generally: see inoculation 2. Also, to introduce infective material into (a plant) or cells or organisms for culture into (a culture medium or a vessel containing one).

1722 *Lond. Gaz.* No. 6045/8 A Child has been inoculated with the Matter. Five.. Children have been inoculated of the Small Pox. **1775** Johnson *Journ. West. Isl., Dunvegan,* He has disarmed it [small-pox] of its terror at Muack, by inoculating eighty of his people. **1799** *Med. Jrnl.* I. 319 With the cow-pox matter were inoculated Mr. Darke's servant, ..[and] Mr. Colborne's three children.. all by a puncture in the left arm. **1871** Tyndall *Fragm. Sci.* (1879) I. v. 145 He proved that the worms inoculate each other. **1886** H. M. Biggs tr. *Hueppe's Methods Bacteriol. Investigation* iv. 171 It [*sc.* the nutrient solution] is then inoculated with a few drops of the mixture of bacteria to be tested. **1920** E. F. Smith *Introd. Bacterial Dis. Plants* ii. 112 In studying a particular disease, the student will.. seek to inoculate those parts of the plant which naturally develop the disease. **1925** [see inoculum]. **1933** K. M. Smith *Rec. Adv. Study Plant Viruses* viii. 196 The plant tissue is macerated.. and then rubbed over the foliage to be inoculated by means of the swab. **1956** *Nature* 18 Feb. 302/2 When White Burley tobacco seedlings in a glass-house are inoculated with the virus from cowpea.. they become systemically infected. **1962** F. J. Baker *Handbk. Bacteriol. Technique* v. 56 When inoculating broth tubes, care must be taken not to spill the contents.

c. *absol.* or *intr.* To perform inoculation.

1765 Gale in *Phil. Trans.* LV. 203 Then inoculate, and repeat the powders. **1789** W. Buchan *Dom. Med.* (1790) 239 Many approve of inoculating on the breast. **1799** Dr. Sims in *Med. Jrnl.* I. 231 Dr. Jenner.. ventured to inoculate with the matter of a putrid sore, with a view of determining if this also had the power of preserving from the contagion of the small-pox. **1891** Greenough White *Philos. Amer. Lit.* iii. 22 (Funk) Zabdiel Boylston.. inoculated for the small-pox with distinguished success.

d. *fig. trans.* To imbue (a person, community, etc.) *with* a feeling, opinion, habit, etc.

1824 W. Irving *T. Trav.* I. 102 My parents had tried in vain to inoculate me with wisdom. **1826** Disraeli *Viv. Grey* ii. vi, I must not inoculate you with my bad spirits. **1868** M. Pattison *Academ. Org.* v. 123 Fox and Wolsey sought.. to inoculate Oxford from within with that classical spirit which could not be forced upon it from without.

4. *Metallurgy.* To add a small quantity of some substance to (metal, esp. iron, about to be poured) in order to produce a smaller grain size or otherwise to modify the microstructure of the cast metal.

1931 *Proc. Inst. Brit. Foundrymen* XXIII. 96 Small grain-size and high density can be.. achieved by 'dosing' or inoculating the alloy so that prior to the main solidification taking place the alloy contains numerous evenly and finely-dispersed nuclei to form centres of crystallisation. **1933** *Jrnl. Iron & Steel Inst.* CXXXVIII. 640 A bath of iron which would normally cast white is prepared and is 'inoculated', by the addition of suitable proportions of nickel and silicon, to cause graphitisation. **1963** C. H. Samans *Metallic Materials Engin.* vi. 316 When it is desired to improve the structure of the cast iron and, consequently, its mechanical properties, the metal often is inoculated just before pouring. **1971** *Daily Tel.* 4 Nov. 5 (Advt.), Semi-continuous casting is standard practice in the [aluminium] industry and, unless the melt is inoculated or grain-refined to produce a fine-grained equiaxed structure, the process has an inherent tendency to grow massive columnar crystals.

†**i'noculated,** *a. Obs. rare.* [f. med. or mod.L. *inoculāt-us* (f. *in-* (in-³) + *oculātus* furnished with eyes) + -ed.] Not having an 'eye' or perforation.

1599 A. M. tr. *Gabelhouer's Bk. Physicke* 34/1 Inoculated Pearles, or Pearles without perforationes. [Glossed on fly-leaf 'unholed'.] **1604** [see next, 1].

i'noculated, *ppl. a.* [f. inoculate + -ed¹.]

1. *Hort.* Engrafted by budding.

1604 R. Cawdrey *Table Alph., Inoculated,* grafted, or vnholed. **1662** Ray *Three Itin.* iii. 182 The old Christmas thorn is now quite dead and gone, but they have several inoculated plants of it about the town. **1679** Evelyn *Kal. Hort.* Sept. (ed. 5) 24 Release Inoculated Buds.

2. *Path.* **a.** Of a person, etc.: Having undergone inoculation. **b.** Of a disease, etc.: Introduced by inoculation.

1722 Nettleton in *Phil. Trans.* XXXII. 214 The Opposers of Inoculation affirm, that two Persons died of the Inoculated Small Pox. **1799** W. Tooke *View Russian Emp.* II. 161 By universal experience we find that of the inoculated only three die out of 1000. **1799** *Med. Jrnl.* I. 10 The inoculated cow-pox is as much milder than the natural, as the inoculated small-pox is milder than the natural. **1873** T. H. Green *Introd. Pathol.* (ed. 2) 229 In those [cases] in which the inoculated liquids contained fewer bacteria and were less active, the process was more protracted.

3. *Metallurgy.* Applied to cast iron whose properties have been improved by inoculation.

1932 *Proc. Inst. Brit. Foundrymen* XXIV. 137 What the author says about the germ theory and inoculated irons is exceedingly interesting. **1956** *Jrnl. Iron & Steel Inst.* CLXXXIV. 89/2 The inoculated cast irons are more elastic, they have smaller damping capacities, and their electrical and magnetic properties are close to those of steels.

i'noculating, *vbl. sb.* [f. as prec. + -ing¹.] The action of the vb. inoculate in its various uses: inoculation.

1598 Florio, *Innoculatione,* an inoculating. *a* **1626** Bacon *New Atl.* (1631) 33 We practise.. all Conclusions of Grafting and Inoculating, as well of Wilde-Trees as Fruit-Trees. **1691** Ray *Creation* i. (1692) 57 Grafting and inoculating, and pruning of Fruit-Trees. **1771** Mrs. Harris in *Priv. Lett. Ld. Malmesbury* I. 231 Inoculation is going on very briskly here.. Is there any inoculating in Spain? **1802** W. Forsyth *Fruit Trees* (1824) 320 The time for inoculating is from the middle of June to the middle of August.

attrib. **1776** J. Adams in *Fam. Lett.* (1876) 189, I could almost wish that an inoculating hospital was opened in every town in New England. **1776** M. Cutler in *Life, Jrnls. & Corr.* (1888) I. 58 The Inoculating Hospital.

inoculation (ɪnɒkju:'leɪʃən). [ad. L. *inoculātiōn-em* engrafting, budding, n. of action f. *inoculāre* to inoculate. Cf. F. *inoculation* (1580 in sense 1, 1752 in sense 2).]

1. a. *Hort.* The insertion of an eye or bud of one plant under the bark of another for the purpose of raising flowers or fruit different from those of the stock; grafting by budding; an instance of this.

1589 Fleming *Virg. Georg.* ii. 21 *note,* Semination, insition, inoculation, or implastration, the three kindes of grafting. **1658** Sir T. Browne *Gard. Cyrus* iv. 172 Nor could we ever make it [mistletoe] grow where nature had not planted it; as we have in vain attempted by inocculation and incision, upon its native or forreign stock. **1709** Addison *Tatler* No. 146 ¶7 Harsh Fruits.. enriched by proper Grafts and Inoculations. **1768–74** Tucker *Lt. Nat.* (1834) II. 161 Gardeners by inoculation cause the trees to bear other than the natural fruits.

b. *transf.* A junction in which the two parts become continuous.

1615 Crooke *Body of Man* 187 Now betweene the hollow and the gate-veines wee know there is no communion vnlesse it bee by the mingling of their mouths in the substance of the liuer; for some of the new writers haue obserued many such inoculations betwixt them in that place.

2. *Path.* The introduction into the body, by puncture of the skin, or through a wound, of the virus or germs of an infectious disease.

a. Originally applied, after 1700, to the intentional introduction of the virus of small-pox in order to induce a mild and local attack of the disease, and render the subject immune from future contagion; also, in 1799, to *vaccine inoculation*, afterwards called vaccination; and in 19th c. to the similar treatment of other infectious or contagious diseases.

1714 E. Timone in *Phil. Trans.* (Abr.) VI. 88 (*title*), An Account of the procuring of the Small Pox by Incision or Inoculation, as it has for some time been practised at Constantinople. **1722** Lady M. W. Montagu *Lett., to C'tess Mar* (1887) I. 338 Accounts of the growth and spreading of the inoculation of the small-pox, which is become almost a general practice, attended with great success. **1732** Arbuthnot *Rules of Diet* 414 It is evident by Inoculation that the smallest quantity of Matter mixed with the Blood produceth the Disease. **1743** Mrs. Delany *Autobiog. & Corr.* (1861) II. 240 In great joy that the inoculation of the girls has been as successful as that of the boys, and they have one fear less to struggle with. **1773** Goldsm. *Stoops to Conq.* ii. Wks. (Globe) 657/1 Since inoculation began there is no such thing to be seen as a plain woman. **1798** Jenner *Causes Variolæ Vaccinæ* 37 The boy was rendered unfit for inoculation from having felt the effects of a contagious fever in a work-house. **1800** *Med. Jrnl.* IV. 253 On the Introduction of the Vaccine Inoculation at Paris. **1856** Miss Mulock *J. Halifax* xxv, Though inoculation and vaccination had made it less fatal among the upper classes. **1866** A. Flint *Princ. Med.* (1880) 1041 As a means of rendering the disease.. mild.. and of preventing pitting, inoculation had been practised from time immemorial in China and Persia.

b. Now also applied to the introduction (accidentally or otherwise) of the virus or germs of any bacterial disease into the body through a wound. Also, the (usually intended) introduction of infective material into a plant or of cells or organisms to be cultured into a culture medium.

1838 *Penny Cycl.* XII. 399/2 *Hydrophobia*.. is the disease occasioned by inoculation with the saliva of a rabid animal. **1861** Bumstead *Ven. Dis.* (1879) 350 The chancroid can be developed upon the head and face by artificial inoculation. **1881** G. M. Sternberg tr. *Magnin's Bacteria* (1883) 265 Anthrax is an infectious disease of animals which may be transmitted to man by inoculation. This occurs, occasionally, from the bite of an insect (fly) which has been feeding upon the carcass of an infected animal; and also from accidental inoculation while handling hides, wool, etc., taken from the victims of anthrax. **1886** H. M. Biggs tr. *Hueppe's Methods Bacteriol. Investigation* iv. 160 Inoculations are made by picking out, with a platinum needle.. a particle from a pure culture.. and introducing it quickly into the solution. **1910** Hiss & Zinsser *Text-bk. Bacteriol.* viii. 141 For the inoculation of solid media and the making of stab cultures, a straight 'needle' or wire should be used. **1920** E. F. Smith *Introd. Bacterial Dis. Plants* iii. iii. 165 The inoculations may be made by spraying or by touching the leaf-tip with an infected platinum needle. **1933** K. M. Smith *Rec. Adv. Study Plant Viruses* viii. 194 The second method of artificial virus transmission is that of inoculation, using this term in its restricted sense of actual application of the virus-containing sap to the plant tissue. **1958** Pelczar & Reid *Microbiol.* viii. 81/1 After inoculation of the media.. and following a suitable period of incubation, it is possible to determine the cultural characteristics of the organism being studied.

c. *fig.* The imbuing of a person *with* feelings, opinions, etc.

1824 Byron *Juan* xv. l, The inoculation Of others with her own opinions. **1864** Bowen *Logic* xiii. 448 We must all begin life without any opinions which we can call our own by any better right than that of passive inheritance or unconscious inoculation. **1876** Mozley *Univ. Serm.* vi. (1877) 124 A new feature of the world.. the popular pursuit of natural beauty, the inoculation of the crowd with it.

3. *Metallurgy.* The addition of an inoculant to molten metal, esp. iron (see inoculate *v.* 4).

1932 *Proc. Inst. Brit. Foundrymen* XXIV. 122 After remelting the graphite particles were restored artificially, when the metal solidified pearlite-flake graphite. The process of putting graphite back into the melt is conveniently referred to as 'inoculation'. **1950** *Jrnl. Iron & Steel Inst.* CLXVI. 260/1 D. J. Reese gave some details of the production and properties of nodular cast iron produced in the U.S.A., using the technique of magnesium inoculation. **1963** B. Harocopos *Princ. Struct. Metall.* viii. 104 The graphite may also be made to appear as spheroids in a ferritic matrix by inoculation with an alloy of silicon, magnesium and zirconium.. and the resulting iron has a U.T.S. of 32 t.s.i., elongation 15%, in the annealed state. **1968** E. N. Simons *Outl. Metall.* iv. 88 In the inoculation of cast iron in Britain calcium silicide is added to the ladle or the cupola spout at the rate of about 120 oz./ton.

4. *attrib.* and *Comb.*, as ***inoculation process***, ***-tuberculosis***; ***inoculation-mad*** adj.

1760 E. Lucas *Jrnls. & Lett.* (1850) 27 But yᵉ people in Charles Town were inoculation mad, I think I may well call it. **1897** *Allbutt's Syst. Med.* II. 20 Inoculation-tuberculosis has occurred in the human being. *Ibid.* 636 Such inoculation process, whichever way induced, is known as vaccination.

inoculative (ɪˈnɒkjʊleɪtɪv, -ətɪv), *a.* [f. L. *inoculāt-* (see INOCULATE) + -IVE.] Characterized by or pertaining to inoculation.
1716 M. DAVIES *Athen. Brit.* II. To Rdr. 2 That Insitive and Inoculative method seems to bid fair for the Cure..of that common Author-Distemper or Companion, call'd φιλοδοξία. **1881** J. SIMON in *Nature* No. 616. 373/2 The rapid multiplication of the tubercle-micrococcus in the blood and tissues of any inoculated animal can be verified both by microscopical observation, and by inoculative experiment. **1887** *Spectator* 3 Sept. 1170 The inoculative cure of patients bitten by mad dogs.

inoculator (ɪˈnɒkjʊleɪtə(r)). Also 7 -er. [a. L. *inoculātor* an engrafter, agent-n. f. *inoculāre* to INOCULATE.] One who or that which inoculates.
1611 FLORIO, *Innestatore*, a graffer, an inoculater. *a* **1626** BACON *New Atl.* (1631) 44 These wee call Inoculators. **1725-6** FREIND *Hist. Physic* (J.), Had John a Gaddesden been now living, he would have been at the head of the inoculators. **1799** *Med. Jrnl.* I. 115 Every one..knows the strenuous opposition which the first inoculators had to encounter, both in England and America, from vulgar prejudice. **1867** BAKER *Nile Tribut.* viii. (1872) 110 Holy relics, that are inoculators of all manner of contagious diseases.

†**inocuˈlatrix.** *Obs. rare*⁻⁰. [fem. of prec.]
1623 COCKERAM II, Shee that Grafteth, *Inocculatrix*.

†**iˈnoculer,** *v. Obs. rare*⁻¹. In 5 en-. [irreg. a. F. *inoculer*.] trans. To inoculate or engraft.
c **1420** *Pallad. on Husb.* v. 130 In cold lond now the figtre plaunte is sette, And graffed in the stook or in the rynde.. And hem tenoculer ek haue in mynde.

iˈnoculist. *rare.* [a. F. *inoculiste* (Littré), f. *inoculer* to INOCULATE: see -IST.] One who is versed in, or advocates, inoculation.
1776 in *Narragansett Hist. Reg.* (1886-7) V. 352 Practitioners and Inoculists may be served with them [*sc.* medicines], if applied for soon. **1886** *Pall Mall G.* 15 May 3/1 M. Pasteur. The great inoculist has explained to Dr. Mott the theory and practice of his discovery.

inoculum (ɪˈnɒkjʊləm). Pl. inocula. [mod.L., f. L. *inoculāre* to INOCULATE *v.*] (A quantity of) infective material used for or capable of inoculating an organism or culture medium.
1902 J. W. H. EYRE *Elem. Bacteriol. Technique* xv. 267 (*heading*) The preparation of the inoculum. **1925** C. H. BROWNING *Bacteriol.* iii. 47 The needle, charged with the inoculum, is introduced into the tube and..the broth..is now said to have been 'inoculated'. **1949** N. G. HEATLEY in H. W. Florey et al. *Antibiotics* I. iv. 212 The reason why small inocula (down to single cells) do not normally grow out was thought to be due to the inhibitory power of a number of substances. **1950** J. C. WALKER *Plant Path.* viii. 347 Since the fungi overwinter on debris, sanitary measures are helpful in reducing spring inoculum. **1970** W. H. SMITH *Tree Path.* xxiii. 243 Early in an epidemic..the absolute rate of increase of disease is small,..as only a limited quantity of inoculum is available. **1973** *Nature* 16 Feb. 456/1 It is highly tumorigenic (inocula of 10^2 cells produce fatal tumours in the animals).

†**iˈnodiate,** *v. Obs.* [f. L. type *inodiāre (f. *in-* (IN-²) + *odi-um* hate; perh. in med.L.; cf. It. *inodiare*, FLORIO) + -ATE³.] *trans.* To bring into odium, render odious or hateful.
1657 W. MORICE *Coena quasi Κοινὴ* Def. xiii. 185, I wish some of them were not more culpable for inodiating Ministers. **16..** SOUTH *Twelve Serm.* (1717) VI. 242 He inflicts them for quite other Ends..partly to inodiate, and imbitter Sin to the chastised Sinner. **1698** *Ibid.* (1727) III. Ded. Abp. Marsh A iij b, Represented, or rather reprobated under the inodiating Character of High Churchmen. **1721** *Addr. Hereford* 10 Feb. in *Lond. Gaz.* No. 5932/1 He hath [never] by inodiating Characters..alienated..Affections.

†**inˈodorate,** *a. Obs.* [IN-³.] Unscented.
1626 BACON *Sylva* §507 Whites are more Inodorate..than Flowers of the same kinde Coloured; As is found in Single White Violets, White-Roses [etc.]. *Ibid.*, Blossoms of trees that are white are commonly inodorate.

†**inˈodorate,** *v. Obs. rare*⁻⁰. [f. ppl. stem of L. *inodōrāre*, f. *in-* (IN-²) + *odōrāre* to give a smell to.] *trans.* To perfume (Cockeram, 1623).
Hence †**inodoˈration.** *Obs. rare*⁻⁰.
1658 PHILLIPS, *Inodoration*, a making to smell, a perfuming.

inodorous (ɪnˈəʊdərəs), *a.* [f. L. *inodōr-us* (f. *in-* (IN-³) + *odōrus* scented, odorous) + -OUS.]
a. Destitute of odour; without smell or scent.
1666 BOYLE *Formes & Qual.* Wks. 1772 III. 111 Moderately dephlegmed oil of vitriol is wont to be inodorous. **1756** C. LUCAS *Ess. Waters* I. 82 No water can be thought pure, but such as is perfectly inodorous. **1796** C. MARSHALL *Garden.* xix. (1813) 377 The single white lilies are very sweet, but the doubles are inodorous. **1871** ROSCOE *Elem. Chem.* 86 Carbon dioxide gas is colourless and inodorous, but possesses a slightly acid taste.
b. Malodorous; having an unpleasant smell. Also *fig.* or *transf.*
1823 *Reading Mercury* in *Spirit of Public Jrnls. M.DCCC.XXIII* (1825) 206 The smell at this time was certainly somewhat inodorous, and was like almost any thing but a nosegay. **1858** *Sat. Rev.* 27 Mar. 308/1 Ceremented in inodorous fallacies, he has gone to corrupt amid old arithmetical dross and the rotting refuse of deceased paradoxes. **1861** C. M. YONGE *Young Step-Mother* viii. 98 Brown, inodorous materials for petticoats, blouses, and trowsers.

Hence **inˈodorously** *adv.*, without smell; **inˈodorousness**, the quality of being without smell (Webster, 1864).
1859 SALA *Gaslight & D.* xviii. 206 Smoke curling up the chimney (not altogether inodorously).

inoffe, obs. form of ENOUGH.

†**inoˈffend,** *v. Obs. rare*⁻¹. [(?) IN-³.] *trans.* (?) Not to offend.
1559 KNOX *First Blast* (Arb.) App. 58 My conscience beareth me reacord that maliciouslie nor of purpose I inoffended your grace.

inoˈffending, *a. rare.* [IN-³.] Unoffending.
1853 KANE *Grinnell Exp.* xiii. (1856) 95 Favoring us with some bear play, snapping at the inoffending icicles.

†**inoˈffensible,** *a. Obs. rare*⁻⁰. [IN-³.]
1611 COTGR., *Inoffencible*, inoffencible, not to be hurt.

inoffensive (ɪnəˈfɛnsɪv), *a.* [IN-³. Cf. mod.F. *inoffensif* (Dict. Acad. 1835).]
1. Doing or causing no harm; harmless, innocuous, unoffending.
1598 [implied in INOFFENSIVELY]. **1646** SIR T. BROWNE *Pseud. Ep.* VI. vi. 305 Wee dye notwithstanding in harmlesse and inoffensive errors. **1655** FULLER *Hist. Camb.* (1840) 213 An inoffensive man for life and conversation..nothing of viciousness could be charged upon him. *a* **1715** BURNET *Own Time* I. IV. 802 The nation had never known such an inoffensive march of an army. **1790** BEATTIE *Moral Sc.* I. ii. v. §316 Useful and inoffensive animals have a claim to our tenderness. **1853** C. BRONTE *Villette* xxvii. (1876) 305, I could not have tormented a being as inoffensive as a shadow.
2. Not objectionable, not obnoxious or offensive; not offending the senses; not a cause of offence.
1622 PEACHAM *Compl. Gent.* xi. (1634) 103 A more delightfull and in-offensive recreation. **1667** MILTON *P.L.* v. 345 For drink the Grape She crushes, inoffensive moust. **1744** BERKELEY *Siris* §9 An inoffensive medicine and agreeable to the stomach. **1876** *Trans. Clin. Soc.* IX. 13 The wound has discharged freely, the discharge being quite healthy and inoffensive.

inoffensively (ɪnəˈfɛnsɪvlɪ), *adv.* [f. prec. + -LY².] In an inoffensive manner; so as not to give offence; without offence; harmlessly.
1598 BP. HALL *Sat.* Postsc. H iv, Tho were shee [Poetry] a more vnworthie Mistresse, I thinke she might be inoffensiuely serued with the broken Messes of our twelue-a-clocke houres. **1646** P. BULKELEY *Gospel Covt.* I. 111 To walk more exactly and inoffensively, considering we have our way so plain before us. **1788** W. EDEN in *G. Rose's Diaries* (1860) I. 76 Ambassadors..who have gone through the same career inoffensively and inefficiently. **1896** MRS. CAFFYN *Quaker Grandmother* 130 She took up her violin which reposed inoffensively in a snug corner.

inoffensiveness (ɪnəˈfɛnsɪvnɪs). [f. as prec. + -NESS.] The quality or condition of being inoffensive; harmlessness.
1641 'SMECTYMNUUS' *Vind. Answ.* ii. 35 But might the complying of our Papists be attributed soly to the inoffensivenesse of our Liturgie. **1663** BOYLE *Usef. Exp. Nat. Philos.* ii. 50 Christ commands his Disciples to learn of Serpents and Pigeons prudence and inoffensiveness. **1750** PRINGLE in *Phil. Trans.* XLVI. 482 What makes the Difference between the stale Urine and other putrid Substances still more specific, is, its Inoffensiveness with regard to Health. *a* **1854** H. REED *Lect. Eng. Hist.* ix. (1855) 285 His offence was nothing more than his pure inoffensiveness, his unresisting meekness.

inofficial (ɪnəˈfɪʃəl), *a. rare.* [IN-³.] Not official; unofficial.
1632 *Star Chamb. Cases* (Camden) 174, I must lay a fyne of 300li upon Martin for dealing soe iniudicially. He was the officiall, but herein inofficiall. **1834** E. EVERETT *Orations* (1850) I. 515 It raised him into a new moral power in the state; an inofficial dictator of principle. **1864** *Reader* No. 99. 635/1 In an inofficial form.

inofficious (ɪnəˈfɪʃəs), *a.* [ad. L. *inofficiōsus*, f. *in-* (IN-³) + *officiōsus* obliging, dutiful, officious: see -OUS. Cf. F. *inofficieux* (1495 in Hatz.-Darm.).]
†**1.** Not ready to do one's duty or 'office'; not inclined to do good offices; disobliging. *Obs.*
1603 B. JONSON *King's Entertainm.* Sp. Genius, Up, thou tame River, wake..Thow drown'st thy selfe in inofficious sleep. **1651** tr. *Life Father Sarpi* (1676) 93 There he acknowledges himself to be severe, inofficious, and hard to please. **1706** PHILLIPS, *Inofficious*, backward in doing one any good Office, or Turn; discourteous, disobliging.
b. *Law.* Not in accordance with moral duty.
1663 *Bullokar's Eng. Expos.*, *Inofficious*, as that Will is called by Civilians, wherein they are omitted, or but slightly provided for, that chiefly ought to be considered. **1765** BLACKSTONE *Comm.* I. xvi. 448 Suggesting that the parent had lost the use of his reason, when he made the inofficious testament. **1785** PALEY *Mor. Philos.* (1818) I. 355 Let not a father hope to excuse an inofficious disposition of his fortune by alleging, that 'every man may do what he will with his own'. **1883** *Wharton's Law Lex.*, *Inofficious testament*, a will not in accordance with the testator's natural affection and moral duties.
2. Without office, function, or operation.
1884 LD. SELBORNE in *Law Times Rep.* L. 314/1 Any other construction..would make either the former or the latter part of the 1st sub-section inofficious and superfluous. **1885** *Ibid.* LII. 404/1 Where the operative part and the recital are at variance, the recital must be treated as inofficious.
Hence **inofficiˈosity** (see above, 1 b); **inoˈfficiously** *adv.*; **inoˈfficiousness**.
1727 BAILEY vol. II, *Inofficiousness*, Backwardness in doing any good Office. **1802-12** BENTHAM *Ration. Judic. Evid.* II. 526 On the part of parent, as well as child, inofficiosity, as the Romanists call it, is indeed always liable to have place. **1856** WEBSTER, *Inofficiously*, not civilly or officiously.

inogen (ˈɪnəʊdʒɛn). Physiol. [f. INO- + -GEN 1.] Hermann's term for a hypothetical complex substance supposed to exist in muscular fibre and to be the energy-yielding substance of muscle.
Supposed to be decomposed during muscular contraction into carbonic and sarcolactic acids and myosin (*Syd. Soc. Lex.* 1886).
1889 H. CAMPBELL *Causation Disease* iv. 22 It [the nervous system] may even be urging them on to some specific effort as when the muscle inogen is exploded.
Hence **inoˈgenic** *a.*, of or pertaining to inogen.

inogh, -oȝh, -oh, -oht, obs. ff. ENOUGH.

inoghe, -oȝe, -oȝhe, -ohe, obs. ff. ENOW.

†**iˈnoil,** var. of ENOIL *v.*, to anoint. *Obs.*
1546-7 CRANMER *Sp. Coron. Edw. VI* in Strype *Life* (1840) I. II. i. 206 The oil, if added, is but a ceremony: if it be wanting, that king is yet..God's anointed, as well as if he was inoiled.

inolfacient (ɪnɒlˈfeɪʃ(ɪ)ənt), *a. rare.* [f. IN-³ + L. *olfacient-em*, pr. pple. of *olfacĕre* to smell: see OLFACTORY.] Not having the power of smell.
1822-34 *Good's Study Med.* (ed. 4) III. 222 As the eyes grow blind and the nostrils inolfaciant by strong stimulants applied to them.

†**ˈinolite.** *Min. Obs.* [f. INO- fibrous + -LITE; named 1801.] = CALC-SINTER (Webster, 1864).

inolith (ˈɪnəʊlɪθ). *Path.* [f. INO- + Gr. λίθος stone.] A calcareous concretion in a fibrous tissue.
1886 in *Syd. Soc. Lex.*

i-nome(n, ME. pa. pple. of NIM *v.*, to take.

†**iˈnominal,** *a. Obs. rare*⁻⁰. [ad. L. *inōminālis* (Gellius), f. *in-* (IN-³) + *ōmen* OMEN; cf. OMINOUS.] Unhappy, unlucky.
1656 in BLOUNT *Glossogr.*

inominous (ɪˈnɒmɪnəs), *a. rare.* [IN-³.] Ill-omened; unfortunate.
1832 W. MACINTOSH *Life J. Sheddon* 32 As a kind of moral provision for such inominous young person, Mr. Sheddon set apart a small property.

inone (ɪnˈwʌn), *v. rare.* [f. IN-¹ + ONE, or the phrase *in one*; used by Pusey, app. after late L. *inūnīre* (Tertullian).] *trans.* To unite, to make one (*with*). Hence **inˈoneing** *vbl. sb.* and *ppl. a.*
1855 PUSEY *Doctr. Real Presence* Note Q. 183 Through the inoneing with the Immortal. *Ibid.* Note S. 321 S. Irenæus himself says..Those [things] which we learn from boyhood, growing up with the soul, are inoned with it. **1860** —— *Min. Proph.* 191 The Prophet uses the two imperatives, *seek Me and live*, inoneing both, man's duty and his reward. **1874** —— *Lent. Serm.* 438 One through the inoneing Spirit.

inooȝ, obs. form of ENOUGH.

†**inoˈpacate,** *v. Obs. rare*⁻⁰. [f. ppl. stem of L. *inopācāre* to overshadow.] 'To make dark.'
1623 in COCKERAM.

†**inoˈpacous,** *a. Obs. rare*⁻⁰. [f. L. *inopācus* + -OUS.] Not opacous, not dark or in shadow.
1656 in BLOUNT *Glossogr.* **1658** in PHILLIPS.

inoperable (ɪnˈɒpərəb(ə)l), *a.* [IN-³; cf. F. *inopérable*.] That cannot be operated on; unfit for an operation.
1886 *Med. News* Apr. 462 An article on the treatment of inoperable cancer. **1897** *Brit. Med. Jrnl.* 17 July 150 To try the value of the serum on selected inoperable cases of malignant disease.

inoperancy (ɪnˈɒpərənsɪ). *rare*⁻¹. [f. IN-³ + OPERANCY.] Failure to operate or function.
1936 T. S. ELIOT *Coll. Poems 1909-1935* 189 Evacuation of the world of fancy, Inoperancy of the world of spirit.

†**inopeˈration.** *Obs.* [ad. late L. *inoperātiōn-em* (Hilary, *a* 400), n. of action f. *inoperāre* to work within.] A working within; in-working.
1620 BP. HALL *Hon. Mar. Clergy* I. §14 Not a cold and feeble preuention, but an effectuall inoperation. **1633** —— *Hard Texts, N.T.* 50 Whosoever, thro' the effectual inoperation of Gods spirit shall improve those graces. **1645** —— *Remedy Discontents* 157 The inoperation of that Holy Spirit from whom every good gift, and every perfect giving, proceedeth.

inoperative (ɪnˈɒpərətɪv), *a.* [IN-³.] Not operative; not working or taking effect in action; in *Law*, without practical force, invalid.
a **1631** DONNE in *Select.* (1840) 204 A dead faith, as all faith is that is inoperative. *a* **1716** SOUTH *Serm.* (1727) VI. iv. 133 Though indeed the divine Knowledge (as all other Knowledge) be of itself inoperative. **1808** SYD. SMITH *Wks.* (1859) I. 114/2 Why is it to be supposed that motives..are inoperative with him alone? **1841** W. SPALDING *Italy & It. Isl.* III. 119 The system..was planned under difficulties which finally made it inoperative. **1885** *Law Times*

LXXVIII. 295/2 The resolutions..not having been so ratified, were inoperative.

Hence **in'operativeness**, the qualilty of being inoperative or of failing in its operation.

1880 MUIRHEAD *Gaius* Dig. 552 The novation put an end to the old obligation even when the new one was inoperative, unless the inoperativeness was due to the fact that the new debtor was a slave. **1883** *Cassel's Fam. Mag.* Aug. 543/2 The inoperativeness of the Canal Boats Act.

inopercular (ɪnəʊ'pɜːkjʊlə(r)), *a. Conch. rare.* [IN-^{3}.] = next.

1864 in WEBSTER. *a* **1884** OWEN is cited in *Cassell's Encycl. Dict.*

inoperculate (ɪnəʊ'pɜːkjʊlət), *a.* [IN-^{3}.] Not having an operculum or lid. **1.** *Conch.* Of or belonging to the *Inoperculata*, a division of *Pulmonifera* containing those univalves, such as snails, whose shell has no operculum.

1835–6 TODD *Cycl. Anat.* I. 114/1 The surface of the body ..covered with a shell..always inoperculate. **1854** WOODWARD *Mollusca* II. 159 One large division of the land-snails is furnished with an operculated shell; the rest are inoperculate, and sometimes shell-less.

2. *Bot.* Of an ascus or sporangium: lacking an operculum and therefore opening by splitting. Also as *sb.*, a fungus having this characteristic.

1879 W. PHILLIPS tr. E. Boudier in *Trans. Woolhope Naturalists' Field Club* (1887) 202 The second [section of the family] I would call *Inoperculate Discomycetes*, or simply *Inoperculæ*, because the exit of the sporidia takes place by a small hole, formed at the extreme summit of the asci, with its margin more or less elevated, but without any appearance of an operculum. **1913** *Trans. Brit. Mycol. Soc.* IV. 402 In the inoperculate species, the spores have a tendency to septation. **1929** *Trans. Brit. Mycol. Soc.* XIV. 267 The epithecium, overlying the hymenium..occurs in several inoperculate genera. **1943** *Mycologia* XXIV. 585 The outstanding characters of this Panamanian discomycete are unlike those of any of the stromatic inoperculates. **1950** E. A. BESSEY *Morphol. & Taxon. Fungi* iii. 45 In this order [*sc.* Chytridiales] the zoospores or motile gametes escape through an exit papilla or tube whose apex softens and permits the motile cells to push out (the inoperculate series), or they escape through a sort of cap that opens like a trap door, the so-called operculum (the operculate series). **1970** J. WEBSTER *Introd. Fungi* i. 25 In the inoperculate chytrids ..the sporangium forms a discharge tube which penetrates to the exterior of the host cell.

inoperculated (ɪnəʊ'pɜːkjʊleɪtɪd), *a.* [IN-^{3}.] = prec.

1836–9 TODD *Cycl. Anat.* II. 378/2 That hermaphrodite condition of the sexual organs common to the inoperculated order. **1854** WOODWARD *Mollusca* II. 160 The in-operculated air-breathers have..rows of very numerous, similar teeth.

†**in'opinable**, *a. Obs.* Also 5 -oppin-. [ad. L. *inopīnābilis* not to be expected, inconceivable, f. *in-* (IN-^{3}) + *opīnābilis* opinable; cf. F. *inopinable* (14th c. in Godef.).] Not opinable; unthinkable, inconceivable; not to be thought of.

1432–50 tr. *Higden* (Rolls) I. 9 Hauenge inoppinable appetite to beholde gestes of antiquite. **1528** ROY *Rede me* (Arb.) 43 Full of crakynge wordes inopinable. *c* **1555** HARPSFIELD *Divorce Hen. VIII* (Camden) 148 This, I say, is inopynable, incredible and a very paradox. **1581** MARBECK *Bk. of Notes* 343 What a wonderful paradoxe and inopinable sentence is this.

Hence †**inopinably** *adv.* [cf. late L. *inopīnābiliter*], inconceivably.

c **1450** *Mirour Saluacioun* 4927 The first [joy] inopynably ware ouere mesure to telle.

†**i'nopinate**, *a. Obs.* [ad. L. *inopīnāt-us*, f. *in-* (IN-^{3}) + *opīnāt-us*, pa. pple. of *opīnārī* to suppose, believe, think.] Not thought of; unlooked for; unexpected.

1598 YONG *Diana* 395 By imagining and hatching in his wicked hart a strange and inopinate treason. **1652** KIRKMAN *Clerio & Lozia* 125 If he is astonished at this inopinate novelty. **1807** tr. *Three Germans* I. 152 The inopinate recovery of his valued companion.

Hence †**inopinately** *adv.* (Bailey, 1730–6).

'inopine, *a. rare.* [ad. L. *inopīn-us* unexpected, f. *in-* (IN-^{3}) + root of *opīnā-rī* to think.] Unexpected.

1880 BLACKMORE *Mary Anerley* xl. (1881) 308 Liable to inopine derangements from excessive activity of mind.

†**i'nopious**, *a. Obs. rare*$^{-1}$. [ad. L. *inopiōs-us*, f. L. *inopia* want, lack: see -OUS.] Lacking wealth or resources; needy.

1656 BLOUNT *Glossogr.*, *Inopious*, poor, needy, destitute. **1675** T. PLUME *Life Hacket* in *Cent. Serm.* 49 Tyrants more commonly oppress the rich than their inopious enemies.

inopportune (ɪnˌɒpə'tjuːn, ɪn'ɒp-), *a.* [ad. late L. *inopportūn-us* unfitting, f. *in-* (IN-^{3}) + *opportūnus* OPPORTUNE. Cf. mod.F. *inopportun*. Rare until 19th c.; no quot. in J. or T.] Not opportune; inappropriate or inconvenient, esp. with regard to time; unsuited to the occasion; unseasonable.

1533 BELLENDEN *Livy* v. (1822) 395 Sic inoportune and cruel servitude..wes nocht commandit to us during the empire of kingis. *a* **1555** LYNDESAY *Tragedy* 402 On ȝow, Prencis, for vndescreit geuyng..And we, for our Inoportune askyng. **1649** JER. TAYLOR *Gt. Exemp.* III. ad sect. xv. 102 An indisposed body, or an inopportune education or evil customes superinduce variety and difference. **1836** T. HOOK *G. Gurney* (L.), No visit could have been more inopportune. **1869** LECKY *Europ. Mor.* I. xi. 311 Turbulent and inopportune in their demands. **1869** *Daily News* 13 Dec., That the proclamation of the dogma of the infallibility of the Pope is a question which would be inopportune to revive.

inopportunely (ɪnˌɒpə'tjuːnlɪ), *adv.* [f. prec. + -LY^{2}.] In an inopportune manner; at an unsuitable or inconvenient time; unseasonably.

a **1631** DONNE *Lett., Sir H. G[oodeere]* (1633) 353 For even that holy exercise [prayer] may not be done inopportunely, no nor importunely. **1796** *Dial. Amusem. Clergymen* 208 (T.) You have taken me, said he, rather inopportunely today. **1885** *Manch. Exam.* 3 Feb. 5/4 The strike..is awkward, and comes inopportunely for the Reichsrath.

inopportuneness (ɪnˌɒpə'tjuːnnɪs). [f. as prec. + -NESS.] The quality or condition of being inopportune; inconvenience or unsuitability of occasion; untimeliness, unseasonableness.

1831 E. E. CROWE *Hist. France* III. x. 314 [Napoleon] saw the inopportuneness, as well as the necessity, of the Russian war. **1878** BAYNE *Purit. Rev.* vii. 276 Rupert marked his sense of the inopportuneness of this request by calling to his own standard the men whom Montrose commanded.

inˌoppor'tunism. [f. as prec. + -ISM.] The practice or habit of acting inopportunely.

1886 *Manch. Exam.* 19 Jan. 5/6 An unmitigated bore, only second to Lord D—in his impracticable inopportunism.

inopportunist (ɪnˌɒpə'tjuːnɪst), *sb.* (*a.*) [f. INOPPORTUNE + -IST: after *opportunist*; cf. F. *inopportuniste*.] One who believes a policy or course of action to be inopportune; *esp.* one who, on that ground, opposed the doctrine of Papal Infallibility at the Vatican Council, 1870; one opposed to the policy of OPPORTUNISTS.

1880 *Daily News* 12 Nov. 4/8 Discontented Republicans who are now associating themselves with that extreme Inopportunist. **1882–3** SCHAFF *Encycl. Relig. Knowl.* II. 1077 Those who opposed the doctrine of papal infallibility ..only from inexpediency, deeming it inopportune..were called also inopportunists. **1885** J. GILLOW *Bibliog. Dict. Eng. Cath.* II. 42 Previous to and during the sitting of the Œcumenical Council of the Vatican, he was a decided Inopportunist.

B. *adj.* Of or belonging to the inopportunists.

1888 *Pall Mall G.* 19 July 11/1 The Inopportunist Party. **1895** PURCELL *Life Manning* II. xvi. 416 A well-known leader of the Inopportunist or Opposition party.

inopportunity (ɪnɒpə'tjuːnɪtɪ). [ad. late L. *inopportūnitās*, in Quicherat: cf. mod.F. *inopportunité* (Dict. Acad. 1835).] The quality or fact of being inopportune; unseasonableness.

1500–20 DUNBAR *Poems* xv. 23 He that dois all his best servyiss May spill it all with crakkis and cryis, Be fowll inoportunitie. **1846** WORCESTER cites *Q. Rev.* **1868** ALCOTT *Tablets* 146 The light..hidden under the bushel of misapprehension, or inopportunity, flames forth at fitting moment. **1894** *Westm. Gaz.* 20 June 1/2 Such inopportunity as there may be in the Conference is not the fault of its organisers.

inoppressive (ɪnə'prɛsɪv), *a. rare.* [IN-^{3}.] Not oppressive; unoppressive.

1627–77 FELTHAM *Resolves* II. iii. 164 If they had the grounds of Morality, even the goodness of Nature would make them in-oppressive. **1832** LEWIS *Use & Ab. Pol. Terms* xvi. 154 Tyranny is properly opposed to mild inoppressive rule.

inoppugnable (ɪnə'pʌgnəb(ə)l), *a. rare.* [IN-^{3}.] Not oppugnable; unassailable.

1885 *N. & Q.* 6th Ser. XI. 279 His statements, as far as they go, are inoppugnable. **1895** JOHN SMITH *Perm. Message Exodus* xi. 156 The inoppugnable might of Jehovah.

†**in'optable**, *a. Obs. rare*$^{-0}$. [ad. L. *inoptābilis*, f. *in-* (IN-^{3}) + *optābilis* desirable.]

1656 BLOUNT *Glossogr.*, *Inoptable*, not to be wished for. **1658** in PHILLIPS.

†**in'opulent**, *a. Obs.* [IN-^{3}.] Not opulent; poor.

1613 SHERLEY *Trav. Persia* 131 This withering peace which you haue with the Turke..is more delighting for the present, then safe for the future: that rest being euer false which is taken amongst inopulent and strong neighbours.

†**i'nopy**. *Obs. rare*$^{-1}$. [ad. L. *inopia* want, n. of quality f. *inops* without resources, helpless: see -Y. Cf. obs. F. *inopie* (Cotgr. 1611).] Absence of resources; indigence, poverty.

1581 T. HOWELL *Deuises* (1879) 252 Two Goddesses to match your Gods there be, Inopie and Impossibilitie.

inorb (ɪn'ɔːb), *v.* [IN-^{2}.] *trans.* To place in an orb or sphere; to enclose or surround with or as with an orb, to encircle.

1847 EMERSON *Poems, Hermione* (1857) 94 Beauty's not beautiful to me, But sceptred genius, aye inorbed, Culminating in her sphere. **1871** R. ELLIS *Catullus* lxiv. 30 Ocean, who earth's vast globe with a watery girdle inorbeth. *Ibid.* 193 Grim brows, with viper tresses inorbed.

†**i'norder**, *v. Obs.* [f. IN-^{2} + ORDER *v.*, after L. *inordināre* to bring into order, arrange, in med.L. to ordain.] *trans.* To order; to ordain.

c **1645** HOWELL *Lett.* I. vi. viii, I have deliver'd Mr. Secretary Cook an account of the whole legation, as your Lord-ship inordred me. **1656** FINETT *For. Ambass.* 205 Therefore we have inordered that he be put in safe custody. **1657** HOWELL *Londinop.* 48 In the reign of Henry the fourth ..it was inordred.

inorderly (ɪn'ɔːdəlɪ), *a.* and *adv. Chiefly Sc.* [f. IN-^{3} + ORDERLY.]

A. *adj.* Not orderly; irregular, disorderly.

1606 G. W[OODCOCKE] tr. *Hist. Ivstine* 125 a, Among these inorderly discords of the Realme. **1885** A. EDGAR *Old Ch. Life Scot.* Ser. I. 167 To him it seemed inorderly: to them it was worse.

B. *adv.* In a disorderly way; irregularly.

1558 *Sc. Acts Mary* (1814) II. 521/1 þe said pretendit proces..and dome wes evill wranguuslie & Inordourlie gevin. **1677** *Rec. Inverness Presb.* (Sc. Hist. Soc.) 84 Persons inorderlie married be delated to the Civill Magistrate.

inordinacy (ɪn'ɔːdɪnəsɪ). Now *rare.* [f. INORDINATE: see -ACY.] The quality or condition of being inordinate; inordinateness; also, an instance or example of this, an inordinate act.

a **1617** P. BAYNE *Lect.* 170 In every affection discerne the inordinacie of it. **1660** *Gentl. Calling* ix. 160 Lest they..be surprized in the midst of their Inordinacies, and have their portion assigned them in weeping and gnashing of teeth. *a* **1714** M. HENRY *Wks.* (1835) I. 307 The inordinacy of thy affections to the world. **1784–5** *Hist. Eur.* in *Ann. Reg.* 37/1 That wantonness of power, and inordinacy of ambition. **1943** C. BROGAN *Who are 'The People'?* xi. 119 It is merely another instance of inordinacy.

†**in'ordinance.** *Obs.* [f. IN-^{3} + ORDINANCE; associated with *inordinate*.] An inordinate action or practice; an excess.

1638 *Penit. Conf.* (1657) 342 It is a necessary duty to cut off enormity and disriegled inordinances. **1673** *Lady's Calling* Pref. 3 Why should they not with the like disdain turn over all sensual inordinances to meer Animals? **1762** GOLDSM. *Cit. W.* cii, How happy..are the English ladies, who never rise to such an inordinance of passion! **1799** R. WARNER *Walk* (1800) 80 That state of desultory warfare in which his own inordinances..perpetually kept him.

in'ordinancy. *rare.* [f. as prec. + -ANCY: prob. confused with *inordinacy*.] = INORDINACY.

a **1617** P. BAYNES *Christian Lett.* (1620) sig. N7^{v}, No such inordinancy of griefe. **1674** *Govt. Tongue* III. §3. 109 It gives..license to all sensual inordinancies. **1679** PULLER *Moder. Ch. Eng.* (1843) 47 The wild inordinancy of them who make their own private principle..the rule of scripture interpretation. **1760–72** H. BROOKE *Fool of Qual.* (1808) I. 10 In order to reform this inordinancy of his desires. **1955** R. NIEBUHR *Self & Dramas of Hist.* (1956) 29 Hobbes.. could regard the..reason..as the cause of the inordinancy of human ambitions.

†**in'ordinary**, *a. Obs. rare.* [IN-^{3}.] Inordinate, extraordinary, unusual.

1606 G. W[OODCOCKE] tr. *Hist. Ivstine* 131 *a*, The remembrance..had more inflamed them to inordinary displeasure against him. **1632** LITHGOW *Trav.* IV. 143 Striving by all inordinary meanes, to bring his new devised plots to perfection.

inordinate (ɪn'ɔːdɪnət), *a.* [ad. L. *inordināt-us* disordered, irregular, f. *in-* (IN-^{3}) + *ordināt-us*, pa. pple. of *ordināre* to order, arrange, regulate.]

1. Not 'ordered'; devoid of order or regularity; deviating from right or rule; irregular, disorderly; not regulated, controlled, or restrained.

1398 TREVISA *Barth. De P.R.* III. xxv. (Add. MS. 27,944), Anon þe puls is swift and þicke quakinge and inordinat. **1485** *Act 1 Hen. VII*, c. 7 Statutes..for the Punition of unlawful and inordinate Huntings in Forests. **1581** J. BELL *Haddon's Answ. Osor.* 414 That the cryme which is inordinate may be reduced to the order of Justice. **1625** FLETCHER *Noble Gent.* II. i, When did ye there keep such inordinate hours? **1692** RAY *Dissol. World* i. (1732) 3 A rude and inordinate heap. **1774** STRANGE in *Phil. Trans.* LXV. 43 From the inordinate course of the Appenines in general, the vulcanic hills of that chain afford no observation so interesting to physical geography. **1898** J. R. ILLINGWORTH *Div. Immanence* iv. §4. 94 To remedy this lawlessness, to restore this inordinate state of humanity to order.

2. Not kept within orderly limits, immoderate, intemperate, excessive.

c **1386** CHAUCER *Pars. T.* ¶340 The clothyng..is cowpable..for the superfluitee, or for the inordinat scantnesse of it. *c* **1425** *Orolog. Sapient.* ii. in *Anglia* X. 342/2 Ouerleyde with a inordinate sorowe and vnskilfulle heuynesse. *c* **1530** *Pol. Rel. & L. Poems* 31 Inordynat bilding causith hasty sale of placys. **1545** BRINKLOW *Compl.* 6 b, The inordinate inhansyng of rentys. *a* **1665** J. GOODWIN *Filled w. the Spirit* (1867) 15 Drunkenness with wine, or inordinate drinking, is altogether inconsistent with a being filled with the Spirit. **1716** ADDISON *Freeholder* No. 30 ¶5 He only taxes us with our inordinate Love of Pudding. **1791** BURKE *Let. Memb. Nat. Assembly* Wks. VI. 31 Their object is to merge all natural and all social sentiment in inordinate vanity. **1840** MISS MITFORD in L'Estrange *Life* (1870) III. vii. 108 Making us pay an inordinate rent for the luxury. **1872** YEATS *Growth Comm.* 284 The prices..were so inordinate.

3. Of persons: Not conforming or subject to law or order, disorderly; unrestrained in passions, feelings, or conduct; immoderate, intemperate.

c **1450** tr. *De Imitatione* III. xiii. 81 O hou shorte, hou inordinat, hou false, hou foule þei all be! **1555** PHILPOT *Let.* in Foxe *A. & M.* (1684) III. 509 The Anabaptists, an inordinate kind of men stirred up by the Devil, to the destruction of the Gospel. **1597** BACON *Ess.*, *Coulers Good & Evill* vii. (Arb.) 149 Sanctuary men which were commonly inordinate men and malefactors. *a* **1684** LEIGHTON *Comm. 1 Pet.* i. 1 Yet were there even then amongst them, as the

writings of the apostles testify, false brethren, and inordinate walkers. **1857** BUCKLE *Civiliz.* I. vii. 341 Inordinate admirers of antiquity. **1871** BROWNING *Pr. Hohenst.* 1824 No more foolish dread O the neighbour waxing too inordinate A rival.

†**4.** *Math.* **a.** ***inordinate proportion***, a 'proportion' or statement of equality of ratios in which the terms are not in regular order. **b.** *Geom.* Of a figure: Irregular; not equilateral and equiangular.

1570 BILLINGSLEY *Euclid* v. def. xix. 136 An inordinate proportionality is, when as the antecedent is to the consequent, so is the antecedent to the consequent: and as the consequent is to an other, so is an other to the antecedent. **1667** H. MORE *Div. Dial.* II. xx. (1713) 151 The Spirits of Men..are as *Isosceles* betwixt the *Isopleuron* and *Scalenum*, not so ordinate a Figure as the one, nor so inordinate as the other. **1691** RAY *Creation* I. (1692) 123 There are only three rectilineous and ordinate figures [triangles, squares, hexagons] which can serve to this purpose; and inordinate or unlike ones must have been not only less elegant and beautiful, but unequal. **1823** CRABB *Technol. Dict.*, *Inordinate proportion*, that in which the order of the terms compared is irregular or disturbed.

†**in'ordinate**, *v. Obs. rare*$^{-1}$. [f. prec.] *trans.* To render inordinate.

1646 GAULE *Cases Consc.* 51 To deprave the will, to inordinate the affections, to perturb the passions.

inordinately (ɪn'ɔːdɪnətlɪ), *adv.* [f. INORDINATE *a.* + -LY^{2}.] In an inordinate manner or degree; in a way that is unruly or disorderly, irregularly; without government or restraint, unrestrainedly, intemperately; beyond measure, immoderately, excessively, extravagantly.

c **1400** *Apol. Loll.* 105 Breþern, we warn ȝow..þat ȝe wiþ draw ȝow fro ilk broþer going inordinatly. *c* **1450** tr. *De Imitatione* I. vi. 8 Whan euer a man coueitiþ eny þing inordinatly, anoon he is unrestid in himself. **1526** TINDALE *2 Thess.* iii. 7 We behaved not oure selves inordinately amonge you. **1547–64** BAULDWIN *Mor. Philos.* (Palfr.) 124 Wine inordinately taken troubleth mans reason. **1597** HOOKER *Eccl. Pol.* v. lxxvii. §10 Ambition..hath been accounted a vice which seeketh after honours inordinately. **1694** KETTLEWELL *Comp. Persecuted* 147 Those things which I..have been the most inordinately fond of. **1736** BUTLER *Analogy* I. iv. 103 Passions inordinately excited. **1836–9** DICKENS *Sk. Boz* (1850) 173/1 He was exceedingly vain, and inordinately selfish. **1859** DARWIN *Orig. Spec.* xi. (1873) 297 Each species tends to increase inordinately.

inordinateness (ɪn'ɔːdɪnətnɪs). [f. as prec. + -NESS.] The quality or condition of being inordinate; want of restraint or moderation; intemperateness, excess; an instance or example of this.

1577 tr. *Bullinger's Decades* (1592) 478 Sinne is an inordinatenesse or peruersenesse of man. **1598** FLORIO, *Inordinatezza*, excesse, inordinatnes, intemperancie. **1633** BP. HALL *Hard Texts, N.T.* 270 Let loose to all inordinatenesse and licentious courses. **1748** HARTLEY *Observ. Man* II. iii. 226 The Irregularity and Inordinateness of the bodily Appetites decline in the same Degrees. **1876** MOZLEY *Univ. Serm.* vii. 148 We have Appetites and Passions which..tend to inordinateness in the indulgence of them.

inordi'nation. [ad. late L. *inordinātiōn-em* disorder, f. *in-* (IN-^{3}) + *ordinātio* a setting in order, ORDINATION.] The condition of being inordinate (in conduct, affections, etc.); inordinateness; an instance or example of this.

1612–15 BP. HALL *Contempl.*, *O.T.* x. iii, Without the gift of continency, a low feed may impaire nature, but not inordination. **1667** *Decay Chr. Piety* xiv. §3. 339 To remove τὴν ἀμετρίαν τῶν παθῶν, the inordination of our passions. **1692** SOUTH 12 *Serm.* (1697) I. 528 The Schoolmen, and Casuists ..go about to clear a Lye from that intrinsick Inordination, and Deviation from right Reason inherent in the Nature of it. **1788** T. TAYLOR *Proclus* I. 66 Corporeal baseness, indeed, arises from material inordination, deformity, and inconvenience. **1883** G. M. HOPKINS *Sermons & Devotional Writings* (1959) 133 The inordination, ugliness of sin in the frame and world of Creator and creature.

inorganic (ɪnɔː'gænɪk), *a.* and *sb.* [f. IN-^{3} + ORGANIC. Cf. F. *inorganique*, and next.]

A. *adj.* **1. a.** Not characterized by having organs or members fitted for special functions; not formed with the organs or instruments of life, or with the organization peculiar to living beings; destitute of organized physical structure: said of inanimate matter and bodies formed of it without vital action.

inorganic world, nature, the material world outside the animal and vegetable kingdoms; the world of matter, with the mechanical and chemical forces to which it is subject.

1794 SULLIVAN *View Nat.* I. 464 We may safely conclude that the mineral kingdom, that assemblage of brute inorganic bodies..has yet distinct families and species. **1796** KIRWAN *Elem. Min.* (ed. 2) I. Pref. 7 The inorganic matter that forms the Earth's surface. **1813** SIR H. DAVY *Agric. Chem.* i. (1814) 29 What can be more delightful than..to examine the progress of inorganic matter in its different processes of change? **1856** DOVE *Logic Chr. Faith* IV. ii. §5. 221 In the inorganic world we observe action and re-action. **1889** A. R. WALLACE *Darwinism* 17 There is a yet deadlier enemy in the forces of inorganic nature.

b. *Chem.* Of elements, compounds, etc.: Not entering into the composition of organized bodies; not formed under the action of the vital forces.

1831 R. KNOX *Cloquet's Anat.* 2 In living bodies there are two kinds of elements, inorganic and organic. The inorganic elements are those which may be obtained by the processes of chemistry from minerals as well as organized bodies. **1832** T. THOMSON *Chem. Org. Bodies* 628 Acids, in general, whether organic or inorganic..act upon sugar in the same manner when assisted by heat. **1864** CARLYLE *Fredk. Gt.* XVI. i. (1872) VI. 137 Innumerable high-dressed gentlemen, gods of this lower world, are gone all to inorganic powder. **1877** WATTS *Fownes' Org. Chem.* (ed. 12) 2 The division of compounds into two distinct branches, inorganic and organic,—formed..the latter only under the influence of a supposed vital force—must therefore be abandoned.

c. ***inorganic chemistry***, that branch of Chemistry which investigates inorganic compounds; the chemistry of mineral substances.

As all organized bodies contain carbon, *organic chemistry* is usually defined as 'the chemistry of the carbon compounds', while *inorganic chemistry* comprises that of all the other elements and their combinations.

[**182.** T. THOMSON (*title*), A System of Chemistry of Inorganic Bodies. Cited in *Penny Cycl.* (1837) VII. 31/2 as *Inorganic Chemistry*.] **1847** CRAIG s.v. *Chemistry*, *Inorganic Chemistry*, is that which investigates inorganic compounds. **1854** *Orr's Circle Sc.*, *Chem.* 383 The limit separating inorganic from organic chemistry is purely conventional.

2. Not furnished with or acting by bodily or material organs; = INORGANICAL 1.

1821 SHELLEY *Prometh. Unb.* I. 135 Speak Spirit! from thine inorganic voice I only know that thou art moving near And love. **1830** MACKINTOSH *Prog. Eth. Philos.* Wks. 1846 I. 161 The theory in its full extent requires a word such as 'inorganic' (if no better can be discovered), extending to all gratification not distinctly referred to some specific organ, or at least to some assignable part of the bodily frame.

3. a. Not belonging or proper to the organism or structure; that does not arise by natural growth; extraneous.

1862 MERIVALE *Rom. Emp.* (1865) III. xxviii. 325 The vitality of European intellect would have thrown off the yoke of an inorganic and alien despotism. **1880** C. E. NORTON *Church Build. Mid. Ages* 229 *note*, The forms of the highly ornamented gables are curiously inorganic.

b. *Philol.*

1861 MAX MÜLLER *Sc. Lang.* 322 These languages will hardly ever agree in what is anomalous or inorganic. **1875** WHITNEY *Life Lang.* v. 93 It all grew out of an inorganic extension of such constructions. *Ibid.* vii. 127 Such a distinction [as that of *rēad*, *rĕad*, *lēad*, *lĕd*, etc.] is wont to be termed 'inorganic', as distinguished from one like *loved* from *love*, which answers just the purpose for which it was at first intended. *Mod.* Feminine words which in Old English ended in a consonant often took in Middle English an inorganic *-e* (derived from the oblique cases), as in OE. *gódnes*, ME. *gōdnesse*, and all nouns in *-nes*.

c. *Path.* ***inorganic murmur***: see quot.

1884 *Cassell's Encycl. Dict.*, *Inorganic cardiac-murmur.* **1891** *Syd. Soc. Lex.* s.v. *Murmur*, *Inorganic Murmurs*, abnormal or superadded heart-sounds which are not due to disease of the heart substance, such as hæmic murmurs. Inorganic murmurs are also said to be due to the irregular action of the musculi papillares in the left ventricle [etc.].

4. Without organization or systematic arrangement.

1843 CARLYLE *Past & Pr.* II. x, That inorganic waste whirlpool.

B. *sb.* An inorganic chemical.

1945 *Chem. & Engin. News* 10 Jan. 103 We offer: inorganics—gallium, germanium, indium metals & salts in quantity. **1968** *New Scientist* 23 May 391/1 The production of inorganics was complemented by the equally distinct manufacture of organic chemicals. **1971** *Nature* 31 Dec. 515/1 Plastics increased in volume by 16·8 per cent a year; basic organics by 13·7 per cent and inorganics by 6·1 per cent.

†**inor'ganical**, *a. Obs.* [f. IN-^{3} + ORGANICAL. Cf. Gr. ἀνόργανος without organs or instruments.]

1. Without organs or instruments; not having, or not acting by, organs. Said of the soul or mind.

1621 BURTON *Anat. Mel.* I. i. II. ix, Many erroneous opinions are about the essence and original of it [the soul].. whether it be organical, or inorganical; seated in the brain, heart or blood; mortal or immortal. *Ibid.*, All three faculties make one Soule, which is inorganicall of it selfe, although it be in all parts, and incorporeall, using their Organs, and working by them. **1643** SIR T. BROWNE *Relig. Med.* I. §36 Nor truely can I peremptorily deny, that the soule in this her sublunary estate, is wholly and in all acceptions inorganicall. **1678** CUDWORTH *Intell. Syst.* I. i. §45. 55 Aristotle should otherwise contradict himself, who had before affirmed, the Intellect to be Separable, Unmixed and Inorganical. *a* **1688** —— *Immut. Mor.* (1731) 135 Though Sense is Passive and Organical, yet Knowledge is Inorganical and an Active Power and Strength of the Mind.

2. = INORGANIC 1.

1674 BOYLE *Eff. Air's Moisture* Wks. III. 799 The moistening particles..exercise a notable..force, even upon inanimate and inorganical bodies. **1685** —— *Effects Mot.* vii. 80 Sonorous motions of the Air..find in bodies inanimate and Inorganicall, such congruous Textures and Dispositions to admit their action. **1690** LOCKE *Hum. Und.* III. vi. §12 We come to the lowest and most inorganical parts of matter.

inorganically (ɪnɔː'gænɪkəlɪ), *adv.* [-LY^{2}.]

†**1.** Without reference to organs or organization. *Obs.*

1676 ALLEN *Address Non-conf.* 101 The whole body of the Nation of the Jews..were..Abraham's Spiritual Seed, and as such were Church matter, and a Church inorganically considered.

2. 'Without organs' (Webster, 1828).

3. Without organization or organized plan.

1853 FROUDE *Short Stud.*, *Forgot. Worthies* (1867) 297 Some unknown gentleman volunteer sat down and chronicled the voyage which he had shared: and thus inorganically arose a collection of writings..striking..for their high moral beauty.

inorganism (ɪn'ɔːgənɪz(ə)m). *rare.* [IN-^{3}, after *inorganic*.] Absence of organization or organic structure.

1882 *Champion of Faith* 169 *heading*, Inorganism and Mind.

†**inor'ganity.** *Obs. rare*$^{-1}$. [f. IN-^{3} + L. *organum*, Gr. ὄργαν-ον organ, instrument + -ITY.] The condition of being without organs.

1643 SIR T. BROWNE *Relig. Med.* I. §36 There is no Organ or Instrument for the rational Soul; for in the brain, which we term the seat of Reason, there is not any thing of moment more than I can discover in the crany of a beast; and this is a sensible, and no inconsiderable argument of the inorganity of the Soul. **1656** BLOUNT *Glossogr.*, *Inorganity*, the want of such [organical] dispositions. **1676** in COLES. **1727** BAILEY vol. II, *Inorganity*, a Deprivation of Organs or Instruments.

inorganizable (ɪn'ɔːgəˌnaɪzəb(ə)l), *a. rare.* [IN-^{3}: cf. mod.F. *inorganisable*.] Not organizable; that cannot be organized.

1883 E. C. MANN *Psychol. Med.* 34 Hyperæmia.. sometimes accompanied by organizable or inorganizable exudates.

inorganization (ɪnˌɔːgənaɪ'zeɪʃən). [IN-^{3}.] Absence of organization; unorganized condition.

1839 POE *Fall House of Usher* Wks. 1864 I. 301 The kingdom of inorganization. **1885** *Science* July 66 The idea of grossness, or inorganization, which the untrained mind applies to the world of matter.

inorganized (ɪn'ɔːgənaɪzd), *a.* [IN-^{3}.] Not organized; not having organization.

1649 *Bounds Publ. Obed.* 5 What it is that forms inorganized people into a Government? **1793** BEDDOES *Calculus* 178 Subject to the laws of inorganized matter. **1856** MRS. BROWNING *Aur. Leigh* III. 250 These tones, inorganized to any tune.

inorga'nography. *rare.* [f. INORGAN(IC + -GRAPHY.] That branch of science which treats of inorganic bodies.

1893 in FUNK.

inoriginate (ɪnə'rɪdʒɪnət), *a.* [IN-^{3}: perh. repr. a Schol.L. *inoriginātus*.] Not originated, not having a beginning.

1852 BP. FORBES *Nicene Cr.* 91 That..the Hutchinsonians..held a doctrine concerning three inoriginate Persons, which, in its legitimate consequences, would have led to a species of Tritheism.

i-norisched, -id, ME. pa. pple. of NOURISH *v.*

†**inorm, -e, inormious, inormitie, inormly, inormous**, obs. (chiefly Sc.) ff. ENORM, etc.

c **1375** *Sc. Leg. Saints*, *Egipciane* 18 Nothire stekis fra goddis mercy of þe syne þe quantyte, na ȝet of It þe Inormyte. *c* **1560** A. SCOTT *Poems* (S.T.S.) xxxiv. 139 The fassoun, and þe fek, ȝe suld it fynd inorme. **1600** J. MELVILL *Diary* (1842) 379 Inormlie grievit and hurt. **1662** GLANVILL *Lux Orient.* ii. 13 What an inormous strength, bad education hath to deprave and pervert well dispos'd inclinations.

inornate (ɪn'ɔːnət), *a.* [ad. L. *inornāt-us*, f. *in-* (IN-^{3}) + *ornāt-us* adorned.] Not ornate; unadorned, plain, simple.

c **1510** BARCLAY *Mirr. Gd. Manners* (1570) A j, To file not with vices nor language inornate. *a* **1834** COLERIDGE *Lit. Rem.* (1838) III. 419 Unperfumed, inornate lays, not redolent of art. **1849** DANA *Geol.* App. i. (1850) 709 Its inornate plications. **1895** SAINTSBURY *Ess. Eng. Lit.* 176 Which can transform words quite as simple and inornate into perfect poetry.

Hence †**inornately** *adv.*

a **1568** '*No woundir is*' 55 in *Bannatyne Poems* (1879) v. 675 My style, inornetly compond.

†**in'orthodox**, *a. Obs. rare.* [IN-^{3}.] Unorthodox.

1657 GAULE *Sapient. Justif.* Ep. Ded., The expressions.. of the Inorthodox. **1698** FRYER *Acc. E. India & P.* 284 The Idle Dreams and Malicious Practises of the Inorthodox.

†**inor'thography.** *Obs. rare.*$^{-1}$ [IN-^{3}.] Incorrect spelling; heterography.

1864 in WEBSTER, citing FELTHAM.

i-nortured, ME. pa. pple. of NURTURE *v.*

'**inosate**, a salt of INOSIC *acid*, q.v.

inosculate (ɪn'ɒskjʊleɪt), *v.* [f. IN-^{2} + L. *ōsculāre* to furnish with a mouth or outlet, e.g. the veins (Cælius Aurelianus), f. *ōsculum*, dim. of *ōs* mouth (also a kiss, whence *ōsculāre*, *-ārī* to kiss).

The transitive uses occur chiefly in the passive voice.]

1. *intr.* Of blood-vessels, etc.: To open into each other, to unite or join by running together; to have connexion terminally; to anastomose.

1683 SNAPE *Anat. Horse* I. xxi. (1686) 44 Interwoven with the Veins, with which yet they do no where inosculate. **1737** BRACKEN *Farriery Impr.* (1757) II. 181 The Veins and Arteries cannot inosculate with one another, to make the Parts adhere. **1754–64** SMELLIE *Midwif.* I. 134 The arteries ..at last end in small capillaries that inosculate with the veins. **1835–6** TODD *Cycl. Anat.* I. 748/2 The arteries of opposite sides inosculate with each other.

2. Of fibres, solid parts, etc.: To unite by interpenetrating or fitting closely into each other.

1713 DERHAM *Phys.-Theol.* V. viii. (1727) 306 This fifth Conjugation of Nerves is branch'd..to the Præcordia also, in some Measure, by inosculating with one of its Nerves. **1816** KIRBY & SP. *Entomol.* (1843) I. 332 Which grooves by means of a most curious apparatus of hooks like those in the laminæ of a feather inosculate into each other. **1835** KIRBY *Hab. & Inst. Anim.* II. xvii. 168 The thigh inosculates with the lower part of..the nameless bone. **1874** CARPENTER *Ment. Phys.* I. ii. §37 (1879) 36 Minute fibrillae, which seem to inosculate with each other, so as to form a network.

3. *trans.* To cause (blood-vessels, or the like) to open into each other; to connect by anastomosis.

1734 W. GIFFARD *Cases Midwif.* lvi. 128 The mouths of its vessels which were before inosculated into the Placenta. **1744** BERKELEY *Siris* §34 Capillary arteries in the trunk, into which are inosculated other vessels of the bark. **1829** SOUTHEY *Sir T. More* I. 171 The vessels of the tumour are ..inosculated into some of the principal veins and arteries.

4. To cause (fibres, or the like) to interpenetrate or pass into each other.

1671 GREW *Anat. Pl.* I. ii. §14 'Tis most probable, that none of their Fibres are truly inosculated, saving perhaps, in the Plexures. **1673** —— *Anat. Roots* iii. §14 They seem.. where they are Braced, to be Inosculated; so as to be pervious one into another. **1713** DERHAM *Phys.-Theol.* IV. iii. 129 The Branches of one of the auditory Nerves..[are] inosculated with the Nerves to go to the Heart and Breast. **1822–34** *Good's Study Med.* (ed. 4) IV. 325 The tumour was so adherent to other organs, and..inosculated with the omentum, that excision was impracticable.

5. *transf.* and *fig.* **a.** *intr.* To pass into; to join or unite so as to become continuous; to blend.

1836 *Blackw. Mag.* XXXIX. 299 Mysticism, pantheism, and scepticism..to use a medical term, inosculate, and lead at last to the same result. **1853** KANE *Grinnell Exp.* vi. (1856) 47 A large strait, called the Waigat..inosculates with the bay. **1854** DE QUINCEY *Autobiog. Sk.* Wks. II. 51 The points ..at which theology inosculates with philosophy. **1874** COUES *Birds N.W.* 371 Data for determination of the line along which the two varieties inosculate. **1874** CARPENTER *Ment. Phys.* II. x. (1879) 429 Our ideas are thus linked in 'trains' or 'series', which..inosculate with each other like the branch lines of a railway.

b. *trans.* To cause to grow together or unite closely so as to become continuous.

1829 STORY *Value Legal Stud.* Misc. Writ. (1852) 505 The civil law..has been adopted, or, if I may say so, inosculated, into the juridical polity of all continental Europe, as a fundamental rule. **1830** *Fraser's Mag.* I. 548 How can you, then,..inosculate yourselves among the heathen—before that day arrives? *a* **1849** H. COLERIDGE *Ess.* (1851) II. 39 The licence lately revived of inosculating the stanzas [of elegiac measure] should be used sparingly.

Hence **in'osculated** *ppl. a.*, grown together.

1883 J. C. BROWN *Forests Eng.* 33 In Epping Forest there are..several curious specimens of 'inosculated' oaks, exhibiting the singular mode of growth so designated, by which two trees are united together.

inosculating (ɪ'nɒskjʊleɪtɪŋ), *ppl. a.* [f. prec. + -ING².] That inosculates; communicating by or as by anastomosis; meeting or running together; uniting so as to become continuous.

1715 TAYLOR in *Phil. Trans.* XXIX. 347 The Radiuses of their inosculating Circles. **1753** N. TORRIANO *Midwifry* 20 There seemed to be inosculating Vessels between the Chorion and Amnion. **1819** CRABBE *T. of Hall* VI, Drear, dark, inosculating lanes. **1854** HOOKER *Himal. Jrnls.* II. xxx. 337 Intersected by innumerable inosculating channels.

inosculation (ɪnɒskjʊ'leɪʃən). [n. of action f. INOSCULATE: cf. L. *ōsculātio vēnārum* the inosculation of blood-vessels (= *ἀναστόμωσις*) in Cælius Aurelianus.] The action of inosculating; the opening of two vessels of an animal body, or of a vegetable, into each other; anastomosis; junction by insertion; hence, applied to the similar junction of fibres, and generally to any branch-system; also to the junction of solid parts which fit into each other, and generally, to the passing of one thing into another. Also *transf.* and *fig.*

1672 *Phil. Trans.* VII. 5133 The Veins..are disposed with them into a certain net-work; whether by Inosculations or bare contact only, we pretend not to determine. **1676** COLE *Ibid.* XI. 604 Mutual inosculations between the contiguous fibres. **1708** *Brit. Apollo* No. 17. 1/2 The Blood did pass by the Inosculation of the Vessels. **1797** BURKE *Regic. Peace* iii. Wks. VIII. 399 This grand junction is an inosculation of the grand trunk [canal]. **1833–6** J. H. NEWMAN *Hist. Sk., Prim. Chr.* 418 The dove-tailings and inosculations of historical facts. **1840** E. WILSON *Anat. Vade M.* (1842) 263 The entire body may be considered as one uninterrupted circle of inosculations, or anastomoses. **1876** E. MELLOR *Priesth.* v. 209 The transition (from the Old to the New Dispensation) was less one of sudden shock than of gentle inosculation.

inosic (aɪ'nɒzɪk), *a. Chem.* [f. a potential **inose* (f. INO- muscle + -OSE) + -IC.] Of the substance of muscle; in ***inosic acid***, an acid found in the mother-liquor of the preparation of creatine from flesh-juice. Its salts are **'inosates**.

1865–72 WATTS *Dict. Chem.* III. 274 Inosic acid is uncrystallisable, easily soluble in water, and has a very agreeable flavour of broth. *Ibid.*, The inosates, heated on platinum-foil, decompose, giving off an odour of roast meat. Inosate of potassium forms elongated quadrilateral prisms. **1878** KINGZETT *Anim. Chem.* 330.

inosin ('aɪnəsɪn). *Chem.* [f. as prec. + -IN.] = INOSITE.

1865–72 WATTS *Dict. Chem.* III. 274 *Inosite* (also) *Inosin.*

inosinic (aɪnə'sɪnɪk), *a. Chem.* [f. prec. + -IC.] In ***inosinic acid***, the earlier name, given by Liebig, of inosic acid. So **ino'sinate** = INOSATE.

1855 MAYNE *Expos. Lex.*, *Inoscinate*, a combination of inoscinic acid with a salifiable base. **1857** G. BIRD *Urin. Deposits* (ed. 5) 108 Creatine and its allies, creatinine and inosinic acid. **1859** *Fownes' Man. Chem.* 551 The mother-liquid from flesh from which the kreatin has been deposited contains, among other things, a new acid, the inosinic, the aqueous solution of which refuses to crystallize.

inosite ('aɪnəʊsaɪt). *Chem.* [f. **inose* (see INOSIC) + -ITE.] A non-fermentable saccharine substance ($C_6H_{12}O_6 + 2H_2O$), isomeric with glucose, discovered by Scherer (1850) in the fluid contained in the cardiac muscular tissue of the ox, and since found in other parts of the body and in several plants. Orig. called *inosin.*

1857 G. BIRD *Urin. Deposits* (ed. 5) 43 Creatine, creatinine, inosinic acid, inosite. **1858** *Penny Cycl.* 2nd Suppl. 133/1. **1859** *Fownes' Man. Chem.* 355 *Inosite*..is identical with phaseomannite, which occurs in unripe beans (*Phaseolus*). **1897** *Allbutt's Syst. Med.* IV. 309 The sugars met with in the urine are dextrose, lactose, and inosite.

inositol (ɪ'nəʊsɪtɒl). *Biochem.* [f. INOSIT(E + -OL.] Modern name of INOSITE: any of the nine stereoisomers of hexahydroxycyclohexane, $(CHOH)_6$; *spec.* that isomer (also called ***meso-inositol*** or ***myoinositol***) which is a member of the vitamin B complex, occurs in many animal organs esp. muscle and (often as its hexaphosphate) in plant leaves and seeds, and promotes the growth of bacteria and yeasts.

1891 ROSCOE & SCHORLEMMER *Treat. Chem.* (new ed.) III. 214 Inositol forms large transparent monosymmetric crystals, which possess a sweet taste and are soluble..in about 6 parts of water, yielding an optically inactive solution. **1936** A. P. MATHEWS *Princ. Biochem.* v. 69 Inositol is found in wheat bran and in many vegetables, where it occurs often in the form of 'phytin', which is the hexa-phosphoric acid-ester of inositol. **1941** *Jrnl. Biol. Chem.* CXL. 465 The ability of substances related to mesoinositol to replace this compound in the nutrition of the mouse and of yeast has been examined. It was found that *d*-inositol, *l*-inositol..[etc.] were inactive for both species. **1948** *Adv. Carbohydrate Chem.* iii. 45 The comparative rarity of the other inositols has justified the general retention of the name inositol to denote *meso*-inositol. **1954** CANTAROW & SCHEPARTZ *Biochem.* vi. 214 No manifestations attributable to inositol deficiency have been recognized in man. This may be due, in part at least, to its synthesis by intestinal bacteria. **1970** R. W. MCGILVERY *Biochem.* xxiv. 599 Phosphatidylinositides are compounds containing residues of inositol, a structural isomer of glucose that can be made from glucose-6-phosphate as inositol-1-phosphate.

inostensible (ɪnɒ'stɛnsɪb(ə)l), *a.* [IN-³.] Not ostensible; unavowed. Hence **ino'stensibly** *adv.*

1791 *Burke's Corr.* (1844) III. 298 The Chevalier..goes to England (inostensibly or ostensibly, as shall be thought best) to act as agent for the princes. **1843** *Tait's Mag.* X. 139 The deterioration..was..progressive and inostensible. **1884** *Homil. Monthly* Oct. 763 Their sympathies have, either obviously or inostensibly, been on the side of the strong.

inotropic (aɪn-, ɪnəʊ'trəʊpɪk, -'trɒpɪk), *a. Physiol.* [ad. G. *inotrop* (T. W. Engelmann 1896, in *Arch. f. ges. Physiol.* LXII. 555): see INO- and -TROPIC.] Modifying the contractility of muscle.

1903 *Sci. Amer. Suppl.* 4 July 22992/3 The author describes..as inotropic such [influences] as lessen or destroy contractibility. **1971** *Nature* 25 June 531/1 An automated system for monitoring both the chronotropic and inotropic effects of chemical and physical agents.

So **i'notropism**, modification of the contractility of muscle.

1902 [see DROMOTROPIC *a.*]. **1971** *Nature* 25 June 531/1 Although inotropism is defined as a change in force, by measuring changes in optical density, we can measure indirectly the relative elongation and contraction of the cells during each contraction cycle.

inou, -ough(e, -ouȝ(e, -ouh, obs. ff. ENOUGH, ENOW.

† **i'nound**, *v. Obs. rare*⁻¹. [a. F. *inonde-r* (13th c. in Hatz.-Darm.), ad. L. *inundāre* to INUNDATE: cf. *surround.*] *trans.* To inundate; to flood. Cf. INUND.

1657 HOWELL *Londinop.* 13 The Thames often inounds the bankes about London.

inouth, var. INWITH *Obs.*, within.

in-ower (ɪn'our). *Sc.* [f. IN *adv.* + *ower*, Sc. form of OVER.] In towards some point; esp. nearer to the fire. (Cf. *atour*, *in-by*.)

1813 W. BEATTIE *Tales* 32 (Jam.) Syne she sets by the spinning wheel, Taks them in-o'er, and warms them weel. **1816** SCOTT *Antiq.* xxvi, The lady carried it in-ower and out-ower wi' her son. **1825–80** JAMIESON s.v., *Come in-oure*, come forward, and join the company. *In-ouer and Out-ouer*, backwards and forwards. **1885** MRS. OLIPHANT *Two Stories Seen & Uns.*, *Open Door* 75 Lord, let that woman there draw him inower.

inoxidable (ɪn'ɒksɪdəb(ə)l), *a. rare.* [IN-³; cf. F. *inoxydable.*] Not oxidable; inoxidizable. Hence **inoxida'bility**.

1841 GROVE *Contrib. Sc.* in *Corr. Phys. Forces* 242 The inoxidability of the anode. *Ibid.* 249 The inoxidable metals. **1871** MERCIER & KING tr. *Verne's Fr. Earth to Moon* viii. 48 Our cannon must be..indissoluble, and inoxydable by the corrosive action of acids.

inoxidizable (ɪnɒksɪ'daɪzəb(ə)l), *a.* [IN-³.] Not oxidizable; that cannot be oxidized; incapable of rusting.

1864 WEBSTER, *Inoxidizable, Inoxydizable.* **1880** W. C. ROBERTS *Introd. Metallurgy* 6 Separating it from precious or inoxidizable metals. **1883** *Fisheries Exhib. Catal.* 76 Ladies' Work Tables..mounted with engraved Argenton or Inoxidisable Metal.

in'oxidize, *v.* [IN-³.] *trans.* To render (iron, etc.) not liable to oxidize; to keep from oxidizing. Hence **in'oxidizing** *vbl. sb.*

1881 *Metal World* No. 3. 35 A new method of protecting iron from the effects of the atmosphere... The inoxydising process consists in coating the cast or wrought-iron objects with a silicate composition. **1883** *Science* I. 103 Paints,.. enamels, galvanizing, electrodepositing, and what is called 'inoxidizing', are among the many systems now in vogue to effect the preservation of iron and steel.

in'oxidized, *a.* [IN-³.] Not oxidized.

1883 R. HALDANE *Workshop Receipts* Ser. II. 411/1 The newly-formed pigment is separated from the inoxidized copper by washing on a sieve.

i-noyed, ME. pa. pple. of NOY *v.*, *Obs.*

† **inoynt, inoynted**, var. *enoint(ed*, obs. forms of ANOINT, ANOINTED.

c **1350** *Horæ de Cruce* in *Leg. Rood* (1871) 224 Cristes body ..In oynt he was wyt aromat holi writ to fulle. **1499** *Promp. Parv.* 262/1 (Pynson) Inoynted, *inunctus.*

inp-: see IMP-, as in *inpale*, *inpane*, etc.

inpale, error for *in pale*: see PALE.

'in-pa,rabola. *Math.* [Cf. IN-CIRCLE.] An inscribed parabola.

inparfit(e, -yt, obs. forms of IMPERFECT *a.*

in pari materia: see IN *Lat. prep.* 21.

† **'in-parish**. *Obs. rare*⁻¹. [See IN *adv.* 12 d.] A parish within city or borough bounds.

a **1677** HALE *Prim. Orig. Man.* II. x. 237 The In-Parishes until the late Fire..have increased from 9 to 10..the 16 Out-Parishes have in that time increased from 7 to 12.

in partibus: see IN *Lat. prep.*

in-parts: see IN *adv.* 12 c.

† **'in-path**. *nonce-wd.* [? f. IN-³, after L. *via invia.*] A way that is no way, an impassable way.

But Stanyhurst may have misunderstood L. *invia* and taken it as = intricate, involved, or internal way.

1583 STANYHURST *Æneis* III. (Arb.) 82 Italy is hence parted by long crosse dangerus inpaths.

in-patient, in-pensioner: see IN *adv.* 12 a.

inpayre, obs. form of IMPAIR.

in pectore: see IN *Lat. prep.*

† **'in-penny**. *Obs.* [f. IN *adv.* 12 + PENNY.] A payment on coming in; entrance-money.

? **13..** *Regist. Monast. Cokesford* (Spelman), De Inpeny et Outpeny, consuetudo talis est in villa de East Rudham.. unum denarium..pro ingressu suo.

'in-pent, *ppl. a.* [f. IN *adv.* 11 b + PENT; cf. IMPENT.] Pent in.

1613–16 W. BROWNE *Brit. Past.* I. iii, Whose in-pent thoughts him long time having pained.

'in-penta,hedron. *Math.* [Cf. IN-CIRCLE.] An inscribed pentahedron.

in-people: see IN *a.* 2.

inpermixt, variant of IMPERMIXT *a. Obs.*

1432–50 tr. *Higden* (Rolls) II. 157 Men inpermixte with other naciones.

in perpetuum: see IN *Lat. prep.*

in-person *attrib.*: see IN *prep.* 18.

inper'suadable, obs. f. IMPERSUADABLE.

1713 in G. Sheldon *Hist. Deerfield, Mass.* (1895) I. 350 She continued inpersuadable to speak.

inpeteous, inphant, inpight, inpliȝe, obs. ff. IMPETUOUS, INFANT, IMPIGHT, IMPLY.

in petto: see PETTO.

in-phase (stress variable), *attrib. phr. Electr.* [f. phr. *in phase* (PHASE *sb.* 3).] That is in phase; of or pertaining to signals that are in phase.

1914 H. PENDER *Amer. Handbk. Electr. Engineers* 1297 The active or in-phase component of the current in a circuit is that component which is in phase with the voltage across the circuit. **1940** *Amat. Radio Handbk.* (ed. 2) xii. 186/1 Besides the desired equal and opposite currents in the two wires, there are two more in-phase currents flowing in the parallel circuit. **1962** A. NISBETT *Technique Sound Studio* 264 If a monophonic signal is fed to an in-phase pair [of loudspeakers] the sound will appear to come from between and behind them. **1968** *Brit. Med. Bull.* XXIV. 253/2 Special techniques, such as in-phase rejection,..were adopted in its design to overcome interference from extraneous voltages.

in-pig (ɪnˈpɪg), *a.* [attrib. use of phrase *in pig*: see IN *prep.* 10 b.] Of a sow: that is in pig; pregnant. Cf. IN-CALF *a.*, IN-FOAL *a.*

1950 *Farming* June 179 In-pig sows can of course receive a proportion of their ration as bulky food. **1959** *Times* 31 Aug. 5/3 For the first time since the..national in-pig and litter tests began..the three major awards..have been won by the same sow. **1969** *Times* 6 Jan. 7/7 The December sample figures for England and Wales indicate a slight cutback south of the Border since September in in-pig gilts, but the number of sows in pig is still rising. **1974** *Listener* 21 Mar. 334/2 Philip had just lost all his pigs from swine vesicular disease, and was meditating buying in-pig gilts and starting again.

in-pile, in-plant, in-process *attrib.*: see IN *prep.* 18.

inplacable, obs. form of IMPLACABLE.

1650 H. MORE in *Enthus. Tri.* (1656) F j b, An inplacable enmity to immorality and foolery.

inˈplume, en-, obs. var. IMPLUME, EMPLUME.

1611 FLORIO, *Impennare*, to enfeather, to enplume. *Ibid.*, *Inpennacchiare*, to infeather, to inplume.

inˈpoison, obs. var. of *enpoison*, EMPOISON.

c **1440** *Promp. Parv.* 262/1 Inpoysyon, or poysnyn.., *intoxico.* **1611** FLORIO, *Inuelenare*, to inpoison, to inuenome.

ˈin-ˌpolygon. *Math.* [Cf. IN-CIRCLE.] An inscribed polygon.

in pontificalibus: see IN *Lat. prep.*

inport, -portable, -portune, -possible, -potence, obs. ff. IMPORT, etc.

in posse: see POSSE.

inpossession, obs. f. IMPOSITION.

in potentia: see POTENTIA.

inpour (ˈɪnpɔə(r)), *sb.* [IN *adv.* 11 d.] A pouring in; inflow, inrush.

1885 *Manch. Exam.* 5 May 5/2 A rush of gas, followed by a tremendous inpour of water. **1893** E. PEACOCK in *Reliquary* Apr. 102 The whole of the period..was harassed by the inpour of barbarians.

inˈpour, *v. rare.* [IN-[1].] *intr.* To pour in.

1885 L. OLIPHANT *Sympneumata* xviii. 269 At every hour of the sweet repose when life inpours.

ˈinˌpoured, *ppl. a.* [IN *adv.* 11 b.] That is poured in.

1651 HOBBES *Leviath.* I. iv. (1839) 27 If it be false to say that virtue can be poured..the words inpoured virtue..are as absurd and insignificant as a round quadrangle. **1864** H. FALCONER in *Reader* 5 Mar. 302/1 The southern end of the lake has been filled up by the deposition of inpoured silt.

ˈinˌpouring, *vbl. sb.* [IN *adv.* 11 c.] The action or fact of pouring in.

1721 R. KEITH tr. *T. à Kempis' Solil. Soul* x. 177, I am like a soured Vessel and wholly unworthy of the Inpouring of thy good Spirit. **1860** PUSEY *Min. Proph.* 225 There shall be one unceasing inpouring of riches.

ˈinˌpouring, *ppl. a.* [IN *adv.* 11 a.] That pours or rushes in.

1853 FARADAY in Bence Jones *Life* (1870) II. 307, I thought it better to stop the inpouring flood. **1884** G. MEREDITH in *Fortn. Rev.* Dec. 738 One among the inpouring passengers.

inpoveryssh, -practicable, -pravable, etc.: see IMP-.

in principio: see IN *Lat. prep.*

inprint, inprinter, inprison, etc., obs. ff. IMPRINT *v.*, IMPRINTER, IMPRISON, etc.

1611 FLORIO, *Impressore*, an inprinter, a stamper. **1658** A. FOX *Wurtz' Surg.* II. xxvii. 179 Splinters will hardly be so broad as to keep the roulers off from in-printing.

†**inpronunciable,** *a. Obs. rare*[−1]. [IN-[3].] Not to be pronounced or uttered; unutterable.

1552 LYNDESAY *Monarche* 6069 With hart it is vnthynkabyll And with toungis Inpronunciabyll.

inproˈportionable, var. IMPROPORTIONABLE.

1634 SIR T. HERBERT *Trav.* 211 Three small plumes short and inproportionable.

in propria persona: see IN *Lat. prep.*

inprynt, -pudence, -pudent, -pugn: see IMPRINT, etc.

inpurple, obs. var. of EMPURPLE.

†**inˈpurtured,** *pa. pple. Obs.* = *importrayed*: cf. IMPORTURAIT.

1526 SKELTON *Magnyf.* 1570 Inpurtured with fetures after your purpose.

ˈin-ˌpushing, *vbl. sb.* [f. *push in* (see IN *adv.* 11 c) + -ING[1].] The action of pushing in.

1884 *Stand. Nat. Hist.* I. Introd. 11 This is accomplished by inpushings of the epiblast at the extremities of the body.

ˈinput, *sb.* [IN *adv.* 11 d.] **1.** A sum put in; a contribution. *Sc.*

1753 *Scots Mag.* Aug. 421/1 An input of four guineas was run for by a white galloway..and a bay mare. **1766** W. GORDON *Gen. Counting-ho.* 11 My account..is debited for my inputs. **1818** SCOTT *Hrt. Midl.* xii, Ilka ane to be liable for their ain input. **1859** W. ANDERSON *Disc.* (1860) 163 The half crown, yea sixpenny, skip-the-plate..in-put of wealthy merchants and landlords..is all made manifest.

2. a. That which is put in or taken in, or which is operated on or utilized by any process or system (either material or abstract).

1893 *Phil. Trans. R. Soc.* B. CLXXXIII. 228 The pressure in the large systemic veins becomes raised during vagus action, because the quantity of blood which passes from them into the right ventricle (which we may refer to as the 'input' of the heart), in a given time, is diminished. **1929** *Prosp. Mona Copper Co.* 6 With Copper at £70 per ton on the basis of an input of 600 tons daily..a gross annual profit of about £100,000 could be expected. **1966** T. LUPTON *Managem. & Social Sci.* iv. 88 To Rice..an organization is an 'open system'. It takes in inputs from the environment, converts them, and sends outputs back into the environment. **1971** *Sci. Amer.* Sept. 111/1 These carcasses are retrieved in the spring, and the meat is considered one of the more flavorsome food inputs. **1971** J. B. CARROLL et al. *Word Frequency Bk.* p. vi, The Corpus is drawn from written, and edited, published materials. There is no direct oral input.

b. Energy supplied to a device or system; *spec.* an electrical signal that enters an electronic device.

1902 *Encycl. Brit.* XXVII. 574/2 The useful return or 'output' at the terminals of a large machine may amount to as much as 95 per cent. of the mechanical energy which forms the 'input'. **1931** *Daily Express* 21 Sept. 7/4 An advanced form of band-pass tuning, providing a special selector circuit between the input from the aerial and the first valve of the set. **1933** E. T. A. RAPSON *Electr. Transmission & Distrib.* xiv. 163 Accurate metering of the power input to and output from the Grid is essential. **1943** C. L. BOLTZ *Basic Radio* xiv. 216 The input is applied between control grid and cathode. **1970** J. EARL *Tuners & Amplifiers* vi. 142 This same switch also receives an input from the a.m. section.

c. *Econ.* The total of resources necessary to production, including raw materials, use of machinery, and manpower, which are deducted from output in calculating assets and profits. (Cf. OUTPUT.) Also *attrib.*

1926 J. D. BLACK *Production Economics* III. xi. 277 The term *input*..will be used..to refer to the amounts of the production elements that are used in turning out any product... In the present illustration, as the inputs of seed increase,..the outputs of grain increase. **1947** *Bull. U.S. Bureau of Labor Statistics* No. 913. 11 Most persons, in using the term 'productivity', have meant the physical output obtained for a given physical input. **1953** STEINER & GOLDNER *Productivity* ii. 5 What do we mean by input? A typical product is a combination of raw materials, machinery, workers' time, power, and many other factors. Each of these is called an input. Input items are combined in the manufacturing process into products or output. Should the unit of input be one worker, or one hour of labor time, or one machine, or a ton of raw materials or a kilowatt hour of electricity? Any of these could be an input although each is different. **1958** *Economist* 15 Nov. 592/3 When the effect of other variables has been allowed for, the farmer is found to be using, even at low inputs, 4s. worth of concentrates to produce a gallon of milk which he sells for 3s. 1½d... Concentrate inputs beyond £45 per cow per year ..have no additional effect..upon milk yield. **1959** *Oxf. Univ. Gaz.* 16 Mar. 796/1 The farmer also uses up large quantities of 'industrial inputs' (equipment, motor fuel, fertilizers, &c.), representing goods and services which could, directly or indirectly, have been exported if the British farmer had not used them, or which, in some cases, have to be imported. **1971** [see *input price* (5 a below)]. **1972** *VAT: Gen. Guide* (H.M. Customs) 16 Those goods and services are called his inputs, and the tax on them is his input tax. **1972** *Accountant* 13 Apr. 471/1 Historically, Britain's indirect taxes had been collectible at a single point and from a restricted clientele; VAT, on the other hand, would be all pervasive. For any person receiving taxable 'inputs', zero-rating would be found preferable, 'if at all possible' to exemption. *Ibid.* 28 Sept. 402/3 Companies with only internal transactions should ensure that they did not lose relief for VAT suffered (input tax).

d. *Computers.* Data or program instructions that are fed into or processed by a computer; also, the physical medium on which these are represented.

1948 *Math. Tables & Other Aids to Computation* III. 7 The 'input' for a computational problem (i.e., the information available before the start of the computation) consists of two kinds of elements: numbers, and 'orders'. *Ibid.* 9 The tapes which contain the input for any problem are classified into three groups. **1949** D. R. HARTREE *Calculating Instruments & Machines* (1950) vii. 80 Input and output for this machine are expressed in standard teletype code, with a coded symbol for the operation required. **1964** A. LYTEL *Fund. Data Processing* viii. 165 Punched paper tape can be read and used as a computer input. **1967** D. WILSON in Wills & Yearsley *Handbk. Management Technol.* iii. 45 It is sometimes necessary to obtain a detailed listing of all the input to determine where the error has occurred. **1973** *Time* 13 Aug. 20/2 Business gave its own donation at the office, with the computer talk of 'inputs'..and 'print-outs'.

e. *Psychol.* The resources of mental and sensory stimuli available to an individual.

1954 *Canad. Jrnl. Psychol.* VIII. 70 The maintenance of normal, intelligent, adaptive behaviour probably requires a continually varied sensory input. **1959** *Amer. Jrnl. Psychiatry* CXV. 1110/1 These studies suggest that maintaining adequate sensory input during space missions will be less of a problem than providing adequate information input. **1972** *Jrnl. Social Psychol.* LXXXVI. 220 Individuals who can tolerate diverse inputs from the environment may not be markedly affected by success or failure.

f. *Linguistics.* (See quot. 1966.) Freq. as ***input string***.

1961 H. A. GLEASON *Introd. Descr. Ling.* (rev. ed.) xii. 173 It is normally stated in the form of rules which may be applied to one of the pair—an *input*—altering it to produce the other—an *output*. **1966** M. PEI *Gloss. Ling. Terminol.* 126 *Input*, in transformational grammar, the term applied to a construction that is transformed into another..which is called the *output* (input: 'he goes'; output: 'he does go', 'he does not go', etc.). **1969** W. A. COOK *Introd. Tagmemic Analysis* ii. 42 The transformational rule is simply a rule of change. This rule has an input string, a rule of change, and an output string. With kernel sentences as input, it is possible to set up a series of optional rules that will produce the output, the derived sentences. **1971** R. FOWLER in *Archivum Linguisticum* II. 136 These rules..are typical of the local transformations which follow base constituent-structure rules on the present grammatical model. Their inputs and outputs are concatenated sets of syntactic.. features, and their effect is to replace or add one feature in one set.

3. A place where, or device through which, an input enters a system, esp. an electronic device.

1929 J. H. MORECROFT *Elem. Radio Communication* vii. 228 Either of these..would give a beat frequency of 50 kc., which is then 'detected' and supplied to the 'input' of the I.F. amplifier. **1933** *Boys' Mag.* XLVII. 108/2 Connect pick-up to 'input' and loud speaker to 'output'. **1946** *Math. Tables & Other Aids to Computation* II. 100 A flip-flop has two inputs and two outputs. **1963** GOULD & ELLIS *Digital Computer Technol.* iv. 33 Data passing from the input to the computer proper, or from this to the output, can be marshalled, sorted and coded..to a large extent independently of the rest of the equipment. **1971** *Hi-Fi Sound* Feb. 105/1 This recorder has inputs for microphone, radio and magnetic and/or ceramic pickup cartridges.

4. The action or process of putting in or feeding in.

1947 *Math. Tables & Other Aids to Computation* II. 356 No means of numerical input or output other than the keyboard and the display panel are provided. **1948** *Ibid.* III. 7 The speed of input is well in balance with the computing speed. **1955** *Sci. Amer.* Jan. 69/3 If a block of iron were magnetized as a single large domain..it..would require the input of a considerable amount of energy. **1964** T. W. MCRAE *Impact of Computers on Accounting* i. 15 The basic idea behind this method of input is to print the characters on the original document in a special type of magnetic ink. **1973** *Nature* 13 Apr. 440/1 What is lacking..is a steady input of information on research and development on other fuels.

5. *attrib.* and *Comb.* **a.** simple attributive, as ***input circuit, device, impedance, price, routine, tape, terminal, transformer, unit.*** **b.** In sense 'constituting input', as ***input current, data, information, signal, voltage.***

1921 *Wireless World* 25 June 214/2 The *input circuit varies according to the receiver circuit to which the connection is made. **1940** *Amat. Radio Handbk.* (ed. 2) iv. 69/1 The first general axiom is to arrange matters so that the output stages are as far as possible from the aerial or input circuits. **1930** FIELD & WEILL *Electro-Plating* 38 Fig. 11. showing the form of the *input and output currents. **1948** *Math. Tables & Other Aids to Computation* III. 7 The Harvard machines use punched cards for most *input data. **1948** *Ann. Computation Lab. Harvard Univ.* XVI. 248 The design of input and output devices for electronic digital computers poses a specialized problem in electrical communications. **1968** *Brit. Med. Bull.* XXIV. 191/1 The basic configuration of any computer consists of a store, a suitable *input and output device, and a control mechanism. **1928** *Times* 23 Mar. 20/1 A certain *input impedance which had the effect of increasing or decreasing the resistance of the tuned circuit. **1949** E. C. BERKELEY *Giant Brains* x. 175 Since the *input information must be carefully verified, we shall need a second magnetic-tape device. **1956** Input information [see BUFFER[2] 1 d]. **1971** *Daily Tel.* 19 May 17/2 *Input prices—the price of basic materials and fuel—have risen by more than 3 p.c. since the start of the year. **1954** *Math. Tables & Other Aids to Computation* VIII. 32 The function of the Ferut *Input Routine is to read information from tape, perform certain alterations on routines or numerical data and store the routines or data in assigned locations in the machine. **1962** *Gloss. Terms Automatic Data Processing (B.S.I.)* 42 *Input routine*, a routine, sometimes stored permanently in the computer, to control the readings of programs and data. **1950** *Mind* LIX. 440 It will seem that given the initial state of the machine and the *input signals it is always possible to predict all future states. **1949** E. C. BERKELEY *Giant Brains* iii. 27 We shall need one register to read the *input tape and to store the number or operation recorded on it. **1919** *Wireless World* Dec. 505/1 It will..be convenient to provide two '*input' terminals, two terminals to which the..accumulator may be connected, and two for ..an external plate battery. **1946** Input terminal [see CONTROL *sb.* 3 f]. **1919** *Wireless World* Dec. 506/1 The leaky grid condenser..is brought into use, the *input transformer ..being isolated. **1962** *Gloss. Terms Automatic Data Processing (B.S.I.)* 81 **Input unit*, that portion of an a.d.p. system used only for input. **1966** B. A. M. MOON *Computer Programming* i. 6 Typical input units are punched card,

paper tape and magnetic tape units. **1940** *Amat. Radio Handbk.* (ed. 2) ii. 28/2 When an A.C. *input voltage is applied to the grid of a valve an amplified A.C. voltage appears across the output load in the anode circuit.

c. Also **input-output** (*input-output, input/output*), usu. *attrib.*

1914 H. PENDER *Amer. Handbk. Electr. Engineers* 961 With large motors it is desirable to use a generator as a load in making an input-output test. **1947** *Math. Tables & Other Aids to Computation* II. 363 Another important element of the automatic computer which affects the compromise is the input-output mechanism. **1953** *Economist* 26 Sept. 870/1 An input-output analysis of the British economic structure.. will be ready by 1956. *Ibid.* 870/2 Mr. Roger Keyes.. recently ordered the suspension of work on American input-output data; the colleagues he left behind..used to share his mistrust of input-output. **1964** GOULD & KOLB *Dict. Social Sci.* 452/2 Input-output tables show the interrelations among the major industry groups of the economy... Tables or matrices are constructed which show the goods-and-services inputs and outputs of each on a 'from-whom to whom' basis. **1964** T. W. MCRAE *Impact of Computers on Accounting* ii. 38 The introduction of magnetic tapes.. facilitates the compact storage and fast input-output of large files. **1967** *Technology Week* 23 Jan. 11/1 (Advt.), Sigma 5 ..does foreground real-time control..and high-speed input/output. **1970** *Sci. Amer.* Oct. 94/2 Ordinarily it is difficult to measure the input-output relations of an ecosystem, particularly those involving nutrients. **1970** *Sunday Times* 29 Nov. 68/6 Input-output tables are brought into play to help estimate that trading profits per vehicle exceed manual pay for the men who make it.

input, *v.* Also 4 yn-, 6 *Sc.* imput(e, 6–7 imputt. [f. IN-[1] or IN *adv.* + PUT *v.*: in earliest quots. after L. *impōnere*; with stress on second syllable in senses 1 and 2, and on first syllable in sense 3.]

†**1.** *trans.* To put on, impose. *Obs.*

1382 WYCLIF *1 Macc.* xi. 13 Ptholome..ynputtide two dyademes to his hed, of Egipt and Asie. —— *Acts* xxviii. 3 Whanne Poul hadde gederid sum multitude of kittingis of vynes, and ynputt on the fyer. **1387–8** T. USK *Test. Love* II. ii. (Skeat) l. 120 That..maner of necessyte be input to gentilmen, that they shulden not varien fro the vertues of their auncestres.

†**2.** To put in, set, or place (in some position). *Sc. Obs.*

1557–75 *Diurnal Occurr.* (Bannatyne Club) 152 Thay.. detrudit the Ministarie of Goddis word, and imputt in thair places preistis to celebrate mess againe. **1593** *Sc. Acts Jas. VI* (1814) 48 (Jam.) It salbe lesum to the said Mr. cunyiour to imputt and outputt forgearis, prentaris, and all vthiris thingis belanging to the said office. **1652** Z. BOYD *Zion's Flowers* (1855) App. 24/2 Quhome I..surrogat substitute and imputte in my full richt tytill and place of the samyn. *a* **1670** SPALDING *Troub. Chas. I* (1829) II. 30 Thay first mell with the five cinque portis, inputtis and outputtis governouris at their plesour.

3. *Computers.* To supply or feed in (data, a program, etc.) *to*; to feed *into*. Pa. pple. **'input**, (less commonly) **'inputted**.

1946 *Nature* 12 Oct. 503/2 These switches are connected up so that for any two-figure argument *x* from 00 to 99, input to the function table, the value of the function for that argument is output in the form of pulse groups on the appropriate digit lines. **1953** A. D. & K. H. V. BOOTH *Automatic Digital Calculators* viii. 62 It is possible to input up to 300 decimal digits per second. *Ibid.* 74 Working instructions do not have to be input after each shut-down. **1964** F. L. WESTWATER *Electronic Computers* vi. 104 Magnetic tape provides a fast means of inputting information. **1965** K. NICOL *Elem. Programming* iii. 14 When all your program has been input and compiled control is transferred from the compiler program to the machine code instructions of your program. **1967** W. F. BAUER in W. J. Karplus *On-Line Computing* iv. 81 He inputs the data directly into the console by electronically filling out a form which the computer provides on the cathode-ray tube. *Ibid.* 80 Data verification is done by the computer's reflecting back to the user on the cathode-ray-tube scope exactly what has been inputted. **1968** *Brit. Med. Bull.* XXIV. 222/1 At convenient intervals, the day lists are input to the computer. **1970** O. DOPPING *Computers & Data Processing* xv. 230 A series of records which are to be input to a computer or have been output from it is called a file.

Hence **'input** *ppl. a.*, **'in,putting** *vbl. sb.* Also **'in,putter**, one who puts in.

Quots. *a* 1578 refer to the imprisonment of James III in Edinburgh Castle by the Scottish lords.

1498 *Acta Dom. Conc.* 320 (Jam.) That the said Thomas.. has done na wrang in the inputting of the saidis gudis in the said tennement again. *a* **1578** LINDESAY (Pitscottie) *Chron. Scot.* (S.T.S.) I. 177 All letteris and commandementis and procliematiounis was gevin and maid in his name, lyke as they war befoir his imputing. *Ibid.*, The lordis..that was his inputtaris. *Ibid.* 178 Desyrand support..quhairby he might be relaxit out of the castell of Edinburgh and to be revengit of his imputtaris. *Ibid.* 183 Certane lordis..quho was the consallouris of the maist pairt of his imputing. **1839** LOCKHART *Ballantyne-Humbug Handled* 34 The whole input stock was gone.

input(e, -putrible, -pytuous, etc.: see IMP-.

'in-,quadric. *Math.* [Cf. IN-CIRCLE.] An inscribed quadric. So **'in-quadri,lateral**, an inscribed quadrilateral.

,in'quaintance. *nonce-wd.*, fancifully used by (and after) Coleridge for 'intimate acquaintance'. So **in'quainted** *ppl. a.*

a **1834** COLERIDGE in *Fraser's Mag.* (1835) XI. 54 Friendships..The sorts, methinks, may be reduced to three. *Ac*quaintance many, and *Con*quaintance few; But for *In*quaintance I know only two—The friend I've mourned with, and the maid I woo! **1840** *Ibid.* XXII. 613 There must be a want of 'inquaintance' (if I may borrow Coleridge's word) with the spirit of Shakspeare's plays. **1849** *Ibid.* XL. 537 Both were intimately acquainted, or rather, in Coleridge's fanciful phraseology, inquainted, with the works of Plutarch and Montaigne.

†**inquart.** *Obs. rare.* [a. F. *inquart* (Littré).] = INQUARTATION.

1683 SALMON *Doron Med.* I. 315 The calcination of Gold by the 'Inquart': The name of Inquart is given to this Immersive calcination of Gold.

in'quartate, *v. rare.* [f. prec. or next: see -ATE[3].] *trans.* To separate (gold) from silver by quartation. Hence **in'quartated** *ppl. a.*

1868 SEYD *Bullion* 214 The inquartated Button obtained is flattened on an anvil.

inquar'tation. *rare.* [? a. F. *inquartation* (Littré).] The process of separating gold from silver by means of nitric acid: see QUARTATION.

1881 in RAYMOND *Mining Gloss.* **1898** *Chamb. Jrnl.* I. 713/1 Many minor processes, such as roasting, scorification, and inquartation, enter into the work done in assay.

inquarter, var. ENQUARTER, to quarter (troops).

in-'quarto. *rare.* [f. phrase *in quarto* (see QUARTO); cf. F. *in-quarto.*] A volume in quarto; a quarto book.

1865 *Pall Mall G.* No. 126. 5/1 To form a thin in-quarto.

inqueir, inquere, obs. Sc. ff. INQUIRE *v.*

†**in'quenchable**, *a. Obs. rare*$^{-1}$. [IN-[3].] Unquenchable.

1577 DEE *Relat. Spir.* I. (1659) 56 Almost for ever buried in a lake of ignorance, and inquenchable flame.

†**in'quered**, *a. Obs. rare*$^{-1}$. [? pa. pple. of **inquere*, a. F. *enqueurer* to put into the heart, to instruct (Godef.); cf. PERQUER.] Instructed. *well inquered*, well-bred, well-mannered.

c **1440** *Promp. Parv.* 521/1 Wel tetchyd, or inqveryd (*K., H.* well condiciond or maneryd, *S.* welle techyd or inqwerdy), *morosus, vel bene morigeratus.*

inquest ('ɪnkwɛst), *sb.* Forms: 3 **anqueste**, 4–5 **enqueste**, 5–7 **enquest**, 5– **inquest**, (6 *Sc.* **-queist**). [a. OF. *enqueste* = Pr. *enquesta*, It. *inchiesta*, Romanic and med.L. *inquesta*, sb. from fem. pa. pple. of Com. Romanic **inquērēre* (L. *inquīrĕre*), It. *inchierere, inchiedere*, Pr. *enquerre, enquerer*, OF. *enquerre*, mod.F. *enquérir* to INQUIRE; analogous to sbs. in *-ata, -ada, -ee*: see -ADE. The spelling with *in-*, though frequent in the 17th c., was not finally established until the 18th c. The pronunciation *in'quest*, whence the aphetic *'quest*, came down to the end of the 17th c.]

1. a. A legal or judicial inquiry to ascertain or decide a matter of fact, esp. one made by a jury in a civil or criminal case. Formerly, a general term for all formal or official inquiries into matters of public or state interest, as fixing of prices, valuation of property with reference to assessments, etc. Now mostly = 'coroner's inquest' (see CORONER 1).

Great Inquest, an appellation sometimes given to the Domesday inquiry and valuation.

α. *c* **1290** *Beket* 387 in *S. Eng. Leg.* I. 117 Þoru an-queste [*v.r.* enqueste] he let þoruȝ þe contreies an-quere Hov muche ech Man scholde paiȝe. *c* **1325** *Poem times Edw. II* (Percy) lxx, Other wit[h] a fals enquest Hang him by the throte. **1393** LANGL. *P. Pl.* C. VI. 57 Clerkes..Sholde noþer swynke ne swete ne swere at enquestes. *c* **1400** *Rom. Rose* 6977 Many tymes I make enquestes..To dele with other mennes thing, That is to me a gret lykyng. **1598** KITCHIN *Courts Leet* (1675) 226 Enquest shall be by custom of the Realm, between party and party. **1641** *Termes de la Ley* 137 b, *Enquest* is that inquiry which is made by Jurors in all causes civill or criminall touching the matter in fact. And such inquirie is either of office or at the mise of the parties. **1655** FULLER *Ch. Hist.* IX. ii. §4 He was indicted upon that Certificat in the County of Middlesex by the common Jury of enquest in the Kings-Bench for that County.

β. **1483** *Cath. Angl.* 196/2 An Inqwest, *Inquesicio, duodena.* **1614** SELDEN *Titles Hon.* 320 If any were distrain'd to bee made Knight, hauing neither in Fee, nor for life, twentie pounds reuenue, and the same were prou'd..by inquest, he should be discharg'd. **1660** R. COKE *Power & Subj.* 193 Indicted of such offences by solemn inquest of lawful men in the Kings Court. **1714** *Fr. Bk. of Rates* 10 We have caused a general Inquest to be made into all the Tolls which are raised upon all the Rivers in Our Kingdom. **1827** HALLAM *Const. Hist.* (1876) I. i. 42 Arbitrary inquests for offences and illegal modes of punishment. **1865** DICKENS *Mut. Fr.* I. iii, There being nothing more to be done until the inquest was held next day. **1874** STUBBS *Const. Hist.* I. ix. 275 The great inquest of all, the Domesday survey. **1882** MISS BRADDON *Mt. Royal* III. iii. 44 You had better go and watch the inquest, and make yourself useful to the coroner.

b. †***Court of Inquest*** (see quot. 1706). †***Halifax inquest***, a summary trial. ***inquest of office***, (*a*) (see quot. 1768); (*b*) 'loosely used of an inquiry into a person's right to the possession of an office held by the government to be forfeited' (*U.S.*).

1597–8 BP. HALL *Sat.* IV. i. 18 Some more strait-lac'd Iuror of the rest, Impannel'd of an Haly-Fax inquest. **1706** PHILLIPS, *The Court of Inquest*, at Guild-hall, London, a particular Court that takes Cognizance of and determines all Complaints preferred for Debt by one Citizen against another under the sum of Forty Shillings. **1768** BLACKSTONE *Comm.* III. xvii. 258 *Inquisition* or *inquest of office*..is an enquiry made by the king's officer..or by commissioners specially appointed, concerning any matter that intitles the king to the possession of lands or tenements, goods or chattels. **1876** DIGBY *Real Prop.* x. §3 (1). 390 The practice is for the Crown to institute an 'inquest of office', usually before commissioners appointed for the purpose, for the purpose of determining whether the tenant died without leaving an heir. **1882** H. ADAMS *J. Randolph* vi. 133 The proceeding was a mere inquest of office under a judicial form.

c. In figurative applications. ***great, last, general inquest***, the last Judgement.

c **1315** SHOREHAM 94 Al desceyved schel he be, Wanne cometh the grete enqueste. **1659** *Gentl. Calling* (1696) 80 If now we proceed to the last part of the Rich man's Duty..we may without an Augur divine the return of that Inquest. **1669** PENN *No Cross* I. iv. §21 In the solemn and general Inquest upon the World. **1784** COWPER *Task* II. 135 It burns down to earth, And in the furious inquest that it makes On God's behalf, lays waste his fairest works. **1885** S. COX *Expos.* Ser. I. ix. 115 The searching inquest of the Judge eternal.

2. a. The body of men appointed to hold a legal inquiry; a jury; now *esp.* a coroner's jury.

c **1305** *Pilate* 196 in *E.E. Poems* (1862) 116 Þenqueste vpe him seide þat he destruyde oure lawe..And ic..Moste nede ȝyue þe dom whan þenqueste sede. **1494** FABYAN *Chron.* VII. 341 The mayre, aldremen, and shryuys, with the sayde enqueste and foure men of euery warde, were chargyd to appere at Westmynster. **1503** *Presentm. Juries* in *Surtees Misc.* (1888) 30 In the presens of all the hole inquest, & many oþer. **1574** tr. *Littleton's Tenures* 79 a, In suche case where the enquest may say their verdit at large. **1623** GOUGE *Serm. Extent God's Provid.* §15 The Coroner and his Inquest comming to view the bodies, found remaining but 63. **1809** BAWDWEN *Domesday Bk.* 623 The inquest say that Gerneber had thirteen acres of wood, and 25 acres of arable land in Irnham. **1863** H. COX *Instit.* II. iii. 345 Where the object is inquiry and information only, the jury is sometimes called an Inquest.

b. ***grand*** or ***great inquest*** = grand JURY; also *transf.*; ***grand*** (or ***great***) ***inquest of the nation***, applied to the House of Commons.

1467 *Ordin. Worcester* xi. in *Eng. Gilds* 382 That the price of ale be sessed at euery lawday by the gret enquest. *Ibid.* xxii. 385 The grete enquest shalle provide..wheþer the pageant shuld go that yere or no. **1629** LYNDE *Via Tuta* 241, I will giue another summons to the prime men, euen of their grand Inquest, who without partiality, will testifie on our behalfe. **1660** *Trial Regic.* 9 Gentlemen, You are the Grand Inquest for the Body of this County of Middlesex. [**1671** F. PHILLIPS *Reg. Necess.* 438 The lower house or Representative of the Commons are but as a Court of grand Enquest to exhibit the grievances of the Nation and the People.] **1691** T. H[ALE] *Acc. New Invent.* p. cxiv, The House of Commons (who are the grand Inquest of the Kingdom). **1752** J. LOUTHIAN *Form of Process* (ed. 2) 193 Adjournment of the Grand Jury. Gentlemen of the Grand Inquest, the Court dismisses you for this Time. **1769** BLACKSTONE *Comm.* IV. xix. 256 An impeachment before the lords by the commons of Great Britain, in parliament, is ..a presentment to the most high and supreme court of criminal jurisdiction by the most solemn grand inquest of the whole kingdom. **1855** MACAULAY *Hist. Eng.* xxii. IV. 748 If he is guilty of partiality, he may be called to account by the great inquest of the nation. **1903** *Daily Chron.* 3 July 7/1 The First Lord of the Admiralty..described it as a grand inquest of the nation.

3. In general sense.

†**a.** An inquiry or question; a questioning.

c **1340** *Gaw. & Gr. Knt.* 1056 For-þy, sir, þis enquest I require yow here, þat ȝe me telle with trawþe, if euer ȝe tale herde Of þe grene chapel. **1671** FLAVEL *Fount. of Life* ii. 32 The grand Inquest of Conscience is: Is God satisfied? **1853** DE QUINCEY *Autobiog. Sk.* Wks. I. 21, I wearied the heavens with my inquest of beseeching looks.

†**b.** A search or investigation in order to find something; a pursuit; a research. In early use, *esp.*, a knightly expedition in pursuit of something or in quest of adventures; a quest. Const. *for* (*of*, *after*). *Obs.*

1470–85 MALORY *Arthur* IX. ii. *heading*, How a damoysel came in to the courte, & desyred a knyght to take on hym an enquest. *c* **1489** CAXTON *Blanchardyn* vi. 25 He founde the foot of the hors of hym for whom he wente in enqueste. **1590** SPENSER *F.Q.* III. ii. 4 To aske..what uncouth wind Brought her into those partes, and what inquest Made her dissemble her disguised kind? **1621** QUARLES *Div. Poems, Esther* (1638) 110 Let strict Inquest and carefull Inquisition In all the Realme be made..For Comely Virgins, beautifull and young. **1651** WALTON *Life Wotton* in *Reliq.* b vij, The City and University were both in a perplext Enquest of the Thieves. *c* **1667** SOUTH *Serm.* (1737) I. vi. 225 This is the laborious and vexatious inquest, that the soul must make after science.

c. Inquiry or investigation (*into* something). Now used *colloq.*, a discussion or investigation of a game, event, etc., after it has taken place.

1625 GILL *Sacr. Philos.* IV. 57 What can the soule and understanding bee busied about, but onely in the enquirie of that trueth and wisedome which God hath manifested in the creature? But whether this inquest shall be immediately after the soules departure from the body, or at the time of restitution..I cannot define. **1645** QUARLES *Sol. Recant.* VII. xxvii, By strict enquest into their sev'rall ways. **1698** FRYER *Acc. E. India & P.* 241 By the Cost and Inquest of this Pious Benefactor, Sweeter Waters are at this time produced. **1837** EMERSON *Amer. Scholar* Wks. (Bohn) II. 178 Let it receive from another mind its truth..without periods of solitude, inquest, and self recovery, and a fatal disservice is done. **1932** *News Chron.* 29 Feb. 8/5 She never in any case holds inquests. You can't make the next shot [in Golf] good by worrying over the last. **1934** *Punch* 3 Jan. 22/3 My intention was to wait for the inevitable inquest and then say..'I don't play much bridge you know.' **1967** J. SYMONS *Man who killed Himself* I. i. 12 'What made you double that heart call?' Clare asked... Mr. Payne wagged a finger. 'Now now. No

inquests.' **1970** *Times* 20 Apr. 1/5 The Apollo 13 astronauts . . tonight left Hawaii to return to Houston where they will soon begin the long inquest into the spacecraft failure.

4. *attrib.* or *Comb.*, as **inquest jury**, a jury of inquiry: see INQUIRY 3; †**inquest-man**, a member of a wardmote inquest (of the city of London); **inquest-room**, the room in which a coroner's inquest is held.

1766 ENTICK *London* IV. 17 Fourteen inquest-men. *Ibid.* 373 This ward . . has 20 wardmote inquest-men. **1825** J. NEWELL *An Enquiry*, etc. 31 Called in the City of London the Inquest Jury, and in the City of Westminster Leet and Annoyance Jury: and which Inquest Jury for its wisdom, usefulness, importance and power to a certain extent is not surpassed by any other. **1845** MRS. NORTON *Child of Islands* (1846) 109 We to the Inquest-Room, to hear in vain, Description of the strong convulsive throes . . By which a struggling life gets rid at last of pain.

†**in'quest**, *pa. pple. Sc. Obs. rare*$^{-1}$. [ad. med.L. *inquest-us* for L. *inquīsītus*: see prec. Used as pa. pple. of *inquere*, INQUIRE; cf. CONQUEST *pa. pple.*] Inquired, questioned.

1566 BP. OF ROSS in Keith *Hist. Ch. Scot.* App. (1734) 135 Hir Majestie maid ane Depesche befoir sche fell seik, bot at this present may nocht be inquest thairof.

†**in'questionably**, *adv. Obs. rare.* [IN-^{3}.] Unquestionably.

a **1641** BP. MOUNTAGU *Acts & Mon.* (1642) 500 Though it be not . . inquestionably to bee beleeved.

in'questual, *a. rare.* [f. med.L. *inquestus* (see prec.), taken as *u*-stem, like L. *quæstus* + -AL^{1}.] Fixed by inquest.

1878 R. W. EYTON *Key to Domesday* 5 There are many cases . . where the inquestual extents of demesnes are either reduced or increased by Domesday.

inquiery, obs. form of INQUIRY.

†**inquie'scential**, *a. Obs. rare*$^{-0}$. [f. IN-^{3} + L. *quiēscentia* rest, QUIESCENCE + -AL^{1}.] Having no rest or quiescence. Hence †**inquie'scentialness** (*rare*$^{-1}$).

1659 D. PELL *Impr. Sea* 425 Amongst the many other sad . . troubles, this of the Mariners inquiescentialness is none of the inferiour ones. If the winds begin . . ten thousand sail . . dance after the musick.

†**in'quiet**, *sb. Obs. rare*$^{-1}$. [f. IN-^{3} + QUIET *sb.*, perh. after L. *inquiēs*, *-quiēt-em*.] Absence of quiet; inquietude; disquiet.

a **1684** LEIGHTON *Serm.* Wks. (1868) 410 Sinful liberty breeds inquiet.

inquiet (ɪn'kwaɪət), *a.* [ad. L. *inquiēt-us*, f. *in-* (IN-^{3}) + *quiētus* QUIET. Cf. F. *inquiet* (16th c. in Hatz.-Darm.).] Not quiet.

†**1.** Restless, turbulent, troublesome. *Obs.*

1382 WYCLIF *2 Thess.* iii. 7 How it bihoueth for to sue vs. For we weren not inquyet among 3ou. *Ibid.* 11 We han herd summe among 3ou for to wandre inquyet, no thing worchinge. **1533** MORE *Debell. Salem* Wks. 961/2 Inquiete vnrestfull wretches. **1552** HULOET, Inquiet, *importunus*.

2. Mentally disturbed; uneasy, anxious. *rare.*

1502 ATKYNSON tr. *De Imitatione* II. vi. 183 An euyll conscience is euer ferefull impacyent and inquyete. *Ibid.* III. xxxiii. 223 Nat to be inquyete of mannes iugement. **1805** tr. *A. La Fontaine's Hermann & Emilia* II. 206 Lebrecht was inquiet, with his hand upon his forehead.

inquiet (ɪn'kwaɪət), *v.* Now *rare*. Also 6 inquyit, (*erron.* enquyet). [a. F. *inquiéter* (12th c.), ad. L. *inquiētāre*, f. *inquiētus*: see prec.] *trans.* To destroy the quiet of; to disquiet.

1. To prevent (a person) from living in peace and quietness; to annoy, molest, harass.

1413 *Pilgr. Sowle* (Caxton 1483) IV. xxxv. 83 Tho that wyllen be besy for to inquyeten and letten the peple by theyr malyce oute of reste and pees. **1530–1** *Act 22 Hen. VIII*, c. 15 His saide subiectes . . shall [not] be sued, vexed, nor inquieted in theyr bodies goodes landes nor cattalles. *a* **1578** LINDESAY (Pitscottie) *Chron. Scot.* (S.T.S.) I. 361 The king inquyrit quho it was that knokit so fast till inquyit him fre his rest. **1697** SIR B. SHOWER *Let. to Convocation-Man* 35 They were frequently and oftentimes arrested and inquieted in their Coming. **1812** SIR R. WILSON *Priv. Diary* I. 6, I passed the night pretty well, but a little inquieted by mosquitoes.

†**2.** To render uneasy; to disquiet; to disturb (in mind). *Obs.* or *arch.*

1486 *Surtees Misc.* (1888) 47 M. John Harington hath been lately inquietid by untrue report maide of hyme. **1494** FABYAN *Chron.* V. cxv. 88 The mystruste that he had in them many tymes inquyeted hym. **1508** FISHER *7 Penit. Ps.* vi. Wks. (E.E.T.S.) 12 Conscyence . . croketh the wyll and enquyeteth the soule. **1540** MORYSINE *Vives' Introd. Wysd.* D b, What . . foolysshenes is it, to inquiete thy mynde, whyles thou studiest to delyte it? **1815** MAD. D'ARBLAY *Let.* 12 June in *Diary* (1846) VII. 189 This delay . . inquieted notre ami. **1828** LANDOR *Imag. Conv.* Wks. 1846 I. 339/1 To fill his bosom with every . . thorny plant that might pierce, blister, or inquiet it.

†**in'quietance.** *Obs. rare*$^{-1}$. [f. INQUIET *v.* + -ANCE: cf. med.L. *quiētāntia*.] = next.

1531 in W. H. Turner *Select. Rec. Oxford* 96 The . . Comissarie demaundyd . . diverse questions . . to the great inquietance of the . . Mayer.

inquietation (ɪnkwaɪə'teɪʃən). *arch.* [a. OF. *inquietation* (1342 in Godef.), ad. med.L. *inquiētātion-em*, n. of action f. *inquiētāre* to INQUIET.] The action of inquieting, disturbing, or molesting; the fact or condition of being inquieted; = next.

1461 *Rolls Parlt.* V. 487/2 Extorcions, Robberies, Murdres been multiplied and contynued within this Reame, to the grete disturbaunce and inquietation of the same. **1530–1** *Act 22 Hen. VIII*, c. 12 Preamble, The inquyetacion and damage of the Kyngs people. **1647** TRAPP *Comm. Matt.* xiii. 23 Thine earnest pantings, inquietations, and desires of better cannot but commend thee much to God. **1684** tr. *Bonet's Merc. Compit.* XIX. 727 The Disease to which a continual inquietation is joined, is terminated within four dayes. [**1878** R. W. DIXON *Hist. Ch. Eng.* I. i. 39 During the same period the complaints of the clergy concerning the inquietation of the times never ceased.]

in'quieting, *vbl. sb.* [f. INQUIET *v.* + -ING^{1}.] The action of disturbing or molesting; the condition of being disturbed or disquieted.

1527 WARHAM *Let. to Wolsey* in Strype *Eccl. Mem.* (1721) I. App. xv. 33 It is a great trouble, vexation, and inquyetyng to be callyd afore your graces commissaries and mine. **1531** in W. H. Turner *Select. Rec. Oxford* 100 Enquyetyng of the Students, and . . greatt hynderans. **1660** R. COKE *Power & Subj.* 201 Without quarrel, inquieting, or vexation of our heirs.

in'quietly, *adv. rare.* [f. INQUIET *a.* + -LY^{2}. Cf. L. *inquiētē*.] In an inquiet or uneasy manner.

1893 VIZETELLY *Glances Back* I. xvi. 313 The duchess, after glancing inquietly at me . . advanced a few paces.

†**in'quietness.** *Obs.* [f. as prec. + -NESS.] The condition of being inquiet; inquietude.

1502 ATKYNSON tr. *De Imitatione* III. xxxiii. 223 Of inordynat loue & vayne drede cometh all inquietnes of herte and dystruccyon of soule. **1516** in Gross *Gild Merch.* II. 381 To the grete trouble, inquietnes and empouerresshement of the same Towne. **1570** BUCHANAN *Admonit.* Wks. (1892) 33 Devysing of generall inquietnes throw yᵉ haill realme.

inquietude (ɪn'kwaɪətju:d). [a. F. *inquiétude* (14th c. in Hatz.-Darm.), or ad. late L. *inquiētūdo*, n. of condition f. *inquiētus* INQUIET *a.*]

†**1.** The fact or condition of being inquieted or having one's quiet disturbed; disturbance. *Obs.*

c **1440** CAPGRAVE *Life St. Kath.* I. 355 Of many thinges was sche sor a-gast, But most of inquietude. *a* **1639** WOTTON *Life Dk. Buckhm.* in *Reliq.* (1651) 104 Having had such experience of his fidelity . . he . . found himself engaged in honour . . to support him . . from any further inquietude. **1748** *Anson's Voy.* II. v. 178 The Commodore . . giving strict orders that they [the female prisoners] should receive no kind of inquietude or molestation whatever. **1797** MRS. RADCLIFFE *Italian* iii. 20 Guard her from inquietude as vigilantly as I have done.

2. *Med.* Restlessness (of the body), caused by pain, uneasiness, or debility.

1597 A. M. tr. *Guillemeau's Fr. Chirurg.* 52/1 Out of the which insueth Inquietude, Agues, Convulsions, *Spasmus*. **1661** LOVELL *Hist. Anim. & Min.* 334 Inquietude, which is a various turning of the body, and members, caused by matter molesting the sentient parts. **1662** STILLINGFL. *Orig. Sacr.* III. iii. §8 The inquietude, aches, and infirmities of old age. **1822–34** *Good's Study Med.* (ed. 4) I. 638 A general soreness over the body, yawning, inquietude, and most of the other concomitants of a febrile incursion. **1875** H. C. WOOD *Therap.* (1879) 476 A narcotic, producing in animals at first inquietude, soon followed by paresis.

†**3.** Restlessness (of a thing). *Obs. rare.*

1790 *Proc. African Assoc.* 19, I was struck with . . the inquietude of his eye.

4. Disturbance of mind; uneasiness, disquietude.

1658 PHILLIPS, *Inquietude*, restlessnesse, want of repose, or quiet of minde. **1695** LD. PRESTON *Boeth.* Pref. 11 We are travelled with Uneasiness, and Inquietude amidst our largest Enjoyments. **1709** STEELE *Tatler* No. 142 ⁋3 The following Letter is what has given me no small Inquietude. **1794** LD. SHEFFIELD in *Ld. Auckland's Corr.* (1862) III. 168, Gibbon is better, but I am by no means without inquietude on his account. **1876** BANCROFT *Hist. U.S.* IV. xxxvii. 593 His forehead was sometimes marked with thought, but never with inquietude.

b. *pl.* Disquieting thoughts; anxieties.

1652 KIRKMAN *Clerio & Lozia* 122 Since I was first molested by these inquietudes for your fair Mistress. **1783** COWPER *Lett.* 29 Sept., Wks. (1876) 140 In the meantime your philosopher . . escapes a thousand inquietudes to which the indolent are subject. **1865** M. ARNOLD *Ess. Crit.* iv. (1875) 176 The very passion of the sister's longing sometimes inspired torturing inquietudes.

†**inquilinate**, *v. Obs. rare*$^{-0}$. [f. ppl. stem of late L. *inquilināre* to be a sojourner: see next.] 'To dwell in a strange place' (Cockeram, 1623).

inquiline ('ɪnkwɪlaɪn), *sb.* (*a.*) *rare.* [ad. L. *inquilīnus* an indweller in a place not his own, a sojourner, lodger, f. *in-* (IN-^{2}) + *colĕre* to dwell. Cf. F. *inquilin* (Cotgr. 1611).]

1. A sojourner, a lodger, an indweller.

a **1641** BP. MOUNTAGU *Acts & Mon.* (1642) 436 Clemens . . and Origen, being both natives or inquilines of Alexandria. **1914** C. MACKENZIE *Sinister St.* II. IV. iv. 926 Half the inquilines of a night and even some of the less transient lodgers ultimately escaped owing her money.

2. *Zool.* An animal which lives in the nest or abode of another; a commensal or guest.

1879 F. H. BUTLER in *Encycl. Brit.* X. 46/1 Besides the larva of the gall-maker, or the householder, galls usually contain inquilines or lodgers, the larvæ of what are termed guest-flies or cuckoo-flies. **1882** *Athenæum* 1 July 19/1 Numerous inquilines of other orders of insects (chiefly beetles) found in ants' nests, which the ants . . never molest, but even take great care of. **1884** *Stand. Nat. Hist.* II. 510 There are several genera of gall-flies which . . are known as guest gall-flies or inquilines.

3. *attrib.* or as *adj.*

1716 M. DAVIES *Athen. Brit.* II. To Rdr. 36 So sung the Inquilin-Muse of Bemerton, Mr. Norris. **1958** *Times Lit. Suppl.* 30 May 299/2 The inquiline figures painted so vigorously by Sir Osbert come to life with extraordinary clarity.

Hence **inqui'linous** *a. Zool.*, living in the nest or abode of another.

1879 F. H. BUTLER in *Encycl. Brit.* X. 46/1 Some saw-flies are inquilinous in the galls of gall-ants.

'inquinate, *v.* [f. ppl. stem of L. *inquināre* to pollute, etc. Cf. obs. F. *inquiner* (1519 in Godef.).] *trans.* To pollute, defile, corrupt.

1542 BECON *Christm. Banquet* in *Early Wks.* (1843) 69 We are . . inquinated, spotted, and defiled. **1646** SIR T. BROWNE *Pseud. Ep.* III. vii. 121 An old opinion it was of that Nation, that the Ibis feeding upon Serpents, that venemous food so inquinated their . . egges within their bodies, that they sometimes came forth in Serpentine shapes. **1661** LOVELL *Hist. Anim. & Min.* 345 False visions are from the vice of the aqueous humour, inquinated by vapours or humours. **1682** SIR T. BROWNE *Chr. Mor.* II. §7 The soul may be foully inquinated at a very low rate, and a man may be cheaply vitious, to the perdition of himself. **1918** H. W. STEED in *19th Cent.* Dec. 987 It is surely enough that some of these stipulations should . . have needlessly protracted the War, without their being allowed to inquinate the peace.

Hence †**'inquinated** *ppl. a.*, polluted, corrupt; **'inquinating** *ppl. a.*

1592 CHETTLE *Kind-harts Dr.* (1841) 15 These impes of iniquitie . . draw whole heapes to hearken to their inquinated cries. **1649** J. H. *Motion to Parl. Adv. Learn.* 39 These inquinated prejudices of education. **1650** tr. *Caussin's Ang. Peace* 85 The inquinated times of the Hebrew Kings. **1914** C. MACKENZIE *Sinister St.* II. IV. iv. 914 Street followed street, each one . . being a little less able to resist the corrosion of a persistently inquinating migration.

inquination (ɪnkwɪ'neɪʃən). Now *rare.* [ad. late L. *inquinātiōn-em* (Vulgate), n. of action from *inquināre* to INQUINATE. Cf. obs. F. *inquination* (Godef.).] The action of polluting, defiling, or corrupting; polluted condition. Also (with *an* and *pl.*), a defilement, a defiling agent. *lit.* and *fig.*

1447 BOKENHAM *Seyntys* (Roxb.) 257 For the kynde of lyht ys . . That . . It dyffoundyth the self wyth owte inquynacyoun. **1582** N. T. (Rhem.) *2 Cor.* vii. 1 Let us cleanse our selves from al inquination of the flesh and spirit. **1626** BACON *Sylva* §676–7 Their Causes, and Axiomes . . are meere Inquinations of Experience, and Concoct it not. **1665** NEEDHAM *Medela Medic.* 410 A venemous Miasma or Inquination affecting the bloud. **1710** T. FULLER *Pharm. Extemp.* 293 It . . obliterates putridinous Inquinations. **1890** J. H. STIRLING *Gifford Lect.* xii. 220 [This] saves God from any derogation of direct intromission with the inquination of sense.

inquirable, enquirable (ɪn'kwaɪərəb(ə)l), *a.* Now *rare.* [f. INQUIRE *v.* + -ABLE.] That may or should be inquired about or into; that admits of or calls for inquiry; open to inquiry. (Chiefly in legal use.) Also with *into*.

α. **1485** *Act 1 Hen. VII*, c. 7 The same . . Disobeysance shall be Felony, enquirable and determinable as is aforesaid. **1535** *Act 27 Hen. VIII*, c. 5 §1 All maner . . things enquirable presentable or determinable before iusticers of peace. **1647** N. BACON *Disc. Govt. Eng.* I. I. (1739) 88 This made the crime enquirable at the common-Law. **1740** *Col. Rec. Pennsylv.* IV. 404 Any Thing of this kind . . is more properly enquirable by others than by us.

β. *a* **1547** *Petit.* in Rye *Cromer* (1889) 53 All suche transpases & offences as be . . Inquyreable in Haven Courts. **1574** J. JONES *Nat. Begin. Grow. Things* 42 So that it wer requisite at Assises, Sessions, and Sinodes, it were inqueereable. **1651** R. SAUNDERS *Plenary Possess.* 9 The Third Question inquirable into is [etc.]. **1670** *Bushell's Case* in *Phenix* (1721) I. 423 An Article inquirable in every Oyer and Terminer. **1766** W. GORDON *Gen. Counting-ho.* 377 The consideration of the note was not inquirable.

†**inquirance, enquirance.** *Obs.* Forms: 5 enquer-, enquiraunce, -ance, inquyrans, 6 inquyr-, inquiraunce, -ance. [In ME. *enquerance* (prob. OF. or AF.), f. *enquerant*, pr. pple. of *enquerre* to INQUIRE: see -ANCE.] Inquiry.

1412–20 LYDG. *Chron. Troy* IV. xxx, Of which thynge . . I wyll my selfe maken enqueraunce. *c* **1449** PECOCK *Repr.* II. viii. 188 Fro enquirancis whi God chesith this place. *c* **1485** *Digby Myst.* (1882) I. 376, I commaunde you all . . after this yong kyng to make good enqueraunce. **1526** TINDALE *Acts* x. 17 The men . . had made inquyraunce for Simons housse. **1567** MAPLET *Gr. Forest* 29 Man mought by art and inquiraunce after these attaine or come vnto knowledge hereof.

in'quirant, en'quirant, *a. nonce-wd.* [irreg. f. INQUIRE, ENQUIRE + -ANT: cf. F. *enquérant*. See also INQUIRENT.] Inquiring.

1822 *Blackw. Mag.* XI. 163 This aspirant, Though observant, enquirant . . betray'd the foot cloven.

inquiration (ɪnkwaɪə'reɪʃən). *dial.* [f. INQUIRE *v.* + -ATION.] Inquiry.

1789 C. SMITH *Ethelinde* III. 136 If so be you would acquaint me where I may make enquiration after your frinds or hern, it would come to the same thing. **1839** C. CLARK *John Noakes* v, If they their inquirations make In winter time, some will Condemn that place as no great shakes. **1850** DICKENS *Dav. Copp.* li. 516 A decent woman as spoke to her about . . making secret inquiration concerning of me and all

at home. **1886** HARDY *Mayor Casterbr.* II. xiv. 196 'Suppose we make inquiration into it, Christopher,' continued Longways; 'and if we find there's really anything in it, drop a letter to them most concerned.'

inquire, enquire (ɪnˈkwaɪə(r)), *v.* Forms: see A. below. [ME. *enquer-e(n.*, a. OF. *enquer-re* (*enquer-ant*), mod.F. *enquér-ir* = Pr. *enquerer*, *enquerre*, It. †*inquierere*, †*inchierere*, *inchiedere*:—late pop.L. type **inquærĕre* for *inquærĕre* (analytical for cl.L. *inquīrĕre*), f. *in-* (IN-[2]) + *quærĕre* to ask. In Eng. the stem-vowel was conformed to the cl.L. in 15th c.; Sc. retained the Fr. form. The prefix began also to be conformed to L. in 14–15th c., but the half-latinized *enquire* still subsists beside *inquire*: cf. *endoss, endorse, indorse*.]

A. Illustration of Forms.

α. 3 anquere, 3–6 enquere, 4 enquer.

c **1290** *Beket* 387 in *S. Eng. Leg.* I. 117 He let þoruȝ þe contreies an-quere [*Harl.* enquere] Hov muche ech Man scholde paiȝe. **1297** R. GLOUC. (Rolls) 7675 King William.. Let enqueri [*v.rr.* enquery, enquere] streitliche [etc.]. *c* **1340** *Cursor M.* 11475 (Trin.) Goop he seide & faste enquere how he is born & where. *c* **1380** *Sir Ferumb.* 2919 þanne of hymen he gan enquer. **1477** EARL RIVERS (Caxton) *Dictes* 67 Enquere and seke to haue vertues. **1535** COVERDALE *1 Sam.* xxiii. 23, I wyl enquere after him.

β. 5–7 inquere, *Sc.* inqueir, 6 inqueere.

14.. *Sir Beues* (MS. M) 1030 A palmers wede thou shalte were, So may thou best after hym inquere. **1487** *Barbour's Bruce* IV. 221 Of thingis that he vald Inqueir. **1512** *Act 4 Hen. VIII*, c. 20 Preamble, [They] caused a Crouner to sit and inquere on the vieu of the Bodies. **1563** WINȜET *Wks.* (1890) II. 57 Perchanse sum man wil inqueir. **1574** Inqueere [see INQUIRABLE β]. **1590** SPENSER *F.Q.* I. i. 31, I chiefly doe inquere [*rimes* heare, neare, weare]. **1663** BUTLER *Hud.* I. i. 131 Whatever Sceptick could inquere for, For every *why* he had a *wherefore*.

γ. 5–6 enquyre, enquier, 5– enquire.

14.. *Chaucer's L.G.W.* 1152 *Dido* (MS. Gg. 4. 27), Of the dedes hath she more enquyrid [4 *MSS.* enquered, *rime* lered]. **1525** LD. BERNERS *Froiss.* II. clxxxviii. [clxxxiv.] 575 Than he was enquyred where he had the wyne. **1596** SHAKS. *Merch. V.* I. i. 183 Goe presently enquire. **1599** —— *Much Ado* I. i. 181 Would you buie her, that you enquier after her? **1667** MILTON *P.L.* III. 571 He stayd not to enquire. **1765** H. WALPOLE *Otranto* iii. 47 Enquire who is without. **1856** (*title*) Enquire within upon Everything.

δ. 5–6 inquyre, 5– inquire.

c **1440** Inquired [see B. 3 b]. **1483** CAXTON *G. de la Tour* F v b, Dylygently inquyred and knowen. **1483** *Cath. Angl.* 196/2 To Inquire. **1567** *Gude & Godlie B.* (S.T.S.) 100 Thair counsell is to seirche and to Inquyre. **1605** BACON *Adv. Learn.* II. i. §5 He inquireth the nature of a commonwealth. **1611** BIBLE *Ps.* xxvii. 4 To inquire in his temple. **1711** ADDISON *Spect.* No. 164 ¶2 To inquire if they had heard any thing. **1850** TENNYSON *In Mem.* iv, Who scarcely darest to inquire.

B. Signification.

†1. *trans.* To search into, seek information or knowledge concerning, investigate, examine. *Obs.*

c **1300** *Beket* 1356 That ȝe with ous sende, A legat to Engelonde: to enquere therof than ende. **1388** WYCLIF *Job* x. 6 That thou enquere my wickidnesse and enserche my synne. **1612** WOODALL *Surg. Mate* Wks. (1653) 8 The use of a Probe.. sometimes to enquire the depth of a wound. **1646** SIR T. BROWNE *Pseud. Ep.* II. iii. 67 The writings of some, and Maps of others, are to be enquired. **1787** *Generous Attachm.* IV. 168 Its propriety [was] enquired with a degree of scrupulosity that would have done honour to the most rigid of the Fathers.

†b. To search (a place). *Obs. rare.*

c **1605** ROWLEY *Birth Merl.* II. i. 292 Do but inquire this forest, I'll go with you. **1615** CHAPMAN *Odyss.* IV. 520 Who can the deeps of all the seas enquire.

2. To seek knowledge of (a thing) by putting a question; to ask about; to request to be told; to ask (something) *of*, Sc. *at* (a person).

a. with simple object. Now less usual.

c **1305** *Pilate* 52 in *E.E.P.* (1862) 112 He wiste wel þe gyle And þe maner enquerede of þe lond. **1388** WYCLIF *Matt.* ii. 16 Aftir the tyme that he had enquerid of the astromyens. *c* **1450** *Merlin* 44 They enquered tidinges of Merlin. *a* **1533** LD. BERNERS *Huon* xxiv. 446 Euer enquyrynge newes for that he sought for. **1548** HALL *Chron., Hen. V*, 76b, Of whom the duke inquired the numbre of his enemies. **1607** SHAKS. *Cor.* III. i. 54 You must enquire your way. **1633** BP. HALL *Hard Texts* 501 To inquire my interpretation of this dreame. **1749** FIELDING *Tom Jones* XVIII. vii, To inquire the character of a servant. **1785** BURNS *Cotter's Saturday Night* vii, The wily mother.. Wi' heart-struck, anxious care, inquires his name. **1805** EMILY CLARK *Banks of Douro* II. 110 Captain O'Dell enquired Mr. Taylor's residence in town. **1812** BYRON *Wks.* (1832) II. 202 Before recurring to my own business I could not help enquiring that of Sheridan.

b. with interrogative clause as object (in indirect or, less frequently, direct oration): To ask, make the inquiry.

c **1290** [see A. α]. **1297** R. GLOUC. (Rolls) 10469 þe king enquerede of is men al, wat hii awei bere? *c* **1380** WYCLIF *Sel. Wks.* III. 312 Wolde God þat alle.. trewe men wolden enquere where it were betre for to fynde goode prestis bi fre almes of þe peple. *c* **1440** *Ipomydon* 110 Men.. Enquered of men of other contre, Of Calabre lond who was kynge. **1523** FITZHERB. *Surv.* 2 It is to be inquered how many feldes are of the demeyns. **1530** PALSGR. 360 We enquyre or demaunde if we haue any parte or porcyon therof. **1611** BIBLE *Matt.* ii. 7 Herod.. enquired of them diligently what time the Starre appeared. **1683** RAY *Corr.* (1848) 132 Visit him, and inquire of him whether he designs to engrave and publish any of those icons. **1747** WESLEY *Prim. Physic* (1762) p. viii, They began to enquire how they might account for these Things. *Ibid.* p. xiv, Is it enquired; But are there not Books enough already? **1824** GALT *Rothelan* III. VII. viii. 76, I will inquire at the servants.. if he has gone out. **1833** HT. MARTINEAU *Berkeley the Banker* I. iv. 93 'May one ask about the forgers?' inquired Fanny.

†c. To ask (a question). *Obs.* (In first quot. with dative of person, or double object.)

a **1400–50** *Alexander* 1110 Enquire me noȝt þat question, for I queth þe it neuer. **1526** *Pilgr. Perf.* (W. de W. 1531) 18 Which forbyddeth ony person to enquyre ony suche questyon.

†3. To seek information from (a person) by putting a question; to address a question to, to question, interrogate; to ask (some one). *Obs.*

a. with personal object only, or const. *of* or *for*.

c **1430** *Freemasonry* 441 They schul enquere every monn ..Ʒef any mon mowe be y-fownde gulty. **1461** *Paston Lett.* No. 409 II. 38, I enqueryd hym of the gydyng of my maystyr yore sone. **1541** R. COPLAND *Guydon's Quest. Chirurg., Man. exam. Lazares* Q iij, Than enquyre hym of his dreames. **1671** MILTON *P.R.* I. 458 Thou no more with pomp and sacrifice Shalt be inquired at Delphos or elsewhere. **1682** DRYDEN *Medal* 164 [The Bible] was fram'd at first our Oracle t' enquire.

b. with subordinate interrogative clause.

c **1440** *Jacob's Well* (E.E.T.S.) 264 þou schalt ben inquired wheþer þou dedyst him for god or for þe world. **1549** *Compl. Scot.* To Rdr. 13 He inquirit annibal, quhat iugement he hed of his philosophour phormion. *a* **1639** SPOTTISWOOD *Hist. Ch. Scot.* v. (1677) 277 Mr. Patrick being enquired.. whether he would submit himself to trial.

4. *intr.* To make search or investigation; to search, seek; to make inquisition. Const. *into*, †*of*, †*after*.

c **1330** R. BRUNNE *Chron.* (1810) 247 þe kyng was [to] enquere of þer wikked dedes. *c* **1386** CHAUCER *Man of Law's T.* 531 This gentil kyng.. thought he wold enquere Depper in this cas. —— *Wife's Prol.* 316 What nedeth thee of me to enquere or spyen? *a* **1500** *Sir Beues* (Pynson) 3424 In eche londe do thou enquere After syr Beuys of Hamptowne. **1590** SPENSER *F.Q.* II. Introd. 4 Of faery lond yet if he more inquyre.. He may it fynd. **1648** D. JENKINS *Wks.* (Table), Briberies, Extortions, Monopolies, ought to bee enquired after by the House of Commons. **1711** ADDISON *Spect.* No. 63 ¶6, I inquired into what they were doing. *a* **1714** SHARP *Serm.* II. ii. (R.), And here two things are to be enquired into. **1864** BRYCE *Holy Rom. Emp.* viii. (1875) 135 He began by inquiring into the character and manners of the Pope.

5. *intr.* To seek information by questioning; to put a question or questions; to ask. (In biblical use often = to consult an oracle, etc.) Const. *of*, also (now Sc.) *at* (the source of information); *about, after*, †*of* (the subject of inquiry). *to inquire after* (a person), to make inquiries about his welfare, etc., to ask how he is.

c **1375** *Cato Major* II. vi. in *Anglia* VII, Enquere not of priuites Of God, ne eke of heuene. *c* **1460** *Play Sacram.* 628 Fast to hym I wold inquere. **1582** N.T. (Rhem.) *Matt.* ii. 8 Goe and inquire diligently of the childe. **1596** SHAKS. *Tam. Shr.* I. ii. 166, I promist to enquire carefully About a schoolemaster. **1600** —— *A.Y.L.* III. iv. 50 You haue oft enquired After the Shepheard that complain'd of loue. **1611** BIBLE *Gen.* xxiv. 57 Wee will call the Damsell, and enquire at her mouth. —— *1 Sam.* xxiii. 2 Dauid enquired of the Lord. —— *1 Chron.* xiii. 3 Let us bring againe the Arke of our God to us: for we enquired not at it in the dayes of Saul. **1613** T. LORKIN *Let.* 8 July in *Crt. & Times Jas. I* (1848) I. 255 Sir Thomas Somerset inquires very kindly after you. *a* **1745** SWIFT (J.), To those who inquired about me, my lover would answer that [etc.]. **1749** FIELDING *Tom Jones* XII. v, We may expect to meet with somebody to inquire of. **1750** JOHNSON *Rambler* No. 45 ¶8 When parents make articles for their children without enquiring after their consent. **1827** KEBLE *Chr. Y.* 17 Sund. Trin. x, Dare not to enquire Of Him whose name is Jealous. **1846** TRENCH *Mirac.* xv. (1862) 256 After this greater offender they inquire now.

b. To make request (*for* a thing); to ask to see a person. Const. *for* (*after*, obs. or arch.).

1500–20 DUNBAR *Poems* xxix. 31, I haif inquyrit in mony a place, For help and confort in this cace. **1603** SHAKS. *Meas. for M.* IV. i. 17 *Duke.* Hath any body enquir'd for mee here to day? .. *Mar.* You haue not bin enquir'd after. **1611** BIBLE *Acts* ix. 11 Inquire in the house of Iudas, for one called Saul of Tarsus.

†6. *trans.* To seek, search for, try to find. esp. with *out* (rarely *forth*): To seek till one finds; to seek out, search out, find out by seeking (often including the notion of *asking*: cf. 3). *Obs.*

1390 GOWER *Conf.* I. 176 Al that I may enquire and seche Of such deceipte, I telle it al. **1450–80** tr. *Secreta Secret.* (E.E.T.S.) 36 Enquere the on that wolle trewly bere thi lettris. **1526** *Pilgr. Perf.* (W. de W. 1531) 3b, Enquyre & seke our lorde, be fixed in hym. **1591** SHAKS. *Two Gent.* II. iv. 186 Goe on before: I shall enquire you forth. **1596** —— *Merch. V.* IV. ii. 1 Enquire the Iewes house out. **1597** *1st Pt. Return fr. Parnass.* IV. i. 1247 Now good Sexton, I am tirde ..with enquiringe you. **1675** MARVELL *Corr.* cclix. Wks. 1872–5 II. 482 To inquire out the Printer and Author. **1725** POPE *Odyss.* VII. 37 Well known to me the palace you enquire. **1751** JOHNSON *Rambler* No. 98 ¶17 He.. would enquire out a trade for his eldest son. **1790** *Norman & Bertha* II. 165 An unhappy chance conducted Bertha to my house.. to enquire out your residence.

†7. *trans.* (or *absol.*) To ask for, demand; to require. *Obs. rare.*

1513 BRADSHAW *St. Werburge* I. 2138 Lamentynge nyght and day his departure As nature enquyred. **1547–64** BAULDWIN *Mor. Philos.* (Palfr.) IV. v, One friend ought not to enquire any vniust thing of another. **1656** H. PHILLIPS *Purch. Patt.* (1676) 85 Any number of pounds inquired.

¶8. (*erron.*) To call, name. *Obs.*

1590 SPENSER *F.Q.* II. x. 12 The which he cald Canutium, for his hyre; Now Cantium, which Kent we comenly inquyre.

†**in'quire, en'quire**, *sb. Obs.* Also 6 inquere, inquyre. [f. prec. vb.] The action, or an act, of inquiring; inquiry.

c **1450** *Merlin* 3 They wende that oure lorde sholde haue no knowynge of their ordenaunce and enquire. **1525** LD. BERNERS *Froiss.* II. clxiii. [clix.] 451 That Betysach was in prison, and that inquyre was made of his dedes. *a* **1547** *Petit.* in Rye *Cromer* (1889) 53 Those trespases and offences that the Kyngs Highnes hath alweys hadd the Inquere and punyssement of. **1600** *Look About You* xxix. in Hazl. *Dodsley* VII. 480 Make thy inquire, where mad Gloster lives. **1638** WILKINS *New World* I. (1684) 142 Whether they are there in a Blessed Estate, or else what means there may be for their Salvation? with many other such Uncertain Enquires.

inquired, enquired (ɪnˈkwaɪəd), *ppl. a. rare.* [f. INQUIRE *v.* + -ED[1].] Sought, investigated, asked, required, etc.: see the verb.

1598 FLORIO, *Inquisito*, examined, enquired. **1684** R. WALLER *Nat. Exper.* 117 If Experience does not reach the very bottom of the enquired Truth, yet it goes hard if it strikes not out some Light.

‖**inquirendo** (ɪnkwaɪˈrɛndəʊ). *Law.* [L. *inquīrendo*, 'by inquiring', abl. gerund of *inquīrĕre* to INQUIRE.] 1. (See quots.)

1607 COWELL *Interpr.*, *Inquirendo*, is an authoritie giuen to a person or persons, to inquire into some thing for the kings aduantage. **1848** WHARTON *Law Lex.*, *Inquirendo*, an authority given to some official person to institute an enquiry concerning the Crown's interests.

2. An investigation.

a **1846** G. DARLEY in B. W. Procter *Procter* (1877) 286 Confound your prose lunatics who leave you no time for inquirendos upon poetic ones! **1897** L. I. GUINEY (*title*) Patrins, to which is added an Inquirendo into the Wit and Other Good Parts of His Late Majesty King Charles the Second.

†**in'quirent**, *a. Obs. rare*[-1]. [ad. L. *inquīrent-em*, pr. pple. of *inquīrĕre* to INQUIRE. Cf. INQUIRANT.] Inquiring.

a **1763** SHENSTONE *Economy* II. 149 Ev'n Delia's eye As in a garden, roves, of hues alone Inquirent, curious.

inquirer, enquirer (ɪnˈkwaɪərə(r)). [f. INQUIRE *v.* + -ER[1].] One who inquires; a seeker, investigator; a questioner, interrogator.

1570–74 BP. COX *Injunct.*, For the Churchwardens and Inquirers. **1605** BACON *Adv. Learn.* I. vii. §6 The most curious man that lived, and the most universal inquirer. **1699** HICKES in *Lett. Lit. Men* (Camden) 283, I pray you.. to let inquirers know that my Book is advanced to the lv. sheet. *a* **1779** WARBURTON *Div. Legat.* IX. Introd., Wks. 1811 VI. 217 Prejudices mislead the Enquirer no less than his passions. **1859** C. BARKER *Assoc. Princ.* iii. 62 These.. virtues.. ever and anon present themselves to the enquirer. **1871** L. STEPHEN *Playgr. Europe* x. (1894) 226 There is one great puzzle in store for the critical inquirer. *Mod.* Numerous inquirers have called during the day.

b. Const. *after, into*, †*of*, etc.

1611 FLORIO, *Inuenitore*,.. a searcher or inquirer out of any thing. **1624** GATAKER *Transubst.* 93 Curious.. enquirers after the workes of those that were before them. **1646** SIR T. BROWNE *Pseud. Ep.* VI. i. 278 Eager enquirers in what day of the month the world began. **1648** W. MOUNTAGUE *Devout Ess.* I. viii. §1. 79 He answereth all sincere inquirers of truth. **1784** COWPER *Tiroc.* 192 Such rhapsodies our shrewd discerning youth Learn from expert inquirers after truth. **1834** J. ANGELL JAMES (*title*) The Anxious Inquirer after Salvation directed and encouraged. **1880** GRANT WHITE *Every-Day Eng.* 76 The inquirers as to the true pronunciation of English are a great multitude.

in'quiress, en'quiress. *rare.* [Short for **inquireress*, f. prec. + -ESS.] A female inquirer.

1810 *Splendid Follies* I. 179 'She's an heiress, my dear lady.' 'Indeed!' replied the enquiress.

inquiring, enquiring (ɪnˈkwaɪərɪŋ), *vbl. sb.* [f. INQUIRE *v.* + -ING[1].] The action of the verb INQUIRE; inquiry.

c **1386** CHAUCER *Man of Law's T.* 790 By witt and subtil enqueryng [*rime* spryng]. **1530** PALSGR. 234/2 Inquyring, *enquisition*. **1546** J. HEYWOOD *Prov.* (1867) 74 But this is a question of olde enqueryng [*rime* hearyng]. **1611** FLORIO, *Inuenimento*,.. an inquiring out.

in'quiring, en'quiring, *ppl. a.* [f. as prec. + -ING[2].] That inquires; disposed to inquire, given to inquiry, inquisitive.

1598 FLORIO, *Inquisitiuo*, enquiring, searching, seeking, inquisitiue, busie. **1702** ROWE *Tamerl.* I. i. 89 Tamerlane Comes like the Proxy of enquiring Heav'n To Judge and to Redress. **1742** RICHARDSON *Pamela* III. 55 Jackey.. now comes in with an inquiring Face. **1850** L. HUNT *Autobiog.* II. xv. 181 Conscientious though not very inquiring Clergymen. **1898** *Daily News* 22 Jan. 2/5 But this world is an inquiring world. This age is an inquiring age.

Hence **in'quiringly, en'quiringly** *adv.*, in an inquiring manner; with a disposition to, or indication of, inquiry.

1644 DIGBY *Mans Soul* (1645) 24 Doubtfull propositions, which the understanding.. maketh inquiringly to informe it self of the truth of them. **1821** *New Monthly Mag.* III. 615 Curiosity has been.. so naturally and so inquiringly awake. **1859** GEO. ELIOT *A. Bede* lii, Dinah looked at him inquiringly.

†**in'quirist.** *Obs. rare.* [f. INQUIRE *v.* + -IST.] An inquirer, questioner.

1748 RICHARDSON *Clarissa* (1811) IV. xlviii. 321 The inquirist keeping himself on the reserve as to his employers. **1750** —— *Corr.* (1804) IV. 123 So kind an enquirist.

†**in'quirous,** *a.* *Obs. rare*⁻¹. [f. INQUIRE + -OUS.] Inquisitive.

1632 LITHGOW *Trav.* VIII. 373 These Savages..were still inquirous, what I was, and whether I went.

inquiry, enquiry (ɪnˈkwaɪərɪ). Forms: α. 5 enquery, 6–7 enquirie, 6– enquiry. β. 6 inquery, -rie, inquyrie, 6–7 inquirie, 7 inquiery, 6– inquiry. [In 15th c. *enquery*, f. *enquere*, INQUIRE *v.* + -Y: subseq. altered to *enquiry, inquiry*, after the vb.] The action, or an act or course, of inquiring.

1. a. The action of seeking, esp. (now always) for truth, knowledge, or information concerning something; search, research, investigation, examination.

α. *c* **1440** *York Myst.* xxxii. 110 It langis to youre lordschippe..As souereyne youre selffe to sitte of enquery. **1581** LAMBARDE *Eiren.* IV. i. (1602) 363 And this description excludeth all meetings, that are onely for Enquirie: in so much as to enquire, and not to heare and determine, is but a half doing. **1662** STILLINGFL. *Orig. Sacr.* III. i. §14, I clearly perceive upon exact enquiry, that to be an animal doth belong to the nature of man. **1719** YOUNG *Revenge* V. ii, Enquiry will discover all. **1782** BURNEY *Hist. Mus.* (1789) II. i. 29 Its Notation seems a subject of enquiry, not unworthy the curiosity of musical readers.

β. **1556** *Aurelio & Isab.* (1608) B vj, The Kyng.. ordeyned, that the processe with diligent inquirie shuld be fornished. *a* **1682** SIR T. BROWNE *Tracts* (1684) 98 Without all doubt and reason for farther inquiry. **1743** J. MORRIS *Serm.* iii. 69 To reject the christian religion without inquiry. **1874** GREEN *Short Hist.* ix. §1. 597 Fields of inquiry which had till then been unknown.

b. (with *pl.*) A course of inquiry, an investigation.

α. **1548** HALL *Chron., Hen. VI* 169 b, To call the empanelles, for thenquiry, as the use and order is. **1646** SIR T. BROWNE *Pseud. Ep.* I. vii. 27 Many simples unknowne to his enquiries. **1709** STEELE *Tatler* No. 6 ¶4 We generally spend the Evening..in Enquiries into Antiquity. **1875** JOWETT *Plato* (ed. 2) V. 424 To make a satisfactory enquiry into what has been said.

β. **1512** *Act 4 Hen. VIII*, c. 20 Preamble, Theire adherentes..caused a Crouner to sit and inquere..and for the inquery therof..caused to be..impanelled such parciall and mysgoverned persons. **1548** HALL *Chron., Hen. VII* 48 He shortly caused inquyries to be made of diverse offences. **1676** RAY *Corr.* (1848) 126 If you still prosecute the same studies and inquiries. **1798** WELLINGTON *Let. to Tippoo Sultaun* in Gurw. *Desp.* (1837) I. 5 You will afford every facility to the conduct of the necessary inquiries. **1868** LOCKYER *Elem. Astron.* iv. (1870) 147 We are now in a position to proceed with our inquiry.

2. a. The action of asking or questioning; interrogation. (In commercial use = DEMAND *sb.*¹ 4.)

1565 GOLDING *Cæsar* v. 116 b, We coulde learne nothinge therof by enquiry. **1572** R. H. tr. *Lauaterus' Ghostes* (1596) 136 That Magike and enquirie of things at the dead, did much displease God. **1611** BIBLE *Prov.* xx. 25 It is a snare to the man..after vowes to make inquirie. **1709** STEELE *Tatler* No. 120 ¶4 Upon Enquiry, I was informed that her Name was Jealousy. **1880** *Daily News* 26 Feb. 3/2 The Stock Exchange settlement begun to-day is the chief cause of the increased inquiry.

b. A question; an interrogation, a query.

1548 HALL *Chron., Hen. VIII* 54 Of his awne frewyll and mynde, without any question or enquiry to him made. **1659** D. PELL *Improv. Sea* Ded. d b, When they were ready to depart, a mutual inquiry was made how that they might meet again. **1715–20** POPE *Iliad* v. 631 Inquiries none they made: the dreadful day No pause of words admits. **1814** W. BROWN *Hist. Prop. Chr. Heathen* II. 30 They made enquiries at him concerning the character of the inhabitants. **1875** SCRIVENER *Lect. Text N.T.* 9 Our reply to this reasonable enquiry is simple, and wholly satisfactory.

3. ***court of inquiry***, a court legally constituted to inquire into and investigate any charge against an officer or soldier of the army, or any transaction in which the conduct of persons may be found to call for proceedings before a court-martial. ***jury of inquiry***, † (*a*) a Grand Jury (also †*jury of inquest*: cf. INQUEST *sb.* 1, quot. 1655) *obs.*; (*b*) a jury summoned to investigate the subject of a writ of inquiry. ***writ of inquiry***, a writ directing an inquiry or inquest; *spec.* that described in quot. 1809.

1588 FRAUNCE *Lawiers Log.* I. xix. 67 b, Each Jury of enquiry ought to conteine twelve in number at the least, and if there bee 18 or more, it shal not bee amisse. Yet the common order with us is to have them of an odde number, as 17, 19, or 21, to the ende..that if they should dissent in opinion..there should bee alwayes one to..cast the ballance. **1800** ADDISON *Amer. Law Rep.* 21 Brackenridge asked the direction of the Court to exhibit a judgment for a penalty in evidence to a jury of enquiry. **1808** WELLINGTON *Let. to Pulteny Malcolm* 12 Nov. in Gurw. *Desp.* (1837) IV. 164 To be examined before the Court of Inquiry. **1809** TOMLINS *Law Dict., Writ of Inquiry of Damages*, a judicial Writ that issues out to the Sheriff upon a judgment by default, in action, of the case, covenant, trespass, trover &c. commanding him to summon a jury to inquire what damages the plaintiff hath sustained *occasione præmissorum.* **1875** *Judicature Act* Ord. xiii. §6 Where the defendant fails to appear..interlocutory judgment may be entered, and a writ of inquiry shall issue to assess the value of the goods and the damages. **1883** *Wharton's Law Lex.* (ed. 7), *Inquiry, Court of*, frequently appointed by the Army authorities to ascertain the propriety of resorting to ulterior proceedings against a person charged before it. The evidence is unsworn.

4. *attrib.* and *Comb.*, as ***inquiry agency, agent, -office, room***, etc.

1850 J. GALLAHER *Western Sk.-Bk.* 243 He came into the inquiry room, and told me..that he had been living in sin. **1888** A. T. PIERSON *Evang. Work* x. 95 Inquiry-rooms will be put where no one can go out without passing their open doors. **1892** KIPLING & BALESTIER *Naulakha* xvii. 204 See here, young woman, do you run a private inquiry agency? **1894** *Daily News* 13 Apr. 7/3 Detectives Croxton and Gentle said that no doubt since 1889 he had been living on inquiry fees. **1897** *Westm. Gaz.* 10 Apr. 7/2 Referring to obstinate South Africa inquiry witnesses. **1901** *Daily News* 5 Feb. 4/4 The Rev. F. B. Meyer..hoped that each church would continue its..band of inquiry-room workers. **1922** *Kelly's Directory Liverpool* 1181/3 Ramage & Kelly private inquiry agents. **1971** K. GOTTSCHALK in B. de Ferranti *Living with Computer* iv. 31 Society is being confronted with.. ultraviolet photography practised by inquiry agents.

†**in'quisible,** *a.* *Obs. rare.* [irreg. f. *inquisite, inquis-ition* + -IBLE.] Capable of being, or liable to be, inquired into; subject to inquisition.

a **1676** HALE *Hist. Placit. Cor.* (1736) I. xxxi. 414 If the body cannot be seen, then it is inquisible before the justices of oyer and terminer.

†**inquisite,** *v.* *Obs.* [f. L. *inquīsīt-*, ppl. stem of *inquīrĕre* to INQUIRE: perh. back-formation from *inquisition.* (It corresponds in form to a L. frequentative of *inquīrĕre*; and also partly to F. *enquêter*, OF. *enquester*, med.L. **inquestāre* to make inquest.)]

1. *trans.* To inquire into, investigate, examine. Also *absol.* To make inquiry.

1674 (*title*) Defensio Legis: Or, the Whole State of England Inquisited and Defended for General Satisfaction. *a* **1734** NORTH *Lives* (1826) III. 195 What rather encouraged them to inquisite the actions of their adversaries. —— *Life Ld. Guildford* (1808) II. 40 (D.) He inquisited with justice and decorum.

2. To proceed against (a person) by inquisition or by the method of the Inquisition.

1639 GENTILIS tr. *Servita's Inquis.* in *Hist. Counc. Trent* (1676) 833 That those which are Inquisited or Cited for Heresie, flying within the State, shall be condemned for four years to Prisons separate from other Prisons. **1651** tr. *Life Father Sarpi* (1676) 22 This is all the remedy that can be had, that such as are so narrowly inquisited may in their recourse to Rome with their Commissions find Justice. *a* **1734** NORTH *Exam.* III. viii. §50 (1740) 621 It is a transcendent Justification to be thus inquisited and in every Respect, acquitted. **1736** CHANDLER *Hist. Persec.* 223 He is farther asked, whether he hath ever been inquisited.

†**inquisite,** *a.* *Obs. rare.* [In form ad. L. *inquīsīt-us*, pa. pple. of *inquīrĕre* to INQUIRE: cf. EXQUISITE; but with active sense.] Inquisitive.

1808 HELEN ST. VICTOR *Ruins of Rigonda* II. 84 [He bent his eyes] in the most firm and inquisite search on his countenance. **1822** 'P. BEAUCHAMP' (G. Grote) *Analysis* 123 When mankind advance a little in knowledge, and become inquisite. [In ed. of 1875 altered to *inquisitive*.]

inquisition (ɪnkwɪˈzɪʃən), *sb.* Forms: 4–7 inquisicion, etc. (with usual interchange in 4–6 of *i* and *y*, *s* and *c* (*sc, ss*), *-on* (*-one*) and *-oun*), 6 enquisicion, 6– inquisition. [a. OF. *inquisition, -icion* (12th c. in Hatz.-Darm.), ad. L. *inquīsītiōn-em* searching into, examination, legal examination, n. of action from *inquīrĕre* to INQUIRE. Cf. It. *inquisizione*, Sp. *inquisicion.*]

1. The action or process of inquiring or searching into matters, esp. for the purpose of finding out the truth or the facts concerning something; search, inquiry, investigation, examination, research; †scrutiny, inspection (*obs.*).

1382 WYCLIF *Acts* xii. 19 Inquicisioun [*gloss* or sekyng] maad of keperis, he comaundide hem for to be brouȝt. *c* **1450** tr. *De Imitatione* I. iii. 5 Meke knowynge of þiself is more acceptable to god þan depe inquisicion of kunnyng. *c* **1450** *Cov. Myst.* (Shaks. Soc.) 82 Stody with meke inquysissyon ..How I xal have knowynge of Godys wylle. **1535** COVERDALE *Ecclus.* xi. 7 Whan thou hast made enquisicion, then refourme righteously. **1570–6** LAMBARDE *Peramb. Kent* (1826) 71 That the reader may be the more justly occasioned to make inquisition of the truth. **1614** RALEIGH *Hist. World* III. (1634) 6 Wherein if he have erred, then is all further inquisition frivolous. **1736** BURKE *Subl. & B.* IV. xxi, The parts..are yet so minute, as to conceal the figure of their component parts from the nicest inquisition of the microscope. **1805** WORDSW. *Prelude* VIII. 536 A simple look Of child-like inquisition now and then Cast upwards on thy countenance. **1897** F. HALL in *Nation* (N.Y.) LXIV. 163/2 Nor has it escaped the inquisition of the curious.

b. with *pl.* An act of inquiring, or process of inquiry; a search, an investigation.

c **1440** *Gesta Rom.* I. xxxviii. 154 (Add. MS.) Anon was made an Inquysicion, who sawe the Erle turne the playse in the disshe. **1627–77** FELTHAM *Resolves* II. xxxi. 223, I will not care for a friend full of Inquisitions. *a* **1677** HALE *Contempl.* II. 190 Make as speedy an Inquisition as thou canst, into thy own state. **1735** BERKELEY *Def. Free-think. Mathem.* §11, I heartily abhor an inquisition in faith. **1878** BOSW. SMITH *Carthage* 295 By a searching inquisition every free-born citizen..had been swept into the ranks.

2. A judicial or official investigation or inquiry, an inquest; also the document recording such inquiry and its result.

1387 TREVISA *Higden* (Rolls) VIII. 295 Kyng Edward made hard inquisicioun aȝenst evel doers, and aȝenst hem þat trespased aȝenst þe crowne, þat manere inquisicioun hiȝte trail-bastoun. **1424** *Paston Lett.* No. 4 I. 13 The seyd Walter and Richard were founden gilty of the seyd trespas by an inquisicion ther of takyn. **1467** in *Eng. Gilds* (1870) 385 By the serche of the Bayllies or by Inquisicion of .xij. men. **1548** HALL *Chron., Hen. VIII* 55 The inquisicion intendid and taken at the cytie of London..afore Thomas Barnewell crouner. **1574** tr. *Littleton's Tenures* 52 b, A man before suche age shall not bee sworne in no jurye nor no inquisition. **1672** PETTY *Pol. Anat.* 342, Ann. 1653, and 1654, there were inquisitions taken of the values which all and every parcel of land in Ireland yielded ann. 1641. **1707** CHAMBERLAYNE *St. Gt. Brit.* III. xi. 375 (*Records in Tower*) Inquisitions post mortem, of infinite advantage upon Trials of Interest or Descent. **1712** *Lond. Gaz.* No. 5074/2 An Inquisition taken..upon View of the dead Body of James Duke of Hamilton. **1767** BLACKSTONE *Comm.* II. xvii. 265 These, not being forfeited till the matter on which they arise is found by the inquisition of a jury, and so made a matter of record. **1839** STONEHOUSE *Axholme* 63 The inhabitants of the Isle or Borderers as they are termed in the Inquisition of 1607. **1840** *Penny Cycl.* XVI. 405/2 Where the king is entitled, upon the occurrence of certain events, to take possession of real or personal property previously belonging to a subject, the facts upon which the king's title accrues must be first ascertained by an inquisition or inquest of office. **1863** H. COX *Instit.* II. x. 546 A defendant may be prosecuted for murder or manslaughter upon an inquisition, which is the record of the finding of a jury sworn to inquire concerning the death of a person *super visum corporis.* **1896** *Law Times* C. 358/1 R. became a lunatic, and was so found by inquisition.

3. *R.C. Ch.* (With capital I.) An ecclesiastical tribunal (officially styled the Holy Office) for the suppression of heresy and punishment of heretics, organized in the 13th century under Innocent III, under a central governing body at Rome called the Congregation of the Holy Office.

The Inquisition existed in Italy, France, the Netherlands, Spain, Portugal, and the Spanish and Portuguese colonies. The Spanish Inquisition, reorganized 1478–83, became notorious in the 16th century for its severities. The Inquisition was abolished in France in 1772, and in Spain finally in 1834. The Congregation of the Holy Office still exists, but is chiefly concerned with heretical literature.

1502 *Ord. Crysten Men* (W. de W. 1506) IV. viii. 189 That letteth malycyously the offyce of the sayd inquysycyon. **1568** V. SKINNER tr. *Montanus* (*title*) A Discovery and Playne Declaration of Sundry Subtill Practices of the Holy Inquisition of Spayne. **1602** WARNER *Alb. Eng.* IX. xliv. (1612) 211 For not they onely die, but die in lingring Torments, who Fault to their Inquisition or their falsed Rytes must doe. **1664** H. MORE *Myst. Iniq.* 439 Many.. were most barbarously abused in the close Prisons of the Inquisition. **1691** *Lond. Gaz.* No. 2724/1 On the 20th Instant..by Order of the Tribunal of the Inquisition at Toledo..Eight Jews were burnt alive. **1756** NUGENT *Gr. Tour, Italy* III. 289 [At Rome] they have an inquisition, but it is neither so severe as those of Portugal and Spain, nor does it exercise its jurisdiction over foreigners. **1855** PRESCOTT *Philip II*, II. ix. (1857) 310 The Spanish Inquisition, with its train of horrors, seemed to be already in the midst of them.

transf. **1771** SMOLLETT *Humph. Cl.* Let. Sir W. Phillips, 10 June, Declaring that it could not be very agreeable to live in a family where an inquisition was established. *a* **1897** H. DRUMMOND *Ideal Life* 86 Without that, life is worse than an enigma: it is an inquisition.

4. *attrib.* and *Comb.*

1612–15 BP. HALL *Contempl., N.T.* I. vi, Egypt is become the sanctuary, Judea the inquisition-house of the Sonne of God. **1644** EVELYN *Diary* 12 Dec., [In Rome] next to this [Hospital] is the Inquisition house and prison, the inside thereof, I thanke God, I was not curious to see. **1766** W. GORDON *Gen. Counting-ho.* 281 To the inquisition-vessel, 22 rials. **1878** TENNYSON *Revenge* ii, I should count myself the coward if I left them..To these Inquisition dogs and the devildoms of Spain. **1891** *Pall Mall G.* 1 July 2/2 There is a reign of more than Inquisition-terror at Santiago.

inqui'sition, *v.* [f. prec. sb.] **a.** *intr.* To make inquisition or investigation. **b.** *trans.* To proceed against by the Inquisition.

1644 MILTON *Areop.* (Arb.) 61 If it come to inquisitioning again, and licencing..it cannot be guest what is intended by som but a second tyranny over learning. **1646** J. HALL *Poems* 2 Or if you into some blind Convent fly Y' are inquisition'd straight for heresie. **1895** *Academy* 29 June 537/3 They bore their testimony..in very aggressive fashion, and so were cruelly inquisitioned and done to death.

inquisitional (ɪnkwɪˈzɪʃənəl), *a.* [f. as prec. + -AL¹. Cf. med.L. *inquīsītiōnālis* (1376 in Du Cange).] Of or pertaining to the Inquisition; of or pertaining to inquisition or inquiry, esp. such as is harsh, strict, or prying; inquisitorial.

1644 MILTON *Areop.* (Arb.) 54 Look..whether those places be one scruple the better, the honester, the wiser, the chaster, since all the inquisitionall rigor that hath bin executed upon books. **1738** WARBURTON *Div. Legat.* I. Ded. 9 To shew them what dismal Effects that inquisitional Spirit ..would have on Literature in general. **1839** J. ROGERS *Antipopopr.* II. II. ii. 119 The Bishop of Leon was an agent in England for the cruel and inquisitional Don Carlos. **1864** SIR M. STEPHENSON in *Athenæum* 3 Sept. 297/2 From its.. vexatious inquisitional character, and uncertainty.

inqui'sitionary, *a.* *rare.* [f. as prec. + -ARY.] = prec.

1846 in WORCESTER.

inqui'sitionist. [f. as prec. + -IST.] An officer of the Inquisition, or one who follows the methods of the Inquisition; an inquisitor.

1882 *St. James's Gaz.* 25 Mar., The Inquisitionists usually did their best to convert a man before they burnt

him. **1899** *Westm. Gaz.* 1 June 2/1 We are familiar with them in religion as persecutors and inquisitionists.

inquisitive (ɪn'kwɪzɪtɪv), *a.* (*sb.*) Forms: 4–6 inquisitif, etc. (with usual interchange of *i* and *y*, *f*, *fe*, *ff*, and *ve*), 5 **enquesitif, inquizitif,** 6– **inquisitive.** [a. OF. *inquisitif*, *-ive* (Godef.), ad. late L. *inquīsītīvus* (Boethius), f. L. *inquīsīt-*, ppl. stem of *inquīrĕre* to INQUIRE: see -IVE. Cf. It. *inquisitivo* (Florio).]

Given to inquiry, questioning, or research; of an inquiring turn of mind; desirous of or eager for knowledge; curious. (Of persons, their dispositions, actions, etc.)

c **1450** *Merlin* 292 Ewein white honde, that was more enquesitif, asked of whens thei were. **1532** MORE *Confut. Tindale* Wks. (1557) 640/1, I purpose not . . to be so curiouse and inquisitive as to enquire whyther [etc.]. **1570** DEE *Math. Pref.* 22 As an Oxe . . no furder carefull or inquisitiue. **1605** BACON *Adv. Learn.* I. v. §11 A natural curiosity and inquisitive appetite. **1654** JER. TAYLOR *Real Pres.* Ep. Ded., To make us humble, apt to learn, inquisitive, and charitable. **1695** WOODWARD *Nat. Hist. Earth* I. (1723) 47 The inquisitive and better Part of Mankind. **1732** BERKELEY *Alciphr.* VI. §8 So many learned, wise and inquisitive men. *a* **1751** LANGLEY *Builder's Jewel* (1757) 26 It will not be in the Power of the most inquisitive Eye to discover the Difference. **1865** GROTE *Plato* Pref. (1875) 7 The number of intellects, independent, inquisitive, and acute is always rare.

b. Often (now usually) in an unfavourable sense: Unduly or impertinently curious; prying.

1529 MORE *Dyaloge* III. Wks. 243/1 The lesse witte the more inquisitife. **1605** BACON *Adv. Learn.* I. Ded. §2 Beholding you not with the inquisitive eye of presumption. *a* **1716** SOUTH *Twelve Serm.* (1717) IV. 70 Inquisitive Persons . . who have a Mind to pry into the Thoughts and Actions of their Neighbour. **1787** A. HAMILTON in *Federalist* No. 12 The genius of our people will ill brook the inquisitive and peremptory spirit of Excise laws. **1832** G. DOWNES *Lett. Cont. Countries* I. 181 This was the most inquisitive old fellow I have ever seen.

fig. *c* **1645** HOWELL *Lett.* (1650) II. v. 7, I pray be cautious of your carriage under that meridian, it is a searching (Inquisitive) air. **1884** *Mag. of Art* VII. 163 A girl in a white figured gown at work, . . white window curtains about her, and the inquisitive light streaming around her.

c. Const. *of*, *after*, *about*, *for*, *into*, †*upon* (the thing which one seeks to know), or with *inf.*, or subordinate interrogative clause.

c **1386** CHAUCER *Miller's Prol.* 56 An housbonde shal nat been Inquisityf Of goddes pryuetee nor of his wyf. *c* **1450** LYDG. & BURGH *Secrees* 1772 *heading*, How a kyng shulde be inquisitiff to knowe diuers Oppynyouns. **1474** SIR J. PASTON in *P. Lett.* No. 745 III. 114 He was passyng inquisytyff howe that I was purveyd for recompensyng off Towneshend. **1477** EARL RIVERS (Caxton) *Dictes* 62 Be not inquisitif vpon other folkis lest they be inquisitif vpon the. **1520** WHITINTON *Vulg.* (1527) 3 b, He is euer inquisytyue of suche maters. **1576** FLEMING *Panopl. Epist.* 178, I would have been inquisitive after things more commendable. **1634** SIR T. HERBERT *Trav.* 149 Not very inquisitive about forreigne affaires. **1655** FULLER *Ch. Hist.* IV. iii. §1 Foraigners there being very inquisitive of them, to be satisfied in the particulars of his devotion. **1676** tr. *Guillatiere's Voy. Athens* 117 We were all of us inquisitive after the famous Temples of Jupiter, Minerva, and Venus. **1693** DRYDEN *Juvenal* xvi. (1697) 390 Inquisitive of Fights, and longs in vain To find him in the Number of the slain. **1699** BENTLEY *Phal.* 246 He was curious and inquisitive into the History of Poetry and the Stage. **1711** ADDISON *Spect.* No. 50 ⁋2 The Upholsterer finding my Friend very inquisitive about these his Lodgers. **1737** WHISTON *Josephus, Antiq.* I. xi. §4 Lot's wife being too nicely inquisitive what would become of it. **1753** HOGARTH *Anat. Beauty* 4 Gentlemen, who have been inquisitive after knowledge in pictures. **1820** LAMB *Elia* Ser. I. *South Sea Ho.*, Some curious finger . . inquisitive to explore the mode of book keeping in Queen Anne's reign.

B. *sb.* An inquisitive person. (By Puttenham applied to the rhetorical figure EROTESIS.)

1589 PUTTENHAM *Eng. Poesie* III. xix. (Arb.) 220 A kinde of figuratiue speach when we aske many questions and looke for none answere, speaking indeed by interrogation, which we might as well say by affirmation. This figure I call the Questioner or inquisitiue. **1685** TEMPLE *Ess.*, *Poetry* Wks. 1731 I. 248 There are no where so many curious Inquisitives, so many Pretenders to Business and State-Imployments.

inquisitively (ɪn'kwɪzɪtɪvlɪ), *adv.* [f. prec. + -LY[2].] In an inquisitive manner; with curiosity to obtain information.

a **1631** DONNE *Lett., to Sir H. G[oodere]* (1633) 353 If at any time I seeme to study you more inquisitively, it is for no other end but to know how to present you to God in my prayers. **1747** LORD LYTTELTON *Observ. St. Paul* Wks. (1774) 304 An age more inquisitively curious into the powers of nature . . than any before it. **1837** DICKENS *Pickw.* ii, Mr. Tupman looked inquisitively in his face. **1865** MISS BRADDON *Sir Jasper* I. ii. 30 The housekeeper watched him inquisitively.

inquisitiveness (ɪn'kwɪzɪtɪvnɪs). [f. as prec. + -NESS.] The quality or character of being inquisitive; disposition to inquire; curiosity to obtain information. Now mostly in unfavourable sense: Excessive, impertinent, or prying curiosity.

1583 GOLDING *Calvin on Deut.* xxviii. 167 When they debate after that maner it is not a simple inquisitiuenes, but a pride . . because they would faine be esteemed. *a* **1586** SIDNEY *Arcadia* (1622) 9 He thought inquisitiuenes an vncomely guest. **1602** MARSTON *Antonio's Rev.* II. ii, Hath he . . No licorish womanish inquisitivenesse? **1748** HARTLEY *Observ. Man* I. iii. 361 Learning and Inquisitiveness diffuse themselves more and more amongst the Nations. **1836** HOR. SMITH *Tin Trump.* (1876) 209 Inquisitiveness—an itch for prying into other people's affairs, to the neglect of our own. **1849** LYTTON *Caxtons* 15 Childhood and genius have the same master-organ in common—inquisitiveness.

inquisitor (ɪn'kwɪzɪtə(r)). Also 6 **inquesytor, inquisiter, enquisitour,** (**-ysy-**), 6–7 **inquisitour,** (**-ysi-**). [a. OF. *inquisiteur* (1404 in Hatz.-Darm.), in AF. *-itour*, ad. L. *inquīsītōr-em* a searcher, detective, spy, inquisitor, examiner; agent-noun from *inquīrĕre* to search into, INQUIRE. Cf. It. *inquisitore*, Sp. *inquisidor*.]

1. One who makes inquisition or inquiry; an inquirer, seeker, investigator; a curious or prying inquirer, an inquisitive person. Const. *of*, *into*.

1504 C'TESS RICHMOND tr. *De Imitatione* IV. xviii. 282 That a man shulde nat be to curious a inquisitor of that holy sacrament. **1525** LD. BERNERS *Froiss.* (1812) II. clxiii. [clix.] 450 Enquisitours . . inquysitours . . enquysytours. **1586** T. B. *La Primaud. Fr. Acad.* (1589) 152 Curious Inquisitors of the causes of all naturall things. **1597** J. PAYNE *Royal Exch.* 18 They . . become rather curiouse inquisitors then Godlie learners. **1665** WALTON *Life Hooker* in *H.'s Wks.* (1888) I. 5 My affection to them made me a diligent inquisitor into many things that concerned him. **1779** H. SWINBURNE in *Crts. Europe close last Cent.* (1841) I. 252 The Grand Duke . . pries into everything, and knows all that passes. This royal inquisitor seems, however, to be very popular. **1841** EMERSON *Misc.* 160 Here comes by a great inquisitor with auger and plumb-line, and will bore an Artesian well through our conventions and theories, and pierce to the core of things.

2. One whose official duty it is to inquire, examine, or investigate, in matters of crime, taxation, etc.

1513 DOUGLAS *Æneis* VI. vii. 17 King Mynos, inquisitour and justice. **1548** HALL *Chron., Hen. VII* 60 b, Hys people, beynge sore vexed with inquysitors, pollers and promoters. **1549** THOMAS *Hist. Italie* 81 b, There be certaine inquisitours, called *Sindici*, sent foorth to refourme extorcions. **1646** SIR T. BROWNE *Pseud. Ep.* I. ii. 6 The subtilty of that Inquisitor shall not present unto God a bundle of calumnies or confutable accusations. **1706** PHILLIPS, *Inquisitor*, a Sheriff, Coroner, etc. having Power to inquire into certain Cases. **1864** D. G. MITCHELL *Sev. Stor.* 231 The three Inquisitors of State were met in their chamber of the Ducal Palace.

†**b.** A detective, informer, or spy. *Obs.*

1580 HOLLYBAND *Treas. Fr. Tong*, *Informateur*, an Informer, an Inquisitour. **1647** R. STAPYLTON *Juvenal* 56 For such a turbut who durst sell or buy, So many inquisitours and informers nigh? **1756–7** tr. *Keysler's Trav.* (1760) I. 114 There are certain officers, called private overseers, who inspect into the offences, clandestine meetings, and other misdemeanors of their fellow-citizens. . . These inquisitors are private, and swear to the faithful execution of their office. **1797** GODWIN *Enquirer* I. xiv. 127 Refrain from acting the spy or inquisitor.

c. *transf.* and *fig.*

1734 FIELDING *Univ. Gallant* II. i, What's that to you, brother? Who made you the inquisitor of my actions? **1878** SIMPSON *Sch. Shaks.* I. 125 While at Rome Stucley and Shelley acted in concert as inquisitors into the lives of the English who happened to come there.

3. An officer of the Inquisition: see INQUISITION 3.

(*Inquisitores ad conquirendos et eruendos hereticos*, 'inquisitors for searching out and rooting out heretics', were first appointed by the Constitution of Theodosius I in 382. *Inquisitores* were sent into the south of France in the 13th c. to extirpate the heresy of the Albigenses. But the name is chiefly associated with the Spanish Inquisition as reconstituted in the end of the 15th c.)

1545 COVERDALE *Def. cert. poor Chr.* Wks. (Parker Soc.) II. 455, I mean euen thee, thou accuser, which . . art called an inquisitor of heresy. *a* **1568** ASCHAM *Scholem.* I. (Arb.) 84 The bloodie Inquisitors in Italie . . their care and charge is . . onelie to watch and ouersee that Christes trewe Religion set no sure footing, where the Pope hath any Iurisdiction. **1611** BIBLE *Transl. Pref.* 6 They will not trust the people with it [the Scripture] . . no not with the Licence of their owne Bishops and Inquisitors. *a* **1745** SWIFT *Pulteney's Answ. Walpole* (Seager), The mercy of a Spanish inquisitor. **1841** BORROW *Zincali* I. x. 1. 171 He . . having been an inquisitor, was doubtless versed in the annals of the holy office. **1856** VAUGHAN *Mystics* (1860) I. 20 One age enrolling the mystic among the saints, another committing him to the inquisitor's torch.

fig. *a* **1680** BUTLER *Rem.* (1759) I. 187 Those fierce Inquisitors of Wit, The Critics, spare no Flesh, that ever writ.

b. ***Inquisitor-General***, the head of the court of Inquisition in certain countries, esp. in Spain. ***Grand Inquisitor***, a director of a court of Inquisition in certain countries.

1659 RUSHW. *Hist. Coll.* I. 78 Gregory the Fifteenth, then Pope, exhorted the Bishop of Conchen Inquisitor-General of Spain, to improve the opportunity. **1711** *Lond. Gaz.* No. 4854/1 The Duke of Anjou has created Cardinal de Giudicis Inquisitor General of Spain. **1840** *Penny Cycl.* XVI. 408/2 Soon after [1482], the pope appointed Thomas de Torquemada, prior of the Dominican convent of Segovia, to the new dignity of inquisitor-general of the kingdom of Castile. **1852** MISS YONGE *Cameos* I. xl. 341 They were to be tried before the grand inquisitor, Guillaume Humbert, a Dominican friar. **1862** LONGF. *Wayside Inn, Torquemada* 4 Torquemada, with his subtle brain, Ruled them as Grand Inquisitor of Spain.

inquisitorial (ɪnkwɪzɪ'tɔərɪəl), *a.* [f. med. L. *inquīsītōri-us* INQUISITORY + -AL[1]: cf. F. *inquisitorial* (1570 in Godef.); also in mod.Sp.]

1. Of or pertaining to an (official) inquisitor or inquisitors; having or exercising the office or function of an inquisitor.

1761–2 HUME *Hist. Eng.* (1806) III. App. Jas. I. 785 An inquisitorial tribunal . . was erected in the kingdom. **1764–7** LD. LYTTELTON *Hen. II*, VI. 101 (Seager) The first proceedings of these inquisitorial commissioners began at Toulouse. **1821** L. MORRISSY (*title*) Development of the Cruel and Dangerous Inquisitorial System of the Church of Rome in Ireland. **1879** FARRAR *St. Paul* I. 5 [Saul] had been selected as the inquisitorial agent of Priests and Sanhedrists because he surpassed his contemporaries in burning zeal for the traditions of the schools.

2. Of the character of an inquisitor; like, or like that of, an inquisitor; offensively or impertinently inquiring, prying.

1796 H. HUNTER tr. *St.-Pierre's Stud. Nat.* (1799) III. 633 This Law is inquisitorial; it obliges Citizens publicly to disclose the secrets of their fortunes. **1814** BYRON *Lara* I. xxiii, With look collected, but with accent cold . . He turned, and met the inquisitorial tone. **1818** SCOTT *Rob Roy* x, Miss Vernon retorted his inquisitorial glance with one of decided scorn. **1868** ROGERS *Pol. Econ.* xxii. (ed. 3) 297 The old hearth-tax was . . said to be inquisitorial, that is, subjected the occupier to frequent and offensive visits.

3. Said of criminal procedure: see quots.

1823 BENTHAM *Not Paul* 350 In modern Rome-bred law, this mode of procedure, in which the parts of judge and prosecutor are performed by the same person, is styled the *inquisitorial.* **1900** *Q. Rev.* Jan. 198 There is the French school [of Criminal Procedure] . . and there is the Anglo-Saxon school . . The one is technically known as the Inquisitorial system, the other as the Accusatorial system. *Ibid.* 220 Two systems of criminal procedure—the inquisitorial or secret system, and the accusatorial or public system.

Hence **inquisi'torially** *adv.*, in an inquisitorial manner, as or like an inquisitor; also **inquisi'torialness**, inquisitorial character.

1830 D'ISRAELI *Chas. I*, III. xiv. 306 The Attorney-General had inquisitorially tampered with Leighton to obtain the names. **1834** *New Monthly Mag.* XL. 62 The repeal of imposts, the vexatiousness and inquisitorialness of which is strongly felt. **1885** L. OLIPHANT *Sympneumata* 195 He rejudges, too, the more inquisitorially, the more uncompromisingly.

†**inquisi'torious,** *a. Obs. rare.* [f. med.L. *inquīsītōri-us* INQUISITORY + -OUS.] = prec. 2.

1641 MILTON *Ch. Govt.* II. Introd., This impertinent yoke of prelaty, under whose inquisitorious and tyrannical duncery no free and splendid wit can flourish.

in'quisitorship. [-SHIP.] The office of Inquisitor: see INQUISITOR 3.

1669 *Lond. Gaz.* No. 404/1 Pressing him to resign into the hands of the Pope the Inquisitorship of Spain. **1840** *Penny Cycl.* XVI. 410/2 In Spain . . during the eighteen years of Torquemada's inquisitorship alone, about 8800 persons were burnt.

in'quisitory, *a.* ? *Obs.* [ad. med.L. *inquīsītōri-us*, f. *inquīsītor*: see above.] = INQUISITORIAL (usually in sense 1).

1639 GENTILIS *Servita's Inquis.* in *Hist. Counc. Trent* (1676) 836 This enterprise of the Fathers Inquisitory was much furthered by the Emperor Frederick the Second . . in the year 1244. **1726** *Wodrow Corr.* (1843) III. 274 In private he rails at the queries, and says he will never give way to the inquisitory method. **1736** CHANDLER *Hist. Persec.* 45 Alexander's inquisitory temper. *Ibid.* 166 He severely rebuked the assessors of the Inquisitory tribunal. **1826** E. IRVING *Babylon* I. II. 125 To escape the violent or mutilating hands of their inquisitory acts, and Expurgatory Indices.

†**in'quisitous,** *a. Obs. rare.* [f. L. ppl. stem *inquīsīt-* (see INQUISITIVE) + -OUS.] = INQUISITIVE.

1658 FRANCK *North. Mem.* (1694) 85 You must have more . . not only for your self, but for those that are more inquisitous. **1716** *Wodrow Corr.* (1843) II. 148 Your brotherly charity towards your most united brethren here disposes you to be inquisitous. **1757** MRS. ELIZ. GRIFFITH *Lett. Henry & Frances* (1767) I. 207 The mind of man, naturally active and inquisitous after truth.

inquisitress (ɪn'kwɪzɪtrɪs). [f. INQUISITOR + -ESS.] A female inquisitor.

1727 *Philip Quarll* 141 This did not a little exasperate the already sufficiently provok'd Inquisitress. **1853** C. BRONTË *Villette* xxvi, Little Jesuit inquisitress as she was, she could see things in a true light. **1897** *Strand Mag.* Christm. No. 634/1 This preliminary settled . . my fair inquisitress asks me how to begin.

inquisitrix. [fem., in L. form, of INQUISITOR: see above and -TRIX.] = prec.

1879 *Cornh. Mag.* Sept. 296 When the inquisitrix is furnished with such a pair of eyes as nature had endowed the Countess Almura withal.

†**inquisi'turient,** *a. Obs. nonce-wd.* [f. L. type **inquīsīturient-em*, pr. pple. of **inquīsīturīre*, desiderative of *inquīrĕre*, *inquīsīt-* to INQUIRE: cf. PARTURIENT, ESURIENT.] Desirous of making inquisition; eager to play the inquisitor.

1644 MILTON *Areop.* (Arb.) 41 This was the rare morsell so officiously snatcht up, and so ilfavourdly imitated by our inquisiturient Bishops.

†**in'quit**, *v. Sc. Obs.* In 6 inquyt(t. [f. IN-[1] + QUIT *v.*] *trans.* 'To redeem from being pledged' (Jam.).
1541 *Aberd. Reg.* V. 17 (Jam.) And requyr him to inborrow and inquytt ane ring of gold quhilk he laid in wed. *Ibid.*, The redemptioun and inquyting of the land.

†**in'quoif**, *v. Obs. rare*⁻⁰. [IN-[2].]
1611 FLORIO, *Inscuffiare*, to inquoife, to inhood.

†**inrace, inras.** *Obs. rare.* [f. IN-[1] + *ras*, RACE, after L. *incursus.*] A rushing upon, inroad, assault.
a **1300** *E.E Psalter* xc. 6 [xci. 5] Fra arwe þat es in daie fleghand..and of inras. *a* **1340** HAMPOLE *Psalter* xc. 6 Of arw fleghand in day..of inras & mydday deuyll. *comm.*, The inras..that is, apert risynge of ill men agayns the.

inraced, *Her.*: see IRRASED.

in'racinate, *v. rare*⁻⁰. [ad. F. *enraciner* (f. *en-*, EN-[1] + *racine* root) + -ATE[3], after DERACINATE.] *trans.* To enroot, to implant.
1882 in OGILVIE.

inradiate, inrage, obs. ff. IRRADIATE, ENRAGE.

in'rag, *v. nonce-wd.* [f. IN-[1] + RAG *sb.*] *trans.* To embody in the form of rags.
1856 *Sat. Rev.* II. 611/2 The popular frenzy of 1851 that for a time incarnated, or rather inragged, him [Guy Fawkes] as a Pope or Cardinal.

†**in'rail**, *v. Obs.* Also 6 **enrail, inrayl.** [f. IN-[1] + RAIL *v.*]
trans. To rail in, enclose with, or as with, a railing. Also *fig.*
1523 SKELTON *Garl. Laurel* 656 The bankes..Enrailid with rosers. **1594** HOOKER *Eccl. Pol.* IV. xiii. (1604) 200 The same if any part doe wilfully violate, it may be reformed and inrayled againe. **1607** F. MASON *Authoritie of Ch.* 9 God hath inrailed their authoritie with certaine bounds and limits which they may not passe. **1724** MACKY *Journ. thro' Eng.* I. xiii. 285 Stairs..inrailed with Iron.
Hence †**'in,railed** *ppl. a.*, railed in.
1682 *Lithgow's Trav.* I. 31 The inrayled [**1632** inravled] image. **1714** GAY *Trivia* II. 74 Where fam'd St. Giles's ancient limits spread, An inrail'd column rears its lofty head.

inrapture, -ravel, obs. ff. ENRAPTURE, -RAVEL.

inravish, -rayl, obs. ff. ENRAVISH, -RAIL.

in re: see IN *Latin prep.* 21 and RE.

†**in'red**, *a. Obs. rare.* [f. IN- *pref.*[4] + RED *a.* and *sb.*[1]] Very red.
a **1225** *Ancr. R.* 402 Jesu Crist..was in-read kundeliche also, ase me weneð. *c* **1425** *Seven Sag.* (P.) 61 The fyrde mayster..was nowthir whyit no blake, And [? *read* an] inred man he was.

†**in'rede**, *v. Obs. rare.* [f. IN-[1] + *rede*, READ *v.*]
1. *trans.* To interpret, explain the meaning of.
c **1315** SHOREHAM 7 That we ne mowe hyt nauȝt i-se, Ne forthe ine bodie inrede.
2. *intr.* To read. Hence **in'reding** *vbl. sb.*
c **1449** PECOCK *Repr.* I. vii. 37 Tho lay persoones, whiche weenen bi her inreding in the Bible forto come into more kunning than thei or alle the men in erthe—clerkis and othere—mowe come to.

'in-,reference. [cf. IN *a.* 2.] A reference understood by only a limited group of people. Cf. IN-JOKE.
1967 *Punch* 15 Feb. 243/2 The pieces..have clearly journeyed from a lost civilisation, although..in-references to..period West End lions, have been omitted. **1968** *Listener* 26 Sept. 421/2 Peel's linking comments are liberally sprinkled with in-references to musicians and to long-playing records destined, one suspects, for infinitesimal sales.

†**inre'flecting,** *ppl. a. Obs. rare*⁻¹. [IN-[2].] That practises inward reflection or study of self.
1614 SYLVESTER *Little Bartas* 645 Man onely hath an inreflecting Knowledge Of his owne selfe (from Nature's onely Colledge).

†**inre'formed**, *a. Obs.* [IN-[3].] Unreformed.
1548 *Privy Council Acts* (1890) II. 164 Being suffred tescape inreformed.

†**inre'fracted**, *a. Obs. rare*⁻¹. [IN-[3].] Unrefracted; without undergoing refraction.
a **1691** BOYLE *Hist. Air* (1692) 73 The light of any planet ..doth descend whole directly and inrefracted unto, or upon our atmosphere.

inregister, obs. form of ENREGISTER *v.*

inremissible, -repealable, -resistable, -resolute, etc., obs. ff. IRREMISSIBLE, etc.

in rerum natura: see IN *Latin prep.* 21.

†**in'rest**, *v. Obs. rare*⁻¹. [f. IN-[1] + REST *v.*; cf. phr. *in rest.*] *trans.* To place (a lance) in rest.
1612 SHELTON *Quix.* III. I. 171 He inrested his Javelin low on the Thigh, and ran with all the Force Rozinante might.

inrest, var. of INNEREST *a. Obs.*, innermost.

inrich(e, etc., obs. forms of ENRICH, etc.

inrigged ('ɪnrɪgd), *a.* [f. IN *adv.* + RIGGED.] Not having the rowlocks outside the boat as in an outrigger.
1884 *West. Morn. News* 28 July 1/4 Four-oared Inrigged Gigs.

in-rigger ('ɪn,rɪgə(r)). [f. IN *adv.* + RIGGER[1] 4.] A boat having the rowlocks formed in the gunwale.
1893 J. H. CLASPER in *Westm. Gaz.* 9 Oct. 7/3 The Düsseldorf boat was an in-rigger—for which orders are very seldom given nowadays.

inright, variant of ENRIGHT *v.*, *Obs.*

†**in'righteous**, *v. Obs. rare.* [f. IN-[1] + RIGHTEOUS *a.*] *trans.* To make righteous. Hence †**in'righteousing** *vbl. sb.*, making righteous.
1578 *Chr. Prayers* in *Priv. Prayers* (1851) 524 Let my heart be made undefiled through thy inrighteousing. **1587** GOLDING *De Mornay* xxx. 483 The death of Jesus..turning ..to our life, his righteousnes to our inrighteousing.

'in,ring, *sb. Sc. Curling.* [f. IN *adv.* 12 d + RING *sb.*] A shot in which the player's stone is made to hit the inside of another stone so as to glance from it and hit the winner, taking it out and lying shot itself: now more usually termed *inwick.*
1789 D. DAVIDSON *Seasons* 169 (Jam.) Syne hurling..Wi' inrings nice and fair He struck the winner frae the cock. *Ibid.* 171 (Jam.) Here stands the winner..Immoveable save by a nice inring. **1824** MACTAGGART *Gallovid. Encycl.* s.v. *Inwick*, To inwick a stone..is different from a common open inring, the two are often confounded with other, but they are quite different.
Hence **inringing** *vbl. sb.*, playing an inring.
1831 in *Blackw. Mag.* XXX. 970 *Wicking*—or *In-ringing*, the prettiest and most scientific point in the game by far.. taking an inner angle off a side-shot, in such a manner as to change and direct the course of your stone upon the one to be projected—or else to effect the same, when the case permitted, by drawing off the said shot.

inring, inripen, obs. ff. ENRING, ENRIPEN.

†**in'rise**, *v. Obs.* [f. IN-[1] + RISE *v.*, after L. *insurgĕre.*] *intr.* To rise; esp. in opposition.
a **1300** *E.E. Psalter* lxxxv[i]. 14 Laverd, wicked in-rase in me. **1382** WYCLIF *Ps.* xxvi[i]. 12 Ther han in risen aȝen me wicke witnessis. —— *Lam.* iii. 61 The lippis of men inrisende to me [1388 risynge aȝens me]. **14..** *MS. Lincoln* A. i. 17 lf. 192 (Halliw.) Sothely fra thythene inryses a gret lufe and what thynge that it trewely towches, it ravesche it utterly to it.
So †**inriser**, one who rises (against).
1382 WYCLIF *Ps.* xliii. 6 [xliv. 5] In thi name we shul dispise inriseris in vs [L. *insurgentes*; 1388 hem that risen aȝen vs].

‖**inro** ('ɪnrəʊ). [Jap., f. Chin. *yin* seal + *lung* basket.] An ornamental nest of boxes, connected by a thin cord, made of lacquer, ivory, or the like, in which seals, medicines, and other necessaries can be carried, formerly worn by the Japanese at the girdle.
1617 W. ADAMS *Let.* 10 Nov. in *Trans. Asiatic Soc. Japan* (1898) XXVI. 207 Your Inro or metsin boxe Skinro told me he would sent it me from Meaco. **1882** *Century Mag.* Dec. 228/2 Gilded pictures of wave, sky, cloud, field, and house, seen on box and tray, *inro* and scroll. **1911** *Connoisseur* Mar. 209/2 Among the *objets d'art* most associated with old Japan are the *inro*, or little medicine cases which the Japanese used invariably to carry about with them. **1960** *Times* 2 Jan. 9/4 Since these garments [*sc.* kimonos] were without pockets, the Japanese carried such belongings as ink, seals, and medicines in lacquer boxes called inros. **1971** *Times Lit. Suppl.* 20 Aug. 998/5 The variety and wit of the subjects used in *inrō* decoration defy description. **1972** *Country Life* 30 Nov. 1500/1 Carved netsuke—the Japanese toggles by which the inro was prevented from falling from the belt.

inroad ('ɪnrəʊd), *sb.* Also 6-8 **inrode.** [f. IN *adv.* 11 d + ROAD *sb.*, in sense 'riding'.]
1. A hostile incursion into a country; a raid or foray.
1548 W. PATTEN *Exp. Scot.* Pref. a j b, Hys grace..soo inuaded the Scottish borders, wasted and burnt Tyuydale and their Marches, that euen yet they forthinke that inrode. **1565-72** COOPER *Thesaurus*, *Incurso*, to inuade, to make inrodes or inuasions on enemies. **1579-80** NORTH *Plutarch* (1676) 745 Demetrius..invaded Laconia with all his Army, and made an inrode to the City of Sparta. **1665** MANLEY *Grotius' Low C. Warres* 77 Several Companies of the King's Souldiers making Inroads, the Country People..took, and without mercy killed them. **1727** POPE *Art Sinking* 72 We never made the least attempt or inrode into their territories. **1776** GIBBON *Decl. & F.* xiv. (1869) I. 311 The provinces were protected by his presence from the inroads of the barbarians. **1867** FREEMAN *Norm. Conq.* I. ii. 36 Aggressive war, as distinguished from mere plundering inroads.
2. *transf.* or *fig.* A powerful or sudden incursion; a forcible encroachment.
1637 C. DOW *Answ. H. Burton* 92 It is a..violent inrode upon the fifth commandement. **1676** tr. *Guillatiere's Voy. Athens* 215 The Ladies..would make another inroad into his Garden. **1740** BUTLER *Serm. bef. Ld. Mayor* Wks. 1874 II. 233 Thus luxury made its inroad, and all the numerous trained evils its attendants. **1798** FERRIAR *Illustr. Sterne* iii. 62 It contains a just account of the first inroads of melancholy. **1830** LYELL *Princ. Geol.* I. 284 We may probably infer some great inroad of the sea at a remote period. **1874** GREEN *Short Hist.* v. §2. 228 They protested against..Papal inroads on the liberties of the Church.
†**3.** An opening or passage in. *Obs. rare.*
1650 BULWER *Anthropomet.* ix. 104 [It] made a shameful inrode or through-passage. **1697** E. LHWYD in *Phil. Trans.* XXVII. 467 Their Coal-works were not Pits sunk like Draw-wells; but great Inroads made into the side of the Hill.

inroad, *v.* Now *rare.* Also 7 **enroad, inrode.** [f. prec. sb.]
†**1.** *trans.* To invade; to make an inroad into.
1625 LISLE *Du Bartas, Noe* 132 A common field where store of cattell grazeth And whence by thousand heads they come our tylth to enroad. **1639** FULLER *Holy War* I. ix. 14 The Saracens..conquered Spain, inroded Aquitain. **1655** —— *Ch. Hist.* III. vii. §14 Robert Bruce..regained Berwick, inroaded England. *a* **1656** USSHER *Ann.* (1658) 668 He.. inroded the Romans as they were fortifying their Camp.
2. *intr.* To make inroads.
1878 *Pop. Sci. Monthly* July 369 A growing liberalization ..is inroading upon the old doctrine of future everlasting punishment.
Hence **inroading** *vbl. sb.* and *ppl. a.* Also **inroader**, one who makes an inroad; an invader.
1611 COTGR., *Voleur*,..a robber, or highway theefe; and an inroder. *a* **1656** USSHER *Ann.* (1658) 674 He was withheld from the inroding of Jerusalem. *a* **1661** FULLER *Worthies, York* III. 230 He had been a great inroder of England. **1855** *N.Y. Tribune* 23 Oct., Its inroading effects upon the mind.

†**in'rogue**, *v. Obs. rare*⁻⁰. [f. IN-[2] + ROGUE *sb.*] *trans.* To make into a rogue.
1611 FLORIO, *Infurfantato*, become a rascall, inrogued.

inrol(l, obs. forms of ENROLL.

inrolled ('ɪnrəʊld), *ppl. a.* [IN *adv.* 11 b.] Rolled or turned inwards; involute.
1881 FARLOW *Marine Algæ* 157 Fertile specimens [of *Hypnea musciformis*] from the West Indies are more robust and do not so frequently have inrolled apices.

'in,rolling, *vbl. sb.* [IN *adv.* 11 c.] A rolling in (e.g. of a great wave).
1546 COVERDALE *Treat. Lord's Supper* Wks. (Parker Soc.) I. 443 To be delivered from these inrollings of perturbations. **1883** *Chicago Advance* 25 Oct., The unexpected inrolling upon him of yet another and heavier wave.

'in,rolling, *ppl. a.* [IN *adv.* 11 a.] That rolls in (as a great wave).
1893 *Treas. Relig. Th.* (N.Y.) XI. 621 What is America to be when this inrolling flood has flowed on and up to the prophesied two hundred millions? **1899** BARING-GOULD *Bk. of the West* II. 300 The king escaped with difficulty before the inrolling stormy sea.

inrolment, obs. form of ENROLMENT.

†**in'romanize**, *v. Obs. rare.* [IN-[2].] *trans.* To include in the Roman church; to Romanize.
1620 BP. HALL *Hon. Mar. Clergy* III. §12 This pope was willing to inromanize the English.

†**'in-,room.** *Obs. rare*⁻¹. [IN *adv.* 12.] An inner room or chamber.
1615 CHAPMAN *Odyss.* v. 302 These two (in an in-room of the cave, Left to themselves).

†**in'root**, *v. Obs. rare*⁻⁰. [IN-[2]. Cf. ENROOT.]
1611 FLORIO, *Irradicare*, to inroote, to take roote.

inrooted, *ppl. a.* [IN *adv.* 11 b; cf. ENROOT *v.*] Deeply rooted, fixed, or established.
1660 tr. *Amyraldus' Treat. conc. Relig.* I. vii. 130 There would be left another not less vehement or less inrooted in us. **1805** *Ann. Rev.* III. 255 It has not the courage of the antient parliaments, because it is less inrooted. **1893** J. PULSFORD *Loyalty to Christ* II. 231 Christ is incipiently becoming the inrooted Righteousness of every man who sees and deplores his inherent sinfulness.

†**inrotu'lation.** *Obs. rare*⁻¹. [ad. med.L. *inrotulātiōn-em*, n. of action f. *inrotulāre* to enrol.] Enrolling or registering; = ENROLMENT 2.
1590 SWINBURNE *Testaments* 221 Where no goodes are bequeathed in the testament, but onely landes, tenements, and hereditaments..and that in such places where neither insinuation, nor inrotulation is necessarie.

inrough, -rowle, obs. ff. ENROUGH, -ROLL.

'in,rubbing, *vbl. sb.* [IN *adv.* 11 c.] The action of rubbing in.
1898 P. MANSON *Trop. Dis.* xxxvii. 584 Limited patches might be treated..by the inrubbing of cassia alata leaves.

'in,run, *sb.* [IN *adv.* 11 d.] **1.** The act of running in; an inrush.
1875 ALEX. SMITH *New Hist. Aberdeensh.* I. 602 A breakwater would have prevented the violent inrun of the sea. **1884** *St. James's Gaz.* 9 Sept. 6/1 One of the most beautiful in-runs that can be found in a day's sail from England.
2. [tr. G. *anlauf.*] In ski-jumping, the distance from the start to the point of taking off; an approach trestle.
1949 F. ELKINS in Elkins & Harper *World Ski Bk.* 103 A group of skiers were preparing their jumping hill for a meet when a small figure was seen leaving the top of the wooden inrun. **1963** *Amer. Speech* XXXVIII. 203 Some of the English terms are literal equivalents of terms used by German-speaking skiers and might be called loan translations...inrun Anlauf.

†inˈrun, *v.*^{1} *Sc. Obs.* In 5–6 -rin, 7 -ryn. [f. IN-^{1} + RUN *v.* (*intr.*), after L. *incurrĕre*.] *trans.* To incur (penalty).

1471 *Act. Audit.* (1839) 12 Vnder all pain & charges he may inrin again þe kingis maieste. **1567** in R. Keith *Hist. Ch. Scot.* (1734) 431 Under all Paine, Charge and Offence that ye and ilk ane of yow may commit and inrin againis his Majestie. **1609** Skene *Reg. Maj.*, *Crimes* v. xix, Na man sould molest or troubill kirk-men..vnder all paine he may inryn against God, and the king.

†inˈrun, *v.*^{2} *Obs. rare*$^{-1}$. [f. IN-^{1} + RUN *v.* (*trans.*).] *trans.* To pierce, stab.

1653 Urquhart *Rabelais* I. xxxv, He inran him at the breast with a hit, which..cut his stomack.

ˌinˈrunning, *vbl. sb.* [IN *adv.* 11 c.] The action of running in. †**a.** Incursion, attack (rendering L. *incursus*). *Obs.*

1382 Wyclif *Ps.* xc[i]. 6 Fro the arwe fleende in dai..fro the inrennyng, and the myddai deuel.

b. Inflowing; the place of inflowing. *rare.*

1859 Tennyson *Elaine* 1379 He went, And at the inrunning of a little brook Sat by the river.

ˈin-ˌrunning, *ppl. a.* [IN *adv.* 11 a.] Running in; running into the land. Also that runs into a river or the sea.

1861 Geikie *E. Forbes* viii. 204 A lonely expanse of grey barren rock and long in-running bays. **1931** *Times Lit. Suppl.* 1 Oct. 738/2 'Australian Literature'..must contribute to the great stream of English literature a new in-running river.

inruption (ˌɪnˈrʌpʃən). [Analytical refashioning of IRRUPTION, emphasizing the prefix *in-*.] A breaking or bursting in.

1809–10 Coleridge *Friend* (1818) II. 63 He must..have the value of his labour reduced to nothing by the inruption of eager competitors. **1881** Ray Lankester in *Encycl. Brit.* XII. 557/2 The true mouth [in an aurelia] then forms by inruption at the opposite pole. **1894** W. Walker *Hist. Congreg. U.S.* 28 The inruption of the officers of the law into their little meeting.

inrush (ˈɪnrʌʃ), *sb.* [IN *adv.* 11 d.] A rushing or pouring in; inflow, influx. *lit.* and *fig.*

1817 Coleridge *Lay Serm.* 396 Compelled to hurry forward, like one who crossing the sands at too late an hour finds himself threatened by the inrush of the tide. **1850** Kingsley *Alt. Locke* vii, The ceaseless in-rush of new images. **1866** G. Macdonald *Ann. Q. Neighb.* xx. (1878) 386 Channels opened for the in-rush of truth into your own mind. **1883** Mrs. Ritchie *Bk. of Sibyls* iii. 174 The animated inrush of tourists.

†ˌinˈrush, *v. Obs.* [IN-^{1}.] *intr.* To rush in.

1610 Holland *Camden's Brit.* I. 443 The Ocean, ready to inrush upon them. *Ibid.* 654 The sea with great violence and assault of waters inrushed upon a little region called Keimes. **1773** J. Ross *Fratricide* II. 17 (MS.) And for the grove by Abel dedicate..The Fiend stalks fast, in-rushes and abides.

ˈinˌrushing, *vbl. sb.* [IN *adv.* 11 c.] A rushing in; inrush.

c **1630** Risdon *Surv. Devon* §225 (1810) 241 The inrushing of the sea's violent breach. **1895** *Papers Ohio Ch. Hist. Soc.* V. 3 Like the inrushing of a whirlwind.

ˈinˌrushing, *ppl. a.* [IN *adv.* 11 a.] Rushing in; entering with force or speed.

1842 Trench *Poems East. Sources* (1851) 108 Hark! a noise is heard without, Then a rude inrushing rout. **1883** *Longm. Mag.* Apr. 625 The powerful inrushing currents from..the storm's centre. **1884** *Ibid.* Apr. 597 Contests arise between the in-rushing masses and the vapours within the spot region.

inrych, obs. form of ENRICH.

†Inˈsabbatist. *Obs. rare.* [f. F. *insabbaté* or med.L. *insabbatus*, *-sab(b)atatus*: see -IST.] A member of the sect of the Waldenses.

The explanation in quot. 1634 is that given by some mediæval writers; but the name is now referred to the peculiar shoe (*sabate* = F. *sabot*, *savate*) worn by the sect; see Du Cange s.v. *Sabatati*, Littré s.v. *Insabbaté*.

1634 E. Knott *Charity Maint.* I. v. §50 They [the Waldenses] denied..the Sabbath, for which cause they were called In-sabbatists. **1804** Ranken *Hist. France* III. II. i, They were supposed falsely to neglect the Sabbath, and called Insabbathists.

So †**Inˈsabbatized** *ppl. a.*, made or become an Insabbatist.

1832 S. R. Maitland *Facts & Documents* 205, I am not, and have not been, an Insabbatized Waldensian.

insaˈccation. *Physiol. rare*$^{-0}$. [noun of action from med.L. *insaccāre* to put into a sack or bag, f. *in-* (IN-^{2}) + *saccus* bag, SACK.]

1855 Mayne *Expos. Lex.*, *Insaccatio*,..the covering or surrounding of the organs with membranes, as the womb, urinary bladder, etc.: insaccation. **1886** in *Syd. Soc. Lex.*

insaciable, etc., obs. ff. INSATIABLE, etc.

in-sack attrib.: see IN *prep.* 18.

†inˈsacred, *a. Obs. rare*$^{-1}$. [IN-^{3}.] Devoid of feelings of reverence, unholy.

1665 Sir T. Herbert *Trav.* (1677) 98 Such is th' insacred famine of a Crown, That it to satisfie..all must go down, Seeing bonds of Blood or Friendship nought avail.

†insaˈcrificable, *a. Obs. rare*$^{-1}$. [ad. L. type **insacrificābilis*, f. *in-* (IN-^{3}) + *sacrificāre* to SACRIFICE; see -ABLE.] Not capable of being sacrificed.

a **1603** T. Cartwright *Confut. Rhem. N.T.* (1618) 631 Hee calleth Christ..insacrificable, or which can not bee sacrificed.

†inˈsafe, *v. Obs. rare*$^{-1}$. [f. IN-^{2} + SAFE *a.*] *trans.* To render safe; to secure, insure.

1628 Feltham *Resolves* II. [I.] ii. 5 In high and mountain'd Fortunes Resolution is necessary to insafe vs from the thefts, and wyles of prosperity.

†inˈsafety. *Obs. rare*$^{-1}$. [IN-^{3}.] Unsafeness; risk.

a **1635** Naunton *Fragm. Reg.* (Arb.) 25 Apprehending the insafety and danger of an inter-mariage with the Bloud-Royall.

insaˈgacity. *rare.* [IN-^{3}.] Want of sagacity.

1808 W. Taylor in *Ann. Rev.* VI. 337 This pamphlet..can have no claim to notice..but for..the insagacity of its predictions.

insalivate (ɪnˈsælɪveɪt), *v.* [IN-^{2}; see SALIVATE.]

1. *trans.* To mix or impregnate (food) with saliva.

1855 Bain *Senses & Int.* II. iv. §22 (1864) 298 We may have a profuse salivation, containing very little of the material that avails for insalivating the food. **1897** *Allbutt's Syst. Med.* III. 401 Food..should be thoroughly masticated and insalivated before it is swallowed.

2. To moisten with saliva.

1884 *Fortn. Rev.* Dec. 807 After experimenting by insalivating fresh subjects..in no single instance was the disease transmitted.

insalivation (ɪnsælɪˈveɪʃən). [IN-^{2}; see SALIVATION, and cf. F. *insalivation* (Littré).] The action of mixing or impregnating food with saliva in the act of mastication.

1833 Dunglison cited by Worcester. **1846–51** Carpenter *Man. Phys.* (ed. 2) 265 This fluid is termed Saliva, and the act by which it is incorporated with the food is termed insalivation. **1866** Huxley *Physiol.* vi. (1872) 144 These processes of mastication, insalivation, and deglutition.

insalubrious (ɪnsəˈl(j)uːbrɪəs), *a.* [f. L. *insalūbri-s* (f. *in-*, IN-^{3} + *salūbris* SALUBRIOUS) + -OUS. Cf. F. *insalubre* (1528 in Hatz.-Darm.), It. *insalubre* (Florio).] Not salubrious; detrimental to health. (Now chiefly of climate or surroundings.)

1638 Sir T. Herbert *Trav.* (ed. 2) 14 It tasts brackish and insalubrious. *Ibid.* 179 The scituation..is low, in a marrish and insalubrious plaine. **1758** W. Battie *Madness* xii. 88 Original Madness..is not necessarily accompanied with any symptoms or succeeded by any effects, that are strictly speaking insalubrious. **1831** Brewster *Nat. Magic* xiii. (1833) 326 Breathing this insalubrious atmosphere. **1854** H. Miller *Sch. & Schm.* xv. (1860) 161/1 He..probably fell a victim, in an insalubrious climate, to old habits, and new rum. **1874** Blackie *Self-Cult.* 49 In hot countries, where insalubrious vapours infest the night.

insalubrity (ɪnsəˈl(j)uːbrɪtɪ). [a. F. *insalubrité* (16th c. in Hatz.-Darm.), It. *insalubrità* (Florio), n. of quality f. *insalubre*; see prec. and -ITY. Cf. L. *salūbritās* SALUBRITY.]

1. Unhealthy character (of locality, climate, etc.); †formerly, unwholesomeness (of food).

1663 Boyle *Usef. Exp. Nat. Philos.* II. ii. 113 There may be ways..to investigate the wholesomness or insalubrity of aliments. **1685** —— *Salub. Air* Pref. 2 The Salubrity and Insalubrity of the Air. **1758** *Monthly Rev.* 476 The insalubrity of their common diet. **1769** R. Price *Obs. Revers. Payments* (1792) II. 378 Proofs of the Insalubrity of marshy Situations. **1834** M. Scott *Cruise Midge* (1863) 56 A climate of the most overpowering heat and fearful insalubrity. **1861** Stanley *East. Ch.* iii. (1869) 89 The rich alluvial plain had a character for insalubrity.

†**2.** Unhealthiness; sickness. *Obs. rare*$^{-1}$.

1668 *Ormonde MSS.* in *10th Rep. Hist. MSS. Comm.* App. v. 79 Your petitioner's former insalubrity and weaknesse of body.

insalutary (ɪnˈsæljuːtərɪ), *a.* [ad. late L. *insalūtāris*, f. *in-* (IN-^{3}) + *salūtāris* SALUTARY. Cf. F. *insalutaire* (16th c. in Littré).] Not salutary.

†**1.** Injurious to health; insalubrious. *Obs.*

1694 Westmacott *Script. Herb.* 36 The too common use of it [sugar]..is insalutary. **1773** Pringle *Disc. Air* 5 Nor did the ancient physicians fail to distinguish..between an insalutary and a wholesome air.

2. Not having a healthy mental or social influence or effect.

1836 Lytton *Athens* (1837) II. 253 Those not insalutary consequences of a free state..their impatience at pecuniary demands [etc.].

insalvability (ɪnsælvəˈbɪlɪtɪ). *rare*$^{-1}$. [ad. L. type **insalvābilitās*, f. *in-* (IN-^{3}) + *salvāre* to save.] Incapability of being saved.

1805 Bp. Watson in *Life* (1818) II. 239 My great objection to the Church of Rome is its uncharitable principle of the insalvability of persons out of its pale.

†inˈsalvable, -eable, *a. Obs. rare*$^{-1}$. [IN-^{3}.] Incapable of being salved.

1608 Middleton *Family of Love* IV. iv. F iv b, To loose Mistrisse Purge for lacke of dexterity, is a disgrace insalueable.

insamble, obs. variant of ENSEMBLE *adv.*

†insame, in same, *adv. phr. Obs.* Also 4 in samen, samyn. [f. IN *prep.* + SAME(N *adv.* (cf. OE. *ætsomne*, *tosomne*); perh. originating in an erroneous notion of the *i-* of I-SAME(N, which is found earlier.] Together, in company. (In late use often a mere expletive.)

13.. *Coer de L.* 4386 Among the toun folk was no game; To counsayl they gaderyd hem insame. *c* **1340** *Cursor M.* 11931 (Fairf.) Ihesu and othir childryn in samyn [*Cott. MS.* samen] went hem by the rever to gamyn. *a* **1400** *Octonian* 47 The emperour with barouns yn-same Rood to Parys. *c* **1440** *Ipomydon* 1555 His modir and he dwellyd insame With moche myrthe, joye and game. *c* **1450** Lonelich *Grail* li. 297 And thus belefen they bothe In-same Pharans and Piers with- Owten blame. *a* **1522** *World & Child* in Hazl. *Dodsley* I. 245, I can many a quaint game, Lo, my top I drive in same. *Ibid.* 247, I am as fresh as flowers in May, I am seemly-shapen in same.

†insaˈmeikle, *adv. phr. Sc.* and north *dial. Obs.* Also inso-. = INSOMUCH.

1483 *Cath. Angl.* 196/2 In so mekylle, *adeo, eatenus.* **1562** Winȝet *Wks.* (1888) I. 42 Insamekle that the sewin diacones ..wes presentit afore the Apostlis. **1588** A. King tr. *Canisius' Catech.* 137 Insameikl that S. Peter..said, ȝe haue slane the authoure of lyf.

insampil, obs. form of ENSAMPLE.

†inˈsanable, *a. Obs.* [ad. L. *insānābilis*, f. *in-* (IN-^{3}) + *sānābilis*, f. *sānāre* to heal. Cf. obs. F. *insanable* (16th c. in Godef.).] That cannot be cured, healed, or remedied; incurable.

1547 Bale *Sel. Wks.* (Parker Soc.) 166 Their own botches are insanable..for the multitude of their mischiefs. **1657** W. Morice *Coena quasi Κοινὴ* Def. xix. 339 They think them..so insanable, that they deserve not to be admonished.

Hence †**insanaˈbility**, the quality of being insanable; incurableness. †**inˈsanableness** (Bailey vol. II, 1727). †**inˈsanably** *adv.*, incurably.

1659 Fuller *App. Inj. Innoc.* III. 18 Not from any insanability in the sore, but from want of seasonable surgery. *a* **1846** Worcester cites *Med. Jrnl.* for *Insanability*.

†insaˈnation. *Obs. rare*$^{-1}$. [f. L. *insānus* INSANE, after L. *sānātio*, f. *sānāre* to heal.] A making or becoming insane; insane condition.

1599 A. M. tr. *Gabelhouer's Bk. Physicke* 347/2 Administre therof to them..and then they shalbe protected agaynste insanation, or maddenes.

insane (ɪnˈseɪn), *a.* (*sb.*) [ad. L. *insān-us* unsound (in mind), f. *in-* (IN-^{3}) + *sānus* healthy, sound in body or in mind, SANE.]

1. Of persons: Not of sound mind, mad, mentally deranged. Also of the mind: Unsound.

1560 Rolland *Crt. Venus* III. 259 Than said Venus with mind almaist Insane. **1721** Bailey, *Insane*, out of Order, mad. **1730–6** —— (folio), *Insane*, out of order as to health; also mad. **1755** Johnson, *Insane*, 1 Mad. **1796** H. Hunter tr. *St. Pierre's Stud. Nat.* (1799) II. 518 They are shut up; and they seldom fail of consequence to become more insane than they were before. **1818** Cruise *Digest* (ed. 2) VI. 72 A man might be sane at the time when two of the witnesses attest, and insane when the third attests. **1842** Dickens *Amer. Notes* (1850) 31/1 The State Hospital for the insane.

b. *absol.* An insane person. Hence (*attrib.* use of the *pl.*), Appropriated to, set apart for, the insane, as ***insane asylum***, ***ward***, etc.

1786 Susannah Haswell *Victoria* II. 67 Every time the sweet insane mentioned the name. **1819** *Metropolis* II. 157 His future fortune and title seem destined for a bold insane. **1828** Webster, *Insane*..2. Used by or appropriated to insane persons; as, an insane hospital. **1873** F. Hall *Mod. Eng.* 127 *note*, We have *sick rooms* and *dying beds*. We qualify an *asylum* as *insane*.

2. Of actions (also colloq. of things): Mad, idiotic, utterly senseless, irrational.

1842 Bischoff *Woollen Manuf.* II. 344 Mr. Alstroemer in 1723 imported a small flock of merinos. It was a hazardous —it appeared to be a presumptuous, and an almost insane attempt. **1869** Sir J. T. Coleridge *Keble* xxi. 534 The insane and excessive passion for athletics.

†**3.** Causing insanity. *Obs.* [So L. *insānus*.]

1605 Shaks. *Macb.* I. iii. 84 Haue we eaten on the insane Root, That takes the Reason Prisoner?

Hence **inˈsanely** *adv.*, in an insane manner, madly. **inˈsaneness**, madness.

1730–6 Bailey (folio), *Insaneness*, unhealthfulness; also madness. **1828** Webster cites Montgomery for *Insanely*. **1849** E. B. Eastwick *Dry Leaves* 72 Plots and conspiracies ..might easily have been formed under our very eyes, while the clue to them was thus insanely withheld. **1891** G. Meredith *One of our Conq.* III. xii. 251 Nataly could not utter all that her insaneness of feeling made her think.

†inˈsanguined, obs. var. ENSANGUINED.

1627 Feltham *Resolves* II. [I.] xciv. (1628) 273 The greatest Prince..comes insanguin'd into the World. **1656** in Blount *Glossogr.*

†inˈsaniate, *v. Obs.* [irreg. f. L. *insānia* insanity + -ATE^3.] *trans.* To make unsound or insane.

1627 Feltham *Resolves* II. [I.] v. (1628) 6 Like a mad Dogg's biting, that not onely wounds the body, but insaniates the soule. *Ibid.* lxiv. 182 Doth not the distemper of the body insaniate the soule?

Hence †**inˈsaniated** *ppl. a.*

1652 S. S. *Weepers* A ij b, A Degenerate, besotted, insaniated, ignorant People. **1665** J. Gadbury *London's Deliv. Pred.* v. 28 An Argument of super-insaniated folly.

†in'sanie. *Obs. rare.* [a. obs. F. *insanie*, ad. L. *insānia*, f. *insānus* INSANE.] Madness.
1572 W. HOLME *Fall Rebell.* (R.), Jack Cade made a brag, With a multitude of people; but.. After a little insanie they fled tag and rag. SHAKS. *L.L.L.* v. i. 28 It insinuateth me of insanie: *ne inteligis domine*, to make franticke, lunaticke. [This is Warburton's conjecture adopted by Theobald: all the orig. edd. have 'infamie'.]

insanify (ɪn'sænɪfaɪ), *v. rare.* [f. L. *insān-us* INSANE + -FY; cf. SANIFY.] *trans.* To make insane. Also *absol.* or *intr.* To cause insanity.
1809 SYD. SMITH *Wks.* (1859) I. 140/2 There may be.. some very respectable men at the head of these maniacs [Methodists], who would insanify them with some degree of prudence, and keep them only half mad, if they could. **1894** *Westm. Gaz.* 16 June 8/1 There is not much virtue in a cup which does not inebriate, if it does insanify.

†in'sanious, *a. Obs. rare.* [f. L. *insānia* (see INSANIE) + -OUS.] Of or pertaining to madness.
1656 S. HOLLAND *Zara* (1719) 94 Leaving our Champion in the most insanious extasie.

insanitary (ɪn'sænɪtərɪ), *a.* [IN-³.] Not sanitary or healthful; injurious to health.
1874 *Standard* 28 Aug., The very insanitary conditions under which these labourers perform their work. **1880** *Macm. Mag.* No. 246. 471 'A pestilent and insanitary area' in the full meaning of the term. **1884** *Athenæum* 5 Apr. 446/2 Models of sanitary and insanitary dwelling-houses. **1884** *Health Exhib. Catal.* p. xxxvi, Specimens of insanitary decorations such as arsenical wall-papers, hangings, etc.
Hence **in'sanitariness,** insanitary condition.
1881 *Standard* 22 Jan. 5/2 It blows over no insanitariness, and wafts with it no germs of fever.

insanitation (ɪnsænɪ'teɪʃən). [IN-³.] Want of sanitation; insanitary condition; absence of sanitary measures or requirements.
1884 *American* IX. 25 Insanitation, he said, did not cause the disease [cholera]. **1896** *Westm. Gaz.* 5 Dec. 2/3 The insufficiency of cottages, the overcrowding and insanitation of the existing supply.

insanity (ɪn'sænɪtɪ). [ad. L. *insānitātem* unhealthiness, unsoundness, disease, n. of quality f. *insānus* INSANE: see -ITY. Cf. mod.F. *insanité* (1863 in Littré).]
1. The condition of being insane; unsoundness of mind as a consequence of brain-disease; madness, lunacy. Orig., called *insanity of mind.*
'A condition of the mind in which a false action of conception or judgment, a defective power of the will, or an uncontrollable violence of the emotions and instincts, have separately or conjointly been produced by disease' (Dr. J. C. Bucknill, *Crim. Lunacy* (1854) 28).
1590 SWINBURNE *Testaments* 36 b, Madfolkes and Lunaticke persons, during the time of their furor or insanitie of minde, cannot make a testament. *a* **1677** HALE *Hist. Placit. Cor.* (R.), There is a partial insanity of mind and a total insanity. This partial insanity seems not to excuse them in the committing of any offence for its matter capital. **1772** *Junius Lett.* lxviii. 355 Did they attempt to produce any evidence of his insanity? **1782** T. ARNOLD (*title*) Observations on the Nature, Kinds, Causes, and Prevention of Insanity. **1827** SCOTT *Highl. Widow* v, The murder of an officer may be.. coloured over with [the plea] of temporary insanity. **1859** *Engineer* VII. 282/2 Two cases of suicide.. In each case the coroner's jury brought in a verdict of temporary insanity. **1865** *Pall Mall G.* 3 Aug. 4/1 The definition of insanity.. as an inability to reason upon the evidence of the senses. **1897** *Dict. Nat. Biog.* LII. 320/2 D. Skae's.. definition of insanity as 'a disease of the brain affecting the mind' is not disputable.
transf. **1784** COWPER *Task* VI. 523 The frenzy of the brain may be redress'd By med'cine well applied, but without grace The heart's insanity admits no cure.
2. Extreme folly or want of sound sense; an instance of this.
1844 EMERSON *Lect., Yng. Amer.* Wks. (Bohn) II. 306 After all the deduction is made for our frivolities and insanities. **1844** STANLEY *Arnold* (1858) II. ix. 162 To lose which.. would be rather our insanity than our misfortune. **1862** H. SPENCER *First Princ.* II. iii. §46 (1875) 159 Did we .. use the term *effect*.. we should be in little danger of falling into the insanities of idealism.
3. *attrib.* and *Comb.*
1892 *Pall Mall G.* 28 May 7/2 One cannot conclude that their insanity rate is remarkably high. **1894** *Daily News* 26 July 9/2 Dr. B——, insanity expert, who had examined the prisoner at the request of the Treasury, said prisoner was now perfectly sane. **1896** *Westm. Gaz.* 6 Nov. 6/3 Eminent nerve and insanity specialists gave evidence.

†in'sanous, *a. Obs. rare*⁻¹. [f. IN-³ + L. *sān-us* sound, healthy + -OUS.] Unhealthy, dangerous to health.
1742 *Lond. & Country Brew.* I. (ed. 4) 16 River-Waters are less liable to be loaded with metallic, petrifying, saline, and other insanous Particles of the Earth, than the Well or Spring-sorts are.

in'sapiency. *rare.* [IN-³.] Want of sapience or wisdom; insipiency.
1876 J. WEISS *Wit, Hum. & Shaks.* v. 177 Polonius hurried to show his insapiency by attributing the craze to love for his daughter.

in'sapient, *a. rare*⁻¹. [IN-³.] Unwise; insipient.
c **1470** HARDING *Chron.* CCXI. ii, In his fyrste yere the lorde Cobham heretike, Confedered with Lollers insapient, Agayne the Churche arose.

†in'sapory, *a. Obs. rare*⁻¹. [irreg. f. IN-³ + L. *sapor* taste + -Y.] Unsavoury.
1665 SIR T. HERBERT *Trav.* (1677) 311 Coho or Coffee.. however ingrate or insapory it seems at first, it becomes grate and delicious enough by custom.

†in'satan, *v. Obs. rare*⁻⁰. [IN-².] *trans.* To possess with or by Satan.
1611 FLORIO, *Insatanire*, to insathan or indiuell.

†in'satanize, *v. Obs. rare*⁻¹. [f. as prec. + -IZE.] = prec.
1857 *Truths Cath. Relig.* (ed. 4) 178 His [Luther's] assertion is 'that Zuinglius, and all who adhere to his doctrine, are insatanized'.

†in'satchel, *v. Obs. rare.* [f. IN-² + SATCHEL, after F. *ensacher*.] (See quots.)
1611 COTGR., *Ensaché*, insachelled, impoaked, put vp into a bag, sachell, or poake. *a* **1693** URQUHART *Rabelais* III. xlii. 344 Papers.. impoaked, insacheled, and put up in Bags.

insatiability (ɪnseɪʃɪə'bɪlɪtɪ). [f. next + -ITY, perh. after F. *insatiabilité* (16th c.), or late L. *insatiābilitās* (Ammianus).] The quality of being insatiable; insatiableness.
1654 COKAINE *Dianea* IV. 275 To please the insatiability of those who deprived me of mine owne. **1750** JOHNSON *Rambler* No. 38 ¶8 An eagerness for increase of possessions deluges the soul, and we sink into the gulphs of insatiability. **1844** H. H. WILSON *Brit. India* III. 311 With the usual short-sightedness of commercial insatiability, they.. joined in the clamour against the East India Company's exclusive privileges. **1846** *Blackw. Mag.* LIX. 405 The.. recklessness, and insatiability of the democrat spirit.

insatiable (ɪn'seɪʃɪəb(ə)l), *a.* Forms: 5-6 insacyable, 5-7 -saciable (5 -sessiabyll, 6 -saciabyll), 6- insatiable. [a. OF. *insaciable* (13th c.; mod.F. *insatiable*), or ad. L. *insatiābilis*, f. *in-* (IN-³) + *satiāre* to SATIATE: see -ABLE.] Not satiable; that cannot be satiated, satisfied, or appeased; that always craves for more; inordinately greedy. Const. *of*, rarely *with.*
a **1420** HOCCLEVE *De Reg. Princ.* 1172 Fy on the, gredynesse insaciable. **1430** LYDG. *S. Margarete* 261 O gredy hounde, lyoun insaciable. **1465** *Paston Lett.* No. 501 II. 180 The dayli contynewyng maleyse of youre insessiabyll enemyes. **1548** HALL *Chron., Hen. VII* 3 b, They dranke the colde water to quenche their importune heate and insaciable thirst. **1607** TOPSELL *Four-f. Beasts* (1658) 383 None but insatiable Beasts or Birds are so affected. **1641** MILTON *Ch. Govt.* I. iii, They are so insatiable of antiquity. **1726** SWIFT *Gulliver* I. viii, My insatiable desire of seeing foreign countries. **1791** COWPER *Iliad* XX. 3 Achilles, glorious Chief Insatiable with war. **1849** MACAULAY *Hist. Eng.* V. I. 532 Insensible to shame, insatiable of notoriety.
b. *fig.* Of things.
1529 MORE *Suppl. Soulys* Wks. 295/2 Gredie golophers he calleth them & insaciable whyrlepoles. **1548** HALL *Chron., Hen. VI* 126 The crie and noyes of this perillous and insaciable warre, was blasted through Europe. **1634** SIR T. HERBERT *Trav.* 192 Overswayed by the insatiable gulph of perdition the Devill. **1857** H. H. WILSON tr. *Rig-veda* III. 446 The insatiable goal whence there is no returning.

insatiableness (ɪn'seɪʃɪəb(ə)lnɪs). [f. prec. + -NESS.] The quality of being insatiable.
1618-29 in Rushw. *Hist. Coll.* (1659) I. 344 It was a mark of Ingratitude and Insatiableness in the Duke, thus to strain the Kings Bounty beyond his intention. **1647** CLARENDON *Ess.* Tracts (1727) 95 Ambition always carries an insatiableness with it, which is a torment to the mind. **1768-74** TUCKER *Lt. Nat.* (1834) II. 358 An inveteracy, and insatiableness of vengeance. **1864** PUSEY *Lect. Daniel* ii. 74 Insatiableness of conquest.

insatiably (ɪn'seɪʃɪəblɪ), *adv.* [f. as prec. + -LY².] In an insatiable manner or degree.
1576 NEWTON *Lemnie's Complex.* (1633) 181 They that bee hungry, devoure meate greedily and insatiably. *a* **1711** KEN *Div. Love* Wks. (1838) 301 Forgive me, if I am insatiably covetous, it is only of thy fruition. **1868** MILMAN *St. Paul's* iii. 47 Insatiably draining away the wealth of the land.

†in'satiacy. *Obs. rare*⁻¹. In 7 insaciacie. [f. INSATIATE: see -ACY 3.] The quality of being insatiate.
1629 GAULE *Holy Madn.* 340 Surfeit yet a while in your hellish Insaciacie.

insatiate (ɪn'seɪʃɪət), *a.* Also 6 insaciate, -cyate, 7 -tiat. [ad. L. *insatiātus* (Statius), f. *in-* (IN-³) + *satiātus*, pa. pple. of *satiāre* to SATIATE.] That is not satiated or satisfied; never satisfied, insatiable. Const. *of*, †*for.*
1509 HAWES *Past. Pleas.* VIII. (Percy Soc.) 30 Wyth brennynge love of insaciate fyre Newe thynges to fynde they set theyr desyre. *a* **1533** LD. BERNERS *Gold. Bk. M. Aurel.* (1546) H vj, The insaciate couetous men are neuer contente. **1616** R. C. *Times' Whistle* v. 1708 The wantonnesse Of their insatiat appetite.. breeds Offensive humors. **1667** MILTON *P.L.* II. 8 Satan.. insatiate to pursue Vain Warr with Heav'n. **1704** HEARNE *Duct. Hist.* (1714) I. 406 Being insatiate for knowledge, he travell'd all over Greece. **1781** GIBBON *Decl. & F.* xxxi. (1869) II. 196 Avarice is an insatiate and universal passion. **1848** BUCKLEY *Homer's Iliad* 246 The Trojans are insatiate of battle. **1860** PUSEY *Min. Proph.* 29 Those who, through their own insatiate desires, are never satisfied.
fig. **1602** MARSTON *Antonio's Rev.* III. iii, Even like insatiate hell, still crying, More.
Hence **in'satiateness** (Bailey vol. II, 1727).

in'satiated, *a. rare.* [IN-³.] Not satiated.
1727 BAILEY vol. II, *Insatiated*, not satisfied or filled. **1759** *Hist. Eur.* in *Ann. Reg.* 51/2 Still insatiated with glory, he determined immediately to set sail again. **1842** MRS. BROWNING *Grk. Chr. Poets* 36 This boon I give instead Unto friend insatiated.

in'satiately, *adv.* [f. INSATIATE + -LY².] In an insatiate or unsatisfied manner.
1509 HAWES *Conv. Swearers* 39 With many aungelles whiche for theyr solace Insacyately do beholde my face. **1633** T. ADAMS *Exp. 2 Peter* ii. 14 Those swinish churls, that insatiately swill up the draff of the world. **1665** SIR T. HERBERT *Trav.* (1677) 321 The better to excuse himself who was so insatiately libidinous.

†insa'tiety. *Obs.* Also 7 insaciety. [a. obs. F. *insacieté, -satieté* (Godef.), ad. L. *insatietās*: see IN-³ and SATIETY.] The condition of being insatiate; unsatisfied desire or demand.
1578 FLORIO *1st Fruites* 66 The temperance and vertue of the one is commendable, the insaciety and wickednes of the other is to be condemned. *a* **1632** T. TAYLOR *God's Judgem.* II. v. (1642) 63 Who knowing his great avarice, caused molten gold to be pour'd downe his throate, deriding his insaciety. *a* **1668** SIR W. WALLER *Div. Medit.* (1839) 136 What an insatiety is there in all these delights.

†insatis'faction. *Obs.* [IN-³.] Absence of satisfaction; unsatisfied condition; dissatisfaction.
1568 NORTH tr. *Gueuara's Diall Pr.* (1619) 609/7 He must beware also that hee shew no countenance to the King of insatisfaction. **1626** BACON *Sylva* §800 It is a Profound Contemplation in Nature, to consider of the Emptinesse.. or Insatisfaction of severall Bodies; And of their Appetite to take in Others. **1656** FINETT *For. Ambass.* 14, I yeelded.. after some discovery of my insatisfaction to be so punctually pressed. *a* **1682** SIR T. BROWNE *Tracts* (1684) 20 With what insatisfaction the most learned Botanists reduce that Plant unto any described by the Ancients.

†insatis'factorily, *adv. Obs. rare.* [IN-³.] In an unsatisfactory way.
1646 SIR T. BROWNE *Pseud. Ep.* I. ii. 6 The displeasure of the Pelagians must needs be irreconcileable, who peremptorily maintaining they can fulfill the whole Law, will insatisfactorily condemne the non-observation of one.

†in'satisfied, *a. Obs. rare.* [IN-³.] Unsatisfied.
1643 T. CASE *Three Serm.* (1644) 69 If any of you.. be any wayes insatisfied.. I advise you to forbear.

†in'sative, *a. Obs. rare*⁻⁰. [f. IN-³ + L. *satīvus* that is sown or planted (cf. L. **insatīvus*, old reading in Pliny XIX. xii. 60 for *in satīvis*).]
1656 BLOUNT *Glossogr.*, *Insative*, that is not planted, sown or grafted; that which coms forth of its own accord. **1658** PHILLIPS, *Insative*, unsown, unplanted, growing voluntarily.

insaturable (ɪn'sætjʊərəb(ə)l), *a.* [In sense 1, ad. L. *insaturābilis* insatiable, f. *in-* (IN-³) + *saturāre* to SATURATE; in 2, f. SATURABLE.]
†1. Insatiable. *Obs.*
1412-20 LYDG. *Chron. Troy* III. xxii, Oh hatefull Tygre passing enuyous, Of aueryce Oh beast insaturable. **1604** TOOKER *Fabric Church* 114 Enemies to all dignitie,.. whose hatred is insaturable. **1631** R. H. *Arraignm. Whole Creature* xiii. §3. 220 The evill will of man is insaturable, his desire insatiable. **1721** in BAILEY. **1755** JOHNSON, *Insaturable* not to be glutted; not to be filled.
2. Not able to be saturated.
1849 *Fraser's Mag.* XL. 454 A solvent of all true oils insaturable in water.

†insa'turity. *Obs. rare.* [IN-³.] **a.** Unsatisfied or unfilled condition. **b.** Unsatisfying quality.
1631 R. H. *Arraignm. Whole Creature* xiii. §3. 205 The insaturity of the Soule of man, taking so little Complacency and Contentation. *Ibid.* xv. §1. 251 The insaturity and insufficiency of all these huskish Vanities, on which our Prodigall eates.

†in'saut, *v. Obs.* In 5 ensaut, ynsawt. [ME. *ensaute*, an altered form of *assaut*, ASSAULT, with change of prefix, due to confusion of *a-*, *an-*, *en-*: cf. ENSAMPLE.] *trans.* To assail contemptuously, insult.
c **1425** *St. Christina* xxiv. in *Anglia* VIII. 129/9 How she ensautid þe worlde, for hit knewe not his creature [= creator]. *c* **1425** *Found. St. Bartholomew's* (E.E.T.S.) 25 The whiche nat oonly to the asker wolde nat yeue but was woonte with scornyng wordes to ynsawt them.

†in'scalable, *a. Obs. rare.* [IN-³.] Incapable of being scaled or climbed; unscalable.
a **1680** BUTLER *Rem.* (1759) I. 417 The opposite Side landward.. might be made as inscalable as the other.

inscape ('ɪnskeɪp), *sb.* [Origin unknown; perh. f. IN *adv.* 12 + SCAPE *sb.*³, or ad. INSHAPE.] Hopkins's word for the individual or essential quality of a thing; the uniqueness of an observed object, scene, event, etc. (see quots.). Hence **'inscape** *v. trans.*; **'inscaped** *ppl. a.*
1868 G. M. HOPKINS *Jrnls. & Papers* (1959) 127 His [*sc.* Parmenides'] feeling for instress, for the flush and fore-drawn, and for inscape is most striking. *Ibid.* 129 The way men judge in particular is determined for each by his own inscape. *Ibid.* 174 Two plants especially with strongly inscaped leaves cover the mountain pastures. *Ibid.* 177 The whole cascade is inscaped in fretted falling vandykes. **1879** —— *Lett. to R. Bridges* (1955) 66 Design, pattern, or what I am in the habit of calling 'inscape' is what I above all aim at

in poetry. Now it is the virtue of design, pattern, or inscape to be distinctive and it is the vice of distinctiveness to become queer. **1886** —— *Let.* 7 Nov. (1956) 373 The essential and only lasting thing left out—what I call *inscape*, that is species or individually-distinctive beauty of style. **1919** R. Fry *Let.* 29 Apr. (1972) II. 450 His [*sc.* G. M. Hopkins's] aesthetic—his 'inscape'; that's what we are after, however much we miss it. **1938** D. Gascoyne *Hölderlin's Madness* 35 All is an inscape And yet separates Thus shelters the Poet. **1944** *Downside Rev.* LXII. 185 The prefix 'in-' of 'inscape' is the operative part. 'Inscape' is the perception that comes only with contraction to a point. The inscape of a scene is not its correspondence with an externally conceived pattern; it is that scene experienced as absolutely unique, knit together in that oneness which is nameable only by relation. **1944** [see INSTRESS *sb.*]. **1945** C. Williams *All Hallows' Eve* vii. 113 He forgot Simon.. he forgot Lester... The inscape of the painting became central. **1948** W. A. M. Peters *G. M. Hopkins* i. 1 'Inscape' is the unified complex of those sensible qualities of the object of perception that strikes us as inseparably belonging to and most typical of it, so that through the knowledge of this unified complex of sense-data we may gain an insight into the individual essence of the object. **1953** W. H. Gardner in G. M. Hopkins *Poems & Prose* 229 *Twindles*.. a portmanteau word inscaping 'twists' and 'dwindles'. **1970** *Country Life* 26 Feb. 484/2 In Manchester there is the fabric of buildings and structures which contribute by their reality to the inscape of the place.

inscenation (ɪnsiːˈneɪʃən). [prob. after G. *inszenierung*.] Theatrical representation, *mise en scène*.

1897 G. B. Shaw in *Sat. Rev.* 13 Nov. 514/2 Maeterlinck's plays, requiring a mystical inscenation in the style of Fernand Knopf, would be nearly as much spoiled by Elizabethan treatment as by Drury Lane treatment. **1900** W. A. Ellis *Life Wagner* I. I. iii. 69 Geyer took an active part in the inscenation of his piece, in which he himself played Painter Klaus. **1963** *Times* 1 Mar. 13/1 A new inscenation of *Trovatore*. **1971** *Times* 8 June 8/2 Britten's setting of the Chester miracle play, and Mr Graham's inscenation of it, strive to recover the rough-and-tumble primitive gusto.

†**inˈscend**, *v. Obs. rare*⁻⁰. [ad. L. *inscendĕre* to ascend, mount, embark, f. *in-* (IN-[2]) + *scandĕre* to climb.]

1604 R. Cawdrey *Table Alph.*, *In[s]cend*, clime vp, or mount vp.

insch, insched, obs. Sc. form of INCH, INSHED.

†**inschool**, *v. Obs. rare*⁻⁰. [IN-[2].]

1611 Florio, *Inscuolare*, to inschoole.

insciciouin, inside, erron. ff. INCISION, INCIDE.

inscience (ˈɪnʃɪəns). Now *rare*. [ad. L. *inscientia* want of knowledge, ignorance, f. *inscient-em* (see next), after *scientia* knowledge, science. Cf. obs. F. *inscience* (15–16th c.), It. *inscienza* (Florio).] The condition of not knowing; want of knowledge; nescience, ignorance.

1578 Banister *Hist. Man* Pref. 5 Rather.. a meane to indurate the cataract of inscience, then to.. take it away. **1579** Lodge *Def. Plays* 5 Are his speeches unperfect? Sauor they of inscience? **1675** J. Smith *Chr. Relig. App.* 3 (L.) Their inscience of the natural cause. *a* **1682** Sir T. Browne *Tracts* (1684) 179 Not to know things without the Arch of our intellectuals.. is.. rather inscience than ignorance in man. **1810** Bentham *Packing* (1821) 179 *note*, On the part of the learned author.. behold still the same pleasantry; or still the same simplicity and inscience. *a* **1896** Benson *Cyprian* (1897) 83 *note*, [His] special pleading is matched by his inscience of every technical law term.

inscient (ˈɪnʃɪənt), *a.*[1] Now *rare*. [ad. L. *inscient-em* unknowing, ignorant, f. *in-* (IN-[3]) + *sciens, scient-*, pr. pple. of *scīre* to know.] Not knowing; lacking knowledge; nescient, ignorant.

1578 Banister *Hist. Man* I. 30 Celsus.. confesseth himselfe inscient, by accomptyng their number uncertaine. **1643** Prynne *Sov. Power of Parlt.* II. Pref. A ij, A Company of seemingly Scient, though really inscient, selfe-conceited Court-Doctors, Priests, and Lawyers. **1898** *Speaker* 10 Dec. 694/2 In the thirties the Oxford mind was inscient.

ˈ**inscient**, *a.*[2] *rare*. [f. IN-[2] + L. *scient-em* knowing.] Having inward knowledge or insight.

1856 Mrs. Browning *Aur. Leigh* IX. 913 Gaze on, with inscient vision toward the sun, And, from his visceral heat, pluck out the roots Of light beyond him.

†**inscienˈtifical**, *a. Obs.* [IN-[3].] Not scientific; unacquainted with science, unlearned.

1660 R. Coke *Justice Vind.* Pref. 9, I would know now of Mr. Hobbs, whether all Arts and Sciences, and Prudent actions, be the Laws of Nature, or not? If they be the Laws of Nature, then is every Inscientifical and Imprudent man, an Unjust man.

ˈ**inscientist**. *nonce-wd.* [cf. INSCIENCE.] A non-scientist.

1909 W. Tuckwell *Pre-Tractarian Oxford* vi. 150 He knew nothing of Science or of Microscopes... So he came to all our Meetings, the one avowed Inscientist amongst us.

†ˈ**inscious**, *a. Obs.* [f. L. *insci-us* not knowing, ignorant (f. *in-*, IN-[3] + *-scius* knowing) + -OUS. Cf. *conscious*.] = INSCIENT *a.*[1]

1633 T. Adams *Exp. 2 Peter* iii. 5 He begins with the dunces, those.. inscious.. wilful ignorants. **1635** Heywood *Hierarch.* VII. *Comm.* 450 The inscious man may be knowne by three things. **1657** Hawke *Killing is M.* 54 His Followers cannot be inscious, what an abhominable and odious crime it is to betray their Lord and Master.

Hence †ˈ**insciously** *adv.*, unwittingly.

1675 Baxter *Cath. Theol.* I. I. 109 Thus insciously he unsaith what laboriously he writeth a book to prove.

inscipient, inscision, -tion, erron. ff. INCIPIENT, INCISION.

insconce, obs. f. ENSCONCE.

inscribable (ɪnˈskraɪbəb(ə)l), *a.* [f. next + -ABLE.] Capable of being inscribed. Hence **inˈscribableness**.

1846 Worcester, *Inscribable*, that may be inscribed. *Dr. Allen.* **1847** Craig, *Inscribableness.* **1879** A. Macfarlane *Princ. Algebra of Logic* 14 The characters 'regular' and 'inscribable in a circle'. *a* **1900** *Mod.* No non-rectangular parallelogram is inscribable in a circle.

inscribe (ɪnˈskraɪb), *v.* [ad. L. *inscrībĕre* to write in or upon, f. *in-* (IN-[2]) + *scrībĕre* to write.]

1. *trans.* To write, mark, or delineate (words, a name, characters, etc.) in or on something; esp. so as to be conspicuous or durable, as on a monument, tablet, etc. (In quot. 1603, with *upon* in indirect passive = passive of sense 2.)

1552 Huloet, Inscribe, *inscribo, intitulo.* **1603** B. Jonson *King's Coron. Entertainm.*, In her hand she holds a sceptre.. and in her lap a little globe, inscribed upon ORBIS BRITANNICUS. **1665** Manley *Grotius' Low-C. Warres* 795 He gave for his word, and inscribed on all his Ensigns this Motto, *Jam aut nunquam*, Now or never. **1781** Cowper *Truth* 28 Inscribed above the portal, from afar Conspicuous as the brightness of a star.. Stand the soul-quickening words—Believe and live. **1864** J. Walker *Faithf. Ministry* 92 We raise the marble and inscribe the flattering epitaph. *Mod.* You must inscribe your name in the Visitors' Book.

fig. *a* **1677** Hale *Prim. Orig. Man.* I. ii. 62 Though there were no such [connatural principles] originally inscribed in the Mind. **1828** Webster, *Inscribe*.. 2. To imprint on; as, to inscribe any thing on the mind or memory.

b. To write or enter the name of (a person) upon an official document or list; to enroll.

1605 B. Jonson *Volpone* I. Wks. (Rtldg.) 177/1 Am I inscribed his heir for certain? **1803** W. Taylor in *Ann. Rev.* I. 353 The French inscribe all their boys on the army-list, and compel every one who cannot raise five and twenty louis, to serve in their turn. **1890** *Spectator* 15 Feb., On Friday, 7th inst., the Duc d'Orléans, eldest son of the Comte de Paris.. demanded to be inscribed on the list of conscripts under the Military Law.

c. *Comm.* To issue a state (or other) loan in the form of shares with registered holders: see INSCRIBED 1 b.

1884 *Pall Mall G.* 18 Aug. 5/2 In Colonial Government stocks, especially those inscribed in London, the rise was rather more than the average.

2. To mark (a surface, column, sheet, etc.) with writing or other characters, esp. in a durable or conspicuous way.

1637 Milton *Lycidas* 106 Like to that sanguine flower inscribed with woe. **1702** Addison *Dial. Medals* ii. (Seager), There is a medal of Heliogabalus inscribed, 'Fides exercitus'. **1713** —— *Guard.* No. 119 ¶5 The two friends made a kind of dial-plate, inscribing it with the four and twenty letters. **1805** Wordsw. *Prelude* II. 149 Though the rhymes were gone that once inscribed The threshold. **1870** Bryant *Iliad* I. VII. 220 Ajax.. who had inscribed And laid it in the helmet.

b. To dedicate (a writing or work of art) *to* a person by a short inscription (placed at the beginning of a writing, or beneath a picture, etc.), less formal than an ordinary dedication.

1645 Boate *Irel. Nat. Hist.* (1652) Ded. A v, I have made bold thus to address.. you, and to inscribe this Work unto your Names, that it may see the light under your joint patronage. **1709** Swift *Advancem. Relig.* Wks. 1755 II. I. 96 The following papers.. being inscribed to your ladyship. **1751** Johnson *Rambler* No. 136 ¶9 An author may with great propriety inscribe his work to him by whose encouragement it was undertaken. **1849** Macaulay *Hist. Eng.* iii. I. 405 The patron to whom a work was inscribed was expected to reward the writer with a purse of gold.

3. *Geom.* To delineate or trace (a figure or line) within a figure, so that some particular points of it lie in the boundary or periphery of that figure.

An angular figure (polygon or polyhedron) is said to be inscribed in another figure when the angular points of the former lie in the bounding line or lines, or surface or surfaces, of the latter. A curved figure (plane or solid) is said to be inscribed in an angular figure when the former touches each of the bounding lines or surfaces of the latter. More rarely, a line is said to be inscribed in a figure when its extremities lie in the boundary of that figure.

1570 Billingsley *Euclid* IV. Introd. 110 It teacheth how a triangle.. may be inscribed within a circle. **1571** Digges *Pantom.*, *Geom. Solids* Ee iij a, Either of bodyes inscribed or circumbscribed. **1662** Stillingfl. *Orig. Sacr.* III. i. §14 When I conceive a Triangle inscribed in a square. *a* **1696** Scarburgh *Euclid* (1705) 165 Therefore in a given square a Circle has been inscribed. **1827** Hutton *Course Math.* I. 373 To inscribe a circle in a regular polygon. **1885** Leudesdorf *Cremona's Proj. Geom.* 185 To inscribe in a given conic a polygon whose sides pass.. through given points.

†**4.** *Sc. Law.* See INSCRIVE.

inscribed (ɪnˈskraɪbd), *ppl. a.* [f. prec.]

1. Written upon or in something. Also *fig.*

1611 Cotgr., *Inscript*, inscribed, intituled, written on. *a* **1677** Hale *Prim. Orig. Man.* IV. iii. 318 Besides this Moral inscribed Law, God Almighty.. gave him a positive Law. **1847** W. C. Burns in *Life* xii. (1870) 318, I gave him two religious books with an inscribed promise to pray for him.

b. Of a state (or other) loan: Issued not in the form of bonds passing from hand to hand, but as shares of which the names of the holders are registered or entered in a list kept at the head office of the issuing state or company.

1882 Bithell *Counting-ho. Dict.*, *Inscribed Stocks*, see *Registered Stocks*. [*Ibid.*, *Registered Stocks* are so called because they are entered with the name of the holder in a Register kept for that purpose at the chief office of the Company or State issuing them.]

2. Marked with writing or other characters. In *Entom.* Having markings resembling letters.

1826 Kirby & Sp. *Entomol.* xlvi. IV. 286 *Inscribed*,.. When the [wing] surface is marked with the resemblance of a letter of any language. Ex. *Noctua Gamma*. **1851** D. Wilson *Preh. Ann.* (1863) II. IV. ii. 209 Inscribed Stones, more or less rudely graven. **1879** Lubbock *Addr. Pol. & Educ.* ix. 173 The Catstane, an inscribed pillar.

3. *Geom.* (See INSCRIBE 3.)

1571 Digges *Pantom.*, *Geom. Solids* V iij b, The square of an equilater triangles syde to the inscribed circles semidimetientes square is as 12 to 1. **1706** Phillips (ed. Kersey), *Inscribed Figures*, those that are drawn within others [etc.]. **1806** Hutton *Course Math.* I. 369 To determine a Triangle, and the Radius of the Inscribed Circle. **1885** Leudesdorf *Cremona's Proj. Geom.* 125 Six points on a conic, taken in any order, may be regarded as the vertices of an inscribed hexagon.

inscriber (ɪnˈskraɪbə(r)). [f. as prec. + -ER[1].] One who inscribes; the writer of an inscription.

1674 Sir G. Mackenzie *Laws & Customs Scotl. Matters Criminal* xix. § 8 (1699) The inscriber was according to the Civil Law, oblidged to find caution. **1782** Pownall *Stud. Antiq.* 48 Characters and.. diagrams.. which Kircher has passed by unnoticed, as though making no part of the inscriber's intention. **1876** S. Manning *Land Pharaohs* 206 Many of the inscribers were Christians. **1894** W. M. Lindsay in *Class. Rev.* Mar. 108/1 Inscriptions, in which a certain amount of illiteracy on the part of the inscribers is at times a disturbing element.

inscript (ˈɪnskrɪpt), *sb.* [ad. L. *inscript-um* that which is written upon anything, an inscription, sb. use of neuter of *inscript-us*: see next.]

1. Something inscribed; an inscription.

1611 Speed *Hist. Gt. Brit.* x. i. §60. 1235 The inducement thereunto, being no more then a namelesse Inscript shuffled, no man knew whence. **1652** Sparke *Prim. Devot.* (1663) 243 What suiting inscript to the Cross belongs. **1882** Col. Yule in *Athenæum* 17 June 765/1 Some time in the sixteenth century.. it is shown by an inscript at the end to have belonged to Symon du Solier, dwelling at Honfleur.

†**2.** *Geom.* A line inscribed in a figure; a chord.

1695 Alingham *Geom. Epit.* 12 The line *AB* is also called an Inscript, and when so applyed, is said to cut the Circle.

†**inˈscript**, *ppl. a. Obs.* [ad. L. *inscript-us*, pa. pple. of *inscrībĕre* to INSCRIBE.] Inscribed.

1432–50 tr. *Higden* (Rolls) V. 11 The name of Ihesu was founde with letters of golde inscripte and wryten in hit. **1592** R. D. *Hypnerotomachia* 16 A shield.. whereupon was inscript in Hebrew, Attic and Latine letters, this sentence.

inscript (ɪnˈskrɪpt), *v. rare.* [f. L. *inscript-*, ppl. stem of *inscrībĕre* to INSCRIBE *v.*; or back-formation from INSCRIPTION.] *trans.* To inscribe. Hence **inˈscripted** *ppl. a.*

1923 *Public Opinion* 16 Feb. 155/3 The statement at the head of this article might usefully be inscripted in all Theological Halls. **1923** *Blackw. Mag.* Feb. 151/1 It does not require inscripted monuments to perpetuate the memory of British deeds.

inˈscriptible, *a. rare.* [f. L. *inscript-us*, pa. pple. of *inscrībĕre* + -IBLE.] = INSCRIBABLE.

a **1696** Scarburgh *Euclid* (1705) 173 Polygons do arise, that are mutually with a Circle, or with one another Inscriptible and Circumscriptible.

inscription (ɪnˈskrɪpʃən). [ad. L. *inscriptiōn-em*, n. of action from *inscrībĕre* to INSCRIBE. Cf. F. *inscription* (Rabelais, 16th c., in Hatz.-Darm.).]

1. The action of inscribing; the action of writing upon or in something. (In quots. *fig.*) *rare*.

a **1652** J. Smith *Sel. Disc.* IX. i. (1821) 410 These we may call the truths of natural inscription. **1748** Hartley *Observ. Man* II. i. 45 The Law of first Inscription.

2. *concr.* That which is inscribed; a piece of writing or lettering upon something; a set of characters or words written, engraved, or otherwise traced upon a surface; *esp.* a legend, description, or record traced upon some hard substance for the sake of durability, as on a monument, building, stone, tablet, medal, coin, vase, etc.

1538 Leland *Itin.* I. 96 Inscription could I find none yn these Stones. **1596** Shaks. *Merch. V.* II. vii. 14, I will suruay the inscriptions, backe againe: What saies this leaden casket? **1667** Evelyn *Diary* 19 Sept., I obtain'd the gift of his Arundelian Marbles, those celebrated and famous inscriptions Greeke and Latine, gather'd with so much cost and industrie from Greece. **1688** R. Holme *Armoury* III. 28/2 Queen Elizabeths shilling had.. this Inscription, *Posui Deum Adjutorem meum.* **1718** Lady M. W. Montagu *Let. to C'tess Bristol* 10 Apr., A brazen column.. was erected.. there is no sign of its having ever had any inscription. **1821** Byron *Two Fosc.* II. i. 226 'Tis perhaps as true as most Inscriptions upon tombs. **1839** *Penny Cycl.* XV. 53/1 It bears on one side the head of Ferdinand with the inscription *Ferdinandvs* [etc.]. **1842** Brande *Dict. Sc.*, etc. 833/1 The

words around the border of the coin form what is termed the *legend*, those in the middle the *inscription*. [B. V. HEAD in *Let.*, Numismatists make no distinction between 'Inscription' and 'Legend'.]

fig. **1643** MILTON *Divorce* Introd. (1851) 11 Nor is this yet the highest inscription that will adorn so religious and so holy a defence as this. **1859** DICKENS *T. Two Cities* I. v, Hunger was the inscription on the baker's shelves written in every small loaf of his scanty stock of bad bread.

3. *spec.* **a.** A short piece of writing placed at the beginning of a book or other composition, descriptive of its nature, contents, authorship, etc.; a title, heading, superscription. (Now *rare* or *Obs.* as distinct from 2.) **b.** A brief dedication of a book or work of art to a person (see INSCRIBE 2 b); the superscription of a letter.

a **1400** *Wyclif's Bible* Gen. Prol. 39 (MS. Trin. Coll. Dubl. A. I. 10) The firste psalme to no man is asigned, for.. what other man is vndirstonden in the firste but the firste geten, that inscripcioun worthili schuld not be necessarie. **1529** MORE *Dyaloge* I. Wks. 174/2 Many bokes be ther that haue false inscripcions, and ar not the bokes of them that they be named by. **1598** FLORIO, *Indice*,.. also the inscription or title of a booke. **1649** *Alcoran* p. vi, Mahomet.. divided it into many Chapters, to which he gave what inscription he thought good: he most commonly intituleth them with words that are in their first line. **1742** RICHARDSON *Pamela* IV. 451 And now-and-then a Letter passes on both Sides, by the Inscription and Subscription of which, they remind one another, that they have been *once* in their Lives at one Church together.

c. In early *Music*, A motto or sign, or combination of both, placed at the beginning of an enigmatical canon, to indicate (often itself enigmatically) the manner of its resolution.

1880 W. S. ROCKSTRO in Grove *Dict. Mus.* s.v., In the second Agnus Dei of his 'Missa L'Ami baudichon', [Josquin des Prés] intimates that the Tenor is to be silent, by the pretty Inscription, 'Agnus secundum non est cum grege.'.. Some of Hobrecht's Inscriptions are very obscure ..'Decimas reddo omnia quæ possideo' shews that the (unwritten) Bass must sing a Tenth below the Discant.

4. *Anat.* A marking upon some organ or part produced by another in contact with it; *esp.* a marking on the fleshy part of a muscle where a tendon crosses it.

1578 BANISTER *Hist. Man* IV. 62 The fift [muscle].. marcheth obliquely towardes the thombe, with many inscriptions, and ceaseth at divers Tendons. *c* **1720** W. GIBSON *Farrier's Guide* I. vi. (1738) 80 Having only Inscriptions answerable to the winding Convolutions of the Brain. **1872** HUMPHRY *Myology* 7 Its fibres are partially interrupted by a tendinous inscription, and it is joined beyond that point by a portion of the muscle arising from the ischium in which there is no tendinous inscription.

5. *Geom.* The action of inscribing one figure in another: see INSCRIBE 3.

1570 BILLINGSLEY *Euclid* IV. Introd. 110 This fourth booke intreateth of the inscription.. of rectiline figures. **1655** STANLEY *Hist. Philos.* I. (1701) 9/2. **1842** DE MORGAN *Diff. & Int. Calc.* 303 It is the condition of a polygon's inscription in a circle that its successive angles should be [etc.].

†**6.** *Civil* and *Sc. Law.* An accusation or challenge at law made under the condition that if it were false, the accuser would undergo the same punishment that would have been inflicted on the accused if found guilty. *Obs.*

Sometimes *inscription* appears to refer to the accusation (see *Inscriptio* in Du Cange), sometimes to the undertaking of the accuser: cf. COTGR. *Fr. Dict.*, '*Inscription en faux*, a challenge of, or exception against the truth of an Euidence; a testimonie or vndertaking to prove it false, entred in Court'.

1479 *Acta Audit.* 93 (Jam.) The said James has drawin himself, landis, and gudis, souerte to the kingis hienes for the said inscriptioune. **1674** SIR G. MACKENZIE *Laws & Cust. of Scotl.* xix. §8 (1699) 227 Which inscription was only necessar in atrocius, but not in lighter crimes. *Ibid.*, Inscriptions were only necessar, to the end the pursuer might be punished, if he were found Guilty of Calumny. **1726** AYLIFFE *Parergon* 24 Inscription is an obligation made in writing whereby the Accuser binds himself to undergo the same Punishment, if he shall not prove the Crime which he objects to the Party accused.. as the Defendant himself ought to suffer, if the same be prov'd.

7. *Comm.* The action of inscribing stock; in *pl.* inscribed stocks: see INSCRIBED 1 b.

1797 *Hist.* in *Ann. Reg.* 85/2 Penury and misery burst forth. The inscriptions, which were at forty, fell to ten; the armies were left without pay. **1809** R. LANGFORD *Introd. Trade* 55 The second description of Russian Stock is called 6 per Cent. Inscriptions. **1884** *Pall Mall G.* 14 Aug. 5/1 The Bank of England.. in its desire to move with the times.. has been undertaking the inscription of a number of colonial loans.

8. *Comb.*

1859 H. L. SMITH in *Archæol. Cant.* XI. 108 Only the labels.. and inscription-plate remain. **1861** F. HALL in *Jrnl. Asiat. Soc. Bengal* 320 Dismissed by the inscription-writer, with nine stanzas of vague encomium.

9. ***inscription maritime*** [Fr.], the French naval system of recruiting; a list of men who may be called to serve in the French navy.

1902 *Encycl. Brit.* XXVII. 499/1 This arrangement is purely for the embodiment of the men of the Inscription Maritime. *Ibid.* XXXI. 103/1 For the purpose of the Inscription Maritime the Newfoundland fisheries were kept up at considerable expense to the nations. **1905** *Westm. Gaz.* 3 Aug. 10/1 A system called 'maritime inscription', which.. furnishes a contingent of about 4,700 naval recruits every year.

inscriptional (ɪnˈskrɪpʃənəl), *a.* [f. prec. + -AL[1].]

†**1.** Bearing an inscription; = INSCRIBED 2. *Obs.*

1778 *Phil. Surv. S. Irel.* 21 In the same nave are three inscriptional Slabs. **1795** J. C. MURPHY *Trav. Portugal* 308 Several ancient inscriptional stones have been found.

2. Of, belonging to, characteristic of, or of the nature of, an inscription or inscriptions.

1822 JAS. TATE in *Parr's Wks.* (1828) VIII. 251 The inscriptional labours of your classical pen. **1880** WARREN *Book-plates* vii. 63 The inscriptional portion of the plate is copied first in italics. **1891** *Spectator* 21 Mar., 'A.S.' is not unfrequently used in inscriptional Latin for 'Anno Salutis'. **1896** RAMSAY in *Expositor* Sept. 195 Criteria derived.. from inscriptional and alphabetical character.

inˈscriptioned (-ʃənd), *a.* *rare.* [f. as prec. + -ED[2].] Furnished with an inscription; = INSCRIBED 2.

1888 *Harper's Mag.* Sept. 641 The marble fount, sculptured and inscriptioned on every surface.

inˈscriptionist. *rare.* [f. as prec. + -IST.] The writer or carver of an inscription.

1861 F. HALL in *Jrnl. Asiat. Soc. Bengal* 3 *note*, The inscriptionist was.. not quite incapable of such an aberration from grammatical orthopraxy. *Ibid.* 16 *note*, The laxity of the inscriptionist.

inˈscriptionless, *a.* [f. as prec. + -LESS.] Devoid of an inscription; having no inscription.

1654 WHITLOCK *Zootomia* 553 Lazarus (whose Receptacle is Inscriptionlesse). **1827** HOOD *Mids. Fairies* xxii, Make tombs inscriptionless—raze each high name. **1852** *Meanderings of Mem.* I. 71 A margin stone I crave Inscriptionless, or chiselled by the wave.

inscriptive (ɪnˈskrɪptɪv), *a.* [f. L. *inscript-*, ppl. stem of *inscrībĕre* to INSCRIBE + -IVE.]

1. Of the nature of an inscription; belonging to or used in inscriptions (quot. 1888).

1740 *Poetry* in *Ann. Reg.* (1772) 208 O! let this column rise, Pure from false trophies and inscriptive lyes. **1807** WORDSW. *Wh. Doe* VII. 214 'God us ayde!'.. Inscriptive legend which I ween May on those holy bells be seen. **1888** BURGON *Lives 12 Gd. Men* I. I. 36 When speaking of inscriptive writing, Routh once remarked [etc.].

†**2.** Bearing an inscription; = INSCRIBED 2. *Obs.*

1740 DYER *Ruins Rome* 79 And vases boss'd and huge inscriptive stones.

Hence **inˈscriptively** *adv.*, by way of an inscription.

1895 *Daily News* 5 Feb. 6/5 Beneath this again are inscriptively quoted the hero's words: 'Thus Sebastopol defends herself'.

†**inˈscriptor.** *Obs. rare.* [? for **inscripture* (ad. late L. *inscriptūra* inscription).] An inscription.

1603 HOLLAND tr. *Plutarch's Mor.* 1089 As Comœdies.. carrie.. ridiculous epigrams or inscriptors.

inˈscriptured, *a.* *rare*[−1]. [f. **inscripture* (see prec.) + -ED[2].] Bearing inscriptions; = INSCRIBED 2.

1881 ROSSETTI *Ball. & Sonn.*, *Church-Porch*, Shake we off the dust we have Upon our feet, lest it defile the stones Inscriptured, covering their sacred bones.

†**inscrive,** *v.* *Obs.* [f. F. *inscriv-*, full stem of *inscrire* = It. *inscrivere*, ad. L. *inscrībĕre*: cf. DESCRIVE.]

1. *trans.* = INSCRIBE 2.

1382 WYCLIF *2nd Prol. Ps.*, Alle the salmyes, that ben inscriued to hym Dauid, pertenen to the sacrament of Crist, for Dauid is seid Crist.

2. *Sc. Law.* *refl.* To undertake, under penalty, to prove (something) false: see INSCRIPTION 6.

Cf. Fr. *s'inscrire en faux*, 'to vndertake that an Euidence, etc., is false; or to vndertake to prove it false or falsified; also to accuse of or charge with falsehood or falsenesse'. (Cotgrave.)

1479 *Acta Audit.* 93 (Jam.) It was allegit be the said James, that the instrument of the said sett.. was falss and offrit him to inscriue him[self] criminally tharto as he aucht of law.

inscroll (ɪnˈskrəʊl), *v.* [f. IN-[1] or [2] + SCROLL.] *trans.* To inscribe or enter upon a scroll.

1596 SHAKS. *Merch. V.* II. vii. 72 Had you beene as wise as bold, Yong in limbs, in iudgement old, Your answere had not beene inscrold. **1898** T. HARDY *Wessex Poems* 131 Drop one plume as pledge that Heaven inscrolls the wrong.

†**inˈscruple,** *v.* *Obs.* *nonce-wd.* [f. IN-[2] + SCRUPLE.] *trans.* To possess with scruples.

1663 *Flagellum or O. Cromwell* (1672) 89 Being inscrupled by some of the Presbyterian Ministers (who were highly incensed at this war).

inscrutability (ɪnskruːtəˈbɪlɪtɪ). [f. next: see -ITY.] The quality of being inscrutable; *transf.* something inscrutable.

1654 W. MOUNTAGUE *Devout Ess.* II. i. §3. 20 These Mysteries.. are Gods own Inscrutabilitie. **1792** G. WAKEFIELD *Mem.* 130 (T.) His theological conceptions were always.. to me.. one of the inscrutabilities of mystery. **1859** KINGSLEY *Misc.* (1860) I. 291 The awe which Nature's grandeur and inscrutability brings with it. **1880** J. CAIRD *Philos. Relig.* i. 31 Reverence, not for a mere blank inscrutability, but for what I can think of as an intelligence essentially the same with my own.

inscrutable (ɪnˈskruːtəb(ə)l), *a.* (*sb.*) [ad. late L. *inscrūtābilis* (Augustine, Hilary), f. *in-* (IN-[3]) + *scrūtārī*, *-āre*, to search or examine thoroughly, to explore: see -ABLE. Cf. F. *inscrutable* (15th c.).]

That cannot be searched into or found out by searching; impenetrable or unfathomable to investigation; quite unintelligible, entirely mysterious.

c **1450** tr. *De Imitatione* III. lv. 131, I haue lerned herby to drede þin inscrutable iugement. **1526** *Pilgr. Perf.* (W. de W. 1531) 32 b, The herte of man is inscrutable, and onely god knoweth it. **1602** WARNER *Alb. Eng.* XIII. lxxix. (1612) 327 O Essence more inscrutable, than all compaierd to it. **1661** COWLEY *Verses & Ess.*, *Cromwell* (1669) 66 The inscrutable mysteries of Eternal Providence. **1732** BERKELEY *Alciphr.* VII. §26 You are a pair of inscrutable, unfathomable, fashionable philosophers. **1838–9** HALLAM *Hist. Lit.* II. II. ii. §27. 77 The doctrine of the Trinity, which theologians agree to call inscrutable, but which they do not fail to define and analyse with the most confident dogmatism. **1870** DISRAELI *Lothair* liii, That countenance was always inscrutable. **1894** H. DRUMMOND *Ascent Man* 155 At the present moment the ultimate origin of Mind is as inscrutable a mystery as the origin of Life.

b. Rarely of things physical, as an abyss: Impenetrable, unfathomable.

1820 LAMB *Elia* Ser. I. *2 Races Men*, Deep holes, inscrutable cavities of the earth. **1858** HAWTHORNE *Fr. & It. Jrnls.* I. 142 The guide.. held his torch down into an inscrutable pit beneath our feet.

B. *sb.* *pl.* Inscrutable things.

1663 SPENCER *Prodigies* (1665) 282 There are Mysteries in Religion, Depths in Providence, Inscrutables in Nature. **1704** DE FOE *Storm* i. 8 The Winds are some of those Inscrutables of Nature, in which humane Search has not yet been able to arrive at any Demonstration.

inˈscrutableness. [f. prec. + -NESS.] The quality or character of being inscrutable.

1727 in BAILEY vol. II. **1828** in WEBSTER. **1851** NICHOL *Archit. Heav.* (ed. 9) 64 The nebulous spots losing all trace of their previous inscrutableness. **1891** *Spectator* 21 Mar., That sense of the mystery and the tragic inscrutableness of human fate which is as modern as it is ancient.

b. An instance of this; something inscrutable.

a **1864** HAWTHORNE *Sept. Felton* (1879) 65 All was a blur, an inscrutableness, a scrawl of unintelligible characters.

inˈscrutably, *adv.* [f. as prec. + -LY[2].] In an inscrutable manner; beyond searching out; unfathomably; quite unintelligibly.

1597 J. PAYNE *Royal Exch.* 6 The essens of the glorioise persons inscrutablie one God. **1818** in TODD. **1828** WEBSTER s.v., The moral government of an infinite being must often be inscrutably dark and mysterious. **1852** M. ARNOLD *Empedocles* 217 Thou.. Watchest us, Nature, throughout, Mild and inscrutably calm.

†**inˈscrute,** *a.* *Obs.* *rare.* [irreg. f. stem of prec., or f. L. *scrūtāt-us* pa. pple.] = INSCRUTABLE.

1639 G. DANIEL *Ecclus.* xviii. 9 For 'tis inscrute: His power, 'bove reach of Mortall to find out. *Ibid.* xxxix. 70 How dare Man question.. His inscrute power?

inscrutive (ɪnˈskruːtɪv), *a.* *rare.* [irreg. f. L. *inscrūtā-re* to search or examine into + -IVE.] Given to scrutiny or investigation.

1882 *Chicago Advance* 22 June 400 What amounts of information these inscrutive young gentlemen of the daily press can evolve from a moderate protoplasm of given information!

insculp (ɪnˈskʌlp), *v.* Now *rare* or *Obs.* Pa. pple. insculpt, insculped. [ad. L. *insculpĕre* to carve or engrave on, f. *in-* (IN-[2]) + *sculpĕre* to carve, or its F. repr. *insculper* (15–16th c. in Godef.). Used at first in pa. pple. *insculpt*, ad. L. *insculpt-us*; the finite vb. may have arisen in part from an analysis of this as *insculp-t* = *insculp-ed*.]

1. *trans.* To carve, engrave, or sculpture (upon something, as a figure or inscription upon stone).

1432–50 tr. *Higden* (Rolls) III. 11 Diuerse carectes to be insculpte in gemmes. **1566** PAINTER *Pal. Pleas.* II. S iv. (N.), More lyvely.. than any forme may be insculped upon metall or marble. **1596** SHAKS. *Merch. V.* II. vii. 57 A coyne that beares the figure of an Angell Stampt in gold, but that's insculpt vpon. **1604** DRAYTON *Moses* I. (R.), Which he insculped in two likely stones, For rareness of invaluable price. **1616** BULLOKAR, *Insculpe*, to cut or carue in. **1665** J. WEBB *Stone-Heng* (1725) 162 By insculping some short Inscription. *Ibid.* 190 They made.. the Architrave.. plain and flat, and thereon insculpt them. **1706** PHILLIPS, *To Insculp*, to engrave, carve, or cut. **1814** SOUTHEY *Carmina Aul.*, etc., Poet. Wks. III. 315 Bearing lyingly the libell'd name Of Lawrence, impudently there insculpt.

fig. **1607** ROWLANDS *Guy Warw.* 5 The wounds and scarrs insculpt upon his flesh. **1668** H. MORE *Div. Dial.* III. xxiii. (1713) 231 Wise Men.. who in Symbols and Parables have insculped the memorials of their Wisdom in the Minds and Memories of rude People.

2. a. To shape artistically by cutting. **b.** To adorn with carved figures or inscriptions; to sculpture (stone, etc.): = CARVE *v.* 5 a, 6 b. Also *fig.*

1578 BANISTER *Hist. Man* I. 15 The inner seate.. of the scull, where Os Cuneale is insculped like the maner of a seat, or stoole. **1653** R. SANDERS *Physiogn.* 254 The ears neatly insculped, of mean bigness. **1665** J. WEBB *Stone-Heng* (1725) 135 Stones.. were insculpt with Antique Runick or Gothick Characters. **1830** W. PHILLIPS *Mt. Sinai* IV. 6 The

sacred Tables..Fresh from their heavenly quarry, and insculpt Of God's own hand immediate.

†**in'sculpt**, *v.* *Obs.* [f. L. *insculpt-*, ppl. stem of *insculp-ĕre*: see prec.] = INSCULP.

1487 *Ann. Barber-Surg. Lond.* (1890) 213 That a tablett of stone shalbe sett up and the Master and Wardeins names insculpted thereon. **1611** SPEED *Hist. Gt. Brit.* VII. x. 248 Therein..their Armes or Atchieuements..are according insculpted from the authoritie of both. **1657** TOMLINSON *Renou's Disp.* 344 Whereon they have insculpted a humane shape.

insculpt, *ppl. a.*: see INSCULP *v.*

†**in'sculption**. *Obs.* Also (*erron.*) -sion. [ad. late L. *insculptiōn-em*, noun of action from *insculpĕre* to INSCULP.] The action of carving or sculpturing upon something; *concr.* a carved figure or inscription. Also *fig.*

1599 *Richmond. Wills* (Surtees) 268 A cup of silver..to be made..with this insculpsion or engravinge therein. **1607** TOURNEUR *Rev. Trag.* I. ii. Wks. 1878 II. 13 For what is it to haue A flattering false insculption on a Toombe, And in men's hearts reproch? **1647** H. MORE *Song of Soul* II. iii. II. xlvi, So forms more stoutly flung Against our spright make deep insculption. **1655** FULLER *Hist. Camb.* 42.

in'sculptor. ? *Obs.* [a. L. type **insculptor*, agent-n. from *insculpĕre*: see prec. Cf. F. *insculpteur* (1584 in Godef.).] One who carves or sculptures a figure, etc. upon something; a sculptor.

1597 A. M. tr. *Guillemeau's Fr. Chirurg.* Bivb/1 The Insculptor or Ingravere, to adorne and imbellishe his laboures. **1727** DART *Canterb. Cathedr.* Pref., The Historian's pen, and the Insculptor's Art.

in'sculpture, *sb.* ? *Obs.* [a. obs. F. *insculpture* (15-16th c. in Godef.), ad. L. type **insculptūra*, f. *insculpĕre*: see -URE.] A figure or inscription carved or sculptured upon something.

1607 SHAKS. *Timon* v. iv. 67 On his Grauestone, this Insculpture which With wax I brought away. **1646** SIR T. BROWNE *Pseud. Ep.* IV. iv. 185 At first (saith he) it was both free and usuall to weare rings on either hand; but..when pretious gems and rich insculptures were added, the custome of wearing them on the right hand was translated unto the left. **1664** H. MORE *Myst. Iniq.* 224 To make up a more gracefull insculpture upon the external Cortex of a Vision.

in'sculpture, *v.* Also en-. [f. IN-² = EN- + SCULPTURE.] *trans.* To carve or sculpture upon something. Hence **in'sculptured** *ppl. a.*

1787 GLOVER *Athenaid* VII. (R.), He surveys, Insculptur'd round, the horrours which befel The house of Laius. **1831** WORDSW. *Yarrow revisited*, etc. Apol. 9 Those Shapes distinct That yet survive ensculptured on the walls. **1834** *Fraser's Mag.* X. 23 The obelisk of the desert, with its insculptured riddles. **1855** BAILEY *Mystic* 6 The myth-insculptured language of the light.

inscyde, obs. (erron.) form of INCIDE *v.*¹

in se: see IN *Lat. prep.*

†**in'sea**, *v.* *Obs. rare.* [f. IN-¹ + SEA *sb.*] *trans.* To enclose with the sea.

c **1611** CHAPMAN *Iliad* XI. 637 There made we halt, and there the sun cast many a glorious beam On our bright armours, horse and foot insea'd together there.

inseal, inseam, obs. ff. ENSEAL, ENSEAM *v.*

†**in'sear**, *v.* *Obs. rare.* [IN-¹ or ² + SEAR *v.*] *trans.* To impress by searing.

1603 *Adv. Don Sebast.* in *Harl. Misc.* II. 371 To report that those natural marks were inseared with a hot iron.

insearch(e, -er, var. of ENSEARCH, -ER, *Obs.*

†**in'searchable**, *a.* *Obs. rare.* [IN-³.] That cannot be searched out; unsearchable.

1647-8 COTTERELL *Davila's Hist. Fr.* (1678) 12 A woman of a most insearchable mind.

†**in'season**, *v.* *Obs. rare.* [f. IN-² + SEASON.] *trans.* To accustom or inure (a plant) to the climate and surroundings; to acclimatize.

1616 SURFL. & MARKH. *Country Farme* 351 That so you may assure your selfe, that his rootes are long since well inseasoned, and haue fully taken with the earth.

'**inseat**. *Sc.* ? *Obs.* Also **inset**. [f. IN *adv.* + SEAT *sb.*] The general living-room in a farmhouse or cottage in Scotland in the 18th c.

1811 AITON *View of Agric. Ayr* 114 That part of the building which served the family for lodging, sleeping, cookery, dairy, etc., denominated the *in-seat*, was about 12 or at most 14 feet square. On larger farms, another of nearly the same dimensions, and which entered through the *in-seat*, was called the *spense*. **18..** W. WATSON *Answ. Unco Bit Want* Poems (1877) 67 (Jam. Supp.) The morn I sall speak to my father, To big us an inset an' spence.

†**insecable**, *a.* *Obs. rare.* [ad. L. *insecābilis*, f. *in-* (IN-³) + *secābilis* that may be cut, f. *secāre* to cut: see -BLE. So F. *insécable* (1570 in Hatz.-Darm.).] Incapable of being cut.

1623 COCKERAM, *Insecable*, not to be cut. **17..** tr. *Voltaire's Wks.* XXVI. 115 (Jod.) If an insecable animal be eternal.

†'**insecate**, *v.* *Obs. rare*⁻⁰. [f. L. *insecāre*: see -ATE³.] *trans.* = INSECT *v.*¹

1623 COCKERAM, *Insecate*, to cut.

insect ('ɪnsɛkt), *sb.* [ad. L. *insectum*, ellipt. for *animal insectum* animal notched or cut into (Pliny), from *insect-us*, pa. pple. of *insecāre* to cut into; a rendering of Gr. ἔντομον insect (Aristotle): cf. ENTOMO-. Cf. F. *insecte* (Du Pinet, 16th c. in Hatz.-Darm.).]

1. A small invertebrate animal, usually having a body divided into segments, and several pairs of legs, and often winged; in popular use comprising, besides the animals scientifically so called (see 2), many other arthropods, as spiders, mites, centipedes, wood-lice, etc., and other invertebrates, as the 'coral-insect'; formerly (and still by the uneducated) applied still more widely, *e.g.* to earthworms, snails, and even some small vertebrates, as frogs and tortoises.

1601 HOLLAND *Pliny* Explan. Words Art, *Insects*, little vermine or smal creatures, which haue (as it were) a cut or diuision betweene their heads and bodies, as Pismires, Flies, Grashoppers, vnder which are comprehended Earth-wormes, Caterpillers [etc.]. **1611** COTGR., *Insecte*, an Insect; a small fleshlesse, and bloudlesse vermine, diuided (in some sort) betweene the head, bodie, and bellie, as an Ant, Fly, Bee, etc.; vnder which, the Earthworme, Caterpiller, etc. be also comprehended. **1646** SIR T. BROWNE *Pseud. Ep.* III. xv. 142 The Scolopendra or hundred footed insect. **1658** tr. *Bergerac's Satyr. Char.* xxvi. 95 Me-thinks I hear an angry frog croak..I use this Author something ill to reduce him to the Insects. **1661** LOVELL *Hist. Anim. & Min.* Introd., Of Insects, few are used as meat, except snailes, which some count most dainty sweet and nourishing meat. **1667** MILTON *P.L.* VII. 476 At once came forth whatever creeps the ground, Insect or Worme. **1732** ARBUTHNOT *Rules of Diet* 252 All Birds which feed upon Worms and Insects. **1754** *Dict. Arts & Sc.* III. 2032 Medusa, in zoology, a genus of naked insects. **1806** PRISCILLA WAKEFIELD *Dom. Recreat.* vii. 97 Desire John to bring in the pan with the sea-insects ..What strange creatures! they are far more like flowers than insects. Therefore they are called sea-anemones. **1863** BATES *Nat. Amazon* iv. (1864) 96 A large hairy spider of the genus Mygale..The Mygales are quite common insects.

2. *Zool.* An animal belonging to the class *Insecta* of *Arthropoda*: see INSECTA 2.

Only gradually restricted from the wider popular use. The earlier quots. here refer to true insects, but their authors would undoubtedly have included other animals under the name.

1601 HOLLAND *Pliny* XI. i. 310 Many and sundrie sorts there be of Insects..and well may they all be called *Insecta*: by reason of those cuts and divisions, which some have about the necke, others in the breast and belly; the which doe goe round and part the members of the bodie, hanging togither only by a little pipe and fistulous conveiance. **1658** PHILLIPS, *An Insect*, the smallest sort of Animal, as a Fly, Bee, or Ant, some think them to be so called, because they have a kind of division, or section, between the head and the belly. *a* **1704** LOCKE *Elem. Nat. Philos.* x. (1754) 38 They are called insects, from a separation in the middle of their bodies, whereby they are, as it were, cut into two parts, which are joined together by a small ligature: as we see in wasps, common flies, and the like. **1753** CHAMBERS *Cycl. Supp.*, *Insects* make one of the classes of animals, the characters of which are, that their body is covered with a sort of bony substance instead of skin, and their heads are furnished with antennae, called horns. Linnæi *Syst. Nat.* p. 83. **1774** GOLDSM. *Nat. Hist.* IV. 137 We may define insects to be little animals without red blood, bones or cartilages, furnished with a trunk or else a mouth, opening lengthwise, with eyes which they are incapable of covering, and with lungs which have their openings in the sides. **1828** STARK *Elem. Nat. Hist.* II. 217 Latreille divides the class of Insects, as now restricted, into eleven orders..The *Parasita* and *Thysanoura*, which Latreille previously arranged with the Arachnides, Dr. Leach first added to the class of Insects. **1862** DARWIN *On Fertil. Orchids* i. 38 Certain orchids require special insects for their fertilization. **1891** L. C. MIALL in *Nature* 10 Sept. 457/1 We understand insects to be animals of small size, furnished with a hard skin and six legs, breathing by branched air-tubes, and commonly provided in the adult condition with wings.

3. *fig.* Applied contemptuously to a person, as insignificant or despicable (sometimes also as annoying, like an insect persistently buzzing around or settling upon one).

1684 OTWAY *Atheist* I. i, We are over-run with a Race of Vermin they call Wits, a Generation of Insects that are always making a Noise. **1707** HEARNE *Collect.* 24 Jan. (O.H.S.) I. 322 He, the little Insect, was recommended to King William. **1798** CHALMERS *Posth. Wks.* (1849) VI. 7 It is not for us, the frail insects of a day..to oppose the feeble powers of our reason to the wonders of Omnipotence. **1813** SCOTT *Trierm.* II. Interl. ii, Insects that skim in Fashion's sky, Wasp, blue-bottle, or butterfly.

4. *attrib.* and *Comb.* **a.** *attrib.* That is an insect, as ***insect breeze***, ***-drone***, ***lamp***, ***locust***, ***pest***, ***vermin***; consisting of insects, as ***insect kind***, ***myriads***, ***quire***, ***race***, ***society***, ***tribe***, ***youth***; resembling or likened to an insect, as ***insect follower***, ***understanding***, ***vexation***; of or belonging to insects, as ***insect egg***, ***fungus***, ***head***, ***larva***, ***life***, ***maggot***, ***origin***, ***parasite***, ***queen***, ***wax***, ***wing***; for insects, as ***insect-box***, ***-cabinet***, ***-repellent***, ***-trap***. **b.** objective, instrumental, etc., as ***insect-collector***, ***control***, ***-destroyer***, ***-eater***, ***-eating*** adj., ***-hunter***; ***insect-borne*** adj., ***-feeding*** adj., ***-fertilizable*** adj., ***-fertilization***, ***-fertilized*** adj., ***-haunted*** adj., ***-pollinated*** adj., ***-proof*** adj.; ***insect-like*** adj. or adv. **c.** Special Combs.: **insect-bed** (see quot.); **insect-feeder**, a creature that feeds on insects; †**insect-flower** (*poet.*), applied to a sea-anemone; **insect-gun**, a small bellows for blowing insect-powder into crevices or sprinkling it upon plants; **insect-net**, a light head-net for catching insects; a butterfly-net; **insect-powder**, a powder (usually prepared from the dried flowers of species of *Pyrethrum*) used to kill or drive away insects.

1893 GEIKIE *Geol.* (ed. 3) 899 These relics of insect life, are so abundant in the calcareous bands [of the British Lias] that the latter are known as *insect-beds. **1909** R. W. BOYCE *Mosquito or Man?* iv. 23 It is Dr. Beauperthuy whom we must regard as the father of the doctrine of *insect-borne disease. **1946** *Nature* 21 Dec. 913/1 Analogy with filariasis elsewhere would suggest that the infection is insect-borne. **1972** *Ibid.* 21 Jan. 135/2 To prevent the spread of insect-borne diseases. **1837** *Lett. fr. Madras* (1843) 140 Many thanks for the *insect-box and pins. **1678** BUTLER *Hud.* III. ii. 1 The learned write, an *insect breeze Is but a mongrel prince of bees, That falls before a storm on cows, And stings the founders of his house. **1843** *Zoologist* I. 342 An *insect-cabinet containing twelve drawers. **1878** SMILES *R. Dick* v. 45 He was an *insect-collector. **1936** *Discovery* Feb. 44/1 The legal insistence on *insect control is lax or non-existent until there is an actual outbreak of some pest causing serious financial loss. **1951** A. W. A. BROWN (*title*) Insect control by chemicals. **1875** KNIGHT *Dict. Mech.*, **Insect-destroyer*, a device for killing noxious insects. **1902** W. DE LA MARE *Songs of Childhood* 30 Is it for fear the birds are flown, And shrills the *insect-drone? **1939** 'N. BLAKE' *Smiler with Knife* xi. 168 The insect-drone of a lawnmower. **1773** WHITE in *Phil. Trans.* LXIV. 201 These birds..*insect-eaters themselves. **1908** *Westm. Gaz.* 22 Feb. 16/1 There is a class of small mammals, mostly of nocturnal habits, that come under the order of Insectivora, or insect-eaters. **1936** *Discovery* July 212/2 Bee-eaters, swallows, swifts, and other insect-eaters. **1872** CARPENTER *Anim. Phys.* iv. 163 *Insect-eating animals obtain their food by means of a long extensible tongue. **1879** LUBBOCK *Sci. Lect.* i. 4 The first observation on insect-eating flowers was made about the year 1768 by our countryman Ellis. **1822-34** *Good's Study Med.* (ed. 4) I. 264 The atmosphere is freighted with myriads of *insect-eggs that elude our senses. **1891** *Daily News* 15 Dec. 5/4 It has been reserved for..Mr. Francis Darwin, to prove conclusively that *insect-fed plants bear heavier and more numerous seeds than unfed ones. **1835-6** TODD *Cycl. Anat.* I. 599/2 The many pointed tuberculous teeth of the *insect-feeders. **1909** *Westm. Gaz.* 23 Apr. 4/2 The migratory, *insect-feeding birds from the South.. begin their nesting work. **1880** A. R. WALLACE *Isl. Life* 473 Many of them require *insect-fertilisation. **1791** E. DARWIN *Bot. Gard.* I. 121 You guard the Mermaid in her briny vale; Feed the live petals of her *insect-flowers. **1751** SMOLLETT *Per. Pic.* (1779) IV. xcv. 159 All those *insect-followers shrink away in the winter of distress. **1897** MARY KINGSLEY *W. Africa* 572, I write by the light of an *insect-haunted lantern. **1857** E. NEWMAN (*title*) The *Insect-hunters or Entomology in Verse. **1897** MARY KINGSLEY *W. Africa* 169, I had to jump at a rock wall, and hang on to it in a manner more befitting an insect than an insect-hunter. **1711** SHAFTESB. *Charac.* (1737) II. 94 Be they of the poorest *insect-kind, such as bees or wasps; 'tis natural to 'em to be rouz'd with fury. **1727-46** THOMSON *Summer* 828 From Menam's orient stream, that nightly shines With *insect-lamps. **1711** SHAFTESB. *Charac.* (1737) III. 156 The contemplation of the *insect-life. **1772** G. WHITE *Let.* 9 Mar. in *Selborne* (1789) II. xii. 147, I..believe that many of the swallow kind..do, *insect-like and bat-like, come forth at mild times. **1929** D. H. LAWRENCE *Pansies* 118 Working men Pale and mean and insect-like, scuttling along And living like lice. **1930** R. CAMPBELL *Adamastor* 55 Faint, insect-like and thin it came, The wistful sound those heroes made. **1658** J. ROWLAND tr. *Moufet's Theat. Ins.* 1125 The *Insect-Locust is like the Lobster, for that cannot be called either flesh or fish. **1747** GOULD *Eng. Ants* 59 Most *Insect Maggots are furnished with a Set of Legs. **1822-34** *Good's Study Med.* (ed. 4) I. 452 Linnæus, who..endeavoured to resolve almost all diseases..into an animalcular or *insect origin. **1853** *Zoologist* XI. 4045 These exceedingly rare *insect-parasites. **1854** *Ibid.* XII. 4179 The galleries or perforations of these *insect-pests. **1911** F. O. BOWER *Plant-Life* 96 In a family (Ranunculaceae) as a rule *insect-pollinated. **1953** J. S. HUXLEY *Evolution in Action* i. 34 Insect-pollinated flowers. **1893** *Jrnl. R. Agric. Soc.* Dec. 823 Ordinary *insect-powders..were quite ineffectual. **1908** *Japan Chron.* 1 July 4/6 It [*sc.* a kind of paper] is said to be capable of being worked into all sorts of patterns, to be *insect-proof and damp-proof. **1946** *Nature* 21 Sept. 417/2 Two insect-proof cubicles in the glasshouse were filled with healthy young turnip and Chinese cabbage plants. **1813** BYRON *Giaour* 388 Rising on its purple wing The *insect-queen of eastern spring [*note*, The blue-winged butterfly of Kashmeer, the most rare and beautiful of the species]. **1818** SHELLEY *Rev. Islam* X. xv, The fish were poisoned in the streams..the *insect race Was withered up. **1953** SCOTT & FISHER *Thousand Geese* v. 50 We had brought effective *insect-repellents, so we were not much troubled by the biting elements of the insect population. **1971** L. PAYNE *Even my Foot's Asleep* xvi. 214 A musky, incense-type perfume..probably an insect repellent. **1887** *Amer. Naturalist* XXI. 501 The plant which I have to notice because of its peculiarity as an *insect-trap. **1728-46** THOMSON *Spring* 60 And some, with whom compared your *insect tribes Are but the beings of a summer's day. **1816** J. GILCHRIST *Philos. Etym.* 105 These cobwebs entangle *insect understandings like their own. **1808** HELEN ST. VICTOR *Ruins Rigonda* II. 109 *Insect vermin which swarmed on the walls. **1750** JOHNSON *Rambler* No. 68 ¶3 *Insect vexations which sting us and fly away. **1853** *Zoologist* XI. 3820 Specimens of the white *insect-wax of China. **1712-14** POPE *Rape Lock* II. 59 Some to the sun their *insect-wings unfold. **1742** GRAY *Ode on Spring* iii, The *insect youth are on the wing, Eager to..float amid the liquid noon.

†**insect**, *a. Obs.* [ad. L. *insect-us*, pa. pple. of *insecāre* to cut into: see prec.] Having the body divided into segments; chiefly in ***insect animals*** = L. *animālia insecta*: see INSECTA.

1589 PUTTENHAM *Eng. Poesie* III. v. (Arb.) 162 So also is the Ante or pismire, and they be but little creeping things, not perfect beasts, but insect, or wormes. *a* **1658** CLEVELAND *Gen. Poems*, etc. (1677) 136 Meeting with the putrid Matter of your Invention, as the Sun produceth Insect Animals. *a* **1677** HALE *Prim. Orig. Man.* IV. ii. 306 Some insect Animals.

†**insect** (ɪnˈsɛkt), *v.*[1] *Obs. rare.* [f. L. *insect-*, ppl. stem of *insecāre* to cut into: cf. *dissect*, *intersect.*] *trans.* To cut into.

a **1652** BROME *Queen & Conc.* III. vii, Down with their weapons, up with their heels, till we insect and rip up the intrails of the cause.

insect (ˈɪnsɛkt), *v.*[2] *nonce-wd.* [f. INSECT *sb.*] *intr.* To hunt or catch insects.

1879 J. BURROUGHS *Locusts & W. Honey* 203 We discovered the bird..insecting in the top of a newly-fallen hemlock.

‖**insecta** (ɪnˈsɛktə), *sb. pl.* [L., pl. of *insectum* INSECT; formerly also, more fully, *insecta animalia* 'cut-waisted animals'.]

†**1.** Formerly used as the plural of INSECT, in its popular application. *Obs.*

[**1577** HARRISON *England* III. vi. (1878) II. 36 The cut or girt wasted (for so I English the word *Insecta*) are the hornets, waspes, bees, and such like. **1601** HOLLAND *Pliny* XI. i. 310 Well may they be called *Insecta*: by reason of those cuts and divisions, which some have about the necke.] **1609** C. BUTLER *Fem. Mon.* Pref., Of all *Insecta* the Bees are chief. **1626** BACON *Sylva* §73 So some *Insecta* which haue Spirit of Life, as Snakes and Silkewormes, are to the touch Cold. **1648** S. MARSHALL *Emmanuel* 23 Sometimes the Lord stirres up other creatures to doe it; the Wind, the Sun, the Stars, nay it may be the very *insecta animalia*..the Rats and Mice, and Frogs, and such poore creatures. **1651** *Raleigh's Ghost* 95 Those living creatures, which are commonly called *insecta*; as flies, gnats, and the like.

†**b.** Also erron. *insectæ*, *insecta's*. Also *fig.*: cf. INSECT *sb.* 3. *Obs.*

1609 B. JONSON *Sil. Wom.* v. *ad fin.*, Take heed of such insectæ hereafter. **1646** J. HALL *Poems* I. 23 Such Individuums as ye? Such *Insecta's*. **1650** —— *Paradoxes* 25 The rayes of these sunnes will..beget abundance of *Insecta's* and Monsters. *a* **1658** CLEVELAND *Lines* Wks. (1687) 354 Such Insecta's, added on To Creatures by Substraction.

2. *Zool.* (With capital initial.) A class of invertebrate animals; formerly (as by Linnæus) made to comprise the whole of the division now called ARTHROPODA, or (as by Latreille) all these except the *Crustacea* and *Arachnida*; now restricted to that division of these otherwise called *Hexapoda*, having the body divided or distinguishable into three regions (head, thorax, and abdomen), with six legs (all borne upon the thorax), and usually two or four wings (but in some cases none); constituting the largest class of *Arthropoda*, and outnumbering all the rest of the animal kingdom, nearly a million species being now known (1988).

1727–41 CHAMBERS *Cycl.*, *Insects*, *Insecta*, in natural history, a smaller sort of animals. **1819** *Pantologia*, *Insecta*, Insects, the fifth class in the Linnæan system of Zoology. **1872** NICHOLSON *Palæont.* 29 The air-breathing classes of the Myriapoda, the Arachnida, and the Insecta or true Insects. **1878** BELL *Gegenbaur's Comp. Anat.* 246 Of pretty much the same form as in the Mandibulate Insecta.

insectan (ɪnˈsɛktən), *a.* [f. INSECTA + -AN: cf. *crustacean*, etc.] Of or belonging to an insect, or to the class *Insecta*.

1888 ROLLESTON & JACKSON *Anim. Life* 493 In a few Crustacea and Insectan larvae. **1893** *Athenæum* 28 Jan. 123/1 The hope of finding a picture of the insectan eye, or an account of the theories of insectan vision, is vain.

insectarian (ɪnsɛkˈtɛərɪən). *nonce-wd.* [f. INSECT *sb.* + *-arian* (after *vegetarian*).] One who feeds on insects. Hence **insecˈtarianism**.

1893 E. A. BUTLER *Our Househ. Insects* 36 The women of Egypt, who, following the precepts of insectarianism, are said to make a savoury dish of the grub by roasting it and serving in butter. *Ibid.* 44 We..sometimes get our bread adulterated with pulverised beetles, and unconsciously become insectarians for the nonce.

insectarium (ɪnsɛkˈtɛərɪəm). Also in anglicized form **insectary** (ˈɪnsɛktərɪ). [f. INSECTA + -ARIUM.] A place for keeping and breeding insects; an entomological vivarium.

1881 W. A. FORBES *Sci. Papers* (1885) 294 A new house in the Zoological Society's Gardens has been opened..an 'Insectarium', or house devoted to the exhibition of living specimens, in their various stages, of the class of Insects. **1888** J. H. COMSTOCK in *Amer. Nat.* Dec. 1129 An Insectary for entomological work.

†**insecˈtation.** *Obs. rare.* [ad.L. *insectātiōn-em* pursuit, pursuing with words, railing, noun of action from *insectārī* to pursue, to rail at.] Railing, calumniation. So †**insecˈtator**, a railer.

a **1535** MORE *Let.* Wks. 1431/2 Stirred by mine owne conscience, (without insectacion, or reproche laieng to any other mans). **1616–61** HOLYDAY *Persius* 288 [Persius] quipping himself first, and afterwards all others, with such an insectation of the new poets and orators, that he spar'd not Nero. **1658** PHILLIPS, *Insectation*, a railing against, as it were a following and prosecuting with evil language. **1706** —— *Insectator*, a Railer, Slanderer..a foul-mouth'd Fellow.

insected (ɪnˈsɛktɪd), *ppl. a. rare.* [f. L. *insectus* (see INSECT *a.*) + -ED[1].] Cut into; divided, as it were, into segments, as an insect.

c **1645** HOWELL *Lett.* (1650) II. vi. 7 We can hardly endure the sting of that small insected animal. **1676** [see INSECTION[1]]. **1826** KIRBY & SP. *Entomol.* xxxviii. III. 4 Its body is insected, being divided as it were into three principal pieces. **1883** KIMBER in *Knowledge* 13 July 22/2 The body [of a sea anemone]..may be..transversely furrowed or insected.

†**inˈsectic**, *a. Obs. rare.* [irreg. f. INSECT *sb.* + -IC.] Of or belonging to an insect; insectan.

1767 G. S. CAREY *Hills of Hybla* 13 A laden ant was passing by, And with her small insectic eye, She look'd upon the abject man.

insecticidal (ɪnsɛktɪˈsaɪdəl), *a.* [f. as next + -AL[1].] Having the property, or the habit, of killing insects.

1857 *National Mag.* II. 205 The insecticidal properties of anæsthetic agents. **1882** *American* V. 57 The numbers of 'insecticidal' ants colonized in their branches. **1894** *Times* 19 June 14/1 Spray-pumps and other insecticidal apparatus.

insecticide[1] (ɪnˈsɛktɪsaɪd). [f. L. *insect-ūm* INSECT + *-cīda*, -CIDE[1], killer.] One who or that which kills insects, an insect-killer; *spec.* a preparation used for destroying insects.

1866 *Sat. Rev.* 24 Mar. 350/2 A rich insecticide is not much, but he is better than that. **1871** L. STEPHEN *Playgr. Europe* ix. (1894) 225 Provided with a good bottle of insecticide. **1887** A. NEWTON in *Encycl. Brit.* XXII. 457/2 [The starling's] character as an insecticide..makes it the friend of the agriculturist. **1894** *Jrnl. R. Agric. Soc.* June 311 Substances likely to prove useful as insecticides.

b. *attrib.* or as *adj.* Having the property of killing insects; insecticidal. (In quot. 1865, *fig.*)

1865 *Sat. Rev.* 25 Nov. 663 Whether Sir George Grey will have recourse to this Parliamentary insecticide powder may be doubted. **1876** *Times* 4 Oct., The section 'Insectologie Générale' embraced..illustrations of the application of insects to ornament, and insecticide preparations of various kinds.

inˈsecticide[2]. [f. as prec. + -CIDE[2].] The killing of insects.

1865 *Sat. Rev.* 14 Oct. 482/2 The patient believer..is bidden..to abjure the inhuman practice of insecticide. *a* **1894** LD. BOWEN in *Daily News* 10 Apr. 6/3 An admirable woman, with perhaps too great a passion for insecticide.

insectiferous (ɪnsɛkˈtɪfərəs), *a.* [f. L. *insect-um* INSECT + -FEROUS.] Producing or containing insects.

1826 KIRBY & SP. *Entomol.* li. IV. 557 It has been observed with respect to insectiferous amber. **1870** T. DE W. TALMAGE *Crumbs Swept Up* 423 The insectiferous water of Galilee.

inˈsectiform, *a.* [f. as prec. + -FORM.] Having the form or appearance of an insect.

1888 A. D. WHITE in *Pop. Sci. Monthly* Feb. 440 Illustrated with the marvelous likenesses of two hundred figured or rather insectiform stones.

insectifuge (ɪnˈsɛktɪfjuːdʒ). [f. as prec. + -FUGE: cf. *vermifuge.*] A substance or preparation used to drive away insects.

In recent Dicts.

insectile (ɪnˈsɛktɪl, -taɪl), *a.*[1] and *sb.* [f. L. *insect-um* INSECT: cf. L. *sectilis*, f. *sectus* cut.]

A. *adj.* Of, pertaining to, or of the nature of an insect; consisting of insects; also *fig.* resembling an insect, infesting like insects. Now *rare.*

a **1626** BACON (J.), Insectile animals, for want of blood, run all out into legs. **1660** STILLINGFL. *Iren.* I. ii. (1662) 68 As he observes from Aristotle in Insectile Animals, the want of blood was the cause they ran out into so many legs. **1667** OLDENBURG in *Phil. Trans.* II. 412 All these [works of Aristotle] are..overwhelmed and degraded by the swarms of Insectile Systemes and dilute Commentaries. **1877** RUSKIN *Fors Clav.* VII. lxxxi. 266 The insectile noise. **1891** *Voice* (N.Y.) 21 May, They [orchards] are not responsible for the insectile armies that may attack them.

†**B.** *sb.* = INSECT *sb. Obs.* (Cf. *reptile.*)

1615 CROOKE *Body of Man* 546 In those creatures which want eye-lids, as Locusts, Lobsters, Crabs, & such like insectiles, nature hath prouided certaine cauities, whereinto in the time of their repose..they receiue their whole eies. **1666** J. SMITH *Old Age* (ed. 2) 264 In those several Transformations and Renovations of the Ant, and Silk-worm, and many such Insectiles.

†**inˈsectile**, *a.*[2] *Obs. rare.* [f. IN-[3] + SECTILE.] Incapable of being cut or divided.

1635 PERSON *Varieties* v. iv. §7 Atoms are little insectile bodies, not unlike the moates which wee see to tumble and rowle about in the sunne beames. **1657–83** EVELYN *Hist. Relig.* (1850) I. 189 Nor can that be destroyed..which, being insectile, has nothing to divide or oppose it.

insectine (ɪnˈsɛktɪn, -aɪn), *a. rare.* [f. L. *insect-um* + -INE[1].] Belonging to or characteristic of an insect.

1853 KANE *Grinnell Exp.* xxxiv. (1856) 307 The something had a crepitating, insectine wriggle.

insection[1] (ɪnˈsɛkʃən). [n. of action f. L. *insect-*, ppl. stem of *insecāre* to cut into: cf. *dissection.*] The action of cutting into, incision; division into sections; *concr.* an incision, division, indentation.

1653 MANTON *Exp. James* i. 21 There must be insection before insition, meekness before ingrafting. **1676** GREW *Anat. Flowers* II. App. §12 The Sides or Edges of the Leaf are..Insected deeply..or with shallow Insections. **1826** KIRBY & SP. *Entomol.* xxviii. III. 4 This character of insection or division into segments, more or less present in almost every insect. **1835–6** TODD *Cycl. Anat.* I. 246/1 The insections or articulations of the body.

†**insection**[2]. *Obs. rare*⁻⁰. [ad. L. *insectio* narration (Aulus Gellius), f. *insecĕre* (var. form of *insequī* to follow), 'to pursue the narration, proceed, relate, declare' (Lewis and Short).]

1623 COCKERAM, *Insection*, a declaration, or long continuance. **1656** BLOUNT *Glossogr.*, *Insection*, a declaration, Treatise, or long continued talk.

†**inˈsective**, *a. Obs. nonce-wd.* [f. L. *insect-um* INSECT + -IVE.] ? Characteristic of insects

a **1834** COLERIDGE in *Fraser's Mag.* (1835) XII. 496 Productivity might be entitled the vegetative, or το φυο-ειδες; the insective, το εντομο-ειδες; and, lastly, the animal, το ιδιωs-ζωικον.

‖**Insectivora** (ɪnsɛkˈtɪvərə), *sb. pl. Zool.* [mod.L., neut. pl. of *insectivorus* insect-eating (sc. *animalia*).]

1. An order of *Mammalia*, comprising numerous small quadrupeds, as the mole, shrew, and hedgehog, most of which feed on insects.

1836 *Penny Cycl.* VI. 306/2 The lateral membranes with which the cheiroptera are furnished are no longer to be found in the insectivora. **1847** CARPENTER *Zool.* §180 It may be affirmed that the Insectivora hold a rank in the Carnivorous division of the Mammalia, analogous to that which the Rodentia take in the Herbivorous. **1888** ROLLESTON & JACKSON *Anim. Life* 363 The eye is..rudimentary or absent in certain burrowing Rodentia and Insectivora.

b. A group of *Cheiroptera*: the insectivorous or insect-eating Bats.

2. *Entom.* In Westwood's classification, A group of *Hymenoptera* which feed on other insects.

insectivore (ɪnˈsɛktɪvɔə(r)). Also **-vor.** [a. mod.F. *insectivore* (Cuvier, 1817), ad. L. *insectivor-us*: see prec.] An insectivorous animal or plant; *spec.* a mammal of the order *Insectivora.*

1863 HUXLEY *Man's Place Nat.* II. 95 The progress of cerebral complexity is traceable through a complete series of steps from the lowest Rodent or Insectivore to Man. **1879** WRIGHT *Anim. Life* 65 Most of the Insectivores live under the ground. **1880** A. R. WALLACE *Isl. Life* II. xvii. 351 Ptilocercus, a feather-tailed arboreal insectivore. **1884** *Cornh. Mag.* Oct. 406 This remarkable insectivore [Venus's fly-trap] appears to be still a new and struggling species, or else an old type on the very point of extinction. **1896** *Brit. Birds* I. 5 Many 'insectivors', when kept in the same aviary with seed-eating birds, swallow quantities of seed.

insectivorous (ɪnsɛkˈtɪvərəs), *a.* [f. mod.L. *insectivor-us* + -OUS: cf. *carnivorous.*] Feeding on insects, insect-eating; applied to several groups of animals, as the *Insectivora* among mammals, and various birds, such as swallows; also to those plants which capture and absorb insects, as the sundew, Venus's fly-trap, etc.

1611 LOVELL *Hist. Anim. & Min.* Introd., Birds, which are..Insectivorous, or feeding upon insects. **1682** LISTER in *Phil. Collect* XII. 166 For this reason we see Insectivorous Birds so solicitous to kill Worms and all other sorts of Insects. **1816** KIRBY & SP. *Entomol.* (1843) I. 221 Those [insects] which are insectivorous only in their larva state may be further subdivided into parasites and imparasites. **1830** LYELL *Princ. Geol.* I. 133 Small insectivorous mammifera, allied to the opossum. **1874** LUBBOCK *Wild Flowers* iv. 102, I cannot pass from this subject without mentioning another insectivorous plant, the genus Sarracenia. **1875** DARWIN (*title*) Insectivorous Plants.

insectology (ɪnsɛkˈtɒlədʒɪ). [a. F. *insectologie* (Bonnet, 1744), f. L. *insect-um* INSECT + -(O)LOGY.] A term formerly used in same sense as ENTOMOLOGY, the science of insects as a branch of Zoology; now usually applied to the study of insects in their economic relations to man, as producers of silk, honey, cochineal, etc., and as agricultural pests or benefactors.

1766 tr. *Bonnet's Contemp. Nat.* IX. ix, I have given the name *insectology* to that part of natural history which has insects for its object: that of *entomology*..would undoubtedly have been more suitable..but its barbarous sound terrify'd me. **1788–9** HOWARD *New R. Cycl.* 1228 *Insectology*, other-wise called Entomology, or a treatise on the science of insects. **1876** *Times* 4 Oct., At the time of its first Exhibition (1865) a division was made for general insectology and one for sericiculture, and the title was assumed of 'Société Centrale d'Agriculture et d'Insectologie'. **1881** *Pop. Sci. Monthly* XIX. 143 At the last exhibition of agriculture and insectology in Paris. **1891** *East. Daily Press* 26 Aug. 6/4 Central Society of Apiculture and Insectology.

So **insec'tologer**, **insec'tologist**, a student of insectology.

1713 DERHAM *Phys.-Theol.* VIII. vi. (1727) 387 *note*, The Insect itself, is (according to the modern Insectologers) of the Ichneumon-Fly Kind. **1815** J. WILSON *Let.* June in *Mem.* vi. (1879) 133 Mr. Laidlaw is an insectologist and poet.

insectual (ɪn'sɛktjuːəl), *a.* [f. INSECT *sb.* + *-ual* as in *conceptual*.] Like an insect, small.

1912 BEERBOHM *Christmas Garland* 61 That swarm of things insectual. **1965** *New Statesman* 26 Nov. 838/3 To him the attacks..are mere 'insectual backbiting'.

insecty ('ɪnsɛktɪ), *a. colloq.* [f. INSECT *sb.* + -Y.] Full of or abounding in insects; of the nature of or consisting of insects.

1859 ALEX. SMITH *Summ. Skye* (1880) 256 The murmuring and insecty air of the moorland. **1889** MISS ORMEROD in *Pall Mall G.* 24 June 3/1 All the papers say that this is going to be an 'insecty' year.

insecure (ɪnsɪ'kjʊə(r)), *a.* [ad. med.L. *insecūr-us*, f. *in-* (IN-^{3}) + *secūrus* SECURE.] Not secure.

1. Not sure; wanting assurance, confidence, or certainty; uncertain; without certainty *of* (something).

1649 JER. TAYLOR *Gt. Exemp.* I. ad sect. ii. 23 The holy Virgin could not but know, that Joseph would be troubled with sorrow, and insecure apprehensions concerning her being with childe. *a* **1694** TILLOTSON *Serm.* (1742) III. 140 Without the providence of God, [we are] continually insecure not only of the good things of this life but even of life itself. **1807** WORDSW. *White Doe* I. 195 But is she truly what she seems? He asks with insecure delight, Asks of himself, and doubts,—and still The doubt returns.

b. *spec.* in *Psychol.*

1935 F. B. HOLMES *Exper. Study Fears of Young Children* xiii. 278 Karl is very insecure and clings to adults. *Ibid.* 284 The fearful children were more frequently described as being dependent upon adults for help..and as appearing generally insecure. **1941** PRITCHARD & OJEMANN in *Jrnl. Exper. Educ.* X. 114/1 The term 'insecurity' and its correlative 'desire for security' appear extensively in child development literature... We need methods by which we can discriminate between the relatively secure and the relatively insecure children. **1947** A. T. JERSILD *Child Psychol.* (ed. 3) vii. 271 In a study of children who were rated by their teachers as being 'insecure', it was found that such children..exhibited a greater tendency to be apprehensive. **1954** A. H. MASLOW *Motivation & Personality* iii. 38 He would not have taken this attitude unless he felt rejected and disliked (insecure). **1960** R. D. LAING *Divided Self* iii. 44 The ontologically insecure person is preoccupied with preserving rather than gratifying himself. *Ibid.* 45 Three forms of anxiety encountered by the ontologically insecure person. **1967** M. ARGYLE *Psychol. Interpersonal Behaviour* i. 29 Individuals who are 'insecure', i.e. uncertain about how to evaluate themselves, are particularly anxious to receive approval from others. *Ibid.* vii. 126 Adolescents, who have only just formed a tentative self-image, are particularly sensitive to the reactions of others, and are 'insecure' in this sense. **1969** W. MAYER-GROSS et al. *Clin. Psychiatry* (ed. 3) xi. 640 Any sudden change..may produce an emotional crisis, especially in the insecure or over-sensitive child.

2. Unsafe; exposed to danger; not firm; liable to give way, fail, or be overcome.

1654 H. L'ESTRANGE *Chas. I* (1655) 56 So in-secure did overmuch security make them. **1706** PHILLIPS, *Insecure*, that is not secure, or out of Danger, unsafe. *a* **1808** HURD (T.), Am I going to build on precarious and insecure foundations? **1849** MACAULAY *Hist. Eng.* ix. II. 406 The insecure and agitated life of a conspirator. **1860** TYNDALL *Glac.* I. x. 66 The ice on the edge..was loose and insecure. **1885** S. COX *Expos.* Ser. I. vi. 81 Outside the defenced cities life and property were insecure.

Hence **inse'cureness** (Bailey vol. II, 1727).

†**inse'cure**, *v. Obs. rare.* [f. prec. adj.] *trans.* To render insecure.

1649 JER. TAYLOR *Gt. Exemp.* IX. §45 A recession from our hopes, and an insecuring our condition. **1675** PENN *Eng. Pres. Interest Disc.* 39 They insecure themselves by making their Friends to be their Enemies.

insecurely (ɪnsɪ'kjʊəlɪ), *adv.* [f. INSECURE *a.* + -LY^{2}.] In an insecure manner or condition; without security; unsafely.

1709 SHAFTESB. *Moralists* I. i. 8 There they chuse to hang, tho ever so insecurely, rather than trust their Strength to bear 'em above Water. **1856** FROUDE *Hist. Eng.* (1858) I. ii. 96 Henry VII sat too insecurely on his throne to venture on a resolute reform.

insecurity (ɪnsɪ'kjʊərɪtɪ). [ad. med.L. *insēcūritās* (Du Cange), f. *in-* (IN-^{3}) + *sēcūrus* free from care, SECURE.] The quality or condition of being insecure; the opposite of security.

1. The condition of not being sure; want of assurance or confidence; (subjective) uncertainty.

1646 SIR T. BROWNE *Pseud. Ep.* IV. xii. 211 It may be easily perceived with what insecurity of truth we adhere unto this opinion.

b. *spec.* in *Psychol.*

1917 GLUECK & LIND tr. *Adler's Neurotic Constitution* (1921) p. x, A sickly girl..in her consciousness of an unusual insecurity leans upon her father and in so doing strives to become superior to her mother. **1932** W. H. BURNHAM *Wholesome Personality* ix. 329 The one outstanding condition menacing the mental health of..every youth, is some form of the emotion of fear, if not acute fear, at least a sense of insecurity. **1937** K. HORNEY *Neurotic Personality* ii. 36 The inner insecurity expressed in this dependence on others is the second feature that strikes us in neurotics on surface observation. **1942** E. FROMM *Fear of Freedom* v. 178 The automatization of the individual in modern society has increased the helplessness and insecurity of the average individual. **1942** B. KLOPFER *Rorschach Technique* III. x. 240 Rorschach signs of insecurity and anxiety, as opposed to signs of a balanced personality structure. *Ibid.* 241 Often the language used by the subject..reveals to some extent open insecurity or anxiety. **1969** R. C. CARSON *Interaction Concepts of Personality* ii. 32 Beyond infancy the experience of anxiety..has the character of a drop in self-esteem or an increase in felt insecurity. **1969** I. STEVENSON *Psychiatric Exam.* iv. 62 Insecurity accompanied by a need to impress the examiner..may also lead the patient to bring forth unnecessary details. **1971** G. E. GARDNER *Emerging Personality* III. vi. 132 First of all, a higher level of anxiety, a greater feeling of insecurity, often appears to beset the nonlearning boy.

2. a. The state or quality of being unsafe; liability to give way, fail, or suffer loss or damage; want of firmness or safety; an insecure state of affairs, a condition of danger.

a **1660** HAMMOND (J.), The unreasonableness and presumption, the danger and desperate insecurity of those that have not so much as a thought..to advance so far as attrition and contrition. **1750** JOHNSON *Rambler* No. 29 ¶7 Reflections on the variableness of fortune, the uncertainty of life, and the insecurity of all human acquisitions. **1822** J. FLINT *Lett. Amer.* 159 The influx of new settlers is greatly prevented by the insecurity of titles. **1853** J. H. NEWMAN *Hist. Sk.* (1873) II. I. i. 42 The insecurity of great prosperity has been the theme of poets and philosophers.

b. with *pl.* An instance or particular case of this; something insecure.

1649 JER. TAYLOR *Gt. Exemp.* I. ad sect. vi. 102 The insecurities and inconveniencies of a strange and new abode are part of the persecution. **1885** S. COX *Expos.* Ser. I. vii. 87 All the insecurities of time.

†**inse'cution.** *Obs. rare.* [ad. late L. *insecūtiōn-em*, n. of action from *insequī* to follow upon, pursue, f. *in-* (IN-^{2}) + *sequī* to follow.] The action of following closely upon; close pursuit.

c **1611** CHAPMAN *Iliad* XI. 524 How deepe the skirmish drew Amongst the Greeks; and with what ruth, the insecution grew. *Ibid.* XXIII. 448 Not the king's own horse gat more before the wheel Of his rich chariot, that might still the insecution feel With the extreme hairs of his tail.

†**in'sedable,** *a. Obs. rare*$^{-0}$. [ad. late L. *insēdābilis* that cannot be stayed or stilled, f. *in-* (IN-^{3}) + *sēdāre* to settle, still.]

1623 COCKERAM, *Insedable*, not to be quieted.

†**insedent.** *Obs. rare.* [f. L. *in-* (IN-^{2}) + *sedēnt-em* sitting. The proper L. form is *insidēnt-em*.] A person sitting upon something.

1594 *2nd Rep. Faust.* in Thoms *E.E. Prose Rom.* (1858) III. 402 There he rode by a little and a little, till he might buckle with the insedent [on an elephant].

†**inse'dulity.** *Obs. rare.* [f. late L. *insēdul-us* (f. *in-*, IN-^{3} + *sēdulus* assiduous, zealous) + -ITY.] Want of sedulousness; carelessness, indolence.

1679 HARBY *Key Script.* ii. 20 Notwithstanding the insedulity of sleepy Inadvertists that mind nothing.

†**in'see,** *v. Obs. rare.* [f. IN-^{1} + SEE *v.* Cf. Goth. *insaihwan* to look upon, behold, MDu. *insien*, Du. *inzien*, Ger. *einsehen*, Sw. *inse*, Da. *indsee*. Prob. largely due to transl. of L. *inspicĕre*, *intuērī*, etc.]

1. *trans.* To look upon; to see.

c **1315** SHOREHAM 155 The merr[i]er hyt hys ine batayle, Thet insykth al the vomen [= foemen] faylle, And falle a-doun.

2. a. *trans.* To see into, have insight into. **b.** *intr.* To have insight (*into*).

1598 GRENEWEY *Tacitus' Ann.* I. iii. (1622) 6 Deeply in-seeing into his lofty and bloudy disposition. **1602** WARNER *Alb. Eng.* XIII. lxxvi. (1612) 316 But none The Vniforme diuersitie of heauens in-sees but One.

inseeing ('ɪn,siːɪŋ), *ppl. a. rare.* [IN *adv.* 11 a.] Seeing into something; having insight.

1590 GREENE *Mourn. Garm.* 3 Philador had so pregnant a wit and such a swift inseeing and reaching capacitie, as it seemed [etc.]. **1611** SPEED *Hist. Gt. Brit.* IX. xxiv. (1632) 1157 His farre reaching and inseeing councell. **1840** LOWELL *Irene* v, In-seeing sympathy is hers, which chasteneth No less than loveth. **1894** G. EGERTON *Keynotes* 20 Her eyes have an inseeing look.

†**inseek,** *v. Obs. rare*$^{-1}$. In 4 **ynseke**. [f. IN-^{1} + SEEK *v.*; rendering L. *inquīrĕre*.] *trans.* To seek after.

1382 WYCLIF *Heb.* xi. 6 He is rewarder of men ynsekinge him.

†**inseer** ('ɪn,siːə(r)). *Obs.* Also 6 **en-**. [IN *adv.* 11 e.] One who sees or looks into something; an investigator, inspector, examiner.

1387-8 T. USK *Test. Love* III. i. (Skeat) l. 25 So this leude booke..lightely by a good inseer maye been vnderstande. *Ibid.* ix. l. 91 Onely this mede I coueite..that euery inseer and herer of this leude fantasie, deuoute horisons and praiers to God the greate iudge yelden, and praien for me. **1535** JOYE *Apol. Tindale* (Arb.) 20 God..is onely the enseer and sercher of herte and mynde.

†**in'seil,** *sb. Obs.* In 1 **inseȝel**, **-seȝl**, **-siȝle**, 2-3 **inseil**, 3 *Orm.* **innseȝȝel**. [OE. *inseȝel* = OFris. *insigel*, *-il* (MDu. *insëgel*), OHG. *insigili* (MHG. *insigele*, *-gil*, Ger. *insiegel*), ON. *innsigli* (Da. *indsegl*), all str. neut. Cf. also (without *in-*) Goth. *sigljo* wk. neut., MHG. *sigel*, Ger. *siegel*, MDu. *zeghel*, Du. *zegel*.

The stem of the word evidently represents L. *sigill-um* 'little sign, figure, or token, seal' (dim. of L. *signum* 'sign, mark, token'), whence OF. *seel*, Eng. SEAL; but the origin of the prefix *in-* in the Teutonic forms is obscure, since no late or med.L. *insigillum* appears. Franck (*Etym. Woorden-bk. Nederl. T.* s.v. *Zegel*) suggests that it may have been taken over in some way from L. *insigne* 'mark, sign', used also in med.L. in sense 'seal'. In the verb, the prefix raises less difficulty; a med.L. *insigillare* actually occurs (though sometimes as a rendering of OE. *inseȝlian*), and *enseeler* is common in OF. (see ENSEAL *v.*).]

A seal; app. orig. the impression made in wax with which a letter, etc. is sealed; also the signet or engraved instrument with which the impression is made.

a **1000** in Thorpe *Charters* (1865) 173 He..brohte insiȝle to me..Ða ageaf ic ðæt insiȝle ðe. *c* **1000** ÆLFRIC *Gloss.* in Wr.-Wülcker 126/2 *Sigillum, uel bulla*, inseȝel. *a* **1100** *Ags. Voc.* ibid. 330/16 *Sigillum*, inseȝl. *a* **1100** *O.E. Chron.* an. 1048 Ða com Sparhafoc..to him mid þæs cynges ȝewrite and inseȝle. *c* **1175** *Lamb. Hom.* 127 Þet inseil þe þe deofel ne mei nefre to breocan þet is þet [loc] þe ðe deofel ne con unlucan. *c* **1200** ORMIN Ded. 260 Sannt Johan sahh upp inn heffne an boc Bisett wiþþ seffne innseȝȝless. *a* **1225** [see INSEIL *v*].

†**in'seil,** *v. Obs.* [OE. *inseȝlian* = OHG. *insigilen*, ON. *innsigla*; med.L. *insigillāre* (Du Cange): see prec.] *trans.* To seal, to impress or secure with a seal, to seal up.

? *a* **1000** *Dom be hatan isene* c. 5 in Schmid *Gesetze* 414 And ga he to and in-seȝliȝe man þa hand, and sece man ofer þæne þriddan dæȝ, swa hwæðer swa heo beo ful swa clæne binnan þam in-seȝle. *c* **1000** *Ags. Gosp.* Matt. xxvii. 66 Soþlice hiȝ ferdon..and inn seȝlodon þone stan mid þam weardum. *c* **1160** *Hatton G.* ibid., And inseȝȝledon þænne stann. *a* **1225** *St. Marher.* 5 He haueð his merk on me inseilet wið his inseil.

inseint, obs. form of ENCEINTE.

†**in'seisin,** *v. Law. Obs.* Also 5 **insesun**, **-yn.** [f. IN-^{1} or ^{2} + SEISIN.] *trans.* To put into seisin or possession; to 'seize' (*of* something). (The opposite of DISSEISIN *v.*)

c **1440** *Promp. Parv.* 262/1 Insesun..in worldely goodys (*K.* insesyn in werdli godys..), *insesino*. **1611** COTGR., *Adherité*, inseisined, put into possession of. *Ibid.*, *Droict de saisine*, the money due vnto the Lo. Censuel, and of the Soyle, by a Purchaser of an Inheritance Censuel, when he is inseisined, and put into possession thereof.

inseity: see *in se* s.v. IN *Lat. prep.*

inselberg ('ɪns-, 'ɪnzəlbɜːg). *Geomorphol.* Also **Inselberg**. Pl. **-bergs, -berge.** [Ger., lit. 'island mountain'.] An isolated hill or mountain which rises abruptly from its surroundings, typically a plain in a hot, dry region.

[**1898** W. BORNHARDT in *Zeitschr. der deutschen geol. Ges.* (*Verhandl.*) L. 71 Näher und ferner in ganz unregelmässiger Vertheilung erheben sich aus ihr die merkwürdigen Inselberge.] **1907** *Q. Jrnl. Geol. Soc.* LXIII. 166 Except around a few clustered 'island-hills' (Insel-bergen) the drainage-gradients throughout this great basin are peculiarly low. **1913** *Rep. Brit. Assoc. Adv. Sci. 1912* 476 A striking feature of these kopjes and inselberge is that they rise at intervals from an apparently level or undulating plain. **1918** *Q. Jrnl. Geol. Soc.* LXXIV. 34 The bare rounded inselberg of gneiss stands alone, like an island in an undulating sea of vegetation. **1937** WOOLDRIDGE & MORGAN *Physical Basis Geogr.* xx. 310 The association of Inselberge and flat rock-plains, with or without a thin veneer of sand or gravel, is..an established fact of observation. **1954** W. D. THORNBURY *Princ. Geomorphol.* xi. 295 Others have applied inselberge rather indiscriminately to any island-like hill which stands conspicuously above its surrounding, such as the so-called sugarloafs of tropical rainy climates. **1960** B. W. SPARKS *Geomorphol.* xi. 257 Many African landscapes.. consist of a series of isolated steep-sided inselbergs rising from an almost flat plain. **1969** BENNISON & WRIGHT *Geol. Hist. Brit. Isles* xii. 272 Two important features of Triassic geography were the hills of Charnwood and the Mendips. These were inselbergs rising above the general level of the Triassic landscape but gradually buried as the deposits accumulated.

inseminate (ɪn'sɛmɪneɪt), *v.* [f. ppl. stem of L. *insēmināre*, f. *in-* (IN-^{2}) + *sēmināre* to sow.]

1. *trans.* To sow in; to cast in as seed. Also *fig.*

1623 COCKERAM, *Inseminate*, to sowe. **1627-77** FELTHAM *Resolves*, II. xix. 200 That Law of Nature..which is so far inseminated in the hearts of all. **1849** *Knife & Fork* 78 He will inevitably..inseminate in the minds of his friends a suspicion on the score of his religion. **1886** B. F. BARRETT in Ravlins *Progr. Th. Gt. Subj.* App. 118 The old falsities are to be uprooted, and the new truths inseminated.

2. To impregnate with semen, by natural or artificial means.

1923 *Vet. Jrnl.* LXXIX. 172 The application of artificial insemination on fox-farms could give a new impetus to the development of this industry... One male could easily inseminate twenty and more females. **1943** *Lancet* 7 Aug. 176/2 To avoid the dangers of in-breeding..the Jockey Club allowed no thorough-bred to be inseminated except by the covering stallion. **1958** *Times* 17 Nov. 15/6 They will now go to A.I. centres and will be used to inseminate a number of Friesian..cows.

insemination (ɪnsɛmɪ'neɪʃən). [n. of action f. prec.] **a.** The action of sowing in; the casting in or implanting of seed, or of germs; also *fig.*

1658 in PHILLIPS. **1682** H. MORE *Annot. Glanvill's Lux O.* 68 Admitting that there is..an orderly insemination of

lapsed Souls into humane Bodies. **1727–41** CHAMBERS *Cycl.*, *Insemination*, one of the four kinds of transplantation in use for the sympathetic cure of certain diseases. It is performed by mixing the medium impregnated with the mumia taken from the patient, with some fat earth, wherein has been sown the seed of a plant appropriate to that disease.. It is supposed the diseases will decline, in proportion as the plant grows. **1893** J. PULSFORD *Loyalty to Christ* II. 94 Earth, Paradise, and Heaven are equally ground.. susceptible of Divine insemination, and capable of yielding the fruits of God. **1896** *Allbutt's Syst. Med.* I. 719 In the last tube [infected with bacteria] the insemination is scantiest.

b. Immission of semen.

1860 TANNER *Pregnancy* iv. 193 Haighton showed that conception does not generally take place in the rabbit till about 50 hours after insemination.

c. = *artificial insemination.*

1923 *Vet. Jrnl.* LXXIX. 171 Apart from this kind of artificial insemination of females with 'natural sperm'.. it is also necessary to indicate the possibility of insemination with the so-called 'artificial sperm'. **1944** *Jrnl. Obstetr. & Gynaecol.* LI. 527/1 One donor was usually used for 4 to 8 inseminations carried out within short intervals from each other. *Ibid.* 528/1 One single insemination with spermatozoa from a donor was followed by pregnancy. **1959** *Chambers's Encycl.* I. 652/1 When the husband is sterile and the wife fertile, insemination with semen obtained from another donor has been used with success. **1974** *Times* 21 Jan. 14/5 Increased beef inseminations may be connected with the subsidized switch out of dairying.

insence, obs. form of INCENSE, INSENSE.

†**in'send**, *v. Obs.* Pa. t. and pple. **insent**. [f. IN-[1] + SEND; tr. L. *immittĕre*. Cf. OE. *onsendan*.] *trans.* To send in; to put in. So †**in'sending** *vbl. sb.*

a **1300** *E.E. Psalter* xxxix. 4 [xl. 3] And he in-sent [L. *immisit*] in mi mouth newe sange. *a* **1340** HAMPOLE *Psalter* xxxiii[i]. 7 In sendes þe aungel of lord in vmgange of dredand him. *Ibid., comm.*, The aungel of lord.. insendis, that is he makis insendynge of goed thoghtis. **1382** WYCLIF *Jas.* i. 21 Receyue ȝe the word insent [*gloss* or ioyned, *v.rr.* in sette, plauntid], that mai saue ȝoure soules.

insenescible (ɪnsɪ'nɛsɪb(ə)l), *a. rare.* [ad. late or med.L. *insenēscibilis* (Gloss. Philox.) not growing old, f. *in-* (IN-[3]) + *senescĕre* to grow old: see -IBLE.] Incapable of growing old.

1851 S. JUDD *Margaret* II. viii. (1871) 279 'Well my lads', said the Deacon, limping in among them with his insenescible smile, 'what have we here?'

insensate (ɪn'sɛnsət), *a.* (*sb.*) Also 6 *erron.* **incensate**. [ad. late L. *insensāt-us* (Tertull., Vulg.), f. *in-* (IN-[3]) + *sensātus* gifted with sense, f. *sensus* sense: see -ATE[2] 2.]

1. Destitute of physical sense or feeling; without sensation, 'senseless', inanimate.

1519 *Interl. Four Elem.* in Hazl. *Dodsley* I. 12 For plants and herbs grow and be insensate. **1538** H. MEDWALL *Nature* (1896) 44/180 Yt shuld neyther fele here nor se But be as other incensate bodys be. **1633** T. ADAMS *Exp. 2 Peter* ii. 13 Thus, like insensate stones, they sink down to their centre. **1799** WORDSW. '*Three Years she grew*' iii, Hers the silence and the calm, Of mute insensate things. **1871** MACDUFF *Mem. Patmos* xviii. 242 Dull, pulseless, unresponsive as the insensate stone.

2. Wanting in mental or moral feeling; devoid of sensibility; unaffected, unmoved; unfeeling. (Of persons, or their qualities, actions, etc.)

1553 T. WILSON *Rhet.* 30b, What is he that is so.. drouping of brain (I will not say) blockheded or insensate that is not moved with suche pleasure. **1612–15** BP. HALL *Contempl., O.T.* XIII. iii, No stone is more hard or insensate than a sinful heart. **1726–46** THOMSON *Winter* 844 The insensate barbarous trade of war. **1859** DICKENS *T. Two Cities* II. i, The heads exposed on Temple Bar with an insensate brutality and ferocity worthy of Abyssinia or Ashantee. **1874** GREEN *Short Hist.* ix. §7. 665 James alone remained stubborn and insensate as of old.

†**b.** With *of*, *to*: Not feeling or perceiving; unconscious of; unaffected by. *Obs.*

1725 POPE *Odyss.* xx. 414 The Suitors souls, insensate of their doom! *c* **1800** K. WHITE *Time* 507 Insensate of the favouring boon. **1813** T. BUSBY *Lucretius* VI. 15 Mortals.. Still live insensate to their happy state.

3. Lacking sense or understanding; unintelligent, stupid, senseless, foolish.

a **1529** SKELTON *Replyc.* Wks. 1843 I. 209 A moche fantasticall frenesy of their insensate sensualyte. **1586** FERNE *Blaz. Gentrie* 94 That incensate custome of Gauelkinde.. tendeth to the destruction of auncient and gentle houses. **1667** MILTON *P.L.* VI. 787 [They] to rebellious fight rallied thir Powers Insensate, hope conceiving from despair. **1725** POPE *Odyss.* IV. 37 Insensate! (with a sigh the king replies) Too long, misjudging, have I thought thee wise! **1839** ALISON *Hist. Europe* (1849–50) VII. xlii. §50. 131 Projects the most insensate [were] formed. **1878** BOSW. SMITH *Carthage* 114 It argues an insensate ignorance on the part of the Romans of what was truly great in their antagonists.

B. as *sb.* An insensate person. [= F. *un insensé*.]

1877 MORLEY *Robespierre* Crit. Misc. Ser. II. 92 Anyone who wishes to make such an opinion into a crime is an insenate. **1878** —— *Diderot* II. 205 A handful of insensates.

†**in'sensate**, *v. Obs. rare.* [f. prec.] *trans.* To render insensate.

1621 BRATHWAIT *Nat. Embassy, Pleasure* Argt. (1877) 5 To the end some thereof might ensnare and insensate the minds.. of the.. Arcadians.

insensately (ɪn'sɛnsətlɪ), *adv.* [f. prec. adj. + -LY[2].] In an insensate manner:

a. Unconsciously; **b.** Unfeelingly; **c.** Senselessly, foolishly.

1863 R. BUCHANAN *Undertones* in *Reader* 26 Dec. 755 Insensately feeling one's way to the sun. **1883** HALL CAINE in *Academy* 26 May 358/1 Byron's own voice was ever heard in his pages.. sometimes sarcastically, brutally, insensately; sometimes pathetically, sadly, despairingly. **1883** *N. & Q.* 20 Oct. 319/2 The debased type known as 'black-letter'.. a type to which the Germans still insensately cling with a devotion which would be admirable if it were not ignorant. **1891** G. MEREDITH *One of our Conq.* I. ix. 164 The insensately infantile interrogation.

in'sensateness. [f. as prec. + -NESS.] The quality or condition of being insensate; want of feeling or sense.

1650 BP. HALL *Balm Gil.* 76 Dost thou not many a time sigh for thine own insensateness? **1867** C. J. SMITH *Syn. & Antonyms* s.v. *Affectibility*, Insensateness.. Unimpressibleness.

†**'in,sense**, *sb. Obs. rare.* In 6–7 **insence**. [f. IN *adv.* 12 + SENSE.] Inner sense; essential meaning.

1502 *Ord. Crysten Men* (W. de W. 1506) I. iii. 17 This solempnyte.. is not of yᵉ insence & necessyte of baptem. **1653** J. TAYLOR (Water P.) *title*, The Essence, Quintessence, Insence.. of Nonsence upon Sence.

insense (ɪn'sɛns), *v. Obs.* exc. *north. dial.* Forms: 5 en-, insens, 5–7 en-, in-, -sence, -cense, -cence, 6– insense. [ME. *ensens(e*, a. OF. *ensenser* to enlighten, to bring into sense, f. *en-* in, into + *sens* sense; afterward assimilated to a L. type **insensāre*. From 17th c. app. only dialectal (chiefly northern), or in writers under dialect influence.] *trans.* To cause (a person) to understand or know something; to inform.

Const. *of*, *with* (rarely *on*, *into*), or with dependent clause; in second quot. with double object.

c **1400** *Beryn* 2213 So was he ful ensensid How he hym wold engyne, as he had purpensid. *Ibid.* 2406, I wold have ensensid ȝewe al the iniquite Of these false marchandis, þat dwellin in þis town. *c* **1450** *St. Cuthbert* (Surtees) 22 Eugeny.. Sent him letters him to ensens Of saynt cuthbert kyth and kynne. **1486** in *Surtees Misc.* (1888) 55 Eternall sapience Did insence me. **1548** UDALL, etc. *Erasm. Par. John* xvi. 96b, Yea and than also the holy goste shall incence you, what to aske and how to aske in my name. **1613** SHAKS. *Hen. VIII*, v. i. 43, I thinke I haue Incenst the Lords o' th' Councell, that he is.. A most Arch-Heretique. **1674** RAY *N.C. Words* 26 To *Insense*, to inform, a pretty word used about Sheffield in York-sh. **1689** *Col. Rec. Pennsylv.* I. 297 Insence yᵉ minds of the good people of this Government. **1797** WOLFE TONE *Autobiog.* (1828) 264 Lewines insensed him a good deal on Irish affairs. **1843** F. E. PAGET *Pageant* 18 Gertrude, so please you.. insense me with the fashions of the sixteenth century. **1846** BROCKETT *N.C. Gloss.* (ed. 3) I. 236 *Insense*, to make to understand. **1849** R. CURZON *Monast. Levant* Introd. 37 The walls.. covered with frescos, served as books to insense the minds of the unlearned with the histories.. of the faith. **1865** S. WILBERFORCE in Burgon *Lives 12 Gd. Men* (1888) II. 34 Pray do insense me. You must know all about it. **1895** J. T. FOWLER in *Durh. Univ. Jrnl.* 16 Feb. 134, I should really be glad to be insensed from the opposite side.

[**insenseless**, error for *is senseless* in Butler *Hud.* II. ii. 394.]

insensibility (ɪnsɛnsɪ'bɪlɪtɪ). [ad. late L. *insensibilitās*, f. *insensibilis*: see -ITY. Cf. F. *insensibilité* (12–13th c. in Littré).] The quality or condition of being insensible; want of sensibility.

I. In passive sense.

1. The quality of being imperceptible, or not appreciable by the senses. *rare.*

1635 HAKEWILL *Apol.* v–vi. 24 For your pretended insensibilitie in Natures decay. **1665** GLANVILL *Scepsis Sci.* xi. 60 Which insensibility of slow motions.. may thus be accounted for; Motion cannot be perceived without the perception of its Terms, viz. The parts of space which it immediately left, and those which it next acquires.

II. In active sense.

2. Incapability, or deprivation, of (physical) feeling or sensation; unconsciousness; a swoon.

c **1510** MORE *Picus* Wks. 12/2 There holdeth me sometyme by almighty god, as it wer euen a swone, and an insensibilitie. **1541** R. COPLAND *Guydon's Quest. Chirurg., Man. exam. Lazares* Q iv b, The insensybylyte of the rotten humours of the outwarde partes. **1692** BENTLEY *Boyle Lect.* i. 28 He will.. dispatch himself resolutely into the State of eternal Sleep and Insensibility. **1774** tr. *Boerhaave's Inst.* III. 409 After a Nerve has been tied.. an Insensibility and Wasting follows in those Parts to which that Nerve was distributed. **1841** LANE *Arab. Nts.* I. 91, I fell from my horse in a state of insensibility. **1879** *Cassell's Techn. Educ.* IX. 143 The carbonic acid is.. heavier than the air.. in breathing it insensibility ensues and ultimately death.

b. Physical insensitiveness (*to* something).

1808 *Med. Jrnl.* XIX. 111 Instances of this insensibility of the system to internal stimuli. **1831** BREWSTER *Nat. Magic* ii. (1833) 29 The insensibility of the eye to particular colours. **1835** W. IRVING *Tour Prairies* 245 Perfect hardihood and insensibility to the changes of the seasons.

3. Incapacity of mental feeling or emotion; incapability of being affected or moved; want of moral susceptibility; apathy, indifference.

1691 HARTCLIFFE *Virtues* 51 So many Circumstances of Insensibility and hardiness of Mind are urged. **1749** FIELDING *Tom Jones* XI. vii, I heard this news with the utmost insensibility. **1796** MORSE *Amer. Geog.* I. 787 The least affliction prompts them to suicide.. and they put an end to their days with great apparent insensibility. **1844** *Mem. Babylonian P'cess* II. 239, I often wonder at my hardheartedness and insensibility, when I reflect on the earnest and affecting entreaties of these dear friends.

b. Const. *of*, *to*.

1692 SOUTH *12 Serm.* (1697) I. 498 An utter insensibility of any good or kindness done him by others. **1802** PALEY *Nat. Theol.* xxvi. (1827) 535/2 One great cause of our insensibility to the goodness of the Creator is the very extensiveness of his bounty. *a* **1853** J. H. NEWMAN *Hist. Sk.* (1873) II. II. iii. 253 Insensibility to the common objects of human cupidity.

insensibilize (ɪn'sɛnsɪbɪ,laɪz), *v. rare*[–0]. [f. L. *insensibil-is* INSENSIBLE + -IZE: cf. *utilize*, etc.] *trans.* To render insensible. Hence **in,sensibili'zation**, the action of rendering or condition of being rendered insensible; **in'sensibilizer**, one who or that which 'insensibilizes'.

1886 *Syd. Soc. Lex.*, *Insensibilisation*, the production of insensibility to pain by means of anæsthetics, alcohols, and narcotic poisons, by hypnotism, and like means, as well as by disease. *Insensibiliser*, an instrument by means of which is produced *Insensibilisation*. **1897** *Allbutt's Syst. Med.* II. 837, I have shewn that it [immunity against snake-venom] depends upon an 'insensibilisation' of the cells in respect of the venom.

insensible (ɪn'sɛnsɪb(ə)l), *a.* (*sb.*) Also (*erron.*) 5–6 incens-, incenc-, -yble, 6–7 incensible. [ad. L. *insensibil-is*, f. *in-* (IN-[3]) + *sensibilis* SENSIBLE, f. *sentīre*, *sens-* to feel. Cf. F. *insensible* (13th c. in Littré).]

I. Passively: Incapable of being perceived.

1. a. Naturally incapable of being perceived by the bodily senses (= IMPERCEPTIBLE a); non-material. Now *rare.*

c **1380** WYCLIF *Wks.* (1880) 469 Bileue is insensible & more trewe þan siche signes; as þis treuþe is insensible þat two & þre maken fyue, & ȝit it is more certeyn þan ony sensible þing heere. **1509** HAWES *Past. Pleas.* XXIII. (Percy Soc.) 106 For though that aungell[s] be invysyble, Inpalpable, and also celestiall, Wythouten substaunce as incencyble. **1581** E. CAMPION in *Confer.* III. (1584) Z ij, His body may be insensible to vs if he will. **1608–33** BP. HALL *Medit. & Vows* (1851) 98 Let my soul.. be raised up to enjoy the insensible society of thy blessed angels. **1851** MANSEL *Proleg. Log.* v. (1860) 167–8 Locke has laid some stress on the fact, that the names which stand for insensible actions and notions, are derived from sensible objects.

b. So small, slight, gradual, or hidden, as not to be perceived by the senses, or by the mind (= IMPERCEPTIBLE b); inappreciable. (The prevailing sense.)

1584 COGAN *Haven Health* ccxvii. (1636) 240 It avoids red choler by urine, and other insensible evacuations. **1625** N. CARPENTER *Geog. Del.* I. ii. (1635) 37 This Inequality, how great soeuer it seeme to the sight is altogether insensible, and bearing no proportion with the huge vastnesse of the Earth. **1664** POWER *Exp. Philos.* I. 29 Exhaled by insensible Transpiration. **1734** tr. *Rollin's Anc. Hist.* (1827) I. 326 Carthage.. grew larger by insensible degrees. **1836** J. M. GULLY *Magendie's Formul.* 214 The temperature of the skin is moderately elevated, and the insensible perspiration increased. **1862** H. SPENCER *First Princ.* I. ii. §9 (1875) 28 There is an insensible transition. *Mod.* Passing by insensible gradations into the next sense.

†**2.** Incapable of being understood; unintelligible; without sense or meaning. (Chiefly in legal use.) *Obs.*

1538 COVERDALE *Ded. Transl. N. Test.*, In many places both base, insensible, and clean contrary, not only to the phrase of our language, but also from the understanding of the text in Latin. **1657–8** *Burton's Diary* (1828) II. 411 The words are insensible and uncertain words. **1767** BLACKSTONE *Comm.* II. xx. 340 If the condition of a bond be impossible.. or be uncertain, or insensible, the condition alone is void, and the bond shall stand single, and unconditional. **1775** T. HUTCHINSON *Diary* 13 Mar. I. 405 Pointed out several inaccuracies and insensible expressions in the New England Bill. **1884** *Law Times* LXXVI. 315/2 The words.. would be insensible, or at any rate superfluous.

II. Actively: Incapable of perceiving.

3. a. Naturally incapable of physical feeling; not having the faculty of sensation. Now *rare.*

c **1400** *Lanfranc's Cirurg.* 24 Þerfore þe ligament is.. incensible, for if þat it hadde be censible, þei myȝten nouȝt han I-susteyned þe traueile and þe meuynge of þe ioyntis. **1581** W. FULKE in *Confer.* III. (1584) Q b, I meane by insensible, voyde of life or sense. *a* **1619** FOTHERBY *Atheom.* II. xii. §3 (1622) 340 Fire, Haile, and Snow, meere insensible things. **1725** SLOANE *Jamaica* II. 310 The stomach of this bird is very muscular, having a thin separable and insensible membrane. **1831** BREWSTER *Nat. Magic* ii. (1833) 13 The insensible spot on the retina is stimulated by a borrowed light.

b. Deprived of sensation; unconscious.

1426 LYDG. *De Guil. Pilgr.* (E.E.T.S.) 9925 Thy body that lyth now blynd & deff, Doom also, and insensyble. **1483** CAXTON *Gold. Leg.* 361 b/2 She knewe not what was sayd ne done aboute her but as unmeuable or as all insensible.. she held her eyen fixed in one place. **1552** HULOET, Insensible, or hauynge no sence or fealynge, as beynge numbe, lyke a dead membre. **1828** SCOTT *F.M. Perth* xxxii, By this staircase the villains conveyed the insensible Prince to the lowest dungeon of the castle. *a* **1859** MACAULAY *Hist. Eng.* xxv. V. 287 He fell down in a fit, and remained long insensible.

c. Incapable of physically feeling or perceiving (something specified). Const. *of*, *to*.

1526 *Pilgr. Perf.* (W. de W. 1531) 61 After the commaundement of our lorde we must be blynde, defe, & dumme, lame & incensyble to all suche thynges. **1640** tr. *Verdere's Romant of Rom.* I. 61 Rendering him insensible of all pain. **1751** EARL ORRERY *Remarks Swift* (1752) 169 The manner of his death was easy, without the least pang or convulsion..Swift was totally insensible of happiness or pain. **1796** PEGGE *Anonym.* (1809) 444 A dog's nose is insensible of cold. **1863** GEO. ELIOT *Romola* v, The martial fury by which men became insensible to wounds.

4. a. Incapable of mentally feeling, perceiving, or being affected by (something specified); unaware, unconscious; not susceptible, unaffected, unmoved, indifferent. Const. *of*, *to*, *subord. cl.*

1612–15 BP. HALL *Contempl., O.T.* x. i, Should I only be insensible of his and the common happiness? **1712** BUDGELL *Spect.* No. 283 ⁋2 Insensible of that Weight and Dignity which a moderate share of Wealth adds to their Characters. **1802** MAR. EDGEWORTH *Moral T.* (1816) I. ix. 66 Insensible of your kindness. **1850** MERIVALE *Rom. Emp.* (1865) I. vi. 277 Their great leader was not insensible how much he owed to their faithful services. **1882** A. W. WARD *Dickens* v. 135 Even Circumlocution Offices are not insensible to the acetous force of satire.

b. Incapable or destitute of feeling or emotion; emotionless, callous, apathetic.

1617 MORYSON *Itin.* I. 236 My conscience was not..so insensible, as it could have passed over the..denying of my faith. *a***1621** BEAUM. & FL. *Thierry & Theod.* IV. ii, Art thou grown Insensible in ill, that thou goest on Without the least compunction? **1683** D. A. *Art Converse* 113 The Phlegmaticks are those the French call properly *Des Apathicks*, without passion or insensible. **1809** MALKIN *Gil Blas* IX. vi. ⁋13 The cold, relentless, insensible, was kindled into the warmest of love's votaries. **1850** MRS. JAMESON *Leg. Monast. Ord.* (1863) 404 He filled the most insensible with terror.

†**5.** Destitute of sense or intelligence; irrational.

*a***1533** FRITH *Answ. Rastel.* Wks. (1573) 27 Are ye so childish and insensible to imagine that ye must yet go through Purgatory, sith ye are already without faulte in his sight. **1598** R. C. *Godly Form Hovseh. Govt.* Ep. Ded. 4 Dumbe & insencible beasts. **1634** SIR T. HERBERT *Trav.* 75 His feare and amazement became greater, and insensible how to qualifie these bloudie stirrings. **1693** *Humours Town* 15 In the Conversation of Brutes, and the Prospect of insensible Animals. **1794** G. ADAMS *Nat. & Exp. Philos.* IV. xi. 486 People stupid and insensible, illiterate and incapable of learning.

†**B.** *sb.* (absol. uses of the adj.) *Obs.*

1. (from A. I.) **a.** Something that cannot be perceived by the senses; a non-material thing. **b.** Something too small or slight to be perceived; something imperceptible or inappreciable.

1656 STANLEY *Hist. Philos.* v. (1701) 159/2 To Insensibles nothing can be added, nothing taken away. This is the nature of Eternal Beings, the like and same ever. **1674** N. FAIRFAX *Bulk & Selv.* 128 By reason of the swarms of insensibles, drilling through their pores or spungholes.

2. (from A. II.) **a.** A thing or person incapable of feeling; an inanimate thing; an apathetic person. **b.** A person destitute of sense, a fool.

*a***1618** SYLVESTER *Tobacco Battered* 470 As of all Insensibles, hath none More Melancholy and Adustion, Then Chimnies have. **1692** DRYDEN *St. Euremont's Ess.* 336 The wise Man of the Stoicks is a vertuous insensible. **1754** RICHARDSON *Grandison* (1812) VI. 405 (D.) What an insensible must have been my cousin, had she not been proud of being Lady Grandison. **1785** COWPER *Let. to Newton* Wks. 1837 XV. 159 Of all the insensibles he ever saw, poor Geary is the most completely stupid. **1802** tr. *A. La Fontaine's Reprobate* II. 198 [Not] a word in favour of that insensible, that savage.

†**in'sensibleness.** *Obs.* [f. prec. + -NESS.] The quality or condition of being insensible.

I. 1. = INSENSIBILITY 1.

*a***1705** RAY (J.), The insensibleness of the pain proceeds rather from the relaxation of the nerves than their obstruction.

II. 2. = INSENSIBILITY 2.

*a***1631** DONNE in Spurgeon *Treas. Dav.* Ps. xxxii. 7 Sometimes by imprinting a holy stupefaction and insensibleness in the person that suffers. **1656** W. D. tr. *Comenius' Gate Lat. Unl.* §310. 85 Of the diseases som caus pain..others numbness and insensibleness. **1692** DRYDEN *St. Euremont's Ess.* 341 He fixed the Cheefest Good in insensibleness.

3. = INSENSIBILITY 3.

*a***1568** COVERDALE *Carrying Christ's Cross* iv. Wks. (Parker Soc.) II. 241 Therefore doth God justly infatuate them, and maketh them foolish, giving them up to insensibleness. **1631** GOUGE *God's Arrows* II. §6. 140 Insensiblenesse of their misery who are in want. **1675** *Art Contentm.* VIII. viii. 218 We betray as much ignorance of our interest, as insensibleness of our obligation. **1715** J. LENG *Serm. Bedington* 20 Our insensibleness for past mercies.

4. Want of sense; insensateness. Cf. prec. 5.

1610 DONNE *Pseudo-Martyr* vi. 176 Was there not some measure of stupid insensiblenesse in him, when he durst not spit in any necessity at his praiers?

†**in'sensiblist.** *nonce-wd.* [f. INSENSIBLE + -IST.] One who professes insensibility or apathy.

1782 MISS BURNEY *Cecilia* IV. ii, Mr. Meadows..since he commenced insensiblist, has never once dared to be pleased, nor ventured for a moment to look in good humour.

insensibly (ɪn'sɛnsɪblɪ), *adv.* [f. INSENSIBLE + -LY^{2}.]

1. In an insensible manner or degree; imperceptibly; unconsciously; *esp.* so slightly or gradually that the action or process is not perceived; by imperceptible degrees.

1584 R. SCOT *Discov. Witchcr.* III. ii. (1886) 33 The wife departeth out of her husbands armes insensiblie. **1639** tr. *Du Bosq's Compl. Woman* I. 21 If insensibly we lay our hand where the paine is, wee likewise bring our tongue unawares, where the passion of the mind is. **1640–4** in Rushw. *Hist. Coll.* III. (1692) I. 638 The other part..will insensibly moulder away. **1667** MILTON *P.L.* VIII. 130 And what if sev'nth to these The Planet Earth, so stedfast though she seem, Insensibly three different Motions move? **1697** DRYDEN *Ess. Virg. Georg.* ⁋2 In a curious Brede of Needle-work, one Colour falls away by..just Degrees, and another rises..insensibly. **1781** GIBBON *Decl. & F.* xvii. (1869) I. 470 The agriculture of the Roman provinces was insensibly ruined. **1851** CARPENTER *Man. Phys.* (ed. 2) 351 The ultimate ramifications of the Arteries pass so insensibly into those of the Veins, that no definite line of demarcation between them can be drawn. **1868** FREEMAN *Norm. Conq.* II. vii. 53 The Witenagemôt insensibly lost its authority.

†**2.** Without sense or understanding; stupidly, irrationally. *Obs. rare.*

*a***1603** in *Liturg. Serv. Q. Eliz.* (Parker Soc.) 682 No doubt he is insensibly blockish.

insensile (ɪn'sɛnsɪl), *a. rare.* [ad. L. *insensil-is* insensible, imperceptible, f. *in-* (IN-^{3}) + *sensilis* SENSILE.] = INSENSIBLE 1.

1822–34 *Good's Study Med.* (ed. 4) III. 367 Species II *Antipathia Insensilis.* Insensile Antipathy.

insensitive (ɪn'sɛnsɪtɪv), *a.* [IN-^{3}.] Not sensitive.

†**1.** Destitute of feeling or consciousness (in general); not sentient; inanimate. *Obs.*

1610 HEALEY *St. Aug. Citie of God* 471 Though man be not insensitive, yet this sence of his..is justly termed rather death then life. *a***1694** TILLOTSON *Serm.* (1743) IX. clxxvi. 4110 This faculty is that which constitutes the difference between sensitive and insensitive creatures. **1713** DERHAM *Phys.-Theol.* IV. i. 85 Sensitive or insensitive Creatures.

2. a. Of an organ or part of the body: Destitute of feeling or sensation; not susceptible of sensuous impressions (esp. those of touch or sight). Const. *to.*

1866 *Sat. Rev.* 21 Apr. 467 A certain degree of sluggishness is inseparable from a skin insensitive to dirt. **1879** HARLAN *Eyesight* iii. 38 One spot on the retina, not very far from the most sensitive portion, is entirely insensitive to light. **1884** *Expositor* Jan. 41 Their optic nerve has shrunk to an insensitive thread. **1898** P. MANSON *Trop. Dis.* xxvii. 432 A painless, insensitive..granulomatous excrescence.

b. *transf.* Of a substance: Not susceptible to a physical influence, esp. that of light or the actinic rays. Const. *to.*

1871 tr. *Schellen's Spectr. Anal.* §35. 129 Most substances absorbed with great avidity rays of certain colors, while they were insensitive to others. **1879** *Cassell's Techn. Educ.* III. 1 The film, which is then totally insensitive to light. **1889** *Anthony's Photogr. Bull.* II. 394 Pure iodide of silver gelatine is for optical sensitizers even quite insensitive.

c. Of a mathematical or physical quantity: (relatively) unaffected in value by variations in some related quantity. Const. *to.*

1968 FOX & MAYERS *Computing Methods for Scientists & Engineers* iii. 31 As r decreases, the results become increasingly insensitive to small changes in the given condition. **1970** *Nature* 25 July 334/2 The energy of interaction turns out to be rather insensitive to $\epsilon(\omega)$ at these frequencies if the layer materials are of similar density.

3. Destitute of, or wanting in, mental or moral sensitiveness; having no quickness of feeling; not susceptible of impression. Const. *to.*

1834 CAMPBELL *Life Mrs. Siddons* II. ii. 49 Insensitive as we have seen her to the slightest joy at the return of her husband. **1881** MRS. C. PRAED *Policy & P.* I. 40 Longleat's insensitive nature.

in'sensitiveness. [f. prec. + -NESS.] The quality of being insensitive; want of sensitiveness.

1838 I. TAYLOR *Home Educ.* 161 To cherish as well animal insensibility (we want the word *insensitiveness*) and self-possession, by arduous field amusements. **1855** —— *Restor. Belief* (1856) 364 It is not insensitiveness of temperament, whence springs the serenity of that brow. **1881** MRS. LYNN LINTON *My Love* III. 44 He had the Pennefather insensitiveness and want of imagination.

†**in'sensuat,** *a. Obs.* var. of INSENSATE *a.* (Cf. *sensuate.*)

1508 KENNEDIE *Flyting w. Dunbar* 321 Insensuat sow, cesse fals Eustase air!

insensuous (ɪn'sɛnsju:əs), *a. rare.* [IN-^{3}.] Not sensuous; that is not an object of sense.

*a***1861** MRS. BROWNING (Webster 1864), That intermediate door Betwixt the different planes of sensuous form And form insensuous.

insented, *Obs.*: see ENCEINTE.

insentience (ɪn'sɛnʃ(ɪ)əns). [f. next: see -ENCE.] The fact or condition of being insentient; insensibility, unconsciousness.

1862 F. HALL *Hindu Philos. Syst.* 102 In the view of all the pandits, there is no emancipation apart from insentience. **1924** J. M. MURRY *Voyage* xii. 224 All was as it must be: happiness for one, pain for another, and for yet another insentience like his own. **1936** D. H. LAWRENCE *Phoenix* 344 The *insentience* of armed, bullying men, in face of living, sentient things. **1951** M. MCLUHAN *Mech. Bride* 13/1 It would be hard to know where to begin to peel back the layers of insentience..in such an ad. **1972** *Sci. Amer.* May 33/1 Whereas the insentience of the viscera has long been received as physiological dogma with a status comparable to the circulation of the blood, the insentience of muscles has often been called in question and probably cannot be regarded as universally accepted even today.

insentient (ɪn'sɛnʃ(ɪ)ənt), *a.* [IN-^{3}.] Not sentient.

1. Destitute of physical feeling, sensation, or consciousness; inanimate.

1764 REID *Inquiry* vi. §6 The qualities or attributes of an insentient inert substance. **1831** *Fraser's Mag.* IV. 77 They are to be hacked and hewed..as if they were of insentient marble. **1884** BROWNING *Ferishtah, Sun* 117 Shall I return it [a stone] thanks, the insentient thing?

2. Devoid of mental feeling; indifferent. *rare.*

1860 RUSKIN *Mod. Paint.* V. 296 Suppose..that he [Giorgione] came down to Venice somewhat recusant, or insentient, concerning the usual priestly doctrines of his day.

in'separabilist. *rare.* [f. L. *insēparābilis* INSEPARABLE + -IST]. One who believes that a religious rite and the spiritual influence held to accompany it are inseparable.

1840 G. S. FABER *Prim. Doctr. Regen.* III. ii. 254 *note*, It is impossible for the Inseparabilist to charge the Separabilist with a hankering after the Doctrine of Reprobation, and yet himself escape the equitable retort of precisely the same charge.

inseparability (ɪnsɛpərə'bɪlɪtɪ). [ad. L. *insēparābilit-ās* (Augustine), f. *insēparābil-is*: see next and -ITY. Cf. F. *inséparabilité* (14–15th c. in Hatz.-Darm.).] The quality or condition of being inseparable.

1623 W. SCLATER *Tythes* 29 In the point of inseparability from their subject. **1662** STILLINGFL. *Orig. Sacr.* III. i. §6 Whence should the Idea of the unity and inseparability of all these perfections come? **1719** WATERLAND *Vind. Christ's Divin.* ix. (1720) 169 We suppose Three Persons to be One God by their Inseparability and the essential Union of the Persons. **1871** FARRAR *Witn. Hist.* ii. 58 The inseparability of the supernatural from the records of Christ's life.

inseparable (ɪn'sɛpərəb(ə)l), *a.* (*sb.*) Also 5–9 *erron.* inseperable. [ad. L. *insēparābilis*, f. *in-* (IN-^{3}) + *sēparābilis* SEPARABLE. Cf. F. *inséparable* (14–15th c. in Hatz.-Darm.).] Not separable; incapable of being separated or disjoined. **a.** Said of two or more united things or persons, or of their connexion or relation.

1398 TREVISA *Barth. De P.R.* XVI. iv. (Add. MS. 27944), Whenne they ben yioynede in a dewe manere the onyng is inseperable, so that they mow nouȝt aftirward be departede atwynne. **1555** EDEN *Decades* 78 The chyldren which god hath giuen vs as pledges of owr inseperable loue. **1571** GOLDING *Calvin on Ps.* lv. 16 They bee inseparable companions, or abyde togither in one lodginge. **1662** GERBIER *Princ.* 20 An inseparable union. **1711** STEELE *Spect.* No. 80 ⁋1 They were inseparable Companions in all the little Entertainments. **1813** J. THOMSON *Lect. Inflam.* 9 The intimate and in some degree inseparable connexion existing between physic and surgery. *a***1852** WEBSTER *Wks.* (1877) III. 342 Liberty and Union, now and for ever, one and inseparable.

b. Said of one member of a combination. Const. *from*, †formerly also *to.*

1504 LADY MARGARET tr. *De Imitatione* IV. xiii. 278 To be with the [= thee] inseparable. **1581** R. GOADE in *Confer.* II. (1584) H iv, This qualitie is not alwayes inseparable. **1620** T. GRANGER *Div. Logike* 67 So originall sinne is inseperable from the mortall body, saving faith..from the Elect regenerated. **1639** tr. *Du Bosq's Compl. Woman* II. 67 Jealousie alwayes..becomes more inseparable to the soule, then Ivy is to..Walls. **1712** STEELE *Spect.* No. 491 ⁋2 Ingratitude is a Vice inseparable to a lustful Man. **1712** BERKELEY *Disc. Pass. Obed.* §16 The miseries inseparable from a state of anarchy. **1860** MRS. CARLYLE *Lett.* III. 23 My inseparable companion during eleven years. **1875** JOWETT *Plato* (ed. 2) I. 406 Fire, which is inseparable from heat, cannot co-exist with cold.

c. ***inseparable accident, attribute, quality***, etc. (*Logic*), an accident, etc. that cannot be separated from its subject. ***inseparable adjunct***, an adjunct that cannot really be separated from its subject, though the subject may be conceived of without it. ***inseparable prefix*** or ***preposition*** (*Gram.*), a prefix found only in combination, and incapable of being used as a separate word: e.g. L. *dis-*, *re-*; Eng. *mis-*, *un-*; Ger. *ge-*, *ver-*, *zer-*.

1551 T. WILSON *Logike* (1580) 6 b, An accident..maie be separated, or it maie not, some maie bee separated from their subjecte, as colde maie bee taken from water, and knowledge from the minde. Other are inseparable, because thei cannot be taken awaie altogether..Heate can not bee taken from fire. **1620** T. GRANGER *Div. Logike* 67 Common qualities, are seperable, or inseperable. *Ibid.* 69 The inseperable qualitie makes a proposition necessary, not reciprocate. **1820** *Mair's Tyro's Dict.* (ed. 10) 414 *Vē* may be reckoned among the inseparable prepositions, which in composition, is sometimes intensive..and sometimes privative. **1843** MILL *Logic* I. vii. §8 Inseparable accidents are properties which are universal to the species but not necessary to it. **1885** W. L. DAVIDSON *Logic Definition* ii. 44 Exception, however, must be made for the case of inseparable accidents ..Neither barking, mewing..nor grunting is more than an accident of the dog, the cat..the pig; but as, wherever we have the animal, we have the corresponding sign, this invariable concomitant becomes an important fact in characterizing and identification.

B. *sb.* Usually *pl.* Things or persons that cannot be separated; inseparable companions.

c **1520** *Wyse chylde & Emperor Adrian* (1860) 11 Shynynge, and heate, the which be inseperables, for the one ne maye be without the other. **1748** RICHARDSON *Clarissa* (1811) V. 278 Which, when a man comes in between the pretended inseparables, is given up. **1771** T. HULL *Hist. Sir W. Harrington* (1797) IV. 189 Except Mr. Renholds, (who is still Sir William's inseparable). **1861** C. P. HODGSON *Resid. Japan* 291 The two swords and fan are inseparables in Japan. **1875** A. R. HOPE *Schoolboy Fr.* 72 In the manner of schoolboy inseparables.

in'separableness. [f. prec. + -NESS.] The quality of being inseparable.

1598 FLORIO, *Indissolubilita*, inseparablenes. a **1631** DONNE in *Select.* (1840) 56 The inseparableness of this union. a **1715** BURNET *Own Time* (1766) II. 137 The inseparableness of the prerogative from the person of the King. **1813** L. HUNT in *Examiner* 31 May 349/2 The supposed inseparableness of Church and State.

inseparably (ɪnˈsɛpərəblɪ), *adv.* [f. INSEPARABLE + -LY².] In an inseparable manner; so as not to be disjoined, or severed; indissolubly.

1490 CAXTON *Eneydos* xiii. 47 The swete flamme of loue esprised in-to the mary and synewes, whiche inseparably goeth thrughe the bones, as depe as the veray hertys roote. **1526** *Pilgr. Perf.* (1531) 156 b, To be vnite or ioyned inseparably to his lorde. **1640** BASTWICK *Lord Bps.* iv. D iij b, They goe inseperably together, like Tobie, and his Dogge. **1758** BLACKSTONE in *Comm.* I. 19 The civil and canon laws, which now came to be inseparably interwoven with each other. **1868** FREEMAN *Norm. Conq.* (1876) II. ix. 423 The city with which their names are inseparably connected.

inseparate (ɪnˈsɛpərət), *a.* [ad. L. *insēparāt-us* (Tertullian), f. *in-* (IN-³) + *sēparātus*, pa. pple. of *sēparāre* to SEPARATE.] Not separate (*from*); united; undivided; hence, often = INSEPARABLE.

1550 [implied in INSEPARATELY]. a **1586** SIDNEY *Astr. & Stella* ci, Ioy, which is inseparate from those eyes. **1606** SHAKS. *Tr. & Cr.* v. ii. 148 This is, and is not Cressid: Within my soule, there doth conduce a fight Of this strange nature, that a thing inseperate, Diuides more wider then the skie and earth. **1607** DAY *Trav. Eng. Bro.* (1881) 75 Enuie and hate Striue in my breast like twinnes inseperate. **1742** WARBURTON *Comm. Pope's Ess. Man* Wks. 1811 XI. 67 That folly and wisdom are the inseparate partage of humanity. **1874** L. MORRIS *Songs two W.* Ser. II. *In the Park* 212 The good which should be, inseparate From the evil things that are. **1887** SWINBURNE *Locrine* I. i. 220 We live linked, inseparate—heart in heart.

b. *Bot.* (See quots., and cf. INSEPARATION.)

1880 GRAY *Struct. Bot.* (ed. 6) 181 Accordingly, Dr. Masters would substitute for coalescence and adnate the term *inseparate*. **1886** *Syd. Soc. Lex.*, *Inseparate*, Masters's term for the condition in which parts of a plant are not separate.

in'separately, *adv.* [f. prec. + -LY².] In an inseparate manner; without separation or severance; inseparably.

1550 CRANMER *Def. Scram.* 96 b, Here sainct Cyrill declareth the dignitee of Christes fleshe, beyng inseperately annexed vnto his diuinitee. **1582** N. T. (Rhem.) *Eph.* v. 29 *note*, So beloued of Christ, and so inseparatly ioyned in marriage with him. **1665** G. HAVERS *P. della Valle's Trav. E. India* 183 Conjoyning so inseparately..their Religion to the Descents or Races of Men. **1704** N. N. tr. *Boccalini's Advt. fr. Parnassus* III. 2 The Splendor..and the good Fortune I at present enjoy, are so inseparately annex'd to this Pirate's power.

insepa'ration. *Bot. rare.* [IN-³.] The congenital union of contiguous organs, viewed as the natural or primitive state; as opposed to *coalescence* or *adnation*, which imply original separation: cf. INSEPARATE b.

1886 in *Syd. Soc. Lex.*

†**in'separized,** *a. Obs. nonce-wd.* [f. IN-³, and assumed vb. **separize* = F. *séparer* to separate.] = INSEPARATE.

a **1618** SYLVESTER *Mem. Mortalitie* xliii, [He] Knew well the cares from Crowns inseparized.

†**'insequent,** *a.*¹ *Obs. rare.* [ad. L. *insequent-em*, pr. pple. of *insequī*, f. *in-* (IN-²) + *sequī* to follow.] Following on, succeeding; subsequent.

c **1620** in Hacket *Abp. Williams* I. (1692) 50 The Storm will gather, and burst out into a greater Tempest, in all insequent Meetings [of parliament]. a **1670** *ibid.* 25 If he had his Apocha or Quietance..he were free from all insequent Demands.

insequent (ˈɪnsɪkwənt, ɪnˈsiːkwənt), *a.*² *Geomorphol.* [f. IN-³ + *-sequent* in CONSEQUENT, SUBSEQUENT *adjs.*] Of a stream, stream valley, or drainage pattern: having a course or form that appears haphazard and exhibits no apparent relation to the form or structure of the land.

1897 W. M. DAVIS in *Science* 2 July 24/1 Then the side streams, growing headwards, are accidentally located; and streams of this class have been called *autogenetic* by McGee. *Insequent* may prove to be a more satisfactory name for such streams, as it is of the same etymological family as *consequent*, *subsequent* and *obsequent*... As *insequent* has proved servicable [*sic*] in my lectures during the past winter, it is now submitted for trial by others. **1939** P. G. WORCESTER *Textbk. Geomorphol.* viii. 155 Streams that develop their valleys on flat-lying sediments or on massive rocks, such as granites, without strong structural control are called insequent streams. **1954** W. D. THORNBURY *Princ. Geomorphol.* v. 114 Insequent valleys are those whose courses are controlled by factors which are not determinable. **1968** R. W. FAIRBRIDGE *Encycl. Geomorphol.* 1075/2 Such a condition, one of literally no structural control, is manifested by an insequent drainage pattern.

inserch(e, obs. form of ENSEARCH *v.*

†**in'sere,** *v. Sc.* Pa. t. and pple. inserit. [ad. F. *insérer*, ad. L. *inserĕre* to INSERT: perh. only in pa. t. and pple.] *trans.* To insert.

1557 *Sc. Acts Mary* (1814) II. App. 605/2 And desyrit this protestatioun to be inserit In þe bukis of parliament. **1563** *Ressoning betuix Crosraguell & Knox* A j a, Amang other godlie lessones..I inserit certane catholick artickles.

†**inse'rene,** *v. Obs. nonce-wd.* [f. IN-³ + SERENE *a.*; or from assumed adj. **inserene* not serene.] *trans.* To render cloudy or not serene; to cloud.

1609 J. DAVIES *Holy Roode* (1878) 18 (R.) Death stood by, Whose gastly presence inserenes my face.

insert (ɪnˈsɜːt), *v.* Also 6–8 incert, *pa. pple.* 6 incert, 7 insert. [f. L. *insert-*, ppl. stem of *inserĕre* to put in, f. *in-* (IN-²) + *serĕre* to join together, put into.]

1. *trans.* To set, put, or place in; to push or thrust in; to fix or fix in; to introduce; to ingraft. Said primarily of putting any solid object into a space which it fits, or fills up; hence to place a thing, as an addition, between the parts of another, as to insert a page or plate into a book; also, to push or put a thing (e.g. a stick, a finger, the point of a knife) into a hole or aperture, whether to remain there, or to be again withdrawn.

1529 MORE *Suppl. Soulys* Wks. 321/1 This soule that bryngeth with hym suche frayle woorkes eyther wrought by themselfe or inserted peraduenture and myxed a myddes of some good and vertuous worke. a **1586** BRADFORD *Wks.* (Parker Soc.) 90 They must needs be condemned if that they be not insert and engrafted into the very true body and natural body of our Saviour Christ. **1638** F. JUNIUS *Paint. of Ancients* 119 To varie the unitie of a stone by inserting such spots into the crust as were not by nature. **1647** H. MORE *Song of Soul* II. iii. II. xxiv, If all to all revert, Each part then into each part is insert. **1658** W. SANDERSON *Graphice* 25 Here a Print of Grotesco should have been inserted. **1782** COWPER *To W. C. Unwin* iii, The bud inserted in the rind.. Adorns..The stock whereon it grows. **1797** BEWICK *Brit. Birds* (1847) I. 277 It inserts its long tongue into the holes through which the ants issue. **1799** *Med. Jrnl.* II. 138 His arm is inflamed from the vaccine matter inserted four days since. **1833** HT. MARTINEAU *Manch. Strike* 110 Boring a hole between two flints in a yard..and inserting therein a daisy. **1840** DICKENS *Barn. Rudge* vii, A..key which he inserted cautiously in the lock..and softly opened the door. **1884** BOWER & SCOTT *De Bary's Phaner.* 514 Slightly thickened fibres, between which wide vessels surrounded by bundle-parenchyma are inserted.

b. To put or introduce (a letter, word, sentence, paragraph, etc.) into a body of written or printed matter, or into a programme; to put as a paragraph, advertisement, or article, into a newspaper or the like; to introduce as a figure or element in a picture, etc.; to include.

1533 MORE *Answ. Poysoned Bk.* I. xi. Wks. 1053/2, I haue good reader, in the exposicion of these woordes of our sauiour inserted the incorporacion of hym and vs together, by the receiuing and eating of his owne body into oures. **1542** LYNDESAY *Herald. Notes* Wks. (E.E.T.S.) v. 609 Vtheris enormities ar incert and registrat in this present buik. **1597** HOOKER *Eccl. Pol.* v. xxxvi. §1 With our Lord's Prayer they would find no fault, so that they might persuade us..not [to] insert it so often into the liturgy. **1647** CLARENDON *Hist. Reb.* I. §125 A short story may not be unfitly inserted. **1676** RAY *Corr.* (1848) 122, I find no more species of birds than what I have already inserted in the Ornithology. **1713** *Lond. Gaz.* No. 5151/4 There was Incerted..in the Gazette, that a Plate..was to be run for. **1818** CRUISE *Digest* (ed. 2) V. 164 Amended and rectified, by inserting the words *St. Stephen's near.* **1855** MACAULAY *Hist. Eng.* xix. IV. 345 We would not consent to insert in them [bills] clauses conferring new privileges on the nobility. **1864** J. H. NEWMAN *Apol.* 107 Something he had inserted into the Magazine.

†**c.** To introduce or ingraft *into* (a family).

1594 J. DICKENSON *Arisbas* (1878) 39 Many Princes.. desirous to insert themselues into [so] royall a kinred.. offered their daughters with large portions. **1610** HOLLAND *Camden's Brit.* (1637) 261 Aetheldred King of England.. inserted into his owne familie by way of adoption Anlaf the Dane.

2. *Anat.*, *Zool.*, *Bot.* To attach; to join at a specified point of attachment. Only in *pa. pple.*

[**1601** HOLLAND *Pliny* I. 310 Where hath she [Nature] placed and inserted the [gnat's] instrument and organ of smelling?] **1828** STARK *Elem. Nat. Hist.* II. 280 Antennæ with six joints, inserted at the internal margin of the eyes. **1851–6** WOODWARD *Mollusca* 25 The muscles of the arms are inserted in a cranial cartilage. **1857** HENFREY *Bot.* §157 When an organ is not adherent to any other circle, but inserted on the receptacle, it is said to be free.

'insert, *sb.* [f. INSERT *v.*, or abbrev. of INSERTION.] Something inserted. **a.** An additional sentence or paragraph added to a proof to be inserted in the 'revise' or 'final'. and **b.** In the U.S. postal service, A paper, circular, etc. placed within the folds of a newspaper, or the leaves of a magazine or book.

1893 in *Funk's Stand. Dict.* **1907** *Installation News* Dec. 1/2 There are three of these loose inserts. One is a pamphlet ..; the second is an advance price sheet [etc.]. **1928** R. B. H. BELL *Life Abundant* 142 This little book would not be complete without an insert on the Art of Prayer.

c. An object of one material around which another material (as concrete, plastic, or metal) sets or solidifies, or which is forced into it after it has set.

1913 G. A. HOOL *Reinforced Concrete Construction* II. iv. 152 These castings are made in convenient lengths and the slot in the bottom makes it possible to place hangers or bolts at any desired location along the length of the insert. The casting can be anchored as securely in the concrete as may be necessary. **1933** L. F. RAHM *Plastic Molding* i. 10 Where the production of work is large enough to justify it, special machines may be developed for the simultaneous staking-in of multiple inserts, instead of molding these in the article. **1934** H. CHASE *Die Castings* iv. 145 Inserts are usually knurled on the surface in contact with metal cast around them. **1967** B. HAROCOPOS tr. *Technol. Gravity Die-Casting* ix. 121 In die-casting, it is possible to produce articles comprising cast-in-place inserts of ferrous metals, bronze, brass or, less frequently, of aluminium. **1968** *Gloss. Formwork Terms* (*B.S.I.*) 16 *Insert*, a piece of timber or other material cast into the concrete surface usually to provide a fixing.

d. A shot inserted into a cinema film, taken after the filming of a particular sequence.

1916 'B. M. BOWER' *Phantom Herd* xvi. 269 He made all of his 'close-ups', his inserts and sub-titles. **1949** A. HUXLEY *Let.* 6 Mar. (1969) 593 Hitchcock..now shoots continuously a whole reel at a time, doing everything without cutting, getting the necessary close-ups and inserts ..by camera movements and movements of the actors. **1957** *B.B.C. Handbk.* 119 Items presented from a central studio may be combined with 'live' or filmed inserts originating from anywhere in Britain. **1965** *Movie* Spring 26 The insert shots representing Hamp's mental images (these recall the joke insert of the mother dropping dead in *Shoot the Pianist*). **1970** *New Yorker* 26 Sept. 123/1 Keaton doesn't care much for inserts. 'I like long takes, in long-shot,' he says. 'Close ups hurt comedy.'

e. Misc. uses.

1922 M. B. HOUSTON *Witch Man* xiv. 180 She glanced quickly through the sheets of paper lying there, even at the insert in the typewriter. **1950** *Jrnl. Acoustical Soc. Amer.* XXII. 655/1 (*heading*) Magnetic insert earphone insertable in the ear of the user... This small telephone receiver is of the earphone type such as is used with hearing aids. **1955** *Gloss. Acoustical Terms* (*B.S.I.*) 24 *Insert earphone*, an earphone of small dimensions associated with a fitting for insertion into the auditory meatus. **1961** *Times* 29 Aug. 13/7 Special inserts telling the story behind this new cigarette are contained in each packet. **1962** *B.B.C. Handbk.* 51 The BBC contributed 116 programmes and received a total of 199 complete programmes or inserts from the network. **1968** *Bodl. Libr. Rec.* VIII. 62 The printing of book-form catalogues is the principal aim of the project; these catalogues are to be maintained up to date by insert sheets. **1970** *Globe & Mail* (Toronto) 26 Sept. 52/1 (Advt.), Men's Leather Palm Wool Gloves. Expertly fashioned of a bulky knit wool with slip-resistant leather palm inserts. **1971** D. POTTER *Brit. Eliz. Stamps* 11 The latest area to have taken up Queen Elizabeth British issues is Western Europe, and the Post Office has responded with overseas agencies and translation inserts in their packaged sets. **1972** *N.Y. Law Jrnl.* 31 Oct. 4/8 Such warranties can be found in many places: in the advertisements of the product, in the circulars or package inserts accompanying it.

insertable (ɪnˈsɜːtəb(ə)l), *a.* [f. INSERT *v.* + -ABLE.] Capable of being inserted; as in ***insertable-tooth saw***, one with removable teeth.

1875 KNIGHT *Dict. Mech.* **1971** *Timber Trades Jrnl.* 14 Aug. 58/1 DCE..will exhibit their Dalmatic insertable filters in a new 'knocked down' kit form on stand 21.

†**in'sertation.** *Obs. rare*⁻⁰. [ad. late L. *insertātiōn-em*, n. of action f. *insertāre*, frequentative of *inserĕre* to INSERT.] = INSERTION.

1623 COCKERAM II, Any thing Added, *Additament, Insertation.*

in'serted, *ppl. a.* [f. INSERT *v.* + -ED¹.] Set or put in; fitted in, ingrafted. **b.** *Entom.* Set deeply; not free. †**c.** *Archit.* (See quot. 1727.)

1598 FLORIO, *Inserito*, set in, put in, ingrafted, added, ioined, mixed, brought in, inserted. **1621** SANDYS *Ovid's Met.* VI. (1626) 109 The combs inserted tooth..Betweene the warp suppress the rising woofe. **1712** POPE *Vertum. & Pomona* 13 Now the cleft rind inserted graffs receives. **1727–41** CHAMBERS *Cycl.* s.v. *Column*, Column inserted, or backed, is that let into a wall, a third or fourth part of its diameter. **1826** KIRBY & SP. *Entomol.* IV. 306 [The head] Inserted, when the head is partly withdrawn within the trunk.

inserter (ɪnˈsɜːtə(r)). [f. INSERT *v.* + -ER¹. See also INSERTOR.] One who inserts.

1611 [see INSERTOR 1]. **1673** H. STUBBE *Further Vind. Dutch War* App. 62 Such clauses or words as are put in to prevent disputes ought not to..prejudice the inserter. **1835** *Tait's Mag.* II. 577 Advertisements..which produce the inserters no adequate return. **1882–3** SCHAFF *Encycl. Relig. Knowl.* I. 280 [Apocrypha] were acknowledged by their inserters not to belong to the canon.

inserting (ɪnˈsɜːtɪŋ), *vbl. sb.* [f. INSERT *v.* + -ING¹.] The action or process of inserting; something inserted. *spec.* = INSERTION 2 b (? *obs.*).

1611 FLORIO, *Insertatione*, an inserting, an insertion. **1623** MEADE in Ellis *Orig. Lett.* Ser. I. III. 150 The King being much disquieted at the inserting of these conditions. **1647** TORSHELL *Design Harmonize Bible* in *Phenix* (1721) I. 103 The greatest variety of transposition and inserting. **1847** WEBSTER *Inserting*, something set in, as lace, etc., into garments. **1879** *N. Y. Fashion Bazar* 22 Nov. 10/2 The latest

is a ruff of fine plaitings of Breton lace, some-times four rows upon a narrow inserting, again put on a shell shape. **1886** *Harper's Mag.* Nov. 836/1 An elaborate trousseau made chiefly of tucks and insertings and edgings.

insertion (ɪn'sɜːʃən). [ad. L. *insertiōn-em*, n. of action f. *inserĕre* to INSERT: cf. F. *insertion* (in sense 2, Paré, 16th c.).]

1. a. The action of inserting, setting or putting in; introduction into or between: see INSERT vb.

1598 FLORIO, *Insertatione*, an intermedling, a grafting, an implying, an insertion. **1675** OGILBY *Brit.* Advt., The Work is capable of Emendation by Insertion. **1750** JOHNSON *Rambler* No. 23 ¶6 In every work of imagination..the insertion of incidents and use of decorations may be varied a thousand ways. **1794** G. ADAMS *Nat. & Exp. Philos.* III. xxx. 204 The progressive motion of the parts from the point of impact is stopped by the insertion of the lead [into the ivory balls]. **1857** DUNGLISON *Med. Lex.* 502 The word *insertion* has likewise been used by pathologists for the act of inoculating or introducing a virus into the body. **1860** TYNDALL *Glac.* I. xxiv. 360, I have tried whether the insertion of a pin would produce the collapse of the bubbles. **1878** L. P. MEREDITH *Teeth* 220 The proper insertion of artificial teeth. *Mod. Newspaper Notice*, Trade notices are charged at the rate of 1/6 per insertion. All communications in reference to the insertion of Advertisements to be sent to the Advertisement Manager.

b. *Astronautics.* = INJECTION 1 d; also **insertion point** = *injection point.*

1962 J. GLENN in *Into Orbit* 192 The computers..had indicated that the insertion of the capsule was good for a minimum of seven orbits. **1962** A. SHEPARD in *Ibid.* 174 During the first four and a half minutes of launch, before we reach the insertion point and the 'Go' or 'No Go' decision as to orbit. **1963** C. MCLAUGHLIN *Space Age Dict.* (ed. 2) 86 Insertion point. That point where a spacecraft acquires a centrifugal force equal to the gravitational field force and goes into orbit.

2. a. That which is inserted; an inserted addition, piece, or part; a word or part inserted in a writing or print; a page inserted in a book; anything inserted in a newspaper, postal packet, etc.

1624 GATAKER *Transubst.* 117 In Fulbertus his workes.. they have with a foule insertion branded them [words] for hereticall. **1682** GREW *Anat. Trunks* I. ii. §1 The Parenchymous Part of the Wood..hath this property, To be disposed into many Rays, or Diametral Insertions, running betwixt so many Lignous Portions, from the Barque to the Pith. **1707** *Curios. in Husb. & Gard.* 37 In the Root..are.. the Skin, the Parenchyma, the Lignous Body, the Insertions, and the Pith. **1742** WEST *Let.* in *Gray's Poems* (1775) 146, I am only sorry you follow the blunders of Broukhusius, all whose insertions are nonsense. **1841** LANE *Arab. Nts.* I. 58 When I find trifling insertions of this kind to be requisite in my translation, I shall not deem it necessary to mention them in a note.

b. *Needlework.* Embroidery or ornamental needlework, made to be inserted or sewed into plain material, for decorative purposes; a piece or detached portion of such work.

c **1840** LADY WILTON *Art of Needlework* xvi. 267 Patterns, without any edging, were seemingly designed for what we should now call 'insertion' work or lace. **1858** SIMMONDS *Dict. Trade*, *Insertions*, narrow strips of lace, embroidered muslin or cambric, sold for inlets in handkerchiefs, dresses, etc. **1864** SALA in *Daily Tel.* 18 June, It was the 'extras' that did the mischief—the *ruches*, the *bouffantes*, the lace, the innumerable yards of 'insertion'. **1881** *Daily News* 22 Aug. 3/2 A white straw hat, trimmed with buff insertion. **1897** *Globe* 18 Feb. 6/3 A band of lace insertion.

3. *Anat., Entom., Bot.* The attachment of a muscle, external organ, etc., as to place or manner.

1578 BANISTER *Hist. Man* I. 17 Some necessary Asperitie, seruing for the insertion of two Muscles. **1651** *Raleigh's Ghost* 109 The connexions or insertions of one threed [of a spider's web] with another..are most strange. **1807** J. G. SMITH *Phys. Bot.* 144 We shall first explain their [leaves'] different situations, insertions, forms, and surfaces. **1870** HOOKER *Stud. Flora* 14 Anthers erect, insertion basal. **1875** BENNETT & DYER *Sachs' Bot.* 167 If the surface of an axial structure..is imagined to be continued through the base of each lateral member, the section forms its Plane of Insertion. An imaginary point in this is considered its organic centre, but does not usually correspond to its geometrical centre; this point may be termed the Point of Insertion. **1883** C. J. WILLS *Mod. Persia* 105 A black mark running from the mane to the insertion of the tail.

4. *Comb.*, as ***insertion stitch***, ***-success***; **insertion loss** *Electr.*, the decrease in the power delivered to a load (or in the voltage across it or the current through it) as a result of the insertion of a four-terminal device or network between it and the source, expressed (usu. logarithmically, in decibels or nepers) in terms of the ratio of the power, etc., without the network in place to that with it; similarly **insertion gain**, the negative of the insertion loss when expressed in logarithmic units.

1930 T. E. SHEA *Transmission Networks & Wave Filters* ii. 49 A negative insertion loss is an insertion gain, and corresponds to an increase in load current amplitude as the result of inserting a network in a circuit. **1964** V. UZUNOGLU *Semiconductor Network Analysis & Design* v. 69 The insertion gain of an amplifier connected between a source and load impedance (both being specified) is defined as $P_{ins} = 10 \log P_{out}/P_{n}$, where P_{n} is the power which would be delivered to the load if the amplifier were removed. **1930** T. E. SHEA *Transmission Networks & Wave Filters* ii. 49 Insertion loss measures the actual change in load current caused by the insertion of a net-work. **1971** KIM & MEADOWS *Mod. Network Analysis* vi. 241 The behavior of a two-port coupling network such as a filter or equalizer..for use in a communication, signal-processing, or control system is frequently studied or specified in terms of an insertion loss defined in terms of voltage or power ratios. **1932** D. C. MINTER *Mod. Needlecraft* 51/2 Various.. insertion stitches may be formed by working an edging stitch, as braid edging or Antwerp edging. **1934** M. THOMAS *Dict. Embroidery Stitches* 128 This simple insertion stitch consists of a row of braid edging stitch worked along both edges of the material to be joined. **1967** *100 Embroidery Stitches* (J. & P. Coats Ltd.) 35 Buttonhole insertion stitch ..consists of groups of four buttonhole stitches worked alternately on each piece of fabric to be joined. **1897** *Allbutt's Syst. Med.* II. 561 The 'insertion-success' of skilled vaccinators is very large, amounting to 97–98 per cent.

Hence **in'sertional** *a.*, of the nature of an insertion; put in as an insertion. **in'sertioned** *ppl. a. Needlework*, ornamented with an insertion; having some ornamental material worked in as an insertion.

1867 *Contemp. Rev.* IV. 325 A sonorous triplet made up by an insertional line. **1894** *Season* X. No. 9. 36/2 The coverlet was of satin, insertioned with linen open thread work.

insertive (ɪn'sɜːtɪv), *a.* [ad. L. *insertīv-us*, f. *insert-*: see INSERT *v.* and -IVE.] Characterized by insertion; of ingrafted origin.

a **1634** RANDOLPH *Poems, Love fondly refused* 42 If the fresh Trunke have sap enough to give That each insertive branch may live. **1727** in BAILEY vol. II. **1881** FAIRBAIRN *Stud. Life Christ* xiv. 247 His sympathy had a strange insertive power.

†**in'sertment.** *Bot. Obs. rare.* [f. INSERT + -MENT.] That which is inserted or placed between; a former term for the *medullary rays*; = INSERTION 2.

1671 GREW in *Phil. Trans.* VI. 3039 The Insertment and Pith, proceeding also from the Plume, as the same in the Root from the Radicle. **1671** —— *Anat. Pl.* ii. §10 The next Part observable in the Root, is the Insertment... In dissecting a Root, I find, that the Cortical Body doth not only environ the Lignous, but is also wedg'd, and in many Pieces inserted into it; and that the said inserted Pieces make not a meer Indenture, but transmit and shoot them-selves quite through as far as the Pith. **1814** *Edin. Rev.* XXII. 257 They were named insertments..and constitute what is vulgarly termed the silver grain of the wood.

†**in'sertor.** *Obs.* Also 6 -our. [agent-n. in L. form from *inserĕre* to INSERT.]

1. = INSERTER, q.v.

1598 FLORIO, *Insertatore*, a medler, an intermedler, a grafter, an insertor [**1611** inserter].

2. Puttenham's name for the figure PARENTHESIS.

1589 PUTTENHAM *Eng. Poesie* III. xii[i]. (Arb.) 180 Your first figure of tollerable disorder is (*Parenthesis*) or by an English name the (Insertour), and is when ye will seeme.. to peece or graffe in the middest of your tale an vnnecessary parcell of speach.

†**in'serve,** *v. Obs. rare*$^{-1}$. [ad. L. *inservīre* to be serviceable, to serve, f. *in-* (IN-^{2}) + *servīre* to serve.] *intr.* To be of service or use *to*; to conduce *to.*

1683 T. HUNT *Def. Charter Lond.* 25 The Duke of Guise ..had inserved to some most detestable Villany, to please the rage or lust of a Tyrant. **1706** in PHILLIPS.

in-service *attrib.*: see IN *prep.* 18.

†**in'serviceable,** *a. Obs. rare.* [IN-^{3}.] Unserviceable.

1607 MARKHAM *Caval.* IV. Ded., Through whome there is ..multitudes of Horses spoyled and made inseruiceable. **1666** J. SMITH *Old Age* (1752) 12 It [age] doth certainly induce such a *cachexia* or ill habit that it renders us inserviceable to our ends.

†**in'servience.** *Obs. rare*$^{-1}$. [f. next: see -ENCE.] Serviceableness, usefulness.

1657 TOMLINSON *Renou's Disp.* 472 Those [supellectuals] ..are more expetible for their ornament..then their inservience.

†**in'servient,** *a. Obs.* [ad. L. *inservient-em*, pr. pple. of *inservīre*, f. *in-* (IN-^{2}) + *servīre* to serve. Cf. *subservient.*]

1. Serving, servile.

1646 SIR T. BROWNE *Pseud. Exp.* I. i. 3 Although their intellectualls had not failed in the theorie of truth, yet did the inservient and brutall faculties controle the suggestion of reason.

2. Serving or subservient *to* some end; serviceable, conducive, assisting.

1646 SIR T. BROWNE *Pseud. Ep.* III. xxi. 158 Any parts inservient to that intention. **1675** E. W[ILSON] *Spadacr. Dunelm.* 41 A *Caput mortuum*..inservient for mixing with cicatrizing Plaisters. **1688** BOYLE *Final Causes Nat. Things* IV. 197 The fabrick of the mouth and other parts inservient to the reception of aliments. **1802** J. JAMIESON *Use Sacr. Hist.* II. III. xi. 331 That part of man's body which is inservient to generation.

b. Accessary *to*, forming an accessary of.

1708 *Phil. Trans.* XXVI. 171 A Brass Pommel, inservient to a Sea-coal Grate, weighing nine Ounces.

†**insess,** *sb. Obs. rare*$^{-1}$. [ad. med.L. *insessus*, f. *insidēre* to sit in; cf. It. *insesso* (Florio).] = INSESSION 1 b.

1657 TOMLINSON *Renou's Disp.* 186 As a Bath is a Lavacre of the whole body..so an Insess of half the body. [**1706** PHILLIPS, *Insessus*, a Bath for the Belly and Lower Parts.]

†**in'sess,** *v. Obs. rare*$^{-1}$. [f. L. *insess-*, ppl. stem of *insidēre* to sit in, dwell in, occupy.] *trans.* To dwell in, inhabit, 'possess'. Cf. INSESSION 3.

a **1641** BP. MOUNTAGU *Acts & Mon.* (1642) 206 Being insessed and acted by the Devill, they babled many lies.

†**in'session.** *Obs.* [ad. late L. *insessiōn-em*, n. of action f. *insidēre* to sit in, f. *in-* (IN-^{2}) + *sedēre* to sit. Cf. It. *insessioni* 'certain bathing medicines' (Florio).]

1. The action of sitting in a bath.

1652 FRENCH *Yorksh. Spa* iv. 49 The second way of using water outwardly is called insession or sitting in water up to the navel. **1684** tr. *Bonet's Merc. Compit.* x. 365 An insession in Bath-waters, and Pumping upon the place affected. [**1855** MAYNE *Expos. Lex.*, *Insessio*, old term for the state of sitting over the vapour of a hot bath; insession.]

b. A bath in which the patient sits with the lower part of the body immersed in water or some other liquid; a hip-bath or sitz-bath.

1559 MORWYNG *Evonym.* 367 Fuchsius and other wryt of fomentacions, apposicions, embroches, litle bags and insessions. **1590** BARROUGH *Meth. Physick* III. xxxviii. (1639) 163 You must release and loosen the reines..with foments, cataplasmes and insessions. **1601** HOLLAND *Pliny* Expl. Words Art, *Insessions* be bathing tubs or vessels halfe full wherein the patient may sit vp to the middle or aboue in some conuenient decoction. **1657** TOMLINSON *Renou's Disp.* 187 Some make Insessions of the decoction of Tripes to cure the exsiccation..of the belly.

2. Inhabitation, indwelling (by a spirit). *rare*$^{-1}$.

a **1641** BP. MOUNTAGU *Acts & Mon.* (1642) 191 The Prophets have by Him Illumination and Insession. He takes possession of their soule, dwelling in them.

insessor (ɪn'sɛsə(r)). *rare.* [a. L. *insessor* (rare), agent-n. f. *insidēre*: see prec.] One who sits in or on.

1835 KIRBY *Hab. & Inst. Anim.* I. Introd. 94 In the different visions of the appearance of the Deity, as the Insessor of the chariot of the cherubim.

‖**Insessores** (ɪnsɛ'sɔəriːz), *sb. pl. Ornith.* [mod.L., pl. of *insessor*, agent-n. from *insidēre* to sit on or upon (in ancient L. found only in the sense 'besetter (of a way, etc.)'.] The Perchers or Perching birds, having feet with three toes in front and one behind, adapted for perching on trees; the name given by Vigors in 1823 to the second Order of Birds in his classification, coinciding nearly with the *Passeres* and *Picæ* of Linnæus.

'Though long accepted without hesitation by most British and many foreign authors, the composite nature of the group has now been recognized, and the use of the name is generally abandoned' (A. NEWTON *Dict. Birds*, 1893).

1823 VIGORS in *Trans. Linn. Soc.* XIV. 405 As the distinctive characters in the other orders are taken from the peculiarities of their feet..I wish to follow the same plan in the present case, and to designate this order by the title of *Insessores* or *Perching Birds.* **1872** NICHOLSON *Palæont.* 395 The Insessores form the largest order of existing birds. **1875** BLAKE *Zool.* 91 In some Insessores it [the carotid artery] is only found on the left side.

insessorial (ɪnsɛ'sɔərɪəl), *a. Ornith.* [f. L. type **insessōri-us* (f. *insessor*: see prec.) + -AL^{1}.] Of or pertaining to the *Insessores*, or Perchers.

1837 *New Monthly Mag.* L. 195 It is in the Insessorial order of birds that the songsters abound. **1874** COUES *Birds N.W.* 321 Claws..hardly more than insessorial, instead of raptorial, in character.

inset ('ɪnsɛt), *sb.* [f. IN *adv.* 11 d + SET *sb.*]

1. A setting in, inflow, influx (of water). †**b.** A place where water flows in, a channel (*obs.*).

1559 in Boys *Sandwich* (1792) 736 By stoppinge of the northe mouthe and diuers other insets. **1875** LYELL *Princ. Geol.* I. II. xx. 498 There are tidal influences combined with the general insets from the Atlantic. **1881** T. G. BOWLES *Flotsam & Jetsam* (1883) 244 The inset into the Bay of Biscay, which..runs at the rate of a mile an hour.

attrib. **1896** *Westm. Gaz.* 20 June 5/2 The Drummond Castle was drawn by a strong inset current to the inner side of the Island of Ushant.

2. That which is set in or inserted.

†**a.** An innate or implanted idea. *Obs. rare.*

1587 GOLDING *De Mornay* Pref. 8 These [witnessings] are common insightes, or insets (as a man may tearme them), namelie the perswasion of the Godhead, the conscience of euil [etc.]. *Ibid.*, Those common and generall Insets haue remained barren in the most part of men.

b. A recess. *rare*$^{-1}$.

1829 J. HODGSON in J. Raine *Mem.* (1858) II. 161 The wall is very perfect..having frequent insets.

c. An extra page or set of pages inserted in a sheet or book (see quot. 1875); an advertisement on a separate leaf inserted in a magazine, etc.

1875 KNIGHT *Dict. Mech.* II. 1189/2 *Inset*,..a certain portion of the printed sheet in 12mo, 24mo, etc., which is cut off before folding and set into the middle of the folded sheet. **1879** *Print Trades Jrnl.* No. 26. 4 A four-page inset with cuts, this portion of the journal is carefully rolled. **1883** C. E. DOBLE in *Academy* 26 May 368/2 My copy..has an inset

of eight pages between pp. 240 and 241. **1892** *Pall Mall G.* 25 June 5/2 To print papers from duplicate plates, with an 'inset'—that is, an extra page gummed in mechanically—whenever desired. **1893** *Bookseller* 201 From two pounds weight of Magazines I have this day taken out fourteen ounces of insets.

d. A smaller map, picture, etc. inserted within the border of a larger one.

1881 *Athenæum* No. 2810. 310/3 The clearness of the maps and their pictorial insets deserves all praise. **1887** *Philips' Handy-vol. Atlas World* Contents, Ireland—Ulster, with inset of Belfast and Environs. **1894** *Nation* (N.Y.) 30 Aug. 161/2 Two admirable maps..with insets indicating the geology, the comparative density of population, and the agriculture of eastern equatorial Africa.

e. A piece of cloth inserted or let into a dress.

1894 *Paris Mode* No. 3. 31/2 An inset at the neck and shoulders, front and back. **1899** *Daily News* 16 Dec. 6/5 The skirt has little insets of lace all round the edge.

in'set, *v.* Also 4 ynsett. Pa. pple. **inset**: in sense 5 also **insetted.** [f. IN-[1] or IN *adv.* + SET *v.*[1] Cf. MDu. and MHG. *insetten*, Du. *inzetten*; MHG. *insetzen*, Ger. *einsetzen*, Da. *indsætte*, Sw. *insätta*.]

†**1.** *trans.* ? To institute, initiate. (Only in OE.: rendering L. *instituĕre*.) *Obs.*

c **900** tr. *Bæda's Hist.* IV. xxiii[i]. (1890) 334 þa seolfan, þe ær þæt mynster heoldon & rehton, heo mid þeodscipum regollices lifes insette & trymede [*etiam hoc disciplinis vitæ regularis instituit*].

†**2.** To set (a person) in office; to appoint. *Obs.*

a **1300** *E.E. Psalter* lxv[i]. 12 þou in-set [L. *imposuisti*] men, mani swa Over our hevedes to be þa. *a* **1572** KNOX *Hist. Ref.* Wks. 1846 I. 357 Commanding the Laird of Killfaunes, insett Provest be the Quene..to cast up the portis of the town.

†**3.** To insert, ingraft. Const. *to*. (= L. *inserĕre*.) *Obs.*

c **1374** CHAUCER *Boeth.* II. pr. iii. 25 (Camb. MS.) So þat wan thise thinges stynten forto sowne in eres, the sorwe þat is insett greueth the thowght. **1382** WYCLIF *2 Macc.* vii. 21 She monestide eche of hem..and ynsettinge mans ynwitt to wommans thouȝt, saide to hem [etc.]. —— *Rom.* xi. 24 Forwhi if thou..aȝens kynde ert inseet in to a good olyue tre, how moche more thei that by kynde, schulen be ynsett to her olyue tre?

4. To set (jewels) in (gold, or the like). *rare*[−1].

1658 W. SANDERSON *Graphice* 69 Thus having inriched you with a Mine of Precious stones, and pearles, with Gold to inset them.

5. To set in, insert; *spec.* to insert as an inset (INSET *sb.* 2 c); to fix an inset in (a sheet), an extra page in (a newspaper), etc.

1890 W. J. GORDON *Foundry* 208 This useful contrivance ..delivering the papers inset, pasted, cut top and bottom, turned out compact as a pamphlet. **1896** *Newsagents' Chron.* 3 Oct. 3/2 Advertisements printed on a sheet which was insetted. **1897** F. C. CONYBEARE in *Expositor* Apr. 302 The numbers inset in my translation indicate the pages of the Armenian text. **1899** *Month* Mar. 328 An excellent map containing three smaller plans inset.

Hence **in'setted** *ppl. a.*

1893 *Westm. Gaz.* 19 Apr. 7/2 The extra cost of carriage consequent upon insetted advertisements in magazines.

inset ('ɪnsɛt), *ppl. a.* [IN *adv.* 11 b.]

†**1.** Implanted, innate, native. *Obs.*

1545 RAYNOLD *Byrth Mankynde* (1564) B iv, The honest ..maintaining of the inset and naturall beautie in a woman. **1594** T. B. *La Primaud. Fr. Acad.* II. *Seneca*, The harth from whence proceedeth all that inset and natiue heate.

2. = INLAID (or ? set with precious stones).

1588 *Wills & Inv. N.C.* (Surtees) II. 179 One lardge Danske chist, with insett worke.

3. Inserted as an inset.

1885 *Pall Mall G.* 11 June 6/1 Each part will contain ten page plates, four illustrations in the text, and one inset plate. **1891** *Times* 14 Apr. 3/2 The map..now includes inset maps containing charts of the mouths of the Zambesi, of Delagoa Bay [etc.].

†**'in,setter**[1]. *Obs.* [app. error for *insitter*, f. IN *adv.* 11 e + SITTER[1].] An indweller; one who resides in the place.

1712 PRIDEAUX *Direct. Ch.-wardens* (ed. 4) 55 These say, that Out-setters, by reason of the Lands which they occupy in the Parish, are as much Parishioners as the In-setters.

insetter[2] ('ɪn,sɛtə(r)). [f. INSET *v.* + -ER[1].] A person who, or device which, insets sheets.

1891 *Pall Mall Gaz.* 27 Oct. 7/2 Compositors, printers,.. stereotypers, insetters. **1960** *Economist* 16 Apr. 275/1 An electronic bulwark called the insetter, which will enable national newspapers to carry full colour pictures—and advertisements—this autumn. *Ibid.*, It is the insetter device that has the job of correcting paper tension and high-speed 'wobble'.

'in,setting, *vbl. sb.* [IN *adv.* 11 c.] **a.** *Printing.* = INDENTION 2. **b.** Insertion, fixing.

1853 RUSKIN *Stones Ven.* II. vii. §20. 247 The cement and various insetting of the balconies. **1867** *Hymns Virg.* 58 *note*, Written without breaks, till near the bottom of p. 131, as marked by the insetting of the even lines here. **1900** *Oxf. Mag.* 7 Mar. 266/2 Explanatory sections—such as might be relegated to footnotes in a modern book—are indicated by small type and insetting.

inseverable (ɪn'sɛvərəb(ə)l), *a.* [IN-[3].] Incapable of being severed or broken; inseparable.

1661 R. L'ESTRANGE *Interest Mistaken* 146 This would seem to imply a more Inseverable Interest than I ayme at. **1841** CATLIN *N. Amer. Ind.* II. lviii. 225 The offence is lost in the inseverable iniquity in which all join. **1880** SIR E. REED *Japan* I. p. xxiv, Ancient and inseverable bonds.

inseverably (ɪn'sɛvərəblɪ), *adv.* [f. prec. + -LY[2].] In an inseverable manner; inseparably.

1640 FULLER *Joseph's Coat* v. (1867) 157 Lest peradventure..we have inseverably been overtaken with the sin of gluttony. **1849** J. WILSON in *Blackw. Mag.* LXVI. 625 What a hand that was which bound the two into one—inseverably! **1882** DALLINGER *Creator* 82 Mind is inseverably associated with neural matter.

insew(e, inseygne, obs. ff. ENSUE, ENSIGN *v.*

†**in'shade,** *v. Obs. rare*[−1]. [f. IN-[2] + SHADE *v.*: cf. ENSHADE.] *trans.* To shade; to tint or vary one colour with another.

1613–16 W. BROWNE *Brit. Past.* I. v. 88 Whose Lilly-white, inshaded with the Rose Had that man seene, who sung th' Eneidos, Dido had in obliuion slept.

†**in'shadow,** *v. Obs. rare*[−0]. [IN-[2].]

1611 FLORIO, *Inombrare*, to inshadow, to darken.

‖**inshallah** (ɪn'ʃɑːlɑː), *int.* Representing Arab. *in šā' Allah* if Allah wills (it), a very frequent pious ejaculation among Muslims.

1857 J. BOWRING *Kingdom & People of Siam* II. xvi. 304 Inshallah! Such promptitude was, I believe, never before exhibited in an Asiatic Court. **1867** 'OUIDA' *Under Two Flags* II. iii. 74 But,—Inshallah! we endure only for a while. .. Allah is great! we can wait. **1909** M. DIVER *Candles in Wind* xviii. 183 Guns—*Inshallah*! The guns of the Maharajah. **1911** T. E. LAWRENCE *Let.* 21 May (1938) 104, I have been photographing this last week—and will more next. Developing too inshallah. **1922** *Ibid.* 20 Nov. 384 I'm hoping to find a regular means of dodging up to London... In a few days, insh'allah. **1959** W. BURROUGHS *Naked Lunch* 40 We aren't a matriarchy here, *Insh'allah*. **1971** *Shankar's Weekly* (Delhi) 11 Apr. 4/2 Nadir Shah Yahya Khan may fancy himself as the Scourge of Dacca. But people's voices wild with pain, Inshallah! surely they will rise again.

†**in'shanked,** *a. Obs. rare*[−0]. [IN-[2].] Having a shank.

1611 FLORIO, *Infustito*, instaked, inshanked.

†**'inshape.** *Obs. rare.* [f. IN *adv.* 12 + SHAPE *sb.*[1]] Inward shape; internal form.

1587 GOLDING *De Mornay* vi. 66 Socrates..taught that God is a minde, and that in the same there is a certaine Inshape, which Inshape as in respect of God, is the knowledge which God hath of himselfe. *Ibid.* xxvii. 423 This marke is..of the very substance and inshape of Religion.

inshave ('ɪnʃeɪv). [f. IN *adv.* 12 + SHAVE.] A tool used by coopers for shaving or planing the inner face of staves.

1875 KNIGHT *Dict. Mech.* 1189/2 *Inshave* (Coopering), a jointer having a convex-edged bit, on which the inner faces of staves are dressed.

†**in'sheaf,** *v. Obs. rare*[−0]. [IN-[2].]

1611 FLORIO, *Immazzettare*, to imbundle, to insheafe, to make into handfuls.

insheath, obs. form of ENSHEATH.

†**in'shed,** *v. Obs.* [f. IN-[1] + SHED *v.*; tr. L. *infundĕre*.]

1. *trans.* To shed or pour something upon; to sprinkle or wet with a liquid.

1382 WYCLIF *Dan.* iv. 22 In dewe of heuene thou shalt be inshed [1388 bished, L. *infunderis*]. —— *Judith* vii. 23 Osias risende, the teris inshed [1388 bisched with teeris, L. *infusus lacrymis*].

2. To shed or pour in; to infuse.

1435 MISYN *Fire Love* 41 Slik swetnes of likynge hete and songe to a lufand saule is insched. *Ibid.* 99 Euer-lastynge lufe gladis & plenteuus lykynge inschedis.

So †**'in,shed** *ppl. a.*; **'in,shedding** *vbl. sb.*

1435 MISYN *Fire Love* 62 Of insched gladnes. **1851** RUSKIN *Stones Ven.* I. xx. (1874) 228 The starred inshedding of light through his vaulted roof.

inshell, enshell (ɪn'ʃɛl, ɛn-), *v. rare.* [f. IN-[1], EN-[1] + SHELL *sb.*] *trans.* To withdraw within the shell. Also *fig.*

1607 SHAKS. *Cor.* IV. vi. 45 Auffidius..Thrusts forth his hornes againe into the world Which were In-shelled, when Martius stood for Rome. **1814** *Prophetess* I. i, The foes Shrink and enshell themselves within their town. **1877** BLACKIE *Wise Men* 302 None In mortal frame enshelled.

†**in'shielder.** *Obs. rare.* [f. *inshield = ENSHIELD *v.* + -ER[1].] One who shields; a protector.

a **1300** *E.E. Psalter* cxx[i]. 5 Laverd in-schilder be Over þe right-hand of þe.

inshining ('ɪn,ʃaɪnɪŋ), *vbl. sb.* [IN *adv.* 11 c.] A shining in; illumination. So **'in,shining** *ppl. a.* [IN *adv.* 11 a], that shines in.

1727 W. MATHER *Yng. Man's Comp.* 412 To receive the Inshining of Grace. **1847** BERNARD BARTON *Select.* (1849) 57 That inshining light which enlightens every regenerate Christian. **1882** *Homiletic Monthly* (U.S.) Oct. 30 Even the inshining of God's Spirit into our hearts still leaves us only men. **1887** ANNA FORBES *Insulinde* 237 The mass of human beings..were better individualised by the inshining moonbeams than by the sparsely scattered lamps.

†**inship** (ɪn'ʃɪp), *v. Obs.* [f. IN-[1] + SHIP *sb.* Cf. MDu. *inscepen*, Du. *inschepen*, Ger. *einschiffen*, Da. *indskibe*, Sw. *inskeppa*.] *trans.* To put into a ship; to ship; to embark.

1591 SHAKS. *1 Hen. VI*, V. i. 49 (Fol. 4) See them guarded, And safely brought to Dover, where inshipp'd [*folios* 1–3 wherein ship'd] Commit them to the fortune of the sea. **1615** DANIEL *Hymen's Tri.* Wks. (1717) 135 When she was thus inshipp'd..she spies a Woman sitting with a Child.

†**in'shirt,** *v. Obs. rare*[−0]. [IN-[2].] *trans.* To clothe in a shirt.

1611 FLORIO, *Incamisciare*, to inshirt, to insmocke.

inshoot ('ɪnʃuːt). *Baseball.* [f. IN *adv.* + SHOOT *sb.*[1]] The act of causing the ball to move rapidly inward, as a ball that is pitched with a curve; a ball which moves thus.

1892 *Outing* (U.S.) Jan. 302/1 An old ball player..taught Harry to pitch and to try some curves and 'in shoots' of his own device. **1897** *Encycl. Sport* I. 74/2 A movement of the hand, an elevation of the head by the latter [*sc.* the catcher], lets the pitcher know that this ball is to be an in-shoot, the other an out-curve. **1904** *Sci. Amer.* 16 July 42/3 The right-handed pitcher delivers his 'outshoot' with much greater effect of incurve at the plate than he can accomplish with his 'inshoot'... The speed of the ball for 'outshoot' and 'inshoot' is the same. **1940** H. L. MENCKEN *Happy Days* 230 When I ventured on an inshoot it was apt to be recovered, not by the catcher, but by the third baseman.

in shore, 'in-'shore, *adv. phr.* (*a.*) [f. IN *adv.* + SHORE. Cf. INLAND *adv.*]

A. *adv.* From seaward in towards the shore; close to the shore.

1748 *Anson's Voy.* II. v. 186 We saw a ship in shore.. plying up the coast. *Ibid.* xi. 251 The two Cutters..were.. sent in shore. **1812** *Sporting Mag.* XXXIX. 87 She was.. driven inshore by some boats. **1856** KANE *Arct. Expl.* II. xxvi. 267, I determined to keep in-shore, in spite of the barricades of ice. **1884** PAE *Eustace* 80 They went closer inshore.

b. *inshore of*: Nearer to the shore than (something else); between (something) and the shore.

1859 in *Merc. Marine Mag.* (1860) VII. 49 The Havilah passing in-shore of the Bombay. **1860** MAURY *Phys. Geog. Sea* (Low) viii. §397 Inshore of..the Black Stream, along the eastern shores of Asia, is found a..current of cold water. **1876** DAVIS *Polaris Exp.* v. 110 The Polaris was anchored just inshore of the largest iceberg.

B. *attrib.* or *adj.* Lying, situated, or carried on near or close to the shore.

1701 in Picton *L'pool Munic. Rec.* (1883) I. 308 Both..y[e] inshore and outward ships. *Ibid.* 309 Those that lay their inshore anchors without buoys. **1798** LD. ST. VINCENT in Nicolas *Nelson's Disp.* 11 May (1845) III. 15 You shall also have some choice Fellows of the in-shore Squadron. **1855** *Cornwall* 13 During the month of August..the principal or inshore fishing begins. **1885** *Times* 25 May 9 The in-shore waters of the Scotch coast are being overfished.

b. Moving or directed in towards the shore.

1882 C. ELTON *Orig. Eng. Hist.* 51 With a high tide and an inshore wind their homes and lives were always in danger of destruction.

†**in'shore,** *v. Obs.* Also 6 enshoar, 7 enshore. [f. IN-[1] + SHORE *sb.*] *trans.* To put on shore; to land.

1577 STANYHURST *Descr. Irel.* in *Holinshed's Chron.* (1807–8) VI. 38 They are no sooner inshored, than they yeeld up their ghosts. **1583** —— *Æneis* I. (Arb.) 29 Theare they were enshoared, wheare thow shalt shortlye see toun wals. *a* **1618** J. DAVIES *Wit's Pilgr.* (1878) 40 Death.. Enshore my Soule neer drownd in flesh, and bloud.

†**'inshot.** *Obs.* [f. IN *adv.* 11 d + SHOT *sb.* Cf. *offshoot*.] A piece shooting or projecting inwards; in quot. applied to a part of the sea running into the land.

1555 W. WATREMAN *Fardle Facions* II. vii. 155 An inshot of the Sea, called the Bosome of Parthia [Persian Gulf].

inshow, obs. variant of ENSUE.

inshrine, inshrowd: see ENSHRINE, -SHROUD.

†**insiccate,** *v. Obs. rare*[−0]. [f. L. type **insiccāre* (prob. in med. or mod.L.: cf. obs. F. *ensecher*), f. *in-* (IN-[2]) + *siccāre* to dry.] *trans.* To dry. So †**insiccated** *ppl. a.*; †**insiccation,** drying.

1623 COCKERAM, *Insiccated*, dryed. **1658** PHILLIPS, *Insiccation*, a drying.

†**insiccated,** *a. Obs. rare*[−0] [f. L. *insiccāt-us* undried + -ED[1].] Undried. (Cockeram, 1623 pt. II.)

insicht, Sc. form of INSIGHT *sb.*[2], *Obs.*

inside (,ɪn'saɪd, 'ɪnsaɪd), *sb.*, *a.*, *adv.*, and *prep.* [f. IN *adj.* (*adv.* used *attrib.*) + SIDE. The opposite of *outside* in all senses.

The two parts appear to have naturally even stress, as in *east side*, *right side*, *top side*, *back side*, with a tendency to a stronger on the sb. part. But when used *attrib.*, or when contrasted explicitly or implicitly with *outside*, and often when followed by *of* and a *sb.*, the main stress is on *in*.]

A. *sb.*

1. a. The inner side or surface; that side of anything which is within, or nearer to the centre, or farther from the outer edge or surface; in a foot-path, the side next to the wall, or away from the road.

1504 in *Eng. Gilds* 327 A tabell yn the syde of the halle.. a bynch yn the yn-syde of the tabell. **1535** COVERDALE *1 Kings* vi. 15 Salomon..buylded the walles on the insyde with Ceder tymber. **1583** HOLLYBAND *Campo di Fior* 333 Rubbing it [my pen] against the inside of my cote. **1613** SHAKS. *Hen. VIII*, III. ii. 78 Look'd he o' th' inside of the Paper? **1662** GERBIER *Princ.* (1665) 30 There is a necessary Magnificence to be exprest on the Front and inside of Princely Buildings, answerable to their greatnesse. **1687** A. LOVELL tr. *Thevenot's Trav.* I. 113 Over the third Gate, in the in-side..is this Inscription. **1703** MOXON *Mech. Exerc.* 193 The two insides of the Joynt-Rule Carpenters use. **1838** T. THOMSON *Chem. Org. Bodies* 600 A very thin coating of the acid is deposited equably upon the inside of the vessel. **1894** *Yellow Bk.* I. 193 They might pass me by now, not even give me the inside of the pavement.

b. *Fencing.* (See quot. 1863.)

1692 SIR W. HOPE *Fencing-Master* 22 When you put-by the thrust, you put it by upon the inside of your Sword. **1863** *Archery, Fencing, & Broadsword* (Rtldg.) 46 It is customary for adversaries, on coming to the Guard, to Engage, or to join blades, on what is called the *inside*, that is, the *right* side; although there are occasions on which it is advisable to engage on the outside, or on the left; otherwise called the *Quarte* or *Tierce* sides.

2. a. The inner part, or the space within something; the interior.

c **1550** CHEKE *Matt.* xxiii. 25 Ie clense ye outward part of ye cup and ye disch, but y insijd is ful of robri and vnstaidnes. **1611** SHAKS. *Wint. T.* IV. iv. 833 Shew the in-side of your Purse to the out-side of his hand, and no more adoe. **1671** MILTON *P.R.* IV.58 So well I have disposed My aery microscope—thou mayest behold, Outside and inside both, pillars and roofs. **1796** MORSE *Amer. Geog.* I. 104 The insides of their dwellings exhibit a complete picture of filth and indolence. **1808** JANE AUSTEN *Let.* 20 Nov. (1952) 233 We mean..to go one night to the play. Martha ought to see the inside of the Theatre once while she lives in Southampton. **1819** R. WOODHOUSE *Let.* 20 Sept. in Keats *Lett.* (1958) II. 165 He parted with me at the Coach door—I had the inside all to myself. **1870** L'ESTRANGE *Miss Mitford* I. ii. 37 The company in the inside [of the coach].. being tolerably quiet. **1891** C. ROBERTS *Adrift Amer.* 6, I had a very varied time and learnt something of the inside of a country. **1969** *Times* 12 Nov. 10/7 It took one war to get a foothold in the treaty ports. That still left the 'inside'.

b. *spec.* (ˌɪnˈsaɪd). The interior of the body; the internal organs, esp. the stomach and bowels; the entrails. (Also in *pl.* in same sense.) *colloq.* and *dial.*

[**1581** SIDNEY *Apol. Poetrie* (Arb.) 21 In the body of his work, though the inside and strength were Philosophy, the skinne as it were and beautie, depended most of Poetrie.] **1741-3** WESLEY *Jrnl.* (1749) 91 It was as if their heart, as if all their inside, as if their whole body was tearing all to pieces. **1840** MARRYAT *Poor Jack* xxx, My insides are out of order. **1855** KINGSLEY *Westw. Ho!* iii, So now away home; my inside cries cupboard. **1893** SELOUS *Trav. S.E. Africa* 143 There was a lot of blood about..and some odd portions of a man's inside.

c. *fig.* Inward nature, mind, thought, or meaning. (Sometimes with humorous suggestion of sense b.)

1599 MASSINGER, etc. *Old Law* I. i. Wks. (Rtldg.) 416/1 Come, come, here's none but friends here, we may speak Our insides freely. *a* **1618** SYLVESTER *Hymn St. Lewis* 133 Rebellious Peers, Who..measuring his in-side by his age, Troubled his State with storms of Civill Rage. **1676** *Phil. Trans.* XI. 554 Sueton. hath drawn to life both the Portraictures and Insides of the XII Cæsars. **1749** CHESTERF. *Lett.* (1792) II. 183 In order to judge of the inside of others, study your own. **1833** LAMB *Elia* Ser. II. *Barrenn. Imag. Fac. Mod. Art*, Conscious of the heroic inside of the noble Quixote.

d. The middle or main portion of a period of time, exclusive of the beginning and end. (In quot. 1890, ***in the inside of*** = 'inside of', within: see C.3.) *colloq.*

1890 CLARK RUSSELL *Ocean Trag.* 74 (Farmer) 'Tain't to be done in the inside of a month. **1891** T. HARDY *Tess* (1892) 204 The Reverend Felix..home for the inside of a fortnight. **1894** *Spectator* 10 Feb. 189 Bishops..in order to come to London for the inside of a week..have to alter a number of arrangements.

e. The inner history, the real facts; also, a person in possession of such information. Phr. ***to be on the inside***, to have knowledge that is not generally available.

1904 W. H. SMITH *Promoters* v. 101 I'll give it to you straight, for I happen to know the inside. **1926** *Flynn's* 16 Jan. 637/1 Also he spills th' info as to how many insides they is; that is, how many bargain counters has one of our gang behind it. **1932** *Daily Express* 28 Jan. 15/5, I have chatted with men who are believed to be on the inside, and they have informed me that there will certainly be changes at forward and in the three-quarter line. **1959** *Economist* 18 Apr. 252/3 This desire to be 'on the inside' is no doubt personal as well as nationalist.

3. (ellipt. use of the adj. or adv.) An inside passenger or place in a coach or other vehicle. *colloq.*

1798 CANNING, etc. *Loves Triangles* 179 in *Anti-Jacobin*, So down thy hill, romantic Ashbourn, glides The Derby dilly, carrying Three Insides. **1837** DICKENS *Pickw.* xxviii, The old gentleman inside..informs the other inside that they're going to change directly; on which the other inside wakes himself up. **1838** SOUTHEY *Lett.* (1856) IV. 550 The four insides of a Dover coach are taken for to-morrow morning. **1890** BOLDREWOOD *Col. Reformer* (1891) 128, I picked myself up and went to help out the insides.

4. In advb. phr. ***inside out*** (ˌɪnsaɪd ˈaʊt), formerly also ***inside outwards*** (usually with the verb *turn*): So that the inner side becomes the outer; so as to expose the inside or interior. Also *fig.*, esp. ***to know*** (something) ***inside out***: to know (it) extremely well.

?*a* **1600** *Tarlton's Jests* (Halliw.) Introd. 22 Could you turne him inside out, You would presentlie see, Squeaking [etc.]. **1681-6** J. SCOTT *Chr. Life* (1747) III. 265 [He] turned them inside-outwards, and revealed their hidden Sense to the World. **1692** WASHINGTON tr. *Milton's Def. Pop.* i. (1851) 32 Though one should turn you topsie-turvy, and in-side out, [you] are but a Grammarian. **1772** H. WALPOLE *Last Jrnls.* (1859) I. 7 Turned their coats inside outwards for luck. **1836** *Penny Cycl.* V. 245/2 The polypes..are so simple in their structure that they may be turned inside out like a glove. **1887** JESSOPP *Arcady* vii. 214. **1921** A. HUXLEY *Let.* 24 Aug. (1969) 201 Maria and I have just come back from.. Rome... What a place! It inspires one at once with a kind of passion to know it utterly and inside out. **1967** N. FREELING *Strike Out* 31 A restaurant—that's a simpler affair, and Marguerite knows it inside out.

5. In various games, a position on the field; a player in that position.

1886 W. ARNOTT in B. James *England v Scotland* (1969) ii. 39 The Corinthians..have perfected the tactics of the three insides. **1901** W. H. PICKERING *Hockey for Ladies* ix. 33 Left inside should be able to shoot for she gets as many chances as any other forward. **1905** E. E. WHITE *How to play Hockey* vii. 47 Touch line tactics make it imperative that the two insides should get out of position. **1935** *Encycl. Sports* 289/1 (*Association Football*) The game is begun by one of the centre-forwards, who usually taps the ball gently to either of his insides. *Ibid.* 517/2 (*Rugby*) One common fault with three-quarters..is running on a slant; it is a pathetic sight to see a fine wing man so bottled by his own 'insides' that he is forced into touch almost as soon as he has the ball. **1967** J. POTTER *Foul Play* vi. 79 George and Boozy moved up on the German insides like a pair of avenging demons.

6. (See quot. 1927.) *U.S.*

1899 B. TARKINGTON *Gentleman from Indiana* i. 11 Presently the 'Herald' announced a news connection with Rouen, and with that, and the aid of 'patent insides', began an era of three issues a week. *Ibid.* xiv. 249 We must buy 'plate matter' instead of 'patent insides'. **1927** *Amer. Speech* II. 242/1 Only in small country papers does one find 'patent insides'. The country editor frequently buys four pages of his paper already printed, filled with 'features', fiction, and advertising. He has only to fill the four remaining pages with local news and advertising.

B. *adj.* **a.** (ˈɪnsaɪd). Situated on or in the inside; of, belonging to, or used for the inside (*lit.* and *fig.*); interior, internal.

Often used technically; esp. in reference to locomotive engines having the driving-gear within the main frame, as ***inside cylinder, framing, gear***. Also, ***inside callipers, tool***, etc. i.e. used for the interior of cylindrical or hollow work.

1611 SHAKS. *Wint. T.* I. ii. 286 Is whispering nothing? Is leaning Cheeke to Cheeke?..Kissing with in-side Lip? **1703** MOXON *Mech. Exerc.* 244 Outside and inside Lathing for Plastring. **1793** SMEATON *Edystone L.* §189 An excellent mortar for under-drawing, and inside work. **1824** E. WEETON *Let.* 31 May–2 June in *Jrnl. of Governess* (1969) II. 276 No consideration could have induced me to travel inside the coach; the guard offered me an inside seat in the night, but I declined it. **1849** THACKERAY *Pendennis* I. xxii. 206 He would not take an inside place in the coach, but sate up behind with his friend the Guard. **1855** D. K. CLARK *Railway Machinery* I. 93/1, $\frac{5}{8}$ inch lap in Sharp's inside-cylinder engines exhausts as well as the $1\frac{1}{4}$ and $1\frac{1}{2}$ inch of lap, which Mr. Sinclair has found necessary in his outside-cylinder engines on the Caledonian Railway. **1857** MRS. GASKELL *Let.* 13 Sept. (1966) 471 We..found to our dismay that there was no inside places. However we got tilted up to the top of the coach behind. **1859** *Engineer* VII. 211/1 The outside cylinder express engines running to Southampton are as steady, under every rate of speed, as any inside cylinder engines in use. *Ibid.* 225/1 The cylinders being bolted to the outside of the inside framing. **1862** in Willis & Clark *Cambridge* (1886) III. 177 The inside fittings of the rooms. **1896** *Allbutt's Syst. Med.* I. 151 An efficient mechanism by which outside variability is used for the maintenance of inside constancy. **1907** F. H. BURNETT *Shuttle* xxiii. 226 We didn't come over on one of the big liners... Took a cheap one, inside cabin, second class. **1959** B. J. FARMER *Murder Next Year* ii. 7 A modern bathroom and an inside w.c. **1963** *Guardian* 7 Mar. 7/2 There are 1,045 berths on this ship, and 16 of them will be available at £35—in four-berth 'inside' cabins on C deck. 'Outside' four-berth cabins cost £55 a berth. **1971** *Ibid.* 1 Dec. 12/5 Some 200,000 families with severely disabled people need improved accommodation because they lack an inside lavatory.

b. Of a person: Employed within a house or building; working indoors. Also *fig.*, and of a person travelling inside a coach (cf. *sb.* 3).

1807 SOUTHEY *Lett. from Eng.* II. xxxvii. 125 These coaches..carry four inside passengers, two outside. **1841** E. HALL *Diary* 17 Dec. in O.A. Sherrard *Two Victorian Girls* (1966) iv. 48, I did feel very lonely and miserable as the coach drove off with the solitary inside passenger. **1886** W. D. HOWELLS *Minister's Charge* xxv. 368 Look at the Blue-book,..it's the apotheosis of farm-boys, mechanics, insidemen, and I don't know what. **1894** *Daily News* 8 Oct. 6/7 Counting the number of hours worked, the outside men are given an equal amount of employment with the inside men. *a* **1900** *Mod. U. S. Newspaper* Advt., Situation wanted as inside man in private family. **1946** K. TENNANT *Lost Haven* (1947) viii. 119 The 'inside men', who fished the lakes ..also appropriated any convenient grassy slope. **1948** 'N. SHUTE' *No Highway* vi. 165 He's an inside man... He's deeply interested in research, and he doesn't concern himself very much with user problems.

c. ***inside edge*** (*Skating*): see EDGE 7b. ***inside track***: in *Racing*, the inner side of a curved track (which is shorter than the outer); hence *fig.* a position of advantage.

1857 *Richmond* (Virginia) *Whig* 5 Sept. 2/1 In a word, 'Gizzard-Foot' has the inside track for the Senatorship. **1867** O. W. HOLMES *Guard. Angel* xviii. (1891) 197 It gave him the inside track, as the sporting men say, with reference to any rivals for the good-will of either of these. **1882** W. JAMES *Let.* 23 Apr. in R. B. Perry *Tht. & Char. W. James* (1935) I. 794 Whoever does it gets the inside track for promotion here on Bowen's withdrawal. **1931** L. STEFFENS *Autobiogr.* IV. xvii. 782 We cannot any more govern them or exploit or have the inside track in them. **1967** *Times Rev. Industry* Mar. 90/3 The real strength of the Labour Party does not lie in Transport House but on the inside track possessed by trade union officials, shop stewards and others, ..all particularly important in influencing the male vote. **1972** *Accountant* 21 Sept. 359/1 At this stage in the contest, President Richard M. Nixon, as the incumbent, clearly enjoys the advantages of the inside track.

d. *fig.* Coming from 'the inside'; inner; not generally available.

1888 *Daily Inter-Ocean* 20 Feb. (Farmer), A secret service officer..claims to have inside information as to the facts in the case. **1896** S. LEAVITT *Our Money Wars* ii. 11 Sometimes a few lines of inside history are worth whole books of that usually printed. **1912** C. MATHEWSON *Pitching in a Pinch* ix. 184 Behind this game is some 'inside' history that has never been written. *c* **1919** H. C. WITWER *Smile a Minute* i. 32 He wanted some inside dope for his paper. **1923** D. L. SAYERS *Whose Body?* xiii, 'Peruvian Oil..hasn't paid a dividend for umpteen years.' 'No..but it's going to. I've got inside information.' **1924** H. CROY *R.F.D. No. 3* 157, I knew a fellow on the inside and we used to pal around together and I got a lot of inside dope. **1932** H. WALPOLE *Fortress* III. 447 John..had been most entertaining. If not of Parliament he was near it enough to have plenty of inside information. **1936** *Discovery* Apr. 129/2 His biography..gives the inside story of Coué in his years of fame. **1938** WODEHOUSE *Code of Woosters* vi. 139, I would be able to get together with Gussie ..and learn the inside dope. **1950** D. RIESMAN et al. *Lonely Crowd* ix. 199 Some inside-dopesters actually crave to *be* on the inside, to join an inner circle or invent one; others aim no higher than to *know* the inside. **1959** *Encounter* Dec. 16/1 The influence of the..gossip-columnists and 'inside dopesters' has steadily risen. **1970** *Daily Tel.* 20 Apr. 17 The newest 'inside' book on the monarchy. **1972** 'H. CARMICHAEL' *Naked to Grave* v. 59, I can get all the credit for an inside story... The way you described it to me is just tailor-made for my column. **1972** P. D. JAMES *Unsuitable Job* iii. 90 If you want the inside dope on Garforth House, you should ask him. **1973** D. LEES *Rape of Quiet Town* i. 10 As soon as they hear I'm from the *Pictorial* they'll fall over themselves to give me the inside gen.

e. Special collocations: **inside centre** *Rugby Football*, the centre playing immediately outside the half-backs; **inside clinch** (see quot.) and cf. CLINCH *sb.*[1]; **inside country** *Austral.* (see quot. 1959); **inside forward**, in association football and hockey, either of the two players, called the inside left or right (see below), of the forward line; the position of such a player; **inside half** = *scrum-half*; **inside job** *slang*, a crime committed in a house, etc., by, or with the help of, a resident or servant, etc., in the building; **inside left, right**, in association football and hockey, a player playing between the outside left or right and the centre forward; the position of such a player; **inside lining** *slang* (see quots.); **inside man** *U.S. slang*, one involved in any of various special roles in a confidence trick or robbery; **inside right** (see *inside left*, above); **inside squatter** *Austral.*, one who lives within the margin of the settlements; **inside stand** *slang* (see quot. 1935).

1936 H. B. T. WAKELAM *Rugby Football* ix. 171 Returning again to outside lines-up, Now and again..we come across a side which, really imitating the five-eighth game, plays two outside-halves, or even an 'inside' and an 'outside' centre. **1960** E. S. & W. J. HIGHAM *High Speed Rugby* ix. 111 When the inside centre receives the ball, he proceeds..to straighten his run. **1969** *Sun-Herald* (Sydney) 13 July 45/5 Barry Honan's play at inside centre was rich encouragement for the side. **1886** *Encycl. Brit.* XXI. 591/2 Inside Clinch. The end [of a rope] is bent close round the standing part till it forms a circle, when it is securely seized..thus making a running eye. **1911** C. E. W. BEAN *'Dreadnought' of Darling* xxxv. 317 But, be the 'inside' country never so tame..there will always be a huge stretch of country 'outside' which cannot by any known means be closely settled. **1959** BAKER *Drum* 119 *Inside country*, well-populated country near or in coastal areas, specifically in contrast to inland or out-back. **1897** *Windsor Mag.* Dec. 25/2 Each of the two inside-forward positions. **1897** *Encycl. Sport* I. 418/1 Try to feed the centre and inside forwards when in your opponent's territory. **1965** *Men's Hockey* (Know the Game) (rev. ed.) 30/1 If the inside forwards are close to the centre, the opposing centre half can cover all three. **1921** E. H. D. SEWELL *Rugby Football* iii. 69 In our view *all* backs should look at the inside half when the ball is being put in the scrum. **1949** *Rugby League Football* ('Know the Game' Series) 8 Scrum half back or inside half. **1969** *Programme* (Llanelli v. Swansea 1 Apr.) 6 Jim Lamb. Mewnwr. Inside-half. **1973** *Sunday Tel.* 18 Mar. 38/2 Smith, for England, was forceful at inside half. **1908** 'O. HENRY' *Gentle Grafter* xi. 142 The police are calling it an inside job. **1924** G. S. DOUGHERTY *Criminal as Human Being* 187 One of my assistants..made an investigation that convinced him an 'inside job' had been committed by the servants. **1925** A. CHRISTIE *Secret of Chimneys* xii. 121 How long have you had the idea that it might be an inside job? **1926** J. BLACK *You can't Win* xxi. 334 It was an inside job..done by the storekeeper to beat his creditors. **1933** D. L. SAYERS *Murder must Advertise* xv. 249 You seem convinced that the murder of Victor Dean was an inside job. **1972** 'M. INNES' *Open House* II. x. 94 Wasn't there something factitious about the whole affair? Didn't it match the hoary old formula of the inside job disguised as an outside job? **1897** *Encycl. Sport* I. 517/1 This is a comparatively easy task for inside right, but by no means so for inside left, who cannot reach out to hit the ball as it is rolled in. **1969** B. JAMES *England v Scotland* ii. 51 Scottish inside-left J. Macpherson..collapsed in a heap. **1851** H. MAYHEW *London Labour* I. 20/1 He was 'going to get an inside-lining' (dinner). **1935** A. J. POLLOCK

Underworld Speaks 61/2 *Inside lining*, an exceptionally good meal. **1935** *Amer. Speech* X. 21/1 (s.v. *Steerer*), *Steerer*, an *inside man* or tipster who locates prospects for robbers or safeblowers. **1937** *N.Y. Times* 22 Dec. 22 *Inside man*, a spy placed in a plant as an employé. **1938** F. D. SHARPE *Sharpe of Flying Squad* xxviii. 288 The 'mug finder' books a room and spots a likely name in the register... When the 'mug's' name is announced in the restaurant by the page, he is followed to the telephone by the 'inside man' and identified. **1940** *Amer. Speech* XV. 119/1 Inside-men are highly specialized workers; they must have a superb knowledge of psychology to keep the mark under perfect control during the days or weeks while he is being fleeced. **1906** *Westm. Gaz.* 16 Mar. 5/1 Bloomer developed into a forward of exceptional skill in the inside-right position. **1969** B. JAMES *England v Scotland* iii. 64 Chadwick provided an opening for inside-right Goodall to score England's second goal. **1881** A. C. GRANT *Bush-Life in Queensland* II. xxxii. 171 Stations were formed for nearly a hundred and fifty miles outside John's run, and he began to regard himself as quite an inside squatter. **1959** BAKER *Drum* 119 *Inside squatter*, a farmer or large land-owner in a fairly well-populated district. **1932** WODEHOUSE *Hot Water* xiii. 227 Oily's got himself into the house, and he's planning to let Soup in when he's good and ready... It's what's known as the inside stand. **1935** *Punch* 4 Dec. 637/3 The 'inside stand', as the business of insinuating a member of a gang into the doomed house is called. **1960** WODEHOUSE *Jeeves in Offing* v. 54 The butler turned out to be one of a gang of crooks, planted in the house to make it easy for them to break in. The inside stand, it's called.

C. *adv.* (ˌɪnˈsaɪd). On or in the inside.

1. a. On the inner side.

1803 NELSON 4 June in Nicolas *Disp.* (1845) V. 79 This Island is bold, too, inside or out. **1806** A. DUNCAN *Nelson* 71 The Goliath.. had the honor to lead inside.

b. *fig.* In a position to have private information. *rare.*

1870 *Congress. Globe* 3 Feb. 1022/1, I ask the gentleman from Ohio to name the ships which he says have been sold for a song. The gentleman is inside on all these matters.

c. *slang.* In prison.

1888 *Referee* 14 Oct. 1/4 There dashes past a once member of the dangerous classes, who has been 'inside' many a time and oft, but who, having run into a bit of ready, will now go straight. **1925** E. WALLACE *King by Night* xxvi. 116 You've been 'inside', and you're going in again unless you can explain.. what you're doing here. **1958** *Listener* 6 Nov. 743/2 Only a very insensitive reader could reach the end of the book without feeling that he had shared the author's daily, even hourly, existence 'inside'—..the effect comprising a powerful, and frequently nauseating, picture of what life in prison, and in a Borstal, is like. **1959** 'L. BRUCE' *Our Jubilee is Death* xvi. 149 She was afraid of me going inside again. **1972** C. DRUMMOND *Death at Bar* ii. 54 Over the years she had been convicted three times, spending in all four years 'inside'.

2. In or into the inner part; within; internally.

1824 E. WEETON *Jrnl.* 21 July (1969) II. 309 The Liverpool fares.. were all 4£ inside and 2£ out. **1847** *Punch* XII. 14 Has he [*sc.* the bus conductor] directions to say ..'Full inside'? **1851** 'NIMROD' *Road* 17 Full, inside, sir. **1866** LATHAM s.v., *Itinerant Showman*, Now then, ladies and gentlemen, walk inside, walk inside! **1875** T. W. HIGGINSON *Hist. U.S.* xi. 93 The houses were kept very clean inside and out. **1905** *19th Cent.* 817 To adopt an elusive bush idiom, the railways bring the country 'inside'. **1930** L. MUNDAY *Mounty's Wife* xvii. 209 After twenty years, almost all of which we had spent 'inside', as the North is always called. **1945** BAKER *Austral. Lang.* 59 When a man from the far interior comes to the city he says he is coming inside. **1957** *Arctic Spotter* (Edmonton, Alberta) Oct. 9 Not once did I meet anyone who was sorry to be 'inside'. **1970** 'D. HALLIDAY' *Dolly & Cookie Bird* v. 66 You didn't know Daddy like I did. He was an awful old softie inside.

3. ***inside of*** (in reference to time): Within the space of; in less than the whole of (a period); before the end of. *U.S.*, *Austral.*, etc. *colloq.*

1839 *Spirit of Times* 27 July 246/1 There are dozens of horses.. that can trot their mile in harness inside of three minutes. **1887** *Hartford Courant* 13 Jan. (Farmer), Both animals had been killed inside of five minutes. **1889** BOLDREWOOD *Robbery under Arms* xi, He knocked the seven senses out of him inside of three rounds. *Ibid.* xxi, I've been pretty quick coming: thirty mile inside of three hours.

D. *prep.* Inside of; on the inner side, or in the inner part, of; within. Now esp. in titles and headlines to indicate special or intimate knowledge.

1791 J. LACKINGTON *Mem.* (1792) 212 The coachman put me inside the carriage. **1840** R. H. DANA *Bef. Mast* xxxv. 133 The captain stood well to the westward, to run inside the Bermudas. **1855** BROWNING *Ch. Roland* xxix, As when a trap shuts—you're inside the den! **1882** W. LARDEN *Sch. Course Heat* 79 We must get rid of the air inside the tube. **1924** A. J. SMALL *Frozen Gold* i. 39, I hear all about it inside twenty-four hours. **1936** J. GUNTHER (*title*) Inside Europe. **1942** R. BENCHLEY (*title*) Inside Benchley. **1972** EVERSON & FITZGERALD (*title*) Inside the city.

Hence †ˈinˌsidely *adv. Obs.*, inwardly.

1803 W. TAYLOR in Robberds *Mem.* I. 457 You say something outsidely rude and insidely civil about its being my choice to edit.

†inˈside, *v. Obs. rare*⁻¹. [ad. L. *insidēre* to sit on: see INSIDENT.] *intr.* To be seated or situated *on* something.

1657 TOMLINSON *Renou's Disp.* 353 On whose summities three.. grateful leafs do inside.

in-side: see IN *adv.* 12 b.

inˈsidedness. *nonce-wd.* [f. INSIDE + -ED + -NESS.] The condition of being inside something else.

1888 DK. ARGYLL in *19th Cent.* Jan. 156 Another kind of outsidedness and insidedness.. namely, the insidedness, the self-containedness, of every organism as a whole with reference to all external forces.

†ˈinsident, *a. Obs.* [ad. L. *insidēnt-em*, pr. pple. of *insidēre* to sit in or on, to inhere or subsist in, f. *in-* (IN-²) + *sedēre* to sit.] Residing or subsisting in; inherent.

1583 BABINGTON *Commandm.* vii. (1637) 68 It is so sweete and so insident to vs which this lawe forbiddeth. **1590** GREENE *Mourn. Garm.* 44 These vices are insident by nature. *a* **1641** BP. MOUNTAGU *Acts & Mon.* (1642) 115 The course of Gods Spirit is.. ingredient and insident, as in good men; or urgent and impellent, as in bad men. **1656** BLOUNT *Glossogr.*, *Insident*, sitting on or in, remaining, continuing.

ˌinside-ˈoutness. [f. *inside out* (INSIDE A. *sb.* 4) + -NESS.] The state of being inside out.

1919 R. BRIDGES in *S.P.E. Tract* II. 40 The insideoutness, topsy-turviness, and preposterousness of Mr. Jones' method is incredible. **1960** *Encounter* XIV. v. 70 The inside-outness Criticus.

insider (ˌɪnˈsaɪdə(r)). [f. INSIDE + -ER¹.] **1.** One who is inside; a person who is within the limits of some place, society, organization, etc.; hence, one in possession of special information, one who is 'in the secret'. Opposed to *outsider*. Also *attrib.* and *Comb.*

In quot. 1957¹ with play on title of Colin Wilson's work *The Outsider*.

1848 W. ARMSTRONG *Stocks* 7 Insiders are those by whom and through whom all transactions are made in and about the Exchange. **1875** POSTE *Gaius* I. (ed. 2) 31 Named outsiders (*exquilini*) as opposed to the burgesses or insiders (*inquilini*). **1885** *Pall Mall G.* 30 June 6/1 Change him from an outsider into an insider (however slight the connection), and the thing is done. **1892** *Nation* (N.Y.) 22 Dec. 468/3 It was possible for insiders to use its revelations in speculation on the Bourse. **1902** H. L. WILSON *Spenders* xxx. 355 Shepler's back of all three [stocks]. The insiders are buying up now, slowly and cautiously, so as not to start any boom prematurely. **1913** *Q. Rev.* July 256 At any rate, as regards the original 10,000 shares bought by Sir Rufus Isaacs, they took part in it as 'insiders' exploiting the ignorance of the public. **1923** F. WALDO *Down Mackenzie through Gt. Lone Land* 248 The Outsider cannot know; the Insider never can make clear to him the grip that holds, the urge that stirs and never sleeps. **1942** *R.A.F. Jrnl.* 2 May 2 Estimates concerning the output of Japanese airplane industry vary. Insiders consider it to be from 1,500 to 2,500 planes a year. **1957** *Observer* 8 Sept. 10/2 They are fools who compare him [*sc.* Anouilh] with Pinero, a born insider who upheld conformity and bade us compromise with imperfection. **1957** C. PEPLER *Riches Despised* ii. 27 To the outsider in fact all these religions would have seemed more or less alike... Indeed the insiders, the Israelites, found themselves all too easily drawn to the high places of the mountains. **1958** *Times Lit. Suppl.* 30 May 293/3 At any moment earnest pedantry may break through to reveal a very young man's novel with nothing much to say and not quite enough 'insider' knowledge to avoid a '*gaffe*'. **1966** *Economist* 12 Feb. 642/2 The main thrust of the Act was to apply to smaller US companies the same financial reporting, proxy-solicitation and insider-trading rules that have long been applied to larger US corporations. **1972** *Observer* 10 Sept. 11/3 The softness of our line compared with that of the US shows up clearly in the area of insider trading. In Britain it is not illegal to use confidential information to make a profit in the stock market. **1973** *Times* 8 June 1/2 The Stock Exchange has reiterated its view that 'insider dealing' in a company's shares should be made a criminal offence. In a memorandum on company law reform presented to the Department of Trade and Industry, it says the police should be empowered to call for the disclosure of true beneficial ownership when they suspect that insider trading has taken place under the cloak of nominee shareholdings.

2. *U.S. slang.* A pocket or pocket-book.

1846 *National Police Gaz.* (U.S.) 12 Sept. 5/1 The mode adopted to get an 'insider' or what may be better understood, the book from an inside coat pocket is as follows. **1896** I. K. FRIEDMAN *Lucky Number* 154 Britch is used to designate the front-pocket; gerve, vest-pocket; insider, inside coat-pocket; [etc.]. **1925** H. LEVERAGE in *Flynn's* 7 Feb. 489/2 *Insider* (a double insider), an inside vest pocket. **1955** D. W. MAURER in *Publ. Amer. Dial. Soc.* xxiv. 115 An *insider* is the long flat wallet carried inside the breast-pocket. **1970** C. MAJOR *Dict. Afro-Amer. Slang* 69 *Insiders*, one's pockets.

†3. An inside passenger. *Obs.*

1854 B. F. TAYLOR *Jan. & June* 170 'No Room For Two!' was the exclamation of some insider, the other morning. **1892** *Harper's Mag.* Jan. 257/1 The exhilarating pace, the smooth roads, and the juxtaposition of the insiders tended, in a high degree, to the promotion of enjoyment.

†inˈsidiary, *a. Obs. rare.* [f. L. *insidiæ* ambushes, ambuscade + -ARY.] = INSIDIOUS.

1625 W. B. *True School War* 18 The sending forth of Bloody, Trecherous, and Insidiarie persons.

†inˈsidiate, *v. Obs.* [f. ppl. stem of L. *insidiārī* to lie in ambush, f. *insidiæ* ambush.]

1. *trans.* To lie in wait for; to plot against.

1624 HEYWOOD *Gunaik.* v. 227 She was ambushed by two Centaures.. who insidiating her virgin chastitie, shee [etc.]. *a* **1632** T. TAYLOR *God's Judgem.* II. ii. (1642) 20 Pretending that he had privately insidiated his father's life. **1651** T. STANLEY *Poems* 109 For this friends insidiate their friends. **1656** —— *Hist. Philos.* v. (1701) 204/2 They.. every hour insidiate our Good.

2. *intr.* To lie in wait; to plot.

1626 W. SCLATER *Exp. 2 Thess.* (1629) 195 Wolues enter or insidiat, not sparing the flocke. **1639** SIR W. BERKLEY *Lost Lady* IV. iii. in Hazl. *Dodsley* XII. 605 She pays the fault of her abusing me, Insidiating with my Milesia's form, To search, and then betray my resolution.

Hence **†inˈsidiating** *ppl. a. Obs.*

1632 HEYWOOD *2nd Pt. Iron Age* IV. Wks. 1874 III. 409 What passionate and insidiating lookes Hee cast on her. **1671** *True Nonconf.* 406 Admitting your meaning to be only of a deliberat insidiating murther.

†insidiˈation. *Obs.* [n. of action from L. *insidiārī* to INSIDIATE.] The action of lying in wait or plotting; a plot; an insidious act.

1612 COTTA *Disc. Dang. Pract. Phys.* II. iv. 111 Who by their insidiation of the proofe of my skill.. prouoked it. **1628** HOBBES *Thucyd.* (1822) 2 The goodness of the land.. made them more obnoxious to the insidiation of strangers. **1668** H. MORE *Div. Dial.* II. xvii. (1713) 139 Industrious Insidiations of other stronger and more crafty Creatures that hunt after their Prey.

†inˈsidiator. *Obs.* [a. L. *insidiātor*, agent-n. from *insidiārī*: see INSIDIATE.] A lier in wait; a plotter.

1539 TAVERNER *Gard. Wysed.* I. 5 b, Such as be manquellours, or insidiatoures of mannes lyfe. **1660** H. MORE *Myst. Godl.* VII. xvii. 358 It is not unconceivable how these invisible Insidiators may so apply themselves. *a* **1677** BARROW *Serm.* (1687) I. x. 132 Both open enemies and close insidiatours.

insidiˈosity. *rare.* [f. L. *insidiōs-us* (see next) + -ITY. Cf. OF. *insidiosité* (Godef.).] Insidious quality, insidiousness.

1873 RUSKIN *Arrows of Chace* (1880) II. 102, [I] solemnly deny the insidiosity of my question.

insidious (ɪnˈsɪdɪəs), *a.* Also 8–9 *erron.* insiduous. [ad. L. *insidiōs-us* cunning, deceitful, f. *insidiæ* ambush: see -OUS. Cf. F. *insidieux* (1420 in Hatz.-Darm.).]

Full of wiles or plots; lying in wait or seeking to entrap or ensnare; proceeding or operating secretly or subtly so as not to excite suspicion; sly, treacherous, deceitful, underhand, artful, cunning, crafty, wily. (Of persons and things.)

1545 JOYE *Exp. Dan.* xi. (R.), There be nowe meruelous subtyle craftinesses exercised by courtes insidiouse wylinesses. **1652** C. B. STAPYLTON *Herodian* 34 All persons good he banish'd as insidious, And kept Buffoones debauched and perfidious. **1692** SOUTH *12 Serm.* (1697) I. 522 A false, insidious Tongue, may whisper a Lye so close, and low. **1725** POPE *Odyss.* XII. 301 The silent fisher casts th' insidious food. **1783** WATSON *Philip III* (1793) I. III. 290 Some deep insidious design against the states. **1853** J. H. NEWMAN *Hist. Sk.* (1873) II. I. ii. 92 A more powerful and insidious enemy. **1878** BATES *Centr. Amer.* ii. 15 For them civilisation is an insidious, but a no less sure and deadly, poison. *Mod.* A victim to an insidious disease.

insidiously (ɪnˈsɪdɪəslɪ), *adv.* [f. prec. + -LY².] In an insidious manner; by secret plotting or artifice; in a subtle or underhand way; slyly, craftily, treacherously, deceitfully.

1545 JOYE *Exp. Dan.* vi. 86 These men insidiously obseruing daniel, espyed him praying and makinge supplicacion to his god. *a* **1626** BACON (J.), The castle of Cadmus was taken by Phebidas.. insidiously and in violation of league. **1779–81** JOHNSON *L.P.*, *Pope* Wks. IV. 40 Those who officiously, or insiduously, quicken his attention to offences. **1844** W. H. MILL *Serm. Tempt. Christ* iii. 62 The reptile, insidiously lying in wait in the dust.

insidiousness (ɪnˈsɪdɪəsnɪs). [f. as prec. + -NESS.] Insidious quality or character; treacherousness, craftiness, subtle deceitfulness.

1677 BARROW *Serm.* (1687) I. v. 65 He hath little of the Serpent, (none of its lurking insidiousness). **1751** JOHNSON *Rambler* No. 174 ¶8 My heart, indeed, acquits me of deliberate malignity, or interested insidiousness. **1846** LUNDIE *Missionary Life in Samoa* 272 The disastrous results of Jesuitical insidiousness.

insight (ˈɪnsaɪt), *sb.*¹ Forms: 3–4 insiht, 3 *Orm.* innsihht, (4–5 insihte), 3–5 insiȝt(e, (3 insiȝht, 4 -syȝht, -syȝt), 4 ensight, 5 ensyght, 5–6 insyght(e, -sighte, 3– insight. [f. IN *adv.* + SIGHT *sb.* Cf. MDu *insicht*, Du. *inzigt*, Ger. *einsicht*, Da. *indsigt*, Sw. *insigt*.

The original notion appears to have been 'internal sight', i.e. with the eyes of the mind or understanding (see IN *adv.* 12 c). Cf. the same use of *in-* in ME. *inwit* (sometimes an equivalent of *insight*), and OE. *inȝehyȝd*, *inȝeþanc*, etc. But subseq. there arose a tendency to analyse the word as sight or seeing *into* a thing or subject, although even so there usually remained the notion of penetrating into things or seeing beneath their surface with the eyes of the understanding.]

†1. a. Internal sight, mental vision or perception, discernment; in early use sometimes, Understanding, intelligence, wisdom. *Obs.*

c **1200** ORMIN 8789 He ȝifeþþ himm.. innsihht tunnderrstanndenn all þatt mann maȝȝ unnderrstanndenn. *Ibid.* 11508 Forr sawle onnfoþ att Drihhtin Godd Innsihht & minndiȝnesse. **1297** R. GLOUC. (Rolls) 6261 Her of þat soþe seggeþ ȝe as bi ȝoure in siȝte. *a* **1300** *Cursor M.* 1565 Sua blind þai war in þair insight, þat reckining cuth þai nan o right. **1340** HAMPOLE *Pr. Consc.* 253 þus þer four lettes his insight þat he knaws noght him-selfe right. *c* **1440** LONELICH *Grail* xxxi. 214 þe wordis.. Whiche that non man vndirstondyn ne Myhte, but Only God thorwh his Insihte. *c* **1491** *Chast. Goddes Chyld.* 47 An Intellectuel vision is callyd whanne the Insighte of the sowle.. is cleerly fastnyd in unbodely substaunce wyth a sothfaste knowynge. **1570** LEVINS *Manip.* 119/42 Insight of knowledge, *scientia*. **1578** *Chr. Prayers* in *Priv. Prayers* (1851) 440 Much better is.. the insight of the mind than the light, or eyesight, of the

body. 1647 H. MORE *Song of Soul* I. II. xxxii, Much he spake where I had no insight.

†**b.** With *in* (*a*, *o*, *on*, *of*): Knowledge of or skill in (a particular subject or department). *Obs.*

*c*1200 ORMIN 3437 Amang þe Calldeowisshe þeod þatt cann innsihht o steorrness. *Ibid.* 7084 Uþwitess..þatt haffden dep innsihht & witt Off fele kinne þingess. *c*1205 LAY. 30497 Insiht he cuðe: a winde and a mone. *c*1430 *Hymns Virg.* (1867) 66 In discrecioun I haue in-siȝt. 1513 MORE in Grafton *Chron.* (1568) II. 810 He..had gotten by great experience..depe insight in pollitique and worldly driftes. 1590 SPENSER *F.Q.* III. iii. 11 Merlin had in Magick more insight Then ever him before, or after, living wight. 1612 BRINSLEY *Lud. Lit.* 174 To follow the Logicke places in Apthonius in a Philosophical discourse, doth require..some insight in Logick. 1640 WILKINS *New Planet* I. (1707) 146 We should examine what particular insight and experience they had in those things.

2. a. The fact of penetrating with the eyes of the understanding into the inner character or hidden nature of things; a glimpse or view beneath the surface; the faculty or power of thus seeing.

*c*1580 SIDNEY *Ps.* XVII. iii, Where silent Night might seeme all faultes to hide, Then was I, by thy searching insight tride. 1683 D. A. *Art Converse* 26 Obstinacy the product either of great Pride or little Insight. 1812 WORDSW. *Sonn., Eve Marriage of Friend*, When the closer view of wedded life Hath shown that nothing human can be clear From frailty, for that insight may the Wife To her indulgent Lord become more dear. 1840 THIRLWALL *Greece* VII. 245 The insight and the effort came too late to be of any avail. 1851–5 BRIMLEY *Ess., Tennyson* 3 Mr. Tennyson is a poet of large compass, of profound insight, of finished skill. 1879 FARRAR *St. Paul* II. 59 That insight which sees at once into the heart of every moral difficulty.

b. With *into* (†*in*).

1581 SIDNEY *Apol. Poetrie* (Arb.) 34 Let but Sophocles bring you Aiax on a stage..and tell mee if you haue not a more familiar insight into anger, then finding in the Schoole-men his *genus* and *difference*? 1586 A. DAY *Eng. Secretary* I. (1625) 47 This by insight had into the very worst and lowest sort of men shall you finde. 1590 GREENE *Orpharion* Wks. (Grosart) XII. 72 You haue a deeper insight in my thoughts then myself. 1674 OWEN *Holy Spirit* (1693) 174 A Spiritual Saving Insight into Spiritual things. 1712 BUDGELL *Spect.* No. 506 ⁋12 Giving her an insight into things she had no notion of before. 1718 *Freethinker* No. 14 ⁋6 This thorough Insight into the Man..makes me disesteem him. 1863 GEO. ELIOT *Romola* (1880) I. Introd. 6 He had gained an insight into all sorts of affairs at home and abroad. 1875 J. H. BENNET *Winter Medit.* I. ix. (1875) 288 Mightily pleased with this little insight into Spanish village life.

c. With *pl.*

1817 COLERIDGE *Biog. Lit.* 187 The representative and reward of our past conscious reasonings, insights, and conclusions. 1832 HT. MARTINEAU *Demerara* ii. 16 His insights into his prospects. 1840 CARLYLE *Heroes* ii. (1872) 48 Glimpses of many things..which were to ripen in a strange way into views, into beliefs and insights one day.

d. *Psychol.* In studies of behaviour and learning, the sudden perception of the solution to a problem or difficulty; applied to animals, giving an indication of their capacity for ideas and reasoning. In *Psychoanalysis*, perception of one's mental condition. Also *attrib.* and in *Comb.*, as ***insight-giving***, ***-learning***, ***therapy***.

1909 W. JAMES *Meaning of Truth* xiii. 260 His insistent desire to have a world of that sort is felt by him to be..an altogether peculiar *insight-giving passion* to which..he would be *stupid* not to yield. 1916 R. M. YERKES *Mental Life Monkeys & Apes* iii. 68 The curve of learning plotted.. would..be described as an ideational, and possibly even as a rational curve; for its sudden drop..to the base line strongly suggests, if it does not actually prove, insight. *Ibid.* 87 This young orang utan..strove persistently, and often vainly, to gain insight. 1925 E. WINTER tr. *Köhler's Mentality of Apes* vii. 194 Since, however, we have to decide whether chimpanzees ever behave with insight, [etc.]. *Ibid.* 198 Hence follows this characteristic: to set up as the criterion of insight, the appearance of a complete solution with reference to the whole lay-out of the field. 1949 *Brit. Birds* XLII. 355 These are not necessarily instances of insight learning, but they do represent persistent attempts to reach the milk when the top of the bottle was no longer visible to the bird. 1949 M. MEAD *Male & Female* 449 Society is the patient. Those who have been in some way hurt or distorted give us many valuable insights into what is wrong with it. 1956 W. H. THORPE *Learning & Instinct in Animals* v. 100 Thus insight-learning seems to be a kind of action by hypothesis, and has often been held to be evidence of ideational processes. 1964 M. ARGYLE *Psychol. & Social Probl.* x. 129 It has been found possible to reduce racial prejudice by means of brief insight-therapy. 1965 A. D. WEISMAN *Existential Core of Psychoanal.* vi. 139 Insight in psycho-analysis often seems to be the *result* of a resolved conflict, not the *cause* of its resolution. 1967 R. R. GREENSON *Technique & Pract. Psychoanal.* I. i. 44 Only rarely does insight lead very quickly to a change in behavior.

†**3. a.** A mental looking *to* or *upon* something; consideration; respect, regard. *Obs.*

13.. *E.E. Allit. P.* B. 1659 He hade so huge an insyȝt to his aune dedes, þat þe power, of þe hyȝe prynce he purely, forȝetes. 1390 GOWER *Conf.* II. 324 Withoute insihte of moderhede..This child withouten noise or cry Sche slou. *Ibid.* III. 19 As they, which none insight hadden, But only to her [= their] drunke fare. 1491 CAXTON *Vitas Patr.* (W. de W. 1495) II. 239 a/1, I am become thus drye and lene by the contynuelle ensyght that I had therupon.

†**b.** A view of a subject; a conspectus. (Cf. F. *aperçu.*) *Obs. rare.*

1581 LAMBARDE *Eiren.* (1602) 3 The First Booke, containing a Theoricke (or insight) of the Office of the Iustices of Peace.

†**4.** Sight (of the bodily eyes); looking; looking in, inspection; a look. *Obs.*

*c*1350 *Will. Palerne* 94 þere walked he a boute þe walles to winne in siȝt. *c*1440 *Promp. Parv.* 262/1 Insyght.., *inspexio*, *circumspeccio*. 1530 PALSGR. 234/2 Insight, *regart.* 1577 G. HARVEY *Letter-bk.* (Camden) 57 That good Sir Thomas More will deyne His cuntryman at first insight So curtously to interteyne. 1586 A. DAY *Eng. Secretary* I. (1625) 81 There will not bee wanting a number that shall bicker for her, from whose insight, you are altogether unable..to convey her. *a*1618 SYLVESTER *Maiden's Blush* 1187 All that ..could fore-tell..by in-sight of sacrificed Heards. 1663 GERBIER *Counsel* 47 He must likewise have a clear insight on the Glasse paines of the Glasier.

†**'insight**, *sb.*² *north. Eng.* and *Sc. Obs.* Also 6 *Sc.* **insicht**. [Of uncertain derivation.

In form the same as prec.; but the sense remains unaccounted for.]

Goods, substance, esp. household furniture.
b. *attrib.* as ***insight gear***.

1522 *Wills & Inv. N.C.* (Surtees 1835) 106, I bequethe to my wife all suche goodes within the house as she brought from Petyngton for her parte of insight. 1523 *St. Papers Hen. VIII*, IV. 44 Sir Rauf Fenwike..and Sir William Heron..have made twoo very good roodes, and have gotten moche insight, catall, horse, and prisoners. 1535 STEWART *Cron. Scot.* II. 28 With wyffe and barnis, insicht and all stoir. *Ibid.* III. 328 Of corne and catell, and of insicht geir. 1536 BELLENDEN *Cron. Scot.* (1821) I. 132 The bestiall drevin away, the cornis and insicht brint. 1561 *Wills & Inv. N.C.* (Surtees 1835) 193, I gyue and bequithe to my doughter Agnes Lilburne the half of my insight & bedding wthin the howse. 1570 LEVINS *Manip.* 119/41 Insight of household, *supellex*. 1592 *Sc. Acts Jas. VI* §125 That nane of them [the commoun sort of people] presume..to beare or vse onie armes..vpon onie their insicht or houshald geare. *a*1670 SPALDING *Troub. Chas. I* (1829) I. 2 [They] begane to rob and spouilzie the earle's tennents..of their haill goods, geir, insight plenishing..and cattell. [1896 *Blackw. Mag.* Aug. 257 It must have been stripped of all 'insight', as our forefathers used to call hangings, carpets and furniture.]

†**in'sight**, *v. Obs. rare*⁻¹. [f. IN-² + SIGHT.] *trans.* To furnish with sight, to give sight to.

1577–87 HOLINSHED *Chron.* II. 19/1 It surpasseth natures course to raise the dead, to lighten or insight the blind.

†**'insighted**, *a. Obs.* [f. INSIGHT *sb.*¹ + -ED².] Having insight: endowed with insight.

1602 WARNER *Alb. Eng.* XIII. lxxvi. (1612) 315 The being of the Soule is to confesse A Deitie, and senselesse such as are insighted lesse. 1610 HOLLAND *Camden's Brit.* 687 Iustus Lipsius, deeply insighted in vnderstanding old Authors. 1642 *Vind. Parlt.* in *Harl. Misc.* (Malh.) V. 272 He, who is not informed, or thoroughly insighted into the truth..is ready to conclude it a fallacy. *a*1684 LEIGHTON *Comm. 1 Pet.* Wks. (1868) 280 One insighted and interested in what he speaks. 1879 G. M. HOPKINS *Let.* 22 Feb. (1955) 71 The thought of the last tercet is truly insighted. 1881 —— *Let.* 16 Sept. (1935) 55 'The Old Bishop' is a fine and insighted picture.

'insightful, *a.* [f. INSIGHT *sb.*¹ + -FUL.] Characterized by insight. Also **'insightfully** *adv.*

1907 GALSWORTHY *Country House* II. i. 104 As if she had been guilty of thoughts too insightful, Mrs Pendyce blushed. 1932 *Brit. Jrnl. Psychol.* Jan. 196 The letters so distorted cannot have been insightfully apprehended. 1934 *Ibid.* July 5 When the problem passes the threshold of insightful understanding these answers are chosen more frequently. 1945 *Jrnl. Compar. Psychol.* XXXVIII. 367 (*title*) The relation of previous experience to insightful problem-solving. 1951 *Mind* LX. 518 Behaviour which we might call 'knowing' or 'insightful'. 1955 *Sci. Amer.* Apr. 109/1 Myers was a goose, but he was also brilliant, insightful and high-minded. 1957 R. K. MERTON *Student-Physician* 177 Physicians and educators have often commented insightfully on their own experiences. 1967 *Language* XLIII. 744 A sensible and insightful account of the history of linguistic thought. 1970 D. L. EMBLEN *Peter Mark Roget* (1971) xv. 276 A remarkably insightful—if somewhat cavalier—critic. 1973 *N. & Q.* Jan. 24/1 Mr. Shippey has written an insightful and in many ways exciting study for the non-specialist university student and teacher.

insign(e, obs. form of ENSIGN *sb.*

†**insignate**, *v. Obs. rare*⁻¹. [f. ppl. stem of late L. *insignā-re* to engrave, f. *in-* (IN-²) + *signāre* to mark.] *trans.* To mark, to engrave.

1653 R. SANDERS *Physiogn.* 227 A mole on or about the ears shews another insignated on the arms.

‖**insigne**, *sb.*: see INSIGNIA.

†**in'signe**, *a. Obs.* Also 8 **insign**. [a. F. *insigne* (15th c. in Hatz.-Darm.), ad. L. *insign-is* distinguished, f. *in-* (IN-²) + *signum* mark, SIGN.] Distinguished, in a good or bad way; eminent, noted, remarkable.

*c*1465 *Eng. Chron.* (Camden 1856) 93 Job thy seruant insygne Whom Sathan not cesethe to sette at care & dysdeyne. 1618 *Time's Store-house* 1742 (L.) Your commendable and insigne enterprise deserveth great recompense. 1623 tr. *Favine's Theat. Hon.* V. i. 50 To massacre the King..by an insigne trechery. 1702 C. MATHER *Magn. Chr.* VII. ii. (1852) 501 It is the cross in the ensign, which does now *insignire*, and render it insign.

‖**insignia** (ɪn'sɪgnɪə), *sb. pl.* Less freq. in sing. **insigne** (ɪn'sɪgniː). [L. *insignia*, pl. of *insigne* 'mark', 'sign', 'badge of office', sb. use of neut. sing. of *insignis*: see prec. Cf. F. *insigne* (Dict. Acad. 1835), and see ENSIGN *sb.*]

1. a. Badges or distinguishing marks of office or honour; emblems of a nation, person, etc.

1648 *Merc. Acad.* No. I. 3 All the *Insignia* of the late Vice-Chancellor and Proctors. 1722 RICHARDSON *Statues, &c. in Italy* 15 A Figure representing the 4 Cardinal Virtues, as having the *Insignia* of them all. *a*1744 POPE *Let. to Swift* (L.), His watch was a present to him from the king of Sicily, whose arms and *insignia* are graved on the inner case. 1810 WELLINGTON in Gurw. *Desp.* (1838) VI. 578, I have received the King's commands to invest you with the Order of the Bath of which I now transmit you the *insignia*. 1869 FREEMAN *Norm. Conq.* III. xi. 46 King Harold..received in due order the insignia of his kingly office.

b. *sing.* **insigne**; a badge, ensign, or emblem.

1774 J. BRYANT *Mythol.* I. 375 The swan was undoubtedly the *insigne* of Canaan. 1794 MATHIAS *Purs. Lit.* (1798) 309 Should the insigne of a Chancellor's authority be borne by a satellite of a French Directory? 1893 G. ALLEN in *Westm. Gaz.* 9 Aug. 3/1 A cross, which was once the instrument of the vilest punishment reserved for slaves, is now..an insigne of knighthood. 1912 R. A. KNOX in *The Blue Bk.* July 124 The seal, and symbol, and secret of Watson is, of course, his bowler. It is not like other bowlers —it is a priestly vestment, an *insigne* of office. 1948 W. R. BENÉT *Reader's Encycl.* 850/1 The men of Lord Louis Mountbatten's Southeastern Asia command wore it [*sc.* the figure of a phoenix] as an insigne in World War II.

¶ *insignia* has been erroneously used as sing., with pl. *-as*.

The erroneous use is discussed by L. Pound in *Amer. Speech* (1956) XXXI. 156 f.

1774 *Trinket* 144 A red coat cockade and shoulder-knot, those irresistible insignias. 1802 WELLINGTON *Mem. Marhatta War* in Gurw. *Desp.* (1837) I. 368 Bajee Rao.. invested himself with every regal *insignia*. 1807 W. H. IRELAND *Mod. Ship of Fools* 182 Bells, ladle, and the fool's cap..Insignias of their liking. 1832 W. IRVING *Alhambra* II. 98 In his hand he bore a slender white wand, the dreaded insignia of his office. 1897 MARY KINGSLEY *W. Africa* 566, I met this morning a big burly chief with his insignia of office —a great stick. 1971 *Times* 24 Dec. 13/2, I saw not a single racer at Sestrière bearing an insignia that seemed out of place.

2. (Usually *fig.* from 1.) Marks or tokens indicative of anything.

1796 ELIZ. HAMILTON *Lett. Hindoo Rajah* II. 72 Families ..in a situation to afford the expensive insignia of sorrow. 1824 W. IRVING *T. Trav.* I. 287 All these insignia announced that the mighty London was at hand. 1831 BREWSTER *Newton* (1855) II. xvii. 155 Before the middle period of his life, Newton was invested with all the insignia of immortality.

insignificance (ɪnsɪg'nɪfɪkəns). (Also 8 *erron.* **-ence**.) [f. INSIGNIFICANT: see -ANCE.] The fact or quality of being insignificant.

1. Want of signification or meaning.

1754 EDWARDS *Freed. Will* I. iii. 15 Such a Man would use these Terms *must*, *irresistible*, &c. with perfect Insignificence and Nonsense.

2. Want of significance, importance, or force; complete unimportance; contemptibility.

1699 GARTH *Dispens.* I. 187 My annals are in mouldy mildews wrought, With easy insignificance of thought. 1755 YOUNG *Centaur* v. Wks. 1757 IV. 216 If we can draw some moral from it, that will abate its insignificance, and give it some little weight. 1793 BEDDOES *Math. Evid.* 27 Mr. Locke has shewn the insignificance of these axioms. 1820 SCOTT *Monast.* xvii, A sufficient apology for a whole life of insignificance. 1872 YEATS *Growth Comm.* 329 The foreign commerce of Cologne sank into insignificance.

insignificancy (ɪnsɪg'nɪfɪkənsɪ). [f. as prec.: see -ANCY.] The quality of being insignificant.

†**1.** The quality of being without signification or meaning; meaninglessness; = INSIGNIFICANCE 1. With *an* and *pl.*, an instance of this. *Obs.*

1651 HOBBES *Leviath.* IV. xlvi. 379 Which Insignificancy of language..hath a quality..to hide the Truth. 1665 GLANVILL *Scepsis Sci.* xviii. 116 The insignificancies and verbal nothings of this philosophy. 1690 LOCKE *Hum. Und.* III. iv. §10 Another Peripatetick Definition..which.. betrays its Uselesness and Insignificancy.

†**2.** Ineffectiveness, futility. *Obs.*

1720 WELTON *Suffer. Son of God* II. xxviii. 729 To confess the Weakness and Insignificancy of their Attempts. 1721 STRYPE *Eccl. Mem.* II. 444 Of the need of discipline, and of the danger or insignificancy of committing it to the bishops, the good King was very sensible.

3. Unimportance; contemptibility; = INSIGNIFICANCE 2. With *an* and *pl.*, An instance or example of this; an unimportant or contemptible thing or person.

1661 *Papers on Alter. Prayer Bk.* 71 Their Arguments were..of another kind of moment, then decency, or indecency, significancy or insignificancy. 1674 R. GODFREY *Inj. & Ab. Physic* Pref., Almost every Mass of Collections or Bundle of Insignificancies, have them [commendatory verses] to perswade the Reader to buy it. 1712 STEELE *Spect.* No. 284 ⁋1 This Affectation in both Sexes makes them Vain of being useless, and take a certain Pride in their Insignificancy. 1821–30 LD. COCKBURN *Mem.* iv. (1874) 185 The charges..were groundless, and were at last reduced to insignificancy. 1831 CARLYLE *Sart. Res.* II. iv, Coming forward..to tread such a one out of sight, as an insignificancy and worm. 1858 —— *Fredk. Gt.* VII. vi. (1872) II. 316 Poor old fellow, these insignificancies..are all I know of him.

insignificant (ɪnsɪgˈnɪfɪkənt), *a.* (*sb.*) [f. IN-[3] + SIGNIFICANT: cf. F. *insignifiant*.]

1. Devoid of signification or meaning; meaningless: of speech, word, gestures, etc.

1651 HOBBES *Leviath.* I. i. 4 The frequency of insignificant speech. **1732** BERKELEY *Alciphr.* VII. §2 Words that suggest no ideas are insignificant. **1751** R. PALTOCK *P. Wilkins* xiv, By signs and gestures, which were very far from being insignificant. **1869–79** AUSTIN *Jurispr.* (ed. 4) II. xliii. 759 The terms 'Law of Things' and 'Law of Persons' are insignificant, i.e. they give no notion of the purpose of the distinction.

2. Devoid of significance, weight, or force.

†**a.** Without efficacy; ineffective. ineffectual.

1627–77 FELTHAM *Resolves* II. xxxiii. 226 Nature..must vary from her self, or by a drowsie sloth be rendered insignificant. **1672** WILKINS *Nat. Relig.* I. xi. (1675) 164 Laws must be insignificant, without the sanction of Rewards and Punishments. **1681–6** J. SCOTT *Chr. Life* (1747) III. 166 All that Christ hath suffered for us will be insignificant to our Discharge from our Obligation to Punishment, unless we repent and amend. *a* **1735** ARBUTHNOT (J.), In a hemorrhage from the lungs..stypticks are often insignificant.

b. Of no importance or moment; immaterial; trivial, trifling; mean, contemptible. (Now usually with some reference to magnitude: cf. 3.)

1658 R. NEWCOURT *Map Lond.* (*title*), Some others whose short and insignificant raignes haue left them buried in oblivion. **1736** BUTLER *Anal.* i. vii, Things seemingly the most insignificant imaginable, are perpetually observed to be a necessary condition to other things of the greatest importance. **1762** GOLDSM. *Cit. W.* lxix, It is insignificant how remote or near..the object of terror may be. **1813** W. TAYLOR *Eng. Synon.* Introd. 20 Nor can it be wholly insignificant to the diffusion and preservation of our language, to have [etc.]. **1855** MACAULAY *Hist. Eng.* xiv. III. 494 The schism which the oaths had produced was, as yet, insignificant. **1879** FROUDE *Cæsar* xiv. 218 The Roman loss was insignificant in this battle.

c. Of a person, in regard to position, character, influence, etc.

1669 CLARENDON *Ess.* Tracts (1727) 126 No man is so insignificant, as that he can be sure his example can do no hurt. **1751–73** JORTIN *Eccl. Hist.* (R.), Jerom wrote against him..and treats him as an insignificant blockhead. **1833** HT. MARTINEAU *Loom & Lugger* II. v. 79 What matters the ruin of one insignificant Frenchman? **1849** MACAULAY *Hist. Eng.* vi. II. 84 Thomas Powis, an insignificant man, who had no qualification for high employment except servility.

3. Small in size; petty; mean.

1748 *Anson's Voy.* I. vi. 64 No other wood has been found than a few insignificant shrubs. **1794** SULLIVAN *View Nat.* II. 17 If Mont Blanc could be transported to the foot of Chimboraço, Chimboraço, all prodigious as it is supposed, would appear of very insignificant dimensions. **1844** THIRLWALL *Greece* VIII. lxvi. 460 Thebes had sunk to an insignificant village.

B. as *sb.* **a.** A word or thing without signification. **b.** An unimportant or contemptible person.

1710 STEELE *Tatler* No. 247 ¶6 If we are the Insignificants that others call us, Where is the Triumph in deceiving us? **1785** TYTLER *Lounger* No. 16 ¶15, I despised the giddy restless insignificants that figured in this perpetual drama. **1816** J. GILCHRIST *Philos. Etym.* 125 A few experiments upon the terminations in question, will probably convince the reader that they are merely connectives; and he will recollect..that connectives are nearly akin to insignificants.

Hence †**insigˈnificantness** (Bailey, 1727).

insignificantly (ɪnsɪgˈnɪfɪkəntlɪ), *adv.* [f. prec. + -LY[2].] In an insignificant manner; so as to signify nothing, or be of no importance; meaninglessly; †without effect, to no purpose (*obs.*).

1651 HOBBES *Leviath.* I. viii. 39 The common sort of men seldome speak Insignificantly. **1676** GREW *Exper. Luctat.* i. §16 As they contain a middle quantity of an Alkaly, they are not insignificantly used against the Stone. *a* **1677** HALE *Prim. Orig. Man.* I. ii. 66 When Birds..are taught to use articulate words, yet they understand not their import..but use them insignificantly. **1691** NORRIS *Pract. Disc.* 153 He has lived insignificantly and wickedly, idly and unaccountably. **1724** DE FOE *Mem. Cavalier* II. 156 Their Swords were extravagantly, and I think insignificantly broad. **1784** COWPER *Task* VI. 320 With all the prettiness of feigned alarm, And anger insignificantly fierce. **1855** KINGSLEY *Westw. Ho* xi. (1890) 95 Raleigh laughed insignficantly; but was silent.

†**insigˈnificate**, *v.* *Obs. rare*[−1]. [irreg. f. INSIGNIFIC-ANT + -ATE[3].] *trans.* To render of no importance, reduce to insignificance.

1676 FOUNTAINHALL in M. P. Brown *Suppl. Decis.* (1826) III. 112 This insignificates their privileges as a burgh royal.

†**insigˈnificative**, *a.* *Obs.* [ad. late L. *insignificātīv-us* (found as a name of the infinitive mood), f. *in-* (IN-[3]) + **significātīvus*, f. *significāre* to SIGNIFY.] Not significative, not denoting by external signs.

1660 JER. TAYLOR *Duct. Dubit.* II. ii. rule 6 §52 They were ineffective and insignificative. **1677** PLOT *Oxfordsh.* 283 Adam..named all living Creatures not by words of a first institution, antecedently insignificative. **1751** tr. *Pernetti's Phil. Lett. Physiognomy* 230 The ordinary sort of the unmeaning [eyes] are not indeed utterly insignificative.

†**inˈsignious**, *a.* *Obs. rare.* [f. L. *insigni-s* distinguished + -OUS.] Distinguished, eminent, notable.

1620 BP. J. KING *Serm.* 26 Mar. 17 This Citty..became ..of more insignious mercy, then the whole earth besides. *a* **1656** USSHER *Ann.* vi. (1658) 120 This insignious Victory was gotten by them, upon the 6 day of Boedromion, the 3 month in the Attic Calendar.

insignis (ɪnˈsɪgnɪs). [a. L. *insignis* remarkable, used as the specific epithet of *Pinus insignis* (D. Douglas in J. C. Loudon *Arboretum et Fruticetum Britannicum* (1838) IV. 2265), the former name of the tree.] The Monterey pine, *Pinus radiata*, which is native to southern California and widely cultivated elsewhere.

[**1866** 'SENILIS' *Pinaceæ* iii. 128 Although not so beautiful as Insignis, yet it [*sc.* the radiated-coned pine] is a useful ornamental Pine.] **1920** C. COLTMAN-ROGERS *Conifers* i. 41 The Insignis is a tree that undoubtedly favours sea air. **1931** E. MAXWELL *Afforestation in Southern Lands* xxxix. 175 The Insignis thrives well under widely different degrees of rainfall. *Ibid.* 179 The quality of Insignis timber varies greatly according to the way it has been grown and its age. **1957** *Handbk. Softwoods* (Forest Prod. Res. Lab.) 41 Pine, radiata... Other names. Insignis pine (general), insignis (S. Africa), Monterey pine (U.S.A.).

†**insignite**, *ppl. a.* *Obs. rare.* [ad. L. *insignīt-us*, pa. pple. of *insignīre* to mark with a sign or badge, distinguish, f. *insignis*: see INSIGNE *a.*] Distinguished. (Construed also as *pa. pple.*)

1432–50 tr. *Higden* (Rolls) V. 169 Constancius..sende hym to Fraunce, whiche havenge mony victoryes þer was insignite mervelleously with a crowne of laurer. **1768–74** TUCKER *Lt. Nat.* (1834) I. 475 Dear doctor, celeberrimous doctor, insignite illustrissim doctor.

†**insigˈnited**, *ppl. a.* *Obs. rare*[−1]. [f. as prec. + -ED[1].] Distinguished with a mark or badge.

1660 WATERHOUSE *Arms & Arm.* 44 A clear proof of the use of Insignited banners amongst the Jewes.

†**insigˈnition.** *Obs. rare*[−1]. [n. of action from L. *insignīre* to distinguish: see INSIGNITE.] A distinguishing mark or ensign.

1660 WATERHOUSE *Arms & Arm.* 42 He will haue their Banners charged with Insignitions of Distinction.

†**insignitor.** *Obs. rare*[−1]. [agent-n. in L. form f. *insignīre* to mark, distinguish: cf. late L. *insignītor* an engraver.] The index-finger.

1597 A. M. tr. *Guillemeau's Fr. Chirurg.* 12 b/1 The Insignitoure, or forefinger, Lat. *Index.*

†**inˈsignity.** *Obs. rare*[−1]. [f. L. *insigni-s*: see INSIGNE *a.* and -ITY.] Distinguished quality; distinction, eminence.

1616 R. C. *Times' Whistle* III. 1126 Ther is an everlasting dignity Of greater worth and more insignity.

†**insignize**, *v.* *Obs. rare*[−1]. [f. as prec. + -IZE.] *trans.* To distinguish.

1678 R. R[USSELL] *Geber* Pref. 1 The specious Titles with which they are insignized.

insignment, obs. form of ENSIGNMENT.

†**inˈsimilar**, *a.* *Obs. rare.* [IN-[3].] Not similar, unlike.

1801 H. SKRINE *Rivers Gt. Brit.* 47 Not insimilar to the rocks of St. Vincent. *Ibid.* 389 The not-insimilar scenic shew of Vauxhall graces the opposite shore.

insimplicity (ɪnsɪmˈplɪsɪtɪ). *rare.* [IN-[3].] Absence or want of simplicity.

1877 *The Survival* 345 A position of pious insincerity, or, shall I say insimplicity. **1897** *Month* Oct. 379 To rid themselves of nineteenth century insimplicity. **1898** *Weekly Reg.* 9 July 49 The insimplicities of the age have to be.. reckoned with.

†**inˈsimulate**, *v.* *Obs.* Also 7 insimulat; *pa. pple.* insimulat. [f. L. *insimulāt-*, ppl. stem of *insimulā-re* to bring a plausible charge against, accuse, f. *in-* (IN-[2]) + *simulāre* to make like, SIMULATE. In sense 2, f. IN-[2] + SIMULATE *v.*]

1. *trans.* To charge, accuse.

1532 MORE *Confut. Tindale* Wks. 340/1 These..heretikes haue of longe whyle neither letted, nor ceased, falsly to insimulate & accuse the churche of god. **1610** J. FORBES *Cert. Rec.* II. xi. (1846) 519 The holy ministrie are insimulat ..as restless and unquiet spirits. **1663** *Flagellum or O. Cromwell* (1672) 38 Not sparing to insimulate his own General the Earl of Manchester of the same prevarications.

2. To feign, simulate. *rare*[−0].

1623 COCKERAM, *Insimulate*, to faine, to dissemble.

†**insimuˈlation.** *Obs.* *rare.* [ad. L. *insimulātiōn-em*, n. of action from *insimulāre*: see prec.] Charge, accusation.

1586 A. DAY *Eng. Secretary* II. (1625) 44 Custome carrying with it selfe any secret insimulation of evill, is not to be followed. **1604** H. JACOB *Reasons* 26 This their insimulation is against none other then Christ him selfe.

insincere (ɪnsɪnˈsɪə(r)), *a.* [ad. L. *insincēr-us* not genuine, adulterated, dishonest, f. *in-* (IN-[3]) + *sincērus* SINCERE.]

1. Not sincere or genuine; assuming a false guise in speech or conduct; dissembling, disingenuous. Said of persons and their actions or behaviour.

1634 CANNE *Necess. Separ.* (1849) 280 We are persuaded they are merely their own dreams, purposely taken up, to countenance by them, if they could, their insincere walking. **1674** MARVELL *Corr.* ccxviii. Wks. 1872–5 II. 424 Things stand as I heare but ticklish and insincere betwixt us and Holland. *a* **1704** T. BROWN *Sat. agst. Wom.* Wks. 1730 I. 56 Alternate smiles and frowns, both insincere. **1745** WESLEY *Answ. Ch.* 12 You make them a close, reserved, insincere deceitful people. **1855** MACAULAY *Hist. Eng.* xxi. IV. 564 The King..was never much inclined to engage in a commerce of insincere compliments.

†**2.** Not pure or genuine; adulterated, unsound.

(The quotations cited in J. and in later Dicts. for this sense have *unsincere* in the originals: see UNSINCERE.)

insincerely (ɪnsɪnˈsɪəlɪ), *adv.* [f. prec. + -LY[2].] In an insincere manner; without sincerity or candour; disingenuously.

1625 BP. MOUNTAGU *App Cæsar* I. iv. 26 For dealing in the case so insincerely and calumniously in their Informations. **1692** LOCKE *3rd Let. Toleration* i. Wks. 1727 II. 310 Speaking insincerely is to speak otherwise than one thinks, let what he says be true or false. **1855** MACAULAY *Hist. Eng.* xii. III. 170 The few Protestants who remained in that part of the country joined in greeting him, and perhaps not insincerely. **1886** H. F. LESTER *Under two Fig Trees* 3, I told Katrina insincerely that it was of no consequence.

insincerity (ɪnsɪnˈsɛrɪtɪ). [f. L. *insincērus* INSINCERE + -ITY: cf. *sincerity*.]

†**1.** Want of purity, corruption. *Obs.*

1548 UDALL, etc. *Erasm. Par. Acts* Pref., If there shal no more insynceritee of doctrine appere in the writynges of theim that will so saie, then [etc.].

2. The opposite of sincerity; the quality of being insincere; dissimulation; an instance of this.

a **1699** STILLINGFL. *Serm.* IV. iii. (R.), Doing all our duties to God in such a manner as our conscience cannot charge us with gross neglect or insincerity. **1792** GOUV. MORRIS in Sparks *Life & Writ.* (1832) II. 231 Manfredi, a statesman of the Italian school, who takes insincerity for wisdom. **1856** FROUDE *Hist. Eng.* II. 232 In him, infinite insincerity was accompanied with a grace of manner which regained confidence as rapidly as it was forfeited. **1885** A. DOBSON *Steele* Introd. 11 He raised his voice unceasingly in condemnation of the fashionable insincerities of his day.

†**inˈsinew**, *v.* *Obs.* Also en-. [f. IN-[2] + SINEW.] *trans.* To furnish with sinews; to innerve; to inspire with vigour or strength.

1597 SHAKS. *2 Hen. IV*, IV. i. 172 All members of our Cause..That are insinewed [*1st Qo.* ensinewed] to this Action. **1611** FLORIO, *Inneruare*, to ensinnew.

†**inˈsinewy**, *a.* *Obs. rare*[−1]. [IN-[3]. Cf. L. *innervis*.] Not sinewy, weak, nerveless.

1653 GAUDEN *Hierasp.* 203 Nothing more loose, spungy, insinnewie, and unsubstantiall, than what ariseth from no higher source than their own brains.

ˈinˌsinking, *vbl. sb.* [IN *adv.* 11 c.] A sinking in; a depression.

1878 BELL tr. *Gegenbaur's Comp. Anat.* 400 An insinking of the surface of the body approaches the point of union of the two halves of the peribranchial space. **1885** J. S. KINGSLEY in *Q. Jrnl. Microsc. Sc.* Oct. 538 That the primary stigma formed by the insinking of the respiratory book is not the functional one of the adult.

†**inˈsinuance.** *Obs. rare*[−1]. [f. next: see -ANCE. Cf. *continuance*.] = INSINUATION.

1647 CLARENDON *Hist. Reb.* III. §261 With some passionate insinuances that, since they opposed a due regulation of their power, there would be no other way but to cut them off root and branch.

insinuant (ɪnˈsɪnjuːənt), *a.* *rare.* [ad. L. *insinuānt-em*, pr. pple. of *insinuāre* to INSINUATE: perh. immed. a. F. *insinuant* (17th c. in Hatz.).]

1. = INSINUATING *ppl. a.* 2; wheedling, ingratiating.

a **1639** WOTTON *Educ.* in *Reliq.* (1672) 80 Plausible, insinuant and fortunate men. **1685** tr. *Gracian's Courtiers Orac.* 258 Novelty is insinuant, and if it be happy, it sets a double value upon what is good. **1839** BAILEY *Festus* xxxi. (1852) 501 The train Of those insinuant tempters.

2. That steals its way in.

1877 BLACKIE *Wise Men* 147 The stony seed Feels the insinuant dew.

insinuate (ɪnˈsɪnjuːeɪt), *v.* Also 6–7 -at. [f. ppl. stem of L. *insinuāre*, f. *in-* (IN-[2]) + *sinuāre* to bend in windings, to curve. Nearly all the Eng. senses were already in Lat.; the fig. senses of the L. were the first to be adopted in Eng.: see 5, 6, 7.]

1. a. *trans.* To introduce tortuously, sinuously, indirectly, or by devious methods; to introduce by imperceptible degrees or subtle means.

1647 H. MORE *Song of S.* III. App., Pref., Nor is it harder to phansie, how these Præexistent Souls insinuate into Seed, Embryos, or Infants, then how Created ones are insinuated. **1671** R. BOHUN *Wind* 146 Open the pores of our bodyes by heat and then insinuate the malignant influences. **1678** CUDWORTH *Intell. Syst.* I. v. 744 These Philosophers concluded concerning Souls, that..they were Insinuated or Introduced into Bodies, in Generations. **1746** BERKELEY *Let. to Prior* 20 May in Fraser *Life* viii. (1871) 316 The insinuating of such salts into the wood. **1809** KENDALL

Trav. III. lxxvi. 185 Trees, which insinuate their roots into the fissures, are seen in all the lower parts of the mountains. **1850** ROBERTSON *Serm.* Ser. III. i. (1872) 3 There are poisons so destructive that a single drop insinuated into the veins produces death in three minutes. **1852** MOTLEY *Corr.* (1889) I. v. 133 Our street was narrow, and the machine could by no possibility be insinuated therein.

fig. **1610** HEALEY *St. Aug. Citie of God* 724 The booke [Malachi] insinuateth the New Testament.

b. *refl.* To introduce oneself, make one's way, or penetrate, by sinuous or subtle ways.

1598 HAKLUYT *Voy.* I. 556 There is ayer also, which insinuating it selfe by passages, and holes, into the very bowels of the earth, doeth puffe vp the nourishment of so huge a fire. **1613** PURCHAS *Pilgrimage* (1614) 513 Mediterranean..in many places he insinuates himselfe within the Land by Gulfes or Bayes, twining his loving armes about. **1759** tr. *Duhamel's Husb.* II. ii. (1762) 206 This wet insinuates itself very easily between the husks. **1865** DICKENS *Mut. Fr.* III. iii, Having insinuated himself into the chamber. **1895** in *Westm. Gaz.* 30 May 2/2 Enormous creepers insinuated themselves everywhere.

†**c.** *intr.* (for *refl.*)

1600 HOLLAND *Livy* XLIV. xli. 1197 The Romanes espied where there was a breach made and lane left between, and there they would insinuate and wind in with their rankes and files. **1666** W. BOYHURST *Loimographia* (1894) 28 The Plague gradually insinuated, and crept downe Holborne and the Strand. **1667** MILTON *P.L.* IV. 348 Close the Serpent sly, Insinuating, wove with Gordian twine His breaded train. **1692** RAY *Dissol. World* iii. (1732) 20 The Water where it could insinuate and make its way. *a* **1774** GOLDSM. *Surv. Exp. Philos.* (1776) II. 209 The air..is forced out of the substances into which it has insinuated.

2. a. *trans.* To introduce (a person) by sinuous, stealthy, or artful ways into some position or relation; esp. *refl.* to worm oneself in, or make one's way sinuously or stealthily into the company, society, favour, affection, etc. of another.

1579 LYLY *Euphues* (Arb.) 134 When their sonnes shall insinuate themselues in the company of flatterers. **1600** HAKLUYT *Voy.* (1810) III. 407, I sent him two sutes of apparell..the better to insinuate myself into his friendship. **1665** *Surv. Aff. Netherl.* 136 Then they petition against strangers..and insinuated their chief Demagogues to the places of greatest Honour and Trust in the Countrey. **1755** *Man* No. 21 ¶6 She knows extremely well how to insinuate herself. **1792** *Anecd. W. Pitt* I. xix. 299 The Duke of Bourbon insinuated himself so adroitly with the young.. King as to establish himself Prime Minister. **1807** ROBINSON *Archæol. Græca* V. xx. 503 Those who, by flattery and other mean arts, were accustomed to insinuate themselves to the tables of other men. **1832** tr. *Sismondi's Ital. Rep.* ix. 198 They insinuated themselves into families to betray them.

†**b.** *intr.* (for *refl.*) To work or wheedle oneself *into*, to ingratiate oneself *with*. *Obs.*

1588 SHAKS. *Tit. A.* IV. ii. 38 To see so great a Lord Basely insinuate, and send vs gifts. *c* **1592** MARLOWE *Massacre Paris* II. iv, Now, Madam, must you insinuate with the King, And tell him that 'tis for his country's good. **1628** GAULE *Pract. The.* (1629) 70 One Angell insinuated to converse with a Woman; and so deceiued her to a desperate Fall. **1656** STANLEY *Hist. Philos.* IV. (1701) 135/2 He soon insinuated into the favour of Dyonysius. **1727** DE FOE *Syst. Magic* I. iii. (1840) 86 With what address he insinuated into her weakest part. **1760-72** H. BROOKE *Fool of Qual.* (1809) III. 13 To keep in fee some discreet..matron, who may insinuate into her acquaintance.

3. a. *refl.* Of an immaterial thing: To instil itself subtly; to win or gain a way for itself *into* men's minds, favour, or notice.

1594 HOOKER *Eccl. Pol.* I. vii. §6 There is no particular evil which hath not some appearance of goodness whereby to insinuate itself. **1662** STILLINGFL. *Orig. Sacr.* I. iv. §2 The novelty and pleasingness of Musick and Poetry did presently insinuate its self into the minds of men. **1776** GIBBON *Decl. & F.* xv. (1869) I. 332 A pure and humble religion gently insinuated itself into the minds of men. **1843** GALLENGA *Italy, Past & Pr.* (1848) I. p. xxviii, That spirit of scholastic erudition which insinuated itself into Italian literature. **1858** CARLYLE *Fredk. Gt.* VII. ix. (1872) II. 340 Saner thoughts begin to insinuate themselves.

†**b.** *intr.* (for *refl.*) *Obs.*

1601 HOLLAND *Pliny* II. 372 Things plausible to the world crept and insinuated farther into the heart of man. **1672** MARVELL *Reh. Transp.* I. 306 To bring them off with Conscience, and (which insinuates into all men) some little Reputation.

†**4.** *trans.* To draw, win, or attract (a person, etc.) subtly or covertly *to* or *unto* something. *Obs.*

1594 J. P. (*title*), Dame Helen Branch, by whose godly and virtuous life virgins are insinuated to virtue, wives to faithfulness, and widows to Christian contemplation (Latham). **1624** HEYWOOD *Gunaik.* III. 143 To reobtaine his principalitie hee insinuated unto his aide Porsenna King of the Tuscans. *a* **1677** BARROW *Wks.* (1686) III. Serm. xxxiii. 364 These [kinds of flattery]..do insinuate our mind, and.. do inveagle to sin more effectually.

5. To introduce, convey, or impart to the mind indirectly, covertly, or privily; to infuse or instil subtly or imperceptibly.

1529 MORE *Dyaloge* I. xxv. 36 a/1 He temperyth hys reuelacyons and in such wyse doth insinuate and inspyre them into the brestys of hys crysten people, that by the secrete instynct of the holy gost, they consent and agre to gether in one. **1553** *Act 1 Mary* Sess. 2. c. 1 §2 A very few persons..deuised first to insinuat a scruple into the King your fathers conscience. **1626** W. SCLATER *Exp. 2 Thess.* (1629) A iv b, On fairest pretenses, to insinuate errour about the time of Christs second comming. **1665** BOYLE *Occas. Refl.* v. ii. (1848) 303 Opportunity to insinuate into the minds of the people, that their Persecutors had rather see men vitious, than inquisitive. **1774** WARTON *Hist. Eng. Poetry* XXX. II. 263 Our Author with much address insinuates to King James the Fourth an exhortation to conjugal fidelity. **1841** D'ISRAELI *Amen. Lit.* (1867) 128 Under Elizabeth favourite phrases were insinuated into the dialect by over-refined travellers. **1862** MAURICE *Mor. & Met. Philos.* IV. ix. §8. 530 In which wisdom was to be insinuated not enforced.

6. To convey (a statement or notion) by indirect suggestion; to hint obliquely: now generally with implication of cunning or underhand action.

1561 THROGMORTON in Tytler *Proofs & Illustr.* VI. 467 Whatsoever the said queen shall insinuate your maj. of him. **1563** WINƷET *Wks.* (1890) II. 10 He can nocht cal it a General Counsel, sa he apperis to insinuat that the haly Fatheris aggreit nocht thare amangis thame selfis. **1596** DALRYMPLE tr. *Leslie's Hist. Scot.* x. 395 Sum wicket persounis clattiris behind backis, and insinuatis, how contrare thair vtilitie was that Jornay. **1692** BP. ELY *Answ. Touchstone* 223 Now that is said to be insinuated which is not expressly prepounded but adumbrated and obscurely indicated. **1732** BERKELEY *Alciphr.* I. §4 Hints and allusions, expressing little, insinuating much. **1772** *Junius Lett.* lxviii. 355 Was it..insinuated to you..that no felony was committed? **1817** COBBETT *Pol. Reg.* 15 Feb. 207 After so much had been said, and so much more had been insinuated, to misrepresent my own particular views. **1825** T. JEFFERSON *Autobiog.* Wks. 1859 I. 67, I..did not think it proper to insinuate any doubt of the fair conduct of his government. **1828** D'ISRAELI *Chas. I*, I. v. 99 [He] delicately insinuated that the marriage would never take place.

absol. **1858** FROUDE *Hist. Eng.* III. xii. 30 He must go beyond the matter and beside it, and insinuate when he was unable to assert.

7. To signify or express indirectly; to give to understand; to hint, suggest, imply. *Obs.* or *arch.*

1533 MORE *Answ. Poysoned Bk.* I. vi. Wks. 1045/1 By these woordes..our Sauiour dyd as the old holye doctours declare, insinuate, and secretelye sygnifye to theym, the meate of hys owne blessed person. **1555** EDEN *Decades* 99 By whiche woordes the poore man seemed to insinuate that he had byn robbed. **1605** WILLET *Hexapla Gen.* 198 It was God that talked with him, and not an angel, as the words of the text insinuate. **1638** F. JUNIUS *Paint. of Ancients* 161 Huge power, which is signified by the scepter; sometimes a sore hurt, which is insinuated by the serpents. **1641** *Marmion Antiquary* I, He did insinuate with his eyes, unto me, I should depart and leave them. **1776** G. SEMPLE *Building in Water* 146 The small Dart at r. insinuates, that only a small Quantity of the Tide comes into the Harbour. **1816** SCOTT *Tales My Landlord* Ser. I. Introd., Our metropolis and mart of gain, whereby I insinuate Glasgow.

8. *Law.* To enter (a deed or document) in an official register; to register; to deliver or lodge for registration. Cf. INSINUATION 6. (F. *insinuer*, late L. *insinuāre*.)

(Still used in the Commissions issued by the Bishop of Winchester to the Deans of Jersey and Guernsey as his Commissaries.)

1529 *Act 21 Hen. VIII*, c. 5 Every suche bysshoppe or ordynary..shall approve insynuate seale and regystre from tyme to tyme the said testamentes. **1602** FULBECKE *2nd Pt Parall.* 32 Such Testaments must be insinuated to the Officiall or Commissarie of the Bishop of the Dioces within foure monethes after the death of the testator: which insinuation is appointed by Law.

Hence **in'sinuated** *ppl. a.*; **in'sinuating** *vbl. sb.*

1605 VERSTEGAN *Dec. Intell.* x. (1628) 338 Borrowed from such before-insinuated languages as haue no dependance on ours. **1643** MILTON *Divorce* Introd. (1851) 4 The suttle insinuating of Error and Custome. **1655** M. CARTER *Hon. Rediv.* (1660) 23 Eminent preferments; which they too often come to, more by insinuated favour, than reall desert. **1828** *Lights & Shades* II. 192 A smile and insinuated sovereign, which purchase my lord's butler.

†**in'sinuate,** *ppl. a. Obs.* [ad. L. *insinuāt-us*, pa. pple. of *insinuāre*: see prec. and -ATE[2].] Insinuated. (Const. as *pa. pple.* or *adj.*)

1534 MORE *Treat. on Passion* Wks. 1292/2 The great mistery of Christes passyon..lyttle and lyttle at sundry seasons to bee sygnifyed and insinuate conueniently to man. **1671** *True Nonconf.* Pref., I thought it worth my pains..to check the tumor of this insinuat boasting.

in'sinuating, *ppl. a.* [f. prec. vb. + -ING[2].]

1. That penetrates by sinuous windings between the particles of a body; subtly penetrating.

1615 J. STEPHENS *Satyr. Ess.* (ed. 2) 170 His wit and apprehension (like the insinuating ayre) will pierce through lesse cranyes then the pores of a mans bodie. **1735** SOMERVILLE *Chase* IV. 369 Th' insinuating Eel, that hides his Head Beneath the slimy Mud. **1744** BERKELEY *Siris* §60 A volatile, smooth, insinuating oil. **1799** tr. *Meister's Lett. Eng.* 165 Black smoak..of the most subtile and insinuating nature.

2. That artfully works his way into company, position, favour, etc.; wily, wheedling, ingratiating. Of persons, their manner, etc.

1591 SHAKS. *1 Hen. VI*, II. iv. 35 Without all colour Of base insinuating flatterie, I pluck this white Rose with Plantagenet. **1592** NASHE *P. Penilesse* (ed. 2) 11 b, Let not a seruile insinuating slaue creepe betwixt your legges into credit with your Lords. **1664** H. MORE *Myst. Iniq.* 209 A more cunning Impostour and insinuating Hypocrite. **1782** COWPER *Progr. Err.* 7 By what unseen and unsuspected arts The serpent Error twines round human hearts..The poisonous, black, insinuating worm. *a* **1859** MACAULAY *Hist. Eng.* xxiii. V. 27 Englishmen of honourable name, distinguished appearance, and insinuating address.

Hence **in'sinuatingly** *adv.*, in an insinuating manner; **in'sinuatingness** (Bailey vol. II, 1727).

1861 G. MEREDITH *E. Harrington* I. vi. 88 He insinuatingly remarked he could jog on all night. **1882** MRS. RIDDELL *Pr. Wales's Garden-Party* 24 'Is your husband very shy, Mrs. Arkley?' enquired the judge's granddaughter, blandly and insinuatingly.

insinuation (ɪnsɪnjuː'eɪʃən). [ad. L. *insinuātiōn-em*, n. of action f. *insinuāre* to INSINUATE: cf. F. *insinuation* (16th c. in Littré).] The action of insinuating.

1. A winding or twisting.

1661 EVELYN *Diary* 15 July, I greately admired at the extravagant turnings, insinuations, and growth of certaine birch trees among the rocks. **1869** J. MARTINEAU *Ess.* II. 3 The infinitely fine insinuations of analysis.

2. Introduction or entrance by winding, indirect, or stealthy motion; creeping or slipping in covertly or stealthily; stealing in.

1614 BP. HALL *Recoll. Treat.* 488 Pleasure is of a winding, and serpentine nature;..Withall, her insinuations are so cunning, that you shall not perceive your excesse, till [etc.]. **1624** DONNE *Serm.* ii. 17 That a Virgin may have a child by the insinuation and practise of the Devill. **1644** BULWER *Chirol.* 114 Omit this benevolent insinuation of the Hand. **1664** EVELYN *Sylva* (1679) 13 These concussions of the Roots, loosning the mould, make room for their more easie insinuations. **1685** BOYLE *Salub. Air* 31 The possible insinuation of Effluvia, that rove in the Air, at the pores of the skin. **1799** KIRWAN *Geol. Ess.* 139 Putrefaction on the one part, and gradual insinuation of stony particles on the other, until the petrifaction is completed. *a* **1806** LD. MACARTNEY *Wks.* II. 365 (Jod.) The resistance of adamant is insufficient to defeat the insinuation of a fibre.

3. The action of stealing into the favour or affections of any one by winning, persuasive, or subtle means; ingratiation. Also, an instance of this, a winning or ingratiating action or speech.

1553 T. WILSON *Rhet.* (1580) 101 A privie twinyng, or close crepyng in, to win favours with muche circumstaunce, called insinuation. **1644** BULWER *Chiron.* 7 When She came to read it, and found not the insinuations of elocution and gesture. **1675** tr. *Machiavelli's Prince* (1883) 181 He..made use of..courtesy and insinuation. **1720** WELTON *Suffer. Son of God* II. xvii. 465 By the Winning Insinuations of His Agreeable Discourses. **1728** MORGAN *Algiers* I. Pref. 2, I never advanced a Step by way of Insinuation, to curry Favour or Affection, as they say, on any Side. **1814** SCOTT *Wav.* xxi, [Her voice] possessed as well the tones which impress awe and conviction as those of persuasive insinuation.

†**b.** *Rhet.* A kind of exordium to a speech designed artfully to win over the hearers. *Obs.*

c **1530** L. COX *Rhet.* (1899) 53 There is yet an other maner, to begyn by insinuacion..he must vse, in stede of a preface, an insinuacion. **1553** T. WILSON *Rhet.* 60 Insinuation must then, and not els, be used, when the judge is greved with us, and our cause hated of the hearers. **1586** A. DAY *Eng. Secretary* I. (1625) 11 We study to winne favour or allowance ..sometimes by insinuation, wherein covertly..we seeke.. to shew that the case is tollerable. **1616** BULLOKAR, *Insinuation*, a cunning speech to creepe into ones fauour.

4. The subtle or insensible instilling of anything into the mind.

1526 *Pilgr. Perf.* (W. de W. 1531) 201 b, Abhorre to admyt in thy mynde y[e] leest insinuacyon or poynt of ony maner of corrupcyon. **1678** CUDWORTH *Intell. Syst.* I. iv. §15. 278 Who by the insinuation of divine truth hath delivered us from such great Errors of mind. **1697** POTTER *Antiq. Greece* II. xiii. (1715) 310 The Mind and Phantasy being pure.. might be the fitter to receive Divine insinuations. **1863** J. G. MURPHY *Comm. Gen.* ii. 17 By the insinuation of a few fundamental and germinant notions into his mind.

5. The suggestion or hinting of anything indirectly, covertly, or by allusion or implication. Also with *pl.*, an indirect or covert suggestion.

1532 MORE *Confut. Tindale* Wks. 819/1 Many other necessary truthes, though they be spoken of in scripture, and some insinuacion made of them..yet [etc.]. **1533** —— *Answ. Poysoned Bk.* IV. viii. Wks. 1112/1 He gaue them an insinuacion and significacion therof, in that he said, And y[t] bred that I shall geue you is my fleshe. **1642** MILTON *Apol. Smect.* Introd., Wks. (1851) 258 A modest title should only informe the buyer what the book containes without furder insinuation. **1664** H. MORE *Myst. Iniq., Apol.* 328 There is not the least insinuation or show of implication that God is the Author of sin. **1727** DE FOE *Syst. Magic* I. iv. (1840) 96 Whether Satan did it thus, or by any other method of insinuation, we are not sure. **1748** *Anson's Voy.* III. vii. 356 Which groundless insinuations had indeed too much weight. **1884** L. J. JENNINGS *Croker Papers* I. x. 287 This insinuation..was promptly met and disposed of at the time.

†**6.** *Law.* The production or delivery of a will for official registration, as a step towards procuring probate. (So in F.; late L. *insinuātio* notification, publication, *Cod. Justin.*) *Obs.*

1529 *Act 21 Hen. VIII*, c. 5 Any..person..whyche.. shall have auctorite or power to take or receyve probacyon insynuacion or approbacion of testament. **1602** [see INSINUATE *v.* 8]. **1706** PHILLIPS, *Insinuation of a Will*.., the first Production of it, or the leaving it in the Register's Hands, in order to its Probate. **1726** AYLIFFE *Parergon* 534 The Insinuation or Registring of Wills is the Publication of Wills at the Acts of Court.

insinuative (ɪn'sɪnjuːeɪtɪv, -ətɪv), *a.* [f. L. *insinuāt-*, ppl. stem of *insinuāre* to INSINUATE + -IVE: cf. F. *insinuatif* (17th c. in Hatz.-Darm.).] Characterized by insinuation, tending to insinuate.

1. Having the tendency or property of stealing into favour or confidence; subtly ingratiating.

1592 BACON *Obs. Libel* i. in *Resuscitatio* (1661) 108 Any Popular, or Insinuative, Carriage of Himself. **1612** T. TAYLOR *Comm. Titus* ii. 14 Preuent the wiles and policies of this tyrant; for he is of a serpentine, creeping, and

insinuatiue nature. **1626** W. SCLATER *Exp. 2 Thess.* (1629) A iv b, First, Proœme insinuatiue, Cap. I. ad Vers. 5. [Cf. prec. 3 b.] **1647** TRAPP *Comm. Matt.* vii. 15 The locusts also ..have faces like women insinuative and flattering. *a* **1656** BP. HALL *Gt. Impostor* (R.), Is a man..plaine dealing? he is rudely uncivill: is he wisely insinuative? he is a flatterer. **1683** CAVE *Ecclesiastici, Athanasius* 93 His Discourse [was] plausible and insinuative. **1768–74** TUCKER *Lt. Nat.* (1834) II. 401 The insinuative force of sympathy and intercourse with other people.

2. Tending to insinuate or gently instil into the mind.

1786 G. CHALMERS *Life De Foe* (1841) 78 Such insinuative instruction as [has] seldom been equalled, but never surpassed.

3. Characterized by or involving insinuation or suggestion; given to or making insinuations; prone to allusive suggestion; suggestive, hinting.

1648 E. SPARKE in *Shute's Sarah & Hagar* (1649) a ij a, None whatsoever extant [writings are] so copious and insinuative in the Application. **1736** LEDIARD *Life Marlborough* II. 223 What a Heap of insinuative Scandal.. is here thrown upon the greatest Man of his Age. **1859** KINGSLEY *Misc.* (1860) II. 35 Not to excite the minds of the public against him by those insinuative or vituperative epithets, which are but adders and scorpions.

Hence **in'sinuatively** *adv.*, in an insinuative manner; **in'sinuativeness**, insinuative quality.

1617 COLLINS *Def. Bp. Ely* II. viii. 309 Not literally, not expressely, but yet insinuatiuely and intentionally. **1657–83** EVELYN *Hist. Relig.* (1850) II. 249 Craftily and insinuatively introduced by the subtlety of Satan. **1727** BAILEY vol. II, *Insinuatingness, Insinuativeness*, insinuating Nature, Engagingness, Winningness. **1837** T. HOOK *Jack Brag* ii, Appeared to be wholly unconscious of his insinuativeness.

insinuator (ɪn'sɪnjuːeɪtə(r)). Also 7 -er. [a. L. *insinuātor*, agent-n. f. *insinuāre* to INSINUATE: see -OR.] One who insinuates. **a.** One who artfully creeps into favour. **b.** One who hints or suggests subtly.

1598 FLORIO, *Insinuatore*, an insinuator, a craftie slie creeper into ones bosome, fauor or mind. **1619** PURCHAS *Microcosmus* lxi. 604 To keepe out the Robber and Cheater, the violent Intruder, and fraudulent Insinuater. *a* **1641** BP. MOUNTAGU *Acts & Mon.* (1642) 416 They were not insinuators with the female sexe. **1741** RICHARDSON *Pamela* xxviii, Why, prythee now, insinuator, said he, say the worst you can. **1748** —— *Clarissa* xlii, This is all you desire at present, creeper-on, insinuator!

insinuatory (ɪn'sɪnjuːətərɪ), *a.* [f. L. *insinuāt-* (see INSINUATE *v.*) + -ORY.] = INSINUATIVE.

1871 MORLEY *Voltaire* iii. (1872) 123 This philosophising is very much more indirect, insinuatory, and furtive.

insinuendo (ɪnsɪnjuː'ɛndəʊ). [A 'portmanteau' blending of INSINUATION and INNUENDO.]

A tasteless word.—R.W.B.

1885 B. MATTHEWS in *Longman's Mag.* Dec. 151 Could I not damn with faint praise and stab with sharp insinuendo? —to use the labor-saving and much-needed word thoughtlessly invented by the sable legislator of South Carolina. **1906** *N. & Q.* 3 Mar. 171/1 An old Yorkshire friend of mine..used the following words frequently. He thought they were good English:—'Disastrophe' = disaster + catastrophe, 'Insinuendo' = insinuation + innuendo. **1909** *Daily Chron.* 9 June 6/7 It was a sable legislator who howled back with scorn the 'insinuendos' of a political opponent. **1921** C. MACKENZIE *Rich Relatives* ix. 216 Anyone more cunning I've never seen. Nasty insinuendos, enough to make anyone sick! **1966** P. MOLONEY (*title*) A plea for Mersey or the gentle art of insinuendo.

insipid (ɪn'sɪpɪd), *a.* (*sb.*) [ad. late L. *insipidus* tasteless, f. *in-* (IN-[3]) + *sapidus* well-tasted, wise, prudent, SAPID: cf. F. *insipide* (15th c. in Hatz.-Darm.). Sense 3 is found in med.L. and the Romanic langs., whence app. in Eng.]

1. Without taste, tasteless; also, having only a very slight taste; without perceptible flavour or flavour sufficient to gratify the palate.

1620 VENNER *Via Recta* vii. 109 There are also some Apples that are insipid, or without taste. **1626** BACON *Sylva* §632 There be Plants that haue their Roots very Hot and Aromaticall; And their Seeds rather Insipide; As Ginger. **1756** C. LUCAS *Ess. Waters* I. 82 No water can be pure that is not quite insipid. **1774** GOLDSM. *Nat. Hist.* (1776) IV. 23 The tame rabbits are larger than the wild ones..but their flesh is not so good, being more insipid and softer. **1811** A. T. THOMSON *Lond. Disp.* (1818) 103 Good and recent yellow wax has a slight odour of honey, is insipid. **1822** IMISON *Sc. & Art* II. 87 The rest of the earths are insipid, and are scarcely at all soluble in water.

b. *Path. insipid diabetes* (*diabetes insipidus*), a form of the disease, distinguished from *saccharine diabetes* (*diabetes mellitus*): see DIABETES.

1879–89 J. M. DUNCAN *Lect. Dis. Wom.* xiii. (ed. 4) 87 In this kind of retention there is frequently, and probably always, a kind of insipid diabetes present.

2. *fig.* Wanting the qualities which excite interest or emotion; uninteresting, lifeless, dull, flat.

(In many early quotations it is doubtful whether the sense meant was 2 or 3.)

16.. EVELYN *Diary* 18 Aug. 1649, In yᵉ coach..went Mrs. Barlow, the King's mistress and mother to yᵉ Duke of Monmouth, a browne, beautifull, bold, but insipid creature. **1710–11** SWIFT *Lett.* (1767) III. 89 This was an insipid snowy day, no walking day. **1723** ORMOND ibid. II. 33, I am still such an insipid correspondent. **1753** HOGARTH *Anal. Beauty* vi. 36 How soon does a face that wants expression, grow insipid, tho' it be ever so pretty. **1845** DISRAELI *Sybil* (1863) 153 Mr. Mountchesney and Lord Milford poured forth several insipid compliments. **1858** LYTTON *What will he do?* I. i, Kisses, though pleasant in private, are insipid in public.

†**3.** Devoid of taste, intelligence, or judgement; stupid, foolish, dull. *Obs.*

1651 BAXTER *Inf. Bapt.* 185, I am sorry..that you should glory in such insipide arguing. **1662** PEPYS *Diary* 29 Sept., 'Midsummer Night's Dream'..is the most insipid ridiculous play that ever I saw. **1665** —— *Ibid.* 15 Jan., To church, where a most insipid young coxcomb preached. **1688** LD. DELAMER *Wks.* (1694) 20 Words and Phrases without Sense Tickle the Ears of insipid people. **1784** COWPER *Task* III. 642 Without it [elegance], all is gothic as the scene To which th' insipid citizen resorts.

†**B.** as *sb.* An insipid person or thing; one who is deficient in sense, spirit, or taste. *Obs.*

a **1700** B. E. *Dict. Cant. Crew, Insipids*, Block-heads. **1727** DE FOE *Syst. Magic* I. iv. (1840) 114 Whether the flights of their insipids are ecstacies of the adored, or of the horrid. **1781** P. KING *Mod. Lond. Spy* 24 It was therefore agreed to class me as an insipid. *a* **1834** LAMB *Final Mem.* i. *To Coleridge* 192 'Tis better not to think of present possibles, that we may not be out of humour with present insipids.

insipidity (ɪnsɪ'pɪdɪtɪ). [f. prec. + -ITY: cf. F. *insipidité* (1572 in Hatz.-Darm.).]

1. The quality of being insipid.

a. Tastelessness.

1611 COTGR., *Insipidité*, insipiditie, wallowishnesse, vnsauourinesse. **1706** PHILLIPS, *Insipidity*, a being insipid, unsavoury. **1740** CHEYNE *Regimen* p. liv, Water being signatur'd by its greatest Fluidity and Insipidity. **1807** T. THOMSON *Chem.* II. 102 Water owes its agreeable taste to the presence of air; hence the insipidity of boiled water.

b. Want of life or spirit, lack of interest, dullness.

1715 tr. *C'tess D'Aunoy's Wks.* 247 The Reason of the Heaviness and Insipidity of my Behaviour. **1796** JANE AUSTEN *Sense & Sens.* xi. (1849) 43 Her insipidity was invariable, for even her spirits were always the same. **1875** WHITNEY *Life Lang.* vii. 113 The..insipidity of words worn out by the use of persons who have put neither knowledge nor feeling into them.

†**c.** Want of taste or judgement; weakness, folly *Obs.*

1603 FLORIO *Montaigne* II. ii. (1632) 191 To teach him his mortalitie, and our insipiditie. **1732** SWIFT *Corr.* Wks. 1841 II. 670 A lieutenant-general of the queen's army that had courage and insipidity enough to hear the poor doctor preach to the bare walls.

2. With *an* and *pl.* An example of insipidity; an insipid person, remark, etc.

1822 CARLYLE *Lett.*, The 'mob of gentlemen' talking insipidities and giving dinners. **1843** MRS. CARLYLE *Lett.* I. 214 Various other men..some other half-dozen insipidities. **1884** *Chr. Commw.* 12 June 833/1 The utterance of a slight insipidity.

insipidly (ɪn'sɪpɪdlɪ), *adv.* [f. INSIPID + -LY[2].] In an insipid manner; tastelessly; dully; †senselessly, foolishly.

1647 CLARENDON *Hist. Reb.* III. §54 This doctrine was insipidly and perniciously urged by them. **1699** GARTH *Dispens.* IV. 46 Demurely meek, insipidly serene. **1799** tr. *Meister's Lett. Eng.* 168 Their pulse is served to table insipidly cooked. **1834** MEDWIN *Angler in Wales* II. 210 Insipidly regular faces. **1876** GEO. ELIOT *Dan. Der.* I. iii, It was a matter of extreme interest to her..that the family life would cease to be entirely, insipidly feminine.

insipidness (ɪn'sɪpɪdnɪs). [f. as prec. + -NESS.] The quality or fact of being insipid; insipidity.

1626 DONNE *Serm.* xxi. 211 Insipidnesse and tastlesnesse in his Palate. **1665–6** *Phil. Trans.* I. 51 The Insipidness of resolved Ice made of Sea Water. **1711** SHAFTESBURY *Charact.* (1737) III. 274 Their remisness, uncorrectness, insipidness, and downright ignorance of all literate art. **1858** HOLLAND *Titcomb's Lett.* viii. 162 Oftentimes, when you are busy with your modest affairs..you will be tempted to repine at their quietness and insipidness.

insipience (ɪn'sɪpɪəns). [a. OF. *insipience* (15th c. in Godef.), ad. L. *insipientia* folly, f. *insipient-em*: see INSIPIENT.] The quality of being insipient; lack of wisdom; unwisdom, foolishness.

c **1422** HOCCLEVE *Jonathas* 228 This Ionathas, this innocent yong man..The ryng hir tooke, of his insipience. **14..** *Songs & Carols* (1847) lviii. 67 Whan..in women be fownd no incypyens; Than put hem in trust and confydens. **1603** FLORIO *Montaigne* III. iii. (1632) 459 All wisedome is unsavourie, that is not conformed to common insipience. **1625** SHIRLEY *Love-tricks* III. v, Your accession is grateful, my most gentle lump of insipience. **1864** KINGSLEY *What then does Newman mean?* 27 Too many prefer the charge of insincerity to that of insipience.

†**in'sipiency.** *Obs. rare*[−0]. [see -ENCY.] = prec. **1727** in BAILEY vol. II.

insipient (ɪn'sɪpɪənt), *a.* and *sb.* Also 6 *erron.* inscip-, incip-, incypyent. [ad. L. *insipient-em*, f. *in-* (IN-[3]) + *sapient-em* wise, SAPIENT.]

A. *adj.* Void of wisdom; unwise, foolish. ? *Obs.* (Now mostly, or wholly, disused to avoid confusion with *incipient*.)

1528 ROY *Rede Me* (Arb.) 97 Braynles and insipient. **1547** BOORDE *Brev. Health* Pref. 2 Fooles and incipient persons. **1576** FLEMING *Panopl. Epist.* 186, I should not only shew my selfe foolish and insipient, but also saucie. **1647** CLARENDON *Contempl.* Tracts (1727) 507 There are very learned men who distinguish and put a great difference between the insipient man and the fool. **1811** *Henry & Isabella* I. 246 The insipient fears of a timid mind.

†**B.** *sb.* An unwise or foolish person. *Obs.*

1494 FABYAN *Chron.* VII. 551 Where the Chylde or insypient drynkyth the swete and delycious wordis unauysydly. **1533** FRITH *Answ. More* (1829) 162 It will go nigh to prove him an insipient, for granting that there is a purgatory. **1633** EARL MANCH. *Al Mondo* (1636) 86 There be certaine Subsapients so worldly wise, as they thinke all other men insipients.

Hence †**in'sipiently** *adv.*, unwisely, foolishly.

1536 BOORDE *Let. to Cromwell* 1 Apr. in *Introd. Knowl.* (1870) Forewords 52 They wolde cause me wrett full incypyently to þe prior of london. **1550** BALE *Apol.* 61 Neyther was Gods servyce therby lefte nor defrauded, as yow insippently write.

insist (ɪn'sɪst), *v.* [ad. L. *insistĕ-re* to stand upon, persist, dwell upon, f. *in-* (IN-[2]) + *sistĕre* to stand: cf. F. *insister* (1336 in Hatz.-Darm.).]

1. *intr.* To stand or rest *on* or *upon.* ? *Obs.*

1598 FLORIO, *Insistere*, to insist..to staie, rest or leane vpon. **1612** BREREWOOD *Lang. & Relig.* xv. 150 No straight line insisteth perpendicularly, on the face or circumference of any special body..except only those that proceed directly to the center of the sphear. **1656** tr. *Hobbes' Elem. Philos.* (1839) 195 Two strait lines meeting in the circumference of a circle and insisting upon equal arches. **1709–29** V. MANDEY *Syst. Math., Geom.* 159 Angles likewise which insist on the Diameter, are all Right Angles. **1812** WOODHOUSE *Astron.* xxxvi. 357 An eclipse caused by the shadow of the globe on which he insists. **1823–79** [see INSISTING *ppl. a.* 1].

2. a. *intr.* To continue steadfastly or persist *in* a course of action, to follow steadfastly *in* (*on*) a person's steps, etc.; to continue with urgency; to persevere. *arch.*

1586 *Let. Earle Leycester* 24 She hath neuerthelesse insisted in her former practises. **1589** NASHE *Ded. Greene's Menaphon* (Arb.) 10 In whose traces..manie other reverent Germaines insisting, have reedified the ruines of our decayed Libraries. **1597** MORLEY *Introd. Mus.* 126 It will be needlesse to insist any longer in teaching him descant. **1638** F. JUNIUS *Paint. of Ancients* 291 To caste our eyes upon Nature, and to insist in her steps. **1680** H. DODWELL *Two Lett.* (1691) 202 Many of the primitive Hereticks..exactly insisted on their footsteps. **1809** *Erskine's Princ. Sc. Law* 207 An action may be defined, a demand regularly made and insisted in..for the attaining or recovering of a right.

†**b.** *trans.* To follow in (a person's steps). *Obs.*

1631 R. H. *Arraignm. Whole Creature* xii. §4. 133 Wee insist their steps, whether crooked or straight.

3. a. *intr.* To dwell at length or with emphasis *on* or *upon* (†*of*, †*in*) a matter; hence, *to insist on* = to assert or maintain persistently. Formerly, also, †to take one's stand *on* (*in*) a point.

1596 DALRYMPLE tr. *Leslie's Hist. Scot.* I. 118 Because we heir haue perchance ouer lang insisted, and haue beine tedious to the reider, in sum particular materis. **1607** SHAKS. *Cor.* III. iii. 17 Let them If I say Fine, cry Fine; if Death, cry Death, Insisting on the olde prerogatiue. **1609** B. JONSON *Case is Altered* I. ii, I cannot now insist Upon particulars. **1611** W. SCLATER *Key* (1629) 131, I haue the longer insisted in this vice, because I see [etc.]. **1630** PRYNNE *Anti-Armin.* 173 On which our Arminians must insist for proofe of their vniuersall redemption. **1713** BERKELEY *Hylas & Phil.* III. Wks. 1871 I. 338, I shall insist no longer on that point. **1793** BURKE *Cond. Minority* Wks. VII. 264 The ruling Jacobins insist upon it, that [etc.]. **1875** JOWETT *Plato* (ed. 2) I. 408 Socrates is not prepared to insist on the literal accuracy of this description.

b. with clause: To maintain persistently or positively *that* a thing is so.

a **1715** BURNET *Own Time* (1725) I. II. 239 Leighton insisted, that it ought to be done for that very reason. **1768** STERNE *Sent. Journ.*, *Case of Delicacy* (1888) 252, I begged a thousand pardons, but insisted it was no more than an ejaculation. **1818** CRUISE *Digest* (ed. 2) V. 489 It was insisted that the testator had restrained the estate of inheritance during her life. **1875** JOWETT *Plato* (ed. 2) IV. 19 Protarchus ..insists that..all pleasures are good.

c. With quoted words.

1888 MRS. H. WARD *R. Elsmere* II. xxxix. 174 'And rather than try,' he insisted, 'you will go on believing [etc.].' **1906** W. S. MAUGHAM *Bishop's Apron* iv. 47 'Do you care for me at all?' he insisted.

4. a. To make a demand with persistent urgency; to take a persistent or peremptory stand in regard to a stipulation, claim, demand, proposal, etc. Const. *on, upon* (formerly *for, against*, or *infin.*).

1623 LD. HERBERT in Ellis *Orig. Lett.* Ser. I. III. 165 That the sayd Kinge of Spaine would never insiste upon obtaininge those priviledges. **1647** CLARENDON *Hist. Reb.* I. §21 This condition should be first humbly insisted on. **1701** C. DAVENANT *Peace & War* I. xi. (1704) I. 244 Those who ..insist for a strange kind of Latitude, and to have Priviledges above the rest of their Fellow Subjects. *a* **1715** BURNET *Own Time* (1725) I. II. 300 They insisted mainly against kneeling at the sacrament of the Lord's Supper. **1749** BP. LAVINGTON *Enthus. Methodists* (1754) I. ii. 34 Her Spouse insisting to play another Game, she lost it. **1778** JOHNSON in *Boswell* 28 Apr., No good and worthy man will insist upon another man's drinking wine. **1875** W. S. HAYWARD *Love agst. World* 77 Since you insist, I cannot help it. **1896** *Law Times* C. 408/1 It is now time to insist on the necessary appointment being made.

b. with *that* and clause.

1676 tr. *Guillatiere's Voy. Athens* 17 We insisted that when we struck and saluted them, the Frigot should hang out either the French or English Colours. **1883** FROUDE *Short Stud.* IV. I. iii. 33 The king insisted that a sacred profession should not be used as a screen for the protection of felony.

insistence (ɪn'sɪstəns). Also 8- **-ance**. [f. INSIST *v.* (or its L. source) + -ENCE. The spelling in *-ance* follows *assistance*, *resistance*, from French: cf. mod.F. *insistance* (Mercier, 1801).] The action of insisting; the fact of being insistent; emphatic or urgent dwelling upon a statement, demand, etc.; also the quality of being insistent; = next.

1611 FLORIO, *Insistenza*, insistence, persistance, an insisting. **1644** DIGBY *Mans Soul* (1645) 111 It requireth no further particular insistance upon it, to shew [etc.]. **1727** *Art Speaking in Publick* 137 (Jod.) The figure called epimone by the Greeks, and which we may call insistance. **1798** W. TAYLOR in *Monthly Rev.* XXVII. 210 His general insistance on tradition. **1863** KINGLAKE *Crimea* (1876) I. ix. 130 A.. tone of insistence bordering at times on intimidation. **1865** M. ARNOLD *Ess. Crit.* vii. (1875) 300 The perpetual insistence on the motive of future rewards and punishments. **1892** MRS. CROSSE *Red letter Days* I. 241 She says with great insistence that her rhymes are meant for rhymes.

insistency (ɪn'sɪstənsɪ). Also **-ancy**. [f. as prec.: see -ENCY.] The quality of being insistent; perseverance in dwelling upon, pressing, or maintaining something; urgency, pertinacity; also, an instance of this.

1859 W. ANDERSON *Disc.* (1860) 236 The faithfulness of the preacher's insistency. **1878** MRS. STOWE *Poganuc P.* iv. (1879) 30 Its ticking began to strike..with a nervous insistancy on her ear. **1881** *Blackw. Mag.* Mar. 400 Sent a gentleman from France to invite him thither with great insistency. **1887** T. HARDY *Woodlanders* xxvii. 189 The terrible insistencies of society.

insistent (ɪn'sɪstənt), *a.* (*sb.*) Also 9 **-ant**. [ad. L. *insistent-em*, pr. pple. of *insistĕre* to INSIST.]

1. Standing or resting on something. *rare.*

1624 WOTTON *Archit.* in *Reliq.* (1672) 19 That the breadth of the Substruction be at least double to the insistent Wall. **1755** JOHNSON, *Insistent*, resting upon anything. *a* **1886** SIR S. FERGUSON *Ogham Inscript.* (1887) 125 Parallel straight lines insistent on and dependent from others.

2. Dwelling firmly on something asserted, demanded, etc.; persistent, urgent. Hence, Enforcing attention, obtruding itself upon the attention.

1868 GEO. ELIOT *Sp. Gipsy* III. 234 The eye of day, The insistent summer sun, seems pitiless. **1876** —— *Dan. Der.* IV. xxx, He got no answer, and..repeated his question in an insistent tone. **1879** FROUDE *Cæsar* xiii. 187 The aristocracy had become more insistent upon the privilege of birth. **1880** T. HARDY *Trumpet-Major* III. xxxii. 56 The solitude was rendered yet more insistent by the silence of the mill-wheel. **1888** *Pall Mall G.* 2 Oct. 1/2 The insistent facts of sin, suffering, and misery. **1893** SELOUS *Trav. S.E. Africa* 50 The natives..were very insistent that I should try and shoot one.

3. *Ornith.* [F. *insistant.*] Applied to the hind toe of birds when it is inserted so high that it touches the ground only with its tip: opposed to *incumbent*.

1886 in *Syd. Soc. Lex.*

B. as *sb.* An insistent person.

1868 KINGLAKE *Crimea* (1877) IV. xiii. 408 Insistants.. approaching him with their urgency. **1881** MRS. C. PRAED *Policy & P.* I. 17 'We don't mean to let you clear out'..cried one of these insistents.

Hence **in'sistently** *adv.*, in an insistent manner, with insistence.

1873 MISS BROUGHTON *Nancy* II. 117 He earnestly and insistantly begs of me to gather all my people..around me. **1876** GEO. ELIOT *Dan. Der.* v. xxxvi, 'Then tell me what better I can do', said Gwendolen, insistently. **1879** H. JAMES *Hawthorne* 114 The interest of the story lies..in the situation which is insistently kept before us.

in'sister, *sb.*^{1} [f. INSIST *v.* + -ER^{1}.] One who insists.

1611 FLORIO, *Insistore*, an insister, a persister. **1641** LD. DIGBY *Sp. Parl.* 19 Jan., 19 The first mover, and insister to have this clause added to the Petition of Right. **1872** *Athenæum* 3 Aug. 145/2 The new President of the Philological Society is a strong insister on the necessity of studying the changes that are in course of working themselves out in living languages.

in-sister, *sb.*^{2}: see IN *adv.* 12 a.

1644 *MS. Acc. St. John's Hosp., Canterb.*, Shee was admitted an in sister.

† **in'sister,** *v. Obs. rare*$^{-0}$. [f. IN-^{1} + SISTER.] *trans.* To make into or admit as a sister.

1611 FLORIO, *Insorellare*, to insister.

insisting (ɪn'sɪstɪŋ), *vbl. sb.* [f. INSIST *v.* + -ING^{1}.] The action of the verb INSIST; insistence.

1598 FLORIO, *Insistenza*, a persisting, an insisting. **1638** F. JUNIUS *Paint. of Ancients* 26 A custome of insisting upon any one intended Imagination. **1866** *Sat. Rev.* 22 Sept. 367/1 There is an altogether unreasonable insisting upon graces and airs and fine manners.

in'sisting, *ppl. a.* [f. as prec. + -ING^{2}.]

1. Resting, superincumbent: cf. INSIST *v.* 1.

1727 BAILEY vol. II s.v., The Angles of any Segment are said to be insisting or standing upon the Arch of another Segment below. **1823** P. NICHOLSON *Pract. Builder* 219 A bressummer, where it resists a transverse insisting weight. **1879** SIR G. SCOTT *Lect. Archit.* I. 146 Making the bases and capitals face in the direction of the insisting arch-rib.

2. That insists; that dwells urgently or pertinaciously upon a point.

1611 FLORIO, *Insistente*, insisting, persisting. **1797** MRS. RADCLIFFE *Italian* xxiii. (1824) 658 A yet more insisting voice. **1832** MOORE *Diary* 1–24 Mar., in *Mem.* (1854) VI. 249 A fancy..which lately took a more serious and insisting shape.

Hence **in'sistingly** *adv.*, with insistence, insistently.

1880 G. MEREDITH *Tragic Com.* xii. (1892) 174 Her father did not let the occasion slip to speak insistingly. **1892** *Blackw. Mag.* CLI. 397/2, 'I forbid you', she called out, insistingly.

in'sistive, *a. rare.* [irreg. f. INSIST + -IVE.] Having the character or quality of insisting.

1649 G. DANIEL *Trinarch., Rich. II*, lii, They many things perpend; and some they Cull Insistive Articles. **1892** *Columbus* (Ohio) *Disp.* 10 Mar., Their women folks are the most brazenly insistive and picturesquely attired fortune tellers in all the world.

† **in'sisture.** *Obs. rare*$^{-1}$. [f. INSIST *v.* + -URE.] A word of obscure use in Shakspere: taken variously in the sense of 'persistency, constancy' (Schmidt), 'regularity, or perhaps station' (Nares); perh. = 'steady continuance' in their path.

1606 SHAKS. *Tr. & Cr.* I. iii. 87 The Heauens themselues, the Planets, and this Center, Obserue degree, priority, and place, Insisture, course, proportion, season, forme.

† **in'site,** *a. Obs.* [ad. L. *insit-us*, pa. pple. of *inserĕre* to engraft, implant: see INSITION.] Implanted; situated within.

1651 WITTIE tr. *Primrose's Pop. Err.* IV. xlviii. 404 They are not insite and naturally placed there. **1656** STANLEY *Hist. Philos.* VI. (1701) 256/2 An insite, connatural, animate, immovable Air, which being moved by the external Air, yieldeth the sense of hearing. **1677** GALE *Crt. Gentiles* IV. 223 Damascene saith..the knowlege or notion of Gods existence is naturally insite and ingenite to us.

† **in'sitiency.** *Obs. rare*$^{-1}$. [f. IN-^{3} + L. *sitient-em*, pr. pple. of *sitī-re* to thirst: see -ENCY.] Freedom from thirst.

1701 GREW *Cosm. Sacra* III. ii. §37 What is more admirable, than..the Insitiency of a Camel, for travelling in the Deserts of Africa?

† **in'sition**^{1}. *Obs.* Also 7 **incision, inscition.** [ad. L. *insitiōn-em*, n. of action f. *inserĕre* to plant in, engraft, f. *in-* (IN-^{2}) + *serĕre* to sow, plant. From similarity of sound, and the use of cutting, formerly mixed up with *incision*.] The action of engrafting, engraftment; *concr.* a graft.

1589 FLEMING *Virg. Georg.* II. 21 *note*, Semination, insition, inoculation..the three kindes of grafting. **1608** WILLET *Hexapla Exod.* 79 The graffing and incision of trees. *a* **1682** SIR T. BROWNE *Tracts* (1684) 45 The rules of insition or grafting. **1691** RAY *Creation* I. (1692) 154 Improved by Transplantation, Stercoration, Insition, Pruning.

b. *transf.* and *fig.*

1601 R. JOHNSON *Kingd. & Commw.* (1603) 144 These acquisitions are as it were incisions or graffings. **1630** PRYNNE *Anti-Armin.* 114 If no Predestination, then no Election, no inscition, no adoption into Christ. **1714** *Phil. Trans.* XXIX. 73 It has, metaphorically, the name of Insition or Inoculation. **1855** W. H. MILL *Panth. Princ.* 201 His ancestry's insition from the Idumean to the Jewish stock.

† **insition**^{2}, obs. erron. form of INCISION.

1653 WALTON *Angler* vii. 150 Cut or make an insition, or such a scar as you may put the arming wyer of your hook into it.

insititious (ɪnsɪ'tɪʃəs), *a.* [f. L. *insitīci-us* (erron. *-ītius*) engrafted, f. *insit-*, pple. stem of *inserĕre*: see INSITION^{1} and -ITIOUS.] Of engrafted or inserted nature; introduced from without.

1639 USSHER *Lett.* (1686) 494 Passages..excepted against as insititious and supposititious. **1679** EVELYN *Sylva* (ed. 3) 28 With insititious fruit. **1716** M. DAVIES *Athen. Brit.* III. *Crit. Hist.* 1 Of our Adscititious School-Books and of Foreign Insititious Translations. **1825** SOUTHEY in *Q. Rev.* XXXIII. 24 The excrescent errors and insititious corruptions were pruned away. **1879** M. PATTISON *Milton* xiii. 171 There are other passages..which have the air of being insititious in the place where they stand.

† **'insitive,** *a. Obs. rare*$^{-1}$. [ad. L. *insitīv-us* engrafted, f. as prec.: see -IVE.] Of or pertaining to insition, engrafting, or inoculation.

1716 M. DAVIES *Athen. Brit.* II. To Rdr. 2 That Insitive and Inoculative method seems to bid fair for the Cure. **1727** BAILEY vol. II, *Insitive*, grafted or put in, not natural.

in situ: see IN *Lat. prep.*

inskonce, -se, inslave, obs. ff. ENSCONCE, ENSLAVE.

† **in'smite,** *v. Obs. rare.* [f. IN-^{1} + SMITE *v.*: after L. *in-cutĕre.*] *trans.* To smite or strike in.

1382 WYCLIF *2 Macc.* xii. 22 And whan the first cumpaignye of Judas appeeride, dreed is ynsmyten [L. *incussus est*] to the enmyes of the presence of God, that biholdith alle thingis.

† **in'smock,** *v. Obs. rare*$^{-0}$. [IN-^{2}.] *trans.* To clothe or envelop in a smock.

1611 FLORIO, *Incamisciare*, to inshirt, to insmocke.

† **insnare, insnarl,** obs. ff. ENSNARE, ENSNARL *v. Obs.*

insobriety (ɪnsəʊ'braɪɪtɪ). [IN-^{3}: cf. It. *insobrietà* (Florio).] Want of sobriety; intemperance (either in general sense, or *spec.* in reference to drinking).

1611 FLORIO, *Insobrieta*, insobrietie, drunkennesse. *c* **1645** HOWELL *Lett.* (1655) III. xxvi. 38 Their spiritual pride, and insobriety in the search of more knowledge. **1652** GAULE *Magastrom.* 198 If the person of the prophecyer or predictor be noted for idolatry..insobriety, covetousness. *a* **1812** ARCH. MACLEAN *Disc.* (1848) 142 This insobriety made him too high for a servant. **1814** W. TAYLOR in *Monthly Mag.* XXXVIII. 213 A feeling of affectation, of insobriety, or flutter.

insociability (ɪnsəʊʃ(ɪ)ə'bɪlɪtɪ). [f. next + -ITY: cf. F. *insociabilité* (Montesq. 1721).] Insociable disposition or state; unsociableness.

1740 WARBURTON *Div. Legat.* v. iv. Wks. 1811 V. 128 Christianity, considered by them as a Sect of Judaism; which had carried its insociability as far, and its pretensions much farther. **1804** W. TENNANT *Ind. Recreat.* (ed. 2) I. 313 A difference of temper and insociability. **1832** LYTTON *Eugene A.* I. vii, By degrees, then, Aram relaxed from his insociability.

insociable (ɪn'səʊʃ(ɪ)əb(ə)l), *a.* Now *rare.* [ad. L. *insociābil-is*, f. *in-* (IN-^{3}) + *sociābilis* SOCIABLE. Cf. F. *insociable* (1564 in Hatz.-Darm.).]

† **1.** That cannot be associated or combined; incapable of union; incompatible. *Obs.*

1581 SAVILE *Tacitus, Agric.* (1662) 184 Prince Nerua.. hath wisely matched and mixed together two things heretofore insociable. **1624** WOTTON *Archit.* in *Reliq.* (1672) 19 Lime and wood are insociable. **1678** CUDWORTH *Intell. Syst.* I. iv. Contents 189 To deny God the honour of His Holiness, His singular, insociable and incommunicable Nature.

2. Not disposed for society or social intercourse; unsociable.

1588 SHAKS. *L.L.L.* v. ii. 809 This austere insociable life. **1626** L. OWEN *Spec. Jesuit.* To Rdr., The pernitious and insociable Societie of the Iesuites. **1653** R. SANDERS *Physiogn.* 171 She is at enmity with her own kindred, insociable. **1865** CARLYLE *Fredk. Gt.* XVI. ix. (1872) VI. 246 In all countries there are insociable fellows, with whom you are obliged to live, though it is difficult.

Hence **in'sociableness** (Bailey vol. II, 1727); **in'sociably** *adv.* (Craig, 1847).

insocial (ɪn'səʊʃəl), *a. rare.* [ad. late L. *insociāl-is*, f. *in-* (IN-^{3}) + *sociālis* SOCIAL.] = prec. 2. Hence **in'socially** *adv.*

1654 tr. *Scudery's Curia Pol.* 164 That long and prodigious Wall, which the Chinaists had erected to separate themselves insocially from the Tartars. **1748** SMOLLETT *Rod. Rand.* (1812) I. 301 An insocial silence ensued.

† **in'sociate,** *a. Obs. rare*$^{-1}$. [f. IN-^{3} + L. *sociāt-us* associated.] Not associated; solitary.

1610 B. JONSON *Hymenæi, Barriers* 16 That the most honour'd state of man and wife, Doth far exceed the insociate virgin life.

insociation (ɪnsəʊʃɪ'eɪʃən, -səʊsɪ-). *rare.* [f. IN-^{2} + L. *sociātiōn-em* union, from *sociāre* to associate, unite.] Intimate association or companionship.

1893 J. PULSFORD *Loyalty to Christ* II. 352 Yet men..can make light of their Father's invitation to the delights of insociation with Himself and with each other.

in so far: see IN *prep.* 39.

† **'insolate,** *ppl. a. Obs.* [ad. L. *insōlāt-us*, pa. pple. of *insōlāre*: see next.] Insolated: see next.

1652 CULPEPPER *Eng. Physic.* 38 The 'insolate' Oyl wherein there hath been three or four Repetitions of Infusion of the top stalks.

insolate ('ɪnsəʊleɪt), *v.* [f. ppl. stem of L. *insōlāre* to place in or expose to the sun, f. *in-* (IN-^{2}) + *sōl* sun.] *trans.* To place in the sun; to expose to the rays of the sun. Hence **'insolated** *ppl. a.*, exposed to the sun's rays.

1623 COCKERAM II, Dried in the Sun, *Insolated.* **1664** EVELYN *Sylva* (1679) 29 The dew that impearls the leaves [of oaks] in May, insolated, meteorizes and sends up a liquor, which is of admirable effect in Ruptures. **1683** SALMON *Doron Med.* I. 110 Some, before boyling, insolate for forty days. **1694** —— *Bate's Dispens.* (1713) 684/1 It is made of the Fruit thereof, being insolated for a long time in Oyl. **1874** GROVE *Corr. Phys. Forces* (ed. 6), Insolated paper retains the power of producing an impression for a very long period.

insolation (ɪnsəʊ'leɪʃən). [ad. L. *insōlātiōn-em*, n. of action from *insōlāre*: see prec.]

The action of placing in the sun; exposure to the sun's rays; sometimes (in mod. use) the action or effect of the sun's rays on a body exposed to them.

1. In general sense. (In quot. 1654, Exposure to daylight, or to the public view.)

1654 H. L'ESTRANGE *Chas. I* (1655) 118 Nature it self, in acts of such uncleannesse..declineth insolation and open view. **1665** BEALE in *Boyle's Wks.* VI. 394, I am almost become confident, that one of my thermometers by such insolation, as may be had in England from our stone walls, hath lost some inches of liquor. **1878** in Sir E. Reed *Japan* (1880) I. 8 The vegetation now begins to develop under a powerful insolation. **1885** *Gardener's Chron.* XXIII. 372 No

where else is the effect of insolation more distinctly observed than in the Arctic regions.

2. In specific senses. **a.** Exposure of some substance to the sun's rays, as for the purpose of drying, bleaching, or maturing.

1612 WOODALL *Surg. Mate* Wks. (1653) 272 *Insolation* is the preparation of simple or compound things by the heat of Sun in the Summer, or a gentle fire in the Winter. **1675** EVELYN *Terra* (1729) 41 Expose it for Insolation a Week or ten Days. **1706** *Phil. Trans.* XXV. 2265 Divers ways of making Salt from Sea-Water; first by insolation only, as Bay Salt. **1886** *Syd. Soc. Lex.*, *Insolation*..In Pharmacy, the drying of substances in the rays of the sun; also, the blanching or bleaching of substances by the same means.

b. Medical treatment by exposure of the body to the sun's rays.

a **1626** BACON *New Atl.* (1631) 32 We vse these Towers, according to their seuerall Heights, and Situations, for Insolation, Refrigeration, Conseruation. **1756** C. LUCAS *Ess. Waters* I. 174 The dry [bath]; such as Insolation, or being exposed to the heat of the sun. **1886** *Syd. Soc. Lex.*, *Insolation*..In Medicine, exposure to the sun's rays as a means of cure.

c. Injurious exposure (of animals or plants) to the sun's rays or to excessive heat; also, disease thus caused: (*a*) sunstroke; (*b*) = HELIOSIS 2.

1758 W. BATTIE *Madness* vii. 47 One case of Consequential Madness..is an effect of Insolation, or what the French call *coup du Soleil*. **1822–34** *Good's Study Med.* (ed. 4) I. 680 Such fever seems less attributable to the reflux of bile into the blood, than to the insolation or solar excitement. **1885** *Century Mag.* XXIX. 661 Disabled in the deserts by insolation produced by excessive heat. **1896** *Allbutt's Syst. Med.* I. 499 In thermic fever or insolation the object is to reduce the temperature. **1898** P. MANSON *Trop. Dis.* xii. 205 Those loosely used terms, sun-stroke, heat-stroke, *coup de soleil*, insolation.

insole (ˈɪnsəʊl). [f. IN *a.* + SOLE *sb.*] **a.** The inner sole of a shoe or boot. **b.** A flat piece of warm or waterproof material laid inside the shoe.

1851–61 MAYHEW *Lond. Labour* II. 34 The soles, if there be a sufficiency of leather, are shaped into insoles for children's shoes. **1880** *Times* 21 Sept. 4/4 Light boots and slippers, called pumps, which have only one sole and no insole. **1890** *Star* 18 Jan. 4/4 Sliced cork is used for insoles.

insolence (ˈɪnsələns), *sb.* Also 5 **-ens**, 6 **-ense**. [ad. L. *insolēntia*, f. *insolēnt-em* INSOLENT: see -ENCE. Cf. F. *insolence* (15th c. in Hatz.-Darm.).]

1. The quality of being insolent, esp. as manifested in action. †**a.** Pride; haughty or overbearing conduct or disposition; arrogance, contempt for inferiors. *Obs.* or blending with b.

c **1386** CHAUCER *Pars. T.* ¶317 Twigges..that cometh of pride..Arrogance. Inpudence. swellynge of herte. Insolence. Elacion. Inpacience. *c* **1470** HARDING *Chron.* Proem. i, My ghoost to kepe from synne and insolence. **1591** SPENSER *Teares Muses* 72 They now, puft vp with sdeignfull insolence, Despise the brood of blessed Sapience. **1607** SHAKS. *Cor.* I. i. 266, I do wonder, his insolence can brooke to be commanded vnder Cominius. **1667** MILTON *P.L.* I. 502 When Night Darkens the Streets, then wander forth the Sons Of Belial, flown with insolence and wine. **1703** ROWE *Fair Penit.* II. i. 553 The rich Man's Insolence. **1769** ROBERTSON *Chas. V.* (1796) III. 262 He began..to treat the citizens with great insolence. *a* **1873** LYTTON *Pausanias* (1876) 35 The contrast between the insolence of the Spartan chief and the courtesy of the Athenians.

b. Offensive contemptuousness of action or speech due to presumption; impertinently insulting behaviour; sauciness.

1668 DAVENANT *Man's the Master* III. i. Wks. 1874 V. 57 'Tell Me by what title thou pretend'st to have Authority to punish her?'..'I ought to do it.'..'That's insolence! Art thou not a servant?' **1683** *Brit. Spec.* 112 When their Insolence was such, as to make Kings the Instruments of their Ambition. **1749** FIELDING *Tom Jones* 33 The generality of those who get their livelihood by people of fashion, contract as much insolence to the rest of mankind, as if they really belonged to that rank themselves. **1830** D'ISRAELI *Chas. I*, III. v. 76 Abbot's behaviour to the highest nobility in the kingdom, was such as to border on insolence. **1861** DUTTON COOK *P. Foster's D.* i, He spoke with such coolness that what he said sounded almost like insolence.

c. with *an* and *pl.* An instance of this; an insolent act; a piece of insolence. Now *rare*.

1491 CAXTON *Vitas Patr.* (W. de W. 1495) 42 The crysten men were constrayned to don in lyke wyse suche insolences with the Arryens. **1607** GRIMSTONE tr. *Goulart's Mem. Hist.* 33 The husband..sees his enemy come who continues his insolences. **1631** GOUGE *God's Arrows* III. §60. 296 Revenging unsupportable insolences and injuries. **1680** MORDEN *Geog. Rect.* (1685) 348 To secure themselves from the Assaults and Insolences of Night Robbers. **1711** SPOTSWOOD in W. S. Perry *Hist. Coll. Amer. Col. Ch.* I. 188 Their Cowardly behaviour..will embolden the Indians to continue their insolences. **1831** LYTTON *Godolphin* 9 For a much smaller insolence than you seem capable of.

d. *transf.* An insolent person.

1741 RICHARDSON *Pamela* (1824) I. 180 Insolence! continued she, this moment, when I bid you, know your duty, and give me a glass of wine.

†**2.** Exultation: cf. INSOLENT 4. *Obs.*

1595 SPENSER *Colin Clout* 621 Her great excellence Lifts me above the measure of my might: That, being fild with furious insolence, I feele my selfe like one yrapt in spright.

†**3.** The condition of being unused or unaccustomed to a thing; inexperience. *Obs.*

1432–50 tr. *Higden* (Rolls) II. 321 Excusenge that thynge by the insolence of the childe [*per insipientiam puerilem*]. ?*a* **1500** *Crt. of Love* 936 Ye shall not find in me suche insolence.

†**4.** The quality or character of being unusual; strangeness, unaccustomedness. *Obs.*

a **1631** DONNE *Ess. Div.* (1651) 128 By the hardness and insolence of the Phrase.

†**ˈinsolence**, *v. Obs. rare*⁻¹. [f. prec. sb.] *trans.* To treat with insolence, behave insolently towards.

1648 *Eikon Bas.* iv. 24 The Bishops, who were first fouly insolenced and assaulted.

†**ˈinsolency.** *Obs.* [ad. L. *insolēntia*: see prec. sb. and -ENCY.]

1. The quality of being insolent; = INSOLENCE 1.

1494 FABYAN *Chron.* v. lxxxvii. 64 After hym shal come a Childe or Childer, that shalbe of suche Insolency and wastynge, that..[they] shall..waste and destroye by theyr folyes all that other noble men hath purchased to their handes. **1547** *Act 1 Edw. VI*, c. 12 §1 For the Repressing of the Insolency and Unruliness of Men. *a* **1577** SIR T. SMITH *Commw. Eng.* (1609) 8 The frailtie of mans nature..cannot abide or beare long that absolute and vncontrolled authoritie, without swelling into too much pride and insolencie. **1650** WELDON *Crt. Jas. I* 62 Those made him proud, overvaluing himselfe, and under-valuing others, and infected with a kinde of insolency. **1698** [R. FERGUSON] *View Eccles.* 34 Acting with that Insolency, which may administer occasion to Sathan and his Instruments to reproach Religion.

b. with *an* and *pl.* = INSOLENCE *sb.* 1 c.

1581 SAVILE *Tacitus, Agric.* (1622) 189 The Britans endure leuies of men and money..if insolencies bee forborne, indignities they cannot abide. **1646** SIR T. BROWNE *Pseud. Ep.* I. i. 4 Vainly attempting not only insolencies, but impossibilities, he deceived himselfe as low as hell. **1680–90** TEMPLE *Ess. Pop. Discont.* Wks. 1731 I. 264 To secure our Trade from the Danger of all Turkish Pyracies, or sudden Insults or Insolencies of our Neighbours. **1698** W. CHILCOT *Evil Thoughts* vi. (1851) 74 The reason of fasting being made a duty, is in order to tame the insolencies of the flesh. **1729** SHELVOCKE *Artillery* v. 355 The Grecians observed them [revels of Bacchus] with the most horrid Excesses and Insolencies imaginable. **1796** MORSE *Amer. Geog.* II. 432 They keep up a small fleet for curbing the insolencies of the piratical states of Barbary.

c. *transf.* = INSOLENCE *sb.* 1 d.

1613 PURCHAS *Pilgrimage* (1614) 760 A truer conversion of the American world, then hitherto our Humorists, or Spanish insolencies have intended.

2. Unusualness: = INSOLENCE *sb.* 3. With *an* and *pl.* An unusual act or occurrence.

1612 DONNE *Lett.* (1651) 123 The D. of Espernon..with 600 horse in his train..came with him into the court: which is an insolency remarkable here. **1649** JER. TAYLOR *Gt. Exemp.* III. Disc. xvi. §5. 58 Every ill example..is a scandall, because it invites others to do the like..taking off the strangenesse and insolency of the act. **1649** G. DANIEL *Trinarch., Rich. II*, xlv, Strange Insolencyes and vnheard of Things..They act. **1663** J. SPENCER *Prodigies* (1665) 131 The History of Præternatural Occurrences..Such insolencies in Nature give us to understand, that the most common rules of Natural Operation are not without exception.

b. Affectedness in the choice of unusual words. [L. *insolentia verborum*.]

1644 BULWER *Chiron.* 33 In the Primitive times of elocution, when eloquence began to flowre and bud, and insolencie was rarely entertained.

insolent (ˈɪnsələnt), *a.* (*sb.*) [ad. L. *insolēnt-em* unaccustomed, unusual, excessive, immoderate, haughty, arrogant, insolent, f *in-* (IN-³) + *solēnt-em*, pr. pple. of *solēre* to be accustomed. Cf. F. *insolent* (R. Estienne, 1549).]

I. †**1.** Proud, disdainful, haughty, arrogant, overbearing; offensively contemptuous of the rights or feelings of others. Said of the powerful, rich, or successful, their actions, etc. *Obs.* or blended with 2.

c **1386** CHAUCER *Pars T.* ¶325 Insolent is he that despiseth in his Iuggement alle othere folk, as to regard of his value and of his konnyng and of his spekyng and of his beryng. **1596** SPENSER *State Irel.* Wks. (Globe) 636/2 Thorough greatnes of their late conquests and seignories they grewe insolent. **1617** MORYSON *Itin.* II. 87 These being neerer..were most insolent upon that City. **1676** tr. *Guillatiere's Voy. Athens* 16 A haughty insolent person who affected to make himself terrible. **1727–38** GAY *Fables* I. xxiv. 26 'What arrogance!' the snail replied; 'How insolent is upstart pride!' **1840** THIRLWALL *Greece* lvi. VII. 189 Antipater was neither insolent nor cruel. **1858** TRENCH *Synon. N.T.* §30 (1876) 101 The boastful in words, the proud in thoughts, the insolent and injurious in acts.

fig. **1822** SHELLEY *Hellas* 344 One star with insolent and victorious light Hovers above its fall. **1830** GALT *Lawrie T.* III. iii. (1849) 93 The insolent and unknown waters which had so swelled the river, shrunk within their banks.

b. *Comb.*, as ***insolent-looking*** adj.

1886 W. J. TUCKER *E. Europe* 198 The numberless Jewish equipages with all those insolent-looking Hebrew women of the Leopoldstadt.

2. Contemptuous of rightful authority; presumptuously or offensively contemptuous; impertinently insulting. Said of those who treat superiors or equals with offensive familiarity or disrespect.

1678 MARVELL *Growth Popery* 4 This last and Insolentest attempt upon the credulity of mankind. **1685** BAXTER *Paraphr. N.T., Matt.* xii. 39–40 God will not gratifie their insolent demand. **1706** PHILLIPS, *Insolent*, saucy, bold, malapert, proud, haughty, disdainful, presumptuous. **1793** BURKE *Policy Allies* Wks. 1842 I. 604 Their revolutionary tribunals, where every idea of natural justice..have been trodden under foot with the most insolent mockery. **1856** FROUDE *Hist. Eng.* (1858) II. vii. 128 Bonner's tongue was insolent, and under bad control. **1884** PAE *Eustace* 69 He is an idle, drunken, insolent fellow.

†**3.** Extravagant, immoderate, going beyond the bounds of propriety. *Obs.*

c **1480** HENRYSON *Mor. Fab.* I. ii, Damesellis wanton, and insolent, That fane wald play, and on the streit be sene. **1568** GRAFTON *Chron.* II. 15 Thurston wasted..the goodes of that place, in lechery, and by other insolent meanes. **1712** STEELE *Spect.* No. 312 ¶2 The constant Pursuit of Pleasure has in it something insolent and improper for our Being. *Ibid.* No. 426 ¶4 All the Extremities of Houshold Expence, Furniture, and insolent Equipage.

†**4.** (?) Swelling, exulting: in good sense. *rare.*

1589 PUTTENHAM *Eng. Poesie* I. xxxi. (Arb.) 77 For dittie and amourous Ode I finde Sir Walter Rawleyghs vayne most loftie, insolent, and passionate.

II. †**5.** Unfrequented. *Obs. rare.*

c **1420** *Pallad. on Husb.* XII. 57 Where is lond vnkept & insolent [*regio insolens et incustodita*] Take from the tronke al clene, vntil so hie As beestis may..Atteyne.

†**6.** Unaccustomed, unwonted, unusual, strange.

1586 PETTIE *Guazzo's Civ. Conv.* To Rdr. A vij, If one chance to derive any word from the Latine, which is insolent to their eares..they forthwith make a jest at it. **1592** R. D. *Hypnerotomachia* 26 Letting passe to speake of the insolent greatnes of the Piramides of Memphis. **1608** A. WILLET *Hexapla Exod.* 468 This is an vnwonted and insolent signification of the word. **1612** BRINSLEY *Lud. Lit.* x. (1627) 164 Words which are insolent, hard and out of use, are to be as warily avoided. **1651** *Fuller's Abel Rediv., Bradford* 181 This favour, though extraordinary and insolent, was thought well bestowed upon him by the whole University. **1665** JER. TAYLOR *Unum Necess.* viii. §3 The phrase is insolent, and the exposition violent.

†**7.** Unused or unaccustomed to a thing; inexperienced. *Obs.*

c **1480** HENRYSON *Orph. & Euryd.* 20 Tendouris to yung and insolent. **1598** MARSTON *Pygmal.* iv. 153 Would euer any erudite Pedant Seeme in his artles lines so insolent?

B. *sb.* An insolent person (in senses 1 and 2).

1595 SHAKS. *John* II. i. 122 Out, insolent, thy bastard shall be King, That thou maist be a Queen, and checke the world! **1639** tr. *Du Bosq's Compl. Woman* II. 61 The salvation of these insolents, seems desperate, their repentance.. Miracles. **1672** J. PHILLIPS *Montelion's Predict.* 10 What Christian will be a Second to such Insolents? **1765** H. WALPOLE *Otranto* v. (1798) 82 Thou art an insolent. **1898** *Academy* 8 Oct. 28/1, I am [acquainted] with insolents, and you are one.

insolently (ˈɪnsələntlɪ), *adv.* [f. prec. + -LY².]

1. In an insolent manner; haughtily overbearingly; with insulting or presumptuous arrogance or contempt.

1494 FABYAN *Chron.* VI. clxiv. 158 Charlys, the sone of Charlys the Ballyd..had rulyd hym insolently, and done in that countrey dyuerse outragyous dedes. **1603** KNOLLES *Hist. Turks* (1638) 301 Thou..dost most insolently and vnaduisedly..propound many conditions of peace, of such qualitie and condition that myne ears scorn to hear the same. **1695** LD. PRESTON *Boeth.* Pref. 8 Afflicted Vertue is insolently stabbed with all manner of Reproaches. **1725** POPE *Odyss.* XVIII. 172 Yon train Of haughty spoilers, insolently vain. **1791** *Gentl. Mag.* 32/2 The gentleman whom he has insolently called Thersites, and the modern Zoilus. *Mod.* A soldier who behaved insolently to his officer.

†**2.** In an unaccustomed or unusual way; strangely. *Obs.*

1664 EVELYN tr. *Freart's Archit.* 133 The interpreter of Hans Bloome names it [*tænia*] the Top of a Pillar, but very insolently; it being indeed the small fascia part of the Doric architrave.

†**ˈinsolentness.** *Obs. rare.* [f. as prec. + -NESS.] The quality of being insolent; insolence, arrogance.

a **1592** GREENE *Selimus* Wks. 1881–3 XIV. 223 And if the Bassaes knew I sought their grace, It would the more increase their insolentnesse. **1727** in BAILEY vol. II.

insolible, obs. form of INSOLUBLE *sb.*

†**inˈsolid**, *a. Obs. rare.* [ad. L. *insolid-us*, f. *in-* (IN-³) + *solid-us* SOLID. Cf. obs. F. *insolide* 'vnsolide, loose, weake, feeble' (Cotgr.), perh. the immed. source.] Not solid; unsubstantial; weak, flimsy, light, unstable.

1618 T. ADAMS *Spir. Eye-salve* Wks. 1862 II. 381 The second defect in the eye is an insolid levity, it it roving, like Dinah's, and ravished abroad. *a* **1658** J. DURHAM *Exp. Revelation* III. ii. (1680) 173 Learning serveth to enable one, in searching for truth, to conceive what is solide or insolide.

insolidity (ɪnsəʊˈlɪdɪtɪ). ?*Obs.* [f. IN-³ + SOLIDITY: cf. prec. and F. *insolidité* (16th c. in Godef.).] Absence of solidity; want of firmness or stability; frailty, flimsiness, weakness.

1578 BANISTER *Hist. Man* I. 3 Notwithstanding the needfulnes of such Insoliditie, it is..as requisite, that the Bones were not continuall. **1660** H. MORE *Myst. Godl.* v. xvi. 201 A demonstration of the insolidity of this Exception. **1827** JARMAN *Powell's Devises* II. 101 Enough has been said ..to shew the insolidity of such a distinction.

†**insolite**, *a. Obs. rare.* (Also 5 -ute, 7 -ete.) [a. F. *insolite* (16th c.), ad L. *insolit-us* unusual, f. *in-* (IN-³) + *solitus* accustomed, from *solēre* to be wont.] Unusual, unaccustomed, strange.

1490 CAXTON *Eneydos* iv. 20 Thyng not acustumed, merueyllous & Insolute. *a* **1622** J. RANDALL *St. Paul's Triumph* Ep. Ded. A, It is no insolete nor unwarrantable

course. **1667** WATERHOUSE *Fire Lond.* 99 Punished with an amazing and insolite judgment.

insolubility (ɪnsɒljuːˈbɪlɪtɪ). [ad. L. type **insolūbilitās* (prob. in mod.L.), f. *insolūbilis* INSOLUBLE: see -ITY. Cf. F. *insolubilité* (1765 in *Dict. Acad.*).] The quality of being insoluble.

†**1.** Incapability of being dissolved; indissolubility. *Obs. rare*⁻¹.

1620 BRENT tr. *Sarpi's Counc. Trent* VII. an.1563 (1676) 627 After he had spoken..of the insolubility of Marriage.

2. Incapability of being solved or unravelled; also, an insoluble problem.

1837 WHEWELL *Hist. Induct. Sc.* (1857) I. 330 The insolubility of this problem. **1851** CARLYLE *Sterling* I. xi. (1872) 65 His health was already very threatening.. rendering the future..an insolubility for him.

3. Incapability of being dissolved in a liquid.

1791 W. NICHOLSON tr. *Chaptal's Elem. Chem.* (1800) III. 87 Its insolubility in the menstruums which usually dissolve resins. **1805–17** R. JAMESON *Char. Min.* (ed. 3) 300 The solubility or insolubility of minerals in the fluxes. **1871** ROSCOE *Elem. Chem.* 212 The greater insolubility of the double chloride.

insolubilize (ɪnˈsɒljʊbɪlaɪz), *v.* [f. L. *insolūbil-is* INSOLUBLE *a.* + -IZE.] *trans.* To render incapable of dissolving. So **inˈsolubilized**, **inˈsolubilizing** *ppl. adjs.*

1897 *Daily News* 4 Oct. 6/4 The colouring matter remaining attached to the paper, and held there by the insolubilised gum. **1904** *Buck's Handbk. Med. Sci.* (rev. ed.) VIII. 351/2 Both the iron and magnesium compounds must be removed from the stomach as soon as possible since the insolubilized arsenic may be again resorbed through the solvent action of the fluids of the body. **1947** *Jrnl. Soc. Chem. Industry* LXVI. 417/2 A small proportion of solids.. became insolubilized during boiling. **1962** J. T. MARSH *Self-Smoothing Fabrics* xx. 333 Hence the main effect of heat is to insolubilise the resin. *Ibid.* vii. 100 This compound had some previous application in Germany as an insolubilising agent for the protein binder in the pigment printing process. **1967** E. CHAMBERS *Photolitho-Offset* xiii. 191 The image consists of an organic resin insolubilised by light. **1971** *Nature* 6 Aug. p. iii (Advt.) The world's most comprehensive selection of insolubilized biochemicals. **1972** *Enzymologia* XLII. 275 Treatment with glutaraldehyde could have insolubilized crystalline catalase in two fashions.

Hence **inˌsolubiliˈzation**, the process of insolubilizing.

1926 *Chem. Abstr.* XX. 838 According to the French pat. 413,007, addition of an organic acid to a bath containing gelatin and CH_2O prevents the insolubilization, which is restored by NH_3. **1946** *Nature* 28 Dec. 925/2 Reactions of rubber and olefinic systems generally with sulphur and other reagents which are known to produce insolubilization. **1971** *Ibid.* 6 Aug. p. iii (Advt.), Supports for the insolubilization of proteins.

insoluble (ɪnˈsɒljuːb(ə)l), *a.* (*sb.*) Also 4–5 -ibil, -ible. [ad. L. *insolūbil-is*, f. *in-* (IN-³) + *solūbilis* SOLUBLE.] Not soluble.

1. That cannot be dissolved, undone, or loosed; indissoluble. Now *rare*.

1382 WYCLIF *Heb.* vii. 16 Lyf insolible [*gloss* or that may not be vndon]. **1561** T. NORTON *Calvin's Inst.* IV. 90 They haue broken..the insoluble bonde wherewith they were bounde to God and to the Chirch. **1605** A. WILLET *Hexapla Gen.* 426 Augustine and Eucherius thinke this knot to be insoluble. **1609** HOLLAND *Amm. Marcell.* XVI. xii. 71 The formost of every ranke in the vaward stood firme and fast, like a strong and insoluble wall. **1695** LD. PRESTON *Boeth.* II. 77 Bound in the insoluble Chains of his Lusts. **1846** GROTE *Greece* I. xvi. (1862) II. 406 The insoluble knot whereby the yoke was attached.

†**b.** Of arguments: Irrefragable, irrefutable. *Obs. rare*.

1533 MORE *Debell. Salem* Wks. 944/2 [To] stand for a sure & an insoluble argument. **1616** BULLOKAR, *Insoluble*, that which cannot be loosed: vnanswerable. **1676** MARVELL *Mr. Smirke* 30 All these contradictory Arguments which either of them had once fancied so insoluble.

2. That cannot be solved, as a difficulty, question, problem, etc.; incapable of being resolved or explained; not susceptible of solution; unsolvable.

1393 LANGL. *P. Pl.* C. XVII. 231 Freres fele sithes..Meuen motifs meny tymes Insolibles and fallaces, That boþe lered and lewed of here by-leyue douten. **1529** MORE *Dyaloge* I. Wks. 165/2 Ye should..haue remayned in an insoluble doute in a matter of the faith. **1634** JACKSON *Creed* VII. iv. §3 The number of insoluble problems is in divinity much greater than in any other faculty. **1738** WARBURTON *Div. Legat.* II. App. Wks. 1811 II. 244 An insoluble question concerning the origin of evil. **1851** D. WILSON *Preh. Ann.* (1863) I. ix. 236 Unsolved, if not insoluble problems. **1875** JOWETT *Plato* (ed. 2) IV. 134 Plato does not treat even this ..class of difficulties as hopeless or insoluble.

3. Incapable of being dissolved in a liquid.

1713 DERHAM *Phys.-Theol.* IV. xi. (1727) 198 That wonderful Faculty of the Stomachs of all Creatures, to dissolve all the several Sorts of Food..even sometimes Things of that Consistency as seem Insoluble. **1791** HAMILTON *Berthollet's Dyeing* I. I. I. ii. 30 It forms an insoluble salt which is precipitated. **1857** G. BIRD *Urin. Deposits* 121 The soluble phosphates..far exceed in quantity the insoluble salts.

4. Of a debt: That cannot be discharged or paid off.

1850 ROBERTSON *Serm.* Ser. I. v. (1881) 76 Remorse is like the clog of an insoluble debt.

B. *sb.* Something insoluble; a difficulty or problem that cannot be solved or explained.

1387 TREVISA *Higden* (Rolls) III. 203 Þan þe iuges sigh þat þe cause was brigous, as it were an insolible, and put it of to a wel longe day. *c* **1440** CAPGRAVE *Life St. Kath.* IV. 1713 To sey of it that it is passyble, Semeth to me a ful gret insolible. **1531** ELYOT *Gov.* III. vi, That good lawes be tourned in to Sophemes and insolubles. **1532** MORE *Confut. Tindale* Wks. 355/1 Tyndalles tryflinge sophisticacions, whyche he woulde shoulde seeme so solempne..insolubles.

Hence **inˈsolubly** *adv.*, in an insoluble manner or degree.

Mod. The affair is insolubly mysterious.

insolubleness (ɪnˈsɒljuːb(ə)lnɪs). [f. prec. + -NESS.] The quality or state of being insoluble.

1672 BOYLE *Hydrost. Disc.* II. v. Wks. 1772 III. 624, I shall return to doctor More, and consider the objection he frames from the supposed insolubleness of it. **1886** *Century Mag.* XXXII. 895 In spite of their perhaps necessary insolubleness. **1890** *Spectator* 15 May, The new questions that arise..have in them an apparent quality of insolubleness.

insolute, erron. form of INSOLITE, *Obs.*

†**insoˈlutive**, *a. Obs. rare*⁻¹. [f. IN-³ + L. *solūt-*, ppl. stem of *solvĕre* to pay + -IVE.] Not able to pay; = INSOLVENT.

1668 WILKINS *Real Char.* 341 A person insolutive, or (as we commonly say) insolvent, is a Bankrupt.

insolvable (ɪnˈsɒlvəb(ə)l), *a.* [IN-³. Cf. F. *insolvable* (1431 in Godef. *Compl.*; in Cotgr.).] Incapable of being solved.

†**1.** That cannot be loosed, unbound, or untied; = INSOLUBLE *a.* 1. *Obs.*

1652 KIRKMAN *Clerio & Lozia* 95 Their souls and hearts were knit in an insolvable knot. *c* **1690** in Somers *Tracts* I. 442 They would scarce apprehend that it could be a more strong or insolvable Bond. **1725** POPE *Odyss.* VIII. 480 To guard with bands Insolvable these gifts, thy care demands.

2. That cannot be solved or explained; = INSOLUBLE 2.

1693 R. W. *Compl. Library* II. 362 The Doctrine..is perplext with an infinite number of Monstrous and insolvable Difficulties. **1741** WATTS *Improv. Mind* I. i. §3 Geometry, wherein there appear some insolvable difficulties. **1884** *Chr. Commw.* 28 Feb. 465/2 Answers are vainly sought to insolvable problems.

3. Incapable of being dissolved; = INSOLUBLE 3.

1823 J. BADCOCK *Dom. Amusem.* 25 Being itself insolvable in any known menstruum.

4. Of a bank note or bill: That cannot be cashed.

1846 HAWTHORNE *Mosses* II. viii. *Earth's Holocaust* 140 A bundle of counterfeit or insolvable bank-notes.

†**5.** Of a debt: That cannot be paid. *Obs. rare*⁻⁰.

1755 JOHNSON, *Insolvable*,..that cannot be paid.

†**6.** Unable to pay one's debts; = INSOLVENT 1.

1648 tr. *Senault's Paraphr. Job* 202 Taking pawnes of those who were insolvable. **1730–6** BAILEY (folio), *Insolvable*, not able to pay.

Hence **insolvaˈbility**, incapability of being solved or explained. **inˈsolvableness**, 'uncapableness of being loosed or resolved' (Bailey vol. II, 1727). **inˈsolvably** *adv.*, insolubly.

1795 G. WAKEFIELD *Reply to 2nd Pt. Age Reason* 42 Something..so insolvably problematical. *a* **1834** COLERIDGE *Lit. Rem.* (1839) IV. 271 As soon as its insolvibility..is proved and accounted for. **1890** *Smithsonian Rep.* 100 A demonstration of the insolvability of this historic problem.

inˈsolvence. *rare.* [f. INSOLVENT *a.*: see -ENCE.] The fact of becoming insolvent.

1793 J. WILLIAMS *Calm Exam.* 88 The..property of a Debtor, whether acquired anterior or posterior to his insolvence.

insolvency (ɪnˈsɒlvənsɪ). [f. INSOLVENT *a.*: see -ENCY.] The state or condition of being insolvent; the fact of being unable to pay one's debts or discharge one's liabilities; an instance of this.

1660 JER. TAYLOR *Duct. Dubit.* III. ii. rule vii. §11. 121 If the Father be under torment or imprisonment for insolvency. *a* **1687** PETTY *Pol. Arith.* (1690) 6 One fifth part was abated for non-valuers or Insolvencies. **1725** *Lond. Gaz.* No. 6388/8 Prisoners..who intend to take the Benefit of the Act of Insolvency. **1788** PRIESTLEY *Lect. Hist.* V. lxiv. 513 If the insolvency of one great merchant, or banker, produce great distress in a country, how dreadful must be the consequence attending the insolvency of such a nation as England! **1841** ELPHINSTONE *Hist. Ind.* II. 61 The king's insolvency..destroyed the credit of his tokens from the first.

b. *transf.* and *fig.* Failure to meet engagements.

1896 *Daily News* 12 Feb. 5/5 Was there ever such a confession of diplomatic insolvency?

insolvent (ɪnˈsɒlvənt), *a.* (*sb.*) [f. IN-³ + SOLVENT, L. *solvent-em* paying.] Not solvent.

1. Unable to pay one's debts or discharge one's liabilities; bankrupt. Said of persons, companies, commercial or financial concerns, estates, etc.

1591 HORSEY *Trav.* (Hakl. Soc.) 246 The..merchants tradinge those countries..became insolvent. **1662** PETTY *Taxes* 57 Why should not insolvent thieves be rather punished with slavery than death? **1781** GIBBON *Decl. & F.* xvii. II. 71 The cruel treatment of the insolvent debtors of the state. **1817** LD. ELLENBOROUGH in *Maule & Selwyn's Rep.* VI. 316 When he knew himself insolvent, and when ruin and bankruptcy were staring him in the face. **1871** MARKBY *Elem. Law* §548 A man may owe more than he is worth, and therefore if a money value is set on his collective legal relations he may be what is called insolvent. **1883** *Law Times* 20 Oct. 409/1 The proceedings connected with the management, in insolvent estates.

†**2.** Not able to be cashed or realized. *Obs.*

1667 *Ormonde MSS.* in *10th Rep. Hist. MSS. Comm.* App. v. 45 Your petitioner received assignments for part of six months' pay for the said troop, part of which assignments proved insolvent. **1728** YOUNG *Love Fame* v. 400 How will the miser startle, to be told Of such a wonder, as insolvent gold?

3. Of, pertaining, or relating to insolvents or insolvency.

1837 HT. MARTINEAU *Soc. Amer.* II. 365 In Philadelphia, from six to eight hundred persons annually take the benefit of the insolvent laws. **1837** THACKERAY *Ravenswing* i, He had been through the Insolvent Court. **1853** WHARTON *Pa. Digest* II. 19 A debtor who has no property whatever is nevertheless entitled to the benefit of the insolvent laws.

B. *sb.* An insolvent debtor.

1725 WATTS *Logic* I. vi. §2 An insolvent is a man that cannot pay his debts. **1767** T. HUTCHINSON *Hist. Mass.* II. i. 65 Creditors of a deceased insolvent shall be paid their full debts. **1883** *Wharton's Law Lex.* (ed. 7) 419 An insolvent as distinguished from a bankrupt, was an insolvent who was not a trader; for originally only a trader could be made bankrupt, in the sense of obtaining an absolute discharge from his debts, while the future estate of an insolvent remained liable for his discharge, even after his discharge.

Hence †**inˈsolventness** (Bailey vol. II, 1727).

in so mekylle, var. INSAMEIKLE, *Sc. Obs.*, insomuch.

‖**insomnia** (ɪnˈsɒmnɪə). Also *β.* 7 in anglicized form **insomnie**; *γ.* 7–9 **insomnium**. [L. *insomnia* sleeplessness, f. *insomnis* sleepless, f. *in-* (IN-³) + *somnus* sleep. Cf. F. insomnie (1680 in Hatz.-Darm.).] Inability to sleep; sleeplessness.

α. **1758** J. S. *Le Dran's Observ. Surg.* (1771) 107 The Patient laboured under *Insomnia*. **1863** READE *Hard Cash* (1864) II. xx. 322 It accused Alfred of headache, insomnia, nightly visions. **1879** F. S. BRIDGES *Round World in six Months* 218 So intolerable was the responsibility, that all these men became afflicted with insomnia, and could scarcely ever rest.

β. **1623** COCKERAM, *Insomnie*, watching, want of power to sleep.

γ. **1694** SALMON *Bate's Dispens.* (1699) 262/1 To ease the Head-ach, correct *Insomniums*, or vehemently to stupify. **1856** KANE *Arct. Expl.* I. xiv. 156, I am so afflicted with the *insomnium* of this eternal night, that I rise at any time between midnight and noon.

insomniac (ɪnˈsɒmnɪæk). [f. INSOMNI(A + -AC.] One who suffers from insomnia. Also *attrib.* or as *adj.*

1908 *Lancet* 8 Feb. 407/2 The urinary secretion is increased, not diminished. The latter phenomenon is, like all the phenomena of sleeplessness, most evident in the neurotic insomniac. **1930** H. CRICHTON-MILLER *Insomnia* ii. 21 Most insomniacs wish it to be believed that the onus of their insomnia lies with their circumstances and environment. **1939** G. GREENE *Lawless Roads* iv. 126 A Pennsylvanian with pouchy insomniac eyes. **1953** E. HYAMS *Gentian Violet* ix. 176 Jim's absence of mind might cause thousands of back-street chemists to have seven instead of four forms to complete when purchasing barbiturates; and compel insomniac neurotics to pass sleepless nights. **1957** P. I. ROSENTEUR *Morpheus & Me* xvi. 270 Our system of individual enterprise has made it possible for anyone, whatever his original social or economic status, to work and worry himself right into the front ranks of the insomniac army. **1959** *Listener* 23 July 121/2 Baghdad has been an insomniac's paradise. **1973** L. MEYNELL *Thirteen Trumpeters* xiv. 214 A Mickey Finn, guaranteed to put the worst insomniac in the world fast asleep in five minutes.

†**inˈsomniate**, *v. Obs.* [irreg. f. L. *in-* (IN-²) + *sommus* sleep + -ATE³.] *trans.* To put to sleep.

a **1657** R. LOVEDAY *Lett.* (1663) 267 A Mercurial Caducæus to insomniate the Argus-eyes of jealous people!

insomnious (ɪnˈsɒmnɪəs), *a. rare.* [ad. L. *insomniōs-us* sleepless, f. *insomnia*: see -OUS.]

Affected with insomnia; sleepless, unable to sleep.

1658 PHILLIPS, *Insomnious*, wanting sleep, also apt to dream. **1730–6** BAILEY (folio), *Insomnious*, troubled with dreams, not sleeping soundly. **1865** GROTE *Plato* (1875) III. xxxvii. 376 Nurses..lull to sleep an insomnious child..by swinging him about in their arms. **1894** *Publisher's Advt.*, Those who sleep well, those who dream, and those who are insomnious.

¶ *Erroneously.* [from L. *insomnium* dream.]

1656 BLOUNT *Glossogr.*, *Insomnious*, troubled with dreams, that dreameth much in his sleep. **1658** [see above]. **1721** BAILEY, *Insomnious*, troubled with Dreams, full of Dreams.

insomnolence (ɪnˈsɒmnələns). *rare.* [IN-³.] The state of being insomnolent; insomnia.

1822 SOUTHEY in *Q. Rev.* XXVI. 315 He brought on a habit of insomnolence and a loathing of food. **1834** —— *Doctor* I. vi. 7 O Doctor, for one of thy comfortable composing draughts!—Two! here's a case of insomnolence! **1842** SIR H. TAYLOR *Edwin the Fair* I. ii, Suspicion's wasting pale insomnolence.

inˈsomnolency. *rare.* [IN-³.] = prec.

a **1843** *Lives Brit. Physic.*, *Harvey* (1857) 57 He was troubled with insomnolency, and would then get up and

walk about his chamber in his shirt, till he was pretty cool, or even till he began to shiver. **1859** R. F. BURTON *Centr. Afr.* in *Jrnl. Geogr. Soc.* XXIX. 40 An impaired appetite, nausea, general debility, and a weary insomnolency..await the patient when the malady has passed away.

in'somnolent, *a.* (*sb.*) *rare.* [IN-³.] Sleepless; unable to sleep; = INSOMNIOUS *a.* In quot. as *sb.* One affected with insomnia.

1892 *Chicago Advance* 12 May, I know that the poor insomnolents will not despise any device for winning sleep.

insomuch (ɪnsəʊ'mʌtʃ), *adv.* [The three words *in so much*, since 16th c. usually written conjunctly.]

1. *absol.* To such an extent or degree; so much, so far. *rare.*

c **1380** WYCLIF *Sel. Wks.* III. 433 Her [priests'] power, gederid togeder, in so myche passiþ power of Petre. **1823** J. BADCOCK *Dom. Amusem.* p. vi, If one fact..has lost a particle of its interest..insomuch is the Editor's design frustrated.

2. ***insomuch as.*** **a.** Inasmuch as, in that, seeing that, since.

1485 CAXTON *Paris & V.* Prol., In so much as I am not French by birth, but born..in the city of Marseilles. *c* **1500** *Adam Bel & Clym of Clough* 489 We besecħe ȝou now, That you graunt vs grace, Insomuche as we be to you comen. **1583** STANYHURST *Æneis* I. (Arb.) 19 In so much as of mankind the Emperor heaunlye And father of thee Gods too thee the auctoritye signed. **1836** *Westm. Rev.* XXIV. 105 To be sure..the present law is inoperative; insomuch as the Universities..contain teachers who have never subscribed this famous confession.

†**b.** = *insomuch that*: see 3. *Obs.*

1579–80 NORTH *Plutarch* (1676) 181 Now this did more encrease..the Peoples good opinion of his sufficiency, and wise conduction of an Army; insomuch as they thought him invincible. **1628** HOBBES *Thucyd.* (1822) 8 Insomuch as never resting they improvd not their power. **1658** EARL MONM. tr. *Paruta's Hist. Wars Cyprus* I. ii. 25 They ran every day through the Territories..insomuch as Bernardo Mollepiero..was so sorely wounded, as he fell down dead off his horseback.

c. To such an extent as, so as: see 1.

1651 HOBBES *Leviath.* I. xii. 54 They attribute their fortune to a stander by, to a lucky or unlucky place [etc.]..insomuch as to believe, they have power to turn a stone into bread [etc.]. **1718** *Freethinker* No. 61 ¶14 The True Breed..is very Alert, insomuch as to pass frequently for a Clan of Intrepids. *a* **1832** BENTHAM *Deontology* (1834) II. 306 In so much and in so far as they are susceptible of becoming [etc.].

3. ***insomuch that***: To such an extent that, so that. (The most usual construction.)

a **1450** *Knt. de la Tour* (1868) 119 In so moche that she had al that she aught to haue by right and of custume. **1535** COVERDALE 1 *Macc.* i. 3 In so moch, yᵗ the worlde stode in greate awe of him. **1568** GRAFTON *Chron.* II. 420 [They] did denie to deliver them, insomuch, that the king openly sayd, that..he would take them without deliveraunce. **1668** WILKINS *Real Char.* 449 There is much more pains required for the remembring of them, than of the Rules themselves; insomuch that many eminent Grammarians have written against Analogy, both in Greek and Latin. **1711** ADDISON *Spect.* No. 60 ¶3 The lover was thunder-struck with his Misfortune, insomuch that in a little time after he lost his Senses. **1833–42** ALISON *Hist. Europe* (1849–50) XIV. xciv. §1. 1 The rain fell in torrents, insomuch that..the soldiers were often ankle-deep in water.

†**4.** With ellipsis of *as*: Inasmuch as, in that: = 2 a. *Obs.*

1600 SHAKS. *A.Y.L.* v. ii. 60, I speake not this, that you should beare a good opinion of my knowledge: insomuch (I say) I know you are. **1605** TIMME *Quersit.* I. v. 20 Among salts, some are earthie..insomuch some of them are fixed, and are of the nature of earth.

insonder: see INSUNDER.

insonorous (ɪnsəʊ'nɔːrəs, now freq. ɪn'sɒnərəs), *a. rare.* [IN-³.] Not sonorous; giving a dull or muffled sound.

1795 *Fortnight's Ramble* 11 An insonorous voice exclaiming, Damn your day-lights, stop the coach! **1889** J. M. ROBERTSON *Ess. Crit. Meth.* 75 The old music-room, with its straitened insonorous instruments.

†**in'soot**, *v. Obs. rare.* In 7 insutt. [IN-².] *trans.* To cover with soot, make sooty.

1611 FLORIO, *Incaliginare, Infuliginire*..to insutt.

insooth, *adv.*, for *in sooth*: see SOOTH *sb.*

insorb (ɪn'sɔːb), *v. rare.* [f. IN-¹ + L. *sorbēre* to suck up.] *trans.* To absorb *into.* So **in'sorbent** *a.*, absorbing in, absorbent.

1756 C. LUCAS *Ess. Waters* I. 44 Perforation so extremely minute..as the insorbent pores of vegetables and animals. *Ibid.* III. 175 He knew that animal bodies..were endued with insorbent pores. **1878** FOSTER *Phys.* II. i. 183 The nutritious digested material is..insorbed into the blood.

†**insor'descent**, *a. R. C. Ch. Obs.* [ad. L. *insordēscent-em*, pr. pple. of *insordēscĕre* to become foul or dirty, f. *in-* (IN-²) + *sordēscĕre* to become dirty, f. *sordēs* dirt, filth.] *lit.* Increasing in filthiness; in quot. *fig.* So †**insor'descence.**

1731 CHANDLER tr. *Limborch's Hist. Inquis.* II. III. xviii. 82 A Man is said to be insordescent in Excommunication, who, after he hath been by Name declared Excommunicate, persists in that Excommunication for a Year. *Ibid.*, He must be deprived of his Benefice for Insordescence.

†**in'sordid**, *a. Obs. rare* [f. IN-³ + SORDID.] Not sordid, unsordid; generous.

1660 WATERHOUSE *Arms & Arm.* 117 For a true Souldier..is a man of liberal and insordid principles.

insorwe(n, variant of ENSORROW *v.*, *Obs.*

‖**insouciance** (ɛ̃susiɑ̃s, *occas.* ɪn'suːsɪəns). [F., f. next: see -ANCE.] Carelessness, indifference, unconcern.

1799 W. G. BROWNE *Trav. Africa*, etc. xxi. 319 Among the poorer class of all countries prevails a kind of *insouciance.* **1847** LONGF. in *Life* (1891) II. 82 Farewell the sweet *insouciance* of lettered ease. **1878** H. M. STANLEY *Dark Cont.* I. xii. 318, I could not help smiling at the diplomatic *insouciance* of this man.

‖**insouciant** (ɪn'suːsɪənt, Fr. ɛ̃susiɑ̃). [F., f. *in-* (IN-³) + *souciant* caring, pr. pple. of *soucier* to care:—L. *sollicitāre* to disturb, agitate.] Careless, indifferent, unconcerned.

1829 SCOTT *Anne of G.* xxix, This insouciant, light-tempered, gay, and thoughtless disposition, conducted René..to a hale and mirthful old age. **1848** MILL *Pol. Econ.* II. ix. §3 (1876) 197 What race would not be indolent and insouciant when things are so arranged that they derive no advantage from forethought and exertion? **1888** *Pall Mall G.* 12 Jan. 2/1 On such subjects, an insouciant agnosticism is the most philosophic attitude.

Hence **in'souciantly** *adv.*, carelessly, with an air of unconcern.

1880 J. HAWTHORNE *Ellice Quentin*, etc. I. 110 Should I..stalk insouciantly through the crowd and up the beach as I was?

insoul, variant of ENSOUL *v.*

†**in'soundable**, *a. Obs. rare.* [IN-³.] Incapable of being sounded; unfathomable.

1600 W. WATSON *Decacordon* (1602) 139 Herein is an insoundable deapth.

†**in'sow**, *v. Obs. rare.* In 4 *north. dial.* insawe. [f. IN-¹ + SOW *v.*, after L. *inserĕre.*] *trans.* To sow in, set in as seed.

c **1340** HAMPOLE *Prose Tr.* 3 This name Ihesu..drawes by þe rote vyces, settys vertus, insawes charytee.

inspan (ɪn'spæn), *v. S. African.* [a. Du. *inspann-en*, f. *in* adv. in + *spannen* to span, stretch, bend, put horses to.] **a.** *trans.* To yoke (oxen, horses, etc.) in a team to a vehicle; to harness (a wagon).

1834 T. BOWKER *Jrnl.* 25 Dec. in *Towards Dict. S. Afr. Eng.* (Dict. S. Afr. Eng. Dict. Committee) (1971) 43 Arrive at [M]erais after sunset find the waggons inspanned ready for going away. **1838** F. OWEN *Diary* (1926) 118 At length, our oxen being inspanned, the waggon being loaded with the chief necessaries belonging to both families..we left the station. **1852** *Blackw. Mag.* LXXI. 294 (Cape Colony) At noon, the cattle, which have been turned out to graze, are 'inspanned', and the march continues. **1880** SIR S. LAKEMAN *Kaffir-Land* 36 The Hottentot drivers inspanned the bullocks. **1883** OLIVE SCHREINER *Story Afr. Farm* II. xii, The waggon..stood 'in-spanned' before the door. **1886** F. H. GUILLEMARD *Cruise 'Marchesa'* I. 191 The agent of the Alaska Commercial Company had kindly provided us with dog-sledges, and we found them 'inspanned' and waiting for us. **1887** RIDER HAGGARD *Jess* xxi, 'Mouti', said John to the Zulu, 'inspan the horses'.

absol. **1863** *Batowin's Hunting in Natal* 182 Inspanned about 3 o'clock. **1893** SELOUS *Trav. S.E. Africa* 93, I determined to inspan and hold on my course to the south.

b. *fig.* or *transf.*

1914 KIPLING in *Georg. Jrnl.* Apr. 373 One man, apparently without effort, inspans the human equivalent of 'three blind 'uns and a bolter' and makes them do miracles. **1928** *Sunday Express* 8 July 10/5 There are hundreds of keen young players with the player's eyesight available for this lining business. Is it beyond the wit and the capacity of the Wimbledon authorities to inspan them? **1939** R. CAMPBELL *Flowering Rifle* I. 15 Our great Victory,..in her car, Which all the way from Portugal to France She inspans in her thundering advance. **1949** *Cape Times* 13 Sept. 8/9 To rescue the Coloured man, all forces will have to be inspanned to raise him economically. **1971** *Rand Daily Mail* 29 June 15 Why, Mrs Barton often gets on the telephone and inspans private householders to help out.

Hence **in'spanning** *vbl. sb.*; also **'inspan** *sb.*, the act of inspanning.

1879 R. J. ATCHERLEY *Trip Boërland* 62, I had been sound asleep at the time of inspanning. *Ibid.* 68 We managed to get along until next morning's sunrise and inspan. **1887** RIDER HAGGARD *Jess* xx, John went..to see the inspanning of the Cape cart.

insparge, insparse, var. INSPERGE, INSPERSE.

in-spawn ('ɪnspɔːn), *a.* [attrib. use of the phrase *in spawn* (cf. IN *prep.* 10 b).] That is about to spawn.

1908 *Westm. Gaz.* 14 Mar. 11/3 Netting the in-spawn dace. **1923** *Daily Mail* 13 Feb. 12 After the fish was landed it disgorged an in-spawn trout of 2 lb.

inspeak (ɪn'spiːk), *v.* [f. IN-¹ + SPEAK *v.* Cf. Ger. *einsprechen.*] *trans.* To speak (something) *into*; to produce in the soul by speech.

1691 E. TAYLOR *Behmen's Theos. Philos.* xx. 31 God inspake again the Ingrafted Word. **1760** LAW *Spir. Prayer* I. 67 When the mercy of God inspoke into Adam a seed of the divine life. **1856** VAUGHAN *Mystics* (1860) II. XI. i. 219 The hidden word of promise, inspoken into all men. **1890** J. PULSFORD *Loyalty to Christ* I. 115 His Spirit in us..will inspeak courage and kindle hope.

Hence **'inspeaking** *vbl. sb.*; **in'spoken** *ppl. a.*

1751 BP. LAVINGTON *Enthus. Method. & Papists* (1754) II. iii. 88 By Visions, In-speakings, Ecstasies [etc.]. **1752** LAW *Spir. Love* II. (1816) 94 Jesus Christ..the inspoken word.

†**in'speakable**, *a. Obs.* [IN-³.] Unspeakable.

1504 LADY MARGARET tr. *De Imitatione* IV. xviii. 282 In sechyng so besily the hye inspekeable thynges. **1548–9** (Mar.) *Bk. Com. Prayer, Collect All Saints' Day*, Those inspeakeable ioyes, whiche thou hast prepared. **1594** GREENE & LODGE *Looking Glass* Wks. (Rtldg.) 126/1 O inspeakable injustice!

Hence †**in'speakably** *adv. Obs.*, unspeakably.

a **1618** RALEIGH *Rem.* (1661) 152 Many other such things, to draw the people to a City inspeakably which leaves behind them much treasure.

'inspeaking, *ppl. a.* [IN *adv.* 11 a.] That speaks within.

1847 B. BARTON *Select.* (1849) 57 That inspeaking word, the voice of his Spirit. **1885** *A Reasonable Faith* 41 To associate the universally inspeaking voice with a Divine Person.

†**in'special**, obs. erron. writing of phrase *in special*, especially; see SPECIAL, and cf. INESPECIAL.

c **1470** HARDING *Chron.* c. ii, The Kynges inspeciall Vnder his rule. **1513** BRADSHAW *St. Werburge* I. 3432 Prepared by the kyng, and ordeyned inspeciall.

So †**inspecially** *adv.* Cf. INESPECIALLY.

1526 in West *Antiq. Furness* (1805) 132 Inspecially for the tythes of certain touns and fermholds. **1557** NORTH tr. *Gueuara's Diall Pr.* 91 b/2 Women..inspeciallye the Princessys and great Ladies.

†**'inspect**, *sb. Obs.* [app. ad. L. *inspectu-s* looking at, inspection, examination, f. ppl. stem of *inspicĕre*: see next. (Stress orig. *in'spect*, in 18th c. *'inspect*: cf. *respect*, *aspect*.)] The act of looking into a matter; inspection, examination.

c **1489** CAXTON *Blanchardyn* lii. 199 Wherupon they fulsone, wythoute eny other inspecte concluded togyder that they sholde departe the nexte daye. **1509** HAWES *Joyf. Medit.* v, O God..In whose inspecte is euery regall se. **1509** —— *Past. Pleas.* VIII. (Percy Soc.) 33 And yf that they had in it inspecte, Than they would it prayse. **1649** ROBERTS *Clavis Bibl.* ii. 18 The Book of life..whose writing is indelible, whose inspect is desirable. **1693** PRIDEAUX *Lett.* (Camden) 158 Matters of fact and matters of law, wᶜʰ private men can never have a clear inspect into. **1730–46** THOMSON *Autumn* 1134 Not so the man of philosophic eye, And inspect sage.

inspect (ɪn'spɛkt), *v.* [f. L. *inspect-*, ppl. stem of *inspicĕre* to look into, inspect, examine, and its frequentative *inspectā-re* to look at, observe, view: cf. mod.F. *inspecter* (1781 in Hatz.-Darm.).]

1. *trans.* To look carefully into; to view closely and critically; to examine (something) with a view to find out its character or condition; now *spec.* to investigate or oversee officially: see INSPECTOR 1.

1623 COCKERAM, *Inspected*, looked into. **1670** SIR SACKVILLE CROW in *12th Rep. Hist. MSS. Comm.* App. v. 16 That mannifacture grows worse daylie, except inspected by one that knowes worke. **1690** CHILD *Disc. Trade* (1694) 8 All men that make it any part of their business to inspect the true nature and principles of trade. **1704** SWIFT *T. Tub* Ded. Posterity, To keep you in an almost universal ignorance of our Studies, which it is your inherent birthright to inspect. **1734** tr. *Rollin's Anc. Hist.* (1827) VII. XVIII. i. 359 He dreaded inspecting the truth. **1788** V. KNOX *Winter Even.* I. II. iii. 128 They inspect some of those conceited writers. **1841** D'ISRAELI *Amen. Lit.* (1867) 608 He inspected nature with the close eye of a naturalist. **1860** TYNDALL *Glac.* 166 Halting at intervals..to inspect the glacier.

†**2.** *intr.* To look closely or carefully; to examine *into* or *among*. *Obs.*

1704 SWIFT *T. Tub* iii, Whoever designs to be a perfect writer must inspect into the books of critics. **1705** FARQUHAR *Twin-Rivals* II. iii, He has declar'd..that he would inspect into all his accounts himself. **1724** SWIFT *Corr.* Wks. 1841 II. 569 That..you would please to inspect among your father's papers. **1799** G. SMITH *Laboratory* II. 8 By inspecting into the figures and inscriptions of the..coins.

Hence **in'spected** *ppl. a.*, **in'specting** *vbl. sb.* and *ppl. a.*; hence **in'spectingly** *adv.*

1697 DRYDEN *Virg. Georg.* III. 738 Th' inspected Entrails cou'd no Fates foretell. **1788** in *Outing* (U.S.) (1894) Apr. 76/1 Places for exercise, and inspecting of arms and accoutrements. **1796–7** *Instr. & Reg. Cavalry* (1813) 262 The inspecting General may be enabled to report the more minutely. **1853** KANE *Grinnell Exp.* xii. 94 [The bear] rose upon his hind palms, and..snuffed the air inspectingly. **1863** A. TYLOR *Educ. & Manuf.* 49 The deplorable account of the state of education in the inspected schools.

inspectable (ɪn'spɛktəb(ə)l), *a.* [f. INSPECT *v.* + -ABLE.] Capable of being inspected.

1816 BENTHAM *Chrestom.* 75 Several such apartments..will in this case be inspectable by one and the same person.

Hence **inspecta'bility.**

1830–1 BENTHAM *Panopt.* App. Wks. 1843 XI. 102/2 Inspectability of the inspectors.

†**inspec'tator.** *Obs. rare*⁻¹. [a. late L. *inspectātor*, agent-n. f. L. *inspectāre* to INSPECT. Cf. F. *inspectateur* (Molière).] = INSPECTOR.

1593 NORDEN *Spec. Brit., Middlesex & Herts* I. Preparative 17 Ouer-curious inspectators that seem to bring with them a preiudicate censure of the worke.

inspection (ɪn'spɛkʃən). In ME. -ci-, -cy-, -oun; also 5 inspexion. [a. F. *inspection*, *-cion* (1290 in

Godef. *Compl.*), ad. L. *inspectiōn-em*, n. of action from *inspicĕre* to look into, INSPECT.]

1. a. The action of inspecting or looking narrowly into; careful scrutiny or survey; close or critical examination; *spec.* official investigation or oversight; see INSPECTOR 1. Const. *of*.

trial by inspection: see quot. 1872. ***valuation of a decimal by inspection***: a process whereby a decimal fraction of a pound sterling is by rapid scrutiny valued in shillings and pence. ***deed of inspectorship***: see INSPECTORSHIP.

1390 GOWER *Conf.* III. 46 His hours of astronomy He kepeth as for that party, Which longeth to the inspection Of love and his affection. **1426** LYDG. *De Guil. Pilgr.* (E.E.T.S.) 10457 Haue her ther-off inspeccyoun, And se her my commyssioun. **1513** BRADSHAW *St. Werburge* I. 626 Consyder the hystory with good inspeccyon. **1568** GRAFTON *Chron.* II. 353 By the inspection of which statute, the sayde newe statute or ordynaunce [etc.] were conceaved in the parliament. **1607** E. GRIMSTONE tr. *Goulart's Mem. Hist.* 74 The olde woman thinking that the inspection of the Urine made me to divine this. **1665** BOYLE *Occas. Refl.* (1848) 18 By the casual flights of Birds, and the Inspection of the Intrails of Beasts, to learn the will of Heaven. **1768** BLACKSTONE *Comm.* III. xxii. 331 Trial by inspection, or examination. *Ibid.* 333 Also, to ascertain any circumstances relative to a particular day past, it hath been tried by an inspection of the almanac by the court. **1830** GRAY *Arithmetic* (1872) 79 To value the decimal of a pound sterling by inspection. **1833** HT. MARTINEAU *Manch. Strike* xii. 128 The account book would be.. open to the inspection of all who could prove themselves to belong to the Union. **1853** KANE *Grinnell Exp.* xxxiv. (1856) 298 It might, on a hurried inspection, be confounded with snow. **1860** TYNDALL *Glac.* I. v. 40 During our inspection of the place. **1861** *Act 24 & 25 Vict.* c. 134 §192 Every Deed or Instrument made or entered into between a Debtor and his Creditors.. relating to the Debts or Liabilities of the Debtor, and his Release therefrom, or the Distribution, Inspection, Management, and winding-up of his Estate. **1869** *Act 32 & 33 Vict.* c. 71 §125 (4) The special resolution, together with the statement of the assets and debts of the debtor, and the name of the trustee appointed, and of the members, if any, of the committee of inspection, shall be presented to the registrar. **1872** *Wharton's Law Lex.* (ed. 5) 488/1 *Trial by Inspection* was resorted to when, for the greater expedition of a cause, some point or issue.. being evidently the object of sense, was decided by the judges of the Court upon the evidence of their own senses. Obsolete. **1876** *Athenæum* 28 Oct. 554/2 A clear distinction is drawn between inspection and examination... Inspection.. undertakes the task of seeing how the school does its daily work. **1883** *Wharton's Law Lex.* (ed. 7) 419/2 Inspection, Deed of.

†**b.** Formerly const. *into* (cf. INSPECT *v.* 2), *in*, *over*, *upon*. *Obs.*

c **1450** *Lenuoye 10 Commandm. Love* in Stowe *Chaucer* (1561) 342 When ye vnto this balade haue inspeccion In my making holde me excusable. **1632** LITHGOW *Trav.* I. 7 To have a quotidian occular inspection, in any obvious object of disastrous misfortune. **1656** CROMWELL *Sp.* 17 Sept. in *Carlyle*, To have a little inspection upon the People thus divided.. into divers interests. **1660** G. WITHERS (*title*) Speculum Speculativum,.. being an Inspection into the Present and Late Sad Condition of these Nations. **1687** A. LOVELL tr. *Thevenot's Trav.* III. 19 There is a Mufty at Surrat, who has the inspection over all that concerns the Mahometan Religion. **1710** *Life Bp. Stillingfleet* 92 To make a due Inspection into the State of his Diocess. *a* **1732** ATTERBURY (J.), Impressions of his perpetual presence with us, and inspection over us. **1739** TULL *Horse-Hoing Husb.* (1740) 233 This Observation.. made by Inspection upon a Glass of Water with Earth in it. **1810** SYD. SMITH *Wks.* (1859) I. 189/1 A close inspection of the master into the studies and conduct of each individual is quite impossible.

†**2.** A sight, spectacle. *Obs. rare.*

c **1430** LYDG. *Min. Poems* (Percy Soc.) 144 Of this terrible doolful inspeccioun [a soul in flames] The peeplis hertys gretly gan abave.

†**3.** Insight, perception. *Obs.*

c **1500** *Prov.* in *Antiq. Rep.* (1809) IV. 406 He hathe a brym breste, and litill inspexion withe all. **1650** R. STAPYLTON *Strada's Low C. Warres* I. 2 An exact knowledge of Councils, and inspection into Cabinets, could not be exspected from one of a sequestred life. **1709** BERKELEY *Th. Vision* Ded., That he should manage a great fortune with that prudence and inspection.. as to shew himself [etc.].

†**4.** A plan of a piece of ground, etc. which has been inspected; a design, survey, view. *Obs.*

1694 R. FRANCK (*title*) Northern Memoirs, Calculated for the Meridian of Scotland.. together with.. several curious and industrious Inspections, lineally drawn from Antiquaries and other noted and intelligible Persons. **1795** *Wythe's Decis.* (U.S.) 119 The line in the surveyor's plat to be the boundary dividing B's inspection and M's tenement.

5. A department or district under an inspector.

1888 *Pall Mall G.* 4 Apr. 5/1 In France.. the forests of the country are first divided into cantonments and then into about 500 inspections. In each inspection there is an inspector, a garde-général, and brigadier.

6. *attrib.* and *Comb.*, as ***inspection-car***, ***-class***, ***-day***, ***-district***, etc.

1753 in *Maryland Hist. Mag.* (1908) III. 366 Which made me apprehend they intended some Opposition to the Inspection Law. **1773** *Ibid.* (1907) II. 358 To compel all the Owners or Makers of Tobacco to send it to certain Inspection Houses whence it cannot be again removed till it is put on Board a Ship. **1791** BENTHAM *Panopt.* I. Postscr. 43 A Chapel.. occupies upon the present plan a considerable portion of the Inspection-Tower. **1865** *Pall Mall G.* 26 Sept. 7/2 Yorkshire contains more coal miners than any other inspection district in the kingdom. *a* **1884** KNIGHT *Dict. Mech.* Suppl. 501/2 *Inspection car*, one used by the officers of a railway while inspecting the track. **1887** *Homeop. World* 1 Nov. 510 Nurses' rooms, with inspection openings commanding all the beds. **1890** *Railways of Amer.* 146 It would require a separate article to give even a brief description of the different kinds of cars which are now used.. Inspection-car, [etc.]. **1903** *Westm. Gaz.* 12 Jan. 7/2 The covering of the electrical inspection box at the Thames-street corner of Bennett's-hill was blown off this morning by the fusing of the wires. **1904** GOODCHILD & TWENEY *Technol. & Sci. Dict.* 311/2 *Inspection chamber*, a chamber at the junction of drains to allow of inspection. **1906** *Daily Chron.* 27 Aug. 3/4 To see that these things are observed.. the firm employs inspection engineers. **1907** *Westm. Gaz.* 13 Nov. 8/2 Free access to the valves and inspection-doors of the crank chamber is given. **1907** *Ibid.* 11 Dec. 3/2, I have found when towing.. that the garage people have a knack of putting difficulties in the way of drivers.. using the inspection pits. **1908** *Ibid.* 2 Apr. 4/2 There are two large inspection doors in the crank-case. **1908** *Installation News* II. 87/2 The straight through type of inspection box should be inserted in the conduit run at short intervals. *Ibid.* 148/2 The other remarkable reductions [in price] are.. Inspection Fittings [etc.]. **1908** *Westm. Gaz.* 20 Nov. 4/2 At the rear it [*sc.* an automobile] has a large inspection-cover. **1909** *Daily Chron.* 18 Sept. 1/6 The houses were flooded by water and filth from the sewers through the stone slabs covering the inspection chambers being displaced by the flood. **1930** *Engineering* 21 Nov. 658/2 The front inspection lamp consists of an electric bulb with the switch above it. **1946** A. PHELPS *I couldn't care Less* x. 76 Improperly secured inspection panels blew off my wings. **1951** *Good Housek. Home Encycl.* 187/1 Cast-iron manhole covers flush with the ground, technically termed 'inspection covers'. **1967** *Gloss. Sanitation Terms* (*B.S.I.*) 26 *Inspection chamber*, a shallow manhole. **1972** M. GILBERT *Body of Girl* iv. 44 An open-fronted workshop.. with two inspection pits.

inspectional (ɪn'spɛkʃənəl), *a.* [f. prec. + -AL[1].] Of, pertaining or relating to inspection; *spec.* that can be read or understood at sight, without further explanation or calculation.

1728 R. MORRIS *Ess. Anc. Archit.* p. xxiii, I must let the Work answer for itself.. being only inspectional. **1851** *Ord. & Regul. R. Engineers* iv. 19 At the Foreign Stations, similar Inspectional Reports are to be made. **1891** *Pall Mall G.* 4 Dec. 6/3 They also suggest.. that the inspectional districts should be of smaller area than at present.

inspective (ɪn'spɛktɪv), *a.* [ad. late L. *inspectīv-us* (Isidore), f. *inspect-*, ppl. stem of *inspicĕre* to INSPECT: see -IVE.]

1. Given to inspection; watchful; attentive.

a **1684** LEIGHTON *Comm. 1 Pet.* iii. 12 They that are most inspective and watchful in this will still be faulty in it. **1797** *Monthly Mag.* III. 522 A certain Chaldaic triad, which is the inspective guardian of the whole of a disordered fabrication. **1827** POLLOK *Course T.* IX, Need was still Of persevering, quick, inspective mood Of mind. **1863** WOOLNER *My Beautiful Lady* III. *Work* 6 Thrushes.. Search dew-gray lawns with keen inspective glance.

†**2.** Concerned with investigation; theoretical. *Obs. rare.*

1609 DOULAND *Ornith. Microl.* 2 Inspective Musicke, is a knowledge censuring and pondering the Sounds formed with naturall instruments, not by the eares, whose iudgement is dull, but by wit and reason. **1660** tr. *Paracelsus' Archidoxis* II. 92, I.. publickly interpret.. the Books of both the Active, and also Inspective Medicine.

inspector (ɪn'spɛktə(r)). Also 7 -er. [a. L. *inspector*, agent-n. from *inspicĕre* to look into, INSPECT. Cf. F. *inspecteur* (*c* 1500 in Hatz.-Darm.).]

1. One who inspects or looks carefully at or into; an overseer, a superintendent; *spec.* an officer appointed to examine into, and supervise or report upon, the working of some department or institution in which numerous persons are employed, or the due observance of certain laws and regulations, as ***inspector of schools***, ***of weights and measures***, ***of factories***, ***mines***, ***explosives***, ***public nuisances***, etc.

1602 F. HERING *Anatomyes* 78 The Eternall, as a carefull Inspector and sincere Judge of them. **1660** MILTON *Free Commw.* Wks. (1851) 433 They.. must raise and manage the publick Revenue, at least with som Inspectors deputed for satisfaction of the People, how it is imploid. **1734** LD. BOLINGBROKE *Let. to Swift* 15 Sept., S.'s Wks. 1841 II. 725, I wrote to you a long letter some time ago.. did the inspectors of private correspondence stop it? **1791** BENTHAM *Panopt.* I. Postscr. 93 An Inspector in his way to the prisoners' Stair-case from the Inspection-Gallery. **1802** A. HAMILTON *Wks.* (1886) VII. 253 When the excise on distilled spirits was established, three different descriptions of officers were instituted.. supervisors, inspectors, and collectors. **1898** *Hazell's Ann.* 208/2 Occasional unannounced visits of the inspector, in lieu of the annual examination.

attrib. **1878** F. S. WILLIAMS *Midl. Railw.* 624 There are a number of.. inspector guards, one of whom is selected to take charge of every excursion train, a duty involving special responsibilities and care. **1898** *Daily News* 30 July 3/1 The lesson to be drawn from the recent cases both of phosphorus and lead poisoning is.. that the inspector system has broken down.

b. One who looks *into* something for information, from curiosity, etc.

1667 PEPYS *Diary* 25 Apr., A severer inspector into his own business and accounts. **1670** MARVELL *Corr.* cliv. Wks. 1872–5 II. 339, I.. must in exchange desire you will not admit many inspectors into my letters. **1774** WALKER *Pronounc. Dict.* Advt., If the inspector should not meet with sufficient information in the Dictionary under the word, let him consult the Principles under the *vowel*, *diphthong*, or *consonant*, he wishes to be explained.

c. An officer of police ranking next below a superintendent and above a sergeant.

1840 *Penny Cycl.* XVIII. 335/2 The number of men of each rank serving in the metropolitan police force, in January, 1840, was as follows:—..73 Inspectors. **1898** *Hazell's Ann.* 529/1 The total strength of the [City of London police] force is 928, consisting of 3 chief inspectors, 15 district inspectors, 22 station inspectors, 12 detective inspectors, 72 sergeants [etc.].

2. *Gr. Antiq.* Used as a translation of Gr. ἐπόπτης, a person fully initiated into the Eleusinian mysteries; = EPOPT.

1818 R. P. KNIGHT *Inquiry Anc. Art. & Myth.* §10. 6 These doctrines were conveyed under allegories and symbols; and.. the completely initiated were called *inspectors*.

3. ***inspector-general***: an officer at the head of a system of inspection, having under him a body of inspectors; a superintendent of a system of inspection.

1702 *Lond. Gaz.* No. 3841/3 Monsieur Puissegure, Inspector-General of their Foot. **1813** WELLINGTON *Lett.* 4 Oct. in Gurw. *Desp.* XI. 159 The inspector general of the infantry fell from his horse. **1859** *Musketry Instr.* 98 The Inspector General of Musketry, being held responsible that the rifle training is conducted efficiently and according to regulation. **1898** *Hazell's Ann.* 530/2 The principal officer of the [Irish] Constabulary is the Inspector-General, resident in Dublin, and who is assisted by a Deputy Inspector-General and three Assistant Inspectors-General.

inspectoral (ɪn'spɛktərəl), *a.* [f. prec. + -AL[1].] Of or belonging to inspectors, inspectorial.

1864 *Daily Tel.* 27 July, Some reform in the system of inspectoral reports might have followed. **1884** *Manch. Exam.* 29 Mar. 5/1 The inadequacy in number of the inspectoral staff.

inspectorate (ɪn'spɛktərət). [mod.f. INSPECTOR: see -ATE[1].]

1. a. The office or function of an inspector; supervision by inspectors. **b.** A body or staff of inspectors. Also *attrib.*

1762 tr. *Busching's Syst. Geog.* IV. 401 Their matrimonial matters, their synods, classes, presbyteries, consistories, and inspectorates, to be determined by them. **1868** G. DUFF *Pol. Surv.* 84 Their attention was next.. drawn to the foreign inspectorate of customs at the Treaty ports. **1898** *Daily News* 14 Apr. 4/6 To ensure the opening up of the inspectorate to experienced teachers. **1899** *Westm. Gaz.* 26 June 2/3 We wish that the County Council had an inspectorate power in the matter.

c. ***inspectorate-general***, the office or function of inspector-general; the personnel of this office.

1883 J. D. CAMPBELL *Fisheries China* 4 (Fish. Exhib. Publ.), Mr. Drew.. Statistical Secretary of the Inspectorate-General. **1890** A. LITTLE tr. *Hosie's China* p. xxv, An Agreement was entered into with the Inspectorate General of Chinese Customs.

2. A district under official inspection; *spec.* the name of the two larger administrative districts of Greenland.

1853 KANE *Grinnell Exp.* vi. (1856) 44 There are but two inspectorates for the Danish coast of Greenland. **1883** *Fortn. Rev.* July 30 The lands were divided into so many districts or inspectorates.

inspectorial (ɪnspɛk'tɔərɪəl), *a.* [f. INSPECTOR + -IAL; after words from L. *-ōri-us* + -AL[1].] Of, pertaining, or belonging to inspectors; having the rank or position of an inspector.

1753 MURPHY *Gray's-Inn Jrnl.* No. 42 His Inspectorial Majesty was pleased to return the following.. Answer. **1863** *Sat. Rev.* XV. 434/1 This remarkable inspectorial execution involves a very peculiar view of the nature and objects of Blue-books. **1884** *American* VIII. 315 Some of the inspectorial features of the English system. **1884** *Times* 21 June 6 In the organization of their inspectorial staff.

inspectorship (ɪn'spɛktəʃɪp). [f. INSPECTOR + -SHIP.] **a.** The office or position of an inspector; inspectorate. Also as a mock title.

1753 C. SMART *Hiliad* Notes, Poems (1810) 51 His Inspectorship has the most notable talent at a motto. **1757** W. THOMPSON *R.N. Advoc.* 52 He was not admitted to his Inspectorship of Dry Stores, till he had passed his Examination. **1864** *Spectator* 20 Aug. 970/2 As for a regular State inspectorship of endowed schools, we shall have it doubtless in Paradise, but not in this world. **1899** *Brit. Med. Jrnl.* 8 July 106 Inspectorships of public health.

b. *attrib.*, as **inspectorship deed** (also ***deed of inspectorship***), see quots. and cf. INSPECTION 1.

1861 *Act 24 & 25 Vict.* c. 134 §191 As to Trust Deeds for Benefit of Creditors, Composition and Inspectorship Deeds executed by a Debtor. **1883** *Wharton's Law Lex.* (ed. 7) 419/2 *Inspectorship, Deed of*, an instrument entered into between an insolvent debtor and his creditors, appointing one or more person or persons to inspect and oversee the winding up of such insolvent's affairs on behalf of the creditors. **1902** *Encycl. Brit.* XXX. 151/2 Estates, however, continued to be wound up under deeds of arrangement, whether in the form of an assignment, or composition, or inspectorship deed. **1959** JOWITT *Dict. Eng. Law* I. 980/2 *Inspectorship, Deed of*,.. the repealed Bankruptcy Act, 1869.

inspectress (ɪn'spɛktrɪs). [f. INSPECTOR + -ESS.] A female inspector.

1785–95 WOLCOTT (P. Pindar) *Lousiad* II. 310 Inspectress General of the royal geer. **1830** *Fraser's Mag.* I. 35 This gifted inspectress of Germany has done us little furtherance with the French. **1881** *Macm. Mag.* XLIV. 488 In company with one of the inspectresses.. I visited one of the Scuole Leopoldine.

inspectrix (ɪn'spɛktrɪks). [a. late L. *inspectrix*, fem. agent-n. f. *inspicĕre*, INSPECT.] = prec.

1715 MRS. J. BARKER *Exilius* I. 97 The Inspectrix of all our Actions. **1896** *Nation* (N.Y.) 28 May 411/3 The inspectrix was appointed because they themselves did the work badly.

†**in'speculate**, *v. Obs. rare*$^{-1}$. [f. IN-^{2} + L. *speculārī* to watch, observe: see SPECULATE.] *trans.* To look upon, behold.

1658 R. FRANCK *North. Mem.* (1694) p. xv, Now I have given you a platform for contemplation which opens the windows of the mind to inspeculate invisible objects.

†**inspecu'lation.** *Obs. rare*$^{-1}$. [f. IN-^{2} + SPECULATION: see prec.] A looking into; introspection.

1650–60 TATHAM *Dramas* (1879) 207 Draw men's souls out by inspeculation.

†**in'sperable**, *a. Obs. rare*$^{-0}$. [ad. L. *insperābilis*, f. *in-* (IN-^{3}) + *sperābilis*, f. *sperāre* to hope.] That cannot be hoped for, beyond hope.

1623 COCKERAM, *Inspirable*, one past all hope, vnlookt for. **1656** BLOUNT *Glossogr.*, *Insperable*, that no man would look or hope for.

†**in'sperge**, *v. Obs.* Also 6 insparge. [ad. L. *inspergĕre* to sprinkle on or in, f. *in-* (IN-^{2}) + *spargĕre* to scatter, sprinkle.] *trans.* To sprinkle on; to scatter on or in. Hence **in'sperged** *ppl. a.*

1599 A. M. tr. *Gabelhouer's Bk. Physicke* 2/2 Make a Quoife, and insparge therin this poulder. **1657** TOMLINSON *Renou's Disp.* 209 Cephalical Powders..insperged in Cotten. **1683** PETTUS *Fleta Min.* I. (1686) 242 The insperged or mixt Copper oars will run together in little Grains.

†**in'sperse**, *v. Obs. rare.* Also 6 -sparse. [f. L. *inspers-*, ppl. stem of L. *inspergĕre.*] = prec.

1577–87 HOLINSHED *Chron.* III. 1162/2 In which albeit thou seest..some good articles insparsed withall, let that nothing mooue thee. **1623** COCKERAM II. To Sprinkle water, *Asperge, Insperse.* **1721** BAILEY, *To Insperse*, to sprinkle upon.

†**in'spersion.** *Obs.* Also 7 *erron.* -tion. [ad. L. *inspersiōn-em*, f. *inspers-us*, pa. pple. of *inspergĕre* to INSPERSE.]

1. The action of sprinkling on; also something sprinkled on.

1568 SKEYNE *The Pest* (1860) 25 In suffumigatioun, brining, or inspersione. *c* **1611** CHAPMAN *Iliad* XI. 452 With sweet inspersion of fit balmes. **1659** STANLEY *Hist. Philos.* XII. (1701) 478/2 By that little inspertion of Unguent. **1668** WILKINS *Real Char.* 244 Mixed Mechanical Operations.. inspersion. **1721** BAILEY, *Inspersion*, a Sprinkling upon.

¶**2.** *erron.* for ASPERSION 6. *Obs.*

1642 ROGERS *Naaman* 290 Thinking their forwardnesse an inspersion to their base backwardnesse.

‖**inspeximus** (ɪn'spɛksɪməs). *Law.* [L., = 'we have inspected': the first word in recital of the inspection of charters, etc.] A charter in which the grantor avouches to have inspected an earlier charter which he recites and confirms. Also *attrib.*

[**1282–3** *Rolls Parlt.* I. 225/1 Carta confirmationis libertatum [sit] sub hac forma: Edwardus &c. Inspeximus Cartam donationis..quam Dominus H. Rex..fecit. **1547–8** MERVYN in Brooke *Abridgem.* (1586) tit. Patentes 97 II. 128 Vn Constat est pledable, contrarie dun Inspeximus, car in lun case le patent remaine, & in lauter il est parde.] **1628** COKE *On Litt.* 225 b, When Littleton wrote, no *constat*, or *inspeximus*, of the king's letters patents were availeable to be shewed forth in court, but the letters patents themselves under seal. **1658** *Coke's Rep.* v. 53 b, It is called *Inspeximus*, because it begins after the King's style with this word *Inspeximus*: and it is called exemplification *a re ipsa*, because the record is thereby exemplified. **1677** PLOT *Oxfordsh.* 332 As appears by an Inspeximus of Q. Elizabeth, granted this Corporation. **1783** WARTON *Hist. Kiddington* 66 *note*, This road is specified, by the names of *strata* and *magna via*, in an Inspeximus-charter of Henry the third to Tarent-abbey in Dorsetshire. **1885** *N. & Q.* 6th Ser. XII. 411/1 An inspeximus consists of a recital that a previous document has been inspected, and a confirmatory regrant thereof.

inspexion, obs. form of INSPECTION.

insphe'ration. *rare*$^{-1}$. [f. prec. + -ATION.] The action of ensphering; enspherement.

1857 HOLLAND *Bay Path* xix, A stranger would have remembered nothing but her eye..that wonderful revelation of character..that inspheration of soul.

insphere, -spheare, variants of ENSPHERE *v.*

in-sphere ('ɪnsfɪə(r)). *Math.* [f. IN-^{1} b + SPHERE *sb.*] A sphere that touches all the faces of a given polyhedron.

1886 G. S. CARR *Synopsis Pure & Appl. Math.* I. II. 890 (Index), In-sphere of a tetrahedron. **1939** H. S. M. COXETER *Ball's Math. Recreations & Ess.* (ed. 11) v. 132 With each of these polyhedra we may associate three concentric spheres: one (the 'circum-sphere') through all the vertices, one touching all the edges, and one (the 'in-sphere') touching all the faces.

†**in'spindle**, *v. Obs. rare*$^{-0}$. [f. IN-^{2} + SPINDLE.] *trans.* To fit on or furnish with a spindle.

1611 FLORIO, *Infusare*, to inspindle, to shaft.

inspinne, var. INCHPIN (sense 1), *Obs.*

1680 SIR. T. BROWNE *Wks.* (1848) III. 468 A dayntie bitt accounted by many, called the inspinne, which may be the *intestinum rectum.*

inspirable (ɪn'spaɪərəb(ə)l), *a.* [f. INSPIRE *v.* + -ABLE (on L. type **inspīrābilis*).] Capable of being inspired (in various senses: see the verb).

1656–72 HARVEY *Morb. Angl.* (J.), To these inspirable hurts, we may enumerate those they sustain from their expiration of fuliginous steams. **1858** BUSHNELL *Nat. & Supernat.* xv. (1864) 515 Inspirable creatures, permeable by God's life, as a chrystal by the light. **1879** H. W. WARREN *Recr. Astron.* xii. 263 It is inspirable by electricity.

So **inspira'bility**, capability of being inspired.

1869 BUSHNELL *Wom. Suffrage* iii. 57 Their religious inspirations, or inspirabilities, put them closer to God.

†**inspi'rado.** *Obs.* [a. Sp. *inspirado* inspired: but it does not appear that the use is taken from Sp.: see -ADO.] A person who imagines himself, or professes, to be inspired.

1664 H. MORE *Myst. Iniq.*, *Apol.* 545 The Sectarian Rabbles that phansy themselves such Inspiradoes. *Ibid.* 562 The boasting Inspiradoes of our Nation.

inspirant (ɪn'spaɪərənt). *rare.* [ad. L. *inspīrānt-em*, pr. pple. of *inspīrāre* to INSPIRE: see -ANT.] One who inspires; an inspirer.

1837 CAROLINE FOX *Jrnl.* 9 Sept. (1882) 20 He presented and read the following lines, which he had written,..Aunt Charles being the inspirant.

inspirate ('ɪnspɪreɪt), *v.* [f. L. *inspīrāt-*, ppl. stem of *inspīrāre* to INSPIRE.] = INSPIRE *v.* (in various senses). Hence **inspirating** *ppl. a.*

1615 CROOKE *Body of Man* 424 Hippocrates speaketh of the aer inspirated or breathed in. **1620** VENNER *Via Recta* Introd. 6 The aire which is inspirated. *a* **1806** K. WHITE *Fragm. Ode Moon* iv, Bland Hope and Fancy ye were there, To inspirate my trance. **1809–10** COLERIDGE *Friend* (1818) I. 170 The most inspirating representation of future bliss, which my mind is capable of comprehending. **1939** L. H. GRAY *Foundations of Lang.* 406 They [*sc.* Hottentot and Bushman] are characterised by inspirated consonants. **1964** P. DELATTRE in D. Abercrombie et al. *Daniel Jones* 48 It [sc. *oui*] can be either expirated or inspirated.

inspiration (ɪnspɪ'reɪʃən). Also 4 yn-, 6 en-. [a. OF. *en-*, *inspiration*, *-cion* (12–13th c. in Hatz.-Darm.), ad. L. *inspīrātiōn-em*, n. of action from *inspīrāre* to INSPIRE.]

I. Literal (physical) senses.

†**1.** The action of blowing on or into. *Obs. rare.*

1513 DOUGLAS *Æneis* XII. Prol. 75 The sulʒe spred hyr braid bosum on breid, Zephyrus comfortabill inspiratioun For till ressaue. **1710** SHAFTESB. *Charac.*, *Enthus.* (1737) I. 28 Their strange voices..are admirably well acted, by the.. Inspiration of Pipes.

2. The action, or an act, of breathing in or inhaling; the drawing in of the breath into the lungs in respiration. (Opp. to EXPIRATION 2.)

1564 BULLEYN *Dial. agst. Pest.* (1888) 37 This is a dispersed Pestilence by the inspiration of ayre. **1607** E. GRIMSTONE tr. *Goulart's Mem. Hist.* 440 That a Priest at Rome lived fortie yeares with the onely inspiration of the aire. **1650** BULWER *Anthropomet.* 79 The Nostrils serve for expiration and inspiration. **1753** N. TORRIANO *Gangr. Sore Throat* 124 A sore Throat, which she received by Inspiration of foul Air. **1774** GOLDSM. *Nat. Hist.* (1776) VII. 59 Upon going down he [the diver] takes in a very long inspiration. **1849–52** TODD *Cycl. Anat.* IV. 1086/2 In Inspiration the lungs are passive. **1872** DARWIN *Emotions* xii. 284 We can draw a full and deep inspiration much more easily through the widely open mouth than through the nostrils.

b. *transf.* A drawing in of air; the absorption of air in the 'respiration' of plants.

1796 MORSE *Amer. Geog.* I. 613 Regular inspirations and expirations of air, by caverns and fissures. **1838** T. THOMSON *Chem. Org. Bodies* 1001 Plants will not live without this nightly inspiration, even though supplied with carbonic acid, provided the oxygen formed by them during the day be constantly withdrawn at the approach of night.

II. Figurative senses.

3. The action of inspiring; the fact or condition of being inspired (in sense 4 or 5 of INSPIRE *v.*); a breathing or infusion into the mind or soul.

a. *spec.* (*Theol.*, etc.) A special immediate action or influence of the Spirit of God (or of some divinity or supernatural being) upon the human mind or soul; said *esp.* of that divine influence under which the books of Scripture are held to have been written.

Various views have been held as to the inspiration of Scripture, such as those of ***verbal inspiration***, according to which every word written was dictated by the Spirit of God; ***plenary inspiration***, according to which the inspiration of the writers extends to all subjects treated of, so that all their statements are to be received as infallibly true; ***moral inspiration***, according to which the inspiration is confined to the moral and religious teaching imparted; ***dynamical inspiration, mechanical inspiration*** (see DYNAMICAL 3).

1303 R. BRUNNE *Handl. Synne* 7746 Þurghe grete þan ynspyracyun, He þoghte so on hys [Christ's] passyun. *a* **1340** HAMPOLE *Psalter* xliv. 2 [xlv. 1] *comm.*, þe vertu of godis inspiracioun. **1387–8** T. USK *Test. Love* II. i. (Skeat) l. 13, I thinke to performe this worke..as my thinne witte, wyth inspyracyon of him that hildeth all grace, woll suffre. **1450–1530** *Myrr. our Ladye* 173 He sente the holy goste on Penthecoste sondaye to enspyracyon of hys dyscyples. **1494** FABYAN *Chron.* v. cxix. 96 Seynt Augustyne..warnyd them by maner of inspyracion, yᵗ sene they wolde not receyue peace of theyr bretherne, they shuld of other receyue warre and wreche. **1526** *Pilgr. Perf.* (1531) 144 b, The inspiracyons of the holy goost. **1526** TINDALE *2 Tim.* iii. 16 All scripture geven by inspiracion of god is proffitable to teache, to improve, to informe, and to instruct in rightewesnes. **1611** BIBLE *Transl. Pref.* 3 The Prophets, who teach us by diuine inspiration. **1692** SOUTH *12 Serm.* (1697) I, The..Principle..was certainly first..fetched up from the very bottom of Hell and utter'd..by particular and immediate inspiration of the Devil. **1793** R. HAWKER (*title*) Evidence of a Plenary Inspiration; a Letter to Mr. T. Porter, in Reply to his Defence of Unitarianism. **1841** *Penny Cycl.* XIX. 429/2 Theologians who hold the theory of plenary but not verbal inspiration. **1860** WESTCOTT *Introd. Study Gosp.* App. B. (ed. 5) 451 The early Fathers teach us that Inspiration is an operation of the Holy Spirit acting through men, according to the laws of their constitution. **1865** M. ARNOLD *Ess. Crit.* ix. 272 The noblest souls of whatever creed..have insisted on the necessity of an inspiration, a living emotion to make moral action pefect. **1896** DK. ARGYLL *Philos. Belief* 370 They warn us that there may be inspirations from below, as well as from above.

b. *gen.* A breathing in or infusion of some idea, purpose, etc. into the mind; the suggestion, awakening, or creation of some feeling or impulse, esp. of an exalted kind.

1651 HOBBES *Leviath.* II. xxix. 169 Why any man should take the law of his country rather than his own Inspiration, for the rule of his action. **1692** DRYDEN *St. Euremont's Ess.* 206 There are some Men, jealous of the Honour of their motions, who refuse all things at the Inspirations of others. **1769** *Junius Lett.* vii. 30 The melancholy madness of poetry, without the inspiration. **1805** FOSTER *Ess.* I. ii. 27 A mind adapted and habituated to converse with the inspirations of nature. **1841–4** EMERSON *Ess.*, *Love* Wks. (Bohn) I. 75 Men have written good verses under the inspiration of passion, who cannot write well under any other circumstances. **1858** HOGG *Life Shelley* II. 416 Inspired with the soft inspiration of strong, sound ale. **1876** MOZLEY *Univ. Serm.* v. (1877) 108 There is inspiration in numbers, in men acting at once and together.

c. The suggestion or prompting (from some influential quarter) of the utterance or publication of particular views or information on some public matter. (Cf. INSPIRE 7, INSPIRED 5.)

1880 *Chr. World* No. 1195. 137 Correspondents..write in the interest, if not at the inspiration of the authorities. **1897** *Daily News* 13 Mar. 3/1 Mr. Goschen said it was not due to inspiration..No idea had been given to the journal.

4. *transf.* **a.** Something inspired or infused into the mind; an inspired utterance or product.

1819 BYRON *Prophecy Dante* IV. 2 Many are poets who have never penn'd Their inspiration. **1871** R. ELLIS *Catullus* lxiv. 321 They..Pour'd grave inspiration, a prophet chant to the future. **1879** SALA in *Daily Tel.* 8 May, Mr. G. F. Boughton's charming figure of 'Priscilla', an inspiration from Longfellow's 'Miles Standish'.

b. An inspiring principle.

1865 MOZLEY *Mirac.* vii. 146 To say that the inspiration of the missionary cause has been the belief in Christian doctrine is almost superfluous. **1869** BALDW. BROWN *Misread Passages* ix. 125 Christian charity, charity which has Christ for its model and inspiration. **1873** BROWNING *Red Cott. Nt.-cap* IV. 682 Whatever motive your own souls supply As inspiration.

5. *Comb.*

1894 *Nation* (N.Y.) 23 Aug. 144/3 Inspiration-like insight.

inspirational (ɪnspɪ'reɪʃənəl), *a.* [f. prec. + -AL^{1}.]

1. Deriving its character or substance from inspiration; under the influence of inspiration; inspired.

1839 J. ROGERS *Antipopopr.* II. xiii. §2. 290 Their formal, official, inspirational, miraculous duty. **1876** PEMBER *Earth's Earliest Ages* (1893) 349 An inspirational address by ..a well-known trance-speaker. **1878** *N. Amer. Rev.* CXXVII. 321 In their inspirational states they [the sacred writers] were sometimes dynamical, sometimes mechanical. **1890** A. LANG in *Longm. Mag.* Jan. 334 The daughter of a distinguished medium and inspirational lecturer.

2. Of, or pertaining to, inspiration.

1888 HORTON *Inspiration & Bible* iv. 104 Inspirational Dogma. **1899** *Daily News* 21 Sept. 7/3 Dr. Pusey recoiled from the very shadow of an appearance of treating the Hebrew and Christian Scriptures as if they stood on the same inspirational level as other Asiatic Scriptures.

3. Imparting inspiration; tending to inspire.

1884 *Harper's Mag.* Jan. 187/2 He [Whittier] is not an inspirational writer. **1895** H. C. MACPHERSON *Carlyle* ix. 160 In the sphere of ethics, Carlyle's influence has been inspirational in the highest sense.

Hence **inspi'rationalist**, a person whose influence is inspirational, or who aims at inspiring others; **inspi'rationally** *adv.*, in an inspirational manner, under the influence of inspiration.

1884 H. JENNINGS *Phallicism* xiv. 148 Bohm wrote inspirationally—that is, altogether from the interior vision. **1895** H. C. MACPHERSON *Carlyle* ix. 152 The influence of the inspirationalist is ever-enduring.

inspi'rationalism. [f. INSPIRATIONAL *a.* + -ISM.] = INSPIRATIONISM.

1911 W. DE MORGAN *Likely Story* 343 Authors who may be said to belong to the school of Inspirationalism. **1961** B. R. WILSON *Sects & Society* I. i. 19 Checks on the possibly disruptive tendencies on [*sic*] radical inspirationalism.

inspi'rationism. [f. as INSPIRATIONAL *a.* + -ISM.] A theory or profession of inspiration.

1881 *Nation* 1 Dec. 433/1 The irresponsible type of inspirationism appears almost only when attended by auditory hallucinations, due to disordered subjective sensations.

inspi'rationist. [f. as prec. + -IST.] A believer in inspiration; one who holds a theory of inspiration. Chiefly with a word qualifying the inspiration, as ***plenary inspirationist***, a believer in plenary inspiration.

1846 Worcester, *Inspirationist*, one who holds to inspiration. *Phren. Jour.* **1867** *Pall Mall G.* No. 693. 11/2 Any verbal inspirationist. **1891** A. J. Harrison *Probl. Chr. & Scepticism* 92 General inspirationists, special inspirationists, plenary inspirationists and verbal inspirationists.

inspi'rationless, *a.* [f. as prec. + -LESS.] Devoid of inspiration.

1896 *Educ. Rev.* 137 Now the order..is not the old-time dead order of inspirationless form.

inspirative (ɪn'spaɪrətɪv, 'ɪnspɪreɪtɪv), *a.* [f. L. *inspīrāt-*, ppl. stem of *inspīrāre* to INSPIRE + -IVE.] Having the quality of inspiring.

1797 T. Park *Sonnets* 4 And pierce afresh each inspirative grove. **1810** F. Dudley *Amoroso* I. Introd. 5 His victories will return with inspirative force to your own bosom. **1831** J. Wilson in *Blackw. Mag.* XXIX. 325 Motionless frozen forests..inspirative in the strangeness of their appareling [of] wild and dreamy thoughts and feelings.

inspirator ('ɪnspɪreɪtə(r)). [a. L. *inspīrātor*, agent-n. from *inspīrāre* to INSPIRE. Cf. F. *inspirateur* (14th c. in Godef. *Compl.*).]

1. One who or that which inspires; an inspirer.

1624 F. White *Repl. Fisher* 337 Subordinate Creators, Inspirators, yea, subordinate Gods. **1848** *Fraser's Mag.* XXXVIII. 185 Inspired by that most glorious of inspirators, a good dinner after a long day's ramble. **1903** K. M. Abbott *Old Paths New Eng.* 99 The first power-loom was set up by Francis Cabot Lowell, the inspirator of cotton manufacture. **1904** *Westm. Gaz.* 19 Nov. 10/3 He might characterise him as the great inspirator of the Opposition.

2. An apparatus for drawing in or inhaling air or vapour. **a.** A kind of injector in a steam-engine. **b.** A kind of respirator: see quot. 1898.

1890 *Daily News* 8 Mar. 3/5 The launch..had broken down owing to the inspirator leaking. **1898** *Voice* (N.Y.) 3 Feb. 6/5 An instrument called the Dight thermal inspirator, which promises to overcome the effects of cold, and make it possible to withstand the most frigid climates.

inspiratory (ɪn'spaɪərətərɪ, 'ɪnspɪreɪtərɪ), *a.* [f. L. *inspīrāt-* (see INSPIRATIVE) + -ORY.] Belonging to or characterized by inspiration or inhalation; serving to draw in the air in respiration.

1773 Hunter in *Phil. Trans.* LXIII. 489 A perpendicular section of the Torpedo a little below its inspiratory openings. **1861** Hulme tr. *Moquin-Tandon* II. v. i. 259 The inspiratory muscles of the thorax. **1878** Foster *Phys.* II. ii. §1. 263 By the inspiratory effort the elastic tissue of the lungs is put on the stretch.

inspiratrix (ɪnspɪ'reɪtrɪks). *rare.* [a. late L. *inspīrātrix*, fem. of *inspirator*: see above.] A female inspirer.

1819 *Blackw. Mag.* IV. 566 The dark-robed Muse of solitary sighs, The inspiratrix—Queen of Elegies.

inspire (ɪn'spaɪə(r)), *v.* Forms: α. 4–7 **enspire**, 5 **enspyr**, 5–6 **enspyre**. β. 4 **ynspyre, -ire**, 4–7 **inspyre**, 6 *Sc.* **inspyr, -ir**, 5– **inspire**. [a. OF. *enspirer, inspirer* (13th c.), *espirer* (12th c. in Littré), ad. L. *inspīrāre* to blow or breathe into, f. *in-* (IN-²) + *spīrāre* to breathe.]

I. Literal (physical) senses.

1. *trans.* To breathe or blow upon or into. *Obs.* or *arch.*

c **1386** Chaucer *Prol.* 6 Whan Zephirus eek with his swete breeth Inspired hath in euery holt and heeth The tendre croppes. **1412–20** Lydg. *Chron. Troy* I. viii. (MS. Cott. Aug. A. IV), And zephirus ful agreable and smoþe þe tendre branchis enspireþ and doþe springe. **1604** R. Cawdrey *Table Alph.*, *Inspire*, breath or blow into. **1649** [see INSPIRED 1]. **1700** Dryden *To D'chess Ormond* 47 A soft Etesian gale But just inspir'd, and gently swell'd the sail. **1704** Pope *Spring* 11 Let my Muse her slender reed inspire. **1708** — *Ode St. Cecilia* 2 Descend, ye Nine!..The breathing instruments inspire. **1784** Cowper *Task* II. 353 He stands, and with swoln cheeks Inspires the News, his trumpet.

†**b.** *intr.* To breathe or blow. *Obs.*

1513 Douglas *Æneis* V. xi. 15 And, that scho [Juno] suld go spedely, The prosper wind gan eftir hir inspyre. **1590** Spenser *F.Q.* II. iii. 30 When the wind emongst them [locks of hair] did inspyre.

†**2.** *trans.* To blow or breathe (air, etc.) upon or into. (In quot. 1536, To 'breathe', utter.) *Obs.*

1536 *Primer Hen. VIII* 145 His dulcetnes hath none enspired, All alone he is to be desired. **1576** Newton *Lemnie's Complex.* (1633) 191 By pestilent diseases and maladies, which..inspireth infection into our bodies. **1590** Spenser *F.Q.* II. ix. 30 An huge great payre of bellowes, which did styre Continually, and cooling breath inspyre. **1598** Sylvester *Du Bartas* II. i. II. *Imposture* 291 With th' air of these sweet words, the wily Snake A poysoned air inspired ..In Eve's frail brest. **1667** Milton *P.L.* IV. 804 Assaying ..if, inspiring venom, he might taint Th' animal Spirits that from pure blood arise. **1697** Dryden *Eneid* VII. 493 Unseen, unfelt, the fiery serpent skims Betwixt her linen and her naked limbs, His baneful breath inspiring as he glides.

b. To breathe (life, a soul, etc.) *in* or *into.* (Cf. Gen. ii. 7.) In later use, *fig.*

1382 Wyclif *Wisd.* xv. 11 He kneȝ not [Him] that made hym, and that enspirede to hym a soule. **1592** Davies *Immort. Soul* IV. xxiv, In their Mother's Wombs..Doth in all Sons of Man their Souls inspire. **1611** Tourneur *Ath. Trag.* v. i. Wks. 1878 I. 137 Inspire new life Into their bodies. **1657** *Lust's Domin.* I. iii. in Hazl. *Dodsley* XIV. 105 Dry your wet eyes; for sorrow wanteth force T' inspire a breathing soul in a dead corse. **1667** Milton *P.L.* x. 785 Least that pure breath of Life, the Spirit of Man Which God inspir'd, cannot together perish With this corporeal Clod. **1860** Hawthorne *Marb. Faun* II. v. 53 Out of his bitter agony, a soul and intellect, I could almost say, have been inspired into him.

†**c.** To produce by blowing or breathing. *Obs.*

c **1420** *Pallad. on Husb.* I. 174 The southern wynd enspirith bettir wyn.

3. *trans.* To breathe in, take into the lungs by breathing, inhale. (Opp. to EXPIRE 1.)

1528 [see INSPIRING *vbl. sb.*]. **1666–72** Harvey *Morb. Angl.* (J.), By means of sulphurous coal smoaks the lungs are stifled and oppressed, whereby they are forced to inspire and expire the air with difficulty, in comparison of the facility of inspiring and expiring the air in the country. **1761** *Descr. S. Carolina* 19 The Air we walk in and inspire. **1800** *Med. Jrnl.* IV. 279 It seems, according to him, forty-three cubic inches are always inspired at once. **1871** Tyndall *Fragm. Sc.* (1879) II. xii. 261 Animals, which inspire oxygen, and expire carbonic acid.

b. *intr.* or *absol.* To draw in the breath.

1661 [see INSPIRING *ppl. a.* 1]. **1767** Gooch *Treat. Wounds* I. 351 The method..is, to make the patient inspire, as much as he possibly can. **1861** F. H. Ramadge *Curab. Consumpt.* 36 When the patient inspired, a slight protrusion took place where the wound had been. **1894** *Times* 5 Mar. 14/4 A man who hunched up his shoulders every time he inspired.

II. Figurative senses.

4. *trans.* To infuse some thought or feeling into (a person, etc.), as if by breathing; to animate or actuate by some mental or spiritual influence.

a. *spec.* (*Theol.*, etc.) Said of God or the Holy Spirit, or of a divinity or supernatural being: To influence or actuate by special divine or supernatural agency; used esp. in reference to the prophets, apostles, and Scripture writers: cf. INSPIRATION 3 a.

a **1340** Hampole *Psalter* cxlvii. 7 Alsone as his gaste enspiris þaire hert. **1375** Barbour *Bruce* IV. 678 Gif that he enspirit war Of him, that all thing euirmar Seis in his presciens. **1387** Trevisa *Higden* (Rolls) I. 189 In þe cop þerof is the temple of Delphicus Apollo; and in þe wyndynge of þe myddel playn is a pitte, oute of þat pitte philosofres were enspired. **1435** Misyn *Fire Love* 9 If paraunter goddis grace to þat þame wald enspyr. *c* **1450** *St. Cuthbert* (Surtees) 897 As god inspired hir forth sho went. **1532** More *Confut. Tindale* Wks. 498/1 As that holi spirite enspired mo then them that wrote, so enspired he the writers in mo thinges then they wrote. **1588** Shaks. *Tit. A.* IV. i. 67. **1651** Hobbes *Leviath.* II. xxix. 169 Such private men as pretend to be supernaturally Inspired. **1718** Watts *Ps.*, 'O *Thou that hear'st'* viii, O may thy Love inspire my Tongue. **1876** J. Parker *Paracl.* I. iii. 20 Few, indeed, may have been inspired to speak the word, but all have been inspired to feel it. **1884** *Nonconf. & Indep.* 7 Feb. 131/2 The Church has decided that writers are inspired who if inspired, have been inspired to suggest to all ordinary judgments that they are not inspired.

b. *gen.* To influence, animate, or actuate (a person) *with* a feeling, idea, impulse, etc.

1390 Gower *Conf.* II. 75 My fader, but I were enspired Through love of you. **1500–20** Dunbar *Poems* lxvi. 93 Experience dois me so inspyre, Of this fals failȝeand warld I tyre. **1530** Tindale *Expos.* (Parker Soc.) 319 He inspired the king that the queen was not his wife. **1638** F. Junius *Paint. of Ancients* Ded. A iij, Feeling my selfe inspired with courage by the signification of your noble desire..I stoutly fell to my taske. **1647** Clarendon *Hist. Reb.* II. §113 Three of the commissioners..were all inspired by the Scots, and liked well all that they pretended to desire. **1709** Berkeley *Th. Vision* Ded., The chief motives that inspire me with the respect I bear you. **1844** Thirlwall *Greece* VIII. 445 That the Romans..only sought to inspire them with a wholesome terror. **1881** Jowett *Thucyd.* I. 198 Poverty inspires necessity with daring.

c. Said of the feeling, influence, etc.

(In quot. 1725, the sense is akin to 2 b.)

1393 Langl. *P. Pl.* C. XVII. 243 As holyness and honeste out of holy churche Spryngeþ and spredeþ and enspireþ þe peuple. **1588** Shaks. *L.L.L.* IV. iii. 229 What zeale, what furie, hath inspir'd thee now? **1725** Pope *Odyss.* III. 451 Long as life this mortal shall inspire. **1818** Shelley *Rev. Islam* VI. ix, Deliberate will Inspired our growing troop. **1863** Geo. Eliot *Romola* lii, She felt it good to be inspired ..by the belief in a heroism struggling for divine ends.

5. To 'breathe in' or infuse (a feeling, thought, principle, etc.) into the mind or soul. Const. †*to* (obs.), *in, into.*

a. *spec.* Of a divine or supernatural being: To impart, communicate, or suggest by special divine or supernatural agency; used esp. in reference to the utterances of prophets and apostles, and the writings of Scripture: cf. INSPIRATION 3 a, INSPIRED 4.

1382 Wyclif *2 Tim.* iii. 16 Al scripture of God ynspyrid is profitable to teche, to arguwe..to reproue, for to lerne in riȝtwysnesse. **1526** *Pilgr. Perf.* (W. de W. 1531) 99 b, It is to suppose that all yᵉ rules of religion were inspired to the holy sayntes & fathers by the holy goost. **1581** Sidney *Apol. Poetrie* (Arb.) 52 The Poet..calleth the sweete Muses to inspire into him a good inuention. *a* **1619** Fotherby *Atheom.* II. xiv. §6. (1622) 360 Yet hath not that spirit the light of vnderstanding, vnlesse the Father of Lights inspire the same into him. **1889** Ruskin *Præterita* III. iv. 163 Melodies which have been, not invented, but inspired to all nations in the days of their loyalty to God, to their prince, and to themselves.

b. *gen.* To infuse (something) into the mind; to kindle, arouse, awaken in the mind or heart (a feeling, idea, impulse, purpose, etc.).

1576 Fleming *Panopl. Epist.* 50 [Which] inspireth into their stomaches such yll beseeming manners. **1683** *Apol. Prot. France* ii. 17 They who inspire into the King such strange Acts. **1718** Lady M. W. Montagu *Let. to C'tess Mar* 10 Mar., Fatima has..an air that inspires, at once, respect and tenderness. **1788** Gibbon *Decl. & F.* xlii. (1869) II. 580 He inspired terror to the enemy and a just confidence to the troops. **1855** Prescott *Philip II*, I. I. vii. 90 He endeavoured to inspire a confidence in others which he was far from feeling himself. **1884** *Manch. Exam.* 26 May 4/7 The course..is calculated to strengthen..the distrust which their erratic career tends to inspire.

6. *absol.* (from 4 or 5).

a **1400** *Gast of Gy* (*Rawl. MS. Poet.* 175 If. 107 b/2), þe spirit enspires whare it will. **1450–1530** *Myrr. our Ladye* 173 *Mater inspirantis*, Mother of hym that enspyreth. **1531** Elyot *Gov.* III. xxiii, I onely exhortynge, and the good spirite inspyringe. **1873** Holland *A. Bonnic.* i. 21 Perfectly self-possessed..commanding, advising, reassuring, inspiring, he was evidently there to do good.

7. *transf.* (from 4 and 5: cf. 1647 in 4 b). *trans.* To suggest or prompt the utterance of particular views or information on some public matter, or to prompt a speaker or writer to such utterance. (See also INSPIRED 5.)

1883 *Manch. Exam.* 29 Oct. 5/2 The abortive *pronunciamentos* which are supposed to have been inspired by the agents of Senor Zorilla's Republican propaganda.

inspired (ɪn'spaɪəd), *ppl. a.* [f. prec. + -ED¹.]

A. *ppl. a.* **1.** Blown on or into; inflated. *Obs.* or *arch.*

1649 G. Daniel *Trinarch., Hen. IV*, cccxx, The French mean-while, with re-inspired Sayles Come to ayde Glendoure.

2. Breathed in; taken into the lungs in breathing; inhaled. (Opp. to EXPIRED 1.)

1649 G. Daniel *Trinarch., Hen. V*, viii, As new-Inspired Ayre. **1753** N. Torriano *Gangr. Sore Throat* 57 General Causes drawn from the inspired Air. **1873** Ralfe *Phys. Chem.* 179 The expired air also occupies a greater volume than the inspired.

3. Actuated or animated by divine or supernatural influence. (In quot. 1667 of a thing, charged with supernatural influence.)

1667 Milton *P.L.* IV. 273 That sweet Grove Of Daphne by Orontes, and th' inspir'd Castalian Spring. **1856** Froude *Hist. Eng.* (1858) II. vii. 183 Archbishops and Cardinals saw an inspired prophetess in a Kentish servant girl. **1875** Jowett *Plato* (ed. 2) I. 282 The poet Pindar and other inspired men.

4. Infused or communicated by divine or supernatural power; having the character of inspiration.

As applied to the Sacred Scriptures, there is now usually a blending of senses 3 and 4, the Word being viewed as still animated by the divine influence which communicated it.

c **1450** Lydg. *Secrees* 220 Thorugh his sugryd Enspyred Elloquence, Kowde of ther tounge make a translacyoun. **1641** Milton *Ch. Govt.* II. Introd. (1851) 146 These abilities, wheresoever they be found, are the inspired guift of God. **1725** Watts *Logic* II. ii. §9 Propositions which are attain'd by this sort of Evidence are called inspired Truths. **1736** Butler *Anal.* II. vii. 352 That those persons were the original proper and sole authors of those books, i.e. that they are not inspired. **1873** H. Rogers *Orig. Bible.* ix. (ed. 3) 419 Inspired in every particle, if not verbally, yet plenarily, from the first verse of Genesis to the last verse of the Apocalypse. **1885** S. Cox *Expos.* Ser. I. iv. 42 Our interpretations of the Inspired Word.

5. *transf.* **a.** Prompted by, or emanating from, an influential (but unavowed) source: said of particular views or information on some public matter, or of a speaker, writer, journal, etc. that publishes such.

1887 *Spectator* 10 Sept. 1201 The North German Gazette contained an inspired article. **1897** *Daily News* 13 Mar. 3/1 It was true that an inspired journal..had given information on this subject.

b. Phr. ***inspired guess***, a guess not based on fact or known information (cf. *educated guess*).

1914 G. B. Shaw *Misalliance* p. xlix, In a single brain.. we get the inspired guess of the man of genius. **1969** J. Argenti *Managem. Techniques* 120 Improving the accuracy of a forecast usually calls for the careful and detailed analysis of past records plus an estimate or an inspired guess as to how future trends will differ from those of the past. **1972** N. Tinbergen in *Proc. R. Soc.* CLXXXII. 389 The effects of other behaviours are so difficult to trace that even now no more than inspired guesses are possible.

B. as *sb.* An inspired person.

1749 Bp. Lavington *Enthus. Methodists* (1754) I. ii. 19 The famous Enthusiast Mrs. Bourignon..assumed the Character of an Inspired.

inspiredly (ɪn'spaɪərɪdlɪ), *adv.* [f. prec. + -LY².] In an inspired manner; by or as by inspiration.

1591 Nashe *Introd. Sidney's Astr. & Stella*, Many courses there be, as Machiavell inspirdly sets downe, which in them selues seem singular and vertuous; but, if a man follow them, they wilbe his vtter subuersion. *a* **1677** Barrow *Serm.* (1686) II. xi. 165 Hath he spoken it, and shall he not make it good? said Balaam inspiredly. **1830** *Blackw. Mag.* XXVII. 840 How inspiredly the Christian poet touches upon each holy theme!

†**inspirement** (ɪn'spaɪəmənt). *Obs.* [f. INSPIRE *v.* + -MENT: cf. OF. *inspirement* (in Gower).]

The act of inspiring, or fact of being inspired; inspiration.

1616 HIERON *Wks.* I. 577 A reuealing before hand, by diuine inspirement, what touching states and commonwealths and particular persons shall ensue. **1677** GILPIN *Demonol.* (1867) 169 The most illiterate errors usually magnify the excellent inspirements and gifts of utterance of their leaders.

inspirer (ɪn'spaɪərə(r)). Also 5 -our. [f. INSPIRE *v.* + -ER[1]. The 15th c. form may repr. an AF. **inspirour*, OF. *inspireur*, for L. *inspīrātōr-em.*] One who or that which inspires.

c **1450** tr. *De Imitatione* III. ii. 65 Speke þou raþer, lorde god, inspirour [L. *inspirator*] & illumynour of prophetes. **1504** ATKYNSON tr. *De Imitatione* III. ii. 196 Thou, good lorde, the inwarde inspirour of all prophetes. **1616** *Rich Cabinet* 125 The gracious illumination of a heauenly Inspirer. **1728** POPE *Dunc.* III. 169 Flow, Welsted, flow! like thine inspirer, Beer. **1795** *Fortnight's Ramble* 60 The Great Supreme inspirer of good. **1873** M. ARNOLD *Lit. & Dogma* (1876) 325 The Bible..is the great inspirer.

Hence **in'spireress** (also, shortened, **in'spiress**: see -ESS), a female inspirer.

1830 W. TAYLOR *Germ. Poetry* I. 249 The poet invokes, as his inspiress, that Joy which results from the contemplation of nature. *Ibid.* II. 495 Echo was his nurse..Venus his inspireress.

inspiring (ɪn'spaɪərɪŋ), *vbl. sb.* [f. INSPIRE *v.* + -ING[1].] The action of the verb INSPIRE; inspiration; breathing in, inhalation; infusion of divine influence, etc.

a **1340** HAMPOLE *Psalter* xvii. 18 Þe inspirynge of his ire is when he says stilly in oure hert, bote if ȝe lefe ȝoure syn..ȝe be tynt men. **1528** PAYNEL *Salerne's Regim.* 2 A ij b, Inspirynge of hotte aier..by breathyng of warme aier, the mattier is warmed and riped. **1529** FRITH *Antith.* Wks. (1829) 313 Christ's law, which is the holy Scripture, came by the inspiring of the Holy Ghost. **1667** *Phil. Trans.* II. 604 How, by inspiring, the Breath is distributed through the Lungs. *a* **1711** KEN *Psyche* Poet. Wks. 1721 IV. 258 To thee from whose Inspirings flow, Our Souls immortal unconfin'd. **1844** MRS. BROWNING *Dead Pan* xiii, Shall..no hero take inspiring From the god-Greek of her lips?

in'spiring, *ppl. a.* [-ING[2].] That inspires.

1. a. Breathing or blowing upon or into something. **b.** Breathing in, inhaling.

1661 WALTON *Angler* I. i. (ed. 3) 9 If the inspiring and expiring Organ of any animal be stopt, it suddenly dies. **1735** POPE *Donne's Sat.* ii. 20 Heav'd by the breath th' inspiring bellows blow: Th' inspiring bellows lie and pant below.

2. Infusing a divine, supernatural, or exalting influence; animating.

1717 POPE *Ep. Jervas* 28 With thee, on Raphaels Monument I mourn, Or wait inspiring Dreams at Maro's Urn. **1790** BURNS *Tam O'Shanter* 105 Inspiring, bold John Barleycorn, What dangers thou canst make us scorn! **1875** JOWETT *Plato* (ed. 2) III. 144 Love, has hitherto been the inspiring influence of modern poetry and romance. **1885** S. COX *Expos.* Ser. I. vii. 83 What promise could be more welcome or more inspiring?

Hence **in'spiringly** *adv.*, in an inspiring manner; so as to inspire or animate.

1800 W. TAYLOR in Robberds *Mem.* I. 332 He has not breathed the air of Helicon so familiarly as the light of nature, or not so inspiringly. **1821** *Examiner* 786/2 The people of France were never thus inspiringly acted upon.

inspirit (ɪn'spɪrɪt), *v.* Also 7 en-. [f. IN-[2] (or EN-) + SPIRIT *sb.*]

1. *trans.* To put spirit, life, or energy into; to quicken, enliven, animate; to cheer, encourage; to incite, stir (*to* something, or *to do* something).

c **1610** SYLVESTER *Tropheis Henry Gt.* 584 The life that late our lives inspirited. **1611** SPEED *Hist. Gt. Brit.* IX. vi. §2. 485 A King..whose entrance like that of the Soule into the Body, did quicken, and enspirite the Realme. **1633** P. FLETCHER *Purple Isl.* XII. lxxxii, Inspiriting dead souls. **1658** *Whole Duty Man* Priv. Devot. (1684) 157 Be thou pleased..to enspirit and enliven this earthly drossy heart. **1673** *Lady's Calling* I. i. §1 Such effect..as should much inspirit the hopes of a new attemt. **1706** ATTERBURY *Serm.* (1723) II. 98 A discreet use of proper and becoming ceremonies..inspirits the sluggish. *a* **1794** SIR W. JONES *Hymn Narayena*, In air, in floods, in caverns, woods, and plains, Thy will inspirits all. **1816** SCOTT *Bl. Dwarf* ii, To inspirit the doubtful courage of his soldiers. **1857** BUCKLE *Civiliz.* I. xii. 686 Those great men, who, by their writings, inspirited the people to resistance.

†**b.** In weaker sense: To animate or inspire (with some spirit), or as some feeling does. *Obs.*

a **1661** FULLER *Worthies* (1840) I. 204 At the siege of Leith ..he was shot in the shoulder, which inspirited him with a constant antipathy against the Scotch. **1814** *Q. Rev.* XI. 92 There can be little doubt that this feeling inspirited Dr. Busby.

2. To fill with, or cause to be possessed by, a 'spirit' or supernatural being.

1675 WOODHEAD, etc. *Paraphr. St. Paul* 103 Whether the effects of those who seem inspirited proceed from a good or a bad spirit. **1826** E. IRVING *Babylon* I. ii. 95 The dragon.. inspiriting the Roman empire, did commence a most savage warfare with the woman. **1839** BAILEY *Festus* xx. (1852) 331 He knew himself a bard ordained, More than inspired, of God, inspirited.

†**in'spiritate**, *a. Obs. rare.* [ad. It. *inspiritato* 'possessed with some diuell or euill spirit', f. *inspiritare* to possess, etc. (Florio), f. *in-* (IN-[2]) + *spirito* SPIRIT.] Possessed with a spirit.

1600 E. BLOUNT *Hosp. Incur. Fools* 158 A woman inspiritate, diabolicall, and stuffed vp euen to the verie gorge with all kinde of flagition and villanie.

in'spiriter. [f. INSPIRIT + -ER[1].] One who or that which inspirits.

1821 *Blackw. Mag.* X. 332 He was the enlivener and inspiriter of conversation.

in'spiriting, *vbl. sb.* [f. as prec. + -ING[1].] the action of the verb INSPIRIT.

1846 DE QUINCEY *Antigone* Wks. 1860 XIV. 213 We may see..a keen attention paid to the inspiriting and dressing of the dialogue. **1880** G. MEREDITH *Tragic Com.* viii. (1881) 132 Alvan, left to himself, had a quiet belief in the.. inspiriting he had given her.

in'spiriting, *ppl. a.* [f. as prec. + -ING[2].] That inspirits; animating, encouraging, cheering.

1795 SOUTHEY *Joan of Arc* x. 209 Joy more inspiriting Fills not the Persian's soul, when sure he deems That Mithra hears propitiously his prayer. **1812** L. HUNT in *Examiner* 14 Sept. 587/2 It is..an inspiriting thing, to see him turn the tables upon Bonaparte. **1897** MARY KINGSLEY *W. Africa* 343 Cheering the paddlers with inspiriting words.

Hence **in'spiritingly** *adv.*

1824 *New Monthly Mag.* XI. 158 The fresh salt breeze blowing inspiritingly upon me.

in'spiritment. *rare.* [f. INSPIRIT + -MENT.] The action of inspiriting, or fact of being inspirited.

1886 MRS. RANDOLPH *Mostly Fools* I. vi. 164 There was an inspiritment which communicated itself even to his horse's hoofs.

inspirometer (ɪnspɪ'rɒmɪtə(r)). [irreg. f. INSPIRE *v.* + -(O)METER.] An instrument for measuring the quantity of air inspired into the lungs.

1882 *Knowledge* 28 July 152 Excuse my mentioning a simple kind of 'inspirometer' which I made.

inspissant (ɪn'spɪsənt). *rare.* [ad. L. *inspissānt-em*, pr. pple. of *inspissāre*, found in pa. pple.: see next.] An inspissating or thickening agent.

1822–34 *Good's Study Med.* (ed. 4) I. 562 Those medicines..were denominated Diluents, Humectants, and Attenuants, while those of an opposite character were called Inspissants. **1857** DUNGLISON *Med. Lex.* 502 *Inspissant*,.. any remedial agent, that renders the blood thicker, directly or indirectly.

†**in'spissate,** *ppl. a. Obs.* [ad. late L. *inspissāt-us* pa. pple. (Vegetius, *c* 420), f. *inspissāre* to thicken: see next.] Inspissated, thickened.

1603 HOLLAND *Plutarch's Mor.* 1006 The aire of rivers being alwaus grosse and heavy, in Winter is more inspissate by reason of the circumstant cold. **1657** *Physical Dict.*, *Inspissate juyce*, is the juyce of some herb boyled to the thickness of honey. *c* **1720** W. GIBSON *Farrier's Dispens.* I. i. (1734) 15 Much safer for Horses..than Scammony and other Gums, and inspissate Juices.

inspissate (ɪn'spɪseɪt, 'ɪnspɪseɪt), *v.* [f. late L. *inspissāre* (Boeth.), f. *in-* (IN-[2]) + *spissāre* to thicken, *spissus* thick.]

1. *trans.* To thicken, condense.

1626 BACON *Sylva* §726 The Sugar doth inspissate the Spirits of the Wine, and maketh them not so easie to resolue into Vapour. **1657** S. PURCHAS *Pol. Flying-Ins.* 141 Manna is first a liquid dew, and after inspissated by a vertue of the tree, or plant on which it falls. **1744** BERKELEY *Siris* §16 Pitch is tar inspissated. **1845** LINDLEY *Sch. Bot.* x. (1858) 170 Whatever tends to inspissate sap..has the property of causing..flower-buds to be produced.

fig. **1732** *Historia Litteraria* III. 249 When the Subject is limpid of it self, he frequently inspissates it, by throwing in a heap of Circumstances not Essential to it. **1884** E. E. HALE *Xmas in Narrag.* v. 117 No method..by which you can inspissate entertainingness into a dull article.

2. *intr.* To become thick or dense, to thicken.

1755 WATHEN in *Phil. Trans.* XLIX. 214 It is..liable to inspissate by heat. **1836** MACGILLIVRAY tr. *Humboldt's Trav.* xvii. 225 Until the yolk..has time to inspissate.

inspissated (see the vb.), *ppl. a.* [f. prec. + -ED[1].] Brought to a thick consistence; thickened.

1655 in *Ref. Commw. Bees* 27 There is..a great difference to be acknowledged between Honey and other inspissated sweetnesses. **1800** HATCHETT in *Phil. Trans.* XC. 387 Inspissated albumen. **1835** KIRBY *Hab. & Inst. Anim.* I. v. 165 The body of polypes is formed of a kind of inspissated mucus.

fig. **1769** JOHNSON in *Boswell* 16 Oct., In the description of night in Macbeth, the beetle and the bat detract from the general idea of darkness,—inspissated gloom.

inspissation (ɪnspɪ'seɪʃən). [ad. med.L. *inspissātiōn-em*, n. of action from *inspissāre* to INSPISSATE.] The action of making, or process of becoming, thick or dense; thickening, condensation; an instance of this.

1603 HOLLAND *Plutarch's Mor.* 1079 What more opposite to subtilization and rarefaction, than inspissation and condensation? **1626** BACON *Sylva* § 919 Wrought by the inspissation of the Aire. **1691** RAY *Creation* II. (1692) 58 The Oyl preserves the Mucilage from Inspissation. **1794** J. HUTTON *Philos. Light*, etc. 193 The greater or lesser degree of inspissation that the oil had suffered. **1874** ROOSA *Dis. Ear* (ed. 2) 122 The secretions are packed in the ear, and.. inspissation of the cerumen is very often caused. **1898** *Allbutt's Syst. Med.* V. 27 The occasional intratubal mucous inspissations of acute bronchitis seen chiefly in children.

fig. **1839** *Blackw. Mag.* XLV. 356 He could imbibe sixteen tumblers of whisky punch, without any other external indication than a slight inspissation of speech.

inspissator ('ɪnspɪseɪtə(r)). [f. INSPISSAT(E *v.* + -OR.] An apparatus for thickening or coagulating serum or other body fluids by heat.

1897 MUIR & RITCHIE *Man. Bacteriol.* ii. 48 (*caption*) Blood serum inspissator. **1928** F. W. TANNER *Pract. Bacteriol.* i. 24 Some media..must be sterilized at low temperatures. For this purpose a serum coagulator, or inspissator, is used. The media are heated at from 57° to 60° C. for different lengths of time. **1951** WHITBY & HYNES *Med. Bacteriol.* (ed. 5) iii. 22 A very rich solid medium may be made by coagulating serum or blood into a solid mass. The coagulation is effected by heating to 75° C. in an inspissator.

inspoken: see INSPEAK.

†**inspreith, -aith.** *Sc. Obs.* Also 5–6 -aich, 7 -eth, -eght. [f. IN *adv.* 12a + SPREATH prey, booty, a. Gael. *spréidh* cattle of any kind.

The sense-history offers difficulties, since the simple *spreith* is not recorded in Sc. in the Gaelic sense of 'cattle', nor in that of 'stock, chattels', which the compound presupposes.]

'Furniture of a house' (Jam.). (Cf. INSIGHT[2].)

1488 *Acta Dom. Concil.* 90 (Jam.) For certane vtheris gudis and inspraich of househald foure skore of merkis. **1563** WINȜET *Four Scoir Thre Quest.* Wks. 1888 I. 114 Togiddir with thair sones, dochtiris, horss, cattell, and all thair insprayth. *c* **1575** *Balfour's Pract.* (1754) 236 It is leasum..to ony persoun to leive in legacie his wapinis, armour, and inspreth of his house to quhom he pleisis.. reservand alwayis to his air his best armour and principal inspreth. **1652** Z. BOYD in *Zion's Flowers* (1855) App. 26/1, I leave to my spouse the use of all my moveable goods as bedding boords and other inspreth for hir hous. **1685–6** *Acc. Depred. on Clan Campbell*, etc. (1816) 35–37 (Jam.) Account of what goods, gear, and inspreght was taken from Duncan McGillespick of Belyie..Inspreght and household plenishing worth 40 *lib.*

†**in'sprent,** *v. Obs. rare*[−1]. [f. IN-[1] + SPRENT *v.* to run, leap, spring.] *intr.* To leap or spring in.

1513 DOUGLAS *Æneis* II. ix. [viii.] 98 The way is maid by fors, and entre brokin, Grekis insprent, the formast haue thai stokin And slane with swerdis.

†**in'sprinkled,** *pa. pple. Obs.* [IN *adv.* 11b.] Sprinkled in.

1671 J. WEBSTER *Metallogr.* xvi. 237 It lieth dry and green in clifts, open caves, and passages, like green frogs insprinkled one in another.

inspunge (ɪn'spʌndʒ), *v. nonce-wd.* [f. IN-[1] or [2] + *spunge*, SPONGE *v.*] *trans.* To confine in a sponging-house.

1837 THACKERAY *Ravenswing* v, On finding himself inspunged for debt in Chancery Lane.

†**in'squadron,** *v. Obs. rare*[−0]. [IN-[2].]

1611 FLORIO, *Insquadronare*, to insquadron. *Ibid.*, *Inschierare*, to introupe, to insquadron.

inst., abbrev. of INSTANT *a.* 2b.

1771 J. WEDGWOOD *Let.* 7 Sept. (1965) 113 Letters of the 3rd 4th and 5th inst. **1954** CROOKS & DAWSON *Dict. Typewriting* (ed. 6) 146 The principal commercial abbreviations beginning with this letter [*sc.* the letter I] are —..Inst. [etc.].

instability (ɪnstə'bɪlɪtɪ). [a. F. *instabilité* (15th c. in Hatz.-Darm.), ad. L. *instabilitāt-em*, f. *instabilis* INSTABLE.] The quality of being unstable; lack of stability in regard to position, condition, or moral qualities; want of steadiness, fixity, or firmness of purpose or character. With *an* and *pl.*, an instance of this.

c **1422** HOCCLEVE *Learn to Die* 863 Fful fewe been, þat.. Konne apparceyue thinstabilitee Of the world. **1548** HALL *Chron.*, *Hen. IV* 15 Some lamentyng the instabilitee of the Englishe people, iudged theim to be spotted with perpetuall infamie. **1640–4** EARL BRISTOL in Rushw. *Hist. Coll.* III. (1692) I. 714 The Scripture telleth us of..the Instability of a Kingdom Divided within it self. **1646** SIR T. BROWNE *Pseud. Ep.* II. vi. 96 Parallels or like relations..by their mutuall concurrences support their solitary instabilities. **1781** C. JOHNSTONE *Hist. J. Juniper* II. 220, I had leisure to reflect on the instability of human happiness. **1783** JOHNSON *Let. to Mrs. Thrale* 21 Oct., Endeavour to reform that instability of attention which your last letter has happened to betray. **1856** STANLEY *Sinai & Pal.* ii. (1858) 125 Nothing conveys..so strong a sense of general instability and insecurity as the recurrence of earthquake. **1878** STEWART & TAIT *Unseen Univ.* vi. §178. 181 Molecular instability, such as water cooled below freezing point.

instable (ɪn'steɪb(ə)l), *a.* Now *rare.* Also 8 **instabile.** [ad. L. *instabil-is*, f. *in-* (IN-[3]) + *stabilis* STABLE. Cf. F. *instable* (14th c. in Hatz.-Darm.).] Not stable; lacking stability; unstable.

1483 [implied in INSTABLENESS]. **1599** MINSHEU II, Instable or vnstable. **1638** CHILLINGW. *Relig. Prot.* I. i. §8. 36 A building cannot be stable, if any one of the necessary pillars thereof be infirme and instable. **1711** E. WARD *Vulgus Brit.* IV. 48 Who would have thought the Rabble were so ingrateful and instable? **1858** LARDNER *Hand-bk. Nat. Phil.*, *Hydrost.*, etc. vii. 130 The equilibrium of a boat may be rendered instable by the passengers standing up in it. **1897** *Allbutt's Syst. Med.* II. 914 Persons of instable nervous system may be less able to withstand such influences [of tobacco].

†**in'stable,** *v. Obs. rare*$^{-0}$. [f. IN-^{2} + STABLE *sb.*] *trans.* To stable (a horse. etc.).

1611 FLORIO, *Installare*, to install, to instable.

†**in'stableness.** *Obs.* [f. INSTABLE *a.* + -NESS.] Unstableness, instability.

1483 CAXTON *Gold. Leg.* 32/2 Me thynketh he myght doo no lasse consyderynge our Instableness. **1618** M. BARET *Horsemanship* I. 46 His hands, being alwaies chocking vpon the snaffle (through the instablenesse of them) will..dull the horses mouth. *c* **1645** HOWELL *Lett.* (1650) II. lviii. 84 Ther cannot be two more pregnant instances of the lubricity and instablenes of mankind.

†**instabu'lation,** *nonce-wd.* [f. IN-^{2} + L. *stabulum*, standing-place, stall, stable.] Installment as in a stable.

1654 GAYTON *Pleas. Notes* I. iii. 11 The..installation..of this Knight Errant, or rather instabulation (for there was no Chappell in the house).

†**in'stagnate,** *v. Obs. rare*$^{-1}$. [f. IN-^{2} + ppl. stem of L. *stagnāre* to STAGNATE.] *intr.* To become stagnant, stagnate.

1656 J. HARRINGTON *Oceana* (1658) 152 So pure and perpetual a stream, as being unable to instagnate is for ever uncapable of corruption.

install (ɪn'stɔːl), *v.*^{1} Also 6-7 **enstall,** 6- **instal.** [ad. med.L. *installā-re*, f. *in-* (IN-^{2}) + *stallum*, cf. OHG. *stal*, *stall-* standing-place, sitting-place: see STALL. Cf. F. *installer* (1349 in Godef. *Compl.*).]

1. *trans.* To invest with an office or dignity by seating in a stall or official seat, as the choir-stall of a canon in a cathedral, or that of a Knight of the Garter or Bath in the chapel of his order, the throne of a bishop, etc. Hence, To instate in an office, rank, etc. with the customary ceremonies or formalities. Often with complemental extension.

1548 HALL *Chron., Hen. VIII* 194 To be had in the more reputacion..he [the Cardinal] determined to be installed or inthronised at Yorke. **1581** J. BELL *Haddon's Answ. Osor.* 5 If you were not already enstalled a brawlyng Byshop. **1628** MEAD in Ellis *Orig. Lett.* Ser. I. III. 271 It is said he shall forthwith be..installed Knight of the Garter. *c* **1645** HOWELL *Lett.* (1650) I. xxxviii. 55 The Bishop of Ostia..consecrates and instals the Pope. **1681-2** WOOD *Life* 15 Feb. (O.H.S.) III. 5 Mr. [Henry] Aldrich student of Ch. Ch., was install'd Canon of the same. **1761** HUME *Hist. Eng.* III. lxi. 322 Cromwell was declared protector; and with great solemnity installed in that high office. **1835** BROWNING *Paracelsus* IV. 118 A sour reproachful glance From those in chief who, cap in hand, installed The new professor scarce a year before. **1880** [see INSTALLANT].

b. By extension: To place in any office or position, esp. one of dignity or authority; to establish in any place or condition.

1647 WARD *Simp. Cobler* 68 Then install some untruth in its roome for your Generall. **1742** YOUNG *Nt. Th.* VI. 317 What station charms thee? I'll install thee there. **1817** COLERIDGE *Biog. Lit.* iii. (1894) 29 It is said that St. Nepomuc was installed the guardian of bridges, because he had fallen over one, and sunk out of sight. **1840** E. FITZGERALD *Lett.* (1889) I. 57, I hope you will soon come home and install yourself in Mornington Crescent. **1878** BOSW. SMITH *Carthage* 397 Having got rid of his namesake ..Hasdrubal installed himself as commander-in-chief. **1888** BRYCE *Amer. Commw.* III. VI. civ. 496 A company of New England Unitarians..installed itself round the piano in the great saloon of the vessel and sang hymns. **1888** MRS. H. WARD *R. Elsmere* I. ii. (1894) 25 His family watched his progress with..amazement, till he announced himself as safely installed at Oxford.

c. In Presbyterian and other Churches of *U.S.* To invest an already ordained minister with a particular pastoral charge.

1788-1888 *Form Govt. Presb. Ch. U.S.A.* I. x. §8 The presbytery has power..to ordain, install, remove, and judge ministers. *Ibid.* xvi. §6 The bishop who is to preside.. addressing himself to the minister to be installed shall propose to him the following or similar questions. **1828** in WEBSTER.

d. To fill (a place) with (an occupant). *Obs. rare.*

1577 STANYHURST *Descr. Irel.* in *Holinshed* (1807-8) VI. 32 His heart being scared with gelousie, and his wits installed with phrenise.

2. To place (an apparatus, a system of ventilation, lighting, heating, or the like) in position for service or use: cf. INSTALLATION 2. [F. *installer.*]

1867 W. W. SMYTH *Coal & Coal-mining* 201 It is apt to be the case, that if one precautionary measure be fully installed, another is neglected,—that when safety lamps are adopted for the entire operations of a mine, the ventilation is no longer a subject of the same attention. **1889** *Science* Feb. 116 This road has recently been installed by the Sprague Electric Railway and Motor Company. *c* **1890** W. H. CASMEY *Ventil. Textile Factories* 16 The heat..caused the warmest part, before the fan was installed, to increase in temperature about 20 degrees.

Hence **in'stalled** *ppl. a.*, **in'stalling** *vbl. sb.*; also **in'staller,** one who installs.

1590 GREENE *Orl. Fur.* Wks. (Rtldg.) 95/1 Nor can there sit within the sacred shrine Of Venus more than one installèd heart. **1610** HOLLAND *Camden's Brit.* II. 109 All Prelates..sit..according to their own ordination, enstalling and promotion. **1611** FLORIO, *Inuestitore*, an inuester, an installer. **1613** DRUMM. OF HAWTH. *Cypress Grove* Wks. (1711) 126 Life is a government and office, wherein man is so long continued, as it pleaseth the Installer. *a* **1649** —— *Irene* ibid. 176 By oaths of princes, at their installing. **1687** BP. CARTWRIGHT in *Magd. Coll. & Jas. II* (O.H.S.) 147 Will you..assist at the Installing of him? **1724** *Lond. Gaz.* No. 6290/3 The two new installed Knights offered together. **1926** Installer [see *check-back*]. **1968** *Listener* 23 May 683/3 It's worth boring the installer with endless questions when you get any new piece of equipment. **1971** *Sci. Amer.* Sept. 25/1 In Chicago I was successively a telephone installer, a postal clerk, [etc.].

†**in'stall, -al,** *v.*^{2} *Obs. rare.* [f. IN-^{2} (?) + STALL *v.* in the sense 'to arrange or fix (a payment)': cf. ESTALL *v.* Perh. influenced in form by INSTALL *v.*^{1}] *trans.* To pay by instalments.

1679 'TOM TICKLEFOOT' *Obs. Trials Wakeman*, etc. 6 To us that know the Methods of the Court, never to pay so much Wages at a time, they always instal such Summs.

install ('ɪnstɔːl), *sb.* [f. INSTALL *v.*^{1}] Something installed or placed in. (Only G. M. Hopkins.)

1871 G. M. HOPKINS *Jrnl.* (1959) 21 Apr. 207 These are not ribs; they are a 'wracking' install made of these two realities—the frets,..and the whiter field of sky shewing between. **1874** *Ibid.* 23 May 244 True bold realism but quite a casual install of woodland. *Ibid.* 245 Happy use of openings, accidental installs, people's feet, hands etc seen through. *c* **1883** —— *Sermons & Devotional Writings* (1959) II. iii. 146 For accidental being, such as that of the broken fragments of things or things purely artificial or chance 'installs', has no true and intrinsic oneness or true self.

installant (ɪn'stɔːlənt), *a.* and *sb.* [ad. med.L. *installānt-em*, pr. pple. of *installāre* to INSTALL.]

a. *adj.* That installs. **b.** *sb.* One who installs.

1880 *Times* 1 July 13/3 The Bishop installant will be the Bishop of Chester. *Ibid.* 19 Oct. 9 Yesterday 15 new Canons were installed..The Bishop was installant. **1895** *N.B. Daily Mail* 13 Nov. 4 Dr. Talbot was yesterday afternoon enthroned in Rochester Cathedral as the hundredth bishop of that diocese. The Bishop of Dover was the installant.

installation (ɪnstɔː'leɪʃən, -stə-). [ad. med.L. *installātiōn-em*, n. of action f. *installāre* to INSTALL. Cf. F. *installation* (1349 in Godef. *Compl.*).]

1. a. The action of installing or fact of being installed; the ceremony of formally inducting (a person) into an ecclesiastical dignity, an order of knighthood, or an official position; hence, formal establishment in any office or position.

1606 HOLLAND *Sueton.* 127 Being nominated to succeede Augur..before his inuesture and installation therein, he was aduanced to the sacerdotall dignitie of a Pontifie. **1726** AYLIFFE *Parergon* 303 So is Installation, in respect of Ecclesiastical Dignities, equivalent unto Collation in respect of simple Benefices. **1823** LINGARD *Hist. Eng.* VI. 215 The cardinal [Wolsey] had invited the nobility of the county to assist at his installation. **1831** BREWSTER *Newton* (1855) I. iv. 69 The Duke of Buckingham's installation as Chancellor of the University of Cambridge. **1840** MACAULAY *Ess., Clive* (1887) 532 The..Nizam came thither..and the ceremony of his installation was performed there with great pomp.

attrib. **1776** ADAM SMITH *W.N.* I. xi. III. (1869) I. 188 In 1309, Ralph de Born, Prior of St. Augustine's, Canterbury, gave a feast upon his installation-day. **1874** GREEN *Short Hist.* vi. §5. 324 On the eve of his installation-feast, he [Wolsey] was arrested on a charge of high treason.

b. In *U.S.* = INSTALMENT 1 b.

1846 in WORCESTER.

2. The action of setting up or fixing in position for service or use (machinery, apparatus, or the like); a mechanical apparatus set up or put in position for use; *spec.* used to include all the necessary plant, materials and work required to equip rooms or buildings with electric light. [F. *installation.*] Also *attrib.*

1882 C. W. SIEMENS in *Nature* XXVII. 69/2 From the experience of large installations, I consider that electricity can..be produced in London at a cost of about one shilling per 10,000 Ampère-Volts. **1882** *Pop. Sci. Monthly* XXI. 578 The final form adopted in electric installations. **1894** H. DRUMMOND *Ascent Man* 365 Childhood in its early stage is a series of installations and trials of the new machinery. **1896** *Allbutt's Syst. Med.* I. 353 This [battery] can be used either in the consulting room or in the patient's home, and is therefore superior to a fixed installation. **1898** *Engineering Mag.* XVI. 48 The installation cost is a matter of estimate. **1908** *Installation News* II. 56/2 Competent to act as installation inspector. **1921** *Dict. Occup. Terms* (1927) §690 *Installation engineer*.., a technical engineer who interviews prospective consumers and points out advantages of electric light or power and advises them as to installation, etc. *Ibid.* §692 Installation inspector. **1962** *Gloss. Terms Automatic Data Processing* (*B.S.I.*) 52 *Installation time*, time spent in installing, commissioning, testing, and approving equipment.

installed, -er, -ing: see after INSTALL *v.*^{1}

instalment^1, **installment** (ɪn'stɔːlmənt). [f. INSTALL *v.*^{1} + -MENT.]

1. The action of installing or fact of being installed; formal induction into an office or dignity; installation.

1589 PUTTENHAM *Eng. Poesie* I. xxiii. (Arb.) 61 At solemne feasts and pompes of coronations and enstallments of honourable orders. **1594** SHAKS. *Rich. III*, III. i. 163 The instalement of this noble Duke, In the seate royall of this famous Ile. **1625** F. MARKHAM *Bk. Hon.* II. x. 80 Chosen to giue a further glory to Coronations and Enstalments. **1661** PEPYS *Diary* 29 Oct., The custom of Lord Mayors going the day of their installment to Paul's. **1767** BLACKSTONE *Comm.* II. xx. 312 In dignities possession is given by installment; in rectories and vicarages by induction. **1836** LD. COCKBURN *Jrnl.* I. 128 Peel..is a most fitting man for this literary honour. His instalment will be made the occasion of a grand party festival.

b. In Presbyterian and other Churches of U.S.A.: The institution of an already ordained minister to a charge; = INDUCTION 4 b. Cf. INSTALL *v.*^{1} 1 c.

1788-1888 *Form Govt. Presb. Ch. U.S.A.* I. xvi. §4 When any minister is to be settled in a congregation, the installment, which consists in constituting a pastoral relation between him and the people of that particular church, may be performed either by the presbytery, or by a committee appointed for that purpose.

c. Establishment in any position, seat, or place.

1646 EVANCE *Noble Ord.* 2 Elyes enstallment, or a large grant of honour to Ely. **1829** I. TAYLOR *Enthus.* x. 296 The instalment of the Inspired Volume in the throne of universal authority. **1863** J. G. MURPHY *Comm. Gen.* ii. 21-2 His instalment in the garden as its owner. **1884** C. F. WOOLSON in *Harper's Mag.* Feb. 375/2 The installment of our twelve selves in these..carriages.

†**2.** A place or seat wherein some one is installed. *Obs. rare.*

1598 SHAKS. *Merry W.* v. v. 67 Each faire Instalment, Coate, and seu'rall Crest, With loyall Blazon, euermore be blest. **1610** HEALEY *St. Aug. Citie of God* XIV. ix. (1620) 482 Here also we see their estate in their immortall future instalment.

instalment^2 (ɪn'stɔːlmənt). Also **install-**. [f. INSTALL *v.*^{2} + -MENT, or f. IN-^{2} + STALMENT. Cf. ESTALLMENT. The spelling *instalment* is now usual in the U.K. and *installment* in the U.S.]

†**1.** The arrangement of the payment of a sum of money by fixed portions at fixed times; = ESTALLMENT. *Obs.*

1732 HEARNE *Otterbourne & Whethamst.* 376 *note*, *Estallamentum* idem est quod *stallamentum*, i.e. Anglice, *stallment* sive *installment*, vel (ut olim efferebant) *estallment*. Id quod liquet ex vocibus *sive assignationes.* **1775** ASH, *Instalment*,..the act of bringing to its proper place in any account, a payment.

2. 'The payment, or the time appointed for payment, of different portions of a sum of money, which, by agreement of the parties, instead of being payable in the gross, at one time, is to be paid in parts, at certain stated times' (Tomlins *Jacob's Law Dict.* 1797).

1776 ADAM SMITH *W.N.* II. ii. (1869) I. 314 This sum ought to have been paid in at several different instalments.

3. a. Each of several parts into which a sum payable is divided, in order to be paid at different fixed times; a part of a sum due paid in advance of the remainder. *attrib.* (freq. in recent use), as ***instalment credit, plan, system,*** etc.

1776 ADAM SMITH *W.N.* II. ii. (1869) I. 314 A great part of the proprietors, when they paid in their first instalment, opened a cash account with the bank. **1796** MORSE *Amer. Geog.* I. 263 Interest on installments of Foreign debt. *Ibid.* II. 380 A loan to be taken up by gradual instalments. **1828** WEBSTER s.v., In large contracts..it is not unusual to agree that the money shall be paid by installments. **1849** LYTTON *Caxtons* II. iii, Your father takes, we say, 50 shares at £50 each, paying only an instalment of £2 a share. **1871** B'NESS BUNSEN in Hare *Life* (1879) II. vii. 418 Königsberg has just paid in the last instalment of the debt she was obliged to incur. **1876** *Los Angeles Daily Herald* 4 Oct. 3/6 Lots for Sale on the Installment Plan. **1887** *Courier-Jrnl.* (Louisville, Kentucky) 18 Jan. 3/7 Installment men and agents generally will find just what they need by addressing Installment Dealers' Supply Co. **1894** *Vermont Agric. Rep.* XIV. 94 They..sell the horse on the installment plan, getting enough down to pay all the horse is worth, and holding notes for the rest. **1895** KIPLING *Day's Work* (1898) 156 'It's the Governor,' said the skipper. 'He's been selling her on the instalment plan.' **1899** SAYCE *Early Israel* vii. 260 The ordinary rate of interest was 20 per cent., paid in monthly instalments. **1904** 'SAKI' *Reginald* 52 They're getting there on the instalment system—so much down, and the rest when you feel like it. **1909** 'O. HENRY' *Roads of Destiny* iii. 47 When they get money they exhibit a strong tendency to spend it..instead of giving it to the instalment man. **1923** R. D. PAINE *Comrades of Rolling Ocean* xi. 187 'This is still a valuable ship,' explained Torrance, 'even if she is floating around the high seas on the installment plan.' **1927** W. E. COLLINSON *Contemp. Eng.* 112 To pay by the instalment system. **1927** *Sat. Even. Post* 24 Dec. 28/2 Upon that premise..is based the vast present-day development of installment selling. **1935** *Economist* 3 Aug. 234/2 The United States itself is the leader of a new, hard, materialistic civilisation..whose priests are the instalment-seller and the advertising expert. **1942** *Short Guide Gt. Brit.* (U.S. War Dept.) 31 *Instalment plan*, hire-purchase system, or hire system. **1948** *Manch. Guardian Weekly* 8 Jan. 4/1 The President says inflation can be beaten..by putting an end to instalment buying. **1952** *Ibid.* 15 May 3/1 The Federal Reserve Board was a little tight-lipped in explaining its move..to suspend controls on hire purchase, or what is known here as instalment credit. **1955** *Times* 15 Aug. 11/5 The Federal Reserve..has expressed mild concern over the rapid rise of consumer instalment (hire purchase) debt. **1965** M. SPARK *Mandelbaum Gate* iv. 104 On his discharge he bought a car on the instalment plan. **1967** *N.Y. Times* (International Edition) 11-12 Feb. 3/3 The measures include..more severe installment purchase restraints and reduction in travel allowances. **1972** *Accountant* 17 Aug. 206/2 Instalment credit..group services and group funding, are the subject of special reviews. **1973** *N.Y. Law Jrnl.* 20 Feb., The assumption of installment payments by appellant did not serve to release decedent.

b. *fig.* A part of something produced or supplied in advance of the remainder; one of several parts supplied or produced at different times.

1823 J. BADCOCK *Dom. Amusem.* 140 The mixture is to be poured on by instalment, as it were. **1856** FROUDE *Hist. Eng.* (1858) II. vii. 194 This was but a slight instalment of lenity. **1858** LYTTON *What will he do?* I. iv, When I had finished the first instalment of the work..my mother grew alarmed for my health. **1862** H. SPENCER *First Princ.* II. ix. §78 (1875) 233 His conclusion may be accepted as a large instalment of the truth.

Instamatic (ɪnstəˈmætɪk). Also with lower case initial. [f. INSTA(NT *a.* + AUTO)MATIC *a.*]

A proprietary name for a type of self-loading camera. Also *fig.*

1962 *Trade Marks Jrnl.* 19 Sept. 1266/1 Instamatic 834,322. Photographic, cinematographic and optical apparatus and instruments, and parts and fittings... Kodak Limited, Kodak House, Kingsway, London, W.C.2; Manufacturers. **1962** *Official Gaz.* (U.S. Patent Office) 11 Dec. TM 68 Eastman Kodak Company, Rochester, N.Y... Instamatic. For Photographic Cameras. **1964** *Ladies' Home Jrnl.* May 3 (Advt.), *Kodak Instamatic* Cameras load instantly, automatically. **1970** N. FLEMING *Czech Point* vi. 70 At six-fifteen the next morning I set out in the car with notebook and Instamatic at the ready. **1973** *Art Internat.* Mar. 58/1 The long tirade looked like nothing so much as a Pinocchio-minded exercise: an easy-thinking, instamatic demonstration of art-destructive politics. **1978** A. WELCH *Bk. Airsports* ii. 32/2 (*caption*) Instamatic cameras are used and fixed to the side of the cockpit. **1984** E. FAIRWEATHER *Only Rivers run Free* i. 1 A soldier lined up his Instamatic for a snapshot of an effigy on the top of an unlit bonfire.

instaminate (ɪnˈstæmɪnət), *a. Bot.* [ad. mod.L. *instaminātus*: see IN-³ and STAMINATE.] Not staminate; not having stamens.

1855 MAYNE *Expos. Lex.*, *Instaminatus*, applied by H. Cassini to the corol in the *Synanthereæ*, when it is not accompanied by perfect male organs: instaminate. **1886** in *Syd. Soc. Lex.*

instamp, obs. form of ENSTAMP.

instance (ˈɪnstəns), *sb.* Forms: 4–6 instaunce, 5 instauns, 5–6 instans, 4– instance. [a. F. *instance* (13th c. in Hatz.-Darm.) eagerness, anxiety, solicitation, a judicial process, a new argument rebutting the reply to a former argument, formerly also an instant of time, ad. L. *instāntia* (1) a being present, presence, (2) urgency, earnestness in supplication, (3) a pleading or process in a court of justice (Ulpian), (4) in med. Schol. L. an objection to a general statement, an instance to the contrary, transl. Gr. ἔνστασις (Buridan, *c* 1350, *In Metaphysicen Aristotelis Quæstiones*: see Prantl): f. *instānt-em* INSTANT *a.*]

I. Urgency; pressure; urging influence.

1. a. Urgency in speech or action; urgent entreaty, solicitation; earnestness; persistence. *arch.*, exc. in phr. ***at the instance of*** (a person), at the solicitation, suit, instigation, or suggestion of.

c **1340** HAMPOLE *Prose Tr.* 26 At þe prayere and instaunce of oþer. **1382** WYCLIF *Judith* iv. 8 Al the puple criede to the Lord with gret instaunce. **1460** CAPGRAVE *Chron.* (Rolls) 176 The Kyng compelled..on the othir party be instauns of the lordes. **1526** TINDALE *Eph.* vi. 18 Watch thervnto with all instance and supplicacion. **1585** T. WASHINGTON tr. *Nicholay's Voy.* I. xix. 23 b, Declaryng unto them..that at the instaunce and request of [etc.]. **1642** ROGERS *Naaman* 31 The instance and unweariednesse of the besieging army hath battered downe the forts. **1664** JER. TAYLOR *Dissuas. Popery* II. ii. §4 The French Embassador.. made instance for restitution of the Chalice to the Laity. **1770** *Junius Lett.* xxxvi. 173 The unhappy man, who yields at last to such personal instance and solicitation. **1851** HUSSEY *Papal Power* i. 29 The Emperor, at the Pope's instance summoned Flavianus to Rome. **1866** DORA GREENWELL, *Ess.* 175 The reverend gentleman labours his point with strong instance and perseverance.

†**b.** rarely ***at (in) the instance of*** (a thing). *Obs.*

1483 CAXTON *Gold. Leg.* 219 b/1 Wherfore maist not thou atte instaunce of my merytes and prayers be meued to pennaunce. **1525** LD. BERNERS *Froiss.* II. lvi. [lviii.] 195, I praye you, in the instaunce of loue and peas, to conuey me to speke with the kynge.

†**c.** *pl.* Urgent entreaties, repeated solicitation. [Cf. F. *instances*.] *Obs.*

1647–8 COTTERELL *Davila's Hist. Fr.* (1678) 34 To satisfy their instances and complaints. *a* **1674** CLARENDON *Hist. Reb.* x. §50 The Parliament made many sharp instances 'that the King might be deliver'd into their hands'. **1737** WHISTON *Josephus, Antiq.* IV. vi. §3 At the earnest instances and fervent intreaties of Balak. **1862** MERIVALE *Rom. Emp.* (1865) IV. xxxvii. 279 Tiberius..thought it decent to interfere for her in a letter; but his instances were sternly rejected.

†**2.** Something which urges or impels; impelling motive; cause. *Obs.*

1594 SHAKS. *Rich. III*, III. ii. 25 Tell him his Feares are shallow, without instance. **1602** —— *Ham.* III. ii. 192 The instances that second Marriage moue, Are base respects of Thrift, but none of Loue. **1665** EVELYN *Corr.* 16 June, His Royal Highness being safe becomes a double instance of rejoicing to us.

II. Instant time.

†**3.** A being present, presence; the present time.

c **1374** CHAUCER *Boeth.* v. pr. vi. 135 (Camb. MS.) þou ne shalt nat demyn it as prescience of things to comyn, but þou shal demyn it moore ryhtfully, þat it is science of presence, or of Instaunce. **1597** SHAKS. *2 Hen. IV.* IV. i. 83 The examples Of euery Minutes instance (present now) Hath put vs in these ill-beseeming Armes.

†**4.** An instant, a moment. *Obs.*

1631 *North's Plutarch, Add. Lives* (1657) 931 Immediatly they pulled out the spill of the Dart, and at that instance he gave up the ghost. **1642** *Perkins' Prof. Bk.* xi. §730. 319 The attornement cannot be so soone done but that there shall bee an instance betweene the grant and the attornement. **1643** SIR T. BROWNE *Relig. Med.* I. §11 Those continued instances of time which flow into thousand yeares. **1674** N. FAIRFAX *Bulk & Selv.* 144 We hold time to be made out of nows or instances.

III. In Scholastic Logic, and derived senses.

†**5.** A case adduced in objection to or disproof of a universal assertion (= med.L. *instantia*, Gr. ἔνστασις). *Obs.*

1573 G. HARVEY *Letter-bk.* (Camden) 115 A marvelous instance Against all dalliance. *c* **1590** MARLOWE *Faust.* v. 134, I am an instance to prove the contrary. **1594** HOOKER *Eccl. Pol.* I. xiv. §2 Against the former of these two constructions instance hath sundry ways been given. **1599** B. JONSON *Cynthia's Rev.* II. i, I can repel that paradox..of those, which hold the face to be the index of the mind..for instance I will now give you the particular and distinct face of every your most noted species of persons. **1605** BACON *Adv. Learn.* I. ii. §3 It is almost without instance contradictory. *Ibid.* II. xiii. §3 To conclude upon an enumeration of particulars, without instance contradictory, is no conclusion, but a conjecture. **1696** PHILLIPS (ed. 5), *Instance*,..a new Objection in School disputes to destroy the Solution which the Respondent has made to the first Argument.

6. a. A fact or example brought forward in support of a general assertion or an argument, or in illustration of a general truth. Hence, any thing, person, or circumstance, illustrating or exemplifying something of a more general character; a case, an illustrative example. Also, in broader sense, a case occurring, a recurring occasion. †***to give*** or ***make instance***; = INSTANCE *v.* 2.

1586 A. DAY *Eng. Secretary* II. (1625) 36, I will but give you an instance of the same. **1600** SHAKS. *A. Y. L.* II. vii. 156 Full of wise sawes, and moderne instances. **1617** MORYSON *Itin.* I. 101 Hee adds, that many miracles are heere done, and first gives instance in the person of the Marques of ——. **1675** BAXTER *Cath. Theol.* II. vi. 117 Did not you confess that they were able..to do the works of common Grace? and that in abundance of instances? *a* **1682** SIR T. BROWNE *Misc. Tracts* (1684) 46 Theophrastus..making instance in the Olive, hath left this Doctrine unto us. **1690** W. WALKER *Idiomat. Anglo-Lat.* 250, I thought him a very great instance of continency. **1790** PALEY *Horæ Paul.* Rom. i. 11 This is an instance of conformity. **1830** D'ISRAELI *Chas. I*, III. iv. 57 Noy..is an instance that mere knowledge is not true wisdom. **1860** ABP. THOMSON *Laws Th.* Introd. 19 Without something more than the mere form, there can be no instance of a law, an instance being the presence of the law in an object capable of containing it. **1874** GREEN *Short Hist.* iv. §4. 189 We may take..a foreign instance to illustrate this fundamental point in our municipal history.

b. ***for instance***: (*a*) for example, as an instance of what has been said.

1657 R. LIGON *Barbadoes* (1673) 19 The proof of this I found by looking on the Stars.., for instance, there is a little Star call'd Auriga [etc.]. **1723** CHAMBERS tr. *Le Clerc's Treat. Archit.* I. 30 It..can never happen, unless in the inside of a Building: for instance, of a Dome, or the like. **1868** LOCKYER *Elem. Astron.* iv. (1870) §326 The daily motion of the Earth is very different in different parts—at the equator and at a pole, for instance. **1885** *Lyell's Stud. Elem. Geol.* (ed. 4) 20 Deposits..are still in progress at many points, as, for instance, at the mouth of the Var.

(*b*) As *sb.*, an example. Freq. in phr. ***to give*** (one) ***a for instance***. *colloq.* (orig. *U.S.*).

1959 in *Amer. Speech* (1962) XXXVII. 202 We'll give you a couple of 'for instances' here... Carpets that sold for $199.95 selling for $129. **1961** *Easton* (Pa.) *Express* 10 July 20/4 A forinstance is the case of a Ring Lardner story he included in an anthology of humorous talks. **1966** *Punch* 25 May 772/3 'Name us a for-instance, Sid, mate,' suggested Jack abstractedly... 'Only now and again the chat round here gets a bit difficult to pin down.' **1978** *New Yorker* 26 June 26/2 'I'll give you a for instance', a man named Irving Goltz told us... 'My real name was Irving. For a while there, they called me Sidney, and then, all of a sudden, they were calling me Sussy. Don't ask me why.'

†**c.** Any particular or point characteristic of or included in something general or abstract; a detail, circumstance. *Obs.*

1649 JER. TAYLOR *Gt. Exemp.* Ep. Ded. 4 All the instances of morality serve man's naturall and politicall ends. **1732** LAW *Serious C.* xvi. (1761) 282 Many people live in all the instances of pride. **1737** WHISTON *Josephus, Hist.* I. vii. §4 Nor did they leave off the instances of their divine worship. *a* **1745** SWIFT *Diffic. knowing one's self* Wks. 1745 VIII. 249 To pursue the heart of man through all the instances of life, in all its several windings and turnings.

†**7.** Something which proves or indicates; a proof, evidence; a sign, token, mark. *Obs.*

1590 GREENE *Mourn. Garm.* (1616) 60 These droppes are not signes of sorrowes, but instances of content. **1593** SHAKS. *Lucr.* 1511 Cheeks neither red, nor pale, but mingled so, That blushing red, no guiltie instance gaue. **1607** HEYWOOD *Wom. Kilde w. Kindn.* Wks. 1874 II. 120 What instance hast thou of this strange report? **1749** FIELDING *Tom Jones* VIII. ix, I beg you to accept a guinea as a small instance of my gratitude. **1791** MRS. RADCLIFFE *Rom. Forest* ii, [She] gave the first instance of her kindness by endeavouring to revive those of her friend.

IV. In legal use, and phrase thence derived. [From L. *instantia* in Ulpian.]

8. a. A process in a court of justice, a suit. ***court of first instance***, court of primary jurisdiction. [Cf. Fr. *tribunal de première instance*.]

1661 BRAMHALL *Just Vind.* vii. 206 To seek for a remedy of these abuses at Rome, was such an insupportable charge, by reason of three instances and three sentences necessary to be obtained. **1681** STAIR *Form of Process* 3 Processes are brought in before the Lords..some in the first instance, some in the second. **1684** SIR G. MACKENZIE *Inst.* IV. iii, If there has been a Debate in the first instance, (for so we call the action before the Decreet). **1692** EARL NOTTINGHAM in *15th Rep. Hist. MSS. Comm.* App. II. 28 The Judges in the first instance are sometimes of the number of the Commissioners upon the Appeale. **1726** AYLIFFE *Parergon* 151 The Instance of a Cause is said to be that Judicial Process, which is made from the Contestation of a Suit, even to the Time of pronouncing Sentence in the Cause, or till the end of three years. **1860** TRENCH *Serm., Rev.* ii. 3 (1861) 174 There lies an appeal to a tribunal of higher instance in Heaven. **1865** *Spectator* 25 Feb. 199 The loser is seldom satisfied with the decision of a Court of first instance. **1888** BRYCE *Amer. Commw.* I. 337 Any court, be it a State court of first instance or the Federal court of last instance.

b. ***instance court***, a branch of the former Admiralty court, having jurisdiction in cases of private injuries to private rights occurring at sea or closely connected with maritime subjects and in contracts of a maritime nature. See ADMIRALTY 4. ***instance side of the court***, a district court of the United States sitting in the exercise of its ordinary jurisdiction in admiralty to determine cases of the same kind.

1802 (*title*) Formulare Instrumentorum: or, a Formulary of..Standing Orders used in the High Courts of Admiralty ..of Prize and Instance. **1846** MᶜCULLOCH *Acc. Brit. Empire* (1854) II. 189 The Court of Admiralty is twofold; the Instance Court, which takes cognisance of contracts made and injuries committed on the high seas; and the Prize Court. **1863** H. COX *Instit.* II. xi. 573 The Instance Court has cognizance of maritime causes arising upon the sea or in parts out of the reach of the common law.

9. *Sc. Law.* See quot. 1693.

1693 STAIR *Inst. Law Scotl.* IV. iii. §22 An Instance is that which may be insisted in at one dyet or course of Probation. **1861** W. BELL *Dict. Law Scot.* s.v. *Diets of Compearance*, The indictment, or the criminal letters, must be called on the precise day to which the accused is cited..otherwise the instance perishes, and a new libel must be raised. *Ibid.*, Where the prosecutor is absent, the Court may desert the diet, and thus the instance will be lost, and no farther proceedings can take place on that libel.

10. Hence, ***in the first instance***: as the first step in proceeding; in the first place.

a **1676** HALE *Hist. Com. Law* i. (1779) 11 The statutes.. were not in the first instance drawn up in the form of acts of parliament; but the petition and the answer were entred in the parliament rolls, and out of both..the act was drawn up. **1850** ROBERTSON *Serm.* Ser. III. viii. 108 The penalty is in the first instance, corrective not penal. **1880** MUIRHEAD *Gaius* IV. §170 The praetor turned his attention to the matter and introduced interdicts of another sort, which we call secondary, because they are had recourse to only in the second instance. *Mod.* I applied to the local post office in the first instance, and then to the Secretary at the General Post Office: I had to write thrice and wait five weeks for an explanation.

instance (ˈɪnstəns), *v.* [f. prec. sb. With sense 1 cf. OF. *instancier* to plead.]

I. †**1.** *trans.* To urge, entreat urgently, importune. *Obs.*

1494 FABYAN *Chron.* VII. 645 The Kynge sent..vnto the forenamed Iohn..& hym by many meanys instaunsyd to leue the company of the lordys. **1515** *Plumpton Corr.* 211, I instaunced & desired you to shew your fatherly kindnes unto my poore wife & me. **1611** FLORIO, *Instare*, to instance, to vrge, to presse with diligence, to importune. **1654** H. L'ESTRANGE *Chas. I* 30 To carry his Majesty their Prince into Spain, to the end he might be enforced, and instanced in the Romish Religion. **1736** [see INSTANCING below].

†**b.** To urge (things). *Obs. rare.*

1606 WARNER *Alb. Eng.* XIV. lxxxix. (1612) 363 So many Incantations, lyes, feares, hopes instanced shee..As lastly did the non-plust Nunne vnto her Charmes agree.

II. 2. *intr.* To cite an instance, to adduce an example in illustration or proof. Const. *in* (the example adduced), rarely *upon* (the matter illustrated); with indirect passive, ***to be instanced in***, to be cited or adduced as an instance. Now *rare*.

1601 R. JOHNSON *Kingd. & Commw.* (1603) 259, I say, that generally (to instance first of all in the Pope) that his catholike majestie, will have him [etc.]. **1624** GATAKER *Transubst.* 8 Hee instanceth in that very particular that wee now treate of. **1649** BP. HALL *Cases Consc.* (1650) 230 It were easie to instance, but charity bids me forbeare. *a* **1670** HACKET *Cent. Serm.* (1675) 549 The victory over death after that bloudy passion, which I shall instance upon in this verse. **1736** BUTLER *Anal.* I. vi. 153 Which is the fallacy instanced in by the ancients. **1789** G. WHITE *Selborne* (1853) II. xxiv. 233 It would be needless to instance in sheep which constantly flock together. **1827** C. WORDSW. *Chas. I* 113 *note*, To instance merely in one short work. **1882** C. SHORT in *Amer. Jrnl. Philol.* III. 151 We will instance in a single writer, Walton.

†**b.** Of a thing: To receive illustration, be exemplified. *Obs. rare.*

a **1667** JER. TAYLOR (Webster 1864), This story doth not only instance in kingdoms, but in families too.

3. *trans.* To illustrate, prove, or show, by means of an instance; to exemplify; to exhibit. Now *rare*.

1608 D. T. *Ess. Pol. & Mor.* 44 b, I coulde instance the truth of this assertion vpon many. **1627** F. E. *Hist. Edw. II* in *Select. fr. Harl. Misc.* (1793) 49 Main reasons are given, probable enough to instance the necessity of his fall. **1769** GOLDSM. *Rom. Hist.* (1776) I. 484 Without uttering a word, or instancing the least civility. **1783** M. W. W. GRENVILLE

Let. to Ld. Temple 28 Mar. in Dk. Buckhm. *Crt. Geo. III* (1853) I. 213 This he instanced in the American war, and in the riots of 1780. **1842–3** GROVE *Correl. Phys. Forces* 34 The above doctrine is beautifully instanced in the experiment of Thilarier.

4. To cite as an instance or example; to mention in illustration. In imperative = 'Take as an instance'; but here perhaps orig. the sb.: cf. WITNESS.

1622 [MISSELDEN] *Free Trade* 64 Other like dispensations of Statutes I might instance. **1645** BOATE *Irel. Nat. Hist.* (1652) 174 Yet it hath happened that..abundance of snow hath fallen, instance that of the year 1635. *a* **1725** POPE *Observ. Homer's Catal.* (Seager), He proceeds to instance several others who..have no farther notice taken of them throughout the poem. **1822** R. G. WALLACE *15 Yrs. India* 304 Some of the customs are curious, but only one or two can be instanced. **18..** H. SPENCER *Induct. Biol.* (L.), The arousing of a thought or feeling, always involves the overcoming of a certain resistance..instance the fact that during nervous prostration [etc.]. **1875** JOWETT *Plato* (ed. 2) I. 148, I may instance olive oil, which is mischievous to all plants.

†**5.** To indicate, point to. *Obs.*

1616 J. LANE *Contn. Sqr.'s T.* viii. 366 Others bethought them that this noble scheone instancd Canac, and Ethelta the queene.

Hence **ˈinstanced** *ppl. a.*; **ˈinstancing** *vbl. sb.* and *ppl. a.*

1606 WARNER *Alb. Eng.* XIV. xci. 370 Not lother, did Æneas, to instancing Dido tell His Cities sack. **1649** BP. HALL *Cases Consc.* IV. v. 437 That worthy Divine did not heedfully observe the great difference betwixt these instanced degrees. **1736** ELIZA STANLEY tr. *Hist. Pr. Titi* 106 There passed between them a little Scuffle of Instancings and Refusings.

†**ˈinstanceable**, *a.* *Obs.* *rare*⁻¹. [f. prec. + -ABLE.] Capable of being instanced or exemplified.

1641 'SMECTYMNUUS' *Vind. Answ.* xiii. 168 You are pleased to say, That..the fault is rare and hardly instanceable. We thinke the contrary is more hardly instanceable.

instancy (ˈɪnstənsɪ). [ad. L. *instāntia*: cf. INSTANCE *sb.*, and see -ANCY.]

1. The quality of being instant; urgency, earnestness, solicitation; pressure, pressing nature.

1515 *Plumpton Corr.* 212, I besech you..to take the payne upon you to make such labor unto Sir John Roclife, that he will, at your instauncie..make a release of that land in Combrig. **1594** HOOKER *Eccl. Pol.* I. x. §14 Those heauenly precepts, which our Lord and Sauiour with so great instancie gaue as concerning peace and vnitie. **1665** R. B. *Comm. 2 Tales* 197 The Autor, upon the instancy of sundry Persons of Quality, had finish'd his Comments. **1841** TRENCH *Parables, Mar. King's Son* (1860) 219 The king..told his servants..to press the message with greater distinctness and instancy. *a* **1894** STEVENSON *St. Ives* xix. (1898) 142 Relieved of the instancy of his fear.

2. The quality of being close at hand; imminence; immediate approach. *rare.*

1658 PHILLIPS, *Instancy*, a being near at hand. **1879** FARRAR *St. Paul* (1883) I. xxx. 601 The supposition that he had spoken of the actual instancy of the day of the Lord.

3. Immediateness, instantaneity. *rare.*

1851 J. CUMMING *Lect. Mirac.* (1854) I. 38 The evidence ..was in the speed and instancy of a process which it usually takes months, or a year, to achieve. **1853** MISS SHEPPARD *Ch. Auchester* II. 54 What riveted the resemblance most was the instancy of their sympathetic communion.

†**4.** = INSTANCE *sb.* 6. *Obs. rare.*

1613 JACKSON *Creed* II. xxi. §7 [That] wee should giue particular instancies of such Martyrs.

†**inˈstand**, *v.* *Obs.* [f. IN-¹ + STAND *v.*, after L. *instāre*: see INSTANT.] *intr.* **a.** To be at hand. **b.** To press closely. (Only in pres. pple. rendering L. *instans.*)

1382 WYCLIF *Gen.* xxxviii. 27 Instondyng the beryng, gemels apereden in the wombe. —— *Judg.* xi. 5 In thoo days fouȝten the sones of Amon aȝens Yrael: the whiche sharpli instoondynge [L. *quibus acriter instantibus*], the more thurȝ birth wenten fro Galaad. —— *1 Esdras* v. 47 In stondende.. the seuenthe moneth..thei camen togidere.

c. To be urgent or pressing, to be importunate.

c **1450** *Mirour Saluacioun* 345 That Adam shuld of the fruyte ete with hir instode Eue. *Ibid.* 241 And yᵗ pilat instode [L. *institisse*] for cristis delyvring.

ˈinˌstanding, *ppl. a.* *rare.* [f. IN *adv.* 11 a + STANDING *ppl. a.*] Standing or projecting inwards.

1878 T. BRYANT *Pract. Surg.* I. 568 Instanding upper front teeth can be trained out.

instant (ˈɪnstənt), *a.* (*adv.*) [a. F. *instant* (14th c. in Hatz.-Darm.) assiduous; at hand, imminent; ad. L. *instānt-em*, pr. pple. of *instāre* to be present, to be at hand; to urge, press upon; to apply oneself to; f. *in-* (IN-²) + *stāre* to stand.]

I. 1. Pressing, urgent, importunate. **a.** Said of persons and their actions.

c **1477** [implied in INSTANTLY 1]. **1494** FABYAN *Chron.* VII. 315 Theyse .iiii. byshoppys..made instaunt labour to the Kynge, for the obseruynge of the popys commaundement. **1555** EDEN *Decades* 58 He was instant to trauayle westwarde by foote. **1560** BIBLE (Genev.) *Luke* xxiii. 23 They were instant with loud voyces, and required that he might be crucified. —— *2 Tim.* iv. 2 Preache the worde: be instant, in season and out of season. **1693** in *Dryden's Juvenal* (1697) 342 He is instant with all Parents, that they permit not their Children, to hear lascivious Words. **1700** TYRRELL *Hist. Eng.* II. 885 The Bishops were instant with the King to make Peace. **1865** TROLLOPE *Belton Est.* xx. 237 He..was more instant in his affection, more urgent in his good office.

b. Of things: Pressing, urgent.

1585 WASHINGTON tr. *Nicholay's Voy.* II. xviii. 52 b, To succour and supply the instant necessities which might happen. **1588** Q. ELIZ. in Ellis *Orig. Lett.* Ser. II. III. 139 Upon this instant extraordinarie occasion. **1642** JER. TAYLOR *Episc.* (1647) 371 Instant necessity..hath ratified it. **1777** BURKE *Let. Sheriffs Bristol* Wks. 1842 I. 209 It would become every man's immediate and instant concern. **1816** SCOTT *Antiq.* xli, I thought there was not such instant haste. **1856** J. H. NEWMAN *Callista* 157 He has instant need of you.

II. 2. a. Now present, or present at the time defined; now (or then) existing or happening. *arch.*

1549 *Compl. Scot.* xiv. 121 Kyng Alexander cam at that instant tyme. **1632** LITHGOW *Trav.* x. 503 This Countries instant Shrieve. *c* **1669** WALLER *To Person of Honour, on his 'British Princes'* 27 Eternity has neither past Nor future.. But is all instant. **1774** GOLDSM. *Nat. Hist.* I. 315 The lower race of animals, when satisfied for the instant moment, are perfectly happy. **1881** *Daily Tel.* 12 Feb., On the 12th of February—this instant Saturday.

b. Said of the current calendar month; now ellipt. as in *the 10th instant*, i.e. the tenth day of the current month. Abbreviated *inst.*

1547 in Tytler *Hist. Scot.* (1864) III. 377, I have appointed friends to convene the 18th day of this instant month. **1583** STOCKER *Hist. Civ. Warres Lowe C.* I. 15 The 20. or 21. of that instant. **1586** A. DAY *Eng. Secretary* I. (1625) 27 On Tuesday being the thirteenth of this instant. **1640–4** in Rushw. *Hist. Coll.* III. (1692) I. 510 The Message received from Your Majesty the seventh of this instant February. **1648** CROMWELL *Let.* 18 Sept. in *Carlyle*, We received yours from Falkirk of the 15th September Instant. **1688** *Lond. Gaz.* No. 2317/1 On the 8th Instant at 5 in the Morning, we discovered a Sail. **1707–8** POPE *Let. to Wycherley* 28 Feb., I have had yours of the 23rd of this instant. **1708** SWIFT *Predict.* Sept., The pope..will die on the 11th instant. **1742** FIELDING *J. Andrews* IV. v, On the —— of this instant October, being Sabbath day. **1817** COBBETT *Pol. Reg.* XXXII. 47 The proprietor of the Courier, on the 2d instant, has these words. *Mod.* In my letter of the 15th inst.

3. Close at hand, impending, imminent.

a **1520** BARCLAY *Jugurth* (Pynson, ed. 2) 82 If I knewe without doute that our sure distruction were instant. **1605** A. WILLET *Hexapla Gen.* 461 Feeling the houre of his death to be instant. **1662** GUNNING *Lent Fast* 77 When now Lent was instant. **1713** STEELE *Guardian* No. 18 ⁋3 The evil which to men in other stations may seem distant, to him is instant and ever before his eyes. **1820** SCOTT *Monast.* iii, Her mind being probably occupied by the instant danger. **1871** BROWNING *Balaust.* 543 The abrupt Fate's footstep instant now.

4. Following immediately. †**a.** Next in order of time, very next. *Obs.*

1613 MARSTON *Insat. C'tess* v. Ij, Vpon the instant morrow of her nuptials.

b. Succeeding or coming without any interval; immediate.

1596 SHAKS. *1 Hen. IV*, IV. iv. 20, I feare the Power of Percy is too weake, To wage an instant tryall with the king. **1605** —— *Lear* I. iv. 268 The shame it selfe doth speake For instant remedy. **1667** MILTON *P.L.* x. 210 Th' instant stroke of Death. **1749** SMOLLETT *Regic.* v. ii, Intelligence important, that demands His instant ear. **1786** BURKE *W. Hastings* Wks. 1842 II. 160 For the sole purpose of creating an instant fortune for the said Sullivan. **1816** ACCUM *Chem. Tests* (1818) 164 An instant milkiness ensues. **1850** MᶜCOSH *Div. Govt.* II. ii. (1874) 163 A particular vital vessel bursts, and instant death follows. **1866** R. W. DALE *Disc. Spec. Occ.* iii. 77 The sailors were in dread of almost instant destruction. *Mod.* The application gave instant relief.

c. Of a processed food: that can be prepared for use immediately. Also *transf.* and *fig.*, hurriedly prepared or carried out, etc.

1912 *Ladies' Home Jrnl.* Oct. 71/4 (Advt.), Instant Postum ..is regular Postum in concentrated form—made in the cup —no boiling required. **1915** E. B. HOLT *Freudian Wish* ii. 87, I wish I had..drunk less of that hot-wash that my wife calls instant coffee. **1924** *Ladies' Home Jrnl.* Oct. 198/1 G. Washington's Delicious Instant Coffee... The coffee ready to drink when dissolved in hot water. **1957** D. KARP *Leave me Alone* xi. 151 Your grand new world of jet airplanes, nylon stockings, frozen food, instant coffee and brain-washing. **1957** *Amer. Speech* XXXII. 313 Instant lather.. instant shaving lather. **1958** *Woman* 18 Oct. 4/3 In these days of 'ready-mix' cakes, 'instant puddings' and other time-saving boons to the busy housewife. **1959** *News Chron.* 26 Sept. 3/5, I tried the new instant tea... I measured out a half teaspoonful of the instant powder, poured on hot water and stirred in milk. *Ibid.* 30 Oct. 6/4 British food firms are being chary about introducing 'instant meals'... Instant bread comes as small frozen pebble shapes which fluff up to fresh crisp rolls after a few minutes in the oven. **1961** H. TRACY *Season of Mists* vii. 84 Sit you down, and I'll make the coffee, nice real instant coffee, none of your messy old grounds. **1962** *Listener* 25 Jan. 185/1 Their habit of producing, on all sorts of occasions, bits of what may be called instant poetry. **1962** J. TERRAINE in *Jrnl. R. United Service Inst.* May 140 There are all too many [historical works] which fall into the category of what I call 'instant history', rapidly composed on the strength of a very fresh approach to the subject, generally devoid of any true period sense, and loaded with comment from false premises. **1963** *Sunday Times* 17 Feb. 29/6 September 3 [*sc.* 1939] is the roundest of capsules: instant peace, instant war, instant history... Instant history may be surface-glossing, but it has a jerky, filmic excitement about it. **1963** *Listener* 7 Mar. 427/3 'This post-war propaganda, piling corpse on corpse, heaping horror on futility, seems bound to fail...' Yet it is back with us now, in the hands of the 'instant historians'. **1965** *Hair Do* July 57/1 Instant curls: for the woman who longs for short, casual curls..the brief luxurious wig is the perfect hair do. **1965** *Punch* 13 Oct. 552/3 A bumper pack of Instant Art for the..young executive—with money. **1966** *Economist* 9 Apr. 161/1 This phrase 'hundred days' is itself out of fashion, because 'instant government' is now condemned as a derogatory term. **1967** *New Scientist* 9 Feb. 352/1 The preparation of instant food is very simple in principle. It consists essentially of precooking the food.. then proceeding to a complete or partial dehydration. **1967** *Observer* 26 Mar. 9 Music and 'instant sex' take subsidiary place to drugs as the real focus of the hippy sub-culture. **1967** U. SEDGWICK *My Learn-to-cook Book* 56 Fruit is an instant food. **1969** *New Yorker* 29 Nov. 167/1 How could Agnew be so confident of the *Register's* objectivity and so certain that it would find the speech worthy of an editorial —tantamount to 'instant analysis'. **1973** *Times* 22 Feb. 1/3 Rising demand for mueslis and instant porridges.

d. ***instant replay*** (U.S.) = *action replay* s.v. ACTION 16.

1973 *Maclean's Mag.* Feb. 80/2 TV instant replay multiplies analysis and assigns error: in the press boxes, after a goal has been scored, sports writers and sportscasters rush to the TV screen for the instant replay, usually shown in slow motion. **1985** *N.Y. Times* 23 Apr. C7/3 There are instant replays, and the running commentary that appears on screen for each play captures the poetry of baseball.

5. as *adv.* (*poet.*) Instantly, at once.

1602 SHAKS. *Ham.* I. v. 94 You my sinnewes, grow not instant Old; But beare me stiffely up. **1667** MILTON *P.L.* VI. 549 Instant without disturb they took Allarm. *a* **1763** SHENSTONE *Elegies* vii. 17 Instant a graceful form appear'd confest. **1813** T. BUSBY *Lucretius* I. 559 Its warmth we instant feel.

instant (ˈɪnstənt), *sb.* [ellipt. use of INSTANT *a.*: cf. med.L. *instans* (Du Cange), F. *instant* (Rabelais, 16th c.).]

I. 1. The point of time now present, or regarded as present with reference to some action or event; hence, point of time, moment.

a **1500** *Sir Beues* 964 (Pynson), They went to the kynge in that instant. **1576** FLEMING *Panopl. Epist.* 63 Which offereth unto me, at this instant, no lesse occasion of musing. **1608** D. T. *Ess. Pol. & Mor.* 31 Green figges, which at that instant were brought from thence. **1610** SHAKS. *Temp.* III. i. 64 The verie instant that I saw you, did My heart flie to your seruice. **1638** F. JUNIUS *Paint. of Ancients* 138 Phantasies..running in the mind at the very instant of conception. **1642** FULLER *Holy & Prof. St.* III. xix. 202 Of all the extent of time, onely the instant is that which we can call ours. **1653** H. COGAN tr. *Pinto's Trav.* xliv. 175, I made him no answer for the instant. **1714** STEELE *Reader* No. 7 (1723) 281 The Monitor of the day following, to wit on the Instant of my present writing. **1715–20** POPE *Iliad* XVII. 777 Fly to the fleet, this instant fly. **1776** GIBBON *Decl. & F.* I. 134 He wished impatiently for death, and hastened the instant of it. *Mod.* Come this very instant!

2. An infinitely short space of time; a point of time; a moment.

1398 TREVISA *Barth. De P.R.* II. xviii. (Add. MS. 27944), An Instant is a duringe that abydith nouȝt, for an Instant is and neuer was nothir shal be. **1570** BILLINGSLEY *Euclid* I. def. iii. 2 An instant in time, is neither tyme, nor part of tyme. **1651** JER. TAYLOR *Holy Dying* iii. §4 (1727) 68 That sorrow..which gives its smart but by instants and smallest Proportions of time. **1690** LOCKE *Hum. Und.* II. xiv. (1695) 94 Such a part of Duration..wherein we perceive no Succession, is that which we may call an Instant. **1713** ADDISON *Cato* I. iii, Every instant I expect him here. **1833** N. ARNOTT *Physics* (ed. 5) II. 82 Owing to the momentum acquired in the first instants. **1891** E. PEACOCK *N. Brendon* II. 68 He was not an instant too soon.

3. Phrases (from 1 and 2). †***at (in) one (an) instant***, at one and the same moment, concurrently. †***at one (an) instant***, in a moment, forthwith, immediately. ***in an instant, on*** (†***upon,*** †***in***) ***the instant***, etc. ***the instant***, elliptically = 'the very instant' or 'moment that', 'as soon as ever'.

1450–1530 *Myrr. our Ladye* 177 The charyte of god.. enflaumed them all in a poynte, momente or instante. **1509** BARCLAY *Shyp of Folys* (1570) 253 In one instant he falles agayne. **1559** W. CUNNINGHAM *Cosmogr. Glasse* 47 It should be midday with us, and them at one instaunt. **1600** SHAKS. *A.Y.L.* III. ii. 225 It is yong Orlando, that tript vp the Wrastlers heeles, and your heart, both in an instant. **1611** BIBLE *Isa.* xxix. 5 It shalbe at an instant suddenly. **1640** tr. *Verdere's Romant of Rom.* I. 17 A great Knight arriving in the instant. *Ibid.* III. 38 The place being on an instant covered with a world of people. **1755** H. WALPOLE *Lett. H. Mann* 15 June, The instant he leaves you, you, all the world, are nothing to him. **1842** GROVE *Corr. Phys. Forces* 78 The instant they are brought into metallic contact, chemical action takes place. **1856** KANE *Arct. Expl.* II. xxii. 217 He ran for it on the instant. **1875** JOWETT *Plato* (ed. 2) I. 224 What, replied Dionysodorus in an instant; am I the brother of Euthydemus?

†**4.** That which is present, or is (as a permanent fact). *Obs. rare.*

1677 GALE *Crt. Gentiles* IV. 285 Eternitie..is but one only fixed permanent *Is* or *Instant*..Eternitie is not a fluent instant, such as they make to be in Time, but 'nunc' or 'instans stans', a standing fixed permanent *Instant*.

II. †**5.** = INSTANCE *sb.* 6. *Obs.*

1560 JEWELL *Corr. Cole* Answ. 2nd Let., Aristotle giveth order to the opponent in many cases to require an instant, as I do now at your hand.

III. †**6.** Urgent entreaty: = INSTANCE *sb.* 1.

1610 HOLLAND *Camden's Brit.* 687 Upon her instant unto the Romans for aide, garisons were set.

IV. 7. An 'instant' beverage (see prec. 4 c); *spec.* instant coffee.

1954 *N.Y. Times Mag.* 19 Sept. VI. 52 The 'instants'.. soluble coffee, soluble cocoa. **1963** 'A. GILBERT' *Ring for Noose* xi. 132 Julie..asked if she could have coffee. 'I'll make you a cup of Instant, dear,' said kind-hearted Sally. **1968** J. PORTER *Dover goes to Pott* iii. 40 She offered the two detectives a cup of coffee..with..the assurance that there

was plenty more instant in the tin. **1973** 'D. HALLIDAY' *Dolly & Starry Bird* i. 4 He had the kettle on and the Instant on the table.

†**'instant**, *v.* *Obs.* [a. OF. *instanter* (1508 in Godef.), f. *instant* INSTANT *a.*]

1. *trans.* To urge, press, solicit, importune (a person); to ask for (a thing) urgently. Also *absol.*

1494 FABYAN *Chron.* VII. 649 Yᵉ Kyng shalbe instauntid to geue yerely vnto his sayd brother, in recompencement of yᵉ sayde duchy .xii. M. li. **1533-4** *Act 25 Hen. VIII*, c. 22 §1 To besech and instant your highnes..to fore se and prouide for the perfit suretie..of your..succession. **1541** PAYNEL *Catiline* xi. 15 b, There was no strete..in all the citie, but Catiline instanted, prouoked, temted, and stered. **1599** SANDYS *Europæ Spec.* (1632) 64 With..teares of love, instanting and importuning no other thing at their hands. **1687** N. JOHNSTON *Assur. Abbey Lands* 89 All the Bishops Instanted the Lords, that they would consent.

2. *intr.* To be close at hand, impend, draw near.

1541 PAYNEL *Catiline* xii. 17 The tyme instantynge to chose the consuls.

†**instan'taneal**, *a.* *Obs. rare*⁻¹. [f. L. type **instāntāne-us* + -AL¹.] = INSTANTANEOUS.

1644 DIGBY *Man's Soul* x. (1645) 100 Names and representations of their instantaneall sight of all things.

instantaneity (ɪnstəntəˈniːɪtɪ). [f. as INSTANTANE-OUS + -ITY; cf. F. *instantanéité* (1737 in Hatz.-Darm.).] The quality of being instantaneous; instantaneousness.

a **1763** SHENSTONE *Ess.* (1765) 12 The flashes of my friend S——..have no sort of claim to be called verses, besides their instantaneity. **1801** W. TAYLOR in *Monthly Mag.* XII. 582 The versatile instantaneity of pantomine scenery. **1882** *Knowledge* No. 12. 241 This apparent instantaneity of the action of gravity.

instantaneous (ɪnstənˈteɪnɪːəs), *a.* [f. L. type **instāntāne-us*, after *mōmentāneus* (prob. in med. or mod.L.: cf. F. *instantané*, 1734 in Hatz.-Darm.), f. *instānt-em* INSTANT; see -EOUS. Cf. *momentaneous*, *simultaneous*.]

1. a. Occurring or operating in an instant; done, completed, or reaching completion without any perceptible lapse of time.

1651 BAXTER *Inf. Bapt.* 194 Justification is a continued Act, and not any Instantaneous act. **1657** REEVE *God's Plea* 29 God's knowledge is instantaneous. **1737** THOMSON *To Mem. Ld. Talbot* 27 His Reason saw, With instantaneous View, the Truth of Things. **1822** IMISON *Sc. & Art* I. 462 The motion of electricity..is so rapid, that it appears to be instantaneous. **1878** LECKY *Eng. in 18th C.* I. i. 30 The effect on the English nation was instantaneous.

b. *Photogr.* Applied to an exposure whose duration is brief and predetermined by means of a shutter mechanism; orig. applied to those sufficiently brief for a moving object to be photographed (in contrast to the time exposures that were usual), and later to those for which the camera may be held in the hand (see quots.). Also *transf.*, applied to a shutter designed for taking such exposures, a photograph taken with one, etc. Now chiefly *Hist.*

1851 *Athenæum* 6 Dec. 1286/2 (*heading*) On the production of instantaneous photographic images. **1858** SUTTON & WORDEN *Dict. Photogr.* 229 Photographs obtained in a fractional part of a second of time are said to be instantaneous. **1867** SUTTON & DAWSON *Dict. Photogr.* 156 Mr. England and others use a guillotine sort of shutter, with a slot across it, which falls immediately in front of the sensitive plate... In some respects this is the best instantaneous shutter that has yet been devised. **1884** *Gaiety Theatre Programme* Oct. in L. de Vries *Victorian Advts.* (1968) 99/3 Superior Sets, comprising..Rectilinear Lens, with Instantaneous Shutter, suitable for taking instantaneous pictures of yachts sailing. **1891** W. E. WOODBURY *Encycl. Photogr.* 356 Instantaneous dry plates are those coated with a very highly-sensitive emulsion that will become sufficiently impressed by the rapid exposure of the image upon it. An instantaneous lens is one that admits a large amount of actinic light. *Ibid.* 357 Instantaneous Photography.—In the very earliest days of photography this term was applied to what would now be considered very slow work indeed. We now usually apply this term when the exposure does not exceed one second. **1902** *Encycl. Brit.* XXXI. 698/2 It [*sc.* an efficient shutter] should be adjustable for variable instantaneous and for prolonged or 'time' exposures. **1939** EMANUEL & DASH *All-in-One Camera-Bk.* 33 It is usual to divide the long series of commonly used exposures into two parts. Exposures of 1/50 or 1/100 second or less belong to the instantaneous group, whereas the slower shutter speeds, such as 1/10 or 1/5 second, and so on, count as time exposures. *Ibid.*, If your hand is reasonably steady you will be able to give an exposure of 1/25 without moving the camera. A picture of this kind, made without the help of a tripod or other fixed support, can be counted as a snap—an instantaneous exposure. **1973** B. JAY *Victorian Cameraman* 57 Instantaneous exposures were not possible when Frith first began his photographic business.

fig. **1867** ELLIS *E.E. Pron.* I. i. 17 Each written word is, as it were an instantaneous photograph of a living thing.

c. Applied to a gramophone record in which the grooves are made directly by the cutting stylus during recording, and to the making of such records.

1937 *Electronics* Sept. 65/3 (Advt.), Disclube protects the delicate sound impressions in the record groove... A 2 oz. bottle of Disclube will be sent..to any person or firm equipped to make instantaneous recordings. **1949** FRAYNE & WOLFE *Elem. Sound Recording* xiv. 263 Besides its commercial applications, instantaneous recording finds considerable use in the home and as an adjunct in some of the educational fields, such as voice and music training, although..magnetic recording is becoming a serious competitor in certain fields. *Ibid.* 270 There is little practical difference between the best instantaneous records and the best pressings..when both are played with good light-weight reproducers.

d. ***instantaneous (water-)heater*** = GEYSER 2.

1935 *Plumber & Decorator* Mar. 57/2 Instantaneous water heaters are of two types—the multi-point, supplying hot water to several taps in different parts of the house; the single-point 'geyser' supplying hot water at the place where it is fixed. **1940** *Chambers's Techn. Dict.* 450/2 Instantaneous water-heater. **1959** *Chambers's Encycl.* VII. 258/1 Instantaneous heaters may be multipoint, supplying hot water to a number of taps, or single point for one tap only.

2. Existing at or pertaining to some particular instant. Chiefly in *Dynamics*, as ***instantaneous axis, centre of rotation.***

1837 BABBAGE *Bridgew. Treat.* App. K. 250 It is to be deduced..from the means of the instantaneous heights of the tide at all intervening periods. **1854** TOMLINSON tr. *Arago's Chem.* 131 Its axis of rotation may change every moment; and this multitude of axes..are called the *instantaneous axes of rotation*. **1886** A. G. GREENHILL *Diff. & Int. Calc.* 241, *I*..is the centre of instantaneous rotation of the right angle.

instan'taneously, *adv.* [f. prec. + -LY².] In an instantaneous manner.

1. In an instant, in a moment; without any perceptible interval between beginning and completion.

1644 DIGBY *Mans Soul* xi. (1645) 117 *margin*, All pure spirits doe worke instantaneously. *a* **1711** KEN *Hymnotheo* Poet. Wks. 1721 III. 156 The Angels..Move Instantaneously from Space to Space, Thought is not quick enough to keep their Pace. **1754** RICHARDSON *Grandison* (1781) II. xxxii. 303 Lady L. is, or seems to be, instantaneously reformed. **1860** TYNDALL *Glac.* II. iii. 242 A vast portion of the sun's rays..can pass instantaneously through a thick sheet of water. **1863** GEO. ELIOT *Romola* xxii, The Florentines..instantaneously rushed between him and his captor.

2. In or at the particular instant.

1849 HERSCHEL *Outl. Astron.* xiii. (1858) 450 It does not follow..that the ellipse thus instantaneously determined will have the same elements as that similarly determined from the arc described in either the previous or the subsequent instant.

instan'taneousness. [f. as prec. + -NESS.] The quality or fact of being instantaneous; instantaneous character or nature.

1727 in BAILEY vol. II. **1828** in WEBSTER. **1859** J. BROWN *Rab & F.* (1862) 22 The mobility, the instantaneousness of that bud [a docked tail] were very funny and surprising. *a* **1871** GROTE *Eth. Fragm.* i. (1876) 6 The rapidity and instantaneousness of a simple feeling.

†**instantany**, *a.* *Obs. rare.* [ad. L. type **instāntāne-us*, or F. *instantané*: see INSTANTANEOUS and cf. *momentany*.] = INSTANTANEOUS.

1608-33 BP. HALL *Medit. & Vows* §107 Instantany motions are more proper for a spirit, than a dull rest. **1649** —— *Cases Consc.* III. x. (1654) 267 An ungrounded conceit of an instantany and entire creation of the world.

‖**instanter** (ɪnˈstæntə(r)), *adv.* [L. adv., urgently, earnestly, in late L. presently, at once.] Immediately, forthwith, at once. (Orig. and still techn. a law term, but now chiefly an emphatic substitute for *instantly*.)

1688 *Ellis Corr.* (1829) I. 365 The information being read, the Bishop would have excused their pleading to it *instanter*. **1813** SIR R. WILSON *Priv. Diary* II. 195 Nothing is done, militarily or politically, that I am not told *instanter*. **1827** JARMAN *Powell's Devises* II. 217 It is therefore in effect a devise of the whole estate *instanter* to B. **1840** HOOD *Kilmansegg, Death* ii, How their souls would sadden instanter. **1883** D. C. MURRAY *Hearts* I. 206 He was at your service *instanter*.

in'stantial, *a.* [f. L. *instāntia* INSTANCE *sb.* + -AL¹.] Of or pertaining to an instance or instances; furnishing an instance. Spec. ***instantial premiss*** (see quot. 1933). Hence **instanti'ality**, the state of being instantial.

1647 M. HUDSON *Div. Right Govt.* II. vi. 110 The Arguments..are partly Instantial, partly Rational. The Instances of Scripture are of two sorts. **1851** T. PARKER *Wks.* (Eng. ed.) VII. 260 A mighty multitude, an instantial, poor, ill-born..and ill-minded too. *a* **1860** —— *Serm.* (Cent.), Instantial cases of this great law of attraction. **1921** W. E. JOHNSON *Logic* I. x. 160 This entirely distinct and peculiar use of the term 'existential' has given rise to endless confusion; and..the term should be entirely discarded and replaced by some such term as *instantial*, or, more accurately, indeterminately instantial. **1922** —— *Logic* II. x. 210 The conclusion is a generalisation of a certain premiss or set of premisses which..may be spoken of as 'the instantial premiss'. **1933** C. A. MACE *Princ. Logic* xii. 243 Induction may be defined as a form of inference in which, given instantial premisses (i.e. premisses concerning 'instances' or particular cases), we draw a conclusion involving some measure of generalization of these premisses. **1961** E. NAGEL *Struct. of Sci.* iii. 31 The above premisses..contain a number of singular or instantial statements. **1966** J. ELLIS in C. E. Bazell *In Memory of J. R. Firth* 81 Contextual meaning is either potential or instantial (or, less unambiguously, 'potential' or 'actual'). *Ibid.*, Between these extremes we might recognize a cline of potentiality/instantiality.

instantiate (ɪnˈstænʃɪeɪt), *v.* [f. INSTANCE *sb.* (L. *instānti(a)* + -ATE³.] *trans.* To represent by an instance. Also **in'stantiative** *a.*, of or pertaining to such instances; **in'stantiating** *ppl. a.*

1946 H. H. PRICE in *Proc. Brit. Acad.* XXXII. 117 This act of recognizing..is at the same time the verifying of a proposition, the discovering of a fact or truth. The proposition in question is an existential proposition (it might also be called an instantiative proposition). **1949** J. R. JONES in *Philos. Rev.* LVIII. 162 He expressly implies that they are instantiated in the concrete things to which they belong. **1951** J. HOLLOWAY *Lang. & Intelligence* ii. 18 Two apples..both instantiate the single universal redness. **1954** I. M. COPI *Symbolic Logic* iv. 100 The instantiating constant '*b*' occurs in the premiss. **1959** P. F. STRAWSON *Individuals* iv. 130 C is a member of a set of complete concepts K, such that all and only the members of K are, in fact, each uniquely instantiated. **1965** A. PLANTINGA in M. Black *Philos. in Amer.* 214 God could instantiate *P* by instantiating P_1. **1972** *Language* XLVIII. 350 Thus the ambiguity of the distinctive-feature relations is mirrored by the ambiguity..of the implementation rule, thereby instantiating one of the chief consequences of the iconic function.

instantiation (ɪnstænʃɪˈeɪʃən). [f. as prec. + -ATION.] The action or fact of instantiating; representation by an instance. Also *attrib.*

1949 J. R. JONES in *Philos. Rev.* LVIII. 162 It is the view that instantiation is necessarily a dyadic relation. **1953** H. H. PRICE *Thinking & Experience* i. 18 It is not easy to see how the doctrine of *universalia in rebus* can make room for this important and familiar notion of instantiation. **1954** A. J. AYER *Philos. Ess.* i. 18 The ∃x..has no descriptive force; it serves only to make an instantiation claim. **1954** I. M. COPI *Symbolic Logic* iv. 98 The instantiation rules *UI* and *EI* must be reformulated. **1956** E. H. HUTTEN *Lang. Mod. Physics* vi. 234 The second alternative, i.e. by instantiation, similarly suggests that we use the law as an empty schema. **1964** M. BLACK *Compan. to Wittgenstein's Tractatus* lxiii. 293 W. [*sc.* Wittgenstein] modifies the convention by demanding that visibly different variables shall be treated *differently* for the purpose of instantiation. **1972** *Language* XLVIII. 343 But a more difficult task also confronts the linguist: discovering the universal laws underlying language as a whole, of which specific rules are instantiations.

instantize (ˈɪnstəntaɪz), *v.* [f. INSTANT *a.* + -IZE.] *trans.* To make (foodstuffs) available in instant form (see INSTANT *a.* 4 c). So **'instantized** *ppl. a.*

1962 R. J. CLARKE in *Proc. 1st Internat. Congr. Food Science & Technol.* (1965) IV. 5 'Instantized' milks, with lowered bulk density are making their appearance. **1970** *Americana Ann.* 58 The department contracted..for the purchase of 'instantized' nonfat dry milk for distribution in welfare programs. **1970** *New Scientist* 24 Dec. 560/1 The formulated, instantised, convenience foods will no longer look like meat, milk, cereal or vegetable.

'instantly, *adv.* [f. INSTANT *a.* + -LY².]

1. Urgently, persistently, with importunity. *arch.*

c **1477** CAXTON *Jason* 29 Whan he had required them instantly and admonested them to doo well he dide doo marche them ayenst their enemyes. **1526** *Pilgr. Perf.* (W. de W. 1531) 86 Labour instauntly, or busyly, & worke with thy handes all that thou mayst. **1526** TINDALE *Luke* vii. 4 They ..besought him instantly. **1577-87** HOLINSHED *Chron.* (1807-8) III. 31 The knights themselves, who uerie instantlie had stood in this error..besought the archbishop to pardon them. **1631** RUTHERFORD *Lett.* xvi. (1862) I. 72 Pray instantly..for this King. **1849** MACAULAY *Hist. Eng.* i. I. 150 Both Houses instantly invited the King to return.

†**b.** Pressingly, so as to press upon. *Obs.*

1638 F. JUNIUS *Paint. of Ancients* 72 Some fierce conquerours..are instantly at their heeles, persecuting, wounding.

†**2.** At this or that very moment; now, just now, just. *Obs.*

c **1485** *Digby Myst.* (1882) IV. 380, I Haue beyne with the Iuge Pilat instantlye. **1596** DALRYMPLE tr. *Leslie's Hist. Scot.* VIII. 138 Our quene is instantlie lychter of a bony barne. **1632** LITHGOW *Trav.* IX. 396 Arriving at Messina.. I encountered with [some Englishmen] who instantly were both come from Malta.

3. In a moment; immediately, forthwith, at once.

1552 HULOET, Instantly, *euestigio*. **1593** SHAKS. *2 Hen. VI*, V. ii. 27 Addresse thee instantly. **1607** TOPSELL *Four-f. Beasts* (1658) 262 Instantly upon the same, came the holy Chariots of Jupiter. **1653** WALTON *Angler* 50 You must do me one courtesie, it must be done instantly. **1794** NELSON 26 July in Nicolas *Disp.* (1845) I. 459 He has never expressed a wish that has not instantly been complied with. **1860** TYNDALL *Glac.* I. xviii. 129 The snow melted instantly wherever it came in contact with the rock.

b. *conjunctively* (with or without *that*, †*as*). The moment that, as soon as.

1793 MRS. E. PARSONS *Woman as she should be* I. 193 The poor lady was actually dead almost instantly that she perpetrated the fatal deed. *Ibid.* II. 84 Almost instantly as I alighted, I fainted. **1827** J. SYMMONS in E. H. Barker *Parriana* (1828) I. 533 Instantly the Doctor was out of his stirrups, 'the calumet of peace' was lighted. **1852** THACKERAY *Esmond* I. 38 He ran across the grass instantly he perceived his mother.

4. Immediately (in position). *rare.*

1849 RUSKIN *Sev. Lamps* iii. §6. 69 Opposite the south-east angle..the dome is seen rising instantly above the apse and transepts.

†**'instantness.** *Obs. rare.* [f. as prec. + -NESS.] The quality of being instant. **a.** Instancy, earnestness. **b.** Immediateness.

1548 UDALL *Erasm. Par. Luke* xi. 106 b, The better to stiere his seruauntes vnto the instauntenesse of praiyng..he added..a parable. **1599** MINSHEU II, Instantness, *instancia*. **1727** BAILEY vol. II, *Instantness*, the Immediateness.

instar (ɪnˈstɑː(r)), *v.* Also 7 **en-**. [IN-[1].]

1. *trans.* To set as a star; to make a star of.

1592 Daniel *Delia* xxvii, Though time do spoyle her of the fairest vaile That euer yet mortallitie did couer; Which shall instarre the needle and the trayle. **1633** Ford *Love's Sacr.* IV. ii, Our heart is high instarr'd in brighter spheres. **1855** Bailey *Mystic*, etc. 100 Grim-tuskèd boar.. Whom ancient myths in the heavenly north instarred.

2. To set or adorn with or as with stars; to stud with stars or brilliants.

1652 Benlowes *Theoph.* I. lxix, Those rayes enstarre the duskie Parts. **1715–20** Pope *Iliad* XVII. 55 The shining circlets of his golden hair.. Instarr'd with gems and gold. **1824** Wiffen *Tasso* XIV. xxxix, The rich flood did all its banks instar With precious stones, enchanting to the sight.

Hence **instarred** (ɪnˈstɑːd), *ppl. a.*, set with stars.

1888 'C. E. Craddock' (Mrs. Murfree) *Despot Broomsedge Cove* vii. (1889) 117 The thickly instarred, moonless sky.

instar (ˈɪnstɑː(r)), *sb. Ent.* [mod.L. (L. H. Fischer *Orthoptera Europæa* (1853) I. 37), a. L. *instar* form, figure, likeness.] Any of the stages in the life of an insect or other arthropod between successive ecdyses, including the stage between hatching from the egg and the first ecdysis; also (and orig.), an individual arthropod at a particular stage.

1895 D. Sharp in *Cambr. Nat. Hist.* V. v. 158 It may be well to adopt a term suggested by Fischer, and call the Insect as it appears at hatching the first instar, what it is as it emerges from the first ecdysis the second instar, and so on. **1925** A. D. Imms *Gen. Textbk. Entomol.* II. 176 The intervals between the ecdyses are known as stages or stadia, and the form assumed by an insect during a particular stadium is termed an instar. **1932** Metcalf & Flint *Fund. Insect Life* vi. 156 The molts occurring during the growing period divide this life stage.. into a number of sharply separated sizes or steps that are called instars. **1964** R. M. & J. W. Fox *Introd. Compar. Ent.* viii. 268 Most spiders provide a cocoon in which the first two instars are spent in passive existence. **1970** *Nature* 24 Oct. 382/1 In Jamaica the fifth instar larvae of the New World hawkmoth.. exhibit four basic colours.

instate (ɪnˈsteɪt), *v.* Also 7–8 **en-**. [f. IN-[2] + STATE *sb.* Cf. *reinstate*.]

1. *trans.* To put (a person) into a certain state or condition; to place in a certain position; to install, establish. Const. *in* (*into*, *to*).

1613 Heywood *Silv. Age* I. Wks. 1874 III. 95 Faire Danaes sonne instated in my throne. **1667** Pepys *Diary* 10 Mar., He will enstate the King of Spayne in the kingdom of Portugall. **1709** Atterbury *Serm.* (1723) II. 258 To have them accepted as holy, and instated in the favour of God. **1833** I. Taylor *Fanat.* iii. 65 The unalterable maxims of rectitude.. being.. firmly instated in their just authority. **1864** E. Sargent *Peculiar* III. 267 Be sure it will not be my fault if she is not at once instated in her rights.

b. with adj. complement.

1633 Heywood *Eng. Trav.* II. Wks. 1874 IV. 32 'Tis enough, that word Alone, instates me happy.

†**2.** To endow or invest (a person) *with*. *Obs.*

1603 Shaks. *Meas. for M.* V. i. 429 For his Possessions.. We doe en-state, and widow you with all, To buy you a better husband. **1614** Lodge *Life Seneca* vi, Before his advancement in Court [he was] plentifully enstated, for his father had left him rich. **1659** T. Wall *Char. Enem. Ch.* 9 The office of a King doth enstate him with power, for the administration of Justice.

†**3.** To confer (a thing) *on* or *upon*. *Obs.*

1641 M. Frank *Serm., 5th on Xmas* (1672) 86 A blessed lot, a goodly heritage, blessedness itself enstated upon him. **1647** *Power of Keys* Pref. 1, The Prime Act of Power enstated by Christ on his Apostles.

Hence **in'stating** *vbl. sb.*

1647 *Power of Keys* i. 4 This formall compleat instating of this power upon them. **1659** Hammond *On Ps.* ii. Paraphr. 9 The instating and setling of David peaceably and triumphantly in his Kingdome.

instatement (ɪnˈsteɪtmənt). Now *rare*. [f. prec. vb. + -MENT.] Instating; establishment.

a **1677** Barrow *Serm.* (1686) II. xxx. 425 Having not onely a just title to what justification doth import, but a real instatement therein. **1746–7** Hervey *Medit.* (1818) 106 We hold our possession of the former; we expect an instatement in the latter. **1877** M. Arnold *Last Ess. Ch.* 47 The instatement of God's kingdom.

in statu nascendi: see IN *Lat. prep.*

in statu pupillari: see IN *Lat. prep.*

†**in'staur**, another form of INSTORE *v.*, *Obs.* = next.

†**in'staurate**, *v. Obs.* [f. L. *instaurāt-*, ppl. stem of *instaurāre*: see INSTORE.] *trans.* To restore, renew; to erect; to supply; = INSTORE *v.*

1583 Stubbes *Anat. Abus.* II. (1882) 81 To instaurate abbeies, prieries, nunries, with other sumptuous edefices. **1635** Mede *Let. to Twisse* 12 Aug., Wks. (1672) IV. 834 To encourage the people lately returned from Captivity, to build their Temple and instaurate their Commonwealth. **1666** J. Smith *Old Age* (ed. 2) 256 It is far more easie.. to overthrow the positive assertions of others than.. to instaurate better in their room.

instauration (ɪnstɔːˈreɪʃən). [ad. L. *instaurātiōn-em*, n. of action f. *instaurāre* to restore: see INSTORE *v.* Cf. F. *instauration* (16th c. in Hatz.).]

1. The action of restoring or repairing; restoration, renovation, renewal.

a **1603** T. Cartwright *Confut. Rhem. N.T.* (1618) 621 At the time of the instauration of all things. **1612** Selden *Notes Drayton's Poly-olb.* xi. 186 If you referre it to instauration of what was discontinued by Wilfrids returne to his Archbishoprique. [**1620** Bacon (*title*) Instauratio Magna. *Ibid.* 35 (Sub-title) Pars Secunda operis quæ dicetur Novum Organum, sive Indicio Vera de Interpretatione Naturæ.] **1625** Bacon *Ess.* Ded. Dk. Buckhm., My Instauration, I dedicated to the King: My Historie of Henry the Seuenth.. to the Prince. *a* **1661** Fuller *Worthies* (1840) I. 135 He gave the first institution, or (as others will have it) the best instauration, to the university of Oxford. **1761** *Biog. Dict., Ld. Bacon* II. 8 At this time he appears to have drawn the first out-lines of his grand instauration of the sciences. **1879** M. Pattison *Milton* vi. 68 Its aim was to realise in political institutions that great instauration of which Bacon dreamed in the world of intelligence.

†**2.** Institution, founding, establishment. *Obs.*

1614 Raleigh *Hist. World* II. (1634) 491 Knowing the instauration of these games to have been in the 408th yeare after Troy. **1631** Heywood *Eng. Eliz.* (1641) 53 The inchoation and instauration of a glorious Church and Commonweal. **1778** Bp. Lowth *Transl. Isaiah* Notes (ed. 12) 213 The instauration and advancement of states.

instaurator (ˈɪnstɔːreɪtə(r)). [a. late L. *instaurātor*, agent-n. f. *instaurāre* to INSTAURATE. Cf. F. *instaurateur* (16th c. in Godef.).] **a.** One who repairs or renews; a restorer. **b.** One who institutes or establishes; a founder.

1660 H. More *Myst. Godl.* v. xvii. 203 Such Enthusiasts and Impostours, who being wholy ignorant of the affairs of the Kingdom of Christ, will yet pretend to be the great Instaurators of his Empire. **1817** Coleridge *Biog. Lit.* I. ix. 152 The first instaurator of the dynamic philosophy in England. **1841** D'Israeli *Amen. Lit.* (1867) 659 A striking evidence how imperfectly the genius of the Instaurator of sciences was comprehended. **1879** M. Pattison *Milton* iv. 46 The great instaurator of all knowledge, Bacon, in preaching the necessity of altering the whole method of knowing, included.. the method of teaching to know.

instead (ɪnˈstɛd), *phrasal comb.* Forms: 3 **ine stude**; 3–4 **in stude**, 4 **in stud**, **in (yn) sted**, 4–5 **in stede**, **in stid**, **in stide**, 6 **in steede**, *Sc.* **in steid**, **(in stayd)**, 6–7 **in steed**, **in steade**, **in stead**; **insteed(e**, 7 **insted**, 7– **instead**. [The two words *in stead* = 'in place', rarely written as one word before 1620, but seldom separately after *c* 1640, exc. when separated by a possessive pronoun or possessive case, as *in my stead*, *in* Duke William's *stead*. Most frequently followed by *of*, in the prepositional phrase *in stead of*, *instead of* (= Fr. *au lieu de*); formerly also *in the stead of*, which is still used dialectally, e.g. in the southern counties of Scotland. See STEAD *sb.*

Of 16 instances of the phrase occurring in the 1623 Folio of Shakspere, 6 are printed conjunctly; but not one of these so occurs in the earlier quartos. The only instance of the conjunct spelling before 1620 is that in 3 Hen. VI, II. vi. 54, where the *True Tragedy* of 1595 has 'Insteed of that', and 1619 'Instead of that'. In all other instances, the earlier reading is *in steed*, or *in stead*. Thus in 1 Hen. IV, v. iii. 8 the 1623 Folio has 'insted of thee', but the Qo. of 1598 'in steed of thee', and the 6 Qos. 1599–1632 'in stead of thee'.]

1. Phrase. ***instead of***, † ***in stead of***: In place of, in lieu of, in room of; for, in substitution for.

α. separately. (Also ***in the stead of*** (obs. or dial.). For *in his stead*, *in his friend's stead*, and the like, see STEAD *sb.*)

(In quot. 1557 *of* is omitted before the inf.)

a **1225** *Ancr. R.* 22 Siggeð a last, ine stude of Benedicamus, 'Requiescant in pace'. **1297** R. Glouc. (Rolls) 4358 Is dragon arerd of golde As in stude of is baner. *a* **1300** *Cursor M.* 1139 In sted o þi noþer sede, Ne sal þe groue bot þorne and wede. *c* **1449** Pecock *Repr.* I. iv. (MS.) 8 b, Hise newe sacramentis wiþ whiche he chargid þe peple of cristen, in stide of.. oold sacramentis. **1485** Caxton *Paris & V.* 53 That he be recommaunded as your son in stede of me. **1551** Robinson tr. *More's Utop.* II. i. (1895) 122 The chykens, assone as they be come owte of the shell, followe men and women in steade of the hennes. **1557** North tr. *Gueuara's Diall Pr.* 231 a/1 In stede to healpe hym to dye well, [he] putteth hym in vayne hope of long lyfe. **1584** R. Scot *Discov. Witchcr.* x. viii. (1886) 148 Either fat, or oile in steed thereof. **1611** Bible *Transl. Pref.* 3 Catholicon the drugge, that it is in stead of all purges. **1639** Fuller *Holy War* i. 2 Pella.. which served them in stead of a little Zoar. **1688** R. Holme *Armoury* III. 407/2 Q.. is a Letter of small use, and put only in stead of C. [**1718** *Freethinker* No. 56 ¶8 In the Stead of the Sanction was Established the famous Concordat.]

β. As one word.

1595 Shaks. *True Trag. Rich. Dk. Yorke* C iv b, Insteed of that [3 Hen. VI. II. vi. 54, In steade whereof], let this supplie the roome. **1612** Brinsley *Lud. Lit.* 101 The translation leadeth the schollar as by the hand, or insteed of his Master. **1634** W. Tirwhyt tr. *Balzac's Lett.* (vol. I.) 42 Thinke you not they made vse of their hands insteede of feete. **1662** Stillingfl. *Orig. Sacr.* I. ii. §10 Preserved in their Temples, which were instead of Libraries to them. **1709** Steele *Tatler* No. 18 ¶1 It was written, This is the Beer, instead of, This is the Bear. **1766** Goldsm. *Vic. W.* iii, Instead of money he gave promises. **1852** Mrs. Carlyle *Lett.* II. 182 We went on the Saturday instead of the Friday. **1892** Gardiner *Stud. Hist. Eng.* 6 They burned instead of burying their dead.

b. *Instead of* may also be used elliptically before a preposition, adverb, adjective, or phrase.

1834 Sir H. Taylor *Autobiog.* (1885) I. 194 People.. called upon to conform to my taste, instead of to read something which is conformable to theirs. **1865** R. W. Dale *Jew. Temp.* Notes (1877) 303 The Law was to be written on the hearts of men instead of on tables of stone. *Mod.* I found the patient worse instead of better. You should be out instead of in, on such a fine day. I found it on the floor instead of in the drawer.

2. Without *of*: In its stead, in stead or in place of the thing mentioned; as a substitute.

1667 Milton *P.L.* XII. 54 To rase Quite out thir Native Language, and instead To sow a jangling noise of words unknown. **1821** Shelley *Dirge for Year* i, Come and sigh, come and weep! Merry hours, smile instead. **1836** J. H. Newman *Par. Serm.* (1837) III. iii. 39 When we look for evidence of his faith.. we discover instead a deadness to all considerations. **1866** Ruskin *Eth. Dust.* 17 The money which the English habitually spend in cutting diamonds.. if it were applied to cutting rocks instead [etc.].

†**in'steadfast**, *a. Obs. rare*[−1]. [IN-[3].] Not steadfast, unsteadfast.

1728 T. Cooke *Hesiod's Theogony* 775 Epimetheus of insteadfast Mind, Lur'd to false Joys, and to the future blind.

instealing (ˈɪnˌstiːlɪŋ), *ppl. a.* [IN *adv.* 11 a.] Stealing in; entering stealthily.

1844 E. B. Elliott *Horæ Apoc.* (1862) I. 293 The awful features of the instealing phantom.

insteam (ɪnˈstiːm), *v. rare.* [f. IN-[2] + STEAM.] *trans.* To furnish or provide with steam.

1891 G. Meredith *One of our Conq.* I. v. 69 They are engines.. insteamed to pursue their infuriate course.

†**'insteep**, *sb. Obs. rare*[−1]. [f. IN-[1] + STEEP *v*: cf. next.] Infusion.

1551 Turner *Herbal* I. B vj a, Mesne gyueth in pouder or pylles from a drame and a halfe to two drammes, and in instepe or infuse from a drame and a halfe vnto iij. drammes and a halfe.

insteep (ɪnstiːp), *v.* Now *rare.* Also 7 **en-**. [f. IN-[1] + STEEP *v.*, after L. *immergĕre*.] *trans.* To immerse; to steep or soak *in*; to imbrue.

1599 Shaks. *Hen. V*, IV. vi. 12 Suffolke first dyed, and Yorke all hagled ouer Comes to him, where in gore he lay insteeped, And takes him by the Beard. **1604** —— *Oth.* II. i. 70 The gutter'd-Rockes, and Congregated Sands, Traitors ensteep'd, to enclogge the guiltlesse Keele. **1611** Florio, *Inmollare*, to ensteepe, to moisten. **1782** Downman tr. *Wormius' Death Song Ragnar Lodbrach*, The hard blue sword insteep'd in gore.

instellation (ɪnstəˈleɪʃən). *rare.* [f. L. *in-* (IN-[2]) + *stella* star + -ATION: cf. *constellation*.] A placing among the stars; a making into a star.

1832 J. Wilson in *Blackw. Mag.* XXXI. 694 Shakspeare has been long enthroned in instellation. **1835** *Ibid.* XXXVII. 287 The instellation of the noblest spirit that ever had its mortal dwelling in a peasant's breast.

instep[1] (ˈɪnstɛp). Also 6 **insteppe**, 7 **-stup**, **-stoppe**, **-stip**. [app. f. IN-[1] + STEP; but the application has not been accounted for. The forms in Cotgr. and Minsheu appear to be corruptions.]

1. a. The upper surface of the human foot between the toes and the ankle.

1530 Palsgr. 234/2 Insteppe of the fote, *col du pie*. **1544** Phaer *Regim. Lyfe* (1546) H ij, On the hyer syde of the insteppe. *Ibid.* (1553) I j a, The veyne.. called saphena.. lieth outwarde beetwene the insteppe and the hele. **1591** Percivall *Sp. Dict.*, *Garganta del pie*, the instep. **1611** Cotgr., *Le montant du pied*, th' instup. **1617** Minsheu, The Instoppe of the foote, *coudepied*. **1624** Massinger *Parl. Love* IV. v, Is not this a pretty foot, And a clean instep? **1777** Sheridan *Trip Scarb.* I. ii, They hurt me just below the instep. **1866** Geo. Eliot *F. Holt* vi, Her own pretty instep, clad in a silk stocking. **1880** Ouida *Moths* I. 10 She always gave her miniature feet and arched insteps their natural play.

b. Phrase. ***high in the instep***, haughty, proud. Now *dial.*

1562 J. Heywood *Prov. & Epigr.* (1867) 164 He is hie in thynstep, his steps may be hie, But to stepe in good steps he stepth nothyng nie. **1580** Hollyband *Treas. Fr. Tong*, *Hautain*, loftie, high in the insteppe. **1617** Moryson *Itin.* II. 26 Now the Gentleman was growne higher in the instep, as appeared by the insolent conditions he required. **1639** Fuller *Holy War* II. viii. (1647) 53 He was too high in the instep to wear another mans shoes. **1828** *Craven Dial.* s.v., 'She is rather high in her instep', she is proud and haughty.

2. a. That part of the hind-leg of a horse which extends from the hock to the pastern-joint. **b.** The corresponding part in the leg of a bird. **c.** In insects: see quot. 1826.

c **1720** W. Gibson *Farrier's Guide* I. vi. (1738) 98 The Instep-bone.. is made up of three Bones. **1751** Chambers *Cycl. Supp.*, *Instep*, in the manege, is that part of a hinder leg of a horse, that corresponds to the shank in the fore-leg. **1783** Lightfoot in *Phil. Trans.* LXXV. 11 The instep [of Motacilla] is covered with seven large imbricated scales. **1826** Kirby & Sp. *Entomol.* xxxiii. III. 385 *Planta* (the Instep). The first joint of the Tarsus is so called when it is remarkably long and broad. It includes the Calx.

3. a. That part of a shoe, stocking, etc., fitting or covering the instep. Hence ***instep-gusset***, ***-hole***, ***-needle***.

c **1615** *Songs Costume* (Percy Soc.) 112 On the feet pinked shooes, Insteps had roses red. **1623** tr. *Favine's Theat. Hon.* III. iv. 360 To weare it on the instup of their Shoes. **1711** Steele *Spect.* No. 48 ¶4, I am mounted in high-heeled Shoes with a glased Wax-leather Instep. **1853** Kingsley *Hypatia* vii. 86 An embroidered shoe, with a large gold cross on the instep. **1880** *Plain Hints Needlework* 48 Cast on 31 stitches, knit a heel, turn it, pick up instep, cast on false instep, and knit the instep gusset and cast off.

b. The arched part of a boot or shoe between the heel and the sole.

1826 *Kaleidoscope* VI. 223/2 A boot-jack of this description..has an equal purchase on the instep and heel. **1913** E. C. Bentley *Trent's Last Case* v. 106 On each [shoe], in the angle between the heel and the instep, he detected a faint trace of red gravel. **1927** 'E. Bramah' *Max Carrados Mysteries* 160 He slyly inserted a nail in the angle of the instep.

4. A part of a hill, a tree trunk, or the like, resembling the human instep in shape or position.

1681 Cotton *Wond. Peake* (ed. 4) 24 At th' instep of just such another Hill, There creeps a Spring that makes a little Rill. **1859** Thoreau *Early Spring in Mass.* 17 Mar. (1881) 163, I know it to be a striped squirrel, and soon see its long unseen striped sides flirting about the instep of an oak. **1862** B. Taylor *Home & Abroad* Ser. II. II. iii. 69 Crossing the insteps of hills, and then into an apparently boundless plain. **1865** Carlyle *Fredk. Gt.* XIX. vii. V. 580 Instep or glacis of the Pirna rock-country.

† **'instep**[2]. *Obs. rare.* [f. the phrase *to step in*: see IN *adv.* 11 d.] The act of stepping in, the first step, the commencement.

1621 Bp. Mountagu *Diatribæ* II. 380 At the first instep into this Chapter. **1624** —— *Gagg* I. 5 Thus in the very insteppe of his pamphlet, he belyeth the Protestant for his opinion. *a* **1641** —— *Acts & Mon.* (1642) 57 Cardinall Baronius..in the very instep into his Apparatus..was much mistaken in Justin Martyr.

instigant ('ɪnstɪgənt). [ad. L. *instigānt-em*, pr. pple. of *instigāre* to INSTIGATE.] One who or that which instigates; an instigator.

1833 *New Monthly Mag.* XXXVIII. 95 Lur'd by his devilish instigant, he tries. **1840** *Tait's Mag.* VII. 26, I look upon our firesides as the instigants of our domestic happiness.

instigate ('ɪnstɪgeɪt), *v.* Pa. pple. -ated; also 7 instigat. [f. L. *instigāt-*, ppl. stem of *instigāre* to urge, set on, incite, f. *in-* (IN-[2]) + **stigāre*: cf. Gr. στίζειν (root στιγ-) to prick.]

1. *trans.* To spur, urge on; to stir up, stimulate, incite, goad (now mostly to something evil).

1542 Boorde *Dyetary* viii. (1870) 245 It doth instygate and lede a man to synne. **1639** Woodall *Wks.* Pref. (1653) 2 Some Noble man, who was instigated thereunto through an excellent and divine power. **1651** Hobbes *Leviath.* III. xlii. 278 To instigate Princes to warre upon one another. **1671** *True Nonconf.* 469 The only motive..whereby Henry was instigat to reject the Pope. **1747** Johnson *Plan Eng. Dict.* Wks. 1787 IX. 185 Commonly, though not always, we *exhort* to good actions, we *instigate* to ill. **1841** Brewster *Mart. Sc.* III. iii. (1856) 204 The proud Duke of Tuscany, instigated no doubt by Galileo, sent Kepler a gold chain. **1855** Browning *Fra Lippo* 316 'Ay, but you don't so instigate to prayer!' Strikes in the Prior. **1875** Jowett *Plato* (ed. 2) IV. 335 You..must not instigate your elders to a breach of faith.

2. To bring about by incitement or persuasion; to stir up, foment, provoke.

1852 Thackeray *Esmond* II. iv, What he and they called levying war was, in truth, no better than instigating murder. **1868** Milman *St. Paul's* iii. 47 The mission of Otho had been instigated by the King.

Hence **'instigated**, **'instigating** *ppl. adjs.*; **'instigatingly** *adv.*, in an instigating manner, so as to instigate.

1611 Cotgr., *Instigué*, instigated, incited, vrged. **1702** De Foe *Reform. Manners* Misc. (1703) 81 How Clito comes from instigating Whore, Pleads for the Man he cuckold just before. **1856** Webster, *Instigatingly*.

instigation (ɪnstɪ'geɪʃən). [ad. L. *instigātiōn-em*, noun of action from *instigāre* to INSTIGATE. Cf. F. *instigation* (1332 in Hatz.-Darm.).] The action of instigating or goading; an urging, spurring, or setting on; incitement, stimulation.

c **1422** Hoccleve *Jereslaus' Wife* Moral., The howndes, þat is to seyn, the wikkid thoghtes, alway berken, & maken swich instigacioun. **1480** Caxton *Chron. Eng.* III. (1520) 26/1 It was denyed hym..by the instygacyon of a lord called Pompei. **1512** *Helyas* (W. de W.) 1 Here begynneth the hystory of the noble Helyas knyght of the swanne newly translated out of frensshe in to englysshe at thynstygacyon of the puyssaunt & illustryouse prynce lorde Edwarde duke of Buckyngham. **1613** Purchas *Pilgrimage* (1614) 362 Alexander..by instigation of wine, and Thais his Concubine,..burned this sometime-Treasure-house of Persia. **1665** Evelyn *Diary* 5 Apr., This terrible warr, begun doubtlesse at secret instigation of the French to weaken the States & Protestant interest. **1762** Jefferson *Corr.* Wks. 1859 I. 181, I should not have accused the Devil, because..hunger, without the addition of his instigations, might have urged them to do this. **1840** Macaulay *Ess., Clive* (1887) 537 Chunda Sahib fell into the hands of the Mahrattas, and was put to death, at the instigation probably of his competitor, Mahommed Ali. **1867** Freeman *Norm. Conq.* (1870) I. v. 264 That this foul deed was done by the instigation, if not by the personal order, of his step-mother.

b. That in which this action is embodied; an incentive, stimulus, spur.

1526 *Pilgr. Perf.* (1531) 34 b, Which illusyon and perylous instigacyon, as soone as it was detected & brought to lyght ..anone it auoyded & was defeted. **1601** Shaks. *Jul. C.* II. i. 49 Speake, strike, redresse. Brutus, thou sleep'st: awake. Such instigations haue beene often dropt, Where I haue tooke them vp. **1710** Addison *Tatler* No. 148 ¶3 When I have seen a young Lady swallow all the Instigations of high Soups, seasoned Sauces, and forced Meats. **1869** Goulburn *Purs. Holiness* ii. 18 The good instigations which from time to time visit your heart.

instigative ('ɪnstɪgeɪtɪv), *a.* [f. L. *instigāt-* (see INSTIGATE *v.*) + -IVE.] Having the quality of instigating; tending to instigate; stimulative.

1642 T. Case *Gods Rising* (1644) 29 In respect of the instigative and directive Office of conscience. **1850** McCosh *Div. Govt.* III. iii. §2. 424 We owe to the instigative feelings a large portion of human energy and activity.

instigator ('ɪnstɪgeɪtə(r)). Also 6-7 -er. [a. L. *instigātor*, agent-n. f. *instigāre* to INSTIGATE. Cf. F. *instigateur* (14th c. in Hatz.-Darm.).] One who instigates or sets on; an inciter, stimulator.

1598 Florio, *Instigatore*, an egger on, a prouoker, a pricker forward, an instigater. **1607** Rowlands *Guy Warw.* 46 Have I..been the instigator unto ought That is unjust in righteous Heavens sight? *c* **1665** Mrs. Hutchinson *Mem. Col. Hutchinson* (1846) 88 The King had another instigator of his own violent purposes..and that was the queen. **1786** Burke *Articles W. Hastings* Wks. 1842 II. 228 Being himself the first mover and instigator of that injustice. **1869** Freeman *Norm. Conq.* (1870) I. App. 653 The chief instigator of the murder.

insti'gatrix. *rare.* [a. L. *instigātrix*, fem. agent-n. f. *instigāre* to INSTIGATE.] A female instigator.

1611 Cotgr., *Stimulatrice*, a stimulatrix, an instigatrix. **1674** Brevint *Saul at Endor* 109 The Woman should be the Instigatrix, or the first Sollicitress. **1902** *Dublin Rev.* July 105 Lady Macbeth, the instigatrix of the murder.

instil, instill (ɪn'stɪl), *v.* [ad. L. *instillāre* to put in by drops, f. *in-* (IN-[2]) + *stillāre* to drop: cf. F. *instiller* (16th c. in Hatz.).]

1. *trans.* To put in by drops; to introduce drop by drop or in small quantities.

1547 Boorde *Brev. Health* ccclxiv, Instyll into the eare the oyle of bitter Almons. **1601** Holland *Pliny* xx. xvii. 66 The juice..dropped or instilled into the head, is good for the paines thereof. **1667** Milton *P.L.* XI. 416 Michael..from the Well of Life three drops instill'd. **1745** Needham *Microsc. Disc.* iii. 26 Then instilling two or three Drops of Water into the Concave Object-Glass. **1891** J. Jacobs *Ess. & Rev., J. H. Newman* 144 A poem's impressiveness, one might say, depends on the number of heart's drops instilled into it. **1900** *Brit. Med. Jrnl.* No. 204. 258 It would be as well to instil eserine before the patient left the hospital.

2. To introduce (some immaterial principle, notion, feeling, or quality) little by little into the mind, soul, heart, etc.; to cause to enter by degrees; to infuse slowly or gradually; to insinuate.

1533 Frith *Answ. More* Wks. (1573) 166/2 As a faythfull preacher by the worde doth instill it into vs by our eares and hearing. **1538** Latimer *Rem.* (1845) 392 Some instilled into him that..he should have suffered afterward for treason. **1667** Milton *P.L.* VI. 269 How hast thou instill'd Thy malice into thousands. **1670** Walton *Lives* III. 160 Instilling into his Soul the seeds of Piety. **1796** Eliz. Hamilton *Lett. Hindoo Rajah* II. 248 These qualities are so carefully instilled at the seminaries of female education. **1895** F. Hall *Two Trifles* 3 Right notions, to be instilled most effectively, must be instilled in childhood.

†**b.** To teach or urge assiduously or stealthily.

1660 Milton *Brief Notes Serm.* ¶1 The humour of returning to our old Bondage, was instill'd of late by some Deceivers. **1806-7** J. Beresford *Miseries Hum. Life* (1826) I. Introd., It wholesomely instils the advantages of frugality.

†**3.** To imbue *with*. *Obs. rare*$^{-1}$.

1644 Milton *Educ.* Wks. (1847) 99/1 Flattery and courtshifts, and tyrannous aphorisms appear to them the highest points of wisdom; instilling their barren Hearts with a conscientious slavery.

Hence **instilled** (-'ɪld) *ppl. a.*, **in'stilling** *vbl. sb.*

1659 Rushw. *Hist. Coll.* I. 101 The instilling thereof into the peoples knowledge by little and little. **1736** Berkeley *Disc. Magistr.*, etc. Wks. III. 430 Bias to good from early principle or instilled opinion.

instile, variant of INSTYLE *v.*

†**in'stillant**, *a. Obs. rare*$^{-1}$. [ad. L. *instillānt-em*, pr. pple. of *instillāre* to INSTIL.] Entering as by instillation; entering gently.

1504 Atkynson tr. *De Imitatione* III. ii. 196 The swete instyllaunt spekynge of his lorde god.

instillation (ɪnstɪ'leɪʃən). [ad. L. *instillātiōn-em*, n. of action from *instillāre* to INSTIL.]

1. The action of instilling; introduction (of a liquid) drop by drop; †the liquid thus instilled.

1608 Topsell *Serpents* (1658) 695 The instillation of this Crocodile, folded up in the Wooll of a black Sheep of the first birth..hath power to drive a quartane Ague. *a* **1619** Fotherby *Atheom.* II. xiv. §5 (1622) 359 He doth it, not by instillation, but by infusion. **1742** Perry in *Phil. Trans.* XLII. 49 Upon the Instillation of Spirit of Vitriol, it deposited a Milk-white greasy Sediment. **1829** Landor *Imag. Conv.* Wks. 1846 II. 47 Let them slumber..in their sunny orchards, without the instillation of that fatal poison. **1879** *St. George's Hosp. Rep.* IX. 483 Notwithstanding the repeated instillation of eserine drops, the pupil was fully dilated from the action of atropine.

transf. and *fig.* **1750** Johnson *Rambler* No. 72 ¶1 Petty qualities..make the draught of life sweet or bitter by imperceptible instillations. **1752** *Ibid.* No. 207 ¶11 The instillations of this frigid opiate.

2. The action of instilling or gradually introducing some feeling, notion, or principle into the mind, soul, or heart; infusion; also, something thus instilled, an insinuation.

c **1540** tr. *Pol. Verg. Eng. Hist.* (Camden) I. 290 Bie the instillation of Godde..reconciliation and concorde forthwith ensewed. **1611** Speed *Hist. Gt. Brit.* VII. xxxviii. (1632) 396 His eare euer opened vnto the instillations of Parasites. **1884** *Bazaar* 22 Dec. 664/1 The painting is thorough, with full instillation of the spirit of the scene portrayed.

instillator ('ɪnstɪleɪtə(r)). [agent-n. in L. form from L. *instillāre* to INSTIL: see -ATOR.] One who instils; an instiller.

a **1834** Coleridge *Lit. Rem.* (1838) III. 403 If the oil-instillator, out of sight and from within, had represented the corrupt nature of man.

instillatory (ɪn'stɪlətərɪ), *a.* [f. L. ppl. stem *instillāt-* + -ORY.] Relating to instillation.

1882 in Ogilvie.

instiller (ɪn'stɪlə(r)). [f. INSTIL *v.* + -ER[1].] One who instils or infuses.

1676 Marvell *Mr. Smirke* 45 Yet that Herod..though he wanted not his instillers, apprehended no Commotion. **1749** P. Skelton *Deism Revealed* viii. (T.), Never was there..so artful an instiller of loose principles as my tutor.

instilment (ɪn'stɪlmənt). [f. INSTIL *v.* + -MENT.] The action of instilling; infusion.

1773 in Johnson ed. 4 (misquoting Shaks. *Ham.* I. v. 64, where the word is Distilment). **1826** Margravine of Anspach *Mem.* I. iii. 81 Mr. Foster was remiss in his instilments of these moral and religious principles. **1850** Hawthorne *Scarlet L.* xx. (1879) 248 The instilment thereof into her mind. **1865** M. Arnold *Ess. Crit.* ii. 71 Persuasion, the instilment of conviction.

†**in'stimulate**, *v. Obs.* [f. ppl. stem of L. *instimulāre*, f. *in-* (IN-[2]) + *stimulāre* to STIMULATE. Cf. obs. F. *instimuler* (16th c. in Godef.).] *trans.* To incite, instigate, stimulate.

1570 Levins *Manip.* 42/3 Instimulate, *instimulare*. **1623** Cockeram, *Instimulate*, to prouoke, pricke forward. **1670** G. H. *Hist. Cardinals* I. I. 24 They are prick'd forward, and instimulated to good deeds by the Divine Spirit.

Hence †**instimu'lation**.

1658 Phillips, *Instimulation*, the same as *Instigation*. **1721** in Bailey.

†**in'stimulating**, *a. Obs. rare*$^{-1}$. [IN-[3].] Not stimulating.

1740 Cheyne *Regimen* 344 Living on..insipid and instimulating Food only, which is the Case of most of the Poor or Indigent.

instinct ('ɪnstɪŋkt), *sb.* Also 6-7 instincte. [ad. L. *instinct-us* instigation, impulse, f. *instinguĕre* to instigate, incite, impel; f. *in-* (IN-[2]) + *stinguĕre* orig. to prick, stick (cf. *distinct*, *extinct*); root *stig-* as in *instigate*. Cf. also F. *instinct* (in 14th c. *instincte*). Formerly stressed *in'stinct*.]

†**1.** Instigation; impulse; prompting. *Obs.*

1412-20 Lydg. *Chron. Troy* II. xii. (1555) Hj/2 Whan that beastes of reason rude and blinde Desyre the same by iust instinct [*MSS.* instymt, instynat, instaunce] of kinde. **1513** More in Grafton *Chron.* (1568) II. 777 Before such great thinges mennes harts (of a secret instinct of nature) misgeveth them. **1529** —— *Dyaloge* I. Wks. 160/2 By the secrete instyncte of the holy gost thei consent and agre together. **1563-87** Foxe *A. & M.* (1684) III. 9 Damasus by the instinct of Hierom appointed Gloria Patri after the Psalms. **1633** Bp. Hall *Hard Texts* 99 He began to have many instincts and strong motions from God. **1710** Prideaux *Orig. Tithes* v. 221 These Tithes..by the instinct of the Devil many have detained them. **1730** A. Gordon *Maffei's Amphith.* 168 This good Woman, following the Instinct of her own Piety [etc.].

2. Innate impulse; natural or spontaneous tendency or inclination. Formerly applicable to the natural tendencies of inanimate things. In modern use associated with sense 3.

1568 Tilney *Disc. Mariage* A vj b, Yea the trees..have a naturall instinct of friendship. **1603** Owen *Pembrokesh.* (1891) 78 A naturalle Instincte engraffed in the stones or lyme..against any wett weather to sweate with great dropps of water. **1663** Butler *Hud.* I. i. 233 To whom our Knight by fast Instinct Of Wit and Temper was so linkt. **1726** Leoni *Alberti's Archit.* I. 41/1 There is a natural instinct in all heavy bodies to lean and press upon the lowest parts. **1845** M. Pattison *Ess.* (1889) I. 9 The instinct of pilgrimage, as it has been said, belongs not exclusively to religion at all. **1874** Symonds *Sk. Italy & Greece* (1898) I. i. 6 Our love of the Alps is..a Teutonic instinct. **1874** Green *Short Hist.* viii. §5. 500 He [Charles I] had..neither the grander nor the meaner instincts of the born tyrant. **1875** Stubbs *Const. Hist.* II. xiv. 107 Edward was by instinct a lawgiver.

3. *spec.* An innate propensity in organized beings (esp. in the lower animals), varying with the species, and manifesting itself in acts which appear to be rational, but are performed without conscious design or intentional adaptation of means to ends. Also, the faculty supposed to be involved in this operation (formerly often regarded as a kind of intuitive knowledge).

1596 Shaks. *1 Hen. IV*, II. iv. 299 Beware Instinct, the Lion will not touch the true Prince: Instinct is a great matter. I was a Coward on Instinct. **1664** Power *Exp.*

Philos. III. 183 Beasts..obey the prescript of their Natures, and live up to the height of that instinct that Providence hath given them. *a* **1677** HALE *Prim. Orig. Man.* I. ii. 48 The instincts of Animals are sensible instincts of a more noble kind and nature than those of Vegetables. **1692** BENTLEY *Boyle Lect.* ix. 314 That he might act, not of necessity, nor blind instinct like the Brutes. **1781** GIBBON *Decl. & F.* xxvi. (1869) II. 10 The operation of instinct is more sure and simple than that of reason. **1871** DARWIN *Desc. Man* I. iii. 100 The very essence of an instinct is that it is followed independently of reason. **1877** BARING-GOULD *Myst. Suffer.* 65 Instinct, the co-ordination and transmission of past experiences.

b. Any faculty acting like animal instinct; intuition; unconscious dexterity or skill.

1597 SHAKS. *2 Hen. IV*, I. i. 86 He that but feares the thing, he would not know, Hath by Instinct, knowledge from others Eyes, That what he feard, is chanc'd. **1768** STERNE *Sent. Journ.* (1778) I. 54 (*Remise Door*) Had not instinct more than reason directed me to the last resource. **1873** BLACK *Pr. Thule* (1874) 6 It was by a sort of instinct that he guided this open boat through the channels. **1873** HAMERTON *Intell. Life* 445 The true instinct of genius.

4. *Comb.*

1845 G. MURRAY *Islaford* 31 None to lull her instinct-dread of harm. **1890** BOLDREWOOD *Col. Reformer* (1891) 312 The scanty pasture provoked the instinct-guided cattle to wander far.

instinct (ɪn'stɪŋkt), *ppl. a.* Usually (in senses 2 and 3 always) const. as *pa. pple.* [ad. L. *instinct-us*, pa. pple. of *instinguĕre* (see prec.): cf. obs. F. *instinct* impelled, constrained (16th c. in Godef.).

Used in sense 2 by Milton, Swift, and Pope; but characterized by Johnson in 1755 as 'a word not in use', and so in Dicts. down to Craig 1847; revived about 1800 in sense 3, which is app. due to a misunderstanding of the meaning in Milton, Swift, and Pope.]

†**1.** Implanted naturally; innate. *Obs.*

1538 STARKEY *England* I. i. 18 Neclygence of man, wych suffryth hys sedys, by nature instincte, by wordly occasyonys to be ouer run. **1628** T. SPENCER *Logick* 34 It moues according vnto the instinct, and inbred disposition of nature.

†**2.** Impelled, moved, excited, inflamed, animated.

1667 MILTON *P.L.* II. 937 The strong rebuff of som tumultuous cloud Instinct with Fire and Nitre. *Ibid.* VI. 752 Forth rush'd..The Chariot..undrawn, It self instinct with Spirit. **1704** SWIFT *Batt. Bks.* Misc. (1711) 228 A new Species of controversial Books..instinct with a most malignant Spirit. *Ibid.* 247 Coffee-house Wits instinct by me, can correct an Author's Stile. **1715-20** POPE *Iliad* XVIII. 442 Full twenty tripods..That plac'd on living wheels..instinct with spirit roll'd From place to place.

3. In recent use: Imbued or charged *with* something, as a moving or animating force or principle.

1797-1803 J. FOSTER *Jrnl.* in *Life & Corr.* (1846) I. 178 Burke's sentences are pointed at the end,—instinct with pungent sense to the last syllable. **1813** SHELLEY *Q. Mab* I. 134 Ianthe's Soul..Instinct with inexpressible beauty and grace. **1821** —— *Def. Poetry* i. in *Ess. & Lett.* (Camelot) 21 Livy is instinct with poetry. **1822** B. CORNWALL *Girl Provence* lx, Through all the palace..Instinct with light, a living splendour ran. **1837** CARLYLE *Fr. Rev.* I. VII. iv, Instinct with life to its finger-ends. **1844** LD. BROUGHAM *A. Lunel* (1872) I. i. 14 Her features were instinct with expression reflecting the spirit within. **1861** TULLOCH *Eng. Purit.* ii. 340 Digressions..instinct with meaning to his audiences. **1878** H. S. WILSON *Alp. Ascents* i. 3 The Matterhorn..instinct with malignant cruelty. **1888** MRS. H. WARD *R. Elsmere* xiv. (1894) 196 The room seemed instinct with a harsh commanding presence.

†**in'stinct,** *v. Obs.* [f. L. *instinct-*, ppl. stem of *instinguĕre* to instigate: see INSTINCT *sb.*]

1. *trans.* To instigate, prompt, impel internally.

1549 CHALONER *Erasm. on Folly* F iij b, The good simple people of the olde golden worlde..lived onely as Nature taught and instincted them. **1663** *Flagellum or O. Cromwell* 6 He Dreamed, or a Familiar rather instincted him and put it into his Head, that He should be King of England. **1694** R. BURTHOGGE *Reason* 40 This false conceit of his being immediately Instincted and moved by the Spirit of God.

2. To implant naturally or as an instinct; to infuse as an animating principle.

1538 [see INSTINCT *ppl. a.* 1]. **1540** RAYNOLD *Byrth Mankynde* IV. ii. (1634) 187 God..hath..instincted such a power and vertue vnto these mortall creatures. **1627** FELTHAM *Resolves* II. [I.] lxiv. (1628) 183 Though I doubt whether I may bee of their opinion, who vtterly take away all reason from Beasts, yet I verily beleeue, these are things, that were neuer instincted in them. **1732** BENTLEY *Pref. Milton's P.L.* a iij, What native, unextinguishable Beauty must be impress'd and instincted through the Whole, which the Defoedation of so many Parts by a bad Printer..could not hinder from shining forth?

3. To perceive by instinct. *nonce-use.*

1865 MRS. WHITNEY *Gayworthys* (1866) 204 There were sugar-plums in her bag, and the children instincted them afar off like flies.

†**in'stinction.** *Obs.* [a. obs. F. *instinction* (15th c.), f. L. type **instinctiōn-em*, n. of action f. *instinguĕre* to instigate: see INSTINCT *sb.*]

1. Instigation; prompting; inspiration.

1490 CAXTON *How to Die* 8 That ofte cometh by instyncyon of the deuyl. **1531** ELYOT *Gov.* I. xiii, Tulli in his Tusculane questyons supposeth, that a poete can nat abundantly expresse verses sufficient and complete..without celestiall instinction. **1534** WHITINTON *Tullyes Offices* II. (1540) 106 By the instynction of nature men were accompanyed togyther. **1633** T. ADAMS *Exp. 2 Peter* i. 20 By his [the Lord's] help and instinction only we preach and expound the prophets. **1670** LASSELS *Voy. Italy* II. 39 St. Gregory..moved by Godly instinction (as John Stow sayth) sent Augustin.

2. Innate or natural impulse; instinct.

1531 ELYOT *Gov.* III. iii, This naturall instinction of creatures unreasonable is necessary and also commendable. **1590** BARROUGH *Meth. Physick* III. lxiii. (1639) 200 There followeth this temperature, an instinction..to lecherie, and driness of the whole body. **1600** F. WALKER *Sp. Mandeville* 96 a, Brute Beastes are led and guided by a naturall instinction and appetite. **1753** *Life Frith* in *Wks.* (1829) 74 In the nature of this young man, being but a child, God had planted marvellous instinctions and love.

instinctive (ɪn'stɪŋktɪv), *a.* (*adv.*) [f. L. *instinct-*, ppl. stem of *instinguĕre* to instigate + -IVE: see INSTINCT *sb.*, and cf. F. *instinctif* (1803 in Hatz.).] Of the nature of instinct; operating by or resulting from instinct or innate prompting.

1649 G. DANIEL *Trinarch., Hen. IV*, c, From Instinctive Causes, and the strict Impresse of Nature, none must Life neglect. **1652** BP. HALL *Invis. World* I. §6 Have we had instinctive intimations of the death of some absent friends..who but our angels hath wrought it? **1718** LADY M. W. MONTAGU *Lett. to C'tess [Bristol]* (1887) I. 240 So powerful is the instinctive fondness natural to parents. **1855** BAIN *Senses & Int.* II. iv. §6 (1864) 267 The alternation of the lower limbs is instinctive in man. **1859** DARWIN *Orig. Spec.* viii. (1878) 205 An action which we ourselves require experience to enable us to perform, when performed by an animal..without experience, and when performed by many individuals in the same way, without their knowing for what purpose it is performed, is usually said to be instinctive. **1861** GEO. ELIOT *Silas M.* xii, Her arms had not yet relaxed their instinctive clutch.

b. *poet.* as *adv.* = *instinctively*.

1715-20 POPE *Iliad* VIII. 544 Swifter than thought the wheels instinctive fly. **1827** POLLOK *Course T.* VII, Instinctive every soul Flew to its clayey part.

instinctively (ɪn'stɪŋktɪvlɪ), *adv.* [f. prec. + -LY².] In an instinctive manner; by instinct; by some innate prompting; without conscious thought or purpose.

1610 SHAKS. *Temp.* I. ii. 148 A rotten carkasse of a Butt, not rigg'd, Nor tackle, sayle, nor mast, the very rats Instinctiuely haue quit it. **1774** GOLDSM. *Nat. Hist.* (1776) VII. 135 At this time the female is instinctively taught that her young ones want relief. **1855** MRS. GASKELL *North & South* xxii. (1897) 187 Margaret..drew her ruffled, luxuriant hair instinctively over the cut. **1870** J. H. NEWMAN *Gram. Assent* II. viii. 279 However sure we are of the accuracy of our instinctive conclusions, we as instinctively put them into words. **1883** FROUDE *Short Stud.* IV. II. vi. 248 The intellect..instinctively dreads lies.

instinc'tivity. *rare*⁻¹. [f. as prec. + -ITY. Cf. F. *instinctivité* (Littré).] The quality of being instinctive; proneness to instinctive action.

1830 COLERIDGE *Table-t.* 2 May §1 There is growth only in plants; but there is irritability, or, a better word, *instinctivity*, in insects.

'instinctless, *a.* [INSTINCT *sb.* + -LESS.] Without or lacking instinct.

1890 W. JAMES *Princ. Psychol.* I. ii. 77 Schrader gives a striking account of the instinctless condition of his brainless pigeons. **1947** A. EINSTEIN *Mus. Romantic Era* xiii. 181 This return [to antiquity]..was no longer inspired by the reverential Classicism of the 18th century, but rather by the indiscriminate and instinctless 'learnedness' of the 19th.

[**instinctly,** *adv.* Error for INSTINCTIVELY.

1855 MRS GASKELL *North & South* xxii Margaret..drew her ruffled, luxuriant hair instinctly [so in ed. 1855; ed. 1897 instinctively] over the cut. Hence in **1871** HOPPE *Engl.-Deutsches Suppl.-Lex.*, **1881** OGILVIE (Annandale), and some later Dicts.]

†**in'stinctment.** *Obs. rare*⁻¹. [f. INSTINCT *v.* + -MENT.] Instigation, prompting, inspiration.

1627-77 FELTHAM *Resolves* II. iii. 162 In obedience to the commands of God, and the Instinctments of Nature.

instinctual (ɪn'stɪŋktjuːəl), *a.* [f. INSTINCT *sb.* (L. *instinctu(s)* + -AL.] Of or pertaining to, involving or depending upon, instinct.

1924 G. KNOX *Land of Afternoon* 294 She possessed the female's instinctual power to project this force. **1925** J. RIVIERE et al. tr. *Freud's Coll. Papers* IV. 62 A stimulus of instinctual origin does not arise in the outside world but from within the organism itself. **1934** H. C. WARREN *Dict. Psychol.* 140/1 *Instinctual fusion*, the theory that every mental process is the result of a fusion of the life instinct and the death instinct. **1937** H. READ *Art & Society* vii. 263 This passage clearly implies an opposition between instinctual (imaginative, creative) activity and practical, mechanical activity. **1945** KOESTLER *Yogi & Commissar* III. iv. 228 Its instinctual root is probably the feeling of insecurity. **1955** J. C. FLÜGEL *Stud. Feeling & Desire* iv. 100 In civilised societies suicide is hardly ever considered as occurring as a result of a natural or instinctual impulse. **1957** R. F. C. HULL tr. *Jung's Coll. Works* I. 132 Here it is not so much a lack of ethical feelings..as an excess of instinctual drives. **1966** R. ARDREY *Territorial Imperative* (1967) ii. 46 The pattern..is common to the species and is instinctual.

†**instinged** (ɪn'stɪŋd), *ppl. a. Obs. rare*⁻⁰. [f. IN-² + STING *sb.*] Furnished with a sting.

1611 FLORIO, *Inuespito*, inwasped, instinged.

instipulate (ɪn'stɪpjʊlət), *a. Bot.* [IN-³.] Not stipulate, having no stipules, exstipulate.

1847 in CRAIG. **1855** in MAYNE *Expos. Lex.*

†**in'stirred,** *a. Obs. rare.* [IN-³.] Unstirred.

1677 FELTHAM *Resolves* I. lxxvii. 118 Like the wind..It disperses Exhalations from the muddy Earth, which would, instirr'd, infect it.

institor ('ɪnstɪtɔː(r)). [a. L. *institor*, agent-n. from *insistĕre* to step upon, to follow, pursue: see INSIST.] A factor or agent; a broker; a retailer, huckster, vendor. (Chiefly in *Rom.* and *Sc. Law.*)

1657 TOMLINSON *Renou's Disp.* 396* Neither the Incolists that make these Pastils, nor the Institors that buy them, mix Goat's blood therewith. **1681** STAIR *Inst. Law Scot.* I. xii. §19 Our custom hath not so fully owned the Roman Law as to institors, as it has as to exercitors. **1754** ERSKINE *Princ. Law Scot.* III. iii. §14 Tho' the *institors* be pupils, and so cannot bind themselves, the prepositor..stands obliged by their deeds. **1858** G. J. BELL *Comm. Laws Scot.* I. vi. §4 (ed. 6) 177 An *Institor* or the person who has the management of a shop, has a presumed authority to bind his principal. [**1880** MUIRHEAD *Gaius* Dig. 509 A *paterfamilias* or owner, who had placed his *filiusfamilias* or slave as *institor* in charge of a shop or other business.]

insti'torial, *a. Rom.* and *Sc. Law.* [f. L. *institōrius* of or belonging to an institor + -AL¹.] Of or pertaining to an institor.

1858 G. J. BELL *Comm. Laws Scot.* I. vi. §4 (ed. 6) 177 As applied to banks, institorial power has raised many questions. *Ibid.*, The public is entitled to trust to the full unlimited institorial power in dealing with any officer placed in the apparent trust of receiving money. **1883** *Wharton's Law Lex.* (ed. 7), *Institorial power*, the charge given to a clerk to manage a shop or store.

insti'torian, *a. Rom. Law.* [f. as prec. + -AN.] = prec.

1853 WHEWELL *Grotius* II. II. xi. §13. 46 Hence we may understand that an exercitorian action (one against ship-owners for the contracts of the captain) and an institorian action, (one against the owner of a trading concern for the contracts of the acting agent,) depend on Natural law. **1880** MUIRHEAD *Gaius* IV. §71 The institorian action is employed when a person has committed the management of a shop or business..to his son or slave, or to some stranger.

institory, *a.* [ad. L. *institōri-us*, f. *institor*: see above.] = INSTITORIAL.

1681 STAIR *Inst. Law Scot.* I. xii. §19 The prætor by the perpetual edict did introduce the Institory Action, in which, by the Contracts of Institors in relation to that wherein they were intrusted, their prepositors are oblieged.

†**institue,** *v. Obs.* Also 4-5 **instue.** [a. F. *instituer* (1219 in Godef. *Compl.*), ad. L. *instituĕre* to INSTITUTE.] *trans.* = INSTITUTE *v.* Hence †**instituing** (**instuing**) *vbl. sb.*

c **1380** WYCLIF *Wks.* (1880) 450 Instuyng wiþ inducting and many oþere mannus lawis weren not to charge. **1382** —— *Heb.* xi. 7 He..is instued [*gloss* or ordeyned] eir of riȝtwysnesse. *c* **1450** *Mirour Saluacioun* 1845 The sacrament instuyd he. **1483** CAXTON *Gold. Leg.* 31/1 Thenne he instiued this holy sacrament. **1525** LD. BERNERS *Froiss.* II. cxiii. [cix.] 326 The emperoure..had institude hym to be..souerayne regarder of the Languefryde. **1529** MORE *Suppl. Soulys* Wks. 318/2 The great..capitayne of goddes people dyd institue and ordayne the great feaste of the dedicacion of the temple. **1611** FLORIO, *Instituire*,..to institue.

institute ('ɪnstɪtjuːt), *sb.*¹ [ad. L. *institūt-um* purpose, design, plan, ordinance, instruction, precept; sb. use of neut. of *institūtus*, pa. pple. of *instituĕre* to INSTITUTE. Cf. F. *institut* (17th c. in Hatz-Darm.). In sense 3, corresp. to F. *institute*, *-s*, ad. late L. *institūta* pl., in sense of cl.L. *institūtiōnes*.]

†**1.** Purpose, design. *Obs.*

a **1520** BARCLAY *Jugurth* (ed. Pynson) 19 a, But nowe wyll I returne to myne institute & purpose concernyng the dyscriptyon of Affrike. **1528** ROY *Rede Me* II. (Arb.) 110 A vowe of folisshnes To accomplysshe Satans institute. *a* **1670** HACKET *Abp. Williams* I. (1692) 118 That which comes to the institute I handle.

2. a. Something instituted; an established law, custom, usage, or organization; an institution.

1546 LANGLEY *Pol. Verg. de Invent.* (*c* **1560**) 95 It is a Godly Institute, and I would that there were mo suche ceremonies to help the pore. **1670** MILTON *Hist. Eng.* II. Wks. (1847) 494/1 Teaching and promoting like a public father the institutes and customs of civil life. **1700** DRYDEN *Sigism. & Guisc.* 518 This law, though custom now diverts the course, As Nature's Institute, is yet in force. **1787** GLOVER *Athenaid* XXVI. 26 Greek institutes require The nearest kindred on the fun'ral stage The dead to lay. **1844** LINGARD *Anglo-Sax. Ch.* (1858) I. i. 31 Veneration for the monastic institute.

†**b.** The act of instituting; institution. *Obs.*

1641 MILTON *Reform.* I. ¶2 Then was..water, sanctify'd by Christ's institute, thought little enough to wash off the original spot. **1657** *Divine Lover* 37 In this contemplatiue way few or none hath appeared since their first institute aboue these hundred yeares.

3. A principle or element of instruction; usually in *pl.*, a digest of the elements of a subject, esp. of jurisprudence. (So in F.) Cf. INSTITUTION 5.

Institutes of Justinian (*Institutiones Justiniani*), an elementary treatise on Roman Law, compiled by order of the Emperor Justinian in 533 A.D., and intended as an introduction to the Pandects. It was based mainly on the ***Institutes of Gaius*** (*Institutiones Gaii*), compiled in the 2nd cent. A.D., long lost, but recovered in 1816. (The Byzantine Greeks explain ἰνστιτοῦτα by εἰσαγωγαί introductions.)

1579 LYLY *Euphues* (Arb.) 112 Thou wilt not beat thy braines about the institutes of the Law. *c* **1590** MARLOWE

Faust. I. 31 Where is Justinian?.. A pretty case of paltry legacies!.. Such is the subject of the institute, And universal body of the law. **1656** BLOUNT *Glossogr., Institute*..a precept, preparing a way to some Art..As Justinians Book of Institutes. **1693** DRYDEN *Persius* v. (1697) 475 Thou art pale, in mighty Studies grown, To make the Stoick Institutes thy own. **1787** JEFFERSON *Writ.* (1859) II. 128, I have read your book..Its learning and its good sense will, I hope, make it an institute for our politicians. **1801** B. RUSH (*title*) Six Introductory Lectures to a Course of Lectures upon the Institutes and Practice of Medicine. **1816** SCOTT *Antiq.* xxxv, I can amuse mysel' very weel with the larger copy of Erskine's Institutes. **1821** JEFFERSON *Autob.* Writ. 1892 I. 58 To compose a new Institute like those of Justinian and Bracton, or that of Blackstone,..would be an arduous undertaking. **1886** *Syd. Soc. Lex., Institutes of medicine*, the explanation or statement of the principles on which medicine is based, being the science called Physiology.

4. a. A society or organization instituted to promote some literary, scientific, artistic, professional, or educational object; also, the building in which the work of such a society is carried on. Freq. with qualifying epithet or as the designation of some particular society or class of societies, as *Literary, Philosophical, Mechanics' Institute*, or (without defining word) esp. as shortened form of ***Women's Institute.*** See also INSTITUTION 7, which is used in the same way.

Apparently at first repr. F. *institut*, the name given to the institution (*Institut National des Sciences et des Arts*) created in France in 1795, to replace the old academies which had been suppressed at the Revolution; after various changes, this now consists of five academies, each devoted to the advancement of a particular branch of literature, science, or art. Thence applied in Great Britain to associations or institutions having somewhat similar aims (though none of them with the comprehensive character and organization of the French Institute); e.g. the Royal Institute of British Architects (founded 1834), Royal Archæological Institute (1843), Royal Institute of Painters in Water Colours, Anthropological Institute, Iron and Steel Institute, Institute of Chartered Accountants, of Actuaries, etc., Royal Colonial Institute, Imperial Institute, etc. Also applied to local institutions for the advancement and dissemination of knowledge, by lectures, reading-rooms, libraries, educational classes, etc, as the Midland Institute, Birmingham, and the various Mechanics' Institutes, founded since 1820, Working Men's Institutes in villages, etc.

1829 *Censor* 87 Lecturing for sixpence a head at the Mechanics' Institute. **1838** *Penny Cycl.* XII. 497/2 Bonaparte..gave a new organization to the National Institute. **1839** *Ibid.* XIV. 127/2 London..Societies and establishments connected with science, literature, and the arts... The Mechanics' Institute, in Southampton Buildings, established in 1823. **1851** HT. MARTINEAU *Hist. Peace* (1877) III. v. v. 263 They established schools, institutes, lecture and reading rooms. **1889** *Harper's Mag.* Mar. 501/1 The title of Member of the Institute is the highest distinction to which a Frenchman of culture can aspire; it is the crowning honour of his career. **1924** KIPLING *Debits & Credits* (1926) 116 She told me there was a whist-drive that afternoon at the Institute. **1939** M. SPRING RICE *Working-Class Wives* v. 111 A woman in another Essex village speaks of 'work for the Institute'. **1959** M. M. KAYE *House of Shade* vi. 74 She misses the Institute and the Girl Guides.

b. In *U.S.* (See quot.)

1890 J. G. FITCH *Notes Amer. Sch. & Training Coll.* 90 By an 'Institute' is meant a sort of normal class, held periodically for the teachers of a district, and furnishing instruction in the art and practice of education, and an opportunity for the discussion of methods. Institutes are, in fact, migratory and occasional academies.

'institute, *sb.*² *Rom.* and *Sc. Law.* [ad. L. *institūt-us* (person) instituted (as heir).] The person to whom an estate is first given in a testament or destination. (See quots.)

1681 STAIR *Inst. Law Scot.* III. viii. §18 Substitution is the nomination of substituted heirs, who take place, failing the institute. **1754** ERSKINE *Princ. Law Scot.* III. viii. §8 The person first called in the tailzie, is the institute; the rest, the heirs of tailzie, or the substitutes. **1861** W. BELL *Dict. Law Scot.* s.v., Where a person executing a settlement dispones his lands to A, whom failing, to B, &c., A is the institute, B, and all who follow him in the destination are heirs, or substitutes. **1880** MUIRHEAD *Ulpian* xxii. §33 Heirs are called..institutes, when their names are mentioned in the testament in the first place, substitutes when in the second or a subsequent place.

†**'institute,** *ppl. a. Obs.* Forms: 4–6 **institut,** 6–7 **institute.** [a. AF. *institut* (Britton), ad. L. *institūt-us*, pa. pple. of *instituĕre*: see next.]

= INSTITUTED. **a.** as *pa. pple.*: see INSTITUTE *v.*

c **1325** *Poem Times Edw. II* 67 in *Pol. Songs* (Camden) 326 Whan this newe parsoun is institut in his churche. *c* **1400** *Apol. Loll.* 51 So no þing be askid for personis of þe kirk to be browt in to þer segis, nor for presthed to be institut. **1502** *Ord. Crysten Men* v. vi. (W. de W. 1506) 406 The lawes, yᵗ haue ben instytute by the sapyence dyuyne. **1532–3** *Act 24 Hen. VIII*, c. 12 §1 Oon Supreme heede and King.. institute and furnysshed by the goodnes and sufferaunce of Almyghtie God with plenarie..power. **1671** *True Nonconf.* G iij, The end, for which Deacons were first institute.

b. as *ppl. a.*

1668 HOWE *Bless. Righteous* (1825) 83 Though this image, in respect of corrupted nature, be supernatural; in respect of institute, and undefiled nature, it was..natural.

institute ('ɪnstɪtjuːt), *v.* [f. L. *institūt-*, ppl. stem of *instituĕre* to set up, establish, found, appoint, ordain, begin, arrange, order, teach. f. *in-* (IN-²) + *statuĕre* to set up, establish: see STATUTE.

The pa. pple. *institut(e* (see prec.) was the earliest part of the vb. adopted, and continued to be used (also as pa. t.) long after the regular *instituted* was also current, being prob. felt to some extent as a shortened form of the latter: cf. the pa. pple. and pa. t. *lit, set, put*, etc.]

1. *trans.* **a.** To set up, establish, found, ordain; to introduce, bring into use or practice.

1483 CAXTON *Cato* E v, Thus hath god Instytuted and ordeyned hit. **1530** PALSGR. 591/2, I instytute, I ordayne a thynge to be done. **1538** STARKEY *England* I. iv. 110 Thys.. was wel consyderyd of them wych fyrst instytute thys law of inherytaunce. **1585** T. WASHINGTON tr. *Nicholay's Voy.* IV. xxix. 152 The famous games called Istmetiques, instituted by Theseus upon envie of those which Hercules had instituted in Olimpe. **1596** SHAKS. *Tam. Shr.* I. i. 8 Heere let vs breath, and haply institute A course of Learning, and ingenious studies. **1678** WANLEY *Wond. Lit. World* v. iii. §9. 474/1 Telesphorus a Grecian, instituted the Lent of seven weeks before Easter. **1732** BERKELEY *Serm. to S.P.G.* Wks. III. 238 This laudable Society, instituted for the Propagation of the Gospel. **1761** JOHNSON *Let. to Baretti* 10 June in *Boswell*, The artists have instituted a yearly exhibition of pictures and statues. **1853** J. H. NEWMAN *Hist. Sk.* (1873) II. I. iii. 107 Honorius the Second instituted the order of Knight Templars to protect the pilgrims.

†**b.** To ordain *that* something shall be, or something *to be. Obs.*

1485 CAXTON *Chas. Gt.* 228 He..Instytuted that al the bysshops..shold..be subget to the bysshop of saynt Iames. **1538** STARKEY *England* I. iv. 136 Wych..was the purpos of the Romaynys, when they fyrst instytute al dyuyne seruyse to be rehersyd in that tong. **1596** DALRYMPLE tr. *Leslie's Hist. Scot.* IV. 230 He Jnstitute, that al thing sulde be done conforme to the rule of Justice. **1631** WEEVER *Anc. Fun. Mon.* 255 Siluester instituted, that..poore people should be prouided for.

†**c.** To order, arrange, put into form, frame. *Obs.*

1538 STARKEY *England* II. ii. 187, I thynk hyt wyl neuer be possybul to instytute our commyn wele wythout thys ordynance brought to passe and put in effect. **1620** T. GRANGER *Div. Logike* 2 The Proposite is the explication of the conceits, or meaning of the minde, instituted or framed according to sound reason. **1627** DONNE *Serm.* v. 47 Therefore does Hester form and institute her Prayer to God so—'Give me boldnesse, O Lord of all power'. *a* **1745** SWIFT *Maxims controlled in Irel.* Wks. 1841 II. 77/1 Before you could institute them [the inhabitants] into a republic.

d. To set in operation, set on foot, initiate, 'start' (a search, inquiry, comparison, etc.).

a **1797** BURKE *Tracts Popery Laws* ii. Wks. IX. 341 They may, at their discretion..break open houses, and institute such search at any hour of the day or night. **1821** J. Q. ADAMS in C. Davies *Metr. Syst.* III. (1871) 84 The results of this inquiry, newly instituted in Spain, have not yet been made known. **1873** MAX MÜLLER *Sc. Relig.* 307 Mythological comparisons instituted by scholars.

2. To establish in an office, charge, or position; to appoint; now, only, to place in a spiritual charge; 'to invest with the spiritual part of a benefice'. Const. *to, into* (*in*), or *absol.*

c **1325**, *c* **1400**, **1532–3** [see INSTITUTE *ppl. a.* a]. **1594** HOOKER *Eccl. Pol.* III. xi. §11 When Timothy was instituted into that office. **1596** SHAKS. 1 *Hen. VI*, IV. i. 162 Cosin of Yorke, we institute your Grace To be our Regent in these parts of France. **1612** DAVIES *Why Ireland*, etc. (1747) 18 To give laws unto a people, to institute magistrates and officers over them. **1639** SLINGSBY *Diary* (1836) 37 Mr. Rhodes was instituted upon a presentation from yᵉ Prebend. **1640** YORKE *Union Hon.* 157 William Seymour..was instituted into the Earldome of Hartford, and Barony of Beauchamp. **1767** BLACKSTONE *Comm.* II. xviii. 277 If the bishop doth not collate his own clerk immediately to the living, and the patron presents..the bishop is bound to institute the patron's clerk. **1804–86** *Bk. Com. Prayer Episc. Ch. U.S., Instit. Ministers*, We by these Presents..do institute you into said Parish, [*or* Church] possessed of full power to perform every Act of sacerdotal Function among the People of the same. **1858** MASSON *Milton* I. 155 Young..was instituted to the united vicarages of St. Peter and St. Mary.

b. *Rom. Law.* To appoint as heir or executor.

1590 SWINBURNE *Testaments* 177 Who so is executor in the first degree, he is saide to be instituted. **1774** S. HALLIFAX *Anal. Rom. Civ. Law* (1795) 38 By the new Law, as reformed by Justinian, all children..were to be instituted or disinherited by name. **1880** MUIRHEAD *Ulpian* xxii. §6 We cannot institute deities as our heirs. *Ibid.* §23 It is unnecessary either to institute or disinherit emancipated children.

†**3.** To ground or establish in principles; to train, educate, instruct. *Obs.*

1538 STARKEY *England* II. ii. 189 Ther schold be wyse men among thys vthe [= youth] to instytute them in the summe of Chrystys Gospel. **1591** SYLVESTER *Du Bartas* I. vii. 307 A painfull School master, that hath in hand To institute the flowr of all the Land. **1656** STANLEY *Hist. Philos.* VIII. (1701) 320/2 Who is there, that being instituted in an honest Family, and ingenuously Educated, is not offended at dishonesty? **1741** MIDDLETON *Cicero* I. i. 48 [Sylla] having been carefully instituted..in all the learning of Greece and Rome. **1784** in Picton *L'pool Munic. Rec.* (1886) 193 Sunday Schools..having been found to be of..advantage to..the children admitted and instituted there. **1831** SIR W. HAMILTON *Discuss., Eng. Univ.* (1852) 396 To imbue his pupils with good principles, and institute them in approved authors.

Hence **'instituting** *vbl. sb.* and *ppl. a.*

1534 MORE *Treat. on Passion* Wks. 1323/2 The instytutynge of that that shoulde be the newe Sacrifice. **1575–85** ABP. SANDYS *Serm.* (Parker Soc.) 242 The presenting, instituting, and inducting of pastors. **1643** MILTON *Divorce* I. ii, His own instituting words.

instituted ('ɪnstɪtjuːtɪd), *ppl. a.* [f. prec. + -ED¹.]

1. Ordained, established, founded.

1647 J. NOYES (*title*) The Temple Measured, or a brief Survey of the Temple Mystical, which is the instituted Church of Christ. **1661** BOYLE *Style of Script.* (1675) 52 An instituted instrument to conveigh revealed knowledge to the studies of it. *a* **1677** HALE *Prim. Orig. Man.* I. i. 24 Till we mutually communicate our thoughts by instituted signs, he knows not what I think or purpose, nor I what he thinks or purposeth. **1736** BUTLER *Anal.* II. i. Wks. 1874 I. 156 An instituted method of instruction, and an instituted form of external Religion. **1837** H. H. WILSON *Sánkhya Káriká* 184 By following instituted observances.

2. Invested with a cure of souls.

1712 PRIDEAUX *Direct. Ch.-wardens* (ed. 4) 24 The repair of the Chancel still lies upon the Parson, whether Appropriator, Impropriator, or instituted Rector. **1804–86** *Bk. Com. Prayer Episc. Ch. U.S., Instit. Ministers*, The Instituted Minister shall proceed to the Communion Service.

instituter ('ɪnstɪtjuːtə(r)). [f. as prec. + -ER¹.] One who institutes (see the vb.); = INSTITUTOR.

1538 STARKEY *England* II. ii. 181 Our old aunceturys, the instytutarys of our lawys..ordeynyd a Connestabul of Englond. **1633** AMES *Agst. Cerem.* II. 317 Artaxerxes was the first instituter of this Feast. **1670** MILTON *Hist. Eng.* III. (1851) 133 The instituter of his youth. **1768–74** TUCKER *Lt. Nat.* (1834) II. 399 A character of wisdom running uniform throughout both in the religion and the Instituter. **1833** I. TAYLOR *Fanat.* ii. 49 The revenge of jealousy seems, to the injured man, to be justified..by the formal instituter of society.

institution (ɪnstɪ'tjuːʃən). [ME. a. OF. *institucion, -tion* (12th c. in Hatz.-Darm), ad. L. *institūtiōn-em*, n. of action f. *instituĕre* to INSTITUTE.]

1. a. The action of instituting or establishing; setting on foot or in operation; foundation; ordainment; the fact of being instituted.

c **1460** FORTESCUE *Abs. & Lim. Mon.* ii. (1885) 113 That oþer [kingdom] beganne bi the desire and institucion of the peple of the same prince. **1591** SPENSER *M. Hubberd* 144 There is no right in this partition, Ne was it so by institution Ordained first. *a* **1631** DONNE *Serm.* viii. 80 Ceremonies.. may be good in their Institution, and grow ill in their Practice. **1776** ADAM SMITH *W.N.* I. iv. (1869) I. 26 Before the institution of coined money..people must always have been liable to the grossest frauds and impositions. **1785** REID *Intell. Powers* II. ix. 276 He was one of the most active members of the Royal Society of London at its first institution. **1839** YEOWELL *Anc. Brit. Ch.* viii. (1847) 77 Societies, whether monastic or secular, are of human, while episcopacy is of divine, institution.

b. *spec.* The establishment or ordination of a sacrament of the Christian Church, esp. of the Eucharist, by Christ. Hence, that part of the office of Baptism, and of the prayer of consecration in the Eucharist, which consists in reciting the words used in institution (more fully ***words, commemoration,*** or ***recital of institution***).

c **1538** BARNES *Sacrament under both Kinds* Wks. (1573) 304/2 Christes ordinaunce is not to receaue the bloud in the body onely, but to receaue the bloud after his institution. **1548** GEST *Pr. Masse* in H. G. Dugdale *Life* App. i. (1840) 122 He reporteth all thee wordes apperteyning to the ryght and ful institution of the sayd supper. **1607** E. GRIMSTONE tr. *Goulart's Mem. Hist.* 433 Hee began then to rehearse the ten commandements..the Lords Prayer, the institution of Baptisme, and of the holy Supper. **1635** PAGITT *Christianogr.* I. iii. (1636) 121 Reciting the words of the Institution: In the night in which he gave himselfe for the life of the world. **1850** NEALE *East. Ch.* I. III. v. 485 The true Eastern doctrine seems to be that there must be co-operation of the words of institution and of the invocation of the Holy Ghost, before the bread and wine become the Body and Blood of Christ.

†**2. a.** The giving of form or order to a thing; orderly arrangement; regulation. **b.** The established order by which anything is regulated; system; constitution. *Obs.*

a **1500** *Mankind* (Brandl 1896) 45/157 A best doth after hys naturall Instytucyone. **1555** W. WATREMAN *Fardle Facions* App. 314 The lawes then perteinyng to the institucion of our citie. **1560** BECON *New Catech* Wks. (Parker Soc.) 7 This book I commend unto you..as.. necessary for the right institution of your life. **1638** RAWLEY tr. *Bacon's Life & Death* (1651) 19 Concerning his Manners, Institution of his Life..there is a general Silence. **1676** tr. *Guillatiere's Voy. Athens* 30 Calogers, which are Monks of the Institution of St. Basil. **1708** SWIFT *Sentim. Ch. Eng. Man* Wks. 1755 II. I. 68 Few states are ruined by any defect in their institution, but generally by the corruption of manners. **1821** SHELLEY *Hellas* Pref., But for Greece..we.. might have arrived at such a stagnant and miserable state of social institution as China and Japan possess.

3. Establishment in a charge or position.

a. *Eccl.* In Episcopal churches, the establishment of a clergyman in the office of the cure of souls, by the bishop or his commissary.

In the Church of England, the investment of the presentee to a living with the spiritual part of his benefice, which is followed by INDUCTION, admitting to the possession of the temporalities of the benefice.

c **1380** WYCLIF *Wks.* (1880) 248 For institucion & induccion he schal ȝeue moche of þis god..to bischopis officers, archdekenes & officialis. **1549** LATIMER *2nd Serm. bef. Edw. VI* (Arb.) 67 There is in thys realme..a greate syghte of laye men wel learned in the scriptures, and of vertuouse and Godly conuersation..let them haue

institution, and gyue them the name of ye cleargye. **1687** W. SHERWIN in *Magd. Coll. & Jas. II* (O.H.S.) 225 [They] have had institutions to small Livings. **1708** *Termes de la Ley, Institution*, is a Faculty made by the Ordinary, by which a Vicar or Rector is approved to be Inducted to a Rectory or Vicarage. **1765** BLACKSTONE *Comm.* I. xi. 390 The clerk so admitted is next to be instituted..which is a kind of investiture of the spiritual part of the benefice; for by institution the care of the souls of the parish is committed to the charge of the clerk. **1804–86** *Bk. Com. Prayer Episc. Ch. U.S., Instit. Ministers*, On the day designated for the new Incumbent's Institution, at the usual hour of Morning Prayer, the Bishop, or the Institutor appointed by him, attended by the new Incumbent, and by all the other Clergy present, shall enter the chancel. **1845** POLSON *Eng. Law* in *Encycl. Metrop* II. 806/1 The institution by the bishop enables the clerk..to enter into his parsonage-house and take his tithes or ecclesiastical dues; but previous to induction he cannot lease them.

b. *Roman Law.* The appointment of an heir.

1880 MUIRHEAD *Ulpian* xxiv. 15 A man cannot legate until he has instituted an heir; for the force and power of the testament begins at the institution.

†**4.** Training, instruction, education, teaching.

1531 ELYOT *Gov.* I. xi, The lytell boke of the most excellent doctour Erasmus Roterodamus..intituled the Institution of a christen prince. **1539** TAVERNER *Gard. Wysed.* I. 8 a, Nature is a thynge of great myghte and efficacye, but surely institution or bringynge up, is moche myghtier. **1607** TOPSELL *Four-f. Beasts* (1658) 245 The Rider must first look to the institution and first instruction of his Horse. **1741** MIDDLETON *Cicero* I. i. 10 As soon as he was capable of a more enlarged and liberal institution, his father brought him to Rome. **1790** HAN. MORE *Relig. Fash. World* (1791) 72 To suppose that piety must be the natural and inevitable consequence of early institution.

†**5.** Usually in *pl.* **a.** Elements of instruction; first principles of a science or art. **b.** A book of first principles, an elementary treatise; = INSTITUTE *sb.* 3. *Obs.*

1537 CRANMER (*title*) The Institution of a Christen man. **1544** (*title*) Instytutions or principall Groundes of the Lawes and Statutes of England. **1561** T. NORTON (*title*) The Institution of Christian Religion, translated into Englysh according to the Authors last Edition. **1603** HOLLAND *Plutarch's Mor.* 923 To compile certaine Institutions of Rhetoricke. **1610** J. GAWEN tr. Trelcatius (*title*) Brief Institution of the Common Places of Sacred Divinitie. **1662** [see INSTITUTIONIST]. **1675** *Art Contentm.* Close § 1. 209 This short institution of the Art of Contentment. **1727–41** CHAMBERS *Cycl.* s.v., Physical or medicinal institutions, are such as teach the necessary præcognita to the practice of medicine, or the cure of diseases. **1800** W. C. BROWN (*title*) Institutions of the Practice of Medicine. Translated from the Latin of Burserius.

6. a. An established law, custom, usage, practice, organization, or other element in the political or social life of a people; a regulative principle or convention subservient to the needs of an organized community or the general ends of civilization.

1551 ROBINSON tr. *More's Utop.* II. i. (1895) 119 Agreyng all together in one tonge, in lyke maners, institucions and lawes. **1594** R. ASHLEY tr. *le Roy's Interchangeable variety Things* 13 b, From them are come many good institutions, Lawes, maners, the art of gouernment. **1691** HARTCLIFFE *Virtues* 410 All Positive Institutions must give way to Moral Duties. **1736** BUTLER *Anal.* II. i. Wks. 1874 I. 156 A society, distinguished..from the rest of the world, by peculiar religious institutions. **1860** THACKERAY *Round. Papers* xvii, I am not going into the slavery question, I am not an advocate for 'the institution'. **1871** R. W. DALE *Commandm.* viii. 196 The institution of property is recognised and sanctioned by the authority of God. **1899** SAYCE *Early Israel* vii. 269 The year of Jubilee was a Babylonian institution.

b. *colloq.* Something having the fixity or importance of a social institution; a well-established or familiar practice or object.

1839 *Times* 18 Feb. in *Spirit Metrop. Conserv. Press* (1840) I. 53 Murder [in Ireland] has become an institution. **1851** THACKERAY *Eng. Hum.* iv. (1858) 226 The pillory was a flourishing institution in those days. **1861** HUGHES *Tom Brown at Oxf.* i. (1889) 8 A great institution of the college..is the buttery-hatch. **1870** MISS BRIDGMAN *R. Lynne* I. xviii. 307 The postman was almost as much an institution at Hampton as the tower-clock. **1899** *Westm. Gaz.* 3 Jan. 3/1 He is..one of the 'institutions' of the place.

7. a. An establishment, organization, or association, instituted for the promotion of some object, esp. one of public or general utility, religious, charitable, educational, etc., e.g. a church, school, college, hospital, asylum, reformatory, mission, or the like; as a literary and philosophical institution, a deaf and dumb institution, the Royal National Life-boat Institution, the Royal Masonic Benevolent Institution (instituted 1798), the Railway Benevolent Institution, etc. The name is often popularly applied to the building appropriated to the work of a benevolent or educational institution.

1707 ATTERBURY *Spittal Serm.* 17 Apr. 14 'Tis not necessary to plead very earnestly in behalf of these Charities ..These, of which you have had an account, are such Wise, such Rational, such Beneficial Institutions. **1764** S. COOPER (*title*) Definitions and Axioms relative to Charity, Charitable Institutions, and the Poor Laws. **1775** J. ADAMS in *Fam. Lett.* (1876) 120 The institutions in New England for the support of religion, morals, and decency exceed any other. **1792** J. LATHAM (*title*) A Plan of a Charitable Institution intended to be established upon the Sea Coast, for the accommodation of Persons afflicted with such Diseases as are usually relieved by Sea Bathing. **1804** (*title*) The Manchester Guide; a brief Historical Description of the Towns of Manchester and Salford..the Charitable and Literary Institutions. **1817** CANNING in *Parl. Deb.* 323 We owed it to our system of public schools and universities. From these institutions was derived..'a due supply of men, fitted to serve their country, both in church and state'. **1864** *Times* 24 Dec., The individual Institutions..endowed and voluntary, for every imaginable condition of want or distress. **1878** JEVONS *Prim. Pol. Econ.* i. 9 He may establish useful public institutions, such as free public libraries, museums, public parks, etc. *Mod. Newspr.*, The testator leaves £10,000 in charitable legacies to various institutions.

b. Often occurring, like INSTITUTE, in the designations of societies or associations for the advancement of literature, science, or art, of technical knowledge, or of special education.

Such are the Royal Institution of Great Britain (incorporated 1800), the British Institution (1805), the London Institution (1806), the Plymouth Institution (1812), the Edinburgh Watt Institution and School of Arts (1821), the Liverpool Institution (1825); the Smithsonian Institution at Washington, U.S. (1830); the Institution of Civil Engineers (1818), Institution of Mechanical Engineers, of Gas Engineers, of Electrical Engineers, etc. Cf. INSTITUTE *sb.* 4.

8. *attrib.* and *Comb.*

1828 SIR D. LE MARCHANT *Rep. Barony Gardner* 167, I had registered her on an institution-book which I superintended at the time. **1892** *Daily News* 19 July 3/5 Epileptics so far advanced in their affliction as to require institution care invariably suffer from varying grades of mental aberration. **1899** A. CLARK *Wood's Oxford* III. 103 In the institution-rolls of the bishops of Lincoln. **1902** *Daily Chron.* 7 May 3/7 Institution life year after year is like pushing a stone uphill. **1905** *Ibid.* 27 Sept. 4/5 To any high-spirited woman, the tyranny of institution life must be almost unbearable. **1930** J. B. PRIESTLEY *Angel Pavement* v. 210 That institution atmosphere..was rather depressing. **1956** [see APPROVED *ppl. a.* 5]. **1960** I. BENNETT *Delinquent & Neurotic Children* iv. 129 Failures in the socialization process..will occur more frequently among institution children. **1963** F. F. LAIDLER *Gloss. Home Econ. Educ.* 48 *Institution administration*, carrying out the management of, or the executive duties concerned with institutions, e.g. Colleges, Hospitals, etc.

institutional (ɪnstɪˈtjuːʃənəl), *a.* [f. prec. + -AL[1].]

1. a. Of, pertaining to, or originated by institution; having the character or function of an institution; furnished with institutions, organized.

1617 COLLINS *Def. Bp. Ely* II. ix. 350 The vnion is very different of the two couples, this hypostaticall, that but institutionall, and arbitrarie, and Sacramentall. **1862** S. LUCAS *Secularia* 346 A departure from the institutional forms which were once common to Western Europe. **1869** TULLOCH in *Contemp. Rev.* X. 245 Such rules..are moral, and not institutional or ritual.

b. *Eccl.* Relating to sacramental institution.

c. Of religion: organized into or finding expression through institutions (a church, ordained ministers, ritual). Cf. INSTITUTIONALISM (*a*).

1908 F. VON HÜGEL *Mystical Element of Relig.* p. vi, The Infinite can still find room for the Historical and Institutional elements in Religion. **1924** A. E. J. RAWLINSON *Authority & Freedom* vi. 136 The Christianity of history is a sacramental and institutional religion. **1941** A. C. BOUQUET *Compar. Relig.* vii. 99 But if the world is unreal, and Deity unknowable, ordinary institutional religion, with its sacrifices and celestial bargaining, becomes a mere fraud.

d. *Linguistics.* (See quots.)

1958 T. HILL in *Orbis* VII. 454 A new branch of systemic linguistics dealing with the types of relation that arise in use between tongues, and between them and their users... As its aim is to confront tongues and communities as social institutions, it might be called *Institutional Linguistics*. **1964** M. A. K. HALLIDAY et al. *Ling. Sci.* i. 16 There is one aspect [of the study of how language works]..which does not strictly fall within 'descriptive linguistics': the study of language in relation to those who use it. This, since it is really the study of language as an institution, is recognized as a separate branch of the linguistic sciences and has come to be known as 'institutional linguistics'. *Ibid.*, Whereas in a descriptive statement we may note..that a speaker has used a transitive and not an intransitive clause.., in an institutional statement we may note that he has spoken English and not French.., that he spoke conversationally and not formally.

2. Dealing with or pertaining to legal institutes or the elements of a subject. Said of writers and works. See INSTITUTION 5, INSTITUTE *sb.* 3.

1765 BLACKSTONE *Comm.* I. Introd. iii. 73 Four volumes of institutes, as he is pleased to call them, though they have little of the institutional method to warrant such a title. **1816** BENTHAM *Chrestom.* 210 How narrow the conception is, which, by the word *rhetoric* has been presented to the authors of the small institutional books above alluded to,——may be seen [etc.]. **1832** AUSTIN *Jurispr.* (1879) I. xv. 392 That leading..distinction which has been assumed by the Roman Institutional Writers. **1885** *Law Times* LXXVIII. 402/2 The law of Scotland was illustrated by decisions and institutional writers.

3. a. Of or pertaining to an organized society, or the building in which its work is carried on.

1882 *Century Mag.* July 458 With the growth of institutional charity comes the creation of a class known as the institutional official. **1892** *Pall Mall G.* 21 Mar. 2/3 No denominational college, as such, is entitled to institutional representation upon the governing body of the University to which it belongs. **1896** *Daily News* 3 Apr. 5/6 The dull monotony of institutional life..has much to answer for in the evil habits contracted by these girls. **1942** *Times Lit. Suppl.* 14 Mar. 127/1 Born in a new country at a time when the desire for freedom from old institutional ways of living ..was burning like a flame in many lands. **1960** I. BENNETT *Delinquent & Neurotic Children* vii. 290 Personality was in some ways similar to that of a deprived institutional child. **1963** F. F. LAIDLER *Gloss. Home Econ. Educ.* 50 *Institutional management*, the study of all branches of the administration of large residential or non-residential establishments, including all branches of food service, menu planning, food purchase, preparation and service, equipment and personnel administration. **1966** R. BARTON (*title*) Institutional neurosis. **1972** *Jrnl. Social Psychol.* LXXXVI. 64 The Christian Conservative has a parallel in the 'Institutional Restraint' type in Gordon's analysis. **1972** *Times* 16 Oct. 12/5 In most cases they no longer require medical or nursing care and suffer mainly from 'institutional neurosis' due to their long stay in the protective environment of the hospital ward.

b. Of advertising, etc.: that lays stress on the business firm or institution rather than on the product itself.

1919 T. RUSSELL *Commercial Advertising* 258 Some manufacturers and commercial firms have used what is called 'institutional advertising': instead of advertising their wares they advertised their firm. **1930** *Harvard Advertising Awards, 1924–28* (Harvard Univ. Grad. School of Business Admin.) 75 In 1923, General Motors..accepted institutional advertising as a business tool. **1957** CLARK & GOTTFRIED *University Dict. Business & Finance* (1967) 10/1 Institutional..Advertising..is aimed at keeping the name of a company or group before the public. **1967** *Economist* 4 Feb. 448/2 A..dignified 'institutional' sales approach.

Hence **insti'tutionally** *adv.*, as an institution.

1857 HODGSON *Let. to Smith* in *Mem.* xv. 214 Long may you flourish institutionally and personally. **1893** *Chicago Advance* 26 Oct., When institutionally abandoned, it [religion] keeps up its constitutional clamor in the human soul.

insti'tutionalism. [f. prec. + -ISM.] The system of institutions; *spec.*, (*a*) the principles of institutional religion; (*b*) the system of housing people in institutions; the characteristics of life in an institution; attachment to such a system.

1862 *Spectator* 29 Mar., The natural reaction which the too cautious, too sober, too pious institutionalism of Oxford has excited in healthy minds. **1886** *Chicago Advance* 25 Feb. 114 Institutionalism engenders helplessness by rewarding it. **1907** *Daily Chron.* 17 Oct. 8/4 There is nothing of 'institutionalism' about life at the Browning Bethany Homes. **1909** G. TYRRELL *Christianity at Cross Roads* Pref. p. xx, The time has come..for a criticism of categories—of the very ideas of religion, of revelation, of institutionalism, of sacramentalism, of theology, of authority, etc. **1909** *Daily Chron.* 28 Oct. 5/3 The great impediment to success in the work of saving fallen women was the machinery of institutionalism. **1927** *Observer* 21 Aug. 7 The Society has set its face against any tendencies towards 'institutionalism', against any attempt..to take children away from their own homes. **1930** W. R. INGE *Christian Ethics & Mod. Probl.* i. 16 The unquestionable advantages which this fanatical institutionalism confers upon the Church as an organisation. **1958** *Times Lit. Suppl.* 19 Sept. 531/1 Institutionalism is usually followed by repeated further stays in institutions.

insti'tutionalist. [f. as prec. + -IST.] **a.** One who writes on legal institutes, or on the elements of a science or art; see INSTITUTIONAL 2. **b.** One who favours the retention of an institution or institutions.

1803–12 BENTHAM *Ration. Jud. Evid.* (1827) II. 389 If the conception entertained by a modern institutionalist be correct. **1816** —— *Chrestomathia* App. § 4 Wks. 1843 VIII. 70 By some Institutionalists, Chemistry..is not considered as included in Natural Philosophy. **1872** COSMO INNES *Scot. Legal Antiq.* i. 6 Our second great institutionalist produced his well-known work. **1920** G. B. SHAW in *New Commonwealth* Suppl. 2 Jan. 3/1 The distinction between the churchman, between the person the Dean of St. Paul's calls the institutionalist, and the genuine out and out Protestant mystic, will always cause a certain division. **1957** O. R. MCGREGOR *Divorce in England* v. 134 'Institutionalists' who insisted on its [*sc.* the matrimonial offence's] retention.

insti,tutionali'zation. [f. INSTITUTIONALIZE *v.* + -ATION.] The condition or state of being or becoming institutionalized; the action of institutionalizing.

1951 E. E. EVANS-PRITCHARD *Social Anthropol.* iii. 49 This order is brought about by the systematization, or institutionalization, of social activities so that certain persons have certain roles in them and so that the activities have certain functions in the general social life. **1964** M. ARGYLE *Psychol. & Social Probl.* vi. 85 The traditional [mental] hospital was run rather like a prison: inmates were treated as if they were incapable of taking an active or responsible place in the community, and it has been found that the longer they have been inside the more they suffer from 'institutionalization'— i.e. they become apathetic.. and become quite dependent on the hospital. **1964** I. L. HOROWITZ *New Sociol.* 21 If we confront problems of social development, we cannot rest content with their institutionalization in one minuscule town. **1969** H. PERKIN *Key Profession* i. 2 The universities are..the institutionalization of innovation in the arts. **1970** G. GREER *Female Eunuch* 234 The alternative is not the institutionalization of parental functions. **1972** *Physics Bull.* Aug. 445/2 The institutionalization of science has brought it, and particularly its R and D aspects, decisively into the realm of government and politics.

insti'tutionalize, *v.* [f. as INSTITUTIONALIST + -IZE.] **a.** *trans.* To render institutional; to convert into or treat as an institution. Freq. as *ppl. a.*

1865 R. H. HUTTON in *Pall Mall G.* 20 Feb. 1 He moralizes finance and commerce, and..institutionalizes

ethics and faith. **1893** *Age* (Melbourne) 25 Nov., The Japanese, who institutionalise the social evil, could hardly agree with the Puritans. **1935** B. MALINOWSKI in M. Black *Importance of Lang.* (1962) 80, I have defined magic as the institutionalized expression of verbal optimism. **1952** W. J. H. SPROTT *Social Psychol.* ix. 187 In some simple societies it [*sc.* homosexuality]..is institutionalized;..those showing a persistent preference for their own sex are given a special position. **1959** *Daily Tel.* 3 Apr. 10/2 Only a firm and institutionalised American commitment to Western Europe could achieve this end. **1962** W. NOWOTTNY *Lang. Poets Use* viii. 200 It means that the tears of the saviour have been metamorphosed into an institutionalized church. **1966** *Listener* 17 Nov. 749/3 That it should issue from a highly institutionalized company should not surprise us. **1971** A. QUINTON in A. Bullock *20th Cent.* 261/2 Marxism, institutionalized in the Communist world, has developed in a direction precisely opposite to the one he hoped for.

b. To house, train, or bring up in an institution; to subject (a person) to institutional life. In *pass.*, to show signs of the influence of institutional life.

1905 J. BURNS in *Daily Chron.* 1 Dec. 4/4 He has been 'institutionalised', and I never yet knew the average man survive that pauperising ordeal. **1924** *Glasgow Herald* 24 May 9 The day of the institutionalised boy or girl is past. **1949** M. MEAD *Male & Female* x. 204 Our techniques for diagnosing or institutionalizing the criminally insane are inadequate. **1959** B. WOOTTON *Social Sci. & Social Path.* iii. 119 In which either a parent had been permanently institutionalized or the child concerned had been sent to live with relatives. **1969** *Daily Tel.* 3 May 21/8 Because he was hopelessly institutionalised he was unable to look after himself when free. **1970** G. F. NEWMAN *Sir, You Bastard* v. 150 Sneed's doctor was sympathetic to his views, and thought the best plan was to put the child in an institution and have another. He offered to go and see Angie and help Sneed to institutionalize the infant. **1971** *Oxford Times* 15 Oct. 1/9 [He] had been in approved schools, prison and mental hospitals for much of his life and had become 'institutionalised'.

c. *Linguistics.* Usu. in *pa. pple.* or as *ppl. a.*: recognized or accepted by the speech community.

1949 J. R. FIRTH in *Trans. Philol. Soc. 1948* 128 It is especially helpful that there *are* things called English words and Arabic words..; indeed, English words and Classical Arabic words are firmly institutionalized. **1961** Y. OLSSON *Syntax Eng. Verb* ii. 24 Punctuation..and spacing..mark off units which are institutionalized, that is to say, recognized by the speech community. **1962** *Listener* 27 Sept. 467/2 Both in grammar and vocabulary Pidgin has deeply engrained distinctive features which are quite institutionalized, as we say.

institutionary (ɪnstɪˈtjuːʃənərɪ), *a.* [f. INSTITUTION + -ARY[1].]

†**1.** Of or pertaining to instruction or elements of instruction; educational. *Obs.*

1646 SIR T. BROWNE *Pseud. Ep.* v. vi. 241 Among the Institutionary rules of youth, he adviseth they might not be permitted to hear Iambicks. *a* **1734** NORTH *Lives* (1826) I. 277 It were well if this institutionary care of parents were always correspondent in the manners of all the children.

2. Of or pertaining to legal institutes.

a **1734** NORTH *Lives* (1826) I. 24 His lordship..used to intermix some institutionary reading with them [law reports].

3. Relating to ecclesiastical institution.

1814 JANE AUSTEN *Mansf. Park* xlvii. (1816) III. 345 Dr. Grant had brought on apoplexy and death by three great institutionary dinners in one week. **1835** *Blackw. Mag.* XXXVIII. 38 Let him establish his pretensions to the honour by the observance of this institutionary process.

4. Of or pertaining to social or political institutions.

1882 H. H. BANCROFT *Centr. Amer.* Pref. 10 Events pure and simple are by no means more important than the institutionary development which they cause or accompany.

†**instiˈtutionist.** [f. as prec. + -IST.] = INSTITUTIST.

1662 H. STUBBE *Ind. Nectar* vii. 133 It is a part of Physical Institutions, and treated on by every English'd Institutionist.

institutionize (ɪnstɪˈtjuːʃənaɪz), *v.* [f. INSTITUTION + -IZE.] *trans.* To render institutional; to institutionalize.

1903 G. TYRRELL *Church & Future* 61 In regarding the 'institutionising' of Christianity as a corruption.. Protestantism seems to me to ignore universal and natural laws. **1903** W. JAMES *Mem. & Stud.* (1911) xiv. 335 The institutionizing on a large scale of any natural combination of need and motive always tends to run into technicality and to develop a tyrannical Machine.

†**ˈinstitutist.** *Obs.* [f. INSTITUTE *sb.* + -IST.] A writer of institutes or elementary instructions.

1666 HARVEY *Morb. Angl.* ix. 77 Green gall the institutists would persuade us, to be an effect of an over-hot Stomach.

institutive (ˈɪnstɪtjuːtɪv), *a.* (*sb.*) [f. as INSTITUTE *v.* + -IVE.]

1. Having the character or quality of instituting; pertaining to the institution of something.

1627 FELTHAM *Resolves* II. [I.] xcviii. (1628) 286 It [the air] does..thrust it still forward, till it passes against institutiue Nature, who made it to incline to the Center. **1645** MILTON *Tetrach.* Wks. (1851) 164 They..must be led back to receive their meaning from those institutive words of God. **1869** J. MARTINEAU *Let.* in *Edin. Rev.* (1893) Oct. 342 The invitations to the institutive dinner were..addressed impartially to some best representatives of the several schools, positive or negative, of philosophical or religious opinion.

†**2.** Characterized by being instituted. *Obs.*

1643 MILTON *Divorce* II. v, It was a penall statute rather then a dispense; and..prefers a speciall reason of charitie, before an institutive decencie. **1651** HOBBES *Govt. & Soc.* v. §12. 82 There are two kinds of Cities, the one naturall.. the other institutive, which may be also called politicall.

†**B.** *sb.* A person or thing that institutes; an institutive agent or cause. *Obs.*

1644 BP. MAXWELL *Prerog. Chr. Kings* ii. 27 This *per me*, by me, Implyeth, Kings are Gods and Christs derivatives, and that God and Christ are their Institutives.

Hence **ˈinstitutively** *adv.*, by institution.

1656 HARRINGTON *Oceana* (1700) 158 It is institutively in the Great Council..tho..it be sometimes exercis'd by the Senat.

institutor (ˈɪnstɪtjuːtə(r)). [a. L. *institūtor*, agent-n. from *instituĕre* to INSTITUTE. Cf. F. *instituteur* (14th c.). See also INSTITUTER.]

1. One who institutes or establishes; a founder; an organizer.

1546 LANGLEY *Pol. Verg. de Invent.* IV. ii. 85 a, There be thre maner of Baptismes..One in water..another in the Holy gost & fyre wherof Christ was institutoure, the third in his blod wherin the Children that Herod slewe were Christened. **1635** PAGITT *Christianogr.* 60 As the institutor speaketh of his body, so also of his blood. **1701** NORRIS *Ideal World* I. ii. 47 The exceeding fewness of those laws of motion whereby the Institutor of nature proceeds in the ordinary course and conduct of it. **1738** WARBURTON *Div. Legat.* I. 85 Institutors of Civil Policy. **1812** LD. ELLENBOROUGH in *Examiner* 28 Dec. 832/2 The defendant was not proved to be the institutor, but only the propagator, of the libel. **1841–4** EMERSON *Essays* Ser. II. iii. (1876) 87 No institution will be better than the institutor.

†**2.** One who teaches; an instructor. *Obs.*

c **1675** A. WALKER (J.), The two great aims which every institutor of youth should mainly and intentionally drive at. **1797** GODWIN *Enquirer* I. i. 3 When a child is born..his institutor ought to..awaken his mind. *a* **1822** SHELLEY *Def. Poetry* in *Ess. & Lett.* (Camelot) 37 To declare whether the fame of any other institutor of human life be comparable to that of a poet.

3. *U.S.* In the American Episcopal Church: A bishop, or a presbyter acting for him, who institutes a minister into a parish or church.

1804–86 *Bk. Com. Prayer Episc. Ch. U.S., Instit. Ministers*, The Bishop, or the Priest who acts as the Institutor, standing within the rails of the Altar.

institutress (ˈɪnstɪtjuːtrɪs). [f. prec., or INSTITUTER + -ESS.] A female institutor.

1786 *Hist. Eur.* in *Ann. Reg.* 141/2 That regulation or compact of which the empress had been institutress. **1827** *Archæol.* XXI. 549 The Queen was then lying in state..at the Convent at Chaillot near Paris, of which she had been the Institutress and Patroness. **1829** SOUTHEY *Sir. T. More* II. 305 An institutress who devotes..her life to this generous purpose.

‖**instiˈtutrix.** *rare.* [fem. (in L. form) of INSTITUTOR: cf. DIRECTRIX.] = INSTITUTRESS.

1706 tr. *Dupin's Eccl. Hist. 16th C.* II. IV. xi. 459 S. Theresa was..the Institutrix of the Reformation of the Carmelite Nuns. **1814** tr. *Klaproth's Trav.* 119 Thou institutrix of this holy sceptre-like mode of sitting.

†**inˈstone,** *v. Obs. rare*[−0]. Also en-. [f. IN-[2] + STONE *sb.*] To turn to stone, to petrify.

1611 FLORIO, *Impetrire*, to instone. *Ibid.*, *Insassire*,..to enstone, to petrifie.

inˈstonement. *rare*[−1]. [f. as prec. + -MENT.] Representation or embodiment in stone.

1839 BAILEY *Festus* xx. (1852) 339 And shew, Like that instonement of divinity, That the whole building doth belong to God.

†**ˈin-stop,** *sb. Obs. rare.* [f. IN *adv.* 12 + STOP *sb.*] (app.) An inside guard.

14.. *Fencing* in *Rel. Ant.* I. 308 The man that wol to the to hond swerd lere bothe close and clere, He most have a goode eye bothe fer and nere, And an in stop, and an owte stop, and an hawke quartere.

†**inˈstop,** *v. Obs. rare*[−1]. [f. IN-[1] + STOP *v.*; cf. Du. *instoppen.*] *trans.* To stop, close up.

1666 DRYDEN *Ann. Mirab.* cxlvii, With boiling Pitch, another near at hand, From friendly Sweden brought, the seams instops.

†**inˈstore,** *v. Obs.* Also 5–7 instaur(e. See also ENSTORE. [ad. L. *instaurāre* to renew, repair, erect, establish, make; OF. *instaurer* (14–15th c. in Godef.). *Instaur* preserved the L. form; *instore* may have followed an OF. or AF. **instorer*; cf. ASTORE, OF. *estaurer*, *estorer*, and RESTORE, OF. *restorer*, from 14th c. *restaurer*.]

1. *trans.* To restore, repair, renew.

α. **1382** WYCLIF *Ezek.* xxxvi. 10 Ruynouse thingis shuln be instorid [*gloss* or maad aȝein]. **1432–50** tr. *Higden* (Rolls) IV. 139 Iohn Hircan destroyede Samaria, whom Herode instorede [HIGDEN *instaurans*, TREVISA bulde] after and callede hit Sebasten. *Ibid.* V. 95 This Aurelius instorede [HIGDEN *restauravit*, TREVISA restored] the cite of Rome in iiij yere. **1563** WIN3ET *Four Scoir Thre Quest.* Wks. 1888 I. 106 Sin is nocht forgeuin..except it quhilk is tane away be instorit.

β. **1607** MARSTON *What you Will* I. i, All things that show or breath Are now instaur'd, saving my wretched brest.

2. To erect, establish, institute, commence. *to instore a battle*, to array a battle, give battle, make war.

α. **1382** WYCLIF *Rom.* xiii. 9 If ther be ony othir maundement, it is instorid in this word, Thou schalt loue thi neiȝbore as thi silf. **1432–50** tr. *Higden* (Rolls) III. 229 Darius instorede a batelle [HIGDEN *bellum indixit*, TREVISA ordeynede werre and bataille] ageyne Anticirus. *Ibid.* IV. 193 Pompeius..instorede [H. *instauravit*, T. arrayed] a batelle ageyne Iulius.

β. **1432–50** tr. *Higden* (Rolls) III. 233 This Xerses.. instaurede a batelle [HIGDEN *bellum instaurat*, TREVISA werred] ageyne the londe of Grece. *Ibid.* VIII. 59 He instaurede [HIGDEN *instauravit*] a place of the ordre Cartusiense at Wytham, nye to Salisbey. *Ibid.* 432.

3. To furnish, provide, supply; to store *with* (*of*).

α. **1432–50** tr. *Higden* (Rolls) VI. 219 Petronax Brixanus.. wente to the mownte Cassyne, and instorede [HIGDEN *instauravit*] that place competentely with goodes and monkes. *c* **1440** *Promp. Parv.* 262/1 Instoron (wythe nedefulle thyngys), *instauro.* **1502** ATKYNSON tr. *De Imitatione* I. xxiii. 173 Instore thy selfe of ryches immortall that shall contynue after thy deth. *a* **1520** BARCLAY *Jugurth* (Pynson, ed. 2) 71 b, For this castell was..plentuously instored with men. *a* **1633** MUNDAY *View Sundry Examples* 79 Of mony and riches sufficiently instored.

β. **1432–50** tr. *Higden* Harl. Contn. (Rolls) VIII. 470 The seide duke..wente to his castelle of Powntefret, whom he instaurede with armes and vitells. *a* **1656** USSHER *Ann.* (1658) 594 Archelaus..Chief priest of Luna, a goddesse of the Comaus in Pontus, instaured with a princely Dynasty.

ˈin-store, *a.* [f. phr. *in store*: cf. IN *prep.* 18.] Of or relating to goods, etc., held in store; that is situated or takes place in a store.

1961 *Progressive Grocer* Oct. 38 The in-store advancement training program is given much credit for the success of Safeway Stores in his division. **1968** *Observer* 22 Dec. 11 What are euphemistically described as 'in-store wastages', can mean, he says, 'losing a whole truckload of stuff before it even gets through the loading bay.' The in-store thief could be someone extracting a little money from each till when it is being cashed up, a 16-year-old on the stocking-counter, or a loading bay hand working in collusion with a truck driver. *Ibid.*, There are no niceties about in-store security. **1972** *Police Rev.* 10 Nov. 1467/2 (Advt.), Investigation of all in-store security.

†**inˈstrange,** variant of ENSTRANGE *v.*, *Obs.*

1586 A. DAY *Eng. Secretary* II. (1625) 10 So pennilesse, and therewithall instranged from all good account.

†**inˈstrangle,** *v. Obs. rare*[−1]. [f. IN-[1] or [2] + STRANGLE.] *trans.* To strangle within something; to stifle.

a **1670** HACKET *Cent. Serm.* (1675) 587 It appears that exhalations and hot air may be instrangled within the bowels of the earth.

inˈstratified, *ppl. a.* [IN *adv.* 11 b] 'Stratified within something else' (Webster, 1828).

a **1828** *Jrnl. Science* cited by Webster.

instreaming (ˈɪnˌstriːmɪŋ), *vbl. sb.* [IN *adv.* 11 c.] The action or fact of streaming in; inflow.

1876 GEO. ELIOT *Dan. Der.* v. xl, Mordecai..seemed to feel a new instreaming of confidence. **1888** *Pop. Sci. Monthly* Jan. 312 The instreaming of the external world through the senses, as impressions.

instreaming (ˈɪnˌstriːmɪŋ), *ppl. a.* [IN *adv.* 11 a.] That streams in; inflowing; inrushing.

1855 EMERSON *Misc.* viii. 64 A power which exists not in time or space, but an instantaneous in-streaming causing power. **1888** BRYCE *Amer. Commw.* III. VI. cix. 575 To furnish homes for instreaming millions of strangers.

inˈstrengthen, *v. rare.* [IN-[1] or [2]. Cf. ENSTRENGTHEN.] *trans.* To strengthen inwardly.

1855 PUSEY *Doctr. Real Presence* Note S. 330 Those who eat are so instrengthened, and are strong with such might from the life-giving food within them. **1860** —— *Min. Proph.* 565 They shall have strength, because God instrengthens them.

instress (ˈɪnstrɛs), *sb.* [f. IN *adv.* 12 + STRESS *sb.*] In the theories of Gerard Manley Hopkins: the force or energy which sustains an inscape (see quots.). Hence **ˈinstress** *v. trans.* and *intr.*; **ˈinstressed** *ppl. a.*; **ˈinstressing** *vbl. sb.*

1868 [see INSCAPE *sb.*]. **1873–4** G. M. HOPKINS *Note-bks. & Papers* (1937) 226 You can without clumsiness instress, throw a stress on/a syllable so supported. **1875** —— *Jrnls. & Papers* Feb. (1959) 263 Standing before the gateway I had an instress which only the true old work gives from the strong and noble inscape of the pointed-arch. **1876** —— *Wr. Deutschland* in *Poems* (1967) 53 His mystery must be instressed, stressed. **1881** —— *Note-bks. & Papers* (1937) 349 This song of Lucifer's was a dwelling on his own beauty, an instressing of his own inscape. **1944** W. H. GARDNER *G. M. Hopkins* i. 11 In the vagaries of shape and colour presented by hills, clouds, glaciers and trees he discerns a recondite pattern—'species or individually-distinctive beauty'—for which he coins the word 'inscape'; and the *sensation* of inscape (or, indeed, of any vivid mental image) is called 'stress' or 'instress'. **1948** W. A. M. PETERS *G. M. Hopkins* i. 14 The original meaning of instress..is that stress or energy of being by which 'all things are upheld'..and strive after continued existence.

†**inˈstrie, -ˈstreye,** *v. Obs. rare.* [f. IN-[1] + *streȝen*, OE. **striéȝan*, *stréȝan* to strew, scatter = Goth. *straujan.* For the phonology cf. DIE *v.*] *trans.* To strew or scatter in or upon something.

c **1420** *Pallad. on Husb.* x. 37 Ther douves donge instrie, And leues of cupresse ek on hit sowe, And ere hit in.

'in-stroke. *rare.* Also instroke. [IN *adv.* 11 d.]

1. A stroke directed inwards; a striking inwards.

1887 A. BIRRELL *Obiter Dicta* Ser. II. 272 In order to win the precious metal you must now work with in-stroke and out-stroke.

2. The stroke which carries the piston away from the crank-shaft and further into the cylinder of an engine.

1902 *Encycl. Brit.* XXVIII. 183/2 Suction during an entire outstroke of the piston;..compression during the following instroke. **1922** GLAZEBROOK *Dict. Applied Physics* I. 320/1 In the Otto cycle the inlet valve usually opens slightly before the end of the in-stroke of the working piston.

†in'strophiate, *v. Obs. rare.* [f. IN-^{2} + L. *strophium* band, headband, chaplet (a. Gr. *στρόφιον*) + -ATE^{3}.] *trans.* To crown with a chaplet; to make into a chaplet; to put on as a headband.

1592 R. D. *Hypnerotomachia* 93 Some [Nymphs] instrophiated with laurel, some with myrtle. *Ibid.* 97 b, Manie had fastened togither diuers broad leaues, instrophiating them with sundrie flowers. **1599** R. LINCHE *Anc. Fiction*, Vpon her head instrophiated a thinne vaile. **1631** R. H. *Arraignm. Whole Creature* Ep. Ded. 4 The former is instrophiated with the Tytle of Gods vpon Earth; The latter lyes subject to the tyranny of Devils in Hell.

†in'struct, *sb. Obs.* [ad. L. *instructu-s*, in med.L. instruction, prompting, impulse, f. *instruct-*, ppl. stem of *instruĕre*: see next.] Instruction.

1529 MORE *Dyaloge* I. Wks. 175/1 Yet hath the churche by secrete instructe of god, reiected the remenaunt. **1642** ROGERS *Naaman* 3 *marg.*, Vse of instruct.

†in'struct, *ppl. a. Obs.* Also 5-6 instructe, (5 yn-), 6 enstruct. [ad. L. *instruct-us*, pa. pple. of *instruĕre* to INSTRUCT. Used as pa. pple. of next, after its introduction.] = INSTRUCTED.

1. Educated; taught; informed.

1440 J. SHIRLEY *Dethe K. James* 25 A mane wele ynstructe yn lawe and letture. *c* **1450** tr. *De Imitatione* III. xliii. 114 þou shalt come ayen instructe in þinges present & þat are to come. **1485** CAXTON *St. Wenefr.* 1 The seid theuith.. also comysed to hym his douȝter for to be instruct & tauȝt. **1533** MORE *Answ. Poysoned Bk.* Wks. 1098/1 Here might Chryst haue enstruct his disciples the trouthe of the eatyng of his fleshe. **1671** MILTON *P.R.* I. 439 Who ever, by consulting at thy shrine, Returned the wiser, or the more instruct To fly or follow what concerned him most?

2. Furnished or equipped *with* something.

c **1470** HARDING *Chron.* XLV. ii, Kymbalyne so was.. Noryshed at Rome, instructe with cheualre. **1538** STARKEY *England* I. ii. 41 So long..as the soule was instructe wyth such vertues as be accordyng to hyr dygnyte. **1615** CHAPMAN *Odyss.* IV. 755 He had neither ship instruct with oars, Nor men to fetch him from those stranger shores.

instruct (ɪn'strʌkt), *v.* Forms: 5-6 instructe, (6 enstructe, *Sc.* instruck; pa. t. instruct), 6- instruct. [f. L. *instruct-*, ppl. stem of *instruĕre* to build, erect, set up, set in order, prepare, furnish, furnish with information, teach, f. *in-* (IN-^{2}) + *struĕre* to pile up, build, etc.: see STRUCTURE, and cf. F. *instruire*. The history in Eng. does not correspond with the sense-development in L.]

I. 1. *trans.* To furnish with knowledge or information; to train in knowledge or learning; to teach, educate.

1526 *Pilgr. Perf.* (W. de W. 1531) 117 b, The examples of holy patriarkes, prophetes, apostles..& holy fathers, enstructeth vs dayly. **1534** WHITINTON *Tullyes Offices* I. (1540) 70 Plato dyd instructe Dyon a sycilyan. **1551** T. WILSON *Logike* (1580) 36 *note*, Had not the Gospel afore instructed me. **1588** SHAKS. *Tit. A.* v. i. 98 Indeede, I was their Tutor to instruct them. **1611** BIBLE *Transl. Pref.* 3 If we be ignorant, they [the Scriptures] will instruct vs. **1713** ADDISON *Cato* I. iv, Who like our active African instructs The fiery steed, and trains him to his hand? **1771** WESLEY *Serm.* ii. div. i. §6 He..instructs the ignorant. **1838** LYTTON *Alice* II. i, Her heart, perhaps, helped to instruct her understanding.

b. To furnish with knowledge or skill *in* an art or branch of study; to educate or train *in* the knowledge of some particular subject; to give methodical teaching to.

1509 HAWES *Past. Pleas.* VI. (Percy Soc.) 25 Besechynge her to enstructe me shortely In her noble science. **1509** BARCLAY *Shyp of Folys* (1874) I. 5 In comon places of the Cyte of Athenes he instruct and infourmed the peple in such doctrynes. **1697** DRYDEN *Virg. Georg.*, III. 261 Let him be Instructed there in Rules of Husbandry. **1745** BUTLER *Serm. Christ-church* Wks. 1874 II. 276 They ought to be instructed and exercised in what will render them useful to society. **1841** BORROW *Zincali* I. iv. II. 294 Procured a teacher to instruct me in latin.

†c. Const. *of, to, with, inf.*, or *clause. Obs.*

1477 EARL RIVERS (Caxton) *Dictes* 7 Instructe hem to haue goode eloquence and to escheue alle vanitees. **1529** MORE *Dyaloge* I. Wks. 123/1 They..were by hym instructed to euerye trewth. **1595** SHAKS. *John* III. i. 68, I will instruct my sorrowes to bee proud. **1611** BIBLE *1 Chron.* xv. 22 He instructed about the song, because he was skilfull. —— *Isa.* xxviii. 26 His God doth instruct him to discretion, and doth teach him. **1628** GAULE *Pract. The.* (1629) 394 That he might instruct him to what he ought. **1749** FIELDING *Tom Jones* VI. v, Books which..would instruct you how to hide your thoughts.

†d. To teach (a thing). (Also with indirect personal obj.) *Obs.*

1623 WEBSTER *Duchess of Malfi* I. i. Wks. (Rtldg.) 62/1 To suspect a friend unworthily Instructs him the next way to suspect you. **1634** SIR T. HERBERT *Trav.* 191 The Brahming ..very readily teach and instruct the perfect way unto damnation. **1670** MILTON *Hist. Eng.* IV. Wks. (1847) 523/1 So perversely then was chastity instructed against the apostle's rule.

2. To impart knowledge to (a person) concerning a particular fact or circumstance; to apprise, inform. Const. †*in, of, with*, or with *subord. cl.*

? a **1500** *Chester Pl.* xiii. 44 Mayster, instruct us in this case, Why this man blynd borne was. **1536** R. BEERLEY in *Four C. Eng. Lett.* 35 Now y wyll ynstrux your grace sumwatt of relygyus men. **1551** T. WILSON *Logike* (1580) 83 Beyng well instructed of his great worthines. **1603** SHAKS. *Meas. for M.* I. i. 81 A powre I haue, but of what strength and nature I am not yet instructed. **1638** SIR. T. HERBERT *Trav.* (ed. 2) 52 Being instructed in the precise time of his Nativity, calculates his fortunes. **1652** H. COGAN tr. *Scudery's Ibrahim* I. v. 103 Instructing my self in the Forms and Ceremonies that are to be observed. **1787** WINTER *Syst. Husb.* 53 Observations instruct me that they [ants] multiply and increase most in cold clayey soils. **1871** MORLEY *Voltaire* (1886) 11 There are, as history instructs us, eras of counsel and eras of execution.

b. *refl.* To acquaint or inform oneself, to acquire information. (= F. *s'instruire.*)

1611 CORYAT *Crudities* Ep. Ded., Any iudicious Reader may by the reading thereof much instruct himselfe with the forme of the Venetian gouernement. **1860** TYNDALL *Glac.* II. xi. 289, I was particularly desirous to instruct myself upon this important head.

c. *Eng. Law.* To give information as a client to a solicitor, or as a solicitor to a counsel; to authorize one to appear as advocate (*Wharton's Law Lex.* 1883). Cf. INSTRUCTION 4 b.

1836 DICKENS *Pickw.* xviii, Having been instructed by Mrs. Martha Bardell, to commence an action against you for a breach of promise of marriage [etc.]. *Ibid.* xxxiv, I am instructed to say that it was put in the plaintiff's parlour-window just this time three years.

3. To furnish with authoritative directions as to action (see INSTRUCTION 4); to direct, command.

1557 N. T. (Genev.) *Matt.* xiv. 8 She beyng before instructed [**1535** COVERD. beynge instructe] of her mother sayed, geue me here Iohn Baptist head in a platter. **1605** SHAKS. *Lear* v. iii. 29 If thou do'st As this instructs thee, thou dost make thy way To Noble Fortunes. **1607** E. GRIMSTONE tr. *Goulart's Mem. Hist.* 436 After they were thoroughly instructed and informed of their charge..wee sent them. *a* **1715** BURNET *Own Time* I. (1725) I. 5 He was very particularly instructed in all the proper methods to gain upon the King's confidence. **1766** GOLDSM. *Vic. W.* vii, It was I that instructed my girls to encourage our landlord's addresses. **1800** *Med. Jrnl.* III. 315, I instructed him to take two grains only of the Digitalis daily.

II. †4. (Chiefly *poet.*) To put in order, put into form; to form; to 'inform'; to make ready, prepare, equip, furnish. *Obs.*

1624 B. HOLYDAY *Serm.* (1626) 29 A body which the breath of the Almighty will instruct with a soule. **1697** DRYDEN *Virg. Georg.* III. 202 Feed him with Herbs, whatever thou canst find, Of generous Warmth; and of salacious kind... Instructed thus, produce him to the Fair. **1718** PRIOR *Solomon* III. 658 The Maids in comely Order next advance; They beat the Timbrel, and instruct the Dance. **1726** AYLIFFE *Parergon* (J.), They speak to the merits of a cause, after the proctor has prepared and instructed the same for a hearing before the judge. **1774** *Westm. Mag.* II. 654 These point the labour, and reward assign, Direct the batt'ry, and instruct the mine.

5. *Sc. Law.* To furnish (a statement) with evidence or proof; to confirm by evidence, vouch, verify; to prove clearly.

1681 STAIR *Inst. Law Scot.* IV. xv. §5 Thirlage of lands to mills of the Kings property is sufficiently instructed by use of coming to the mill, and paying the insucken multures. **1727** P. WALKER *Life Peden* 12 (Jam.) It was also a day of very astonishing apparitions..which I can instruct the truth of. **1755** *Guthrie's Trial* 206 (Jam.) None should charge this sin on themselves or others, unless they can prove and instruct the charge according to Christ's example. **1868** *Act 31 & 32 Vict.* c. 101 §85 An extract retour or decree of general service..instructing the propinquity of such person to the party who died last vest. **1883** *Law Rep.* 9 App. Cases 98 *note*, If the defender had been able to instruct by evidence the averments he has placed on record.

instructable, obs. variant of INSTRUCTIBLE.

instructed (ɪn'strʌktɪd), *ppl. a.* [f. INSTRUCT *v.* + -ED^{1}; taking the place of INSTRUCT *ppl. a.*]

1. Educated; taught; informed.

1552 HULOET, Instructed, *catechisatus, instructus, ornatus ..catechumenus.* Instructed in good maners, *moratus.* **1553** EDEN *Treat. Newe Ind.* (Arb.) 33 Magellanus sent with them .vii. men well instructed. **1611** BIBLE *Ecclus.* xxvi. 14 There is nothing so much worth, as a mind well instructed. **1671** MILTON *Samson* 757 With more cautious and instructed skill. **1712** STEELE *Spect.* No. 539 ¶1, I can dance very well .. I..never exert my instructed Charms till I find I have engaged a Pursuer. *a* **1871** GROTE *Eth. Fragm.* iv. (1876) 77 As society becomes more instructed.

†2. Furnished, fitted out, equipped; drawn up in order, arrayed. *Obs.*

1552 [see 1]. **1596** DALRYMPLE tr. *Leslie's Hist. Scot.* x. 430 An Jnglis nauie to the number of xvj verie weil instructet schipis. **1613-16** W. BROWNE *Brit. Past.* II. iv, Instructed swarmes Of men immayl'd. **1666** DRYDEN *Ann. Mirab.* clxiii, Instructed ships shall sail to quick commerce.

Hence **in'structedly** *adv.*; **in'structedness.**

1628 BP. HALL *Old Relig.* 116 A commendation of the well instructednesse of those people. **1873** MORLEY *Struggle Nat. Educ.* xii. 116 It would be a most substantial gain if our labouring class in England could all talk as articulately, as rationally, and as instructedly..as you may trust the labouring class in Scotland to do.

instructer (ɪn'strʌktə(r)). [f. INSTRUCT *v.* + -ER^{1}.] One who instructs. (Formerly frequent; now usually INSTRUCTOR.)

1535 COVERDALE *Isa.* xxx. 20 Thine instructer fleyth not farre from the. **1579** GOSSON *Sch. Abuse* (Arb.) 32 We should haue an instructer at our elbowes. **1611** BIBLE *Gen.* iv. 22 Tubal-Cain an instructer of euery artificer in brasse and iron. **1779-81** JOHNSON *L. P., Pope* Wks. IV. 4 Impressed with such veneration for his instructer. **1807** G. CHALMERS *Caledonia* I. i. 3 The instructer of nations. **1826** J. F. COOPER *Mohicans* (1829) I. x. 130 The imperfect nomenclature of his provincial instructers.

[**instructess,** misprint for INSTRUCTRESS.]

in'structible, *a. rare.* Also 7 -able. [f. L. *instruct-*, ppl. stem (see INSTRUCT *v.*) + -IBLE.] Capable of being instructed, open to instruction.

1603 FLORIO *Montaigne* I. lvi. (1632) 175 As children propose their essayes, instructable, not instructing. **1611** COTGR., *Endoctrinable*, docible, teacheable, instructable. **1618** BACON *Submission to Ho. Lords* (T.), A king..whose heart is instructible for wisdom and goodness.

instructing (ɪn'strʌktɪŋ), *vbl. sb.* [f. INSTRUCT *v.* + -ING^{1}.] The action of the vb. INSTRUCT; instruction.

1557 *Order Hospitalls* C, For the better instructinge of your Worships touching the Government herein. **1581** SIDNEY *Apol. Poetrie* (Arb.) 48 Hee dooth not onely farre passe the Historian, but, for instructing, is well nigh comparable to the Philosopher. **1670** EACHARD *Cont. Clergy* 62 Instead of a sober instructing the people in those eminent and excellent graces.

attrib. **1831** CARYLE *Sart. Res.* II. iii, Though the Soldier wears openly..his butchering-tool, nowhere, far as I have travelled, did the Schoolmaster make show of his instructing-tool.

instructing (ɪn'strʌktɪŋ), *ppl. a.* [f. as prec. + -ING^{2}.] That instructs, or gives instruction or information; instructive.

1581 SIDNEY *Apol. Poetrie* (Arb.) 35 Thought not historicall acts, but instructing Parables. *a* **1688** W. CLAGETT *17 Serm.* (1699) 81 How instructing ought to be our profession. **1754** RICHARDSON *Grandison* (1810) VI. lii. 347 'See my dear young ladies', said the happy and instructing Mrs. Shirley..'the reward of duty, virtue, and obedience'. **1802** MAR. EDGEWORTH *Moral T.* (1816) I. xiv. 112 Instructing narrative. **1893** *Westm. Gaz.* 3 Oct. 6/1 He went with Instructing-constable B—— and searched the prisoner C——'s house.

instruction (ɪn'strʌkʃən). [a. OF. *in-, enstruction, -cion* (1348 in Hatz.-Darm.), mod.F. *instruction*, ad. L. *instructiōn-em*, n. of action f. *instruĕre* to INSTRUCT.]

1. The action of instructing or teaching; the imparting of knowledge or skill; education; †information.

1506 GUYLFORDE *Pilgr.* (Camden) 30 There was no processyon, nor shewynge, nor instruccion of the holy places. **1548** HALL *Chron., Hen. V* 80 b, Bryng up my lytle infant..that.. by your instruction, he may prove pollitike. **1589** PUTTENHAM *Eng. Posie* I. x. (Arb.) 39 The instruction of morall doctrines. **1662** STILLINGFL. *Orig. Sacr.* II. iv. §4 We see what care God took for the instruction of his people in a time of so generall an Apostacy. **1781** GIBBON *Decl. & F.* xxvii. III. 12 The faith of a soldier is commonly the fruit of instruction, rather than of inquiry. **1861** *Times* 29 Aug., The old antithesis between 'instruction' and 'education' still continues to perplex scrupulous minds.

2. The knowledge or teaching imparted. With *an* and *pl.* An item of knowledge imparted; an instructive rule, a precept, a lesson.

1412-20 LYDG. *Chron. Troy* I. vi. (MS. Cott. Aug. A. iv), Whan sche hadde þus..ȝoue instruccion Pleyn doctrine and informacion How he schal skape þe dangeris by and by. *c* **1449** PECOCK *Repr.* Prol. 1 He ȝeueth instruccioun of correpcioun and of correpting. **1526** *Pilgr. Perf.* (W. de W. 1531) 5 Moralytees and instruccyons of good maner and pollicy. **1662** STILLINGFL. *Orig. Sacr.* I. iv. §1 All the Philosophy and instruction they had, was from their Poets, and was all couched in verse. **1796** MISS BURNEY *Camilla* I. 67 She gave her various instructions how to set off her person to most advantage. **1873** L. FERGUSON *Disc.* 41 It is good..to profit by the instructions of the pulpit.

†3. Knowledge imparted concerning a particular fact or circumstance; information. With *an* and *pl.*, An item of information imparted or acquired, an account, a narrative. *Obs.*

1425 W. PASTON in *P. Lett.* No. 5. I. 19, I sende yow copies and a trewe instruccion of the seyd matier. **1513** MORE *Rich. III* Wks. 69/2 The messenger sent back wt thanks, & some secret instruccion of ye protectors mind. **1548** HALL *Chron., Hen. V* 77 b, Or thei from thence departed, thei had knowledge and true instruccion that the Dolphyn..was reculed. **1655** FULLER *Ch. Hist.* IX. ii. §21 May they..(if having the conveniences of leisure, and instructions) be pleased to perfect this my Catalogue.

4. a. A making known to a person what he is required to do; a direction, an order, a mandate

(oral or written). Now usu. *pl.*: Directions, orders.

1433 LYDG. *Leg. S. Edmund* III. 993 (Horstm.) Affter the fourme off his Instruccioun He folwed theffect off his auysioun. **1494** FABYAN *Chron.* VI. clx. 152 Whan Lewys had gyuen answere.. and geuen vnto theym other instruccions, he sent them forthe agayn. **1513** MORE in Grafton *Chron.* (1568) II. 771 Some of the company had.. secret instruction.. to take hym. **1640–4** in Rushw. *Hist. Coll.* III. (1692) I. 620 We read the fourth Article of our Instructions to the whole Company. *a* **1715** BURNET *Own Time* II. (1725) I. 242 He had an instruction to pass an act of indemnity. **1725** N. ROBINSON *Th. Physick* 287 If these Instructions.. be but punctually attended to, he need not fear any Returns of his Cholic Pains. **1860** TYNDALL *Glac.* I. xxvii. 215 My voice could be heard, and my instructions understood.

b. Direction given to a solicitor or counsel.

a **1734** NORTH *Life Ld. Guilford* (1808) I. 196 An attorney .. said that he had given the serjeant his fee, and instructions over night, to move for him. **1768** BLACKSTONE *Comm.* III. iii. (1809) 29 A counsel is not answerable for any matter by him spoken, relative to the cause in hand, and suggested in his client's instructions. **1837** DICKENS *Pickw.* xxxiv, Attorneys.. from that spot can whisper in the ear of the leading counsel in the case, any instructions that may be necessary during the progress of the trial.

c. *Computers.* An expression in a program or routine, or a sequence of characters in a machine language, which specifies an operation (esp. a basic operation) and freq. also one or more operands, and results in its performance by the computer.

1947 GOLDSTINE & VON NEUMANN in J. von Neumann *Coll. Wks.* (1963) V. 82 The control scans the coded instruction in the selectron memory as a rule linearly. **1948** *Math. Tables & Other Aids to Computation* III. 121 The terms defined in the following short glossary are used in their technical sense in this discussion... 2. Word: A group of digits.. stored in coded form in a single memory position. .. 5. Instruction: A word directing the machine to perform a particular operation. **1949** D. R. HARTREE *Calculating Instruments & Machines* (1950) 67 A single instruction of this type specifies two locations, one in the store and one in the arithmetical unit, and an operation. **1951** [see COMMAND *sb.* 1 d]. **1958** M. PHISTER *Logical Design Digital Computers* xi. 342 An instruction (also called a command or an order) is a computer word which identifies which of a limited number of operations the computer is to carry out, and the computer functions by executing a sequence of these instructions, one at a time. **1959** E. M. MCCORMICK *Digital Computer Primer* x. 139 The number of instructions which can be executed by a computer represents a compromise between the designer's and user's requirements. The fewer the instructions, the easier it is to design and build the machine, but the more difficult (at least time-consuming) it is to code for it. *Ibid.* 141 Some computers have two separate instructions in one word... However, most computers, binary or decimal, use one instruction per word. **1962** B. A. GALLER *Lang. Computers* xii. 193 In the IBM 650 computer, for example, a typical [machine] instruction might be 1512150123 in which the first two digits (15) indicate that the contents of the location specified by the next four digits (1215) are to be added to the lower half of the accumulator register. The next four digits (0123) give the address of the location in storage in which the next instruction to be executed is stored. **1967** [see COMMAND *sb.* 1 d]. **1969** P. B. JORDAIN *Condensed Computer Encycl.* 253 The word instruction is preferable to the words command and order, sometimes used synonymously. Command should be reserved for electrical signals. **1970** O. DOPPING *Computers & Data Processing* vi. 98 When local control units have their own instructions, these instructions can be called commands to distinguish them from the instructions to the central control unit.

5. *attrib.*, as ***instruction book***.

1895 *Montgomery Ward Catal.* 123/2 Tissue Paper Flower Outfits... Containing.. 12 half sheets assorted tissues,.. and instruction book. **1926–7** *T. Eaton & Co. Catal.* Fall & Winter 300/3 Easy Method Instruction Books for Various Instruments. **1970** *Which?* Aug. 237/1 The instruction books generally gave good information for setting up and using the machines.

instructional (ɪnˈstrʌkʃənəl), *a.* [f. prec. + -AL[1].]

1. Of or pertaining to instruction or teaching; educational.

1801 W. TAYLOR in *Monthly Mag.* XII. 585 The most satisfactory account of the instructional state of France. **1850** *Tait's Mag.* XVII. 595/2 From the want of a sufficient instructional machinery. **1873** *Daily News* 4 Aug., The instructional cooking college at Aldershot. **1898** *Westm. Gaz.* 28 Mar. 7/3 The training brig *Wanderer*.. leaving Portsmouth Harbour under sail with a crew of boys for the first instructional cruise of the season to-day.

2. Conveying instruction or information.

1832 *Examiner* 566/1 It contains no instructional matter as to the framing of bills. **1882** W. SHARP *D. G. Rossetti* 415 A sonnet meant to convey an instructional idea.

3. spec. ***instructional film*** (also ellipt.), *set*, *television* (U.S.).

1933 (*title*) Guide to instructional and educational films available for use by educational and social organisations in Great Britain (Central Information Bureau for Educational Films). **1944** R. MANVELL *Film* I. 36 The case of the close-up in documentary.. is rather different... So also is the obvious importance of close-up in the instructional film, where processes are being explained and emphasised. **1959** HALAS & MANVELL *Technique Film Animation* 13 We are seeing a considerable expansion of the animated film into every kind of use from the television commercial to the highly specialized instructional film. **1962** *Listener* 25 Jan. 193/1 The earnest reportage, the non-theatrical instructionals, and the forward-looking films. **1971** *Jrnl. Gen. Psychol.* Jan. 59 Kazsuk and Bartley supported these findings in a subsequent investigation of the effect of instructional sets on brightness matching. **1972** *Jrnl. Social Psychol.* LXXXVI. 155 For individual cooperative choices, instructional set.. and trial blocks.. were significant. **1966** *Sat. Rev.* (U.S.) 19 Nov. 88 After more than a decade of intensive effort and the expenditure of hundreds of millions of dollars, instructional television seems to have arrived. **1968** *Economist* 21 Dec. 31/3 The receiving stations will still fill the rest of the day with instructional television (which is what ITV stands for in America) of a quality which Mr. McGeorge Bundy of the Ford Foundation has described as staggeringly mediocre.

inˈstructionary, *a. rare.* [f. as prec. + -ARY.] = prec.

1861 *Times* 7 Oct., It is important that a model and instructionary farm should pay.

instructive (ɪnˈstrʌktɪv), *a.* [f. L. *instruct-*, ppl. stem (see INSTRUCT *v.*) + -IVE. Cf. F. *instructif, -ive* (14th c. in Godef. *Compl.*).] Having the character or quality of instructing; conveying instruction or knowledge.

1611 FLORIO, *Instruttiuo*, instructiue. **1615** J. STEPHENS (*title*) Essays and Characters Ironicall and Instructive. **1653** R. SANDERS *Physiogn.* 156 This Chapter shall be more instructive than what hath been spoken of it elsewhere. **1708** *Brit. Apollo* No. 104. 1/2 To Peruse those Instructive writings. **1738** JOHNSON *Van. Hum. Wishes* 50 Once more, Democritus, arise on earth, With cheerful wisdom and instructive mirth. **1848** W. H. BARTLETT *Egypt to Pal.* xx. (1879) 440 The structure of these sepulchres.. is instructive in regard to the prevalent method of burial.

b. Denoting the case used in some languages, e.g. the Ugro-Finnish group, to express means.

1857 *Trans. Philol. Soc.* 34 Nominative.. genitive.. dative .. instructive.. affective. **1890** C. N. E. ELIOT *Finnish Gram.* 22 The instructive is formed by simply adding the letter *n* to a root, and expresses the means by which anything is done. **1896** [see INESSIVE *a.*]. **1954** PEI & GAYNOR *Dict. Ling.* 102 *Instructive*, in certain languages (e.g., Finno-Ugric languages), a case having the same denotation as the English *by means of*.

instructively (ɪnˈstrʌktɪvlɪ), *adv.* [f. prec. + -LY[2].] In an instructive manner; so as to instruct; †by way of instruction.

1631 *Celestina* Ep. Ded. A iij b, It is written reprehensively and not instructively. **1719** D'URFEY *Pills* I. 359 Whilst Books Instructively do Science raise. **1875** WHITNEY *Life Lang.* viii. 145 No exercises of reason.. are so closely and instructively parallel as these two.

instructiveness (ɪnˈstrʌktɪvnɪs). [f. as prec. + -NESS.] The quality of being instructive.

1661 BOYLE *Style of Script.* (1675) 130 The pregnant instructiveness of the Scripture. **1875** MAINE *Hist. Inst.* viii. 226 A phenomenon of little interest and of no instructiveness. **1886** *Manch. Exam.* 18 Jan. 5/5 An experiment.. which is full of instructiveness for the country at large.

instructor (ɪnˈstrʌktə(r)). Also 5–6 -our. [a. L. *instructor* preparer (in med.L., teacher), agent-n. from *instruĕre* to INSTRUCT. Orig. in AF. form *instructour* = F. *instructeur* (14th c. in Godef. *Compl.*).] One who instructs; a teacher.

1460 CAPGRAVE *Chron.* (Rolls) 260 Thei were principal instructouris of heretikes. **1530** PALSGR. Epistle to King (1852) 7 Maister Gyles Dewes, somtyme instructour to your noble grace in this selfe tonge. **1576** FLEMING *Panopl. Epist.* 213 To the end hee might winne Heraclitus to be his instructour. **1583** HOLLYBAND *Campo di Fior* 53 The most famous instructor of children. **1693** DRYDEN *Juvenal* Ded. (1697) 61 Horace is somewhat the better Instructor of the two.. his Instructions are more general; Juvenal's more limited. **1715** DE FOE *Fam. Instruct.* I. i. (1841) I. 29 The Spirit is the secret instructor. **1873** *Act 36 & 37 Vict.* c. 77 §13 A permanent staff, consisting of an officer, and of so many seamen instructors as may seem fit. **1875** JOWETT *Plato* (ed. 2) V. 397 Let the judgment of them rest with the instructor of youth.

transf. **1879** MᶜCARTHY *Own Times* II. xxix. 369 Such history.. is of little value as an instructor in the lessons of the times and events it deals with.

b. *spec.* in American colleges: A college teacher inferior in rank to a professor; variously = Reader, Teacher, Lecturer, or Tutor, in an English college or university.

1722 in B. Peirce *Hist. Harvard Univ.* (1833) 232 Voted.. that Mr. Judal Monis be *improved* as an instructor of the Hebrew language in the College. **1873** in *Sci. Amer.* (1973) May 11 There are at present 500 students, and the faculty consists of 40 professors and instructors. **1891** *Univ. Chicago Official Bull.* I. 11 Lecturers and teachers.. shall be classified as follows... (6) The Instructor. **1900** *Harvard Univ. Catal.* 1899–1900, 17 Lecturers and Instructors. **1947** [see *full professor* (FULL *a.* 12 d)].

Hence **instrucˈtorial** *a.*; **inˈstructorship**, the office or post of an instructor.

1882–3 *Schaff's Encycl. Relig. Knowl.* III. 2344 Recently the instructorship has been changed to a professorship. **1890** *Pall Mall G.* 23 Oct. 1/3 To found, or aid in founding, an instructorship in road engineering. **1952** Instructorial [see *assistant professor*].

instructress (ɪnˈstrʌktrɪs). [f. INSTRUCTOR or -ER + -ESS.] A female instructor. Also *fig.*

1630 BRATHWAIT *Eng. Gentl.* III. 75 Education is the Seasoner or instructresse [*ed.* 1641 *mispr.* instructess] of Youth, in principles of knowledge [etc.]. **1742** RICHARDSON *Pamela* IV. 38 You must allow me to look upon you as.. my Instructress. **1825** LYTTON *Falkland* 28 To be the instructress of an infant, a Mother should be its playmate. **1845** R. W. HAMILTON *Pop. Educ.* ix. (ed. 2) 229 It will be said, that the Church of the Country is the proper instructress of the people.

†**inˈstructrice.** *Obs. rare*[−1]. [f. INSTRUCTOR, after fem. forms from F. in *-rice*.] = prec.

1531 ELYOT *Gov.* III. iii, Knowledge also, as a perfeyte instructrice and mastresse.. declareth by what meane the sayd preceptes of reason.. may be well vnderstande.

†**ˈinstrumency.** *Obs. rare.* [irreg. f. INSTRUMENT, after sbs. in -ENCY from adjs. in -ENT.] = INSTRUMENTALITY I.

1675 WOODHEAD, etc. *Paraphr. Heb.* 11 Deliverances.. done by the instrumency of the angels.

instrument (ˈɪnstrəmənt), *sb.* [a. F. *instrument* (14th c.; the earlier form was *estrument*), or ad. L. *instrūment-um* provision, apparatus, furniture, an implement or tool, a document, f. *instruĕre* to fit out, equip, INSTRUCT.]

1. a. That which is used by an agent in or for the performance of an action; a thing with or through which something is done or effected; anything that serves or contributes to the accomplishment of a purpose or end; a means.

1340 HAMPOLE *Pr. Consc.* 3139 Bot þat fire.. es An instrument of Goddes ryghtwysnes. **1387–8** T. USK *Test. Love* III. vi. (Skeat) I. 52 Ye han in your bodie diuers members, and fiue sondrie wittes,.. whiche thynges as instrumentes ye vsen, as your handes apart to handle. *c* **1477** CAXTON *Jason* 37 Spekyng with the mouth whiche is instrument of the dischargyng and discouering of hertes. *c* **1532** DU WES *Introd. Fr.* in Palsgr. 987 This verbe *am* the which is an instrument wherby we do expresse by our wordes all verbes passives. **1570** T. NORTON tr. *Nowel's Catech.* (1853) 180 Faith is not the cause but the instrument of justification. **1605** SHAKS. *Lear* V. iii. 171 The Gods are iust, and of our pleasant vices Make instruments to plague vs. **1675** BAXTER *Cath. Theol.* I. I. 107 Properly an Instrument is an efficient cause moved by the principal to an effect above its proper virtue. **1776** ADAM SMITH *W.N.* IV. i. (1869) II. 2 Among the Tartars.. cattle are the instruments of commerce. **1807** T. THOMSON *Chem.* (ed. 3) II. 521 The importance of the salts as chemical instruments is very much connected with their solubility in water. **1846** WRIGHT *Ess. Mid. Ages* II. xix. 259 At all periods of English history, songs and ballads were the popular instruments equally of libel and of praise.

b. A person made use of by another person or being, for the accomplishment of a purpose. (In mod. use often taken as *fig.* from 2: cf. *tool*.)

a **1340** HAMPOLE *Psalter* xliv. 2 *comm.*, His instrument, whaim he ledis as he will. *c* **1386** CHAUCER *Man of Law's T.* 272 Thou madest Eua brynge vs in seruage.. Thyn Instrument so.. Makestow of wommen whan thou wolt bigile. **1548** HALL *Chron.*, *Hen. V* 68 The duke of Burgoyn was a convenient organe and a necessary instrument to conveigh his desires to his purpose. **1611** SHAKS. *Wint. T.* I. ii. 415 He sweares, As he had seen't, or beene an Instrument To vice you to't. **1661** BRAMHALL *Just Vind.* iii. 43 God used him as an instrument to reform his Church. **1726** SWIFT *Gulliver* I. v, I would never be an instrument of bringing a free and brave people into slavery. **1867** BRIGHT *Sp. America* 29 June (1876) 144 To do honour to a most eminent instrument in the achievement of that freedom. **1896** *Daily News* 28 Apr. 3/1 The divergence between Mr. Chamberlain and his instrument in South Africa has been no less marked.

2. a. A material thing designed or used for the accomplishment of some mechanical or other physical effect; a mechanical contrivance (usually one that is portable, of simple construction, and wielded or operated by the hand); a tool, implement, weapon. Also applied to devices whose primary function is to respond to a physical quantity or phenomenon, esp. by registering or measuring it, rather than to accomplish an effect, and which may function with little direct human intervention and be of complicated design and construction.

Now usually distinguished from a *tool*, as being used for more delicate work or for artistic or scientific purposes: a workman or artizan has his *tools*, a draughtsman, surgeon, dentist, astronomical observer, his *instruments*. Distinguished from a *machine*, as being simpler, having less mechanism, and doing less work of itself; but the terms overlap.

1375 BARBOUR *Bruce* XVII. 342 The ynglis host.. With Instrumentis on seir maneris, As scaffatis, ledderis, and coueryngis, Pykis, howis, and ek staff-slyngis. *c* **1391** CHAUCER *Astrol.* Prol. ¶ 1 Conclusions apertenyng to the same instrument [Astrolabe]. **1432–50** tr. *Higden* (Rolls) I. 357 Berenge in theire honde an instrumente callede a sparth. **1530** PALSGR. 234/2 Instrument of any handy crafte, *ovtil.* **1592** SHAKS. *Rom. & Jul.* v. iii. 200 Here is a Frier, and Slaughter'd Romeos man, With Instruments vpon them fit to open These dead mens Tombes. **1611** BIBLE *2 Sam.* xxiv. 22 Here be oxen for burnt sacrifice, and threshing instruments. **1634** SIR T. HERBERT *Trav.* 147 A Crossebowe,.. not comparable to the Gun (an instrument they now make practice of). **1658** W. SANDERSON *Graphice* 68 Take a needle or small pointed Instrument, heated in a Candle. **1672** PETTY *Pol. Anat.* (1691) 49 An Instrument to measure the Motion of the Wind. **1672** [see BAROMETER]. **1774** M. MACKENZIE *Maritime Surv.* 74 The other Distances may be got sufficiently exact by Intersections of a good Needle, without any other Instrument to take the Angles. **1839** [see INDICATOR 3]. **1843** J. CLASON *Serm.* xi. 189 Instruments of torture are unknown. **1845** *Encycl. Metrop.* IV. 68/1 By the term *Electroscope* we understand an instrument which enables us to observe the presence of free electricity. **1864** *Rep. Brit. Assoc. Adv. Sci. 1863* 147 Electric currents are most simply compared by 'electro-dynamometers' (20)——instruments which, unlike galvanometers, are practically independent of the intensity of the earth's magnetism. **1876** [see INDICATOR 3]. **1884** *List of Subscribers* (London & Globe Telephone Co.), The

newest and most improved Telephonic Instruments and Apparatus. *Ibid.*, Subscribers..must not allow non-subscribers to use their instruments for the transmission of messages. **1888** S. R. BOTTONE *Electr. Instrument Making* (ed. 2) 116 Ammeters.—These instruments are intended to measure the amount of current in ampères passing through any given circuit. **1889** PREECE & MAIER *Telephone* xxix. 464 An instrument of such marvellous sensitiveness as the telephone. *a* **1900** *Mod.* A case of mathematical instruments. The surgeon had to use instruments. **1910** R. W. A. BREWER *Art of Aviation* xvi. 213 Other instruments will be carried to indicate the speed of the machine relatively to the air and to the land. **1924** P. J. RISDON *Wireless* xxxviii. 304 These bells are kept ringing until the operator gets to his instruments, adjusts his headpiece and is ready to receive the direction signals giving the position of the vessel in distress. **1947** E. W. F. FELLER *Instrument & Control Manual* xii. 280 The primary purpose of an emergency instrument is to sound an alarm or shut down equipment upon some abnormal operation. **1950** A. MARCUS *Radio Servicing* xiii. 585 The vacuum-tube voltmeter..is rapidly becoming one of the most useful instruments employed in radio servicing. **1957** *Encycl. Brit.* XII. 447/1 Instruments which make a record on paper of the magnitude of an electrical quantity with time are available in considerable variety. **1959** K. ULLYETT *Jaguar Compan.* x. 170 Polished figured walnut instrument panel features revolution counter and speedometer..and separate instruments for oil pressure, water temperature, fuel gauge and ammeter. **1963** GODDARD & BROWN *Pract. Chem.* iii. 57 In modern analytical techniques, heavy reliance is placed upon the use of instruments, such as pH-meters, potentiometric titrators,..spectrographs, polarimeters, refractometers, etc. **1967** D. P. DAVIES *Handling Big Jets* viii. 231 The attitude indicator is the primary flight instrument for turbulence flying.

†**b.** *collect.* Apparatus. (A Latinism.) *Obs.*

1671 MILTON *P.R.* III. 388 Much ostentation vain of fleshy arm, And fragile arms, much instrument of war.

3. *spec.* A contrivance for producing musical sounds, by the vibrations of some solid material (as strings, reeds, rods, membranes, etc.), or of a body of air in a pipe or tube.

Musical instruments are commonly classified as WIND *instruments*, STRINGED *instruments*, and *instruments of* PERCUSSION (most REED *instruments* being classed under *wind instruments*): see these words.

c **1290** *S. Eng. Leg.* I. 225/191 As a fiþele his wynges furde ..Muriere Instrument neuere nas þan his wyngen were! **13..** *E.E. Allit. P.* B. 1081 Aungelles with instrumentes of organes & pypes. *c* **1381** CHAUCER *Parl. Foules* 197 Of Instreumentis of strengis in a-cord Herde I so pleye, and rauyshyng swetnesse. *c* **1400** MAUNDEV. (Roxb.) xix. 88 Next..gase all þe mynistralles..with all maner of instruments of music. *a* **1533** LD. BERNERS *Huon* li. 172, I am a mynstrell as thou seest here by myne instrumentes. **1540** in *Old City Acc. Bk.* in *Archæol. Jrnl.* XLIII, Pd to yᵉ clarke for playeng of yᵉ yensterment iiijᵈ. **1604** SHAKS. *Oth.* III. i. 6 Are these I pray you, winde Instruments? **1796** JANE AUSTEN *Pride & Prej.* vi. (1813) 20, I am going to open the instrument, Eliza, and you know what follows. **1815** —— *Emma* (1870) III. x. 287 She..put the music aside, and..closed the instrument. **1863** LONGF. *Wayside Inn* Prel. 271 The instrument on which he played Was in Cremona's workshops made.

†**4.** A part of the body having a special function; an organ. *Obs.*

c **1386** CHAUCER *Wife's Prol.* 149 In wyfhode I wol vse myn Instrument As frely as my makere hath it sent. *c* **1400** tr. *Secreta Secret., Gov. Lordsh.* (E.E.T.S.) 79 Cold water dronkyn yn wynter..destruys þe Instrumentis of þe brest, & harmys þe longys. **1572** J. JONES *Bathes of Bath* II. 18a, Instrument, or organ [of taste] is a skinne pellicle, or philme, stretched in the over part of the tongue. **1656** RIDGLEY *Pract. Physick* 28 Whatsoever is troublesome to the instruments of breathing. **1718** J. CHAMBERLAYNE *Relig. Philos.* (1730) I. xiii. §1 Among all the Instruments which Animals use, those of the external Senses are least of all known to us.

5. a. *Law.* A formal legal document whereby a right is created or confirmed, or a fact recorded; a formal writing of any kind, as an agreement, deed, charter, or record, drawn up and executed in technical form, so as to be of legal validity.

1483 CAXTON *Gold. Leg.* 257/1 It ought to be myn for I haue therof an Instrument publyque. **1494** FABYAN *Chron.* VII. 344 The sayde lordys shewyd an instrument or wrytynge, at yᵉ which hynge many labellys with sealys, as the Kynges seale, syr Edwarde hys sonnys seale, wᵗ many other of the nobles of the lande. **1523** LD. BERNERS *Froiss.* I. clxxiv. 211 Of this ordynaunce and bondes there were made instrumentes publykes, and letters patentes, seyled by bothe Kynges. **1570** BUCHANAN *Admonit.* Wks. (1892) 28 Yᵉ cardinall Betoun quha be ane fals instrument had taken yᵉ suppreme authoritie to himself. **1607** TOPSELL *Four-f. Beasts* (1658) 214 There were present at the sight hereof seven publick notaries, which called witnesses, and made instruments thereupon. **1660** *Trial Regic.* 45 We shall show that Instrument, that was made under the Hand, and Seal, of the Prisoner at the Bar, as well as others, for Execution of the King: that Bloody Warrant. **1767** BLACKSTONE *Comm.* II. ix. 142 We may observe, in Madox's collection of antient instruments, some leases for years of a pretty early date. **1827** HALLAM *Const. Hist.* (1876) II. x. 245 The instrument under which he [Cromwell] took his title accorded to him no unnecessary executive authority. **1845** MᶜCULLOCH *Taxation* II. vi. §3 (1852) 284 The payment of the proper duty is made essential to the validity of an instrument. **1866** CRUMP *Banking* v. 104 Where an instrument is drawn in a careless way, in the form of a promissory note, and accepted, and indorsed as a bill of exchange.

b. *Sc. Law.* A formal and duly authenticated record, drawn up by a notary-public, of any transaction; hence *to ask, give, take instruments.*

1535 LYNDESAY *Satyre* 2832 (Bannatyne MS.) To that, my lordis, planely we disconsent; Notar, thairof I tak ane instrument. **1540** *Sc. Acts Jas. V*, c. 81 Gif the Notar and Scribe of courte refusis to giue instrumentes, actes, or notes to ony persones desirand the samin, he sall tine his office. **1572** BUCHANAN *Detect. Mary* F ij (Jam.), Upon the quhilk ..the said aduocate askit an act of Court and Instrumentis, and desyrit of the Justice proces conform thairto. *a* **1693** URQUHART *Rabelais* III. xxiii, We will take Instrument formally and authentically extended, to the end he be not, after his Decease declared an Heretick. **1814** SCOTT *Wav.* l, The Baron of Bradwardine then took instruments..bearing that all points and circumstances of the act of homage had been *rite et solenniter acta et peracta.* **1897** *Johnston of Warriston's Diary* (Scot. Hist. Soc.) 96 *note*, Instruments are the formal and duly authenticated narrative by a Notary public of *res gestae* of which a person interested desires to preserve a record. The practice of taking instruments is now confined for the most part to Church Courts.

6. *attrib.* and *Comb.*, as ***instrument-maker***, ***-making*** (usually scientific instruments), etc.; ***instrument-carrying*** adj.; **instrument board** = *instrument panel*; **instrument panel**, a surface on which gauges, dials, etc., of measuring or indicating instruments are grouped together (as in a motor vehicle or aircraft).

1917 'CONTACT' *Airman's Outings* 18 Not till a pilot can fly his bus unconsciously does he keep place without repeated reference to the throttle and *instrument-board. **1926** *Amer. Speech* I. 686/1 Automobile nomenclature... Instrument board [American], facia board [English]. **1930** P. WHITE *How to fly Airplane* iv. 65 The first endeavor of the pilot-instructor is to familiarize the beginner with..the functions of the various controls, and with the instrument board. **1935** *Discovery* Feb. 44/2 The Leningrad University Observatory is stated to be building a high-altitude *instrument-carrying rocket for stratospheric work. **1959** *Daily Tel.* 1 May 1/1 The programme will certainly enable Britain to put three or four instrument-carrying satellites into space. **1876** PREECE & SIVEWRIGHT *Telegraphy* 294 The *instrument counters and floors. *a* **1691** BOYLE *Hist. Air* (1692) 99 Made by a skilful Mathematical-*Instrument-maker. **1770** BARRINGTON in *Phil. Trans.* LXI. 294, I.. directed two rain-gages..to be made by your instrument-maker. **1836** DUBOURG *Violin* ix. (1878) 269 The Italian renown for *instrument-making attained its climax by the productions of..Straduarius and Guamerius. **1933** *Discovery* Feb. 59/2 An *instrument panel..is incorporated in the camera. **1935** *Economist* 7 Dec. 1140/1 The use of plastics in the motor accessory field will undoubtedly increase considerably in the future... Another noteworthy development with which plastics are connected is the combination instrument panel... By grouping all the instruments in a single panel the space saved can be utilised to give larger storage pockets. **1958** W. R. BARRETT et al. in H. W. Cremer *Chem. Engin. Pract.* V. 126 Large [air-compressor] installations usually have an instrument panel on which are fitted all pressure gauges and a temperature indicator. **1972** E. H. J. PALLETT *Aircraft Instruments* iii. 43 A more effective and standardized grouping has now been adopted; this is known as the 'basic T'... It constitutes a system by which various items of related flight information can be placed in certain standard locations in all instrument panels. **1876** PREECE & SIVEWRIGHT *Telegraphy* 280 The upper and lower rows of terminals are used for the 'Up' and 'Down' line wires: the two intermediate rows are '*Instrument' terminals.

b. With reference to the use of, esp. dependence on, instruments in the flying of aircraft, as ***instrument conditions***, ***runway***, ***weather***; **instrument flying**, flying in which the pilot makes no observation of the ground but depends entirely on the instruments in the aircraft; so ***instrument flight***; similarly **instrument approach** or **landing**, an approach (APPROACH *sb.* 13) or landing in which the pilot depends entirely on instruments and a ground-based radio guidance system (an ***instrument landing system***).

1947 *Engineering News-Record* 16 Oct. 532/3 Runway E, for instrument approach is 10,000 ft. long and will be paved 8,000 × 200 ft. **1957** *Encycl. Brit.* I. 230/1 During World War II another system was developed for instrument approaches. This..used a talk-down technique. **1957** Instrument conditions [see *instrument landing* below]. **1943** Instrument flight [see *instrument flying* below]. **1956** W. A. HEFLIN *U.S. Air Force Dict.* 270/2 *Instrument flight*, a flight made by using instruments, without visual reference to the ground. **1928** STERLING & KRUSE *Radio Manual* xiii. 506 While instrument flying may enable a pilot to keep his craft at a safe altitude and in a generally correct direction, the hazard of getting far away from the course..is ever present. **1943** *Instrument Flight* (U.S. Bureau of Aeronautics (Navy Dept.)) p. iii, Instrument flying is as logical and easy as contact flying. **1938** *Proc. IRE* XXVI. 681 At present, the major airlines are planning to install a number of instrument landing systems. **1942** J. B. HOAG *Basic Radio* xxxiv. 288 At certain airports, a radio wave is transmitted..to provide a glider path for 'blind' or instrument landing. **1957** *Encycl. Brit.* I. 230/1 In the United States the Civil Aeronautics administration developed a system for landing approaches under instrument conditions, commonly known as ILS (instrument landing system). **1947** *Shell Aviation News* CXIII. 3/1 It will have three runways: an instrument runway (8,500 ft. × 250 ft.) and two non-instrument runways. **1951** *Gloss. Aeronaut. Terms* (*B.S.I.*) III. 23 *Instrument runway*.., a runway..equipped with non-visual aids for take-off and landing. **1949** *Britannica Bk. of Year 1948* 37/1 Seventy-nine per cent. of all aircraft..landed during instrument weather with no traffic delays.

instrument (ˈɪnstrəmənt, ɪnstruːˈmɛnt), *v.* [f. prec. sb.: cf. F. *instrumenter* (1440 in Hatz.-Darm.). For the pronunciation cf. COMPLIMENT *v.*]

1. *Law.* **a.** *intr.* To draw up an instrument (see prec. 5). **b.** *trans.* To address an instrument to, petition by means of an instrument.

1719 *Descr. Parish of Deer* in Alex. Smith *Aberdeensh.* (1875) 1065 The presbitry instrumented in terms of the act of parliament, to make patent doors for them. **1752** J. LOUTHIAN *Form of Process* (ed. 2) 74 When the sixty Days are run, and no Indictment execute, then the Prisoner instruments the Lord Advocate..and thereafter presents a Petition.. for Letters of Liberation.

2. *Mus.* To arrange or score (a piece of music) for instruments, esp. for an orchestra.

1822 *Blackw. Mag.* XII. 443 These he hastily wrote down upon scraps of paper, and next morning arranged them; or, to make use of his own term, instrumented them. **1845** E. HOLMES *Mozart* 136 Mozart..is deep in a 'Miserere'..to contain three choruses, a fugue, and a duet, and to be instrumented for a large orchestra. **1878** E. PROUT in Grove *Dict. Mus.* I. 35 *note*, The Te Deum and Acis were instrumented by Mendelssohn.

3. *trans.* To equip or provide with instruments (for measuring, recording, controlling, etc.).

1949 *Trans. Soc. Instrument Technol.* I. v. 21/1 The extent of instrumentation..is greater than it is in comparable British plants, although the most modern of these are just as comprehensively instrumented as their opposite numbers in the U.S.A. **1959** *Instrument Pract.* XIII. 194/1 The methods [of analysis] are used specifically for production control and merely to instrument them for laboratory use may be to daily unnecessarily halfway. **1961** *New Scientist* 16 Mar. 661/1 The system will be equipped throughout for automatic control and instrumented for safety. **1962** *B.S.I. News* Feb. 27/2 The whole equipment will be scientifically instrumented. **1962** F. I. ORDWAY et al. *Basic Astronautics* iv. 125 Explorer II..was instrumented primarily to detect and measure high-energy gamma rays. **1970** *Physics Bull.* Mar. 107/1 It would be too costly to instrument and monitor the whole process.

So ˈ**instrumented** *ppl. a.*, equipped with or using instruments.

1947 *Shell Aviation News* CIX. 13/1 In a large hangar there [is]..the completely instrumented fuselage of a modern bomber. **1954** *Trans. Soc. Instrument Technol.* VI. 47/1 An analysis of the total number of instruments employed on a well-instrumented ironmaking plant. **1957** *Times* 10 Oct. 10/1 The first fully instrumented satellite was planned for launching in March. **1967** *Guardian* 19 Oct. 1/7 The Russian success in carrying out the first instrumented landing on another planet. **1972** *Lebende Sprachen* XVII. 72/2 This is the launch day scheduled for UK-3, the third British-instrumented satellite to be lifted into orbit by an American scout rocket.

instrumental (ɪnstruːˈmɛntəl), *a.* and *sb.* [a. F. *instrumental* (Oresme, 14th c.), ad. med.L. *instrūmentālis*: see INSTRUMENT *sb.* and -AL[1].]

A. *adj.*

1. a. Of the nature of an instrument (material or subservient); serving as an instrument or means; contributing to the accomplishment of a purpose or result.

1398 TREVISA *Barth. De P.R.* III. xx[i]. (Add MS. 27944), The cause material and instrumental [L. *instrumentalis*] is in the tonge. **1478** *Househ. Ord.* (1790) 44 No fees of plate nor sylver, but it be in his instrumental tools perused by occupation. **1576** FLEMING *Panopl. Epist.* To Rdr. ¶v b, The service of his naturall abilities, and the use of his instrumentall powers. **1583** STUBBES *Anat. Abus.* II. (1882) 59 We giue unto God..the cheefest rule in all things, all other creatures being but the instrumentall, or secundarie causes. **1697** tr. *Burgersdicius his Logic* I. xvii. 65 The Instrumental Cause is that which subserves the principal Cause in its Effecting. **1766** FORDYCE *Serm. Yng. Wom.* (1767) II. xi. 137 The instrumental duties of religion, as they are usually termed. **1848** H. ROGERS *Ess.* (1874) I. vi. 322 The art of persuasive argumentation will, like every other instrumental art, be capable of abuse.

b. Const. *to*, *in*; †*inf.*; rarely †*of*, †*for*.

1650 JER. TAYLOR *Holy Living* (J.), Prayer, which is instrumental to every thing. **1655** HARTLIB *Ref. Silk-worm* To Rdr., Then would all hands be set a-work, and every one would become instrumentall to serve himselfe and his Neighbours in Love. **1663** DRYDEN *Wild Gallant* IV. i, You have been instrumental, I hear, of my Preferment. **1666** PEPYS *Diary* 28 Apr., My Lady Castlemaine is instrumental in this Matter. **1722** SEWEL *Hist. Quakers* (1795) I. Pref. 9, I was prepared to be instrumental for such a work as this. **1736** BUTLER *Anal.* I. iii. Wks. 1874 I. 57 Instrumental in bringing about revolutions. **1873** SYMONDS *Grk. Poets* i. 17 Zeal for greater rigour of thought was instrumental in developing a new vehicle of language in the creation of a prose style. **1881** J. SIMON in *Nature* XXIV. 372/1 When the life of either man or brute is to be made merely instrumental to the establishment of a scientific truth.

c. Serving well for the purpose; serviceable, useful; effective, efficient. Now *rare* or *Obs.*

1602 SHAKS. *Ham.* I. ii. 48 The Head is not more Natiue to the Heart, The Hand more Instrumentall to the Mouth. **1672** MARVELL *Reh. Transp.* I. 26 How instrumental soever the Captain hath been, the General usually carries away the honour of the Action. **1674** *Essex Papers* (Camden) 249 My Lord Conway & Sʳ Arthʳ Forbese have bin instrumentall & usefull to me herein. **1709** SWIFT *Advancem. Relig.* Wks. 1755 II. I. 115 It would be very instrumental to have a law made. **1782** PRIESTLEY *Corrupt. Chr.* I. II. 175 Those truths which are most instrumental.

2. Of, pertaining to, performed with, or arising from, a material instrument; due to the instrument (as *instrumental error*).

1644 NYE *Gunnery* II. (1647) 47 The degree in the Circle, that was cut in the Circle of the Instrument, when you made your Instrumentall observation. **1760** PEMBERTON in *Phil. Trans.* LI. 921 The instrumental construction proposed by Mr. Collins will very readily give the true latitude. **1797** DOWNING *Disord. Horned Cattle* 129 All instrumental methods of extraction I wish to avoid as much as possible. **1830** HERSCHEL *Stud. Nat. Phil.* 125 We are obliged to have recourse to instrumental aids. **1858** —— *Outl. Astron.* (ed. 5) iii. §141 Such inquiries constitute the theory of instrumental

errors. **1876** *Clin. Soc. Trans.* IX. 70 No instrumental treatment had taken place that day.

3. a. Of Music: Performed on, or composed for, an instrument or instruments. (Opp. to *vocal.*)

1509 HAWES *Past. Pleas.* XVI. *heading*, Of musike: mundain, humayn, and instrumental. **1597** HOOKER *Eccl. Pol.* v. xxxviii. §2 They which..require the abrogation of instrumentall musique. **1641** EVELYN *Diary* 5 Oct., His three daughters entertained us with rare music, vocal and instrumental. **1667** MILTON *P.L.* IV. 686 With Heav'nly touch of instrumental sounds In full harmonic number joind. **1891** *Times* 8 Oct. 7/4 When these alone sing, the balance is better kept by omitting the instrumental parts.

b. Of the nature of, or belonging to, a musical instrument. *rare.*

a **1683** WALTON *Angler* i. (1886) 15 The nightingale.. breathes such sweet loud music out of her little instrumental throat. *a* **1822** SHELLEY *To Constantia Singing* iii, The blood and life within those snowy fingers Teach witchcraft to the instrumental strings.

†**4.** *Old Physiol.* Having a special vital function; that is a bodily organ; organic. (Cf. INSTRUMENT *sb.* 4.) *Obs.*

1533 ELYOT *Cast. Helthe* (1541) 10b, Members instrumentall [are] The stomake: The raines: The bowelles: All the great synewes. **1578** BANISTER *Hist. Man* IV. 44 A Muscle..is an instrumentall part of the body. **1607** TOPSELL *Four-f. Beasts* (1658) 266, I wish all Farriars..to know the causes of all diseases, as well in the parts similar as instrumental.

5. *Gram.* The name of a case in the declensions of some languages (as Sanskrit and Slavonic), denoting that *with* or *by* which something is done.

Called also 'the ablative of the instrument', and by early authors of English Sanskrit grammars *causative*, and *implementive*. The Skr. name is *karaṇa* means, instrument.

1806 CAREY *Sungskrit Gram.* 864 Of the instrumental case after the verb. **1813** W. TAYLOR in *Monthly Rev.* LXXI. 476 Several Slavonian dialects..have seven cases, the six cases of the Latins, and an instrumental case. **1874–5** PAPILLON *Man. Comp. Philol.* (1877) 106 In both languages [Greek and Latin] we shall find remnants of both locative and instrumental forms. **1879** WHITNEY *Sanscrit Gram.* §283 Many instrumental constructions..call in translation for other prepositions than 'with' or 'by'; yet the true instrumental relation is usually to be traced.

6. *Law.* = INSTRUMENTARY *a.* 3. *rare.*

1790 DALLAS *Amer. Law Rep.* I. 209 Instrumental witnesses are always called upon.

7. *Psychol.* A term used to describe the type of learning where a particular response is the instrument by which the organism is taught to alter its environment.

1940 HILGARD & MARQUIS *Conditioning & Learning* iii. 51 When the occurrence of the reinforcement is contingent upon the organism's behavior the procedure may be termed instrumental conditioning. *Ibid.* 52 As a reference experiment for instrumental reward training we may select a study by Grindley. **1956** B. R. BUGELSKI *Psychol. of Learning* iv. 58 'Instrumental' learning covers all other types. It is called 'instrumental' because the organism is learning how to affect its environment to bring about some change. **1964** M. ARGYLE *Psychol. & Social Probl.* x. 128 Instrumental learning consists of the blind stamping-in of rewarded responses. **1969** R. H. SCHUSTER in D. P. Hendry *Conditioned Reinforcement* viii. 194 The complication of three factors is necessary—simple association, instrumental reinforcement, and a decay process. *Ibid.* 195 Whether the stimuli precede or follow an instrumental response. **1971** J. L. GEWIRTZ in R. Glaser *Nature of Reinforcement* viii. 288 He assumes that instrumental conditioning might be more effective for the acquisition of responses connoting complex skills. **1972** *New Yorker* 26 Aug. 32/1 Edward L. Thorndike ..is credited with the first rigorous investigation of trial-and-error, or instrumental, learning.

B. *sb.*

†**1.** That which is instrumental to some end or purpose (see A. 1); an instrument, means. *Obs.*

[**1597** A. M. tr. *Guillemeau's Fr. Chirurg.* Q, To demonstrate, not only the materialle and formal principles, but the Instrumentalles.] **1605** BACON *Adv. Learn.* II. i. §10 Unto the deepe, fruitefull, and operative studie of many Scyences..Bookes be not the only Instrumentals. **1643** SIR J. SPELMAN *Case of Affairs* 11 Through the concurrence of those that are the instrumentals of His restraint.

†**2.** An 'instrumental' part of the body (see A. 4); a bodily organ. *Obs.*

1541 R. COPLAND *Guydon's Quest. Chirurg.* etc., As to the seconde questyon that asketh why they [members] be called organykes & instrumentalles. **1564** P. MOORE *Hope Health* I. iv. 7 Some other partes in the body be called.. instrumentalles and vnlyke partes.

3. *Gram.* The instrumental case, 'the ablative of the instrument' : see A. 5.

1806 CAREY *Sungskrit Gram.* 35 There are seven cases, viz. the Nominative, Accusative, Instrumental [etc.]. **1824** HEARD *Russ. Gram.* §9 There are six cases in the Russian Language: the Nominative, the Accusative, the Genitive, the Dative, the Instrumental, the Prepositional. **1879** SWEET *Anglo-Sax. Rdr.* (ed. 2) Introd. 48 Adjectives have the three genders of nouns, and the same cases, with the addition of the instrumental. **1879** WHITNEY *Sanscrit Gram.* §278 The instrumental is originally the *with*-case: it denotes adjacency, accompaniment, association—passing over into the expression of means and instrument (*with* and *by*).

4. (See quot. 1945.)

1940 *Swing* July 17/1 Bob Mersey's *Blue Ink* is another slightly *Wham*-like instrumental. **1945** *Music Library Assoc. Notes* 2nd Ser. VII. 1. 45/1 *Instrumental*, composition written for instrumental performance, solo or group. Also, any performance without benefit of a vocal. **1949** L. FEATHER *Inside Be-Bop* i. 9 Dizzy..changed it from a slow ballad to a jump-tempo instrumental. **1972** *Jazz & Blues* Sept. 11/3 'Jump' instrumentals, normally featuring the tenor of Herb Hardesty.

instrumentalism (ɪnstruːˈmɛntəlɪz(ə)m). *Philos.* [f. INSTRUMENTAL *a.* + -ISM.] The pragmatic theory of John Dewey (1859–1952) that thought exists as an instrument of adjustment to the environment; *spec.* that terms of thought and meaning are relative to the function they perform and that their validity or truth is determined by their efficacy.

1909 *Philos. Rev.* XVIII. 396 By instrumentalism is meant that element of pragmatism which has grown out of the application of the evolutionary method to logical problems. **1929** J. DEWEY *Experience & Nature* iv. 151 'Instrumentalism' is a theory not about personal disposition and satisfaction in knowing, but about the proper objects of science. **1931** A. WOLF in W. Rose *Outl. Mod. Knowl.* 549 Pragmatism, instrumentalism, and fictionism..treat beliefs as instruments of life, and to be valued accordingly. **1948** B. RUSSELL *Human Knowl.* 75 There is another kind of 'meaning', which gives occasion for pragmatism and instrumentalism. **1968** J. J. C. SMART *Between Sci. & Philos.* v. 142 Instrumentalism does allow theoretical concepts to be quite free constructions of the theorist.

instruˈmentalist. [f. INSTRUMENTAL + -IST.]

1. a. One who plays on a musical instrument; a performer of instrumental music. (Opp. to *vocalist.*)

1823 *Herald* in *Spirit Pub. Jrnls.* (1824) 108 There are many aspiring instrumentalists who protest boldly against the monopoly. **1864** H. SPENCER *Illustr. Univ. Progr.* 26 Uniting the now separate offices of poet, composer, vocalist, and instrumentalist. **1871** *Athenæum* 2 Dec. 727 This body of vocalists and instrumentalists.

b. A composer of instrumental music. *rare.*

1880 W. S. ROCKSTRO in Grove *Dict. Mus.* II. 572 The age in which he [Beethoven] lived produced more than one instrumentalist of the highest order.

2. An advocate of the use of instrumental music in public worship. *nonce-use.*

1882–3 in Schaff *Encycl. Relig. Knowl.* 1961 An injunction is more than a permission, which is all for which most instrumentalists contend.

3. *Philos.* One who advocates the theory of instrumentalism. Also *attrib.*

1909 *Philos. Rev.* XVIII. 397 From the instrumentalist standpoint, the inquiry, *What is reality*? appears..futile. **1913** W. CALDWELL *Pragmatism & Idealism* i. 17 Professor Dewey has also written many..short studies upon the application of an instrumentalist conception of philosophy to education and to social questions. **1940** B. RUSSELL *Inquiry into Meaning & Truth* viii. 154 There are some schools of philosophy—notably the Hegelians and the instrumentalists—which deny the distinction between data and inferences altogether. **1965** J. D. NORTH *Measure of Universe* App. 421 It would be misleading to describe the views represented in this book as 'pragmatist' or 'instrumentalist'.

instrumentality (ˌɪnstruːmənˈtælɪtɪ). [f. as prec. + -ITY.]

1. The quality or condition of being instrumental; the fact or function of serving or being used for the accomplishment of some purpose or end; agency.

1651 BAXTER *Inf. Bapt.* 332 They say Their own Faith is Physically the efficient instrumentall cause of their own forgiveness and justification; Yea that it is a Passive Reception of Christ himself (by the said Physicall instrumentality). **1692** RAY *Dissol. World* iii. (1732) 9 By the Intervention and Instrumentality of second Causes. **1747** BUTLER *Serm. Ho. Lords* Wks. 1874 II. 292 Civil government is that part of God's government..which he exercises by the instrumentality of men. **1849** MACAULAY *Hist. Eng.* vii. II. 254 An interest was established in the army by the instrumentality of Churchill.

2. with *pl.* That which serves or is employed for some purpose or end; a means, an agency.

a **1677** HALE *Prim. Orig. Man.* IV. ii. 295 God needed not the subsidiary Instrumentalities of Nature to compleat his Work. **1833** I. TAYLOR *Fanat.* I. 11 The moral and intelligent instrumentality..is nothing else than the vital force which animates each single believer. **1838** GLADSTONE *State in Rel. Ch.* iv. (L.), From that liability to abuse with which state power is charged, no human instrumentality is exempt. **1875** MAINE *Hist. Inst.* ix. 255 One of the most powerful instrumentalities in the historical transformation of the civilised world.

†**instruˈmentalize,** *v. Obs.* [f. as prec. + -IZE.]

1. *trans.* To make or render instrumental to some end; to fashion into an instrument; to organize.

1594 CAREW *Huarte's Exam. Wits* To Rdr., Hee instrumentalized their braine in such sort, as they might receiue it with ease. *Ibid.* (1616) 50 If a reasonable soule informe a well instrumentalized bodie..his knowledge comes little behind that of the subtillest deuill. **1629** T. ADAMS *Medit. Creed* Wks. 1862 III. 147 God first instrumentalised a perfect body, and then infused a living soul.

2. To measure or reckon by means of instruments.

1610 W. FOLKINGHAM *Art of Survey* II. iv. 53 If the place cannot bee brought within view, instrumentalize the tract at Randon. *Ibid.*, To instrumentalize a distance, first point-forth two competent stations, and from the first quantulate the angle betwixt the marke and second station.

instrumentally (ɪnstruːˈmɛntəlɪ), *adv.* [f. INSTRUMENTAL *a.* + -LY[2].]

1. In an instrumental manner; in the way of instrumentality. **a.** As an instrument or means; by being employed for some purpose.

1581 SHERWIN in *Confer.* I. (1584) Eiv, Faith iustifieth instrumentally. **1608** A. WILLET *Hexapla Exod.* 41 Angels.. may instrumentallie pronounce the blessings of God. **1711** G. CARY *Phys. Phylactick* 146 God..Excommunicates Efficiently, the Clergy do it Instrumentally, as his Instruments. *a* **1795** BURKE *Popery Laws* iii. I. Wks. IX. 362 They will argue, that the end being essentially beneficial, the means become instrumentally so. **1871** *Daily News* 1 Feb., To acknowledge it..as instrumentally capable of bringing about the meeting of a 'National Assembly'.

b. By the agency of another thing or person; by an instrument or means.

1612 T. TAYLOR *Comm. Titus* iii. 1 The spirit indeed doth it principally, but by the word in the ministery instrumentally. *a* **1631** DONNE *Ess.* (1651) 141 They must do it instrumentally by others. *a* **1871** in Spurgeon *Treas. Dav.* Ps. xxxiii. 18–19 She never knew to whom she was instrumentally indebted for this timely and merciful assistance.

2. a. By means of a (material or legal) instrument.

1611 FLORIO, *Instrumentalmente*, by deed, instrument, euidence or writing, instrumentally. **1633** T. JAMES *Voy.* 69, I tooke the height of it instrumentally. **1760** PEMBERTON in *Phil. Trans.* LI. 910 A problem..proposed, and solved instrumentally upon a globe. **1807** HUTTON *Course Math.* II. 7 In the Third Method, Or Instrumentally, as suppose by the log. lines on one side of the common two-foot scales.

b. With or upon a musical instrument.

1716 *Lond. Gaz.* No. 5487/3 Mr. Purcell's Te Deum will be vocally and instrumentally performed. **1795** MASON *Ch. Mus.* i. 27 The earlier Fathers of the Church..condemned musical Devotion when instrumentally accompanied. **1876** GRANT *Burgh Sch. Scotl.* II. xiii. 373 Schools..in which the music of the church was taught vocally and instrumentally.

3. *Gram.* In or by the instrumental case.

1846 M. MONIER-WILLIAMS *Elem. Gram. Sanscrit Lang.* 160 Instrumentally Dependent..those [compounds] in which the relation of the first word (being in the crude) to the last is equivalent to that of an instrumental case.

†**instruˈmentalness.** *Obs.* [f. as prec. + -NESS.]

= INSTRUMENTALITY 1.

1655 SIR H. VANE *Retired Man's Medit.* 360 For their greater instrumentalnesse unto Satan, in rage, fiercenesse and cruelty. *a* **1660** HAMMOND (J.), The instrumentalness of riches to works of charity.

†**instruˈmentar,** *a. Sc. Obs.* [f. INSTRUMENT: see -AR[2].] = INSTRUMENTARY *a.* 3.

c **1575** *Balfour's Practicks* (1754) 383 Albeit the remanent of the witnessis instrumentar, beand of greiter nombre, depone or say aganis the samin.

†**instrumenˈtarian,** *a. Obs. rare.* [f. next + -AN.] = next, 2.

1649 BULWER *Pathomyot.* I. vi. 29 The passions aptly obey the instrumentarian parts.

instrumentary (ɪnstruːˈmɛntərɪ), *a.* [f. INSTRUMENT + -ARY; cf. F. *instrumentaire* (15th c.).]

†**1.** Of the nature of or serving as an instrument or means (= INSTRUMENTAL *a.* 1); of or belonging to an instrument or means. *Obs.*

a **1617** BAYNE *On Eph.* (1658) 151 This opinion maketh the divine properties become instrumentary faculties, as it were to a finite nature. **1642** *Declar. Lords & Comm.* 3 Aug. 6 Made use of..as instrumentary and subservient to it. **1657** M. LAWRENCE *Use & Pract. Faith* 83 Faith doth not justifie by merit..but onely by the instrumentary application of Christ's righteousness.

†**2.** Serving for some particular vital function; organic: = INSTRUMENTAL *a.* 4. *Obs.*

1564 P. MOORE *Hope Health* I. iv. 7 All other instrumentarie members besides these foure, are lesse principall. **1638** A. READ *Chirurg.* ii. 9 The veines and arteries are instrumentary parts.

3. *Sc. Law.* Of or relating to a deed or legal instrument; in phr. ***instrumentary witness***, one who witnesses a deed. (Cf. INSTRUMENTAR.)

1722 W. FORBES *Instit. Law Scot.* II. 176 Witnesses in written Contracts, called Instrumentary witnesses. **1773** ERSKINE *Instit. Law Scot.* (ed. 2) IV. ii. §5. 666 Offered to be proved by the oaths of the procurator and instrumentary witnesses. **1868** *Act 31 & 32 Vict.* c. 101 §139 It shall be competent for any female person..to act as an instrumentary witness in the same manner as any male person.

instrumentation (ˌɪnstruːmɛnˈteɪʃən). [a. F. *instrumentation* (1835 in *Dict. Acad.*), f. *instrumenter*: see INSTRUMENT *v.* and -ATION.]

1. a. *Mus.* The composition or arrangement of music for instruments, esp. for an orchestra (usually with reference to the art or skill shown by the composer in adapting the parts to the various instruments); orchestration.

1845 E. HOLMES *Mozart* 222 The cantatas..possess not only all the dignity of Gluck, but an instrumentation far more brilliant and spirited. **1875** OUSELEY *Mus. Form* ii. 4 To supply the harmonies, the counterpoints, and even the Instrumentation. **1880** W. S. ROCKSTRO in Grove *Dict. Mus.* II. 567 The most prominent characteristics of good Instrumentation are (I.) Solidity of Structure, (II.) Breadth of Tone, (III.) Boldness of Contrast, (IV.) Variety of Colouring.

¶ **b.** Erroneously used for: Performance of instrumental music; playing on instruments (with reference to style).

1856 RUSKIN *Mod. Paint.* IV. v. xix. §6 *note*, Finished instrumentation by an adequate number of performers, exquisite acting, and sweetest singing, might be secured.. at a fourth part of the cost. **1893** *Yorksh. Post* 14 Dec. 8/2 The choruses were admirably sung.. The instrumentation was excellent.

2. The use of a scientific, surgical, or other instrument; operation with an instrument.

1874 VAN BUREN *Dis. Genit. Org.* 34 The first principle of instrumentation in the urethra is to avoid the use of force. **1881** *Nature* No. 622. 516/2 Intensely black diffraction rings round each, and several fainter ones, fewer as the quality of instrumentation is raised. **1884** D. G. MITCHELL *Bound Together, Highways & Parks* 248 Something more is needed than the Engineer, stiff with his instrumentation and his equations and his economies of line.

3. Operation, or provision, of instruments or means; instrumental agency, instrumentality.

1858 BUSHNELL *Nat. & Supernat.* iv. (1864) 91 Having nature as their field and the tool-house of their instrumentations. *Ibid.* xii. 376 Otherwise we have no sufficient instrumentation, for our human use or handling of so great a fact. **1883** D. C. MURRAY *Hearts* III. 140 If I am caught, whether by your instrumentation or not, I shall tell what I know.

4. The design, construction, and provision of instruments for measurement, control, etc.; the state of being equipped with or controlled by instruments; also, such instruments collectively. orig. *U.S.*

1931 *Instruments* Jan. 11 Mr. Schroeder's book.. fills an even greater need than that filled by our industrial instrumentation manual. **1932** M. F. BÉHAR *Man. Instrumentation* I. p. xi, I confidently predict the early recognition of Instrumentation as a distinct branch of engineering and as a distinct field of scientific management. **1944** *Jrnl. R. Aeronaut. Soc.* XLVIII. 153 The paper.. emphasised quite clearly that instrumentation was coming more and more to the fore in the testing of aircraft. **1949** [see INSTRUMENT *v.* 3]. **1952** [see AUTOMATIZE *v.* 2]. **1958** *Engineering* 28 Mar. 387/2 As the age of automation develops it is bound to bring with it increased instrumentation and increased efforts to measure both more rapidly and more accurately by systems of remote control. **1959** *Daily Tel.* 13 Mar. 15/6 The instrumentation on the ground and in the missile recorded the flight satisfactorily. **1959** *Instrument Pract.* XIII. 195/1 In America we find a marked trend towards the instrumentation of a variety of physico-chemical estimations, such as phosphate and sulphur assays. **1963** B. FOZARD *Instrumentation Nucl. Reactors* xiii. 157 Instrumentation of a nuclear power reactor is commonly undertaken on a very large scale. **1973** *Physics Bull.* May 273/3 Josephson's work.. has sparked off very fruitful developments in the instrumentation field, leading for example to highly sensitive voltage detectors.

instru'mentist. *rare.* [f. INSTRUMENT + -IST; cf. F. *instrumentiste* (Littré).] = INSTRUMENTALIST 1.

1609 DOULAND *Ornith. Microl.* 14 By sounding the sounds [of a song] only, which belongs to Instrumentists.

instru'mento-, comb. form (from L. *instrumentum*), used with sb. in sense 'instrumental', with adj. in sense 'instrumentally'.

1872 COHEN *Dis. Throat* 12 One.. can hardly realize the extent to which this instrumento-mania has run rampant. **1898** *Daily News* 10 Feb. 5/2 A 'realistic instrumento-descriptive' opera.

instue, variant of INSTITUTE *Obs.*, to institute.

†**in'stupefying,** *ppl. a. Obs. rare.* [IN-². Cf. L. *instupēre* to be numb.] Stupefying.

1834 *Tait's Mag.* I. 586 Previous uses.. had filled it with hebetative and instupifying qualities.

†**in'style,** *v. Obs.* Also 6–8 **instile.** [f. IN-² + STYLE *sb.* or *v.* See also ENSTYLE.] *trans.* (with *complemental obj.*) To call by the style or name of; to style, denominate, entitle.

1596 DRAYTON *Legends* iv. 664 Him She instil'd *Defender of the Faith.* **1615** G. SANDYS *Trav.* 145 The Christians of the West, for the recovery of the Holy Land (so by them instiled). **1626** JACKSON *Creed* VIII. ix. §1 Abraham.. was instiled the friend of God. **1714** GAY *Sheph. Week* Proeme, Knowing no age so justly to be instiled Golden, as this of our sovereign lady Queen Anne. **1759** MARTIN *Nat. Hist. Eng.* II. 116 We antiently instile Mongst sundry other Things, a Wonder of our Isle.

†**in'suave,** *a. Obs. rare.* [ad. L. *insuāv-is* unpleasant, f. *in-* (IN-³) + *suāvis* sweet, SUAVE. Cf. F. *insuave.*] Not suave or sweet; unpleasant.

1657 TOMLINSON *Renou's Disp.* 503 It admitted of no sugar, but many insuave and.. useless things. **1657** *Physical Dict., Insuave,* unpleasant.

insuavity (ɪn'swævɪtɪ). *rare.* [ad. L. *insuāvit-ās*, f. *insuāvis*: see prec. and SUAVITY. Cf. F. *insuavité* (Littré).] Lack of suavity or sweetness; unpleasantness; surliness.

1621 BURTON *Anat. Mel.* I. iv. I. (1624) 186 All fears.. discontents, imbonities, insuavities are swallowed up.. in this Irish sea, this Ocean of misery. **1657** TOMLINSON *Renou's Disp.* 54 By reason of its ill odor and insuavity. **1878** T. HARDY *Return Native* III. v. ii. 123 It partly explained the insuavity with which the woman greeted him.

insubduable (ɪnsʌb'djuːəb(ə)l), *a. rare.* [IN-³.] That cannot be subdued; invincible.

1865 BUSHNELL *Vicar. Sacr.* II. i. 103 The insubduable fires of hate.

†**in'subid,** *a. Obs. rare*⁻⁰. [ad. L. *insubid-us* (post-cl.) stupid, foolish.]

1656 BLOUNT *Glossogr., Insubid,* rash, without consideration, heady.

insubjection (ɪnsʌb'dʒɛkʃən). *rare.* [IN-³.] Want of subjection; the state of not being subject to authority or control.

1818 TODD, *Insubjection*, state of disobedience to government. **1847** BUSHNELL *Chr. Nurt.* II. ii. (1861) 255 Some appearance of irritability, or insubjection. **1878** H. G. GUINNESS *End of Age* (1880) 23 The eternal state dates from death's destruction, and in it insubjection is unknown.

insubmergible (ɪnsʌb'mɜːdʒɪb(ə)l), *a.* [IN-³.] That cannot be submerged or sunk under water.

1808 SYD. SMITH *Wks.* (1859) I. 100/1 Religion.. is so buoyant and so insubmergible—that it may be made, by fanatics, to carry with it any degree of error. **1822** *New Monthly Mag.* V. 382 One of the company in this insubmergible passage-boat. **1883** *Fisheries Exhib. Catal.* 19 Collapsible Insubmergible Dinghys for Fishing Smacks.

insubmersible (ɪnsʌb'mɜːsɪb(ə)l), *a. rare.* [IN-³; perh. after F. *insubmersible* (1775 in Hatz.-Darm.).] = prec.

1865 ESQUIROS *Cornwall* 169 The English expect a life-boat to be insubmersible. **1879** D'ANVERS tr. *J. Verne's Fur Country* II. iv. 197 A wandering island, with a solid insubmersible foundation.

insub'mission. *rare.* [IN-³.]

Want of submission; unsubmissiveness; insubordination.

1828 in WEBSTER.

insubmissive (ɪnsʌb'mɪsɪv), *a.* [IN-³.] Not submissive; not disposed to submit; unyielding to power or authority; unsubmissive.

1841 *Mem. W. Ferrier* iv. 350 Multitudes are at once insubmissive and despondent. **1878** SWINBURNE *Poems & Ball.* Ser. II. 17 Thine unbowed, bright, insubmissive head.

insubordinate (ɪnsə'bɔːdɪnət), *a.* (*sb.*) [IN-³; cf. F. *insubordonné* (1789 in Hatz.-Darm.).] Not subordinate. **a.** Not obedient to the orders of superiors; prone to insubordination.

1849 COBDEN *Speeches* 86 To keep down a very restless and insubordinate population; but why restless and insubordinate? **1864** *Daily Tel.* 23 Sept., A motley crew of insubordinate adventurers. **1897** P. WARUNG *Tales Old Regime* 37 To be insubordinate was to commit the unpardonable sin.

b. Not subordinate in altitude; not inferior.

1868 MILMAN *St. Paul's* 398 Those adjacent buildings soar to an insubordinate height.

B. *sb.* One who is insubordinate.

1886 SIR F. H. DOYLE *Remin.* 45 In managing his subordinates (insubordinates I should rather call them). **1896** *Westm. Gaz.* 25 Feb. 2/1 He.. was court-martialled, and came near being shot. But.. [he] had early become a past master of chess.. The staff were unable to face a sudden curtailment of their only recreation, and the insubordinate was spared.

Hence **insu'bordinately** *adv.*, in an insubordinate, unsubmissive, or refractory manner.

18.. in Jas. Grant *Hist. India* (1876) I. xli. 209/1 The king's troops.. loudly and insubordinately uttered the old complaint of want of beef.

insubordination (ɪnsəbɔːdɪ'neɪʃən). [IN-³; perh. after F. *insubordination* (1788 in Hatz.-Darm.).]

The fact or condition of being insubordinate; absence of subordination or submission; resistance to or defiance of authority; refusal to obey orders; refractoriness, disobedience.

1790 BURKE *Fr. Rev.* Wks. V. 381 All the disorders arising from idleness, luxury, dissipation, and insubordination. **1797** COLLINGWOOD in Alison *Europe* xxii. (1854) IV. 22 If you attempt to excite insubordination in my ship, I will.. throw you into the sea. **1840** THIRLWALL *Greece* VII. lvii. 228 Antigonus complained of Cassander's insubordination. **1894** H. NISBET *Bush Girl's Rom.* 19 He was punished for insubordination, until at last in desperation he made his escape to the bush.

†**insub'sistence.** *Obs. rare.* [IN-³.] Lack or want of subsistence.

1651 tr. *Life Father Sarpi* (1676) 36 Although he might well discern an insubsistence, and that the Cardinal Protector was not much incensed by any instances against him upon those accusations.

†**insub'sistent,** *a. Obs. rare.* [IN-³.] That does not subsist.

1654 JER. TAYLOR *Real Pres.* 260 What they cannot be to themselves, they cannot be to others, in matter of supply and subsistence; it being a contradiction to say, insubsistent subsistencies.

insubstantial (ɪnsʌb'stænʃəl), *a.* [ad. late and med.L. *insubstāntiāl-is*, f. *in-* (IN-³) + *substāntiālis* SUBSTANTIAL. Cf. F. *insubstantiel* (16th c. in Littré).]

1. Not existing in substance or reality; not real; imaginary, illusive; non-substantial.

1610 SHAKS. *Temp.* IV. i. 155 The great Globe it selfe, Yea, all which it inherit, shall dissolue, And like this insubstantiall Pageant faded Leaue not a racke behinde. **1820** LAMB *Elia* Ser. I. *South-Sea Ho.*, Peradventure the very names, which I have summoned up before thee, are fantastic, insubstantial. **1865** SEELEY *Ecce Homo* (1866) 136 It was no insubstantial city, such as we fancy in the clouds.

2. Void of substance; not of stout or solid substance; unsubstantial. Also *fig.*

1607 MARKHAM *Caval.* IV. (1617) 36 The errors and inconueniences which doe necessarily belong to such insubstantiall instructions. *a* **1774** W. HARTE tr. *à Kempis, Vision* Note 36 (R.) Nothing in the event is more fragil and insubstantial [than a spider's web]. **1827** HARE *Guesses* (1859) 460 The multitude of indistinct, insubstantial words, which have been driven across our language from foreign regions. *a* **1861** MRS. BROWNING *Lett. R. H. Horne* (1877) II. lii. 83 A common cough striking on an insubstantial frame began my bodily troubles.

insubstantiality (ˌɪnsʌbstænʃɪ'ælɪtɪ). [f. prec. + -ITY.] The quality of being insubstantial; unsubstantiality.

1827 HARE *Guesses* (1859) 436 No wonder that such houses are soon overthrown, nay, that they topple ere long through their own insubstantiality. **1891** G. MEREDITH *One of Conq.* II. iv. 76 No metaphors, no similes, nor flowery insubstantiality. *a* **1898** J. CAIRD *Fundamental Ideas Chr.* I. iv. 87 It [pantheism] means, not the divinity, but rather the nothingness and insubstantiality of the world.

†**insub'stantiate,** *a. Obs. rare.* [IN-³.] Not composed of (material) substance.

1621 BRATHWAIT *Nat. Emb., Blasphemie* Argt. (1877) 35 God.. incomprehensible in his works, indiuisible, in his substance insubstantiate.

insubstantiate (ɪnsʌb'stænʃɪeɪt), *v. rare.* [f. IN-² + L. *substāntia* SUBSTANCE + -ATE³: cf. *incarnate, incorporate.*] *trans.* To embody or manifest in (material) substance.

1865 J. GROTE *Explorat. Philos.* I. iv. 58 A mind or reason so far insubstantiated or embodied.

So **insubstanti'ation**, embodiment.

1867 SALA *Waterloo to Penins.* II. 227 It is the insubstantiation of 'nada'—the home of nothing. There is nothing to eat, nothing to drink, nothing to wear, nothing to sit or lie upon.

insub'vertible, *a. rare.* [IN-³.] Incapable of being subverted.

1806 *Simple Narrative* II. 70 The champion of immutable truth, and the insubvertible law of Nature. **1821** COLERIDGE *Lett.* Jan. (1836) I. 155 If the premises be, as I.. am convinced they are—insubvertible.

†**in'succate,** *v. Obs. rare*⁻⁰. [f. L. *insuccāre*, properly *insūcāre* (Columella), f. *in-* (IN-²) + *succus, sūcus* juice: see -ATE³.] *trans.* To soak, steep. So †**insu'ccation**, the action of soaking or steeping. *Obs.*

1623 COCKERAM, *Insuccate*, to make wet. **1664** EVELYN *Sylva* (1679) 8 Concerning the medicating, and insuccation of Seeds. **1706** PHILLIPS, *Insuccation* (in the Apothecaries Art), the moistening of Aloes, or other Drugs, with the Juice of Violets, or Roses, etc.

insuccess (ɪnsʌk'sɛs). [IN-³. Cf. F. *insuccès* (1802 in Hatz.).] Want of success; unsuccess.

1646 C. SPELMAN in *Spelman's De non temer. Eccl.* (ed. 4) To Rdr. b ij, View the insuccesse of Sacrilegious persons. **1661** FELTHAM *Resolves* II. lxxviii. 357 The insuccess of an Affair.. how it alters quite the sound that Fames lowd Trumpet makes! **1738** WEDDELL *Voy. up Thames* 94 Tired with his Insuccess. **1900** *Contemp. Rev.* Jan. 144 Their insuccesses have conferred no great gains on our adversary.

†**insuc'cessful,** *a. Obs.* [IN-³.] Not successful; unsuccessful.

1646 C. SPELMAN in *Spelman's De non temer. Eccl.* (ed. 3) To Rdr. a iij b, Although he was not so happy as with Saint Peter at once to convert thousands, yet was he not with him so insuccessefull, as to fish all night and catch nothing. **1683** SALMON *Doron Med.* I. 99 It will prove insuccessful.

Hence †**insuc'cessfulness.** *Obs.*

1648 JENKYN *Blind Guide* i. 6 The totall insuccessefulnesse of your Ministry. **1672** GREW *Philos. Hist. Pl.* §4 The acknowledged.. Insuccessfulnes of any Mens Undertakings.

†**insuc'cessive,** *a. Obs. rare.* [IN-³.] Without succession in time.

1678 GALE *Crt. Gentiles* III. 158 The Eternitie of God is insuccessive and indivisible.

†**insuc'cessively,** *adv. Obs.* [IN-³.] Without success, unsuccessfully.

a **1650** MAY *Satir. Puppy* (1657) 86 Griev'd that the Verses were so insuccessively left in Peel's Lodging.

insucken ('ɪnˌsʌk(ə)n), *a. Sc. Law.* [f. IN *prep.* + SUCKEN.] Situated within a certain *sucken*, or jurisdiction having its own mill; astricted to a certain mill in the servitude of thirlage.

1681 STAIR *Inst. Law Scot.* II. vii. §7 Infeftment in a mill, with the astricted multures.. and forty years possession of paying the insucken multures was found to constitute the thirlage. **1773** ERSKINE *Inst. Law Scot.* (ed. 2) II. ix. §20. 314 The duties payable by those who come voluntarily to the mill are called *outsucken*, or *out-town multures*; and those that are due by tenants within the sucken, *in-town* or *insucken multures*.. The rate of insucken [multure] is frequently a peck in the boll, and at some mills considerably higher. **1861** W. BELL *Dict. Law Scot.* s.v., Insucken multures are the multures exigible from the suckeners, or parties astricted to the mill.

insuction (ɪn'sʌkʃən). *rare*. [f. IN *adv.* 11 d + SUCTION.] The action of sucking in.
1883 A. STEWART *Nether Lochaber* liii. 337 The capture and insuction of its ordinary food. **1895** PARKES *Health* 141 The in-suction caused by fires within the house.

†**in'sudate**, *a. Obs. rare*. [ad. L. *insūdāt-us*, pa. pple. of L. *insūdāre*, f. *in-* (IN-²) + *sūdāre* to sweat; cf. *exudate*.] 'Accompanied with sweating' (Nares); laborious. So †**insu'dation**, sweating; severe labour, such as to cause sweating. *rare*.
1609 HEYWOOD *Brit. Troy* VI. ciii, And such great victories attaind but seild, Though with more labours and insudate toyles. **1669** *Addr. hopeful Yng. Gentry Eng.* 107 All this without anxious solicitudes, laborious insudations, or more than common Stock of comprehension or contrivance.

insue, obs. form of ENSUE.

insuetude ('ɪnswiːtjuːd). *rare*. [ad. L. *insuētūdo* (post-class.), f. *insuētus* unaccustomed; cf. *consuetude*, *desuetude*.] The quality of not being in use; unaccustomedness.
1824–46 LANDOR *Imag. Conv.* Wks. I. 258/2 Absurdities and enormities are great in proportion to custom or insuetude.

†**in'suffer**, *v. Sc. Obs.* [app. ad. OF. *ensoufrir* (Godef.), f. *en-*, EN-¹ (IN-²) + *soufrir* to SUFFER.] *trans.* To suffer.
c **1470** HENRY *Wallace* VII. 443 In all the warld na grettar payne mycht be, Than thai with in insufferit for [*MS.* sor] to duell, That euir was wrocht, bot purgatory or hell. **1536** BELLENDEN *Cron. Scot.* (1821) I. Proheme Cosm. p. x, Bot thou mon first insuffer mekill pine.

insufferable (ɪn'sʌfərəb(ə)l), *a.* [f. IN-³ + SUFFERABLE; perh. ad. obs. and dial. F. *insouffrable*.] Not sufferable; that cannot be borne or endured; insupportable, intolerable, unbearable.
1533 BELLENDEN *Livy* V. (1822) 425 To be irkit with owre ithand and insuffirabil lauboure. **1657** R. LIGON *Barbadoes* (1673) 9 We found so great, so insufferable heat, as you will hardly imagine that bodies..could indure. **1693** DRYDEN *Juvenal* Ded. (1697) 22 Now Age has overtaken me; and Want, a more insufferable Evil..has wholly disenabl'd me. **1712** STEELE *Spect.* No. 429 ⁋2 A vain Person is the most insufferable Creature living in a well-bred Assembly. **1827** KEBLE *Chr. Y.*, *Convers. Paul*, Still gazing, though untaught to bear Th' insufferable light. **1845** JAMES *A. Neil* II. vi, This insolence is insufferable.
Hence **in'sufferableness**, the quality or condition of being insufferable.
1586 A. DAY *Eng. Secretary* I. (1625) 67 By the indignity, unjustnesse, wickednesse, insufferablenesse,..that thereof ensueth. **1889** *Cape Law Jrnl.* 196 Any one who..out of insufferableness (or insupportableness) withdraws himself from the marriage bond, or goes away and leaves his spouse, with the intention not to return to her again, leaves the innocent party free to re-marry.

insufferably (ɪn'sʌfərəblɪ), *adv.* [f. prec. + -LY².] In an insufferable manner or degree; beyond endurance; intolerably, unbearably.
1625 K. LONG tr. *Barclay's Argenis* IV. xii. 278 Hee grew most insufferably insolent over good men. **1692** SOUTH *12 Serm.* (1697) II. 288 So insufferably have these Impostors poysoned the Fountains of Morality. **1716** ADDISON *Drummer* I. i, He's most insufferably witty upon us about this story of the drum. **1849** MACAULAY *Hist. Eng.* iii. I. 379 This mode of travelling..by Englishmen of the present day would be regarded as insufferably slow.

insuffice (ɪnsə'faɪs), *v. nonce-wd.* [f. IN-³ + SUFFICE *v.*, after *insufficient*.] *intr.* To fail to suffice; to be insufficient.
1847 LD. G. BENTINCK *Let.* 30 Aug. in Disraeli *Life* xxiii. 448 She [Ireland] imported three millions sterling worth of breadstuffs, which insufficed to prevent one million, or say half a million, of the people from dying of starvation.

insufficience (ɪnsə'fɪʃəns). Now *rare*. Also 5 -ens. [a. OF. *insufficience* (14th c., Oresme), ad. late L. *insufficientia*: see next and -ENCE. Cf. INSUFFISANCE.]
†**1.** Of a person: = INSUFFICIENCY 1. *Obs.*
1432–50 tr. *Higden* (Rolls) I. 5 To comprehende the knowledge of whom oure insufficience [L. *modicitas*] sufficethe not. **1460** CAPGRAVE *Chron.* (Rolls) 147 The Pope ..anulled the eleccion of the bischop for insufficiens. **1521** *Bradshaw's St. Werburge* 1st Bal. Author 11 Whiche knowe full well myn insufficience. **1611** SHAKS. *Wint. T.* I. i. 16. **1672** BAXTER *Bagshaw's Scand.* ii. 19, I doubt whether they would not reject him for utter Ignorance and insufficience. *a* **1797** H. WALPOLE *Mem. Geo. II* (1847) III. i. 17 He had heard of his own all-sufficience; he knew our insufficience.
2. Of a thing: = INSUFFICIENCY 2. Now *rare*.
1486 *Surtees Misc.* (1888) 54 Gyve not your eye Oonely to this citie of insufficience. **1597** *Compl. Buik D. Wedderburne* (Scot. Hist. Soc.) 98 Becaus of the insufficience of tua barrellis salmond he sauld me. **1623** in *N. Shaks. Soc. Trans.* (1885) 499 Benifitt of excepcion to thuncertainties and all other thimperfeccions and insufficiences of the said bill. *a* **1711** KEN *Hymnotheo* Wks. 1721 III. 259 While I the World, and thee, my God, compare, I nothing find but insufficience there. **1882** *Mind* Apr. 294 Another defect which partly explains the insufficience of his Psychology.

insufficiency (ɪnsə'fɪʃənsɪ). [ad. late L. *insufficientia* (Tertullian), n. of quality f. *insufficientem*: see next and -ENCY.] The quality or condition of being insufficient.
†**1.** Of a person: Inability to fulfil requirements; unfitness, incapacity, incompetence. *Obs.* or *arch.*
1526 *Pilgr. Perf.* (W. de W. 1531) 1 b, Ascrybe it..to my insuffycyency and ignoraunce. **1597** HOOKER *Eccl. Pol.* v. xxxi. §3 His aptnesse or insufficiency otherwise than by reading to instruct the flock. **1624** *Nottingham Rec.* IV. 391 We present Maister Wylleam Borrowes, Vsher of the Free Scoole, for his insuficientie. **1742** RICHARDSON *Pamela* IV. 80 His Lady is always accusing herself to me of Awkwardness and Insufficiency; but not a Soul who sees her can find it out. **1751** EARL ORRERY *Remarks Swift* (1752) 7 When he appeared as a candidate for the degree of Batchelor of Arts, he was set aside on account of insufficiency. **1767** WILKES *Corr.* (1805) III. 211 The office he bears with the utmost discredit to himself, and with equal disgrace and insufficiency to the public.
b. with *pl.* An example of this.
1756 C. LUCAS *Ess. Waters* I. Pref., It will enable the public to detect their insufficiencies. **1773** MRS. CHAPONE *Improv. Mind* (1774) II. 15 A due sense of his own faults and insufficiencies. **1850** TENNYSON *In Mem.* cxii, I, who gaze with temperate eyes On glorious insufficiencies, Set light by narrower perfectness.
2. Of a thing: Deficiency in effectiveness, force, quality, or amount; inadequacy.
1531 ELYOT *Gov.* I. i, The wordes, publike and commune, which be borowed of the latin tonge, for the insufficiencie of our owne langage. **1632** *Star Chamb. Cases* (Camden) 135 For the insufficiencie of the plea Mr. Brome did taxe costes at 20ˢ. **1769** ROBERTSON *Chas. V* (1796) III. x. 241 He now felt the insufficiency of his own resources. **1814** CHALMERS *Evid. Chr. Revel.* i. 12 There is an insufficiency of data. **1860** TYNDALL *Glac.* II. xiii. 296 These experiments..prove the insufficiency of the theory.
3. Physical incapacity or impotence; inability of a bodily organ to do its work. Also *attrib.*
1714 STEELE *Lover* No. 40 (1723) 227 The Marriage afterwards being declared Null, by Reason of his Insufficiency. **1866** A. FLINT *Princ. Med.* (1880) 334 The existence of so-called relative insufficiency of the valves. **1886** *Syd. Soc. Lex.*, *Insufficiency*,..inability to perform normal work. Usually applied to imperfect action of the valves of the heart. **1897** *Allbutt's Syst. Med.* IV. 555 According to this view the nervous and insufficiency theories are combined.

insufficient (ɪnsə'fɪʃənt), *a.* (*sb.*) [a. OF. *insufficient* (14th c., Oresme; cf. INSUFFISANT), or ad. L. *insufficient-em*, f. *in-* (IN-³) + *sufficient-em* SUFFICIENT.] Not sufficient.
†**1.** Of a person: Of inadequate ability or qualification; unfit; incompetent. *Obs.*
c **1386** CHAUCER *Sompn. T.* 252 Holde ye thanne me or elles oure Couent To praye for yow been insufficient? *c* **1430** LYDG. *Min. Poems* (Percy Soc.) 240 Which of mysilfe am insufficient To rekne or count. **1494** FABYAN *Chron.* II. xlviii. 31 The .ii. sonnes beforenamed of Lud were to yonge or insuffycyent for to take on hande so great a charge. **1562** LD. BACON in Strype *Ann. Ref.* (1709) I. xxvi. 256 Some of those that were ministers were much insufficient. **1596** SPENSER *State Irel.* Wks. (Globe) 647/2 Soe as the bishop.. may justly rejecte them as incapable and insufficient. **1657** *Burton's Diary* (1828) II. 58 An ordinance for the ejection of scandalous, ignorant, and insufficient ministers and schoolmasters.
†**b.** Not having enough of some thing; inadequately provided with money, possessions, etc.
1426 LYDG. *De Guil. Pilgr.* (E.E.T.S.) 10739 They be mor Rude than am I, And mor ek insuffycyent Off konnyng, as by jugement. **1427–8** *Waterf. Arch.* in *10th Rep. Hist. MSS. Comm.* App. v. 294 If ony of the saide citsayns be insufficiente..in the saide actione of dette. **1591** LAMBARDE *Archeion* (1635) 211 Then shall that Clarke both make Fine to the King, and satisfie the partie hurt (if he be able)..But if the Clarke be insufficient, then is the Sheriffe himselfe to answer for him. **1620** J. WILKINSON *Coroners & Sherifes* 2 Hee is insufficient in lands.
2. Of a thing: Deficient in force, quality, or amount; lacking in what is necessary or requisite; inadequate. ***insufficient answer***: see quot. 1848.
1494 FABYAN *Chron.* VII. 314 The maters of obieccion were, by hym and his courte, thought insuffycient. **1586** A. DAY *Eng. Secretary* II. (1625) 120 Men..whose demeanors are to vertue wholly insufficient. **1642** ROGERS *Naaman* 581 Who beleeve not promises according to the intention of them: They make them weaker and insufficienter then they are. **1692** DRYDEN *Eleanora* Ded., But a single hand is insufficient for such a harvest. **1772** *Junius Lett.* lxviii. 347 Even these provisions were found insufficient. **1848** WHARTON *Law Lex.* s.v. *Insufficiency*, An answer in Chancery is said to be insufficient when it does not specifically reply to the specific charges in the bill. **1879** HARLAN *Eyesight* viii. 115 Good artificial light is much to be preferred to insufficient daylight.
†**b.** Wanting in strength or stability. *Obs.*
1703 MOXON *Mech. Exerc.* 243 The reason of so many insufficient Buildings, is the using of the Morter, as soon as 'tis made.
B. *sb.* †**1.** Insufficiency. *Obs.*
1494 FABYAN *Chron.* VII. 301 Consyderynge the insuffycyent of Englysshe men & other. *Ibid.* VII. 549 The sayde kynge Rycharde, knowynge his owne insuffycient, hath..renouncyd and geuen vp the rule and gouernaunce of this lande.
†**2.** An unfit or incompetent person. *Obs.*
1654 WHITLOCK *Zootomia* 433 Some of Abilities..have been no more esteemed than worthlesse Insufficients.
Hence †**insu'fficientness**, personal unfitness, incompetence, incapacity.
c **1585** CARTWRIGHT in R. Browne *Answ.* 93 Giuing the people warning of their corruptions and insufficientnesse. **1727** in BAILEY vol. II.

insu'fficientism. *Med.* [f. prec. + -ISM.] 'The doctrine which regards drugs as insufficient for the cure of disease and regards as the basis of all treatment the *Expectant method*' (*Syd. Soc. Lex.* 1886). Hence **insu'fficientist**, 'a believer in insufficientism' (ibid.).

insufficiently (ɪnsə'fɪʃəntlɪ), *adv.* [f as prec. + -LY².] In an insufficient manner or degree; inadequately; not enough.
1526 *Pilgr. Perf.* (W. de W. 1531) 178 b, Better it is to prayse her though insufficiently, than to holde my tonge from her prayses. **1532–3** *Act 24 Hen. VIII*, c. 1 Hydes and tanned lether..vntruly, insufficiently, and deceiuably tanned. **1641** MILTON *Animadv.* iii. Wks. (1847) 60/2 As insufficiently, and..as imprudently did they provide by their contrived liturgies. **1875** JOWETT *Plato* (ed. 2) V. 336 If he [man] be insufficiently or ill educated he is the most savage of earthly creatures.

†**in'suffisance.** *Obs.* [a. F. *insuffisance* (1337 in Godef. *Compl.*), f. *insuffisant*: see next and -ANCE; cf. INSUFFICIENCE.] = INSUFFICIENCE 1; personal unfitness or incompetency.
1387–8 T. USK *Test. Love* I. ix. (Skeat) l. 14 To declare that thy insuffisaunce is no maner letting. *c* **1400** MAUNDEV. (1839) xxxi. 315 For myn unable insuffisance now I am comen Hom (mawgree my self) to reste. **1502** *Ord. Crysten Men* (W. de W. 1506) IV. vii. 186 That he may supplye the insuffysaunce of his confessoure.

†**in'suffisant**, *a. Obs.* [a. F. *insuffisant* (not recorded till 1474), f. *in-* (IN-³) + *suffisant* SUFFISANT, pr. pple. of *suffire* to suffice; cf. INSUFFICIENT.] Insufficient; not sufficing; incompetent.
1387 TREVISA *Higden* (Rolls) VII. 227 Þe child was insuffisant to so grete a charge. *c* **1400** MAUNDEV. (1839) xxix. 293 What may ben y now to that man to whom alle the World is insuffisant. *c* **1450** *Mirour Saluacioun* 4566 Thaire witnesse ware insuffissant ilkone.

insufflate ('ɪnsʌfleɪt), *v.* [f. L. *insufflāt-*, ppl. stem of *insufflāre* (post-cl.), f. *in-* (IN-²) + *sufflāre* to blow upon. Cf. F. *insuffler* (14–15th c.).]
1. *trans.* To blow or breathe in.
1657–83 EVELYN *Hist. Relig.* (1850) II. 5 He..infusing or insufflating..a rational soul, capable of immortality.
b. *spec.* To breathe upon catechumens, or on the water of baptism: see next 1 b.
2. *Med.* To blow (air, gas, etc.) into some opening or cavity of the body; to treat by insufflation.
1670 H. STUBBE *Plus Ultra* 95 Bartholin evidenced the same thing by a pair of bellows, or tube and winde insufflated. **1897** *Allbutt's Syst. Med.* IV. 682 The most convenient plan is first to insufflate the nose with iodoform.

insufflation (ɪnsʌ'fleɪʃən). [ad. L. *insufflātiōn-em* (post-class.), n. of action f. *insufflāre*: see prec. Cf. F. *insufflation* (14th c. in Hatz.-Darm.).]
1. The action of blowing or breathing on or into.
1621 AINSWORTH *Annot. Pentat.*, *Gen.* ii. 7 This showeth man's spirit not to be of the earth..but of nothing, by the insufflation of God. *a* **1726** W. REEVES *Serm.* (1729) 346 Christ by His second insufflation reinspired the same Spirit, when breathing on His Apostles, He said, Receive ye the Holy Ghost. **1835** KIRBY *Hab. & Inst. Anim.* I. Notes 365 The immediate insufflation, if I may so use the term, of the Deity.
b. *spec.* Blowing or breathing upon a person or thing to symbolize the influence of the Holy Spirit and the expulsion of evil spirits; a rite of exorcism used in the Roman, Greek, and some other churches.
1580 FULKE *Retentive True Faith* 168 Insufflations, that is blowing vpon. **1647** JER. TAYLOR *Lib. Proph.* v. 87 The custom of exorcisme and insufflation. **1660** Z. CROFTON *Fasten. Peter's Fetters* 59 Putting Cream and Honey into the mouth of the baptized; insufflation, and spitting at the Devil and the World. **1706** tr. *Dupin's Eccl. Hist. 16th C.* II. v. 47 Then he [Cassander] undertakes to justify Exorcism and Insufflation, as well as the Renunciation, and the Profession of Faith, and the other Ceremonies of Baptism. **1839** J. H. NEWMAN *Ess.* I. *Prosp. Angl. Ch.* 284 Insufflations and stoles with crosses on them complete their notion of the ancient religion. **1882–3** SCHAFF *Encycl. Relig. Knowl.* I. 2022 Exorcism, accompanied by breathing upon the baptismal waters (insufflation).
2. The blowing or breathing (*of* something) in; in *Med.* the blowing of air, etc. into the lungs, or of gas, vapour, or powder into or on some part of the body.
1823 CRABB *Technol. Dict.*, *Insufflation* (Med.), the blowing into any cavity. **1849–52** TODD *Cycl. Anat.* IV. 1046/2 Insufflation in the dead body is not the movement of inspiration in the living subject. **1876** BARTHOLOW *Mat. Med.* (1879) 4 By the method of insufflation solid medicinal agents in a finely-divided state are applied to various parts of the respiratory tract. **1887** J. W. BURGON in *Fortn. Rev.* Apr. 593 With the insufflation of his soul, Adam received also the grace of the Holy Spirit. **1897** *Allbutt's Syst. Med.* IV. 681 The insufflation of iodoform..has given good results. **1898** *Ibid.* V. 198 Violent inspiratory efforts..and..consequent insufflation of infective secretion into healthy lung.

3. The condition of being inflated or distended with air.

1866 A. FLINT *Princ. Med.* (1880) 244 The names *acute emphysema* and *insufflation* are given to a dilatation of the air-cells frequently met with in the lungs of those who have suffered from severe dyspnœa during the last days or hours of life. **1877** ROBERTS *Handbk. Med.* (ed. 3) I. 171 The lungs are in many cases the seat of acute insufflation.

insufflator (ˈɪnsʌfleɪtə(r)). [agent-n., in L. form, from INSUFFLATE.] A contrivance for insufflating. **a.** An instrument for blowing air into the lungs or for injecting powders into a cavity, a wound, etc. **b.** A kind of injector for blowing air into a furnace.

1872 COHEN *Dis. Throat* 192 Astringent powders may be propelled upon the parts..from the insufflator of Rauchfuss. **1886** *Syd. Soc. Lex.*, *Ribemont-Dessaigne's Insufflator*, an instrument for inflating the lungs in an asphyxiated newborn child. **1897** *Allbutt's Syst. Med.* IV. 682 To insufflate the nose with iodoform by means of Kabierski's insufflator.

†**in'suitable**, *a.* *Obs.* *rare*⁻¹. [IN-³.] Not suitable; unsuitable. Hence †**insuita'bility**.

1612 SHELTON *Quix.* IV. x. 411 The inequalitie and the insutability of his armes, and his graue manner of proceeding. **1692** BURNET *Rochester* 73 Many rites of the Jewish worship seemed to him insutable to the Divine Nature.

†**'in-suitor.** *Sc. Law. Obs.* [f. IN *adv.* 12a + SUITOR.] A suitor (in a Baronial Court) dwelling within the Barony.

?*a***1600** *Forme Of Baron Courts* i §3 in Skene *Reg. Maj.* (1609) 100 Then the Serjand aucht to gar call the soytours anes simplie: First the out soytours [*marg.* dwelland out-with the Baronie] of the court, gif there any be, and syne the in soytours. —— *Balfour's Practicks* (1754) 38 The in-suitaris.

‖**insula** (ˈɪnsjuːlə). Pl. -æ. [L. *insula* an island, a block of buildings.]

1. *Rom. Antiq.* A block of buildings; a square or space mapped out or divided off.

1832 GELL *Pompeiana* II. 54 The whole group or *insula* of public buildings. **1893** *Archæologia* LIII. 539 The entire square, *Insula* iv., of which the *forum* and *basilica* form the greater part. *Ibid.* 570 The unexcavated portion of this *insula* has been reserved. **1899** *Daily News* 1 Nov. 8/3 Those who..would build their blocks as high as those insulæ which darkened the sunlit spaces of ancient Rome.

2. *Anat.* **a.** The central lobe of the cerebrum; the lobule of the corpus striatum or Sylvian fissure, the Island of Reil. **b.** See quot.

1886 *Syd. Soc. Lex.*, *Insula*, in Anatomy, the Island of Reil; also, a term applied to a clot of blood floating in serum.

†**'insulan, -ane.** *Obs. rare.* [ad. L. *insulān-us*, f. *insula* island.] An islander.

1460 CAPGRAVE *Chron.* (Rolls) 207 He is a insulane, therefor he doth no subjeccioune onto no man. **1585** T. WASHINGTON tr. *Nicholay's Voy.* I. xv. 15b, Secretly assembling certaine number of souldiers and Insulans.

'insulant, *a.* and *sb.* [f. assumed L. *insulāre + -ANT.] †**A.** *adj.* Insulating (electrically). *Obs. rare.*

1803 *Med. Jrnl.* IX. 239 Which so modifies the carbon as to produce a substance totally insulant.

B. *sb.* Any substance or medium which insulates (electrically, thermally, etc.).

1934 in WEBSTER. **1946** *Electronic Engin.* XVIII. 280/1 The growth of the electronics and high frequencies industries has been phenomenal. With this growth there has been a demand for more efficient insulants. **1959** *Times* 27 Apr. (Rubber Industry Suppl.) p. viii/5 The best thermal insulant is a vacuum. *Ibid.*, Most thermal insulants..work on the principle of trapped air. **1971** *Engineering* Apr. 112/1 (Advt.), A dense yet feather-light carpet of pure mineral fibre... A natural thermal and acoustic insulant.

insular (ˈɪnsjʊlə(r)), *a.* (*sb.*) [ad. L. *insulār-is*, f. *insula* island: see -AR¹. Cf. F. *insulaire*.]

A. *adj.* **1. a.** Of or pertaining to an island; inhabiting or situated on an island.

1611 COTGR., *Insulaire*, Insular, Iland-like; of, or belonging to, an Iland. **1669** GALE *Crt. Gentiles* I. II. vi. 73 In ancient times..they called every Insular Prince by the name of Neptune. **1796** BURKE *Regic. Peace* i. Wks. VIII. 151 The names and other..signs of approximation, rather augmented than diminished our insular feuds. **1867** FREEMAN *Norm. Conq.* I. ii. 29 The insular Teutons showed themselves the most zealous of missionaries.

b. *Phys. Geog.* Of climate: Of the moderate or temperate kind which prevails in situations surrounded and tempered by the sea.

1830 LYELL *Princ. Geol.* I. 97 An alteration from what has been termed an 'insular' to an 'excessive' climate. **1880** HAUGHTON *Phys. Geog.* iii. 118 The term 'Insular Climate' has been always given to climates in which the annual range of temperature is small. **1885** R. H. SCOTT *Elem. Meteorol.* 344 Hence comes the subdivision of climates into insular or moderate, and continental or excessive. The west coasts of continents enjoy insular..climates.

2. Of the nature of an island; composing or forming an island.

1662 STILLINGFL. *Orig. Sacr.* I. ii. §4 That the Tyre mentioned by Sanchoniathon was not the famous Insular Tyrus, but some other Tyre. **1830** LYELL *Princ. Geol.* I. 228 The alleged exposure of certain insular rocks in the Bothnian and other bays. **1879** D. M. WALLACE *Australas.* i. 1 A description of the great insular land—Australia.

3. a. *transf.* Detached or standing out by itself like an island; insulated. **b.** *Bot.* 'Situated alone, applied to galls which occur singly on a leaf' (*Cent. Dict.* 1890). **c.** *Path.* ***insular sclerosis.*** 'Moxon's term for *Sclerosis, disseminated*' (*Syd. Soc. Lex.* 1886). **d.** *Anat.* (see quot. 1886).

1886 *Syd. Soc. Lex.*, *Insular*, relating to an *Insula*, or to the Island of Reil. **1891** *Lancet* 3 Oct. 780 We are inclined to think that the evidence of insular sclerosis is not quite convincing. **1897** *Allbutt's Syst. Med.* II. 932 In insular sclerosis the tremor is completely absent during rest.

4. a. Pertaining to islanders; *esp.* having the characteristic traits of the inhabitants of an island (e.g. of Great Britain); cut off from intercourse with other nations, isolated; self-contained; narrow or prejudiced in feelings, ideas, or manners.

1775 JOHNSON *Journ. West. Isl.*, *Coriatachan*, The relief given to the mind in the penury of insular conversation by a new topick. **1829** LYTTON *Disowned* xxxv, Percy Bobus, with true insular breeding, took up the newspaper. **1847** JAMES *J. Marston Hall* ix, My English accent, and my insular notions, as he called them. **1849** MACAULAY *Hist. Eng.* ix. II. 427 They were a race insular in temper as well as in geographical position. **1856** MRS. BROWNING *Aur. Leigh* VI. 1 The English have a scornful insular way Of calling the French light. **1870** LOWELL *Study Wind.* 252 Without ceasing to be English, he has escaped from being insular. **1890** BOLDREWOOD *Col. Reformer* (1891) 136, I am not sufficiently insular to deny a foreign nobility all the graces and virtues that add lustre to our own.

b. *Palæogr.* (See quots.)

1908 W. M. LINDSAY *Contractions in Early Latin Minuscule MSS.* 1 The most fertile source of error..is the unfamiliarity of the writers with the contractions used in the Irish or pre-Carolingian script... The correct term is Insular, for English MSS. are included and Welsh too. **1913** F. W. HALL *Compan. Classical Texts* 167 Insular hands..i.e. Irish and Anglo-Saxon; a peculiar type of the half-uncial developed in the sixth century. **1960** G. A. GLAISTER *Gloss. Bk.* 195/1 *Insular hand*, the name given to the Hiberno-Saxon script widely used in England until the Norman Conquest for non-Latin texts. Its origins may be traced to 6th-century Ireland. An example is the first London Charter, 1066, which may be seen in the Guildhall Library. **1960** E. A. LOWE *Eng. Uncial* 14 By Insular symptoms we mean features and practices peculiar to Anglo-Saxon (and Irish) scribes. **1971** T. A. M. BISHOP *Eng. Caroline Minuscule* p. xiii, The most extensive repertories of Insular abbreviations in Caroline minuscule are MSS. of probably Continental origin.

B. *sb.* An inhabitant of an island; an islander.

1744 BERKELEY *Siris* §109 It is much to be lamented that our insulars..grow stupid or dote sooner than other people. **1845** in J. Pye *Patron. Brit. Art* v. 206 Generous insulars of our country. **1886** *Longm. Mag.* VII. 517 A nimbleness foreign to us phlegmatic, deliberate insulars.

'insula,rism. [f. prec. + -ISM.] The quality of being insular, or of having the character which is developed by living on an island detached from free intercourse with other people; esp. narrowness of ideas, feelings, or outlook.

1880 *Blackw. Mag.* Feb. 142 The intolerant insularism and contempt of other people, which is one of the great national characterstics of Englishmen. **1880** J. NICHOL *Byron* 210 Unless we wrap ourselves in an insolent insularism, we are bound at least to ask..the meaning of their concurrent testimony. **1888** H. S. MERRIMAN *Young Mistley* II. vii. 101 This curse of 'insularism' militates against England.

insularity (ɪnsjuːˈlærɪtɪ). [f. as prec. + -ITY; cf. F. *insularité* (Littré).]

1. The state or condition of being an island, or of being surrounded by water.

1790 *Cook's Voy.* I. Pref. 5 He discovered the Society Islands, determined the Insularity of New Zealand. **1802** PINKERTON *Geog.* (L.), The insularity of Britain was first shown by Agricola, who sent his fleet round it. **1891** J. WINSOR *Columbus* xviii. 425 If Varnhagen's opinion..be accepted as knowledge of the time, the insularity of Cuba was necessarily proved even at that early day.

2. The condition of living on an island, and of being thus cut off or isolated from other people, their ideas, customs, etc.; hence, narrowness of mind or feeling, contractedness of view.

1755 H. WALPOLE *Mem. Geo. II* 12 Dec., [Lord Barrington] owned..that our foreign dominions do take off from our insularity..on the other hand, their connection with us takes away the insularity of Hanover. **1861** *Sat. Rev.* XI. 251/2 Guilty of an insularity in their pictures of English politics which the real course of those politics has rarely justified. **1893** EARL DUNMORE *Pamirs* II. 135 The proverbial insularity of the average Briton.

'insula,rize, *v. rare.* [f. as prec. + -IZE.] *trans.* To render insular or represent as an island.

1891 J. WINSOR *Columbus* App. 650 We find the peninsula made by the St. Lawrence and the Atlantic insularized from the beginning of the seventeenth century. **1894** —— *Cartier to Frontenac* 58 Sebastian Münster contented himself with insularizing a region which he associated with the earlier Cortoreal.

'insularly, *adv.* [f. as prec. + -LY².] After the manner of an island or islander.

1856 in WEBSTER. **1867** H. KINGSLEY *Silcote of S.* xlvii. (1876) 347 Are you insularly stupid? **1882** *Standard* 17 Mar. 4/8 Of whose virtues these 'brumous isles' are insularly ignorant.

insulary (ˈɪnsjʊlərɪ), *a.* and *sb.* Now *rare* or *Obs.* [ad. L. *insulāris* INSULAR: see -ARY².]

A. *adj.* = INSULAR.

1642 HOWELL *For. Trav.* (Arb.) 46 Great Britaine having also most of Her trade intrinsique, with many other Insulary advantages. **1651** EVELYN *Char. Eng.* Misc. (1805) 150 These are the natural effects of parity..insulary manners. **1716** CHETWODE *Let. to Secretary Stanhope* 29 June in Earl Stanhope *Hist. Eng.* II. p. lvi, This is a mean insulary spirit. **1799-1805** S. TURNER *Anglo-Sax.* I. III. v. 195 Ethelbert.. at length succeeded to that insulary predominance among the Anglo-Saxon kings, which they called the Bretwalda.

B. *sb.* An inhabitant of an island; an islander.

1585 T. WASHINGTON tr. *Nicholay's Voy.* II. vii. 37b, In al those Ilands..after the common opinion of the Insularies. **1718** OZELL tr. *Tournefort's Voy.* I. 136 The Samians whose ships were painted red according to the old custom of the Insularies. **1861** SALA in *Temple Bar Mag.* III. 157 You are not wholly an insulary.

insulate (ˈɪnsjʊlət), *a.* Now *rare.* [ad. L. *insulāt-us*, f. *insula* island: see -ATE² 2. Cf. F. *insulé* (Littré).] Detached, isolated, INSULATED; *spec.*: see quot. 1826.

1712 J. JAMES tr. *Le Blond's Gardening* 166 Trees that are insulate or detached..so as you may walk round about them. **1723** CHAMBERS tr. *Le Clerc's Treat. Archit.* I. 110 An Order of Insulate Columns with a Corridor..behind. **1803** J. KENNY *Society* 73 Man, mere man, bare, insulate, unknown. **1826** KIRBY & SP. *Entomol.* IV. 340 *Nervures.. Insulate*, discoidal nervures that are entirely unconnected with any others, or with the base of the wing.

insulate (ˈɪnsjʊleɪt), *v.* [f. L. *insula* island + -ATE³, or *insulāt-us* adj. (see prec.). The verb *insulāre is not recorded in late or med.L., but may have existed in the latter or in Renascence L.; the corresp. It. *isolāre* 'to reduce into an island' (Florio) is known in 16th c.]

1. *trans.* To make into an island by surrounding with water; to convert into an island.

1538 LELAND *Itin.* I. 5 The Ryver of Avon so windeth aboute Oundale Toune that it almost insulatithe it, savyng a litle by West North West. **1610** HOLLAND *Camden's Brit.* I. 586 Trent..turneth aside his streame Northward..and so almost insulateth or encompasseth Burton. **1774** PENNANT *Tour Scotl. in 1772*, 56 The river..forming two branches, and insulating the ground. **1851** D. WILSON *Preh. Ann.* (1863) I. i. 32 Ere Britain had been insulated from the continent.

2. *transf.* and *fig.* To cause (a thing, person, etc.) to stand detached from its surroundings; to separate or detach from its fellows or the rest; to set or place apart; to isolate.

1785 in Picton *L'pool Munic. Rec.* (1886) II. 258 It would greatly tend..to the ornament..of this town if the Exchange was insulated. **1786** JEFFERSON *Writ.* (1859) II. 39 To insulate ourselves, to retire from all aid, and to wrap ourselves in the mantle of self-sufficiency. **1809** WELLINGTON in Gurw. *Desp.* (1837) IV. 444 If General Cuesta and Venegas leave Madrid upon their left, I must march by the Escurial, or insulate myself entirely from them. **1809-10** COLERIDGE *Friend* (1818) III. 90 Tendency to individualize, embody, insulate. **1833** HT. MARTINEAU *Three Ages* iii. 95 Thrown into an atmosphere of corruption for want of room to insulate him. **1849** MURCHISON *Siluria* iii. (1867) 53 The black schists of this age are there insulated by a powerful dislocation. **1854** H. ROGERS *Ess.* II. i. 64 By insulating it from its context.

3. *Electr.* and *Heat.* To cut off or isolate from conducting bodies by the interposition of non-conductors, so as to prevent the passage of electricity or heat. Also (*Acoustics*) used with reference to sound.

1742 J. T. DESAGULIERS *Diss. Electr.* 2 They must be insulated, that is, they must not be suspended from..any Bodies but what are Electricks *per se.* **1755** B. MARTIN *Mag. Arts & Sc.* III. vii. 325 His Apparatus was perfectly insulated [*mispr.* insurated] (or suspended) by silken Strings, and had no Communication with the Earth. **1816** J. SMITH *Panorama Sc. & Art* II. 203 A person is equally insulated when he stands upon a stool with glass legs, or is suspended by silken cords from a ceiling. **1827** FARADAY *Chem. Manip.* xxiv. 631 Insulate the substances whose electricity is to be examined. **1870** POPE *Electr. Tel.* i. (1872) 20 The cells of a battery should always be thoroughly insulated from each other. **1927** DAVIS & KAYE *Acoustics of Buildings* ix. 178 The practice rooms have been so satisfactorily insulated, that it is impossible to hear any sound either through the floors or the partitions. **1955** *Oxf. Jun. Encycl.* XI. 175/2 The need for insulating floors against noise has long been understood.

†**4.** *Chem.* and *Phys.* To free from combination with other elements; to isolate. *Obs.*

1830 HERSCHEL *Stud. Nat. Phil.* 92 We are sometimes compelled to acknowledge the existence of elements different from those already..known, though we cannot insulate them. **1834** MRS. SOMERVILLE *Connex. Phys. Sc.* xix. (1849) 178 He insulated each coloured ray, and finding that it was no longer capable of decomposition [etc.].

insulated (ˈɪnsjʊleɪtɪd), *ppl. a.* [f. prec. + -ED¹.]

1. Made into an island; surrounded by water.

1776 GIBBON *Decl. & F.* (1869) I. i. 19 Britain was viewed in the lights of a distinct and insulated world. **1789** WOLCOTT (P. Pindar) *Expost. Odes* xiii. Wks. 1812 II. 245 Like some lone insulated Rock am I. **1820** SCOTT *Monast.* v, The bridge-keeper..resided with his family in the second and third stories of the tower, which, when both drawbridges were raised, formed an insulated fortalice in the midst of the river. **1856** KANE *Arct. Expl.* I. xviii. 225

Greenland, however insulated it may ultimately prove to be, is in mass strictly continental.

2. *transf.* and *fig.* Placed or standing in a detached position; standing apart; separated from intercourse with others; solitary, isolated.

1727–41 CHAMBERS *Cycl.*, *Insulate*, or *Insulated*, a term applied to a column, or other edifice which stands alone, or free and detached from any contiguous wall, &c. like an island in the sea. **1774** PENNANT *Tour Scotl. in 1772*, 39 Insulated pyramidal hills. **1781** COWPER *Let. to W. Unwin* 26 Nov. To be content with an insulated life. **1790** BURKE *Fr. Rev.* Wks. V. 37 In the case of separate insulated private men. **1837** HT. MARTINEAU *Soc. Amer.* II. 102 The accusation has arisen out of some insulated case. **1859** G. MEREDITH *R. Feverel* xii, Like every insulated mortal.

3. Electrically cut off from (the earth or other conducting bodies) by being surrounded with non-conductors. Also used with reference to heat and sound (cf. INSULATE *v.* 3).

1772 H. CAVENDISH in *Phil. Trans. R. Soc. 1771* LXI. 650 Any number of bodies, insulated and communicating with each other by conducting substances. **1777** T. CAVALLO *Compl. Treat. Electr.* 3 A body resting intirely upon non-conductors is said to be insulated. **1791** READ in *Phil. Trans.* LXXXI. 195, I had purposely placed a large glass bowl, upon an insulated table, in the room, to catch the falling electricity. **1834** MRS. SOMERVILLE *Connex. Phys. Sc.* xxviii. (1849) 312 Bodies surrounded with non-conductors are said to be insulated, because, when charged, the electricity cannot escape. **1871** TYNDALL *Fragm. Sc.* (1879) II. xvi. 446 Between the two principal carbons is placed a third insulated rod of the same material. **1964** W. MARKFIELD *To Early Grave* (1965) x. 176 An appetizing store, where..you can take home their potato salad in an insulated bag. **1970** *Guardian* 24 Aug. 14/2 Insulated containers for the fruit and food trade. **1970** C. DUERDEN *Noise Abatement* vii. 115 Construct a special sound insulated chamber. **1974** A. ROSS *Bradford Business* 75 A length of insulated cable..snaked across the floor to a three-pin socket.

ˈinsulating, *ppl. a.* [f. as prec. + -ING[2].] That insulates; *spec.* that does not conduct electricity or heat; that protects wires, or an electrified body, from conducting bodies. Also used with reference to sound. ***insulating stool***, one with glass legs, or other non-conducting supports to insulate a body placed on it.

1767 J. PRIESTLEY *Hist. & Present State Electr.* 200 Upon the subject of insulating bodies, he observes, that when cakes of sulphur..are made use of for this purpose, they ought to be well cooled before they are used. **1787** CAVALLO in *Phil. Trans.* LXXVIII. 8 The second plate B..is furnished with an insulating handle. **1816** J. SMITH *Panorama Sc. & Art* II. 219 The insulating stool..is..a mahogany board with glass feet, which are varnished like other insulating supports that are made of glass. By standing upon this stool, the human body may be insulated. **1874** F. HALL in *Scribner's Mag.* VI. 465/2 The insulating and depressing genius of their religion. **1881** MAXWELL *Electr. & Magn.* I. 36 The electrification of a body placed in a perfectly insulating medium. **1893** *Funk's Stand. Dict.*, Insulating tape. **1910** *Hawkins' Electr. Dict.*, 219/1 *Insulating tape*, tape, usually adhesive, rendered non-conducting by being saturated with an insulating compound, for the purpose of covering..exposed parts of insulated electrical conductors. **1927** DAVIS & KAYE *Acoustics of Buildings* ix. 171 Suitable insulating material can be..interposed between columns, girders, cross-beams etc., to counteract the transmission of sound. **1940** *Chambers's Techn. Dict.* 451/1 *Insulating oils*, special types of oil..used for oil-immersed transformers, circuit-breakers, etc. **1945** *Archit. Rev.* CVI. 308 Roof of steel decking covered with half-inch insulating board and mineral-faced felt. **1955** *Oxf. Jun. Encycl.* VIII. 399/1 The defence against noise lies in planning wisely..and also in using sound insulating and sound absorbing materials. **1963** H. R. CLAUSER *Encycl. Engin. Materials* 352/1 The selection of the proper insulating varnish for an electrical unit, such as a motor, generator, solenoid coil, or a transformer, is becoming of increasing importance as the efficiency and ratings of electrical units are improved.

insulation (ɪnsjuːˈleɪʃən). [n. of action f. INSULATE *v.*: see -ATION.] The action of insulating, the fact or condition of being insulated.

1. The action of surrounding by water or making into an island; the fact of being made insular. Also, an island.

1848 E. BRYANT *California* xi. 157 The waters surrounding these insulations could be traced between them as far as the eye could reach. **1851** RICHARDSON *Geol.* ii. 21 The insulation of peninsulas by the destruction of the isthmus which previously connected them with the mainland. **1871** *Scribner's Monthly* II. 7 Their smooth sides, uniform width and height..considered in connection with the courses which had wrought their insulation, excited our wonder and admiration.

2. *transf.* and *fig.* The action of placing apart or detaching from other things; the state or condition of standing alone or cut off; *concr.* an insulated object.

1798 G. WAKEFIELD *Reply Bp. of Landaff's Addr.* 4 An absolute insulation..from the reasonable benefits of society. **1829** I. TAYLOR *Enthus.* ix. 224 This sort of meditative insulation is the ultimate and natural issue of all enthusiastic piety. **1849** ROBERTSON *Serm.* Ser. I. xv. 221 There are two kinds of solitude: the first consisting of insulation in space.

3. a. The action of insulating electrically or physically; the condition of being isolated by non-conductors so as to prevent the passage of electricity, heat, or sound. Also the degree in which a body is insulated, as *partial*, *imperfect*, *total* insulation.

1767 J. PRIESTLEY *Hist. & Present State Electr.* 515 It is advisable that there should be no sharp edges or angles about the rubber [of the electrical machine], for that would make the insulation of it..ineffectual. **1822** IMISON *Sc. & Art* I. 327 The upper end of the glass is covered and lined with sealing-wax..to make its insulation more perfect. **1827** FARADAY *Chem. Manip.* xvii. 465 The insulation of substances is frequently required in electro-chemical investigation. **1876** PREECE & SIVEWRIGHT *Telegraphy* 265 Having ascertained the total insulation of the circuit, the insulation per mile is found by multiplying the total insulation by the mileage of line. **1896** *Electr. Rev.* 6 Mar. 41 Higher Voltage demands better insulation. **1913** *Chem. Abstr.* VII. 689 (*heading*) Incombustible and refractory materials for insulation from sound, heat and cold. **1955** *Oxf. Jun. Encycl.* VIII. 399/2 Double partitions, ..'floating floors',..and independent or suspended ceilings are all forms of construction used for sound insulation. **1972** L. L. DOELLE *Environmental Acoustics* xiv. 173 Bare concrete slab ..gives satisfactory insulation against airborne noises.

b. *concr.* Insulating or non-conductive material.

1870 R. M. FERGUSON *Electr.* 280 The insulation.. consists of four layers of gutta-percha. **1892** *Suppl. to Lightning* 7 Jan., *Insulation*, insulating material put on to a conductor to prevent as far as possible the escape of electricity. **1927** DAVIS & KAYE *Acoustics of Buildings* ix. 171 Felt-like insulation may..be introduced into the..structure of the building, to assist in isolating noise. **1969** *Sears Catal.* Spring/Summer 963 Fiber glass insulation..keeps water hotter and jacket cooler.

4. *Comb.*, as ***insulation material***, ***meter***, ***resistance***, ***tape***, ***test***, ***tester***.

1876 PREECE & SIVEWRIGHT *Telegraphy* 266 If, for instance, a wire gives 12°, the constant being 43°, 4387 will be the insulation resistance. **1889** EDISON in *Daily News* 7 Nov. 5/7 The operation of time upon the insulation material which surrounds these wires. **1903** *Whittaker's Electr. Engineer's Pocket-Bk.* 276 (*heading*) Insulation tests. **1909** *Cent. Dict.* Suppl., Insulation-meter. **1920** *Talking Machine News & Jrnl. Amusements* Feb. 77/2 Electrical insulation tape in a metal horn. **1923** *Nature* 13 Jan. 63/2 The 'Meg' insulation tester.., a remarkably light and cheap megger.

insulative (ˈɪnsjʊleɪtɪv, -ətɪv), *a.* [f. INSULAT(E *v.*: see -IVE.] Of, pertaining to, or as insulation.

1945 *Sci. News Let.* 23 June 397/3 The insulative concretes vary in weight from one-third to one-half that of ordinary gravel concrete. **1971** *Nature* 4 June 331/1 The fur was very spiny with virtually no soft underfur and thus probably offers little insulative protection. This may be an adaptation to the tropical environment. **1973** *Ibid.* 26 Jan. 240/1 Their fur is less than half as long..and has a correspondingly lower insulative quality.

insulator (ˈɪnsjʊleɪtə(r)). [agent-n. in L. form, from INSULATE *v.*: see -OR.] One who or that which insulates; *e.g.* a body or substance that entirely or to a great degree prevents the passage of electricity or heat between contiguous bodies; a non-conductor; *spec.* a contrivance, usually made of glass or porcelain, for supporting or carrying telegraph or telephone wires, or power lines, without carrying off the current. Also used with reference to sound.

1801 *Encycl. Brit.* Suppl. I 605/1 Mr. Volta..and others ..have attempted to shew how these substances are preferable..to more perfect insulators. **1814** G. J. SINGER *Elem. Electr.* III. iii. 278 Insulation may..be partially preserved by coating all the glass insulators with sealing wax. **1845** J. O. N. RUTTER *Hum. Electr.* iii. 31 Glass is not the most perfect insulator (non-conductor); but in practice it is the most useful. **1847** BRETT & LITTLE *Compendium Improvements Electr. Telegraphs* 22 The insulators are made of earthenware, and secured direct to the poles. **1876** PREECE & SIVEWRIGHT *Telegraphy* 185 Seeing, however, that the insulators have little more than the weight of the wire to withstand, except at the terminal posts, no trouble is experienced in suiting the form of insulator to this. **1885** WATSON & BURBURY *Math. Th. Electr. & Magn.* I. 183 Non-conducting spaces may be occupied by actual substances, called non-conductors, insulators, or dielectrics ..such as dry air and other gases, wood, &c. **1927** DAVIS & KAYE *Acoustics of Buildings* ix. 173 The usual principle is to have double walls..and to fill the space..with sound absorbents or insulators. **1950** KNUDSEN & HARRIS *Acoustical Designing in Archit.* xi. 246 If the porous blocks are not plastered, they may be very poor insulators: sound 'leaks' through the interstices. **1957** *Encycl. Brit.* XIV. 115I/1 On steel tower transmission lines the lightning voltage which can exist on the conductors..depends on the lightning flashover value of the supporting insulators.

b. *attrib.* and *Comb.*

1876 PREECE & SIVEWRIGHT *Telegraphy* 159 Insulator breaking is the main evil which has been met with on roads. *Ibid.* 210 A small aperture..is previously cut in the middle; through this the insulator bolt and nut are placed.

ˈinsulet. *nonce-wd.* [f. L. *insul-a* island + -ET[1]. An Anglo-Latin *insulētum* is given by Du Cange; cf. also It. *isoletta*, F. *îlette*, *îlet* islet.] An islet.

1622 DRAYTON *Poly-olb.* xxvii, And Fulney at her back, a pretty insulet.

insulin (ˈɪnsjʊlɪn). *Biochem.* Also †**insuline**. [f. L. *insul-a* island (because it is produced by the islets of Langerhans) + -IN[1].] **1.** A polypeptide hormone (the amino-acid composition differing slightly from species to species) which is concerned with carbohydrate metabolism in man and some other vertebrates, being produced by the islets of Langerhans and having effects that include the removal of sugar from the blood (so that a deficiency of insulin causes diabetes mellitus) and the promotion of protein synthesis and fat storage.

The name *insulin(e)* was proposed for the hormone on three separate occasions, each time independently: see quot. 1926.

[**1909** J. DE MEYER in *Archivio di Fisiol.* VII. 96 Le produit de la sécrétion interne du pancréas (non denommé encore).., s'il dérive, comme nous le pensons, des ilots de Langerhans pourrait être appelé *Insuline*.] **1914** E. A. SCHÄFER *Introd. Study Endocrine Glands* 84 The results of pancreas-extirpation and pancreas-grafting can..be best explained by supposing that the islet-tissue produces an autacoid substance which passes into the blood and affects carbohydrate metabolism and carbohydrate storage in such a manner that there is no undue accumulation of glucose in the blood. Provisionally it will be convenient for description purposes to refer to this hypothetical autacoid as insuline. **1916** —— *Endocrin Organs* xvii. 128 The islet tissue produces an autacoid which passes into the blood and affects carbohydrate metabolism... Provisionally it will be convenient to refer to this hypothetical autacoid as insuline. **1922** F. G. BANTING et al. in *Proc. & Trans. R. Soc. Canada* XVI. v. 27 (*heading*) The preparation of pancreatic extracts containing insulin. **1922** F. G. BANTING et al. in *Amer. Jrnl. Physiol.* LXII. 175 Purified alcoholic extracts of pancreas, for which we suggest the name *insulin*, when injected subcutaneously into normal rabbits cause the percentage of sugar in the blood to fall within a few hours. **1923** A. E. HOUSMAN *Let.* 16 May (1971) 213 When I saw the invention of Insulin I..expected to hear you were cured already. **1926** E. A. SCHÄFER *Endocrine Organs* (ed. 2) II. xlix. 343 To this autacoid the name insulin is applied. [*Note*] The term was introduced by de Meyer (Arch. di fisiol., vii., 1909). In ignorance of this it was employed as a convenient term to denote the autacoid of the islet tissue in the first edition of this work, published in 1916. It was independently adopted by the Toronto workers [*viz.* F. G. Banting et al.] in 1922. **1956** *Arch. Biochem. & Biophysics* LXV. 427 The amino acid sequences in pig and sheep insulins were compared with that of cattle insulin... The only differences found were in the three residues occupying positions 8, 9, and 10 in the glycyl chain. **1959** *Ann. N.Y. Acad. Sci.* LXXXII. 340 Most commercial preparations are mixtures of beef and pork insulin. **1968** PASSMORE & ROBSON *Compan. Med. Stud.* I. xxv. 43/1 Insulin promotes all the known pathways of glucose disposal and transformation including glycogen storage, fat formation, total oxidation and the use of the hexose-monophosphate pathway.

2. *attrib.* and *Comb.*, as **insulin shock**, hypoglycæmia resulting from excessive insulin in the body, producing nervousness, weakness, sweating and in extreme cases coma, **insulin coma; insulin (shock) treatment**, a treatment for mental illness consisting of a course of artificially produced insulin comas (see quot. 1951).

1942 M. DICKENS *One Pair of Feet* viii. 167 A policeman, who had mistaken an Insulin coma for a drunken stupor. **1959** *Times* 26 Mar. 15/5 Not for them the hashish-dream and the insulin-coma. **1972** *Chem. Abstr.* LXXVII. 135684 After more than 45 min in an insulin coma, administration of glucose..to the affected animals did not interrupt the coma. **1925** *Ann. Clin. Med.* III. 381/1 In diabetics whose blood sugars were high, that is above 300 mgm., symptoms of insulin shock frequently have been observed when their blood sugars were rapidly reduced to within usual normal range. **1936** *Jrnl. Nerv. & Mental Dis.* LXXXV. 504 Insulin shock stimulates metabolism in general and liver function in particular. **1938** *Arch. Neurol. & Psychiatry* (Chicago) XXXIX. 1 (*heading*) Insulin shock treatment of schizophrenic patients. **1951** F. HOPKINS in E. N. Chamberlain *Text-bk. Med.* ix. 692 Insulin shock treatment ..consists of the induction of coma by the injection of insulin. When the optimum dose for the individual case has been ascertained, a coma is induced each day for five or six days a week until a course of 50 or thereabouts has been given. **1958** H. BECKMAN *Drugs* xxxiv. 351/2 Epinephrine is used adjuvantly in combating insulin shock. **1940** *Ann. Internal Med.* XIV. 393 The insulin treatment of schizophrenia owes its origin to an accidental observation made by Sakel in his treatment of morphine addicts. **1958** I. MURDOCH *Bell* xxvi. 302 Catherine had been having insulin treatment and was continually under the influence of drugs.

Hence **ˈinsulinase** [-ASE], an enzyme or enzyme system that breaks down insulin; **ˈinsulinized** *ppl. a.*, treated with insulin.

1928 *Amer. Jrnl. Physiol.* LXXXIV. 571 In both of these fishes the normal sugars are often even lower than the reduced sugars of the insulinized trout, scup and menhaden. **1949** MIRSKY & BROH-KAHN in *Arch. Biochem.* XX. 8 Pending further investigation, it is proposed..to characterize the active principle in these extracts as 'insulinase'. **1959** *Metabolism* VIII. 99 The liver is rich in an enzyme system designated 'insulinase', which causes cleavage of insulin; this system may be comprised of more than one enzyme. **1966** *Chem. Abstr.* LXV. 1157 The increased sensitivity of aged humans and animals towards hypoglycemics is probably due to decreased insulinase activity. **1969** *Physiol. Chem. & Physics* I. 355 (*heading*) The subsequent accumulation of labeled glucose by insulinized frog muscle at 0°C.

insulite (ˈɪnsjʊlaɪt). *Electr.* [f. *insul-*, in INSULATE + -ITE.] The trade name of an artificially made insulating or non-conducting substance.

1882 *Athenæum* 13 May 607/1 Dr. Fleming has patented a new insulating material..to which is given the name of 'Insulite'. **1883** *Chamb. Jrnl.* 728 Insulated by means of caps of insulite, which is formed by driving paraffine oil into sawdust at great pressure.

†**inˈsulphured,** *ppl. a. Obs.* Also en-. [IN-[2].] Charged with sulphur.

c **1611** CHAPMAN *Iliad* x. 7 Or opes the gulfy mouth of war with his ensulphur'd hand. **1615** G. SANDYS *Trav.* 265 Meere heate Of aire insulphur'd makes the Patient sweate.

†**in'sulsate**, *a.* *Obs. rare.* [irreg. f. as next + -ATE².] = next, 1.

1652 GAULE *Magastrom.* xxvi, The kind of words..and the insulsate phrase, doe openly bewray themselves to containe nothing else but mere toyes and impostures.

in'sulse, *a.* Now *rare.* [ad. L. *insulsus*, f. *in-* (IN-³) + *salsus* witty, lit. salted, pa. pple. of *salĕre*, f. *sal* salt.]

1. Lacking wit or sense; dull, insipid, stupid; senseless, absurd.

1609 BP. W. BARLOW *Answ. Nameless Cath.* 142 Neither insulse nor insulting, either Pamphlets or Replies. **1641** MILTON *Prel. Episc.* 10 Not to speak of the insulse, and ill-layd comparison. **1642** —— *Apol. Smect.* Introd., Wks. (1851) 259 An insuls and frigid affectation. **1732** BERKELEY *Alciphr.* VI. §14 In our times a dull Man is said to be insipid or insulse. **1772** NUGENT tr. *Hist. Friar Gerund* I. vii. 173 He said that Martial was insulse in respect to Catullus.

2. *lit.* Tasteless, insipid, dull or flat in taste.

1675 EVELYN *Terra* (1729) 28 Some Plants are very brisk and quick, others insulse and flat. **1699** —— *Acetaria* (1729) 146 It may be too sharp, if it exceed a grateful Acid; too insulse and flat, if the Profusion be extreme. **1772** NUGENT tr. *Hist. Friar Gerund* IV. ix. 196 An insipidity enough to make salt itself insulse.

†**in'sulsed**, *a.* *Obs.* [f. as prec. + -ED¹.]

Unsalted; fresh, freshly made.

1597 A. M. tr. *Guillemeau's Fr. Chirurg.* 42 b/2 Remedyes made..of insulsed and freshe Butter. **1599** —— tr. *Gabelhouer's Bk. Physicke* 177/1 Halfe a pinte of leane, & insulsede hennes broth. *Ibid.* 265/1 Take a freshe, and insulsede Cheese.

†**in'sulsely**, *adv.* *Obs.* [f. INSULSE + -LY².]

Senselessly, stupidly.

1637 C. DOW *Answ. H. Burton* 167 So grosse an error so insulsly expressed.

in'sulsity. Now *rare.* [ad. L. *insulsitās*, n. of quality f. *insulsus* INSULSE.] The quality of being 'insulse'; stupidity, senselessness.

1623 COCKERAM, *Insulsitie*, folly. **1643** MILTON *Divorce* II. iii, To justifie the councells of God and Fate from the insulsity of mortall tongues. **1651** *Fuller's Abel Rediv., Melancthon* 235 The insulsitie and blockishnesse of the man. **1658** PHILLIPS, *Insulsity*, unsavoriness,..also folly, bluntness of wit. **1900** *Speaker* 3 Mar. 598/1 That quality [humour] in him saves the (unavoidably expurgated) Falstaff, and Shallow, and Fluellen from insulsity.

insult ('ɪnsʌlt), *sb.* [a. F. *insult* (1380 in Godef.) now *insulte*, or ad. late L. *insultus*, f. *in-* (IN-²) + *saltus* leap, after *insultāre*; see next.]

1. a. An act, or the action, of attacking or assailing; attack, assault, onset (*lit.* and *fig.*). *arch.* †**b.** *Mil.* An open and sudden attack or assault without formal preparations: cf. INSULT *v.* 4 b (*obs.*).

1603 HOLLAND *Plutarch's Mor.* 618 Talking of the instances, the insults, the intercidences, communities of diseases, and all to shew..that we know the words and tearmes of physick. **1610** F. HERING *Cert. Rules Contagion* (1625) C iij, The venyme, by a second insult and incounter surpriseth..the Heart, and caryeth away the Patient. **1697** POTTER *Antiq. Greece* III. xx. (1715) 152 To defend them against the Insults of Winds and Waves. **1710** STEELE *Tatler* No. 174 ¶10 We sufficiently cover from all Insults both our Siege and Convoys. **1726** CAVALLIER *Mem.* I. 48 The others were obliged to retire into fenced Cities, for fear of our Insults. **1808** SCOTT *Marm.* VI. ii, Many a rude tower and rampart there Repelled the insult of the air. **1844** H. H. WILSON *Brit. India* II. 448 The enterprising pirate, Kanhoji Angria, by whom the trade of the Company was subjected to repeated insult and plunder during the first thirty years of the eighteenth century.

†**c.** *fig.* A 'leaping in'; an inrush. *Obs. rare.*

1652 GAULE *Magastrom.* 201 It [the acquisition of prophecy] is a free, sudden, extraordinary insult, or illapse.

d. *Med.* Anything which tends to cause disease in or injury to the body or to disturb normal bodily processes; also, the resulting reaction, lesion, or injury.

[Cf. quots. 1603, 1610 for sense 1.] **1904** STEDMAN *Dunglison's Dict. Med. Sci.* (ed. 23) 581/1 *Insult*, injury; trauma exciting a morbid process. **1959** S. DUKE-ELDER *Parson's Dis. Eye* (ed. 13) xvii. 228 The avascularity of the sclera and the lack of reaction of its dense fibrous tissues to insult whether traumatic or infective, make diseases of this tissue relatively rare. **1961** *Acta Psychiatrica et Neurol. Scand. Suppl.* CL. 110 Patients with cerebro-vascular insults. *Ibid.* 112 It was possible that the insult had been provoked by the anti-hypertensive therapy. **1962** HARRIS & GRUBER in A. Pirie *Lens Metabolism Rel. Cataract* 373 Changes in the level of inorganic and organic phosphate within the lens may follow certain metabolic insults. *Ibid.* 375 The older the lens, the less is it able to withstand the insult which cold induces. **1970** G. R. TAYLOR *Doomsday Bk.* vii. 158 The US population was exposed to 'severe chronic lead insult' (insult being a technical term in medicine). **1971** *Nature* 23 July 276/2 Left handedness may be caused by neurological insults associated with prenatal or birth trauma. **1971** *Sci. Amer.* Oct. 118/2 Congenital heart abnormalities are the most serious of the commoner defects. Often caused by rubella or similar insults in the early months of pregnancy, they affect about one birth in 60.

2. An act, or the action, of insulting (in sense 1 or 2 of vb.); injuriously contemptuous speech or behaviour; scornful utterance or action intended to wound self-respect; an affront, indignity, outrage. Freq. in phr. ***to add insult to injury***.

1671 MILTON *P.R.* III. 190 Try'd in humble state..By tribulations, injuries, insults, Contempts, and scorns, and snares, and violence. *a* **1743** SAVAGE (J.), The ruthless sneer that insult adds to grief. **1748** E. MOORE *Foundling* V. v. 60 This is adding Insult to Injuries. **1751** EARL ORRERY *Remarks Swift* (1752) 121 The voyage to the Houyhnhnms is a real insult upon mankind. **1769** *Junius Lett.* xii. 48 They did not dare to offer a direct insult to their understanding. **1805** *Deb. Congress U.S.* 31 Jan. 1072 It was adding insult to injury, and expenses to both, as it regarded the claimants. **1807** *Ibid.* 18 Nov. 933 Were the laws of a free and respectable State to be evaded by such shameful expedients as these? This was adding insult to injury. **1820** BYRON *Mar. Fal.* II. i, 'Twas a gross insult. **1853** H. T. RILEY tr. *Phædrus' Fables* 429 You wanted to revenge the sting of a tiny insect with death; what will you do to yourself who have added insult to injury? **1874** GREEN *Short Hist.* vii. §8. 433 The young prince who..plucked them in insult by the beard. **1876** E. MELLOR *Priesth.* viii. 364 To talk of 'orders' without 'fitness' in a spiritual kingdom is an insult both to God and man. **1928** A. HUXLEY *Point Counter Point* ix. 155 It shocked him that one should lie in bed while other people were up and working. To get up late was somehow to add insult to injury. **1970** B. SPOCK *Decent & Indecent* 19 The behavioural sciences then added insult to injury. Psychologists have given man the impression that he responds like a laboratory rat. **1972** *Times* 12 Dec. 22/7 They submitted defective contracts, made arithmetical errors adding up to several thousand pounds and, to add insult to injury, charged their fees on the wrong and higher scale.

†**3.** The act of leaping upon; 'covering'. *Obs.*

1697 DRYDEN *Virg. Georg.* III. 99 The Mother Cow must wear a low'ring Look..The Bull's Insult at Four she may sustain.

4. Used *attrib.* in expressions denoting contests in verbal insult, characteristic of U.S. Blacks.

1964 *Amer. Folk Music Occasional* I. 81 One of the standard routines of both the Negro and blackface minstrel show was the insult-dialogue. Though this theatrical expression is no longer widely current, this kind of dialogue has retained an interest... Here..is an insult-routine used in a street corner situation. **1968** P. OLIVER *Screening Blues* vi. 246 Dr Abrahams makes acknowledgment of the dozens as played by young Negroes in the army but had not himself noted much use of the insult game among females or adults generally. **1969** *Language* XLV. 602 The children I studied engaged in constant verbal play..(for instance, their ritualized insult game).

insult (ɪn'sʌlt), *v.* [ad. L. *insultāre* to leap at or on, assail, insult. Cf. F. *insulter* (14th c. in Littré), possibly the immediate source.

Insultāre may be viewed either as freq. of *insilīre* to leap upon, f. *in-* (IN-²) + *salīre* to leap, or as a compound of *in-* + *saltāre* freq. of *salīre*. Cotgrave 1611 has (F.) *Insulter*, 'to insult, crow, vaunt, or triumph over; to wrong, reproach, affront; contemne; also, to rebound, reioyce at, leape for ioy'. The Fr. intrans. constr. takes *à*, L. has the dative, or *in* with accus.]

1. *intr.* To manifest arrogant or scornful delight by speech or behaviour; to exult proudly or contemptuously; to boast, brag, vaunt, glory, triumph, esp. in an insolent or scornful way. †**a.** *absol.*

a **1592** H. SMITH *Wks.* (1866–7) I. 439 Let no man insult beyond the lists of humility. *a* **1619** DANIEL *Funeral Poem* Poems (1623) 24 They know how, The Lyon being dead euen Hares insult. **1637** R. HUMPHREY tr. *St. Ambrose* II. 2 Those that much insult, and solace themselues in sounding forth a trumpet. **1670** DRYDEN *1st Pt. Conq. Granada* III. i, Then proudly she insults, and gives you Cares And Jealousies. **1674** MILTON *Samson* 113 My enemies who come to stare At my affliction, and perhaps to insult.

b. Const. *over*, *upon*, *on*, *against*, rarely *at* (the object of scorn or triumph). *Obs.* or *arch.*

1570–6 LAMBARDE *Peramb. Kent* (1826) 164 What was it else for this proud Prelate, thus to insult over simple men? **1583** FULKE *Defence* xvii. 512 You shall have little lust hereafter to insult against mine ignorance. **1586** A. DAY *Eng. Secretary* II. (1625) 89 When injuriously..we insult upon a mans doings. **1597** HOOKER *Eccl. Pol.* V. xxi. §4 Because they insist so much and so proudly insult thereon. **1617** MORYSON *Itin.* III. 288 Nothing is more frequent, then for little girles to insult over their brothers much bigger then they, reproving their doings. **1621** BURTON *Anat. Mel.* II. iii. II. (1651) 318 Let no *filius terræ*, or upstart, insult at this which I have said. **1690** DRYDEN *Amphitryon* Ep. Ded., They are not apt to insult on the Misfortunes of their Countrymen. **1699** BENTLEY *Phal.* 425 Will the Examiner insult upon that Great Man, as he has done upon Me? **1711** ADDISON *Spect.* No. 171 ¶5 There are many who..insult over an aking Heart. **1785** PALEY *Mor. Philos.* (1818) II. 97 Whilst the infidel..insults over their credulous fears. **1857** DE QUINCEY *S. Parr* Wks. 1862 V. 185 We all know that it was not in his nature to insult over the fallen.

†**c.** Const. *in*, *of*, *on* (the occasion of boasting). *Obs.* [= L. with abl.]

1589 NASHE *Ded. Greene's Menaphon* (Arb.) 13 England might have long insulted in his wit. **1608–11** BP. HALL *Occas. Medit.* §92 (T. Suppl.) Too many insult in this just punishment, who have deserved more. **1630** *R. Johnson's Kingd. & Commw.* 575 [It] insulteth of two Summers, temperature of Aire, with duplicitie of increase. *a* **1653** GOUGE *Comm. Heb.* vii. 111 They much insult on this, that they have such priests as offer up a real..sacrifice. **1666** PEPYS *Diary* 16 June, The Dutch do mightily insult of their victory, and they have great reason.

2. *trans.* To assail with offensively dishonouring or contemptuous speech or action; to treat with scornful abuse or offensive disrespect; to offer indignity to; to affront, outrage.

1620 E. BLOUNT *Horæ Subs.* 101 Insult them [servants] not too much, and reduce them not to ouer-great subiection. **1696** PHILLIPS (ed. 5), *To Insult*, to afflict one that is already afflicted, to reproach him with his Misery, to rejoyce over it. *a* **1713** SHAFTESB. *Misc. Refl.* I. ii. Wks. 1749 III. 45 The sacred Pomp trodden under-foot, insulted. **1771** *Junius Lett.* lxvii. 330 When you do not insult the man you have betrayed. **1823** LAMB *Elia* Ser. II. *Poor Relation*, [He] insults you with a special commendation of your window-curtains. **1849** MACAULAY *Hist. Eng.* iii. I. 400 What-ever the canting Roundhead had regarded with reverence was insulted.

b. To triumph over contemptuously.

1775 JOHNSON *Journ. West. Isl., Ostig* 268 The Welsh, two hundred years ago, insulted their English neighbours for the instability of their Orthography.

†**3.** *intr.* To make an attack or assault (*lit.* and *fig.*). *Obs.*

1638 SIR T. HERBERT *Trav.* (ed. 2) 296 In whose road wee found thirty or forty Frigads of Mallabar men of warre, who durst not insult upon their numbers, but choose rather to avoyd. **1662** J. CHANDLER *Van Helmont's Oriat.* 292 If a stinking muscilage inclining to bitterness doth arise, there is a giddiness of the head; and that more strongly insulting, doth stir up an Apoplexy. **1670** MILTON *Hist. Eng.* II. Wks. (1851) 86 Having recover'd much Territory about Rhine, where the German inrodes before had long insulted.

4. *trans.* To attack, assault, assail (now only *fig.* in general sense). †**b.** *spec.* (*Mil.*) To attack openly and suddenly without formal preparations.

1697 DRYDEN *Virg. Georg.* III. 370 The spumy Waves..March onwards, and insult the rocky Shoar. **1727** A. HAMILTON *New Acc. E. Ind.* I. x. 100 Having no Fleet at Sea, the Portugueze insulted his Sea-coasts. **1729** SHELVOCKE *Artillery* v. 396 The Tower appearing..Cæsar ..ordered his Army to advance up to it, and insult it. **1775** MONTGOMERY in Sparks *Corr. Amer. Rev.* (1853) I. 492, I propose amusing Mr. C. with a formal attack, erecting batteries, &c., but mean to insult the works, I believe towards the Lower Town, which is the weakest part. **1853** STOCQUELER *Mil. Encycl.*, *Insult (to)*, in a military sense, is to attack boldly and in open day, without going through the slow operations of trenches. **1853** JAMES *Agnes Sorel* (1860) I. 4 A group of night-ramblers walked along insulting the ear of night with cries.

†**5.** *intr.* To leap wantonly, frisk. *Obs. rare.*

1652 GAULE *Magastrom.* 249 A goat..began to insult with strange voyce and gesture.

Hence **in'sulted** *ppl. a.*, treated with contemptuous abuse, outraged.

1781 CRABBE *Library* 271 Insulted reason fled the grov'ling soul. **1855** MACAULAY *Hist. Eng.* xviii. IV. 153 If a rude word were spoken of him..he might vindicate his insulted dignity both by civil and criminal proceedings.

insultable (ɪn'sʌltəb(ə)l), *a.* *rare.* [f. prec. vb. + -ABLE. Cf. F. *insultable* (St. Simon, in Littré).]

Capable of being insulted; open to insult; quick to feel insult.

1841–4 EMERSON *Ess.*, *Exper.* Wks. (Bohn) I. 186 The chagrins which the bad heart gives off..treason or insult whatever is threatenable and insultable in us. **1868** ALCOTT *Tablets* 71 Civility has not completed its work if it leaves us unsocial, morose, insultable.

†**in'sultance.** *Obs. rare.* [f. as next: see -ANCE.]

Insulting action or behaviour.

1615 CHAPMAN *Odyss.* IX. 635 Instantly I staid our ores, and this insultance vsede; Cyclop! thou shouldst not haue so much abusde Thy monstrous forces.

So †**in'sultancy.** *Obs.*

1655 M. CARTER *Hon. Rediv.* (1660) 23 The Commonwealth in generall, much prejudiced by the insultancy of such mungrele spirits.

in'sultant, *a.* *rare.* [ad. L. *insultānt-em*, pr. pple. of *insultāre*; see INSULT *v.* Cf. F. *insultant* (17th c. in Littré).] Insulting.

1627 E. F. *Hist. Edw. II* in *Select. fr. Harl. Misc.* (1793) 45 A kind of insultant triumphing tyranny, far unworthy the nobility of her sex and virtue, she makes her poor condemned adversary..attend her progress. **1866** BICKERSTETH *Yesterday, To-day, and For ever* VIII. 376 Meanwhile for thy insultant ambassage..Cherub, abide in chains.

insultation (ɪnsʌl'teɪʃən). *Obs.* or *arch.* [a. F. *insultation* (1370 in Godef.), or ad. L. *insultātiōn-em*, n. of action f. *insultāre* to INSULT. Exceedingly common in 17th c.]

1. The action, or an act, of insulting (in sense 1 or 2 of vb.); scornful triumph or boasting; injuriously contemptuous speech or behaviour; insult.

1513 BRADSHAW *St. Werburge* I. 2245 Sayenge with insultacyon Trowe ye to be spared from punyshment this day. **1534** MORE *Godly Medit.* Wks. 1417/2 Almighty god, take from me..al delite of exprobacion, or insultation against anye parson in their affliccion and calamitie. **1631** GOUGE *God's Arrows* III. §80. 336 Insultations over the Church of Christ in her calamities. **1683** BURNET tr. *More's Utopia* (1685) 6 Insultation against any in their Affliction or Calamity. **1755** S. WALKER *Serm.* ii, Distressing Groans, woful Curses and blasphemous Insultations. **1849** J. MORISON in *Life* xxiv. (1898) 286 Insultation over my person,..calumniation of my character.

†**2.** Attack, assault. *Obs.*

1596 FITZ-GEFFRAY *Sir F. Drake* (1881) 55 Like as abroade with unresisted armes He tam'd his foes prowde insultations. **1615** *Trade's Incr.* in *Harl. Misc.* (Malh.) III. 292 The benefits [of commerce] allayed by insultation of pirates. **1615** T. ADAMS *Blacke Devill* 36 Here will I stay the insultation of thy proud waves. **1656–7** *Rhode Island Col. Rec.* (1856) I. 342 Your wisdoms may know the inhuman insultations of these wild creatures.

insulter (ɪnˈsʌltə(r)). [f. INSULT *v.* + -ER¹.] One who insults, in various senses: see the verb.

1592 SHAKS. *Ven. & Ad.* 550 Her lips are conquerors, his lips obey, Paying what ransom the insulter willeth. **1714** ROWE *Jane Shore* I, Man, the merciless Insulter..who rejoices in our sex's weakness. **1750** WARBURTON *Doctr. Grace* Pref., The Defender of Religion should not imitate the insulter of it in his modes of disputation. **1889** STEVENSON *Master of B.* 111 How was he to smile back on the deceiver and the insulter?

insulting (ɪnˈsʌltɪŋ), *vbl. sb.* Now *rare* exc. as gerund. [f. as prec. + -ING¹.] The action of the verb INSULT: **a.** Scornfully triumphing over another (*obs.* or *arch.*), or treating him with contemptuous abuse; with *pl.* a scornful boast, an insult. **b.** Assaulting, attacking; an assault.

1628 WITHER *Brit. Rememb.* II. 1189 To reprove With proud insultings. **1660** MILTON *Free Commw.* Wks. (1851) 445 Let them but hear the Insolencies, the Menaces, the Insultings of our newly animated common Enemies. **1837** S. R. MAITLAND *Twelve Lett.* (1841) 86 The incessant mocking, bantering, and insulting of the papists.

inˈsulting, *ppl. a.* [f. as prec. + -ING².] That insults (see the verb).

1591 SHAKS. *1 Hen. VI,* I. ii. 138 Now am I like that prowd Insulting Ship, Which Cæsar and his fortune bare at once. **1697** DRYDEN *Virg. Georg.* IV. 14 Far from the Cows and Goats insulting Crew. **1781** GIBBON *Decl. & F.* xxx. III. 150 The captive wife of Alaric..was reduced to implore the mercy of the insulting foe. **1855** MACAULAY *Hist. Eng.* xx. IV. 402 His enemies rejoiced with vindictive and insulting joy.

insultingly (ɪnˈsʌltɪŋlɪ), *adv.* [f. prec. + -LY².] In an insulting manner; so as to insult; with scornful abuse, or treatment that wounds self-respect.

1623 R. BERNARD (*title*) Looke beyond Luther, or an Answere to that Question so often and so insultingly proposed by our adversaries, asking vs where this our Religion was before Luther's time. **1660** R. COKE *Power & Subj.* 68 In the Fable of the Logg which Jupiter gave the Frogs for their King; when they became fearless of it, every one jumped insultingly upon it. *a* **1711** KEN *Hymns Evang.* Poet. Wks. 1721 I. 140 Insultingly the wretch they toss, and gore. **1856** OLMSTED *Slave States* 288 Virginia now insultingly spurns from her councils all who suggest that slavery is ever to be eradicated.

†**insultment.** *Obs. rare.* [f. INSULT *v.* + -MENT.] The action of insulting; contemptuous triumph; insult.

1611 SHAKS. *Cymb.* III. v. 145 He on the ground, my speech of insultment ended on his dead bodie.

†**inˈsume,** *v. Obs.* [f. IN-² + L. *sūmĕre* to take; cf. *assume, consume.* (*Insūmĕre* was used in L., but not in this sense, its nearest use being 'to take to oneself'.)] *trans.* To take in, absorb.

1675 EVELYN *Terra* (1729) 16 Animals in preparing Chyle, transmute, alter, and insume what is only their proper Aliment. *Ibid.* 25 It facilitates their being insum'd, assimilated, and made apt to pass into Nourishment. **1733** J. TULL *Horse-Hoing Husb.* 6 Roots..do not Insume what is disagreeable, or Poison to them.

So †**inˈsumption,** the action or process of taking in, absorption. *Obs.*

1675 EVELYN *Terra* (1729) 9 Earth..produces no Vegetable..without Water to dissolve and qualify it for Insumption.

†**inˈsunder,** *adv. Obs.* [The phrase *in sunder,* analytical alteration of ASUNDER, ME. *on sundre,* OE. *on sundran,* written as one word. See SUNDER.] = ASUNDER.

1526 *Pilgr. Perf.* (W. de W. 1531) 290 But it sholde brast insonder. **1551** TURNER *Herbal* I. B v, Garlyke..breaketh insundre grosse humores. **1598** HAKLUYT *Voy.* I. 54 Some of these Tabernacles may quickely be taken asunder, and set together againe..Other some cannot be taken insunder.

insunk (ˈɪnsʌŋk), *ppl. a.* [from *sink in*: see IN *adv.* 11 b.] Sunk in.

1877 E. G. SQUIER *Peru* (1878) 212 They are all ascended by insunk stairs.

‖**insuper, in super** (ɪnˈs(j)uːpə(r)), *adv. Obs.* [L., = on the top, from above, over and above, over; f. *in* in + *super* over, above.] Over; ***to stand in super***, to stand over, remain over, be carried forward as a balance or unsettled claim.

1624 *Act 21 Jas. I,* c. 2 That the same haue beene duely in charge to his Maiestie, or the late Queene Elizabeth, or haue stood in Super of Record within the said space of threescore yeares. *Ibid.,* Deemed, construed, or taken to be a putting in charge, standing in Super, or taking, or answering the Farme Rents, Reuenues or Profits, by, or to his Maiestie. *Ibid., marg.,* The King's Title required by this Act to bee within 60 yeares, ought to accrew vpon a verdict or demurrer, and not vpon a bare putting in charge, or standing in Super. **1672** *Cowell's Interpr., In super,* is a Word used by Auditors in their Accounts in the Exchequer, when they say so much remains *in super* to such an Accountant, that is, so much remains due upon such an Account. **1706** in PHILLIPS (ed. Kersey). **1708** in *Termes de la Ley.*

insuperability (ɪnˌsjuːpərəˈbɪlɪtɪ). [f. next: see -ITY.] The quality of being insuperable; incapability of being 'got over' or overcome.

1721 BAILEY, *Insuperability,* Invincibleness. **1822** J. W. CROKER in *C. Papers* 25 Aug. (1884), I do not believe in the insuperability of objections of that class. **1883** *Longm. Mag.* Sept. 525 A further difficulty, amounting to insuperability.

insuperable (ɪnˈsjuːpərəb(ə)l), *a.* (*sb.*) [ad. L. *insuperābilis,* f. *in-* (IN-³) + *superābilis,* f. *superāre* to overcome, surmount. Cf. obs. F. *insuperable* (14th c. in Godef., and still in Cotgr. 1611), which was perh. in part the immediate source.]

†**1.** That cannot be overcome or vanquished; unconquerable, invincible. *Obs.* or merged in 3.

c **1340** HAMPOLE *Perfect Living* viii. Wks. 1895 I. 31 Þi luf es Insuperabel, when na thyng þat es contrary til gods lufe ouercomes it. **1398** TREVISA *Barth. De P.R.* XVI. xvii. (Tollem. MS.), Þis ston makeþ men insuperable, þat þey may not be ouercome [*insuperabiles et invictos*]. **1490** CAXTON *Eneydos* xii. 44 Folke insuperable..and inuyncible in armes. **1603** HOLLAND *Plutarch's Mor.* 637 Three hundred thousand fighting men..all invincible soldiers, and appointed with armes insuperable. **1678** CUDWORTH *Intell. Syst.* I. iv. §26. 444 To be able to effect..all those things..argues an insuperable Power. **1737** WHISTON *Josephus, Antiq.* XI. iii. §3, Wine is the..most insuperable of all things. **1857** H. H. WILSON tr. *Rig-veda* III. 26 Insuperable, foe-surpassing, give food to the institutor of this sacrifice.

2. That cannot be surmounted or passed over.

1660 H. MORE *Myst. Godl.* III. iii. 63 Whether we..admire the height of some insuperable and inaccessible Rock or Mountain. **1667** MILTON *P.L.* IV. 138 Over head up grew Insuperable highth of loftiest shade, Cedar, and Pine, and Firr, and branching Palm. **1777** ROBERTSON *Hist. Amer.* I. I. 24 Such an insuperable barrier was placed between the two temperate regions. **1853** J. H. NEWMAN *Hist. Sk.* (1873) II. I. iv. 202 There is no insuperable gulf between themselves [Christians] and the rest of mankind. **1865** SWINBURNE *Poems & Ball., Anactoria* 307 The insuperable sea.

3. *fig.* (from 1 and 2). Of difficulties, hindrances, etc.: That cannot be 'got over' or overcome; unconquerable, invincible; forming an impassable barrier to action, insurmountable.

1657 *Burton's Diary* (1828) II. 199 Your debts are insuperable upon you. **1711** COTES in Rigaud *Corr. Sci. Men* (1841) I. 262 The want of his sight is certainly an insuperable disadvantage to him in several respects. **1744** BIRCH *Life Boyle* B.'s Wks. 1772 I. p. lxxiii, On account of his insuperable disinclination to entering into holy orders. **1820** W. IRVING *Sketch Bk.* I. 51 An insuperable aversion to all kinds of profitable labour. **1856** SIR B. BRODIE *Psychol. Inq.* I. IV. 129 Having been overcome by a sense of insuperable drowsiness. **1869** FARRAR *Fam. Speech* iv. (1873) 121 The difficulties of this kind are insuperable.

4. That cannot be surpassed, 'beaten', or excelled; unsurpassable.

1849 RUSKIN *Sev. Lamps* vi. §10. 172 The strength..which maintains its sculptured shapeliness for a time insuperable. **1856** —— *Mod. Paint.* III. IV. xii. §16 The perfection of both these passages, as far as regards truth and tenderness of imagination, is quite insuperable. **1878** —— *Notes Turner* 9 His most wonderful work in his own special manner,—in the perfect pieces of it insuperable.

B. as *sb.* An insuperable hindrance. *nonce-use.*

1782 COWPER *Lett.* Wks. 1837 XV. 118 All these are so many insuperables in the way.

Hence **inˈsuperableness** = INSUPERABILITY.

1727 BAILEY vol. II, *Insuperableness,* invincibleness.

insuperably (ɪnˈsjuːpərəblɪ), *adv.* [f. prec. + -LY².] In an insuperable manner, or so as not to be overcome; unconquerably; insurmountably.

1675 BAXTER *Cath. Theol.* II. I. 9 Some say, that he [God] decreed to predetermine men insuperably to the forbidden act. **1681** GREW *Museum* 282 The latter, being so insuperably hard hinders the splitting of it. **1751** JOHNSON *Rambler* No. 180 ¶8 Many who toil through the intricacy of complicated systems are insuperably embarrassed with the least perplexity in common affairs. **1838–9** HALLAM *Hist. Lit.* III. III. v. §32. 252 From its nature it [the poem] is insuperably wearisome. **1880** WATSON *Prince's Quest* (1892) 65 An island of the middle sea In watery barriers bound insuperably.

insupportable (ɪnsəˈpɔətəb(ə)l). [a. F. *insupportable* (14–15th c.), or ad. eccl.L. *insupportābil-is* (Hilary), f. *in-* (IN-³) + *supportāre* to carry, SUPPORT: see SUPPORTABLE.]

1. That cannot be supported, endured, or borne; insufferable; unbearable.

1530 PALSGR. 316/2 Insupportable, nat able to be sustayned, *insupportable.* **1585** T. WASHINGTON tr. *Nicholay's Voy.* IV. xxxvi. 160 b, Constrained to insupportable tributes. **1600** HOLLAND *Livy* XL. xlv. 1088 A suddaine and insupportable storme and tempest. **1661** COWLEY *Ess., Cromwell* (1684) 65 The insupportable Insolence of an ignorant Mountebank. **1791** MRS. RADCLIFFE *Rom. Forest* ix, Her distress became insupportable. **1859** GEO. ELIOT *A. Bede* xvii, I..find them concur in the experience that great men are over-estimated and small men are insupportable.

b. That cannot be supported or sustained by grounds or reasons; unjustifiable, indefensible.

1649 SIR E. NICHOLAS in *N. Papers* (Camden) 144 His destruccion wilbe soe much yᵉ more insupportable and inexcusable. **1663** GERBIER *Counsel* 47 When a Plummer sets pounds of Candles used about his Sauder, that trick prove as insupportable as that of one, who..set in his Bill to have paid a hundred pound for Mustard.

†**2.** That cannot be sustained; irresistible.

1590 SPENSER *F.Q.* I. vii. 11 He gan advaunce With huge force and insupportable mayne. **1693** *Mem. Ct. Teckely* II. 151 Ordinarily the Turks, who are insupportable with good Fortune, have little courage under bad. **1697** POTTER *Antiq. Greece* III. i. (1715) 3 They were the most pugnacious and insupportable of Mankind.

insuˈpportableness. [f. prec. + -NESS.] The quality of being insupportable or unbearable.

a **1586** SIDNEY *Arcadia* II. (1622) 99 Then fell she to so pitifull a declaration of the insupportablenesse of her desires, that [etc.]. **1670** G. H. *Hist. Cardinals* I. II. 50 The Prelates are not permitted to complain of their grievances, of the insupportableness of their [the Pope's nephews] Pensions. **1689** *Col. Rec. Pennsylv.* I. 313 My Severall Letters of Complaint of yᵉ Insupportableness of it are Witnesses. **1889** *Cape Law Jrnl.* 191 [see INSUFFERABLENESS].

insuˈpportably, *adv.* [f. as prec. + -LY².] In an insupportable degree or manner; insufferably; †irresistibly.

1671 MILTON *Samson* 137 Safest he who stood aloof, When insupportably his foot advanc't. **1679** *Hist. Jetzer* 1 A Person very learned..but withall of a haughty spirit, and insupportably proud. **1781** COWPER *Lett.* Wks. 1837 XV. 82 People imagine they should be happy in circumstances which they would find insupportably burthensome in less than a week. **1864** tr. *Vambery's Trav. Centr. Asia* 182 The weather was insupportably hot.

insupposable (ɪnsəˈpəʊzəb(ə)l), *a.* [IN-³.] That cannot be supposed.

1668 HOWE *Bless. Righteous* (1825) 194 It was an insupposable thing they should be ignorant. *a* **1848** R. W. HAMILTON *Rew. & Punishm.* vii. (1853) 325 An infinite act against a finite nature is insupposeable. **1899** *Expositor* Nov. 425 A moments consideration of 2 Corinthians should suffice to show how utterly insupposable this is.

insuppressible (ɪnsəˈprɛsɪb(ə)l), *a.* [IN-³.] That cannot be suppressed; incapable of suppression; irrepressible.

1610 HEALEY *St. Aug. Citie of God* 787 The will is such a foe to the passion, and the passion to the will, that they are for ever in-suppressible. **1748** SMOLLETT *Rod. Rand.* lx. (1804) 432 Seized with insuppressible sorrow at the prospect of my misery he burst into tears. **1755** YOUNG *Centaur* iii. Wks. 1757 IV. 178 He shall find, that truth..however..injured, wounded, suppressed, is insuppressible, victorious, immortal. **1880** SWINBURNE *Stud. Shaks.* ii. (ed. 2) 155 The beloved disciple of that insuppressible divine, the immortal and most reverend vicar of Meudon.

Hence **insuˈppressibly** *adv.,* in a manner not to be suppressed (Webster, 1856).

insuppressive (ɪnsəˈprɛsɪv), *a. rare.* [IN-³.] Insuppressible.

1601 SHAKS. *Jul. C.* II. i. 134 But do not staine The euen vertue of our Enterprize, Nor th' insuppressiue Mettle of our Spirits. **1742** YOUNG *Nt. Th.* VII. 390. **1778** HAN. MORE *Florio* I. 178 Though Florio tried a thousand ways, Truth's insuppressive torch would blaze. **1844** BROWNING *Colombe's Birthday* II, The best Of her good pageant seemed its standers-by With insuppressive joy on every face!

insurable (ɪnˈʃʊərəb(ə)l), *a.* [f. INSURE *v.* + -ABLE.] Capable of being, or proper to be, insured (in sense 5 of the verb); sufficient to form a ground for insurance (esp. in phr. ***insurable interest***).

1810 BENTHAM *Packing* (1821) 51 Situation not being insurable, either at the Equitable or the Amicable. **1813** *Chron.* in *Ann. Reg.* 302 At..the period of the insurance..he was not in insurable health. **1848** ARNOULD *Mar. Insur.* (1866) I. I. iii. 49 The parties..are presumed to have an insurable interest in the property specified. **1884** *Pall Mall G.* 15 Jan. 1/2 Freight will no longer be insurable, or, if insurable, allowance will be made in the amount recovered for the expenses which the owner would have incurred, but did not in point of fact incur, in earning the freight.

Hence **insuraˈbility,** the quality of being insurable.

1884 *Law Times Rep.* LI. 244/2 Written opinions..as to the insurability or uninsurability of the life of..Harvey.

insurance (ɪnˈʃʊərəns). [Variant of ENSURANCE, with change of prefix as in INSURE.]

†**1.** The action or a means, of ensuring or making certain: = ENSURANCE 1. *Obs.*

1660 WILLSFORD *Scales Comm.* Ded. A iij, The acceptance of my former Labours hath given me faire hopes of an Insurance for these. **1678** N. HOMES in Spurgeon *Treas. Dav.* cxliv. 15 To have God to be our Jehovah is the insurance of happiness to us. *a* **1788** MICKLE *Inq. Bramin Philos.* (R.), An offering grateful to their gods, as the most acceptable insurance of the divine protection.

†**2.** = ASSURANCE 3. *Obs. rare.*

1706 FARQUHAR *Recruit. Officer* II. i, *Silv.* Shall I venture to believe public report? *Plume.* You may, when 'tis backed by private insurance.

†**3.** Betrothal, affiance, troth-plighting, engagement to marry: = ENSURANCE 2. *Obs.*

a **1553** UDALL *Royster D.* IV. vi. (Arb.) 70 Dyd not I knowe afore of the insurance Betweene Gawyn Goodlucke, and Christian Custance?

4. *Comm.* **a.** The act or system of insuring property, life, etc.; a contract by which the one party (usually a company or corporation) undertakes, in consideration of a payment (called a *premium*) proportioned to the nature of the risk contemplated, to secure the other against pecuniary loss, by payment of a sum of money in the event of destruction of or damage to property (as by disaster at sea, fire, or other accident), or of the death or disablement of a person; the department of business which deals

with such contracts. Also called ASSURANCE (and in 17th c. sometimes ENSURANCE).

Assurance is the earlier term, used alike of marine and life insurance before the end of 16th c. Its general application is retained in the titles and policies of some long-established companies (e.g. the London Assurance Corporation). *Insurance* (in 17th c. also ENSURANCE) occurs first in reference to fire (1635 in INSURE *v.* 4), but soon became coextensive with *assurance*, the two terms being synonymous in Magens 1755 (see ASSURANCE 5). *Assurance* would probably have dropped out of use (as it has almost done in U.S), but that Babbage in 1826 (see quot.) proposed to restrict *insurance* to risks to property, and *assurance* to life insurance. This has been followed so far that *assurance* is now rarely used of marine, fire, or accident insurance, and is retained in Great Britain in the nomenclature and use of the majority of life insurance companies. But in general popular use, *insurance* is the prevalent term. Mr. T. B. Sprague, followed by others, considers *assurance, assure, assurer*, etc., the proper words for the action of the company or persons undertaking the risk, *insurance, insure, insurer*, etc., for that of the person paying the premium. This would be in some respects a useful distinction, if it could be carried out; but it would leave the members of mutual societies at once *assurers* and *insurers*.

1651 [see sense 5]. **1663** PEPYS *Diary* 1 Dec., Money was taken up upon bottomary and insurance, and the ship left by the master and seamen upon rocks where..she must perish. **1665** MANLEY *Grotius' Low C. Warres* 80 The Covenant of preventing Danger (commonly called Insurance) frequent among Merchants, added a Shadow of Law; whereby the incertainty of the Event is usually transferred to another, with some certain Reward. **1693** E. HALLEY in *Phil. Trans.* XVII. 602 By what has been said, the Price of Insurance upon Lives ought to be regulated. **1711** *Act 10 Anne* c. 26 (*title*) An Act for laying additional Duties on Hides and Skins..Gilt and Silver Wire, and Policies of Insurance. *Ibid.* §68 Any writing commonly called a Policy of Assurance or Insurance. **1755** MAGENS (*title*) Essay on Insurances. *Ibid.* I. 12 On June the 1st he sent aboard Ten Bales marked M, No. 1 to 10, which cost One Thousand Pounds; and on that Day he had Insurance done to that Value under the general expression of Merchandize. **1786** JEFFERSON *Writ.* (1859) II. 26 Making further inquiry as to the premium of insurance at L'Orient for vessels bound to or from America. **1817** W. SELWYN *Law Nisi Prius* (ed. 4) II. 869 A policy of insurance is the instrument in which the terms of this agreement are set forth. **1826** BABBAGE *Assur. of Lives* Pref. *note*, The terms *insurance* and *assurance* have been used indiscriminately for contracts relative to life, fire, and shipping; as custom has rather more frequently employed the latter term for those relative to life, I have in this volume entirely restricted the word *assurance* to that sense. If this distinction be admitted *assurance* will signify a contract dependent on the duration of life, which must either happen or fail; and *insurance* will mean a contract relating to any other uncertain event which may partly happen or partly fail. **1848** ARNOULD *Mar. Insur.* (1866) I. I. i. 3 Marine Insurance..in its essential nature is a contract of indemnity. **1853** A. FARR in *Reg. General's 12th Rept.* Appendix p. xvii, The phrase 'Life Insurance' is in every respect preferable to 'Life Assurance'. **1872** *Wharton's Law Lex.* s.v., The practice of marine insurance is older than insurance against fire and upon lives. While all fire and life insurances are made at the risk of companies..a large proportion of marine insurances is made at the risk of individuals called under-writers. **1893** RELTON *Fire Insur. Companies* 6 It having been decided that the Court [created by 43 Eliz. c. 12] had no jurisdiction in the case of Life Insurances, it is evident that it could not have had any in the case of Fire Insurances, which..did not exist in Great Britain when the Act was passed.

b. The sum paid for insuring; the premium.

1666 *Lond. Gaz.* No. 100/3 The Insurance upon our Convoy to the Levant is very high. **1806** HUTTON *Course Math.* I. 127 To find the insurance on 107*l*, for 117 days, at 4¾ per cent. per annum. **1833** HT. MARTINEAU *Loom & Lugger* I. i. 12 Upon the payment of an insurance of ten per cent. *Mod.* His Insurance falls due this month.

c. The sum to be recovered in case of the occurrence of the contingency; the amount for which property or life is insured.

1838 DE MORGAN *Ess. Probab.* 227 The present value of such an insurance as the preceding.

†**d.** Short for *insurance-office*. *Obs. rare.*

1722 DE FOE *Col. Jack* (1840) 54 One Stewart..kept a wager-office and insurance.

e. The act or system of insuring employed persons against sickness or unemployment, esp. in accordance with the National Insurance Acts of 1911, 1920, 1946, and 1965, which require certain wage-earners to make weekly payments supplemented by their employers, in return for which they are entitled to State assistance in sickness, unemployment, etc.

1878, etc. [see *National Insurance* s.v. NATIONAL *a.* 5]. **1911** *Times* 28 Mar. 10/3 The preparation of the Sickness and Invalidity Insurance Bill. *Ibid.* 5 May 14/3 If he had divided his bill into two—one dealing with unemployment and one with invalidity insurance. *Ibid.* 14/5 The burden imposed by State insurance must necessarily fall on manufacturers. **1911** *Act 1 & 2 Geo. V.* c. 55. 337 National Health Insurance. **1912** [see sense 5]. **1920** *Act 10 & 11 Geo. V.* c. 30 §48 (1) This act may be cited as the Unemployment Insurance Act, 1920.

5. *attrib.* and *Comb.* (in sense 4 a), as ***insurance adjuster, agency, agent, broker, commissioner, company, man, office, officer, policy, premium, rate***; (sense 4 e) ***insurance act, benefit, card, committee, stamp***.

1651 CULPEPPER *Astrol. Judgem. Dis.* (1658) 176 When the matter..remains still within the lungs..there's but little security of life: and I am confident never a one of the Colledge keeps an insurance office for such a businesse, nor will ensure thereupon at 50 per cent. **1680** (*title*) (Br. Mus. 816 m. 10./67) An advertisement from the Insurance Office for houses at the Backside of the Royal Exchange. **1755** Insurance premium [see ASSURANCE 5]. *a* **1776** R. JAMES *Diss. Fevers* (1778) 24 An insurance broker, in Castle Alley, near the Royal Exchange. **1781** COWPER *Friendship* 106 Like Hand-in-Hand insurance plates, Most unavoidably creates The thought of conflagration. **1784** in H. M. Brooks *Days of Spinning-Wheel in New Eng.* (1886) 62 The Gentlemen forming this Insurance Company, whose names are inserted in each Policy. **1841-4** EMERSON *Ess.*, *Self-Reliance* Wks. (Bohn) I. 36 The insurance-office increases the number of accidents. **1866** C. N. EMERSON *Internal Revenue Guide* 73 Insurance agents shall pay ten dollars. **1869** 'MARK TWAIN' *Innoc. Abr.* xxxviii. 409 If her [*sc.* Smyrna's] 'crown of life' had been an insurance policy, she would have had an opportunity to collect on it. **1874** B. F. TAYLOR *World on Wheels*, etc. II. ii. 199 He was an insurance agent—a retired doctor, who growing weary of saving lives with pills, had taken to insuring lives with policies. **1879** *Harper's Mag.* July 215 The insurance men..would insure the lives of the hands who were at work there. **1881** *Instructions to Census Clerks* (1885) 83 Insurance Company's officer, manager, actuary, secretary,..clerk. **1883** 'MARK TWAIN' *Life on Mississippi* xliii. 436 Insurance-agency business, you know; mighty irregular. **1889** *Cent. Dict.*, *Insurance commissioner*, in some of the United States, a State officer who in behalf of the public maintains a supervision over the affairs of insurance companies. **1896** *Allbutt's Syst. Med.* I. 484 The rapid, nervous, palpitating 'insurance heart', so constantly observed among candidates for life assurance. **1899** *Westm. Gaz.* 11 Apr. 2/2 To determine whether we cannot agree together to reduce our respective insurance-rates. **1911** *Act 1 & 2 Geo. V.* c. 55 §15 The regulations made by the Insurance Commissioners. *Ibid.*, The Insurance Committee for each county or county borough. *Ibid.* §115 This Act may be cited as the National Insurance Act, 1911. **1912** *Chemist & Druggist* LXXX. 950/2 Cards and stamps for health insurance under the National Insurance Act are now procurable at post offices. **1912** *Punch* 31 July 99/3 Mr. Masterman has laid it down that it is the wife's duty, and not that of the husband, to lick the servants' insurance stamps. **1913** *Ibid.* 15 Jan. 49/1 As the 15th of January approaches, bringing fulfilment of 9d. for 4d. through operation of Insurance Act. *Ibid.* 13 Aug. 148/3 Somebody come to see about an insurance card or something. **1915** W. OWEN *Let.* 22 June (1967) 189 Am feeling quite independent of Insurance Policies just now. **1923** D. H. LAWRENCE *Birds, Beasts, & Flowers* 86 Ah Phoenix, Phoenix, John's Eagle! You are only known to us now as the badge of an insurance Company. **1926** FOWLER *Mod. Eng. Usage* 741/1 The injustice of throwing on the landlord in whose house they happen to be resident the cost of a large additional insurance benefit for those who are sick. **1929** J. B. PRIESTLEY *Good Companions* I. i. 32 He..threw an insurance card and some money on the table. **1930** *Morning Post* 7 Aug. 11 The employers at four factories agreed to take upon themselves the charge of the insurance stamp which the men refuse to pay. **1933** Insurance agent [see CONFIDENCE *sb.* 10]. **1933** *Radio Times* 14 Apr. 98/1 Meltonian Cream..is..an insurance policy for shoes. **1934** Insurance adjuster [see ADJUSTER]. **1945** N. L. MCCLUNG *Stream runs Fast* xii. 99 But one day, an insurance man, hearing that Wes had sold his drug store came out to offer him an agency, and Wes became an agent for the Manufacturers' Life Insurance Company. **1958** *Listener* 23 Oct. 634/2 The insurance officer denied that this was an industrial accident. **1961** *Ibid.* 10 Aug. 219/2 An insurance adjuster who also acts as a private detective. **1972** J. GORES *Dead Skip* (1973) xiv. 101 Harvey E. Wyman was red-faced and jovial... He was also, unlike so many small insurance agents Ballard had met, very smart. **1973** W. MCCARTHY *Detail* i. 56 You should check the people you choose more carefully... They must also have special diets. Just an insurance policy.

†**in'surancer.** *Obs.* See also ENSURANCER. [f. prec. + -ER[1].] One who gives 'insurance' or assurance; one who insures or makes sure.

1685 DRYDEN *Thren. August.* 186 The vain Insurancers of life [physicians]. **1742** BLAIR *Grave* 188 The far-famed sculptor, and the laurell'd bard, Those bold insurancers of deathless fame, Supply their little feeble aids in vain.

insurant (ɪnˈʃʊərənt). [f. INSURE *v.* + -ANT[1].] One who effects or obtains an insurance (whether on his own life or that of another); the person to whom an insurance policy is issued.

1853 W. FARR in *Reg. General's 12th Rep.* App. p. xvii, The Insuree performs two functions; which are separated when a third party (Insurant) procures the policy and pays the premium. Under one aspect the same person is the *Insuree*, under another he is the *Insurant*. **1883-6** *Post Off. Insurance Regulations*, All amounts due in respect of Insurances or Annuities will be credited to the Insurants' or Annuitants' Savings Bank accounts. **1894** *Westm. Gaz.* 10 Mar. 2/3 By the 'Natural Premium System' the premium payable increases with the age of the insurant.

†**in'surde,** *v. Obs. rare.* [ad. OF. *ensourd-re* to arise, spring up, partly assimilated to the L. prototype *insurgĕre*: see INSURGE *v.*] *intr.* To arise, spring up; = INSURGE 1.

1521 WOLSEY *Let. to Hen. VIII* in *St. Papers* I. 86 Suche ambiguities as mought insurde of and upon the said article.

insure (ɪnˈʃʊə(r)), *v.* [Variant of ENSURE (with substitution of IN-[2] for EN-[1]), orig. used in all the senses of that word; now established in sense 4 (cf. ENSURE 7), and fairly common in senses 5 and 6.]

†**1.** *trans.* To make (a person) sure (*of* a thing); to give security to (a person) for the fulfilment of something: cf. ASSURE *v.* 9, ENSURE *v.* 1, 2. *Obs.*

c **1440** *Promp. Parv.* 262/2 Insuryn, or make suere, *assecuro*. **1681-6** J. SCOTT *Chr. Life* (1747) III. 21 Thus Christ..hath taken the most effectual Care to insure the mutual Performance of this everlasting Covenant to both Parties..to insure God of our performing our Part..and to insure us of God's performing his Part.

†**2.** To pledge one's credit to (a person), or to the truth of (a statement); to tell (a person) confidently (that something is so); to guarantee: = ASSURE *v.* 10, ENSURE *v.* 3, 4. *Obs.*

c **1460** *Towneley Myst.* xxi. 36 His self shalle not excuse hym; To you I insure it. **1509** BARCLAY *Shyp of Folys* (1874) II. 329 The glas shall shewe the the same I the insure. **1533** FRITH *Answ. More* Wks. (1573) 115/2, I insure you, I neither will nor can cease to speake. *c* **1560** T. PRESTON *Cambyses* in Hazl. *Dodsley* IV. 220, I insure you he is a king most vile and pernicious.

†**3.** To engage by a pledge or contract, esp. for or by marriage; to betroth, espouse: = ASSURE *v.* 4, ENSURE *v.* 5. *Obs. rare.*

1530 PALSGR. 592/1, I insuer a man or woman by maryage.

4. *Comm.* To secure the payment of a sum of money in the event of loss of or damage to property (esp. by casualty at sea, or by fire, or other accident), or of the death or disablement of a person, in consideration of the payment of a premium and observance of certain conditions; to effect an insurance upon. Said either of the person who pays the premium, or of the office or underwriters who undertake the risk. For the latter many offices and writers prefer *assure* (now esp. in reference to life insurance). The object of the vb. is either **a.** the amount secured, or **b.** the property or life, sometimes the person: see quots.

In 17th c. also ENSURE (sense 7). For usage as to *insure* and *assure* see further under INSURANCE 4.

a. **1635** *Draft of Petition to King* (P.R.O.) (Walford *Encycl. Insur.* III. 439), Authorising your petitioner to ensure all your majesty's subjects whatsoever for soe much of their estates combustible as they themselves shall conceive in danger of Fire, not taking above 12*d.* per centum yearly for soe much soe insured. **1663** PEPYS *Diary* 30 Nov., As much more insured upon his ship and goods as they were worth. **1688** *Lond. Gaz.* No. 2322/4 Where all Persons may Insure an Hundred Pound on a Brick House, for Six Shillings for one Year. **1838** DE MORGAN *Ess. Probab.* 214, 2*l.* 13*s.* 6*d.* is the premium for insuring 100*l.* at the end of the year in which a life of 30 fails. **1857** *Chambers' Inform.* II. 557/1 An individual..incurring a risk in behalf of another, or having a large claim upon him in the form of debt, can insure upon the life of that person such a sum as would be sure to cover all loss in the event of..death.

b. **1635** [see a]. **1665** PEPYS *Diary* 18 May, Was before the King..discoursing about insuring some of the King's goods. **1680** *Lond. Gaz.* No. 1514/4 Samuel Vincent Esq.; and Doctor Nicolas Barbon, and others, have lately made Propositions in Print for Insuring Houses from Fire. **1682** *Ibid.* No. 1683/4 The City of London are about to Insure Brick-houses at 48*s.* and 7*d.* per Cent. **1711** ADDISON *Spect.* No. 5 ¶3, I hope that he has been wise enough to insure his House. **1753** SMOLLETT *Ct. Fathom* (1784) 126/2 He had granted his bond, and been at the expence of insuring his life for the money. **1817** W. SELWYN *Law Nisi Prius* (ed. 4) II. 878 Goods were insured on board a vessel on a voyage from Liverpool to Palermo. **1870** T. R. SPRAGUE in *Jrnl. Inst. Actuaries* XVI. 77 The more correct distinction I believe to be that a man *insures* the life of himself or of some other person, or his house, or his ship [etc.], and that the Office *assures* to him in each of these cases a sum of money payable in certain contingencies. Hence the Office is called the *assurer* or *assurers*, and the man the *assured*; while we may speak either of the life *assured* or the life *insured*, also of the sum *assured* or the sum *insured*, according as we take the point of view of the Office or of the individual. **1883** *Chambers' Encycl.* V. 603/1 In order to insure a life, the insurer must either himself be 'the life', or must have a pecuniary interest in the life.

c. *absol.* or *intr.* To undertake insurance risks; to effect an insurance.

1651 [see INSURANCE 5]. **1680** *Argts. for insuring Houses from Fire* (Walford *Encycl. Insur.* III. 446), Neither would a man..be disquieted with the too late advice of his friends, every one blaming, and asking *why did he not insure?* Or be tormented by his own thoughts with the *wish I had insured*. **1693** LEYBOURN *Panarithmologia* (Walford I. 487), Suppose you ship £300 of goods for Jamaica..you go to the Assu. Office behind the Royal Exchange in Lond., and there acquaint the clerk you will insure for £200 or £250, or, if you will, the whole £300..upon such ship for so much goods as you have on board. **1828** WEBSTER s.v., This company insures at 3 per cent, or at a low premium. **1858** LD. ST. LEONARDS *Handy-Bk. Prop. Law* v. 29 The tenant's neglect to insure, or his insuring in an office..not authorised by his lease.

d. (Cf. INSURANCE 4 e.)

1911 *Act 1 & 2 Geo. V* c. 55 §1 All persons so insured (in this Act called 'insured persons').

5. *trans.* To make certain, to secure, to guarantee (some thing, event, etc.): = ASSURE *v.* 5, 7 a, ENSURE *v.* 8, 9.

1681-6 [see sense 1]. **1809** W. IRVING *Knickerb.* VII. xiii. (1849) 450 Such supineness insures the very evil from which it shrinks. **1821** MRS. SHERWOOD *Hist. Geo. Desmond* 19 He had insured for me the situation of a writer on the Bengal establishment. **1849** RUSKIN *Sev. Lamps* vi. §8. 170 Want of care in the points which insure the building's endurance. *a* **1862** BUCKLE *Civiliz.* viii. (1873) 462 An ardour which could hardly fail to insure success.

6. To make safe, to secure, to guarantee (*against, from*): = ASSURE *v.* 1 c, ENSURE *v.* 6.

1724 SWIFT *Drapier's Lett.* Wks. 1755 V. II. 122, I cannot say, I would insure it from the hands of the common hangman. **1825** JEFFERSON *Autobiog.* Wks. 1859 I. 107 A recurrence to these letters now insures me against errors of memory. *a* **1864** J. D. BURNS *Mem. & Rem.* (1879) 361 The evidence of trials past does not insure them against trials that may come.

Hence **in'suring** *vbl. sb.* (usually in sense 4).

1646 W. BRIDGE *Saints Hiding-pl.* (1647) 17 But there is an Insuring-Office set up in the Gospel, as to the venture of our eternities. **1681** *Lond. Gaz.* No. 1668/4 The City of London have published their Intentions to Insure Houses from Fire, which may delay some Persons from Insuring. **1703** T. N. *City & C. Purchaser* 83 The Friendly Society of London, for Insuring of Houses. **1815** *Zeluca* III. 59 She had done with the insuring system.

insured (ɪnˈʃʊəd), *ppl. a.* [f. INSURE *v.* + -ED¹.] Assured, guaranteed, etc.: see the verb. Usually *absol.* (in sense 4 of the verb): The person (or persons) to whom an insurance upon property is to be paid on the occurrence of loss or damage, or upon whose death or disablement a (life or accident) insurance becomes due; = ASSURED B.

1681 *Lond. Gaz.* No. 1668/4 A Paper..which shews that the Insured cannot have greater advantage from the City. **1755** MAGENS *Insurances* I. 7 With this particular Obligation..that the Insured shall neglect or omit nothing that may be for the Interest of the Insurer, whose Right is properly to be set forth and defended. **1842** *Sir J. A. Park's Mar. Insur.* (ed. 8) II. xxiv. 987 No insurance shall take place till the premium be actually paid by the insured, his heir, or their agent or agents. **1870** [see INSURE *v.* 4b]. **1883** *Wharton's Law Lex.* s.v. *Insurance*, Undertaking to pay specified sums upon the death of the insured.

insuree (ɪnʃʊəˈriː). [f. INSURE *v.* + -EE: cf. *insurer*.] A person whose life (or property) is insured. (Correlative to INSURER 2; identical with INSURER 3, but from a different point of view.)

1853 W. FARR in *Reg. General's 12th Rep.* App. p. xvii, Two parties are concerned, the person who grants (Insurer) and the person whose life is in the policy (Insuree). *Ibid.* p. xxi, In Mutual Societies the insurees are partners. **1857** *Chambers' Inform.* II. 557/2.

insurer (ɪnˈʃʊərə(r)). [f. INSURE + -ER¹. See also ENSURER.] One who or that which insures.

1. One who or that which makes sure or certain, guarantees, etc.: see the verb. Now *rare* in *gen.* sense, exc. as transferred from 2.

1654 W. MOUNTAGUE *Devout Ess.* II. xi. §3. 231 This befals them, when beautie..proves an insurer of the lastingness of this life. **1687** DRYDEN *Hind & P.* I. 148 Faith is the best insurer of thy bliss. **1754** HAY *Ess. Deformity* 25 O Temperance!.. Thou Prolonger of Life! Thou Insurer of Pleasure! Thou Promoter of Business! **1880** PREBLE *Hist. of Flag* 164 The mysterious Scandinavian standard..the supposed insurer of victory..was on board his [Sweyn's] ship. **1894** *Forum* (N.Y.) 659 A democratic form of government is no better than an aristocratic or a monarchical form as an insurer against our human nature.

2. *Comm.* One who contracts, in consideration of the payment of a premium, to indemnify a person against pecuniary loss in the event of destruction of or damage to property, or against a particular event (see INSURE *v.* 4); an underwriter. Also called *Assurer* (*Assuror*), which is preferred by many in connexion with life insurance.

1654–1660 [see ENSURER]. **1663** PEPYS *Diary* 1 Dec., His ship..is brought by one sent for on purpose by the insurers, into the Thames, with her cargo. **1680** *Lond. Gaz.* No. 1517/4 The said Insurers have agreed, That such persons as shall subscribe..shall have the like benefit of a years purchase. **1692** LUTTRELL *Brief Rel.* (1857) II. 635 That instead of the common insurers on the Exchange, who take from £10 to £40 per cent., that his majestie be the insurer him-selfe at £5 per cent. **1755** MAGENS *Insurances* I. 7 The Intent and Meaning of those who pay a valuable Consideration for Insurance, is, that the Insurers shall stand in their Place and Stead. **1817** W. SELWYN *Law Nisi Prius* (ed. 4) II. 941 But if a ship..does all in her power to rejoin the convoy, this will be considered as a sufficient compliance with the warranty, so as to render the insurers liable. **1842** *Sir J. A. Park's Mar. Insur.* (ed. 8) I. i. 33 The insurers were held liable for an accident which happened to the goods on board the lighters. **1899** H. W. MANLEY in *Insurance Rec.* 1 Dec. 563 According to the principles of the construction of the English language, the insurer is the one who insures, that is, in life and fire insurance, the company.

3. One who insures (his own or another's) life, or who pays for the insurance of his property from loss at sea, fire, etc.

In order to distinguish this from the prec. sense, insurance offices, etc., usually employ the term *assured* or *insured*; *insuree, insurant* have also been substituted, or 2 and 3 distinguished as *assurer* (*-or*) and *insurer*: see note to INSURANCE 4.

1753 *Scots Mag.* Apr. 164/2 Every..insurer shall be entitled to have the premium which was paid.., imputed for insuring any other house. **1766** ENTICK *London* IV. 262 Every insurer signs a deed of settlement, by which he is not only insured, but insures all that have signed that deed, from losses in their houses by fire. **1812** H. & J. SMITH *Rej. Addr.*, *Tale Drury L.*, The Hand-in-Hand the race begun, Then came the Phœnix and the Sun, Th' Exchange, where old insurers run, The Eagle, where the new. **1857** *Chambers' Inform.* II. 559/2 The great bulk of insurers are between 27 and 40, the time about which men in this country begin to feel the responsibilities of a family. **1879** *Cassell's Techn. Educ.* I. 187 Lloyd's was originally a coffee-house at which insurers and underwriters met.

insurge (ɪnˈsɜːdʒ), *v.* Now *rare.* Also 6 ensourge. [ad. L. *insurgĕre* to rise upon or to, f. *in-* (IN-²) + *surgĕre* to rise. In form and sense partly through Fr.: cf. (in sense 1) OF. *s'insurgir* (1414 in Godef.), and (in sense 3) mod.F. *s'insurger* (16th c. in Godef. *Compl.*).]

†**1.** *intr.* To arise, spring up. (= OF. *ensourdre, s'insurgir*). *Obs.*

1523 WOLSEY *Let. to Hen. VIII* in *St. Papers* I. 117 The manyfolde difficulties which have insurged. **1527** *Ibid.* I. 240 If in the communicacion or debating therof..ther shulde insurge any doubte or difficulte..she wolde so interpone her auctorite. **1532** HEN. VIII *Proclam. abolishing power of Pope* (ed. 2, 1535, in Soc. Antiq., *Procl.* I. 78), We ..perceyuyng rightwel what great reste, quietnes, and tranquilite of consciens & manyfold other commodities might insurge & arise vnto them. **1548** HALL *Chron., Edw. IV* 223 That there should insurge hereafter, no newe commocion within the realme again. **1576** NEWTON *Lemnie's Complex.* (1633) 192 And not this discommodity alone, but certaine other sickly and foule affections insurge thereupon.

†**2.** *intr.* Of the sea: To surge or rush in *upon*.

1534 *Act 26 Hen. VIII*, c. 9 The flud and rage of the sea ..insurgyng vppon suche decayed tenementes in times of tempest.

†**3.** *intr.* To rise in opposition or insurrection *against*; to make insurrection, revolt. *Obs.*

1532 MORE *Confut. Tindale* Wks. 724/1 All the heretikes that rebelle againste it, nor all the tyrauntes vppon earth that ensourge & oppugne it [the Church]. *c* **1540** tr. *Pol. Verg. Eng. Hist.* (Camden) I. 183 Cuthredus..beinge endamaged with manie injuries by the Mercians..insurged mannefullie againste them. **1548** UDALL *Erasm. Par. Luke* Pref. 3b, Antichriste followyng the steppes of his father Lucifer.. also hath ensourged against heauen. **1577–87** HOLINSHED *Chron.* I. 42/1 The chiefe cause of the Britains insurging against the Romans. *c* **1610** J. MELVILLE in Morison *A. Melville* vii. (1898) 84 He, insurging with graitter bauldnes & force of langage buir out the mater.

4. *trans.* To stir up; to raise in tumult, hostility, or insurrection. *Obs* exc. as *nonce-wd.*

1796 *Monthly Rev.* XX. 568 You insurge the people. **1883** *Encycl. Brit.* XVI. 498/2 He [Miranda] saw a good deal of Pitt, who had determined to make use of him to 'insurge' the Spanish colonies.

Hence **in'surged** *ppl. a.*

1548 HALL *Chron., Hen. VIII* 230b, The Kynges highnes was credebly certefied of this new insurged insurrection.

†**in'surge**, *sb. Obs. rare*⁻¹. [f. INSURGE *v.*] A heaving or rising; an upheaval.

c **1555** HARPSFIELD *Divorce Hen. VIII* (Camden) 177 She was tossed and tumbled by the rageous insurges of the seas, of the wind and water.

insurgence (ɪnˈsɜːdʒəns). [f. as next: see -ENCE; cf. mod.F. *insurgence* (Littré).] The action of rising against authority; a rising, revolt.

1847 LEWES *Hist. Philos.* (1867) II. 88 Certain to give way before the necessary insurgence of Reason insisting on freedom. **1863** GEO. ELIOT *Romola* lxxi, There was a moral insurgence in the minds of grave men against the Court of Rome. **1868** —— *Sp. Gipsy* 291 His many-voiced self.. Whose hungry needs..Made loud insurgence.

insurgency (ɪnˈsɜːdʒənsɪ). [f. next: see -ENCY.] The quality or state of being insurgent; the tendency to rise in revolt; = prec.

1803 *Edwin* III. 174 The internal insurgency he feared not putting a speedy termination to by the vigour of his proceedings. **1822** *Examiner* 273/2 The consequence.. would be riot, insurgency, and rapine. **1833** *Blackw. Mag.* XXXIII. 731 The Insurgency was not put down. **1856** GRINDON *Life* xvi. (1875) 204 Good books alleviate care, repress the insurgency of evil passions. **1879** G. MEREDITH *Egoist* III. ix. 173 The circumstance of its prevailing successfulness..heaped stores of insurgency in the Celtic bosom.

insurgent (ɪnˈsɜːdʒənt), *a.* and *sb.* [ad. L. *insurgent-em*, pr. pple of *insurgĕre* to rise up: see INSURGE *v.* and -ENT. Cf. obs. F. *insurgent* sb. (now *insurgé*).]

A. *adj.* **1.** Rising in active revolt. Also *fig.*

1814 SCOTT *Wav.* xxxviii, A broad white ensign.. announced that the garrison was held by the insurgent adherents of the House of Stewart. **1845** LD. CAMPBELL *Chancellors* (1857) I. vi. 112 The insurgent barons dictated whatever clauses they deemed desirable. **1847** LEWES *Hist. Philos.* (1867) II. 13 The insurgent mind of Abelard took up the same position. **1849** C. BRONTE *Shirley* xi, Its electric passage left her veins kindled, her soul insurgent.

2. Of the sea or a flood: Surging up or rushing in.

1849 M. ARNOLD *Mycerinus* 40 Some force..Bears earth, and heaven, and men, and gods along Like the broad volume of the insurgent Nile. **1893** NORMAN GALE *Country Muse*, *Requiescam*, The loss..Of no more hearing rebel waves Insurgent on the shore.

B. *sb.* One who rises in revolt against constituted authority; a rebel who is not recognized as a belligerent.

1765 FALCONER *Demagogue* 377 His sanction will dismay, And bid th' insurgents tremble and obey. **1801** WELLINGTON *Mem. Seringapatam* in Gurw. *Desp.* (1837) I. 348 In regard to the insurgents in Malabar, the war against them cannot be carried on at all without assistance. **1812** G. CHALMERS *Dom. Econ. Gt. Brit.* 164 [Why] it was, that the vast strength of Britain did not beat down the colonial insurgents, not in one campaign, but in three. **1851** GALLENGA *Italy* 133 He acceded to all the immediate demands of the insurgents.

insur'gescence. *rare.* [f. L. type **insurgesc-ĕre*, inceptive of *insurgĕre* to rise up + -ENCE.] Tendency to rise in insurrection.

1881 SYMONDS *Renaiss. Italy* (1898) IV. v. 244 This insurgescence of all classes..threatened the very fabric of society.

insuring: see under INSURE *v.*

insurmountable (ɪnsəˈmaʊntəb(ə)l), *a.* [IN-³; perh. after F. *insurmontable* (Cotgr. 1611).] That cannot be surmounted, overcome, or passed over.

1696 PHILLIPS (ed. 5), *Insurmountable*, that cannot be overcome by Labour and Industry. *a* **1704** LOCKE (J.), This difficulty is insurmountable, 'till I can make simplicity and variety the same. **1797** MRS. RADCLIFFE *Italian* vi, The angles of the insurmountable walls which fenced the garden from the precipices below. **1848** LYTTON *Harold* VII. iv, The rock is well nigh insurmountable to those who know not the passes. **1849** MACAULAY *Hist. Eng.* vi. II. 150 Perhaps those prejudices might not prove insurmountable. **1876** T. HARDY *Ethelberta* (1890) 292 Between himself and her there was that kind of division which is more insurmountable than enmity.

Hence **insurmounta'bility** (Craig, 1847); **insur'mountableness**, the state or quality of being insurmountable (Bailey vol. II, 1727); **insur'mountably** *adv.*, so as not to be surmounted or overcome; 'invincibly, unconquerably' (J. 1755).

1860 MILL *Repr. Govt.* (1865) 62/2, I do not think that the people of England have deserved to be, without trial, stigmatized as insurmountably prejudiced against anything which can be proved to be good either for themselves or for others.

insur'passable, *a. rare.* [IN-³.] Incapable of being surpassed.

1859 J. C. HOBHOUSE (Ld. Broughton) *Italy* xvii. II. 137 *note*, The effect was instantly discovered to be insurpassable.

insurrect (ɪnsəˈrɛkt), *v. rare.* [f. L. *insurrect-*, ppl. stem of *insurgĕre* to rise up (see INSURGE *v.*); in sense 2, a back-formation from next.]

†**1.** *intr.* To arise. *Obs.*

1658 R. FRANCK *North. Mem.* (1694) 202 From whence there insurrect such pernicious Vapours, as nauseate the Air.

2. To rise in insurrection or revolt.

1821 BYRON *Diary* 9 Jan., They mean to *insurrect* here.. though I don't think them in force or heart sufficient to make much of it. **1887** *Spectator* 1 Oct. 1303 The people are in spirit in insurrection, yet they do not insurrect.

insurrection (ɪnsəˈrɛkʃən). Also 5 -rexyon, 5–6 -rec(c)ion, -yon, 6 -rexsion. [a. F. *insurrection*, ad. rare L. *insurrectiōn-em*, n. of action f. *insurgĕre*: see INSURGE.]

1. The action of rising in arms or open resistance against established authority or governmental restraint; with *pl.*, an instance of this, an armed rising, a revolt; an incipient or limited rebellion.

1459 *Rolls of Parlt.* V. 346/2 He [Jack Cade]..wrote letters to many Citees..to have made a comon insurrection. **1461** *Paston Lett.* No. 401 II. 27 Yll dysposed persones, defame..me..how that I intend to make insurexyones contrari unto the law. **1535** COVERDALE *Ezra* iv. 19 This cite of olde hath made insurreccion agaynst kynges. **1548** HALL *Chron., Rich. III* 38 Other dyd secretely move and sollicite the people to rise and make an insurrecion. **1577–87** HOLINSHED *Chron.* I. 98/2 The remnant of the Britains therefore withdrew..into Cornwall, and into Wales, out of which countries they oftentimes brake out, and made insurrections vpon the Saxons. **1687** A. LOVELL tr. *Thevenot's Trav.* I. 277 The Moors made an Insurrection, and made one Osman their first Dey. **1855** MILMAN *Lat. Chr.* IV. ix. (1864) II. 418 The people broke out in instant insurrection, declared their determination to renounce their allegiance. **1858** BUCKLE *Civiliz.* (1873) II. viii. 593 Insurrections are generally wrong; revolutions are always right.

b. *fig.*

1641 MILTON *Ch. Govt.* I. vi, If God afterward gave, or permitted this insurrection of Episcopacy, it is to be fear'd he did it in his wrath. **1780** BLAIR *Serm.* (ed. 3) II. ii. 35 He [who hath no rule over his spirit] lies open to every insurrection of ill-humour. **1887** LOWELL *Democr.* 15 It is not the insurrections of ignorance that are dangerous, but the revolts of intelligence.

2. The action of rising up; upheaval. *rare.*

1864 RUSKIN *Arrows of Chace* (1880) I. 264 Every winter, the whole glacier surface rises to replace the summer's waste, not with progressive wave..but with silent level insurrection, as of ocean tide, the gray sea-crystal passes by.

insurrectional (ɪnsəˈrɛkʃənəl), *a.* [f. prec. + -AL¹: cf. F. *insurrectionnel* (1798 in *Dict. Acad.*).] Of, pertaining to, or of the nature of insurrection.

1801 LD. CAMPBELL *Let.* Apr. in *Life* (1881) I. 66 Ministers are..exceedingly alarmed at the insurrectional spirit which has shown itself in different parts of the country. **1832** *Examiner* 556/2 To excite at Rheims an insurrectional movement. **1883** *Pall Mall G.* 16 May 1/1 Russia did not interfere even by encouraging insurrectional bands.

Hence **insu'rrectionally** *adv.*, in an insurrectional way, from an insurrectional point of view.

1848 *Tait's Mag.* XV. 525 Paris was laid down on a map insurrectionally. Her strong and weak points were explained. **1880** G. MEREDITH *Tragic Com.* viii. (1881) 141 He was insurrectionally notorious in morals and menacingly in politics.

insurrectionary (ɪnsəˈrɛkʃənərɪ), *a.* (*sb.*) [f. as prec. + -ARY.]

1. Of, pertaining to, or of the nature of insurrection; addicted to insurrection.

1796 BURKE *Regic. Peace* iv. Wks. IX. 44 On their murderous insurrectionary system, their own lives are not sure for an hour. **1837** CARLYLE *Fr. Rev.* III. III. i, This huge Insurrectionary Movement.. has swept away Royalty, Aristocracy, and a King's life. **1891** *Spectator* 13 June, As a ..fact, London is the least insurrectionary of cities.

2. *humorous.* Tending to raise itself.

1864 LOWELL *Fireside Trav.* 28 A sign-board presented at either end an insurrectionary bottle. *Ibid.* 211 His trousers working up.. above his knees, an insurrectionary movement which I also was unable to suppress in my own.

B. *sb.* A person who engages in insurrection.

1893 *Nation* (N.Y.) 9 Feb. 95/3 All Spanish traditions of law and order are so bound up with Catholicism that religious innovators, like the Protestant missionaries, necessarily seem insurrectionaries.

†**insuˈrrectioner.** *Obs. rare.* [See -ER[1].] = prec. B.

a **1734** NORTH *Exam.* (1740) 418 What had the people got if the Parliament.. had colleagued with Venner and other insurrectioners?

insuˈrrectionism. [See -ISM.] The principle of revolt against constituted authority.

1890 G. B. SHAW *Fab. Ess. Socialism* 192 They welcome Socialism, insurrectionism, currency craze. *Ibid.* 193 A piece of unpractical catastrophic insurrectionism.

insurrectionist (ɪnsəˈrɛkʃənɪst). [f. INSURRECTION + -IST.] One who takes part in an insurrection, or who advocates revolt against authority.

1845 WHITTIER *Pr. Wks.* (1889) II. 266 The insurrectionists were speedily crushed into subjection. **1855** MILMAN *Lat. Chr.* VI. 125 Not indeed that such insurrectionists were likely to look with much respect on the exorbitant wealth of the clergy. **1882** *19th Cent.* Oct. 552 A few of the more energetic spirits muster courage to rise up against the system, and these become insurrectionists.

attrib. **1899** *Literary Guide* 1 Nov. 172/2 We cannot altogether bless this perky and insurrectionist attitude.

insurrectionize (ɪnsəˈrɛkʃənaɪz), *v.* [f. as prec. + -IZE.]

1. *trans.* To raise in insurrection.

1822 *Examiner* 195/1 A conspiracy formed to insurrectionize Poland. **1851** SIR F. PALGRAVE *Norm. & Eng.* I. 552 The deposed Count Bernard insurrectionized the country.

2. *intr.* To make insurrection; to rise in insurrection.

1841 GEN. P. THOMPSON *Exerc.* (1842) VI. 44 That ceasing to be a 'slave class' they might insurrectionize no more.

†**insuˈrrectious,** *a. Obs. rare.* [f. INSURRECTION: see -OUS.] Given to insurrection, turbulent, unruly.

1631 J. DONE *Polydoron* 125 None excelleth another but in good and vertuous actions or in suppressing insurrectious passions.

†**insuˈrrective,** *a. Obs. rare.* [f. L. *insurrect-*, ppl. stem of *insurgĕre* (see INSURGE) + -IVE.]

Prone to insurrection; of insurgent character.

1593 NASHE *Christ's T.* (1613) 28 They are no winds but insurrectiue sins, which so possesse the waues with the spyrite of raging. *Ibid.* 155 Thys didst thou to mortifie thy insurrectiue masse of corruption.

‖**insurrecto** (ɪnsʌˈrɛktəʊ). [Sp.] An insurgent or rebel. Also *attrib.* or as *adj.*

1907 *Cablenews* (Manila, Philippines) 21 Aug. 5/7 Villa, then Colonel of the insurrecto army. **1910** *Sat. Even. Post* 15 Oct. 17/2 I'll declare an amnesty for him and all his insurrectos. **1930** J. DOS PASSOS *42nd Parallel* I. 1 Up to where them insurrectos was afightin' fit to kill. **1947** *Sat. Even. Post* 8 Mar. 18/3 Later he saw a bit of fighting in the Philippines, north of Manila, against Aguinaldo's insurrectos.

†**insuˈrrector.** *Obs. rare.* [a. med. or mod.L. *insurrector*, agent-n. from *insurgĕre* to INSURGE.]

An insurgent.

[*a* **1458** T. GASCOIGNE *Loci e Libro Veritatum* (1881) 174 Homines qui vocabantur insurrectores occiderunt duos episcopos in Anglia.] **1658** R. FRANCK *North. Mem.* (1694) 87 A strong citadel..erected on purpose to reduce insurrectors. **1667** WATERHOUSE *Fire Lond.* 26 Popular rages to seize upon Insurrectors.

insusceptibility (ɪnsəsɛptɪˈbɪlɪtɪ). [f. next: see -ITY.] The quality of being insusceptible; want of susceptibility.

1821 COLERIDGE in *Blackw. Mag.* X. 249 The object is identified with the subject, both positively by the act of the subject, and negatively by insusceptibility of outness in the object. **1822–34** *Good's Study Med.* (ed. 4) I. 655 The same kind of insusceptibility to the action of the contagion of yellow fever. **1884** *Congreg. Year Bk.* 69 Insusceptibility to the touch and inspiration of goodness and truth.

insusceptible (ɪnsəˈsɛptɪb(ə)l), *a.* [IN-[3]; perh. after F. *insusceptible* (16th c. in Littré).] Not susceptible; not able or apt to receive impressions; not liable to be affected or influenced by something or in some way.

a. Const. *of* (an action, process, or condition).

1603 HOLLAND *Plutarch's Mor.* 1043 It is not altogether insusceptible of mutation. **1742** FIELDING *J. Andrews* I. v, You shall never persuade me that your heart is so insusceptible of affection. **1821** SHELLEY *Hellas* Pref., The subject..is insusceptible of being treated otherwise than lyrically. **1899** R. H. CHARLES *Eschatol.* x. 378 Souls in Sheol were conceived as insusceptible of ethical progress.

b. Const. *to* (an influence or agency).

1808 *Med. Jrnl.* XIX. 197 In others, vaccine inoculation did not take effect; consequently they were not rendered insusceptible to the infection of the small-pox. **1877** BROCKETT *Cross & Cr.* 264 Insusceptible to all those influences..which so powerfully affect most peoples. **1898** *19th Cent.* XLIV. 1000 The one, heavy, slow, insusceptible to violent passion.

c. *ellipt.* without construction.

1830 *Fraser's Mag.* I. 577 Coarse animal passion and animal craft, at once energetic and insusceptible. **1880** MACCORMAC *Antisept. Surg.* 83 This number of insusceptible or, as I may call them, not poisonable people, must be left out of account. **1898** P. MANSON *Trop. Dis.* vii. 142 To remove the entire population of the neighbourhood with the exception of the insusceptible.

insuˈsceptive, *a. rare*[−1]. [IN-[3].] = prec.

1752 JOHNSON *Rambler* No. 198 ¶9 The sailor was wholly insusceptive of the softer passions.

†**insuˈspect,** *a. Obs.* [IN-[3].] Unsuspected; not to be suspected. So †**insuˈspected** *a. Obs.*, unsuspected, of which one has no suspicion.

1606 BIRNIE *Kirk-Buriall* xiii. D j b, The constant silence of the insuspect auncients does testifie their misknowledgment and disclamation of the same. **1646** SIR T. BROWNE *Pseud. Ep.* II. ii. 58 Their penetrating natures, their invisible paths, and insuspected effects, are very considerable.

†**insuˈsurrate,** *v. Obs. rare*[−0]. [f. L. *insusurrāt-*, ppl. stem of *insusurrāre*: see next.] *trans.* 'To whisper one in the ear' (Bailey, 1727).

†**insusuˈrration.** *Obs. rare.* [ad. L. *insusurrātiōn-em*, n. of action f. *insusurrāre*, f. *in-* (IN-[2]) + *susurrāre* to murmur, whisper. Cf. SUSURRATION.] A whispering in the ear; an insinuation.

1614 JACKSON *Creed* IV. III. viii. §3 The Spirit sometimes instils some drops of this gladsome ointment into our souls by soft insusurrations in silent night. **1653** *Legenda Lignea* Pref. A iv b (L.), The other party insinuates their Roman principles by whispers and private insusurrations. **1721** in BAILEY. **1755** in JOHNSON.

†**inˈswak,** *v. Sc. Obs.* [f. IN-[1] + SWAK *v.*] *trans.* To cast in with force, to dash in.

1513 DOUGLAS *Æneis* IX. viii. 150 Mezentyus the grym.. The blak fyre blesis of reik inswakkis [*infert*] he.

inswamp (ɪnˈswɒmp), *v. rare.* [f. IN-[1] + SWAMP *sb.*] *trans.* and *intr.* To plunge into a swamp.

1775 ADAIR *Amer. Ind.* 315 The violent exercise of running a great distance under the violent rays of the sun.. would not allow him to inswamp. *Ibid.* 386 [They] take an oblique course, till they inswamp themselves again, in order to conceal their tracks.

inswarming (ˈɪnˌswɔːmɪŋ), *ppl. a.* [IN *adv.* 11 a.]

Swarming in, entering in swarms.

1892 *Chicago Advance* 17 Nov., Inswarming thousands from the older countries.

inswathe, variant of ENSWATHE *v.*

insweeping (ˈɪnˌswiːpɪŋ), *ppl. a.* [IN *adv.* 11 a.] Sweeping in.

1883 *Home Missionary* (U.S.) Aug. 155 Whether this insweeping migration is to foreignize us. **1897** *Westm. Gaz.* 20 Apr. 6/2 From the high cliff a man had seen..little imploring hands raised above the insweeping waves.

insweeten, variant of ENSWEETEN *v., Obs.*

inswell (ɪnˈswɛl), *v. rare.* [f. IN-[1] + SWELL *sb.* or *v.*] *trans.* To cause a swell in; to swell.

a **1774** FERGUSSON *Poems, Exped. Fife* 19 Boreas regains his strength To wake new tempests and inswell our seas.

inswept (ˈɪnswɛpt), *a.* [f. IN *adv.* + SWEPT *ppl. a.*] Of the frame of a motor vehicle: narrowed at the forward end or at the side.

1907 *Westm. Gaz.* 12 Nov. 12/3 The frames will be inswept from the dash. **1908** *Ibid.* 30 Jan. 4/1 The frame.. is inswept in front and gracefully upturned in the rear.

†**inˈswined,** *ppl. a. Obs.* = INHOGGED.

1611 FLORIO, *Inporchito*, inswined, become a hogge.

inswinger (ˈɪnˌswɪŋə(r)). *Cricket.* [IN *adv.*]

A ball bowled with a swerve or swing from the off to leg in its flight; also, the bowler of such a ball. So **ˈinswing**, the swerve or swing imparted to such a ball; a ball bowled in this manner; as vb., to bowl an inswinger; hence **ˈinˌswinging** *ppl. a.*

1920 *Times* 29 May 7/2 He [*sc.* Mr. Robertson-Glasgow] again seemed to rely too much on his 'inswinger' on the leg side, and he would surely do very much better if he could be certain of pitching his inswinging ball on the off stump. **1920** E. R. WILSON in P. F. Warner *Cricket* 67 The first right-handed 'in-swinger'..who was in-swinging as early as 1895. **1924** N. CARDUS *Days in Sun* 49 Jacques, of Hampshire..was a bowler commanding an in-swinging flight and an off-break. *Ibid.* 254 Nor would it be accurate to describe this ball as an in-swinger, for the true in-swinger swings from almost the first few yards of its flight through the air. **1927** *Observer* 17 Apr. 17/3 Last year he [*sc.* Mr. Allom] specialised in the 'inswing'. **1933** *Times* 28 Jan. 11/5 The leg-theory has been bowled in this country for a number of years, starting with 'in-swing' bowling. **1953** R. WARNER *Escapade* 74 He bowls in-swingers himself, though as a matter of fact he takes most of his wickets with his leg-breaks. **1955** *Times* 5 July 4/1 D. J. Smith, in spite of an in-swinger's action, was making the ball move from leg, and C. S. Smith was finding umpire Pothecary hard to satisfy. **1958** *Times* 22 Oct. 14/1 As it is, it may be many a long day before he has better figures as a medium-pace inswinger. **1962** *Times* 2 Aug. 3/3 Buxton, who bowled his inswing deceptively.

insygne, obs. form of ENSIGN *v.*

insykth, ME. 3rd pers. sing. of INSEE *v.*

insytation, obs. form of INCITATION.

1525 LD. BERNERS *Froiss.* II. xcix. [xcv.] 292 By insytacion of the duke of Irelonde.

†**int,** *sb. Obs.* [Origin obscure.] ? A sharper.

1631 BRATHWAIT *Whimzies* 12 (N.) His nipps, ints, bungs, and prinados. **1658** —— *Honest Ghost, Chym. Ape* 231 Flankt were my troups with bolts, bands, punks, and panders, Pimps, nips and ints, Prinados.

in't, arch. abbreviation of *in it.*

1610 SHAKS. *Temp.* I. ii. 304 Goe take this shape And hither come in't. **1742** RICHARDSON *Pamela* III. 246 The Devil's in't if you won't put that down. **1842** BROWNING *Soliloquy Span. Cloister* viii, Ope a sieve and slip in in't [*rime* print].

i'n't, i'nt, obs. abbreviation of *isn't, is not.*

1742 RICHARDSON *Pamela* III. 363 Your Lady's gone with them, i'n't she? *Ibid.* IV. 116 No indeed; it i'n't worth while. **1797** MRS. A. M. BENNETT *Beggar Girl* (1813) III. 30 That's game, i'nt it, maum?

intablature, obs. form of ENTABLATURE.

†**inˈtable,** *v. Obs. rare*[−1]. [f. IN-[1] + TABLE *sb.*; cf. ENTABLE.] *trans.* To enter in a table.

1611 SPEED *Hist. Gt. Brit.* IX. xii. §81 The names of the first twentie and sixe..you shall finde intabled in our Map of Barkeshire.

inˈtabulate, *v. rare.* [f. ppl. stem of med.L. *intabulāre*, f. *in-* (IN-[2]) + *tabula* TABLE.] *trans.* To enter or inscribe in a table or list.

1656 BLOUNT *Glossogr.*, *Intabulate*, to write in tables. **1894** *Athenæum* 22 Sept. 378/3 We learn [from the Evesham 'Officium Ecclesiasticum', *c* 1300]..that the abbot was formally 'intabulated' to the service of the kitchen for the weeks of Easter, Whitsuntide, and Christmas.

†**intabuˈlation.** *Obs. rare*[−0]. [ad. L. type **intabulātio*, n. of action from med.L. *intabulāre*, in sense of L. *tabulātio* planking or flooring over.]

1658 PHILLIPS, *Intabulation*, a laying on of boards or planks.

intack, dial. form of INTAKE *sb.*

intact (ɪnˈtækt), *a.* [ad. L. *intact-us*, f. *in-* (IN-[3]) + *tactus*, pa. pple. of *tangĕre* to touch. Cf. F. *intact* (17–18th c. in Godef. *Compl.*).]

Untouched; not affected by anything that injures, diminishes, or sullies; kept or left entire; unblemished; unimpaired.

c **1450** *Mirour Saluacioun* 4966 Thi maydenhode intacte inmaculat eurelastinge. **1721** in BAILEY. **1815** J. W. CROKER in *C. Papers* (1884) I. iii. 67 No mischief..had been done, except to one old china jar..The gallery was perfectly intact. *a* **1862** BUCKLE *Civiliz.* (1869) III. ii. 86 The principles on which Church authority is based remained intact. **1877** K. JOHNSTON *Africa* v. (1878) 62 Tunis..has retained the character of an oriental city almost intact.

Hence **inˈtactness**, the quality or condition of being intact.

1890 E. H. HANKIN in *Nature* 11 Dec. 121/2 The intactness of the leucocytes in these special cases.

‖**intacta** (ɪnˈtæktə). [fem. of L. *intactus* (see INTACT *a.*).] A shortening of L. *virgo intacta* a woman of inviolate chastity, used as adj. to denote: unaffected, not spoiled or sullied, esp. in *fig.* senses.

1941 H. G. WELLS *You can't be too Careful* III. xvi. 198 Edward Albert attempted an ironical whistle, but Mrs Butter held her position, intacta. **1960** A. WEST *Trend is Up* (1961) vi. 244 There's no sex angle to it. The kid is *intacta*, so's the woman for that matter. **1966** *New Statesman* 25 Feb. 255/3 The *People's* $5\frac{1}{2}$ million readers found their favourite Sunday paper *intacta* this week: the carefully balanced mixture of sex, exposure and sport..had not been tampered with.

†**inˈtactible,** *a. Obs. rare*[−0]. [IN-[3].] 'Not perceptible to the touch' (J.); = next.

1623 COCKERAM, *Intactible*, not to bee touched. **1658–1706** in PHILLIPS. **1755** in JOHNSON; and in mod. Dicts.

inˈtactile, *a. rare.* [ad. L. *intactil-is*, f. *in-* (IN-[3]) + *tactilis* TACTILE. Cf. F. *intactile* (16th c. in Hatz.-Darm.).] Not tactile or capable of being touched; intangible.

1659 STANLEY *Hist. Philos.* XIII. (1701) 556/1 Emptiness, or Uacuum..is understood..chiefly from being of an intactile Nature, and void of all Solidity. **1886** *Syd. Soc.*

Lex., *Intactile*, that cannot be recognised by the sense of touch, impalpable.

intagliated (ɪnˈtæljeɪtɪd), *ppl. a.* [f. It. *intagliat-o*, pa. pple. of *intagliare* to engrave (f. *in-* (IN-^{2}) + *tagliare* to cut: cf. ENTAIL *v.*^{1}) + -ED^{1}.] Carved on the surface; engraved in or as in intaglio; incised.

1782 WARTON *Hist. Kiddington* 25 A species of astroite, or starry-stone..deeply intagliated or engraven like a seal. **1825** T. D. FOSBROKE *Encycl. Antiq.* (1843) II. 763/1 Arms upon plate are in use as early as the thirteenth century, but only intagliated, or engraved in 1334. **1884** C. T. DAVIS *Bricks & Tiles* xv. (1889) 452 Clay, plaster-of-Paris..is pressed into the mould, so that the intagliated lines in this will appear upon the plaque or tile.

†inˈtagliature. *Obs. rare*$^{-1}$. In 6 **intaliature.** [ad. It. *intagliatura* carving, engraving, f. *intagliare*: cf. prec.] = INTAGLIO 1.

1599 R. LINCHE *Fount. Anc. Fict.* Tij, Engraued with exquisite and rare intaliature.

intaglio (‖inˈtaʎo, ɪnˈtæljəʊ), *sb.* Pl. **intaglios** (7 **entaglos**, 8 **intaglio's**), *rarely* **intagli** (inˈtalji). Also 7–8 *erron.* **intaglia**; *pl.* **-as**. [It., = engraving, engraved work, a carving (pl. *intagli*), f. *intagliare* to cut in, engrave: see INTAGLIATED.]

1. a. A figure or design incised or engraved; a cutting or engraving in stone or other hard material.

1644 EVELYN *Diary* 1 Mar., A chaplet of admirable invention, the intaglias being all on fruit-stones. **1662** J. BARGRAVE *Pope Alex. VII* (1867) 125 The cutt is certainly a very very ancient *intaglia* (as they use to call such cutts at Rome)..pronouncing it almost with a *ll—intallia.* **1682** WHELER *Journ. Greece* II. 202 Antient Entaglos or Figures, cut on several sorts of precious Stones. **1715** LEONI *Palladio's Archit.* (1742) II. 23 The Architrave..has many fine Intaglias. **1858** HAWTHORNE *Fr. & It. Jrnls.* I. 101 There is a profile there..an intaglio in the solid rock. **1858** O. W. HOLMES *Aut. Breakf.-t.* xi. 105 All its reliefs and intaglios have electrotyped themselves in the medallions that hang round the walls of your memory's chamber.

fig. and *transf.* **1686** PLOT *Staffordsh.* 192 The *rilieve* raies of one Trochite, always lying in the *intagli* or furrows between two protuberant raies of the other. **1886** SYMONDS *Renaiss. It., Cath. React.* (1898) VII. viii. 24 Boccaccio's clear-cut intaglios from life and nature.

b. The process or art of carving or engraving in a hard material; incised carving as opposed to carving in relief; the condition or fact of being incised. Chiefly in phrase ***in intaglio***, as opposed to *in rilievo* or *in relief*. Also *fig.*

1762–71 H. WALPOLE *Vertue's Anecd. Paint.* (1786) I. 276 Another gem with the head of Edward VI. cameo on one side, and intaglia on the other. **1816** J. DALLAWAY *Stat. & Sculpt. Anc.* v. 298 In every period of the Grecian celebrity the art of intaglio has been cultivated as a branch of sculpture. **1853** KANE *Grinnell Exp.* xxi. (1856) 166 It was startling to see the evidences of a travel nearly six years old, preserved in *intaglio* on a material so perishable. **1857** BIRCH *Anc. Pottery* (1858) I. 15 Bricks were impressed with a stamp on which hieroglyphics were cut in intaglio, so as to present them in relief on the surface of the brick. **1869** LUBBOCK *Preh. Times* viii. 268 The animals..are represented, not in relief, but intaglio; not by a mound, but by an excavation.

fig. **1813** MAR. EDGEWORTH *Patron.* I. xvi. 269 A woman's accomplishments..ought to be..more in intaglio than in cameo.

2. a. Anything ornamented with incised work; esp. a precious stone having a figure or design cut on its surface, an incised gem. Opposed to *cameo*.

1654 EVELYN *Mem.* 23 Oct., One of the rarest collections of achates, onyxes, and intaglios, that I had ever seene. **1704** ADDISON *Italy* (1733) 179 We meet with the Figures..on Antique Intaglio's and Medals. **1797** HOLCROFT *Stolberg's Trav.* (ed. 2) III. lxiv. 5 The collection of..gems, both cameos and intaglios, is considerable. **1864** C. W. KING *Gnostics* 56 The Jasper..is..employed for the *intagli* connected with the Mithraic idea. **1872** HUXLEY *Physiol.* x. 244 An intaglio, or medal on which the head is hollowed out.

b. A mould of something to be cast or struck in relief; a countersunk die.

1825 J. NICHOLSON *Operat. Mechanic* 616 When the casts, or intaglios, are first taken from the mould, they are not very firm. **1873** BURTON *Hist. Scot.* I. ii. 49 The use of intaglios to make up ecclesiastical seals.

3. *attrib.* and *Comb.* ***intaglio cylinder, engraving, impression, method, principle, printer, process, type, work***; **intaglio print**, an impression of a plate cut in intaglio; **intaglio printing**, the group of processes used to print intaglio plates; **intaglio-rilevato** [It., lit. raised or relieved intaglio] = CAVO-RILIEVO.

1859 *Abridgments of Specifications relating to Printing* (Patent Office) 354 The invention consists..in producing intaglio-graphic printing and other plates from forms of intaglio types by taking a casting in plaster of Paris, or other suitable material. *a* **1877** KNIGHT *Dict. Mech.* II. 1192/1 *Intaglio-type*, a process..depending upon the production of a friable surface of oxide of zinc on a metallic plate under hydraulic pressure... At drying, the surface is brushed over,..leaving an intaglio impression. **1886** R. A. M. STEVENSON tr. *Delaborde's Engraving* iii. 55 It is his [*sc.* Finiguerra's] invention..of the art of printing intaglio engravings, or rather of the art of engraving itself, that has made him immortal. **1888** C. T. JACOBI *Printers' Vocab.* 66 *Intaglio*, printing, such as from copper-plate—the reverse of 'relief' printing. **1914** E. H. RICHTER *Prints* i. 8 The different intaglio processes produce their blacks in different ways. **1917** E. POUND *Lustra* 181 Give up the intaglio method? **1921** *Dict. Occup. Terms* (1927) §529 *Intaglio printer*..places metal intaglio cylinder in position in machine, sets roll of paper and adjusts machine for even printing. **1930** D. STRANG *Printing of Etchings & Engravings* 1 The term 'etchings' will often..be intended to include all the other processes which are commonly employed by the artist in the making of intaglio prints. **1933** T. S. BARBER in W. Atkins *Art & Pract. Printing* IV. i. 8 Printing was done by the intaglio method of inking and wiping. **1959** *Chambers's Encycl.* V. 341/2 Intaglio work, when the design is cut into the block or plate. **1965** ZIGROSSER & GAEHDE *Guide to Collecting Orig. Prints* iv. 46 Intaglio Process... A general term descriptive of all techniques employing the intaglio principle of duplication, where the design is incised below the surface of the plate. **1967** V. STRAUSS *Printing Industry* i. 28/1 Intaglio printing is the name of a process family comprising a variety of printing methods which all use printing-image carriers with the printing areas sunken, or embedded, in the depth of the carrier material. **1972** W. CHAMBERLAIN *Thames & Hudson Man. Etching & Engraving* i. 11 In the context of intaglio printmaking, the term 'etching' normally refers to both the action of corroding lines, etc. into a metal plate with acid, and the inked, paper impression taken from the surface of the plate.

intaglio (ɪnˈtæljəʊ), *v.* [f. prec.] *trans.* To engrave with a sunk pattern or design; to represent or execute in intaglio.

1847 *Tait's Mag.* XIV. 383 Vestiges of pre-Adamite existence found filagreed into fossils, or intaglioed in stones. **1854** BADHAM *Halieut.* 234 Forms of various fossil fish.. Niobe-like, converted into stone; or intaglioed in a calcareous matrix. **188.** *Art. Jrnl.* VIII. 46 (Cent.) The device intaglioed upon it [a finger-ring] is supposed to be flowers bursting from the bud.

intail, -aile, -ayle, obs. ff. ENTAIL *sb.* and *v.*

†inˈtailed, *ppl. a. Obs. nonce-wd.* [f. IN-^{1} + TAIL + -ED.] Joined by the tails (with allusion to Judg. xv. 4).

1628 in Rushw. *Hist. Coll.* (1659) I. 586 So that you might guess there might be a double Plot..to set on fire the frame and estate of this Commonwealth: And one of these intailed Foxes was Mr. Manwaring.

intake (ˈɪnteɪk), *sb.* orig. *Sc.* and *north. dial.* Forms: 6- **intack**, (6–7 **-tacke**), 8- **intake** (*Sc.* **-tak**). [IN *adv.* 11 d; cf. *take in*, TAKE *v.*]

1. a. The act of taking in or receiving from outside; that which is taken in, an amount or quantity received internally.

1808–18 JAMIESON, *Intake*, the bringing in of the crop. **1854** *Phemie Millar* 161 With her..downright intake in the shape of meat and drink. **1886** STEVENSON *Dr. Jekyll* ii. (ed. 2) 22 Mr. Hyde shrank back with a hissing intake of the breath. **1896** *Allbutt's Syst. Med.* I. 143 Both the oxygen intake and the output of carbon dioxide in normal and fevered animals were compared. **1940** *Economist* 9 Nov. 590/1 Thanks to the heavy intake of raw wool this year..it has been possible to meet military and almost all export requirements without stinting the home consumer. **1955** *Times* 10 May 18/3 The intake of orders for the first four months is higher than ever before. **1971** *Nature* 2 July 63/3 Thus there is the intake and evaluation in one computerized centre of duplicate magnetic tapes from many sources.

b. (One of) a group of entrants to the army, a school, a trade, etc.

a **1943** B. WEBB *Our Partnership* (1948) ii. 79 It was.. among educational ladders..the most elaborate in its organisation of 'intakes' and promotions. **1943** *Times* 10 Dec. 2/1 That is evident from the moment when new intakes arrive and at once are interviewed by the..commanding officer. **1946** *News Chron.* 8 Aug. 1/4 It is understood that they will be part of the new intake of the U.S. Army. **1958** *Technology* May 66/2 The intake pattern can be worked out for transfer at appropriate stages. **1970** *Nature* 28 Nov. 798/1 The school should be functioning by 1975, with an intake of 100 students.

2. (Chiefly *north. dial.*) A piece of land taken in from a moorland, common, etc.; an inclosure.

[*c* **1330** *Selby Cartul.* II. 14 Ibidem est quoddam yntauk de feodo prædicto quod vocatur le Munkebank.] **1523** FITZHERB. *Surv.* viii. 8b, The lordes..haue gyuen lycence to dyuers of their tenauntes..to take in newe intackes or closes out of the commens. **1536** in Speed *Hist. Gt. Brit.* IX. xxi. §98 (1611) 1022 That all Intacks, Inclosys syth Anno quarto Henrici septimi be pullyd downe. **1641** BEST *Farm. Bks.* (Surtees) 28 Wee..keepe them [sheep] togeather in some well fenced place, as..the Newe Intacke in the towne becke. **1787–9** WORDSW. *Even. Walk* 49 When horses in the sunburnt intake stood. **1862** *Life amongst Colliers* 8 A nice garden..led to a ha-ha dividing it from a large pasture, known as the Intack.

attrib. and *Comb.* **1664** in *Lex Scripta Isle of Man* (1819) 150 Poor People, as Cotlers, Intack-holders, Prentices, and the like. **1832** *Spec. Yorksh. Dial.*, Te sell t' awd intack barley.

3. The place where water is taken into a channel or pipe from a river or other body of water, to drive a mill, or supply a canal, waterworks, etc. Also *attrib.*, as ***intake crib, tunnel, well.***

? *a* **1800** *State, Leslie of Powis* etc. 157 (Jam.) The water for driving the machinery of said new work is taken from the river above..the cruive-dike..the intake of this water is within the bounds of the cruive-fishing property. **1804** TARRAS *Poems* 40 (Jam.) Water-wraiths at in-tack drear. **1866** *Times* 8 Aug. 9/5 The first improvement was effected by carrying its intake up the river to Lea bridge. **1887** *Spectator* 9 July 921/1 Riparian towns above the intake of the Water Companies. **1892** *Chicago Advance* 28 Jan., An ice blockade at the port-holes had prevented the passage of the water into the intakes. **1909** *Daily Chron.* 21 Jan. 1/7 A fire which occurred at the construction works of a waterworks intake crib on Lake Michigan. **1909** *Westm. Gaz.* 21 Jan., This new intake tunnel was thrust further out into the lake. **1964** R. PERRY *World of Tiger* xi. 160 A tiger had attacked a tapir at a reservoir near Kuala Lumpur, and ..both had fallen into the dry 'intake' well.

4. a. *Mining.* The airway by which a current of air is introduced into a mine. Also *attrib.*

1851 GREENWELL *Coal-trade Terms Northumb. & Durh.* 32 *Intake*, the airway along which the fresh air is conducted into a place, district, or mine. **1867** W. W. SMYTH *Coal & Coal-mining* 219 The 'returns' are generally made to mount over the intake drifts. **1881** RAYMOND *Mining Gloss.* s.v., Downcast..is more appropriate for a shaft; Intake for an adit. **1894** *Westm. Gaz.* 23 Aug 7/1 He did not see how it was possible for fire-damp to have accumulated in the main intake air roads.

b. Short for ***air-intake*** (AIR *sb.*^{1} B. II).

1946 *Flight* 1 Aug. 115/2 (*caption*) A Heinkel single-jet proposal with the intake between two nacelles. **1959** *Listener* 30 July 164/1 He dealt with the ice that started forming on the engine intakes of the Vickers Vimy machine.

5. A narrowing or abrupt contraction made in the width of a tube, a stocking, etc.; the point at which this is made.

1808–18 JAMIESON, *Intake*..2. A contraction, in sewing. **1875** M^{c}ILWRAITH *Guide Wigtownshire* 14 The monument ..after a series of intakes, is formed into a clustered column. **1880** *Plain Hints Needlework* 29 One-third of the foot is the length of the ankle, from the last intake or decreasing.

6. *Sc.* A 'take in', an imposition. Also, one who 'takes in', a cheat.

1808–18 JAMIESON, *Intake*,..4. A fraud, a swindling trick. 5. A swindler. **18..** *Edinburgh* II. 118 (Jam.) Some even made so bold as to call him an in-tak and an adventurer. **1832** *Fraser's Mag.* V. 2 What was the lottery but an intake? **1860** W. ARNOT *Laws fr. Heaven* 281 The counterpart is a terrible truth—it is more cursed to be an intake than to be taken in.

7. *attrib.* and *Comb.* (see also 3 and 4 above).

1921 *Dict. Occup. Terms* (1927) §449 *Intake man*, grain intake man (grain milling); at a signal from men on ship, barge, etc., alongside wharf that suction pipe is inserted in grain, starts air pump, which draws up grain through pipe by suction. **1940** *Chambers's Techn. Dict.* 451/2 *Intake belt course*, a projecting course of stone or bricks, serving as an intake at a place where the thickness of a wall is diminished. **1941** *B.B.C. Gloss. Broadc. Terms* 15 *Intake report*, analysis summarizing the content of broadcasts directed to listeners in a particular country, in its own language, from a selected number of stations. **1957** *Times* 2 July (Agric. Suppl.) p. vi/2 A typical old barn now houses the grain intake pit, cleaner, pre-dry bin, continuous dryer, and sectional storage bins. **1958** *U.S. Dept. Agric. Yearbk. 1957* 760/2 *Intake rate*, the rate, usually expressed in inches per hour, at which rain or irrigation water enters the soil. **1961** B. FERGUSSON *Watery Maze* v. 127 Those ports on the West Coast which had become intake valves for our life's blood from across the Atlantic. **1966** Intake chimney [see CORDTEX]. **1972** *Classification of Occupations & Directory Occupational Titles* (Department of Employment) III. 478/1 *Intakeman* (grain, sugar and similar materials). Checks supplies of grain, sugar and similar materials into storage silos, transfers materials to processing departments and maintains stock records.

†ˌinˈtake, *v. Sc. Obs.* [IN-^{1}; see *take in*, TAKE *v.*] *trans.* **a.** To take or gather in. **b.** To take by force of arms, capture.

1572 *Satir. Poems Reform.* xxxiii. 271 Ryue out the Mures; the bestialls gers intak. *c* **1647** R. BAILLIE *Lett.* (1775) II. 265 Having..no artillery at all fit for intaking any strong house.

ˈinˌtaker. *north. dial.* [IN *adv.* 11 e.] **†1.** One who 'takes in' or receives stolen property. *Obs.*

1421 *Act 9 Hen. V*, c. 7 Diverses persones larons & felons appellez Intakers & Outputters demourantz deinz la franchise de Ridesdale. **1607** COWELL *Interpr.*, *Intakers* be a kind of theeves, so called because they..did receive in such booties of catell or other things as the outparters brought in unto them.

2. (See quot. 1921.)

1921 *Dict. Occup. Terms* (1927) §368 *Drawer*, drawer-in, ..healder, in-taker,..attaches weaving beam to drawing-in frame, and draws each warp yarn, separately, with a hook, through eye (or loop) of heald, and through dent of reed in loom. **1960** *Classification of Occupations* (General Register Office) 49/3 In-taker.

ˈinˌtaking, *vbl. sb.* [IN *adv.* 11 c.]

†1. The action of capturing or taking by force of arms. [= Ger. *einnahme*, *einnehmung*.] *Sc. Obs.*

1637 R. MONRO *Exp. Scots Regim.* II. 13 Captaine Robert Stewart..was preferred before the In-taking of Virtzberg, having beene before the Battaile of Lipsigh. **1891** *Cornh. Mag.* Apr. 348, I have held two and twenty towns, and I have been at the intaking of thirty-one [Archaism temp. Edw. III].

†2. The taking in of moorland into cultivation. *Sc. Obs.*

1812 SOUTER *Agric. Surv. Banffs.* App. 49 The reasons of ebb-ploughing, at intaking, are to retain the dung as near the surface as possible.

3. The action of taking in or receiving from outside (esp. in senses 1 a, b of INTAKE *sb.*).

1905 C. KERNAHAN *Visions* 283 The soft intaking of a baby's breath. **1959** *Listener* 5 Mar. 402/2 A period of intensive learning—of intaking rather than outputting. **1966** I. JEFFERIES *House-Surgeon* iv. 88, I just went to the intaking chief.

†inˈtaminate, *v. Obs. rare*$^{-0}$. [f. ppl. stem of med.L. *intāmināre*, f. *in-* (IN-^{2}) + L. **tāmināre* to violate: see CONTAMINATE.] *trans.* To defile. So **†inˌtamiˈnation**, defilement.

1623 COCKERAM, *Intaminate*, to defile. **1658** PHILLIPS, *Intamination*, a defiling or polluting.

†**in'taminated**, *a. Obs. rare*⁻¹. [f. L. *intāmināt-us* uncontaminated (f. *in-*, IN-³ + pa. pple. of **tāmināre*: see prec.) + -ED¹.] Uncontaminated, uncorrupted, pure.

a **1695** WOOD *Ath. Oxon.*, *F. Junius* (1721) II. 603 Whose Inhabitants use the antient and intaminated Frisic Language.

intangibility (ɪnˌtændʒɪ'bɪlɪtɪ). [f. next + -ITY. Cf. mod.F. *intangibilité* (Littré).] **a.** The quality of being intangible.

1847 in CRAIG. **1848** *Fraser's Mag.* XXXVII. 99 There is an intangibility about all the charges that are made against her. **1885** CLODD *Myths & Dr.* II. vii. 184 Its [his shadow's] intangibility feeds his awe and wonder.

b. Inviolability.

1783 C. J. FOX *Memorials & Corr.* (1853) II. 102, I beg of gentlemen to be aware of the lengths to which their arguments upon the intangibility of this charter may be carried. **1929** *Times* 13 Aug. 10/2 There has been too much talk..of the intangibility of the Young Plan.

intangible (ɪn'tændʒɪb(ə)l), *a.* and *sb.* [ad. med.L. *intangibil-is*, f. *in-* (IN-³) + L. *tangibilis* TANGIBLE: cf. F. *intangible* (1508 in Godef. *Compl.*).] **A.** *adj.* **a.** Not tangible; incapable of being touched; not cognizable by the sense of touch; impalpable.

1640 WILKINS *New Planet* II. (1684) 148 A Man should be still in danger of knocking his head against every Wall and Pillar; unless it were also intangible, as some of the Peripateticks affirm. **1717** CLARKE *Leibnitz Papers* Reply iv. §45. 151 The Means by which Two Bodies attract each other, may be invisible and intangible. **1845** MᶜCULLOCH *Taxation* III. iii. (1852) 476 The proportion of monied and other moveable and all but intangible property..has increased ten-fold, since the accession of George I. **1871** TYNDALL *Fragm. Sc.* (1879) I. iii. 76 The assumption of this wonderful intangible aether. **1880** MUIRHEAD *Gaius* II. §14 Incorporeal [things] are those that are intangible..such as an inheritance, a usufruct.

b. *fig.* That cannot be grasped mentally.

1880 *Mem. John Legge* 127 To the irreligious man all this is intangible, unintelligible. **1898** RAMSAY *Was Christ born in Bethlehem?* 20 This abstract and rather intangible argument must yield to the demonstration of hard facts.

B. *sb.* Anything intangible; spec. (in *pl.*) = *intangible assets*, i.e. assets (e.g. goodwill, rights, etc.) which cannot easily or precisely be measured.

1914 *Cycl. Amer. Govt.* III. 496/1 The term 'personal property'..includes..visible property and intangibles. **1930** *Economist* 29 Mar. 710/1 Net tangible assets may be defined as total assets less 'intangibles' (goodwill, patents, etc.), current liabilities, and funded debt. **1933** *Discovery* Oct. 313/2 Scientific changes were coming in so thick and fast that other factors in social life—the intangibles of credit, the improvements in political and international ideas—were unequal to the task of accommodating them. **1949** *Here & Now* (N.Z.) Oct. 30/3 The intangibles—the many local developments—being not reducible to statistics, the food of all bureaucracy, count for nothing. **1957** *Economist* 19 Oct. (Suppl.) 1/2 The success of individual motor producers will depend mainly upon intangibles such as the success of their design policy.

Hence **in'tangibleness**; **in'tangibly** *adv.*, so as to be intangible.

1678 CUDWORTH *Intell. Syst.* I. v. 769 That which is extended also, but penetrably and intangibly which is space or vacuum. **1828** WEBSTER, *Intangibleness*, the quality of being intangible. **1887** E. F. BYRRNE *Heir without Heritage* II. v. 91 The most intangibly delicate sense of duty.

in'tangle, -ment, obs. ff. ENTANGLE, -MENT.

†**in'tangle**, *a. Obs. rare*⁻¹. [IN-¹.] In a tangle; entangled.

1642 HOWELL *For. Trav.* 40 His observations will lye confusedly huddled up, like a skeine of intangle silk.

in'tarissable, *a. rare.* [a. F. *intarissable* (Cotgr.), f. *in-* (IN-³) + *tarissable*, f. *tarir*, *tarissant* to dry up.] Not to be dried up, inexhaustible.

1656-81 BLOUNT *Glossogr.*, *Intarissable*, not to be withered or dryed up. **1859** MRS. SCHIMMELPENNINCK *Princ. Beauty* IV. v. §6 That intarissable fountain of gushing joy.

intarsia (ɪn'tɑːsɪə). Also -io. [It. *intarsio.*] = TARSIA. Also *attrib.*, *transf.* and *fig.* So **intarsiatore** (ɪnˌtɑːsɪə'tɔəreɪ), a worker in intarsia; **intarsiatura** (ɪnˌtɑːsɪə'tʊərə), pl. **-e**, = INTARSIA.

1863 A. JAMESON *Legends of Monastic Orders* (ed. 3) 275 The fine intarsiatura in the Choir of San Francesco di Assisi. **1867** *Ecclesiologist* XXVIII. 216 Hidden under the intarsio pavement. **1868** C. C. PERKINS *Italian Sculptors* 262 A celebrated wood-carver and 'intarsiatore' named Luchino Bianchini..helped them to carve the presses for the sacristy. *Ibid.*, Luchino Bianchini..made the woodwork about its great portal, as well as the intaglios and intarsiature of the choir at San Lodovico. **1892** A. M. CLERKE *Familiar Stud. Homer* x. 266 Some rusty dagger-blades..skilfully ornamented in coloured metallic intarsiatura. **1894** *Daily News* 6 Dec. 5/2 Humorous intarsia showing Polyphemus.. feeling the backs of the sheep. **1896** *Q. Rev.* Oct. 471 The intarsias of the choir-stalls of S. Maria Maggiore at Bergamo. **1906** *Westm. Gaz.* 4 July 2/1 The Brunellese looked critically at the intarsia chests of drawers. **1913** MRS. H. WARD *Mating of Lydia* IV. xix. 389 The gleaming reflections on lacquer and intarsia, on ebony or Sèvres. **1919** H. F. JONES *Samuel Butler* II. 67 The seats of the stalls in the church of Santa Maria Maggiore at Bergamo are ornamented with intarsia work. **1945** *Burlington Mag.* Aug. 191/2 The treatment of the *intarsia* is closely paralleled in the panelling of coeval rooms in Swiss museums. **1957** *Textile Terms & Defs.* (Textile Inst.) (ed. 3) 54 *Intarsia.* (1) Weft-knitted plain, rib or purl fabrics containing designs in two or more colours... (2) A motif design in stitch and/or colour. **1958** *Listener* 11 Sept. 388/3 Of the poems, with their tessellated intarsia of natural scenery, natural passion and liturgical imagery, perhaps the most revealing on the subject of Zhivago's destiny is the first. **1970** *Times* 28 Feb. (Sat. Suppl.) p. vii/4 The most startling form of marquetry was perspective picture making in wood, known as intarsia. **1973** *Guardian* 10 Apr. 13/3 Sweater with intarsia thistle motif.

†**in'tastable**, *a. Obs. rare*⁻¹. [IN-³.] Incapable of being tasted.

a **1711** GREW (J.), Something which is invisible, intastable, and intangible..existing only in the fancy, may produce a pleasure superiour to that of sense.

†**in'taxable**, *a. Obs. rare.* [IN-³.] That cannot be taxed or charged with something.

1631 I. CRAVEN *God's Tribvnall* 16 The Lord of Hosts, whose..iustice [is] intaxable, anger intollerable.

intechni'cality. *rare.* [IN-³.] Want of technicality; something not technically correct.

1821 *New Monthly Mag.* I. 618 Every power must be for ever on the alert, to detect intechnicalities, to fence with witnesses, to puzzle or persuade phlegmatic jurors.

†**'integent**, *a. Obs. rare*⁻¹. [ad. L. *integent-em*, pr. pple. of *integĕre*, f. *in-* (IN-²) + *tegĕre* to cover.] That covers; covering.

1661 LOVELL *Hist. Anim. & Min.* 319 As for the parts, they are dissimilar, *sc.* the basis and point, or similars external, as the fat, integent membran.

integer ('ɪntɪdʒə(r)), *a.* and *sb.* [a. L. *integer* untouched, intact, entire, f. *in-* (IN-³) + *tag-*, *teg-*, root of *tangĕre* to touch. Cf. F. *intègre* (1567 in Hatz.-Darm.), and ENTIRE.]

A. *adj.* (Now *rare* or *Obs.*)

†**1.** Having no part taken away or wanting; whole, entire: = INTEGRAL A. 3. *Obs.*

a **1509** WOLSEY *Let. to Hen. VII* in *Lett. Rich. III* (Rolls) I. App. 443 Wher I seyd that the emperors m...he dote of thre hunderyth thousan..should..have the seyd integyr dote in effect and equyvalen..[*MS. imperf.*]

†**2.** Marked by moral integrity; honest, upright. *Obs.*

1644 VICARS *God in Mount* 108 The face of their best and most integer proceedings.

3. *Math.* Denoting a whole thing or number of whole things; denoted by a whole number; 'whole', not fractional: = INTEGRAL A. 4 a. Now *rare* or *Obs.*

1660 BOYLE *New Exp. Phys. Mech.* xii, I had..found that ..14 and 1 be the nearest of small integer numbers that express the proportion between the specifick gravities of quicksilver and water. **1806** HUTTON *Course Math.* I. 52 A whole or integer number may be expressed like a fraction, by writing 1 below it, as a denominator. **1833** HERSCHEL *Astron.* ii. 79 To keep the reckoning of the integer days correct..is the object of the calendar.

B. *sb.* **1.** *Math.* A number or quantity denoting one or more whole things or units; a whole number or undivided quantity. Opp. to *fraction.*

1571 DIGGES *Pantom.* IV. v. V ij b, The containing circles Semidimetient being very nighe $11\frac{18}{21}$ for exactly nether by integer nor fraction it can be expressed. **1675** OGILBY *Brit.* Pref. 4 Not regarding the Fractional Parts of a Mile, but taking the lesser Integer. **1831** CARLYLE *Sart. Res.* III. xi, The Fraction will become..an Integer. **1875** TODHUNTER *Alg.* (ed. 7) lii, Theory of Numbers. Throughout the present Chapter the word *number* is used as an abbreviation for *positive integer*.

2. A particular quantity of any kind (as money, weight, length, etc.) taken as the unit of measurement. Now *rare* or *Obs.*

1822 J. FLINT *Lett. Amer.* 50 The dollar is the integer of money in the United States. **1827** FARADAY *Chem. Manip.* iii. 67 Two integers..the pint and the cubic inch. **1868** SEYD *Bullion* (1880) 146 The Carat serves as the Integer.

3. *gen.* (often with allusion to 1): A whole or entire thing or entity, either as complete in itself, or as the sum of its parts or elements.

a **1848** R. W. HAMILTON *Rew. & Punishm.* v. (1853) 202 The soul is the integer of the man. **1859** HELPS *Friends in C.* Ser. II. II. viii. 150 You would never amongst you all make up the noble integer. **1875** E. WHITE *Life in Christ* I. iii. (1878) 23 Death is followed by the speedy dissipation of the combined elements which formed the organism..The Integer, the Animal which resulted from the former combination, is no more. **1899** R. C. TEMPLE *Univ. Gram.* 4 Functionally a word is either—(1) An integer, or a sentence in itself.

ˌ**integra'bility.** [f. next: see -ITY.] The fact or character of being integrable; capability of being integrated.

1816 *Edin. Rev.* XXVII. 93 The theorem, which is called the *Criterion of Integrability*. **1816** tr. *Lacroix's Diff. & Int. Calculus* 337 Ascertaining whether the proposed equation satisfies the condition of integrability. **1882** *Nature* XXVI. 310 This definition..satisfies as well the condition of integrability as the differential equation of motion.

integrable ('ɪntɪgrəb(ə)l), *a.* [f. L. *integrā-re* to make whole, INTEGRATE + -BLE.] Capable of being integrated. **a.** *Math.*: see INTEGRATE *v.* 3.

1727-41 CHAMBERS *Cycl.* s.v. *Calculus*, The differential quantity to be integrated..must.. be reduced to an integrable finite, or an infinite series. **1809** IVORY in *Phil. Trans.* XCIX. 349 The expressions..are all integrable with respect to one of the variable quantities they contain. **1882** J. B. STALLO *Concepts Mod. Physics* 107 *note*, When their equations are integrable.

b. *gen.*: see INTEGRATE *v.* 2.

1855 H. SPENCER *Princ. Psychol.* (1870) I. 298 Dispersed atoms of integrable matter. *Ibid.* (1872) I. III. vi. 330 To the lowest living things, the integrable matter is everywhere present.

integral ('ɪntɪgrəl), *a.* and *sb.* [ad. late L. *integrāl-is*, f. *integer*, *integr-*: see INTEGER and -AL¹. Cf. F. *intégral* (Oresme, 14th c.); It. *integrale* 'entire, consisting of entirenesse' (Florio).

'*Integralis pars*', and '*partium integralium*, quæ si conveniant, totum exstat', occur in a 6th c. Comment. on Cicero *de Invent. Rhet.*, in Suringar *Hist. Crit. Scholiast. Latin.* (1834) pp. 248, 222.]

A. *adj.*

1. Of or pertaining to a whole. Said of a part or parts: Belonging to or making up an integral whole; constituent, component; *spec.* necessary to the completeness or integrity of the whole; forming an intrinsic portion or element, as distinguished from an adjunct or appendage. (Cf. INTEGRANT.) (Formerly distinguished from *essential*: see quots. 1697, 1727.)

1551 T. WILSON *Logike* 39 b, The integral partes, which make perfect the whole, and cause the bignesse thereof. *a* **1639** W. WHATELEY *Prototypes* II. xxvi. (1640) 43 The parts integrall, viz. as the severall members of the matter, head, heart, &c. in man. **1651** N. BACON *Disc. Govt. Eng.* II. xv. (1739) 79 In a mixt Commonwealth they [kings] are integral Members. **1697** LOCKE *2nd Vind. Reas. Chr.* 247 (Seager) Integral parts..are contradistinguished to essential; and signify such parts, as the thing can be without, but without them will not be so complete and entire as with them. **1727-41** CHAMBERS *Cycl.*, *Integral*, or *Integrant*, is applied by the schoolmen, to those parts which are necessary to the integrity of a whole... In which sense they stand contradistinguished from *essential* parts... The arms, legs, etc. are *integral* parts; body and soul *essential* parts of a man. **1786** BURKE *W. Hastings* Wks. 1842 II. 220 Forming no legal or integral part of the government. **1862** GOULBURN *Pers. Relig.* III. x. (1873) 238 Recreation must form an integral part of human life. **1867** FREEMAN *Norm. Conq.* I. ii. 69 A dependency of the British Crown..not an integral part of the United Kingdom. **1923** GLAZEBROOK *Dict. Appl. Physics* V. 165/1 This cylinder has an open-ended steel barrel with integral fins. **1958** *Chambers's Techn. Dict.* 987/1 *Integral stiffeners*, the stiffening ridges left when an aircraft skin panel is machined from a solid billet. **1968** *Gloss. Formwork Terms* (*B.S.I.*) 16 *Integral facing*, a special facing concrete or mortar cast simultaneously with the backing concrete so as to be monolithic with it. **1972** [see INTEGRALLY *adv.* b].

2. Made up of component parts which together constitute a unity; in *Logic*, said of a whole consisting of or divisible into parts external to each other, and therefore actually (not merely mentally) separable. Now *rare* or *Obs.* exc. in technical use.

1588 FRAUNCE *Lawiers Log.* I. vi. 33 The whole Integrall cannot bee affirmed of any one of his parts, for a part is not the whole. **1628** T. SPENCER *Logick* 203 An Integrall whole is not in each part, neither according to their whole essence, nor vertue, and therefore it is no wayes predicated of the singular parts. **1649** JER. TAYLOR *Gt. Exemp.* II. vi. §19 In every Christian there are three parts concerning this integral Constitution, body and soul, and Spirit. **1725** WATTS *Logic* I. vi. §10 As an integral Whole is distinguish'd into its several Parts by Division, so the Word Distribution is most properly used when we distinguish an universal Whole into its several Kinds of Species. *Ibid.*, Logicians have sometimes given a mark or sign to distinguish when it is an integral whole, that is, divided into its parts and members, or when it is a genus, an universal whole, that is, distributed into its species and individuals. **1836-7** SIR W. HAMILTON *Metaph.* xxxvii. (1859) II. 340 The Integral or, as it ought to be called Integrate whole (*totum integratum*), is composed of integrant parts (*partes integrantes*) which are either homogeneous, or heterogeneous. **1864** BOWEN *Logic* iv. 67 *note*, The Essential or Physical whole is that which consists of Matter and Form, or substance and accident, as its essential parts. The characteristic of this whole is that, as its parts do not exist out of each other, they cannot be separated except in Thought..The Mathematical or Integral whole, on the other hand, has parts which are external to each other, so that they can be divided asunder. **1945** H. D. SMYTH *Gen. Acct. Devel. Atomic Energy Mil. Purposes* xii. 132 Two 'integral experiments' (experiments on assembled or integrated systems comprising fissionable material, reflector, and perhaps moderator also) may be described. **1953** C. WALLACE *Photographer's Pocket-Bk.* 112 In modern colour materials the colours are achieved by building up on a suitable base..an 'integral tri-pack' of three separate emulsions.

3. a. Having no part or element separated, taken away, or lacking; unbroken, whole, entire, complete. Now somewhat *rare.* [= mod.F. *intégral.*]

1611 FLORIO, *Integrale*, whole or integrall. **1626** BACON *Sylva* §344 All Locall Motion keepeth Bodies Integrall, and their Parts together. **1651** BIGGS *New Disp.* ¶238 Thorow the integral porous pelt. **1659** D. PELL *Impr. Sea* 484 Their hearts are not integral, and entire in prayer. **1794** MATHIAS *Purs. Lit.* (1798) 157 Excerpta of Writers whose integral works are lost for ever. **1862** LYTTON *Str. Story* II. 15 Who

could expect that every link in a madman's tale would be found integral and perfect?

b. Of things immaterial.

1651 JER. TAYLOR *Serm. for Year* I. iv. 51 Repent with an integral, a holy and excellent repentance. **1656** EARL MONM. *Advt. fr. Parnass* 281 They are thought by them to merit their Princes integral love. **1847** R. W. HAMILTON *Sabbath* v. (1848) 181 It is felt that, if we would retain Christianity, we must hold fast the full, the integral, sabbath.

†**c.** *Gram.* Applied by Wilkins to a word or part of speech denoting a complete notion; see B. 3. *Obs.*

1668 WILKINS *Real Char.* 305 They supply the room either, 1. Of some Integral word, as Pronouns, or 2. Of some Sentence or complex part of it, as Interjections.

4. *Math.* **a.** That is, or is denoted by, an integer, or involves only integers; consisting of a whole number or undivided quantity; not fractional, or not involving a fraction.

1658 PHILLIPS s.v., In Arithmetick integral numbers are opposed to fraction[s]. **1674** JEAKE *Arith.* (1696) 15 To express the true content of any Number Integral. **1812** J. SMYTH *Pract. of Customs* (1821) 286 The fractional part of a foot..is to be given up in favour of the importer, and the duties to be charged only upon the integral feet. **1816** tr. *Lacroix's Diff. & Int. Calculus* 185 *Q* being a rational and integral function of *x*. **1875** TODHUNTER *Algebra* (ed. 7) xxxvi. §516 When *n* has any value positive or negative, integral or fractional.

b. Relating to or involving integrals (see B. 4); obtained by, belonging to, or proceeding by integration.

integral calculus: the calculus of integrals (see B. 4); that branch of the infinitesimal calculus which deals with the finding and properties of integrals of functions (in this restricted sense, the inverse of the differential calculus, and corresponding to the 'inverse method of fluxions' in the Newtonian calculus), also used to include the solution of differential equations, and parts of the theory of functions and other branches of the higher mathematics. ***integral sign*** = *sign of integration*: see B. 4 a, and INTEGRATION 2.

1727–41 CHAMBERS *Cycl.* s.v. *Calculus*, The *integral Calculus*..is the inverse of the differential one. *Ibid.*, Suppose ∫ the sign of the sum, or integral quantity. **1802** WOODHOUSE in *Phil. Trans.* XCII. 95 Expressions deduced from the true integral equations. **1875** C. P. BUCKINGHAM *Diff. & Int. Calc.* (1880) §157 The..problem of the integral calculus is to pass from a given differential of a function to the function itself. **1881** MAXWELL *Electr. & Magn.* I. 21 In the expression under the integral sign only the finite values ..are to be considered. **1887** R. A. ROBERTS *Int. Calc.* 1 The principal object of the Integral Calculus is to find the value of a function of a single variable when its differential coefficient is given.

c. Applied to the entire or total amount of a continuous quantity (*e.g.* curvature) taken between definite limits, and thus expressible by a definite integral (see B. 4 a).

1879 THOMSON & TAIT *Nat. Phil.* I. I. §10 The *integral curvature*, or *whole change of direction* of an arc of a plane curve, is the angle through which the tangent has turned as we pass from one extremity to the other.

d. *integral domain*: see DOMAIN *sb.* 4 d.

B. *sb.*

1. Something entire or undivided; a whole, either as wanting no part, or as made up of parts: see A. 2, 3. *Obs.* exc. as *transf.* from 4 = total sum.

1620 T. GRANGER *Div. Logike* 177 A tree, a body, an house ..are totall Integrals, whose integritie, or wholenesse..is made of their parts. **1657** TOMLINSON *Renou's Disp.* 9 In the third genus are contained all Animals whether Integrals or In-parts. **1784** J. BARRY in *Lect. Paint.* iv. (Bohn 1848) 152 Any other conjunction of parts forming an integral or whole. **1834** LANDOR *Exam. Shaks.* Wks. 1846 II. 299/2 No more.. than breaking an eggshell is breaking an egg, the shell being a part, and the egg being an integral. **1881** *Nature* No. 625. 582 What is seen in a sun-spot is the integral, as it were, of all that is taking place..in many thousand miles of solar atmosphere.

†**2.** An integral part or element; a constituent, component: see A. 1. *Obs.*

1658–9 *Burton's Diary* (1828) III. 557 We must, therefore, be very circumspect in the materials of the other House. Let us, therefore, look to the integrals in this building. *a* **1677** HALE *Prim. Orig. Man.* I. i. 21 Anatomy can give us the Position..of all the several Integrals of the Body of Man or Beast. *Ibid.* IV. viii. 372 They all make up a most magnificent and stately Temple, and every Integral thereof full of wonder. **1680** BAXTER *Answ. Stillingfl.* 82 Doth not every good Law and Rule distinguish between *Essentials*, *Integrals*, and *Accidents*, and make more Accidents than are Integrals, and Integrals, than are Essentials? **1685** —— *Paraphr. N.T., 1 Cor.* xii. 14 So wise, as besides the Essentials of Christianity, to know all the Integrals.

†**3.** *Gram.* Applied by Wilkins to those words or parts of speech which of themselves express a distinct notion, as distinct from those which express relations between notions. *Obs.*

1668 WILKINS *Real Char.* III. i. §2 By Integrals or Principal words, I mean such as signifie some entire thing or notion. **1688** R. HOLME *Armoury* III. 251/2. **1845** STODDART *Gram.* in *Encycl. Metrop.* I. 124/1 Wilkins includes under the term *integral* both the noun and the verb.

4. *Math.* **a.** (of a function): That quantity of which the given function is the differential or differential coefficient (corresponding to the fluent of a given fluxion in Newton's method); so called because it may be regarded as the whole sum of a series of consecutive values assumed by an infinitesimal function (differential) of the variable while the latter changes continuously from any one value to any other. When such *limits* of variation are fixed or determinate, it is called a ***definite integral***: see quot. 1877. An integral is denoted by the sign ∫ (originally a long *s*, for L. *summa* sum); in a definite integral the inferior and superior limits are indicated at the bottom and top of the sign, thus $\int_a^b$. (Formerly sometimes applied to the quantity from which a given 'finite difference' or 'increment' is derived, as in quot. 1763; cf. quot. 1831 s.v. INTEGRATE *v.* 3.) **b.** (of a differential equation, or a system of such equations): An equation or system of equations from which the given equation or system can be derived by differentiation. (In relation to a system of equations, any quantity which that system makes constant is sometimes called its integral.)

1727–41 CHAMBERS *Cycl.* s.v. *Calculus*, ∫*ydx* will denote the sum, or integral of the differential *ydx*. **1763** EMERSON *Increments* p. vii, Some Increments have no integrals, but what infinite series afford. **1802** WOODHOUSE in *Phil. Trans.* XCII. 90 The integral or fluent of *Px*· is that function from which *Px*· is derived. **1877** B. WILLIAMSON *Int. Calc.* (ed. 2) vi. §91 The expression $\int_{x_0}^{X}\phi(x)dx$ is called the *definite integral* of $\phi(x)dx$ between the limits x_0 and *X*, and represents the limit of the sum of the infinitely small elements $\phi(x)dx$, taken between the proposed limits... In contradistinction, the name *indefinite integrals* is often applied to integrals..in which the form of the function is merely taken into account, without regard to any assigned limits. **1881** MAXWELL *Electr. & Magn.* I. 27 The double integrals destroy each other.

integralism (ɪn'tɛgrəlɪz(ə)m). [f. INTEGRAL *a.* 1 + -ISM.] A name sometimes adopted for a philosophical or political, etc., doctrine or theory which involves the concept of an integral whole.

1871 S. P. ANDREWS *Primary Synopsis Universology* xii. 178 Integralism is the new and final philosophy; the all-sided and complete reconciliation of all possible sectarian divisions in all spheres; not as extinguishing individual differences, but as softening, co-ordinating, and utilizing them. **1939** *Times* 18 Feb. 17/4 The counterpart of the Nazi movement—Integralism—has its supporters. **1964** D. G. MACRAE in J. H. Plumb *Crisis in Humanities* 127 By 'integralism' is meant a set of beliefs that involve one in claiming that social structures form a 'seamless web' in which every institution and social position is linked to every other and is part of a unique, interconnected configuration. **1969** D. M. SMITH *Italy* (ed. 2) VII. xxi. 255 The Rome party congress of 1906 had recorded a victory for 'integralism'.. yet revolutionary socialism continued to spread.

integralist (ɪn'tɛgrəlɪst), *sb.* [f. INTEGRAL *a.* 1 + -IST.] One who favours a policy or doctrine of integralism. Also *attrib.* or as *adj.* Cf. INTEGRIST.

1907 I. ZANGWILL *Ghetto Comedies* 412 Russia is to be saved..by the Integralists, who alone maintain the purity of the Social Revolutionary programme. **1922** *Glasgow Herald* 23 Jan. 11 The so-called 'integralists' who held that every good Catholic should see eye to eye with the Holy Father in everything. **1930** *Times Educ. Suppl.* 3 May 197/2 The schools or coteries of the last few decades—the symbolists, ..integralists,..and so forth. **1938** *Sun* (Baltimore) 12 May 1/1 To smash completely the outlawed integralist Greenshirt organization. **1967** C. SETON-WATSON *Italy from Liberalism to Fascism* vii. 267 His [*sc.* Ferri's] contribution to the restoration of party unity was..inspired by the 'integralist' formula of 'Neither to right nor to left, but straight ahead'. *Ibid.* xi. 437 So far from being an integralist, he had during his years at Bologna come under suspicion of modernist sympathies. **1968** R. K. MERTON *Social Theory* (rev. ed.) III. xv. 529 He [*sc.* Sorokin] adopts an 'integralist' conception of truth.

integrality (ɪntɪ'grælɪtɪ). [prob. ad. med.L. **integrālitās*, f. *integrālis* INTEGRAL: see -ITY; cf. F. *integralité* (Cotgr.), It. *integralità* 'a whole entire masse' (Florio, 1611).] The condition of being integral (see prec. A. 3); wholeness, entirety, completeness: = INTEGRITY 1.

1611 COTGR., *Integralité*, integralitie, wholeness. **1627** DONNE *Serm.* cviii. IV. 476 Here is the latitude, the Totality, the Integrality of the means of salvation. **1651** BIGGS *New Disp.* ¶239 What God made and ordained in its integrality. **1728** EARBERY tr. *Burnet's State Dead* I. 87 There the Integrality that gives Denomination to the Species is to be found. **1838** GLADSTONE *State in Rel. Ch.* (1839) 173 Establishing the independence and integrality of the nation as a collective body. **1853** *Tait's Mag.* XX. 265 The maintenance of the Empire of the Sultans in its integrality is necessary.

integrally ('ɪntɪgrəlɪ), *adv.* [f. as prec. + -LY[2]. Cf. med.L. *integrāliter* entirely, wholly.] **a.** In an integral manner; as a whole, in its entirety; completely, entirely, wholly.

1471 RIPLEY *Comp. Alch.* II. v. in Ashm. (1652) 136 When the Erth ys integrally yncynerat. **1649** JER. TAYLOR *Gt. Exemp.* II. Disc. viii. 74 We should choose vertue..and pursue it integrally and make it the businesse of our lives. **1816** BENTHAM *Chrestom.* App. ii. Wks. 1843 VIII. 188 The only part of speech which is perfectly simple in its import, and at the same time integrally significant, is the noun-substantive. **1850** LYNCH *Theo. Trin.* x. 200 The more an individual is integrally a man, the more may he know of man.

b. As an integral whole: see INTEGRAL A. 1.

a **1680** CHARNOCK *Attrib. God, God a Spirit* (1682) 116 Whatsoever is compounded of many parts, depends either essentially or integrally upon those parts. **1936** COLVIN & STANLEY *Turning & Boring Pract.* ix. 131 Gisholt lathes have been materially changed in design and construction. Headstocks are now cast integrally with the bed. **1952** S. E. RUSINOFF *Forging & Forming Metals* iv. 55 Small steam hammers have the anvil and frame cast integrally, but large hammers have a separate anvil. **1972** *Sci. Amer.* Jan. 49/2 (Advt.), An integral peak-reading meter lets you optimize record level without using a scope. Options include a 5 to 30 foot loop adaptor, an interrupting voice channel, and an inverter for 12 or 28 VDC..all integrally mounted.

integrand ('ɪntɪgrænd). *Math.* [ad. L. *integrand-us*, gerundive of *integrāre* (see INTEGRATE *v.*): see -AND[2].] An expression that is to be integrated.

1897 H. F. BAKER *Abel's Theorem* xviii. 561 The integrand of the Abelian integral u_r is single-valued on the Riemann surface. **1937** *Proc. Cambr. Philos. Soc.* XXXIII. 374 It is natural to approximate by expanding the integrand in powers of *z*. **1968** FOX & MAYERS *Computing Methods for Scientists & Engineers* ix. 178 We illustrate this process..by considering the computation of the integral $I = \int_0^1 (0{\cdot}92 \cosh x - \cos x)\,dx$... Table 9.3 gives the tabulated values of the integrand and its differences.

integrant ('ɪntɪgrənt), *a.* (*sb.*) [ad. L. *integrānt-em*, pr. pple. of *integrāre*: see INTEGRATE *v.* Cf. F. *intégrant* (1690 in Hatz.-Darm.).]

Of parts: Making up or contributing to make up a whole, constituent, component; essential to the completeness of the whole: = INTEGRAL A. 1.

integrant parts, in F. *parties intégrantes*, is etymologically more correct than the usual *integral parts*.

1637 GILLESPIE *Eng. Pop. Cerem.* III. viii. 186 The Church consisteth of two integrant parts, *viz.* Pastors and Sheepe. **1651** CHARLETON *Ephes. & Cimm. Matrons* II. (1668) 38 An Appendix, or rather an integrant part of his fellow. **1727** [see INTEGRAL A. 1]. **1773** HORSLEY in *Phil. Trans.* LXIV. 246 Imagine the integrant particles of A to be equal in quantity of matter and bulk..to the integrant particles of B, severally. **1794** BURKE *Rep. Lords' Jrnls.* Wks. 1842 II. 598 These judges..are no integrant and necessary part of that court. **1836–7** [see INTEGRAL A. 2]. **1849** KEMBLE *Saxons in Eng.* II. II. vi. 235 There is no reason to suppose that the ceorls did not form an integrant part of the shire-moot. **1875** H. C. WOOD *Therap.* (1879) 91 Iron constitutes a necessary integrant portion of the red blood-corpuscles.

B. *sb.* That which integrates; a component.

1824 COLERIDGE *Aids Refl.* (1848) I. 261 It is the differentia of immortality, of which the assimilative power of faith and love is the integrant, and the life in Christ the integration. **1827** COLEBROOKE *Misc. Ess.* (1837) I. 389 The aggregate and its integrants are utterly different.

integraph ('ɪntɪgrɑːf, -æ-). [ad. F. *intégraphe* (B. Abdank-Abakanowicz 1885, in *La Lumière électr.* 17 Oct. 111/1), f. *intégral* INTEGRAL *a.* and *sb.*, *intégrer* to INTEGRATE *v.*: see -GRAPH.] Any of various kinds of apparatus which mechanically draw a curve representing the variation in the integral of some given curve or function as a limit or parameter varies.

1885 *Min. Proc. Inst. Civil Engin.* LXXXII. 162 The machines that he [*sc.* B. Abdank-Abakanowicz] had called briefly 'Integraphs' traced these curves mechanically. **1902** *Encycl. Brit.* XXX. 582/1 While an integrator determines the value of a definite integral, hence a mere constant, an integraph gives the value of an indefinite integral, which is a function of *x*. **1927** *Jrnl. Franklin Inst.* CCIII. 64 Mechanical integrators usually evaluate the definite integral between given fixed limits... The present machine, which we have called an integraph, since it records the result of an integration in the form of a plot or graph, has therefore been developed to evaluate *F*(*x*) against *x* from the expression $F(x) = \int_a^x f_1(x)f_2(x)dx$ where f_1 and f_2 are known functions, formal or empirical. **1931** *Ibid.* CCXII. 77 The Photo-Electric Integraph..extends the range of practical solution of mathematical problems through its usefulness in the evaluation of integrals having a variable parameter within the integrand. **1961** S. FIFER *Analogue Computation* IV. xxv. 968 The development of the harmonic analyzer is closely associated with the development of two devices, (1) the planimeter,..and (2) the integraph, which draws a graph of the indefinite integral of a function.

integrate ('ɪntɪgrət), *a.* [ad. L. *integrāt-us*, pa. pple. of *integrāre*: see next.] **1.** Made up, as a whole, of separate (integrant) parts, composite; belonging to such a whole; complete, entire, perfect: = INTEGRAL A. 2, 3.

1485 [implied in INTEGRATELY]. **1599** B. JONSON *Cynthia's Rev.* II. iv, Exceeding wittie and integrate [said of a joke]. **1697** tr. *Burgersdicius his Logick* I. xiv. 46–7 An Integral Whole is that which has Part out of Part... This Whole termed Mathematical; because Quantity is of Mathematical Consideration: Vulgarly, Integral, more properly Integrate. **1836–7** [see INTEGRAL A. 2]. **1837–8** SIR W. HAMILTON *Logic* iii. (1866) III. 51 We may consider Logic either as a universal, or as an integrate whole. **1888** J. T. GULICK in *Linn. Soc. Jrnl.* XX. 249/2 A transition from Integrate Fecundity to Segregate Fecundity usually takes place at a point in the history of evolution intermediate between the formation of an incipient variety and a strongly marked species. **1898** *Daily News* 20 Apr. 5/5 The people of Spain are for the war to keep integrate their possessions in Cuba.

2. *Psychol.* Of, pertaining to, or designating people with strong eidetic imagery (particularly in the theories of Jaensch).

1930 O. OESER tr. *Jaensch's Eidetic Imagery* III. 93 In these individuals functions that later are separate still interpenetrate one another to a high degree and influence each other. That is why we call them 'integrate'. The

integrate type is an earlier one from the evolutionary point of view. *Ibid.* 105 The integrate and disintegrate types are true fundamental forms of human existence corresponding, in a sense, to the fundamental forms discovered by biology. **1931** *Brit. Jrnl. Psychol.* July 94 When the child is in an integrate state, it should not be forced to behave in a disintegrate manner. **1943** H. READ *Educ. through Art* IV. iv. 81 Younger children and primitive peoples belong to an earlier evolutionary type which Jaensch calls 'integrate'.

integrate ('ɪntɪgreɪt), *v.* [f. ppl. stem of L. *integrāre* to make whole, f. *integer*, *integr-* whole.]

1. a. *trans.* To render entire or complete; to make up, compose, constitute (a whole): said of the parts or elements. ? *Obs.*

1638 CHILLINGW. *Relig. Prot.* I. ii. §159. 117 The particular doctrines which integrate Christianity. **1654** JER. TAYLOR *Real Pres.* 153 Matter and form are substances, and those that integrate all physical and compound substances: but till yesterday it was never heard that accidents could. *a* **1716** SOUTH *Twelve Serm.* (1744) II. 294 Did men consider .. how many such good actions are required to integrate and perfect a legal righteousness.

b. To complete or perfect (what is imperfect) by the addition of the necessary parts.

1675 R. BURTHOGGE *Causa Dei* 125 Vertues..that Integrate the Humane Nature, without which it would be Lame, Imperfect, Defective. **1822–56** DE QUINCEY *Confess.* (1862) 58 The fragmentary contribution of one being integrated by the fragmentary contributions of others. **1858** GLADSTONE *Homer* III. 297 The two sets of Phœnician reports are in this way oddly brought to integrate one another.

2. a. To put or bring together (parts or elements) so as to form one whole; to combine into a whole. (Sometimes with allusion to 3.)

1802 *Edin. Rev.* I. 214 Time performs the office of integrating the infinitesimal parts of which this progression is made up. **1840** J. H. GREEN *Vital Dynam.* 103 Tending to integrate all into one comprehensive whole. **1861** J. G. SHEPPARD *Fall Rome* i. 36 This immense variety of 'peoples, nations, and languages' which Rome had integrated into a coherent whole.

b. To bring (racially or culturally differentiated peoples) into equal membership of a society or system; to cease to segregate (racially). Also *intr.*, to become integrated. (See INTEGRATION 1 c.)

1948 *Richmond* (Virginia) *Times-Dispatch* 5 Aug. 1/8 (*headline*) Democrats 'integrate' Negroes for campaign. **1949** W. E. BARKER in *Jrnl. Racial Affairs* I. 1. 25 In the same way it can be seen that were South Africa to try to integrate her widely differing races, she would only create far greater problems than such a policy could ever solve. **1962** *Daily Tel.* 2 Aug. 10/2 It might be supposed that in doing these things for its people [i.e. of Tristan da Cunha], something had also been done to them: that they had..been 'integrated'. Not so. They want to go home, with an intensity and unanimity of desire. **1964** MRS. L. B. JOHNSON *White House Diary* 10 June (1970) 163 A girl who was one of the first students to be integrated at Little Rock was praised by her counselor. **1964** L. NKOSI *Rhythm of Violence* 46 Why don't Indians in this country ever 'integrate'? **1966** *New Statesman* 22 Apr. 575/1 Those children who came knowing some English integrated well, but, when we threw those who knew none into the maelstrom, they sank... No one was going to integrate without first being able to communicate. **1969** *Times* 30 Apr. 8/3 The Americans intend to make the scheme permanent..but we advised the experiment to see how well they integrate. **1972** *Nature* 24 Mar. 133/1 Old people, sick people and isolated people need access to a telephone if they are to be fully integrated with the rest of society.

3. a. *Math.* To find or calculate the integral of (a function or equation): see INTEGRAL B. 4. Also *absol.* to perform the operation of integration.

to integrate by parts: see INTEGRATION 2.

1727–41 CHAMBERS *Cycl.* s.v. *Calculus*, Any variable or flowing quantity can be differenced; but, *vice versa*, any differential cannot be integrated. **1778** PLAYFAIR in *Phil. Trans.* LXVIII. 334 To integrate such equations. **1790** WILDBORE *ibid.* LXXX. 520 The product of a particle of the body into the square of its distance from such axis, when integrated through the whole body. **1802** WOODHOUSE *ibid.* XCII. 94 To integrate these differential equations. **1804** *Ibid.* XCIV. 266 Multiply each side by $d\theta$, and integrate. **1831** BREWSTER *Nat. Magic* xi. (1833) 294 To integrate innumerable equations of finite differences. **1885** WATSON & BURBURY *Math. Th. Electr. & Magn.* I. 1 Integrating by parts between $x = x_1$ and $x = x_2$.

b. *transf.* and *fig.*; *spec.* to indicate or register the mean value, or the total sum of all the portions or elements, of some physical quantity: see INTEGRATING *ppl. a.* below.

1864 WEBSTER, *Integrate*..2. To indicate the whole; to give the sum or total; as, an integrating anemometer; that is, one that indicates or registers the entire action or motion of the wind in a given time. **1876** *Trans. Victor. Inst.* 24 Integrate a moral phenomenon between limits *a* and *b*, your result is a good action. **1881** *Nature* No. 625. 582 We not only integrate through the depth of the atmosphere, but also over the whole surface of the star..This is equivalent to the superposition of innumerable separate spectra.

Hence '**integrating** *vbl. sb.* and *ppl. adj.*

integrating spectroscope, a spectroscope in which the slit receives light from all parts of a luminous object and blends it all together to form a single united spectrum: opposed to *analysing spectroscope*; ***integrating circuit*** Electr., a circuit whose output is the integral, with respect to time, of the input; ***integrating factor*** Math., an expression by which a differential equation may be multiplied to turn it into an exact equation (and therefore integrable as it stands); ***integrating meter***, a meter which indicates the total amount of one quantity (e.g. electric charge passed) by effectively integrating, with respect to time, another (e.g. electric current).

1654 WHITLOCK *Zootomia* 555 The Universe, whereof he is an Integrating part. **1859** G. BOOLE *Treat. Differential Equations* iv. 55 To every differential equation of the form $Mdx + Ndy = 0$, pertain an infinite number of integrating factors, all of which are included under a single functional expression. **1874** L. STEPHEN *Hours in Library* (1892) II. vii. 215 There is a continuous series of integrating and disintegrating processes. **1898** *Daily News* 15 Feb. 8/4 All the instruments, with the exception of the integrating spectroscope, were most successful. **1902** *Encycl. Brit.* XXX. 597/1 All the above forms of house meters are called continuously integrating meters, in that the operation of recording or obtaining the time-integral of the current or power is continuous. **1943** *Gloss. Terms Electr. Engin.* (*B.S.I.*) 75 *Integrating frequency meter* (master frequency meter), an instrument for integrating the number of cycles through which the supply voltage has passed, and enabling this to be compared with the number through which it would have passed had the frequency been maintained at the prescribed value. **1948** L. JÁNOSSY *Cosmic Rays* ii. 43 Some authors make use of an integrating circuit which allows [one] to read the average counting rate at any instant. **1952** E. MOLLOY *Electr. Instruments* 37 The induction disc principle is now adopted as the basic pattern for all types of alternating current integrating meters throughout the world. **1961** H. J. REICH *Functional Circuits & Oscillators* iv. 18 Integrating circuits find applications in..electronic instruments and controls,..in analog computers and in circuits for the generation of linearly rising voltages. **1962** T. M. APOSTOL *Calculus* II. v. 241 A differential equation may have more than one integrating factor. **1973** M. WOODHOUSE *Blue Bone* iii. 24 The integrating Dekatron counter I was designing.

'**integrated**, *ppl. a.* [f. INTEGRATE *v.*, or f. L. *integrāt-us* ppl. a., INTEGRATE + -ED.]

a. Combined into a whole; united; undivided. Also of a personality in which the component elements combine harmoniously.

a **1586** SIDNEY *Arcadia* (1613) 571 A certaine *Pulchra puella profecto* elected and constituted by the integrated determination of all this topographical region. *a* **1661** FULLER *Worthies, Lancashire* II. (1662) 120 The integrated and incorporate Rector unto whom the parsonage was appropriated. **1847** H. ROGERS *Ess.* I. v. 262 The mind.. cannot comprehend them at a glance, and feel at once their integrated force, but must examine them in detail by successive acts of mind. **1941** *Brit. Jrnl. Psychol.* Apr. 298 Among the individuals studied..it was possible to distinguish..*integrated* personalities, in which conflicting drives had been reconciled and were now functioning in harmony with each other. **1945** *Psychol. Rev.* LII. 65/2 Later we shall see that an integrated personality does indeed have a kind of 'autonomy' which gives it a certain limited immunity to the Law of Effect. **1950** O. H. MOWRER *Learning Theory & Personality Dynamics* I. ii. 59 When, however, opposing impulses are more nearly matched, the submerged one is likely to exert its influence..by diminishing the smoothness and efficiency of the main stream of integrated behavior. **1954** G. W. ALLPORT *Nature of Prejudice* v. xx. 339 What vanishes in an integrated personality are the racial bogies and traditional scapegoats who have nothing, really, to do with life's woes. **1963** A. HERON *Towards Quaker View of Sex* v. 48 Idealism can be a sign of spontaneous and selfless devotion in an integrated personality. **1973** *Lancet* 24 Feb. 441/2 The plaintiff was well integrated and had learned to live with the problem.

b. Uniting in one system several constituents previously regarded as separate; ***integrated circuit***, a small unit or package which is made as a single indivisible structure (such as a chip) and is electrically equivalent to a conventional circuit of many separate components.

1947 F. C. SIMMONS in *Jrnl. Forestry* XLV. 347/2 At the roadside, or at the using plant, the electric chain-saw, or one of the highly efficient circular-saw cutting-up plants,..can divide these tree lengths into raw material for the products to which they are best suited. This type of logging, which we call 'integrated logging' should result in higher returns from the logging job. **1954** WEBSTER Add., *Integrated logging*, a system of logging planned to remove in one cutting all usable timber and to separate the primary products and distribute them to industries where they will bring the highest returns. **1958** J. T. WELLMARK in *Aviation Age Res. & Devel. Technical Handbk.* 1958–1959 F-6/1 One promising technique uses the 'integrated electronic device' concept. *Ibid.*, The true 'integrated device' can do the jobs of both active and passive components. **1959** *IRE Trans. Electronic Computers* VIII. 103/1 Some specific examples of integrated logic circuits..are shown in the figures below. **1962** *Electronics, Reliability & Microminiaturization* I. 184/1 In integrated circuits the [circuit] element may be a region in a block of the material rather than a separate device. **1962** A. BATTERSBY *Guide to Stock Control* x. 96 Looking ahead in the field of Integrated Data Processing, we can foresee the situation in which the machine will prepare the advice note and invoice, classify and analyse the sales, calculate ROL and ROQ for each item and go on to send out orders automatically. **1964** *Times Rev. Industry* Apr. 49/2 It will be an integrated mill—trees will go in one end and fine paper will emerge from the other. **1967** *Times Rev. Industry* Mar. 46/1 Where once the circuit designer had to employ comparatively large components mounted on some sort of backing sheet..now he can often put in an integrated circuit, in which the separate components are commonly created in miniscule form on the surface of thin wafers of silicon by complex processing. **1969** A. C. TICKLE *Thin-Film Transistors* i. 3 The first advanced all-thin-film integrated circuit, in which *both* active and passive devices were produced by thin-film deposition techniques, was produced by Weimer in 1965. It was designed for scanning an image sensor and contained 360 thin-film transistors, 180 diodes, 360 resistors, and 180 capacitors. **1970** F. C. FITCHEN et al. *Electronic Integrated Circuits* i. 4 The monolithic integrated circuit is an IC whose [circuit] elements are formed in situ upon or within a semiconductor substrate with at least one of the elements formed within the substrate... In a multichip integrated circuit, the elements are formed on or within two or more semiconductor chips that are separately attached to a substrate. **1970** 'J. EARL' *Tuners & Amplifiers* i. 16 The majority of Class B and Class AB amplifiers..are of the so-called 'integrated' kind. This means that the preamplifiers and control unit..are built into the same housing—usually on the same chassis—as the power amplifiers and that a common power supply feeds both sections. **1973** *Physics Bull.* May 297/3 The continual recurrence of the same names in different fields of study is ..in no way to be confused with, or used to justify, the contemporary rush to some illusory 'integrated science' concept.

c. Of institutions, groups, etc., which are not divided by considerations based on race or culture (see INTEGRATE *v.* 2 b).

1948 *Richmond* (Virginia) *Times-Dispatch* 5 Aug. 1/8 This will be an integrated rather than a segregated operation. **1956** *N.Y. Times* 1 Oct., Approximately 2,400,000 Negro and 6,500,000 white pupils remained in segregated classes. Integrated school districts numbered 780; segregated numbered 3,000. **1958** *Newsweek* 29 Sept. 22 (*title*) Integrated schools or none. **1959** *Spectator* 11 Sept. 319/1 The newly integrated junior high school at Little Rock re-opened, but not before three bombs had gone off. **1965** B. SWEET-ESCOTT *Baker St. Irreg.* vi. 167 My assignment at A.F.H.Q. was with the planners. It was my first introduction to a really integrated staff... It was difficult to have a word in private with any of the British members of it because it was a rule that Americans and British should share rooms. **1974** *Times* 14 Jan. 12/4 Southern schools are now more integrated than their northern counterparts.

'**integrately**, *adv. rare.* [f. INTEGRATE *a.* + -LY[2].] As an undivided whole; entirely.

1485 in *Proc. Suffolk Inst. Archæol.* V. 63 [I wyll that] ye forseid iiij pecs of londe & j pece of medwe w[t] her pertynencs integratly remayn onto myn sone Robrte. *Ibid.*, Than I wyll ye seyd mesuage pece of londe & pece of woode w[t] her pertynencs remayn holly and integratly on to ye forseyd John.

integration (ɪntɪ'greɪʃən). [ad. L. *integrātiōn-em* (in L. only in sense 'renewal, restoration to wholeness'), n. of action from *integrāre* to INTEGRATE. Cf. mod.F. *intégration* (1700 in Hatz.-Darm.).] The action or process of integrating.

1. a. The making up or compostion of a whole by adding together or combining the separate parts or elements; combination into an integral whole: a making whole or entire. (Often opposed to *differentiation*; sometimes with allusion to sense 2.)

1620 T. GRANGER *Div. Logike* 178 The Integrall in Logike ..respecteth..integration whereby the totall is made a totall of all his members together. **1658** PHILLIPS, *Integration*, a making whole, or restoring. **1846** GROTE *Greece* I. xxi. II. 201 Their first permanent arrangement and integration was delayed for three centuries and accomplished at last only by the taste of Peisistratus. **1855** H. SPENCER *Princ. Psychol.* (1872) I. III. x. 376 Out of co-ordination, there grows up integration. **1873** G. HENSLOW *Evol. Liv. Things* x. 129 Physical conditions will ever give rise to differentiation in Beings, together with its concomitant phenomenon, integration.

b. *Psychol.* The combining of diverse parts into a complex whole; a complex state the parts of which are distinguishable; the harmonious combination of the different elements in a personality. Also *attrib.*

1855 H. SPENCER *Princ. Psychol.* III. xiv. 481 Progress in integration has been a necessary accompaniment of progress in speciality and complexity. **1893** J. M. BALDWIN *Elem. Psychol.* 36 Integration, therefore, represents a structural change in the direction both of simplicity and of complexity. **1931** *Brit. Jrnl. Psychol.* July 25 A more adequate psychological theory..speaks of the 'integration' of the constituent sensations into a perception. **1937** L. T. HOPKINS *Integration* i. 2 Integration must be the shorthand word to describe the process involved in this intelligent ongoing, interacting, adjusting behavior. **1938** L. P. THORPE *Psychol. Found. Personality* ix. 434 Perhaps we are warranted then in using the word integration with the understanding that it stands for a wholeness in personality which gives direction to the coordination of parts. **1943** H. READ *Educ. through Art* IV. iv. 81 Jaensch's next step is to relate his classification to the degree of integration which the individual establishes between his mental imagery and the external world. **1963** LANGNER & MICHAEL *Life Stress & Mental Health* xvi. 460 Integration involves the incorporation of the 'thou shalt nots' as well as the 'thou shalts', the acceptance of the middle-class rules of the game as well as the goal of winning.

c. The bringing into equal membership of a common society those groups or persons previously discriminated against on racial or cultural grounds.

1940 T. J. HAARHOFF *S. Afr. & Crisis Mod. Civilization* 19 For the great task that awaits us in South Africa is a task of integration, of making the Union into a unity. **1949** *Jrnl. Racial Affairs* I. 1. 25 Although..assimilation would destroy the racial differences in South Africa, it would necessitate the prior integration of the cultures—a very difficult and uncertain process. Apart from that one argument, there is practically no other logical reason in support of either racial or cultural integration. **1951** J. D. L. KRUGER *Bantustan: Study in Pract. Apartheid* iii. 15 In fact it is difficult if not impossible to think of a single aspect of integration which could be regarded as beneficial to the white population. **1955** *Ann. Amer. Acad. Pol. & Social Sci.* CCCII. 25/1 The frontier for race relations has been shifting more and more to the housing field... The degree of integration in the schools now depends very largely on the residential pattern. **1968** *Listener* 26 Dec. 855/3, I define integration not as a flattening process of assimilation but as equal opportunity accompanied by cultural diversity in an atmosphere of

mutual tolerance. **1970** *Times* 23 Mar. 13/3 It seemed that all we had to do to achieve integration was to sit down at enough lunch counters together.

2. *Math.* The operation of finding the integral of a given function or equation (see INTEGRAL B. 4); the inverse of differentiation.

integration by parts: integration by means of the formula $\int udv = uv - \int vdu$, where u and v are any functions of the same variable. ***constant of integration***: an arbitrary constant which must be added to get the complete expression for an integral. ***sign of integration***: the sign ∫ denoting an integral (see INTEGRAL B. 4 a).

1727–41 CHAMBERS *Cycl.* s.v. *Calculus*, The integration is known to be justly performed, if the quantity found..being differenced, produce that proposed to be summed. **1837** BREWSTER *Magnet.* 173 A fluxionary equation..by the integration of which the curve may be constructed. **1877** B. WILLIAMSON *Int. Calc.* (ed. 2) vi. §90 The process of integration may be regarded as that of finding the limit of the sum of the series of values of a differential $f(x)dx$, when x varies by indefinitely small increments from any one assigned value to another... For example, in seeking the area of a curve, we conceive it divided into an indefinite number of suitable elementary areas, of which we seek to determine the sum by a process of integration.

integrational (ɪntɪˈgreɪʃənəl), *a.* [f. INTEGRATION + -AL.] Of or pertaining to integration.

1937 G. W. ALLPORT *Personality* (1938) III. xiii. 354 From each condensed portrait (called by the experimenter 'integrational hypothesis'), the judges predicted what responses the eight subjects would make. **1957** V. W. TURNER *Schism & Continuity in Afr. Soc.* p. xxi, Ndembu ritual..compensates for the integrational deficiencies of a politically unstable society. **1960** J. B. CARROLL in Saporta && Bastian *Psycholinguistics* (1961) 339/2 She tested decoding....and encoding functions with respect to semantic, grammatical, and integrational responses.

integrationist (ɪntɪˈgreɪʃənɪst), *sb.* and *a.* [f. INTEGRATION + -IST.] **A.** *sb.* An adherent or advocate of integration, esp. political or racial.

1955 *N.Y. Times* 1 June 29/3 The initial reaction, including segregationists and integrationists, overridingly stressed the court's ruling. **1956** *Atlantic Monthly* Nov. 49/1 It is because there the adolescent and 'unprejudiced' mind can be reached that the integrationists have chosen the Southern schools as their primary target. **1959** *Listener* 27 Aug. 305/1 It is becoming less and less possible for the 'integrationists' to paper over the cracks by references to General de Gaulle's 'silences'. **1963** *Economist* 23 Feb. 695/2 This racial appeal is disliked by integrationists. **1971** *Black Scholar* Jan. 52/1 In the work of black authors who are integrationists a tacitly separatist or ethnically independent element appears frequently.

B. *adj.* Of, or pertaining to, persons or policies favouring integration, esp. political or racial.

1956 *Newsweek* 21 May 17/1 A political unknown named Sumter Lowry, who ran on the single plank of preserving segregation, got 130,000 votes. An integrationist candidate got 5,000. **1958** *Times* 11 Nov. 8/1 The solitary list is strongly integrationist, and is led by Azem Ouali, a prominent member of the Algeria-Sahara public safety committee. **1968** *Ann. Amer. Acad. Pol. & Social Sci.* CCCLXXVI. 199/2 These Negroes fervently embraced an integrationist ideology. **1973** *Black World* Mar. 34 The integrationist tendencies of the Negro intellectuals. **1973** E. BULLINS *Theme is Blackness* 4 The militant integrationist syndrome.

integrative (ˈɪntɪgreɪtɪv), *a.* [f. L. *integrāt-*, ppl. stem (see INTEGRATE *v.*) + -IVE.] Having the quality of integrating; tending to integrate.

1862 H. SPENCER *First Princ.* II. xiii. §105 (1875) 304 This chapter opened by briefly specifying the conditions under which Evolution is integrative only. **1879** W. E. HEARN *Aryan Househ.* 262 Public opinion, and afterwards positive law, forbad that any Hellen, or any Quirite, should be reduced to slavery. But the integrative tendency went no further. **1906** C. S. SHERRINGTON (*title*) The integrative action of the nervous system. **1937** [see DOMINATIVE *a.* 1 c]. **1937** G. W. ALLPORT *Personality* (1938) II. v. 138 Whatever condition makes for mental health is called 'integrative', whatever condition makes for mental difficulty is called 'disintegrative'. **1953** J. S. HUXLEY *Evolution in Action* iv. 91 What we may call integrative emotions, like love. **1957** M. BANTON *W. Afr. City* ix. 179 Up to this point the integrative effects of the companies have been stressed. **1967** *Amer. Pol. Sci. Rev.* LXI. 91 Far from finding a stagnation of integrative processes since 1958, I would argue that.. European integration may have moved into full gear only *since* 1958. **1972** *World Archaeol.* III. 231 He [*sc.* V. G. Childe] saw culture as an essentially integrative device.

integrator (ˈɪntɪgreɪtə(r)). [a. L. *integrātor*, n. of action from *integrāre* to INTEGRATE. (In L. only in sense 'renewer'.)] One who or that which integrates; *spec.* an instrument for indicating or registering the total amount or mean value of some physical quantity, as area, temperature, etc.: see INTEGRATE *v.* 3 b.

1876 W. THOMSON in *Proc. R. Soc.* XXIV. 269, I have made many attempts to plan a mechanical integrator which should give solutions by successive approximations... We have the instrument founded on my brother's disk-, globe-, and cylinder-integrator. **1879** THOMSON & TAIT *Nat. Phil.* I. I. 497, I have made many attempts to plan a mechanical integrator which should give solutions by successive approximations. **1884** S. P. THOMPSON *Dynamo-Electr. Machinery* iv. 59 Fig. 48 gives the curve as integrated..for me from Fig. 47 by the aid of the very ingenious curve integrator of Mr. C. Vernon Boys. **1898** *Daily News* 24 Jan. 5/6 The photographs, including those taken with the integrator, are very good. **1931** *Jrnl. Franklin Inst.* CCXII. 450 There has been an enormous change in technique since the time when Sir William Thomson first suggested..that the integrators developed by his brother could be connected together and thus forced to produce solutions of differential equations. **1938** *Math. Gaz.* XXII. 343 Integrators... Any continuously variable gear can act as an integrating mechanism. **1955** T. L. MARTIN *Electronic Circuits* 618 Waveform relationships in integrators and differentiators. **1964** *Ann. N.Y. Acad. Sci.* CXV. 571 Until recently, analog computers have depended on the use of relays for mode control, switching, and resetting of integrators.

†**inˈtegre**, *a.* *Obs. rare.* [a. F. *intègre* (1567 in Hatz.-Darm.) = Pr. *integre*, Sp. and It. *integro*, ad. L. *integr-um* (nom. *integer*) whole: see INTEGER.] Having the character of integrity; upright, honest, sincere.

1526 ABP. LEE *Let. to Wolsey* (*MS. Cott. Vesp. C. III.* lf. 213), Your innocent, integre and at all points unblamefull mynd towards his Mageste.

†**inˈtegrious**, *a.* *Obs. rare.* [irreg. f. F. *intègre* or L. *integer*, *integr-* (see INTEGER) + -I-OUS; (as if from a L. *integris.*) Cf. INTEGROUS.] Marked by integrity. Hence †**inˈtegriously** *adv.*

1658 SLINGSBY *Diary* (1836) 201 Such was their integrious candor and intimacy to me in my greatest extremes. *Ibid.* 208 Being so integriously grounded, as it admitted no alloy or mixture with By-respects or self-interests.

integripallial (ɪntɛgrɪˈpælɪəl), *a.* *Zool.* Also **integro-**. [f. L. *integri-*, regular comb. form of *integer* whole + *palli-um* cloak + -AL[1]. The form *integro-* is not in accordance with L. analogies.] Having the pallial line not broken or indented; applied to a division of lamellibranchiate molluscs, in which the siphons are small or absent. Also **integriˈpalliate** *a.* (Opp. to *sinupallial*, *-ate.*)

1862 DANA *Elem. Geology* 192 This division, the sinupallial, was far less common in the Silurian than the integripallial, or that in which the tube was wanting. **1875** BLAKE *Zool.* 270 The integropalliate Siphonida. **1877** HUXLEY *Anat. Inv. Anim.* viii. 481 Hence the distinction of integripalliate and sinupalliate as applied to the Lamellibranchs which have the pallial line evenly rounded or notched. **1882** OGILVIE, *Integropallial.*

integrist (ˈɪntɪgrɪst). Also **intégriste**. [F. *intégriste.*] = INTEGRALIST. Hence **ˈintegrism** = INTEGRALISM.

1907 *Dublin Rev.* Jan. 38 The Carlists and Integrists, who muster half a dozen deputies between them. **1938** *Downside Rev.* LVI. 154 Benedict XV..told Cardinal Billot that he wanted to hear no more talk of 'integrism'. He demanded that..where Rome had not decided, all should be free to state their views without being attacked as heretical. **1969** R. MANHEIM tr. *Corbin's Creative Imagination in Ṣūfism* Introd. 41 We shall let Ibn 'Arabī describe the encounter between the integrist Aristotelian master and the young man. **1970** J. ARDAGH *New France* xi. 577 The tradition of integrism will not die easily in France. *Ibid.*, The unreconciled integrists represent only a small proportion of practising Catholics. **1971** *Month* May 146/2 [The] silent assembly of *intégristes* at Versailles in November 1970. *Ibid.* July 17/1 The French *intégriste* who attended one of the sessions and refused the kiss of peace.

†**integritive** (ɪnˈtɛgrɪtɪv), *a.* *Obs. rare*[−1]. [irreg. f. INTEGRITY + -IVE: cf. *quantitive* = *quantitative.*] Marked by integrity; upright, sincere.

1784 BURNS *Comm.-pl. Bk.* Aug., To maintain an integritive conduct towards our fellow-creatures.

integrity (ɪnˈtɛgrɪtɪ). [ad. L. *integritās* wholeness, entireness, completeness, integrity, chastity, purity, f. *integer*, *integr-* whole, INTEGER. Perh. in part a. F. *integrité* (*c*1420 in Hatz.-Darm.).]

1. The condition of having no part or element taken away or wanting; undivided or unbroken state; material wholeness, completeness, entirety.

1533 MORE *Answ. Poysoned Bk.* Wks. 1095/1 Not yͤ sacrifice nor oblacion, whyche to the integritie therof requyreth both the formes. *a* **1677** HALE *Prim. Orig. Man.* I. iii. 93 Are there not among men some that want the integrity of their Limbs? **1756–82** J. WARTON *Ess. Pope* (ed. 4) I. III. 101 The poem before us is by no means destitute of a just integrity, and a lucid order. **1833** LYELL *Princ. Geol.* III. 192 The integrity of the cones..shows that the country has not been agitated by violent earthquakes. **1838** SIR W. HAMILTON *Logic* xxiv. (1866) II. 2 Method, considered in its integrity, consists of two processes,—Analysis and Synthesis. **1868** G. DUFF *Pol. Surv.* 44 To work for the integrity of the Ottoman Empire, and at the same time to promote its dismemberment, is to stultify one's-self. **1870** F. R. WILSON *Ch. Lindisfarne* 68 The walls were standing.. though not in their integrity.

†**b.** Something undivided; an integral whole.

1620 T. GRANGER *Div. Logike* 110 They be privatives of Originall integrities. *Ibid.* 111 They are somethings, *id est*, pravities contrarie to created integrities.

2. The condition of not being marred or violated; unimpaired or uncorrupted condition; original perfect state; soundness.

c **1450** *Mirour Saluacioun* 4316 When he [Christ] was borne savyng his moders integritee [*glossed* hir maydenhod]. **1550** BALE *Apol.* 122 (R.) In these and other lyke factes, was faythes integrite broken, whych is the true maydenhede of yͤ soule. **1561** T. NORTON *Calvin's Inst.* II. 114 He did but restore the law to her integritie. **1638** F. JUNIUS *Paint. of Ancients* 118 Why the integritie of workmanship is now adayes put down by false and adulterate wayes. **1650** BULWER *Anthropomet.* 224 Natures constant provision to preserve virginal integrity. **1783** JOHNSON *Let. to Mrs. Thrale* 19 June, This prayer, that I might try the integrity of my faculties, I made in Latin verse. **1881** WESTCOTT & HORT *Grk. N.T.* Introd. §85 Any investigation of the ultimate integrity of the text.

3. In moral sense. †**a.** Unimpaired moral state; freedom from moral corruption; innocence, sinlessness. *Obs.*

1561 T. NORTON *Calvin's Inst.* I. 54 In this integritie, man had freewil, wherby if he would he might haue atteined eternall life. **1622** T. SCOTT *Belg. Pismire* 1 Adam in his integritie should have wrought, but without wearinesse. **1675** TRAHERNE *Chr. Ethics* 55 In his corruption, he might possibly retain a sence of that nature and life, which he enjoyed in his integrity. **1678** OWEN *Mind of God* ii. 41 The State of Integrity.

b. Soundness of moral principle; the character of uncorrupted virtue, esp. in relation to truth and fair dealing; uprightness, honesty, sincerity.

1548 HALL *Chron.*, *Hen. VI* 185 b, So much estemed..for his liberalitie, clemencie, integritie, and corage. **1599** *Life More* in Wordsw. *Eccl. Biog.* (1853) II. 157 That he might reserve the integritie of a good conscience. **1611** BIBLE *Prov.* xix. 1 Better is the poore that walketh in his integritie, then he that is peruerse in his lippes, and is a foole. **1639** S. DU VERGER tr. *Camus' Admir. Events* 12 Who for a kingdome would not have blemished her integrity. **1795** *Gentl. Mag.* 543/1 In integrity of heart and uprightness of intention he was excelled by few. **1850** McCOSH *Div. Govt.* III. i. (1874) 276 Mankind do, in fact, trust in a person known to be of thorough integrity, that he will always be upright.

integro-differential (ˌɪntɪgrəʊdɪfəˈrɛnʃəl), *a.* *Math.* [ad. It. *integro-differenziale* (V. Volterra 1909, in *Atti d. r. Accad. dei Lincei: Rendiconti* (*Classe di sci. fisiche*) XVIII. I. 167).] Involving both integral and differential quantities.

1914 *Trans. Amer. Math. Soc.* XV. 215 A large part of the theory of integral and integro-differential equations may be reduced to the corresponding theory of algebraic and differential equations by the introduction of convenient symbolism. **1923** *Bull. Amer. Math. Soc.* XXIX. 210 Integro-differential invariants of one-parameter groups of Fredholm transformations. **1930** M. LONG tr. *Volterra's Theory of Functionals* 31 As it has the characters of both integral and differential equations, it will be called an integro-differential equation. **1958** E. M. GRABBE et al. *Handbk. Automation, Computation, & Control* I. ix. 18 The method..is applicable to 'integro-differential equations' such as the following: $a_0dx/dt + a_1x + a_2\int_0^t xdt = f(t)$. **1964** N. N. HANCOCK *Matrix Analysis of Electr. Machinery* v. 70 The fundamental equations of an electro-dynamic system are inherently integro-differential equations.

integropallial, -palliate, irreg. var. INTEGRI-.

†**ˈintegrous**, *a.* *Obs. rare.* [f. L. *integer*, *integr-* + -OUS.] Marked by integrity; = INTEGRE, INTEGRIOUS.

1657 W. MORICE *Coena quasi Κοινή* Def. xx. 174 That an action be good, the cause ought to be integrous.

†**ˈintegrum.** *Obs.* [a. L. *integrum*, neut. of *integer* whole: see INTEGER.] = INTEGER B. 1, 2.

1594 BLUNDEVIL *Exerc.* I. vii. (1636) 20 What is Integrum? Any thing that is whole, and not broken, or divided into parts: as one whole yard, a pound, a shilling. *Ibid.* viii. 28 So shall yo find that 20 Integrums being multiplied by $\frac{5}{12}$ do make $\frac{100}{12}$, that is to say 8 Integrums and $\frac{4}{12}$. **1637** JACKSON *Serm. Man's Comf.* §28 These qualifications differ no more from Abraham's faith than fractions or parcels do from their proper integrums. **1681** H. MORE *Exp. Daniel* 311, I first considered the Integrum which was to be distributed into these seven parts.

†**integuˈmation.** *Obs.* *rare*[−1]. [Shortened from *integumentation*, q.v.] The formation of integuments.

1816 *Edin. Encycl.* XI. 13 (*heading*), Of integumation in Reptiles [cf. quot. 1809 s.v. INTEGUMENTATION]. **1817** *Blackw. Mag.* I. 187 Their..secretion and excretion, integumation, generation, and hybernation. **1828** WEBSTER, *Integumation*, that part of physiology, which treats of the integuments of animals and plants. *Encyc.*

integument (ɪnˈtɛgjʊmənt), *sb.* [ad. L. *integument-um* covering, f. *integĕre* to cover.] That with which anything is covered, enclosed, or clothed; a covering, investment, coating.

a. In general sense. (Now usually either *fig.* from, or with humorous allusion to, next sense.)

c **1611** CHAPMAN *Iliad* XXII. 446 Many and much in price Were those integuments they wrought t'adorn thy exequies. **1658** PHILLIPS, *Integument*, a covering, a garment to cover with. **1695** WOODWARD *Nat. Hist. Earth* I. (1723) 13 This Stratum is still expanded at Top of all; serving, as it were, for a common Integument to the rest. **1827** T. HAMILTON *Cyril Thornton* (1845) 99 His nether integuments were of dark plush. **1837–9** HALLAM *Hist. Lit.* III. III. iii. § 99. 84 To throw away those integuments of sense which hide us from ourselves. **1847–8** H. MILLER *First Impr.* xi. (1857) 175 Let us..strip the vast landscape here of its upper integuments, coat after coat.

b. *spec.* The natural covering or investment of the body, or of some part or organ, of an animal or plant; a skin, shell, husk, rind, etc.

1664 EVELYN *Sylva* (1679) 20 The Trees..which are expos'd to the North, with an hard, dark, rougher, and more mossie Integument. **1671** GREW *Anat. Pl.* i. §17 So far common with the Coats of the Bean, as to be like those, an Integument. **1713** ADDISON *Guardian* No. 102 ¶7 What the anatomists call one of the Integuments of the body. **1807** J. E. SMITH *Phys. Bot.* v. 25 Under the Cellular Integument we find the Bark. **1831** CARLYLE *Sart. Res.* II. iii, It had a

faculty called Memory, and could be acted-on through the muscular integument by appliance of birch-rods.

in'tegument, *v. rare.* [f. prec. sb.] *trans.* To furnish with an integument; to cover, invest.
1883 *Chamb. Jrnl.* 690 His gaunt frame was merely integumented with yellow flesh.

integumental (ɪntɛgjuːˈmɛntəl), *a.* [f. as prec. + -AL¹.] Of or belonging to the integument.
1836–9 TODD *Cycl. Anat.* II. 500/2 The density of the integumental covering. **1861** BUMSTEAD *Ven. Dis.* (1879) 110 The integumental together with an insignificant portion of the mucous layer.

integumentary (ɪntɛgjuːˈmɛntərɪ), *a.* [f. as prec. + -ARY.] Of or belonging to the integument; of the nature of an integument; cutaneous.
1841–71 T. R. JONES *Anim. Kingd.* (ed. 4) 138 Primary involution of the integumentary membrane. **1846** WORCESTER cites *Penny Mag.* **1862** H. W. BELLEW *Mission Afghanistan* 211 An aggravated form of Lepra, that affected the entire integumentary surface. **1869** E. A. PARKES *Pract. Hygiene* (ed. 3) 547 The large class of integumentary diseases.

integumen'tation. *rare.* [f. as prec. + -ATION.] The action of covering or condition of being covered with an integument; integumented condition.
1809 *Edin. Encycl.* I. 841/1 Those membranes that form the universal covering of the external surface, with their appendages..are here..denominated the Organs of Integumentation. [**1846** WORCESTER, *Integumentation*, that part of physiology which treats of integuments.] **1864** WEBSTER, *Integumentation*, act of covering with integuments; state of being thus covered.

'in-,teinds. *Sc.* [IN *adv.* 12 a.] Teinds or tithes on lands within certain bounds.
1621 *Sc. Acts Jas. VI* (1816) IV. 635/1 Þe teindschevis of þe toun Landis territorie and boundis of the burgh of Lanerk Callit þe inteyndis of þe said burgh of lanerk.

inteir, -ly, obs. Sc. form of ENTIRE, -LY.

†**in'tellable**, *a. Obs.* (chiefly *Sc.*) [f. IN-³ + TELL *v.* + -ABLE.] That cannot be 'told' or counted; innumerable.
1537 LYNDESAY *Deplor. Q. Magdalene* 60 Hir hie lynage, nor Riches intellebill. **1563** WINȜET *Four Scoir Thre Quest.* Wks. 1888 I. 92 We may bring intellable testimoneis theirof. **1575** LANEHAM *Let.* (1871) 44 So frequent, so intellabl, & of such continuauns in the spending.

intellect (ˈɪntɪlɛkt), *sb.* [ad. L. *intellectus* (*u* stem) a perceiving, discerning, discernment, understanding, meaning, sense, signification, f. ppl. stem of *intellegĕre*: see INTELLIGENT. Cf. It. *intelletto* (Boccaccio), F. *intellect* (13th c., Brunetto Latino); but the word was little used in F. or Eng. before the 16th c.]
1. That faculty, or sum of faculties, of the mind or soul by which one knows and reasons (excluding sensation, and sometimes imagination; distinguished from *feeling* and *will*); power of thought; understanding. Rarely in reference to the lower animals.
c **1386** CHAUCER *Knt.'s T.* 1945 Oonly the intellect with outen moore That dwelled in his herte syk and soore Gan faillen when the herte felte deeth [Boccaccio *Teseide* x. cxi, Sol nello intelletto e nel cuore]. —— *Sec. Nun's T.* 339 Right as a man hath sapiences three Memorie, Engyn, and Intellect also. **1398** TREVISA *Barth. De P.R.* III. iii. (Add. MS. 27944), As þe yee is in þe body, so is þe intellect vndirstondinge in þe soule. **1588** SHAKS. *L.L.L.* v. i. 64 It reioyceth my intellect, true wit. **1593** —— *Rich. II*, v. i. 28 Hath Bullingbrooke Depos'd thine Intellect? **1667** MILTON *P.L.* VI. 351 All Heart they live, all Head, all Eye, all Eare, All Intellect, all Sense. *a* **1677** HALE *Prim. Orig. Man.* I. i. 28 The proper Acts of the Intellect are Intellection, Deliberation, and Determination or Decision. **1696** PHILLIPS, *Intellect*, that Faculty of the Soul which is usually called the Understanding. **1773** MONBODDO *Language* (1774) I. I. iv. 45 The faculty by which it [the mind] operates singly, and without participation of the body, I call *intellect*. **1862** DARWIN *Fertil. Orchids* i. 46 To test the intellect of moths I tried the following little experiment. **1870** BLAINE *Encycl. Rur. Sports* (ed. 3) §851 The elephant..has given instances of what may be termed intellect that the horse does not possess. **1888** RUSKIN *Præterita* III. iii. 93 The.. elasticity and acuteness of the American intellect.
2. *transf.* †**a.** An intellect embodied; a being possessing understanding; an 'intelligence', a spirit. *Obs.* **b.** Intellect embodied; a person of a great intellect; also, intellectual persons collectively.
1602 MARSTON *Antonio's Rev.* III. i. Wks. 1856 I. 105 Thou royal spirit of Andrugio, where ere thou hoverst (Ayrie intellect). *c* **1645** MILTON *Sonn. Detract. cert. Treat.*, The subject new: it walked the town awhile, Numbering good intellects; now seldom pored on. **1665** BOYLE *Occas. Refl.* IV. vi. (1848) 207 How little will humane Intellects, without Revelation, discover of that manifold Wisdome of God. **1732** BERKELEY *Alciphr.* IV. §19 It is more improper to say of God, He is an intellect or intelligent Being, than to say of a reasonable soul that it is an angel. **1831** CARLYLE *Sart. Res.* I. iii, He stood-up in full coffee-house..where all the Virtuosity, and nearly all the Intellect of the place assembled of an evening. **1838** DE QUINCEY *Shaks.* Wks. 1863 xv. 69 This transcendent poet, the most august amongst created intellects. **1856** MASSON *Ess., Shaks. & Goethe* 22 To say that he [Shakespeare] was the greatest intellect that ever lived, is to bring the shades of Aristotle and Plato, and Bacon and Newton..grumbling about us.
3. *pl.* Intellectual powers; mental faculties; 'wits', 'senses'. Very common in 17–18th c. Now *arch.* or *vulgar.*
1698 VANBRUGH *1st Pt. Æsop* I. Wks. (Rtldg.) 370/1, I know he's modest, but I likewise know His intellects are categorical. **1751** JOHNSON *Rambler* No. 95 ¶18 My judgment embarrassed, and my intellects distorted. **1751** SMOLLETT *Per. Pick.* (1779) IV. xcv. 157 A man of sound intellects. **1799** E. HOME in *Phil. Trans.* 166 He was weak in his intellects. **1814** MAD. D'ARBLAY *Wanderer* I. 390 Her faculties are all disordered: her very intellects, I fear, are shaken. **1832** HT. MARTINEAU *Demerara* i. 12 Mark had never been very bright in his intellects during his best days. **1837–9** HALLAM *Hist. Lit.* (1847) III. vii. §48. 159 To ask, why this Don Quixote..should have been more likely to lose his intellects by reading romances than Cervantes himself.
†**4.** Understanding; comprehension. *Obs. rare.*
c **1470** HARDING *Chron.* Proem. iii, And some in Frenche they made, for intellecte Of men that could no Latyn vnderstande.
†**5.** That which one is to understand by something; the sense, meaning, signification, purport (of a word or passage). *Obs. rare.*
1520 WHITINTON *Vulg.* (1527) 6 Which verbe dothe accorde with the intellecte or significacyon & not with the voyce. **1588** SHAKS. *L.L.L.* IV. ii. 137, I will looke againe on the intellect of the Letter, for the nomination of the partie writing [*mispr.* written] to the person written vnto.

†**'intellect**, *v. Obs. rare.* [f. prec. sb.] *trans.* **a.** To give to understand; to inform. **b.** To understand (in a particular way); to interpret.
1599 R. LINCHE *Fount. Anc. Fict.* Bbij, Which intellecteth vs..that Iudges and such like officers..ought continually striue by all endeuours to suppresse wrongs. *Ibid.* E, These Stations are many times thus intellected: by the Spring is meant Venus; the Summer signifies Ceres.

,intellec'tation. *rare.* [f. INTELLECT *v.* or *sb.* + -ATION: cf. *sensation, cerebration.*] The action or exercise of the intellect; = INTELLECTION.
1855 *Tait's Mag.* XXII. 139 Forms..necessarily dissimilar to the simple fictions of a simple age, when human intellectation was more direct.

'intellected, *a. rare.* [f. INTELLECT *sb.* + -ED².] Endowed with intellect or understanding.
1791 COWPER *Odyss.* x. 297 In head, in voice, In body, and in bristles they became All swine, yet intellected as before. **1827** *Examiner* 264/1 A cold-blooded half-intellected Lord.

inte'llectible, *a. Philos.* [ad. med.L. *intellectibilis*, f. L. *intellect-*, ppl. stem of *intellegĕre*: see INTELLIGENT and -IBLE. (Cf. also *sensible.*)] †**a.** Capable of understanding; = INTELLECTIVE *a.* 1. **b.** Capable of being apprehended by the intellect alone (not by the senses) = INTELLIGIBLE A. 3.
1557 NORTH tr. *Gueuara's Diall Pr.* 215 a/2 Chilo the philosopher..dysputed, that the world..had an intellectible and sensible soule. **1583** STUBBES *Anat. Abus.* I. (1877) 35 When the Lord our God, a spirituall, intellectible, vnderstanding substance. **1857** MAURICE *Mor. & Met. Philos.* III. i. §13. 9 Things intelligible have a close connection with the intellectible.

†**inte'llectile**, *a. Obs. rare.* [f. L. *intellect-*, ppl. stem of *intellegĕre* + -ILE: cf. *ductile, fictile, pensile, sectile*, etc.] Of, pertaining to, or characterized by, intellect; intellectual.
1677 GALE *Crt. Gentiles* IV. 37 By how much the more immaterial, spirital & intellectile our joys are, by so much the more agreable they are to our Spirits. *Ibid.* 274 The proper good of every intellectile Nature is Beatitude.

intellection (ɪntɪˈlɛkʃən). [ad. late and med.L. *intellectiōn-em* (in late L. only = Synecdoche; frequent in Schol. med.L.), n. of action from *intellegĕre* to understand: see INTELLIGENT. Cf. F. *intellection* (in 13–14th c. tr. Boethius; but otherwise app. not till 17th c.; not in Cotgr. 1611).]
1. The action or process of understanding; the exercise or activity of the intellect; *spec.* simple apprehension, as distinct from imagination.
1614 JACKSON *Creed* IV. vi. §3 If..the will know the good to which it tends..by understanding, to will either formally is or essentially includes such an act as we call *intellection*. **1625** *Ibid.* v. xv. §2 Intellection, or vnderstanding is said to be of Vniversalls, not of Particulars. **1650** CHARLETON *Paradoxes* 133 The intellect..doth by the act of intellection acquire the figure of the object understood. **1678** CUDWORTH *Intell. Syst.* I. i. §45. 55 Aristotle..somewhere plainly determines, that there is no Intellection without Corporeal Phantasms. **1704** NORRIS *Ideal World* II. iii. 183 They who explain the manner of human understanding by material effluvias and emanations from bodies, seem to leave no room for any distinction between intellection and imagination. **1837–9** HALLAM *Hist. Lit.* IV. IV. iii. §34. 81 No follower of Descartes has more unambiguously than this author distinguished between imagination and intellection. **1856** DOVE *Logic Chr. Faith* v. i. 256 The form of our thought is..determined by the laws of our intellection.
†**b.** Applied *spec.* to the kind of immediate knowledge or intelligence ascribed to divine or angelic beings: cf. INTUITION. *Obs.*
1628 T. SPENCER *Logick* 8 In this, mans knowledge differs from the knowledge that is in God and the Angels: in that they behold the things in themselues, as they are in themselues, distinct each from other: they doe not know one thing lesse knowne, by the light and reflection of another thing, that is better knowne: wherefore their knowledge, is called intellection, ours is called rationalitie. *a* **1680** CHARNOCK *Attrib. God* (1834) I. 525 Some therefore have called God, not *intellectus*, understanding, because that savours of a faculty; but *intellectio*, intellection. **1732** BERKELEY *Alciphr.* IV. §19 As reason is of kind peculiar to man, so by intellection he [Picus] understands a kind or manner of knowledge peculiar to angels.
c. (with *pl.*) A particular act of understanding; sometimes, the permanent mental result of such an act; a conception, notion, idea.
1579 FULKE *Heskins' Parl.* 172 We stande vpon..the trueth of thinges naturall, which either sense or first intellections doth manifestly approue vnto vs. **1678** CUDWORTH *Intell. Syst.* I. iv. §18. 353 The Prince and Ruler over all the Celestial Gods, whom he affirmeth to be a Mind understanding himself and converting his Cogitations or Intellections into himself. **1731** *Hist. Litteraria* I. 382 The internal Actions are the Intellections and Volitions. **1839** B. H. SMART *Way out Metaph.* 25 An intellection having once occurred, remains with us as a notion or something known. **1847** LEWES *Hist. Philos.* (1867) II. 626 Any conception of Biology which excluded the sensations, instincts, and intellections would be monstrously truncated.
†**d.** The faculty of understanding; intellect.
c **1449** PECOCK *Repr.* I. xiii. 67 Thei puttiden al her motyue in her affeccioun or wil forto so trowe; and not in her intelleccioun or resoun. **1504** ATKYNSON tr. *De Imitatione* III. v. 199 Some other ther be that haue theyr intelleccyon or reason clerely illumyned. **1529** *Will of Hollonde* (Somerset Ho.), Being hole in mynde & of perfite intellection. **1647** H. MORE *Song of Soul* II. ii. III. ix, Yet intellection Or higher gets, or at least hath some sent Of God. **1744** BERKELEY *Siris* §254 That which acts naturally is not intellection, but a certain power of moving matter, which doth not know but only do. **1797** *Monthly Mag.* III. 515 [They] possess intellection themselves from the Father, so far as they energize intellectually, being moved by ineffable counsels.
†**e.** That which is obtained by the exercise of the intellect; understanding, information. *Obs.*
?*c* **1470** G. ASHBY *Active Policy Prince* 391 Countreies.. disposed to insurreccion, Wherof ye may haue intelleccion Redyng Cronicles. **1509** HAWES *Past. Pleas.* v. (Percy Soc.) 24 Who knewe gramer wythout impediment Shoulde perfytely have intelleccion Of a lytterall cense and moralyzacion.
†**2.** Meaning, intention, purpose, 'mind'.
c **1400** *Beryn* 2473 She..byhete me frendshippe outward by hir chere But inward it was contrary hir intelleccioune.
†**3.** *Gram.* and *Rhet.* The figure SYNECDOCHE.
1549 COVERDALE, etc. *Erasm. Par. Heb.* 10, I sayed after this intelleccion, that Leuy, who came of Abraham, gaue tithes vnto Melchisedech. **1553** T. WILSON *Rhet.* 92 b, Intellection, called of the Grecians Synecdoche, is a trope, when wee gather or judge the whole by the parte, or part by the whole.

intellective (ɪntɪˈlɛktɪv), *a.* and *sb.* [ad. late L. *intellectīv-us* (Augustine, Boethius), f. *intellect-*, ppl. stem of *intellegĕre* (see INTELLIGENT) + -IVE. Cf. F. *intellectif* (13th c.), perh. the immed. source.]
A. *adj.* **1.** Having the faculty of understanding; possessed of intellect. Applied, after Aristotle, to one of the parts of the soul (ψυχή).
c **1480** HENRYSON *Orpheus & Eurydice* 428 The pairte intelletyfe Off mans saule. **1509** HAWES *Past. Pleas.* XXII, Beastes, with soules [*printed* fowles] sensatiue, And man also, with soule intellectyue. **1643** R. O. *Man's Mort.* iii. 10 Aristotle [divides the Soul] into vegetative, sensetive, motive, appetitive, intellective. **1775** HARRIS *Philos. Arrangem.* Wks. (1841) 280 A being intellective and rational. **1843** MILL *Logic* III. v. (1856) I. 394 *note*, The Greek philosophers acknowledged several kinds of ψυχή, the nutritive, the sensitive, and the intellective. **1873** M. ARNOLD *Lit. & Dogma* 401 So far as our being is æsthetic and intellective.
†**2.** Characterized by a high degree of understanding; intelligent: = INTELLECTUAL A. 3 b.
1509 HAWES *Past. Pleas.* (Percy Soc.) 43 So famous poetes did us endoctrine Of the ryght way for to be intellectyfe. **1599** HAKLUYT *Voy.* II. I. 235 In my iudgment there is not a beast so intellectiue as are these Eliphants. **1632** LITHGOW *Trav.* VI. 284 Made manifest to the intellective Reader.
3. Of or pertaining to understanding, or the understanding; that is a function or attribute of the intellect; having to do with, or relating to, the intellect: = INTELLECTUAL A. 1.
1477 EARL RIVERS (Caxton) *Dictes* 15 b, She is reputed for dede for she leseth the intellectif lyffe. **1583** STUBBES *Anat. Abus.* I. (1877) 107 They mortifie the vitall spirits and intellectiue powers. *a* **1638** MEDE *Wks.* (1672) I. *Dæmoniacks* 29 From some weakness of the Brain or Intellective faculty. **1745** J. MASON *Self-Knowl.* III. x. (1853) 223 Strengthening the intellective and reflective Faculties. *c* **1826** COLERIDGE *Rem.* (1836) III. 38 Confine the term reason to the highest intellective power. **1837** *Blackw. Mag.* XLI. 258 We now proceed to consider the act of our Intellective Faculty, in the most distinguished and complex operation which our mind performs, namely, in reasoning.
†**4.** Apprehensible by the intellect alone (not by the senses): = INTELLECTIBLE b. *Obs.*
1644 MILTON *Educ.* Wks. (1847) 99/1 The most intellective abstractions of logic and metaphysics. **1656** HOBBES *Lib., Necess. & Chance* (1841) 107 The knowledge of vision, (which doth not produce the intellective objects, no more than the sensitive vision doth produce the sensible objects).
†**b.** *Gram.* Of a noun: Denoting something apprehensible only by the intellect; 'abstract'.
1823 *Monthly Mag.* LVI. 302 Though all intellective nouns are certainly appellative, it does not necessarily follow that we are without other appellatives.

†**B.** *sb. Obs. rare.*

1. Intellective faculty; intellect, understanding.

1560 ROLLAND *Crt. Venus* I. 71 Sa far as I can efter my Fantasie, I will yow schaw be my Intellectiue, How thay war cled.

2. *Gram.* An abstract noun: see A. 4 b.

1823 *Monthly Mag.* LVI. 300 Intellectives, the names of subjects contemplated solely by the mind..as of mental emotions, affections, and qualities, not regarded with substances..Grammarians have called them abstract nouns.

intellectively (ɪntɪˈlɛktɪvlɪ), *adv. rare.* [f. prec. + -LY².] In relation to the intellect; †in quot. 1602, Intelligibly.

1602 WARNER *Alb. Eng.* IX. xliv, Not intellectively to write, is learnedly they troe. **1839** BAILEY *Festus* ix. (1852) 121 In man thus, as composed of thrice three forms Intrinsic; first, corporeally, blood, Body, and bones; next, intellectively, Imagination, judgment, memory; And thirdly, spiritually, mind and soul, And spirit.

intellectual (ɪntɪˈlɛktjuːəl), *a.* and *sb.* [ad. L. *intellectuāl-is*, f. *intellectu-s*, partly through F. *intellectuel* (Brunetto Latino, 13th c.).]

A. *adj.* **1. a.** Of, or belonging to, the intellect or understanding. (In quot. 1531 = INTELLECTIVE *a.* 1.)

1398 TREVISA *Barth. De P.R.* I. xvi. (Add. MS. 27944), God is..welle of goodnes and of riȝtiousnesse, intellectual siȝt & vertue, þat comeþ of non oþer. **1531** ELYOT *Gov.* III. xxiv, The thirde parte of the soule is named the parte intellectuall or of understandynge. **1624** GATAKER *Transubst.* 97 By contemplation with intellectual eyes. **1654** WHITLOCK *Zootomia* 214 Easy Credulity, which is the third cause of Intellectuall slavery. **1725** POPE *Odyss.* xx. 414 Pallas clouds with intellectual gloom The Suitors souls, insensate of their doom! **1845** MAURICE *Mor. Philos.* in *Encycl. Metrop.* 652/1 That sense of intellectual lordship whereby a man is able to feel that he has that in him of which nature may present many likenesses, but to which it can offer no parallel. **1850** ROBERTSON *Serm.* Ser. III. iv. 43 An intellectual conception of the Almighty. **1878** MORLEY *Carlyle* 171 All unveracity, torpid or fervid, breeds intellectual dimness.

b. Qualifying a descriptive noun: That is such in relation to the intellect.

1731 CHANDLER tr. *Limborch's Hist. Inquis.* II. 28 He who is a concealed Heretick in this sense is generally called an Heretick purely intellectual. **1786** A. SEWARD *Let.* 25 Mar. (1811) I. 130 Those who are not interested in its anecdotes, can have little intellectual curiosity and no imagination. **1881** *Atlantic Monthly* May 597/1 He talked in a way..lively enough to sap his own intellectual integrity. **1891** A. JAMES *Diary* 24 June (1965) 216 Owing to my curious, given my inheritance and surroundings, complete absence of intellectual curiosity. **1891** W. JAMES *Let.* 21 Sept. in R. B. Perry *Tht. & Char. of W. James* (1935) II. 174 What a strange thing an intellectual *atmosphere* is! **1896** —— *Will to Believe* (1897) 9 Mr. Balfour gives the name of 'authority' to all those influences, born of the intellectual climate, that make hypotheses possible or impossible for us. **1899** *Q. Rev.* Jan. 29 The intellectual aristocracy of the thirteenth century had conquered. **1903** G. B. SHAW *Man & Superman* II. 50 That tone of intellectual snobbery. **1933** *Week-end Rev.* 11 Feb. 142/1 Intellectual integrity is necessary precisely in proportion as it is difficult. **1939** L. MACNEICE *Autumn Jrnl.* xii. 49 Spiritually bankrupt Intellectual snobs. **1965** H. A. GLEASON *Ling. & Eng. Gram.* 35 In the intellectual climate of the late nineteenth century this was most attractive. **1971** D. CRYSTAL *Ling.* iv. 187 We must..take account of the intellectual climate of the time.

c. That appeals to or engages the intellect; requiring the exercise of understanding.

1834 MACAULAY *Ess., Pitt* (1851) 286 Almost every intellectual employment has a tendency to produce some intellectual malady. **1871** FREEMAN *Norm. Conq.* (1876) IV. xviii. 216 Skill in the more intellectual branches of warfare.

d. ***intellectual property*** (Law), a general name for property (such as patents, trademarks, and copyright material) which is the product of invention or creativity, and which does not exist in a tangible, physical form.

1845 WOODBURY & MINOT *Rep. Cases Circuit Court of U.S.* (1847) I. 57 Only in this way can we protect intellectual property, the labors of the mind, productions and interests as much a man's own..as the wheat he cultivates. **1919** *Readers' Guide Periodical Lit. 1915–19 Cumul.* IV. 1582/1 (*heading*) Property, intellectual. See Patents. **1968** *Convention World Intellectual Property Organiz.* Art. 2 (viii) 3 in *Parl. Papers 1970–71* (1970) IX. 649 'Intellectual property' shall include the rights relating to:—literary, artistic and scientific works,..—industrial designs,—trademarks, [etc.]. **1987** *Independent* 26 June 1/6 The proposal..is part of a Bill reforming the law of copyright and intellectual property.

†**2.** Apprehensible only by the intellect or mind, non-material, spiritual; apprehended by the intellect alone (as distinguished from what is perceived by the senses), ideal. *Obs.*

1398 TREVISA *Barth. De P.R.* II. ii. (Add. MS. 27944), An aungel is substancia intellectual, alwey menable, free, and bodiles, seruinge god by grace & not bi kynde. *c* **1491** *Chast. Goddes Chyld.* 47 An intellectual vision is callyd whanne the Insighte of the sowle by a wonderfull myghte of god is cleerly fastnyd in unbodely substaunce. **1526** *Pilgr. Perf.* (W. de W. 1531) 270 b, Of the intellectuall visyon, saynt Thomas gyueth example of the holy wryters of the scripture. **1605** BACON *Adv. Learn.* I. vi. §4 To descend from spirits and intellectual forms to sensible and material forms. **1704** NORRIS *Ideal World* II. iv. 271 By intellectual objects I mean those objects which the mind perceives, without having any such impressions made upon the body. **1711** POPE *Temp. Fame* 10 A train of phantoms in wild order rose, And, joined, this intellectual scene compose.

†**3. a.** Characterized by or possessing 'intellection', understanding, or intellectual capacity; intelligent. *Obs.* exc. as in b.

1483 CAXTON *Gold. Leg.* 25/1 (R. Suppl.) The heuen intellectuel ben thaungellis, and thaungellis ben called heuen by yᵉ reason of dignity, and of their understanding. **1599** DAVIES *Nosce Teipsum, Hum. Knowl.* iii, When their reason's eye..Could haue approch't th' eternall light as neere As the intellectual angels could haue done. **1664** H. MORE *Myst. Iniq.* ix. 26 [Angels] to whom Origen pronounces Good men equal, nor allows the glorious Stars, though they were intellectual, to be worshipped. **1667** MILTON *P.L.* II. 147 Who would loose, Though full of pain, this intellectual being? **1797** MRS. RADCLIFFE *Italian* xvii, It appeared as if the strength of his intellectual self had subdued the infirmities of the body.

b. Possessing a high degree of understanding; given to pursuits that exercise the intellect.

1819 BYRON *Juan* I. xxii, But—oh! ye lords of ladies intellectual, Inform us truly, have they not hen-peck'd you all? **1860** TYNDALL *Glac.* II. xvi. 311 The interest which the intellectual public of England take in the question. **1876** MISS BRADDON *J. Haggard's Dau.* II. 35 Priscilla cast away her velvet head-band, reckless of the little mourning brooch ..which confined it on her intellectual brow.

B. *sb.* †**1.** The intellectual faculty or part of man; the intellect, mind. *Obs.*

1599 MARSTON *Sco. Villanie* III. viii, The bright glosse of our intellectuall Is fouly soyl'd. **1602** *2nd Pt. Return fr. Parnass.* III. iv. 1344 How ere my dulled intellectuall, Capres lesse nimbly then it did a fore. **1661** GLANVILL *Van. Dogm.* xiii. 124 The corporal Machine; which even on the most sublimate Intellectuals is dangerously influential. **1667** MILTON *P.L.* IX. 483 The Woman, opportune to all attempts, Her Husband..not nigh, Whose higher intellectual more I shun.

2. *pl.* Intellectual faculties; mental powers; 'wits'; = INTELLECT *sb.* 3. *arch.*

1615 J. STEPHENS *Satyr. Ess.* 285 He is a fellow as much beholding to his five senses, as to his intellectuals. *c* **1645** EVELYN *Diary* 29 Sept. an. 1635 Retaining her intellectuals ..to the very article of her departure. **1713** SWIFT *Frenzy Denny* Wks. 1755 III. I. 144 The gentleman is of good condition, sound intellectuals, and unerring judgment. *a* **1732** T. BOSTON *Crook in Lot* (1805) 15 Some are weak to a degree in their intellectuals. *a* **1834** LAMB *Lett.* x. *to Southey* 96 Your fear for Hartley's intellectuals is just and rational. **1847** DE QUINCEY *Secr. Societies* Wks. 1863 VI. 237, I keep her intellectuals in a state of exercise, nearly amounting to persecution.

3. *pl.* Things pertaining to the intellect.

1650 BAXTER *Saints' R.* IV. xi. Add. (1662) 823 A Copious Digression, which I will not now Characterize either as to the Intellectuals or Morals. **1882** SCHAFF *Encycl. Relig. Knowl.* II. 1707/1 Forgetting that orthodoxy in the department of religion, of intellectuals, may be divorced from orthodoxy in life and conduct.

4. An intellectual being; a person possessing or supposed to possess superior powers of intellect: see A. 3, 3 b.

1652 BENLOWES *Theoph.* II. v, First race of Intellectuals. **1813** BYRON *Jrnl.* in Moore *B.'s Wks.* (1836) II. 271 Canning is to be here, Frere and Sharpe,—perhaps Gifford. ..I wish I may be well enough to listen to these intellectuals. **1847** J. J. RUSKIN *Let.* 2 Sept. in M. Lutyens *Ruskins & Grays* (1972) vi. 50, I want you to stand well with Lockhart and the Intellectuals. **1884** A. A. WATTS *Life A. Watts* I. 124 The silent person who astonished Coleridge at a dinner of intellectuals. **1898** *Daily News* 30 Nov. 5/1 Proceeding to refer to the so-called intellectuals of Constantinople, who were engaged in discussion while the Turks were taking possession of the city. **1903** *Sat. Rev.* 19 Dec. 760/2 We are compelled to rank higher the mind of the average young man of fashion than the mind of the average 'intellectual' at those literary tea-parties. **1931** [see CULTURE *sb.* 5 d]. **1937** [see BRAIN TRUST, BRAINS TRUST]. **1960** *Times Lit. Suppl.* 12 Aug. 513/2 The English have a great respect for brute facts; and the intellectual in politics often looks to them like a man busily engaged in brushing unpleasant facts under the carpet. **1974** *Times* 15 Feb. 15/8 Russian history has set a pattern of alienated intellectuals.

intellectualism (ɪntəˈlɛktjuːəlɪz(ə)m). [f. prec. + -ISM. Cf. Ger. *intellectualismus* in sense 1.]

1. *Philos.* The doctrine that knowledge is wholly or mainly derived from the action of the intellect, i.e. from pure reason.

1829 SIR W. HAMILTON *Discuss., Philos. Uncondit.* (1852) 4 Rationalism (more properly Intellectualism) has, from his [Leibnitz's] time, always remained the favorite philosophy of the Germans. **1848** R. I. WILBERFORCE *Incarnation* xiv. (1852) 401 The opposite system, which may be called Intellectualism..To Locke's principle, 'Nihil in intellectu nisi quod prius fuerit in sensu', he [Leibnitz] added, 'nisi ipse intellectus'. **1854** FERRIER *Inst. Metaph.* x. (1856) 288 A middle course between two extremes, by which the Scylla of an excessive sensualism is avoided on the one hand, and the Charybdis of an extravagant intellectualism on the other.

2. The exercise of the intellect alone; devotion to merely intellectual culture or pursuits.

1838 GLADSTONE *State in Rel. Ch.* (1839) 317 The advocates of this theory often deprecate, in words, a mere naked intellectualism. **1859** I. TAYLOR *Logic in Theol.* 309 Courting whatever diversions I can find in a sensuous, or a frivolous life, or in a cold intellectualism. **1873** M. ARNOLD *Lit. & Dogma* (1876) 275 Religion is no intellectualism, but righteousness.

inteˈllectualist. [f. as prec. + -IST.] A devotee of the intellect or understanding; in *Philos.* one who holds that knowledge is wholly or mainly derived from the action of the intellect, i.e. from pure reason. Now freq. attrib. or as adj.

1605 BACON *Adv. Learn.* I. v. §6 Upon these intellectualists, which are notwithstanding commonly taken for the most sublime and divine philosophers, Heraclitus gave a just censure, saying, Men sought truth in their own little worlds, and not in the great and common world. **1666** BP. S. PARKER *Platonick Philos.* 59 These pure and Seraphick Intellectualists forsooth despise all sensible knowledge, as too gross and material for their nice and curious Faculties. **1802** LD. CAMPBELL *Let.* Aug. in *Life* (1881) I. 92, I gain admission to the richest banquet ever served up to the longing intellectualist. **1831** *Fraser's Mag.* III. 582 Mr. Godwin is an Intellectualist, and his reasoning is speculative, a mode of ratiocination which makes a man doubt. **1865** LECKY *Rationalism* (1878) II. 318 The intellectualist and the art critic were replaced by men of saintly lives but of persecuting zeal. **1881** *Nation* (N.Y.) XXXII. 791 The great quarrel between the Intellectualists and the Sensationalists in vision.

attrib. **1857** T. E. WEBB *Intellect. Locke* iv. 71 The views which have influenced Locke's Intellectualist opponents from the time of Stillingfleet and Leibnitz to the present. **1890** W. JAMES *Princ. Psychol.* II. xxii. 325 The traditional intellectualist philosophy has always made a great point of treating the brutes as wholly irrational creatures. **1941** J. S. HUXLEY *Uniqueness of Man* ii. 76 Men..of an intellectualist and academic type.

Hence **inteˌllectuaˈlistic** *a.*, pertaining to intellectualists or intellectualism; **inteˌllectuaˈlistically** *adv.*

1887 T. WHITTAKER in *Mind* July 455 What may be called spiritualistic or intellectualistic pantheism. **1890** *Athenæum* 5 July 34/1 It became completely overshadowed by the intellectualistic-speculative. **1907** W. JAMES *Pragmatism* iii. 121 Yet dark tho they be in themselves [*sc.* the words *God, free-will*, etc.], or intellectualistically taken, when we bear them into life's thicket with us the darkness *there* grows light about us. **1909** —— *Pluralistic Universe* ii. 72 The substituted conceptions are treated intellectualistically, that is as mutually exclusive and discontinuous. **1927** L. STEIN *A.B.C. of Æsthetics* i. 10 No one can get much good out of my book who reads it intellectualistically.

intellectuality (ɪntɪlɛktjuːˈælɪtɪ). [ad. late L. *intellectuālitās* (Tertullian), f. *intellectuālis*: cf. It. *intellettualità* (Florio).] The quality or state of being intellectual; intellectual power or ability.

1611 FLORIO, *Intellettualita*, intellectuality. **1664** H. MORE *Myst. Iniq.* 420 We may see how Fire is a symbol of Intellectuallity. **1667** —— *Div. Dial.* IV. xxxiii. (1713) 386 If you would but once vouchsafe to bow down your Metaphysical Intellectualities to these meaner Theories. **1701** BEVERLEY *Apoc. Quest.* 44 In the Former Parts of Prophecy the Prophetick Symbols, and Emblems have exceeded the Sensibility, and even Intellectuality of the Events. **1821** *Blackw. Mag.* X. 89 A dispute..about the superior intellectuality of the profession. **1863** MRS. C. CLARKE *Shaks. Char.* x. 255 It remained for Shakespeare to assert in behalf of his sisterhood a claim to the higher endowments of intellectuality. **1874** LISLE CARR *Jud. Gwynne* I. i. 20 The whole space was..lighted up with passion and intellectuality.

b. *transf.* An embodiment of intellectual ability; an intellectual person (or one so reputed).

1866 CARLYLE *Edw. Irving* in *Remin.* (1881) I. 141 Irving ..used to give breakfasts to intellectualities he fell in with.. They were but stupid intellectualities.

intellectualization (ɪntɪˌlɛktjuːəlaɪˈzeɪʃən). [f. next + -ATION.] The action of intellectualizing, or condition of being intellectualized.

1821 *Blackw. Mag.* X. 677 At the time when the Edinburgh Review made its appearance, there existed, among all ranks and orders in this country, a general intellectualization. **1873** H. SPENCER *Stud. Sociol.* xv. (1877) 372 A superficial intellectualization is to be secured at the cost of a deep-seated demoralization. **1887** *Harper's Mag.* Oct. 807/2 Is this intellectualization of women beginning to show, in the conversation of women when they are together, say in the hours of relaxation?

intellectualize (ɪntɪˈlɛktjuːəlaɪz), *v.* [f. INTELLECTUAL *a.* + -IZE.]

1. *trans.* To render intellectual; to give an intellectual character or quality to.

c **1819** COLERIDGE in *Rem.* (1836) II. 131 Shakespeare.. brings forward no subject which he does not moralize or intellectualize. **1821** *Blackw. Mag.* X. 525 It makes literature popular, and refines and intellectualizes life. **1877** E. CAIRD *Philos. Kant* II. xiii. 506 Leibnitz intellectualised perception just as Locke sensualised the conceptions of the understanding.

absol. **1843** *Blackw. Mag.* LIII. 594 The bent of Sir Joshua's mind was to elevate, to dignify, to intellectualize.

b. *intr.* for *refl.* To become intellectual.

1897 A. BIRRELL in *Daily News* 8 Nov. 6/7 If they considered the characteristics of the poetry of that day and its progress down to the present time, he thought they could not fail to see that it had intellectualised a great deal.

2. *intr.* [after *moralize*.] To exercise the intellect; to talk or write intellectually; to reason, philosophize.

1827 *Blackw. Mag.* XXI. 516 Yet could I sit and moralize, and intellectualize, for hours at this window.

Hence **inteˈllectualized** *ppl. a.*, **inteˈllectualizing** *vbl. sb.* and *ppl. a.*

1829 SOUTHEY *Sir T. More* II. 368 Whatever may be pleaded for its soothing and intellectualizing effects. **1831** *Blackw. Mag.* XXX. 345 The march-of-mind mechanics, the intellectualized artificers. **1854** E. G. HOLLAND *Mem. Jos. Badger* iv. 46 This intellectualizing on great vital facts. **1881** SHAIRP *Asp. Poetry* vii. 202 One sentiment, one

emotion, simple, passionate, unalloyed with intellectualising or analysis.

intellectually (ɪntɪˈlɛktjuːəlɪ), *adv.* [f. as prec. + -LY[2]: cf. late L. *intellectuāliter*, F. *intellectuellement* (1570 in Hatz.-Darm.).] In an intellectual manner; by means of, or in relation to, the intellect; mentally. Also used with an adj. as a quasi-Comb. (†In first quot. = Spiritually, as opposed to 'bodily'.)

1398 TREVISA *Barth. De P.R.* II. ii. (W. de W. 27944), Aungelis..beþ nouȝt bodiliche longe, noþir brood, noþir þicke, but þey beþ intellectualliche nyȝ and present. **1571** DIGGES *Pantom.* III. Defin. P iv b, Intellectually ye may thus conceyue a Sphere to be made. *a* **1677** HALE *Prim. Orig. Man.* IV. viii. 372 Man..is able to perform that duty intellectually and intentionally. **1701** NORRIS *Ideal World* I. iv. 204 When I reason intellectually I have oftentimes that intuitive evidence which is the ground of demonstration. **1859** J. A. SYMONDS *Let.* Oct. (1967) I. 211, I want to get Puller to organize a club with me, introducing 5 other intellectually-pursuited men. **1860** FROUDE *Hist. Eng.* V. 391 He was considered by the ultras as timid and intellectually weak. **1884** *Manch. Exam.* 26 May 6/2 It is frivolous to ask whether woman is intellectually the equal of man. **1923** J. S. HUXLEY *Ess. Biologist* i. 8 Intellectually-minded men. **1941** *Mind* L. 236 Mr. Clive Bell in his excellent and intellectually snobbish book *Civilization*.. makes this blunder. **1951** M. MCLUHAN *Mech. Bride* 58/2 The intellectually creative man with whom the future of mankind always rests.

inteˈllectualness. [f. as prec. + -NESS.] The quality or character of being intellectual; intellectuality.

1854 THOREAU *Walden* 16 Is it impossible to combine the hardiness of these savages with the intellectualness of the civilized man?

†**inteˈllectuate.** *Obs. nonce-wd.* [f. L. *intellectu-s* INTELLECT + -ATE[1].] Intellectual character or position.

1600 TOURNEUR *Transf. Met.* Epil. iii, Or else my sight gin's to abate, And's reaued of it's intellectuate.

intelligence (ɪnˈtɛlɪdʒəns), *sb.* Also 5–6 -ens. [a. F. *intelligence* (12th c. in Hatz.-Darm.), ad. L. *intelleg-*, *intelligentia* understanding, from *intellegent-em* INTELLIGENT: see -ENCE.]

1. The faculty of understanding; intellect.

1390 GOWER *Conf.* III. 378 He, which..thilke intelligence In mannes soule resonable Hath shape to be perdurable. *c* **1450** *Cov. Myst.* xxvii. (Shaks. Soc.) 273 It excedyth myn intellygens. **1591** SPENSER *Teares Muses* 255 A stonie coldnesse hath benumbd the sence..And dimd with darknesse their intelligence. **1664** POWER *Exp. Philos.* III. 158 To say, this Polary direction proceeds from itself, is to put a Soul, or Intelligence, at least, into the Stone. **1802** PALEY *Nat. Theol.* iv. §3 (1819) 49 There being no difference, as far as argument is concerned, between an intelligence which is not exerted, and an intelligence which does not exist. **1830** HERSCHEL *Stud. Nat. Phil.* 4 He is led to the conception of a Power and an Intelligence superior to his own.

2. Understanding as a quality of admitting of degree; *spec.* superior understanding; quickness of mental apprehension, sagacity. (Said also in reference to animals.)

c **1430** LYDG. *Min. Poems* (Percy Soc.) 9 God the ffulfylle withe intelligence. ? **1507** *Communyc.* (W. de W.) A ij, O man deuoyde of intellygence Open thyne eeres unto my call and crye. **1508** DUNBAR *Poems* iv. 34 He spairis no lord for his piscence, Na clerk for his intelligence. **1568** GRAFTON *Chron.* I. Ep., That some learned Englisheman of good intelligence would..confute such errors. **1780** BURKE *Sp. Econ. Ref.* Wks. 1842 I. 232 We can proceed with confidence, because we can proceed with intelligence. **1837** *Penny Cycl.* IX. 350/1 Baron Cuvier..observes [of elephants] that.. he never found their intelligence surpass that of a dog nor of many other carnivorous animals. **1847** CARPENTER *Zool.* §202 The Common Seal..is readily domesticated, and shows great intelligence and attachment to Man. **1872** YEATS *Techn. Hist. Comm.* 428 It is clear that intelligence has ever proved itself superior to ignorance.

3. a. The action or fact of mentally apprehending something; understanding, knowledge, cognizance, comprehension (*of* something). Now *rare* or *Obs.*

c **1450** *Mirour Saluacioun* 3680 To whayme..Crist gaf.. Grace of the haly gast and eke of tonges intelligence. ? *c* **1530** *Crt. of Love* 5, I write, as he that none intelligence Of metres hath, ne floures of sentence. **1552** ABP. HAMILTON *Catech.* (1884) 46 It helpis us to the trew intelligence of the scripture. **1620** T. GRANGER *Div. Logike* 2 God doth not reason..but with one simple apprehension, or intelligence he knowes all things. **1790** HAN. MORE *Relig. Fash. World* (1791) 75 A disposition to enjoy them, arising from an intelligence of their nature, and a reverence for their value. **1819** SHELLEY *Peter Bell* v. xi, Of lakes he had intelligence; He knew something of heath and fell.

†**b.** ? A branch of knowledge, department of science. *Obs.*

1390 GOWER *Conf.* III. 90 Mathematique of his science Hath yet the thridde intelligence Full of wisdom and of clergie And cleped is geometrie.

4. a. An impersonation of intelligence; an intelligent or rational being; esp. applied to one that is or may be incorporeal; a spirit.

[**1398** TREVISA *Barth. De P.R.* II. ii. (Add. MS. 27944), Spiritis þat beþ also I-clepid intelligencie [Lat. pl.], beþ ful of schappis & liknes þat nediþ to haue knowlech & konnynge.] **1589** PUTTENHAM *Eng. Poesie* I. iii. (Arb.) 23 The diuine intelligences or good Angels. **1667** MILTON *P.L.* VIII. 181 How fully hast thou satisfi'd mee, pure Intelligence of Heav'n, Angel serene! **1685** BOYLE *Enq. Notion Nat.* 53 The School Philosophers..teach, the Cœlestial Orbs to be moved or guided by Intelligences, or Angels. **1756** NUGENT *Montesquieu's Spir. Laws* (1758) I. i. 1 The intelligences superior to man have their laws. **1829** SOUTHEY *Sir T. More* I. 11 A correspondent degree of wickedness may effect a communion with evil Intelligences. **1836–7** SIR W. HAMILTON *Metaph.* (1877) I. iii. 50 Man, as a thinking and cogniting intelligence.

b. An embodiment of intelligence; a person of superior intellect. *rare.*

1824 MISS MITFORD *Village* Ser. I. (1863) 177 'Really', said Charles Grover, our intelligence—a fine old steady judge..'they are no better than so many old women'.

5. a. Interchange of knowledge, information, or sentiment; mutual conveyance of information; communication, intercourse. Now *rare* or *Obs.*

1531 ELYOT *Gov.* III. xxiv, Also intelligence is nowe used for an elegant worde, where there is mutuall treaties or appoyntementes, eyther by letters or message. **1549** *Compl. Scot.* ix. 78 Ane prince of athenes callit circisus..hed secret intelligens vitht xerxes kyng of perse. **1560** BIBLE (Genev.) *Dan.* xi. 30 He shal euen returne, & haue intelligence with them that forsake the holie couenant. **1614** RALEIGH *Hist. World* I. (1634) 120 That they might repayre to each other and keepe intelligence by River. **1664** BUTLER *Hud.* II. iii. 848 [Constellations] as they came from hence, With us may hold Intelligence. **1717** LADY M. W. MONTAGU *Let. to Pope* 12 Feb., They took it into their heads..that he was of intelligence with the enemy. **1720** MRS. MANLEY *Power of Love* (1741) 250 They were of Intelligence together. **1855** MILMAN *Lat. Chr.* VII. vi. (1864) IV. 190 Denunciations of ..the barbarity of these..who were accused of secret intelligence and confederacy with the Mohammedans.

fig. **1650** FULLER *Pisgah* II. iv. 106 Whence he concluded that this river entertained an underground intelligence with that fountain.

†**b.** esp. applied to the communication of spies, secret or private agents, etc. *Obs.*

1587 FLEMING *Contn. Holinshed* III. 1372/1 Diuerse aduertisements thereof sent..by other good meanes and intelligences from hir ambassadors and seruants residing in other countries. **1695** TEMPLE *Hist. Eng.* 565 He practis'd private Intelligences in the Danish Court. **1696** PHILLIPS (ed. 5), *Intelligence*,..the Correspondence that Statesmen and Merchants hold in Foreign Courts and Countreys.

†**6.** A relation or footing of intercourse between persons or parties; a good (or other) understanding *between* or *with*. *Obs.*

1597–8 BACON *Ess., Followers* (Arb.) 32 That ill intelligence that we many times see between great personages. **1601** R. JOHNSON *Kingd. & Commw.* (1603) 262 With the king of Polonia hee hath not any negotiation, save good intelligence. **1661** BRAMHALL *Just Vind.* vi. 146 Intestine discord between the King and his Barons, bad intelligence with Neighbour-Princes. **1696** PHILLIPS (ed. 5), *Intelligence*,..the Union and Amity between two or more Persons that rightly understand one another. **1734** tr. *Rollin's Anc. Hist.* (1827) VII. XVI. §6. 43 He sent an embassy..to renew the good intelligence between them. **1827** SCOTT *Napoleon* VIII. 405 Having made the truce with Joachim..it was to last no longer than his good intelligence with her ally.

fig. **1605** BACON *Adv. Learn.* I. iv. §11 The sciences.. which have had better intelligence..with the imagination.. than with..reason, are.. astrology, natural magic, and alchemy. **1642** FULLER *Holy & P. State* II. viii. 77 Well did the Poets feigne Pallas Patronesse of arts and armes, there being ever good intelligence betwixt the two Professions.

7. a. Knowledge as to events, communicated by or obtained from another; information, news, tidings; *spec.* information of military value.

c **1450** *Cov. Myst.* xiii. (Shaks. Soc.) 125 The aungel Gabryel apperyd hym to, That hese wyff xulde conseyve he ȝaff hym intelligence. **1509** HAWES *Past. Pleas.* XXXVI. (Percy Soc.) 190 We anone to our lady Pacience Will geve of you perfyte intelligence. **1613** PURCHAS *Pilgrimage* (1614) 830, I suspend [belief] till some eye-intelligence of some of our parts have testified the truth. **1695** TEMPLE *Hist. Eng.* (1699) 5 These were the Men from whom Cæsar drew his best Intelligence concerning the Country. **1714** LADY M. W. MONTAGU *Let. to Wortley Montagu* 24 Sept., I fear her intelligence is not at all to be depended on. **1799** G. HARRIS *Diary* 4 Apr. in Wellington *Disp.* (1837) I. 24 If our intelligence is true, his [*sc.* Tippoo Sultaun's] whole army are in a complete state of terror. **1818** JAS. MILL *Brit. India* II. v. v. 485 Intelligence poured in from all quarters, that one place after another was assailed. **1880** MCCARTHY *Own Times* IV. xlix. 29 The most accurate source of intelligence in all matters of public interest. **1899** *McClure's Mag.* Mar. 473/2 The swift single cruisers, the purveyors of intelligence. **1925** FRASER & GIBBONS *Soldier & Sailor Words* 125 'Intelligence', *i.e.* information of military value. The use of the word as a military technical term dates from the 16th Century, but in the War of 1914–18 it was used to denote specially the department of the General Staff dealing with information. **1974** *Times* 15 Jan. 14/3 The first question that everybody asked was why the intelligence of the Arab armies massing on the borders..was misread?

†**b.** *pl.* A piece of information or news. *Obs.*

1592 T. HENAGE *Let.* in *Sir H. Unton's Corr.* (Roxb.) 268 The busines of procuringe the intelligences of the world. **1654–66** LD. ORRERY *Parthenissa* (1676) 529 The just gods.. have sent me an Intelligence. **1682** LUTTRELL *Brief Rel.* (1857) I. 231 For the suppressing all the weekly intelligences and other libells. **1707** J. CHAMBERLAYNE *St. Gt. Brit.* II. xi. 147 The Keeper [of the Paper Office] hath in his Charge all the publick Papers..all Letters, Intelligences, Negotiations of the Queen's publick Ministers abroad. **1750** [R. PALTOCK] *Life P. Wilkins* xl. (1883) 114/2, I sent for Nasgig to obtain some intelligences I wanted to be informed of.

c. The obtaining of information; the agency for obtaining secret information; the staff of persons so employed, secret service. Cf. INTELLIGENCER.

1602 MARSTON *Antonio's Rev.* IV. i. Wks. 1856 I. 117 When will the Duke holde feed Intelligence, Keepe warie observation in large pay? **1617** MORYSON *Itin.* II. 240 We have here the worst intelligence, of any Instruments that any Prince in Christendome doth imploy in so waighty a businesse. **1668** PEPYS *Diary* 14 Feb., Secretary Morrice did this day in the House..say that he was allowed but £700 a-year for intelligence. **1697** DAMPIER *Voy.* I. 133 To land some Men purposely to get Prisoners for intelligence. **1915** KIPLING *France at War* 21 The Intelligence with its stupefying photo-plans of the enemy's trenches. **1949** A. CHRISTIE *Crooked House* xii. 95 A person who has something to hide can't really afford to talk *at all*. The blokes knew that in Intelligence during the war. **1957** [see COURIER *sb.* 1 b]. **1963** A. ORLOV *Handbk. Intelligence* i. 10 Stalin in 1932 ordered intelligence to discontinue sending him quarterly surveys of foreign countries. **1974** *Listener* 31 Jan. 142/1 Tizard has managed to get it through that someone should be seconded to British Intelligence for a while.

d. *Comb.* (sense 7 c) ***intelligence agency***, ***corps***, ***officer***, ***operator***, ***service***; **intelligence department**, a department of a state organization or of a military or naval service whose object is to obtain information (esp. by means of secret service officers or a system of spies); **Intelligence Office** (*U.S.*), 'an office or place where information may be obtained, particularly respecting servants' (Webster, 1864).

1951 *Intelligence Agency [see *C.I.A.* s.v. C III. 3]. **1960** J. BLISH *Galactic Cluster* 116 This intelligence agency is my sole source of income... I have every right to operate a private investigation bureau. **1963** A. ORLOV *Handbk. Intelligence* i. 7 The American intelligence agencies monitor as many as five million words daily from foreign radio broadcasts alone. **1898** *Westm. Gaz.* 24 Sept. 5/2 (France) Colonel Picquart then presided over the spy department, known in polite language as the *Intelligence Bureau. **1961** *Intelligence Corps [see *intelligence operator* below]. **1974** P. MCCUTCHAN *Call for Simon Shard* xiv. 132 Hedge had been in the war, a captain in the Intelligence Corps. **1875** *Encycl. Brit.* II. 573/1 The *Intelligence Department [of the Army] ..under a Deputy-Adjutant-General. **1888** *Times* (weekly ed.) 3 Feb. 9/1 An intelligence department—that is, a department which gathers information of every class and character to enable the administration in that department to use their Services if called upon. **1895** *Whitaker's Almanack* 230 Naval Intelligence Department. **1928** W. S. MAUGHAM *Ashenden* i. 2 The Colonel..was known in the Intelligence Department..by the letter R. **1611** COTGR., *Intelligencier*.. an *intelligence-giuer; a spy. **1692** BENTLEY *Boyle Lect.* iii. 102 Berosius set up his *Intelligence Office at Cos. **1856** OLMSTED *Slave States* 31 Much like Intelligence Offices, being large rooms partly occupied by ranges of forms. **1885** *Pall Mall G.* 6 Mar. 7/1 The Survey and *Intelligence officers are again busy in all directions. **1901** *Westm. Gaz.* 31 Dec. 10/1 You are intelligence officer to the new cavalry brigade. **1914** R. BROOKE in E. Marsh *Rupert Brooke* (1918) 132 Intelligence Officer in H.M.S. *Vengeance*. **1946** E. M. ZACHARIAS (*title*) Secret mission: the story of an intelligence officer. **1961** *Times* 12 Sept. 2/6 The Intelligence Corps... Vacancies exist for training in the trades of:—Staff *Intelligence Operator and Counter Intelligence Operator. **1930** B. MIALL tr. *Berndorff's Espionage* i. 16 At Nice..he continued to work for the French *Intelligence Service. **1932** R. H. B. LOCKHART *Mem. Brit. Agent* IV. iii. 234 A Colonel in our Intelligence Service. **1956** A. L. ROWSE *Early Churchills* 262 Of this Marlborough, whose intelligence-service was always of the first order, was well aware. **1974** *Listener* 31 Jan. 142/1 The Führer..said he had a secret weapon. Immediately Neville Chamberlain..asked the Intelligence Services what the secret weapon was.

8. *attrib.* and *Comb.*, as **intelligence quotient** [ad. G. *intelligenz-quotient* (W. L. Stern, 1912)], a number arrived at by means of intelligence tests and intended to express the degree of intelligence of an individual in relation to the average for the age-group, which is fixed at 100; abbrev. *I.Q.* (I. III); so **intelligence test, tester, testing**.

1921 C. BURT *Mental & Scholastic Tests* 151 If a child's mental age be divided by his chronological age, the quotient will state what fraction of ability the child actually possesses. .. This fraction may be termed..the child's '*intelligence quotient'. **1922** R. S. WOODWORTH *Psychol.* xii. 274 Brightness or dullness can also be measured by the intelligence quotient. **1944** H. READ *Educ. Free Men* iii. 13 Truth, we say, is not found exclusively in the possession of those with a high 'intelligence quotient'. **1953** *Sci. News* XXIX. 45 Isolated concepts, from sex-motivation to intelligence quotients, are taken up, puffed up, and what may be limited but useful notions become ridiculed, because of the disproportionate importance attached to them. **1971** *Nature* 2 Apr. 306/1 The worship of the Intelligence Quotient, mercifully a-dying, is still not entirely dead. **1972** KAGAN & HAVEMANN *Psychol.* (ed. 2) xiv. 473 The intelligence quotient, or I.Q., is simply the relationship of mental age to chronological age; it is obtained by the formula I.Q. = MA/Chronological age × 100... This is the general principle for computing the I.Q. on the Stanford-Binet. In actual practice..the I.Q. is usually determined from tables that make it possible to compare the child's raw score with the scores made by other children of the same age. This latter method is also the one used with all other intelligence tests... This statistical method of computing the I.Q. is valuable because the concept of mental age..is not meaningful for adults. **1914** *Eugenics Rev.* Apr. 42 General ability, estimated by *intelligence tests, is largely hereditary. **1957** *Technology* Mar. 10/1 The trade school, however, is well equipped to sort wheat from chaff—each candidate is given the latest types of intelligence and aptitude tests. **1927** A. HUXLEY *Proper Stud.* 65 The *intelligence-testers would isolate..the sum of the activities of the whole mind. **1962** H. J. EYSENCK *Know your own I.Q.* 31 From the point of view of the intelligence tester it is very undesirable to have mixed groups to deal with. **1972** J. L. DILLARD *Black English* i. 28 Some intelligence testers..have suffered from lack of valid information about Black English in standard sources on American dialects. **1919** *Elem. School Jrnl.* Sept. 26 (*title*)

*Intelligence testing as an aid to supervision. **1958** [see *child welfare* (CHILD *sb.* 22)]. **1972** J. L. DILLARD *Black English* i. 28 An intelligence-testing procedure which is completely invalid because of its cultural and linguistic bias.

†**in'telligence**, *v. Obs.* [f. prec.]

1. *trans.* **a.** To bring intelligence of (an event, etc.). **b.** To bring tidings to (a person); to inform.

1593 NASHE *Christ's T.* (1613) 70 Thy little soule to Heauen must be sent, to intelligence the calamity of Ierusalem. **1637** WOTTON in *Reliq.* (1672) 75 They were freshly intelligenced from thence. **1642** T. CASE *God's Rising* (1644) 5 Gedaliah, when Intelligenct by Jonathan.. of a bloody massacre contrived against him.

2. *intr.* To convey intelligence; to tell tales. (Cf. INTELLIGENCING *ppl. a.* 1.)

1616 BEAUM. & FL. *Scornf. Lady* III. i, If you stir far in this, I'le have you whipt, your ears nail'd for intelligencing o' the pillory, and your goods forfeit.

intelligenced (-ənst, *poet.* -ənsɪd), *a.* [f. prec. sb. + -ED².] **a.** Having understanding, intelligent. **b.** Furnished with information, informed.

1602 WARNER *Alb. Eng.* XIII. lxxix. (1612) 327 More we purpos'd to haue pen'd: Which to intelligenced Men, more daring, we commend. **1605** BACON *Adv. Learn.* II. xxiii. §22 Haue priuacye and conuersation with some one friend.. well intelligenced in euery seuerall kinde. **1889** *Sat. Rev.* 17 Aug. 177/2 The dust.. thrown in the eyes of persons better intentioned than intelligenced.

intelligencer (ɪn'tɛlɪdʒənsə(r)). [f. INTELLIGENCE *sb.* + -ER: perh. after obs. F. *intelligencier* 'an Intelligencer; an intelligence-giuer; a spy' (Cotgr.); cf. It. *intelligentiere* 'an intelligencer' (Florio).] One who conveys intelligence or information: **a.** *spec.* One employed to obtain secret information, an informer, a spy, a secret agent.

1581 SAVILE *Tacitus, Agric.* (1622) 184 Being depriued by intelligencers and spies of the commerce of hearing and speaking together. **1596** NASHE *Saffron Walden* 124 The hellish detested Iudas name of an Intelligencer. **1644** CHAS. I. in Ellis *Orig. Lett.* Ser. II. III. 317 Wee desire you to keep forth Scouts and Intelligencers to give you timely advertisement, if he shall advance Westward. **1658** OSBORN *Adv. Son* (1673) 85 It is an Office unbecoming a Gentleman to be an Intelligencer, which in real truth is no better than a Spie. **1788** JEFFERSON *Writ.* (1859) II. 444 He has no diplomatic character whatever, but is to receive eight thousand livres a year, as an intelligencer. **1796** BURKE *Regic. Peace* ii. Wks. VIII. 241 All the spies, all the intelligencers, actually or late in function. **1874** MOTLEY *Barneveld* I. i. 68 He was all-sufficient as a spy and intelligencer.

b. A bringer of news; a messenger; an informant; a newsmonger.

1632 LITHGOW *Trav.* IX. 386 They are curious, and great lovers of novelties.. great intelligencers, and lovers of histories. **1633** T. ADAMS *Exp. 2 Peter* iii. 6 He [Noah] sends out his intelligencers, the raven and the dove. **1651** C. CARTWRIGHT *Cert. Relig.* I. 21 Think ye, that those ministring Angels who are called Intelligencers, give them no intelligence? **1712** STEELE *Spect.* No. 427 ¶2 The many Stories which every Body furnishes her with.. make her the general Intelligencer of the Town of all that can be said by one Woman against another. **1780** COWPER *Lett.* 10 Dec., Wks. 1837 XV. 62 My intelligencer with respect to Lady Cowper's legacy proved to be mistaken. **1863** *Pilgrimage Prairies* II. 3 Bryce and I eagerly followed our intelligencer to assure ourselves of the truth of his report.

c. *fig.* Applied to things.

a **1586** SIDNEY *Arcadia* II. Wks. 1725 I. 203 Whose eyes, being his diligent intelligencers, could carry unto him no other news, but discomfortable. **1649** BULWER *Pathomyot.* I. iii. 13 The Nerves.. are the Intelligencers and way of conveyance untill they come into the moveable parts. **1687** SETTLE *Refl. Dryden* 76 Oliver's Nose was no doubt a wonderful intelligencer. **1769** E. HARGROVE *Knaresbro.* ii. (1798) 99 The subscription book to this library is of great use as an intelligencer to know what company are at the place. **1877** DOWDEN *Stud. Lit.* (1890) 247 The avenues between the senses and the imagination are traversed to and fro by swift and secret intelligencers.

†**d.** As the title of a newspaper, or other publication. *Obs.*

1641 R. BRATHWAIT (*title*) Mercurius Britannicus: or, the English Intelligencer. **1659** (*title*) The Parliamentary Intelligencer. **1728** *Swift's Lett.* (1766) II. 89 Desire her to shew it to the author of the Intelligencer, and to print it if he thinks fit. **1801** F. BARRETT (*title*) The Magus, or Celestial Intelligencer; being a complete system of Occult Philosophy.

†**in'telligencing**, *ppl. a. Obs.* [f. INTELLIGENCE *v.* or *sb.* + -ING².]

1. Conveying intelligence or information; playing the intelligencer or spy.

1608 CHAPMAN *Byron's Consp.* II. Plays 1873 II. 203 You much wrong me To thinke me an intelligencing instrument. **1611** SHAKS. *Wint. T.* II. iii. 68 A most intelligencing bawd. *a* **1711** KEN *Edmund* Poet. Wks. 1721 II. 160 Happy the Prince.. Who is omniscient in his Royal sphere, By a diffus'd intelligencing Ear.

2. Acting as an 'intelligence': cf. quot. 1685 s.v. INTELLIGENCE *sb.* 4.

1669 COKAINE *Poems, Elegie Eliz. Reppington* 76 Begetting harmony to emulate What the Intelligencing Spirits create By motion of the Spheres.

intelligency (ɪn'tɛlɪdʒənsɪ). Now *rare.* [ad. L. *intelligentia*: see INTELLIGENCE and -ENCY.]

1. = INTELLIGENCE *sb.* 1.

1871 BROWNING *Pr. Hohenst.* 598 Omniscience with intelligency.

2. = INTELLIGENCE *sb.* 4.

1652 BENLOWES *Theoph.* Pref., Super-cœlestials are Intelligencies altogether Spiritual and Immortal. **1720** WATERLAND *Eight Serm.* 88 The very Angels.. those bright Intelligencies, glorious Ministers of the Court of Heaven. *a* **1844** R. BALMER *Lect. & Disc.* (1845) II. 113 Heaven, the dwelling place of incorporeal intelligencies. **1865** BROWNLOW NORTH *Ourselves* (1866) 101 Every created intelligency must have answered, 'No one'.

†**3.** = INTELLIGENCE *sb.* 5. *Obs.*

1598 J. D. tr. *Le Roy's Aristotles Politiqves* 74 To permit no banquets, assemblies, intelligencies, nor any like thing. **1711** SHAFTESB. *Misc. Refl.* III. ii. *note*, From Flocks, Herds, and other natural Assemblages.. to human Intelligencys and Correspondencys.

†**4.** = INTELLIGENCE *sb.* 7 b. *Obs.*

1675 EARL OF ESSEX *Lett.* (1770) 32, I give you thanks for the divers intelligencies you send me. **1748** RICHARDSON *Clarissa* (1811) I. xxvi. 181 He cannot come at these intelligencies fairly.

intelligent (ɪn'tɛlɪdʒənt), *a.* and *sb.* [ad. L. *intelleg-*, *intelligent-em*, pr. pple. of *intellegĕre* (later *intelligĕre*) to see into, perceive, understand, f. *inter* between, within + *legĕre* to bring together, gather, pick out, choose, catch up, catch with the eye, read. Cf. F. *intelligent* (Cotgrave, 1611).]

A. *adj.* **1.** Having the faculty of understanding; possessing intelligence or intellect.

1598 FLORIO, *Intelligente*, intelligent, knowing, vnderstanding, skilful. **1615** J. STEPHENS *Satyr. Ess.* 128 Philosophy hath divided our soules faculty; and makes the Intelligent part our principall essence. **1736** BUTLER *Anal.* I. iii. 62 The work of an intelligent mind. **1830** HERSCHEL *Stud. Nat. Phil.* 5 When he contemplates.. the thoughts, acts, and passions of this his sentient intelligent self. **1881** DARWIN *Vegetable Mould* ii. 97 If worms have the power of acquiring some notion, however rude, of the shape of an object and of their burrows, as seems to be the case, they deserve to be called intelligent. **1890** C. L. MORGAN *Anim. Life & Intelligence* ix. 372, I regard the bees in their cells.. as workers of keen perceptions and a high order of practical intelligence. But I do not.. believe that they reason upon the phenomena they deal with so cleverly. Intelligent they are; but not rational.

2. Having a high degree or full measure of understanding; quick to understand; knowing, sensible, sagacious.

1509 HAWES *Past. Pleas.* XI. (Percy Soc.) 40 O what pleasure to the intelligent It is to knowe and have perceyveraunce Of theyr connyng. *a* **1626** BACON (J.), It is.. in order of nature for him to govern that is the more intelligent. **1647** CLARENDON *Hist. Reb.* I. §199 How acceptable soever to grave and intelligent Persons. **1678** CUDWORTH *Intell. Syst.* I. iv. §14. 258 The more intelligent of the Greekish pagans did frequently understand by Zeus that supreme unmade Deity who was the maker of the world. **1796** BURKE *Regic. Peace* ii. Wks. VIII. 150 By far the most intelligent statesmen. **1837** *Penny Cycl.* IX. 61/2 The spaniels.. and the hounds which comprise the most useful and intelligent dogs. **1849** MACAULAY *Hist. Eng.* i. I. 83 After the fashion of intelligent and well educated gentlemen.

Comb. **1830** MOORE *Mem.* (1854) VI. 143 A fine.. intelligent-spoken old fellow. **1863** MRS. CARLYLE *Lett.* III. 168 He is a good, intelligent-looking man.

b. Of action, speech, etc.: Showing a high (or fair) degree of understanding.

1842 CALHOUN *Wks.* IV. 66 [They] tell us, in language too intelligent to be mistaken, that they intend [etc.]. **1891** *Speaker* 2 May 534/1 All who take an intelligent interest in the growth of education.

3. That understands or knows (a particular thing, circumstance, or subject); cognizant *of*; acquainted *with*; versed *in*.

1546 *St. Papers Hen. VIII*, XI. 95 A conspiracion.. in the wich the said Secretary shold be intelligent. **1652** H. COGAN tr. *Scudery's Ibrahim* III. i. 32 They were intelligent with your carrying away. **1653** —— *Scarlet Gown* 133 He is.. most intelligent in the Civil and Cannon Lawes. **1665** G. HAVERS *P. della Valle's Trav. E. India* 57 Skill'd in the Indian Tongue, and perfectly intelligent of these matters. **1667** MILTON *P.L.* VII. 427 Part.. rang'd in figure, wedge thir way, Intelligent of seasons, and set forth Thir Aierie Caravan. **1791** COWPER *Iliad* II. 1040 She ceased; her Hector heard intelligent. **1858** *Sat. Rev.* VI. 606/2 Those who are capable of fairness.. susceptible of justice, intelligent of liberty.

†**4.** 'Bearing intelligence, giving information, communicative' (Schmidt *Shaks. Lex.*). *Obs.*

1605 SHAKS. *Lear* III. i. 25 Seruants.. Which are to France the Spies and Speculations Intelligent of our State. *Ibid.* III. v. 12 An intelligent partie to the aduantages of France. *Ibid.* III. vii. 12 Our Postes shall be swift, and intelligent betwixt vs. **1611** —— *Wint. T.* I. ii. 378 Do you know, and dare not? Be intelligent to me.

5. Of a device or machine: able to vary its behaviour in response to varying situations and requirements and past experience; *spec.* (esp. of a computer terminal) having its own data-processing capability; incorporating a microprocessor. Cf. DUMB *a.* 7 c.

1969 C. MACHOVER in Fairman & Nievergelt *Pertinent Concepts Computer Graphics* 182 Because economical general purpose computers are now available, the 'intelligent' terminal almost always uses such a computer for both a refresh memory and the other functions. **1978** *Pract. Computing* July–Aug. 55/3 Also available on the Tandberg TDV-2114, an intelligent terminal with stand-alone computing capability, is the Logica Commercial BASIC. **1979** *Financial Times* 19 Feb. 15/7 The emphasis of the market will continue to shift from large machines to terminals (particularly so-called 'intelligent terminals' which include some computing power). **1983** *McGraw-Hill Yearbk. Sci. & Technol. 1984* 21/1 Intelligent mobile robots can be used in space as planetary exploratory vehicles. **1984** *Times* 20 Mar. 14/8 The 'intelligent pig'.. enabled engineers to monitor the national gas grid system for defects. **1985** *Computing Equipment* Sept. 46/4 Anyone with a personal computer can now produce labels, nameplates, tags and tickets, in-house, using the plug compatible Intacs 5200 series intelligent imprinters. **1986** *Keyboard Player* Apr. 27/1 An intelligent masterkeyboard.. allows control, via MIDI, of up to eight synthesizers in all registrations.

B. *sb.* **1.** An intelligent or rational being; = INTELLIGENCE 4. **b.** A person of intelligence. Now *rare.*

1601 GILL *Trinity* in *Sacr. Philos.* (1625) 218 An Infinite intelligible, cannot be conceived of an Infinite intelligent, but by an Infinite action of the understanding. **1669** GALE *Crt. Gentiles* I. I. i. 3 God.. must of necessitie also be the first intelligent. **1719** WATERLAND *Vind. Christ's Div.* ix. (1720) 172 Unless one infinite Intelligent be made up of Unintelligents or finite Intelligents. **1892** *Athenæum* 2 July 26/2 Karpoff and Garin.. depict to us the self-conscious troubles and failures of our 'intelligents' in search of rest for their souls.

†**2.** One who is cognizant of something; a recipient of intelligence or information; a hearer. *Obs.*

1508 FISHER *7 Penit. Ps.* Prol., That the intellygentes of the sayd sermons may be gladder in the path of ryghtwysness.

†**3.** One who conveys intelligence or information; an intelligencer; a spy. *Obs.*

1600 W. WATSON *Decacordon* (1602) 65 By.. apprehension of their messengers, or some of their inferior intelligents. **1643** *5 Yrs. K. James* in *Harl. Misc.* (Malh.) V. 352 The Irish.. hearing of these misdemeanors, for they have their intelligents here also, began to grow obstinate. **1751** tr. *Beau-Philosopher* 60, I had been Fool enough to have believed the heavenly Intelligent [= angel].

intelligential (ɪntɛlɪ'dʒɛnʃəl), *a.* [f. L. *intelligentia* INTELLIGENCE + -AL¹. (Cf. the It. in quot. 1611.)]

1. Of, belonging to, relating to, or treating of, intelligence or intellect: = INTELLECTUAL A. 1.

1611 FLORIO, *Intelegentiale*, intelligentiall, intelectuall. **1647** CRASHAW *Poems* 164 We vow to make brave way Upwards, and press on for the pure intelligential prey. **1667** MILTON *P.L.* IX. 190 The Devil enterd, and his brutal sense, ..soon inspir'd With act intelligential. **1814** CARY *Dante, Paradise* XXIV. 132, I in one God believe;..Nor demonstration physical alone, Or more intelligential and abstruse, Persuades me to this faith. **1873** M. ARNOLD *Lit. & Dogma* i. (1876) 45 Indications.. of a true law of our being on its æsthetic and intelligential side.

2. Possessing, or of the nature of, intelligence: = INTELLECTUAL A. 3, INTELLIGENT A. 1.

1646 GAULE *Cases Consc.* 115 Though Devills be intelligentiall Creatures. **1792** MARY WOLLSTONECR. *Rights Wom.* iv. 163 An intelligential creature who is not to receive but acquire happiness. **1876** BLACKIE *Songs Relig. & Life* 17 First Thought, first Word, first Deed, these three, Intelligential Trinity, That was, and is, and is to be.

3. Relating to or conveying intelligence or news.

1883 *Century Mag.* XXVI. 692 The New York telegraph office, radiates 250,000 miles of intelligential nerves to ten thousand minor centers in America.

†**intelli'gentiary**, *a.* and *sb. Obs.* Also 6 -ci-. [f. as prec. + -ARY.]

A. *adj.* = INTELLIGENTIAL 3.

1590 WOTTON *Let. to Ld. Zouch* 20 Nov. in *Reliq.* (1685) 591 What the Intelligentiary Letters of Ausburg, Lyons and Venice bring, Mr. Osborn, I know, fails not to advertise.

B. *sb.* = INTELLIGENCER.

1577–87 HOLINSHED *Scot. Chron.* (1805) I. 72 There were sent over into France certeine intelligenciaries to move some conspiracie.

intelligently (ɪn'tɛlɪdʒəntlɪ), *adv.* [f. INTELLIGENT *a.* + -LY².] In an intelligent manner; with intelligence, sagaciously, sensibly.

1671 BOYLE *Usef. Math. to Nat. Philos.* Wks. 1772 III. 429 The knowledge of celestial bodies is not well to be attained, nor.. the theories proposed of them to be intelligently judged of, without arithmetick and geometry. **1790** BEATTIE *Moral Sc.* I. II. i. §412 In affirming that the universe proceeds from chance, it would appear, that atheists mean, either that it has no cause at all, or that its cause did not act intelligently, or with design, in the production of it. **1867** in Anderson *Missions Amer. Bd.* II. xxxvi. 325 They.. discuss and vote as intelligently.. as the missionary fathers. **1883** H. DRUMMOND *Nat. Law in Spir. W.* v. (1884) 144 A doctrine which, intelligently enforced, ought to appeal to all men with convincing power.

intelligentsia (ɪntɛlɪ'dʒɛntsɪə; formerly also ɪntɛlɪ'gɛntsɪə). Also (formerly) **intelligenzia**. [f. Russ. *intelligéntsiya*, ad. L. *intelligentia* INTELLIGENCE *sb.*] The part of a nation, orig. in pre-revolutionary Russia, that aspires to intellectual activity; the class of society regarded as possessing culture and political initiative.

1907 M. BARING *Year in Russia* vii. 77 They [*sc.* the revolutionaries] fear that if the question of a Republic is brought forward there will be a general massacre of the educated bourgeoisie, the so-called 'Intelligenzia'. **1910** —— *Landmarks Russian Lit.* iii. 68 Chekov has depicted the pessimism and the ineffectiveness of the 'intelligenzia'. **1914** *Round Table* Dec. 115 The importance and meaning of the so-called *intelligentsia*. **1916** H. G. WELLS *Mr. Britling* I. ii. 62 They are the sort of equivalent of the Russian Intelligentsia, an irresponsible middle class with ideas. **1921** A. HUXLEY *Let.* 31 May (1969) 197 The English colony [at

Florence] is a queer collection; a sort of decayed provincial intelligentsia. **1922** C. E. M. JOAD *Highbrows* vi. 224 Those waifs and strays of the intelligentsia who had resolutely refused to participate in the war. **1922** C. SIDGWICK *Victorian* xxviii. 211 He told me ..that he belonged to the Intelligentsia and that he was out to shoot capitalists. **1924** GALSWORTHY *White Monkey* I. ix, It was not the intelligentsia, but just intellectual society, which was gathered there. **1940** WODEHOUSE *Eggs, Beans & Crumpets* 75 It was a painful shock to the intelligentsia.. when they discovered that their old friend was not going to prove the geyser of easy money they had anticipated. **1949** I. T. SANDERS *Balkan Village* i. 7 The intelligentsia, as they were called by the [Bulgarian] peasants, were the most influential group in the community... I was sure to find several of them playing cards... The mayor..could watch..the municipal building... The priest could look..to the church just beyond. The village doctor's husband was near in case his wife needed him. **1956** R. REDFIELD *Peasant Society & Culture* ii. 61 To the administrative and cultural intermediaries between local life and wider life the word 'intelligentsia' has long been applied. **1971** H. SETON-WATSON in A. Bullock *20th Cent.* 139/1 The revolutionary propensity of the intelligentsia has been definitely correlated with the extent of the cultural gap between the educated élite and the mass of the people.

intelligibility (ɪnˌtɛlɪdʒɪˈbɪlɪtɪ). [f. next: see -ITY.]

1. The quality or character of being intelligible; capability of being understood; comprehensibility.

1678 CUDWORTH *Intell. Syst.* I. v. 718 The very essence of truth here is this clear perceptibility or intelligibility. **1788** H. WALPOLE *Dram. Compos.* in *Walpoliana* (ed. 2) I. 42 Thence a comedy always loses some of its beauties..and some of its intelligibility. **1869** HUXLEY in *Sci. Opinion* 5 May 505/2 An essay of exquisite clearness and intelligibility. **1895** F. HALL *Two Trifles* 30 Its convenience and instant intelligibility.

b. *transf.* An intelligible thing: = INTELLIGIBLE B. *rare.*

1610 HEALEY *St. Aug. Citie of God* 317 Plato..averreth the antiquity of that opinion that affirmed the essence of intelligibilities onely. **1651** BIGGS *New Disp.* ¶ 290 Phantasie obtruded in the species of Intelligibilities.

†**2.** Capacity of understanding; intelligence. (Cf. next 1.) *Obs. rare.*

a **1680** GLANVILL (J.), The soul's nature consists in intelligibility.

intelligible (ɪnˈtɛlɪdʒɪb(ə)l), *a.* (*sb.*) [f. L. *intellegi-*, *intelligibil-is*, f. *intellegĕre* to understand + -IBLE.]

†**1.** Capable of understanding; able to understand; intelligent. *Obs.*

1382 WYCLIF *Wisd.* vii. 23 The spirit of vnderstonding.. alle thingus beholdende, and that taketh alle intelligible spiritis [1388 able to vndurstonde: Vulg. *intelligibiles*]. **1509** HAWES *Past. Pleas.* I. xii, He must enclyne..to determine, And set his hert to be intelligible. *a* **1613** OVERBURY *A Wife*, etc. (1638) 124 A meere Scholer is an intelligible Asse. **1669** GALE *Crt. Gentiles* I. III. iii. 38 Plato supposeth the Universe ..a living intelligible creature. **1744** in G. Sheldon *Hist. Deerfield* (*Mass.*) (1895) I. 535 A very Intellegable man about thirty years of age. **1777** E. BADLAM in *New Eng. Hist. & Gen. Reg.* (1848) II. 49 The Mohawks are the most intelligible, as they live among the English in Caughnawaga.

2. Capable of being understood; that may be apprehended by the intellect; comprehensible.

1509 HAWES *Past. Pleas.* XLIII. (Percy Soc.) 211 Whose fame renowmed is ful openly..In flamynge tongues to be intellygyble. **1549** *Compl. Scot.* To Rdr. 16, I hef vsit domestic scottis langage, maist intelligibil for the vlgare pepil. *a* **1610** HEALEY *Theophrastus* (1636) To Rdr., The hardest wordes are made intelligiblest. **1732** BERKELEY *Alciphr.* III. §8 What you say now is very intelligible. **1754** SHERLOCK *Disc.* (1759) I. i. 58 A Rule of Action must be plain and intelligible. **1875** JOWETT *Plato* (ed. 2) V. 194 The aim of our institutions is easily intelligible to any one.

b. Of a person in reference to his words.

1655 FULLER *Ch. Hist.* II. ii. §73 Aidan, who naturally spoke Irish, was not intelligible of his English Congregation. **1841** D'ISRAELI *Amen. Lit.* (1867) 105 Calvin deemed that to render the people intelligent their instructor should be intelligible. *Mod.* He spoke so fast as to be hardly intelligible. He is not a very intelligible writer.

3. *Philos.* Capable of being apprehended only by the understanding (not by the senses); objective to intellect. (Opp. to *sensible.*) (Cf. INTELLECTIBLE.)

1398 TREVISA *Barth. De P.R.* II. ii. (Add. MS. 27944), An aungel, by resoun of þe spiritualte of his substaunce perceyueþ in hymself al fourmes intelligibil. **1534** MORE *Treat. on Passion* Wks. 1344/1 The sanctifying of the misticall sacrifice, and the translacion or chaunging of it from thynges sensible to thynges intelligible. **1638** F. JUNIUS *Paint. of Ancients* 18 Our mind..maketh up the conceivable or intelligible things out of the sensible. **1701** NORRIS *Ideal World* I. i. 12 When we say the Intelligible world, the meaning is..a world of a nature purely spiritual and intellectual, and such as is not sensible, but intelligible only. **1856** VAUGHAN *Mystics* (1860) I. 54 The presumption of those who place sense above intelligence—who think that they can storm the Intelligible by the Sensible.

B. *sb.* That which is intelligible; an object of intellect or understanding; *spec.* in *Philos.* (see A. 3).

1601 GILL *Trinity* in *Sacr. Philos.* (1625) 218 An Infinite intelligible, cannot be conceived of an Infinite intelligent, but by an Infinite action of the understanding. **1659** STANLEY *Hist. Philos.* III. II. 118 The philosophy which is of incorporealls, and intelligibles, and immaterialls, and eternalls..is firmly established. **1681–6** J. SCOTT *Chr. Life* (1747) III. 634 This divine Word..is itself the Image of God, the most ancient of all Intelligibles, and next to the most High. **1788** T. TAYLOR *Proclus* I. 44 The ancient theologists..affirmed that the soul was of a certain middle nature and condition between intelligibles and sensibles. **1847** LEWES *Hist. Philos.* (1867) I. 23 Draw off the mind from Sensible things and conduct them to Intelligibles.

inˈtelligibleness. [f. prec. + -NESS.] The quality of being intelligible; intelligibility.

1611 FLORIO, *Intelligibilita*, intelligiblenesse. **1660** H. MORE *Myst. Godl.* I. i. 2 Intelligibleness adds this further requisite also to a Mystery, that it thereby becomes Communicable to such as are fitly prepared to be instructed therein. **1698** S. CLARKE *Script. Just.* xvi. 85 Because of the commodiousness, coherence, consistence, intelligibleness and smoothness thereof. **1827** HARE *Guesses* (1859) 437 The primary requisite of a style is its intelligibleness: that is to say, it must be capable of being understood.

intelligibly (ɪnˈtɛlɪdʒɪblɪ), *adv.* [f. as prec. + -LY^{2}. (Cf. late L. *intellegibiliter*, Augustine.)]

1. In an intelligible manner; so as to be capable of being understood; comprehensibly.

1607 E. GRIMSTONE tr. *Goulart's Mem. Hist.* 434 The Maide talked plainly and intelligibly with her. **1711** ADDISON *Spect.* No. 165 ¶ 6 When he writes for Money he knows how to speak intelligibly enough. **1794** SULLIVAN *View Nat.* II. xlvii. 344 Do not many head lands, shoals, islands, speak most intelligibly to us, and say, we are but remnants of lands, rudely torn from other shores? **1855** MACAULAY *Hist. Eng.* xvi. III. 708 They..drew up a paper in which they very intelligibly hinted that this was their wish.

†**2.** In relation to the understanding; as an object of intellect. (Opp. to *sensibly*; cf. INTELLIGIBLE A. 3.) *Obs.*

1660 R. COKE *Justice Vind.* 2 There are many things intelligible, which are not sensible; as time does, every article of it, intelligibly pass away, not sensibly. **1701** NORRIS *Ideal World* I. i. 8 By the Ideal world I understand that world which is intelligibly what this is sensibly, the eternal model and exemplar of all created essence.

intelligize (ɪnˈtɛlɪdʒaɪz), *v. rare.* [irreg. f. L. *intellegĕre* to understand + -IZE.] **a.** *intr.* To exercise the intelligence or intellect; to think. **b.** *trans.* To take into the intellect.

1803 *Edin. Rev.* I. 261 They [forms of thought]..exist *a priori*, and independently of all experience in the subject who intelligizes. **1890** *Scott. Leader* 1 July 6 Hume lived in a society of highly-cultivated men, whose scholarship was assimilated and intelligized.

†**inˈtelliment.** *Obs. rare*$^{-1}$. [? corruption of *intendiment* after *intelligence*.] = INTENDMENT 3.

c **1537** *Thersites* in *Four Old Plays* (1848) 78 He that forgeue Mary Mawdalene hyr synne, Make the hyghest of all thy kynne. In this wordes is double intellimente, Wouldest thou haue me hanged, mother, veramente?

Intelsat (ˈɪntɛlsæt). Also **INTELSAT**. [An acronym f. the name of the organization, *In*ternational *Tel*ecommunications *Sat*ellite Consortium.] **a.** An international organization of member countries formed in 1964 to establish and operate a worldwide system of commercial communication satellites. **b.** A communication satellite owned by this organization.

1966 *Aviation Week* 7 Mar. 125/3 International Telecommunications Satellite Consortium (Intelsat) is already on the road to becoming a profit-making venture by 1970. It now includes 48 nations... U.S.'s Communications Satellite Corp. serves as manager for the consortium. **1967** *Wall Street Jrnl.* 6 Jan. 4/3 The successful weekend orbiting of Intelsat II. **1969** *Listener* 5 June 779/1 In communications we have accepted INTELSAT, for example, a global organisation which runs the satellite communications system. **1971** *New Scientist* 3 June 552/1 The settlement now reached mostly meets the criticism.. that Intelsat was American dominated. **1972** *Sci. Amer.* Sept. 111/1 The latest Intelsat has a capacity of 5,000 voice channels or 12 television channels.

†**inˈtemerable,** *a.* *Obs. rare*$^{-1}$. [ad. L. *intemerābil-is* inviolable, f. *in-* (IN-^{3}) + **temerābilis*, f. *temerāre* to violate.] Inviolable, incorruptible.

1657 J. GOODWIN *Triers Tried* 2 Both infallibility of judgement, and intemerable faithfulnesse, in matters of Faith and supernatural concernment.

intemerate (ɪnˈtɛmərət), *a.* [ad. L. *intemerāt-us*, f. *in-* (IN-^{3}) + *temerātus*, pa. pple. of *temerāre* to violate.] Inviolate, undefiled, unblemished.

1491 CAXTON *Vitas Patr.* (W. de W. 1495) I. vii. 10a/1 Our sauyour wyth his intemerate & holy moder. **1495** *Trevisa's Barth. De P.R.* I. (W. de W.) 7 The moost pure, moost intermerate..and moost vertuouse vyrgyne. **1502** ARNOLDE *Chron.* (1811) 161 [We] wyl not suffer our intemerat and inviolate feyth in no maner of promesse to be corrupte or defilled. **1657** REEVE *God's Plea* Ep. Ded. 1 A Gentleman of intemerate fame, and unblemished reputation. **1864** E. SARGENT *Peculiar* II. 254 You mean to make her your wife, and the wife of Corberry Ratcliff must be intemerate. **1893** *Tablet* 21 Oct. 651 The absolute sinlessness of Mary, as well as her intemerate virginity.

Hence **inˈtemerately** *adv.*, in an intemerate or inviolate manner; purely. **inˈtemerateness**, the quality of being intemerate or undefiled; purity.

1607 DONNE *Poems, etc., Let. to Sir H. Goodeere* (1633) 362 They [my letters] shall therefore ever keepe the sincerity and intemeratenesse of the fountaine whence they are derived. *a* **1631** —— *Serm.* li. 520 He cannot take the water so sincerely, so purely, so intemerately from the channell as from the fountaine head.

†**inˈtemerated,** *a. Obs.* [f. as prec. + -ED^{1}.] = INTEMERATE.

1608 J. KING *Serm. St. Mary's* 29 That leaueth an aspersion of scandall vpon his sacred and intemerated name. *a* **1670** HACKET *Abp. Williams* I. (1692) 224 Which made him much contest to keep regal majesty intemerated. **1682** H. MORE *Annot. Lux O.* 269 Intemerated youth.

†**intemeˈration.** *Obs. rare.* [f. INTEMERATE (or its source): see -ATION. (Late L. has *temerātio* in sense 'forging'.)] Inviolate condition.

1660 JER. TAYLOR *Duct. Dubit.* III. iii. rule 1 §17 This immunity and intemeration of holy things as well as holy persons.

†**inˈtemper,** *v.* *Obs. rare*$^{-1}$. [IN-^{2}: cf. ENTEMPER.] *trans.* To immix.

1627 H. BURTON *Baiting Pope's Bull* 4 The judicious Reader may therein discerne notable artifice, intempering strong poyson as it were in a payre of Italian or Spanish perfumed gloues.

inˈtemperable, *a. rare*$^{-1}$. [ad. L. *intemperābil-is* not to be moderated, f. *in-* (IN-^{3}) + *temperāre* to mingle in due proportion, to TEMPER.]

Incapable of being moderated or kept within bounds.

1898 *Blackw. Mag.* Jan. 135/1 A ruler so wilful, so everlastingly boyish and intemperable.

Hence **inˈtemperably** *adv.*, in an intemperable manner, without moderation or restraint.

1897 F. THOMPSON *New Poems* 48 Round and round in bacchanal rout reel the swift spheres intemperably.

†**inˈtemperacy.** *Obs. rare.* [f. INTEMPERATE: see -ACY; cf. *obstinacy*, etc. (But perh. a misprint for *intemperancy*.)] Intemperateness.

1541 R. COPLAND *Galyen's Terapeut.* 2 Bij, It is necessarye that the curacyon of the thynges that are put fer fro theyr naturall beynges by some intemperacy be made by thynges of contrary vertue.

intemperament (ɪnˈtɛmpərəmənt). *rare.* [f. IN-^{3} + TEMPERAMENT: perh. repr. a mod.L. **intemperāmentum*.] An untempered or distempered condition (esp. of the body, blood, etc.).

1698 FRYER *Acc. E. India & P.* 311 Fevers..that accompany Catarrhs, from the Intemperament of the Spirable Parts. **1822–34** *Good's Study Med.* (ed. 4) I. 231 But whether [Cholera is] dependent upon an intemperament of the atmosphere or upon specific contagion, is by no means ascertained. *Ibid.* IV. 364 The disease [diabetes] is dependent upon a dyscrasy or intemperament of the blood.

intemperance (ɪnˈtɛmpərəns). [a. F. *intempérance* (Oresme, 14th c.), ad. L. *intemperantia* (in senses 1 and 2 below), f. *in-* (IN-^{3}) + *temperantia* TEMPERANCE.] Want of temperateness; the opposite of temperance.

†**1.** Intemperateness, inclemency, severity of the air, weather, or climate. *Obs.*

1432–50 tr. *Higden* (Rolls) II. 291 Knowenge by the planetes the intemperaunce of wedre. **1482** *Monk of Evesham* (Arb.) 97 He was sum what dyssesyd and peynyd only by the intemperans of the eyre as in coolde and in hete. **1538** STARKEY *England* I. ii. 47 The body, yf hyt be not strong, sone..by intemperance of ayr, labur, and trauayle, ys oppressyd and ouerthrowne. **1676** tr. *Guillatiere's Voy. Athens* 309 That the intemperance of that Wind might produce no rheums. **1697** POTTER *Antiq. Greece* II. xx. (1715) 423 When the Season through its coldness and intemperance forc'd the Mariners to stay at Home. **1707** *Curios. in Husb. & Gard.* 40 The Trunk..hinders those Juices from being lost or corrupted..by the Intemperance of the Air.

2. Lack of moderation or restraint; excess in any kind of action; immoderation; *spec.* excessive indulgence of any passion or appetite.

1547 BOORDE *Brev. Health* ccxiv. 73 b, Intemperance is a great vyce, for it doth set every thynge out of order. **1553** BRENDE *Q. Curtius* VIII. 151 b, He..would haue striken Clitus that was yet raging with thintemperaunce of his toung. **1601** MUNDAY & CHETTLE *Death Earl Huntington* IV. iii. in Hazl. *Dodsley* VIII. 303 No church nor chapel, abbey, nunnery, Are privileg'd from his intemperance. **1667** MILTON *P.L.* VI. 472 Some..by violent stroke shall die,..by Intemperance more In Meats and Drinks, which on the Earth shal bring Diseases dire. **1765** H. WALPOLE *Otranto* iv. (1798) 71 Your feeling, Isabella, is warm; but..I never knew it betray you into intemperance. **1849** MACAULAY *Hist. Eng.* vii. II. 196 But the intemperance of his bigotry was thought amply to atone for the intemperance of all his other passions. **1880** *Plain Hints Needlework* 39 Intemperance in any thing is bad. If young girls will read for several hours consecutively..can they wonder that such intemperance brings its own punishment? **1883** S. C. HALL *Retrospect* I. 246 It will now be difficult to credit the intemperance of language to which he gave way.

b. with *pl.* An instance of this, an intemperate act or an excess.

1613–18 DANIEL *Coll. Hist. Eng.* (1626) 17 Hee inflicted exact punishment on all intemperances of his people. **1807** *Life Fielding* in *Tom Jones* I. p. xiii, The intemperances of his early parts of life put a check by their consequences, to the progress of his success.

3. *spec.* Immoderate indulgence in intoxicating drink; addiction to the use of intoxicants.

(In early use always contextually qualified.)

1617 MORYSON *Itin.* III. 156 My protection from large drinking,..and so for that time avoided any great

intemperance. **1725** DE FOE *Voy. round World* (1840) 204 Drank large quantities of punch..and by their intemperance inflamed their blood. **1793** *Friendly Addr. to Poor* 8 Of such men intemperance in drinking is the general fault. **1794** S. WILLIAMS *Vermont* 158 The difficulty of procuring a large quantity of this liquor, prevented any general intemperance. **1841** *Temperance Lancet* 18 Sept., To awaken the deadened sensibility of the Christian world to the crying evils of *intemperance*. **1881** *Med. Temp. Jrnl.* XLVI. 114 It appears then, that intemperance is far more common on the male than the female side.

† **in'temperancy.** *Obs.* [ad. L. *intemperāntia*: see prec. and -ANCY.]

1. = INTEMPERANCE 1.

1540 RAYNOLD *Byrth Mankynde* II. vii. (1643) 136 The intemperancie and mutation of the ayre and weather, may be cause of aborcement. **1599** HAKLUYT *Voy.* II. 70 The intemperancy of the scalding ayre in that hot countrey. **1669** WORLIDGE *Syst. Agric.* (1681) 44 We cannot pretend to an Intemperancy of Climate for neither Hemp nor Flax.

2. = INTEMPERANCE 2.

1532 TINDALE *Wks.* (1573) 227 To auoyde..yᵉ great heape of vices that spring of intemperancy. **1555** W. WATREMAN *Fardle Facions* II. iv. 144 A manne ought to be ware of the intemperauncy of women. **1678** OWEN *Mind of God* iii. 93 Immixed with that intemperancy of reviling other men.

b. = INTEMPERANCE 2 b.

1608 D. T. *Ess. Pol. & Mor.* 98 b, That for a while, he would beare with the intemperancies of his wife. **1645** MILTON *Tetrach.* Introd., Wks. (1851) 138 Not knowing.. why I should be subject..to the intemperancies of this mans preaching choler. **1662** BP. HOPKINS *Fun. Serm.* (1685) 96 They appeal to reason for their judge, which commonly by their debauches and intemperancies, they..so corrupt that it will not discern the truth.

3. = INTEMPERANCE 3. (But always with qualification.)

1586 FERNE *Blaz. Gentrie* 128 Their wonderfull excesse and intemperancie in drinking. **1619** R. HARRIS *Drunkard's Cup* B b, Intemperancies of this nature. **1620** VENNER *Via Recta* ii. 23 These are..the commodities of wine..that a meane and frugality be had in the vse of it, not intemperancy and drunkennes.

† **in'temperant,** *a.* and *sb. Obs. rare.* [ad. L. *intemperānt-em*, f. *in-* (IN-^{3}) + *temperānt-em*, pr. pple. of *temperāre* to qualify, moderate, temper: see -ANT.]

A. *adj.* Wanting moderation or self-restraint; incontinent, intemperate.

1542 UDALL *Erasm. Apoph.* (1877) 15 Soche as be intemperaunt, that is: foloers of their naughtie appetites and lustes. **1598** J. D. tr. *Le Roy's Aristotles Politiques* 377 They which begin so yong to haue the company and vse of men are more intemperant.

B. *sb.* One who is intemperate, esp. in the use of alcoholic liquors.

1882 in ANNANDALE (Suppl.), citing Dr. B. W. Richardson.

Hence **in'temperantly** *adv.*, in an intemperate manner.

1561 T. NORTON *Calvin's Inst.* IV. 58 He that behaueth himselfe intemperantly..geueth euil example to his brethren. **1596** DALRYMPLE tr. *Leslie's Hist. Scot.* I. 111 To truble hail the Republik, gif the king leiuet intemperantlie, and by the boundes of his office.

intemperate (ɪn'tɛmpərət), *a.* [ad. L. *intemperāt-us* untempered, inclement, immoderate, f. *in-* (IN-^{3}) + *temperātus*, pa. pple. of *temperāre* to TEMPER. Primarily, as derived from a passive pple., applied to things, actions, etc.; thence transferred to persons = *intemperant.*]

1. Not temperate, excessive, extreme; esp., of climate or weather, inclement, severe. Now *rare*.

intemperate zone, the Torrid or Frigid zone, as opposed to the Temperate zone.

1526 *Pilgr. Perf.* (W. de W. 1531) 107, I wyll..not departe for all this intemperate heate. **1591** SYLVESTER *Du Bartas* I. iii. 502 The two intemperate zones. **1690** LEYBOURN *Curs. Math.* 463 The Zones are either Temperate or Intemperate, and the Intemperate are either Cold or Hot. *c* **1817** HOGG *Tales & Sk.* II. 139 A cold intemperate mind.

2. Of persons, their actions, or habits: Without temperance or moderation; going beyond due bounds; immoderate, unbridled; violent.

1508 KENNEDIE *Flyting w. Dunbar* 522 Traitour, tyran intemperate. **1590** SPENSER *F.Q.* II. vii. 60 Vnto all that liue in high degree, Ensample be of mind intemperate. **1688** *Col. Rec. Pennsylv.* I. 271 Many intemperate Speeches and passages happend. **1777** WATSON *Philip II* (1839) 187 The most unhappy consequences, which would otherwise have arisen from the intemperate zeal of the reformers. **1799** HOOK in Gurw. *Wellington's Desp.* (1837) I. 40 General Baird requested permission to withdraw his intemperate appeal. **1875** HELPS *Ess., Choice & Managem. Agents* 76 You will often find that men who are intemperate in speech are cautious in writing.

3. Characterized by or addicted to excessive indulgence in a passion or appetite.

c **1430** LYDG. *Min. Poems* (Percy Soc.) 258 Unfructuous talkyng, intemperat diete. **1522** MORE *De quat. Noviss.* Wks. 100 Through intemperate liuing driue our self in sicknes. **1603** SHAKS. *Meas. for M.* v. i. 98 His concupiscible intemperate lust. **1665** MANLEY *Grotius' Low C. Warres* 239 Several Diseases raged among them, springing chiefly from intemperate Drinking. **1846** RUSKIN *Mod. Paint.* II. III. I. ii. §4 Men are held intemperate, only when their desires overcome or prevent the action of their reason; and they are indeed intemperate in the exact degree in which such prevention or interference takes place.

b. *spec.* Given to the immoderate use of intoxicating drink; addicted to drinking.

1677 TEMPLE *Cure of Gout* Wks. 1720 I. 145, I do not allow the pretence of Temperance to all such as are seldom or never drunk..Men may..be intemperate every Day, without being drunk perhaps once in their Lives. **1688** R. HOLME *Armoury* III. 294/2 Intemperate persons..care not which End goes first so they can get Drink. **1790–3** BEATTIE *Moral Sc.* III. iii. §3 (R.) Men, habitually intemperate, justly forfeit the esteem of their fellow-citizens; because they disqualify themselves for every duty. **1846** G. E. DAY tr. *Simon's Anim. Chem.* II. 254 A man..of a muscular frame and good constitution, but of intemperate habits.

† **in'temperate,** *v. Obs. rare*$^{-1}$. Pa. pple. in 7 intemperate. [f. prec.: see -ATE^3.] *trans.* To render intemperate; to disorder, distemper.

1654 T. WHITAKER *Blood of Grape* 92 The fifth age is virill, and the *media* between young and old age; yet doth it not so participate of either, as to affect, or intemperate it [*ed.* 1638 *p.* 44 as that it is intemperate, or infected thereby].

in'temperately, *adv.* [f. INTEMPERATE *a.* + -LY^2.] In an intemperate manner or degree; without moderation; immoderately, excessively.

1576 A. HALL *Acc. of Quarrell* (1815) 34 Hall intemperately sware he would never performe the same. **1620** VENNER *Via Recta* Introd. 3 *marg.*, Aire intemperately cold. **1620** T. GRANGER *Div. Logike* 53 Wine intemperately drunke, corrupteth the memorie. **1744** *Phil. Trans.* XLIII. 136 In Africa..the Soil is as intemperately hot as the Climate. **1765** H. WALPOLE *Otranto* v. (1834) 243 Frederic ..flung the door intemperately against Manfred, and bolted it inwards. **1775** ADAIR *Amer. Ind.* 117 That evil habit of using spirituous liquors intemperately, which they have been taught by the Europeans. **1858** DORAN *Crt. Fools* 96 To laugh intemperately on very small occasion for it.

in'temperateness. Now *rare.* [f. as prec. + -NESS.] The quality of being intemperate.

1. Excessive or extreme character of air or climate; inclemency, severity; = INTEMPERANCE 1.

1555 EDEN *Decades* 75 Theyr countenaunces doo declare the intemperatenes of the ayer and region of Dariena. **1617** MORYSON *Itin.* III. 77 The foresaid intemperatenesse of cold pressing great part of Germany..they use hot stoves. **1685** BOYLE *Salub. Air* 51 Divers Diseases..referr'd to manifest Intemperatenesses of the air, in point of heat, cold, Moisture. **1764** HARMER *Observ.* XVIII. viii. 351 The intemperateness of the weather however obliged them..to desist.

2. Want of moderation, excess in any action, esp. in passion or indulgence; = INTEMPERANCE 2.

1571 GOLDING *Calvin on Ps.* lix. 6 David was..cleere from all troublesome intemperatnes. **1614** BP. HALL *Heaven upon Earth* §7 For a Christian to excuse his intemperatenesse..and to say, I am borne cholericke, sullen, amorous, is an Apologie worse then the fault. **1653** MANTON *Exp. James* i. 26 The quality of men's religion may be discerned by the intemperateness of their language. **1880** G. MEREDITH *Tragic Com.* (1881) 307 [He] was getting to purer fires through his coarser when the final intemperateness drove him to ruin.

† **in'temperature.** *Obs.* [a. obs. F. *intempérature* 'intemperature or distemperature of the bodie, vnseasonablenesse or foulenesse of weather' (Cotgr.), f. *in-* (IN-^{3}) + *température.*]

1. Inclemency, severity, distemperature of the air, weather, etc.; = prec. 1.

1563–87 FOXE *A. & M.* (1596) 309/1 For the great heat and intemperature of the weather. **1684** T. BURNET *Th. Earth* II. 194 The same excesses and intemperature of the seasons. **1725** N. ROBINSON *Th. Physick* 198 How the different Gravities of this Element [Air], and its several Variations, of hot, cold, dry, and moist Intemperatures, cause Diseases. **1753** JOHNSON in *Adventurer* No. 115 ¶8 Whether we owe it to the influences of the constellations, or the intemperature of seasons. **1815** tr. *Duc de Levis' Eng. 19th Cent.* I. 19 The most delicate women are seen exposing themselves to the intemperature of a humid atmosphere. **1820** *Sporting Mag.* VI. 159 These were not the only extraordinary effects of the late intemperature.

2. Abnormal or distempered condition of the body; intemperament.

1559 MORWYNG *Evonymus* 154 It amendeth the cold intemperature of the cheaste. **1660** tr. *Amyraldus' Treat. conc. Relig.* II. v. 229 He would have hindred the intemperature of the humors. **1727** BRADLEY *Fam. Dict.* s.v. *Head-ache*, There is an Head-Ach, which proceeds from the Intemperature of the Brain, which Intemperature being cold and moist, predominates therein. **1799** CORRY *Sat. Lond.* (1803) 38 Plato..observes, that the moral intemperature of cities and the corruption of manners, originate in the bad example of others to youth.

3. Intemperateness of action or passion; = INTEMPERANCE 2.

1589 WARNER *Alb. Eng.* VI. xxx. (1612) 156 Our owne intemprature doth worke in vs our owne vnrest.

† **in'tempered,** *a. Obs.* [IN-^{3}. Cf. F. *intempéré.*] = INTEMPERATE 1; inclement, severe.

1556 *Aurelio & Isab.* (1608) E viij, The heatte of the herte maketh you to take the intemperede and horribill winter for hotte somer.

‖ **intemperies** (ɪntɛm'pɛriːz). [L. *intemperiēs* intemperateness, f *in-* (IN-^{3}) + *temperiēs* temperature, temper.] Disordered condition of the body, dyscrasy; rarely, of the weather.

1676 WISEMAN *Chirurg. Treat.* II. iii. 173 In the Cure of an Ulcer with a moist Intemperies..you are to mix Corroboratives of an astringent faculty. **1707** FLOYER *Pulse-Watch* 99 From the several Cacochymias, the several Intemperies are produc'd, as *Calida, Frigida, Humida, Sicca. Ibid.* 276 The Pulse will show..the hot or cold Intemperies of any Part [etc.]. **1886** *Syd. Soc. Lex.*, *Intemperies*, a derangement of the constitution of the weather. Also, the same as *Dyscrasia*.

† **in'temperous,** *a. Obs. rare*$^{-1}$. [irreg. f. stem of *intemper-ate*, etc. + -OUS.] = INTEMPERATE.

a **1618** SYLVESTER *Panaretus* 269, I..rather would, hearts so intemperous Should not enjoy me, than imploy mee thus.

† **in'tempery.** *Obs. rare*$^{-1}$. [ad. F. *intempérie* = It. *intemperie*, ad. L. *intemperiēs*, *intemperiæ* (see above).] = INTEMPERIES.

1676 T. GARENCIERES *Coral* 63 A feaver is a hot intempery.

† **intem'pestious,** *a. Obs. rare*$^{-1}$. An erroneous form (or perh. misprint) for **intempestivous* = next. (Cf. INTEMPESTUOUS.)

1548 HALL *Chron., Rich. III* 53 Lykewyse his armie muche marveled and no lesse mourned for his sodeyne and intempestious absence.

intempestive (ɪntɛm'pɛstɪv), *a.* [ad. L. *intempestīv-us*, f. *in-* (IN-^{3}) + *tempestīvus* seasonable, TEMPESTIVE. Cf. F. *intempestif, -ive* (1579 in Hatz.).] Untimely, unseasonable, inopportune.

1548 [implied in INTEMPESTIVELY]. **1604** *Supplic. Masse Priests* viii, The disturbance that might have growne by such intempestive troubles. **1608** A. WILLET *Hexapla Exod.* 420 An intempestiue and vnseasonable confession of the truth. **1621** VENNER *Baths of Bathe, Tobacco* (1637) 364 Reproving the too too licentious, liberall, and intempestive taking of it [tobacco]. **1765** GALE in *Phil. Trans.* LV. 202 The hemorrhages were produced by an injudicious intempestive use of hot alexipharmic medicines. **1891** *Cornh. Mag.* Sept. 274 Break out into loud and intempestive laughter. **1891** E. CASTLE *Consequences* III. II. xx. 106 What intempestive freak brought the girl..at such a moment?

Hence **intem'pestively** *adv.*, unseasonably.

1548 W. PATTEN *Exp. Scotl.* Perorat. P ij, So intempestiuely to tell that tale. **1650** CHARLETON *Paradoxes* Ep. Ded. 6 Had I not been intempestively drawne upon the Stage.

† **intempe'stivity.** *Obs.* [ad. L. *intempestīvit-ās*, f. *in-* (IN-^{3}) + *tempestīvitās* seasonableness, TEMPESTIVITY. Cf. F. *intempestivité* (Littré).] Unseasonableness, untimeliness.

1654 GAYTON *Pleas. Notes* III. ix. 127 They were either guilty of Intempestivity and unseasonablenesse, or else of want of Worth and Glory. *a* **1656** HALES *Serm. Eton* i. (1673) 4 A vice which they call ἀκαιρία, Intempestivity, an indiscretion by which unwise and unexperienced men see not what befits times, persons, occasions.

intem'pestuous, *a. rare*$^{-1}$. An erroneous form (or perh. misprint) for **intempestivous* = INTEMPESTIVE. (Cf. INTEMPESTIOUS.)

1885 STEVENSON *Dynamiter* vii. 105 Visitors..arrived..at intempestuous hours of night or morning.

† **intemple,** obs. variant of ENTEMPLE.

1673 H. MORE *Appendix* 28 The Godhead indeed is hypostatically intempled in the humane nature of Christ.

in'temporal, *a.* [IN-^{3}.] Not temporal; eternal, everlasting. Hence **in'temporally** *adv.*

1656 STANLEY *Hist. Philos.* v. (1701) 207/2 When divested of Matter, and Spiritualiz'd, their Will is only fed with intemporal spiritual good. *Ibid.* IX. 424/1 They..inhabit Eternity, which is..always being, because it always was, is, and shall be intemporally in the divine Mind. **1911** J. WARD *Realm of Ends* xiv. 306 The intemporal world of ideas. **1962** tr. *J. L. Borges's Labyrinths* (1964) 262 There was no other instant than the intemporal one of the crickets.

† **intena'bility.** *Obs.* [f. next + -ITY.] The character of being 'intenable'; incapacity of being held or defended.

1644 PRYNNE & WALKER *Fiennes's Trial* 46 The weaknesses, defects, and intenability of the Castle. *Ibid.* 83 What should be judged uttermost extremity in regard of men, Ammunition, victuals, or intenability of any Fort, to justifie the Governour's surrender of it to the enemy?

† **in'tenable,** *a. Obs.* [IN-^{3}.] That cannot be held or maintained; untenable.

1738 WARBURTON *Div. Legat.* I. 335 The Doctrine was preached up..but intenable by Reason. **1752** —— *Wks.* (1811) IX. Serm. xiii. 252 Intenable pretensions.

intend (ɪn'tɛnd), *v.* Forms: *α.* 3–8 **entend**, 4–6 **entende**; *β.* 4–7 **intende**, 5– **intend.** (Also 6, *3rd pers. sing.* **intent.**) [ME. a. F. *entend-re*, in 14–15th c. also *intendre*, to stretch, extend, strain, direct one's thoughts or faculties, to hear, understand, expect, occupy oneself (also *refl.*):—L. *intendĕre* to stretch out or forth, to strain, direct, spread out, increase, turn one's attention, purpose, endeavour, maintain, assert; in med.L., also, to understand, interpret, f. *in-* (IN-^{2}) + *tendĕre* to stretch, to TEND.

The extensive and complex development of senses in L. and OF. is reflected also in English. But the chronological

appearance of the senses here does not accord with their original development; those first taken over from French in 13–14th c. being figurative uses, far removed from the literal sense, which was only adopted directly from L. about or after 1600. As an attempt at chronological order would only end in chaos, a logical arrangement, according in the main with the development as gathered from all three languages, is here followed. But the history of some senses is obscure: see VI. The sense of early quotations is also often difficult to determine.]

I. To stretch out, extend, expand, increase, intensify. [A group of senses of late introduction, immediately from Latin.]

†**1.** *trans.* To stretch forth, extend; to point forwards. *Obs.*

1601 GILL *Trinity* in *Sacr. Philos.* (1625) 223, I will onely intend my finger to some very few. **1615** G. SANDYS *Trav.* (1670) 94 The Camelion..swiftly intending his tongue of a marvellous length..wherewith he preys upon flyes. **1633** P. FLETCHER *Purple Isl.* v. xxvii, Upon whose tops spear-men their pikes intending, Watch there.

†**2.** *intr.* To stretch, extend (in position). *Obs.*

1594 *2nd Rep. Faustus* in Thoms *E.E. Prose Rom.* (1858) III. 335 Out of which are two and thirty marvellous good stone bridges, intending to either side of the city.

†**3.** *trans.* To stretch, strain, make tense; to expand, dilate. *lit.* and *fig. Obs.*

1658 ROWLAND *Moufet's Theat. Ins.* 992 A thin skin, which being..shaken or intended, it must make a sound. *a* **1677** HALE *Prim. Orig. Man.* I. i. 29 'Tis by this..the Lungs are intended or remitted. **1678** CUDWORTH *Intell. Syst.* I. iv. §13. 221 As when a bow is successively intended and remitted. **1697** BP. PATRICK *Comm. Exod.* iv. 21 The last word (Cavad) intends and increases the Sense. **1740** CHEYNE *Regimen* 314–5 We may..have an innate, inherent Power to intend or remit our Wills *in infinitum*. **1837** SIR W. HAMILTON *Metaph.* xliii. (1870) II. 472 When we intend the vital powers above the suitable degree we occasion a hindrance, a pain.

†**4.** To increase the intensity of, to intensify. *Obs.*

1603 SIR C. HEYDON *Jud. Astrol.* xii. 293 The Moone.. intendeth or remitteth her influence at one time more then an other. **1647** JER. TAYLOR *Lib. Proph.* i. 14 The Church hath power to intend our Faith but not to extend it. **1705** C. PURSHALL *Mech. Macrocosm* 297 A small quantity of *Aqua Vitae* sprinkled upon the Freezing Mixture, wonderfully intends its Force.

†**b.** *intr.* To become more intense. *Obs.*

1654 H. L'ESTRANGE *King Chas. I* (1655) 98 Having certain intelligence from his correspondents..that the heat did rather intend then relax.

II. To strain or direct (the eyes, mind, thoughts, words, efforts, etc.). [L. *intendere oculos, animum, curas, eruditionem*, etc.]

5. *trans.* To direct (the eyes, mind, etc.), *to, into, towards* something. Now a conscious Latinism.

14.. *Aungeles Song* 13 in *Hoccleve's Wks.* III. p. li, To his pleasaunce hire hertes to intende. **1502** ATKINSON tr. *De Imitatione* III. lxiv. 258 Myn iyen intendynge into the, I truste fullye in the, my lorde god. **1509** HAWES *Past. Pleas.* XXVII. (1845) 130 His power to entende Ageynst all suche rebelles contrarious. **1607** HIERSON *Wks.* I. 209 Dauids longing was entended vnto both. **1711** HEARNE *Collect.* (O.H.S.) III. 181 He..blam'd himself that he could not intend his Mind in yᵉ Prayers. **1877** PATMORE *Unknown Eros* (1890) 1 Intend thine eye Into the dim and undiscovered sky.

†**6.** *intr.* and *trans.* To direct one's course, make one's way; to proceed on (a journey, etc.). (L. *intendere, intendere iter.*) *Obs.* or *arch.*

c **1425** *Found. St. Bartholomew's* (E.E.T.S.) 61 With othir men that intendid to the same place. **1476** SIR J. PASTON in *P. Lett.* No. 776 III. 162 Iff ye entende hyddrewarde. **1528** LYNDESAY *Dreme* 372 Up, throuch the Watter, schortlie we intendit, Quhilk invirons the Erth. **1596** DALRYMPLE tr. *Leslie's Hist. Scot.* x. 341 He thairfor leiueng the Quene at Neoporte..intendis the hie way to Scotland. **1608** SHAKS. *Per.* I. ii. 116 Tyre, I now look out from thee then, and to Tarsus Intend my travel. **1611** BIBLE *Transl. Pref.* 2 Assured that the course which he intended made much for the glory of God. **1638–48** G. DANIEL *Eclog.* ii. 31 Wee may intend at Something, and arrive In ken of the faire Port at which wee drive. **1682** SOUTHERNE *Loyal Brother* I. i, Your royal Mother, with the fair Semanthe, Intend this way. **1744** HARRIS *Three Treat.* Wks. (1841) 47 As if..a company of travellers, in some wide forest, were all intending for one city. **1774** D. JONES *Jrnl.* (1865) 108 Set out about eleven o'clock..intending the nearest course for the river Ohio. *a* **1832** CRABBE *Birth Flattery* i, Guide him to Fairy-land, who now intends That way his flight.

†**b.** *intr.* To start on a journey, to set out. (Sometimes app. ellipt. for 'intend to go or start', purpose a journey: cf. 18.) *Obs.*

[**1596** SHAKS. *1 Hen. IV*, IV. i. 92 The King himselfe in person hath set forth, Or hither-wards intended speedily.] **1646** in *12th Rep. Hist. MSS. Comm.* App. v. 2 Hee is at Newcastle and intends for France. **1666** *Lond. Gaz.* No. 47/2 She is preparing for her journey, and suddenly intends to Cleve. **1700** PENN in *Pa. Hist. Soc. Mem.* IX. 16 The first fair day I intend down. **1749** WESLEY *Wks.* (1872) II. 155 Pray let us know when you or your brother intend for this Kingdom. **1817** BYRON *Wks.* (1837–40) III. 356, I intend for England this spring, where I have some affairs to adjust.

†**7.** *trans.* **a.** To direct, level, aim (something) *against* some one. **b.** To refer, attribute, ascribe (a thing) *to* some one. *Obs.*

1615 J. STEPHENS *Satyr. Ess.* 167 Hee haunts the Authours company, recites the worke, intends it to some third person, and after he hath damnd the thing in question, he refers himselfe to the right owner. *a* **1734** NORTH *Life Francis North* (1742) 215 Many Complaints were intended against him, and such as were thought well enough grounded.

III. To strain, direct, or bend the attention; to attend to; to attend. [An obsolete group of senses from OF., ultimately from L. *intendere* = *intendere animum*.]

†**8.** *intr.* To direct the mind or attention; to pay heed; to exert the mind, devote attention, apply oneself assiduously. Const. *to, unto*, rarely *about, on, at. Obs.*

a. c **1374** CHAUCER *Troylus* III. 375 (424) Eche to his owene nede gan entende. —— *Boeth.* I. pr. ii. 4 (Camb. MS.) She entendynge to me ward with alle the lookynge of hyr eyen seyde [etc.]. *c* **1450** *Merlin* 23 In the menetyme that they entended a-boute this mater, come Merlyn to Blase. *c* **1477** CAXTON *Jason* 61 Iason..entended gladly unto the dubbyng and making of his shippe. **1523** LD. BERNERS *Froiss.* I. ccxxxv. 330 Haue mercy, and entend on the delyuerance of the kyng my husbande. **1589** PUTTENHAM *Eng. Poesie* I. iii. (Arb.) 23 They were the first that entended to the obseruation of nature and her works.

β. **1432–50** tr. *Higden* (Rolls) I. 81 Somme peple tylle the erthe..somme intende to sapience and discipline. *c* **1450** tr. *De Imitatione* III. vi. 71 Loue is circumspecte,..not intendyng to veyn þinges. *c* **1530** in *Pol. Rel. & L. Poems* (1866) 31 A man that Intendyth to mynstrels, shalle soone be weddyd to poverte. **1547–64** BAULDWIN *Mor. Philos.* (Palfr.) 123 It is a foolishnesse to intend much to dreames. **1613** PURCHAS *Pilgrimage* III. xvi. 279 They sometimes intend to their owne dreames.

†**b.** *refl.* To devote oneself; *pass.* To be devoted. Const. *to. Obs.*

1503 HAWES *Examp. Virt.* VII. xxxviii, Euery true crysten man sholde to To god intended with lyberalyte. **1568** GRAFTON *Chron.* II. 371 All the knightes and squiers.. entended and prepared themselves to nothing, but..to be of the one parte or the other. **1627** FELTHAM *Resolves* II. [I.] xxvi. (1628) 83 To what can we intend our selues, wherein there is not a Deuill to intrap vs?

†**c.** *absol.*

1549–62 STERNHOLD & H. *Ps.* xxxiii[i]. 18 But loe the eyes of God entend And watch to ayde the iust. **1603** OWEN *Pembrokeshire* (1891) 25 The saied Earle..ought not to intende or meddle within the said Lordship of Kemes.

†**9.** To apply oneself *to do* something; to endeavour, to strive. *Obs.*

c **1385** CHAUCER *L.G.W.* 1155 (*Dido*) Al the longe day they tweye Entendedyn to spekyn & to pleye. **1471** RIPLEY *Comp. Alch.* Ep. ii. in Ashm. (1652) 111 Intending over all thing.. his precepts tenne..to keep. **1582** MUNDAY *Eng. Rom. Life* in *Harl. Misc.* (Malh.) II. 195 She could not intend to speake to them, being troubled with so many other suters. **1589** PUTTENHAM *Eng. Poesie* I. xxxi. (Arb.) 74 No man or very few entended to write in any laudable science. **1590** BARROUGH *Meth. Physick* I. xxiii. (1639) 39 That he..may with all his power intend to amend it. **1674** tr. *Scheffer's Lapland* 85 Blocks, upon which..they divide their flesh, fish, or other things they intend to make ready.

†**10.** *intr.* To give auditory attention; to give ear, listen, hearken. *Obs.*

c **1380** *Sir Ferumb.* 5325 'Balan', said he, 'to me entende'. **1450–1530** *Myrr. our Ladye* 48, I entended to them & gaue them answeres. **1481** CAXTON *Myrr.* III. ix. 152 Now entende ye of the kynge tholomeus and of the werkes of somme other philosophres. **1568** GRAFTON *Chron.* II. 371 If it please you to returne againe hether, then we will gladly entend to your treatie.

†**b.** *trans.* To give ear to; to hearken to, hear. [F. *entendre*.] *Obs.*

c **1450** *Merlin* 310 Sche ne a-tended to no-thinge but to be-holde and entende what songe thei seiden. **1549** LATIMER *3rd Serm. bef. Edw. VI* (Arb.) 95 Manye begyn to praye, and sodaynelye caste awaye prayer..as thoughe God coulde not entend them, or had somewhat els to do.

†**11.** *intr.* To give personal attendance; to be in attendance or waiting; to attend. *Obs.*

c **1386** CHAUCER *Merch. T.* 656 Seynte Marie how may this be That Damyan entendeth nat to me. **1390** GOWER *Conf.* III. 100 Eche in his office Entendeth to don him service. **1469** *Househ. Ord.* (1790) 94 All suche persons as shall entend aboute the Duchesse. **1576** *Tyde Taryeth no man* (Collier) 3 At hand to approche the Players intend. **1644** CROMWELL *Let.* 1 Sept. in *Carlyle*, I wish that one of your number..may intend and appear at that Committee.

†**b.** *trans.* To attend on or to, minister to. *Obs.*

c **1500** *For to serve Lord* in *Babees Bk.* (1868) 373 Hit moste be awayted and well entended by servitours yf drinke be asked. *a* **1533** LD. BERNERS *Gold. Bk. M. Aurel.* (1546) R v b, The malady was greuous..and also he was not well intended. **1633** T. STAFFORD *Pac. Hib.* II. vi. (1810) 301 The great trouble it would bee to our selves to intend you.

†**12.** *trans.* To turn one's thoughts to, fix the mind on (something); to attend to; to occupy oneself with; to look after. *Obs.*

a. **1429** in Rymer *Fœdera* (1710) X. 424 Eretikes there that entenden the Subversion of the Christien Feith. **1483** CAXTON *G. de la Tour* C viij, They entended wel other thynges than to saye theyr matyns. **1592** HARVEY *Four Lett.* 13, I have smal superfluity of leysure to entend such businesse.

β. **1432–50** tr. *Higden* (Rolls) III. 87 Those schepardes.. appelede to that kynge..; and when that kynge intendede oon [*in unum intenderet*] of theyme, an other did slee the kynge. **1482** *Monk of Evesham* (Arb.) 102 So bode al moste. x. days with owte any mete intendyng only the benefitys of god and the exhortacion of hys brethyrne. **1526** *Pilgr. Perf.* (W. de W. 1531) 1 b, Euery religious persone sholde intende the perfeccyon of his soule. **1617** MORYSON *Itin.* III. 239 The Plebeans intended Traffique and Shop-keeping. **1667** MILTON *P.L.* II. 457 Intend at home..what best may ease The present misery. **1694** COLLIER *Ess. Mor. Subj.* I. (1703) 210 The Priest is supposed only to intend the Affairs of Religion. **1784** COWPER *Tiroc.* 660 Too busy to intend a meaner care.

IV. To apprehend, and kindred sense. [An obsolete group of senses from OF.: also in med.L.]

†**13.** *trans.* To have understanding of (something); to understand or apprehend *that* something is; also, in early use, to understand (a person). *Obs.*

a **1300** *Cursor M.* 23896 (Gött.) Here i haue a littel spend In word, efter þat i entend. *c* **1430** *Syr Gener.* (Roxb.) 9266 Generides gan tho to entend That Segryne aspied here fleeyng. *c* **1450** LONELICH *Grail* xlii. 547 Of On thing thou me Entende. **1606** WARNER *Alb. Eng.* XIV. lxxxiii. 347 The ancient Irish Manners..if conferd with Egypts, Thence may be intended hadd. **1620** MARKHAM *Farew. Husb.* II. xix. (1668) 107 It is to be intended the voyage is seldome long, but from neighbour to neighbour.

†**14.** *intr.* To have or come to an understanding; to agree together; to be in accord. [F. *s'entendre*.]

1421 in Rymer *Foedera* (1710) X. 462 Then myght they togeder entende ayeins Miscreants. **1429** *Ibid.* 424 The Men of Armes and Archers, that have Entended with the said Cardinal. **1509** HAWES *Past. Pleas.* XIV. xiv, Musyke hath them so set in concorde, That all in one may right well entende.

†**15.** *trans.* and *intr.* To apprehend, conceive; to think, estimate, have an opinion; to judge. *Obs.*

c **1570** *Pride & Lowl.* (1841) 15 Which, then well understood, wyl not deceave, Nor suffer us to erre, as I entend. **1586** A. DAY *Eng. Secretary* I. (1625) 5 One that sometimes intended not a little of his owne invention. *Ibid.*, The woman..began hereupon..to waxe coy, and to intend great matter of her selfe. *Ibid.* II. 118 Men vain-gloriously minded, or arrogantly otherwise intending of their owne proper services. **1638** FORD *Fancies* V. i, *Liv.* Before our sleeping hour, you vow? *Troy.* I do, Before we ought to sleep. *Liv.* So I intend too.

†**16.** *trans.* To understand as in the view or sense of the law; to construe, interpret, or hold legally. Cf. INTENDMENT 4. *Obs.*

1613 SIR H. FINCH *Law* (1636) 479 That which is found by the oath of twelue men is intended true till it be reuersed, but it may as well be intended that there is an errour in the Record. **1642** *Perkins' Prof. Bk.* iii. §191. 85 He shall be punished for his first entrie. For it cannot be intended that his entrie was unto any other intent but to steale the cup. **1768** BLACKSTONE *Comm.* III. xiii. 219 If such market or fair be on the same day with mine, it is *prima facie* a nusance to mine, and there needs no proof of it, but the law will intend it to be so. **1798** BOY *Amer. Law Rep.* (1809) I. 48 Nothing shall be intended to be within the jurisdiction [of inferior courts] but what is expressly given.

V. To bend the mind to something to be done; to purpose, design, mean. [The chief current group of senses. From OF.]

17. *intr.* To have a purpose or design; to be minded or resolved (in some defined way). *Obs.*, exc. as an absol. use of 18.

1390 GOWER *Conf.* III. 213 Mote every worthy prince entende Betwene the simplesse of pite And the foolhaste of cruelte. **1497** BP. ALCOCK *Mons Perfect.* E j, And so I entende all my lyf. *c* **1529** in *Life Fisher* F.'s Wks. (E.E.T.S.) II. p. lx, Inventions are nowe devised against me that neuer entended but honestly. **1587** M. GROVE *Pelops & Hippod.* (1878) 78 Let me heare from you, how that you doe entend. **1656** S. HOLLAND *Zara* (1719) 87 [They] have cause to guess that he intends rather to a bloody War, then a Wanton Tilt.

18. *trans.* To have in the mind as a fixed purpose; to purpose, design. (The chief current sense.)

a. with *inf. phr.* or *subord. clause.*

a. **1413** *Pilgr. Sowle* (Caxton 1483) IV. xxx. 78 Flaterers.. only entenden to plese for the tyme. **1494** FABYAN *Chron.* I. ii. 8 Eneas..entendyd to haue sauyd from deth yᵉ fayre Polixena. **1559** W. CUNNINGHAM *Cosmogr. Glasse* 141 To morrow..I entende to consume in teaching you necessarye principles. **1628** DIGBY *Voy. Medit.* (1868) 27, I sett sayle for Zant, where I entended to sell the corne. **1650** SIR E. NICHOLAS in *N. Papers* (Camden) 200 The King, entending to make an escape from the Scotts. **1775** ADAIR *Amer. Ind.* 241 The man he entended to enslave.

β. c **1374** CHAUCER *Troylus* V. 478 Intendestow that we shul here bleve? **1529** MORE *Suppl. Soulys* Wks. 332/2 In dede he intendeth to goe ferther. **1590** SHAKS. *Mids. N.* II. i. 138 How long within this wood intend you stay? **1624** HEYWOOD *Gunaik.* 207 Alcippus intended to abrogate and adnichilate their lawes. **1657** R. LIGON *Barbadoes* (1673) 22 We were compelled to stay longer in the Island than we intended. **1818** CRUISE *Digest* (ed. 2) VI. 375 He intended his son should have it in remainder for his life only. **1875** W. S. HAYWARD *Love agst. World* 79 What do you intend to do?

b. with *simple obj.*, alone or with complemental extension.

c **1450** tr. *De Imitatione* II. iv. 44 If þou intende ner seke no þinge elles but þe plesing of god & þe profit of þy neiȝbore, þou shalt haue inwarde liberte. **1509** HAWES *Past. Pleas.* XIX. (Percy Soc.) 87 It was for fere ye dyde some yll entende. **1535** COVERDALE *Prov.* iii. 29 Intende no hurte vnto thy neghboure. **1548** HALL *Chron., Hen. VIII* 61 If suche a thinge were entended, they coulde not tell who woulde take their parte. **1601** SHAKS. *Jul. C.* III. i. 151, I know not Gentlemen what you intend. **1606** —— *Tr. & Cr.* II. ii. 39 You know an enemy intends you harme. **1634** SIR T. HERBERT *Trav.* 200 An Ile where not long agoe the English merchants entended a Plantation. **1693** DRYDEN *Juvenal* (1697) 382 He intended an Invective against a Standing Army. **1781** COWPER *Lett.* 27 Nov., We both wish it may have the effect you intend. **1795** BURKE *Corr.* IV. 380 A measure better intended than considered. **1857** MISS S. WINKWORTH tr. *Tauler's Serm.* xxv. 386 They..remain a prey to their besetting sin of always seeking and intending themselves. **1875** GLADSTONE *Glean.* (1879) VI. 224 We intend going to Rome. **1885** S. COX *Expos.* Ser. I. i. 9 We intended no neglect.

c. with indirect passive.

1651 HOBBES *Leviath.* II. xxx. 175 This is intended should be done. **1662** *Bk. Com. Prayer* Pref., The evils that were

intended to be remedied. **1818** BENTHAM *Ch. Eng.* ii. 159 Was it thus intended and commanded by him to be drunken?

19. *trans.* To design (a thing) for some purpose; to destine (a thing or person) to a fate or use; to purpose to bestow or give; to mean (a thing) *to be* or *to do* something.

a. with prep. or conj. phr., or dative, as compl.

1590 SHAKS. *Mids. N.* III. ii. 12 A Play, Intended for great Theseus nuptiall day. **1603** —— *Meas. for M.* III. i. 58 Lord Angelo hauing affaires to heauen Intends you for his swift Ambassador. **1662** GERBIER *Princ.* Ep. Ded., The Place of Surveyor Generall was also intended to me (after late Inigo Jones). **1701** PENN in *Pa. Hist. Soc. Mem.* IX. 47, I intend him the island under some moderate conditions. **1748** RICHARDSON *Clarissa* (1811) I. xli. 309 Your father intends you six suits..at his own expense. **1812–16** J. SMITH *Panorama Sc. & Art* I. 320 The threads of screws are differently formed, according to..the use for which they are intended. **1875** JOWETT *Plato* (ed. 2) I. 112 The whole composition is intended as an attack upon Pittacus. *Mod.* The second son is intended for the army, and the third for the bar.

†**b.** with complemental obj. *Obs.*

a **1648** LD. HERBERT *Life Hen. VIII* (1683) 146 The Building was intended most ample and magnificent. **1659** *Burton's Diary* (1828) IV. 356 Your vote makes it clear that you intend them a legislature. **1726** AYLIFFE *Parergon* 370 If the Person bearing the same protests that he does not thereby intend himself a Monk, 'tis otherwise.

c. with *inf.*

1729 BUTLER *Serm. Hum. Nat.* Wks. 1874 II. 3 The several members..were intended to be instruments of good ..to the whole body. **1853** RUSKIN *Stones Ven.* II. vi, This we suppose to be all the pleasure that architecture was ever intended to give us. **1884** CHURCH *Bacon* 143 They intended him now to come to the bar to receive his sentence.

20. To design to express; to signify by one's words; to mean. † ***to intend at***, to mean for.

1572 J. JONES *Bathes of Bath* I. 1 b, The propertie of every definicion is, to shew..to the sences, the matter entended. **1625** BACON *Ess., Unity Relig.* (Arb.) 429 Fraile Men, in some of their Contradictions, intend the same thing. **1647** N. BACON *Disc. Govt. Eng.* I. lxi. (1739) 119 Glanvil.. frequently toucheth upon the King's Court of Pleas, which cannot be intended at the Court of Lords. **1676** HOBBES *Iliad* Pref. (1686) 1 By Profit I intend not here any Accession of Wealth. **1783** M. CUTLER in *Life, Jrnls. & Corr.* (1888) II. 211 Consumption, by which the Physicians intend a disorder of the lungs. **1853** TALFOURD *Castilian* I. i, You intend my husband? **1857** MAURICE *Ep. St. John* i. 1 Do I understand something different by Ethics? No; I intend the same thing.

†**b.** Of words, etc.: To mean; to signify; to indicate. *Obs.*

?*c* **1530** *Crt. of Love* 1370 *Domini est terra*; this Laten intent, The god of Love hath erth in governaunce. **1565** *Satir. Poems Reform.* i. 677 Owtbraythinge Envye, debayte, and stryffe entendes nothinge ells but civill myscheffe. **1602** MARSTON *Antonio's Rev.* IV. iii, What intend these plaints? **1749** FIELDING *Tom Jones* I. ix. *note*, This word..intends persons without virtue or sense. **1847** R. W. HAMILTON *Sabbath* i. (1848) 12 The word..generally intends a sacred appropriation of a particular time.

†**c.** To designate as something; to call. *rare.*

a **1599** SPENSER *F.Q.* VII. vi. 9 Vesper, whom we the Euening-starre intend. **1605** CHAPMEN *All Fooles* Plays 1873 I. 122 *Gost.* You haue a forward, valiant eldest Sonne ..*Mar.* I know not wherein you intend him so.

VI. Senses of uncertain position or origin; mostly due to literalism of translation from L. or F.

†**21.** *trans.* To expect. *Obs.* [OF. *entendre* = F. *attendre*.]

c **1374** CHAUCER *Troylus* IV. 1621 (1649) þere lyuyth lady non..þat be-trayed were or wo-begon As I þat al treuthe in ʒow entende. **1485** CAXTON *Paris & V.* 69 She neuer entended to here tydynges of hyr loue Parys.

†**22.** To assert, maintain; to pretend; to claim. [cf. L. *eam sese intendit esse.*]

c **1570** *Marr. Wit & Science* IV. i. in Hazl. *Dodsley* II. 360 Friend Wit, are you the man indeed, which you intend? **1593** SHAKS. *Lucr.* 121 For then is Tarquine brought vnto his bed, Intending wearinesse with heauie sprite. **1594** —— *Rich. III*, III. v. 8, I can counterfeit the deepe tragedian.. Tremble and start at wagging of a straw: Intending deepe suspition. **1633** T. ADAMS *Exp. 2 Peter* i. 20 Alchymists that labour to make gold by projection, intend that there is natural gold. **1634** SIR T. HERBERT *Trav.* 153 The Title of Universall Bishop: though..Bishops formerly in that Sea from Lynus..to this Boniface never intended it.

†**23.** *Sc. Law.* To maintain or prosecute (an action, etc.) in legal form. *Obs.*

15.. *Acts Sederunt* 3 (Jam.) By the same Act their are libertie grantit to all personis quho might be prejudgit be the saidis prescriptiouns..to intend their actiouns within the space of thretten yeirs. *a* **1578** LINDESAY (Pitscottie) *Chron. Scot.* (S.T.S.) I. 286 Hie on novayis could gett them [bulls] proclametit nor durst nocht intend the same ffor feir of the Hepburnes. **1690** *Andros Tracts* I. 144 All Actions intended upon Informations of Intrusions..must have had their Decision at the Ordinary Courts of Common Law.

†**24.** *intr.* To tend or incline. *Obs.*

1509 BARCLAY *Cyt. & Uplondyshm.* (Percy Soc.) p. lxvii, To what vices that princes most intend That dare these fooles solemnize and commende. **1587** GOLDING *De Mornay* vii. 91 The wil intendeth rather to commaund than to obey, and vnto freedom rather than bondage. **1597** SHAKS. *2 Hen. IV*, I. ii. 9 The braine of this foolish compounded Clay-man, is not able to inuent any thing that intends [*Fols.* tends] to laughter. **1640** G. ABBOTT *Job Paraphr.* 245 The raine, which is heavie of it selfe, and intends downward.

25. *trans.* To superintend, direct. Cf. INTENDANT.

[app. allied to 12.]

1791 COWPER *Odyss.* VIII. 314 Nine arbiters, appointed to intend The whole arrangements of the public games. **1831** E. IRVING *Exp. Revelat.* I. 58 According to their several spheres of creation and providence which they occupy and intend.

†**in'tend**, *sb. Obs.* [f. INTEND *v.*] = INTENT.

1526 TINDALE *Acts* x. 29, I axe you therfore; for what intend have ye sent for me? **1607** *Schol. Disc. agst. Antichr.* I. ii. 71 This answer of a good intend is meerly cauillous. **1649** BP. REYNOLDS *Hosea* iv. 57 In pursuance of other ends and intends.

†**in'tendable**, *a. Obs.* Forms: 4–5 en-, 6–7 in-. See also INTENDIBLE. [a. OF. *entendable* understandable, understanding, intelligent, attentive (12th c. in Godef.), f. *entendre*: see INTEND. In sense 3, from L. *intendĕre*: see INTENDIBLE.]

1. Devoting attention; attentive, assiduous.

1390 GOWER *Conf.* III. 157 Nought entendable To holde upright his kinges name. **1481** CAXTON *Godfrey* 286 An holy woman and entendable to good werkes.

2. Understandable; = INTENDIBLE 1.

c **1570** *Pride & Lowl.* (1841) 43 Which is not to be thought nor intendable.

3. Averrable; = INTENDIBLE 2.

1628 COKE *On Litt.* 52 b, His warrant is intendable in law of an actuall liverie.

†**in'tendance**[1]. *Obs.* Also 4–6 **entendaunce**, 7 *erron.* **intendants**. [a. OF. *entendance* (12th c. in Godef.) attention, etc., f. *entendre*, *entendant*, to INTEND.] Application of the mind; attention.

1390 GOWER *Conf.* III. 359 All freshe I sigh hem springe and daunce, And do to love her entendaunce. **1450–1530** *Myrr. our Ladye* 10 All the wordes of thys holy seruyce oughte to be sayde or songe wyth entendaunce therto. *c* **1540** HYRDE *Vives' Instr. Chr. Wom.* (1592) Bij, The maide whom wee would have specially good requireth all intendance both of Father and Mother. **1575** TURBERV. *Faulconrie* 325 When a hawke hath bene recovered of some great greefe by good keeping and intendance. **1611** W. SCLATER *Key* (1629) 95 It were long to recite all their deuout intendants, all their strict obseruances.

intendance[2] (ɪn'tɛndəns). [a. F. *intendance* (1595 in Godef. *Compl.*), f. *intendant* INTENDANT *sb.*: see -ANCE.] The function of an intendant; superintendence, direction; intendancy; *spec.* a department of the French public service, or the officials conducting it, as the war commissariat, etc.

1739 CIBBER *Apol.* (1756) II. 90 Which province..was the only one we car'd to trust to his particular intendance. **1839** JAMES *Louis XIV*, IV. 291 The real intendance of public buildings was held by the famous Mansard. **1862** M. HOPKINS *Hawaii* 250 They stipulated..that the Roman Catholic schools should be exclusively under the intendance of inspectors professing that faith. **1880** KINGLAKE *Crimea* VI. v. 95 The French Intendance and the English Commissariat must meet as best they might the huge accession of wants.

b. The official quarters or office of an intendant.

1895 G. PARKER in *Atlantic Monthly* (U.S.) Mar. 301 There was yet an hour before I was to go to the *intendance*.

intendancy (ɪn'tɛndənsɪ). Also 6 -encie. 7–9 -ency. [f. INTENDANT *sb.*: see prec. and -ANCY. In sense 2, ad. Sp. *intendencia*.]

1. The office, position, or function of an intendant; a body of intendants.

1598 J. D. tr. *Le Roy's Aristotles Politiques* 172 The fourth [of the kinds of governments is]..a perpetuall military intendencie by tribe. **1645** EVELYN *Diary* 25 Jan., Hence we went to see Dr. Gibbs..who had some intendency in an Hospital built on the Via Triumphalis [Rome]. **1670** COTTON *Espernon* III. XI. 548 Under colour of some Commission of his Intendancy. **1762** tr. *Busching's Syst. Geog.* III. 619 Each..is vested with the intendancy of some interior districts. **1825** CARLYLE *Schiller* App. ii. (1872) 265 The theatre of that town..owes to him its foundation, and its maintenance through his long Intendancy. **1870** *Daily News* 27 Sept., The intendancy had orders to proceed to Lagny.

b. *fig.* Superintendence.

1727 WARBURTON in *Tracts* (1789) 118 The Atomist Lucretius, whose cold Philosophy had formally excluded all Intendency of a superior Mind.

2. A district in Spanish America under the control of an intendant (*intendente*).

[**1808** PIKE *Sources Mississ.* III. App. (1810) 4 The foregoing nine administrations or intendencias, the kingdom of Leon, and the province of Nuevo San Ander.. form, as I believe, the whole political government of the vice-roy of Mexico.] **1810** *Edin. Rev.* XVI. 98 The intendancy of Guanaxuato has 568 inhabitants to the square league. **1836** MACGILLIVRAY tr. *Humboldt's Trav.* xxvi. 395 The silver..was deposited in the provincial treasuries established in the chief places of the intendancies.

intendant (ɪn'tɛndənt), *sb.* Also 7–9 -ent. [a. F. *intendant* (1591 in Hatz-Darm.), ad. L. *intendent-em*, pr. pple. of *intendĕre*; cf. INTEND *v.* 25.]

1. One who has the charge, direction, or superintendence of a department of public business, the affairs of a town or province, the household of a prince or nobleman, etc.; a superintendent, a manager. Used originally and chiefly as the title of certain public officers in France and elsewhere; often repr. Fr. *intendant* or the corresponding term in other languages.

Among the officials thus denoted are: (*a*) The functionary who formerly administered a French province, according to the system introduced under Richelieu in the 17th cent., called also *intendant of justice, police, and finances.* (*b*) The second officer in Canada during the French rule, possessing civil and maritime jurisdiction. (*c*) In Mexico, the principal officer of the treasury or of the district, exercising administrative and some judicial authority (Sp. *intendente*).

a. As a French, Spanish, or other foreign title.

1652 EVELYN *St. France* (R.), Subordinate to him are four other intendents. *a* **1674** CLARENDON *Hist. Reb.* XV. §153 The Intendant of the Province [of Nismes], who is the Supreme Minister in all Civil Affairs throughout the whole Province. **1676** tr. *Guillatiere's Voy. Athens* 395, I saw the Vizier..talking to..his Kiaia, or Intendant of his house. **1744** A. DOBBS *Hudson's Bay* 21 The Intendant of Canada wanted to discover these Countries from thence. **1803** M. CUTLER in *Life, Jrnls. & Corr.* (1888) II. 121 The violation of the Spanish treaty by the Governor and Intendent at New Orleans. **1812** BRACKENRIDGE *Views Louisiana* (1814) 89 The mode of carrying on the Indian traffic..was by monopolies, in which the interest of the governor or intendant was alone consulted. **1862** MERIVALE *Rom. Emp.* (1865) IV. xxxviii. 341 The provincial administration, with its..judicial and fiscal intendants, and the whole apparatus of official tyranny. **1871** SMILES *Charac.* iv. (1876) 116 Having served as an intendant of the army in Switzerland under Massena.

b. In English (or American) use.

1696–7 EVELYN *Corr.* 20 Jan., Sir Christopher Wren, his Majesties Surveyor and Intendent of his Buildings. **1776** *Rhode Isl. Col. Rec.* (1862) VII. 572 There shall be two persons annually appointed by this General Assembly, as intendants of trade. **1796** MORSE *Amer. Geog.* I. 678 Charleston was..divided into 13 wards, which choose as many wardens, from whom the citizens elect an Intendant of the city. **1844** DISRAELI *Coningsby* V. vi, The Marquess.. appointed him..Intendant of his household.

c. *fig.*

1760–72 H. BROOKE *Fool of Qual.* (1809) IV. 20 The intendant of his principles, or the former of his manners.

2. ***Intendant-General***, a chief or supreme intendant.

1701 *Lond. Gaz.* No. 3716/3 Monsieur de Bagnols has received a Commission from Spain, to be Intendant-General of Justice and the Finances in these Provinces. **1812** WELLINGTON *Let. to I. de Carvajal* 27 Dec. in Gurw. *Desp.* (1838) X. 11, I recommend that there should be an Intendant General appointed to each of these armies.

3. The administrator of an opera house or theatre (cf. G. *intendant*); see also quot. 1903.

1903 R. HUGHES *Mus. Guide* I. 174/2 *Intendant*,.. director, conductor. **1958** *Spectator* 1 Aug. 166/1 The vital demarcation between *intendant* and administrator is overgrown by the cult of the amateur run riot. **1961** *Times* 30 Jan. 14/2 In each city, the fortunes of opera, ballet, and drama depend largely on an intendant who occupies his position for a comparatively few years before moving elsewhere. **1966** *New Statesman* 18 Nov. 758/2 Very often the Intendants hardly understand the meaning of the word 'choreography',..and automatically scrap each ballet at the end of the season. **1973** *Times* 11 Apr. 12/5 In most of the big towns the Intendant can attract the audience he needs only with a fairly rapid turnover of plays.

Hence **in'tendantism**, the system of governing by intendants; **in'tendantship**, the office or position of an intendant, intendancy.

1889 *Athenæum* 5 Oct. 451/2 We believe that it is not the revival, but the invention, of intendantism that is to be attributed to the seventeenth century. **1892** *Daily News* 12 Sept. 5/3 The first performance of a grand opera..was given by order of Frederick II, under the intendantship of George Wenzeslaus von Knobelsdorff.

in'tendant, *a.* [In sense 1, later form of ENTENDANT; in sense 2, f. INTEND *v.* + -ANT.]

†**1.** Attentive, paying attention. *Obs.*

c **1440** *Gesta Rom.* I. xv. 52 (Add. MS.) The kyng commaundide..that all shulde be intendaunte to kyng leyre ..as to hym selfe. **1581** LAMBARDE *Eiren.* I. ix. (1602) 47 These..bee charged to be diligently intendant about the execution of all and singular the premisses.

2. Intending. *rare.*

1882–3 SCHAFF *Encycl. Relig. Knowl.* III. 1891 Intendant communicants.

intended (ɪn'tɛndɪd), *ppl. a.* (*sb.*) [f. INTEND *v.* + -ED[1].]

1. Purposed to be done or accomplished; designed, meant; designed to be what is denoted by the noun (cf. INTENDING *ppl. a.* b); done on purpose, intentional.

1586 A. DAY *Eng. Secretary* I. (1625) 67 In Epistles Exhorting or Perswading, the intended vertue of goodnesse of every thing is more amply set forth by the opposite evill. **1594** J. DICKENSON *Arisbas* (1878) 37 You may prosecute your entended iourney. **1643** SIR T. BROWNE *Relig. Med.* Pref. §1 A ful and intended Copy of that Piece which was most imperfectly and surreptitiously published before. **1703** MOXON *Mech. Exerc.* 31 Hammer it down to your intended Thickness. **1772** *Junius Lett.* lxviii. 341, I say this, with-out the least intended disrespect to the learned author. **1868** FREEMAN *Norm. Conq.* II. viii. 304 His intended bride sprang by direct..descent from the stock of the great Ælfred.

†**2.** Stretched out or forth, outstretched; extended; increased in force or intensity, strained.

1590 SPENSER *F.Q.* I. xi. 38 With sharpe intended sting. **1592** R. D. *Hypnerotomachia* 58 b, I did take great pleasure with my intended admiration, in seeing of such.. sumpteousnes. **1647** H. MORE *Song of Soul* II. i. I. xviii. 9 My strong intended voice all the wide world shall fill. **1667**

MILTON *P.L.* IX. 45 Unless an age too late, or cold Climat, or Years, damp my intended wing Deprest.

†**3.** Of a person: Minded, resolved, having the purpose; ***to be intended***, to intend, to purpose. *Obs.*

1576 FLEMING *Panopl. Epist.* 87 By this little crop, judge you..and how they are intended. **1586** DAY *Eng. Secr.* (1625) 138 O that you are intended..to marry unto him my neece, your yongest daughter upon a sudden. **1625** K. LONG tr. *Barclay's Argenis* (1638) 425 Being now furiously intended of her death, she hastened, and yet often stucke at it. **1657** W. RAND tr. *Gassendi's Life Peiresc* I. 102 He was intended to return into France, and to lay his bones by the bones of his Father Julius.

B. *colloq.* as *sb.* An intended husband or wife.

1767 *Woman of Fashion* II. 61 Continually taken up with his precious Intended. **1807** W. IRVING *Salmag.* 4 Apr., I see her doubting, hesitating, stand..And sigh for her intended in his place. **1838** DICKENS *Nich. Nick.* xii, What is the reason that men fall in love with me..and desert their chosen intendeds?

Hence **in'tendedness**, the quality or fact of being intended.

1800 W. TAYLOR in *Monthly Mag.* X. 8 The perpetual tendency (or rather *intendedness*) of each and all toward (*for*) progressive improvement.

intendedly (ɪn'tɛndɪdlɪ), *adv.* [f. prec. + -LY².] By intention, intentionally, designedly.

*a***1641** BP. MOUNTAGU *Acts & Mon.* (1642) 89 Iacob, by Iudah, meaneth..not so intendedly, that particular Tribe. **1648** MILTON *Tenure Kings* 7 Power to execute, not accidentally but intendedly, the wrath of God upon evill doers. **1748** RICHARDSON *Clarissa* (1811) VI. ix. 45, I was going towards her, with a countenance intendedly changed to love and softness. **1818** J. H. FRERE *Let.* in Smiles *Mem. J. Murray* (1891) II. xx. 24 The expression was ambiguous, and I fancied that it was intendedly so. **1972** *Daily Tel.* 3 Feb. 14 Your implication that priests present at the illegal, though intendedly peaceful, protest march have no right to be 'mixed up' with their people is absurb.

intendence (ɪn'tɛndəns). *arch.* [f. INTEND *v.*: see -ENCE.] The paying of attention, attendance; spec. ***writ of intendence and respondence***, in 13–15th c., a writ under the Great Seal in favour of one who received an appointment from the King, ordering all persons concerned to be *intendentes et respondentes* to him, i.e. to attend and respond to his requests.

Also called by Sir T. D. Hardy (*Rot. Litt. Pat.* 1835 Introd. 6) *writ de intendendo*; the English formula occurs in 1448 (Willis & Clark *Arch. Hist. Camb.* I. 399) as 'to be attending, helping, and councelling'. See also INTENTIVE *a.* 1 quot. 1835.

1687–8 in *Sarum Church-w. Acc.* (ed. Swayne, 1896) 348 W. Surman labour and intendence upon plummer, carpenters. **1881** F. S. HAYDON in *Cal. Pat. Rolls 1 Edw. I*, in *42nd Rep. D.K.R.* 610 Mandate of intendence and respondence addressed to the sheriffs of Oxford [etc.] and to the bailiffs in the cities and burghs..in favour of Roger de Wanton and John de Swineford..to hold pleas of the market [etc.]. **1895** *Eng. Hist. Rev.* Apr. 217 Edward I. addressed writs of intendence and respondence in his favour.

intendency, -ent: see INTENDANCY, -ANT.

intender (ɪn'tɛndə(r)). Also 6 in-, entendour. [f. INTEND *v.* + -ER¹. With the form *entendour* cf. OF. *entendeour, -eor* (13th c. in Godef.), mod.F. *entendeur* understander, hearer.]

1. One who intends or purposes.

1513 MORE *Rich. III* (1883) 22 Well perceyuyng that the intendours [**1568** GRAFTON entendours] of suche a purpose wolde rather haue hadde theyr harneys on theyr backes. **1627–77** FELTHAM *Resolves* I. xxxii. 56, I will rather bless them, as instruments than condemn them, as not intenders. **1660** *Plea Ministers Sequest.* 8 He cannot deny us to be pretenders (and intenders too) to Godliness. **1667** WATERHOUSE *Fire Lond.* 148 An intender of Publique charity.

†**2.** A claimant, pretender. *Obs.*

1640 YORKE *Union Hon.* 185 Henry of Spaine, son of King John the Intender.

intender, var. of ENTENDER *v.*, to make tender.

†**in'tendible**, *a. Obs.* Forms: 5 en-, 7 in-. See also INTENDABLE. [In sense 1, a. F. *entendible* (14th c. in Godef.) 'conceiuable, intellegible, understandable' (Cotgr.), f. *entendre* to understand, after a L. type **intendibilis*; in sense 2, from juristic sense of L. *intendĕre* to aver, assert, maintain.]

1. Understandable, conceivable, intelligible.

1489 CAXTON *Faytes of A.* I. i. 1 The most playn and entendible langage. *Ibid.* (ad fin.), I hope..that it shal be entendyble & understanden to euery man.

2. *Law.* Capable of being averred or maintained.

1613 SIR H. FINCH *Law* (1636) 51 So a plea in a barre which is intendible at the Common Law cannot be maintained by a matter of custome or by Statute law. *c* **1630** in Rushw. *Hist. Coll.* (1659) I. 52 It is not intendible, that the Parliament should disadvantage themselves, in point of their priviledge.

†**in'tendiment.** *Obs.* [ad. med.L. *intendimentum* understanding, f. *intendĕre* to INTEND.]

1. Understanding; = INTENDMENT 1.

1528 LYNDESAY *Dreme* 799 Efter my sempyll intendiment ..I sall declare the suith and verrayment. **1590** SPENSER *F.Q.* III. v. 32 She of heerbes had great intendiment.

2. Intention, purpose; = INTENDMENT 5.

1595 MARKHAM *Sir R. Grinvile* xxxix, If armes preuent not heauens intendiment. **1602** R. T. *Five Godlie Serm.* 157 Christ..being the complement of the Lawe, and the intendiment of the Gospel. **1608** MACHIN & MARKHAM *Dumb Knight* I. i. in Hazl. *Dodsley* X. 129 And what are you or your intendiments?

3. Attention, attentive consideration.

1590 SPENSER *F.Q.* I. xii. 31 Till well ye wote by grave intendiment, What woman, and wherefore, doth me upbrayd With breach of love and loialty betrayd.

intending (ɪn'tɛndɪŋ), *vbl. sb. rare.* [f. INTEND *v.* + -ING¹.] The action of the vb. INTEND; intention, attention, stretching, etc.; a purpose.

*a***1536** *Calisto & Melibæa* in Hazl. *Dodsley* I. 63 God reward thee for thy gentle intending. **1611** FLORIO, *Intendimento*,..a purpose, an intendment or intending. **1876** MAUDSLEY *Physiol. Mind* i. 6 An unavoidable intending of the mind to the realities of nature.

intending (ɪn'tɛndɪŋ), *ppl. a.* [f. as prec. + -ING².] That intends; having intentions.

1660 FULLER *Mixt Contempl.* (1841) 233 Such as are sensible..that their well-intending simplicity hath been imposed on. **1802** PALEY *Nat. Theol.* x. §2 (1819) 143 The intending mind of a Creator.

b. Qualifying the agent-noun corresponding to an inf. after the verb *intend*; hence, by extension, with other sbs. used proleptically: Purposing to be, that is (such) in intention.

1788 BURKE *Sp. agst. Hastings* Wks. XIII. 124 If he gave the Nabob over to an intending murderer [etc.]. **1876** GEO. ELIOT *Dan. Der.* xi, Marriageable men, or what the new English calls 'intending bridegrooms'. **1884** *Athenæum* 19 Jan. 90/3 Intending subscribers should communicate with the author.

Hence **in'tendingly** *adv.*, with intention, intentionally.

1678 CUDWORTH *Intell. Syst.* I. iii. §37. 162 We do not act fatally only, but electively and intendingly.

intendment (ɪn'tɛndmənt). Forms: α. 4–7 **entend(e)ment.** β. 6–7 **intende-**, 6– **intendment.** [a. F. *entendement* understanding, formerly also, meaning, interpretation, view, opinion, end, intention (12th c. in Hatz.-Darm.), f. *entendre*: see INTEND *v.*, and cf. INTENDIMENT.]

†**1.** The faculty or action of understanding. *Obs.*

c **1374** CHAUCER *Troylus* IV. 1668 (1696) Mannes hed ymagynen ne kan Nententement considere..This cruwel peynes of þis sorwful man. *c* **1384** —— *H. Fame* II. 475 More clere entendement Nas never yit y-sent. **1413** *Pilgr. Sowle* (Caxton) v. i. (1859) 74 His werkes ben infynyte..so that none entendement ne may them vnderstande. *a* **1420** HOCCLEVE *De Reg. Princ.* 1963 Mi maister Chaucer, flour of eloquence, Mirour of fructuous entendement. **1553** T. WILSON *Rhet.* A iij, By corruption of this our fleshe mans reason and entendement were both overwhelmed. **1601** GILL *Trinity* in *Sacr. Philos.* (1625) 218 The intendment of man worketh nothing in the thing conceived.

†**2.** Way of understanding (something); conception or interpretation of a matter; view. In later use passing into 4. *Obs.*

1390 GOWER *Conf.* III. 105 He saith in his entendement, That yet there is an element Above the foure. **1485** CAXTON *Paris & V.* 91 After thentendement of somme men. **1548** BODRUGAN (Adams) *Epit. King's Title* Pref. in *Compl. Scot.* (1872) App. iv. 248 Such plentie of writers..could not by any entendement so fully consent vpon any vntruth. **1625** DONNE *Serm.* xii. 113 The whole Congregation is, oftentimes, in common entendment conformable, and well setled in all matters of Doctrine. **1630** SANDERSON *Serm.*, *ad Mag.* II. 258 To take away a Mans substance..is..to common intendment all one as to take away the very Life itself.

3. Meaning conveyed or intended; signification; import. Now *rare* or *Obs.*

double entendement, 'double meaning', the equivocal use of a word or phrase which has two senses. Cf. DOUBLE ENTENDRE, and see DOUBLE *a.* 2.

1390 GOWER *Conf.* I. 179 A tale of greet entendement I thenke telle for thi sake. *c* **1399** *Pol. Poems* (Rolls) II. 13 The pes..schal with wordes pleine, Withouten eny double entendement Be treted. **1548** HALL *Chron.*, *Hen. VI* 172 Fye on doble entendement. **1610** GUILLIM *Heraldry* I. i. (1611) 5 Words of large intendment and signification. **1767** *Poetry* in *Ann. Reg.* 235 Studious to expound Their dark intendment. **1879** *N. & Q.* 5th Ser. XII. 344 A phrase of sinister and odious intendment.

4. *Law.* The construction put upon anything by the common law; the sense in which the law understands a thing; true meaning as fixed by law.

common intendment, customary or reasonable interpretation, as determined by the law. (Cf. 2.)

1574 tr. *Littleton's Tenures* 119 The righte of fee simple is in abeiance, that is to say alonely in the remembrance, entendemente and consideration of the lawe. *a* **1577** SIR T. SMITH *Commw. Eng.* (1609) 117 The Ordinary (which is the Bishop by common intendment). **1613** SIR H. FINCH *Law* (1636) 354 A man may be a Knight that hath no freehold: So cannot an Earle or Lord by common entendement. **1747** CARTE *Hist. Eng.* I. 295 All the possessions..which had been always either in express terms, or by common intendment of law understood to be exempted. **1780** M. MADAN *Thelyphthora* I. 165 With respect to the moral intendment of those laws. **1885** *Law Rep.* 14 Q. Bench Div. 250 Every intendment ought to be made in favour of long continued usage. **1897** BRYCE *Impr. S. Africa* 155 Britain still claimed that they were, in strict intendment of law, British subjects.

†**5.** The act or fact of intending; will, purpose, intent; that which is intended, an intention; a design, project. *Obs.*

1450–80 tr. *Secreta Secret.* (E.E.T.S.) 35 He owith to be a man of good feith and trewe, and wijs to know thyn entendement. *c* **1470** HARDING *Chron.* CCXI. ii, [He] was full lyke It to haue destroyed by theyr entendment. **1599** SHAKS. *Hen. V*, I. ii. 144 We..feare the maine intendment of the Scot. *c* **1630** RISDON *Surv. Devon* (1714) II. 261 The Spaniards had Intelligence of his Intendments. *a* **1703** BURKITT *On N.T.*, *Heb.* x. 4 The intendment of our Apostle in these words, is to prove that [etc.]. **1804** FESSENDEN *Democr.* (1806) I. 165 To state the motives and intendments, In constitutional amendments.

†**b.** The purpose, design, or object of anything. *Obs.*

1626 JACKSON *Creed* VIII. xiii. §1 The Law, whose true intendment alwayes is to make all men willing to doe to others, as they desire should bee done unto them. **1680** BURNET *Rochester* (1692) 112 Friendship and Converse were among the Primitive Intendments of Marriage. **1732** NEAL *Hist. Purit.* I. 414 It was not the intendment of the Act of Supremacy, to invest any new powers in the Crown.

†**6.** Tendency, inclination; also, the general character or nature (of a thing). *Obs.*

1509 HAWES *Joyf. Medit.* xi, To auaryce he had entendement. **1586** A. DAY *Eng. Secretary* I. (1625) 23 The Epistles..bee commonly without addition at all, either of praise or mislike, or any other intendment. **1620** T. GRANGER *Div. Logike* 56 The Sunne hardeneth clay..from the nature of the clay, not intendment in the Sunne.

†**7.** A charge, an office of supervision. *Obs.*

1638 FORD *Fancies* I. i, Well he merited Th' intendments o'er the gallies at Leghorn, Made grand collector of the customs there.

†**in'tenebrate**, *v. Obs.* [f. late or med.L. type **intenebrāre*, f. *in-* (IN-²) + *tenebrāre* to make dark, f. *tenebræ* darkness: cf. It. *intenebrare* 'to endarken' (Florio), OF. *entenebrer* (13th c. in Godef.).] *trans.* To darken; to render obscure.

1618 WOTTON in *Reliq.* (1672) 251 No more then a pretty conjecture intenebrated by Antiquity. **1656** BLOUNT *Glossogr.*, *To intenebrate* (*intenebro*), to endarken or obscure.

So †**intene'bration**, darkening, obscuration.

1656 HOBBES 6 *Less.* iii. Wks. 1845 VII. 240 There is within you some special cause of intenebration. **1658** PHILLIPS, *Intenebration*, a darkning or obscuring.

intenerate (ɪn'tɛnəreɪt), *v.* Now *rare.* [f. L. type **interenāre*, f. *in-* (IN-²) + *tener* tender: see -ATE³. Cf. It. *intenerire*, OF. *entendrir* to become tender.] *trans.* To make tender, soften, mollify (*lit.* and *fig.*).

1595 DANIEL *Sonn.* x, Thou pow'r that rul'st the confines of the night..Intenerate that heart that sets so light The truest love that ever yet was seen! **1631** BRATHWAIT *Whimzies, Metall-man* 62 Elixate your antimonie; intenerate your chrysocoll. **1637** BP. HALL *Remedy Prophanenesse* II. §13 Feare intenerates the heart, making it fit for all gracious impressions. **1668** *Phil. Trans.* III. 699 M. Garenciers observes of Sugar, how it intenerates the flesh. **1753** JOHNSON *Pr. & Medit.* 23 Apr. in *Boswell*, I hope they intenerate my heart. **1811** *Self Instructor* 536 To intenerate the hairs of wool. **1872** W. R. GREG *Enigmas Life* iv. 172 Prolonged abstinence from food..purifying, and intenerating the devotional part of our nature.

Hence **intenerated, in'tenerating** *ppl. adjs.*

a **1711** KEN *Hymnotheo* Poet. Wks. 1721 III. 42 Mov'd by no Intenerating cries. **1822–34** *Good's Study Med.* (ed. 4) I. 30 Perhaps, in refined and intenerated society, in the larger number, there is..disease of a..fatal character. *a* **1861** D. GRAY *Poet. Wks.* (1874) 135 The teeming South Breathes life and warm intenerating balm.

in'tenerate, *ppl. a. rare.* [f. L. type **interenātus*, pa. pple.: see prec.] Intenerated, softened.

1846 WORCESTER cites RICHARDSON.

inteneration (ɪntɛnə'reɪʃən). Now *rare.* [n. of action f. prec. vb.: see -ATION.] The action of intenerating, or fact of being intenerated; softening.

1626 BACON *Sylva* §58 Restauration of some Degree of Youth; and Inteneration of the Parts. **1664** EVELYN *Pomona* i. (1729) 55 The pleasanter or plumper and larger Apple being the effect of some Inteneration. **1822** KITCHINER *Cook's Oracle* 70–1 The due degree of inteneration [of meat] may be ascertained, by its yielding readily to the pressure of the finger.

†**in'tenible**, *a. Obs. rare.* [f. IN-³ + L. type **tenibilis*, f. *tenēre* to hold. Cf. INTENABLE.] Incapable of holding or containing.

1601 SHAKS. *All's Well* I. iii. 208 In this captious, and intenible [*Fol.* 1 intemible] Siue, I still poure in the waters of my loue.

intensate (ɪn'tɛnseɪt), *v. rare.* [f. L. type **intensāre* (f. *intens-us* INTENSE, or as freq. of *intendĕre* to stretch) + -ATE³ 7.] *trans.* To make intense; to intensify. Hence **in'tensated** *ppl. a.*

1831 CARLYLE *Misc. Ess.*, *Early Germ. Lit.* (1872) III. 202 Like an infinitely intensated organ of Speech. **1837** —— *Fr. Rev.* III. v. i, In colours all intensated, the sublime, the ludicrous, the horrible succeed one another. **1856** EMERSON *Eng. Traits* iv. 58 To intensate the influences that are not of race. **1870** WHITTIER in Pickard *Life* (1894) II. 567 Perhaps a sense of insecurity in their possession..intensates the love I feel for them.

intensation (ɪntɛnˈseɪʃən). *rare.* [n. of action from prec.] A making intense, intensification; intensified condition.

1826 CARLYLE in Froude *Life* (1882) I. 372 The breath of life (*selon* Herder) is but a higher intensation of light and electricity. **1833** —— *Misc. Ess., Diderot* (1872) V. 39 Cooks ..who..cause the patient, by successive intensations of their art, to eat with new and ever-new appetite.

intensative (ɪnˈtɛnsətɪv), *a.* and *sb. rare.* [f. L. *intensāt-, ppl. stem of **intensāre* + -IVE: see INTENSATE, and cf. -ATIVE.]

A. *adj.* = INTENSIVE *a.* 4.

1870 SPURGEON *Treas. Dav.* Ps. lxv. 13 The intensative particle..*aph*..yea. **1880** B. NICHOLSON in *Athenæum* 18 Dec. 815/1 [In Shaks. *Mids. N.* v. i. 59] 'wondrous' is not an attributive of 'snow', but an intensative attributive of 'strange'.

B. *sb.* = INTENSIVE B.

1853 G. J. CAYLEY *Las Alforjas* xvii. II. 79, I also took occasion to use 'plus bêtes que des philosophes' as an intensative of common folly. **1880** *N. & Q.* 6th Ser. II. 324 'Infernal' used as an Intensative.

intense (ɪnˈtɛns), *a.* Also 5 intens. [a. F. *intense*, ad. L. *intens-us* 'stretched, strained, tight, violent', rarely 'intent', pa. pple. of *intendĕre*: see INTEND *v.* In origin a doublet of INTENT *a.*, q.v.]

Etymologically, Stretched, strained, high-strung. Hence:

1. Of a quality or condition: Raised to or existing in a strained or very high degree; very strong or acute; violent, vehement, extreme, excessive; of colour, very deep; of a feeling, ardent (cf. also 3).

c **1400** MAUNDEV. (Roxb.) xiv. 65 þe north..whare comounly es mare intense cold þan in oþer placez. **1435** MISYN *Fire of Love* i. 2 Sum tyeme more & more intens, & sum tyeme les. **1625** HART *Anat. Ur.* I. iii. 33 Vrines not of so high intense a colour. **1667** EVELYN *Diary* 4 Apr., The cold so intense that there was hardly a leaf on a tree. **1708** J. PHILIPS *Cyder* I. 10 Titan then exerts His Heat intense, and on our Vitals preys. **1816** ACCUM *Chem. Tests* (1818) 288 The colour is a pure intense indigo blue. **1857** RUSKIN *Pol. Econ. Art* 48 The..intensest possible type of the greatest error which nations and princes can commit. **1883** *Hardwich's Photogr. Chem.* (ed. Taylor) 240 The black colour is even more intense than an experienced chemist would have anticipated.

2. *transf.* Of a thing: Having some characteristic quality in a very high degree; intensely forcible, bright, hot, etc.

1653 R. SANDERS *Physiogn.* 242 A middle voice, betwixt intense and remiss. **1707** FLOYER *Physic. Pulse-Watch* 357 The intense Pulse is great and frequent. **1802** PALEY *Nat. Theol.* xix. §3 (1819) 289 A supply of poison, intense in quality, in proportion to the smallness of the drop. **1821** SHELLEY *Adonais* xx, Th' intense atom glows A moment, then is quenched. **1852** M. ARNOLD *Self-defence* iv, From the intense, clear, star-sown vault of heaven, Over the lit sea's unquiet way. **1873** BLACK *Pr. Thule* xxvii, The yellow stars grew more intense overhead.

b. *spec.* in *Photography*: = DENSE *a.* 3.

1879 *Cassell's Techn. Educ.* III. 143 Beginners often make their negatives too intense.

3. Of personal, esp. mental, action, etc.: Strained or strenuously directed to some end; intent, eager, earnest, ardent. (Often not distinguished from 1.)

1645 MILTON *Tetrach.* Wks. (1851) 155 Somtime slackning the cords of intense thought and labour. **1744** BERKELEY *Siris* §86 Cruel vigils, occasioned either by sickness or by too intense application of mind. **1797** MRS. RADCLIFFE *Italian* xi, Vivaldi listened with intense attention. **1849** MACAULAY *Hist. Eng.* iv. I. 464 They looked with intense anxiety towards England. **1851** CARPENTER *Man. Phys.* (ed. 2) 444 A state of unusual activity, either from intense thought, from prolonged exertion, or from continued anxiety. **1874** SIDGWICK *Meth. Ethics* II. v. §3. 172 A man may live a very intense life if he be passionately devoted to field-sports or beetles. **1882** OUIDA *Maremma* I. vii. 155 Her voice gave intensest passion and longing to the words.

4. Of a person: †**a.** Having the thoughts strenuously directed to some end; intent *upon* (*about*) something. *Obs.* **b.** Feeling, or susceptible to, intense emotion or affection. Also, manifesting intense emotion or excitability, esp. in æsthetic or intellectual contexts.

1640 W. BRIDGE *True Souldiers Convoy* 14 A man is saide to be a sleepe when he is so intense about one busines that hee doth not regard another. **1677** W. HUBBARD *Narrative* 33 They were so intense upon the Project they were about. **1724** DE FOE *Mem. Cavalier* (1840) 48 We found the elector intense upon the strengthening of his army. **1817** KEATS *Let.* 28 Dec. (1931) I. 76, I..went..to see 'Death on the Pale Horse'. It is a wonderful picture, when West's age is considered; but there is nothing to be intense upon, no women one feels mad to kiss, no face swelling into reality. **1830** MACKINTOSH 12 Oct. in *Life* (1836) II. 476 'The intense school' may be defined as always using the strongest possible word on every possible occasion. **1871** FARRAR *Witn. Hist.* iii. 103 Even Pagan hatred never surpassed..the deep gloom and scorching glare of the intense Tertullian. **1879** W. D. HOWELLS in *Atlantic Monthly* Jan. 38/2 'Why Miss Blood you are intense!' 'I don't know what you mean by that,' said Lydia. 'You like to take things seriously. You can't bear to think that people are not the least in earnest, even when they least seem so.' **1880** G. DU MAURIER *Eng. Soc. at Home* pl. 49 Fair Æsthetic (suddenly, and in deepest tones, to Smith, who has just been introduced to take her in to Dinner). 'Are you *Intense*?' **1897** H. ELLIS *Stud. Psychol. Sex* I. 88 Miss M., aged 29, the daughter of English parents (both musicians) who were both of what is described as 'intense' temperaments. **1925** *Punch* 6 May 487 *Intense Lady.* 'Tell me—have you ever been psyched?'

5. *transf.* Of language, aspect, etc.: Expressing or manifesting intense feeling, purpose, etc.

1684 EARL ROSCOMMON *Ess. Transl. Verse* 344 Sublime or low, unbended or intense, The sound is still a Comment on the Sense. **1838** MACAULAY *Diary* in Trevelyan *Life* (1876) II. vii. 32 The expression singularly intense and stern. **1860** MOTLEY *Netherl.* (1868) I. vi. 322 It is also instructive to observe the intense language.

†**6.** Tending strongly; prone. *Obs. rare.*

1620 VENNER *Via Recta* viii. 172 In sleep, the spirits are more intense to concoction.

†**inˈtensed,** *ppl. a. Obs. rare.* [f. L. *intensus* (see INTENSE *a.*) + -ED[1].] Intensified.

a **1658** CLEVELAND *Obseq.* 51 Thou desired'st to..beard the Truth with as intens'd a Zeal, As Saints upon a fast Night quilt a Meal.

intensely (ɪnˈtɛnslɪ), *adv.* [f. INTENSE *a.* + -LY[2].] In an intense degree or manner.

1. In a very high degree; very greatly, strongly, or deeply; violently, vehemently; extremely.

1646 SIR T. BROWNE *Pseud. Ep.* III. xxi. 161 They intensly heat the aire above their surface. **1698** FRYER *Acc. E. India & P.* 53 *note*, Intensely cold Anights. **1712** ADDISON *Spect.* No. 303 ¶1 There are some which glow more intensely, and dart a stronger Light than others. **1805** WORDSW. *Prelude* XII. 177, I loved whate'er I saw: nor lightly loved, But most intensely. **1897** MARY KINGSLEY *W. Africa* 560 Sticky, slippery mud, intensely sticky, and intensely slippery.

b. With intense feeling, expression, etc.

1860 RUSKIN *Mod. Paint.* V. VI. x. 93 Titian will only paint a fan or a wristband intensely, never a flower. **1886** E. DOWDEN *Shelley* I. ii. 41 He lived intensely in his own imaginings, wise or idle, beautiful or feebly extravagant.

†**2.** With strenuous effort, attention, or exertion; eagerly, earnestly, intently. *Obs.* or merged in 1.

a **1614** DONNE *Βιαθανατος* (1644) 112 To doe even that, so intensly, as we neglect our office of Society. **1659** MILTON *Rupt. Commw.* Wks. (1851) 400, I began to consider more intensly thereon than hitherto I have bin wont. **1743** J. DAVIDSON *Æneid* IV. 35 Trojans intensely ply their work. **1856** SIR B. BRODIE *Psychol. Inq.* I. III. 84 He had had his thoughts intensely fixed for a considerable time on an.. imaginary object.

intenseness (ɪnˈtɛnsnɪs). [f. as prec. + -NESS.] The quality of being intense.

1. Very high or great degree; violence, intensity.

a **1614** DONNE *Βιαθανατος* (1644) 60 Though it merited not salvation, yet it diminished the intensnesse of Damnation. **1677** GALE *Crt. Gentiles* IV. 39 The vehemence and intensenesse of any pleasure is proportionable to the energie, power and activitie of the subject which is affected with such pleasure. **1768** BARRINGTON in *Phil. Trans.* LVIII. 60 The intenseness of the cold, which he.. experienced. **1829** I. TAYLOR *Enthus.* viii. 189 Proofs of the energy, purity and intenseness of practical Christianity among a large number of those who made profession of the name.

2. Strained quality, strenuousness of action or thought. (In later use not distinguished from 1.)

1642 T. GOODWIN *Heart of Christ in Heaven* 16 The Hebrew phrase likewise signifies an urgencie, vehemencie, and intensenesse of some act. *a* **1665** J. GOODWIN *Filled w. the Spirit* (1867) 229 They do not frequently, and with intenseness of mind, consider the abundance of evil that is in it. **1727** SWIFT *Art Polit. Lying* Wks. 1755 III. I. 122 Too great a zeal and intenseness in the practice of this art. **1779–81** JOHNSON *L.P., Cowley* Wks. II. 7 Cambridge, where he continued his studies with great intenseness. **1819** WIFFEN *Aonian Hours* (1820) 22 With a more melancholy tenderness, And more subdued intenseness, I would scan All scene.

intensification (ɪnˌtɛnsɪfɪˈkeɪʃən). [n. of action from INTENSIFY: see -FICATION.] The action of intensifying; intensified condition.

1847 LEWES *Hist. Philos.* (1867) II. 73 An intensification of power by its economy of effort and definiteness of aim. **1864** *Reader* 9 Apr. 450/1 The combustion is accompanied by a great intensification of the heat. **1880** GRANT WHITE *Every-Day Eng.* 46 Reduplication is..perhaps the earliest mode of expressing intensification of interest.

b. *spec.* in *Photography*: The thickening or increasing of the opacity of the film of a negative.

1879 *Cassell's Techn. Educ.* IV. 359/1 It will be better to employ distilled water..in all parts of the process until the development and intensification are completed. **1883** *Hardwich's Photogr. Chem.* (ed. Taylor) 382 The plate should be washed and dried previous to its being intensified, should intensification be found necessary.

inˈtensifier (-faɪə(r)). [f. next + -ER[1].] Something that intensifies; an intensifying agent: *spec.* **a.** *Photogr.* (see next, 1 b); **b.** *Gram.* = INTENSIVE *sb.*; **c.** = *hydraulic intensifier* (s.v. HYDRAULIC *a.* and *sb.* A. 2); **d.** = *image intensifier* (s.v. IMAGE *sb.* 8).

1835 *New Monthly Mag.* XLIII. 293 There are many intensifiers, I say, to the passion of love; such as pride, jealousy, poetry. **1878** SPURGEON *Treas. Dav.* Ps. cvii. 4 Solitude is a great intensifier of misery. **1883** *Hardwich's Photogr. Chem.* 382 One of the oldest Collodion intensifiers. **1892** *Lockwood's Dict. Mech. Engin.* (ed. 2) 429 *Intensifier*, a device frequently employed in place of the hydraulic accumulator, for converting a low water pressure into a higher. **1915** E. H. BARTON *Introd. Mech. Fluids* xii. 191 In connection with an hydraulic pressure system an intensifying accumulator or intensifier may be used. In this device a piston works in the low-pressure cylinder and a connected piston rod, or ram, in the high-pressure cylinder. .. The pressure is magnified in the ratio of the areas of ram and piston. *Ibid.*, The intensifier presents an analogy to the hydraulic press. **1931** G. STERN *Meaning & Change of Meaning* 338 Intensifiers used ironically instead of downtoners. 'A lot you know about that!' **1939** L. M. MYERS *Electron Optics* viii. 449 The term amplifier, in contradistinction to converter, indicates an increase in intensity. With the same reasoning we might term the device an image intensifier. Perhaps the term intensifier may be the best of all. However, we shall employ the usually accepted term converter, because there does exist a conversion effect. **1940** C. C. FRIES *Amer. Eng. Gram.* 205 The pressure to add *-ly* to intensifiers modifying adjectives is especially strong in Standard English. **1951** W. EMPSON *Struct. Complex Words* i. 26 The modern feeling about *quite* is entirely different from that about a discredited intensifier (*awfully*, *frightfully*). **1959** *Proc. IRE* XLVII. 907/2 Although the resolution obtainable is obviously much too low for military use, it is still of interest to the nuclear physicist as a simple and inexpensive intensifier for scintillation photography. **1964** *Language* XL. 39 Intensifier is the name given here to a small class of modifiers, e.g. *mere*, *utter.* **1970** R. H. WARRING *Fluids for Power Syst.* i. 17 Intensifiers are almost invariably used for the production of pressures over 50 000 psi. **1971** G. ANSRE in J. Spencer *Eng. Lang. W. Afr.* 162 The word classes: adjective, quantifier, specifier, pluraliser and intensifier respectively.

intensify (ɪnˈtɛnsɪfaɪ), *v.* [f. L. *intens-us* INTENSE + -FY: corresp. to a L. type **intensificāre* after *sanctificāre*, etc.: see -FY.

In a note to quot. 1817, Coleridge says: 'I am aware that this word occurs neither in Johnson's Dictionary nor in any classical writer. But the word, 'to intend', which Newton and others before him employ in this sense, is now so completely appropriated to another meaning, that I could not use it without ambiguity: while to paraphrase the sense, as by *render intense*, would often break up the sentence and destroy that harmony of the position of the words with the logical position of the thoughts, which is a beauty in all composition, and more especially desirable in a close philosophical investigation. I have therefore hazarded the word, *intensify*; though, I confess, it sounds uncouth to my own ear'.]

1. a. *trans.* To render intense, to give intensity to; to augment, strengthen, heighten, deepen, etc.

1817 COLERIDGE *Biog. Lit.* I. vii. 126 The will itself by confining and intensifying the attention may arbitrarily give vividness or distinctness to any object whatsoever. **1855** DICKENS *Lett.* (1880) I. 410 Her uneasiness will be greatly intensified. **1863** GEO. ELIOT *Romola* xxxiii, The unknown labyrinth around..seemed to intensify his sense of loneliness. **1873** TRISTRAM *Moab* ii. 34 The aurora..was all orange-red, with grand streaks intensifying the rays occasionally.

b. *Photogr.* To make the chemically affected parts of (a negative) more dense or opaque, so as to produce a stronger contrast of light and shade.

1861 in *Circ. Sc.* I. 161/1 The negative will require to be intensified. **1883** [see INTENSIFICATION b].

2. *intr.* To become intense, to grow in intensity.

1853 C. BRONTE *Villette* xi, His expectant, vigilant, absorbed, eager look never wore off: it rather intensified. **1896** R. G. MOULTON *Lit. Study Bible* xv. 370 There is no relief: the action intensifies.

Hence **inˈtensified**; **inˈtensifying** *ppl. a.*, esp. in ***intensifying screen***, a fluorescent screen placed in contact with the film or plate when a radiograph is taken in order to increase the effect on it of the X-rays.

1862 LYTTON *Str. Story* I. 239 Thought too can travel in trance, and in trance may acquire an intensified force. **1863** GEO. ELIOT *Romola* lxv, There was an intensifying flash and energy in his countenance. **1866** R. W. THOMAS *Mod. Pract. Photogr.* 14 (*heading*) Intensifying solution. **1878** W. ABNEY *Treat. Photogr.* x. 71 These intensifying solutions may be applied to the image either before or after fixing. **1879** [see DEVELOPER b]. **1883** H. SPENCER in *Contemp. Rev.* XLIII. 14 An intensified life, which may be summed up as—great labour, great profit, great expenditure. **1903** PUSEY & CALDWELL *Pract. Application Röntgen Rays* vi. 144 The ratio of the exposure necessary with a single intensifying screen and photographic plate to that which is necessary with the same plate without the screen is about 1 to 4 or 5. **1940** K. S. LOW *Metall. & Industr. Radiol.* iv. 30 Intensifying screens when placed in contact with the film will by fluorescence under the action of x-radiation supplement the action of x-rays on the film, and thus shorten exposure periods. **1968** *Kodak Med. X-Ray Catal.* 8 High speed, fine grain X-ray film for use with intensifying screens.

intension (ɪnˈtɛnʃən). [ad. L. *intensiōn-em* stretching, straining, n. of action from *intendĕre* to stretch: see INTEND, INTENSE, and cf. INTENTION, which is etymologically a doublet of this.]

1. The action of stretching, tension; straining. ? *Obs.*

1603 HOLLAND *Plutarch's Mor.* 395 There be in musicke many divers tunes and different intensions of the voice, which the musicians call harmonies. **1626** BACON *Sylva* §181 The Industry of the Musitian hath produced two other Meanes of Straining, or Intension of Strings, besides their Winding vp. **1661** LOVELL *Hist. Anim. & Min.* 359 From great intension of the voice. **1858** HOGG *Life Shelley* I. 56 His voice..was intolerably shrill, harsh..of the most cruel intension.

2. Strenuous exertion of the mind or will; earnest attention, intentness; resolution, determination.

a **1619** W. COWPER in Spurgeon *Treas. Dav.* Ps. cxix. 131 A vehement intension of his spirit. **1676** HALE *Contempl.* I. 456 While with great intension of mind we gaze upon the End. **1822** *Examiner* 251/1 Resolution here means, a bending up, an intension of the spirits. **1860** *Cornh. Mag.* I. 675 Suddenly I found myself springing to my feet, and listening with an agony of intension.

3. Increase of degree or force; augmentation, intensification. (Opp. to *remission*.) [Cf. Schol.L. *intensio et remissio formæ*, in Peter of Ailly *a* 1400, Prantl IV. 105.]

1610 HEALEY *Vives' Comm. St. Aug. Citie of God* (1620) 420 He directly affirmeth, that essence admitteth neyther intension nor remission, more or less. **1615** CROOKE *Body of Man* 574 Parts of the Eares which serue as well for the reception of the sound into them, as also for the intension thereof. **1658** W. SANDERSON *Graphice* 48 Brightness is the Intension of Light. **1751** HARRIS *Hermes* Wks. (1841) 174 Some of these quantities and qualities are capable of intension and remission. **1842** MANNING *Serm., Sins of Infirmity* (1848) I. 231 The mind cannot without a strain be ever at one pitch..it must have its intervals of intension and remission.

b. In *Evolution*: see INTERGENERATION. Cf. INTENSIVE 7.

4. Degree, esp. notable degree, of some quality, etc.; intensity, depth, strength, force. Often contrasted with *extension* in sense of width of range.

1604 T. WRIGHT *Passions* v. §4. 29 In all the obiects of delight, we may find a certaine intension of goodnes and a certaine extension. **1638** F. JUNIUS *Paint. of Ancients* 326 The pictures..having vehemencie and intension, seeme to be forcibly expressed. **1651** JER. TAYLOR *Serm. for Year* I. iv. 48 It may be of universal efficacie, large in the extension of parts, deep in the intension of degrees. **1855** H. SPENCER *Princ. Psychol.* II. II. vi. 50 *note*, Intension being synonymous with intensity. **1888** *19th Cent.* May 718 The essence of farming on virgin soils is extension; on old land it is intension. **1898** S. J. ANDREWS *Chr. & Antichr.* i. 8 The hostile kingdoms should not only increase in extension, but also increase in intension.

5. *Logic.* The internal quantity or content of a notion or concept, the sum of the attributes contained in it; the number of qualities connoted by a term (= COMPREHENSION 4, CONNOTATION 2 b; opp. to EXTENSION 8 b). Cf. INTENSIVE *a.* 3.

1836-60 SIR W. HAMILTON *Logic* viii, The Internal Quantity of a notion,—its Intension or Comprehension, is made up of..the various characters connected by the concept itself into a single whole in thought. **1851** MANSEL *Proleg. Log.* vi. (1860) 203 Formal distinctness as regards the intension or comprehension of the concept. **1876** JEVONS *Logic Prim.* v. §23. 22 In putting steam before ship we have greatly reduced the extension of the term. But we have increased its intension, because steam-ship means all that ship does, and more, for it means that the ship is moved by steam power.

intensional (ɪnˈtɛnʃənəl), *a.* *Philos.* [f. INTENSION 5 + -AL.] Related or pertaining to the intension, or the attributes contained in a concept. Cf. EXTENSIONAL *a.* 2.

1883 F. H. BRADLEY *Princ. Logic* 162 Dismissing for the present the intensional reading, let us consider interpretation in *Extension*. **1903** B. RUSSELL *Princ. Math.* vi. §66. 67 Thus every predicate (provided it can be sometimes truly predicated) gives rise to a class. This is the genesis of classes from the intensional standpoint. **1949** S. I. HAYAKAWA *Lang. in Thought & Action* (1952) xv. 253 By intensional orientation, 'capitalist', 'Bolsheviks,', 'farmers', and 'working men' 'are' what we *say* they are. **1956** A. CHURCH *Introd. Math. Logic* (rev. ed.) I. 28 We shall not have occasion to use variables whose values are propositions, but we would suggest the term intensional propositional variable for these. **1970** *Philos. Q.* XX. 52 The star notation can be made the groundwork of a system of intensional propositional logic in which a wide class of formal principles can be proved.

intensionalist (ɪnˈtɛnʃənəlɪst), *a.* and *sb.* *Philos.* [f. prec. + -IST 3 b.] **A.** *adj.* Of or pertaining to the intensional attributes of a concept. **B.** *sb.* One who considers a concept from the standpoint of its inner attributes.

1948 *Mind* LVII. 198 No one, I think, ever intended to deny the interdependence of meaning and deducibility in this sense..although some 'intensionalists' have spoken as if it *were* denied. *Ibid.*, The confusion just described is a mild and limited form of what we might describe as the 'intensionalist error'. **1962** *Times Lit. Suppl.* 16 Mar. 187/3 In a level-headed and sometimes ingenious discussion..the authors show themselves uncompromisingly 'intensionalist'. **1963** R. CARNAP in P. A. Schilpp *Philos. R. Carnap* 919 The basic ideas underlying my intensionalist thesis are simple.

intensionality (ɪntɛnʃəˈnælɪtɪ). *Philos.* [f. INTENSIONAL *a.* + -ITY.] The state or fact of being intensional. Cf. EXTENSIONALITY.

1937 A. SMEATON tr. *Carnap's Logical Syntax of Lang.* IV. §71. 259 The difference between the extensionality and intensionality of a language has nothing to do with the difference between the formal and the material treatment. **1944** K. GÖDEL in P. A. Schilpp *Philos. B. Russell* 138 Chwistek..has shown that the system of simple types becomes contradictory if one adds the 'axiom of intensionality' which says (roughly speaking) that to different definitions belong different notions.

intensionally (ɪnˈtɛnʃənəlɪ), *adv.* *Philos.* [f. INTENSIONAL *a.* + -LY².] By way of intension, in an intensional manner.

1883 F. H. BRADLEY *Princ. Logic* 161 If again you emphasize the connection of the differences, you take the judgment intensionally. **1903**, etc. [see EXTENSIONALLY *adv.*]. **1953** K. BRITTON *J. S. Mill* vi. 189 This judgement also must be understood intensionally: i.e. as a connexion of universals which holds without reference to the mere spatio-temporal positions of the instances. **1970** *Philos. Q.* XX. 43 We may take it that the expression so obtained is formally valid intensionally.

intensitive (ɪnˈtɛnsɪtɪv), *a.* (*sb.*) *rare.* [irreg. f. INTENSITY + -IVE.] = INTENSATIVE, INTENSIVE.

1817 G. S. FABER *Eight Dissert.* (1845) II. 197 Intensitive reduplication. **1835** *New Monthly Mag.* XLIV. 5 The small voice of the nightingale..seems an intensitive and a low burthen to the general anthem of the earth. **1879** L. STEPHEN *Hours in Library* Ser. III. 167 The highest epithet applicable to Jeffrey is 'clever', to which we may prefix some modest intensitive.

intensity (ɪnˈtɛnsɪtɪ). [f. INTENSE + -ITY: cf. F. *intensité* (1743 in Hatz.-Darm.).]

1. a. The quality of being intense; a strained or very high degree (*of* a quality, condition, or action, or of the characteristic quality *of* something); extreme force, strength, depth, brightness, etc.

1665 BOYLE *Exp. Hist. Cold, Defic. Weather-glasses* Wks. 1772 II. 497 Susceptible of such an intensity of cold. **1791** BURKE *App. Whigs* Wks. VI. 202 The number engaged.. only augments the quantity and intensity of the guilt. **1824** LANDOR *Imag. Conv.* Wks. 1846 I. xii. 51/2 In England great crimes escape through the intensity of law; in Italy small ones through its relaxation. **1834** MEDWIN *Angler in Wales* I. 90 The water from the intensity of its blue, must be very deep. **1834** *Phil. Trans. R. Soc.* CXXIV. 222 The term intensity..is immediately referable to..the operation of either a part, or the whole of the total force in a given direction up to the point of discharge. **1846** RUSKIN *Mod. Paint.* I. II. II. ii. §3 Nature exhibits her hues under an intensity of sunlight which trebles their brilliancy. **1879** [see SATURATION 4]. **1933** L. BLOOMFIELD *Lang.* ix. 156 The second more specialized type of connotation..is intensity. The most characteristic intense forms are exclamations. **1939** BROOKS & WARREN *Understanding Poetry* II. 167 The effect of this condensation in poetry is a sense of greater intensity than is usually found in prose fiction. **1961** J. H. GOODIER *Dict. Painting & Decorating* 143 *Intensity*, the purity of a colour, sometimes called the 'saturation' or, in American terminology, the 'chroma'.

b. High-strung quality of personal feeling or emotion; strenuous energy of action.

1830 SOUTHEY *Life Bunyan* in *Pilgr.* 38 This led him to search the Bible and dwell upon it with an earnestness and intensity which no determination of a calmer mind could have commanded. **1837** DICKENS *Pickw.* ii, He..looked at the stranger for several seconds with a stern intensity. **1876** GEO. ELIOT *Dan. Der.* ii, She might have done so with an agreeable sense that she was living with some intensity and escaping humdrum. **1876** LOWELL *Among my Bks.* Ser. II. *Wordsw.* 243 In proportion to the intensity needful to make his nature thoroughly aglow is the very high quality of his best verses. **1896** G. F. STOUT *Analytic Psychol.* I. I. v. 110 The word 'intensity' in..psychology..is usually regarded as synonymous with the liveliness or vivacity of which Hume has so much to say.

c. with *pl.* An instance of this quality; an intense condition.

1847 BUSHNELL *Chr. Nurt.* II. viii. (1861) 388 Over-dosing in the spiritual intensities of religion. *a* **1849** POE *Blackwood Article* Wks. 1864 IV. 232 What everybody else calls the intensities.

2. a. The degree or amount of some quality, condition, etc.; force, strength, energy; degree of some characteristic quality, as brightness, etc.; *esp.* in *Physics*, as a measurable quantity.

1794 J. HUTTON *Philos. Light*, etc. 291 The light of greatest intensity, which is supposed to be white. **1796** KIRWAN *Elem. Min.* (ed. 2) I. 26 Denoting the degrees of intensity of some particular qualities by figures. **1831** BREWSTER *Optics* xxii. 200 To compare the polarising intensities of different crystals. **1881** MAXWELL *Electr. & Magn.* I. 168 The force on a small charged body is proportional to its own charge, and the force per unit of charge is called the Intensity of the force.

b. *Photogr.* = DENSITY 4; cf. INTENSE *a.* 2 b.

1855 HARDWICH *Photogr. Chem.* viii. 111 With the intensity of a picture..the developing fluid is largely concerned.

3. *attrib.* and *Comb.*

1844 in H. M. Noad *Lect. Electr.* (ed. 2) ix. 401 The trifling decomposing effect from the intensity-inductor. *a* **1877** KNIGHT *Dict. Mech.* II. 1192/1 An intensity battery is one in which the elements are coupled up together, to give a current known as high-tension. **1927** E. G. RICHARDSON *Sound* x. 238 Beside the frequency limits there are intensity limits to the sounds which the ear can perceive. **1932** D. JONES *Outl. Eng. Phonetics* (ed. 3) xxxi. 277 Contrast-emphasis may be applied to almost any word, but intensity-emphasis can only be applied to certain words expressing qualities which are measurable. **1940** *Chambers's Techn. Dict.* 452/1 *Intensity modulation*, modulation of a luminosity of the fluorescent screen of a cathode ray tube by variation of the current carried in the beam. **1947** *Radiology* XLIX. 284/2 Our data also suggest that an intensity factor exists. Daily exposures of very short duration over long periods of time should therefore be avoided. **1964** J. C. CATFORD in D. Abercrombie et al. *Daniel Jones* 31 Fricative *hiss*,.. intensity-modulated by voice. **1972** *Science* 16 June 1236/1 The audio frequency Doppler signals from the detector were amplified sufficiently to provide a 30- to 40-volt signal for intensity-modulating the cathode-ray tube.

intensive (ɪnˈtɛnsɪv), *a.* (*sb.*) [a. F. *intensif, -ive* (14–15th c. in Hatz.-Darm.) = It. *intensivo*, med. or mod.L. *intensīv-us*, f. *intens-*, ppl. stem of *intendĕre* to stretch, strain: see INTEND, INTENSE. Late L. had the parallel *extensīvus* EXTENSIVE.]

A. *adj.* †**1.** Of very high degree or force, vehement: = INTENSE *a.* 1. *Obs.*

1526 *Pilgr. Perf.* (W. de W. 1531) 283 It shall be to euery chrysten man or woman more intensyue and feruent than is the naturall loue. **1598** YONG *Diana* 225 It was strange to see what intensiue loue euery one did beare vs. **1621** BURTON *Anat. Mel.* I. iii. III, A very intensive pleasure follows the passion or displeasure. **1687** *Death's Vis.* viii. 74 Call yonder Planet, Mercury, Whom such intensive Heat Will not Evaporate.

†**2.** Strenuously directed *upon* something (quot. 1605); strained, earnest, eager, intent; = INTENSE *a.* 3. *Obs.*

1605 BACON *Adv. Learn.* II. xi. §3 Fascination is the power and act of Imagination, intensive upon other bodies, than the bodie of the Imaginant. *a* **1628** PRESTON *Mt. Ebal* (1638) 5 It is nothing else but an intensive bending of the mind unto Christ. *a* **1639** WOTTON *Paralell* in *Reliq.* (1651) 3 Being almost tyred..with that assiduous attendance, and intensive circumspection. **1669** WOODHEAD *St. Teresa* I. Pref. 12 Intensive thinking is tedious, and tires.

3. a. Of, relating, or pertaining to intensity, or degree of intrinsic strength, depth, or fullness, as distinguished from external spatial extent or amount; of or pertaining to logical intension.

1604 T. WRIGHT *Passions* v. 293 In every obiect of delight there is a certaine intensive goodnes and perfection, and there is an extensive. **1626** JACKSON *Creed* VIII. vi. §7 The intensive infinity of the satisfaction for the sinnes of the world. **1641** LD. BROOKE *Eng. Episc.* I. i. 3 Concomitants, we may call, that almost illimited power, both Intensive, in sole Ordination; Jurisdiction..As also Extensive, over so vast a Diocesse. **1649** JEANES *Wks. Heaven on Earth* in Spurgeon *Treas. Dav.* Ps. cxlv. 7 There must be an intensive greatness in our praises, in regard of the degree, fervour and heat of them. **1698** KEILL *Exam. Th. Earth* (1734) 169 The part immerged of each Cylinder, bears the same proportion to the whole Cylinder, that the intensive gravity of the Cylinder bears to the intensive gravity of the Fluid. **1798** W. TAYLOR in *Monthly Rev.* XXV. 585 Were we endeavouring to characterize this work, in the dialect peculiar to Professor Kant, we should observe, that its *intensive*, like its *extensive*, magnitude is small. **1845-6** TRENCH *Huls. Lect.* Ser. I. iv. 58 The record of an intensive as well as extensive development. **1877** E. CAIRD *Philos. Kant* II. xi. 442–3 In all phenomena the Real has intensive quantity or degree.

b. Having the quality or character of intensity.

1836 J. GILBERT *Chr. Atonem.* vi. (1852) 167 Justice is an intensive exercise of holiness. **1836-7** SIR W. HAMILTON *Metaph.* xxiv. (1859) II. 100 Hearing is, however, much less extensive in its sphere of knowledge or perception than sight; but in the same proportion is its capacity of feeling or sensation more intensive. **1899** *Q. Rev.* Oct. 492 Friends whose reciprocal intensive criticism fanned each other's interest into flame.

4. Having the property of making intense; intensifying; esp. in *Gram.*, expressing intensity; giving force or emphasis; = INTENSATIVE.

1608 TOPSELL *Serpents* (1658) 630 Aristophanes deriveth it from 'Alpha', an intensive particle, and 'Spizo', which signifieth 'to extend'. **1751** HARRIS *Hermes* Wks. (1841) 175 These comparatives..seem sometimes to part with their relative nature, and only retain their intensive. **1820** *Mair's Lat. Dict.* 414 *Vē*..is sometimes intensive..and sometimes privative. **1882** FARRAR *Early Chr.* I. 448 *note*, The τις is intensive.

5. a. *Econ.* Applied to methods of cultivation, fishery, etc., which increase the productiveness of a given area: opposed to *extensive* in which the area of production is extended.

1832 CHALMERS *Pol. Econ.* x. 324 The removal..of the tithes, gives scope both to a more extensive and a more intensive agriculture. **1865** *Times* 15 Apr., Ruin stares in the face the occupier whose farm premises are inadequate to the requirements of an 'intensive cultivation'. **1889** *Nature* 3 Oct. 558/2 The necessity for increased food productions calls for intensive methods. **1899** *19th Cent.* No. 264. 300 There is little probability of their escaping from being caught..on account of the intensive fishery.

b. Suffixed to sbs. to form adjs. with the sense 'intensively using the thing specified', as ***capital-intensive, labour-intensive***.

1957 K. A. WITTFOGEL *Oriental Despotism* vi. 218 The replacement of labor-intensive irrigation farming by labor-extensive cattle breeding. **1959** *Listener* 22 Oct. 666/1 We have the highly capital-intensive process of textile manufacture. **1970** *Times* 2 June (Container Suppl.) p. iii/4 The latest sophisticated container systems add up to a capital-intensive system of some magnitude. **1972** *Guardian* 29 June 15/5 The developing world..is beginning to see the case for labour-intensive farming. **1973** *Nature* 6 Apr. 378/2 Economies of scale have been operating in capital-intensive and graduate-intensive industries like chemicals, oil, electric power, steel, and computers. *Ibid.* 382/3 Intelligence-intensive biology would take its place alongside this intelligence-intensive cosmology.

6. *Med.* Applied to a method of inoculation in which the intensity or strength of the matter introduced is increased in successive operations.

1888 *Pall Mall G.* 4 Sept. 4/2 He mistook the phials, and made the first inoculation with the intensive matter which should be used for the second. **1894** *Lancet* 3 Nov. 1049 A guinea-pig which had undergone 'intensive treatment' with Dr. Viquerat's serum had died ' stuffed full of tubercle'. **1897** *Allbutt's Syst. Med.* II. 709.

7. Subject to intensification; characterized by being intensified.

1888 J. T. GULICK in *Linn. Soc. Jrnl.* (Z.) XX. 197 A discussion of the principles of Intensive Segregation, under which name I class the different ways in which other principles combine with Segregation in producing Divergent Evolution.

8. ***intensive care***: a form of medical treatment in which a patient is kept under concentrated and special observation; so ***intensive-care unit***, etc.

1963 *Lancet* 19 Jan. 169/2 Our medical staff found the medical intensive-care unit so valuable that they requested ..a separate surgical intensive-care unit. **1965** *Math. in Biol. & Med.* (Med. Res. Council) I. 40 He felt that patient monitoring was essential in the operating theatre and the intensive-care unit. **1965** *Listener* 16 Sept. 401/1 We would like to see intensive-care units in all large modern hospitals. **1967** *Spectator* 11 Aug. 159/2 This method of dealing with a serious cardiac emergency..is known as intensive care. **1972** J. GORES *Dead Skip* (1973) ii. 14 Bart's at Trinity Hospital in intensive care, a single-bed room with a private nurse. **1973** J. GOODFIELD *Courier to Peking* x. 123 First, one of the general wards..and then to our new intensive care unit.

B. *sb.* Something that intensifies; *spec.* in *Gram.* an intensive word or prefix: see 4.

1813 W. TAYLOR *Eng. Synon.* 38 *Ætzen* or *ætschen* is to eat into, to corrode; it is the intensive of the verb *to eat.* **1860** MARSH *Eng. Lang.* 570 The use of mere sound as an accompaniment and intensive of sense. **1888** SKEAT *Etym. Dict.* s.v. *To-* prefix, Examples of the addition of *al* [= *all*] as an intensive, meaning 'wholly'.

intensively (ɪnˈtɛnsɪvlɪ), *adv.* [f. prec. + -LY².] In an intensive manner.

1. In a high degree, intensely. Now *rare.*

1604 T. WRIGHT *Passions* II. i. 51 It sheweth them very intensively. *a* **1643** J. SHUTE *Judgem. & Mercy* (1645) 167 Thou didst more intensively hate them, and multiply their sorrowes. **1706** PHILLIPS, *Intensively*, extremely, excessively, in the highest degree. **1882** *Nature* 23 Mar. 481/2 The covered flowers being less intensively coloured than the others.

†**2.** With strained effort; earnestly, assiduously, intently. *Obs.*

1612–15 BP. HALL *Contempl., N.T.* IV. xi, Let us wait reverently, and intensively upon this Bethesda of God, that when the Angell shall descend and move the water, our soules may be cured. **1637** GILLESPIE *Eng. Pop. Cerem.* II. vii. 28 Against them they contend more remissely, against us more intensively. *c* **1655** ALG. SIDNEY in *19th Cent.* (1884) Jan. 61 Theire desires are most intensively placed upon one object.

3. In relation to intensity or degree of intrinsic force: opp. to EXTENSIVELY 2.

1642 tr. *Ames' Marrow Div.* 200 This administration differs from the former, both intensively and extensively. **1652** FRENCH *Yorksh. Spa* ii. 28 The fire is not great extensively, but intensively, because it is kept within a narrow compass. **1657** W. MORICE *Coena quasi Κοινὴ* Diat. vi. 308 To enlarge an impost and burden extensively, to lessen the sense thereof intensively. **1877** in Dawson *Orig. World* xv. 339 The same power..has continued to operate in intensively as well as extensively increasing activity.

4. In regard to logical intension.

1674 OWEN *Holy Spirit* (1693) 144 Intensively or Subjectively. **1864** BOWEN *Logic* viii. 234 Interpreted Intensively, this Judgment [*Man is an animal*] signifies that all the attributes of *animal* are contained in or among—form a part of—the attributes of *man.*

intensiveness (ɪnˈtɛnsɪvnɪs). [f. as prec. + -NESS.] The quality or condition of being intensive; vehemence, intensity.

a **1656** USSHER *Ann.* (1658) 207 The heat thereof was encreased by the intensivenesse of the Sun. **1656** JEANES *Fuln. Christ* 221 This love is for its intensivenesse, motion upwards unto heaven..compared unto fire. **1704** NORRIS *Ideal World* II. iii. 151 Accomplishments..that consist in the extensiveness of thought carry it in the public vogue before those that consist in the intensiveness of it. **1892** SCHÄFFLE *Imposs. Soc. Democr.* 277 Peasant industry carried on with growing intensiveness.

intent (ɪnˈtɛnt), *sb.* Forms: 3–6 **entent, entente,** (5 **ententte**); 4–6 **intente,** (7 **intentt**), 3– **intent.** [ME. had two forms: (1) *entent, intent,* a. OF. *entent* intention, application:—L. *intent-us* a stretching out, in late L. attention, intention, f. *intent-*, ppl. stem of *intendĕre* to INTEND; (2) *entente, intente,* a. OF. *entente* intention, thought, desire, purpose, etc.:—pop.L. **intenta* sb. from fem. of *intentus* pa. pple. (analogous to sbs. in *-ata*, etc.), from same vb. In ME. *entent* appears to be more frequent, and *entente* disappears before 1500; but in the pl. *ententes*, the two forms were indistinguishable, and it is not possible to separate them in sense. The form with *in-* is rare before 1400, while *en-* is rarely found after 1550. They were equally common *c* 1500.]

1. The act or fact of intending or purposing; intention, purpose (formed in the mind). Formerly also, in more general sense, Will, inclination; that which is willed, pleasure, desire (cf. 4). Now chiefly in legal phraseology, and in the expressions ***with intent to*** (*hurt*, etc), ***with good*** or ***malicious intent***, etc.

a **1225** *Ancr. R.* 386 Haue, in al þet tu dest, on of þeos two ententes, oðer bo togederes. *a* **1300** *Cursor M.* 2636 Agar.. ham til hir lauedi went And serued hir wit god entent. *c* **1375** *Sc. Leg. Saints, Bertholomeus* 279, I ame redy, lo, to fulfill al þine entent, & sacrify to þi mawnment. *c* **1400** *Destr. Troy* 11364, I haue takon intent þo traitours to sle. *c* **1460** *Play Sacram.* 120 My curat waytheth vpon me to knowe myn entent. **1526** TINDALE *Heb.* iv. 12 And iudgeth the thoughtes and the intentes off the herte. **1553** T. WILSON *Rhet.* (1580) 31 We maie advise hym, to continue in his good entent. **1570** T. NORTON tr. *Nowel's Catech.* (Parker Soc.) 204 Men ought not to be beneficial and liberal, of intent to get thanks. **1660** *Trial Regic.* 9 In the case of the King; His life was so precious, that the Intent was Treason by the Common Law. *a* **1716** SOUTH *Twelve Serm.* (1744) II. 112 It was Josephus's intent by this device to slubber over the massacre of these innocents. **1769** BLACKSTONE *Comm.* IV. iii. 35 The bare intent to commit treason is many times actual treason. **1818** CRUISE *Digest* (ed. 2) VI. 496 In a will, the intent and meaning of the devisor was to be observed, and the law would make construction of the words to satisfy his intent. **1843** JAMES *Forest Days* ii, They were rushing upon the old peasant with no very merciful intent. **1875** JOWETT *Plato* (ed. 2) V. 142 He who wounds with intent to kill..shall be tried as if he had succeeded. **1896** DK. ARGYLL *Philos. Belief* 408 Christian ethics..insists on a purity enthroned in the thoughts and intents of the heart. **1897** *Daily News* 13 Feb. 4/6 Sent to five years' penal servitude for wounding a man with intent.

†**b.** Design, plan, project, scheme. *Obs.*

c **1386** CHAUCER *Man of Law's T.* 49 In swich place as thoughte hem auantage ffor hire entente they take hir herbergage. *c* **1400** *Sowdone Bab.* 625 Isres in his fals ententes Purposed treson and sorowe. **1513** MORE in Grafton *Chron.* (1568) II. 795 To propose their entent of which they would to none other person any part disclose. **1665** MANLEY *Grotius' Low C. Warres* 103 Subtle in the managing of the Intents of that Noble and great-spirited Young-man. **1830** JAMES *Darnley* xxxviii, The nobles joining in his intent, showered their largess upon their retainers.

†**2.** Attention, heed; intent observation. *Obs.*

c **1320** R. BRUNNE *Medit.* 43 Take gode entent How petyr and iohne from hym he sent. *c* **1400** tr. *Secreta Secret., Gov. Lordsh.* (E.E.T.S.) 105 þe Iew wolde noght loke aȝeyn, no gyf entent to his sawes. *c* **1477** CAXTON *Jason* 12 He behelde her with grete entente. *c* **1570** *Pride & Lowl.* (1841) 9 And it beheld with full and whole intent. **1704** STEELE *Lying Lover* II. (1747) 40 Betty, do you see with what Intent.. Penelope gazes yonder?

†**3.** Intent or assiduous effort, endeavour. *Obs.*

a **1340** HAMPOLE *Psalter* xvi. 7 Wiþ stalworth entent i adressid my prayere til þe. *c* **1374** CHAUCER *Anel. & Arc.* 28 The peple blisful al and somme..him to honouren dide al her intent. *a* **1450** *Le Morte Arth.* 3691 To please god Alle that I maye I shalle here-After do myne entente. **1483** *Cath. Angl.* 197/1 An Intente,..*opera.*

†**4.** Mind, or an act of the mind; understanding; the mental faculties generally; frame of mind, will, spirit; perception, judgement; what is in the mind, notion, opinion, or thought of any kind. *Obs.*

a **1300** *Cursor M.* 365 (Gött.) þe world i calle wid min ententis þe mater of foure elementis. *c* **1375** *Sc. Leg. Saints, Egipciane* 121 Quhene gudmen suld to faste begyne, of syne to clenge þare entent. *c* **1386** CHAUCER *Man of Law's T.* 824 She taketh in good entente The wyl of Crist. **1390** GOWER *Conf.* III. 150 Her dethe and his living She chose with all her hole entent. **1420** in Ellis *Orig. Lett.* Ser. III. I. 68 Vp on the beste wyse that we cowde deuyse aftir owr simple ententes. *c* **1470** HENRY *Wallace* I. 370 Sic fantasye fell in his entent. **1513** BRADSHAW *St. Werburge* I. 7, I..cast in myne intent How I myght spende the tyme conuenyent. **1623** LISLE *Ælfric on O. & N. Test.* Pref. 5 Hereby grew..the second error..worse (to their intent) then the first.

†**5.** Meaning; import; purport. *Obs.*

1303 R. BRUNNE *Handl. Synne* Prol. 174 To turne it fro þat speche away In to laten..þat þe Inglis mot know þe entente. *Ibid.* 976 Of þys tale ys alle þe entent To kepe weyl þe commaundement. **1495** *Act 11 Hen. VII*, c. 8 So obscure derke and diffuse that the true entent of the makers therof cannot perfitely be undrestond. **1572** FORREST *Theophilus* 347 in *Anglia* VII, The some and entent of hys hole requeste. *a* **1676** HALE *Contempl.* II. 57 It is more Large and Spacious than the intent of the Text bears.

†**b.** *Law* = INTENDMENT 4. *Obs.*

1574 tr. *Littleton's Tenures* 17 b, Hee that shall haue the lande..shall haue the same lande after the Entent of the surrender. **1608** W. BRADSHAW *Unreason. Separ.* 26 What obedience doe they promise to the Prelates in the intent of the Law, but onely in things that they shall judge honest and Lawfull. **1767** BLACKSTONE *Comm.* II. 476 They not being goods, wares, or merchandize, within the intent of the statute, by which a profit may be fairly made.

6. An end purposed; the object of an action, etc.; aim, purpose. *rare* or *Obs.* exc. as in c.

c **1340** HAMPOLE *Prose Tr.* 10 Ffor þat entent anely [þay] are for to lowte. **1375** BARBOUR *Bruce* III. 206 Thai come weill till thar entent. *c* **1385** CHAUCER *L.G.W.* Prol. 78 That nys nothyng the entent of myn labour. *c* **1440** *Jacob's Well* (E.E.T.S.) 79 Whanne..þe ende & þe entent is, for to don þerby ony dedly synne, þanne is þat desyre..dedly synne. **1523** LD. BERNERS *Froiss.* I. cxl. 167 He thought by their meanes the soner to come to his entent. **1655** CULPEPPER, etc. *Riverius* xv. iii. 412 Juyce of the Knot-grass may be used to the same intent. **1754** CHATHAM *Lett. Nephew* iv. 22, I highly recommend the end and intent of Pythagoras's injunction. **1863** KINGLAKE *Crimea* (1876) I. iv. 60 Some outward and visible figure or sign to which the multitude could point as the symbol of its great intent.

†**b.** In phrases, as ***to what intent, to that intent, for this intent,*** etc. Esp. in the conjunctional phrase ***to*** (†***for***) ***the intent*** (***that***): to the end (that), in order (that). *Obs.*

1390 GOWER *Conf.* I. 180 [He] axeth hem to what entente Thei have here ferste feith forsake. *a* **1450** *Knt. de la Tour* (1868) 161 Y wolde that the tyme were come ayen to that entent to encrece the worship of alle goode. *c* **1460** FORTESCUE *Abs. & Lim. Mon.* ix. (1885) 130 But this is writun only to the entent, þat it be wel vnderstande, how [etc.]. **1470–85** MALORY *Arthur* II. xvii, I did it to this entent that it sholde better thy courage. **1513** MORE *Rich. III* (1883) 7 [He] forethought to be king..And thei deme, that for thys intente, he was gladde of his brothers death. **1523** LD. BERNERS *Froiss.* I. clx. 195 To the entent they somwhat to-breke and to-opyn the archers. **1526** TINDALE *John* xiii. 28 That wist noo man at the table for what intent he spake vnto hym. **1569** J. ROGERS *Gl. Godly Loue* (1876) 179 To the intente that they two may dwell together. **1611** BIBLE *John* xi. 15 To the intent yee may beleeue. **1703** MAUNDRELL *Journ. Jerus.* (1732) 24 To the intent that I might give some light, for the better deciding [etc.].

c. ***to*** (***for***) ***all intents and purposes*** (less usually ***to all intents***): in regard to any end or object, for all practical purposes, 'practically'.

1546 *Act 37 Hen. VIII*, c. 9 §1 To all intents, constructions, and purposes. **1555** RIDLEY *Wks.* (Parker Soc.) 19, I would know, whether that Christ's words, spoken upon the cup, were not as mighty in work, and as effectual in signification, to all intents, constructions, and purposes (as our Parliament men do speak), as they were, spoken upon the bread? **1629** STRAFFORD *Let.* in *Slingsby's Diary* (1836) 321 Your self [being] as formerly vice president to all intentts. **1709** ADDISON *Tatler* No. 96 ¶2 Whoever resides in the World without having any Business in it..is to me a Dead Man to all Intents and Purposes. **1856** RUSKIN *Mod. Paint.* IV. v. xiii. §5 The materials are so hardened and knit together that to all intents and purposes they form one solid mass. **1879** M. ARNOLD *Ess., Porro unum* 162 The rest of the nation consists, for all intents and purposes, of one immense class.

†**7.** The subject or theme to be treated in an argument or discourse. *Obs.*

c **1460** *Play Sacram.* 6 We be ful purposed wᵗ hart & wᵗ thowght Off oure mater to tell yᵉ entent. **1594** J. DICKENSON *Arisbas* (1878) 41 Leauing this digression, I will returne to the proposed entent of my discourse. **1638** F. JUNIUS *Paint. of Ancients* 198 It is better wee should pursue our intent, by comparing that carefull diligence of the ancients [etc.]. **1670** E. BORLASE *Lathom Spaw* 45 From whence this Patient received so much benefit: But to our intent.

†**b.** *Sc. Law.* A cause in litigation. *Obs.*

c **1575** *Balfour's Practicks* (1754) 373 Efter that the partie has chosin ane certain nombre of witnessis for preiving of his intent he may not..desire ony ma nor thame allanerlie quhom he has chosin.

intent (ɪnˈtɛnt), *a.* [ad. L. *intent-us* bent on (something), strained, attentive, earnest, eager, pa. pple. of *intendĕre* to INTEND; cf. OF. *intent* intended, attentive, assiduous.

Intent and *intense* are etymologically doublets, *intentus* and *intensus* being two forms of the L. pple.; but already in L. *intensus* was (like the simple *tensus*) more restricted to the physical sense 'stretched, strained', hence 'intense, violent', while *intentus* was extended to the notion of 'mentally or nervously on the stretch, intent, eager, attentive'. In the modern langs. this differentiation has been made more complete. So with *intention, intension.*]

1. Having the mind strenuously bent upon something; earnestly attentive, sedulously occupied, eager, assiduous; bent, resolved.

a. Const. *on, upon*; formerly *to* (*at*) or *inf.*

1610 *Hymne* in Farr *S.P. Jas. I* (1848) 28 How intent our prayers to heare. **1654–66** EARL ORRERY *Parthen.* (1676) 15 If I endeavoured to preserve a life she is so intent to destroy. **1660** R. COKE *Power & Subj.* 37 The third are..always intent upon robbery. **1661** BRAMHALL *Just Vind.* iv. 87 The Court of Rome so potent, so prudent, so vigilant, so intent to their own advantage. **1674** tr. *Scheffer's Lapland* 107 Women in the absence of men, are very intent for some weeks at catching fish. **1764** GOLDSM. *Trav.* 329 Intent on high designs, a thoughtful band. **1866** KINGSLEY *Herew.* i, They had met him riding along, intent upon his psalter. **1888** J. INGLIS *Tent Life Tigerland* 345 Intent on securing what seemed to be a good head of horns.

b. Without const.

1704 POPE *Windsor For.* 138 The patient fisher takes his silent stand, Intent, his angle trembling in his hand. **1835** LYTTON *Rienzi* x. viii, He stood, with folded arms, musing and intent.

Comb. **1899** *Westm. Gaz.* 19 Oct. 1/3 An alert, very intent-looking man.

2. Of the faculties, looks, etc.: Directed with strained or keen attention; earnest, eager, keen; intense. Const. *on, upon* (†*to*).

1606 BRYSKETT *Civ. Life* 276 The Intellective soule.. being once freed from the bodie..is altogether bent and intent to contemplation. **1709** STEELE *Tatler* No. 38 ¶11 The intent Application with which he pursues Trifles. **1756** C. LUCAS *Ess. Waters* II. 199 The eye is intent upon watching the changes. **1830** D'ISRAELI *Chas. I*, III. vi. 79 So intent was his elegant mind on those treasures of literature and art. **1849** C. BRONTE *Shirley* ii. 20 His eyes are large.. their expression is intent and meditative.

†**3.** Intensely active. Opposed to *remiss. Obs.*

1650 SIR T. BROWNE *Pseud. Ep.* (ed. 2) 312 The streams from either side..arise or fall according to the motion in those parts, and the intent or remisse operation of the first exciting causes.

†**inˈtent**, *v. Obs.* Also 3–6 **en-**. [In branch I, ME. a. OF. *entente-r* to intend, attempt (14th c. in Godef.), ad. L. *intentāre* to stretch out towards, direct, threaten with, attack, accuse, freq. of *intendĕre* to INTEND. In sense 4, a. F. *intenter* (14th c.), to institute (a legal process) = med.L. *intentāre lītem*; in sense 5, app. directly from L. *intentāre*.]

I. 1. *intr.* To direct the mind or attention, to give heed, to attend; to be intent.

13.. *K. Alis.* 2834 Whiles the people of the toun Ententid to Permeneon. **1475** *Bk. Noblesse* (Roxb.) 11 [He] ententid about the defence and saufegarde of the gret cite of Acres.

1611 Speed *Hist. Gt. Brit.* ix. ix. (1632) 626 The King now wholly intented vpon encrease of treasure.

b. *trans.* To attend to.

14.. *Prose Leg.* in *Anglia* VIII. 148 Ententynge þat þe apostel seiþ. *c* **1500** *New Notbroune Mayd* 433 in Hazl. *E.P.P.* III. 18 My comaundement Neuer tentente.

2. *intr.* and *trans.* To intend, purpose.

a **1300** *Cursor M.* 26793 Sli[k] penance mai ha na f[r]o, Man dos intent at eft misdo. **1450–1530** *Myrr. our Ladye* 77 To aske therby all thynges that he entented shulde be asked therby. **1494** Fabyan *Chron.* iv. lxviii. 46 He expulsed..his fader Herculeus Maxymyanus yt ententyd agayne to haue been Emperoure. **1523** Ld. Berners *Froiss.* I. ccxxxv. 331 To lerne what their enemyes entented. **1577–87** Holinshed *Scot. Chron.* (1805) I. 196 Donald..had understanding what these outlawes intented.

3. *trans.* To make an attempt on; to try to seize.

c **1400** *Sowdone Bab.* 550 Ferumbras than gan to assaye, If he myght that praye entente.

II. 4. *trans.* To institute (a legal action). *Sc.*

15.. *Acts Sederunt* 6 (Jam.) The saidis Lordis declaris that the samen sal not prejudge ony persone..of thair lawful defences..aganis ony actioun to be intentit heireftir at his Majesties instance. **1673–4** *Lauderdale Papers,* He heard that she hade given orders to intent a law suit against him. **1737** J. Chamberlayne *St. Gt. Brit.* ii. ii. iv. 376 (*Scotland*), The Lord Advocate..intents no Processes of Treason, except by Warrant of Privy-Council.

5. To accuse. **b.** To level (an accusation). *rare.*

1613 W. Browne *Brit. Past.* Pref. Verses (N.), They were her errors, whilst she intented Browne. **1695** J. Sage *Article* Wks. 1895 I. 389 The accusation was intented against the Queen.

†**in'tentable,** *a.* *Obs.* *rare*$^{-0}$. [ad. late L. *intentābil-is*, f. *in-* (in-^{3}) + **tentābilis*, f. *tentāre* to try, to tempt.]

1656 Blount *Glossogr.*, *Intentable*, that cannot be tempted.

†**inten'tation.** *Obs. rare.* [ad. L. *intentātiōn-em* stretching out, in late L. (Tertull., v.r. *intentio*) accusation, n. of action f. *intentāre*: see intent *v.*] An accusation; a threatening.

1612–15 Bp. Hall *Contempl., O.T.* xix. ii, Witnesses come forth, and agree in the intentation of the crime. **1656** Blount *Glossogr.*, *Intentation*, a menacing or threatening.

†**in'tented,** *ppl. a.* *Obs.* [f. intent + -ed.]

1. = intent *a.* 2.

1633 P. Fletcher *Elisa* ii. xlii, So did she quake, And with intented eyes upon them gazed.

2. Intended, purposed.

1624 Sanderson *Twelve Serm.* (1632) 444 If my intented course led me that way.

3. Legally instituted.

1639 Drumm. of Hawth. *Queries of State* Wks. (1711) 177 Whether it be lawful to proscribe and forfeit country-men, professing one religion, without process intented or law?

†**in'tentfully,** *adv.* *Obs.* *rare*$^{-1}$. [f. **intentful* (f. intent *sb.* + -ful) + -ly^{2}. But perh. a scribal corruption.] Attentively.

c **1410** Love *Bonavent. Mirr.* xii. 29 (Gibbs MS.) Þei fonden hym syttyng emonge doctoures of lawe heryng hem ententfully [*Sherard MS.* & *W. de Worde*, ententifly].

†**intential,** *a.* *Obs. rare.* [irreg. f. intent *sb.* + -ial.] Of or belonging to the intent or meaning: cf. intent *sb.* 5.

?*c* **1470** G. Ashby *Active Policy Prince* 39 Poems 14 Thaugh all thynges be nat..swetely englisshed..I byseche you hertely to excuse it, So that I kepe intential substance.

†**in'tentible,** *a.* *Obs.* In 5 en-. [a. OF. *en-, intentible* (Godef.), f. L. type **intentibilis*, f. ppl. stem of *intendĕre* to intend: see -ible.] Understandable, intelligible.

1491 Caxton *Vitas Patr.* (W. de W. 1495) i. xlix. 96 b/1, I haue now a voys ententyble; and I was late dompe.

intention (ɪn'tɛnʃən), *sb.* Forms: α. 4–6 **entencion**, (-cy-, -one, -oun(e), 5–6 -tion, (-oun), 5 -sioun, 6 -syon. β. 5–6 **intencion**, (-cy-, -one, -oun(e), 5– **intention**. [a. OF. *en-, intencion, -ciun, -tion, -çon* stretching, intensity, will, thought, opinion, etc. (12th c. in Hatz.-Darm.), ad. L. *intentiōn-em* stretching, straining, effort, attention, application, design, purpose, etc., n. of action from *intendĕre* to intend. A doublet of *intension*; see note to intent *a.*]

I. General senses.

†**1.** The action of straining or directing the mind or attention to something; mental application or effort; attention, intent observation or regard; endeavour. *Obs.* (but cf. 7 b).

c **1400** *Rom. Rose* 4701 Now sette wel thyn entencioun, To here of love discripcioun. *c* **1450** tr. *De Imitatione* iii. xxx. 99 Neuere to relesse þe soule fro intencion of heuenly þinges. **1481** Caxton *Myrr.* i. iv. 12 Therfore he [God] gaf to hym [man] witte and reson to haue entencion to hym. **1526** *Pilgr. Perf.* (W. de W. 1531) 160 Attencion or intencyon for our purpose here is onely the attendaunce study & diligence yt man or woman gyueth to theyr dede. **1599** B. Jonson *Cynthia's Rev.* i. v, My soule (Like one that lookes on ill-affected eyes) Is hurt with mere intention on their follies. **1647** Sprigge *Anglia Rediv.* i. ii. (1854) 9 Which petition the king refusing, he pressed with that instance and intention..till at last he tendered the same upon the pommel of his saddle. **1651** *Fuller's Abel Rediv., Bolton* 589 Being advised by Phisitians..to break off the strong intention of his study, he rejected their counsell. **1690** Locke *Hum. Und.* ii. xix. §1 When the Mind with great Earnestness, and of Choice, fixes its View on any Idea..it is that we call Intention or Study. **1749** Bp. Lavington *Enthus. Methodists* (1754) I. ii. 39 Disease caused perhaps by..deep Intention of Thought.

†**2.** The action or faculty of understanding; way of understanding (something); the notion one has of anything. Also, the mind or mental faculties generally; cf. intent *sb.* 4. *Obs.*

1340 Hampole *Pr. Consc.* 4521 Þe Iewes and cristen men..Sal þan thurgh even entencion Assent in Crist als a religion. **1390** Gower *Conf.* II. 77 Resonable entencion, The which out of the soule groweth And the vertue fro vice knoweth. **1483** Caxton *G. de la tour* L iv b, I wylle answere after myn aduys and intencion. **1500–20** Dunbar *Poems* ix. 114, I synnit in consaiving thochtis jolie, Vp to the hevin extolling myne ententioun. **1526** *Pilgr. Perf.* (W. de W. 1531) 161 b, Ye the idyot may haue..his entencyon fully set to desyre the lyfe eternall.

†**3.** The way in which anything is to be understood; meaning, significance, import. *Obs.* or blending with 5.

1387–8 T. Usk *Test. Love* iii. ii. (Skeat) I. 140 For necessary & necessite been wordes of mokel intencion. **1638** F. Junius *Paint. of Ancients* 310 That from thence gathering the full intention of the conceit, wee might..rightly apprehend the whole argument. **1668** Culpepper & Cole *Barthol. Anat.* i. iii. 6 If we will beleive Galen..Whose Intention Rodeletius interprets to be, that the Fat doth only releive famished persons. [**1871** B. Taylor *Faust* (1875) I. Notes 230 The intention of the passage was sufficiently clear. **1885** S. Cox *Expos.* Ser. i. ii. 22 The story of every man has a religious intention and significance.]

4. The action of intending or purposing; volition which one is minded to carry out; purpose. †*of intention*, on purpose, intentionally (*obs.*).

c **1375** *Sc. Leg. Saints, Placidas* 229 Of his synnis repentyng, As man of gud entencione. **1430** Lydg. *St. Margaret* 381 Men supposyng..There was closed grete tresour and rychesse, Brak the vessel, of entencyoun. **1552** Abp. Hamilton *Catech.* (1884) 29 We suld keip the commands of God with ane rycht intencioun. **1601** R. Johnson *Kingd. & Commw.* (1603) 264 There is not that disposition and good intention, which ought to be betwixt so neere a couple. **1645** Slingsby *Diary* (1836) 166 Having it once in his intention to go to Bristol. *a* **1780** Johnson in *Boswell* Apr. an. 1753, [At one time, Johnson said to Beauclerk] You never open your mouth but with intention to give pain. **1841** Lane *Arab. Nts.* I. 59 Our actions are judged good or evil, according to our intention. **1887** Fowler *Princ. Mor.* ii. v, Intention, as distinguished from motive, on the one side, and the action itself, on the other, may be defined as the volition immediately preceding the overt act.

5. a. That which is intended or purposed; a purpose, design.

1375 Barbour *Bruce* x. 527 It wes his entencioune Till put him in-to auenture. *c* **1430** *Pilgr. Lyf Manhode* iii. xxxii. (1869) 153 It is wel..myn entencioun þat þou make me þer of collacioun. **1654** Whitlock *Zootomia* 203 It is a saying among Divines, that Hell is full of good Intentions, and Meanings. **1748** F. Smith *Voy. Disc.* I. 118 It was not the Intention that the Ships should go higher up. **17..** Johnson in *Boswell* Apr. an. 1775, Sir, Hell is paved with good intentions. **1771** Wesley *Serm.* ii. ii. §9 'Hell is paved' saith one 'with good intentions'. **1818** Cruise *Digest* (ed. 2) V. 167 Sir W. Blackstone thought the deed of uses sufficient evidence of the intention of the parties.

b. *colloq.* in *pl.* Purposes in respect of a proposal of marriage.

[**1751** Smollett *Per. Pic.* IV. ii.] **1796** Jane Austen *Pride & Prej.* xxxiv, Colonel Fitzwilliam had made it clear that he had no intentions at all, and..she did not mean to be unhappy about him. **1852** *Punch* 27 Mar. (Cartoon), *Mr. Bull.* Now, Sir, don't let us have any more Derby Dilly Dallying. What are your Intentions towards Miss Britannia? **1884** Flor. Marryat *Under the Lilies* xxxiii, 'Why! I'm just about to ask you your intentions!' 'Don't! please! For I am married.'

6. a. Ultimate purpose; the aim of an action; †that for which anything is intended (*obs.*).

c **1410** Hoccleve *Mother of God* 52 Cryst of thee hath deyned for to take Flessh and eek blood for this entencioun Vp on a crois to die for our sake. **1484** Caxton *Fables of Æsop* ii. iii, To consydere and loke wel to what entention the yeft is gyuen. **1556** *Aurelio & Isab.* (1608) E iij, To none other intension, than onele to begille them. **1652** French *Yorksh. Spa* iv. 48 It..serves as effectually..for most intensions that almost any Physick is prescribed for. **1773** Reid *Aristotle's Log.* ii. §2 (1788) 25 The intention of the categories is to muster every object under ten heads. **1878** Morley *Crit. Misc.* Ser. i. *Carlyle* 201 One thing to estimate the intention and sincerity of a movement, when it first stirred the hearts of men, and another thing to pass sentence upon it in the days of its degradation.

b. In literary criticism: the aim or design which a critic detects in a writer's work.

1946 Wimsatt & Beardsley in *Sewanee Rev.* LIV. 469 Intention has obvious affinities for the author's attitude toward his work, the way he felt, what made him write. **1959** *Times Lit. Suppl.* 20 Feb. 97/1 Intention, in Mr. Wimsatt's use of the word, does not mean what it means in Dr. Richards's distinction between sense, tone, feeling, and intention... It means what we might have reason to think that the author thought he was up to.

7. †**a.** Stretching, tension: = intension 1. *Obs.*

1580 Lyly *Euphues* (Arb.) 383 As Musitians tune their strings who..either by intention, or remission, frame them to a pleasant consent. **1616** *Rich Cabinet* 123 So doe we vnbend bowes..lest continuall intention should boow the bowe, or breake the string. **1654** Gataker *Disc. Apol.* 57 By intention of speech a vein opening in my Lungs caused such a flux of blood.

b. Straining, bending, forcible application or direction (*of* the mind, eye, thoughts, etc.). (Akin to 1, but with more of the notion of *tension* as in 7.)

1638 F. Junius *Paint. of Ancients* 206 We shall doe well to breath our selves now and then..by unbending the intention of our thoughts. **1659** *Gentl. Calling* iv. §13 Not being able to endure so much seriousness and intention of mind. *a* **1716** South *Twelve Serm.* (1744) X. 326 The toil and labour, and racking intention of the brain. **1862** Thoreau *Excurs., Autumnal Tints* (1863) 262 It required a different intention of the eye in the same locality, to see different plants.

†**8.** Intensification: = intention 3. *Obs.*

1603 Holland *Plutarch's Mor.* 69 Morall vertue..tempereth the remission and intention..of the passions. **1638** F. Junius *Paint. of Ancients* 276 Brightnesse may bee sayd to bee nothing else but an intention of Light. **1758** J. S. *Le Dran's Observ. Surg.* (1771) Dict., *Typus*, is the Order of Fevers consisting of Intention and Remission.

†**9.** Inclination, tendency. *Obs.*

1594 Plat *Jewell-ho.* ii. 35 If it continew longe in a pewter sawcer, it hath an intention towardes ceruse.

II. Specific uses.

10. *Surg.* and *Med.* **a.** An aim or purpose in a healing process; hence, a plan or method of treatment. [med.L. *curationis intentio*, transl. ὁ τῆς ἰάσεως σκοπός Galen (ed. Kühn I. 385).] *arch.*

c **1400** *Lanfranc's Cirurg.* 18 Al þe entencioun of a surgian, how diuers þat it be, it is on [of] þre maners, þe first is vndoynge of þat, þat is hool, þe secunde to hele þat, þat is broke, þe .iij. is remeuynge of þat, þat is to myche. **1541** R. Copland *Guydon's Formul.*, etc. S j, In the cure of colde apostemes be iij intencyons. The fyrste is to egall the mater antecedent. The seconde is the conioynt mater. And ye thyrde is to correct ye accydentes. **1701** T. Fuller (*title*) Pharmacopœia Extemporanea; or, a body of Select Medicines, answering most intentions of cure. **1727–41** Chambers *Cycl.*, *Intention* or *Intension*, in medicine, that judgment, or method of cure, which a physician forms to himself from a due examination of symptoms. **1822–34** *Good's Study Med.* (ed. 4) IV. 378 Some of the indications of the disease, however, have given rise to a much bolder intention.

b. *spec.* in ***first intention***, the healing of a lesion or fracture by the immediate re-union of the severed parts, without granulation; ***second intention***, the healing of a wound by granulation after suppuration.

1543 Traheron *Vigo's Chirurg.* (1586) 130 b, Solution of continuitie in the flesh may be restored by the waie of the first intention. **1767** Gooch *Treat. Wounds* I. 130 The first intention belongs to incised wounds, and is performed, by bringing their lips, as much as possible, into contact..The second intention is accomplished, by promoting digestion, and regeneration of the loss of substance. **1813** J. Thomson *Lect. Inflam.* 125 The first [mode] is by adhesion without granulation; this Galen termed re-union by the first intention; the second is re-union by granulation..re-union by the seond intention. **1859** J. Brown *Rab & F.* ii. (1862) 26 The wound healed 'by the first intention'.

11. *Logic.* The direction or application of the mind to an object; a conception formed by directing the mind to some object; a general concept. ***first intentions***, primary conceptions of things, formed by the first or direct application of the mind to the things themselves; e.g. the concepts of *a tree, an oak.* ***second intentions***, secondary conceptions formed by the application of thought to first intentions in their relations to each other; e.g. the concepts of *genus, species, variety, property, accident, difference, identity.*

The introduction of these terms is due to the early Latin translation of Avicenna, in which the Arabic *ma‘qūlāt* 'perceptions, notions', pl. of *ma‘qūl* 'what is perceived by the intellect, intelligible, known', is rendered by *intentiones.* Thus tr. Avicenna *Metaph.* I, 2 (Prantl II. 321) Subjectum vero logicæ, sicut scisti, sunt intentiones intellectæ secundo [*al-ma‘qūlāt al-þāniyah*], quæ apponuntur intentionibus primo intellectis [*al-ma‘qūlāt al-ūlā*], secundum quod per eas pervenitur de cognito ad incognitum. Hence in Albertus Magnus (1193–1280) *Metaph.* I; I, 1 (Opp. ed. Jammy, Lugd. 1651, III. 3/1) Scientiæ logicæ non considerant ens et partem entis aliquam, sed intentiones secundas circa res per sermonem positas, per quas viæ habentur veniendi de noto ad ignotum. Pacius (*Aristot. Organ.*, 1584) identifies *intentio* with *notio* 'notion': 'prima notio seu prima intentio'.

1550 Bale *Image Both Ch.* ii. Pref. 2 b, Subtiltees, seconde intencyons, intrinsecall moodes. **1551** Robinson tr. *More's Utopia* ii. vi. (1895) 185 Our newe Logiciens..were neuer yet able to fynde out the seconde intentyons; in so muche that none of them all coulde euer see man hymselfe in commen, as they call hym. **1638** Rouse *Heav. Acad.* ii. 15 For things of the second intention, to discern them we ascend above Sense unto Reason, and see them with our Understandings. **1646** Sir T. Browne *Pseud. Ep.* i. iii. 9 Not attaining the..second intention of the words. **1852** Mansel *Notes Aldrich's Logic* (ed. 2) 20 First Intentions, as conceptions of things, are predicable of the individuals conceived under them..Second Intentions are not so predicable..When Genus is said to be predicable of Species, it is not meant that we can predicate the one second Intention of the other, so as to say, 'Species is Genus'; but that the first intention 'animal' is predicable of the first intention 'man'; the relation of the one to the other being expressed by the second intentions 'genus' and 'species'. For this reason, Logic was said [by Avicenna] to treat of *second intentions applied to first.* **1864** Bowen *Logic* v. 112.

12. *Theol.* **a.** One of the three things necessary, according to the Schoolmen, to the effectual administration and validity of a Sacrament, the two others being *matter* and *form*: see quots.

1690 SHADEWELL *Am. Bigot* v. *ad fin.*, I vill pronounce de Words of de maarriage without intention, and den it is no marriage. **1726** AYLIFFE *Parergon* 103 The doctrine of the Schools is, That a Sacrament requires Matter, Form, and Intention. *Ibid.*, I am at a loss to know what the Intention of a Sacrament is, unless it be what the Church requires to be done therein, according to the Council of Florence. **1842–71** HOOK *Ch. Dict.* 397 The following is the eleventh canon of the Council of Trent:—'If any shall say that there is not required in the ministers while they perform and confer the sacraments, at least the intention of doing what the Church does, let him be accursed'. **1869** HADDAN *Apost. Success.* viii. (1879) 267 Popes like Alexander VIII. may tell us..that a minister invalidates a rite by withdrawing his interior intention from it,..soberer schoolmen..limit the required intention to nothing more at the least than a virtual intention to do as the Church does.

b. *R.C. Ch.* ***special*** or ***particular intention***, a special purpose or end for which mass is celebrated, prayers are offered up, etc. as the spiritual welfare of some person, etc.

1849 ROCK *Ch. of Fathers* I. i. 76 Like ourselves, the Anglo-Saxons often celebrated mass for a particular intention. **1886** *Echo* 30 Nov., In the Communion Service a '*special intention*' was made known by the introduction of words implying that the 'sacrifice was received in memory' of the dead. **1890** LOUISA DOBRÉE *Stories Sacram.*, *Blanche's Baptism* 20, I gave you all my intentions at Mass that morning, and said the *Te Deum* for you. **1895** *Catholic Mag.* July 184 Our Mother General..gives us the intention for the next day's Communion. **1966** *New Statesman* 22 Apr. 608/1 The text of the Mass itself, with its special intention in capitals.

13. *Roman Law.* (See quot.)

1880 MUIRHEAD *Gaius* IV. §41 The clauses of a formula are these,—the demonstration, the intention, the adjudication, and the condemnation.. The intention is the clause in which the pursuer embodies his demand; for example, thus: 'Should it appear that Numerius Negidius ought to give ten thousand sesterces to Aulus Agerius'.

†**14.** *Rhet.* Intensification of force or meaning; the use of a word to such an end. (L. *intentio*, Aul. Gell.; Gr. ἐπίτασις, Dion. Hal.) *Obs.*

1678 PHILLIPS (ed. 4), *Intention*,..in Rhetorick it is the repetition of the same word in a contrary sense, as *Una salus victis nullam sperare salutem*.

15. Special Comb.: **intention movement** [tr. G. *intentionsbewegung* (O. Heinroth)], a movement or action on the part of an animal which itself performs no function except to reveal or signal that a further movement or action may follow or is contemplated; **intention tremor**, a tremor which is manifested when a voluntary action is performed.

[**1910** O. HEINROTH in *Jrnl. für Ornith.* LVIII. 122 Eine Modifikation des eigentlichen Locktones, wie sie kurz vor dem Auffliegen hervorgebracht und dann mit den oben beschriebenen Intentionsbewegungen verbunden wird, ist ein langes und fein ausklingendes 'Hu'.] **1950** K. Z. LORENZ in *Symposia Soc. Exper. Biol.* IV. 242 We know of two phyletically distinct ways, by which non-social, mechanically effective endogenous activities may develop into social releasers: in one case the so-called 'intention movement' (*Intentionsbewegung*, Heinroth), in the other the so-called 'displacement activities'. *Ibid.* 243 Intention movements..are..very reliable indicators for the present 'mood' of an animal. **1953** N. TINBERGEN *Herring Gull's World* xvii. 153 A bird may rapidly change from pecking to the intention-movement of brooding. **1961** A. J. BERGER *Bird Study* v. 136 The first intention movement preceding walking or hopping often is a 'bow'. **1887** VICKERY & KNAPP tr. *A. von Strümpell's Textbk. Med.* 593 The tremor in multiple sclerosis comes on only with intended movements, 'intention tremor'. **1969** *Times* 8 Feb. 4/1 All but one suffered from defects in their nervous systems. The commonest of these seems to have been intention tremors, which are tremors occurring when a voluntary movement is made.

†**in'tention**, *v. Obs.* *rare*$^{-0}$. [f. prec., after It. *intenzionare*, f. *intenzione*: cf. F. *intentionner* (1690 in Hatz.-Darm.).] To have an intention.

1611 FLORIO, *Intentionare*, to intention.

intentional (ɪnˈtɛnʃənəl), *a.* (*sb.*) [ad. med.L. *intentiōnālis* (Herveus Natalis *De Intent.*, *c* 1300), f. *intentiōn-em* INTENTION: cf. F. *intentionnel* (Palsgr. 1530).]

A. *adj.* **1.** Of or pertaining to intention or purpose; exisiting (only) in intention. ***intentional fallacy***: in literary criticism, the fallacy that the meaning or value of a work may be judged or defined in terms of the writer's intention.

1530 PALSGR. 316/2 Intencyonall belongyng to the intent, *intencionel*. **1602** in Moryson *Itin.* II. (1617) 247 Where wee see faith and dutie onely intentionall *in origine*. *a* **1695** W. D. *Dissuas. Cursing* in *Boyle's Wks.* (1772) VI. 31 These intentional sins, for being ineffectual against others, divest not the being criminal in themselves. **1754** RICHARDSON *Grandison* I. xxvi. 186 Her heart overflows with sentiments of gratitude on every common obligation and even on but intentional ones. **1818** CRUISE *Digest* (ed. 2) VI. 154 The second will never operated, it was only intentional. **1946** WIMSATT & BEARDSLEY in *Sewanee Rev.* LIV. 482 The question of 'allusiveness', for example,..is certainly one where a false judgement is likely to involve the intentional fallacy. **1948** [see AFFECTIVE *a.* 7 c]. **1954** W. K. WIMSATT *Verbal Icon* i. 6 It is not so much a historical statement as a definition to say that the intentional fallacy is a romantic one. **1958** *Listener* 9 Oct. 578/2 A studied defence of what has been labelled—and dismissed—as the 'intentional fallacy'.

2. Done on purpose, resulting from intention; intended. Rarely of an agent: Acting with intention.

16.., *a* **1677** [implied in INTENTIONALLY]. *a* **1729** ROGERS (J.), The glory of God is the end which every intelligent being is bound to consult, by a direct and intentional service. **1744** HARRIS *Three Treat.* Wks. (1841) 7 There is, too, another alteration..which..is equally wanting; and that is with respect to the epithet, 'intentional or voluntary'. **1824** SYD. SMITH *Wks.* (1867) II. 41 We accuse nobody of intentional misrepresentation. **1828** SCOTT *F.M. Perth* ii, Considering this as an intentional insult. *a* **1862** BUCKLE *Civiliz.* (1873) III. v. 306 An intentional suppression of facts. **1863** J. G. MURPHY *Comm. Gen.* ii. 5 Man is the only intentional cultivator.

3. *Scholastic Philos.* Pertaining to the operations of the mind; mental; existing in or for the mind.

intentional species, appearances or images supposed to be emitted by material objects so as to strike the senses and produce sensation.

1624 F. WHITE *Repl. Fisher* 452 The thought of man is a spirituall or intentionall motion and action, and not a substantiall thing. **1647** H. MORE *Poems* 277 Let him..with uncessant industry persist Th' intentionall species to mash and bray In marble morter. **1678** CUDWORTH *Intell. Syst.* I. i. §14. 15 It is evident, that Empedocles did not suppose Sensations to be made by intentional Species or Qualities. **1694** R. BURTHOGGE *Reason* 79 Colours, Sounds, Sapors, Time..are Intentional things, things that, as such, have only an *esse Objectivum*, an *esse Cognitum*, as the School-men phrase it. **1704** NORRIS *Ideal World* II. vii. 344 Some philosophers talk of..intentional species, and of their successive generating and spawning each other, after their first emission from the object, throughout the several points of the medium.

4. *Heb. Gram.* Applied by some to the use of the Future or Imperfect tense (in some cases marked by a special form) of the Hebrew verb to express intention; also called *cohortative*: e.g. in Gen. xi. 7.

1892 DAVIDSON *Hebr. Gram.* 60 *note*, Both the Jussive and Cohortative are comprehended by Ewald under the name *Voluntative*; for Cohortative Böttcher prefers to use the term *Intentional*.

†**B.** *sb.* An appearance or phenomenon which has no substantial or concrete existence. *Obs.*

1658 W. SANDERSON *Graphice* 4 The sight is the subject of Forms without a Body; which are called, *Intentionalls*. **1697** tr. *Burgersdicius his Logic* I. iii. 5 To a true Being..are oppos'd..3dly. Appearances, or as they commonly say, Intentionals, as the Rain-bow, Colours appearing, Species's and Spectres of the Senses and Understanding, and other things whose Essence only consists in their Apparition.

intentionalism (ɪnˈtɛnʃənəlɪz(ə)m). [f. INTENTIONAL *a.* + -ISM.] The doctrine that a literary work or some other work, etc., is the result of conscious intention or design. So **in'tentionalist**, one who propounds such a doctrine; **intentiona'listic** *a.*, of, pertaining to, or characterized by intentionalism.

1878 W. AFFLECK tr. *Janet's Final Causes* I. vi. 215 God has come forth from Himself as well in pantheism as in creationism or intentionalism. **1946** WIMSATT & BEARDSLEY in *Sewanee Rev.* LIV. 485 Allusiveness in poetry is one of several critical issues by which we have illustrated the more abstract issue of intentionalism. *Ibid.* 486 Allusiveness would appear to be in some recent poems an extreme corollary of the romantic intentionalist assumption. **1952** *Essays in Crit.* II. I. 106 But does the 'intentionalist' assert that no lyric can ever be abstracted from a longer work? **1954** W. K. WIMSATT *Verbal Icon* i. 11 The use of biographical evidence [in criticism] need not involve intentionalism. **1958** *Listener* 16 Oct. 595/1 There is a suspicious silence on the whole issue of intentionalism among the classical English critics. **1958** I. P. HUNGERLAND *Poetic Discourse* vi. 162 The Intentionalists have neglected such situations. **1958** M. C. BEARDSLEY *Aesthetics* 27 There are other critics who tend to shift back and forth between the work and its creator, never quite clear in their own minds when they are talking about the one or the other. They mingle the evidences of intention with the evidences of accomplishment, and sometimes decide what the work is or means primarily on external evidence. This is to practice intentionalistic criticism.

intentionality (ɪnˌtɛnʃəˈnælɪtɪ). [ad. Schol.L. *intentiōnālitās* (Herveus Natalis, *c* 1300, *De Intent.*, lf. 7 b), f. *intentiōnālis* INTENTIONAL: see -ITY.] The quality or fact of being intentional.

1611 FLORIO, *Intentionalita*, intentionalitie. **1651** HOBBES *Leviath.* I. iv. 12 Intentionality..and other insignificant words of the School. **1780** BENTHAM *Princ. Legisl.* vii. §6 In every transaction..which is examined with a view to punishment there are four articles to be considered..3. the intentionality that may have accompanied it. **1823** —— *Not Paul* 229 Perfect consciousness, fixed intentionality, predetermined perseverance. *a* **1834** COLERIDGE *Rem.* (1836) II. 180 Observe the consciousness and the intentionality of his wit.

intentionally (ɪnˈtɛnʃənəlɪ), *adv.* [f. INTENTIONAL *a.* + -LY^{2}.] In an intentional manner or relation. †**a.** In respect of the mind or its workings; by the action of the mind (*obs.*). †**b.** In respect of intention or purpose, as opposed to performance (*obs.*). **c.** With intention, on purpose.

16.. CARYL in Spurgeon *Treas. Dav.* Ps. xci. 13 His meaning is, thou shalt intentionally tread upon them like a conqueror. [*a* **1661** FULLER *Worthies* I. (1662) 29 Surely, not intentionly, but accidentaly.] **1665** BOYLE *Occas. Refl.* II. xi. (1848) 133 They think, That for a Man to be otherwise than Intentionally Religious before his Hair begin to change Colour, were not only to lose the priviledges of Youth, but to incroach upon those of old Age. *a* **1677** HALE *Prim. Orig. Man.* II. iv. 155 Some things are found out casually or accidentally; some things intentionally. *Ibid.* IV. viii. 372 Man above all visible Creatures is able to perform that duty intellectually and intentionally. **1720** DE FOE *Capt. Singleton* i. (1840) 11, I was guilty of the fact intentionally.. but providence..always frustrated my designs. **1820** SCORESBY *Acc. Arctic Reg.* I. App. 46 This observation was intentionally made at a different hour almost every day. **1875** JOWETT *Plato* (ed. 2) I. 370, I never intentionally wronged any one.

†**in'tentionary**, *a.* and *sb. Obs.* [f. INTENTION + -ARY.] **A.** *adj.* **a.** = INTENTIONAL *a.*

1647 CLARENDON *Contempl. Ps.* Tracts (1727) 496 We give no ear, no serious and intentionary hearkening to it. **1684** *Depos. Cast. York* (Surtees) 266 A combiner with and intentionary introducer of Popery.

b. According to legal intent or intendment.

1647 N. BACON *Disc. Govt. Eng.* II. xxxix. (1739) 173 The intentionary sense of the Statute..although not within the explicite words of that Law.

B. *sb.* One who does something with 'intention': cf. INTENTION 12.

1619 W. SCLATER *Exp. 1 Thess.* (1630) 246 Not lesse blame-worthy are our superstitious Votaries or Intentionaries, that walke out of Gods Church, to the Shrines of Saints, and..the Holy Land.

†**in'tentionate**, *a. Obs.* *rare*$^{-1}$. [f. INTENTION + -ATE^{2}: cf. F. *intentionné* (16th c. in Hatz.-Darm.).] Having, or characterized by, intention; intentional, intended.

1631 R. H. *Arraignm. Whole Creat.* Ep. Ded. 8 Mooving the minde of the admirer or intentionate observer.

†**in'tentionated**, *a. Obs. rare.* [f. as prec. + -ED^{1}.] = INTENTIONED.

1620 SHELTON *Quix.* IV. xxiv. 196 So christianly a Father and Daughter..to see to, so well intentionated. *c* **1690** *Consid. Raising Money* 9 It will be readily granted by all wise and well-intentionated Persons.

†**in'tentionately**, *adv. Obs.* *rare*$^{-1}$. [f. INTENTIONATE *a.* + -LY^{2}.] Intentionally.

1609 BP. W. BARLOW *Answ. Nameless Cath.* 135 The same doctrine..which wrought in others the sauour of death; not intentionately from the Subject, but occasionately by the vice of the Obiect.

intentioned (ɪnˈtɛnʃənd), *a.* [f. INTENTION *sb.* + -ED^{2}.] Having intentions (of a specified kind).

1667 W. BROWNE tr. *Gomberville's Polexander* IV. v. 333 To let her know they were loyally intentioned. **1729** SWIFT *Let. M'Culla's Project* Wks. 1841 II. 97/1 Those who are honest and best-intentioned. **1818** CRUISE *Digest* (ed. 2) III. 457 The Lord Chief Justice's system was very great and noble, and very equitably intentioned. **1825** CARLYLE *Schiller* II. (1845) 111 So occupied and so intentioned, he continued to reside at Weimar. **1898** J. R. TRUMBULL *Hist. Northampton, Mass.* I. 2 A spirit of thrift undoubtedly permeated the best intentioned of them.

in'tentionless, *a. rare.* [-LESS.] Without intention; purposeless.

1887 *Harper's Mag.* Nov. 931 He began..to lose himself in intentionless plausibilities. **1894** *Athenæum* 10 Nov. 634/2 The surviving life of old Japan here depicted [is] unknowing, probably, and intentionless of its own charm.

intentive (ɪnˈtɛntɪv), *a. Obs.* or *arch.* Forms: α. 3–5 **ententif**, 4–5 **-yf**, **-yve**, 5 **-ife**, **-yfe**, 6 **-ive**. β. 5–6 **intentif**, **-yf**, **-ife**, 6– **intentive**. [a. OF. *en-*, *intentif*, *-ive* (12th c. in Godef.), ad. late L. *intentīvus*, f. *intent-*, ppl. stem of *intendĕre* to INTEND: see -IVE.]

1. Of persons: Devoting earnest attention or pains; paying regard or attention; attentive, heedful, assiduous, intent. Const. *to*, *about*, *on*, *upon*, or *inf.*

α. *c* **1290** [implied in INTENTIVELY]. *c* **1374** CHAUCER *Troylus* II. 789 (838), I loue oon which is most ententyf To seruen wel vnwery and vnfeynid. —— *Boeth.* I. pr. iii. 6 (Camb. MS.) They ben ententyf abowte sarpuleris or sachels. *c* **1430** *Pilgr. Lyf Manhode* I. cxxiv. (1869) 66 Wel me liketh þat ententyf to my wordes þou hast ben. **1491** CAXTON *Vitas Patr.* (W. de W. 1495) I. xlix. 97 a/2 Lete your eeres by ententif and dylygente to me. *a* **1563** BALE *Sel. Wks.* (Parker Soc.) 113 Is not Chrysostom an ententive doctor?

β. **1523** SKELTON *Garl. Laurel* 942 Intentyf, aye And dylygent. **1548** HALL *Chron.*, *Hen. VII* 54 b, The Kynge.. was so vigilant, so circumspect and so intentive. *a* **1635** NAUNTON *Fragm. Reg.* (Arb.) 30 He was wholly intentive to the service of his Mistris. **1658** BROMHALL *Treat. Specters* III. 227 They..going nearer privily..the servants being intentive, flew upon them. **1670** *Famous Concl. wherein Clement VIII was elected Pope* 10 Montalto..was..intentive to continue his solicitation. [**1835** SIR T. HARDY in *Rot. Litt. Pat.* Introd. 6 (tr. Writ, 4 John, *De intendendo*) We command you to be intentive to him in all things as our Seneschal, and to execute his commands.]

2. Of the faculties, thoughts, actions, looks, etc.: Intently bent or directed.

c **1386** CHAUCER *Pars. T.* ¶707 Ententif desir to byen thyng espiritueel. **1475** *Bk. Noblesse* (Roxb.) 70 The saide Cirus employed..intentife besynesse in..labourage of his londis. **1555–8** PHAER *Æneid* II. C iij b, They whusted all, and fixt with eies ententiue did behold. *a* **1592** GREENE *Jas. IV*, II. ii, His too intentive trust to flatterers. **1637** HEYWOOD *Royal Ship* 22 My purpose, which is fully intentive upon brevity. **1655** H. VAUGHAN *Silex Scint.* II. *Rainbow* 7 The youthful world's gray fathers..Did with intentive looks watch every hour For thy new light. **1725** POPE *Odyss.* VI. 80 Blushes ill-restrained betray Her thoughts intentive on the

bridal-day. **1844** ALB. SMITH *Adv. Mr. Ledbury* xlii. (1886) 129 Many..were at breakfast..with such intentive appetites, that they took no notice of the courteous salute.

in'tentively, *adv. Obs.* or *arch.* [f. prec. + -LY^2.] In an intentive manner; with earnest attention or application; earnestly, heedfully, intently.

c **1290** *Beket* 504 in *S. Eng. Leg.* I. 121 Kniȝtes and oþure ..beden seint Thomas ententifliche: þat he þat word forbere. **1340** *Ayenb.* 210 And acsi wisliche and diligentliche þet is ententifliche and perseuerantliche. *c* **1374** CHAUCER *Boeth.* III. pr. xii. 81 (Camb. MS.) For as I trowe thow ledyst now moore ententyfly thyne eyen to loken the verray goodes. *c* **1400** *Beryn* 239 The knyȝt with his meyne went to se the wall..Devising ententiflich the strengthis al a-bout. **1481** CAXTON *Godfrey* clxxxiii. 268 Alle they of oure hooste behelde them moche ententyfly. **1593** NASHE *Christ's T.* (1613) 145 The Phylosopher that too intentiuely gaz'd on the stars, stumbled and fell into a ditch. *a* **1619** FOTHERBY *Atheom.* II. ix. §1 (1622) 295 The end of the Mathematicks, is, to leade vs men intentiuely to consider of the nature of God. **1711** STEELE *Spect.* No. 6 ¶3, I looked intentively upon him.

in'tentiveness. *Obs.* or *arch.* [f. as prec. + -NESS.] The quality or fact of being intentive; closeness of attention; intentness.

1561 T. NORTON *Calvin's Inst.* IV. 78 He doth..speake.. of suche praiers as require a more earnest intentiuenesse. **1612–15** BP. HALL *Contempl., N.T.* IV. xxiv, Their care and intentivenesse is truly commendable; they came to comfort her, they do what they came for. **1685** R. LOWMAN *Descr. Fireworks Coron.* 1 The Earnestness of Expectation and Intentiveness of what was..to succeed.

intently (ɪn'tɛntlɪ), *adv.* [f. INTENT *a.* + -LY^2. ME. had the kindred form *ententely*, *intentily*, ?after F. *ententement* attentively, or reduced from *ententifly*: cf. *jolifliche*, *jollily*.] In an intent manner; with strained attention or close application; earnestly, eagerly.

α. **1375** BARBOUR *Bruce* I. 613 He lukyit the Seyle ententily. *c* **1425** WYNTOUN *Cron.* VIII. xviii. 129Ðe Brws it lukyd ententely.

β. **1635** J. HAYWARD tr. *Biondi's Banish'd Virg.* 123 So intently were all her thoughts busied in chastizing them. **1695** LD. PRESTON *Boeth.* IV. 182 When I consider intently thy Reasons. **1772** HURD *Prophecies* (1788) l. iii. 66 Intently prosecuting one entire scheme. **1838** LYTTON *Alice* 29 Intently gazing on the scene below. **1871** H. AINSWORTH *Tower Hill* I. iii, ''Tis mere fancy', he rejoined, after listening for a moment intently.

†**in'tentment.** *Obs. rare.* [f. INTENT *v.*: cf. OF. *ententement* intention, wish.] Intention.

1624 HEYWOOD *Captives* III. i. in Bullen *O. Pl.* IV, To invert my good intentements, turne this nest I built for prayer unto a bedd of sinnes.

intentness (ɪn'tɛntnɪs). [f. INTENT *a.* + -NESS.] The quality or condition of being intent; strained or fixed attention; close mental application.

1642 BP. REYNOLDS *Israel's Petit.* 15 It doth intimate an Intentnesse of the Church upon that point. **1692** LOCKE *Educ.* Wks. 1812 IX. 62 Intentness of thought upon something else. **1755** VISC. PARKER in *Phil. Trans.* XLIX. 368, I found by his intentness, that he saw something extraordinary. **1817** J. SCOTT *Paris Revis.* (ed. 4) 145 This business..was carried on with an intentness that seemed to have no distraction towards any other consideration. **1880** MISS BRADDON *Just as I am* II. 119 A tone and look that indicated intentness of purpose.

†**in'tenuate**, *a. Obs. rare*$^{-1}$. [f. IN-^{2} + L. *tenuāt-us*, pa. pple. of *tenuāre* to make thin: cf. ATTENUATE.] Thinned, thin.

1471 RIPLEY *Comp. Alch.* II. i. in Ashm. (1652) 135 Whych..makyth intenuate thyngs that were thyk also.

†**in'tepidate**, *v. Obs. rare.* [f. IN-^{2} + ppl. stem of L. *tepidāre*, f. *tepidus* lukewarm, TEPID.] *trans.* To render lukewarm, to discourage.

a **1631** DONNE *Serm.* IV. cii. 359 It slackens us, enfeebles and intepidates our Zeal. **1670** G. H. *Hist. Cardinals* II. III. 189 To leave a person..without any reward, would but discourage and intepidate the rest.

inter (ɪn'tɜː(r)), *v.* Forms: *α.* 4–5 **entir, -tyre,** 4–6 **-tere, -tyr,** 4–7 **-ter, -terre,** 5 **-tire, -tiere, -tyer(e,** 5–6 **-tier,** 7 **-terr.** *β.* 5 **intyr, yntyr,** 6 **intere,** 6–8 **-terre,** 7–8 **-terr,** 5– **inter.** [ME. a. OF. *enterre-r* (11th c. in Littré) = Pr., Sp. *enterrar*, It. *interrare*, prob. late pop.L. *interrāre* (in med.L. 11th c.), f. *in-* (IN-^{2}) + *terra* earth, for cl. L. *inhumāre*, INHUME.]

1. *trans.* To deposit (a corpse) in the earth, or in a grave or tomb; to inhume, bury.

α. **1303** R. BRUNNE *Handl. Synne* 6390 Þe sone..come home to þe enteryng. **1375** BARBOUR *Bruce* XIX. 224 Thar, with gret solempnite And with gret dule, entyrit wes he. *c* **1425** WYNTOUN *Cron.* VIII. xxiii, In þe kyrk of Dwnfermlyne Hys Body wes enteryd syne. **1470–85** MALORY *Arthur* X. li, Thenne the kynge lete entyere them in a chappel. **1513** MORE in Hall *Chron., Edw. V* (1548) 14b, His body and head wer enterred at Wyndesore. **1523** LD. BERNERS *Froiss.* I. cccxiv. 482 To be entred with the greatter solemnytie. **1601** SHAKS. *Jul. C.* III. ii. 81 The euill that men do, liues after them, The good is oft enterred with their bones. *a* **1631** DONNE *Poems* (1650) 35 Dead and enterr'd.

β. **1499** *Promp. Parv.* 140/2 (Pynson) Entyryn or intyryn dede men. **1565–73** COOPER *Thesaurus* s.v. *Componere*, To bury or interre. **1587** *Mirr. Mag., Albanact* xlii, To interre the dead. **1687** A. LOVELL tr. *Thevenot's Trav.* I. 58 Being come to the Burying-place where the Corps is to be Interr'd, they take it out of the Coffin. **1711** ADDISON *Spect.* No. 164 ¶10 She..was interred according to her Request. **1755** *Capt. P. Drake* i. 3 Staying but one Day after the Battle to inter Lord Dungan. **1849** MACAULAY *Hist. Eng.* vi. II. 44 James..had not ventured to inter his brother with the rites of the Church of Rome.

b. *transf.* and *fig.*

1601 ? MARSTON *Pasquil & Kath.* III. 123, I will interre my selfe in Ploydens coffin. **1601** CORNWALLIS *Ess.* II. xxviii. (1631) 24 O Signieur..give me leave to interre myself in your armes. **1651** tr. *De las-Coveras' Hist. Don Fenise* 136, I resolved to enterre my selfe alive in this desert. **1742** YOUNG *Nt. Th.* I. 137 Yet man, fool man! here buries all his thoughts; Interrs celestial hopes without one sigh.

†**2.** Said of a tomb: To enclose the corpse of.

1631 MILTON *Epit. Marchioness Winchester* 1 This rich marble doth inter The honoured wife of Winchester.

†**3.** To place (*anything*) in the ground; to cover up with soil; = BURY *v.* 3. *Obs.*

1601 HOLLAND *Pliny* II. 17 It is very good to enterre and couer with mould round about the leaues, now one, and then another. **1664** EVELYN *Sylva* (1679) 19 Be circumspect never to interr your stem deeper than you found it standing. **1695** WOODWARD *Nat. Hist. Earth* (1702) 13 How these Sea-shells..became interr'd in the bowels of the Earth. **1727–41** CHAMBERS *Cycl.* s.v., Gardeners also Interr, or earth up, sellery, endive, and lettice, to blanch, or whiten..them.

†**inter**, *sb. Sc. Obs. rare*$^{-1}$. In 6 **entire, -tyre.** [f. prec. vb.] = INTERMENT.

1513 DOUGLAS *Æneis* VI. ii. 151 Til his funerale entire [*ed.* 1553 entyre], or sacrifice, Do bring the blak beistis.

†**inter**, obs. form of ENTER *v.*

1494 *Acc. Ld. High Treas.* (Dickson) I. 250 To Jhone Lame quhen he interit, xviijs.

‖**inter** ('ɪntə(r)), *prep.* The L. preposition = 'between', 'among', occurs in a few Latin phrases occasional in Eng., e.g. ***inter alia***, amongst other things (less usually ***inter alios***, amongst others, other persons); ***inter nos***, between ourselves; ***inter partes*** (Law), of an action: relevant only to the two parties in a particular case (see quots. 1966); of a deed or the like: made between two parties; ***inter se***, between or among themselves; ***inter vivos***, between living persons (esp. of a gift as opposed to a legacy). (†Rarely with English object.)

a **1641** BP. MOUNTAGU *Acts & Mon.* (1642) 293 The great garboyles *inter Herod and his sons. **1665** SIR T. HERBERT *Trav.* (1677) 195 Three errant Monks..make strange discoveries as well as descriptions of places; and **inter alia* of Cambalu. *a* **1670** HACKET *Abp. Williams* II. (1693) 152 The Lords produce *inter alios*, John Duke of Lancaster. **1872** J. A. H. MURRAY *Synops. Hor. Paul.* 1 A Narrative called the Acts of the Apostles, purporting to furnish (*inter alia*) memoirs of portions of the life of St. Paul. **1896** LELY *Stat. Pract. Util.* 39 *note*, By the letters patent the governors include (inter alios) the archbishops and bishops. **1714** SWIFT *Hor. Sat.* II. vi, Where all that passes **inter nos* Might be proclaimed at Charing-cross. **1790** M. CUTLER in *Life, Jrnls. & Corr.* (1888) I. 459 This request is *inter nos*, and [I] wish my name may not be mentioned. **1816** MAULE & SELWYN *Rep. Cases King's Bench* III. 308 A deed **inter partes* cannot operate as a release to strangers. **1906** *Daily Colonist* (Victoria, B.C.) 16 Jan. 10/2 Mr. Bodwell.. contended that this must not be considered an action inter partes; in form it may have been, but in substance it was a propounding of the will. **1960** *Times* 4 Aug. 11/5 On July 19 the injunction was granted in an *inter partes* form. **1966** BLACK & BROWN *Outl. Eng. Law* VI. xvii. 160 In modern terms actions are either *Actions in Rem* or *Actions in Personam* or *Inter Partes*. *Ibid.* 161 An action..*inter partes* produces a judgment which is binding only as between the parties to the case and not upon third parties. **1968** *Law Rep.* 106 The old common law rule that in an indenture inter partes the covenantee must be named as a party to the indenture to take the benefit of an immediate grant or the benefit of a covenant. **1971** *Mod. Law Rev.* XXXIV. VI. 605 The Court gives decisions on preliminary points of law.. when such questions are referred to it by municipal courts or tribunals in the course of proceedings *inter partes*. **1845** FORD *Handbk. Spain* I. 223 The 'little wars' which Spaniards wage **inter se*. **1888** G. F. STOUT *Stud. Philos. & Psychol.* (1930) i. 42 Forms of combination among presentations other than those by which sense-perceptions are connected *inter se*. **1971** *Mod. Law Rev.* XXXIV. VI. 598 Suppose that..the *inter se* doctrine of Commonwealth relations had emerged as a credible body of legal principle. **1972** *Times* 14 Mar. 12/2 The essential link between members of a volunteer unit was not their contractual relationship *inter se* but their common military service to the Crown. **1837** T. LEWIN *Pract. Treat. Law Trusts & Trustees* vi. 86 The Bank of England cannot be made a trustee, for the Company will not enter notice of instruments **inter vivos* upon their books. **1949** W. B. LEACH *Cases Law of Wills* 30 In 1931 decedent had created a large inter vivos trust. **1955** *Times* 8 June 4/3 Transfer of property through inheritance or *inter vivos* gifts or settlements should reckon as realization. **1963** *Economist* 16 Mar. 976/1 Death duties are ..largely avoided by transfers *inter vivos*. **1969** *Daily Tel.* 1 Oct. 20/6 Half the Seafield 'empire' is owned by Lord Reidhaven following his mother's foresight in transferring the property outside the *inter vivos* period, which exonerates the assets from death duty. **1972** *Accountant* 28 Sept. 381/3 Benefits..should be mentioned in reply to the question in the Inland Revenue Affidavit about gifts *inter vivos*.

inter., inter ('ɪntə(r)), abbrev. of INTERMEDIATE *a.* = *intermediate examination* (in arts, etc.), often used in ordinary colloquial speech.

1891–2 *London Univ. Guide* 29 Inter. Arts Honours. *Ibid.* 40 Inter. Science and Prel. Sci. Exams. **1913** W. OWEN *Let.* 28 Sept. (1967) 199 He was a student of Nottingham College, but failed to pass Inter-Arts. **1948** L. WALMSLEY *Master Mariner* II. i. 134 He had entered for a degree in science, had passed his 'inter' with the same ease as he'd passed his matric, and was sitting for his final in the coming term.

inter-, *prefix.* The Latin preposition and adv., *inter* 'between, among, amid, in between, in the midst', entered into combination with verbs, adjs., and sbs., as in *intercēdĕre* to go between, intercede, *intercipĕre* to seize on the way, intercept, *interdīcĕre* to interpose in speech, interdict, *interjacĕre* to throw between, interject, *interpōnĕre* to put between, interpose, *intervenīre* to come between, intervene, *intercalāris* intercalary, *interdigitālis* lying between the fingers, *interfluus* flowing between, *intermedius* intermediate, *intermūrālis* between walls; *interamnium* a place between rivers, *intercilium* the space between the eyebrows, *intercolumnium* the space between two columns, *internuntius* a messenger between, *interregnum* the time between two reigns, *intervallum* the space between two ramparts, interval. Some of these uses received great extension in late L. and the Romanic languages.

Of all these classes representatives are found in English, the earlier derived through French, the later often immediately from Latin. The Fr. form of the prefix is *entre-*, and it was with *entre-* or *enter-*, as in *entrechange*, *entercourse*, *enterfere*, that these words were taken into ME., and new compounds formed in Eng. itself: see ENTER-. But, between the 15th and 17th centuries, *entre-*, *enter-* gradually yielded to the L. *inter-*; *entertain* and *enterprise*, with their derivatives, being now the only relics of the earlier form. On the pattern of the words from L., many new derivatives have been formed from L. (or Gr.) elements: esp. the adjs. formed on the type (rare in L.) of *inter-mūr-ālis*: see 4 below.

In some cases English received from Latin and French both the simple word and its *inter-* compound: such are *change*, *inter-change*, *commune*, *inter-commune*, *view*, *inter-view*, *column*, *inter-column*. By extension from such compounds, *inter-* became a living prefix, freely used to form new compounds upon verbs, nouns, and adjs., not merely of Latin and French, but of native English origin, as in *inter-twine*, *inter-talk*, *inter-brain*, *inter-tidal*. Finally, the same process which produced such adjs. as *anti-slavery*, *anti-vaccination*, *anti-war* (see ANTI- 4), has produced the adjs. *inter-college*, *inter-island*, *inter-town*, *inter-university*.

The following are the uses of the prefix as an English formative element.

I. In adverbial or adjectival relation to the second element.

1. Prefixed to verbs, participles, vbl. sbs., and ppl. adjs., to form verbs, etc.

These are entered here in the uninflected form as verbs, but some of them are exemplified only in the form of participles or vbl. sbs. As a rule, wherever there is a verb compounded with *inter-*, the usual derivatives (vbl. sb. and ppl. a. in *-ing*, agent-n. in *-er*) are possible. Some of the verbs may be regarded as formed from sbs., e.g. *intercloud*, *-dash*, *-layer*, *-mesh*, *-net*, *-word*. The stress is on the radical element.

a. Denoting 'Between or among other things or persons; between the parts of, in the intervals of, or in the midst of, something; together *with*; between times or places, at intervals, here and there': as ***interbreathe*** (***interbreathing*** vbl. sb.), ***-chase***, ***-check***, ***-circle***, ***-cloud***, ***-come***, ***-crust***, ***-curl***, ***-dash***, ***-distinguish*** (also ***interdistinguishable*** adj.), ***-file*** (***interfiling*** vbl. sb.), ***-fillet***, ***-flash***, ***-forge***, ***-gild*** (in pa. pple. ***-gilt***), ***-insert***, ***-involve***, ***-layer***, ***-lie*** (in pres. pple. ***-lying***), ***-lighten***, ***-lot***, ***-mention***, ***-pave***, ***-peal***, ***-receive***, ***-rule***, ***-set***, †***-situate***, ***-smile***, ***-sole***, ***-squeeze***, ***-tinge***, ***-trace***, ***-whistle***, ***-word***. With an intr. verb, *inter-* sometimes stands in prepositional relation to a following noun, the verb thus becoming trans. with the noun as obj.; as ***interwend*** (to wend or pass between).

Such formations with ENTER- are found in 15th c., and with *inter-* from 16th c.: cf. INTERPLACE. Words of this form are much used by S. Daniel *c* 1600.

1818 KEATS *Endym.* II. 664 He..exhaled asphodel, And rose, with spicy fannings *interbreathed. *a* **1834** COLERIDGE *Notes & Lect.* (1874) 318 A harshness unrelieved by any lyrical *inter-breathings. **1620** T. ROBINSON *Mary Magd.* I. 37 The Chrystall windowes too, were *interchast With Iacynths, Diamonds, and Sappheirs blew[e]. **1821** BYRON *Cain* I. i. 453 Sorrow, *Intercheck'd with an instant of brief pleasure. **1821** SOUTHEY *Vis. Judgem.* I. 54 The regions of Paradise, sphere within sphere *intercircled. **1595** DANIEL *Civ. Wars* IV. xxv, None the least blacknes *interclouded had So faire a day. **1606** *Proc. agst. Garnet* Rrjb, Notwithstanding the pope's *intercoming to make himself a party in the quarrel. **1578** BANISTER *Hist. Man* I. 21 These Spondils are..obliquely cut, and *intercrusted with

Cartilages. a1586 SIDNEY *Arcadia* I. (1622) 59 Queene Helen, whose Iacinth haire..*intercurled by art (like a fine brooke through golden sands) had a rope of faire pearle. 1780 COWPER *Table Talk* 538 A prologue *interdash'd with many a stroke, An art contriv'd to advertise a joke. 1657 W. RAND tr. *Gassendi's Life Peiresc* I. 196 Figures..white, in a black Sea, *interdistinguished with a certain.. yellowishnesse. 1950 J. LAWLER *H. W. Wilson Co.* vii. 111 Specially trained women..handle the task of *interfiling the metal linotype slugs. *Ibid.* 112 The Production Department staff interfiles the new and old slips of copy. 1962 Y. MALKIEL in Householder & Saporta *Probl. Lexicogr.* 15 Interfiling..of authentic word cards. 1967 COX & DEWS in Cox & Grose *Organiz. Bibliogr. Rec. by Computer* II. 16 Anonymous works are frequently interfiled by title in author catalogues. 1967 C. J. DUNCAN *Ibid.* 41 The insertion of special sorts or 'pi-characters' has been the traditional interfiling solution adopted. 1868 BROWNING *Ring & Bk.* I. 138 A Latin cramp enough..But *interfilleted with Italian streaks. 1857–8 SEARS *Athan.* xvii. 144 Nothing hinders the *interflashings of the sunshine. a1641 BP. MOUNTAGU *Acts & Mon.* (1642) 408 With these..orthodoxall confessions some Pagan impieties..were *interforged. 1684 *Lond. Gaz.* No. 1980/4 A Silver Hilted Sword *Intergilt with Gold. 1622 MABBE tr. *Aleman's Guzman d'Alf.* II. 41 Stories..not fit to be *inter-inserted with this. 1865 MASSON *Rec. Brit. Philos.* 232 A logic that should profess to..*interinvolve the thought of nothing..with the thought of Absolute Being. 1816 W. SMITH in J. Phillips *Mem.* (1844) 82 The surface of this rock..is very narrow and *interlayered with clay. 1595 DANIEL *Civ. Wars* IV. xxxiv, Yet now in this so happie a meane while And *interlightning times thy vertues wrought. 1933 *Bulletin* (Sydney) 22 Nov. 28/1 '*Interlotting', a practice gratuitously rendered by woolbrokers, consists in selecting a number of what would be star lots, and bracketing them into one big lot to sell as such. 1878 LAWRENCE tr. *Cotta's Rocks Class.* 379 Subordinate *interlying beds of limestone. 1898 P. MANSON *Trop. Diseases* xxxi. 481 The comparatively smooth-sided and deep interlying sulci permitting limited movement. 1640 H. GRIMSTON in Rushw. *Hist. Coll.* III. (1692) I. 122 There is scarce any..Complaint..wherein we do not find him *intermentioned, and as it were twisted into it. 1598 YONG *Diana* 86 A faire broade court..*interpaued all ouer with Lozanges of Allablaster and blacke Marble. 1832 [R. CUTTERMOLE] *Beckett* 175 See it burst..Midst *interpealing thunders. 1864 WEBSTER, **Interreceive*, to receive between or within. 1875 *Ure's Dict. Arts* III. 368 It is ruled over in squares, each of about twelve inches. These are again *interruled with small squares. 1609 DANIEL *Civ. Wars* VIII. lxvii, This barrier..*inter-set, to keepe his forwardnes Backe. 1597 A. M. tr. *Guillemeau's Fr. Chirurg.* 17 b/2 The little compressione must be *intersituated betweene the stitches. 1622 MABBE tr. *Aleman's Guzman d'Alf.* II. 65 By some *inter-smilings, and casting of his eyes. 1889 *Pall Mall G.* 25 Apr. 7/2 Boots *intersoled with brown paper. a1658 CLEVELAND *Wks.* (1687) 248 Where never prying Sun.. Could..*intersqueeze a Ray. 1850 NEALE *Med. Hymns* (1867) 60 'Tis *intertinged with golden specks. 1610 W. FOLKINGHAM *Art of Survey* I. ix. 20 Spungy and boggy grounds must be *intertraced..with Trenches of some eighteene inches breadth. 1881 BLACKMORE *Christowell* (1882) II. iii. 36 The windings of the great hills, as they *interwend each other. 1762 *Gentl. Mag.* 185 [He] hems and *interwhistles (*hearts of oak*). 1818 J. MILL *Brit. India* (1858) I. 347 His gloss or commentary, *interworded with the text.

b. Denoting 'Between or among themselves or one another; with each other; mutually, reciprocally, alternately (in a *vbl. sb.*, mutual, reciprocal), together': as in ***interaccuse, -arch, -assure, -balance, -bring, -charge, -chase, -chequer, -circulate, -clash, -clasp, -crystallize, -debate,*** †***-devour, -grapple, -indicate, -influence*** (vbl. sb. ***-influencing***), ***-jangle, -justle, -lend, -loop, -mason, -mat, -match, -maze, -meet, -melt, -minister, -net, -oscillate, -pervade, -pledge, -plight, -pour, -quarrel, -rime, -salute, -shade, -shift, -strive, -talk, -thread, -tie, -vary, -wed, -weld, -wish, -worry, -wrap***; also INTERMINGLE, -MARRY, -WEAVE, etc. With a trans. verb, *inter-* sometimes = 'each other reciprocally' as obj., the resulting verb thus becoming intr.; as ***interchase*** to chase each other, ***-choke, -clasp, -confound,*** †***-enjoy, -touch***: also INTERDESPISE, etc.

These appear in 16th c.; see *intersalute* in 1506, *inter-justle* in 1591. De Quincey (*Logic Pol. Econ.*, 1844, 18 note) says: 'The late Mr. Coleridge suggested, and by his own example sanctioned, the use of the preposition *inter* for expressing cases of reciprocal action, or, in his language, of interaction. Thus the verb *interpenetrate*, when predicated of the substances A and B, implied that by an equal action and reaction, each penetrated the other..But, even as a justifiable English usage, it may be found occasionally in Shakspere, and much more frequently in Daniel, a writer of the same age'. The stress is on the radical element.

1610 DONNE *Pseudo-M.* viii. 236 The same falshoods, of which they *inter-accuse one another. 1875 H. JAMES *R. Hudson* ii. 63 The great Northhampton elms *interarched far above. a1631 DONNE *Poems* (1633) 194 But we by a love, so much refin'd..*Inter-assured of the mind, Care lesse, eyes, lips, hands to miss. 1867 *Contemp. Rev.* VI. 13 The complexities of its *interbalanced forces. 1613 DONNE *Eclogue* 26 Dec., Poems (1633) 131 Blest payre of Swans, oh may you *interbring Daily new joyes, and never sing. 1610 —— *Pseudo-M.* vii. 214 The maine point, with which we *intercharge one another. a1711 KEN *Edmund* Poet. Wks. 1721 II. 239 Retirement and Converse may *inter-chase. 1666 J. SMITH *Old Age* (1752) 192 The innumerable branches of the veins and arteries and their several wonderful *interchasings. 1660 N. INGELO *Bentivolio & Urania* I. (1682) 4 *Intercheckered like great beds of flowers and fresh grass-plats in a large Garden. 1622 SIR W. ALEXANDER in Sidney *Arcadia* III. 332 Pyrocles..not able to abide the *interchoaking of such extremities. 1805 W. TAYLOR in *Monthly Mag.* XX. 512 Two nations whose literature *inter-circulates. 1897 MARY KINGSLEY *W. Africa* 346 Pouring down their waters in swirling, intermingling, *interclashing currents. 1868 G. STEPHENS *Runic Mon.* I. 185 *Interclasping rings riveted within each other. 1821 LAMB *Elia* Ser. I. *Quaker's Meet.*, 'Boreas, and Cesias, and Argestes loud'..with their *interconfounding uproars. 1879 RUTLEY *Study Rocks* x. 91 These..commonly occur side by side or *inter-crystallised. 1598 I. D. tr. *Le Roy's Aristotle's Pol.* 175 Which question is *interdebated *pro & contra*, affirmatiuely and negatiuely. 1603 FLORIO *Montaigne* II. xii. (1632) 314 Without them, men would *enterdevour one another. 1898 ZANGWILL *Dreamers Ghetto* xv. 459 Old sea-fights with *inter-grappling galleys. 1860 W. J. C. MUIR *Pagan or Christian?* 6 Civilization and Architecture approximately *inter-indicate one the other. 1921 E. SAPIR *Lang.* viii. 184 In many such cases it is perfectly clear that there could have been no dialectic *interinfluencing. 1961 L. F. BROSNAHAN *Sounds of Lang.* x. 215 Genetic and linguistic interinfluencing of such groups favours the reverse trend. 1599 DANIEL *Musoph.* xxxvii, The diuers disagreeing Cords Of *inter-iangling Ignorance. 1591 SYLVESTER *Du Bartas* I. i. 359 Th' *inter-justling of each others forces. 1968 *Listener* 5 Sept. 319/2 Two of the very few important libraries which do not '*inter-lend' are those of Oxford and Cambridge. 1891 MISS DOWIE *Girl in Karp.* 224 The regular *interlooping of that soft even wool. 1883 *Harper's Mag.* Apr. 698/2 Curiously *intermasoned were the stone and brick work. 1768–74 TUCKER *Lt. Nat.* (1834) II. 414 Whether the roots of corn be not so *intermatted with it, that he shall pluck up both together. 1677 R. CARY *Chronol.* II. I. I. xiv. 127 The several *Intermatchings..that were betwixt the two Neighbour Kingdoms. 1686 tr. *Heliodorus' Æthiop. Advent.* I. (1753) 7 The great quantity of reed and cane..stands before them as their bulwark, and therein they have cut out so many ways, *intermazed one within another. a1577 GASCOIGNE *Dan Bartholomew*, Upon her cheekes the lillie and the rose, Did *intermeet wyth equall change of hew. 1879 G. MEREDITH *Egoist* v. (1889) 37 Where the gentle dints were faintly *intermelting even during quietness. 1883 A. S. HERSCHEL in *Nature* XXVII. 458/2 The marvellous maze of *internetted motions. 1842 DE QUINCEY *Philos. Herodotus* Wks. 1862 VIII. 178 Afterwards..it *inter-oscillated with the Roman stadium. 1863 DRAPER *Intell. Devel. Europe* vi. (1865) 137 The Stoics conclude that the soul is mere warm breath, and that it and the body mutually *interpervade one another. 1651 DAVENANT *Gondibert* I. v. 63 We *interpledg, and bind each others heart. 1880 LANIER *Poems, Crystal* 27 To..*inter-plight Your geniuses with our mortalities. 1862 T. ARCHER *Let.* in J. Macfarlane *Mem.* ix. (1867) 254 Oh for half an hour with you to *interpour mind and heart. 1820 KEATS *Hyper.* II. 141 At war, at peace, or *inter-quarrelling. 1881 *Athenæum* 20 Aug. 229/2 The Italian *rispetto* consists of a stanza of *interrhyming lines ranging from six to ten in number. 1506 in *Mem. Hen. VII* (Rolls) 286 They *inter-saluted the one the other and departed. 1897 *Daily News* 21 Sept. 2/3 Emotions of rejoicing and resignation are subtly *intershaded. 1883 G. MEREDITH *Sonn. Shakspere* i, Full of speech and *intershifting tales. 1606 DANIEL *Queen's Arcadia* I. i. 37 Montanus and Acrysius *interstriue How farre their seuerall Sheep-walkes should extend. 1640 HERRICK *Hesper., Mrs. Eliz. Wheeler*, Amongst the myrtles as I walked, Love and my sighs thus *intertalked. 1877 BLACKIE *Wise Men* 113 A complex web, where thread Still crosses thread, an *interthreaded maze. 1633 J. DONE *Hist. Septuagint* 49 A Girdle of Flowers, and Tussies of all Fruits, so *inter-tyed and following together so well. a1631 DONNE *Poems* (1633) 12 They *intertouched as they did passe. 1864 WEBSTER, **Intervary*, to alter or vary between; to change. 1818 J. BROWN *Psyche* 76 First cousins..Are consequently always reckon'd Freer to *interwed than second. a1859 DE QUINCEY *On the Mythus* Posth. Wks. 1891 I. 44 Lacunæ arising in these *interwelded stories. a1631 DONNE *Poems* (1633) 232 (*The curse*) What Tyrans and their subjects *interwish..all ill, which all Prophets, or Poets spake. 1678 R. L'ESTRANGE *Seneca's Mor.* (1685) 407 What a shame is it for Men to *Enterworry one another. 1871 PROCTOR *Light Sc.* 7 The folds of the curtain *interwrapping and forming a series of graceful curves.

2. Prefixed in adjectival relation to substantives, or in adverbial relation to adjectives.

a. With sbs. of action or condition, denoting 'Performed or subsisting between things or persons, esp. between each other, mutual, reciprocal'; with adjs., 'mutually, reciprocally': as in ***inter-absorption, -acquaintanceship, -affiliation, -agreement, -association, -availability, -behaviour, -celebration, -chaff, -circulation, -citizenship, -civilization, -cohesion, -colonization, -combat, -combination, -comparison, -complexity, contradiction, -crystallization, -culture, -differentiation, -dispensation, -entanglement, -federation, -fertility, -gesture, -gossip, -habitation, -incorporation, -independence, -influence, judgement, -laudation, -match, -mobility, -modification, -mutation, -pressure, -racialism, -repulsion, -responsibility, -reticulation, -right, -sale, -sterility, -subsistence, -substitutability, -substitution, -tesselation, -wish; inter-available, -behavioural, -comparable, -complimentary, -contradictory, -fertile, -hostile, -inhibitive, -measurable, -proportional, -repellent, -responsive, -sterile, -substitutable, -visible*** adjs.

These go back to 16th c.: see INTER-AFFAIR (1563), INTERMARRIAGE (1579). The main stress is on the radical element.

1872 *Daily News* 29 July, There will be at first a common lack of *inter-acquaintanceship. 1887 *National Rev.* Mar. 59 As to the expediency of their *inter-affiliation [i.e. of Labour Registries]. 1849 H. MAYO *Truths Pop. Superst.* ii. 34 All of these..instances agree in another important respect; which ..*inter-agreement separates them as a class from death-trance. *Ibid.* v. 77 An endless current of images..suggested ..by their own *inter-associations. 1894 *Harper's Mag.* Mar. 554 This..interassociation and interdependence of the flower and the insect. 1920 *Glasgow Herald* 1 July 6 The issue of a circular cancelling the *inter-availability of practically all railway tickets between Scotland and England. 1923 *Ibid.* 27 Jan. 11 The deputation intends..to press for the inter-availability of these tickets on all systems. 1935 *Punch* 21 Aug. 204/3 'Interavailability of Tickets between the G.W., L.M.S. and L. & N.E. Companies'.— *G.W.R. Pamphlet.* 1972 *Daily Tel.* 26 Feb. 2/6 Tickets are *inter-available and British Rail fares will now reflect the London Transport increase. 1939 *Mind* XLVIII. 111 Linguistic phenomena are forms of *inter-behaviour with stimulus objects. 1952 W. J. H. SPROTT *Social Psychol.* I By social situation is meant what might be called the 'inter-behaviour' of one human being with one or more other human beings. 1938 J. R. KANTOR in *Jrnl. Philos.* XXXV. 449 The *interbehavioral hypothesis signifies that all human phenomena..consist of the concrete interbehavior of specific individuals with things. 1939 *Mind* XLVIII. 111 The inter-behavioural hypothesis encourages us properly to evaluate every form of scientific and logical work. 1921 *Spectator* 26 Mar. 391/2, I should be glad to see inter-communion, but not, under present circumstances, *inter-celebration. 1969 *Daily Tel.* 30 May 20/6 For inter-celebration of services there must be a solution of the problems over the ministry which the proposals evaded. 1886 *Harper's Mag.* Dec. 32 In the way of *interchaff we rustics could hold a good front. c1814 COLERIDGE *Rem.* (1836) III. 73 By an eternal περιχώρησις or mysterious *intercirculation. 1876 BANCROFT *Hist. U.S.* VI. 33 A recommendation that *inter-citizenship should be confined to the white man. 1798 W. TAYLOR in *Monthly Rev.* XXVI. 561 Institutions which have favoured the *inter-civilization of nations. 1841 DE QUINCEY *Homer & Homeridæ* Wks. 1857 VI. 333 That sort of natural *intercohesion. 1827 G. HIGGINS *Celtic Druids* 92 The..intermixture or *inter-colonization which may have taken place between the two countries. 1609 DANIEL *Civ. Wars* I. lii, They both in order of the field appear,..And at the point of *intercombate were. 1866 *Athenæum* 23 July 838/1 Changes..made by the *intercombination, in varying proportions, of a few proximate elements. 1883 C. WRAGGE in *Nature* (1884) 4 Feb. 326/2 They [ozone papers] would give results more *inter-comparable, if uniformly exposed. 1861 MAX MÜLLER *Sc. Lang.* Ser. I. v. (1864) 174 By comparative grammar; that is to say, by an *intercomparison of the grammatical forms of language. 1847 DE QUINCEY *Sp. Mil. Nun* xx. Wks. 1863 III. 62 *note*, After these *intercomplexities had arisen between all complications and interweavings of descent. 1836 *Fraser's Mag.* XIII. 78 [They] then accomplished the following *intercomplimentary canticle. 1897 MARY KINGSLEY *W. Africa* 439 You would stun him with the seeming *inter-contradiction of some, and utter pointlessness of the rest. 1819 W. TAYLOR in *Monthly Mag.* XLVII. 389 There are many *intercontradictory articles among the thirty-nine. 1879 RUTLEY *Study Rocks* x. 90 The *intercrystallisation which probably gives rise to the compound-specific character of some felspars. 1881 *Scribner's Mag.* Aug. 542 Blending the politics..art and letters of the several European countries..in proportion to the growth of travel and *interculture. 1647 SALTMARSH *Spark. Glory* (1847) 190 All that pure administration of Ordinances and Gifts..is but a middle or *interdispensation betwixt God and his. 1865 MASSON *Rec. Brit. Philos.* 226 Their present *inter-entanglement. 1885 FROUDE *Oceana* xiii. (1886) 224 *Interfederation of the Australian States..may, and perhaps will, be raised as a hustings cry in England. 1916 *Mem. N.Y. Bot. Garden* VI. 352 Two seedling varieties derived from the same variety may be *inter-fertile to some degree. 1971 J. Z. YOUNG *Introd. Study Man* xxvii. 387 Leopard frogs (*Rana pipiens*) from the north and south of the United States are only partially interfertile when they are crossed. 1924 *Genetics* IX. 36 The *inter-fertility relationships of these 27 classes are indicated. 1953 *Jrnl. Gen. Microbiol.* VIII. 72 Some forty strains of *Bact. coli*.. which either out-cross with K-12 mutants or show inter-fertility. a1641 BP. MOUNTAGU *Acts & Mon.* (1642) 284 By secret glances and mutuall *intergestures. 1836 *Blackw. Mag.* XXXIX. 149 *note*, Fabricated upon..the *intergossip of ambassadors. 1817 G. S. FABER *Eight Dissert.* II. v. (1845) I. 191 He dwelt visibly among the Apostle's countrymen.. the verb, which he employs to describe this *interhabitation. 1890 *Scribner's Mag.* Jan. 29/2 *Interhostile points of view. 1893 FAIRBAIRN *Christ in Mod. Theol.* II. i. I. 306 This *inter-incorporation of the Person with the office and of the office with the Person. *Ibid.* ii. II. 414 The complete separation or *inter-independence of God and the world. 1948 *Q. Rev.* Apr. 180 The cant *inter-influence among all English-speaking countries has been considerable. 1959 C. L. WRENN *Word & Symbol* (1967) 17 Oghams and Runes came into use at about the same period..and the possibility of their mutual relationship and inter-influence has continued to tease the brains of scholars. 1960 PARTRIDGE *Charm of Words* i. 23 This interinfluence is unavoidable. 1883 MAUDSLEY *Body & Will* III. iii. 267 An impairment of the *interinhibitive functions. 1879 G. MEREDITH *Egoist* xxxiii. (1889) 325 They had so knit themselves together with the pelting of their *interlaudation. 1652 C. B. STAPYLTON *Herodian* XIV. 116 If once this Royall *Intermatch were done,..The World might Govern'd be betwixt them twain. a1866 J. GROTE *Exam. Util. Philos.* xviii. (1870) 295 *Inter-measurable qualities of happiness. 1864 WEBSTER s.v., The *intermobility of the particles of matter. 1844 DE QUINCEY *Logic Pol. Econ.* 140 From the balance or *intermodification between the two. 1877 HALDEMAN *Etymol.* 17 (Cent.) When [mutation] occurs between vowels we may term it *intermutation. 1858 CARLYLE *Fredk. Gt.* IV. iii. (1872) I. 294 Intolerable *interpressure and consequent battle. 1880 CLEMINSHAW *Wurtz' Atom. The.* 3 The numbers..are *interproportional for all kinds of combinations. 1931 *Amer. Speech* VII. 78 A writer in the *Congregationalist* says '*Interracialism, like love, service, and brotherhood, is a splendid word which has been cheapened by overuse.' How many acquaintances have you whose diction suffers from over-use of the word interracialism? 1844 DE QUINCEY *Logic Pol. Econ.* i. §2. 18 They are not, to borrow a word from Coleridge, *inter-repellent ideas. 1851 —— *Ld. Carlisle on Pope* Wks. 1863 XII. 31 *note*, No doctoring..

could disguise their essential *inter-repulsion. 1873 Contemp. Rev. XXII. 92 The.. continuous *inter-responsibility of the mental and bodily life. 1906 Macm. Mag. Apr. 434 The mystic net-work, *inter-responsive as a delicate system of nerves. 1955 R. Blesh Shining Trumpets (ed. 3) ii. 30 It is a thing.. as sensitively inter-connected and inter-responsive, as the branches of a tree. 1852 Dana Crust. I. 143 Gradations and *inter-reticulations among groups. a 1668 Sir W. Waller Div. Medit. (1839) 25 Thou art in a common world, wherein every person hath an *inter-right with thee. 1894 Daily News 21 Mar. 2/7 There was.. a power of *intersale, within certain limits, between the companies that took water from the Thames. 1916 Mem. N.Y. Bot. Garden VI. 352 It was found that at least three varieties are strongly *inter-sterile. 1956 Nature 21 Jan. 142/1 The mating type of the hybrid shows no change, that is, the hybrid males remain intersterile with O females, as in the original strain H. 1899 Q. Rev. Oct. 419 The *intersterility test has broken down. 1872 H. Macmillan True Vine iii. 94 The inseparable *intersubsistence between Christ and His people. 1954 I. M. Copi Symbolic Logic vii. 224 Of the list of elementary valid argument forms.. the last ten were equivalences whose *intersubstitutability was assumed. 1957 P. Geach Mental Acts 90 We cannot define synonymy as a supreme degree of equivalence, intersubstitutability salva veritate in all contexts. 1954 I. M. Copi Symbolic Logic iii. 44 The list contains all those logical equivalences which are certified as *intersubstitutable. 1957 P. Geach Mental Acts 101 In an 'extensional' logic.. predicates or relative terms would be freely intersubstitutable provided that they held good of the same objects. 1886 Bible Soc. Rec. (N.Y.) Oct. 147 The *inter-substitution of the kindred mutes, b for p, and p for b. 1847 De Quincey Protestantism Wks. 1862 VII. 113 The coherencies, tendencies, and *intertesselations (to use a learned word) of the whole. 1856 Webster, *Intervisible,.. mutually visible, or able to be seen the one from the other;—said of stations. 1668 Davenant Epithal. xii, Those *inter-wishes you did make In dream.

b. With sbs. (chiefly concrete), denoting 'Situated or occurring between things, or in the midst of something; intermediate, intervening': as in **intercalm** (an interval of calm), **-canal** (a canal forming a connexion between two others), **-chapter** (an intermediate chapter), **-division**, †**-light** (1624), **-limitation**, †**-mask**, **-piece**, **-scene**, **-thing**, **-while**; also INTERMEAN, INTERSPACE, etc.

In these the main stress is now on inter-.

1822 Beddoes Brides' Trag. III. iii, The roar has ceased: the hush of *intercalm Numbs with its leaden finger Echo's lips. 1887 Sollas in Encycl. Brit. XXII. 413/2 These canals are the '*intercanals' of Haeckel, now generally known by their older name of incurrent canals. 1834 Southey Doctor I. 105, I will call them *Interchapters. 1882 Saintsbury Short Hist. Fr. Lit. Pref. 8 Notes or interchapters have been inserted between the several books. 1710 Norris Chr. Prud. iii. 106 Many other *inter-divisions between these. 1624 Heywood Gunaik. VIII. 370 Hee affirmed the Galaxia.. to be a meere reflex of the Sunne, and no *inter-light arising from the Starres. 1848 Blackw. Mag. LXIV. 512 Shore is exactly the *interlimitation of land and sea. 1678 (title) The Traitor to Himself, or Man's Heart his Greatest Enemy, a Moral Interlude.. with *Intermaskes of Interpretation at the close of each several Act. 1853 Miss Sheppard Ch. Auchester I. 334 The chorale so grave and powerful, with its *interpieces so light and florid. 1888 Amer. Jrnl. Philol. Oct. 348 Epirrhemation.. then follows an *inter-scene. a 1657 R. Loveday Lett. (1663) 261, I have suffered such an amphibious *interthing betwixt health and sickness, as it has pos'd me to christen it. 1891 V. C. Cotes 2 Girls on Barge 136 A single Sunday of home comfort for her cramped wanderings in the *interwhile.

c. With adjs. as INTERMIDDLE.

II. In prepositional relation to the sb. expressed or implied in the second element.

3. Prefixed to sbs., forming sbs., with the senses **a.** 'Space, distance, or part between...', esp. in architectural terms, after L. intercolumnium INTERCOLUMN, as **inter-dentil**, **-glyph**, **-joist**, **-modillion**, **-mutule**, **-quarter**, **-spiral**; also **inter-world**; **b.** 'Period or interval of time between', in words formed on the analogy of INTERREGNUM, as **inter-papacy**, **-parliament**. See also INTERKING, INTERPILASTER.

The stress is on the radical part, but with a monosyllable tends to rest on inter-.

1823 P. Nicholson Pract. Build. Gloss. 586 *Inter-dentils, the space between dentils. 1875 Encycl. Brit. II. 404/1 The *interglyphs are each one-seventh of the whole tablet or triglyph. 1823 P. Nicholson Pract. Build. Gloss. 586 *Inter-joist, the space between joists. 1723 Chambers tr. Le Clerc's Treat. Archit. I. 94 The Corinthian *Inter-modillions consist of 41 Minutes and a quarter. c 1863 Dict. Archit. (Archit. Publ. Soc.) III. 149/1 The temple to Ceres at Pœstum has no mutules or triglyphs. The example at Albano has no *intermutules. 1901 R. Sturgis Dict. Archit., Intermutule, the space between two mutules, as in an architrave. 1687 S. Hill Cath. Balance 63 They have had not only very many, but also.. very long *Interpapacies. 1678 Marvell Growth Popery 22 During this *Inter-Parliament.. five Judges places either fell, or were made vacant. 1823 P. Nicholson Pract. Build. Gloss. 586 *Inter-quarter, the space between two quarters. 1831 Fraser's Mag. IV. 281 The size and shape of the eye of the volute.. the greater or lesser depth of the *interspirals. 1603 Holland Plutarch's Mor. 781 Imagining, that they are run hither.. out of.. other worlds; or imaginarie *inter-worlds [L. intermundia, Gr. μετακόσμια] and spaces betweene.

4. Prefixed to adjs. (originally, and most frequently, of Latin origin), in prepositional relation to the sb. implied (as inter-acinous, 'that is inter acinos, between the acini': cf. ANTI- 3, INFRA- 1), or sometimes to a phrase consisting of the adj. + a sb. (as inter-accessory 'between accessory processes').

For the etymology of the second element, see the simple words ACCESSORY, ACINOUS, etc. Ancient Latin had only a very few examples of this formation, as intermūrālis, interamnus, interdigitālis, interlūnis, intermēstris; but their number in modern times, chiefly since 1600, and esp. since 1800, is very great, and they are formed freely when needed. Logically they are composed of inter + L. sb. stem + adj. suffix; but, as the adj. suffix is the same that is used in forming an adj. from the simple word (e.g. nation-al, inter-nation-al, collegi-ate, inter-collegi-ate), they have the form of being composed of inter + adj., and in some later formations, as interhuman, intercapillary, interaccessory, intermolar, this is actually their structure. The main stress is on the radical part.

a. Denoting 'Situated, placed, or occurring locally, between or among (what is implied in the second element)': in modern scientific and other terms (chiefly of Anatomy and Zoology), as **interantennal**, **-antennary** (between the antennæ), **-apophysial**, **-capillary**, **-cavernous**, **-consonantal**, **-corallite** (see CORALLITE 2), **-corpuscular**, **-coxal**, (see COXA 2), **-cuspidal**, **-cystic**, **-electronic**, **-epimeral**, **-fibrillar** (**-ary**), **-fibrous**, **-filamentar**, **-follicular**, **-ligamentary** (**-ous**), **-mandibular**, **-marginal**, **-membranous**, **-mesenterial** (**-ic**), **-micellar**, **-molar**, **-morainic**, **-muscular**, **-nebular**, **-papillary**, **peduncular**, **-spheral**, **-spicular**, **-staminal**, **-sternal**, **-systematical**, **-tentacular**, **-trabecular**, **-ureteral**, **-vesicular**, **-villous** adjs. See also interaccessory, interacinous, etc. in 6; INTERALVEOLAR, -ARTICULAR, -CELLULAR, etc., among the main words.

1852 Dana Crust. I. 283 The six *interantennary front teeth. 1887 Syd. Soc. Lex., *Interapophysial, situated between apophyses. 1847–9 Todd Cycl. Anat. IV. 115/2 The red corpuscles.. exude thence into the *intercapillary texture. 1890 Webster, *Inter-cavernous. 1968 Passmore & Robson Compan. Med. Stud. I. xxi. 9/1 The two cavernous sinuses intercommunicate across the midline by means of the anterior and posterior intercavernous sinuses. 1931 Amer. Speech VII. 19 His *inter-consonantal u is perhaps Southern. 1839–47 Todd Cycl. Anat. III. 857/1 Developed in the *inter-corpuscular tissue. 1871 Herschel Outl. Astron. (ed. 11) 497 Every *intercuspidal arc. 1964 J. W. Linnett Electronic Struct. Molecules i. 12 In chromium.. the six electrons are spread among the five 3d and one 4s orbital to reduce the effect of *inter-electronic repulsion. 1877 Huxley Anat. Inv. Anim. vi. 309 By reason of the calcification of the *inter-epimeral and intersternal membranes. 1883 MacAlister tr. Zeigler's Pathol. Anat. I. §143 A swollen and semi-liquid condition of the *interfibrillar substance. 1896 Allbutt's Syst. Med. I. 191 A peculiar form of *interfibrillary degeneration of the muscles of the tongue. 1882 J. Paton in Encycl. Brit. XIV. 384/1 Pressing the combined lime and *interfibrous matter out of the tissue. 1883 Ray Lankester in Encycl. Brit. XVI. 689/1 Solid permanent *inter-filamentar junctions. 1888 Syd. Soc. Lex., *Inter-follicular, situated between follicles. 1968 J. H. Burn Lect. Notes Pharmacol. (ed. 9) 88 Thyrocalcitonin is a hormone formed in the interfollicular cells of the thyroid gland. 1872 Cohen Dis. Throat 56 An *inter-ligamentous rima corresponding to the length of the cords. 1872 Humphrey Myology 43 *Intermandibular [muscles].. passing transversely.. from one side of the lower jaw to the other beneath it. 1858 Phil. Trans. R. Soc. CXLVIII. 280 *Inter-marginal cavities [of sponges]. 1900 E. R. Lankester Treat. Zool. III. xiv. 246 In some genera intermarginal plates occur between these two series. 1907 J. H. Parsons Dis. Eye x. 171 The palpebral conjunctiva is said to commence at the anterior margin of the edge of the lid, but from this point to the posterior margin of the edge (the intermarginal strip) and for about 2 mm beyond (to the sulcus subtarsalis) there is a transitional zone. 1887 G. C. Bourne in Q. Jrnl. Microsc. Sc. Aug. 34 The *intermesenterial chambers or entocœles. 1877 Huxley Anat. Inv. Anim. iii. 153 The *intermesenteric chambers in the Actinozoon. 1937 Chem. Abstr. XXXI. 5155 The diam. of the *inter-micellar spaces decreases considerably on shrinkage. 1962 J. T. Marsh Self-Smoothing Fabrics xv. 257 They.. concluded that the resin must be in the inter-micellar spaces of the cellulose. 1839–47 Todd Cycl. Anat. III. 387/1 The *intermolar eminence of the tongue in certain Rodents. 1894 J. Geikie Gt. Ice Age (ed. 3) xxxv. 593 The *inter-morainic lakes which occupy similar positions at the base of the Alps in North Italy. 1957 G. E. Hutchinson Treat. Limnol. I. i. 90 A few inter-morainic bogs still exist but the lakes in general have disappeared. 1929 J. H. Jeans Universe around Us ii. 142 The vast stretches of *internebular space. 1957 Jrnl. Brit. Interplanetary Soc. XVI. 22 Calculations on the feasibility of long-range interstellar travel—including internebular journeys. 1887 Syd. Soc. Lex., *Interpapillary. 1898 J. Hutchinson Archives Surg. IX. 317 The interpapillary processes of the epithelium. 1839–47 Todd Cycl. Anat. III. 673/1 The depression.. which separates them is the ..*interpeduncular space. 1881 Mivart Cat 271 They issue from the cerebral surface in the interpeduncular space between the crura and cerebri. 1883 Nature 8 Feb. 350/1 As the particles of the spheres decrease in heat momentum, those of *interspheral space increase. 1870 Hooker Stud. Flora 68 Disk obscure or of *interstaminal glands. 1877 *Intersternal [see inter-epimeral]. 1783 Sir W. Herschel in Phil. Trans. LXXIII. 276 The probability of many stars being.. solitary, or, if I may use the expression, *intersystematical. 1888 Rolleston & Jackson Anim. Life 236 A ciliated *intertentacular tube. 1879 Rutley Study Rocks xi. 192 An irregular network of fibrous *intervesicular matter. 1890 Billings Med. Dict. I. 710/2 *Intervillous lacunæ, irregular vascular spaces connected with the maternal blood-vessels, surrounding the fœtal villi in the placenta. 1962 Gray's Anat. (ed. 33) 115 In the early stages of placental development the blood in the foetal vessels is separated from the maternal blood in the intervillous space.

b. Denoting 'Intervening or happening in the time or period between...': as in **inter-artistic**, **-conciliary**, **-equinoctial**, **-menstrual**, **-paroxysmal**, **-sessional**, **-testamental** adjs. See also **interadventual**, **intermealary** in 6; and cf. 5 b.

1883 Eng. Illustr. Mag. Nov. 89/2 The late Georgian or early Victorian age which might fairly be designated.. the *inter-artistic period. 1620 Brent tr. Sarpi's Hist. Council Trent (1676) 545 To write.. *interconciliary times by way of Annals. a 1795 F. Balfour in Asiat. Res. (W. 1828), Spring and autumn I have denominated equinoctial periods. Summer and winter I have called *inter-equinoctial intervals. 1853 Mrs. Sheppard Ch. Auchester III. 265 The Spirit moving upon the face of the waters before the *intermomentary light. 1853 Kane Grinnell Exp. xxvii. (1856) 226 The *inter-paroxysmal yell. 1897 Allbutt's Syst. Med. III. 162 The interparoxysmal periods of chronic gout. 1956 Jrnl. Theol. Stud. VII. 292 Professor Stauffer.. is apt to find in the N.T. references to lost *intertestamental literature [etc.]. 1973 Times Lit. Suppl. 7 Dec. 1516/2 Dr Vermes begins by ransacking the inter-testamental and rabbinic literatures (especially the Dead Sea Scrolls, the Targumim and the Palestinian Talmud).

c. Denoting 'Subsisting, carried on, taking place, or forming a communication, between ...'; hence, sometimes, 'Belonging in common to, or composed of elements derived from, different things (of the kind indicated by the second element)': as in **inter-African**, **-American**, **-cameral**, **-Caribbean**, **-clerical** (between clergymen), **-coastal**, **-collegiate**, **-confessional**, **-cultural**, **-denominational**, **-dialectal**, **-ecclesiastical**, **-ethnic**, **-generational**, **-governmental**, **-human**, **-parliamentary**, **-perceptual**, **-professional**, **-racial** (so **-racially** adv.), **-regimental**, **-regional**, **-religional**, **-religious**, **-territorial** adjs. See also intercivic, etc., in 6, and INTERCONTINENTAL, etc., among the main words. The prototype of this class was INTERNATIONAL (Bentham, 1780).

1956 Nature 25 Feb. 366/2 An *Inter-African Committee for Social Sciences. 1960 Guardian 6 Oct. 10/6 An expression of inter-African solidarity. 1973 Black World May 61/2 Those whom the truth would incriminate hid behind the made-in-Hilton Hotel masks of amnesty, reconciliation and inter-African dialogue. 1938 Sun (Baltimore) 5 Dec. 2/5 In this and in other matters of *inter-American interest, I anticipate working with the representatives of Ecuador. 1961 Ann. Reg. 1960 532 The Inter-American system is incompatible with any form of totalitarianism. 1964 Illustr. London News 18 Jan. 81 President Johnson.. sent his Assistant Secretary of State for Inter-American Affairs.. to the Canal Zone. 1972 Buenos Aires Herald 4 Feb. 7/1 Bruno Quijano met yesterday with Charles Meyer, assistant secretary of state for inter-American affairs. 1973 Sunday Advocate-News (Barbados) 25 Feb. 13/7 Barbados strongly opposes any case of racial discrimination.. and for this reason opposes the admission of Portugal in the Inter American system. 1929 Times 29 Oct. 16/1 Nobody believes that the question will.. go to the *intercameral conference before the Special Session ends. 1935 Economist 13 July 62/2 The Public Utility Holding Company Bill.. has been returned to the Senate, which has sent it to an inter-cameral conference. 1971 Jamaican Weekly Gleaner 10 Nov. 5/5 Mr. Arnold Foote.. lauded the function as a 'gesture of *inter-Caribbean friendship'. 1973 Caribbean Contact Jan. 6/3, I believe that this magazine would help bridge the gap between Caribbean peoples and so foster inter-Caribbean harmony. 1868 Examiner 1 Feb. 65 A breach of *inter-clerical amity. 1927 Contemp. Rev. Oct. 493 Already in *inter-coastal traffic New York is surpassed. 1969 Jane's Freight Containers 1968–69 57/2 Intercoastal Services via the Port of New York. 1884 Durham Univ. Jrnl. 29 Mar. 15 The *Inter-collegiate [Boat-] Race. 1900 G. C. Brodrick Mem. & Impress. 357 Another change.. was the inroad made upon the College system by the introduction of intercollegiate lecturing. 1892 Cheyne Founders O.T. Crit. Pref. (1893) 9 Sound Biblical criticism is neither German nor English, neither Lutheran, nor Anglican, nor Presbyterian, but international and *interconfessional. 1937 Theology XXXV. 347 Our present consideration of *intercultural contacts. 1955 Sci. Amer. Apr. 84/2 In the interest of intercultural understanding various U.S. Government agencies have hired anthropologists. 1972 Ibid. Nov. 82/1 If pictorial recognition is universal, do pictures offer us a lingua franca for intercultural communication? 1893 Chicago Advance 13 July, An increase in international and *interdenominational fellowship. 1894 Daily News 7 Nov. 8/7 The establishment of friendly workers' areas under the management of Interdenominational Committees. 1959 M. Schlauch Eng. Lang. in Mod. Times i. 28 An *inter-dialectal survey. 1920 Q. Register Nov. 339 A great moment of international and *inter-ecclesiastical opportunity. 1959 H. Wolff in Anthropol. Ling. Mar. 34 (title) Intelligibility and *inter-ethnic attitudes. 1971 Sunday Nation (Nairobi) 11 Apr. 13/3 There was one section of the population in Uganda, inter-ethnic in composition, which was not using English as the primary qualification for professional ascent. This section was the armed forces of Uganda. 1964 S. Lieberson in J. A. Fishman Readings Sociol. of Lang. (1968) 551 We find *intergenerational linguistic unity of nationality groups is less than the unity within the immigrant groups themselves. 1968 Listener 29 Feb. 259/1 The intergenerational differences amount to a mutation. 1971 Black Scholar June 29/2 The black revolution will then become an intergenerational revolution. 1927 Glasgow Herald 20 Jan. 8 When it came to negotiation, agreement could not be obtained by *inter-Governmental intervention. 1946 J. S. Huxley Unesco ii. 48 This important group of human activities.. has never previously been adequately dealt with by any inter-governmental organisation. 1969 Jane's Freight Containers 1968–69 142/3 Some of the problems requiring action at the inter-governmental level.. have been indicated above. 1973 Times 21 May 4/7 The inter-governmental

convention establishing the European University Institute was signed by the six founding members of the Community in April, 1972. **1881** *Standard* 21 May 3/4 An account..of a..case of *inter-human osseous transplantation. **1892** *Times* (weekly ed.) 2 Sept. 5/2 The *Interparliamentary Conference [shall] be requested to influence the insertion of arbitration clauses in all international treaties. **1898** *Times* 16 Dec. 5/7 About a couple of years ago an inter-Parliamentary peace conference on disarmament was held at Budapest. **1932** W. T. Stace *Theory of Knowledge & Existence* vii. 160 What it is or is not during *inter-perceptual periods makes no difference to me as a practical person. **1934** *Mind* XLIII. 151 Why must we believe that causation continues to operate during inter-perceptual intervals? **1960** *Times* 15 Feb. 11/7 The third *Interprofessional Conference in March will examine some cardinal moral issues. **1971** *Optometry Today* (Amer. Optometric Assoc.) 13 Naturally, interprofessional referrals are a two-way street. **1888** *Scot. Leader* 20 Aug. 5 *Interracial conflict in Louisiana. Twenty niggers slain. **1892** Stevenson & L. Osbourne *Wrecker* viii. 123 Chinatown..drew and held me; I could never have enough of its ambiguous, interracial atmosphere. **1905** *Athenæum* 30 Sept. 430/1 Inter-racial cordiality. **1953** E. H. Brookes *S. Afr. in Changing World* v. 105 Thus the services of Americans to South Africa in the interracial field are spanned across a century. **1960** *Spectator* 22 July 128 There is a large, brand-new 'inter-racial' hotel. **1968** *Blues Unlimited* Dec. 12 The local interracial Dirty Blues Band. **1972** *Publishers Weekly* 7 Feb. 37 (Advt.), Grace Halsell.. describes what happens to interracial couples when they are joined in a love affair or marriage. **1964** *Punch* 26 Aug. 290/1 Anger..fomented internally and directed *inter-racially. **1972** *Publishers Weekly* 14 Aug. 40/2 He hustled a basketball scholarship, lost it for dating interracially. **1883** *Manch. Exam.* 20 Nov. 5/4 The results of the *inter-regimental matches..the shooting exhibiting great improvement. **1945** *Interregional [see expressway]. **1962** H. R. Loyn *Anglo-Saxon Eng.* ii. 77 Gold was the essential commodity for interregional exchange in the Mediterranean context. **1894** *Forum* (N.Y.) Sept. 61 *Inter-religious good-will is a manifest help to the study of comparative theology. **1888** *Philadelphia Ledger* 4 Dec. (Cent.), An *inter-territorial convention of the north-western Territories. **1964** *Ann. Reg. 1963* 102 Agreement..that joint authorities..would continue to provide services on an inter-territorial basis was reached. **1967** *Economist* 17 June 1234/2 The main points of the treaty are: the establishment of an East African development bank; interterritorial tariffs on goods originating in one country and exported to another, [etc.].

d. Loosely used to denote 'Situated, occurring, carried on, etc., between the parts or divisions of...', and hence erroneously 'within...' (properly expressed by intra-): as in *inter-asteroidal*, *-coccygeal*, *-cranial*, *-imperial*, *-mercurial*, *-parenchymal*, *-trinitarian*: see 6.

5. a. Prefixed to sbs., forming adjs., with the sense 'Situated, distributed, occurring, carried on, plying, etc. between...'; usually of communication, commerce, athletic contests, or the like: as in ***inter-arrival***, ***-bank***(*s*), ***-borough***, ***-bourse*** (between different stock-exchanges), ***-brigade*** (between brigades), ***-caste***, ***-centre***, ***-church***, ***-city*** (also *absol.*), ***-class***, ***-club***, ***-company***, ***-county***, ***-dealer***, ***-district***, ***-electron***, ***-empire***, ***-faith***, ***-family***, ***-fibre***, ***-hemisphere***, ***-island***, ***-library***, ***-nucleon***, ***-office***, ***-particle***, ***-party***, ***-school***, ***-species***, ***-stream***, ***-street***, ***-team***, ***-town***, ***-trial***, ***-union***, ***-university*** (***-'varsity***), ***-valve***, ***-village***, ***-zone***, etc., etc. See also inter-cell, interstate (*a* 1845 in *U.S.*). **b.** Rarely, in the same sense as 4b: as in ***inter-epidemic***, ***-whiff***.

These are app. all of 19th c. or 20th c. origination, and may be formed at pleasure. For their form and analysis, see what is said under the analogous anti- *pref.* 4. The main stress is on the radical word; but, when this is a monosyllable, tends to shift to *inter-*.

1962 J. Riordan *Stochastic Service Syst.* i. 3 For this, as for the Poisson, the intervals between demands (*inter-arrival intervals) are independent random variables. **1968** P. A. P. Moran *Introd. Probability Theory* iii. 179 Much more complicated queueing systems with general inter-arrival and service time distributions are considered. **1907** *Daily Chron.* 29 Sept. 9/2 The *Inter-Banks Team Race, in which sixteen banks in London were represented. **1966** *Economist* 12 Nov. 718/2 The big broker in unsecured 'interbank' sterling deposits. **1973** *Daily Tel.* 9 Feb. 21 Overnight money in the interbank market rose to a peak of 13 p.c. earlier this week. **1905** *Westm. Gaz.* 8 Nov. 5/1 The officials of the *inter-borough railways. **1928** *Daily Express* 19 May 9/5 The first inter-borough competition of its kind ever organised in London. **1893** *Daily News* 29 June 2/5 *Interbourse securities are not perceptibly affected. **1898** *Westm. Gaz.* 17 May 8/1 The shares are of £4 each..for convenience of inter-bourse dealing. **1897** *Westm. Gaz.* 16 July 7/2 An *inter-brigade competition by volunteer teams of sixteen. **1908** *New Reformer* II. 62 It is a case of *inter-caste and inter-provincial marriage. **1925** E. S. Jones *Christ of Indian Road* xiii. 243 We sat down to an intercaste dinner —a hundred high-caste Hindus, a hundred outcastes, a hundred Indian Christians, a few Mohammedans, and several of us of the West. **1964** *Ann. Reg. 1963* 358 Among social measures which came into force were the banning of polygamy and permission for inter-caste marriages. **1946** *Nature* 20 July 97/2 Each centimetre on the plotting-board of the apparatus corresponds with 'the cone *intercentre distance', that is, the distance between the centre of one foveal cone and that of its next-door neighbours. **1970** *New Scientist* 31 Dec. 596 Saturation signalling involves a large volume of inter-centre communication. **1905** *Daily Chron.* 22 Nov. 1/7 At an *inter-Church Conference in New York 17,000,000 Church members of all denominations were represented. **1926** *Brit. Weekly* 22 July 327/1 Dr. Clark has toured the world to build this inter-church, international organisation. **1909** *Westm. Gaz.* 3 June 14/1 In the first *inter-city match played between Edinburgh and Glasgow. **1940** A. L. Albert *Electr. Communication* (ed. 2) vii. 174 Connections are made between the two exchanges by means of toll lines... In some locations this has been designated intercity service. **1955** *Railway Mag.* May 334/1 The 9 a.m. 'Inter-City' from Paddington averaged 18¼ min. late at Snow Hill. **1968** *Daily Tel.* 12 Nov. 26/7 A three-months' trial scheme..was introduced by British Railways on inter-city trains in September. **1970** A. Dekker *Divers Diamonds* xxii. 145 The GPO intercity microwave link towers. **1972** *Guardian* 13 Mar. 13/1 The expression 'Inter-City' was a British invention and its success is demonstrated by the adoption of the title in such countries as Germany, Japan, Holland, and now the United States, to describe express business trains. **1973** *Times* 29 Oct. 14/8 On the inter-city to Sunderland I was one of the first people in the dining car. **1909** *Post-Intelligencer* (Seattle) 18 Apr. 1/2 The *interclass crews and girls' crews work at other hours during the day. **1950** T. H. Marshall *Citizenship & Social Class* I. iv. 57 A divided educational system, by promoting both intra-class similarity and inter-class difference, gave emphasis..to a criterion of social distance. **1971** P. J. Keating *Working Classes in Victorian Fiction* iii. 71 A romance of corrupted character and inter-class love. **1972** *Listener* 27 July 107/2 Venice was untouched by the inter-class antagonisms..that troubled the domestic peace of other states. **1890** *Daily News* 3 Feb. 3/5 An *inter-club race. **1895** *Ibid.* 30 Jan. 5/5 A set of rules..for governing inter-club and *inter-county matches. **1968** *N.Y. Times* 19 Feb. 60 It appears to be technically feasible to use a central computer to record and report *interdealer quotations. **1970** *Washington Post* 30 Sept. D 11/4 The following..are representative interdealer prices. **1964** J. W. Linnett *Electronic Struct. Molecules* i. 11 Clearly, for the lowest energy state, it is advantageous to reduce *inter-electron repulsion as much as possible. **1896** Chamberlain *Sp.* 8 June, The laws regulating *inter-Empire commerce. **1897** *Allbutt's Syst. Med.* II. 185 The longer duration of the *inter-epidemic periods since 1856. **1967** *Economist* 6 May 574/2 It is joining with 39 other firms and an *interfaith group to provide 1,500 new jobs. **1970** *Toronto Daily Star* 24 Sept. 37/1 An interfaith group which supports tough anti-obscenity laws. **1973** *Jewish Chron.* 2 Feb. 13/5 The Israel Interfaith Committee. **1946** *Nature* 10 Aug. 204/2 The successful production of hybrid plants from interspecific, intergeneric, and even *inter-family crosses has naturally led to investigation of the events which occur in some of the crosses which habitually fail. **1965** J. E. Cross in *English Studies* Apr. 96 The provincial and interfamily strife..between..Deira and Bernicia. **1962** J. T. Marsh *Self-Smoothing Fabrics* iv. 39 In a fabric with a high cover factor, *i.e.* a tightly woven material, the friction between fibres is apt to be high enough to restrict *inter-fibre movement. **1895** C. Dixon in *Fortn. Rev.* Apr. 648 Migratory species [of birds] that are neither Inter-polar nor *Inter-hemisphere. *Ibid.* 653 Families and groups which I have ventured to describe as Interhemisphere..with a more or less dominant equatorial base, spreading both north and south. **1859** *Sandwich Islands 1 cent postage stamp*, *Interisland Hawaiian Postage. Uku Leta. **1891** *Daily News* 1 Jan. 5/5 To serve as an inter-island steamer in the South Seas. **1928** J. A. McMillen (*title*) Selected articles on *interlibrary loans. **1938** *Times* 1 Jan. 10/1 All England and Wales is now covered by schemes for the inter-library lending of books. **1968** *Language* XLIV. 211 The publications..are available to any American library on inter-library loan. **1953** *Physical Rev.* XCI. 1529/2 The meson theory, which predicts strong *internucleon interactions. **1934** Webster, *Inter-office. **1938** *Times* 29 Sept. 19/1 War Loan..was being quoted 95 middle in inter-office dealings. **1969** *New Yorker* 20 Sept. 181/1 An interoffice memo cast in cablese. **1972** *Accountant* 6 Apr. 456/1 On the sports side, it was hoped to revive the inter-office cricket tournament and play matches with other students' societies and the law students. **1946** *Nature* 6 July 13/1 The resistance increased, indicating that the width of the *inter-particle contacts had diminished. **1953** *Physical Rev.* XCI. 1527 The leading term..depends only on the interparticle distances. **1962** W. B. Thompson *Introd. Plasma Physics* vii. 148 The simple theory presented here may be extended by including in a phenomenological way the effect of interparticle collisions. **1909** *Westm. Gaz.* 8 Mar. 2/1 A break in the party seems inevitable. The issue of this *inter-party struggle will be one of great moment for South Africa. **1957** C. Hunt *Guide to Communist Jargon* xxx. 103 He [*sc.* Marx] held that, under the capitalist system, parliaments were simply the instruments by means of which the bourgeoisie maintained its domination, and that inter-party conflicts within this framework had no real significance. **1895** *Westm. Gaz.* 25 July 3/3 The encouragement of *inter-school matches. **1920** *Proc. Amer. Soc. Hort. Sci. 1919* 50 (*heading*) *Inter species pollination of plums. **1962** *Punch* 14 Mar. 443/1 The possible consequences of inter-species communication between man and dolphin. **1902** Webster Suppl., **Interstream* a. (Phys. Geog.), between streams. **1968** D. S. Simonett in R. W. Fairbridge *Encycl. Geomorphol.* 559 Many geomorphologists today use the term [*sc.* interfluve] for the interstream area to imply a discrete landscape or geomorphic unit. **1895** *Pop. Sci. Monthly* Apr. 756 The history of cheap *interstreet transportation in New York. **1897** *Westm. Gaz.* 26 Apr. 5/1 International, inter-club, *inter-team, inter-college, or inter-school contests. **1892** *Daily News* 23 Feb. 4/6 For the development of the telephone in London with an *inter-town service all over the country. **1971** *Jrnl. Gen. Psychol.* Jan. 125 Within each order, 21 plates consisting of three different spatial arrangements of each level of number were also shown randomly with an *intertrial interval of 10 seconds. **1972** *Jrnl. Social Psychol.* Dec. 225 The timer was preset so that the signals for all shock options were of three seconds duration, with a 15-second intertrial interval. **1969** *Daily Tel.* 10 Feb. 19/5 Because of bitter *inter-union rivalry, the original purpose of the strike..has become almost totally obscured. **1973** *Times* 17 Jan. 16/8 Eliminating the possibility of inter-union disputes in one factory. **1870** John Morgan *University Oars*, Wordsworth..legitimately to be looked upon as the father of the *inter-university [rowing] match. **1874** *Graphic* 4 Apr. 327/3 Contemporaneous with the boat race are several other Inter-University contests. **1891** Chas. Wordsworth *Ann. Early Life* 56 Encouraged by the example of the inter-university cricket match, which had taken place in 1827, we talked over the possibility of getting up a similar competition in rowing. **1956** *Nature* 3 Mar. 405/1 In 1944 the Secretary of State for the Colonies invited British universities to set up an Inter-University Organization to assist the development of higher education in the Colonies. **1970** *Internat. & Compar. Law Q.* XIX. 1. 181 Dr. Verheul is now Head of the private international law department of the T.M.C. Asser Institute in The Hague, an inter-university institute which is engaged in comprehensive documentation in the field of international law. **1909** *Cent. Dict.* Suppl., **Inter-valve*, in steam-engines, noting the space which is between the throttle- and slide-valves. **1921** *Wireless World* 2 Apr. 17/2 The 5-step Amplifier, with intervalve resistance couplings, is of the usual type. **1921** *Ibid.* 14 May 120/1 Substitute an intervalve transformer for your telephone transformer. **1885** *Whitaker's Alm.* 400/2 Oxford, for the third year in succession, won the *inter-'varsity match against Cambridge. **1897** *Westm. Gaz.* 8 Mar. 9/3 The Inter-'Varsity sports. **1949** M. Mead *Male & Female* 413 The biggest *inter-village economic exchange. **1844** Kinglake *Eothen* xii. (1878) 162 Speaking in short *inter-whiff sentences. **1960** *Inter-zone [see dust *v.*[1] 12c]. **1961** *Times* 8 June 5/2 They gained a 5–1 winning lead over Denmark in the inter-zone final.

6. The following adjectives (mostly *Anat.*) belonging to the uses mentioned in 4, are given here as being of subordinate importance, but not self-explanatory. For those of greater importance see their alphabetical places. **interac'cessory**, situated, as a muscle, between accessory processes of the vertebræ. **interacinar** (-'æsɪnə(r)) = *interacinous*. **interacinous** (-'æsɪnəs), situated or occurring between or among the acini of a gland. **interad'ventual**, intervening between the first and second Advents. **inter'andean**, situated between or among the Andes. **interary'tenoid**, situated between the arytenoid cartilages of the larynx. **interaste'roidal** *Astron.*, situated within the orbits of the asteroids. **inter'astral**, situated or taking place between or among the stars. **inter'atrial**, situated between the atria of the heart; **interau'ricular**, 'situated between the auricles of the heart' (*Syd. Soc. Lex.* 1887). **inter-Au'stralian**, existing or carried on between the different Australian colonies. **intercana'licular**, situated between or among minute canals. **inter-'cardinal**, of points of the compass: lying midway between the cardinal points; also as *sb.* **interca'rotic**, **interca'rotid**, situated between the two carotid arteries. **inter'carpal**, situated or occurring between the bones of the carpus. **inter'cerebral**, situated between the cerebral hemispheres, or between two cerebral ganglia. **intercivic** (-'sɪvɪk), existing or carried on between fellow-citizens. **intercoccygeal** (-kɒk'sɪdʒiːəl), **intercoc'cygean**, situated or occurring between portions of the coccyx. **inter'coracoid**, situated between the coracoid processes of the shoulder-blades. **inter'cortical**, situated within the (or a) cortex (properly *intracortical*). **inter'cosmic**, **-ical**, situated or existing between worlds. **inter'cotyloid**, existing between the cotyloid cavities of the hip-joints. **inter'cranial**, situated within the skull (properly *intracranial*). **inter'cultural** *Agric.*: see quot. **interepi'thelial**, situated between or among cells of the epithelium. **interfra'ternal**, existing or carried on between brothers. **inter'genic** [genic *a.*], taking place or existing between neighbouring genes. **intergyral** (-'dʒaɪərəl), situated between gyri or convolutions of the brain. **interhemi'cerebral**, situated between the hemispheres of the brain. **interhemis'pheric**, situated between two hemispheres, esp. those of the brain. **interim'perial**, carried on between or connecting the various countries of the (British) Empire. **inter'insular**, carried on or plying between islands. **interlati'tudinal**, situated between particular parallels of latitude. **interma'mmillary**, situated or placed between the breasts. **inter'mastoid**, extending between the mastoid processes of the temporal bones of the skull. †**inter'mealary**, **-iary**, held or performed between meals. **inter'membral**, subsisting (as a relation) between members or limbs, as ***intermembral homology***. **intermeningeal** (-miː'nɪndʒiːəl), occuring between two of the investing membranes of the brain. **inter'mental**, taking place between different minds. **intermer'curial** *Astron.* (properly *intra-*), situated within the orbit of Mercury. **intermeta'carpal**, situated between the bones of the metacarpus; so also **intermeta'tarsal**. **inter'montane**, situated between mountains (Webster, 1828). **inter'ocular**, situated or occurring between the eyes. **inter'olivary**, 'situated between the olivary bodies' (*Syd. Soc. Lex.*). **inter'optic**, situated between the optic lobes of the brain.

inter'palpebral, situated between the eyelids. **interparenchymal** (-pə'rɛŋkɪməl) *Biol.*, situated within the parenchyma, e.g. of an infusorian (properly *intraparenchymal*). **inter'pectoral**, situated between the two sides of the breast. **inter'petalary** *Bot.*, 'situated between petals' (Worcester, citing Smith). **inter'petaloid** *Zool.*, situated between petaloid parts, as in an echinoderm. **interphalangeal** (-fə'lændʒiːəl), situated between two successive phalanges of a finger or toe. **inter'planar** *Cryst.*, existing between the planes of a crystal lattice. **interplical** (-'plaɪkəl), situated between folds (see PLICA 2). **interpopu'lational**, occurring or existing between populations or groups. **inter'portal**, existing or carried on between ports, esp. those of the same country. **interproto'plastic** *Biol.*, situated between, or connecting, masses of protoplasm. **inter'proximal** *Dentistry*, situated between adjacent teeth; on or affecting the surfaces bounding such a region. **inter'pupillary**, existing between the pupils of the eyes. **intersciatic** (-saɪ'ætɪk), situated or extending between the hip-bones (see SCIATIC). **intersynap'ticular** *Zool.*, situated between the synapticulæ or cross-bars of actinozoan corals. **inter'tarsal** *Anat.*, situated between the bones of the tarsus. **inter'tidal**, inhabiting the sea-shore between the limits of low and high tide. **inter'tonic**, occurring between two tones or stresses. **intertrini'tarian**, taking place between the persons of the Trinity. **intertrochan'teric**, situated between two trochanters; *spec.* applied to a line or ridge between the greater and lesser trochanter of the femur. **intertu'bercular**, placed or situated between tubercles. **inter'tubular**, situated between tubes or tubuli. **inter'ungular**, **inter'ungulate**, situated between the hoofs (e.g. in sheep). **interva'rietal**, formed or obtained from, or occurring between, (members of) different varieties (VARIETY 6 b). **inter'veinal** *Bot.*, situated or occurring between the veins of a leaf. **inter'xylary** *Bot.*, situated within the secondary xylem. **interzoœcial** (-zəʊ'iːʃɪəl), intervening between or among the zoœcia of a polyzoan. **interzygapophysial** (-zɪgəpəʊ'fɪzɪəl), situated between the zygapophyses or articular processes of the vertebræ. **interzygomatic** (-zɪgəʊ'mætɪk), lying between the zygomatic arches of the skull.

1900 *Bull. Johns Hopkins Hosp.* XI. 205/2 *Interacinar cell islets have been studied by Harris and Gow. **1961** *Lancet* 29 July 258/2 A high prevalence of pancreatic arteriosclerosis ..could have caused the associated insular and interacinar fibrosis and hyalinisation. **1876** tr. *Wagner's Gen. Pathol.* 271 Indurating inflammations, in which *inter-acinous, inter-lobular, connective tissue increases in quantity. **1886** WARFIELD in *Expositor* Dec. 441 This *inter-adventual period is..to be a period of conflict. **1870** J. ORTON *Andes & Amazons* II. xxxiv. (1876) 444 The *interandean plateau. **1872** COHEN *Dis. Throat* 47 The arytenoids, separated from each other by a fissure known as the *inter-arytenoid incisure. **1873** CHASE in *Proc. Amer. Phil. Soc.* XIII. 156 *Interasteroidal planets. **1882** 'N. GREENE' *Thousand years Hence* 110 The wide *interastral ocean. **1892** *Working Men's College Jrnl.* Oct. 118 The method of interastral communication, if ever one is discovered. **1911** STEDMAN *Med. Dict.* 431/1 **Interatrial*, between the atria of the heart. **1967** G. M. WYBURN et al. *Conc. Anat.* iii. 89/1 On the interatrial septum there is a shallow depression, the fossa ovalis. **1889** *Pall Mall G.* 15 Nov. 1/3 Did you..urge *inter-Australian federation as the first step to Imperial Federation? **1897** *Allbutt's Syst. Med.* II. 234 In these cases the *intercanalicular tissue is little altered. **1909** WEBSTER, *Intercardinal, adj.—n., an intercardinal point. **1961** F. H. BURGESS *Dict. Sailing* 121 *Inter-cardinal points*, the half-cardinals. **1969** *Gloss. Terms Magnetic Compasses & Binnacles (B.S.I.)* 5 *Inter-cardinal points.* These are north-east, south-east, south-west, north-west and may be marked with the capital letters NE, SE, SW, and NW respectively. **1884** HOLDEN *Anat.* (ed. 5) 486 The *intercarotic ganglion. **1885** —— *Hum. Osteol.* 124 The bones of the first row.. form, with the bones of the second row, an important moveable joint, which we call the '*intercarpal'. **1895** G. ALLEN *Woman who did* xvii, It is the last word of the *intercivic war. **1857** BULLOCK *Cazeaux's Midwif.* 25 These *inter-coccygeal articulations are similarly constructed. **1902** *Proc. Zool. Soc.* II. 215 Cortex [of the sponge] fibrous throughout,..without *intercortical cavities. **1924** R. M. OGDEN tr. *Koffka's Growth of Mind* ii. 55 According to Edinger, morphological changes in the brain are indicated by..the growth of intercortical pathways. **1933** J. ROSETT *Intercortical Syst. Human Cerebrum* iv. 26 In the course of cerebral evolution the intercortical systems increase in number and in bulk. **1883** A. WINCHELL *World-Life* 49 (Cent.) The doctrine of attenuated matter scattered through the *intercosmical spaces of organized systems. **1859** TODD *Cycl. Anat.* V. 168/2 The great *intercotyloid distance gives to their gait its peculiar waddle. **1878** E. L. STURTEVANT (*title*) *Intercultural Tillage. **1878** *Pop. Sci. Monthly* July 376 By 'intercultural tillage', Dr. Sturtevant means tilling, stirring the soil, while the plant is growing. **1899** SAYCE *Early Israel* i. 55 The tribes..plunged into *interfraternal war. **1941** *Cold Spring Harbor Symp. Quant. Biol.* IX. 161/1 The breaks of minute rearrangements would in all probability differ from them in being only *intergenic. **1951** G. H. BOURNE *Cytol. & Cell Physiol.* (ed. 2) v. 225 It.. assumes that there are no non-genic portions of the chromosome (matrix, intergenic connexions). **1968** *Canad. Jrnl. Genetics & Cytol.* X. 50 A UV-sensitive mutant of *Aspergillus rugulosus* unrelated to intergenic crossing over. **1884** *Pall Mall G.* 10 Oct. 11/2 The schooner was in the usual style of the *inter-insular boats, foully dirty. **1882** *Knowledge* 7 July 91 If we..divide it into six *interlatitudinal zones or belts. **1652** URQUHART *Jewel* Wks. (1834) 244 Most of the young ladies..had his effigies in a little oval tablet of gold hanging 'twixt their breasts, and held..that metamazion, or *intermammillary ornament, a necessary outward pendicle. **1864** *Reader* 9 July 52/1 Greater proportionate development of the zygomatic and *intermastoid diameters. **1622** MABBE tr. *Aleman's Guzman D'Alf.* II. 240 In her banquets, feasts and other *inter-mealary-intertainments. *a* **1652** BROME *Mad Couple* v. ii. Wks. 1873 I. 92 Noonings, and *intermealiary Lunchings. **1876** tr. *Wagner's Gen. Pathol.* 316 *Inter-meningeal apoplexy. **1887** F. R. STOCKTON *Borrowed Month* 225 That congruent *intermental action of the intellect of two persons. **1871** tr. *Schellen's Spectr. Anal.* lii. 233 The search for *intermercurial planets. **1881** MIVART *Cat* 102 An *inter-metacarpal ligament. **1887** *Syd. Soc. Lex.*, *Intermetatarsal arteries..I. ligaments. **1826** KIRBY & SP. *Entomol.* IV. 316 Antennæ..*Interocular..When inserted any where between the eyes. **1881** LE CONTE *Sight* 109 Equal to the interocular distance. **1892** A. DUANE tr. *Fuchs' Textbk. Ophthalm.* xii. 467 That part of the cornea and of the scleral conjunctiva which ordinarily is not covered by the lids is called the *interpalpebral zone... When the eyes are a little screwed together..the interpalpebral zone diminishes in size. **1934** E. WOLFF *Path. Eye* ii. 29 Pinguecula, or interpalpebral spot, is a slightly raised yellowish area placed next to the inner or outer margin of the cornea. **1854** OWEN *Skel. & Teeth* in *Circ. Sc., Organ. Nat.* I. 222 In the goose and duck tribes..the *interpectoral ridge extends from the prominent part of the coracoid margin backwards. **1884** *Science* IV. 223 (Cent.) The *interpetaloid spaces [on parts of recent and fossil crinoids] are plain, and devoid of sculpture. **1897** *Allbutt's Syst. Med.* III. 82 The *interphalangeal joints of the fingers swell. **1932** *Amer. Mineralogist* XVII. 549 (*caption*) The values given are the calculated *interplanar spacings. **1948** K. LONSDALE *Crystals & X-Rays* iii. 77 There is now, however, no way of measuring interplanar angles. **1970** A. J. C. WILSON *Elem. X-Ray Crystallogr.* ii. 19 All the interplanar spacings capable of producing lines in an X-ray powder photograph can be obtained by consideration of the distance between successive planes of the lattice points. **1900** *Proc. U.S. Nat. Museum* XXIII. 398 The term *interplical ridge has been applied to the summit of the radial convexities of the wing and interplical groove the bottom of the alternating concavities. **1903** *Phil. Trans. R. Soc.* B. CXCV. 161 The thickened chitin bands, which..are in contact by those edges directed towards the interplical space, are here divaricated. **1971** *Listener* 30 Dec. 907 There are no known IQ tests which are capable of overcoming the **inter*populational cross-cultural barrier. **1971** *McGraw-Hill Yearbk. Sci. & Technol.* 253 Interpopulational developmental comparisons..helped to clarify what in the past seemed to be an aberrant course of leaf development. **1881** SIR W. HUNTER in *Encycl. Brit.* XII. 764/1, 32 millions represent *interportal, and 25 millions foreign trade. **1888** *Engineer* 21 Dec. 517 Competition by foreigners in the interportal trade of the East. **1898** *Pop. Sci. Monthly* LIII. 856 The *interprotoplastic threads have so far received no conclusive interpretation. **1897** E. C. KIRK *Amer. Textbk. Operative Dentistry* iii. 97 The counteraction of the tongue and cheek..drives the finer particles of the food into the *interproximal spaces. **1908** G. V. BLACK *Operative Surg.* 211 (*heading*) Interproximal wear and its treatment. *Ibid.* 213 If there has been much loss of inter-proximal gum tissue ..watch the case for a few weeks. **1960** KERR & ASH *Oral Path.* vii. 115 Interproximal caries involve all of the teeth, but the molars and bicuspids are involved more frequently than the incisors. **1972** S. GARFIELD *Teeth* iv. 88 The small spaces between adjacent teeth around the contact points are called Contact Areas or Interproximal Spaces. *Ibid.* ix. 133 Inside the ridges between the roots of each adjacent tooth the bone is called Interproximal Bone. **1907** J. H. PARSONS *Dis. Eye* xxvi. 525 With an *interpupillary distance of 60 mm. this angle is about 2°. **1962** L. S. SASIENI *Princ. & Pract. Optical Dispensing* v. 106 (*heading*) Inter-pupillary distance. **1866** HUXLEY *Preh. Rem. Caithn.* 143 The excessively narrow *intersciatic diameter which characterises the Australian male pelvis. **1887** G. C. BOURNE in *Q. Jrnl. Microsc. Sc.* Jan. 303 Ligaments passing down through the *intersynapticular spaces. **1878** BELL *Gegenbaur's Comp. Anat.* 488 It moves on an *intertarsal joint. **1883** RAY LANKESTER in *Encycl. Brit.* XVI. 648/1 The Limpet being a strictly *intertidal organism. **1909** *Cent. Dict.* Suppl., *Intertonic. **1953** K. JACKSON *Lang. & Hist. in Early Brit.* II. 268 Syncope of intertonic syllables in Vulgar Latin. **1882–3** SCHAFF *Encycl. Relig. Knowl.* I. 465 We cannot conceive of such a self-reduction of the Logos without suspending the *intertrinitarian process. **1890** —— *Creed Revis.* 3 In the single eternal intertrinitarian procession of the Spirit. **1836–9** TODD *Cycl. Anat.* II. 814/1 Approximated..to the posterior *intertrochanteric line. **1855** HOLDEN *Hum. Osteol.* (1878) 195 The posterior 'inter-trochanteric ridge', is mainly for the support of the great trochanter. **1893** *Jrnl. Anat. & Physiol.* XXVII. 260 The level which is expressed by our *inter-tubercular line. **1967** G. M. WYBURN et al. *Conc. Anat.* ii. 53/1 The muscle is inserted..into the lateral lip of the intertubercular groove on the front of the humerus. **1847–9** TODD *Cycl. Anat.* IV. 570/2 The *intertubular substance. **1854** OWEN *Skel. & Teeth* in *Circ. Sc., Organ. Nat.* I. 265 A small portion of human dentine, showing the tubuli..in the inter-tubular substance. **1897** *Allbutt's Syst. Med.* IV. 354 The intertubular substance [of the kidney] shares in the inflammatory process. **1870** ROLLESTON *Anim. Life* Introd. 44 Glands..according to the locality in which they are situated, known as anal, inguinal, *interungular, and preputial. **1885** *Syd. Soc. Lex.* s.v. *Gland*, *Interungulate G., the *Canalis biflexus*. **1916** *Mem. N.Y. Bot. Garden* VI. 352 No essential differences were noted in *intervarietal fertility and fruitfulness. *Ibid.*, Intervarietal crosses. **1951** *New Biol.* XI. 115 In *Paramecium aurelia* there are seven varieties, and each variety contains types I and II... Intervarietal mating takes place very rarely and then only between type I of one variety and type II of the other. **1934** WEBSTER, *Interveinal. **1946** *Nature* 9 Nov. 663/2 The virus strain used produced a bright yellow interveinal mottle in the tomato. **1970** *Bot. Gaz.* CXXXI. 152/1 This strip [of leaf] was five interveinal areas wide at the upper margin. **1889** *Ann. Bot.* III. 293 The phloëm-islands, or *interxylary phloëm-strands, are formed centripetally by certain portions of the normal cambium. **1969** K. ESAU *Phloem* vi. 213 In..the interxylary or included phloem, the cambium ..forms periodically some phloem increments towards the interior of the stem so that the phloem becomes embedded in the xylem. **1884** *Nature* 24 July 306/2 The arrangement of the *interzoœcial pores may frequently give great assistance, and these are considered the equivalents of the rosette-plates. **1872** MIVART *Elem. Anat.* 40 A strong *interzygapophysial ridge may connect together the pre and post-zygapophyses of each side of a vertebra. **1870** ROLLESTON *Anim. Life* 7 The *interzygomatic diameter is in all Rodents the widest transverse cranial diameter.

inter-absorption, -accessory, -accuse, -acinous, -acquaintance: see INTER- *pref.*

interacinar: see INTER- *pref.* 6.

interact ('ɪntərˌækt), *sb.* [f. INTER- 3 + ACT *sb.*, after F. *entr'acte* in same sense.] The interval between two acts of a play; a short performance between two acts, an interlude; hence, an intermediate employment. *attrib.*

1750 CHESTERF. *Lett.* (1774) I. clxxxvii. 563 Play..is only the 'inter-acts' of other amusements. **1831** *Soc. Life Eng. & For.* 181 The *Aminta* of Tasso, a complete pastoral drama, accompanied by choruses and interacts of music. **1873** E. FITZGERALD *Lett.* (1889) I. 360 The Choruses..still serving to carry on the Subject of the Story in the way of Inter-act. **1908** *Daily Chron.* 3 July 3/5 At the 'private' or roofed theatres, the performance of interact music was the rule. **1909** *Morning Leader* 29 May 4/6 At the 'private theatres', such as the Blackfriars, they not only had interacts but interact music.

interact (ɪntər'ækt), *v.* [INTER- 1 b.] *intr.* To act reciprocally, to act on each other.

1839 BAILEY *Festus* xviii. (1852) 238 Is it not a fact That saints and demons ofttimes interact? **1856** EMERSON *Eng. Traits, Lit.* Wks. (Bohn) II. 115 The two..styles of mind.. are ever in counterpoise, interacting mutually. **1871** TYNDALL *Fragm. Sc.* (1879) II. vi. 83 The grain and the substances which surround it interact. **1967** M. ARGYLE *Psychol. Interpersonal Behaviour* viii. 144 Children and adolescents are very limited in their social techniques, and may be able to interact with other children, and parents, but not with other adults... Most mental patients apart from schizophrenics are able to interact, but are much less successful in forming permanent relationships. **1972** *Jrnl. Social Psychol.* LXXXVII. 7 Very few *S*s [*sc.* subjects] left their chair in order to interact with *E* [*sc.* the examiner]; those who did were ignored.

Hence **inter'acting** *ppl. a.*, acting reciprocally.

1851–5 BRIMLEY *Ess., Tennyson* 63 A more complex machinery of interacting events. **1873** SYMONDS *Grk. Poets* ix. 295 A play of Shakspere or Goethe overwhelms us by the force and frequence of combined and interacting motives.

interaction (ɪntər'ækʃən). [f. INTERACT *v.*, after *action*.] Reciprocal action; action or influence of persons or things on each other. *spec.* in *Physics*, referring to the action between atomic and subatomic particles. Also *attrib.*

1832 I. TAYLOR *Saturday Even.* (1833) 86 The reaction, or rather *interaction*, which at present is going on between readers and writers. **1852** *Fraser's Mag.* XLV. 264 The results of the interaction of so many different agencies. **1883** G. ALLEN in *Gentl. Mag.* Oct. 313 The close interaction between the vegetable and animal worlds. **1930** *Proc. R. Soc.* A. CXXIX. 4 The simplified interaction which couples the nuclear system and the electron. **1951** T. PARSONS et al. in Parsons & Shils *Toward Gen. Theory Action* II. iv. 190 The specific interaction systems of ego. **1955** H. B. G. CASIMIR in W. Pauli *Niels Bohr* 130 The electrostatic interaction energy is e^2/a where a is a distance between electrons. **1959** *Listener* 9 July 52/1 There are four distinct types of force through which the manifold transformations of matter and energy arise. These forces are known as the strong, the electromagnetic, the weak and the gravitational interactions. **1964** *Language* XL. 242 An interaction cycle between the mother and child that amounts to a pair of reciprocal transformations. **1967** M. ARGYLE *Psychol. Interpersonal Behaviour* vii. 128 If A presents himself as an upper-class person but B reacts to him as a working-class person, interaction will not proceed smoothly.

Hence **inter'actional** *a.*, of, belonging to, or characterized by, interaction.

1886 J. F. SMITH in *Encycl. Brit.* XXI. 412/1 The sum of being consists of the two systems of substantial forms and interactional relations.

interactionism (ɪntər'ækʃənɪz(ə)m). *Philos.* [f. INTERACTION + -ISM.] The theory that in the causal relations between mind and body the causal influence runs in both directions, in sensation from body to mind and in volition from mind to body. So **inter'actionist** *sb.*, an adherent of interactionism; *adj.*, of or pertaining to this doctrine.

1902 *Pop. Sci. Monthly* 459 Interactionism has to maintain, in this concrete form of the 'survival theory', that the mental process as such is an aid to evolution. **1903** C. A. STRONG *Why the Mind has a Body* 5 Whether this interactionist tendency in biology be significant or ephemeral, we need not inquire. *Ibid.* 23 What the interactionist..takes for an action of mind on body is..an action of the brain upon the rest of the body. *Ibid.* 33 Interactionism seems almost to necessitate two juxtaposed realities exchanging influences, and thus to imply a metaphysical dualism. **1934** *Brit. Jrnl. Psychol.* Jan. 273 The annoyance may not be a response to being struck with a pin... We will not try here to settle the quarrel between

such a parallelistic interpretation and the interpretation of an interactionist. **1941** *Mind* L. 86 He argues for interactionism, as against psychophysical parallelism. **1956** J. O. URMSON *Philos. Analysis* II. vii. 110 One [metaphysician] advocates psycho-physical parallelism, the other interactionism. **1972** *Jrnl. Social Psychol.* Aug. 214 Pursuing the explanations of the symbolic interactionist somewhat further, Mead's theory suggests.. maximum category overlap.

interactive (ɪntər'æktɪv), *a.* [f. INTERACT *v.*, after *active.*] **1.** Reciprocally active; acting upon or influencing each other.

1832 I. TAYLOR *Saturday Even.* (1833) 333 The Infinite Excellence.. comprising Interactive Causes which must have products possessing absolutely no affinity with any thing exterior to itself. **1879** H. W. WARREN *Recr. Astron.* xii. 257 Yet its interactive atoms can give four hundred millions of light-waves a second. **1972** *Computers & Humanities* VI. 195 A method which will provide the student with a rapid interactive feedback. **1972** *Science* 2 June 1019/1 A complicated and interactive set of physical, chemical, biological and human processes act in concert to yield a spectrum of measured values.

2. Pertaining to or being a computer or other electronic device that allows a two-way flow of information between it and a user, responding immediately to the latter's input.

1967 *IEEE Trans. Human Factors in Electronics* VIII. 1/1 Multiple-access, on-line interactive man-computer systems. **1971** *IEEE Trans. Electron Devices* XVIII. 618/2 We can see that even from this simplified description of the composition of interactive terminals, a wide variety of disciplines are called upon to establish a successful interaction between man and the computer system. **1973** C. W. GEAR *Introd. Computer Sci.* iv. 153 The input to the typewriter system is in the interactive mode. **1981** *Event* 9 Oct. 28/4 *Interactive video*, TV screens equipped with computer-linked press-buttons for instant Q&A verdicts on the show—asked in the studio and answered in your own home. **1983** *Listener* 22 Sept. 34/2 It would include local and national news, sport and finance, but also interactive teleshopping, telebanking and a host of special offers and giveaways to members of the club. **1985** *Personal Computer World* Feb. 196/1 Educationalists recognise interactive video as being potentially more accessible to teachers than the micro.

Hence **inter'actively** *adv.*, by means of an interactive system; in a way characteristic of such a system.

1970 *Computers & Humanities* V. 24 It would be especially interesting to make this sort of investigation interactively, using some kind of terminal. **1973** *Physics Bull.* Aug. 497/1 A computer program, *Trace*,.. can be interrogated interactively to show how store movements have progressed. **1978** *Sci. Amer.* Apr. 26/1 Using a satellite to transmit data, voice, full-motion and freeze-frame video, and facsimile documents—all interactively—Satellite Business Systems (SBS) has undertaken a pace-setting experiment in advanced communications for geographically dispersed organizations.

interadditive (ɪntər'ædɪtɪv). *nonce-wd.* [f. INTER- 2a + ADDITIVE.] Something added or inserted between or among other things.

c **1819** COLERIDGE *Shaks. Notes* in *Rem.* (1836) II. 147, I.. understand it as a parenthesis, an interadditive of scorn.

interadventual, -affiliation, etc.: see INTER-.

†**inter-a'ffair.** *Obs. rare.* [INTER- 2a.] ? An affair or business between two parties.

1563 *Homilies* II. *Matrimony* Xxxxiij, For the merchaunte man, excepte he firste be at composition with his factor, to vse his interaffares [*later edd.* interfairs] quietlye, he wyll neyther stirre his shyppe to sayle nor yet wyll lay handes vpon his marchandyse.

inter-African: see INTER- *pref.* 4c.

inter-agent (ɪntər'eɪdʒənt). [f. INTER- 2a + AGENT.] An intermediate agent; a go-between, intermediary. So **inter-'agency.**

1728-31 GORDON *Tacitus, Hist.* II. xcix. II. 151 By the interagency of Rubrius Gallus, the mind of Cecina came to be shaken. *Ibid.* IV. lxxxvi. II. 299 Domitian is believed to have tried, by secret interagents, to corrupt the fidelity of Cerialis. **1835** KIRBY *Hab. & Inst. Anim.* (1852) II. 178 To believe that they may be inter-agents by which the Deity acts upon animal organizations and structures to produce all their varied instincts. **1837** LOCKHART *Scott* xxxvii, Had Scott never possessed any such system of inter-agency as the Ballantynes supplied. **1969** *R. & E. Coordinator* (Res. & Engin. Council Graphic Arts Industry) Apr. 4/1 The Government uses millions of microfiche internally for storage and retrieval systems and for interagency communications. **1973** *Times* 24 May 8/4 On July 5, 1970, Mr Nixon said, he appointed Mr Hoover chairman of an inter-agency committee to discuss a need for better intelligence operations.

†**'interail, -all,** obs. forms of ENTRAIL.

1508 *Burgh Rec. Edinburgh* (1869) I. 114 Nolt heids nowmyllis nor interallis of thair flesche. **1610** G. FLETCHER *Christ's Vict.* II. xlviii, When zephyrs breath'd into their watry interall.

inter alia: see INTER *Lat. prep.*

inter-allied (ɪntərə'laɪd, -'ælaɪd), *a.* [f. INTER- 1b + ALLIED.] Existing or constituted between allies or allied forces. So **inter-ally** (-'ælaɪ), *a.*

1919 J. M. KEYNES *Econ. Consequences Peace* 96 The supreme authority is to be in the hands of an Inter-Allied Rhineland Commission. *Ibid.* 240 The settlement of inter-Ally indebtedness. **1925** A. TOYNBEE *Survey Internat. Affairs 1920-23* 1 The four Treaties.. had provided for the establishment of a number of inter-Allied bodies to perform temporary or permanent executive duties. **1942** W. S. CHURCHILL in *Hutchinson's Pict. Hist. War* 18 Mar.-9 June 30/2 The task of national self-preservation and of inter-allied duty. **1973** *Times* 29 Oct. 15/2 This public airing of an inter-allied dispute on a day of acute international tension was tactless to say the least.

interalveolar (ɪntəræl'viːələ(r)), *a. Phys.* [INTER- 4a.] **1.** Situated between the alveoli or air-cells of the lungs.

1834 J. FORBES *Laennec's Dis. Chest* (ed. 4) 157 There was no infiltration or extravasation of air into the inter-alveolar tissue. **1896** *Allbutt's Syst. Med.* I. 185 Atrophy of blood-vessels and interalveolar connective tissue.

2. Situated between the alveoli or sockets of the teeth of a sea-urchin.

1877 HUXLEY *Anat. Inv. Anim.* ix. 576 Beside the inter-alveolar muscles already described.

‖**interambulacrum** (-'eɪkrəm). *Zool.* Pl. **-acra.** [INTER- 3.] One of the imperforate plates occupying the intervals of the ambulacra or perforate plates in the shells of echinoderms. Hence **interambu'lacral** *a.*, of or pertaining to interambulacra; situated between ambulacra.

1870 ROLLESTON *Anim. Life* 225 Quadrangular reticulations, formed by the 'interambulacral' ossicles. **1877** HUXLEY *Anat. Inv. Anim.* ix. 569 Two series of interambulacral plates, those in the middle of each interambulacrum being hexagonal.

inter-American: see INTER- *pref.* 4c.

interamnian (ɪntər'æmnɪən), *a.* [f. L. *Interamnium* sb. (f. *interamnus* lying between two rivers, f. *inter* between + *amnis* river) + -AN.] Lying between rivers, like Mesopotamia; enclosed by rivers.

1774 J. BRYANT *Anc. Myth.* III. 26 Supposed to be confined to one narrow interamnian district. **1819** G. PAXTON *Illustr. Script.* (1842) I. 111 Leaving Babel on the inter-amnian region in which it was built.

inter'animate, *v. rare.* [INTER- 1b.] *trans.* To animate mutually. Hence **interani'mation,** mutual animation.

a **1631** DONNE *Poems, Ecstasy* (1650) 43 When love with one another so Interanimates two souls. **1925** I. A. RICHARDS *Princ. Lit. Crit.* xxxi. 237 Conflicts, resolutions and interanimations. **1966** *English Studies* XLVII. 200 The interanimation of the complex parts.

interantennal, -antennary: see INTER- *pref.*

†**interarbo'ration.** *Obs. rare*$^{-1}$. [f. INTER- 2a + L. *arbor* tree + -ATION.] Intermixture of the branches of trees on opposite sides.

1658 SIR T. BROWNE *Gard. Cyrus* iv. 177 Though the inter-arboration do imitate the Areostylos or thin order.

interarch, etc.: see INTER- *pref.*

inter-arrival, -atrial, -availability, -available, -bank(s): see INTER- *pref.* 5, 6, 2a, 5.

interarticular (ˌɪntərɑː'tɪkjuːlə(r)), *a.* [f. INTER- 4a + L. *articul-us* joint.] Lying or prevailing between the contiguous surfaces in a joint.

1808 BRODIE in *Phil. Trans.* XCVIII. 306 An inter-articular cartilage is here interposed between the tibia and the fibula. **1872** HUXLEY *Phys.* vii. 167 Separated by independent plates of cartilage, which are termed inter-articular. **1877** —— *Anat. Inv. Anim.* vi. 311 The.. excessive narrowing of the interarticular regions of the sterna.

interartistic, -arytenoid, -association, -assure, -asteroidal, -astral, etc.: see INTER-.

interatomic (ˌɪntərə'tɒmɪk), *a.* [INTER- 4a.] Existing or acting between atoms.

1863 TYNDALL *Heat* ii. §17 (1870) 23 The material theory supposes.. a subtle fluid stored up in the inter-atomic spaces of bodies. **1889** *Nature* 19 Sept. 509/2 From the motions of the heavenly bodies down to the minutest interatomic movements in chemical reactions.

interaulic (ɪntər'ɔːlɪk), *a. nonce-wd.* [f. INTER- 4a + L. *aula* hall, court: see AULIC.] 'Existing between royal courts' (Webster).

a **1864** MOTLEY (cited in Webster), Interaulic politics.

interau'ricular, etc.: see INTER- *pref.*

interaxis (ɪntər'æksɪs). *Archit.* Pl. **-axes** (-'æksiːz). [INTER- 3.] The space between the axes. So **inter'axal** *a.*, of or pertaining to the space between the axes, situated between the axes.

1842-76 GWILT *Archit.* §2842 The walls.. are placed centrally upon the axes.. The doors, windows, niches, and the like are then placed centrally in the interaxes. *Ibid.* §2843 An illustration of the principles of interaxal division from the.. Villa Capra, near Vicenza, by Palladio.

interbalance *v.*, etc.: see INTER- *pref.*

†**inter'bastate,** *v. Obs. rare*$^{-1}$. [f. Fr. *interbaster* to quilt: see -ATE[3] 6.] *trans.* To sew between (cotton, etc.) so as to keep in place; to quilt. Hence †**interba'station,** quilting.

1657 TOMLINSON *Renou's Disp.* 210 This medicinal Powder interbastated in Cotten. **1666** J. SMITH *Old Age* 184 The word [*tpr*] is a Metaphor taken from interbastation, patching or piecing, sewing or clapping close together.

†**inter'baste,** *v. Obs. rare.* [a. F. *interbaste-r*, f. INTER- 1a + *baster* to BASTE.] = prec.

1611 COTGR., *Interbasté*, interbasted; basted, or quilted betweene. **1612** *Ench. Med.* 162 Let it [a powder] bee couered ouer with red sarsnet, and inter-bast it, and so apply it.

interbed (ɪntə'bɛd), *v.* [INTER- 1a.] *trans.* To embed amongst or between, to interstratify.

c **1806** D. WORDSWORTH *Jrnl.* (1941) I. 252 These two islands.. were intermingled with the water, I might say interbedded and interveined with it. **1858** GEIKIE *Hist. Boulder* xi. 208 The strata interbedded among the Coal-seams. **1879** RUTLEY *Study Rocks* xiii. 270 Crystalline schists, with which rocks serpentine is very commonly associated and interbedded.

Hence **inter'bedded,** interstratified; **inter'bedding,** interstratification.

1872 W. S. SYMONDS *Rec. Rocks* iv. 116 The highest inter-bedded igneous rocks. **1879** RUTLEY *Study Rocks* iv. 32 In the interbedding of lava-flows.

inter-behaviour, -behavioural: see INTER- *pref.* 2a.

interbellum (ɪntə'bɛləm), *a.* Also **interbella.** [f. INTER- 4b + L. *bellum* war.] Of or with reference to a period between two wars, e.g. between the wars of 1914-18 and of 1939-45. So **inter'belline** *a.*

1940 BEERBOHM *Mainly on the Air* (1946) 82, I feel sure that even in the inter-bella period a river would have done Bloomsbury no end of good. **1958** *Oxf. Mag.* 22 May 454/1 The interbelline English Don.. did his best not to take 'Eng. Lit.'.. too seriously. **1961** *Ann. Reg. 1960* 462 Nathalie Sarraute.. was noticeably closer than he to the English experimental novel of the interbelline years. **1969** P. ANDERSON in Cockburn & Blackburn *Student Power* 231 The German emigration, coming from a philosophical culture that was quite distinct from the parish-pump positivism of interbellum Vienna, avoided this island.

interblend (ɪntə'blɛnd), *v.* Pa. pple. **-blended, -blent.** [INTER- 1a, 1b.]

†**1.** *trans.* To interpose opaquely. *Obs. rare*$^{-1}$.

1591 SYLVESTER *Du Bartas* I. iv. 774 Sometimes thy thick Orb thow dost inter-blend Twixt Sol and us, toward the later end.

2. To blend intimately; to intermingle.

a **1849** J. C. MANGAN *Poems* (1859) 432 Night is interblent with day. **1861** GEIKIE *E. Forbes* viii. 208 Notices of plants, insects, minerals, and rocks, are interblended with remarks upon the peculiarities of his breakfast. **1888** R. BUCHANAN *City of Dream* VIII. 169 The lilies and the roses interblent.

3. *intr.* To blend or mingle with each other.

1856 MASSON *Ess., De Quincey* 467 Where παθησις at its utmost thrill and ecstasy interblends with the highest and most daring ποιησις. **1872** E. H. SEARS *Fourth Gospel* (1874) 100 The first and second [divisions of the Apocalypse] inter-blend imperceptibly with each other.

Hence **inter'blending** *ppl. a.*

1892 E. C. STEDMAN in *Century Mag.* Apr. 826 Inter-blending vibrations. **1896** W. GLADDEN in *Papers Ohio Ch. Hist. Soc.* VII. 134 The natural and supernatural are not separated but interblending realms.

interblending (ɪntə'blɛndɪŋ), *vbl. sb.* Also 6 **enterblinning.** [f. prec. + -ING[1].] A blending or mingling intimately; intermingling.

1591 SYLVESTER *Du Bartas* I. ii. 402 But till To-morrow, leave the enter-blinning Of rocky Mounts, and rowling Waves so wide. **1836** J. GILBERT *Chr. Atonem.* vi. (1852) 170 The unperceived interblending of cases.. in all their bearings mutually opposite. **1866** FELTON *Anc. & Mod. Gr.* I. II. i. 277 The interblending of these elements by land and sea.

inter-borough: see INTER- *pref.* 5.

inter-bourse: see INTER- *pref.* 5.

†**inter'brace,** *v. Obs. rare.* [f. INTER- 1b + BRACE *v.*[1]] *trans.* To embrace mutually.

1592 G. HARVEY *Four Lett.* Sonn., To interbrace each other with delight.

interbrachial (-'breɪkɪəl), *a.* (*sb.*) *Zool.* [f. INTER- 4a + L. *brachi-um* arm: cf. BRACHIAL.] Situated between the 'arms' or rays of an echinoderm: = INTERAMBULACRAL, INTERRADIAL. Also as *sb.* An interbrachial part or member.

1877 W. THOMSON *Voy. Challenger* II. ii. 66 Towards the base of the interbrachial groove. **1895** *Athenæum* 28 Dec. 906/1 This was specially the case with regard to the inter-brachials.. and joints [of a fossil crinoid].

'inter-brain. *Anat.* [INTER- 2b.] The middle brain; = DIENCEPHALON.

1887 *Syd. Soc. Lex.*, *Inter-brain*, the *Thalamencephalon*.

interbranchial (-'bræŋkɪəl), *a. Zool.* [INTER- 4a.] Situated between the branchiæ or gills.

1880 GÜNTHER *Fishes* 139 The interbranchial clefts have sometimes nearly the same extent as the branchial arches.

interbreathe, -bring, etc.: see INTER-.

interbreed (ɪntəˈbriːd), *v.* [INTER- 1 b.]

1. *intr.* Of animals of different race or species: To breed with each other.

1864 *Reader* No. 86. 235/3 Capable of fertile interbreeding. **1889** A. R. WALLACE *Darwinism* 2 Rooks always produce rooks, and crows produce crows, and they do not inter-breed. **1896** *Blackw. Mag.* May 683 Some interbreeding races.

2. *intr.* or *absol.* To cause animals to interbreed; *spec.* to practise breeding between the members of two stocks.

1859 DARWIN *Orig. Spec.* iii. (1872) 55 The good effects of inter-crossing, and the ill effects of close interbreeding.. come into play. **1870** A. L. ADAMS *Nile Valley & Malta* 47 No doubt the ferocious propensities of the feline race may be overcome by constant interbreeding. **1886** C. SCOTT *Sheep-farming* 22 There is much prejudice in many quarters against breeding in-and-in,—that is, inter-breeding too closely between members of the same family.

3. *trans.* To breed (offspring) from individuals of different species or races; to cross-breed. Also *fig.*

1865 MASSON *Rec. Brit. Philos.* 62 Effects interbred between them and a particular sentiency in the midst of them. **1889** *Pall Mall G.* 24 June 2/1 Miserable inhabitants, inter-bred from Chinese, Portuguese, Malay, Indian, and unknown human jetsam.

Hence **interˈbreeding** *vbl. sb.* and *ppl. a.*

[See examples above.]

intercadence (-ˈkeɪdəns). *Path.* [INTER- 2 a.] 'An irregular rhythm of the pulse, so that there seems to be now and then an additional interposed pulsation' (*Syd. Soc. Lex.* 1887).

1857 in DUNGLISON *Med. Lex.*

intercadent (-ˈkeɪdənt), *a.* [INTER- 2 a.] Irregular or uneven in rhythm; *spec.* in *Path.* Characterized by intercadence (see prec.).

1837 CARLYLE *Misc., Mirabeau* (1872) V. 237 The bitter ugliness, the intercadent step, the trenchant breathless blown-up precipitation. **1887** *Syd. Soc. Lex., Intercadent*, exhibiting the phenomena of intercadence.

†**inˈtercalar,** *a. Obs.* Also 6 -or, 7 -air. [ad. L. *intercalār-is*: see INTERCALATE. Cf. F *intercalaire* (14th c. in Godef.).] = INTERCALARY 1.

1582 N. LICHEFIELD tr. *Castanheda's Conq. E. Ind.* 93 They haue their day which they do call Intercalor, which is of 40 houres. **1603** HOLLAND *Plutarch's Mor.* 1292 Reputing the third of these intercalar daies to be desasterous and dismall. **1653** H. COGAN *Diod. Sic.* 6 The Egyptians have five intercalair days. **1699** LOCKE *Let. to Sloane* 2 Dec. in Fox Bourne *Life* (1876) II. xv. 477 The remedy which I offer is that the intercalar day should be omitted the next year, and so the ten next leap years following.

†**intercaˈlarian,** *a. Obs. rare*$^{-1}$. [f. L. *intercalāri-us* + -AN.] = INTERCALARY 1.

1690 LEYBOURN *Curs. Math.* 467 To make up their Year of 365 days, they add at the end of the Year 5 Intercalarian days.

†**intercaˈlarity.** *Obs. rare*$^{-0}$. [f. INTERCALARY *a.* + -ITY.] 'The burden of a song; the putting between, as the burden is between the verses' (Blount, 1656).

intercalarium (ˌɪntəkəˈlɛərɪəm). *Zool.* Pl. **-ia.** Also **interˈcalare, interˈcalary.** [mod.L., neut. sing. of L. *intercalārius* INTERCALARY *a.*]

1. An element found between adjacent neural arches in the vertebral column of elasmobranchs and certain other fishes.

1887 *Proc. Zool. Soc.* 31 Intercalaria are absent in the hæmal tube [of the shark, *Carcharodon rondeletii*]. **1922** J. F. DANIEL *Elasmobranch Fishes* iii. 49 Each dorsal intercalary [is perforated] by the dorsal root of the same [*sc.* spinal] nerve. **1925** J. S. KINGSLEY *Vertebr. Skeleton* 28 (*caption*) Intercalaria. *Ibid.*, The ring with arches is called the centrum, the one without is an intercentrum or intercalare. **1967** *Jrnl. Linn. Soc. (Zool.)* XLVII. 186 In *Polyodon*, dorsal intercalaries may be absent in the abdominal region, but they are usually present in the caudal.

2. In cypriniform fishes, an ossicle forming part of the Weberian apparatus linking the inner ear with the swimbladder.

1893 *Phil. Trans. R. Soc.* B. CLXXXIV. 83 Like the scaphium [in Macrones] the intercalarium consists of ascending and horizontal processes united at nearly a right angle. **1962** K. F. LAGLER et al. *Ichthyol.* viii. 248 These ossicles are derived from the apophyses of anterior vertebrae; the hindmost of them, the tripus, touches the anterior wall of the gas bladder and is connected with a ligament to the next bone, the intercalare. **1970** *Amer. Mus. Novitates* No. 2428. 16 The intercalarium is attached to the tripus by a very dense, elongate ligament.

intercalary (ɪnˈtɜːkələrɪ), *a.* [ad. L. *intercalāri-us* or *intercalāri-s*, f. *intercalāre* to INTERCALATE.]

1. Of a day, days, or month: Inserted at intervals in the calendar in order to bring an inexact reckoning of the year into harmony with the solar year.

In the Jewish, Greek and Roman calendars, intercalary days or months were necessary chiefly to adapt the lunar to the solar reckoning of time. Since the reform of the calendar by Julius Cæsar (B.C. 46), an intercalary day (now Feb. 29) is required only once in 4 years; see BISSEXTILE and LEAP-YEAR.

1614 RALEIGH *Hist. World* II. iii. §6. 255 Ve Adar was an intercalarie Moneth, added, some yeares, vnto the other twelue, to make the Solarie and Lunarie yeare agree. *a* **1660** HAMMOND *19 Serm.* viii. Wks. 1684 IV. 607 An..intercalary day between two months. **1777** ROBERTSON *Hist. Amer.* (1783) III. 180 Those, which were properly intercalary days ..were devoted wholly to festivity and pastime. **1850** MERIVALE *Rom. Emp.* (1865) II. xx. 407 An intercalary month of twenty-three days was inserted. **1881** E. B. TYLOR *Anthropol.* 334 They..added to the 12 solar months of 30 days 5 intercalary days to make 365.

absol. *a* **1834** LAMB *Misc. Wks.* (1871) 451 The intercalaries and other subtle problems he will do well to omit.

b. Of a year: Having intercalated days or an additional month.

1648 LIGHTFOOT *Glean. Ex.* 20 Every third yeare was leape yeare, or intercalary of a moneth added of 33 dayes, which was called Veadar. **1699** *Phil. Trans.* XXI. 358 For Forty Years space there should be no Bissextile or intercalary Years, or as we call them Leap-years, inserted in the Calendar. **1876** *Prayer-bk. Interleaved* 69 The 54 weeks of an intercalary Jewish year.

†**2.** Of a line or stanza: Inserted at intervals in a composition; of the nature of a refrain. *Obs.*

1659 HAMMOND *On Ps.* cvii. Paraphr. *heading*, Having a double burthen or intercalary verse oft recurring. **1778** LOWTH *Isaiah* Prel. Diss. 32 The third line of the intercalary stanza. *a* **1803** BEATTIE *Virg. Past.* viii. *note*, This inter-calary line, (as it is called by the commentators,) which seems to be intended as a chorus or burden to the song.

3. Of the nature of an insertion between the original or ordinary members of a series or parts of a whole; interpolated, intervening.

1798 W. TAYLOR in *Monthly Rev.* XXVII. 489 We have now to mention two volumes of intercalary matter. **1858** CARLYLE *Fredk. Gt.* II. xiv. (1872) I. 137 Sigismund.. seventh and last of the Intercalary Kaisers. **1882** BITHELL *Counting-Ho. Dict.* (1893) 154 An Intercalary dividend is not distributed at any fixed date, and in this respect it differs from what is properly called an Interim dividend. **1888** H. R. REYNOLDS *Comm. John* II. 147/2 The closing words of our Lord's public ministry, delayed by the intercalary remarks of the evangelist.

b. *spec.* in various sciences, as (*a*) of geological strata: Lying between the normal strata of the series; (*b*) of biological types: Intermediate in structure, but not transitional; (*c*) of vegetable growth: Of the nature of new parts inserted among the old.

1846 OWEN *Anat. Vertebr.* I. iii. 67 But whatever modifications these dermal and intercalary spines present above, the same are usually repeated below. **1875** BENNETT & DYER tr. *Sachs' Bot.* 179 Internodes..formed at a later period by further differentiation and intercalary growth. **1877** HUXLEY *Anat. Inv. Anim.* iii. 166 That these ancient corals represent an intercalary type between the Hexacoralla and the Octocoralla. **1884** BOWER & SCOTT *De Bary's Phaner.* 261 The bundles of the leaf-trace and intercalary bundles.

intercalate (ɪnˈtɜːkəleɪt), *v.* [f. L. *intercalāt-*, ppl. stem of *intercalāre* to proclaim the insertion in the calendar of (a day, etc.), f. *inter* between, among + *calāre* to proclaim solemnly: cf. CALENDS. Cf. F. *intercaler* (1570 in Hatz.-Darm.).]

1. *trans.* To insert (an additional day, days, or month) in the calendar in order to bring the current reckoning of time into harmony with the natural solar year. Also *absol.*

1614 RALEIGH *Hist. World* II. iii. §6. 256 Intercalating in ..each eighth yeare one whole moneth. *a* **1654** SELDEN *Table-t.* (Arb.) 119 Twas the manner of the Jews (if the Year did not fall out right..) to intercalate a Month, and so to have, as it were, two Februarys. **1812** WOODHOUSE *Astron.* xliv. 456 To interpose, or to intercalate a day in a month previous to March. **1850** MERIVALE *Rom. Emp.* II. xx, He writes to his friends at Rome to entreat them to hinder the pontiffs from intercalating in that year.

2. *transf.* **a.** To insert or interpose something additional, extraneous, or out of the ordinary course, between the ordinary members of any series or the successive parts of any whole; to interpolate. Chiefly in *passive.*

1824 J. JOHNSON *Typogr.* II. 52 Matter..which is intercalated after the work is gone beyond the proper place for it. **1833** LYELL *Princ. Geol.* III. 45 It has become necessary to intercalate new groups of an age intermediate between those first examined. **1837** CARLYLE *Fr. Rev.* III. I. i, Into the body of the poor Tatars execrative Roman History intercalated an alphabetic letter; and so they continue Tartars, of fell Tartarean nature, to this day. **1874** SAYCE *Compar. Philol.* ii. 94 A noun of number being actually intercalated into the root itself. **1877** R. F. LITTLEDALE in *Academy* 3 Nov. 425/3 Spasmodic episodes of fussy attention, intercalated in habitual neglect.

b. *Geol.* in *pass. pple.* Interstratified, interbedded with the original series.

1847–8 H. MILLER *First Impr.* xix. (1857) 332 Harder beds of rock, intercalated with the softer ones. **1863** A. C. RAMSAY *Phys. Geog.* i. (1878) 15 Marine mud and sand, accumulated bed upon bed, intercalated here and there with strata of limestone.

3. *intr.* To become part of a sequence or array as an extraneous interpolation; to become intercalated *in* or inserted *into*.

1960 UBBELOHDE & LEWIS *Graphite* vi. 141 The easy exchange that is observed between halogen atoms when iodine monochloride or monobromide intercalate in graphite lends some support to this suggestion. **1970** *Nature* 24 Oct. 322/2 The dye, ethidium bromide, which intercalates into DNA, binds to tRNA chiefly at one site. **1973** *Sci. Amer.* Apr. 22/1 Large numbers of ethidium bromide molecules can intercalate in a nicked duplex loop or a linear duplex.

†**inˈtercalate,** *ppl. a. Obs. rare*$^{-1}$. [ad. L. *intercalāt-us*, pa. pple.: see prec.] = INTERCALATED *ppl. a.*

1690 LEYBOURN *Curs. Math.* 466 b, They add 5 Intercalate Days at the end of their Year.

intercalate (ɪntəˈkæleɪt), *sb.* [f. the vb.] **a.** An atom or molecule, or a substance, that enters between the layers of the crystal lattice of another substance, esp. graphite. Freq. *attrib.*

1964 *Proc. R. Soc.* A. CCLXXIX. 291 Fuller understanding of interaction forces between the intercalates and the macro-aromatic molecules is..needed to interpret some highly interesting properties of crystal compounds in the direction of the *c* axis. **1966** *Ibid.* CCXCI. 332 Short range order within any single layer of intercalate clearly resembles that in a liquid or glass. **1968** *Ibid.* CCCIV. 26 Entry of intercalate molecules from the edge of basal planes of crystallites must be kept sufficiently slow to mitigate mechanical strains..before the intercalate has spread uniformly through any layer. **1971** *Nature* 2 July 43/2 Hindrances to charge wandering across the layers in the *c*-axis direction of such crystal compounds must depend extensively on the electron affinity and the local repulsion potentials of the intercalate molecules.

b. A compound formed by foreign atoms or molecules entering between the layers of a crystal lattice, esp. of graphite.

1968 *Proc. R. Soc.* A. CCCIV. 26 First sequence intercalates may eventually be formed on saturation. **1969** *Ibid.* CCCIX. 300 For preparing intercalates with quite low anion uptakes..the mounted specimen was actually immersed in concentrated nitric acid.

intercalated (ɪnˈtɜːkəleɪtɪd), *ppl. a.* [f. INTERCALATE *v.* + -ED[1].] Inserted or introduced between the members of an existing series. **a.** Of an additional day, month, or space of time; hence *transf.* of something written or spoken, etc.; interpolated.

1845 DARWIN *Voy. Nat.* v. (1879) 84 An intercalated period of subsidence, of which we have no evidence. **1846** JOYCE *Sci. Dial., Astron.* xiii. 97 The intercalated day was called *bis sexto calendas Martii.* **1849** LONGF. *Kavanagh* xxvii. Pr. Wks. 1886 II. 396 Dreamy little pauses of silence, and intercalated sighs. **1883** EDERSHEIM *Life Jesus* (ed. 6) II. 529 What follows seems an intercalated sentence.

b. Of material things; *esp.* geological strata.

1849 MURCHISON *Siluria* iv. 84 The intercalated beds of fossiliferous grits. **1863** LYELL *Antiq. Man* viii. (ed. 3) 138 The liquefaction of underlying or intercalated snow and ice. **1876** PAGE *Adv. Text-bk. Geol.* xi. 194.

intercalation (ɪntɜkəˈleɪʃən). [ad. L. *intercalātiōn-em*, n. of action f. *intercalāre* in INTERCALATE. Cf. F. *intercalation* (15th c.).]

1. The insertion of an additional day, days, or month into the ordinary or normal year; the result of this, an intercalated day or space of time.

1577 HARRISON *England* III. xiv. (1878) II. 98 Our intercalation for the leape yere is somewhat too much by certeine minuts. **1609** HOLLAND *Amm. Marcell.* XXVI. i. 285 The Romanes..had transferred upon the priests the power and authoritie of Intercalation. **1764** HARMER *Observ.* ix. 28 The middle of April falls almost perpetually with the Jewish month Abib or Nisan, even without those extraordinary Intercalations the Dr. speaks of. **1876** G. F. CHAMBERS *Astron.* 440 Caesar, by way of securing the intercalation as a matter of precedent, made his initial year, 45 B.C., a leap year.

2. *transf.* The insertion of any addition between the members of an existing or recognized series; interposition or interjection (of something additional or foreign); the occurrence of a layer or bed of a different kind between the regular strata of a series; also with *an* and *pl.*, the thing or matter thus interjected: an interpolation.

1648 HAMMOND *Serm.* iii. Wks. 1684 IV. 484 Intercalations of mercy. *a* **1656** HALES *Gold. Rem.* (1688) 346 When you come to any imperfection to leave him and supply his wants by intercalation of some other author. **1841** TRIMMER *Pract. Geol.* 216 The intercalation of a new system of rocks between the carboniferous and Silurian. **1852** H. ROGERS *Ecl. Faith* (1853) 256 To say that the intercalation of miracles in the world's history is also according to law. **1880** A. R. WALLACE *Isl. Life* ix. 174 Successive intercalations indicative of more than one period of glaciation. **1882** F. DARWIN in *Nature* 20 Apr. 581 Increase of length by turgescence and the intercalation of solid matter.

intercalative (ɪnˈtɜːkəleɪtɪv, -ətɪv), *a.* [f. L. *intercalāt-* (see INTERCALATE *v.*) + -IVE.] That intercalates; *spec.* of a language, characterized by inserting modifying elements in the body of a word.

1882 in OGILVIE. **1887** C. W. HUTSON *Begin. Civiliz.* ii. 23 The intercalative system of the Red Men of America being only a variety of agglutination.

intercalatory (ɪnˈtɜːkələtərɪ), *a. rare.* [f. as prec. + -ORY.] = INTERCALARY.

1610 HEALEY *St. Aug. Citie of God* 547 This month [February] was called nothing but the intercalatory month. **1795–8** T. MAURICE *Hindostan* (1820) I. I. v. 153 It [the Metonic cycle]..has in it seven intercalatory months.

†**intercale,** *v. Obs.* Also 7 -call. [ad. L. *intercalāre* or F. *intercaler.*] = INTERCALATE *v.*

1613 PURCHAS *Pilgrimage* II. iv. 102 [They] were constrained everie second or third yeare to intercale, or

adde, as in Leape-yeare one moneth of 22 dayes. **1728** NEWTON *Chronol. Amended* i. 76 The Greeks..varied the manner of intercaling the three months in the Octaeteris. **1826** J. R. BEST *Four Years France* 320 They intercale, after the wheat..a crop of haricots or French beans.

†**inter'calender**, *v. Obs. rare*⁻¹. [f. INTER- 1 a + CALENDAR *v.*] = INTERCALATE.

1590 L. LLOYD *Dial. Daies* 65 Of these sixe houres, every fourth yeare one naturall daye is here intercalendered.

inter-cameral, -cardinal, -Caribbean, -caste, -cavernous, -celebration: see INTER- *pref.* 4 c, 6, 4 c, 5, 4 a, 2 a.

intercanalicular, -capillary, -carpal, etc.: see INTER- *pref.*

intercartilaginous (-kɑːtɪ'lædʒɪnəs), *a. Anat.* [INTER- 4 a.] Situated between cartilages.

1872 COHEN *Dis. Throat* 56 An inter-ligamentous rima..and an inter-cartilaginous rima. **1880** M. MACKENZIE *Dis. Throat and Nose* I. 519 Situated on the inter-cartilaginous portions of the trachea.

inter'catenated, *a. rare.* [INTER- 1 b.] Chained to each other; interchained.

1830 J. WILSON in *Blackw. Mag.* XXVII. 921 People..built up, of a quantity of intercatenated ideas given to them.

†**inter'ceasing,** *vbl. sb. Obs. rare.* [INTER- 1 a.] The action or condition of ceasing during an interval; a temporary cessation.

c **1450** *Mirour Saluacioun* 4358 Neure ony entercessing of contynuel punysshing. **1583** GOLDING *Calvin on Deut.* Pref. 1 So little ought the long interceassing of so great a benefite ..to make us to hold scorn of it. **1596** *Edw. III*, v. i. 76 We do proclaim a rest And interceasing of our painful arms.

intercede (ɪntə'siːd), *v.* Also 7 -ceed(e. [ad. L. *intercēd-ĕre* to come between, intervene, interfere, become surety for, in med.L. also to interpose on some one's behalf, to intercede; f. *inter* between + *cēdĕre* to go. Cf. F. *intercéder* (late 16th c.).]

1. *intr. Rom. Hist.* Of the tribunes: To interpose a veto.

1581 SAVILE *Tacitus, Hist.* III. ix. (1591) 175 Tertullinus Tribune of the people interceded (*note*, interposed his negative). **1600** HOLLAND *Livy* VI. 245 At the first their lawes were crossed by the interceding of their brethren Tribunes. **1747** MIDDLETON *Rom. Senate* 160. **1853** MERIVALE *Rom. Rep.* viii. (1867) 216 The senators could not oppose it by argument; but they gained one of the tribunes to *intercede* against it.

†**2.** To come *between*, in time, space, or action; to intervene. *Obs.*

1578 BANISTER *Hist. Man* I. 13 Betwixt yᵉ hollow, and the same Process, intercedeth [*printed* -cideth] a certaine soft and mouable Gristle. **1612** SELDEN *Illustr. Drayton's Poly-olb.* i. 21 From this time till the Norman conquest; 'twixt which intercedes cc.lxx.ix. yeares. **1620** T. GRANGER *Div. Logike* 109 When one thing mooveth, and another is mooved, motion intercedeth. **1633** HART *Diet of Diseased* III. xxx. 368 The distance alleaged..to interceed betwixt the bullet and the party thereby offended. **1677** R. CARY *Chronol.* II. i. I. vii. 108 Between the first..and the last.. there do intercede 51 Years. **1692** RAY *Dissol. World* II. iv. (1732) 127 The Beds of Sand interceeding between these Rows of Shells. **1799** KIRWAN *Geol. Ess.* 43 The vallies that intercede between them.

†**b.** To pass or exist *betwixt* persons. *Obs.*

1630 LORD *Banians* 10 With the courtesies interceding betwixt Man and Wife. **1679** JENISON *Popish Plot* 13 Betwixt whom and myself, there had interceeded several Offices of strict Friendship.

†**3.** *trans.* To come, pass, or lie between; to intervene between. *Obs.*

1614 SELDEN *Titles Hon.* II. i. 177 The time which interceded Henry the first and K. John. **1671** NEWTON in Rigaud *Corr. Sci. Men* (1841) II. 310, 6·6, the number equally interceding those limits, 6·3, and 6·9. **1728** PEMBERTON *Newton's Philos.* 352 The strongest reflection is made at those surfaces, which intercede transparent bodies differing most in density. **1799** KIRWAN *Geol. Ess.* 94 The hollows that interceded the abrupted masses.

†**4.** *intr.* To intervene by way of obstruction or prevention; to come in the way. *Obs.*

a **1661** FULLER *Worthies, Worcestershire* III. (1662) 172 He was challenged at Verona by an Italian..whom he had slain at the second weapon, had not some seasonably interceded. **1673** MARVELL *Reh. Transp.* II. 195 Subjects are bound..to obey the Magistrate Actively in all things where their Duty to God intercedes not.

5. *intr.* To interpose on behalf of another or others.

1606 HOLLAND *Sueton.* 266 Himselfe affrighted as it were with the rigorous cruelty of that punishment, would intercede in these words. **1612–15** BP. HALL *Contempl., O.T.* XXI. viii, I heare not one man open his mouth to intercede for the offender. **1656** BRAMHALL *Replic.* ii. 116 The Emperour and other Roman Catholick Princes interceded with her for the displaced Bishops. **1671** MILTON *Samson* 920, I to the lords will intercede, not doubting Their favourable ear, that I may fetch thee From forth this loathsome prison-house. **1704** ATTERBURY *Serm. 1 Tim.* ii. 1, 2, 3. 10 Our Interceding with God in the behalf of Kings and all that are in Authority. **1839** KEIGHTLEY *Hist. Eng.* II. 30 More requested him to intercede with the King. **1841** LANE *Arab. Nts.* I. 111 The Family of the favoured Prophet shall intercede for me.

†**b.** *trans.* To obtain (a thing) by intercession.

c. To intercede with (a person). *Obs. rare.*

1632 J. HAYWARD tr. *Biondi's Eromena* 172 Your Highnesse: whom I humbly beseech to intercede some remission for me. **1698** in *Col. Rec. Pennsylv.* I. 543 Had I known you had been interceded about it.

Hence **inter'ceding** *vbl. sb.* and *ppl. a.*

1600 [see above 1]. **1611** FLORIO, *Intercedente*, interceeding, suing or going betweene. **1656** EARL MONM. *Advt. fr. Parnass.* 336 The offers and intercedings of these noble men. **1657** W. RAND tr. *Gassendi's Life Peiresc* II. 26 The difference of the interceding Meridians might be calculated. **1848** R. I. WILBERFORCE *Incarnation* xiv. (1852) 414 The operations of the interceding Word and sanctifying Spirit.

†**inter'cedence.** *Obs. rare*⁻¹. [f. next: see -ENCE.] Intervention.

1640 BP. REYNOLDS *Passions* xxxiv. 408 The acts of the soule are educ'd immediately in it selfe, without the Intercedence of any organ whereby sensitive faculties work.

†**inter'cedent,** *a.* and *sb. Obs.* [ad. L. *intercēdent-em*, pr. pple. of *intercēdĕre*.]

A. *adj.* Coming between; intervening.

1578 BANISTER *Hist. Man* I. 32 A Cartilage also is intercedent, which..holdeth..them together. **1610** HEALEY *St. Aug. Citie of God* Argt. 9 Some years passed..before I could..finish..by reason of many intercedent affaires. **1657–83** EVELYN *Hist. Relig.* (1850) I. 170 Her [the Soul's] objects need no intercedent organ or medium between it and the faculty. **1727** in BAILEY vol. II. **1775** in ASH.

B. *sb.* An intercessor.

a **1661** HOLYDAY *Juvenal* 12 Some she-intercedents did obtain pardon of great informers for some offenders.

interceder (ɪntə'siːdə(r)). [f. INTERCEDE *v.* + -ER¹.] One who intercedes; an intercessor; a go-between; one who intervenes.

a **1656** USSHER *Ann.* (1658) 421 He had promised them to be an interceder with the Senate. **1675** *3 Inhumane Murthers* 2 Whether her Daughter had been an Interceder between him and his Sweet-Heart..is not certainly known. **1843** LYTTON *Last Bar.* IV. vi, Warwick listens to no interceders between himself and his passions.

intercell ('ɪntə,sɛl), *a.* [INTER- 5.] = next.

1847–9 TODD *Cycl. Anat.* IV. 120/1 Fluid intercell substance is nothing more than non-solidified blastema.

intercellular (ɪntə'sɛljʊlə(r)), *a.* [INTER- 4 a.] Situated between or among cells. Hence **inter'cellularly** *adv.*, between cells.

1835 LINDLEY *Introd. Bot.* (1848) I. 150 Only two cells form an intercellular passage, not three or four. **1845** TODD & BOWMAN *Phys. Anat.* I. 92 The intercellular substance is not exactly white fibrous tissue. **1875** BENNETT & DYER *Sachs' Bot.* 93 The fibro-vascular bundle consists at first of similar cells combined without intercellular spaces. **1935** E. A. BESSEY *Text-bk. Mycol.* (1939) x. 251 The mycelium is long, slender and branching, growing intercellularly within the host. **1950** J. C. WALKER *Plant Path.* viii. 346 The fungus develops in the epidermal wall..and it also proceeds intercellularly.

intercellulary (ɪntə'sɛljʊlərɪ), *a.* = prec.

1874 COOKE *Fungi* (1875) 265 These organs originate from the intercellulary tubes of the brown tissue.

intercensal (ɪntə'sɛnsəl), *a.* [Improperly f. INTER- 4 b + L. *censu-s* CENSUS + -AL¹: the etymological form would be *intercensual*: see CENSUAL.] Of, or belonging to the interval between two censuses, occurring between two censuses.

1887 *Leeds Mercury* 3 Feb. 4/6 The rate of growth during the intercensal period has been the same as in the decade preceding 1881. **1891** *Athenæum* 20 June 803/3 Methods.. suggested for estimating the population of towns in intercensal years. **1894** *Times* 6 Jan. 12/1 The average annual rate of growth in the last intercensal period.

intercentral (ɪntə'sɛntrəl), *a. Phys.* [INTER- 4 a.]

a. Situated between the centra of the vertebræ: see CENTRUM. **b.** Connecting, or relating to the connexion of, nerve-centres: see CENTRE *sb.* 7 a.

1870 ROLLESTON *Anim. Life* 21 These vertebrae..being articulated simply by ball and shallow socket joints on their centra and intercentral fibrocartilaginous discs. **1878** *Smithsonian Rep.* 419 *note*, A nerve tubule..has the same properties whether it be of intercentral or peripheral significance. **1887** *Syd. Soc. Lex.*, *Intercentral nerves*, nerve fibres which connect ganglionic centres, as in co-ordinated movements.

‖**inter'centrum.** *Comp. Anat.* [f. INTER- 3 + CENTRUM.] A wedge-shaped or chevron-shaped process, generally situated between the centra, occurring on the ventral aspect of the vertebral column in many Vertebrates, and especially in Reptiles; = HYPAPOPHYSIS.

1878 E. D. COPE in *Amer. Naturalist* XII. 319 The basal portions of the chevron bones are continued throughout the greater part of the vertebral column in the Permian genera *Clepsydrops, Metarmasaurus* and *Epicaudylus*, forming elements to which I have given the name of intercentra. **1891** BOULANGER in *Proc. Zool. Soc. Lond.* 115 [Treated as synonymous with *Hypapophysis*]. **1897** EADOW in *Phil. Trans.* CLXXXVII B. 24.

intercept ('ɪntəsɛpt), *sb.* [ad. L. *intercept-um*, neut. of *interceptus*: see next. In sense 4 and perh. in sense 1, from INTERCEPT *v.*]

1. An interception. *spec.* of a ball passed or thrown to an opponent.

1821 J. BANIM *Damon & Pythias* IV. ii, This hand has cast An intercept between him and the block! **1954** in WEBSTER Add. **1960** T. MCLEAN *Kings of Rugby* xi. 143 Meredith made an intercept.

2. *Math.* The part of a line lying between two points at which it is intersected by lines or planes.

1864 in WEBSTER. **1878** GURNEY *Crystallogr.* 18 The lengths..which are cut off by the plane..from the axes are called its intercepts. **1882** C. SMITH *Conic Sect.* (1885) 15 To find the equation of a straight line in terms of the intercepts which it makes on the axes.

3. *Navigation.* The angular difference between the calculated and the observed zenith distances of a heavenly body.

1901 J. R. WALKER *Explanation Method Obtaining Position at Sea* 15 Let the difference between the calculated and observed zenith distance be *k* miles nearer (say) at the first observation and *l* miles further at the second. Let the extremities of these intercepts be A and B. **1939** *Geogr. Jrnl.* XCIV. 254 Nowadays the best way of obtaining latitude and longitude with a theodolite is the quadrantal and intercept method. **1969** G. RICHARDS *Sextant Observations* iii. 92 The difference in value between the true altitude and the tabulated altitude is the intercept, and it can be 'Towards' (the body) or 'Away' (from the body).

4. A conversation, message, code, etc., that is picked up or discovered by the use of a concealed microphone, by listening to a radio communication, etc.; a device for achieving this.

1942 *Sun* (Baltimore) 10 Dec. 1/3 Distributing these copied excerpts to Government departments and officials who might have an interest in such 'intercepts', as they are called. **1945** *Ibid.* 30 Nov. 3 In the War Department..the intercepts were shown only to Secretary Henry L. Stimson, [etc.]. **1958** *Manch. Guardian* 13 Jan. 4 The 'intercepts' (transcripts of recordings obtained by wire-tapping)..were used as evidence in the hearing. **1967** 'W. HAGGARD' *Conspirators* xii. 123 We can't monitor every wavelength round the clock..but we've picked up one or two intercepts between Kaunas and this diplomat. **1972** R. LUDLUM *Osterman Weekend* i. 32 Intercepts have been placed on all telephones. **1973** *N.Y. Times* 22 June 35 Given torrents of intercepts..cryptanalysts could not reach a solution for thousands of years.

†**intercept,** *ppl. a. Obs. rare.* [ad. L. *intercept-us*, pa. pple. of *intercipĕre*: see next.] Intercepted. **a.** as *pa. pple.* **b.** as *adj.*

c **1391** CHAUCER *Astrol.* II. §39 Thay mene the arch meridian þat is contiened or intercept [*v.r.* except] by-twixe the cenyth and the equinoxial. **1715** DE MOIVRE in *Phil. Trans.* XXIX. 338 A Curve whose Ordinates..are equal to the Tangents of their respective intercept Arcs.

intercept (ɪntə'sɛpt), *v.* Also 6 enter-. [f. L. *intercept-*, ppl. stem of *intercipĕre*, f. *inter* between + *capĕre* to take, seize. Cf. F. *intercepter* (Cotgr. 1611).]

1. *trans.* To seize, catch, or carry off (a person, ship, letter, etc.) on the way from one place to another; to cut off from the destination aimed at.

a **1548** HALL *Chron., Hen. VII* 28 b, Which goyng prevely out..roade about the walles to viewe and see their strength, was sodeynly intercepted and taken of hys enemies. **1560** DAUS tr. *Sleidane's Comm.* 409 b, Letters..sent at this time to the Princes confederated and others, but intercepted. **1593** SHAKS. *3 Hen. VI*, II. i. 114, I..Marcht toward S. Albons, to intercept the Queene. *a* **1661** FULLER *Worthies* (1840) II. 515 He wrote Postils on the Proverbs, and other sermons, which the envy of time hath intercepted from us. **1709** STEELE *Tatler* No. 44 ¶7 Sir John Leak, who lies off of Dunkirk, had intercepted several Ships. **1847** PRESCOTT *Peru* (1850) II. 233 He also posted a large body..to watch the movements of the enemy, and to intercept supplies. **1868** E. EDWARDS *Ralegh* I. xii. 233 The utmost endeavour was to be made to intercept and capture the homeward bound fleets.

fig. *c* **1540** tr. *Pol. Verg. Eng. Hist.* (Camden) I. 162 Beinge intercepted bie deathe, [he] lefte this worcke to be accomplished to his successor Oswaldus.

b. To stop the natural course of (light, heat, water, etc.); to cut off (light) *from* anything.

1545 JOYE *Exp. Daniel* x. (R.), God will shortely intercept your brethe..if ye repent not. **1665** GLANVILL *Scepsis Sci.* xix. 124 Like paint on Glass, which intercepts and dyes the light. *a* **1711** KEN *Div. Love* Wks. (1838) 302 Ah, Lord! there is a dark cloud of ignorance spread over my soul, that intercepts thy beams. **1821** CRAIG *Lect. Drawing* iv. 233 To shadow the parts..from which the light is intercepted. **1856** STANLEY *Sinai & Pal.* xiv. 465 A blue curtain is drawn across the top to intercept the rain admitted through the dome.

†**c.** To interrupt, break in upon (esp. a narrative or a person speaking). *Obs.*

1581 J. BELL *Haddon's Answ. Osor.* 299 Whom the Pope with open mouth entercepted most arrogantly saying [etc.]. **1588** SHAKS. *Tit. A.* III. i. 40 In some sort they are better than the Tribunes, For that they will not intercept my tale. **1644** SIR E. DERING *Prop. Sacrif.* bb, Some will intercept me with a question. **1759** JOHNSON *Rasselas* xxxviii, I could not listen without intercepting the tale.

d. To stop, check, or cut off (passage or motion) from one place to another.

1596 SPENSER *State Irel.* Wks. (Globe) 661/1 Garrisons.. allwayes readye to intercept his going or coming. **1683** *Brit. Spec.* 251 A Fleet of English Vessels, sent out..to intercept his passage. **1838** THIRLWALL *Greece* II. 313 To destroy the bridges, and intercept the return of Xerxes. **1855** MACAULAY *Hist. Eng.* xvi. III. 636 He was seized with an apprehension that his flight might be intercepted.

†**e.** *absol.* or *intr. Obs.*

1612 ROWLANDS *Knaue Harts* 23 Till that Death doe intercept, Now we are borne, we must, and will be kept. **1647** N. BACON *Disc. Govt. Eng.* I. lxi. (1739) 120 Thefts belonged to the Sheriff's Court; and (if the Lords Court intercepts not) all batteries and woundings. **1682** WHELER

Journ. Greece VI. 409 As soon as we were come up, a Cloud of Snow intercepted between us and the most charming Prospect my Eyes ever beheld.

2. To cut off or stop (a person or thing) from accomplishing some purpose; to prevent, stop, hinder. Const. *from* (*inf.*). Now *rare* or *Obs.*

1576 FLEMING *Panopl. Epist.* 314, I was intercepted and hindered with most grievous and sorrowfull thoughtes. **1594** SHAKS. *Rich. III*, IV. iv. 137 O she, that might haue intercepted thee By strangling thee..From all the slaughters (wretch) that thou hast done. *a* **1626** BACON *Maxims & Uses Com. Law* ii. (1636) 7 The party altogether prevented and intercepted to come by his right. **1700** DRYDEN *Meleager & Atalanta* 33 He tramples down the spikes and intercepts the year. **1784** COWPER *Task* I. 514 Snug inclosures in the sheltered vale, Where frequent hedges intercept the eye. **1793** JEFFERSON *Writ.* (1859) IV. 95 We have been intercepted entirely from the commerce of furs with the Indian nations.

b. To check, prevent, or cut off (the operation or effect of an event, action, faculty, etc.).

1581 MULCASTER *Positions* xxxvii. (1887) 149 The embush, which lyeth still in waite to intercept our possession. **1591** SHAKS. *1 Hen. VI*, I. iv. 14 To intercept this inconuenience, A Peece of Ordnance 'gainst it I haue placed. **1618** BOLTON *Florus* (1636) 84 The Victory was intercepted by tempest, and the tryumph miscarried by Shipwracke. **1754** SHERLOCK *Disc.* (1759) I. iv. 158 A very thick Film over [his eyes] intercepts all sight. **1843** J. MARTINEAU *Chr. Life* (1867) 286 Causes less excusable also intercept its influence.

3. To mark off or include (a certain space) between two points or lines; hence, to contain, enclose. *spec.* in *Math.* (see INTERCEPT *sb.* 2).

1571 DIGGES *Pantom.* I. xxxi. K j a, I fynde 10 partes in my scale of altitudes, intercepted with the perpendicular lyne. **1647** LILLY *Chr. Astrol.* iv. 37, I conclude that the Signe ♈ is intercepted; for so we say when a Signe is not upon any of the cuspes of Houses, but is included betwixt one House and another. **1686** W. HARRIS tr. *Lemery's Course Chem.* (ed. 3) 390 The pores of Silver being very near one another, and of a much greater number, do intercept less solid matter, and consequently it must be lighter. **1760–72** tr. *Juan & Ulloa's Voy.* (ed. 3) I. 14 The number of degrees intercepted between the magnetic and true north of the world. **1793** SMEATON *Edystone L.* 184 The whole time intercepted betwixt the first stroke upon the Rock, and leaving the Lighthouse compleat, was 3 years, 9 weeks, 3 days. **1827** HUTTON *Course Math.* I. 317 Any two parallel chords intercept equal arcs.

4. To cut off (one thing) *from* (another), or (elliptically) from sight, access, etc. †Also with *of*.

1662 H. MORE *Philos. Writ.* Pref. Gen. 13 There being other properties in Body that intercepted from it the capacity of perceiving. **1697** DAMPIER *Voy.* I. 478 These Bays are intercepted, or divided from each other, with as many little rocky points of Woodland. **1700** DRYDEN *Flower & Leaf* 220 Thick as the college of the bees in May, When swarming o'er the dusky fields they fly..and intercept the sky. **1765** STERNE *Tr. Shandy* VII. xl, When I saw the gate which intercepted the tomb, my heart glowed within me. **1814** CHALMERS *Posth. Wks.* (1849) VI. 197 The glass which now intercepts from the eye of the mind the realities of the future world.

intercepted (ɪntəˈsɛptɪd), *ppl. a.* [f. prec. + -ED¹.] Caught or stopped by the way, cut off, etc.: see the verb.

1623 COCKERAM, *Intercepted*, taken by the way. **1665** BOYLE *Occas. Refl.* IV. xi. (1848) 235 A private Whisper, or the Intimation from..an intercepted Letter. **1700** DRYDEN *Sigism. & Guisc.* 118 A glimmering and malignant light..A twilight of an intercepted day. **1888** J. INGLIS *Tent Life Tigerland* 133 Still lagoons of intercepted flood water.

b. *spec.* in *Math.* of part of a line or curve. (Cf. INTERCEPT *sb.* 2.)

1702 RALPHSON *Math. Dict.* App. Conic Sections 10 In a Parabola..the intercepted Axes ED, EO. **1706** PHILLIPS, *Intercepted Arcs* or *Intercepted Diameters*, a Term in Conick Sections, the same as *Abscissæ*. **1837** WHEWELL *Hist. Induct. Sc.* (1857) I. 153 The intercepted portion of a circumference.

†**inter'cepter.** *rare.* [f. as prec. + -ER¹.] One who intercepts, an INTERCEPTOR.

1601 SHAKS. *Twel. N.* III. iv. 242 Thy intercepter, full of despight..attends thee at the Orchard end. **1611** [see INTERCEPTOR]. **1880** LEWIS & SHORT *Latin Dict.*, *Interceptor*, an intercepter, usurper, embezzler.

inter'cepting, *vbl. sb.* [f. as prec. + -ING¹.] The action of the vb. INTERCEPT in its various senses; interception.

1598 FLORIO, *Intercetti*, interceptings of forfaited goods. **1611** *Ibid.*, *Intercettione*, an intercepting, a preuenting. **1603** KNOLLES *Hist. Turks* (1638) 197 [He] laid strong ambushes for the intercepting of his enemies. **1614** BP. HALL *Epist.* III. x, His life..he accounts lent to him, that he may give it for his master: the intercepting of whose harmes, he holds both his duty and honor. **1711** *Fingall MSS.* in *10th Rep. Hist. MSS. Comm.* App. v. 142 [He] offered his service towards the intercepting of that great convoy. **1881** *Athenæum* 1 Oct. 425/2 The intercepting of the letter.

inter'cepting, *ppl. a.* [f. as prec. + -ING².] That intercepts, in senses of the vb.

intercepting carrier: see quot. 1865. ***intercepting trap***, in house-drainage, a trap placed at or near the outfall into a main sewer, generally connected with a system of ventilation.

1665 GLANVILL *Scepsis Sci.* xiii. 76 We may as well say that the Sun is the Cause of the Shadow, which is the effect of the intercepting Opacity. **1826** KIRBY & SP. *Entomol.* IV. 346 *Intercepting*,..when the trochanter intervenes between the thigh and the coxa, so as entirely to separate them. **1853** KANE *Grinnell Exp.* xvi. (1856) 125 We were forced to cut through some intercepting ice. **1865** *Standard* 11 July, The plaintiff..is what is called..an *intercepting carrier*; that is to collect parcels, pack all for one town in one package and forward them to the agent in that town who delivers them..paying the Company by tonnage rates.

interception (ɪntəˈsɛpʃən). [ad. L. *interceptiōn-em*, n. of action f. *intercipĕre* to INTERCEPT: see -TION. Cf. F. *interception* (16th c., Paré).]

1. a. The action of intercepting; seizing or stopping (a person or thing) in the way; the fact of being intercepted or stopped; an instance of this.

1599 SHAKS. *Hen. V*, II. ii. 7 The King hath note of all that they intend, By interception, which they dreame not of. **1611** SPEED *Hist. Gt. Brit.* VII. iv. (1623) 205 The King holding himselfe now sure from all interceptions. **1615** G. SANDYS *Trav.* 22 Such dispersed encounters, such long pursuites, interception of scouts [etc.]. **1700** TYRRELL *Hist. Eng.* II. 892 There were..great Plunderings and Robberies committed in the Marches, which they only termed Interceptions or Seizures. **1868** E. EDWARDS *Ralegh* I. xxvii. 683 He had recourse to the interception of letters written by and to Lady Ralegh.

b. The cutting off of anything in its natural course, action, extent, etc., *esp.* of light.

1624 WOTTON *Archit.* I. in *Reliq.* (1651) 267 The Pillars..will, by interception of the Sight, somwhat in appearance diminish the breadth. **1653** GATAKER *Vind. Annot. Jer.* 41 The interception of the light of the Sun..arises from the interposition of the body of the Moon. **1790** BEATTIE *Moral Sc.* I. I. II. §33 Silence is the effect of a total interception of the voice. **1860** TYNDALL *Glac.* II. iii. 244 The interception of radiant heat.

†**c.** *Med.* The interruption of the motion or passage of bodily humours. *Obs.*

1597 A. M. tr. *Guillemeau's Fr. Chirurg.* 40b/1 Any derivatione, revulsione, interceptione, or evacuatione of anye matter. **1615** CROOKE *Body of Man* 43 The interception of the Vrine is mortall. **1661** LOVELL *Hist. Anim. & Min.* 333 The rabies..is a madnesse..it's cured, by interception [etc.]. [**1855** MAYNE *Expos. Lex.*, *Interceptio*,..formerly applied to a kind of remedy when the motion of the humours, and especially of the blood was interrupted: interception.]

d. The action of closing in on and trying to destroy an enemy aircraft or missile. Also *attrib.*

1941 in R. W. Zandvoort et al. *Wartime English* (1957) 102 The toll of enemy raiders increases as the R.A.F. improves its methods of interception. **1955** *Bull. Atomic Sci.* Mar. 79/2 There is a great deal more that can be done to set up an effective warning and interception system. **1955** *Sci. News Let.* 15 Oct. 243/1 Once in the air, the missile's miniature radar and its own electronic computer—a baby version of the one that launched it—would keep it on an interception course. **1958** C. C. ADAMS et al. *Space Flight* 64 Surface-to-surface and intercontinental missiles are, generally, a means for delivering atomic and hydrogen bombs as a sort of 'interception-proof' air weapon.

2. The fact of containing or enclosing between points, lines, or boundaries; inclusion. *rare.*

1665 BOYLE *Exp. Hist. Cold* ix. §1 Made up of icy fragments cemented together, with the interception of considerable cavities filled with air. *Mod.* The line between the points of interception.

inter'ceptive, *a.* [f. ppl. stem of L. *intercipĕre*: see INTERCEPT *v.* and -IVE.] Having the quality of intercepting.

1819 FOSTER *Pop. Ignorance* (1834) 143 The awful interceptive lines of that other arrangement. **1860** RUSSELL *Diary India* I. 291, I repaired once more to the Dilkoosha only to find the dust more hopelessly interceptive than before. **1881** *Argosy* XXXII. 148 To peer round obstructing pyramids of plants or interceptive dishes of grapes.

inter'ceptor. [a. L. *interceptor*, agent-n. f. *intercipĕre* to INTERCEPT.] **a.** One who or that which intercepts.

1598 FLORIO, *Intercettore*, a preuenter, a forestaller, an encrocher, an interceptor [**1611** intercepter]. **1790** ANNA M. JOHNSON *Monmouth* III. 116 She..followed her furious interceptor to the house. **1884** *Health Exhib. Catal.* 50/1 Sewer Gas Interceptors..Grease Interceptors. Mud Interceptors. **1894** H. D. LLOYD *Wealth agst. Commw.* 375 People had been digging oil wells for 20 years that all the value might flow into the bank accounts of a few interceptors.

b. *Aeronaut.* A fast aircraft which is designed specifically for the interception of hostile aircraft. Also *attrib.*, as ***interceptor fighter***, ***'plane***.

1930 *Flight* 27 June 691/2 For a normal fighter, tanks to carry fuel for a flight of..2½ hours are sufficient. The new class of 'interceptor fighters' require even less endurance than that. **1934** *Times* 26 June *Air Suppl.* p. xvi/1 The modern interceptor was evoked by the fast day bomber. **1935** *Economist* 12 Oct. 708/1 There is no direct defence against air attack—'the bomber will always get through'—there never can be an adequate force of interceptor 'planes. **1948** 'N. SHUTE' *No Highway* xii. 294 One of the jet interceptor fighters coming into squadron use. **1966** *Electronics* 17 Oct. 104 The considerations will be presented in terms of a typical modern interceptor system. **1973** *Times* 14 May 12/6 The Warsaw Pact is also superior in light bombers, interceptors, and ground attack aircraft.

inter'ceptress. *rare*⁻¹. [f. INTERCEPTOR + -ESS.] A female interceptor.

1889 *Universal Rev.* Sept. 37 The interceptress soon would lack her eyes.

intercerebral, etc.: see INTER- *pref.*

†**inter'cess,** *v. Obs.* [f. L. *intercess-*, ppl. stem of *intercēdĕre* to INTERCEDE.] **a.** *intr.* To intercede. **b.** *trans.* To intercede with.

1556 HEYWOOD *Spider & F.* Q ij, But natures zeale I set to intercesse To you for me without moe wordes of me. **1589** WARNER *Alb. Eng.* II. Prose Add. (1612) 331 With great terrour and deuotion intercessing the Gods. **1624** GEE *Foot out of Snare* 32 They earnestly intercessed our Lady for him.

†**interce'ssation.** *Obs. rare.* [INTER- 2 b.] Cessation for the time; intermission.

1659 H. MORE *Immort. Soul* (1662) 125 If there was ever any intercessation of them [perceptive functions] in the astonishments of Death. **1680** —— *Apocal. Apoc.* 170 The intercessation of Paganism, when the Empire becomes Christian. **1681** —— *Exp. Dan.* VI. 185 An Intercessation of War is intimated.

intercession (ɪntəˈsɛʃən), *sb.* [ad. L. *intercessiōn-em*, n. of action f. *intercēdĕre* to INTERCEDE. Cf. F. *intercession* (Godef. *Compl.*).

Sense 1 does not occur in ancient L.; it is found in F. from 15th c.]

I. 1. The action of interceding or pleading on behalf of (*rarely* against) another; entreaty, solicitation, or prayer for another; mediation.

1534 TINDALE *Rom.* xi. 2 What the scripture sayth by the mouth of Helias, how he maketh intercession to God agaynst Israel. **1548** HALL *Chron.*, *Hen. VIII* 141 b, I will send to the kyng, and make humble intercession for your pardon. **1588** D. ROGERS in Ellis *Orig. Lett.* Ser. II. III. 145 Certaine goodes..confiscated the day before I came, were by my quicke intercession all released. **1659** WILLSFORD *Scales Comm.*, *Archit.* 36, I will here interpose a few lines betwixt them and the copy, as an intercession for the Printer, who is less culpable. **1725** DE FOE *Voy. round World* (1840) 79 It was upon my seeming intercession that he gave consent. **1865** DICKENS *Mut. Fr.* I. viii, He came back to make intercession for his sister.

b. *spec.* in religious use: Intercessory prayer.

1508 DUNBAR *Poems* viii. 26 Pray now for him..And for his saull mak intercessioun Unto the Lord that hes him bocht so deir. **1526** TINDALE *Heb.* vii. 25 He ever liveth to make intercession for vs. **1534** —— *1 Tim.* ii. 1, I exhorte therfore that..prayers, supplicacions, intercessions, and gevynge of thankes be had for all men. **1645** USSHER *Body Div.* (1647) 350 We are also bound to pray like-wise for others; which kinde of prayer is called Intercession. **1726** LAW *Serious C.* xxi, Intercession is a great and necessary part of christian Devotion. **1782** PRIESTLEY *Corrupt. Chr.* I. IV. 377 Justinian [made] use of the intercession of the virgin. **1848** R. I. WILBERFORCE *Incarnation* ix. (1852) 214 We are to address God only through Him whose Intercession as man is the ground of our hope.

†**c.** Loosely used for a petition or pleading on one's own behalf. *Obs.*

1500–20 DUNBAR *Poems* xiii. 54 Thair cumis ȝung monkis ..Thay ar so humill of intercessioun, All mercyfull wemen thair eirandis grantis. *a* **1548** HALL *Chron. Hen. VII* 45 b, He was content at his intercession to departe. **1742** FIELDING *J. Andrews* IV. xv, Unbuttoning his coat at the intercession of the company.

II. In other senses, repr. ancient L. *intercessio*.

2. *Rom. Hist.* The action of interposing a veto: cf. INTERCEDE *v.* 1.

1573–80 BARET *Alv.* I 202 To make Intercession, to let, *intercedo*. **1747** MIDDLETON *Rom. Senate* 160 The general law of these intercessions was, that any magistrate might inhibit the acts of his equal, or inferior. **1753** CHAMBERS *Cycl. Suppl.*, *Intercession*,..was used in antient Rome, for the act of a tribune of the people, or other magistrate, by which he inhibited the acts of other magistrates; or even in the case of the tribunes, the decrees of the senate. **1843** *Penny Cycl.* XXV. 202/1 In this year [B.C. 394] we meet with the first instance of the intercession (veto) of one tribune rendering the resolution of his colleagues void.

†**3.** A coming or existing among or between; interposition, intervention. *Obs.*

1605 TIMME *Quersit.* I. v. 20 Whose extreames, to wit, fixed and volatile, of the sulphurus salt or the niterus..are coupled together by intercession. **1638** WILKINS *New World* iii. (1707) 30 The Bones..and the Flesh..are not joined together but by the Intercession of Membranes.

4. *Rom. Law.* (See quot.)

1875 POSTE *Gaius* III. (ed. 2) 399 Intercession is the assumption of liability for the debt of another person by negotiation or contract with his creditor.

¶**5.** = INTERCESSATION; intermission. *Obs.*

1572 *Latimer's Serm. Lord's Prayer* iii. 8 We must call upon God without intercession. —— *Serm. Lincoln* iii. 87 We must pray at all times without intercession [*ed.* 1562 intermission *in both cases*]. **1661** *Except. agst. Liturgy* 7 Whence are caused many unnecessary intercessions and abruptions. *a* **1683** OWEN *Expos. Heb.* (1790) III. 394 There was an intercession of its administration for seventy years.

†**inter'cession,** *v. Obs. rare*⁻¹. [f. prec. sb.: cf. OF. *intercessionner* (Godef.).] *intr.* To make intercession.

1593 NASHE *Christ's T.* (1613) 49 Violently, eagerly haue I intercessioned vnto her, to gather herselfe vnto mee.

intercessional (ɪntəˈsɛʃənəl), *a.* [f. as prec. + -AL¹.] Of or pertaining to intercession.

1845 J. A. JAMES in *Ess. Chr. Union* iv. 207 That touching intercessional petition.

intercessionary (ɪntəˈsɛʃənərɪ), *a.* [f. as prec. + -ARY.] Employed in intercession.

1861 LYTTON & FANE *Tannhäuser* 109 Thine intercessionary Saint while now For thee she sues about the Throne of Thrones.

†**inter'cessionate**, *v.* *Obs.* [f. as prec. + -ATE[3] 7.]

1. *intr.* To make intercession; = INTERCEDE *v.*

1593 NASHE *Christ's T.* (1613) 105 They haue but one houre to intercessionate for their soules. **1598** TOFTE *Alba* (1880) 67 Yet Ile not leaue to intercessionate, To her hard Breast, for my too gentle Hart. **1623** COCKERAM, *Intercessionate*, to intreat for one.

2. *trans.* To intercede with, entreat.

1594 NASHE *Terrors Night* G iij b, They..neuer ceased extensiuely to intercessionate God for his speedie recouerie.

†**inter'cessionment.** *Obs.* *rare*$^{-1}$. [f. INTERCESSION *v.* + -MENT.] Making of intercession; intercession.

1593 NASHE *Christ's T.* (1613) 187 With one vnited intercessionment, thus reconcile your selues vnto him.

intercessive (ɪntə'sɛsɪv), *a.* [ad. late L. *intercessīv-us* (Cassian), f. *intercess-*, ppl. stem of *intercēdĕre* to INTERCEDE: see -IVE.] Characterized by intercession; intercessory.

1624 HEYWOOD *Gunaik.* III. 155 By Polycrita's intercessive intreaties surprized Diognetus scapes with life. **1814** MRS. J. WEST *Alicia de Lacy* I. 215 The delightful music of praise and intercessive prayer.

intercessor (ɪntə'sɛsə(r)). [a. L. *intercessor*, agent-n. from *intercēdĕre* to INTERCEDE. In sense 1 not used in ancient L., but in OF. *entrecessor* (13th c.), *intercesseur* (16th c.).]

1. One who intercedes or interposes on behalf of another; a mediator.

1482 *Monk of Evesham* (Arb.) 91 The whyche schulde be deuowt and meke intercessours to god bothe for hym that byn a lyue and for hym that byn dede. **1665** MANLEY *Grotius' Low C. Warres* 360 He would advise with the King, to whom he would also be an Intercessor, for attaining such things as related to the Peace. **1667** MILTON *P.L.* III. 219 On mans behalf Patron or Intercessor none appeerd. **1769** ROBERTSON *Chas. V* (1796) III. x. 220 Charles..eluded a demand made by such powerful intercessors. **1868** FREEMAN *Norm. Conq.* II. vii. 103 Beorn was persuaded to undertake the office of intercessor with the King on Swegen's behalf.

b. In religious use: One that intercedes with God for man; a Mediator.

1526 *Pilgr. Perf.* (W. de W. 1531) 178 And that we sholde make the holy sayntes in heuen our intercessours. *a* **1540** BARNES *Wks.* (1573) 337/1 If you wyll bee Christes, make hym alonely your mediatour and your intercessour to the father of heauen. **1664–94** SOUTH *Twelve Serm.* II. 73 Some great Umpire, and Intercessour, to open him a new way of access to God. **1703** S. CLARKE *Evid.* Prop. xiii. (R.), It cannot be thought unreasonable..that a mediator or intercessor should be appointed between God and man. **1856** MRS. CONANT *Eng. Bible Transl.* iv. (1881) 29 Saint worship..had substituted, for the one Mediator, a countless army of intercessors in the Saints of the Romish Calendar.

†**2.** One who intervenes between parties; an intermediary; a go-between. *Obs.*

1554 *Act 1 & 2 Ph. & Mary* c. 8 §25 We..make most humble Suit unto your Majesties to be likewise Means and Intercessors, that all Occasions of Contention..may..be abolished. **1578** T. N. tr. *Conq. W. India* 362 By intercessors he was assured unto the Duke of Beiar his brothers daughter. **1598** FLORIO, *Intercessore*, an intercessour, one..that sues, that goes betweene,..a mediator.

3. *Eccles.* (See quot.) *Obs.*

1727–41 CHAMBERS *Cycl.* s.v., *Intercessor* is also a term heretofore applied to such bishops, as, during the vacancy of a see, administered the bishoprick, till a successor to the deceased bishop had been elected..The third council of Carthage calls these *interventors*.

intercessorial (ɪntəsɛ'sɔərɪəl), *a.* [f. as next + -AL[1].] Of or pertaining to an intercessor.

1776 BP. HORNE *Comm. Psalms* ii. 8. **1860** PUSEY *Min. Proph.* 538 The priest's office was to stand before the Lord, his intercessorial office to offer gifts and sacrifices for sin. **1863** LE FANU *Ho. by Churchyard* (ed. 2) II. 197 A kind of graceful, intercessorial relation to the object of his highly prudent passion.

intercessory (ɪntə'sɛsərɪ), *a.* [f. L. type **intercessōri-us*, f. *intercessor*, in OF. *intercessoire*: see -ORY.] Having the function or purpose of intercession; that intercedes or pleads for others.

1576 FLEMING *Panopl. Epist.* To Rdr. ¶v b, Of letters.. Intercessorie, Commendatorie..there be sundrie sortes. **1720** EARBERY *Mod. Fanat.* 39 The Lord's Prayer has an intercessory petition for our enemies. **1782** PRIESTLEY *Corrupt. Chr.* I. II. 161 His solemn intercessory prayer before his death. **1841** TRENCH *Parables* (1860) 323 It is here intercessory prayer, prayer for the needs of others, in which we are bidden to be instant.

interchaff, etc.: see INTER- *pref.*

†**interchain**, *v.* *Obs.* *rare.* Also 7 enter-. [INTER- 1 b.] *trans.* To chain or link one to another.

1590 SHAKS. *Mids. N.* II. ii. 49 (Qo. 1600) Two bosomes interchained with an oath So then two bosomes, and a single troth. **1603** FLORIO *Montaigne* II. xi. (1632) 237 Vices, errors ..for the most part entertaine and enterchaine them-selves one with another. *a* **1649** DRUMM. OF HAWTH. *Poems* Wks. (1711) 13/1 This moon, that sun, Those lesser fires..Be but the same, which under Saturn's reign Did the serpentine seasons interchain.

interchange ('ɪntətʃeɪndʒ), *sb.* Also 6–7 enter-, (6 -chaunge). [a. OF. *entrechange* (Godef.), f. *entrechangier*: see INTERCHANGE *v.*] The act or fact of interchanging.

1. a. The act of exchanging reciprocally; giving and receiving with reciprocity; reciprocal exchange (*of* commodities, courtesies, ideas, etc.) between two persons or parties.

1548 LD. SOMERSET *Epist. Scots* B j b, What can be more offered and more profered, then entercourse of merchaundises, enterchaunge of mariages. **1594** SHAKS. *Rich. III*, v. iii. 99 Ample enterchange of sweet Discourse. **1611** —— *Wint. T.* I. i. 30 With enter-change of Gifts, Letters, louing Embassies. **1632** HEYWOOD *1st Pt. Iron Age* III. Wks. 1874 III. 309 In hostile enter-change Of warlike blowes. **1791** COWPER *Odyss.* VIII. 463 With nimble interchange They pass'd it [the ball] to each other. **1804** EARL LAUDERD. *Publ. Wealth* (1819) 353 Promoting an interchange of commodities betwixt two countries. **1885** *Manch. Exam.* 28 Feb. 6/1 There was a remarkable interchange of courtesies between the two Houses of Parliament to-night.

b. *Cytology.* Reciprocal exchange of chromosome segments, esp. between non-homologous chromosomes.

1927 *Jrnl. Genetics* XVIII. 198 In other words, chromosomes I and IX seem to have undergone interchange of a terminal segment in the ancestry of the isomorphic *B* strain. **1963** LEWIS & JOHN *Chromosome Marker* I. iii. 66 Individuals which are heterozygous for an interchange are known as interchange heterozygotes. **1968** R. RIEGER *Gloss. Genetics & Cytogenetics* 440 An interchange of segments between homologous chromosomes is called 'fraternal', while one between nonhomologous chromosomes is called 'external'.

2. The change of each of two (or more) things, conditions, etc. for the other, or of one thing, etc. for another; the taking by each of the place or nature of the other.

1581 T. WATSON *Centurie of Loue* xlix. (Arb.) 85 How faine my soule an interchaunge would make Twixt this her present State and Limbo Lake. **1638** DRUMM. OF HAWTH. *Irene* Wks. (1711) 169 What gain you by your enterchange of war for peace? **1830** HERSCHEL *Stud. Nat. Phil.* 318 The experiments..are all perfectly explained by Prevost's theory of reciprocal interchange. **1885** CLODD *Myths & Dr.* I. v. 91 Lower races still ascribe power of interchange to man and brute.

3. Alternate or varied succession in time, order, or space; alternation, vicissitude.

1559 *Mirr. Mag.*, *Warwick* ii, My fame and shame her [Fortune's] shift full oft hath shaked, By enterchaunge alow and vp aloft. **1581** J. BELL *Haddon's Answ. Osor.* 481 b, As after light, followeth darkenesse, and after Calme come Clowdes: even so the whole course of this lyfe, hath his continuall enterchaunges. **1633** EARL MANCH. *Al Mondo* (1636) 8 In the courses of my life I haue had interchanges: the world it selfe stands upon vicissitudes. **1667** MILTON *P.L.* IX. 115 Sweet interchange Of Hill and Vallie, Rivers, Wood and Plaines, Now Land, now Sea. **1847** J. WILSON *Chr. North* (1857) II. 1 How endless the interchange of woods and meadows. **1874** SYMONDS *Sk. Italy & Greece* (1898) I. v. 87 Red anemones..with interchange of blue and lilac buds.

4. *attrib.* in reference to the passage of traffic from one railway line to another, as *interchange-service*, *station*, etc.

1887 *Pall Mall G.* 14 Apr. 9/1 The fares and rates to be.. charged in respect of through booking and interchange service. **1892** *Daily News* 7 June 6/1 Nearly 4,000 persons availed themselves of the interchange station with the Great Eastern Company's Chingford line at Hackney.

5. A road junction designed so that traffic streams do not intersect.

1944 *Sun* (Baltimore) 6 Dec. 7-o An accident on the Pennsylvania Turnpike near the New Stanton interchange. **1954** HEWES & OGLESBY *Highway Engin.* viii. 207 An interchange not only offers grade separation between the two traffic arteries, but in addition provides easy routes for vehicles transferring from one through facility to the other. **1958** H. M. SHERRARD *Austral. Road Pract.* xix. 365 Much ingenuity has been displayed in the design of such intersections or 'traffic interchanges'. **1962** *Amer. Speech* XXXVII. 267 A multilevel freeway interchange. **1967** *Gloss. Highway Engin. Terms* (*B.S.I.*), *Interchange*, a general term for a grade-separated junction of roads which provides free flow between them. **1968** *Listener* 29 Aug. 267/3 It was an important junction and interchange. **1970** *Daily Tel.* 14 Nov. 1/7 The Berrygrove interchange of the A41 and the M1. **1973** D. WESTHEIMER *Going Public* ix. 127 A four-mile long..traffic jam..backing up to the San Diego Freeway interchange.

interchange (ɪntə'tʃeɪndʒ), *v.* Also 4–7 enter-, (4 entre-, 5 entyr-), 4–6 -chaunge. [a. OF. *entre-changier* to change, disguise (Godef.), f. *entre-* (INTER- 2) + *changier*, *changer* to CHANGE.]

1. *trans.* Of two persons or parties: To exchange (commodities, gifts, courtesies, words, etc.) with each other; to give and receive in reciprocity.

c **1374** CHAUCER *Troylus* III. 1319 (1368) Sone affter this, spake they of sundry thinges..And pleying enterchaungeden hir ringes. **1534** MORE *Comf. agst. Trib.* II. Wks. 1170/1 Wyshed I..that wee hadde more often enterchanged words, and parted the talkyng betwene vs. **1593** SHAKS. *Lucr.* 70 The sovereignty of either being so great, That oft they interchange each other's seat. **1624** CAPT. SMITH *Virginia* IV. 142 Then we interchanged presents. **1661** BOYLE *Style of Script.* (1675) 140 The texts of the Bible interchange light with one another. **1708** J. PHILIPS *Cyder* II. 73 Amicable Talk, and moderate Cups Sweetly interchang'd. **1820** W. IRVING *Sketch Bk.* I. 20 There were repeated cheerings and salutations interchanged between the shore and the ship. **1849** MACAULAY *Hist. Eng.* ix. II. 543 They..interchanged opinions freely, and interchanged also good offices in perilous times. **1884** *Contemp. Rev.* Oct. 509 The great object now, is not to conquer, but to produce and interchange.

b. Of one person or party: To exchange (something) *with* another person.

1566 DRANT *Horace, Sat.* I. ix. E ij, I thoughte to interchaunge a worde. **1610** HEALEY *St. Aug. Citie of God* III. xvi. (1620) 121 Soone after perished hee himself, hauing enterchanged a many wounds with his foe. **1673** *Lady's Call.* I. v. §1 It do's in a sort communicate and enterchange properties with him. **1805** SIR E. BERRY 13 Oct. in Nicolas *Disp. Nelson* (1846) VII. 118 *note*, I interchanged signals with His Majesty's Ship, L'Aimable. **1853** J. H. NEWMAN *Hist. Sk.* (1873) II. I. ii. 49 The Romans interchanged embassies with its sovereign in the reign of..Justin the younger.

2. To put each of (two things) in the place of the other; to transpose or make an exchange between; †also, to exchange (one thing) *for* another; †to change (clothes).

c **1374** CHAUCER *Boeth.* III. pr. ii. 51 (Camb. MS.) And ther ben folk þat entrechaungen the causes and the endes of thyse forseyde goodes As they þat desyren rychesses to han power and delytes. **1593** SHAKS. *3 Hen. VI*, IV. vii. 3 Once more I shall enterchange My wained state, for Henries Regall Crowne. **1676** TEMPLE *Let. to Sir J. Williamson* 3 Apr., Greffier Fagel came to me from the States, to desire me, That I would interchange the Swedish Passports and theirs, which were both in my Hands. **1855** PUSEY *Doctr. Real Presence* Note G. 87 Our Saviour interchanged the names: and to the Body gave the name of the symbol, and to the symbol that of the Body. **1861** WRIGHT *Ess. Archæol.* II. xvi. 76 *L* and *r* were constantly interchanged in the languages of the middle ages. **1875** OUSELEY *Harmony* iii. 52 It is allowable occasionally to interchange dissonant notes in a fundamental discord.

3. To cause (things) to follow each other alternately or in succession; to alternate.

1561 T. NORTON *Calvin's Inst.* II. 146 As if they should quarell with God..for that his wil was to haue enterchanged courses betwene winter and sommer, betwene day and nighte. **1600** FAIRFAX *Tasso* XV. liv, Not as elsewhere now sunshine bright, now showres, Now heat, now cold, there enterchanged weare. **1874** SYMONDS *Sk. Italy & Greece* (1898) I. i. 9 Some sad and sombre moments should be interchanged with hours of merriment.

b. *intr.* To alternate *with*; †to change or become by turns.

1483 *Cath. Angl.* 116/1 To Entyrchaunge, *alternor*. *a* **1586** [see INTERCHANGING *ppl. a.*]. **1626** BACON *Sylva* §697 Those [Insecta] that Enterchange from Wormes to Flyes in the Summer, and from Flies to Wormes in the Winter. **1822–34** *Good's Study Med.* (ed. 4) I. 611 Quartan ague.. occasionally interchanges with dysentery.

interchangea'bility. [f. next + -ITY.] The quality of being interchangeable; interchangeableness.

1805 in W. PERRY *Dict.* **1884** *American* VIII. 313 The principle of the interchangeability of parts in machine construction. **1886** SYMONDS *Renaiss. It., Cath. React.* (1898) VII. ix. 78 The interchangeability of types in living creatures.

interchangeable (ɪntə'tʃeɪndʒəb(ə)l), *a.* (*adv.* and *sb.*) Also 5–7 enter-, 5–6 -chaungeable. [a. OF. *entrechangeable* (Godef.): see INTERCHANGE *v.* and -ABLE. Mod.F. has *interchangeable* (1870 in Littré *Suppl.*) perh. from English.]

†**1.** Given, done, caused, or exhibited, by each side to the other; mutual, reciprocal. *Obs.*

c **1450** *Mirour Saluacioun* 2999 Eure [= ever] enterchaungable envy. **1542–3** *Act 34 & 35 Hen. VIII*, c. 18 Indentures interchangeable, sealed with the seales of suche parties. **1571** DIGGES *Pantom.* IV. Defin. T j b, Proportion is a mutuall or enterchangeable relation of two magnitudes. **1594** J. DICKENSON *Arisbas* (1878) 83 Shedding teares, enterchaungeable tokens of their mutuall ioy. **1665** G. HAVERS *P. della Valle's Trav. E. India* 77 They have great correspondence by interchangeable Ambassies and Presents.

†**b.** as *adv.*: Mutually; = INTERCHANGEABLY 1.

1465 in Tytler *Hist. Scot.* (1864) II. 388 Ather of yhe pairtis hes geffyn till udiris, yair bodily aithis..and enterchangable, set to yair selis. **1496** *Newminster Cartul.* (Surtees) 196 Y[e] said Alex. and Robert enterchaungeable hath set to our seales. **1644** SLINGSBY *Diary* (1836) 128 Hereupon articles were drawn and interchangeable signed.

†**2. a.** Of two or more things: Coming or following in place of each other; alternating, successive, varying. *Obs.*

1561 T. NORTON *Calvin's Inst.* III. ii. (1634) 269 Therefore of necessity distrust and good hope must by enterchangeable courses reigne in thy minde. **1586** A. DAY *Eng. Secretary* I. (1625) 26 They have their Consuls, Tribunes, Pretors..and other interchangeable offices, as sometimes had Rome. **1658** SIR T. BROWNE *Gard. Cyrus* iv. 181 Darknesse and light hold interchangeable dominions, and alternately rule the seminal state of things. **1783** W. F. MARTYN *Geog. Mag.* I., Interchangeable vicissitudes of sunshine and rain.

†**b.** Of one thing: Subject to change from one condition, state, etc. to another; changeable. *Obs.*

1573–80 BARET *Alv.* I 203 The Interchangeable course of pleasure, *laboris ac voluptatis vicissitudo.* **1607** TOPSELL *Four-f. Beasts* (1658) 79 Very beautifull to behold, by reason of the variable and interchangeable skin, being full of spots. **1749** F. SMITH *Voy. Disc.* II. 43 Interchangeable Weather, from one Day excessive hot..changing to another Day intensely Cold.

3. Of two things: Capable of being put or used in the place of each other; admitting an exchange of place or function. Also, of one

thing: That may change places *with* some other thing.

a **1569** KINGESMYLL *Confl. Satan* (1578) 38 Thou art saued, thou art delivered, for these are interchangeable wordes, one self-same in speach. **1768–74** TUCKER *Lt. Nat.* (1834) II. 282 Personality is what makes a man to be himself, can never be divested..nor is interchangeable with that of any other creature. **1879** *Cassell's Techn. Educ.* IV. 205/1 In this process heat and time are, to a certain extent, interchangeable commodities. **1888** *Glasgow Even. Times* 27 Aug. 4/2 A convertible driving phaeton, fitted with interchangeable seats. **1897** F. HALL in *Nation* (N.Y.) LXIV. 105/2 Not one..recognizes it [*for the nonce*] as interchangeable with 'for the occasion'.

b. Capable of being exchanged or bartered.

1826 T. TOOKE *State of Currency* 87 Commodities which are interchangeable with other countries.

c. as *sb.* in *pl.*

1823 LAMB *Lett.* xii. *to Wordsworth* 111 A, B and C make a party. A dies. B not only loses A, but all A's part in C. C loses A's part in B, and so the alphabet sickens by subtraction of interchangeables.

interˈchangeableness. [f. prec. + -NESS.] The condition of being interchangeable; liability to interchange; alternation, variation.

1627 BP. HALL *Art Div. Medit.* viii, Being, without all interchangeablenesse, bent vpon the same discourse, the mind must needs grow weary. **1652–62** HEYLIN *Cosmogr.* II. (1682) 56 After much vicissitude and interchangeableness of affairs. **1810** HUSKISSON *Currency* 144 Nothing but its interchangeableness with cash can now restore [the credit of paper]. **1878** EDISON in *N. Amer. Rev.* CXXVI. 529 Having proper regard for the perfect interchangeableness of the various working parts of the apparatus.

interchangeably (ɪntəˈtʃeɪndʒəblɪ), *adv.* [f. as prec. + -LY^{2}. Cf. OF. *entrechangeablement.*]

1. By way of exchange, reciprocity, or return between two parties, or of mutual correspondence between things; mutually, reciprocally, respectively. Now *rare*; formerly freq. in the wording of legal compacts (see quots.).

[**1351** *Treaty betw. England & France* (Godef.), En tesmoing de les choses les chivalers..ont mis enterchangeablement lours seaulx a ceste presente cedule.] *c* **1375** *Sc. Leg. Saints, Machor* 1087 Eftire all þe cumpany has kissit entrechangeably. **1495** *Act 11 Hen. VII*, c. 39 *Preamble*, [Indentures] Yeven enterchaungeably aswel under the seale of oure seid Sovereign Lord, as the seale of the seid Edmond. **1547** *Newminster Cartul.* (Surtees) 315 The seyd partyez..enterchaungeably haue putt theyr Seales. **1637** HEYWOOD *Dialogues* i. Wks. 1874 VI. 96 Mate ..is a word That Sailers interchangeably afford To one another. **1710** STEELE *Tatler* No. 199 ¶7 To which we have interchangeably set our Hands, Hearts, and Seals, this 17th of July 1710. **1786** JEFFERSON *Writ.* (1859) I. 514, I put several together myself, taking the pieces at hazard..and found them to fit interchangeably in the most perfect manner. **1854** DE QUINCEY *Autobiog. Sk.* Wks. II. 283 Defiances..carried on interchangeably between barn-door cocks.

2. Alternately, in turn, one after the other.

1483 *Cath. Angl.* 116/1 Entirchawngeably, *alternatim.* **1581** LAMBARDE *Eiren.* IV. xix. (1588) 598 It is very likely that therupon the same [Sessions] were first kept interchangeably at two sundry townes. **1669** EVELYN *Diary* 9 July, There follow'd divers panegyric speeches both in prose and verse, interchangeably pronounc'd by the young students plac'd in the rostrums. **1710** STEELE *Tatler* No. 179 ¶8 Along the Gravel Walk, I have ranged interchangeably the Bay, the Mirtle, the Orange. **1744** A. DOBBS *Hudson's Bay* 12 All the Month of December was interchangeably three or four Days cold, and then a temperate Frost.

b. *Her.* (See quot.)

1882 CUSSANS *Her.* viii. (ed. 3) 129 When Charges are placed in parallel lines, so that the head of each appears between the tails of two others..they are said to be *Interchangeably posed.*

c. With interchange of state, condition, colour, etc.

1776 BP. HORNE *Comm. Psalms* lxviii. 13 The bright and beautiful plumage of an eastern dove, glistering interchangeably, as with silver and gold.

3. By way of interchange of two (or more) things, each taking the place of the (or an) other; hence of the use of words: synonymously, indifferently. Also const. *with.*

1587 GOLDING *De Mornay* xv. 250 Thus haue we three Articles which follow interchaungeably one another Insomuch that he which proueth any one of them, doth prooue them all three. **1636** PRYNNE *Unbish. Tim.* 126 [He] twice together cals him, interchaingably, both a Bishop and Elder. **1860** PUSEY *Min. Proph.* 150 Israel, the house of Israel, the Virgin of Israel, the sanctuaries of Israel, occur interchangeably as the object of Amos's Prophecy. **1873** EARLE *Philol. Eng. Tongue* (ed. 2) §516 *Thereof* is used interchangeably with *of it* in 1 Kings vii. 27.

interchanged (ɪntəˈtʃeɪndʒd), *ppl. a.* [f. INTERCHANGE *v.* + -ED^{1}.] Mutually or reciprocally exchanged; †alternated, successively varied (*obs.*).

1567 MAPLET *Gr. Forest* 3 b, Golden Berill..whose interchaunged greene colour resembleth almost the wan and yelow colour of Golde. **1581** J. BELL *Haddon's Answ. Osor.* 266 b, A certeine continuall order and enterchaunged course of the world. **1589** WARNER *Alb. Eng.* VII. xxxiv. (1612) 166 To his Grome himselfe was Grome, By interchaunged rayment. **1697** J. WOODWARD *Relig. Soc. Lond.* iii. (1701) 130 That by their interchanged counsels and exhortations they might the better maintain their integrity. **1885** *Athenæum* 17 Oct. 502/3 Deserted wives, interchanged babies..make up an oft-told tale.

†**interˈchangement.** *Obs.* [f. as prec. + -MENT.] = INTERCHANGE *sb.* 1.

1601 SHAKS. *Twel. N.* V. i. 162 A Contract of eternall bond of loue..Strengthned by enterchangement of your rings. **1796** *Plain Sense* I. 133 Interchangement of sentiments. *Ibid.* II. 113 The interchangement of the common-place civilities.

interˈchanger. [f. as prec. + -ER^{1}.] **1.** One who interchanges: see the verb.

1861 THORNBURY *Turner* (1862) I. 398 He saw no reason why the mere interchanger of commodities should get more by them than the planter from whose land they had come.

2. A heat exchanger.

1896 A. J. WALLIS-TAYLER *Refrigerating & Ice-Making Machinery* viii. 136 An interchanger was also sometimes provided, wherein the air that had done duty in the storage or cold chambers was utilised for further reducing the temperature of the compressed air. **1949** M. DAVIES *Physical Princ. Gas Liquefaction* vi. 86 The tubular type of interchanger carrying the compressed gas through a pipe mounted within a wider one which carries the expanded gas, is..more common..than the Hampson Spiral.

interˈchanging, *vbl. sb.* [f. as prec. + -ING^{1}.] The action of the vb. INTERCHANGE, in various senses; mutual or alternate exchanging.

c **1374** CHAUCER *Boeth.* I. met. v. 14 (Camb. MS.) Whi suffres thow þat slydynge fortune torneth so grete entrechaunginges of thinges? *Ibid.* IV. met. iv. 102 They moeuen..crwel batayles and wylnen to perise by entrechaungynges [*Add. MS.* -ynge] of dartes. **1553** GRIMALDE *Cicero's Offices* I. ii. (1558) 19 When he was sent to Rome aboute the enterchanging of prisoners. **1559** MORWYNG *Evonym.* Pref., The Art of enterchaunging of metalles. **1622** BACON *Hen. VII* 236 Hee had withall a strange kind of Interchanging of large and inexpected Pardons with seuere Executions. **1895** *Athenæum* 10 Aug. 185/1 There is one rule enunciated by Collier for the interchanging of the vowels.

interˈchanging, *ppl. a.* [f. as prec. + -ING^{2}.] That interchanges, in senses of the vb.

a **1586** SIDNEY *Arcadia* II. Wks. 1725 I. 212 With some interchanging changes of fortune, they begat of a just war, the best child, Peace. **1660** JER. TAYLOR *Duct. Dubit.* II. i, By this relation and interchanging reason it is necessary that those laws should be distinguished from all others. **1839** BAILEY *Festus* xix. (1852) 277 The interchanging universe Of sense and substance.

intercharge, -chase, -check, etc.: see INTER-.

interchondral (-ˈkɒndrəl), *a. Anat.* [f. INTER- 4 a + Gr. χόνδρ-ος cartilage + -AL^{1}.] Situated or occurring between cartilages, esp. those of the ribs.

1887 *Syd. Soc. Lex., Interchondral articulations,* the joints between the corresponding margins of the sixth, seventh, and eighth ribs.

inter-church, -city, -class, -coastal: see INTER- *pref.* 5, 4 c.

†**interˈcide,** *v.*^{1} *Obs. rare.* [ad. L. *intercīdere* to cut through, f. *inter* between + *cædĕre* to cut.]

a. = INCIDE *v.*^{1} 2. **b.** To interrupt, intermit.

1541 R. COPLAND *Guydon's Quest. Chirurg.*, The syxth vtylyte that Galyen putteth is to entrebreake, and intercyde the matter. *a* **1641** BP. MOUNTAGU *Acts & Mon.* (1642) 112 Then was not the Scepter utterly departed from Iudah,.. but onely intercided for a season.

†**interˈcide,** *v.*^{2} *Obs. rare*$^{-1}$. [ad. L. *intercidĕre* to fall between, fall through, f. *inter* between + *cadĕre* to fall.] *intr.* To fall through, fall to the ground, come to nothing.

1637 R. HUMPHREY tr. *St. Ambrose* Pref., The travels of very many did utterly intercide and perish.

†**inˈtercidence.** *Obs. rare*$^{-1}$. [f. next: see -ENCE.] The fact of being intercident.

1603 HOLLAND *Plutarch's Mor.* 618 Talking of the instances, the insults, the intercidences, communities of diseases, and all to shew..that we know the words and tearmes of physick.

†**inˈtercident,** *a. Obs.* [ad. L. *intercident-em*, pr. pple. of *intercidĕre*: see INTERCIDE *v.*^{2}]

1. *Med.* Of days in an illness: Falling between the critical and judicial days.

1603 SIR C. HEYDON *Jud. Astrol.* xxi. 424 In these 20 daies ..the septenaries be Criticall, the quaternaries, iudiciall: all the rest, intercident, and of least force. **1685** BOYLE *Enq. Notion Nat.* vi. 226 She [Nature] rouses herself up to make a crisis..on improper, and, as Physicians call them, intercident days, such as the third, fifth, ninth.

2. *Path.* Of the pulse: cf. INTERCADENCE.

(Littré has F. *intercédent* in this sense.)

1665 HARVEY *Adv. agst. Plague* 3 In a Malign Pestilent Feaver [the pulse is] thick, low, languid..quavering and intercident.

So †**interciˈdental** *a.* = prec. 1. *Obs.*

1658 CULPEPPER *Astrol. Judgem. Dis.* 22 Another time is called Intercidental, which is a time falls out between the Judicial dayes and Critical. **1671** BLAGRAVE *Astrol. Physic* 22 The intercidental time or divident part of the circle is not so dangerous, as the judicial time or part.

†**interciˈpation.** *Obs. rare.* [irreg. f. L. *intercip-ĕre* to INTERCEPT + -ATION.] = INTERCEPTION.

1583 FOXE *A. & M.* 989/2 Excusing the delay of yᵉ money, as wel as he could, by intercipation, or other causes by the way incident.

†**interˈcipient,** *a.* and *sb. Med. Obs.* [ad. L. *intercipient-em*, pr. pple. of *intercipĕre* to INTERCEPT.] **A.** *adj.* That intercepts or stops the flow of humours.

1684 tr. *Bonet's Merc. Compit.* III. 90 It is safer in the beginning to apply our selves to revulsive, diverting and intercipient Medicines.

B. *sb.* An application which stops the flow of humours.

1656 RIDGLEY *Pract. Physick* 45 Intercipients must be laid upon the part affected. **1684** tr. *Bonet's Merc. Compit.* XV. 529 Some..use Intercipients in a Periodical difficulty of Breathing.

intercircle, etc.: see INTER- *pref.*

†**interˈcise,** *ppl. a. Arith. Obs. rare.* Also -scise. [ad. L. *intercis-us*, pa. pple. of *intercīdere*: see next.] Broken at intervals, interrupted.

c **1430** *Art Nombryng* (E.E.T.S.) 13 Naturelle progressioun ay begynnethe with one, and Intercise or broken progressioun, omwhile begynnythe with one, omwhile with twayne. *Ibid.* 14 Whan the progressioun interscise endithe in ode..as .1. 3. 5.

†**interˈcision.** *Obs.* [ad. L. *intercīsiōn-em*, n. of action f. *intercīdere*: see INTERCIDE *v.*^{1}. Cf. obs. F. *intercision* (Godef.).]

1. The action of cutting through; section, intersection. Also with *an*: A cross-section.

1578 BANISTER *Hist. Man* I. 9 Seuered..from the Cuneall bone, as also from the vpper iawe, by the intercision of that Seame. **1623** COCKERAM II, A Cutting through the middest, *Intercision.* **1726** LEONI tr. *Alberti's Archit.* III. 6/1 This visual Pyramid shou'd be cut off in some one part, that the Painter may in this part express with his lines and tints, the circumferences and colours which this Intercision gives him. Thus the person who views the painted Superficie, beholds a certain Intercision of the Pyramid. Picture then is an intersection of the visual Pyramid. *Ibid.* III. 8/2 Fixing the place of the Intercision with..a perpendicular line, I form the Intercision of all the Lines which that perpendicular meets with.

2. The action of cutting off the course of, stopping, or interrupting, esp. temporarily; the fact of being interrupted or ceasing for a time.

1625 BP. MOUNTAGU *App. Cæsar* I. ii. 16, I have bin assured, that Arminius did hold..not only Intercision for a Time, but also Abscision..for ever. **1646** SIR T. BROWNE *Pseud. Ep.* VII. xii. 361 By cessation of Oracles..we may understand their intercision, not abscission or consummate desolation; their rare delivery not a totall dereliction. **1660** JER. TAYLOR *Duct. Dubit.* IV. i. rule iii. §9 If the course and continuance of the outward act be interrupted, and then proceeded in again, when the cause of the intercision is over.

b. With *an* and *pl.*

a **1631** DONNE *Serm.* (Alford) IV. cv. 420 They came..to a stopping, to an intercision, to an interruption of the water. **1659** PEARSON *Creed* VI. 564 After these intercisions, the throne of David was continued. **1681** BAXTER *Answ. Dodwell* iv. 35 If there were an intercision of an hundred years. **1813** [see INTERCURSATION].

3. Falling away, failing. (Cf. INTERCIDE *v.*^{2})

1647 TRAPP *Comm. Matt.* vii. 27 Yet from intercision, prolapsion, from utter and irrecoverable falling away, they are freed, because founded upon a Rock. **1649** JER. TAYLOR *Gt. Exemp.* II. Disc. viii. 80 The greatest danger is of fainting and intercision. **1651** J. GOODWIN *Red. Redeemed* i. §8 An intercision or failing of such interposals and actings.

intercity, -civic, -clash, -clasp, -class, etc.: see INTER- *pref.*

†**interˈclassis.** *Obs. rare*$^{-1}$. [f. INTER- 2 b + CLASSIS 4.] An intermediate smaller 'classis', or case of book-shelves in a library.

1678 W. DILLINGHAM *Let.* in Willis & Clark *Cambridge* III. 464 There may be very well an interclassis against the midst of every window as high as the soyle of it..to come as farr out as the higher classes.

interclavicle (ɪntəˈklævɪk(ə)l). *Anat.* [f. INTER- 3 + CLAVICLE.] A **T**-shaped or rod-like dermal bony plate lying on the under side of the sternum and attached to the clavicles, in lizards, crocodiles, and the lower mammals.

1870 ROLLESTON *Anim. Life* 36 Those 'parosteal' bones which are developed from the skin..and form the important bones known as 'clavicle' and 'interclavicle'. **1881** MIVART *Cat* 470 There are no epicoracoids or interclavicle.

interclavicular (ˌɪntəkləˈvɪkjʊlə(r)), *a. Anat.* [INTER- 4 a.] Lying between the clavicles; esp. in ***interclavicular bone*** (= prec.), ***ligament, notch.***

1831 R. KNOX *Cloquet's Anat.* 199 Inter-clavicular Ligament,..a very distinct fasciculus, placed transversely above the upper extremity of the sternum, between the heads of the two clavicles. **1870** ROLLESTON *Anim. Life* Introd. 53 One [air-sac] on either side of the azygos interclavicular sac. **1872** MIVART *Elem. Anat.* 471 The inter-clavicular is formed by the coalescence of what was at first a pair of sacs.

interclerical, -cloud, etc.: see INTER- *pref.*

interclose, var. ENTERCLOSE, *Obs.*, a partition.

†**interˈclose,** *v. Obs. rare.* [f. INTER- 1 a + CLOSE *v.*, after next.] *trans.* To shut up; to enclose within.

1592 *Sc. Acts Jas. VI*, c. 156 Bigging of dikes for interclosing of the saidis common passages. **1611** FLORIO, *Interchiudere*, to interclose or shut in betweene. **1680** BOYLE

Produc. Chem. Princ. IV. Wks. 1772 I. 638, I see not why it should be impossible for art to interclose some very minute and restless particles, which, by their..incessant motions, may keep a metalline body in the state of fluidity.

Hence **inter'closed** *ppl. a.*; **inter'closing** *vbl. sb.* Also † **inter'closure.**

1611 FLORIO, *Interchiuso*, enterclosed, shut betweene. *Ibid.*, *Interchiusione*, an enterclosing or shutting betweene. *Ibid.*, *Interchiusura*, an enterclosure, a shutting betweene.

† **inter'clude,** *v. Obs.* Also 6 enter-. [ad. L. *interclūd-ĕre*, f. *inter* between + *claudĕre* to close.]

1. *trans.* To close, shut up, block (a passage); to prevent the passage of.

1526 *St. Papers Hen. VIII*, VI. 546 Mutual concurraunce ..canne not be hadde if the wayes of Ambassiadours be intercluded. **1575** TURBERV. *Faulconrie* 225 The passage of those spirites beeing shutte up and intercluded, the creature whatsoever it be muste dye. **1669** W. HOLDER *Elem. Speech* 113 Like as the voice is sometimes intercluded by a hoarseness. **1683** SNAPE *Anat. Horse* IV. xvi. (1686) 176 Muscles set..to interclude the passage.

2. To shut up, enclose, confine within bounds.

1524 WOLSEY *Let. to Pace* in Strype *Eccl. Mem.* (1721) I. App. xii. 23 Thinking to interclude themperors folks betwene both companies. **1632** LITHGOW *Trav.* x. 434 Such I say, interclude their doctrine, betweene the thatch and the Church-wall tops. **1806** *Simple Narrative* II. 73 To bind yourself in the fetters invented by interested men, to interclude the rights of nature?

3. To shut off, cut off *from.*

1569 STOCKER tr. *Diod. Sic.* I. xix. 27/2 Antigone.. thinking to enterclude Alcete from his footemen. **1614** RALEIGH *Hist. World* II. v. iii. §1. 360 Demetrius..was soone intercluded from the Town, by those that lay in ambush. **1621** SANDERSON *Serm.* I. 26, I would be loth to interclude the hope of repentance from any sinner.

Hence **inter'cluding** *vbl. sb.*

1586 A. DAY *Eng. Secretary* II. (1625) 83 *Parenthesis*, an intercluding of a sentence..commonly set betweene two halfe circles, as thus ( ). **1691** RAY *Creation* I. (1692) 63 Nothing but the intercluding of the Air.

† **inter'clusion.** *Obs.* [ad. L. *interclūsiōn-em*, n. of action f. *interclūdĕre*: see prec.] The action of the vb. INTERCLUDE; shutting up.

1623 COCKERAM, *Interclusion*, a shutting vp of a sluce. **1671** *True Nonconf.* 443 The first act of hostility, by the interclusion of passages, was done by these of Zurich. **1798** BISSET *Burke* I. 411 (Jod.) The interclusion of commerce.

† **inter'clusive,** *a. Obs. rare*$^{-0}$. [f. ppl. stem of L. *interclūdĕre* + -IVE.] 'Enclosed, shut in, stopped' (Blount *Glossogr.* 1656).

intercoccygeal, -college, etc.: see INTER-.

intercolline (ɪntə'kɒlaɪn), *a. Geol.* [f. INTER- 4 a + L. *collis* a hill, *collīnus* relating to a hill.] Lying between hills; applied by Sir Charles Lyell to the hollows lying between hills formed by accumulation of erupted volcanic matter.

1858 LYELL in *Phil. Trans.* CXLVIII. 739. **1859-65** PAGE *Handbk. Geol. Terms* (ed. 2) 258 Such *intercolline* spaces abound in all volcanic regions of sub-aërial origin.

intercolonial (ˌɪntəkəʊ'ləʊnɪəl), *a.* [f. INTER- 4 c + COLONIAL. Cf. F. *intercolonial* (1871 in Littré *Suppl.*).] Existing, carried on, etc. between different colonies.

1843 J. OSBORNE *Guide Madeiras* 199 (*heading*) Intercolonial voyages. **1859** CORNWALLIS *New World* I. 319 Half-a-dozen other inter-colonial steamers. **1864** *Sat. Rev.* 31 Dec. 800/2 The outbreak of an angry intercolonial quarrel between Victoria and New South Wales. **1881** *Times* 31 Dec. 9/4 The attitude of the Natal colonists was.. inconsistent with an intercolonial union. **1905** *Daily Chron.* 14 July 5/5 The Intercolonial Railway to Montreal.

Hence **interco'lonially,** *adv.*

1855 in HYDE CLARKE *Eng. Dict.*

† **intercolo'nnation.** *Obs. rare.* [var. of INTERCOLUMNIATION, after It. *intercolonnato* 'entercollumned or set with pillars betweene' (Florio).]

1782 JEFFERSON *Notes Virginia* (1787) 254 A portico.. tolerably just in its proportions..save only that the intercolonnations are too large.

inter'colour, *v. rare.* [f. INTER- I a + COLOUR *v.*] *trans.* To intersperse with colours.

1607 TOPSELL *Four-f. Beasts* (1658) 79 The whole body [is] so admirably intercoloured with variety that it is in vain for the wit or art of man once to go about to endevour the emulous imitation thereof.

ˌ**inter'column.** *Arch.* ? *Obs.* [ad. L. *intercolumnium* (f. *inter* between + L. *columna* COLUMN); in OF. *entrecolumpne* (1464 in Godef. *Compl.*), F. *entrecolonne* (1547 ibid.), It. *intercolonnio* (Florio).] The space between two columns.

1665 J. WEBB *Stone-Heng* (1725) 42 Architects assign the Intercolumn of it, to exceed three Diameters. **1708** *New View Lond.* II. 360/1 The Intercolumns are the Commandments, very neatly done in gold Characters on Black. **1766** ENTICK *London* IV. 60 The intercolumns are painted in imitation of porphyry. **1823** P. NICHOLSON *Pract. Build.* 586. **1934** H. P. CLUNN *Face of London* (ed. 5) 28 The City of London Club, built in 1832-3 with..a Doric order of seven inter-columns.

interco'lumnal, *a. Anat. rare.* [f. as next + -AL[1].] = next (sense 2).

1835-6 TODD *Cycl. Anat.* I. 5/1 These fibres..have been termed intercolumnal bands.

intercolumnar (ˌɪntəkəʊ'lʌmnə(r)), *a.* [f. mod.L. type **intercolumnāris*, f. INTER- 4 a + L. *columna* COLUMN: cf. F. *intercolumnaire* (Littré).]

1. *Arch.* Lying or placed between two columns.

1862 R. H. PATTERSON *Ess. Hist. & Art* 76 The doors, windows, columns, and intercolumnar spaces. **1876** S. BIRCH *Egypt* 41 Sarcophagi and intercolumnar slabs.

2. *Anat.* Extending between the columns of the external abdominal rings.

1842 E. WILSON *Anat. Vade M.* 250 Upon escaping at the external abdominal ring, it receives the intercolumnar fascia.

† **interco'lumnary,** *a. Arch. Obs. rare.* [f. as prec. + -ARY: cf. COLUMNARY.] = prec. (sense 1).

1665 J. WEBB *Stone-Heng* (1725) 58 The other intercolumnary, or void Spaces.

† **intercolum'nation.** *Arch. Obs.* Variant of INTERCOLUMNIATION. [cf. COLUMNATION.]

1664 EVELYN *Acc. Archit.* in *Freart's Archit.* 131 Intercolumnation signifies the distance or voyd between Pillar and Pillar. **1726** LEONI *Alberti's Archit.* II. 129/1 This new Arch may quite fill up the old intercolumnation, or aperture between the Ribs. **1757** LANGLEY *Builder's Jewell* 25 The proper Intercolumnations, or just Distances, that the Columns of every Order must be placed in from each other.

† **inter'columned,** *ppl. a. Obs. rare*$^{-0}$.

1611 FLORIO, *Intercolonnato*, enter-collumned, or set with pillars betweene.

interco'lumniary, *a. Arch. rare.* [f. as next + -ARY.] = INTERCOLUMNAR I.

1663 CHARLETON *Chor. Gigant.* 23 Where are those three Entrances? or how should we distinguish them from the other intercolumniary, or void spaces? **1849** FREEMAN *Archit.* I. iv. 75 The intercolumniary walls.

intercolumniation (ˌɪntəkəʊlʌmnɪ'eɪʃən). [f. L. *intercolumni-um* INTERCOLUMN + -ATION.]

1. The space between two adjacent columns or pillars in a building: = INTERCOLUMN.

1624 WOTTON *Archit.* in *Reliq.* (1651) 229 The distance, or Intercolumniation (which word Artificers doe usually borrow) may be neer four of his own Diameters. **1657** R. LIGON *Barbadoes* (1673) 103 Dorique Pillars Archt from one to another, and in each intercolumniation a square stud of stone. **1761** *London & Environs* II. 195 The columns are massy, and the intercolumniation large. **1829** LANDOR *Wks.* (1846) I. 483/1 The proportions of porticoes, of columns, of intercolumniations.

2. The placing of columns, with reference to the space between them.

1847 SMEATON *Builder's Man.* 246 That intercolumniation in which the columns are placed two diameters and a quarter from each other. **1880** *Academy* 21 Aug. 139/3 His explanation of the closer intercolumniation at the angles..is obviously fallacious.

intercom ('ɪntəkɒm). Also **inter-com, inter-comm** (with hyphen), **intercomm.** [Colloq. abbrev. of INTERCOMMUNICATION.] A system of intercommunication by radio or telephone between or within aircraft, offices, vehicles, etc. Also *attrib.*

1940 C. OLSSON in Michie & Graebner *Their Finest Hour* iv. 61 The others behind me were gossiping as usual on their 'intercoms'. **1941** [see DECK *sb.*[1] 3 e]. **1941** *War Illustr.* 20 Oct. 215/1 The rear gunner, I remember, called up on the inter-com., and said, 'I hope you chaps see the next one before I do.' *Ibid.* 30 Dec. 383/1 Unable to talk to the others over the 'intercom.' because my mouthpiece was not working, I stuck to the controls. **1942** T. RATTIGAN *Flare Path* I. 101 He even moaned to me over the intercomm. because he'd shot down a Messerschmitt. **1943** *Electronic Engin.* XVI. 140 A is valve set for three-fold communication: tank-commander; tank-tank; intercomm. in tanks. **1949** *Ibid.* XXI. 109 Electricians will welcome new chapters on Intercoms (loudspeaking telephones). **1951** J. STEINBECK *Log from 'Sea of Cortez'* (1958) p. xxv, An intercom phone between the basement and the upstairs office. **1964** M. MCLUHAN *Understanding Media* II. xxiv. 236 The close teamwork and tribal loyalty now demanded by electrical intercom again puts the Japanese in positive relation to their ancient traditions. **1967** [see INTERCOMMUNICATION 4]. **1972** G. DURRELL *Catch me a Colobus* iv. 73 The intercom system that we have all over the zoo. **1972** J. POTTER *Going West* 8 The intercom announced the departure of Flight BA 531.

intercombat, -come, etc.: see INTER- *pref.*

intercombination (ˌɪntəkɒmbɪ'neɪʃən). [f. INTER- + COMBINATION.] (See INTER- 2 a.) *spec.* in *Physics*, an electronic transition between atomic states of different multiplicities (i.e. having different spin quantum numbers); also *ellipt.* for **intercombination line,** a spectral line so produced.

1930 RUARK & UREY *Atoms, Molecules & Quanta* xx. 705 When intercombination lines occur, the intensity rules considered in this section must be modified. **1934** O. W. RICHARDSON *Molecular Hydrogen* iii. 46 There may be intercombination lines between the singlet and triplet states but if so they must be very faint. **1937** J. W. T. SPINKS tr. *Herzberg's Atomic Spect. & Atomic Struct.* ii. 79 Terms of the triplet system of He practically do not combine with the terms of the singlet system, and conversely. That is, a prohibition of intercombinations is observed. **1941** *Rev. Mod. Physics* XIII. 75 Intercombinations may occur with appreciable intensity only if the molecule contains some heavier atoms. **1950** *Discussions Faraday Soc.* IX. 16 To identify spectroscopically the long-lived luminescence and converse absorption bands as intercombinations, use is made of the characteristics of the spin-orbit coupling process. **1970** G. K. WOODGATE *Elem. Atomic Struct.* vii. 132 When S changes one speaks of intercombination lines.

inter'common, *v.* Forms: 5 entercomen, entrecomon, entyrcomyn, 7 entercommon, 6- intercommon, (6 *Sc.* -oun, -one). [ad. AF. *entrecomuner* (Godef.), f. *entre-* (INTER- 1 b) + *comuner* to COMMON, COMMUNE; see these verbs, and cf. INTERCOMMUNE.]

† **1.** *intr.* To have intercourse, common dealings, or relations *with* others, or with each other; to associate *with* or together (cf. COMMON *v.* 4); *esp.* in *Sc. Law*, to have correspondence or dealings *with* (outlaws, etc.). *Obs.*

c **1430** LYDG. *Hors, Shepe & G.* (Roxb.) 26 That one lacketh, nature hath geue to another..Entercomen therefore as broder doth with broder. **1448** *Leg. March.* c. 3 in *Scot. Stat.* (1844) I. App. iv. 305/2 þat na maner of persoun..sal intercomoun with ony Inglis man or woman. **1583** GOLDING *Calvin on Deut.* xi. 63 Mony..is that thing whereby men intercommon among themselues. **1592** *Sc. Acts Jas. VI*, c. 144 Nane of our Soveraine Lordis lieges sal presume to receipt, supplie, or intercommoun with them [traitors, etc.]. **1675** PENN *Eng. Pres. Interest* 15 The Brittains and Saxons began to grow tame to each other, and intercommon amicably.

† **2.** *intr. Sc.* To hold conversation or discourse *with*; to take counsel *together.* (Cf. COMMON *v.* 6.)

1536 BELLENDEN *Cron. Scot.* (1821) I. 194 The moder, desiring to bring hir sonnis to concord, tuke freindis to intercommone on thir debaitis. **1578** *Sc. Acts Jas. VI* (1814) III. 105 To confer treat and intercommone with thame vpoun the confirmatioun of all testamentis within this realme.

3. *intr.* To share in the use of the same common. (Cf. COMMON *v.* 9.)

1598 KITCHIN *Courts Leet* (1675) 210 Inhabitants cannot prescribe to Intercommon. **1679** BLOUNT *Anc. Tenures* 145 When Horned Beasts of several adjoyning Parishes do promiscuously intercommon together. **1694** COLLIER *Ess. Mor. Subj.* I. (1703) 118 Where there are no Inclosures, all People may intercommon, without Preference or Ceremony. **1767** BLACKSTONE *Comm.* II. iii. 33 Common because of vicinage..is where the inhabitants of two townships, which lie contiguous to each other, have usually intercommoned with one another. **1874** SIR G. JESSEL in *Law Rep.* Eq. Cas. XIX. 160 The end parish in this case could by no means intercommon with the parish at the other end.

† **4.** *intr.* To share or participate *with* others, or mutually. (Cf. COMMON *v.* 3.) *Obs.*

1626 BACON *Sylva* § 55 The Spirits of the Wine, doe prey vpon the Roscide Juyce of the Body, and inter-common with the Spirits of the Body, and so deceiue and rob them of their Nourishment. *a* **1661** FULLER *Worthies, Hartfordsh.* II. (1662) 22 He lived and dyed Childlesse, entercommoning therein with many Worthies, who are..either improlifick, or have Children *in genitorum vituperium*. *Ibid.*, *London* 197 He and hogs did in some sort entercommon both in their diet and lodging.

† **5.** *trans. Sc. Law.* To denounce by 'letters of intercommuning'; hence, to prohibit (a person) from intercourse or communication; to outlaw. (Cf. INTERCOMMONING *vbl. sb.* 2.) *Obs.*

a **1715** BURNET *Own Time* (1766) II. 17 The numbers and desperate tempers of those who were intercommoned. **1717** DE FOE *Mem. Ch. Scot.* I. 8 Citing Paul Meffen of Dundee, before them, and he not appearing, was intercommoned; that is, every one was forbid to harbour, or relieve him, or converse with him, on severe Penalties.

† **inter'common,** *sb. Obs.* Also 5 entircomyn, entercomen. [f. prec.] The act, practice, or right of intercommoning (esp. in sense 3).

1449 in Rymer *Foedera* (1710) XI. 244 Have.. Entircomyn in the Landez Pasturez and Medues. *c* **1470** HARDING *Chron.* CXL. i, The Soudan toke a trewce w[t] Kyng Richard..to bye all marchandise, And sell and passe saufly thitherward To the sepulcre..With entercomen, as then it did suffice. **1655-6** in J. C. Hodgson *Hist. Northumberland* (1897) IV. 138 [The award of the arbitrators..confirmed to] the tenants of the town of Anick intercommon on Acomb fell.

inter'commonable, *a. rare.* [f. INTERCOMMON *v.* + -ABLE, after COMMONABLE.] That may be used in common; commonable.

1807 VANCOUVER *Agric. Devon* (1813) 274 For enclosing and cultivating those intercommonable lands, which at this time occupy so large a portion of the area of the district.

inter'commonage. [f. as prec. + -AGE, after COMMONAGE.] The practice of sharing with others, esp. of using common pasture.

1628 LE GRYS tr. *Barclay's Argenis* 355 This enter-commonage; this confusion; not friends, not brothers, doe long with quiet endure. **1807** VANCOUVER *Agric. Devon* (1813) 102 The extensive downs and commons, open to a general intercommonage of the stock belonging to the inhabitants at large. **1883** *Law Rep.* 11 Q. Bench Div. 697 The value of the land..unaffected by the right of inter-commonage.

†**inter'commoned**, *ppl. a. Obs.* [f. as prec. + -ED[1].] **a.** Held in intercommonage. **b.** *Sc. Law.* Denounced in a writ or letters of intercommuning; outlawed: see the verb.

a **1715** BURNET *Own Time* (1765) II. 104 Those desperate intercommoned men who..wander about inflaming one another. **1768–74** TUCKER *Lt. Nat.* (1834) II. 78 Between the provinces of nature and chance, there lies a tract claimed by both, or shared in common between them..Within this intercommoned tract [etc.].

inter'commoner. [f. as prec. + -ER[1], after COMMONER.] **1.** One who participates with others, esp. in the use of common pasture. Chiefly in *pl.*

c **1550** *Disc. Common Weal Eng.* (1893) 124 Wheare men are intercominers in comon feildes. *a* **1638** MEDE *Wks.* (1677) 20 Laying both courts into one hath made the Jews and Gentiles intercommoners. **1807** VANCOUVER *Agric. Devon* (1813) 275 A part of this common has been..wrested from the intercommoners at large, and now constitutes the character of open common-field, or of Lammas ground.

2. *Sc. Law.* = INTERCOMMUNER 1.

1567 *Sc. Acts Jas. VI*, c. 21 That the receipter..and intercommoner with sik persones, salbe called..as airt and pairt of thir thifteous deidis.

inter'commoning, *vbl. sb.* [f. as prec. + -ING[1].]

1. The action of sharing, participating, or associating with others; *esp.* that of using the same common pasture.

a **1577** GASCOIGNE *Ferd. Ieronimi* Wks. (1587) 236 Wee finde by experience, that such secrete entercomoning of ioyes dooeth encrease delight. **1658** OSBORN *Jas.* Wks. (1673) 522 No Lord of a Rich Mannor would accept the offer of one more poor, upon the condition of enter-commoning. *a* **1668** SIR W. WALLER *Div. Medit.* (1839) 86 It was just with God..to turn his majesty to grass, to have his dwelling, and intercommoning with the beasts of the field. **1727** BRADLEY *Fam. Dict.* s.v. *Common.* **1883** SIR N. LINDLEY in *Law Rep.* 11 Q. Bench Div. 702 At some time or other rights of intercommoning over the lands were acquired.

2. *Sc. Law.* ***writ of intercommoning***: see INTERCOMMUNING 2.

a **1715** BURNET *Own Time* (1823) II. 101 Upon that great numbers were outlawed: and a writ was issued out, that was indeed legal, but very seldom used, called intercommoning: because it made all that harboured such persons..to be involved in the same guilt.

intercommunal (ɪntə'kɒmju:nəl), *a.* [f. INTER- 4 c + COMMUNAL *a.*] Existing or occurring between communities or races. Hence **inter'communalism.**

1909 in WEBSTER. **1960** S. FOOT *Emergency Exit* xii. 98 The inter-communal strife was at its worst. Turk and Greek were going for each other. **1971** *Black Scholar* June 51/1 With the establishment of society through inter-communalism, the entire social contract must be altered. **1973** *Black World* Dec. 19/2 We believe in intercommunalism—the relatedness of all people. **1974** *Black Panther* 9 Feb. 8/3 The Maryland Pen Intercommunal Survival Collective is calling for a community-based united front to halt the injustices and tortures before it is too late.

intercommune, *v.* Now *rare* or *Obs.* Forms: 4 entre-, 5 entercomune, 6 entre-, 7–8 intercommune. [a. AF. *entrecomuner*: see INTERCOMMON *v.*, and cf. COMMUNE *v.* The earlier stress was app. *'commune*, in later examples prob. *co'mmune.*]

1. *intr.* To have mutual communion; to hold discourse or conversation with each other or with another. (Cf. COMMUNE *v.* 6.)

c **1374** CHAUCER *Troylus* IV. 1326 (1354) The nature of þe pes mot nedes dryue, That men moste entrecomunen y-fere. **1387–8** T. USK *Test. Love* I. v. (Skeat) l. 7 Raddeste thou neuer howe Paris of Troye and Helaine loued togider, and yet had they not entrecommuned of speche. **1623** T. SCOT *Highw. God* 51 Let not man presume to intercommune with God. **1833** [see INTERCOMMUNING *vbl. sb.* 1].

†**2.** To have intercourse, relations, or connexion, esp. in *Sc. Law*, with rebels or denounced persons.

c **1374** [see INTERCOMMUNING *vbl. sb.* 1]. *c* **1449** PECOCK *Repr.* I. x. 49 How fer..he schal strecche him silf..and not entercomune with eny other craft in conclusions and treuthis. **1555** W. WATREMAN *Fardle Facions* II. xi. 241 That parte of Arabia..wher it entrecommuneth with Jewry on the one side, and with Egipt on the other. *a* **1639** SPOTTISWOOD *Hist. Ch. Scot.* VI. (1677) 376 The Noblemen ..came in and made offer of their service, giving surety not to reset nor intercommune with the Rebels. **1681** *Proclam.* in Wodrow *Hist. Ch. Scot.* (1722) II. App. 78 That ye.. prohibit and discharge all our subjects..to reset, supply, or intercommune with the said Earl. **1828** COL. YOUNG in *Bentham's Wks.* (1843) XI. 8 They cannot eat or drink, intermarry and intercommune together.

†**3.** To participate in the use of the same pasture or the like. *Obs.*

1601 HOLLAND *Pliny* I. 272 Their very concurrents..who would intercommune with them, and rob them of their prey.

†**4.** *trans. Sc.* To denounce by letters or writ of intercommuning; hence, to prohibit 'intercommuning with'. (Cf. INTERCOMMON *v.* 5.) *Obs.*

168. in Somers *Tracts* I. 386 Not daring to appear, he is denunced and intercommuned. **1681** *Lond. Gaz.* No. 1648/4 Preachers..Excommunicated, Intercommuned, or Declared Fugitives upon a Process intented against the said Tennants. *c* **1730** BURT *Lett. N. Scotl.* (1818) II. 12 For atrocious crimes..the chief or laird was condemned in absence and intercommuned, as they call it, or outlawed.

Hence **intercommune** *sb.*, an act of intercommuning; mutual communion or conversation.

1820 COLERIDGE *Lett. to J. H. Green* 14 Jan. (1895) 704, I must therefore defer our philosophical intercommune till the Sunday after.

intercommuned, *ppl. a. Sc. Law.* Now *Hist.* [f. prec. (sense 4) + -ED[1].] Denounced in letters of intercommuning; prohibited from being communicated with or entertained; outlawed.

1680 HICKES *Spir. Popery* 63 Mr. Welsh and other Traiterous, Intercommuned, and Rebellious Preachers. **1816** SCOTT *Old Mort.* xiii, You saw and entertained him, knowing him to be an intercommuned traitor. **1895** CROCKETT *Men Moss Hags* xvii. 119 The dragoons.. searched every nook and corner for intercommuned fugitives.

inter'communer. [f. as prec. + -ER[1].]

1. *Sc. Law.* One who holds intercourse or correspondence with a person denounced by law. Now *Hist.*

1620 in Row *Hist. Kirk* (Wodrow Soc.) 270 The intercommuners and resetters of jesuits. **1737** J. CHAMBERLAYNE *St. Gt. Brit.* 418 (*Scotland*) Resetters of thieves or intercommuners with them..are guilty of Felony. **1849** JAS. GRANT *Kirkaldy of Gr.* xv. 147 Denounced those who had intercourse with them, as intercommuners with rebels.

†**2.** One who conducts negotiations between parties; a mediator. *Obs. rare*[−1].

1638 R. BAILLIE *Lett.* 22 July, We agreed, on condition that..the intercommuners should engage their honour.. that in the meantime there should no munition at all..be put into the house.

intercommunicable (ˌɪntəkə'mju:nɪkəb(ə)l), *a.* [f. INTERCOMMUNICATE *v.*, after COMMUNICABLE.] Capable of or suitable for intercommunication.

1822 *Edin. Rev.* XXXVI. 537 This matter is not intercommunicable from one person to another. **1854** DE QUINCEY *Autobiog. Sk.* Wks. II. 83 Any pronunciation whatever that should be articulate, apprehensible, and intercommunicable, such as might differentiate the words.

Hence ˌ**interco**ˌ**mmunica'bility.**

1884 *19th Cent.* Feb. 336 The intercommunicability of Scarlatina and Diphtheria (under certain conditions).

intercommunicate (ˌɪntəkə'mju:nɪkeɪt), *v.* Also 6–7 enter-. [f. ppl. stem of Anglo-Lat. *intercommūnicāre* to have intercourse with each other (1401 in Du Cange); see INTER- 1 b and COMMUNICATE, and cf. F. *entrecommuniquer* (16th c.).]

1. *intr.* To communicate mutually, hold communication with each other; to have mutual intercourse; to have free passage into each other.

1586 [see INTERCOMMUNICATION 1]. **1706** PHILLIPS, *To intercommunicate*, to communicate mutually, or one with another. **1835–6** TODD *Cycl. Anat.* I. 530/2 The branchial chambers intercommunicate both above and below this septum. **1870** ROLLESTON *Anim. Life* 45 The anterior and posterior surfaces of the bodies of the vertebræ.. intercommunicate. **1874** HELPS *Soc. Press.* x. 143 Lest we should live in sets, and should not intercommunicate freely.

2. *trans.* To communicate, impart, or transmit to and from each other.

1603 HOLLAND *Plutarch's Mor.* 1170 The raies..receive one from another, and intercommunicate the lights, as they be sent to and fro. **1633** EARL MANCH. *Al Mondo* (1636) 200 When the faculties both of will and understanding doe intercommunicate their ravishments.

Hence **interco'mmunicated, -ing** *ppl. adjs.*

1852 G. WILSON *Reid* v. 102 It is placed in connection by means of intercommunicating fibres. **1853** *Q. Rev.* Sept. 329 A prepared and intercommunicated dialogue. **1891** W. M. RAMSAY in *Athenæum* 5 Sept. 327/3 Without actually seeing the country it is difficult to comprehend thoroughly the relation of its parts and the intercommunicating routes.

intercommunicate (-kə'mju:nɪkət), *ppl. a.* [f. as prec.: see -ATE[2].] = INTERCOMMUNICATED; characterized by reciprocal communication.

1851 RUSKIN *Mod. Painters* II. III. i. iv. §11 Such difference is secured in the feelings as shall make fellowship itself more delightful, by its inter-communicate character.

intercommunication (-kəmju:nɪ'keɪʃən). Also 6–7 enter-. [ad. Anglo-Lat. *intercommūnicātio* (1406 in Du Cange): see INTERCOMMUNICATE *v.* and COMMUNICATION.]

1. The action or fact of communicating with each other; intercourse.

1586 T. BRIGHT *Treat. Melancholy* xii. 56 These haue each of them, but one quality: fire hote, ayer moist..if they should haue twaine, then must they needes either entercommunicate, or two qualities concurre with the firste matter: entercommunication is there none: for then should they not be the elements of other things seeing they should be elements of ech other. **1829** SOUTHEY *Lett.* (1856) IV. 149 When you and I had more leisure for an inter-communication, of which I have..made profitable use. **1846** GROTE *Greece* II. iii. II. 362 Those causes which tended to bring about increased Hellenic intercommunication.

2. The mutual imparting of ideas or information; interchange of speech; mutual conference.

1603 FLORIO *Montaigne* II. xii. (1632) 251 Even in beasts, that have no voice at all,..we easily inferre there is some other meane of entercommunication. **1833** L. RITCHIE *Wand. by Loire* 255 A brief question, and a monosyllable in reply, was their only intercommunication. **1871** DARWIN *Desc. Man* I. ii. 58 Ants have considerable powers of intercommunication by means of their antennæ.

3. Passage to and fro by connecting channels or lines of communication.

1866 OWEN *Anat. Vertebr.* I. vii. 510 The free intercommunication between the basal spaces into which the auricles open.

4. *attrib.* Cf. INTERCOM.

1911 M. HIRD in L. Weaver *House & its Equipment* 124 With an 'intercommunication' system of telephones in the house, room after room can be..easily 'rung up'. **1967** *Lebende Sprachen* XII. 137/1 *Intercommunication system* (*intercom*), a system of wiring which enables two-way communication between teacher and student(s).

interco'mmunicative, *a. rare.* [f. INTERCOMMUNICATE *v.*, after COMMUNICATIVE.] Characterized by, or adapted for, intercommunication.

a **1641** BP. MOUNTAGU *Acts & Mon.* (1642) 3 This Church ..is made up out of many diverse Portion,..inter-communicative one with another. **1868** *Daily Tel.* 24 Mar. 4/1 That stir and intercommunicative talk..which marks that honourable members are in a state of special curiosity. **1885** G. MEREDITH *Diana* II. i. 10 Charm, wit, ardour, intercommunicative quickness, and kindling beauty.

interco'mmunicator. *rare.* [f. as prec., after COMMUNICATOR.] An agent or means of intercommunication.

1855 in HYDE CLARKE *Eng. Dict.* **1880** *Academy* 24 Dec. 459 A monthly periodical intended as an 'intercommunicator' for antiquaries, bibliophiles and other investigators.

intercommuning, *vbl. sb.* [f. INTERCOMMUNE *v.* (q.v. for stress) + -ING[1].]

1. Mutual conversation, discourse, or intercourse.

c **1374** CHAUCER *Boeth.* II. pr. vii. 44 (Camb. MS.) [For] defawte of vn-vsage and entrecomunynge of marchaundise. **1574** WHITGIFT *Def. Aunsw.* II. Wks. (Parker Soc.) I. 260 Participation and intercommuning of the churches together, by councils and assemblies. **1833** L. RITCHIE *Wand. by Loire* 220 To be selected for his intercommunings by a man like him..was something.

2. *Sc. Law.* The holding of intercourse or having dealings with a person legally proscribed. ***letter*** (or ***writ***) ***of intercommuning***: a letter issued by the Privy Council, or other authority, prohibiting intercourse with the person or persons named in it. Now *Hist.*

1646 BP. MAXWELL *Burd. Issach.* in *Phenix* (1708) II. 300 Upon the same Remonstrance goeth out a Writ, which there they call Letters of Intercommuning..the Intent is, that none of the King's Subjects commune or confer with him.. otherwise, the Intercommuner is to be judg'd and reputed to be a Rebel of the same guiltiness. **1761–2** HUME *Hist. Eng.* (1806) V. lxvi. 59 Several writs of intercommuning were now issued against the hearers and preachers in conventicles. *a* **1806** FOX *Hist. Jas. II*, ii. (1808) 110 Letters had been issued by government, forbidding the intercommuning with persons who had neglected, or refused, to appear before the privy council, when cited for the above crimes.

†**b.** ***under intercommuning***: proscribed by letters of intercommuning. *Obs.*

1679 *Lond. Gaz.* No. 1406/2 Whereas there are several Persons under Caption and Intercommuning in the said Shire for several Causes [etc.].

intercommunion (-kə'mju:nɪən, -jən). [f. INTER- 2 a + COMMUNION.]

1. Communion or fellowship one with another; intimate intercourse.

a **1761** LAW *The. Relig.* II. (R.), To prevent any intimate connections, or..an entire intercommunion with the idolatrous religions round them. **1839** YEOWELL *Anc. Brit. Ch.* Pref. (1847) 4 Unity and intercommunion of the various branches of the visible church of Christ. **1875** STUBBS *Const. Hist.* III. xix. 371 The Reformation had suspended religious intercommunion.

2. The mutual action or relation between things in regard to functions.

1817 COLERIDGE *Biog. Lit.* 57 The incomprehensibility.. of intercommunion between substances that have no one property in common. **1872** H. MACMILLAN *True Vine* vi. 259 There is nothing to hinder the intercommunion of vital substances and impulses between the branch and the vine. **1875** JOWETT *Plato* (ed. 2) III. 419 When all these studies reach the point of intercommunion and connection with one another.

3. Participation in the sacrament of Holy Communion by members of different religious denominations.

1921 [see *inter-celebration* s.v. INTER- 2 a]. **1931** W. TEMPLE *Thoughts on Probl. of Day* iii. 99 It is perfectly clear that the authors of the Memorandum never contemplated such action as formal Intercommunion. **1936** A. M. RAMSEY *Gospel & Catholic Ch.* i. 8 To the one 'intercommunion' is meaningless without unity of outward order; to the other 'intercommunion' seems the one sensible and Christian way towards unity. **1966** *Church of Eng. Newspaper* 3 June, The laity expressing disquiet at what may generically be described as 'acts of inter-communion'. **1971** *World Council of Churches: Faith & Order, Louvain* 63 The whole area of question has generally been referred to in the past as the question of 'intercommunion', but that one word cannot cover the whole range and has become seriously ambiguous. It will be better to find terms which can exactly describe the

different practices and their ecclesiological significance, among which the term 'intercommunion' may find its precise and particular place. **1973** *Times* 17 May 21/3 (*heading*) Bishops a stumbling block in intercommunion talks.

intercommunity (-kəˈmjuːnɪtɪ). [f. INTER- 2 a + COMMUNITY.] The quality of being common to various parties; the condition of having things in common or of participating in the same things.

1587 FLEMING *Contn. Holinshed* III. 1576/2 The frogs, who..would needs (as misliking their present intercommunitie of life)..sue to Jupiter for a king. **1747** LD. LYTTELTON *Obs. Convers. Paul* 30 The Genius of Paganism allowed an Intercommunity of Worship. **1830** MACKINTOSH *Eth. Philos.* Wks. 1846 I. 9 The intercommunity of the technical terms of science in Europe having been..broken down by the Germans. **1847** R. W. HAMILTON *Sabbath* iii. (1848) 86 Hospitality and alms succeeded to intercommunity of property.

intercomparison, -complexity, etc.: see INTER-, *pref.*

intercondylar (-ˈkɒndɪlə(r)). [f. INTER- 4 a + L. *condylus*, a. Gr. κόνδυλος knuckle.] Situated between condyles or rounded bone-ends.

1884 in *Cassell's Encycl. Dict.* **1887** *Syd. Soc. Lex.*, *Intercondylar line*, a transverse line on the lower end of the femur separating the patellar fossa from the popliteal fossa. *Intercondylar notch*, the deep notch which separates the condyles of the femur behind.

intercondyloid (-ˈkɒndɪlɔɪd), *a. Anat.* [See prec. and CONDYLOID.] = prec.

1836–9 TODD *Cycl. Anat.* II. 167/1 The intercondyloid notch. **1854** OWEN *Skel. & Teeth* in *Circ. Sc., Organ. Nat.* I. 225 They are separated by an 'intercondyloid' tract, from the fore part of which there usually rises an intercondyloid tuberosity.

interconfessional, -confound: see INTER-.

interconnect (-kəˈnɛkt), *v.* [INTER- 1 b.] *trans.* To connect each with the other; to connect by reciprocal links. Chiefly in *pa. pple.*

1865 MASSON *Rec. Brit. Philos.* 27 The different departments of speculative inquiry are obviously interconnected. **1889** *Minutes Congr. Council U.S.* 64 Among the ancients religion and the state were closely interconnected and dependent on each other. **1895** *Atlantic Monthly* Aug. 225 These are all interconnected by a network of canals.

ˌintercoˈnnectedness. [f. *interconnected*, pa. pple. of INTERCONNECT *v.* + -NESS.] The property or state of being interconnected.

1922 A. G. HOGG *Redemption from this World* vi. 191 We labour hardest to perceive the interconnectedness of events. **1952** *Mind* LXI. 285 Logical interconnectedness..is the mark of genuine knowledge. **1952** S. SPENDER *Learning Laughter* xi. 149 The inter-connectedness of Western and Eastern influences. **1959** *Africa* Apr. 142 The interconnectedness of political and ritual status.

intercoˈnnector. [f. INTERCONNECT *v.* + -OR.] Something that interconnects, *spec.* (see quot. 1940).

1930 *Engineering* 13 June 771/3 The substitution of a supply from Ardnacrusha..has necessitated the erection of a sub-station..into which three of the inter-connectors from Fleet-street to Pigeon House Fort are looped. **1940** *Chambers's Techn. Dict.* 452/1 *Interconnector*, a feeder which serves to interconnect two substations or generating stations, and along which energy may flow in either direction. **1962** *Newnes Conc. Encycl. Electr. Engin.* 598/2 An attempt to adjust..power flow only on the tie between two generating stations will result in an undesirable change of power on the remainder of the inter-connectors. **1971** *Nature* 13 Aug. 470/1 (*caption*) Photograph of four diodes in a monolithic array... Contact is made to the devices by aluminium interconnectors.

interconnexion, -connection (-kəˈnɛkʃən). [INTER- 2 a.] Mutual connexion.

1822–56 DE QUINCEY *Confess.* (1862) 232 A little attention will show the strictness of the inter-connection. **1857–8** SEARS *Athan.* 10 It is not likely that two realms of being lie closely proximate..and yet have no inter-connexion.

inter-consonantal: see INTER- *pref.* 4 a.

intercontiˈnental, *a.* [INTER- 4 c.] **a.** Situated or subsisting between, or connecting, different continents; including persons of different continents.

1855 in HYDE CLARKE *Eng. Dict.* **1887** *Times* (weekly ed.) 1 July 11/4 Interoceanic Canals and intercontinental railways. **1894** *Chicago Advance* 25 Oct. 121/1 As a consequence of its inter-continental position..Corinth early became celebrated for its wealth and luxury. **1896** *Curr. Hist.* (Buffalo, N.Y.) VI. 675 An intercontinental combination of Fenians, Russian Nihilists in the U.S. and anarchists.

b. Capable of travelling or of being sent from one continent to another; esp. in the designation *intercontinental ballistic missile* (abbrev. *I.C.B.M.*).

1956 *Spaceflight* I. 22/2 The terrible threat implicit in the alliance of inter-continental ballistic missiles and thermonuclear warheads, to which the whole world will stand utterly defenceless, is evident for all to see. **1957** *Jane's Fighting Ships 1957–58* 478 The combination of Regulus I guided missiles and submarines has given the United States Navy an intercontinental missile capability today instead of in the years to come. **1968** *Times* 16 Dec. 7/2 The second stage of the Saturn V rocket, with a thrust of one million lb., was comparable with the thrust of the Atlas rocket first developed as an inter-continental ballistic missile. **1969** *Guardian* 23 June 10/2 The Russians did not have a true intercontinental bomber until 1954.

interconversion (ɪntəkənˈvɜːʃən). [INTER- 2 a + CONVERSION.] The process of converting each of two or more things into the other(s).

1865 *Fortn. Rev.* I. 441 It shall be shown..in what these molecular movements themselves consist..and how their mutual interconversion is effected. **1911** *Ann. Rep. Progr. Chem.* VIII. 65 The interconversion of the hydroxy-acids was realised in accordance with the following scheme. **1946** *Nature* 2 Nov. 610/2 These reaction systems..which must include the interconversions of dietary, bacterial and protozoan protein, through the agency of ciliates. **1970** P. J. WHEATLEY *Chem. Consequences Nucl. Spin* iv. 80 The half-life of interconversion [of ortho- and para-hydrogen] is not known accurately.

interconvert (ɪntəkənˈvɜːt), *v.* [f. INTER- 1 b + CONVERT *v.*, or as back-formation from prec.] *trans.* To convert into one another.

1953 S. F. MASON *Hist. Sci.* xviii. 167 The ordinary and extraordinary rays were interconverted when the crystals were placed at right angles. **1955** *Sci. News Let.* 7 May 297/1 Other enzymes in the muscle interconvert these two forms [of phosphorylase] and keep them in equilibrium. **1971** *Sci. Amer.* Aug. 47/1 Lester Friedman and John G. Miller..'interconverted' *R*-carvone and *S*-carvone into their enantiomers and then back again.

interconvertible (-kənˈvɜːtɪb(ə)l), *a.* [INTER- 2 a.] Mutually convertible; interchangeable.

1802–12 BENTHAM *Ration. Judic. Evid.* (1827) III. 219 Such evidentiary fact and such principal fact are interconvertible expressions. **1882** *Cornh. Mag.* June 715 A belief..that everything in nature is interconvertible. **1895** B. KIDD *Soc. Evolut.* ix. 264 The two being often used as interconvertible terms by anthropologists.

Hence **interconvertiˈbility; interconˈvertibly** *adv.*

1811–31 BENTHAM *Logic* ix. Wks. 1843 VIII. 270 As if the two appellatives were..synonymous and interconvertibly employable. **1883** J. A. FARRER in *Cornh. Mag.* XLVII. 466 The interconvertibility of Zeus, or Odin, or Indra with the animal creation.

intercooler (ˈɪntəkuːlə(r)). Also **inter-cooler.** [INTER- 2 b.] An apparatus for cooling gas heated by compression, esp. before it is compressed a second time (as in a multi-stage compressor or the cylinders of a super-charged engine).

1900 *Engin. Mag.* XIX. 679 A complete system of jacket water and a very large intercooler are used, the total capacity of the machine being 3,000 cubic feet of free air per minute compressed to 125 pounds' pressure. **1903** [see AFTERCOOLER]. **1932** CHATFIELD & TAYLOR *Airplane & its Engine* (ed. 2) viii. 234 Compressing air by a supercharger.. increases its temperature considerably and it is sometimes desirable to cool this air before it reaches the engine. This is accomplished by means of an intercooler which usually takes the form of a small radiator inserted in the air passage between the super-charger and the engine. **1944** [see AFTERCOOLER]. **1963** A. W. FARRALL *Engin. for Dairy & Food Products* viii. 202 The booster compressor..discharges its gas into an intercooler, which in turn is piped to the suction of a standard high-pressure refrigeration machine. **1970** *Motor Boat & Yachting* 16 Oct. 39/2 By installing a type of heat exchanger, called an intercooler, the mixture leaving the turbo-charger is cooled before it enters the cylinder and this increases the efficiency.

intercooling (ˈɪntəkuːlɪŋ), *vbl. sb.* Also **inter-cooling** (with hyphen). [f. the vb. *intercool* contained in prec. + -ING[1].] The cooling of gas between successive compressions; the use of an intercooler.

1902 G. D. HISCOX *Compressed Air* xii. 187 The value of proper intercooling. **1923** J. M. FORD *Compressor Theory & Pract.* viii. 153 The intercooling of the air or gas..is imperfect in that the temperature is not reduced to the initial value between the several stages. **1951** COHEN & ROGERS *Gas Turbine Theory* i. 7 If..the compression process is carried out in two or more stages with intercooling, the work of compression may be reduced appreciably. **1970** *Commercial Motor* 25 Sept. 56/3 Output of about 350 bhp, naturally aspirated, would be possible with 600 bhp when turbocharged with inter-cooling.

Hence (as a back-formation) **ˈintercool** *v. trans.*, to equip or provide with an intercooler; **ˈintercooled** *ppl. a.*

1944 E. W. F. FELLER *Air Compressors* x. 348 (*caption*) Power saved by intercooling a multistage centrifugal compressor. **1947** *Shell Aviation News* No. 109. 22/3 A wide range of performance at both moderate and high altitudes is provided by the..inter-cooled and after-cooled supercharger. **1970** *Motor Boat & Yachting* 16 Oct. 39/2 A number of diesel engines these days are offered in turbo-charged form, which pushes up their horsepower, and then intercooled as well as turbocharged for a further increase in power. **1971** *Engineering* Apr. 103 (Advt.), The five stage intercooled turbo compressors absorb 1555 bhp delivering 22,700 Kg/hr.

intercoracoid, -corallite, -cosmic, etc.: see INTER- *pref.*

intercorrelate (ɪntəˈkɒrɪleɪt), *v.* [f. INTER- 1 b + CORRELATE *v.*] *trans.* and *intr.* To correlate with one another.

1909 *Amer. Jrnl. Psychol.* XX. 368 We find..that efficiency in marking A's on a sheet of printed capitals, efficiency in finding circles or hexagons or isosceles triangles on a sheet of printed geometrical forms and efficiency in finding misspelled words are in adults all very closely intercorrelated (to ·8 or more), but are by no means so closely correlated to general intellect. **1955** T. H. PEAR *English Social Differences* 11 These [types] are so intercorrelated that they can be separated only abstractly. **1970** *Jrnl. Gen. Psychol.* LXXXII. 171 If the DAS correlates as highly with each of these scales as they intercorrelate with each other, then it could be argued that the DAS measures anxiety in general rather than death anxiety in particular. **1971** *Nature* 25 June 538/1 Faculty responses to each of these items were highly intercorrelated. **1972** *Jrnl. Social Psychol.* LXXXVII. 69 Tests were intercorrelated, and factor analyses carried out.

intercorrelation (ˌɪntəkɒrɪˈleɪʃən). *Statistics.* [f. INTER- 2 a + CORRELATION.] Correlation (sense 1 c) that relates each of a number of variates with one another.

1901 *Psychol. Rev.* VIII. 540 The laboratory mental tests show little inter-correlation in the case of college students. **1904** *Amer. Jrnl. Psychol.* XV. 92 The three observations of the same objective series presented the extraordinarily small inter-correlation of 0·22. **1922** *Jrnl. Exper. Psychol.* V. 68 Intercorrelations of a number of variables may be efficiently solved on the adding machine by means of transmutation of gross scores into class numbers with the aid of standard grouping tables. **1935** [see FACTORIALLY *adv.*]. **1961** *Lancet* 12 Aug. 359/2 Inter-correlations were calculated between the four types of test set. **1970** *Jrnl. Gen. Psychol.* LXXXIII. 125 The usual statistical information regarding the tests was obtained, including means, standard deviations,..and inter-correlations.

Hence **ˌintercorreˈlational** *a.*

1970 *Jrnl. Gen. Psychol.* LXXXIII. 157 These additional data..plus the original measures were subjected to an intercorrelational analysis.

intercortical: see INTER- *pref.* 6.

intercostal (-ˈkɒstəl), *a.* and *sb.* [ad. mod.L. *intercostāl-is*, f. INTER- 4 a + L. *costa* rib: see COSTAL. Cf. F. *intercostal* (1536 in Hatz.-Darm.).]

A. *adj.* Situated between the ribs. **a.** *Anat.* with reference to the ribs of the body.

1597 A. M. tr. *Guillemeau's Fr. Chirurg.* 19/2 Betweene the ribbes and the intercostalle muscles. **1615** CROOKE *Body of Man* 356 The midriffe and the intercostall muscles. **1741** A. MONRO *Anat.* (ed. 3) 224 The Channel for the intercostal Vessels is not to be found. **1800** *Med. Jrnl.* IV. 343 The intercostal nerve was considered by many physicians of this century, as a continuation of the *nervus vagus*. *Mod.* He is suffering from intercostal rheumatism.

b. *transf.*; esp. in shipbuilding.

1658 EVELYN *Fr. Gard.* (1675) 150 The change of their colour, and the intercostal yellowness, which is a sufficient index of their maturity. **1869** SIR E. REED *Shipbuild.* i. 7 A keelson with intercostal plates. **1890** W. J. GORDON *Foundry* 66 Such a keel is 'intercostal'.

B. *sb. pl.* Intercostal parts. **a.** *Anat.* The intercostal muscles, nerves, arteries, etc.

1681 tr. *Willis' Rem. Med. Wks.* Vocab., *Intercostals*.. nerves, so called, because..they run between the ribs. *c* **1720** W. GIBSON *Farrier's Guide* I. iii. (1738) 22 The Intercostals compose all the Flesh that we observe to fill up the Spaces between the Ribs. **1872** HUXLEY *Phys.* iv. 86 Two sets of muscles, called intercostals. **1899** *Month* Mar. 311 The ball..has wounded one of the intercostals.

b. *transf.* in shipbuilding.

1883 NARES *Constr. Ironclad* 5 The parts between the frames being called intercostals.

Hence **interˈcostally** *adv.*

1874 THEARLE *Naval Archit.* 93 Two longitudinals are fitted above the turn of the bilge, where the floor plates do not extend. Each of these is worked intercostally between all the frames. *Ibid.* 118 The stringer being connected to both the bottom plating and bracket by pieces of angle-iron worked intercostally.

interˌcosto-ˈhumeral, *a. Anat.* [f. comb. form of prec. + HUMERAL.] Connected with the intercostal parts and the humerus.

1842 E. WILSON *Anat. Vade M.* 423 The first intercosto-humeral nerve is of large size. **1868** HOLDEN *Anat.* (ed. 3) 224 The perforating branch of the second intercostal nerve ..is larger than the others, and is called the 'intercosto-humeral', because it supplies the integuments of the arm.

intercotyloid, -county, etc.: see INTER- *pref.*

intercourse (ˈɪntəkɔəs), *sb.* Also 5–7 **entercourse**, (6 **-cours**). [a. OF. *entrecours* exchange, commerce (Godef.; in AF. also *-course*), f. *entrecorre* to run between:—L. *intercurrĕre*: see INTERCUR, COURSE. Cf. the L. abl. *intercursu* 'by intervention', and med.L. *intercursus*.]

1. Communication to and fro between countries, etc.; mutual dealings between the inhabitants of different localities. In early use exclusively with reference to trade, and hence sometimes = commerce, traffic; now in more general sense.

a. **1494** FABYAN *Chron.* VII. 368 She..besought the Kynge that his marchauntes myght vse their entercourse into Flaundres as they before tymes had done. *a* **1548** HALL *Chron., Hen. VIII* 60 b, Straungiers..take the lyvinge from all the artificers, and the entercourse from all merchauntes. **1584** COGAN *Haven Health* ccxvii. (1636) 239 God hath divided his blessings, that..one Country might have entercourse with an other. **1623** BINGHAM *Xenophon* 57 They had free entercourse of trade one with another. **1669**

GALE *Crt. Gentiles* I. I. iv. 23 Their vicinitie, and mutual entercourses, made the Jews passe under their neighbors names.

β. **1473** *Rolls Parlt.* VI. 65/1 The..Company..have had and used free and frendely communication and intercurse of Marchaundise with his Subgetts. **1599** HAKLUYT *Voy.* II. 178 He wil not but maintaine yt faith promised her, & the intercourse in due force. **1656** *Burton's Diary* (1826) I. 181 The intercourse merchants are many of them traders into the Spanish countries, which are your enemies. *Ibid.*, Whether the city or the merchants of the intercourse should pay it. **1803** *Med. Jrnl.* X. 405 The almost innumerable means of intercourse now introduced into most parts of this island. **1863** LYELL *Antiq. Man* 40 It is clear that the Ohio mound-builders had commercial intercourse with the natives of distant regions.

2. a. Social communication between individuals; frequent and habitual contact in conversation and action; dealings.

1547–64 BAULDWIN *Mor. Philos.* V. iii. (Palfr.), Men, between whom happeneth to be entercourse or familiarity. **1652–62** HEYLIN *Cosmogr.* Introd. (1682) 7 That civil Entercourse, and mutual Society which the nature of Mankind doth most delight in. *a* **1714** BURNET *Hist. Ref.* I. II. 244 For justifying himself, he [Sir Thomas More] wrote a full account of all the intercourse he had with the Nun and her complices. **1751** JOHNSON *Rambler* No. 160 ¶6 Those with whom time and intercourse have made us familiar. **1852** DICKENS *Let. to Mrs. Watson* 5 Aug., We looked forward to years of unchanged intercourse.

b. With *of* (= in respect of, as regards).

1613 PURCHAS *Pilgrimage* (1614) 163 Amongst all which was peace, but no intercourse of marriages in differing Sects. **1641** J. JACKSON *True Evang. T.* III. 174 [They] have friendly and mutuall entercourse of affections, actions, customes, habits.

c. *pl.* Now *rare.*

1742 RICHARDSON *Pamela* IV. 220 Disengaging myself from all Intercourses that have given you Uneasiness. **1748** HARTLEY *Observ. Man.* I. iii. 311 Their former Intercourses with the Israelites. **1804** A. RANKEN *Hist. France* III. I. v. 75 New scenes, objects and intercourses enlarged his views. **1855** HT. MARTINEAU *Autobiog.* (1877) II. 446 My hours are now best spent in affectionate intercourses.

d. Sexual connexion.

1798 MALTHUS *Popul.* I. ii. (1806) I. 21 *note*, An illicit intercourse between the sexes. **1804** ABERNETHY *Surg. Obs.* 143 Propagated by promiscuous intercourse. **1919** M. K. BRADBY *Psycho-Anal.* III. ix. 118 Witches were examined during their trials for evidence of their fleshly intercourse with the devil. **1922** JOYCE *Ulysses* 402 He..did not scruple ..to attempt illicit intercourse with a female domestic. **1963** A. HERON *Towards Quaker View of Sex* i. 6 The incidence of extra-marital intercourse is great. **1973** S. FISHER *Female Orgasm* i. 26 Some of the decline in intercourse frequency and responsiveness..may be caused by the..physiological decline of their husbands.

3. Communion between man and that which is spiritual or unseen.

1561 T. NORTON *Calvin's Inst.* II. 145 He suffered other nations to walke in vanitie, as though they had not any entercourse or any thing to do with him. **1597** HOOKER *Eccl. Pol.* V. xxiii. §1 His heavenly inspirations and our holy desires are as so many Angels of entercourse and commerce betweene God and us. **1649** ROBERTS *Clavis Bibl.* 354 The sweet entercourse and communion betwixt God, and his Church. **1727** DE FOE *Hist. Appar.* Introd. (1840) 2 It does not follow that there is no intercourse or communication between the world of spirits and the world we live in. **1860** PUSEY *Min. Proph.* 605 A devout intercourse with God.

†**4.** Communication of ideas; discourse, conversation, discussion. *Obs.* (exc. as included in 2).

1570–6 LAMBARDE *Peramb. Kent* (1826) 421 After some entercourses, and when they had agreed upon a plat of their businesse. **1611** SPEED *Hist. Gt. Brit.* VI. xl. §4. 144 After much inter-course, and many intreaties passed, at length.. he accepted their offer. **1660** R. COKE *Power & Subj.* 259 To these may be added a profound Judgement in the affaires both of Church & State, how much it appeared in the former, appears in the entercourse between him and Master Hinderson. **1692** RAY *Dissol. World* 38 This Tradition.. which they could not receive from the Greek Philosophers or Poets, with whom they had no entercourse.

†**5. a.** Intercommunication between things or parts.

1626 BACON *Sylva* §700 We see plainly what an Intercourse there is between the Teeth, and the Organ of the Hearing, by the taking of the end of a Bow between the Teeth, and striking upon the String. **1634** SIR T. HERBERT *Trav.* 95 This Caspian Sea, which..has no commerce or entercourse with any Sea, except..it be subterranean. **1661** BOYLE *Spring of Air* I. v. (1682) 12 When the Mercurial Cylinder..has at the other end of it Air, kept from any Entercourse with the Atmosphere. **1787** BEST *Angling* (ed. 2) 126 Those [rivers] that have a more immediate intercourse with the sea, participate of its influences, and have the same vicissitudes.

†**b.** A means or way of intercommunication.

1660 BOYLE *New Exp. Phys. Mech.* xli. 333 We thought fit to open..an intercourse betwixt the Air in the Receiver, and that without it. **1781** *Hist. Eur.* in *Ann. Reg.* 14/1 Smaller armed vessels..master of all the channels and intercourses, as well as of the adjoining sea.

†**6.** Passage in; entrance. *Obs.*

1598 STOW *Surv.* xxv. (1603) 226 A doore of entercourse into this garden. **1658** EVELYN *Fr. Gard.* (1675) 293 Where both the sun and air have free entrecourse.

7. Continuous interchange or exchange *of* (letters, etc.). Now *rare.*

1576 FLEMING *Panopl. Epist.* 130, I will not write..what I thinke toucheing the weale publique..because the intercourse of suche letters are daungerous. **1667** MILTON *P.L.* IX. 238 This sweet intercourse Of looks and smiles. **1729** BUTLER *Serm. Forgiveness* Wks. 1874 II. 106 The first offence..becomes the occasion of entering into a long intercourse of ill offices. **1818** JAS. MILL *Brit. India* II. v. i. 344 An active intercourse of letters and messengers ensued. **1828** D'ISRAELI *Chas. I*, II. ii. 54 These letters were afterwards followed by an intercourse of civilities.

†**8.** Interchange of one thing with another; alternation. *Obs.*

1571 GOLDING *Calvin on Ps.* xix. 2 The orderly intercourse of dayes and nightes so fitly succeding. **1613** PURCHAS *Pilgrimage* II. viii. (1614) 137 Yet had the Kingdome of Judah their entercourses of corruption and reformation, according as they had good or bad kings. **1621** QUARLES *Argalus & P.* (1678) 14 The entercourses Of whose mixt fortunes taught her tender heart To feel the self-same joy, the self-same smart. **1655** H. VAUGHAN *Silex Scint.*, *Man* i, Birds like watchful clocks the noiseless date, And inter-course of times divide.

9. †**a.** The fact of coming between or intervening; intervention; an intervening course or space; an interval. *Obs.*

a **1586** SIDNEY *Arcadia* VI. (1590) 487 The Arcadian plaines, beautified by the intercourse of many forrests. **1589** NASHE *Anat. Absurd.* Ep. Ded. 3 But from such entercourse of excuse, let my vnschooled indignities conuert themselves to your courtesie. **1645** PAGITT *Heresiogr.* (1662) 8 Three courses of meat, but between them there was an entercourse, for the king accused a man of treason and cut off his head and returned again.

†**b.** Intervention on the part of some agent.

1586 FERNE *Blaz. Gentrie* 67 By the intercourse of the Kinges royall assent adhibited by the hande of his heralde. **1603** SIR C. HEYDON *Jud. Astrol.* To Rdr. 6 [It] is effected immediately by the..arme of God, without the intercourse of naturall causes. **1646** J. GREGORY *Notes & Obs.* (1650) 115 If we betake our selves to this other way, one onely entercourse of Omnipotency will serve the turne.

†**inter'course**, *v.* *Obs. rare.* [f. prec. sb.]

1. *intr.* To run through, run across.

1597 GERARDE *Herbal* II. liii. §1. 272 Two colours occupying halfe the flower, or intercoursing the whole flower with streakes and orderly streames. **1611** FLORIO, *Intercorrere*, to entercourse or run.

2. To have intercourse *with.*

1571 HANMER *Chron. Irel.* (1633) 53 Entercoursing with domesticall and forraigne students.

intercoxal, -cranial, etc.: see INTER- *pref.*

intercrop (ɪntə'krɒp), *v.* [INTER- 1.] To raise a crop among plants of a different kind, usually using the space between rows. Hence **inter'cropping** *vbl. sb.*; **'intercrop** *sb.*, a crop so raised.

1898 W. ROBINSON *Eng. Flower Garden* (ed. 6) v. 94 Some kind of inter-cropping would give an excellent result in the flower garden also. **1935** H. F. MACMILLAN *Tropical Planting & Gardening* (ed. 4) iv. 30 The inter-crop or catch-crop may retard the growth of the principal crop. **1945** in R. W. Zandvoort et al. *Wartime English* (1957) 133 In a West-country orchard..rows of inter-cropped potatoes flourish beneath the fruit trees. **1951** J. S. DOUGLAS *Hydroponics* vi. 89 Any well-planned hydroponicum will allow plenty of scope for careful intercropping. **1966** WEBSTER & WILSON *Agric. in Tropics* x. 230 An intercrop is clearly undesirable on account of competition for soil moisture. **1969** G. WRIGLEY *Tropical Agric.* (ed. 2) ii. 119 The production of an acre inter-cropped was equivalent to an acre and a half cultivated in a pure stand.

intercross ('ɪntəkrɒs, -krɔːs), *sb.* [INTER- 2 a.] An instance of cross-breeding or cross-fertilization.

1859 DARWIN *Orig. Spec.* iv. 101 Both in the vegetable and animal kingdoms, an occasional intercross with a distinct individual [*ed.* 1873, between distinct individuals] is a law of nature.

intercross (ɪntə'krɒs, -krɔːs), *v.* [INTER- 1 b.]

1. *trans.* **a.** To cross each other (also *intr.* for *refl.*). **b.** To lay or place across each other.

1711 SHAFTESB. *Charac.* (1737) III. 184 Various shapes and colours agreeably mixt, and rang'd in lines, intercrossing without confusion. **1817** COLERIDGE *Lay Serm.* in *Biog. Lit.* (1882) 379 A vast idol, framed of iron bars intercrossed, which formed..an immense cage. **1821** LAMB *Elia* Ser. I. *St. Valentine*, This is the day on which.. Valentines cross and intercross each other at every street and turning. **1858** G. MACDONALD *Phantastes* iv. 37 Golden and red..fires crossed and intercrossed each other.

2. *intr.* Of plants or animals of different stocks or species: To breed or propagate with each other. Also *trans.* in *pass.*

1859 DARWIN *Orig. Spec.* iv. 101 If..all hermaphrodites do occasionally intercross with other individuals [etc.]. **1863** BATES *Nat. Amazon* i. (1864) 15 Ants..are thus enabled to intercross with members of distant colonies. **1878** DARWIN in *Life & Lett.* (1887) III. 162 The..offspring must intercross one with another. **1880** —— in *Nature* XXI. 207/1 The almost universal sterility of species when intercrossed.

Hence **inter'crossing** *vbl. sb.* and *ppl. a.*

1859 DARWIN *Orig. Spec.* iv. 96 On the Intercrossing of Individuals. **1876** *Times* 4 Oct., Inter-crossing and overlapping lines of light. **1878** BELL *Gegenbaur's Comp. Anat.* 395 In others the muscular layer is..composed of intercrossing bands.

intercrural (ɪntə'krʊərəl), *a.* *Anat.* [INTER- 4 a.] Situated between the crura, legs, or limbs, of the body, or of some part of it: see CRUS 2.

a **1693** URQUHART *Rabelais* III. xviii. 148 It is my intercrural Pudding. **1839–47** TODD *Cycl. Anat.* III. 673/1 The depression..which separates them, is the intercrural.. space. **1856–8** W. CLARK *Van der Hoeven's Zool.* II. 739 Inter-crural membrane mostly small or none. **1888** ROLLESTON & JACKSON *Anim. Life* 415 Intercrural cartilages which are placed intervertebrally.

intercrust, -crystallize, -curl, etc.: see INTER- *pref.*

intercrystalline (ɪntə'krɪstəlaɪn), *a.* [INTER- 4 a.] Situated or occurring between crystals, esp. those which form a metal.

1901 *Phil. Trans. R. Soc.* A. CXCV. 295 Where the quantity of impurity present is sufficiently great, this eutectic can be seen under the microscope forming an intercrystalline cement. **1923** GLAZEBROOK *Dict. Appl. Physics* V. 361/2 Intercrystalline cracking near the melting-point sometimes takes place under very low stresses. **1962** *Science Survey* III. 329 The final failure of the metal is essentially mechanical and it usually occurs by the propagation, through the body of the metal, of inter-crystalline (or intergranular) cracks.

inter-cultural: see INTER- *pref.* 4 c.

†**inter'cur**, *v.* *Obs.* Also 6 entercorre, 6–7 intercurre. [ad. L. *intercurrĕre*, f. *inter* between + *currĕre* to run; in early use, through OF. *entrecorre* (Godef.).]

1. *intr.* To run, come, or pass *between* persons or things.

1527 *St. Papers Hen. VIII*, I. 237, I was sent as your Lieutenant, being alwaies propice and redy to entercorre, as a lovyng mynister, for the encrease of amyte bitwene Your Highnes and hym. **1545** RAYNOLD *Byrth Mankynde* I. x. (1634) 36 Like as the earth doth intercurre and intermingle it selfe between and among the small fibres..of rootes. **1625** USSHER *Answ. Jesuit* 468 The first beginning..is a sanctified heart, the last end the seeking of Gods glorie, and faith working by loue must intercurre betwixt both.

2. To come between, or in the course of; to intervene, come in the way.

c **1555** HARPSFIELD *Divorce Hen. VIII* (Camden) 99 Because it [their untrue assertion] doth often intercurre in their book, we will here make answer for the whole. **1592** BABINGTON *Notes Genesis* xxi. (1637) 71 Matrimony ceaseth not to bee the holy ordinance of God, though these troubles ..intercurre. **1677** R. CARY *Chronol.* II. II. I. x. 207 With this Series of Years..doth intercur another Succession of High Priests.

Hence †**inter'curring** *ppl. a.*, intervening.

1611 SPEED *Hist. Gt. Brit.* IX. xi. §47. 661 Wee will hasten now to the last Act..onely we will first remember some intercurring matters.

intercurrence (ɪntə'kʌrəns). [f. next: see -ENCE.] Intervention; an intervening occurrence.

1603 HOLLAND *Plutarch's Mor.* 1335 There may be providence, and the least intercurrence of fortune. **1661** BOYLE *Phys. Ess., Hist. Fluid.* xvi, We may proceed to consider what fluidity salt-petre is capable of without the intercurrence of a liquor. **1682** SIR T. BROWNE *Chr. Mor.* I. §29 To be sagacious in such intercurrences is not Superstition, but wary and pious Discretion. **1897** *Allbutt's Syst. Med.* IV. 401 Epithelial casts are also occasionally found, and must be held to indicate the intercurrence of tubal catarrh.

So †**inter'currency**. *Obs. rare*$^{-1}$.

1670 H. STUBBE *Plus Ultra* 40 The intercurrencies of irregular and unknown particles, like to moats in..a Glass.

intercurrent (ɪntə'kʌrənt), *a.* (*sb.*) [ad. L. *intercurrent-em*, pr. pple. of *intercurrĕre* to INTERCUR.] That runs or comes between.

1. †**a.** Of material things: Coming in between others; lying or situated between. *Obs.*

1656 W. D. tr. *Comenius' Gate Lat. Unl.* §41. 17 The Cardinal winds..with their middle, and the other intercurrent ones. **1665** HOOKE *Microgr.* 160 Some very easie way of separating the pulp or intercurrent juices. **1682** GREW *Veget. Roots* §39 Yielding to the intercurrent Fibres of the Parenchyma. *c* **1685** E. HALLEY in *Naval Chron.* VIII. 119 This shoalness of the sea, and the intercurrent continents, are the reason.

b. Of time, the course of events: Intervening.

1611 SPEED *Hist. Gt. Brit.* VIII. iii. §16. 385 By many his intercurrent actions..he may iustly be cleared of that imputation. **1614** RALEIGH *Hist. World* III. (1634) 16 A longer space of time intercurrent. **1677** R. CARY *Chronol.* II. II. III. xx. 268 The intercurrent dispositions of the Times under the Persian and Macedonian, Ægyptian Monarchies. **1883** F. W. H. MYERS *Ess., Mod., Mazzini* (1885) 3 Alfieri —his republicanism strangely complicated by an intercurrent passion for high-born dames. **1887** F. ROBINSON *New Relig. Med.* 82 The Book of Job affords a sufficient refutation; no intercurrent paradox meets us there.

†**c.** Of messengers: Passing to and fro between parties. *Obs. rare*$^{-1}$.

1665 MANLEY *Grotius' Low C. Warres* 663 The Embassadors could not be drawn to agree..Nor was there any better progress by intercurrent Messengers.

2. *spec.* in *Med.* **a.** Of a disease: Occurring during the progress of another disease. Also, Recurring at intervals. Formerly (of a fever), Happening at any period of the year, as distinguished from those confined to particular seasons.

1684 tr. *Bonet's Merc. Compit.* VI. 189 Some Fevers may deservedly be reckoned among the Intercurrent. **1857** DUNGLISON *Med. Lex.* 554 Intercurrent Pneumonia. **1869** E. A. PARKES *Pract. Hygiene* (ed. 3) 493 The low intercurrent inflammations which occur in scurvy. **1877** ERICHSEN *Surgery* I. 11 Slow recoveries, often interrupted by intercurrent diseases.

b. Of the pulse: Having an extra beat.

1707 FLOYER *Physic. Pulse-Watch* 49 An intercurrent Pulse is unequal in Crebrity, when one Pulse happens more

than usual. **1857** DUNGLISON *Med. Lex.* 503 The pulse in such cases [of intercadence] is said to be intercurrent.

† **B.** *sb.* An intervening circumstance or event; an incident. *Obs. rare*⁻¹.

1603 HOLLAND *Plutarch's Mor.* 1224 Fortune..having diversified..our enterprise, like a plaie or enterlude, with many dangerous intercurrents, was assistant and ran with us.

Hence **inter'currently** *adv.*, in an intercurrent manner.

1885-8 FAGGE & PYE-SMITH *Princ. Med.* (ed. 2) I. 175 Examples of relapse occurring 'intercurrently'.

intercur'sation. *rare.* [n. of action from L. *intercursāre*, freq. of *intercurrĕre*: see INTERCUR.] The action of running between, or coming in the way of anything.

1813 T. BUSBY *Lucretius* v. Comm. xviii, Scheinerus asserts that they [the scintillations of the stars] proceed from the intercisions of their several species darting to the eye, which he attributes to vaporous intercursations.

†**inter'cursitor.** *Obs. rare*⁻¹. [INTER- 1 a + CURSITOR.] A messenger between parties.

1603 HARSNET *Pop. Impost.* xxii. 144 An Intelligencer or Intercursitor betweene them, that may in a trice relate to the one what the other hath done or said.

inter'cut, *v.* Also 7 enter-. [INTER- 1 a.] *trans.*

†**1.** To cut into, to divide by, or as by, cutting; to intersect. *Obs. rare.*

1611 FLORIO, *Intercidere*, to entercut. **1660** HOWELL *Parly Beasts* i. 5 The Countrey..so intercutt, and indented with the Sea, or fresh navigable Rivers. **1725** BRADLEY *Fam. Dict.* s.v. *Garden*, Gardens whose Level and Grounds are intercut with Descents of Terrasses.

2. *Cinematogr.* To insert (a scene or shot) into an existing one by cutting. Const. *with.* Also *intr.* and *transf.*

1953 K. REISZ *Technique Film Editing* i. 33 Inter-cut with a number of slow-moving shots of Kerensky proudly ascending the stairway, are separate titles describing Kerensky's rank. **1954** *Encounter* Aug. 52/1 Frank Norris.. employed the method of ironic contrast, intercutting the death of a destitute widow from starvation with descriptions of the sumptuous dinner given by a rail-road-king obliquely responsible for her condition. **1957** MANVELL & HUNTLEY *Technique Film Music* ii. 38 The military advance to drum taps and trumpet, beautifully intercut in track and picture to a rising string crescendo for the masses. **1958** *Listener* 6 Nov. 750/2 There was an intrusive guitar, an impromptu balladist, a ticking clock, and much elaborate montage, inter-cutting street voices with voices on the radio. **1962** *Ibid.* 27 Sept. 474/2 *La Notte* abounds with high-angled shots intercut with the reverse low angles which create a complex of vertiginous effects. **1970** I. C. JARVIE *Towards Sociol. of Cinema* ix. 128 Resnais..intercuts scenes from the heroine's memories..with her present *affaire.*

Hence **inter'cutting** *vbl. sb.*

1611 FLORIO, *Intercisione*, a cutting off or betweene, an entercutting. **1953** K. REISZ *Technique Film Editing* ii. 133 The explosion itself is conveyed by the rapid intercutting of frames of the submarine and of a cone of water thrown up by a depth-charge. **1966** *Punch* 9 Nov. 692/1, I intended to do all the characters' complete dialogue before I attempted inter-cutting (the TV phrase).

†**in'tercutal,** *a. Obs.* [f. L. *intercus, -cutem*, absol. for *aqua intercus* 'intercutal water', dropsy, (f. *inter* between, within + *cut-em* skin) + -AL¹.] In *intercutal water*, dropsical fluid.

1650 ASHM. *Chym. Collect., Arcanum* (ed. 3) 194 The second borders upon the dropsie, and is the corruption of intercutal Water. **1684** tr. *Bonet's Merc. Compit.* VIII. 295 Vesicatories let out the intercutal water plentifully.

†**intercu'taneous,** *a. Obs.* [f. late L. *intercutāne-us* (see prec. and CUTANEOUS) + -OUS. Cf. F. *intercutané* (Littré).] Situated between the skin and flesh; subcutaneous. Also, lying between the bark and stem of a tree.

1651 BIGGS *New Disp.* ¶241 Some intercutaneous part, which the Physitian commands to be wounded. **1664** EVELYN *Sylva* 55 If it [a tree] lye prostrate with the bark on, which is a receptacle for a certain intercutaneous worm that accelerates its decay. *Ibid.* (1776) 363 The intercutaneous moisture endangers the tree.

intercystic, -dash, etc.: see INTER- *pref.*

†**'interdeal,** *sb. Obs.* Also enter-. [f. INTER- 2 a + DEAL *sb.*²; or from INTERDEAL *v.*] Mutual dealing, negotiation; intercourse; ado.

1591 SPENSER *M. Hubberd* 785 Thereto [he] doth his Courting most applie To learne the enterdeale of Princes strange. **1596** —— *State Irel.* Wks. (Globe) 628/2 The trading and interdeale with other nations rounde about. **1605** SYLVESTER *Du Bartas* II. iii. IV. *Captains* 1013 That Form of Rule is a right Common-weal Where all the People have an Enterdeal. **1612** T. JAMES *Jesuit's Downf.* 44 The Iesuits haue continuall enterdeale with the Civill Magistrates, with Heretickes, and men of a suspected Religion.

inter'deal, *v.* [f. INTER- 1 b + DEAL *v.*] *intr.* To deal or negotiate mutually.

1601 DANIEL *Civ. Wars* VI. xxxvi, Yorke & his side could not, while life remaynd, Though thus disperst, but worke and interdeale. **1808** W. TAYLOR in *Ann. Rev.* VI. 304 The great mass of emigrants would be young merchants..who would intermarry, as well as interdeal with the Hindoos.

Hence †**inter'dealing** *vbl. sb.* = INTERDEAL *sb.*; also †**inter'dealer**, a negotiator, a mediator.

1611 SPEED *Hist. Gt. Brit.* IX. xi. §15. 654 By the continuall interdealings of the Prelates..the kindling displeasures were for the present allayed. **1613-18** DANIEL *Coll. Hist. Eng.* (1626) 54 He was a friend to them both, and would gladly bee an interdealer for concord.

interdebate, -denominational, -dentil: see INTER- *pref.*

interdefinable (ɪntədɪ'faɪnəb(ə)l), *a. Logic.* [f. INTER- 2 a + DEFINABLE *a.*] Of constants, etc.: that can be defined interchangeably with each other. Hence **interdefina'bility**, the state or quality of being interdefinable; **interdefi'nition**, one of two or more definitions that are interchangeable.

1948 AMBROSE & LAZEROWITZ *Fund. Symbolic Logic* iii. 41 With the exception of '~', which is absolutely primitive, all the symbols for the logical constants are inter-definable. *Ibid.* 36 The possibilities of interdefinition of the relatively primitive constants. **1951** *Mind* LX. 265 The interdefinability of the constants of the system. **1955** A. N. PRIOR *Formal Logic* i. 9 Evaluation of truth-functional forms, and the inter-definability of truth functions. **1958** H. B. CURRY et al. *Combinatory Logic* I. v. 155 (*heading*) Interdefinability of simple combinators. **1965** *Philos. Rev.* LXXIV. 522 'Ought' and 'must' are interdefinable. **1972** H. B. CURRY et al. *Combinatory Logic* II. xiii. 222 In §2 we considered interdefinitions among the basic arithmetical combinators.

interdental (ɪntə'dɛntəl), *a.* and *sb.* [INTER- 4 a.]

A. *adj.* **1.** Situated or placed between the teeth (of a person or animal, or of a toothed wheel).

1874 KNIGHT *Dict. Mech., Gear-cutting Machine*, one for making cog-wheels by cutting out the interdental material. **1878** T. BRYANT *Pract. Surg.* I. 555 Moon's splint therefore seems to be the best interdental one we possess.

2. *Phonology.* Pronounced by placing the tip of the tongue between the teeth.

1877 SWEET *Handbk. Phonetics* §145 French (t) and (d) are dental, often also interdental. **1887** COOK tr. *Sievers' O.E. Gram.* 104, ð and þ originally denote without distinction the interdental spirant which is now represented in Eng. by th. **1933** L. BLOOMFIELD *Lang.* vi. 98 Contact..can be made against the edges of the upper teeth (interdental position). **1943** K. L. PIKE *Phonetics* II. vii. 123 An interdental sound is one in which the tip of the tongue is placed between the upper and lower teeth.

B. *sb. Phonology.* A sound formed by placing the tip of the tongue between the teeth.

1953 C. E. BAZELL *Ling. Form* iv. 45 The distribution of voiced and voiceless inter-dentals in English is quite different from that of other voiced/voiceless pairs. **1961** R. B. LONG *Sentence & its Parts* xix. 430 This obstruction can occur..at the front teeth, as for the interdentals.

interdentally (ɪntə'dɛntəlɪ), *adv.* [f. INTERDENTAL *a.* + -LY².] In an interdental position; between the teeth.

1910 *Practitioner* Jan. 115 The neck of the tooth..is embraced by a thin shallow flap of gum, continuous interstitially (interdentally) with the gum pad. **1939** I. BIRSCHFELD *Toothbrush* i. 4 Irregular occlusal openings to the interproximal spaces developed, through which food was forced interdentally.

interdepartmental (ɪntədiːpɑːt'mɛntəl), *a.* [INTER- 4 c.] Carried on or forming a communication between or among departments. Hence **interdepart'mentally** *adv.*

1895 *Daily News* 25 May 4/6 An interdepartmental Committee, composed of representatives of the Treasury, the Post Office, and the Colonial Office. **1901** *Westm. Gaz.* 7 June 2/2 This is the bane of Government offices, both departmentally and interdepartmentally. **1906** *Ibid.* 30 Oct. 2/1 But there are strong grounds for believing that the question of the attitude of the Government towards the proposals now before the Berlin Conference has not been made a Cabinet question; in other words, that it has been dealt with interdepartmentally. **1963** *Times* 18 Apr. 9/4 One result is that interdepartmentally External Affairs staff frequently display a lack of understanding of other departments and programmes. **1966** *Economist* 10 Dec. 1155/1 In actual fact the case is still being argued interdepartmentally.

interdepend (ˌɪntədɪ'pɛnd), *v.* [INTER- 1 b.] *intr.* To depend upon each other mutually.

1848 HARE *Guesses* (1867) 482 Bringing them [atoms] to coalesce and interdepend. **1888** *Voice* (N.Y.) 15 Mar., Under the state all rights and duties are mutual—they interdepend.

interdependence (ˌɪntədɪ'pɛndəns). Also -ance. [INTER- 2 a.] The fact or condition of depending each upon the other; mutual dependence.

1822 COLERIDGE *Lett., Convers.*, etc. II. 97 Unfitness for a state of moral and personal union and life-long interdependence. **1825** —— *Aids Refl.* (1858) I. App. C. 412 In social and political life this acme is inter-dependence; in moral life it is independence. **1878** HUXLEY *Physiogr.* Pref. 6 Knowledge respecting natural phenomena and their inter-dependence.

ˌ**interde'pendency.** [INTER- 2 a.] = prec.

1838 *Fraser's Mag.* XVII. 665 An interdependency of the will revealed as a fact..to the power of consciousness. **1848** R. I. WILBERFORCE *Incarnation* iii. (1852) 43 That interdependency of structure, which unites the different portions of an organic agent into a co-ordinate whole. **1889** MIVART *Truth* 493 The interrelations and interdependencies which exist between the various orders of creatures inhabiting this planet.

interdependent (ˌɪntədɪ'pɛndənt), *a.* [INTER- 2 a.] Dependent each upon the other; mutually dependent.

1817 COLERIDGE *Biog. Lit.* (1882) 57 Which..stand..in interdependent connection with everything that exists. **1879** H. SPENCER *Data Ethics* i. §2. 5 Conduct is a whole..an aggregate of inter-dependent actions performed by an organism.

Hence **interde'pendently**, in an inter-dependent manner, in mutual dependence.

1884 H. SPENCER in *Contemp. Rev.* June 773 A conception of [society] as having a natural structure in which all its institutions, governmental, religious, industrial, commercial, etc., etc., are inter-dependently bound. **1890** *Scribner's Mag.* Jan. 21 The buildings were interdependently combined.

interdespise (-dɪ'spaɪz), *v. rare.* [INTER- 1 b.] *trans.* To despise mutually, feel mutual contempt for (each other); also *absol.*

1840 DE QUINCEY in *Tait's Mag.* VII. 38 They met, they saw, they interdespised. **1893** FAIRBAIRN *Christ in Mod. Theol.* I. ii. II. i. 232 The two great masters..cordially inter-despised each other.

interdestructive (ˌɪntədɪ'strʌktɪv), *a.* [INTER- 2 a.] Mutually destructive.

1805 W. TAYLOR in *Ann. Rev.* III. 245 There can be no such thing as unproductive capital; the terms are inter-destructive. **1813** —— in *Monthly Mag.* XXXV. 215 The document concerning Paradise, and the document concerning the Deluge, are inter-destructive.

Hence **interde'structiveness**, mutual destructiveness.

1817 GODWIN *Mandeville* II. 103 There are antipathies, and properties interchangeably irreconcilable and destructive to each other..I had found this true opposition and interdestructiveness in Clifford.

interdevour, etc.: see INTER- *pref.*

inter-dialectal: see INTER- *pref.* 4 c.

†**inter'dice.** *Carpentry. Obs.* Forms: 7 **enterdese, enter-, interdice,** 8 **enter-, intertise, -duce.** [Derivation obscure.

The OF. *entretoise* (app. of same meaning):—late L. **intertensa* 'something stretched between', would in Eng. normally assume the form **entertese*, of which the recorded *enterdese* and *entertise* seem to be corruptions. The form *enterdese* seems to have been further corrupted into *enter-*, *interdise*, and perverted by pseudo-etymology into *enter-*, *interduce*, as if from L. *dūcĕre* to lead; while *entertise*, *interties*, have suggested the formation of the mod. synonym INTERTIE.]

A horizontal piece of timber connecting two vertical pieces; an INTERTIE.

1617 *MS. Acc. St. John's Hosp., Canterb.*, Payd for the laing in of two selles and laing in of enterdeses at Owsbanes houss. **1663** GERBIER *Counsel* 67 Interdices and Braces seven inches and five inches. **1703** MOXON *Mech. Exerc.* 141 The Binding Intertises, or indeed, more properly Inter-duces. *Ibid.* 160 *Enterduce*, or *Entertise*. **1703** T. N. *City & C. Purchaser* 183 *Inter-ties, -duces*,..are those smaller pieces of Timber that lie Horizontally betwixt the Summers. **1734** *Builder's Dict.*, Interties, Interduces.

interdict ('ɪntədɪkt), *sb.* Forms: α. 3 **entredit,** 4 **enterdite.** β. 5 **interdite.** γ. 5 **interdicte,** 7– **interdict.** [ME. a. OF. *entredit* (13th c. in Hatz.-Darm.), in 14th c. *intredit*, mod.F. *interdit*, ad. L. *interdictum* (from *interdictus*, pa. pple. of *interdīcĕre* to INTERDICT) to which the Eng. word was conformed in 16th c. The order in which the senses have been adopted in Eng. is the reverse of that in which they orig. arose.]

1. *gen.* An authoritative prohibition; an act of forbidding peremptorily.

a **1626** BACON (J.), Among his other fundamental laws, he did ordain the interdicts and prohibitions touching entrance of strangers. **1671** MILTON *P.R.* II. 369 These are not Fruits forbidden, no interdict Defends the touching of these viands pure. **1824** W. IRVING *T. Trav.* I. 217, I put a positive interdict on my rooms being exhibited. **1841** MYERS *Cath. Th.* III. xii. 46 Irrepressible instincts and interdicts of the Conscience and the Reason.

2. *Law.* **a.** *Roman Law.* A provisional decree of the prætor, in a dispute of private persons relating to possession, commanding or (more usually) forbidding something to be done.

1611 FLORIO, *Interdittione*..Also an iniunction made by the Magistrate, an interdict. **1652** NEEDHAM tr. *Selden's Mare Cl.* 87 Ulpian saith, against that man who hath cast a Dam or Pile into the Sea, an Interdict is allowed him who perhaps may bee endamaged thereby. **1681** STAIR *Inst. Law Scotl.* IV. xxvi. §1 These actions [possessory] are like the interdict in the Roman law, *uti possidetis.* **1880** MUIRHEAD *Gaius* IV. §140 They are called decrees when he orders something to be done, as when he commands that something shall be produced or restored; interdicts, when he prohibits something to be done.

b. *Sc. Law.* 'An order of the Court of Session, or of an inferior court, pronounced, on cause shown, for stopping any act or proceedings complained of as illegal or wrongful' (Bell *Dict. Law Scotl.*); corresponding to an INJUNCTION in English Law.

1810 *Act 50 Geo. III*, c. 112 §41 Bills of suspension and interdict shall with respect to caution remain as at present. **1876** *Act 39 & 40 Vict.* c. 70 §31 An interim interdict, although appealed against, shall be binding till recalled.

3. *R.C. Ch.* An authoritative sentence debarring a particular place or person (esp. the former) from ecclesiastical functions and privileges.

1297 R. GLOUC. (Rolls) 10297 þou hast nou..þe pope bisout þat he relesi þe entredit. *Ibid.* 10393 Drede in eche half was vpe þis king Ion Of mansinge & entredit, & al so of is fon. **1390** GOWER *Conf.* I. 259 This pope..Hath sent the bulle of his sentence With cursinge and enterdite. **1481** CAXTON *Reynard* xxviii. (Arb.) 70, I shall..sende there an Inderdicte that noman shal rede ne syngen ne crystene chyldren ne burye the deede ne receyue sacramente. **1682** BURNET *Rights Princes* v. 177 He requires them to put the whole Kingdom under an Interdict. **1769** ROBERTSON *Chas. V* (1796) III. xii. 423 Those Bulls and Interdicts..made the greatest Princes tremble. **1815** ELPHINSTONE *Acc. Caubul* (1842) I. 265 He..stopped the usual call to prayers, and suspended all the ceremonies of religion, as if the country were under an interdict. **1885** *Catholic Dict.* (ed. 3) s.v., Interdicts are divided into local, personal, and mixed. In the first kind a place is interdicted, so that no divine office may be celebrated or heard in it, either by the inhabitants or by strangers. By the second kind persons are interdicted, so as to be debarred from using the sacraments or exercising the functions prohibited, in whatever place they may be. By the mixed kind both place and persons are directly interdicted—*e.g.* a city and its inhabitants.

4. *attrib.* and *Comb.*

1875 POSTE *Gaius* IV. (ed. 2) 642 The mortgagor had by a legal fiction usucapion-possession, the mortgagee had interdict-possession. **1884** *Pall Mall G.* 16 Feb. 7/2 One of the Glendale men who was imprisoned in connection with the well-known interdict case. **1898** S. EVANS *Holy Graal* 28 The Interdict difficulty had pressed hardly on former legations against the heretics.

interdict (ɪntə'dɪkt), *v.* Forms: α. 3–4 **entredite**, 4–6 **enterdite, -dyte**, (4–5 **entir-, entyr-**). β. 5–7 **interdyte**, 6 **intredite, interdite**. γ. 6– **interdict**. [ME. *entredite-n*, f. *entredit* INTERDICT *sb.*, after OF. *entredire*, pa. pple. *entredit*, ad. L. *interdīcere*, *interdict-um* to interpose by speech, forbid by decree, f. *inter* between + *dīcĕre* to say, speak; subseq. conformed, first in prefix, and finally in stem, to the L. ppl. stem *interdict-*. As in the sb., the specific ecclesiastical sense was the earliest in Eng. use.]

1. *trans.* To declare authoritatively against the doing of (an action) or the use of (a thing); to forbid, prohibit; to debar or preclude by or as by a command.

1502 *Ord. Crysten Men* (W. de W. 1506) II. xv. 123 All foule thoughtes & carnalle desyres to us ben interdyted and defended. **1581** J. BELL *Haddon's Answ. Osor.* 68 As well bycause the Gospell interditeth it, as also bycause reason reclaimeth agaynst it. **1592** *Nobody & Someb.* in Simpson *Sch. Shaks.* (1878) I. 329 What traitrous hand dares interdict our way? **1631** GOUGE *God's Arrows* III. §94. 359 Clement 8. had sent..two Bulls, to interdict all claime or title to the Crown of England. **1725** POPE *Odyss.* XIX. 250 Firm wisdom interdicts the soft'ning tear. **1844** H. H. WILSON *Brit. India* III. 461 All proceedings against the Rawal were..positively interdicted. **1865** LIVINGSTONE *Zambesi* Pref. 8 The Portuguese interdict all foreign commerce.

2. To restrain (a person) by authority from the doing or use of something; to forbid to do something; to debar or preclude from something. (With the legal instances cf. INTERDICTION 3 and INTERDICT *sb.* 2.) Const. *from*, †*of*, †*to do* something; also with double obj. (a person a thing).

c **1575** *Balfour's Practicks* (1754) 186 Ony persoun may..be interdictit fra alienation, dispositioun, or making of ony takkis of ony his landis and heritage, bot be expresse consent and assent of certane of his kinnismen and freindis, quhome he pleisis to name. **1575–85** ABP. SANDYS *Serm.* (Parker Soc.) 204 Who..will exclude thee out of his kingdom, interdict thee his tabernacle. **1581** *Sc. Acts Jas. VI* (1597) c. 118 That the person, at quhais instance the vther is interdited or inhibite produce the said interdiction and inhibition..to the Clerke of the Schire. **1600** HOLLAND *Livy* XXV. 548 They judged him to bee a banished man..and interdicted the use of water and of fire. **1653** H. COGAN tr. *Pinto's Trav.* xxvii. 107 They interdicted that great Court from proceeding any further against them. **1713** STEELE *Englishman* No. 9. 57 In Italy..Women are..interdicted the Pleasures of Society and Conversation. **1815** *Zeluca* II. 244 She is interdicted transmitting remembrance to old friends. **1856** FROUDE *Hist. Eng.* II. ix. 313 The clergy were interdicted from indulging any longer in the polemics of theology. **1876** *Act 39 & 40 Vict.* c. 70 Sch. A, To interdict the defender from [etc.] and to grant interim interdict. **1880** MUIRHEAD *Gaius* I. §128. 49 A person who, on account of crime..has been interdicted fire and water, forfeits his civic privileges.

3. *Eccl.* To cut off authoritatively from religious offices or privileges; to lay (a place or person) under an interdict: see INTERDICT *sb.* 3.

c **1290** *Beket* 1714 in *S. Eng. Leg.* I. 155 And entre-diten al engelond. **1297** R. GLOUC. (Rolls) 10184 þis bissopes..entreditede al þis lond, & walis al so, þat noþing of cristendom þer inne nere ido. *c* **1386** CHAUCER *Pars. T.* ⁋892 The prest scholde be enterdyted that dede such a vilonye to terme of al his lyf. **1480** CAXTON *Chron. Eng.* VII. (1520) 81 b/1 For the woundynge of a Cardynall he enterdyted all the cyte of Rome. **1530** TINDALE *Pract. Prel.* Wks. (Parker Soc.) II. 295 Then was the land interdicted many years. **1556** *Chron. Gr. Friars* (Camden) 2 That yere the londe was enterdyted. **1660** R. COKE *Power & Subj.* 147 Alexander not only allows the Conquerors pretensions to the Crown of England, but interdicts all those who should oppose him. **1700** TYRRELL *Hist. Eng.* II. 901 The Legate..Interdicted the University of Oxford. **1885** [see INTERDICT *sb.* 3].

†**inter'dict**, *ppl. a. Obs.* Also 5 **-dyte, -dicte**. [ad. L. *interdict-us*, pa. pple. of *interdīcere* (see prec.); cf. F. *interdit, -e*.] Interdicted: construed as pa. pple. of INTERDICT *v.*

1432–50 tr. *Higden* (Rolls) I. 85 Hit was interdicte [HIGDEN *interdictum fuit*, TREVISA was forbode]..to kynge Alexander, that he scholde not entre in to Babylon. *c* **1440** *Promp. Parv.* 262/2 Interdyte, *interdictus*. **1484** CAXTON *Fables of Poge* (1889) 6 A place whiche is prophane or Interdicte. *a* **1593** MARLOWE *Faust.* 763 Both he and thou shall stand excommunicate, And interdict from church's privilege.

inter'dicted, *ppl. a.* [f. INTERDICT *v.* + -ED[1].] Forbidden, prohibited; debarred, precluded: see the verb. **a.** Of things.

1565 T. STAPLETON *Fortr. Faith* II. 160 He..hongred not after the interdicted frute, as Adam did. **1667** MILTON *P.L.* VII. 47 Charg'd not to touch the interdicted Tree. **1751** JOHNSON *Rambler* No. 163 ⁋5 Fruitless attempts to catch at interdicted happiness. **1865** TYLOR *Early Hist. Man.* vi. 146 Occasion to obliterate interdicted words.

b. Of persons: *spec.* in *Law* (see INTERDICTION 3).

1637 RUTHERFORD *Lett.* (1862) I. 299 Let me be His interdicted heir. **1754** ERSKINE *Princ. Sc. Law* (1809) 108 Reduction..may be brought not only by the heirs of the interdicted person, and by the interdictors, but by the interdicted person himself. **1863** BURTON *Bk. Hunter* 344 An interdicted pastor, wandering over the desolate moors. **1880** MUIRHEAD *Ulpian* xix. §5 *note*, It was denied to the interdicted spendthrift.

inter'dicting, *vbl. sb.* Forms: see INTERDICT *v.* [-ING[1].] The action of the verb INTERDICT; interdiction. (Now *rare* exc. as gerund.)

c **1380** WYCLIF *Sel. Wks.* III. 361 Suspendingis, enterditingis, cursingis, and reisingis of croiserie. **1480** CAXTON *Chron. Eng.* cxlvii. 126 They pronounced the generall enterdytyng thurghout al englond so that the chirch dores were shytte. **1523** LD. BERNERS *Froiss.* I. ccxii. 260 The pope shall..gyue generall sentences of cursynge, and suspencion of enterdytynge to renne vpon vs. **1530** TINDALE *Pract. Prelates* in *Expos. & Notes* (Parker Soc.) 295 When neither the interdicting neither that secret subtilty holp [etc.].

interdiction (ɪntə'dɪkʃən). Also 5–6 **enterdiccion**, 6 **interdiccion**. [ad. L. *interdictiōn-em*, n. of action from *interdīcĕre* to INTERDICT. In its earliest form agreeing with an OF. type **entrediction*: cf. INTERDICT *sb.* and *v.*] The action of interdicting, or fact of being interdicted.

1. The action of forbidding by or as by authority; authoritative or peremptory prohibition.

1579 J. STUBBES *Gaping Gulf* A vj b, Against those interdictions in the law which seeme to compas in no more but the Canaanites Iebusites [etc.]. **1656** W. MONTAGUE *Accompl. Wom.* 133 Freedom extinguishes desire, and interdiction kindles it. **1738** WARBURTON *Div. Legat.* I. 208 This Interdiction of sepulchral Rites. **1827** HALLAM *Const. Hist.* (1876) I. iii. 113 This act operated as an absolute interdiction of the catholic rites.

2. *Eccl.* The issuing of an interdict; the action of laying (a place, etc.), or condition of being laid, under an interdict: see INTERDICT *sb.* 1.

1494 FABYAN *Chron.* VII. 318 Of the maner of this Enterdiccion of this lande haue I seen dyuerse opynyons. **1592** tr. *Junius' Revel.* xiii. 16 To use most violent interdictions, and to shoot out cursings. **1670** G. H. *Hist. Cardinals* II. I. 112 Several poor Bishops are rendred subject to interdictions and censures. *c* **1750** SHENSTONE *Ruined Abbey* 218 The wily Pontiff scorns not to recall His interdictions.

3. *Law.* **a.** *Sc. Law.* A restraint imposed upon a person incapable of managing his own affairs on account of unsoundness of mind, improvidence, etc. **b.** = INTERDICT *sb.* 2 a, b. **c.** *Rom. Law.* ***interdiction of fire and water***: a sentence of banishment or outlawry forbidding the supply to the person sentenced of fire and water or the necessaries of life.

c **1575** *Balfour's Practicks* (1754) 186 All publicatiounis and interdictiounis aught and sould be maid..quhair the persoun interdictit dwellis. **1579–80** NORTH *Plutarch* (1676) 961 So were Brutus and Cassius, and all their friends condemned, with interdiction of water and fire. **1581** *Sc. Acts Jas. VI* (1597) c. 118 That all inhibitiones and interdictiones to be raised hereafter for quhatsumever cause..be..produced..to the Schireffe clerk of the Schire, quhair the persone interdited or inhibit dwellis. **1681** [see INTERDICTOR]. **1754** ERSKINE *Princ. Law Scotl.* I. vii. §32 Judicial interdiction is imposed by a Sentence of the Court of Session. **1861** W. BELL *Dict. Law Scot.*, *Interdiction* is a system of judicial, or of voluntary restraint, provided for those who, from weakness, facility, or profusion, are liable to imposition... *Voluntary interdiction* is imposed by the sole act of the interdicted person, who, being conscious of his facility, lays himself under this restraint... *Judicial interdiction* is imposed by sentence of the Court of Session; generally proceeding on an action at the instance of a near kinsman of the facile person. [See also INTERDICTOR, quot. 1861.] **1867–8** *Act 31 & 32 Vict.* c. 64 §16 The particular registers of inhibitions and interdictions throughout Scotland shall be discontinued. **1880** MUIRHEAD *Gaius & Ulpian* Digest 472 Citizenship..was lost..by..interdiction of fire and water, which practically was outlawry.

4. The interruption of supply operations by aerial bombing. Freq. *attrib.*

1944 *B.B.C. War Rep.* 1 Nov. (1946) xiv. 283 The enemy railways were harassed day and night by what was known as 'interdiction'—or, in other words, rail-cutting by air attack. **1955** *Bull. Atomic Sci.* Feb. 56/3 The inability of the Air Force interdiction campaign—Operation Strangle—to bring about the collapse of Communist armies in Korea has obscured the true potential of air interdiction. **1963** *Listener* 21 Feb. 331/1 Overwhelming air support, invaluable as it was in an interdiction role, sometimes proved a clumsy weapon when used in close co-operation with ground forces. **1966** *Guardian* 26 Sept. 9/1 Using a bombing technique known as 'interdiction in depth', Navy planes had destroyed two locomotives, 225 goods wagons. **1973** *Times* 19 Apr. 18/8 Sensitive Washington spokesmen do not like the term bombing. They find it jarring. In Vietnam it was interdiction, armed reconnaissance and protective reaction.

interdictive (ɪntə'dɪktɪv), *a. rare.* [f. L. *interdict-*, ppl. stem (see prec.) + -IVE.] = INTERDICTORY.

1609 BP. W. BARLOW *Answ. Nameless Cath.* 185 It was an hasty rashnesse..to award a sentence so resolutely Interdictiue. **1641** MILTON *Animadv.* xiii. Wks. (1851) 230 A timely separation from the flock by that interdictive sentence.

interdictor (ɪntə'dɪktə(r), -ɔː(r)). [a. late L. *interdictor* forbidder (Tertull.), agent-n. from *interdīcere* to INTERDICT.] **a.** One who interdicts. **b.** *Sc. Law.* (See quot. 1861.)

1681 STAIR *Inst. Law Scotl.* I. vi. §37 Our custom hath interdictions, whereby persons, acknowledging their own weakness..do therefore bind themselves, that they shall not act without the consent of those persons, interdictors therein mentioned. **1754** ERSKINE *Princ. Law Scotl.* I. vii. §34 All deeds, done..without the consent of his interdictors..are subject to reduction. **1861** W. BELL *Dict. Law Scotl.* s.v. *Interdiction*, Voluntary interdiction..is usually executed in the form of a bond, whereby the granter obliges himself to do no deed which may affect his estate, without the consent of certain persons therein named, technically called interdictors... Onerous or rational deeds, granted by the interdicted person, are effectual without the consent of the interdictors. **1888** *Life D. McLaren* II. xvii. 68 Lord Gifford decided in favour of the interdictors.

interdictory (ɪntə'dɪktərɪ), *a.* [ad. late L. *interdictōri-us*, f. *interdictor*: see prec. and -ORY.] Having the quality or effect of interdicting; belonging to or conveying interdiction; prohibitory.

1755 JOHNSON, *Interdictory*, belonging to an interdiction. *Ainsworth.* **1786** *Antiq.* in *Ann. Reg.* 107/1 The effect of that abomination..was interdictory. **1844** R. WARDLAW *Proverbs* (1869) II. xliv. 116 There is nothing interdictory of the use of it. **1855** MILMAN *Lat. Chr.* (1864) II. III. v. 20 Interdictory statutes declared marriages with Jews and heathens not only invalid but adulterous.

interdifferentiation: see INTER- *pref.*

interdiffuse (ɪntədɪ'fjuːz), *v.* [INTER- 1 a.] *trans.* To diffuse between or among other things. So **interdiffusion** (-dɪ'fjuːʒən), diffusion between or among other things, or each other; mutual diffusion. **interdiffusive** (-dɪ'fjuːsɪv) *a.*, tending to mutual diffusion; hence **interdi'ffusiveness**.

a **1859** G. WILSON *Relig. Chem.* (1862) 14 That property of interdiffusiveness among elastic fluids. **1864–72** WATTS *Dict. Chem.* II. 812 This mixture or interdiffusion likewise takes place when the gases communicate with each other through minute pores or apertures of insensible magnitude. **1882** OGILVIE cites *North. Brit. Rev.* for *Interdiffuse*.

interdigit (ˌɪntə'dɪdʒɪt). [f. INTER- 3 a + L. *digit-us* finger, DIGIT.] The part of the hand (or foot) between the roots of the adjacent digits.

1875 H. C. WOOD *Therap.* (1879) 454 This is rubbed in night and morning for three days, especially to the interdigits and wrists.

interdigital (ɪntə'dɪdʒɪtəl), *a.* [ad. L. *interdigitālis*, f. *inter* + *digitus* finger.]

1. Situated between, or connecting, digits (fingers or toes).

1836–9 TODD *Cycl. Anat.* II. 519/1 Up to the second or third month of intra-uterine life an interdigital membrane exists. **1874** COUES *Birds N.W.* 645 Anterior toes all long; the interdigital webs broad. **1875** H. C. WOOD *Therap.* (1879) 326 The interdigital membrane of the frog.

2. *Electronics.* Having the form of or consisting of two similar series of parallel strips, those of each series forming part of a single structure and interdigitating with those of the other series: used of a kind of transducer.

1967 *IEEE Trans. Electron. Devices* XIV. 185/2 The operation of an interdigital pattern whose fundamental frequency was 15 MHz has been observed at odd integral multiples up to the seventh on AT-cut quartz. **1968** *Ibid.* XV. 586 (*heading*) Frequency response of an interdigital transducer for excitation of surface elastic waves. **1972** *Sci. Amer.* Oct. 52/3 In recent years the technology of acoustic waves has expanded rapidly with the development of the interdigital transducer, an efficient type of transducer for converting the electrical signal into an acoustic surface wave and reconverting the acoustic wave back into an electrical signal.

interdigitate (ɪntə'dɪdʒɪteɪt), *v.* Chiefly *Anat.* [f. INTER- 1 b + L. *digit-us* finger + -ATE[3]: cf. DIGITATE *v.*]

1. *intr.* To interlock like the fingers of the two hands when clasped; to project or be inserted alternately between each other, as processes of a

muscle, etc.; to inosculate by reciprocal serrations.

1847–9 TODD *Cycl. Anat.* IV. 737/2 An equal number of similar processes..with which they interdigitate. **1855** R. OWEN *Lectures on the Comparative Anat. & Physiol. of the Invertibrate Animals* (ed. 2) i. 7 The groups of characters that are essential to the true definition of a plant and an animal interdigitate, so to speak, in that low department of the organic world from which the two great branches rise and diverge. **1870** ROLLESTON *Anim. Life* 193 It [the posterior retractor] inter-digitates very freely with the protractor pedis. **1887** *Lancet* 24 Sept. 604/1 This strapping ..is fenestrated, and cut into strips that interdigitate. **1893** BURDON-SANDERSON *Pres. Addr. Brit. Assoc.*, Questions.. which here, though they do not overlap, at least interdigitate.

2. *trans.* To cause to interlock or inosculate in this way. In *Geol.* = INTERSTRATIFY *v.* 1.

1864 in WEBSTER. **1882** in OGILVIE. **1969** BENNISON & WRIGHT *Geol. Hist. Brit. Isles* viii. 160 In north Devon marine and non-marine beds occur in the same sequence. They are interdigitated due to alternating expansions and contractions of the area of marine deposition. **1974** *Sci. Amer.* Feb. 64/1 The last step..involves interdigitating a set of thick filaments in the spaces between the thin filaments.

Hence **interˈdigitating** *ppl. a.*

1875 ROMANES in *Life* (1895) 25 Interposing a great number of interdigitating cuts in the course of the spiral.

interdigitation (ˌɪntədɪdʒɪˈteɪʃən). Chiefly *Anat.* [n. of action f. prec.: see -ATION.] The action or condition of interdigitating; *concr.* an interdigitating structure, or one of a number of interdigitating processes.

a **1864** OWEN cited in Webster. **1872** MIVART *Elem. Anat.* 24 When bones are immovably joined by an interdigitation of their irregularly shaped margins, they are said to be joined by suture. **1874** COUES *Birds N.W.* Introd. 10 The boundary line..in these latitudes is a zig-zag of interdigitations.

interdine (ɪntəˈdaɪn), *v.* [INTER- 1 a.] *intr.* Of members of different castes and tribes: to eat a meal together.

1932 G. S. GHURYE *Caste & Race in India* iv. 73 Evidently interdining, like intermarrying, was a mark of equality. **1933** RAHMAT ALI *Now or Never* (1934) 4 We [*sc.* Muslims] do not inter-dine [with Hindus]; we do not inter-marry. **1960** KOESTLER *Lotus & Robot* II. x. 228 In India, inter-marriage, and even inter-dining, between different castes was unthinkable.

interdisciplinary (ɪntəˈdɪsɪplɪnərɪ, -ˈplɪn-), *a.* [INTER- 4 c.] Of or pertaining to two or more disciplines or branches of learning; contributing to or benefiting from two or more disciplines.

1937 *Jrnl. Educ. Sociol.* Dec. 251 Programs of study submitted should provide..for training of an inter-disciplinary nature. **1956** J. LOTZ in L. White *Frontiers of Knowledge in Study of Man* 217 There is also considerable interest in interdisciplinary studies involving structural linguistics. **1957** E. BOTT *Family & Social Network* ii. 35 Ten years ago interdisciplinary research was very much in vogue. **1965** *Listener* 18 Nov. 788/2 The work..is again interdisciplinary and does not fall into any of the established academic categories. **1970** *Guardian* 12 Nov. 5/6 The academic policies put forward—essentially a two-year general interdisciplinary degree. **1972** *Language* XLVIII. 487 Child language acquisition has proved to be one of the more important interdisciplinary areas of the past decade.

interdispensation, -distinguish, -district, division, etc.: see INTER- *pref.*

interdite, -dyte, obs. var. INTERDICT *sb.* and *v.*

†**interˈditement.** *Obs.* [f. *interdite*, earlier form of INTERDICT *v.* + -MENT. (Possibly from an OF. original.)] = INTERDICTION 2.

1530 PALSGR. 234/2 Interditement, *interdissement.* **1583** FOXE *A. & M.* 594/1 Vnder payne of interditement, suspending and excommunication.

inter-dominion (ɪntədəʊˈmɪnjən), *a.* [f. INTER- 5 + DOMINION 2 b (*c*).] Occurring, or carried on, between the self-governing dominions of the British Commonwealth.

Used esp. in Australia and N.Z.

1949 *Australia 1949* 776/1 Totalisator investments for the three days of the Auckland Inter-Dominion Championships totalled £506,498/10/-. **1950** *Sydney Morning Herald* 12 Jan. 10/7 Sir Nigel will now go to Melbourne for the inter-Dominion championships in February. **1966** *Weekly News* (N.Z.) 27 Apr. 39 (*caption*) Australian and New Zealand crews competed for an interdominion championship under conditions similar to those at the Cowes Regatta. **1968** *Wanganui* (N.Z.) *Chron.* 15 Nov. 6/9 The 1971 inter-Dominion championship series have been allocated to the New Zealand Metropolitan Trotting Club.

interduce, variant of INTERDICE *Obs.*

†**interˈduct.** *Obs. rare*$^{-0}$. [ad. L. *interduct-us* interpunctuation, f. *inter* between + *duct-us* leading, f. *dūcĕre* to lead.] (See quot.)

1656 BLOUNT *Glossogr.*, *Interduct*, a space between full sentences in printing or writing.

intere, obs. form of ENTIRE.

inter-ecclesiastical: see INTER- *pref.* 4 c.

inter-electrode (ˌɪntərɪˈlɛktrəʊd), *a.* *Electr.* Also interelectrode. [INTER- 5.] Existing between two or more electrodes; said esp. of electrical quantities pertaining to the space between electrodes.

1922 GLAZEBROOK *Dict. Appl. Physics* II. 902/1 Certain types of valve are constructed to reduce the inter-electrode capacity to a minimum. **1925** E. B. WEDMORE *Electr. Engineers' Data Bks.* III. 162 For high frequency amplification it is desirable to use valves having a low interelectrode capacity and also a low amplification factor. **1930** *Daily Express* 9 Sept. 11/1 The new..Valve has a greater effective amplification because its inter-electrode capacity is lower. **1962** W. B. THOMPSON *Introd. Plasma Physics* v. 76 In order to relate the resistance to the resistivity of the plasma, the tube was filled with a solution of known conductivity and the inter-electrode resistance measured. **1964** CHODOROW & SUSSKIND *Fund. Microwave Electronics* ii. 19 When the cathode is heated, the negative charge of the emitted electrons depresses the potential in the interelectrode region.

inter-electron: see INTER- *pref.* 5.

†**inteˈrempt**, *ppl. a.* *Obs. rare.* [ad. L. *interempt-us*, pa. pple. of *interimĕre*: see next.] Destroyed. (Const. as pa. pple.)

1561 *Queen Esther* (1862 Collier), Wherby good order may sone be interempte.

†**inteˈremption.** *Obs. rare.* [ad. late L. *interemptiōn-em* (Tert.), n. of action from *interimĕre* to cut off, destroy, slay, f. *inter* (INTER-) + *emĕre* to buy, orig. to take.] Destruction, slaughter.

1656 BLOUNT *Glossogr.*, *Interemption*, a killing or slaying. **1664** H. MORE *Myst. Iniq.* 290 Nor was it seasonable to take notice of..his utter and final perdition, he being to revive again after his first Interemption.

inter-entanglement, -epidemic, -epimeral, -epithelial: see INTER- *pref.*

interepte, obs. corrupt f. INTERRUPT *v.*

†**interˈequitate**, *v.* *Obs. rare*$^{-0}$. [ad. ppl. stem of L. *interequitāre* to ride between, f. *inter* between + *equitāre* to ride.] (See quot.)

Hence †**interˌequiˈtation.**

1656 BLOUNT *Glossogr.*, *Interequitate*, to ride between. **1658** PHILLIPS, *Interequitation*, a riding between.

†**interess**, *sb.* *Obs.* Also 5–6 **enteres(se, en-, intresse.** [ME. and AF. *interesse*, a. med.L. *interesse* compensation for loss, compensatory payment, sb. use of L. *interesse* to be between, to differ, make a difference, to concern, be of importance. Cf. Pr., It., Ger. *interesse*, Sp. *interes* sb.; the OF. sb. was *interest*: see INTEREST *sb.*]

1. The relation of being legally concerned or having part (in the ownership or possession of anything); legal concern, title, or claim; = INTEREST *sb.* 1.

[**1387–8** *Rolls Parlt.* III. 246/2 Si ascun pretende d'avoir droit ou interesse en ycelles [forfaitures], sue au Conseil si lui semble a faire.] **1430–1** *Ibid.* IV. 376/2 That.. Proclamation be made..that alle ye persones yat pretende any interresse to object ayens yat partie yat pretendith hym to be mulire [etc.]. **1473** SIR J. PASTON in *P. Lett.* No. 732 III. 100 That my moodre be agreable to the same, by cawse of th' entresse that she hathe for my brother William, whyche shall nott be off age thys vij. yeer. **1491** *Act 7 Hen. VII*, c. 2 §5 The right title and interesse that they..have in the same. **1523** LD. BERNERS *Froiss.* I. xx. 28 All rightis and enteresses that euery baron had in Scotlande, was than clene forgyuen. **1659** *England's Conf.* 6 The House of Commons ..had..asserted their interess in the Militia.

b. *transf.* Concern, part, share *in* (anything). = INTEREST *sb.* 1 d, e.

c **1374** CHAUCER *Fortune* 71 The heuene hath proprete of sykyrnesse, This world hath euer resteles trauayle; Thy laste day is ende of myn intresse [*v. rr.* interesse, intersse, encresse] In general, this reule may nat fayle. **1430–40** LYDG. *Bochas* Prol. 39 Though woe with ioye have an intresse. *Ibid.* I. i. (1544) 1 b, The soyle embroyded ful of sumer floures Where wedes wicked had none interesse. **1569** MURRAY in H. Campbell *Love Lett. Mary Q. Scots* (1824) 58 The trial of the said Quenis interes in the murder of the King our soverane Lordis father. **1663** BP. PATRICK *Parab. Pilgr.* (1667) 287 There he found a discourse of the Nature of Ioy..of the Interess that our Animal Spirits have in it.

2. The relation of advantage or profit; benefit; = INTEREST *sb.* 2, 2 b.

1452 RICH. DK. YORK *Charges agst. Dk. Somerset* (MS. Cott. Vesp. C. xiv. lf. 40) For the grete welfare and the comen availle and interesse of your mageste Roiall and of this youre noble roialme. **1611** SPEED *Hist. Gt. Brit.* IX. xiv. §11 Such oftentimes is the corruption of humane nature, that it will..thrust the pietie due to our Countrey vnder the inferiour respect of particular interesses. **1613** SHERLEY *Trav. Persia* 83 To embarke you in dangerous enterprises for others interesses. **1632** J. HAYWARD tr. *Biondi's Eromena* 120 In a noble minde one generous act prevailes more than all wordly interesses. **1657** HEYLIN *Hist. Ref.* I. II. iii. 32 That they should lay aside their particular interesses, to center all together upon one design. **1678** CUDWORTH *Intell. Syst.* I. ii. §21. 84 That it is also the Interess of Civil Sovereigns and of all Common-wealths, that there should neither be Deity nor Religion, the Democritick Atheists would perswade in this manner.

b. Self-interest; = INTEREST *sb.* 5.

1678 CUDWORTH *Intell. Syst.* I. v. 847 These are the men, who afterwards Argue from Interesse also against a God and Religion.

3. Injury; compensation for injury; = INTEREST *sb.* 9. [Cf. med.L. *damna et interesse*, F. *dommages et intérêts.*]

1489 CAXTON *Faytes of A.* III. xi. 191 He is holden as he was byfore to suche damages and Interesses that he hathe doon unto hym by wronge hande.

4. Interest on money, usury; = INTEREST *sb.* 10.

1529 HEN. VIII *Instruct. Orator Rome* (MS. Cott. Vit. B. XI. lf. 74 b), Which money..shalbe truely repayde with interesse. **1548** UDALL *Erasm. Par. Luke* xix. 153 He.. would haue streightely required it together with the encrease of entresse. **1716** *Let. to Dk. Montrose* 19 Nov. in Scott *Rob Roy* Introd., He carries..my books and bonds for entress, not yet paid, along with him.

†**inteˈress**, *v.* *Obs.* Pa. pple. **interessed, -est.** [f. INTERESS *sb.*: cf. F. *intéresser* to invest with a share, etc.; earlier, to injure, hurt, damage (15th c. in Godef.), f. L. *interesse.*]

1. *trans.* To invest (a person) with a right to or share in something; to admit to a privilege; = INTEREST *v.* 1. Chiefly in *pass.*, *to be interessed*, to have a right or share.

1577–87 HOLINSHED *Chron.* (1807) II. 35 The sonnes of king Malcolme were aided..to obteine the crowne of Scotland, whereunto they were interessed. **1602** WARNER *Alb. Eng.* Epit. (1612) 378 Who..disclaiming all other Titles as litigious, interessed himselfe here by the only Title of Conquerour. **1605** SHAKS. *Lear* I. i. 87 To whose yong loue, The Vines of France, and Milke of Burgundie, Striue to be interest. **1617** HIERON *Wks.* II. 102 Man, in his first estate..was in fauour with God, and interessed into the attendance of angels. **1657** AUSTEN *Fruit Trees* II. 59 The soule sees it selfe interessed in the kingdome and all the riches and treasures of it. **1674** PLAYFORD *Skill Mus.* I. xi. 47 To teach them to those who have been interessed in my house.

2. To cause to be objectively concerned; to affect, implicate, to involve; = INTEREST *v.* 2. Chiefly in *pass.*

1570 EARL LENNOX *Let.* in H. Campbell *Love Lett. Mary Q. Scots* (1824) 229 Hir richt dewtie to ȝow and me, being the parteis interest. **1617** J. WOODFORD in *Buccleuch MSS.* (Hist. MSS. Comm.) I. 199 [This] could not be done without interessing the honour of some, which was not to be touched. **1622** MISSELDEN *Free Trade* 89 In the East India Action certainely the Kings Honour is interessed. **1627** *Lisander & Cal.* III. 50 A suspicion that she was interest in the discourse. **1663** BOYLE *Usef. Exp. Nat. Philos.* II. ii. 30 Being unwilling to interesse the reputation of Holy Writ.. in the doubtful contentions of Naturalists.

3. To affect injuriously; to injure, endamage.

1598 GRENEWEY *Tacitus' Ann.* III. ii. (1622) 66 Whereof being conuicted, he could not be interessed, if he could purge himselfe of the latter crimes. **1599** *Burgh Rec. Aberdeen* (Spald. Cl.) II. 181 Dyvers of the cuntriemen and of the inhabitantis of this burght ar grytumlie intrest in the wynter day, throw the insufficiencie and hoillis in the said calsey. **1607** E. GRIMSTONE tr. *Goulart's Mem. Hist.* 127 [She] was found interessed in the heart with certaine imposthumes and two stones.

4. To cause to take an active part, to rouse to action, to engage; *refl.* to take part (F. *s'intéresser*); = INTEREST *v.* 4.

1623 MASSINGER *Dk. Milan* I. i, The wars so long continued..Have interess'd, in either's cause, the most Of the Italian princes. **1693** DRYDEN *Juvenal* Ded. (1697) 17 He might have gain'd the Victory for us Christians, without interessing Heaven in the Quarrel. **1711** SHAFTESB. *Charac.* (1737) II. III. ii. 416 That which interesses and engages men as Good.

5. To affect with a feeling of concern; *refl.* To concern oneself. *pass.* To be concerned.

1664 MARVELL *Corr.* Wks. 1872–5 II. 173 No Prince in Christendom doth interess Himself more in your Majestie's health..than my Master. **1697** DRYDEN *Æneid* Ded., To love our native country..to be interessed in its concerns, is natural to all men.

Hence †**inteˈressing** *vbl. sb.*, admitting (*into* a position, etc.).

a **1655** VINES *Lord's Supp.* (1677) 342 The interessing of Christ into pre-eminence.

†**inteˈressed**, *ppl. a.* *Obs.* [f. INTERESS *v.* + -ED[1].] = INTERESTED.

1598 FLORIO, *Interessato*, interessed, toucht in honor, or reputation. **1635** J. HAYWARD tr. *Biondi's Banish'd Virg.* 79 We were with interessed kindnesse conveniently accomodated in the Castle of the poope. **1640** BP. HALL *Humb. Remonstr.* 3 There are not more eyes in these three interessed kingdomes, than are now bent on you. **1647** CLARENDON *Hist. Reb.* VII. §19 The most interressed, passionate, or prejudicate Person. **1707** *Reflex. upon Ridicule* 70 It ought to divert the Indifferent, without wounding the Interess'd.

intereˈssee. *rare.* [f. INTERESS *v.* + -EE[1]; F. *intéressé.*] One who is interested or concerned (in something); an interested party.

1610 W. FOLKINGHAM *Art of Survey* title-p., For euery other Interessee in the Profits or Practise deriued from the compleate Survey of Manours, Lands, &c. **1826** BENTHAM in *Westm. Rev.* VI. 450 By rendering conveyances.. somewhat less unintelligible to parties and other interessees.

†**inteˈressent.** *Obs.* *rare*$^{-1}$. [ad. med.L. *interessent-em*, pr. pple. of L. *interesse*: see INTEREST.] = prec.

c **1677** *List of Ships* in Marvell *Growth Popery* (1678) 66 The Interessents are really damaged,..to the value of 759*l.*

‖**inte'resse 'termini.** *Law.* [med.L., = interest of term or end.] A right of entry on a leasehold estate, acquired through a demise.

[**1628** COKE *On Litt.* 345 b, Interesse is vulgarly taken for a terme or chattle reall, and more particularly for a future tearme, in which case it is said in pleading, that he is possessed *De interesse termini.*] **1658** tr. *Coke's Rep.* v. 124 (1826) III. 253 Such *interesse termini* cannot by disseisin or feoffment be divested. **1809** TOMLINS *Jacob's Law Dict.* s.v. *Interest,* The bare lease..gives him [the lessee] a right of entry on the tenement, which right is called his interest in the term, or *interesse termini.* **1893** *Law Times Rep.* LXVIII. 428/2 The plaintiff having only an *interesse termini,* and never having been in possession, he could not maintain..an action for trespass.

†**inte'ressor.** *Obs. rare.* [a. med.L. *interessor* (Du Cange), f. *interesse* to be among.] A partner, a fellow.

1672 PETTY *Pol. Anat.* xi. Tracts (1769) 357 Why may not the rents of the same be actually sent, without prejudice to the other three parts of the interessor[s] thereof?

interest ('ɪntərɪst, -ɛst), *sb.* Also 5 **entrest,** 6 **enterest,** 6–7 **intrest,** (7 **int'rest**). [An alteration of the earlier INTERESS, app. after the cognate F. *interest* (1290 in Godef.), mod.F. *intérêt,* app. a sb. use of L. *interest* it makes a difference, concerns, matters, is of importance, 3rd pers. sing. pres. indic. (used impersonally) of the vb., of which the infinitive *interesse* was used as a sb. in med.L., and in the other Romanic langs. and ME.

There is much that is obscure in the history of this word, first as to the adoption of L. *interest* as a sb., and secondly as to the history of the OF. sense 'damage, loss'. No other sense is recorded in Fr. until the 16th c. As this was not the 15th c. sense of Eng. *interess(e,* it is curious that the form of the French word should have affected the Eng. The relations between the sense-development in French and English in 16–17th c. are also far from clear.]

I. 1. The relation of being objectively concerned in something, by having a right or title to, a claim upon, or a share in.

a. The fact or relation of being legally concerned; legal concern *in* a thing; esp. right or title to property, or to some of the uses or benefits pertaining to property; = INTERESS *sb.* 1.

1450 *Rolls Parlt.* V. 185/1 Noon of youre Liege peple hafuyng interest, right or title, of or in ony of the premisses. **1478** SIR J. PASTON in *P. Lett.* No. 814 III. 222 He never knywe..that I hadde any clayme or entrest in the maner off Heylesdon. **1523** FITZHERB. *Surv.* 7 b, Their tytell and interest grewe by enherytaunce. **1571** *Wills & Inv. N.C.* (Surtees 1835) 352, I gyue to John Stephen..all my quarrell geare..& my whole interest and good will of my Quarrell. **1593** SHAKS. *2 Hen. VI,* III. i. 84 All your Interest in those Territories Is vtterly bereft you. **1628** COKE *On Litt.* 345 b, *Interesse*..in legall vnderstanding extendeth to Estates, Rights and Titles, that a man hath of, in, to, or out of Lands, for he is truly said to haue an interest in them. **1653** HOLCROFT *Procopius, Goth. Wars* IV. 139 They transport many Families to the Francks, who plant them in desert Countries, and upon that ground pretend an interest to the Island. **1767** BLACKSTONE *Comm.* II. xx. 323 The estates exchanged must be equal in quantity; not of value..but of interest; as fee-simple for fee-simple. **1858** LD. ST. LEONARDS *Handy Bk. Prop. Law* xv. 101 You should always, before granting a lease, consider what interest you have in the estate.

fig. **1549** COVERDALE, etc. *Erasm. Par. Jude* 22 We in beleuing the Gospell, haue through Baptisme escaped Satans enterest. **1600** SHAKS. *A.Y.L.* v. i. 8 *Clow.* But Awdrie, there is a youth heere in the Forrest layes claime to you. *Awd.* I, I know who 'tis: he hath no interest in mee in the world. **1632** J. HAYWARD tr. *Biondi's Eromena* 39 One who next the King his Father, claimed greatest interest in P——, for having bred him up from his infancie. *a* **1680** BUTLER *Eleph. in Moon* I. 165 Proud of his Int'rest in the Glory Of so miraculous a Story.

b. Right or title to spiritual privileges.

1607 HIERON *Wks.* I. 482 A freedome it is from the bondage of Sathan..giuing an interest into Gods fauour. **1675** TRAHERNE *Chr. Ethics* 53 Tho all eternity were full of treasures..and our interest to all never so perfect. *a* **1716** SOUTH *Twelve Serm.* (1744) II. 149 Let him impartially ask himself..what evidences he has of his..interest in the second Covenant.

c. Right or title to a share in something; share, part.

c **1586** C'TESS PEMBROKE *Ps.* CII. xv, Thou art one, still one: Tyme, interest in thee hath none. **1594** SHAKS. *Rich. III,* II. ii. 47 Ah so much interest haue [I] in thy sorrow, As I had Title in thy Noble Husband. **1611** TOURNEUR *Ath. Trag.* I. ii. Wks. 1878 I. 19 The honestie of your conuersation makes me request more int'rest in your familiaritie. **1635** J. HAYWARD tr. *Biondi's Banish'd Virg.* 72, I am sorry that her love hath so small interest in you. **1781** COWPER *Conversat.* 74 A Persian..begg'd an interest in his frequent prayers.

†**d.** Participation or share in doing something or the production of some result. *Obs.*

1660 BOYLE *New Exp. Phys. Mech.* xxiii. 184 Suspecting that..the Figure of the Vessel might have an interest in this odde Phænomenon. **1671** FLAVEL *Fount. Life* v. 12 Great is the Interest of Words in this doctrine. **1709** F. HAUKSBEE *Phys. Mech. Exp.* v. (1719) 145 A signal Demonstration of the Influence and Interest of the Air in these Phænomena. *a* **1748** WATTS (J.), Endeavour to adjust the degrees of influence, that each cause might have in producing the effect, and the proper agency and interest of each therein.

e. *esp.* A pecuniary share or stake in, or claim upon anything; the relation of being a part-owner of property, a shareholder or bondholder in a commercial or financial undertaking, or the like.

1674 tr. *Martiniere's Voy. N. Countries* 2 To address myself to a Friend of mine who had a principal interest in that affair, and to desire his Mediation to the Company. **1767** BLACKSTONE *Comm.* II. xxx. 460 A practice of insuring large sums without having any property on board, which were called insurances, *interest or no interest.* **1824** J. MARSHALL *Const. Opin.* (1839) 345 The Planter's Bank of Georgia is not the state of Georgia, although the state holds an interest in it. **1863** KINGLAKE *Crimea* (1876) I. xiv. 239 He was a buyer and seller of those fractional and volatile interests in trading adventures which go by the name of 'shares'. **1890** BOLDREWOOD *Miner's Right* (1899) 73/1 We had..bought up all the 'interests', that is, shares, half shares, and quarter shares, on or near the supposed run of gold that we had struck.

2. a. The relation of being concerned or affected in respect of advantage or detriment; esp. an advantageous relation of this kind.

a **1533** LD. BERNERS *Gold Bk. M. Aurel.* Let. v. (R.), Without interest we commit sinne, seeyng peyne commyng withall. **1600** E. BLOUNT tr. *Conestaggio* 55 There was none in Lisbone but had some interest in this warre, who so had not his sonne there, had his father;..the traders..did venture their wealth in it. **1611** SHAKS. *Cymb.* IV. ii. 365 What's thy interest In this sad wracke? **1639** T. BRUGIS tr. *Camus' Mor. Relat.* 269 By reason of the double interest of pleasure and profit. **1766** GOLDSM. *Vic. W.* viii, I have an interest in being first to deliver this message, as I expect for my reward to be honoured with Miss Sophia's hand as a partner. **1780** BURKE *Corr.* (1844) II. 369 No people ought to be permitted to live in a country, who are not permitted to have an interest in its welfare. **1815** J. W. CROKER in *C. Papers* (1884) I. iii. 66 Castlereagh says what interest has Fouché now to tell a lie? **1849** MACAULAY *Hist. Eng.* vi. II. 39 Persons who were bound by strong ties of interest to the government.

b. That which is to or for the advantage of any one; good, benefit, profit, advantage.

1579 FENTON *Guicciard.* III. 129 Caried with ambicious respectes touching their interests and desires particular. **1605** SHAKS. *Macb.* I. ii. 64 No more that Thane of Cawdor shall deceiue Our Bosome interest. **1691** NORRIS *Pract. Disc.* 11 Is not every thing almost reckoned Profitable only so far as it conduces to some Temporal Interest? **1724** SWIFT *Drapier's Lett.* iii. Wks. 1761 III. 48 His profit is preferred, not only before the interest, but the very safety and being of a great Kingdom. **1745** BURKE *Corr.* (1844) I. 17 One who has our interest at heart. **1843** J. CLASON *Serm.* v. 85 He thought it to his temporal interest to do it. **1855** PRESCOTT *Philip II,* II. vii. (1857) 278 His devotion to the interests both of the king and of religion. **1884** *Law Times* LXXVII. 20/1 It is the interest of the keeper of an asylum to retard or conceal the recovery of his patient.

c. ***in the interest*** (***interests***) ***of***: on the side of what is advantageous or beneficial to.

1716 ADDISON *Freeholder* No. 4 ¶1 The Women of our Island, who are the most eminent for Virtue and good Sense, are in the Interest of the present Government. **1727** SWIFT *Country Post* Wks. 1755 III. I. 175 She had betrayed us, and was in the interest of the kite aforesaid. **1771** GOLDSM. *Hist. Eng.* I. 347 The party in the interests of Lewis began to lose ground. **1802** MAR. EDGEWORTH *Moral T.* (1816) I. xiii. 105 He did not choose to keep a clerk who was not in his interests. **1858** DE QUINCEY *Wks.* IX. Pref. 10 *note,* 'In the interest' (to use a slang phrase just now coming into currency) of enlightened patriotism. **1884** *Manch. Exam.* 27 May 5/1 In the interests of humanity there is no need to regret the change.

3. A thing in which one has an interest or concern.

1618 BOLTON *Florus* III. xix. (1636) 236 Very many striving together whose prisoner he should bee, the prey was torne in peeces while they wrangled about that interest. **1659** D. PELL *Impr. Sea* 384 Many times your interests are seised on by storms, sometimes by Pyrats. **1678** CUDWORTH *Intell. Syst.* I. iv. §31. 476 The Supreme God is saluted, as the Great Wonder of the World, and Interest of Mankind. **1835** I. TAYLOR *Spir. Despot.* VI. 267 Religion is in a secondary yet not an unimportant sense an interest of the present life. **1850** CARLYLE *Latter-d. Pamph.* iii. 2 Colonies excite more attention at present than any of our other interests.

4. A business, cause, or principle, in which a number of persons are interested; the party interested in such a business or principle; a party having a common interest; a religious or political party, business connexion, etc.

1674 *Essex Papers* (Camden) I. 246 He will be regarded as yᵉ great patron of yᵉ protestant Interest. **1679** in Puller *Moder. Ch. Eng.* (1843) 290 [This] would greatly strengthen the Protestant interest. **1714** POPE *Let. to the Hon.* —— 8 June, He said that I was enter'd into a cabal with Dean Swift and others to write against the Whig Interest. **1725** DE FOE *Voy. round World* (1840) 28 Caballing and forming an interest among the men. **1735** BOLINGBROKE *Lett. Stud. Hist.* ii. (1752) 39 The notion of creating a new, that is, a moneyed interest, in opposition to the landed interest. **1830** D'ISRAELI *Chas. I,* III. iv. 38 The cabinet was divided by two opposite interests. **1891** *Leeds Merc.* 27 Apr. 4/7 The banking interest in the City is known to be averse to the change. **1893** *Daily News* 28 Feb. 4/7 Mr. Gladstone..said that interests were always awake, while the country too often slumbered and slept.

5. Regard to one's own profit or advantage; selfish pursuit of one's own welfare; = SELF-INTEREST.

1622 MABBE tr. *Aleman's Guzman d'Alf.* II. xx. 4 a, Loue, interest, and feare, are those three ropes that halter Iustice. **1639** S. DU VERGER tr. *Camus' Admir. Events* 13, I love you without interest, without pretence, and without any other desire, then to see you. **1734** tr. *Rollin's Anc. Hist.* V. 25 The more she was above interest the more she abandoned herself to ambition. *a* **1839** PRAED *Poems* (1864) II. 102 The coil That interest flings upon our hearts.

6. Influence due to personal connexion; power of influencing the action of others; personal influence *with* (†*in*) a person or body of persons. ***to make interest,*** to bring personal influence to bear.

[**1596** SHAKS. *Merch. V.* III. ii. 224 Lorenzo and Salerio, welcome hether, If that the youth of my new interest heere Haue power to bid you welcome.] **1600** E. BLOUNT tr. *Conestaggio* 202 Those magistrates were mechanicke men, in whom feare hath a more interest, then the respect of a King. **1653** *Act Govt. Commw.* 45 Several persons of Interest and Fidelity in this Commonwealth. **1676** tr. *Guillatiere's Voy. Athens* 365 Her interest with him is such, that she governs him absolutely. **1709** STRYPE *Ann. Ref.* I. ii. 50 Early interest was made with Elizabeth for the continuance of the old religion. **1723** *True Briton* No. 56. 488 The Author *made no Interest* (as the Phrase goes), That is to say, was so Civil to..his Cotemporaries, as to suppose they were qualify'd to *hear* and *see* for *themselves.* **1761** HUME *Hist. Eng.* II. xxxvi. 293 To raise the people in the counties..where his interest lay.

7. a. The feeling of one who is concerned or has a personal concern in any thing; hence, the state of feeling proper to such a relation, or a particular form or instance of it; a feeling of concern for or curiosity about a person or thing.

1771 MACKENZIE *Man Feel.* vii. (1803) 9 There are certain interests, which the world supposes every man to have. **1811** *Ora & Jul.* IV. 115 No one ever appeared to take an interest about us. **1836** JAS. GRANT *Rand. Recoll. Ho. Lords* xvi. 385 The issue of the debate is regarded by him with an interest of no ordinary intensity. **1846** RUSKIN *Mod. Paint.* I. II. IV. iv. §28 He who can take no interest in what is small, will take false interest in what is great. **1853** LYTTON *My Novel* I. xi, I should be glad..to see you take a little more interest in duties which..you may be called upon to discharge. **1879** MORLEY *Burke* x. 209 The contentiousness is not..rapid enough to hold the interest of a practical assembly. **1898** A. W. W. DALE *Life of R. W. Dale* i. 8 He was a man with wide interests.

b. *transf.* of things: Power of exciting this feeling, interesting character or quality.

1821 MACKINTOSH *Bacon & Locke* Wks. 1846 I. 321 The confutation of Sir Robert Filmer..has long lost all interest. **1875** JOWETT *Plato* (ed. 2) IV. 135 Questions of great interest. **1884** GLADSTONE *Sp. Edin.* 30 Aug., There was one feature in that struggle..which gave it an interest—a finishing interest—if not a higher interest than any other. **1886** *Manch. Exam.* 3 Nov. 3/1 The *Quarterly* for October is exceptionally strong in literary interest, but the interest is not wholly of a pleasant kind. **1895** F. HALL *Two Trifles* iii, A short article on a province of English philology which is, to me..one of interest.

8. The fact or quality of mattering or being of importance (as belonging to things); concernment, importance.

1809–10 COLERIDGE *Friend* (1865) 35 The conscience..is already violated when to moral good or evil we oppose things possessing no moral interest. **1845** MᶜCULLOCH *Taxation* III. i. (1852) 415 However important, these, after all, are matters of subordinate interest.

II. Senses related to med.L. *interesse,* as used by Matthew Paris *a* 1259, and frequently from 13th c. (see Du Cange), in the phrase *damna et interesse,* in French legal phraseology *dommages et intérêts,* the indemnity due to any one for the damage and prejudice done to him. Cf. OF. *interest* (1290 in Godef.) in sense 'damage', also recompense for damage done or caused, 'damages'. In sense 10 F. *interest* (now *intérêt*) occurs in Rabelais, 1535.

†**9. a.** Injury, detriment. **b.** Compensation for injury, 'damages'. (F. *dommages et intérêts* (see Littré, *Intérêt* 2ᵉ), med.L. *damna et interesse.*) *Obs. rare.*

[*a* **1259** MATT. PARIS *Chron.* 612 (Du Cange) Propter usuras, pœnas, & Interesse. **1274** *Acquittance to Edw. I* (Rymer *Fœdera* II. 34) Tam super principali quam super custibus dampnis & interesse refundendis Domui nostrae.] **1489** [see 'damages and Interesses' in INTERESS sb. 3].

c **1575** *Balfour's Practicks* (1754) 178 The awner..hes gude richt and just actioun aganis the with-halder of the saidis landis or gudis, for the damnage, skaith and interest quhilk he may sufficientlie prove that he sustenit throw the wanting of the proffeitis of the saidis landis or gudis. *Ibid.* 179 He sall be haldin to pay to the uther partie the foirsaid pane, as damnage and interest. **1603** FLORIO *Montaigne* II. xii. (1632) 293 How can this [be done]..without extreme interest and manifest derogation from his divine greatnesse? **1607** E. GRIMSTONE tr. *Goulart's Mem. Hist.* 14 Untill the full payment of the fines, charges, damage and interest adjudged, as well to the King; as to the said parties.

10. a. Money paid for the use of money lent (the *principal*), or for forbearance of a debt, according to a fixed ratio (*rate per cent.*).

Interest is paid at fixed intervals, usually once or twice in the year. ***simple interest*** is the interest paid on the principal as lent. ***compound*** (†***compounded***) ***interest*** (***interest upon interest***), is the interest eventually paid on a principal periodically increased by the addition of each fresh amount of interest as it becomes due and remains unpaid. Interest in this sense was formerly called *usury,* a name still applied when interest is charged at a rate beyond what is considered legitimate or just.

In med.L. *interesse* (Interest) differed from *usura* (Usury) in that the latter was avowedly a charge for the use of money, which was forbidden by the Canon Law; whereas originally '*interesse* refers to the compensation which under the Roman Law, was due by the debtor who had made default. The measure of compensation was *id quod interest,* the difference between the creditor's position in consequence of the debtor's laches and the position which might reasonably have been anticipated as the direct consequence of the

debtor's fulfilment of his obligation'. This compensation was always permissible when it could be shown that such loss had really arisen (*damnum emergens*). At a later period, *lucrum cessans*—loss of profit through inability to reinvest—was also recognized as giving a claim to *interesse*; both cases appear to be included in the formula *damna et interesse*. The *interesse* was originally a fixed sum specified in the contract; but a percentage reckoned periodically, so as to correspond to the creditor's loss, was afterwards substituted (as sometimes in England in the first half of the 13th cent.). Interest in the modern sense was first sanctioned by law (though apparently under cover of the mediæval theory) by 37 Hen. VIII, c. 9 (see quot. 1545); this statute was repealed in 1552, but re-enacted in 1571. (See W. J. ASHLEY *Engl. Econ. Hist. Middle Ages* II. 397, 466, and I. S. LEADAM in *Dict. Pol. Econ.*, 1896, II. 429.)

[**1529** see INTERESS *sb.* 4: 'money repayde with interesse'.] **1545** *Act 37 Hen. VIII*, c. 9 §3 Be it also enacted..that no person or persons..by way or meane of any corrupte bargayne, loone, eschaunge, chevisaunce, shifte, interest of any wares..accepte or take, in lucre or gaynes, for the forbearinge or givinge daye of payment of one hole yere of and for his or their money..above the sume of tenne poundes in the hundred. **1555** W. WATREMAN *Fardle Facions* I. v. 71 It was not thought to bee Justice, that the man o warre..should for an enterest of lone, bee throwen into prisone. **1573–80** BARET *Alv.* I. 205 To borow monie vpon interest to paie my debt. **1577** in *Rec. Convent. Roy. Burghs* (1870) I. 50 Ane hundreth and aucht merkis to pay for one ȝeris interest thairof, according to the raitt of tuelf for the hundreth. **1586** T. B. *La Primaud. Fr. Acad.* (1589) 497 Interest, or profit of monie, when as it hath been alwaies unpleasant in the sight of God, who forbiddeth all kinde of usurie whatsoever it be. **1590** RECORDE, etc. *Gr. Artes* (1640) 604 Interest is the summe reckoned for the lending or forbearance of the Principall for any termes or time. Interest simple is that which is counted from the Principall onely. Interest compound is that which is counted for the Principall, together with the Arrerage. **1598** I. D. tr. *Le Roy's Aristotle's Politiqves* 52 Men haue now inuented interest in steed of vsury. **1632** MASSINGER *City Madam* I. iii, Built with other men's moneys Ta'en up at interest. **1660** WILLSFORD *Scales Comm.* 59 Decimall Tables of compounded Interest. **1767** BLACKSTONE *Comm.* II. xxx. 454 When money is lent on a contract to receive..an increase by way of compensation for the use; which is generally called interest by those who think it lawful, and usury by those who do not so. **1806** HUTTON *Course Math.* I. 127 Compound interest, called also Interest upon Interest, is that which arises from the principal and interest, taken together, as it becomes due. **1878** JEVONS *Prim. Pol. Econ.* vi. 52 When the rate is above five or six per cent., it will be to some extent not true interest, but compensation for the risk of losing the capital altogether. **1879** J. T. ROGERS in *Cassell's Techn. Educ.* IV. 14/1 Interest is the reward which a man obtains for allowing another to use his property. **1881** N. T. (R.V.) *Matt.* xxv. 27 At my coming I should have received back mine own with interest [**1611** usury].

b. *fig.* esp. in phr. ***with interest***, with increase or augmentation.

1589 NASHE *Pasquill & Marf.* 11 When I lacke matter to talke of, I may resort hether [to the Exchange] to take vp a little newes at interest. **1596** SHAKS. *1 Hen. IV*, IV. iii. 49 You shall haue your desires, with interest. **1601** ? MARSTON *Pasquil & Kath.* II. 30, I doe returne your wish With ample interest of beatitude. **1724** DE FOE *Mem. Cavalier* (1840) 131 He paid the imperialists with interest. **1850** W. IRVING *Goldsmith* xxxviii. 364 The latter..returned the blows with interest. **1890** *Spectator* 24 May 715/1 They never seem to have put out their ideas to interest, but kept them wrapped up in napkins till they forgot their existence.

11. *attrib.* and *Comb.*, as (sense 4) ***interest-bound*** adj.; (sense 7) ***interest-awaking***, ***-compelling*** adjs.; (sense 10) ***interest-bearing***, ***charge***, ***-equalization***, ***policy***, ***-rate***; ***interest-free*** adj.; **interest group**, a group of individuals possessing a common identifying interest; **interest-money** = sense 10.

1618 *Barnevelt's Apol.* C iij b, The interest-money came to that height, that the State of the whole seemed desperate. **1673** KIRKMAN *Unlucky Citizen* 212 He were better to pay interest-money. **1818** BENTHAM *Ch. Eng.* p. xviii, The seductive influence of sinister interest, and interest-begotten prejudice. **1848** ARNOULD *Mar. Insur.* (1866) I. I. v. 217 An interest policy is one that shows by its form that the assured has a real, substantial interest in the thing insured. **1894** W. T. STEAD in *Westm. Gaz.* 7 May 2/1 The watchword of the Coxeyite agitation is 'Death to the interest-bearing bond!' **1895** *Outing* (U.S.) XXVI. 343/2 Johann received the interest money gruffly. **1901** *Daily Chron.* 18 Nov. 6/3 The 'great retrograde, tyrannical, interest-bound party'. **1902** *Ibid.* 17 July 6/4 Its interest-awaking value. **1902** *Ibid.* 6 Aug. 3/2 As interest-compelling ..as the amour of a mediæval queen. **1908** A. F. BENTLEY *Process Govt.* xii. 300 The deeper-lying interest groups of society. **1936** WIRTH & SHILS tr. *Mannheim's Ideology & Utopia* III. i. 136 The hitherto constantly emphasized interest-bound nature of political thought. **1943** E. BLUNDEN *Return to Husbandry* iii. 18 This demands ample credit of an interest-free nature. **1957** M. SWAN *Brit. Guiana* iv. 78 Houses which had been built with interest-free loans or with other forms of estate assistance. **1959** E. POUND *Thrones* xcviii. 42 Byzance lasted longer than Manchu because of an (%) interest-rate. **1962** *Economist* 25 Aug. 685/2 The authors see signs of change..in the growth of interest-group organisations. **1963** *Daily Tel.* 2 Oct. 23/8 The interest-equalisation tax to raise the cost of foreign borrowing in New York. **1964** R. WILKINSON *Gentlemanly Power* iv. 48 The parliamentary Conservative party has come to represent different interest-groups, farmers.. manufacturers, small professional men..stockbrokers, shopkeepers and elderly widows. **1966** *Times* 28 Feb. (Canada Suppl.) p. vii/5 The United States's interest-equalization tax of 15 per cent, to be paid by any United States resident buying foreign stocks. **1972** *Sat. Rev.* (U.S.) 6 May 38/3 The company store charged exorbitant prices, but extended interest-free credit. **1974** *Times* 18 Feb. 14/5 It may..be difficult with such a budget deficit to prevent interest rates from rising.

interest ('ɪntərɪst, -ɛst), *v.* [An alteration of the earlier INTERESS *v.*, after INTEREST *sb.*

(It has been suggested that the change might be partly due to confusion with *interes-t* = *interess-ed* pa. t. of INTERESS; cf. *hoise, hoist, graff, graft, infeoff, infeft*.)]

1. *trans.* To invest (a person) with a share in or title to something, esp. a spiritual privilege. Const. *in* (†*to, into, unto*).

1610 DONNE *Pseudo-Martyr* 152 Sufficient cause to intitle and interest a man in the crowne of martyrdome. **1614** T. ADAMS *Devil's Banquet* 56 Depriuing them of some comfort or right, which the inuiolable Law of God, hath interested them to. **1615** CHAPMAN *Odyss.* xv. 326 Aurora ravish'd him ..And interested him amongst the Gods. *a* **1639** W. WHATELEY *Prototypes* I. xx. (1640) 203 Let us strive to interest ourselves into Gods blessing on the godly. *Ibid.* xxi. 264 Benefits..to him that interests himselfe to them by getting into Christ. **1834** J. BROWN *Lett. Sanctif.* I. 220 The interesting a sinner in the atoning sacrifice of the Redeemer, takes away the irritating power of the divine law. *a* **1864** J. D. BURNS *Mem. & Rem.* (1879) 338 By faith we become interested in the propitiation.

2. To cause (a person) to have an objective interest or concern in the progress or fate of a matter; to involve; chiefly in pass. ***to be interested***.

1608 D. T. *Ess. Pol. & Mor.* 2 b, When they think he is not interested in the cause, or induced by any priuate obligation. **1620** BRENT tr. *Sarpi's Hist. Council Trent* (1676) 451 All was concluded..without interesting the Popes authority. **1656** BAXTER *Reformed Pastor* iv. 74 They will..interest piety itself with their faults. **1727** LARDNER *Wks.* (1838) I. 157 Pilate finding they interested their religion in this cause, and that they were resolute in it, became afraid he must.. submit to them. **1781** GIBBON *Decl. & F.* xxviii. III. 79 The emperor himself was interested not to deface the splendour of his own cities. **1886** *Law Rep.* 32 Ch. Div. 48 The landlord..is interested in seeing that the liquidators discharge their duty properly.

3. Of a thing: To concern; to affect; to relate to. *rare* or *Obsolescent*.

1638 DIGBY *Lett. conc. Relig.* ii. (1651) 9 Their private opinions..doe not interest our beliefs. **1798** MALTHUS *Popul.* IV. xii. (1806) II. 497 The subject..interests the question of human happiness so nearly. **1813** SIR R. WILSON *Priv. Diary* II. 161 The news of the morning principally interested the Crown Prince. **1864** *Scotsman* 10 Dec., It is matter for deep regret that..the case..has so little interested those whom it most interests.

4. To cause (any one) to take a personal interest, share, or part in (a scheme, business, etc.); to induce to participate *in*; to engage *in*. *refl.* To take active part *in*.

1630 CAPT. SMITH *Trav. & Adv., Disc. Voy. Guiana* 49 After his returne for England, he endeavoured by his best abilities to interest his Countrey and state in those faire Regions. **1647** *Manifesto* 10 June in *Carlyle's Cromwell*, They seek to interest in their design the City of London. **1691** T. H[ALE] *Acc. New Invent.* 2 Their first interesting themselves in this undertaking. **1702** ADDISON *Dial. Medals* (J.), This was a goddess who used to interest herself in marriages. *Mod.* I do not feel called upon to interest myself in his behalf.

5. To affect with a feeling of concern; to stimulate to cause sympathetic feeling; to excite the curiosity or attention of. (Prob. a back-formation from INTERESTED *ppl. a.* 3.)

[**1748** *Anson's Voy.* III. vi. 348 They did not appear to be at all interested about us.] **1780** BENTHAM *Princ. Legisl.* xviii. §57 By what other means should an object engage or fix a man's attention, unless by interesting him? **1791** MRS. RADCLIFFE *Rom. Forest* ix, She had been too much interested by the events of the moment. **1830** GALT *Lawrie T.* IV. viii. (1849) 172 Something in his appearance..interested my attention. **1866** G. MACDONALD *Ann. Q. Neighb.* i. (1878) 6, I wanted to interest myself in it. **1868** DICKENS *Lett.* (1880) II. 334 Your account of the first night interested me immensely.

interesta'bility. *rare*$^{-1}$. [f. **interest-able* (f. INTEREST *v.*): see -ITY.] Capability of being interested.

1811 W. TAYLOR in Robberds *Mem.* (1843) II. 343 It did not again absorb all my interestability.

interested ('ɪntərɪstɪd), *ppl. a.* [f. INTEREST *v.* + -ED[1].]

1. Concerned, affected; having an interest, concern, or share in something.

1828 WEBSTER s.v., One interested in the funds. An interested witness. *a* **1834** J. BROOKS in D. A. Wells *Burden & Strength* (1864) 34 Substitute skilful, intelligent, interested free labor for unskilled, ignorant, and uninterested slave labor. **1844** WILLIAMS *Real Prop.* (1877) 207 The evidence of interested persons is now received, and its value estimated according to its worth. **1887** MOLONEY *Forestry W. Afr.* vi. 126 With an issue to the interested of having..to pay freight only on good marketable stuff.

2. Influenced by considerations of personal advantage; moved by self-interest; self-seeking, self-interested. (The opposite of *disinterested*.)

1705 STANHOPE *Paraphr.* I. 34 Dissembled or interested Homage of Rulers or Rabbies. **1771** MACKENZIE *Man Feel.* lv. (1803) 91 The world is, in general, selfish, interested, and unthinking. **1855** THACKERAY *Newcomes* II. 213 The wretched consequences of interested marriages. **1855** MACAULAY *Hist. Eng.* xxi. IV. 555 He was generally thought interested and grasping.

3. Characterized by a feeling of concern, sympathy, or curiosity.

1665 PEPYS *Corr.* 4 Sept., No day hath passed..without my most interested wishes for your health. **1729** BUTLER *Serm.* Wks. 1874 II. Pref. 23 The very idea of an interested pursuit necessarily presupposes particular passions or appetites. **1753** SMOLLETT *Ct. Fathom* (1784) 18/1 He thought she would..have betrayed some interested symptom; that her face would have undergone some favourable suffusion. **1806** SURR *Winter in Lond.* (ed. 3) III. 35 'Is he alive?' said Belloni with interested emotion. *Mod.* They found in me an interested auditor.

interestedly ('ɪntərɪstɪdlɪ), *adv.* [f. prec. + -LY[2].] In an interested manner; through self-interest; with interest or concern.

1765 EARL BUCKINGHAM in *Lett. C'tess Suffolk* (1824) II. 307 Lamenting that others interestedly refuse me any return for what I in some sort interestedly did. **1782** R. CUMBERLAND *Anecd.* (1787) I. 9. **1827** *Hist. Eur.* in *Ann. Reg.* 277/1 The interestedly slow movements of the ordinary tribunals. **1859** LANG *Wand. India* 258, I do not speak interestedly. I have as much already on my hands as I can perform, if not more. **1886** MISS BROUGHTON *Dr. Cupid* I. vii. 114 A figure whose manœuvres are interestedly watched by the rest of the company.

interestedness ('ɪntərɪstɪdnɪs). [f. as prec. + -NESS.] The quality or condition of being interested; esp. of being moved by interested motives (the opposite of *disinterestedness*).

1711 SHAFTESB. *Charac.* (1737) II. II. II. §2. 140 The Affections which..constitute whatever we call Interestedness or Self-Love. **1757** H. WALPOLE *Mem. Geo. II*, Apr., His [Pitt's] ambition was glaring; his interestedness not even specious. **1788** A. MACDONALD *Misc. Serm.* (1790) 50 Too much interestedness in the affairs of our neighbour is less supportable than absolute indifference. **1882** J. HAWTHORNE *Fort. Fool* I. xxi, The passion, wholly free..from any lower form of interestedness.

'interester. *rare.* [f. INTEREST *v.* + -ER[1].] One who interests; in quot. 1701, †One who interests himself in behalf of others.

a **1701** SEDLEY *Grumbler* I. Wks. 1778 II. 206 *Gri.* Pray who are they that say so? *Ari.* Some persons who interest themselves in your behalf. *Gri.* I don't care a rush for them. The world is full of nothing but these interesters, who at the bottom value us no more, than John-a-Nokes and Tom-a-Styles.

interesterification (ˌɪntərɛstɛrɪfɪ'keɪʃən). [f. INTER- 2 a + ESTERIFICATION.] The exchange of alkoxy or acyl groups between an ester and another compound, sometimes used to modify the properties of margarine and other fats.

1941 T. P. HILDITCH *Industr. Chem. Fats & Waxes* (ed. 2) IV. ii. 305 Suggestions have..been made..with the objects either of interchanging the acyl radicals between the triglyceride molecules of the mixture of fats used, or of introducing a certain amount of butyroglycerides into the margarine fats. Brief reference may be made to these 'interesterification' processes. **1961** *Times Rev. Industry* July 8/2 Interesterification..brings about a molecular rearrangement in the fat. This manifests itself in changes both in melting characteristics and crystal type.

Hence (as a back-formation) **ˌintere'sterify** *v. trans.* and *intr.*, to subject to or undergo interesterification; **ˌintere'sterified** *ppl. a.*

1950 KIRK & OTHMER *Encycl. Chem. Technol.* V. 817 Some esters will interesterify with methanol at 100°C. or lower with no catalyst added. **1958** C. PLACEK in *Mod. Chem. Processes* V. 84/2 In baking performance, directly interesterified lard has all the desirable properties of vegetable shortening. *Ibid.* 88/3 Until operating conditions (equilibrium) are reached, material appearing at the end of the run is usually not interesterified to the desired point and is recycled after catalyst separation.

interesting ('ɪntərɪstɪŋ), *ppl. a.* [f. INTEREST *v.* + -ING[2]. Formerly, and still dialectally, *inte'resting*.] That interests.

†**1.** That concerns, touches, affects, or is of importance; important. *Obs.*

1711 SHAFTESB. *Charac.* (1737) II. II. II. §2. 155 That Passion which is esteem'd peculiarly interesting; as having for its Aim the Possession of Wealth. **1769** *Junius Lett.* (1804) I. 2 In defence of what they thought most dear and interesting to themselves. **1773** MRS. CHAPONE *Improv. Mind* (1774) I. 112 A woman..thought meanly of in points the most interesting to her honour. **1813** SIR R. WILSON *Priv. Diary* II. 460 It is extremely interesting that at this time you should be well informed.

2. Adapted to excite interest; having the qualities which rouse curiosity, engage attention, or appeal to the emotions; of interest.

1768 STERNE *Sent. Journ.* (1778) I. 48 (*Remise Door* i.) It was a face of about six and twenty..it was not critically handsome, but there was that in it, which..attached me much more to it—it was interesting. **1781** GIBBON *Decl. & F.* xxxi. III. 202 The interesting and original picture of the manners of Rome. **1843** BETHUNE *Sc. Fireside Stor.* 37 A long and interesting conversation. **1849** MACAULAY *Hist. Eng.* i. I. 66 The Irish..were distinguished by qualities which tend to make men interesting rather than prosperous. **1882** M. ARNOLD in *19th Cent.* Aug. 222 All knowledge is interesting to a wise man, and the knowledge of nature is interesting to all men.

3. (*to be*) ***in an interesting condition***, ***situation***, ***state***: (to be) pregnant; also, ***to be interesting***; ***interesting event***: a birth.

1748 SMOLLETT *R. Random* II. lxix. 335 So that I cannot leave her in such an interesting situation, which I hope will produce something to crown my felicity. **1838** DICKENS *Nickleby* (1839) xxix. 286 Mrs. Lenville (who, as has been before hinted, was in an interesting state). **1848** [see SITUATION 7 b]. **1899** *Westm. Gaz.* 27 June 6/3 'Interesting event' at Peterhof. Another daughter! **1928** W. B. MAXWELL *We Forget because we Must* II. iii. 44 I'm afraid I seem to make heavy weather of my interesting condition. **1930** GALSWORTHY *On Forsyte 'Change* 171 Winifred, beginning

to be 'interesting', owing to the approach of a little Dartie, kept her eyes somewhat watchfully on 'Monty'. **1970** K. GILES *Death in Church* ii. 49 Her little maid got into An Interesting Condition and the young fellow was willing to solemnise it.

'interestingly, *adv.* [f. prec. + -LY².]

a. In an interesting manner, so as to interest. **1811** SHELLEY *St. Irvyne* VII. Pr. Wks. 1888 I. 174 The thrilling accents of her interestingly sweet voice. **1821** CAMPBELL in *New Monthly Mag.* I. 387 None of them appeal more interestingly to the heart. **1888** BURGON *Lives 12 Gd. Men* II. 83 Another friend.. writes thus interestingly concerning him.

b. Used as a sentence adverb. **1972** *Times* 13 May 10/4 Interestingly Balanchine is no longer called a director of New York City Ballet. **1973** *Nature* 18 May 118/1 Interestingly, the results presented were not in accord with the rather precise quantum calculations.

'interestingness. [f. as prec. + -NESS.] The quality of being interesting. **1759** ADAM SMITH *Mor. Sent.* II. VI. §3. 107 [The axe] the emblem of having been beheaded, which is engraved under those [heads].. sheds a real dignity and interestingness over their characters. **1881** *19th Cent.* May 788 The interestingness of commonplace lives is insisted on. **1884** *Spectator* No. 2903. 212 The *Times* under his management failed in interestingness.

'interestless, *a. rare.* [f. INTEREST *sb.* + -LESS.] Devoid of interest. **1886** *Sat. Rev.* 17 July 103 The passionless, humourless, interestless 'analysis'.

inter-ethnic: see INTER- *pref.* 4 c.

interface ('ɪntəfeɪs), *sb.* [f. INTER- 2 b + FACE.]

1. A surface lying between two portions of matter or space, and forming their common boundary. **1882** BOTTOMLEY *Hydrost.* 13 The term *interface* denotes a face of separation, plane or curved, between two contiguous portions of the same substance. **1883** G. CHRYSTAL in *Encycl. Brit.* XV. 264/1 The interface of the two liquids in the axial line.

2. *transf.* and *fig.* **a.** A means or place of interaction between two systems, organizations, etc.; a meeting-point or common ground between two parties, systems, or disciplines; also, interaction, liaison, dialogue. **1962** M. MCLUHAN *Gutenberg Galaxy* 141 (*heading*) The interface of the Renaissance was the meeting of medieval pluralism and modern homogeneity and mechanism. **1962** *Evening Star* (Washington, D.C.) 18 Aug. 1/6 Interface.. seems to mean the liaison between two different agencies that may be working on the same project. *Ibid.* 1/7 The Defense Communications Agency.. was made responsible for the resolution of interface problems. **1964** A. BATTERSBY *Network Analysis* viii. 116 Interfaces: events should be established at stages where the work passes from one department to another—these stages are known as interfaces. **1965** H. I. ANSOFF *Corporate Strategy* (1968) vi. 107 Functional organizations, such as research, development, finance, and marketing, have a strong interface with the outside environment. **1965** *Internat. Sci. & Technol.* Oct. 30/1 The advantages of high-speed transport were piddled away at the nodes or interfaces: from bus to train, train to train, city terminal to airport terminal, check-in counter to loading gate, and so on. **1967** *Technology Week* 23 Jan. 75/1 The interface across which the engineer-scientist and the biologist can interact is a broad one. **1967** *Times Rev. Industry* Feb. 27/1 The third interface between government and the marketing system is with the intermediate firm supplying either other intermediate firms or the consumer. **1967** *Economist* 16 Sept. p. ix/1 The North Sea and Channel ports form the biggest frontiers in world trade—or the biggest interface, in the language of the modern transport man, meaning the place where the greatest quantity of international cargo changes its mode of transport. **1970** *Nature* 23 May 684/1 The interface between physics and music is of direct relevance to.. the psychological effects of hearing. **1970** *Interior Design* Dec. 767/4 Educationalists are convinced that the need for the interface of lecturer and student will not diminish. **1972** *Sci. Amer.* Nov. 51/3 The issue of insanity as a defense in criminal cases.. is at the interface of medicine, law and ethics.

b. (An) apparatus designed to connect two scientific instruments, devices, etc., so that they can be operated jointly. **1964** *Ann. N.Y. Acad. Sci.* CXV. 574 The collection of components which connects the analog and digital computers to each other, and which controls and converts the data, is generally termed the 'interface'. **1966** *Electronics* 3 Oct. 130 If a flight carries special equipment, then modular interfaces can easily be designed to adapt the general-purpose computer to the equipment. **1973** T. ALLBEURY *Choice of Enemies* xvi. 79 Programs are written in a computer language... If you wanted to use one of the IBM languages on an ICL machine, you'd have to have what's called an interface to make the two different things compatible. **1973** *Physics Bull.* Apr. 242/3 Scobie and Wellum.. have built interfaces for two pulse height analysers.

interface ('ɪntəfeɪs), *v.* [f. the sb.]

1. a. *trans.* To connect (scientific equipment) *with* or *to* so as to make possible joint operation. **1969** *Computers & Humanities* IV. 76 Professor Louis Delatte.. publishes.. various computer-prepared indices to classical texts, using a Selectric typewriter interfaced with his own local computer. **1969** *Physics Bull.* Sept. 367/2 The prospect of interfacing each device specifically with each computer on each application becomes formidable in these circumstances in terms of effort and cost. This is avoided using the CAMAC technique of interfacing the device to the dataway, via a module, and the dataway to the computer, via the controller. **1970** *Sci. Jrnl.* Mar. 17/4 Their movements were monitored by a series of illuminated photoconductor cells, which were interfaced to the PDP-8/S computer. **1973** *Nature* 6 Apr. 402/2 A 'Perkin-Elmer 900' and a 'Hewlett Packard 7610A' chromatograph,.. interfaced with a 'Perkin-Elmer PEP-1' gas chromatography data system, were used. **1973** *Physics Bull.* Apr. 240/2 The memory uses 'static' circuitry and no clocking is required which makes it easy to use and interface to any system.

b. *intr.* for *pass.* **1969** *New Yorker* 11 Jan. 42 Inflated space units, which have to 'interface'—a space-age verb meaning, roughly, to coordinate—with equipment in the cabin. **1971** *Physics Bull.* Jan. 42/3 The minimum system can be attached to 16 devices..; the largest can 'interface' with about 2000 remote sensing/control devices.

2. *intr.* To come into interaction *with*. **1967** M. MCLUHAN *Medium is Massage* 88 A strange bond often exists among antisocial types in their power to see environments as they really are. This need to interface, to confront environments with a certain anti-social power, is manifest in the famous story 'The Emperor's New Clothes'. **1968** *Lebende Sprachen* XIII. 4/1 Before turning to a discussion of how this management system.. interfaces with functional organization let us try to define what we mean by project management. **1973** *LSA Bull.* Mar. 14 Mr. Hamp, the LSA delegate to UNESCO, reported on ways which he felt the Linguistic Society could interface with the United States National Commission.

interfacial (ɪntə'feɪʃ(ɪ)əl), *a.* [f. INTER- 4 a + L. *faci-es* face: cf. FACIAL.] Included between two faces of a crystal or other solid, as in ***interfacial angle***, the dihedral angle included between two faces. **1837** J. D. DANA *Min.* 14 The interfacial angle.. M:T is an oblique angle, while P:T = 90°. **1877** E. S. DANA *Text-bk. Min.* 3 In the descriptions of crystals three kinds of angles may come under consideration, *solid, plane,* and *interfacial.*

interfacing ('ɪntəˌfeɪsɪŋ), *vbl. sb.* [f. INTER- 2 a + FACING *vbl. sb.*; cf. INTERFACE *v.*] The action of the verb INTERFACE; also *concr.* (see quot. 1964). Also *attrib.* or as *ppl. a.* **1964** MARGOLIS *Compl. Bk. Tailoring* 180 An inter-facing is a reinforcing or shaping fabric used between the outer fabric and the facing or the lining. **1968** J. IRONSIDE *Fashion Alphabet* 89 Very similar to interlining but interfacing is usually only placed along edges or in collars, cuffs, etc. **1968** *Lebende Sprachen* XIII. 4/1 There will be a large or small group, depending on the complexity of the interfacing problems. *Ibid.* 104/1 (*heading*) Terms in PERT planning interfacing network. **1969** *Physics Bull.* Sept. 367/1 The use of a common highway permits many sources and acceptors of data (devices) to be connected to the computer.. via the CAMAC compatible modules. This type of interfacing would be unnecessary.. if the number of devices were small and the computer had sufficient input-output channels which were already matched to each device.

interfaction: see INTERFATION.

interfair, -fayer, erron. ff. INTER-AFFAIR.

inter-faith, -family: see INTER- *pref.* 5.

†**inter'falk**, *v. Obs. rare*⁻¹. [f. INTER- 1 a + *-falk*, as in DEFALK, q.v.] *trans.* To interrupt, break into. **1621** MOLLE *Camerar. Liv. Libr.* II. ix. 101 The great joy that tooke him being interfalcked with sighes.

†**inter'farce**, *v. Obs. rare*⁻¹. [f. INTER- 1 a + FARCE *v.*¹ 6.] *trans.* To stuff in between. **1566** DRANT *Horace* To Rdr. 3, I haue interfarced.. much of myne owne deuisinge.

interfare, obs. form of INTERFERE.

interfascicular (-fə'sɪkjʊlə(r)), *a. Anat.* and *Bot.* [INTER- 4 a.] Situated between fascicles or 'bundles' of tissue. **1836–9** TODD *Cycl. Anat.* II. 118/2 In the interfascicular cellular tissue of the muscles. **1875** BENNETT & DYER *Sachs' Bot.* 573 An interfascicular cambium is formed by divisions in the intermediate cells of the medullary rays. **1897** *Allbutt's Syst. Med.* II. 454 Overgrowth of interfascicular connective tissue.

†**inter'fation.** *Obs. rare*⁻⁰. [ad. L. *interfātiōn-em*, n. of action f. *interfārī* to interrupt in speaking, f. *inter* + *fārī* to speak.] (See quot.) **1656** BLOUNT *Glossogr.*, *Interfaction*, an interrupting of one tale, a speaking whilst another speaks. **1658** PHILLIPS, *Interfaction* [ed. **1678** *Interfation*].

interfeat: see ENTERFEAT.

†**inter'fection.** *Obs. rare.* [ad. L. *interfectiōn-em*, n. of action from *interficĕre* to kill: cf. obs. F. *interfection* (Godef.).] **a.** Killing or slaying. **b.** In *Alchemy* (see quot. 1727). *c* **1450** *Mirour Saluacioun* 2396 Yᵗ thay.. shuld.. cesse of his interfectionne [*glossed* slaghtere]. **1656** BLOUNT *Glossogr.*, *Interfection*, murder, a killing or slaying. **1727** BRADLEY *Fam. Dict.* s.v. *Elixir*, In the space of twenty Hours, the Elixir will reduce the Gold into its primitive Matter, and become very black. This is what they call Interfection, and what we simply call Resolution.

†**inter'fector.** *Obs.* [a. L. *interfector*, agent-n. f. *interficĕre* to kill. Cf. obs. F. *interfecteur* (Godef.).] **a.** A slayer, murderer. **b.** *Astrol.* A death-bringing planet. **1450** *Pol. Poems* (Rolls) II. 232 His interfectours blessed might thei be. **1647** LILLY *Chr. Astrol.* lxvii. 409 It pre-notes.. death.. when the malevolent Interfector comes to the degree of the Zodiack wherein the Lord of the ascendant was. **1658** [see INTERFICIENT]. **1660** H. MORE *Myst. Godl.* VII. xv. 344 When the ἀφέτης comes to the place of the ἀναιρέτης, that is, the Emissor unto the place of the Interfector, then wo be to the brat.. born under so unlucky Starrs; for there is no remedie but he must die the death.

interfederation: see INTER- *pref.* 2 a.

interfemoral (-'fɛmərəl), *a. Anat.* [INTER- 4 a.] Extending between the femora or thighs (chiefly of the membrane between the thighs of a bat). **1828** STARK *Elem. Nat. Hist.* I. 69 Tail slender, half enveloped in the interfemoral membrane. **1835–6** TODD *Cycl. Anat.* I. 598/2 A tail for the support and extension of the interfemoral membrane is found in the insectivorous Bats. **1875** BLAKE *Zool.* 54 The tail and the web-skin connecting the hind-legs, and called the 'interfemoral' web.

interfenestral (-fɪ'nɛstrəl), *a. Arch. rare.* [f. INTER- 4 a + L. *fenestra* window.] Placed between windows. **1851** RUSKIN *Stones Ven.* I. xv. §9 A northern apse is a southern one with its inter-fenestral piers set edgeways.

interfenestration (-fɛnɪ'streɪʃən). *Arch.* [INTER- 2 a: see prec., and cf. *inter-columniation.*] The spacing of the windows of a building. **1823** P. NICHOLSON *Pract. Build.* 586 *Inter-fenestration*, the space between windows. **1846** *Civil Eng. & Archit. Jrnl.* IX. 329 The vertical interfenestration is not so good as the horizontal, owing to there being too many tiers of windows, and they are put too closely together. **1859** *Building News* V. 1136 *Interfenestration*—a term now suggested.. as a useful correlative to 'intercolumniation', inasmuch as it refers to the spacing of the windows.

interfere (ɪntər'fɪə(r)), *v.* Forms: α. 6 **entrefyer**, 6–7 **enterfere**, 7 **-fear(e, -feer, -feir(e, -faire, -fare, -fayr, -fire.** β. 6 **interfier**, 6–7 **-feir**, 7 **-feer(e, -vere, -fare, -fyre**, 7– **interfere.** [a. OF. *s'entreférir* to strike each other, f. *entre-* INTER- 1 b + *férir*:—L. *ferīre* to strike; mod.F. has *interférer* (from English) in scientific use. The forms in *-fare, -fire, -vere*, etc. are app. popular corruptions arising while the word was only known in sense 1 (which is also given by Cotgr. for the OF. word), but the first of these may have been regarded by some as f. INTER- 1 + FARE *v.*¹]

1. *intr.* Of a horse: To strike the inside of the fetlock with the shoe or hoof of the opposite foot (= CUT *v.* 27); to knock one leg against another. Said also of the feet. (Rarely of persons.) α. **1530** PALSGR. 538/1 My horse entrefyereth all redy, I feare me the jade wyll fayle me, or I come to my journayes ende, *mon cheual entretaille desja* [etc.]. **1562** J. HEYWOOD *Prov. & Epigr.* (1867) 215 My horse to weare greate breeches is now asynde: Why? to kepe him from enterferyng behynde. **1607** MARKHAM *Caval.* VI. (1617) 65 If your horse.. doth enterfaire or hew one leg vpon another. **1635** VALENTINE *Foure Sea-Serm.* 58 The feet of both crosse and enterfere, and fall foule one with the other. **1684** *Lond. Gaz.* No. 1929/4 She [a mare] enterfears a little behind. β. **1578** COOPER *Thesaurus*, *Terere calcem calce*, In an horse to interfier [*earlier edd.* enterfier]. **1616** SURFL. & MARKH. *Country Farme* 145 If the horse interfering doe wound himselfe vpon his hinder feet. **1687** *Lond. Gaz.* No. 2290/4 A black.. Colt.. intervering behind. **1725** BRADLEY *Fam. Dict.* s.v. *Shoeing of horses*, For those Hoofs that Interfere [etc.]. **1883** *Harper's Mag.* Oct. 726/1 If he 'interferes', there is a multiplicity of boots and pads to protect every irritated point.

2. a. *intr.* Hence, of things generally: To strike against each other; to come into physical collision; to collide or clash, so as to hamper or hinder each other; to get in each other's way, cross each other's path. Now chiefly in *Physics*, of waves of light, heat, sound, etc.: To exercise reciprocal action so as to increase, diminish, or nullify the natural effect of each (cf. INTERFERENCE 2). Also in *Broadcasting*: to transmit a signal which is received simultaneously *with* the signal sought; to cause or emit interference (sense 5 a). **1613** R. CAWDREY *Table Alph.* (ed. 3), *Enterfire*, to strike one another. **1620** T. SCOTT *God & King* (1633) 4 With eyes staring.. teeth grating and interfering. **1692** BENTLEY *Boyle Lect.* vii. 232 The Atoms being various moved.. must needs knock and interfere. **1801** T. YOUNG in *Phil. Trans.* (1802) 35 The reflection from the depressed point will so interfere with the reflection from the fixed point. **1860** TYNDALL *Glac.* II. i. 230 Two systems of sonorous waves can be caused to interfere and.. to destroy each other. **1904** in J. Erskine-Murray *Handbk. Wireless Telegr.* (1907) x. 179 From 11.27 till noon the receiving ship 'Hancock'.. and the experimental station in building §75.. interfered continually. **1928** L. S. PALMER *Wireless Princ. & Pract.* iii. 49 Stations transmitting on the same wavelength but lying in different directions from the receiving station can be prevented from interfering. **1940** L. R. LOHR *Television Broadcasting* iii. 37 If television images were capable of being received beyond the horizon, the received images.. would interfere with the transmissions of other stations. **1960** *Which?* Apr. 72/2 Does it [*sc.* the vacuum cleaner] interfere with radio or TV?

†**b.** *fig.* Of persons and things: To come into non-physical collision or contact, to clash in opinions, tendencies, etc. *Obs.*

a **1644** WESTFIELD *Serm., Ps.* cvi. 19–20 (1646) 62 They tell us of divisions among our selves: it is a wonder to see how they interferre, and strike one on another, in the point of worshipping of Images. **1698** S. CLARK *Script. Just.* viii. 36 These two Places would enterfere and contradict one another. **1761** HUME *Hist. Eng.* III. lxi. 323 The two republics were not inflamed by any national antipathy, and their interests very little interfered. **1836** J. GILBERT *Chr. Atonem.* v. (1852) 137 When public duty and private feeling interfere..then justice calls for punishment.

†**3.** *intr.* To run into each other, cross each other's paths; to intercross, intersect. *Obs.*

1647 [see INTERFERING *vbl. sb.*]. **1655** FULLER *Ch. Hist.* IX. iii. §38 Though at first there was a reall difference..in their opinions, yet..afterwards they did so interfere amongst themselves, that it is almost impossible to banke, and bound their severall absurdities. **1668** CULPEPPER & COLE *Barthol. Anat.* III. xi. 154 The Fibres of the Head do so interfere and cross one another, that [etc.]. **1693** J. CLAYTON in *Phil. Trans.* XVII. 791 The Heads of the Branches of the Rivers interfere and lock one within another. **1725** DE FOE *Voy. round World* (1840) 258 It is impossible to describe how the sound, crossing and interfering, mingled itself, and the several voices sunk one into another.

4. a. Of things, actions, etc.: To come into collision or opposition, so as to affect the course of.

1662 STILLINGFL. *Orig. Sacr.* I. iii. §5 Where they do not enterfere with the history of Scripture. **1771** *Junius Lett.* lvii. 296 No scruples of conscience to interfere with his morality. **1885** F. TEMPLE *Relat. Relig. & Sc.* vii. 199 It is not the purpose of Revelation to interfere with the course of nature.

b. Of persons: To meddle *with*; to interpose and take part in something, esp. without having the right to do so; to intermeddle. Also with *indirect passive.*

1632 T. NASH *Quaternio* 269 Let not the husbandman enterfare with the citizen, nor the citizen with the husbandman. **1782** PRIESTLEY *Corrupt. Chr.* I. I. 117 He frequently interfered with the disputes. **1846** R. W. DALE in *Life* ii. (1898) 33 Methodists are interfered with in their work. **1875** JOWETT *Plato* (ed. 2) I. 370 Cannot you hold your tongue..and no one will interfere with you?

c. *Chess.* Of a piece: to obstruct the line of action of another piece. (Cf. INTERFERENCE 1 b.)

1913 A. C. WHITE *Sam Loyd* 303 The White pieces can interfere in all kinds of ways with the Black pieces, and the Black pieces can interfere with each other with varied and beautiful results. **1926** H. WEENINK *Chess Probl.* 38 It will be noticed that..Re6 in turn interferes with the line of force of the Bg4, shutting off its command of d7 and c8. **1930** WHITE & HUME *Valves & Bi-Valves* 139 The moves of the checking Valve interfere, not..on an actual line of the Black Queen, but on her possible (potential) line of check next move. **1937** T. R. DAWSON *Caïssa's Wild Roses in Clusters* vi. 24/2 One Black piece..interferes on two squares on the line of another piece... Each of two Black pieces..interferes with the other.

d. Const. *with*: to molest or assault sexually.

1948 D. BALLANTYNE *Cunninghams* (1963) iii. 22 The former Mayor..who was kicked out of his church for interfering with a youngster in a Sunday School class. **1956** L. MCINTOSH *Oxford Folly* viii. 119 'All the girls I used to fall for,' said Julian, 'were incredibly beautiful, and as hard as nails. But they tolerated me, because I was much too timid ever to "interfere" with them.' **1968** A. MACLEOD *Dam* v. 51 She had reason to suspect that Sandra had been 'interfered' with. **1972** *Observer* 3 Sept. 33/1 In a few cases, like Byron's, a nanny sexually 'interfered' with her charge.

5. To interpose, take part, so as to affect some action; to intervene. Const. *in.*

1743 POCOCKE *Descr. East* I. III. i. 133 A Sheik Arab, who lives here, has really all the power, whenever he pleases to interfere. **1794** MRS. RADCLIFFE *Myst. Udolpho* xxviii, Montoni and the rest of the party interfered and separated them. **1794** S. WILLIAMS *Vermont* 291 The Governor of New York by letters to them and otherwise interfered in the business. **1844** LD. BROUGHAM *Brit. Const.* viii. (1862) 102 They may interfere in elections by the use of corrupt means to bribe or intimidate the electors. **1856** FROUDE *Hist. Eng.* (1858) I. i. 29 Parliament interfered to protect employers against their labourers.

6. *U.S. Football.* To interpose between the player with the ball and a would-be tackler so as to help the former. *Baseball.* To obstruct a runner between two bases; also, to obstruct a catcher or fielder who is trying to take or throw the ball. (Cf. INTERFERENCE 1 c.)

1920 W. CAMP *Football without a Coach* 51 The full-back and the right half must interfere for their companion. **1969** *Official Baseball Rules* 39 The batter..is entitled to first base without liability to be put out..when..the catcher or any fielder interferes with him.

†**interfere**, *sb. Obs. rare*⁻¹. In 6 enterfyre. [f. prec. vb.] The action of interfering: see prec. 1.

1523 FITZHERB. *Husb.* §109 Enterfyre, is a sorance, and cometh of yll shoynge, and appereth ofte both behynde and before, betwene the fete agaynst the fetelockes.

interference (ɪntəˈfɪərəns). [irreg. f. prec. vb. + -ENCE, after derivatives of L. *ferre*, e.g. *difference.* Cf. mod.F. *interférence.*]

1. a. The action or fact of interfering or intermeddling (*with* a person, etc., or *in* some action).

1783 BURKE *9th Rep. Aff. India* I. Wks. XI. 26 The interference of government was introduced by this act in two ways. **1804** W. TENNANT *Ind. Recreat.* (ed. 2) II. 247 This tax..with the collection of which the British have avoided all interference..is farmed out. **1874** GREEN *Short Hist.* vi. §4. 305 England..withdrew from any active interference in the struggles of the Continent.

b. *Chess.* Obstruction of the line of action of one piece by another. Also *attrib.*

1913 A. C. WHITE *Sam Loyd* 303 There are many forms of interference play which have nothing to do with avoiding stalemate... But interference has a far wider scope than the cutting off of one White man by another. **1926** H. WEENINK *Chess Probl.* 39 In both problems there is mutual interference of the black Rook and Bishop. **1931** G. HUME in A. C. White *Probl. by my Friends* 210 By forgoing the interference of the Black Bishop with the Black Pawn, a second flight-square has been obtained. **1947** T. R. DAWSON *Caïssa's Fairy Tales* 7/2 Rc4, which is Black interference permitting 2 Sb6 mate... The interference and pin ideas create nice new task record objectives. **1963** J. BOCHKOR tr. *Bán's Tactics of End-Games* II. 115/2 We can also make use of line interference by sparing a hostile piece that is closing a line and is thus harmful to its own camp.

c. *U.S. Football.* (*a*) The act of interposing between a runner and a tackler to obstruct the latter; (*b*) see quot. 1895; (*c*) a player or players who obstruct the tackler or tacklers. *Baseball.* The act of obstructing a runner between two bases.

1894 *Outing* (U.S.) XXIV. 112/2 The special feature of American Rugby arises from the principle of interference to aid the man running with the ball. **1895** G. J. MANSON *Sporting Dict.* 61 *Interference*, using the hands or arms in any way to obstruct or hold a player who has got the ball. **1920** W. CAMP *Football without a Coach* 59 To amount to anything at all interference must be perfectly timed... On a play between tackle and guard..the interference must reach that point prepared to take care of the tackle, the guard and even the backfield men, too. **1922** D. CANFIELD *Rough-Hewn* xxvi. 241 Where *was* the ball? Sometimes it came straight through and the next minute on the same formation swung outside—and Neale uselessly buried under the interference. **1927** H. G. SALSINGER in *Secrets of Baseball* 147 Interference plays, too, are scored as they probably have been made. **1969** *Official Playing Rules Nat. & Amer. Football Leagues* 68 Interlocked interference means the grasping of one and another by, or encircling body to any degree with, hands or arms by offensive players.

d. Sexual assault or molestation.

1968 M. CULPAN *Vasiliko Affair* v. 63 You'll get the pathologist to examine the body. But I'd say no interference. **1972** J. SYMONS *Bloody Murder* xii. 160 Before the War..the rape would have been mentioned delicately. 'Any sign of—interference?' **1973** 'D. SHANNON' *No Holiday for Crime* (1974) ii. 27 Not raped, for ninety-nine per cent sure—no interference.

2. *Physics.* The mutual action of two waves or systems of waves, in reinforcing or neutralizing each other, when their paths meet or cross.

Orig. introduced to designate phenomena observed in the mutual action of two rays of light, before the establishment of the undulatory theory; subsequently extended to sound-waves, the undulations on the surface of water, etc.

[**1802** T. YOUNG in *Phil. Trans.* 388 It occurred to me, that their cause must be sought in the interference of two portions of light.] **1830** HERSCHEL *Stud. Nat. Phil.* 260 This principle, which is known in optics by the name of the interference of the rays of light. **1831** BREWSTER *Optics* xv. §84. 135 The doctrine of interference is in complete accordance with the theory of undulation. **1834** MRS. SOMERVILLE *Connex. Phys. Sc.* xxv. (1849) 264 Darkness results from the interference of two undulations of light. **1873** W. LEES *Acoustics* I. iii. 28 The sound-waves proceeding from the prongs of the fork neutralizing each other—an effect known as interference.

3. The action of interfering (of a horse): see INTERFERE *v.* 1.

In mod. Dicts.

4. *U.S.* The conflict of claims arising when two applications are made for a similar patent.

attrib. **1888** *Scribner's Mag.* Aug. 190/2 An application for a patent which, after an interference litigation with Edison, was finally issued to Maxim.

5. Various scientific and technical senses.

a. *Broadcasting* and *Telecommunications.* Disturbance of the transmission or reception of signals by the intrusion of extraneous signals; hence, signals collectively or radiation which causes such disturbance, or the effects by which it is perceived (e.g. unwanted sounds in radio reception).

1887 *Electrician* 7 Oct. 462/1 Strong signals were received on the copper [telephone] wires, although they were completely isolated from any possible interference. **1888** *Operator & Electr. World* XII. 140 (*heading*) Dynamo current interference with telephone systems and means of relief. **1899** *Electrician* 17 Nov. 106/2 Before beginning the experiments, Mr. Marconi wrote to the Commission stating that he had an instrument which would render interference practically impossible. **1902** *Windsor Mag.* May 720/2 Two messages were sent, one in English and one in French. Both were received at the same time on the same wire at Poole.. without the least interference. **1926** *Encycl. Brit.* I. 459/1 The atmosphere is nearly always filled with vagrant radio waves which enter the receiving set, producing noises called 'interference'. **1932** R. W. HALLOWS *Finding Foreign Stations* xiv. 113 Other kinds of apparatus which are apt to radiate interference are refrigerators..and flashing signs. **1943** A. L. ALBERT *Fund. Telephony* xiii. 314 When two or more telephone circuits parallel each other, electric energy may be transferred from one to the other, causing.. inductive interference. **1962** J. H. & P. J. REYNER *Radio Communication* viii. 311 The interference is conducted by the mains..to the point where the receiver is located. **1964** R. F. FICCHI *Electr. Interference* ii. 9 Interference is an electrical disturbance created by equipment in one part of a system which is carried into equipment in another part of the system, causing malfunctioning of the latter part. **1966** *B.B.C. Handbk.* 133 On the television screen the interference is seen as patterns of lines, white flashes or bands of light. **1967** E. L. GRUENBERG *Handbk. Telemetry & Remote Control* xi. 11 Some of the remedies for interference are the use of shielded line between signal source and input section of the data-acquisition equipment, [etc.].

b. *Engin.* (i) The collision of the tips of the teeth of one gear-wheel with the flanks of those of the mating wheel which occurs if the teeth are not cut to a suitable profile.

1914 A. E. INGHAM *Gearing* i. 32 If, however, pinions having a low number of teeth are constructed, they are much more undercut below the base line than is consistent with strength or with tooth contact. This 'undercut' or 'interference' is clearly shown in Fig. 11. **1926** BRADFORD & EATON *Machine Design* viii. 149 Contact will have taken place between the tip of the driven tooth and the radial flank of the driving-gear tooth. Since the latter is not the conjugate involute of the former the two curves will not run together and interference takes place. **1948** PARKINSON & DAWNEY *Gears* iv. 39 (1) Involute interference..is avoided by making the whole working profile of involute form, (2) tip interference..is avoided by making the diameter of the spur pinion a sufficient amount smaller than that of the internal gear. **1966** G. W. MICHALEC *Precision Gearing* xi. 591 It is important to avoid even the most isolated interference points because they cause wear that results in rapid degradation of precision quality.

(ii) The amount by which the external dimension of a part exceeds the internal dimension of the part into which it has to fit.

[**1919**: see *interference fit* below.] **1930** L. S. MARKS *Mech. Engineers' Handbk.* (ed. 3) 896 In Table 47 is given a summary of the allowances, allowances plus tolerance, and average interferences for the various classes of fits, as recommended tentatively by the A.S.A. Interference here denotes negative allowance. **1950** T. NUTTALL *Nat. Cert. Workshop Technol.* xv. 124 The force required to pass in the shaft will be much greater with the maximum interference; for this reason the modern tendency is to specify very close limits for both hole and shaft when interference fits are required. **1969** M. HASLEHURST *Manuf. Technol.* xiii. 320 This gives a maximum interference of 0·056 mm and a minimum interference of 0·025 mm.

c. *Genetics.* The action of one cross-over in reducing or increasing (orig. only reducing) the chance of a second cross-over occurring along the same chromosome, the effect being generally proportional to distance.

1916 H. J. MULLER in *Amer. Naturalist* L. 288 In a sense, then, the occurrence of one crossing-over interferes with the coincident occurrence of another crossing-over in the same pair of chromosomes, and I have accordingly termed this phenomenon 'interference'. **1969** G. W. BURNS *Sci. Genetics* vii. 115 Interference appears to be unequal in different parts of a chromosome... In general, interference appears to be greatest near the centromere and at the ends of a chromosome.

d. *Aeronaut.* (See quot. 1940.)

1932 *Gloss. Aeronaut. Terms* (*B.S.I.*) (Proofs) III. 3 *Interference*, the aerodynamic influence of two or more bodies on one another. **1940** *Chambers's Techn. Dict.* 452/2 *Interference*, the aerodynamic influence of one body upon another. Usually, the head resistance, or drag, of two bodies placed close together will be greater than the total of their separate drags, because of interference.

e. *Biol.* and *Med.* The action of a virus of one kind in inhibiting a virus of another kind in the same host.

1937 *Jrnl. Path. & Bacteriol.* XLIV. 420 In plant viruses the phenomenon of interference is only seen in connection with those viruses that are generically related. **1970** PASSMORE & ROBSON *Compan. Med. Stud.* II. xviii. 108/2 If the viruses are inoculated at different times, the second may not replicate. This is known as interference.

f. *Philol.* (See quot. 1953.) Also *attrib.*

1940 *Language* XVI. iii. 219 Thus, in describing the difficulty of pronouncing foreign sounds (5), there is no mention of the interference of the speaker's native phonemic habits. **1953** U. WEINREICH *Lang. in Contact* i. 1 Those instances of deviation from the norms of either language which occur in the speech of bilinguals as a result of their familiarity with more than one language..will be referred to as interference phenomena. *Ibid.* 11 In speech, interference is like sand carried by a stream; in language, it is the sedimented sand deposited on the bottom of a lake. **1962** W. F. MACKEY in J. A. Fishman *Readings Sociol. of Lang.* (1968) 569 The foregoing characteristics of degree, function, and alternation determine the interference of one language with another in the speech of bilinguals. Interference is the use of features belonging to one language while speaking or writing another. *Ibid.* 570 In the speech of bilinguals the pattern and amount of interference is not the same at all times and under all circumstances... Interference also varies with the style of discourse used—descriptive, narrative, conversational, etc. **1964** E. PALMER tr. *Martinet's Elem. Gen. Ling.* v. 160 Interference..may have the result of increasing the range of phoneme variation. **1965** *Amer. Speech* XL. 63 Galinsky deals less with regular interference phenomena than with occasional borrowings of language-conscious individuals. **1972** J. L. DILLARD *Black English* i. 36 *Interference* is the term for the influence of one's native language on a language acquired later.

6. *attrib.* or *Comb.*, as (chiefly senses 2 and 5) ***interference pattern***; **interference figure**, the figure produced when a section of crystal, appropriately cut, is viewed in converging polarized light; **interference fit** *Engin.*, a fit between two mating parts for which, within the specified tolerances, there is always an interference between them; **interference-free** *a.*, not causing or not affected by interference; **interference fringe**, one of a series of alternate light and dark bands produced by a diffraction-grating (FRINGE 2 g); †**interference preventer**,

an apparatus for reducing interference at a radio receiver; **interference spectrum**, the spectrum produced by a diffraction-grating (DIFFRACTION 1); so *interference colour, phenomena, screen*, etc.; **interference suppressor**, an electrical device designed to prevent or reduce the production of interference by the apparatus to which it is fitted.

1879 ROOD *Chromatics* iv. 50 Colours produced in this way are called '*interference colours'. **1881** *Nature* No. 622. 515 The well-known *interference extinction of undulation evolving precisely-formed rings of darkness. **1919** *Engineer* 23 May 511/2 The following three classes of fit would be needed, *i.e.*, running fits, transition fits, and *interference fits. **1973** A. PARRISH *Mech. Engineer's Ref. Bk.* vii. 31 The magnitude of the interference fit will depend upon the conditions required, i.e. axial, torsional or radial holding ability. **1950** *Engineering* 3 Feb. 140/2 A range of waterproofed and *interference-free [electrical] components is being produced. **1965** *B.B.C. Handbk.* 49 Reception in the overcrowded medium- and long-wave bands continues to be difficult in many areas, in marked contrast to the interference-free reception which VHF can provide. **1933** *Discovery* May 151/2 As a typical example, I need only mention the *interference patterns which appear when light from one source can travel to a screen along two different paths. **1973** *Nature* 12 Oct. 297/1 The only consistent difference between cross-over and non-cross-over events, apart from the presence or absence of an exchange of homologous segments of chromatids, is in their interference pattern. **1905** *Interference preventer [see ATMOSPHERICS *sb. pl.*]. **1914** R. STANLEY *Text-bk. Wireless Telegr.* xix. 292 Marconi patented an interference preventer which involved the use of two aerials and a rotating machine. **1890** *Anthony's Photogr. Bull.* III. 368 An apparatus for holding an *interference screen. **1860** TYNDALL *Glac.* I. xi. 76 The sun.. surrounded by a glory of *interference spectra. **1951** *Gloss. Terms Plastics Industry (B.S.I.)* 41 *Interference suppressor. **1966** *B.B.C. Handbk.* 133 It has for some years been compulsory for all new vehicles and stationary engines using spark ignition to have interference suppressors fitted.

interferent (ɪntəˈfɪərənt), *a. rare.* [f. as prec. + -ENT.] Interfering.

1876 RUSKIN *Fors Clav.* VI. lxix. 293 The little pyramid of a child.. would have been too symmetrical, but for the interferent light in the dog.

interferential (-fɪəˈrɛnʃəl), *a.* [f. INTERFERENCE, after *differential*, etc.] Of, pertaining to, or operating by, wave-interference: *spec.* belonging to interference of light-waves.

1880 PICKERING *Dimens. Fixed Stars* 14 The interferential refractometer [used] in measuring the index of refraction of gases. **1896** *Daily News* 18 Dec. 6/6 With the exception of a few examples of Professor Lippmann's interferential method.. colour in photography has represented little else but failure.

interferer (ɪntəˈfɪərə(r)). [f. INTERFERE *v.* + -ER[1].] **a.** One who interferes.

1803 W. TAYLOR in *Ann. Rev.* I. 284 At length the mass of interferers are convinced that the thing is reasonable. **1850** L. HUNT *Autobiog.* I. vii. 289 Nothing but gentlemen in distress, and hard landlords, and generous interferers.

b. *U.S. Football.* One who interposes between a runner and a tackler.

1897 *Encycl. Sport* I. 424/2 Interference.. once established,.. the query was immediately raised of how much aid the interferers could give the runner. **1922** D. CANFIELD *Rough-Hewn* xxvi. 243 Neale could see Rogers rock a second, undecided, on tip-toe; side-step an interferer; and then shoot his body like a projectile into the play.

interfering (ɪntəˈfɪərɪŋ), *vbl. sb.* [-ING[1].] The action of the vb. INTERFERE, in various senses.

1562 [see INTERFERE *v.* 1]. **1607** TOPSELL *Four-f. Beasts* (1658) 319 Enterfering is a grief that cometh sometimes by ill shooing.. and there is no remedy but shooing him with shooes made thin and flat on the outside, and narrow and thick within. **1642** ROGERS *Naaman* 228 Our base enterfeering with God in his holy wayes. **1647** H. MORE *Poems* Notes 390 No enterfaring or cutting of circles as in Tycho's [system], where the course of the Sunne cuts Mars his circuit. *a* **1677** HALE *Prim. Orig. Man.* IV. ii. 303 The casual Coalition of the Universe by the motion or interfering of Atoms. **1677** R. CARY *Chronol.* II. I. xiv. 127 The several Intermatchings and Interfarings that were betwixt the two Neighbour Kingdoms. **1682** BUNYAN *Holy War* (Cassell) 201 There were no jars,.. no interferings.. in the town of Mansoul. **1793** BURKE *Policy Allies* Wks. VII. 155 It is not the interfering or keeping aloof, but iniquitous intermeddling.. which is praised or blamed.

b. *attrib.* ***interfering shoe*** (see above 1607).

1678 *Lond. Gaz.* No. 1301/4 A black pacing Gelding, shod of his hinder feet with interfering shoes.

interfering (ɪntərˈfɪərɪŋ), *ppl. a.* [f. as prec. + -ING[2].] **a.** That interferes, in senses of the vb.

1580 HOLLYBAND *Treas. Fr. Tong*, *Cheval qui s'entr[et]aille*, interfeiring in an horse, when a man or horse in going galleth or rubbeth one foote against an other. **1614** *Jrnls. Ho. Comm.* 5 May I. 474/1 That some like interfyring Horses, that the faster they go, the more they lame themselves. **1661** BOYLE *Style of Script.* (1675) 95 Books.. replenish'd with interfering passages and contradictions. **1718** ROWE tr. *Lucan* VIII. 466 Our War no interfering Kings demands, Nor shall be trusted to Barbarian Hands. **1801** SOUTHEY *Thalaba* III. i, Thy life.. so saved by interfering Heaven. **1802** T. YOUNG in *Phil. Trans.* 387 The light becomes.. least intense in the intermediate state of the interfering portions. **1885** G. MACDONALD *Diary of an Old Soul* 10 Apr., Might I but scatter interfering things— Questions and doubts, distrust and anxious pride. *Mod. colloq.* 'I do not like her in the house, she is so interfering'.

b. That causes or constitutes interference (sense 5 a).

1914 R. STANLEY *Text-bk. Wireless Telegr.* xix. 292 If the International Rules are duly observed an interfering station should be one which considers itself out of range. **1954** E. MOLLOY *Radio & Television Engineers' Ref. Bk.* XXXIII. 10 As with all forms of interference, the effect will largely depend upon the ratio of the levels of the interfering signal to the picture signal.

Hence **interˈferingly**, **interˈferingness**.

1847 CRAIG, *Interferingly.* **1874** HELPS *Soc. Press.* xvi. (1875) 225 The fussiness and interferingness of mankind. **1894** *Cornh. Mag.* Jan. 82 [He] has come very interferingly into the nursery.

interferogram (ɪntəˈfɪərəʊgræm). [f. INTERFER(E *v.* + -O + -GRAM.] A pattern formed by the interference of radiation, esp. one represented in a photograph or diagram.

1921 *Trans. Optical Soc.* XXII. 185 Fig. 12 represents an interferogram as seen on one of the lens interferometers described, the thick lines representing dark bands. **1949** *Jrnl. R. Aeronaut. Soc.* LIII. 637/2 The interferograms give the density variation across the mixing zone. **1959** *Physics of Fluids* II. 165 (*caption to photograph*) Monochromatic interferograms taken simultaneously at λ = 4122 A and 5463 A of an ionizing shock wave in argon... The fringes move upward with increasing refractivity. **1965** E. B. BROWN *Mod. Optics* viii. 440 The intensity plots.. are referred to as interferograms, and the interferometers used in this fashion are often called interferometer modulators. **1966** D. G. BRANDON *Mod. Techniques Metallogr.* 27 For first-order interference at λ = 5,500 Å with a high refractive index oil between the plates.. the cone angle *a* that can be tolerated is.. about 25°, corresponding to a 0·65 *NA* objective, and critical illumination can be used to form the interferogram.

interfeˈrometer. [f. INTERFERE + (O)METER] Any instrument in which the interference of waves (e.g. of light) from a common source is employed to make precise measurements of (linear or angular) length or displacement in terms of the wavelength.

1897 *Physical Rev.* IV. 480 An application of the Michelson 'interferometer' to the measurement of the small linear movements of the electrometer disk. **1897** *Phil. Mag.* XLIV. 91 To these two methods of measuring angular motions we must now add a third, the interferometer method, first suggested by Michelson. **1899** LD. RAYLEIGH in *Nature* LIX. 533/1 As one of the few who have used the interferometer in observations involving high interference, I should like to make a remark or two. **1899** T. PRESTON *Ibid.* 605/2 The 'structure' revealed by the interferometer in the light emitted by a source placed in a strong magnetic field. **1921** *Discovery* July 181/2 Betelgeux, the size of which was measured in December last at Mount Wilson by interferometer methods, has a diameter of 273,000,000 miles. **1932** HARDY & PERRIN *Princ. Optics* xxviii. 592 These interferometers are often used in the analysis of a mixture of gases to determine the proportion in which the components are present. **1957** *New Scientist* 15 Aug. 14/1 At the Cambridge radio-observatory four aerials with a total area of one acre are placed at the corners of a rectangle to form a double interferometer which was used in 1954 to plot the positions of nearly 2,000 radio stars. **1969** C. A. RONAN *Invisible Astron.* vi. 83 For mapping radio sources.. the radio interferometer has become widely adopted. This is based on the same principles as that of the stellar interferometer.., and at its simplest uses two antennae separated by as large a distance as is convenient, the signals being fed into an electronic mixing unit and then passed to the radio telescope receiver.

attrib. **1899** J. C. SHEDD in *Phys. Rev.* July, An Interferometer Study of Radiations in a Magnetic Field.

interferometric (ˌɪntəfɛrəʊˈmɛtrɪk), *a.* [f. prec. + -IC, after *barometric*, etc.] Of or pertaining to interferometry; employing or of the nature of an interferometer.

1932 HARDY & PERRIN *Princ. Optics* xvii. 378 Lens-bench methods [of measuring aberrations of lenses], the Hartmann method, and the interferometric method yield this information in different ways. **1951** *Engineering* 18 May 589/1 Dr. J. S. Courtney-Pratt has used interferometric methods to study the uniformity and thickness of thin films adsorbed on solid surfaces. **1954** *Oxf. Univ. Gaz.* 15 June 1036/1 Spectra for the interferometric determination of wavelengths. **1957** *New Scientist* 24 Oct. 11 An interferometric radio telescope consists of two separate aerials each joined to the same receiver whose output measures, in effect, the difference in the distances from the source to each of the aerials. **1974** *Times* 12 Jan. 14/7 He carried interferometric methods to an extreme degree of precision.

Hence **ˌinterferoˈmetrically** *adv.*, by means of interferometry.

1959 *Physics of Fluids* II. 166/2 Photomultiplier observations through 4122-A and 4515-A interference filters show the appearance of peak luminosity to be closely associated with the attainment of interferometrically observable ionization. **1972** *McGraw-Hill Yearbk. Sci. & Technol.* 388/2 Along with the recent development of stable lasers.. have come interferometrically ruled gratings practically free of 'ghosts'. **1973** *Physics Bull.* May 307/3 The longitudinal and transverse curvatures of a plate subjected to a bending moment are determined interferometrically.

interferometry (ˌɪntəfəˈrɒmɪtrɪ). [INTERFEROMETER: see -METRY.] The action or art of measuring interference phenomena; the study and use of the interferometer.

1911 C. BARUS in *Publ. Carnegie Inst. Washington* CXLIX. I. p. iii, I came across a principle of interferometry which seemed of sufficient importance to justify special investigation. **1946** *Nature* 12 Oct. 519/2 It is possible to evaluate an approximate crystal lattice spacing with visible light waves by virtue of multiple beam interferometry. **1950** *Endeavour* IX. 196 Multiple-beam interferometry offers a delicate method of detecting extremely small imperfections in surfaces. **1962** *Punch* 29 Aug. 298/2 The distinguished custodian of Jodrell Bank is well up in the cepheid variables, interferometry and the Laplace hypothesis. **1971** *Physics Bull.* July 397/2 Several of these laboratories.. are now using laser interferometry for calibration purposes.

interferon (ɪntəˈfɪərɒn). *Biol.* [f. INTERFER(E *v.* + *-on*.] A protein released by an animal cell, usu. in response to the entry of a virus, which has the property of inhibiting further development of viruses of any kind in the animal (or in others of the same species).

1957 ISAACS & LINDENMANN in *Proc. R. Soc.* B. CXLVII. 263 To distinguish it from the heated influenza virus we have called the newly released interfering agent 'interferon'. **1961** *New Scientist* 13 July 81/1 It looks as if.. interferon is capable of blocking the multiplication of virtually all the animal viruses that have been tested. **1961** *Lancet* 23 Sept. 680/2 Recently there has been growing evidence that interferon may play an important part in recovery from virus infections. **1963** *Ann. Reg. 1962* 393 The investigation of Interferon, a chemical substance produced in men and animals and believed to act as the body's first line of defence against a wide range of virus infections, passed a critical stage in May 1962. **1968** B. D. DAVIS et al. *Princ. Microbiol. & Immunol.* IV. xxvi. 789 Purified interferons from various sources consist of small proteins usually stable at low pH... Interferons are not virus-specific but cell-specific in both their production and their effects. **1970** PASSMORE & ROBSON *Compan. Med. Stud.* II. xviii. 109/2 Interferon has many of the properties of an ideal antiviral agent but its present clinical applications are limited by difficulties associated with the production of large quantities of purified human interferon and the assessment of its activity in man.

inter-fertile, -fertility: see INTER- *pref.* 2 a.

inter-fibre, interfile *v.*: see INTER- *pref.* 5, 1 a.

interfibrillar, -ary, -fibrous: see INTER- 3 a.

†**interˈficient**, *a. Obs. rare.* [ad. L. *interficient-em*, pr. pple. of *interficĕre* to kill.] Killing, destroying. (Cf. INTERFECTOR b.)

1647 LILLY *Chr. Astrol.* lxvii. 409 Behold.. who.. afflicts him, and is the interficient Planet. **1658** PHILLIPS, *Interfectour*, an interficient or destroying Planet, and which is placed in the eighth house (in a Nativity).

interfilamentar, -fillet, -flash: see INTER-.

interˈfinger, *v. Geol.* [INTER- 1 b.] *intr.* Of strata, sediments, etc.: to interdigitate (*with*). So **interˈfingering** *ppl. a.*

1921 A. W. GRABAU *Textbk. Geol.* II. xxxvi. 441 (*caption*) The source of the black mud is the land on the south from which it was repeatedly washed into the sea, interfingering with clastics derived from the east. **1960** *New Scientist* 23 June 1609/1 Detailed geological mapping of interfingering and overlapping lava flows. **1965** G. J. WILLIAMS *Econ. Geol. N.Z.* xiii. 205/2 The granitic facies of the Hawks Crag Breccia nearby and the interfingering facies containing both granite and greywacke components were quickly found to contain uranium minerals. **1971** *Nature* 28 May 247/1 The lower part of this lacustrine sequence interfingers with about 20 m of fluvio-deltaic sediments.

inter-firm, *a.* [INTER- 5.] Carried on between two or more business firms.

1949 *Collier's Year Bk.* 132 The rulings.. disapproved secondary boycotts affecting interfirm activities. **1961** *Times* 2 May 2/5 The growing volume of interfirm comparison work. **1964** *Economist* 21 Mar. 1067/1 Confidential interfirm comparisons. **1967** *Ibid.* 7 Jan. 24/3 What sort of mergers, and what sort of inter-firm co-operation, does Britain want? **1972** *Times* 31 Oct. 25/2 'Interfirm comparison' is one of those rare animals, a management technique which the British have managed to sell to the Americans.

Interflora (ɪntəˈflɔərə). Name of the Florists' Telegraph Delivery Association, an international agency which organizes the delivery of flowers to order; also the trade name of the British branch of this association.

1949 *Sell's Directory of Registered Telegraphic Addresses* 795/2 Taylor William (florist),.. Worthing, Sussex. Interflora Worthing. **1951** G. LEWIS in *Mod. Florist* xxiii. 229 The four large groups.. are closely connected and compose the overall organisation Interflora, set up in 1946 to control and develop the interchange of overseas orders. **1960** L. JOHNS in *Retail Florist's Handbk.* xxii. 250 The clearing house at Interflora headquarters is an impressive sight. **1966** *Guardian* 4 Oct. 8/2, 22 million Interflora orders were sent world-wide last year. **1971** N. FREELING *Over High Side* I. 51 The ladies of Belgrave Square had sent long emotional telegrams and Interflora wreaths. **1972** F. WARNER *Maquettes* 30, I arrange bouquets for Interflora.

interflow (ˈɪntəfləʊ), *sb.* [INTER- 2: cf. next.] †**1.** A flowing between; a channel or strait. *Obs.*

1610 HOLLAND *Camden's Brit.* II. 215 They [islands] are severed.. by a narrow enterflow of the Sea betweene.

2. A flowing into each other; intermingling.

1865 *Cornh. Mag.* June 647 The delicious interflow of the soft purity of the sky and the bright tranquillity of the lake. **1867** FROUDE *Short Stud., Sci. Hist.* 19 In the subtle interflow of good and evil.. Shakspeare is true to real experience. **1883** D. H. WHEELER *By-Ways Lit.* vii. 110 We know too little of the human interflow and communion during the unhistoric periods.

interflow (ɪntəˈfləʊ), *v.* [f. INTER- 1 + FLOW *v.*; in sense 1 after L. *interfluĕre* to flow between.] **1.** *intr.* To flow between. *rare.*

1610 HOLLAND *Camden's Brit.* 12 What way the current cold Of Northern Ocean with strong tides doth interflow and swell. **1848** LYTTON *Arthur* x. c, Till light at last From skies long hid, wide silvering, interflows.

†**b.** *trans.* (with obj. governed by the prep.)

1610 HOLLAND *Camden's Brit.* II. 60 Where it interfloweth France and Britain, it is properly called the British Sea.

2. *intr.* To flow into each other; to intermingle.

1844 [see INTERFLOWING below]. **1859** WHITTIER *Overheart* v, The earthquake and the storm are God's, And good and evil interflow. **1880** G. MEREDITH *Tragic Com.* (1881) 172 The thousand varying shades of her motions and her features interflowing like a lighted water.

Hence **inter'flowing** *vbl. sb.* and *ppl. a.*

1610 HOLLAND *Camden's Brit.* I Severed from the continent of Europe by the interflowing of the Ocean. **1674** JOSSELYN *Voy. New Eng.* 220 The streight of Magellan, where there are many Islands distinguished by an interflowing Bay. **1844** MRS. BROWNING *Lady Geraldine* xl, The subtle interflowings Found in Petrarch's sonnets. **1898** *Expositor* June 440 Intermingling clouds and interflowing waves.

interfluence (ɪn'tɜːfluːəns). *rare.* [f. as next: see -ENCE] The fact of being interfluent or flowing into each other.

1817 COLERIDGE *Lay Serm.* in *Biog. Lit.* (1882) 397 *note*, The circulations counterpoise each other, or rather they are neutralized by interfluence.

interfluent (ɪn'tɜːfluːənt), *a.* [ad. L. *interfluent-em*, pr. pple. of *interfluĕre* to flow between.]

1. Flowing between. Now *rare.*

1651 HOWELL *Venice* 186* Girt about with the waters of the interfluent Hadrian Sea. **1664** BOYLE *Exp. Cold* iii. Wks. 1772 II. 503 Whether the spring of the air depend..upon the agitation of some interfluent subtile matter. **1877** BLACKIE *Wise Men* 73 The cosmic water's subtle-streaming force, Interfluent, circumfluent.

2. Flowing into each other, intermingling; in which there is an interflow.

1872 G. MACDONALD *Wilf. Cumb.* I. x. 137 A world of shadows and sunny streaks, kept ever in interfluent motion. **1885** E. C. STEDMAN in *Century Mag.* XXIX. 508 The interfluent, luxurious pentameter couplet, revived by Hunt and Keats. **1894** *Forum* (N.Y.) Nov. 284 To draw the mystic line dividing his science from his poetry would be a difficult matter. The two were interfluent streams.

interfluous (ɪn'tɜːfluːəs), *a.* [f. L. *interflu-us*: see -OUS.] = prec.

1656 BLOUNT *Glossogr.*, *Interfluous*, that flows or runs between. **1818** SHELLEY *Woodman & Night.* ii, One nightingale in an interfluous wood. **1876** BROWNING *Pacchiarotto* 252 If wealth would become but interfluous, Fill voids up with just the superfluous.

interfluve ('ɪntəfluːv). [Back-formation from next.] A region lying between (the valleys of) adjacent watercourses, esp. one between the valleys of a dissected upland.

1902 in WEBSTER Suppl. **1913** *Bull. Geol. Soc. Amer.* XXIV. 206 In an early stage of the new cycle the fault-line scarp will be highest near the incised valleys of transverse streams, and it may remain for a time undeveloped on the interfluves. **1937** *Geogr. Jrnl.* LXXXIX. 356 A cross-section of a typical portion of deltaic country from river to interfluve. **1956** D. L. LINTON *Sheffield* 29 Here are some eighty or more square miles where dips are gentle and the grits build broad tabular interfluves swathed in peat and separating deep valleys with benched sides. **1968** R. W. FAIRBRIDGE *Encycl. Geomorphol.* 559 *Interfluve*... Many geomorphologists today use the term for the interstream area to imply a discrete landscape or geomorphic unit, composed of uni- or polycyclic slope facets. Interfluve almost always appears in a phrase explicitly or implicitly denoting its dissection.

interfluvial (ɪntə'fluːvɪəl), *a.* [f. INTER- 4 a + FLUVIAL *a.*] Situated between (the valleys of) adjacent watercourses.

1830 *New Monthly Mag.* III. *Hist. Reg.* Jan. 6/2 Returning from Bagdad across the interfluvial country, he took up his quarters at Hillah. **1903** *Sci. Amer. Suppl.* 14 Feb. 22679/1 A deposit of the flooded rivers during a stage of abundant ice melting, with considerable redistribution over the interfluvial upland areas by winds. **1933** *Antiquity* VII. 27 Beech Bottom and the Verulamium Devil's Dyke were relics of a transverse *limes* covering the whole tract of interfluvial country. **1971** [see HUM *sb.*[4]].

†'**interflux.** *Obs. rare.* [INTER- 2 a.] Flowing between or in the midst.

1657 W. RAND tr. *Gassendi's Life Peiresc* I. 6 A very straight yet exceeding pleasant valley, enriched by the Interfluxe of the same River Gapell.

†'**interfoil.** *Obs. rare.* [f. INTER- 3 + FOIL *sb.*[1]] An interposed leaf.

1674 GREW *Anat. Pl.* iv. §17 Sometimes, besides Surfoyls, there are also many Interfoyls set betwixt the Leaves, from the Circumference to the Center of the Bud.

interfold (ɪntə'fəʊld), *v.* Also 6–7 enter-. [f. INTER- 1 b + FOLD *v.*] *trans.* (and *refl.*) To fold together or within each other; to involve in common folds.

1579 J. STUBBES *Gaping Gulf* F j b, The weale and well doing of Christes church, of a Christien state, and of a good princes person, are so enterfolded, as whatsoeuer is agaynst one is agaynst all. **1587** FLEMING *Contn. Holinshed* III. 1294/1 The figure of a serpent, interfolding it selfe: in the middest whereof did sit a dooue. **1621** MOLLE *Camerar. Liv. Libr.* II. xv. 121 Hauing their fingers enter-folded together. **1631** *Celestina* II. 127 The skirts of my Petticoate..did so often interfold themselves betweene my feet. **1772** JACKSON in *Phil. Trans.* LXIII. 9 Interfolding the ends of one or more pieces..with each other. **1841** LONGF. *Childr. Lds. Supp.* 172 Kneels before the Eternal's throne; and, with hands interfolded, Praises..the only giver of blessings.

interfoliaceous (-fəʊlɪ'eɪʃəs), *a. Bot.* [INTER- 4 a. Cf. F. *interfoliacé.*] Situated alternately between a pair of opposite leaves.

1760 J. LEE *Introd. Bot.* III. xxi. (1765) 218 *Interfoliaceous*, such as come out between the opposite Leaves, but are placed alternately. **1785** *Gentl. Mag.* LV. I. 431 Peduncles or flower-stalks, numerous, interfoliaceous, opposite. **1880** GRAY *Struct. Bot.* (ed. 6) 417/1 *Interfoliaceous*, between the leaves of a pair, as the stipules of Rubiaceae.

interfoliar (-'fəʊlɪə(r)), *a. Bot.* [f. INTER- 4 a. + FOLIAR.] Situated between the leaves.

1835 LINDLEY *Introd. Bot.* (1848) I. 234 The interfoliar parts are undeveloped.

inter'foliate, *v.* [f. INTER- 1 a + L. *foli-um* leaf + -ATE[3]. Cf. mod.F. *interfolier.*] *trans.* To interleave (a book). Hence **inter'foliated** *ppl. a.*

1696 EVELYN *Let. to Place* 17 Aug., So much [correction] as I conceive is necessary, I will take care to send you with your interfoliated copy. **1888** *Scribner's Mag.* Oct. 443 He interfoliates the piano score with blank leaves.

inter-follicular: see INTER- *pref.* 4 a.

interforce, -fraternal: see INTER- *pref.*

inter'fretted, *ppl. a. Her.* [f. INTER- 1 b + FRETTED *ppl. a.*[2] 2.] = INTERLACED.

1828–40 BERRY *Encycl. Herald.* I. Gloss., *Interfretted*, or *Interlaced*, is said of any bearings linked together, one with the other.

†**interfri'cation.** *Obs. rare*[−1]. [f. INTER- 2 a + FRICATION.] = next.

1747 FRANKLIN *Conjecture* Wks. 1887 II. 106 By this motion there must be a constant interfrication of its constituent solid parts.

inter'friction. *rare*[−1]. [f. INTER- 2 a + FRICTION.] Rubbing together.

1847 DE QUINCEY *Sp. Mil. Nun* xvi 41 Kindling a fire by interfriction of dry sticks was a secret almost exclusively Indian.

interfrontal (-'frʌntəl), *a. Anat.* and *Zool.* [f. INTER- 4 a + FRONTAL. Cf. F. *interfrontal* (Littré).] Situated between the right and left frontal bones, or portions of the frontal bone, or of the 'front' of an insect.

1855 MAYNE *Expos. Lex.*, *Interfrontalis*, applied by Robineau-Desvoidy to two pieces, more or less developed, in the *Myodariæ* [an order of *Diptera*]..at the anterior part of the front and which are sometimes interposed between the frontal portions in their whole length: interfrontal.

interfulgent (-'fʌldʒənt), *a. rare.* [ad. L. *interfulgĕnt-em* (Livy); see INTER- 1 a and FULGENT.] Shining among or between.

1721 in BAILEY. **1755** in JOHNSON. **1891** *Harper's Mag.* Jan. 218/2 He caught the interfulgent rays amongst the sycamore leaves.

interfuse (ɪntə'fjuːz), *v.* [f. L. *interfūs-*, ppl. stem of *interfundĕre*, f. *inter* between + *fundĕre* to pour: cf. *infuse*, etc.]

1. *trans.* To permeate or intersperse (a thing) *with* an infusion or mixture of something else.

1593 NASHE *4 Lett. Confut.* 32 Thou interfusest delight with reprehension. **1599** HAKLUYT *Voy.* II. II. 89 The kingdom of China is in all parts thereof interfused with commodious riuers. **1846** HAWTHORNE *Mosses* I. i. 16 Abundantly interfused with Greek and Latin quotations. **1876** BLACK *Madcap V.* vii. 57 The wonderful light greens of the Spring foliage seemed to be interfused with a lambent sunshine.

2. To pour in, infuse (one thing *through* or *throughout* another).

1667 MILTON *P.L.* VII. 89 This which yeelds or fills All space, the ambient Aire wide interfus'd, Imbracing round this florid Earth. **1784** COWPER *Task* v. 148 Ice upon ice, the well-adjusted parts Were soon conjoined, nor other cement ask'd Than water interfused to make them one. **1798** WORDSW. *Tintern Abbey* 96 A sense sublime Of something far more deeply interfused, Whose dwelling is the light,.. And the blue sky, and in the mind of man. **1863** WHITTIER *A. Rykman's Prayer* 154 Through chaos, doubt and strife, Interfuse Thy calm of life.

3. To fuse or blend (things) together. In *pass.*

1853 DE QUINCEY *Autobiog. Sk.* Wks. I. 54 The sorrow.. and the devotion..were profoundly interfused. **1865** E. BURRITT *Walk Land's End* 450 Here their different orders of intellectual and scholastic architecture may be seen intermixed but not interfused. **1870** LOWELL *Study Wind.* 37 The character and its intellectual product are inextricably interfused.

4. *intr.* Of two things: To fuse or blend with each other.

1851 H. MELVILLE *Whale* xli. 203 His torn body and gashed soul bled into one another; and so interfusing, made him mad. **1870** YEATS *Nat. Hist. Comm.* 120 South of the Tropic of Capricorn the products of the torrid and temperate zones interfuse.

5. *trans.* Of one thing: To penetrate or permeate and blend with.

1876 J. WEISS *Wit, Hum. & Shaks.* viii. 252 The genius which interfused the plays. **1881** H. JAMES *Portr. Lady* xlix, She had become deeply, tenderly acquainted with Rome; it interfused and moderated her passion.

Hence **inter'fusing** *ppl. a.* Also '**interfuse** *sb.*

1881 G. ALLEN *Evolutionist at Large, Microsc. Brains*, The whole universe is clearly to them [ants] a complicated picture made up entirely of infinite interfusing smells. **1887** *Century Mag.* Feb. 586 A chalice choicely fit For Truth's and Beauty's perfect interfuse.

interfusion (-'fjuːʒən). [n. of action f. prec.; cf. FUSION and eccl.Lat. *interfūsio.*] The action of interfusing; the fact of being interfused.

1817 COLERIDGE *Biog. Lit.* (1882) 182 The interfusion of the same throughout the radically different. **1840** THIRLWALL *Greece* lv. VII. 113 The extent to which the interfusion actually took place..was by no means small. **1851** D. WILSON *Preh. Ann.* (1863) II. IV. iv. 264 The interfusion of the Celtic and Norse races. **1872** LIDDON *Elem. Relig.* ii. 45 This eternal interfusion of force with matter.

intergalactic (ɪntəgə'læktɪk), *a.* [INTER- 4 a.] Situated between the galaxies; of, pertaining to, or occupying the regions between galaxies.

1928 *Nature* 6 Oct. 556/1 In other words, in interstellar or intergalactic space. **1930** R. A. MILLIKAN *Sci. & New Civilization* iv. 106 We think that the atom-building processes that give rise to the observed cosmic rays can take place only under the extreme conditions of temperature and pressure existing in interstellar, or intergalactic, space. **1953** J. S. HUXLEY *Evolution in Action* i. 13 The whole of space intergalactic as well as interstellar. **1969** *Times* 29 May 12/8 Extremely far away even by intergalactic standards. **1971** *Nature* 29 Jan. 305/2 At these energies both the interstellar and the intergalactic gas should become gradually opaque.

interganglionic (-gæŋglɪ'ɒnɪk), *a. Anat.* [INTER- 4 a.] Situated between or connecting ganglia, as the nerves of the sympathetic system.

1835–6 TODD *Cycl. Anat.* I. 765/1 The whole of these inter-ganglionic cords are in contact along the median line.

†**in'tergatory.** *Obs.* A syncopated form of INTERROGATORY *sb.* So **intergatour.**

1589 R. HARVEY *Pl. Perc.* I Tush Perceuall, hath no felicitie in these captious Intergatories. **1596** SHAKS. *Merch. V.* v. i. 298 Let vs goe in, And charge vs there vpon intergatories, And we will answer all things faithfully. **1603** B. JONSON *Sejanus* I. ii, Harmless Intergatories, but Conceits. **1632** BROME *Novella* II. i. Wks. 1873 I. 121 You must answer To these intergatories. **1678–96** PHILLIPS (ed. 5), *Intergatories*, or *Interrogatories*, in Common Law. **1685** in *15th Rep. Hist. MSS. Comm.*, App. VIII. 135 The first peaper..did give a ryse for generall intergatoures.

inter'generant, *a. Biol.* [INTER- 2 a.] = next.

1888 [see next].

intergenerating (-'dʒɛnəreɪtɪŋ), *ppl. a.* [INTER- 1 b; cf. prec.] Generating or breeding with each other; interbreeding. So **intergeneration.**

1888 J. T. GULICK in *Linn. Soc. Jrnl.* (*Z.*) XX. 200 An Intergenerant, or Intergenerating Group, is a group of individuals so situated and so endowed that they freely cross with each other. *Ibid.* 216, I now call the certainty that some form of divergent transformation will arise when intergeneration is prevented, the principle of Intension.

inter-generational: see INTER- *pref.* 4 c.

interge'neric, *a.* [INTER- 4 c.] Formed or obtained from (individuals of) different genera.

1921 *Genetics* VI. 380 Intergeneric crosses between genera only distantly related. **1926** *Jrnl. Agric. Res.* XXXIII. 101 (*heading*) Intergeneric hybrids in Aegilops, Triticum, and Secale. **1946** *Nature* 10 Aug. 204/2 The successful production of hybrid plants from interspecific, intergeneric and even interfamily crosses. **1973** W. J. BEAN *Trees & Shrubs Hardy in Brit. Isles* (ed. 8) II. 103 It is difficult to agree..that these plants [*sc.* varieties of *Erica cinerea*] are intergeneric hybrids between the bell-heather and *Calluna vulgaris.*

intergenic: see INTER- *pref.* 6.

intergenital (-'dʒɛnɪtəl), *a. Zool.* [INTER- 4 a.] Situated between genital structures; applied to a ring of plates in echinoderms, outside and between the genital plates (*Syd. Soc. Lex.*).

1878 BELL *Gegenbaur's Comp. Anat.* 204 Five pieces (intergenital plates) are attached to, and partly intercalated between these.

intergential (-'dʒɛnʃəl), *a.* [f. INTER- 4 a + L. *gens, genti-* people, nation + -AL[1].] Between nations; international.

1873 H. A. WISE *7 Decades Union* 253 To secede would make the war intergential.

†**in'tergerine,** *a. Obs. rare*[−1]. [ad. *intergerīnus*, erron. reading of L. *intergerīvus*, f. *intergerĕre* to carry between; cf. *intergeriēs* a party-wall, partition.] Of the nature of a partition-wall; dividing one space from another.

1709 BLAIR in *Phil. Trans.* XXVII. 117 The Intergerine Walls or Sides, whereof they are compos'd.

†**intergern** (-'gɜːn), *v. Obs. rare*[−1]. [f. INTER- 1 + *gern* GIRN *v.*[1]] *intr.* To snarl back.

1608 SYLVESTER *Du Bartas* II. iv. *Decay* 938 The angry beast [the badger] to his best chamber flies And angled there sits grimly intergerning.

intergesture, -gild: see INTER- *pref.* 2 a, 1 a.

interglacial (-'gleɪʃ(ɪ)əl), *a. Geol.* [INTER- 4 b; introduced in German in 1865 by Heer (*Urwelt des Schweiz*, p. 532).] Lying between glacial

periods; formed or occurring between two such periods. Also *absol.*, an interglacial period.

1867 LYELL *Princ. Geol.* (ed. 10) I. 196 The interval of milder weather, marked by the decrease of snow and ice in the Alps, has been called by Prof. Heer the Inter-glacial Period. **1873** J. GEIKIE *Gt. Ice Age* Pref. 10 None of these gravels in my opinion are post-glacial, but all must be relegated to pre-glacial and inter-glacial times. **1875** CROLL *Climate & T.* xv. 238 Our limited knowledge of warm inter-glacial periods. *Ibid.* i. 22, I have given the reasons which induce me to believe that coal is an inter-glacial formation. **1881** G. ALLEN *Vignettes fr. Nat.* xv. 154 Among the subsisting drift of glacial and interglacial rivers. **1922** *Bull. Geol. Soc. Amer.* XXXIII. 421 In the terraces corresponding to the First Interglacial of the Alps he holds that there is no Scandinavian material. **1939** G. CLARK *Archaeol. & Society* v. 137 An extra long gap, which.. would be equivalent to the Mindel-Riss inter-glacial. **1970** I. CORNWALL *Ice Ages* iii. 69 This down-cutting formed the bench..on which the deposits of the following Interglacial were laid down.

Hence **inter'glacialism**, the theory of interglacial periods; **inter'glacialist**, one who holds this view.

1881 W. B. DAWKINS in *Nature* XXIII. 309 Dr. James Geikie takes his stand upon the glaciated mountains of Scotland, and..pushes glacialism and interglacialism to an extreme. **1893** SIR H. H. HOWORTH *Glacial Nightmare* II. 459 The interglacialists are not agreed among themselves as to the number of the ice periods.

interglandular (-'glændjʊlə(r)), *a.* *Anat.* [INTER- 4 a.] Lying between glands.

1873 T. H. GREEN *Introd. Pathol.* (ed. 2) 161 A secondary process..resulting from the irritation of the inter-glandular growth. **1897** *Allbutt's Syst. Med.* II. 765 The inter-glandular substance is softened.

interglobular (-'glɒbjʊlə(r)), *a.* *Anat.* [INTER- 4 a.] Situated between globules (of dentine).

1859 J. TOMES *Dental Surg.* 302 The part corresponding to the interglobular space is occupied by dense tissue. **1870** tr. *Stricker's Man. Histol.* xv. (N. Syd. Soc.) 470 The inter-globular substance [of the tooth] is..a structure tolerably widely distributed.

Interglossa (ɪntə'glɒsə). [f. INTER- + Gr. γλῶσσα tongue.] An artificial auxiliary language devised by Lancelot Hogben (b. 1895).

1943 L. HOGBEN *Interglossa* 7 The author of *Interglossa* does not flatter himself with the hope that it will ever become the common language of international communication. **1946** H. JACOB *On Choice of Common Lang.* iii. 36 The potential extent of the Interglossa vocabulary will be many times greater than the number of terms contained in its vocabulary. **1954** PEI & GAYNOR *Dict. Ling.* 103 *Interglossa*, an artificial language proposed by Hogben, based on Greek and Latin roots with a system of syntax resembling that of Chinese.

interglyph, inter-governmental: see INTER- *pref.* 3 a, 4 c.

intergradation (-grə'deɪʃən). [INTER- 2 a: cf. next.] The action or fact of passing into, or approximating to, each other by degrees.

1874 TRIPPE in Coues *Birds N.W.* 145 The intergradation, however, is by no means as perfect as that between the two latter races. **1874** COUES *Birds N.W.* 281 The complete intergradation of the two forms.

'intergrade, *sb.* [INTER- 2 b.] An intermediate grade or stage.

1889 S. H. SCUDDER *Butterflies New Engl.* 160 The intergrades found throughout the belt forming the northern boundary of the typical alope and the southern boundary of the typical nephele seem to be far more easily explainable on the hypothesis of hybridism. **1896** *Brit. Birds* I. 193 The intergrades between the olive and ruddy mottled types are the commonest.

inter'grade, *v.* [INTER- 1 b.] *intr.* To pass into another form by intervening grades.

1874 T. M. TRIPPE in Coues *Birds N.W.* 145 *Junco hyemalis*, a. *aikeni*, intergrades with the following form, though not as intimately as that does with the succeeding. **1884** COUES *Key N.A. Birds* 79 We treat as specific any form that we do not know or believe to intergrade.

intergranular (-'grænjʊlə(r)), *a.* [INTER- 4 a.] Situated between or among granules, or between granular structures, as the inner nuclear layer of the retina. Also, occurring between granules or grains; intercrystalline.

1875 H. WALTON *Dis. Eye* p. xxviii, The granular and intergranular layers are absent. **1897** *Allbutt's Syst. Med.* IV. 392 Fat cells, which are found most abundantly in the granular and intergranular layers of the retina. **1932** *Jrnl. Iron & Steel Inst.* CXXV. 680 Intergranular corrosion of a chromium-nickel steel. **1946** *Nature* 24 Aug. 275/1 It is suggested that the migrations responsible for metasomatism occur partly by ionic diffusion through the crystal lattices and partly by molecular and/or ionic diffusion through the interstices ('intergranular film' of Wegmann) between the minerals. **1962** *Science Survey* III. 329 The final failure of the metal is essentially mechanical and it usually occurs by the propagation, through the body of the metal, of intercrystalline (or intergranular) cracks. **1971** *Nature* 30 July 327/1 It is quite likely that fluids have been able to flow through these rocks by means of both intergranular and fracture channels.

intergrapple: see INTER- *pref.* 1 b.

†**inter'grated**, *ppl. a.* *Obs. rare*⁻⁰. [INTER- 1 b.] Cross-grated.

1611 COTGR., *Entreillizé*, intergrated, thick lattised, crosse-barred. **1611** FLORIO, *Intralciamenti*, any kind of grate or entergrated workes of Osiers or Willowes.

intergroup ('ɪntəgruːp), *a.* [INTER- 5.] Situated, distributed, carried on, etc., between groups. Also as *sb.* So **inter'grouping** *vbl. sb.* and (as a back-formation) **inter'group** *v.*

1883 W. ROBINSON *Eng. Flower Garden* p. cx/2 Breadth of mass and intergrouping. **1931** *Economist* 11 Apr. 783/1 The formation of an 'intergroup' for mutual benefit in connection with the coming contest at the polls. **1936** *Discovery* May 160/1 Inter-group relations..are cemented by an elaborate exchange of gifts. **1943** WYNDHAM LEWIS *Let.* 17 Aug. (1963) 365 The inter-group and inter-racial quarrels seem to grow in number. **1965** *Math. in Biol. & Med.* (Med. Res. Council) III. 87 (*caption*) The centres are at points representing the average intergroup distance. **1970** G. F. NEWMAN *Sir, You Bastard* i. 17 The fifteen recruits.. were moved and taught en masse, intergrouped with students further advanced and those who followed them in. **1972** *Accountant* 17 Aug. 191/2 Inter-group dividends may thus be paid gross.

inter'grow, *v.* *rare.* [INTER- 1.]

1. *intr.* To grow intermixed with each other.

1891 *Dublin Rev.* July 194 These can intergrow, yet preserving distinct individuality.

2. *trans.* To intersperse or cover in parts with a growth (of something): only in *pass. pple.*

1891 ATKINSON *40 Yrs. Moorland Parish* 159 All that was not moorland was a series of swampy marshes, inter-grown rather than overgrown with wood and forest.

intergrowth ('ɪntəgrəʊθ). [INTER- 2 a.] The growing (of things) into each other.

1844 DE QUINCEY *Finlay's Hist. Greece* Posth. Wks. 1891 II. 86 Forest trees of the elder generation..begin to thicken with the intergrowth of a younger shrubbery. **1873** HAMERTON *Intell. Life* VII. i. (1875) 227 Real marriage is a long slow intergrowth, like that of two trees planted quite close together in the forest. **1885** *Encycl. Brit.* XVIII. 260/2 The complex incrustations and intergrowths of sessile forms. **1894** *Naturalist* 68 The brown mica is in part in parallel intergrowth with the white.

intergyral, -habitation: See INTER- *pref.*

interhæmal (-'hiːməl), *a.* (*sb.*) *Anat.* [INTER- 4 a.] Situated between hæmal spines.

1846 OWEN *Comp. Anat. Vetebr.* I. *Fishes* iii. 67 Both interneural and interhæmal spines are, in the osseous fishes, commonly shaped like little daggers, plunged in the flesh up to the hilt. **1880** GÜNTHER *Fishes* 351 A dorsal and anal fin supported by interneural and interhæmal spines.

b. as *sb.* An interhæmal bone or spine.

1880 GÜNTHER *Fishes* 53 The anterior being..destined to support a series of interhæmals.

interhemicerebral, -hemisphere, -eric; -human: see INTER- *pref.*

interhyal (-'haɪəl), *a.* (*sb.*) *Anat.* [f. INTER- 4 a + HY(OID) + -AL[1].] Situated between two parts of the hyoid arch of a fish.

1884 *Stand. Nat. Hist.* (1888) III. 21 The lower part of the [hyoid] arch retains its connection with the upper part, in fishes, by means of an interhyal piece.

b. as *sb.* An intermediate bone or cartilage in the hyoid arch.

1888 ROLLESTON & JACKSON *Anim. Life* 93 The remaining portion of the embryonic hyoidan cartilage gives origin to the interhyal or stylohyal [etc.].

†**in'terial**, *a.* *Obs.* [irreg. f. L. *inter* between, within, *interior* INTERIOR, inner: cf. med.L. *interia* intestines, entrails, and INFERIAL.] Inward, internal, interior.

1432-50 tr. *Higden* (Rolls) III. 469 Ye moue batelles exterialle to men where hit is so that ye haue not victory of your enmyes interialle. *Ibid.* IV. 119 A disease of his partes interialle [*dolor viscerum*]. **1542** BOORDE *Dyetary* xix. (1870) 278 Good..for all the interyall membres of man. **1547** —— *Brev. Health* Pref. 4 The interial partes.

Hence †**in'terially** *adv.*, inwardly, internally.

1432-50 tr. *Higden* (Rolls) I. 53 Colde..makethe men more of body..moore hoote interially [*interius calidiores*], and by that moore bolde.

interim ('ɪntərɪm), *adv.*, *sb.*, and *adj.* [L. *interim* adv., in the meantime, meanwhile, f. *inter* between + advb. ending *-im*.]

‖**A.** *adv.* In the meantime, meanwhile. (Also AD INTERIM, PER INTERIM, q.v.)

1580 G. HARVEY *3 Proper Lett.* in Haslewood *Eng. Poets & Poesy* (1815) II. 265 *Interim*, credit me, I dare geue no Preceptes. *a* **1641** BP. MONTAGU *Acts & Mon.* (1642) 83 Which yet is so meant; unlesse interim the same spirit expound them, which did dictate them. **1775** BENEDICT ARNOLD *Let.* 23 May (Amer. Archives) (Cent.), I hope some gentleman will soon be appointed in my room here.. Interim, I am, gentlemen, your most obedient servant. **1804** *Something Odd* II. 139 Interim, take courage, and make your calculations anew.

B. *sb.*

1. An intervening time, interval of time; the meantime: now usually in phr. *in the interim* = A.

1563-87 FOXE *A. & M.* (1684) III. 935 He knew not what in this interim should be done against England. **1579-80** NORTH *Plutarch* (1676) 918 The Wars that fell out in the interim were a hindrance. **1601** SHAKS. *Jul. C.* II. i. 64 Betweene the acting of a dreadfull thing, And the first motion, all the Interim is Like a Phantasma, or a hideous Dreame. **1609** W. M. *Man in Moone* (1849) 13 Physicke is not taken at al times and seasons, continually without interim. **1615** G. SANDYS *Trav.* 123 After all sung ioyntly, at interims praying to themselues. **1665** MANLEY *Grotius' Low C. Warres* 183 In the interim of these Affairs, Collonel Schenck took by Surprize Bonne. **1795** WASHINGTON *Lett.* Writ. 1892 XIII. 79 If nothing in the interim casts up. **1822** HAZLITT *Table-t.* Ser. II. vii. (1869) 140 We imagine all sorts of pleasures in the interim. **1876** MOZLEY *Univ. Serm.* iii. 63 There is an interim provided during which the religious view of death can work in the mind calmly.

†**2.** Something done in an interval; an interlude. *by interims*: at intervals. *Obs.*

1588 SHAKS. *L.L.L.* I. i. 172 This childe of fancie that Armado hight, For interim to our studies shall relate, In high-borne words the worth of many a Knight. **1591** SYLVESTER *Du Bartas* I. vi. *margin*, Made to the Image of God..not all at once, but by interims, first his Body, and then his reasonable Soule. **1633** T. JAMES *Voy.* 44 It did (by *interims*) snow and blow.

3. a. A temporary or provisional arrangement, adopted in the meanwhile.

1558 in Strype *Ann. Ref.* (1824) I. II. App. iv. 397 What order be fit..as an *interim*? **1589** *Hay any Work* B b, This may serue for an aunswere.., by way of an Interim. **1791** BURKE *Let. Memb. Nat. Assembly* Wks. VI. 46 Even before it could be done in due form, the chiefs of the nation did not attempt themselves to exercise authority so much as by *interim*. **1864** FROUDE *Short Stud.*, *Sci. Hist.* 28 The reconciliation of parties..is no tinkered-up truce or convenient Interim.

b. *Ch. Hist.* (with capital *I.*) A provisional arrangement for the adjustment of religious differences between the German Protestants and the Roman Catholic Church (of which there were three promulgated, one in 1541 and two in 1548) pending a settlement by a General Council.

1548 SIR P. HOBY *Let. Dk. Somerset* 9 July, The Emperor, the diet being now finished, converteth his whole study to the setting forth of the *interim*. *Ibid.*, The three townes, Constance, Argentine, and Lynda..have not yet granted unto the *interim*. **1560** DAUS tr. *Sleidane's Comm.* 302 The Emperour..leaving all hope of a counsell, begynneth to set forth his Interim..Bucer refuseth to subscribe to the Interim. The Pope himselfe condemneth the Interim. **1681** BURNET *Hist. Ref.* II. I. 86 They drew up all the Points of Religion in a Book, which was best known by the name of the *Interim*, because it was to last during that Interval, till a General Council should meet in Germany. **1732-8** NEAL *Hist. Purit.* (1822) I. 55. **1848** J. WATERWORTH *Canons Counc. Trent* (new ed.) p. cxxvi, Charles promulgated, in the Diet of Augsburgh, on the 15th of May, 1548, the celebrated formulary called the *interim*. **1857** PUSEY *Real Presence* i. (1869) 62 The 'Interim' then proposed for the acceptance of the Catholics and Lutherans was.. drawn up by Gropper.

†**4.** An intervening space, interval. *Obs.*

1650 BULWER *Anthropomet.* 79 In the interim being annexed on both sides to the bone of the Genæ.

5. An interim dividend.

1930 *Daily Express* 6 Nov. 14/2 An interim of 5 per cent. actual was declared in May. **1935** *Economist* 14 Sept. 527/2 Associated Portland Cement had decided to pay the first interim in its history, at the rate of 5 per cent. **1964** *Financial Times* 10 Feb. 8/1 On Wednesday an interim is expected from Triplex Holdings.

C. *adj.* Done, made, provided, occurring, etc. in or for the meantime; provisional, temporary. Formerly also of time: Intervening.

1604 DEKKER *Honest Wh.* Wks. 1873 II. 78 How shall the *interim* houres by us be spent? *a* **1734** NORTH *Exam.* I. iii. §67 (1740) 173 Amusements only to consume the *interim* Time. **1808** BENTHAM *Sc. Reform* 112 To regulate all matters relating to interim possession. **1858** LD. ST. LEONARDS *Handy Bk. Prop. Law* xii. 75 The Court has power to make interim orders for payment of alimony for the wife. **1869** *Bradshaw's Railway Manual* XXI. 247 The interim dividend of gross receipts. **1882** BITHELL *Counting-Ho. Dict.* (1893) 154 Interim dividends are permissible only when the finances of a Company are in so sound a condition as to place the annual balance beyond doubt. **1905** *Daily Chron.* 21 June 4/3 The Committee should..be invited to present an interim Report. **1950** T. S. ELIOT *Cocktail Party* III. 145 We have just drawn up an interim report. **1968** J. LOCK *Lady Policeman* xviii. 149 A four-week interim order was made so that enquiries could continue. **1972** *Accountant* 17 Aug. 197/1 What would happen if that same company deferred the interim dividend.

Interimist ('ɪntərɪmɪst). *Ch. Hist.* [f. prec. 3 b + -IST.] One who accepted or advocated one of the Interims: see prec. B. 3 b.

1560 J. DAUS tr. *Sleidane's Comm.* 313 b *note*, Two sacrifices of Christ after these interimistes. **1614** BP. HALL *No Peace with Rome* iii, Those honest and good-natured men..Cassander, Fricius, the Interimists, and that namelesse Apologist of the French. *a* **1640** JACKSON *Creed* X. xxi. §9 Some interimists or labourers for reconciliation betwixt the Church of Rome and of England. **1674** *Ch. & Crt. of Rome* 5 For instance, Erasmus, Cassander,..the Interimists,..&c.

interimistic (ˌɪntərɪ'mɪstɪk), *a.* [f. prec. + -IC, or from INTERIM + -ISTIC. Cf. G. *interimistisch.*]

1. Done, occurring, etc. in or for the interim; provisional: = INTERIM C.

1859 *Ecclesiologist* XX. 345 Only one unintelligible word struck us, and that is 'interimistic' [Review of P. A. Munch's *Cathedral of Throndheim*]. **1875** POSTE *Gaius* II. Comm. (ed. 2) 228 In its origin *Bonorum possessio* was probably only the provisional or interimistic possession granted to one of the parties in a suit of *Hereditatis petitio*. **1878** SEELEY *Stein* II. 438 The Interimistic National Representation from April 1812 to March 1815.

2. *Ch. Hist.* Belonging to the Interimists; pertaining to or in accordance with the Interim: see INTERIM B. 3 b.

1885 R. W. DIXON *Hist. Ch. Eng.* III. 98 *note*, The Emperor had strongly urged upon the ambassadors the settling of a form of religion agreeable to the Interimistic doctrine.

So †**interi'mistical** *a.* = prec.; **interi'mistically** *adv.*, (in quot.) in the interim, meanwhile (= INTERIM A).

1643 T. GOODWIN, etc. *Apol. Narrat.* 24 We had.. during this inter[i]misticall season, tentations, yea provocations enough to have drawn forth such a spirit. **1658** MANTON *Meat out of the Eater* Wks. 1871 V. 407 God hateth those *iniquos syncresismos*, profane mixtures and *inter[i]mistical* designs. **1890** J. H. STIRLING *Gifford Lect.* x. 177 Before coming to Anselm, it is to the Fathers that we must interimistically pass.

inter-imperial: see INTER- *pref.* 6.

‖**Interimsethik** ('ɪntərɪmzˌeːtɪk). *Theol.* Also in anglicized forms **interim-ethic, interim ethic.** [G. (Schweitzer, 1901, 1906) *interims-*, comb. form of *interim*, provisional, temporary + *ethik* ethics, ethical values, principles.] The moral principles laid down by Jesus, interpreted as formulated for the guidance of men expecting the imminent end of the world; hence, a code of behaviour for use in a specific, temporary situation.

1910 W. MONTGOMERY tr. *Schweitzer's Quest Historical Jesus* xix. 352 What this repentance, supplementary to the law, the special ethic of the interval before the coming of the kingdom (*Interimsethik*) is,.. He explains in the Sermon on the Mount. [**1915** A. HALL *Jesus & Christianity in 20th Cent.* iii. 43 Schweitzer.. perceives the difficulty, and endeavours to overcome it by describing this side of the message and character of Jesus as 'the ethic of the interim'.] **1918** *Encycl. Relig. & Ethics* X. 733/1 Many NT students argue that the ethics of Jesus is conditional, an *Interimsethik*, and was proclaimed in indissoluble connexion with the eschatological expectation of a state of perfect blessedness to be supernaturally brought about. **1946** R. KNOX tr. *Epistles & Gospels* 270 But Matthew makes it more plain than Luke that we are not merely dealing with what Schweitzer called an *interimsethik*, a scale of values only appropriate to a world which is shortly to go up in smoke. **1947** G. SEAVER *Albert Schweitzer* II. xiii. 183 Our Lord's teaching was an *interim-ethic*, that is to say it was conditioned by His conviction of the nearness of the supernatural Kingdom. **1960** N. SYKES *Sixty Yrs. Since* 7 It was in the light of this eschatology that all the ethical teaching of the Gospels must be understood.. and the whole was an *Interimsethik*. **1961** *Times Lit. Suppl.* 17 Feb. p. x/3 He also points out.. that their advocacy of toleration was intended only as an *Interimsethik*, until reconciliation.. had been attained. *Ibid.* p. xii/3 Schweitzer's thorough-going eschatology and his consequent estimate of the ethical teaching of Jesus as *Interimsethik*. **1964** M. RATTER *Schweitzer* 116 The teaching of Jesus is seen to be an 'Interim Ethic'.

†**interi'nation.** *Obs.* In 5 **interynacion.** [a. F. *intérination*, var. of *entérination*, n. of action from *in-*, *entériner* to render (an act) definitive or valid by juridical ratification, f. OF. *enterin* entire, complete, deriv. of *entier* entire, whole. Cf. med.L. *interināre*, *interinātio* (Du Cange).] Ratification, confirmation.

1489 CAXTON *Faytes of A.* III. xiv. 199 Yf he deyed within the fyrst monethe of the yere after the Interynacion of hys offyce, hys heyre myght haue an actyon for to demande the hole payement of hys wages.

interincorporation, -independence, -indicate: see INTER- *pref.*

interindividual (-ɪndɪ'vɪdjuːəl), *a.* [INTER- 5.] Subsisting, carried on, taking place, or forming a communication between, individuals. So **interindi'vidually** *a.*

1922 JOYCE *Ulysses* 651 The converse domain of interindividual relations. **1951** T. PARSONS et al. in Parsons & Shils *Toward Gen. Theory Action* I. i. 24 These selections cannot be inter-individually random in a social system. **1953** N. TINBERGEN *Herring Gull's World* xvi. 122 The female's posture is identical with the submissive posture which the species has developed for other kinds of inter-individual conflict. **1965** *Philos. Rev.* LXXIV. 181 According to Kant interindividual inferences concerning existence are impossible by analytic means. **1971** *Jrnl. Gen. Psychol.* Oct. 175 The actual conditioning procedures should be introduced only after interindividual differences have been reduced to a minimum.

inte'rinement. *rare.* [a. F. *intérinement*, obs. var. *entérinement* ratification, f. *entériner*: see prec. sb.] = INTERINATION.

1883 H. JUTA tr. *Van der Linden's Inst. Holland* 75 The lower court of the nearest town to which also this confirmation (interinement) must be committed. *Note*, *Interinement*, when the domiciliary judge certifies in favour of the applicant whose petition he was directed to investigate.

inter-influence: see INTER- *pref.* 1 b, 2 a.

interinhibition, -insert, -insular, -involve: see INTER- *pref.*

interionic (ɪntəraɪ'ɒnɪk), *a.* [INTER- 4 a.] Existing or occurring between ions.

1903 *Nature* 19 Nov. 65 The interionic forces.. probably exert an effect even at dilutions at which the inter-molecular forces are negligible. **1929** *Jrnl. Chem. Soc.* 1487 The influence of interionic attractions. **1965** PHILLIPS & WILLIAMS *Inorg. Chem.* I. v. 153 The observed interionic distances and the sums of the radii for the alkali halides with the NaCl structure are given in Table 5. VII.

interior (ɪn'tɪərɪə(r)), *a.* and *sb.* Also 5 **-ore**, 6 **-oure**, 6–9 **-our.** [a. L. *interior* inner, comparative adj. from *inter* (superlative *intimus*). Cf. F. *intérieur*, 16th c. (also rare *interior*, 15th c.). Our earliest instance is in a transl. from Fr.; the early spelling followed words from AF. *-our* = F. *-eur*. Cf. the parallel *inferior*. Opposed in all senses and uses to *exterior*.]

A. *adj.*

1. a. Situated more within, or (usually, simply) within, something; belonging to or connected with the inside; = INNER *a.* 1 a, INTERNAL *a.* 1.

interior angle (*Geom.*): any one of the angles included between the sides of a rectilineal figure within the figure; also, an angle included between a straight line falling upon two other straight lines and either of the latter on the side towards the other. ***interior planets***: Mercury and Venus, whose orbits are within that of the earth (more usually called INFERIOR). ***interior screw, side, slope***: see quots.

1490 CAXTON *Eneydos* xiii. 47 Dydo wyth her suster Anne .. loked In to the entraylles Interiores of the bestes there slayne, For to fuldo the sacryfyce. **1513** BRADSHAW *St. Werburge* I. 3400 Her.. interiour vesture. **1578** LYTE *Dodoens* III. xii. 333 All colde diseases of the interior or inner partes. **1651** HOBBES *Leviath.* I. vi. 23 Sense is Motion in the organs and interiour parts of mans body. **1706** PHILLIPS s.v. *Polygon*, *Interior Polygon*, the main Body of the Work or Place, excluding the Out-works. *Ibid.* s.v. *Talus*, *Talus Interiour* or *Inward Talus*, the Steepness of the Rampart, or other Work on the in-side. **1723** WOODWARD *Nat. Hist. Earth* i. (ed. 3) 3 Cole-pits and the like.. displayed to sight the interiour parts of it. **1756** R. SIMSON *Euclid* I. Prop. xvi, If one side of a triangle be produced, the exterior angle shall be greater than either of the interior opposite angles. *Ibid.* xxxii, The three interior angles of any triangle are equal to two right angles. **1853** STOCQUELER *Mil. Encycl.*, *Interior flanking angle* is formed by the curtain and line of defence .. *Interior side* is the line of the curtain produced to the two oblique radii of the front, or a line drawn from the centre of one bastion to that of the next. *Interior slope* is the inclination towards the inner part of a work given to the earth forming the rampart or parapet. **1863** TYNDALL *Heat* v. §160 (1870) 135 Also accomplishes what we may call *interior* work. **1875** KNIGHT *Dict. Mech.*, *Interior Screw*, one cut on an interior or hollow surface, as of a nut, burr, or taphole.

b. rarely with *to*: Situated within or on the inner side of (something).

1816 T. L. PEACOCK *Headlong Hall* vi, The library.. which was interior to the music-room. **1867** SMYTH *Sailor's Word-bk.*, *Inferior Planets*, this name.. is applied to Mercury and Venus, because they revolve in orbits interior to the earth's path.

c. Situated within and at a distance from the coast, or frontier of a country, etc.; inland; belonging to the interior.

1777 SIR W. JONES *Ess. Poetry East. Nat.* in *Poems* 177 In the interiour parts of the empire. **1796** MORSE *Amer. Geog.* I. 160 Proximity to the Bay of Fundy, and principal interiour settlements of the province. **1856** KANE *Arct. Expl.* I. x. 114 To learn something of the interior features of the country. **1895** *Westm. Gaz.* 9 Sept. 2/1 He knew of no other interior chief who had even attempted the half that Khama had accomplished in the advancing of his people towards the goal of civilisation. **1897** MARY KINGSLEY *W. Africa* 636 Coomassie.. if properly managed for a few years, will become a great interior market, attracting to itself the routes of interior trade.

d. *Entom.* Situated nearer to the body or to the median line.

1862 KIRBY & SP. *Entomol.* IV. 339 *Interior* [*margin*], the inner margin of the wing, or that next the body.

2. Existing within limits figured as spatial; belonging to the inner relations or intrinsic nature of anything.

a. Internal, domestic: as opposed to *foreign*.

1768 P. THICKNESSE (*title*) Useful Hints to those who make the Tour of France, including Account of the Interior Police of that Kingdom. **1818** JAS. MILL *Brit. India* II. IV. v. 198 The interior trade, or that from place to place within the country. **1841** *Penny Cycl.* XX. 264/2 (Russia) The administration.. is conducted by the.. Ministry of foreign affairs, Ministry of interior affairs, or home department [etc.].

b. Inner, as distinct from what appears on the surface or is publicly declared.

1775 *Hist. Eur.* in *Ann. Reg.* 44/1 He was thwarted and overruled by what in the cant phrase is called the interior cabinet. **1790** SIR J. REYNOLDS *Disc.* xv. (1876) 100 To draw out the interior principles of our art. **1791** BURKE *Let. Memb. Nat. Assembly* Wks. VI. 61 The exterior or interiour purposes of the French monarchy. **1849** MACAULAY *Hist. Eng.* ii. I. 241 There was to be no interior cabinet. All the thirty were to be entrusted with every political secret, and summoned to every meeting.

3. a. Belonging to or existing in the mind or soul; mental or spiritual, as distinguished from that which is bodily; 'inward': = INNER *a.* 2, INTERNAL *a.* 3.

1513 BRADSHAW *St. Werburge* I. 1304 Wherby he perceyued the great holynesse Of blessed saynt Cead and interyor deuocyon. **1548** HALL *Chron., Edw. IV* 219 Peraventure.. that her interior iye sawe privily, and gave to her a secrete monicion of the greate calamities. *c* **1566** J. ALDAY tr. *Boaystuau's Theat. World* T iv, To exercise his fancie and other interior senses. **1651** C. CARTWRIGHT *Cert. Relig.* I. 298 They doe not deny but that it may be called a Sacrament, and that some interiour Grace is conferred by it. **1754** RICHARDSON *Grandison* (1781) V. xlii. 260 A number of people, of high interior worth. **1852** H. ROGERS *Ess.* I. vii. 337 One or two extracts.. give the key to his whole interior history. **1899** FINDLAY in *Expositor* Feb. 90 The outcome of the interior, spiritual action of Christ upon human society.

†**b.** Inwardly conceived or felt. *Obs.*

a **1548** HALL *Chron., Hen. IV* 25 The Earle of Northumberland.. began secretely to communicate his interior imaginacions and privie thoughtes with Richard Scrope. **1610** *Death Rauilliack* in *Harl. Misc.* (Malh.) III. 110 We thinke it an interior loue to our countri-men to haue an abstract of the most occurences that hapned since.

c. Devoted to spiritual things; pious, devout.

1854 J. H. NEWMAN *Lect. Hist. Turks* 257 An apposite illustration of what I mean by an 'interior' people, if I may borrow a devotional word to express a philosophical idea. **1863** *Home & For. Rev.* II. 274 So pious, so contemplative, and so interior a spirit. **1879** W. G. WARD *Ess.* (1884) II. x. 9 Difference.. between the interior and the worldly man respectively.

4. Special collocations, as **interior monologue** (cf. F. *monologue intérieur*), a form of writing in which the inner thoughts of a character are presented; **interior spring** (also **interior-sprung**) **mattress**, one with coiled springs within.

1922 tr. V. Larbaud in *Criterion* I. 103 It is of course especially in the interior monologues.. that sexual instinct and erotic revery emerge. **1933** JOYCE *Let.* 17 Mar. (1966) III. 270 The other [is] going to Rome to lecture on the Interior Monologue. **1952** A. WILSON *Emile Zola* iii. 66 The Impressionist approach which he [*sc.* Zola] used could have led to a development of the interior monologue, as it did for Tolstoy. **1971** *Guardian* 27 May 8/7 Eight ward-inmates of an old people's home describe themselves in interior monologue that rambles on. **1959** *Spectator* 9 Oct. 498/2 A fridge, interior spring mattresses, even a bath. **1948** BINNIE & BOXALL *Housecraft* (ed. 4) xvii. 197 Interior sprung beds .. may occasionally be turned from side, to side or from end to end. **1951** *Good Housek. Home Encycl.* 187/2 Interior-sprung mattresses do not require such frequent turning. **1961** *Countryman* LVIII. 601 The stretcher felt like an interior-sprung mattress.

B. *sb.*

1. a. The interior part of anything; the inside.

1828 SCOTT *F.M. Perth* xvii, The Prince.. acquainted with its interior, ran up stairs. **1858** HAWTHORNE *Fr. & It. Jrnls.* I. 264 The interior.. we found very impressive, dim with the light of stained and painted windows. **1861** M. PATTISON *Ess.* (1889) I. 46 In the booths which lined the interior of the court. **1878** HUXLEY *Physiogr.* 188 Deep-seated in the interior of the earth.

b. That part of a country, island, or continent, lying at a distance from the frontier or coast; the inland parts; an inland region.

1796 BURKE *Regic. Peace* ii. Wks. VIII. 228 Her frontier was terrible, her interiour feeble. **1803** SYD. SMITH *Wks.* 38 Our first acquaintance with the interior of many countries. **1868** G. DUFF *Pol. Surv.* 89 The Chinese merchants purchase goods and take them to other ports or the interior. **1883** *Chambers' Cycl.* I. 565 Western Australia.. rests on desert sandstone, which also stretches north and eastward far into the interior. *Ibid.* VII. 251 (Papua) In the interior are abundance of fine timber trees. **1887** MOLONEY *Forestry W. Afr.* 159 Sierra Leone.. connected with a wide-spread Interior also largely Mohammedan.

c. The inside of a building or room, esp. in reference to the artistic effect; also, a picture or representation of the inside of a building or room. Also, in a theatre, a 'set' consisting of the inside of a building or room. (Usually with *an* or in *pl.*).

1829 H. FOOTE *Compan. to Theatres* 57 A few interiors, two or three streets, and about the same number of country views, would last as stock scenery for several seasons. **1858** GEO. ELIOT *Jrnl.* 20 May in J. W. Cross *George Eliot's Life* (1885) II. viii. 40 The two interiors of Westminster Abbey by Ainmueller admirable. **1864** *Realm* 22 June 7 Everything that brings nature into our interiors deserves encouragement. **1891** *Anthony's Photogr. Bull.* IV. 88 Many points must be borne in mind by the brain behind the lens to direct and then supplement its work, especially in the studio and with interiors. **1898** W. ARCHER *Theatr. 'World' 1897* 180 Mr. and Mrs. Alfred Wigan at the Olympic, made great strides towards realism in the dressing of modern plays and setting of everyday 'interiors'. *a* **1900** *Mod.* A photographer noted for his success with interiors. **1916** J. R. TOWSE *Sixty Yrs. Theater* ii. 23 There were no elaborate and costly interiors, no enclosed box scenes, flats and wings were shifted before the eyes of the spectators. **1966** J. POTTS *Footsteps on Stairs* (1967) i. 9 She does the most divine interiors.

d. The internal parts of the body, esp. the digestive system. *colloq.*

1835 DICKENS *Let.* 4 Nov. (1965) I. 87 A.. Pill—which.. is performing such singular evolutions in my interior. **1906** JOYCE *Let.* 18 Oct. (1966) II. 183 It [*sc.* wine] had not the least effect upon.. 'my interiors'. **1922** —— *Ulysses* 622 Mr Bloom.. noticed when he stood up that he had two flasks of presumably ship's rum sticking one out of each pocket for the private consumption of his burning interior.

2. Inner nature or being; inward mind; soul, character. Now chiefly with *of*.

1596 SHAKS. *Merch. V.* II. ix. 28 Not learning more then the fond eye doth teach, Which pries not to th' interior. **1690** NORRIS *Beatitudes* (1694) I. 146 The regulation of the outward Behaviour, not much regarding the Sanctity of the Interiour. **1715** JANE BARKER *Exilius* I. 97 The Strangeness of the Adventure.. gave a pleasing Surprize to my whole Interiour. **1794** PALEY *Evid.* I. iii. (1817) 51 It is in our own books that the detail and interior of the transaction must be sought for. **1847** L. HUNT *Men, Women & B.* II. x. 231 Her letters from the Levant are so much in the interior of Turkish taste and feeling. **1865** MOZLEY *Mirac.* ii. 230 *note*,

There were difficulties in the interior of the subject of induction which were not yet solved.

3. The internal or 'home' affairs of a country or state; the department concerned with these: in the titles ***Secretary, Department of the Interior***, used in U.S. and the Dominion of Canada, and ***Minister of the Interior***, used in reference to most foreign countries, as France, Germany, Italy, etc.

(Corresponding to the Home Office, and Home Secretary, in Great Britain, and to the Colonial Office and Colonial Secretary in most British Colonies.)

1838 *Penny Cycl.* X. 418/2 The cabinet council of the king [of France] consists of eight ministers for the following departments:—1, Finance; 2, the Interior; 3, Justice [etc.]. **1899** *Whitaker's Almanac* 484 (Canada) Sec. of State, Railways & Canals, Finance, Justice, Interior, Public Works, Agriculture, etc. *Ibid.* 583 (United States of A.) Sec. of State, Treasury, War, Navy, Interior, Agriculture.

interior decoration (ɪn'tɪərɪə dɛkə'reɪʃən). [f. INTERIOR *sb.* 1 c + DECORATION 1.] The planned co-ordination for artistic effect of colours and furniture, etc., in a room or building. So **interior 'decorator**, one who practises interior decoration. Also **interior-'decorate** *v. trans.*, to paint and furnish (a room or the inside of a building) in accordance with an artistic design; ***interior-decorated*** ppl. adj.; ***interior decorating*** vbl. sb. Also *attrib.* and *fig.* (see also quot. 1926).

1807 T. HOPE (*title*) Household furniture and interior decoration. **1861** C. M. YONGE *Young Step-Mother* vii. 83 She was..too fond of out-of-door occupation, to regard interior decoration as one of the domestic graces. **1867** D. R. HAY (*title*) The interior decorator, being the laws of harmonious coloring adapted to interior decorations. **1906** *Dress* Oct. p. xxvi/1, I am a student of interior decoration —have had splendid success in this direction. It will pay you to consult me as to your plans for home beautifying. **1921** W. S. MAUGHAM *Circle* II. 51 Arnold should have been an interior decorator. **1926** MAINES & GRANT *Wise-Crack Dict.* 9/2 *Interior decorator*, bartender. **1930** E. FERBER *Cimarron* xxiii. 373 Fascinating little..interior decorating shops. **1933** *Burlington Mag.* Aug. p. xv/1 Arranging flowers for interior decoration. **1935** *Discovery* Nov. 326/2 Ideal for interior decoration work. **1935** S. LEWIS *It can't happen Here* ii. 24 The bar-room had been professionally interior-decorated by a young New York gentleman. **1943** F. L. WRIGHT *Autobiogr.* (1945) III. 160 John was to regale the inner man, interior-decorate him. **1950** E. H. GOMBRICH *Story of Art* iv. 77 The painters and interior decorators of Pompeii obviously drew freely on the stock of inventions made by the great Hellenistic artists. **1960** *House & Garden* July 4/3, I wonder if there are any courses in Interior Decorating that can be studied at home. I am thinking of starting a small interior decorating business. **1967** E. SHORT *Embroidery & Fabric Collage* i. 18 Texture is a factor which plays a very important part in modern architecture and interior decoration. **1972** L. P. BACHMANN *Ultimate Act* i. 9 The library..was as interior-decorated as the rest of the house.

interior design (ɪn'tɪərɪə dɪ'zaɪn). [f. INTERIOR *sb.* 1 c + DESIGN *sb.* 7.] The design of the interior of a building, including wallpaper, furniture, fittings, etc., according to artistic and architectural criteria. So **interior designer**, one whose business is to plan such interiors. Cf. prec. entry.

1927 T. P. BENNETT *Archit. Design in Concrete* 13 The effect of this adjustment of proportion and detail upon interior design is..in some ways more fundamental than the effect on the new proportions upon exterior designs. **1938** *Decorative Art* p. xxxii, The favourable attention of all leading Interior Designers can be secured..through a single publication, 'Interior Design and Decoration'. **1957** *Encycl. Brit.* XII. pl. x (*caption*) Living room by Ain, Johnson and Day, showing relationship of interior and exterior design. **1962** H. STEPHENSON *Design & Decoration in Home* 7 There is more to interior design than just putting furniture in a room and paint on a wall. **1967** E. SHORT *Embroidery & Fabric Collage* iii. 64 Good interior designers sometimes go as far as having carpets specially designed and manufactured. **1972** *Guardian* 17 May 9/4 She turned to interior design.

interiority (ɪntɪərɪ'ɒrɪtɪ). *rare.* [ad. med.L. *interiōritās*, f. *interior*: see -ITY. (In mod.F. *intériorité*.)] **a.** The quality or state of being interior or inward. **b.** Inner character or nature; an inner element.

1701 NORRIS *Ideal World* I. vi. 391 What St. Augustine.. inculcates concerning both the interiority, and the community of truth. **1704** *Ibid.* II. xiii. 549 Some of his expressions..relate to the interiority of Truth. **1803** *Edin. Rev.* I. 261 Interiority and exteriority, by which is meant the distinction of the attributes of an object as originally existing in itself or as acquired from without. **1818** BP. JEBB in C. Forster *Life* II. (1836) 140 Those deep *interiorities* (if I may be allowed the expression), which will ever be the refreshment and delight of the most pious worshippers. **1884** H. W. BEECHER *Plymouth Pulpit* 19 Mar. 496 (Cent.) He had been a breaker of the law in its essential spirit, in its interiority, all the way through. **1890** W. JAMES *Princ. Psychol.* II. xvii. 43 It is surely subjectivity and interiority which are the notions *latest* acquired by the human mind. **1934** E. BOWEN *Cat Jumps* 51 Voices came out from some dark interiority. **1941** *Theology* XLII. 156 The characteristic of the new period was, as Hegel put it, interiority. **1967** *Listener* 26 Oct. 552/1 Alan Bates as Gabriel Oak suffers..from Schlesinger's reluctance to suggest, as Hardy might put it, interiority. **1973** *Times Lit. Suppl.* 2 Nov. 1348/4 For all its imaginative ambitiousness, the volume lacks a certain human interiority.

interiorize (ɪn'tɪərɪəraɪz), *v.* [f. INTERIOR *a.* + -IZE.] *trans.* To connect with the soul, as distinguished from the body; also, to locate within the mind.

1906 *Academy* 20 Oct. 392/2 To 'interiorise' the struggle, to place it on the stage of the soul, with eternity for background. **1916** STANFORD & FORSYTH *Hist. Mus.* xvi. 329 The second [feature in American life] is the interiorizing and democratic habit-of-mind which partly connotes the term *Americanism.* **1934** *Mind* XLIII. 89 In so far as habits of co-operation have convinced the child at a later age of the necessity of not lying, rules will become comprehensible and interiorised. **1937** G. W. ALLPORT *Personality* (1938) p. viii, From this point of view culture is relevant only when it has become *interiorized* within the person as a set of personal ideals, attitudes, and traits. **1971** *Jrnl. Gen. Psychol.* Apr. 206 The child interiorizes what he already understands.

Hence **interiori'zation.**

1941 *Theology* XLII. 156 To discover anew the meaning of authority *in* their immanent freedom, by making it itself immanent within them by a process of interiorization. **1956** *Scottish Jrnl. Theol.* IX. 74 Hence he is unable to rise to the thought of suffering as the gift of divine love, as a sacramental medium through the purifying effect of which man attains a deeper realisation and interiorisation of God. **1961** J. N. FINDLAY *Values & Intentions* i. 40 Our talk about thoughts, decisions, etc., is always largely an 'interiorization' of our talk about words. **1966** L. JONES in A. Chapman *New Black Voices* (1972) 465 The Black man must seek a Black politics, an ordering of the world that is beneficial to his culture, to his interiorization and judgment of the world. **1971** *Jrnl. Gen. Psychol.* Apr. 206 Since these interiorizations are not sufficient for the child, he gradually proceeds to representations based upon more logical.. principles of operation.

interiorly (ɪn'tɪərɪəlɪ), *adv.* [f. INTERIOR *a.* + -LY².]

1. In or on the inside; with respect to the interior; internally, inside, within.

1758 JENTY in *Phil. Trans.* L. 551, I found the lungs closely adhering to the ribs laterally, and posteriorly and interiorly close to the pericardium. **1804** CARLISLE *ibid.* XCV. 14 The skeleton..is placed interiorly, where the bulk of the animal admits of the bones being sufficiently strong. **1856** OLMSTED *Slave States* 386 Not more than twelve feet square, interiorly. **1894** BARING-GOULD *Queen of L.* I. ix. 98 The van was divided interiorly into compartments.

2. In, or with respect to, the inner or intrinsic nature of a thing; inwardly; intimately.

1633 J. DONE *Hist. Septuagint* (1685) 180 The Divine vertue that sustains and interiourly nourisheth all things. **1682** SIR T. BROWNE *Chr. Mor.* III. §15 To see ourselves interiourly, we are fain to borrow other Mens Eyes. **1866** *Reader* No. 159. 29/3 Exteriorly difficult and interiorly dangerous.

3. In, or with respect to, the inner nature, mind, or soul; inwardly; mentally or spiritually.

1609 BIBLE (Douay) *Lev.* i. comm., As the soule must interiorly worship God in spirite and veritie; so the bodie must also honour him exteriorly. **1657** *Divine Lover* 67 If I hold my peace I shall interiorlie be tormented with insupportable bitternesse. **1750** CHESTERF. *Lett.* (1792) III. ccxxix. 39 Interiorly most people enjoy the inferiority of their (?) friends. **1863** MRS. C. CLARKE *Shaks. Char.* xix. 481 Interiorly, morally, he is immeasurably below him. **1874** H. W. BEECHER in *Chr. World Pulpit* V. 140/2 There is given to men interiorly a moral constitution which is illumined by the direct influence of the Divine soul acting on ours.

in'teriorness. *rare.* [f. as prec. + -NESS.] = INTERIORITY *a.*

1895 *Thinker* VII. 157 This doctrine of the interiorness or coinherence of the Son in the Father.

†in'teriously, *adv. Obs. rare.* [app. f. L. *interius* adv. inwardly, within + -LY².] Inwardly.

1513 BRADSHAW *St. Werburge* II. 1298 This forsayd erle of his benignite Interiously louynge holy religion.

inteript(e, obs. corrupt form of INTERRUPT.

interisland: see INTER- *pref.* 5.

†inte'rition. *Obs. rare*⁻⁰. [ad. L. *interitiōn-em*, n. of action from *interīre* to go to ruin, perish.]

1656 BLOUNT *Glossogr.*, *Interition*, a decaying, a perishing. **1658** in PHILLIPS.

inter'jacence. *rare.* [f. INTERJACENT: see -ENCE.] The fact of lying between.

1864 in WEBSTER.

interjacency (ɪntə'dʒeɪsənsɪ). [f. as prec. + -ENCY.] The quality, condition, or state of being interjacent or of lying between; also, an instance of this, something lying between.

1646 SIR T. BROWNE *Pseud. Ep.* VII. xvii. 377 Its fluctuations are but motions..which winds, stormes, shoares, shelves, and every interjacency irregulates. **1651** BIGGS *New Disp.* ¶197 In demonstration..it is accounted impossible to go on from one extreame to another, without a mean, and that mean wholly deny all interjacency. **1773** *Connect. Col. Rec.* (1887) XIV. 475 The Interjacency of two Provinces between your Seat of Government and the Places to which you would now extend your Jurisdiction.

interjacent (ɪntə'dʒeɪsənt), *a.* [ad. L. *interjacēnt-em*, pr. pple. of *interjacēre*, f. *inter* between + *jacēre* to lie.] Lying or existing between; intervening, intermediate.

1594 in Row *Hist. Kirk* (Wodrow Soc.) 159 That a fast be keeped..the two last Sabbaths of June, with exhortations and prayers in the interjacent week dayes. **1597** A. M. tr. *Guillemeau's Fr. Chirurg.* 23/2 The whole interiacent skinne might be cleane therof severed. **1614** RALEIGH *Hist. World* IV. i. §7 (1634) 471 In spight of all the nations interjacent. **1628** JACKSON *Creed* IX. xl. §11 The time interjacent betwixt the great feast..and the pentecost following. **1691** RAY *Creation* I. (1692) 176 What should take away the sight of these Ships from each other, but the gibbosity of the interjacent Water? **1695** ALINGHAM *Geom. Epit.* 47 Add to each the interjacent angle. **1840** DE QUINCEY *Style* II. Wks. 1860 XI. 222 A great resisting mass, interjacent between Greece and the..enemies to the far north east. **1858** CARLYLE *Fredk. Gt.* IV. v. (1872) I. 308 He issued from Stettin; took the interjacent outpost places.

interjaculate (ɪntə'dʒækjʊleɪt), *v.* [f. INTER- 1 a + ppl. stem of L. *jaculārī* to throw, dart: cf. EJACULATE.] To ejaculate in the midst of a conversation; to interject (an ejaculation).

1854 THACKERAY *Newcomes* vii, 'O Dieu! que n'ai-je pu le voir?' interjaculates Mademoiselle.

interjaculatory (ɪntə'dʒækjʊlətərɪ), *a.* [f. prec.: see -ORY.] Expressed in parenthetical ejaculations.

1827 *Blackw. Mag.* XXI. 642 A sudden squall that smites a large dinner-party mute, or into interjaculatory admiration. **1871** T. A. TROLLOPE *Durnton Abbey* III. i. 6 A liberal amount of interjaculatory commentary.

interjangle: see INTER- *pref.* 1 b.

†inter'ject, *ppl. a. Obs. rare*⁻¹. [ad. L. *interject-us*, pa. pple. of *interjicĕre*: see next.] Interjected: used as pa. pple. of next.

1578 BANISTER *Hist. Man* I. 21 A thick crust of Cartilage interiect and put betwene them.

interject (ɪntə'dʒɛkt), *v.* [f. L. *interject-*, ppl. stem of *interjicĕre* (*-jacĕre*) to throw or cast between, f. *inter* between + *jacĕre* to throw.]

1. *trans.* To throw or cast in between; to introduce abruptly; to insert, interpolate, interpose.

1588 A. KING tr. *Canisius' Catech.* H vij, Thay war interiectit betuix ye accomplissing of ye course of ye sone and ye moone. **1624** T. SCOTT *Belg. Souldier* 3 Some.. temporizing Parasite may interiect these doubts. **1684** tr. *Bonet's Merc. Compit.* VI. 217 If..as soon as [blood]..were let, without any stay interjected, Sweat were raised. **1791** BEDDOES in *Phil. Trans.* LXXXI. 64 When the latter is interjected between the strata, or squeezed up through fissures. **1874** S. COX *Pilgr. Ps.* iii. 59 He can interject a mere play upon words. **1882** MASSON *Carlyle* in *Macm. Mag.* XLV. 248 She interjected one of her bright and witty remarks.

b. To remark parenthetically or as an interruption.

1791 BOSWELL *Johnson* 6 Apr. an. 1775, Moody interjected in an Irish tone and with a comick look, 'Ah! poor George the Second'. **1822** W. TAYLOR in *Monthly Mag.* LIII. 103 'Ridiculous', interjected I. **1881** MISS BRADDON *Asph.* I. 172 'I have been at home so little, you see', she interjected with a piteous air.

†c. In *passive*: To be interposed or situated between; to lie or occur between; to intervene.

1578 BANISTER *Hist. Man* I. 27 That cauitie or hollow, interiected betwene them, is a seat for the Muscle. **1633** EARL MANCH. *Al Mondo* (1636) 15 It [death] is but a point of time interjected betwixt two extremes. **1746–7** *Act 20 Geo. II*, c. 43 §15 In case such lands are interjected between two shires. **1752** *Stewart's Trial* in *Scots Mag.* (1753) July 333/2 High ground interjected betwixt him and the deponent.

†2. *intr.* for *refl.* **a.** To cross one another, as two lines. **b.** To come between; to intervene, interpose. *Obs. rare.*

1598 SYLVESTER *Du Bartas* II. ii. IV. *Columnes* 356, I never see their glances inter-ject In Triangle, Sextile, or Square aspect, Now milde, now moody; but methinks I see [etc.]. **1646** BUCK *Rich. III* 61 The confluence of Souldiers interjecting rescued him. **1676** WISEMAN *Chirurg. Treat.* V. ix. 375 The Sagittall [Suture] which usually begins at that point where these Lines interject.

Hence **inter'jected** *ppl. a.*, thrown or cast between, interpolated; placed or lying between, interposed; **inter'jecting** *vbl. sb.*, the action of interpolating or interposing.

1590 BARROUGH *Meth. Physick* Pref. (1639) 5 The interjecting of these few lines. *a***1619** W. COWPER in Spurgeon *Treas. Dav.* Ps. li. 11 They see not his merciful face by reason of many interjected veils. **1650** BULWER *Anthropomet.* 164 The Scapula..grows prominent with the interjected Muscules. **1880** MUIRHEAD *Gaius* IV. §129 The employment of such interjected clauses may go even further.

interjection (ɪntə'dʒɛkʃən). [a. F. *interjection* (13–14th c. in Hatz.-Darm.), ad. L. *interjectiōn-em*, n. of action from *interjicĕre*: see prec.]

1. The utterance of ejaculations expressive of emotion; an ejaculation or exclamation.

*c***1430** *Pilgr. Lyf Manhode* III. vii. (1869) 139 This interieccioun sorweful wer-inne is no thing that lusteth. **1576** FLEMING *Panopl. Epist.* 332 Hee beginneth his letter with an interjection of joye, or a kinde of speache importing his inwarde gladnesse. **1626** BACON *Sylva* §721 A Continued Expulsion of the Breath, with the loud Noise, which maketh the Interjection of Laughing. **1816** J. SCOTT *Vis. Paris* Pref. (ed. 5) 23 People have exclaimed their joy and astonishment so often, that, being no longer able to keep up the proper climax of interjection, they [etc.]. **1850** THACKERAY *Mr. & Mrs. Berry* ii, A!—note of interjection.

2. *Gram.* A natural ejaculation expressive of some feeling or emotion, used or viewed as a Part of Speech.

So called because, when so used, it is interjected between sentences, clauses, or words, mostly without grammatical connexion. But the interjection *O* is often construed with the vocative or nominative of address, and *alas, hey, hurrah, woe*, etc. with the prep. *for* or *to* and an object. Beside the simple interjections, as *ah!, oh!, ha!, ho!, hulloa!, psha!, whew!*, and the like, substantives, adjectives, adverbs, and short phrases or sentences are often used interjectionally; e.g. *marry!, fiddlesticks!, fiddle-de-dee!, the devil!, O dear!, dear me!, well, well!, Gad's 'ooks!, God ha' mercy!, bless my soul!*

1530 PALSGR. 149 Interjection be suche as serve to expresse the passyons and the affections of the mynde. **1599** SHAKS. *Much Ado* IV. i. 22 How now! interiections? why then, some be of laughing, as ha, ha, he. **1712** STEELE *Spect.* No. 400 ¶4 Much Care and Concern for the Lady's Welfare ..expressed by an Interjection, an Ah, or an Oh, at some little Hazard in moving or making a Step. **1786–1805** H. TOOKE *Purley* 31 The dominion of speech is erected upon the downfall of Interjections. **1871** EARLE *Philol. Eng. Tongue* §193 The interjection may be defined as a form of speech which is articulate and symbolic but not grammatical.

†**b.** Something that has the effect of an interjection, in expressing emotion. *Obs.*

1649 JER. TAYLOR *Gt. Exemp.* III. xv. 85 He rent his garments, which was the interjection of the Country.

3. The action of interjecting or interposing anything; also, something interposed.

1598 FLORIO, *Intergettione*, a putting betweene, an Interiection. **1643** HERLE *Answ. Ferne* 33 That third estate of the Peeres..becomes the best conjunction by being an interjection betweene them. **1658** PHILLIPS, *Interjection*, a casting between. **1881** PRES. ARTHUR *Message to Congress* 6 Dec. 5/8 The interjection of any foreign guarantee might be regarded as a superfluous and unfriendly act.

b. An interpolated remark or exclamation; an interruption.

1896 *Daily News* 31 Mar. 7/4 *Prisoner.* This is too bad—flesh and blood can't stand it. *Mr. de R——.* You don't do yourself any good by these interjections.

†**4.** *Rhet.* = PARENTHESIS. *Obs.*

1678 PHILLIPS (ed. 4), *Interjection*,..also a figure in Rhetorick and Grammar, being the same with Parenthesis, and otherwise called Interruption.

interjectional (ɪntəˈdʒɛkʃənəl), *a.* [f. prec. + -AL¹.]

1. Of the nature of something interjected or thrown in between or among other remarks.

1788 CUMBERLAND *Observer* No. 116 ¶19 This simply turns upon Saint Mark's interjectional observation, not noticed by Saint Matthew in his account. **1818** SCOTT *Hrt. Midl.* xlii, 'And Effie?—and Effie, dear father?' was an eager interjectional question which Jeanie repeatedly threw in among her expressions of joyful thankfulness. **1839** *New Monthly Mag.* LVI. 547 Interrupted..by interjectional observations.

2. Of, belonging to, or of the nature of an interjection in language.

1761 STERNE *Tr. Shandy* III. xi, Dr. Slop..was just beginning to return my uncle Toby the compliment of his whu—u—u, or interjectional whistle. **1824** SCOTT *Redgauntlet* ch. vii, A number of interjectional sounds uttered with a strange variety of intonation. **1860** FARRAR *Orig. Lang.* (1865) 36 Some onomatopoetic or interjectional root.

Hence **interˈjectionally** *adv.*, in an interjectional way; as an interjection.

1837 CARLYLE *Fr. Rev.* II. IV. vii, His Troopers..respond interjectionally. **1840** *Fraser's Mag.* XXII. 306 'I do pity you', replied the ordinary, interjectionally. **1875** RENOUF *Egypt. Gram.* 56 The crude form of the verb appears sometimes to be used interjectionally. **1882** SERJT. BALLANTINE *Exper.* xxxvii. 355, I rarely kept a diary, and only interjectionally, at long intervals and for short periods.

interjectionalize (ɪntəˈdʒɛkʃənəlaɪz), *v.* [-IZE.] *trans.* To make into an interjection.

1871 EARLE *Philol. Eng. Tongue* §208 By the sixteenth century this 'all hail!'..having lost all construction, was completely interjectionalised.

interjectionary (ɪntəˈdʒɛkʃənərɪ), *a.* [f. INTERJECTION + -ARY.] Characterized by interjection; interjectory.

1797 B. SWIFT (W. R. Paterson) *Tormentor* 91 Crying into the deaf night that has had so many interjectionary confidences from us all. **1858** CARLYLE *Fredk. Gt.* VI. vi. II. 85 Friedrich Wilhelm's inarticulate, interjectionary utterances. **1888** *Cornh. Mag.* Feb. 166 The most perfunctory and interjectionary and spasmodic of observations.

interjector (ɪntəˈdʒɛktə(r)). [agent-n. from L. *interjicĕre* to INTERJECT.] One who interjects or interpolates.

1891 *Pall Mall G.* 3 June 6/1 The interjector always gets the worst of it in an encounter with an old parliamentary hand.

interjectory (ɪntəˈdʒɛktərɪ), *a.* [f. as INTERJECT *v.* + -ORY.] Characterized by interjection; interruptive; interpolated; interjectional.

1859 G. MEREDITH *R. Feverel* xix. II. 37 'The smallest occasional doses', Mrs. Caroline remarked, to an accompaniment of interjectory eyebrows and chins from all her younger daughters. **1859** *Sat. Rev.* 19 Mar. 336/1 [He] mars the even flow of an opening speech by restless interjectory comments. **1894** *Harper's Mag.* Feb. 404/1 Broken with interjectory sentences.

Hence **interˈjectorily** *adv.*, interjectionally, interruptedly.

1891 G. MEREDITH *One of our Conq.* II. iii. 62 A tale.. narrated interjectorily among the by-ways of the City.

interjectural (ɪntəˈdʒɛktjʊrəl), *a.* [f. as next + -AL¹.] Of the nature of what is interjected or thrown in parenthetically; interjectional.

1775 SHERIDAN *Rivals* II. i, He..rapped out a dozen interjectural oaths. **1881** 'BASIL' *Love the Debt* vii, Interjectural asides to the donkey he drove.

†**interˈjecture.** *Obs. rare*⁻¹. [ad. L. *interjectūra* an insertion, f. ppl. stem of *interjacĕre* to INTERJECT: see -URE.] Interposition.

1578 BANISTER *Hist. Man* I. 22 They are together committed like vnto the superiour Vertebres, saue that.. they lacke the interiectur of Cartilages.

†**interˈjoin,** *v. Obs. rare*⁻¹. [INTER- 1 b: cf. L. *interjungĕre*, OF. *entrejoindre.*] *trans.* To join one with another, to join reciprocally.

1607 SHAKS. *Cor.* IV. iv. 22 So fellest foes..shall grow deere friends And inter-ioyne their yssues.

interjoist, -judgement, -justle: see INTER-.

interˈjunction. *rare*⁻⁰. [n. of action from L. *interjungĕre* to interjoin.] A mutual joining.

1836 in SMART.

interkinesis (ɪntəkaɪˈniːsɪs). *Cytology.* [ad. F. *intercinèse* (V. Grégoire 1905, in *La Cellule* XXII. 226): see INTER- 2 b and KINESIS.] A stage which sometimes intervenes between the first and second divisions of meiosis; also, any stage between mitoses.

1906 *Jrnl. R. Microsc. Soc.* 283 The daughter-chromosomes..preserve their autonomy during the interkinesis. **1925** E. B. WILSON *Cell* (ed. 3) i. 28 The central body..retains its morphological identity during the interkinesis or vegetative (non-mitotic) condition of the cell. **1965** PENNY & WAERN *Biol.* xlii. 775 In some cases the chromosomes decondense as in ordinary mitosis, and there is a brief pause before the second division commences. This stage, if it occurs, is called interkinesis.

Hence **interkiˈnetic** *a.*

1927 *Protoplasma* II. 189 The interkinetic nuclear substance is devoid of any structural element. **1931** J. GRAY *Text-bk. Exper. Cytol.* viii. 141 A 'resting' or inter-kinetic nucleus in the living condition is usually optically homogeneous. **1960** L. PICKEN *Organization of Cells* iv. 101 (*heading*) The interphasic, interkinetic, 'resting', or non-mitotic nucleus.

†**ˈinterˌking.** *Obs. rare*⁻¹. [A rendering of L. *interrex.*] = INTERREX.

1533 BELLENDEN *Livy* (1822) 262 The patricianis war convenit to cheis ane Interking, becaus na man aucht to convene the senate without he war clothit with public office.

interknit (ɪntəˈnɪt), *v.* [INTER- 1 b.]

1. *trans.* To knit each into the other; to intertwine, interweave.

1805 SOUTHEY *Madoc* II. xi, Here they..infix the ready piles, Or interknitting them with oziers, weave The wicker wall. **1825** —— *Tale Paraguay* I. xix, These strongly interknit they closed around With basket-work of many a pliant bough. **1885** *Athenæum* 23 May 666/3 A little girl.. with fingers interknit in her lap.

2. *intr.* To intertwine.

1818 KEATS *Endym.* I. 812 Nor with aught else can our souls interknit So wingedly.

Hence **ˈinterknit** *ppl. a.*

1885 *Athenæum* 18 Apr. 512 [He] lets his interknit fingers lie in his lap.

†**ˈinterˌknot,** *sb. Obs. rare*⁻⁰. In 7 enter-. [INTER- 2 a.] A knot which interknits or ties together.

1611 FLORIO, *Internodo*, an enterknot.

interknot (ɪntəˈnɒt), *v.* Also 7 enter-. [INTER- 1 b.] *trans.* To knot together.

1611 FLORIO, *Internodare*, to enterknot or knit. **1888** L. HEARN *Chita* II. i, Millennial oaks interknotted their python roots below its surface. *Ibid.* iii, Ropes are unrolled and interknotted into a line.

†**interˈknow,** *v. Obs.* Also 7 enter-. [INTER- 1 b.] *trans.* To know mutually.

1603–52 [see ENTERKNOW]. **1612–15** BP. HALL *Contempl., O.T.* XIX. v, How familiarly do these prophets inter-know one another.

Hence **interˈknowledge**, mutual or reciprocal knowledge.

a **1626** [see ENTERKNOWLEDGE]. *a* **1656** BP. HALL *Recap. Whole Disc.* (R.), See them in mutuall interknowledge, enjoying each other's blessednesse.

interlace (ɪntəˈleɪs), *v.* Forms: 4–7 entrelace, 4–6 enter-, 6 interlase, 6–7 enter-, 6– interlace. [ME. *entrelace*, a. F. *entrelace-r* (OF. *-ier*), f. *entre-* (ENTER-, INTER- 1) + *lacer* to LACE.]

1. *trans.* To unite two (or more) things by intercrossing laces, strings, or threads; hence, to connect or bind together intricately; to entangle, involve, mix up. (*rare* in physical sense.)

c **1374** CHAUCER *Boeth.* III. pr. xii. 82 (Camb. MS.) The hows of dydalus so entrelaced þat it is vn-able to be vnlaced. **1481** CAXTON *Myrr.* I. v. 27 The vii artes..ben in such wise entrelaced that they may not be auctorised that one without that other. **1578** BANISTER *Hist. Man* VIII. 110 With these nerues, the vj coniugation of brayne is interlaced and mingled. **1791** COWPER *Odyss.* XXIII. 237, I..fashion'd the whole bed..beneath Close interlaced with purple cordage strong. **1878** HUXLEY *Physiogr.* 62 Ice..is built up of crystalline particles interlaced together.

2. a. To draw two series of threads, withes, or other things, across each other, passing each alternately above and below the other, as in weaving; but implying a simpler and less elaborate arrangement than *interweave.*

1523 LD. BERNERS *Froiss.* I. ccccxx. 736 Enterlase your staues ouer your armes, one within another. *a* **1649** DRUMM. OF HAWTH. *Poems* 95 Trees, pleasant trees..Now interlace your trembling tops above. **1694** WESTMACOTT *Script. Herb.* 76 Linnen cloth is that which we call flax..curiously twisted, enterlaced, and conjoyned. **1768–74** TUCKER *Lt. Nat.* (1834) I. 594 The boughs..had matted themselves together, or been interlaced by persons of an unlucky shrewdness. **1857** W. COLLINS *Dead Secret* iii. (1861) 86 Her fingers..interlaced themselves mechanically. **1874** BOUTELL *Arms & Arm.* iii. 51 Head-pieces formed of brass mail—of rings or chainwork, which might be interwoven or interlaced.

b. *fig.* To intermix with constant alternation; to alternate; to interweave.

1576 FLEMING *Panopl. Epist.* 28 The meeting of us, twoe old acquainted friends, and interlacing of talke and communication. **1581** J. BELL *Haddon's Answ. Osor.* 28 b, Amongest these are enterlaced some of the royall bloud. **1644** MRQ. WORC. in Dircks *Life* vi. (1865) 77 You were pleased so to interlace terror and comfort. **1882** FARRAR *Early Chr.* II. 391 The two are inextricably interlaced. A righteous life is the result of faith, and faith is deepened by a righteous life.

†**3.** To interweave one thing or set of things into another; to introduce as by interweaving; to insert, interpolate. Chiefly *fig.* or *transf. Obs.*

1532 MORE *Confut. Barnes* Wks. 739/2 His goodly doctrine interlaced here and there by the waye. **1551** T. WILSON *Logike* 21 In the seconde Proposition, there bee certaine Negatives enterlaced. **1593** SHAKS. *Lucr.* 1390 Here and there the Painter interlaces Pale cowards marching on with trembling paces. **1598** GRENEWEY *Tacitus' Ann.* I. iii. (1622) 6 Yet he interlaced some things among, touching his attire and behauiour. *a* **1677** BARROW *Serm.* Wks. 1687 I. vi. 77 That we do with all our occupations and all occurrences interlace devout ejaculations of prayer and praise.

4. To cross, vary, or diversify a thing *with* interwoven or intermixed elements; to intersperse, mingle, or mix *with*. Chiefly *transf.* and *fig.*

1531 ELYOT *Gov.* III. xxv. (1880) II. 398 Admytte that some histories be interlaced with leasynges. **1594** ? GREENE *Selimus* Wks. 1881–3 XIV. 270 There our ioyes are interlaced with feares. **1611** CORYAT *Crudities* 335 Faire pillars of blacke marble, interlaced with pretty white vaines. **1634** SIR T. HERBERT *Trav.* 61 Mosaicke worke, enterlaced with Arabian characters out of their Alcoran. **1699** DAMPIER *Voy.* II. III. 109 Yet is it interlaced with pleasant Valleys and large Plains. *c* **1730** BURT *Lett. N. Scotl.* (1818) I. 157 When the natives drink plentifully of it [common ale], they interlace it with brandy or usky. **1827** CARLYLE *Misc., Richter* (1872) I. 10 Interlaced with..quips, puns, and even oaths. **1872** BLACK *Adv. Phaeton* xxix, Beautiful green meadows interlaced with streams.

5. *intr.* for *refl.* **a.** To cross each other intricately, as if woven together; to lie between each other in opposite directions, like the fingers of the two interlaced hands.

1596 SPENSER *F.Q.* V. iii. 23 As roses did with lilies interlace. **1848** CARPENTER *Anim. Phys.* 21 Tissue consisting of fibres crossing and interlacing in every direction. **1855** LYNCH *Rivulet* LXXXV. vii, As skies are seen more sweetly clear Through boughs that interlace. **1895** J. WINSOR *Mississ. Basin* 179 Where the sources of the Roanoke and James interlace with those of the Kanawha.

†**b.** To mix oneself up, to become entangled or involved. *Obs. rare.*

c **1380** WYCLIF *Sel. Wks.* III. 164 If freres enterlasen, þo synne is more perilouse. **1602** WARNER *Alb. Eng.* XI. lxi. (1612) 271 Yeat interlace we shall among the loue of her and him.

6. *Television.* (*trans.*) To present (scanning lines) so that alternate lines of a picture form one sequence and are followed by the intervening lines in a second sequence; to present (dots) similarly so that several fields of regularly spaced dots go to form each picture. Also, to combine (two or more fields), or form (a picture or raster), in this way. Freq. as pa. pple. Cf. also INTERLACED *ppl. a.*

1927 M. LATOUR *Brit. Pat. 267,513*, The elements of the image transmitted by each system AB are..the ones within the others, or interlacing each other. **1936** [see FRAME *sb.* 12 c]. **1955** D. G. FINK *Color Television Standards* iii. 92 Dot interlace, in which minute dots..of different primary colors, produced adjacent to each other during the color-scanning process, are interlaced in various repeated and prearranged sequences. **1966** G. H. HUTSON *Television Receiver Theory* I. xii. 187 If these conditions are met the resulting raster must be interlaced. **1967** [see FIELD *sb.* 16 d]. **1972** *Sci. Amer.* Sept. 132/2 Every other line is scanned in just under a sixtieth of a second and the missing lines are interlaced in the next sixtieth of a second.

interlace (ˈɪntəleɪs), *sb.* [f. the vb.] The action or result of interlacing.

1904 GOODCHILD & TWENEY *Technol. & Sci. Dict.* 312/2 *Interlace.* This relates to the crossing of warp and weft, the order of the interlacing in a weave prescribing the structure of the cloth. **1923** *Daily Mail* 19 Mar. 1 The upturned brim has fancy straw interlace, giving a ribbon effect. **1936** A. W. CLAPHAM *Romanesque Archit.* iii. 61 The acanthus-scroll.. commonly has a stem composed of three strands, a trick of the carver which was probably inherited from the universal use of the triple strand interlace in Italy at an earlier date. **1948** N. GRAY in *Papers Brit. Sch. Rome* XVI. 116 The cross is carved with a foliage pattern on one side..and an interlace

on the other. **1973** *Country Life* 29 Nov. 1761/1 Strap-work and interlace patterns on plain velvet.

b. *spec.* in *Television* (see INTERLACE *v.* 6).

1936 O. S. PUCKLE tr. *M. von Ardenne's Television Reception* i. 5 The line component and the frame component of scanning are regularly recurrent, the interlace being derived from the fractional relationship between line and frame frequencies. **1937** *Electronics* June 15/2 At the end of each half-frame or 'interlace', the frame synchronizing impulses are imposed in a similar manner. **1961** *Listener* 2 Nov. 725/3 The television service reopened on June 7, 1946, using the pre-war system (405-lines, 25 pictures per second with 2:1 interlace, positive modulation and AM sound). **1966** G. H. HUTSON *Television Receiver Theory* I. xii. 192 The alternate scanning field is ½ line late in starting. This causes very poor interlace.

inter'laced (ɪntə'leɪst, 'ɪntəleɪst), *ppl. a.*

a. In senses of the vb. spec. in *Her.* see quot. 1766 and cf. INTERFRETTED.

1593 Q. ELIZ. *Boeth.* IV. met. vi. 97 So Interlaced looue renewes The eternall courses all. **1598** FLORIO, *Intercalare uerso,..a verse interlaced.* **1766** PORNY *Heraldry* Gloss., *Interlaced*..is applied in blazoning Annulets, Rings, Crescents, etc., that are linked together in the same manner as are the links of a chain. **1830** R. KNOX *Béclard's Anat.* 51 Bundles of parallel or interlaced threads. **1874** BOUTELL *Arms & Arm.* x. 189 True mail armour of interlaced rings.

b. *Television.* Applied to scanning in which the lines or the dots of the picture are interlaced (see INTERLACE *v.* 6), so that each is built up from two or more fields; composed or combined in this way.

1935 R. W. HUTCHINSON *Television Up-to-Date* v. 131 It has been suggested that a system of interlaced scanning, as it is called, should be adopted: in this, lines 1, 3, 5, 7, etc., would first be scanned, and then the intermediate ones, 2, 4, 6, 8, and so on. **1936** O. S. PUCKLE tr. *M. von Ardenne's Television Reception* i. 21 With the resulting 50 pictures per second, the flicker of the interlaced picture is almost entirely avoided. **1953** H. A. CHINN *Television Broadcasting* i. 5 In order to conserve bandwidth without sacrificing freedom from flicker, the standard television system employs a system of interlaced scanning. **1961** *New Scientist* 26 Jan. 199/3 The British system transmits 25 complete pictures per second, forming each from 405 horizontal lines laid down in two interlaced sequences of 202½ lines each.

Hence **inter'lacedly** *adv.*, in an interlaced manner.

a **1641** BP. MOUNTAGU *Acts & Mon.* (1642) An infallible concatenation of causes depending interlacedly one upon another. **1830** T. ROSCOE *Tourist Switz. & Italy* 154 These were to be declaimed, as it may be termed, interlacedly; that is, a piece of Noah, a piece of Cæsar, and a piece of Pantaloon.

interlacement (ɪntə'leɪsmənt). Also 7 enter-. [f. INTERLACE *v.* + -MENT. Cf. F. *entrelacement* (12th c. in Hatz.-Darm.).]

1. The action of interlacing or condition of being interlaced; alternate crossing of threads, lines, or branches; also *concr.*, an interlaced arrangement or structure.

1603 FLORIO *Montaigne* II. xii. (1632) 300 The wheelings, the windings, and enterlacements of the celestiall bodies. **1831** R. KNOX *Cloquet's Anat.* 421 Whence there results an interlacement resembling mat-work. **1851** CARPENTER *Man. Phys.* (ed. 2) 324 Formed..by the interlacement or anastomosis of their minutest branches. **1881** W. G. PALGRAVE *Phra-Bat* in *Macm. Mag.* XLV. 33 The dense interlacement of the bamboo thicket.

2. Complicated or intricate intermingling.

1872 GEO. ELIOT *Middlem.* IV. 202 There might be such an interlacement of poor Peter's former and latter intentions. **1891** *Spectator* 4 Apr., Below Cape de Verde.. the interlacement of nationalities is exceedingly complicated.

interlacery (ɪntə'leɪsərɪ). [f. INTERLACE *v.* + -ERY: cf. *tracery.*] Something interlaced; interlaced threads, tendrils, etc.; interlaced work.

1865 *Reader* 28 Oct. 480/1 That produced in the boggy districts was full of minute fibrous interlacery. **1895** CLARK RUSSELL *Good Ship Mohock* viii. 176, I stood behind the interlacery of the main shrouds watching them.

interlacing (ɪntə'leɪsɪŋ), *vbl. sb.* [f. INTERLACE *v.* + -ING¹.] The action of the verb INTERLACE; interlacement, intermingling.

1532 MORE *Confut. Barnes* VIII. Wks. 747/1 He laboureth with interlacing of his heresies and hys rayling, to make such confusion in the matter. **1593** NASHE *Christ's T.* (1613) 146 Your pinches, your purles, your floury iaggings, superfluous enterlacings. **1685** COTTON tr. *Montaigne* II. 354 To range the carriages and interlacings of the heavenly bodies of differing colours about the axis of necessity, according to Plato. **1809** MALKIN *Gil Blas* VII. xii. ¶ 12 With a copious interlacing of additions and corrections. **1875** FORTNUM *Majolica* ix. 76 Pieces having a decoration..with interlacings and other ornaments in manganese and blue. **1927** *Jrnl. Genetics* XVIII. 182 There is interlacing of the chromatids. **1935** R. W. HUTCHINSON *Television Up-to-Date* v. 132 Both Baird and E.M.I. have experimented with interlacing. **1936** *Proc. IRE* XXIV. 573 The difference between the amplitude of the alternate discharges is somewhat critical for perfect interlacing. **1974** J. ROBINSON *Penguin Bk. Sewing* xii. 328/2 Interlacing..consists of horizontal stitches interlaced with the herring bone stitch.

inter'lacing, *ppl. a.* [f. as prec. + -ING².] That interlaces; crossing intricately; intertwining, interweaving, intermingling.

1738 GLOVER *Leonidas* II. Poems (1810) 31/2 Pomegranates, purple mulberry, and fig, From interlacing branches mix their hues And scents. **1835-6** TODD *Cycl. Anat.* I. 250/1 Composed of a series of interlacing fibres. **1842-76** GWILT *Encycl. Archit.* Gloss., *Interlacing Arches*, semicircular arches as in an arcade, the mouldings of which intersect each other, as frequently seen in Norman architecture. **1884** *Athenæum* 16 Aug. 216/3 The interlacing sculpture met their eye in many of the churches and churchyards.

interlacustrine (ɪntələ'kʌstrɪn), *a.* [f. INTER- 4 a + LACUSTRINE *a.*] Lying between lakes.

1900 *Geogr. Jrnl.* Feb. 179 This region forms part of the great interlacustrine plateau. **1958** E. WINTER in Middleton & Tait *Tribes without Rulers* 158 The other Interlacustrine kingdoms of which the best known is Buganda.

inter'laid, *ppl. a.* [f. INTERLAY *v.* + -ED¹.] Laid or inserted between; interposed.

1856 KANE *Arct. Expl.* I. ix. 92 *note*, The cliffs were of.. limestone, with interlaid and inferior sandstones.

interlamellar (ɪntə'læmɪlə(r)), *a. Zool.* [INTER- 4 a.] Situated between or among lamellæ (*e.g.* of the gills).

1846 DANA *Zooph.* iv. (1848) 46 Opposite interlamellar spaces in the visceral cavity. **1888** ROLLESTON & JACKSON *Anim. Life* 130 The space between the two lamellae, i.e. outer and inner, of each gill, is the 'interlamellar' space, and examination shows that it is crossed by numerous 'interlamellar' junctions.

interlamellation (ɪntəlæmɪ'leɪʃən). [INTER- 2 a.] A placing, or being placed, in alternate lamellæ or layers.

1879 RUTLEY *Study Rocks* x. 103 An admixture or interlamellation of albite and orthoclase.

interlaminar (ɪntə'læmɪnə(r)), *a. Anat.* [INTER- 4 a.] **1.** Situated between laminæ or plates.

1831 R. KNOX *Cloquet's Anat.* 186 Yellow ligaments.. occupy the interlaminar spaces of the vertebræ.

2. Situated or occurring between the reinforcing layers or components of a laminate or composite.

1963 *Symposium Standards for Filament-Wound Reinforced Plastics, 1962* (Amer. Soc. Testing Materials STP 327) 17 In this method, a bending test is conducted with a short span to induce failure in horizontal ('interlaminar') shear. **1964** *Plastics Inst. Trans. & Jrnl.* XXXII. 292/2 Creep effects in the composite thus become limited principally to the resin interlaminar planes. **1966** K. L. LOWENSTEIN in L. Holliday *Composite Materials* v. 200 The consensus of opinion is that failure [of composites] occurs by interlaminar shear, *i.e.* fracture of resin between reinforcing fibres followed, as a secondary step, by the fracture of individual fibres themselves. **1971** *New Scientist* 8 July 70/1 Composites of [carbon] fibres in resin having the expected high tensile strength and modulus..had a low interlaminar shear strength of only 2500 lb/sq in.

interlaminate (ɪntə'læmɪneɪt), *v.* [INTER- 1 a.] *trans.* To insert in or between alternate laminæ or plates.

1816 W. SMITH *Strata Ident.* 17 Clay, interlaminated with stony nodules. **1849** DANA *Geol.* iii. (1850) 241 Interlaminated with thin calcareous seams or plates.

Hence **interlami'nation**, the action of interlaminating; also, an interlaminated formation.

1864 in WEBSTER. **1876** PAGE *Adv. Text-bk. Geol.* xiii. 218 With occasional interlaminations of fissile grey sandstone. **1879** RUTLEY *Study Rocks* x. 90 Orthoclase and albite occur together in infinitesimal interlaminations of the two species.

interlanguage ('ɪntəlæŋgwɪdʒ), *sb.* [INTER- 2 a.] An artificial auxiliary language. Also *attrib.*

1927 E. S. PANKHURST *Delphos* vii. 86 The Interlanguage cannot be the creation of Governments. **1928** O. JESPERSEN *Internat. Lang.* I. 45 The Delegation and the Ido academy have left their indelible mark on the inter-language movement. **1929** T. C. MACAULAY in *S.P.E. Tract* (1930) XXXIV. 462 Interlanguage will have no idiomatic tradition of its own. **1960** E. DELAVENAY *Introd. Machine Transl.* iv. 47 Georges Mounin rightly distinguishes between pseudolanguages—of which Esperanto is the classic example—intended to be *speakable*, and inter-languages, designed for use as auxiliary languages, such as the *interlingua* of Peano or that of Gode and Blair.

inter'language, *a.* [INTER- 5.] Between or relating to two languages.

1953 U. WEINREICH *Lang. in Contact* i. 8 Interference resulting from such inter-language identification. **1964** E. A. NIDA *Towards Sci. Transl.* vii. 147 In an attempt to describe these interlanguage and intercultural factors, we must reckon with differences of time.

interlap (ɪntə'læp), *v.* [f. INTER- 1 b + LAP *v.*] *intr.* To lap over, or rest one upon another. Hence **inter'lapping** *vbl. sb.* and *ppl. a.*

1889 *Electric Rev.* 8 Mar. 281/2 In case of any serious accident, the whole of the mains can, by one turn of a screw, be disconnected from the dynamos, the interlapping pieces all dropping out. **1892** *Eng. Illustr. Mag.* Sept. 886 The logs were laid generally with the small ends towards the end of the raft, and interlapped so as to give strength. **1895** *Treas. Relig. Th.* (N.Y.) Oct. 443 Any classification..is attended with difficulty because of the variations and interlappings.

inter'lapidate, *v. nonce-wd.* [f. L. *inter-* between + L. *lapid-em* stone: cf. *interfoliate.*] *trans.* To fit in between each other like stones in a building.

1814 COLERIDGE *Let. to Justice Fletcher* 2 Nov. in *Ess. Own Times* (1850) 698 Combinations of the mechanics and lower craftsmen..interlapidated and cemented as they all are, each in the club of his own trade.

'interlapse. *rare*⁻¹. [INTER- 2 a.] The lapse of time between any two events; an intervening space (of time).

a **1658** HARVEY (J.), These dregs are calcined into such salts, which, after a short interlapse of time, produce coughs.

†inter'laqueate, *a. Sc. Obs. rare*⁻¹. [ad. med.L. *interlaqueāt-us* (Du Cange), f. *inter-* (INTER- 1 b) + *laqueātus* entangled, after F. *entrelacé.*] Entangled.

1560 ROLLAND *Crt. Venus* I. 419 [Thy] minde it is sa Interlaqueat..in the Net of lufe Prophane.

interlard (ɪntə'lɑːd), *v.* Also 6-7 enter-. [a. F. *entrelarder* (12th c. in Hatz.-Darm.), f. *entre-* (INTER- 1 a) + *larder* to LARD.]

†1. *trans.* To mix with alternate layers of fat: said in the passive voice of natural intermixture; in *Cookery*, to insert strips of fat, bacon, etc. into (lean meat) before cooking; to lard. *Obs.*

a **1533** LD. BERNERS *Gold. Bk. M. Aurel.* (1546) I v b, Flesshe oughte not to be..so fatte that it cloie the stomacke: but meane and enterlarded. **1555** EDEN *Decades* 26 Peacockes and phesauntes [lose their taste] except they bee interlarded beefore they bee rosted. **1622** DRAYTON *Poly-olb.* xxvi. (1748) 371 Whose [the salmon's] grain doth rise in flakes with fatness interlarded. *c* **1720** W. GIBSON *Farrier's Guide* I. iv. (1738) 50 These Muscles are interlarded with a considerable deal of Fat. **1741** *Compl. Fam. Piece* I. ii. 153 Take a good Buttock of Beef, interlarded with great Lards rolled up in Savoury Spice and sweet Herbs.

†b. To intermix (fat) in lean meat. *Obs.*

1649 *Alcoran* 88 We forbad the Jews to eat..of the fat of beasts, except of such as is interlarded in the flesh.

†2. *transf.* To intermingle or intermix (a thing) *with* alternate or inserted layers or portions of something else. *Obs.*

1632 LITHGOW *Trav.* VIII. 369 Grey Marble, interlarded with white Alabaster. **1777** STEWART in *Phil. Trans.* LXVII. 487 It was found throughout interlarded (if I may be allowed the expression) with the purest metal.

3. *fig.* To diversify by intermixture or interjection; to mix, mingle, or intersperse *with.*

1563-87 FOXE *A. & M.* (1596) 920/1 To interlard a tale of untruth, with some parcell of truth nowe and then among. **1590** GREENE *Mourn. Garm.* (1616) 1 The gifts of the minde so interlarded with the excellence of all vertues. **1670** G. H. tr. *Hist. Cardinals* II. III. 196 [He] enterlards the fury of his heart..with a counterfeit modesty and goodness. *a* **1694** TILLOTSON *Serm.* xxii. (1742) II. 81 When men use to interlard all their careless talk with oaths. **1708** J. PHILIPS *Cyder* II. (R.), They interlard their native drinks with choice Of strongest brandy. **1752** FIELDING *Amelia* I. iii, A volley of dreadful oaths, interlarded with some language, not proper to be repeated. **1820** SCOTT *Monast.* xiv, The high-flown and ornate compliments with which the gallant knight of the sixteenth century interlarded his conversation. **1841** LEVER *C. O'Malley* xxxv. 191 He would interlard his meditation by passages of scripture. **1872** MINTO *Eng. Prose Lit.* Introd. 29 There is a tolerably unanimous public opinion against interlarding English composition with foreign words.

b. Said of the ingredient.

c **1654** FLECKNOE *Relat. 10 Yrs. Trav.* 105 Latin..rather serves to *interlard* other Languages, than to make an intire meal of discourse. **1695** CONGREVE *Love for L.* IV. xix, Lying is a figure of speech that interlards the greatest part of my conversation. **1867** MISS BRADDON *Aur. Floyd* x. 97 Slangy technicalities of the turf had interlarded the poor girl's brain-sick babble.

†4. To interpolate, interpose. *Obs.*

1545 RAYNOLD *Byrth Mankynde* 6 Plenty of flesshe enterlardyng and entermyngling it selfe with the muskles. **1565** JEWEL *Repl. Harding* (1611) 456 Here M. Harding.. hath interlarded a long Fable of his owne. **1589** PUTTENHAM *Eng. Poesie* II. xiii[i] (Arb.) 136 Your fourth [verse] of one bissillable, and two monosillables interlarded. **1601** HOLLAND *Pliny* XXXIV. viii. II. 497, I will not ouerpasse the multitude of others, but interlard (as it were) and disperse them among. **1668** CULPEPPER & COLE *Barthol. Anat.* I. xxxvi. 80 An innumerable company of..Veins, and Arteries, among which Blood out of the Vessels seems to be shed and interlarded. **1755** CARTE *Hist. Eng.* IV. 28 Boyish speeches in which he often interlarded the words O tempora, O mores.

†5. To smear internally (*with* something). *Obs.*

1632 LITHGOW *Trav.* v. 182 Jarres..whose insides are all interlarded with pitch to preserve the earthen vessells.

Hence **inter'larded** *ppl. a.*, **inter'larding** *vbl. sb.*

1581 MULCASTER *Positions* xxxvii. (1887) 157 With some enterlarding of towardnes and learning. *a* **1648** DIGBY *Closet Opened*, Shred half a pound of the belly-part of interlarded Bacon. **1759** STERNE *Tr. Shandy* II. v, He was voluble;—the eternal interlardings of 'your Honour', with the respectfulness of Corporal Trim's manner. **1845** *Woman's Will* III. i, Hell and the devil! will you never have done with these interlardings?

†'interlard, *sb. Obs. rare.* [f. prec. vb.] The fat or *omentum* of a beast.

c **1440** *Promp. Parv.* 262/2 Interlarde, of fet flesche, *abdomen.* **1557** *Primer*, *Lauds* A viij, My soule shal be satisfied as it wer with interlarde and fatnesse.

†interlar'dation. *Obs. rare*⁻¹. [f. INTERLARD *v.* + -ATION.] The action of interlarding; something interlarded.

1728 MORGAN *Algiers* I. vi. 207 In spite of my frequent Interlardations, I fear some Epicureans may think [this Preamble] dry Feeding.

interlardment (ɪntə'lɑːdmənt). [f. as prec. + -MENT.] = prec.

1748 RICHARDSON *Clarissa* (1811) III. xiv. 89 This gives me an appetite to oblige thee by interlardment. **1852** R. S. SURTEES *Sponge's Sp. Tour* xxvi, A..cap—curious in microscopic punctures and cherry-coloured ribbon interlardments.

interlatitudinal, -laudation, -layer: see INTER- *pref.*

interlay (ɪntə'leɪ), *v.* Pa. t. and pple. -laid. [f. INTER- 1 a + LAY *v.*]

1. *trans.* To lay between or among; to interpose.

1609 DANIEL *Civ. Wars* IV. lxx, This Chayne of Nature might be interlay'd Betweene the Father and his high intents. **1624** WOTTON *Archit.* in *Reliq.* (1651) 225 That certain Courses or Ledges of more strength then the rest, be interlayed. **1850** MRS. BROWNING *Hector in Gard.* vii, And the meadow turf, cut finely, Round them laid and interlaid.

2. To furnish or vary *with* something placed or inserted between; also *fig.*

1613 PURCHAS *Pilgrimage* (1614) 457 The walls of red marble shined like fire, interlaid with gold. **1631** BRATHWAIT *Eng. Gentlew.* (1641) 289 The one interlayeth affection with too much passion, the other with too much dissimulation. **1652–62** HEYLIN *Cosmogr.* III. (1673) 79/1 Composed of Marble, and everywhere enterlaid with Gold.

interlay ('ɪntəleɪ), *sb.* [Back-formation f. the vb.] That which is intercalated; esp. in *Printing.*

1901 *Westm. Gaz.* 10 Oct. 2/2 A delicate Chantilly lace mounted over cream satin, with an interlay of cream chiffon. **1940** *Chambers's Techn. Dict.* 453/2 *Interlay*, paper inserted between a printing plate and its mount in order to raise the plate to type height. **1948** H. MISSINGHAM *Student's Guide Commercial Art* II. 82 *Interlay*, paper placed between the mount and the metal plate to raise those portions of the block, representing usually the dark tones and solids.

interlayer ('ɪntə,leɪə(r)), *sb.* and *a.* [f. INTER- + LAYER *sb.*] **A.** *sb.* [INTER- 2 b.] A layer situated between two other layers.

1936 *Brit. Pat.* 453,578, The polymer..is..dried in vacuo and may be mixed with a suitable amount of an appropriate plasticiser..compressed to form a block either of rectangular or of cylindrical shape, and..cut into sheets ready for use as a laminated safety glass interlayer. **1960** *Nature* 16 July 262/1 The laboratory introduction of aluminium interlayers into montmorillonite and vermiculite produced clays that resembled the chloritized soil clays in their 14-Å spacing. **1962** L. S. SASIENI *Princ. & Pract. Optical Dispensing* xiii. 329 The three laminae are joined under heat and pressure, and if one or both of the layers of glass are broken by impact..the pieces of glass remain adherent to the interlayer. **1972** *Soil Sci.* CXIII. 172/2 It was anticipated that the removal of interlayer liquid in K-saturated illite might be similar to montmorillonite and vermiculite, where entire interlayers are usually lost abruptly.

B. *adj.* [INTER- 5.] Situated or occurring between two layers.

1956 *Nature* 4 Feb. 239/2 A flake of magnesium vermiculite, which has been partially dehydrated to the phase containing single sheets of interlayer water molecules. **1970** *Proc. Soil Sci. Soc. Amer.* XXXIV. 201/1 Interlayer swelling of the soil clays.

interleaf ('ɪntəliːf), *sb.* Pl. leaves. [INTER- 2 b.]

1. An extra leaf inserted between the regular leaves of a book, usually blank to receive notes or additional matter; also *transf.* matter such as is written on such a leaf.

1741 RICHARDSON *Pamela* lix, My little book of select devotions, with my notes in the inter-leaves. **1832** R. H. FROUDE *Rem.* (1838) I. 257 All his interleaves and margins are scribbled over with lug-sails. **1856** MASSON *Ess., Story* 1770. 199 Here the reader must permit me a little Essay or disquisitional Interleaf on the character and writings of Chatterton. **1898** S. COLVIN *Advt. Flor. Pict. Chron.* 2/1 His text..comprises 42 pages of Introduction and 79 Interleaves facing the drawings.

2. *Bot.* A leaf developed between the ordinary leaves of a plant.

1868 *Rep. U.S. Commissioner Agric.* (1869) 573 The stunting of the shoots and grapes, the curling and premature fall of the leaves, the development of interleaves, and cracking and drying of the berries.

interleaf (ɪntə'liːf), *v.* [f. prec.] = INTERLEAVE *v.* Hence **inter'leafed** *ppl. a.*, **inter'leafing** *vbl. sb.*

1733 A. HILL *Let.* 24 Oct. Wks. 1753 I. 156, I will interleaf your part, if you send it me. **1739** —— in *Richardson's Corr.* (1804) I. 34 The interleafed volumes of Plain Dealers and Prompters. **1876** ROCK *Text. Fabr.* ii. 8 The curious example of such gauzy interleafings in the manuscript of Theodulph. **1900** *Westm. Gaz.* 26 Jan. 10/2 He proposes to 'interleaf' his parliamentary duties with agreeable studies.

interleague (ɪntə'liːg), *v.* Now *rare.* Also 6 enter-. [f. INTER- 1 b + LEAGUE *v.* But perh. a perversion of the phrase *to enter league*: see quot. 1579.] *intr.* and *refl.* To enter into or form a league *with* another, or with each other.

[**1579** LYLY *Euphues* (Arb.) 49, I studied euer since my first comming to Naples to enter league with such a one as might direct my steps.] **1590** LODGE *Euphues' Gold. Leg.* (1880) M iv, See..howe Fortune and loue haue interleagued themselues to be..thy foes. **1593** NASHE *Christ's T.* (1613) 60 [He] there enter-leagued himselfe with Eleazar. **1606** MARSTON *Sophonisba* I. i. A iv b, So fearefully will I take vengeance: I'le interleague with Scipio.

Hence **inter'leagued** *ppl. a.*

1844 LYTTON tr. *Schiller's Poems & Ball., Fridolin* I. 86 Their strength the Fire, the Water gave, In interleagued endeavour.

interleave (ɪntə'liːv), *v.* [f. INTER- 1 a + LEAF *sb.*[1] (pl. *leaves*).]

1. *trans.* To insert leaves, usually blank, between the ordinary leaves of (a book).

1668 WOOD *Life* (O.H.S.) II. 140 Interleaving the book, he added to it [etc.]. **1712** ADDISON *Spect.* No. 547 ¶2 Having the two last volumes in large paper interleaved for her own private use. **1839** J. G. LOCKHART *Let.* in Smiles *Mem. J. Murray* (1891) II. xxxiv. 453 He is going to interleave his copy and annotate largely. **1874** BLACKIE *Self-Cult.* 21 The young student cannot begin too early the practice of interleaving certain books.

2. *transf.* and *fig.* To insert or introduce something at regular intervals between (things) or between the parts of (a thing). Const. *with.*

1822–56 DE QUINCEY *Confess.* (1862) 143 Any feasible plan for interleaving days of hardship with days of ease. **1861** H. R. REYNOLDS in *Life* vii. (1898) 176 We do vary and curtail and interleave the liturgy with free prayer and psalmody. **1878** A. H. GREEN, etc. *Coal* ii. 42 Towards the north..the rock becomes interleaved with shale and sandstone.

b. With inverted construction. Const. *in.*

1802 T. S. SURR *Splendid Misery* III. 49 The transparent *Fashions of London and Paris*..not unaptly interleaved in *Les Études de la Nature.*

interleaved (ɪntə'liːvd), *ppl. a.* [f. prec. + -ED[1].] Having (blank) leaves inserted.

1698 *Phil. Trans.* XX. 458 An interleav'd Catalogue in the Bodleian Library. **1787** SIR J. HAWKINS *Johnson* 175 An interleaved copy of Bailey's dictionary in folio he [Dr. Johnson] made the repository of the several articles. **1888** BURGON *Lives 12 Good Men* II. x. 263 An interleaved copy ..annotated throughout by himself.

interleaving (ɪntə'liːvɪŋ), *vbl. sb.* [f. as prec. + -ING[1].] The insertion of (blank) leaves; interfoliation.

1885 *Athenæum* 6 June 724/3 The usual plan is..to publish your inferior sketches in very large type with liberal interleaving. **1899** *Speaker* 30 Dec. 339/1 Pusey owned a Hebrew Bible with large folio interleavings.

inter-lend, *v.*: see INTER- *pref.* 1 b.

interlevel ('ɪntəlɛvəl). *Linguistics.* [INTER- 2 a.] A 'level' of language serving to relate other linguistic levels (see quots.).

1961 M. A. K. HALLIDAY in *Word* XVII. 269 Context is an interlevel in a different sense, since it relates language to something that is not language. **1963** R. M. W. DIXON *Ling. Sci. & Logic* i. 23 An interlevel will itself contain theories which will perform the necessary level-relating. **1964** R. H. ROBINS *Gen. Ling.* p. xix, Both treat phonology as an 'interlevel' serving to relate statements made at the level of grammar with those made at the level of phonetics. **1966** J. ELLIS in C. E. Bazell *In Memory of J. R. Firth* 79 This classification of levels is represented by the diagram showing the levels of substance form and situation and interlevels of phonology/graphology and context.

†**inter'libel**, *v.* *Obs.* *rare*$^{-0}$. [f. INTER- 1 b + LIBEL *v.*] *trans.* To libel (one another). Hence †**inter'libelling** *vbl. sb.*, libelling of one another.

a **1626** BACON *Ch. Controv.* in *Resuscit.* (1661) 165 My Lords of the Clergy have none Intelligence with this interlibelling.

inter-library: see INTER- *pref.* 5.

interlie, -ligamentary, -light, -lighten, -limitation: see INTER- *pref.*

interline (ɪntə'laɪn), *v.*[1] Also 5–6 enterlyne, 6–7 -line. [In sense 1 app. ME. ad. med.L. *interlīneāre* (1278 in Du Cange), f. *inter* between + *līnea* LINE *sb.*[1]; cf. OF. *entreligneure*, *interlineure* interlinear insertion (14th c. in Godef.; = med.L. *interlīneātūra*), F. *interligner* vb. (formerly *entreligner*, Cotgr.); also *interligne* and *entreligne* sb. (16th c. in Hatz.-Darm.). But sense 1 also comes close to that of the unconnected L. *interlinĕre* to smear between, write between, which the English word may have been taken by some to represent (cf. INTERLINEATE). Later senses are partly transferred from the first, partly derived from various senses of LINE *sb.*[1] and *v.*[1]]

1. *trans.* To insert additional words between the lines of (a written, esp. a legal, document). Chiefly *pass.*, const. *with.*

1421 *Will Hen. V* in *Rolls Parlt.* IV. 299/2, I have.. written hit in hast with myn owen hande, þus enterlynit and blotted as hit is. **1563** A. NOWELL in *Lett. Lit. Men* (Camden) 20 The coopie..was interlined and sumwhear blotted. **1598** KITCHIN *Courts Leet* (1675) 441 A Deed raced or interlined. **1658** WILLSFORD *Secrets Nat.* 198 The Printer ..is the lesse culpable, the Copy being much interlin'd. **1726** SHELVOCKE *Voy. round World* 32 Written by several hands, and interlin'd in a great many places. **1823** J. BADCOCK *Dom. Amusem.* 39 Write with ordinary ink on common topics, and interline this with the important secret intelligence meant to be conveyed.

fig. **1597** MIDDLETON *Wisd. Solomon* xvii. 16 But thou with sorrow interlines his song. *a* **1631** DONNE in *Select.* (1840) 51 Though he interline it with other studies..yet the text itself..will shine through and appear.

†**b.** To add interlineary glosses to. *Obs.*

1676 MARVELL *Mr. Smirke* 40 No man ought to cheat another though to the true beliefe: Not by Interlining the Scripture. Not by false Quotation of Scripture, or of a Father.

†**c.** To interpolate or extend (a narrative, etc.) with new matter. *Obs.*

1611 SPEED *Hist. Gt. Brit.* VII. xxi. §5. 301 With such lauish enlargements haue those Writers enterlined the deeds of Gods Saints. **1654** H. L'ESTRANGE *Chas. I* (1655) 208 Where the series of the story is not enterlined nor disturbed with matters independent, and of a different kind.

2. To insert (a word or words) between the lines in a written document; also, loosely, between word and word (quot. 1681).

1589 *Pappe w. Hatchet* C ij, To raze out good Greeke, and enterline bad Latine. **1671** F. PHILLIPS *Reg. Necess.* 399 The word Executor being interlined. **1681** STAIR *Inst. Law Scot.* IV. xlii. §19 Superinduction..of Monosyllabs or short words, as when *No* or *Not* is interlined, not between Line and Line,..but between word and word. **1875** STUBBS *Const. Hist.* III. xviii. 59 These words were found interlined in Richard's grant. **1882–3** SCHAFF *Encycl. Relig. Knowl.* I. 278/2 Words accidentally omitted were also placed in the margin, or interlined.

3. *absol.* or *intr.* **a.** To make interlinear insertions.

1576 FLEMING *Panopl. Epist.* 254 To interline here for necessitie, there for exornation. **1654** WHITLOCK *Zootomia* Pref. a v b, His fault that could never take..his Hand off, but was still mending, disliking, interlining. **1733** SWIFT *On Poetry* 88 Blot out, correct, insert, refine, Enlarge, diminish, interline. **1858** LD. ST. LEONARDS *Handy Bk. Prop. Law* xviii. 143 If you obliterate, interline, or make any other alteration in your will after it is executed, you must re-execute your will..as if it were an original will.

†**b.** To come between the lines. In quots. *fig.*

1633 G. HERBERT *Temple, Longing* ix, Indeed the world's thy book, Where all things have their lease assign'd: Yet a meek look Hath interlin'd. **1655** H. VAUGHAN *Silex Scint.* II. *White Sunday* x, As in night's gloomy page One silent star may interline.

†**4.** *trans.* To write or print in alternate lines. *Obs.*

1692 LOCKE *Educ.* Wks. 1812 IX. 159 By this way of interlining Latin and English one with another.

†**5.** To mark with lines, esp. of various colours.

1572 BOSSEWELL *Armorie* II. 61 This serpente is but halfe a foote of lengthe, and enterlined with white spottes. **1657** *Lust's Domin.* I. i. in Hazl. *Dodsley* XIV. 99 For each contracted frown A crooked wrinkle interlines my brow. **1661** LOVELL *Hist. Anim. & Min.* 62 Their skinnes..being white, spotted, and changeably interlined like diverse flowers.

†**6.** To place or insert something in lines between or among (something else). Const. *with.*

1600 DYMMOK *Ireland* (1843) 32 Vpon eyther syde of the vauntguarde..marched wings of shott, enterlyned with pikes. **1655** H. VAUGHAN *Silex Scint.* I. Pref. (1858) 7 They are interlined with many virtuous and some pious mixtures. **1660** T. WATSON in Spurgeon *Treas. Dav.* Ps. ci. 1 Mercy interlined with judgment.

†**b.** With the thing placed between as object.

1724 DE FOE *Mem. Cavalier* (1840) 143, I saw the foot.. interlined among the horse. **1736** LEDIARD *Life Marlborough* I. 498 The Enemy being re-inforced with some Squadrons, and having interlined some Infantry with them, moved again towards the Allies.

Hence **inter'lined** *ppl. a.*

1601 CHESTER *Love's Mart.* xciii, The white-veind enterlin'd-stone Achates. **1828** WEBSTER s.v., An interlined word..an interlined manuscript.

interline (ɪntə'laɪn), *v.*[2] Also 5 enterlyne. [f. INTER- 1 a + LINE *v.*[2]] *trans.* To insert a second or inner lining between the stuff and ordinary lining of (a garment).

1480 *Wardr. Acc. Edw. IV* (1830) 148 A doublet..lined with Holand clothe and interlined with busk. **1483** *Wardr. Acc.* in *Antiq. Rep.* (1807) I. 41 A doublet of grene satyn enterlyned with..busk, and lyned with..Holand cloth. **1690** C. HATTON in *H. Corr.* (Camden) II. 160 Let yᵉ linning of yᵉ cloake be sent to yᵉ taylor to interline yᵉ coat. **1894** *Chicago Advance* 6 Sept., Skirts of dresses are now so generally lined and interlined, that they become too heavy for comfort..if made of weighty material.

†**interline**, *sb.*[1] *Obs.* *rare*$^{-1}$. In 6 enterlyne. [f. prec.] Inner lining.

c **1570** *Pride & Lowl.* (1841) 19 Of silk it had a costly enterlyne.

interline ('ɪntə,laɪn), *sb.*[2] [INTER- 2 b.] An intermediate line.

1721 BAILEY, An *Interline.* **1886** G. M. CRAWFORD in *Fortn. Rev.* July 11 There is a network of wrinkles at the temple, and lines and interlines about the brow and side of the nose.

interline (ɪntə'laɪn), *a.* [f. INTER- 5 + LINE *sb.*[2]] Of or pertaining to transport: using more than one route, service, etc.

1946 T. C. BIGHAM *Transportation* iii. 96 Service may be local or interline. **1957** *Encycl. Brit.* XVIII. 940 (*heading*) Joint or interline rates. **1969** *Jane's Freight Containers 1968–69* 48/1 The New York Port District may be likened to the centre of a web of gleaming steel rails..of ten long-haul railroads which, through interline connections, serve the entire nation, Canada and Mexico. **1970** *Daily Tel.* 30 June 24 Logically the first flight after the official connecting time would be the correct interline connection.

interlineal (-ˈlɪniːəl), *a.* [INTER- 4 a. Cf. obs. F. *interlineal* (1584 in Godef.).]

†**1.** = INTERLINEAR A. 1. *Obs.*

1526 *Pilgr. Perf.* (W. de W. 1531) 238 In this commaundement, as yᵉ glose interlineal sayth, is understande & forbydden [etc.]. **1612** BRINSLEY *Lud. Lit.* 236 If you take the ordinary interlineall Translation. **1687** A. LOVELL tr. *Thevenot's Trav.* II. 106 Several Alcorans Translated in Persian, nevertheless that is but an interlineal Translation, word for word, and without any Sence. **1826** SYD. SMITH *Wks.* (1869) 523 Whether very close interlined translations are helps in learning a language.

2. Disposed in alternate lines.

1851 RUSKIN *Stones Ven.* I. xxvi. §2 The merely ocular charm of interlineal opposition of colour.

Hence **interˈlineally** *adv.*

1612 BRINSLEY *Lud. Lit.* 240 The Greeke text is set downe both in Greek Characters, and also in Latine letters interlineally, directly ouer the head of the Greek words.

interlinear (-ˈlɪniːə(r)), *a.* and *sb.* Also 5 -liniare, 6 -lyniare. [ad. med.L. *interlīneār-is*, f. *inter* between + *līnea* LINE: cf. LINEAR; perh. immed. ad. F. *interlinéaire* (earlier *entrelinaire*; 13–14th c. in Hatz.-Darm.).]

A. *adj.* **1.** Written or printed between the lines.

Interlinear Gloss, Anselm's gloss on the Vulgate, placed in MSS. between the lines of the Latin text, while the *Ordinary Gloss* by Walafrid Strabo occupied the top and side margins, and the commentary of Nicholas de Lyra filled the lower part of the page. ***interlinear system*** (see HAMILTONIAN *a.* a. and quots. there).

c **1440** *Jacob's Well* 267 þe glose interliniare seyth, þat it is noȝt worthy god to be mercyfull to hym þat is cruel & vnmercyfull. **1532** MORE *Confut. Barnes* VIII. Wks. 758/2 He shall see that Lire, and the ordinarye glose, and the interlyniare glose also, doe declare [etc.]. **1625** S. WARD in *Abp. Ussher's Lett.* (1686) 330 He shewed me the Psalter in Hebrew MS. interlinear with a Latin Translation. **1774** WARTON *Hist. Eng. Poetry* (1840) I. Diss. ii. 103 At Trinity College in Cambridge there is an Hebrew Psalter with a Normanno-Gallic interlinear version. **1880** MUIRHEAD *Gaius* Introd. 11 He has often incorporated in his text what ..were merely marginal or interlinear glosses.

fig. **1812** CRABBE *Tales, Patron* 256 He sometimes saved his cash, By interlinear days of frugal hash.

2. Of a book: Having the same text in different languages printed in alternate lines. ? *Obs.*

1624 BEDELL *Lett.* vi. 107 In the Interlineary Bible set forth by the authoritie of King Philip..the Hebrew Text is reformed.

†**B.** *sb.* = INTERLINEATION. *Obs. rare*⁻¹.

1597–8 BP. HALL *Sat.* IV. i. 8 Scoring the margent with his blazing stars, And hundreth crooked interlinears.

interˈlinearily, *adv. rare.* [f. INTERLINEARY + -LY².] In an interlinear manner; between, or as between, the lines.

1627 BP. HALL *Gt. Impostor* Wks. 503 Certaine common principles..together with this law, interlinearily written in the tables of the heart. **1660** S. FISHER *Rusticks Alarm* Wks. (1679) 593 Doctrines..interlinearily refuted before.

interˈlinearly, *adv.* [f. INTERLINEAR + -LY².] = prec.

1846 in WORCESTER [citing Bp. Hall: but cf. quot. 1627 in prec. word, which Worcester has not entered]. Hence in mod. Dicts. **1906** *Hibbert Jrnl.* Apr. 682 A distinction that is indeed repeatedly suggested interlinearly in Mr Mallock's pages. **1955** C. E. WRIGHT in *Bald's Leechbook* Pref. 11 One manuscript, the later of the two, is a volume of small format ..(glossed interlinearly).

interlineary (ɪntəˈlɪniːərɪ), *a.* and *sb.* Also 8 *erron.* -liniary. [ad. med.L. *interlīneāris*: see INTERLINEAR and -ARY².]

A. *adj.* **1.** = INTERLINEAR 1.

1605 A. WILLET *Hexapla Gen.* 174 The interlinearie glosse. **1625** USSHER in *Lett. Lit. Men* (Camden) 133 That which hath the Saxon interlineary translation inserted, is the old Roman Psalterium. **1764** *Mem. G. Psalmanazar* 260, I contented myself with the interliniary versions of Pagninus, Arius Montanus, and other interpreters. **1865** *Athenæum* No. 1987. 725/3 An interlineary translation.

fig. *a* **1631** DONNE *Serm.* xlv. 455 Thou heardst two Sermons..besides thine interlineary week Lectures.

2. = INTERLINEAR 2. ? *Obs.*

1641 J. JACKSON *True Evang. T.* II. 94 The interlineary Bible of Arias Montanus concurres with our best and latest English Translation of K. James. **1642** FULLER *Holy & Prof. St.* III. xviii. 200 Christopher Plantin, by printing of his curious interlineary Bible in Antwerp.

B. *sb.* **1. a.** An interlinear version. **b.** *fig.* Something interposed like an interlinear gloss or translation.

[**1377** LANGL. *P. Pl.* B. XI. 297 If false latyn be in þe lettre þe lawe it inpugneth, Or peynted par enterlinarie [or] parceles ouer-skipped.] **1644** MILTON *Areop.* (Arb.) 64 The infinit helps of interlinearies, breviaries, synopses, and other loitering gear. **1670** BROOKS *Wks.* (1867) VI. 437 Sincerity is not a single grace, but the source of all graces, and the interlineary that must run through every grace.

2. *ellipt.* for **a.** the Latin interlinear version of the Bible by Arias Montanus (1568–72); **b.** the Interlinear Gloss on the Vulgate.

1659 BP. WALTON *Consid. Considered* 197 The Vulgar Latin..He esteems..the best in the whole collection, except the Interlineary. **1677** W. HUGHES *Man of Sin* II. i. 5 Lyranus and the Interlineary saith, Peter was crucified, not by the Romans, but by the Jews. **1685** POCOCK *Hosea* ii. 62 In the Interlineary we have *vilitatem ejus*, her vileness or baseness.

interlineate (-ˈlɪniːeɪt), *v. rare.* [f. ppl. stem of med.L. *interlīneāre* to INTERLINE *v.*¹ Cf. F. *interlinéer* (Littré). In mod. use perh. backformation from INTERLINEATION. By Cockeram app. connected with L. *interlinĕre*, f. *linĕre* to smear.] *trans.* and *absol.* = INTERLINE *v.*¹ Also *fig.*

[**1623** COCKERAM II, To Deface, *Interlineate.*] **1693** BEVERLEY *True St. Gosp. Truth* 18 And therefore is the Gospel..constantly interlineated with Christ, and his Spirit. **1875** LIGHTFOOT *Comm. Col. & Philem.* (1876) 280 When therefore the Greek text came to an end, the scribe's work was done, for he could no longer interlineate.

Hence **interˈlineated** *ppl. a.*

1877 W. S. GILBERT *Foggerty's Fairy* (1892) 260 The badly-scrawled, interleaved, and interlineated manuscript. **1882–3** SCHAFF *Encycl. Relig. Knowl.* I. 732 There appeared in 1640 the interlineated Psalter by John Spelman.

interlineation (-lɪniːˈeɪʃən). [n. of action f. prec.; see -ATION. Cf. F. *interlinéation* (Littré).] The insertion of a word or words between the lines of a writing; the word or words so inserted.

1692 *New Jersey Archives* (1881) II. 63 Before ye execution of ye originall Deed there was this interlineation inserted..betweene the Thirty eighth and thirty nynth Lines. **1698** G. HICKES in *Lett. Lit. Men* (Camden) 268 The manner of interlineation in many places shews that the Latin exemplars were first written. **1779–81** JOHNSON *L.P., Pope* Wks. IV. 32 A former copy, more varied, and more deformed with interlineations. **1877** DOWDEN *Shaks. Prim.* ii. 18 In Shakspere's will the only mention of his wife occurs in an interlineation.

interˈlinement. *rare.* [f. INTERLINE *v.*¹ + -MENT.] = INTERLINEATION.

1887 TENNANT *Notary's Man.* (ed. 5) 18 All blank spaces, erasures or interlinements duly verified by the notary in the margin thereof.

interˈliner. *rare.* [f. as prec. + -ER¹.] One who interlines.

1652 COLLINGES *Caveat for Prof.* xiv. (1653) 66 Papists, who are known depravers of Antiquity, and interliners of the Fathers.

Interlingua (ɪntəˈlɪŋgwə). Also **interlingua**. [f. INTER- + L. *lingua* tongue.] An artificially devised international language; *spec.* one promoted by the International Auxiliary Language Association of New York.

Several invented languages have been so named.

1922 A. L. GUÉRARD *Short Hist. Internat. Lang. Movement* v. 127 Those which, like Neutral, Ido, Interlingua, present themselves as the collective work of some 'Academy' bear..the mark of one master mind. **1927** E. S. PANKHURST *Delphos* iv. 38 'Interlingua is the standard of the insurrection against the routine of red tape and the tyranny of the ancient grammarian', thus wrote Kerchoffs, the first director of the Volapük Academy, in 1886. Giuseppe Peano..was presently to translate those words into a language scheme, and to adopt Interlingua as its title. **1928** O. JESPERSEN *Internat. Lang.* I. 45 This 'interlingua' is now employed in the publication of *Academia pro Interlingua.* **1953** J. B. CARROLL *Study of Lang.* iv. 127 A recent attempt to rationalize an artificial language by making maximal use of elements common to the most widely used natural languages is Interlingua, the work of the International Auxiliary Language Association of New York. **1955** *Sci. News Let.* 29 Jan. 79/2 Interlingua is a language composed of elements common to Spanish, Portuguese, French, Italian and other Romance languages. *Ibid.* 22 Oct. 258/2 Interlingua is no overnight creation of one linguist or even one group of linguists. No one sat down and theorized as to what an international language should be. Instead three decades ago, in 1924, an ambassador-to-be, a chemist, several radio engineers, several educators, editors and linguistic experts started a long and detailed inquiry into what an international language should be. **1956** J. WHATMOUGH *Lang.* iv. 59 An interlingua needs more than expletives and exclamations. **1960** [see INTERLANGUAGE *sb.*].

interlingual (-ˈlɪŋgwəl), *a.* [INTER- 4 a.] Between or relating to two languages. So **interˈlingually** *adv.*

In quot. 1931 *spec.* = of or relating to an artificial interlanguage (cf. INTERLANGUAGE *sb.*).

1854 R. G. LATHAM *Native Races Russian Emp.* 331 A question of international (or, rather, interlingual) copyright. **1862** *Sat. Rev.* XIV. 683/2 A practice of publishers in France, regarding interlingual literary matters. **1931** *Mod. Lang. Notes* XLVI. 18 Those who..have paid little attention to the interlingual movement. **1941** P. B. GOVE *Imaginary Voy. Prose Fiction* I. i. 8 The term is in some degree interlingual; occasionally to German writers it seems so apposite that it is not translated. **1951** W. EMPSON *Struct. Complex Words* xxi. 397 The confusion of translation equivalents is so great that many students have been warned against the interlingual dictionary. **1958** J. BERRY in J. A. Fishman *Readings Sociol. of Lang.* (1968) 741 Is it.. preferable to follow the orthographic practice of the trade language or that of an interlingual notational inventory such as The Africa Script? **1964** *Language* XL. 243 A minimum of inter-lingual interference. **1966** *Publ. Amer. Dial. Soc.* XLVI. 5 Whenever two interlingually identified forms are similar in sound and..meaning,..we have a homologous diamorph.

interlinguist (-ˈlɪŋgwɪst). [INTER- 2 a.] One versed in or an adherent of an interlanguage or interlanguages.

1928 O. JESPERSEN *Internat. Lang.* I. 12 What then we interlinguists are thinking of, is..what another inventor of an artificial language, Bollack, took as his motto: The second language to everybody. **1934** *N. & Q.* 8 Sept. 168/1 The true interlinguist..contends that a suitable auxiliary language must be an efficient medium for the communication of thought internationally. **1947** H. JACOB *Planned Auxiliary Lang.* I. i. 31 Leopold Einstein, a well-known interlinguist.

interlinguistic (-lɪŋˈgwɪstɪk), *a.* [INTER- 4 a.] **1.** Intermingling in speech.

1879 G. MEREDITH *Egoist* xviii. (1889) 167 Not a colloquy but a chasing, impossible to say which flies, which follows, or what the topic, so interlinguistic are they and rapidly counterchanging.

2. Of or relating to an interlanguage; between or relating to two languages.

1947 H. JACOB *Planned Auxiliary Lang.* III. xiv. 131 For the purposes of interlinguistic discussion they have been termed the naturalistic school and the autonomistic school. **1962** P. S. RAY in J. A. Fishman *Readings Sociol. of Lang.* (1968) 756 We might speak, instead of 'closure' and 'opening', of intra-linguistic and inter-linguistic uniformity.

interlinguistics (-lɪŋˈgwɪstɪks). [INTER- 2 a.] The study of the relationships of two or more languages, e.g. for the purpose of devising an interlanguage. Hence **interlinguiˈstician** = INTERLINGUIST.

1931 O. JESPERSEN in H. N. Shenton et al. *Internat. Communication* iii. 95 A new science is developing, Interlinguistics. **1934** *N. & Q.* 8 Sept. 168/1 The new or coming science of 'interlinguistics' is based upon certain fundamental principles of its own. **1938** *Encycl. Brit. Bk. of Yr.* 673/2 In recent years, interlinguisticians have been feeling their way to an average, as it were, of existing languages. **1947** H. JACOB *Planned Auxiliary Lang.* I. iii. 70 In interlinguistics the term *pleonastic endings* has been used to describe specific grammatical terminations. **1953** M. WEINREICH in J. A. Fishman *Readings Sociol. of Lang.* (1968) 394 As the raw material..is drawn from the most divergent sources: Persian.., Arabic, Slavic, Greek, several Romance languages, Teutonic, Jewish inter-linguistics should prove the comparativist's delight.

interlining (-ˈlaɪnɪŋ), *sb.* [INTER- 1 a: cf. INTERLINE *v.*²] An inner lining placed between the stuff and ordinary lining of a garment.

1881 C. C. HARRISON *Woman's Handiwork* I. 76 Lay the work upon the interlining of canton flannel, and turn the edges down. **1892** *Gentlew. Bk. Sports* I. 215, I have fine steel chainmail placed between two folds of doeskin, as interlining to my corduroy (fencing) jacket. **1959** [see IRON-ON *a.*]. **1974** J. ROBINSON *Penguin Bk. Sewing* v. 133 Interlining..used in tailoring..consists of the introduction of a section of tailor's canvas, Vilene, [etc.]..to stiffen the fabric.

interlining (-ˈlaɪnɪŋ), *vbl. sb.* [f. INTERLINE *v.*¹ + -ING¹.] = INTERLINEATION.

1467 *Paston Lett.* No. 575 II. 307, I had thought to have wretyn the letter..newe, by cause of the foule wrytyng and interlynyeng. **1586** A. DAY *Eng. Secretary* II. (1625) 128 Without any often blurring or enterlining. **1684** BAXTER *Pref. Hale's True Relig.* A iij, Only the Latin Verses, and an enterlining or two, are his own hand. **1735** SWIFT *Let.* Wks. 1824 XVIII. 277 You see, by my many blottings and interlinings, what a condition my head is in.

fig. **1651** JER. TAYLOR *Serm. for Year* I. viii. 92 Mingle it with false principles, and interlinings of our own.

†**interˈlining**, *ppl. a. Obs. rare.* [f. INTERLINE *v.*¹ + -ING².] That interlines: in quots. *fig.*

a **1658** CLEVELAND *Gen. Poems* (1677) 40 Reforming Tweed Hath sent us Runts even of her Churches breed, Lay interlining Clergy. **1661** R. W. *Conf. Charac., Pragm. Pulpit-filler* (1860) 83 So that I may justly..with illustrious Cleaveland, call him a lay interlining clergyman.

interlink (ɪntəˈlɪŋk), *v.* [INTER- 1 b.] *trans.* To link (two or more things) to one another, or (one thing) *with* something else. Often *fig.* Hence **interˈlinkage**; **interˈlinking** *vbl. sb.* and *ppl. a.*

1587 GOLDING *De Mornay* xi. (1617) 159 The interlinking of all things together. *a* **1626** DAVIES *Orchestra* (ad fin.), Many an incomparable lovely pair With hand-in-hand were interlinked seen. **1695** DRYDEN *Observ. Art Paint.* §69 These are two Chains which are interlink'd. **1761** KINNERSLEY in *Phil. Trans.* LIII. 95 Square iron nail rods, ..connected together by interlinking joints. **1809–10** COLERIDGE *Friend* (1837) II. 23 The interests of the proprietors were interlinked. **1863** MISS BRADDON *Eleanor's Vict.* II. iv. 54 With the memory of the past, was interlinked the face and figure of Launcelot Darrell. **1895** J. WINSOR *Mississ. Basin* 204 To find interlinking natural canals. **1904** *Westm. Gaz.* 3 Dec. 16/3 The phenomena to be seen in the living being, their inter-linkage, their apparent adaptation to an end. **1930** *Times* (Empire Press No.) 31 May p. xi/4 An Empire broadcasting system... A total problem that includes both interlinkage with the United States and [etc.]. **1957** V. W. TURNER *Schism & Continuity in Afr. Soc.* x. 301 The..values shared by all Ndembu are prominently displayed..in the ritual association of those who have suffered regardless of their kinship or other interlinkages.

interlink (ˈɪntəlɪŋk), *sb.* [INTER- 2 b.] An intermediate or connecting link.

a **1834** COLERIDGE *Rem.* (1838) III. 402 A longer time and more interlinks are requisite.

interlobate (-ˈləʊbət), *a.* [INTER- 4 a.] Situated between loops or lobes, esp. in *Geol.* between the terminal lobes of a glacier-moraine.

1881–2 T. C. CHAMBERLIN in *Rep. U.S. Geol. Surv.* (1883) 313 (Funk) A peculiar morainic type to which the term intermediate or interlobate moraines will be applied. **1889** *Amer. Sci. Assoc.* in *Nature* 3 Oct. 558 The terminal loops meet on opposite sides of large interlobate moraines.

interlobular (-ˈlɒbjʊlə(r)), *a. Anat.* and *Path.* [INTER- 4 a. Cf. F. *interlobulaire* (Littré).]

Situated or occurring between the lobes of any organ.

1834 J. FORBES *Laennec's Dis. Chest* (ed. 4) 141 There are two kinds of emphysema of the lungs, the vesicular or pulmonary properly so called, and the interlobular. **1836–9** TODD *Cycl. Anat.* II. 493/2 The plastic mass..fills up the interlobular fissures. **1881** MIVART *Cat* 188 The portal veins end by minute vessels, which surround and penetrate the lobules of the liver (whence..called interlobular veins).

inter'local, *a. rare.* [INTER- 4 b.] Existing between place and place. Hence **inter'locally** *adv.*

1850 *Tait's Mag.* XVII. 772/2 In a few years means of transit by steam will no doubt exist interlocally in all parts of the world. **1920** A. C. PIGOU *Econ. of Welfare* II. vi. 171 So soon as people become thoroughly familiarised with town-planning, local patriotism and inter-local emulation will make resort to external pressure from the central Government no longer necessary.

interlocate ('ɪntələʊˌkeɪt), *v.* [INTER- 1 a.] *trans.* To place between other things, or between one another; to intercalate.

1851 KITTO *Bible Illustr.* Morn. Ser. (1857) IV. 54 The stones are so irregularly interlocated as to show that they belong to the restorations from old materials. **1853** *Jrnl. R. Agric. Soc.* XIV. I. 235 There are thin beds of the silica rock interlocated with seams of blue limestone.

interlocation (-ləʊ'keɪʃən). *rare.* [INTER- 2 a. Cf. obs. F. *interlocation* (Cotgr.).]

1. A placing between, interposition; also, something placed between.

1611 COTGR., *Interlocation*, an interlocation, interplacing, interposition. **1672** VILLIERS (Dk. Buckhm.) *Rehearsal* v. (Arb.) 127 As likewise your Eclipse of the Sun is caus'd by an interlocation of the Moon, betwixt the Earth and Sun. **1834** SOUTHEY *Doctor* I. 104, I will not..call these intervening chapters either Interpellations, or Interpositions, or Interlocations, or Intervals.

2. An intermediate location, settlement, or place.

1890 DOANE in *Mission Herald* (Boston) June 226 [By canoe] I reach the ends and interlocations of my bishopric.

interlock (ɪntə'lɒk), *v.* [INTER- 1 b.]

1. a. *intr.* To engage with each other by partial overlapping or interpenetration of alternate projections and recesses.

1632 LITHGOW *Trav.* v. 190 The branches grow so straight, and interlocking as though they were kept by Arte. **1802** PALEY *Nat. Theol.* xx. (1830) 257 The attracting syrup, the rows of strong prickles, their position so as to interlock, the joints of the leaves [etc.]. **1831** R. KNOX *Cloquet's Anat.* 84 The edges of the bones..are merely placed together without interlocking by means of denticulations. **1853** C. BRONTË *Villette* xxvii, I felt my fingers work and my hands interlock.

b. *spec.* (*U.S.*) said of the head-streams of rivers which lie between each other, but flow in different directions.

[**1693** T. CLAYTON in *Phil. Trans.* XVII. 791 The Heads of the Branches of the Rivers interfere and lock one within another..after the manner that an Indian explained..to me, when..he clapt the Fingers of one Hand 'twixt those of the other, crying, they meet thus.] **1749** L. EVANS *Map Pensilv.* in J. Winsor *Mississ. Basin* (1895) 241 This Branch [of the Susquehannah] interlocks with the Branches of Allegeny and the North Branch of Potomack. **1808** PIKE *Sources Mississ.* II. (1810) 135 At five o'clock arrived at the dividing ridge between the waters of the Osage and Arkansaw..the dry branches of which interlock within 20 yards of each other. **1876** BANCROFT *Hist. U.S.* II. xxxii. 300 By way of the Ottawa and the rivers that interlock with it.

c. *fig.* Of immaterial things.

1859 DARWIN *Orig. Spec.* vi. (1873) 134 These representative species often meet and interlock. **1861** L. L. NOBLE *Icebergs* 25 The twilight, that..neutral ground, where gloom and splendor interlock and wrestle.

2. *trans.* To lock or clasp within each other. Chiefly *pass.*

1807 VANCOUVER *Agric. Devon* (1813) 239 Their branches so interlocked..and covered with..tree moss, that the feeble foliage and diminutive fruit they produce, are scarcely visible. **1831** R. KNOX *Cloquet's Anat.* 168 They [bones] are interlocked, if the general mechanism of the region is insufficient to maintain this solidity. **1853** KANE *Grinnell Exp.* xlii. (1856) 384 It had so interlocked itself with other ice-fields of different diameters, that to the eye it became a part of a great plain. **1879** *Cassell's Techn. Educ.* IV. 65/1 The scales hook into each other..and thus the fibres become inextricably interlocked.

fig. **1861** F. HALL in *Jrnl. Asiat. Soc. Bengal* 6 *note*, Words which rigorous euphony would interlock are sometimes found asunder. **1893** A. OGLE *Marq. D'Argenson* 161 Interlocked with the political battle, there proceeded a spiritual conflict.

3. *Railways.* To connect (the levers for working a system of signals, switches, etc.) in such a manner by catches, bars, bolts, or the like, that they cannot be operated independently of each other, but only in such a manner as to secure agreement in their position. Also *intr.* for *pass.*

1874 R. C. RAPIER *Signals Railw.* 23 Switches and signals ..are said to be interlocked when the movement of a signal to safety cannot be commenced until after the necessary movement of the switches has been completed, and also the movement of the switches cannot be commenced until after all the signals concerned by them have first been set fully to danger. *Ibid.* 26 If a signal had to interlock with several sets of switches, say for example, ten or twelve [etc.]. *Ibid.* 32 When a lever is required to interlock with several others, it is fixed only once by its own lock. **1889** G. FINDLAY *Eng. Railway* 67 In 1856 a successful attempt was made by Mr. John Saxby to concentrate and interlock the levers working both points and signals.

4. *Cinemat.* To connect (the electric motors of cameras or the like) electrically in such a way that they rotate in synchronism with one another.

1928 *Trans. Soc. Motion Picture Engin.* XII. 704 It has been necessary..to develop a motor drive equipment which will satisfactorily interlock the camera and the recording machine... It is essential that the interlock should hold.. during acceleration and deceleration. **1931** B. BROWN *Talking Pictures* ix. 206 Where we have cameras working in conjunction with sound recorders..there is absolute necessity for both devices to be inter-locked or driven together, so that sound and photograph are always exactly in phase. **1953** L. J. WHEELER *Princ. Cinematogr.* ii. 68 When all was ready to take the scene the camera was interlocked with the sound recorder so that, on starting up, both camera and recorder would rotate in synchronism.

Hence **inter'locked** *ppl. a.*; **inter'locking** *vbl. sb.* and *ppl. a.*; also **inter'locker**, one who or that which interlocks.

1854 OWEN *Skel. & Teeth* in *Circ. Sc., Organ. Nat.* I. 165 The tail is encased in a sheath of..interlocked ossicles. *Ibid.* 192 The firm interlocking of the ordinary vertebræ. **1854** WOODWARD *Mollusca* II. 245 A hinge furnished with interlocking teeth. **1874** R. C. RAPIER *Signals Railw.* 23 The first interlocking of switches and signals took place at East Retford Junction, in the year 1852. *Ibid.* 47 The interlocking apparatus. **1889** G. FINDLAY *Eng. Railway* 67 In 1859 the first interlocking frame was fixed on the London and North Western Railway..In 1873..13,000 interlocked levers were in use on that railway. **1896** *Columbus* (Ohio) *Disp.* 6 Jan. 5/2 An annunciator has been put in between Mound street and the interlocker at the crossing of the T. & O.C., C., H.V. & T. and Cincinnati division of the Pan Handle, for the purpose of announcing trains approaching the crossing from the south. **1899** SAYCE *Early Israel* ii. 77 The same interlocking of Amorite and Hittite..meets us also on the monuments of Egypt.

interlock ('ɪntəlɒk), *sb.* (*a.*) [f. prec. vb.]

A. *sb.* **1.** *rare.* **a.** The fact or condition of being interlocked. **b.** An interlocked portion of an estate, etc.

1874 BUSHNELL *Forgiven. & Law* iv. 237 Modes of false opinion that have no show of interlock save in their common opposition to God. **1877** BURROUGHS *Taxation* 356 A junior patentee has the right to pay on the interlock, and a sale of the whole tract..is void as to the part within the interlock.

2. a. *Cinemat.* Synchronism between two or more electric motors (e.g. in a camera and in sound-recording apparatus); also, the mechanism by which this is effected. Freq. *attrib.*

1928 [see INTERLOCK *v.* 4]. **1931** B. BROWN *Talking Pictures* ix. 206 Gaumont coupled the armature of his projector motor, and using a common power supply, obtained synchronism. To-day we use a similar type of arrangement known as the 'electrical interlock'. **1938** *Motion Picture Sound Engin.* (Acad. Motion Pict. Arts & Sci.) viii. 118 Another commonly used driving system employs the Selsyn type of motor and is known as the interlock system. This is virtually an electrical gear system, whereby all the motors connected together on several separated units will start together, come up to speed at the same rate, and continue to run at identical speeds. *Ibid.* 119 Field rheostats for each motor are located in one place and all speeds are adjusted to maintain interlock at the estimated camera and recorder loads. **1949** FRAYNE & WOLFE *Elem. Sound Recording* xxiv. 477 Because the three-phase interlock windings are inter-connected with the d-c windings voltage appears on the interlock circuit as soon as the d-c leads are excited. **1962** E. L. LEVITAN *Animation Technique* I. 70/1 The process whereby the picture reel and the sound track are run and projected at the same time is called the interlock.

b. A mechanism for preventing a set of operations from being performed in any but the prescribed sequence.

1934 in WEBSTER. **1945** *Rev. Sci. Instruments* XVI. 57/2 There are two mechanical interlocks on the controls... The selector switch is locked so that it cannot be moved unless the Variac is set to zero. **1955** *Archit. Rev.* CXVII. 142/3 The most important piece of equipment associated with lift doors is the inter-lock, an electro-mechanical device which ensures that the lift cannot move until both car and landing doors are locked in position. **1958** *Engineering* 28 Feb. 261/3 To prevent incorrect operation, electrical interlocks are provided to ensure that the hopper can only be tilted when all the pressing rams are clear and the box is open..and that the ejection door cannot be closed until the final pressing ram has been withdrawn. **1958** *Newnes Compl. Amat. Photogr.* 54 It is common nowadays for even simple cameras to have a shutter-film wind interlock which prevents blank negatives or double exposures. **1963** B. FOZARD *Instrumentation Nucl. Reactors* xiii. 170 Interlocks must be fitted to ensure that the chambers cannot be inserted under high flux conditions.

B. *attrib.* or *adj.* Esp. designating woven material in which the stitches are woven together.

1928 *Daily Mail* 25 July 3/6 (Advt.), The merits of Meridian Interlock Underwear. **1935** *Economist* 23 Nov. 1003/1 Considerable progress..was made with the development of spun yarns for..pyjama cloths and for underwear fabric manufactured on circular interlock knitting machines. **1969** *Sears Catal.* Spring/Summer 26 Cardigan sweater interlock knit of Orlon acrylic.

interlocular (-'lɒkjʊlə(r)), *a. Zool.* [INTER- 4 a.] Situated between loculi or chambers, as in shells or corals.

1888 G. J. HINDE in *Geol. Jrnl.* XLIV. 209 The internal cavity of the corallites is divided into a series of closed longitudinal chambers or interlocular spaces.

†**interlo'cute**, *v. Obs. rare.* [f. L. *interlocūt-*, ppl. stem of *interloquī*: see next.] *intr.* To talk *with*, hold conversation *with*.

1621 BP. MOUNTAGU *Diatribæ* III. 539 Cleon..is brought in interlocuting with Agoracritus.

interlocution (-ləʊ'kjuːʃən). Also 7 **-loquution.** [ad. L. *interlocūtiōn-em*, n. of action f. *interloquī*, f. *inter* between + *loquī* to speak. Cf. F. *interlocution* (1549 in Godef. *Compl.*).]

1. The action (on the part of two or more persons) of talking or replying to each other. **a.** Talk, conversation, discourse, dialogue.

a **1534** W. DE WORDE (*title*), An Interlocucyon, with an Argument betwyxt Man and Woman, whiche of them could prove most excellent. *a* **1548** HALL *Chron.* (1809) 291 Al the whole daye was consumed in doutfull communicacion and earnest interlocution. **1638** BROME *Antipodes* II. ii. Wks. 1873 III. 260 You hold interloquutions with the Audients. **1681** FLAVEL *Meth. Grace* iii. 46 That treaty requires interlocution betwixt both the parties concerned in it. **1756–82** J. WARTON *Ess. Pope* II. XII. 340 He is for ever introducing these little interlocutions, which give his satires and epistles an air so lively and dramatic. **1864** W. C. HAZLITT *Early Pop. Poetry* I. Introd. 14 Productions..for the most part in the form of dialogues or interlocutions.

†**b.** An alternate reading or speaking, as in making responses, or reading alternate verses of the Psalms. *Obs.*

1597 HOOKER *Eccl. Pol.* v. xxxvii. §1 Rehearsall of them [the Psalms]..done by interlocution, and with a mutuall returne of sentences from side to side. **1643** *True Informer* 35 Then wee proceed by holy alternatif interlocutions (whereby wee heare our selves speak as well as the Minister) to some effectuall short prayers.

†**c.** Manner of intercommunication. *Obs.*

1670 *Conclave wherein Clement VIII was elected Pope* 12 There arose no small fluctuation and confusion amongst them..from the diversity of their interlocution.

†**2.** The action of replying; a reply, response.

1597–8 BACON *Ess., Discourse* (Arb.) 22 A good continued speech without a good speech of interlocution sheweth slownesse; and a good reply or second speech, without a good set speech sheweth shallownesse and weaknes. **1661** *Grand Debate* 83 Indeed Abraham did so, when Gods interlocution answering the first Prayer, called him to vary his request. **1782** PRIESTLEY *Corrupt. Chr.* II. VIII. 127 The people..made small interlocutions or responses.

†**3.** The action of interrupting (one's own or another's) speech; an interruption; a parenthetical utterance or section. *Obs.*

1592 tr. *Junius on Rev.* vii. 1 This whole chapter is a certaine interlocution. **1604** CAWDREY *Table Alph.*, *Interlocution*, interrupting of anothers speech. **1655** FULLER *Ch. Hist.* IV. i. §9 Lest their interlocutions should hinder the intireness of our Discourse, take them Verbatim in a Dialogue. **1683** BP. PATRICK *Prov.* xxix. Argt., A speech broken off by interlocutions, and instilled by parts, penetrates deeper than that which is continued.

†**4.** *Law.* An intermediate decree before final decision: see INTERLOCUTORY *a.* 3.

1706 PHILLIPS, *Interlocution*,..in a Law-sense, the determining some small Matter in a Tryal till such time as the principal Cause be fully known. **1726** AYLIFFE *Parergon* 65 The Judge ought by an Interlocution to enjoin new Answers. *Ibid.* 149 Some new Incident..may emerge..on which the Judge ought to proceed by Interlocution.

interlocutive (-'lɒkjʊtɪv), *a. rare.* [f. as INTERLOCUTE *v.*: see -IVE.] Characterized by interlocution (see prec. 1 b); responsive.

1842 G. S. FABER *Provinc. Lett.* (1844) II. 74 The Breviary..is a public interlocutive service, requiring a Priest and a Reader and a Congregation.

interlocutor¹ (-'lɒkjʊtə(r)). Also 6–7 **-our**, 6 **-loquutor.** [f. L. type **interlocūtor*, agent-n. f. *interloquī*: see INTERLOCUTION, and cf. F. *interlocuteur* (16th c. in Godef. *Compl.*).]

a. One who takes part in a dialogue, conversation, or discussion. In *pl.* the persons who carry on a dialogue.

1514 BARCLAY *Cyt. & Uplondyshm.* (Percy Soc.) 3 Interlocutoures be Amyntas and Faustus. **1559** W. CUNNINGHAM *Cosmogr. Glasse* 1 The Interloquutors: Philonicus, Spondæus. *a* **1670** HACKET *Abp. Williams* I. (1693) 20 An assiduous Overseer and Interlocutor at the Afternoon Disputations of the Under Graduates. **1699** BENTLEY *Phal.* 279 The Interlocutors in this Dialogue, are Socrates and one Minos an Athenian, his Acquaintance. **1763** J. BROWN *Poetry & Mus.* vi. 108 'Tis probable that He [Thespis] was the first Declaimer or Interlocutor to his own Choir. **1849** MACAULAY *Hist. Eng.* vi. II. 69 Dryden had done him the honor to make him a principal interlocutor in the dialogue on dramatic poesy. **1875** JOWETT *Plato* (ed. 2) V. 7.

b. With *poss. pron.* One who enters into or takes part in conversation with another.

1848 THACKERAY *Van. Fair* li. (end) 'It's you, Moss, is it?' said the Colonel, who appeared to know his interlocutor. **1859** GEO. ELIOT *A. Bede* ii, Your true rustic turns his back on his interlocutor. **1863** MRS. C. CLARKE *Shaks. Char.* ii. 50 Celia..always checks the career of her wit, when it curvets beyond the comfort of her interlocutor.

c. The compère in a troupe of nigger minstrels; the man in the middle of the minstrel line who questions the end men.

1880 E. JAMES *Amat. Negro Minstrel's Guide* 2 Interlocutor or Middle Man, in the Center. **1884** [see

BANJOIST]. **1957** W. C. HANDY *Father of Blues* xxi. 276 Henry Troy acted as the interlocutor, with Tom Fletcher and Laurence Deas as end men.

interlocutor² (-ˈlɒkjʊtə(r)). *Sc. Law* Also 6, 8 -loquitur, -tor, 6–7 -loquutour. [a. F. *interlocutoire* interlocutory, ad. L. *interlocūtōrium*: see next, and cf. DECLARATOR. The occasional spelling *interloquitur* appears to imply an identification with the L. verbal form *interloquitur* 'he pronounces an interim sentence'.] A judgement or order of a court or of the Lords Ordinary, signed by the pronouncing or presiding judge.

'Interlocutors, correctly speaking, are judgments or judicial orders pronounced in the course of a suit, but which do not finally determine the cause. The term, however, in Scotch practice, is applied indiscriminately to the judgments or orders of the Court, or of the Lords Ordinary, whether they exhaust the question at issue or not' (Bell *Dict. Law Scotl.* 1861).

1533 BELLENDEN *Livy* III. (1822) 272 This Appius..or evir ony place wes gevin to Virginius to answere to the peticioun, he gaif his interloquitur [*Boyndlie MS.* interlocutour] aganis Virginia. **1560** ROLLAND *Crt. Venus* IV. 285 Scho was put to honour Aboue Venus be Interloquutour Of the Assise furth geuin be thair sentence. **1639** in Row *Hist. Kirk* (Wodrow Soc.) 525 Protests that all acts, sentences, decreets, interlocutors, to be pronunced, be in themselves null, voyd, and ineffectuall. **1746–7** *Act 20 Geo. II*, c. 43 §14 Decrees, Sentences, Interloquitors, Judgments, Executions, or Proceedings relating to any Civil or Criminal Cause in any such Court. **1818** CRUISE *Digest* (ed. 2) V. 34 The House of Lords ordered, that the interlocutor complained of in the appeal should be reversed; and that the interlocutor of the Lord Ordinary should be affirmed.

interˈlocutorily, *adv. rare.* [f. next + -LY².] In the way of an interlocutory decree (see next, A. 3); provisionally.

1620 BRENT tr. *Sarpi's Hist. Counc. Trent* (1676) 128 Decreeing interlocutorily the occurring differences.

interlocutory (-ˈlɒkjʊtərɪ), *a.* and *sb.* Also 7 -loquutory. [ad. L. type **interlocūtōri-us*: see INTERLOCUTION and -ORY. Cf. F. *interlocutoire* (13th c. in Hatz.).]

A. *adj.* **1.** Of the nature of, pertaining to, or occurring in, dialogue or conversation.

1597 HOOKER *Eccl. Pol.* v. xxxix. §1 These interlocutorie formes of speech. **1626** W. FENNER *Hidden Manna* (1652) A iv b, He knowes that interloquutory swearing is a sinne. **1678** CUDWORTH *Intell. Syst.* I. iii. §17. 161 Another.. plastick power in the soul,..in sleep or dreams..frames interlocutory discourses betwixt it self and other persons. **1763** J. BROWN *Poetry & Mus.* iv. 42 The Episode or interlocutory Part would be also sung. **1868** E. EDWARDS *Ralegh* I. xix. 388 The interlocutory form must be preserved.

b. Of a person: Taking part in a conversation.

1866 HOWELLS *Venet. Life* xvii. 252 The barber here prattles on with a freedom..respected by the interlocutory *conte* under his razor.

2. Spoken intermediately, interjected into the main course of speech.

1821 SCOTT *Kenilw.* xvii, A few of Leicester's interlocutory sentences ran as follows: 'Poynings, good morrow, and how does your wife and fair daughter?' ..'Adams, your suit is naught: the Queen will grant no more monopolies'. **1854** MOTLEY *Corr.* (1889) I. vi. 169 Making all his interlocutory observations in a most musical voice. **1864** *Lond. Rev.* 18 June 641 Interlocutory observations addressed to his unfortunate and joyless partner.

3. *Law.* Pronounced during the course of an action; not finally decisive of a case or suit; esp. in ***interlocutory decree, judgement, order.*** Also, relating to a provisional decision in a case.

1590 SWINBURNE *Testaments* 9 Of Iudiciall sentences there bee two sortes, the one *interlocutory*, the other *definitiue*. An interlocutory sentence, is a decree giuen by the iudge, betwixte the beginning and ending of the cause, touching some incident or emergent question. **1626** DONNE *Serm.* xxvii. 271 All the Judgments of the world are but Interlocutory Judgments, There is a finall Judgment. **1665** MANLEY *Grotius' Low C. Warres* 489 Not by a setled and perpetual Law, but in the manner of an Interloquutory Edict. **1707** CHAMBERLAYNE *St. Gt. Brit.* II. xv. 222 In case any Person be aggriev'd by any Sentence or Interlocutory Decree..he may appeal to the High Court of Admiralty. **1881** LD. JAMES in *Times* 12 Apr. 4/2 He did not intend to dispose of anything finally on the present occasion, but only to deal with the case as upon an interlocutory application.

B. *sb.* †**1.** *Law.* An interlocutory decree. *Obs.*

1620 BRENT tr. *Sarpi's Hist. Counc. Trent* (1676) 314 The Decrees of the Judge which they call Interlocutories. **1694** FALLE *Jersey* iv. 105 No Appeal is admitted in Matters of less Value; nor in Interlocutories, nor in Criminal Causes. *a* **1758** SIR G. LEE in F. T. Pratt *Law Contraband* (1856) 67 By Interlocutory the Judge condemned ship and cargo as lawful prize. **1774** BP. HALLIFAX *Anal. Rom. Civil Law* (1795) 125 Appeals..within 15 days from the Sentence, if it be definitive, or 10 days, if it be an Interlocutory.

†**2.** A discussion. *Obs.*

1708 MOTTEUX *Rabelais* v. xvi. (1737) 72 These..tedious Interlocutories, Examinations and Appointments.

†**3.** = INTERLOCUTOR¹. *Obs.*

1697 in W. S. Perry *Hist. Coll. Amer. Col. Ch.* I. 36 (Lambeth Conference) Interlocutories. C..Thomas Lᵈ Archbishop of Canterbury. L..Henry Lᵈ Bishop of London [etc.].

interlocutress (-ˈlɒkjuːtrɪs). [f. INTERLOCUTOR¹ + -ESS.] A female interlocutor.

1858 HOGG *Shelley* II. 328, I..asked..the fair interlocutresses for some samples of the nightly dialogue. **1880** H. JAMES *Mme. de Mauves* 105 Longmore felt a revival of interest in his interlocutress.

So **interˈlocutrice**, **interˈlocutrix**, repr. the French and Latin forms of the feminine.

1848 C. BRONTË *J. Eyre* xiv, Have the goodness to serve her as auditress and interlocutrice. **1860** MRS. BYRNE *Undercurrents* I. 27 The man moved from the wall towards his interlocutrix. **1868** *Pall Mall G.* 28 Mar. 11 His interlocutrix will not have Mrs. Guinevere for the brand-mark of the sex. **1892** *Nation* (N.Y.) 22 Dec. 481/1 'Would it not have been better', suggested his interlocutrice.

interloˈpation. *nonce-wd.* [f. next + -ATION.] The action of interloping or intruding within the domain of another.

1803 MARY CHARLTON *Wife & Mistress* III. 278 Her domestic plans having been rather discomposed by the interlopation of three or four people in the house and premises. **1881** *Edinburgh Courant* No. 30318. 2 His interlopation is a sad blow to Mrs. Netherby.

interlope (ɪntəˈləʊp), *v.* [Evidently f. INTER- 1 + *lope*, dial. form of LEAP *v.*, as in *land-loper*, or the cognate MDu. and LG. *lôpen*, Du. *loopen*, to run.

See note below.]

1. *intr.* 'To run between parties and intercept the advantage that one should gain from the other; to traffick without a proper licence; to forestall; to anticipate irregularly' (J.); to intrude within the domain or sphere of action of another; to intrude *upon* (with *indirect passive*).

1603–27 [see INTERLOPING *ppl. a.*]. **1615** *Minutes Court East Ind. Co.* 22 Feb. (MS.), To examine all suspected personns that intend interlopinge into the East Indies or Muscovy. **1641** HEYLIN *Help to Hist.* (1680) 304 The Rivers and Courtneys held the Title long: as now the Cavendishes may do..But how long any of them held it, and who they were that interloped we shall..see [etc.]. **1691** T. HALE *Acc. New Invent.* p. xcvii, Patents that interloped in the Conservacy of the River. **1713** C'TESS WINCHELSEA *Misc. Poems* 209 My Industry, he cries, is all the Cause; Sometimes I interlope, and slight the Laws. **1775** C. JOHNSTON *Pilgrim* 106 Not chusing to be interloped upon by their servants. **1801** COLERIDGE *Sibyl. Leaves* II. 215 Idle Hope And dire Remembrance interlope To vex the feverish slumbers of the mind. **1818** SHELLEY *Rev. Islam* IX. xxvii, Though some envious shade may interlope Between the effect and it. **1833** M. SCOTT *Tom Cringle* xi. (1859) 252 The colours were never blended in the same set, no blackie ever interloped with the browns.

†**2.** *trans.* To introduce improperly or out of place; to foist in; to intercalate. *Obs.*

a **1641** BP. MOUNTAGU *Acts & Mon.* (1642) 515 Aaron.. interloped onely a typicall Priesthood for a time unto the Jewes. **1641** HEYLIN *Hist. Episc.* II. (1657) 27, I know the antiquaries of that Church have interloped an Anacletus between these two. **1659** —— *Cert. Epist.* 301 Grotius interlopes the following passage.

†**3.** To intrude upon, to interfere with. *rare.*

1701 C. WOLLEY *Jrnl. N. York* (1860) 44 Which legal faculties and professions..should not be interlop'd and undermin'd by persons of any other faculties.

[*Note.* The actual history of the words *interlope, interloper*, is somewhat obscure. Our earliest examples belong to the end of the 16th c. No form nor cognate of these words is found in any other language until after 1700, when the English sb. was adopted in Fr. as *interlopre* (Savary *Dict. de Comm.* 1723), now *interlope*, applied to a ship, and to a limited extent in Du. and LG. (*enterlopen* in Halma, 1758–61, *enterloper* in *Bremisches Wbch.* 1767). In Du. *enterlooper* is expressly stated in 1768 to be 'van de Engelse ontleend', borrowed from English, and is explained to mean the same thing as the proper Du. term *lorrendraaijer*, used from the end of the 16th c. *Interlope, interloper* were thus of English formation. About 1600, *interlopers, intermeddlers, stragglers, straggling Englishmen*, occur as appellations of the same class of persons (see INTERLOPER 1 a, 1603, INTERMEDDLER c., 1601). Some of these synonyms suggest connexion with *land-loper*, 'vagabond, vagrant, straggler', in common use before 1580 in place of the earlier *land-leaper* (1362–1621), *lope* being the form of *leap* in eastern and some north-midl. dialects (= north. dial. *loup, lowp*). It seems probable therefore that the two elements of *interloper* are identical with those of *inter*-meddler and land-*loper* respectively; at least, this seems more likely than that the word should have been compounded of the L. and Engl. prefix *inter-* and the Du. or LG. *lôpen, loopen* to run, *lôper, looper* runner, a combination which could not well have arisen in England, and of which we have no historical indication in any foreign parts where English and Dutch traders came in contact. The earliest known references to the practices of interlopers are in connexion with the Russia Company; see Sir E. A. Bond's Introduction to *Russia at close of 16th c.* (Hakl. Soc. 1856) p. xxi. *seqq.* But the word soon became a well-known term in connexion with the trade of the East India Company, chartered in 1600.]

†**interlope**, *sb. Obs. rare.* [f. prec. vb.] The act of interloping.

1645 P. PELHAM in *Hull Lett.* (1886) 66, I desire you to write at large of your sufferings by interlope to the Speaker, and to the Committee of Examinations.

interloper (ɪntəˈləʊpə(r)). [See INTERLOPE *v.* F. *interlope* (in 1723 *interlopre*) is from English.]

1. a. *orig.* An unauthorized trader; one who trespasses on the rights or privileges of any trade monopoly (see quot. 1896); †a ship engaged in unauthorized trading (*obs.*).

c **1590** H. LANE in Hakl. *Voy.* (1599) I. 375 From those parts the Muscouites were furnished out of Dutchland by enterlopers with all arts and artificers, and had few or none by vs. **1603–27** HORSEY *Trav.* etc. (Hakl. Soc.) 290 All interloperes and straglyng Englishemene lyving in that contrey weare gathered togather and appoynted to be transported. *a* **1615** DONNE *Ess.* (1651) 66 Such..who are but Interlopers, not staple Merchants, nor of the Company. **1627** MINSHEU *Duct. Ling.* (ed. 2), Interlopers in trade. **1658** PHILLIPS, *Interlopers*, in Common Law, are those that without legal authority, intercept the trade of a company, as it were Interleapers. **1685** LUTTRELL *Brief Rel.* (1857) I. 326 The judges..gave judgment in the case of the East India Company and the interloper. **1725** *Brice's Weekly Jrnl.* 9 July 1 Three Dutch Vessels, call'd interlopers, were taken in the Sea of Mexico by the Spanish Men of War. **1777** ROBERTSON *Hist. Amer.* (1783) III. 327 To station ships.. upon the coasts of those provinces to which interlopers most frequently resorted. **1896** W. A. S. HEWINS in *Dict. Pol. Econ.* II. 436/2 Interlopers were persons who, not being members of the companies chartered by the crown, nor having a license from them, traded on their own account to the countries to which the companies had the sole trade.

b. *transf.* One who, esp. for his own profit, thrusts himself into any position or affair, which others consider as pertaining solely to themselves.

(Quot. 1632 is intermediate in sense between a. and b.)

1632 *New Hampshire Prov. Papers* (1867) I. 49 The sayed Hollanders as interlopers fell into the middle, betwixt the sayed plantations. **1642** HOWELL *For. Trav.* viii. (Arb.) 44 In the Court of Spain there are likewise such Interlopers, and I have known divers Dutch Gentlemen grosly guld by this cheat. **1655** SIR E. NICHOLAS in *N. Papers* (Camden) II. 162 Yᵉ Queene must necessarily be offended for any man to be an interloper, and to meddle with thinges which belonged not to them and thereby to crosse her designes. **1816** SCOTT *Antiq.* i, The coach was calculated to carry six regular passengers, besides such interlopers as the coachman could pick up by the way. **1884** *Law Times Rep.* LI. 747/1 He was a mere interloper, and we were entitled to use force to keep him out of our premises.

†**2.** An intercepter (*of* something). *Obs. rare*⁻¹.

1670 MILTON *Hist. Eng.* v. *Edgar*, The King..resolv'd not only to recover his intercepted right, but to punish the interloper of his destind spouse.

†**interˈloperie.** *Obs. rare.* [f. INTERLOPER: see -ERY.] The practice of interloping; the trade of interlopers.

1612–13 JOHN WHEELER in *Buccleuch MSS.* (Hist. MSS. Comm.) I. 122 [Our Company (*i.e.* the Merchant Adventurers) languishes,] for the town of Amsterdam, in maintaining the Interloperie, sucketh the very heart-blood from us.

interloping (-ˈləʊpɪŋ), *vbl. sb.* [f. INTERLOPE *v.* + -ING¹.] The action of the vb. INTERLOPE; *esp.* unauthorized trading within the sphere of action of a chartered company.

1615 [see INTERLOPE *v.*]. **1641** MILTON *Animadv.* ii. Wks. (1851) 206 You should have given so much honour then to the word preach't, as to have left it to Gods working without the interloping of a Liturgy baited for them to bite at. **1698** FRYER *Acc. E. India & P.* 89 Not only the Jews..but other monied Gentlemen in England might be tempted to set up for Interloping. **1727** A. HAMILTON *New Acc. E. Ind.* II. xxxiii. 15, I, having three or four large Ships at Bengal, was reckoned a Criminal guilty of that unpardonable Sin of Interlopping. **1868** ROGERS *Pol. Econ.* ix. (1876) 82 Of course these monopolists could not prevent smuggling, or, as the East India Company called it, 'interloping'.

attrib. **1658–9** *Burton's Diary* (1828) IV. 107 The question now is, whether the interloping question shall prevail. **1675** TEMPLE *Let. Mercht. Advent.* 26 Mar., Wks. 1731 II. 331 The Liberty or Connivance given..to the interloping Trade. **1767** T. HUTCHINSON *Hist. Mass.* II. i. 116 A ship fitted out..in the interloping trade.

interloping (-ˈləʊpɪŋ), *ppl. a.* [f. as prec. + -ING².] That interlopes, or is an interloper.

1603–27 HORSEY *Trav.* (Hakl. Soc.) 228, I procured unto the Company of merchants the fredom of all their howses in Musco [etc.]... All the interlopinge merchants tradinge in those countries without leave of the Company, beinge 29, wear delivered into my handes to transport into England. **1633** PRYNNE *Histriom.* II. 995, I have..compleatly finished this my Histrio-Mastix..(as well as..other Interloping Imployments would permit). **1664** POWER *Exp. Philos.* I. 60 The whole Heart with both Auricles and both Ventricles, the one manifestly preceding the pulse of the other..and without any interloping perisystole at all. **1753** SMOLLETT *Ct. Fathom* (1784) 169/2 The quack; who..had long looked upon him in the odious light of an interloping rival. **1871** B. TAYLOR *Faust* (1875) II. II. iii. 134 Enchaining The interloping witch's son. **1885** *Pall Mall G.* 23 July 10/2 We shall oppose you in Parliament because we think these interloping lines are an evil generally.

interlot, *v.*: see INTER- *pref.* 1 a.

†**interˈlucate**, *v. Obs. rare*⁻⁰. [f. ppl. stem of L. *interlūcāre*, f. *inter* between + *lux, lūc-em* light.] To lop or thin a tree.

1623 COCKERAM, *Interlucate*, to cut boughs.

interlucation (-luːˈkeɪʃən). *rare.* [ad. L. *interlūcātiōn-em* (Pliny), n. of action f. *interlūcāre*: see prec.] The action of thinning a tree or wood.

1656 BLOUNT *Glossogr.*, *Interlucation*, a cutting off boughs, where they let or hinder the light. **1664** EVELYN *Sylva* (1776) 472 For interlucation, remove Exuberant branches..where the boughs grow too thick and cumbersome, to let in Sun and Air. *Ibid.* (1679) Advt., Let them read for..*interlucation*, thinning and disbranching of a

wood. **1887** *Rep. U.S. Sec. Agric., Forestry* 221 (Funk) By interlucations we imitate, assist, anticipate nature in this process of elimination.

interlucent (-'l(j)uːsənt), *a. rare.* [ad. L. *interlūcēnt-em*, pr. pple. of *interlūcēre*: see INTER-1 a and LUCENT.] Shining between.

1727 in BAILEY, vol. II. **1829** LANDOR *Imag. Conv.* Wks. 1846 II. 251/2 A fillet of pale sapphire and interlucent gold. **1860** C. SANGSTER *Hesperus*, etc. 14 The burning incense of the sun Rolled up the interlucent space.

†**interluci'dation.** *Obs. rare*$^{-1}$. [f. INTER- 2 a + L. *lucidus* shining; cf. *elucidation*.] Mutual or reciprocal illumination.

1652 BENLOWES *Theoph.* IV. xxii, Here, oft's an Enterview in Heat, and Might By Inter-lucidations from above Twining Embraces with 's ensphearing arm of love!

interlude ('ɪntəl(j)uːd), *sb.* Forms: 4–7 **enterlude,** (4 **entirlodie, entyrlude,** 5 **-lute**), 5– **interlude,** (6 **-lud**). [ad. med. (Anglo-)Lat. *interlūdium* (Du Cange), f. *inter-* (INTER- 2) + *lūdus* play, possibly after an AF. **entrelude*.]

1. A dramatic or mimic representation, usually of a light or humorous character, such as was commonly introduced between the acts of the long mystery-plays or moralities, or exhibited as part of an elaborate entertainment; hence (in ordinary 17–18th c. use) a stage-play, esp. of a popular nature, a comedy, a farce. Now (after Collier; see quot. 1831) applied as a specific name to the earliest form of the modern drama, as represented by the plays of J. Heywood.

1303 R. BRUNNE *Handl. Synne* 8993 Entyrludes or syngynge, Or tabure bete or oþer pypynge. **13..** *Gaw. & Gr. Knt.* 472 Wel bycommes such craft vpon cristmasse, Laykyng of enterludez, to laȝe & to syng. **1494** FABYAN *Chron.* VI. clxxii. 167 He dyd on hym yᵉ abyt of a mynstrell, & with his instrument of musyke he entred the tentes.. of the Danys.. shewynge there his enterludes and songes. **1501** DOUGLAS *Pal. Hon.* II. 410 At eis thay eit with interludis betwene. *a* **1553** UDALL *Royster D.* Prol. (Arb.) 10 Our Comedie or Enterlude, which we intende to play, Is named Royster Doyster in deede. **1588** *Marprel. Epist.* (Arb.) 11 Your first book was a proper Enterlude, called Gammar Gurtons needle. **1619** DALTON *Countrey Just.* xxiii. (1630) 63 There shall be no.. Enterludes Common Plays or other unlawful exercises of pastimes. *a* **1677** HALE *Prim. Orig. Man.* IV. viii. 361 As the inconsiderate part of Mankind please themselves with beholding of Interludes, or Cock-fighting, or Bear-baiting. **1759** FRANKLIN *Ess.* Wks. 1840 III. 491 Thus, harlequin-like, he could play contrary parts in the same interlude. **1831** J. P. COLLIER *Hist. Dram. Poetry* II. 384 John Heywood's dramatic productions.. are neither Miracle-plays nor Moral-plays, but what may be properly and strictly called Interludes. **1865** T. WRIGHT *Hist. Caricat.* xvi. (1875) 277 The word *interlude* remained long in our language as applied to such short and simple dramatic pieces as we may suppose to have formed the drolleries of the mysteries. **1887** LOWELL *Old Eng. Dram.* (1892) 5 The Interludes may have served as training-schools for actors.

†**b.** *transf.* or *fig.* Any performance or action compared to a play. *Obs.*

1375 BARBOUR *Bruce* x. 145 Now may ȝe heir.. Interludys and Iuperdys, þat men assayit on mony vis Castellis and pelis for till ta. **1581** J. BELL *Haddon's Answ. Osor.* 437 b, He suppeth out of the Challice: in such wise neverthelès as that not so much as a croome of this supper, or apish Enterlude rather, cann come to the peoples share. **1641** MILTON *Reform.* I. (1851) 6 Sencelesse Ceremonies which wee onely retaine.. as an Enterlude to set out the pompe of Prelatisme. **1651** N. BACON *Disc. Govt. Eng.* II. xxxvii. (1739) 167 He did no more than shape a Garment to serve the present Interlude, neither fit to the body, nor easy to be worn.

2. An interval in the performance of a play; the pause between the acts, or the means (dramatic or musical) employed to fill this up. Also *fig.*

1660 WILLSFORD *Scales Comm.* Pref. A v, A Tragedy of Cares, or a Comedy of Errours,..; yet Penury in the Interludes often provokes noble minds to act ignoble things. **1700** DRYDEN *Cock & Fox* 325 Dreams are but interludes which fancy makes; When monarch reason sleeps, this mimic wakes. **1717** BERKELEY *Jrnl. Tour Italy* 25 Jan., Wks. 1871 IV. 535 We went to see a play, with interludes of music. **1828** CARLYLE *Misc.*, *Goethe's Helena* (1872) I. 169 Such is Helena, the interlude in Faust. **1829** LONGF. in *Life* (1891) I. 169 It seems more like an interlude in the drama of life than a part of the play.

b. *Music.* An instrumental piece played between the verses of a psalm or hymn, or in the intervals of a church-service, etc.

1838 *Penny Cycl.* XII. 507/1 *Interlude*, a brief piece of church music for the organ.. generally produced *ex tempore*, and played after each stanza, except the last, of the metrical psalm. **1873** HALE *In His Name* viii. 72 The interludes which had been arranged to be played on the great organ. **1880** *Grove's Dict. Mus.* II. 7/2 A good extempore Interlude was regarded as no unfair test of an Organist's ability.

3. *transf.* **a.** An interval in the course of some action or event; an intervening time or space of a different character or sort.

1751 JOHNSON *Rambler* No. 156 ¶10 Variegated with interludes of mirth. **1802** MAD. D'ARBLAY *Lett.* 16 Apr., We were confined to the inn, except for the interlude of the custom-house. **1865** LIVINGSTONE *Zambesi* vii. 169 All night long it is boil and eat, roast and devour, with a few brief interludes of sleep. **1890** SWINBURNE *Stud. Prose & Poetry* (1894) 223 A ghastly.. wilderness of salt marshes, with interludes of sterile meadow and unprofitable vineyard.

b. *pl.* Pieces of material of a different kind inserted at intervals.

1890 *Daily News* 31 Jan. 6/2 A brown silk dress, made with interludes of green velvet and sleeves of velvet.

4. *Comb.*, as ***interlude-maker, -play, -player, -rimer*** (***rhymer***); ***interlude-like*** adj. and adv.; ***interlude-wise*** adv.

1552 HULOET, Enterlude maker, *comicus*. Enterlude players, *ludij, ludiones*. **1561** T. NORTON *Calvin's Inst.* IV. 118 Then Baptisme may enterludelike and in sport be ministred of boies when they plaie. *Ibid.* IV. xix. (1634) 729 Deacons, whom they institute onely for their enterlude-like playes. **1609** HOLLAND *Amm. Marcell.* XXVIII. iv. 342 Unto the Enterlude-rhymer. **1626** BERNARD *Isle of Man* (1627) N v, As it were interlude-wise.

interlude ('ɪntəl(j)uːd), *v.* [f. prec.]

†**a.** *intr.* To act, perform a play (*obs.*).

b. *intr.* To come between, as an interlude. **c.** *trans.* To interrupt, as with an interlude.

1608 MIDDLETON *Mad World* v. i. 27 There are certain players come to town, sir, and desire to interlude before your worship. **1830** LAMB *Album Verses, Album Lucy Barton*, Blameless wit.. Sometimes mildly interluding Amid strains of graver measure. **1887** *Harper's Mag.* LXXV. 583 Their conversation was interluded with snatches of songs.

Hence †**interluding** *vbl. sb.*, acting, stage-playing. Also †**interluder**, a player in an interlude.

1612 T. TAYLOR *Comm. Titus* ii. 15 Iesting, interluding, and stage representations. **1625** B. JONSON *Staple of N.* III. (*intermean*), Is 't not a fine sight, to see all our children made Enterluders? *a* **1626** MIDDLETON *Mayor of Queenborough* v. i. 68 Country comedians, interluders, sir, desire.. leave to enact in the town-hall.

interludial (ɪntə'l(j)uːdɪəl), *a.* [f. INTERLUDE *sb.* + -IAL.] Of, pertaining to, or of the nature of an interlude.

1884 *Encycl. Brit.* XVII. 94/1 Admitted for interludial purposes in a fabrication styled *intermezzo* that was played between the acts of a serious composition, comedy became [etc.]. **1922** S. GREW *Art of Player-Piano* 75 The interludial figure is extended to lead into a *forte*.

†**inter'luency.** *Obs. rare*$^{-1}$. [f. L. *interluent-em*, pr. pple. of *interluĕre* to flow between, f. *inter* between + *luĕre* to wash; see -ENCY, and cf. *influency*.] A flowing between.

a **1677** HALE *Prim. Orig. Man.* II. vii. 193 Those parts of Asia and America which are now dis-joyned by the interluency of the Sea, might have been formerly.. contiguous to each other.

interlunar (ɪntər'l(j)uːnə(r)), *a.* [f. INTER- 4 b + LUNAR, after L. *interlūnium* INTERLUNE; cf. F. *interlunaire* (16th c. in Littré).] Pertaining to the period between the old and new moon.

1598 I. D. tr. *Le Roy's Aristotles Politiques* 361 Betweene the interlunar spaces. **1671** MILTON *Samson* 89 Dark And silent as the moon, When she deserts the night, Hid in her vacant interlunar cave. **1794** SULLIVAN *View Nat.* I. 399 Towards the end of the interlunar interval. **1843** CARLYLE *Past & Pr.* II. vii, Our interlunar obscuration is to cease.

So †**inter'lunary** *a., Obs.*

1594 R. ASHLEY tr. *Le Roy's Interchangeable Var. Things* 12/2 The moone.. is seene alwaies towards the west betweene the interlunary spaces. **1646** SIR T. BROWNE *Pseud. Ep.* IV. xiii. 228 If we adde the two Ægyptian dayes in every moneth, the interlunary and plenilunary exemptions, the Eclipses of Sunne [etc.]. **1656** in BLOUNT *Glossogr.*

interlunation (-luː'neɪʃən). [See prec. and LUNATION.] The period between the old and new moon; *fig.* a blank or dark interval.

1813 JEFFREY *Let.* in Cockburn *Life* II. lxiv, This interlunation of your parliamentary course. *a* **1822** SHELLEY *Def. Poetry* Pr. Wks. 1888 II. 34 The vanishing apparitions which haunt the interlunations of life. **1854** J. D. BURNS *Vision Prophecy* 201 The great interlunation of its mind.

interlune. *rare*$^{-1}$. Also in L. form **interlunium.** [a. F. *interlune*, or ad. L. *interlūnium*, f. *inter* between + *lūna* moon.] = prec.

1561 EDEN *Arte of Navig.* II. xi. 38 b, The tyme that she is so [invisible], is called *Interlunium*. **1835** *Fraser's Mag.* XI. 186 Where pines.. Shut out the blessed moon, As 'twere the lightless interlune.

inter'lusory, *a. rare*$^{-1}$. [f. L. *interlūs-*, ppl. stem of *interlūdĕre* to play between + -ORY.] Appearing and disappearing sportively.

1853 DE QUINCEY *Autobiog. Sk.* Wks. I. 27 The half-sportive interlusory revealings of the symbolic tend to the same effect.

interly, -lych, obs. forms of ENTIRELY.

intermammillary, -mandibular: see INTER-.

inter-marginal: see INTER- *pref.* 4 a.

intermarriage (ɪntə'mærɪdʒ). Also 6–7 **enter-.** [INTER- 2 a.]

1. The action or fact of intermarrying; union in or connexion by marriage. **a.** Of two persons, or of one person *with* another. Now only in legal phraseology = 'Marriage', in ordinary use.

1579 J. STUBBES *Gaping Gulf* C iij b, If entermariages emongst themselues in theyr owne family, can not stay this furye of theyrs. **1580** MRS. STUBB in *Lett. Lit. Men* (Camden) 42 Your poor subjects said wife hath, by many arguments since their entermarriage [etc.]. **16..** in Somers *Tracts* I. 551 That no Man shall be liable to any Action for any Debt contracted by his Wife during their Inter-marriage. **1692** *Wicked Contriv. S. Blackhead* in *Select. fr. Harl. Misc.* (1793) 523 Persons, who were present at the inter-marriage of the said Ann to the said Robert Young. **1709** STEEL *Tatler* No. 9 ¶2 A Liberty our Family has.. from an Inter-Marriage with a Daughter of Mr. Scoggin. **1800** WEEMS *Washington* ii. (1877) 11 From his intermarriage with this charming girl. **1848** WHARTON *Law Lex.* 302/1 A bond given by a husband to his intended wife, upon a condition not to be performed in his life-time.. would not be extinguished by the inter-marriage; for marriage extinguishes such contracts only as are for debts or things which are due in *præsenti*.

b. Marriage between members of different families, castes, tribes, nations, or societies, as establishing a connexion between such families, etc.

1602 WARNER *Alb. Eng.* Epit. (1612) 367 Through continued supplies of their owne nation.. intermarriages, and confederacies with ours. *a* **1635** NAUNTON *Fragm. Reg.* (Arb.) 25 Apprehending the insafety and danger of an inter-marriage with the Bloud-Royall. **1695** TEMPLE *Hist. Eng.* Introd. (R.), The Normans began generally, by force of intermarriages.. to use the English tongue. **1798** COLEBROOKE *Misc. Ess.* (1873) II. 163 A third set of Indian classes originate from the intermarriages of the first and second set. **1841** BORROW *Zincali* I. iii. II. 274 It is.. by intermarriage alone that the two races will ever commingle. **1893** P. C. MOZOOMDAR in Barrows *World's Parlt. Relig.* I. 347 In 1851 the first intermarriage was celebrated. Intermarriage in India means the marriage of persons belonging to different castes.

2. *loosely.* Marriage between persons (or interbreeding between animals) nearly related; consanguineous marriage or breeding.

[**1875** W. RIDLEY *Kámilarói* 162 The effects of these [native Australian] rules, in passing every family through each of the four classes in as many generations, and in preventing the intermarriage of near relations, will appear on inspection of this pedigree.] **1882** J. P. IRVINE in *Quain's Dict. Med.* 384/2 Intermarriage certainly predisposes to disease.. Breeders of first-class animals practise intermarriage, and thereby develop speed, quality, and endurance in the offspring.

inter'marriageable (-dʒəb(ə)l), *a. rare.* [f. prec. + -ABLE.] Capable of intermarrying.

1899 *19th Cent.* July 53 It is of the essence of the existing constitution of intermarriageable groups.. to narrow the range of individual marriage.

intermarry (ɪntə'mærɪ), *v.* Also 6–7 **enter-.** [INTER- 1 b.]

1. *intr.* To contract matrimony, to enter into marriage; to marry. **a.** Said of a couple; hence of one person (*with* another). Now only in legal phraseology, in which it is the ordinary word for the intransitive use.

1574 tr. *Littleton's Tenures* 6 a, Issues that come of the donees after the fowerth degree.. may betwixt them by yᵉ law of holy church inter marye. *a* **1626** BACON *Max. & Uses Com. Law* ix. (1636) 37 If the feme be disseised and intermarry with the disseisor. **1650** *Bury Wills* (Camden) 224 My desire is that she shall not entermarry with any, but live singly. **1721** *St. German's Doctor & Stud.* 70 One of the men entermarrieth with the woman, and alieneth the land. **1823** *Act 4 Geo. IV*, c. 76 §22 If any Persons.. shall knowingly and wilfully intermarry without due Publication of Banns, or License.. obtained. **1855** MOTLEY *Dutch Rep.* (1861) II. 286 She was then to intermarry with Norfolk.

b. Of members of different families, castes, tribes, nations, or societies, in reference to the connexion thus formed between such families, etc.

1611 SPEED *Hist. Gt. Brit.* IX. xx. §66. 974 Neighbour-Kings reputed it safe to enter-marry with his Family. **1665** MANLEY *Grotius' Low C. Warres* 962 The Hollanders obtaining a garrison there, intermarried with the Native Women. **1701** SWIFT *Contests Athens & Rome* iii. Misc. (1731) 37 About the middle of the fourth century from the building of Rome, it was declared lawful for nobles and plebeians to intermarry. *a* **1789** MICKLE *Inq. Bramin Philos.* (R.), As the Gentoo tribe never intermarry, India may properly be said to contain four different nations. **1899** SAYCE *Early Israel* i. 53 The Israelites intermarried with the older population.

c. To marry with each other.

1839–40 W. IRVING *Wolfert's R.* (1855) 15 The inhabitants of the Hollow were of the primitive stock, and had intermarried, and bred in and in, from the earliest time of the province. **1843** BETHUNE *Sc. Fireside Stor.* 113 They had married, and intermarried, till nearly the whole inhabitants of the place were in some way or other connected.

2. *trans.* To join in marriage, to marry (those who are of different races); in quot. *fig.* (*rare.*)

1863 HAWTHORNE *Our Old Home* 82 Without any attempt at intermarrying it [the old custom or institution] with modern fashions.

Hence **inter'marrying** *vbl. sb.* and *ppl. a.*

1843 *Manning & Granger's Rep.* V. 697 Since the intermarrying of the plaintiffs, a *sci. fa.* had issued to recover the judgment. **1881** *Athenæum* 16 Apr. 528/2 Suppose the people of Middlesex and the people of Surrey to represent two intermarrying but exogamous classes.

inter-mask, -mason, -mastoid: see INTER-.

intermat (ɪntə'mæt), *v.* [INTER- 1 b.] *trans.* and *intr.* To mat together.

1904 GOODCHILD & TWENEY *Technol. & Sci. Dict.* 312/2 *Intermat* (Textile Manufac.), the term applied to the felting or shrinking of cloths, the fibres intermatting or felting

together. **1927** *Daily Express* 18 Apr. 3/7 As the hair grows, it is worked into a kind of felt by intermatting it.

‖**intermaxilla** (ˌɪntəmæk'sɪlə). *Anat.* Pl. **-æ.** [mod.L., f. INTER- 3 + MAXILLA.] Each of two bones situated between the maxillary bones of the upper jaw, in man small and soon fusing with these, but in most mammals large, distinct, and situated in front of them (thus more often called *premaxillæ* or *premaxillary bones*).

1882 in OGILVIE (Annandale). **1887** in *Syd. Soc. Lex.*

†**inter'maxillar,** *a. Anat. Obs. rare.* [INTER- 4 a.] = next.

1801 *Med. Jrnl.* V. 566 Mr. Fischer..asserts..that there is no trace of an intermaxillar bone in the human species, the rimula semilunaris having only a very distant analogy with it.

intermaxillary (ˌɪntə'mæksɪlərɪ, -mæk'sɪlərɪ), *a.* (*sb.*) *Anat.* and *Zool.* [INTER- 4 a.]

a. Situated between the maxillæ (i.e. the chief bones of the upper jaw in Vertebrates, or the cephalic appendages so called in Insects and Crustaceans); as in ***intermaxillary bone*** (= INTERMAXILLA), ***intermaxillary apodeme.*** **b.** Belonging or attached to the intermaxilla; as ***intermaxillary teeth*** (in mammals, the incisors).

1826 KIRBY & SP. *Entomol.* III. xxxiv. 431 Unless it be synonymous with the *intermaxillary arcade* of Marcel de Serres. **1836–9** TODD *Cycl. Anat.* II. 48/2 The intermaxillary bone is excessively small in Ant-eaters. **1870** ROLLESTON *Anim. Life* 6 Teeth are never found [in Mammals] elsewhere than upon the mandibular, maxillary and intermaxillary bones. **1877** HUXLEY *Anat. Inv. Anim.* vi. 312 The intermaxillary apodeme..developed from the connecting membrane of the two maxillary somites. **1886** *Syd. Soc. Lex., Intermaxillary gland,* a convoluted tubular gland found in Amphibia.

B. as *sb.* Short for *intermaxillary bone,* etc.

1834 MCMURTRIE *Cuvier's Anim. Kingd.* 215 The Herrings have two well-marked characters in the narrow and short intermaxillaries, that constitute but a small portion of the upper jaw. **1870** ROLLESTON *Anim. Life* 6 The intermaxillaries, in relation with which the upper incisors are first developed.

intermealary, -measurable: see INTER-.

†**inter'mean,** *sb. Obs. rare.* Also 7 enter-. [f. INTER- 2 b + MEAN *sb.* Cf. OF. *entremoyen* (1328 in Godef.).] An intermediate part, act, etc.; something introduced between the parts of something else, as a dialogue between the acts of a play; an interlude.

1599 MINSHEU *Sp. Dict., Intermedio,* the intermeanes. **1611** FLORIO, *Intramezzamento,* an entermeane. **1625** B. JONSON *Staple of N.* I, The first Intermean after the first act. **1801** STRUTT *Sports & Past.* III. ii. §6. **1834** SOUTHEY *Doctor* I. 104, I reject the designation of Intermeans, though it hath the sanction of great Ben's authority.

†**intermeate,** *v. Obs. rare*$^{-0}$. [f. ppl. stem of L. *intermeāre,* f. *inter* between + *meāre* to go, pass.] (See quot.) So †**interme'ation.** *Obs. rare*$^{-0}$.

1656 BLOUNT *Glossogr., Intermeate (intermeo),* to go or flow between, to pass through. **1658** PHILLIPS, *Intermeation,* a passing between.

intermeddle (ɪntə'mɛd(ə)l), *v.* Forms: α. 4–6 entremedle, (-el), 5–6 -meddle, 5–7 entermedle, (-el), 6–7 -meddle. β. 5–7 intermedle, (6 -el, intremedle, intermeddyl), 6– intermeddle. [ME. *entremedle,* a. AF. *entremedle-r,* = OF. *entremesler,* F. *entremêler,* f. *entre-,* L. *inter-* + AF. *medler* (Britton), OF. *mesler* to MEDDLE.]

†**1.** *trans.* To 'meddle' or mix together; to intermingle; to intermix. Const. *with. Obs.*

c **1384** CHAUCER *H. Fame* III. 1034 With shrippes bret-ful of lesenges Entremedled with tydynges. *c* **1430** *Pilgr. Lyf Manhode* II. lix. (1869) 98 Bushes thorny..and thikke entermedled. *c* **1450** *Merlin* 164 The bateilles were entermedled that oon with the tother. **1494** FABYAN *Chron.* VII. 449 [King Edward] made clayme to the hole crowne of Fraunce..and..entermedelyd the armys of Englande with the armys of Fraunce. **1577** B. GOOGE *Heresbach's Husb.* II. (1586) 72 b, Entermedling the greater with the lesser. **1599** SANDYS *Europæ Spec.* (1632) 239 Their Liturgy is intermedled much with singing. **1658** BROMHALL *Treat. Specters* I. 40 He might intermeddle some holy discourse out of holy Writ. **1733** MADDOX *Vind. Ch. Eng.* 155 Some keep precisely the Order of the Book, others intermeddle Psalms in Metre.

†**b.** To interpose. *Obs.*

1577–87 HOLINSHED *Scot. Chron.* (1805) II. 117 He wrote to pope Innocent..praying him to intermeddle his authority by sending some legat into Scotland. **1581** J. BELL *Haddon's Answ. Osor.* 474 b, Constantine..entermedled his authoritye in the pacyfying of quarells.

†**2.** *refl.* To mix oneself up *with*; to take part, concern oneself, interfere: = next. *Obs.*

1483 CAXTON *Cato* B v, Hyt is grete presumpsion for to entremeddle hym ne to enquere of the counceyl of other. **1494** FABYAN *Chron.* VII. 391 That no cytezyn shulde entermedle hym with ye sayd straungers. **1559** ABP. HETHE in Strype *Ann. Ref.* (1824) I. II. App. vi. 406 Her highness may not entermeddle her self with the same. **1594** T. B. *La Primaud. Fr. Acad.* II. 159 If reason intermeddle and mingle it selfe with them, it will be so troubled, that it will not be able to iudge as it ought of those things.

3. *intr.* To concern or occupy oneself *with* or *in*; to have to do *with*; to take part *in*; to meddle, interfere; *esp.* to concern oneself with what is none of one's business, to meddle or interfere impertinently.

c **1477** CAXTON *Jason* 16 b, All they sette hand on their swerdes and came for to entremedle with Jason. **1491** *Act 7 Hen. VII,* c. 16 §1 If..any othre persone..hath intermedled with theym. **1542–3** *Act 34 & 35 Hen. VIII,* c. 10 §2 Diuers other persons..entermedlynge with the same crafte or occupacion, hauing little experience therein. **1561** T. NORTON *Calvin's Inst.* IV. 39 The see of Rome was alway ready to entermedle. **1639** GENTILIS *Servita's Inquis.* (1676) 877 The Ministers of Christ, to whom is severely forbidden to entermeddle in it. **1683** *Lond. Gaz.* No. 1856 1 Because several Carriers..intermeddle with, and intrude upon the Office of the Post-Master General. **1785** BURKE *Nabob Arcot's Debts* Wks. IV. 198 The board of control had no right whatsoever to intermeddle in the business. **1834** MACAULAY *Ess., Pitt* (1854) 306 Fox would certainly intermeddle with that department. **1877** BLACK *Green Past.* xviii. (1878) 149 It was not to be expected that a woman should be constantly intermeddling in affairs of which she could not possibly be a fair judge.

†**inter'meddled,** *ppl. a. Obs.* [f. prec. + -ED[1].] Intermingled, intermixed.

1595 DANIEL *Civ. Wars* IV. xiv, And onely tell the worst of euery raigne; And not the intermedled good report. *a* **1617** P. BAYNE *On Eph.* (1658) 52 Predestination would bee an intermedled action; partly grace partly Justice.

inter'meddlement. [f. as prec. + -MENT. Cf. OF. *entremeslement* (Godef.).] An act, or the action, of intermeddling; impertinent interference.

1836 SIR J. Y. SIMPSON in *Life* iv. (1873) 76, I hate the intermeddlements of these folks yclept doctors. **1879** [LINGHAM] *Science Taste* v. 178 Our nervous intermeddlement in continental affairs.

intermeddler (ɪntə'mɛdlə(r)). Also 7 enter-. [f. as prec. + -ER[1].] One who intermeddles. †**a.** One who concerns himself or has to do with something. *Obs.* in *gen.* sense.

1576 HUMPHREY *Let. to Ld. Burghley* in Strype *Ann. Ref.* (1824) I. App. xxviii. 518 Wherin I was no open intermedler, but only a private solicitor. **1577** NORTHBROOKE *Dicing* (1843) 12 When they come to be citizens, and intermedlers in matters of the common welth.

†**b.** An intermediary. *Obs.*

1630 LENNARD tr. *Charron's Wisd.* (1658) 49 It is the great Intermedler and Huckster, by it we traffick. **1886** *Law Times* LXXX. 168/2 Before that time attorneys-at-law were not recognised as legal intermeddlers.

c. *spec.* One who meddles or interferes with what is none of his business; a meddler; in early use = INTERLOPER.

1601 JOHN WHEELER *Treat. Comm.* 11 With an expresse restraint of all Straglers and Entermedlers, that might disturbe, or impeach their trade. **1611** COTGR., *Entremetteur,*..an intermedler, or dealer in other mens causes, or controuersies. **16..** R. L'ESTRANGE (J.), There's hardly a greater pest to government and families, than officious tale-bearers, and busy intermeddlers. **1702** *Eng. Theophrast.* 130 Busy bodies and intermedlers are a dangerous sort of people to have to do withal. **1876** BLACK *Madcap V.* xxv. 236 You know, Violet, what intermeddlers get as a rule.

inter'meddlesome, *a. rare*$^{-0}$. [f. INTERMEDDLE *v.* + -SOME.] 'Prone to intermeddle; meddlesome'. Hence **inter'meddlesomeness.**

1864 in WEBSTER.

intermeddling (ɪntə'mɛdlɪŋ), *vbl. sb.* Forms: see the verb. [f. as prec. + -ING[1].] The action of the verb INTERMEDDLE.

†**1.** Intermingling. *Obs.*

1591 SYLVESTER *Du Bartas* I. iii. *margin,* The intermedling of the Earth and Sea, and of the commodities thence arising, and contrariwise of the confusion that would follow, if they were separated.

2. Concerning oneself, having to do *with*; interference. **b.** *esp.* Impertinent interference; meddling.

1531 ELYOT *Gov.* III. i, That parte of iustyce is contayned in intremedlynge, and somtyme is voluntary, somtyme involuntary intermedlynge. **1607** HIERON *Wks.* I. 287 So great an euill, as is the entermedling with the seales of Gods couenant. **1705** HEARNE *Collect.* 20 Nov. (O.H.S.) I. 87 The Dutchess of Marlborough's Intermeddling. **1752** CARTE *Hist. Eng.* III. 349 To give the duke a discharge for all his intermeddlings with the publick money. **1884** H. A. TAINE in *Contemp. Rev.* Oct. 525 Nothing is more destructive than the unrestricted intermeddling of the State.

inter'meddling, *ppl. a.* [f. as prec. + -ING[2].] That intermeddles. †**1.** Intermingling. *Obs.*

1595 [implied in INTERMEDDLINGLY].

2. Interfering, meddlesome.

1804 RANKEN *Hist. France* III. II. 287 It showed the intermeddling spirit of the Church. **1825** BENTHAM *Ration. Rew.* 110 All governments have been more or less infected with that intermeddling disposition.

Hence **inter'meddlingly** *adv.,* †(in quot.) with intermingling, promiscuously (*obs.*).

1595 *Polimanteia* (1881) 11 They are all so intermedlingly inwrapped each in other states, that scarse anie knoweth how to escape himselfe.

'intermede. [a. F. *intermède* (Molière, 17th c.), ad. It. *intermedio,* ad. L. *intermedium,* neuter of *intermedius* adj.: see INTERMEDIUM.]

†**1.** Something that serves as a means of some action between other things; a medium: = INTERMEDIUM 3. *Obs.*

1791 HAMILTON *Berthollet's Dyeing* I. ii. 28 The title Mordant is applied to those substances which serve as intermedes between the colouring particles and the stuff to be dyed, either for the purpose of facilitating or of modifying their combination. **1794** J. HUTTON *Philos. Light,* etc. 225 The electrical fluid..is made to leap from one conducting body to another, through a short space, without any sensible intermede, or through a rare transparent fluid. **1796** PEARSON in *Phil. Trans.* LXXXVI. 438 Copper may be united to steel without the intermede of any other metal.

2. An intermediate performance, interlude: = INTERMEDIUM 2. Now current only in alien form *intermède* (ɛ̃tɛrmɛd).

1820 T. MITCHELL *Aristoph.* I. 247 A short *intermede* relieves the time, while the two disputants are absent fetching their oracles. **1887** *Gentl. Mag.* June 540 The singularly appropriate *intermède* arranged by Beaumarchais for performance between the acts of his 'Eugenie'. **1931** *Times Lit. Suppl.* 6 Aug. 606/2 The inclusion between the first and second acts of an *intermède* of song and dance. **1970** *Oxf. Compan. Mus.* (ed. 10) 517/2 It was as *intermezzo* or *intermède* that the comic opera grew up.

intermedia, plural of INTERMEDIUM.

intermediacy (ɪntə'miːdɪəsɪ). *rare.* [f. INTERMEDIATE *a.*: see -ACY.] The state of being intermediate; intermediateness; intermediate agency, intervention.

1713 DERHAM *Phys.-Theol.* IV. iii. (1727) 126 (*note*), In Birds, the auditory Nerve is affected by the Impressions made on the Membrane, by only the Intermediacy of the Columella. **1836** T. HOOK *G. Gurney* III. 177, I had..fallen into a purgatorial state of intermediacy between sleeping and waking. *c* **1840** SIR W. HAMILTON *Logic* App. II. 430 To preserve the order of intermediacy, so that..we assign the middle place to the middle term.

inter'medial, *a.* and *sb.* [f. L. *inter medi-us* intermediate + -AL[1]: cf. L. *mediāl-is* MEDIAL.]

A. *adj.* **1.** = INTERMEDIATE *a.* (in various uses).

1599 SANDYS *Europæ Spec.* (1632) 237 That service intermediall which he requires at his hand. **1613** M. RIDLEY *Magn. Bodies* 27 At the poles, or any intermediall part. **1679** BURNET *Hist. Ref.* I. 351 In the Record there is no mention of any intermedial prorogation. **1704** NORRIS *Ideal World* II. vii. 340 All the intermedial spaces between the earth and the heavens. **1852** TH. ROSS *Humboldt's Trav.* II. xx. 251 It was ..supposed that, wherever mountains are divided into parallel chains, the intermedial or central ridge must be more elevated than the others. **1942** *Mind* LI. 80 Part II is a systematic and richly illustrated description of generic and special forms, of inter-medial and intra-medial forms.

2. = INTERMEDIARY *a.* 1.

1649 JER. TAYLOR *Gt. Exemp.* Pref. §3 That end, to which they are fitted with organs and intermediall appetites. **1660** —— *Duct. Dubit.* III. iii. rule 6 §15 Temporal things are not ordained to minister to spiritual intermedial things. **1846** MRS. GORE *Eng. Char.* (1852) 135 To manage the intermedial negotiations..requires no trifling exercise of vicarial tact.

B. *sb.* = INTERMEDIATE *sb.*

1605 TIMME *Quersit.* I. xvi. 80 The antimonials, from the intermedials (that is to say, from things partly good and partly malignant) receive a worse nature. **1625** USSHER *Answ. Jesuit* 435 The Pope is appealed vnto, any intermediall whatsoeuer omitted. **1654** JER. TAYLOR *Real Pres.* 224 His body is in none of the intermedials.

†**inter'median,** *a. Obs. rare*$^{-0}$. [f. L. *intermedi-us* intermediate + -AN: cf. L. *mediān-us* MEDIAN.] = INTERMEDIATE *a.*

1656 BLOUNT *Glossogr., Intermedian,* that lieth, or is between two.

†**inter'mediant,** *a. Obs. rare*$^{-1}$. [? corruption of *intermediate,* after words of ppl. origin in -ANT.] Intervening, intermediate.

1716 M. DAVIES *Athen. Brit.* III. *Dissert. Phys.* 6 Commerce with the Phenicians, and other conterminous Countrys and intermediant Nations.

intermediary (ɪntə'miːdɪərɪ), *a.* and *sb.* [f. med.L. type **intermediāri-us,* f. *intermedium*: cf. F. *intermédiaire* (1678 in Hatz.-Darm.), perh. the immediate source.]

A. *adj.* **1.** Acting or of the nature of action between two persons, parties, etc.; serving as a means of interaction; mediatory.

1818 HALLAM *Mid. Ages* iii. II. (1855) I. 457 Without an intermediary power between the doge and the patrician multitude. **1869** ROGERS *Note Adam Smith's W.N.* I. I. i. 6 Such a system tends to eliminate intermediary agents.

2. Situated or occurring between two things (in space, time, degree, or character); intermediate.

1788 *New Lond. Mag.* 537 Whether the Shamoys..may not form with our goats some intermediary race. **1799** *Hist. Eur.* in *Ann. Reg.* (1800) 28/2 A plan or project..for an intermediary government was presented by Chazal. **1823** H. J. BROOKE *Crystallogr.* 67 Decrements have been already defined to be either simple, mixed, or intermediary. **1875** BLAKE *Zool.* 36 The canines..are separated from the molars by a large diastema or intermediary vacancy. **1882** J. HAWTHORNE *Fort. Fool* I. xxi, During this intermediary stage of her life.

B. *sb.* **1.** One who acts between others; an intermediate agent; a go-between middleman, mediator.

1791 GOUV. MORRIS in Sparks *Life & Writ.* (1832) I. 357 He thinks the Emperor will become the intermediary. **1831** SOUTHEY in *Q. Rev.* XLV. 441 They serve as intermediaries between the labourers, who want instruments of labour, and the possessors of those instruments. **1866** ROGERS *Agric. & Prices* I. xxvii. 652 None were intermediaries to the producer and consumer. **1883** *Manch. Guard.* 10 Oct. 4/6 The prisoner had been speculating largely on the Stock Exchange through an intermediary.

2. Something acting between persons or things, a medium, means; also *abstr.* Action as a medium, mediation, agency (*of* something).

1859 SALA *Tw. round Clock* (1861) 183 Mysteriously transmitting them through the intermediary of glib Jew boys with curly heads. **1880** *Daily Tel.* 8 Oct., We are the only European people who teach practical geometry through the recondite intermediary of Euclid's 'Elements'.

3. Something intermediate between others; an intermediate form or stage.

1865 *Intell. Observ.* No. 37. 11 No intermediaries were known. **1890** *Anthony's Photogr. Bull.* III. 121 The equalizing of these two extremes and their intermediaries is the work of the photographer.

intermediate (ɪntəˈmiːdɪət), *a.* and *sb.* [ad. med.L. *intermediāt-us*, f. L. *intermedi-us*: cf. *mediate*, *immediate*, and F. *intermédiat* (*a* 1519 in Godef. *Compl.*).]

A. *adj.* **1.** Coming or occurring between two things, places, etc.; 'holding the middle place or degree between two extremes' (J.); interposed, intervening.

a. in spatial position: Situated in the middle place, or between two things or places.

1646 SIR T. BROWNE *Pseud. Ep.* III. xix. 154 The two extremes would sufficiently performe the office of sight without the help of the intermediate eyes. **1665** HOOKE *MicrSogr.* 64 All the intermediate points between F and D. **1710** STEELE *Tatler* No. 179 ¶6 The intermediate Spaces are filled up with large Sashes. **1828** STARK *Elem. Nat. Hist.* II. 163 Four antennæ, the intermediate two short. **1884** F. J. BRITTEN *Watch & Clockm.* 124 Intermediate Wheel..a toothed wheel used to connect two others.

b. Occurring or coming between two points of time or events.

intermediate state (*Theol.*), the condition of souls after death and before resurrection; hence, Hades or the place of departed spirits.

1623 COCKERAM, *Intermediate speech*, a thing spoken betwixt. **16..** SOUTH *Serm.* (1717) V. 126 There was no Vacancy, or intermediate Chasm of Time, between the Arian Poyson ceasing, and the Popish Ferment beginning to infest the Church. **1748** HARTLEY *Observ. Man* I. iii. 350 He fixes all the most remarkable intermediate Events. **1777** PRIESTLEY *Matt. & Spir.* (1782) I. xxi. 279 The doctrine of an intermediate state is now retained by few. **1827** HARE *Guesses* Ser. I. (1838) 11 Most idle then are all disquisitions on the intermediate state, founded on the assumption that the soul, when apart from the body, has no perceptions. **1858** SEARS *Athan.* II. iv. 199 He did not tarry with them during the intermediate time.

c. in serial order, *e.g.* of numbers, or in logical or causal succession.

1641 WILKINS *Math. Magick* I. iv. (1648) 24 And in the like manner are we to conceive of the other intermediate divisions. **1790** PALEY *Horæ Paul.* i. (1849) 5 The intermediate steps through which the conclusion is deduced. **1821** J. Q. ADAMS in C. Davies *Metr. Syst.* III. (1871) 75 The intermediate measures were different. **1875** JOWETT *Plato* (ed. 2) IV. 8 The intermediate links which occur..in the passage from unity to infinity.

d. in amount, degree, rank, nature, or character.

Formerly applied to a class of passenger accommodation in steam ships, intermediate between 'saloon' and 'steerage'; now superseded by 'second class'. Also *intermediate education, school.*

1665 HOOKE *Microgr.* 58 The two principal colours, Scarlet and Blue, and all the intermediate ones which arise from the composition and dilutings of these two. **1720** WELTON *Suffer. Son of God* I. ix. 217 'Twas determined.. there should be something Intermediate and Woven, in the Corporeal and Spiritual Nature of Man, of a Third Sort. **1823** J. D. HUNTER *Captiv. N. Amer.* 7 A squaw of an intermediate stature. **1842** E. LAZARUS *Let.* 19 July in N. E. Eliason *Tarheel Talk* (1956) 278 There are the primary & the intermediate schools, & the high-school. **1860** TYNDALL *Glac.* II. i. 228 The vibrations which excite the other colours are intermediate between these two extremes. **1875** JOWETT *Plato* (ed. 2) III. 100 That middle state..intermediate between aristocracy and oligarchy. **1882** W. D. HAY *Brighter Britain* I. ii. 57 It doesn't matter twopence *how* you go out, whether saloon, intermediate, or steerage, so far as your future prospects are concerned. **1886** KIPLING *Plain Tales from Hills* (1888) 120 The four constables saw him safe to Umritsar in an 'intermediate' compartment. **1889** *Act 52–54 Vict.* c. 40 (*title*) An Act to promote Intermediate Education in Wales..sect. 1. This Act may be cited for all purposes as the Welsh Intermediate Education Act, 1889. *Ibid.* sect. 17 The expression 'intermediate education' means a course of education which does not consist chiefly of elementary instruction..but which includes instruction in Latin, Greek, the Welsh and English language and literature,..mathematics, natural and applied science. **1893** *Harper's Mag.* Apr. 806 Oh, she was a rose half-budded, in the intermediate school, And her face and form I studied twice as much as task or rule. **1945** C. V. GOOD *Dict. Educ.* 223 Intermediate school: a school that enrolls pupils in intermediate grades, usually comprising the fourth, fifth, and sixth years of schoolwork. **1974** *Times* 1 Apr. (Yorkshire & Humberside Suppl.) p. i/2 Yorkshire and Humberside is classified as an 'intermediate area'. As such, while enjoying the benefits of financial inducements available to incoming and expanding industry, it does not rank for the benefits available in the other two types of aided regions.

e. in position or function: Intervening between persons or parties.

1783 BURKE *9th Rep. Aff. India* Wks. XI. 87 The Company might suffer above, the Natives might suffer below; the intermediate party must profit to the prejudice of both. **1855** MACAULAY *Hist. Eng.* xx. IV. 426 How much of it was embezzled by intermediate agents.

2. Specific techn. uses.

a. *Petrol.* Of a rock: having a silicate content that falls between that of the acidic and that of the basic rocks (cf. ACIDIC *a.* 2, BASIC *a.* 2b); often *spec.* having a silicate content between 52 and 66 per cent by weight.

1888 J. J. H. TEALL *Brit. Petrogr.* viii. 253 The basic rocks shade into the intermediate rocks, and these again into the acid rocks, in the most gradual manner. **1892** F. H. HATCH *Text-bk. Petrol.* (ed. 2) vi. 107 In respect to the percentage of silica, igneous rocks fall naturally into four groups, viz.:—(1) An acid group with 65–80% of silica... (2) An intermediate group with 55–70% of silica... (3) A basic group with 45–60% of silica... (4) An ultrabasic group with silica between 35 and 50%. **1909** *Ibid.* (ed. 5) III. i. 152 Arranged in the order of their silica contents, the plutonic rocks can be divided into three groups: 1. Acid, with silica contents above 66 per cent. 2. Intermediate, with silica contents between 66 and 52 per cent; and 3. Basic, with silica contents below 52. **1939** A. JOHANNSEN *Descr. Petrogr. Ign. Rocks* (ed. 2) I. 181 (*gloss.*) *Intermediate rocks*, rocks intermediate between the 'acid' and 'basic' groups. Syn. Neutral rocks, medio-silicic. Cf. Acid. **1968** B. BAYLY *Introd. Petrol.* vi. 53 The second system is chemical rather than mineralogical, being based on the weight percentage of SiO_2 in the rock; thus if SiO_2 percentage is: over 66, rock is acid; 52–66, rock is intermediate; 45–52, rock is basic; under 45, rock is ultrabasic.

b. *Nuclear Physics.* Applied to neutrons with less energy than fast neutrons but more than thermal neutrons, and also to nuclear reactors in which such neutrons are the chief cause of fission.

1947 *Rep. U.S. Atomic Energy Commission* A-4315 (*title*) A multi-group method for computing critical masses of intermediate piles. **1949** *Nucleonics* Dec. 41/1 Intermediate piles may operate with neutrons at any energy level between thermal and fission or even at several different energy levels. **1956** GLASSTONE *Princ. Nucl. Reactor Engin.* i. 15 In nuclear reactor work, the term *fast neutrons* is applied to neutrons having energies of about 0·1 Mev, i.e., 10^5 ev, or more. Those with energies from 10^5 ev down to 1 ev are called intermediate neutrons. **1959** L. F. CURTISS *Introd. Neutron Physics* i. 18 Less information has been accumulated about intermediate neutrons than about neutrons of lower energies because of [the] difficulty of finding efficient detectors. **1966** *McGraw-Hill Encycl. Sci. & Technol.* XI. 358/1 An example of an intermediate reactor is the first propulsion reactor for the submarine USS *Seawolf*. The fuel core consisted of enriched uranium with beryllium as a moderator.

3. Specific collocations: **intermediate boson**: see BOSON; **intermediate frequency** *Electronics*, the frequency to which an incoming carrier wave is converted by the frequency changer of a superheterodyne receiver; abbrev. *I.F.*; **intermediate host** *Zool.*, an organism infected by a parasitic animal which then goes on to complete its life cycle in another host; **intermediate-range**, used *attrib.* of a ballistic missile of medium range (less than 'intercontinental').

1924 *Proc. IRE* XII. 540 Three intermediate frequency amplifiers. **1947** D. G. FINK *Radar Engin.* x. 504 The [radar receiver] system which avoids the foregoing difficulties is the superheterodyne, which introduces an initial change from radio frequency to a lower frequency (intermediate frequency) followed by a high-gain amplification at this frequency. **1968** B. P. LATHI *Communication Syst.* iii. 202 The advantage of conversion to an intermediate frequency is that to receive different stations it is necessary to tune only the first stage (and the local oscillator). All of the amplification is achieved at a constant intermediate frequency and needs no tuning. **1878** *Jrnl. R. Microsc. Soc.* I. 377 The ultimate form assumed by the larvae whilst still within the body of the intermediate host. **1892** [see HOST *sb.*[2] 3]. **1901** *Practitioner* Mar. 273 It is parasitic in man and in a certain genus of mosquito (Anopheles); the former is its intermediate host and the latter its definitive host. **1925** A. D. IMMS *Gen. Textbk. Ent.* III. 365 The latter issue from the galls and are divisible into winged *gallicolæ migrantes* (migrantes), which fly to the intermediate host, and *gallicolæ non-migrantes* which remain on the spruce and give rise to further fundatrices. **1971** E. R. & G. A. NOBLE *Parasitol.* (ed. 3) xxiv. 528/1 As a generalization, there is less host specificity when there are two intermediate hosts than when only one is employed. **1956** *Newsweek* 30 Jan. 27/1 Developing a 1,500-mile intermediate-range ballistic missile (IRBM) is now largely a question of 'straightforward engineering'. **1957** *Economist* 30 Nov. 774/2 The Polaris, the intermediate range ballistic missile to be launched from submarines. **1959** *Listener* 18 June 1053/1 Intermediate-range ballistic missiles—in other words, medium-range rockets.

B. *sb.* **1. a.** Something intermediate or intervening (in position, time, succession, degree, or character); a middle term; a nexus between two things.

1650 ELDERFIELD *Tythes* 339 My eye upon the main, diverts and takes me off from..giving all I think of the intermediates. **1784** J. BARRY in *Lect. Paint.* vi. (Bohn 1848) 217 The association or dissociation of colours with or without those intermediates of compound, half, or broken colour. **1792** T. TAYLOR *Proclus* I. Dissert. 71 Infinite intermediates cannot intervene between two finite terms. **1809–10** COLERIDGE *Friend* (1818) III. 123 By no intermediate could they be preserved in lasting adhesion. **1870** HOOKER *Stud. Flora* 120 All the so-called species are connected by intermediates.

b. *Math.* A syzygetic function of two quantics of the same order.

1858 CAYLEY in *Math. Papers* (1889) II. 515.

c. *Chem.* and *Biochem.* A compound which after being produced by one reaction participates in another; *esp.* one manufactured from naturally occurring materials for use in the synthesis of dyes, plastics, or other substances.

1919 E. DE B. BARNETT *Coal Tar Dyes* I. ii. 29 Aniline. —This is the most important intermediate, and is invariably manufactured by the reduction of nitrobenzole. *Ibid.* 31 Factories preparing their own intermediates. **1938** *Nature* 30 July 203/2 Mr. F. P. Garvan's appreciation of the dependence of the United States on Germany for dyes, intermediates, photographic chemicals, medicinals, etc., led him to organize the Chemical Foundation. **1953** *Nature* 27 June 1160/2 (*heading*) Occurrence of hydroxylamine in lake waters as an intermediate in bacterial reduction of nitrate. **1961** *Times* 30 May (I.C.I. Suppl.) p. xvi/1 All of them are 'intermediates'—the raw materials of other products such as Terylene or plastics. **1962** J. HINE *Physical Org. Chem.* (ed. 2) vii. 163 In most of the S_N1 reactions that have been studied kinetically the carbonium ion is a very reactive intermediate that is rapidly transformed into the final product. **1962** [see HOMOCYSTEINE].

2. A person who intervenes between others.

1879 FARRAR *St. Paul* II. 445 Representing God as a Being so far removed..that they could only approach him through a series of angelic intermediates. **1888** BRYCE *Amer. Commw.* II. III. lxiv. 470 Rendering a little homage to decency by seeking to do it through intermediates.

intermediate (ɪntəˈmiːdɪeɪt), *v.* Also 7 **enter-.** [f. INTER- 1 + MEDIATE *v.*]

†**1.** *intr.* To come in or occur between, to intervene. *Obs.*

1652 FRENCH *Yorksh. Spa* xv. 113 The full proportion [must] be not taken at once, but at several times, exercise intermediating.

†**2.** To come in among others in the way of action; to interfere, interpose. *Obs.*

1610 HOLLAND *Camden's Brit.* I. 135 They had an opinion, that she intermediated in humane affaires. **1611** FLORIO, *Intermediare*, to enter-mediate. **1638** FORD *Lady's Trial* V. i, I'll tell you what conditions threaten danger Unless you intermediate. **1694, 1716** [see INTERMEDIATING below].

3. To act between others; to mediate.

1624 BP. MOUNTAGU *Immed. Addr.* 118 It is either because they will not intermediate for vs..Or because they cannot. **1838** MOORE *Diary* 26 May in *Mem.* (1856) VII. 226 Leaving the whole conduct of the death-bed scene to an abbé, who intermediated. **1872** HUXLEY *Phys.* viii. 190 To intermediate between these agents and the nerves of sight and hearing.

4. *trans.* To join by parts of intermediate character. *rare.*

1880 WALDSTEIN *Pythag. Rhegion* 27 In poor work, the muscles, joints, &c...are not intermediated—they seem put together; while in good work..all flows together, as in nature.

Hence **interˈmediating** *ppl. a.*, interposing, acting as an intermediary.

1694 tr. *Milton's Lett. State, to Charles Gustavus* May an. 1655, That you would..by interposing your intermediating Authority, endeavour to avert the horrid Cruelty of this Edict. **1716** M. DAVIES *Athen. Brit.* II. 382 That the Son.. proceeded Naturally and Necessarily from the Father without his Intermediating Fiat or Creating Volition. **1866** J. H. NEWMAN *Let. Pusey* (ed. 2) 90 It is the Divine Presence which is the intermediating Power by which we reach her [Mary] and she reaches us.

intermediately (ɪntəˈmiːdɪətlɪ), *adv.* [f. INTERMEDIATE *a.* + -LY[2].]

1. In an intermediate position or relation; in the intervening space, time, etc.; between two things in position, succession, degree, or other relation.

1730–6 BAILEY (folio), *Intermediately*, lying in a manner between. **1822–34** *Good's Study Med.* (ed. 4) III. 223 This last case is given by Dr. Darwin, whom the patient had intermediately consulted. **1877** BURROUGHS *Taxation* 153 He stands intermediately between the producer and consumer.

2. By intermediate agency; indirectly: opp. to *immediately*.

1755 JOHNSON, *Intermediately*, by way of intervention. **1796** MORSE *Amer. Geog.* I. 755 Were the council..chosen by the people, instead of being intermediately chosen by electors. **1822–34** *Good's Study Med.* (ed. 4) II. 256 An abscess that has..discharged its contents immediately or intermediately into the intestinal canal.

interˈmediateness. [f. as prec. + -NESS.] The state of being intermediate; intermediacy.

1854 GEO. ELIOT tr. *Feuerbach's Essence Christianity* xii. 123 Thoughts of intermediateness and dependence. **1909** W. R. SORLEY *Interpretation of Evolution* 28 The characteristics of life, indeed,..have a certain appearance of intermediateness. **1958** P. A. M. DIRAC *Princ. Quantum Mech.* (ed. 4) i. 13 The probability of a particular result for the state formed by superposition is not always intermediate between those for the original states..so there are restrictions on the 'intermediateness' of a state formed by superposition.

intermediation (ɪntəmiːdɪˈeɪʃən). [n. of action from INTERMEDIATE *v.*, or f. INTER- 2a +

MEDIATION.] The action of intermediating; interposition, intervention, mediation.

1602 FULBECKE *Pandectes* 62 By the agreement of frends or intermediation of others. **1651** JER. TAYLOR *Clerus Dom.* 35 There can be no reason..why God will accept the intermediation of one man for many. **1798** PENNANT *Hindoostan* I. 39 They worship God alone, without image or intermediation. **1854** J. SCOFFERN in *Orr's Circ. Sc., Chem.* 213 The intermediation of a non-conducting material. **1885** *Manch. Exam.* 24 Jan. 5/4 Why..should not a client be able to consult a barrister without the intermediation of a solicitor?

intermediator (ɪntəˈmiːdɪeɪtə(r)). [f. INTER- 2 a + MEDIATOR, or f. INTERMEDIATE *v.*, after *mediator.*] One who or that which intermediates; a mediator.

1522 J. CLERK in Ellis *Orig. Lett.* Ser. III. I. 313 Intermediators in bryngyng that to passe. **1864** in WEBSTER. **1872** HUXLEY *Phys.* viii. 191 The epidermis..is the intermediator between the nerve and the physical agent. **1873** TRISTRAM *Moab* i. 8 Attached himself to us as a sort of intermediator in various negotiations.

intermediatory (ɪntəˈmiːdɪətərɪ), *a.* [f. INTERMEDIATE *v.* + -ORY.] Having the function of intermediating; mediatory.

1851 *Fraser's Mag.* XLIV. 608 Animosities are softened by the intermediatory offices of an unpremeditated libation.

intermedin (ɪntəˈmiːdɪn). *Physiol.* Also -ine. [a. G. *intermedin* (Zondek & Krohn 1932, in *Klin. Wochenschr.* 5 Mar. 406/1), f. mod.L. (*pars*) *intermed(ia* the intermediate part (of the hypophysis) + -IN[1].] = *melanocyte-stimulating hormone.*

1932 *Q. Cumulative Index Medicus* XI. 900/1 Red coloring of European minnow as test of intermedin from pars intermedia. **1948** G. H. PARKER *Animal Colour Changes* vi. 194 The intermedine system in amphibians is assumed to operate in the following manner. **1963** M. FINGERMAN *Control Chromatophores* vi. 103 Two general types of intermedin have been found. **1964** E. J. W. BARRINGTON in Pincus & Thimann *Hormones* IV. v. 327 The particular hormone involved, formerly known as intermedin, or B-substance, but now more usually termed melanocyte-stimulating hormone, or MSH.

intermedio-lateral (ɪntəˌmiːdɪəʊˈlætərəl), *a. Anat.* Also **intermediolateral**. [ad. mod.L. *intermedio-lateralis*, f. mod.L. *intermedio-*, comb. form of L. *intermedius* intermediate + L. *lateralis* lateral.] Both intermediate and lateral: applied *spec.* to the tract of nerve cells which constitutes the lateral grey column of the spinal cord.

[**1859** J. L. CLARKE in *Phil. Trans. R. Soc.* CXLIX. 446 This tract..was first pointed out by myself in 1851. I shall call it, on account of its position, the *tractus intermedio-lateralis*.] **1875** *Encycl. Brit.* I. 866/2 Lockhart Clarke described an intermedio-lateral group of nerve cells. **1906** *Fifth Rep. Carnegie Trust Scotland* 20 Pathology of the intermedio-lateral tract of the spinal cord. **1972** J. MINCKLER *Introd. Neuroscience* xxii. 382 The pre-ganglionic fibers arise in the intermediolateral column of cells of the ventral horn from segments T1 to L2.

†**interˈmedious**, *a. Obs. rare.* [f. L. *intermedi-us* intermediate + -OUS.] = INTERMEDIATE *a.* Hence †**interˈmediously** *adv. Obs. rare.*

1657 W. MORICE *Coena quasi Κοινή* Def. xv. 233 The Sacrament..may be adjumental intermediously. **1678** CUDWORTH *Intell. Syst.* I. iv. §36. 596 There was..Nothing Intermedious, or that could possibly be Thrust in between them. *Ibid* v. 851 A Tension of the Intermedious Air or Æther.

intermedium (ɪntəˈmiːdɪəm). Pl. **-ia**, **-iums**. Also 7 **enter-**. [a. L. *intermedium*, neuter of *intermedius*, f. *inter* between + *medius* mid, middle: cf. MEDIUM.]

1. Something intermediate in position; an intervening space, interval of space. ? *Obs.*

1611 COTGR., *Entredeux*, an intermedium, or interual. **1804** WATT in *Phil. Trans.* XCIV. 310 When no such intermedium occurred, there was invariably a division in the middle of the vein.

2. Something intermediate in time; an intervening action or performance (? *obs.*); †*esp.* one between the parts or acts of a play, an interlude.

1589 NASHE *Addr. Gentl. Stud.* in *Greene's Menaphon* (Arb.) 15 Silenus, when nodding on his Asse..made his moist nosecloth, the pausing intermedium, twixt euerie nappe. **1611** FLORIO, *Intermedio*,..Intermedium, the musike that is, or shewes that are betweene the acts of a play. **1658** BURBURY *Hist. Christ. Alessandra Queen Swedland* 456 Musical Playes..with rare changes of scenes, intermediums of dances, and most exquisite musick. **1838** CHALMERS *Wks.* XIII. 256 A long intermedium of many transitions and arguments.

b. An intervening time, interval of time. ? *Obs.*

1611 COTGR., *Entrecesse, sans*, without intermission, intermedium, rest, pause. **1617** in *Crt. & Times Jas. I* (1849) I. 413 Sudden mutations, without any intermedium. **1757** WASHINGTON *Lett.* Writ. 1889 I. 427 The French and Indians..repeating the stroke..sending down parties in the intermedium to discover our motions.

3. An intermediate agent, intermediary, medium; *esp.* in earlier *Chem.* and *Physics*, a substance serving as a means of some natural action or process; also *abstr.* intermediate agency, mediation (*of*).

1660 HICKERINGILL *Jamaica* (1661) 28 Growing immediately out of the bole or body of the Tree, and..admitting not so much as the intermedium or usherage of a twig. **1660** tr. *Amyraldus' Treat. conc. Relig.* III. i. 307 Between God and the Conscience of man there is no intermedium. **1756** C. LUCAS *Ess. Waters* I. 71 Oils [are] insoluble in water, without some proper intermedium. **1791** COWPER *Priv. Corr.* (1824) II. 273 The obliging request of a lady, and of a lady who employed you as her intermedium. **1825** J. NICHOLSON *Operat. Mechanic* 726 Uniting the silver by the intermedia of slips of rolled tin. **1839** *John Bull* 18 Aug. in *Spirit Metrop. Conserv. Press* (1840) II. 302 Through the intermedium of one person. **1884** *American* VII. 218 The pabulum for the realization of this knowledge can only be afforded through the intermedium of books.

b. With mixture of sense 1: An intervening medium serving to transmit energy through space.

1805 *Edin. Rev.* VII. 118 The hypothesis of an æther or other invisible *intermedium.* **1830** HERSCHEL *Stud. Nat. Phil.* 23 The communication of an impulse to such a distance, by any solid intermedium we are acquainted with, would require, not moments, but whole years. **1842** GROVE *Corr. Phys. Forces* 49 A molecular action of the gas or intermedium through or across which they are transmitted.

4. *Comp. Anat.* [sc. *os.*] A bone of the carpus, situated between the ulnare and radiale (hence also called *os centrale*), or the corresponding bone of the tarsus between the tibiale and fibulare.

1878 BELL *Gegenbaur's Comp. Anat.* 488 An intermedium is united with a tibiale to form an astragalus. **1887** in *Syd. Soc. Lex.*

†**interˈmell**, *v. Obs.* (or rare archaism). Forms: 4 **entremelle**, 5–6 **entermel(l**, 5–6 (chiefly *Sc.*), 9 (*arch.*) **intermel(l**. [a. OF. *entremelle-r*, var. of *entremesler*, mod.F. *entremêler* to INTERMEDDLE.]

1. *trans.* To mix together, intermingle: = INTERMEDDLE 1.

1387–8 T. USK *Test. Love* I. v. (Skeat) l. 14 That is a thinge enclosed vnder secretnes of priuitie, why twey persons entremellen hertes after a sight. **1413** *Pilgr. Sowle* (Caxton) v. ii. (1859) 75 With lusty prymerosys and lylyes entermellyd. **1509** FISHER *Fun. Serm. C'tess Richmond* Wks. (1876) 305 The lyfe of this wretched world whiche is alway entermelled with moche bytternes. **1866** J. B. ROSE tr. *Ovid's Met.* 258 Fame, who her facts with fictions intermells.

2. *refl.* To concern oneself: = next.

1550 CROWLEY *Epigr., Fools* 32 They thyncke it becometh them well, In euery mans matter them selfe to entermel.

3. *intr.* To concern oneself, have to do *with*; to meddle, interfere: = INTERMEDDLE 3.

c **1470** HENRYSON *Mor. Fab.* IV. (*Fox's Conf.*) i, This foxe ..Quhilk durst na mair with wayting intermell. **1480** CAXTON *Chron. Eng.* liv. 38 So that hym self no thyng entermelled, but only bare the name of kyng. **1560** ROLLAND *Crt. Venus* II. 172 To Intermell we will not with sic thing. **1599** MARSTON *Sco. Villanie* III. ix. 221 To bite, to gnaw, and boldly intermell With sacred things.

Hence †**interˈmelling** *vbl. sb.*, intermingling.

1413 *Pilgr. Sowle* (Caxton) v. i. (1859) 72 Who that had herd the song that was among the Angels, by wonderfull entermellynge, and full swete accord.

†**interˈmell**, *sb. Obs.* [f. prec. vb.: cf. OF. *entremesle*, *entremelle.*] An intermingling; a mixed engagement or combat, melée.

1489 *Barbour's Bruce* x. 145 (MS. E) Now may ye her, giff that ye will, Entremellys, and juperdiss, That men assayit mony wyss. **1535** STEWART *Cron. Scot.* (1858) I. 144 And syne or that intermell wes done, The greit battell on euerie syd did jone.

†**intermellé**, *a. Obs.* [? a. OF. *entremellé.*] Intermingled, in confusion.

1375 BARBOUR *Bruce* XIV. 215 In-to the toune all comonly Thai enterit bath Intermelle. Thair mycht men felloune slauchtir se.

intermelt, -member, etc.: see INTER- *pref.*

interment (ɪnˈtɜːmənt). Forms: see INTER *v.* [f. INTER *v.* + -MENT.] The action of interring or burying in the earth; burial.

c **1330** R. BRUNNE *Chron.* (1810) 327 After þe enterment þe kyng tok his way To þe South. **1390** GOWER *Conf.* II. 319 In worship of her susters minde She made a riche enterement. *c* **1440** *Promp. Parv.* 140/2 Entyrement, or yntyrment, *funerale.* **1576** FLEMING *Panopl. Epist.* 39 His interrement shuld not be withstoode. **1656** STANLEY *Hist. Philos.* I. VI. 111 The solemn rites after my enterrement. **1709** STRYPE *Ann. Ref.* I. xxxvi. 368 At the interrement of the Dutchess. **1797** MRS. RADCLIFFE *Italian* vi, The body was..carried on an open bier to the place of interment. **1808** PIKE *Sources Mississ.* III. 266 The solemnity of the interment, agreeably to the ritual of the Spanish Church.

intermental, -mention: see INTER- 6, 1 a.

intermesh (ɪntəˈmɛʃ), *v.* [f. INTER- 1 b + MESH *v.* 3 b.] *intr.* Of gears, etc.: to mesh or interlock with one another. Also *fig.*

1909 in WEBSTER. **1928** *Daily Tel.* 27 Mar. 7 (Advt.), The light yarns are vibrated to cause them to intermesh in the fabric. **1948** M. J. HERSKOVITS *Man & his Works* xiv. 215 To achieve some expression of the unities in culture by indicating how trait and complex and pattern..intermesh, as the gears of some machine to constitute a smoothly running, effectively functioning whole. **1955** J. G. DAVIS *Dict. Dairying* (ed. 2) 153 The cylinders have square-cut threads which intermesh. **1957** G. E. HUTCHINSON *Treat. Limnol.* I. iii. 201 These chains form an intermeshed net and run in any direction in the free liquid. **1971** *Flying* Apr. 92/3 Medical records..are not yet intermeshed with airman records. **1971** T. F. MITCHELL in *Archivum Linguisticum* II. 39 It should perhaps be said again that the aspects of meaning we are distinguishing intermesh and often meet in one text, in one sentence, even in one word or syllable.

†**ˈintermess**, later variant of ENTREMESS, something served between the courses at a banquet: also *fig. Obs.*

1658 EVELYN *Fr. Gard.* (1675) 102 Eaten in Lent in pease-pottage, and intermesses at the best tables. **1690** —— *Let. Lady Sunderl.* 4 Aug., Mem. (1819) II. 255 To these I likewise added my little history of Chalcography, a treatise of the perfection of paynting..with some other intermesses which might divert within dores. **1725** BRADLEY *Fam. Dict.* s.v. *Gruel*, There are those who prepare an Inter-mess of Gruel or Milk-pottage in the following manner. **1748** MRS. S. HARRISON *House-Keeper's Pocket-Bk.* ii. (ed. 4) 9 Inter-Messes, or odd Dishes for small Families, now in Season.

interˈmessage, *sb. rare.* [INTER- 2 a.] A message conveyed between two persons or places. So **interˈmessage** *v. trans.*, to exchange messages with; **interˈmessenger** (†**-messager**), a messenger between two persons or places.

1560 DAUS tr. *Sleidane's Comm.* 363 The matter was treated betwene them by letters and intermessagers. **1691** WOOD *Ath. Oxon.* II. 644 He was often posting to London upon intermessages and fatigues. *a* **1732** T. BOSTON *View Covt. Grace* (1771) 23 An inter-messenger between God and Israel. **1882** 'N. GREENE' *Thousand Years Hence* 110 Those whom as yet we are only permitted to intermessage.

intermetacarpal, -metatarsal: see INTER-.

intermetallic (ɪntəmɪˈtælɪk), *a.* Also **inter-metallic** (with hyphen). [f. INTER- 4 c + METALLIC *a.* and *sb.*] Applied to compounds formed from two or more metals. Hence as *sb.*, an intermetallic compound.

1900 *Rep. Brit. Assoc. Adv. Sci. 1900* 131 Most students of alloys are now convinced that they often contain definite chemical compounds, yet these 'intermetallic' compounds are still passed over in silence by..books on descriptive chemistry. **1923** U. R. EVANS *Metals & Metallic Compounds* I. 198 Inter-metallic compounds are rarely—if ever—formed between two metals belonging to the same group of the periodic table. **1937** *Chem. & Industry* XV. 677/1 A consideration of the formulæ of typical intermetallic compounds..shows at once that their formation is not governed by the simple rules of valency. **1956** *Nature* 10 Mar. 487/1 Its analysis is complicated by the presence of..intermetallics. **1962** SIMPSON & RICHARDS *Junction Transistors* iii. 36 E.g. InP and GaAs among the intermetallic compounds. **1967** *New Scientist* 27 Apr. 209/2 Intermetallics are compounds of two or more metals, and are commonly found in alloys. **1972** *Sci. Amer.* Aug. 46/3 They have successfully synthesized intermetallic compounds in which the hydrogen is held in the form of hydrides.

intermete, variant of ENTERMETE *v.*, *Obs.*

intermewed (ɪntəˈmjuːd), *ppl. a. Falconry.* ? *Obs.* Also 6–8 **enter-**. [f. OF. *entremué* (Godef.) half-moulted (L. type **intermūtātus*) + -ED.]

Applied to a hawk after her first 'mewing' or moulting, and before receiving her next coat, when she becomes a 'white hawk'.

1598 FLORIO, *Amutata*, an entermewed hauke. **1615** LATHAM *Falconry* (1633) 37 The intermewed Haggard is more able and strong to resist the course of nature. *Ibid.* (Words explaned), *Intermewed* is from the first exchange of a Hawkes coat, or from her first mewing, till she come to be a white Hawke. **1679** *Lond. Gaz.* No. 1436/4 Lost of his Majesties..between Windsor and Burnham, an Entermewed Jass Faulcon, having newly Mewed her long Feathers, with the Kings Varvels. **1828** SEBRIGHT *Hawking* 33. [Erroneously explained.]

So **interˈmewing** *vbl. sb. rare*[−0].

1678 PHILLIPS (ed. 4), *Intermewing* (among Faulconers) is from the first exchange of the Hawks Coat till she turn white, and is so called from the first Mewing.

intermewer (ɪntəˈmjuːə(r)). *Falconry.* ? *Obs.* Also 6–7 **entermewer**, 7 *erron.* **intermure**. [f. as prec. + -ER.] A hawk of the second year, after her first 'mewing' or moulting, and before she has the full third year's coat.

1575 TURBERV. *Faulconrie* 32 They are called Entermewers or hawkes of the first cote that is from the middle of May till..December. Those hawkes are called Entermewers for that they cast the old and have new feathers and they prove very good and hardie hawkes. **1680** *Lond. Gaz.* No. 1491/4 A Tercel Gentle an Intermewer, lost a Month since in Staffordshire. *a* **1682** SIR T. BROWNE *Tracts* 118. **1727** BRADLEY *Fam. Dict.* s.v. *Hawk*, The second [year] an Intermewer, the third a white Hawk.

fig. *a* **1613** OVERBURY *A Wife* (1638) 117 The fourth and fift, she's an intermewer, preies for herselfe, and ruffles all she reaches.

‖**intermezzo** (ɪntəˈmɛdzəʊ, -mɛtsəʊ). Pl. **-i** (-iː), **-os** (-əʊz). Also 9 **intermez.** [It. *intermezzo*, more popular form of *intermedio*: see INTERMEDE. With the form *intermez*, cf. obs. F. *intermèze*, *-mèse* (16th c. in Littré), ad. the Italian word.]

1. a. A short dramatic, musical, or other performance, of a light and pleasing character, introduced between the acts of a drama or opera (or, subsequently, in the latter half of the 18th c., performed independently, and merging in

the Opera Buffa). **b.** A short movement serving as a connecting link between the main divisions of a large musical work, instrumental or vocal; sometimes used for an independent piece of similar character.

1771 [see BAD *a.* 1 c]. [**1811** BUSBY *Dict. Mus.* (ed. 3), *Intermezzi* (Ital.), the name given by the Italians to interludes, or detached dances, introduced between the acts of an opera.] **1834** BECKFORD *Italy* II. 213 (Stanf.) The entertainment ended with a sort of intermez. **1840** *Penny Cycl.* XVI. 441/2 s.v. *Opera*, In July, 1703, Italian *intermezzi*, or 'interludes and musical entertainments of singing and dancing', were performed at York Buildings. **1880** W. S. ROCKSTRO in Grove *Dict. Mus.* II. 8 Almost all the earlier Italian plays were relieved by Intermezzi. **1883** *Pall Mall G.* 12 Oct. 4/1 The composer's predilection for instrumental music has shown itself in the so-called intermezzos which are freely interspersed through the three sections.

2. *transf.* An interval; an 'episode'.

1851 CARLYLE *Sterling* III. iv. (1872) 198 A little intermezzo of ramble was not unadvisable. **1875** *N. Amer. Rev.* CXX. 264 The purgatorial intermezzo of the Catholic church. **1897** *Q. Rev.* Oct. 356 Impatient, bewildered, expectant in an atmosphere of intermezzo.

†**intermicate,** *v. Obs. rare*⁻⁰. [f. ppl. stem of L. *intermicāre*, f. *inter* between + *micāre* to glitter.]

'To shine between' (Cockeram, 1623). So †**intermiˈcation,** 'a shining between' (Phillips, 1658).

inter-micellar: see INTER- *pref.* 4 a.

†**interˈmiddle,** *a. Obs.* [f. INTER 2 c + MIDDLE *a.*, after L. *intermedius.*] = INTERMEDIATE.

1613 M. RIDLEY *Magn. Bodies* 54 In the intermiddle spaces.

intermigration (-maɪˈgreɪʃən). [INTER- 2 a.] Interchange of abode or habitat; reciprocal migration.

a **1677** HALE *Prim. Orig. Man.* II. vii. 200 Though the Continent be but one, as to point of Access and mutual Intercourse and possibility of Intermigrations. **1859** DARWIN *Orig. Spec.* xii. (1873) 333 Serving as a bridge.. for the intermigration of their inhabitants. **1880** A. R. WALLACE *Isl. Life* 422 One of the routes by which that intermigration of American and European animals and plants was effected.

interminability (ɪnˌtɜːmɪnəˈbɪlɪtɪ). [f. next: see -ITY.] The quality of being interminable; interminableness.

1681 FLAVEL *Meth. of Grace* xxv. 437 We know that essential interminability is the incommunicable property of God. **1805** *Monthly Mag.* XX. 417 The immensity, the apparent interminability of the forests. **1862** T. A. TROLLOPE *Lent. Journey* xii. 196 All previous experiences of interminability were exceeded by the interminableness of the ascent to Fermo.

interminable (ɪnˈtɜːmɪnəb(ə)l), *a.* [a. F. *interminable* (14th c., Oresme), or ad. late L. *interminābilis* (Tertull.), f. *in-* (IN-³) + *termināre* to TERMINATE: see -ABLE.] That cannot be bounded or ended; boundless; endless. (In mod. use freq. exaggerative, implying impatience or disgust at the length of something.)

c **1374** CHAUCER *Boeth.* v. pr. vi. 133 (Camb. MS.) Eternite.. is parfyt possession.. of lyf Intermynable. *c* **1450** tr. *De Imitatione* III. lxi. 143, I am þe wey undefoulid, þe trouþe infallible, þe lyf intermynable. **1520-30** SKELTON *Prayer to the Father* 1 O radiant Luminary of lyght interminable Celestial Father. **1681** FLAVEL *Meth. Grace* viii. 175 Your fellowship with Christ is interminable, and abides for ever. **1727-46** THOMSON *Summer* 691 Plains immense Lie stretch'd below, interminable meads And vast savannahs. **1830** D'ISRAELI *Chas. I*, III. xi. 227 Two able men arguing by two opposite standards of judgment, may open an interminable controversy. **1860** MOTLEY *Netherl.* (1868) I. i. 2 A writing-table covered with heaps of interminable despatches.

b. *absol.* ***the Interminable***, the Infinite.

1671 MILTON *Samson* 307 As if they would confine the Interminable, And tie him to his own prescript, Who made our laws to bind us, not himself.

inˈterminableness. [f. prec. + -NESS.] The quality of being interminable; endlessness.

1682 H. MORE *Annot. Glanvill's Lux O.* 59 The.. interminableness of those Torments which after this life shall incessantly vex the impious. **1817** COLERIDGE *Lay Serm.* 342 Interminableness of object with perfect indifference of means. **1894** *Blackw. Mag.* Jan. 143 The seeming interminableness of a Canadian city's streets.

interminably (ɪnˈtəmɪnəblɪ), *adv.* [f. as prec. + -LY².] In an interminable manner; without end or limit; endlessly.

1447 BOKENHAM *Seyntys* (Roxb.) 132 Wych wyth jhu thi sone.. Now lyvyst and regnyst intermynabylly. **1612-15** BP. HALL *Contempl., N.T.* IV. xiii, A kingdome restored magnificently, interminably. **1701** NORRIS *Ideal World* I. ii. 102 Totally and intirely as well as interminably existing. **1813** SHELLEY *Q. Mab* VI. 18 Will yon vast suns roll on Interminably? **1858** HAWTHORNE *Fr. & It. Jrnls.* (1882) I. 23 Hall after hall opened interminably before us.

†**inˈterminant,** *ppl. a. Obs. rare*⁻⁰. [f. IN-³ + L. *termināntem*, pr. pple. of *termināre* to TERMINATE.] 'Boundless, borderless, uncertain' (Blount *Glossogr.* 1656).

interminate (ɪnˈtɜːmɪnət), *a.* Now *rare.* [ad. L. *interminātus*, f. *in-* (IN-³) + *terminātus* ended, TERMINATE *ppl. a.* Cf. F. *interminé* (16th c.).]

1. That is without end or limit; endless, boundless, infinite.

1533 BELLENDEN *Livy* IV. (1822) 386 Quhen Servilius had conquest, be thir wourdis, interminate loveing and favoure of all the pepill. **1615** CHAPMAN *Odyss.* VII. K v b, Within a thicket I reposde.. and found.. a sleepe interminate. *a* **1677** HALE *Prim. Orig. Man.* II. iv. 159 The very same supineness and negligence.. for interminate Ages. **1677** GALE *Crt. Gentiles* IV. 142 Sin is interminate and infinite, but good terminate and finite, as the Pythagoreans hold. **1852** BP. FORBES *Nicene Cr.* 35 There is one Principle of all things.. unbegotten, indestructible,.. interminate.

b. *Arith.* ***interminate decimal***, a fractional number that cannot be exactly expressed by tenths, tenths of tenths, and so on, but either repeats, as $\cdot\dot{3} = \frac{1}{3}$, circulates, as $\cdot\dot{1}4285\dot{7} = \frac{1}{7}$, or continues without any definite order, as the decimal in the square root of 2, 3, 5 or other non-square number, in the value of π, etc.

1726 COLSON in *Phil. Trans.* XXXIV. 163 In this last Example the Numbers are what I call interminate, or Approximations only. **1866** *Arithm. Irish Nat. Schools* 178 We cannot always obtain an exact quotient, when we divide one number by another:—in such a case, what is called an interminate, or.. a recurring, or circulating decimal is produced.

†**2.** quasi-*adv.* Without end, always. *Obs.*

1556 ABP. PARKER *Ps.* cxxxi. 384 Be meeke: flee pryde.. From this tyme forth interminate.

†**interminate,** *v. Obs. rare.* [f. ppl. stem of L. *interminārī*, f. *inter* between + *minārī* to threaten; cf. obs. F. *interminer* (Godef.).] *trans.* To threaten, menace (a thing). Hence †**interminated** *ppl. a.*

a **1631** DONNE *Serm.* xxxv. 347 In all those three Evangelists where this fearful Denunciation is interminated. *a* **1656** BP. HALL *Rem. Wks.* (1660) 163 But enough, enough of these dolefull accents of these interminated judgments.

†**inˈterminated,** *a. Obs.* [f. as INTERMINATE *a.* + -ED, or f. IN-³ + TERMINATED.] = INTERMINATE *a.*

a **1734** NORTH *Exam.* I. iii. §54 (1740) 155 The Author's Directory, that is a Parcel of confused, interminated, Scandals upon the Court. **1738** GLOVER *Leonidas* II. 243 Throughout the interminated surface throws Its rays abroad. **1746** AKENSIDE *Hymn Naiads* 281 O'er the peopled earth and o'er The interminated ocean.

†**ˌintermiˈnation.** *Obs.* [ad. L. *interminātiōn-em*, n. of action f. *interminārī*: see INTERMINATE *v.* and cf. obs. F. *intermination* (Godef.).] The action of threatening or menacing; commination; a threat or menace.

1526 *Pilgr. Perf.* (W. de. W. 1531) 205 b, God.. in paradyse gaue the commaundement to Adam, vnder this interminacyon and thrette. *a* **1631** DONNE *Serm.* cvii. IV. 452 Here is no Malediction no Intermination mingled in Gods first Act. **1684** HOCKIN *Gods Decrees* 304 What method imaginable more persuasive.. than the divine promises and interminations are.

†**interˈmind,** *v. Obs. rare*⁻¹. [INTER- 1.] *trans.* ? To remember at intervals; to recall.

1571 GOLDING *Calvin on Ps.* Ep. Ded. 6 Hee might recover newe strength and cheerfulnesse, by interminding Gods former promises and benefites.

interˈmine, *v. rare.* [f. INTER- 1 + MINE *v.* or *sb.*] *trans.* To intersect with mines or veins.

1622 DRAYTON *Poly-olb.* xxviii. (R.), Her earth with allom veins so richly intermin'd. **1850** *Tait's Mag.* XVII. 682/1 Her bosom yet was intermined with ice.

intermingle (ɪntəˈmɪŋg(ə)l), *v.* Also 6-7 **enter-**, 6 **-mengle.** [f. INTER- 1 + MINGLE *v.*]

1. *trans.* To mingle (two or more things) together, so that each is mixed with the other; also, to introduce and mix (an element) *with* another or *among* other things.

c **1470** HENRYSON *Mor. Fab.* II. (*Town & C. Mouse*) xxx, Swa intermynglit is aduersitie With eirdlie joy. **1555** EDEN *Decades* 143 Let vs nowe entermyngle certeyne smaule thynges amonge these great matters. **1577** VAUTROUILLIER *Luther on Ep. Gal.* 231 In his exhortation he intermingleth threatnings and promises. **1687** A. LOVELL tr. *Thevenot's Trav.* I. 221 Houses built of black and white Stones intermingled. **1712** STEELE *Spect.* No. 272 ¶1 Crowds of forlorn Coquets who intermingle themselves with other Ladies. **1803** W. TAYLOR in *Ann. Rev.* I. 419 A cause of displacing and intermingling the people. **1842** H. ROGERS *Ess.* I. i. 36 Fuller has intermingled a great deal of gossip and rubbish with his facts.

2. To intersperse (a thing) *with* some other element; †to variegate.

1553 EDEN *Treat. Newe Ind.* (Arb.) 20 Popingiayes of white colour intermingled with seuen variable coloures. **1649** ROBERTS *Clavis Bibl.* 161 The highest Prosperity of Gods people, is (like Chequer-work) intermingled with Crosses and Calamities. **1807** *Med. Jrnl.* XVII. 423 The vinegar the patient had swallowed, intermingled with the mucus of the stomach. **1875** JOWETT *Plato* (ed. 2) V. 371 It will be proper to have hymns and praises of the Gods intermingled with prayers.

3. *intr.* To mingle together or *with* something.

1626 BACON *Sylva* §270 Visibles doe not intermingle, and confound one another,.. but Sounds doe. **1664** POWER *Exp. Philos.* II. 115 You shall see.. the Water and it confusedly to intermingle one with the other. **1784** COWPER *Task* I. 347 Shadow and sunshine intermingling quick. **1879** WALLACE *Australas.* i. 9 Farther east this flora intermingles with that of Australia and Polynesia.

interˈmingled, *ppl. a.* [f. prec. + -ED¹.] Mingled with each other or with some other thing.

1586 A. DAY *Eng. Secretary* I. (1625) 10 Histories,.. and other intermingled actions not of any in particular, but of all in generall. **1607** TOPSELL *Four-f. Beasts* (1658) 358 Of divers and sundry intermingled colours, both white, black and red. **1711** POPE *Temp. Fame* 18 There trees, and intermingl'd temples rise. **1849** LONGF. *Building of Ship* 131 Soon.. Were heard the intermingled sounds Of axes and of mallets.

Hence **interˈmingledly** *adv.*

1601 DENT *Pathw. Heaven* (1603) 15 Intermingledly joined together in all the faculties of the soule and body.

interˈmingledom. *nonce-wd.* [f. as next + -DOM.] = next.

1753 RICHARDSON *Grandison* (1883) IV. vi. 52 Filled with bits and ends of ribands, patterns, and so forth.. with intermingledoms of goldbeater's skin, plasters for a cut finger.

interˈminglement. *rare.* [f. INTERMINGLE *v.* + -MENT.] An intermingling.

1873 SYMONDS *Grk. Poets* viii. 240 The intermingement of debauchery with a spirit of true piety. **1883** A. STEWART *Nether Lochaber* liii. 334 An ugly intermingiement of black and dark grey.

intermingling (-ˈmɪŋglɪŋ), *vbl. sb.* [-ING¹.] The action of the vb. INTERMINGLE.

1576 FLEMING *Panopl. Epist.* To Rdr. ¶5 The tediousnesse of studie, is to be assuaged with some intermingling of delight. **1601** DENT *Pathw. Heaven* (1831) 13 This intermingling of grace and corruption in the Soul. **1862** GOULBURN *Pers. Relig.* i. II. (1873) 41 The intermingling of devotion with action.

interˈmingling, *ppl. a.* [f. as prec. + -ING².] That intermingles.

1808 J. BARLOW *Columb.* II. 440 Its portal gleams With various gems intermingling beams.

interminister: see INTER- *pref.* 1 b.

interministerial (-mɪnɪˈstɪərɪəl), *a.* [INTER- 4 b: cf. next.] **1.** Belonging to a period between two ministries.

1861 MAY *Const. Hist.* (1863) I. ii. 126 The provisional character of this inter-ministerial government.

2. Involving the participation of two or more ministers or of the representatives of two or more departments of state; constituted from members of different departments of state.

1937 *Times* 30 Dec. 10/1 After a day of almost incessant inter-Ministerial consultation.. the Government decided to take a firm line with the strikers. **1967** *Economist* 29 Apr. 477/1 A secret report on the labour market by the commissioner-general for national planning, M. Francois-Xavier Ortoli, is to be discussed by a special interministerial committee within the next 10 days. **1970** *Nature* 8 Aug. 544/2 In most countries.. there is an inter-ministerial committee for science and technology.

‖**interministerium** (-mɪnɪˈstɪərɪəm). *rare.* [f. INTER- 3 + L. *ministerium* MINISTRY; formed by Walpole, app. after INTERREGNUM.] The period intervening between two ministries.

1743 H. WALPOLE *Let. to H. Mann* 31 July, The Regency are so temporizing and timid, especially in this Inter-ministerium, that [etc.]. **1750** —— *Lett.* (1857) II. 233 The Inter-ministerium still exists; no place is filled up. **1756** —— *Corr.* (1837) I. 351 After an interministerium of seventeen days Mr. Pitt has this morning accepted the government as secretary of state. **1890** *Dict. Nat. Biog.* XXI. 185/1 The long interministerium ended in George's acceptance of the coalition administration.

†**interˈmise.** *Obs.* [var. of ENTERMISE, with prefix in L. form: cf. INTERMIT *v.*²] Intervention, mediation, agency.

1612 NAUNTON in *Buccleuch MSS.* (Hist. MSS. Comm.) I. 118 By the noble and Christian intermise of Sir H. Nevyll, there is a concentration made between my Lords of Pembroch and Rochester. **1673** S. C. *Art of Complaisance* 144 Either by ourselves, or the means and intermise of our friends. **1715** M. DAVIES *Athen. Brit.* I. 172 Vorstius, whom he [James I.] desir'd the States to turn out of his Professorship, by the Intermise of his Ambassador Sir Ralph Winwood.

†**interˈmisle,** var. of INTERMELL *v.*: cf. OF. *entremesler*.

a **1641** BP. MOUNTAGU *Acts & Mon.* (1642) 385 Herod.. brought in a new hotchpotch Religion, consisting of Judaisme and Paganisme intermisled.

†**interˈmiss.** *Obs. rare*⁻¹. [ad. L. *intermissus* (Pliny), intermission, f. *intermittĕre* to INTERMIT *v.*¹] Interval.

1627 E. F. *Hist. Edw. II* (1680) 94 Which for a time.. enforc'd their absence; in which short intermiss, the King relapseth to his former errour.

intermission¹ (ɪntəˈmɪʃən). [ad. L. *intermissiōn-em*, n. of action f. *intermittĕre* to INTERMIT *v.*¹ Cf. F. *intermission* (1413 in Hatz.-Darm.).]

1. a. The fact of intermitting, giving over, or ceasing for a time; a temporary pause, cessation, or breach of continuity in an action, state, etc.

(freq. in phr. ***without intermission***). *spec.* in *Path.*, of a fever or the pulse.

1526 *Pilgr. Perf.* (W. de W. 1531) 88 Euermore to praye without intermyssyon or ceasynge. **1576** Fleming *Panopl. Epist.* 86 Your friende Anthonie, kindleth coles of furious outrage continually, and maketh no intermission. **1590** Swinburne *Testaments* 39 In this case is the testament voide, vnlesse that it may bee prooued, that there was intermission of furor the same time. **1600** Shaks. *A.Y.L.* II. vii. 32 And I did laugh, sans intermission, An houre by his diall. **1613** Purchas *Pilgrimage* (1614) 741 They saw a whirle-winde take up the water..into the aire, three houres together with little intermission. **1769** Robertson *Chas. V* (1796) III. xii. 392 The gout after a longer intermission than usual returned. **1791** Cowper *Iliad* I. 118 Neither end, nor intermission of his heavy scourge. **1869** Phillips *Vesuv.* viii. 226 This eruption lasted two nights and two days without intermission.

b. Temporary cessation, respite, relief, rest, pause. Const. *from* something. Now *rare.*

1576 Fleming *Panopl. Epist.* 63 Your overwearied heart, which brayeth after intermission and rest from..great matters. **1667** Milton *P.L.* II. 802 They..Afresh with conscious terrors vex me round That rest or intermission none I find. **1756** Burke *Subl. & B.* I. v, He often gives himself some intermission from such melancholy reflections. **1834** Medwin *Angler in Wales* I. 232 We had hardly a moment's intermission from rain.

2. The lapse of a space of time between events or periods of action; the time during which action temporarily ceases; interval; †vacation, recess. *spec.* = the interval between the parts of a play, film, concert, etc. (chiefly *U.S.*).

1563–7 Buchanan *Reform. St. Andros* Wks. (1892) 13 The medicinis lesson, quha sal reid on to ix houris; and fra ix to ten salbe intermission. **1660** Milton *Free Commw.* Wks. (1847) 448/1 The grand council, which..should sit perpetually (unless their leisure give them now and then some intermissions or vacations). **1704** Swift *Mech. Operat. Spir.* Misc. (1711) 286 Chusing their Time in those Intermissions while the Preacher is at Ebb. **1854** E. G. Holland *Mem. Jos. Badger* xv. 310 At the intermission many strangers flocked around me. **1927** *N.Y. World* 24 July, *Intermission*, interval. **1933** H. Footner *Ring of Eyes* xv. 104 When the curtain descended for the intermission, [etc.]. **1955** Keepnews & Grauer *Pict. Hist. Jazz* xvi. 197 Nick Rongetti..loved to join the intermission pianist. **1956** B. Holiday *Lady sings Blues* (1973) iii. 37 In between ups, ..there was Garland Wilson at the piano for intermission. **1961** *Listener* 7 Dec. 1002/2 *Rocco* does have an intermission, but when a film is [etc.].

†**3.** An omission in the course of a narrative.

a **1635** Naunton *Fragm. Reg.* (Arb.) 41 Having..toucht [this subject] somewhat, which I would not, if the equity of the Narration would have admitted an intermission.

4. An interruption or break of continuity in a wall, line of cliffs, or similar material formation.

1624 Wotton *Archit.* in *Reliq.* (1651) 223 Wals are either entire and continuall, or intermitted; and the Intermissions be either Pillars or Pylasters. **1663** Charleton *Chor. Gigant.* 19 Intermissions made by Columns or Pillars. **1853** Kane *Grinnell Exp.* xxxi. (1856) 270 After a mile or two of intermission, the high cliffs rise up again in abutments.

†**inter'mission**[2]. *Obs. rare.* [f. intermit *v.*[2], after prec.]

1. Mediation, intervention; = intermise.

1647 Lilly *Chr. Astrol.* liii. 372 They shall agree without Suit of law, but not without intermission of a third party or more. **1670** Heylin *Hist. Presbyt.* 126 That no other.. Towns..shall in any part meddle by way of friendly intermission tending to an accord.

2. Interposition, intervention (of a thing).

1628 T. Spencer *Logick* 100 Aristotle sayth, that this opposition is made by it selfe, and wants the intermission of a third: for no power can put a third thing betweene being and not being. **1667** Marvell *Corr.* lxxviii. Wks. 1872–5 II. 222 The third day that the Lords have, without intermission of any other businesse, continued upon the question.

intermissive (ɪntəˈmɪsɪv), *a.* [f. L. *intermiss-*, ppl. stem of *intermittĕre* to intermit *v.*[1] + -ive.]

Of the nature of, pertaining to, intermission; intermittent; coming at intervals.

1586 Ferne *Blaz. Gentrie* Ep. Ded., To the reading whereof, as in the place of an intermissiue delectation, I did something addicte myselfe. **1656** Stanley *Hist. Philos.* viii. (1701) 328/2 Again, of Offices, some are continual, as, to live vertuously; some intermissive, as, to question, answer, walk, and the like. **1682** Sir T. Browne *Chr. Mor.* iii. §23 Make Pleasure thy Recreation or intermissive Relaxation, not thy Diana, Life and Profession. **1822–34** *Good's Study Med.* (ed. 4) I. 427 In some instances..this failure of the voice has been more or less permanent or intermissive.

†**inter'mist,** *ppl. a. Obs. rare.* [ad. L. *intermist-us*, pa. pple. of *intermiscēre*: see intermixed.]

Intermixed.

1538 Leland *Itin.* II. 94 Crosselettes of Golde many intermist in one yn a Feld..Gules. **1637** R. Humphrey tr. *St. Ambrose* II. 13 The standing corne..hath some small sprinkling of wilde oates intermist.

intermit (ɪntəˈmɪt), *v.*[1] [ad. L. *intermittĕre* to leave off (*trans.* and *intr.*), f. *inter* between + *mittĕre* to send, let go, put.]

1. *trans.* To leave off, give over, discontinue (an action, practice, etc.) for a time; to suspend.

1576 Fleming *Panopl. Epist.* 327 *note*, Occasions of intermitting the writing of letters. **1594** Hooker *Eccl. Pol.* I. iii. §2 If nature should intermit her course, and leaue altogether..for a while, the obseruation of her own lawes. **1609** Bible (Douay) *Ezek.* xlv. 9 Intermitte ye iniquitie and robberies, and doe judgement and justice. **1684–5** Boyle *Min. Waters* sect. vi. 106 To intermit it sometimes for a year or two,..and then to return to the use of it. **1761** Hume *Hist. Eng.* II. xxx. 171 The king had seemed willing, during some time, to intermit the blows which overwhelmed him. **1875** M. Pattison *Casaubon* 464 When seriously urged to intermit his application, and allow himself a holiday.

†**b.** To interrupt, cause intermission to (a person or action, or the course of anything). *Obs.*

a **1542** [see intermitted]. **1563–87** Foxe *A. & M.* (1684) III. 614, I had thought to have treated this matter at large, but even now I am intermitted and otherwise letted. **1667** Milton *P.L.* ix. 223 Casual discourse..which intermits Our dayes work. **1704** Hearne *Duct. Hist.* (1714) I. 386 The consular State..was afterwards retrenched by the Tribunes of the People; then intermitted by the Decemviri, and Military Tribunes.

†**c.** To omit, leave out, pass over, let slip. *Obs.*

1563–87 Foxe *A. & M.* (1596) 68/1 As touching the line and order of the Roman bishops hitherto intermitted. *a* **1645** Heywood & Rowley *Fort. by Land & Sea* iv. i. H.'s Wks. 1874 VI. 412 They that intermit advantages, Must know occasions head is bald behind. **1671** Hobbes *Three papers* Wks. 1845 VII. 437 Square numbers (beginning at 1) intermit first two numbers, then four, then six [etc.]. **1692** Luttrell *Brief Rel.* (1857) II. 676 Orders are sent to the docks to work night and day without intermitting Sunday or holydayes.

2. *intr.* To cease or stop for a time (†const. *from*, or *inf.*); to be intermittent.

1571 Hanmer *Chron. Irel.* (1633) 67 To intermit a while from speaking of these learned men. **1609** Bible (Douay) *1 Kings* xv. 21 He intermitted to build Rama. **1633** Bp. Hall *Hard Texts* 347 He doth not intermit to furnish me continually with his good spirit. **1748** *Anson's Voy.* I. viii. 87 The winds every now and then intermitted. **1773** Johnson *Let. to Boswell* 5 July in *Boswell*, Let me know the exact time when your Courts intermit. **1871** J. R. Nichols *Fireside Science* 11 A spring which intermits as often as every three minutes.

b. *spec.* in *Path.* of a fever (pain, etc.) or of the pulse.

1626 [see intermitting *ppl. a.*]. **1665** Boyle *Occas. Refl.* II. xi, Physitians are wont..to tell us, That Feavers which intermit are devoid of Danger. **1749** Fielding *Tom Jones* v. viii, The last application..had brought the fever to intermit. **1796** Burke *Regic. Peace* i. Wks. VIII. 85 Because the pulse seems to intermit, we must not presume that it will cease instantly to beat. **1872** Darwin *Emotions* xiii. 340 A man who by continually watching his own pulse, at last caused one beat out of every six to intermit. **1878** E. J. Trelawny *Rec. Shelley*, etc. (1887) 205 His sadness intermitted, and his cold fits alternated with hot ones. **1897** *Allbutt's Syst. Med.* IV. 432 There are instances of the tumour intermitting, that is being prominent at one time and not distinguishable at another.

†**intermit,** *v.*[2] *Obs.* [A re-fashioning of entermete, after L. *intermittĕre*: see prec.]

1. *refl.* To concern or occupy oneself, etc.; = entermete 1.

c **1340** Hampole *Prose Tr.* 25 Þei intermettid hem with worldely besynes. **1502** Atkinson tr. *De Imitatione* I. xi. 160 It is one speciall meane to acquyre pease, nat to intermytte vs of the wordes & werkes of those that attayne nat to vs. **1548** Hall *Chron., Hen. VII* 49 b, Because Bisshoppes.. dyd not..intermit them selves with the serche and punyshment of suche..offences.

b. *intr.* = entermete 1 b; = intromit 3.

1456 in Sir W. Fraser *Wemyss of W.* (1888) II. 74 Sene the said Schir Andro intermittit vith the said landis of Inchmertin. **1540** *Act 32 Hen. VIII*, c. 14 The lorde admiralle..shall [not] in any wise intermitte ne meddle with the liberties of the .v. portes. *a* **1548** Hall *Chron., Hen VII* 23 [He] never intermitted with the affayres of Flaunders.

2. *trans.* To interpose, put between; to introduce, admit; = intromit 1.

c **1540** tr. *Pol. Verg. Eng. Hist.* (Camden, No. 29) 4 Charles saylyng..with a prosperous winde, intermitting no delaye. **1658** W. Sanderson *Graphice* 86 A long prospective Trunk..through which, the visible radiations..are intermitted, falling upon a paper. **1676** Hobbes *Iliad* (1677) 295 As when in war a pause we intermit.

intermitotic (ɪntəmaɪˈtɒtɪk), *a. Cytology.* Also **inter-mitotic.** [f. inter- 4 b + mitotic *a.*]

Occurring or existing between mitoses; capable of dividing again. Also *absol.*, a cell which is capable of dividing again.

1942 E. V. Cowdry *Probl. Ageing* (ed. 2) xxiv. 627 The daughter epidermal cells that retain a basal location..are comparatively undifferentiated and may be called vegetative intermitotics. *Ibid.*, The cells that are formed from vegetative intermitotics, and begin to differentiate may also be intermitotic with lives extending from one mitosis to the next. Their lives are, however, different insofar that they exhibit increasing specialization. Consequently they may be designated differentiating intermitotics. **1948** W. Andrew tr. *E. D. P. de Robertis's Gen. Cytol.* xii. 324 Cowdry has classified cells into four groups on the basis of their degree of differentiation and ability to divide. The first group, vegetative intermitotic cells, comprises those undifferentiated cells which have the capacity to multiply continually. **1962** L. von Sallmann et al. in A. Pirie *Lens Metabolism Rel. Cataract* 449 The intermitotic, or turnover, time was estimated as 19 days for the equatorial zone..of the lens epithelium of young rats. **1964** G. H. Haggis et al. *Introd. Molecular Biol.* i. 13 The appearance of the inter-mitotic nucleus in living cells. **1968** M. W. Strickberger *Genetics* ii. 13 As compared to the period of active mitosis.. the interphase or 'intermitotic' period of most cells is usually many times longer.

intermitted (ɪntəˈmɪtɪd), *ppl. a.* [f. intermit *v.*[1] + -ed[1].] Broken off or stopped for a time; interrupted.

a **1542** Wyatt *Death C'tess Pembroke* Poems (1810) 421/2 Yet once againe, my Muse, I pardon pray, Thine intermitted song if I repeate. **1615** G. Sandys *Trav.* 242 Ætna..yet smoking..and vomiting intermitted flames. **1713** Young *Last Day* II. 13 Again the trumpets intermitted sound Rolls the wide circuit of creation round. **1873** Mrs. Whitney *Other Girls* xiv. 187 The heavy bell swung out slow, intermitted peals.

Hence **inter'mittedly** *adv.*, in an intermitted, broken, or interrupted manner.

1829 Scott *Demonol.* i. 42 The cry of a distant pack of hounds, sounding intermittedly. **1846** Dana *Zooph.* (1848) 509 Polyps intermittedly coralligenous at base.

intermittence (ɪntəˈmɪtəns). Also **-ance.** [a. F. *intermittence* (1740 in Hatz.-Darm.): see intermittent and -ence.]

1. The fact of intermitting; discontinuance or cessation for a time.

1796 H. Hunter tr. *St.-Pierre's Stud. Nat.* (1799) I. 185 The intermittence of certain fountains..which flow only at particular hours of the day. **1830** Lyell *Princ. Geol.* I. xix. 339 A long intermittance of activity in the principal volcano. **1865** Mill *Pol. Econ.* (ed. 6) iv. vii. §2 The progress..will take place more rapidly, and with fewer intermittences and aberrations. **1876** Bartholow *Mat. Med.* (1879) 318 Hyoscyamia renders the movements of the heart regular; daturia often produces intermittence and arrest of action.

2. Alternation, intermittent sequence.

1860 Tyndall *Glac.* i. v. 41 A wonderful intermittence of gloom and glare.

intermittency (-ˈmɪtənsɪ). [f. next: see -ency.]

1. The quality or condition of being intermittent; intermission.

1662 J. Chandler *Van Helmont's Oriat.* 329 Every Being in Nature operates..without cessation, rest, intermittency, and trouble. **1821** *Examiner* 50/1 The intermittency which is occasionally attendant upon slow fever. **1892** *Illustr. Lond. News* 21 May 630/3 The rain kept up with cheerful intermittency.

2. Special Comb.: **intermittency effect** *Photogr.*, the difference in the density of an emulsion when it is exposed intermittently from that resulting from a continuous exposure (the total light received being the same in both cases).

1907 Sheppard & Mees *Investigations Theory Photogr. Process* II. vi. 223 The intermittency effects are all in good agreement with this view, since the reverse reaction would have the greater effect, (*a*) the longer the pause, and (*b*) the more numerous the pauses, a pause being the period of no illumination. **1958** H. Baines *Sci. of Photogr.* xiv. 172 Another phenomenon now known to be closely connected with reciprocity failure is the intermittency effect.

intermittent (ɪntəˈmɪtənt), *a.* (*sb.*) [ad. L. *intermittent-em*, pr. pple. of *intermittĕre* to intermit[1]; cf. F. *intermittent* (1598 in Godef. *Compl.*).]

A. *adj.* That intermits or ceases for a time; coming at intervals; operating by fits and starts.

a. *spec.* in *Path.* of the pulse, of a fever, etc. ***intermittent claudication***: see claudication.

1603 Holland *Plutarch's Mor.* 1277 Beating..now and than like intermittent pulses. **1609** —— *Amm. Marcell.* xxxi. xii. 420 Fits of an intermittent ague. **1625** Hart *Anat. Ur.* I. iii. 33 How canst thou..tell whether it be an intermittent or continuall feauer? **1796** Burke *Regic. Peace* ii. Wks. VIII. 214, This disorder was not in its nature intermittent. **1834** J. Forbes *Laennec's Dis. Chest* (ed. 4) 487 The pulse small, hard and intermittent. **1876** tr. *Wagner's Gen. Pathol.* 131 Intermittent fever is not contagious.

b. In other technical collocations. ***intermittent movement*** (see quot. 1959); ***intermittent sterilization***, a microbiological procedure which accomplishes sterilization without using the high temperatures required to kill spores outright, and which involves alternately maintaining the materials to be sterilized at a temperature high enough to kill vegetative cells and at a much lower temperature during which germination of spores occurs (producing new vegetative cells to be killed during the next high-temperature period).

1893 tr. *W. Migula's Introd. Pract. Bacteriol.* ii. 41 The test-tubes containing the blood serum may be now subjected to 'fractional or intermittent sterilisation', by exposing them for an hour a day for eight days to a temperature of 58°C. **1959** W. S. Sharps *Dict. Cinematogr.* 104/1 *Intermittent movement*, the term used for the method of film transport in a camera, projector or printer, whereby the film is moved intermittently and only exposed to light when stationary. **1969** S. T. Lyles *Biol. Micro-organisms* v. 130 Intermittent sterilization may be accomplished by boiling or steaming in the autoclave at O pressure.

c. In general use.

1675 Ogilby *Brit.* 36 A Village with an intermittent Market. **1706** Phillips, *Intermittent Stitch* (in Surgery), a kind of Stitch made at certain separate Points in the sowing of transverse or cross Wounds. **1858** *Merc. Marine Mag.* V. 374 The new Light is intermittent every half minute. **1872** Nicholson *Palæont.* 35 The work of rock-deposition is an intermittent process.

B. *sb. Path.* An intermittent fever. Also *fig.*

1693 *Phil. Trans.* XVII. 720 Quotidian, Tertian and Quartan Intermittents. *Ibid.* 721 That no body dies of an Intermittent but in the Cold Fit. **1772–84** Cook *Voy.* (1790) I. 270 Mr. Sporing also, and a sailor..were seized with the deadly intermittent. **1869** E. A. Parkes *Pract. Hygiene* (ed. 3) 70 The air of marshes is the sole cause of intermittents. **1872** O. W. Holmes *Poet Breakf.-t.* iv. 118 Struggling with the chills and heats of his artistic intermittent.

intermittently (-ˈmɪtəntlɪ), *adv.* [f. prec. + -LY².] In an intermittent manner; with intervals of cessation; by fits and starts.

1833 MRS. BROWNING *Prometh. Bound* Poems 1850 I. 157 From my restless eyes Drop by drop intermittently A trickling stream of tears supplies My cheeks. **1874** W. PAGE-ROBERTS *Law & God* (1876) 10 The evils which continuously or intermittently afflict humanity.

interˈmitter¹. *rare*⁻¹. [f. INTERMIT *v.*¹ + -ER¹.] One who intermits or discontinues (some action or practice) for a time.

1598 FLORIO, *Intermettitore*, an intermitter, a delayer of time. **1647** TRAPP *Comm. Jude* 19 *Who separate*..The Arabick renders it, Intermitters, sc. of Church-worships.

†**interˈmitter².** *Obs. rare*⁻⁰. [f. INTERMIT *v.*² + -ER¹.] One who interferes or intervenes.

1611 FLORIO, *Intermettitore*, an intermitter, an interposer.

intermitting (ɪntəˈmɪtɪŋ), *ppl. a.* [f. INTERMIT *v.*¹ + -ING².] = INTERMITTENT; *spec.* in *Path.* = INTERMITTENT A. a.

1626 *Art. agst. Dk. Buckhm.* in Rushw. *Hist. Coll.* (1659) I. 352 Great distempers, as..Raving, Fainting, an intermitting pulse. **1643** MILTON *Divorce* I. vii, Cheerefulnesse..in a thousand outward and intermitting crosses. **1761** HUME *Hist. Eng.* II. xxxvii. 316 Cardinal Pole had long been sickly, from an intermitting fever. **1794** S. WILLIAMS *Vermont* 29 Such kinds of intermitting springs are to be found in great numbers on the sides of all high mountains. **1899** tr. *Von Jaksch's Clin. Diagn.* i. (ed. 4) 59 Remitting and intermitting attacks, and cases of fever with short periods of apyrexia.

†**b.** Marked by an intermission (of fever). *Obs.*

1657 J. COOKE tr. *Hall's Cures* 181 The intermitting day she had the following glyster.

intermittingly (-ˈmɪtɪŋlɪ), *adv.* [-LY².] In an intermitting manner; intermittently.

1654 W. MOUNTAGUE *Devout Ess.* II. vi. §2. 113 These grains or motes..in that eye..suffering it to look up but intermittingly. **1818** SHELLEY *Let. to Peacock* 20 Nov., It.. rises and falls intermittingly. **1860** MAURY *Phys. Geog. Sea* (Low) xvi. §704 In March it blows intermittingly, and with hard squalls.

intermix (ɪntəˈmɪks), *v.* Also 7 enter-. [opp. f. INTERMIXT, taken as pa. pple. of an Eng. vb. repr. L. *intermiscēre*: see COMMIX, MIX.]

1. *trans.* To mix together, mix intimately, intermingle.

1562 *Jack Juggler* in Hazl. *Dodsley* II. 110 Therefore intermix honest mirth in such wise That your strength may be refreshed. **1568** GRAFTON *Chron.* I. To Rdr., The same is not intermixed with foreine affayres. **1630** PRYNNE *Anti-Armin.* 149 They are promiscuously entermixed one with the other. **1667** MILTON *P.L.* VIII. 54 Hee, she knew, would intermix Grateful digressions, and solve high dispute With conjugal Caresses. *a* **1763** SHENSTONE *Elegies* xiii. 36 Fool that I was..To let suspicion intermix a fear. *a* **1864** HAWTHORNE *Amer. Note-Bks.* (1879) I. 228 It is not wise to intermix fantastic ideas with the reality.

2. *intr.* To be or become mixed together; to mix, blend, or associate intimately.

1722 WOLLASTON *Relig. Nat.* ix. 214 Here bodily wants and affections..do intermix with human affairs. **1727** BRADLEY *Fam. Dict.* s.v. *Bezoar stone*, It's conveyed..into the Duodenum where it intermixes with the chyle. **1846** JOYCE *Sci. Dial.* xvi. 244 Do not the hot and cold water intermix?

Hence **interˈmixing** *vbl. sb.* and *ppl. a.*

1690 WAGSTAFFE *Answ. Sherlock's Case Alleg.* 13 Through all the Authors Shufflings and Intermixings, we are got to this Point. **1815** *Zeluca* III. 27 The ordeal to which she delusively put his intermixing proprieties.

intermixed, intermixt (ɪntəˈmɪkst), *ppl. a.* [orig. *intermixt*, ad. L. *intermixt-us*, pa. pple. of *intermiscēre* to mix among, intermingle, f. *inter* between, among + *miscēre* to mix, mingle. After the formation of the vb. *intermix*, *intermixt* was treated as its pa. pple. and gradually spelt *intermix'd*, *intermixed*: cf. COMMIXED.] Mixed together, intimately mixed, intermingled.

a. In form **intermixt**: const. as pa. pple. or adj.

1555 EDEN *Decades* 87 Lynen intermyxt with golde. **1578** LYTE *Dodoens* IV. xxx. 487 Of a brownishe colour, intermixt with white. **1643** MILTON *Divorce* II. x, In respect of returning to her former Husband after an intermixt Marriage. **1755** MAGENS *Insurances* I. 203 Relating to Naval, mercantile or intermixt Affairs.

β. In form **intermixed.** (In quot. 1630, Of a mixed or intermediate character.)

1598 FLORIO, *Intermisto*, intermixed..mixt among or betweene. **1630** LENNARD tr. *Charron's Wisd.* III. xvii. §3 (1670) 471 Magistrates are intermixed persons, placed between the Sovereign and private men. **1635** *Grammar Warre* C v, The intermixed..and secret hidden words were giuen him.

Hence **interˈmixedly, interˈmixtly** *adv.*, with intermixture, promiscuously.

a **1586** SIDNEY *Arcadia* III. (1598) 348 Making..prettie knots, which tyed together the names of Musidorus and Pamela, sometimes entermixedly changing them to Pammidorus and Musimela. **1596** H. CLAPHAM *Briefe Bible* I. 70 Neither..falling alone, or successiuely to the Iudges, but togither or intermixtly with them. **1672** NEWTON in *Phil. Trans.* VII. 5101 Perhaps..the Colours may be also seen intermixedly reflected from them. **1684** H. MORE *Answer* 64 Stones..laid confusedly and intermixtly one by another.

†**interˈmixt,** *v. Obs. rare.* [f. L. ppl. stem *intermixt-*: see prec. and cf. *admixt, commixt* vbs.] = INTERMIX *v.*

1551 ROBINSON tr. *More's Utop.* II. ix. (1895) 295 They sing prayses vnto God, whiche they intermixt [L. *interstinguunt*] with instrumentes of musick.

†**interˈmixtion.** *Obs.* Also 6 -myxtyon, 7 -mixion. [n. of action f. L. *intermixt-*, ppl. stem of *intermiscēre*: see prec.] = next.

a **1520** BARCLAY *Jugurth* (1557) 56 b, Without intermixtion of other occupacion. **1529** MORE *Dyaloge* II. xii. 66 a/2 Wythout intermyxtyon of obstynate heresyes. **1640** BP. REYNOLDS *Passions* xxiv. 249 By a wise intermixtion of feare and caution. **1664** POWER *Exp. Philos.* I. 63 Intermixtion with the moist Air.

intermixture (ɪntəˈmɪkstjʊə(r)). [f. as prec. + -URE: cf. L. *mixtūra* MIXTURE.]

1. The action of intermixing or fact of being intermixed; intimate mixture (of two or more things together, or of one thing *with* another).

1592 WARNER *Alb. Eng.* (title-p.), With Intermixture of Histories and Inuention. **1658** T. WALL *Charact. Enem. Ch.* 43 Confused and incongruous intermixture of the different kinds of prayer. **1672** NEWTON in *Phil. Trans.* VII. 5098 This Whiteness is produced by a successive Intermixture of the Colours, without their being assimilated. **1778** *Eng. Gazetteer* (ed. 2) s.v. *Norwich*, From the intermixture of its houses with trees, it is called a city in an orchard. **1874** GREEN *Short Hist.* vii. §7. 418 In the intermixture of tragedy and comedy..the dramas of England and Spain are remarkably alike.

2. *concr.* or quasi-*concr.* Something, or a quantity or portion *of* something, intermixed with or added to something else.

1586 WARNER *(title)* The First and Second Parts of Albion's England..with Historicall Intermixtures, Inuention, and Varietie. **1681–6** J. SCOTT *Chr. Life* (1747) III. 306 They profane and desecrate her Worship with those sinful Intermixtures they infuse into it. **1845** CARLYLE *Cromwell* (1872) I. i. 16, I have seen a fifth edition with foreign intermixtures. **1864** BRYCE *Holy Rom. Emp.* xii. (1875) 188 It is at least probable that her population [Venice] never received an intermixture of Teutonic settlers.

intermobility: see INTER- *pref.*

intermodal (ɪntəˈməʊdəl), *a.* Also inter-modal (with hyphen). [f. INTER- + MOD(E *sb.* 4 + -AL.] Of the conveyance of goods: making use of differing modes of transport during the journey between the place of dispatch and the destination. Hence **interˈmodally** *adv.*

1963 A. H. NORLING *Future U.S. Transportation Needs* (NASA Rep. N-64-25006) VIII-4 The elimination of the wasteful, duplicative handling now required in the intermodal transfer of goods will call for the increased use of containerized shipments. **1967** *Containerization* (McKinsey & Co.) 27 Low-cost intermodal transfer makes it economic to switch modes to take advantage of the lowest cost alternative. **1968** *Economist* 14 Sept. p. xxxiv, The sea-going container will fit nicely into the big aircraft, and hey presto we have real 'intermodal' transport. **1969** *Jane's Freight Containers 1968–69* 3/2 This subject is part of the legal issues arising in connection with combined or inter-modal transport in general. **1970** *Commercial Motor* 25 Sept. 133/1 The exhibition is by no means limited to container traffic and equipment, but will deal with all the intermodal systems currently available. **1970** *Times* 16 Sept. (Road Haulage Suppl.) p. vii/8 By the mid 1970s, more than 1 m. containers will be circulating intermodally on an international basis. **1971** JOHNSON & GARNETT *Econ. of Containerisation* i. 11 It [*sc.* containerization] has been standardised, making it intermodal: i.e. a container can be carried by almost any mode of transport and easily transhipped between modes. **1972** *Times* 29 Sept. 20/6 The association gives a warning that attempts to take over small ports are likely to result in 'some quite extraordinary distortions of the inter-modal transport patterns'.

intermodification, -modillion: see INTER- *pref.*

intermodulation (ˌɪntəmɒdjuːˈleɪʃən). *Electr. Engin.* [f. INTER- 2 a + MODULATION.]

Modulation of the sinusoidal components of a signal or wave-form by one another, a kind of distortion that produces new components with frequencies equal to the sums and differences of those already present. Freq. *attrib.*, esp. in ***intermodulation distortion***.

1931 *Inst. Radio Engin. Year Bk.* 50 Intermodulation is the production, in a non-linear circuit element, of frequencies corresponding to the sums and differences of the fundamentals and harmonics of two or more frequencies which are transmitted to that element. **1940** *Chambers's Techn. Dict.* 454/1 Intermodulation distortion. **1950** K. HENNEY *Radio Engin. Handbk.* (ed. 4) xvii. 854 These frequencies resulting from intermodulation are generally inharmonic or discordant and also likely to fall in the middle or upper portion of the audio range, both of which conditions make them quite objectionable. **1958** *Engineering* 31 Jan. 160/2 If two musical tones are applied, both appear at the output with all their combination tones (intermodulation products). **1964** R. F. FICCHI *Electr. Interference* iii. 24 The mixing of at least two signals in a nonlinear device which causes intermodulation distortion and results in the generation of harmonics should not be permitted. **1971** *Sci. Amer.* Sept. 178/1 (Advt.), That's 250 watts..over the whole power-pushin' listening range. Right through from 20 Hz to 20,000 kHz [*sic*] with total harmonic and intermodulation distortion at less than 0·1%!

intermolar: see INTER- *pref.*

intermolecular (ɪntəməʊˈlɛkjʊlə(r)), *a.* [INTER- 4 a.] Situated, existing, or occurring between the molecules of a body or substance. Hence **intermoˈlecularly** *adv.*, between molecules.

1843 GROVE *Contrib. Sci.* in *Corr. Phys. Forces* (1874) 304 Believing that all electrical phenomena are intermolecular changes of the bodies. **1874** HARTWIG *Aerial W.* v. 50 The intermolecular spaces of the various humours are filled with it. **1882** VINES in *Nature* 19 Oct. 595/1 Swelling-up is then the expression of the taking-up of water into the meshes of the molecular reticulum, where it is retained by intermolecular capillarity. **1936, 1971** [see INTRAMOLECULAR *a.*]. **1973** *Nature* 13 Apr. 473/2 In a condensed phase, initially formed vibrational excited 'states' are coupled intra- and inter-molecularly..to a quasi-continuum of other vibrational 'states'.

intermontane (ɪntəˈmɒnteɪn), *a.* [f. INTER- 4 a + MONTANE *a.*] Situated or lying between mountains. Also **ˈintermont, interˈmountain** *adjs.*

1807 J. MEASE *Geol. Acct. U.S.* 59 Whatever of saline.. the soil of the upland contains, is thus floated or rolled along to the low lands, and constitutes with proportional diversity and mixture, the intermontane soil. **1828** WEBSTER, Intermontane. **1900** *Congress. Rec.* 24 Jan. 1147/2 Polygamy ..was taught by the Mormon Church throughout the whole of the intermountain country as a religious duty. **1901** *Science* 8 Mar. 396/1 The erosion of narrow valleys in the floor of the weak-rock intermont peneplains. **1902** *Encycl. Brit.* XXV. 362/2 The inter-montane basins and the piedmontese plains that slope eastward from the Rocky Mountains in middle latitudes are treeless. **1903** *Science* 12 June 950/1 The study of the anthropology of the Indian races in this intermountain region. **1911** J. L. MYRES *Dawn of History* iv. 91 We are..concerned..with the intermont plains and upland valleys which sustained the old Medes and Persians. **1920** L. V. PIRSSON *Textbk. Geol.* (ed. 2) I. 269 Intermontane Plateaus. **1927** *Glasgow Herald* 21 May 8 This fungus..attacks both the green or Oregon and the blue or Colorado Douglas [fir], as well as the intermountain variety. **1936** *Geogr. Jrnl.* LXXXVII. 27 Coarse detritus which came to rest in the intermont basins. **1959** WOOLDRIDGE & MORGAN *Outl. Geomorphol.* (ed. 2) xx. 285 Plains are here in a much less dominant rôle; we have an intermont-basin landscape as compared with a true Inselberge landscape. **1962** G. MACEWAN *Blazing Old Cattle Trail* xxv. 167 Ranching of western Canada's prairie, foothill and inter-mountain ranges was just two or three decades old. **1965** G. J. WILLIAMS *Econ. Geol. N.Z.* xviii. 297/1 The Tertiary-filled intermontane basin is 50 miles long and averages 15 miles in width.

inter-morainic: see INTER- *pref.* 4 a.

intermundane (ɪntəˈmʌndeɪn), *a.* [f. INTER- 4 a + L. *mund-us* world, *mundān-us* of or belonging to the world; cf. L. *intermundia*, in next.]

1. Situated, or present, between different worlds.

a **1691** BOYLE *Hist. Air* (1692) 1 The air..is so different from the æther..in the intermundane or interplanetary spaces. *a* **1704** LOCKE *Elem. Nat. Phil.* ii. (1754) 7 The vast distance, between these great bodies, are call'd intermundane spaces. **1766** G. CANNING *Anti-Lucretius* II. 91 To intermundane regions they were hurl'd.

2. Existing between worlds reciprocally.

1858 G. MACDONALD *Phantastes* xii. 134 Worlds cannot be without an intermundane relationship.

†**interˈmundial,** *a. Obs. rare.* [f. L. *intermundia* (pl.) the spaces between the worlds + -AL¹.] = INTERMUNDANE. So †**interˈmundian** *a.*

1670 H. STUBBE *Plus Ultra* 40 Neither the constitution of our Atmosphear..and air, nor the intermundial Æther. *a* **1711** KEN *Edmund* Poet. Wks. 1721 II. 123 Alot a sep'rate intermundian Space For the fond youthful self-denying Race. —— *Hymnotheo* ibid. III. 223 One intermundian God must be profess'd.

‖**interˈmundium.** [A mod. sing. of L. *intermundia*: see prec.] A space between two worlds.

1812 COLERIDGE in *Southey's Omniana* II. 81 The confine, the *intermundium*, as it were, of existence and non-existence. **1817** —— *Biog. Lit.* (1882) 15 The former rest content between thought and reality, as it were in an *intermundium*.

interˈmural, *a. rare*⁻⁰. [ad. L. *intermūrāl-is*, f. *inter* between + *mūr-us* wall, *mūrāl-is* pertaining to a wall, mural.] Situated between walls.

1656 in BLOUNT *Glossogr.* **1658** PHILLIPS, *Intermural space*, a space between two walls.

†**interˈmure,** *v. Obs.* Also 7 enter-. [f. INTER- 1 a + L. *mūr-us* wall.] *trans.* To inclose between walls, to wall in.

1606 FORD *Fame's Memorial* E j, A bulwarke intermur'd with walls of Brasse, A like can neuer bee, nor euer was. **1611** FLORIO, *Intermurare*, to entermure or wall. **1611** SPEED *Hist. Gt. Brit.* VI. xvii. §5. 97 This Wall..was made of stakes driuen deepe into the ground..and with Turfe and Earth intermured as a Rampire or Bulwarke. **1628** FORD *Lover's Mel.* I. i, Her bosom yet Is intermured with ice.

intermure, *sb.*: see INTERMEWER.

intermuscular (ɪntəˈmʌskjʊlə(r)), *a.* *Anat.* [INTER- 4 a.] Situated between muscles, or between muscular fibres.

1822–34 *Good's Study Med.* (ed. 4) IV. 218 Bichat.. remarked, that the intermuscular tissue is almost everywhere without [fat]. **1878** BELL *Gegenbaur's Comp. Anat.* 496 The ribs themselves lie in the intermuscular ligaments.

†**interˈmusculary**, *a.* *Obs.* = prec.

1650 CHARLETON *Paradoxes* Prol. 11 Intumescence, from the distension of its vessels, membranes and intermusculary Capacities.

intermutation: see INTER- *pref.* 2 a.

intermutual (ɪntəˈmjuːtjuːəl), *a.* [INTER- 2 a; a pleonastic strengthening of *mutual*, used by some writers.] Mutual, reciprocal.

1595 DANIEL *Civ. Wars* III. xxxiv, A solemne oth religiously they make By intermutuall vowes protesting there This neuer to reueale. **1627** FELTHAM *Resolves* II. [I.] xvi. (1628) 49 An entire chaine of intermutuall amity. **1850** *Fraser's Mag.* XLI. 578 There was, of course, much intermutual laudation. **1858** POLSON *Law & L.* 194 An intermutual change of familiar jokes.

interˈmutually, *adv.* [f. prec. + -LY², or f. INTER- 2 a + MUTUALLY: see prec.] Mutually, reciprocally.

1601 DANIEL *Civ. Wars* VI. lxxxi, Proclaym'd with ioyfull acclamations, And intermutually there ratifide. **1671** FLAMSTEED in Rigaud *Corr. Sci. Men* (1841) II. 113 My distempers and affairs of late have been so intermutually urgent. **1840** *Fraser's Mag.* XXII. 65 The use the various sciences are intermutually.

So **intermutualness**. *rare*⁻¹.

1627 FELTHAM *Resolves* II. [I.] lxxxv. (1628) 244 When Paires keepe themselues in a moderate intermutualnesse, each constant to the other.

intermutule: see INTER- *pref.* 3 a.

intern (ɪnˈtɜːn), *a.* and *sb.* Also 6–9 **interne**. [a. F. *interne* (14th c. in Littré) = It. *interno*, ad. L. *intern-us* inward, internal, f. *in* adv. + *-ternus* suffix, as in *ex-ternus*, *sempi-ternus*, etc.]

A. *adj.* (Now only *poet.* or *arch.*)

1. = INTERNAL A. 1.

1578 BANISTER *Hist. Man* VII. 90 Euery where this Membran Pleura is two fold.. the one interne, the other externe. **1658** R. WHITE tr. *Digby's Powd. Symp.* (1660) 89 Within a living body, such as is man's, the intern spirits do aid. **1865** GIDLEY *Aletes* 133 Its stubborn fibres thrill'd with some intern commotion.

2. = INTERNAL A. 2.

1610 B. JONSON *Alch.* IV. i, Your predicaments, substance and accident, Series, extern and intern, with their causes, Efficient, material, formal, final. **1645** HOWELL *Dodona's Gr.* 3 The midland towns are most flourishing.. which shews that her riches are interne and domestick. **1703** T. N. *City & C. Purchaser* 8 In Architecture 'tis us'd to signifie an intern Support to the Superstructure. **1856** MRS. BROWNING *Aur. Leigh* VIII. 548 But innermost Of the inmost, most interior of the interne, God claims his own.

3. = INTERNAL A. 3.

1600 FAIRFAX *Tasso* IX. xl, The Soldan stroue his rage interne To satisfie with blood of Christians spild. **1645** HOWELL *Dodona's Gr.* 70 He being a Spirit ought to be serv'd in spirit, and chiefly with intern worship. **1683** E. HOOKER *Pref. Pordage's Mystic Div.* 78 O the incredibl intern exercitations and extern exertions of the veri visibl form of som Persons!

B. *sb.* Also **interne**. 'An inmate, as of a school; especially, an assistant resident physician or surgeon in a hospital, usually a student or recent graduate, acting in the absence of the attending physician or surgeon.' ('A recent use from Fr.', *Cent. Dict.*). Now usu., a recent medical graduate who is working under supervision in a hospital (and often living there) as part of his training, prior to entering general practice or becoming a resident. (Broadly equivalent to a houseman in Great Britain.) Also *transf.*, used of individuals in other professions (esp. teaching) who are receiving practical experience under supervision. Chiefly *U.S.*

Freq. pronounced with stress on first syllable.

[**1699** M. LISTER *Journey to Paris* (ed. 3) 74 Monsieur du Pes Surgeon Interne of the Hôtel-dieu.] **1879** in WEBSTER Suppl. **1889** *Kansas City* (Missouri) *Times & Star* 16 Oct., Convalescent women and young nurses are given too much freedom with the internes. **1890** W. JAMES *Princ. Psychol.* I. x. 385 His brother, Dr. Jules Janet.. was *interne* at the Salpêtrière Hospital. **1914** M. GERRY *Masks of Love* 123 The young interne.. had alarmed them. **1938** *Amer. Speech* XIII. 228/1 *Resident* ranks over *intern* by reason of experience, but both are medical school graduates studying in the hospital. **1955** W. GADDIS *Recognitions* I. i. 41 Physicians, technicians, and internes X-rayed the boy from every possible angle. **1961** J. HELLER *Catch-22* (1962) xviii. 175 In the morning a helpful young English intern popped in to ask him about his liver. **1963** A. BEALES *Educ. under Penalty* I. ii. 18 In the field of lay education the loss caused by the dissolution was less than formerly supposed, since the monasteries had long ceased, most of them, to teach any but interns. **1967** MRS. L. B. JOHNSON *White House Diary* 14 Mar. (1970) 497 One intern was giving remedial reading. **1969** *Eugene* (Oregon) *Register-Guard* 3 Dec. 1A/3 Representing Springfield teachers are Rita Castleberry, Lee Elementary School instructor; Roy Van Horn, principal at Mt. Vernon Elementary School, and Moore, who is intern teacher supervisor at Lee Elementary School. **1970** *Toronto Daily Star* 24 Sept. 31/6 (Advt.), Broderick Crawford.. gives young intern Steve Brooks some food for thought. **1972** *Nature* 4 Feb. 291/2 Doctor of medicine and intern of the hospitals of Lyon, in 1908 Professor Lacassagne entered the Laboratory of Histology to work under the direction of Claudius Regaud.

Hence **inˈternship**, **interneship**, the position or station of an intern; the period of such a position. Chiefly *U.S.*

1904 *Jrnl. Amer. Med. Assoc.* 13 Aug. 469/2 From one to two years of what might be called practical apprenticeship is the privilege sought by the earnest [medical] student. To gain this privilege he.. delays for the period of his interneship his start in the world and his establishment in his profession. **1924** *Scribner's Mag.* Feb. 183/1 My father, who had the practice.. told me the story in professional confidence... I was at that time just finishing my internship. **1934** A. WOOLLCOTT *While Rome Burns* 46 The fiery young doctor, in the days of his interneship, had already tasted the experience of spending two months in the lockup. **1938** *Internships & Residences in N.Y. City, 1934–1937* p. xxvii, An internship is a period of service as a member of the hospital staff while residing in the hospital and receiving a period of formal education subsequent to graduation from medical school. **1948** *Training of a Doctor* (B.M.A.) xxxii. 127 This prescribed period of compulsory pre-registration house-appointments corresponds to the post known in America as an 'internship', and the period is called ' the intern year'. **1957** KENDALL & SELVIN in R. K. Merton *Student-Physician* 155 Nearly every medical student is required to take an internship when he has completed medical school, regardless of his plans for his later career. **1968** *Globe & Mail* (Toronto) 17 Feb. 50 (Advt.), The internship plan for the training of elementary school teachers. **1968** *New Scientist* 14 Nov. 388/2 One suggestion is very similar to the principle of our sandwich systems, under the more anaesthetised name of an 'internship'. **1971** *Black Scholar* June 62/1 (Advt.), An individually tailored, accelerated career program which begins with a two-year internship and leads to positions of increasing responsibility in the developing countries. **1971** *Nature* 1 Oct. 301/1 The money will be used to establish internships in federally funded laboratories for some 420 young unemployed scientists and engineers who hold advanced degrees.

intern (ɪnˈtɜːn), *v.* Also 7 **interne**. [In sense 1, ad. It. *internere* 'to enter, goe, or passe in', *internare* 'to enter or pearce into ones minde secretly' (Florio, 1598); in sense 2, a. F. *interne-r* (18th c. in *Dict. Trévoux*); these vbs. from It. *interno*, F. *interne*: see prec.; in sense 4, f. the *sb.*]

†**1.** *intr.* To enter or pass in; to become incorporated or united with another being. *Obs.*

1606 BRYSKETT *Civ. Life* 131 Now wak'd thou art among the heau'nly spirits, Where blessed soules interne within their maker... Seeming to infer that she was now interned or become inward in the contemplation of her maker.

2. *trans.* To confine within the limits of a country, district, or place; to oblige to reside within prescribed limits without permission to leave them. Also *fig.* Hence **inˈterned** *ppl. a.*

1866 *Pall Mall G.* 31 Jan. 9 Certain prisoners in a foreign country were described as having been 'interned'. The word, we venture to think, supplies a want. **1867** *Standard* 3 June 3/1 All Poles interned in Russia will be allowed to return to their homes. **1874** W. E. HALL *Rights Neutrals* ii. 83 To disarm troops crossing the neutral frontier and to intern them till the conclusion of peace. **1884** LOWELL *Wks.* (1890) VI. 108 Calderon retains a Spanish accent, and is accordingly interned (if I may Anglicise a French word) in that provincialism which we call nationality.

3. To send (merchandise, goods, etc.) into the interior of a country. *U.S.*

4. (Usu. pronounced with stress on first syllable.) *intr.* To act as an intern. *U.S.*

1933 S. KINGSLEY *Men in White* I. i. 24 You interned here? **1969** *Eugene* (Oregon) *Register-Guard* 3 Dec. 5D/1 He.. interned at Cook County Hospital in Chicago for one year. **1971** 'D. SHANNON' *Murder with Love* (1972) v. 83 Harlow interned at the General... He had the makings of a very fine surgeon.

internal (ɪnˈtɜːnəl), *a.* and *sb.* [ad. late med.L. *internāl-is* (f. *intern-us*: see -AL¹): cf. obs. F. *internel* (15–16th c. in Godef.), It. *internale* (Florio). Opposed in all senses to *external*.]

A. *adj.* **1. a.** Situated or existing within or in the interior of something; of or pertaining to the inside (e.g. of the body); inward.

internal angle (Geom.) = *interior angle*: see INTERIOR A. 1. ***internal contact***: see quot. 1867. ***internal object***: in *Psychoanalysis*, the inward image formed of an object invested with the emotional energy which would normally have been expended on the object itself.

1590 SPENSER *F.Q.* III. x. 59 That doth with curelesse care consume the hart,.. Cros-cuts the liver with internall smart. **1607** E. GRIMSTONE tr. *Goulart's Mem. Hist.* 394, I did conjecture that this disease grewe from some internall cause. **1660** BARROW *Euclid* I. Ax. xiii, If a right line BA falling on two right lines AD, CB, make the internal angles on the same side, BAD, ABC, less than two right angles. **1794** S. WILLIAMS *Vermont* 103 When all naturalists shall have visited and examined the internal parts [of the country]. **1804** W. TENNANT *Ind. Recreat.* (ed. 2) I. 49 The internal navigation is conducted by the natives. **1821** J. Q. ADAMS in C. Davies *Metr. Syst.* III. (1871) 166 The capacity of a ship .. is ascertained by its internal cubical dimensions. **1855** MACAULAY *Hist. Eng.* xiv. III. 400 He was tormented by a cruel internal disease. **1867** SMYTH *Sailor's Word-bk.*, *Internal contact*.. in a transit of Mercury or Venus.. occurs when the planet is just within the sun's margin. **1940** *Internat. Jrnl. Psycho-Anal.* XXI. 280 (*title*) Temper tantrums in early childhood in their relation to internal objects. **1949** *Brit. Jrnl. Med. Psychol.* XXII. 13 Thus we see the internal object represents also the child himself. **1973** H. SEGAL *Introd. Work M. Klein* (new ed.) ii. 12 These internal objects are not 'objects' situated in the body or the psyche: like Freud, Melanie Klein is describing unconscious phantasies which people have about what they contain.

b. *Anat.* Situated away from the surface of the body, or nearer the median line: in names of vessels, nerves, etc. correlated with others called *external* (see EXTERNAL A. 1 b).

1842 E. WILSON *Anat. Vade M.* (ed. 2) 103 The Internal Lateral Ligament has no connection with the articulation of the lower jaw. *Ibid.* 348 The Internal iliac Vein is formed by vessels which correspond with the branches of the internal iliac artery. **1872** MIVART *Elem. Anat.* 182 On its inner side is a projection called the internal tuberosity. **1881** —— *Cat* 213 The Internal Iliac, or hypogastric artery, dips down into the pelvis.

c. Of a remedy: To be taken internally.

1799 *Med. Jrnl.* II. 300 He recommends external warmth .. but not internal stimulants.

2. a. Pertaining to the inner nature or relations of anything, as distinguished from its relations to things external to itself; belonging to the thing or subject in itself; intrinsic. *spec.* in *Philos.*, as ***internal property***, ***relation***: a property or relation which belongs essentially to an object or proposition.

internal evidence: evidence derived from what is contained in the thing itself (opp. to *external evidence*: see EXTERNAL A. 4).

1607 E. GRIMSTONE tr. *Goulart's Mem. Hist.* 393 This made mee to doubt, whether one by internall principles, and of their owne corruption, might not become madde. **1632** MASSINGER & FIELD *Fatal Dowry* IV. i, All the internal quality and habiliment of the soul. **1651** BAXTER *Inf. Bapt.* 73 It is a two-fold respect of one and the same Church; one as to the internal Essence, the other as to the external manner of existing. **1657** W. RAND tr. *Gassendi's Life Peiresc* I. 132 The internall goodness of the *Solidus*.. decreasing. **1769** *Junius Lett.* xxvii. 127 The conduct of this minister carries with it an internal and convincing evidence against him. **1818** HALLAM *Mid. Ages* (1855) I. i. I. 2 *note*, It is by no means deficient in internal probability. **1871** FREEMAN *Hist. Ess.* Ser. I. i. 26 The internal evidence for some statements renders them highly probable. **1883** F. H. BRADLEY *Princ. Logic* 432 As the material supplied is in each case different, so again the product is not the same. In one case the whole precedes and is followed by its internal relations. **1920** G. E. MOORE in *Proc. Aristotelian Soc.* XX. 40 (*title*) External and internal relations. *Ibid.* 41 And I shall maintain that, if we give to the assertion that a relation is 'internal' the meaning which this proposition would give to it, then.. *some* relations are 'internal'. **1922** tr. *Wittgenstein's Tractatus* 4. 122 Instead of property of the structure I also say 'internal property'; instead of relation of structures 'internal relation'. **1937** A. SMEATON tr. *Carnap's Logical Syntax of Lang.* v. §79. 304 The numerous discussions and controversies about external and internal properties and relations. **1959** R. WOLLHEIM *F. H. Bradley* iii. 92 The most important of them all, the doctrine of Internal Relations. **1966** *Amer. Philos. Q.* III. 45/1 This forces one to acknowledge that a thing changes when what it is related to changes. In short one is involved with *internal relations*.

b. Of or pertaining to the domestic affairs of a country, as distinguished from its relations with foreign countries. ***internal revenue*** (*U.S.*): revenue derived from duties and taxes imposed on domestic trade and commerce; inland revenue.

1795–8 WELLINGTON in Gurw. *Desp.* (1837) I. 3 Internal tranquillity prevailed throughout the Company's possessions. **1796** *Deb. Congress U.S.* 26 Feb. 379 Mr. W. Smith moved the order of the day on the report of the Committee of Ways and Means on the Internal Revenue. **1849** MACAULAY *Hist. Eng.* i. I. 132 The colony had its own internal disputes, both national and religious. **1860** MOTLEY *Netherl.* (1868) II. ix. 60 To glance at the internal politics of the Republic. **1873** *Newton Kansan* 2 Jan. 2/1 The most important bills.. are those reducing the internal revenue force. **1875** STUBBS *Const. Hist.* III. xviii. 243 In the task of defence against foreign foes and in the maintenance of internal peace. **1959** *Chambers's Encycl.* VII. 417/1 In the United States collection is made by the Bureau of Internal Revenue. **1972** *Lebende Sprachen* XVII. 34/1 US internal revenue—BE inland revenue.

c. Of a student: That has studied in one of the colleges of a university, as distinguished from an *external* student who is examined by the university but has studied elsewhere.

1898 *Daily News* 20 July 6/3 Sir A. Rollit also tried to get rid of the words 'Each certificate and diploma shall state whether the candidate has passed as an internal or as an external student'.

3. Of or belonging to the inner nature or life of man; pertaining to the mind or soul; mental or spiritual; inward; subjective.

1509 HAWES *Past. Pleas.* XXIV. (*title*), Of the five internall wittes. **1608** D. T. *Ess. Pol. & Mor.* 15 b, Passions are certaine internall acts, and operations of our soule. *a* **1631** DRAYTON *Q. Margaret to De La Poole* 11 No object greets my soules internall eies, But divinations of sad Tragedies. **1671** MILTON *Samson* 1334 *Off.* Regard thyself; this will offend them highly. *Sams.* Myself! my conscience, and internal peace. **1764** GOLDSM. *Trav.* 270 Praise too dearly lov'd or warmly sought, Enfeebles all internal strength of thought. **1869** J. MARTINEAU *Ess.* II. 110 Sensations and ideas are both internal.

†**4.** Intimate. *Obs. rare*⁻⁰.

1616 BULLOKAR, *Internall*, inward: verie deerely esteemed, or familiar with one.

5. Special collocations: **internal clock**, a person's innate sense of time; = *biological clock*; **internal-combustion**, used *attrib.* to designate any engine in which combustion of the fuel takes place inside it in the chamber where the force is developed (or a part continuous with it); also

fig.; **internal conversion** *Physics*, (*a*) the process whereby the whole energy of a gamma-ray photon emitted by a nucleus is given up to an orbital electron, causing its emission from the atom; (*b*) (see quot. 1972[2]); **internal energy**, the energy possessed by a physical system in consequence of the positions and relative motions and interactions of its component parts: a function of its state (usu. of undefined absolute magnitude) such that any change in the function is equal to the sum of the heat absorbed by the system and the work done on it; **internal friction**, resistance to the deformation or flow of a substance that occurs inside it with the production of heat, and arises from the relative motion of adjacent parts; **internal medicine** = MEDICINE *sb.*[1] 1 (in the 'more restricted sense'); **internal phloem** (see quot. 1933); **internal pressure**, the pressure which exists within a fluid arising from intermolecular attraction; **internal secretion** *Physiol.* [tr. F. *sécrétion interne* (C. Bernard *Leçons sur les Propriétés physiol. des Liquides de l'Organisme* (1859) II. xvii. 408)], any secretion that is delivered into the internal environment of the body, esp. into the blood stream; *spec.* a hormone; also, the process of secreting in this manner; **internal stress**, stress that arises inside a substance (e.g. as a result of differential heating of different parts) and is not imposed from without; **internal wave**, any transverse wave occurring within a fluid either along the interface between layers of different density or within a layer having a vertical density gradient.

1960 I. JEFFERIES *Dignity & Purity* vi. 123, I suppose he works according to his own internal clock. **1974** *Guardian* 28 Jan. 8/3 If a programme is on too late for our internal clocks, we would almost rather it were not shown at all. **1884** H. C. F. JENKIN in *Heat in its Mech. Applications* (Inst. Civil Engin.) (1885) 105 The internal combustion engine..is really the fore-runner of the gas-engine. **1921** W. H. BERRY *Mod. Motor Car Pract.* i. 14 In effect liquid fuel made the internal combustion motor practicable for locomotive purposes, its essential qualities being that it can be easily stored and carried, and be readily converted into an explosive gas ignitable within the cylinder. **1949** D. G. SHEPHERD *Introd. Gas Turbine* i. 1 The gas turbine, in common with other forms of internal combustion engines, converts heat into work by a cycle using a gas as the working medium, the processes being compression, addition of heat and expansion, and requiring continuous flow of the gas during these changes of state. **1951** M. MCLUHAN *Mech. Bride* 113/2 What Kipling was to the aggressive British imperialists, these ads are to our domestic economy. They act as a sort of firing spark in the internal combustion engine. **1967** E. DELMAR-MORGAN *Maintenance Inboard Engines* i. 19 Within the broad category of the internal-combustion engine there are the spark-ignition engine (petrol and paraffin) and the compression ignition (diesel). **1927** *Proc. R. Soc.* A. CXVI. 491 (*heading*) The internal conversion of γ-rays. **1927** *Proc. Cambr. Philos. Soc.* 718 The homogeneous groups in the β-ray spectra are due to the conversion of the γ-rays, and the intensities of these groups depend not only on the intensities of these γ-rays but also on the extent to which they are converted, that is the magnitude of the internal conversion coefficient. **1949** P. PRINGSHEIM *Fluorescence & Phosphorescence* iii. 272 Since no light emission accompanies the transition from the higher electronic state to the emitting state, the transition must correspond to a process of internal conversion. **1955** R. D. EVANS *Atomic Nucleus* i. 23 The second general class of nuclear transitions which invariably result in X-ray-emission spectra is the internal-conversion transitions... Internal conversion..often predominates over γ-ray emission if the nuclear excitation energy is small and the angular-momentum change is large. **1959** *Q. Rev.* XIII. 5 The strong fluorescence indicates that internal conversion does not take place as often as would be expected. **1972** H. A. ENGE et al. *Introd. Atomic Physics* xii. 386 Internal conversion competes with gamma emission, and the ratio of the probabilities of the two processes depends strongly upon the multipolarity. **1972** C. H. J. WELLS *Introd. Molecular Photochem.* iii. 34 Internal conversion (ic) is the term given to the radiationless process whereby a molecule transfers from one electronic state to another electronic state of the same multiplicity. **1887** *Encycl. Brit.* XXII. 480/1 Since the gas had neither gained nor lost heat, and had done no work, its internal energy was the same at the end as at the beginning of the experiment. **1921** A. W. JUDGE *Automobile & Aircraft Engines* ii. 60 The internal energy of a given quantity of gas depends only upon its temperature. **1927** H. S. TAYLOR *Elem. Physical Chem.* ii. 64 The internal energies of the gas in the two states may include the energy resultant from such factors as motion and position of the molecules, molecular attraction, intra-molecular forces, intra-atomic vibrations, chemical and other unknown forces. We therefore note that the absolute magnitudes..are not ascertainable. The change of internal energy, ΔU, is definite and measurable. **1966** *McGraw-Hill Encycl. Sci. & Technol.* VII. 209/1 The change in internal energy is fixed by the initial and final states, and is independent of the path by which the change in state is accomplished. **1972** A. L. RUOFF *Introd. Materials Sci.* iv. 159 The change in internal energy associated with stress, electric and magnetic fields is due to the work done on the material. **1849** *Trans. Cambr. Philos. Soc.* VIII. 297 The internal friction of the water. **1860** *Phil. Mag.* XIX. 20 The internal friction of gases. **1875** *Encycl. Brit.* III. 39/2 The compressed gas expanded to twice its volume, and the work of expansion..was soon converted into heat by the internal friction of the gas. **1922** GLAZEBROOK *Dict. Appl. Physics* I. 351/1 The characteristics of the internal friction of fluids when the general motion is eddying or turbulent. **1931** [see *internal wave* below]. **1958** *Jrnl. Iron & Steel Inst.* CXC. 93/2 Stress relaxation across grain boundaries and phase interfaces, an important source of internal friction, is considered. [**1894** GOULD *Dict. Med.* 735/1 On the European continent it is customary to divide medicine into internal and external, the former implying the restricted sense of the term, or the study of diseases of internal organs.] **1904** STEDMAN *Dunglison's Dict. Med. Sci.* (ed. 23) 583/2 *I[nternal] medicine*, that branch of medicine which has to do with diseases of the body not amenable to operative treatment; medicine as contrasted with surgery. **1968** TALSO & REMENCHIK (*title*) Internal medicine, based on mechanisms of disease. **1933** *Tropical Woods* XXXVI. 3 Internal Phloem.—Primary phloem internal to the primary xylem. (To replace *Intraxylary Phloem.*) **1953** K. ESAU *Plant Anat.* xii. 268 In angiosperms the internal phloem is initiated somewhat later than the external. **1967** S. BROIDO-ALTMAN tr. *Fahn's Plant Anat.* xi. 167 The internal phloem may be present as separate strands on the border of the pith. **1911** *Trans. Faraday Soc.* VII. 94 It is therefore immaterial ..whether we fix our attention on the internal pressure or on the thermal pressure, which acts in the opposite sense. **1940** GLASSTONE *Text-bk. Physical Chem.* vii. 472 The internal pressure of naphthalene is about 3600 atm., so that the forces of cohesion in liquids are evidently very large. **1973** A. W. ADAMSON *Textbk. Physical Chem.* iv. 151 The internal pressure is zero for an ideal gas and for most real gases it is small compared to *P* [*sc.* the measured pressure]. **1895** *Brit. Med. Jrnl.* 10 Aug. 341/1 On the other hand, some secreted materials are not poured out upon an external surface at all, but are returned to the blood. These may be termed internal secretions. **1921** I. G. COBB *Organs Internal Secretion* (ed. 3) i. 19 The term hormone is in more or less general use to denote an internal secretion. **1924** A. LIPSCHÜTZ *Internal Secretions Sex Glands* p. vi, Prof. Starling suggested the term 'hormone' for the active principles of those internal secretions which act as chemical messengers. **1926** J. S. HUXLEY *Ess. Pop. Sci.* 203 Claude Bernard introduced physiology to the general idea of internal secretion. **1941** R. G. HOSKINS *Endocrinol.* i. 20 Usually, however, formal credit for first demonstrating the process of internal secretion is given to Claude Bernard, who in 1848 reported the discovery that sugar stored in the liver in the form of glycogen is discharged as dextrose directly into the blood rather than through the ducts of the organ after the fashion of an ordinary secreting gland. The term 'internal secretion' is no longer applied to substances like sugar, but is restricted to those having a more specific regulatory function. **1966** W. S. HOAR *Gen. & Compar. Physiol.* ii. 34 As a matter of fact, the first internal secretion conclusively demonstrated was the hormone secretion produced by the wall of the gut. **1904** GOODCHILD & TWENEY *Technol. & Sci. Dict.* 313/1 Internal stress. **1906** *Jrnl. Iron & Steel Inst.* LXXII. 608 (*heading*) Internal stresses and strains in iron and steel. **1923** GLAZEBROOK *Dict. Appl. Physics* V. 344/1 Carpenter and Edwards argue that in quenching steel these internal stresses cause internal straining of the metal. **1950** *Jrnl. Iron & Steel Inst.* CLXIV. 166/2 In a partially transformed steel, the volume changes accompanying transformation presumably set up a system of internal stresses. **1931** *Rapports et Proc.-Verb. des Réunions Conseil Perm. Internat. Explor. Mer* LXXVI. 5 (*heading*) On internal waves. *Ibid.* 10 Free internal waves must abate owing to internal friction and eddy-viscosity. **1966** *McGraw-Hill Encycl. Sci. & Technol.* XIV. 417/2 Internal waves have been found in the atmosphere as lee waves (waves in the wind stream downwind from a mountain) and as waves propagated along an inversion layer. **1966** R. W. FAIRBRIDGE *Encycl. Oceanogr.* 402 Internal waves are sub-surface waves found between layers of different density or within layers where vertical density gradients are present. They can exist in any stratified fluid and can be caused by flow over an irregular bottom, atmospheric disturbances, tidal forces, and shear flow.

B. *sb.* **1.** *pl.* The inward parts or organs; 'inwards', entrails.

1834 JAS. WILSON *Let.* in *Mem.* v. (1859) 177 We.. counted his teeth and compared his internals with those of the common species.

†**2.** *Med.* (usually in *pl.*) A medicine or remedy to be taken internally. *Obs.*

1694 SALMON *Bate's Dispens.* (1713) 361/1 It is mostly used as an Internal in the Venereal Disease and all its Retinue. **1704** F. FULLER *Med. Gymn.* Pref. (1711) 2 Internals do indeed make up the far greatest part of the Means of Cure. *Ibid.* (1718) 4 Without the Use of Internals.

3. Something belonging to the thing in itself; an intrinsic or essential attribute, quality, etc. (Usually, now always, in *pl.*)

1652 GAULE *Magastrom.* 80 Why should the planets have such influences upon externalls and accidentalls, that had none upon the internalls and essentialls? **1697** tr. *Burgersdicius his Logic* I. xviii. 71 The Internal of Oratory is to speak Ornately, and Accommodately to persuade; the External to persuade. **1709** SACHEVERELL *Serm.* 5 Nov. 10 The Exterior Fences to Guard the Internals of Religion. **1884** *Chr. Commw.* 20 Mar. 536/2 The real sweets of life.. belong to the internals and subjectives of existence.

†**4.** (Usually in *pl.*) The inner nature, soul, spirit. *Obs.*

a **1635** NAUNTON *Fragm. Reg.* (Arb.) 15 As for externals she was full blown, so was she for her internals grown ripe, and seasoned with adversity. **1651** tr. *Life Father Sarpi* (1676) 102 The Father Fulgentio that understood the internals of the Father by a long practise. **17..** tr. *Swedenborg's New Jerus.* §223 Man is so created, that as to his internal he cannot die.

Hence **in'ternalness**, inwardness (Bailey vol. II, 1727).

internality (ɪntəˈnælɪtɪ). [f. prec.: see -ITY.] The quality or fact of being internal; inwardness.

1813 W. TAYLOR *Eng. Synonyms* 193 The internality of action which accompanies the signification of the word [*grow*]. **1877** HUXLEY *Anat. Inv. Anim.* viii. 473 All ligaments are external, and their internality or externality is in respect of the hinge line. **1895** J. KIDD *Moral. & Relig.* vi. 233 What specially concerns us meanwhile is the internality of these ideals, the fact that both lie within the self.

b. with *pl.* An internal quality or characteristic.

1879 MOMERIE *Personality* IV. (1886) 103 It is inconceivable how any number of associated internalities can ever produce the idea of externality.

internalization (ɪnˌtɜːnəlaɪˈzeɪʃən). [f. next + -ATION.] The action or process of internalizing; an instance of this.

1883 *Century Mag.* 479 Beauty is the joyful internalisation of outwardness. **1890** J. H. STIRLING *Gifford Lect.* iv. 69 Nature is but the externalization of thought:—thought but the internalization of Nature. **1942** *Internat. Jrnl. Psycho-Anal.* XXIII. 8 (*title*) A contribution to the problem of sublimation and its relation to processes of internalization. **1952** GERTH & MARTINDALE tr. *Weber's Anc. Judaism* IV. xii. 328 For Jeremiah this internalization..went hand in hand with the formation of quite modest external hopes. **1954** T. GRYGIER *Oppression* I. i. 8 Civilization takes certain measures to check it [*sc.* aggression]. The most important is the introjection or internalization of aggressiveness. **1964** M. ARGYLE *Psychol. & Social Probl.* i. 20 Such people often behave differently when away from the group—they are showing overt compliance without internalization, and we should only speak of learning taking place when there is also internalization. **1970** P. KELVIN *Bases of Social Behaviour* ix. 281 'Internalization' here refers to the process and condition whereby the norms of the group or society become the individual's own norms, whether of behaviour or of values. **1971** *Sci. Amer.* Sept. 192/3 One method of fostering the incorporation of technology assessment into their decisional processes would involve the internalization of costs. **1973** *Nature* 20 Apr. 488/1 The most economical way of controlling both pollution and congestion in cities must depend on what the economists call an internalization of the externalities—making the motorist bear not merely the costs of operating his vehicle but the costs of what he does to other people.

internalize (ɪnˈtɜːnəlaɪz), *v.* [f. INTERNAL + -IZE.] **a.** *trans.* To make internal; to give an inward or subjective character to. *spec.* in *Psychol.*, to transfer to a subjectively formed image (the emotions connected with some object) (see also INTROJECT *v.*); to adopt or incorporate as one's own (the values, etc., of a social group).

1884 *Chicago Advance* 14 Feb., Many of us..internalize it [religion] too much. **1942** *Internat. Jrnl. Psycho-Anal.* XXIII. 15/1 The atonement for guilt is here carried out by internalizing the attacked external object. **1950** BETTELHEIM & SYLVESTER in P. Greenacre et al. *Psychoanal. Study Child* V. 330 While their own actions are motivated by 'what will get by'..they demand that he himself be guided by 'what is right'... The child who tries to internalize these discrepant demands is confronted by a seemingly insoluble conflict. **1958** M. ARGYLE *Relig. Behaviour* v. 42 The suggestion that Protestants internalize the super-ego to a greater extent. **1960** KOESTLER *Lotus & Robot* II. viii. 203 The chances are that his aggressive impulses..will be internalized and deflected against himself. **1968** J. M. ZIMAN *Public Knowl.* v. 77 He must internalize the scientific attitude so that he cannot even conceive of, say,..recording the epoch of an eclipse by reference to the age of the reigning monarch. **1971** *Black Scholar* June 7/1 Some [black women] even internalize white society's low regard for black men.

b. *Linguistics.* To acquire knowledge of (a set of rules in a given language): used esp. of the language-learning procedures of a child.

1965 [implied in quots. for INTERNALIZED *ppl. a.*]. **1968** CHOMSKY & HALLE *Sound Pattern Eng.* 3 The person who has acquired knowledge of a language has internalized a system of rules. **1971** D. CRYSTAL *Ling.* iii. 104 We have mastered ('internalized' is a word often used here) a technique for breaking each new sentence up.

c. *Econ.* To incorporate (costs) as part of the internal cost structure, esp. 'social' costs, resulting from the use or manufacture of a particular product.

1971 *Sci. Amer.* Aug. 44/3 The first is the alteration of the ground rules and incentives under which the market operates by such devices as taxes, subsidies, and judicial actions to internalize (i.e., make explicit) social costs. *Ibid.* Sept. 194/2 A consideration of means whereby the legal system can internalize costs that power companies have been allowed to treat as external and therefore to exclude from their cost-benefit calculations.

internalized (ɪnˈtɜːnəlaɪzd), *ppl. a.* [f. the vb.] Made internal, acquired or mastered internally. Also in other senses of the vb.

1932 A. STRACHEY tr. *Klein's Psycho-Anal. Children* vii. 169 The boy could not maintain this alliance with a cruel external super-ego against his id and his internalized objects. **1942** *Internat. Jrnl. Psycho-Anal.* XXIII. 9/2 The connection between her phantasies about internalized objects and her artistic productivity. **1959** *Psychiatry* XXII. 290 The successfully treated patient comes to be his own critic, using in relation to himself evaluations previously consensually validated with the therapist and hence perpetuating the relationship in an internalized form. **1964** M. ARGYLE *Psychol. & Social Probl.* iv. 54 There is considerable evidence that the stronger the forces which are restraining aggression—whether external fear of punishment or internalized anxiety about aggression—then the more remote the displaced aggression will be. **1965** N. CHOMSKY *Aspects of Theory of Syntax* 21 Few hearers may be aware..that their internalized grammar..provides at least three structural descriptions for this sentence. **1965** H. A. GLEASON *Ling. & Eng. Gram.* 476 This means strengthened competence in the student's internalized grammar of literary English. **1968** CHOMSKY & HALLE *Sound Pattern Eng.* 3 New utterances..are formed and interpreted by the same grammar, the same internalized system of rules. **1971** *Sci. Amer.* Sept. 194/2 The company may merely pay the internalized costs (whether they are in

the form of a judgment for damages, a tax or a negotiated payment), absorbing the payment or passing it on to customers.

internally (ɪn'tɜːnəlɪ), *adv.* [f. INTERNAL *a.* + -LY^2.] In an internal manner; inwardly.

1. In, on, or with respect to, the inside or interior (of a country, a house, etc., or esp. of the body).

1597 A. M. tr. *Guillemeau's Fr. Chirurg.* 14/1 A wounde, cleansed, as well externallye as internallye. **1660** R. COKE *Power & Subj.* 71 By which [military discipline] nations are protected from foreign enemies..religion, justice, peace, learning &c. are internally preserved. **1758** WRIGHT in *Phil. Trans.* L. 598 Salt of steel, taken internally. **1831** R. KNOX *Cloquet's Anat.* 267 This muscle..is situated internally of the preceding and above it. **1866** J. G. MURPHY *Comm. Exod.* xxvi. 1 The mansion..consists internally of a pavilion or set of ten curtains.

2. With respect to the inner nature or relations of anything, esp. the internal affairs of a country, a state, etc.

1791 BURKE *Th. French Aff.* Wks. VII. 54 There never was seen so strong a government internally as that of the French municipalities. **1826** DIGBY *Broadst. Hon.* (1829) I. I. 251 Foreign enemies..to be prevented from preying upon each internally agitated state. **1864** BOWEN *Logic* iv. 93 A Concept is internally Distinct when we can fully enumerate and clearly distinguish from each other all its original and essential Marks. **1867** FREEMAN *Norm. Conq.* I. iii. 105 Such communities..were..internally self-governed from the beginning.

3. In, or with respect to, the mind or soul; mentally or spiritually.

1646 SIR T. BROWNE *Pseud. Ep.* VII. iv. 345 That which is internally presented unto the understanding. **1665** MALL *Offer F. Help* 95 Satan works externally..but lust internally. **1766** GOLDSM. *Vic. W.* xxiv, Would you have me applaud to the world what my heart must internally condemn? **1872** O. W. HOLMES *Poet Breakf.-t.* vi. (1885) 136, I smiled internally.

internarial (ɪntə'nɛərɪəl), *a. Anat.* [f. INTER- 4 a + L. *nāri-s* nostril + -AL^1.] Situated between the nostrils.

1866 OWEN in *Reader* No. 163. 152/2 This internarial tubercle.

internasal (ɪntə'neɪzəl), *a. Anat.* [f. INTER- 4 a + L. *nās-us* nose: see NASAL.] Situated between the divisions of the nose, or the nostrils: = prec.; more properly INTRANASAL.

1866 OWEN in *Reader* No. 163. 152/2 Upon the internasal tubercle. **1878** BELL *Gegenbaur's Comp. Anat.* 546 The internasal septum..separates the nasal cavity into two portions.

internation (ɪntə'neɪʃən). *U.S.* [n. of action from INTERN *v.*] The action of 'interning': see INTERN *v.* 3.

1885 *U.S. Cons. Rep.* No. 53½. 282 (Cent.) Importations and internations which are made from the 1st of April..through the frontier custom-house of Paso del Norte.

international (ɪntə'næʃənəl), *a.* (*sb.*) [INTER- 4.]

A. *adj.* **1. a.** Existing, constituted, or carried on between different nations; pertaining to the relations between nations.

1780 BENTHAM *Princ. Legisl.* xvii. §25 The law may be referred to the head..of *international* jurisprudence. *Note.* The word *international*, it must be acknowledged, is a new one; though, it is hoped, sufficiently analogous and intelligible. It is calculated to express, in a more significant way, the branch of law which goes commonly under the name of the *law of nations*. **1801** W. TAYLOR in *Monthly Mag.* XI. 646 A Comprehensive System of Civic Morality and International Obligation. **1814** SCOTT *Wav.* vi, Without being aware that the payment was an international concern. **1838–9** HALLAM *Hist. Lit.* II. II. iv. §86. 173 The great science of international law, the determining authority in questions of right between independent states. **1861** GOSCHEN *For. Exch.* 11 The first element which we have to consider in discussing the Foreign Exchanges is to be found ....in international indebtedness. **1861** *Engineer* XI. 94/3 The Commissioners for the International Exhibition of 1862 propose to invite..tenders for the erection of the buildings. **1872** *Daily News* 3 Oct. 2 What was international law? It was once very happily defined in the *Times* as the limit of the conscience of the strongest. **1888** *Pall Mall G.* 22 June 6/2 An International yacht race was decided yesterday at Amsterdam in the North Sea. **1948** *Written Statement U.K.* 11 Dec. in *I.C.J. Pleadings* I. v. 25 Does the United Nations possess international personality? **1959** R. A. GRAHAM *Vatican Diplomacy* vii. 185 After 1870... Could the papacy..be properly regarded as a member of the international community of the law of nations? This was tantamount to asking whether the papacy had 'international personality'. **1963** T. TULLETT *Inside Interpol* ii. 22 What is, in actual fact, an 'international criminal'? The definition of this type of wrongdoer is not based on any legal concept.. but simply on practical convenience. **1970** D. W. GREIG *Internat. Law* iii. 73 The brief statement that an international person is an entity having the power of independent action on the international plane has the obvious advantage of including not only states, but also communities like 'protected states'. **1971** *Mod. Law Rev.* XXXIV. VI. 599 A country may be sovereign in the sense that it satisfies the international law criteria for independent statehood and is recognized as independent by the international community. *Ibid.* 613 The sovereignty of the United Kingdom as an international person has been abridged..a..formidable camel for a court to swallow. **1974** *Times* 15 Feb. 14/1 Renegotiation of our membership of the European Community..will add yet another uncertainty to international relations.

b. (with capital *I.*) Belonging to the International Working Men's Association: see B. b.

1880 WOOLSEY *Communism & Socialism* 133 The essence of the International movement was a federal association, a combination of movements in part already begun, with the social end in view of raising the operatives up over against the employers and capitalists. **1881** T. KIRKUP in *Encycl. Brit.* XIII. 189/1 The International Working Men's Association, commonly called the 'International', was formed at London in 1864. **1887** *Ibid.* XXII. 215/1 In 1869 they founded the 'social democratic working men's party', and..sent representatives to the International congress at Basel.

c. Applied to various units of physical quantities (now mostly obsolete) agreed upon by different nations, and in some cases forming part of the formal name of a unit, so as to distinguish it from a unit numerically similar but differently defined; ***international system* (*of units*)** (usu. with capital initials) [tr. F. *système international d'unités*], a system of physical units (together with a set of prefixes indicating multiplication or division by a power of ten) based on the metre, kilogramme, second, ampere, kelvin, candela, and mole as independent basic units, with each of the derived units defined in terms of these without any multiplying factor.

Quot. 1932 represents an isolated and fortuitous use of *international system of units*, unrelated to the later Système International.

1893 *Electrician* 29 Sept. 578/2 To distinguish these units as now defined from the definitions given by previous meetings or Congresses, they are denominated the 'international' ohm, the 'international' ampere, &c. **1908** *Nature* 29 Oct. 678/2 The international ohm is the resistance offered to an unvarying electric current by a column of mercury at the temperature of melting ice, 14·4521 grams in mass, of a constant cross-sectional area, and of a length of 106·300 centimetres. *Ibid.* 679/1 The difference between the ohm and the international ohm remains a matter for experiment. **1909** *Engineering* 17 Sept. 397/2 The British Committee..now have the honour to submit..that the name 'International Candle' be adopted. **1924** A. W. SMITH *Electr. Measurements* (ed. 2) i. 3 In practical measurements the electron current is measured in international amperes. **1932** *Phil. Mag.* XIV. 292 The international system of [electrical] units differs but little from the practical system, and the two may be taken as identical for the present purpose. **1934** *Brit. Inst. Radiol. Year Bk.* 39 The International Unit of X-radiation shall be called the 'Röntgen'. **1937** *Discovery* Sept. 285/2 Last month, the first international conference on acoustics met in Paris... Thanks in particular to the conciliatory attitude of the delegates of Germany and the United States the 'phon' and the 'decibel' become international units. **1938** G. P. HARNWELL *Princ. Electr. & Electromagn.* 602 It is evident that 1 international volt is equal to 1·00043 absolute volts, 1 international joule is equal to 1·00034 absolute or mechanical joules, etc. [**1957** *Proc.-Verb. du Comité Internat. Poids et Mesures*, *1956* 81 Après discussion, la Commission adopte la dénomination de 'Système International d'Unités'.] **1957** *Nature* 21 Dec. 1388/1, 1 A. becomes, by definition, equal to 10^{-10} m. exactly. It may be recalled that the value λ_R = 6438·4696 A. was adopted as the spectroscopic reference standard in 1907 and thereby became the means of defining the international angstrom ——the unit that has since served for all spectroscopic measurements of wave-length. **1961** *Ibid.* 21 Jan. 196/2 Among other scientific resolutions adopted by the Conference [*sc.* the eleventh General Conference of Weights and Measures] are the following... Approval of a detailed list of the international system of units (designation *SI*) founded on six basic units (metre, kilogram, second, ampere, degree Kelvin and candela). **1967** A. J. LISSAMAN *Metrology* i. 5 The U.K., U.S.A., Canada, Australia, New Zealand and South Africa have agreed to adopt an international yard based upon the metre. **1971** P. VIGOUREUX *Units & Standards for Electromagn.* ii. 11 The hour, the day and the year, so long established and in such common use, will undoubtedly outlive the International System.

2. Special collocations: **international baccalaureate**: see BACCALAUREATE 1 b; **International Brigade**, a body of volunteers, raised internationally by foreign Communist parties, although open to non-Communists, with the purpose of fighting for the Republic in the Spanish Civil War of 1936–39; also *transf.*; hence **International Brigader**; **international code**, a code of signals by which seamen of all nations can hold communication at sea; **international copyright**, the protection of literary and artistic property by international agreement, particularly the Berne Convention of 1885, which led to the foundation of the International Copyright Union, and the Universal Copyright Convention of 1952; **International Court of Justice**, a judicial court of the United Nations which replaced the Cour Permanente de Justice in 1945; **international date-line**, the date-line (see DATE *sb.*^{2} 8) in the Pacific Ocean; **international driving licence, permit**, a licence allowing the holder to drive a specified class of vehicle in foreign countries; **international Gothic**, name given to a style of Gothic art which spread across western Europe in the late 14th and early 15th centuries; also called *international style*; **International Monetary Fund**, an organization having a monetary pool on which member nations can draw, established in 1945 to promote international trade and stabilization of currencies; **international orange**, a bright orange colour, visible from a great distance; **International Phonetic Alphabet**, a set of phonetic symbols for international use, introduced in the late 19th century by the International Phonetic Association: constructed on the basis of the Roman and Greek alphabets with the addition of some special symbols and diacritical marks; **international style**, name given to a naturalistic style of twentieth-century architecture associated esp. with Walter Gropius (1883–1969) and his associates; also (*rare*) = *international Gothic*; **international unit**, (*a*) *Physics* (see sense A. c above); (*b*) *Biol.* and *Med.*, a unit of activity or potency of sera, hormones, vitamins, etc., defined individually for each substance in terms of the activity of a standard quantity or preparation.

1937 'G. ORWELL' *Let.* 9 May in *Coll. Ess.* (1968) I. 267 Owing partly to an accident I joined the POUM militia instead of the International Brigade, which..meant that I have never seen the Madrid front. **1968** K. MARTIN *Editor* x. 214 The International Brigade..came from every part of Europe and America. **1968** *N.Y. Rev. Books* 11 Apr. 42/3 Genuine American patriots must..work for the downfall of American imperialism even if this means joining international brigades should the Vietnamese request them. **1972** *N.Y. Times* 3 Nov. 2/2 Well-known as a writer, Mr. Popovic studied philosophy in Paris before World War II and later fought in the International Brigades during the Spanish Civil War. **1949** KOESTLER *Promise & Fulfilment* vi. 57 This same argument..has served the Soviet Government as a constant pretext for refusing to admit.. International Brigaders..into Soviet territory. **1885** H. PAASCH *From Keel to Truck* 161/1 *Signal*,..international code of signals. **1961** F. H. BURGESS *Dict. Sailing* 121 *International code of signals*, the system of signals adopted for use between ships and shore stations of all nations, with simplicity of use in coding and decoding in any language. **1838** *Act 1 & 2 Vict.* c. 59 An act for securing to Authors, in certain Cases, the Benefit of International Copyright. **1844** *Act 7 & 8 Vict.* c. 12. §1 Which Act [*sc.* 1 & 2 Vict. c. 59] is herein-after, for the sake of Perspicuity, designated as 'the International Copyright Act'. **1894** in H. Paasch *From Keel to Truck* (ed. 2) (title-page), Protected by International Copyright. **1901** *Empire Rev.* May 364 A book is subject to national copyright..and also to international copyright in the several countries admitting that right. **1942** *Times Lit. Suppl.* 14 Nov. 559/3 The last International Copyright Convention, signed at Berne in 1908, afforded a very considerable degree of protection to the literary and artistic property belonging to the nationals of those countries which signed it. **1971** E. P. SKONE JAMES *Copinger & Skone James on Copyright* (ed. 11) xxiv. 435 International copyright is concerned with treaties or conventions between nations requiring their signatories to respect, in their own countries, the copyright of nationals of other signatories. **1945** *Times* 10 Sept. 2/5 The nomination of candidates to the posts of Judge of the International Court of Justice. **1972** *Mod. Law Rev.* XXXV. I. 52 In the North Sea Continental Shelf Cases the International Court of Justice had the opportunity of considering this phenomenon. **1973** *Times* 15 May 6/4 Mr van der Stoel is in favour of increasing the powers of the International Court of Justice at The Hague so that countries which accept its jurisdiction in principle cannot, as Iceland has done recently and France now threatens to do, disregard the court's competence to judge a case which may turn out wrongly for them. **1910** *Encycl. Brit.* II. 134/1 The so-called 'International Date Line'..is..practically only due to American initiative. **1957** VON ENGELN & NETSCHERT *Gen. Geogr.* iv. 71/2 The international date line does not coincide with 180° meridian.. but zigzags to give portions of the same political territories the same date. **1966** MRS. L. B. JOHNSON *White House Diary* 2 Nov. (1970) 453 Sometime in the dark hours over the Pacific we had crossed the International Dateline. **1931** *Automobile Assoc. Foreign Touring Guide* 19 The International Driving Permit acts as a driving licence in all the countries recognising the International Certificate for Motor Vehicles. **1966** R. E. PICKERING *Himself Again* x. 67 Do you have an international driving licence? **1966** A. A. RANDALL *Flashpoint* ii. 41 The two men book a passage on the Car Sleeper Express from Boulogne to Narbonne... You bring the Car Temporary Exportation Certificate, International Driving Permits and Insurance Green Card. **1951** M. DAVIES *Nat. Gallery Catal. Earlier Italian Schools* 280 They [*sc.* works by Master of the Bambino Vispo] are somewhat related to Lorenzo Monaco in style, and are even more markedly in the 'International Gothic' current. **1959** P. & L. MURRAY *Dict. Art & Artists* 199 Masolino may have worked under Ghiberti on the First Baptistry Doors..and this would explain his normal International Gothic style. **1961** H. E. SCOTT tr. *Chiarelli's European Painting 15th Cent.* 10 In international Gothic painting there is a contrast between a growing interest in naturalism..and..a transference of natural forms into abstract figures which are frankly decorative and heraldic. **1970** *Oxf. Compan. Art* 584/1 International Gothic..first distinguished by Louis Courajod in 1892. *Ibid.* 584/2 International Gothic was nurtured in the cosmopolitan courts of France and Burgundy from the soil of the French aristocratic court style. **1944** H. MORGENTHAU in *U.N. Monetary & Financial Conference* p. iii, The International Monetary Fund agreed upon at Bretton Woods will help remedy this situation [*sc.* economic tactics which contribute to world-wide depression and war]. **1955** *Times* 4 July 13/4 The International Monetary Fund has agreed to a change in the par value of the Nicaraguan cordoba from five to seven a United States dollar. **1957** *Economist* 21 Dec. 1075/2 The British Government this week decided to extend for 12 months its $738,530,000 standby credit with the International Monetary Fund. **1936** *Proc. IRE* XXIV. 28

Skeleton towers should be painted throughout their height with.. alternate bands of chrome yellow or international orange. **1958** *Colour Index* (Soc. Dyers & Colourists) (ed. 2) IV. 4323 International Orange 2221... C.I. Pigment Orange 21. **1967** 'G. CARR' *Lewker in Tirol* vi. 85 The cagoule is in the colour we call 'international orange'... It is the colour that can best be seen from a distance, so that climbers in difficulties can quickly be found and rescued. **1969** *New Yorker* 12 Apr. 110/3 The dial is coated with a luminous orange paint called International Orange, a psychedelic color that is glaringly visible against the milky-white experiment. **1898** *Mod. Q. Lang. & Lit.* I. I. 69/2 It is of the utmost importance that, for the more advanced students of languages, we should adopt an international phonetic alphabet. **1912** *Princ. Internat. Phonetic Assoc.* 1 In 1888, after consulting the opinion of its members, the Association drew up an *International Phonetic Alphabet*, by means of which the pronunciation of any language may be accurately represented. **1962** A. C. GIMSON *Introd. Pronunc. Eng.* iv. 35 The International Phonetic Alphabet.. provides symbols to denote the sound types occurring in languages. **1964** J. DOWNING *Initial Teaching Alphabet* p. ix, Some educational reformers.. favour an alternative type of 'rational orthography' or 'systematized notation' such as the International Phonetic Alphabet. **1932** HITCHCOCK & JOHNSON *Internat. Style* i. 20 There is, first, a new conception of architecture as volume rather than mass. Secondly, regularity rather than axial symmetry serves as the chief means of ordering design. These two principles, with a third proscribing arbitrary applied decoration, mark the productions of the international style. **1937** *Archit. Rev.* LXXXI. 133/2 This natural phenomenon, specifically variegated in each of these regions, constitutes a severe impediment in considering the rational mode of design as quickly resulting in a so-called 'International Style'. **1937** *Time* 8 Feb. 32/1 Walter Gropius, one of the founders of the concrete-pipe-and-plate-glass school of architectural modernism known as the 'International Style'. **1950** E. H. GOMBRICH *Story of Art* xiii. 178 Until round about 1400, art in different parts of Europe had developed on similar lines. .. The style of the Gothic painters and sculptors of that period is known as the International Style. **1922** *Internat. Conf. Standardisation of Sera & Serological Tests 1921* (League of Nations) 6 The Sub-Committee for investigating methods for testing the potency of anti-diphtheritic and anti-tetanic sera considers it both possible and desirable to fix for both these sera an antitoxin unit which could be generally accepted and acknowledged as an International Unit. **1944** L. E. H. WHITBY *Med. Bacteriol.* (ed. 4) xxv. 234 Staphylococcus: an 'international unit' is the specific antitoxic activity contained in 0·5 mg. of dry standard serum preserved at the National Institute of Medical Research, London. **1961** *Brit. Med. Dict.* 1500/2 *International unit of male hormone*, the specific activity contained in 0·1 milligram of pure androsterone... *International unit of vitamin C*, the antiscorbutic activity contained in 0·05 mg. of pure ascorbic acid. **1970** *Daily Tel.* 12 Oct. 3/2 The Medical Research Council now requires that all influenza vaccines should contain 600 of the new international units of virus to each human dose.

B. *sb.* **a.** A person belonging to two different nations (*e.g.* native of one and resident in another). Also, one who takes part in an international contest; the contest itself.

1870 *Pall Mall G.* 8 Dec. 12 The bitterness against the neutrals is fearful, and will make the social position of all internationals very painful. **1890** *North British Daily Mail* 7 Apr. 6/6 Their goal was again and again besieged in a way never before seen at the close of an international. **1895** *Westm. Gaz.* 7 Feb. 7/2 He has already taken part in eight international matches. This does not, of course, compare with the record of several other internationals. **1905** A. CONAN DOYLE *Return of Sherlock Holmes* 330 The defeat of the Light Blues may be entirely attributed to the unfortunate absence of the crack International, Godfrey Staunton, whose want was felt at every instant of the game. **1942** *R.A.F. Jrnl.* 30 May 33 It was like.. Wembley or Hampden Park after an international. **1959** *Times* 21 Sept. 3/6 The British Lions were given but a faint hope of defeating the world champion All Blacks in the fourth and final international of their tour at Eden Park yesterday. **1971** *Leader* (Durban) 7 May 1/2 Efforts were being made for the Mauritian team to play a series of games including 'internationals' against South African Indian, Coloured and African elevens. **1973** *Times* 7 Feb. 15/4 It is no wonder, she feels, that so many former internationals never stay on in the sport.

b. (with capital *I*; also **Internationale**) = International Working Men's Association; *spec.* **First International**, founded in London by Karl Marx in 1864 for promoting the joint political action of working classes in all countries, and dissolved in Philadelphia in 1876; **Second International**, an organization founded in Paris in 1889 to celebrate the 100th anniversary of the French Revolution; **Third International**, founded at Moscow in 1919 by delegates from twelve countries to promote communism and support the Russian Revolution, and dissolved in 1943; also called **Communist International** (abbrev. COMINTERN); **Fourth International**, founded in 1936 by followers of Trotsky. Also, a member or adherent of any of these; cf. A. 1 b.

1871 *Observer* 9 Apr. 6/4 Most of the decrees are the work of illiterate members of the *Internationale*; they consist of candid attacks on the rights of property,.. such as you may expect from vulgar Socialists. **1871** G. M. HOPKINS *Let.* 2 Aug. (1935) 27, I feel inclined to begin by asking whether you are secretary to the International... I am always thinking about the Communist future. **1872** MRS. LYNN LINTON *Joshua Davidson* 153 In the International and in other political societies which abound among the working men. **1887** T. KIRKUP in *Encycl. Brit.* XXII. 214/1 Of the International Marx was the inspiring and controlling head from the beginning. **1919** Communist International [see COMMUNIST 1 b]. **1919** G. B. SHAW *Matter with Ireland* (1962) 193 The number of branches of The International formed in France in the 1860s by the police agents of Napoleon III must have filled the Castle with envy. **1920** B. RUSSELL *Pract. & Theory Bolshevism* 6, I do not believe that the methods of the Third International can lead to the desired goal. **1935** C. ISHERWOOD *Mr. Norris changes Trains* vi. 89 My association with.. the representatives of the Third International.. have even excited favourable comment in certain quarters in Moscow. **1937** E. SNOW *Red Star over China* iv. 154 In 1920, M. Martin, an energetic and persuasive representative of the Third International.. came to Shanghai. **1950** THEIMER & CAMPBELL *Encycl. World Politics* 430/1 Trotsky's adherents in a number of countries, recruited from discontented left-wing communists, tried to found a Fourth International. *Ibid.* 430/2 The Fourth International, a shadowy organization which held conferences in Paris in 1936 and 1948. **1951** W. PICKLES in *Political Q.* XXII. 335 June 30th, 1951.. was the fourth occasion in less than 100 years on which a Socialist International has been founded.. and the longest-lived of these ancestors, the Second International of 1889, survived for only 25 years. **1959** *Chambers's Encycl.* VII. 684/1 The first International spread rapidly, sections being founded in France, Belgium, Germany, Switzerland, Italy, Spain and other countries. **1967** N. McINNES in R. P. Arnot et al. *Impact Russ. Revolution* 85 The Communist International having been disbanded by Stalin in 1943, the only socialist international in existence was the Fourth, demonstrating again that Trotskyism was the last refuge of several of socialism's discarded illusions. **1968** K. MARTIN *Editor* xi. 234 'I tell you,' he [*sc.* Trotsky in 1937] said, 'that in three to five years from now the Fourth International will be a great force in the world.' **1969** *Listener* 27 Mar. 429/1 If the ILP had joined the Communist International, as its French and German equivalents did, and as the Scottish divisional council wanted it to, a powerful Communist Party might have come into existence on British soil. **1972** *Guardian* 10 Mar. 3/2 The Fourth International (FI) arose after the disintegration under Stalin of the Third International.

c. *pl.* International bonds.

1909 *Westm. Gaz.* 17 Sept. 12/2 Internationals featureless.

d. ***The International*** = next.

1912 *Songs for Socialists* (Fabian Soc.) 2 The International. **1928** A. HUXLEY *Point Counter Point* xxiii. 413 Organized singing of the International.

Internationale (-næʃ(ɪ)əˈnɑːl, ‖ɛ̃tɛrnasjɔnal). [Fr. (sc. *chanson* song).] A revolutionary hymn composed by Eugène Pottier in 1871 and adopted by French socialists and subsequently by others. Also *fig.*

[**1912** H. M. HYNDMAN *Further Reminisc.* 124 We all left Paris regretfully, with the strains of 'L'Internationale' ringing in our ears.] **1920** S. LEWIS *Main St.* i. 9 A Russian Jewess who sang the Internationale. **1933** *Morning Post* 30 Mar. 11/3 Communists.. waved red flags and sang the 'Internationale'. **1938** I. GOLDBERG *Wonder of Words* p. vii, This *internationale* of poverty in a West-End slum. **1949** I. DEUTSCHER *Stalin* xii. 491 The Internationale, the hymn of the Labour movement of the world. **1974** *Times* 7 Mar. 16/8 Cardew had intended to end the programme with the *Internationale*.

interˈnationalism. [f. INTERNATIONAL *a.* (*sb.*) + -ISM.]

International character or spirit; the principle of community of interests or action between different nations; *spec.* (with capital *I*) the doctrine or principles of the International Working Men's Association.

1851 M. TUPPER in D. Hudson *Martin Tupper* (1949) x. 121 [President Fillmore.. received me] very kindly and cordially, and avowing himself a great lover of my works and my Internationalism. **1877** M. M. GRANT *Sun-Maid* xi, Its internationalism was the feature that struck you first. **1886** *Pall Mall G.* 26 Aug. 3/2 If this should be the sole fruit of this year's conference the interests of internationalism in labour will have been very considerably advanced. **1888** SIR C. MONCRIEFF *ibid.* 11 Sept. 4/1 On a par with most of the others which internationalism has devised for the welfare of Egypt. **1895** *Thinker* VIII. 536 Internationalism is the only virtue that comports with peace. **1898** *Daily News* 27 July 6/2 The preacher of the Four Commandments (non-Resistance, Chastity, Labour, Universal Brotherhood, otherwise Internationalism). **1955** *Times* 17 May 10/7 Internationalism seems to have become by now an accepted thing even in trades far less easily internationalized than ours. **1971** *World Archaeol.* III. 226 In Childe's view, it was .. the Iron Curtain which abruptly severed this age-old tradition of internationalism. **1973** *Times* 16 Apr. 4/6 No city has done more than Coventry since the war to further the cause of internationalism.

interˈnationalist. [f. as prec. + -IST.] **a.** An advocate of or believer in internationalism; *spec.* a member of or sympathizer with the International Working Men's Association. **b.** One versed in international law.

1864 WEBSTER, *Internationalist*, one who advocates the principles of international law. **1876** FAWCETT *Pol. Econ.* (ed. 5) II. xi. 285 The idea most prevalent amongst Internationalists, and other modern Socialists, is the immediate purchase of the land by the state. *a* **1882** *N. Brit. Rev.* (O.), In the days of Elizabeth, the publicists of England, both as constitutionalists and internationalists, in so far as international law was then understood, had nothing to fear from a comparison with their continental rivals. **1916** A. HUXLEY *Let.* 19 Mar. (1969) 94, I get extraordinarily irritated with some of these Internationalists, who conscientiously object. **1955** H. HODGKINSON *Doubletalk* 60 In practice it is enough to discover what the USSR considers her own interests to be to show to the 'proletarian internationalist' his own. **1965** M. BRADBURY *Stepping Westward* i. 47 They were avaricious internationalists, evidently, their legs turned nutmeg by a sun that had come to find them daily in different places. **1973** *Listener* 17 May 636/1 A little-known Maoist organisation known as the Internationalists, founded in Vancouver in March 1963.

c. *attrib.* or as *adj.*

1941 J. S. HUXLEY *Uniqueness of Man* xiv. 288 The nationalistic element in socialized religion will be subordinated or adjusted to the internationalist. **1955** KOESTLER *Trail of Dinosaur* 190 Socialism has lost its claim to represent the internationalist trend of humanity.

Hence **internationaˈlistic** *a.*

1930 A. FLEXNER *Universities* i. 13 This present-day world, compounded of tradition, good and bad, racial mixtures, nationalistic and internationalistic strivings. **1973** M. TRUMAN *Harry S. Truman* x. 204 Arthur Vandenberg, leader of the internationalistic Republicans, fulminated against what was happening in Poland.

internatioˈnality. [f. as prec. + -ITY.] International quality, condition, or character.

1864 *Daily Tel.* 7 June, Of course, a French race-course is not like an English one. Internationality is not yet so perfect. **1881** T. HARDY *Laodicean* III. VI. v. 262 From a representative of the new aristocracy of internationality to a representative of the old aristocracy of exclusiveness. **1881** J. PAGET *Addr. Intern. Med. Congr.* in *Nature* No. 614. 308 Let our internationality be a clear abiding sentiment, to be, as now, declared and celebrated at appointed times, but never to be forgotten.

interˈnationalize, *v.* [f. as prec. + -IZE.] *trans.* To render international in character or use; *spec.* in *mod. Politics*, to bring (a country, territory, etc.) under the combined government or protection of two or more different nations.

1864 WEBSTER, *Internationalize*, to make international; to cause to affect or pertain to the mutual relations of two or more nations; as, to internationalize a war. **1883** *Contemp. Rev.* June 769 An earnest appeal to the Government at Berlin to unite with England in internationalizing the Congo. **1884** *19th Cent.* Oct. 627 Comte, Mill, and Herbert Spencer have internationalised the word [Sociology]. **1885** *Spectator* 30 May 693/2 The Suez Canal must be internationalised and confided to the Khedive. **1897** STEAD in *Contemp. Rev.* Sept. 431 An internationalising of the peoples.. based not on competition but on co-operation.

Hence **interˌnationaliˈzation**, the action of internationalizing.

1871 *Contemp. Rev.* Dec. 95 Internationalisation is even now a great, though as yet but insufficiently recognised actuality. **1882** E. DICEY in *19th Cent.* Aug. 173 The internationalisation, if I may use the word, of Egypt. **1884** *Times* (weekly ed.) 31 Oct. 19/2 Questions affecting the internationalization of the Congo, the Niger, and other fields of commerce.

interˈnationally, *adv.* [f. as prec. + -LY².] In an international manner; between or among different nations; with reference to the mutual relations of two or more nations.

1864 ADM. FITZROY in *Leis. Hour* 32/2 Internationally there is now.. regular meteorologic correspondence. **1883** SIR C. DILKE *Sp. Ho. Comm.* 11 May, They had no case internationally against the Government of Spain. **1891** *Law Times* XCI. 225/1 A contract by a foreigner with a rebel State which has not been internationally recognised.

interne, variant of INTERN *a.*

inter-nebular: see INTER- *pref.* 4 a.

†**internecate,** *v. Obs. rare*⁻⁰. [f. ppl. stem of L. *internecāre* to kill off, destroy.] (See quot.) So †**interneˈcation.**

1623 COCKERAM, *Internecate*, to kill all. *Internecation*, a slaughter where none escape.

interneciary (ɪntəˈniːʃɪərɪ), *a. rare.* [f. L. *interneci-um* (see below) + -ARY.]

= INTERNECINE.

1846 WORCESTER cites MACKINTOSH.

internecinal (ɪntəˈnɛsɪnəl), *a. rare.* [f. L. *internecīn-us* INTERNECINE + -AL¹.] Destructive, deadly; = INTERNECINE 1. ***internecinal war***, war to the death.

1846 WORCESTER cites *Qu. Rev.* **1862** MERIVALE *Rom. Emp.* (1865) VII. lx. 260 The Jews could not have maintained their internecinal war against Rome, had not their social system been very different. **1875** —— *Gen. Hist. Rome* lxx. (1877) 575 He proclaimed internecinal war against the Christian Society.

internecine (ɪntəˈniːsɪn, -saɪn), *a.* [ad. L. *internecīn-us* murderous, destructive, f. *internecium* slaughter, destruction, f. *internecāre*: see next.

App. first used as a rendering of L. *internecīnum bellum*, in Butler's Hudibras (to which also is due the unetymological pronunciation, instead of *inˈternĕcine*). On this authority entered by Johnson in his Dictionary, with an incorrect explanation, due to association with words like *interchange*, *intercommunion*, etc. in which *inter-* has the force of 'mutual', 'each other'. From J. the word has come into later dictionaries and 19th c. use, generally in the Johnsonian sense.]

1. *orig.* Deadly, destructive, characterized by great slaughter. ***internecine war***, war for the sake of slaughter, war of extermination, war to the death.

1663 BUTLER *Hud.* I. i. 774 Th' Ægyptians worshipp'd Dogs, and for Their Faith made internecine [*ed.* 1674 fierce and zealous] war. **1843** GLADSTONE *Glean.* V. i. 60 Rome has written on her banners.. the alternatives only of internecine war or absolute surrender. **1853** KINGSLEY *Hypatia* Pref. 9 Contending against that Gospel in which it had recognised

. . its internecine foe. **1878** Bosw. Smith *Carthage* 170 The war was henceforward, in the literal sense of the word, internecine.

2. *esp.* (In modern use.) Mutually destructive, aiming at the slaughter or destruction of each other.

1755 Johnson, *Internecine*, endeavouring mutual destruction. **1837** Carlyle *Fr. Rev.* I. iii. iv, The real death-grapple of war and internecine duel, Greek meeting Greek. **1859** Tennent *Ceylon* II. 24 An internecine war now raged for years in Ceylon. **1868** Kingsley *Christm. Day* 62 Living things Compete in internecine greed. **1875** Bennett & Dyer *Sachs' Bot.* 833 'The internecine war', he [Nägeli] says, 'is obviously most severe between the species and races that are most nearly related'. **1882** Farrar *Early Chr.* I. 556 Eight thousand Zealots, who stabbed each other in internecine massacre.

internecion (ɪntəˈniːʃən). *rare.* [ad. L. *internecĭōn-em* massacre, slaughter, f. *internecāre* to kill, destroy, f. *inter* (as in *interīre* to perish, *interficĕre* to destroy) + *necāre* to kill.]

Destruction, slaughter, massacre.

1610 Bp. Carleton *Jurisd.* 240 Hauing had their whole army brought vnto Internecion at Abdua. **1658** Phillips, *Internecion*, a making a universal slaughter, or utter destroying. *a* **1677** Hale *Prim. Orig. Man.* ii. ix. 215 By the Spaniards in the West Indies, the numbers of Internecions and Slaughters would exceed all Arithmetical Calculation.

b. *improp.* Mutually deadly conflict.

1893 *Westm. Gaz.* 19 June 2/1 Unless biassed by such paltry prejudice as that of religious or racial internecion.

internecive (ɪntəˈniːsɪv), *a. rare.* [ad. L. *internecīvus*, a (scribal) var. of *internecīnus* INTERNECINE.] = INTERNECINE 2.

1819 Syd. Smith *Wks.* (1859) I. 255/2 An internecive war between the gamekeepers and marauders of game. **1847** Grote *Greece* II. xxxi. IV. 210 The precise index of that growing internecive hostility. **1853** G. S. Faber *Reviv. Fr. Emp.* 51 The latter scenes of this internecive war.

†**interˈnect,** *v. Obs.* [ad. L. *internect-ĕre* to bind to each other, f. *inter* between + *nectĕre* to tie, knot.] *trans.* To interconnect. (In quot. humorously pedantic.) So †**interˈnexion, -ˈnection** *Obs.*, mutual connexion; interconnexion.

1654 W. Mountague *Devout Ess.* II. iv. § 1. 54 He coupled his own goodness and mans evils, by so admirable an internection that ev'n the worst parts of the chain drew some good after them. **1708** Motteux *Rabelais* v. xxiii, Your frequently experimented Industry internected with perdiligent Sedulity, and sedulous Perdiligence.

internee (ɪntɜːˈniː). [f. INTERN *v.* 2 + -EE¹.] One who is interned; an interned person.

1918 *Rep. Detenus & Internees Bengal* 2 in *Parl. Papers* (Cd. 9198) VIII. 106 The cases of the State prisoners and internees. **1920** *Observer* 5 Dec. 13/4 Lorries with military guards . . removed the internees to the camp. **1941** Wodehouse *Let.* 13 Aug. in *Performing Flea* (1953) 179 We are elderly internees, most of us with corns and swollen joints. **1972** *Daily Tel.* 4 Mar. 32/6 A policy to end imprisonment without trial by a phased programme of releases of every detainee and internee.

internet: see INTER- *pref.* 1 b.

interneural (ɪntəˈnjʊərəl), *a.* (*sb.*) *Anat.* and *Zool.* [f. INTER- 4 a + Gr. νεῦρον nerve: see NEURAL.] 'Situated between nerves, or between neural spines or arches' (*Syd. Soc. Lex.*); applied *spec.* to the dermal spines or bones supporting the dorsal fin-rays in fishes (cf. INTERSPINAL). **b.** as *sb.* (*pl.*) = Interneural spines.

1846 [see INTERHÆMAL]. **1854** Owen *Skel. & Teeth* in *Circ. Sc., Organ. Nat.* I. 182 The rest of the fins are single and median in position, and are due to folds of the skin, in which certain dermal bones are developed for their support . . those along the upper surface of the fish are called 'interneural spines' . . those on the under surface are the 'interhæmal spines'. **1880** Günther *Fishes* 53 A series of flat spines called interneurals, to which the spines and rays of the dorsal fins are articulated, are supported by the neural spines.

interneuron (ɪntəˈnjʊərɒn). *Physiol.* Also interneurone. [f. INTER(NUNCIAL *a.* + NEURON.]

Any of the neurons which transmit nerve impulses from receptor neurons to effector neurons; an internuncial neuron.

1939 R. Lorente de Nó in *Jrnl. Neurophysiol.* II. 402 Following the example of Prof. Gerard the simple term 'interneuron' will henceforth be used instead of the rather cumbersome designation 'internuncial neuron'. **1963** S. Ochs in E. E. Selkurt *Physiol.* v. 104 (*caption*) Sensory fibers terminate upon interneurons within the spinal cord which, by multiple branches, engage a large number of motoneurons. **1971** *Jrnl. Exper. Biol.* LV. 727 The DCMD (descending contralateral movement detector) neurone is a monocular visual interneurone . . which sends a large axon down the contralateral connective to the thoracic ganglia. **1971** Villee & Dethier *Biol. Princ. & Proc.* xx. 619 Interneurons are those that connect two or more neurons. They usually lie wholly within the central nervous system.

interneuronal (ɪntənjʊəˈrəʊnəl), *a. Physiol.* [Partly f. prec. + -AL, partly f. INTER- 4 a + NEURONAL *a.*] **a.** Of, pertaining to, or affecting an interneuron. **b.** Occurring or existing between neurons.

1948 E. Gardner *Fund. Neurol.* viii. 174 The afferent tracts of the cord evolve from such interneuronal pools. **1952** J. D. Hardy et al. *Pain Sensations* i. 15 Lorente de Nó . . inferred that all interneuronal connections fall into two categories. **1959** *Jrnl. Amer. Chem. Soc.* LXXXI. 4347/1 In quite a few of the compounds analgesic activity is accompanied by marked interneuronal blocking action. **1969** *New Scientist* 6 Feb. 278/1 The *specificity* of this interneuronal communication, every neuron making contact with other, often carefully specified, neurons.

†**interˈnex,** *v. Obs. rare.* [f. L. *internex-*, ppl. stem of *internectĕre* to bind together: cf. *annex, connex.*] = INTERNECT *v.*

a **1618** Sylvester *Panaretus* 725 Their Vice and Vertues them so inter-nex, That scarce can one distinguish their Effects.

†**internigrant,** *a. Obs.* [ad. L. *internigrānt-em* ppl. a., from a verbal type **internigrāre* to be black at intervals.] So †**interniˈgration.**

1656 Blount *Glossogr.*, *Internigrant*, having black interlaced among other colours. **1658** Phillips, *Internigration*, a mingling of black.

internist (ɪnˈtɜːnɪst). *U.S.* [f. *intern(al medicine* + -IST.] A general physician; also, a specialist in internal medicine.

1904 *Science* 29 Apr. 696/1 Many internists ('general physicians') of experience and authority. **1910** [see HYPOPARATHYROID *a.*]. **1918** *Nation* (N.Y.) Feb. 170/1 A maternity bureau composed of expert obstetricians and competent internists. **1961** *Brit. Jrnl. Clin. Pract.* June 510/2 The role of the internist is different. He grasps intuitively the whole of the patient—the 'gestalt'—and combines the various organic findings. **1970** *Sci. Amer.* Mar. 60/3 The British surgeon is a consultant who sees only patients referred to him by a general practitioner or internist. **1972** *Science* 5 May 489/1 The use of anti-depressants by general practitioners, internists and psychiatrists.

†**inˈternity.** *Obs. rare.* [f. L. *intern-us* INTERNAL + -ITY; cf. *externity.*] The quality of being internal, inwardness; something internal.

1760–72 H. Brooke *Fool of Qual.* (1792) V. 189 The internity of his ever-living light kindled up an externity of corporal irradiation.

internment (ɪnˈtɜːnmənt). [f. INTERN *v.* 2 + -MENT.] **a.** The action of 'interning'; confinement within the limits of a country or place.

1870 *Spectator* 24 Dec. 1534 Two months' imprisonment or internment in a fortress. **1871** *Daily News* 30 Jan., It may be hoped that internment in their own capital is all the confinement the army of Paris will have to submit to.

b. *attrib.*, as **internment camp**, a detention camp for prisoners of war and aliens.

1916 *Daily Colonist* (Victoria, B.C.) 26 July 1/3 Brandon, Man. July 25.—The internment camp here is to be closed at the end of this month. **1941** *Star* 10 Apr. 8/3 A revolt at an internment camp at Vernet les Bains.

interno-, mod. combining adverbial form of L. *internus* INTERNAL: as in **interno-medial** (ɪnˌtɜːnəʊˈmiːdɪəl), **interno-ˈmedian,** *adjs. Entom.*, situated within the median vein or nervure, or between the internal and median nervures, of the wing.

1826 Kirby & Sp. *Entomol.* III. 374 Anal Area. All that part of the wing which in Diptera lies between the interno-medial nervure . . and the posterior margin. *Ibid.* 376 The Interno-medial Nervure. The fourth principal nervure.

internodal (ɪntəˈnəʊdəl), *a. Bot.* and *Zool.* [f. INTER- 4 a + L. *nōdus* (:— *gnōdus*) knot, NODE: cf. *nodal.*] Situated between nodes; belonging to or constituting an internode.

1835 Lindley *Introd. Bot.* (1848) I. 167 The vascular connection of the internodal spaces. **1853** G. Johnston *Nat. Hist. E. Bord.* I. 86 He who is musically inclined converts an internodal piece [of *Angelica sylvestris*] into a whistle or flute.

internode (ˈɪntənəʊd). [ad. L. *internōdium* (see below).]

1. *Bot.* That part of a stem or branch intervening between two of the nodes or knots from which the leaves arise.

1667 *Phil. Trans.* II. 486 Canes, so big, that they can make as many Barrels of them, as they have internodes or Joynts. **1727** Bradley *Fam. Dict.* s.v. *Carnation*, Cutting half thro' a joint, and splitting the Internode upwards half way to the other Joint above it. **1863** Darwin in *Life* (1892) 314 The climbing of all plants yet examined is the simple result of the spontaneous circulatory movement of the upper internodes.

2. *Zool.* and *Anat.* A slender part (as a bone, or a portion of the neural cord of an arthropod, or of the stem of a polyzoan) intervening between two nodes or joints; each bone of a finger or toe.

1722 Quincy *Lex. Physico-Med.* (ed. 2) 2 Descending over the first Internode of the said Finger. **1744** Parsons *Muscular Motion* i. 26 *note* in *Phil. Trans.* XLIII, That they divide them [muscular fibres] thus into Bladders at equal Internodes, we must deny. **1826** Kirby & Sp. *Entomol.* IV. xxxvii. 9 At the union of the [neural] chords . . a knot or ganglion is usually formed, and an alternate succession of internodes and ganglions commonly follows to the end. **1870** Rolleston *Anim. Life* 73 The Polyzoary is plant-like, erect, calcareous, dividing dichotomously, the internodes articulating by flexible chitinous bands. **1885** F. Warner *Phys. Expression* ix. 155 The individual bones of the fingers and thumb are termed 'internodes'.

†**interˈnodial,** *a. Obs. rare.* [f. next + -AL¹.] = INTERNODAL. So †**interˈnodian** *a.*

1657 Tomlinson *Renou's Disp.* 270 Its root extends itself with internodian genicles. **1658** Sir T. Browne *Gard. Cyrus* iii. 158 The internodial parts of Vegetables . . are contrived with more uncertainty.

‖**internodium** (ɪntəˈnəʊdɪəm). Pl. **-ia.** Now *rare.* [L., f. *inter* between + *nōdus* knot; cf. *intercolumnium, interlunium*, etc.: see INTER- 3.] = INTERNODE. (*erron.* A joint.)

1644 Evelyn *Diary* 17 Nov., At the internodium of the transept rises yᵉ cupola. **1664** Power *Exp. Philos.* i. 31 The Wasp-Locust . . hath two horns, made of five or six internodium's very pretty to behold. **1681** tr. *Willis' Rem. Med. Wks.* Vocab., *Internodia*, between the joynts or knots, as the spaces in a ratoon cane between the joynts or knots. **1699** 'Misaurus' *Honour Gout* in *Harl. Misc.* (1809) II. 47 When that same tophous mass shall lodge in the internodia of your Worship's bones. **1856–8** W. Clark *Van der Hoeven's Zool.* I. 83 Shaft with jointed axis, nodes horny . . internodia stony.

internuclear (-ˈnjuːkliːə(r)), *a. Anat.* [INTER- 4 a.]

1. a. Situated between nuclei. **b.** Situated between the two nuclear layers of the retina.

1878 A. M. Hamilton *Nerv. Dis.* 274 The internuclear spaces were filled with wavy connective tissue. **1881** Mivart *Cat* 293 The inter-granular, or internuclear layer.

2. *Physics.* Existing between atomic nuclei.

1946 *Nature* 17 Aug. 224/1 The carbon chain must then be coiled to the same extent if normal internuclear distances are to be maintained. **1949** Koestler *Insight & Outlook* xi. 156 The integrative tendencies in the various forms of attracting or binding forces: internuclear, gravitational, electromagnetic, and so on. **1962** *Science Survey* III. 36 Typical known values for atomic masses and approximate values for typical inter-nuclear distances.

3. *Phonetics.* Situated between nuclei.

1961 Y. Olsson *On Syntax Eng. Verb* ii. 23 In pre-, inter-, and post-nuclear sections, 4/S-units and 4/o-units may occur in various combinations.

inter-nucleon: see INTER- *pref.* 5.

†ˈ**internunce¹.** *Obs.* Also **-nonce.** [a. F. *internonce* (16–17th c. in Hatz.-Darm.), ad. L. *internuntius* (*-nuncius*): see INTERNUNCIUS.] = INTERNUNCIO.

1647 Hammond *Power of Keys* iv. 100 He was call'd . . *Apostolus* also, an intercessor or internunce betwixt them. **1661** Evelyn *Fumifugium* Misc. Writ. (1805) I. 217 The internunce and interpreter of prudence. **1686** *Expos. Doctr. Ch. Eng.* xxxiv, Complaint was made . . first to the Internonce, then to his Holiness himself. [**1847** Disraeli *Tancred* vi. xi, I shall make a representation to the Internonce at Stambool.]

†ˈ**internunce².** *Obs. rare.* [ad. L. *internuntium* medium, means: see prec.] Medium of intercommunication.

1674 Evelyn *Navig. & C.* § 19 Intelligence is convey'd by the Inter-nunce of Pidgeons trained up for the purpose.

internuncial (ɪntəˈnʌnʃ(ɪ)əl), *a.* [f. as next + -AL¹.] Having the function of conveying messages between two parties, etc.; used *fig.* of the nerves as the organs of communication between different parts of the system.

1845 Todd & Bowman *Phys. Anat.* I. 205 The threads of fibrous matter which pass to or from it are called nerves. The latter are internuncial in their office. **1860** Spencer *Ess., Social Org.* I. 305 In the simplest organisms, there is no 'internuncial apparatus' as Hunter styled the nervous system. **1874** Carpenter *Ment. Phys.* i. ii. § 44 (1879) 44 A Nervous system, whose action may be purely internuncial, —that of calling forth Muscular movements in respondence to the impressions made by external agencies.

interˈnunciary, *a. rare.* [f. L. *internunti-us* (see below) + -ARY.] Of or pertaining to an internuncio, messenger, or interpreter.

1847 *Blackw. Mag.* LXI. 314 He interlarded his internunciary discourse with a continual annotation of asides.

internunciate (-ˈnʌnʃɪeɪt), *v. rare*⁻⁰. [f. ppl. stem of L. *internuntiāre* (*-nunciāre*) to send messengers to and fro between.] *intr.* To convey messages between two parties.

1656 Blount *Glossogr.*, *Internunciate*, to go in message between two parties.

So **internunciˈation** (*rare*⁻⁰); **interˈnunciatory** *a.*, relating to the conveyance of messages.

1658 Phillips, *Internuntiation*, a going or sending of a message between several parties. **1890** Dakyns *Xenophon* I. p. cxxi. *note*, All these internunciatory stories reveal a side of Greek character . . which I hardly know how to name.

†**interˈnunciess.** *Obs. rare.* [irreg. f. INTERNUNCE¹ or INTERNUNCIO + -ESS.] A female internuncio or messenger.

c **1611** Chapman *Iliad* xv. 140 Iris that had place Of internunciess from the Gods.

internuncio (ɪntəˈnʌnʃɪəʊ). Also 7 **-tio.** [ad. It. *internunzio*, in Florio *internuntio* 'a messenger

that goeth betweene man and man'; ad. L. *internuntius* (*-nuncius*): see next.]

1. A messenger between two parties.

1641 MILTON *Animadv.* xiii. Wks. (1851) 243 They onely are the internuntios or the go-betweens of this trim devis'd mummery. *a* **1656** USSHER *Ann.* (1658) 428 Thoas..being sent from Rhodes by Dinon to Perseus as an internuncio. **1769** BURKE *Corr.* (1844) I. 196 Townshend being a mutual friend, and having been..an internuncio between you.

2. An official representative or ambassador of the Pope at a foreign court in an interval during which there is no nuncio, or at a minor court to which no nuncio is sent.

1670 G. H. *Hist. Cardinals* II. III. 204 The Abbot was declar'd Internuntio to Brussels. **1682** *News fr. France* 37 The Old resolute Pope sent a Courier to France to the Internuntio with a Bull of Excommunication. **1705** *Lond. Gaz.* No. 4130/2 The Pope's Inter-Nuncio, who resides at Brussels, is lately come hither. **1892** J. MORRIS *Cath. Eng.* 21 The Internuncio at Brussels wrote to the Propaganda.

3. A minister representing a government, esp. that of Austria, at the Ottoman Porte.

1700 RYCAUT *Hist. Turks* III. 195 The Polish Internuntio, who from the beginning of the War had been kept under restraint at Constantinople, was now upon exchange for a Turk of quality, again set at Liberty. **1815** *Tweddell's Rem.* 316 *note*, The Austrian minister residing at the Othman Porte, with the peculiar title of 'Internuncio'.

Hence **inter'nuncioship**, the office or function of an internuncio or go-between.

1748 RICHARDSON *Clarissa* (1811) V. 6 Several billets passed between us..by the internuncioship of Dorcas.

‖**inter'nuncius.** [L. in med. spelling, for cl.L. *internuntius*, f. *inter* between + *nuntius* messenger.] = prec. 1.

1675 BROOKS *Gold. Key* Wks. 1867 V. 176 They desired an *Internuncius*, a man like themselves, who might be as a mediator to go betwixt God and them. **1825** R. CUTHBERTSON *Lect. Revelation* i. 10 No ordinary minister..ever occupied the place of an internuncius between Christ and other prophets. **1867** LEGGE *Confucius* (1877) 244 Trying to see the master without using the services of an *internuncius*.

internuptial (ɪntəˈnʌpʃəl), *a.* [f. INTER- 2 or 4 + L. *nuptiæ* nuptials, marriage: cf. *nuptial*.]

1. Pertaining to intermarriage.

1850 GROTE *Greece* II. lvii. VII. 197 A quarrel..about some alleged wrong in cases of internuptial connection.

2. Intervening between two marriages or married states.

1885 F. HALL in *Nation* (N.Y.) XL. 257/1 Some few months of his internuptial disconsolateness. **1896** *Edin. Rev.* July 65 During the internuptial period some insight can be gained into the character of Sheridan.

†**inter'nuptials,** *sb. pl. Obs.* [f. as prec., after *nuptials*.] = INTERMARRIAGE 1 b.

1654 H. L'ESTRANGE *Chas. I* (1655) 7, I have heard some ..passionately ascribe Englands calamities to those internuptials, and fetch that ireful stroke of divine Iustice.. from his marrying a Lady of mis-belief.

interoceanic (ˌɪntərəʊʃiːˈænɪk), *a.* [INTER- 4 b.] Situated between oceans; connecting two oceans, as a strait or canal. So **inter'ocean** *a.*

1850 *Clayton-Bulwer Treaty* 19 Apr. 8 Interoceanic communication. **1855** HYDE CLARKE *Eng. Dict.*, *Interoceanic*. **1856** *Sat. Rev.* II. 651/1 Englishmen ought to anticipate the difficulty by insisting on due security for the Inter-Oceanic passage. **1858** SIMMONDS *Dict. Trade*, *Interoceanic*, lying between two seas; a communication connecting two oceans—as a railway, road, etc. **1891** J. WINSOR *Columbus* App. 573 [They] had been misled by the broad estuary of the La Plata to think that it was really an inter-oceanic passage. **1913** *Chambers's Jrnl.* Jan. 22/2 The isthmus..became a centre of attraction for interocean transit. **1969** *Jane's Freight Containers 1968–1969* 93/1 Parcel Tankers, Inc. Agent: Interocean Steamship Corp.

interoceptor (ˌɪntərəʊˈsɛptə(r)). *Physiol.* [perh. f. INTER(IOR *a.* and *sb.* + -O + RE)CEPTOR, after EXTEROCEPTOR.] Any sensory receptor which receives stimuli arising within the body, or *spec.* within the viscera. So **intero'ceptive** *a.*

1906 C. S. SHERRINGTON *Integrative Action Nervous Syst.* ix. 317 This [inner] surface of the animal may be termed the intero-ceptive. *Ibid.* 352 Spinal shock hardly at all affects the nervous reactions of the intero-ceptors (visceral system). **1930** L. T. TROLAND *Princ. Psychophysiol.* II. IV. xiii. 14 The visceral or interoceptive systems include those for the feelings of hunger, thirst, nausea. **1940** FRAENKEL & GUNN *Orientation of Animals* (1961) iii. 33 The interoceptors in the alimentary canal which are responsible for belly-aches. **1971** D. J. AIDLEY *Physiol. Excitable Cells* xv. 307 Exteroceptors are sensitive to stimuli originating outside the body, and interoceptors are excited by stimuli inside the body. **1972** C. H. HOCKMAN *Limbic Syst. Mechanisms & Autonomic Function* viii. 128/2 Intracellular recording in awake, sitting squirrel monkeys have shown a differential effect of interoceptive and exteroceptive inputs on the excitability of hippocampal neurons.

interocular, -olivary: see INTER- *pref.* 6.

inter-office: see INTER- *pref.* 5.

interoperable (ˌɪntərˈɒpərəb(ə)l), *a.* [f. INTER- 2 a + OPERABLE *a.*] Able to operate in conjunction.

1969 *Nature* 29 Nov. 839/1 Skynet is inter-operable with the IDCSP system and is intended to be inter-operable with its successor now in view. **1970** *Sci. Jrnl.* Mar. 13 In other respects the two nations' forces are working in parallel and Skynet [the Royal Navy's military satellite communications system] is compatible and interoperable with the US Defence Communication Satellite system. **1970** *Fremdsprachen* XIV. 220/1 Sometime in the mid-1970s the communications..will not only be interoperable among themselves, but with United States, Canadian and Australian services also.

interopercle (ˌɪntərəʊˈpɜːk(ə)l). *rare*⁻⁰. Anglicized form of INTEROPERCULUM.

interopercular (ˌɪntərəʊˈpɜːkjʊlə(r)), *a. Ichthyol.* [f. next + -AR; cf. *opercular*.] Belonging to, or of the nature of, an interoperculum, chiefly in ***interopercular bone*** = INTEROPERCULUM.

1854 OWEN *Skel. & Teeth* in *Circ. Sc.*, *Organ. Nat.* I. 178 The appendage in question consists of four bones; the one articulated to the tympanic pedicle is called 'preopercular' ..; the other three are, counting downwards, the 'opercular',..the 'subopercular',..the 'interopercular'. **1897** GÜNTHER in Mary Kingsley *W. Africa* 700 Part of the interopercular margin is spiny.

‖**interoperculum** (ˌɪntərəʊˈpɜːkjʊləm). *Ichthyol.* [INTER- 2 b.] One of the four bones normally forming the gill-cover, esp. in teleostean and ganoid fishes; usually situated below the præoperculum, and partly between this on one side and the operculum and suboperculum on the other.

1855 in MAYNE *Expos. Lex.* **1871** DARWIN *Desc. Man* II. xii. 10 The male has its mouth and interoperculum fringed with a beard of stiff hairs. **1888** ROLLESTON & JACKSON *Anim. Life* 93 A series of membrane bones well developed in *Teleostei* and *Ganoidei* are attached to the posterior edge of the hyomandibular and quadrate bones. These are the prae-operculum, the operculum, the sub-operculum, and the inter-operculum. They close in laterally the branchial cavity.

interoptic, -oscillate: see INTER- 6, 1 b.

interorbital (ɪntərˈɔːbɪtəl), *a. Anat.* [INTER- 4 a.] Situated between the eye-sockets.

1852 DANA *Crust.* I. 420 Front abruptly narrower than interorbital breadth. **1859** R. F. BURTON *Centr. Afr.* in *Jrnl. Geog. Soc.* XXIX. 314 The bridge of the nose is rarely flat, though not without a deepening in the interorbital portion, and the eyes are wide apart. **1880** GÜNTHER *Fishes* 38 The space across the forehead, between the orbits, is called the interorbital space.

interosculant (ɪntərˈɒskjʊlənt), *a.* [INTER- 2 a: cf. next.] Interosculating; forming a connecting link (see quot.).

1855 KINGSLEY *Glaucus*, *Peachia hastata*, Belonging to what the long-word-makers call an 'interosculant' group, —a party of genera and species which connect families scientifically far apart.

interosculate (ɪntərˈɒskjʊleɪt), *v.* [f. INTER- 1 b + OSCULATE, f. L. *ōsculāre, -ārī*, to kiss.] *intr.* **a.** To interpenetrate or inosculate with each other. **b.** To form a connecting link between two groups (as between different genera or species of animals or plants).

1882 in OGILVIE (Annandale). **1885** *Trans. Geol. Soc.* 10 Caverns which have yielded palæolithic tools interosculating with relics of several extinct Mammalian species. **1896** G. ALLEN in *Westm. Gaz.* 18 Dec. 1/3 'Sir Nicholas Lombard's set' forms a well-marked nucleus in the interosculating system of London Society.

interosculation (ˌɪntərɒskjuːˈleɪʃən). [n. of action from prec.] The action or fact of interosculating. **a.** Interpenetration of two things or sets of things; inosculation. **b.** Connexion of two things (e.g. distinct species) by something intermediate.

1883 G. ALLEN in *Knowledge* 6 July 1/2 The hawkweeds.. display just this close interosculation of species. **1889** GEIKIE in *Nature* 19 Sept. 487/2 The dovetailing and interosculation of boulder-clay with aqueous deposits are explained by the relation of the ice to the surface over which it flowed.

interosseal (ɪntərˈɒsiːəl), *a. Anat.* [f. as next + -AL¹.] = next.

1805 CARLISLE in *Phil. Trans.* XCVI. 11 Interosseal muscles, which close the rays. **1831** R. KNOX *Cloquet's Anat.* 694 The Interosseal Artery..comes from the posterior part of the ulnar..and is always of considerable size.

interosseous (ɪntərˈɒsiːəs), *a. Anat.* [f. INTER- 4 a + L. *os, oss-* bone, *osse-us* bony + -OUS. Cf. mod.L. *interossei* pl. the interosseous muscles.] Situated between bones; said of various ligaments, muscles, nerves, and vessels.

1745 *Phil. Trans.* XLIII. 408 The interosseous Ligament of the *Os Pubis*. **1759** *Ibid.* LI. 783, I afterwards electrified ..the interosseous muscles. **1840** G. V. ELLIS *Anat.* 428 The posterior interosseous artery, arising from the common interosseous trunk opposite the tubercle of the radius in the front of the forearm, passes to the posterior part above the interosseous membrane. **1872** MIVART *Elem. Anat.* 303 The fibula and the interosseous membrane connecting that bone with the tibia.

interpage (ɪntəˈpeɪdʒ), *v.* [INTER- 1.] *trans.* To print or insert on intermediate pages.

1858 *Sat. Rev.* V. 541/2 An abridgment of the story ..(interpaged with the original). **1880** *Athenæum* 25 Dec. 867/2 The play..is to be published in the original, with an interpaged English translation. **1888** *Ibid.* 24 Nov. 707/1 [In the first Shakspeare folio] 'Troilus and Cressida' is interpaged between histories and tragedies.

†**inter'pale,** *v. Obs.* [f. INTER- 1 + PALE *v.*]

1. *trans.* To divide by pales, as in Heraldry; to alternate in vertical divisions.

1553 BRENDE *Q. Curtius* VI. P iij, He ware upon his head a Diademe of purple, interpaled with white.

2. = IMPALE *v.* 2.

a **1657** LOVELACE *Lucasta* (1864) 10 Interpale their browes with flourishing bayes.

inter-palpebral, papacy, -papillary, -parenchymal: see INTER- *pref.*

interparenthetical (ɪntəpærɪnˈθɛtɪkəl), *a.* [f. INTER- 4 a + *parenthesis*, after *parenthetical*.] Enclosed within parentheses. So **interparen'thetically** *adv.*, by way of parenthesis.

1852 SMEDLEY *L. Arundel* vi. 53 And be it observed interparenthetically that we use the theatrical metaphor advisedly. **1877** *World* VII. 54 A long involved interparenthetical sentence which may be comprehensible on paper requires a tremendous effort to read aloud.

interparietal (-pəˈraɪɪtəl), *a.* (*sb.*) *Anat.* [INTER- 4 a.] Situated between the right and left parietal bones of the skull.

1835–6 TODD *Cycl. Anat.* I. 254/2 The interparietal suture of the human skull. *Ibid.* 473/2 The interparietal bone..is considerable in the dogs. **1886** *Syd. Soc. Lex.* s.v., Romiti and others consider that the interparietal bone of mammals is represented in man by the whole of the upper squamous and non-cartilaginous part of the occipital bone.

B. *sb.* The interparietal bone; in fishes, 'the median bone of the posterior part of the roof of the skull, now generally called *supraoccipital*' (*Cent. Dict.*).

interparlance, -parlee, -parley, obs. forms of ENTERPARLANCE, etc.

1610 W. FOLKINGHAM *Art of Survey* II. iii. 51 By opportunity for..intercourse of passage for Commerce, and interparlée for Converse.

interparliament, -ary, -paroxysmal: see INTER- *pref.*

inter partes: see INTER L. prep.

inter-particle, -party: see INTER- *pref.*

†**inter'pass,** *v. Obs.* Also 5 entir-. [ME. a. OF. *entrepasser* to pass; in later use prob. independently f. INTER- 1 + PASS *v.*] *intr.* To pass between, to pass from one to another.

c **1450** *Merlin* 407 Gawein hym smote in entirpassinge thourgh the helme to the sculle. **1591** HORSEY *Trav.* (Hakluyt Soc.) 265 Some imbassages hathe interpassed of late years more abusivly then comodious. **1620** SHELTON *Quix.* IV. xxxi. 242 Divers Compliments..did mutually interpass between Don Alvaro and Don Quixote.

b. To come to pass meanwhile.

1613–18 DANIEL *Coll. Hist. Eng.* (1621) 47 Many skirmishes interpassed..but in the end a treaty of peace was propounded.

†**interpa'ssation.** *Obs. rare*⁻⁰. [n. of action from INTERPASS *v.* (in sense 'to pass between'): cf. OF. *entrepassé* 'interlaced' (in Godef.).]

1706 PHILLIPS (ed. Kersey), *Interpassation* (among Apothecaries), the stitching of Bags at certain distances, to prevent the Drugs contained therein from falling together in a heap.

†**inter'pause,** *v. Obs. rare.* In 6 enter-. [f. INTER- 1 + PAUSE *v.*] *intr.* To pause in the midst of something.

1534 MORE *Comf. agst. Trib.* Wks. 1169/2 In talkynge so longe together withoute enterpausyng betwene. *Ibid.*, Manye woordes..spoken..without enterpausing.

†**'interpause,** *sb. Obs. rare*⁻¹. [INTER- 2 a.] A pause between or in the course of something.

1599 DANIEL *Civ. Wars* v. lxxvi, Giuing an interpause to pride and spight, Which breath'd but to break out with greater might.

interpave, -peal, -pectoral, -peduncular: see INTER- *pref.*

interpel (ɪntəˈpɛl), *v.* Now only in *Sc. Law.* Also 4 **enterpele,** 7 **interpell (-peal).** [ad. L. *interpellā-re* to interrupt by speaking, f. *inter* between + *pellāre*, secondary form of *pellĕre* to drive. Cf. F. *interpeller* (14th c. in Godef.).]

†**1.** *trans.* To appeal to; to petition. *Obs.*

1382 WYCLIF *Deut.* xxv. 7 She shal enterpele [Vulg. *interpellabit*] the more men thurȝ birth [1388 sche schal axe the greetere men in birthe]. **1591** R. BRUCE *Eleven Serm.* N v b, So every one of you..interpel God continuallie, be importune suiting.

†**2.** To interrupt (a person) in speaking; to break in on or disturb. *Obs.*

1541 ELYOT *Image Gov.* 165 The emperour..interpelled Lupus, and commaunded hym to enter into his narracion. *a* **1637** B. JONSON *Underwoods, Eupheme* ix. 70 Why should my tongue, or pen Presume to interpell that fulnesse? *c* **1645** HOWELL *Lett.* I. vi. i, No more now, for I am interpell'd by many businesses. **1647** H. MORE *Song of Soul* I. III. xxxi, Here one of us began to interpeal Old Mnemon.

3. *Sc. Law.* To intercept, cut off, prevent.
1722 A. PENNECUIK *Hist. Blue Blanket* 77 (Jam.) Interpelling the judges of justiciary from proceeding against them for their riot. **1809** *Erskine's Princ. Sc. Law* 74 The notification must be also made at the bride's, in order to interpel persons from contracting with her. **1856** *Act 19 & 20 Vict.* c. 91 §1 An arrestment executed to attach the effects of a debtor, as in the hands of a person out of Scotland, shall not be held to have interpelled such person from paying to the original creditor.

interpellant (ɪntə'pɛlənt). [a. F. *interpellant*, pr. pple. of *interpeller*, ad. L. *interpellāre*: see prec.]
One who addresses an interpellation (in the French or other foreign Chamber).
1869 *Pall Mall G.* 9 July 5 None of the interpellants are enemies to the dynasty. **1899** *Daily News* 13 July 5/6 The interpellant in to-day's sitting of the Reichstag.

interpellate (ɪn'tɜːpɪleɪt, ɪntə'pɛleɪt), *v.* [f. ppl. stem of L. *interpell-āre*: see INTERPEL.]
†**1.** *trans.* To interrupt (a person) in speaking; hence, to break in on or interrupt (a process or action). *Obs.*
1599 A. M. tr. *Gabelhouer's Bk. Physicke* 302/1 Applye.. a green Oaken leafe theron, and that will interpellate the resanatione therof as longe as ther is anye venoum therin.
2. To address an interpellation to (a minister in the French or other Chamber). Also *absol.*
1874 LADY HERBERT tr. *Hübner's Ramble* (1878) II. iv. 329, I have been told that when thus interpellated, these.. have not always refused their advice. **1885** *Law Times* 28 Mar. 384/1 The Government will be interpellated upon the subject at an early date. **1898** *Daily News* 8 Sept. 5/5 M. Mirman, another Socialist, will interpellate on Colonel Henry's suicide.

†**interpellate**, *ppl. a. Obs. rare.* [ad. L. *interpellāt-us*, pa. pple. of *interpellāre*: see INTERPEL.] Appealed to; interrupted.
1447 BOKENHAM *Seyntys* (Roxb.) 161 Cryst, wych iuge was interpellat,.. ageynys hyr sustrys acusacyoun He fonde a resonable excusacyoun. **1604** R. CAWDREY *Table Alph.*, *Interpellate*, disturbed, hindered.

interpellation (ˌɪntəpɛ'leɪʃən). [ad. L. *interpellātiōn-em*, n. of action from *interpellāre*: see INTERPEL. The English uses became obsolete before 1700; it has been re-introduced from Fr. in sense 5 in the 19th c.] The action of interpellating or of interrupting by question or appeal.
†**1.** The action of appealing to or entreating; pleading, intercession. *Obs.*
1526 *Pilgr. Perf.* (W. de W. 1531) 243 Makyng.. interpellacyon & pletynge for vs before yᵉ father of heuen. **1542** BECON *Pathw. Prayer* in *Early Wks.* (Parker Soc.) 169 By the importunity of her interpellation and hearty request. **1612** AINSWORTH *Annot. Ps.* iv. 2 Appeale, interpellation or intercession. **1650** JER. TAYLOR *Holy Living & Dying* II. ii. §4 (1870) 348 For whose interest the Spirit makes interpellations with groans and sighs unutterable. *a* **1670** HACKET *Cent. Serm.* (1675) 1012 The personal complaint of the Souls under the Altar, and not the interpellation of their injuries.
†**2.** A summons, citation. *Obs.*
1599 FENTON *Guicciard.* III. 140 To put the Duke of Myllan in contumacie, it were necessarie to haue interpellation. **1726** AYLIFFE *Parergon* 180 In all Extra-judicial Acts, one Citation, Monition, or Extra-judicial Interpellation is sufficient.
†**3.** The action of breaking in upon with speech or otherwise; interruption. *Obs.*
1611 SPEED *Hist. Gt. Brit.* IX. vi. §23. 490 The Archbishop had enjoyed the same for a long time, without interpellation or disturbance. **1640** BP. HALL *Episc.* Ep. Ded. 5, I had need to crave pardon of your Majestie for the boldnesse of this interpellation. **1647** H. MORE *Song of Soul* I. II. xliv, Good Sir, I crave pardon If so I chance to break that golden twist You spin, by rude interpellation. **1668** —— *Div. Dial.* II. x. (1713) 119 So frequent and palpable Interpellations in humane affairs would take away the Usefulness of both. **1829** LANDOR *Wks.* (1846) II. 23/2 Such writers have confined their view.. to.. sophistic reasonings, and sarcastic interpellations. **1834** [see INTERLOCATION 1].
4. *Sc. Law.* Prevention, hindrance. Cf. INTERPEL 3.
1814 *Act. 54 Geo. III*, c. 137 §3 *margin*, Arrestments at Market Cross, &c. no sufficient interpellation.
5. The action of interrupting the order of the day (in the French or other foreign legislative Chamber) by asking from a Minister an explanation of some matter belonging to his department.
It may lead to a debate and division, and thus answers both to 'asking a question' in the British House of Commons, and to a 'motion for the adjournment of the House' in order to call attention to a matter of urgency.
1837 CARLYLE *Fr. Rev.* I. III. iii, He is standing at bay: alone; exposed to an incessant fire of questions, interpellations, objurgations. **1861** *Sat. Rev.* 22 June, The last invention in this way is the word 'interpellation'. When an Opposition member of a foreign Parliament asks a question of a Minister, he is said to 'put an interpellation'. **1867** *Morn. Star* 28 Jan., If you put a question in the House of Commons you cannot have a debate. But an 'interpellation' is really equivalent to our 'motion'. It always opens with a long speech, and usually leads to a long debate. **1893** *Nation* (N.Y.) 9 Feb. 99/3 The interpellations already announced are numerous.

interpellator (ˌɪntəpɛ'leɪtə(r)). [a. L. *interpellātor*, agent-n. from *interpellāre*: see INTERPEL.] One who interpellates: †**a.** An interrupter (*obs.*). **b.** One who addresses an interpellation.
1623 COCKERAM, *Interpellator*, which interrupts. **1859** *Sat. Rev.* VIII. 568/1 The Cabinet is enjoying rest from the awkward interruptions of Parliamentary interpellators. **1881** *Daily News* 8 Nov. 5/5 Rumours circulated by extreme Radical journals that he was only a complaisant interpellator.

†**inter'pend**, *ppl. a. Obs. rare.* [f. INTER- 1 + PEN *v.*[1] (pa. pple. *penned*, *pen'd*, *pent*).] Shut in, confined, or enclosed between.
1621 G. SANDYS *Ovid's Met.* IV. (1626) 76 Thus, while they [the Meneïdes] corners seeke, thin films extend From lightned lims, with small beams inter-pend [*tenuesque includunt brachia pennæ*]. [The 'small beams' are the long slender metacarpal bones between which the 'thin film' of a bat's wing is stretched.]

inter'pendent, *a.* (*sb.*) [INTER- 2 a.]
†**1.** Hanging between two things, courses, etc.; hesitant, undecided. *Obs. rare.*
1708 *Brit. Apollo* No. 12. 2/2, I am still interpendent.
2. = INTERDEPENDENT. *rare.*
1855 BAILEY *Mystic*, etc. 57 Interpendent harmonies of song.
†**B.** *sb.* One who hangs between; one who belongs to neither of two parties. (In quot. with play on *Independent.*) *Obs.*
1647 WARD *Simp. Cobler* 37, I am neither Presbyterian, nor plebsbyterian, but an Interpendent.

inter'penetrable, *a.* [INTER- 2 a.] Capable of mutual penetration.
1860 J. YOUNG *Prov. Reason* 74 It is not in the nature of things, that these qualities should be interpenetrable or convertible.

interpenetrant (ɪntə'pɛnɪtrənt), *a.* [f. INTER- 2 a + L. *penetrānt-em*, pr. pple. of *penetrāre* to penetrate.] Interpenetrating.
1839 BAILEY *Festus* vi. (1852) 81 With these.. I mix and serve All with each order interpenetrant. **1881** L. FLETCHER in *Nature* XXV. 49/2 The twin plane of the two interpenetrant tetrahedra.

interpenetrate (ɪntə'pɛnɪtreɪt), *v.* [INTER- 1.]
1. *trans.* To penetrate between the parts or particles of (anything); to penetrate thoroughly; to pass through and through, permeate, pervade.
1818 SHELLEY *Eugan. Hills* 313 Living things.. And my spirit.. Interpenetrated lie By the glory of the sky. **1825** COLERIDGE *Statesm. Man.* (1858) I. App. B. 458 It follows, that reason.. must be interpenetrated by a power, that represents the concentration of all in each. **1834** MEDWIN *Angler in Wales* I. 59 The water is everywhere interpenetrated by air, which the fishes breathe. **1872** HUXLEY *Phys.* vi. 144 The food.. thus becomes interpenetrated.. with the salivary fluid. **1883** *Contemp. Rev.* Nov. 645 Greeks, Romans, Arabs, and Levantines interpenetrating the country.
b. *intr.*
1879 D. M. WALLACE *Australas.* xiv. 269 Owing to the great amount of sea which interpenetrates among the islands.
2. *intr.* To penetrate each other; to unite or mingle by mutual penetration.
1809–10 COLERIDGE *Friend* (1850) I. xiii. 119 Law and religion thus interpenetrating neutralized each other. **1820** SHELLEY *Vis. of Sea* 120 At one gate They encounter, but interpenetrate. **1870** BALDW. BROWN *Eccl. Truth* 278 No order keeps to itself, they all interlock and interpenetrate.
b. *trans.* To penetrate reciprocally.
1843 TRENCH *Five Serm. Cambr.* 43 Sin and suffering do ever interpenetrate one another. **1873** SYMONDS *Grk. Poets* ii. 61 The influence of love and harmony kept the elements joined and interpenetrated. **1875** CROLL *Climate & T.* xiii. 219 The polar current and the Gulf-stream are mutually interpenetrated. **1884** *Expositor* Jan. 18 Two main spheres of thought.. overlapping and interpenetrating each other.
3. *Arch.* (*trans.* and *intr.*) To appear as if penetrating or passing through a moulding, etc. See INTERPENETRATION 3.
1840 WILLIS in Gwilt *Archit.* (1876) 933 Knobs.. which really represent the Gothic base of a square mullion on the same plinth with the hollow chamfered mullion, and interpenetrating with it. **1864** BOUTELL *Her. Hist. & Pop.* xxx. (ed. 3) 451 Their shafts interpenetrating the mouldings of the panels and tracery.
Hence **inter'penetrating** *ppl. a.*
1873 SYMONDS *Grk. Poets* xii. 409 They blend and mingle in a concord of separate yet interpenetrating beauties. **1888** *Spectator* 22 Sept. 1292 The extreme complexity of the various interpenetrating systems of law under which the American citizen lives makes him a slave to lawyers.

interpenetrate (ɪntə'pɛnɪtrət), *ppl. a.* [f. INTER- 1 b + L. *penetrāt-us* penetrated.]
Interpenetrated. (Const. as *pa. pple.*)
1877 BLACKIE *Wise Men* 303 That true world above.. Peopled with stars, and interpenetrate By native glory.

interpenetration (ˌɪntəpɛnɪ'treɪʃən). [INTER- 2 a.] The action of interpenetrating or fact of being interpenetrated.
1. The action of penetrating between or among; the passing through and through; deep or thorough penetration.
a **1822** SHELLEY *Ess. & Lett., Def. Poetry* i. (Camelot) 35 It is.. the interpenetration of a diviner nature through our own. **1875** MAINE *Hist. Inst.* ii. 58 There has certainly been nothing like an intimate interpenetration of ancient Irish law by Christian principle. **1880** A. R. WALLACE *Isl. Life* I. ix. 184 The interpenetration of the sea into any part of the great continents.
2. Mutual penetration; diffusion of each through the other.
1809–10 COLERIDGE *Friend* (1818) III. 150 That union and interpenetration of the universal and the particular, which must ever pervade all works of decided genius and true science. **1857** KINGSLEY *Misc., Gt. Cities* II. 339 A complete interpenetration of city and of country. **1877** LE CONTE *Elem. Geol.* xvi. (1879) 158 Regions or zones in latitude.. shade insensibly into one another by interpenetration.
3. *Arch.* The intersection of two forms; *spec.* an independent continuation of mouldings or other members past their intersection, so that the identity of a member is preserved after it has partly coincided with another or has been altogether swallowed up in it.
1840 WILLIS in Gwilt *Archit.* (1876) 933 In many Flamboyant examples, small knobs and projections may be observed, and on a superficial view might pass for mere unmeaning ornaments, but will be found explicable upon this system of interpenetration. **1848** T. RICKMAN *Archit.* App. p. lviii, It has also the interpenetration of mouldings. **1879** SIR G. SCOTT *Lect. Archit.* I. 53 The groined or intersecting vault formed by the interpenetration of two demi-cylinders.

interpenetrative (ɪntə'pɛnɪtreɪtɪv), *a.* [INTER- 2 a.] Intimately or reciprocally penetrative.
1860 O. W. HOLMES *Elsie V.* (1861) 175 Such a mutually interpenetrative consciousness there was between the father and the old physician. **1875** G. MACDONALD *St. George & St. Michael* (1878) 47 The interpenetrative power of feeling.
Hence **inter'penetratively** *adv.*
a **1834** COLERIDGE *Lit. Rem.* (1839) IV. 197 The philosophic principle, that can only act immediately, that is, interpenetratively, as two globules of quicksilver, and co-adunatively.

inter-perceptual: see INTER- *pref.* 4 c.

interpermeate (ɪntə'pɜːmiːeɪt), *v.* [INTER- 1 b.] To pervade or penetrate reciprocally. Hence **interperme'ation.**
1909 in *Cent. Dict.* Suppl. **1926** *Blackw. Mag.* Oct. 518/2 It [*sc.* the Vital Principle] came into being by the inter-permeation of air and water. **1954** *Jrnl. Theol. Stud.* V. 54 It is surely more intelligible to postulate a personal unity in which persons coinhere and interpermeate in a way unknown to us on earth.

interpersonal (ɪntə'pɜːsənəl), *a. Psychol.* [f. INTER- 4 c + PERSONAL *a.* 5.] Between persons; *spec.* a term introduced by H. S. Sullivan (1892–1949) to describe behaviour between people in any encounter. So **interperso'nality**, the state or fact of being interpersonal; **inter'personally** *adv.*, in an interpersonal manner.
1842 CAROLINE FOX *Mem.* 30 May (1883) 195 Talking over phrenology, mesmerism, and interpersonal influence. **1938** H. S. SULLIVAN in *Psychiatry* I. 121 Psychiatry seeks to discover and formulate the laws of human personality... Its peculiar field is the study of interpersonal phenomena. Personality is made manifest in interpersonal situations, and not otherwise. It is to the elucidation of interpersonal relations, therefore, that psychiatry applies itself. **1946** C. MORRIS *Signs, Lang. & Behavior* 39 (*heading*) The interpersonality of the language sign. **1947** P. L. HARRIMAN *Dict. Psychol.* 184 *Interpersonal relationships*, the reciprocal influences which persons exert upon one another in primary (face-to-face) social groups. **1949** M. MEAD *Male & Female* x. 212 The specific interpersonality of the sexual act. *Ibid.* ii. 39 Using the understanding not interpersonally but personally. **1959** H. BONNER *Group Dynamics* II. iii. 90 An important feature of interpersonal aggression is that it is usually accompanied by the members' insight into their own behavior. **1962** U. WEINREICH in Householder & Saporta *Probl. in Lexicogr.* 43 Lexicography as a descriptive (rather than a normative) discipline must also take the criterion of interpersonality seriously. **1963** *Dissertation Abstr.* XXIII. 3484/1 He was impulsive, emotionally and interpersonally immature, and not emancipated from his parents. **1964** M. ARGYLE *Psychol. & Social Probl.* xv. 183 Sociological field studies of neighbourhoods, factories and families can disclose facts about inter-personal behaviour and relationships. **1971** M. COOK (*title*) Interpersonal perception. *Ibid.* 11 That area of social psychology—variously called interpersonal perception, person perception and impression formation. **1972** *Jrnl. Social Psychol.* LXXXVI. 177 The 15-year-old boy.. was involved in interpersonal conflicts with his stepfather.

interpervade, -petalary, -petaloid: see INTER- *pref.*

interpetiolar (ɪntə'pɛtɪələ(r)), *a. Bot.* [f. INTER- 4 a + PETIOLE: see PETIOLAR.] Situated between petioles, or between a petiole and the axis. Also **inter'petiolary** *a.*
1830 LINDLEY *Nat. Syst. Bot.* 50 Leaves opposite.. with interpetiolar stipulæ. *Ibid.* 203 The interpetiolary stipules and seeds of Rubiaceæ. **1843** *Penny Cycl.* XXV. 451/1 The umbels of small flowers interpetiolar or disposed alternately along a common pedicle.

interphalangeal, -piece: see INTER- 6, 2 b.

interphase ('ɪntəfeɪz), *sb.* and *a.* [f. INTER- + PHASE.] **A.** *sb.* [INTER- 2 b.] **1.** *Cytology.* [a. G.

interphase (H. Lundegårdh 1912, in *Arch. f. mikrosk. Anat.* LXXX. 27).] A stage in the cycle of nuclear division which intervenes between one mitosis and the next; also, a stage between the first and second division of meiosis. Also *attrib.* or as *adj.*

1913 *La Cellule* XXIX. 308 For the excellent term 'interphase' we are indebted to Lundegårdh. **1932** C. D. DARLINGTON *Recent Adv. Cytol.* iv. 90 The chromosomes may form two daughter-nuclei at the poles and pass into a resting stage, the interphase. **1961** *Lancet* 26 Aug. 488/1 Any X chromosomes in excess may produce a sex-chromatin body in the interphase nucleus. **1968** M. W. STRICKBERGER *Genetics* ii. 13 As compared to the period of active mitosis..the interphase or 'intermitotic' period of most cells is usually many times longer. *Ibid.* 21 The chromosomes pass into a short interphase before the second meiotic division begins.

2. *Physical Chem.* The region between two phases in which the properties are significantly different from the bulk properties of either phase.

1933 *Phil. Mag.* XVI. 849 In recent years attention has been concentrated once more on the electro-chemistry of the interphase between mercury and an aqueous solution containing electrolytes. *Ibid.* 864 The surface tension of a liquid-liquid interphase is defined in such a way as to be applicable to any desired boundary in an interphase of finite thickness. **1955** E. J. PRYOR *Introd. Mineral Dressing* xvii. 428 In the solid-fluid interphase, forces of each phase meet and merge through a transition stage. **1970** BOCKRIS & REDDY *Mod Electrochem.* I. i. 2 An interface formed by two phases..is an apparent surface because..there is a *region* in which there is a continuous transition from the properties of one phase to the properties of the other. If one aims to refer specifically to this three-dimensional transition region, then it is more appropriate to use the term interphase. **1972** BOCKRIS & DRAŽIĆ *Electro-Chem. Sci.* ii. 22 An interphase is a less sharply definable region, which will range over at least two molecular diameters, but may extend over thousands of ångströms.

B. *adj.* [INTER- 5.] **1.** Occurring or existing between two phases or states of matter.

1933 *Jrnl. Chem. Physics* I. 8/1 The equilization [*sic*] of spreading force *f* in different phases within one field may take place in 3 ways: (a) Interphase mobility by which adatoms cross the phase boundary [etc.]. **1959** *Times* 22 Jan. 2/5 (Advt.), The work will include calculation of interphase reactions in which water or steam is normally one phase. **1967** B. P. NICOLSKY et al. in G. Eisenman *Glass Electrodes for Hydrogen* vi. 175 We shall agree to regard the interphase potential as the electrical potential of the solid phase as compared with the liquid one.

2. *Electr. Engin.* Applied to an inductor used to connect two or more polyphase rectifiers so that they operate in parallel with the current divided between them.

1935 *Gen. Electric Rev.* XXXVIII. 499/1 Polyphase rectifiers usually have an interphase transformer which serves to divide the anodes into two or more groups which operate in parallel. **1952** ERIKSON & BRYANT *Electr. Engin.* xxiv. 431 The presence of the interphase transformer is necessary to allow conduction in two tubes..at any given time. **1970** J. SHEPHERD et al. *Higher Electr. Engin.* (ed. 2) xxv. 804 By the addition of an inter-phase reactor to the simple 6-phase connexion it is possible to obtain rectifier action with the smoothness of normal 6-phase rectification and the utilization factor of 3-phase rectification.

interphasic (ɪntəˈfeɪzɪk), *a.* *Cytology.* [f. prec. + -IC.] Of or pertaining to interphase.

1948 W. ANDREW tr. *E.D.P. de Robertis's Gen. Cytol.* vii. 134 Every cell passes..through two periods: one being interphasic or metabolic and the other being mitotic, or a period of division. **1960** [see INTERKINETIC *a.*].

ˌinterpheˈnomenon. *Physics.* Pl. **-phenomena.** [INTER- 2 b.] Reichenbach's name for a phenomenon that cannot (even in principle) be inferred or demonstrated straightforwardly from observations in accordance with the laws of classical physics. Hence used for any unobserved phenomenon.

1944 H. REICHENBACH *Philos. Found. Quantum Mech.* I. §6. 21 We..shall consider as unobservable all those occurrences which happen between the coincidences, such as the movement of an electron, or of a light ray from its source to a collision with matter. We call this class of occurrences the interphenomena. Occurrences of this kind are introduced by inferential chains of a much more complicated sort; they are constructed in the form of an interpolation within the world of phenomena, and we can therefore consider the distinction between phenomena and interphenomena as the quantum mechanical analogue of the distinction between observed and unobserved things. **1956** —— *Direction of Time* v. §25. 217 The terms 'particle' and 'wave' both belong to the language of interphenomena. They assert something about what happens between the localized phenomena. **1956** E. H. HUTTEN *Lang. Mod. Physics* v. 195 In classical physics..the unobserved phenomena are supposed to follow the same laws as the observed phenomena. The idealised character of measurement in classical theory allows us to speak about these interphenomena. *Ibid.*, The uncertainty principle makes it impossible to introduce interphenomena.

interphone (ˈɪntəfəʊn). orig. *U.S.* [f. INTER- 2 a + PHONE *sb.*[2]] An intercommunication system whereby telephones are used to connect points within a small area, as a building, aeroplane, etc.

1942 *Time* 20 Apr. 25/2 During the same fracas, the pilot inquired over the [Flying] Fortress interphone: 'Are you firing at the enemy?' **1958** J. CANNAN *And be a Villain* v. 118 Pelly was speaking on his interphone. **1961** 'B. WELLS' *Day Earth caught Fire* viii. 119 He was urgently dialling his interphone. **1962** *Punch* 5 Dec. 816/1 You'll need a Home Interphone, to communicate with the party in the other rooms.

interpilaster (ˌɪntəpɪˈlæstə(r)). *Arch.* [INTER- 3] The space between two pilasters.

1823 P. NICHOLSON *Pract. Build.* 513 Unless there should be imposts, or continued cornices, in the inter-pilasters. **1859** W. H. GREGORY *Egypt* II. 361 With a square window in every third interpilaster.

So **interpiˈlastering** *sb.* (in same sense).

1828 ELMES *Metrop. Improv.* 102 To accommodate them [pilasters] and their interpilasterings, to the openings of the windows.

†**interˈplace,** *v.* *Obs.* [INTER- 1 a, b.] *trans.* **a.** To place between or in the midst of; to insert, interpose. **b.** To place between each other or alternately. (Only in *pass.*)

1548 GEST *Pr. Masse* in H. G. Dugdale *Life* App. i. (1840) 132 Here am I demaunded wether I suppose the Epystell and Gospell interplaced in the Masse to be godly..or no. **1609** DANIEL *Civ. Wars* VII. liv, The Powre of Lords (thus inter-plact Betwixt the height of Princes, and the State). **1650** FULLER *Pisgah* III. iv. 323 Besides these gates, Jerusalem was beautified and fortified with many towers proportionably interplaced. **1678** NORRIS *Coll. Misc.* (1699) 127 Solitude and company are to have their turns, and to be interplaced.

Hence **interplaced** *ppl. a.*; **interplacing** *vbl. sb.*

1567 MAPLET *Gr. Forest* 8 b, A Gem..hath his best beautifying in the varietie and interplacing of colours. **1599** MINSHEU *Sp. Dict., Tramontár,* to be hidden by the interplacing or comming betweene of some hill or mountaine. **1603** DANIEL *Panegyr.* Wks. (1717) 339 Strength..to stand Against all th' interplac'd Respondences Of Combinations.

interplait (ɪntəˈplæt), *v.* Also **-plat.** [INTER- 1 b.] *trans.* To plait together; to intertwine, interweave; to intermix in plaits *with.* Hence **interplaited** *ppl. a.*

1822 BEWICK *Mem.* 11 The whins on each side drawn together to grow interplatted at the tops so as to form an arched kind of roof. **1884** *Cassell's Fam. Mag.* Apr. 311/2 On the shoulders a small interplaited chenille cape. **1886** W. J. TUCKER *E. Europe* 224 The long thick plaits of raven-black glossy hair..were prettily inter-plaited with coloured ribbons.

interplanar: see INTER- *pref.* 6.

interplane (ˈɪntəpleɪn), *a.* *Aeronaut.* [f. INTER- 5 + PLANE *sb.*[3]] Situated between or connecting the upper and lower 'planes' or wings of a biplane.

1916 H. BARBER *Aeroplane Speaks* 96 Interplane struts..have to keep the lifting surfaces or 'planes' apart. **1920** *Blackw. Mag.* Nov. 565/1 Great lanky beasts with double interplane engines, heavy bombers of freak aspect. **1969** K. MUNSON *Pioneer Aircraft 1903–14* 152/2 The rigid construction of the wings needed no tie-wires, the sole bracing consisting of two I-type interplane struts on each side.

interplanetary (-ˈplænɪtərɪ), *a.* [INTER- 4 a.] Situated between the planets. Also, existing between planets or pertaining to travel between planets.

a **1691** BOYLE *Hist. Air* (1692) 1 The air..is different from the æther (or vacuum) in the..interplanetary spaces. **1842** GROVE *Corr. Phys. Forces* (1874) 124 Unless the matter or ether in the interplanetary spaces be infinitely elastic. **1880** HAUGHTON *Phys. Geog.* i. 5 Meteoric stones, which enter the earth's atmosphere from the interplanetary spaces. **1897** *Pearson's Mag.* July 116/1 Cylinder followed cylinder in its interplanetary flight. **1901** *Daily News* 7 Jan. 5/1 Dreams of inter-planetary communication. **1931** D. LASSER *Conquest of Space* 13 Ignorance and prejudice..surround the 'interplanetary rocket' question. **1936** 'J. BEYNON' *Planet Plane* iii. 28 Mr. Curtance is going to try to win the Keuntz Prize for the inter-planetary flight. **1943** C. S. LEWIS *Perelandra* vi. 91 In obscure works of 'scientifiction', in little Interplanetary Societies and Rocketry Clubs. **1950** *Jrnl. Brit. Interplanetary Soc.* IX. 300 Should be able to take the Interplanetary Age, when it comes, without hysteria. **1957** *Economist* 2 Nov. 377 The artificial satellite circling the earth was to be a proud reminder of the distance covered along the road from the wooden plough to the inter-planetary rocket. **1960** *Analog Science Fact/Fiction* Oct. 30/1 Maybe they were bravely defending their own planet by hunting down an interplanetary raider. **1962** [see COSMIC *a.* 3 b].

interplant (ɪntəˈplɑːnt, -æ-), *v.* [f. INTER- 1 a + PLANT *v.*] *trans.* To plant (land) so that it is occupied by a mixture of plant species; to plant (a specified crop) *with* another crop. Hence **interˈplanting** *vbl. sb.* So **ˈinterplant** *sb.*, a plant growing among others of different species.

1927 *Daily Tel.* 11 May 3/4 Included in the 1,442 acres of rubber were 98 acres which were interplanted with coffee. **1942** *R.A.F. Jrnl.* 30 May 27 Fill every inch of space by inter-planting one crop with another. This principle has already been illustrated by interplanting early potatoes with winter greens. **1950** *N.Z. Jrnl. Agric.* LXXX. 539/1 Other interplants are chiefly peaches. **1966** WEBSTER & WILSON *Agric. in Tropics* x. 230 Interplanting with suitable crops, in a manner which maintains fertility and avoids competition, may be profitable. **1969** G. WRIGLEY *Tropical Agric.* (ed. 2) ii. 119 On the fertile soils of East Africa bananas are interplanted with coffee. **1971** *Countryman* LXXVI. iv. 109 Interplant them with dark purple tulips, or white splashed with purple, to give spring interest.

interplat, variant of INTERPLAIT.

interplay (ˈɪntəpleɪ), *sb.* [INTER- 2 a.] Reciprocal play, free interaction; mutual operation of two things or agents in influencing each other's action or character.

1862 DANA *Man. Geol.* 45 The two [series of winds] pass into one another in mutual interplay. **1870** LOWELL *Among my Bks.* Ser. I. (1873) 343 That interplay of plot and character which makes Shakespeare more real..than other dramatists. **1885** CLODD *Myths & Dr.* II. xii. 228 Explanation of the operations of nature was impossible while man had no..knowledge of the interplay of its several parts.

So **interplay** *v. intr.*, to exert mutual influence.

1890 *Amer. Missionary* (N.Y.) Dec. 403 Let these two institutions advance together, play and interplay upon and within each other.

†**interplea.** *Obs. rare.* [INTER- 2 b.] A dilatory plea.

1631 BRATHWAIT *Whimzies, Undersheriffe* 99 No interplea nor demurre will serve; he must timely prevent the occasion ..and make the undersheriffe his friend. *a* **1641** BP. MOUNTAGU *Acts & Mon.* (1642) 279 Without admitting interplea of consideration.

interplead (ɪntəˈpliːd), *v.* Also 6–7 **enterple(a)de.** [ad. AF. *enterpleder* = F. *(s')entreplaider*: see INTER- 1 a, b and PLEAD *v.*]

1. *intr.* In *Law*: To litigate with each other in order to determine some point in dispute in which a third party is concerned.

[**1357** *Pat. Roll 30 Edw. III, Hilary* (1585) 5 b, A certein iour en propre persone denterpleder pur le garde de corps.] **1567** STAUNFORD *Expos. Kings Prerog.* 57 Forasmuche as the kinge is brought in doubt to whiche of them his hyghnesse maye make liuerie, they therefore muste firste enterplede, and when by enterpleder the priuitie of the bloode is tried beetweene them, then his highnesse oughte to make the liuerye to him that is tryed to bee the nexte heire. **1670** BLOUNT *Law Dict., Enterplede,* signifies to discuss or try a Point incidentally falling out, before the Principal Cause can be determined. **1768** [see INTERPLEADER[1]]. **1848** WHARTON *Law Lex.* s.v. *Interpleader,* The ordinary decree is, that the defendants do interplead, and the plaintiff then withdraws from the suit.

†**2.** *trans.* To plead or allege in excuse or defence; to raise as a plea. *Obs.*

1594 [see INTERPLEADING below]. **1716** M. DAVIES *Athen. Brit.* II. 245 So that for bewilder'd Arians to interplead their near related Sabellian Labyrinths, is but the despairing shifts of wilful obstinacy and reprobate ignorance.

Hence **interˈpleading** *vbl. sb.*

1594 NASHE *Unfort. Trav.* 28 No interpleading was there of opposite occasions, but backe I must returne. **1613** SIR H. FINCH *Law* (1636) 335 In euery enterpleading, an office must bee found for both. And if one be found heire of full age, and after another within age, the enterpleading shall not stay till the full age of the second, because the other was found heire first. **1837** LD. COTTENHAM in Mylne & Craig *Rep.* II. 21 That rule, if in favour of the interpleading, would not be decisive. *Ibid.* 22 Sir John Leach..refused an injunction in an interpleading suit by a broker.

interpleader[1] (ɪntəˈpliːdə(r)). *Law.* Also 6–7 **enterple(a)der,** 7 **interpleder.** [a. AF. *enterpleder* (see prec.), inf. used subst.] A suit pleaded between two parties to determine a matter of claim or right, on which the action of a third party depends, esp. to determine to which of them livery or payment ought to be made.

[**1516** FITZHERB. *La Grande Abridgem.* 226 b, Le title de enterpleder.] **1567** [see INTERPLEAD 1]. **1607** COWELL *Interpr., Enterpleder.* **1668** HALE *Pref. Rolle's Abridgm.* 5 Garnishment and Interpleder were large titles at Common Law, but now much out of use. **1768** BLACKSTONE *Comm.* III. xxvii. 448 There is likewise a bill of interpleader; where a person who owes a debt or rent to one of the parties in suit, but, till the determination of it, he knows not to which, desires that they may interplead, that he may be safe in the payment. **1831** *Act 1 & 2 Will. IV,* c. 58 A suit in equity..usually called a bill of interpleader.

b. *attrib,* as *interpleader act, case, issue, order.*

1848 WHARTON *Law Lex.* s.v., *Interpleader act,* 1 & 2 Wm. IV., c. 58. **1883** *Ibid.* (ed. 7) 428/1 Appeals in interpleader cases. **1857** KERR *Blackstone* III. xx. 322 He may apply to the court or a judge for relief under the statute 1 & 2 Will. IV. c. 58, called the Interpleader Act. *Ibid.* xxvi. 454 If both parties appear, an interpleader issue, to try the right of property, is directed.

interpleader[2]. [f. INTERPLEAD *v.* + -ER[1].] One who interpleads.

1846 in WORCESTER; and in later Dicts. [But it is doubtful whether the word is more than a dictionary assumption due to a misunderstanding of prec.]

interpledge: see INTER- *pref.* 1 b.

interpleural (ɪntəˈplʊərəl), *a.* *Anat.* [f. INTER- 4 a + Gr. πλευρά ribs, side: see PLEURAL.] Situated between the pleuræ of the right and left lungs; as *interpleural space.*

1879 HOLDEN *Anat.* (ed. 4) 122 A space is left between them [the right and left pleuræ] extending from the sternum to the spine..This interval is called by anatomists the interpleural space.

†**interpley, -ply,** *v.* *Sc. Obs. rare.* [f. INTER- 1 + *pley,* PLEA *v.*] *intr.* = INTERPLEAD 1.

c **1470** HENRYSON *Fables* (*Dog, Scheip & Wolf*) 45 (Bann. MS.) The law sayis it is rycht perelouss Till interply [*MS. Harl.* Till enter in pley] befoir a juge suspect.

interplical: see INTER- *pref.* 6.

interplicate (ɪn'tɜːplɪkeɪt), *v. rare.* [f. ppl. stem of L. *interplicāre* (Statius), f. *inter* between + *plicāre* to fold; cf. *implicate*, etc.] *trans.* To fold between or together; to interfold. Hence **in'terplicated** *ppl. a.*; also † **interpli'cation**.

1623 COCKERAM, *Interplicate*, to fold vp betweene. **1658** PHILLIPS, *Interplication*, a folding between. **1884** H. D. TRAILL *New Lucian* 192 Coil by coil he will unroll the interplicated mass.

interplight: see INTER- *pref.* 1 b.

interpluvial (ɪntə'pluːvɪəl), *a.* and *sb.* [f. INTER- 4 b + PLUVIAL *a.*] **A.** *adj.* Designating any of the periods of generally drier conditions in equatorial latitudes during the geological past (esp. the Pleistocene) which alternated with pluvial periods in a cycle which may be correlated with or related to the better-known cycle of interglacial and glacial periods in more polar latitudes. **B.** *sb.* An interpluvial period.

1907 *Bull. Geol. Soc. Amer.* XVIII. 362 The time when a thesis occurs is a thesial epoch, which may be described as interglacial, or interfluvial, and so forth, when the agents which modify the earth's surface are considered, or as intervegetal, interpluvial, and so forth, when other phases are considered. **1931** L. S. B. LEAKEY *Stone Age Cultures Kenya Colony* ii. 13 During the dry inter-pluvial periods.. the lakes in the Rift Valley dried up. *Ibid.*, One would expect that the prehistoric tribes moved to the high land.. during the inter-pluvials. **1940** *Geogr. Jrnl.* XCVI. 333 There have been very long wet and dry phases, the so-called pluvials and interpluvials. **1957** G. E. HUTCHINSON *Treat. Limnol.* I. i. 133 Such deposits are supposed to be the result of water-borne material, washed toward the pan in pluvial times, becoming cemented during the following interpluvial. *Ibid.*, Interpluvial periods of deflation. **1963** D. W. & E. E. HUMPHRIES tr. *Termier's Erosion & Sedimentation* i. 9 In Equatorial Zones it is now suspected that the pluvial phases were hot times and interpluvial (dry) phases were equivalent to the glacial epochs. **1973** *Nature* 16 Mar. 187/1 It seems.. that the tectonic movement which caused the tilting of the Ubeidiya Formation occurred some time within the Mindel-Riss Interpluvial and is younger than 640,000 yr.

† **'interpoint**, *sb. Obs. rare*⁻¹. [INTER- 2 b.] A point or 'stop' inserted between words.

1684 N. S. *Crit. Enq. Edit. Bible* xv. 147 The novelty of points, errors, interpoints, and the addition of Vowels and Accents [in Hebrew Bibles].

interpoint (ɪntə'pɔɪnt), *v.* [INTER- 1 a.] **a.** *trans.* To put a point or points between (words); to interpunctuate; to furnish (writing, etc.) with points between the words, to punctuate. Also *fig.* **b.** *intr.* or *absol.* To insert a point or points.

1595 DANIEL *Civ. Wars* II. lxxxvii, Her hart commands her words should pass out first, And then her sighes should interpoint her words. **1635** HEYWOOD *Hierarch.* VII. 442 Their words were By interpointing so disposed to beare A Double sence. **1660** H. MORE *Myst. Godl.* I. x. 29 There is no evasion from this interpretation the Syriack.. interpointing betwixt (*I say unto thee*) and (*To day*). **1897** SIR H. MAXWELL (*title*) Sixty Years a Queen. Embossed in Interpointed Braille [Type for the Blind].

Interpol ('ɪntəpɒl). [abbrev. of *Inter*national *pol*ice.] The International Criminal Police Commission (founded in 1923), with headquarters in Paris.

1952 SÖDERMAN & O'CONNELL *Mod. Criminal Investigation* (ed. 4) ii. 24 All national bureaus of the ICPC have adopted the telegraphic address of 'Interpol'. **1955** *Times* 7 July 7/5 They have issued the description of a man of about 45.. whom they would like to interview. This has been circulated through the international police organization, Interpol, since it is thought likely that the man may have gone abroad. **1957** *Times* 24 June 10/2 Wire-tapping was one of the subjects discussed at the Lisbon meeting of the International Criminal Police Commission (Interpol) which ended yesterday. **1958** *Daily Mail* 31 July 1/5 British police last night sent a call to Interpol, the international police organisation, for help in solving the riddle of a British airman whose father believes he is still alive 15 years after he was shot down over Germany. **1964** J. CRAMER *World's Police* VI. 442 The word 'Interpol' was originally the telegraphic address of the I.C.P.O. but it became so well known that it is now part of the official title of the organization.

interpolability (ɪn,tɜːpələ'bɪlɪtɪ). [f. INTERPOLAB(LE *a.* + -ILITY.] The state or quality of being interpolable.

1938 *Nature* 12 Nov. 852/2 Attention is paid everywhere to interpolability, and the volume ends with a number of tables of interpolation coefficients. **1971** T. F. MITCHELL in *Archivum Linguisticum* II. 46 Other points of contrast with the other examples include the interpolability before *off* of the 'adverbial' forms *straight* or *right*, the substitutability of *away* for *off*, [etc.].

interpolable (ɪn'tɜːpələb(ə)l), *a.* [f. L. *interpolāre* to INTERPOLATE + -ABLE.] Capable of being interpolated; suitable for interpolation.

a **1871** DE MORGAN cited in OGILVIE (Annandale) Suppl.

interpolant (ɪn'tɜːpələnt). *Math.* [f. L. *interpolant-em*, pres. pple. of *interpolāre* (see INTERPOLATE *v.*), or INTERPOL(ATE *v.* + -ANT¹.]

A value or expression (given or calculated) used in finding some other value by interpolation.

1920 *Tracts for Computers* II. 17 Forward difference formulae, central difference formulae and Lagrangian formulae, when the interpolants are spaced equally apart are really different aspects of the same process, i.e. running a parabola of the (*n*-1)th order through *n* points. **1946** *Phil. Mag.* XXXVII. 260 A function value interpolated in this way may indeed be more accurate than any of the eight values used to obtain it. For in a perfect table the rounding-off errors of the eight interpolants have uniform probability distributions between − 0·5 and 0·5 in units of the last decimal, and it may be shown that the probability of the resulting error of the interpolate is very nearly normally distributed with standard deviation 0·12. **1965** A. RALSTON *First Course Numerical Analysis* iii. 57 An important advantage of finite-difference interpolation formulas.. would seem to be the property.. that enables a term to be added to them merely by adding one tabular point and computing an additional row of differences... This enables us to generate a sequence of interpolants each involving one more tabular point than the previous one.

interpolar (-'pəʊlə(r)), *a.* (*sb.*) [INTER- 4 a.]

Situated between the poles (of a galvanic battery, etc.).

1870 R. M. FERGUSON *Electr.* 115 If interruptions be made in the interpolar wire. **1896** *Allbutt's Syst. Med.* I. 351 Some of the results.. may be due to interpolar electrolytic actions in the tissues traversed by the current. **1898** P. MANSON *Trop. Dis.* viii. 147 The extremities [of the plague bacillus] taking on a deeper colour than the interpolar part.

b. as *sb.* An interpolar wire.

1882 MINCHIN *Unipl. Kinemat.* 222 In the case of linear flow in an interpolar between two points.

interpolary (ɪn'tɜːpələrɪ), *a. Math.* [f. INTERPOL-ATE *v.* + -ARY¹.] Pertaining to interpolation.

1890 in *Cent. Dict.*

† **in'terpolate**, *ppl. a. Obs.* [ad. L. *interpolāt-us*, pa. pple. of *interpolāre*: see next.] Interpolated. **a.** Interrupted, intermittent. **b.** Added surreptitiously; inserted.

With earliest quots. cf. INTERPOLATE *v.* 5 and obs. F. *fièvre interpolée* (Godef.).

1547 BOORDE *Brev. Health* cxxxvii. 50 b, A symple interpolate fever doth infest a man ones a day. A doble interpolate fever doth infest a man twyse a day. **1653** A. WILSON *Jas. I*, 125 In the interpolate Fits of Agues. **1651** BAXTER *Inf. Bapt.* 155 Though the place be most express for Infant Baptism, and the Book ancient, yet it is either spurious or interpolate. **1669** *Addr. hopeful yng. Gentry Eng.* 23 On publick [affairs], their interpolate jealousies.. every where bring in growing discontents and murmurings.

interpolate (ɪn'tɜːpəleɪt), *v.* [f. ppl. stem of L. *interpolāre* to furbish up, to alter, f. *inter* (INTER- 1 a) + *-polāre*, related to *polīre* to POLISH.]

† **1.** *trans.* To polish or furbish up; to put a fresh gloss on. *Obs. rare.*

1623 COCKERAM, *Interpolate*, to polish. **1706** PHILLIPS (ed. Kersey), *To Interpolate* (properly to bring old things to a new form), to new vamp,.. to alter or falsify an Original.

2. a. To alter or enlarge (a book or writing) by insertion of new matter; *esp.* to tamper with by making insertions which create false impressions as to the date or character of the work in question.

1612 SELDEN *Illustr. Drayton's Poly-olb.* xi. (R.), You admit Cæsar's copy to be therein not interpolated. *a* **1661** FULLER *Worthies, Cornwall* I. (1662) 211 A Manuscript of Sir Ralph Hoptons.. interpolated with his own hand. **1709** *Phil. Trans.* XXVI. 398 They had no more Allowance to alter them than they had to alter and interpolate the Text of the Author himself. **1846** WRIGHT *Ess. Mid. Ages* I. viii. 258 The poem of Beowulf.. has been much interpolated by Christian transcribers. **1873** CLARK & WRIGHT *Macbeth* (Clar. Press ed.) p. xii, We are inclined to think that the play was interpolated after Shakspeare's death.

b. *transf.* To adulterate, temper, or modify, by new or foreign additions.

1834 *Blackw. Mag.* XXXVI. 69 It was judged sufficient to interpolate, as it were, the hostile people by colonizations from Rome. **1862** LYTTON *Str. Story* I. 212 The strange notions with which he was apt to interpolate the doctrines of practical philosophy.

3. a. To introduce (words or passages) into a pre-existing writing; *esp.* to insert (spurious matter) in a genuine work without note or warning.

1640 BP. HALL *Episc.* II. xi. 157 Words which no Vedelius can carp at as interpolated. **1699** BENTLEY *Phal.* Introd. 22 The same Person has interpolated four Passages more. **1791** BOSWELL *Johnson* an. 1751, In these he [Lauder] interpolated some fragments of Hog's Latin translation of that poem. **1876** BANCROFT *Hist. U.S.* II. xxx. 243 It interpolated into the statute-book the exclusion of papists from the established equality.

b. *transf.* To insert or introduce (something additional or different) between other things, or in a series; to intercalate.

1802–12 BENTHAM *Ration. Evid.* Wks. 1843 VI. 237 You may.. oblige me to interpolate a number.. of intermediate causes. **1837** WHEWELL *Hist. Induct. Sc.* (1857) I. 101 By interpolating a month of 30 days. **1839** MURCHISON *Silur. Syst.* I. iii. 28 A great thickness of sandstone is there interpolated between the magnesian limestone and the carboniferous strata. **1843** MILL *Logic* III. xii. §3 Future experience may.. interpolate another link.

c. (With the words spoken as object.) To interpose orally.

1881 MRS. J. H. RIDDELL *Senior Partner* I. vii. 151 'I have not a word to say against Effie,' began.. Robert... 'If ye had, ye'd best not say it before me,' interpolated his father. **1908** *Smart Set* June 142/1 'I suppose I may claim some eminence as physicians go.' 'Top notch of the whole bunch, dad!' interpolated Keene. **1922** JOYCE *Ulysses* 614 What year would that be about? Mr Bloom interpolated.

4. *intr.* or *absol.* To make insertions or interpolations.

1720 GAY *Poems* (1745) II. 107 Criticks in Classicks oft interpolate, But ev'ry word of thine is fix'd as fate. **1768–74** TUCKER *Lt. Nat.* (1834) II. 329 Have not other writers elsewhere interpolated, invented, and forged? **1845** GRAVES *Rom. Law* in *Encycl. Metrop.* II. 773/1 They were to select all that was best, with permission to alter and interpolate.

† **5.** *trans.* To interrupt by an interval. (Only in *pass.*: cf. INTERPOLATE *ppl. a.*) *Obs. rare.*

a **1677** HALE *Prim. Orig. Man.* I. iii. 79 This motion even of the Heavenly Bodies themselves seems to be partly continued and unintermitted.. partly interpolated and interrupted. *Ibid.* 96 The alluvion of the Sea upon those Rocks might not be eternally continued, but interpolated.

6. *Math.* To insert an intermediate term or terms in a series (see INTERPOLATION 3 b). With the series, or now usually the term, as *obj.* Also *absol.* or *intr.*, to use or perform interpolation. Also *fig.*

1796 HUTTON *Math. Dict.* I. 640/2 A general theorem for Interpolating any term is as follows. **1882** OGILVIE s.v., To interpolate a number or a table of numbers. **1888** *Encycl. Brit.* XXIX. 8/2 The reciprocal of a number of five figures is therefore taken out at once, and two more figures may be interpolated for as in logarithms. **1905** [see EXTRAPOLATE *v.* 2 b]. **1928** *Monthly Notices R. Astron. Soc.* LXXXVIII. 506 The Lagrangian method of interpolating to fixed subdivisions of an interval. **1968** FOX & MAYERS *Computing Methods for Scientists & Engineers* i. 11 Interpolating for $y(2{\cdot}5)$, from given values at $x = 2$ and $x = 3$, the formula gives $y(2{\cdot}5) = 22y(3)/35 + 18y(2)/35$.

Hence **in'terpolated** *ppl. a.*; **in'terpolating** *vbl. sb.* and *ppl. a.*

a **1677** HALE *Prim. Orig. Man.* I. v. 113 That Individual hath necessarily a concomitant succession of interpolated Motions. **1695–6** T. SMITH in *Lett. Lit. Men* (Camden) 239, I.. found it to bee the interpolated copy of Symeon Metaphrastes. **1796** HUTTON *Math. Dict.* I. 641/1 This series for the interpolated term will break off, and terminate. **1838** *Penny Cycl.* XII. 508/1 Generally speaking.. the interpolated values are as correct as the tabular ones. **1851–9** WHEWELL in *Man. Sci. Enq.* 67 This way of finding the exact time of high water (or low water) from observations made every five or every ten minutes.. is called 'interpolating'. **1875** OUSELEY *Mus. Form* 109 Bar 24 is an interpolated bar to prolong the cadence.

interpolate (ɪn'tɜːpələt), *sb. Math.* [f. L. *interpolāt-us*, pa. pple. of *interpolāre* (see INTERPOLATE *v.*): see -ATE¹ b.] A value arrived at by interpolation.

1920 *Tracts for Computers* II. 17 As a rule the interpolation formulae work, but once in a while bitter experience forces us up against cases in which increasing the number of differences.. is quite ineffectual as a method of obtaining accurate interpolates. **1932** *Proc. Edin. Math. Soc.* III. 56 For example, a linear interpolate $u_{0.683}$ can be computed from u_0 and u_1 as $u_{0.683} = 0{\cdot}317u_0 + 0{\cdot}683u_1$. **1946** [see INTERPOLANT]. **1956** F. B. HILDEBRAND *Introd. Numerical Analysis* ii. 35 If more reliable interpolates are desired, it is clearly necessary to make use of more information than that consisting merely of tabulated values (ordinates) of a function, corresponding to two successive abscissas.

interpolation (ɪn,tɜːpəʊ'leɪʃən). [a. F. *interpolation* (Cotgr., 1611), or ad. L. *interpolātiōn-em*, n. of action f. *interpolāre*: see INTERPOLATE *v.* and -ATION.]

† **1.** The action of furbishing or polishing up.

1623 COCKERAM, *Interpolation*, a polishing. **1656** BLOUNT *Glossogr.*, *Interpolation*, a new dressing or polishing a thing, a scowring or furbishing. **1678** CUDWORTH *Intell. Syst.* I. iv. §16. 281 Some may still suspect, all this to have been.. but a Refinement and Interpolation of Paganism.

2. a. The action of interpolating a writing, or a word, etc. therein (cf. senses 2 and 3 of the vb.); the condition or fact of being interpolated.

1612 SELDEN *Illustr. Drayton's Poly-olb.* iv. 73 Our Chronologies, which are by transcribing, interpolation, misprinting.. now and then strangely disordered. **1720** WATERLAND *Eight Serm.* 64 Any pretence of Forgery or Interpolation does but expose the Man that makes it. **1838** SIR W. HAMILTON *Logic* xxxiv. (1866) II. 194 Rules, by which the authenticity or spuriousness, the integrity or interpolation, of a writing is to be judged. **1851** HUSSEY *Papal Power* iii. 149 This end was carried out by interpolations and falsification of ecclesiastical documents.

b. With *pl.* An interpolated word or passage.

1675–6 EVELYN *Let. to Aubrey* Feb. (R.), I beseech you to accept or pardon these trifling interpolations, which I have presumed to send you. **1711** STEELE *Spect.* No. 78 ¶6 That the word Oxford was an Interpolation of some Oxonian instead of Cambridge. **1849** W. IRVING *Mahomet* viii. (1853) 42 Both were pronounced errors and interpolations of the expounders. **1867** FREEMAN *Norm. Conq.* I. v. 306 *note*, That the name Aulaf is an interpolation in the text.

3. a. The action of introducing or inserting among other things or between the members of any series. Also with *an* and *pl.*: An insertion.

1849 MURCHISON *Siluria* viii. 171 The interpolation of fossiliferous.. rocks. **1860** PHILLIPS *Life* 207 The Permian series contains some Mesozoic interpolations. **1864** BOWEN *Logic* ix. 295 The vice [reasoning in a circle] is usually concealed by the interpolation of intermediate propositions. **1875** OUSELEY *Mus. Form* ii. 17 An expansion of a regular four-bar phrase of two strains, formed by the interpolation of an additional strain.

b. *Math.* The process of inserting in a series an intermediate number or quantity ascertained by

calculation from those already known. Freq. *attrib.*

1763 EMERSON *Meth. Increments* iv, The Differential Method of Mr. Sterling, which he applies to the summation and interpolation of series. **1816** PLAYFAIR *Nat. Phil.* II. 85 The manner of finding an equation between the time and any quantity determined by observations, made at given intervals of time, is called the Method of Interpolation. *Ibid.* 220 The most useful interpolations are, when the time is one of the unknown quantities [etc.]. **1816** tr. *Lacroix's Diff. & Int. Calculus* 551 One of the principal uses of the Calculus of Differences consists in the Interpolation of Series. **1872** [see EXTRAPOLATION]. **1888** *Encycl. Brit.* XXIII. 13/1 All tables of proportional parts may be regarded as interpolation tables. **1928** *Monthly Notices R. Astron. Soc.* LXXXVIII. 511 The interpolation formula known as Bessel's but really discovered by Newton. **1968** FOX & MAYERS *Computing Methods for Scientists & Engineers* viii. 147 Moreover the 'interpolation coefficients'.. are available in tabular form,.. and our interpolation process is reasonably straightforward. **1970** O. DOPPING *Computers & Data Processing* xvi. 256 The computer calculates a first approximation to the desired address by interpolation between the known minimum and maximum values of the argument.

†**4.** Interposition of time; interval. *Obs.* (So F. *interpolation* in Godef.)

1615 CROOKE *Body of Man* 55 The mutation or change of bloud into a bone, cannot be accomplished but by long interpolation and many meane alterations.

in'terpolative, *a. rare.* [f. as INTERPOLATE *v.* + -IVE.] Having the effect of interpolation.

1817 BENTHAM *Swear not at all* Wks. 1843 V. 201 Liberty of making amendments:—amendments omissive, interpolative, substitutive.

Hence **in'terpolatively** *adv.*, in the way of interpolation.

1836 G. S. FABER *Reply Husenbeth* 44 *note*, This..he effects by interpolatively forcing him to say what, in truth, he never did say.

interpolator (ɪn'tɜːpəleɪtə(r)). [a. L. *interpolātor*, agent-n. f. *interpolāre* to INTERPOLATE. Cf. F. *interpolateur* (1671 in Godef.).] **1.** One who interpolates.

1659 PEARSON *Creed* (1839) 243 What the interpolator of Gregory Nyssen's Homily produceth, he confesseth taken from apocryphal writings. **1699** BENTLEY *Phal.* 463 The Interpolator borrow'd it, and clapt it in here. **1807** G. CHALMERS *Caledonia* I. II. iii. 259 It was denominated by Nennius, or his interpolator, *Provincia Lodonesie.* **1868** FREEMAN *Norm. Conq.* II. App. 528 An interpolator would surely have taken care to insert the more famous stories.

2. A mechanical contrivance for securing correct retransmission from a submarine cable of any consecutive letter-elements having the same sign.

1902 *Encycl. Brit.* XXXIII. 226/2 The special form of curb sender mentioned, termed the 'Interpolator'. **1958** *Economist* 1 Nov. 425 (Advt.), The Interpolator is the essential part of the mechanism used to re-form signals automatically at the end of their journey through a long cable, before they are sent into another.

3. *Engin.* A device or apparatus which, when fed with a set of datum points defining a curve, produces a continuous output for guiding a tool over the curve.

1953 *IRE Trans. Industr. Electronics* I. 29 The interpolator output provides a continuous angular rotation whose instantaneous angular position represents the radius vector of the machine tool's cutter locus. **1961** S. FIFER *Analogue Computation* IV. xxx. 1279 The function of the analogue interpolator is to compute a continuous curve from the discrete set of digital information and to position a mechanical lathe accordingly. **1973** tr. *W. Simon's Numerical Control Machine Tools* ii. 43 The cost of the control equipment located on the machine tool itself is considerably reduced, since the machine no longer has its own interpolator.

interpolatory (ɪn'tɜːpələtərɪ), *a.* [f. INTERPOLAT(E *v.* + -ORY².] Serving to interpolate.

1946 *Mind* LV. 201, I would suggest approaching the matter from the Quantum Analogue angle and boldly taking the line that the latter were Interpolatory expressions. **1965** W. S. ALLEN *Vox Latina* iii. 72 The interpolatory nature of the '*gnus*' passage.

†**interpole,** *v. Obs. rare*⁻¹. [ad. L. *interpol-āre*: see INTERPOLATE. Cf. F. *interpoler* (1740 in *Dict. Acad.*).] = INTERPOLATE *v.* 2 c.

1677 COLLINS in Rigaud *Corr. Sci. Men* (1841) II. 457 How to add or interpole progressions of squares, cubes, or of any other ranks of numbers.

interpole ('ɪntəpəʊl). *Electr.* [INTER- 2 b.] In an electric motor or generator having a commutator, each of a set of auxiliary poles situated between the main poles and connected in series with the armature, the function of which is to facilitate commutation of the current by cancelling the induced e.m.f. in the coils that tends to hinder it.

1907 H. H. NORRIS *Introd. Study Electr. Engin.* x. 280 The function of the commutating or 'inter' pole is to produce a reversing field for the coil undergoing commutation. **1927** H. H. BROUGHTON *Electr. Winders* iii. 82 Sparkless commutation can be obtained by means of interpoles alone. **1964** R. F. FICCHI *Electrical Interference* vii. 108 If interpoles or compensating windings are introduced in the design, the commutation process will usually become more efficient and interference will be minimized.

†**inter'polish,** *v. Obs. rare.* Also 7 enter-. [INTER- 1 a.] *trans.* To polish here and there or at intervals.

1609 BIBLE (Douay) *Exod.* xxv. 25 Thou shalt make..a crowne enterpolished [Vulg. *interrasilis*], foure fingers high. **1641** MILTON *Ch. Govt.* I. v, Yet all this will not fadge, though it be cunningly interpolisht by some second hand with crooks and emendations.

interpolitical (-pəʊ'lɪtɪkəl), *a.* [f. INTER- 4 c + Gr. πόλις city, state, after POLITICAL.] Pertaining to the relations between (Greek) cities or states.

1846 GROTE *Greece* II. ii. II. 341 We are compelled to use a word such as interpolitical to describe the transactions between separate Greek cities. **1876** G. W. COX *Gen. Hist. Greece* III. i. 271 The Athenians were..fully justified by Hellenic interpolitical law in excluding the Megarians from their ports.

inter'polity. *rare*⁻¹. [f. INTER- 2 a + Gr. πολιτεία citizenship, POLITY.] Mutual citizenship.

1849 LYTTON *Caxtons* II. XIII. lxvi, You, whose whole theory is an absolute sermon upon emigration, and the transplanting and interpolity of our species.

interpolymer ('ɪntə,pɒlɪmə(r)). *Chem.* [INTER- 2 b.] (See quot. 1966.)

1936 *Chem. Abstr.* XXX. 6478/2 Mixts. of polymers or interpolymers of these compds. **1950** *Thorpe's Dict. Appl. Chem.* (ed. 4) X. 87/2 The product is not a mixture of polymers A-A-A-A-A-A-... with B-B-B-B-B-B-..., but an interpolymer, e.g. A-B-A-A-A-B-A-A-..., the order in which the units are arranged not being readily determinable. **1955** *Jrnl. Polymer Sci.* XVIII. 129 A general method of producing graft and block interpolymers between elastomers is therefore indicated. **1966** M. L. MILLER *Struct. Polymers* ix. 426 Polymers made up of molecules containing two or more types of monomer units are called copolymers or interpolymers... The terms 'copolymer' and 'interpolymer' are essentially equivalent but the term 'interpolymer' is more restrictive because it implies an intimate distribution of monomer units in the molecule while the term 'copolymer' has no such implication.

Hence **inter'polymerize** *v. trans.* and *intr.*, to combine so as to form an interpolymer; **,interpolymeri'zation.**

1950 *Thorpe's Dict. Appl. Chem.* (ed. 4) X. 87/2 Vinyl acetate is interpolymerised with vinyl chloride to give plastics which are lower softening and more soluble than polyvinyl chloride. *Ibid.* 88/1 There are monomers..which do not give high molecular-weight polymers by themselves but may readily interpolymerise with a second component. .. Interpolymerisation may even be effected in cases where neither component is separately polymerisable.

interpone (ɪntə'pəʊn), *v.* Also 6 enter-, entre-. [ad. L. *interpōnĕre* to place between, etc.; *refl.* to interfere, f. *inter* between + *pōnĕre* to place, put.] *trans.* and *refl.* = INTERPOSE *v. Obs.* exc. in ***interpone one's authority*** (in *Sc. Law*).

1523 WOLSEY in Fiddes *Wolsey* Collect. (1726) 68 Offering unto me to interpone their authorities..therein to the utter-most. **1528** GARDINER in Pocock *Rec. Ref.* I. lii. 137 Interponing himself as *mediatorem pacis.* **1533** BELLENDEN *Livy* I. (1822) 34 He colleckit all thir odd dayis togidder, and interponit thame with monethis intercalaris ilk XXIV yeris anis. **1599** THYNNE *Animadv.* (1875) 53 Yf I shall interpone my opynione, I wolde more willingly.. receve Surrey. **1678** CUDWORTH *Intell. Syst.* I. iv. §36. 624 Porphyrius interponed it [his Psyche], betwixt the Father and the Son, as a middle between both. **1752** J. LOUTHIAN *Form of Process* (ed. 2) 273 When Application is made to the Sheriff, to interpone his Authority to a Baron's Decreet. **1868** *Act 31 & 32 Vict.* c. 101 §107 The Lord Ordinary is hereby authorized..to interpone his authority to such minute and acceptance. **1880** MUIRHEAD *Ulpian* xi. §25.

†**inter'ponent.** *Obs. rare.* [ad. L. *interpōnent-em*, pr. pple. of *interpōnĕre*: see prec.] One who or that which interposes.

1592 *Nobody & Someb.* in Simpson *Sch. Shaks.* (1878) I. 279 Murall interponents twixt the world And their proceedings. **1638** HEYWOOD *Lucrece* I. ii. Wks. 1874 V. 171 Lop downe these interponents that withstand The passage to our throne.

†**interponi'bility.** *Obs. rare*⁻¹. [f. **interponible* (f. INTERPONE): see -ITY.] Capacity of being interposed.

1734 tr. *Barrow's Math. Lect.* x. 176 Space is nothing else but the mere Power, Capacity, Ponibility, or (begging pardon for the Expressions) Interponibility of Magnitude.

interpopulational: see INTER- *pref.* 6.

interportal: see INTER- *pref.* 6.

interposal (ɪntə'pəʊzəl). [f. next + -AL¹.]

1. The act of placing or causing to come between; = INTERPOSITION 1.

1625 JACKSON *Creed* V. iv. §4 Affluence or abundance of things desired without interposall of indigence. **1651** *Fuller's Abel Rediv., Bradford* 182 He was..without any interposall of time, chosen Fellow of Pembrooke Hall. **1691-8** NORRIS *Pract. Disc.* (1711) III. 167 Nothing that may by its interposal hinder that immediate contact. **1893** F. HALL in *Nation* (N.Y.) LVI. 274/2 The interposal of a word or words between *to* and the infinitive.

2. Intervention, interference; = INTERPOSITION 2.

1607 *Hist. Sir J. Hawkwood* iv. 7 To prevent the Interposal of any envious Person. **1742** RICHARDSON *Pamela* IV. 306 My Friends indiscreet Interposals incensed me. **1845** *N. Brit. Rev.* III. 321 Their well-timed interposal in favour of the ejected families.

interpose (ɪntə'pəʊz), *v.* Also 7 enter-. [a. F. *interposer* (14th c. in Godef.), f. L. *inter* between + F. *poser* to place (see POSE); substituted for L. *interpōnĕre* (see INTERPONE) by form-association with inflexions and derivatives of the latter, as *interposition*, etc.; cf. *compose*, *depose*, *dispose*. Cf. also F. *entreposer* (12-13th c. in Hatz.-Darm.), in OF. to place alternately or intermixedly.]

I. 1. a. *trans.* To place between (in space or time); to put or set between or in an intermediate position; to cause to intervene. Often with implication of obstruction or delay; cf. 3.

1599 MINSHEU *Sp. Dict.*, *Interpuesto*, interposed, put betwixt. **1602** FULBECKE *1st Pt. Parall.* 25 He is not bound to doe any seruice either in his owne person, or by any other person interposed during his minority. **1647** MAY *Hist. Parl.* I. viii. 89 Much time was interposed betweene the severall proceedings against this Earle of Strafferd. **1665** HOOKE *Microgr.* 75 Darkning..a colour, is onely interposing a multitude of dark or black spots among the same ting'd parts. **1796** MORSE *Amer. Geog.* I. 37 Only a small part of the convexity of the globe is interposed between us and the sun. **1870** ROLLESTON *Anim. Life* 129 The portions of the pseud-haemal system which were interposed between the digestive tract and the dorsal surface.

†**b.** To place (things) with intervals, or in alternation, to cause to alternate. *Obs.*

1602 WARNER *Alb. Eng.* Epit. (1612) 356 The other [wall] of Pyles and Tymber strongly and artificially interposed. **1691** BAXTER *Nat. Ch.* xv. 72 God can..interpose days with nights, and Summers with Winters.

c. *Chess.* To move (a man) so as to obstruct the line of action of an opposing piece, esp. when the latter is giving check. Also *absol.*, or with the interposed man as subject.

1761 E. HOYLE *Ess. Game of Chess* 2, 6 B. The Queen gives Check. W. The Bishop interposes. **1765** R. LAMBE *Hist. Chess* 107 If the B. Bp. instead of retreating, checks your K. you must interpose your Bp. **1808** J. H. SARRATT *Treat. Game of Chess* I. 49 If he interpose his King's Knight, you must take his Rook with your Queen. **1844** W. LEWIS *Treat. Game of Chess* 19 Sometimes a piece or pawn, which before was out of play, may be interposed, and force the piece that checks to retire. **1861** *Chambers's Encycl.* II. 799/2 The king ..must either move out of check or interpose some one of his subjects, unless the checking piece can be captured. **1876** *Encycl. Brit.* V. 593/1 If..the king, being thus in check, cannot move to another square..and there is no piece or pawn which can be interposed, and the checking piece or pawn cannot be taken, then it is 'checkmate'. **1950** *Hoyle's Games Modernized* (ed. 20) 366 The player may..interpose one of his own men between the King and the attacking piece.

2. To place or station oneself between; to come between in position, to stand in the way. †**a.** *refl.*

1601 SHAKS. *Jul. C.* II. i. 98 What watchfull Cares doe interpose themselves Betwixt your Eyes, and Night? **1632** J. HAYWARD tr. *Biondi's Eromena* 145 Two hundred of them falling into a close order, interposed themselves between them. *a* **1745** SWIFT (J.), Human frailty will too often interpose itself among persons of the holiest function.

b. *intr.* (for *refl.*)

1615 G. SANDYS *Trav.* 121 We offering to returne to the other, which he fearing, interposed. **1638** SIR T. HERBERT *Trav.* (ed. 2) 161 The river Syndery interposing. **1746-7** HERVEY *Medit.* (1818) 272 The earth interposing with its opaque body, intercepted the solar rays. **1844** H. H. WILSON *Brit. India* III. 69 Three columns..moved to the right, as if intending to interpose between the lines and the town.

3. *trans.* To put forth or introduce (action, authority, etc.) in the way of interference or intervention.

1606 HOLLAND *Sueton.* 13 The Senate came not betweene nor interposed their authoritie to stop the course intended against him. **1798** MRQ. WELLESLEY in Owen *Desp.* (1877) 42 Our arbitration..will be both acceptable and efficacious whenever it shall be interposed. **1822** LAMB *Elia* Ser. II. *Detached Th. Bks.*, Expecting every moment when he [the owner] shall interpose his interdict.

4. To put oneself forward or interfere in a matter; to step in between persons at variance or in a person's behalf; to intervene. †**a.** *refl. Obs.*

1603 KNOLLES *Hist. Turks* (1638) 29 The Patriark and other princes..seeing the danger..had interposed themselues. **1606** HOLLAND *Sueton.* Annot. 36 Noble Dames, who in old time..interposed themselves as *Mediatrices*, betweene the Romans and Sabines. **1625** USSHER in *Lett. Lit. Men* (Camden) 133 If he interpose himself seriouslye herein. **1658** EARL MONM. tr. *Paruta's Wars of Cyprus* 28.

b. *intr.*

1611 SHAKS. *Wint. T.* v. iii. 119 Please you to interpose (fair Madam) Kneele, And pray your Mothers blessing. **1656** BRAMHALL *Replic.* iv. 159 It is no innovation for our Kings to interpose in ecclesiasticall affairs. **1710** ADDISON *Tatler* No. 224 ¶3, I shall not interpose in their Quarrel. **1791** COWPER *Iliad* VI. 19 None interposed To avert his woeful doom. **1874** GREEN *Short Hist.* II. §7. 100 The Archbishop interposed between the rival claimants to the crown.

5. a. *trans.* To introduce between other matters, or between the parts of a narrative, as an interruption or digression; to say or pronounce as an interruption.

1605 BACON *Adv. Learn.* II. iv. §4 That all the fables and fictions of the poets were but pleasure and not figure, I interpose no opinion. **1647** N. BACON *Disc. Govt. Eng.* xxxiii. 80, I shall desire leave to enterpose this parenthesis ensuing, before I proceed. *a* **1687** PETTY *Pol. Arith.* iv. (1691) 65 To interpose a jocular, and perhaps ridiculous

digression. 1783 GIBBON *Misc. Wks.* (1814) II. 265-6 The Historian, who, without interposing his own sentiments, has delivered a simple narrative of authentic facts. 1817 MOORE *Lalla R.* (1824) 171 The Princess..was about to interpose a faint word of objection. 1828 SCOTT *F.M. Perth* xiii, 'Do not injure an innocent man', interposed the Prince.

b. *absol.* or *intr.* To interrupt, make a digression.

1667 MILTON *P.L.* XII. 270 Here Adam interpos'd. O sent from Heav'n, Enlightner of my darkness! *a*1873 E. DEUTSCH *Rem.* (1874) 77 We must here interpose for a moment. 1875 JOWETT *Plato* (ed. 2) I. 185 Here Ctesippus, the lover of Cleinias, interposes in great excitement.

II. †**6. a.** *trans.* To come or be in the way of (a person or thing); to intercept; to obstruct. *Obs.*

1615 J. STEPHENS *Satyr. Ess.* 152 We have no liberty..to judge;..when Discontents do trouble us. They interpose our brightest eminence of wisedom no otherwise than cloudes darken the Sunnes glory. 1624 HEYWOOD *Gunaik.* v. 258 All the theeves and robbers that interposed him in his way to Athens. 1671 R. BOHUN *Wind* 278 The great Rivers interposing us, together with..many other difficulties.

†**b.** To lie between (places); to part, separate.

1615 G. SANDYS *Trav.* 46 Arabia felix which stretcheth out into the South sea, interposing the Persian and Arabian Gulphs. *Ibid.* 207 Phœnicia is a province of Syria, interposing the sea and Galily.

Hence **inter'posed** *ppl. a.*; **inter'posing** *vbl. sb.*

1602 ANTHONY HEBORNE in *Archpriest Controv.* (Camden) II. 224 Some other interposed..dealers in this business. 1626 JACKSON *Creed* VIII. ii. §5 Interposed flashes of this day starr's brightnesse. 1657 R. LIGON *Barbadoes* (1673) 5 We often lose sight of them, by interposing of the waves. 1659 MILTON *Civ. Power* Wks. (1851) 329 Those ends which he can likely pretend to the interposing of his force therin. 1730 SAVERY in *Phil. Trans.* XXXVI. 301 No interposed Body..(unless it is magnetical)..was ever known..to impede or divert any of the Effects of a Magnet. 1860 TYNDALL *Glac.* I. vi. 43 The ridges..with their interposed fissures.

†**interpose**, *sb. Obs. rare.* [f. prec. vb.] Interposition, interposal.

1610 HOLLAND *Camden's Brit.* I. 154 Countries are divided by Geographers..Naturally, according to the course of Rivers, and interpose of Mountains. 1663 J. SPENCER *Prodigies* (1665) 117 Dangerous humors..which, without the wise interpose of State-Physicians, presage ruine to the whole. *Ibid.* 139 Upon the interpose of such impediments.

interposer (ɪntə'pəʊzə(r)). [f. as prec. + -ER¹.] One who or that which interposes or intervenes.

1596 SHAKS. *Merch. V.* III. ii. 329 No bed shall ere be guilty of my stay, Nor rest be interposer twixt vs twaine. 1617 COLLINS *Def. Bp. Ely* II. x. 535 Princes should be interposers in Ecclesiasticall affairs. 1685 F. SPENCE tr. *Varillas' Ho. Medicis* 172 Some affairs that could not be negotiated by an interposer. 1836 J. GILBERT *Chr. Atonem.* iii. (1852) 69 The occasions of interposition are widely different, as well as the circumstances of the interposer.

interposing (ɪntə'pəʊzɪŋ), *ppl. a.* [f. as prec. + -ING².] That interposes (in senses of the vb.).

1621 G. SANDYS *Ovid's Met.* XV. (1626) 311 So Zancle once on Italie confind; Till interposing waues their bounds disioynd. 1647 MAY *Hist. Parl.* I. i. 7 Without any interposing authority. 1725 POPE *Odyss.* X. 521 My interposing train For mercy pleaded. 1836 KEBLE in *Lyra Apost.* (1841) 57 So dreary seem'd Death's interposing veil.

Hence **inter'posingly** *adv.*, in an interposing manner, by way of interposition.

1845 *Whitehall* 277 Said the president, interposingly.

†**inter'posit**, *sb. Obs. rare.* [ad. L. *interpositum*, neut. of pa. pple. of *interpōnĕre* to place between: see INTERPONE.] A place to which goods are brought for distribution; an entrepôt.

*a*1827 W. MITFORD cited in Webster (1828).

†**inter'posit**, *v. Obs. rare*$^{-1}$. [f. L. *interposit-*, ppl. stem of *interpōnĕre*: see INTERPONE; cf. *deposit* vb.] *trans.* (?) To put forth, advance.

1678 R. R[USSELL] *Geber* II. i. I. iii. 28 Some, who are Slaves, loving Money..are afraid to interposit the necessary charges.

interposition (ˌɪntəpəʊ'zɪʃən). [a. F. *interposition*, OF. also *-icion* (12th c. in Hatz.-Darm.), ad. L. *interpositiōn-em*, n. of action from *interpōnĕre* to INTERPONE. Not derivationally related to INTERPOSE, but associated with it in OF. by contact of form, and adoption of *-poser* as virtual representative of L. *-pōnĕre*; cf. *composition*, *disposition*, etc.] The action of the vb. INTERPOSE.

1. The action of placing something or oneself between; the fact of being placed or situated between; intervention.

1412-20 LYDG. *Chron. Troy* I. v. (MS. Digby 230) lf. 38b/1 So þe mone haþ made diuisioun By here sodein interposicioun. 1527 R. THORNE in Hakluyt *Voy.* (1589) 252 If..the sea did extend, without interposition of land. 1586 W. WEBBE *Eng. Poetrie* (Arb.) 56 One verse either immediatly, or by mutuall interposition, may be aunswerable to an other. 1741 T. ROBINSON *Gavelkind* ii. 11 Without the Interposition of a Female Parent. 1840 DICKENS *Barn. Rudge* lviii, He made the cell..black by the interposition of his body. 1864 BRYCE *Holy Rom. Emp.* ii. (1875) 8 The sovereign's person..was removed further from the subject by the interposition of a host of officials.

b. An instance of this; sometimes quasi-*concr.*, that which is interposed.

1650 CROMWELL *Lett.* 4 Sept. in *Carlyle*, The enemy..gathered towards the Hills; labouring to make a perfect interposition between us and Berwick. 1665 SIR T. HERBERT *Trav.* (1677) 58 A Narrative..which though it may appear too great an interposition to our travel, will..I hope find acceptance. 1671 MILTON *P.R.* III. 222 A shelter and a kind of shading cool Interposition, as a summer's cloud. 1696 WHISTON *The. Earth* IV. (1722) 353 The Seasons were..without any quick Interpositions of Day and Night to disturb them. 1834 [see INTERLOCATION].

2. The action of interfering or intervening in a matter; intervention between persons or in a person's behalf; interference, mediation. With *an* and *pl.*, an instance of this.

1461 *Paston Lett.* No. 415 II. 50 Lete sum interposicion go a twix you and my mastres your moder. 1603 FLORIO *Montaigne* II. xii. (1632) 248 Nature in generall disavoweth her [Reason's] jurisdiction and interposition. 1670 in Somers *Tracts* I. 8 The Pacification was effected wholly by Interposition of the English Commissioners. 1696 WHISTON *The. Earth* IV. (1722) 303, I take [it] to be a Miraculous Interposition very worthy of God. 1769 *Junius Lett.* i. 10 By the immediate interposition of Providence. 1769 ROBERTSON *Hist. Chas. V* (1796) III. xii. 401 His interpositions in her favour became more cold. 1875 MAINE *Hist. Inst.* ix. 255 The interposition of the Praetor and the acceptance of his mediation expanded into the Administration of Justice in the Roman State. 1877 SPARROW *Serm.* xxii. 298 In the matter of religion, man needs the direct interposition of divine authority.

†**3.** A parenthesis; a digression. *Obs.*

1553 T. WILSON *Rhet.* (1580) 171 Some use so many interpositions, bothe in their talke and in their writyng, that thei make their saiynges as darke as helle.

interpositive (-'pɒzɪtɪv), *a.* and *sb.* [a. F. *interpositif* (Godef.), ad. L. type **interpositīvus*, f. ppl. stem of *interpōnĕre*: see INTERPONE.]

a. *adj. Bot.* Characterized by being placed between certain structures. †**b.** *sb.* Something interposed.

1650 HUBBERT *Pill Formality* 87 Having a form of godliness, but denying the power thereof..this interpositive (*but*) eclipseth the brightness and glory that mens actions did before seem to carry with them. 1855 MAYNE *Expos. Lex.*, *Interpositivus*,..applied to stamens situated between the divisions of a simple perianth..interpositive.

†**'interpost.** *Obs. rare*$^{-1}$. [a. F. *entrepôt*, formerly *entrepost*, ad. L. *interpositum*: see INTERPOSIT *sb.*] A commercial centre, an entrepôt.

1695 MOTTEUX *St. Olon's Morocco* 141 Cadiz is the Interpost to all the Traffick of England and Holland.

†**inter'posure.** *Obs.* [f. INTERPOSE *v.* + -URE; cf. *composure*, *disposure*, *exposure*.] The action of interposing; interposition, interposal.

1627 FELTHAM *Resolves* I. xx. (1677) 37 Though other interposures do eclipse her; yet this is a principal. 1653 H. COGAN tr. *Pinto's Trav.* x. 31 The Mahometan Merchant, that he might the more easily redeem me, used the interposure of a man born in the Country. 1689 DILLINGHAM *Myst. Iniq.* 13 The..Interposure of several Parliaments for removing the Grounds of our Differences and Animosities, by an Indulgence. 1733 WATTS *Philos. Ess.* IX. ii. (1734) 206 To represent the great Engine of this visible World, as moving onward in its appointed Course, without the continual interposure of His Hand.

interpour: see INTER- *pref.* 1 b.

interprater. *nonce-wd.* [f. INTER- 2 a + PRATER.] One who prates at intervals.

1591 LYLY *Sapho* IV. iii, You are no interpreter, but an interprater, harping always upon love, till you be as blind as a harper.

†**inter'prease**, *v. Obs. rare*$^{-1}$. [f. INTER- 1 a + *prease*, PRESS *v.*] *intr.* To press in between.

1615 CHAPMAN *Odyss.* IV. 896, I may interprease, Waylay, and take him.

interprement: see INTERPRETAMENT.

interpressure: see INTER- *pref.* 2 a.

interpret (ɪn'tɜːprɪt), *v.* Forms: 4-7 **interprete**, (5 **-pritt**), 6 *Sc.* **interpreit**, (**enterprit**), (7 **enterpret**), 6- **interpret**. Pa. pple. **interpreted**; also 5 **interpred**, 6 **interpret**. [a. F. *interpréter* (13th c. in Littré), or immed. ad. L. *interpretārī* to explain, expound, translate, understand, also in pass. sense, to be explained, mean, f. *interpres*, *-pret-em* an agent, explainer, expounder, translator, dragoman, f. *inter* between + root corresp. to Skr. *prath-* to spread abroad.]

1. a. *trans.* To expound the meaning of (something abstruse or mysterious); to render (words, writings, an author, etc.) clear or explicit; to elucidate; to explain. †Formerly, also, To translate (now only contextually, as included in the general sense).

1382 WYCLIF *Dan.* v. 16, I herde of thee, that thou mayst interprete derke thingis, and vnbynde bounden thingis. —— *Matt.* i. 23 His name shal be clepid Emanuel, that is interpretid [*gloss* or expounid], God with vs. 1483 CAXTON *Gold. Leg.* 295 b/1 Leuy is interpred assumpte or applyed or putte to. 1513 DOUGLAS *Æneis* IX. Prol. 74 My lewitnes..Schup to enterprit..Thys maist renownit prince of poetry. 1588 A. KING tr. *Canisius' Catech.* 81 Quhilk wordis yᵉ kirk hes so diligentlie interpret. 1617 MORYSON *Itin.* I. 242 We returned againe to him, with our Muccaro to interpret our words. 1737 WHISTON *Josephus, Antiq.* Diss. i, According to his usual way of interpreting authors, not to the words but to the sense. 1857 H. MILLER *Test. Rocks* ii. 76 Be it enough for the geologist rightly to interpret the record of creation. 1863 FAWCETT *Pol. Econ.* II. i. 119 The law interprets..his wishes with regard to the disposal of his property.

b. To make out the meaning of, explain to oneself.

1795 COWPER *Pairing Time Antic.* 6 The child who knows no better, Than to interpret by the letter A story of a cock and bull. 1866 GEO. ELIOT *F. Holt* i. (1868) 14 That her knowledge of the youth of nineteen might help her little in interpreting the man of thirty-four. 1892 WESTCOTT *Gospel of Life* 294 It is a final fact of our nature that we must interpret the phenomena of human life.

c. In recent use: To bring out the meaning of (a dramatic or musical composition, a landscape, etc.) by artistic representation or performance; to give one's own interpretation of; to render.

1880 *Athenæum* 25 Dec. 876/1 The two female characters ..were interpreted with striking success. 1888 MRS. H. WARD *R. Elsmere* II. xii, She was playing Wagner, Brahms, and Rubinstein, interpreting all those passionate voices of the subtlest moderns.

d. To obtain significant information from (a photograph), used esp. of aerial photographs taken for military purposes.

1950 A. LEE *Soviet Air Force* vii. 154 Photographs, developed in mobile front-line vans, were interpreted and the main points signalled..to army and corps headquarters. 1958 C. B. SMITH *Evidence in Camera* i. 21 Although the art of interpreting air photographs had been developed quite a long way in the First World War, in the summer of 1939 there was precisely one experienced interpreter.

2. a. To give a particular explanation of; to expound or take in a specified manner. Also, To construe (motives, actions, etc.) favourably or adversely. (In quot. 1709, To attribute *to*.)

*c*1380 WYCLIF *Serm.* Sel. Wks. I. 206 As princes of prestis, and Phariseis joyned wiþ hem, wolen interprete Goddis lawe, aff hem shal it be taken. 1484 CAXTON *Curial* 4b, To make false relacion ne to interprete euyl my worde. 1549 *Compl. Scot.* To Rdr. 17 Interpreit my intentione fauorablye. 1613 PURCHAS *Pilgrimage* (1614) 89 King of Moab, who being besieged..sacrificed his eldest sonne: which yet some interprete of the eldest sonne of the King of Idumæa. 1626 DONNE *Serm.* iv. 35 As thou wouldst be well interpreted by others interpret others well. 1651 HOBBES *Leviath.* II. xxiii. 124 No Commission that can be given them, can be interpreted for a Declaration [etc.]. 1709 MRS. MANLEY *Secret Mem.* (1736) IV. 141 The Difficulty of Access was often interpreted to, what she was not at all guilty of, Pride. 1741 MIDDLETON *Cicero* I. vi. 457 Commonly interpreted of those of Alexandria. 1758 SMOLLETT *Hist. Eng.* (1800) II. 227 This transaction was interpreted into a bribe. 1856 FROUDE *Hist. Eng.* (1858) I. v. 393 Each of them perhaps interpreted their engagements by their own wishes or interests.

†**b.** To render, explain, or translate by a specified term. *Obs.*

1530-1 *Act 22 Hen. VIII*, c. 13 No person..being a common Baker, Brewer..shall be interpreted or expounded handicrafts men. 1605 VERSTEGAN *Dec. Intell.* iii. (1628) 80 Friga is also interpreted for Venus. 1690 TEMPLE *Ess.*, *Gardens Epicurus* 29 All the sorts of their Mala, which we interpret Apples.

3. *absol.* or *intr.* To make an explanation; to give an exposition; *spec.* to act as an interpreter or dragoman. †Formerly, also, in general sense, To translate.

1382 WYCLIF *1 Cor.* xii. 30 Wher alle speken with langages? wher alle interpreten [*gloss* or expownen]? 1576 FLEMING *Panopl. Epist.* 253 To interprete out of the Greeke tongue into the Latine. 1588 R. PARKE tr. *Mendoza's Hist. China* 285 Euery one wil construe and interpret thereon at his pleasure. 1638 SIR T. HERBERT *Trav.* (ed. 2) 38 Pe-unes ..ready..to serve you, either to interpret, to runne, go arrands or the like. 1667 MILTON *P.L.* XI. 33 Unskilful with what words to pray, let mee, Interpret for him. 1860 HAWTHORNE *Marb. Faun* (Tauchn.) II. vii. 82 Each must interpret for himself.

†**4.** *intr.* To signify, to mean. *Obs.*

1614 SELDEN *Titles Hon.* 107 Sophi by all likelyhood was giuen him with regard to his reformd profession, as the word interprets.

Hence **in'terpreted** *ppl.a.*; **in'terpreting** *vbl. sb.* and *ppl. a.*

1382 WYCLIF *1 Cor.* xii. 10 Interpretynge [*gloss* or expownyng] of wordis. *c*1500 *Melusine* 64 Aftir the interpretyng made by you of her owne name. 1659 PEARSON *Creed* (1839) 313 An interpreted and an intended unction of our Saviour. 1892 *Pall Mall G.* 17 Mar. 2/3 He [Freeman] was an interpreting historian.

†**in'terpret**, *sb. Obs. rare*$^{-1}$. [ad. L. *interpretem*, or F. *interprète* (14th c. in Littré).] An interpreter.

1585 JAS. I *Ess. Poesie* (Arb.) 29 The heauenly Poets..Dame Naturs trunchmen, heauens interprets trewe.

interpretable (ɪn'tɜːprɪtəb(ə)l), *a.* [ad. late L. *interpretābilis* (Tert.), f. *interpretārī* to INTERPRET: see -BLE. Cf. obs. F. *interpretable* (Godef.).]

1. Susceptible of interpretation, explicable.

1611 FLORIO, *Interpetrabile*, interpretable. 1672 STILLINGFLEET *Idol. Ch. Rome* (ed. 2) 37 The letter of the Scripture as interpretable by every private mans reason. 1852 *Tait's Mag.* XIX. 552 It had a real, vocal, interpretable language. 1859 I. TAYLOR *Logic in Theol.* 49 They are facts that are not interpretable by consciousness.

2. Capable of being interpreted or construed in a specified manner.

1650 *Vind. Hammond's Addr.* 34 'Tis not..intelligible to me, how those words..should be..interpretable to any further sense. **1722** WOLLASTON *Relig. Nat.* i. 12 Covering the head with a hat..is in itself an indifferent thing, and people by usage or consent may make it interpretable either way. **1816** COLERIDGE *Statesm. Man.* 357 The words of St. John..are in their whole extent interpretable of the understanding. **1862** H. SPENCER *First Princ.* II. iii. §47 (1875) 163 Such alleged further forms are interpretable as generated by the primary form.

Hence **interpreta'bility**, **in'terpretableness**, the quality of being interpretable; **in'terpretably** *adv.*, in an interpretable manner.

1679 J. GOODMAN *Penit. Pardoned* I. iii. (1713) 60 Whereas the habits were voluntarily contracted, the effects are interpretably so too. **1685** H. MORE *Cursory Reflexions* 18 The Natural Interpretableness of the Apocalypse that way. **1854** G. BOOLE *Investigation Laws of Tht.* 67 The same conditions of interpretability. **1898** FRASER *Reid* v. 66 The uniformity and therefore interpretability of nature. **1956** E. H. HUTTEN *Lang. Mod. Physics* ii. 64 It is not translatability but interpretability in terms of an empiricist language that can establish meaning.

†**in'terpretament**. *Obs. rare.* Also *erron.* interprement. [ad. L. *interpretāment-um*, f. *interpretārī* to INTERPRET: see -MENT. Cf. obs. F. *interpretement.*] Interpretation.

1645 MILTON *Tetrach.* (1851) 216 This bold interpretament..cannot stand a minute with any competent reverence to God or his law. **1802** KNOX & JEBB *Corr.* I. 47 The Hebraisms..are peculiarly susceptible of useful interprement.

interpretant (ɪn'tɜːprətənt). *Philos.* [f. INTERPRET *v.* + -ANT[1].] Peirce's term for the effect of a proposition, or sign-series, upon its interpreter, the person who understands it; thus, the meaning, in one sense.

c **1905** C. S. PEIRCE *Coll. Papers* (1931) I. III. 147 Now the relation of every sign to its object and interpretant is plainly a triad. *a* **1910** W. JAMES *Some Probl. Philos.* (1911) iv. 71 The interpretants are then substituted for the sensations, which thus get rationally conceived. **1939** *Mind* XLVIII. 480 The class of interpretations of the kind described in L will be called the *interpretant* of that sign. **1946** C. MORRIS *Signs, Lang. & Behavior* i. 17 The disposition of an interpreter to respond, because of the sign,..will be called an interpretant. **1947** H. REICHENBACH *Elem. Symbolic Logic* vii. 280 These psychological processes are sometimes called the *interpretant* of a sentence. **1964** *Language* XL. 234 The relationship between linguistic signs and their users, the relationship which Morris calls the 'interpretant'.

†**in'terpretate**, *ppl. a. Obs. rare.* [ad. L. *interpretāt-us*, pa. pple. of *interpretārī* to INTERPRET.] Interpreted; understood.

1526 *Pilgr. Perf.* (1531) 95 Without yᵉ knowlege or lycence expresse of theyr souerayne, or at leest interpretate.

in'terpretate, *v.* Now *rare* or *Obs.* Also 6 enter-. [f. L. *interpretāt-*, ppl. stem of *interpretārī* to INTERPRET.] = INTERPRET *v.*

c **1522** BP. R. FOX in Ellis *Lett.* Ser. II. II. 8, I beseche your good lordship favorably & beningly to interpretate & take the premisses. **1534** WHITINTON *Tullyes Offices* I. (1540) 64 This temperaunce that we enterpretate so as I haue sayd. **1685** BOYLE *Enq. Notion Nat.* 407, I hope that any.. Expressions..will be interpretated with congruity to the Title and avowed Scope of this Treatise. *a* **1763** BYROM *Crit. Rem. Horace* (R.), When they take interpretating pains, Sometimes the difficulty still remains. **1866** T. WRIGHT in *Intell. Observ.* No. 50. 110 To interpretate..the inscription of the Newton Stone.

interpretation (ɪn,tɜːprɪ'teɪʃən). Also 4–6 **-cioun, -cion(n)e, -cyon,** 5 **enterpretacioun, (-teysoun).** [a. F. *interprétation* (12th c. in Hatz.-Darm.), or immed. ad. L. *interpretātiōn-em*, n. of action from *interpretārī* to INTERPRET; cf. AF. *entrepretacion* (Godef. *Compl.*). The form *enterpreteysoun* represents an OF. semi-popular form in *-aison*, after *raison, saison*, etc.; cf. AF. *interpretiso(u)n* (like *orison, venison*).

1292 BRITTON II. viii. §3 Pur ceo voloms qe a nous soint les dotaunces et les deloyaunces moustrez, et qe par nous soint fetes les interpretisouns.]

1. a. The action of interpreting or explaining; explanation, exposition. †*by interpretation*, inferentially; = INTERPRETATIVELY.

Interpretation of Nature, a phrase used by Bacon to denote the discovery of natural laws by means of induction.

1382 WYCLIF *2 Pet.* i. 20 Ech prophecie of scripture is not maad bi propre interpretacioun. **1529** MORE *Dyaloge* I. Wks. 141/2 In the interpretacion we may paraduenture styck, Is it not so? **1605** BACON *Adv. Learn.* II. xiv. §1 For the real and exact form of judgement, we refer ourselves to that which we have spoken of the interpretation of nature. **1692** SOUTH *12 Serm.* (1697) I. 441 Neither can he Will the Means, but he must Vertually, and by Interpretation at least, Will the End. **1765** BLACKSTONE *Comm.* I. Introd. 58 It may not be amiss to add a few observations concerning the interpretation of laws. **1869** HUXLEY in *Sci. Opin.* 21 Apr. 464/2 The knowledge..requisite for the just interpretation of geological phenomena.

†**b.** The faculty or power of interpreting. *Obs.*

1526 TINDALE *1 Cor.* xii. 10 To won is geven the vtteraunce off wisdom..To another the interpretacion off tonges. **1552** ABP. HAMILTON *Catech.* (1884) 46 The gift of the haly spirit, callit *interpretatio sermonum*, the interpretation of wordis.

c. The technique of obtaining information from a photograph, esp. an aerial photograph. Cf. INTERPRET *v.* 1 d.

1948 CARLING & ROSS *Brit. Surg. Pract.* V. 276 The interpretation of the pyelogram may be difficult. **1958** C. B. SMITH *Evidence in Camera* i. 21 Interpretation was supposed to be a job that any Station Intelligence Officer could be trained for in a week or two.

2. a. An explanation given; a way of interpreting or explaining; †a comment, a commentary (*obs.*).

1390 GOWER *Conf.* I. 145 Of..straunge interpretations, Problemes and demaundes eke His wisedome was to finde and seke. *c* **1450** *Mirour Saluacioun* 1027 After of this dreme herd he swilk interpretacionne. **1535** JOYE *Apol. Tindale* (Arb.) 42 Nether is the interpretacion of that worde resurreccion my priuate interpretacion. **1582** C. CARLILE *Disc. Peter's Life* (title-p.), An interpretation upon the Second Epistle of S. Paule to the Thessalonians, the second chapter. **1651** LILLY *Chas. I* (1774) 251 The ambiguity of oracles, and their ambodextrous interpretations. **1732** BERKELEY *Alciphr.* VI. §25 He..ridiculed allegorical interpretations. **1866** G. MACDONALD *Ann. Q. Neighb.* xi. (1878) 191 Perhaps I may have put a wrong interpretation on the passage.

b. Construction put upon actions, purposes, etc.

1387 TREVISA *Higden* (Rolls) VII. 153 ȝe auȝt for to soften þe opinicuns of fonde men wiþ better interpretacioun. **1608** D. T. *Ess. Pol. & Mor.* 56 Wee are bounde to give our neighbours proceedings a charitable interpretation. **1692** DRYDEN *St. Euremont's Ess.* 94 Whatsoever Interpretation Tacitus has given of so prudent a Design. **1709** ADDISON *Tatler* No. 108 ⁋3 They give mean Interpretations and base Motives to the worthiest Actions. **1874** MRS. OLIPHANT *Mak. Florence* x. (1877) 257 Things he had done which no charitable interpretation could explain away.

c. The representation of a part in a drama, or the rendering of a musical composition, according to one's conception of the author's idea.

1880 *Athenæum* 25 Dec. 876/1 The part of Cassandra..is capable of more various interpretation than that of her rival.

3. The way in which a thing ought to be interpreted; proper explanation; hence, Signification, meaning.

c **1400** tr. *Secreta Secret., Gov. Lordsh.* 106 Bytokenynge or enterpreteysoun of wordes ys so as þe esprit of word, and þe endytynge ys þe body, and þe writynge ys þe clethynge of wordys and spekynge. **1551** T. WILSON *Logike* (1580) 49 To whom the interpretation of a Noune doeth agre, to the same also the Noune it selfe agreeth. **1845** POLSON *Eng. Law* in *Encycl. Metrop.* 822/1 Our law..claims to determine the interpretation and effect of every deed or will executed here. **1867** MAURICE *Patriarchs & Lawg.* i. (1877) 34 Man finds his meaning and interpretation in God.

†**4.** The action of translating; a translation or rendering of a book, word, etc. *Obs.*

1382 WYCLIF *Prol. Joshua*, If the oold oonliche interpretacioun plese to hem. **1447** BOKENHAM *Seyntys* (Roxb.) 44 Aftyr the reulys of interpretacyon Anne is as myche to seyn as grace. **1526** TINDALE *John* i. 2 Thou shalt be called cephas: which is by interpretacion, a stone. **1646** SIR T. BROWNE *Pseud. Ep.* VI. i. 279 Whatsoever Interpretations there have beene since, have been especially effected with reference unto..the Greeke and Hebrew text.

5. *attrib.*: **interpretation clause**, a clause in an Act of Parliament which defines the meaning of certain terms for the purposes of the Act.

1897 *Bouvier's Law Dict.* I. 1107/2. **1971** *Halsbury's Statutes Eng.* (ed. 3) XXXII. 363 *Interpretation sections.* Most modern Acts contain an interpretation clause which states the meanings which particular expressions used in the Act in question are to bear or include.

Hence **in,terpre'tational** *a.*, of or pertaining to interpretation.

1867 LIGHTFOOT in *Contemp. Rev.* V. 407 *note*, In its interpretational purpose..the work of Basilides would present a parallel to the exposition of Papias.

interpretative (ɪn'tɜːprɪteɪtɪv), *a.* [f. L. *interpretāt-*, ppl. stem of *interpretārī* to INTERPRET + -IVE. Cf. F. *interprétatif* (1752 in Hatz.-Darm.) and obs. F. *interprétativement* (Godef. *Compl.*).]

1. Having the character, quality, or function of interpreting; serving to set forth the meaning (*of* something); explanatory, expository.

1569 J. SANFORD tr. *Agrippa's Van. Artes* xcvii. 171 b, The true diuinitee..also is deuided in two partes: for the one is Propheticall, the other Interpretatiue. *a* **1638** MEDE *Rever. God's Ho.* i. Wks. (1672) II. 344 That interpretative expression used in the New Testament of the Lord's descent upon Mount Sinai. **1737** WATERLAND *Eucharist* 98 These are not mere Allusions to the Sacrifices of the Old Testament, but they are interpretative of them. **1755** JOHNSON *Pref. Dict.* ⁋48 The rigour of interpretative lexicography requires that the explanation, and the word explained, should be always reciprocal. **1865** M. ARNOLD *Ess. Crit.* iii. 80 The grand power of poetry is its interpretative power. **1882** *Harper's Mag.* LXV. 57 One of the new interpretative composers. **1884** *American* VII. 337 All that is fairly implied in it as interpretative of the Constitution.

2. Deduced or deducible by interpretation or inference; inferential, constructive, implicit, virtual. *arch.* or *Obs.*

1610 DONNE *Pseudo-martyr* 349 This is accounted an interpretatiue periury. *a* **1614** —— *Βιαθανατος* (1644) 151 Though concurrence of Examples, and either an expresse or interpretative approbation of them..bee equivalent to a Rule. *a* **1659** BP. BROWNRIG *Serm.* (1674) I. xxvii. 352 'Tis an implicit, virtual, interpretative Atheism and Denial. **1798** in Dallas *Amer. Law Rep.* II. 250 Constructive, or interpretative treasons, must be the dread and scourge of any nation that allows them. **1870** J. H. NEWMAN *Gram. Assent* II. vii. 204, I will call simple assent *material* certitude; or, to use a still more apposite term for it, *interpretative* certitude.

in'terpretatively, *adv.* [f. prec. + -LY[2].] In an interpretative manner. **a.** By way of interpretation.

1670 BLOUNT *Law Dict.* s.v. *Emparlance*, Kitchin says, If he imparl, or pray continuance..where praying continuance is spoken interpretatively. **1691** BEVERLY *Thous. Years Kingd. Christ* 36 The Four Mettals and Beasts, (Interpretatively Kingdoms). **1950** E. E. EVANS-PRITCHARD *Ess. Social Anthropol.* (1962) i. 22 He then lives the experiences over again critically and interpretatively in the conceptual categories and values of his own culture. **1969** *Daily Tel.* 17 Dec. 10/8 It was already obvious that we were to be treated to playing which was free of all technical cares, and which developed interpretatively with disciplined spontaneity.

†**b.** By inference, constructively, implicitly. *Obs.*

1600 W. WATSON *Decacordon* (1602) 171 The seculars.. meddle no way in any thing..whereby a premunire can be incurred, no not so much as interpretatively. **1691** NORRIS *Pract. Disc.* 89 To be Singular in any of our Actions, is interpretatively and in effect, to prefer our own Sense and Judgement, before that of the World. **1720** WATERLAND *Eight Serm.* 135 The revealing his Nature, and Character, and personal Perfections..were interpretatively so many qualifying Clauses or Exceptions.

interpretativeness (ɪn'tɜːprɪtətɪvnɪs). [f. INTERPRETATIVE *a.* + -NESS.] The quality or condition of being interpretative.

1932 *Mind* XLI. 216 The several associations of 'meaning' with intellectual interpretativeness, value-carrying, and purposefulness are being confounded. **1957** D. L. BOLINGER in *Publ. Amer. Dial. Soc.* XXVIII. 26 The interpretativeness may be indicated merely by accent.

†**in'terpre,tator.** *Obs.* [a. late L. *interpretātor* (Tert.), agent-n. f. *interpretārī* to INTERPRET.] An interpreter.

1432–50 tr. *Higden* (Rolls) II. 419 Aylon, of the tribe of Zabulon..whom the lxxᵗⁱ interpretatores do not annumerate. *Ibid.* V. 397 Austyn did londe in..Kente.. with..certayne interpretators taken from Fraunce. **1533–4** *Act 25 Hen. VIII*, c. 12 Henry Golde toke vpon him to be interpretatour thereof. **1621** BURTON *Anat. Mel.* I. i. II. vii, Those imaginary dreams..of which Artemidorus, Cardanus and Sambucus, with their several interpretators, have written great volumes.

interpreter (ɪn'tɜːprɪtə(r)). Forms: 4–7 **inter-, enterpretour, -or,** 6– **interpreter.** [ME. *interpretour*, AF. form of OF. *interpreteeur*, *-teur*, also *entrepreteur* (Godef.), ad. late L. *interpretātōr-em* (Tert.), agent-n. f. *interpretārī* to INTERPRET. In 16th c. conformed to agent-nouns in *-er*, like *speak-er*: see -ER[1] 2.]

1. One who interprets or explains. †**a.** An official or professional expounder of laws, texts, mysteries, etc.; a commentator. *Obs.*

c **1400** *Apol. Loll.* 32 God seiþ bi Ysaie..þin enterpretors han brokyn þe lawe aȝenis Me. *c* **1440** *Promp. Parv.* 262/2 Interpretowre, or expownere, *interpres.* **1534** MORE *Comf. agst. Trib.* II. Wks. 1177/1 All the olde holye enterpretours, haue construed the scripture agaynst them. **1535** COVERDALE *Num.* xxii. 5 Balaam the sonne of Beor, which was an interpreter. **1605** BACON *Adv. Learn.* I. v. §10 They convert their labours to aspire to certain second prizes: as to be a profound interpreter or commenter. **1678** BUNYAN *Pilgr.* I. 23 Then said Christian to the Interpreter, Expound this matter more fully to me.

b. One who interprets a particular thing, or interprets something in a particular way; one who explains or puts a construction upon the meaning or purposes of a person. Also *transf.* of things.

1531 ELYOT *Gov.* Proheme, I..beseche your hyghnes to dayne to be..defendour of this litle warke agayne the assaultes of maligne interpretours. **1613** SHAKS. *Hen. VIII*, I. ii. 82 What we oft doe best, By sicke Interpreters..is Not ours, or not allow'd. **1638** *Penit. Conf.* vii. 191 Tears are a Penitents best Interpreter. **1833** BREWSTER *Nat. Magic* ii. 17 We have supposed that the spectator..is a faithful interpreter of the phenomena presented to his senses. **1857** PUSEY *Real Presence* ii. (1869) 185 Our prayers are the interpreters of the articles. **1875** JOWETT *Plato* (ed. 2) I. 117 The Poets and the Sophists, who are their interpreters. **1884** CHURCH *Bacon* ix. 225 Great ideas and great principles need their adequate interpreter..if they are to influence the history of mankind.

†**c.** Formerly a frequent title of books explaining the meaning of technical terms or unusual words. *Obs.*

1607 COWELL (*title*) The Interpreter: or booke containing the Signification of Words. **1623** COCKERAM (*title*) The English Dictionarie: or, an Interpreter of hard English Words. **1672** MANLEY *Cowell's Interpreter* Pref., I have reserved to it the former Name, and call it The Interpreter, which is most proper, as opening those obscure terms which otherwise are with great difficulty understood.

d. One who interprets (sense 1 d) photographs.

1950 A. LEE *Soviet Air Force* ii. 55 Large flying units.. had photographic interpreter specialists. **1958** [see INTERPRET *v.* 1 d].

2. One who translates languages. †**a.** A translator of books or writings (*obs.*).

c **1400** tr. *Secreta Secret., Gov. Lordsh.* 48 Iohan þat translatyd þis book..ful wys, & leel enterpretour of

langages. **1494** FABYAN *Chron.* I, The Hebrews..accompt for yᵉ sayd terme iii. M ix. C. sixty and iii yeres; the seuenty Interpretours rekyn v. M. C. lxxx. and xix. yeres. **1535** COVERDALE *Pref. Apocrypha*, The other prayer and songe.. haue I not founde amonge eny of the interpreters, but onely in the olde latyn texte, which reporteth it to be of Theodotios translacion. **1797** W. JOHNSTON tr. *Beckmann's Invent.* II. 398 This error has been occasioned by the seventy interpreters.

b. One who translates the communications of persons speaking different languages; *spec.* one whose office it is to do so orally in the presence of the persons; a dragoman.

1382 WYCLIF *1 Cor.* xiv. 28 If ther be not an interpretour, be he stille in the chirche. **1535** COVERDALE *Gen.* xlii. 23 They knew not that Ioseph vnderstode it, for he spake vnto them by an interpreter. **1600** HOLLAND *Livy* XXVII. xliii. 660 The letters [were] read by an enterpretour. **1752** LOUTHIAN *Form of Process* (ed. 2) 212 In Cases where the Prisoner and Witnesses, do not understand the British Language, Interpreters must be procured and sworn, as follows. **1838** THIRLWALL *Greece* xii. II. 109 Psammetichus..consigned a number of Egyptian boys to their care, to be instructed in the Greek language, so as to form a permanent class of interpreters.

†**3.** One who makes known the will of another; a title of Mercury as messenger of the gods. (L. *interpres divum* Virgil.) *Obs.*

1490 CAXTON *Eneydos* xvi. 61 Iupyter..called to hym Mercuryus, whiche ys interpretour of the goddes. **1667** MILTON *P.L.* III. 657 Uriel, for thou..The first art wont his great authentic will Interpreter through highest Heav'n to bring, Where all his Sons thy embassie attend. **1678** CUDWORTH *Intell. Syst.* I. iv. §32. 487 She [Minerva] performing the office of an Interpreter and Introducer to the Gods when it is needful.

†**4.** *Rhet.* An explanation of one expression by another; = SYNONYMY. (L. *interpretatio.*) *Obs.*

1589 PUTTENHAM *Eng. Poesie* III. xix. (Arb.) 223 The Greekes call it Sinonimia..the Latines..called it by a name of euent, for (said they) many words of one nature and sence, one of them doth expound another. And there-fore they called this figure the Interpreter.

5. *Computers.* **a.** A machine that prints on a punched card fed into it the alphabetic or numerical equivalent of the pattern of holes.

1936 *Office Machine Man.* Dec., The Interpreter which interprets the information punched into the card and prints such information in figures along the top edge of the card. **1949** E. C. BERKELEY *Giant Brains* iv. 47 The chief IBM punch-card machines are: the key punch, the verifier, the sorter, the interpreter, the reproducer, the collator, the multiplying punch, the calculating punch, and the tabulator. **1970** O. DOPPING *Computers & Data Processing* iii. 54 If the cards have no text, a special machine, an 'interpreter', can be used to read the cards and print their contents on the top line.

b. An interpretive routine (see INTERPRETIVE *a.* b).

1954 *Computers & Automation* Dec. 15/2 *Interpreter*, an executive routine which, as the computation progresses, translates a stored program expressed in some machine-like pseudo-code into machine code and performs the indicated operations, by means of subroutines, as they are translated. **1958** GOTLIEB & HUME *High-Speed Data Processing* xiv. 291 If a complete translation of the program is prepared *before* the initiation of its operation the system is a compiler; if the pseudo-code is retranslated each time it is used during operation, the system is an interpreter. **1964** [see INTERPRETIVE *a.* b].

interpretership (ɪnˈtɜːprɪtəʃɪp). [f. prec. + -SHIP.] The office or position of an interpreter; esp. of an official interpreter in the administration of law or government.

1845 STOCQUELER *Handbk. Brit. India* (1854) 311 Officers must pass an examination in Hindoostanee before they are eligible for an adjutancy or interpretership. **1860** A. L. WINDSOR *Ethica* vi. 290 It seems..as though the imagination had arrogated to itself the rights of interpretership to the great social world about it. **1879** *Academy* 5 Apr. 307/1 Men who have achieved the feat of qualifying for interpreterships in..seven or eight Oriental languages.

†**in'terpretess.** *Obs.* [Variant of INTERPRETRESS, prob. euphonic.] A female interpreter.

1717 LADY M. W. MONTAGU *Let. to C'tess Mar* 18 Apr., The Greek lady..was my interpretess [*some later edd.* -tress]. **1792** MAD. D'ARBLAY *Diary* V. VIII. 352 She had been his interpretess here on his arrival.

interpretive (ɪnˈtɜːprɪtɪv), *a.* [f. INTERPRET *v.* + -IVE, after words in which *t* belongs to the L. ppl. stem, as *assertive*.] **a.** = INTERPRETATIVE.

1680 FILMER *Patriarcha* iii. §15 (1884) 66 '*Le roy le veult*' is the interpretive phrase. **1839** BAILEY *Festus* xix. (1852) 284 Confounding text and comment, with no rule Interpretive. **1953** D. CECIL in W. de la Mare *Private View* p. vi, In his critical essays, Mr. de la Mare had not the scope for his interpretive genius to display itself so freely. **1955** *Bull. Atomic Sci.* June 218/3 There will be some 200 to 300 supplementary and interpretive books on atomic energy provided by American publishers. **1966** J. J. KATZ *Philos. of Lang.* iv. 111 Both the phonological and semantic components are, therefore, purely interpretive. **1966** MEIER & ELLIOTT (*title*) From plantation to ghetto: an interpretive history of American negroes. **1969** A. B. CALLOW (*title*) American urban history: an interpretive reader with commentaries. **1970** A. CAMERON et al. *Computers & O.E. Concordances* 107, I will admit that what follows will be interpretive. **1971** *World Archaeol.* III. 197 The field of interpretive functions which archaeologists call upon their pottery collections to sustain. **1973** *Studies in Eng. Lit.: Eng. Number* (Tokyo) 65 This is a highly controversial analysis, and has been much criticized by the so-called Interpretive Semanticists.

b. *Computers.* Applied to a routine that executes a source program by translating each instruction into machine language and then executing it (by means of subroutines) before proceeding to the next instruction; of or pertaining to the operation of such a routine.

1951 M. V. WILKES et al. *Preparation of Programs for an Electronic Computer* I. iv. 34 There are in the library a number of subroutines which, when called in, execute series of operations according to sets of parameters in the store... These subroutines are usually called in by the method used for the closed type, the parameter following the orders which call in the routine. The routines do, however, form a distinct class, and have been labelled 'interpretive'. **1957** W. D. BELL *Managem. Guide Electronic Computers* viii. 148 The availability of already established libraries is an important consideration in selecting a data system. And then there are 'interpretive routines', 'pseudo coding', 'compilers', and many other specialized programming methods and techniques. **1964** F. L. WESTWATER *Electronic Computers* ix. 143 As the number of subroutines available increased.. whole programs could be written without any machine code being necessary. The coded orders were read in and a special routine (called the interpretive program or 'interpreter') selected each required subroutine in turn. **1970** O. DOPPING *Computers & Data Processing* xix. 306 Nowadays, the interpretive systems are used mainly for simulating a computer *B* using another computer *A* with other programming characteristics.

Hence **in'terpretively** *adv.*, inferentially.

a **1665** J. GOODWIN *Filled w. the Spirit* (1867) 285 To know..that God is able to enlighten..is interpretively or constructively to know that he hath a Spirit to give.

in,terpre'torial, *a. rare.* [f. INTERPRETER, after L. adjs. in *-ōrius* (instead of the full *interpretatorial*).] Of or pertaining to an interpreter.

1865 D. F. RENNIE *Peking & Pekingese* I. 185 Mr. Douglass..has lately arrived in Peking for interpretorial duty.

interpretress (ɪnˈtɜːprɪtrɪs). [f. INTERPRETER + -ESS.] A female interpreter.

1775 ADAIR *Amer. Ind.* 327 They..were so polite as to order their black interpretress to bid our red couriers tell us, they thanked us for our friendly offer. **1859** KINGSLEY *Misc.*, *Raleigh* I. 12 Interpretress of the will and conscience of the people of England. **1865** M. ARNOLD *Ess. Crit.* iii. (1875) 123 Poetry is the interpretress of the natural world and she is the interpretress of the moral world.

†**interprice, -ise, -ize, -yse,** obs. ff. ENTERPRISE *sb.*

a **1548** HALL *Chron.*, *Hen. V* an. 6 (R.), Kynge Henry not myndynge..to leaue his interprice vnperformed, sent the Duke of Clarence to the sea coaste. **1567** *Satir. Poems Reform.* v. 17, I grant ȝour interpryse was gude. **1601** R. JOHNSON *Kingd. & Commw.* (1603) 254 To undergoe once more another interprize for the kingdome of England.

†**interprise, -yse,** obs. ff. ENTERPRISE *v.*, to undertake.

1573 *Satir. Poems Reform.* xlii. 185 Thay that..did the mater Interpryse. **1601** R. JOHNSON *Kingd. & Commw.* (1603) 97 They..never interprised to forsake their limited habitations. *a* **1605** MONTGOMERIE *Sonn.* xiii, In thair spheirs thay dar not interpryse For to appeir lyk planeits, as they ar.

†**interpro'duce,** *v. Obs. rare.* Also 7 enter-. [INTER- 1 b.] *trans.* To produce mutually.

1603 FLORIO *Montaigne* III. xii. (1632) 602 His inventions enflame, follow and enter-produce one another. **1685** COTTON *Montaigne* III. 484 His inventions heat, pursue, and interproduce one another.

interproportional, -protoplastic: see INTER- *pref.* 2 a, 6.

interpro'vincial, *a.* [INTER- 4 b.] Lying, extending, or carried on, between different provinces; pertaining to the mutual relations of two or more provinces.

1839 *Times* 21 Mar. in *Spirit Metropol. Conserv. Press* (1840) I. 122 It would leave..her interprovincial communication between Fredericton and Quebec unbroken. **1851** KITTO *Daily Bible Illustr.* (1867) VIII. LII. ii. 432 Disputes were continually arising between the Roman governors about their interprovincial rights. **1883** *Daily News* 13 Sept. 4/6 Questions..involving new taxes, public loans, interprovincial canals and railways. **1888** *Mag. Amer. Hist.* Jan 26 The representatives of the five chief provinces of the Dominion, at the Interprovincial conference in Quebec.

interproximal: see INTER- *pref.* 6.

interpubic (ɪntəˈpjuːbɪk), *a.* [INTER- 4 a.] Situated between the right and left pubic bones.

1836–9 TODD *Cycl. Anat.* II. 262/2 The ossification of the interpubic fibro-cartilage. **1857** BULLOCK *Cazeaux' Midwif.* 23 A considerable thickness of the interpubic ligament fills up the interval.

interpulse (ˈɪntəpʌls), *a.* and *sb.* Also **inter-pulse.** [f. INTER- + PULSE *sb.*[1]] **A.** *adj.* [INTER- 5.] Existing or occurring between one pulse and the next.

1948 G. N. GLASOE in Glasoe & Lebacqz *Pulse Generators* iv. 119 For such a succession of pulses, it is generally desired that the interpulse intervals, as well as the pulses, be of controlled duration. **1962** SIMPSON & RICHARDS *Physical Princ. Junction Transistors* xvii. 444 The interpulse period must be long enough to allow C_1 to replenish its charge before another sweep begins. **1966** *Jrnl. Exper. Psychol.* LXXI. 881/1 As the interpulse intervals increase the threshold for the gap monotonically increases. **1971** *Jrnl. Gen. Psychol.* LXXXIV. 86 It is possible that pairs of photic pulses of the proper durations and appropriate interpulse intervals would provide impairment of visual resolution. **1971** *Sci. Amer.* Jan. 50/1 The amplitude of the pulses from the objects was observed to be very uneven, but the interpulse spacing was quite regular.

B. *sb. Astr.* [INTER- 3.] A weaker pulse occurring between the main pulses of radiation from some pulsars.

1969 *Nature* 8 Feb. 525/2 The interpulse trails the main pulse by 14·0 ms. **1971** *New Scientist* 1 July 6/2 In many pulsars..there is a weak 'interpulse' roughly halfway between main pulses.

'interpunct, *sb. rare.* [f. INTER- 2 a + L. *punct-us* point.] A point between words in writing.

1898 *Amer. Jrnl. Philol.* XIX. 92 The general character of the alphabet used in each inscription is always noted, as well as..the presence or lack of interpuncts.

†**inter'punct,** *v. Obs. rare*⁻¹. [f. L. *interpunct-*, ppl. stem of *interpungĕre* to place points between: see next.] *trans.* To mark with points inserted between words or clauses.

1626 DONNE *Serm.* lxxiii. 737 As the originall copies are distinguished and interpuncted now.

interpunction (ɪntəˈpʌŋkʃən). [ad. L. *interpunctiōn-em*, n. of action from *interpungĕre*, f. *inter* between + *pungĕre* to prick, etc.] The insertion of points between words, clauses, or sentences; punctuation. **b.** *concr.* A point inserted in writing.

1617 COLLINS *Def. Bp. Ely* To Rdr. 12 Marring and monstrifying anothers directest meaning, with his own most prodigious interpunctions. **1626** DONNE *Serm.* lxxiii. 738 We find no reason to depart from that Distinction and Interpunction of these words which our owne Church exhibits to us. **1764** *Phil. Trans.* LIV. 425 The earlier Greeks also used the first kind of interpunction. **1894** *Thinker* VI. 297 In regard to the vocalization and interpunction of the Hebrew text.

fig. *a* **1640** JACKSON *Creed* XI. xxi. §2 Our life is full of interpunctions or commas: death is but the period or full point.

interpunctuate (ɪntəˈpʌŋktjuːeɪt), *v.* [INTER- 1 a.] *trans.* and *absol.* To insert the points between words and clauses; to punctuate. Also *fig.*

1850 *Fraser's Mag.* XLII. 701 They remind one of the nightmares which occasionally interpunctuate the festivities of the Christmas week. **1853** W. KAY in *Missionary* III. 241 The notorious use of *vel* was what made it unnecessary to interpunctuate. **1891** *Black & White* 12 Dec. 770 2 Sir William Harcourt is a man of humour, and inter-punctuates the serious business of his speech with conspicuous laughter.

interpunctu'ation. [INTER- 2 a.] = INTERPUNCTION.

1717 BERKELEY *Jrnl. Tour Italy* 7 Jan., Wks. 1871 IV. 513 The first [book] had inter-punctuations, the other none. **1827** BEDDOES *Poems* p. lxxi, I have communicated the lines, with a strict regard even to the interpunctuation, exactly as I received them. **1881** *Contemp. Rev.* Mar. 486 Epistles to his eldest daughter on her interpunctuation.

interpupillary: see INTER- *pref.* 6.

†**inter'puzzle,** *v. Obs. rare*⁻¹. [INTER- 1 b.] *trans.* To entangle, make intricate, confuse.

1650 B. *Discolliminium* 29 To trouble and interpuzle all our present proceedings.

interquarrel, -quarter: see INTER-.

interquartile (ɪntəˈkwɔːtaɪl), *a. Statistics.* [f. INTER- 5 + QUARTILE *sb.*] Situated between the first and third quartiles of a distribution.

1882 F. GALTON in *Rep. Brit. Assoc. Adv. Sci. 1881* 245 This gave the upper and lower 'quartile' values, and consequently the 'interquartile' range (which is equal to twice the 'probable error'). **1944** *Mind* LIII. 175 Does a statistical description in terms of mean, mean deviation, interquartile range, describe well enough the individuals we have examined? **1952** *New Biol.* XII. 23 The interquartile range will be about 7 per cent of the median. That is to say, if we take 101 teeth, and arrange them in order for the particular length measured, the difference in length between the 26th and the 76th will be about 7 per cent of the length of the 51st.

inter-racial, -racialism: see INTER- *pref.* 4 c, 2 a.

interradial (ɪntəˈreɪdɪəl). *Zool.* [INTER- 4 a.] **a.** *adj.* Situated between radii or rays, as in an echinoderm. **b.** *sb.* An interradial part.

1870 ROLLESTON *Anim. Life* 143 In the inter-radial space ..is seen the madreporic tubercle. *Ibid.* 226 One of the interradial septa. **1877** W. THOMSON *Voy. Challenger* II. ii. 95 The excretory opening is on a small interradial papilla.

Hence **inte'rradially** *adv.*

1870 ROLLESTON *Anim. Life* 224 One of the interradially-placed circumoral plates. **1888** ROLLESTON & JACKSON *Anim. Life* 190 Five sets of spines..project over this area interradially.

inte'rradiate, *v. rare.* [INTER- 1 b.] To radiate into each other. Hence **inte'rradiating** *ppl. a.*; also **interradi'ation**.

1851–5 BRIMLEY *Ess.*, *Tennyson* 74 A mighty cataract, with..its dazzling interradiation of changing forms and colours. **1858** G. MACDONALD *Phantastes* xii. 134 The community of the centre of all creation suggests an interradiating connexion and dependence of the parts.

‖**interradius** (ɪntə'reɪdɪəs). *Zool.* Pl. **-radii** (-'reɪdɪaɪ). [mod.L., f. INTER- 3 + RADIUS *sb.*] An interradial space or part, as in an echinoderm; a secondary ray or radiating part lying between two primary rays in some Hydrozoa.

1870 ROLLESTON *Anim. Life* 142 The Echinodermata.. move in locomotion indifferently in the direction of any one radius or inter-radius. **1878** BELL *Gegenbaur's Comp. Anat.* 101 In Cestum..the form of the body has become that of a band, from its having grown in the direction of two similar interradii.

interramal (ɪntə'reɪməl), *a. Ornith.* [INTER- 4 a.] Situated between the rami or branches of the lower jaw.

1874 COUES *Birds N.W.* 466 Interramal space broad and very long, extending nearly to the end of the bill.

interramicorn (ɪntə'ræmɪkɔːn). *Ornith.* [f. L. *inter* between + *ramus* branch + *cornu* horn; lit. 'interramal horn'.] A separate piece of the horny sheath of the bill situated between the rami of the lower jaw in the albatross, etc.

1866 COUES in *Proc. Philadelphia Acad.* 176 *Diomedea exulans.* The 'interramicorn' forms the gonal element of the bill. *Ibid.* 179, 181, 185.

interramifi'cation. *rare*$^{-1}$. [INTER- 2 a.] Intermingling of branches or branch-like parts.

1825 COLERIDGE *Aids Refl.* (1858) I. App. C. 404 As the corals approach the conchylia, this interramification decreases.

†**inte'rraneous**, *a. Obs. rare.* [f. mod.L. *interrāneus*, f. L. *in-* (IN-²) + *terra* earth, after *subterrāneus*.] (See quot.)

1855 MAYNE *Expos. Lex.*, *Interraneus*, applied by Mirbel to plants which grow and vegetate in the very bosom of the earth..; interraneous.

interreceive, -reconciliation: see INTER-.

interred (ɪn'tɜːd), *ppl. a.* [f. INTER *v.* + -ED¹.] Laid in a grave; buried.

c **1440** *Promp. Parv.* 140/2 Entyryd, or intyryd.., *funeratus.* **1610** FLETCHER *Faithf. Shepherdess* II. ii, The sweet rest of these interred bones. **1613** PURCHAS *Pilgrimage, India* (1864) 53 With enterred hopes, and dispossession of their liues. **1665** J. WEBB *Stone-Heng* (1725) 92 Epitaphs, containing..the famous Deeds of the interred. *Mod.* The recently interred body.

inte'rregal, *a. rare.* [INTER- 4 c.] Subsisting between kings.

1855 MOTLEY *Dutch Rep.* I. II. i. 261 The isolated execution of an interregal conspiracy, existing for half a generation. **1868** *Fortn. Rev.* July 90 The so-called international law of the past is a misnomer..being a code of kings not of nations, an interregal, not an international, system.

†**inte'rregency.** *Obs. rare.* [f. next: see -ENCY.] The tenure of an interrex or interregent; an interreign.

1600 [see INTERREGNUM 1]. **1620** E. BLOUNT *Horae Subs.* 226 Romulus being dead, there succeeded him, after one yeeres interregency, Numa Pompilius. **1674** in BLOUNT *Glossogr.* (ed. 4).

†**inte'rregent.** *Obs. rare.* [INTER- 2 b; after *interrex*.] = INTERREX.

1600 HOLLAND *Livy* I. xvii. 13 The Interregent [*interrex*] having called a generall parliament [etc.]. *Ibid.* v. 201 When as..the Consuls had resigned their office, M. Furius Camillus was created Interregent.

interregimental: see INTER- 4 c.

interregnal (ɪntə'rɛgnəl), *a.* [f. next, after REGNAL.] Belonging to or of the nature of an interregnum. Also *fig.*

1649 NEEDHAM *Case Commw. Stated* (1650) 86 Those Interregnall Controversies, which have risen betwixt Competitors by way of Election. **1856** LEVER *Martins of Cro' M.* 578 It was that interregnal period between the time when the Castle parties included the first gentry of the land, and that later era [etc.].

‖**interregnum** (ɪntə'rɛgnəm). Pl. **-regna, -regnums.** [L., f. *inter* (INTER- 3) + *regnum* REIGN *sb.*; cf. next.]

†**1.** Temporary authority or rule exercised during a vacancy of the throne or a suspension of the usual government. *Obs.*

1579–80 NORTH *Plutarch* (1612) 63 The Romaines call this manner of regiment in vacation *Interregnum*: as you would say, rule for the time. **1600** HOLLAND *Livy* I. 13 The governement upon this occasion was (as is still at this day) called *Interregnum*. [*Margin*] The Interregencie. **1641** SIR E. DERING *Sp. on Relig.* 21 June ix. Divb, As one government goes out, I could see another come in, and that without an *Interregnum* of Commissioners. **1770** LANGHORNE *Plutarch* (1879) I. 69/2 This occasional administration the Romans call an *Interregnum*.

2. The interval between the close of a king's reign and the accession of his successor; any period during which a state is left without a ruler or with a merely provisional government.

1590 L. LLOYD *Consent of Time* 31 The Hebrewes had none to gouerne them 8 yeeres after (so long *inter regnum* continued). **1649** ROBERTS *Clavis Bibl.* 228 There was an Inter-regnum or vacancie of the Royal seat in Judah. **1727–41** CHAMBERS *Cycl.* s.v., In hereditary kingdoms, as England, there are properly no interregnums. **1765** BLACKSTONE *Comm.* I. xviii. 470 The king..is made a corporation to prevent in general the possibility of an *interregnum* or vacancy of the throne. **1888** BRYCE *Amer. Commw.* I. xxvi. 397 Such a risk of interregna is incidental to all systems.

3. A cessation or suspension of the usual ruling power; a period of freedom *from* some authority. Also *fig.*

1648 JENKYN *Blind Guide* Pref. A ij b, All that time was an *interregnum* of his reason. **1656** COWLEY *Misc.*, *Chronicle* ix, Thousand worse Passions then possest The *Inter-regnum* of my Breast. Bless me from such an Anarchy. **1832** LEWIS *Use & Ab. Pol. Terms* v. 38 A day's interregnum of lawlessness—during which the Sovereign slept. **1879** FARRAR *St. Paul* I. 153 They were at the moment enjoying a sort of interregnum from Roman authority.

4. A breach of continuity; an interval, pause, vacant space.

1659 T. PECKE *Parnassi Puerp.* 30 But all the Interregnum, she was chaste: Yet not for vertue's Love, but her own sake. **1750** H. WALPOLE *Lett. to Mann* 19 Nov., Such is the Interregnum of our politics! **1829** LYTTON *Disowned* xvi, One could be merry till bed-time without an interregnum. **1860** MAURY *Phys. Geog. Sea* (Low) xvi. §699 The coming of this interregnum which they call the changing of the monsoons.

interreign ('ɪntəreɪn). Now *rare*. Also 6 **-regne**, 6–7 **-reigne**, **-raign(e.** [f. INTER- 3 + REIGN, after L. *interregnum* (see prec.), or F. *interrègne* (14th c. in Hatz.-Darm.); the latter may be the immediate source.]

†**1.** = INTERREGNUM 1. *Obs.*

1533 BELLENDEN *Livy* I. (1822) 30 This governance..wes callit the Interregne; that is to say, the vacance betwix the deith of ane king, to the electioun of ane uthir. **1600** HOLLAND *Livy* III. viii. 93 P. Valerius Poplicola, the third day of his Interreigne or Regencie for the time, createth Consuls. **1611** SPEED *Hist. Gt. Brit.* VIII. vii. (1632) 426 Sauing the small Inter-Raignes of these three Danish Kings.

2. = INTERREGNUM 2. Now *unusual.*

1586 J. HOOKER *Girald. Irel.* in *Holinshed* II. 162/2 They ..confer togither how they may in this inter-reigne win the spurs, and be vtterlie deliuered from the English gouernement. **1689** *Def. Liberty agst. Tyrants* 74 Succession was tollerated to avoid..contentions, interraigns, and other discommodities of Elections. **1775** PLANTA in *Phil. Trans.* LXVI. 139 The confusions, divisions, and interreigns which frequently distracted the empire. **1828** THIRLWALL & HARE tr. *Niebuhr's Hist. Rome* (1855) I. 265 It very easily.. happened that the outgoing magistrates did not complete the election, and that an interreign took place.

fig. *a* **1854** H. REED *Lect. Brit. Poets* iv. (1857) 116 The literary interreign between Chaucer and Spenser.

†**inte'rreigning**, *ppl. a. Obs. rare.* [f. INTER- 1 + REIGNING, after prec.] Reigning in the interval; interregnal.

1657–83 EVELYN *Hist. Relig.* (1850) I. 365 A passing over of divers inter-reigning princes between Cyrus and Alexander. **1793** HELY tr. *O' Flaherty's Ogygia* II. 372 They..include the inter-reigning space among them [24 years].

interrelate (ˌɪntərɪ'leɪt), *v.* [INTER- 1 b.] *trans.* To bring into relation to each other. Also *intr.*

1888 S. V. CLEVENGER in *Amer. Naturalist* XXII. 616 Spaces..filled with fibrils and cells that interrelate these and other functions complexly. **1895** *Educat. Rev.* Nov. 365 Wise men of experience think it desirable to interrelate the subjects of the curriculum. **1964** R. JOHNSTON in *Oceanogr. & Marine Biol.* II. 100 Because the conductivity-chlorinity relationship has been shown to be somewhat variable, one cannot interrelate density, chlorinity and conductivity. **1964** M. MCLUHAN *Understanding Media* (1967) II. xiv. 149 Money becomes..the principal means of interrelating the ever more specialist activities of literate society. **1973** *Times Lit. Suppl.* 23 Mar. 320/3 The essays do not interrelate very adequately.

interrelated (ˌɪntərɪ'leɪtɪd), *ppl. a.* [INTER- 1 b.] Mutually related or connected.

1827 I. TAYLOR *Transm. Anc. Bks.* (1859) 207 The interrelated, and the mutually attestative evidence of thousands of witnesses. **1880** BASTIAN *Brain* 26 Another set of inter-related nerve-cells.

Hence ˌ**interre'latedness**.

1865 MASSON *Rec. Brit. Philos.* 259 The demonstrable inter-relatedness of both.

interrelation (ˌɪntərɪ'leɪʃən). [INTER- 2 a.] Mutual or reciprocal relation.

1848 J. H. NEWMAN *Loss & Gain* 181 The limits of each opinion as he held it, and the inter-relations of opinion with opinion. **1855** I. TAYLOR *Restor. Belief* (1864) 4 The interrelation and dependence, one upon another, of moral, religious, and political questions. **1889** MIVART *Truth* 493 The interrelations and interdependencies which exist between the various orders of creatures.

So ˌ**interre'lationship**, mutual relationship.

1867 MACFARREN *Harmony* iii. (1876) 105 Whose interrelationship results from their common reference to the keynote. **1892** *Class. Rev.* July 317/2 The interrelationship of the MSS...having thus been very plausibly determined. **1879** MARY KINGSLEY *W. Africa* 211 The inter-relationship of these two subjects may not seem on the face of it very clear, but inter-relationships of customs very rarely are.

†**inter-religion.** *Obs. rare.* [INTER- 2 b.] = INTERIM *sb.* 3 b.

1620 BRENT tr. *Sarpi's Hist. Counc. Trent* (1676) 308 Cæsar also, in the Decree of the Inter-religion, was forced to yield to this.

interreligional, -religious, etc.: see INTER-.

interrenal (ɪntə'riːnəl), *a.* and *sb. Anat.* [f. INTER- 4 a + L. *rēn-es* kidneys: see RENAL.]

a. *adj.* Situated between the kidneys. **b.** *sb.* An interrenal body.

1893 in *Funk's Stand. Dict.* **1902** *Nature* 18 Sept. 516 On the interrenal bodies of Plagiostomes, by M. Ed. Grynfeltt. **1929** *Physiol. Abstr.* XIII. 530 The interrenal organ is essential to life in Selachians. **1940** *Chambers's Techn. Dict.* 455/2 *Interrenal body*, in selachian Fish, a ductless gland which lies between the kidneys and corresponds to the cortex of the suprarenal gland of higher Vertebrates. **1965** LEE & KNOWLES *Animal Hormones* iv. 69 The term adrenal cortex can be retained for all the vertebrate classes, but in the fish in view of the anatomical position the synonym interrenal may be preferred.

inter-repellent: see INTER- *pref.*

interrer (ɪn'tɜːrə(r)). [f. INTER *v.* + -ER¹.] One who inters; a burier.

1611 COTGR., *Entereur*, an Interrer, or burier. **1623** DRUMM. OF HAWTH. *Cypress Grove* Wks. (1711) 117 Death is the violent estranger of acquaintance..the interrer of fame. **1833** THIRLWALL in *Philol. Museum* II. 529 To expose him to such interrers as befit a wretch like him.

inter-responsive: see INTER- *pref.* 2 a.

‖**interrex** ('ɪntərɛks). Pl. **-reges** (-'riːdʒiːz). [L., f. *inter* between (INTER- 2 b) + *rex* king.] One who holds the supreme authority in a state during an interregnum.

In ancient Rome, an *interrex* was appointed to hold office between the death of a king and the election of his successor; the title was continued under the Republic to denote officers appointed to hold the comitia when the consulate happened to be vacant.

1579–80 NORTH *Plutarch* (1612) 308 The regents at that time called *Interreges.* **1590** L. LLOYD *Consent of Time* 682 This time in Fraunce were appointed two chiefe gouernours called *Interreges.* **1741** MIDDLETON *Cicero* I. vi. 521 The administration fell into the hands of an *Interrex*; a provisional Magistrate [etc.]. **1796** MORSE *Amer. Geog.* II. 287 Upon the king's demise the regal authority is then vested in the..primate of Poland, as interrex or regent. **1838–42** ARNOLD *Hist. Rome* II. xxv. 9 They resigned therefore, and the comitia were held by an interrex. **1855** LEWIS *Cred. Early Rom. Hist.* xii. §49 II. 204 The proposition for the appointment of an interrex..is mentioned by Livy.

interright, -rime: see INTER- *pref.* 2 a, 1 b.

interring (ɪn'tɜːrɪŋ), *vbl. sb.* [f. INTER *v.* + -ING¹.] The action of burying; interment, burial.

1303 [see INTER *v.* 1]. *c* **1375** *Sc. Leg. Saints, Theodera* 792 To se þat monkis enteryng. **1387** in *Eng. Gilds* (1870) 43 At his masse and his enteryinge. **1597** HOOKER *Eccl. Pol.* v. xli. §2 These Processions..were first begun for the interring of holy Martyrs. **1753** CHAMBERS *Cycl. Supp.* s.v. *Burial*, Interring appears to be the older practice.

interrogable (ɪn'tɛrəgəb(ə)l), *a.* [f. L. *interrogā-re* to INTERROGATE: see -ABLE.] Capable of being interrogated. So **in,terroga'bility**, capability of being interrogated.

1802–12 BENTHAM *Ration. Judic. Evid.* (1827) II. 169 For the purpose of justiciability (*vivâ voce* interrogability included). *Ibid.* III. 408 The person..being forthcoming and interrogable.

interrogant (ɪn'tɛrəgənt). [ad. L. *interrogānt-em*, pr. pple. of *interrogāre*: see next. Cf. F. *interrogant* (Cotgr. 1611).] = INTERROGATOR¹.

1647 LILLY *Chr. Astrol.* xxvii. 172 The Interrogant would know the cause why. **1807** *Edin. Rev.* IX. 279 It is always uncertain if the native has seized the idea of the interrogant. **1889** A. B. BRUCE *Kingd. God* ii. (1891) 71 The first evangelist makes Christ, in answer to His interrogants, at once announce the original law of marriage.

†**in'terrogate**, *sb. Obs. rare* Also **-rogat.** [ad. L. *interrogāt-um*, neut. of the pa. pple. of *interrogāre* (see next), used as sb. Perh. immed. a. F. *interrogat* (16th c. in Hatz.-Darm.).] A question; an interrogation.

1633 J. DONE *Hist. Septuagint* 169 The interrogats also of the King; and the Answers which were giuen him. **1649** BP. HALL *Cases Consc.* III. x. (1654) 270 Referring the *ventura* (things to come) to the following interrogate.

†**in'terrogate**, *ppl. a. Obs. rare.* [ad. L. *interrogāt-us*, pa. pple. of *interrogāre*: see next.] Interrogated, asked about; that is in question.

1625 *Impeachm. Dk. Buckhm.* (Camden) 38 Hee hath bin Skipper of the interrogate shipp..three yeeres.

interrogate (ɪn'tɛrəgeɪt), *v.* Also 5 **enter-**. Pa. t. and pple. **-ated** (8 *Sc.* **interrogate**). [f. L.

interrogāt-, ppl. stem of *interrogāre*, f. *inter* between, at intervals + *rogāre* to ask.]

1. a. *trans.* To ask questions of, to question (a person), esp. closely or in a formal manner; to examine by questions.

1483 CAXTON *Cato* D iv, They wold yet haue enterrogated hym but to them he sayd, speke no more to me for I..haue moche thynges to doo. **1626** J. PORY in Ellis *Orig. Lett.* Ser. I. III. 241 Those..knaves would by way of confession interrogate her Majestie. **1753** in *Stewart's Trial* App. 17 And being also further interrogate for the pannel, depones, That [etc.]. **1768** STERNE *Sent. Journ.* (1778) II. 20 (*Hotel at Paris*) Eugenius..had drawn me aside to interrogate me. **1855** MACAULAY *Hist. Eng.* xx. IV. 469 The Turkey merchants themselves were called in and interrogated. **1875** JOWETT *Plato* (ed. 2) IV. 236 [He] begs him to interrogate Theaetetus.

fig. **1701** NORRIS *Ideal World* I. v. 324 We often interrogate her [Truth] without knowing what it is which we demand of her. **1794** SULLIVAN *View Nat.* II. xliv. 245 Many..had not an opportunity to interrogate nature. **1875** HELPS *Ess., Organ. Daily Life* 182 Carefully interrogating my memory, I recollected that [etc.].

b. With dep. clause expressing the question.

a **1684** KNATCHBULL *Annot. Texts N. Test.* (1693) 312 The 'Catechumeni'..were interrogated by the Priest, whether they did believe in the Resurrection of the dead. **1721** *Wodrow Corr.* (1843) II. 585 They had conversed with the brethren, whom they interrogate, what they meant by the many other things they had to except against. **1785** J. ADAMS *Diary* 31 Jan., Wks. 1851 III. 389 He interrogated me, whether I had any correspondents in Holland.

†**2.** To ask about (something). *Obs. rare.*

1600–9 ROWLANDS *Knave of Clubs* 37 As on the way I Itinerated, A Rurall person I Obuiated, Interrogating times Transitation. **1698** FRYER *Acc. E. India & P.* 132 Interrogating the State of Europe, the Government, Policy, and Learning.

3. *absol.* or *intr.* To ask questions, to make inquiries; *spec.* in *Law* (see INTERROGATORY B. 1).

1622 BACON *Hen. VII* 244 By his Instructions..touching the Queene of Naples, it seemeth hee could Interrogate well touching Beautie. **1843** BETHUNE *Sc. Fireside Stor.* 39 It became not her to interrogate. **1883** *Law Times* 20 Oct. 407/2 The leave of the court to interrogate must be obtained.

b. With question quoted. (Cf. 1 b.)

a **1660** HAMMOND (J.), His proof will be retorted by interrogating, Shall the adulterer and the drunkard inherit the kingdom of God? **1824** L. MURRAY *Eng. Gram.* (ed. 5) I. 420 We may answer, by interrogating on our part; Do not those same poor peasants use the Lever and the Wedge? **1824** MISS FERRIER *Inher.* xxxvi, 'What am I to understand ..Miss St. C.?' interrogated he.

4. *trans.* **a.** To cause (a transponder, or a vehicle or craft fitted with one) to transmit a signal, usually coded to give information about the device or its surroundings, by transmitting a triggering signal to it.

1945 R. WATSON-WATT in *Nature* 15 Sept. 319/2 The 'H' and 'Oboe' systems, in which the primary radio pulses 'interrogating' the mobile craft automatically release from it a series of reinforced, coded, and conveniently frequency-displaced reply pulses. **1951** *Engineering* 3 Aug. 151/3 The aircraft would carry a transponder which, when interrogated would give the aircraft's identity and possibly other information such as height. **1953** *Electronic Engin.* XXV. 416/1 As the balloon ascends into the upper air, its airborne transponder is interrogated from the ground station by radar pulses. **1960** *Electronics Weekly* 23 Nov. 20/1 It..allows the control stations to interrogate each repeater for checking its operational condition. **1961** *Observer* 19 Feb. 11/1 The Russians have said they will 'interrogate' the rocket every five days. **1970** *Sci. Jrnl.* Apr. 52/1 Orbiting satellites interrogate the moving platforms.. as they pass over them, using a coded VHF signal, and receive back the data measured by sensors carried by the platforms.

b. To cause (a computer memory or memory element) to give a signal that corresponds to or reveals information contained in it.

1964 T. W. MCRAE *Impact of Computers on Accounting* i. 7 A system whereby one can interrogate any record (or group of records) directly without having to process all of the previous records is called a random access storage system. **1971** *Nature* 19 Mar. 156/2 It is now possible, in principle, for the user to interrogate the computer store directly. **1971** *Publishers' Weekly* 9 Aug. 25/3 The customer's file will be interrogated to determine his credit status. **1972** *Nature* 31 Mar. 206/1 The memories are interrogated (read) by much lower voltage signals.

Hence **in'terrogated** *ppl. a.* (also *absol.*), questioned; obtained by interrogation; **in'terrogatedness**, the quality of evidence obtained by interrogation; **in,terroga'tee**, one who is interrogated; **in'terro,gatingly** *adv.*, in a questioning manner.

1802–12 BENTHAM *Ration. Jud. Evid.* II. iv. §6 Abstract terms..of which some are already in use, others have been constructed for the purpose..4. Suggestedness..5. Unsuggestedness..6. Interrogatedness: if a conjugate of so harsh a form may, for the purpose of the moment, be endured. **1816** —— *Extract fr. Prop. Const. Code* (1830) 34 For falsity committed in this Judicatory the interrogatee is responsible. **1860** ELLICOTT *Life Our Lord* vii. 312 The interrogated now assuming the character of the interrogator. **1886** MISS LINSKILL *Haven under Hill* II. xvi. 210 'Well?' said Mrs. Stanmere interrogatingly. **1964** D. F. GALOUYE *Counterfeit World* i. 11 'I won't answer any questions,' Siskin said... The pollster frowned. 'You must. You are an officially registered interrogatee.'

interrogating (ɪn'tɛrəgeɪtɪŋ), *ppl. a.* [f. INTERROGAT(E *v.* + -ING[2].] Of a radio signal: intended to cause a transponder to emit a signal.

1946 *Jrnl. Inst. Electr. Engin.* XCIII. IIIA. 332/1 In the earliest radar beacon systems the responder replied on the same frequency as the radar interrogating pulse. **1953** *Electronic Engin.* XXV. 416/1 The interrogating pulses are received by the balloon-borne unit.

interrogation (ɪn,tɛrəʊ'geɪʃən). [a. F. *interrogation* (13th c. in Godef. *Compl.*), or ad. L. *interrogātiōn-em*, n. of action f. *interrogāre* to INTERROGATE.]

1. a. The action of interrogating or asking questions; a questioning; †request (*obs.*).

1551 BP. GARDINER *Explic.* 80 He opposith by interrogation, and would be aunswered. **1590** SWINBURNE *Testaments* 116 The testator maie lawfullie make his executor not onelie of his owne accorde without interrogation, but also at the intreatie or request of an other. **1632** LITHGOW *Trav.* x. 472 The Inquisitor made interrogation, of what difficulties, errors, or mis-beliefe I had. **1769** *Junius Lett.* (1804) I. 63, I could, by malicious interrogation, disturb the peace of the most virtuous man in the kingdom. **1825** J. NEAL *Bro. Jonathan* III. 177 If your heart were not pure..you would not be so ready to meet a deathbed interrogation.

b. With *an* and *pl.* A question. In quot. 1386 perh. = Syllogism, = L. *interrogātio* in Cicero.

c **1386** CHAUCER *Miller's T.* 8 His fantasye Was turned for to lerne Astrologye, And koude a certeyn of conclusions To demen by Interrogacions. **1526** *Pilgr. Perf.* (W. de W. 1531) 185 b, [That] all the interrogacyons or questyons made to vs be of fayth. **1563–87** FOXE *A. & M.* (1596) 105/1 The tenor of his questions or interrogations. **1700** S. L. tr. *Fryke's Voy. E. Ind.* 335 Some preliminary interrogations, why I would not settle there? **1861** GEO. ELIOT *Silas M.* i, He was trembling at this strange interrogation.

2. *Gram.* and *Rhet.* Questioning, or a question, as a form of speech.

c **1532** DU WES *Introd. Fr.* in Palsgr. 994 The interrogation negatyve, as, Am not I? **1589** PUTTENHAM *Eng. Poesie* III. xix. (Arb.) 220 There is a kinde of figuratiue speach when we aske many questions and looke for none answere, speaking..by interrogation, which we might as well say by affirmation. **1661–98** SOUTH *Twelve Serm.* III. 5 The words in the Text (by an usual way of speech) under an Interrogation couching a Positive Assertion. **1824** L. MURRAY *Eng. Gram.* (ed. 5) I. 513 Though Interrogations may be introduced into close and earnest reasoning, exclamations belong only to strong emotions of the mind.

b. ***point*** (***mark, note***) ***of interrogation***, also ***interrogation-point*** (and, formerly, *interrogation*): the symbol used in writing or printing to indicate a question, in most European languages placed at the end of the sentence and having the form ? or ;. Also *fig.*

In Spanish, it is placed both before and after the question, in the former case inverted as in *¿Quien sabe?* who knows? A point of interrogation is also sometimes placed before a word or phrase, to query its correctness, existence, etc.

1598 FLORIO, *Iterogatiuo punto*, a point of interrogation. **1633** J. CLARKE *2nd Praxis* 38 Secondly, you must marke all the poynts, commaes, colons, interogations, &c. **1706** PHILLIPS, *Interrogation*, or *Note of Interrogation*..which in Greek is thus expressed (;) and thus (?) in Latin. **1748** J. MASON *Elocut.* 23 The Common Stops or Points are these: A Comma (,), Semi-colon (;)..Interrogation (?), Admiration (!). **1888** J. A. NOBLE in *Academy* 3 Nov. 283/3 We are compelled to read them..with a greater number of mental notes of interrogation. **1889** W. B. YEATS *Let.* 7 May (1954) 125, I have no theories about her. She is simply a note of interrogation. **1895** *How to get Married* 74 It is a mistake to be inquisitive. A walking interrogation-point is never a pleasant companion. **1897** G. B. SHAW *Our Theatres in Nineties* (1932) III. 130 The ending of the play is not on the face of it particularly tragic: the alleged 'note of interrogation' is a sentimental fancy. **1931** H. G. WELLS *Work, Wealth & Happiness of Mankind* (1932) xv. 747 The note of interrogation which is born in the nature of every human being has been released. **1944** —— *'42 to '44* 116 No battle is a foregone conclusion, and so I must end with a note of interrogation. Will this thing be done now, rapidly?

3. The process of obtaining a signal from a transponder by transmitting an appropriate 'interrogating' signal to it; also, an interrogating signal.

1946 *Jrnl. Inst. Electr. Engin.* XCIII. IIIA. 487/2 The earlier varieties of I.F.F. all used direct interrogation. *Ibid.*, Each display..showed one echo fixed in position for each aircraft, due to its station's own interrogation. **1947** L. N. RIDENOUR *Radar Syst. Engin.* viii. 258 The interrogations were at 10 cm, the replies at 1·5 m. **1959** K. HENNEY *Radio Engin. Handbk.* (ed. 5) xix. 112 The moving craft sends out the interrogation and the beacon returns the reply. **1966** *Guardian* 19 Aug. 16/6 The new Interrogation Recording and Location System..to be embodied in future Nimbus satellites. **1970** *Sci. Jrnl.* Apr. 52/2 Direct interrogation of the package is made from the satellite using normal VHF interrogation telecommunications.

4. *attrib.* (sense 1), as ***interrogation centre, room***.

1973 *Freedom* 2 June 3/1 Always there are the Chicago-style shootings from passing cars, the churches bombed or burned, the homes gutted by fire and watching over it all the army with its own State-sponsored violence, the interrogation centre, the beatings-up, [etc.]. **1944** *Sat. Even. Post* 15 July 19, I went into the interrogation rooms with these pilots and listened to the laconic reports they were relating to the Intelligence officers. **1971** 'O. BLEECK' *Thief who painted Sunlight* (1972) ix. 79 We were in one of those small, brown interrogation rooms at Homicide South. **1972** H. C. RAE *Shooting Gallery* iii. 142 Surely, sir, you've *seen* them round here, in the Interrogation Room, at the desk?

interro'gational, *a.* [f. prec. + -AL[1].] Of the nature of an interrogation; interrogative.

1880 F. HALL *Doctor Indoctus* 24 Why the interrogational 'how are we'?

interrogative (ɪntə'rɒgətɪv), *a.* and *sb.* [ad. late L. *interrogātīv-us*: see INTERROGATE *v.* and -IVE. Cf. F. *interrogatif, -ive* (1507 in Godef.).]

A. *adj.*

1. Of, pertaining to, or of the nature of questioning; having the form or force of a question.

1597 HOOKER *Eccl. Pol.* v. lxiii. §3 The Baptisme, which saveth vs, is..ἐπερώτημα, an interrogative triall of a good conscience towards God. **1661–98** SOUTH *Twelve Serm.* III. 5 Nor does this Interrogative way of Expression import only a bare Negation of the Thing. **1711** J. GREENWOOD *Eng. Gram.* 209 The substantive comes before the verb except in an Interrogative sentence. **1853** KINGSLEY *Hypatia* xxviii. 354 Miriam made interrogative signs, which Pelagia understood as asking her whether she was alone. **1875** JOWETT *Plato* (ed. 2) IV. 152 The Platonic ideas are tested by the interrogative method of Socrates.

2. *Rhet.* and *Gram.* Of a word or form: Employed in asking a question.

interrogative pronouns, the pronouns *who? which? what? whether?* ***interrogative adverbs***, such as *where? when? why? wherefore?* ***interrogative point*** = INTERROGATION 2 b.

1520 WHITINTON *Vulg.* (1527) 6 Nownes interrogatyue as *quis, uter.* **1530** PALSGR. 80 Of the pronownes interrogatives. *c* **1532** DU WES *Introd. Fr.* in Palsgr. 994 The conjugation interrogative, as, Am I? *suis je?* **1589** PUTTENHAM *Eng. Poesie* II. iv. [v.] (Arb.) 89 His comma, colon and interrogatiue point. **1620** T. GRANGER *Div. Logike* 250 The interrogative particle, whether. **1845** STODDART *Gram.* in *Encycl. Metrop.* I. 186/1 The..interrogative form of the verb.

3. Given to asking questions; inquisitive. *rare.*

1709 STEELE *Tatler* No. 140 ¶11 Such Interrogative Gentlewomen are to be answered no other Way than by Interrogation. **1836** DICKENS *Sk. Boz* iv, He is a tall, thin, bony man, with an interrogative nose, and little restless perking eyes.

B. *sb.* **1.** An interrogation, a question. *rare.*

1581 SIDNEY *Apol. Poetrie* (Arb.) 30 These men..with a scornefull interogatiue, doe..aske. **1601** HOLLAND *Pliny* II. 295 Olenus Calenus..intended by subtill interrogatiue to translate the benefit thereof to his owne natiue countrey of Tuscane. **1847** JEFFREY *Let.* in Cockburn *Life* II. cxciv, I do expect and require an answer to all these interrogatives.

2. *Gram.* A word or form employed in asking a question; esp. an interrogative pronoun.

1530 PALSGR. Introd. 29 Relatyves as *qui* or *lequel*; interrogatyves as *qui.* **1533** UDALL *Flowres* 104 (R.) For al voices that are relatiues, may sometimes be interrogatiues, as whan they aske a question. **1763** LOWTH *Eng. Gram.* (1838) 39 *Who, which, what*, are called Interrogatives, when they are used in asking questions. **1875** WHITNEY *Life Lang.* v. 96 They [relatives] are demonstratives and interrogatives put to a new use.

interrogatively (ɪntə'rɒgətɪvlɪ), *adv.* [f. prec. + -LY[2].] In an interrogative manner; by way of interrogation; as a question.

1571 GOLDING *Calvin on Ps.* lvi. 8 Some reade..the verse interrogatiuely. **1609** W. BIDDULPH in T. Lavender *Trav.* (1612) B j b, That which Persius speaketh interrogatiuely, I vnderstand positiuely. **1751** HURD *Notes Ep. Augustus* (R.), Mr. Pope..seems to have read the lines interrogatively. **1876** MISS BRADDON *Dead Men's Shoes* i, A girl whom the passers by look at interrogatively.

interrogator[1] (ɪn'tɛrəgeɪtə(r)). [a. late L. *interrogātor*, agent-n. f. *interrogāre* to INTERROGATE; cf. F. *interrogateur* (1549 in Hatz.-Darm.).] **1.** One who interrogates; a questioner.

1751 HARRIS *Hermes* I. viii. 153 *note*, Retrenching by an ellipsis all the rest, which rest the interrogator is left to supply from himself. **1779–81** JOHNSON *L.P., Prior* Wks. III. 138 He was examined before a committee..Mr. Stanhope, and Mr. Lechmere were the principal interrogators. **1865** LIVINGSTONE *Zambesi* xxvii. 559 When we tried to fancy ourselves in the position of the interrogator.

2. A radio or radar transmitter designed to transmit interrogating signals to a transponder; also (more fully ***interrogator-responsor, -responder***), one that in addition receives the resulting signals from the transponder.

1945 *Nature* 15 Sept. 324/1 Pulses from an airborne or shipborne interrogator. **1945** *Electronic Engin.* XVII. 735/3 Aircraft and other moving vehicles could now carry small questioning transmitters ('interrogators'). **1946** *Jrnl. Inst. Electr. Engin.* XCIII. IIIA. 331/2 (*heading*) Introduction of an independent interrogator-responder system. **1947** A. ROBERTS *Radar Beacons* ii. 28 An interrogator-responsor can be so designed as to be useful as a radar. **1962** *Aeroplane & Commercial Aviation News* 29 Mar. 27/1 The aerial system ..was delivered in February and the interrogator-responsor is now being shipped. An airborne transponder is also being obtained.

†**inte'rrogator**[2]. *Sc. Obs.* [ad. F. *interrogatoire*; see next and cf. INTERLOCUTOR[2].] = INTERROGATORY B. 1. See also INTERGATOUR.

1561 *St. Andrews Kirk-sess. Reg.* (1889) 108 Examinat upon the generall interrogatouris of the law, he purgis hym [self]. **1609** SKENE *Reg. Maj.* 66 The veritie of the mater sall be tryed before the Justitiar, be sundrie interrogatouris and answers made thereto.

interrogatory (ɪntə'rɒgətərɪ), *a.* and *sb.* [ad. late L. *interrogātōri-us*: see INTERROGATE *v.* and

-ORY. Cf. F. *interrogatoire* (1422 in Hatz.-Darm.).]

A. *adj.* = INTERROGATIVE *a.* ***interrogatory point*** (see INTERROGATION 2 b).

1576 FLEMING *Panopl. Epist.* To Rdr. ¶v b, Of letters.. Interrogatori, Dehortatorie..there be sundrie sortes. *a* **1668** DAVENANT *Masque* Wks. (1673) 362 My Priviledges are an ubiquitary..interrogatory..immunity over all the privy lodgings. **1824** L. MURRAY *Eng. Gram.* (ed. 5) I. 407 Of the Interrogatory point. **1866** GEO. ELIOT *F. Holt* xlii, Hinted at in a mild interrogatory manner.

B. *sb.* **1.** An interrogation, a question; *spec.* in *Law*: A question formally put, or drawn up in writing to be put, to an accused person or a witness. (In 16–17th c. freq. in phr. ***to examine upon interrogatories***). See also INTERGATORY.

1533 in More *Apol.* xlv. Wks. 915/1 If he can by interrogatories and questions be drieuen to confesse anye thing. **1566** PAINTER *Pal. Pleas.* I. 42 He was..examined vpon interrogatories to bewraye the rest of the conspiratours. **1669** WOODHEAD *St. Teresa* I. xxxv. 265 He willed me to examine myself well upon this one Interrogatory. **1681** NEVILE *Plato Rediv.* 106 A more pertinent Interrogatory could never have been made by Plato, or Aristotle. **1751** JOHNSON *Rambler* No. 177 ¶3, I was bewildered by an unseasonable interrogatory. **1849** MACAULAY *Hist. Eng.* v. I. 562 A paper of interrogatories was laid before him by order of the Privy Council. **1898** *Encycl. Laws Eng.* (Renton) VII. 41 The Common Law Procedure Act, 1854, for the first time enabled interrogatories to be administered in actions in the superior Courts of Law.

2. Examination or questioning (of an accused person). *rare.* [= F. *interrogatoire*, It. *interrogatorio*.]

1827 HALLAM *Const. Hist.* (1876) I. i. 55 A tribunal.. proceeding by modes of interrogatory unknown to the common law. **1831–3** E. BURTON *Eccl. Hist.* xiv. (1845) 320 If the parties accused still confessed themselves Christians upon the third interrogatory, he ordered them to be put to death.

Hence **inte'rrogatorily** *adv.* = INTERROGATIVELY.

1625 BP. MOUNTAGU *App. Cæsar* II. xviii. 242 We.. propose it in Baptisme interrogatorily unto God-fathers and God-mothers. *c* **1866** ELIHU BURRITT *Descr. Locomotive*, And now he shouts, interrogatorily, All right?

interrogatrix (ɪnˌtɛrəʊ'geɪtrɪks). [fem., in L. form, corresp. to *interrogator*.] A female interrogator.

1859 tr. *Bengel's Gnomon* I. 466 The temptation was not great if you consider only the interrogatrix.

†**interrogue, -roge,** *v. Obs.* [a. OF. *interroguer* (1389 in Hatz.-Darm.; mod.F. *interroger*), ad. L. *interrogāre*.] = INTERROGATE *v.*

1484 CAXTON *Fables of Æsop* (1889) 253 They.. Interroged hym why he had slayne that man. *a* **1521** *Helyas* xxx. Nj, Whan the noble knight..had interrougued and questioned the duchesse.

in terrorem: see IN *Lat. prep.*

interrule: see INTER- *pref.* 1 a.

†**inte'rrupt,** *ppl. a. Obs.* Also 5 inteript, 6 -repte. [a. OF. *interrupt*, ad. L. *interrupt-us*, pa. pple of *interrumpĕre*: see next.] Interrupted, in various senses: see the verb. In quot. 1667, Forming an interval or breach between two parts of something. Usually construed as *pa. pple.*

1412–20 LYDG. *Chron. Troy* IV. xxix. (MS. Digby 230) lf. 130/2 Free eleccioun Not interrupte by mediacioun Of brocage. *c* **1450** *Merlin* 105 Ne therfore shull ye nothynge be inteript. ? *a* **1500** *Colyn Blowbols Test.* 206 in Hazl. *E.P.P.* I. 102, I wold they shold for no thing Be interupt of their possessouns. **1502** *Ord. Crysten Men* (W. de W. 1506) IV. xxiii. E e iij, Such wyll may be interrepte [*se peut interrompre*] and deuysed in many maners. **1549** LATIMER *4th Serm. bef. Edw. VI* (Arb.) 122 Prayer is neuer interrupte but by wickednes. **1667** MILTON *P.L.* III. 84 Our adversarie, whom no bounds Prescrib'd, no barrs of Hell..nor yet the main abyss Wide interrupt, can hold.

interrupt (ɪntə'rʌpt), *v.* Also 5 **interepte, interipte, intrippe,** 6 **interrup(p)e;** *pa. t.* 5 **enterrupte, interrupte,** 6 (*Sc.*) **interup.** [f. L. *interrupt-*, ppl. stem of *interrump-ĕre* to break asunder, break off (a speech or the like), f. *inter* between + *rumpĕre* to break: cf. CORRUPT.

With the form *interrup, -uppe*, cf. CORRUP, -UPPE.]

1. *trans.* To break in upon (an action, process, or condition, *esp.* speech or discourse); to break the continuity of (something) in time; to break off, to hinder the course or continuance of, cause to cease or stop (usually temporarily).

a **1420** HOCCLEVE *De Reg. Princ.* 1231 For as moche as it nat to me sit, Your tale for to interrupte or breke. **1526** SKELTON *Magnyf.* 257 Who made you so bolde to interrupe my tale? **1538** STARKEY *England* I. ii. 35, I wyl not interrupt your communycatyon now in the myddys. **1599** H. BUTTES *Dyets drie Dinner* D ij, They hinder, disturbe, and interrupt the course..of other mens matters. **1615** G. SANDYS *Trav.* 18 Not one of us but had his sleepe interrupted by fearfull dreames. **1673** TEMPLE *United Prov.* i. 5 Flanders was erected into a County, which changed the Title of Forester for that of Count, without interrupting the Succession. **1783** WATSON *Philip III*, II. (1839) 103 The army of the states was at hand to interrupt his operations. **1838** JAMES *Robber* iv, Do not let anything which has passed to-day interrupt our friendship. **1861** W. BELL *Dict. Law Scot.* 471/2 The acts whereby..prescriptions may be legally interrupted, and in effect put an end to.

b. To break the continuity of (something) in space or serial order; to make an interval or breach between the parts of (something continuous); to stand in the way of, obstruct (*e.g.* a view).

1647 CLARENDON *Hist. Reb.* II. §41 There being neither Tree nor Bush to interrupt his Charge. **1679** OWEN *Christologia* vi. (1831) 65 As a beam interrupted from its continuity unto the sun is immediately deprived of light. **1774** PENNANT *Tour Scotl. in 1772*, 166 The land is so interrupted with rocks, that the natives, instead of the plough are obliged to make use of the spade. **1794** MRS. RADCLIFFE *Myst. Udolpho* i, They interrupt my prospects.

2. To break in upon (a person) while doing something, *esp.* speaking; to hinder from proceeding with some action; to cause to stop (usually temporarily) in what one is doing.

1413 *Pilgr. Sowle* I. xvi. (1859) 17 There roose vp soone a lady and enterrupte me of my wordes. *c* **1430** ? LYDG. *Stans. Puer* 69 (Lamb. MS. 853) Intrippe no man where so þat þou wende, No man in his tale [1450–60 *MS. Harl.* 2251 Interrupt nat..None other mans tale]. **1578** T. N. tr. *Conq. W. India* 40 The poore Indians durst not once interrupt them. **1639** T. BRUGIS tr. *Camus' Mor. Relat.* 302 It were a grosse incivility to interrupt them in their conversation. **1709** STEELE *Tatler* No. 45 ¶8 Florio, who never interrupted any Man living when he was speaking. **1887** RUSKIN *Præterita* II. xii. 421, I could not bear being interrupted in anything I was about.

3. *absol.* or *intr.* (from 1 or 2). (Also quasi-*trans.* with the words spoken as object = to say in interruption.)

1412–20 LYDG. *Chron. Troy* V. xxxviii, (MS. Digby 230) lf. 188 b/2 Ther shal no man reclayme ne sei nay, Interrupte ne make no delay. **1667** MILTON *P.L.* IX. 512 As one who sought access, but feard To interrupt, side-long he works his way. **1828** SCOTT *F.M. Perth* xxv, 'Ay, truly', interrupted the glover; 'and I so counselled and commanded thee'. **1875** JOWETT *Plato* (ed. 2) I. 220 By Zeus, said Ctesippus, interrupting, I only wish that you would give me some proof. *Ibid.* 224 Please not to interrupt, my good friend.

†**4.** *trans.* To hinder, stop, prevent, thwart. **a.** an action, etc. *Obs.*

1497 BP. ALCOCK *Mons Perfect.* B iij, This holy ghost interrupte this desyre, and apperyd. **1548** HALL *Chron., Edw. IV* 242 b, To the onely intent, that the mariage should herafter, neither be interrupted nor broken. **1632** J. HAYWARD tr. *Biondi's Eromena* 141 The neighbours would have been awaked, and so the execution of their designes interrupted.

†**b.** a person, etc., in or from some action. Const. *of* or with *inf. Obs.*

1464 *Mann. & Househ. Exp.* (Roxb.) 184, I schal nat interepte heme deweryng is lyffe. **1481** CAXTON *Myrr.* I. xiii. 41 Ther is noman that coude interrupte hym of ony thing that he wolde preue. **1604** JAS. I *Counterbl.* (Arb.) 102 To interrupt them of their due function. **1624** BP. HALL *Hon. Mar. Clergy* Ded., Satan enuying me this happinesse, interrupts me by the malice of an importunate Aduersarie.

†**5.** To infringe, suspend (a law). *Obs.*

1430–40 LYDG. *Bochas* IV. v. (1554) 103 b, Al their statutes by which thei were made fre He interrupted of force and not of right. **1587** GOLDING *De Mornay* xxxiii. 536 God created nature, and hath giuen it a Lawe, which Lawe he wil haue it to follow. Neuerthelesse somtimes..he interrupteth it,..to make vs to know yͭ he is Lord of nature.

†**6.** To cut short, put an end to, destroy. *Obs.*

1570 *Satir. Poems Reform.* xx. 176 The Cup, Quhairwith oft tymes, for saikles crymes, Mennis lyues he Interup. **1608** TOPSELL *Serpents* (1658) 686 So soon as a great Crocodile is discovered, there is such watch and care taken to interrupt and kill him for hope of the reward, that he cannot long escape alive.

interrupt (ɪntə'rʌpt), *sb. Computing.* [f. the vb.]

1. The action (usu. automatic) of interrupting the execution of a program as a result of the need for the immediate execution of another program, after which the original program is automatically resumed.

1957 *Computers & Automation* VI. 17/2 The interrupt feature of the 1103A will no doubt be embodied in many future computers. **1967** *Technology Week* 23 Jan. 11/1 (Advt.), Sigma 5 can deal with foreground real-time interrupts in 6 microseconds. **1969** P. B. JORDAIN *Condensed Computer Encycl.* 257 Some interrupts are initiated by the computer operator when he wants to give a command, or by a remote user who wishes to request service. **1970** O. DOPPING *Computers & Data Processing* vi. 106 In older computers, the response to an error discovered by the built-in checks was usually to stop... In modern machines, the response usually is an interrupt..which automatically gives a branch to a special routine for analyzing and, if possible, correcting the error. *Ibid.* ix. 126 During these time intervals, the computer can run a background program which is not a real-time job. When a transaction has been input, perhaps over a telecommunication line, an interrupt signal causes the CPU to hand over control to the real-time program. When the transaction is dealt with.., a return jump to background takes place.

2. Special Comb.: **interrupt handler**, a routine that deals with interrupts and returns control to the main program afterwards; so **interrupt handling** *vbl. sb.*

[**1963** *Information Processing Jrnl.* II. 209/2 The IBM 7070 STRETCH machine requires, by its speed and design, some resident routine, monitor, or interruption handler.] **1966** *Proc. IEEE* LIV. 1812 (*heading*) A method of processor selection for interrupt handling in a multiprocessor system. **1978** H. LORIN in J. Belzer et al. *Encycl. Computer Sci. & Technol.* XI. 399 The function of the interrupt handler is to save the registers and other status information about the interrupted program..so that the program can be resumed at its point of disruption at some time in the future. **1982** P. E. BURTON *Dict. Minicomputing & Microcomputing* 139 The interrupt handler processes interrupt signals from peripheral devices and resolves contentions for the services of the CPU. **1985** *Personal Computer World* Feb. 169/3 Probably the most surprising and most useful..is WHEN, which incorporates interrupt-handling into a program.

interrupted (ɪntə'rʌptɪd), *ppl. a.* [f. INTERRUPT *v.* + -ED[1].] Broken in upon; broken off; having its course hindered or continuity broken; made discontinuous: see the verb.

1552 HULOET, Interrupted, *interpellatus.* **1592** DANIEL *Delia* ii, Sigh out a Storie of her cruell deedes, With interrupted accents of despaire. **1607** SHAKS. *Cor.* III. i. 249 Whose Rage doth rend Like interrupted Waters, and o're-beare What they are vs'd to beare. **1748** DODSLEY *Preceptor* (1763) I. p. xliv, Express..Sorrow by a low, flexible interrupted Voice. **1879** *St. George's Hosp. Rep.* IX. 605 The patient recovered under daily application of the interrupted current.

b. *Bot.* (and *Zool.*) Having smaller, or otherwise differing, members (*e.g.* leaflets in a compound leaf, or spikelets in an inflorescence) in the intervals between the others in a series; also, having a gap or void interval, discontinuous (as a linear marking): see next b.

1855 MAYNE *Expos. Lex.*, *Interruptus, Bot.*, broken in respect to uniformity: interrupted. **1861** MISS PRATT *Flower. Pl.* VI. 269 Interrupted Club-moss. **1866** *Treas. Bot.*, *Interrupted*, when any symmetrical arrangement is destroyed by local causes: a leaf is interruptedly pinnated when some of the pinnæ are much smaller than the others, or wholly wanting.

c. *Mus.* ***interrupted cadence***: an alteration of the perfect cadence, in which the full close is deferred or evaded by the use of some other chord (usually that of the sixth of the key) instead of that of the tonic.

1811 BUSBY *Dict. Mus.* (ed. 3), *Interrupted*, a term applied by theorists to those closes or cadences in which the base, instead of falling or rising from the fifth to the key-note, passes to some other, and interrupts the full close, or final cadence. **1877** STAINER *Harmony* xii, The interrupted cadence consists of a temporary delay of the perfect cadence. **1880** C. H. H. PARRY in Grove *Dict. Mus.* I. 291 The form of Interrupted cadence generally quoted as typical is that in which the chord of the dominant, instead of proceeding to the harmony of the tonic as the mind is led to expect, is followed by the chord of the 6th of the key, or sub-mediant.

inte'rruptedly, *adv.* [f. prec. + -LY[2].] In an interrupted manner; with interruptions or void intervals; discontinuously.

1663 BOYLE *Exp. Hist. Colours* I. iii. §19 The incident light that meets with a grosser liquour..will have its beams either refracted, or imbibed, or else reflected more or less interruptedly than they would be, if the body had been unmoistened. *a* **1708** BEVERIDGE *Thes. Theol.* (1711) III. 38 Not interruptedly, but constantly. **1817** BYRON *Manfred* III. iv, Interruptedly..the fitful song Begun and died upon the gentle wind.

b. *Bot.* (and *Zool.*) With smaller or otherwise different members in the intervals between the others: see prec. b.

1753 CHAMBERS *Cycl. Supp.* s.v. *Leaf* (*Pinnated*), The interruptedly pinnated, in which the folioles are irregular and unequal in size or situation. **1846** DANA *Zooph.* (1848) 215 Cellules interruptedly uniseriate. **1870** HOOKER *Stud. Flora* 108 *Spiræa ulmaria*..leaves interruptedly pinnate. *Ibid.* 290 *Galeopsis Ladanum*..leaves..interruptedly serrate or subentire.

interrupter, -or (ɪntə'rʌptə(r)). Also 6 -our(e. [In form α, a. L. *interruptor*, agent-n. from *interrumpĕre*: cf. F. *interrupteur*; in β, f. INTERRUPT *v.* + -ER[1].] **a.** One who interrupts: see the vb.

α. **1511–12** *Act 3 Hen. VIII*, c. 10 The seid interruptoures and letters therof to be brought to Gaole. **1552** HULOET, Interruptour, *interpellator.* **1602** WARNER *Alb. Eng.* x. lviii. (1612) 254 Wherefore our Queene her interruptors sent. **1797** MAD. D'ARBLAY *Diary & Lett.* VI. 141 Princess Augusta declined any interruptors.

β. **1573–80** BARET *Alv.* L 342 A disturber, or letter of other: an interrupter. **1654–66** LD. ORRERY *Parthen.* (1676) 203 To seek out the high interrupter of it. **1771** MRS. DELANY *Life & Corr.* Ser. II. I. 382 We were so busy no interrupters were admitted. **1804** H. K. WHITE *Let. to B. Maddock* in *Rem.* (1819) I. 135 The companion of my walks —the interrupter of my evening studies. **1869** *Daily News* 16 Apr., This rebuke was loudly cheered by Mr. Aytoun's interrupters.

b. A device for interrupting an electric current.

1851 C. CIST *Cincinnati* 302 It has been represented that Prof. Locke had merely invented a new species of 'electrical interrupter'. **1881** S. P. THOMPSON *Electr. & Magn.* x. §398 The interruptors of induction coils are usually self-acting. **1881** *Sci. American* XIX. 388 If a Helmholtz interrupter be employed to make and break the primary circuit.

c. *attrib.* **interrupter gear**, a timing device attached to machine-guns in aeroplanes to prevent the discharge of bullets when the propeller is in the line of fire. Also *transf.*

1928 C. F. S. GAMBLE *Story N. Sea Air Station* x. 150 The Fökker monoplane, which was equipped with a mechanical interrupter gear. **1932** *Discovery* Oct. 323/2 A very great advance..has been made in reducing the attrition of fabrics during washing, by an invention of the Research Association, called the Interrupter Gear. **1940** *Flight* 4 Jan.

characteristics proper to the other sex. Also *absol.* as *sb.*, an intersexual individual.

1916 [see INTERSEXUALITY]. **1917** R. GOLDSCHMIDT in *Endocrinology* I. 438 With the male of race P, all would-be females will be high grade intersexuals, almost transformed into males. **1926** J. S. HUXLEY *Ess. Pop. Sci.* 51 Intersexual males—*i.e.* animals which have started as males and been forced to finish their development as females. **1962** D. J. B. ASHLEY *Human Intersex* xxi. 289 When the diagnosis of an intersexual state is deferred. **1965** *Punch* 10 Nov. 691/1 The intersexual goats are sterile. **1970** *Guardian* 7 Jan. 7/3 With ..intersexuals, the problem begins at birth, for in rare cases it is uncertain from the genital organs whether a baby is a boy or a girl.

intersexuality (ˌɪntəsɛksjuːˈælɪtɪ). *Biol.* [ad. G. *intersexualität* (R. Goldschmidt 1915, in *Biol. Centralblatt* XXXV. 566): see INTER- 2 b and SEXUALITY.] The state or condition of being intersexual; intersexual character.

1916 R. GOLDSCHMIDT in *Amer. Naturalist* L. 708 It seems advisable to use another term for these forms, which in general represent a definite step between the two sexes. The phenomenon shall therefore be called intersexuality. Further experiments now proved that intersexuality segregates, F_2 giving normal and intersexual animals. **1930** G. R. DE BEER *Embryol. & Evolution* iii. 22 A series of degrees of intersexuality can be established from very slight to complete sex-reversal. **1965** *Punch* 10 Nov. 691 Goat-breeders have tried to maximise hornlessness..but in so doing they have unwittingly increased the frequency of the gene for intersexuality. **1966** K. L. MOORE *Sex Chromatin* xiv. 229 Intersexuality occurs about as frequently in cattle, swine and goats as it does in humans.

inter-shade: see INTER- *pref.*

intershock (ɪntəˈʃɒk), *v. rare.* Also 7 enter-. [f. INTER- 1 b + SHOCK *v.*, in sense 1 after F. *s'entrechoquer* (1564 in Thierry).]

† **1.** *trans.* To strike or attack mutually. *Obs.*

1603 FLORIO *Montaigne* I. xlvii. (1632) 153 When with vehemence they come to entershocke one another. **1605** DANIEL *Philotas* Wks. (1717) 372 What Discontentments will there still arise In such a Camp of Kings, to intershock Each others Greatness.

2. *intr.* To strike together, collide.

1650 EARL MONM. tr. *Senault's Man bec. Guilty* 227 Pleasures do enter-shock, and always leave some of our senses in languishment. **1886** SHELDON tr. *Flaubert's Salammbo* xiv. 395 The elephants' carcases, driven by the wind, intershocked, like an archipelago of black rocks floating on the water.

Hence **inter'shocking** *vbl. sb.* So † **'intershock** *sb.* [cf. obs. F. *entrechoc*]. *rare*$^{-0}$.

1611 COTGR., *Entrechoc*, an intershocke; a mutuall or interchangeable rushing one vpon another. **1652** URQUHART *Jewel* Wks. (1834) 264 There was concerning it such an intershocking of opinions. **1706** PHILLIPS, *Intershock*, a clashing, or striking of one thing against another.

intershoot (ɪntəˈʃuːt), *v.* [INTER- 1 a.] **a.** *intr.* To shoot or glance at intervals. **b.** *trans.* To shoot or dart between or among; to variegate at intervals (chiefly in pa. pple. *intershot*, *const. with*: cf. SHOT *ppl. a.*).

1845 WORDSW. *Suggested by Bird of Paradise* 21 Hues.. intershooting, and to sight Lost and recovered, as the rays of light Glance on the conscious plumes. **1845** FABER *Rosary*, etc. 56 A long broad lake of meadow-grass..intershot with gold and green. **1890** *Chicago News* 29 Oct., The fires of the eruption intershot the dense smoke.

intersidereal (ˌɪntəsaɪˈdɪəriːəl), *a.* [f. INTER- 4 a + L. *sīdus, sīder-* star: see SIDEREAL.] Situated or occurring between the stars: = INTERSTELLAR.

1656 tr. *Hobbes' Elem. Philos.* Wks. 1839 I. 445 Besides the stars..they may be all comprehended under the name of intersidereal bodies. **1862** SIR H. HOLLAND *Ess.* i. 18 Those inter-planetary and inter-sidereal distances.

† **inter'silient**, *a. Obs. rare.* [f. L. type **intersilient-em*, pr. pple. of **intersilīre* to leap or spring between, f. *inter* between + *salīre* to leap.] Emerging suddenly in the midst of something.

1647 WARD *Simp. Cobler* 50 Parliaments, Senates or accountable Commissions, must have power to consult and execute against intersilient dangers and flagitious crimes, prohibited by the light of Nature.

† **inter'sist**, *v. Obs. rare*$^{-0}$. [ad. L. *intersist-ĕre* to stop between.]

1623 COCKERAM, *Intersist*, to stay betweene.

† **'intersited**, *ppl. a. Obs. rare.* [f. L. *intersit-us* put between, interposed, pa. pple. of *interserĕre* set between + -ED[1].] Placed or situated between; interposed.

1578 BANISTER *Hist. Man.* I. 22 The soft Cartilage intersited betwene their bodyes, is so much the greater and thicker.

intersituate, -smile: see INTER- *pref.* 1 a.

intersocial (ɪntəˈsəʊʃəl), *a.* [f. INTER- 4 c + L. *socius* companion: see SOCIAL.] Existing between associates; social.

1852 ROGET *Thesaurus* Introd. (1892) 27 *note*, I have.. ventured to introduce the adjective *intersocial*, to express the active voluntary relations between man and man. **1864** *Realm* 6 Apr. 8 The pressure of intersocial criticism. **1883** *Longm. Mag.* July 262 They have..entered on the condition of inter-social citizens.

† **inter'soil**, *v. Agric. Obs.* [f. INTER- 1 b + SOIL *sb.*] To mix one kind of soil with another.

1610 W. FOLKINGHAM *Art of Survey* I. x. 33 We would endeuour..to make seuerall Soyles serue interchangeably.. by inter-soyling or seasoning the one with the other. **1688** R. HOLME *Armoury* III. 334/1. **1725** in BRADLEY *Fam. Dict.*

intersole, *sb.* variant of ENTRESOL.

intersole, *v.*: see INTER- *pref.* 1 a.

intersomnial (ɪntəˈsɒmnɪəl), *a.* [f. INTER- 4 d + L. *somni-um* dream + -AL[1]: more properly *intrasomnial.*] Occurring in the midst of a dream. So **inter'somnious** *a.*, 'between sleeping and waking' (Worcester 1846, citing *Dublin Rev.*).

1849 H. MAYO *Truths Pop. Superst.* iv. 69 The ghostly and intersomnial communications..have been announcements of the deaths of absent parties.

in'tersonant, *a. rare*$^{-0}$. [ad. L. *intersonānt-em*, pr. pple. of *intersonāre* to sound between or among.] 'Sounding between' (Ogilvie).

† **inter'sour**, *v. Obs.* [f. INTER- 1 a + SOUR *v.* or *a.*] *trans.* To intermix sourness in or with.

1599 DANIEL *Let. Octavia* Wks. (1717) I. 81 Fear..held back something from thee full of Sweet, To intersour unsure Delights the more.

intersow (ɪntəˈsəʊ), *v.* Pa. pple. -sown. [INTER- 1 a: cf. *interseam, interseminate.*]

1. *trans.* To sow, or *fig.* to scatter or sprinkle, among or between other things; = INTERSPERSE 1.

1605 CAMDEN *Rem.* (1636) 40 Here amongst, the Brittans have left divers of their words intersowed.

2. To furnish (ground, etc.) with seed or the like sown or scattered among or between other things, or at intervals; const. *with*: = INTERSPERSE 2.

1725 BRADLEY *Fam. Dict.* s.v. *Planting*, The remainder of the Ground may be inter-sow'd with Ash-Keys. **1856** R. A. VAUGHAN *Mystics* (1860) II. VIII. ix 97 The very dust is dazzling and priceless, intersown with the sapphire, the sardonyx, the emerald of heaven.

interspace (ˈɪntəspeɪs), *sb.* [INTER- 2 b.]

1. A space between two things; intermediate or intervening space, interval.

c **1420** *Pallad on Husb.* II. 88 Yf diches plese, hem make, and thre feet depe..Thyn entre space in oon maner thou kepe. **1611** FLORIO, *Intermezzo*,..an interspace. **1658** SIR T. BROWNE *Gard. Cyrus* ii. 41 [The crown] was framed.. with an intersection in the middle from the main crossing barres, and the interspaces, unto the frontal circle, continued by handsome network-plates. **1726** LEONI *Alberti's Archit.* II. 41/2 The Ancients..made a grate of brass..and filled up the interspaces of this grate..with a transparent sort of stone. **1817** COLERIDGE *Zapolya* IV. iii, Our messengers are posted With such short interspace, that fast as sound Can travel to us, we shall learn the event. **1866** LAING *Preh. Rem. Caithn.* 32 Consisting of concentric circular walls with cells or chambers in the interspaces between the walls.

2. A space of time between two events, etc.; an interval of time.

1629 MAXWELL tr. *Herodian* (1635) 186 The inter-space betwixt the past and present Celebrity, exceeded the longest Age of Men. *a* **1670** HACKET *Abp. Williams* I. (1693) 27 To gather up more at the Interspaces of Leisure, then others do at their Study. **1820** *Blackw. Mag.* VI. 379 Men..separated by the interspace of ages. **1879** FARRAR *St. Paul* (1883) 575 During one of those little interspaces of repose and hope which occur in even the most persecuted lives.

interspace (ɪntəˈspeɪs), *v.* [INTER- 1.] *trans.* To put a space or interval between; to occupy or fill the space or interval between.

1847 BUSHNELL *Chr. Nurt.* II. iii. (1861) 282 Intelligent feeding, which is interspaced by rest. **1886** H. JAMES *Bostonians* II. II. xxi. 58 He bagan to interspace his visits considerably, and at last made them very rare. **1889** HORTON *Inspir. & bible* vi. 143 It is necessary sometimes to interspace, if we may so term it, the Biblical records.

interspatial (ɪntəˈspeɪʃ(ɪ)əl), *a.* [f. L. type **interspati-um* as = *interspace* + -AL[1]: cf. SPATIAL.] Of or belonging to an interspace, *esp.* in *Entom.* to one of the interspaces or areas between the veins on an insect's wing. Hence **inter'spatially** *adv.*, in relation to an interspace.

† **'interˌspeaker.** *Obs. rare.* [INTER- 2 a.] One who holds a colloquy with another; an interlocutor. So † **'interspeaking** *ppl. a.* (*rare*$^{-0}$).

1586 T. B. *La Primaud. Fr. Acad.* I. To Rdr., The chiefe scope and drift of these Interspeakers. **1594** *Ibid.* II. 1 The forespeach of the interspeakers in this Academy, wherein is handled the cause of their future discourses. **1611** FLORIO, *Interparlante*, enterspeaking.

inter-species: see INTER- *pref.* 5.

interspe'cific, *a.* [f. INTER- 4 c + SPECIFIC, as adj. from *species.*] Existing or prevailing betwen different species. Also, formed or obtained from (individuals of) different species.

1889 *Nature* XXXIX. 287/1 As the description of the relations of organs characterized the physiology of the individual, so that of interspecific adaptations is the physiology of the race. **1913** *Amer. Naturalist* XLVII. 243 Interspecific hybrids seldom show the typical Mendelian behavior. **1946** [see INTERGENERIC *a.*]. **1968** H. HARRIS *Nucleus & Cytoplasm* v. 93 If somatic cells derived from the two species of animal are fused together with inactivated virus, the resultant interspecific hybrids not only multiply, but actually over-grow the two parent cells.

Hence **interspe'cifically** *adv.*, between species, from one species to another.

1970 *Nature* 10 Oct. 189/2 The number of cellular enzymes known to differ interspecifically, for example, between mouse and man, is increasing rapidly.

† **'interspeech.** *Obs.* [INTER- 2 a.] Speech between or among a number of persons; colloquy.

1579 FENTON *Guicciard.* x. (1599) 453 Peradventure..it was more profitable with these enterspeeches to stay the kings armie. **1656** BLOUNT *Glossogr.* s.v. *Deipnosophists*, That title, importing a Conference, Discourse or inter-speech among wise men at a supper.

inter'spersal. *rare.* [f. next + -AL[1].] = INTERSPERSION.

1893 *Athenæum* 11 Mar. 314/1 To vary the somewhat monotonous succession of the thirty Pipe Rolls..by the judicious interspersal of these unique fragments.

intersperse (ɪntəˈspɜːs), *v.* Also 6 **entersparse.** [f. L. *interspers-*, ppl. stem of **interspergĕre* (found only in pa. pple. *interspersus*), f. *inter* between + *spargĕre* to scatter, sprinkle.]

1. *trans.* To scatter or sprinkle between or among other things; to place here and there in the course of something; to mingle dispersedly or at intervals.

c **1645** HOWELL *Lett.* II. lxix. (1655) II. 100 You should do well to intersperse among them some eucharistical ejaculations and doxologies. **1712** ADDISON *Spect.* No. 315 ¶3 That particular Art which he [Milton] has made use of in the interspersing of all those Graces of Poetry, which the Subject was capable of receiving. **1856** KINGSLEY *Lett.* (1878) I. 413, I like the way in which you have interspersed local traditions and stories.

2. To furnish, adorn, or diversify (a thing) *with* other things scattered about, placed here and there, or mingled at intervals.

1566 ADLINGTON *Apuleius* 51 A man of midle age hauing his bearde entersparsed with gray heares. **1645** EVELYN *Diary* 7 Feb., Various colour'd cinders..some like pitch.. other metaliq, interspers'd with innumerable pumices. **1781** GIBBON *Decl. & F.* xxiv. (1869) I. 687 The face of the country was interspersed with groves. **1796** C. MARSHALL *Garden.* xix. (1813) 378 Rich crimson grains interspersed with black berries. **1858** THACKERAY *Virgin.* iv, Harry had proceeded in his narrative after his own fashion, interspersing it with many youthful ejaculations.

b. Rarely said of the things intermingled.

1796 MORSE *Amer. Geog.* I. 172 A prodigious number of islands intersperse that mighty river.

interspersed (ɪntəˈspɜːst), *ppl. a.* [f. prec. + -ED[1].] Scattered, or placed here and there, between or among other things; dispersedly mingled.

1664 POWER *Exp. Philos.* II. 133 The particles..with interspersed Vacuities. *a* **1711** KEN *Edmund* Poet. Wks. 1721 II. 332 Short Sleeps, and watchful Care, Alternated with interspersed Prayer. **1863** LYELL *Antiq. Man* 12 Large heaps of oysters, and other marine shells, with interspersed stone implements.

Hence **inter'spersedly** (-ɪdlɪ) *adv.*, in an interspersed manner; here and there among other things.

1664 POWER *Exp. Philos.* II. 119 Aetherial Atoms may be interspersedly diffused through all our Elements. **1861** MUSGRAVE *By-roads* 241 Producing corn, flax, and beet-root, interspersedly with carrots, potatoes, and dwarf beans.

interspersion (ɪntəˈspɜːʃən). [n. of action f. INTERSPERSE; cf. *aspersion, dispersion.*] The action of interspersing or condition of being interspersed; dispersion among other things; an intermingling here and there.

1658 PHILLIPS, *Interspersion*, a sprinkling or scattering between. **1662** STILLINGFL. *Orig. Sacr.* III. ii. §15 The ground of divisibility of bodyes is the interspersion of a disseminated Vacuum. **1712** ADDISON *Spect.* No. 387 ¶13 This Interspersion of Evil with Good, and Pain with Pleasure, in the Works of Nature, is very truly ascribed by Mr. Locke..to a moral Reason. **1811** PINKERTON *Petral.* I. 132 The interspersion of a few crystals..of felspar or felsite. **1865** E. BURRITT *Walk Land's End* 409 A picturesque interspersion of church towers, villages, hamlets, and the half-revealed faces of stately mansions.

interspheral: see INTER-.

inter'sphere, *v.* [INTER- 1 b.] **a.** *trans.* To bring within the sphere one of another. **b.** *intr.* To come each within the sphere or orbit of the other.

1887 *Chicago Advance* 28 Apr. 259/4 The interests of men and women are so intersphered that whatever affects one reacts upon the other. **1889** *Harper's Mag.* Feb. 466/2 Their lines shall intersphere or soon or late, And move together to the journey's end. **1896** LADY H. SOMERSET *Addr. Brit. Wom. Temp. Assoc.* 1 June, That intersphering of the world life with our own, is already the practical realization of many.

inter-spicular: see INTER- *pref.*

interspinal (ɪntəˈspaɪnəl), *a. Anat.* [INTER- 4 a: in mod.L. *interspīnālis*.] = INTERSPINOUS.

1831 R. KNOX *Cloquet's Anat.* 186 Interspinal Ligaments . . These ligaments occupy the intervals of the spinous processes in the back. **1888** ROLLESTON & JACKSON *Anim. Life* 94 The dorsal and anal fins [of the Perch] are supported by a series of bones, 'fin-bearers' or 'interspinal' bones.

interspinous (ɪntəˈspaɪnəs), *a. Anat.* [INTER- 4 a.] Situated between the spines or spinous processes of vertebræ.

1842 E. WILSON *Anat. Vade M.* (ed. 2) 97 The interspinous ligaments are thin and membranous. **1881** MIVART *Cat* 54 Adjacent spinous processes are also connected together by membranes . . called interspinous ligaments.

b. *spec.* in *Ichthyol.* Situated between the spines of the vertebræ of a teleostean fish, so as to support the dorsal fin.

1839–47 TODD *Cycl. Anat.* III. 845/2 Interspinous bones . . embedded in the flesh of the back. **1870** ROLLESTON *Anim. Life* Introd. 32 The inter-spinous bones and fin-rays of more highly organized fish.

inter-spiral: see INTER- *pref.*

†**interspiˈration.** *Obs.* [ad. L. *interspīrātiōn-em*, n. of action from *interspīrāre*: see next.] A taking breath between; a breathing space, a momentary pause or rest.

1623 COCKERAM, *Interspiration*, a breathing betweene. **1635** BRATHWAIT *Arcad. Pr.* 29 These interspirations minister new matter to their distemper'd humour to worke on. **1656** H. MORE *Enthus. Tri.* To Rdr. A iv b, That there may be a due time of Interspiration betwixt the ending of the serious and the entring into the merry passages.

†**interˈspire,** *v. Obs. rare*$^{-1}$. [ad. L. *interspīrāre*, f. *inter* between + *spīrāre* to breathe.] *intr.* To take breath between; to pause, take rest.

1647 H. MORE *Song of Soul* II. App. lxxiii, And now I do awhile but interspire, A torrent of objections 'gainst me beat. **1721** in BAILEY.

interˈsprinkle, *v.* [INTER- 1 a.] *trans.* To sprinkle here and there, or at intervals; to intersperse. Hence **interˈsprinkled** *ppl. a.*

1842 ALISON *Europe* (1849–50) XI. lxxvi. §74. 480 Luxuriant valleys, intersprinkled with hamlets, vineyards, and flower-gardens. **1898** HORTON *Commandm. Jesus* viii. 136 The modest purple of the intersprinkled violets.

intersqueeze: see INTER-.

interstadial (ɪntəˈsteɪdɪəl), *sb.* and *a. Geol.* [a. G. *interstadial*, ad. F. *interstadiaire* adj. (A. Penck et al. 1894, in *Bull. de la Soc. d. Sci. nat. de Neuchâtel* XXII. 81): see INTER- and STADIAL.] **A.** *sb.* A minor period of ice retreat during a glacial period, less pronounced than an interglacial. **B.** *adj.* Pertaining to or characteristic of such a period.

1914 W. B. WRIGHT *Quaternary Ice Age* vii. 156 It is, of course, extremely difficult to distinguish between interstadial and interglacial. This can only be done with certainty when the flora of the deposit in question indicates an oscillation of the snow-line of too great a magnitude to be regarded as interstadial. **1922** *Bull. Geol. Soc. Amer.* XXXIII. 421 Baltic interstadial (= Achen recession). **1946** L. D. STAMP *Britain's Struct.* xiv. 163 Arkell attributes the Aurignacian buried channel period to an 'interstadial' period in the midst of the Fourth or Final Glaciation rather than to the Third Interglacial. **1953** *Proc. Prehist. Soc.* XIX. 181 The additional notch at about 5 m. may correspond to the Epi-Monastirian beach of the First Interstadial of the Last Glaciation. **1968** ERICSON & WOLLIN *Ever Changing Sea* iv. 139 We may be living during a short interval of mild climate, or interstadial, within the last ice age. **1969** *Proc. Geol. Soc.* Aug. 155 Includes Upton Warren interstadial complex. **1973** *Times Lit. Suppl.* 1 June 607/3 (Advt.), The evidence for high interstadial sea levels.

ˈinterstage, *a.* [INTER- 5.] Situated or occurring between successive stages of an apparatus.

1929 R. F. YATES *ABC of Television* v. 89 This interstage shielding is further insurance against audio-frequency regeneration. **1933** A. HUND *High-Frequency Measurement* viii. 255 This happens . . when interstage transformers are used in amplifiers. **1958** W. R. BARRETT et al. in H. W. Cremer *Chem. Engin. Pract.* V. 125 The interstage relief valves protect the compressor against excessive interstage pressures. **1970** V. O. STOKES *Radio Transmitters* xi. 147 The most suitable method of interstage coupling when driving a final amplifier in a grounded-cathode arrangement is a Π circuit. **1972** *Physics Bull.* Oct. 583/1 In the manufactured version of this pump the interstage pressure is raised to about 0·1 Torr.

inter-staminal: see INTER- *pref.*

interstate, inter-state (ˈɪntəˌsteɪt), *a.* and *sb.* orig. *U.S.* [INTER- 5.] Lying, extending, or carried on between independent states, or between states belonging to a Union, Federation, etc. Also as *sb.*, a road between states.

Interstate Commerce Act, an Act of Congress, passed Feb. 4, 1887, to regulate the commerce between the different States, establishing a body of commissioners for the administration of the law.

a **1845** JOSEPH STORY cited in Worcester. **1862** J. M. LUDLOW *Hist. U.S.* 36 The Supreme Court has exclusive jurisdiction in all questions of constitutional, international, and (if I may venture the term) interstate law. **1876** BANCROFT *Hist. U.S.* VI. xxvi. 34 When inter-state rights were to be confided to the members of each state. **1887** *Daily News* 11 Jan. 6/5 To await the action of Congress upon the Inter-State Commerce Bill. **1887** *Statutes at Large U.S.A.* XXIV. 383 A Commission is hereby created and established to be known as the Inter-State Commerce Commission. **1899** C. M. DEPEW ibid. 5 June 2/2 Trusts are purely State, and not inter-State affairs. **1928** *Manch. Guardian Weekly* 31 Aug. 75/1 The problem of inter-State legal aid was bound to throw light upon the larger question of international legal aid. **1943** WYNDHAM LEWIS *Let.* 21 Aug. (1963) 367, I hate to think how much inter-state competition there is going to be after this war. **1953** A. UPFIELD *Murder must Wait* iv. 30 Such matters as State boundaries [in Australia] and inter-State jealousies wouldn't register with Bony. **1968** *Globe & Mail* (Toronto) 3 Feb. 33/5 Here in Georgia where Inter-state 75 slices through the heart of a peanut, cotton and general farming area. *Ibid.* 17 Feb. B2/3 The U.S. Food and Drug Administration proposes to ban the interstate shipment of products containing carbon tetrachloride because of health hazards. **1969** *Jane's Freight Containers 1968–69* 115/1 During 1967, the Interstate Commerce Commission approved the merger of the company with the Chicago Great Western Railway. **1969** *Sydney Morning Herald* 24 May 35/4 (Advt.), Interstate carrier requires hauliers. **1971** *Sunday Australian* 8 Aug. 8/3 Builders and interstate truckdrivers, always high on the bankruptcy lists, continue to provide more than their share of debtors. **1971** D. E. WESTLAKE *I gave at the Office* (1972) 84 The shipments . . traveled via truck on Interstate 40 and US 64 to a small town near Little Rock. **1972** *Times of India* 28 Nov. 10/7 Referring to inter-state disputes, Dr. Gajendragadkar urged the government to set up an inter-state council under Art. 263 to deal with such disputes instead of attempting to solve them on a political plane. **1973** J. M. WHITE *Garden Game* 173 The five-hour drive along Interstate 10 from Phoenix to Los Angeles. **1973** *Sun-Herald* (Sydney) 26 Aug. 73/4 As NSW champion she would have been the first player picked in the State team for the interstate series.

inter-ˈstation, *a.* [INTER- 5.] Occurring (in a radio) between two stations or tuning positions.

1937 [see QUIETING *vbl. sb.* 2 a]. **1940** *Chambers's Techn. Dict.* 456/1 *Inter-station interference*, interference which arises from the presence of another transmitter on the same (or on an adjacent) wavelength as that to which a receiver is tuned. **1946** C. A. QUARRINGTON *Mod. Pract. Radio & Television* I. xxvii. 225 Another unpleasant inter-station noise is experienced when tuning off one station and when tuning on to the next. **1970** J. EARL *Tuners & Amplifiers* i. 24 Other features found in tuner-amplifiers . . are automatic mono/stereo switching . . and an inter-station muting device which in the 'on' position deadens the audio channels on weak signals . . and on noise signals between stations, thus making it possible to tune over the f.m. band without the annoyance of a high background noise, the tuner audio channels only being activated when a transmission of a useable strength is tuned.

interstellar (ɪntəˈstɛlə(r)), *a.* [INTER- 4 a.] Situated between the stars; occupying or passing through the regions of space between the stars. Also, relating to matter or to travel in interstellar space; occurring in such regions.

1626 BACON *Sylva* §354–5 The Interstellar Skie . . hath . . so much Affinity with the Starre, that there is a Rotation of that, as well as of the Starre. **1674** BOYLE *Excell. Theol.* II. iv. 178 The inter-stellar part of heaven, which several of the modern Epicureans would have to be empty. **1821** SHELLEY *Hellas* 771 The sapphire floods of interstellar air. **1862** R. H. PATTERSON *Ess. Hist. & Art* 10 This efflux occasions a thrill, or vibratory motion, in the ether which fills the interstellar spaces. **1880** PROCTOR *Poetry Astron.* xi. (1881) 378 A comet arriving from remote interstellar space. **1926** A. S. EDDINGTON *Internal Constitution of Stars* xiii. 377 Fixed calcium lines . . are formed either in an envelope surrounding the whole system or during the passage of the light through interstellar space. *Ibid.* 379 The question . . arises whether, granting that there is a cloud extending through interstellar space, the fixed lines are produced uniformly during the transit of the light from the star to the earth. **1930** *Astrophysical Jrnl.* LXXII. 199 A star at a distance of 200 parsecs from the sun should show an interstellar K line of intensity 2. **1936** S. ROSSELAND *Theoret. Astrophysics* xxiii. 345 An intensive study of interstellar absorption is a necessary feature of stellar spectroscopy. **1937** *Physical Rev.* LII. 762/1 A third hypothesis . . seems to point toward a physical relationship between space reddening (presumably caused by interstellar dust) and the formation of the spectral line. **1937** WHIPPLE & GREENSTEIN in *Proc. Nat. Acad. Sci.* XXIII. 178 The energy density in the galactic nucleus will be considerably increased, resulting in an increased temperature and emission for the interstellar particles. **1946** A. HUXLEY *Let.* 18 Mar. (1969) 539 People either wanted to talk about themselves, their job and their country; or else they couldn't stick to the point at issue, but wandered off into interstellar space. **1950** [see COSMONAUTICS]. **1950** O. STRUVE *Stellar Evolution* II. 106 All indications are that interstellar matter can and does condense into protostars which later form real stars. **1952** LOVELL & CLEGG *Radio Astron.* ii. 34 The current belief about the remaining mass is that it is concentrated in the dust and gas which permeates interstellar space. By terrestrial standards this interstellar material is highly attenuated. **1953** *Mag. Fantasy & Sci. Fiction* I. II. 95 The cruiser *Ilkor* had just gone into her interstellar over-drive beyond the orbit of Pluto. **1966** *McGraw-Hill Encycl. Sci. & Technol.* VII. 221/1 Interstellar lines can be distinguished from the stellar atmospheric lines by their extreme narrowness. **1969** *Times* 16 Jan. 4/7 Measurements of the radio signals from sulphur hydride may be a valuable check of estimates of the amount of sulphur in interstellar space. **1973** *Times* 28 Dec. 10/8 Amino acids . . are formed when three of the chemicals known to be present in the interstellar clouds . . are mixed in a flask and subjected to an electric spark.

interˈstellary, *a.* [INTER- 4 a.] = prec.

1856 in WEBSTER: hence in later Dicts.

inter-sterile: see INTER- *pref.* 2 a.

intersterility, -sternal: see INTER- 2 a, 4 a.

interstice (ɪnˈtɜːstɪs, ˈɪntəstɪs). Also 7 pl. **intersticies.** [ad. L. *interstiti-um* space between, f. **interstit-*, ppl. stem of *intersistĕre*, f. *inter* between + *sistĕre* to stand; cf. F. *interstice* (14th c.).]

1. a. An intervening space (usually, empty); *esp.* a relatively small or narrow space, between things or the parts of a body (freq. in *pl.*, the minute spaces between the ultimate parts of matter); a narrow opening, chink, or crevice.

1603 HOLLAND *Plutarch's Mor.* 848 When it is carried to the interstice or place between the browes, the very seat of reason. **1646** SIR T. BROWNE *Pseud. Ep.* II. v. 87 When the ayery intersticies are filled, and as much of the salt of the ashes as the water will imbibe is dissolved. *a* **1697** AUBREY *Nat. Hist. Surrey* (1719) I. 45 The great wooden Bridge (over the Thames) hath twenty Interstices. **1756** C. LUCAS *Ess. Waters* I. 56 The interstices of water are always found full of air. **1833** HT. MARTINEAU *Three Ages* iii. 89 He found an interstice, through which he could slip half-a-dozen burnt almonds. **1839** STEPHENS *Man. Brit. Coleoptera* 47 Elytra striated, interstices finely punctulated.

fig. **1653** J. HALL *Paradoxes* 16 Democracie . . is . . indeed an interstice of government, rather than government. **1876** MOZLEY *Univ. Serm.* vi. 132 Side currents are perpetually . . slipping into the empty interstices of his thoughts.

b. *Physics.* The space between adjacent atoms or ions in a crystal lattice. Cf. INTERSTITIAL *a.* 2 e.

1933 [see INTERSTITIAL *a.* 5]. **1940** F. SEITZ *Mod. Theory Solids* xiv. 496 The interstices of metals forming substitutional alloys usually are much smaller than the atomic size. **1942** SNEED & MAYNARD *Gen. Inorg. Chem.* xlvii. 1108 The interstices in a metal lattice are small, hence only the smallest metalloid atoms, C, N, B and H, can form such compounds and solid solutions. **1972** GROSS & WISEALL *Princ. Phys. Chem.* xix. 39 The holes or interstices formed between the layers of spheres in close-packed structures are of two different types, (a) tetrahedral interstices and (b) octahedral interstices.

2. a. An intervening space of time; an interval between actions. Now *rare*.

1639 SALTMARSH *Policy* lxxxi. 69 Long inter-regnums or interstices in government is the Winter and ill Season of a State. **1688** SEDLEY *Proc. in Eng.* Wks. 1722 I. 184 There must be some Interstice, some space of time, before they who deposed a King can set up another. **1726** AYLIFFE *Parergon* 179, I will endeavour to point out the Interstices of Time, which ought to be between one Citation and another. **1862** GOULBURN *Pers. Relig.* III. x. (1873) 239 Who look to the little intervals and interstices of work as so much time which may be freely wasted.

b. *spec.* in *Canon Law* (*pl.*) The intervals required between the reception of the various degrees of holy orders.

1745 A. BUTLER *Lives Saints, Norbert* (1847) VI. 119 The irregularity committed in his receiving the holy orders of deacon and priest at the same time, without observing the interstices prescribed by the canons. **1885** *Catholic Dict.* (ed. 3) 454/2 A bishop cannot dispense with the interstices in ordaining candidates coming to him from another diocese.

Hence **intersticed** *a.*, having interstices; also, fitted at intervals *with* something. *rare.*

1848 LYTTON *Harold* v. vii, Through the intersticed columns of the fane Edith saw the large shadow of a man. **1888** *Voice* (N.Y.) 6 Sept., His bare back was inflamed with scourges intersticed with pieces of lead and bone.

†**interˈstinct,** *a. Obs. rare.* [ad. L. *interstinct-us*, pa. pple. of *interstinguĕre* to separate, f. *inter* between + *stinguĕre* (cf. DISTINCT).] Divided, separated (in quot. 1684 = DISCRETE 1 c).

1623 COCKERAM, *Interstinct*, diuided, separated. **1684** tr. *Bonet's Merc. Compit.* XVIII. 601 The interstinct or discrete [Small Pox] come with a Shivering and Coldness.

†**interˈstinctive,** *a. Obs. rare*$^{-1}$. [f. as prec. + -IVE.] Serving to divide or mark off. *interstinctive point*, a punctuation-mark.

1696 WALLIS *Lett. to Dr. Smith* 8 Sept. in *Aubrey's Anecd.* (1813) I. 78 [To see] whether the notes of Parenthesis ( ) be used: and what care is taken of the interstinctive points,;:.

interstitial (ɪntəˈstɪʃəl), *a.* and *sb.* [f. L. type **interstitiālis*, f. *interstitium* INTERSTICE + -AL[1].]

A. *adj.* **1.** Of the nature of an interstice; forming interstices.

1646 SIR T. BROWNE *Pseud. Ep.* II. i. 55 In oyled paper . . the interstitial divisions being continuated by the accession of oyle, it becommeth more transparent. **1751** JOHNSON *Rambler* No. 108 ¶7 Those interstitial vacancies which intervene in the most crowded employment. **1830** KATER & LARDN. *Mech.* ii. 17 The volume [of a body] consists partly of material particles, and partly of interstitial spaces. **1846** DANA *Zooph.* iv. (1848) 76 The interstitial spaces between adjoining polyps.

2. a. Of a thing: Pertaining to, existing in, or occupying interstices.

1665 HOOKE *Microgr.* 96 According as these pores are more or greater in respect of the interstitial bodies. **1709** *Phil. Trans.* XXVI. 264 When there is a larger quantity of Interstitial Air to remove. **1879** RUTLEY *Study Rocks* x. 130 The hornblendic matter merely appearing as little interstitial specks between the magnetite granules.

b. *Anat. interstitial tissue*, the fine connective tissue lying between the cells of other tissue. *interstitial organs*, smaller organs of the body situated between larger ones.

1835-6 TODD *Cycl. Anat.* I. 510/1 The interstitial tissue varies according to the age and temperament of the individual. **1876** tr. *Wagner's Gen. Pathol.* 239 In the interstitial or subpleural pulmonary tissue.

c. *Entom.* Situated in the interstices or spaces between the striæ, e.g. on the elytra of beetles.

1900 D. SHARP *Biol. Centr. Amer., Coleoptera* II. I. 620 The peculiar interstitial punctuation [of the elytra] making it recognizable at a glance.

d. Occupying an interval in time or order.

1841 E. HAWKINS *Silver Coins* (1887) 245 Edward IV, in his interstitial usurpation. **1859** GLADSTONE *Glean.* (1879) II. 147 'The Brook', with its charming interstitial soliloquy ..will..always rank among Mr. Tennyson's happy efforts.

e. *Physics.* Situated between the normally occupied points of a crystal lattice. Cf. sense 5.

1938 *Trans. Faraday Soc.* XXXIV. 851 Motion..is possible by jumps of ions from one interstitial position to the neighbouring one... An interstitial ion takes the place of a neighbouring lattice ion. **1940** F. SEITZ *Mod. Theory Solids* xiv. 496 Semi-conductors, such as zinc oxide, that have interstitial atoms. **1966** C. R. TOTTLE *Sci. Engin. Materials* iv. 92 There may be interstitial atoms present in a lattice as impurities.

3. Of a physical or morbid process: Taking place in the interstices of a body; *spec.* in *Phys.* Affecting the internal structure of an organ or part by acting in its interstices or on its interstitial tissue; as ***interstitial absorption, emphysema, growth***.

interstitial pregnancy, that in which the development of the ovum takes place in that portion of the Fallopian tube which passes through the uterine wall.

1807 M. BAILLIE *Morb. Anat.* (ed. 7) 220 This change [in the liver] must arise from a process which takes place through its whole substance, and seems to be what Mr. Hunter has called the interstitial absorption. **1845** TODD & BOWMAN *Phys. Anat.* I. 121 Bone..grows in an interstitial manner after being originally deposited. **1858** J. H. BENNET *Nutrition* iv. 100 The variable activity of interstitial nutritive changes, rapid in the child, slow in the aged. **1877** ROBERTS *Handbk. Med.* (ed. 3) I. 391 Interstitial pneumonia runs a very chronic course.

4. Having interstices. *rare.*

1855 BAILEY *Mystic*, etc. 25 The interstitial net of death.

5. Containing atoms or ions in interstitial positions: cf. sense 2e.

1933 W. H. & W. L. BRAGG *Crystalline State* I. vii. 158 The atoms of H, N, C, or B are placed in the interstices of the metallic structures... Such structures are called *Einlagerungsstrukturen* by Hägg, and will be referred to here as 'interstitial structures'... All hydrides and nitrides [of transition elements], and some carbides, fall within the first category of interstitial compounds. **1948** *Acta Crystallogr.* I. 180/1 A large number of metals form metal-like phases with hydrogen, boron, carbon, nitrogen, and occasionally oxygen... Following suggestions of Hägg, these phases are generally regarded as interstitial solutions of the small, light elements in the metals. **1967** B. L. SHAW *Inorg. Hydrides* xi. 101 It is now known that the metal lattice often does change when the hydrogen is absorbed so that the term 'interstitial hydride' is not a good one.

B. *sb. Physics.* An interstitial atom or ion.

1961 *Physical Rev.* CXXIV. 669/2 If the interstitial is displaced slightly from its position in configuration '*B*' toward surrounding crowdion, 'body-centred' or '*A*' interstitial positions the calculations show that the interstitial returns to its position in configuration '*B*'. **1969** [see DISLOCATION 1 e]. **1972** *Physics Bull.* July 400/1 At the temperatures relevant to the operation of fast reactors both vacancies and interstitials, produced as a consequence of radiation damage, are able to migrate under thermal activation.

interstitialcy (ɪntəˈstɪʃəlsɪ). *Physics.* [f. INTERSTITIAL *a.* + -CY, after *vacancy*.] A kind of imperfection in a crystal lattice, characterized by an interstitial atom able to displace an atom from an adjacent lattice position so that it becomes the interstitial in its turn, able to displace another atom.

1950 F. SEITZ in *Acta Crystallogr.* III. 361/1 The lattice imperfection which is the inverse counterpart of a lattice vacancy is an interstitial atom which moves by jumping into a normal lattice site and forces the atom that is there into a neighboring interstitial site... We shall term it an interstitialcy. *Ibid.* 361/2 The interstitial atom associated with a passing interstitialcy at any point in its migration may be either an *A* atom or a *B* atom. **1956** *Physical Rev.* CI. 1210/2 The effects discussed here may be useful in distinguishing experimentally between interstitialcy and vacancy migration in other crystals. **1967** F. C. BROWN *Physics of Solids* x. 315 In the silver halides the interstitial ion moves by an interstitialcy mechanism. **1968** J. R. MANNING *Diffusion Kinetics for Atoms in Crystals* i. 6 Two jumps of the interstitialcy are required to move an atom from one lattice site to another.

interstitially (ɪntəˈstɪʃəlɪ), *adv.* [f. INTERSTITIAL *a.* and *sb.* + -LY².] In an interstitial manner; in or through interstices.

1794 G. ADAMS *Nat. & Exp. Philos.* IV. xlix. 351 [Invisible fire] exists..in two modes, interstitially and organically. **1870** BENTLEY *Bot.* 19 By the incorporation of new matter in its substance, or interstitially. **1913** F. H. HUMPHRIS *Electro-Therapeutics for Practitioners* xvi. 115 Antiseptic chemicals..interstitially diffused throughout the growth. **1938** *Trans. Faraday Soc.* XXXIV. 851 Some ions exist interstitially within the normal lattice. **1965** *Nuclear Instruments & Methods* XXXVIII. 158/2 Interstitially located impurities. **1972** *Sci. Amer.* Nov. 45/1 In silver halide many cations wander interstitially through the lattice.

†**inter'stitiated**, *ppl. a. Obs.* [f. med.L. *interstitiāt-us* (f. *interstiti-um*: see INTERSTICE and -ATE²) + -ED¹.] Situated as or in interstices.

1665 HOOKE *Microgr.* 96 Whether it have any interstitiated pores or vacuities.

†**inter'stition.** *Obs. rare*⁻¹. [ad. L. *interstitiōn-em*, n. of action f. *intersistĕre*: see INTERSTICE.] = INTERSTITIUM.

1390 GOWER *Conf.* III. 94 The ferste Periferie.. Engendreþ Myst..The dewes and þe ffrostes hore After þilke Intersticion In which þei take impression. **1623** COCKERAM, *Interstition*, a ceasing, a pawsing.

†**inter'stitious**, *a. Obs.* [f. L. *interstiti-um* + -OUS.] Having the quality of an interstice.

1592 R. D. *Hypnerotomachia* 21 The streight cheekes and sides of the doore, with an interstitious aspect, inwardly carved with as great cunning as the rest.

‖**interstitium** (ɪntəˈstɪʃɪəm). *Obs.* Pl. **-stitia**, (†**-a's**), **-stitiums.** [L.; see INTERSTICE.]

1. Of space: = INTERSTICE 1.

1597 A. M. tr. *Guillemeau's Fr. Chirurg.* 42b/1 Noe concavity or interstitium of muscles. **1665** HOOKE *Microgr.* 94 The small pores, or interstitia..betwixt the Globules, I plainly saw. **1698** FRYER *Acc. E. India & P.* 37 Curtains fringed with Battlements from one to the other; in whose Interstitiums whole Culverin are traversed. **1706** BAYNARD in Sir J. Floyer *Hot & Cold Bath* II. 252 It must be granulated and corn'd that the Air may lodge in the Interstitia's.

2. Of time: = INTERSTICE 2.

1624 T. SCOTT *2nd Pt. Vox Pop.* 45 This *interstitium* or twi-light of Treatie, or suspence betweene Warre and Peace. **1650** FULLER *Pisgah* III. vi. 421 There was an Interstitium, or distance of seventy years between the destruction of Solomon's, and erection of Zorobabel's Temple. **1704** SWIFT *Mech. Operat. Spir.* Misc. (1711) 288 The Interstitia are duly fill'd up by the Preacher, to prevent too long a pause.

interstrain, inter-strain (ˈɪntəstreɪn), *a. Biol.* [f. INTER- 5 + STRAIN *sb.*¹] Occurring or existing between one strain (STRAIN *sb.*¹ 7) and another; formed by crossing two strains.

1950 *Amer. Jrnl. Bot.* XXXVII. 631/1 Exceptions to the relatively ready inter-strain crossability among the strains hybridized were 109 × 105 and 109 × 110. **1955** *New Biol.* XIX. 52 Livesay's interstrain F_1 hybrids should be genetically uniform. **1965** *Jrnl. Gen. Microbiol.* XLI. 7 The progeny of inter-strain crosses.

interstratification (-ˌstrætɪfɪˈkeɪʃən). [INTER- 2 a.] The condition or fact of being interstratified; an interposed formation or deposit.

1855 in HYDE CLARKE *Eng. Dict.* **1872** W. S. SYMONDS *Rec. Rocks* ix. 104 The repeated interstratification of the Caradoc slates with..igneous rocks. **1876** PAGE *Adv. Text-bk. Geol.* xiv. 259 In the lower Coal-measures we have frequent interstratifications of trap-tuff and ash.

interstratify (-ˈstrætɪfaɪ), *v.* [INTER- 1 b.]

1. *trans.* in *pass.* Of geological strata: To be alternated, or interspersed, *with* other strata.

1822 G. YOUNG *Geol. Surv. Yorksh. Coast* (1828) 57 The flint is not interstratified with the chalk. **1845** DARWIN *Voy. Nat.* xi. (1873) 249 The soil here consists of ice and volcanic ashes interstratified. **1863** LYELL *Antiq. Man* ix. (ed. 3) 155 Interstratified with this gravel..are beds of sand, loam, and clay. **1876** PAGE *Adv. Text-bk. Geol.* iii. 73 Lava and ashes will be interstratified and mingled with the sedimentary matter.

2. *intr.* To lie as strata between other strata.

1880 *Libr. Univ. Knowl.* (U.S.) XI. 467 Sandstone, iron ore, limestone and fire-clay interstratify with the coal.

Hence **inter'stratified** *ppl. a.*, placed as a stratum between other strata.

1849 MURCHISON *Siluria* iii. 49 This..formation contains many interstratified bands of..materials. **1876** DARWIN in *Life & Lett.* (1887) III. 214 Many irregular beds of interstratified drift.

inter-stream, -street: see INTER- *pref.* 5.

interstrial (ɪntəˈstraɪəl), *a.* [f. INTER- 4 a + L. *stria* streak + -AL¹.] Situated between striæ or streaks, e.g. on an insect's wing; = INTERSTITIAL 1 c.

interstriation (ˌɪntəstraɪˈeɪʃən). *Nat. Hist.* [INTER- 2 a.] An intermediate striation, streak, or linear marking.

1849 DANA *Geol.* App. i. (1850) 719 Its delicate ridges or interstriations.

intersturb, erron. form of INTERTURB *v.*

intersubjective (ɪntəsəbˈdʒɛktɪv), *a. Philos.* [INTER- 4 c.] Existing between conscious minds. Hence **intersub'jectively** *adv.*, in an intersubjective manner; **intersubjec'tivity**, the fact or state of being intersubjective.

1899 J. WARD *Naturalism & Agnosticism* II. 170 It seems to depend upon three elements or conditions which are consequences of intersubjective intercourse. **1925** J. E. TURNER *Theory Direct Realism* iv. 44 Intersubjective communication. **1934** M. BLACK tr. *Carnap's Unity of Sci.* iii. 42 It will be proved..that the physical language is inter-subjective and can serve as a *universal* language. *Ibid.* iii. 51 In such a case p will be said to have sense (for those persons) inter-subjectively. **1938** *Mind* XLVII. 133 Propositions about private experiences are intersubjectively understood. **1938** C. MORRIS *Found. Theory of Signs* § 12. 125 The thesis of the potential intersubjectivity of every meaning. **1945** K. R. POPPER *Open Soc.* II. xxiii. 205 Scientific objectivity can be described as the inter-subjectivity of scientific method. **1945** *Psychol. Rev.* LII. 258/2 Concepts which are to be of value to the factual sciences must be definable by operations which are..intersubjective and repeatable. **1956** *Essays in Crit.* VI. 10 The validation for the new myth philosophy.. plunges, in the vast reservoir of racial unconsciousness, for an intersubjective base for universality. **1957** C. LA DRIÈRE in N. Frye *Sound & Poetry* 97 The acknowledged intersubjectivity of meaning is a kind of objectivity. **1963** R. CARNAP in P. A. Schilpp *Philos. R. Carnap* 52 One of the most important advantages of the physicalistic language is its intersubjectivity, i.e., the fact that the events described in this language are in principle observable by all users of the language. **1967** W. SELLARS *Philos. Perspectives* xv. 371 Universals are..identities not only with respect to their many instances, but also with respect to the many minds which think in terms of them... This inter-subjective and inter-linguistic character must be accounted for by any adequate theory of abstract entities.

intersubstance, -substitutability, -substitutable, -substitution: see INTER- *pref.*

intersu'sception, *Path.*, erron. for INTRO- or INTUS-SUSCEPTION.

[**1756** A. MONRO in *Ess. Phys. & Lit.* II. 353 (*heading*) Remarks on Procidentiæ Ani, Intersusceptio, Inflammation, and Valvula of the Intestines.] **1793** J. HUNTER in *Trans. Med. & Chir.* I. 103 (*heading*) Observations on Intersusception.

inter-synapticular, -systematical: see INTER- *pref.*

intertain(e, -tayn(e, obs. ff. ENTERTAIN *v.*

inter-talk: see INTER- *pref.*

intertangle (ɪntəˈtæŋg(ə)l), *v.* Also 6 enter-. [INTER- 1 b.] *trans.* To tangle together; to intertwine confusedly or inextricably. Hence **inter'tangled** *ppl. a.*, **inter'tangling** *vbl. sb.* and *ppl. a.*

1589 PUTTENHAM *Eng. Poesie* II. ii. (Arb.) 80 Elegie, Epitaph, Epigramme or such meetres, of plaine concord not harmonically entertangled. *Ibid.* II. xi[i]. (Arb.) 120 All which parts are discouered in this figure: loue by the serpents amorous entertangling. **1612** *Two Noble K.* I. iii, To water Their intertangled roots of love. **1820** SHELLEY *Witch Atl.* xxv, Intertangled lines of light. *a* **1849** POE *W.W. Lord* Wks. 1864 III. 169 Its veriest common-places are intertwined and inextricably intertangled.

†**inter'tangle**, *sb. Obs.* In 6 enter-. [INTER- 2 a.] = next; *spec.* an intricate system of rimes.

1589 PUTTENHAM *Eng. Poesie* II. x[i]. (Arb.) 100 Concord in Plaine compasse..Entertangle.

intertanglement (ɪntəˈtæŋg(ə)lmənt). [f. prec. vb. + -MENT.] Intertangled state or condition; also quasi-*concr.*, something intertangled.

1817 COLERIDGE *Lay Serm.* in *Biog. Lit.* (1882) 372 The foodful plants..whose slender surface-roots owe their whole stedfastness to their inter-tanglement. **1846** MRS. GORE *Eng. Char.* (1852) 82 All the intertanglements of pink, blue, and lilac, devised by haberdashers for the perdition of the female kind. **1877** BLACKIE *Wise Men* 242 The strange Wild intertanglement of sound with sound Which we call language.

intertarsal, -team: see INTER- *pref.* 6, 5.

†**inter'tear**, *v. Obs.* Also enter-. [INTER- 1 b.] *trans.* To tear or rend mutually.

1603 FLORIO *Montaigne* II. xi. (1632) 240 All are pleased to see them [beasts]..enterteare one another. **1647** TRAPP *Comm. Matt.* v. 9 The wicked are apt (as dogs) to intertear and worry one another. **1649** S. CLARKE *Lives Fathers, P. Martyr* (1854) 582 Rather to hazard the loss of his life, than to suffer Christians thus to intertear one another.

interteign, -tein(e, -tene, -teny, etc., obs. ff. ENTERTAIN *v.*

intertentacular: see INTER-.

†**inter'tenure.** *Obs. rare*⁻¹. [a. obs. F. *entretenure*, f. *entretenir* to maintain, ENTERTAIN.] Maintenance.

1536-7 STARKEY *Let. to King* in *St. Papers Hen. VIII* 463 The intertenure of amyte wyth vtward pryncys.

intertergal (-ˈtɜːgəl), *a. Zool.* [INTER- 4 a.] Situated between adjacent terga or tergites of an arthropod.

1888 E. A. MINCHIN in *Microsc. Sc.* XXIX. III. 230 A cuticle continuous with that of the intertergal membrane.

inter-territorial, -tesselation, -testamental: see INTER- *pref.*

†**inter'tex**, *v. Obs.* [ad. L. *intertexĕ-re*, f. *inter* between + *texĕre* to weave.] *trans.* To weave together, interweave, intertwine.

1578 BANISTER *Hist. Man* IV. 49 Fibres..so intertexed and wouen together, as that one from another..cannot be disioyned. *a* **1637** B. JONSON *Underwoods, Epithal.* 60 See how with Roses, and with Lillies shine, The bright Brides path..this Paire doth intertexe! **1666** HARVEY *Morb. Angl.* iv. 39 The heart..consisting of robust fibres variously intertext.

intertexture (ɪntə'tɛkstjʊə(r)). [f. L. *intertext-*, ppl. stem of *intertexĕre* (see prec.) + -URE: cf. TEXTURE.]

1. The action of interweaving; the fact or condition of being interwoven.

1649 JER. TAYLOR *Gt. Exemp.* I. Ad sect. v. §8 Like vowels pronunciable by the intertexture of a consonant. **1779-81** JOHNSON *L.P., Pope* Wks. IV. 17 He always considered the intertexture of the machinery with the action, as his most successful exertion of the poetical art. **1841** DE QUINCEY *Wks.* (1857) VI. 388. **1855** WESTCOTT *Canon N. Test.* ii. §7 (1881) I. 105 The same intertexture of the narratives of St. Matthew and St. Luke..characterise[s] the great mass of Justin's references to the Gospel-history.

2. quasi-*concr.* An intertwined or interwoven structure.

1651-3 JER. TAYLOR *Serm. for Year* I. xxiii. 302 They knew how to make them roare aloud with a slovenly and wanton word..as is to be seen in the intertextures of Aristophanes Comedies. **1666** J. SMITH *Old Age* (ed. 2) 112 There are several vessels appointed for that purpose, and many admirable..intertextures of them all. **1779-81** JOHNSON *L.P., Akenside* Wks. IV. 291 The sense is carried on through a long intertexture of complicated clauses. **1784** COWPER *Task* I. 111 Intertexture firm Of thorny boughs. **1893** TRAILL *Soc. Eng.* Introd. 21 That endless intertexture of institutions of which contemporary society is made up.

interthing, -thread, -tidal: see INTER-.

intertie ('ɪntətaɪ), *sb.* [INTER- 2 b: but orig. variant of INTERDICE, arising from viewing the forms *inter-ties, interties* as plural.] (See quots.)

1703-34 [see INTERDICE]. **1823** P. NICHOLSON *Pract. Build.* 225 *Intertie*, a horizontal piece of timber, framed between two posts, in order to tie them together. **1847** SMEATON *Builder's Man.* 249 *Intertie*, small pieces of timber, placed horizontally between and framed into vertical pieces to tie them together.

intertie, v., intertinge: see INTER- *pref.*

inter'tillage. *U.S.* [INTER- I.] Intercropping. So **inter'tilled** *a.*

1912 L. A. MOREHOUSE in *Bull. Bureau Plant Industry, U.S. Dept. Agric.* No. 260. 55 The alfalfa roots give some trouble at times, especially with the first cultivations of an intertilled crop, but this difficulty does not seem to be encountered when the cantaloupe or the cucumber is selected as the initial crop in the rotation. *Ibid.* 60 Regular intertillage can not be omitted without incurring losses. **1914** *Rep. Brit. Assoc. Adv. Sci.* 270 The intertilled crop has in many sections largely taken the place of fallow. **1973** *Times Lit. Suppl.* 21 Dec. 1572/3 The schemes of the Altai region to replace fallow and grass with intertilled crops (sugar-beet, maize, and fodder beans).

intertissued (ɪntə'tɪʃjuːd), *ppl. a.* Also 7 enter-. [f. OF. *entretissu* interwoven (15-16th c. in Godef.) + -ED[1].] Interwoven.

1599 SHAKS. *Hen. V,* IV. i. 279 The enter-tissued Robe of Gold and Pearl. **1652** BENLOWES *Theoph.* Postill for Author, Your first Love is pure; Whose ev'ry dresse Is intertissued Wit and Holinesse. **1806-7** J. BERESFORD *Miseries Hum. Life* (1826) VII. Introd., Those exquisite paradoxes in feeling wherewith the texture of my fibres is so mystically intertissued. **1863** W. LANCASTER *Præterita* 120 Purple vetches dazzling some sere pine With intertissued bravery.

intertonic, -touch, -town, -trabecular, -trace: see INTER- *pref.*

intertrade ('ɪntətreɪd). [INTER- 2 a.] Reciprocal trade. Also *attrib.*

1915 E. CARPENTER *Healing of Nations* xi. 168 Merchants and dealers came in and effected the exchange, and so an intertrade has sprung up. **1929** *Daily Tel.* 15 Jan. 6/4 The variations in the curve of consumer demand are much less than the curve of inter-trade demand.

inter'trading, *vbl. sb.* Also 7 enter-. [INTER- I b.] Mutual dealing, reciprocal trade.

1605 DANIEL *Queen's Arcadia* III. i. 74 Have had no inter-trading with the rest Of Men, nor yet will have. **1611** FLORIO, *Intercomertio*, an enter-trafficke, an enter-trading or comerce.

†**inter'traffic,** *sb.* *Obs.* Also enter-. [INTER- 2 a.]

Traffic between two or more persons or places; reciprocal commerce or intercourse.

a **1603** T. CARTWRIGHT *Confut. Rhem. N.T.* (1618) 192 The Saints..haue found a ladder to go up and downe for entertraffike between them and these upon earth. **1603** DANIEL in Florio *Montaigne*, Whom neither Ocean, Desarts, Rockes nor Sands Can keepe from th' intertraffique of the minde. **1611** [see prec.] **1640** G. WATTS tr. *Bacon's Adv. Learn.* VI. i. 261 Tongues might be enrich and perfected by mutuall intertrafique one with another.

†**inter'traffic,** *v.* *Obs. rare*[-1]. Also enter-. [INTER- I b.] *intr.* To trade together.

1603 J. DAVIES *Microcosmos* (1878) 61 And intertrafficke with them, tunne for pound. **1611** FLORIO, *Intertrafficare*, to entertraffike or trade.

intertranslatable (ɪntətrɑːn'sleɪtəb(ə)l, -æ-), *a.* [INTER- 2 a.] Capable of being translated from one language to another and vice versa. Also *transf.* Hence **intertransla'bility**.

a **1866** J. GROTE in *Jrnl. Philol.* (1872) IV. 58 We assume that all languages are pretty accurately intertranslatable. **1951** *Mind* LX. 93 There is thus no genuine intertranslateability. **1960** W. V. O. QUINE *Word & Object* ii. 76 An illusion that our so readily intertranslatable sentences are diverse verbal embodiments of some inter-

cultural proposition or meaning. **1969** *Canad. Jrnl. Linguistics* XV. 47 From these (and other) approaches, therefore, we are forcefully reminded that linguistics now has more facets than ever—and that we must be on guard to maintain a degree of integration and inter-translatability among its schools.

intertran'spicuous, *a. rare.* [INTER- 2 a.] Transpicuous between or through each other.

1821 SHELLEY *Prometh. Unb.* IV. 246 Ten thousand orbs involving and involved, Sphere within sphere..Yet each inter-transpicuous.

intertransverse (-trɑːns'vɜːs, -æ-), *a. Anat.* [INTER- 4 a.] Situated between the transverse processes of the vertebræ.

1831 R. KNOX *Cloquet's Anat.* 257 These muscles..are not placed in two rows, each inter-transverse space containing only one. The first occupies the interval which exists between the transverse processes of the first lumbar, and the last dorsal vertebra. **1881** MIVART *Cat* 54 Adjacent transverse processes are also connected together by fibrous bands termed the inter-transverse ligaments.

So **intertrans'versal, intertrans'versary** *adjs.*

1855 MAYNE *Expos. Lex.*, Intertransversal.

intertrial: see INTER- *pref.*

intertribal (ɪntə'traɪbəl), *a.* [INTER- 4 c.] Existing or carried on between different tribes.

1862 *N. Brit. Rev.* Aug. 204 Intertribal wars broke out, and anarchy succeeded. **1865** MCLENNAN *Prim. Marriage* (1876) 39 In an intertribal marriage one tribe loses a woman, the other acquires one. **1897** MARY KINGSLEY *W. Africa* 542 Sometimes representatives..from several tribes meet together and discuss intertribal difficulties.

†**intertri'gation.** *Obs. rare*[-1]. [f. next + -ATION.] Mutual friction.

1651 BIGGS *New Disp.* ¶196 In the intertrigation of their own hypotheses they contradict themselves.

‖**intertrigo** (ɪntə'traɪgəʊ). *Path.* [L. (for *interterigo*), f. **interter-ĕre* to rub against each other.] Inflammation caused by the rubbing of one part of the surface of the skin against another.

1706 PHILLIPS, *Intertrigo*, a fleaing of the Skin that proceeds from a violent motion, especially Riding, a Gall, or Chase. **1799** HOOPER *Med. Dict.*, *Intertrigo*, an excoriation about the anus, groins, axilla, or other parts of the body, attended with inflammation and moisture. **1876** DUHRING *Dis. Skin* 91 Dusting Powders play quite an important part in the management of certain..inflammatory disorders, as in erythema, intertrigo, and eczema.

†**inter'trike,** *v. Sc. Obs. rare.* Also -tryik. [INTER- I + ? L. *tricāri* to make or start difficulties, to play tricks, f. *tricæ* perplexities, quirks, tricks.] *trans.* ? To intermeddle with, to perplex.

1513 DOUGLAS *Æneis* I. Prol. 490 Bot laith me war, but other offence or cryme, Ane burell [*MSS.* bruitell, brimell, *ed.* 1710 rural] body suld intertrike my ryme. **1535** STEWART *Cron. Scot.* III. 499 As now me think it is nocht meit With thame my storie for to intertryik, Without sum thing that tha war mercatlike.

intertrinitarian, -trochanteric: see INTER-.

intertrochlear (-'trɒkliːə(r)), *a.* [INTER- 4 a.] Situated in the middle of the trochlear or pulley-like surface of a joint.

1870 ROLLESTON *Anim. Life* 24 At the distal end of the bone, a little above the external intertrochlear notch. **1887** E. D. COPE *Orig. Fittest* 348 The development of distinct facets in the cubito-carpal articulation, and of a tongue and groove ('intertrochlear crest') in the elbow-joint.

intertropical (ɪntə'trɒpɪkəl), *a.* [f. INTER- 4 a + TROPICAL.] Of or pertaining to regions between the tropics; tropical.

1794 G. ADAMS *Nat. & Exp. Philos.* IV. lii. 474 Jamaica, St. Domingo, Sumatra, and most other intertropical islands, are furnished with mountains. **1830** LINDLEY *Nat. Syst. Bot.* 66 Trees or shrubs, mostly intertropical. **1864** R. F. BURTON *Dahome* II. 187 The tribes of intertropical Africa.

intertrude (-'truːd), *v. rare.* [ad. late L. *intertrūdĕre*, f. *inter* between + *trūdĕre* to thrust: cf. INTRUDE.] *trans.* To thrust in between, introduce intrusively.

1809 COLERIDGE *Let. to Southey* Dec. in *Lett.* (1895) 556 The *whole* passage was inserted, and intertruded after the rest was written. *a* **1834** —— *Anima Poetæ* (1895) 6 Mackintosh intertrudes not introduces his beauties.

intertubercular, -tubular: see INTER- *pref.*

†**inter'turb,** *v. Obs.* [ad. L. *interturbā-re*, f. *inter* between + *turbā-re* to disturb.] *trans.* To disturb by interruption.

1554 LD. DARNLEY in Ellis *Orig. Lett.* Ser. II. II. 250 Being afraid, with thes my superflous woordes to interturbe ..Your Highnes. **1590** FENNE *Frutes* 36 b, The Ambassadors of Greece so vehemently interrupted and interturbed his speech. **1659** O. WALKER *Oratory* 12 Skipping and withdrawing themselves out of sight, or interturbing some matter.

Hence †**inter'turber**, a disturber, a troubler.

1538 HEN. VIII *Let. to Wyatt* 4 May (R.), The world percase fantazing us to be an interturber of the peace, rather than an indifferent mediator.

†**intertur'bation.** *Obs.* [ad. L. *interturbātiōn-em*, n. of action from *interturbā-re*: see prec.] Disturbance, interruption.

1624 MEDE *Let. to Wood* Wks. (1672) III. 594 Hourly molested with such occasions of interturbation as the place and solemnity brings. **1657** TOMLINSON *Renou's Disp.* Pref., Obnoxious to..nocturnal interturbations.

intertwine (ɪntə'twaɪn), *v.* [INTER- I b.]

1. *trans.* To twine (two or more things) together, or entwine (one thing) with another; to unite by twining; to interlace, intertwist, interweave.

1641 TRAPP *Theologia Theol.* 357 The word..signifieth thoughts so perplexed and inter-twined one within another, that there is no way out almost. **1671** MILTON *P.R.* IV. 405 Under some concourse of shades, Whose branching arms thick intertwin'd might shield From dews and damps of night his shelter'd head. **1799** WORDSW. *Infl. Nat. Obj.* 6 From my first dawn Of childhood didst thou intertwine for me The passions that build up our human soul. **1800** *Hart-leap Well* I. xxii, Flowers of stature tall With trailing plants and trees were intertwined. **1841** BORROW *Zincali* I. viii. I. 131 They are busied at their morning's occupation, intertwining..the gold and silk on the tambour. **1882** FARRAR *Early Chr.* II. 93 Faith and works in this sense are in fact inseparably intertwined.

2. *intr.* for *refl.* To twine or become entwined with one another.

1782 J. SCOTT *Ecl. Rural Scenery Poems* 99 O'er my darken'd casement intertwine The fragrant briar, the woodbine, and the vine. **1794** COWPER *Needless Alarm* 16 Horrid brambles intertwine below. **1851** NICHOL *Archit. Heavens* (ed. 9) 46 Intertwining and forming a most curious and complex network.

3. *trans.* To twine round and involve. *rare.*

1717 CROXALL tr. *Ovid's Met.* VI. (R.), Fresh flow'rs, which twists of ivy intertwine. **1847** EMERSON *Poems, Dæmonic Love* II, Their cords of love so public are, They intertwine the farthest star.

Hence **inter'twined** *ppl. a.*

a **1680** T. BROOKS in Spurgeon *Treas. Dav.* Ps. xciv. 12 My..ensnared, intertwined, and perplexed thoughts. **1862** SMILES *Engineers* III. 224 The surface-ground..containing the intertwined roots of heather and long grass.

'intertwine, *sb. rare.* [f. prec.] = next.

1812 COLERIDGE *Lit. Rem.* (1836) I. 340 Oft are the flowers of the bind-weed mistaken for the growth of the plant, which it chokes with its intertwine. **1817** —— *Lay Serm.* in *Biog. Lit.* (1882) 399 They were twined at the very root, and could not grow or thrive but in intertwine.

intertwinement (ɪntə'twaɪnmənt). [f. as prec. + -MENT.] The fact of intertwining; intertwined state or condition; also quasi-*concr.*, an intertwined formation.

1840 J. ROBERTSON *Let. in Life* vi. (1887) 80 The present perplexed intertwinements of my path. **1883** *Pall Mall G.* 31 Mar. 4/1 Gorse and heather growing in intricate intertwinement form superb cushions of gold and purple blossom. **1889** *Archæol. Inst. Jrnl.* No. 181. 27 The guilloche, that rope intertwinement, consisting of two bands or strings twisted over each other in a continued series.

intertwining (ɪntə'twaɪnɪŋ), *vbl. sb.* [f. as prec. + -ING[1].] The action of the vb. INTERTWINE.

1836 MACGILLIVRAY tr. *Humboldt's Trav.* vii. 93 A first attempt to penetrate into this pass was rendered unsuccessful by..the intertwining of lianas and thorny plants. **1843** RUSKIN *Mod. Paint.* I. II. ii. iii. §5. 145 So again in the Rhymer's Glen..note the intertwining of the shadows across the path. **1852** TH. ROSS *Humboldt's Trav.* II. xxii. 332 None knew better than the Caribs the intertwinings of the rivers. **1899** F. A. WOOD in *Amer. Jrnl. Philol.* XX. 254 There are many intertwinings of meaning within any related group of words.

inter'twining, *ppl. a.* [f. as prec. + -ING[2].] That intertwines; interlacing, interweaving. Hence **inter'twiningly** *adv.*, so as to intertwine.

1823 E. MOOR *Suffolk Words* 120 Running a line of hazel or other flexible wands intertwiningly along the top of a hedge. **1827-44** WILLIS *Lazarus & Mary* 26 The intertwining locks of that bright hair. **1844** H. H. WILSON *Brit. India* III. 95 An intricate net-work of intertwining reeds and brushwood.

intertwist (ɪntə'twɪst), *v.* [INTER- I b.] *trans.* To twist one within another; to twist together; to intertwine, intertangle.

a **1659** [implied in INTERTWISTED below]. **1797** GODWIN *Enquirer* I. i. 1 In society the interests of individuals are intertwisted with each other. **1822** LAMB *Elia* Ser. I. Roast Pig, A bundle of virtues and vices, inexplicably intertwisted. **1865** G. MEREDITH *Rhoda Fleming* xxxiii. (1890) 289 Mrs. Sumfit then intertwisted her fingers. **1872** BLACK *Adv. Phaeton* xv, A long lane of silver, intertwisting itself with millions of gleaming lines.

Hence **inter'twisted** *ppl. a.*; **inter'twisting** *vbl. sb.* and *ppl. a.*; **inter'twistingly** *adv.* (Webster, 1856).

a **1659** HERLE *David's Song of 3 Parts* in Spurgeon *Treas. Dav.* Ps. xcv. 1 The third and last intertwisted string, or part in the musick. **1753** HOGARTH *Anal. Beauty* x. 58 The more pleasing turns and intertwistings of the lines. **1797** E. M. LOMAX *Philanthrope* 274 The poplar's intertwisting boughs. **1830** *Fraser's Mag.* I. 591 Not full of philosophical knottinesses and metaphysical intertwistings. **1847** DICKENS *Haunted M.* i, The intertwisted chain of feelings and associations.